THE AMERICAN HERITAGE

STUDENT

dic•tion•ar•y

HOUGHTON MIFFLIN COMPANY

BOSTON • NEW YORK

Words are included in this Dictionary on the basis of their usage. Words that are known to have current trademark registrations are shown with an initial capital and are also identified as trademarks. No investigation has been made of common-law trademark rights in any word, because such investigation is impracticable. The inclusion of any word in this Dictionary is not, however, an expression of the Publisher's opinion as to whether or not it is subject to proprietary rights. Indeed, no definition in this Dictionary is to be regarded as affecting the validity of any trademark.

Library of Congress Cataloging-in-Publication Data

The American heritage student dictionary.

p. cm.
ISBN 0-395-55857-3
1. English language—Dictionaries, Juvenile. [1. English language—Dictionaries.]
I. Houghton Mifflin Company. II. Title: Student dictionary.
PE1628.5.A45 1994
423—cd20 93-32433
CIP

Manufactured in the United States of America

Table of Contents

Editorial and Production Staff

EDITORIAL STAFF

Vice President, Director of Lexical Publishing
Margery S. Berube

Senior Lexicographer
David A. Jost

Project Director
Joseph P. Pickett

Senior Coordinating Editor
Kaethe Ellis

Executive Editor
Robert B. Costello

Managing Editor
Marion Severynse

Editors
Martha F. Phelps
Donna Cremans (Physical Science)
Joseph M. Patwell (Word Histories)

Contributing Editors
Rebecca A. Parker
Laura P. Chesterton (Synonym Paragraphs)

Pronunciations
Ann-Marie Imbornoni

Etymologies
David M. Weeks

Assistant Editor
Michael H. Choi (Life Science)

Editorial Staff Consultants
Jim A. Craig, Paul G. Evenson,
Nina Judith Katz, Ann Marie Menting,
David R. Pritchard, Susan E. Schwartz

Science Consultants
Elizabeth A. Jordan, David C. Roberts

Editorial Assistants
Kenneth C. Carpenter, Rachel King,
Lily Moy (Citations Clerk),
Beth Gately Rowen, Hanna Schonthal,
Donna Whiting

Administrative Assistants
Jennifer L. Crawford, Margaret M. May,
Alisa Stepanian

PRODUCTION STAFF

Production and Manufacturing Manager
Christopher Leonesio

Production Supervisor
Patricia McTiernan

Senior Art and Production Coordinator
Margaret Anne Miles

Database Production Supervisors
Scott Brigante, Michael Rosenstein

Database Keyboarding Supervisor
Miriam E. Palmerola

Database Keyboarding
Raymond V. Coffey, Lori Galvin,
Britney K. Gress, M. Madeleine Newell,
Meredith B. Phelan

Manufacturing Supervisor
Greg Mroczek

Production Coordinator
Nancy Priest

Production Assistants
Christina M. Granados, Donna Muise

Administrative Assistants
Elaine A. Gottlieb, Lauren B. Hunnewell,
Gladymir Veillard

Text Design
Textart, Inc.
Creatives, Inc.

Introduction

We have made *The American Heritage Student Dictionary* for you, students in grades 6 through 9. It is a completely new book. The entry list is based on the books, magazines, encyclopedias, and other printed materials actually read by students of your age. We carefully examined every entry in the previous edition and revised most entries to be easier to understand or to reflect how words are used today. We designed the Dictionary to be informative, easy to use, and fun to read. Here are some of the things the Dictionary can help you do:

Keep up-to-date. Your Dictionary contains the very latest vocabulary. It has roughly 5,000 new words—words such as *African-American*, *neurotransmitter*, *laptop*, and *wetland*. It also has thousands of new senses added to existing words, as the computer sense of *mouse*.

Expand your vocabulary. One hundred Synonym Paragraphs identify words with similar meanings and distinguish the shades of meaning among groups of related words.

Learn about the history of words. Etymologies provide useful information on the origins of 6,000 words in a simple, straightforward style. More than 60 Word History Notes tell in detail the stories of words of particular interest. You can follow the trail of words that have come into English through several different languages. You can discover why words with the same spelling have different meanings and how words with very different spellings sometimes go back to the same word in an ancient language.

Understand words by understanding their parts. Over 80 Word Building Notes help you to understand difficult words. Some Notes show how prefixes and suffixes affect the meanings of various words. Other Notes show how words with a common root, such as the *–pose–* in *compose* and *transpose*, have a central meaning that is a result of a common origin in an ancient language.

Get advice on how to write well. Nearly 100 Usage Notes point out common problems that every writer must deal with and give advice on how to solve them. What is the difference between *credible* and *credulous* or *affect* and *effect*? Should you always say *Whom am I speaking to*? Or is *Who am I speaking to* acceptable? The Usage Notes answer these and many other questions.

Learn how things have different names in different places. Did you know that you get the same sandwich whether you order a *hoagie* in Philadelphia, a *poor boy* in New Orleans, or a *bomber* in upstate New York? Regional Notes identify words that are used in certain regions of the country and add spice to our language.

Learn more about people and places. An entirely new program of biographical entries includes accomplished men and women of many different backgrounds. In addition, Biographical Notes tell the stories of many key figures in history. A series of Geographical Notes explains how the 50 U.S. states got their names. Still other Notes provide information about important places in a rapidly changing world.

See for yourself. The definitions in this Dictionary are illustrated by 2,000 photographs and drawings that not only make it easier to understand what words mean, but also make you want to see more! These and other useful features make *The American Heritage Student Dictionary* a book that will increase your knowledge about words and excite your curiosity to learn more. So read and enjoy!

Elements of the Dictionary

entry word

bea•con (bē′kən) *n.* **1.** A guiding or warning signal, such as a lighthouse located on a coast. **2.** A radio transmitter that sends a guidance signal for aircraft. **3.** A source of guidance or inspiration: *Her achievements were a beacon to others.* **4.** A fire set as a signal or warning of an enemy's approach. [First written down about 725 in Old English and spelled *bēacen.*]

sense number

definition

Marginal Art

caption

beaker
Measuring liquid into a beaker

bead (bēd) *n.* **1.** A small, often round piece of glass, wood, plastic, or other material that is pierced for placing on a string or wire. **2. beads.** A necklace of beads on a string. **3. beads.** A rosary. **4.** A small round object, such as a drop of moisture: *beads of sweat on one's forehead.* **5.** A small knob of metal located at the muzzle of a rifle or pistol and used in taking aim. *—tr. & intr.v.* **bead•ed, bead•ing, beads.** To furnish with or collect into beads: *bead the collar around a sweater; water beading on the soda can.* ***—idiom.*** **draw a bead on.** To take careful aim at. [First written down about 725 in Old English and spelled *gebed*, prayer.]

part-of-speech label

beak (bēk) *n.* **1.** The hard, horny, projecting structure forming the mouth of a bird; a bill. **2.** A similar, often horny, part in other animals. Turtles and octopuses have beaks. **3.** A projecting part that resembles a bird's beak. [First written down before 1250 in Middle English and spelled *bec*, from Latin *beccus*, of Celtic origin.]

etymology

beak•er (bē′kər) *n.* **1.** A cylindrical glass container with a pouring lip, used especially in laboratories. **2.** A large drinking cup with a wide mouth. [First written down about 1380 in Middle English and spelled *bekir*, from Medieval Latin *bicārium.*]

ber•ke•li•um (bər kē′lē əm *or* bûrk′lē əm) *n. Symbol* **Bk** A radioactive metallic element produced artificially from americium, curium, or plutonium. It has 9 isotopes with mass numbers ranging from 243 to 250 and half-lives ranging from 3 hours to 1,380 years. Atomic number 97. See table at **element.** [First written down in 1950 in Modern English, after *Berkeley*, California.]

symbol

Table cross-reference

be•sides (bĭ sīdz′) *adv.* **1.** In addition; also: *We had dinner and a late-night snack besides.* **2.** Moreover; furthermore: *It was time to go; besides, I was getting bored.* *—prep.* **1.** In addition to: *Dentists do other things besides drilling cavities.* **2.** Other than; except for: *There's nothing to eat here besides a little cheese.* —SEE NOTE at **together.**

Note cross-reference

Synonyms: besides, too, also, likewise, furthermore. These adverbs mean in addition to something else. **Besides** often introduces something that reinforces what has gone before it: *We don't feel like cooking; besides, there is no food in the house.* **Too** is the most casual, used in everyday speech: *If you're going to the library today, I'd like to go too.* **Also** is more formal than **too**: *Al is usually very friendly, but he is also capable of bearing a grudge.* **Likewise** is even more formal: *Their parents were likewise attending the ceremony.* **Furthermore** often stresses the clause following it as more important than the preceding clause: *I don't want you to go to that place; furthermore, I forbid it.*

Synonym Paragraph

Mary McLeod Bethune

Be•thune (bə tho͞on′ *or* bə thyo͞on′), **Mary McLeod.** 1875–1955. American educator and reformer. In 1935 she founded the National Council of Negro Women, serving as its president until 1949.

biographical entry

bet·ter[1] (bĕt′ər) *adj.* Comparative of **good. 1.** Greater in excellence or higher in quality than another of the same kind: *Which of the twins is the better skater?* **2.** More useful, suitable, or desirable: *I know a better way to go.* **3.** Larger; greater: *It took the better part of an hour to get there.* **4.** Healthier than before: *Many days passed before I began to feel better.* —*adv.* Comparative of **well[2]. 1.** In a more excellent way: *He sings better than his father.* **2.** To a greater extent or larger degree: *I like fish better when it's broiled.* **3.** More: *The play was first performed better than 20 years ago.* —*n.* **1.** The superior of two: *Both are good, but which is the better?* **2.** A superior: *I leave the delicate work to my betters.* —*v.* **bet·tered, bet·ter·ing, bet·ters.** —*tr.* **1.** To surpass or exceed: *The old record stood until another athlete bettered it.* **2.** To make better; improve: *The purpose of education is to better ourselves.* —*intr.* To become better: *Conditions bettered with time.* —***idioms.*** **better off.** In a better condition: *With vaccines, people are better off than they were years ago.* **for the better.** Resulting in or aiming at an improvement. **had better.** Ought to; must: *We had better leave before dark.* [First written down about 725 in Old English and spelled *betera.*] —SEE NOTE.
❑ *These sound alike.* **better[1], bettor** (one who bets).

bet·ter[2] (bĕt′ər) *n.* Variant of **bettor.**

be·twixt (bĭ twĭkst′) *adv. & prep.* Between. —***idiom.*** **betwixt and between.** In an intermediate position; neither wholly one thing nor another.

BeV *abbr.* An abbreviation of billion electron volts.

big (bĭg) *adj.* **big·ger, big·gest. 1.** Of great size, number, quantity, or extent; large: *a big house; a big city; a big appetite.* See Synonyms at **large. 2.a.** Grown-up; adult: *Most big people are kind to young children.* **b.** Older: *Big brothers and sisters must look out for the little children in a family.* **3.** Prominent; influential: *a big banker.* **4.** Of great significance; momentous: *a big day in my life; practice for the big game.* **5.** Loud; resounding: *a big voice.* **6.** Full of self-importance; boastful: *a big talker.* —*adv.* With an air of self-importance; boastfully: *talk big about what one is going to do.* —***idiom.*** **big on.** Enthusiastic about; partial to: *She's big on volleyball.* [First written down about 1300 in Middle English, perhaps of Scandinavian origin.] —**big′ness** *n.*

big-heart·ed (bĭg′här′tĭd) *adj.* Generous; kind. —**big′-heart′ed·ly** *adv.* —**big′-heart′ed·ness** *n.*

big·horn (bĭg′hôrn′) *n., pl.* **big·horn** or **big·horns.** A wild mountain sheep of western North America, having large curving horns in the male; the Rocky Mountain sheep.

bi·o·eth·ics (bī′ō ĕth′ĭks) *n.* (*used with a singular verb*). The study of the problems of behavior and conduct in biological and medical research.

Bish·kek (bĭsh′kĕk *or* bēsh′kĕk). Formerly **Frun·ze** (frōōn′zə). The capital of Kirghiz, in the north-central part of the republic west of Alma-Ata, Kazakhstan. Population, 604,000.

Bk The symbol for the element **berkelium.**

breath·er (brē′*th*ər) *n. Informal.* A short period of rest.

breth·ren (brĕ*th*′rən) *n.* A plural of **brother** (sense 2).

bron·to·saur (brŏn′tə sôr′) or **bron·to·sau·rus** (brŏn′tə sôr′əs) *n.* A very large dinosaur that lived in swamps and streams and fed on plants during the Jurassic period. [First written down in 1879 in Modern English and spelled *brontosaurus* : Greek *brontē*, thunder + Greek *sauros*, lizard.]

Marginal Note

Usage: better[1]

The phrase *had better*, meaning "must, ought," is acceptable only as long as the *had* or *'d*, the contraction of *had*, is present. You can say *You had better do it* or *You'd better do it* but not *You better do it.*

bighorn

pronunciation
inflected forms
idioms
homophones
homograph
abbreviation entry
run-on entry
usage label
geographical entry
symbol entry
sense-specific cross-reference
Marginal Note reference
cross-reference
illustrative examples
status label
variant

Guide to Using the Dictionary

This Guide is designed to help you find and understand the information contained in this Dictionary.

Guidewords

This dictionary has just one alphabetical list. It presents all entries, including single words, phrases, hyphenated compounds, abbreviations, proper names, prefixes, and suffixes. To help you find the word you want to look up, we have put a pair of boldface guidewords at the top of each page in this book:

bravura / break

The guideword to the left of the slash represents the first boldface entry on that page. The guideword to the right of the slash represents the last boldface entry on that page. Thus, the entry words *bravura* and *break* and all entries that fall between them are listed on the page that has these guidewords.

The Entry Word

The word or phrase you look up in the dictionary is called an *entry word* or an *entry*, or sometimes a *main entry*. The entry words are printed in boldface a little to the left of the rest of the column. They are listed in alphabetical order. Words that begin with the same letter are put into alphabetical order using their second letter, or, if the first two letters are the same, the third letter, and so on, as is shown in the list below:

beagle
beak
beaker
beam

Some entries consist of more than one word. These may be written as phrases, such as *water buffalo* and *water color*, or as hyphenated compounds, such as *baby-sit* and *heavy-duty*. Such phrases and compounds are listed in alphabetical order as if they were written as one word.

Superscript Numbers

Some words have identical spellings but different meanings and histories. These words, called *homographs*, are entered separately. Each has a superscript, or raised, number printed after the entry word:

sole^1 (sōl) *n.* **1.** The bottom surface of the foot. **2.** The bottom surface of a shoe or boot, often excluding the heel.
sole^2 (sōl) *adj.* **1.** Being the only one; single; only: *Her sole purpose in coming is to see you.* **2.** Belonging or relating exclusively to one person or group: *She took sole command of the ship.*
sole^3 (sōl) *n., pl.* **sole** or **soles.** Any of various flatfishes related to the flounders and used as food.

Syllabication

Entry words of more than one syllable are divided into syllables by centered dots:

clas•si•cal (klăs′ĭ kəl) *adj.*

Inflected and derived forms are also divided into syllables:

clas•si•fy (klăs′ə fī′) *tr.v.* **clas•si•fied, clas•si•fy•ing, clas•si•fies. 1.** To arrange in classes or assign to a class; sort; categorize: *A librarian classifies books according to subject matter.* **2.** To designate (information) as available only to authorized persons. **—clas′si•fi′a•ble** *adj.* **—clas′si•fi′er** *n.*

At entries that consist of two or more words, centered dots are omitted for words that are divided into syllables at their own place as main entries in the Dictionary:

Con•es•to•ga wagon (kŏn′ĭ stō′gə) *n.*

Thus, the word *wagon*, which is a separate entry, has no centered dots at the entry for *Conestoga wagon*.

The syllabication of an entry word reflects the traditional practices of printers and editors in breaking words at the end of a line. Pronunciations are divided into syllables according to the way a word is pronounced. Therefore, the syllabication of an entry word may not match that of its pronunciation:

serv•ice (sûr′vĭs) *n.*

Variants

Some words have two or more different spellings. The variant spelling or spellings are shown in boldface after the entry word. The word *or* indicates that both spellings are used with equal frequency:

> **ad•vis•er** or **ad•vi•sor** (ăd vīʹzər) *n.*

The word *also* joining an entry word and variant form indicates that the variant form is used less frequently than the main entry word:

> **an•es•the•sia** also **an•aes•the•sia** (ănʹĭs **thēʹ**zhə) *n.*

Variants that do not fall immediately before or after their main entry word in alphabetical order are entered at their own alphabetical places:

> **an•aes•the•sia** (ănʹĭs **thēʹ**zhə) *n.* Variant of **anesthesia.**

British variants. A number of variants consist of spellings preferred in England and other parts of the United Kingdom. These variants, such as *defence* and *colour,* have the label *Chiefly British*. They are entered at their own alphabetical places but are not given as variants at the entries to which they refer:

> **de•fence** (dĭ **fĕnsʹ**) *n. & v. Chiefly British.* Variant of **defense.**

Parts of Speech

The following italicized labels indicate parts of speech:

adj.	adjective
adv.	adverb
conj.	conjunction
def. art.	definite article
indef. art.	indefinite article
interj.	interjection
n.	noun
prep.	preposition
pron.	pronoun
v.	verb

Plurals are indicated by the label *pl.* The label *pl.n.* appears at entries for words, such as *clothes* and *cattle,* that are only used in the plural.

These italicized labels are used for the traditional classification of verbs:

tr.	transitive
intr.	intransitive
aux.	auxiliary

A transitive verb is a verb that requires a direct object to complete its meaning. *Enforce* and *foster* are examples of transitive verbs. An intransitive verb never takes an object; verbs such as *rejoice* and *tremble* are intransitive. Many verbs, of course, can be transitive or intransitive depending on how they are used. An auxiliary verb, such as *have* or *may,* is used with another verb to make a tense, mood, or voice.

The labels for word elements are:

pref.	prefix
suff.	suffix

Entries that are abbreviations, such as *A.M.* and *blvd.*, are labeled *abbr.*

Certain entries do not carry part-of-speech labels. They include contractions (*I'll*), symbols (*I*², the symbol for *iodine*), trademarks (*Band-Aid*), and biographical and geographical entries (George *Washington* or *Washington*, D.C.).

Parts of Speech in Combined Entries

Many words can be used as more than one part of speech. For example, *paint* can be both a verb (as in *to paint a wall*) and a noun (as in *a gallon of paint*). In such cases, the different parts of speech are defined in a single entry called a *combined entry.* In an entry of this kind, each part of speech receives its own part-of-speech label. Each part of speech that follows the first part of speech is preceded by a dash.

If a piece of information, such as a pronunciation or a status label, appears before the first part of speech in an entry, that piece of information applies to all parts of speech in that entry. Labels and pronunciations appearing after a part of speech apply to that part of speech only. Some entries, such as *rebel,* have a different syllabication and pronunciation for each part of speech.

> **re•bel** (rĭ **bĕlʹ**) *intr.v.* **re•belled, re•bel•ling, re•bels. 1.** To refuse loyalty to and oppose by force an established government or a ruling authority. **2.** To resist or defy an authority or a generally accepted convention: *rebelled against wearing a tie in summer.* —*n.* **reb•el** (**rĕbʹ**əl). A person who rebels or is in rebellion.

Inflected Forms

An inflected form of a word differs from the main entry form by the addition of a suffix or by a change in the normal spelling of the main entry. Thus, the verb *walk* forms its past tense, *walked,* by the addition of the suffix *–ed,* and *swim* forms its past tense *swam* by changing its spelling.

In this Dictionary, inflected forms are

given in full. They appear in boldface, are syllabicated, and have pronunciations when necessary. An inflected form immediately follows the part-of-speech label or the number of the definition to which it applies.

Principal parts of verbs. The principal parts of verbs are entered in this order: *past tense*, *past participle*, *present participle*, and *third person singular present tense.*

> **fly**[1] (flī) *v.* **flew** (flo͞o), **flown** (flōn), **fly•ing, flies** (flīz).

When the past tense and the past participle are identical, one form represents both. For example, *walked* is the past tense and past participle of the verb *walk*:

> **walk** (wôk) *v.* **walked, walk•ing, walks.**

Comparison of adjectives and adverbs. Adjectives and adverbs that form the comparative and superlative degrees by adding *–er* and *–est* show these forms in full immediately after the part-of-speech label:

> **high** (hī) *adj.* **high•er, high•est. 1.a.** Being a relatively great distance above a certain level, as above sea level or the surface of the earth: *These high mountains are over 15,000 feet.* . . . *—adv.* **higher, highest.** At, in, or to a high position, level, or degree: *Hawks fly high in the sky.*

Irregular comparative and superlative forms are also given in full:

> **good** (go͝od) *adj.* **bet•ter** (bĕt′ər), **best** (bĕst).

Plural forms of nouns. Regular plurals formed by adding the suffixes *–s* or *–es* to a noun are not normally shown in this Dictionary, but irregular plurals are always shown following the label *pl.*:

> **mouse** (mous) *n., pl.* **mice** (mīs).

When a noun has a regular and an irregular plural form, both forms appear, with the most common form shown first:

> **cer•e•brum** (sĕr′ə brəm *or* sə rē′brəm) *n., pl.* **cer•e•brums** or **cer•e•bra** (sĕr′ə-brə, sə rē′brə).

Regular plurals are also shown when spelling might be a problem:

> **po•ta•to** (pə tā′tō) *n., pl.* **po•ta•toes.**

Sometimes inflected forms apply only to certain senses of a word. In such cases, the inflected form appears in boldface after the sense number or letter to which it applies:

> **fly**[1] (flī) *v.* **flew** (flo͞o), **flown** (flōn), **fly•ing, flies** (flīz). *—intr.* . . . **7.** *past tense and past participle* **flied.** In baseball, to hit a fly ball.

From this example you can see that the verb *fly* usually has the past tense *flew* and the past participle *flown*, but when used in baseball it has *flied* as its past tense and past participle.

Separate Entries for Inflected Forms

Irregular inflected forms involving a change in spelling of the main form of a word are entered separately when they fall more than one entry away from the main entry form. Thus, *flew*, the past tense of *fly*, and *men*, the plural of *man*, both have their own entries:

> **flew** (flo͞o) *v.* Past tense of **fly**[1].
>
> **men** (mĕn) *n.* Plural of **man.**

The Dictionary does not normally give separate entries for inflected forms of words ending in *–y*, such as *berry*, *happy*, and *carry*, because forms such as *berries*, *happiest*, and *carried* entail a regular, easily recognized change in spelling. However, this Dictionary does enter inflected forms of words having only one syllable ending in *–y*, because the change in spelling affects the base form of the word:

> **dri•est** (drī′ĭst) *adj.* A superlative of **dry.**
>
> **spied** (spīd) *v.* Past tense and past participle of **spy.**

Labels

This Dictionary uses labels to identify words and meanings whose use is limited in some way—to a particular style of expression, for example, or to a geographical region. When a label applies to all parts of an entry it appears before the first part of speech:

> **snitch** (snĭch) *Slang. v.* **snitched, snitch•ing, snitch•es.** *—tr.* To steal (something of little value): *snitch candy.* *—intr.* To tell on someone; turn informer: *snitched on his brother.* *—n.* **1.** A thief. **2.** An informer. **—snitch′er** *n.*

Thus the positioning of the label *Slang* in the preceding example means that both the noun and verb senses of the word are slang.

A label may apply only to a single part of speech, in which case it follows the part-of-speech label. Sometimes a label applies only to a single definition or subdefinition, in which case it follows the sense number or letter to which it applies:

> **hot** (hŏt) *adj.* **hot•ter, hot•test.** . . . **7.** *Informal.* Most recent; new or fresh: *a hot piece of news.*

In this entry, the label *Informal* applies only to sense 7.

Status Labels

Status labels indicate that an entry word or a definition is limited to a particular level or style of usage. All words and definitions not restricted by such a label should be regarded as appropriate for use in all contexts.

Non-Standard. This, the most restrictive label in the Dictionary, applies to forms and usages that educated speakers and writers consider unacceptable:

> **ir•re•gard•less** (ĭr′ĭ gärd′lĭs) *adv. Non-Standard.* Regardless.

Slang. This label indicates a style of language that uses extravagant, often humorous expressions as a means of making an effect. Some forms of slang occur in most educated speech but not in formal discourse. An example of a word labeled *Slang* follows:

> **rin•ky-dink** (rĭng′kē dĭngk′) *Slang. adj.* **1.** Old-fashioned; worn-out. **2.** Of cheap or poor quality. **3.** Unimportant.

Informal. Words that people use commonly in conversation and in informal writing but not in formal writing are identified by the label *Informal.* Informal words are ones you might use in a letter to a friend but should not use in a letter to a teacher, business, or newspaper, for example:

> **fish•y** (fĭsh′ē) *adj.* **fish•i•er, fish•i•est.** **1.** Tasting, resembling, or smelling of fish. **2.** Cold or expressionless: *a fishy stare.* **3.** *Informal.* Inspiring doubt or suspicion: *something fishy about that excuse.* **—fish′i•ness** *n.*

Offensive. This label is reserved for words and expressions that are not only derogatory and insulting to the person to whom they are directed but are also a discredit to the one using them.

Temporal Label

The Temporal label *Archaic* signals words or senses that once were common but are now rare:

> **fain** (fān) *adv.* Willingly or gladly. *—adj. Archaic.* Willing or glad.

English-Language Labels

These labels identify an entry as a form whose use is restricted to specific areas of the English-speaking world:

> **lor•ry** (lôr′ē *or* lŏr′ē) *n., pl.* **lor•ries.** *Chiefly British.* A motor truck.

> **bairn** (bârn) *n. Scots.* A child.

Cross-References

A cross-reference is a word referring you to another word. It signals that more information can be found at another entry. A cross-reference is helpful in avoiding the repetition of information at two entries, and also serves to indicate where further discussion of a word occurs.

The word referred to in a cross-reference appears in bold type and is preceded by a short phrase:

> **bade** (băd *or* bād) *v.* A past tense of **bid.**

This cross-reference tells you that *bade* is a past tense of the word *bid.* This indicates that more information about the entry can be found at *bid.*

A cross-reference referring to only one sense of a word having more than one sense contains that sense number:

> **tzar** (zär *or* tsär) *n.* Variant of **czar** (sense 1).

This cross-reference tells you that *tzar* is a variant spelling of *czar,* but refers only to sense 1.

Some cross-references refer to tables. The word or words in bold type tell you where the table can be found:

> **Mes•o•zo•ic** (mĕz′ə zō′ĭk *or* mĕs′ə zō′-ĭk) *adj.* Of, belonging to, or being the third era of geologic time, including the Triassic, Jurassic, and Cretaceous Periods. . . . See table at **geologic time.**

Other cross-references refer you to a note that appears at another entry:

> **huge** (hyo͞oj) *adj.* **hug•er, hug•est.** Of great size, extent, or quantity; tremendous: *a huge iceberg; a huge difference.* See Synonyms at **large.**

> **brook**[1] (bro͝ok) *n.* A small natural stream of fresh water. [First written down about 847 in Old English and spelled *brōc.*] —See Note at **run.**

These cross-references tell you that there is more information about the word in a note at another entry.

Order of Senses

Entries having more than one sense are arranged with the central meanings first. The central meaning of a word will most often be the meaning you are seeking. In addition, senses and subsenses that are related in meaning are grouped together. For example, in the entry for *nice* shown below, the commonly sought meaning "Good; pleasant; agreeable" appears first and the less common sense "Able to notice small differences" comes as sense 6b:

> **nice** (nīs) *adj.* **nic•er, nic•est. 1.** Good; pleasant; agreeable: *a nice play to stay.* **2.** Having a pleasant appearance; attractive: *a nice dress.* **3.** Courteous and polite; considerate: *It's nice of you to help.* **4.** Morally upright; respectable. **5.** Done with skill and delicacy: *a nice bit of work.* **6.a.** Requiring the ability to notice small differences: *a nice distinction.* **b.** Able to notice small differences: *a nice ear for music.* **7.** Used as an intensive with *and*: *nice and warm.*

Division of senses. Letters that appear in bold type before senses show that two or more subsenses are closely related:

> **prin•ci•pal** (prĭn′sə pəl) *adj.* First or foremost in rank, degree, or importance; chief: *the principal character in the story.* —*n.* **1.** A person who holds a leading position, especially the head of an elementary school or high school. **2.** A main participant, as in a business deal. **3.a.** A financial holding as distinguished from the interest or revenue earned from it. **b.** A sum of money owed as a debt, on which interest is calculated.

When an entry has more than one part of speech, the definitions are numbered in separate sequence beginning with each new part of speech:

> **dream** (drēm) *n.* **1.** A series of mental images, ideas, and emotions occurring during sleep: *awake from a happy dream.* **2.** A daydream. **3.** A state of abstraction; a trance: *wandering about in a dream.* **4.** A hope or an aspiration: *dreams of world peace.* **5.** Something especially gratifying, excellent, or useful: *The new car runs like a dream.* —*v.* **dreamed** or **dreamt** (drĕmt), **dream•ing, dreams.** —*intr.* **1.** To have a dream while sleeping. **2.** To daydream: *dreaming of far-off places.* **3.** To consider as feasible or practical: *I wouldn't even dream of going.* —*tr.* **1.** To have a dream of during sleep: *Did it storm last night, or did I dream it?* **2.** To conceive of; imagine: *We never dreamed it might snow so hard.* **3.** To pass (time) idly or in daydreaming.

Usage phrases. Some noun entries have added information that tells you whether the word takes a singular or plural verb or whether it can take either a singular or a plural verb. This information appears as a usage phrase in italics before the sense or part of speech that it applies to:

> **ge•net•ics** (jə nĕt′ĭks) *n.* **1.** *(used with a singular verb).* The branch of biology that deals with the principles of heredity and the variation of inherited characteristics among similar or related organisms. **2.** *(used with a plural verb).* The genetic makeup of an individual or a group.

In the entry *genetics* above, the usage phrase tells you that sense 1 takes a singular verb only and sense 2 takes a plural verb only.

Forms That Apply to Specific Senses

Information such as an inflected form that applies only to a particular sense or subsense is shown after the number or letter of that sense or subsense:

> **broth•er** (brŭ*th*′ər) *n., pl.* **broth•ers. 1.** A boy or man having the same mother and father as another person. **2.** Often **brethren** (brĕ*th*′rən). **a.** A person who shares common ancestors, a common allegiance to a country, or a common purpose with another or others. **b.** A fellow member of a group, such as a profession, fraternity, or labor union. **3.** A member of a men's Christian religious order who is not a priest.

In this entry the plural form *brethren* applies only to the second sense of brother. For the other senses, the plural is *brothers.*

Some nouns have senses in which they are usually used in the plural. In these cases, the boldface plural form of the noun appears just before the definition to show you that it is used in the plural:

> **jack** (jăk) *n.* . . . **5.a. jacks.** *(used with a singular or plural verb).* A game in which each player in turn bounces and catches a small ball while picking up small six-pointed metal pieces with the same hand.

In this entry, the sense of *jack* that refers to the game occurs only in the plural form *jacks.*

The same style is used for any change in

the form of a word as it shifts from one sense to another:

> **Af•ghan** (ăf′găn′ *or* ăf′gən) *adj.* Of or relating to Afghanistan or the Afghans. —*n.* **1.** A native or or inhabitant of Afghanistan. **2. afghan.** A colorful wool blanket or shawl knitted or crocheted in squares, circles, or other designs.

Here the boldface lowercase form of the word appears just before the definition it applies to, telling you that in this sense the word only occurs in the lowercase form *afghan.*

Illustrative Examples of Definitions

In addition to giving clear definitions of words, this Dictionary also gives you thousands of examples showing how a word is used in context. These examples are especially useful for illustrating figurative senses of a word, transitive and intransitive verbs, and multiple senses of very common words:

> **a•round** (ə round′) *adv.* **1.** On all sides or in all directions: *We drove around looking for a parking place.* **2.** In a circle or circular motion: *The skater spun around twice.* **3.** In circumference: *a pond two miles around.* **4.** In or toward the opposite direction: *The horse turned around and ran toward the barn.* **5.** From one place to another; here and there: *wander around.* **6.** In or near one's current location: *He waited around all day.* **7.** To a specific place or area: *when you come around again.* **8.** Approximately; about: *Around 20 rafts floated down the Rio Grande.*

> **do**[1] (dōō) *v.* **did** (dĭd), **done** (dŭn), **do•ing, does** (dŭz). —*tr.* **1.** To perform, carry out, or accomplish: *Do a good job. Do your duty.* **2.a.** To create, produce, or make: *do a painting; do a report.* **b.** To create or produce for an audience: *The actors did a new play.* **3.** To bring about; effect: *Crying won't do any good.* **4.** To put into action; exert: *I'll do everything in my power to help you.* **5.** To deal with as is necessary; take care of: *do one's hair; do the dishes.* **6.** To render or give: *do a favor.* **7.** To work at for a living: *What work do you do?* **8.** To work out the details of; solve (a problem): *I did this equation.* **9.a.** To travel (a specified distance): *do a mile in 15 minutes.* **b.** To travel at a speed of: *He was only doing 50 on the highway.* **10.** To be sufficient or convenient for; suffice: *This room will do us very nicely.* **11.** *Informal.* To serve (a prison term). *Both did time for theft.* —*intr.* **1.** To behave or conduct oneself; act: *You did well on the test.* **2.** To get along; manage; get on: *The new student is doing well.* **3.** To serve a purpose: *That old coat will do for now.* **4.** Used instead of a preceding verb: *She reads as much as I do.*

Idioms

An *idiom* is a group of words whose meaning as a group cannot be understood from the meanings of the individual words in the group. In this Dictionary, idioms are defined at the entry for the first important word in the phrase. For example, *walk on air* is defined at *walk.*

In this Dictionary, idioms appear at the very end of the definitions of an entry in alphabetical order. Each idiom is shown in boldface. A single idiom is preceded by the introductory label ***idiom.*** A series of idioms is identified by the label ***idioms.*** Verbs especially form many idioms with adverbs or prepositions, as this example shows:

> **take** (tāk) *v.* **took** (to͝ok), **tak•en** (tā′kən), **tak•ing, takes.** . . . —***idioms.*** **take advantage of. 1.** To put to good use; avail oneself of: *take advantage of the sale.* **2.** To use unfairly and selfishly; exploit: *They took advantage of our friendship just to get a ride to the movies.* **take after.** To resemble in appearance, temperament, or character: *He takes after his grandfather.* **take apart.** To divide into parts; disassemble: *We had to take the chair apart to refinish it.* **take back.** To retract something stated or written: *I took back my promise when I saw I had been cheated.* **take care.** To be careful: *Take care when you cross the street.* **take care of.** To assume responsibility for the maintenance, support, or treatment of: *I'm taking care of the puppy now.* **take charge.** To assume control or command. **take effect.** To become operative, as under law or regulation: *The new rules are to take effect today.* **take five** or **take ten.** *Slang.* To take a short rest or break, as of five or ten minutes. **take for. 1.** To regard as: *Many take him for a genius.* **2.** To consider mistakenly: *The teacher took me for my sister.* **take for granted. 1.** To consider as true, real, or forthcoming; anticipate correctly: *took it for granted that he would pass the test.* **2.** To underestimate the value of. **take hold. 1.** To seize, as by grasping. **2.** To become established: *The new shrubs took hold on the hill.*

This Dictionary lists only nonliteral or unusual senses of idioms. Thus in the example below *back out,* meaning "to retire or withdraw from something," is defined in that sense, but not in the sense "to leave a parking lot in reverse." You should be able to figure out this latter meaning of the phrase by the meanings of the two words themselves, and therefore we do not define it:

back (băk) *n.* . . . **—idioms. back down.** To withdraw from a stand that one has taken: *There was an argument because neither side was willing to back down.* **back off.** To retreat or retire, as from a dangerous position. **back out.** To retire or withdraw from something: *They accepted the invitation but backed out at the last minute.* **back up. 1.** To make a copy of (a computer program or file). **2.** To accumulate: *Traffic backed up at the intersection.* **behind (one's) back.** When one is not present: *Don't talk about me behind my back.*

Etymology

Many entries in this Dictionary have etymologies that show when a word was first written down in English and, in many cases, what language or languages it came from. The etymology appears in brackets near the end of the entry.

school[1] (sko͞ol) *n.* **1.** An institution for teaching and learning. . . . [First written down before 899 in Old English and spelled *scōl*, from Latin *schola*, from Greek *skholē*.]

The etymology begins by giving the date when the word was first written down in the English language. This date is the best evidence we have for knowing when a word entered the language. Most words are used in conversation before someone writes them down, so the actual date when a word was first used in English is in many cases somewhat earlier. By knowing the date of a word's first written occurrence you can know how old a word is. In the example given above, you can see that *school*[1] is a very old word, first recorded in a document that scholars have determined was written before the year 899. Other words, such as scientific terms or terms used in technology, are relatively young. Many have existed for only a few decades.

The second piece of information in an etymology tells you whether the date of a word's first occurrence is in Old English, Middle English, or Modern English, since these are the three main divisions of the history of the English language. The word *school*[1] goes back to Old English, which lasted from about 450 until about 1100, or before English was much influenced by French.

The third piece of information presented in an etymology is the form of the word as it appeared when it was first written down. Thus, the word for "school" in Old English was spelled *scōl*. The original spelling is given so that you can see how the word has changed since its first appearance. If an etymology does not provide an original spelling, this means that the word's original spelling is the same as its present spelling. If a word originally had a different meaning from the one it has today, we also provide that meaning as a gloss:

deer (dîr) *n., pl.* **deer.** Any of various hoofed mammals, such as the elk and the white-tailed deer, that chew their cud and usually have antlers in the males. [First written down before 899 in Old English and spelled *dēor*, beast.]

This etymology tells you that the word *deer* originated in Old English but meant "beast," that is, any animal. The word's meaning has since narrowed to refer only to certain kinds of beasts.

Most words have come into English from other languages, and this information is given next in the etymology. Thus, in the example of *school*[1] presented above, the speakers of Old English got their word from the Latin word *schola*, which itself came from a Greek word, *skholē*. So our modern word *school*[1] ultimately goes back to ancient Greek but shows the influence of Latin as well.

Words that come from compound words in other languages can best be understood by breaking down the compound into its parts. In the etymology, a colon introduces these parts, as in the following example:

con•tain (kən tān′) *tr.v.* **con•tained, con•tain•ing, con•tains. 1.** To have within; hold: *Orange juice contains vitamin C.* . . . [First written down before 1300 in Middle English and spelled *conteinen*, from Latin *continēre* : *com-*, together + *tenēre*, to hold.]

Here you can see that our word *contain* goes back to the Latin compound *continēre*. This compound has two parts: the prefix *com-*, meaning "together," and the verb *tenēre*, meaning "to hold." So from an analysis of its history the word *contain* means basically "to hold together." Thus, a box might contain or "hold together" many different things.

Run-On Entries

This Dictionary includes many additional words formed from an entry word by the addition of a suffix and located at the end of the entry. These run-on entries are obviously related to the main entry word and have the same essential meaning, but they have different endings and different parts of speech. Run-on entries appear in boldface followed by a part-of-speech label. Syllabication and stress are indicated on all run-on words of more than one syllable, and pronunciations are given where needed.

> **re•gret•ful** (rĭ grĕt′fəl) *adj.* Full of regret; sorrowful or sorry. **—re•gret′ful•ly** *adv.* **—re•gret′ful•ness** *n.*

When two or more run-on forms have the same part of speech, they are separated by a comma and have a single part-of-speech label:

> **rap•id** (răp′ĭd) *adj.* **rap•id•er, rap•id•est.** Fast; swift: *rapid progress; walking with rapid strides.* . . . **—ra•pid′i•ty** (rə pĭd′ĭ tē), **rap′id•ness** *n.* **—rap′id•ly** *adv.*

Homophones

Some words, such as *cent, scent,* and *sent,* sound the same, but have different spellings and meanings. These words are called *homophones.* To help you keep track of these words, the Dictionary provides a list of words that sound alike at the end of each entry for a homophone. The homophones are listed in alphabetical order with the main entry word first, preceded by the phrase *These sound alike.* Each homophone following the main entry in the list has a word or phrase enclosed in parentheses that identifies its meaning. Proper nouns and foreign words are not entered as homophones.

> **row**[1] (rō) *n.* **1.** A series of persons or things placed next to each other, usually in a straight line: *a row of poplar trees.* **2.** A line of adjacent seats, as in a theater. **3.** A succession without a break or gap in time: *won the title for three years in a row.* **4.** A continuous line of buildings along a street. [First written down in 940 in Old English and spelled *rāw.*]
> ❑ *These sound alike:* **row**[1] (series), **rho** (Greek letter), **roe**[1] (fish eggs), **roe**[2] (small deer), **row**[2] (use oars).

In the entry *row*[1], you can see that the words *row*[1], *rho, roe,* and *row*[2] all sound alike.

Synonym Paragraphs

This Dictionary has 100 Synonym Paragraphs that list and describe words that have similar meanings. Each Paragraph follows the entry for the central word of each synonym group. The Paragraphs are introduced by the heading *Synonyms* and the synonyms themselves appear in boldface. A list of antonyms, or words with meanings opposite those of the synonyms, appears when applicable in boldface at the end of the Paragraph.

There are two kinds of Paragraphs. The first gives a central meaning shared by the synonyms in the list, and illustrative examples for each word:

> Synonyms: **help, aid, assist.** These verbs mean to contribute to fulfilling a need, furthering an effort, or achieving a purpose. **Help** and **aid** are the most general: *A new medicine has been developed to help* (or *aid*) *digestion.* **Help** often means to aid in an active way: *I'll help you move the sofa.* **Assist** often means to play a secondary role in aiding: *A few of the students assisted the professor in researching the data.*

The second kind explains the varying shades of meaning that distinguish the synonyms and shows how these words are used in context:

> Synonyms: **obstinate, stubborn, mulish, headstrong.** These adjectives mean determinedly unwilling to yield. **Obstinate** means unreasonably rigid and difficult to persuade: *Jenny is obstinate about doing things in her own way.* **Stubborn** and **mulish** can mean perversely unyielding by nature: *Robert is too stubborn to admit he was wrong. It's mulish of you to refuse to look at the map until after we're lost.* **Headstrong** means stubbornly, often recklessly willful: *That headstrong child will never follow advice.* Antonyms: **cooperative, flexible.**

Every word that is discussed in a Synonym Paragraph has at its own entry a cross-reference to the entry that has the Synonym Paragraph. Thus, the entry for *headstrong* has a cross-reference to the Synonym list presented at *obstinate*:

> **head•strong** (hĕd′strông′ *or* **hĕd′**-strŏng′) *adj.* **1.** Inclined to insist on having one's own way; stubbornly and recklessly willful: *a proud and headstrong person.* See Synonyms at **obstinate.**

Marginal Notes

In the margins of this Dictionary you will find a variety of notes providing fuller information about individual words. These notes describe how words are and should be used, where words come from, and how their meanings can be deciphered from an understanding of their parts. Some notes supply additional information about certain entries—information that is too extensive to be included in a definition. The words *See Note* at the end of an entry direct you to a note in the margin discussing that entry.

In the text of the notes, words that appear in boldface are entry words in this Dictionary. Words that are discussed in the note but for some reason have not been entered in the Dictionary appear in italic.

Usage Notes. Some words are easily confused with others or present difficulties in how they should be used. These entries have Usage Notes that provide explanations and offer advice on how to avoid or solve usage problems. Here is a typical Usage Note:

Usage: affect¹

The words **affect** and **effect** look and sound similar. Their meanings, however, are very different. The verb **affect** means "to influence": *That decision will affect my whole life.* The verb **effect** means "to make happen": *We effected some helpful changes.* The noun **effect** can mean "a result" or "an influence," but only the verb **affect** means "to influence."

When a word is discussed in a Usage Note in the margin next to an entry elsewhere in the book, it has a cross-reference to that entry. Thus, at *effect* you are directed to the note at *affect¹*, where *effect* is also discussed.

ef•fect (ĭ fĕkt′) *n.* **1.** Something brought about by a cause or an agent; a result: *The effect of advertising should be an increase in sales.* . . . [First written down about 1350 in Middle English, from Latin *effectus*, past participle of *efficere*, to accomplish : *ex-*, out + *facere*, to make.] —SEE NOTE at **affect¹**.

Word Histories. In addition to etymologies, this Dictionary provides paragraphs that tell the story of many words that have an interesting past. Some notes explain how a word has moved from one language to another before coming into English. Others explain how words that are spelled differently in fact have a common origin. Still others explain the processes by which words change or develop new meanings. An example of a Word History Note can be found at the entry *quick*:

Word History: quick

When your father yells up the stairs at you to "look alive," you know he means to "be quick." **Quick** comes from the Old English adjective *cwic*, pronounced [kwĭk], which means "alive." This sense is now obsolete except in the phrase *the quick and the dead*, which means "the living and the dead." In Middle English the word *quik* develops the senses "lively, active, swift," which is what your father wants you to be in the first place. A similar development takes place in French. The French adverb *vite* means "quickly," and it comes from the Latin word *vīta*, meaning "with life." The Latin word *vīta* is also the source of **vital** and **vitamin**.

Word Building Notes. Word Building Notes help you understand how word parts are joined together to make longer, more complex words. There are two kinds of Word Building Notes: Affix Notes and Word Root Notes. Affix Notes show how prefixes and suffixes are attached to words to make new words. These notes often describe the history of the affix, which in many cases goes back to Latin or Greek:

Word Building: trans–

The prefix **trans–** goes back to the Latin prefix *trāns–*, from the Latin preposition *trāns*, meaning "across, beyond, through." Many of the most common English words beginning with **trans–** are derived from Latin words or elements, as in **transfer**, **transfuse**, **translate**, **transmit**, **transpire**, and **transport**. Another large group of words has **trans–** in combination with English adjectives, as in **transatlantic**, **transcontinental**, **transoceanic**, **transpacific**, and **transpolar**, with the meaning "across" or "through" a particular geographic element.

Word Root Notes describe how Greek and Latin roots form the heart of many words that have different but related meanings:

Word Building: compose

The word root *–pose–* in English comes from the French verb *poser*, "to put." **Compose** therefore literally means "to put together" (using the prefix *com–*, "with, together"); **propose** is literally "to put forward" (*prō*, "forward, in front"); **expose** means "to put out" (*ex–*, "out, out of"); **impose** is literally "to put upon" (*im–*, a form of *in–²*, "in, on"). French developed from Latin, and the French verb *poser* is a replacement of an earlier Latin verb *ponere.* The past participle of *ponere* is *positus*, from which is formed the Latin noun *positio*, "position." It is from this Latin noun that we form the English noun forms that correspond to the verbs, that is, **composition**, **proposition**, **exposition**, **imposition**.

Regional Notes. One of the most interesting aspects of English is that things are often called by different names in different places. Regional Notes discuss terms that are limited to certain areas of the United States. For example, the word *dragonfly* is common throughout the United States for this insect, but in some areas other names are used as well, as the note at *dragonfly* reveals:

Regional Note: dragonfly

People have different names for the same thing depending on where they live. What most people in the United States call a **dragonfly** is known by other names in various parts of the country. In the southern states the most common term is *snake doctor* because of the folk belief that dragonflies care for snakes. In the middle part of the United States we find the name *snake feeder.* In some parts of the South some people call it a *mosquito hawk* or a *skeeter hawk.* People in some parts of the northern states call it a *darning needle* or a *devil's darning needle.* Those in coastal New Jersey call it a *spindle*, and in Northern California they say *ear sewer* (from the belief that it could sew up ears).

Many of these regional terms, such as *snake doctor*, are not used in Standard English and so have not been entered at their own place in the Dictionary.

Other Notes. Biographical Notes tell a more detailed story about the accomplishments of important people, such as Thomas Jefferson and Ida B. Wells, identified at certain entries.

Geographical Notes tell how the 50 U.S. states and the Canadian provinces and territories came to have the names they do. Other geographical notes provide background information for geographical names that might present difficulty, as *Union of Soviet Socialist Republics*, for example.

Science Notes supply background information and often dispel commonly held misconceptions about terms used in science, such as *acid rain* and *vitamin.*

Pronunciation

The pronunciation, which is enclosed in parentheses, appears immediately after the boldface entry word. If an entry word and a variant of that entry word have the same pronunciation, the pronunciation follows the variant. If the variant or variants do not have the same pronunciation as the entry word, pronunciations follow the forms to which they apply. If a word has more than one pronunciation, the pronunciations are separated within the parentheses by *or*. All pronunciations given are acceptable in all circumstances. When more than one pronunciation is given, the first is assumed to be the most common, but often they are equally common. Differing pronunciations are given within an entry wherever necessary, as when there is a change in part of speech and in other special cases.

A full Pronunciation Key appears on page xix. A shorter form of this Key appears in a block in the margin of every other page. The set of symbols used is designed to enable the user to reproduce a satisfactory pronunciation with no more than a quick reference to the Key.

Stress

In this Dictionary, stress, or the relative degree of emphasis with which the syllables of a word (or phrase) are spoken, is indicated in three different ways. An unmarked syllable has the weakest stress in the word. The strongest, or *primary*, stress is marked with a bold mark (**ʹ**). The syllable that receives the primary stress is set in boldface type. An intermediate level of stress, here called *secondary*, is marked with a lighter mark (ʹ). Words of one syllable show no stress mark, since there is no other stress level to which the syllable is compared.

Pronunciation Key

A list of the pronunciation symbols used in this Dictionary is given here in the column headed **Symbols**. The column headed **Examples** contains words chosen to illustrate how the symbols are pronounced. The letters that correspond in sound to the symbols are shown in boldface.

The nonalphabetical symbol (ə) is called *schwa*. It is used to represent a reduced vowel, a vowel that receives the weakest level of stress within a word. The schwa sound varies, sometimes according to the vowel it is representing and often according to the sounds surrounding it:

a•bun•dant (ə **bŭn′**dənt)
mo•ment (**mō′**mənt)
civ•il (**sĭv′**əl)
pro•pose (prə **pōz′**)
grate•ful (**grāt′**fəl)

Note that the consonants *l* and *n* in English can constitute complete syllables by themselves. Some examples of words in which syllabic *l* and *n* occur are **needle** (nēd′l), **rattle** (răt′l), **sudden** (sŭd′n), and **rotten** (rŏt′n).

Foreign Symbols. These symbols are used infrequently in this Dictionary, but they do occur, primarily in some foreign place names and expressions. The sound represented by (œ) is made in the front of the mouth. To make the (œ) sound the lips must be rounded, as if you are going to make the sound (ō), but instead you make the sound (ā). The sound represented by (ü) is also made in the front of the mouth. To make the (ü) sound the lips must also be rounded, as if you are going to make the sound (o͞o), but instead you make the sound (ē). The sound represented by (KH) is made in the back of the mouth. This sound is similar to a (k), but the air is forced through continuously, not stopped as with a (k). And the symbol (N) shows that the preceding vowel is nasalized—that is, air escapes through the nose (as well as the mouth) when you say it. Strictly speaking, English does not have nasal vowels, but it does have nasal consonants such as *m* and *n*.

Symbols	Examples
ă	p**a**t
ā	p**ay**
âr	c**are**
ä	f**a**ther
b	**b**i**b**
ch	**ch**ur**ch**
d	**d**ee**d**, mill**ed**
ĕ	p**e**t
ē	b**ee**
f	**f**i**f**e, **ph**ase, rou**gh**
g	**g**a**g**
h	**h**at
hw	**wh**oop
ĭ	p**i**t
ī	p**ie**, b**y**

Symbols	Examples
îr	d**ear**, d**eer**, p**ier**
j	**j**u**dge**
k	**k**i**ck**, **c**at, pi**que**
l	**l**id, needl**e**
m	**m**u**m**
n	**n**o, sudd**en**
ng	thi**ng**
ŏ	p**o**t
ō	t**oe**
ô	c**augh**t, p**aw**, f**o**r
oi	n**oi**se
o͝o	t**oo**k

Symbols	Examples
o͞o	b**oo**t
ou	**ou**t
p	**p**o**p**
r	**r**oa**r**
s	**s**au**c**e
sh	**sh**ip, di**sh**
t	**t**igh**t**, stopp**ed**
th	**th**in
th	**th**is
ŭ	c**u**t
ûr	**ur**ge, t**er**m, f**ir**m, w**or**d, h**ear**d
v	**v**al**v**e

Symbols	Examples
w	**w**ith
y	**y**es
z	**z**ebra, **x**ylem
zh	vi**s**ion, plea**s**ure, gara**ge**
ə	**a**bout, it**e**m, ed**i**ble, gall**o**p, circ**u**s
ər	butt**er**

Foreign Symbols

œ	*French* f**eu**
ü	*French* t**u**
KH	*Scottish* lo**ch**
N	*French* bo**n**

Capitalization, Punctuation, and Style Guide

This section of the Dictionary sets forth the basic points of style used in written and printed American English. The rules for the correct use of capital letters, punctuation marks, numbers, and italics or underlining are grouped together under headings and subheadings for easy reference. Each rule is illustrated with an example phrase or sentence.

At the end of this Guide you will find a brief section on the styling of bibliographical information. If you want to know more about any of the points discussed in the Guide, you should consult your grammar or composition textbook or one of the many style manuals available for writers and researchers.

Capitalization

Rules for capitalization

Capitalize the names of geographical entities, such as cities, states, and countries, and geographical features, such as rivers, mountains, and lakes:

Boston	Arctic Circle	Middle East	Connecticut River
Minnesota	Western Hemisphere	Gulf Coast	Lake Geneva
Brazil	South Pole	the South	Blue Ridge Mountains
Mountain States	Torrid Zone	the Midwest	Pacific Ocean

But do not capitalize directions:

We live ten miles west of Philadelphia.

Capitalize titles or their abbreviations when used with a person's name:

Governor Richards   Senator Garcia   Dr. Lin   President Clinton

Capitalize words showing a familial relationship when used with a person's name:

Uncle Bob
Grandmother Burrows
but
her uncle, Robert Smith
my grandmother, Dora Burrows

Capitalize words derived from proper names:

We ate at a Hungarian restaurant.
She is French.

Capitalize the names of nationalities, languages, religions, and tribes:

Canadian	Maori
Spanish	Bantu
Old English	Roman Catholic Church

Capitalize the names of months, holidays, and holy days:

Monday	Passover
January	Ramadan
Labor Day	Easter

Capitalize the names of specific school subjects when followed by a number:

History I
Geography 101

Capitalize the names of councils, congresses, organizations and their members, and historical periods and events:

the Free and Accepted Masons
a Mason
the Republican Party
the House of Representatives
the Potsdam Conference
the Battle of Bull Run
the Harlem Renaissance
the Middle Ages

Capitalize the names of streets, highways, buildings, bridges, and monuments:

Fifth Avenue
Route 9
World Trade Center
Vietnam Veterans Memorial
Golden Gate Bridge

Capitalize the first word and all words except conjunctions and prepositions of four letters or fewer and articles in the titles of documents and literary, dramatic, artistic, and musical works:

the novel *To Kill a Mockingbird*
the short story "The Necklace"
Bill of Rights
Robert Frost's poem "The Road Not Taken"
the play *A Raisin in the Sun*
Bartok's *Concerto for Orchestra*
an article entitled "The Exports of Italy"
Picasso's *Guernica*

Capitalize the first word of each main topic and subtopic in an outline:

I. Types of libraries
  A. Large public library
  B. Bookmobile
  C. School library
II. Library services

Capitalize the first word in the greeting and closing of a letter:

Dear Marcia,
Dear Ms. Olsen:
Your friend,
Sincerely yours,

Capitalize the first word of a direct quotation:

The candidate said, "Actions speak louder than words."
Who said "I think, therefore I am"?

Punctuation

End marks

A *period* (.) ends a declarative or imperative sentence. A *question mark* (?) follows an interrogative sentence. An *exclamation point* (!) is used after an exclamatory sentence and after an interjection that expresses strong feeling.

The scissors are on my desk. (declarative)
Look up the spelling of that word. (imperative)
How is the word spelled? (interrogative)
This is your best poem so far! (exclamatory)
Wow! We've just won the essay prize. (interjection)

Apostrophe

To form the possessive of a singular noun, add an apostrophe and *s*:

sister-in-law's   family's   Agnes's

To form the possessive of a plural noun that does not end in *s*, add an apostrophe and *s*:

women's   mice's   sisters-in-law's

To form the possessive of a plural noun that ends in *s*, add an apostrophe only:

sisters'   families'   Joneses'

Use an apostrophe and *s* to form the plural of letters, numerals, symbols, and words that are used as words:

s's   *i*'s   *2*'s   *'s
Fill in the questionnaire with *yes*'s and *no*'s.

Use an apostrophe in contractions in place of dropped letters:

isn't (is not)   they've (they have)   it's (it is)

Colon

Use a colon to separate the hour from the minute:

7:30 P.M.   8:15 A.M.

Use a colon after the greeting in a business letter:

Dear Mrs. Trimby: Dear Sir or Madam:

Use a colon before a list introduced by words such as *the following* or *these*:

Call the following: Hester, Wanda, Doyle, and Carl.

But do not use a colon after a verb or a preposition:

Next year I am taking English, history, and math.
He arrived with a suitcase, a coat, and an umbrella.

Comma

Use commas to separate words in a series:

Clyde asked if we had any apples, peaches, or grapes.

Use commas between two or more adjectives that come before a noun unless the adjectives are used together to express a single idea:

He had a solid, heavy gait.
but
The bird had shiny yellow feathers on its head.

Use a comma to separate the independent clauses in a compound sentence:

Some students were at lunch, but others were studying.

Use commas after words, phrases, and clauses that come at the beginning of sentences:

No, you cannot avoid the deadline.
Following the applause, the speaker continued.
When you are in doubt, ask for advice.

Use commas to separate interrupters such as *of course*, *however*, and *by the way* from the rest of the sentence:

Maureen, of course, was late for the bus again.
The driver, however, had forgotten the directions.

Use commas to set off an appositive from the rest of the sentence when the appositive is not necessary to the meaning of the sentence:

Texas, the Lone Star State, borders Mexico.
(The appositive is extra, not needed for meaning.)
but

The writer Charles Dickens created complex plots.
(The appositive is necessary to the meaning.)

Use commas to set off a nonessential phrase or clause—one that adds optional information not necessary to the meaning of the sentence. If a phrase or clause is essential, do not use commas:

Emily Dickinson, who was born in 1830, was a poet.
(The clause is not necessary to the meaning.)
The man who read the poem is my father.
(The clause is necessary to the meaning.)

Use a comma to set off a word in direct address:

Thank you, Joe, for your help.
How was your trip, Mom?

Use a comma to separate the month and day from the year. Use a comma to separate the year from the rest of the sentence. Do not use commas if a specific day is not included:

January 12, 1994, was the date of the banquet.
but
Halley's Comet appeared last in April 1986.

Use a comma after an interjection that expresses emotion:

Oh, I didn't see you there!

Use a comma to set off short quotations and sayings:

Jo told him, "Come tomorrow for dinner."
"I don't know if I can," he said, "but maybe I will."

Use a comma between the names of a city and a state in an address. If the address is within a sentence, also use a comma after the name of the state. Do not use a comma before the ZIP code:

Does Chicago, Illinois, have the world's tallest building?
Denise lives at 10 Palm Court, Lima OH 45807-3212.

Use a comma after the greeting in a personal letter and after the closing in all letters:

Dear Deena,
Sincerely yours,

Semicolon

Use a semicolon to connect independent clauses that are closely related in thought or have commas within them:

There were five movie tickets left; Ed needed six.
He bought nuts, dates, and figs; we ate them all.

Use a semicolon to join two independent clauses when the second clause begins with an adverb such as *however, therefore*, or *consequently*:

It was growing dark; however, there were no clouds.

Hyphens, Dashes, and Parentheses

Use a hyphen to join the parts of compound numbers, to join two or more words that work together as one adjective before a noun, or to divide a word at the end of a line:

thirty-two   long-range plans
Raphael is known as one of Italy's many magnificent painters.

Use a dash to show a sudden change of thought:

The sky grew dark—it might mean snow.

Use parentheses to enclose unnecessary information:

Geraldine was reelected (once more) as treasurer.

Quotation marks

Use quotation marks to set off titles of short stories, articles, songs, poems, and book chapters:

"The Party" (short story)
"Crewelwork" (article)
"America" (song)
"If" (poem)
"Saxon Art" (chapter)

Use quotation marks to enclose direct quotations:

"What was Berlin like during the war?" she asked.
Eleanor Roosevelt said, "We must do the things we think we cannot do."

Numbers

Spell out numbers *zero* through *ten* and *first* through *tenth* and numbers at the beginning of a sentence. Use numerals for numbers over *ten* or *tenth*:

My team has 25 players.
Two hundred people were in the audience.
There are 147 apartments in my building.
It happened in the tenth century B.C.
He came in 14th out of 200.

Italics

Titles of books, magazines, newspapers, long musical works and poems, plays, works of art, movies, and TV series are italicized:

In a Pickle (book)
Miami Herald (newspaper)
Requiem (musical work)
As You Like It (play)
Mona Lisa (painting)
Nature (TV series)

Use italics to indicate a word, number, or letter used as such:

The word *straight* has two *t*'s.
A *6* looks like an inverted *9*.

Use italics to distinguish the New Latin names of genera and species in botany and zoology:

Homo sapiens (human being)
Phaseolus vulgaris (string bean)

Use italics to set off the names of ships, planes, and often spacecraft:

U.S.S. *Kitty Hawk*
Spirit of St. Louis
Voyager II

In word processed, typewritten, or handwritten copy, as in an essay or a book report, italics are indicated by underlining:

Melville's <u>Moby Dick</u>

the movie <u>The Wizard of Oz</u>

Bibliography

The basic organization of a bibliography is alphabetical. If the author's name is not given, list the title first, and alphabetize it by the first important word of the title.

Books

List the author's name (last name first), the book title, the city where the publisher is located, the publisher's name, and the year of publication. Note the punctuation.

Winkler, Connie. *The Computer Careers Handbook.* New York: Arco Publishing, 1983.

Encyclopedia articles

List the author's name (last name first), then the title of the article (in quotation marks). Next, give the title of the encyclopedia (in italics or underlined), and the year of publication of the edition you are using. Note the punctuation.

Shields, Dianne. "Learning Disabilities." *The World Book Encyclopedia.* 1992 ed.

If the author of the article is not given, begin your listing with the title of the article.

"Rhododendron." *New Encyclopaedia Britannica.* 1991 ed.

Magazine and newspaper articles

When listing an article from a magazine or newspaper, give the information in the following order: author, article title, magazine or newspaper title, volume number, date, section number, and pages. A colon always precedes the page numbers. Note the punctuation in the examples below.

MAGAZINE: Clift, Eleanor. "Battle Scars." *Newsweek* 8 Feb. 1993: 22.

NEWSPAPER: Wright, Patricia. "The Power of Political Art." *Daily Hampshire Gazette* 4 March 1993, sec. 3: 19, 21.

If the author of the article is not given, begin your listing with the title of the article.

"Ultrasound Computer Gives Look Inside Heart." *Boston Globe* 16 March 1993:12.

A a

a[1] or **A** (ā) *n., pl.* **a's** or **A's.** **1.** The first letter of the English alphabet: *There are three a's in alfalfa.* **2.** Something shaped like the letter A. **3. A.** The best or highest grade: *get an A on a report; grade A eggs.* **4. A.** In music, the sixth tone in the scale of C major. **5.** The first in a series or group: *row A in a theater.* **6. A.** One of the four types of blood in the ABO system.

a[2] (ə; ā *when stressed*) *indef. art.* **1.** One: *I didn't say a single word.* **2.** The same: *Birds of a feather flock together.* **3.** Any: *A cat will always eat fish.* **4.** An example of a kind of: *Water is a liquid.* —See Note at **article.**

a[3] (ə) *prep.* In each; for each; per: *once a month; ten dollars a trip.*

a–[1] *pref.* A prefix that means without or not: *amoral; atypical.* —See Note.

a–[2] *pref.* A prefix that means: **1.** On or in: *abed; aboard.* **2.** In the direction of: *astern.* **3.** In a particular condition: *afire.*

Aa•chen (ä'kən *or* ä'KHən). A city of western Germany near the Belgian and Dutch borders. Charlemagne may have been born here in 742. Population, 239,801.

aard•vark (ärd'värk') *n.* A burrowing mammal of Africa having long claws and a long, sticky tongue with which it feeds on insects.

Aar•on (âr'ən *or* ăr'ən). In the Bible, the elder brother of Moses who helped lead the Hebrews out of Egypt.

AB (ā'bē') *n.* One of the four types of blood in the ABO system.

A.B. *abbr.* An abbreviation of Artium Baccalaureus (Bachelor of Arts).

ab•a•ca (ăb'ə kä') *n.* A plant resembling the banana that is native to the Philippines and has broad leaves and long stalks.

ab•a•ci (ăb'ə sī') *n.* A plural of **abacus.**

a•back (ə băk') *adv.* By surprise: *I was taken aback by his angry words.*

ab•a•cus (ăb'ə kəs) *n., pl.* **ab•a•cus•es** or **ab•a•ci** (ăb'ə sī'). A computing device consisting of a frame holding parallel rods with sliding beads. The abacus is used in China, Japan, and Korea.

a•baft (ə băft') *adv.* Toward a ship's stern: *It was fast sailing with the wind abaft.* —*prep.* Toward the stern from: *The cargo hatch is abaft the mainmast.*

ab•a•lo•ne (ăb'ə lō'nē) *n.* Any of various edible mollusks that have a large shallow shell lined with mother-of-pearl.

a•ban•don (ə băn'dən) *tr.v.* **a•ban•doned, a•ban•don•ing, a•ban•dons. 1.** To leave and not intend to return; desert: *abandon a sinking ship.* **2.** To give up completely; stop trying to accomplish: *They abandoned the attempt to climb the mountain.* See Synonyms at **yield. 3.** To yield (oneself) to an impulse or emotion: *Don't abandon yourself to despair.* —*n.* A yielding to one's impulses or emotions: *We skied down the hill with abandon.* —**a•ban'don•ment** *n.*

a•ban•doned (ə băn'dənd) *adj.* **1.** Deserted or given up; forsaken: *During the snowstorm the highway was littered with abandoned cars.* **2.** Wicked or immoral: *an abandoned life.*

a•base (ə bās') *tr.v.* **a•based, a•bas•ing, a•bas•es.** To lower in rank, dignity, or reputation; humble or degrade: *Lying abases one's reputation.* —**a•base'ment** *n.*

a•bash (ə băsh') *tr.v.* **a•bashed, a•bash•ing, a•bash•es.** To make ashamed or uneasy; embarrass: *The teacher was abashed by her careless mistake.*

a•bate (ə bāt') *v.* **a•bat•ed, a•bat•ing, a•bates.** —*tr.* To reduce in amount, degree, or intensity: *The horse galloped around the curve without abating his speed.* —*intr.* To become less in degree or intensity: *The storm abated.* —**a•bate'ment** *n.*

ab•bess (ăb'ĭs) *n.* A nun who is the head of a convent.

ab•bey (ăb'ē) *n., pl.* **ab•beys. 1.** A monastery or convent. **2.** A church that once belonged to a monastery, especially in Great Britain.

ab•bot (ăb'ət) *n.* A monk who is the head of a monastery.

abbr. *abbr.* An abbreviation of abbreviation.

ab•bre•vi•ate (ə brē'vē āt') *v.* **ab•bre•vi•at•ed, ab•bre•vi•at•ing, ab•bre•vi•ates.** —*tr.* **1.** To reduce (a word or group of words) to a shorter form by leaving out some of the letters: *abbreviate* hour *to* hr. **2.** To shorten: *abbreviate a long explanation.* —*intr.* To use abbreviations or shorten by abbreviation: *No one will understand your writing if you abbreviate so much.* [First written down before 1425 in Middle English and spelled *abbreviaten,* to shorten, from Late Latin *abbreviāre* : *ad-,* to + *breviāre,* to shorten.]

ab•bre•vi•a•tion (ə brē'vē ā'shən) *n.* **1.** The act or process of abbreviating; abridgement: *His abbreviation of the story left out many details.* **2.** A shortened form of a word or group of words, for example, *Mr.* for *Mister* and *U.S.A.* for *United States of America.*

ABC (ā'bē sē') *n., pl.* **ABC's. 1.** The alphabet. Often used in the plural: *learn one's ABC's.* **2.** The basic facts of a subject. Often used in the plural: *After learning the ABC's of arithmetic most students are ready for algebra.*

ab•di•cate (ăb'dĭ kāt') *v.* **ab•di•cat•ed, ab•di•cat•ing, ab•di•cates.** —*tr.* To give up (power or responsibility) formally: *abdicate the throne.* —*intr.* To give up power or responsibility: *The king abdicated to allow his son to take over.* —**ab'di•ca'tion** *n.* —**ab'di•ca'tor** *n.*

ab•do•men (ăb'də mən *or* ăb dō'mən) *n.* **1.a.** In human beings and other mammals, the front part of the body from below the chest to about where the legs join, containing the stomach, intestines, and other vital organs. **b.** The corresponding part of other vertebrates: *the green abdomen of a garter snake.* **2.** The last part of the body of an insect, an arachnid, or a crustacean: *A bee's stinger is in its abdomen.* [First written down in 1541 in Modern English, from Latin *abdōmen,* belly.]

ab•dom•i•nal (ăb dŏm'ə nəl) *adj.* Of, in, or relating

Word Building: a–[1]

The basic meaning of the prefix **a–** is "without." For example, **achromatic** means "without color." Before vowels and sometimes *h*, **a–** becomes *an–*: **anaerobic**. Many of the words beginning with this prefix are used in science, such as **aphasia**, **anoxia**, and **aseptic**. It is important not to confuse **a–** with other prefixes, such as **ad–**, that begin with the letter *a*.

aardvark

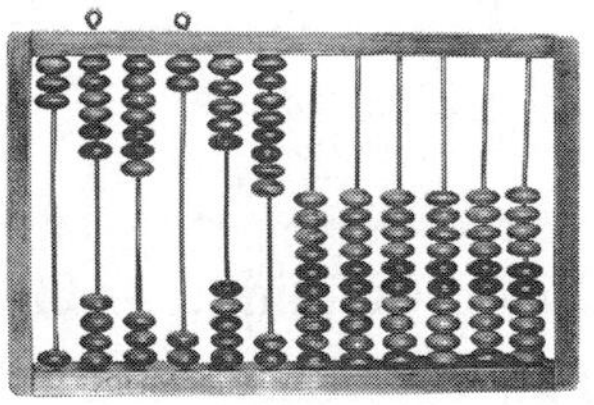

abacus

ă	pat	oi	boy
ā	pay	ou	out
âr	care	ŏŏ	took
ä	father	ōō	boot
ĕ	pet	ŭ	cut
ē	be	ûr	urge
ĭ	pit	th	thin
ī	pie	*th*	this
îr	pier	hw	whoop
ŏ	pot	zh	vision
ō	toe	ə	about
ô	paw	N	*French* bon

Aberdeen Angus

Word Building: –able

The suffix **-able**, which forms adjectives, comes from the Latin suffix *–ābilis*, meaning "capable or worthy of." Thus a **likable** person is one who is capable of or worthy of being liked. The suffix **–ible** is closely related to **–able** and has the same meaning, as in **flexible**. Since they sound exactly alike, it is important to consult your dictionary when spelling words that end in this suffix.

to the abdomen: *abdominal muscles.* —**ab•dom′i•nal•ly** *adv.*

ab•duct (ăb dŭkt′) *tr.v.* **ab•duct•ed, ab•duct•ing, ab•ducts.** To carry away by force; kidnap.

ab•duc•tor (ăb dŭk′tər) *n.* **1.** A person who abducts; a kidnapper. **2.** A muscle that draws an arm or leg away from a line that runs down the middle of the body or the middle of a hand or foot.

a•beam (ə bēm′) *adv.* **1.** Directly opposite the middle of a ship's side. **2.** At right angles to the keel of a ship.

a•bed (ə bĕd′) *adv.* In bed: *She lay abed with a cold.*

A•bel (ā′bəl). In the Bible, the son of Adam and Eve who was killed by his elder brother, Cain.

Ab•e•na•ki (ä′bə nä′kē *or* ăb′ə năk′ē) *n., pl.* **Abenaki** or **Ab•e•na•kis. 1.** A member of any of various Native American peoples of northern New England and southeast Canada. **2.** Either of the Algonquian languages of the Abenaki.

Ab•er•deen (ăb′ər dēn′). A city of northeast Scotland on the North Sea. It is known as "the Granite City" because stone from local quarries is used in many of its buildings. Population, 212,542.

Aberdeen An•gus (ăng′gəs) *n.* A breed of black hornless cattle originally developed in Scotland and raised chiefly for beef.

ab•er•rant (ă bĕr′ənt) *adj.* Differing from what is normal, right, or typical: *aberrant behavior.*

ab•er•ra•tion (ăb′ə rā′shən) *n.* **1.** A departure or a differing from what is normal, right, or typical: *Wearing a tie to work is an aberration for him.* **2.** A mental disorder or lapse. **3.** A deviation in the normal structure or number of chromosomes in an organism. **4.** The failure of a lens, mirror, or telescope to bring rays of light coming from a source, such as a star, to a single focus, causing a distorted or blurred image. **5.** The apparent change in the position of a celestial object caused by the motion of the earth during the time it takes for light from the object to reach an observer on earth.

a•bet (ə bĕt′) *tr.v.* **a•bet•ted, a•bet•ting, a•bets.** To encourage or help: *They have abetted our efforts to build a new gym.* —**a•bet′ment** *n.*

a•bet•tor or **a•bet•ter** (ə bĕt′ər) *n.* A person who encourages or helps someone else.

a•bey•ance (ə bā′əns) *n.* A state or condition of being put off to a later time; a postponement or temporary suspension: *Let's hold the plan in abeyance until we know more about the details.*

ab•hor (ăb hôr′) *tr.v.* **ab•horred, ab•hor•ring, ab•hors.** To feel disgust or hatred for; regard with horror or loathing: *I abhor getting into needless arguments.* —**ab•hor′rer** *n.*

ab•hor•rence (ăb hôr′əns *or* ăb hŏr′əns) *n.* **1.** A feeling of disgust or hatred: *an abhorrence or prejudice.* **2.** Something regarded with disgust or loathing: *Cheating in any form is an abhorrence.*

ab•hor•rent (ăb hôr′ənt *or* ăb hŏr′ənt) *adj.* Causing disgust or loathing; hateful; horrible: *an abhorrent crime.*

a•bide (ə bīd′) *v.* **a•bode** (ə bōd′) or **a•bid•ed, a•bid•ing, a•bides.** —*tr.* **1.** To put up with; bear; tolerate: *Most gardeners can't abide weeds.* **2.** To wait patiently for; await. —*intr.* **1.** To remain; stay: *Abide with me until the storm passes.* **2.** To live in a place; reside; dwell: *The happy couple abide in that old house.* **3.** To last; endure: *Generations come and go, but the earth abides.* —***idiom.*** **abide by.** To submit to; comply with: *We abided by the terms set forth in the agreement.* [First written down before 1200 in Old English and spelled *ābīdan.*] —**a•bid′er** *n.*

a•bid•ing (ə bī′dĭng) *adj.* Continuing; lasting; permanent: *The doctor had an abiding faith in good nutrition.*

Ab•i•djan (ăb′ĭ jän′). The capital and largest city of Ivory Coast, in the southern part of the country on an enclosed lagoon of the Gulf of Guinea. Population, 1,500,000.

Ab•i•lene (ăb′ə lēn′). A city of west-central Texas west-southwest of Fort Worth. Abilene was founded in 1881 with the coming of the railroad. Population, 106,654.

a•bil•i•ty (ə bĭl′ĭ tē) *n., pl.* **a•bil•i•ties. 1.** The power to do something: *Monkeys don't have the ability to speak.* **2.** A skill or talent: *a famous violinist of great musical ability.*

–ability or **–ibility** *suff.* A suffix that means ability, preference, or appropriateness for some action or condition: *acceptability; accessibility.*

ab•ject (ăb′jĕkt′ *or* ăb jĕkt′) *adj.* **1.** Deserving contempt; base: *an abject coward.* **2.** In a low condition; miserable; wretched: *Medieval serfs lived in abject poverty.* —**ab′ject′ly** *adv.* —**ab•ject′ness** *n.*

ab•jure (ăb jo͝or′) *tr.v.* **ab•jured, ab•jur•ing, ab•jures.** To vow to give up; renounce; repudiate: *New citizens adjure allegiance to their former country.* —**ab′ju•ra′tion** *n.* —**ab•jur′er** *n.*

ab•la•tion (ă blā′shən) *n.* The carrying off of excess heat by the melting away of the outer surface of a nose cone or heat shield of a rocket or spacecraft as it reenters the atmosphere.

a•blaze (ə blāz′) *adj.* **1.** On fire; in flames; blazing: *The barn was ablaze.* **2.** Brightly shining: *During the celebration the sky was ablaze with fireworks.* —**a•blaze′** *adv.*

a•ble (ā′bəl) *adj.* **a•bler, a•blest. 1.** Having the power, ability, or means to do something: *He is able to work part-time after school.* **2.** Capable; talented: *Most cats are extremely able hunters.* [First written down about 1375 in Middle English, from Latin *habēre*, to handle.] —**a′bly** *adv.*

–able or **–ible** *suff.* A suffix that means: **1.** Capable of or likely to be affected by a certain action: *breakable; washable.* **2.** Worthy of a certain action: *honorable.* **3.** Inclined to a certain action: *variable.* —See Note.

a•ble-bod•ied (ā′bəl bŏd′ēd) *adj.* Physically strong and healthy.

able-bodied seaman *n.* A sailor certified and experienced in all the duties of a merchant seaman.

able seaman *n.* An able-bodied seaman.

a•bloom (ə blo͞om′) *adj.* In bloom; flowering.

ab•lu•tion (ə blo͞o′shən) *n.* A washing of the body, especially as part of a religious ceremony. Often used in the plural.

ab•ne•gate (ăb′nĭ gāt′) *tr.v.* **ab•ne•gat•ed, ab•ne•gat•ing, ab•ne•gates.** To renounce or give up; deny (something) to oneself: *A nun must abnegate the luxuries of life.*

ab•ne•ga•tion (ăb′nĭ gā′shən) *n.* A giving up one one's rights, interests, or desires; self-denial.

ab•nor•mal (ăb nôr′məl) *adj.* Differing from what is considered normal, usual, or expected, not standard or ordinary: *flooding caused by an abnormal amount of rain.* —**ab•nor′mal•ly** *adv.*

ab•nor•mal•i•ty (ăb′nôr măl′ĭ tē) *n., pl.* **ab•nor•mal•i•ties. 1.** The condition of not being normal. **2.** Something that is not normal: *I wear glasses because of abnormalities in my eyes.*

a•board (ə bôrd′) *adv.* On, onto, or in a ship, train, or other passenger vehicle. —*prep.* On, onto, or in: *life aboard ship.*

a•bode (ə bōd′) *v.* A past tense and a past participle of **abide.** —*n.* The place where one lives; a home. [First written down about 1200 in Middle English and spelled *abod*, home, from *abiden*, to wait, abide.]

a•bol•ish (ə bŏl′ĭsh) *tr.v.* **a•bol•ished, a•bol•ish•ing, a•bol•ish•es.** To put an end to; do away with:

Let's abolish the regulation that forbids eating in the study hall.

ab•o•li•tion (ăb′ə **lĭsh′**ən) *n.* **1.** The act or state of abolishing: *Many people favor an abolition of smoking.* **2.** Often **Abolition.** The abolishing of slavery in the United States.

ab•o•li•tion•ist (ăb′ə **lĭsh′**ə nĭst) *n.* **1.** A person who favors abolishing a custom, law, or practice. **2.** Often **Abolitionist.** A person who favored the abolition of slavery in the United States.

A-bomb (ā′bŏm′) *n.* An atomic bomb.

a•bom•i•na•ble (ə **bŏm′**ə nə bəl) *adj.* **1.** Causing disgust or hatred; detestable; horrible: *an abominable crime.* **2.** Thoroughly unpleasant or disagreeable: *The cold, windy day was abominable weather for a hike.* [First written down in 1340 in Middle English, from Latin *abōminārī*, to abhor.] **—a•bom′i•na•bly** *adv.*

abominable snowman *n.* A hairy animal that has been reported to exist in the Himalaya Mountains and is supposed to resemble a human being.

a•bom•i•nate (ə **bŏm′**ə nāt′) *tr.v.* **a•bom•i•nat•ed, a•bom•i•nat•ing, a•bom•i•nates.** To detest; abhor: *He abominates most modern architecture.*

a•bom•i•na•tion (ə bŏm′ə **nā′**shən) *n.* **1.** A feeling of hatred or disgust: *an abomination of cruelty.* **2.** Something that causes hatred or disgust: *Many of these ugly concrete buildings are abominations.*

ab•o•rig•i•nal (ăb′ə **rĭj′**ə nəl) *adj.* **1.** Of or relating to aborigines: *aboriginal customs.* **2.** Having existed in a region from the earliest times; native; indigenous: *aboriginal plants.* —*n.* An aboriginal plant or animal.

ab•o•rig•i•ne (ăb′ə **rĭj′**ə nē) *n.* A member of a group of people who are the first known to have lived in a region. [First written down in 1547 in Modern English, from Latin *aborīgines*, original inhabitants : *ab-*, from + *orīgō*, beginning.]

a•bort (ə **bôrt′**) *v.* **a•bort•ed, a•bort•ing, a•borts.** —*intr.* **1.** To give birth to an embryo or fetus before it has developed enough to survive. **2.** To end something, such as a rocket launch, before it is completed. —*tr.* **1.** To cause to be born at a stage of development too early to allow survival. **2.** To end before completion: *Heavy fog forced the pilot to abort the landing.*

a•bor•tion (ə **bôr′**shən) *n.* **1.** The birth of an embryo or fetus before it is developed enough to survive; miscarriage. **2.** Deliberate ending of a pregnancy and expulsion of an embryo or fetus that is incapable of survival. **3.** Something that fails to develop properly or come to completion as expected.

a•bor•tive (ə **bôr′**tĭv) *adj.* **1.** Not successful; fruitless: *an abortive revolution.* **2.** Partially or imperfectly developed: *an abortive organ.* **—a•bor′tive•ly** *adv.*

ABO system (ā′bē′ō′) *n.* A system for classifying human blood that uses four groups, A, B, AB, and O, to determine compatibility for transfusion.

a•bound (ə **bound′**) *intr.v.* **a•bound•ed, a•bound•ing, a•bounds. 1.** To be full; teem: *The forest abounds in wildlife.* **2.** To be present in large numbers; be plentiful: *Books abound on the library shelves.*

a•bout (ə **bout′**) *adv.* **1.** Approximately; roughly: *The river is about 600 yards wide.* **2.** Almost; nearly: *The new highway is just about completed.* **3.** To and fro: *Great waves tossed the ship about.* **4.** To or in a reverse direction: *Instantly the shark turned about.* **5.** In no particular direction: *We wandered about all afternoon.* **6.** Everywhere; all around: *looking about for a hiding place.* —*prep.* **1.** Concerning; having to do with; relating to: *stories about animals; the need to be careful about handling broken glass.* **2.a.** On the point of. Followed by the infinitive with *to*: *We are just about to go.* **b.** *Informal.* Anywhere near intending: *I'm not about to do anything he asks.* **3.** Near; close to: *She is about my size.* **4.a.** On all sides of; all around: *Thick fog is all about our boat.* **b.** Over different parts of; around: *a bear lumbering about the woods.* —*adj.* In circulation; astir: *School's closed, and there's no one about.* [First written down about 880 in Old English and spelled *onbūtan* : *on*, in + *būtan*, outside.]

a•bout-face (ə **bout′fās′**) *n.* **1.** The act of turning the body to face in the opposite direction, especially in a military drill. **2.** A change to an opposite attitude or opinion: *The candidate's abrupt about-face on that issue startled everyone.* —*intr.v.* **a•bout-faced, a•bout-fac•ing, a•bout-fac•es.** To do an about-face.

a•bove (ə **bŭv′**) *adv.* **1.** In or to a higher place; overhead. *Clouds floated above.* **2.** In an earlier part of a book, article, or other written piece: *in remarks quoted above.* —*prep.* **1.** Over or higher than: *seagulls hovering just above the waves; a tree that rises above the others.* **2.a.** Higher in rank, degree, or number: *The President is above all military officers.* **b.** Too honorable to undertake: *He is above telling a lie.* **3.** Farther on than; beyond: *The road is closed above the bridge.* **4.** Beyond the level or reach of: *The noise was audible above the music.* —*adj.* Appearing or stated earlier: *the above figures.* [First written down about 890 in Old English and spelled *abufan* : *a-*, on + *būfan*, above.]

above all *adv.* Over and above everything else: *truth above all.*

a•bove•board (ə **bŭv′**bôrd′) *adv. & adj.* Without deceit or trickery; open; honest: *In a democracy all dealings of government should be aboveboard.* [First written down in 1616 in Modern English and spelled *above-board*, originally a gamblling term referring to the fact that when gamblers' hands were above the board or gaming table, they could not engage in trickery, such as changing cards, below the table.]

ab•ra•ca•dab•ra (ăb′rə kə **dăb′**rə) *n.* **1.** A word once thought to have magical powers, especially of healing. **2.** Meaningless talk; foolish chatter.

a•brade (ə **brād′**) *tr.v.* **a•brad•ed, a•brad•ing, a•brades.** To rub off by scraping; wear down by rubbing: *Flowing water abrades rocks in a stream.*

A•bra•ham (ā′brə hăm′). In the Bible, the first patriarch of the Hebrew people. He was the husband of Sarah and the father of Isaac.

ab•ra•sion (ə **brā′**zhən) *n.* **1.** The act or process of scraping off or rubbing away. **2.** An injury in which part of the skin has been scraped or rubbed away: *abrasions on the knees from a bicycle spill.*

ab•ra•sive (ə **brā′**sĭv *or* ə **brā′**zĭv) *adj.* **1.** Causing a rubbing away or wearing off: *Sand is an abrasive substance.* **2.** Causing friction or resentment in people: *an abrasive personality.* —*n.* A substance used in rubbing, grinding, or polishing. **—a•bra′sive•ly** *adv.* **—a•bra′sive•ness** *n.*

a•breast (ə **brĕst′**) *adv.* Side by side in a line: *The band marched up the street four abreast.* ***—idiom.*** **abreast of** or **abreast with.** Up to date with: *keeping abreast of the latest news.*

a•bridge (ə **brĭj′**) *tr.v.* **a•bridged, a•bridg•ing, a•bridg•es. 1.** To reduce the length of; condense: *abridge a long novel by leaving out some chapters.* **2.** To limit; curtail: *The law was ruled unconstitutional because it abridged the rights of citizens.* [First written down about 1300 in Middle English and spelled *abregen*, from Late Latin *abbreviāre*, to shorten.]

a•bridg•ment also **a•bridge•ment** (ə **brĭj′**mənt) *n.*

ă	**p**a**t**	oi	**b**oy
ā	**p**a**y**	ou	**out**
âr	**c**are	ŏŏ	**t**oo**k**
ä	**f**a**ther**	ōō	**b**oo**t**
ĕ	**p**e**t**	ŭ	**c**u**t**
ē	**b**e	ûr	**u**r**ge**
ĭ	**p**i**t**	th	**th**in
ī	**p**ie	*th*	**th**is
îr	**p**ier	hw	**wh**oop
ŏ	**p**o**t**	zh	vi**s**ion
ō	**t**oe	ə	**a**bout
ô	**p**aw	N	*French* bo**n**

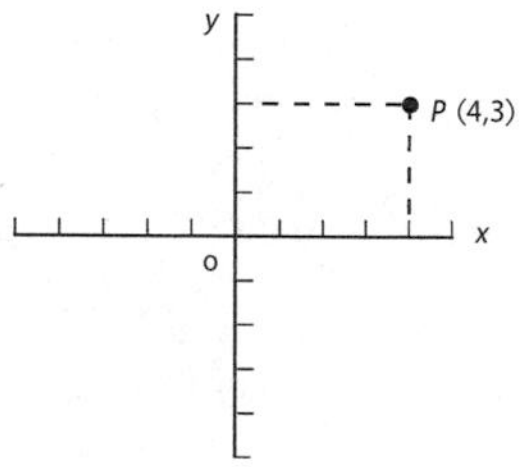

abscissa
P, abscissa 4; ordinate 3

1. The act of abridging or the condition of being abridged: *an abridgment of freedom.* **2.** An abridged version of something, such as a book or an article.

a•broad (ə **brôd′**) *adv. & adj.* **1.** Out of one's country; in or to foreign places: *traveling abroad.* **2.** Broadly or widely: *The wind scattered seeds abroad.* **3.** In circulation: *With rumors abroad soon the whole town was in an uproar.*

ab•ro•gate (ăb′rə gāt′) *tr.v.* **ab•ro•gat•ed, ab•ro•gat•ing, ab•ro•gates.** To annul (a law or privileges, for example); abolish: *War abrogated the treaty between the countries.* **—ab′ro•ga′tion** *n.*

a•brupt (ə **brŭpt′**) *adj.* **1.** Unexpected; sudden: *an abrupt change in temperature.* **2.** Very steep: *The path ends in an abrupt descent to the water.* **3.** Short and brief so as to suggest rudeness or displeasure; brusque: *an abrupt answer made in anger.* [First written down in 1583 in Modern English, from Latin *abruptus*, past participle of *abrumpere*, to break off : *ab-*, away + *rumpere*, to break.] **—a•brupt′ly** *adv.* **—a•brupt′ness** *n.*

ab•scess (**ăb′**sĕs′) *n.* A mass of pus that forms at one place in the body and is surrounded by inflamed tissue.

ab•scessed (**ăb′**sĕst′) *adj.* Having an abscess: *an abscessed tooth.*

ab•scis•sa (ăb **sĭs′**ə) *n., pl.* **ab•scis•sas** or **ab•scis•sae** (ăb **sĭs′**ē). The distance of a point from the y-axis on a graph. It is measured parallel to the x-axis in the Cartesian coordinate system.

ab•scond (ăb **skŏnd′**) *intr.v.* **ab•scond•ed, ab•scond•ing, ab•sconds.** To leave quickly and secretly and hide oneself, especially to avoid arrest: *The cashier absconded with the money.*

ab•sence (**ăb′**səns) *n.* **1.** The state of being away: *Soccer practice was cancelled because of the coach's absence.* **2.** The period during which one is away: *an absence of four days.* **3.** A lack: *Rumors spread in the absence of reliable information.*

ab•sent (**ăb′**sənt) *adj.* **1.** Not present; not on hand: *Two students are absent today.* **2.** Lacking; missing: *Scales are absent in eels.* **3.** Not paying attention; absorbed in thought: *The dazed boy had an absent look on his face.* *—tr.v.* (ăb **sĕnt′**). **ab•sent•ed, ab•sent•ing, ab•sents.** To keep (oneself) away: *I absented myself from work because of illness.* [First written down about 1382 in Middle English, from Latin *absēns*, present participle of *abesse*, to be away : *abs-*, *ab-*, away + *esse*, to be.]

ab•sen•tee (ăb′sən **tē′**) *n.* A person who is absent. *—adj.* **1.** Absent. **2.** Not in residence: *an absentee landlord.*

ab•sen•tee•ism (ăb′sən **tē′**ĭz′əm) *n.* Habitual failure to appear, especially for work or other regular duty.

ab•sent•ly (**ăb′**sənt lē) *adv.* As if lost in thought: *stared absently out the window.*

ab•sent-mind•ed (ăb′sənt **mīn′**dĭd) *adj.* Tending to be lost in thought and to forget what one is doing; forgetful or preocuppied. **—ab′sent-mind′ed•ly** *adv.* **—ab′sent-mind′ed•ness** *n.*

ab•sinthe also **ab•sinth** (**ăb′**sĭnth) *n.* A strong green alcoholic liquor that is flavored with wormwood and anise.

ab•so•lute (**ăb′**sə lo͞ot′) *adj.* **1.** Complete; total: *absolute silence.* **2.** Not limited in any way: *absolute monarchy; absolute freedom.* **3.** Without reservation; utter: *absolute confidence in the teacher.* **4.** Not to be doubted; positive: *absolute proof.* [First written down about 1380 in Middle English, from Latin *absolūtus*, unrestricted, past participle of *absolvere*, to absolve : *ab-*, away + *solvere*, to loosen.] **—ab′so•lute′ness** *n.*

ab•so•lute•ly (**ăb′**sə lo͞ot′lē *or* ăb′sə **lo͞ot′**lē) *adv.* Completely; perfectly: *I am absolutely certain. Stand absolutely still.*

absolute pitch *n.* **1.** The precise pitch of a tone as established by its frequency. **2.** The ability to recognize or sing any tone heard; perfect pitch.

absolute temperature *n.* Temperature measured relative to absolute zero.

absolute value *n.* The value of a number without regard to its sign. For example, +3 and −3 each have the absolute value of 3.

absolute zero *n.* The temperature at which all molecules cease to move and at which no heat energy is present, equal to −459.67°F or −273.15°C.

ab•so•lu•tion (ăb′sə **lo͞o′**shən) *n.* The formal forgiveness of a sin by a priest.

ab•so•lut•ism (**ăb′**sə lo͞o′tĭz′əm) *n.* A form of government in which the ruler has unlimited power.

ab•solve (əb **zŏlv′** *or* əb **sŏlv′**) *tr.v.* **ab•solved, ab•solv•ing, ab•solves.** **1.** To clear of blame of guilt: *Evidence absolved the suspect of being involved in the crime.* **2.** To grant formal forgiveness to (someone) for sins committed. **3.** To release, as from a promise, duty, or obligation: *Paying off the loan absolved her of any obligation to the bank.* [First written down before 1425 in Middle English and spelled *absolven*, from Latin *absolvere*.] **—ab•solv′a•ble** *adj.* **—ab•solv′er** *n.*

ab•sorb (əb **sôrb′** *or* əb **zôrb′**) *tr.v.* **ab•sorbed, ab•sorb•ing, ab•sorbs.** **1.** To take in; soak up: *A paper towel absorbed the water.* **2.** To take in and make a part of something: *Plants absorb energy from the sun. New York absorbed many immigrants.* **3.** To take in or receive without transmitting or reflecting: *Thick curtains absorb sound.* **4.** To receive or withstand with little effect or reaction: *The car bumper absorbed the force of the collision.* **5.** To occupy the full attention of: *Homework completely absorbed her thoughts.* **6.** To take up completely: *My job after school absorbs all of my time.* **7.** To assume the burden of: *Many businesses absorb the extra costs of mailing.* [First written down about 1425 in Middle English, from Latin *absorbēre*, to swallow up : *ab-*, away + *sorbēre*, to suck.] **—ab•sorb′er** *n.*

ab•sorbed (əb **sôrbd′** *or* əb **zôrbd′**) *adj.* Completely interested: *The absorbed look on their faces indicated they enjoyed hearing the story.*

ab•sorb•ent (əb **sôr′**bənt *or* əb **zôr′**bənt) *adj.* Capable of absorbing: *absorbent cotton.* *—n.* A substance that is capable of absorbing.

ab•sorb•ing (əb **sôr′**bĭng *or* əb **zôr′**bĭng) *adj.* Holding one's interest or attention; engrossing: *an absorbing novel.* **—ab•sorb′ing•ly** *adv.*

ab•sorp•tion (əb **sôrp′**shən *or* əb **zôrp′**shən) *n.* **1.** The act or process of absorbing: *Absorption of food is essential to living matter.* **2.** Close, undivided attention: *absorption in an exciting TV program.*

absorption spectrum *n.* A spectrum produced when light or other radiation passes through a gas or liquid that absorbs only certain wavelengths, resulting in a distinctive pattern of light and dark bands that indicates what chemical element or compound is present.

ab•stain (ăb **stān′**) *intr.v.* **ab•stained, ab•stain•ing, ab•stains.** To keep from doing something by one's own choice; refrain: *He abstains from eating meat.* **—ab•stain′er** *n.*

ab•ste•mi•ous (ăb **stē′**mē əs) *adj.* Eating and drinkng in moderation; sparing. **—ab•ste′mi•ous•ly** *adv.*

ab•sten•tion (ăb **stĕn′**shən) *n.* **1.** The practice of abstaining: *Abstention from candy helps prevent cavities.* **2.** An act of abstaining, especially the withholding of a voice at an election: *one vote for, two against, and four abstentions.*

ab•sti•nence (ăb′stə nəns) *n.* The act or practice of abstaining, especially by giving up certain drinks or foods. **—ab′sti•nent** *adj.*

ab•stract (ăb **străkt′** *or* **ăb′**străkt′) *adj.* **1.** Thought of apart from any particular object or thing. For example, *goodness* is an abstract noun and *softness* is an abstract quality. **2.** Difficult to understand: *Your complicated explanation is too abstract for me.* **3.** In art, concerned with designs or shapes that do not realistically represent any person or thing: *an abstract painting full of strange shapes.* —*n.* (**ăb′**străkt′). A brief summary of the main points of a text: *read a short abstract of the speech.* —*tr.v.* (ăb **străkt′**). **ab•stract•ed, ab•stract•ing, ab•stracts. 1.** To take away; remove. **2.** To think of (a quality, for example) apart from any particular instance or thing: *abstract a law of nature from a laboratory experiment.* **3.** To make a summary of: *It was not easy to abstract his article.* **—*idiom.* in the abstract.** In theory but not necessarily in practice: *In the abstract, canoeing is relaxing, but we found it to be hard work.* [First written down before 1398 in Middle English, from Latin *abstractus*, past participle of *abstrahere*, to draw away : *abs-*, *ab-*, away + *trahere*, to draw.] **—ab•stract′ly** *adv.* **—ab•stract′ness** *n.*

ab•stract•ed (ăb **străk′**tĭd) *adj.* Lost or deep in thought; absent-minded. **—ab•stract′ed•ly** *adv.*

ab•strac•tion (ăb **străk′**shən) *n.* **1.** The act or process of considering something, such as a quality apart from particular instances or things. **2.** An idea or quality thought of apart from any particular instance or thing: *abstractions hard to understand.* **3.** Absent-mindedness: *In his abstraction, he didn't say hello.* **4.** An abstract work of art.

ab•struse (ăb **stro͞os′**) *adj.* Hard to understand: *abstruse theories of atomic interaction.* **—ab•struse′ly** *adv.* **—ab•struse′ness** *n.*

ab•surd (əb **sûrd′** *or* əb **zûrd′**) *adj.* Plainly not true or contrary to common sense; ridiculous: *It would be absurd to walk backward all the time.* **—ab•surd′ly** *adv.* **—ab•surd′ness** *n.*

ab•surd•i•ty (əb **sûr′**dĭ tē *or* əb **zûr′**dĭ tē) *n.* **1.** The state of being absurd; foolishness. **2.** An absurd action, thing, or idea.

A•bu Dha•bi (ä′bo͞o **dä′**bē). The capital of the United Arab Emirates, in eastern Arabia on the Persian Gulf. Abu Dhabi has enormous oil revenues. Population, 242,975.

a•bun•dance (ə **bŭn′**dəns) *n.* A great amount or quantity; a plentiful supply: *The heavy spring rains gave us an abundance of water for the summer.*

a•bun•dant (ə **bŭn′**dənt) *adj.* **1.** Existing in great supply; very plentiful: *Abundant rainfall swelled the rivers.* **2.** Rich; abounding: *a forest abundant in oak trees.* [First written down about 1380 in Middle English and spelled *aboundant*, from Latin *abundāns*, present participle of *abundāre*, to overflow.] **—a•bun′dant•ly** *adv.*

a•buse (ə **byo͞oz′**) *tr.v.* **a•bused, a•bus•ing, a•bus•es. 1.** To use improperly; misuse: *abuse a special privilege.* **2.** To hurt or injure by treating badly; mistreat: *abused his eyesight by reading in poor light.* **3.** To attack or injure with words; revile: *The candidates abused each other in sharp debate.* —*n.* (ə **byo͞os′**). **1.** Improper use; misuse: *drug abuse.* **2.** Harsh or severe treatment: *The truck received a lot of abuse when we moved the furniture.* **3.** A corrupt practice or evil custom: *Needlessly berating an assistant is an abuse of power.* **4.** Insulting language: *Baseball umpires take a lot of abuse from the crowd.* [First written down about 1425 in Middle English and spelled *abusen*, from Latin *abūtī* : *ab-*, away + *ūtī*, to use.] **—a•bus′er** *n.*

a•bu•sive (ə **byo͞o′**sĭv) *adj.* **1.** Using coarse and insulting language: *abusive remarks.* **2.** Wrongly treated or incorrectly used: *the abusive powers of a dictator.* **—a•bu′sive•ly** *adv.* **—a•bu′sive•ness** *n.*

a•but (ə **bŭt′**) *v.* **a•but•ted, a•but•ting, a•buts.** —*intr.* To touch at one end or side; be adjacent: *Our fence abuts on our neighbor's property.* —*tr.* To border on; be next to: *The garage abuts the house.*

a•but•ment (ə **bŭt′**mənt) *n.* **1.** A support for the end of a bridge, arch, or beam. **2.** The point where a support joins the thing it is supporting.

a•buzz (ə **bŭz′**) *adj.* **1.** Filled with a buzzing sound. **2.** Filled with activity or talk.

a•bys•mal (ə **bĭz′**məl) *adj.* Too deep to be measured; bottomless: *abysmal despair; abysmal ignorance.* **—a•bys′mal•ly** *adv.*

a•byss (ə **bĭs′**) *n.* A very deep and large hole; a seemingly bottomless space: *The scientists sent a probe into the abyss of the volcano.* [First written down before 1398 in Middle English and spelled *abissus*, from Greek *abussos*, bottomless : *a-*, without + *bussos*, bottom.]

Ab•ys•sin•i•a (ăb′ĭ **sĭn′**ē ə). Ethiopia.

ac or **AC** *abbr.* An abbreviation of alternating current.

Ac The symbol for the element **actinium.**

a•ca•cia (ə **kā′**shə) *n.* **1.** Any of several mostly tropical trees with feathery leaves and clusters of small usually yellow flowers. **2.** The locust tree of North America.

acad. *abbr.* An abbreviation of: **1.** Academic. **2.** Academy.

ac•a•dem•ic (ăk′ə **dĕm′**ĭk) *adj.* **1.** Of or relating to a school or college: *an academic degree.* **2.** Relating to studies that are liberal or general rather than technical or vocational: *History and languages are academic studies.* **3.** Merely theoretical; having no practical purpose: *The scientists raised many academic points.* **—ac′a•dem′i•cal•ly** *adv.*

ac•a•de•mi•cian (ăk′ə də **mĭsh′**ən *or* ə kăd′ə **mĭsh′**ən) *n.* A member of an academy or a society for promoting literature, art, science, and other studies.

a•cad•e•my (ə **kăd′**ə mē) *n.*, *pl.* **a•cad•e•mies. 1.** A school for a special field of study: *a naval academy.* **2.** A private high school. **3.** An association of educated persons or scholars for the purpose of advancing knowledge. [First written down in 1474 in Middle English and spelled *achadomye*, the school where Plato taught, from Greek *Akadēmia*.]

A•ca•di•a (ə **kā′**dē ə). A region and former French colony of eastern Canada, chiefly in Nova Scotia but also including New Brunswick, Prince Edward Island, Cape Breton Island, and the coastal area from the St. Lawrence River south into Maine. The descendants of the Acadians who migrated to southern territories, including Louisiana, came to be known as Cajuns.

A•ca•di•an (ə **kā′**dē ən) *adj.* Of or relating to Acadia or its people, language, or culture. —*n.* **1.** A French settler of Acadia. **2.** A Cajun.

a•can•thus (ə **kăn′**thəs) *n.*, *pl.* **a•can•thus•es** or **a•can•thi** (ə **kăn′**thī′). **1.** Any of various plants of the Mediterranean region with large spiny leaves and showy white or purplish flowers. **2.** Decoration in the form of acanthus leaves, as the carving on the capital of a Corinthian column.

a cap•pel•la (ä′ kə **pĕl′**ə) *adv.* In music, without instrumental accompaniment: *a duet sung a cappella.*

ac•cede (ăk **sēd′**) *intr.v.* **ac•ced•ed, ac•ced•ing, ac•cedes. 1.** To consent; agree; yield: *I acceded to her request and went in spite of my cold.* **2.** To come or succeed to a public office or position: *The winning candidate acceded to the presidency.*

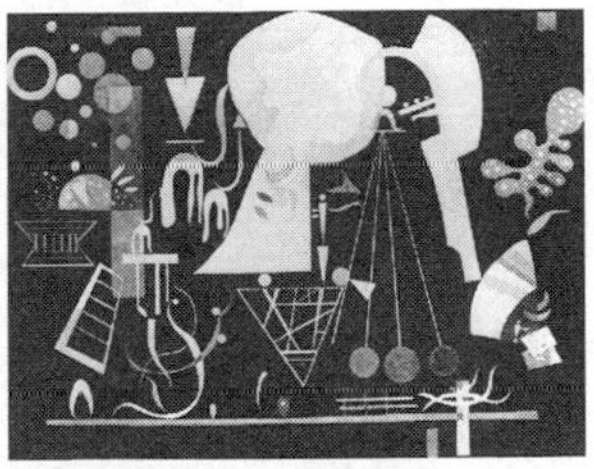

abstract
Abstract painting *Tensions Relaxed No. 838* by Wassily Kandinsky (1866–1944)

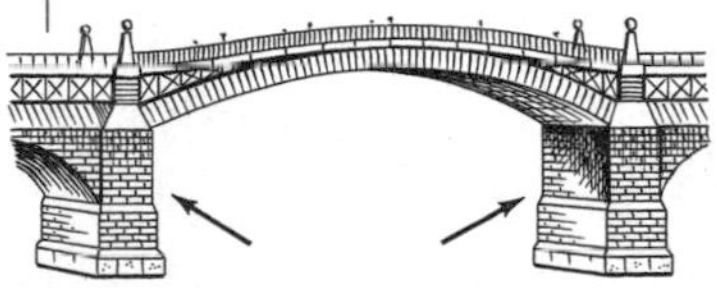

abutment
Arched bridge

ă	pat	oi	**boy**
ā	**pay**	ou	**out**
âr	**care**	o͝o	**took**
ä	father	o͞o	**boot**
ĕ	pet	ŭ	cut
ē	**be**	ûr	**urge**
ĭ	pit	th	**thin**
ī	**pie**	*th*	**this**
îr	**pier**	hw	**whoop**
ŏ	pot	zh	vision
ō	**toe**	ə	about
ô	**paw**	N	*French* bon

ac•cel•er•an•do (ä chĕl′ə **rän′**dō) *adj. & adv.* In music, gradually becoming faster.

ac•cel•er•ate (ăk **sĕl′**ə rāt′) *v.* **ac•cel•er•at•ed, ac•cel•er•at•ing, ac•cel•er•ates.** —*tr.* **1.** To cause to go faster; speed up: *accelerate one's pace to a run.* **2.** In physics, to change the speed or direction of (a moving body): *A falling object accelerates 32 feet per second per second near the earth's surface.* **3.** To cause to happen earlier; hasten: *Eating a lot of candy may accelerate tooth decay.* —*intr.* To increase in speed; quicken: *The car accelerated on the downhill slope.* [First written down about 1525 in Modern English, from Latin *accelerāre* : *ad-*, intensive prefix + *celerāre*, to quicken.]

ac•cel•er•a•tion (ăk sĕl′ə **rā′**shən) *n.* **1.** The act or process of accelerating; an increase in speed. **2.** The rate of change in the speed or direction of a moving body with respect to time.

ac•cel•er•a•tor (ăk **sĕl′**ə rā′tər) *n.* **1.** A device that controls the speed of a machine, especially the pedal that increases the flow of fuel to the motor of an automobile or truck. **2.** A substance that increases the rate of a chemical reaction. **3.** Any of various devices for increasing the speed and energy of charged atomic particles such as protons or electrons. Accelerators are often used to bombard atomic nuclei causing them to release new particles and energy.

ac•cel•er•om•e•ter (ăk sĕl′ə **rŏm′**ĭ tər) *n.* An instrument that measures and indicates acceleration, often used in aircraft and spacecraft.

ac•cent (**ăk′**sĕnt′) *n.* **1.** The stress or force with which a speaker utters one or more syllables of a word compared with the other syllables of the word. In the word *butter* the accent is on the first syllable. **2.** An accent mark. **3.** A style of speech or pronunciation that is typical of a certain region or country: *She speaks with a French accent.* **4.** A special feature or distinguishing quality; an emphasis: *cooking with an accent on hot spices.* **5.a.** A special stress given to a musical note within a measure or phrase. **b.** A mark indicating that this is to be done. **6.** Rhythmical stress given to a word or syllable in a line of poetry. —*tr.v.* (**ăk′**sĕnt′ *or* ăk **sĕnt′**). **ac•cent•ed, ac•cent•ing, ac•cents. 1.** To stress in speech or in music: *accent the first syllable of a word; accent every third note.* **2.** To place an accent mark over. **3.** To give emphasis or prominence to; accentuate: *Her speech accented the accomplishments made over the last decade.* [First written down before 1398 in Middle English, from Latin *accentus*, accentuation : *ad-*, to + *cantus*, song.]

accent mark *n.* **1.** A mark showing accent or stress uttered in one or more syllables of the pronunciation of a word. **2.** In certain foreign languages, and in English words borrowed from such languages, a mark placed over a letter to indicate a certain feature of pronunciation. For example, in the word *exposé* the final *e* is pronounced like the *a* in *state.* **3.** A mark indicating rhythmical stress in a line of poetry.

ac•cen•tu•ate (ăk **sĕn′**cho͞o āt′) *tr.v.* **ac•cen•tu•at•ed, ac•cen•tu•at•ing, ac•cen•tu•ates. 1.** To give prominence to; stress or emphasize: *A red background accentuates the letters of a stop sign.* **2.** To pronounce with a stress or an accent. **3.** To mark with an accent mark. —**ac•cen′tu•a′tion** *n.*

ac•cept (ăk **sĕpt′**) *v.* **ac•cept•ed, ac•cept•ing, ac•cepts.** —*tr.* **1.** To receive (something offered): *accept a birthday gift.* **2.** To admit to a group: *They accepted me as a new member of the club.* **3.** To regard as proper or right: *Both sides accepted the judge's ruling.* **4.** To regard as correct or true; believe in: *We accepted your explanation of what happened.* **5.** To put up with; endure: *You can accept the situation or do something to change it.* **6.** To say "yes" to; answer affirmatively: *I accept your invitation.* **7.** To take up; assume: *You must accept responsibility for your own actions.* —*intr.* To receive something offered. [First written down about 1380 in Middle English and spelled *accepten*, from Latin *accipere* : *ad-*, to + *capere*, to take.]

ac•cept•a•ble (ăk **sĕp′**tə bəl) *adj.* **1.** Worthy of being well received; welcome; agreeable: *an acceptable meal.* **2.** Adequate to satisfy a need, requirement, or standard; satisfactory: *Her work in chemistry is acceptable, but she could do better.* —**ac•cept′a•bil′i•ty** *n.* —**ac•cept′a•bly** *adv.*

ac•cep•tance (ăk **sĕp′**təns) *n.* **1.** The act of taking something offered: *the acceptance of a new job.* **2.** Favorable reception; approval: *Acceptance of seat belts among the public has greatly reduced injuries in car accidents.* **3.** Belief in something as true; agreement: *Acceptance of the theory has been slow.*

ac•cess (**ăk′**sĕs) *n.* **1.** The act of entering; entrance: *gain access through the basement.* **2.** The right to enter, reach, or use: *We have access to secret information.* **3.** A way of approaching or reaching: *The only access to the pond is by a dirt road.* —*tr.v.* **ac•cessed, ac•cess•ing, ac•cess•es.** To find and make available (data) from a computer. [First written down about 1300 in Middle English and spelled *acces*, from Latin *accēdere*, to arrive : *ad-*, to + *cēdere*, to come.]

access code *n.* A code that allows a user access to a computer and data stored in it.

ac•ces•si•ble (ăk **sĕs′**ə bəl) *adj.* **1.** Capable of being reached or approached: *The lake is easily accessible from the highway.* **2.** Capable of being obtained: *The information is accessible on our computer.* —**ac•ces′si•bil′i•ty** *n.* —**ac•ces′si•bly** *adv.*

ac•ces•sion (ăk **sĕsh′**ən) *n.* **1.** An increase; an addition: *The museum has been improved by the accession of new fossils.* **2.** Something added: *The library's latest accession is a new encyclopedia.* **3.** The act of coming to power or high office: *the king's accession to the throne.*

ac•ces•so•ry (ăk **sĕs′**ə rē) *n., pl.* **ac•ces•so•ries. 1.** Something that is beyond what is needed but adds to the usefulness or appearance of something else: *a car full of accessories including a radio; a red scarf worn as an accessory with a black coat.* **2.** A person who is not present at the time a crime is committed but who aids a criminal either before or after a crime is committed. —*adj.* Helping or adding to something more important: *The camera does not include accessory items like a flash.* [First written down in 1414 in Middle English and spelled *accessorie*, from Medieval Latin *accessor*, helper.]

ac•ci•dent (**ăk′**sĭ dənt) *n.* **1.** Something that happens without being planned or known in advance: *Our meeting was a lucky accident.* **2.** An unexpected and undesirable event; a mishap: *an automobile accident.* **3.** Chance or coincidence: *She ran into an old friend by accident.* [First written down about 1380 in Middle English, from Latin *accidere*, to happen : *ad-*, to + *cadere*, to fall.]

ac•ci•den•tal (ăk′sĭ **dĕn′**tl) *adj.* Happening without being expected or intended: *the accidental discovery of gold in a river.* —*n.* In music, a sharp, flat, or natural that is not in the key signature. —**ac′ci•den′tal•ly** *adv.*

ac•ci•dent-prone (**ăk′**sĭ dənt prōn′) *adj.* Tending to have accidents.

ac•claim (ə **klām′**) *tr.v.* **ac•claimed, ac•claim•ing, ac•claims. 1.** To greet with loud approval; praise; applaud: *The new movie has been acclaimed by all the critics.* **2.** To announce with approval; hail: *Newspapers acclaimed the returning astronauts.*

—*n.* Loud or enthusiastic praise, applause, or approval.

ac•cla•ma•tion (ăk'lə mā'shən) *n.* **1.** Enthusiastic praise or applause; acclaim. **2.** An enthusiastic voice vote of approval taken without making an actual count.

❑ *These sound alike:* **acclamation, acclimation** (adaptation).

ac•cli•mate (ə klī'mĭt *or* ăk'lə māt') *tr. & intr.v.* **ac•cli•mat•ed, ac•cli•mat•ing, ac•cli•mates.** To adapt or become adapted to new climate conditions or surroundings.

ac•cli•ma•tion (ăk'lə mā'shən) *n.* The process of acclimating or condition of being acclimated.

❑ *These sound alike:* **acclimation, acclamation** (acclaim).

ac•cli•ma•tize (ə klī'mə tīz') *tr. & intr.v.* **ac•cli•ma•tized, ac•cli•ma•tiz•ing, ac•cli•ma•tiz•es.** To acclimate. **—ac•cli'ma•ti•za'tion** (ə klī'mə tĭ zā'shən) *n.*

ac•co•lade (ăk'ə lād' *or* ăk'ə läd') *n.* **1.** An expression of approval; praise: *That movie received the Academy Award and other accolades.* **2.** A ceremonial giving of knighthood, marked by a tap on the shoulder with the flat of a sword. [First written down in 1623 in Modern English, from Old French *acoler*, to embrace.]

ac•com•mo•date (ə kŏm'ə dāt') *v.* **ac•com•mo•dat•ed, ac•com•mo•dat•ing, ac•com•mo•dates.** —*tr.* **1.** To do (someone) a favor; oblige; help: *I shall try to accommodate you in this matter.* **2.** To provide with lodging or living space: *accommodate guests at a hotel.* **3.** To have room for; hold: *an airport built to accommodate the largest planes.* **4.** To adjust or adapt; make fit: *We must accommodate ourselves to changing conditions.* See Synonyms at **adapt.** —*intr.* To become adjusted, as the eyes do in focusing on objects at a distance.

ac•com•mo•dat•ing (ə kŏm'ə dā'tĭng) *adj.* Inclined or ready to give assistance; helpful and obliging: *an agreeable and accommodating manner.* **—ac•com'mo•dat'ing•ly** *adv.*

ac•com•mo•da•tion (ə kŏm'ə dā'shən) *n.* **1.** The act of accommodating or the state of being accommodated; adjustment: *His accommodation to suburban life was a painful experience.* **2.** A favor or convenience, especially a loan of money. **3. accommodations. a.** Room and board; lodging: *We requested accommodations at the inn for two nights.* **b.** Seats on a train, airplane, ship, or other means of transportation. **4.** Adjustment by the lens of the eye in focusing on objects at differing distances.

ac•com•pa•ni•ment (ə kŭm'pə nē mənt *or* ə kŭmp'nē mənt) *n.* **1.** Something that goes along with or supplements something else: *Crackers are a good accompaniment to soup.* **2.** A musical part played as support or embellishment, especially for a soloist.

ac•com•pa•nist (ə kŭm'pə nĭst *or* ə kŭmp'nĭst) *n.* A musician who plays an accompaniment.

ac•com•pa•ny (ə kŭm'pə nē *or* ə kŭmp'nē) *tr.v.* **ac•com•pa•nied, ac•com•pa•ny•ing, ac•com•pa•nies. 1.** To go along with: *The dog accompanied him through the woods.* **2.** To occur or happen in connection with: *Heat accompanies fire.* **3.** To cause to be attended by; supplement: *The teacher accompanied the lesson with slides.* **4.** To play a musical accompaniment for: *Can you accompany this song on the guitar?*

ac•com•plice (ə kŏm'plĭs) *n.* A person who helps another do something wrong or illegal.

ac•com•plish (ə kŏm'plĭsh) *tr.v.* **ac•com•plished, ac•com•plish•ing, ac•com•plish•es.** To carry out; achieve; complete: *We accomplished our goal of building a greenhouse.* [First written down about 1380 in Middle English and spelled *accomplisshen*, from Old French *acomplir*, from Latin *complēre*, to fill out.]

ac•com•plished (ə kŏm'plĭsht) *adj.* **1.** Carried out; completed; finished: *an accomplished mission.* **2.** Skilled because of practice or study; expert: *an accomplished musician.*

ac•com•plish•ment (ə kŏm'plĭsh mənt) *n.* **1.** The act of carrying out; completion: *the accomplishment of a task.* **2.** Something accomplished; an achievement: *The first walk on the moon was a huge accomplishment in technology.* **3.** A skill acquired through training and practice: *Singing and painting are among the actor's many accomplishments.*

ac•cord (ə kôrd') *v.* **ac•cord•ed, ac•cord•ing, ac•cords.** —*tr.* To give; grant: *Citizens are accorded certain rights by our Constitution.* —*intr.* To be in agreement or harmony: *Your ideas accord with mine.* —*n.* **1.** Agreement; harmony: *His ideas are in accord with mine.* **2.** A formal act of agreement; settlement between conflicting parties: *The strikers and the employers reached an accord.* ***—idiom.*** **of (one's) own accord** or **on (one's) own accord.** By one's own choice or wish; voluntarily: *The children returned of their own accord.* [First written down before 1121 in Middle English and spelled *accorden*, ultimately from Latin *cor*, heart.]

ac•cor•dance (ə kôr'dns) *n.* Agreement; keeping: *Play the game in accordance with the rules.*

ac•cord•ing•ly (ə kôr'dĭng lē) *adv.* **1.** In keeping with what is known, stated, or expected: *Learn the rules and act accordingly.* **2.** Therefore; consequently: *The student was sick; accordingly, the teacher called the parents.*

ac•cord•ing to (ə kôr'dĭng) *prep.* **1.** As stated or indicated by; on the authority of: *According to the weather report, it will rain tomorrow.* **2.** In keeping with; in agreement with: *Proceed according to instructions.* **3.** As determined by: *a list arranged according to the first letter of each word.* **4.** In proportion to: *Salt is added according to the amount of water used.*

ac•cor•di•on (ə kôr'dē ən) *n.* A wind instrument with keys and a bellows from which air can be forced to pass over reeds that create tones. —*adj.* Having folds like the bellows of an accordion: *a skirt with accordion pleats.* [First written down in 1831 in Modern English, from German *Akkordion*, from Old French *acorder*, to be in harmony.]

ac•cost (ə kôst' *or* ə kŏst') *tr.v.* **ac•cost•ed, ac•cost•ing, ac•costs.** To come up to and speak to, often in an bold way: *A stranger accosted me for a quarter to make a phone call.*

ac•count (ə kount') *n.* **1.** A written or spoken description of events; a narrative: *The explorers gave an exciting account of their adventures.* **2.** A set of reasons; an explanation: *Give an account for your strange behavior.* **3.** A record or written statement of business dealings or money received or spent: *A bookkeeper kept the accounts of the company.* **4.** A business arrangement, as with a bank or store, in which money is kept, exchanged, or owed: *a savings account in the local bank; a charge account at the drugstore.* **5.** A customer or client of a company or store: *an advertising agency with several accounts that are big manufacturing companies.* **6.** Importance; standing; worth: *Most gossip is of little account.* —*tr.v.* **ac•count•ed, ac•count•ing, ac•counts.** To believe to be; consider; regard: *The judge was accounted fair and wise.* ***—idioms.*** **account for. 1.** To give the reason for; explain: *How do you account for your absence from practice?* **2.** To be the reason for: *Bad weather accounted for the delay in their arrival.* **on account.** On credit: *I*

accolade

accordion

ă	pat	oi	boy
ā	pay	ou	out
âr	care	o͝o	took
ä	father	o͞o	boot
ĕ	pet	ŭ	cut
ē	be	ûr	urge
ĭ	pit	th	thin
ī	pie	*th*	this
îr	pier	hw	whoop
ŏ	pot	zh	vision
ō	toe	ə	about
ô	paw	N	*French* bon

bought this coat on account. **on account of.** Because of; for the sake of: *We were late on account of the traffic jam. Don't stay home on account of me.* **on no account.** Under no circumstances: *On no account should you touch live wires.* [First written down about 1300 in Middle English, from Latin *computāre,* to sum up.]

ac•count•a•ble (ə **koun′**tə bəl) *adj.* Expected or bound to answer for one's actions; responsible: *Senators are accountable to the people who elect them.* **—ac•count′a•bil′i•ty** *n.*

ac•count•ant (ə **koun′**tənt) *n.* A person who keeps or inspects financial records, as of a business, government agency, or person.

ac•count•ing (ə **koun′**tĭng) *n.* The occupation or methods of keeping financial records, as of a business or government agency.

ac•cou•ter or **ac•cou•tre** (ə **ko͞o′**tər) *tr.v.* **ac•cou•tered, ac•cou•ter•ing, ac•cou•ters** or **ac•cou•tred, ac•cou•tre•ing, ac•cou•tres.** To equip with clothing and equipment, especially for a particular purpose: *The explorers were completely accoutered for outdoor living.*

ac•cou•ter•ments or **ac•cou•trements** (ə **ko͞o′**-tər mənts *or* ə **ko͞o′**trə mənts) *pl.n.* **1.** Articles of clothing or equipment; trappings: *boots, breeches, and other accouterments of riding.* **2.** A soldier's equipment, including bedding and a backpack, but not including clothing and weapons.

ac•cou•tre (ə **ko͞o′**tər) *tr.v.* **ac•cou•tred, ac•cou•tre•ing, ac•cou•tres.** Variant of **accouter.**

ac•cou•tre•ments (ə **ko͞o′**tər mənts *or* ə **ko͞o′**-trə mənts) *pl.n.* Variant of **accouterments.**

Ac•cra (**ăk′**rə *or* ə **krä′**). The capital and largest city of Ghana, in the southeast part of the country on the Gulf of Guinea. Accra has been an important economic center since the completion of the railroad in 1923. Population, 859,640.

ac•cred•it (ə **krĕd′**ĭt) *tr.v.* **ac•cred•it•ed, ac•cred•it•ing, ac•cred•its. 1.** To regard as the work of; ascribe or attribute: *The discovery of radium is accredited to Marie Curie.* **2.** To approve or record as having met certain standards: *This high school has been accredited by the state.* **3.** To send or appoint (an ambassador, envoy, or other representative) with official standing.

ac•cred•i•ta•tion (ə krĕd′ĭ **tā′**shən) *n.* Recognition of a school, a hospital, or an agency of having met certain standards.

ac•cre•tion (ə **krē′**shən) *n.* **1.** The process of increasing in size as a result of being added to or growing: *The accretion of rust in the pipes will eventually block the flow of water.* **2.** Something added that produces such an increase: *Accretions of mineral deposits in the cave developed into these large structures.*

ac•cru•al (ə **kro͞o′**əl) *n.* **1.** The process of accruing; increase: *Education leads to an accrual of knowledge.* **2.** Something that has accrued.

ac•crue (ə **kro͞o′**) *intr.v.* **ac•crued, ac•cru•ing, ac•crues. 1.** To come to someone as a gain or an addition: *Interest accrues in my savings account.* **2.** To increase or come about as a result of growth: *Our knowledge of disease has accrued from scientific research.* [First written down in 1440 in Middle English and spelled *acreuen,* ultimately from Latin *accrēscere,* to grow : *ad-,* to + *crēscere,* to arise.]

ac•cu•mu•late (ə **kyo͞om′**yə lāt′) *v.* **ac•cu•mu•lat•ed, ac•cu•mu•lat•ing, ac•cu•mu•lates.** *—tr.* To gather together; pile up; collect: *By working hard and spending little he accumulated a great deal of money.* See Synonyms at **gather.** *—intr.* To increase: *During the storm deep piles of snow accumulated on the sidewalk.* [First written down in 1529 in Modern English, from Latin *accumulāre,* from *cumulus,* heap.]

ac•cu•mu•la•tion (ə kyo͞om′yə **lā′**shən) *n.* **1.** The collection or amassing of something: *a collection of seashells created by accumulation over many years.* **2.** An accumulated amount or mass of something: *the weekly accumulation of rubbish.*

ac•cu•ra•cy (**ăk′**yər ə sē) *n.* **1.** Freedom from error or mistake; correctness: *check the results for accuracy.* **2.** Exactness; precision: *the accuracy of the clock.*

ac•cu•rate (**ăk′**yər ĭt) *adj.* **1.** Free from errors or mistakes; correct: *accurate answers.* **2.** Exact; precise: *an accurate description; an accurate method of measurement.* [First written down in 1612 in Modern English, from Latin *accūrāre,* to do with care.] **—ac′cu•rate•ly** *adv.* **—ac′cu•rate•ness** *n.*

ac•curs•ed (ə **kûr′**sĭd *or* ə **kûrst′**) also **ac•curst** (ə **kûrst′**) *adj.* **1.** Under a curse; damned. **2.** Hateful or detestable: *the accursed trade in ivory.* **—ac•curs′ed•ly** *adv.* **—ac•curs′ed•ness** *n.*

ac•cu•sa•tion (ăk′yo͞o **zā′**shən) *n.* **1.** A statement or formal declaration that a person is guilty of wrongdoing: *The lawyer presented a written accusation against the suspected criminal.* **2.** The act of accusing or the state of being accused with wrongdoing: *False accusation is a serious offense.*

ac•cu•sa•tive (ə **kyo͞o′**zə tĭv) *adj.* Of or relating to the grammatical case in languages like Latin that indicates the direct object of a verb or the object of a preposition. *—n.* The accusative case.

ac•cuse (ə **kyo͞oz′**) *tr.v.* **ac•cused, ac•cus•ing, ac•cus•es. 1.** To make a declaration charging (someone) with wrongdoing: *The lawyers accused them of polluting the river.* **2.** To find at fault; blame: *She accused her little brother with messing up her room.* [First written down about 1300 in Middle English and spelled *acusen,* from Latin *accūsāre.*] **—ac•cus′er** *n.*

ac•cused (ə **kyo͞ozd′**) *n.* The defendant or defendants in a criminal case: *The accused were taken to trial for theft.*

ac•cus•tom (ə **kŭs′**təm) *tr.v.* **ac•cus•tomed, ac•cus•tom•ing, ac•cus•toms.** To make familiar with; get (someone) used to: *Growing up in Florida had accustomed her to hot weather.*

ac•cus•tomed (ə **kŭs′**təmd) *adj.* Usual; habitual; familiar: *The researcher presented his discovery with his accustomed modesty.* ***—idiom.*** **accustomed to.** Used to; in the habit of: *Farmers are accustomed to working long days.*

ace (ās) *n.* **1.** A playing card with one figure of its suit in the center. **2.** A person who can do something very well or is an expert in some field: *That senior is our school team's pitching ace.* **3.** In tennis, a point scored when one's opponent fails to return a serve. **4.** A fighter pilot who has destroyed a number of enemy planes. *—tr.v.* **aced, ac•ing, ac•es. 1.** To serve an ace against (an opposing player) in tennis. **2.** To achieve a grade of A on: *ace a quiz in French.* ***—idiom.*** **ace in the hole.** A hidden advantage or resource kept in reserve until needed. [First written down before 1250 in Middle English and spelled *as,* from Latin, unit.]

ac•e•tate (**ăs′**ĭ tāt′) *n.* **1.** A salt or ester of acetic acid: *lead acetate.* **2.** Cellulose acetate or a product, such as a fabric or fiber, derived from it.

a•ce•tic acid (ə **sē′**tĭk) *n.* A clear pungent acid composed of carbon, hydrogen, and oxygen with the formula $C_2H_4O_2$. It occurs naturally in vinegar and is also produced commercially from ethyl alcohol and from wood. It is used as a solvent, in making rubber and plastics, and in photographic chemicals.

ac•e•tone (**ăs′**ĭ tōn′) *n.* A compound composed of carbon, hydrogen, and oxygen with the formula

C_3H_6O. It is a colorless, strong-smelling liquid that vaporizes easily, burns very readily, and is widely used as a solvent.

a•cet•y•lene (ə sĕt′l ēn′ *or* ə sĕt′l ən) *n.* A colorless very flammable gas composed of carbon and hydrogen with the formula C_2H_2. It is used to cut through metal and can be burned to produce light.

a•ce•tyl•sal•i•cyl•ic acid (ə sēt′l săl′ĭ sĭl′ĭk) *n.* Aspirin.

ache (āk) *intr.v.* **ached, ach•ing, aches. 1.** To hurt with or feel a dull steady pain: *My tooth aches. I ache all over.* **2.** To want very much; long; yearn: *I am aching to get home.* —*n.* **1.** A dull, steady pain: *Growing pains often appear as aches in the legs.* **2.** A feeling of sadness or longing. [First written down about 1000 in Old English and spelled *acan*.]

a•chieve (ə chēv′) *tr.v.* **a•chieved, a•chiev•ing, a•chieves. 1.** To succeed in accomplishing, producing, or gaining: *We achieved our goal.* **2.** To get to, reach, or attain by effort: *achieve fame as a tennis player.* See Synonyms at **reach.** [First written down about 1300 in Middle English and spelled *acheven*, from Old French *(venir) a chef*, (to come) to a head.] —**a•chiev′er** *n.*

a•chieve•ment (ə chēv′mənt) *n.* **1.** The act or process of attaining or accomplishing something: *The achievement of voting rights for women was the main focus of her life.* **2.** Something that has been achieved, especially as an outstanding accomplishment: *The development of the computer is a great achievement in technology.*

achievement test *n.* A test to measure how much a person has learned, especially at a particular grade level.

A•chil•les (ə kĭl′ēz) *n.* In Greek mythology, a Greek hero of the Trojan War who is killed by an arrow shot into his heel, the only part of his body in which he can be wounded.

A•chil•les′ heel (ə kĭl′ēz) *n.* A weak point or vulnerable place: *Poor defense is the Achilles' heel of their team.*

Achilles tendon *n.* A strong tendon at the back of the leg connecting the calf muscles with the bone of the heel.

ach•ro•mat•ic (ăk′rə măt′ĭk) *adj.* **1.** Refracting white light without breaking it up into the colors of the spectrum: *an achromatic telescope.* **2.** Lacking color; colorless.

achromatic lens *n.* A combination of lenses that forms an image in which the various colors of the spectrum that compose white light meet at a single focus.

ach•y (ā′kē) *adj.* **ach•i•er, ach•i•est.** Filled with aches; having an ache: *Flu is usually accompanied by an achy feeling.*

ac•id (ăs′ĭd) *n.* Any of a class of substances that when dissolved in water are capable of reacting with a base to form salts and release hydrogen ions. Acids can be identified by the fact that they turn blue litmus paper red and have a characteristic sour taste. —*adj.* **1.** Of, relating to, or containing an acid: *an acid solution.* **2.** Having a sour taste: *Lemons have an acid taste.* **3.** Sharp and biting; scornful or sarcastic: *an acid remark.* [First written down in 1626 in Modern English, from Latin *acidus*, sour.] —**ac′id•ly** *adv.* —**ac′id•ness** *n.*

a•cid•ic (ə sĭd′ĭk) *adj.* **1.** Of, relating to, or containing an acid: *acidic ions.* **2.** Tending to form an acid.

a•cid•i•fy (ə sĭd′ə fī′) *tr. & intr.v.* **a•cid•i•fied, a•cid•i•fy•ing, a•cid•i•fies.** To make or become acid: *Vinegar acidifies water. Milk becomes sour when it acidifies.*

a•cid•i•ty (ə sĭd′ĭ tē) *n.* The condition, quality, or degree of being acid: *The acidity of some soils is very high.*

acid rain *n.* Rain, snow, or other precipitation containing a high amount of acidity that is the result of emission into the atmosphere of polluting substances that form acid in water vapor. Acid rain is usually composed of a solution of sulfuric or nitric acid. —See Note.

acid test *n.* A situation that provides a decisive test.

ac•knowl•edge (ăk nŏl′ĭj) *tr.v.* **ac•knowl•edged, ac•knowl•edg•ing, ac•knowl•edg•es. 1.** To admit the existence or truth of: *acknowledge one's mistakes.* **2.** To recognize the standing or authority of: *The teacher was acknowledged as an authority on butterflies.* **3.a.** To express thanks for: *acknowledge a favor.* **b.** To recognize and reply to: *acknowledge the cheers of the crowd.* **4.** To state that one has received: *The college acknowledged my application with a postcard.* [First written down in 1481 in Middle English and spelled *aknowlechen*, probably blend of *knowlechen*, to acknowledge, and *aknouen*, to recognize (from Old English *oncnāwan*, to know).]

ac•knowl•edg•ment or **ac•knowl•edge•ment** (ăk nŏl′ĭj mənt) *n.* **1.** Something done or given in answer to or recognition of another's gift, favor, or message: *send an acknowledgment of an invitation.* **2.** The act of admitting the existence or truth of something; recognition: *His smile was acknowledgment that I had passed the test.*

ac•me (ăk′mē) *n.* The highest point; greatest degree; peak: *the acme of perfection.*

ac•ne (ăk′nē) *n.* A condition in which the oil glands of the skin become clogged and infected, often causing pimples to form, especially on the face.

ac•o•lyte (ăk′ə līt′) *n.* **1.** A person who assists a priest in the celebration of a Christian religious ceremony, especially a Mass. **2.** An assistant, an attendant, or a follower.

ac•o•nite (ăk′ə nīt′) *n.* **1.** Any of various poisonous plants having blue, purple, or yellowish flowers shaped somewhat like a hood. **2.** A poisonous drug prepared from wolfsbane, formerly used to relieve pain and inflammation.

a•corn (ā′kôrn′ *or* ā′kərn) *n.* The nut of an oak tree, having a hard shell set in a woody base. [First written down about 1000 in Old English and spelled *æcern*.]

a•cous•tic (ə ko͞o′stĭk) also **a•cous•ti•cal** (ə ko͞o′stĭ kəl) *adj.* **1.** Relating to sound, the sense of hearing, or the science of sound: *the acoustic quality of a concert hall.* **2.** Designed to absorb or direct sound: *an acoustic ceiling.* **3.** Of or relating to a musical instrument that does not use electronic amplification of its sound: *an acoustic guitar.* —**a•cous′ti•cal•ly** *adv.*

a•cous•tics (ə ko͞o′stĭks) *n.* **1.** *(used with a singular verb).* The scientific study of sound and its transmission. **2.** *(used with a plural verb).* The structural features of a room or building that determine how well sounds can be heard in it: *The acoustics of the concert hall were improved by lowering its ceiling.*

ac•quaint (ə kwānt′) *tr.v.* **ac•quaint•ed, ac•quaint•ing, ac•quaints. 1.** To inform: *Acquaint us with your plans as soon as possible.* **2.** To make familiar: *Let me acquaint myself with the facts of the case.* [First written down before 1200 in Middle English and spelled *aqueinten*, from Medieval Latin *adcognitāre*, to make known to.]

ac•quain•tance (ə kwān′təns) *n.* **1.** Knowledge gained from experience: *I have an acquaintance of Chinese painting.* **2.** A person whom one knows but who is not a close friend: *We have many acquaintances in the neighborhood.* —***idiom.* make (someone's) acquaintance.** To get to know someone. —**ac•quain′tance•ship′** *n.*

ac•quaint•ed (ə kwān′tĭd) *adj.* **1.** Known to one or

acid rain

Sulfur dioxide and nitrogen oxide are gases that are given off when coal, gasoline, and oil are burned in automobiles, factories, and power plants. In the atmosphere, these compounds combine with water vapor to form highly corrosive sulfuric and nitric acids. Prevailing winds carry these acids away from the industrial areas where they originate, and they fall to earth as **acid rain**. Acid rain is most common in the northeast United States and Canada, but it is spreading into the Midwest and South. It damages forests and soils and pollutes lakes and rivers, killing fish and other aquatic life. Adding lime to affected lakes has failed to neutralize their acidity. The Clean Air Act of 1990 sets limits on power-plant emissions of sulfur dioxide in the United States, with the goal of reducing acid rain pollution by the year 2000.

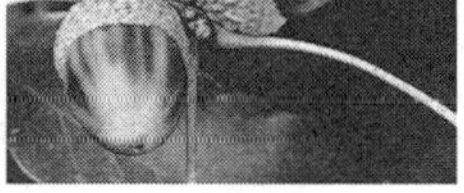

acorn

ă	**pat**	oi	**boy**
ā	**pay**	ou	**out**
âr	**care**	o͝o	**took**
ä	**father**	o͞o	**boot**
ĕ	**pet**	ŭ	**cut**
ē	**be**	ûr	**urge**
ĭ	**pit**	th	**thin**
ī	**pie**	*th*	**this**
îr	**pier**	hw	**whoop**
ŏ	**pot**	zh	**vision**
ō	**toe**	ə	**about**
ô	**paw**	N	*French* **bon**

Acropolis
As reconstructed
by Friedrich Ritter von Thiersch
(1852–1921)

each other: *We've been acquainted for years.* **2.** Informed; familiar: *I am not acquainted with her novels.*

ac•qui•esce (ăk′wē **ĕs′**) *intr.v.* **ac•qui•esced, ac•qui•esc•ing, ac•qui•esc•es.** To agree or yield without protest; consent quietly: *acquiesce to a demand; acquiesce in a decision.*

ac•qui•es•cence (ăk′wē **ĕs′**əns) *n.* Submission without protest; quiet agreement.

ac•qui•es•cent (ăk′wē **ĕs′**ənt) *adj.* Agreeing or submitting without protest. **—ac′qui•es′cent•ly** *adv.*

ac•quire (ə **kwīr′**) *tr.v.* **ac•quired, ac•quir•ing, ac•quires.** To get to have; gain; obtain: *acquire knowledge; acquire new skills.* [First written down in 1601 in Modern English, from Latin *acquīrere*, to add to : *ad-*, to + *quaerere*, to seek, get.] **—ac•quir′a•ble** *adj.*

ac•quired immunity (ə **kwīrd′**) *n.* Immunity to a disease that develops from the presence of antibodies in the blood, as after an attack of the disease or vaccination against it.

ac•quire•ment (ə **kwīr′**mənt) *n.* **1.** The act or process of acquiring: *the acquirement of property by inheritance.* **2.** A skill or an ability gained by effort or experience; an attainment: *a talented student of many acquirements.*

ac•qui•si•tion (ăk′wĭ **zĭsh′**ən) *n.* **1.** The act or process of acquiring: *The museum's acquisition of a large art collection took many years.* **2.** Something acquired, especially as an addition to a collection or one's possessions: *the museum's newest acquisitions to its art collection.*

ac•quis•i•tive (ə **kwĭz′**ĭ tĭv) *adj.* **1.** Eager to acquire things, especially possessions: *an acquisitive collector of books.* **2.** Tending to acquire information: *the acquisitive mind of a scientist.* **—ac•quis′i•tive•ly** *adv.* **—ac•quis′i•tive•ness** *n.*

ac•quit (ə **kwĭt′**) *tr.v.* **ac•quit•ted, ac•quit•ting, ac•quits. 1.** To free or clear from a formal accusation of wrongdoing: *A jury acquitted the suspect of the crime.* **2.** To conduct (oneself); behave: *The firefighters acquitted themselves bravely during the crisis.* **—ac•quit′ter** *n.*

ac•quit•tal (ə **kwĭt′**l) *n.* The freeing of a person from an accusation of wrongdoing by the judgment of a court: *The jury's vote of not guilty resulted in the defendant's acquittal.*

a•cre (**ā′**kər) *n.* **1.** A unit of area used in measuring land, equal to 43,560 square feet or 4,047 square meters. See table at **measurement. 2. acres.** Property in the form of land. [First written down about 975 in Old English and spelled *æcer.*]

a•cre•age (**ā′**kər ĭj *or* **ā′**krĭj) *n.* Land area measured in acres: *a national park of vast acreage.*

a•cre-foot (**ā′**kər **fo͝ot′**) *n.* The volume of water that will cover an area of one acre to a depth of one foot; 43,560 cubic feet or about 1,233 cubic meters of water.

ac•rid (**ăk′**rĭd) *adj.* **1.** Harsh or bitter to the sense of taste or smell: *Acrid smoke from the blazing chemical plant filled the air.* **2.** Sharp or biting in tone or manner; nasty: *acrid comments of discontent.* **—ac′rid•ly** *adv.* **—ac′rid•ness** *n.*

ac•ri•mo•ni•ous (ăk′rə **mō′**nē əs) *adj.* Bitter or stinging in language or tone; caustic; ill-natured: *acrimonious exchanges among the candidates.* **—ac′ri•mo′ni•ous•ly** *adv.* **—ac′ri•mo′ni•ous•ness** *n.*

ac•ri•mo•ny (**ăk′**rə mō′nē) *n.* Bitterness or ill-natured sharpness in manner or language: *sudden outbursts or acrimony between jealous partners.*

ac•ro•bat (**ăk′**rə băt′) *n.* A person who can perform athletic feats requiring great agility and balance, such as swinging on a trapeze or walking a tightrope. [First written down in 1825 in Modern English, from Greek *akrobatein*, to walk on tiptoe.]

ac•ro•bat•ic (ăk′rə **băt′**ĭk) *adj.* Of, relating to, or suggestive of an acrobat or acrobatics: *an acrobatic dive into the pool.* **—ac′ro•bat′i•cal•ly** *adv.*

ac•ro•bat•ics (ăk′rə **băt′**ĭks) *n. (used with a singular or plural verb).* **1.** The art or performance of an acrobat. **2.** A display of great skill and agility: *the singer's vocal acrobatics.*

ac•ro•nym (**ăk′**rə nĭm′) *n.* A word or name formed from the first letters or syllables of other words. *Radar* is an acronym from *ra*dio *d*etection *a*nd *r*anging. *OPEC* is an acronym from *O*rganization of *P*etroleum *E*xporting *C*ountries. [First written down in 1943 in Modern English : Greek *akros*, high, top + Greek *onuma*, name.]

a•crop•o•lis (ə **krŏp′**ə lĭs) *n.* **1.** The high, fortified part of an ancient Greek city. **2. Acropolis.** The hill in Athens on which the Parthenon stands.

a•cross (ə **krôs′** *or* ə **krŏs′**) *prep.* **1.** On, at, or from the other side of: *a house across the road.* **2.** From one side of to the other: *a bridge across a river.* **3.** So as to cross; over; through: *draw lines across the paper.* *—adv.* **1.** From one side to the other: *The bridge swayed as they drove across.* **2.** On or to the opposite side: *We came across by ferry.* [First written down before 1200 in Middle English and spelled *acrois*, from Anglo-Norman *an croiz*, crosswise.]

a•cros•tic (ə **krô′**stĭk *or* ə **krŏs′**tĭk) *n.* A poem or series of lines in which certain letters, usually the first in each line, spell out a name, phrase or message.

a•cryl•ic (ə **krĭl′**ĭk) *n.* **1.** An acrylic resin. **2.** A paint made with acrylic resin. **3.** An acrylic fiber.

acrylic acid *n.* A colorless strong-smelling liquid with the formula $C_3H_4O_2$ that combines easily with other substances to form acrylic resins and is soluble in alcohol and water.

acrylic fiber *n.* Any of a number of synthetic fibers derived from acrylic acid and used in making certain long-wearing fabrics.

acrylic resin *n.* Any of a number of tough, clear plastics derived from acrylic acid and used in making paints and automobile parts.

act (ăkt) *n.* **1.** Something done; a deed: *an act of bravery.* **2.** The process of doing something: *Police caught the robber in the act of stealing.* **3.a.** A performance for an audience, often forming part of a longer show: *a comedian's act.* **b.** One of the main divisions of a play or other dramatic work: *a play in three acts.* **4.** An insincere pretense; a false show: *His buying you flowers was just an act to look good in front of others.* **5.** A law, especially one enacted by a legislative body: *an act of Congress.* *—v.* **act•ed, act•ing, acts.** *—intr.* **1.** To do something; perform an action: *By acting quickly, we prevented the fire from spreading.* **2.** To serve or function: *One of the older students acted as teacher. The heart acts like a pump.* **3.** To behave; conduct oneself: *She acts like a born leader.* **4.** Perform in a dramatic presentation: *act in a play.* **5.** To put on a false show; pretend: *He tried to look brave, but he was only acting.* **6.** To have an effect: *The medicine acts soon after it is taken.* *—tr.* **1.** To play the part of; perform as: *She acted Juliet in the play.* **2.** To behave like: *act the fool.* **3.** To behave as suitable for: *Act your age.* ***—idioms.*** **act on** or **act upon.** To do something as a result of: *I finally acted on my doctor's advice and gave up chocolate.* **act out.** To perform in or as if in a play; dramatize: *act out a story.* **act up. 1.** To misbehave: *The children were acting up all day, and their mother was upset.* **2.** To work improperly; malfunction: *The furnace was acting up and the radiators stayed cold.* [First written down about 1380 in Middle English, from Latin *agere,* to do.] **—act′a•ble** *adj.*

ACTH (ā′sē′tē **āch′**) *n.* A hormone secreted by a lobe of the pituitary gland. It stimulates the adrenal glands to produce cortisone and related hormones.

act•ing (**ăk′**tĭng) *adj.* Serving temporarily or in place of another person: *the acting principal.* —*n.* The occupation or performance of an actor or actress.

ac•tin•ic radiation (ăk **tĭn′**ĭk) *n.* A form of radiation, such as ultraviolet rays or x-rays, that can cause chemical changes in an object that it strikes.

ac•ti•nism (**ăk′**tə nĭz′əm) *n.* The action or property in radiant energy that produces chemical changes, as the effects of actinic radiation on photographic film.

ac•tin•i•um (ăk **tĭn′**ē əm) *n. Symbol* **Ac** A highly radioactive metallic element somewhat like radium, found in uranium ore and used as a source of alpha rays. Atomic number 89. See table at **element.**

ac•tion (**ăk′**shən) *n.* **1.a.** A thing done; a deed: *take responsibility for one's actions.* **b.** Behavior; conduct. Often used in the plural: *amusing actions.* **c.** A tendency toward vigorous activity: *a man of action.* **2.** The process or fact of doing something: *firefighters springing into action; an emergency requiring immediate action.* **3.** The series of events in a play or story: *The action of the play takes place in a castle.* **4.** A physical change, as in position, mass, or energy, that an object or system undergoes: *the action of a sail in the wind.* **5.a.** The way in which something works or acts, often upon a larger system: *the action of the liver in digestion.* **b.** The effect of this: *the corrosive action of acid on metal.* **6.** The operating parts of a mechanism: *the action of a piano.* **7.** Battle; combat: *send the troops into action.* **8.** A lawsuit.

action verb *n.* A verb that expresses action. Action verbs are either transitive, as *activate* (*Electricity activates the fan's motor*) or intransitive, as *run* (*The fan's motor runs on electricity*).

ac•ti•vate (**ăk′**tə vāt′) *tr.v.* **ac•ti•vat•ed, ac•ti•vat•ing, ac•ti•vates. 1.** To make active; set in operation or motion: *The motor is activated by a battery.* **2.** To start or accelerate a chemical reaction in, as by heating. **3.** To make (a substance) radioactive. **—ac′ti•va′tion** *n.*

ac•tive (**ăk′**tĭv) *adj.* **1.** Moving or tending to move about; engaged in physical action: *Nurses are more active than office workers.* **2.** Performing or capable of performing an action or process; functioning; working: *an active volcano.* **3.** Taking part or requiring participation in activities: *an active member of the club.* **4.** Full of energy; busy: *an active and useful life; an active mind.* **5.** Causing action or change; effective: *active efforts for improvement.* **6.** In grammar, of or relating to the active voice. —*n.* **1.** The active voice in grammar. **2.** A verb form in the active voice. **—ac′tive•ly** *adv.* **—ac′tive•ness** *n.* —See Note at **verb.**

active duty *n.* Military service with full pay and regular duty.

active immunity *n.* Immunity from a disease as a result of the production of antibodies by an organism.

active voice *n.* In grammar, a form of a verb that shows that the subject is performing or causing the action expressed by the verb. In the sentence *John bought the book, bought* is in the active voice.

ac•tiv•ist (**ăk′**tə vĭst) *n.* A person who believes in or takes part in direct action to bring about changes in government, social conditions, or a cause.

ac•tiv•i•ty (ăk **tĭv′**ĭ tē) *n., pl.* **ac•tiv•i•ties. 1.** The condition or process of being active; action: *mental or physical activity.* **2.** A particular kind of action or behavior: *the nesting activities of birds.* **3.** A planned or organized thing to do, as in a school subject or social group: *Outside activities usually make school more fun.* **4.** Vigorous movement or action; liveliness: *The department store was a scene of great activity.*

ac•tor (**ăk′**tər) *n.* **1.** A person who acts a part in a play, motion picture, or television program. **2.** A person or group that takes part in or accomplishes something: *England, France, and Spain were actors in the colonizing of North America.*

ac•tress (**ăk′**trĭs) *n.* A woman who is an actor.

Acts of the Apostles (ăkts) *pl.n.* (*used with a singular verb*). A book of the New Testament giving a history of the early Christian Church.

ac•tu•al (**ăk′**cho͞o əl) *adj.* Existing or happening in fact; real: *Actual sales greatly exceeded estimated sales.*

ac•tu•al•i•ty (ăk′cho͞o **ăl′**ĭ tē) *n., pl.* **ac•tu•al•i•ties.** Real existence or circumstance; reality; fact: *The human dream of walking on the moon has become an actuality in our time.*

ac•tu•al•ly (**ăk′**cho͞o ə lē) *adv.* In fact; really.

ac•tu•ar•y (**ăk′**cho͞o ĕr′ē) *n., pl.* **ac•tu•ar•ies.** A person who estimates risks and calculates rates and premiums for an insurance company.

ac•tu•ate (**ăk′**cho͞o āt′) *tr.v.* **ac•tu•at•ed, ac•tu•at•ing, ac•tu•ates. 1.** To put into action or motion: *Stepping on a pedal actuates the brake.* **2.** To cause or inspire to act; motivate: *His remarks actuated a heated discussion.* **—ac′tu•a′tion** *n.* **—ac′tu•a′tor** *n.*

a•cu•i•ty (ə **kyo͞o′**ĭ tē) *n.* Keenness of mind; sharpness of perception; acuteness: *With great acuity the doctor diagnosed the patient's problem.*

a•cu•men (ə **kyoo′**mən *or* **ăk′**yə mən) *n.* Quickness and wisdom in making judgments; keen insight: *The owner's business acumen permitted the store to grow rapidly.*

ac•u•punc•ture (**ăk′**yo͝o pŭngk′chər) *n.* The practice originating in traditional Chinese medicine in which thin needles are inserted into the body at specific points in order to relieve pain, treat a disease, or anesthetize parts of the body during surgery. [First written down in 1684 in Modern English : Latin *acus,* needle + English *puncture.*]

a•cute (ə **kyo͞ot′**) *adj.* **1.** Keen; perceptive: *an acute sense of hearing; an acute awareness of one's surroundings.* **2.** Sharp and intense: *A toothache can cause acute pain.* **3.** Developing suddenly and having a short but severe course: *acute appendicitis.* **4.** Very serious; critical: *an acute lack of funds.* **5.** High in pitch; shrill: *the acute sounds of a bat's cry.* [First written down before 1398 in Middle English, from Latin *acuere,* to sharpen.] **—a•cute′ly** *adv.* **—a•cute′ness** *n.*

acute accent *n.* **1.** A mark (´) indicating how a vowel is pronounced; in the word *cliché* the final *e* is pronounced like the *a* in *game.* **2.** A mark (´) indicating metrical stress in poetry.

acute angle *n.* An angle whose measure in degrees is between 0° and 90°.

ad (ăd) *n.* An advertisement.

❑ *These sound alike:* **ad, add** (combine to form a sum).

A.D. *abbr.* An abbreviation of Anno Domini (in the year of the Lord; that is, after the birth of Jesus).

ad– *pref.* A prefix that means toward or to: *adsorb.* —See Note.

ad•age (**ăd′**ĭj) *n.* A short proverb or saying generally considered to be wise and true; for example, "Haste makes waste" is an adage.

a•da•gio (ə **dä′**jō *or* ə **dä′**jē ō′) *adv.* In music, slowly. —*adj.* In music, slow.

Ad•am (**ăd′**əm). In the Bible, the first man and the husband of Eve.

activist

Protesting the building of a toxic waste storage facility

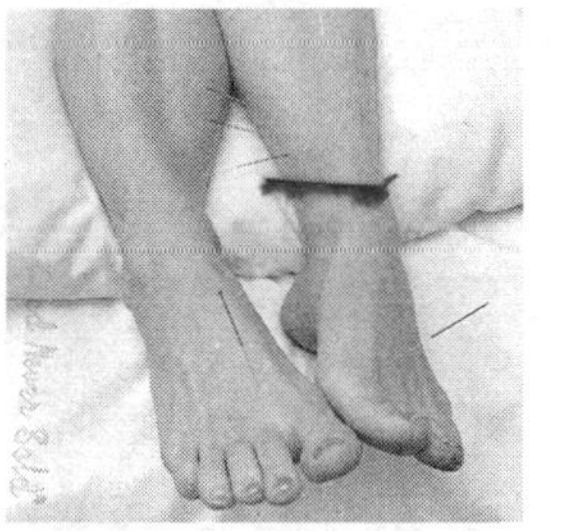

acupuncture

Word Building: ad–

The prefix **ad–** comes from the Latin preposition *ad,* meaning "to, toward, on top of." In Latin, this preposition became a prefix, and when it was followed by *c, f, g, l, n, r, s,* or *t,* it became *ac, af, ag, al, an, ar, as,* or *at,* respectively. Thus Latin *ad–* is easy to see in English words such as **adhere, admit,** and **adverse,** but it is not so obvious in words such as **affix, apply,** and **attend.**

ă	pat	oi	boy
ā	pay	ou	out
âr	care	o͝o	took
ä	father	o͞o	boot
ĕ	pet	ŭ	cut
ē	be	ûr	urge
ĭ	pit	th	thin
ī	pie	*th*	this
îr	pier	hw	whoop
ŏ	pot	zh	vision
ō	toe	ə	about
ô	paw	N	*French* bon

Abigail Adams
Detail of portrait by Gilbert Stuart (1755–1828)

John Adams
Detail of portrait by Gilbert Stuart (1755–1828)

John Quincy Adams
Detail of 1864 portrait by George Peter Alexander Healy (1813–1894)

ad•a•mant (ăd′ə mənt) *adj.* Firm and unyielding; not giving in easily: *Our parents were adamant and showed no sign of yielding in their decision.* [First written down in 1387 in Middle English, from Greek *adamas*, hard steel, diamond.] **—ad′a•mant•ly** *adv.*

Ad•ams (ăd′əmz), **Abigail Smith.** 1744–1818. American writer whose many letters provide a vivid picture of life in colonial Massachusetts. Abigail Adams was the First Lady of the United States (1797–1801) as the wife of John Adams.

Adams, John. 1735–1826. The first Vice President (1789–1797) and second President (1797–1801) of the United States. He helped draft the Declaration of Independence and the U.S. Constitution.

Adams, John Quincy. 1767–1848. The sixth President of the United States (1825–1829). After his presidency he served in the House of Representatives (1831–1848), where he strongly opposed slavery.

Adams, Samuel. 1722–1803. American Revolutionary leader who incited Bostonians to rebel against Great Britain. He was a member of the First and Second Continental Congresses and signed the Declaration of Independence.

Ad•am's apple (ăd′əmz) *n.* The lump at the front of the throat where a part of the larynx projects forward, most noticeably in men. [First written down in 1755 in Modern English, from Hebrew *tappuach hā-ādām*, swelling of the man.]

a•dapt (ə dăpt′) *v.* **a•dapt•ed, a•dapt•ing, a•dapts.** *—tr.* **1.** To change or adjust for a certain purpose: *They adapted the old truck for use as a camper.* **2.** To make fit or suitable for a particular use or situation: *Her parents could not adapt themselves to living on an island.* *—intr.* To become adjusted: *The polar bear has adapted well to the Arctic climate.* [First written down before 1425 in Middle English and spelled *adapten*, from Latin *adaptāre* : *ad-*, to + *aptāre*, to fit.]

Synonyms: **adapt, accommodate, adjust, conform.** These verbs all mean to change something to make it suitable. *Human beings can adapt themselves to a great variety of climates. I cannot accommodate myself to the new rules. If you adjust your seat belt you will be more comfortable. He wore shorts to school the first day but later conformed to the dress code.*

---

a•dapt•a•ble (ə dăp′tə bəl) *adj.* Able to change or be adjusted to fit in with new or different uses or situations: *an adaptable schedule that is easy to rearrange; an adaptable person.* **—a•dapt′a•bil′i•ty** *n.* **—a•dapt′a•ble•ness** *n.*

ad•ap•ta•tion (ăd′ăp tā′shən) *n.* **1.** The act or process of adapting; change or adjustment to meet new conditions: *The friendly student's adaptation to a new school was easy and quick. The water wheel permitted adaptation of water power for the driving of early machinery.* **2.** Something that is produced by being adapted: *The movie was an adaptation of a story written by Charles Dickens.* **3.** The alteration or adjustment of a body part or type of behavior that fits an animal or plant for a particular way of living: *Wings are an adaptation of the forelimbs of a bird for flight.*

a•dapt•ed (ə dăp′tĭd) *adj.* Fitted or suitable, especially for a certain purpose: *claws well adapted for digging.*

a•dapt•er also **a•dap•tor** (ə dăp′tər) *n.* **1.** A device for putting together different parts of an apparatus that otherwise would not fit together. **2.** A device for putting a machine or a piece of equipment to a different use.

a•dap•tive (ə dăp′tĭv) *adj.* **1.** Capable of or resulting from adaptation: *Adaptive changes in the penguin allow it to move swiftly underwater.* **2.** Tending to adapt easily: *an adaptive good nature.*

add (ăd) *v.* **add•ed, add•ing, adds.** *—tr.* **1.** To combine (two or more numbers) to form a sum: *If one adds 6 and 8 the total is 14.* **2.** To join or unite so as to increase, change, or improve something: *add a suffix to a word; add an annex to a building.* **3.** To say or write as something extra; say further: *Give directions and add a word of caution.* *—intr.* **1.** To find a sum in arithmetic: *Most store clerks can add in their heads.* **2.** To cause an increase or addition: *He adds to his savings each week.* ***—idioms.*** **add up.** To be reasonable; make sense: *What she said did not add up.* **add up to.** To amount to: *A group of friends and some music add up to a good time.* [First written down about 1380 in Middle English and spelled *adden*, from Latin *addere*.]

❑ *These sound alike:* **add, ad** (advertisement).

Ad•dams (ăd′əmz), **Jane.** 1860–1935. American social reformer and pacifist who founded Hull-House, which provided cooperative housing for working women, in Chicago (1889). She shared the 1931 Nobel Peace Prize.

ad•dax (ăd′ăks′) *n.* A large antelope of Arabia and North Africa, having a heavy body and long spirally twisted horns.

ad•dend (ăd′ĕnd′ *or* ə dĕnd′) *n.* A number or quantity to be added to another number. For example, in 9 + 2 = 11, the numbers 9 and 2 are addends.

ad•den•dum (ə dĕn′dəm) *n., pl.* **ad•den•da** (ə dĕn′də). **1.** An appendix to a book or document. **2.** Something to be added; an addition.

ad•der (ăd′ər) *n.* **1.** Any of several poisonous snakes of northern Europe and Asia; a viper. **2.** Any of several nonpoisonous snakes of North America, such as the hognose. **3.** A puff adder. [First written down about 950 in Old English and spelled *nædre*, altered to Middle English *(an) addre*, from the phrase *(a) naddre*, a snake.]

ad•dict (ə dĭkt′) *tr.v.* **ad•dict•ed, ad•dict•ing, ad•dicts.** To cause (someone) to become dependent on the use of a habit-forming substance, especially a narcotic drug. *—n.* (ăd′ĭkt). **1.** A person who has an uncontrollable craving for a harmful, habit-forming substance, especially a narcotic drug. **2.** A person who is deeply devoted to or very enthusiastic about something: *a baseball addict.* [First written down in 1534 in Modern English, from Latin *addīcere*, to sentence : *ad-*, to + *dīcere*, to adjudge.]

ad•dict•ed (ə dĭk′tĭd) *adj.* **1.** Dependent on a harmful, habit-forming substance, especially a narcotic drug. **2.** Disposed or devoted, as by habit or interest: *addicted to gossiping on the phone; addicted to a radio program.*

ad•dic•tion (ə dĭk′shən) *n.* The condition of being addicted, especially dependence on harmful, habit-forming drugs.

ad•dic•tive (ə dĭk′tĭv) *adj.* Causing addiction; habit-forming: *Watching television can become an addictive pastime.*

Ad•dis Ab•a•ba (ăd′ĭs ăb′ə bə *or* ä′dĭs ä′bə bä′). The capital and largest city of Ethiopia, in the center of the country on a plateau more than 8,000 feet (2,440 meters) above sea level. Population, 1,408,068.

ad•di•tion (ə dĭsh′ən) *n.* **1.** The act, process, or operation of adding two or more numbers. **2.** The act or process of adding something extra to a thing: *the addition of seasoning to food.* **3.** An added thing, part, or person: *My new baby brother is an addition to our family.* ***—idioms.*** **in addition.** Also; as well as: *We ate at a restaurant and saw a movie in addition.* **in addition to.** Along with; besides: *In* *addition to riding her bike, she played her guitar this morning.* —SEE NOTE at **together.**

ad•di•tion•al (ə dĭsh′ə nəl) *adj.* Added; extra; more: *The instructions are incomplete and we need additional information to finish the project.* **—ad•di′tion•al•ly** *adv.*

ad•di•tive (ăd′ĭ tĭv) *n.* A substance added in small amounts to something in order to improve its performance or quality, preserve its usefulness, or make it more effective: *a food additive to prevent spoiling.* —*adj.* Marked by or involving addition.

additive inverse *n.* Either one of a pair of numbers, such as +7 and −7, whose sum is zero (0).

ad•dle (ăd′l) *tr. & intr.v.* **ad•dled, ad•dling, ad•dles. 1.** To make or become mixed up, confused, or muddled: *The shouting and pushing of the crowd addled my sense of direction. My sense of direction addled in the confusion.* **2.** To make or become spoiled: *Heat addled the eggs. The eggs addled in the heat.*

ad•dress (ə drĕs′) *tr.v.* **ad•dressed, ad•dress•ing, ad•dress•es. 1.** To speak to: *The police officer addressed the speeder in low tones.* **2.** To give a speech to: *The President will address the nation on TV.* **3.** To direct to a particular person, group, or place: *The teacher's remarks were addressed to the new students.* **4.** To refer to directly; call; greet: *Address the judge as "Your Honor."* **5.** To put a destination on (a piece of mail) to show where it should go: *address an envelope.* **6.** To direct the efforts or attention of (oneself): *The committee addressed itself to plans for a new town hall.* **7.** To deal with: *We must address this problem.* —*n.* **1.** (*also* ăd′rĕs′). **a.** The place where a person lives or where a business is located: *your home address.* **b.** The information on a piece of mail, indicating where it is to be delivered. **2.** A formal speech: *The President's inaugural address outlined plans for the economy.* **3.** A way of speaking or behaving: *a woman of polite address.* **4.** A number, label, or other symbol identifying a particular location where information is stored in the memory of a computer. [First written down before 1325 in Middle English and spelled *adressen*, to direct, from Old French *addresser.*]

ad•dress•ee (ăd′rĕ sē′ *or* ə drĕs′ē′) *n.* The person to whom a letter or package is addressed.

ad•duce (ə do͞os′ *or* ə dyo͞os′) *tr.v.* **ad•duced, ad•duc•ing, ad•duc•es.** To offer as a reason; give as an example or means of proof: *The defendant was unable to adduce evidence to support his innocence.*

A•den (ăd′n *or* äd′n). The largest city of Yemen, in the southern part of the country on the **Gulf of Aden,** an inlet of the Indian Ocean. It has been one of the chief ports of southern Arabia since ancient times. Population, 271,600.

ad•e•nine (ăd′n ēn′ *or* ăd′n ĭn) *n.* A base that is a component of DNA and RNA.

ad•e•noi•dal (ăd′n oid′l) *adj.* Of or relating to the adenoids.

ad•e•noids (ăd′n oidz) *pl.n.* Masses of glandular tissue, similar to that of lymph nodes, located in the nose above the throat. When swollen they may obstruct breathing and make speech difficult.

a•dept (ə dĕpt′) *adj.* Very skillful and effective; proficient: *Tailors are adept at sewing. The inventor was an adept mechanic.* See Synonyms at **proficient.** —*n.* (ăd′ĕpt′). A person who is highly skilled; an expert. [First written down before 1691 in Modern English, from Latin *adipīscī,* to attain : *ad-*, to + *apīscī,* to grasp.] **—a•dept′ly** *adv.* **—a•dept′ness** *n.*

ad′e•qua•cy (ăd′ĭ kwə sē) *n.* The condition of being adequate; sufficiency or suitability.

ad•e•quate (ăd′ĭ kwĭt) *adj.* **1.** As much as is needed for a particular purpose; sufficient; enough: *adequate supplies to meet our needs.* **2.** Barely satisfactory or sufficient: *That student's skills are just adequate to pass the test.* [First written down before 1617 in Modern English, from Latin *adaequāre,* to equalize : *ad-*, to + *aequāre,* to make equal (from *aequus,* equal).] **—ad′e•quate•ly** *adv.* **—ad′e•quate•ness** *n.*

ad•here (ăd hîr′) *intr.v.* **ad•hered, ad•her•ing, ad•heres. 1.** To stick or hold fast: *The wallpaper adheres to the wall.* **2.** To remain devoted; support: *adhere to one's religious beliefs.* **3.** To carry out something, such as a plan, without changes; hold firmly: *They adhered to the original plan* [First written down in 1597 in Modern English, from Latin *adhaerēre* : *ad-*, to + *haerēre,* to stick.]

ad•her•ence (ăd hîr′əns *or* ăd hĕr′əns) *n.* **1.** The process or condition of adhering or sticking fast: *the gum's annoying adherence to my shoe.* **2.** Faithful attachment or loyalty; devotion: *adherence to one's principles.*

ad•her•ent (ăd hîr′ənt *or* ăd hĕr′ənt) *n.* A loyal supporter or faithful follower: *Adherents of conservatism oppose most increases in government spending.* —*adj.* Sticking or holding fast; clinging.

ad•he•sion (ăd hē′zhən) *n.* **1.** The process or condition of sticking fast or adhering. **2.** Loyal attachment or devotion. **3.** A condition in which body tissues that are normally separate grow together.

ad•he•sive (ăd hē′sĭv *or* ăd hē′zĭv) *adj.* **1.** Tending to hold fast to another material; sticky. **2.** Coated with glue or other sticky substance: *an adhesive label.* —*n.* **1.** An adhesive substance, such as paste or glue. **2.** Adhesive tape. **—ad•he′sive•ness** *n.*

adhesive tape *n.* A tape coated on one side with a sticky substance.

ad hoc (ăd hŏk′ *or* ăd hōk′) *adv. & adj.* For a specific purpose or case: *a committee formed ad hoc to deal with the problem; an ad hoc meeting.*

ad•i•a•bat•ic (ăd′ē ə băt′ĭk *or* ā′dī ə băt′ĭk) *adj.* Occurring without gain or loss of heat: *The passage of sound through air is approximately adiabatic.* **—ad′i•a•bat′i•cal•ly** *adv.*

a•dieu (ə dyo͞o′ *or* ə do͞o′) *interj.* An expression used to say good-bye; farewell. —*n., pl.* **a•dieus** or **a•dieux** (ə dyo͞oz′ *or* ə do͞oz′). A farewell: *say one's adieus upon leaving.* [First written down about 1385 in Middle English, from Old French *a dieu,* (I commend you) to God.]

❑ *These sound alike:* **adieu, ado** (fuss).

ad in•fi•ni•tum (ăd ĭn′fə nī′təm) *adv.* Without limit; forever; endlessly: *talk on ad infinitum.*

ad•i•os (ăd′ē ōs′ *or* ä′dē ōs′) *interj.* An expression used to say good-bye; farewell. [First written down in 1837 in Modern English, from Spanish *adiós,* probably translated from French *à dieu.*]

ad•i•pose (ăd′ə pōs′) *adj.* Of, relating to, or consisting of animal fat; fatty.

Ad•i•ron•dack Mountains (ăd′ə rŏn′dăk′). A group of mountains in northeast New York between the St. Lawrence River valley in the north and the Mohawk River valley in the south. The range is part of the Appalachian system and rises to 5,344 feet (1,629.9 meters).

adj. *abbr.* An abbreviation of adjective.

ad•ja•cent (ə jā′sənt) *adj.* **1.** Next to; adjoining: *I can hear all the noise from the room adjacent to mine.* **2.** Lying near or close; nearby; neighboring: *the city and adjacent farm lands.* **—ad•ja′cent•ly** *adv.*

adjacent angle *n.* Either of a pair of angles that have a vertex and a side in common so that they are located next to each other.

adjacent side *n.* A side of a right triangle next to the given angle.

ad•jec•ti•val (ăj′ĭk tī′vəl) *adj.* Of, relating to, or

Jane Addams
Photographed in the 1890's

addax

ă	**pat**	oi	**boy**
ā	**pay**	ou	**out**
âr	**care**	o͝o	**took**
ä	**father**	o͞o	**boot**
ĕ	**pet**	ŭ	**cut**
ē	**be**	ûr	**urge**
ĭ	**pit**	th	**thin**
ī	**pie**	*th*	**this**
îr	**pier**	hw	**whoop**
ŏ	**pot**	zh	**vision**
ō	**toe**	ə	**about**
ô	**paw**	N	*French* **bon**

Usage: adjective

Words that modify nouns are called **adjectives**. If an adjective precedes a noun, it is called an **attributive** adjective. In the phrase *a blue coat, blue* is an attributive adjective. If an adjective follows a noun and a linking verb, such as *be, grow,* or *seem,* the adjective is called a **predicate adjective**, as in the sentence *The sky grew dark.*

admiral
Red admiral

adobe
Taos pueblo, Taos, New Mexico

functioning as an adjective: *an adjectival phrase.* **—ad′jec•ti′val•ly** *adv.*

ad•jec•tive (ăj′ĭk tĭv) *n.* In grammar, a word used to modify a noun by describing it or limiting or adding to its meaning. For example, in the sentence *The young boy is very tall, young* and *tall* are adjectives. In English, adjectives usually appear before the noun they modify, but with verbs such as *act, seem,* and *be,* they often appear after the verb, as in *The mouse acts nervous. The cat seems happy. The horse is thirsty.* —*adj.* Adjectival: *the adjective position.* —See Note.

ad•join (ə join′) *v.* **ad•joined, ad•join•ing, ad•joins.** —*tr.* To be next to or connected with; share a boundary with: *The bath adjoins the bedroom.* —*intr.* To be side by side or connected: *These rooms adjoin.*

ad•join•ing (ə joi′nĭng) *adj.* Next to or connected with; alongside: *a bedroom and adjoining bath; a row of adjoining houses.*

ad•journ (ə jûrn′) *v.* **ad•journed, ad•journ•ing, ad•journs.** —*tr.* To bring (a meeting or session) to a close, putting off further business until later: *The judge adjourned the trial for the holidays.* —*intr.* **1.** To stop proceedings until a later time; break up: *The court adjourned for the weekend.* **2.** To move from one place to another: *The dinner guests adjourned to the living room.* [First written down before 1338 in Middle English and spelled *ajournen,* from Old French *ajourner* : *a-,* to + *jour,* day (from Late Latin *diurnum,* from Latin *diurnus,* daily, from *diēs,* day).]

ad•journ•ment (ə jûrn′mənt) *n.* **1.** The act of adjourning or the state of being adjourned. **2.** The time during which a legislature or a court is not in session.

ad•judge (ə jŭj′) *tr.v.* **ad•judged, ad•judg•ing, ad•judg•es. 1.** To determine, rule, or declare by law: *The accused thief was adjudged guilty.* **2.** To award by law: *The injured motorist was adjudged damages for medical costs.*

ad•junct (ăj′ŭngkt′) *n.* A separate, less important thing added to something: *The card shop is an adjunct of the bookstore.*

ad•ju•ra•tion (ăj′ə rā′shən) *n.* A solemn command or an earnest appeal: *a judge's adjuration to a witness to tell the whole truth.*

ad•jure (ə jo͝or′) *tr.v.* **ad•jured, ad•jur•ing, ad•jures. 1.** To command solemnly. **2.** To ask or entreat earnestly: *I adjure you on your honor to keep my secret.*

ad•just (ə jŭst′) *v.* **ad•just•ed, ad•just•ing, ad•justs.** —*tr.* **1.** To change, set, or regulate in order to improve or make suitable: *I adjusted the seat belts in the car to fit the child.* See Synonyms at **adapt. 2.** To bring the parts of (a mechanism, for example) into a more effective arrangement: *The mechanic adjusted the carburetor on my car.* **3.** To change or adapt to suit existing circumstances or conditions: *Some wild animals do not adjust themselves to living in a cage.* **4.** To decide how much is to be paid on (an insurance claim). —*intr.* To become accustomed or adapt: *We can adjust to living in a smaller apartment.* [First written down about 1380 in Middle English and spelled *ajusten,* from Old French *ajoster* : from Latin *ad-,* to + Latin *iuxtā,* near.] **—ad•just′er** *n.* **—ad•just′a•ble** *adj.*

ad•just•ment (ə jŭst′mənt) *n.* **1.** The act of adjusting or the state of being adjusted: *Winter weather requires an adjustment to colder temperature.* **2.** The state of being adjusted: *valves in proper adjustment.* **3.** A means by which a device can be adjusted: *Our TV set has several adjustments to regulate the color of the picture.* **4.** A settlement of a claim or debt.

ad•ju•tant (ăj′ə tənt) *n.* **1.** An army officer who acts as an assistant to a commanding officer. **2.** A helper or assistant. **3.** An adjutant stork.

adjutant stork *n.* Any of several very large storks of India and Africa having soft down.

ad-lib (ăd lĭb′) *v.* **ad-libbed, ad-lib•bing, ad-libs.** —*tr.* To make up (words, music, or actions) while performing: *ad-lib a joke.* —*intr.* To make up words, music, or actions while performing: *The actor forgot his lines and ad-libbed.* —*n.* (ăd′lĭb′). A line, speech, action, or passage of music made up on the spot. —*adj.* Made up on the spot; improvised: *an ad-lib remark.* [First written down in 1919 in Modern English, from Latin *ad libitum,* at pleasure.]

ad•min•is•ter (ăd mĭn′ĭ stər) *v.* **ad•min•is•tered, ad•min•is•ter•ing, ad•min•is•ters.** —*tr.* **1.** To direct the affairs of; manage: *The mayor administers the city government.* **2.a.** To give or deal out; dispense: *A judge administers justice.* **b.** To give and supervise: *administer a test.* **3.** To give formally or officially: *administer an oath of office.* **4.** To settle (an estate); take charge of (property). —*intr.* To be helpful; contribute: *The Red Cross administered to the needs of the flood victims.*

ad•min•is•trate (ăd mĭn′ĭ strāt′) *tr.v.* **ad•min•is•trat•ed, ad•min•is•trat•ing, ad•min•is•trates.** To administer.

ad•min•is•tra•tion (ăd mĭn′ĭ strā′shən) *n.* **1.** The act or process of directing the affairs of a business, school, or other institution; management. **2.** The people who manage an institution or direct an organization: *Our school administration is made up of the principal and a staff of teachers.* **3.** Often **Administration.** The executive branch of a government, especially the President of the United States and the cabinet. **4.** The time that a chief executive is in office or that a government is in power: *Many civil rights laws were enacted during the Johnson administration.* **5.** The act of administering: *administration of justice; administration of an oath.*

ad•min•is•tra•tive (ăd mĭn′ĭ strā′tĭv *or* ăd mĭn′ĭ strə tĭv) *adj.* Of or relating to government or management: *a manager with administrative ability; the President and other administrative officers of the government.* **—ad•min′is•tra′tive•ly** *adv.*

ad•min•is•tra•tor (ăd mĭn′ĭ strā′tər) *n.* **1.** A person in charge of directing or managing affairs; an executive. **2.** A person appointed by a court to manage the property left by a dead person: *Our family's lawyer is the administrator of my grandfather's estate.*

ad•mi•ra•ble (ăd′mər ə bəl) *adj.* Worthy of admiration; excellent: *Honesty is an admirable quality.* **—ad′mi•ra•ble•ness** *n.* **—ad′mi•ra•bly** *adv.*

ad•mi•ral (ăd′mər əl) *n.* **1.** The commanding officer of a navy or fleet of ships. **2.a.** A rank in the U.S. Navy or Coast Guard that is above vice-admiral and below Admiral of the Fleet. **b.** An officer in the U.S. Navy or Coast Guard ranking above a captain, including admiral, vice admiral, and rear admiral. **3.** Any of various brightly colored butterflies. [First written down in 1297 in Middle English and spelled *amiral,* from Arabic *'amīr a 'ālī,* high commander.]

Admiral of the Fleet *n.* **1.** The highest rank in the U.S. Navy. **2.** An officer holding this rank.

ad•mi•ral•ty (ăd′mər əl tē) *n., pl.* **ad•mi•ral•ties. 1.** The body of law or the court that deals with matters involving ships and the sea. **2. Admiralty.** The department of the British government that once was in charge of naval affairs.

ad•mi•ra•tion (ăd′mə rā′shən) *n.* **1.** A feeling of pleasure, wonder, or approval: *The tourists gazed at the Grand Canyon in admiration.* **2.** An object of great wonder or respect: *The ballerina was the admiration of younger dancers.*

ad•mire (ăd mīr′) *tr.v.* **ad•mired, ad•mir•ing, ad•mires. 1.** To look at or regard with wonder, pleasure, and delight: *admire a beautiful picture.* **2.** To have a high opinion of; feel great respect for: *People admire her ability as a musician.* [First written down about 1590 in Modern English, from Latin *admīrārī*, to wonder at : *ad-*, at + *mīrārī*, to wonder.] **—ad•mir′ing•ly** *adv.*

ad•mis•si•ble (ăd mĭs′ə bəl) *adj.* **1.** Accepted or permitted; allowable: *Admissable evidence in court must be based on fact.* **2.** Worthy of admission; having the right or permission to use: *Children are not admissible to the museum without an adult.* **—ad•mis′si•bil′i•ty** *n.* **—ad•mis′si•bly** *adv.*

ad•mis•sion (ăd mĭsh′ən) *n.* **1.** The act of allowing to enter or join: *Congress must approve the admission of new states to the Union.* **2.a.** The power or right to enter: *Admission to public school is open to all children.* **b.** Acceptance and entry of an applicant into a school, profession, club, or position: *He received a letter of admission from the college.* **3.** A price charged or paid to enter a place: *The spectators paid an admission of two dollars each.* **4.** An acknowledgment of the truth; a confession: *an admission of guilt.*

ad•mit (ăd mĭt′) *v.* **ad•mit•ted, ad•mit•ting, ad•mits.** *—tr.* **1.** To acknowledge or confess to be true or real: *I must admit that you are right. Never admit defeat.* **2.a.** To allow or permit to enter: *This pass will admit one person free.* **b.** To accept and take in as a new member, student, or patient: *The hospital admitted the accident victim.* **3.** To have room for: *The harbor is large enough to admit many ships at once.* *—intr.* **1.** To allow the possibility: *That problem admits of no solution.* **2.** To allow access: *The screen door admits to the porch.* [First written down before 1387 in Middle English and spelled *admitten*, from Latin *admittere* : *ad-*, to + *mittere*, to send.]

ad•mit•tance (ăd mĭt′ns) *n.* **1.** Permission or right to enter: *The sign said "no admittance."* **2.** The act of admitting: *gained admittance with a key.*

ad•mit•ted•ly (ăd mĭt′ĭd lē) *adv.* By general admission; without denial: *They all agreed that they were admittedly scared.*

ad•mix•ture (ăd mĭks′chər) *n.* **1.** The act of mixing. **2.** Something formed by mixing; a combination, mixture, or blend: *An admixture of flour and water makes paste.* **3.** Something added in mixing.

ad•mon•ish (ăd mŏn′ĭsh) *tr.v.* **ad•mon•ished, ad•mon•ish•ing, ad•mon•ish•es. 1.** To criticize for a fault in a kind but serious way: *The uncle admonished the twins for their lateness.* **2.** To advise, warn, urge, or caution: *She admonished us to be careful on the ice.* **—ad•mon′ish•ment** *n.*

ad•mo•ni•tion (ăd′mə nĭsh′ən) *n.* A gentle criticism or friendly warning: *Remember the doctor's admonition to keep the bandage dry.*

ad•mon•i•to•ry (ăd mŏn′ĭ tôr′ē) *adj.* Given or expressing a warning; urging caution: *an admonitory word of advice.*

a•do (ə do͞o′) *n.* Fuss; bother: *They said their goodbyes and set off quickly without further ado.*
❑ *These sound alike:* **ado, adieu** (farewell).

a•do•be (ə dō′bē) *n.* **1.** A brick made of clay and straw that is dried in the sun. **2.** Clay or soil from which such bricks are made. **3.** A building made with such bricks. [First written down in 1739 in Modern English, from Spanish, from Arabic *aṭ-ṭūbah*, brick.]

ad•o•les•cence (ăd′l ĕs′əns) *n.* **1.** The period of growth and physical development that leads from childhood to adulthood. **2.** A period of change and development to maturity: *the adolescence of the computer industry.*

ad•o•les•cent (ăd′l ĕs′ənt) *adj.* Of, relating to, or going through adolescence: *an adolescent youngster.* *—n.* A boy or girl, especially a teenager, in the stage of growth and development between childhood and adulthood. [First written down in 1459 in Middle English, from Latin *adolēscere*, to grow up.]

A•don•is (ə dŏn′ĭs *or* ə dō′nĭs) *n.* **1.** In Greek mythology, a young man loved by the goddess Aphrodite for his beauty. **2.** A very handsome and often vain young man.

a•dopt (ə dŏpt′) *tr.v.* **a•dopt•ed, a•dopt•ing, a•dopts. 1.** To take (a new member) into one's family through legal means and treat as one's own: *Our neighbors adopted a baby girl.* **2.** To take and make one's own: *Samuel Clemens adopted the name Mark Twain.* **3.a.** To accept and use or follow: *adopt a suggestion; adopt new methods.* **b.** To pass by vote or approve officially: *adopt a new constitution for our state government.* **4.** To put on; assume: *Some people adopt a confident air to hide their uneasiness.* **5.** To take on; acquire: *English has adopted the Italian word "concerto" and many other foreign words.* [First written down before 1500 in Middle English and spelled *adopten*, from Latin *adoptāre* : *ad-*, to + *optāre*, to choose.] **—a•dopt′a•ble** *adj.* —SEE NOTE.

a•dop•tion (ə dŏp′shən) *n.* **1.** The act of adopting or the condition of being adopted: *the adoption of a child; the adoption of new methods.* **2.** The state of being adopted; official approval: *The new building code finally gained the town council's adoption.*

a•dop•tive (ə dŏp′tĭv) *adj.* Related by adoption: *Some children have adoptive parents.* —SEE NOTE at **adopt.**

a•dor•a•ble (ə dôr′ə bəl) *adj.* **1.** Delightful; lovable; charming: *an adorable puppy.* **2.** Worthy of worship or adoration. **—a•dor′a•ble•ness** *n.* **—a•dor′a•bly** *adv.*

ad•o•ra•tion (ăd′ə rā′shən) *n.* **1.** Worship of God or of a divine being. **2.** Great and devoted love: *Many famous screen actors have enjoyed the adoration of millions of fans.*

a•dore (ə dôr′) *tr.v.* **a•dored, a•dor•ing, a•dores. 1.** To love deeply and devotedly; idolize: *The girl adored her mother.* See Synonyms at **revere. 2.** To like very much: *Audiences everywhere adore the circus.* **3.** To worship as divine. [First written down about 1375 in Middle English and spelled *adouren*, from Latin *adōrāre*, to pray to : *ad-*, to + *ōrāre*, to pray.] **—a•dor′er** *n.* **—a•dor′ing•ly** *adv.*

a•dorn (ə dôrn′) *tr.v.* **a•dorned, a•dorn•ing, a•dorns.** To decorate with something beautiful or ornamental: *The table was adorned with flowers.* **—a•dorn′er** *n.*

a•dorn•ment (ə dôrn′mənt) *n.* **1.** The act of adorning; decoration: *jewelry worn for personal adornment.* **2.** Something that adorns or beautifies; an ornament or a decoration: *They wore no jewels or other adornments.*

ad•re•nal (ə drē′nəl) *adj.* **1.** Of, relating to, or derived from the adrenal glands. **2.** Near or on the kidney. *—n.* An adrenal gland.

adrenal gland *n.* Either of two endocrine glands, located one above each kidney, that produce adrenaline and certain other hormones.

a•dren•a•line (ə drĕn′ə lĭn) *n.* A hormone secreted by the adrenal glands that quickens the heartbeat, raises blood pressure, and thereby prepares the body for vigorous action, as in response to danger or other stress. It is also prepared synthetically and used to treat asthma.

A•dri•at•ic Sea (ā′drē ăt′ĭk). An arm of the Med-

Usage: adopt

The words **adopted** and **adoptive** are similar in appearance, but they refer to different situations. Someone who is **adopted** has been taken into a family by legal means and raised as the child of that family. The word **adoptive** means "adopting" or "having adopted" and refers to the family who has adopted a child.

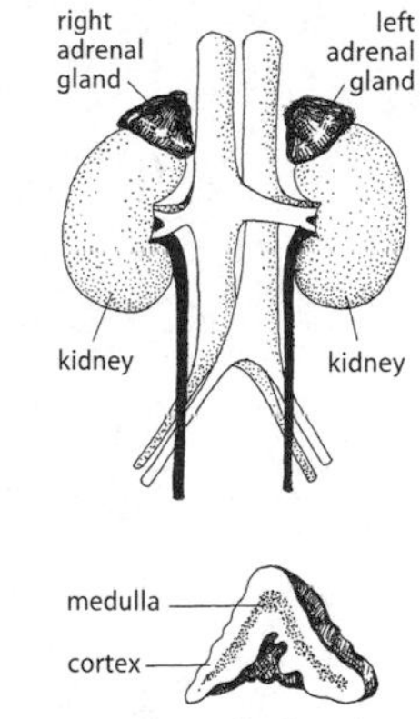

adrenal gland

ă	pat	oi	boy
ā	pay	ou	out
âr	care	o͝o	took
ä	father	o͞o	boot
ĕ	pet	ŭ	cut
ē	be	ûr	urge
ĭ	pit	th	thin
ī	pie	*th*	this
îr	pier	hw	whoop
ŏ	pot	zh	vision
ō	toe	ə	about
ô	paw	N	*French* bon

iterranean Sea between Italy and the Balkan Peninsula.

a•drift (ə drĭft′) *adv. & adj.* **1.** Drifting or floating without direction: *a boat set adrift for weeks in the middle of the lake.* **2.** Without direction or purpose: *The editorial department was adrift until a new supervisor was hired.*

a•droit (ə droit′) *adj.* Skillful or clever at doing or handling something difficult: *an adroit answer to a complicated question.* **—a•droit′ly** *adv.* **—a•droit′ness** *n.*

ad•sorb (ăd sôrb′ *or* ăd zôrb′) *tr.v.* **ad•sorbed, ad•sorb•ing, ad•sorbs.** To take up and hold (a gas, liquid, or dissolved substance) in a thin layer of molecules on the surface of a solid substance: *A dye is adsorbed in a tightly held layer on the surface of cloth fiber.*

ad•sorp•tion (ăd sôrp′shən *or* ăd zôrp′shən) *n.* The process of adsorbing or the condition of being adsorbed.

ad•u•late (ăj′ə lāt′) *tr.v.* **ad•u•lat•ed, ad•u•lat•ing, ad•u•lates.** To praise too much; flatter.

ad•u•la•tion (ăj′ə lā′shən) *n.* Too much praise; flattery: *The leader sought respect, not adulation.*

ad•u•la•to•ry (ăj′ə lə tôr′ē) *adj.* Praising or flattering too much: *an adulatory biography that avoided mention of the President's mistakes.*

a•dult (ə dŭlt′ *or* ăd′ŭlt) *n.* **1.** An animal or a plant that is fully grown and developed. **2.** A person of legal age, usually 18 or 21 years old, having the right to vote, hold property, and fulfill certain duties: *All adults should vote in an election.* *—adj.* **1.** Fully developed; mature: *an adult cat and her kittens.* **2.** Intended or suitable for mature persons: *adult education.* [First written down in 1531 in Modern English, from Latin *adultus*, from *adolēscere*, to grow up.]

a•dul•ter•ant (ə dŭl′tər ənt) *n.* A substance used to adulterate something.

a•dul•ter•ate (ə dŭl′tə rāt′) *tr.v.* **a•dul•ter•at•ed, a•dul•ter•at•ing, a•dul•ter•ates.** To reduce the quality of (something) by adding impure, inferior, or improper substances: *adulterate milk with water.* [First written down in 1531 in Modern English, from Latin *adulterāre*.]

a•dul•ter•a•tion (ə dŭl′tə rā′shən) *n.* **1.** The act or process of adulterating something: *a regulation forbidding the adulteration of milk with water.* **2.** A product or substance that has been adulterated.

a•dul•ter•er (ə dŭl′tər ər) *n.* A person who commits adultery.

a•dul•ter•ess (ə dŭl′trĭs *or* ə dŭl′tər ĭs) *n.* A woman who commits adultery.

a•dul•ter•ous (ə dŭl′tər əs) *adj.* Relating to or guilty of adultery. **—a•dul′ter•ous•ly** *adv.*

a•dul•ter•y (ə dŭl′tə rē *or* ə dŭl′trē) *n., pl.* **a•dul•ter•ies.** Voluntary sexual intercourse between a married person and someone who is not the person's spouse. [First written down about 1415 in Middle English and spelled *adulterie*, from Latin *adulter*, adulterer.]

a•dult•hood (ə dŭlt′hood′) *n.* The time or condition of being fully grown and developed; maturity.

adv. *abbr.* An abbreviation of adverb.

ad•vance (ăd văns′) *v.* **ad•vanced, ad•vanc•ing, ad•vanc•es.** *—tr.* **1.** To move (something) forward, onward, or ahead: *In checkers players advance their pieces one square at a time.* **2.** To aid the growth or progress of; promote: *Scientific research advances knowledge.* **3.** To raise in rank or position: *advance a soldier from private to sergeant.* **4.** To put forward; propose or offer: *advance a theory.* **5.a.** To move ahead to a later time: *Advance your watch one hour in the spring.* **b.** To move from a later to an earlier time: *advance a deadline from June to May.* **6.** To make higher; put up or raise: *advance the price of gasoline by 20 cents.* **7.** To lend or pay (money) ahead of time: *The company advanced him a week's pay.* *—intr.* **1.** To move forward, onward, or ahead: *A cat advanced toward the bird.* **2.** To make progress; improve or grow: *We are advancing in our studies.* **3.** To rise in rank or position: *The police officer advanced from sergeant to lieutenant.* **4.** To increase in amount or value: *As costs advance prices go up.* *—n.* **1.** Forward or onward movement: *the rapid advance of fire through the forest.* **2.** A forward step; an improvement or a development: *recent advances in science.* **3.** A loan or payment made ahead of time: *Can you get an advance on your allowance?* **4.** An increase in price, amount, or value: *an advance of a nickel a gallon in gasoline.* **5. advances.** Approaches or efforts made to win someone's friendship or favor: *advances to make up after a quarrel.* *—adj.* **1.** Made or given ahead of time: *advance warning.* **2.** Going before: *the advance guard.* ***—idioms.*** **in advance.** Ahead of time; beforehand: *Make your travel plans in advance.* **in advance of.** In front of; ahead of: *She skied in advance of us, showing us the way.* [First written down before 1200 in Middle English and spelled *avauncen*, from Latin *abante*, from before.]

ad•vanced (ăd vănst′) *adj.* **1.** Highly developed or complex; beyond in progress: *an advanced technology.* **2.** At a level higher than others: *an advanced student; advanced courses.* **3.** Far along in course or time: *illness in its advanced stages; advanced age.*

ad•vance•ment (ăd văns′mənt) *n.* **1.** The act of advancing or the condition of being advanced. **2.** A forward step; an improvement or a development: *new advancements in science.* **3.** A promotion: *opportunity for advancement to a higher position.*

ad•van•tage (ăd văn′tĭj) *n.* **1.** A beneficial factor or feature: *Museums and libraries are some of the advantages of city life.* **2.** Benefit or profit: *She learned from her mistake, turning it to her advantage.* **3.** A favorable or preferred position: *Their early start gave them the advantage.* ***—idiom.*** **to advantage.** To good effect; favorably: *The summer job let him display his talents to advantage.* [First written down about 1300 in Middle English and spelled *avauntage*, from Old French *avant*, before, from Latin *abante*, from before.]

ad•van•ta•geous (ăd′vən tā′jəs) *adj.* Profitable; favorable; useful; beneficial: *an advantageous location.* **—ad′van•ta′geous•ly** *adv.* **—ad′van•ta′geous•ness** *n.*

ad•vent (ăd′vĕnt′) *n.* **1.** The coming of a new person or thing: *before the advent of the airplane.* **2. Advent.** The birth or coming of Jesus. **3. Advent.** The period including the four Sundays before Christmas, observed by Christians as a time of prayer and penitence. [First written down in 963 in Old English, from Latin *adventus*, arrival, from *advenīre*, to come to : *ad-*, toward + *venīre*, to come.]

Ad•vent•ist (ăd′vĕn′tĭst *or* ăd vĕn′tĭst) *n.* A member of a Christian denomination that believes Jesus's Second Coming and the end of the world are near. **—Ad′vent′ism** *n.*

ad•ven•ti•tious (ăd′vĕn tĭsh′əs) *adj.* **1.** Acquired by accident; added by chance. **2.** In zoology and botany, appearing in an unusual place or in an irregular manner: *a plant with adventitious shoots.*

ad•ven•ture (ăd vĕn′chər) *n.* **1.** A bold, dangerous, or risky undertaking: *They set out on a daring adventure in the wilderness.* **2.** An unusual, exciting, or memorable experience: *Going to the art museum is always an adventure.* **3.** Excitement, danger, or discovery arising from bold action or new experience: *in search of adventure.* *—v.* **ad•ven•tured, ad•ven•tur•ing, ad•ven•tures.** *—intr.* To go in search of new or exciting experiences. —*tr.* To venture; risk. [First written down before 1200 in Middle English and spelled *aventure,* from Latin *advenīre,* to arrive.]

ad•ven•tur•er (ăd **vĕn′**chər ər) *n.* **1.** A person who seeks or has adventures. **2.** A person who seeks wealth in dangerous undertakings or by less than honest means: *The prospector was an old adventurer.*

ad•ven•ture•some (ăd **vĕn′**chər səm) *adj.* Bold; daring; adventurous.

ad•ven•tur•ess (ăd **vĕn′**chər ĭs) *n.* A woman who seeks to gain money or social position by scheming.

ad•ven•tur•ous (ăd **vĕn′**chər əs) *adj.* **1.** Fond of adventure; seeking new experience; willing to take risks: *adventurous youths hiking in the wilderness.* **2.** Full of adventure or risk: *the pioneer's adventurous journey.* **—ad•ven′tur•ous•ly** *adv.* **—ad•ven′tur•ous•ness** *n.*

ad•verb (**ăd′**vûrb) *n.* In grammar, a word used to modify a verb, an adjective, or another adverb. For example, in the sentences *They left early, The peacock is very pretty,* and *The dog ran very fast,* the words *early, very,* and *fast* are adverbs.

ad•ver•bi•al (ăd **vûr′**bē əl) *adj.* **1.** Used as an adverb: *an adverbial phrase.* **2.** Of or relating to an adverb: *an adverbial form.* **—ad•ver′bi•al•ly** *adv.*

ad•ver•sar•y (**ăd′**vər sĕr′ē) *n., pl.* **ad•ver•sar•ies.** An opponent or enemy: *The lawyers for the two sides were adversaries.*

ad•verse (ăd **vûrs′** *or* **ăd′**vûrs′) *adj.* **1.** Not favorable; hostile: *adverse criticism; an adverse decision.* **2.** In an opposite direction: *Adverse currents pushed against the boat.* [First written down about 1385 in Middle English, from Latin *advertere,* to turn toward : *ad-,* toward + *vertere,* to turn.] **—ad•verse′ly** *adv.* **—ad•verse′ness** *n.*

ad•ver•si•ty (ăd **vûr′**sĭ tē) *n., pl.* **ad•ver•si•ties.** Great misfortune; hardship.

ad•vert (ăd **vûrt′**) *intr.v.* **ad•vert•ed, ad•vert•ing, ad•verts.** To call attention; refer: *advert to a problem.*

ad•ver•tise (**ăd′**vər tīz′) *v.* **ad•ver•tised, ad•ver•tis•ing, ad•ver•tis•es.** —*tr.* **1.** To call public attention to (a product or business), as by placing a notice in a newspaper: *Manufacturers advertise their products.* **2.** To make known; call attention to: *Mistakes in arithmetic advertised the student's carelessness.* —*intr.* To give public notice of something, as something wanted or offered for sale: *The building's owner advertised in the newspaper for a tenant.* [First written down before 1425 in Middle English and spelled *advertisen,* from Old French *advertir,* to notice.] **—ad′ver•tis′er** *n.*

ad•ver•tise•ment (ăd′vər **tīz′**mənt *or* ăd **vûr′**-tĭs mənt) *n.* A public notice, as in a newspaper or on television, to call attention to a product, a meeting, or an event.

ad•ver•tis•ing (**ăd′**vər tī′zĭng) *n.* **1.** The act of calling public attention to a product, a meeting, or an event. **2.** The business of preparing and distributing advertisements: *Many people are employed in advertising.* **3.** Advertisements considered as a group: *How much advertising does the magazine have?*

ad•vice (ăd **vīs′**) *n.* **1.** Opinion about how to solve a problem; guidance: *The pupil sought advice from the teacher.* **2.** Information or a report, especially when communicated from a distance. Often used in the plural: *advices from our ambassador in India.*

ad•vis•a•ble (ăd **vī′**zə bəl) *adj.* Worth recommending or suggesting; wise; sensible: *Driving fast in the rain is not advisable.* **—ad•vis′a•bil′i•ty** *n.* **—ad•vis′a•bly** *adv.*

ad•vise (ăd **vīz′**) *v.* **ad•vised, ad•vis•ing, ad•vis•es.** —*tr.* **1.** To give advice to: *The doctor advised the patient to get some rest.* **2.** To recommend: *Our mechanic advised a complete overhaul of the car's motor.* **3.** To inform; notify: *The radio advised us of the coming storm.* —*intr.* **1.** To offer advice. **2.** To consult; confer: *advised with one's associates.* [First written down about 1300 in Middle English and spelled *avisen,* from Old French *avis,* advice.]

ad•vised (ăd **vīzd′**) *adj.* **1.** Thought out; considered: *a poorly advised decision.* **2.** Informed; notified: *Police kept motorists advised of all new developments in road conditions.*

ad•vis•ed•ly (ăd **vī′**zĭd lē) *adv.* With careful consideration; deliberately.

ad•vise•ment (ăd **vīz′**mənt) *n.* Careful consideration: *Our lawyers took the matter under advisement to see if we had a case.*

ad•vis•er or **ad•vi•sor** (ăd **vī′**zər) *n.* **1.** A person who offers advice, especially officially or professionally: *The local doctor served as the school's health adviser.* **2.** A teacher who advises students in selecting courses and planning careers.

ad•vi•so•ry (ăd **vī′**zə rē) *adj.* **1.** Having the power to advise: *an advisory committee.* **2.** Relating to or containing advice: *an advisory report.* —*n., pl.* **ad•vi•so•ries.** A report giving information and especially a warning: *a weather advisory.*

ad•vo•ca•cy (**ăd′**və kə sē) *n.* Active support, as of an idea, a cause, or a policy.

ad•vo•cate (**ăd′**və kāt′) *tr.v.* **ad•vo•cat•ed, ad•vo•cat•ing, ad•vo•cates.** To be or speak in favor of; recommend; urge: *advocate changes in the law controlling air pollution.* —*n.* (**ăd′**və kĭt *or* **ăd′**və kāt′). **1.** A person who supports or speaks in favor of a cause: *an advocate of animal rights.* **2.** A lawyer. [First written down in 1340 in Middle English and spelled *advocat,* lawyer, from Latin *advocāre,* to summon for counsel : *ad-,* toward + *vocāre,* to call.] **—ad′vo•ca′tion** *n.* **—ad′vo•ca′tor** *n.*

advt. *abbr.* An abbreviation of advertisement.

adz or **adze** (ădz) *n.* A tool resembling an ax, used for shaping wood. [First written down before 830 in Old English and spelled *adesa.*]

Aegean Sea. An arm of the Mediterranean Sea off southeast Europe between Greece and Turkey. Most of the **Aegean Islands** belong to Greece.

ae•gis also **e•gis** (**ē′**jĭs) *n.* **1.** Protection or care: *an expanse of land under the aegis of the state.* **2.** Sponsorship or patronage: *a conference under the aegis of the United Nations.*

Ae•ne•as (ĭ **nē′**əs) *n.* In Greek and Roman mythology, the Trojan warrior and son of Aphrodite who escapes during the fall of Troy and wanders for seven years before settling in Italy.

Ae•o•lus (**ē′**ə ləs) *n.* In Greek mythology, the god of the winds.

ae•on (**ē′**ŏn′ *or* **ē′**ən) *n.* Variant of **eon.**

aer– *pref.* Variant of **aero–.**

aer•ate (**âr′**āt) *tr.v.* **aer•at•ed, aer•at•ing, aer•ates. 1.** To expose to the circulation of the air: *We opened the windows to aerate the little cottage, which had been closed up all winter.* **2.** To supply or charge (a liquid) with air or another gas, such as carbon dioxide. **3.** To supply with oxygen: *The lungs aerate the blood.* **—aer•a′tion** *n.* **—aer′a′tor** *n.*

aer•i•al (**âr′**ē əl *or* ā **îr′**ē əl) *adj.* **1.** Of, in, or caused by air: *aerial currents.* **2.** Of, for, or by aircraft: *aerial reconnaissance.* **3.** High; lofty. **4.** Growing in air without underground support: *aerial roots.* —*n.* (**âr′**ē əl). An antenna, as for a radio or television. **—aer′i•al•ly**

aer•i•al•ist (**âr′**ē ə lĭst) *n.* An acrobat who performs on a tightrope or trapeze.

aer•ie or **aer•y** also **ey•rie** or **eyr•y** (**âr′**ē *or* **îr′**ē) *n., pl.* **aer•ies** also **eyr•ies. 1.** The nest of an eagle or other predatory bird, built on a cliff or other high

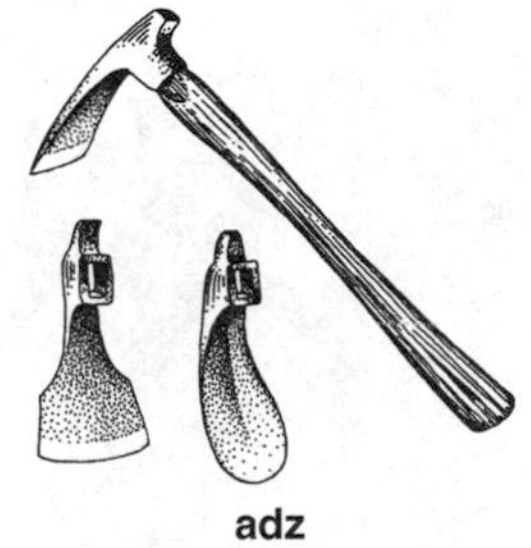

adz

Carpenter's adz (*top*), shipbuilder's adz (*bottom left*), and curved-blade adz (*bottom right*)

aerialist

ă	pat	oi	boy
ā	pay	ou	out
âr	care	ŏŏ	took
ä	father	ōō	boot
ĕ	pet	ŭ	cut
ē	be	ûr	urge
ĭ	pit	th	thin
ī	pie	*th*	this
îr	pier	hw	whoop
ŏ	pot	zh	vision
ō	toe	ə	about
ô	paw	N	*French* bon

aerobics

Aesop

Usage: affect[1]

The words **affect** and **effect** look and sound similar. Their meanings, however, are very different. The verb **affect** means "to influence": *That decision will affect my whole life.* The verb **effect** means "to make happen": *We effected some helpful changes.* The noun **effect** can mean "a result" or "an influence," but only the verb **affect** means "to influence."

place. **2.** A house or stronghold built on a height. ❑ *These sound alike:* **aerie, airy** (breezy).

aero– or **aer–** *pref.* A prefix that means: **1.** Air or atmosphere: *aerodynamics; aeroplane.* **2.** Gas: *aerosol.* **3.** Aviation: *aeronautics.* [First written down before 1393 in Middle English, from Greek *aēr*, air.]

aer•obe (âr′ōb′) *n.* An aerobic organism that requires oxygen to live.

aer•o•bic (â rō′bĭk) *adj.* **1.** Needing or using oxygen: *aerobic organisms.* **2.** Relating to exercise that improves the body's ability to use oxygen: *aerobic dancing.*

aer•o•bics (â rō′bĭks) *n.* *(used with a singular or plural verb).* A system of physical exercises that involves calisthenics, dance routines, and other conditioning to promote use of oxygen by the body.

aer•o•drome (âr′ə drōm′) *n.* *Chiefly British.* Variant of **airdrome.**

aer•o•dy•nam•ic (âr′ō dī năm′ĭk) also **aer•o•dy•nam•i•cal** (âr′ō dī năm′ĭ kəl) *adj.* Of or relating to aerodynamics. **—aer′o•dy•nam′i•cal•ly** *adv.*

aer•o•dy•nam•ics (âr′ō dī năm′ĭks) *n.* *(used with a singular verb).* **1.** The scientific study of the motions of and forces associated with air and other gases, especially as they interact with objects moving through them. **2.** The interaction of a moving object with the atmosphere: *the aerodynamics of a new car design.*

aer•ol•o•gy (â rŏl′ə jē) *n.* Meteorology that is based on the study of the entire atmosphere rather than just the part that is close to the earth's surface.

aer•o•nau•tic (âr′ə nô′tĭk) also **aer•o•nau•ti•cal** (âr′ə nô′tĭ kəl) *adj.* Of or relating to aeronautics or aircraft. **—aer′o•nau′ti•cal•ly** *adv.*

aer•o•nau•tics (âr′ə nô′tĭks) *n.* *(used with a singular verb).* **1.** The design and construction of aircraft. **2.** The theory and practice of aircraft navigation.

aer•o•pause (âr′ō pôz′) *n.* The level of the atmosphere above which aircraft cannot fly.

aer•o•plane (âr′ə plān′) *n.* *Chiefly British.* Variant of **airplane.**

aer•o•sol (âr′ə sôl′ *or* âr′ə sŏl′) *n.* **1.** A mass of very fine particles of a liquid or solid suspended in a gas: *Mist and fog are aerosols.* **2.** A substance, such as a paint, an insecticide, or a hair spray, packaged under pressure for use in this form. **3.** An aerosol can.

aerosol can *n.* A can containing a liquid, such as paint or a deodorant, packaged under pressure with a gas to be released in a spray.

aer•o•space (âr′ō spās′) *adj.* **1.** Of or relating to Earth's atmosphere and the space beyond. **2.** Of or relating to the science and technology of flight.

aer•y (âr′ē *or* îr′ē) *n.* Variant of **aerie.**

Ae•sir (ā′sîr′ *or* ā′zîr′) *pl.n.* The gods of Norse mythology.

Ae•sop (ē′səp *or* ē′sŏp′). Sixth century B.C. Greek storyteller who is traditionally considered the author of *Aesop's Fables,* including "The Tortoise and the Hare."

aes•thete or **es•thete** (ĕs′thēt) *n.* **1.** A person who is very sensitive to beauty, as in art. **2.** A person who pretends to be very sensitive to beauty.

aes•thet•ic or **es•thet•ic** (ĕs thĕt′ĭk) *adj.* **1.** Of or relating to the aethetics. **2.** Of or relating to the appreciation of beauty: *the aesthetic quality of a dining room.* **3.** Very sensitive to beauty, especially in art.

aes•thet•ics or **es•thet•ics** (ĕs thĕt′ĭks) *n.* *(used with a singular verb).* The branch of philosophy that deals with the nature and expression of beauty, as in art.

Aet•na (ĕt′nə), **Mount.** Mount Etna.

AF *abbr.* An abbreviation of: **1.** Air force. **2.** Audio frequency.

a•far (ə fär′) *adv.* Far away; far off: *saw the bird afar off.* **—*idiom.* from afar.** From a long distance: *We could only glimpse the boat from afar.*

af•fa•ble (ăf′ə bəl) *adj.* Easy to speak to; pleasant; friendly. **—af′fa•bil′i•ty** *n.* **—af′fa•bly** *adv.*

af•fair (ə fâr′) *n.* **1.** A matter of concern: *Their argument was a private affair.* **2.** An occurrence, an action, an event, or a procedure: *Building a skyscraper is a long and costly affair.* **3. affairs.** Matters of business interest or public concern: *affairs of state.* **4.** A social gathering: *The ball was a glittering affair.* **5.** A thing or an object: *The new boat is not a very large affair.* **6.** A brief romantic relationship between two people. [First written down before 1300 in Middle English and spelled *afer*, from Old French *a faire*, to do.]

af•fect[1] (ə fĕkt′) *tr.v.* **af•fect•ed, af•fect•ing, af•fects. 1.** To have an influence on; bring about a change in: *The drought has affected the fruit crop.* **2.** To touch or move the emotions of: *The movie affected us deeply.* **3.** To attack or infect: *Arthritis affects many older people.* [First written down in 1410 in Middle English, from Latin *afficere* : *ad-*, to + *facere*, to do.] —SEE NOTE.

af•fect[2] (ə fĕkt′) *tr.v.* **af•fect•ed, af•fect•ing, af•fects. 1.** To put on a false show of; pretend to have: *He affected indifference, though he was hurt by the remark.* **2.** To like; prefer: *She affects hats with wide brims.* [First written down before 1425 in Middle English and spelled *affecten*, from Latin *affectāre*, to strive after, from *afficere*, to affect, influence.]

af•fec•ta•tion (ăf′ĕk tā′shən) *n.* Artificial behavior adopted to impress others; pretense.

af•fect•ed[1] (ə fĕk′tĭd) *adj.* **1.** Acted upon, influenced, or changed: *the affected business in this recession.* **2.** Acted upon in an injurious way, as by disease or malfunction: *The affected toes were numbed by frostbite.*

af•fect•ed[2] (ə fĕk′tĭd) *adj.* Speaking or behaving in an artificial way to make an impression: *an affected tone of voice.* **—af•fect′ed•ly** *adv.* **—af•fect′ed•ness** *n.*

af•fect•ing (ə fĕk′tĭng) *adj.* Touching the emotions; moving: *an affecting tale of woe.*

af•fec•tion (ə fĕk′shən) *n.* A fond or tender feeling toward someone or something; fondness.

af•fec•tion•ate (ə fĕk′shə nĭt) *adj.* Having or showing affection; tender; loving. **—af•fec′tion•ate•ly** *adv.*

af•fer•ent (ăf′ər ənt) *adj.* Directed or leading toward a central organ or part of an organism: *an afferent nerve.*

af•fi•ance (ə fī′əns) *tr.v.* **af•fi•anced, af•fi•anc•ing, af•fi•anc•es.** To promise in marriage: *The lovers were affianced to each other.*

af•fi•da•vit (ăf′ĭ dā′vĭt) *n.* A written declaration made under oath before a notary public or other authorized officer.

af•fil•i•ate (ə fĭl′ē āt′) *v.* **af•fil•i•at•ed, af•fil•i•at•ing, af•fil•i•ates.** *—tr.* To associate or join, as with a larger or more important body: *The local unit of the Red Cross is affiliated with the national organization.* *—intr.* To become connected or associated: *The two unions voted to affiliate.* *—n.* (ə fĭl′ē ĭt *or* ə fĭl′ē āt′). A person or an organization associated or joined with a larger or more important body: *Our company has affiliates in Europe as well as the United States.* [First written down in 1761 in Modern English, from Medieval Latin *affīliāre*, to adopt : Latin *ad-*, to + Latin *fīlius*, son.]

af•fin•i•ty (ə fĭn′ĭ tē) *n., pl.* **af•fin•i•ties. 1.** A natural attraction; a liking: *Our dog has an affinity for* *young children.* **2.** A similiarity based on relationship: *The twins have a closer affinity than most members of their family.* **3.** A chemical attraction by which atoms combine with atoms of other elements to form compounds. [First written down about 1303 in Middle English and spelled *affinite*, from Latin *affīnis*, related by marriage.]

af•firm (ə fûrm′) *tr.v.* **af•firmed, af•firm•ing, af•firms. 1.** To declare positively; say firmly: *She affirmed her intention to run for the Senate seat.* **2.** To give approval or validity to; confirm: *The appeals court affirmed the lower court's ruling.*

af•fir•ma•tion (ăf′ər mā′shən) *n.* **1.** The act of affirming; assertion. **2.** Something declared to be true.

af•fir•ma•tive (ə fûr′mə tĭv) *adj.* Affirming that something is true, as with the answer *yes: an affirmative response.* —*n.* **1.** A word or statement of agreement or assent. **2.** The side in a debate that supports the question being debated. —***idiom.*** **in the affirmative.** Expressing agreement; saying "yes." —**af•fir′ma•tive•ly** *adv.*

affirmative action *n.* A policy or program that actively attempts to correct past discrimination by improving the opportunities for women and members of minority groups in employment and education.

af•fix (ə fĭks′) *tr.v.* **af•fixed, af•fix•ing, af•fix•es. 1.** To fasten to something; attach: *affix a label to a package* **2.** To add at the end; append: *I affixed my name at the end of my letter.* —*n.* (ăf′ĭks′). A syllable or group of syllables that is added at the beginning or the end of a word or word part to change its meaning or make another word; a prefix or suffix.

af•flict (ə flĭkt′) *tr.v.* **af•flict•ed, af•flict•ing, af•flicts.** To cause distress to; cause to suffer: *Human beings are afflicted with many diseases.* [First written down before 1393 in Middle English and spelled *afflighten*, from Latin *afflīgere*, to knock down.]

af•flic•tion (ə flĭk′shən) *n.* **1.** A condition of pain or distress. **2.** A cause of pain or suffering: *Scurvy used to be a common affliction among sailors.*

af•flu•ence (ăf′lo͞o əns *or* ə flo͞o′əns) *n.* A plentiful supply of goods or money; wealth.

af•flu•ent (ăf′lo͞o ənt *or* ə flo͞o′ənt) *adj.* Having plenty of money, property, or possessions; prosperous; rich. —**af′flu•ent•ly** *adv.*

af•ford (ə fôrd′) *tr.v.* **af•ford•ed, af•ford•ing, af•fords. 1.** To be able to pay for: *By saving we can afford a new TV set.* **2.** To be able to give or spare: *I am too busy to afford the time just now.* **3.** To give or furnish; provide: *This window affords a view of the mountains.* **4.** To be able to do without harming oneself: *Anyone can afford to be kind.* [First written down before 1387 in Middle English and spelled *aforthen*, from Old English *geforthian*, to carry out.]

af•fray (ə frā′) *n.* A noisy quarrel or brawl.

af•fright (ə frīt′) *tr.v.* **af•fright•ed, af•fright•ing, af•frights.** To frighten; terrify.

af•front (ə frŭnt′) *tr.v.* **af•front•ed, af•front•ing, af•fronts.** To insult intentionally or openly. —*n.* An intentional insult or offense.

Af•ghan (ăf′găn′ *or* ăf′gən) *adj.* Of or relating to Afghanistan or the Afghans. —*n.* **1.** A native or inhabitant of Afghanistan. **2. afghan.** A colorful wool blanket or shawl knitted or crocheted in squares, circles, or other designs. **3.** A large, slender dog with long, thick hair, a pointed snout, and drooping ears.

af•ghan•i (ăf găn′ē *or* ăf gä′nē) *n.* The basic monetary unit of Afghanistan.

Af•ghan•i•stan (ăf găn′ĭ stăn′). A mountainous landlocked country of southwest-central Asia east of Iran. Kabul is the capital and the largest city. Population, 13,051,358.

a•fi•cio•na•do (ə fĭsh′ē ə nä′dō) *n., pl.* **a•fi•cio•na•dos.** An enthusiastic admirer; a devotee.

a•field (ə fēld′) *adv.* **1.a.** Away from one's usual environment; to or at a distance: *The children wandered far afield in search of butterflies.* **b.** Off or away from the subject: *The witness's remarks went farther afield.* **2.** In or on the field: *The geologist preferred working afield to reading papers in the office.*

a•fire (ə fīr′) *adv. & adj.* On fire or as if on fire; burning: *The leader's ideas set the people afire. The room was afire.*

a•flame (ə flām′) *adv. & adj.* In flames or as if in flames; flaming: *The spark set the chimney aflame. The house is aflame.*

AFL-CIO *abbr.* An abbreviation of American Federation of Labor and Congress of Industrial Organizations.

a•float (ə flōt′) *adv. & adj.* **1.** In a floating condition: *The raft was afloat on the lake.* **2.** On a boat or ship; at sea. **3.** In circulation: *Talk of a change in managers is afloat.* **4.** Flooded: *The basement was afloat.*

a•flut•ter (ə flŭt′ər) *adj.* In a flutter; excited; agitated.

a•foot (ə fo͝ot′) *adv. & adj.* **1.** On foot; walking: *They traveled afoot. We were afoot and arrived much later.* **2.** In the process of happening; astir: *Something strange is afoot.*

a•fore (ə fôr′) *adv. & prep.* A dialectal variant of **before.**

a•fore•men•tioned (ə fôr′mĕn′shənd) *adj.* Mentioned before.

a•fore•said (ə fôr′sĕd′) *adj.* Spoken of earlier.

a•fore•thought (ə fôr′thôt′) *adj.* Planned beforehand; premeditated: *with malice aforethought.*

a•foul of (ə foul′) *prep.* **1.** In entanglement with: *The anchor fell afoul of the fishing lines.* **2.** In trouble with: *ran afoul of the law.*

Afr. *abbr.* An abbreviation of: **1.** Africa. **2.** African.

a•fraid (ə frād′) *adj.* **1.** Filled with fear; fearful: *afraid of the dark.* **2.** Reluctant; hesitant: *not afraid of work.* **3.** Full of concern; regretful: *I'm afraid you don't understand.* [First written down about 1300 in Middle English and spelled *affraied*, from Old French *esfraier*, to disturb.]

A-frame (ā′frăm′) *n.* A house built on a frame shaped like the letter A.

a•fresh (ə frĕsh′) *adv.* Anew; again: *We must start afresh.*

Af•ri•ca (ăf′rĭ kə). The second-largest continent, lying south of Europe between the Atlantic and Indian oceans.

Af•ri•can (ăf′rĭ kən) *adj.* Of or relating to Africa or its peoples, languages, or cultures. —*n.* **1.** A native or inhabitant or Africa. **2.** A person of African descent.

Af•ri•can-A•mer•i•can or **African American** (ăf′rĭ kən ə mĕr′ĭkən) *n.* An American of African ancestry. —**Af′ri•can-A•mer′i•can** *adj.*

African violet *n.* A popular houseplant, originally from Africa, with usually purplish flowers and velvety leaves.

Af•ri•kaans (ăf′rĭ käns′ *or* ăf′rĭ känz′) *n.* A language that developed from 17th-century Dutch and is the official language of South Africa.

Af•ri•ka•ner (ăf′rĭ kä′nər) *n.* An Afrikaans-speaking South African of European ancestry, especially one descended from 17th-century Dutch settlers.

Af•ro (ăf′rō) *n., pl.* **Af•ros.** A hairstyle in which the hair is rounded, thick, and tightly curled. —*adj.* African in style or origin.

A-frame

ă	pat	oi	boy
ā	pay	ou	out
âr	care	o͝o	took
ä	father	o͞o	boot
ĕ	pet	ŭ	cut
ē	be	ûr	urge
ĭ	pit	th	thin
ī	pie	*th*	this
îr	pier	hw	whoop
ŏ	pot	zh	vision
ō	toe	ə	about
ô	paw	N	*French* bon

agave

Af•ro-A•mer•i•can (ăf′rō ə mĕr′ĭ kən) *adj.* Of or relating to Americans of African ancestry or to their history or culture. —*n.* An American of African ancestry.

Af•ro-A•si•at•ic (af′rō āzhē ăt′ĭk) *n.* A family of languages spoken in northern Africa and southwest Asia, including the Semitic and ancient Egyptian languages. —**Af′ro-A′si•at′ic** *adj.*

aft (ăft) *adv. & adj.* Toward or near the stern of a ship or an aircraft: *going aft; the aft cabin.* [First written down before 1325 in Middle English and spelled *afte*, back, from Old English *æftan*, behind.]

af•ter (ăf′tər) *prep.* **1.** Behind in place or order: *all in a row, one after another.* **2.** In pursuit of: *running after the fire engine.* **3.** About; concerning: *I asked after you.* **4.** At a later time than: *They arrived after dinner.* **5.** Past the hour of: *five minutes after three.* **6.** With the same name as; in honor of: *named after his grandfather.* —*adv.* **1.** At a later time: *We left shortly after.* **2.** Behind; in the rear: *First came the tractor and then the wagon came rumbling after.* —*adj.* **1.** Later; following: *in after years.* **2.** Nearer a ship's stern: *the after quarter.* —*conj.* Following the time that: *We can eat after we get home.* [First written down before 735 in Old English and spelled *æfter*.]

after all also **af•ter•all** (ăf′tər ôl′) *adv.* In spite of everything; nevertheless.

af•ter•birth (ăf′tər bûrth′) *n.* The placenta and fetal membranes expelled from the uterus shortly after birth.

af•ter•burn•er (ăf′tər bûr′nər) *n.* A device in a jet engine that increases its power by injecting extra fuel into the hot exhaust gases.

af•ter•deck (ăf′tər dĕk′) *n.* The part of a ship's deck near or toward the stern.

af•ter•ef•fect (ăf′tər ĭ fĕkt′) *n.* An effect that follows its cause after some delay, especially a delayed bodily or mental response to something: *The driver's nervousness was an aftereffect of the accident.*

af•ter•glow (ăf′tər glō′) *n.* **1.** Light that remains after its source has disappeared, as the atmospheric glow that remains for a short time after sunset. **2.** A comfortable feeling after a pleasant experience.

af•ter•im•age (ăf′tər ĭm′ĭj) *n.* An image that persists after the original source is no longer active: *the afterimage one sees after the flash of a camera.*

af•ter•life (ăf′tər līf′) *n.* Life or existence after death.

af•ter•math (ăf′tər măth′) *n.* A consequence or result, especially of a disaster or misfortune: *the aftermath of a hurricane.*

af•ter•noon (ăf′tər no͞on′) *n.* The part of the day from noon until sunset.

af•ter•shock (ăf′tər shŏk′) *n.* A less powerful quake coming after an earthquake.

af•ter•taste (ăf′tər tāst′) *n.* A taste that remains in the mouth after the substance that caused it is no longer there.

af•ter•thought (ăf′tər thôt′) *n.* An idea that occurs to a person after something, such as an event or a decision, has passed.

af•ter•ward (ăf′tər wərd) also **af•ter•wards** (ăf′tər wərdz) *adv.* At a later time; subsequently.

Ag The symbol for the element **silver** (sense 1). [From Latin *argentum*, silver.]

a•gain (ə gĕn′) *adv.* **1.** Once more; anew: *If you don't win, try again.* **2.** To a previous place or position: *They left home but went back again.* **3.** Furthermore; moreover. **4.** On the other hand: *They might go, and again they might not.* —***idiom.* again and again.** Often; repeatedly. [First written down before 830 in Old English and spelled *ongeagn*, against.]

a•gainst (ə gĕnst′) *prep.* **1.** In a direction or course opposite to: *sailing against the wind.* **2.** So as to come into contact with: *waves washing against the shore.* **3.** In hostile opposition or resistance to: *struggling against prejudice.* **4.** Contrary to: *against my better judgment.* **5.** In contrast to: *dark colors against a light background.* **6.** As a defense or safeguard from: *wearing gloves against the cold.* **7.** To the account or debt of: *drew a check against my bank balance.* [First written down before 1160 in Middle English and spelled *againes*, from Old English *ongeagn*.]

Ag•a•mem•non (ăg′ə mĕm′nŏn′) *n.* In Greek mythology, the king of Mycenae and leader of the Greeks in the Trojan War.

A•ga•na (ə gä′nyə *or* ä gä′nyä). The capital of Guam, on the western coast of the island. Population, 896.

a•gape (ə gāp′ *or* ə găp′) *adv. & adj.* In a state of wonder or surprise: *The dazzling tricks of the magician set the audience agape.*

a•gar (ā′gär′ *or* ä′gär′) also **a•gar-a•gar** (ā′gär ā′gär′ *or* ä′gär ä′gär′) *n.* A gelatinous material obtained from certain seaweeds, used as the base on which bacteria are grown and in medicine as a mild laxative.

Ag•as•siz (ăg′ə sē), **(Jean) Louis (Rodolphe).** 1807–1873. Swiss-born American naturalist noted for his study of fossil fish and for recognizing that ice ages had occurred in the Northern Hemisphere.

ag•ate (ăg′ĭt) *n.* **1.** A type of quartz found in various colors that are arranged in bands or in cloudy patterns. **2.** A marble used in games that is made of this quartz or of glass.

a•ga•ve (ə gä′vē *or* ə gā′vē) *n.* Any of several tropical American plants having a tall flower stalk and large, thick leaves that are often the source of a fiber used for making rope or sacks.

age (āj) *n.* **1.** The length of time during which a person or thing has existed; a lifetime or lifespan: *Elephants are known for their great age.* **2.** One of the stages of life: *the age of adolescence.* **3.** The time in life when a person is allowed to assume adult rights and responsibilities, usually at 18 or 21 years. *Children are under age.* **4.** The condition of being old; old age. **5.** Often **Age.** A distinctive period of history: *the space age.* **6. ages.** A long time: *It took ages to clean up after dinner.* —*v.* **aged, ag•ing, ag•es.** —*tr.* **1.** To cause to grow old: *The crisis seemed to age the President.* **2.** To allow to mature or become flavorful: *They aged the wine in oak casks.* —*intr.v.* **1.** To become or look old: *The flimsy house aged poorly through the years.* **2.** To allow time for alcoholic beverages, cheese, or meat to mature or become flavorful. [First written down about 1275 in Middle English, from Latin *aetās*.]

-age *suff.* A suffix that means: **1.** Collection; mass: *leafage; mileage.* **2.** Condition; state: *patronage.* **3.** Charge or fee: *postage.* **4.** Residence or place: *orphanage.* **5.** Act or result: *breakage; spoilage.*

ag•ed (ā′jĭd) *adj.* **1.** Old; elderly. **2.** (ājd). Having reached the age of: *a child aged five.* **3.** (ājd). Ripe; mature: *aged cheese.* —*n.* Elderly people considered as a group: *Many of the aged continue to exercise.*

age•ism (ā′jĭz′əm) *n.* Discrimination based on age, especially against elderly people, as in regard to employment and housing.

age•less (āj′lĭs) *adj.* **1.** Seeming never to grow old: *an ageless grandparent.* **2.** Existing forever; eternal: *ageless stories of daring and adventure.* —**age′less•ly** *adv.* —**age′less•ness** *n.*

a•gen•cy (ā′jən sē) *n., pl.* **a•gen•cies. 1.** A person or thing that helps achieve an end; a means. **2.** A business or service authorized to act for others: *a real estate agency.* **3.** A governmental department of administration or regulation: *the agency that administers the recycling program.*

a•gen•da (ə jĕn′də) *n., pl.* **a•gen•das.** A list of things to be considered or done, as a program of business at a meeting.

a•gent (ā′jənt) *n.* **1.** A person with the power or authority to act for another: *a ticket agent; a publicity agent.* **2.** A representative of a government or a governmental department: *an FBI agent.* **3.** A means by which something is done or caused: *Wind and rain are agents of erosion.* [First written down in 1471 in Middle English, from Latin *agere,* to do.]

age-old (āj′ōld′) *adj.* Very old; ancient: *an age-old story.*

ag•glom•er•ate (ə glŏm′ə rāt′) *tr. & intr.v.* **ag•glom•er•at•ed, ag•glom•er•at•ing, ag•glom•er•ates.** To make or form into a rounded mass: *Heat and pressure have agglomerated much of the earth's rock.* —*adj.* (ə glŏm′ər ĭt). Gathered and shaped into a rounded mass. —*n.* (ə glŏm′ər ĭt). **1.** A jumbled mass of things heaped together. **2.** A volcanic rock consisting of rounded and angular fragments fused together.

ag•glom•er•a•tion (ə glŏm′ə rā′shən) *n.* **1.** The act or process of massing things together: *the continual agglomeration of rocks at the foot of the cliff.* **2.** A jumbled mass; an agglomerate.

ag•glu•ti•nate (ə glo͞ot′n āt′) *v.* **ag•glu•ti•nat•ed, ag•glu•ti•nat•ing, ag•glu•ti•nates.** —*tr.* **1.** To join together, as with glue. **2.** To cause (red blood cells or bacteria) to clump together. —*intr.* To undergo agglutination.

ag•glu•ti•na•tion (ə glo͞ot′n ā′shən) *n.* **1.** The joining together of distinct parts. **2.** A process in which red blood cells or bacteria clump together into a mass. **3.** The mass formed in this way.

ag•gran•dize (ə grăn′dīz′ *or* ăg′rən dīz′) *tr.v.* **ag•gran•dized, ag•gran•diz•ing, ag•gran•diz•es.** To make greater, as in power or influence. —**ag•gran′dize•ment** (ə grăn′dĭz mənt) *n.* —**ag•gran′diz′er** *n.*

ag•gra•vate (ăg′rə vāt′) *tr.v.* **ag•gra•vat•ed, ag•gra•vat•ing, ag•gra•vates.** **1.** To make worse: *aggravate an injury.* **2.** To irritate; provoke: *Our constant noise aggravated the neighbors.* [First written down in 1471 in Middle English and spelled *aggravate,* weighed down, from Latin *aggravāre,* to weigh down : *ad-,* to + *gravāre,* to burden (from *gravis,* heavy).] —**ag′gra•vat′ing•ly** *adv.* —**ag′gra•va′tor** *n.*

ag•gra•va•tion (ăg′rə vā′shən) *n.* **1.** The act or process of aggravating. **2.** Irritation; annoyance.

ag•gre•gate (ăg′rĭ gĭt) *adj.* Gathered into or considered together as a whole; total. —*n.* **1.** A total or whole; a gross amount. **2.** The mineral materials, such as sand and stone, used to make concrete. —*tr. v.* (ăg′rĭ gāt′). **ag•gre•gat•ed, ag•gre•gat•ing, ag•gre•gates.** **1.** To gather into a mass, sum, or whole. **2.** To amount to; total. —***idiom.* in the aggregate.** Taken as a whole; considered collectively. [First written down about 1400 in Middle English and spelled *aggregat,* from Latin *aggregāre,* to add to : *ad-,* to + *gregāre,* to collect (from *grex,* flock).] —**ag′gre•gate•ly** *adv.* —**ag′gre•gate•ness** *n.*

ag•gre•ga•tion (ăg′rĭ gā′shən) *n.* **1.** The collecting of separate things into one mass or whole. **2.** The group or mass collected.

ag•gres•sion (ə grĕsh′ən) *n.* **1.** The action of launching an unprovoked attack on another country. **2.** Hostile action or behavior.

ag•gres•sive (ə grĕs′ĭv) *adj.* **1.** Given to hostile behavior: *an aggressive person.* **2.** Vigorous; energetic: *an aggressive campaign to promote physical fitness.* —**ag•gres′sive•ly** *adv.* —**ag•gres′sive•ness** *n.*

ag•gres•sor (ə grĕs′ər) *n.* A person or country that attacks another without cause or justification.

ag•grieved (ə grēvd′) *adj.* **1.** Treated wrongly; offended: *The aggrieved worker wrote a letter of complaint to her boss.* **2.** Feeling distress; troubled: *She tried to comfort her aggrieved friend.*

a•ghast (ə găst′) *adj.* Shocked or horrified, as by something terrible.

ag•ile (ăj′əl *or* ăj′īl′) *adj.* **1.** Able to move quickly and easily; nimble: *an agile mountain climber.* **2.** Mentally alert: *She has an agile mind.* [First written down in 1581 in Modern English, from Latin *agilis,* from *agere,* to drive, do.] —**ag′ile•ly** *adv.* —**ag′ile•ness** *n.*

a•gil•i•ty (ə jĭl′ĭ tē) *n.* The quality or condition of being agile; nimbleness.

ag•i•tate (ăj′ĭ tāt′) *v.* **ag•i•tat•ed, ag•i•tat•ing, ag•i•tates.** —*tr.* **1.** To shake or stir up violently: *The storm agitated the sea.* **2.** To disturb; upset: *Our quarrel agitated everyone present.* —*intr.* To stir up public interest in a cause: *agitate for civil rights.* [First written down in 1449 in Middle English and spelled *agitat,* agitated, from Latin *agitāre,* to agitate.] —**ag′i•tat′ed•ly** *adv.*

ag•i•ta•tion (ăj′ĭ tā′shən) *n.* **1.** The act of agitating. **2.** Great emotional disturbance or excitement. **3.** Energetic action to arouse public interest in a cause.

ag•i•ta•tor (ăj′ĭ tā′tər) *n.* **1.** A person who is active in stirring up interest in a cause. **2.** A mechanism that stirs or shakes, as in a washing machine.

a•gleam (ə glēm′) *adv. & adj.* Brightly shining.

a•glit•ter (ə glĭt′ər) *adv. & adj.* Glittering; sparkling: *eyes aglitter with excitement.*

a•glow (ə glō′) *adv. & adj.* Glowing brightly: *a room aglow with lights.*

ag•nos•tic (ăg nŏs′tĭk) *n.* A person who believes that there can be no proof that God exists, but does not deny the possibility that God exists. —*adj.* Relating to or being an agnostic. —**ag•nos′ti•cal•ly** *adv.*

ag•nos•ti•cism (ăg nŏs′tĭ sĭz′əm) *n.* The belief that there can be no proof either that God exists or that God does not exist.

Ag•nus De•i (ăg′nəs dē′ī′ *or* än′yo͞os dā′ē) *n.* **1.** The Lamb of God; Jesus. **2.** A prayer to Jesus that is part of the Mass and begins with the words "Agnus Dei." **3.** A musical composition for this prayer.

a•go (ə gō′) *adv. & adj.* **1.** Gone by; past: *two years ago.* **2.** In the past: *They lived there long ago.*

a•gog (ə gŏg′) *adv. & adj.* Full of eager anticipation; greatly excited.

ag•o•nize (ăg′ə nīz′) *intr.v.* **ag•o•nized, ag•o•niz•ing, ag•o•niz•es.** To be in extreme pain or suffer great distress: *agonize over a decision.*

ag•o•niz•ing (ăg′ə nī′zĭng) *adj.* Causing great pain or anguish: *an agonizing decision.* —**ag′o•niz′ing•ly** *adv.*

ag•o•ny (ăg′ə nē) *n., pl.* **ag•o•nies.** Intense and prolonged pain or suffering.

ag•o•ra (ăg′ər ə) *n., pl.* **ag•o•rae** (ăg′ə rē′) or **ag•o•ras.** The marketplace of an ancient Greek city, used as a meeting place.

a•gou•ti (ə go͞o′tē) *n., pl.* **a•gou•tis.** A burrowing rodent of tropical America, related to and resembling the guinea pig.

a•grar•i•an (ə grâr′ē ən) *adj.* **1.** Relating to or concerning farmland or its ownership: *agrarian countries.* **2.** Relating to farming or farmers; agricultural.

a•gree (ə grē′) *v.* **a•greed, a•gree•ing, a•grees.** —*intr.* **1.** To have or share the same opinion; concur: *I agree with you.* **2.** To consent: *A smart in-*

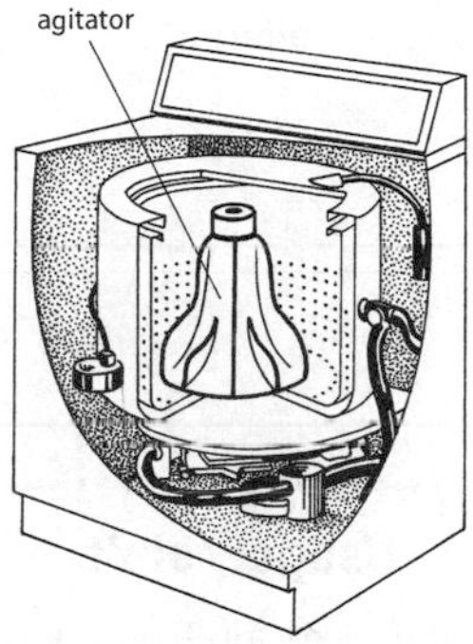

agitator
Cutaway view of a washing machine

ă	pat	oi	boy
ā	pay	ou	out
âr	care	o͝o	took
ä	father	o͞o	boot
ĕ	pet	ŭ	cut
ē	be	ûr	urge
ĭ	pit	th	thin
ī	pie	*th*	this
îr	pier	hw	whoop
ŏ	pot	zh	vision
ō	toe	ə	about
ô	paw	N	*French* bon

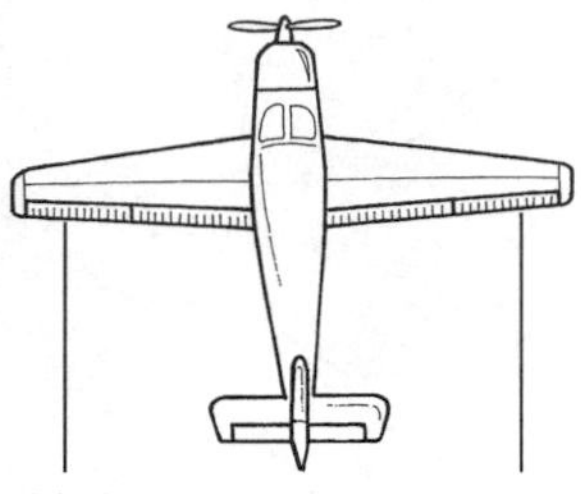

aileron

Usage: ain't

The word **ain't** has a long history of use as a contraction of *am not, are not, is not, has not,* and *have not. Ain't,* however, is not acceptable for use in formal writing or speaking. Instead of *ain't* use *I'm not, aren't, isn't, hasn't,* and *haven't.*

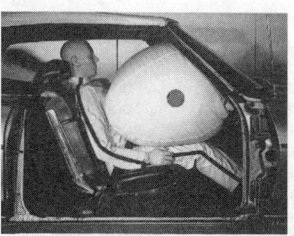

air bag
Inflated air bag

vestor would never agree to such a crazy scheme. **3.** To be in harmony or accord: *The two versions of the story do not agree.* **4.** To come to an understanding or a settlement: *The jury could not agree on a verdict.* **5.** To be suitable, pleasing, or healthful: *Onions do not agree with me. The wet climate here does not agree with many people.* **6.** In grammar, to correspond in number, gender, case, or person: *In this sentence the verb agrees with the subject.* —*tr.* To grant or concede: *My parents agreed that we should go.* [First written down about 1385 in Middle English and spelled *agreen,* from Old French *agreer* : Latin *ad-,* to + Latin *grātus,* pleasing.]

a•gree•a•ble (ə grē′ə bəl) *adj.* **1.** Pleasing; pleasant: *an agreeable smell.* **2.** Willing to agree or consent: *The teacher was agreeable to the suggestion.* **—a•gree′a•ble•ness** *n.* **—a•gree′a•bly** *adv.*

a•gree•ment (ə grē′mənt) *n.* **1.** Harmony of opinion: *The neighboring countries were in agreement and signed a treaty.* **2.** An arrangement or understanding between two parties: *an agreement between states over water rights.* **3.** In grammar, correspondence between words in gender, number, case, or person.

ag•ri•busi•ness (ăg′rə bĭz′nĭs) *n.* The business of producing, processing, and distributing agricultural products.

agric. *abbr.* An abbreviation of: **1.** Agricultural. **2.** Agriculture. **3.** Agriculturist.

ag•ri•cul•tur•al (ăg′rĭ kŭl′chər əl) *adj.* Of or relating to farming; concerned with agriculture. **—ag′ri•cul′tur•al•ly** *adv.*

ag•ri•cul•ture (ăg′rĭ kŭl′chər) *n.* The science, art, and business of cultivating the soil, producing useful crops, and raising livestock; farming. [First written down about 1440 in Middle English, from Latin *agrīcultūra* : *ager,* field + *cultūra,* cultivation.]

ag•ri•cul•tur•ist (ăg′rĭ kŭl′chər ĭst) *n.* A farmer or other expert in farming.

a•gron•o•my (ə grŏn′ə mē) *n.* The study of soil and the improvement of crop production; scientific farming. **—a•gron′o•mist** *n.*

a•ground (ə ground′) *adv. & adj.* Stranded in shallow water or on a reef or shoal: *During the storm the ship ran aground near shore.*

agt. *abbr.* An abbreviation of agent.

a•gue (ā′gyo͞o) *n.* **1.** A fever, like that of malaria, accompanied by periods of chills and sweating. **2.** A chill or fit of shivering.

ah (ä) *interj.* An expression used to show surprise, delight, pity, or other emotions.

a•ha (ä hä′) *interj.* An expression used to show satisfaction, pleasure, or triumph: *Aha! I've got you now!*

a•head (ə hĕd′) *adv.* **1.** At or to the front: *Let's move ahead to the front of the bus.* **2.** In advance: *To get tickets, you have to phone ahead.* **3.** For the future: *plan ahead.* **4.** Forward or onward: *The train moved ahead.* **—*idiom.* be ahead.** To be winning or in a superior position: *Our team is ahead by two goals.*

ahead of *prep.* **1.** In front of: *the path ahead of us.* **2.** At an earlier time than: *She arrived ahead of us.* **3.** More successful than: *Your class is ahead of ours in mathematics.*

a•hem (ə hĕm′) *interj.* An expression used to attract attention or to express doubt or warning.

a•hoy (ə hoi′) *interj.* An expression used to hail a ship or person or to attract attention.

AI *abbr.* An abbreviation of artificial intelligence.

aid (ād) *v.* **aid•ed, aid•ing, aids.** —*intr.* To provide help or assistance. —*tr.* To provide help or assistance to: *aid a friend in distress.* See Synonyms at **help.** —*n.* **1.** Help; assistance: *foreign aid.* **2.** An assistant or a helper. **3.** A device that helps or is helpful: *a hearing aid; visual aids used in teaching.* [First written down before 1400 in Middle English and spelled *aiden,* from Latin *adiūtāre.*] **—aid′er** *n.*

❑ *These sound alike:* **aid, aide** (helper).

aide (ād) *n.* **1.** An assistant or helper: *a Presidential aide.* **2.** An aide-de-camp.

❑ *These sound alike:* **aide, aid** (help).

aide-de-camp (ād′dĭ kămp′) *n., pl.* **aides-de-camp.** A military officer acting as secretary and assistant to a general.

AIDS (ādz) *n.* A severe disorder caused by HIV, a virus that attacks and breaks down the body's immune system, thereby making the body more susceptible to infections and diseases. The virus can be transmitted through bodily fluids such as semen and blood. [First written down in 1982 in Modern English, from *a(cquired) i(mmune) d(eficiency) s(yndrome).*]

ai•grette or **ai•gret** (ā grĕt′ *or* ā′grĕt′) *n.* **1.** A tuft of upright plumes or feathers, especially those from an egret's tail. **2.** An arrangement of jewels that resembles these feathers.

ai•ki•do (ī′kē dō′ *or* ī kē′dō) *n.* A Japanese method of self-defense in which one's opponent is made to lose balance.

ail (āl) *v.* **ailed, ail•ing, ails.** —*intr.* To be ill: *Their grandmother has been ailing for months.* —*tr.* To cause pain; make ill: *A high temperature is a sure sign that something is ailing you.* [First written down about 940 in Old English and spelled *eglian,* from *egle,* troublesome.]

❑ *These sound alike:* **ail, ale** (strong beer).

ai•lan•thus (ā lăn′thəs) *n.* Tree-of-heaven.

ai•le•ron (ā′lə rŏn′) *n.* A small section of the back edge of an airplane wing that can be moved up or down to control the plane's rolling and banking movements.

ail•ment (āl′mənt) *n.* A mild illness or disease: *a heart ailment.*

aim (ām) *v.* **aimed, aim•ing, aims.** —*tr.* To direct (a weapon or remark, for example) at someone or something. —*intr.* **1.** To direct a weapon: *She aimed carefully at the target.* **2.** To determine a course: *aim for a better education.* **3.** To propose; intend: *aim to solve a problem.* —*n.* **1.a.** The pointing of a weapon at a target: *take careful aim.* **b.** The ability of a person to hit a target: *The hunters' aim was perfect.* **2.** Purpose; goal: *My aim is to be an actor.* [First written down about 1300 in Middle English and spelled *aimen,* from Latin *aestimāre,* to estimate.]

aim•less (ām′lĭs) *adj.* Without direction or purpose: *We spent an aimless afternoon strolling in the park.* **—aim′less•ly** *adv.* **—aim′less•ness** *n.*

ain't (ānt). *Non-Standard.* Contraction of *am not, is not, are not, has not,* or *have not.* [First written down in 1778 in Modern English, contraction of *am not.*] —SEE NOTE.

Ai•nu (ī′no͞o) *n., pl.* **Ainu** or **Ai•nus. 1.** A member of a native people of Japan now living on its northernmost islands and on islands in the possession of Russia. **2.** The language of the Ainu.

air (âr) *n.* **1.** The colorless, odorless, tasteless mixture of gases that surrounds the earth. Air contains about 78 percent nitrogen and 21 percent oxygen, with the remaining part being made up of argon, carbon dioxide, neon, helium, and other gases. **2.** The open space above the earth: *a photograph taken from the air.* **3.** Transportation by aircraft: *travel by air; ship goods by air.* **4.** The appearance or manner of a person or thing: *The judge has a very dignified air.* **5. airs.** An affected, unnatural way of acting, intended to impress people: *She is putting on airs by speaking with an accent.* **6.** A melody or

tune. *—v.* **aired, air•ing, airs.** *—tr.* **1.** To expose to the air so as to dry, cool, or freshen; ventilate: *air a blanket.* **2.** To express publicly: *air one's grievances.* *—intr.* To become fresh or cool by exposure to the air: *give the room a chance to air out.* *—idioms.* **in the air.** Abroad; prevalent: *rumors in the air.* **off the air.** Not being broadcast. **on the air.** Being broadcast. **up in the air.** Not yet decided; uncertain. [First written down before 1200 in Middle English, from Greek *aēr*.]

❑ *These sound alike:* **air, e'er** (ever), **ere** (before), **heir** (inheritor).

air bag *n.* A safety device in an automobile, consisting of a bag that inflates in a collision to prevent a passenger or the driver from pitching forward.

air base *n.* A base for a military aircraft.

air bladder *n.* A sac in most fishes and various animals and plants that is filled with air and functions to maintain buoyancy or to aid respiration or hearing.

air•borne (âr′bôrn′) *adj.* **1.** Carried or transported by air: *airborne troops.* **2.** In flight; flying: *Drinks are served shortly after the plane is airborne.*

air brake *n.* A type of brake, often used on large trucks or trains, that is operated by the power of compressed air.

air•brush (âr′brŭsh′) *n.* A small spray gun used to apply paints, inks, or dyes to a surface, as in painting or drawing. *—tr.v.* **air•brushed, air•brush•ing, air•brush•es.** To spray with an airbrush.

air-con•di•tion (âr′kən dĭsh′ən) *tr.v.* **air-con•di•tioned, air-con•di•tion•ing, air-con•di•tions. 1.** To ventilate (an enclosed space) by means of an air conditioner or air conditioners. **2.** To provide with air conditioning.

air-con•di•tioned (âr′kən dĭsh′ənd) *adj.* Having air conditioning: *an air-conditioned theater.*

air conditioner *n.* A device, especially a cooling device, that regulates the temperature and humidity of the air in an enclosure.

air conditioning *n.* **1.** A system of air conditioners. **2.** The condition of the air produced by a system of air conditioners.

air-cooled (âr′ko͞old′) *adj.* Cooled by having air blown on it: *an air-cooled engine.*

air•craft (âr′krăft′) *n., pl.* **aircraft.** A machine or device, such as an airplane, helicopter, glider, or dirigible, that is capable of flying.

aircraft carrier *n.* A naval ship designed to serve as a seagoing air base, having a long flat deck on which aircraft can take off and land.

air•drome (âr′drōm′) *n.* An airport or landing field.

air•drop (âr′drŏp′) *n.* A delivery, as of supplies or troops, by parachute from aircraft in flight. *—tr. & intr.v.* **air•dropped, air•drop•ping, air•drops.** To drop or be dropped from an aircraft in flight.

Aire•dale (âr′dāl′) *n.* A large terrier of a breed having a wiry tan and black coat.

air•field (âr′fēld′) *n.* A place, usually with paved runways, where aircraft can take off and land.

air•flow (âr′flō′) *n.* A flow of air, especially the air currents caused by the motion of an aircraft, an automobile, or a similar object.

air•foil (âr′foil′) *n.* A part, such as an aircraft wing or propeller blade, designed to control direction or provide lift by changing how air flows around its surface.

air force or **Air Force** *n.* The branch of a country's armed forces in charge of fighting war by using aircraft.

air•glow (âr′glō′) *n.* A faint glow seen in the night sky, held to be due to chemical changes caused by radiation from the sun striking the upper atmosphere.

air gun *n.* A gun that is discharged by compressed air.

air hammer *n.* A pneumatic drill.

air hole *n.* A hole through which air can pass, as in the ice on a river or lake.

air•i•ly (âr′ə lē) *adv.* In a light or airy manner; gaily; jauntily.

air•i•ness (âr′ē nĭs) *n.* The state or quality of being airy.

air•ing (âr′ĭng) *n.* **1.** Exposure to the air as for drying, cooling, or freshening. **2.** Public expression or discussion: *an airing of unpopular views.*

air lane *n.* A regular route of travel for aircraft.

air•less (âr′lĭs) *adj.* **1.** Having no air: *The moon is airless.* **2.** Lacking fresh air; stuffy: *a cramped and airless room.*

air letter *n.* A sheet of paper for writing a letter that can be folded to form an envelope and has an imprinted airmail stamp.

air•lift (âr′lĭft′) *n.* A system of transporting troops or supplies by aircraft, especially when surface routes are blocked. *—tr.v.* **air•lift•ed, air•lift•ing, air•lifts.** To transport by aircraft when ground routes are blocked.

air•line (âr′līn′) *n.* A company that transports passengers and freight by air.

air•lin•er (âr′lī′nər) *n.* A large commercial passenger plane.

air lock *n.* **1.** An airtight chamber in which air pressure can be regulated to allow passage between two areas of unequal pressure. **2.** A bubble or pocket of air in a pipe that stops the flow of fluid.

air•mail (âr′māl′) *tr.v.* **air•mailed, air•mail•ing, air•mails.** To send (a letter, for example) by airmail. *—adj.* Of, relating to, or for use with airmail: *an airmail letter.* *—n.* or **air mail. 1.** The system of transporting mail by aircraft. **2.** Mail transported by aircraft.

air•man (âr′mən) *n.* **1.** The pilot or other crew member of an aircraft. **2.** An enlisted person of the lowest rank in the U.S. Air Force.

airman first class *n.* An enlisted person in the U.S. Air Force ranking next below a sergeant.

air mass *n.* A large body of air that has approximately the same temperature and humidity throughout.

air mattress *n.* A sack that can be inflated and used as a mattress.

air mile *n.* A unit of distance in air navigation equivalent to a nautical mile, 6,076 feet (1,852 meters).

air piracy *n.* The hijacking of aircraft in flight; skyjacking.

air•plane (âr′plăn′) *n.* Any of various vehicles that are capable of flight, are held aloft by the force of air flowing around its wings, and are driven by jet engines or propellers.

air plant *n.* An epiphyte.

air pocket *n.* A downward current of air that makes an aircraft lose altitude suddenly.

air•port (âr′pôrt′) *n.* A level area for aircraft to take off and land, equipped with a control tower, hangars, refueling equipment, and accommodations for passengers and cargo.

air•pow•er or **air power** (âr′pou′ər) *n.* The military power of a nation for carrying on war in the air.

air pressure *n.* The force that air exerts per unit of area of a surface.

air pump *n.* A pump used to compress air or to cause it to flow.

air raid *n.* An attack by military aircraft usually armed with bombs.

air rifle *n.* A rifle from which pellets are propelled by compressed air.

air rights *pl.n.* The rights to use airspace, especially

aircraft carrier
U.S.S. *Ranger*

Airedale

air pump

ă	pat	oi	boy
ā	pay	ou	out
âr	care	o͝o	took
ä	father	o͞o	boot
ĕ	pet	ŭ	cut
ē	be	ûr	urge
ĭ	pit	th	thin
ī	pie	*th*	this
îr	pier	hw	whoop
ŏ	pot	zh	vision
ō	toe	ə	about
ô	paw	N	*French* bon

Alabama

The state of **Alabama** is named for a Native American people who inhabited the region when European explorers arrived. The name is sometimes translated "people who clear away thickets" and is taken by some as evidence that the Native Americans cultivated their land. The French first gave the name to the Alabama River and the state later took its name from the river.

Alaska

The state of **Alaska** gets its name from an Aleut word meaning "the mainland." The Aleut live mostly on the Aleutian Islands, and their word for *mainland* refers to the Alaska Peninsula, the narrow part of the mainland that juts out toward the islands. Before 1867, when it was purchased from Russia by the United States, the territory was known as "Russian America."

albatross

above an existing structure, such as a building or road.

air sac *n.* An air-filled space in the body, especially an alveolus of a lung or one of the spaces in a bird's body connecting the lungs and bone cavities.

air shaft *n.* A passage for letting fresh air into a tunnel, building, or other structure.

air•ship (âr′shĭp′) *n.* A self-propelled aircraft that is lighter than air; a dirigible.

air•sick (âr′sĭk′) *adj.* Suffering from airsickness: *an airsick passenger.*

air•sick•ness (âr′sĭk′nĭs) *n.* Nausea and discomfort caused by the motions of an aircraft during flight.

air•space or **air space** (âr′spās′) *n.* **1.** The space in the atmosphere above a particular section of the earth. **2.** The space occupied by an aircraft in flight.

air speed *n.* The speed of an aircraft relative to the speed of the air it is traveling through.

air•strip (âr′strĭp′) *n.* A flat, clear area that serves as an airfield, usually only temporarily or in emergencies.

air•tight (âr′tīt′) *adj.* **1.** Allowing no air or other gas to pass in or out: *an airtight seal.* **2.** Having no weak points; sound: *an airtight excuse.*

air•time (âr′tīm′) *n.* The time that a radio or television station is broadcasting.

air-to-air (âr′tə âr′) *adj.* Passing between aircraft while flying, as a rocket launched by one aircraft at another.

air•waves (âr′wāvz′) *pl.n.* The media used for broadcasting radio and television signals.

air•way (âr′wā′) *n.* **1.** A passage through which air circulates, as in ventilating a mine. **2.** A route for aircraft; an air lane.

air•wor•thy (âr′wûr′*thē*) *adj.* **air•wor•thi•er, air•wor•thi•est.** In fit condition for flight: *an airworthy plane.* **—air′wor′thi•ness** *n.*

air•y (âr′ē) *adj.* **air•i•er, air•i•est. 1.** Open to the air: *The house was airy and full of light.* **2.** Lighthearted; merry: *airy songs.* **3.** Light as air; delicate: *airy silk.* **4.** Unreal or impractical; without substance: *airy schemes.*

❑ *These sound alike:* **airy, aerie** (nest).

aisle (īl) *n.* **1.** A passageway between rows of seats, as in a church or theater. **2.** A similiar passageway, as between counters in a department store. [First written down about 1370 in Middle English and spelled *ele*, from Latin *āla*, wing of a building.]

❑ *These sound alike:* **aisle, I'll** (I will), **isle** (island).

a•jar (ə jär′) *adv. & adj.* Partially open: *Leave the door ajar.* [First written down about 1500 in Middle English and spelled *on char* : *on*, in + *char*, turn (from Old English *cierr*).]

A•jax (ā′jăks′) *n.* In Greek mythology, a Greek hero of great strength and courage who fights against Troy.

AK *abbr.* An abbreviation of Alaska.

a•kim•bo (ə kĭm′bō) *adv. & adj.* With the hands on the hips and the elbows bent outward: *stood akimbo before beginning the exercises.* [First written down in 1611 in Middle English and spelled *in kenebowe*.]

a•kin (ə kĭn′) *adj.* **1.** Related by blood. **2.** Derived from the same origin: *The word "maternal" is akin to the word "mother."*

Ak•ron (ăk′rən). A city of northeast Ohio south-southeast of Cleveland. The first of its many rubber factories was established in 1869 by B.F. Goodrich (1841–1888). Population, 223,019.

Al The symbol for the element **aluminum.**

AL *abbr.* An abbreviation of Alabama.

–al[1] *suff.* A suffix that means of, relating to, or characterized by: *adjectival; postal.*

–al[2] *suff.* A suffix that means action or process: *denial; arrival.*

Ala. *abbr.* An abbreviation of Alabama.

Al•a•bam•a (ăl′ə băm′ə). A state of the southeast United States west of Georgia. It was admitted as the 22nd state in 1819. The southern section of Alabama was claimed by the United States as part of the Louisiana Purchase (1803). Montgomery is the capital and Birmingham the largest city. Population, 4,062,608. —See Note.

al•a•bas•ter (ăl′ə băs′tər) *n.* Any of various smooth, hard, translucent minerals that are white, tinted, or banded, and consist mainly of salts of calcium.

à la carte also **a la carte** (ä′lə kärt′ *or* ăl′ə kärt′) *adv. & adj.* With a separate price for each item on the menu: *Meals in many high-priced restaurants are à la carte.*

a•lack (ə lăk′) *interj.* An expression used to show sorrow, regret, or alarm.

a•lac•ri•ty (ə lăk′rĭ tē) *n.* Speed and willingness in acting or responding: *The messenger carried out the assignment with alacrity.*

al•a•me•da (ăl′ə mē′də *or* ăl′ə mā′də) *n.* A shaded public walk lined with trees.

Al•a•mo (ăl′ə mō′). A chapel built after 1744 as part of a mission in San Antonio, Texas. During the Texas Revolution against Mexican rule some 182 people were besieged here from February 24 to March 6, 1836. All the rebels were killed.

à la mode (ä′lə mōd′ *or* ăl′ə mōd′) *adj.* **1.** According to or in the style or fashion; fashionable. **2.** Served with ice cream: *apple pie à la mode.*

a•larm (ə lärm′) *n.* **1.** Sudden fear caused by a sense of danger: *There is no cause for alarm.* **2.** A warning of approaching danger: *Rumors that the boiler broke were only a false alarm.* **3.** A device sounded to warn people of danger: *a fire alarm; a burglar alarm.* **4.** An alarm clock. *—tr.v.* **a•larmed, a•larm•ing, a•larms. 1.** To fill with alarm; frighten: *The loud noise alarmed the children.* See Synonyms at **frighten. 2.** To warn of approaching danger. [First written down about 1380 in Middle English, from Old Italian *all'arme*, to arms.]

alarm clock *n.* A clock that can be set to sound a bell or buzzer at a certain time in order to wake a person up.

a•larm•ing (ə lär′ming) *adj.* Causing great fear of anxiety: *The wind is increasing at an alarming rate.* **—a•larm′ing•ly** *adv.*

a•larm•ist (ə lär′mĭst) *n.* A person who frightens others needlessly or for little reason.

a•la•rum (ə lär′əm *or* ə lăr′əm) *n.* A warning or an alarm, especially a call to arms.

a•las (ə lăs′) *interj.* An expression used to show sorrow, regret, or grief.

A•las•ka (ə lăs′kə). A state of the United States in extreme northwest North America, separated from the other mainland states by British Columbia, Canada. It was admitted as the 49th state in 1959 and is the largest state of the Union. The extensive territory was purchased from Russia in 1867 for $7,200,000. Juneau is the capital and Anchorage the largest city. Population, 551,947. **—A•las′kan** *adj. & n.* —See Note.

Alaskan malamute *n.* The malamute.

Alaska Standard Time *n.* Standard time in the ninth time zone west of Greenwich, England, used for example in Alaska and Hawaii.

alb (ălb) *n.* A long, white linen robe with tapered sleeves that fit closely at the wrist, worn by a priest at Mass.

Alb. *abbr.* An abbreviation of Albanian.

al•ba•core (ăl′bə kôr′) *n., pl.* **al•ba•core** or **al•ba•**

cores. A large ocean fish that is one of the main sources of canned tuna.

Al•ba•ni•a (ăl **bā′**nē ə *or* ăl **bān′**yə). A country of southeast Europe on the Adriatic Sea northwest of Greece. Albania has had close ties with communist countries since 1944. Tiranë is the capital and the largest city. Population, 2,841,300.

Al•ba•ni•an (ăl **bā′**nē ən *or* ăl **bān′**yən) *adj.* Of or relating to Albania or its people, language, or culture. —*n.* **1.** A native or inhabitant of Albania. **2.** The Indo-European language of Albania.

Al•ba•ny (**ôl′**bə nē). The capital (since 1797) of New York, in the eastern part of the state on the west bank of the Hudson River. The early 17th-century Dutch settlement Fort Orange was renamed Albany when the English took control in 1664. Population, 101,082.

al•ba•tross (**ăl′**bə trôs′ *or* **ăl′**bə trŏs′) *n., pl.* **alba-tross** or **al•ba•tross•es. 1.** A large, web-footed sea bird with a hooked beak and very long wings. **2.** An obvious handicap or great burden: *the albatross of too many responsibilities.* [First written down in 1672 in Modern English, probably alteration of *alcatras*, pelican, from Arabic *al-ġaṭṭās*.]

al•be•it (ôl **bē′**ĭt *or* ăl **bē′**ĭt) *conj.* Even though; although: *They proposed an imaginative, albeit somewhat impractical, idea.*

Al•ber•ta (ăl **bûr′**tə). A province of western Canada between British Columbia and Saskatchewan. It joined the Canadian confederation in 1905. Edmonton is the capital and the largest city. Population, 2,237,724. —See Note.

al•bi•nism (**ăl′**bə **nĭz′**əm) *n.* **1.** Absence of normal skin, hair, and eye coloring. **2.** The condition of being an albino.

al•bi•no (ăl **bī′**nō) *n., pl.* **al•bi•nos.** A person or animal born lacking normal coloring, so that the skin and hair are white and the eyes have pink or blue irises and deep red pupils. [First written down in 1777 in Modern English, from Portuguese, from Latin *albus*, white.]

al•bum (**ăl′**bəm) *n.* **1.** A book with blank pages on which to mount such things as photographs or stamps or to collect autographs. **2.** A phonograph record sold in a jacket. [First written down in 1651 in Modern English, from Latin *album*, blank tablet, from *albus*, white.]

al•bu•men (ăl **byōō′**mən) *n.* **1.** The white of an egg, consisting mostly of albumin dissolved in water. **2.** Albumin.

al•bu•min (ăl **byōō′**mĭn) *n.* Any of several simple proteins that dissolve in water, are coagulated by heat, and are found in egg white, blood serum, milk, and various plant and animal tissues.

Al•bu•quer•que (**ăl′**bə kûr′kē). A city of central New Mexico on the upper Rio Grande southwest of Santa Fe. It was founded in 1706. Population, 384,736.

al•che•mist (**ăl′**kə mĭst) *n.* A person who practices alchemy.

al•che•my (**ăl′**kə mē) *n.* A medieval system of chemistry that had among its aims the changing of common metals into gold and the preparation of a potion that gives eternal youth.

al•co•hol (**ăl′**kə hôl′ *or* **ăl′**kə hŏl′) *n.* **1.** Any of a large number of colorless, flammable organic compounds that contain the radical −OH, especially ethanol, the form that occurs in wines and liquors. **2.** Alcoholic beverages in general. [First written down in 1543 in Modern English, from Medieval Latin *alcohol*, fine metallic powder, from Arabic *al-kuḥl*.]

al•co•hol•ic (ăl′kə **hô′**lĭk *or* ăl′kə **hŏl′**ĭk) *adj.* **1.** Of, containing, or resulting from alcohol, especially ethanol: *the alcoholic odor of an antiseptic.* **2.** Suffering from alcoholism. —*n.* A person who suffers from alcoholism. **—al′co•hol′i•cal•ly** *adv.*

al•co•hol•ism (**ăl′**kə hô lĭz′əm *or* **ăl′**kə hŏ lĭz′əm) *n.* **1.** Excessive drinking of or addiction to alcoholic beverages. **2.** The diseased conditions, mainly of the nervous and digestive systems, that result from this.

Al•cott (**ôl′**kət *or* **ôl′**kŏt), **Louisa May.** 1832–1888. American writer who is best known for her largely autobiographical novel *Little Women* (1868–1869).

al•cove (**ăl′**kōv′) *n.* A small room opening on a larger one without being separated from it by a wall or door.

Ald. *abbr.* An abbreviation of alderman.

Al•deb•a•ran (ăl **dĕb′**ər ən) *n.* A binary star in the constellation Taurus. It is one of the brightest stars.

al•der (**ôl′**dər) *n.* Any of various trees or shrubs having rounded leaves and rough bark and growing in cool damp places.

al•der•man (**ôl′**dər mən) *n.* A member of the governing body of a city or town.

ale (āl) *n.* A fermented, bitter alcoholic beverage similar to but heavier than beer.

❑ *These sound alike:* **ale, ail** (be ill).

a•lee (ə **lē′**) *adv.* Away from the wind; to leeward.

a•lert (ə **lûrt′**) *adj.* **1.** Watchful; attentive; vigilant: *A good driver must remain constantly alert.* **2.** Mentally quick; perceptive; intelligent: *an alert child.* —*n.* **1.** A warning signal against danger or attack. **2.** The period during which one must obey this signal. —*tr.v.* **a•lert•ed, a•lert•ing, a•lerts. 1.** To warn of approaching danger. **2.** To make aware of: *alert the public to the need for pollution control.* **—*idiom.* on the alert.** Watchful and prepared: *The police are on the alert to prevent vandalism.* [First written down in 1618 in Modern English, from Italian *all'erta*, on the lookout.] **—a•lert′ly** *adv.* **—a•lert′ness** *n.*

A•leut (ə **lōōt′** *or* **ăl′**ē ōōt′) *n., pl.* **Aleut** or **A•leuts. 1.** A member of a Native American people inhabiting the Aleutian Islands. **2.** Either of two languages, related to Eskimo, spoken by the Aleuts. **—A•leu′tian** (ə **lōō′**shən) *adj.*

Aleutian Islands. A chain of rugged volcanic islands of southwest Alaska curving about 1,200 miles (1,931 kilometers) west from the Alaska Peninsula and separating the Bering Sea from the Pacific Ocean. The islands were purchased from Russia by the United States in 1867.

ale•wife (**āl′**wīf′) *n., pl.* **ale•wives** (**āl′**wīvz′). A fish related to the herring, commonly found off the Atlantic coast of North America.

Al•ex•an•der the Great (ăl′ĭg **zăn′**dər). 356–323 B.C. King of Macedonia (336–323) and conqueror of Asia Minor, Syria, Egypt, Babylonia, and Persia.

Al•ex•an•dra (ăl′ĭg **zăn′**drə). 1872–1918. Last czarina of Russia (1894–1917) as the wife of Nicholas II. After the Bolshevik revolution, she and her family were imprisoned and executed.

Al•ex•an•dri•a (ăl′ĭg **zăn′**drē ə). **1.** A city of northern Egypt on the Mediterranean Sea at the western tip of the Nile Delta. It was founded by Alexander the Great in 332 B.C. The lighthouse at Alexandria was one of the Seven Wonders of the World. Population, 2,821,000. **2.** A city of northern Virginia on the Potomac River opposite Washington, D.C. George Washington helped survey the city in 1749. Population, 111,183.

Al•ex•an•dri•an (ăl′ĭg **zăn′**drē ən) *adj.* **1.** Of or relating to Alexandria. **2.** Of or relating to Alexander the Great.

al•fal•fa (ăl **făl′**fə) *n.* A plant with three leaflets and purplish flowers, grown as feed for cattle and other livestock. [First written down in 1845 in Modern English, from Spanish, from Arabic *al-faṣfaṣah*.]

Al•fred (**ăl′**frĭd) Known as "Alfred the Great." 849–

Alberta

The territory of **Alberta** was named in 1882 by the Scottish Marquis of Lorne (1845–1914), the Governor General of Canada from 1878 to 1883. He named the territory after his wife, Princess Louise Caroline Alberta, daughter of Prince Albert and Queen Victoria of Great Britain.

Louisa May Alcott

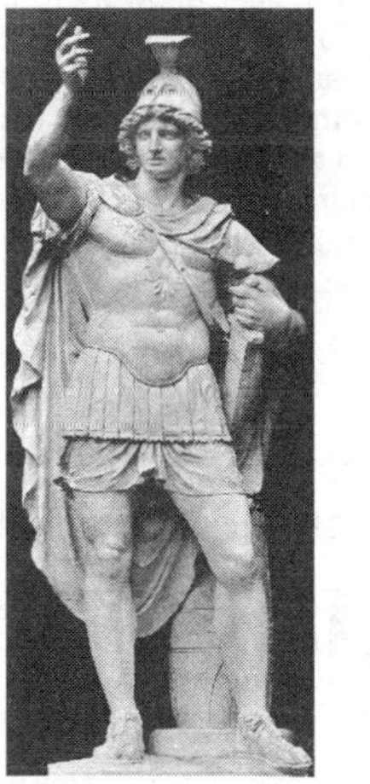

Alexander the Great

ă	pat	oi	boy
ā	pay	ou	out
âr	care	ŏŏ	took
ä	father	ōō	boot
ĕ	pet	ŭ	cut
ē	be	ûr	urge
ĭ	pit	th	thin
ī	pie	*th*	this
îr	pier	hw	whoop
ŏ	pot	zh	vision
ō	toe	ə	about
ô	paw	N	*French* bon

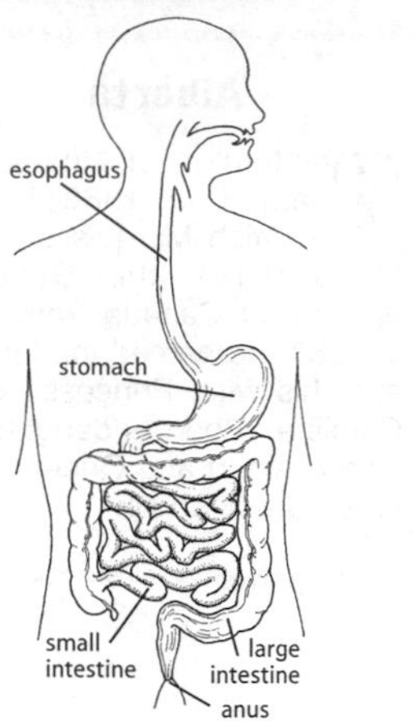

alimentary canal

Word History: alimony

The words **alimentary**, **alimony**, and **alumnus** are all relatives. They all come from the Latin verb *alere*, "to nourish, raise, rear." The noun *aliment*, "nutrition, nourishment," comes from that Latin verb, and the adjective *alimentary*, "pertaining to nutrition," comes from the noun *aliment*. *Alimony* is "allowance for the support or nourishment of a former spouse." An *alumnus* or an **alumna**, literally "one who has been brought up or nourished," is a graduate from a school that is one's **alma mater**, "a nourishing mother."

Word History: alkali

Many English words that begin with the spelling *al–* are borrowed from Arabic, where *al–* means "the." Many of these words are in the subjects of chemistry and mathematics, to which Arab scientists made important contributions in the early Middle Ages. Thus **alkali** is from *al-qalīy*, "the ashes." **Alchemy** is from *al-kīmiyā*, "the science of chemistry" (from Greek *khēmeia*, "transmutation.") **Algebra** is from *al-jabr*, "the science of reconnecting or restoring broken parts." And **alcove** comes from *al-qubbah*, "the vault."

899. King of the West Saxons (871–899) who defeated the Danes and helped unite England.

al•fres•co (ăl **frĕs′**kō) *adv. & adj.* In the fresh air; outdoors.

alg. *abbr.* An abbreviation of algebra.

al•ga (**ăl′**gə) *n., pl.* **al•gae** (**ăl′**jē). Any of various green, red, or brown organisms that lack true roots, stems, and leaves, grow mostly in water, and range from single cells to large spreading seaweeds.

al•ge•bra (**ăl′**jə brə) *n.* A branch of mathematics that deals with the relations and properties of quantities by the use of letters and other symbols to represent unknown numbers, especially in equations, in order to solve problems. [First written down in 1551 in Modern English, from Arabic *al-jabr*, the (science of) reuniting, bone-setting.]

al•ge•bra•ic (ăl′jə **brā′**ĭk) *adj.* Of, relating to, or used in algebra: *an algebraic equation.*

Al•ge•ri•a (ăl **jîr′**ē ə). A country of northwest Africa on the Mediterranean Sea west of Tunisia and Libya. Algeria gained its independence from France in 1962. Algiers is the capital and the largest city. Population, 16,948,000.

Al•giers (ăl **jîrz′**). The capital and largest city of Algeria, in the north on the **Bay of Algiers**, an arm of the Mediterranean Sea. Population, 1,523,000.

Al•gon•qui•an (ăl **gŏng′**kwē ən *or* ăl **gŏng′**kē ən) *n., pl.* **Algonquian** or **Al•gon•qui•ans.** A family of Native American languages spoken over a large area of North America, including Ojibwa, Cree, and Blackfoot. **—Al•gon′qui•an** *adj.*

Al•gon•quin (ăl **gŏng′**kwĭn *or* ăl **gŏng′**kĭn) *n., pl.* **Algonquin** or **Algon•quins. 1.** A Native American people living along the Ottawa River in Canada. **2.** A member of this people. **3.** The Algonquian language of this people.

al•go•rithm (**ăl′**gə rĭ*th*′əm) *n.* A mathematical rule or process for computing a desired result: *an algorithm used in a computer program.*

Al•ham•bra (ăl **hăm′**brə). A citadel and palace on a hill overlooking Granada, Spain. Built by Moorish kings in the 12th and 13th centuries, the Alhambra is the finest remaining example of Moorish architecture in Spain.

A•li (ä **lē′**). 600?–661. Muslim caliph (656–661) after whose assassination Islam was divided into Sunnite and Shiite sects.

a•li•as (**ā′**lē əs *or* **āl′**yəs) *n.* An assumed name used to conceal a person's real identity. *—adv.* Otherwise named: *William Blake alias James Flynn.*

al•i•bi (**ăl′**ə bī′) *n., pl.* **al•i•bis. 1.** A claim made by an accused person of not being present when a crime was committed. **2.** *Informal.* An excuse: *No more of your alibis!*

a•li•en (**ā′**lē ən *or* **āl′**yən) *adj.* **1.** Belonging to or coming from another country; foreign. **2.** Not natural; unfamiliar; strange: *Having lived in the city, he found the suburb an alien place.* **3.** Inconsistent or opposed; contradictory: *an idea wholly alien to my philosophy.* *—n.* **1.** A person living in one country while remaining a citizen of another; a foreigner. **2.** A being from outer space: *In the movie, Earth is invaded by aliens.* [First written down before 1338 in Middle English, from Latin *aliēnus*, from *alius*, other.]

al•ien•ate (**āl′**yə nāt′ *or* **ā′**lē ə nāt′) *tr.v.* **al•ien•at•ed, al•ien•at•ing, al•ien•ates. 1.** To lose the friendship or support of; estrange: *A barking dog tends to alienate the neighbors.* **2.** To cause to become emotionally withdrawn or isolated: *Treating people as if they were just numbers in a computer will only alienate them.* **—al′ien•a′tor** *n.*

al•ien•a•tion (āl′yə **nā′**shən *or* ā′lē ə **nā′**shən) *n.* The act of alienating or the condition of being alienated: *After two weeks of alienation, they made up and became friends again.*

a•light[1] (ə **līt′**) *intr.v.* **a•light•ed** or **a•lit** (ə **lĭt′**), **a•light•ing, a•lights. 1.** To come down and settle gently: *A bird alighted on the branch.* **2.** To get off; dismount: *Passengers alighted from a train.* [First written down about 1000 in Old English and spelled *ālīhtan.*]

a•light[2] (ə **līt′**) *adj.* **1.** Lighted; lit up: *eyes alight with excitement.* **2.** On fire; burning: *The discarded match was still alight.* [First written down before 1200 in Middle English, from Old English *ālīhtan*, to illuminate.]

a•lign also **a•line** (ə **līn′**) *v.* **a•ligned, a•lign•ing, a•ligns** also **a•lined, a•lin•ing, a•lines.** *—tr.* **1.** To arrange in a straight line: *The chairs were aligned in two rows.* **2.** To ally (oneself) with one side, as of an argument or cause: *The allies usually align themselves behind the same position in foreign policy.* **3.** To adjust (a device, mechanism, or some of its parts) in order to produce a proper relationship or condition: *The mechanic aligned the wheels of my car.* *—intr.* To fall into line: *The soldiers aligned.*

a•lign•ment also **a•line•ment** (ə **līn′**mənt) *n.* **1.** The act of arranging in a straight line. **2.** Arrangement or position in a straight line: *perfect alignment of the teeth.* **3.** The policy of allying with a certain group of nations: *The governments of oil-producing nations followed a policy of alignment.* **4.** The process of aligning a device or mechanism or the condition of being aligned: *A mechanic must perform an alignment on the car.*

a•like (ə **līk′**) *adj.* **1.** Having close resemblance; similar: *Mother and daughter are very much alike.* **2.** Exactly or nearly exactly the same: *Parts for plumbing must be alike to fit.* *—adv.* In the same way or manner or to the same degree: *We must try to treat everyone alike.*

al•i•men•ta•ry (ăl′ə **mĕn′**tə rē *or* ăl′ə **mĕn′**trē) *adj.* Of or relating to food, nutrition, or digestion: *the alimentary tract.*

alimentary canal *n.* The tube or passage of the body of an animal that extends from the mouth to the anus and through which food passes and is digested and wastes are eliminated. In human beings, it includes the pharynx, esophagus, stomach, and intestines.

al•i•mo•ny (**ăl′**ə mō′nē) *n., pl.* **al•i•mo•nies.** An amount of money that a court orders a divorced person to pay as support to a former spouse. —See Note.

a•line (ə **līn′**) *v.* Variant of **align.**

a•line•ment (ə **līn′**mənt) *n.* Variant of **alignment.**

al•i•phat•ic (ăl′ə **făt′**ĭk) *adj.* Of or relating to an organic chemical compound in which the carbon atoms are linked together in straight chains rather than in rings.

a•lit (ə **lĭt′**) *v.* A past tense and a past participle of **alight**[1].

a•live (ə **līv′**) *adj.* **1.** Having life; living: *The frog was alive, and swam off as we drew near.* **2.** In existence or operation; not extinct or inactive: *Keep your hopes alive.* **3.** Full of life; animated; alert: *The audience came alive when the rock star began to sing.* **4.** Now living: *the oldest person alive.* **—*idiom.*** **alive to.** Aware of; sensitive to: *He is usually alive to the moods of others.* **—a•live′ness** *n.*

al•ka•li (**ăl′**kə lī′) *n., pl.* **al•ka•lis** or **al•ka•lies. 1.** A strong base or hydroxide, such as ammonia or lye, that is soluble in water, neutralizes acids, and forms salts with them. Alkalis turn red litmus paper blue. **2.** A salt or mixture of salts that neutralizes acids and is found in arid soils. [First written down about 1395 in Middle English, from Arabic *al-qalīy*, ashes of saltwort.] —See Note.

alkali metal *n.* Any of a group of soft white metals that melt at low temperature, have a low density, and are highly reactive. They include lithium, sodium, potassium, rubidium, cesium, and francium.

al•ka•line (ăl′kə lĭn *or* ăl′kə līn′) *adj.* **1.** Of, relating to, or containing an alkali. **2.** Capable of neutralizing an acid; basic.

al•ka•line-earth metal (ăl′kə lĭn ûrth′ *or* ăl′kə līn′ûrth′) *n.* Any of a group of metallic elements that includes beryllium, magnesium, calcium, strontium, barium, and radium.

al•ka•lin•i•ty (ăl′kə lĭn′ĭ tē) *n.* The alkali concentration or alkaline quality of a substance.

al•ka•lize (ăl′kə līz′) *tr. & intr.v.* **al•ka•lized, al•ka•liz•ing, al•ka•liz•es.** To make or become alkaline or an alkali.

al•ka•loid (ăl′kə loid′) *n.* Any of a class of alkaline organic compounds that contain nitrogen, including nicotine, quinine, and morphine. Many of these compounds are derived from plants.

all (ôl) *adj.* **1.** The total number of: *All the windows are open.* **2.** The whole of: *We spent all day in the museum.* **3.** The utmost possible of: *In all seriousness, I think you should apply for the job.* **4.** Every: *He enjoys all manner of cooking.* **5.** Any: *proven beyond all doubt.* **6.** Nothing but; only: *all skin and bones.* —*n.* Everything one has: *The winning team gave their all.* —*pron.* **1.** The whole amount: *All of the flowers grew.* **2.** Each and every one: *All aboard the ship were saved.* —*adv.* **1.** Wholly; entirely: *The instructions are all wrong.* **2.** Each; apiece: *a score of five all.* —***idioms.*** **all along.** From the beginning; throughout: *They saw through my disguise all along.* **all but.** Nearly; almost: *The patient all but fainted.* **all in all.** Everything being taken into account: *All in all, she's a good athlete.* **all of.** *Informal.* Not more than: *I was gone for all of an hour.* **all that.** *Informal.* To the degree expected: *It's not all that hard.* **at all.** **1.** In any way: *I couldn't sleep at all.* **2.** To any extent; whatever: *not at all sorry.* **in all.** Altogether: *The two buses held 100 passengers in all.* [First written down about 725 in Old English and spelled *eall.*]
❑ *These sound alike:* **all, awl** (pointed tool).

Al•lah (ăl′ə *or* ä′lə) *n.* God, especially in Islam.

all-A•mer•i•can (ôl′ə mĕr′ĭ kən) *adj.* **1.** Typical of the best in the United States: *an all-American hero.* **2.** In sports, chosen as the best amateur in the United States at a particular position or event: *an all-American fullback.* **3.** Composed entirely of American elements or materials: *The orchestra played an all-American program.* —*n.* An all-American athlete.

al•lan•to•is (ə lăn′tō ĭs) *n., pl.* **al•lan•to•i•des** (ăl′ən tō′ĭ dēz′). A membranous sac that develops from the lower end of the alimentary canal of the embryos of reptiles, birds, and mammals. In mammals it takes part in forming the placenta and umbilical cord.

all-a•round (ôl′ə round′) also **all-round** (ôl′round′) *adj.* **1.** Able to do many or all things well: *an all-around athlete.* **2.** Comprehensive in extent: *an all-around education.*

al•lay (ə lā′) *tr.v.* **al•layed, al•lay•ing, al•lays.** **1.** To lessen; reduce; relieve: *allay pain.* **2.** To set to rest; calm: *allay one's fears.* —**al•lay′er** *n.*

all clear *n.* A signal, usually by siren, that an air raid, threat of a tornado, or other danger is over.

al•le•ga•tion (ăl′ĭ gā′shən) *n.* A statement made without proof.

al•lege (ə lĕj′) *tr.v.* **al•leged, al•leg•ing, al•leg•es.** To declare to be true, usually without offering proof: *The indictment alleges that the mayor took bribes.* —**al•leg′a•ble** *adj.* —**al•leg′er** *n.*

al•leged (ə lĕjd′ *or* ə lĕj′ĭd) *adj.* Stated to be as described but without proof: *The alleged thief turned out to be innocent.* —**al•leg′ed•ly** (ə lĕj′ĭd lē) *adv.*

Al•le•ghe•ny Mountains (ăl′ĭ gā′nē) also **Al•le•ghe•nies** (ăl′ĭ gā′nēz). A mountain range forming the western part of the Appalachian Mountains. The range extends about 500 miles (805 kilometers) from northern Pennsylvania to southwest Virginia and rises to approximately 4,862 feet (1,483 meters) in northeast West Virginia.

Allegheny River. A river rising in north-central Pennsylvania and flowing about 325 miles (523 kilometers) northwest and southwest, finally joining the Monongahela River at Pittsburgh to form the Ohio River.

al•le•giance (ə lē′jəns) *n.* Loyalty or devotion, as to one's country, a ruler, or a cause: *pledge allegiance to the United States.*

al•le•gor•i•cal (ăl′ĭ gôr′ĭ kəl *or* ăl′ĭ gŏr′ĭ kəl) *adj.* Of or containing allegory: *In the allegorical tale, the old woman represents wisdom.* —**al′le•gor′i•cal•ly** *adv.*

al•le•go•ry (ăl′ĭ gôr′ē) *n., pl.* **al•le•go•ries.** A story, play, or picture in which characters or events stand for ideas or principles.

al•le•gret•to (ä′lĭ grĕt′ō) *adv. & adj.* In music, in a manner slightly slower than allegro.

al•le•gro (ə lĕg′rō *or* ə lā′grō) *adv. & adj.* In music, in a quick lively manner.

al•lele (ə lēl′) *n.* Any of the possible forms in which a gene can occur.

al•le•lu•ia (ăl′ə lo͞o′yə) *interj.* Hallelujah.

Al•len (ăl′ən), **Ethan.** 1738–1789. American Revolutionary soldier whose troops, the Green Mountain Boys, helped capture Fort Ticonderoga from the British (1775).

al•ler•gen (ăl′ər jən) *n.* A substance, such as pollen, that causes an allergy.

al′ler•gen′ic (ăl′ər jĕn′ĭk) *adj.* Causing an allergy. —**al′ler•gen′i•cal•ly** *adv.*

al•ler•gic (ə lûr′jĭk) *adj.* **1.** Of or caused by an allergy: *an allergic reaction.* **2.** Having an allergy: *a person allergic to tomatoes.* **3.** *Informal.* Having a dislike; averse: *allergic to hard work.* —**al•ler′gi•cal•ly** *adv.*

al•ler•gist (ăl′ər jĭst) *n.* A physician who specializes in the diagnosis and treatment of allergies.

al•ler•gy (ăl′ər jē) *n., pl.* **al•ler•gies.** A disorder in which exposure to a substance or to an environmental influence, such as pollen or cat dander, causes an abnormal and often violent reaction that may include difficulty in breathing, sneezing, watering of the eyes, and skin rashes. [First written down in 1911 in Modern English, from German *Allergie* : Greek *allos*, other + Greek *ergon*, action.]

al•le•vi•ate (ə lē′vē āt′) *tr.v.* **al•le•vi•at•ed, al•le•vi•at•ing, al•le•vi•ates.** To make more bearable; relieve; lessen: *Medicine will alleviate the pain.* [First written down before 1425 in Middle English and spelled *alleviaten*, from Late Latin *alleviāre*, to lighten : Latin *ad-*, to + *levis*, light.] —**al•le′vi•a′tion** *n.* —**al•le′vi•a′tor** *n.*

al•ley (ăl′ē) *n., pl.* **al•leys.** **1.** A narrow street or passageway between or behind buildings. **2.** A path between flowerbeds or trees in a garden or park. **3.** A bowling alley. —***idiom.*** **up (one's) alley.** *Informal.* Suitable to one's interests or abilities. [First written down in 1360 in Middle English and spelled *alei*, from Old French *aller*, to walk, from Latin *ambulāre*.]

alley cat *n.* A homeless cat that wanders through city streets and alleys.

al•ley•way (ăl′ē wā′) *n.* A narrow passage between buildings.

All Fools' Day (ôl fo͞olz) *n.* April Fools' Day.

Ethan Allen

alley
Bowling alley

ă	pat	oi	boy
ā	pay	ou	out
âr	care	o͝o	took
ä	father	o͞o	boot
ĕ	pet	ŭ	cut
ē	be	ûr	urge
ĭ	pit	th	thin
ī	pie	*th*	this
îr	pier	hw	whoop
ŏ	pot	zh	vision
ō	toe	ə	about
ô	paw	N	*French* bon

alligator
American alligator

alluvial fan

All•hal•lows (ôl′hăl′ōz) *n.* All Saint's Day.

al•li•ance (ə lī′əns) *n.* **1.** A formal agreement or union between nations, organizations, or individuals: *Britain and France sealed their alliance with a treaty.* **2.** A connection based on marriage, friendship, or common interest: *There is a strong alliance between cousins in that family.*

al•lied (ə līd′ *or* ăl′īd′) *adj.* **1.** Joined together in an alliance: *the allied countries of Europe.* **2.** Similar; related: *Biology and medicine are allied sciences.* **3. Allied.** Of or relating to the allied countries, especially the countries that fought against Germany and its allies in World War I and World War II.

al•li•ga•tor (ăl′ĭ gā′tər) *n.* **1.** Either of two large reptiles having tough skin, sharp teeth, and powerful jaws. An alligator's snout is blunter than that of the crocodile. **2.** Leather made from the hide of an alligator. [First written down in 1623 in Modern English and spelled *allegater*, alteration of Spanish *el lagarto*, the lizard, from Latin *lacertus*.]

alligator pear *n.* An avocado.

all-im•por•tant (ôl′ĭm pôr′tnt) *adj.* Very important; vital; crucial: *all-important efforts to keep the peace.*

al•lit•er•a•tion (ə lĭt′ə rā′shən) *n.* The repetition of the same consonant sounds for poetic or rhetorical effect.

al•lit•er•a•tive (ə lĭt′ə rā′tĭv *or* ə lĭt′ər ə tĭv) *adj.* Showing or characterized by alliteration: *an alliterative phrase.*

all-night (ôl′nīt′) *adj.* **1.** Continuing all night: *an all-night radio program.* **2.** Open all night: *an all-night diner.*

al•lo•cate (ăl′ə kāt′) *tr.v.* **al•lo•cat•ed, al•lo•cat•ing, al•lo•cates.** To set aside for a particular purpose; allot: *allocate part of one's allowance for going to the movies.* **—al′lo•ca′tion** *n.*

al•lot (ə lŏt′) *tr.v.* **al•lot•ted, al•lot•ting, al•lots.** **1.** To distribute or parcel out: *The profits of the business were allotted equally to each partner.* **2.** To assign a portion for a particular purpose; allocate: *We allotted 20 minutes for each speaker in the discussion.* **—al•lot′ter** *n.*

al•lot•ment (ə lŏt′mənt) *n.* **1.** The act of allotting. **2.** Something allotted: *The soldiers' allotment of coffee was reduced during the winter.*

al•lo•trope (ăl′ə trōp′) *n.* Any of the different structural forms that a chemical element may have. Charcoal, graphite, and diamond are allotropes of carbon.

al•lo•trop•ic (ăl′ə trŏp′ĭk *or* ăl′ə trō′pĭk) *adj.* Of or having allotropes.

al•lot•ro•py (ə lŏt′rə pē) *n.* The existence of different forms of the same chemical element, each form having a different structure of atoms.

all out *adv.* With every possible effort; vigorously: *studied all out and got an A in the course.*

all-out (ôl′out′) *adj.* Using all available resources; vigorous: *an all-out effort.*

all over *adv.* **1.** Over the whole area or extent: *a cloth embroidered all over with roses.* **2.** Everywhere: *searched all over for the keys.* **3.** In every respect; utterly.

al•low (ə lou′) *tr.v.* **al•lowed, al•low•ing, al•lows.** **1.** To let do or happen; permit: *We do not allow eating in the library. Please allow me to finish.* **2.** To let have; permit to have: *We allowed ourselves a treat.* **3.** To let in; permit the presence of: *We do not allow the dog upstairs.* **4.** To make provision for; assign: *The schedule allows time for a break before the second speaker.* **5.** To admit; concede; grant: *I'll allow that some mistakes have been made.* **6.** To give as a discount or in exchange: *The store allowed me $20 on my old typewriter.* ***—idiom.*** **allow for.** To take into consideration and make a provision for: *Our plans allow for changes in the weather.*

al•low•a•ble (ə lou′ə bəl) *adj.* Capable of being allowed; permissible. **—al•low′a•bly** *adv.*

al•low•ance (ə lou′əns) *n.* **1.** The act of allowing. **2.** An amount, as of money or food, given at regular intervals or for a specific purpose: *a weekly allowance of five dollars; a travel allowance.* **3.** A price reduction given in exchange for used merchandise: *an allowance of $500 on one's old car.*

al•loy (ăl′oi′ *or* ə loi′) *n.* **1.** A metal made by mixing and fusing two or more metals, or a metal and a nonmetal, to obtain desirable qualities such as hardness, lightness, and strength: *Pewter is an alloy of copper, antimony, and lead.* **2.** An inferior metal mixed with a more valuable one: *This ring is not pure gold; there is some alloy in it.* **3.** Something added that lowers quality or value: *contentment without the alloy of regret.* *—tr.v.* (ə loi′ *or* ăl′oi′). **al•loyed, al•loy•ing, al•loys.** **1.** To combine (metals) to form an alloy. **2.** To lessen the quality or value of by adding something inferior: *My excitement was alloyed with doubts.* [First written down before 1325 in Middle English and spelled *alay*, from Latin *alligāre*, to bind together : *ad-*, to + *ligāre*, to bind.]

all-pur•pose (ôl′pûr′pəs) *adj.* Useful in many ways: *an all-purpose thread.*

all right *adj.* **1.** Satisfactory; in good condition: *The tires are old but all right.* **2.** Average; mediocre: *This work is all right, but it could be better.* **3.** Correct: *These figures are perfectly all right.* **4.** Not injured; safe: *Are you all right?* *—adv.* **1.** In a satisfactory way: *The motor was running all right.* **2.** Very well; yes: *All right, I'll go.* **3.** Without a doubt: *That's him, all right!*

all-round (ôl′round′) *adj.* Variant of **all-around.**

All Saints' Day (sānts) *n.* November 1, observed by Christians as a feast in honor of all the saints.

All Souls' Day (sōlz) *n.* November 2, observed by Roman Catholics as a day of prayer for the souls in purgatory.

all•spice (ôl′spīs′) *n.* **1.** The fragrant strong-flavored berries of a tropical American tree, dried and used as a spice. **2.** The tree that bears such berries.

all-star (ôl′stär′) *adj.* Made up entirely of star performers: *an all-star cast.* *—n.* A person chosen for an all-star team, cast, or other group.

all the same *adv.* Nevertheless; anyway: *It was hard, but I managed all the same.*

all-time (ôl′tīm′) *adj.* Unsurpassed until now; of all time: *set an all-time attendance record.*

al•lude (ə lo͞od′) *intr.v.* **al•lud•ed, al•lud•ing, al•ludes.** To refer to something indirectly; mention something casually or in passing: *It is considered impolite to allude to how much money a person has.* [First written down in 1533 in Modern English, from Latin *allūdere*, to play with : *ad-*, to + *lūdere*, to play (from *lūdus*, game).]

al•lure (ə lo͝or′) *tr.v.* **al•lured, al•lur•ing, al•lures.** To attract; entice; tempt: *I was allured to the movie by the ads.* *—n.* Strong attraction; fascination: *the allure of sailing.* **—al•lur′er**

al•lu•sion (ə lo͞o′zhən) *n.* **1.** The act of alluding; indirect reference. **2.** An instance of indirect reference: *allusions to Greek mythology in the poems.*

al•lu•sive (ə lo͞o′sĭv) *adj.* Containing or making allusions; suggestive. **—al•lu′sive•ly** *adv.* **—al•lu′sive•ness** *n.*

al•lu•vi•a (ə lo͞o′vē ə) *n.* A plural of **alluvium.**

al•lu•vi•al (ə lo͞o′vē əl) *adj.* Of, relating to, or found in alluvium: *rich alluvial deposits at the mouth of the river.* *—n.* Alluvial soil.

alluvial fan *n.* A fan-shaped mass of alluvium deposited by a river at a place where its flow becomes less swift.

al•lu•vi•um (ə lo͞o′vē əm) *n., pl.* **al•lu•vi•ums** or **al•lu•vi•a** (ə lo͞o′vē ə). Sand, silt, mud, or other matter deposited by flowing water, as in a riverbed, a river delta, or a flood plain.

al•ly (ə lī′ *or* ăl′ī) *tr.v.* **al•lied, al•ly•ing, al•lies.** To join or unite for a specific purpose: *The United States allied itself with the Soviet Union during World War II.* —*n., pl.* **al•lies. 1.** A person or country that is allied to another. **2. Allies. a.** The nations, including Russia, France, Great Britain, and the United States, that were allied against the Central Powers during World War I. **b.** The nations, including Great Britain, France, the Soviet Union, and the United States, that were allied against the Axis during World War II. [First written down about 1300 in Middle English and spelled *allien*, from Latin *alligāre* : *ad-*, to + *ligāre*, to bind.]

Al•ma-A•ta (ăl′mə ä′tə *or* əl mä′ə tä′). The capital of Kazakhstan, in the southeast part of the republic near the Chinese border. It was founded in the 1850's. Population, 1,068,000.

al•ma ma•ter or **Al•ma Ma•ter** (ăl′mə mä′tər *or* äl′mə mä′tər) *n.* **1.** The school, college, or university that a person has attended. **2.** The song or anthem of a school, college, or university. [First written down in 1710 in Modern English : Latin *alma*, nourishing + Latin *mater*, mother.]

al•ma•nac (ôl′mə năk′ *or* ăl′mə năk′) *n.* **1.** A book published once a year including calendars with weather forecasts, astronomical information, tide tables, and other related information. **2.** A book published once a year containing lists, charts, tables, and other information in many different fields. [First written down before 1388 in Middle English and spelled *almenak*, from Medieval Latin *almanach*.]

Al Ma•nam•ah (ăl′ mə năm′ə). Manama.

al•might•y (ôl mī′tē) *adj.* All-powerful; omnipotent: *almighty God.* —*n.* **Almighty.** God. —**al•might′i•ly** *adv.* —**al•might′i•ness** *n.*

al•mond (ä′mənd *or* ăm′ənd) *n.* **1.** An oval edible nut having a soft light-brown shell. **2.** The tree that bears such nuts.

al•mo•ner (ăl′mə nər *or* ä′mə nər) *n.* A person who gives out alms, as for a king or a monastery.

al•most (ôl′mōst′ *or* ôl mōst′) *adv.* Slightly short of; nearly: *almost done but not quite.*

alms (ämz) *pl.n.* Money or goods given to the poor as charity. [First written down before 810 in Old English and spelled *ælmesse*, from Greek *eleēmosunē*, from *eleēmōn*, pitiful, from *eleos*, pity.]

alms•house (ämz′hous′) *n.* A public home for the poor; a poorhouse.

al•ni•co (ăl′nĭ kō′) *n.* Any of several alloys of aluminum, cobalt, copper, iron, nickel, and often other metals, used in making strong permanent magnets.

al•oe (ăl′ō) *n.* **1.** Any of various tropical plants, chiefly of Africa, having thick spiny-toothed leaves and red or yellow flowers. **2. aloes.** *(used with a singular verb).* A bitter medicinal drug made from the dried juice of these plants, used as a laxative. **3.** Aloe vera. [First written down about 950 in Old English and spelled *aluwe*, from Greek *aloē*.]

aloe ver•a (vĕr′ə *or* vîr′ə) *n.* **1.** An aloe native to the Mediterranean region. **2.** The juice or gel obtained from the leaves of this plant, widely used in cosmetics and drugs for its soothing and healing properties.

a•loft (ə lôft′ *or* ə lŏft′) *adv.* **1.** In or into a high place; high or higher up: *Jet planes fly thousands of feet aloft.* **2.** In or toward a ship's upper rigging.

a•lo•ha (ə lō′ə *or* ə lō′hə) *interj.* An expression used as a greeting or farewell. It is the Hawaiian word for "love."

a•lone (ə lōn′) *adj.* **1.** Apart from the company of anyone else: *She returned to the room and found she was alone.* **2.** Being without anyone or anything else; only: *The teacher alone knows when the quiz will be given.* —*adv.* **1.** Without others: *She likes to travel alone.* **2.** Without aid or help: *I can lift the rock alone.* —***idiom.*** **leave well enough alone** or **let well enough alone.** To be satisfied with things as they are and not try to change them. —**a•lone′ness** *n.*

Synonyms: **alone, solitary, lonesome, lonely.** These adjectives describe being apart from others. **Alone** means lacking a companion but not necessarily feeling unhappy about it: *I walked alone on the beach while my brother went surfing.* **Solitary** often means being physically apart from others by choice: *She thoroughly enjoyed her solitary dinner.* **Lonesome** means wishing for a companion: *Tom thought the goldfish looked lonesome in its glass bowl.* **Lonely** often means sad at being by oneself: *Jill felt lonely while all her friends were away on vacation.*

a•long (ə lông′ *or* ə lŏng′) *prep.* **1.** Over the length of: *walked along the path.* **2.** On a line or course close to; beside: *trees growing along the river.* **3.** In accordance with: *Congress was split along party lines.* —*adv.* **1.** Forward; onward: *The train moved along, crossing the plains.* **2.** As a companion: *Bring your friend along.* **3.** As an associate piece; together: *packed her binoculars along with her hiking boots.* **4.** On one's person; in hand: *He took a camera along.* —SEE NOTE at **together.**

a•long•side (ə lông′sīd′ *or* ə lŏng′sīd′) *adv.* At or near the side; to the side; side by side: *The car drove alongside the fence.* —*prep.* By the side of; side by side with: *The boat pulled up alongside the dock.*

a•loof (ə lo͞of′) *adj.* Distant, reserved, or indifferent in manner: *an aloof manner.* —*adv.* At a distance but within view; apart; withdrawn: *The new student stood aloof from the others.* —**a•loof′ly** *adv.* —**a•loof′ness** *n.*

a•loud (ə loud′) *adv.* **1.** With the voice: *Read the story aloud.* **2.** In a loud tone; loudly: *If we speak aloud, it will awaken the baby.*

alp (ălp) *n.* A high mountain.

al•pac•a (ăl păk′ə) *n., pl.* **alpaca** or **al•pac•as. 1.** A South American mammal related to the llama, having long silky wool. **2.** Cloth made from the wool of this mammal. **3.** A stiff glossy fabric woven from this wool and other fibers. [First written down in 1792 in Modern English, from American Spanish, from Aymara *allpaca*.]

al•pen•horn (ăl′pən hôrn′) *n.* A curved wooden horn used by herders in the Alps to call cows to pasture.

al•pen•stock (ăl′pən stŏk′) *n.* A long staff with an iron point used by mountain climbers.

al•pha (ăl′fə) *n.* **1.** The first letter of the Greek alphabet, written Α, α. In English it is represented as *A, a.* **2.** The first one; the beginning.

alpha and omega *n.* **1.** The first and the last. **2.** The most important part of something.

al•pha•bet (ăl′fə bĕt′) *n.* **1.** The letters used to represent the different sounds of a language, arranged in a set order. **2.** A system of characters or symbols representing sounds or things.

al•pha•bet•i•cal (ăl′fə bĕt′ĭ kəl) also **al•pha•bet•ic** (ăl′fə bĕt′ĭk) *adj.* **1.** Arranged in the order of the alphabet: *In a dictionary the words are listed in alphabetical order.* **2.** Based on or using an alphabet: *an alphabetic system of writing.* —**al′pha•bet′i•cal•ly** *adv.*

al•pha•bet•ize (ăl′fə bĭ tīz′) *tr.v.* **al•pha•bet•ized, al•pha•bet•iz•ing, al•pha•bet•iz•es.** To arrange in alphabetical order. —**al′pha•bet′i•za′tion** (ăl′fə bĕt′ĭ zā′shən) *n.* —**al′pha•bet•iz′er** *n.*

aloe vera

alpaca

ă	pat	oi	boy
ā	pay	ou	out
âr	care	o͝o	took
ä	father	o͞o	boot
ĕ	pet	ŭ	cut
ē	be	ûr	urge
ĭ	pit	th	thin
ī	pie	*th*	this
îr	pier	hw	whoop
ŏ	pot	zh	vision
ō	toe	ə	about
ô	paw	N	*French* bon

altar

Usage: altogether

The word **altogether** and the phrase *all together* sound alike, but their meanings differ. **Altogether** means "completely": *I was altogether amazed by her actions. All together* means "with everybody or everything together or acting at the same time": *My friends and I went all together. All together* can be used only if you can rephrase the sentence and separate *all* and *together* by other words: *The books lay all together in a heap. All the books lay together in a heap.*

al•pha•nu•mer•ic (ăl′fə no͞o **mĕr′**ĭk *or* ăl′fə nyo͞o **mĕr′**ĭk) *adj.* Consisting of or using letters and numbers: *an alphanumeric computer code.*

alpha particle *n.* A positively charged particle that consists of two protons and two neutrons bound together. It is identical with the nucleus of a helium atom.

alpha ray *n.* A stream of alpha particles.

al•pine (**ăl′**pīn′) *adj.* **1.** Of, relating to, living on, or growing in high mountains: *Laurel is an alpine plant.* **2. Alpine.** Of or relating to the Alps.

Alps (ălps). A mountain system of south-central Europe, about 500 miles (805 kilometers) long and 100 miles (161 kilometers) wide, curving in an arc from the Mediterranean Sea through Italy, France, Switzerland, Germany, Austria, and along the Adriatic coast into Albania.

al•read•y (ôl **rĕd′**ē) *adv.* By this time: *They are late and should be here already.*

al•right (ôl **rīt′**) *adv. Non-Standard.* All right.

Al•sace (ăl **săs′**). A region and former province of eastern France west of the Rhine River.

Al•sace-Lor•raine (ăl′săs′lô **rān′**). A region of northern France that was annexed by Germany in 1871 and returned to France in 1919.

Al•sa•tian (ăl **sā′**shən) *adj.* Of or relating to Alsace or to its inhabitants or culture. —*n.* **1.** A native or inhabitant of Alsace. **2.** *Chiefly British.* A German shepherd.

al•so (**ôl′**sō) *adv.* **1.** In addition; besides: *The label lists the ingredients and also gives nutritional information.* See Synonyms at **besides. 2.** Likewise: *If you will stay, I will also.* —*conj.* And in addition: *Many students studied French and math, also music and drawing.* [First written down around 1000 in Old English and spelled *ealswā*, entirely so.] —SEE NOTE at **not.**

al•so-ran (**ôl′**sō răn′) *n.* **1.** A horse that does not come in first, second, or third in a race. **2.** A person or thing that is defeated in a race, election, or other competition; a loser.

alt. *abbr.* An abbreviation of: **1.** Alternate. **2.** Altitude.

Alta. *abbr.* An abbreviation of Alberta.

Al•tai Mountains or **Al•tay Mountains** (**ăl′**tī′). A mountain system of central Asia, mostly in eastern Kazakhstan and south-central Russia. It rises to 14,783 feet (4,508.8 meters).

al•tar (**ôl′**tər) *n.* **1.** A table or similar structure in a church or temple, used in religious ceremonies. **2.** A raised place, such as a block of stone or mound of earth, used to make sacrifices to a god. [First written down about 1000 in Old English, from Latin *altāre*.]

❑ *These sound alike:* **altar, alter** (change).

altar boy *n.* A boy or a man who helps a cleric in the performance of a religious service.

al•tar•piece (**ôl′**tər pēs′) *n.* A painting, carving, or similar work of art behind and above an altar in a church.

al•ter (**ôl′**tər) *v.* **al•tered, al•ter•ing, al•ters.** —*tr.* **1.** To change or make different: *We altered our plans for the weekend.* **2.** To adjust (a garment) for a better fit: *You will have to have this jacket altered.* **3.** To castrate or spay (a cat, dog, or other animal). —*intr.* To change or become different: *Since their trip abroad, their whole outlook has altered.* [First written down about 1385 in Middle English and spelled *alteren*, from Medieval Latin *alterāre*, from Latin *alter*, other.] **—al′ter•a•ble** *adj.* **—al′ter•a•bly** *adv.*

❑ *These sound alike:* **alter, altar** (table for worship).

al•ter•a•tion (ôl′tə **rā′**shən) *n.* **1.** The act or process of changing or altering: *Alteration of the school took several months.* **2.** A change: *many alterations to a suit.*

al•ter•ca•tion (ôl′tər **kā′**shən) *n.* A noisy angry quarrel.

alter ego *n.* **1.** An intimate friend or constant companion. **2.** Another side of oneself; a second personality.

al•ter•nate (**ôl′**tər nāt′) *v.* **al•ter•nat•ed, al•ter•nat•ing, al•ter•nates.** —*intr.* **1.** To occur in turns: *Showers alternated with sunshine.* **2.** To pass back and forth from one state, action, or place to another: *alternate between hope and despair.* —*tr.* To do, perform, or use in turns: *We alternated shoveling and raking the topsoil.* —*adj.* (**ôl′**tər nĭt). **1.** Occurring in turns; succeeding each other: *alternate periods of rain and drought.* **2.** Every other; every second: *She works on alternate days of the week.* **3.** In place of another: *an alternate route.* —*n.* (**ôl′**tər nĭt). A person acting in place of another. [First written down in 1599 in Modern English, from Latin *alternāre*, from *alternus*, by turns, from *alter*, other.]

al•ter•nate angle (**ôl′**tər nĭt) *n.* One of a pair of angles, both interior or both exterior but not adjacent, formed on opposite sides of a line that crosses two other lines. When the two lines are parallel, the alternate angles are equal.

al•ter•nate•ly (**ôl′**tər nĭt lē) *adv.* In alternate order; in turn: *The crowd alternately booed and cheered.*

al•ter•nat•ing current (**ôl′**tər nā′tĭng) *n.* An electric current that reverses its direction of flow at regular intervals.

al•ter•na•tion (ôl′tər **nā′**shən) *n.* Regular and repeated change between two or more things: *the alternation of the seasons.*

al•ter•na•tive (ôl **tûr′**nə tĭv) *n.* **1.** One of two or more possibilities from which to choose: *We had two alternatives: to continue driving or wait for the storm to pass.* **2.** A choice between two or more possibilities: *The alternative is between hard work or failure.* See Synonyms at **choice. 3.** A remaining choice: *You leave me no alternative but to go without you.* —*adj.* Allowing a choice between two or more possibilities: *I can suggest two alternative plans.* **—al•ter′na•tive•ly** *adv.*

al•ter•na•tor (**ôl′**tər nā′tər) *n.* An electric generator that makes alternating current.

al•though also **al•tho** (ôl ***th*ō′**) *conj.* Regardless of the fact that; even though.

al•tim•e•ter (ăl **tĭm′**ĭ tər) *n.* An instrument that measures and indicates the height at which an object, such as an aircraft, is located.

al•ti•tude (**ăl′**tĭ to͞od′ *or* **ăl′**tĭ tyo͞od′) *n.* **1.** The height of a thing above a reference level, usually above sea level or the earth's surface. **2.** In astronomy, the angle between a line aimed at the horizon and a line aimed at a celestial object: *a star at an altitude of 18°.* **3.** The perpendicular distance from the base of a geometric figure, such as a triangle, to the opposite vertex, side, or surface. [First written down about 1386 in Middle English, from Latin *altitūdō*, from *altus*, high.]

al•to (**ăl′**tō) *n., pl.* **al•tos. 1.** A low female singing voice; a contralto. **2.** A countertenor. **3.** The range between soprano and tenor. **4.** A singer whose voice lies within this range. **5.** A part written in this range. **6.** An instrument whose sound falls within this range.

al•to•cu•mu•lus (ăl′tō **kyo͞o′**myə ləs) *n.* A round, fleecy white or gray cloud formation.

al•to•geth•er (ôl′tə **gĕ*th*′**ər) *adv.* **1.** Completely: *Soon the noise faded away altogether.* **2.** With all included or counted: *Altogether there are 36 teachers in the school.* **3.** On the whole; with everything

considered: *Altogether it was a successful field trip.* —SEE NOTE.

al•to•stra•tus (ăl′tō strā′təs *or* ăl′tō străt′əs) *n.* A cloud formation that extends in bluish or gray sheets or layers.

al•tru•ism (ăl′troo ĭz′əm) *n.* Concern for the welfare of others. **—al′tru•ist** *n.*

al•tru•is•tic (ăl′troo ĭs′tĭk) *adj.* Showing concern for the welfare of others: *After the earthquake some altruistic doctors treated patients without charge.* **—al′tru•is′ti•cal•ly** *adv.*

al•um (ăl′əm) *n.* Any of various crystalline salts in which a metal such as aluminum or chronium is combined with another metal such as potassium or sodium, especially aluminum potassium sulfate, $AlK(SO_4)_2$, used in dyeing and sometimes in medicine to stop bleeding from a small cut.

a•lu•mi•na (ə lo͞o′mə nə) *n.* Any of several forms of aluminum oxide, Al_2O_3, such as bauxite or corundum, that occur naturally and are used in aluminum production and in ceramics and electrical insulation.

al•u•min•i•um (ăl′yə mĭn′ē əm) *n. Chiefly British.* Variant of **aluminum.**

a•lu•mi•num (ə lo͞o′mə nəm) *n. Symbol* **Al** A lightweight silvery-white metallic element that is easily shaped and conducts electricity well. Atomic number 13. See table at **element.** [First written down in 1812 in Modern English : *alumin(a)* + *-(i)um,* chemical element suffix.]

a•lum•na (ə lŭm′nə) *n., pl.* **a•lum•nae** (ə lŭm′nē′). A woman who has graduated from a certain school, college, or university.

a•lum•nus (ə lŭm′nəs) *n., pl.* **a•lum•ni** (ə lŭm′nī′). A man who has graduated from a certain school, college, or university. [First written down in 1645 in Modern English, from Latin, pupil, from *alere,* to nourish.]

al•ve•o•lus (ăl vē′ə ləs) *n., pl.* **al•ve•o•li** (ăl vē′ə-lī′). **1.** Any of the tiny air-filled sacs in the lungs from which oxygen passes into the blood and which, in turn, receive carbon dioxide; an air sac. **2.** A small bodily pit or cavity, such as a tooth socket in the jawbone. **—al•ve′o•lar** (ăl vē′ə lər) *adj.*

al•ways (ôl′wāz *or* ôl′wĭz) *adv.* **1.** On every occasion; without exception: *I always leave at six o'clock.* **2.** For all time; forever: *They will always be friends.* **3.** At any time; in any event: *If the bus is late we can always walk.* [First written down about 1350 in Middle English and spelled *alweis,* from Old English *ealne weg.*]

a•lys•sum (ə lĭs′əm) *n.* A garden plant related to the mustard plant having small yellow or white flowers.

Alz•heim•er's disease (älts′hī mərz *or* ălts′-hī mərz) *n.* A disease of the nervous system, marked by deterioration of memory and other mental activity. [First written down in 1912 in Modern English after Alois *Alzheimer* (1864–1915), German neurologist.]

am[1] (ăm) *v.* First person singular present tense of **be.**

am[2] or **AM** *abbr.* An abbreviation of amplitude modulation.

Am The symbol for the element **americium.**

Am. *abbr.* An abbreviation of: **1.** America. **2.** American.

a.m. *abbr.* An abbreviation of ante meridiem (before noon).

A.M. *abbr.* An abbreviation of: **1.** Ante meridiem (before noon). **2.** Artium magister (Master of Arts).

AMA *abbr.* An abbreviation of American Medical Association.

a•mal•gam (ə măl′gəm) *n.* **1.** An alloy of mercury with other metals. **2.** A combination or mixture.

a•mal•ga•mate (ə măl′gə māt′) *v.* **a•mal•ga•mat•ed, a•mal•ga•mat•ing, a•mal•ga•mates.** *—tr.* **1.** To unite to make a unified whole; merge: *The company amalgamated several of its shops under one manager.* **2.** To alloy (a metal) with mercury. *—intr.* **1.** To be combined; consolidate: *Many different peoples amalgamated to form the United States.* **2.** To blend with another metal. **—a•mal′ga•ma′tor** *n.*

a•mal•ga•ma•tion (ə măl′gə mā′shən) *n.* **1.** The process of amalgamating. **2.** A consolidation or merger, as of businesses.

am•a•ni•ta (ăm′ə nī′tə *or* ăm′ə nē′tə) *n.* Any of various related mushrooms, many of which are very poisonous.

a•man•u•en•sis (ə măn′yo͞o ĕn′sĭs) *n., pl.* **a•man•u•en•ses** (ə măn′yo͞o ĕn′sēz). A person who is employed to write down what another says or to copy manuscripts.

am•a•ranth (ăm′ə rănth′) *n.* Any of various plants having showy purple, greenish, or crimson flowers.

Am•a•ril•lo (ăm′ə rĭl′ō *or* ăm′ə rĭl′ə). A city of northern Texas east of Albuquerque, New Mexico. The city grew after the coming of the railroad in 1887. Population, 157,615.

am•a•ryl•lis (ăm′ə rĭl′ĭs) *n.* Any of several plants of tropical America having large, funnel-shaped, reddish or white flowers.

a•mass (ə măs′) *tr.v.* **a•massed, a•mass•ing, a•mass•es.** To gather; accumulate: *amass wealth; amass knowledge.* **—a•mass′a•ble** *adj.* **—a•mass′er** *n.*

am•a•teur (ăm′ə tûr′ *or* ăm′ə cho͝or′ *or* ăm′-ə tyo͝or′) *n.* **1.** A person who engages in art, science, or sport for enjoyment rather than as a profession or for money. **2.** A person who does something without professional skill: *The fact that the window was not level showed that it was the work of an amateur.* *—adj.* **1.** Of or relating to an amateur: *an amateur gymnast.* **2.** Made up of amateurs: *an amateur orchestra.* **3.** Not skillful; amateurish: *an amateur performance.* [First written down in 1784 in Modern English, from Latin *amātor,* one who loves.]

am•a•teur•ish (ăm′ə tûr′ĭsh *or* ăm′ə cho͝or′ĭsh) *adj.* Done or performed as one would expect of an amateur rather than a professional. **—am′a•teur′-ish•ly** *adv.* **—am′a•teur′ish•ness** *n.*

am•a•to•ry (ăm′ə tôr′ē) *adj.* Of, relating to, or expressive of love: *an amatory look.*

a•maze (ə māz′) *tr.v.* **a•mazed, a•maz•ing, a•maz•es.** To fill with surprise or wonder; astonish: *The size of the skyscrapers amazed the tourists.* See Synonyms at **surprise.** **—a•maz′ed•ly** (ə mā′zĭd lē) *adv.*

a•maze•ment (ə māz′mənt) *n.* Great surprise; astonishment.

Am•a•zon (ăm′ə zŏn′ *or* ăm′ə zən) *n.* **1.** In Greek mythology, a member of a race of women warriors. **2.** Often **amazon.** A tall, vigorous, and strong-willed woman.

Am•a•zo•ni•an (ăm′ə zō′nē ən) *adj.* **1.** Of or relating to the Amazon River or the region it drains. **2.a.** Of or relating to the Amazon warriors. **b.** Often **amazonian.** Resembling an Amazon; vigorous or aggressive.

Amazon River. The second-longest river in the world, flowing about 3,900 miles (6,275 kilometers) from northern Peru across northern Brazil to the Atlantic Ocean.

am•bas•sa•dor (ăm băs′ə dər *or* ăm băs′ə dôr′) *n.* **1.** A diplomatic official of the highest rank who represents a government in another country. **2.** A messenger or representative: *a goodwill ambassador.*

am•ber (ăm′bər) *n.* **1.** A hard, translucent, light or

amaranth

ă	pat	oi	boy
ā	pay	ou	out
âr	care	o͝o	took
ä	father	o͞o	boot
ĕ	pet	ŭ	cut
ē	be	ûr	urge
ĭ	pit	th	thin
ī	pie	*th*	this
îr	pier	hw	whoop
ŏ	pot	zh	vision
ō	toe	ə	about
ô	paw	N	*French* bon

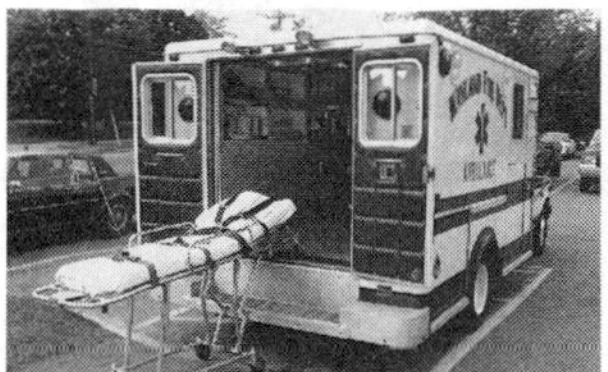

ambulance

brownish-yellow fossil resin used for making jewelry and ornaments. **2.** A brownish-yellow. *—adj.* **1.** Made of amber: *an amber necklace.* **2.** Brownish yellow: *amber light.* [First written down in 1365 in Middle English and spelled *ambre*, from Arabic *'anbar*, ambergris, amber.]

am•ber•gris (ăm′bər grĭs′ *or* **ăm′**bər grēs′) *n.* A grayish waxy material formed in the intestines of sperm whales, often found floating at sea or washed ashore. It is used in making perfumes.

am•bi•ance also **am•bi•ence** (ăm′bē əns *or* äN **byäNs′**) *n.* The atmosphere or mood surrounding a person, place, or thing: *the exotic ambiance of Paris streets.*

am•bi•dex•trous (ăm′bĭ **dĕk′**strəs) *adj.* Able to use both hands equally well. **—am′bi•dex′trous•ly** *adv.* **—am′bi•dex′trous•ness** *n.*

am•bi•gu•i•ty (ăm′bĭ **gyo͞o′**ĭ tē) *n., pl.* **am•bi•gu•i•ties. 1.** The condition of having two or more possible meanings. **2.** Something that is ambiguous: *There were several ambiguities in their conflicting statements.*

am•big•u•ous (ăm **bĭg′**yo͞o əs) *adj.* Having two or more possible meanings or interpretations; unclear; vague: *A number of ambiguous sentences made the report hard to understand.* See Synonyms at **vague.** **—am•big′u•ous•ly** *adv.* **—am•big′u•ous•ness** *n.*

am•bi•tion (ăm **bĭsh′**ən) *n.* **1.a.** A strong desire to achieve something: *The student's ambition was to become a great scientist.* **b.** The object or goal desired: *My ambition is to be the best dancer in the show.* **2.** Initiative; drive: *Champion athletes must be people of great energy and ambition.* [First written down in 1340 in Middle English and spelled *ambicioun*, from Latin *ambitiō*, from *ambīre*, to go around (for votes).]

am•bi•tious (ăm **bĭsh′**əs) *adj.* **1.** Full of ambition; eager to succeed: *The ambitious new worker learned very quickly.* **2.** Full of desire; eager: *The new doctor was ambitious for success.* **3.** Requiring great effort; challenging: *ambitious goals; an ambitious schedule.* **—am•bi′tious•ly** *adv.* **—am•bi′tious•ness** *n.*

am•biv•a•lence (ăm **bĭv′**ə ləns) *n.* The existence of two conflicting feelings at the same time: *His hesitation to join the band was evidence of his ambivalence.*

am•biv•a•lent (ăm **bĭv′**ə lənt) *adj.* Showing or feeling conflicting feelings about someone or something: *She was ambivalent about taking the job on the night shift.* **—am•biv′a•lent•ly** *adv.*

am•ble (**ăm′**bəl) *intr.v.* **am•bled, am•bling, am•bles.** To walk or move along at a slow leisurely pace: *We ambled aimlessly down the street.* *—n.* An ambling gait, as of a horse. **—am′bler** *n.*

am•bro•sia (ăm **brō′**zhə *or* ăm **brō′**zhē ə) *n.* **1.** In Greek mythology, the food of the gods, thought to give immortality. **2.** Something highly pleasing to one's taste or smell. [First written down in 1555 in Modern English, from Greek, from *ambrotos*, immortal.] **—am•bro′sial** *adj.* **—am•bro′sial•ly** *adv.*

am•bu•lance (**ăm′**byə ləns) *n.* A specially equipped vehicle used to transport sick and injured people.

am•bu•la•to•ry (**ăm′**byə lə tôr′ē) *adj.* Able to walk; not confined to one's bed: *an ambulatory patient.*

am•bus•cade (**ăm′**bə skād′ *or* ăm′bə **skād′**) *n.* An ambush. *—tr.v.* **am•bus•cad•ed, am•bus•cad•ing, am•bus•cades.** To ambush. **—am′bus•cad′er** *n.*

am•bush (**ăm′**bo͝osh) *n.* **1.** A surprise attack made from a concealed position: *The soldiers at the rear of the column fell victims of an ambush.* **2.** The concealment from which such an attack is made: *The tiger crouches in ambush.* *—tr.v.* **am•bushed, am•bush•ing, am•bush•es.** To attack from a concealed position: *The soldiers hid among the rocks to ambush the pursuing forces.* [First written down about 1300 in Middle English and spelled *embushen*, to ambush, from Old French *embuschier*.]

a•me•ba (ə **mē′**bə) *n.* Variant of **amoeba.**

a•me•bic dysentery or **a•moe•bic dysentery** (ə **mē′**bĭk) *n.* A disease caused by eating food or drinking water containing amoebas and characterized by diarrhea and nausea.

a•me•lio•rate (ə **mēl′**yə rāt′) *tr. & intr.v.* **a•me•lio•rat•ed, a•me•lio•rat•ing, a•me•lio•rates.** To make or become better; improve: *Lower taxes will ameliorate the conditions for hiring new workers.* **—a•me′lio•ra′tion** *n.* **—a•me′lio•ra′tor** *n.*

a•men (ā **mĕn′** *or* ä **mĕn′**) *interj.* An expression used at the end of a prayer or a statement to express approval. [First written down before 1000 in Old English, from Late Latin *āmēn*, from Hebrew *'āmēn*, verily.]

A•men also **A•mon** (**ä′**mən) *n.* In Egyptian mythology, the god of life and reproduction, represented as a man with the head of a ram.

a•me•na•ble (ə **mē′**nə bəl *or* ə **mĕn′**ə bəl) *adj.* **1.** Willing to yield or cooperate; agreeable: *I am amenable to your suggestion.* **2.** Responsible; answerable; accountable: *We are all amenable to the law.* **—a•me′na•bil′i•ty, a•me′na•ble•ness** *n.* **—a•me′na•bly** *adv.*

a•mend (ə **mĕnd′**) *tr.v.* **a•mend•ed, a•mend•ing, a•mends. 1.** To change for the better; improve: *I amended my earlier proposal to make it clearer.* **2.** To change or add to (a legislative motion, law, or constitution).

a•mend•ment (ə **mĕnd′**mənt) *n.* **1.** A legally adopted change or addition to a law or body of laws: *Giving voting rights to women was accomplished in an amendment to the Constitution.* **2.** The act of changing for the better; improvement: *Some treaties have provisions for amendment.*

a•mends (ə **mĕndz′**) *pl.n.* *(used with a singular or plural verb).* Something given or done to make up for an injury or insult: *By offering to pay for the repairs, they hoped to make amends for the damage.* [First written down before 1300 in Middle English and spelled *amendes*, from Old French, plural of *amende*, reparation.]

a•men•i•ty (ə **mĕn′**ĭ tē *or* ə **mē′**nĭ tē) *n., pl.* **a•men•i•ties. 1. amenities.** Polite social behavior; courtesies. **2.** Something that provides or increases physical comfort; a convenience: *an apartment with all the amenities of modern living.* **3.** The quality of being pleasant and agreeable: *the amenity of vacationing in the countryside.*

Amer. *abbr.* An abbreviation of:. **1.** America **2.** American.

Am•er•a•sian (ăm′ə **rā′**zhən *or* ăm′ə **rā′**shən) *n.* A person of American and Asian descent. **—Am′er•a′sian** *adj.*

A•mer•i•ca (ə **mĕr′**ĭ kə). **1.** The United States. **2.** The land areas and islands of North America, South America, Mexico, and Central America included in the Western Hemisphere.

A•mer•i•can (ə **mĕr′**ĭ kən) *adj.* **1.** Of or relating to the United States of America or its people, language, or culture: *American literature.* **2.** Of or relating to North or South America, the West Indies, or the Western Hemisphere: *American geology.* **3.** Of or relating to any of the Native American peoples: *American herbal medicine.* *—n.* A native or inhabitant of the United States or the Americas.

A•mer•i•ca•na (ə mĕr′ə **kä′**nə *or* ə mĕr′ə **kăn′**ə) *n.* A collection of things relating to American history, folklore, or geography.

American cheese *n.* A smooth mild white or yellow cheddar cheese.

American eagle *n.* The bald eagle.
American English *n.* English as used in the United States.
American Indian *n.* A Native American. —**A•mer′i•can-In′di•an** *adj.*
A•mer•i•can•ism (ə mĕr′ĭ kə nĭz′əm) *n.* **1.** A word or phrase originating in or peculiar to American English. **2.** A custom, trait, or tradition originating in the United States. **3.** Allegiance to the United States and its customs and institutions.
A•mer•i•can•ize (ə mĕr′ĭ kə nīz′) *tr.* & *intr.v.* **A•mer•i•can•ized, A•mer•i•can•iz•ing, A•mer•i•can•iz•es.** To make or become American in manner, customs, or speech. —**A•mer′i•can•i•za′tion** (ə mĕr′ĭ kə nĭ zā′shən) *n.*
American Revolution *n.* The war fought from 1775 to 1783 between Great Britain and the American colonies in which the colonies won independence.
American Sa•mo•a (sə mō′ə). A U.S. territory in the southern Pacific Ocean northeast of Fiji made up of the eastern Samoan islands. Pago Pago is the capital. Population, 32,279.
American Sign Language *n.* An American system of communication for the hearing-impaired that employs manual signs.
American Spanish *n.* The Spanish language as used in the Western Hemisphere.
am•er•i•ci•um (ăm′ə rĭsh′ē əm) *n.* *Symbol* **Am** A radioactive metallic element produced by bombarding plutonium with neutrons. It has isotopes with mass numbers ranging from 237 to 246 and half-lives ranging from 25 minutes to 7,950 years. Atomic number 95. See table at **element.**
Am•er•in•di•an (ăm′ə rĭn′dē ən) also **Am•er•ind** (ăm′ə rĭnd′) *n.* A Native American. —**Am′er•in′di•an** *adj.*
am•e•thyst (ăm′ə thĭst) *n.* **1.** A purple or violet form of transparent quartz used as a gemstone. **2.** A purple or violet color. [First written down before 1300 in Middle English and spelled *amatist*, from Greek *amethustos* : *a-*, not + *methuein*, to be drunk (from the belief that it was a remedy for drunkenness).]
a•mi•a•ble (ā′mē ə bəl) *adj.* Friendly; good-natured: *an amiable laugh.* —**a′mi•a•bil′i•ty, a′mi•a•ble•ness** *n.* —**a′mi•a•bly** *adv.*
am•i•ca•ble (ăm′ĭ kə bəl) *adj.* Characterized by friendliness and good will; friendly: *an amicable discussion.* —**am′i•ca•bil′i•ty, am′i•ca•ble•ness** *n.* —**am′i•ca•bly** *adv.*
a•mid (ə mĭd′) also **a•midst** (ə mĭdst′) *prep.* Surrounded by; in the middle of: *The swimmer's head appeared amid the waves.*
a•mid•ships (ə mĭd′shĭps′) also **a•mid•ship** (ə mĭd′shĭp′) *adv.* In or toward the middle part of a ship: *The cabin passengers lived amidships.* —*prep.* In the middle part of.
a•midst (ə mĭdst′) *prep.* Variant of **amid.**
a•mi•go (ə mē′gō) *n., pl.* **a•mi•gos.** A friend. [First written down in 1837 in Modern English, from Spanish, from Latin *amīcus*.]
a•mine (ə mēn′ *or* ăm′ēn) *n.* Any of a group of organic compounds formed from ammonia (NH_3) by substituting organic radicals for one or more of the ammonia's hydrogens.
a•mi•no acid (ə mē′nō *or* ăm′ə nō′) *n.* Any of a large number of organic compounds that contain carbon, oxygen, hydrogen, and nitrogen and that form proteins. Certain essential amino acids cannot be produced by the body and must be obtained from food.
a•mir (ə mîr′ *or* ā mîr′) *n.* Variant of **emir.**
A•mish (ä′mĭsh *or* ăm′ĭsh) *n.* **1.** An orthodox Anabaptist religion, most of whose followers live in southeast Pennsylvania. **2.** The followers of this religion considered as a group. —*adj.* Of or relating to this religion or its followers.
a•miss (ə mĭs′) *adv.* & *adj.* In an improper or defective way: *Your work is going amiss. Something is amiss when the train is this late.*
am•i•ty (ăm′ĭ tē) *n., pl.* **am•i•ties.** Peaceful relations, as between nations; friendship.
Am•man (ä män′ *or* ä′män). The capital and largest city of Jordan, in the north-central part of the country. The area has been inhabited since prehistoric times. Population, 777,500.
am•me•ter (ăm′mē′tər) *n.* An instrument that measures an electric current and indicates its strength in amperes.
am•mo•nia (ə mōn′yə) *n.* **1.** A colorless gas, with a strongly irritating odor, that is composed of nitrogen and hydrogen and has the formula NH_3. It is used to manufacture fertilizers, explosives, and plastics. **2.** A solution of ammonia in water; ammonium hydroxide.
ammonia water *n.* Ammonium hydroxide.
am•mo•ni•um (ə mō′nē əm) *n.* An ion, with the formula NH_4+, that consists of four hydrogen atoms bound to a single nitrogen atom and that has a single positive charge. Its compounds are similar to those of alkali metals.
ammonium chloride *n.* A white crystalline salt that consists of an ammonium ion and a chloride ion bound together. It is used in dry cells, as a soldering flux, and in metal finishing.
ammonium hydroxide *n.* A solution of ammonia in water. It is often used as a general cleanser; ammonia water.
ammonium nitrate *n.* A colorless crystalline salt composed of ammonium ions and nitrate ions bound together. It is chiefly used in fertilizers.
am•mu•ni•tion (ăm′yə nĭsh′ən) *n.* **1.** Projectiles such as bullets, shells, and shot, that can be fired from guns. **2.** Explosive objects, such as bombs or rockets, that are used as weapons. **3.** Something that is used to attack or defend an argument or point of view: *The Senator's improper conduct gave opponents ammunition during the election campaign.*
am•ne•sia (ăm nē′zhə) *n.* A partial or total loss of memory, especially when caused by shock, brain injury, or some form of mental or physical illness. [First written down in 1786 in Modern English, from Greek *amnēsia*, forgetfulness, probably from *amnēstia* : *a-*, not + *mimnēskein*, to remember.]
am•nes•ty (ăm′nĭ stē) *n., pl.* **am•nes•ties.** A pardon for past offenses. [First written down in 1605 in Modern English, from Latin *amnestia*, from Greek *amnēstos*, not remembered : *a-*, not + *mimnēskein*, to remember.]
am•ni•on (ăm′nē ən *or* ăm′nē ŏn′) *n., pl.* **am•ni•ons** or **am•ni•a** (ăm′nē ə). A sac of thin tough membrane containing a watery liquid in which the embryo of a reptile, bird, or mammal is suspended.
am•ni•ot•ic (ăm′nē ŏt′ĭk) *adj.* Of, relating to, or within the amnion: *A fetus develops in a sac of amniotic fluid.*
a•moe•ba also **a•me•ba** (ə mē′bə) *n., pl.* **a•moe•bas** or **a•moe•bae** (ə mē′bē) also **a•me•bas** or **a•me•bae** (ə mē′bē). A very small one-celled organism that has an indefinite changing shape. [First written down in 1855 in Modern English, from Greek *amoibē*, change.] —**a•moe′bic** (ə mē′bĭk) *adj.*
amoebic dysentery *n.* Variant of **amebic dysentery.**
a•mok (ə mŭk′ *or* ə mŏk′) *adv.* Variant of **amuck.**
A•mon (ä′mən) *n.* Variant of **Amen.**
a•mong (ə mŭng′) also **a•mongst** (ə mŭngst′) *prep.* **1.** In the midst of; surrounded by: *an oak among*

ă	pat	oi	boy
ā	pay	ou	out
âr	care	ŏŏ	took
ä	father	ōō	boot
ĕ	pet	ŭ	cut
ē	be	ûr	urge
ĭ	pit	th	thin
ī	pie	*th*	this
îr	pier	hw	whoop
ŏ	pot	zh	vision
ō	toe	ə	about
ô	paw	N	*French* bon

amphitheater
Théâtre Antique, Orange, France

amphora
c. 540 B.C.
Greek amphora by Exekias (fl. 550–525 B.C.)

the pines. **2.** In the company of: *among friends.* **3.** In the number or class of: *I count myself among the lucky ones.* **4.** By many or all of: *a custom popular among the Greeks.* **5.** With portions to each of: *The soda was shared among them.* **6.** Each with the other: *The dogs were fighting among themselves.* —SEE NOTE at **between.**

a•mor•al (ā môr′əl *or* ā mŏr′əl) *adj.* Not admitting of moral distinctions or judgments; neither moral nor immoral: *Nature is amoral.* **—a′mo•ral′i•ty** (ā′mô răl′ĭ tē) *n.* **—a•mor′al•ly** *adv.*

am•o•rous (ăm′ər əs) *adj.* **1.** Strongly attracted to love, especially sexual love: *an amorous young knight.* **2.** Feeling or expressing love: *an amorous look.* **3.** Of or associated with love: *an amorous poem.* [First written down about 1303 in Middle English, from Latin *amor,* love.] **—am′or•ous•ly** *adv.* **—am′or•ous•ness** *n.*

a•mor•phous (ə môr′fəs) *adj.* **1.** Lacking definite form or shape: *an amorphous mass of mud and rock.* **2.** Not made of crystals: *Glass is an amorphous substance.* **—a•mor′phous•ly** *adv.* **—a•mor′phous•ness** *n.*

am•or•tize (ăm′ər tīz′ *or* ə môr′tīz′) *tr.v.* **am•or•tized, am•or•tiz•ing, am•or•tiz•es.** To pay back (a debt) by setting money aside regularly in a fund that accumulates interest. **—am′or•ti•za′tion** (ăm′ər tĭ zā′shən) *n.*

A•mos (ā′məs) *n.* **1.** A Hebrew prophet of the eighth century B.C. **2.** A book of the Bible in which Amos denounces greed and social injustice.

a•mount (ə mount′) *n.* **1.** The total of two or more quantities: *The amount of your bill is $8.72.* **2.** A number; a sum. **3.** Quantity: *a meager amount of rainfall.* —*intr.v.* **a•mount•ed, a•mount•ing, a•mounts. 1.** To add up in number or quantity: *Total sales for the day amounted to $655.* **2.** To add up in significance or effect: *Our effort to convince them didn't amount to much.* **3.** To be equivalent: *In some cases, disobeying orders amounts to treason.* [First written down about 1275 in Middle English and spelled *amounten,* to ascend, from Old French *amonter,* from Latin *ad montem,* to the hill.]

a•mour (ə mo͝or′) *n.* A love affair, especially an illicit one.

amp (ămp) *n. Informal.* **1.** An ampere. **2.** An amplifier, especially one used to amplify music.

am•per•age (ăm′pər ĭj *or* ăm′pîr′ĭj) *n.* The strength of an electric current expressed in amperes.

am•pere (ăm′pîr′) *n.* A unit of electric current, equal to a flow of one coulomb per second. [First written down in 1881 in Modern English, after André Marie *Ampère* (1775–1836), French physicist.]

am•per•sand (ăm′pər sănd′) *n.* The character or sign (&) representing *and.*

am•phet•a•mine (ăm fĕt′ə mēn′ *or* ăm fĕt′ə mĭn) *n.* **1.** A colorless liquid composed of carbon, hydrogen, and nitrogen and having the formula $C_9H_{13}N$. From it are derived a number of drugs that act to stimulate the central nervous system. **2.** A drug derived from amphetamine.

am•phib•i•an (ăm fĭb′ē ən) *n.* **1.a.** A cold-blooded animal that has a backbone and moist skin without scales, such as a frog, toad, or salamander. Most amphibians lay eggs in water and their young breathe with gills in early life but develop lungs and breathe air as adults. **b.** An animal living both on land and in water, such as the crocodile or beaver. **2.** A vehicle that is capable of traveling both on land and in water. **3.** An aircraft that is capable of taking off from and landing on either land or water.

am•phib•i•ous (ăm fĭb′ē əs) *adj.* **1.** Able to live both on land and in water. **2.** Capable of traveling both on land and in water: *an amphibious vehicle.* **3.** Launched from the sea with navy, air, and land forces against an enemy on land: *an amphibious operation.* [First written down in 1643 in Modern English, from Greek *amphibios* : *amphi-,* both + *bios,* life.] **—am•phib′i•ous•ly** *adv.* **—am•phib′i•ous•ness** *n.*

am•phi•bole (ăm′fə bōl′) *n.* Any of a large group of minerals composed of a silicate joined to various metals, such as calcium, magnesium, iron, or sodium.

am•phi•the•a•ter (ăm′fə thē′ə tər) *n.* **1.** An oval or round structure having tiers of seats rising gradually outward from an open space, or arena, at the center. **2.** A level area surrounded by ground that slopes upward.

am•pho•ra (ăm′fər ə) *n., pl.* **am•pho•rae** (ăm′fə rē′) or **am•pho•ras.** A tall earthenware jar with two handles, used by the ancient Greeks and Romans to store wine or oil.

am•ple (ăm′pəl) *adj.* **am•pler, am•plest. 1.** Of large or great size, amount, extent, or capacity: *a rich nation with ample food for all.* **2.** Large in degree, kind, or quantity: *an enormous stadium with ample space for large crowds.* **3.** More than enough: *ample evidence to get a conviction.* **4.** Sufficient for a particular need: *ample provisions for a week of camping.* [First written down in 1437 in Middle English, from Latin *amplus.*] **—am′ple•ness** *n.*

am•pli•fi•ca•tion (ăm′plə fĭ kā′shən) *n.* **1.a.** The act or result of amplifying, enlarging, or extending. **b.** An increase in the magnitude or strength of an electric current, a force, or another physical quantity. **2.** An expansion of a statement or idea: *The report is an amplification of the committee's views.*

am•pli•fi•er (ăm′plə fī′ər) *n.* A device, especially an electronic device, that produces amplification of an electric signal.

am•pli•fy (ăm′plə fī′) *tr.v.* **am•pli•fied, am•pli•fy•ing, am•pli•fies. 1.** To produce amplification of: *A public-address system amplifies a speaker's voice.* **2.** To add to (something spoken or written); expand; make complete: *amplify earlier remarks.*

am•pli•tude (ăm′plĭ to͞od′ *or* ăm′plĭ tyo͞od′) *n.* **1.** Greatness of size; extent. **2.** Abundance; fullness. **3.** One half the full extent of a vibration, oscillation, or wave. For example, the distance between the position of rest and the highest swing of a pendulum is its amplitude; thus a pendulum swinging through an angle of 90 degrees has an amplitude of 45 degrees. **4.** The peak strength of an alternating electric current in a given cycle.

amplitude modulation *n.* A system of radio transmission in which the amplitude of the carrier wave is adjusted so that it is proportional to the sound or other information that is to be transmitted.

am•ply (ăm′plē) *adv.* More than sufficiently; generously, liberally: *Marie Curie's ambitions were amply satisfied.*

am•pu•tate (ăm′pyo͞o tāt′) *tr.v.* **am•pu•tat•ed, am•pu•tat•ing, am•pu•tates.** To cut off (a part of the body), especially by surgery. [First written down in 1638 in Modern English, from Latin *amputāre,* to cut around : *ambi-,* around + *putāre,* to cut.] **—am′pu•ta′tion** *n.* **—am′pu•ta′tor** *n.*

am•pu•tee (ăm′pyo͞o tē′) *n.* A person who has had a limb or limbs removed by amputation.

Am•ster•dam (ăm′stər dăm′). The constitutional capital and largest city of the Netherlands, in the western part of the country northeast of The Hague. It is linked to the North Sea by a ship canal. Population, 676,439.

amt. *abbr.* An abbreviation of amount.

a•muck (ə mŭk′) also **a•mok** (ə mŭk′ *or* ə mŏk′) *adv.* In a wild manner, with intent to do violence or kill: *The frightened bear ran amuck slashing at its* *captors.* [First written down in 1672 in Modern English, from Malay *amok.*]

am•u•let (ăm′yə lĭt) *n.* A charm worn to ward off evil or injury, especially one worn around the neck.

A•mund•sen (ä′mənd sən *or* ä′mo͝on sən), **Roald.** 1872–1928. Norwegian explorer who in 1911 became the first person to reach the South Pole.

A•mur River (ä mo͝or′) also **Hei•long Jiang** (hā′-lông′ jyäng′). A river of northeast Asia flowing about 1,800 miles (2,896 kilometers) mainly along the border between China and Russia.

a•muse (ə myo͞oz′) *tr.v.* **a•mused, a•mus•ing, a•mus•es. 1.** To entertain agreeably; divert: *The explorer amused us with adventure stories.* **2.** To cause to laugh or smile by giving pleasure: *The kitten's antics amused everyone.* **—a•mus′a•ble** *adj.* **—a•mus′er** *n.*

a•muse•ment (ə myo͞oz′mənt) *n.* **1.** The state of being pleasantly entertained: *They were too overcome with amusement to say a word.* **2.** Something that amuses or entertains: *The carnival provides amusement for everyone.*

amusement park *n.* A commercially operated park that offers rides, games, and other forms of entertainment.

a•mus•ing (ə myo͞o′zĭng) *adj.* Pleasantly entertaining or comical: *an amusing trick.* **—a•mus′ing•ly** *adv.*

am•y•lase (ăm′ə lās′ *or* ăm′ə lāz′) *n.* Any of various enzymes that are present in saliva, in pancreatic juice, or in parts of plants and convert starches to sugars, as in digestion.

an (ən; ăn *when stressed*) *indef. art.* The form of *a* used before words beginning with a vowel or with an unpronounced *h: an elephant; an hour.* —See Note at **article.**

–an *suff.* A suffix that means: **1.** Born in or being a citizen of: *American; Mexican.* **2.** Belonging to, associated with, or expert in: *Unitarian; librarian; electrician.* **3.** Of, relating to, or resembling: *Herculean; Shakespearean.*

An•a•bap•tist (ăn′ə băp′tĭst) *n.* A member of a Christian movement supporting baptism as a sign of faith, the Bible as the primary religious authority, and separation of church and state. **—An′a•bap′-tist** *adj.*

anabolic steroid *n.* Any of a group of synthetic hormones that promote the storage of protein and the growth of tissue, sometimes used by athletes to increase muscle size and strength.

a•nab•o•lism (ə năb′ə lĭz′əm) *n.* The phase of metabolism in which simple substances are combined to form the complex materials found in living tissue. **—an′a•bol′ic** (ăn′ə bŏl′ĭk) *adj.*

a•nach•ro•nism (ə năk′rə nĭz′əm) *n.* **1.** The placing of something in a time other than its proper or historical time. **2.** Something that is out of its proper time: *Cavalry is an anachronism in modern warfare.* [First written down before 1646 in Modern English, from Late Greek *anakhronismos* : Greek *ana-*, back + Greek *khronos*, time.]

a•nach•ro•nis•tic (ə năk′rə nĭs′tĭk) *adj.* Out of proper time; misplaced chronologically: *One anachronistic detail in the play is having General Washington get a message by telegraph.* **—a•nach′-ro•nis′ti•cal•ly** *adv.*

an•a•con•da (ăn′ə kŏn′də) *n.* A large nonpoisonous tropical American snake that coils around and crushes its prey. [First written down in 1768 in Modern English, perhaps from Singhalese *henakandayā*, a kind of snake.]

a•nae•mi•a (ə nē′mē ə) *n.* Variant of **anemia.**

a•nae•mic (ə nē′mĭk) *adj.* Variant of **anemic.**

an•aer•obe (ăn′ə rōb′ *or* ăn âr′ōb′) *n.* An anaerobic bacterium or other microorganism that can live where there is no atmospheric oxygen.

an•aer•o•bic (ăn′ə rō′bĭk *or* ăn′âr ō′bĭk) *adj.* Living or growing where there is no atmospheric oxygen: *anaerobic bacteria.* **—an′aer•o′bi•cal•ly** *adv.*

an•aes•the•sia (ăn′ĭs thē′zhə) *n.* Variant of **anesthesia.**

an•aes•the•si•ol•o•gist (ăn′ĭs thē′zē ŏl′ə jĭst) *n.* Variant of **anesthesiologist.**

an•aes•the•si•ol•o•gy (ăn′ĭs thē′zē ŏl′ə jē) *n.* Variant of **anesthesiology.**

an•aes•thet•ic (ăn′ĭs thĕt′ĭk) *adj. & n.* Variant of **anesthetic.**

a•naes•the•tist (ə nĕs′thĭ tĭst) *n.* Variant of **anesthetist.**

a•naes•the•tize (ə nĕs′thĭ tīz′) *v.* Variant of **anesthetize.**

an•a•gram (ăn′ə grăm′) *n.* **1.** A word or phrase formed by changing the order of the letters of another word or phrase. **2. anagrams.** A game in which players form words by changing the order of a group of letters or by adding to them.

a•nal (ā′nəl) *adj.* Of, relating to, or near the anus. **—a′nal•ly** *adv.*

anal. *abbr.* An abbreviation of: **1.** Analogous. **2.** Analogy. **3.** Analysis.

an•al•ge•si•a (ăn′əl jē′zē ə *or* ăn′əl jē′zhə) *n.* A condition, most often produced by a drug, in which a person remains conscious but has reduced sensitivity to pain.

an•al•ge•sic (ăn′əl jē′zĭk *or* ăn′əl jē′sĭk) *n.* A drug that produces analgesia; a painkiller: *Aspirin is a common analgesic.* —*adj.* Of or causing analgesia.

an•a•log (ăn′ə lôg′ *or* ăn′ə lŏg′) *n. & adj.* Variant of **analogue.**

analog computer also **analogue computer** *n.* A computer in which numbers are represented by continuously varying physical quantities such as wavelengths, electric currents, or voltages. Analog computers have been largely replaced by digital computers.

a•nal•o•gous (ə năl′ə gəs) *adj.* Similar or parallel in certain ways: *The relation between addition and subtraction is analogous to that between multiplication and division.* **—a•nal′o•gous•ly** *adv.* **—a•nal′o•gous•ness** *n.*

an•a•logue also **an•a•log** (ăn′ə lôg′ *or* ăn′ə lŏg′) *n.* **1.** Something that bears an analogy to something else. **2.** An organ in a plant or an animal that is similar in function to one in another kind of plant or animal. —*adj.* **1.** Often **analog.** Of or relating to analog computers. **2.** Often **analog.** Of or relating to a device that uses continuously varying physical quantities to represent data. For example, the position of the hands of a clock is an analog representation of time or the level of a mercury thermometer is an analog representation of temperature.

analogue computer *n.* Variant of **analog computer.**

a•nal•o•gy (ə năl′ə jē) *n., pl.* **a•nal•o•gies. 1.** Similarity in some respects between things that are otherwise unlike. **2.** An explanation of something by comparing it with something similar: *The author uses the analogy of a beehive when describing the city.* [First written down before 1425 in Middle English and spelled *analogie*, from Greek *analogos*, proportionate.]

a•nal•y•sis (ə năl′ĭ sĭs) *n., pl.* **a•nal•y•ses** (ə năl′ĭ sēz′). **1.** The separation of something into its parts in order to determine its nature: *An analysis of the theory shows it is based on faulty evidence.* **2.a.** The separation of a substance into its parts, usually by chemical means, for the study and identification of each component. **b.** A written report of the infor-

Roald Amundsen

anaconda
South American giant anaconda

ă	**pat**	oi	**boy**
ā	**pay**	ou	**out**
âr	**care**	o͝o	**took**
ä	**father**	o͞o	**boot**
ĕ	**pet**	ŭ	**cut**
ē	**be**	ûr	**urge**
ĭ	**pit**	th	**thin**
ī	**pie**	*th*	**this**
îr	**pier**	hw	**whoop**
ŏ	**pot**	zh	**vision**
ō	**toe**	ə	**about**
ô	**paw**	N	*French* bon

mation obtained in this way. **3.** Psychoanalysis. [First written down in 1581 in Modern English, from Greek *analusis*, a dissolving : *ana-*, throughout + *luein*, to loosen.]

an•a•lyst (ăn′ə lĭst) *n.* **1.** A person who performs an analysis. **2.** A psychoanalyst.

an•a•lyt•ic (ăn′ə lĭt′ĭk) or **an•a•lyt•i•cal** (ăn′ə lĭt′ĭ kəl) *adj.* Of or relating to analysis: *analytical chemistry.* **—an′a•lyt′i•cal•ly** *adv.*

analytical balance *n.* A precision balance, used in chemistry for weighing quantities as small as 1/10,000 of a gram.

analytic geometry *n.* The use of algebra to solve problems in geometry. In analytic geometry, geometric figures are represented by algebraic equations and plotted using coordinates.

an•a•lyze (ăn′ə līz′) *tr.v.* **an•a•lyzed, an•a•lyz•ing, an•a•lyz•es. 1.** To separate into parts in order to determine what something is or how it works: *They analyzed the ore and found gold in it.* **2.** To examine in detail: *analyze past expenses to make a budget for next year.* **3.** To psychoanalyze. **—an′a•lyz′a•ble** *adj.* **—an′a•ly•za′tion** (ăn′ə lĭ zā′shən) *n.* **—an′a•lyz′er** *n.*

an•a•pest (ăn′ə pĕst′) *n.* **1.** In poetry, a metrical foot consisting of two short syllables followed by one long syllable, as in *seventeen.* **2.** A line of poetry using this meter.

an•a•phase (ăn′ə fāz′) *n.* The stage of mitosis and meiosis in which the doubled set of chromosomes separates into two identical groups that move to opposite sides of the cell.

an•ar•chic (ăn är′kĭk) or **an•ar•chi•cal** (ăn är′kĭ kəl) *adj.* **1.** Of, relating to, or promoting anarchy. **2.** Lacking order or control; lawless: *the anarchic society of America's wild frontier.* **—an•ar′chi•cal•ly** *adv.*

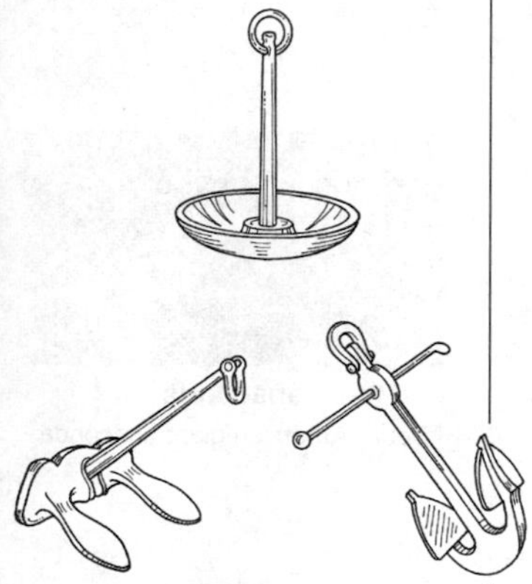

anchor
Top: Mushroom
Bottom: Stockless (*left*) and admiralty (*right*)

an•ar•chism (ăn′ər kĭz′əm) *n.* **1.** The theory that all forms of government lessen individual freedom and should be replaced by small cooperative groups of people. **2.** Rejection of all forms of coercive organization or authority.

an•ar•chist (ăn′ər kĭst) *n.* A person who advocates or supports anarchism. **—an′ar•chis′tic** *adj.*

an•ar•chy (ăn′ər kē) *n., pl.* **an•ar•chies. 1.** Absence of any governmental authority. **2.** Disorder and confusion resulting from lack of authority: *For several days after the hurricane the region was in a state of anarchy.* [First written down in 1539 in Modern English, from Greek *anarkhos*, without a ruler : *an-*, without + *arkhos*, ruler.]

A•na•sa•zi (ä′nə sä′zē) *n., pl.* **Anasazi.** A member of a Native American people living in the southwest United States from about A.D. 100. The Pueblo peoples are descendants of the Anasazi.

a•nath•e•ma (ə năth′ə mə) *n., pl.* **a•nath•e•mas. 1.** A formal ban, curse, or excommunication imposed by a church. **2.** A strong denunciation or condemnation. **3.** A person or thing that is intensely disliked: *The idea of working sloppily on an experiment was anathema to her.*

a•nath•e•ma•tize (ə năth′ə mə tīz′) *tr.v.* **a•nath•e•ma•tized, a•nath•e•ma•tiz•ing, a•nath•e•ma•tiz•es.** To proclaim an anathema on; denounce; curse. **—a•nath′e•ma•ti•za′tion** (ə năth′ə mə tĭ zā′shən) *n.*

An•a•to•li•a (ăn′ə tō′lē ə *or* ăn′ə tōl′yə). The Asian part of Turkey, between the Mediterranean Sea and the Black Sea.

an•a•tom•i•cal (ăn′ə tŏm′ĭ kəl) also **an•a•tom•ic** (ăn′ə tŏm′ĭk) *adj.* **1.** Of or relating to anatomy or dissection: *anatomical comparison of similar fish.* **2.** Relating to the structure of an organism as opposed to its functioning: *an anatomical abnormality.* **—an′a•tom′i•cal•ly** *adv.*

a•nat•o•mist (ə năt′ə mĭst) *n.* A person who specializes in anatomy.

a•nat•o•mize (ə năt′ə mīz′) *tr.v.* **a•nat•o•mized, a•nat•o•miz•ing, a•nat•o•miz•es. 1.** To cut apart or dissect (an organism) in order to study its structure parts. **2.** To perform a detailed analysis of: *The students anatomized the novel.* **—a•nat′o•mi•za′tion** (ə năt′ə mĭ zā′shən) *n.*

a•nat•o•my (ə năt′ə mē) *n., pl.* **a•nat•o•mies. 1.** The structure of an animal or a plant or any of its parts: *Bones and muscles are part of the human anatomy.* **2.** The scientific study of the shape and structure of living things: *Anatomy has revealed many of the body's secrets to modern medicine.* **3.** The dissection of a plant or an animal in order to study its structure. **4.** The human body: *the rugged anatomy of an athlete.* [First written down before 1398 in Middle English and spelled *anatomie*, from Greek *anatomē*, dissection : *ana-*, up, apart + *tomē*, a cutting.]

–ance *suff.* A suffix that means: **1.** State or condition: *resemblance.* **2.** Action: *compliance.*

an•ces•tor (ăn′sĕs′tər) *n.* **1.** A person from whom one is descended, especially if of a generation earlier than a grandparent: *His ancestors came to America from China.* **2.** An organism or a type of organism, either known or supposed to exist, from which later organisms evolved: *The mammoth is an ancestor of the modern elephant.* **3.** A forerunner; a predecessor: *The harpsichord is an ancestor of the piano.* [First written down about 1300 in Middle English and spelled *auncestre*, from Latin *antecessor*, predecessor : *ante-*, before + *cēdere*, to go.]

an•ces•tral (ăn sĕs′trəl) *adj.* Of, relating to, or evolved from an ancestor or ancestors: *an ancestral trait.* **—an•ces′tral•ly** *adv.*

an•ces•try (ăn′sĕs′trē) *n., pl.* **an•ces•tries. 1.** A line of descent; lineage. **2.** Ancestors considered as a group: *My ancestry lived in Russia.*

an•chor (ăng′kər) *n.* **1.** A heavy object attached to a boat or ship by a cable and dropped overboard to keep the vessel in place, either by its weight or by catching on the bottom. **2.** A rigid point of support, as for securing a rope or cable. **3.** Something that helps one feel secure: *Listening to music has been my anchor in tough times.* **4.** An anchorman or anchorwoman. *—v.* **an•chored, an•chor•ing, an•chors.** *—tr.* **1.** To hold fast or secure by or as if by an anchor. **2.** To act as an anchorman or anchorwoman on (a news broadcast) or in (a relay race). *—intr.* To drop anchor or be held by an anchor. [First written down before 899 in Old English and spelled *ancor*, from Latin *ancora*, from Greek *ankura*.]

an•chor•age (ăng′kər ĭj) *n.* **1.** A place where ships can anchor: *a safe anchorage in the harbor.* **2.** The action of anchoring or the condition of being held by an anchor.

An•chor•age (ăng′kər ĭj). A city of southern Alaska south-southwest of Fairbanks. The largest city in the state, it was founded in 1915. Population, 226,338.

an•cho•rite (ăng′kə rīt′) *n.* A person who for religious reasons has withdrawn from society to live alone; a hermit.

an•chor•man (ăng′kər măn′) *n.* **1.** In radio and television, a man who narrates or coordinates a news broadcast in which several correspondents give reports. **2.** A man who is the last member of a relay team in a race.

an•chor•per•son (ăng′kər pûr′sən) *n.* An anchorman or an anchorwoman.

an•chor•wom•an (ăng′kər wo͝om′ən) *n.* **1.** In radio and television, a woman who narrates or coordinates a news broadcast in which several correspon-

dents give reports. **2.** A woman who is the last member of a relay team in a race.

an•cho•vy (ăn′chō′vē *or* ăn **chō′**vē) *n., pl.* **anchovy** or **an•cho•vies.** A small sea fish related to the herring, often salted and canned. [First written down in 1596 in Modern English, from Spanish *anchova*, probably from Greek *aphuē*.]

an•cient (**ān′**shənt) *adj.* **1.** Very old; aged: *the ancient giant sequoias of the California forests.* **2.** Of or relating to times long past, especially the historical period before the fall of Rome in A.D. 476. —*n.* **1.** A very old person. **2. Ancients.** The Greeks or Romans of ancient times. [First written down about 1390 in Middle English and spelled *auncien*, from Old French : Latin *ante*, before + *-ānus*, adjective and noun suffix] **—an′cient•ly** *adv.* **—an′cient•ness** *n.*

ancient history *n.* **1.** History from earliest times to the fall of Rome in A.D. 476. **2.** *Informal.* Common knowledge, especially of a recent event that has lost its original importance.

an•cil•lar•y (**ăn′**sə lĕr′ē) *adj.* Serving as help or support but not of first importance: *an ancillary pump.*

-ancy *suff.* Condition or quality: *buoyancy.*

and (ənd *or* ən; ănd *when stressed*) *conj.* **1.** Together with or along with; as well as: *The weather is clear and crisp.* **2.** Added to; plus: *Two and two makes four.* **3.** As a result: *Go, and you will enjoy yourself.* **4.** To: *Try and find it.* —SEE NOTE at **both.**

An•da•lu•sia (ăn′də **lōō′**zhə *or* ăn′də **lōō′**zhē ə). A region of southern Spain on the Mediterranean Sea, the Strait of Gibraltar, and the Atlantic Ocean.

an•dan•te (än **dän′**tā) *adv. & adj.* In music, moderately slow.

An•der•sen (**ăn′**dər sən), **Hans Christian.** 1805–1875. Danish writer of fairy tales, including "The Princess and the Pea" and "The Ugly Duckling."

An•der•son (**ăn′** dər sən), **Marian.** 1897–1993. American contralto who was the first Black singer to perform at New York City's Metropolitan Opera (1955).

An•des (**ăn′**dēz). A mountain system of western South America extending more than 5,000 miles (8,045 kilometers) along the Pacific coast from Venezuela to Tierra del Fuego. The Andes rise at many points to more than 22,000 feet (6,710 meters).

and•i•ron (**ănd′**ī′ərn) *n.* One of a pair of metal supports for holding up logs in a fireplace.

and/or (**ăn′dôr′**) *conj.* Used to indicate that either *and* or *or* may be used to connect words, phrases, or clauses depending upon what meaning is intended, as in the sentence *Thin the paint with turpentine and/or linseed oil.*

An•dor•ra (ăn **dôr′**ə *or* ăn dŏr ə). A tiny independent country of southwest Europe between France and Spain in the eastern Pyrenees. Andorra la Vella is the capital. Population, 38,051.

An•drew (**ăn′**drōō), Saint. Died about A.D. 60. One of the 12 Apostles.

An•dro•cles (**ăn′**drə klēz′) *n.* In Roman legend, a slave spared in the arena by a lion that remembered him as the man who had once pulled a thorn from its paw.

an•dro•gen (**ăn′**drə jən) *n.* A hormone, such as testosterone, that acts in the development and maintenance of masculine physical characteristics. **—an′dro•gen′ic** (ăn′drə **jĕn′**ĭk) *adj.*

an•droid (**ăn′**droid′) *n.* A robot that is created from biological materials and resembles a human being. [First written down about 1727 in Modern English : Greek *anēr*, man + English *-oid*, -like.]

An•drom•a•che (ăn **drŏm′**ə kē) *n.* In Greek mythology, the brave and faithful wife of Hector, captured by the Greeks at the fall of Troy.

An•drom•e•da (ăn **drŏm′**ĭ də) *n.* **1.** In Greek mythology, a princess who is offered as a sacrifice to a sea monster and marries Perseus after he kills the monster. **2.** A constellation in the Northern Hemisphere.

an•ec•dote (**ăn′**ĭk dōt′) *n.* A short account of an interesting or humorous event. [First written down in 1686 in Modern English, from Greek *anekdotos*, unpublished : *an-*, not + *ek-*, out + *dotos*, given.] **—an′ec•dot′al** *adj.* **—an′ec•dot′al•ly** *adv.*

a•ne•mi•a also **a•nae•mi•a** (ə **nē′**mē ə) *n.* A diseased condition in which the blood cannot carry enough oxygen to the body tissues. It can be caused by lack of hemoglobin, too few red blood cells, or poorly formed red blood cells. [First written down before 1824 in Modern English and spelled *anaemia*, from Greek *anaimia* : *an-*, without + *haima*, blood.]

a•ne•mic also **a•nae•mic** (ə **nē′**mĭk) *adj.* **1.** Of, relating to, or suffering from anemia. **2.** Lacking vitality; weak: *an anemic economic recovery.*

an•e•mom•e•ter (ăn′ə **mŏm′**ĭ tər) *n.* An instrument that measures the speed of the wind.

a•nem•o•ne (ə **nĕm′**ə nē) *n.* **1.** Any of various plants having lobed leaves and cup-shaped white, purple, or red flowers. **2.** A sea anemone.

a•nent (ə **nĕnt′**) *prep.* Regarding; concerning; about.

an•er•oid barometer (**ăn′**ə roid′) *n.* A barometer that measures changes in atmospheric pressure by means of the expansion and contraction of an elastic disk that covers a chamber in which there is a partial vacuum.

an•es•the•sia also **an•aes•the•sia** (ăn′ĭs **thē′**zhə) *n.* A condition in which some or all of the senses, especially the sense of touch, stop functioning or are greatly diminished. This condition can be produced by disease or intentionally by the administration of drugs or acupuncture.

an•es•the•si•ol•o•gist also **an•aes•the•si•ol•o•gist** (ăn′ĭs thē′zē **ŏl′**ə jĭst) *n.* A physician whose specialty is anesthesiology.

an•es•the•si•ol•o•gy also **an•aes•the•si•ol•o•gy** (ăn′ĭs thē′zē **ŏl′**ə jē) *n.* The medical study of anesthetics, their effects, and their use.

an•es•thet•ic also **an•aes•thet•ic** (ăn′ĭs **thĕt′**ĭk) *adj.* **1.** Relating to, resembling, or causing anesthesia. **2.** Lacking sensation or feeling; insensitive. —*n.* A drug that causes anesthesia. **—an′es•thet′i•cal•ly** *adv.*

a•nes•the•tist also **a•naes•the•tist** (ə **nĕs′**thĭ tĭst) *n.* A person specially trained to administer anesthetics.

a•nes•the•tize also **a•naes•the•tize** (ə **nĕs′**thĭ tīz′) *tr.v.* **a•nes•the•tized, a•nes•the•tiz•ing, a•nes•the•tiz•es** also **a•naes•the•tized, a•naes•the•tiz•ing, a•naes•the•tiz•es.** To put into a condition of anesthesia, especially by means of a drug: *They anesthetized the injured dog in preparation for surgery.* **—an•es′the•ti•za′tion** (ə nĕs′thĭ tĭ **zā′**shən) *n.*

an•eu•rysm also **an•eu•rism** (**ăn′**yə rĭz′əm) *n.* A swelling in a weakened part of an artery or vein, caused by disease or injury.

a•new (ə **nōō′** *or* ə **nyōō′**) *adv.* Over again: *ready to start anew.*

an•gel (**ān′**jəl) *n.* **1.** One of the immortal beings serving as attendants or messengers of God. **2.** A guardian spirit. **3.** A kind and lovable person. **4.** *Informal.* A person who provides financial support for something, especially a stage play. [First written down before 1300 in Middle English, from Greek *angelos*, messenger.]

An•gel•a Me•ri•ci (ăn′jə lə mə **rē′**chē), Saint. 1474–1540. Italian Roman Catholic nun who founded the Ursuline order (1535).

Marian Anderson
Photographed in 1943

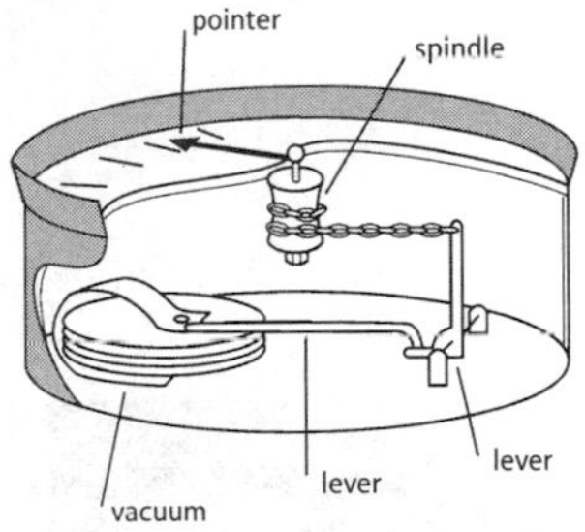

aneroid barometer

ă	pat	oi	boy
ā	pay	ou	out
âr	care	ŏŏ	took
ä	father	ōō	boot
ŏ	pot	ŭ	cut
ē	be	ûr	urge
ĭ	pit	th	thin
ī	pie	*th*	this
îr	pier	hw	whoop
ŏ	pot	zh	vision
ō	toe	ə	about
ô	paw	N	*French* bon

angelfish

Angora goat

An•ge•le•no (ăn′jə **lē′**nō) *n., pl.* **An•ge•le•nos.** A native or inhabitant of Los Angeles, California.

an•gel•fish (**ān′**jəl fĭsh′) *n.* Any of several tropical fishes having a flattened body and bright coloring or showy markings.

angel food cake *n.* A light, white, spongy cake made with stiffly beaten egg whites, sugar, and flour.

an•gel•ic (ăn **jĕl′**ĭk) also **angelical** (ăn **jĕl′**ĭ kəl) *adj.* **1.** Of or relating to angels. **2.** Resembling an angel, as in goodness, kindness, or purity.

An•ge•lus also **an•ge•lus** (**ăn′**jə ləs) *n.* **1.** In the Roman Catholic Church, a devotional prayer at morning, noon, and sunset in celebration of the Annunciation. **2.** A bell rung as a call to recite this prayer.

an•ger (**ăng′**gər) *n.* A feeling of great displeasure or hostility toward someone or something; rage; wrath: *surprise and then anger at being cheated.* —*tr. & intr.v.* **an•gered, an•ger•ing, an•gers.** To make or become angry: *I was angered by his rudeness. She angers slowly.* [First written down about 1250 in Middle English, from Old Norse *angr*, sorrow.]

Synonyms: **anger, rage, fury, indignation.** These nouns refer to different degrees of strong displeasure. **Anger** is the most general: *He wasn't shouting but we could sense his anger at the mix-up.* **Rage** and **fury** mean strong and often destructive anger: *They'll go into a rage when they find out who wrecked their car. In her fury at being teased, Amy threw Jo's books down the stairs.* **Indignation** is anger at something wrongful, unjust, or evil: *The ugly incident aroused the whole town's indignation.*

an•gi•na (ăn **jī′**nə *or* **ăn′**jə nə) *n.* **1.** A condition, such as a severe sore throat, marked by painful spasms. **2.** Angina pectoris.

angina pec•to•ris (**pĕk′**tər ĭs) *n.* A severe tightening and pain in the chest, often extending into the left shoulder and arm. It generally results from an insufficient supply of blood to the heart muscle, usually because of coronary disease.

an•gi•o•sperm (**ăn′**jē ə spûrm′) *n.* Any of a large group of plants that have flowers and produce seeds enclosed in an ovary or a fruit; a flowering plant.

an•gle[1] (**ăng′**gəl) *intr.v.* **an•gled, an•gling, an•gles. 1.** To fish with a hook and line. **2.** To try to get something by using schemes or tricks: *By posing as a reporter, the tourist angled for a chance to meet the President.* [First written down about 1380 in Middle English and spelled *anglen*, from Old English *angel*, fishhook.]

an•gle[2] (**ăng′**gəl) *n.* **1.** A geometric figure formed by two lines that begin at a common point or by two planes that begin at a common line. **2.** The space between such lines or planes, measured in degrees. **3.** The difference in direction between two such lines or planes, measured especially in degrees. **4.** A projecting corner, as of a building: *The angle of the building blocked our view.* **5.** The place, position, or direction from which an object is presented to view; point of view: *a funny-looking hat from any angle.* **6.** A particular part or phase, as of a problem; an aspect: *studying every angle of the question.* —*v.* **an•gled, an•gling, an•gles.** —*tr.* To move or hit at an angle: *angling the camera for a clearer view.* —*intr.* To turn or proceed at an angle: *The road angles sharply at the river.* [First written down about 1450 in Middle English, from Latin *angulus*.]

An•gle (**ăng′**gəl) *n.* A member of a Germanic people who settled in England in the fifth and sixth centuries A.D. and together with the Jutes and Saxons formed the Anglo-Saxon peoples.

angle iron *n.* A length or iron or steel bent into a right angle to be used as a support.

angle of incidence *n.* The angle formed by a ray or wave, as of light or sound, striking a surface and a line perpendicular to the surface at the point of impact.

angle of reflection *n.* The angle formed by a ray or wave, as of light or sound, reflected from a surface and a line perpendicular to the surface at the point of reflection.

angle of refraction *n.* The angle formed by the path of refracted light or other radiation and a line drawn perpendicular to the refracting surface at the point where the refraction occurred.

an•gler (**ăng′**glər) *n.* **1.** A person who fishes with a hook and line. **2.** An anglerfish.

an•gler•fish (**ăng′**glər fĭsh′) *n.* A deep-sea fish having a flap of skin hanging from a slender projection over its large mouth. The flap acts as bait to attract smaller fish.

an•gle•worm (**ăng′**gəl wûrm′) *n.* An earthworm, especially when used as fishing bait.

An•gli•can (**ăng′**glĭ kən) *adj.* Of, relating to, or characteristic of the Anglican Church. —*n.* A member of the Anglican Church.

Anglican Church *n.* The Church of England and those churches in other nations that are in agreement with it.

An•gli•can•ism (**ăng′**glĭ kə nĭz′əm) *n.* The beliefs, practices, and form of organization of the Anglican Church.

An•gli•cize (**ăng′**glĭ sīz′) *tr.v.* **An•gli•cized, An•gli•ciz•ing, An•gli•ciz•es. 1.** To adapt (a foreign word) to use in English, especially by changing its spelling or pronunciation: *The Greek name Odysseus, or Ulixes in Latin, was Anglicized as Ulysses.* **2.** To make English or similar to English in some form, style, or character of custom or habit.

an•gling (**ăng′**glĭng) *n.* The act or sport of fishing with a hook and line.

An•glo (**ăng′**glō) *n., pl.* **An•glos.** *Informal.* An Anglo-American, especially a white resident of the United States who is not of Hispanic descent.

Anglo– *pref.* A prefix that means English: *Anglo-American; Anglo-Saxon.*

An•glo-A•mer•i•can (**ăng′**glō ə **mĕr′**ĭ kən) *n.* An American, especially an inhabitant of the United States, who is of English descent. —*adj.* **1.** Of, relating to, or between England and America, especially the United States. **2.** Of or relating to Anglo-Americans.

An•glo-French (**ăng′**glō **frĕnch′**) *adj.* Of, relating to, or between England and France, or their peoples. —*n.* The dialect of Old French spoken by Anglo-Normans.

An•glo-Nor•man (**ăng′**glō **nôr′**mən) *n.* **1.** One of the Normans who lived in England after the Norman conquest of England in 1066 or a descendant of these settlers. **2.** The dialect of Old French, derived chiefly from Norman French, that was used by the Anglo-Normans. **—An′glo-Nor′man** *adj.*

An•glo-Sax•on (**ăng′**glō **săk′**sən) *n.* **1.** A member of one of the Germanic peoples, the Angles, the Saxons, and the Jutes, who settled in Britain in the fifth and sixth centuries A.D. **2.** Any of the descendants of these people, who were the main people in England until the Norman Conquest in 1066. **3.** Old English. **4.** A person of English ancestry. **—An′glo-Sax′on** *adj.*

An•go•la (ăng **gō′**lə *or* ăn **gō′**lə). A country of southwest Africa on the Atlantic Ocean north of Namibia. The country gained its independence from Portugal in 1975. Luanda is the capital and the largest city. Population, 8,140,000.

An•go•ra (ăng **gôr′**ə) *n.* **1.** An Angora goat. **2.** An

Angora cat. **3.** An Angora rabbit. **4. angora.** Yarn or cloth made from the hair of an Angora goat or rabbit.

Angora cat *n.* A long-haired domestic cat.

Angora goat *n.* Any of a breed of domestic goat having long silky hair.

Angora rabbit *n.* Any of a breed of domestic rabbit having long, soft, usually white hair.

an•gry (ăng′grē) *adj.* **an•gri•er, an•gri•est. 1.** Feeling or showing anger: *an angry customer; an angry expression.* **2.** Seeming to threaten: *angry dark storm clouds.* **3.** Inflamed: *an angry wound.* **—an′gri•ly** *adv.* **—an′gri•ness** *n.*

ang•strom (ăng′strəm) *n.* A unit of length equal to one hundred-millionth (10^{-8}) of a centimeter. It is used mainly in measuring wavelengths of light and shorter electromagnetic radiation. [First written down in 1906 in Modern English and spelled *Ångström,* after Anders Jonas *Ångström* (1814–1874), Swedish physicist.]

an•guish (ăng′gwĭsh) *n.* Strong pain or suffering of mind or body; torment; torture: *They were in anguish until their lost puppy was found.* [First written down before 1200 in Middle English and spelled *angwisshe,* from Latin *angustiae,* distress.]

an•guished (ăng′gwĭsht) *adj.* Feeling, expressing, or caused by anguish: *the anguished faces of people whose homes were destroyed by the hurricane.*

an•gu•lar (ăng′gyə lər) *adj.* **1.** Having, forming, or consisting of an angle or angles: *an angular point.* **2.** Measured by an angle: *angular distance.* **3.** Bony and lean: *an angular face.* **4.** Lacking grace or smoothness: *an angular gait.* **—an′gu•lar•ly** *adv.*

an•gu•lar•i•ty (ăng′gyə lăr′ĭ tē) *n., pl.* **an•gu•lar•i•ties.** The condition or quality of being angular.

an•hy•dride (ăn hī′drīd′) *n.* **1.** A chemical compound formed from another by the removal of water. **2.** An oxide that reacts with water to form a base or an acid.

an•hy•drous (ăn hī′drəs) *adj.* Lacking water, especially water of crystallization: *Many crystals, like diamond and quartz, are anhydrous.*

an•i•line also **an•i•lin** (ăn′ə lĭn) *n.* A colorless, oily, poisonous liquid derived from coal tar and benzene and used in making dyes, rubber, drugs, and varnishes. *—adj.* Derived from aniline.

an•i•mad•ver•sion (ăn′ə măd vûr′zhən *or* ăn′ə măd vûr′shən) *n.* Hostile criticism or a remark that directs criticism or blame.

an•i•mal (ăn′ə məl) *n.* **1.** An organism that is able to move itself from place to place, is limited in how large it can grow, uses specialized sensory organs to recognize and respond to external stimuli, and eats plants and other animals because it cannot make its own food. **2.** An animal organism other than a human being: *Primitive humans had to protect themselves from the animals.* **3.** A person whose bearing or behavior suggests an animal as distinguished from a human being; a brutish person. *—adj.* **1.** Relating to, characteristic of, or derived from animals: *animal behavior; animal fat.* **2.** Relating to the physical or sensual nature of humans rather than to the mind or soul: *animal vitality.* [First written down about 1330 in Middle English, from Latin, from *anima,* spirit.]

an•i•mal•cule (ăn′ə măl′kyo͞ol) *n., pl.* **an•i•mal•cules.** An animal of very small or microscopic size, such as an amoeba or a paramecium.

animal husbandry *n.* The care and breeding of domestic animals such as cattle and horses.

animal kingdom *n.* The category of living organisms that includes all animals.

animal rights *pl.n.* The idea or claim that animals should be protected from pain and torment, especially in laboratory experimentation.

an•i•mate (ăn′ə māt′) *tr.v.* **an•i•mat•ed, an•i•mat•ing, an•i•mates. 1.** To give life to; cause to come alive: *Spring rain animates the grass and plants.* **2.** To give interest or vitality to: *The party was animated by the band's music.* **3.** To inspire or motivate: *The soldiers were animated by the noblest patriotism.* **4.** To produce as an animated cartoon: *Many children's stories have been animated by motion picture companies.* *—adj.* (ăn′ə mĭt). **1.** Living: *The seabed is full of animate objects that grow out of the sand.* **2.** Belonging to the class of nouns that stand for living things: *The word "dog" is animate; the word "car" is inanimate.*

an•i•mat•ed (ăn′ə mā′tĭd) *adj.* **1.** Lively: *The band leader's personality was energetic and animated.* **2.** Designed so as to appear alive and move in a lifelike manner: *animated puppets.* **—an′i•mat′ed•ly** *adv.*

animated cartoon *n.* A motion picture in which a series of photographed drawings give the impression of motion by slight changes in the shapes of the drawings.

an•i•ma•tion (ăn′ə mā′shən) *n.* **1.** The condition or quality of being alive; liveliness; vitality. **2.** The process or processes by which an animated cartoon is prepared. **3.** An animated cartoon.

a•ni•ma•to (ä′nē mä′tō) *adj.* In music, animated or lively. *—adv.* In music, in a lively animated way.

an•i•ma•tor (ăn′ə mā′tər) *n.* An artist or a technician who works at making animated cartoons.

an•i•mism (ăn′ə mĭz′əm) *n.* A belief that natural objects, such as trees, waterfalls, and mountains, and natural forces, such as wind and the tide, have souls.

an•i•mos•i•ty (ăn′ə mŏs′ĭ tē) *n., pl.* **an•i•mos•i•ties.** Hatred, enmity, or hostility that is shown openly: *There was much animosity between the two nations even before war broke out.*

an•i•mus (ăn′ə məs) *n.* **1.** A feeling of animosity; hatred: *animus among bitter rivals.* **2.** An intention or a purpose; a motive behind an action.

an•i•on (ăn′ī′ən) *n.* An ion that has a negative charge and moves toward the positive electrode in electrolysis.

an•ise (ăn′ĭs) *n.* **1.** An herb related to parsley, having small licorice-flavored seeds. **2.** The seeds of this plant, used for flavoring.

anise seed or **an•i•seed** (ăn′ĭ sēd′) *n.* The seed of the anise plant.

An•jou (ăn′jo͞o′ *or* äɴ zho͞o′). A historical region and former province of northwest France in the Loire River valley. It became part of France in the 1480's.

An•ka•ra (ăng′kər ə *or* äng′kər ə). The capital of Turkey, in the west-central part of the country southeast of Istanbul at an elevation of about 3,000 feet (915 meters). Ankara replaced Istanbul as the capital in 1923. Population, 1,877,755.

an•kle (ăng′kəl) *n.* **1.** The joint formed by the tibia and fibula of the lower leg with the talus of the foot. **2.** The slender part of the leg just above this joint. [First written down about 1350 in Middle English and spelled *ancle,* partly from Old English *anclēow,* and partly of Scandinavian origin.]

an•kle•bone (ăng′kəl bōn′) *n.* The main bone of the ankle; the talus.

an•klet (ăng′klĭt) *n.* **1.** A bracelet or chain worn around the ankle. **2.** A short sock reaching to just above the ankle.

An•na I•va•nov•na (ä′nə ē vä′nəv nə). 1693–1740. Empress of Russia who ruled from 1730 until 1740.

an•nals (ăn′əlz) *pl.n.* **1.** A record of events written in the order of their occurrence, year by year. **2.** A descriptive account or record; a history: *the annals of the American Revolution.*

An•nap•o•lis (ə năp′ə lĭs). The capital of Maryland, in the central part of the state on an inlet of Ches-

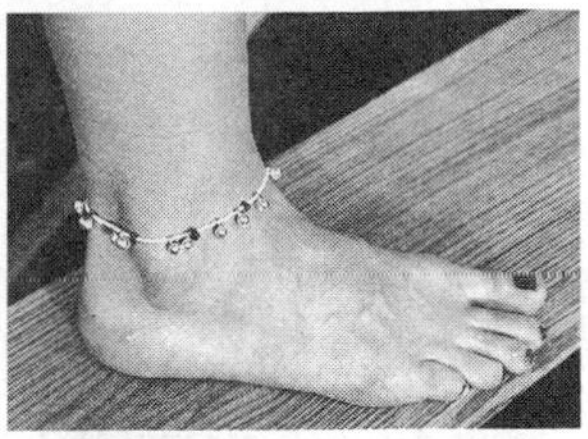

anklet

ă	pat	oi	boy
ā	pay	ou	out
âr	care	o͝o	took
ä	father	o͞o	boot
ĕ	pet	ŭ	cut
ē	be	ûr	urge
ĭ	pit	th	thin
ī	pie	*th*	this
îr	pier	hw	whoop
ŏ	pot	zh	vision
ō	toe	ə	about
ô	paw	ɴ	*French* bon

Anne

apeake Bay south-southeast of Baltimore. It was settled in 1649. Population, 33,187.

Anne (ăn). 1665–1714. Queen of Great Britain and Ireland (1702–1714) who was the last monarch of the Stuart line.

an•neal (ə nēl′) *tr.v.* **an•nealed, an•neal•ing, an•neals.** To treat (glass or a metal) by heating and slow cooling in order to toughen and reduce brittleness: *anneal hammered copper.*

an•ne•lid (ăn′ə lĭd) *n.* Any of various worms or related animals, such as an earthworm or a leech, having a soft, elongated, segmented body.

an•nex (ə nĕks′ *or* ăn′ĕks′) *tr.v.* **an•nexed, an•nex•ing, an•nex•es. 1.** To add or join to, especially to a larger or more significant thing: *The new gym is to be annexed to the school.* **2.** To add (territory) to an existing country or other area: *The city is trying to annex two of the suburbs.* —*n.* (ăn′ĕks′). An extra building that is added to another bigger building and used for some related purpose: *the library annex.*

an•nex•a•tion (ăn′ĭk sā′shən) *n.* The act of annexing: *Germany's annexation of Czechoslovakian territory during World War II.*

an•ni•hi•late (ə nī′ə lāt′) *tr.v.* **an•ni•hi•lat•ed, an•ni•hi•lat•ing, an•ni•hi•lates. 1.** To destroy completely; wipe out. **2.** To defeat severely; vanquish. [First written down in 1525 in Modern English, from Late Latin *annihilāre* : Latin *ad-*, to + Latin *nihil*, nothing.] —**an•ni′hi•la′tion** *n.*

an•ni•ver•sa•ry (ăn′ə vûr′sə rē) *n., pl.* **an•ni•ver•sa•ries. 1.** The yearly returning of the date of an event that happened in an earlier year: *a wedding anniversary.* **2.** A celebration on this date. [First written down before 1200 in Middle English and spelled *anniversarie*, from Latin *anniversārius*, returning yearly : *annus*, year + *vertere*, to turn.]

an•no Dom•i•ni (ăn′ō dŏm′ə nī′ *or* ăn′ō dŏm′ə nē) *adv.* In a specified year since the birth of Jesus. Used chiefly in abbreviated form: *A.D. 500.*

an•no•tate (ăn′ō tāt′) *tr.v.* **an•no•tat•ed, an•no•tat•ing, an•no•tates.** To furnish (a written work) with explanatory notes: *Many textbooks are annotated with notes in the margin.* —**an′no•ta′tor** *n.*

an•no•ta•tion (ăn′ō tā′shən) *n.* **1.** The act or process of annotating. **2.** An explanatory note: *an annotation in the margin.*

an•nounce (ə nouns′) *v.* **an•nounced, an•nounc•ing, an•nounc•es.** —*tr.* **1.** To bring to public notice; give formal notice of: *The principal announced a change in our schedule.* **2.** To make known the presence or arrival of: *The doorman announced us by telephone.* **3.** To serve as an announcer of: *announced hockey games on television.* —*intr.* To serve as an announcer on radio or television. [First written down in 1483 in Middle English and spelled *announcen*, from Latin *annūntiāre*, to report to, from *nūntius*, message.]

an•nounce•ment (ə nouns′mənt) *n.* **1.** The act of announcing. **2.** A public declaration to make known something that has happened or that will happen; an official statement: *An announcement concerning the policy changes will be made soon.* **3.** A printed or published notice: *Read this announcement.*

an•nounc•er (ə noun′sər) *n.* A person who announces, especially a person who introduces a show, makes comments, or reads news on radio or television.

an•noy (ə noi′) *tr.v.* **an•noyed, an•noy•ing, an•noys.** To bother or irritate: *The children's screaming annoyed the neighbors.* [First written down about 1275 in Middle English and spelled *anoien*, from Old French *anoier*, from Latin *in odio*, odious.] —**an•noy′er** *n.*

an•noy•ance (ə noi′əns) *n.* **1.** Irritation or displeasure: *Much to my annoyance, the bus was late.* **2.** Something causing trouble or irritation; a nuisance: *Heartburn is a relatively minor annoyance.*

an•noy•ing (ə noi′ĭng) *adj.* Troublesome or irritating: *an annoying habit.* —**an•noy′ing•ly** *adv.* —**an•noy′ing•ness** *n.*

an•nu•al (ăn′yo͞o əl) *adj.* **1.** Occurring or done every year; yearly: *an annual medical examination.* **2.** Of, relating to, or determined by a year's time: *I was offered an annual income of $30,000.* **3.** Living and growing for one year or season: *annual plants.* —*n.* **1.** A periodical published yearly; a yearbook. **2.** A plant that grows, flowers, produces seeds, and dies in a single year or season. [First written down before 1382 in Middle English and spelled *annuel*, from Late Latin *annuālis*, from Latin *annus*, year.] —**an′nu•al•ly** *adv.*

annual ring *n.* One of the layers of wood formed each year in a tree trunk or other woody stem, showing as a ring-shaped band in cross section.

an•nu•i•ty (ə no͞o′ĭ tē *or* ə nyo͞o′ĭ tē) *n., pl.* **an•nu•i•ties. 1.a.** An amount of money paid at regular intervals. **b.** A sequence of such payments. **2.** An investment on which one receives fixed payments during one's lifetime or for a certain number of years. [First written down about 1412 in Middle English and spelled *annuite*, from Medieval Latin *annuitās*, from Latin *annuus*, yearly, from *annus*, year.]

an•nul (ə nŭl′) *tr.v.* **an•nulled, an•nul•ling, an•nuls.** To make or declare void; nullify; cancel: *The court annulled their marriage.*

an•nu•lar (ăn′yə lər) *adj.* Forming or shaped like a ring. —**an′nu•lar•ly** *adv.*

annular eclipse *n.* A solar eclipse in which the moon blocks all of the sun except for a bright ring around the edge of the sun.

an•nul•ment (ə nŭl′mənt) *n.* **1.** The act of annulling. **2.** A legal declaration stating that a marriage was never valid.

an•nun•ci•a•tion (ə nŭn′sē ā′shən) *n.* **1.** The act of announcing: *The annunciation of the new policy stirred up controversy.* **2. Annunciation.** In the New Testament, the angel Gabriel's announcement to the Virgin Mary that she was to become the mother of Jesus. **3.** The Christian feast on March 25 celebrating this event.

an•ode (ăn′ōd′) *n.* **1.** The positively charged electrode of an electrolytic cell or electron tube. **2.** In a battery or other device that is supplying current, the negatively charged terminal.

an•o•dyne (ăn′ə dīn′) *n.* **1.** A medicine that relieves pain. **2.** Something that soothes or comforts.

a•noint (ə noint′) *tr.v.* **a•noint•ed, a•noint•ing, a•noints. 1.** To apply oil, ointment, or a similar substance to: *The nurse anointed the burn with salve.* **2.** To put oil on in a religious ceremony as a means of making pure or holy: *anoint a king.* —**a•noint′ment** *n.*

a•nom•a•lous (ə nŏm′ə ləs) *adj.* Differing from what is normal or common; abnormal. —**a•nom′a•lous•ly** *adv.* —**a•nom′a•lous•ness** *n.*

a•nom•a•ly (ə nŏm′ə lē) *n., pl.* **a•nom•a•lies.** Something that is unusual, irregular, or abnormal: *Flooding is an anomaly in desert regions of Africa.* [First written down in 1571 in Modern English, from Greek *anōmalos*, uneven.]

a•non (ə nŏn′) *adv.* **1.** At another time; later. **2.** In a short time; soon.

anon. *abbr.* An abbreviation of anonymous.

an•o•nym•i•ty (ăn′ə nĭm′ĭ tē) *n., pl.* **an•o•nym•i•ties.** The condition of being anonymous: *The donor made a large contribution on the condition of anonymity.*

a•non•y•mous (ə nŏn′ə məs) *adj.* **1.** Nameless or unnamed: *The prize was awarded by a panel of anonymous judges.* **2.** Having an unknown source: *The anonymous letter was sent without a return address.* [First written down in 1601 in Modern English, from Greek *anōnumos*, nameless : *an-*, without + *onuma*, name.] **—a•non′y•mous•ly** *adv.*

a•noph•e•les (ə nŏf′ə lēz′) *n.* Any of various mosquitoes that transmit malaria to human beings.

an•o•rex•i•a (ăn′ə rĕk′sē ə) *n.* Loss of appetite, especially as a result of disease or psychological disorder. [First written down in 1626 in Modern English, from Greek : *an-*, without + *orexis*, appetite.]

anorexia nerv•o•sa (nûr vō′sə) *n.* A disorder usually occurring in young women that is characterized by an abnormal fear of becoming obese, a persistent aversion to food, and severe weight loss.

an•oth•er (ə nŭth′ər) *adj.* **1.** Additional; one more: *another cup of coffee.* **2.** Different: *These baseball players have been another team since they got a new coach.* **3.** Some other: *We'll discuss this at another time.* **4.** New or similar but not exactly the same: *The coach thinks this batter is another Babe Ruth.* *—pron.* **1.** An additional one: *I had a drink of water and then another.* **2.** Something or someone different: *A baby is one thing to take care of; a 6-year-old is another.* **3.** One of a group of things: *for one reason or another.*

an•ox•i•a (ăn ŏk′sē ə) *n.* A lack of enough oxygen reaching body tissues, caused by failure of the blood to absorb oxygen or of the lungs to transmit oxygen to the blood.

ans. *abbr.* An abbreviation of: **1.** Answer. **2.** Answered.

an•swer (ăn′sər) *n.* **1.** A spoken or written reply, as to a question, request, or letter: *I wrote weeks ago but never got an answer.* **2.** An act that serves as a reply or response: *Their answer was to ignore me.* **3.a.** A solution or result, as to a problem: *We all got the right answer to that problem.* **b.** The correct solution or response: *Our teacher read the answers to the quiz.* *—v.* **an•swered, an•swer•ing, an•swers.** *—intr.* **1.** To respond in words or action: *Answer to your name when it is called.* **2.** To be liable or accountable: *You will have to answer for this mess.* **3.** To match or correspond: *a car answering to this description.* *—tr.* **1.** To reply to: *answer a letter.* **2.** To respond correctly to: *I can't answer the question.* **3.** To fulfill the demands of: *A good rest answered the weary traveler's needs.* **4.** To match or correspond to: *That dog answers the description of the one you're looking for.* [First written down about 725 in Old English and spelled *andswaru*.]

Synonyms: answer, respond, reply, retort. These verbs refer to different kinds of reactions. **Answer, respond,** and **reply** mean to speak, write, or act in response to something: *Please answer my question. I didn't expect the President to respond personally to my letter. The visiting team scored three runs and the home team replied with two of their own.* **Retort** means to answer verbally in a quick, sharp, or witty way: *"My shoes may not be new, but at least they're clean!" Terry retorted.*

an•swer•a•ble (ăn′sər ə bəl) *adj.* **1.** Responsible; accountable; liable: *You are answerable for the money in the account.* **2.** Capable of being answered or proved wrong: *scientific questions not wholly answerable.* **—an′swer•a•ble•ness** *n.*

an•swer•ing machine (ăn′sər ĭng) *n.* A tape recorder attached to a telephone to record messages from callers.

answering service *n.* A business that answers a person's telephone calls and reports on the calls received.

ant (ănt) *n.* Any of various insects that live in highly organized colonies, often digging and tunneling in the ground or wood. Most ants are wingless; only the males and queens have wings. [First written down before 899 in Old English and spelled *æmete*.]

❑ *These sound alike:* **ant, aunt** (sister of one's parent).

ant. *abbr.* An abbreviation of antonym.

ant– *pref.* Variant of **anti–.**

–ant *suff.* A suffix that means: **1.** Performing a certain action or being in a certain state: *defiant; flippant.* **2.** A person or thing that performs or causes a certain action: *coolant; deodorant.*

ant•ac•id (ănt ăs′ĭd) *adj.* Capable of neutralizing an acid; basic. *—n.* A substance that neutralizes acids or counteracts acidity, especially one used to neutralize excess stomach acid.

an•tag•o•nism (ăn tăg′ə nĭz′əm) *n.* **1.** Unfriendly feeling; hostility: *antagonism among rival factions.* **2.** Opposition, as between conflicting principles or forces.

an•tag•o•nist (ăn tăg′ə nĭst) *n.* **1.** A person who opposes and actively competes with another; an adversary. **2.** Either of a pair of drugs or other substances that neutralize each other in the body: *An antitoxin is the antagonist of a toxin.* **3.** A muscle that resists or counteracts another muscle, as by relaxing while the opposite one contracts.

an•tag•o•nis•tic (ăn tăg′ə nĭs′tĭk) *adj.* **1.** Opposed; contending: *antagonistic points of view.* **2.** Unfriendly; hostile: *an antagonistic attitude.* **—an•tag′o•nis′ti•cal•ly** *adv.*

an•tag•o•nize (ăn tăg′ə nīz′) *tr.v.* **an•tag•o•nized, an•tag•o•niz•ing, an•tag•o•niz•es.** To earn the dislike of; provoke a feeling of irritation in: *Don't antagonize the dog by teasing it.*

An•ta•na•na•ri•vo (ăn′tə năn′ə rē′vō *or* än′tə nä′nə rē′vō). The capital and largest city of Madagascar, in the east-central part of the country. It was founded in the 17th century. Population, 700,000.

Ant•arc•tic (ănt ärk′tĭk) *adj.* Of, relating to, or in the regions surrounding the South Pole: *the Antarctic climate.* *—n.* Antarctica and its surrounding waters.

Ant•arc•ti•ca (ănt ärk′tĭ kə *or* ănt är′tĭ kə). A continent lying chiefly within the Antarctic Circle and surrounding the South Pole. About 95 percent of Antarctica is covered by a thick layer of solid ice.

Antarctic Circle. The parallel of latitude approximately 66 degrees 33 minutes south. It forms the boundary between the South Temperate Zone and South Frigid Zone.

Antarctic Ocean. The waters surrounding Antarctica, the southernmost extensions of the Atlantic, Pacific, and Indian oceans.

ant bear *n.* A large anteater of South America having a black band on the chest and a large bushy tail.

an•te (ăn′tē) *n.* In poker, a bet that each player must make to begin or stay in the game. *—tr.v.* **an•ted** or **an•teed, an•te•ing, an•tes. 1.** To put (one's stake) into the pool in poker. **2.** To pay: *After lunch we anteed up the bill.*

ante– *pref.* A prefix that means: **1.** Prior to; earlier: *antedate; antediluvian.* **2.** In front of: *anteroom.*

ant•eat•er (ănt′ē′tər) *n.* **1.** Any of several long-snouted tropical American mammals that feed on ants and other insects, which they catch with a long sticky tongue. **2.** Any of several similar animals, such as the aardvark.

an•te•bel•lum (ăn′tē bĕl′əm) *adj.* Belonging to the

anteater

ă	pat	oi	boy
ā	pay	ou	out
âr	care	o͝o	took
ä	father	o͞o	boot
ĕ	pet	ŭ	cut
ē	be	ûr	urge
ĭ	pit	th	thin
ī	pie	*th*	this
îr	pier	hw	whoop
ŏ	pot	zh	vision
ō	toe	ə	about
ô	paw	N	*French* bon

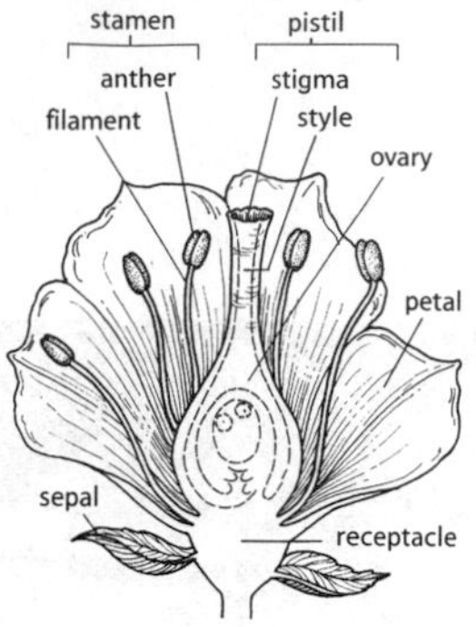

anther

Susan B. Anthony
Photographed in 1896
by Theodore C. Marceau
(1868?–1922)

Susan Brownell Anthony

Women could not vote at the beginning of the 19th century, and married women had no rights over their own property, earned wages, or children. Susan B. **Anthony** worked for legislation to change this. She petitioned for such laws as the Married Women's Property Act, passed in New York State in 1860. By 1900 almost all states had passed similar acts protecting the property, wages, and guardianship rights of married women. Anthony also worked for women's right to vote, remaining active in suffrage organizations until her death, at which time she was known as the unofficial leader of the woman suffrage movement.

period prior to the Civil War: *an antebellum mansion.*

an•te•ce•dent (ăn′tĭ **sēd′**nt) *adj.* Going before; preceding; prior. —*n.* **1.** A person or thing that precedes another. **2.** An occurrence or event prior to another. **3. antecedents.** A person's ancestors: *I do not know my antecedents beyond my grandparents.* **4.** The word, phrase, or clause to which a pronoun refers. In the sentence *My cousin arrived yesterday and I took her to the park,* the word *cousin* is the antecedent of *her.* —**an′te•ce′dent•ly** *adv.*

an•te•cham•ber (**ăn′**tē chăm′bər) *n.* A waiting room at the entrance to a larger room.

an•te•date (**ăn′**tĭ dāt′) *tr.v.* **an•te•dat•ed, an•te•dat•ing, an•te•dates. 1.** To be of an earlier date than: *This novel antedates the writer's poetry.* **2.** To give (something) a date earlier than the actual date; date back: *Management antedated the union's contract to the first of the year.*

an•te•di•lu•vi•an (ăn′tĭ də **lo͞o′**vē ən) *adj.* **1.** Occurring before or belonging to the period before the Biblical Flood. **2.** Very old; antiquated: *The horse and buggy is an antediluvian way of travel.*

an•te•lope (**ăn′**tl ōp′) *n., pl.* **antelope** or **an•te•lopes. 1.** Any of various swift-running, often slender, horned mammals of Africa and Asia. **2.** An animal similar to a true antelope, especially the pronghorn of western North America. [First written down in 1417 in Middle English and spelled *antelope,* a heraldic beast, from Late Greek *antholops.*]

an•te me•rid•i•em (ăn′tē mə **rĭd′**ē əm) *adv. & adj.* Before noon. [First written down in 1563 in Modern English : Latin *ante,* before + *meridiem,* accusative of *meridiēs,* noon.]

an•ten•na (ăn **tĕn′**ə) *n., pl.* **an•ten•nae** (ăn **tĕn′**ē). **1.** One of a pair of long, slender, segmented structures growing on the head of an insect or a crustacean such as a lobster or shrimp. Most antennae are organs of touch, but some are sensitive to odors and other stimuli. **2.** *pl.* **an•ten•nas.** A metallic device for sending and receiving radio or television signals. [First written down in 1646 in Modern English, from Latin *antenna,* sail yard.]

an•te•pe•nult (ăn′tē **pē′**nŭlt′ *or* ăn′tē pĭ **nŭlt′**) *n.* The third syllable from the end of a word, as *te* in *antepenult.*

an•te•ri•or (ăn **tîr′**ē ər) *adj.* **1.** Placed in front; located forward: *a small anterior room leading to the main hall.* **2.** Prior in time; earlier. **3.a.** In lower animals, situated toward or near the front or head. **b.** In higher animals, such as human beings, on, near, or toward the surface of the body on which the abdomen is found.

an•te•room (**ăn′**tē ro͞om′ *or* **ăn′**tē ro͝om′) *n.* An antechamber.

an•them (**ăn′**thəm) *n.* **1.** A song of praise or loyalty: *a national anthem.* **2.** A piece of music set to words from the Bible. [First written down before 899 in Old English and spelled *antefn,* from Late Greek *antiphōnos,* sounding in answer.]

an•ther (**ăn′**thər) *n.* The pollen-bearing part at the upper end of the stamen of a flower.

ant•hill (**ănt′**hĭl′) *n.* A mound of earth or sand formed by ants in digging or building a nest.

an•thol•o•gy (ăn **thŏl′**ə jē) *n., pl.* **an•thol•o•gies.** A collection of writings, such as poems or stories, by various authors.

An•tho•ny (**ăn′**thə nē), **Susan Brownell.** 1820–1906. American feminist leader and suffragist whose work led to laws that gave married women legal rights over their children, property, and wages. In 1869 she helped found the National Woman Suffrage Association. —See Note.

an•thra•cite (**ăn′**thrə sīt′) *n.* A hard shiny coal that has a high carbon content. It burns with a clean flame without smoke.

an•thrax (**ăn′**thrăks′) *n.* An infectious disease of mammals, mainly cattle and sheep, that can also be transmitted to human beings. It is caused by bacteria and is usually fatal.

an•thro•poid (**ăn′**thrə poid′) *adj.* Resembling a human being: *Gorillas and chimpanzees are anthropoid apes.* —*n.* An anthropoid ape. [First written down in 1832 in Modern English : Greek *anthrōpos,* person + English *-oid,* -like.]

an•thro•po•log•i•cal (ăn′thrə pə **lŏj′**ĭ kəl) *adj.* Of or relating to anthropology. —**an′thro•po•log′i•cal•ly** *adv.*

an•thro•pol•o•gist (ăn′thrə **pŏl′**ə jĭst) *n.* A scientist who specializes in anthropology.

an•thro•pol•o•gy (ăn′thrə **pŏl′**ə jē) *n.* The scientific study of the origin, the behavior, and the physical, social, and cultural development of human beings.

anti– or **ant–** *pref.* A prefix that means: **1.** Opposite: *antihero.* **2.** Opposing: *anti-Semitism.* **3.** Counteracting: *antibiotic.* —See Note.

an•ti•a•bor•tion (ăn′tē ə **bôr′**shən) *adj.* Opposed to induced abortions.

an•ti•air•craft (ăn′tē **âr′**krăft′) *adj.* Designed for defense, especially from a position on the ground, against attack by aircraft: *antiaircraft missiles.*

an•ti•bal•lis•tic missile (ăn′tĭ bə **lĭs′**tĭk) *n.* A missile designed to intercept and destroy a ballistic missile in flight.

an•ti•bi•ot•ic (ăn′tĭ bī **ŏt′**ĭk) *n.* A substance, such as penicillin or streptomycin, produced by certain fungi, bacteria, and other organisms, that is capable of destroying or weakening harmful microorganisms. Antibiotics are widely used in the treatment and prevention of diseases. —*adj.* Of or relating to antibiotics: *an antibiotic drug.*

an•ti•bod•y (**ăn′**tĭ bŏd′ē) *n.* A protein produced in the blood or tissues in reaction to a specific antigen. Antibodies are capable of acting against these foreign substances and provide immunity against certain microorganisms and toxins.

an•tic (**ăn′**tĭk) *adj.* Odd; ludicrous: *antic behavior.* —*n.* An odd or extravagant act or gesture; a caper or prank. Often used in the plural. [First written down in 1529 in Modern English and spelled *antike,* from Italian *antico,* ancient, old-fashioned, from Latin *antīquus,* former, old.]

an•ti•christ (**ăn′**tĭ krīst′) *n.* **1.** An enemy of Christ. **2.** In early Christianity, the great enemy who was expected to set himself up against Christ in the last days before the end of the world.

an•tic•i•pate (ăn **tĭs′**ə pāt′) *tr.v.* **an•tic•i•pat•ed, an•tic•i•pat•ing, an•tic•i•pates. 1.** To foresee or consider in advance: *We hadn't anticipated such a crowd at the zoo.* **2.** To deal with in advance: *Store owners anticipated the storm by boarding up their windows.* **3.** To look forward to, especially with pleasure; expect. See Synonyms at **expect.** [First written down in 1532 in Modern English, from Latin *anticipāre,* to take before : *ante-,* before + *capere,* to take.] —**an•tic′i•pa′tor** *n.*

an•tic•i•pa•tion (ăn tĭs′ə **pā′**shən) *n.* **1.** Expectation, especially happy or eager expectation: *She looked forward to vacation with great anticipation.* **2.** Foreknowledge or apprehension: *Our anticipation of the rise in oil prices was mistaken.*

an•ti•cler•i•cal (ăn′tē **klĕr′**ĭ kəl) *adj.* Opposed to the influence of the church or the clergy in political affairs.

an•ti•cli•mac•tic (ăn′tē klī **măk′**tĭk) *adj.* Of, relating to, or accompanied by an anticlimax. —**an′ti•cli•mac′ti•cal•ly** *adv.*

an•ti•cli•max (ăn′tē **klī′**măks′) *n.* **1.** A decline or letdown viewed as a disappointing contrast to what has gone before: *The rest of the story was an anticlimax to the scene in the courtroom.* **2.** A less important or trivial event that follows a series of significant ones: *Rain showers were an anticlimax to the full force of the hurricane.*

an•ti•cline (ăn′tĭ klīn′) *n.* A fold of rock layers that slope upward on both sides to a common crest. —**an′ti•cli′nal** (ăn′tē **klī′**nəl) *adj.*

an•ti•co•ag•u•lant (ăn′tē kō **ăg′**yə lənt) *n.* A substance that prevents or slows coagulation of the blood.

an•ti•cy•clone (ăn′tē **sī′**klōn′) *n.* A system of winds that spiral outward around a region of high atmospheric pressure, circling clockwise in the Northern Hemisphere and counterclockwise in the Southern Hemisphere.

an•ti•do•tal (ăn′tē **dōt′**l) *adj.* Of, resembling, or serving as an antidote.

an•ti•dote (**ăn′**tĭ dōt′) *n.* **1.** A substance that counteracts the effects of poison. **2.** Something that relieves or counteracts something: *Baking soda is often used as an antidote to indigestion.* [First written down before 1425 in Middle English, from Greek *antidoton* : *anti-*, against + *didonai*, to give.]

An•tie•tam (ăn **tē′**təm). A creek of north-central Maryland emptying into the Potomac River. The Civil War Battle of Antietam (or Sharpsburg) was fought along its banks on September 17, 1862.

an•ti•freeze (**ăn′**tĭ frēz′) *n.* A substance added to a liquid, such as water, to lower its freezing point.

an•ti•gen (**ăn′**tĭ jən) *n.* A substance that stimulates the production of an antibody when introduced into the body. Antigens include toxins, bacterial cells, and foreign blood cells.

An•tig•o•ne (ăn **tĭg′**ə nē) *n.* In Greek legend, the daughter of Oedipus and Jocasta who performs funeral rites over her brother's body in defiance of her uncle, the king of Thebes.

an•ti•grav•i•ty (ăn′tē **grăv′**ĭ tē) *n.* A supposed physical force that counteracts gravity.

An•ti•gua and Bar•bu•da (ăn **tē′**gə ănd bär **bōō′**də). A country in the northern Leeward Islands of the Caribbean Sea, made up of three small islands. It became independent in 1981. St. John's is the capital. Population, 72,000.

an•ti•he•ro (**ăn′**tē hîr′ō) *n., pl.* **an•ti•he•roes.** A main character in a novel, play, or other work, who lacks traditional heroic qualities, such as courage.

an•ti•her•o•ine or **an•ti-her•o•ine** (ăn′tē **hĕr′**ō ĭn) *n.* A main character in a novel, play, or other work, who lacks traditional qualities of a heroine, such as fortitude.

an•ti•his•ta•mine (ăn′tē **hĭs′**tə mēn′ *or* ăn′tē **hĭs′**tə mĭn) *n.* Any of various drugs that relieve symptoms of allergies or colds by interfering with the production or action of histamine in the body.

an•ti•knock (**ăn′**tĭ nŏk′) *n.* A substance added to gasoline to reduce pounding or clanking in an engine.

An•til•les (ăn **tĭl′**ēz). The islands of the West Indies except for the Bahamas, separating the Caribbean Sea from the Atlantic Ocean.

an•ti•log (**ăn′**tē lôg′ *or* **ăn′**tē lŏg′) *n.* An antilogarithm.

an•ti•log•a•rithm (ăn′tē **lô′**gə rĭ*th*′əm *or* ăn′tē **lŏg′**ə rĭ*th*′əm) *n.* The number that corresponds to a given logarithm. For example, $10^3 = 1000$, so $3 = \log 1000$ and $1000 = \text{antilog } 3$.

an•ti•ma•cas•sar (ăn′tē mə **kăs′**ər) *n.* A small cover placed on the backs or arms of chairs or sofas to keep them from getting dirty.

an•ti•mat•ter (**ăn′**tĭ măt′ər) *n.* A supposed form of matter identical to physical matter except that its atoms are made of positrons, antiprotons, and antineutrons.

an•ti•mis•sile (ăn′tē **mĭs′**əl) *adj.* Designed to intercept and destroy another missile in flight: *an antimissile system.*

an•ti•mo•ny (**ăn′**tə mō′nē) *n.* *Symbol* **Sb** A metalloid element, the most common form of which has a hard, extremely brittle, blue-white crystalline texture. Antimony occurs chiefly in combination with other elements and is used to strengthen alloys. Atomic number 51. See table at **element.** [First written down about 1425 in Middle English and spelled *antimonie*, from Medieval Latin *antimōnium.*]

an•ti•neu•tri•no (ăn′tē nōō **trē′**nō *or* ăn′tē nyōō **trē′**nō) *n., pl.* **an•ti•neu•tri•nos.** The antiparticle of the neutrino.

an•ti•neu•tron (ăn′tē **nōō′**trŏn′ *or* ăn′tē **nyōō′**trŏn′) *n.* The antiparticle of the neutron.

an•ti•nu•cle•ar (ăn′tē **nōō′**klē ər *or* ăn′tē **nyōō′**klē ər) *adj.* Opposed to the use of nuclear energy for military purposes or for generating electricity.

an•ti•par•ti•cle (ăn′tē **pär′**tĭ kəl) *n.* Either of a pair of atomic particles, such as a positron and an electron, that have the same mass and lifetime, but are exactly opposite in electric charge and magnetic properties.

an•ti•pas•to (än′tē **päs′**tō) *n., pl.* **an•ti•pas•tos** or **an•ti•pas•ti** (än′tē **päs′**tē). A dish of assorted appetizers.

an•tip•a•thy (ăn **tĭp′**ə thē) *n., pl.* **an•tip•a•thies.** **1.** A feeling of dislike or opposition: *Some people always express antipathy to new ideas.* **2.** A person or thing that causes such dislike.

an•ti•per•spi•rant (ăn′tē **pûr′**spər ənt) *n.* A preparation applied to the skin to reduce or prevent perspiration.

an•tip•o•dal (ăn **tĭp′**ə dəl) *adj.* **1.** Of, relating to, or situated on opposite sides of the earth. **2.** Exactly opposite; diametrically opposed: *antipodal theories.*

an•tip•o•des (ăn **tĭp′**ə dēz′) *pl.n.* **1.** Two places on directly opposite sides of the earth: *The North Pole and the South Pole are antipodes.* **2.** Two things that are exact opposites: *Punishment and forgiveness are antipodes.*

an•ti•pov•er•ty (ăn′tē **pŏv′**ər tē) *adj.* Created or intended to reduce poverty: *antipoverty programs.*

an•ti•pro•ton (ăn′tē **prō′**tŏn′) *n.* The antiparticle of the proton.

an•ti•quar•i•an (ăn′tĭ **kwâr′**ē ən) *adj.* Of or relating to antiquarians or the study of antiquities. —*n.* A person who studies, collects, sells, or buys relics and ancient works of art.

an•ti•quar•y (**ăn′**tĭ kwĕr′ē) *n., pl.* **an•ti•quar•ies.** An antiquarian.

an•ti•quate (**ăn′**tĭ kwāt′) *tr.v.* **an•ti•quat•ed, an•ti•quat•ing, an•ti•quates.** To make obsolete or old-fashioned.

an•ti•quat•ed (**ăn′**tĭ kwā′tĭd) *adj.* Too old to be useful, suitable, or fashionable.

an•tique (ăn **tēk′**) *adj.* **1.** Belonging to, made in, or typical of an earlier period: *antique furniture.* **2.** Of or belonging to ancient times, especially those of ancient Greece or Rome: *the antique legend of the founding of Rome.* **3.** Very old; old-fashioned: *an antique style of writing.* —*n.* Something having special value because of its age, especially a work of art or handicraft that is over 100 years old: *The writing table was a treasured antique.* —*tr.v.* **an•tiqued, an•tiqu•ing, an•tiques.** To give the appearance of an antique to: *an antiqued chair.* [First written down in 1530 in Modern English, from Latin *antīquus.*] —**an•tique′ly** *adv.* —**an•tique′ness** *n.*

an•tiq•ui•ty (ăn **tĭk′**wĭ tē) *n., pl.* **an•tiq•ui•ties.** **1.** Ancient times, especially the times before the Mid-

Word Building: anti–

The prefix **anti–** goes back to Greek *anti*, meaning "against." **Anti–** is so recognizable and its meaning is so clear that it is frequently used to make up new words. For example, the meanings of words such as *anticrime* and *antipollution* are easy to guess, even without a definition. Sometimes, when followed by a vowel, **anti–** becomes *ant–*: **antacid**.

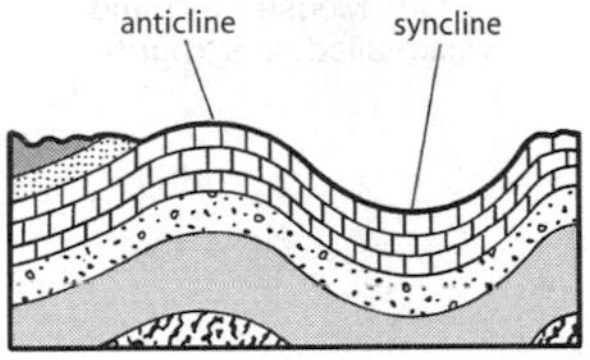

anticline

antimacassar

ă	pat	oi	boy
ā	pay	ou	out
âr	care	ŏŏ	took
ä	father	ōō	boot
ĕ	pet	ŭ	cut
ē	be	ûr	urge
ĭ	pit	th	thin
ī	pie	*th*	this
îr	pier	hw	whoop
ŏ	pot	zh	vision
ō	toe	ə	about
ô	paw	N	*French* bon

antler

Top: Reindeer
Bottom: Moose (*left*) and white-tailed deer (*right*)

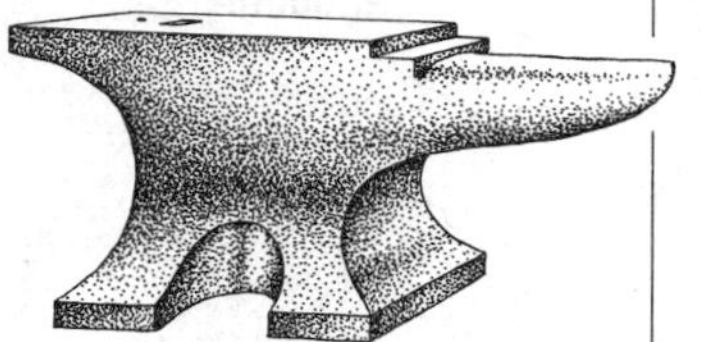

anvil

Blacksmith's anvil

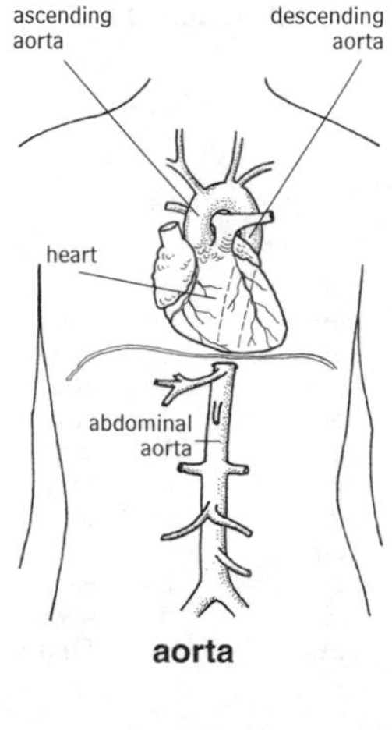

aorta

dle Ages: *The pyramids of ancient Egypt belong to antiquity.* **2.** The people of ancient times, especially the writers of those times: *an invention unknown to antiquity.* **3.** The quality of being old: *a carving of great antiquity.* **4.** Something, such as a relic, that dates from ancient times. Often used in the plural: *That museum has a collection of many antiquities from ancient Greece.*

an•ti-Sem•i•tism (ăn′tē **sĕm′**ĭ tĭz′əm) *n.* Prejudice against or hostility toward Jews. **—an′ti-Se•mit′ic** (ăn′tē sə **mĭt′**ĭk) *adj.*

an•ti•sep•tic (ăn′tĭ **sĕp′**tĭk) *adj.* **1.** Preventing infection, fermentation, or rot by stopping the growth and activity of microorganisms. **2.** Free of microorganisms: *Surgery is done under antiseptic conditions.* —*n.* An antiseptic substance or agent, such as alcohol or boric acid. [First written down in 1751 in Modern English : Greek *anti-*, against + Greek *sēptikos*, putrefying.] **—an′ti•sep′ti•cal•ly** *adv.*

an•ti•slav•er•y (ăn′tē **slā′**və rē *or* ăn′tē **slāv′**rē) *adj.* Opposed to or against slavery.

an•ti•so•cial (ăn′tē **sō′**shəl) *adj.* **1.** Avoiding the society or company of others; not sociable: *an antisocial recluse.* **2.** Opposed to or interfering with society: *Criminal acts are aggressive antisocial behavior.* **—an′ti•so′cial•ly** *adv.*

an•ti•tank (ăn′tē **tăngk′**) *adj.* Designed for use against tanks or other armored vehicles: *an antitank weapon.*

an•tith•e•sis (ăn **tĭth′**ĭ sĭs) *n., pl.* **an•tith•e•ses** (ăn **tĭth′**ĭ sēz′). **1.** Direct contrast; opposition: *Your behavior stands in antithesis to your beliefs.* **2.** The direct or exact opposite: *Hope is the antithesis of despair.* **3.** In speech or writing, the placing together of sharply opposed ideas.

an•ti•tox•in (ăn′tē **tŏk′**sĭn) *n.* **1.** An antibody formed in response to and capable of acting against a biological toxin, such as one produced by bacteria. **2.** A serum containing antibodies, obtained from the blood of an animal or person that has had a particular disease or was immunized against infection from the disease.

an•ti•trades (**ăn′**tĭ trādz′) *pl.n.* The westerly winds that blow at a level above the trade winds of the tropics.

an•ti•trust (ăn′tē **trŭst′**) *adj.* Opposing or regulating trusts or similar business monopolies considered not in the best interests of the public: *antitrust laws that prevent unfair business practices.*

an•ti•ven•in (ăn′tē **vĕn′**ĭn) *n.* **1.** An antitoxin that counteracts the venom of a snake, scorpion, or other venomous animal. **2.** A human or animal serum containing such an antitoxin.

an•ti•vi•ral (ăn′tē **vī′**rəl) *adj.* Destroying or slowing the growth and reproduction of viruses.

an•ti•war (ăn′tē **wôr′**) *adj.* Opposing war: *an antiwar demonstration.*

ant•ler (**ănt′**lər) *n.* **1.** A horny growth on the head of a deer, moose, elk, or other related animal, usually having one or more branches. Antlers grow usually only on males, and are shed and grown again from year to year. **2.** A branch of such a growth. [First written down before 1398 in Middle English and spelled *aunteler*, from Old French *antoillier* : Latin *ante-*, in front + Latin *oculāris*, of the eye.]

ant lion *n.* An insect whose larva digs holes to trap ants and other insects for food.

an•to•nym (**ăn′**tə nĭm′) *n.* A word having a sense opposite to a sense of another word; for example, *thick* is an antonym of *thin.*

ant•sy (**ănt′**sē) *adj.* **ant•si•er, ant•si•est.** *Slang.* Uneasy; anxious; restless.

Ant•werp (**ăn′**twərp). A city of northern Belgium north of Brussels. It is one of Europe's busiest ports. Population, 490,524.

A•nu•bis (ə **nōō′**bĭs *or* ə **nyōō′**bĭs) *n.* In Egyptian mythology, a jackal-headed god who conducts the dead to judgment.

a•nus (**ā′**nəs) *n., pl.* **a•nus•es.** The opening at the lower end of the alimentary canal through which solid waste is excreted.

an•vil (**ăn′**vĭl) *n.* **1.** A heavy block of iron or steel, with a smooth flat top on which metals are shaped by hammering. **2.** The incus. [First written down about 1000 in Old English and spelled *anfilte.*]

anx•i•e•ty (ăng **zī′**ĭ tē) *n., pl.* **anx•i•e•ties.** **1.** A feeling of uneasiness and distress about something in the future; worry: *The settlers were filled with anxiety about food supplies in the coming winter.* **2.** Eagerness or earnestness, often marked by uneasiness: *the pianist's anxiety to play well.*

anx•ious (**ăngk′**shəs *or* **ăng′**shəs) *adj.* **1.** Having a feeling of uneasiness; worried: *They were anxious about the upcoming exam.* **2.** Marked by uneasiness or worry: *anxious moments.* **3.** Eagerly earnest or desirous: *anxious to begin.* [First written down in 1623 in Modern English, from Latin *ānxius*, from *angere*, to torment.] **—anx′ious•ly** *adj.* **—anx′ious•ness** *n.*

an•y (**ĕn′**ē) *adj.* **1.** One or some; no matter which; of whatever kind: *Take any book you want. Do you have any information on Chinese cooking?* **2.** No matter how many or how few; some: *Are there any oranges left?* **3.** Every: *Any dog likes meat.* —*pron. (used with a singular or plural verb).* Any person or thing or any persons or things; anybody or anything: *We haven't any left. Any of the teachers can help you.* —*adv.* At all: *The patient doesn't feel any better.* [First written down about 725 in Old English and spelled *ǣnig.*] —See Note at **she.**

an•y•bod•y (**ĕn′**ē bŏd′ē *or* **ĕn′**ē bŭd′ē) *pron.* Any person; anyone. —*n.* A person of importance: *Everybody who is anybody came to the party.*

an•y•how (**ĕn′**ē hou′) *adv.* **1.** In any case; at any rate; anyway: *The twins were sick, but they didn't want to go anyhow.* **2.** Just the same; nevertheless; anyway: *You may know these words, but study them anyhow.*

an•y•more (ĕn′ē **môr′**) *adv.* **1.** Any longer; at the present: *Do they make this style anymore?* **2.** From now on: *We promised not to shout in the library anymore.*

an•y•one (**ĕn′**ē wŭn′) *pron.* Any person; anybody. —See Note at **she.**

an•y•place (**ĕn′**ē plās′) *adv.* Anywhere: *I can go any place I like.*

an•y•thing (**ĕn′**ē thĭng′) *pron.* Any object, occurrence, or matter whatever. —*adv.* To any degree or extent; at all: *Is your bike anything like mine?* ***—idiom.*** **anything but.** By no means; not at all: *This room is anything but warm.*

an•y•time (**ĕn′**ē tīm′) *adv.* At any time: *Anytime we come inside we should wipe our feet.*

an•y•way (**ĕn′**ē wā′) *adv.* **1.** In any case; at least: *I don't know if the book is lost or stolen; anyway, it's gone.* **2.** In any manner whatever: *Get the job done anyway you can.* **3.** Just the same; nevertheless; anyhow: *The ball was slippery, but the fielder caught it anyway.*

an•y•where (**ĕn′**ē wâr′) *adv.* **1.** To, in, or at any place: *They travel anywhere they want to.* **2.** At all: *We aren't anywhere near finished.*

A-OK (ā′ō **kā′**) *adj. Informal.* Perfectly OK.

A-one (**ā′wŭn′**) *adj. Informal.* First-class; excellent.

a•or•ta (ā **ôr′**tə) *n., pl.* **a•or•tas** or **a•or•tae** (ā **ôr′**tē). The main artery of the body, starting at the left ventricle of the heart and branching to carry blood to all the organs of the body except the lungs.

a•pace (ə pās′) *adv.* At a rapid pace; swiftly: *The building of the new hospital is proceeding apace.*

A•pach•e (ə păch′ē) *n., pl.* **Apache** or **A•pach•es. 1.** A member of a Native American people of the southwestern United States. **2.** Any of the Athabaskan languages of the Apache.

a•part (ə pärt′) *adv.* **1.** Away from another in time or position: *two trees about ten feet apart.* **2.** In or into separate pieces; to pieces: *The wagon fell apart as it crashed into the rocks.* **3.** One from another: *Can you tell the puppies apart?* **4.** Aside or in reserve: *set money apart for a vacation.* —*adj.* Set apart; isolated: *Unusually strong winds made this storm one apart from the others.* **—a•part′ness** *n.*

apart from *pref.* Other than; aside from: *Apart from a few showers we had fine weather on our vacation.*

a•part•heid (ə pärt′hīt′ *or* ə pärt′hāt′) *n.* An official policy of the Republic of South Africa involving legal and economic discrimination against nonwhites. It is now gradually being abandoned. [First written down in 1947 in Modern English, from Afrikaans : Dutch *apart*, separate + *-heid*, -hood.]

a•part•ment (ə pärt′mənt) *n.* A room or group of rooms to live in.

apartment building *n.* A building divided into apartments.

apartment house *n.* An apartment building.

ap•a•thet•ic (ăp′ə thĕt′ĭk) *adj.* Feeling or showing little or no interest; uninterested; indifferent: *Adults who are apathetic about politics should not complain about poor government.* **—ap′a•thet′i•cal•ly** *adv.*

ap•a•thy (ăp′ə thē) *n.* Lack of feeling or interest; indifference: *Apathy among our friends made it difficult to organize the skiing trip.* [First written down in 1603 in Modern English, from Greek *apathēs*, without feeling : *a-*, without + *pathos*, feeling.]

a•pat•o•saur (ə păt′ə sôr′) or **a•pat•o•sau•rus** (ə păt′ə sôr′əs) *n.* A brontosaur.

ape (āp) *n.* **1.** Any of various large tailless primates, as the gorilla, chimpanzee, or orangutan. **2.** A monkey. **3.** A person who imitates or mimics. —*tr.v.* **aped, ap•ing, apes.** To imitate the actions of; mimic: *Many comedians ape the speech and mannerisms of public figures.* [First written down about 700 in Old English and spelled *apa*.] **—ap′er** *n.*

Ap•en•nines (ăp′ə nīnz′). A mountain system extending about 840 miles (1,352 kilometers) from northwest Italy to the southern tip of the mainland. The Apennines rise to 9,560 feet (2,915.8 meters).

a•pé•ri•tif (ä pĕr′ĭ tēf′) *n.* An alcoholic drink taken before a meal to stimulate the appetite.

ap•er•ture (ăp′ər chər) *n.* **1.** A hole or an opening: *an aperture in the wall.* **2.** The diameter of the opening through which light can pass into a camera, telescope, or other optical instrument. [First written down probably before 1425 in Middle English, from Latin *apertūra*, from *aperīre*, to open.]

a•pex (ā′pĕks) *n., pl.* **a•pex•es** or **a•pi•ces** (ā′pĭ sēz′*or* ăp′ĭ sēz′). **1.** The peak or highest point of something: *The runner won many victories at the apex of her great career.* **2.** The highest point of a geometric figure; a vertex. [First written down in 1601 in Modern English, from Latin.]

a•pha•sia (ə fā′zhə) *n.* The loss of some or all of the ability to express and understand ideas, resulting from damage to the brain. **—a•pha′sic** (ə fā′zĭk *or* ə fā′sĭk) *adj. & n.*

a•phe•li•on (ə fē′lē ən *or* ə fēl′yən) *n., pl.* **a•phe•li•a** (ə fē′lē ə). The point farthest from the sun in the orbit of a planet, a comet, or an artificial satellite. [First written down in 1676 in Modern English, from New Latin *aphēlium* : Greek *apo-*, away + Greek *hēlios*, sun.]

a•phid (ā′fĭd *or* ăf′ĭd) *n.* Any of various small, soft-bodied insects that feed by sucking sap from plants.

aph•o•rism (ăf′ə rĭz′əm) *n.* A short saying expressing a general truth; for example, "The only way to have a friend is to be one" is an aphorism.

aph•ro•dis•i•ac (ăf′rə dĭz′ē ăk′ *or* ăf′rə dē′zē ăk′) *n.* A drug or food that stimulates sexual desire. —*adj.* Sexually stimulating.

Aph•ro•di•te (ăf′rə dī′tē) *n.* In Greek mythology, the goddess of love and beauty, identified with the Roman Venus.

A•pi•a (ə pē′ə *or* ä′pē ä′). The capital of Western Samoa in the southern Pacific Ocean. Population, 33,170.

a•pi•ar•y (ā′pē ĕr′ē) *n., pl.* **a•pi•ar•ies.** A place where bees and beehives are kept, especially as a source of honey.

a•pi•ces (ā′pĭ sēz′ *or* ăp′ĭ sēz′) *n.* A plural of **apex.**

a•piece (ə pēs′) *adv.* To or for each one; each: *Give them an apple apiece.*

ap•ish (ā′pĭsh) *adj.* **1.** Resembling an ape. **2.** Foolishly imitative. **3.** Silly, ridiculous: *an apish grin.* **—ap′ish•ly** *adv.* **—ap′ish•ness** *n.*

a•plen•ty (ə plĕn′tē) *adj.* In abundance: *We'll have water aplenty when the floods come.*

a•plomb (ə plŏm′ *or* ə plŭm′) *n.* Self-confidence; poise; assurance: *Our teacher handled the situation with aplomb.*

APO or **A.P.O.** *abbr.* An abbreviation of Army Post Office.

a•poc•a•lypse (ə pŏk′ə lĭps′) *n.* **1. Apocalypse.** The Book of Revelation. **2.** A prophecy or revelation, especially about the end of the world.

a•poc•a•lyp•tic (ə pŏk′ə lĭp′tĭk) *adj.* **1.** Of or relating to a prophecy or revelation. **2.** Involving or indicating widespread devastation.

A•poc•ry•pha (ə pŏk′rə fə) *n. (used with a singular or plural verb).* **1.** The fourteen Biblical books not included in the Old Testament by Protestants as being of doubtful authorship and authority. Eleven of these books are accepted by the Roman Catholic Church. **2.** Various early Christian writings excluded from the New Testament.

a•poc•ry•phal (ə pŏk′rə fəl) *adj.* **1.** Of doubtful origin; false: *Folk legend is full of apocryphal stories of animals coming to the aid of humans in distress.* **2.** Of or relating to the Apocrypha. **—a•poc′ry•phal•ly** *adv.*

ap•o•gee (ăp′ə jē) *n.* **1.** The point farthest from the earth in the orbit of the moon or an artificial satellite. **2.** The highest point; apex. [First written down in 1594 in Modern English, from Greek *apogaios*, far from the earth : *apo-*, away + *gaia*, earth.]

A•pol•lo (ə pŏl′ō) *n.* In the Greek and Roman mythology, the god of prophecy, music, medicine, and poetry, sometimes identified with the sun.

a•pol•o•get•ic (ə pŏl′ə jĕt′ĭk) *adj.* Expressing or making an apology: *The student's excuse was offered with an apologetic smile.* **—a•pol′o•get′i•cal•ly** *adv.*

a•pol•o•gist (ə pŏl′ə jĭst) *n.* A person who argues in defense or justification of an idea or cause: *The park ranger was an apologist for conservation.*

a•pol•o•gize (ə pŏl′ə jīz′) *intr.v.* **a•pol•o•gized, a•pol•o•giz•ing, a•pol•o•giz•es. 1.** To make an apology; say one is sorry: *Did he apologize for being late?* **2.** To make a formal defense or justification in speech or writing. **—a•pol′o•giz′er** *n.*

a•pol•o•gy (ə pŏl′ə jē) *n., pl.* **a•pol•o•gies. 1.** A statement expressing regret for an offense or fault: *make an apology for being late.* **2.** A defense or justification, as of an idea or cause: *Her letter to the*

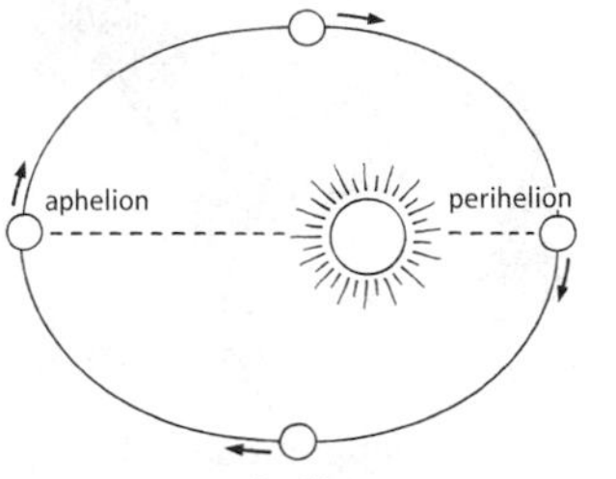

aphelion

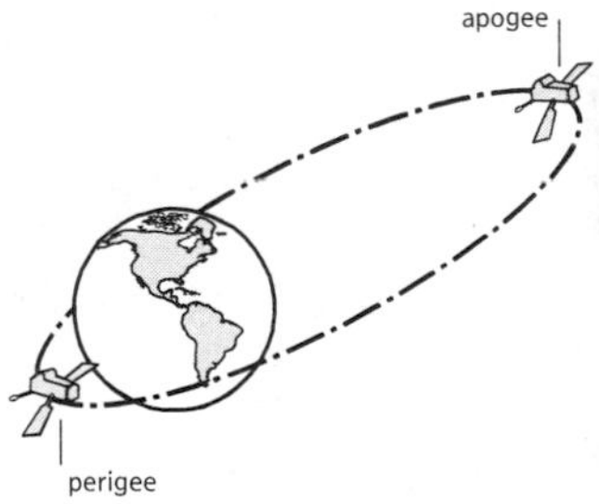

apogee

ă	pat	oi	boy
ā	pay	ou	out
âr	care	ŏŏ	took
ä	father	ōō	boot
ĕ	pet	ŭ	cut
ē	be	ûr	urge
ĭ	pit	th	thin
ī	pie	*th*	this
îr	pier	hw	whoop
ŏ	pot	zh	vision
ō	toe	ə	about
ô	paw	N	*French* bon

appaloosa
Dreamfinder,
National Grand Champion

editor is an apology for animal rights. **3.** An inferior substitute: *That short note was a poor apology for a letter.* [First written down in 1533 in Modern English and spelled *apologie*, from Greek *apologia* : *apo-*, away + *logos*, speech.]

ap•o•plec•tic (ăp′ə **plĕk′**tĭk) *adj.* Of, resembling, causing, or affected with apoplexy. **—ap′o•plec′ti•cal•ly** *adv.*

ap•o•plex•y (**ăp′**ə plĕk′sē) *n.* A condition in which a blood vessel in the brain breaks or becomes blocked, often resulting in loss of muscular control, paralysis, unconsciousness, or death.

a•pos•ta•sy (ə **pŏs′**tə sē) *n., pl.* **a•pos•ta•sies.** A giving up of one's religious faith, political beliefs, or loyalty.

a•pos•tate (ə **pŏs′**tāt′ *or* ə **pŏs′**tĭt) *n.* A person who abandons or forsakes religious faith, political principles, or loyalty, as to a cause.

a•pos•tle (ə **pŏs′**əl) *n.* **1.** Often **Apostle.** One of the twelve original disciples of Jesus. **2.** A missionary of the early Christian Church: *St. Patrick, the apostle of Ireland.* **3.** A person who leads or strongly supports a cause or movement: *an apostle of government reform.*

A•pos•tles' Creed (ə **pŏs′**əlz) *n.* A Christian creed traditionally thought to have been written by the 12 Apostles.

ap•os•tol•ic (ăp′ə **stŏl′**ĭk) *adj.* **1.** Of, relating to, or at the same time as the 12 Apostles. **2.** Of or relating to the pope as successor to Saint Peter: *apostolic authority.*

a•pos•tro•phe (ə **pŏs′**trə fē) *n.* A mark (') used to indicate the omission of a letter or letters from a word or phrase, as in *aren't,* or to show the possessive case, as in *Tom's hat* or certain plurals, especially those of numbers and letters, as in *A's.* [First written down in 1530 in Modern English, from Greek *apostrophos* : *apo-*, away + *strephein*, to turn.]

a•poth•e•car•ies' measure (ə **pŏth′**ĭ kĕr′ēz) *n.* A system of liquid volume measure used in pharmacy.

apothecaries' weight *n.* A system of weights used in pharmacy.

a•poth•e•car•y (ə **pŏth′**ĭ kĕr′ē) *n., pl.* **a•poth•e•car•ies.** A person trained in the preparation of drugs and medicines; a pharmacist. [First written down about 1387 in Middle English and spelled *apotecarie*, from Late Latin *apothēcārius*, clerk, from Greek *apothēkē*, storehouse.]

ap•o•thegm (**ăp′**ə thĕm′) *n.* A short and witty instructive saying; a maxim.

a•poth•e•o•sis (ə pŏth′ē **ō′**sĭs) *n., pl.* **a•poth•e•o•ses** (ə pŏth′ē **ō′**sēz′). **1.** The elevation to divine rank or status; deification: *the apotheosis of a Roman emperor.* **2.** A glorified ideal or example: *The dancer was considered the apotheosis of grace.*

app. *abbr.* An abbreviation of: **1.** Apparatus. **2.** Appendix. **3.** Appointed. **4.** Apprentice.

Ap•pa•la•chi•a (ăp′ə **lā′**chē ə *or* ăp′ə **lăch′**ē ə). A region of the eastern United States including the Appalachian Mountains. Appalachia is known for its diverse folk culture, which includes long traditions of music and dance. **—Ap′pa•la′chi•an** *adj.*

Appalachian Mountains. A mountain system of eastern North America extending about 1,600 miles (2,574 kilometers) southwest from eastern Canada to central Alabama. The Appalachians rise to 6,684 feet (2,038.6 meters).

ap•pall (ə **pôl′**) *tr.v.* **ap•palled, ap•pall•ing, ap•palls.** To fill with horror and amazement; shock: *My mother was appalled when she saw the mess we made in the backyard.*

ap•pall•ing (ə **pô′**lĭng) *adj.* Causing fear or dismay: *the appalling working conditions of miners in the last century.* **—ap•pall′ing•ly** *adv.*

ap•pa•loo•sa (ăp′ə **lōō′**sə) *n.* A breed of horse having a spotted rump, originally bred in northwest North America.

ap•pa•ra•tus (ăp′ə **rā′**təs *or* ăp′ə **răt′**əs) *n., pl.* **ap•paratus** or **ap•pa•ra•tus•es. 1.** The means by which some function or task is performed: *Congress has a complicated apparatus for making laws.* **2.** A device or mechanism for a particular purpose: *a laboratory full of scales and other scientific apparatus.* **3.** A group or system of organs that perform a certain function: *The dolphin has a sensory apparatus much like sonar.*

ap•par•el (ə **păr′**əl) *n.* Clothing; attire: *The clothing store has a separate department for children's apparel.* —*tr.v.* **ap•par•eled, ap•par•el•ing, ap•par•els** or **ap•par•elled, ap•par•el•ling, ap•par•els.** To dress or clothe: *The queen was richly appareled in velvet robes.*

ap•par•ent (ə **păr′**ənt *or* ə **pâr′**ənt) *adj.* **1.** Readily understood or seen; obvious: *for no apparent reason.* **2.** Appearing as such but not necessarily so; seeming: *an apparent advantage.* **—ap•par′ent•ly** *adv.* **—ap•par′ent•ness** *n.*

ap•pa•ri•tion (ăp′ə **rĭsh′**ən) *n.* **1.** A ghost; a specter. **2.** An eerie sight.

ap•peal (ə **pēl′**) *n.* **1.a.** An urgent or earnest request: *an appeal for help.* **b.** A request of a person to decide something in one's favor: *I wanted to go and made an appeal to my parents.* **2.** The power of attracting or of arousing interest: *The waterfront has great appeal for tourists.* **3.a.** The transfer of a legal case from a lower court to a higher court for a new hearing. **b.** A case so transferred. **c.** A request for a new hearing. —*v.* **ap•pealed, ap•peal•ing, ap•peals.** —*intr.* **1.** To make an urgent or earnest request: *I appeal to you to help us.* **2.** To be attractive or interesting: *That fine automobile appealed to the buyer.* **3.** To make or apply for a legal appeal. —*tr.* To make or apply for a legal appeal of (a case). [First written down before 1338 in Middle English and spelled *apel*, from Latin *appellāre*, to entreat.]

ap•peal•ing (ə **pē′**lĭng) *adj.* Attractive or interesting: *appealing clothes.*

ap•pear (ə **pîr′**) *intr.v.* **ap•peared, ap•pear•ing, ap•pears. 1.** To come into view: *A ship appeared on the horizon.* **2.** To come before the public: *The violinist has appeared in two concerts.* **3.** To seem or look: *The Senator appears to be in good health.* **4.** To present oneself formally before a court of law: *The criminal appeared before the judge.* [First written down about 1275 in Middle English and spelled *aperen*, from Latin *appārēre* : *ad-*, to + *pārēre*, to show.]

ap•pear•ance (ə **pîr′**əns) *n.* **1.** The act of appearing; a coming into sight: *the sudden appearance of storm clouds on the horizon.* **2.** The act of coming into public view: *nine years since the pianist's last personal appearance.* **3.** The way something or someone looks or appears; outward aspect: *A neat appearance helps to make a good impression.* **4.** A semblance, especially a false show: *The frightened soldier was only keeping up an appearance of bravery.* **5. appearances.** Outward indications; circumstances: *By all appearances you would never know that she was famous.*

ap•pease (ə **pēz′**) *tr.v.* **ap•peased, ap•peas•ing, ap•peas•es. 1.** To calm or pacify, especially by giving what is demanded: *The baby sitter appeased the startled baby with a bottle.* **2.** To satisfy; relieve: *Several glasses of water appeased his thirst.* [First written down about 1300 in Middle English and spelled *appesen*, from Old French *apesier* : Latin *ad-*, to + Latin *pāx*, peace.] **—ap•peas′er** *n.*

ap•pease•ment (ə **pēz′**mənt) *n.* **1.** An act of appeasing or a condition of being appeased. **2.** A policy of attempting to avoid war by meeting the demands of a threatening nation.

ap•pel•lant (ə pĕl′ənt) *n.* A person who appeals a court decision. —*adj.* Of or relating to a legal appeal; appellate.

ap•pel•late (ə pĕl′ĭt) *adj.* Having the legal power to hear appeals and to reverse previous court decisions: *an appellate court.*

ap•pel•la•tion (ăp′ə lā′shən) *n.* A name or title: *The telephone company was known by the appellation "Ma Bell."*

ap•pend (ə pĕnd′) *tr.v.* **ap•pend•ed, ap•pend•ing, ap•pends.** To attach; add: *The editor appended an index to the history book.*

ap•pend•age (ə pĕn′dĭj) *n.* **1.** Something appended or attached: *The handle on a coffee cup is a useful appendage.* **2.** A part or organ of the body that hangs or projects from another part: *A finger is an appendage of the hand.*

ap•pen•dec•to•my (ăp′ən dĕk′tə mē) *n., pl.* **ap•pen•dec•to•mies.** The removal of the appendix by surgery.

ap•pen•di•ces (ə pĕn′dĭ sēz′) *n.* A plural of **appendix.**

ap•pen•di•ci•tis (ə pĕn′dĭ sī′tĭs) *n.* Inflammation of the appendix.

ap•pen•dix (ə pĕn′dĭks) *n., pl.* **ap•pen•dix•es** or **ap•pen•di•ces** (ə pĕn′dĭ sēz′). **1.** A section at the end of a book containing additional material, tables, or other information relating to the subject of the book. **2.** The tubular projection attached to the large intestine near where it joins the small intestine. [First written down in 1542 in Modern English, from Latin, from *appendere*, to hang upon.]

ap•per•tain (ăp′ər tān′) *intr.v.* **ap•per•tained, ap•per•tain•ing, ap•per•tains.** To belong as a function or part; have relation: *the policies of government that appertain to economic reform.*

ap•pe•tite (ăp′ĭ tīt′) *n.* **1.** The desire for food or drink. **2.** A strong desire for something: *an appetite for learning.* [First written down about 1303 in Middle English and spelled *apetit*, from Latin *appetītus*, strong desire, from *appetere*, to strive after.]

ap•pe•tiz•er (ăp′ĭ tī′zər) *n.* A food or drink taken before a meal to arouse the appetite.

ap•pe•tiz•ing (ăp′ĭ tī′zĭng) *adj.* Stimulating or appealing to the appetite; tasty: *an appetizing meal.* **—ap′pe•tiz′ing•ly** *adv.*

ap•plaud (ə plôd′) *v.* **ap•plaud•ed, ap•plaud•ing, ap•plauds.** —*tr.* **1.** To express praise or approval of, as by clapping the hands: *applaud the actors.* **2.** To praise; approve: *My parents applauded my decision to study physics.* —*intr.* To express approval, especially by clapping the hands: *The audience applauded for ten minutes.* [First written down about 1475 in Middle English and spelled *applauden*, from Latin *applaudere* : *ad-*, to, for + *plaudere*, to clap.] **—ap•plaud′a•ble** *adj.* **—ap•plaud′er** *n.*

ap•plause (ə plôz′) *n.* **1.** Praise or approval expressed by the clapping of hands: *The guitarist's performance was cheered with loud applause.* **2.** Public approval: *The vaccine for polio received applause from doctors everywhere.*

ap•ple (ăp′əl) *n.* **1.** A firm rounded edible fruit having thin red, yellow, or green skin. **2.** The tree that bears such fruit. —***idiom.*** **apple of (one's) eye.** A person or thing that is especially liked or loved: *Her grandson is the apple of her eye.*

apple butter *n.* A dark-brown spread, somewhat like butter in consistency, made of stewed apples and spices.

ap•ple•jack (ăp′əl jăk′) *n.* **1.** Brandy distilled from hard cider. **2.** An alcoholic drink made from hard cider that has been frozen.

ap•ple•sauce (ăp′əl sôs′) *n.* Apples stewed to a pulp and sweetened.

ap•pli•ance (ə plī′əns) *n.* A machine, such as a toaster or dishwasher, used to perform a household task.

ap•pli•ca•ble (ăp′lĭ kə bəl *or* ə plĭk′ə bəl) *adj.* Capable of being applied; appropriate: *The new rule is not applicable in your case.* **—ap′pli•ca•bly** *adv.* **—ap′pli•ca•bil′i•ty** *n.*

ap•pli•cant (ăp′lĭ kənt) *n.* A person who applies for something: *an applicant for a job.*

ap•pli•ca•tion (ăp′lĭ kā′shən) *n.* **1.** The act of applying: *Careless application of paint left several bare spots on the wall.* **2.** Something that is applied, such as a medicine or a cosmetic: *a thick application of salve on a burn.* **3.** A method of applying or using; a specific use: *the application of science to industry.* **4.** The capacity of being usable; relevance: *Geometry has practical application to flying an airplane.* **5.** Careful work and attention; diligence: *Their application was rewarded by good grades in school.* **6.a.** A request, as for a job or admittance to a school. **b.** The form or document upon which such a request is made.

ap•pli•ca•tor (ăp′lĭ kā′tər) *n.* An instrument for applying something, such as medicine or glue.

ap•plied (ə plīd′) *adj.* Put into practice; used in a particular way: *The new yacht was designed using applied physics.*

ap•pli•qué (ăp′lĭ kā′) *n.* A decoration, design, or trimming made by sewing or attaching pieces of one material to the surface of another. —*tr.v.* **ap•pli•quéd, ap•pli•qué•ing, ap•pli•qués.** To put on or apply as appliqué: *appliqué a monogram on a coat.*

ap•ply (ə plī′) *v.* **ap•plied, ap•ply•ing, ap•plies.** —*tr.* **1.** To put on, upon, or to: *apply a little bit of glue to the paper.* **2.** To put to or adapt for a special use: *The Red Cross applied all its money to medical supplies.* **3.** To put into action: *apply the brakes.* **4.** To use (a special word or phrase) in referring to someone or something: Underground Railroad *was the name applied to the system that helped fugitive slaves escape.* **5.** To devote (oneself or one's efforts) to something: *The students applied themselves to their homework.* —*intr.* **1.** To be pertinent or relevant: *This rule for quiet in the library does not apply during a fire drill.* **2.** To request employment, acceptance, or admission: *Several people applied for the same job. Many high-school students applied to college.* [First written down about 1380 in Middle English and spelled *applien*, from Latin *applicāre*, to affix : *ad-*, to + *plicāre*, to fold together.] **—ap•pli′er** *n.*

ap•point (ə point′) *tr.v.* **ap•point•ed, ap•point•ing, ap•points.** **1.** To select or designate for an office, position, or duty: *appoint a new police chief.* **2.** To decide on or set by authority: *appointed three o'clock for the next meeting.* **3.** To furnish; equip: *The playroom was appointed with sturdy furniture.* [First written down about 1385 in Middle English and spelled *appointen*, from Old French *a point*, to the point.] **—ap•point′er** *n.*

ap•point•ee (ə poin′tē′ *or* ăp′oin tē′) *n.* A person who is appointed to an office, position, or duty.

ap•point•ive (ə poin′tĭv) *adj.* Relating to or filled by appointment: *an appointive office.*

ap•point•ment (ə point′mənt) *n.* **1.a.** The act of appointing to an office or position: *The appointment of a school principal is an important decision.* **b.** The office or position to which a person has been appointed: *Our principal accepted the appointment as superintendent.* **2.** An arrangement for a meeting at a particular time or place: *I called the dentist to change the time of my appointment.* **3. appointments.** Furnishings, fittings, or equipment: *tables,*

ă	pat	oi	boy
ā	pay	ou	out
âr	care	ŏŏ	took
ä	father	ōō	boot
ĕ	pet	ŭ	cut
ē	be	ûr	urge
ĭ	pit	th	thin
ī	pie	*th*	this
îr	pier	hw	whoop
ŏ	pot	zh	vision
ō	toe	ə	about
ô	paw	N	*French* bon

chairs, lamps and other appointments of the room.

Ap•po•mat•tox (ăp′ə măt′əks). A town of south-central Virginia southwest of Richmond. Confederate general Robert E. Lee surrendered to Union general Ulysses S. Grant at **Appomattox Courthouse** on April 9, 1865, ending the Civil War.

ap•por•tion (ə pôr′shən) *tr.v.* **ap•por•tioned, ap•por•tion•ing, ap•por•tions.** To divide and assign according to some plan or proportion; allot: *apportion money for several departments.*

ap•por•tion•ment (ə pôr′shən mənt) *n.* The act of apportioning or the condition of being apportioned: *the apportionment of taxes to pay for expenses of running the town government.*

ap•po•site (ăp′ə zĭt) *adj.* Appropriate or relevant.

ap•po•si•tion (ăp′ə zĭsh′ən) *n.* **1.** The act of placing side by side or next to each other. **2.a.** In grammar, a construction in which a noun or noun phrase is placed with another noun as a further explanation or description. **b.** The relationship between such nouns or noun phrases. For example, *Rufus* and *the scientist* are in apposition in the sentence *Rufus, the scientist, made another discovery.* **—ap′po•si′tion•al** *adj.* **—ap′po•si′tion•al•ly** *adv.*

ap•pos•i•tive (ə pŏz′ĭ tĭv) *adj.* Of, relating to, or being in apposition: *an appositive phrase.* *—n.* A noun or phrase that is in apposition with another noun. In the sentence *My friend the chemist works in a laboratory,* the appositive is *the chemist.*

ap•prais•al (ə prā′zəl) *n.* **1.** The act or an instance of setting a value or price: *The carpenter's appraisal for installing a new door took only a few minutes.* **2.** An official or expert estimate of something, as for quality or worth.

ap•praise (ə prāz′) *tr.v.* **ap•praised, ap•prais•ing, ap•prais•es. 1.** To set a value on; fix a price for: *The jeweler appraised the customer's ring.* **2.** To estimate the quality, amount, or size of; judge: *The captain appraised the condition of the scuba gear and found it was excellent.* [First written down before 1420 in Middle English and spelled *appreisen,* from Late Latin *appretiāre* : Latin *ad-*, to + Latin *pretium,* price.] **—ap•prais′er** *n.* **—ap•prais′ing•ly** *adv.*

ap•pre•cia•ble (ə prē′shə bəl) *adj.* Capable of being noticed or measured; noticeable: *an appreciable difference in the newly painted house.* **—ap•pre′cia•bly** *adv.*

ap•pre•ci•ate (ə prē′shē āt′) *v.* **ap•pre•ci•at•ed, ap•pre•ci•at•ing, ap•pre•ci•ates.** *—tr.* **1.** To recognize the worth, quality, or importance of; value highly: *The citizens of the new democracy appreciate their freedoms.* **2.** To be aware of or sensitive to; realize: *I appreciate the difficulty of your situation.* **3.** To be thankful for: *The neighbors appreciated our help.* *—intr.* To rise in price or value: *The value of the painting has appreciated over the last ten years.* [First written down in 1655 in Modern English, from Late Latin *appretiāre,* to appraise.] **—ap•pre′ci•a′tor** *n.*

Synonyms: appreciate, value, prize, treasure, cherish. These verbs mean to have a favorable opinion of someone or something. **Appreciate** means to judge highly in comparison with something else: *That awful restaurant certainly taught me to appreciate home cooking.* **Value** means to have a high opinion of something's importance or worth: *A true democracy values the free exchange of ideas.* **Prize** often suggests feeling pride in owning something: *Steve prizes the movie star's autograph so highly that he is making a frame for it.* **Treasure** and **cherish** both mean to care for attentively and affectionately: *Susan treasures that quilt—it has been in her family for generations. A solid friendship is something to cherish.*

---

ap•pre•ci•a•tion (ə prē′shē ā′shən) *n.* **1.** Recognition of the worth, quality, or importance of something: *Your appreciation of her accomplishments has meant a lot to her.* **2.** Gratitude; gratefulness: *They expressed their appreciation with a gift.* **3.** Awareness of artistic values; understanding and enjoyment: *showing a great appreciation of music and sculpture.* **4.** A rise in value or price: *Appreciation of land value has made some farmers wealthy.*

ap•pre•cia•tive (ə prē′shə tĭv *or* ə prē′shē ā′tĭv) *adj.* Showing or feeling appreciation: *applause of an appreciative audience.* **—ap•pre′cia•tive•ly** *adv.*

ap•pre•hend (ăp′rĭ hĕnd′) *tr.v.* **ap•pre•hend•ed, ap•pre•hend•ing, ap•pre•hends. 1.** To take into custody; arrest: *Police officers apprehended the suspect.* **2.** To grasp mentally; understand: *We tried to apprehend the implications of her theory.* **3.** To look forward to fearfully; anticipate with anxiety. [First written down before 1398 in Middle English and spelled *apprehenden,* from Latin *apprehendere,* to seize : *ad-*, to + *prehendere,* to grasp.] **—ap′pre•hend′er** *n.*

ap•pre•hen•sion (ăp′rĭ hĕn′shən) *n.* **1.** Fear or dread of what may happen; anxiety about the future: *The fall in prices caused apprehension among the investors.* **2.** The ability to understand; understanding. **3.** The act of capturing; an arrest: *apprehension of a criminal.*

ap•pre•hen•sive (ăp′rĭ hĕn′sĭv) *adj.* Anxious or fearful; uneasy: *apprehensive about the future.* **—ap′pre•hen′sive•ly** *adv.* **—ap′pre•hen′sive•ness** *n.*

ap•pren•tice (ə prĕn′tĭs) *n.* **1.** A person who works for another without pay in return for instruction in a craft or trade. **2.** A person, usually a member of a labor union, who is learning a trade. **3.** A beginner. *—tr.v.* **ap•pren•ticed, ap•pren•tic•ing, ap•pren•tic•es.** To place as an apprentice: *In earlier times many children were apprenticed to craftsmen.* [First written down in 1307 in Middle English and spelled *apprentis,* from Latin *apprehendere,* to seize.]

ap•pren•tice•ship (ə prĕn′tĭs shĭp′) *n.* **1.** The condition of being an apprentice. **2.** The period during which one is an apprentice: *He acquired many skills in his long apprenticeship as an editor.*

ap•prise (ə prīz′) *tr.v.* **ap•prised, ap•pris•ing, ap•pris•es.** To cause to know; inform: *Please apprise your teacher of the principal's message.*

ap•proach (ə prōch′) *v.* **ap•proached, ap•proach•ing, ap•proach•es.** *—intr.* To come near or nearer in place or time: *As spring approached, our work neared completion.* *—tr.* **1.** To come near or nearer to (someone or something) in place or time: *The speaker approached the microphone. Our doctor is approaching retirement.* **2.** To come close to in quality, appearance, or other characteristics; approximate: *What could approach the beauty of this lake?* **3.** To begin to deal with or work on: *We approach the task with eagerness.* **4.** To make a proposal to; make overtures to: *I approached the owner for a job.* *—n.* **1.** The act of approaching: *The captain had to be cautious in his approach to the dock. Flocks fly southward at the approach of winter.* **2.** A way or method of dealing or working with someone or something: *a new approach to the problem.* **3.** A way of reaching a place; an access: *the approach to the bridge.* [First written down about 1300 in Middle English and spelled *approchen,* from Late Latin *appropiāre* : Latin *ad-*, to + Latin *propius,* nearer.] **—ap•proach′er** *n.*

ap•proach•a•ble (ə prō′chə bəl) *adj.* **1.** Capable of being reached; accessible: *a small town approachable only through a mountain pass.* **2.** Easy to talk to; friendly: *an approachable person.* **—ap•proach′a•bil′i•ty** *n.*

ap•pro•ba•tion (ăp′rə **bā′**shən) *n.* **1.** The act of approving, especially officially; approval: *The bill to protect the marsh received the approbation of all.* **2.** Praise; commendation: *not a murmur of approbation or blame.*

ap•pro•pri•ate (ə **prō′**prē ĭt) *adj.* Suitable for a particular person, condition, occasion, or place; proper: *What are the appropriate clothes for this occasion?* —*tr.v.* (ə **prō′**prē āt′). **ap•pro•pri•at•ed, ap•pro•pri•at•ing, ap•pro•pri•ates. 1.** To set apart for a particular use: *Congress appropriated money for education.* **2.** To take possession of exclusively for oneself, often without permission: *Another spectator appropriated my seat when I got up for a drink of water.* **—ap•pro′pri•ate•ly** *adv.* **—ap•pro′pri•ate•ness** *n.* **—ap•pro′pri•a′tor** *n.*

ap•pro•pri•a•tion (ə prō′prē **ā′**shən) *n.* **1.** The act of appropriating to oneself or to a specific use. **2.** Public funds set aside for a specific purpose: *Congressional appropriations for disaster relief.*

ap•prov•al (ə **prōō′**vəl) *n.* **1.** Favorable regard: *The voters expressed their approval by voting for our mayor again.* **2.** An official consent or sanction: *The article was published with the approval of the editors.* ***—idiom.*** **on approval.** For examination or trial by a customer without the obligation to buy: *We bought our new car on approval.*

ap•prove (ə **prōōv′**) *v.* **ap•proved, ap•prov•ing, ap•proves.** —*tr.* **1.** To confirm or consent to officially; sanction; ratify: *The Senate approved the treaty.* **2.** To regard favorably; consider right or good: *The country approved the President's decision to fund more medical research.* —*intr.* To feel, voice, or demonstrate approval: *The Puritans did not approve of card playing or other amusements on Sunday.* [First written down about 1300 in Middle English and spelled *approven*, to show to be true, from Latin *approbāre* : *ad-*, to + *probāre*, to test (from *probus*, good).]

ap•prov•ing•ly (ə **prōō′**vĭng lē) *adv.* In a manner that expresses approval: *Our teacher nodded approvingly.*

approx. *abbr.* An abbreviation of: **1.** Approximate. **2.** Approximately.

ap•prox•i•mate (ə **prŏk′**sə mĭt) *adj.* Almost exact or accurate: *the approximate height of the building.* —*v.* (ə **prŏk′**sə māt′). **ap•prox•i•mat•ed, ap•prox•i•mat•ing, ap•prox•i•mates.** —*tr.* To come close to; be nearly the same as: *The temperatures of the Mediterranean Sea approximate those of Caribbean waters.* —*intr.* To come near or close in degree, nature, or other characteristic. **—ap•prox′i•mate•ly** *adv.*

ap•prox•i•ma•tion (ə prŏk′sə **mā′**shən) *n.* Something that is almost, but not quite, exact, correct, or true: *This table contains metric approximations of measures in yards, feet, and inches.*

ap•pur•te•nance (ə **pûr′**tn əns) *n.* **1.** Something added to another, more important thing; an appendage; an accessory: *The television set is an appurtenance of modern living.* **2. appurtenances.** Equipment, such as clothing or tools, used for a specific purpose; gear: *a tent, cooking utensils, and other appurtenances of camping.* **3.** In law, a right, privilege, or property that belongs with a principal property and goes along with it in case of sale or inheritance.

Apr. or **Apr** *abbr.* An abbreviation of April.

a•pri•cot (**ăp′**rĭ kŏt′ *or* **ā′**prĭ kŏt′) *n.* **1.** A juicy yellow-orange fruit similar to a peach. **2.** The tree that bears such fruit. **3.** A yellowish orange. [First written down in 1551 in Modern English and spelled *abrecock*, ultimately from Latin *praecoquus*, ripened early : *prae-*, before + *coquere*, to ripen.]

A•pril (**ā′**prəl) *n.* The fourth month of the year in the Gregorian calendar, having 30 days. [First written down about 1375 in Middle English, from Latin *aprīlis*.]

April Fools' Day (fōōlz) *n.* April 1, traditionally celebrated as a day for playing practical jokes.

a•pron (**ā′**prən) *n.* **1.** A garment worn over the front of the body and usually tied in the back to protect the clothes. **2.** The paved strip in front of an airport hangar or terminal. **3.** The part of the stage in a theater that is in front of the curtain. [First written down in 1307 in Middle English, from *an apron*, alteration of *a napron*, from Old French *naperon*, from Latin *mappa*, napkin.]

ap•ro•pos (ăp′rə **pō′**) *adj.* Relevant or fitting: *The teacher's explanation was apropos to the story we read.* —*adv.* At an appropriate time. —*prep.* Concerning; regarding: *Apropos our appointment, I'm afraid I can't make it.*

apropos of *prep.* With regard to: *The candidate told a funny story apropos of politics.*

apse (ăps) *n.* A semicircular, usually domed, projection of a building, especially the end of a church in which the altar is located.

apt (ăpt) *adj.* **1.** Exactly suitable; appropriate: *The alert student gave an apt reply.* **2.** Having a tendency; inclined: *Most people are apt to accept the advice of an expert.* **3.** Quick to learn: *an apt student with high grades.* [First written down about 1350 in Middle English, from Latin *aptus*, past participle of *apere*, to fasten.] **—apt′ly** *adv.* **—apt′ness** *n.*

apt. *abbr.* An abbreviation of apartment.

ap•ti•tude (**ăp′**tĭ tōōd′ *or* **ăp′**tĭ **tyōōd′**) *n.* **1.** A natural ability or talent: *She has a remarkable aptitude for mathematics.* **2.** Quickness in learning and understanding: *a student with high grades showing unusual aptitude.*

aptitude test *n.* A test used to measure a person's ability to learn some particular skill or acquire information.

A•qa•ba (**ä′**kə bə *or* **ăk′**ə bə), **Gulf of.** An arm of the Red Sea between the Sinai Peninsula and northwest Saudi Arabia.

aq•ua (**ăk′**wə *or* **ä′**kwə) *n., pl.* **aq•uae** (**ăk′**wē *or* **ä′**kwī′) or **aq•uas. 1.** Water. **2.** A light bluish green.

aq•ua•cul•ture (**ăk′**wə kŭl′chər) also **aq•ui•cul•ture** (**ăk′**wĭ kŭl′chər) *n.* The growing and harvesting of plants or fish in an artificial body of water.

Aq•ua-Lung (**ăk′**wə lŭng′). A trademark for an underwater breathing apparatus.

aq•ua•ma•rine (ăk′wə mə **rēn′**) *n.* **1.** A transparent blue-green variety of beryl, used as a gemstone. **2.** A pale blue to light greenish blue.

aq•ua•plane (**ăk′**wə plăn′) *n.* A board on which a person stands and rides while it is towed over the water by a motorboat. —*tr.v.* **aq•ua•planed, aq•ua•plan•ing, aq•ua•planes.** To ride on an aquaplane. **—aq′ua•plan′er** *n.*

aqua re•gi•a (**rē′**jē ə *or* **rē′**jə) *n.* A fuming corrosive mixture of nitric acid and hydrochloric acid, used for testing metals and dissolving gold and platinum.

a•quar•i•um (ə **kwâr′**ē əm) *n., pl.* **a•quar•i•ums** or **a•quar•i•a** (ə **kwâr′**ē ə). **1.** A tank or other container, such as a glass bowl, filled with water for keeping and displaying fish or other animals and plants. **2.** A place where such animals and plants are displayed to the public.

A•quar•i•us (ə **kwâr′**ē əs) *n.* **1.** A constellation in the Southern Hemisphere near Pisces. **2.** The eleventh sign of the zodiac in astrology.

a•quat•ic (ə **kwăt′**ĭk *or* ə **kwŏt′**ĭk) *adj.* **1.** Consisting of, relating to, or being in water: *Lily pads grow in an aquatic environment.* **2.** Living or growing in or on the water: *The whale is an aquatic mammal,*

apricot

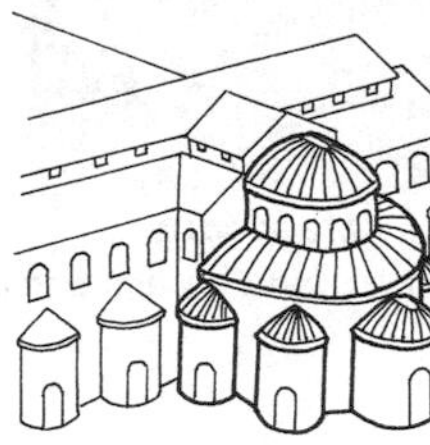

apse

ă	pat	oi	boy
ā	pay	ou	out
âr	care	ŏŏ	took
ä	father	ōō	boot
ĕ	pet	ŭ	cut
ē	be	ûr	urge
ĭ	pit	th	thin
ī	pie	*th*	this
îr	pier	hw	whoop
ŏ	pot	zh	vision
ō	toe	ə	about
ô	paw	N	*French* bon

aqueduct
Pont du Gard, near Nîmes, France

arabesque
Carla Stallings in *Concerto Barocco*

and seaweeds are aquatic plants. **3.** Taking place in or on the water: *diving and other aquatic sports.*

aq•ue•duct (ăk′wĭ dŭkt′) *n.* **1.** A large pipe or channel that carries water from a distant source. **2.** A structure that supports such a pipe or channel across low ground or a river. [First written down in 1538 in Modern English, from Latin *aquaeductus* : *aquae*, of water + *ductus*, a leading.]

a•que•ous (ā′kwē əs *or* ăk′wē əs) *adj.* Of, resembling, containing, or dissolved in water: *an aqueous solution of salt and water.*

aqueous humor *n.* A clear fluid that fills the space between the cornea and lens of the eye.

aq•ui•cul•ture (ăk′wĭ kŭl′chər) *n.* Variant of **aquaculture.**

aq•ui•fer (ăk′wə fər) *n.* An underground layer of sand, gravel, or spongy rock that collects water.

aq•ui•line (ăk′wə līn′ *or* ăk′wə lĭn) *adj.* **1.** Curved or hooked like an eagle's beak: *an aquiline nose.* **2.** Of, relating to, or resembling an eagle. [First written down in 1646 in Modern English, from *aquilīnus*, from *aquila*, eagle.]

A•qui•nas (ə kwī′nəs), Saint **Thomas.** 1225–1274. Italian monk, theologian, and philosopher.

A•qui•no (ä kē′nō), **Corazón Cojuangco.** Born 1933. Philippine political leader who became president of the country in 1986.

Ar The symbol for the element **argon.**

AR *abbr.* An abbreviation of Arkansas.

–ar *suff.* A suffix that means of, relating to, or resembling: *angular; linear.*

Ar•ab (ăr′əb) *n.* **1.** A member of a Semitic people inhabiting Arabia. **2.** A member of an Arabic-speaking people. **—Ar′ab** *adj.*

ar•a•besque (ăr′ə bĕsk′) *n.* **1.** A ballet position in which the dancer stands on one leg with the other leg extending straight back. **2.** An ornamental pattern of interwoven flowers, leaves, or geometric forms.

A•ra•bi•a (ə rā′bē ə) also **A•ra•bi•an Peninsula** (ə rā′bē ən). A peninsula of southwest Asia between the Red Sea and the Persian Gulf. It includes the countries of Saudi Arabia, Yemen, Oman, the United Arab Emirates, Qatar, Bahrain, and Kuwait.

Arabian horse *n.* Any of a breed of swift horse native to Arabia.

Arabian Sea. The northwest part of the Indian Ocean between Arabia and western India. It is an important trade route between India and the West.

Ar•a•bic (ăr′ə bĭk) *adj.* Of or relating to Arabia, the Arabs, or their language or culture. *—n.* A Semitic language consisting of many dialects that is spoken in many countries in southwestern Asia and northern Africa.

Arabic numeral *n.* One of the numerical symbols 1, 2, 3, 4, 5, 6, 7, 8, 9, or 0. They are called Arabic numerals because they were introduced into western Europe from sources of Arabic scholarship.

ar•a•ble (ăr′ə bəl) *adj.* Fit for cultivation.

a•rach•nid (ə răk′nĭd) *n.* Any of a group of animals that resemble insects but have eight rather than six legs, no wings or antennae, and a body divided into two rather than three parts. Spiders and scorpions are arachnids.

Ar•a•gon (ăr′ə gŏn′). A region and former kingdom of northeast Spain. It was united with Castile in 1479 to form the core of modern Spain.

Ar•al Sea (ăr′əl). An inland sea between southern Kazakhstan and northwest Uzbekistan east of the Caspian Sea. The diversion of water from its major sources has greatly reduced the size of the Aral Sea.

Ar•a•ma•ic (ăr′ə mā′ĭk) *n.* The Semitic language originally of the ancient Syrians and Mesopotamians that was spoken throughout Southwest Asia from the 7th century B.C. to the 7th century A.D.

A•rap•a•ho (ə răp′ə hō′) *n., pl.* **Arapaho** or **A•rap•a•hos. 1.** A member of a Native American people living in Oklahoma and Wyoming. **2.** The Algonquian language of the Arapaho.

Ar•a•rat (ăr′ə răt′), **Mount.** A mountain peak of extreme eastern Turkey near the Iranian border rising to about 16,945 feet (5,168 meters). It is the traditional resting place of Noah's ark.

Ar•au•ca•ni•an (ăr′ô kā′nē ən) *n.* A family of languages of a group of Native American peoples of Chile and Argentina. **—Ar′au•ca′ni•an** *adj.*

Ar•a•wak (ăr′ə wäk′) *n., pl.* **Arawak** or **Ar•a•waks. 1.** A member of a Native American people formerly living in the West Indies and now living chiefly in northeast South America. **2.** The Arawakan language of the Arawak.

Ar•a•wa•kan (ăr′ə wä′kən) *n., pl.* **Arawakan** or **Ar•a•wa•kans.** The largest and most important group of languages of Native American peoples, spoken in a wide region of the Amazon basin. **—Ar′a•wa′kan** *adj.*

ar•bi•ter (är′bĭ tər) *n.* **1.** A person chosen to judge a dispute; an arbitrator. **2.** A person or thing having the power to ordain or judge at will: *Willingness of the public to accept new styles is the final arbiter of the fashion world.*

ar•bi•trar•y (är′bĭ trĕr′ē) *adj.* **1.** Based on a whim, impulse, or chance, not on reason or law: *Drawing numbers out of a hat was an arbitrary way to select the captain of the team.* **2.** Not limited by law; despotic: *The dictator's arbitrary government jailed many of his political opponents.* **—ar′bi•trar′i•ly** (är′bĭ trâr′ə lē) *adv.* **—ar′bi•trar′i•ness** *n.*

ar•bi•trate (är′bĭ trāt′) *v.* **ar•bi•trat•ed, ar•bi•trat•ing, ar•bi•trates.** *—tr.* **1.** To decide as an arbitrator: *arbitrate the boundary dispute between the two neighbors.* **2.** To submit to judgment by arbitration: *Management and labor agreed to arbitrate their differences.* *—intr.* **1.** To serve as an arbitrator: *Even strong nations must allow others to arbitrate between them.* **2.** To submit a dispute to arbitration.

ar•bi•tra•tion (är′bĭ trā′shən) *n.* The process of referring the issues in a dispute to an impartial person or group for judgment or settlement: *Many disputes between labor and management are settled by arbitration.*

ar•bi•tra•tor (är′bĭ trā′tər) *n.* **1.** A person chosen to settle a dispute or controversy. **2.** A person having the ability or power to make authoritative decisions; an arbiter.

ar•bor (är′bər) *n.* A shaded bower, often made of latticework on which vines or other climbing plants grow: *a grape arbor; a rose arbor.* [First written down before 1300 in Middle English and spelled *erber*, from Old French *erbier*, garden, from *erbe*, herb.]

Arbor Day *n.* A day observed in many areas by planting trees, often occurring in the spring.

ar•bo•re•al (är bôr′ē əl) *adj.* **1.** Relating to or resembling a tree. **2.** Living in trees: *monkeys, lemurs, and other arboreal animals.* [First written down before 1667 in Modern English, from Latin *arbor*, tree.] **—ar•bo′re•al•ly** *adv.*

ar•bo•re•tum (är′bə rē′təm) *n., pl.* **ar•bo•re•tums** or **ar•bo•re•ta** (är′bə rē′tə). A place for the study and exhibition of growing trees, especially rare trees.

ar•bor•vi•tae (är′bər vī′tē) *n.* Any of several evergreen trees or shrubs having small leaves, often planted in hedges.

ar•bu•tus (är byōō′təs) *n.* A trailing plant having evergreen leaves and fragrant pink or white flowers that bloom in early spring.

arc (ärk) *n.* **1.** Something shaped like a curve or

arch: *the arc of a rainbow.* **2.** A continuous part of a circle or other curve. **3.** A stream of brilliant light or sparks produced when an electric current jumps across the gap between two electrodes separated by a gas. *—intr.v.* **arced** or **arcked** (ärkt), **arc•ing** or **arck•ing** (är′kĭng), **arcs. 1.** To form an arc. **2.** To take or follow a curved path: *The shooting star arced across the sky.*
❑ *These sound alike:* **arc, ark** (ship).

ar•cade (är **kād′**) *n.* **1.** A series of arches supported by columns or pillars. **2.** A roofed passageway, especially one with shops on either side. **3.** A store or room that has coin-operated games.

Ar•ca•di•a (är **kā′**dē ə). A region of ancient Greece in the Peloponnesus. According to popular legend, its relatively isolated inhabitants lived a simple, pastoral life.

Arc de Tri•omphe (ärk′ de trē **ôɴf′**) *n.* An arch in Paris, built to celebrate the victories of Napoleon I.

arch[1] (ärch) *n.* **1.a.** A curved structure that spans an open space and supports a roadway, ceiling, or similar load, so that the weight of the load is borne by the sides. **b.** A monument built in this form. **2.** Something curved like an arch: *the arch of leaves overhanging the lane.* **3.** Any of various arch-shaped structures of the body: *the arch of the foot.* *—v.* **arched, arch•ing, arch•es.** *—tr.* **1.** To cause to form an arch or a similar curve: *The cat arched its back.* **2.** To supply with an arch: *The builders arched the entrance to the store.* **3.** To span: *The bridge arched the river.* *—intr.* To extend in an arch: *The bridge arched across the river.* [First written down about 1300 in Middle English, from Latin *arcus.*]

arch[2] (ärch) *adj.* **1.** Chief; principal: *our arch rivals.* **2.** Mischievous; roguish: *an arch reply.* [First written down in 1547 in Modern English, from *arch-*, chief, from Greek *arkhi-.*] **—arch′ly** *adv.* **—arch′ness** *n.*

arch– *pref.* A prefix that means principal or chief: *archdiocese; archenemy.*

ar•chae•o•log•i•cal or **ar•che•o•log•i•cal** (är′kē ə **lŏj′**ĭ kəl) *adj.* Of or relating to archaeology. **—ar′chae•o•log′i•cal•ly** *adv.*

ar•chae•ol•o•gist or **ar•che•ol•o•gist** (är′kē **ŏl′**ə jĭst) *n.* A person who studies or is an expert in archaeology.

ar•chae•ol•o•gy or **ar•che•ol•o•gy** (är′kē **ŏl′**ə jē) *n.* The scientific recovery and study of the remains of past human activities, such as burials, buildings, tools, and pottery.

ar•chae•op•ter•yx (är′kē **ŏp′**tər ĭks) *n.* An extinct bird found as a fossil and having certain of the characteristics of a reptile, such as teeth.

ar•cha•ic (är **kā′**ĭk) *adj.* **1.** Of, relating to, or characteristic of a very early, often primitive, period: *archaic fish.* **2.** Not current; antiquated: *archaic laws to regulate horse-drawn traffic.* **3.** Of or relating to words that were once common but are now used chiefly to suggest an earlier style: Methinks *is an archaic word meaning "It seems to me."* [First written down before 1804 in Modern English and spelled *archaical*, from Greek *arkhaios*, ancient, from *arkhē*, beginning.] **—ar•cha′i•cal•ly** *adv.*

ar•cha•ism (**är′**kē ĭz′əm *or* **är′**kā ĭz′əm) *n.* An archaic word or expression.

arch•an•gel (**ärk′**ān′jəl) *n.* An angel of high rank.

arch•bish•op (ärch **bĭsh′**əp) *n.* A bishop of the highest rank, heading an archdiocese or church province.

arch•dea•con (ärch **dē′**kən) *n.* A church official, especially of the Anglican Church, in charge of business and other affairs in a diocese.

arch•di•o•cese (ärch **dī′**ə sĭs *or* ärch **dī′**ə sēs′) *n.* The area under an archbishop's jurisdiction.

arch•duch•ess (ärch **dŭch′**ĭs) *n.* **1.** The wife or widow of an archduke. **2.** A princess of the former Austrian royal family.

arch•duke (ärch **do͞ok′** *or* ärch **dyo͞ok′**) *n.* A prince of the former Austrian royal family.

arched (ärcht) *adj.* **1.** Forming an arch or a curve like that of an arch: *the arched dome of the night sky.* **2.** Provided, made, or covered with an arch: *an arched bridge.*

arch•en•e•my (ärch **ĕn′**ə mē) *n.* A chief or most important enemy: *France was the archenemy of Britain in Colonial America.*

ar•che•o•log•i•cal (är′kē ə **lŏj′**ĭ kəl) *adj.* Variant of **archaeological.**

ar•che•ol•o•gist (är′kē **ŏl′**ə jĭst) *n.* Variant of **archaeologist.**

ar•che•ol•o•gy (är′kē **ŏl′**ə jē) *n.* Variant of **archaeology.**

arch•er (**är′**chər) *n.* A person who shoots with a bow and arrow.

arch•er•y (**är′**chə rē) *n.* **1.** The sport or skill of shooting with a bow and arrow. **2.** A group of archers.

ar•che•type (**är′**kĭ tīp′) *n.* An original model or form after which other, similar things are patterned: *The Wright brothers' first plane served as the archetype for later airplanes.*

Ar•chi•me•des (är′kə **mē′**dēz). 287?–212 B.C. Greek mathematician, engineer, and inventor. He discovered formulas for the area and volume of various geometric figures.

ar•chi•pel•a•go (är′kə **pĕl′**ə gō′) *n., pl.* **ar•chi•pel•a•goes** or **ar•chi•pel•a•gos. 1.** A large group of islands. **2.** A sea in which there is a large group of islands.

ar•chi•tect (**är′**kĭ tĕkt′) *n.* **1.** A person who designs and directs the construction of buildings and other large structures. **2.** A person who plans or designs a project, especially one that requires long hard work: *The delegates to the Constitutional Convention were the architects of the Constitution.* [First written down in 1563 in Modern English, from Greek *arkhitektōn* : *arkhi-*, principal, chief + *tektōn*, builder.]

ar•chi•tec•tur•al (är′kĭ **tĕk′**chər əl) *adj.* Of or relating to architecture. **—ar′chi•tec′tur•al•ly** *adv.*

ar•chi•tec•ture (**är′**kĭ tĕk′chər) *n.* **1.** The art and occupation of designing and directing the construction of buildings and other large structures. **2.** A style of building: *Many government buildings in Washington, D.C. are patterned on classical architecture.* **3.** Buildings and other large structures: *the hulking architecture of the New York City skyline.* **4.** The orderly arrangement of parts; structure: *the architecture of a story.*

ar•chi•trave (**är′**kĭ trāv′) *n.* A horizontal piece supported by the columns of a building in classical architecture.

ar•chive (**är′**kīv′) *n.* **1.** A place where records and documents of historical interest are kept. Often used in the plural: *We went to the film archives to research silent movies.* **2.** A collection of such records and documents. Often used in the plural. **—ar•chi′val** *adj.*

arch•way (**ärch′**wā′) *n.* **1.** A passageway under an arch. **2.** An arch that covers or encloses an entrance or passageway.

–archy *suff.* A suffix that means a kind of rule or government: *oligarchy.*

arc lamp *n.* A lamp in which an electric current crosses between electrodes separated by a gas and generates an arc that produces light.

arc•tic (**ärk′**tĭk *or* **är′**tĭk) *adj.* Extremely cold; frigid: *arctic weather.* *—n.* A warm waterproof overshoe.

arch[1]
Arc de Triomphe, Paris, France

archery

ă	pat	oi	**boy**
ā	pay	ou	**out**
âr	care	o͝o	**took**
ä	father	o͞o	**boot**
ĕ	pet	ŭ	**cut**
ē	be	ûr	**urge**
ĭ	pit	th	**thin**
ī	pie	*th*	**this**
îr	pier	hw	**whoop**
ŏ	pot	zh	vision
ō	toe	ə	about
ô	paw	ɴ	*French* bon

arena
Boston Garden

Aristotle

Arizona

The name **Arizona** comes to us through Spanish from the Basque word *arizonac*, meaning "good oaks." A Basque-speaking Spaniard applied this name to the site of a large silver deposit.

[First written down about 1400 in Middle English and spelled *artic*, northern, from Greek *arktikos*, from *arktos*, bear, the northern constellation Ursa Major.]

Arc•tic (ärk′tĭk *or* är′tĭk). A region between the North Pole and the northern timberlines of North America and Eurasia. **—Arc′tic** *adj.*

Arctic Archipelago. A group of more than 50 large islands of Northwest Territories, Canada, in the Arctic Ocean between North America and Greenland.

Arctic Circle. The parallel of latitude approximately 66 degrees 33 minutes north. It forms the boundary between the North Temperate and North Frigid zones.

Arctic Ocean. The waters surrounding the North Pole between North America and Eurasia. The smallest ocean in the world, it is covered by ice throughout the year.

Arc•tu•rus (ärk to͝or′əs *or* ärk tyo͝or′əs) *n.* The brightest star in the northern sky. It is in the constellation Boötes

ar•dent (är′dnt) *adj.* **1.** Expressing or full of warmth of passion, desire, or other emotion; passionate: *an ardent plea to preserve the marsh.* **2.** Strongly enthusiastic; extremely devoted; eager: *an ardent defender of the free press.* [First written down before 1333 in Middle English and spelled *ardaunt*, from Latin *ārdēre*, to burn.] **—ar′dent•ly** *adv.*

ar•dor (är′dər) *n.* **1.** Great warmth or intensity of passion, desire, or other emotion. **2.** Intense enthusiasm or devotion; zeal: *the driving ardor of a reformer.*

ar•du•ous (är′jo͞o əs) *adj.* Demanding great effort; difficult: *arduous training; an arduous task.* **—ar′du•ous•ly** *adv.* **—ar′du•ous•ness** *n.*

are (är) *v.* **1.** Second person singular present tense of **be. 2.** First, second, and third person plural present tense of **be.** [First written down before 830 in Old English and spelled *earun.*]

ar•e•a (âr′ē ə) *n.* **1.a.** A section or region, as of land: *an industrial area full of factories; the Los Angeles area including its suburbs.* **b.** A part or section, as of a building: *The cafeteria is an eating area for employees.* **2.** A surface, especially a part of the earth's surface: *a mountainous area.* **3.** The extent of a surface or plane figure as measured in square units: *The area of a rectangle is the product of the lengths of two adjacent sides.* **4.** A range, as of activity or study: *the area of medical research.*

Area Code also **area code** *n.* A three-digit number assigned to a telephone area and used when placing a call to that area from outside of it.

ar•e•a•way (âr′ē ə wā′) *n.* **1.** A small sunken area allowing access or light and air to basement doors or windows. **2.** A passageway between buildings.

a•re•na (ə rē′nə) *n.* **1.** The space in the center of an ancient Roman amphitheater where athletic contests and other spectacles were held. **2.** A modern building for presenting sports events. **3.** An area of conflict or activity: *The new candidate stepped into the political arena.* [First written down in 1600 in Modern English, from Latin *arēna*, sand, a sand-strewn place of combat in an ampitheater.]

aren't (ärnt *or* är′ənt). **1.** Contraction of *are not*: *They aren't there anymore.* **2.** Contraction of *am not.* Used in questions: *I'm properly dressed for school, aren't I?*

Ar•es (âr′ēz) *n.* In Greek mythology, the god of war, identified with the Roman Mars.

Ar•gen•ti•na (är′jən tē′nə). A country of southeast South America stretching about 2,300 miles (3,701 kilometers) from its border with Bolivia to southern Tierra del Fuego, an island it shares with Chile. Argentina proclaimed its independence from Spain in 1816. Buenos Aires is the capital and the largest city. Population, 27,947,446.

Ar•go (är′gō′) *n.* In Greek mythology, Jason's ship in his search for the Golden Fleece.

ar•gon (är′gŏn′) *n. Symbol* **Ar** A colorless, odorless element that is an inert gas, used in electric light bulbs. See table at **element.**

Ar•go•naut (är′gə nôt′) *n.* In Greek mythology, any of the men who sail with Jason in search of the Golden Fleece.

ar•go•sy (är′gə sē) *n., pl.* **ar•go•sies. 1.** A big sailing merchant ship. **2.** A fleet of such ships. [First written down in 1577 in Modern English and spelled *ragusa*, from Italian *ragusea*, vessel of Ragusa (Dubrovnik, in southern Croatia).]

ar•got (är′gō *or* är′gət) *n.* The jargon or slang of a particular class or group of persons, often used to conceal meaning from outsiders.

ar•gue (är′gyo͞o) *v.* **ar•gued, ar•gu•ing, ar•gues.** *—tr.* **1.** To give reasons for or against (something, such as an opinion or proposal); debate: *The lawyer argued the case in court.* **2.** To prove or attempt to prove by reasoning; maintain: *I argued that the vacant lot should be turned into a park.* **3.** To give evidence of; indicate: *Her vocabulary argues that she has read a lot.* **4.** To persuade or influence, as by presenting reasons: *He would not let us argue him into leaving early.* *—intr.* **1.** To put forth reasons for or against something: *argue against building a new airport.* **2.** To engage in a quarrel; dispute: *The twins seldom argued with each other.* [First written down about 1303 in Middle English and spelled *arguen*, from Old French *arguer*, from Latin *arguere*, to make clear.] **—ar′gu•a•ble** *adj.* **—ar′gu•a•bly** *adv.* **—ar′gu•er** *n.*

ar•gu•ment (är′gyə mənt) *n.* **1.** A quarrel or dispute: *an argument over who goes first.* **2.** A discussion of differing points of view; a debate: *a scientific argument.* **3.** A statement in support of a position; a reason: *an argument for going.*

ar•gu•men•ta•tive (är′gyə mĕn′tə tĭv) *adj.* **1.** Given to or liking to argue: *an argumentative person.* **2.** Containing or full of arguments: *an argumentative paper.* **—ar′gu•men′ta•tive•ly** *adv.* **—ar′gu•men′ta•tive•ness** *n.*

Ar•gus (är′gəs) *n.* In Greek mythology, a giant with one hundred eyes.

ar•gyle also **ar•gyll** (är′gīl′) *n.* **1.** A knitting pattern made up of diamond shapes in contrasting colors. **2.** A sock knit in such a pattern. [First written down in 1899 in Modern English, after Clan Campbell of *Argyle, Argyll*, a former county of western Scotland, originally from the pattern of their tartan.]

a•ri•a (ä′rē ə) *n.* A piece written for a solo singer accompanied by instruments, as in an opera, a cantata, or an oratorio.

Ar•i•ad•ne (ăr′ē ăd′nē) *n.* In Greek mythology, the daughter of King Minos and Pasiphaë who helps Theseus escape from the Minotaur's labyrinth.

ar•id (ăr′ĭd) *adj.* **1.** Having little or no rainfall; dry; parched: *an arid desert; an arid wasteland.* **2.** Lifeless; dull: *a long arid book.* **—a•rid′i•ty** (ə rĭd′ĭtē), **ar′id•ness** *n.* **—ar′id•ly** *adv.*

Ar•ies (âr′ēz *or* âr′ē ēz′) *n.* The first sign of the zodiac in astrology.

a•right (ə rīt′) *adv.* Properly; correctly.

A•rik•a•ra (ə rĭk′ər ə) *n., pl.* **Arikara** or **A•rik•a•ras. 1.** A member of a Native American people of North Dakota. **2.** The Caddoan language of the Arikara.

a•rise (ə rīz′) *intr.v.* **a•rose** (ə rōz′), **a•ris•en** (ə rĭz′ən), **a•ris•ing, a•ris•es. 1.** To get up: *He arose from his chair to greet me.* **2.** To come into being; appear: *Take advantage of opportunities as they arise.* **3.** To ascend; move upward: *Mist arose from* *the lake.* **4.** To result; proceed: *The breakdown arose from some temporary defect.*

ar•is•toc•ra•cy (ăr′ĭ **stŏk′**rə sē) *n., pl.* **ar•is•toc•ra•cies. 1.a.** A social class based on inherited wealth, status, and sometimes titles. **b.** A government controlled by such a class. **2.** A group considered superior to others: *the aristocracy of local landowners.*

a•ris•to•crat (ə **rĭs′**tə krăt′ *or* **ăr′**ĭs tə krăt′) *n.* **1.** A member of the aristocracy or nobility. **2.** A person or thing with the tastes, preferences, or other characteristics of the aristocracy. **3.** A person who favors government by the aristocracy. [First written down in 1789 in Modern English, from Greek *aristokratia*, aristocracy : *aristos*, best + *kratos*, power.]

a•ris•to•crat•ic (ə rĭs′tə **krăt′**ĭk *or* ăr′ĭs tə **krăt′**ĭk) *adj.* **1.** Of, relating to, or characteristic of the aristocracy: *aristocratic manners.* **2.** Having an aristocracy as a form of government: *aristocratic city-states of ancient Greece.* **—a•ris′to•crat′i•cal•ly** *adv.*

Ar•is•to•te•li•an (ăr′ĭ stə **tē′**lē ən *or* ə rĭs′tə **tē′**lē ən) *adj.* Of or relating to the Greek philosopher Aristotle or his philosophy. *—n.* **1.** A follower of Aristotle or his teachings. **2.** A person who is guided by experience or tends to be scientific in methods or thought. **—Ar′is•to•te′li•an•ism** *n.*

Ar•is•tot•le (**ăr′**ĭ stŏt′l). 384–322 B.C. Greek philosopher who wrote works on logic, the natural sciences, politics, and poetry.

a•rith•me•tic (ə **rĭth′**mĭ tĭk) *n.* **1.** The study of numbers and their properties under the operations of addition, subtraction, multiplication, and division. **2.** Calculation using these operations. *—adj.* **ar•ith•met•ic** (ăr′ĭth **mĕt′**ĭk) or **ar•ith•met•i•cal** (ăr′ĭth **mĕt′**ĭ kəl). Of or relating to arithmetic; according to the rules of arithmetic: *arithmetic computations.* [First written down about 1250 in Middle English and spelled *arsmetike*, from Greek *arithmētikē (tekhnē)*, (the art) of counting, from *arithmein*, to count.] **—ar′ith•met′i•cal•ly** *adv.*

a•rith•me•ti•cian (ə rĭth′mə **tĭsh′**ən) *n.* A person who specializes in the study of arithmetic.

arithmetic mean *n.* An average of a set of quantities obtained by adding all the quantities and dividing the result by the number of quantities in the set.

arithmetic progression *n.* A sequence of numbers such as 1, 3, 5, 7, 9 . . . or 14, 9, 4, −1 . . . in which the difference between any successive pair of numbers is the same.

Ariz. *abbr.* An abbreviation of Arizona.

Ar•i•zo•na (ăr′ĭ **zō′**nə). A state of the southwest United States west of New Mexico on the Mexican border. It was admitted as the 48th state in 1912. The area was acquired by the United States in 1848 through a treaty with Mexico. Phoenix is the capital and the largest city. Population, 3,677,985. —SEE NOTE.

ark (ärk) *n.* **1.** In the Bible, the ship built by Noah for survival during the Flood. **2.** The Ark of the Covenant. **3.** A cabinet in a synagogue in which the scrolls of the Torah are kept; the Holy Ark. [First written down before 830 in Old English and spelled *arc*, from Latin *arca*, chest.]

❑ *These sound alike:* **ark, arc** (part of a curve).

Ark. *abbr.* An abbreviation of Arkansas.

Ar•kan•sas (**är′**kən sô′). A state of the south-central United States north of Louisiana and bordered on the east by the Mississippi River. It was admitted as the 25th state in 1836. The region passed to the United States in 1803 as part of the Louisiana Purchase. Little Rock is the capital and the largest city. Population, 2,362,239. —SEE NOTE.

Ar•kan•sas River (**är′**kən sô′ *or* är **kăn′**zəs). A river of the south-central United States rising in central Colorado and flowing about 1,450 miles (2,333 kilometers) to the Mississippi River in southeast Arkansas. It was an important trade and travel route in the 19th century.

Ark of the Covenant *n.* In the Bible, the chest containing the Ten Commandments on stone tablets, carried by the Hebrews during their wanderings in the desert.

Ar•ling•ton (**är′**lĭng tən). A county and city of northern Virginia across the Potomac River from Washington, D.C. It is the site of **Arlington National Cemetery**, where American war dead and other prominent figures are buried. Population, 170,936.

arm[1] (ärm) *n.* **1.a.** Either of the upper limbs of the human body, connecting the hand and wrist to the shoulder. **b.** The forelimb of an animal, as of an ape or a bear. **2.** A part that branches or seems to branch from a main body: *an arm of the sea; the arm of a starfish.* **3.** Something designed to cover or support a human arm: *the arm of a shirt; the arm of a chair.* **4.** Authority or effect that extends or seems to extend from a main source: *the long arm of the law.* ***—idioms.*** **an arm and a leg.** An excessively high price: *charged me an arm and a leg for the antiques.* **at arm's length. 1.** With the arm extended straight out from the body: *The art dealer held the picture at arm's length and looked at it.* **2.** At a distance; not on friendly or intimate terms: *A shy person often keeps acquaintances at an arm's length.* **with open arms.** In a very friendly manner: *welcomed friends with open arms.* [First written down about 725 in Old English and spelled *earm.*] **—armed** *adj.*

arm[2] (ärm) *n.* **1.** A weapon, especially a firearm: *the troops stacked the arms and made camp.* **2. arms.** Warfare or military power: *The besieged city could not be taken by force of arms.* **3. arms.** A design or emblem used as an identifying mark, as by a family or nation. *—v.* **armed, arm•ing, arms.** *—tr.* **1.** To equip with weapons or other means of defense: *The governor of the young colony armed civilians during the emergency.* **2.** To equip or provide with something necessary or useful: *Many people do not arm themselves with the facts before getting into an argument.* **3.** To make ready; prepare: *arm the mechanism of a trap.* *—intr.* To prepare for war, as by amassing weapons and training soldiers: *As the countries armed, the leaders reached a settlement.* ***—idiom.*** **up in arms.** Very upset; angry: *The whole neighborhood was up in arms when the mayor closed the fire station.* [First written down before 1250 in Middle English and spelled *armes*, weapons, from Latin *arma.*]

ar•ma•da (är **mä′**də *or* är **mā′**də) *n.* A big fleet of warships. [First written down in 1533 in Modern English, from Spanish, from Medieval Latin *armāta.*]

ar•ma•dil•lo (är′mə **dĭl′**ō) *n., pl.* **ar•ma•dil•los.** Any of several burrowing mammals of southern North America and South America, having a covering of jointed bony plates. [First written down in 1577 in Modern English, from Spanish, diminutive of *armado*, armored, from Latin *armāre*, to arm, from *arma*, arms.] —SEE NOTE.

Ar•ma•ged•don (är′mə **gĕd′**n) *n.* **1.** In the Bible, the site of the final battle between good and evil, to occur at the end of the world. **2.** A decisive conflict.

ar•ma•ment (**är′**mə mənt) *n.* **1.** The weapons, ammunition, and other equipment to fight a war or skirmish. **2.** All the military forces and war equipment of a country. Often used in the plural. **3.** Preparation for war: *Armament is a function of national security in time of war.*

Arkansas

The state name **Arkansas** comes from *akansea*, the Illinois name for the Quapaw, the Native American people living along the Arkansas River. The final *s* was added to the name by French explorers to make the word plural when referring to this group. The pronunciation, with the final *s* silent, comes from the French.

armadillo
Nine-banded armadillo

Word History: armadillo

The Spanish word **armadillo** literally means "a little armored animal." It comes from the adjective *armado*, "armed, armored," and the suffix *–illo*, which forms *diminutives*, words that express youngness, smallness, or affection. **Peccadillo**, "a minor flaw or fault," is another word formed with the same suffix. Other diminutive endings in English are *–let*, as in **booklet**, *–ette*, as in **kitchenette**, and *–ling*, as in **duckling** and **darling** (from the adjective **dear** plus the suffix *–ling*).

ă	pat	oi	**boy**
ā	pay	ou	**out**
âr	care	ŏŏ	took
ä	father	ōō	boot
ĕ	pet	ŭ	cut
ē	be	ûr	urge
ĭ	pit	th	**thin**
ī	pie	*th*	**this**
îr	pier	hw	**wh**oop
ŏ	pot	zh	vision
ō	toe	ə	about
ô	paw	N	*French* bon

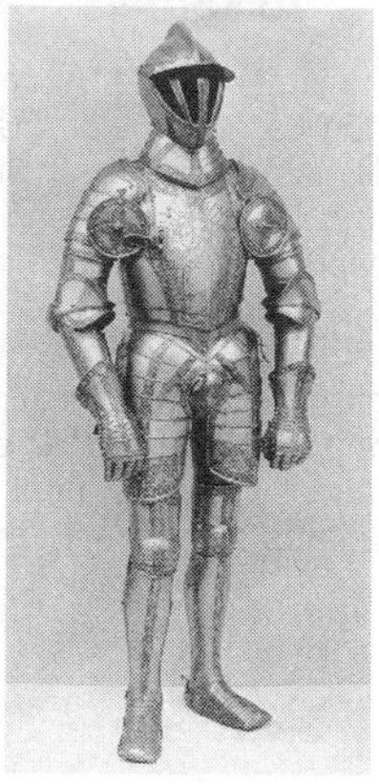

armor
16th-century German

Neil Armstrong

arrowhead
8000–10,000 B.C.

ar•ma•ture (är′mə chər) *n.* **1.a.** A rotating part of an electric motor or generator, consisting of wire wound around an iron core. **b.** A piece of soft iron connecting the poles of a magnet. **c.** The part of an electromagnetic device, such as a relay, buzzer, or loudspeaker, that moves or vibrates. **2.** A framework, especially one used as a support for clay sculpture. **3.** A part or an organ on an animal or a plant that serves for offense or defense. A porcupine's quills are its armature. **4.** Armor.

arm•band (ärm′bănd′) *n.* A piece of cloth worn around the upper arm, often as a sign of mourning.

arm•chair (ärm′châr′) *n.* A chair with supports on the sides for one's arms. —*adj.* Remote from the field of action: *an armchair detective.*

armed forces (ärmd) *pl.n.* The military forces of a country.

Ar•me•ni•a (är mē′nē ə *or* är mēn′yə). A region and republic of Asia Minor south of Georgia. It was formerly a kingdom that extended into northeast Turkey and northwest Iran. Armenia was part of the Soviet Union from 1921 to 1991. Yerevan is the capital. Population, 3,317,000.

Ar•me•ni•an (är mē′nē ən *or* är mēn′yən) *adj.* Of or relating to Armenia, or its people, language, or culture. —*n.* **1.** A native or inhabitant of Armenia. **2.** A person of Armenian ancestry. **3.** The Indo-European language of the Armenians.

arm•ful (ärm′fo͝ol′) *n.* As much as one or both arms can hold: *an armful of flowers.*

arm•hole (ärm′hōl′) *n.* An opening in a garment for an arm.

ar•mi•stice (är′mĭ stĭs) *n.* A temporary stop of fighting by mutual agreement; a truce. [First written down in 1707 in Modern English, from New Latin *armistitium* : Latin *arma*, arms + Latin *-stitium*, a stopping.]

Armistice Day *n.* Veterans Day as observed before 1954.

arm•let (ärm′lĭt) *n.* **1.** A band worn on the arm for ornament or identification. **2.** A small arm, as of the sea.

ar•mor (är′mər) *n.* **1.** A covering worn to protect the body in battle. **2.** A protective covering, such as the bony plates covering an armadillo or the metal plates on tanks or warships. **3.** The armored vehicles of an army. —*tr.v.* **ar•mored, ar•mor•ing, ar•mors.** To cover or protect with armor: *armor a warship.*

ar•mored (är′mərd) *adj.* **1.** Covered with or having armor: *tanks and other armored vehicles.* **2.** Equipped with armored vehicles: *an armored division of the Marines.*

ar•mor•er (är′mər ər) *n.* **1.** A person or business that makes or repairs weapons. **2.** An enlisted person in charge of maintenance and repair of the small arms of a military unit.

armor plate *n.* A specially made hard steel plate designed to withstand enemy fire and protect warships, military aircraft, and armored vehicles.

ar•mor•y (är′mə rē) *n.*, *pl.* **ar•mor•ies.** **1.** A storehouse for weapons; an arsenal. **2.** A building that serves as the headquarters of a military reserve force. **3.** A weapons factory.

ar•mour (är′mər) *n.* & *v. Chiefly British.* Variant of **armor.**

arm•pit (ärm′pĭt′) *n.* The hollow place under the arm at the shoulder.

arm•rest (ärm′rĕst′) *n.* A support for the arm, as one on a chair or couch.

Arm•strong (ärm′strông′), **Neil Alden.** Born 1930. American astronaut who became the first person to walk on the moon (July 20, 1969).

ar•my (är′mē) *n.*, *pl.* **ar•mies.** **1.** A large body of people organized and trained for warfare on land. **2.** Often **Army.** The entire military land forces of a country. **3.** Often **Army.** The largest unit in a country's army, consisting of two or more corps: *the Ninth Army of the U.S. Army.* **4.** A large group of people organized for a cause: *An army of construction workers built the bridge.* **5.** A large group, as of people or animals: *An army of shoppers appeared for the sale.* [First written down about 1387 in Middle English and spelled *armee*, from Latin *armāta*, from *armāre*, to arm.]

ar•ni•ca (är′nĭ kə) *n.* **1.** Any of various plants having yellow flowers that resemble daisies. **2.** A medical preparation made from these flowers, used to treat sprains and bruises.

Ar•nold (är′nəld), **Benedict.** 1741–1801. American Revolutionary general who unsuccessfully tried to surrender West Point to the British for 20,000 pounds (1780).

a•ro•ma (ə rō′mə) *n.*, *pl.* **a•ro•mas.** A pleasant characteristic smell; a fragrance. See Synonyms at **scent.** [First written down before 1200 in Middle English and spelled *aromat*, aromatic substance, from Old French, from Latin *arōmata*, aromatic herbs, from Greek.]

ar•o•mat•ic (ăr′ə măt′ĭk) *adj.* Having an aroma; fragrant: *the aromatic scent of roses.* —**ar′o•mat′i•cal•ly** *adv.*

a•rose (ə rōz′) *v.* Past tense of **arise.**

a•round (ə round′) *adv.* **1.** On all sides or in all directions: *We drove around looking for a parking place.* **2.** In a circle or circular motion: *The skater spun around twice.* **3.** In circumference: *a pond two miles around.* **4.** In or toward the opposite direction: *The horse turned around and ran toward the barn.* **5.** From one place to another; here and there: *wander around.* **6.** In or near one's current location: *He waited around all day.* **7.** To a specific place or area: *when you come around again.* **8.** Approximately; about: *Around 20 rafts floated down the Rio Grande.* —*prep.* **1.** On all sides of: *There are trees around the field.* **2.** So as to encircle or enclose: *He wore a belt around his waist.* **3.** All about; throughout: *The reporter looked around the room.* **4.** On or to the farther side of: *the house around the corner.* **5.** Close by; near: *She lives right around here.* **6.** So as to pass or avoid: *How can we get around the problem?* **7.** Approximately at: *I woke up around seven.*

a•rous•al (ə rou′zəl) *n.* The act of arousing or the condition of being aroused.

a•rouse (ə rouz′) *tr.v.* **a•roused, a•rous•ing, a•rous•es.** **1.** To awaken from or as if from sleep: *The baby's crying aroused me from my nap.* **2.** To stir up; stimulate; excite: *Their comments about the movie aroused my interest.* —**a•rous′a•ble** *adj.* —**a•rous′er** *n.*

ar•peg•gi•o (är pĕj′ē ō′ *or* är pĕj′ō) *n.*, *pl.* **ar•peg•gi•os.** **1.** The playing of the tones of a chord in succession rather than all at once. **2.** A chord played or sung in this way.

ar•que•bus (är′kə bəs *or* är′kwə bəs) *n.* Variant of **harquebus.**

ar•raign (ə rān′) *tr.v.* **ar•raigned, ar•raign•ing, ar•raigns.** To summon before a court of law to answer a charge or indictment: *The suspect was arraigned on charges of fraud.* —**ar•raign′er** *n.* —**ar•raign′ment** *n.*

ar•range (ə rānj′) *v.* **ar•ranged, ar•rang•ing, ar•rang•es.** —*tr.* **1.** To put in a specific order or relation: *Arrange these words alphabetically.* **2.** To plan or prepare for: *A travel agent arranges transportation for tourists.* **3.** To come to an agreement about: *The dealers arranged prices for the items.* **4.** To prepare an arrangement of (music): *He arranged the piano piece for orchestra.* —*intr.* **1.** To come to an agreement: *The company arranged with the union to grant more holidays.* **2.** To make preparations; plan: *We arranged for a cab to pick us up at the train station.*

ar•range•ment (ə rānj′mənt) *n.* **1.** The act of arranging: *The arrangement of a time and place for the meeting was quite difficult.* **2.** The manner or style in which things are arranged: *The arrangement of ideas in the essay was clear and logical.* **3.** A collection or set of things that have been arranged: *a flower arrangement.* **4.** An agreement: *We have an arrangement about who cooks dinner and who washes the dishes.* **5.** A plan or preparation. Often used in the plural: *Make arrangements for a vacation.* **6.** A version of a musical composition that differs from the original in style or use of instruments: *a jazz arrangement of a popular tune.*

ar•rant (ăr′ənt) *adj.* Thoroughgoing; out-and-out: *an arrant coward.* —**ar′rant•ly** *adv.*

ar•ras (ăr′əs) *n., pl.* **ar•ras.** A tapestry or wall hanging.

ar•ray (ə rā′) *tr.v.* **ar•rayed, ar•ray•ing, ar•rays. 1.** To put in an orderly arrangement, as troops. **2.** To dress up, especially in fine clothes; adorn: *The dancers were arrayed in red velvet.* —*n.* **1.** An orderly arrangement: *an array of data.* **2.** An impressively large number or group: *The cast for the play is a formidable array of talent.* **3.** Clothing or finery: *The prince and princess were clad in rich array.* —**ar•ray′er** *n.*

ar•rears (ə rîrz′) *pl.n.* **1.** An unpaid or overdue debt: *You have arrears of $23.00.* **2.** The state of being behind in fulfilling payments or an obligation: *After this is paid they will no longer be in arrears.*

ar•rest (ə rĕst′) *tr.v.* **ar•rest•ed, ar•rest•ing, ar•rests. 1.** To seize and hold under authority of law: *The police arrested the thief.* **2.** To stop the progress of; check: *The antibiotic arrested the spread of the infection.* **3.** To capture and hold; engage: *The exciting chapter arrested the reader's attention.* —*n.* The act of arresting or the state of being arrested. [First written down in 1375 in Middle English and spelled *aresten*, from Old French *arester* : Latin *ad-*, to + Latin *restāre*, to stand still.]

ar•rest•ing (ə rĕs′tĭng) *adj.* Capturing and holding the attention; striking: *the actor's arresting performance.* —**ar•rest′ing•ly** *adv.*

ar•rhyth•mi•a (ə rĭ*th*′mē ə) *n.* An irregular beating of the heart.

ar•ri•val (ə rī′vəl) *n.* **1.** The act of arriving: *the arrival of the passengers at the airport.* **2.** The attainment of a goal or an objective: *The principal's arrival at a decision came after much thought.* **3.** A person or thing that has arrived: *the newest arrivals at the video store.*

ar•rive (ə rīv′) *intr.v.* **ar•rived, ar•riv•ing, ar•rives. 1.** To reach a destination; come to a place: *They arrived in the city on time.* **2.** To come; take place: *Spring arrived early this year.* **3.** To achieve success or fame: *She has finally arrived as an artist.* —***idiom.* arrive at.** To reach through effort or a process: *The jury arrived at a decision.* [First written down before 1200 in Middle English and spelled *ariven*, from Old French *ariver* : Latin *ad-*, to + Latin *rīpa*, shore.]

ar•ri•ve•der•ci (ä rē′vĕ dĕr′chē) *interj.* An expression used to say farewell.

ar•ro•gance (ăr′ə gəns) *n.* The quality or condition of being arrogant.

ar•ro•gant (ăr′ə gənt) *adj.* **1.** Excessively and unpleasantly proud of oneself: *a conceited arrogant person.* **2.** Marked by excessive pride: *an arrogant refusal to listen to others.* See Synonyms at **proud.** —**ar′ro•gant•ly** *adv.*

ar•ro•gate (ăr′ə gāt′) *tr.v.* **ar•ro•gat•ed, ar•ro•gat•ing, ar•ro•gates.** To take, claim, or assume for oneself without right: *The President cannot arrogate the power of Congress to declare war.* —**ar′ro•ga′tion** *n.*

ar•row (ăr′ō) *n.* **1.** A straight thin shaft with a pointed head at one end and feathers at the other, meant to be shot from a bow. **2.** Something similar in shape, as a sign or mark used to indicate direction. [First written down before 800 in Old English and spelled *earh*.]

ar•row•head (ăr′ō hĕd′) *n.* The pointed removable tip of an arrow.

ar•row•root (ăr′ō ro͞ot′ *or* ăr′ō ro͝ot′) *n.* **1.** An edible easily digested starch made from the root of a tropical American plant. **2.** The plant that has such roots, having long leaves and white flowers.

ar•roy•o (ə roi′ō) *n., pl.* **ar•roy•os. 1.** A small stream. **2.** A dry gulch in the southwest United States, formed by a stream. [First written down in 1807 in Modern English, from Spanish, from Latin *arrūgia*, mine.]

arroyo
Canyon de Chelly National Monument, Arizona

ar•se•nal (är′sə nəl) *n.* **1.** A building for the storage, manufacture, or repair of arms or ammunition. **2.** A stock of weapons.

ar•se•nic (är′sə nĭk) *n.* **1.** *Symbol* **As** A brittle, gray, metalloid element that occurs chiefly in combination with other elements. Arsenic forms poisonous compounds with oxygen and is used in making alloys, semiconductors, solders, and certain medicines. See table at **element. 2.** A highly poisonous compound of arsenic in the form of a white, odorless, tasteless powder, used especially as an insecticide and herbicide. [First written down before 1393 in Middle English and spelled *arsenik*, from Greek *arsenikon*, a yellowish pigment.]

ar•son (är′sən) *n.* The crime of intentionally setting fire to a building or other property. —**ar′son•ist** *n.*

art[1] (ärt) *n.* **1.** Human effort to imitate, change, or counteract nature: *The beauty of this park owes more to art than to nature.* **2.a.** The creation or production of something that is considered beautiful, as in painting, sculpture, poetry, or music. **b.** The study of these activities, especially the study of the visual arts: *I took art in school.* **c.** A work or works resulting from these activities, as a painting or a piece of sculpture: *an exhibit of modern art.* **3.** A practical skill; a craft: *the art of sewing.* **4.** The body of knowledge of a particular field: *the art of medicine; the industrial arts.* **5. arts.** The liberal arts; the humanities: *a college of arts and sciences.* **6. arts.** Artful devices; stratagems; tricks. [First written down about 1250 in Middle English, from Latin *ars*.]

art[2] (ärt) *v. Archaic.* Second person singular present tense of **be.**

art deco
Chrysler Building, New York City

art dec•o also **Art Dec•o** (dĕk′ō) *n.* A style of decoration that originated in the 1920's, using geometrical patterns, bold colors, and plastic and glass.

Ar•te•mis (är′tə mĭs) *n.* In Greek mythology, the goddess of the moon and the hunt, identified with the Roman Diana.

ar•te•ri•al (är tîr′ē əl) *adj.* **1.** Of, relating to, or resembling an artery or arteries. **2.** Bright red and charged with oxygen; not venous: *arterial blood.* **3.** Serving as a main route of transportation: *This highway is the arterial route through town.* —**ar•te′ri•al•ly** *adv.*

ar•te•ri•ole (är tîr′ē ōl′) *n.* A small artery, especially one leading into capillaries.

ar•te•ri•o•scle•ro•sis (är tîr′ē ō sklə rō′sĭs) *n.* A diseased condition in which the walls of the arteries become thickened and hard and interfere with the circulation of the blood.

ar•ter•y (är′tə rē) *n., pl.* **ar•ter•ies. 1.** Any of a branching system of blood vessels that carry blood

ă	pat	oi	**boy**
ā	pay	ou	**out**
âr	care	o͝o	**took**
ä	father	o͞o	**boot**
ĕ	pet	ŭ	**cut**
ē	be	ûr	**urge**
ĭ	pit	th	**thin**
ī	pie	*th*	**this**
îr	pier	hw	**wh**oop
ŏ	pot	zh	vision
ō	toe	ə	about
ô	paw	N	*French* bon

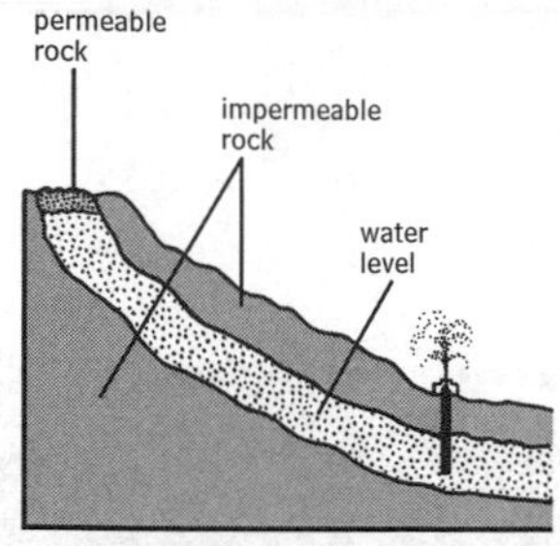

artesian well

Chester A. Arthur

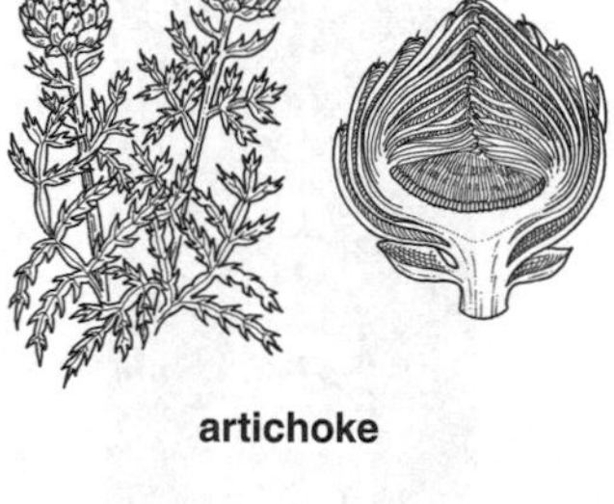
artichoke

Usage: article

The words **a**, **an**, and **the** are known as **articles**. **A** and **an**, the **indefinite articles**, refer to any one. *I want an apple* means that I do not care which apple I get. The form *a* is used before a word beginning with a consonant sound, however it may be spelled (*a frog, a university*). The form *an* is used before a word beginning with a vowel sound (*an orange, an hour*). **The**, the **definite article**, refers to something or someone specific or definite: *I want the apple that you dipped in honey.*

away from the heart to various parts of the body. **2.** A major transportation route from which other routes branch. [First written down before 1398 in Middle English and spelled *arterie*, from Greek *artēria.*]

ar•te•sian well (är **tē′**zhən) *n.* A deep well that passes through hard impermeable rock and reaches water that is under enough pressure to rise to the surface without being pumped.

art•ful (**ärt′**fəl) *adj.* **1.** Showing art or skill; skillful: *an artful cook.* **2.** Crafty; cunning: *an artful peddler.* **—art′ful•ly** *adv.* **—art′ful•ness** *n.*

ar•thrit•ic (är **thrĭt′**ĭk) *adj.* Of, relating to, or suffering from arthritis: *an arthritic joint.* —*n.* A person affected with arthritis.

ar•thri•tis (är **thrī′**tĭs) *n.* Inflammation and stiffness of a joint or joints in the body.

ar•thro•pod (**är′**thrə pŏd′) *n.* Any of numerous invertebrate animals having a segmented body, jointed legs or wings, and an external skeleton.

ar•thro•scope (**är′**thrə skōp′) *n.* An instrument used to examine the interior parts of a joint.

Ar•thur (**är′**thər) *n.* A legendary king of sixth-century Britain who gathers his knights at the Round Table and holds court at Camelot. **—Ar•thu′ri•an** (är **thŏŏr′**ē ən) *adj.*

Arthur, Chester Alan. 1829–1886. The 21st President of the United States (1881–1885). He supported legislation to regulate the appointments of federal officials.

ar•ti•choke (**är′**tĭ chōk′) *n.* **1.** The unopened flower head of a plant similar to the thistle, covered with thick fleshy scales and eaten as a vegetable. **2.** The plant that bears such a flower head. [First written down in 1530 in Modern English and spelled *archicokk*, from Old Spanish, *alcarchofa*, from Arabic *al-ḫaršūf.*]

ar•ti•cle (**är′**tĭ kəl) *n.* **1.** A written piece that forms an independent part of a publication; a report; an essay: *read an article about sports in the newspaper.* **2.** A section or an item of a written document: *an article of the Constitution.* **3.** An individual thing; an item: *A bed is an article of furniture.* **4.** In grammar, any of a class of words that are used to introduce nouns and to specify their application. In English the indefinite articles are *a* and *an* and the definite article is *the.* [First written down before 1200 in Middle English, from Latin *articulus*, part, diminutive of *artus*, joint.] —SEE NOTE.

ar•tic•u•late (är **tĭk′**yə lĭt) *adj.* **1.** Spoken clearly and distinctly: *a radio announcer's articulate speech.* **2.** Capable of speaking clearly and effectively: *Teachers and lawyers must be articulate people.* **3.** Having the power of speech. **4.** Consisting of sections connected by joints: *Legs of most animals are articulate.* —*v.* (är **tĭk′**yə lāt′). **ar•tic•u•lat•ed, ar•tic•u•lat•ing, ar•tic•u•lates.** —*tr.* **1.** To utter (a speech sound or sounds) distinctly; enunciate: *Children begin to articulate words around age two.* **2.** To express verbally: *Our leader articulated the feelings of the group.* —*intr.* **1.** To speak clearly and distinctly. **2.** To be jointed; form a joint: *the bones that articulate in the shoulder.* **—ar•tic′u•late•ly** *adv.* **—ar•tic′u•late•ness** *n.* **—ar•tic′u•la′tor** *n.*

ar•tic•u•la•tion (är tĭk′yə **lā′**shən) *n.* **1.** The act or process of speaking clearly; enunciation: *Good articulation is essential for a radio broadcaster.* **2.** A point at which things join or are joined. **3.** A method or manner of joining. **4.** A joint between bones or similar parts.

ar•ti•fact (**är′**tə făkt′) *n.* An object produced by human handiwork, especially an item of primitive art.

ar•ti•fice (**är′**tə fĭs) *n.* **1.** A clever device or stratagem; a ruse. **2.** Deception; trickery.

ar•tif•i•cer (är **tĭf′**ĭ sər) *n.* A skilled worker; a person who practices a craft.

ar•ti•fi•cial (är′tə **fĭsh′**əl) *adj.* **1.** Made by human beings rather than occurring in nature: *an artificial sweetener; artificial flowers.* **2.** Not genuine or natural; affected: *an artifical display of tears and distress.* [First written down about 1390 in Middle English, from Latin *artificium*, craftsmanship, from *artifex*, craftsperson.] **—ar′ti•fi′ci•al′i•ty** (är′tə fĭsh′ē **ăl′**ĭ tē) *n.* **—ar′ti•fi′cial•ly** *adv.*

artificial intelligence *n.* **1.** The ability of a machine or computer program to perform tasks normally thought to require intelligence, such as problem solving, discrimination among single objects, and response to spoken commands. **2.** The branch of computer science concerned with the development of machines having this ability.

artificial respiration *n.* Any of several methods by which a living person who has stopped breathing may be revived. These methods usually involve forcing air rhythmically in and out of the lungs.

ar•til•ler•y (är **tĭl′**ə rē) *n.* **1.** Large mounted guns, such as cannons, that are operated by crews. **2.** The branch of an army that specializes in the use of such guns.

ar•til•ler•y•man (är **tĭl′**ə rē mən) *n.* A soldier in the artillery.

ar•ti•san (**är′**tĭ zən) *n.* A person skilled in making a certain product; a craftsperson. [First written down in 1538 in Modern English, from Italian *artigiano*, from Latin *artītus*, skilled in the arts.]

art•ist (**är′**tĭst) *n.* **1.** A person who produces works of art, especially in the fine arts such as painting, sculpture, or music. **2.** A person who works in one of the performing arts, such as dancing or acting. **3.** A person who shows skill and creativity in an occupation or pastime: *That surgeon is a real artist.*

ar•tis•tic (är **tĭs′**tĭk) *adj.* **1.** Of or relating to art or artists: *acclaimed by all artistic circles.* **2.** Sensitive to beauty: *an artistic temperament.* **3.** Showing skill and good taste: *an artistic flower arrangement.* **—ar•tis′ti•cal•ly** *adv.*

art•ist•ry (**är′**tĭ strē) *n.* **1.** Artistic quality or workmanship: *the subtle artistry of a poem.* **2.** Artistic ability: *a painter of superb artistry.*

art•less (**ärt′**lĭs) *adj.* **1.** Free from deceit; guileless: *an artless child.* **2.** Not artificial; natural: *the artless beauty of a sunset.* **—art′less•ly** *adv.* **—art′less•ness** *n.*

art nou•veau often **Art Nou•veau** (är′ nōō **vō′** *or* ärt′ nōō **vō′**) *n.* A style of decoration and architecture first popular in the 1890's, using curved lines and flower shapes.

art•work (**ärt′**wûrk′) *n.* **1.a.** The production of decorative or artistic objects: *Artwork in this potter's studio goes on every day.* **b.** The decorations or objects so made: *The archaeologists saved the artwork on the walls of the cave.* **2.** The illustrations and decorative parts of a book or other publication as distinct from the text.

ar•um (**ăr′**əm *or* **âr′**əm) *n.* **1.** Any of serveral plants having arrow-shaped leaves. **2.** Any of several related plants, such as the calla.

-ary *suff.* A suffix that means: **1.** Of or relating to: *legendary.* **2.** One that related to or is connected with: *boundary.*

Ar•y•an (**âr′**ē ən *or* **ăr′**ē ən) *n.* **1.** An Indo-Iranian. **2.** A member of the prehistoric people who spoke the language from which the Indo-European languages developed. **3.** A member of any of the peoples speaking an Indo-European language. **4.** In Nazi ideology, a non-Jewish Caucasian, especially one of a Nordic type supposed to be superior to other peoples. [First written down in 1839 in Modern English and spelled *Arian*, from Sanskrit *ārya-*, noble, Aryan.] **—Ar'y•an** *adj.*

as (ăz; əz *when unstressed*) *adv.* **1.** Equally: *You won't easily find someone as nice.* **2.** For instance: *large cats, as tigers and lions.* *—conj.* **1.** To the same degree or quantity that; equally with: *sweet as sugar.* **2.** In the same way that: *When in Rome, do as the Romans do.* **3.** At the same time that; while: *They smiled as their eyes met.* **4.** Since; because: *I wanted to stay home, as I was ill.* **5.** Though: *Nice as it is, I don't want it.* **6.** In accordance with which; a fact that: *The sun is hot, as everyone knows.* *—pron.* That; who; which: *I got the same grade as you did. We brought such things as were necessary.* *—prep.* **1.** The same as; like: *They treated the old car as an honored relic of the past.* **2.** In the role or function of: *The diplomat was acting as a peacemaker.* ***—idioms.*** **as is.** *Informal.* Just the way it is; without changes: *If you leave the bottle on the shelf as is, it will tip and fall.* **as it were.** In a manner of speaking: *The hikers were explorers, as it were, until it began to rain.* **as much.** All that; the same: *I might have guessed as much.*

As The symbol for the element **arsenic** (sense 1).

as•a•fet•i•da (ăs'ə **fĕt'**ĭ də) *n.* A brownish resin with a very unpleasant odor, obtained from various Asian plants and formerly used in medicine.

as•bes•tos (ăs **bĕs'**təs *or* ăz **bĕs'**təs) *n.* Any of several fibrous mineral forms of magnesium silicate that are resistant to heat, flames, and chemical action. Some forms have been shown to contribute to certain lung diseases. For this reason, asbestos is no longer used in making insulation, fireproofing material, and brake linings. [First written down before 1100 in Middle English and spelled *abestus*, from Greek *asbestos*, unquenchable.]

as•cend (ə **sĕnd'**) *v.* **as•cend•ed, as•cend•ing, as•cends.** *—intr.* **1.** To go or move upward; rise: *The balloon ascended rapidly.* **2.** To move to a higher rank or level: *The prince ascended to the throne and so became king.* *—tr.* **1.** To climb to or toward the top of: *The climbers ascended the mountain.* **2.** To come to occupy: *The queen ascended the throne upon the death of her father.* [First written down before 1382 in Middle English and spelled *ascenden*, from Latin *ascendere* : *ad-*, to + *scandere*, to climb.]

as•cen•dan•cy also **as•cen•den•cy** (ə **sĕn'**dən sē) *n.* Dominance in position or power: *Britain lost ascendancy in the United States after the Revolution.*

as•cen•dant also **as•cen•dent** (ə **sĕn'**dənt) *adj.* Coming into a position of power or influence: *Rome was the ascendant power in Europe before the Middle Ages.* ***—idiom.*** **in the ascendant.** Rising in power or influence.

as•cend•ing (ə **sĕn'**dĭng) *adj.* Moving, going, or growing upward: *in ascending order of importance; a tree with ascending branches.* **—as•cend'ing•ly** *adv.*

as•cen•sion (ə **sĕn'**shən) *n.* **1.** The act or process of ascending. **2. Ascension.** In Christian theology, the bodily rising of Jesus into heaven after his death and resurrection.

Ascension Day *n.* The 40th day after Easter, on which the Christian feast of the Ascension of Jesus is observed.

as•cent (ə **sĕnt'**) *n.* **1.** The act of ascending or moving up: *the first stages of the rocket's ascent through the atmosphere.* **2.** An upward slope: *The goats climbed the steep ascent to the mountain pasture.* **3.** The act or process of rising from a lower level, degree, or status; development: *the industrialist's ascent to the upper class.*

❑ *These sound alike:* **ascent, assent** (agreement).

as•cer•tain (ăs'ər **tān'**) *tr.v.* **as•cer•tained, as•cer•tain•ing, as•cer•tains.** To find out: *ascertain the truth.* **—as'cer•tain'a•ble** *adj.* **—as'cer•tain'a•bly** *adv.* **—as'cer•tain'ment** *n.*

as•cet•ic (ə **sĕt'**ĭk) *n.* A person who renounces comforts and pleasures in order to practice rigid self-denial, often as an act of religious devotion. *—adj.* Relating to or characteristic of an ascetic; self-denying; austere: *Most hermits lead an ascetic life.* **—as•cet'i•cal•ly** *adv.*

as•cet•i•cism (ə **sĕt'**ĭ sĭz'əm) *n.* Ascetic practice or discipline.

ASCII (**ăs'**kē) *n.* A standard code used in many computers to convert letters, numbers, and symbols into binary numbers, allowing computers made by different manufacturers to exchange information.

As•cle•pi•us (ə **sklē'**pē əs) *n.* In Greek mythology, the god of medicine.

a•scor•bic acid (ə **skôr'**bĭk) *n.* A compound of carbon, hydrogen, and oxygen, having the formula $C_6H_8O_6$, found in citrus fruits, tomatoes, potatoes, and leafy vegetables; vitamin C. Lack of ascorbic acid in the diet can cause scurvy.

as•cot (**ăs'**kət *or* **ăs'**kŏt') *n.* A wide necktie or scarf tied so that the broad ends are laid flat, one on top of the other, and pinned together. [First written down in 1908 in Modern English, after the racetrack near *Ascot*, England.]

as•cribe (ə **skrīb'**) *tr.v.* **as•cribed, as•crib•ing, as•cribes.** To think of (something) as belonging to or coming from a specific cause, origin, or source; attribute: *The farmers ascribed their poor harvest to drought. Most scholars ascribe the poem to Chaucer.* **—as•crib'a•ble** *adj.*

as•crip•tion (ə **skrĭp'**shən) *n.* **1.** The act of ascribing. **2.** A statement that ascribes something to someone or something.

a•sep•tic (ə **sĕp'**tĭk *or* ā **sĕp'**tĭk) *adj.* Free from living microorganisms causing infection: *aseptic surgical methods.* **—a•sep'ti•cal•ly** *adj.*

a•sex•u•al (ā **sĕk'**sho͞o əl) *adj.* **1.** Neither male nor female; sexless: *an asexual organism such as an ameba.* **2.** Not involving sex organs or the union of sex cells: *asexual reproduction.* **—a•sex'u•al•ly** *adv.*

as for *prep.* With regard to; concerning: *As for me, I'll stay.*

As•gard (**ăs'**gärd' *or* **äz'**gärd') *n.* In Norse mythology, the heavenly dwelling place of the gods.

ash[1] (ăsh) *n.* **1.** The grayish-white powdery residue left when something is burned. **2.** The fine particles of solid matter thrown out of a volcano in an eruption. **3. ashes.** Human remains, especially after cremation. [First written down before 800 in Old English and spelled *æsce.*]

ash[2] (ăsh) *n.* **1.** Any of various trees related to the olive having feathery leaves, winged seeds, and strong tough wood. **2.** The wood of such a tree, used for making tool handles, baseball bats, and other sports equipment. [First written down about 725 in Old English and spelled *æsc.*]

a•shamed (ə **shāmd'**) *adj.* **1.** Feeling shame or guilt: *You should be ashamed for losing your temper.* **2.** Reluctant through fear of shame or embarrassment: *Don't be ashamed to ask for help.* **—a•sham'ed•ly** (ə **shā'**mĭd lē) *adv.*

A•shan•ti (ə **shăn'**tē *or* ə **shän'**tē) *n., pl.* **Ashanti** or **Ashan•tis.** A member of a people of Ghana.

ash•can or **ash can** (**ăsh'**kăn') *n.* A large metal receptacle for ashes or trash.

ash•en[1] (**ăsh'**ən) *adj.* Resembling ashes; pale: *ashen gray; turn ashen with fear.*

ash•en[2] (**ăsh'**ən) *adj.* Of, relating to, or made from the wood of the ash tree.

Ash•kha•bad (ăsh'kä **bäd'**). The capital of Turk-

art nouveau

Building in Barcelona, Spain, designed by Antonio Gaudí (1852–1926)

ascot

ă	pat	oi	**boy**
ā	pay	ou	**out**
âr	care	o͝o	**took**
ä	father	o͞o	**boot**
ĕ	**pet**	ŭ	**cut**
ē	be	ûr	**urge**
ĭ	pit	th	**thin**
ī	pie	*th*	**this**
îr	**pier**	hw	**whoop**
ŏ	**pot**	zh	vision
ō	**toe**	ə	about
ô	**paw**	N	*French* bon

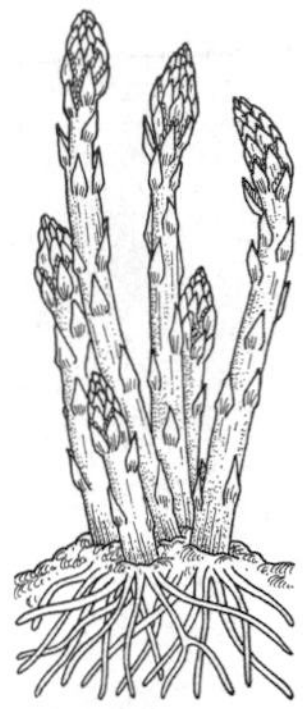
asparagus

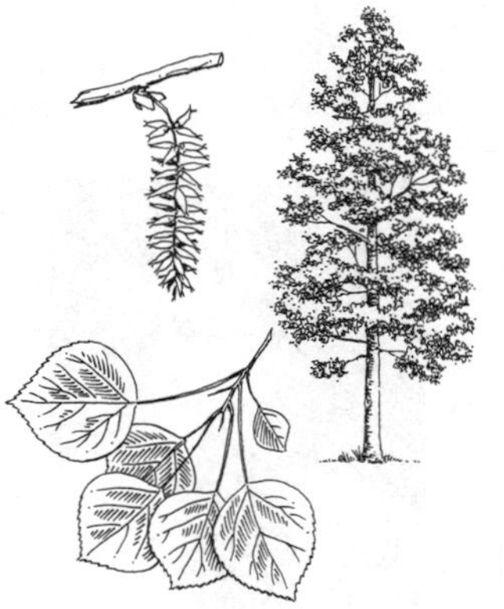
aspen
Quaking aspen

menistan, in the south-central part of the republic near the Iranian border. It was founded in 1881. Population, 356,000.

a•shore (ə shôr′) *adv.* **1.** To or onto the shore: *go ashore.* **2.** On land: *The sailors spent the day ashore.*

ash•tray (ăsh′trā′) *n.* A small receptacle for tobacco ashes.

Ash Wednesday *n.* The first day of Lent, when many Christians receive a mark of ashes on the forehead as a sign of penitence and mortality.

ash•y (ăsh′ē) *adj.* **ash•i•er, ash•i•est. 1.** Relating to, resembling, or covered with ashes. **2.** Having the color of ashes; ashen.

A•sia (ā′zhə *or* ā′shə). The world's largest continent, covering an area between Europe and Africa to the west and the Pacific Ocean to the east.

Asia Minor. A peninsula of western Asia between the Black Sea and the Mediterranean Sea, occupying the Asian part of Turkey.

A•sian (ā′zhən *or* ā′shən) *adj.* Of or relating to Asia or its peoples, languages, or cultures. —*n.* **1.** A native or inhabitant of Asia. **2.** A person of Asian descent.

Asian American *n.* A U.S. citizen or resident of Asian descent.

A•si•at•ic (ā′zhē ăt′ĭk) *adj.* Asian: *an Asiatic plant.*

a•side (ə sīd′) *adv.* **1.** To or toward one side: *step aside; draw the curtain aside.* **2.** Apart: *a day set aside for relaxation.* **3.** In reserve: *money put aside for a vacation.* **4.** Out of one's thoughts or mind: *put one's fears aside.* —*n.* A remark spoken by a character in a play that the other actors on stage are not supposed to hear.

aside from *prep.* Apart from; except for: *Aside from a miracle, nothing can save their team from losing.*

as if *conj.* **1.** In the same way that it would be if: *She ran as if she would never tire.* **2.** That: *It seemed as if the day lasted forever.*

as•i•nine (ăs′ə nīn′) *adj.* Stupid or silly: *an asinine remark.* **—as′i•nine′ly** *adv.*

ask (ăsk) *v.* **asked, ask•ing, asks.** —*tr.* **1.** To put a question to: *My friend asked me if I had ever been to St. Louis.* **2.** To seek an answer to: *You learn to ask the right questions as you become an experienced detective.* **3.** To make a request to or for: *She asked me for help. I asked a favor of him.* **4.** To invite: *Why don't we ask them to our house for lunch?* **5.** To charge: *They are asking 20 dollars for this book.* **6.** To expect or demand: *Riding in a car all day is asking a great deal of a small child.* —*intr.* **1.** To make a request: *I asked for help.* **2.** To make inquiries: *We asked about the train schedule.* [First written down before 725 in Old English and spelled *āhsian.*]

Synonyms: ask, inquire, question, examine, quiz. These verbs all mean to seek information. **Ask** and **inquire** are the most general: *We stopped at the gas station and asked for directions to the stadium. Rosa went into the store to inquire about the "Help Wanted" sign in the window.* **Question** often means to ask a series of questions: *The lawyer questioned the witness in great detail about the robbery.* **Examine** often means to question in order to test someone's knowledge: *All of their real estate agents have been examined and licensed by the state board.* **Quiz** means to question students in an informal test: *The teacher will quiz us tomorrow on the multiplication tables.* **Antonym: answer.**

a•skance (ə skăns′) *adv.* **1.** With a sidelong glance. **2.** With distrust or disapproval: *The reporter looked askance at such rumors.*

a•skew (ə skyōō′) *adv. & adj.* Out of line; crooked; awry: *Wind knocked the sign askew.*

ASL *abbr.* An abbreviation of American Sign Language.

a•slant (ə slănt′) *adv.* At a slant: *The trees stood aslant on the hill.* —*adj.* Slanting: *a shaft of moonlight aslant on the floor.* —*prep.* Obliquely over or across: *lights from the traffic shining aslant the wall.*

a•sleep (ə slēp′) *adj.* **1.** Sleeping: *You must have been asleep when the phone rang.* **2.** Numb: *My foot is asleep.* —*adv.* Into a sleep: *The campers fell asleep quickly after their long hike.*

as long as *conj.* **1.** Since: *As long as you're offering, I accept.* **2.** On the condition that: *I'll go on the camping trip as long as you lend me a tent.*

as of *prep.* On; at: *The assignment is due as of Friday.*

asp (ăsp) *n.* Any of several poisonous snakes of Africa, Asia, and Europe, especially a small cobra of northern Africa and southwest Asia.

as•par•a•gus (ə spăr′ə gəs) *n.* **1.** The young tender stalks of a cultivated plant related to the lily, cooked and eaten as a vegetable. **2.** The plant that has such stalks. [First written down before 1398 in Middle English and spelled *asperages,* from Greek *asparagos.*]

as•par•tame (ăs′pər tām′ *or* ə spär′tām′) *n.* An artificial sweetener, about 200 times as sweet as sugar, containing four calories per gram.

A.S.P.C.A. *abbr.* An abbreviation of American Society for the Prevention of Cruelty to Animals.

as•pect (ăs′pĕkt) *n.* **1.** A particular facial expression: *a judge of grim aspect.* **2.** The way in which something can be viewed by the mind; an element or a facet: *In prescribing a treatment, the doctor considered all aspects of the patient's history.* **3.** Appearance; look: *the barren aspect of the desert.* **4.** A position facing or commanding a given direction; exposure: *a bright sunny room with a southern aspect.* [First written down about 1385 in Middle English, from Latin *aspectus,* a view : *ad-,* at + *specere,* to look.]

as•pen (ăs′pən) *n.* Any of several poplar trees having small rounded leaves that flutter in the lightest of breezes.

as•per•i•ty (ă spĕr′ĭ tē) *n.* Harshness of manner; irritability: *a note of asperity in one's voice.*

as•per•sion (ə spûr′zhən *or* ə spûr′shən) *n.* A damaging or slanderous report or remark: *The comment cast aspersions on my motives.*

as•phalt (ăs′fôlt′) *n.* **1.** A thick, sticky, dark-brown mixture of petroleum tars used in paving, roofing, and waterproofing. Asphalt is obtained in the refining of petroleum or is found in natural beds. **2.** A paving material composed of sand, small stones, gravel, and asphalt. —*tr.v.* **as•phalted, as•phalt•ing, as•phalts.** To pave or coat with asphalt. [First written down before 1398 in Middle English and spelled *aspalt,* from Greek *asphaltos.*]

as•pho•del (ăs′fə dĕl′) *n.* Any of several plants of the Mediterranean region having white or yellow flowers.

as•phyx•i•a (ăs fĭk′sē ə) *n.* Death or loss of consciousness caused by a lack of oxygen.

as•phyx•i•ate (ăs fĭk′sē āt′) *intr. & tr.v.* **as•phyx•i•at•ed, as•phyx•i•at•ing, as•phyx•i•ates.** To undergo or cause to undergo asphyxia; suffocate: *Without air the bugs in the jar will asphyxiate. The thick smoke nearly asphyxiated us.* **—as•phyx′i•a′tion** *n.* **—as•phyx′i•a′tor** *n.*

as•pic (ăs′pĭk) *n.* A jelly made from gelatin and chilled meat juices or vegetable juices and served as a garnish or as a molded dish.

as•pi•rant (ăs′pər ənt *or* ə spīr′ənt) *n.* A person who desires or strives for a particular position or honor: *an aspirant to high position and power.*

as•pi•rate (ăs′pə rāt′) *tr.v.* **as•pi•rat•ed, as•pi•rat•ing, as•pi•rates. 1.** To remove (a liquid or gas) from a body cavity by suction, as by using an aspirator: *aspirate the lungs.* **2.** To pronounce (a vowel or word) with a puff of breath, as in *help.* —*n.* (**ăs′**pər ĭt). **1.** The sound of the letter *h* as in *help.* **2.** The puff of air accompanying or following certain speech sounds, as that accompanying *p* in *peach.*

as•pi•ra•tion (ăs′pə **rā′**shən) *n.* **1.a.** A strong desire, as for the realization of an ambition or ideal: *the student's aspiration to become a doctor.* **b.** An object of such desire; an ambitious goal: *To become a surgeon was my friend's aspiration.* **2.** The process of removing a liquid or gas from a body cavity by suction. **3.** The pronunciation of certain speech sounds with a puff of breath, especially at the beginning of a word, as *h* in *hurry.*

as•pi•ra•tor (**ăs′**pə rā′tər) *n.* A suction pump, especially a small one used to draw fluids from body cavities.

as•pire (ə **spīr′**) *intr.v.* **as•pired, as•pir•ing, as•pires.** To have a great ambition; desire strongly: *aspire to become a good player; aspire to great knowledge.* [First written down before 1400 in Middle English and spelled *aspiren,* from Latin *aspirāre,* to desire : *ad-,* toward + *spirāre,* to breathe.] **—as•pir′er** *n.*

as•pi•rin (**ăs′**pər ĭn *or* **ăs′**prĭn) *n.* **1.** A white, crystalline compound of carbon, hydrogen, and oxygen in the proportions $C_9H_8O_4$, commonly used as a drug to relieve fever and pain; acetylsalicylic acid. **2.** A tablet of aspirin.

ass (ăs) *n., pl.* **ass•es** (**ăs′**ĭz). **1.** Any of several hoofed mammals related to the horse, but smaller and having longer ears, as the donkey. **2.** A silly or stupid person.

as•sa•gai (**ăs′**ə gī′) *n.* Variant of **assegai.**

as•sail (ə **sāl′**) *tr.v.* **as•sailed, as•sail•ing, as•sails.** To attack physically or with words: *The candidate assailed her opponents with strong criticism.* **—as•sail′a•ble** *adj.* **—as•sail′er** *n.*

as•sail•ant (ə **sā′**lənt) *n.* A person who assails someone; an attacker.

as•sas•sin (ə **săs′**ĭn) *n.* A person who kills someone by surprise attack, especially one who kills a public official or other prominent figure for political reasons. [First written down in 1531 in Modern English, from Medieval Latin *assassīnus,* from Arabic *ḥaššāš,* hashish user.]

as•sas•si•nate (ə **săs′**ə nāt′) *tr.v.* **as•sas•si•nat•ed, as•sas•si•nat•ing, as•sas•si•nates.** To murder (a public figure) by surprise attack, usually for political reasons. **—as•sas′si•na′tion** *n.* **—as•sas′si•na′tor** *n.*

as•sault (ə **sôlt′**) *n.* **1.** A violent physical or verbal attack: *The tanks made an assault upon the town. The senator launched an assault upon the corrupt politicians.* **2.** An unlawful attempt or threat to injure another physically. —*tr.v.* **as•sault•ed, as•sault•ing, as•saults.** To attack vigorously: *The troops assaulted the fort.* [First written down before 1200 in Middle English and spelled *assaut,* from Latin *assultus,* from *assilīre,* to jump on.] **—as•sault′er** *n.*

assault and battery *n.* An illegal act in which a threat of attack on another person is carried out.

as•say (**ăs′**ā′ *or* ă **sā′**) *n.* **1.** A chemical analysis of something, especially an ore or a drug. **2.** A specimen or sample subjected to an assay. —*v.* (ă **sā′** *or* **ăs′**ā′). **as•sayed, as•say•ing, as•says.** —*tr.* **1.** To analyze (an ore or alloy) to find out the quantity of gold, silver, or other metal in it. **2.** To test and evaluate; assess: *We assayed the chances of success and decided to make the film.* **3.** To attempt; try: *In spite of the dangers she still assayed the difficult journey.* —*intr.* To be shown by an assay to contain some ingredient: *The ore assayed at 1 percent uranium.* **—as•say′er** *n.*

as•se•gai or **as•sa•gai** (**ăs′**ə gī′) *n., pl.* **as•se•gais** or **as•sa•gais.** A light spear, often with an iron tip, used by southern African peoples.

as•sem•blage (ə **sĕm′**blĭj) *n.* **1.** A collection of persons or things: *The mayor spoke before a large assemblage in the town square.* **2.** The act of gathering or fitting together.

as•sem•ble (ə **sĕm′**bəl) *v.* **as•sem•bled, as•sem•bling, as•sem•bles.** —*tr.* **1.** To bring together as a group: *The teachers assembled their classes in the auditorium.* See Synonyms at **gather. 2.** To perform the assembly of; put together: *The mechanic assembled the engine.* —*intr.* **1.** To come together; gather; congregate: *A group of friends assembled at the corner.* **2.** To fit together: *The unit assembles quite easily.* [First written down before 1325 in Middle English and spelled *assemblen,* from Old French *assembler* : Latin *ad-,* to + Latin *simul,* together.] **—as•sem′bler** *n.*

as•sem•bly (ə **sĕm′**blē) *n., pl.* **as•sem•blies. 1.** A group of persons gathered together for a common purpose. **2. Assembly.** A legislative body: *the State Assembly.* **3.a.** The process of putting together a number of parts to make up a complete unit: *Assembly of a new car usually takes less than a day.* **b.** A set of parts that work together as a unit; an apparatus: *the steering assembly of a truck.*

assembly line *n.* An arrangement in which articles are assembled in successive stages, passing from worker to worker or machine to machine, often on some kind of conveyor.

as•sem•bly•man (ə **sĕm′**blē mən) *n.* A member of a legislative assembly.

as•sem•bly•wom•an (ə **sĕm′**blē wo͝om′ən) *n.* A woman member of a legislative assembly.

as•sent (ə **sĕnt′**) *intr.v.* **as•sent•ed, as•sent•ing, as•sents.** To express agreement: *Everyone's parents assented to the class trip.* —*n.* Agreement, as to a proposal, especially in a formal or impersonal manner: *The prime minister desired the king's assent.*

❑ *These sound alike:* **assent, ascent** (rising).

as•sert (ə **sûrt′**) *tr.v.* **as•sert•ed, as•sert•ing, as•serts. 1.** To state or declare positively; claim: *By opposing the bill, the senators asserted their independence from business leaders.* **2.** To insist upon recognition of; defend or maintain: *The lawyer asserted the defendant's right to a fair trial.* ***—idiom.*** **assert (oneself).** To express oneself boldy or forcefully. **—as•sert′er, as•ser′tor** *n.*

as•ser•tion (ə **sûr′**shən) *n.* **1.** The act of asserting. **2.** A positive statement or claim, especially one for which no proof is offered: *His assertions of innocence were later found to be true.*

as•ser•tive (ə **sûr′**tĭv) *adj.* Bold and self-confident, especially in putting forward one's opinions: *She was assertive in her request for a raise.* **—as•ser′tive•ly** *adv.* **—as•ser′tive•ness** *n.*

as•sess (ə **sĕs′**) *tr.v.* **as•sessed, as•sess•ing, as•sess•es. 1.** To estimate the value of (property) for taxation: *The apartment building was assessed at several million dollars.* **2.a.** To set the amount of (a tax, fine, or other payment): *assess a tax for road repairs.* **b.** To charge (a person) with a tax, fine, or other special payment. *Each member of the team will be assessed five dollars for new equipment.* **3.** To analyze and determine the significance, importance, or value of; estimate; evaluate: *Our teacher has special skills in assessing problems of learning.* [First written down in 1423 in Middle English, from Latin *assidēre,* to sit by as an assistant judge

assembly line
Robots welding on an automobile assembly line in Fenton, Missouri

ă	**pat**	oi	**boy**
ā	**pay**	ou	**out**
âr	**care**	o͝o	**took**
ä	**father**	o͞o	**boot**
ĕ	**pet**	ŭ	**cut**
ē	**be**	ûr	**urge**
ĭ	**pit**	th	**thin**
ī	**pie**	*th*	**this**
îr	**pier**	hw	**whoop**
ŏ	**pot**	zh	**vision**
ō	**toe**	ə	**about**
ô	**paw**	N	*French* **bon**

: *ad-*, next to + *sedēre*, to sit.] —**as•sess′a•ble** *adj.*

as•sess•ment (ə sĕs′mənt) *n.* **1.** The act of assessing. **2.** An amount assessed: *Property owners paid an assessment for street repairs.*

as•ses•sor (ə sĕs′ər) *n.* An official whose job it is to assess the tax value of property.

as•set (ăs′ĕt′) *n.* **1.** A valuable quality or possession: *An agreeable personality is a great asset.* **2.** **assets.** All the property owned by a person or business that has monetary value and may be applied directly or indirectly to the payment of debts. [First written down in 1531 in Modern English, from Anglo-Norman *asez*, enough : Latin *ad-*, to + Latin *satis*, enough.]

as•sev•er•ate (ə sĕv′ə rāt′) *tr.v.* **as•sev•er•at•ed, as•sev•er•at•ing, as•sev•er•ates.** To declare seriously or positively; affirm.

as•sid•u•ous (ə sĭj′o͞o əs) *adj.* Diligent; industrious: *an assiduous worker.* —**as•sid′u•ous•ly** *adv.* —**as•sid′u•ous•ness** *n.*

as•sign (ə sīn′) *tr.v.* **as•signed, as•sign•ing, as•signs.** **1.** To set apart for a particular purpose; designate: *assign a day for the test.* **2.** To select for a duty or office; appoint: *a group of firefighters assigned to the industrial area of the city.* **3.** To give out as a task; allot: *The teacher assigned homework to all of us.* **4.** To regard as belonging; ascribe; attribute: *We sorted the rocks by assigning them to different categories.* [First written down about 1300 in Middle English and spelled *assignen*, from Latin *assignāre* : *ad-*, to + *signāre*, to mark (from *signum*, sign).] —**as•sign′a•ble** *adj.* —**as•sign′er** *n.*

as•sign•ee (ə sī′nē′ *or* ăs′ĭ nē′) *n.* A person to whom some property, rights, or interest is transferred by law.

as•sign•ment (ə sīn′mənt) *n.* **1.** The act of assigning: *The work was divided among us by assignment.* **2.** Something assigned, especially a task or job: *What's the chemistry assignment for tomorrow?* See Synonyms at **task.** **3.** A post of duty to which one is assigned: *The journalist will take an assignment outside the United States.*

as•sim•i•late (ə sĭm′ə lāt′) *v.* **as•sim•i•lat•ed, as•sim•i•lat•ing, as•sim•i•lates.** —*tr.* **1.** To take in and convert (nutrients) into living tissue: *The body assimilates protein.* **2.** To take in; incorporate; absorb: *immigrants striving to assimilate the culture of their new homeland.* **3.** To take into the cultural or social tradition of a group: *The United States assimilated immigrants of many nationalities.* **4.** To alter (a speech sound) by assimilation. —*intr.* **1.** To be taken in and converted into living tissue. **2.** To be taken into the mind: *technological changes that are difficult to assimilate.* **3.** To be taken into a group: *Many ethnic groups assimilated rapidly.* [First written down before 1425 in Middle English and spelled *assimilaten*, from Latin *assimilāre*, to make similar to : *ad-*, to + *similis*, like.] —**as•sim′i•la′tor** *n.*

as•sim•i•la•tion (ə sĭm′ə lā′shən) *n.* **1.** The act or process of assimilating: *assimilation of immigrants in the new country.* **2.** In biology, the process by which nourishment is changed into living tissue; constructive metabolism. **3.** In linguistics, the process by which a sound is modified to resemble a nearby sound. For example, the prefix *in-* becomes *im-* in *impossible* by assimilation.

As•sin•i•boin (ə sĭn′ə boin′) *n., pl.* **Assiniboin** or **As•sin•i•boins.** **1.** A member of a Native American people of northeast Montana and the adjacent area of Canada. **2.** The Siouan language of the Assiniboin.

as•sist (ə sĭst′) *tr. & intr.v.* **as•sist•ed, as•sist•ing, as•sists.** To help; aid: *Our friends assisted us in repairing the roof. I assisted in editing the videotape.* See Synonyms at **help.** —*n.* **1.** An act of giving aid; help: *give someone a quick assist.* **2.a.** In baseball, an act of fielding or throwing the ball that enables a runner to be put out. **b.** A pass that enables a teammate to score, as in basketball or hockey. [First written down in 1426 in Middle English and spelled *assisten*, from Latin *assistere* : *ad-*, next to + *sistere*, to stand.] —**as•sist′er** *n.*

as•sis•tance (ə sĭs′təns) *n.* Help; aid: *The government provided financial assistance to farmers.*

as•sis•tant (ə sĭs′tənt) *n.* A person who assists; a helper: *the President's special assistant.* —*adj.* Acting under the authority of another person: *an assistant curator.*

as•sizes (ə sī′zĭz) *pl.n.* A court session held periodically in each of the counties of England and Wales.

assn. *abbr.* An abbreviation of association.

assoc. *abbr.* An abbreviation of: **1.** Associate. **2.** Association.

as•so•ci•ate (ə sō′shē āt′ *or* ə sō′sē āt′) *v.* **as•so•ci•at•ed, as•so•ci•at•ing, as•so•ci•ates.** —*tr.* **1.** To bring together in one's mind or imagination; connect: *We associate the theater with Broadway and New York.* **2.** To connect (oneself) with a cause, group, or partnership: *Many large companies associate themselves with the charity.* —*intr.* **1.** To join in or form a union or other combination. **2.** To keep company: *How long have you been associating with those people?* —*n.* (ə sō′shē ĭt *or* ə sō′sē ĭt *or* ə sō′shē āt′ *or* ə sō′sē āt′). **1.** A partner or colleague: *my business associate.* **2.** A companion; a comrade. **3.** A member who has only partial status: *an associate of the museum society.* —*adj.* (ə sō′shē ĭt *or* ə sō′sē ĭt *or* ə sō′shē āt *or* ə sō′sē āt′). **1.** Joined with another and having equal or nearly equal status; sharing in responsibility or authority: *an associate judge.* **2.** Having only partial status: *an associate member of a club.* [First written down before 1425 in Middle English and spelled *associaten*, from Latin *associāre* : *ad-*, to + *socius*, companion.] —**as•so′ci•a′tor** (ə sō′shē ā′tər *or* ə sō′sē ā′tər) *n.*

as•so•ci•a•tion (ə sō′sē ā′shən *or* ə sō′shē ā′shən) *n.* **1.** The act of associating: *The author made a striking new association of ideas.* **2.** A partnership or friendship: *a close association with old schoolmates.* **3.** A group of people joined together for a common purpose or interest: *a trade association; a teachers' association.* **4.** An idea or a train of ideas triggered by another idea or by a thought, feeling, or sensation: *What associations does the word* whale *bring to your mind?*

association football *n. Chiefly British.* Soccer.

as•so•ci•a•tive (ə sō′shē ā′tĭv *or* ə sō′sē ā′tĭv *or* ə sō′shə tĭv) *adj.* **1.** Of, characterized by, resulting from, or causing association. **2.** In mathematics, of or relating to the associative property or an operation that has the associative property. —**as•so′ci•a′tive•ly** *adv.*

associative property *n.* In mathematics, a law that the combinations by which numbers are added or multiplied will not change their sum or product. For example, $2 + (3 + 4)$ will give the same sum as $(2 + 3) + 4$. $(2 \times 3) \times 5$ will give the same product as $2 \times (3 \times 5)$.

as•so•nance (ăs′ə nəns) *n.* **1.** Similarity in sound, especially the repetition in poetry of the same vowel sounds. **2.** A partial rhyme in which the stressed vowel sounds are the same but the consonants are different, as in *tent* and *sense.*

as•sort (ə sôrt′) *tr.v.* **as•sort•ed, as•sort•ing, as•sorts.** To separate into groups according to kinds; classify: *assort books by author.* —**as•sort′er** *n.*

as•sort•ed (ə sôr′tĭd) *adj.* Consisting of various kinds: *shirts of assorted sizes; assorted screws.*

Usage: assure

The words **assure**, **ensure**, and **insure** all mean "to make secure or certain," but **assure** and **insure** have more specific meanings as well. Of the three, only **assure** can mean "to cause to feel sure": *assured the queen of his loyalty.* **Insure** is the only one used in the commercial sense of "to guarantee persons or property against risk," as in *insured the car.*

as•sort•ment (ə sôrt′mənt) *n.* A collection of various kinds; a variety: *people with an unusual assortment of skills; an assortment of vegetables.*

asst. *abbr.* An abbreviation of assistant.

as•suage (ə swāj′) *tr.v.* **as•suaged, as•suag•ing, as•suag•es. 1.** To make less burdensome or painful: *Maybe your kind words will assuage their sorrow.* **2.** To satisfy; appease: *assuage one's thirst.* **3.** To pacify; calm: *Our apologies assuaged their anger.* **—as•suage′ment** *n.*

as•sume (ə so͞om′) *tr.v.* **as•sumed, as•sum•ing, as•sumes. 1.** To take for granted; suppose: *Let's assume that our guests will come on time.* **2.** To take upon oneself; undertake: *We assume responsibility for keeping the playground clean.* **3.** To undertake the duties of: *The new governor assumes office in January.* **4.** To take over; seize: *She assumed control of the project during the crisis.* **5.** To take on; put on: *assume a disguise.* **6.** To feign; pretend: *always assuming an air of indifference.* [First written down before 1420 in Middle English and spelled *assumen*, from Latin *assūmere* : *ad-*, to + *sūmere*, to take.] **—as•sum′a•ble** *adj.* **—as•sum′a•bly** *adv.* **—as•sum′er** *n.*

as•sumed (ə so͞omd′) *adj.* **1.** Fictitious; adopted: *an assumed name.* **2.** Taken for granted: *an assumed fact.*

as•sum•ing (ə so͞o′mĭng) *adj.* Taking too much for granted; presumptuous; arrogant.

as•sump•tion (ə sŭmp′shən) *n.* **1.** The act of assuming. **2.** An idea or a statement accepted as true without proof: *Let's start with the assumption that all people have equal rights under the law.* **3. Assumption. a.** In Christian theology, the bodily taking up of the Virgin Mary into heaven. **b.** A Christian feast on August 15 commemorating this.

as•sur•ance (ə sho͝or′əns) *n.* **1.** The act of assuring or the state of being assured. **2.** A statement or indication that inspires confidence; a guarantee: *The debtor gave the bank solemn assurance that the debt would be paid.* **3.** Confidence; certainty: *We had no assurance that the car was in good condition.* **4.** Self-confidence: *The veteran actor played the part with complete assurance.*

as•sure (ə sho͝or′) *tr.v.* **as•sured, as•sur•ing, as•sures. 1.** To declare positively: *I can assure you that the train will be on time.* **2.** To cause to feel sure; convince: *She assured me of her good intentions.* **3.** To make certain; ensure: *The bank lent us the money to assure the success of the business.* **4.** To give confidence to; reassure: *The doctor assured me that I would recover quickly.* —SEE NOTE.

as•sured (ə sho͝ord′) *adj.* **1.** Confident: *an assured manner.* **2.** Certain; guaranteed: *an assured success.* **—as•sur′ed•ly** (ə sho͝or′ĭd lē) *adv.*

As•syr•i•a (ə sîr′ē ə). An ancient empire of western Asia in the upper valley of the Tigris River. In the ninth through seventh centuries B.C. the empire extended from the Mediterranean Sea across Arabia and Armenia. **—As•syr′i•an** *adj. & n.*

As•tar•te (ə stär′tē) *n.* In ancient Phoenician mythology, the goddess of love and fertility.

as•ta•tine (ăs′tə tēn′ *or* ăs′tə tĭn) *n. Symbol* **At** A radioactive metalloid element that resembles iodine in some of its properties and is usually produced artificially from bismuth. It is highly unstable, with many isotopes, the most stable one having a half-life of about 8 hours. Atomic number 85. See table at **element.**

as•ter (ăs′tər) *n.* Any of various plants having white, purplish, or pink flowers resembling daisies. [First written down in 1706 in Modern English, from Greek *astēr*, star.]

as•ter•isk (ăs′tə rĭsk′) *n.* A symbol (*) used in printed and written matter to indicate an omission or a reference to a footnote, for example. [First written down before 1387 in Middle English, from Greek *asteriskos*, diminutive of *astēr*, star.]

a•stern (ə stûrn′) *adv. & adj.* **1.** Behind a ship or boat. **2.** At or toward the rear of a ship or boat. **3.** With the stern foremost; backward.

as•ter•oid (ăs′tə roid′) *n.* Any of numerous small, often irregularly shaped bodies that orbit the sun, chiefly in the region between Mars and Jupiter. They range in size from about one mile to several hundred miles in diameter.

asth•ma (ăz′mə *or* ăs′mə) *n.* A chronic respiratory disease that is often caused by an allergy and is marked by tightness of the chest with coughing and difficulty in breathing. [First written down before 1398 in Middle English and spelled *asma*, from Greek *asthma*.]

asth•mat•ic (ăz măt′ĭk *or* ăs măt′ĭk) *adj.* **1.** Of or relating to asthma. **2.** Having asthma: *an asthmatic child.* —*n.* A person with asthma.

as though *conj.* As if: *They looked as though they were enjoying themselves.*

a•stig•ma•tism (ə stĭg′mə tĭz′əm) *n.* A structural defect of an eye or a lens that prevents rays of light from converging at a single point, producing indistinct or imperfect images. **—as′tig•mat′ic** (ăs′-tĭg măt′ĭk) *adj.*

a•stir (ə stûr′) *adj.* **1.** In motion; moving about: *The miners' camp was astir after the news of the gold discovery.* **2.** Having gotten out of bed; up.

as to *prep.* **1.** With regard to: *There is much controversy as to nuclear energy.* **2.** According to: *The fabrics were arranged as to color.*

a•ston•ish (ə stŏn′ĭsh) *tr.v.* **a•ston•ished, a•ston•ish•ing, a•ston•ish•es.** To fill with wonder; amaze; surprise: *The results of the experiment astonished the researchers.* See Synonyms at **surprise.** [First written down before 1300 in Middle English and spelled *astonien*, from Old French *estoner* : Latin *ex-*, out + Latin *tonāre*, to thunder.]

a•ston•ish•ing (ə stŏn′ĭ shĭng) *adj.* Greatly surprising; amazing: *an astonishing discovery.* **—a•ston′ish•ing•ly** *adv.*

a•ston•ish•ment (ə stŏn′ĭsh mənt) *n.* Great surprise; amazement: *our astonishment at seeing a shooting star.*

As•tor (ăs′tər), **Nancy Witcher Langhorne.** Viscountess Astor. 1879–1964. American-born British politician. In 1919 she became the first woman to sit in the House of Commons, serving until 1945.

a•stound (ə stound′) *tr.v.* **a•stound•ed, a•stound•ing, a•stounds.** To astonish and bewilder: *The rise in stock prices astounded investors.* See Synonyms at **surprise.** [First written down in 1600 in Modern English, from Middle English *astoned*, past participle of *astonen*, to astonish.]

a•stound•ing (ə stoun′dĭng) *adj.* Surprising; amazing: *an astounding success.* **—a•stound′ing•ly** *adv.*

a•strad•dle (ə străd′l) *prep.* Astride; astride of: *astraddle a horse.*

as•tra•khan (ăs′trə kən) *n.* **1.** The curly or wavy fur of young lambs from Russia. **2.** A fabric with curly looped pile, made to resemble this fur. [First written down in 1766 in Modern English, from *Astrakhan* in southwest Russia.]

as•tral (ăs′trəl) *adj.* Of, relating to, coming from, or resembling the stars; stellar.

a•stray (ə strā′) *adv.* Away from the proper goal or path: *led astray by bad advice.*

a•stride (ə strīd′) *adv.* **1.** With the legs on each side: *riding astride on a horse.* **2.** With the legs wide apart. —*prep.* With a leg on each side of; bestriding: *The cowboy sat astride the horse's back.* **—idiom. astride of.** Astride: *She stood astride of the fallen tree.*

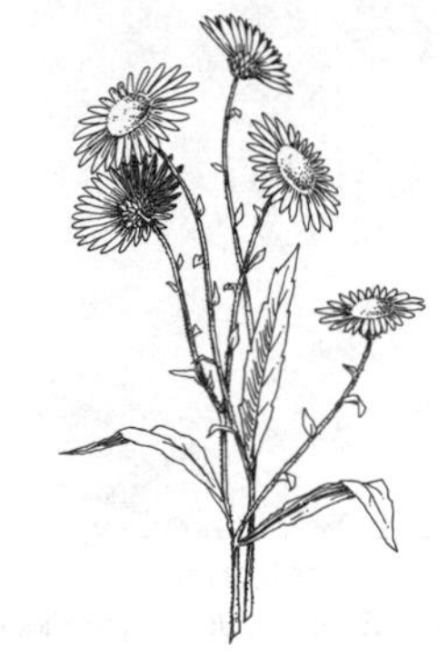

aster

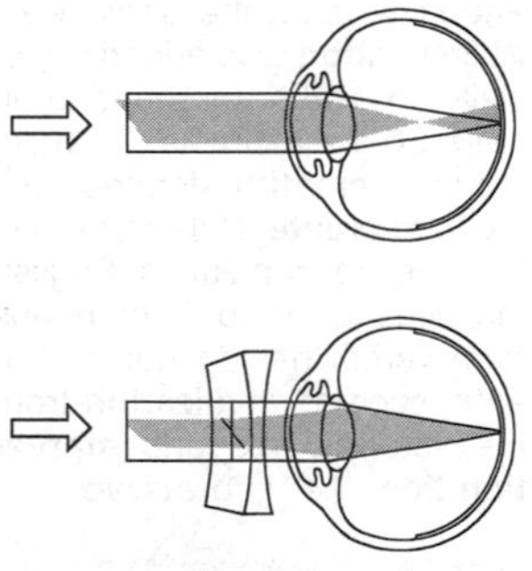

astigmatism

Top: Before correction
Bottom: After correction

ă	pat	oi	boy
ā	pay	ou	out
âr	care	o͝o	took
ä	father	o͞o	boot
ĕ	pet	ŭ	cut
ē	be	ûr	urge
ĭ	pit	th	thin
ī	pie	*th*	this
îr	pier	hw	whoop
ŏ	pot	zh	vision
ō	toe	ə	about
ô	paw	N	*French* bon

astronaut
Edwin E. Aldrin, Jr., on the moon

Word Building: –ation

The very common noun suffix **–ation** comes from a Latin suffix that is added to a verb and changes that verb to a noun. In English, the suffix **–ation** is used the same way. At first **–ation** was added especially to verbs that ended in **–ate**. So, for example, we have the noun **creation**, formed from the verb **create**. But **–ation** has become so popular in English that it is used to form nouns from verbs that do not end in **–ate**, such as **civilization** from the verb **civilize** and **starvation** from the verb **starve**.

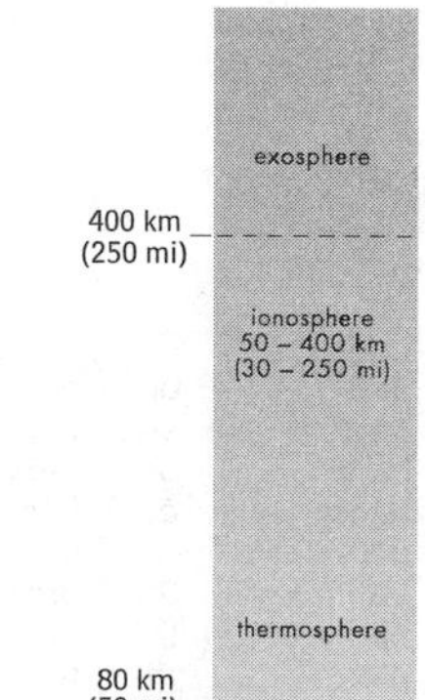

atmosphere

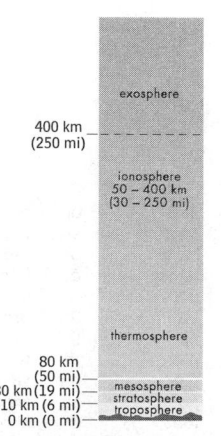

as•trin•gent (ə strĭn′jənt) *adj.* Having the property of drawing together or contracting tissues. —*n.* A substance, such as alum, that draws together or contracts body tissues and thus checks the flow of blood or other secretions. **—as•trin′gen•cy** *n.* **—as•trin′gent•ly** *adv.*

astro– *pref.* A prefix that means: **1.** Star: *astrophysics.* **2.** Celestial body or bodies: *astrometry.* **3.** Outer space: *astronaut.*

astrol. *abbr.* An abbreviation of: **1.** Astrologer. **2.** Astrological. **3.** Astrology.

as•tro•labe (ăs′trə lāb′) *n.* A medieval instrument formerly used to determine the altitude of the sun and other celestial bodies.

as•tro•log•i•cal (ăs′trə lŏj′ĭ kəl) *adj.* Of or relating to astrology: *astrological predictions.* **—as′tro•log′i•cal•ly** *adv.*

as•trol•o•gy (ə strŏl′ə jē) *n.* The study of the positions of the stars and planets in the belief that they influence the course of human affairs and natural occurrences on earth. **—as•trol′o•ger** *n.*

as•trom•e•try (ə strŏm′ĭ trē) *n.* The scientific measurement of the positions and motions of celestial bodies.

astron. *abbr.* An abbreviation of: **1.** Astronomer. **2.** Astronomical. **3.** Astronomy.

as•tro•naut (ăs′trə nôt′) *n.* A person trained to serve as a member of the crew of a spacecraft. [First written down in 1929 in Modern English : Greek *astron,* star + Greek *nautēs,* sailor.]

as•tro•nau•tics (ăs′trə nô′tĭks) *n. (used with a singular or plural verb).* The science and technology of space flight. **—as′tro•nau′tic, as′tro•nau′ti•cal** *adj.*

as•tron•o•mer (ə strŏn′ə mər) *n.* A person who specializes in astronomy.

as•tro•nom•i•cal (ăs′trə nŏm′ĭ kəl) also **as•tro•nom•ic** (ăs′trə nŏm′ĭk) *adj.* **1.** Of or relating to astronomy. **2.** Too large to be easily imagined; immense: *The budget for running the federal government is astronomical.* **—as′tro•nom′i•cal•ly** *adv.*

astronomical unit *n.* A unit of length equal to the mean distance of Earth from the sun, about 93 million miles (150 million kilometers), used to measure distances between planets and stars.

astronomical year *n.* A solar year.

as•tron•o•my (ə strŏn′ə mē) *n.* The science that deals with the study of the sun, moon, planets, stars, and all other celestial bodies. Astronomy studies the composition, motion, relative position, energy, and size of the universe and the objects in it. [First written down before 1200 in Middle English and spelled *astronomie,* from Greek *astronomia* : *astron,* star + *-nomia,* field of study.]

as•tro•phys•ics (ăs′trō fĭz′ĭks) *n. (used with a singular verb).* The branch of astronomy that deals with the physical processes, such as energy generation and transmission, that occur in stars, galaxies, and interstellar space. **—as′tro•phys′i•cal** *adj.*

As•tro•Turf (ăs′trō tûrf′). A trademark for an artificial ground covering that resembles grass.

as•tute (ə sto͞ot′ *or* ə styo͞ot′) *adj.* Having or showing keen judgment; shrewd: *The reporter was an astute observer. Before advising us the carpenter made an astute appraisal of the blueprints.* **—as•tute′ly** *adv.* **—as•tute′ness** *n.*

A•sun•ción (ä so͞on′syôn′). The capital and largest city of Paraguay, in the southern part of the country near the Argentinian border. It is Paraguay's chief port. Population, 455,517.

a•sun•der (ə sŭn′dər) *adv.* **1.** Into separate parts or groups: *A tornado tore the house asunder.* **2.** Apart from each other in position or direction: *The curtains were drawn asunder.*

as well as *conj.* And in addition: *warm as well as sunny.* —*prep.* In addition to: *The principal as well as the teachers attended the meeting.*

a•sy•lum (ə sī′ləm) *n.* **1.** A hospital or shelter for people with physical or mental disorders. **2.** A place of refuge: *I sought asylum from the raging storm in an old shed.* **3.** Protection and immunity from extradition granted to a political refugee from another country.

a•sym•met•ri•cal (ā′sĭ mĕt′rĭkəl) also **a•sym•met•ric** (ā′sĭ mĕt′rĭk) *adj.* Not symmetrical; lacking symmetry. **—a′sym•met′ri•cal•ly** *adv.*

a•sym•me•try (ā sĭm′ĭ trē) *n.* Lack of symmetry or balance.

at (ăt; ət *when unstressed*) *prep.* **1.** In or near the position or location of: *at home; at the center of the room.* **2.** To or toward the direction or goal of: *look at us; jump at the chance.* **3.** On, near, or by the time or age of: *at noon.* **4.** In the state or condition of: *He's at peace with himself.* **5.** In the activity or field of: *skilled at playing chess; good at math.* **6.** Because of: *rejoice at victory.* **7.a.** Dependent upon: *at your mercy.* **b.** According to: *at the judge's discretion.* **8.** In the rate, extent, or amount of: *at 40 miles per hour; at two dollars a gallon.* **9.** Through; by way of: *Come in at the side entrance.*

At The symbol for the element **astatine.**

at•a•vism (ăt′ə vĭz′əm) *n.* The reappearance in a strain of organisms of a hereditary trait that has been absent for several generations, generally as a result of a chance recombination of genes.

at•a•vis•tic (ăt′ə vĭs′tĭk) *adj.* Reappearing after an absence of several generations; being an atavism.

a•tax•i•a (ə tăk′sē ə) also **a•tax•y** (ə tăk′sē) *n.* Loss or lack of muscular coordination. **—a•tax′ic** *adj.*

ate (āt) *v.* Past tense of **eat.**
❑ *These sound alike:* **ate, eight** (number).

–ate[1] *suff.* A suffix that means: **1.** Characterized by: *Latinate.* **2.** One that is characterized by: *laminate.* **3.** Rank; office: *rabbinate.* **4.** To act upon in a specified manner: *insulate.*

–ate[2] *suff.* A suffix that means a salt or an ester of a specified acid whose name ends in *-ic*: *acetate.*

at•el•ier (ăt′l yā′) *n.* An artist's studio.

a tem•po (ä tĕm′pō) *adv. & adj.* In music, returning to the original tempo.

Ath•a•bas•kan (ăth′ə băs′kən) *n.* A group of languages of Native American people of the western United States and Canada and parts of Alaska. Apache and Navajo are two important Athabaskan languages. **—Ath′a•bas′kan** *adj.*

a•the•ism (ā′thē ĭz′əm) *n.* Disbelief in or denial of the existence of God.

a•the•ist (ā′thē ĭst) *n.* A person who does not believe in or denies the existence of God. **—a′the•is′tic** *adj.*

A•the•na (ə thē′nə) *n.* In Greek mythology, the goddess of wisdom and the arts, identified with the Roman Minerva.

Ath•ens (ăth′ənz). The capital and largest city of Greece, in the eastern part of the country near an arm of the Aegean Sea. It was at the height of its cultural achievements and imperial power in the fifth century B.C. Athens became the capital of modern Greece in 1834. Population, 885,737.

ath•er•o•scle•ro•sis (ăth′ə rō sklə rō′sĭs) *n.* A diseased condition in which a deposit of fatty material accumulates on the interior walls of the arteries, making them narrower.

ath•lete (ăth′lēt′) *n.* A person who is trained for or naturally good at sports requiring physical strength, endurance, and coordination. [First written down before 1425 in Middle English and spelled *athletez,* from Greek *athlētēs,* contestant, from *athlein,* to contend.]

ath•lete's foot (ăth′lēts) *n.* A contagious skin disease caused by parasitic fungi. It usually attacks the feet, causing the skin to itch, blister, and crack.

ath•let•ic (ăth lĕt′ĭk) *adj.* **1.** Of, relating to, or for athletics or athletes: *athletic ability; an athletic club.* **2.** Physically strong; muscular: *an athletic build.* See Synonyms at **muscular.** **—ath•let′i•cal•ly** *adv.*

ath•let•ics (ăth lĕt′ĭks) *n. (used with a singular or plural verb).* Athletic activities; sports.

athletic supporter *n.* An elastic support for the male genitals, worn during athletic activities.

a•thwart (ə thwôrt′) *adv.* **1.** From side to side across. **2.** At right angles to the center line of a ship or boat. *—prep.* **1.** Across: *threw the rope athwart the dock.* **2.** Across the center line or course of: *a tug pushing athwart the ocean liner.* **3.** Contrary to; against: *spending habits quite athwart their meager income.*

–ation *suff.* A suffix that means: **1.** Action or process: *strangulation.* **2.** The state, condition, or quality of: *starvation.* **3.** The result of an action or process: *discoloration.* —SEE NOTE.

–ative *suff.* A suffix that means of, relating to, or associated with: *talkative; authoritative.*

At•lan•ta (ăt lăn′tə). The capital and largest city of Georgia, in the northwest part of the state. It was founded in 1837 and almost entirely destroyed by fire on November 15, 1864, before the start of Union general William Tecumseh Sherman's march to the sea. Population, 394,017.

At•lan•tic Ocean (ăt lăn′tĭk). The world's second-largest ocean, divided into the **North Atlantic** and the **South Atlantic.** It extends from the Arctic in the north to the Antarctic in the south between the eastern Americas and western Europe and Africa.

Atlantic Standard Time *n.* Standard time in the fourth time zone west of Greenwich, England, used, for example, in Puerto Rico and Nova Scotia.

At•lan•tis (ăt lăn′tĭs) *n.* A fabled island or continent of ancient times, said to have sunk beneath the sea during an earthquake.

at•las (ăt′ləs) *n., pl.* **at•las•es.** A book or bound collection of maps. [First written down in 1589 in Modern English, after *Atlas*, legendary king of northern Africa, sometimes identified with, or considered descended from, the Titan Atlas.]

At•las (ăt′ləs) *n.* In Greek mythology, a Titan who supports the heavens on his shoulders as punishment for revolt against Zeus.

Atlas Mountains. A mountain range of northwest Africa extending from southwest Morocco to northern Tunisia. It rises to 13,665 feet (4,167.8 meters).

ATM *abbr.* An abbreviation of: **1.** Automated teller machine. **2.** Automatic teller machine.

at•mos•phere (ăt′mə sfîr′) *n.* **1.** The mass of gases that surrounds Earth or some other celestial body and is held by the force of gravity. The atmosphere of Earth is rich in nitrogen; that of Venus is mainly carbon dioxide. **2.** A unit of pressure equal to the pressure of the air at sea level, about 14.7 pounds per square inch. **3.** The air or climate of a place: *the dry atmosphere of the desert.* **4.** A general feeling or mood: *the library's quiet atmosphere.* [First written down in 1677 in Modern English, from New Latin *atmosphaera* : Greek *atmos*, vapor + Latin *sphaera*, sphere.]

at•mos•pher•ic (ăt′mə sfĕr′ĭk *or* ăt′mə sfîr′ĭk) also **at•mos•pher•i•cal** (ăt′mə sfĕr′ĭ kəl *or* ăt′mə sfîr′ĭ kəl) *adj.* Of, relating to, in, or from the atmosphere: *atmospheric disturbances; atmospheric flight.* **—at′mos•pher′i•cal•ly** *adv.*

atmospheric pressure *n.* Pressure caused by the weight of the air. At sea level it has an average value of one atmosphere but reduces with increasing altitude.

at•mos•pher•ics (ăt′mə sfĕr′ĭks *or* ăt′mə sfîr′ĭks) *n. (used with a singular verb).* Electromagnetic radiation produced by natural disturbances in the atmosphere, such as lightning.

at. no. *abbr.* An abbreviation of atomic number.

a•toll (ăt′ôl′ *or* ăt′ŏl′ *or* ā′tôl′ *or* ā′tŏl′) *n.* A coral island or a string of coral islands and reefs forming a ring that nearly or entirely encloses a lagoon. [First written down in 1625 in Modern English and spelled *atollon*, perhaps ultimately from Tamil *aṭar*, to be close together, thick, crowded.]

at•om (ăt′əm) *n.* **1.a.** The smallest unit of an element, consisting of protons and neutrons in a dense central nucleus surrounded by moving electrons. The number of protons equals the number of electrons so the entire structure is electrically neutral. Atoms remain intact in chemical reactions, except for the removal, transfer, or exchange of certain electrons. **b.** A unit of this kind regarded as a source of nuclear energy. **2.** A bit or jot: *There is not an atom of truth in that statement.* [First written down in 1477 in Middle English and spelled *attome*, from Greek *atomos*, indivisible, atom : *a-*, not + *tomos*, cuttable (from *temnein*, to cut).] —SEE NOTE.

atom bomb *n.* A nuclear bomb that explodes by the nearly instantaneous release of energy from the fission of heavy atomic nuclei, as of uranium or plutonium, in an uncontrolled chain reaction.

a•tom•ic (ə tŏm′ĭk) *adj.* **1.** Of or relating to atoms. **2.** Using or produced by atomic energy; nuclear: *an atomic power plant.*

atomic age *n.* The present age considered as the time of the discovery and use of atomic energy; the nuclear age.

atomic bomb *n.* An atom bomb.

atomic clock *n.* An extremely precise clock that is regulated by atomic vibrations.

atomic energy *n.* Nuclear energy.

atomic mass *n.* The mass of an atom, usually expressed in atomic mass units.

atomic mass unit *n.* A unit of mass equal to $\frac{1}{12}$ the mass of the most abundant kind of carbon atom; approximately 1.6604×10^{-24} gram.

atomic number *n.* The number of protons in the atomic nucleus of a chemical element.

atomic theory *n.* The theory that all matter is made up of atoms and that atoms are the smallest possible units of matter.

atomic weight *n.* The average weight of an atom of an element, usually expressed relative to the most abundant isotope of carbon, which is assigned 12 atomic mass units.

at•om•ize (ăt′ə mīz′) *tr.v.* **at•om•ized, at•om•iz•ing, at•om•iz•es. 1.** To break apart or separate into atoms. **2.** To reduce (a liquid) into a fine spray. **—at′om•i•za′tion** (ăt′ə mĭ zā′shən) *n.*

at•om•iz•er (ăt′ə mī′zər) *n.* A device for producing a fine spray, especially of a perfume or medicine.

atom smasher *n.* An atomic particle accelerator.

a•ton•al (ā tō′nəl) *adj.* In music, having no key or tonality. **—a•ton′al•ly** *adv.*

a•to•nal•i•ty (ā′tō năl′ĭ tē) *n., pl.* **a•to•nal•i•ties.** The absence of a tonal center and of harmonies using a diatonic scale.

a•tone (ə tōn′) *intr.v.* **a•toned, a•ton•ing, a•tones.** To make amends for a sin, fault, or other wrong: *atone for bad manners by apologizing.* [First written down about 1300 in Middle English and spelled *atonen*, to be reconciled, from *at one*, in agreement : *at*, at + *one*, one.]

a•tone•ment (ə tōn′mənt) *n.* **1.** The act of atoning; amends. **2. Atonement.** In Christianity, the sacrifice and death of Jesus to redeem mankind.

atom

Everything in the universe is made up of **atoms**. An atom is incredibly tiny. The smallest bacterium that can be seen with an ordinary microscope contains about one trillion atoms. Each atom consists of even tinier particles. **Protons** and **neutrons** form the nucleus, a minute region at the center of the atom. If a hydrogen atom were about four miles in diameter, its nucleus would be about the size of a tennis ball. Outside the nucleus, the atom is mostly empty space. **Electrons** zip through this space at fantastic speeds, completing billions of trips around the nucleus each millionth of a second. The rapid motion of the electrons makes an atom act as if it were solid, just as the rapidly whirling blades of a fan prevent a stick from being shoved through them.

atomizer
Perfume atomizer

ă	pat	oi	boy
ā	pay	ou	out
âr	care	ŏŏ	took
ä	father	ōō	boot
ĕ	pet	ŭ	cut
ē	be	ûr	urge
ĭ	pit	th	thin
ī	pie	*th*	this
îr	pier	hw	whoop
ŏ	pot	zh	vision
ō	toe	ə	about
ô	paw	N	*French* bon

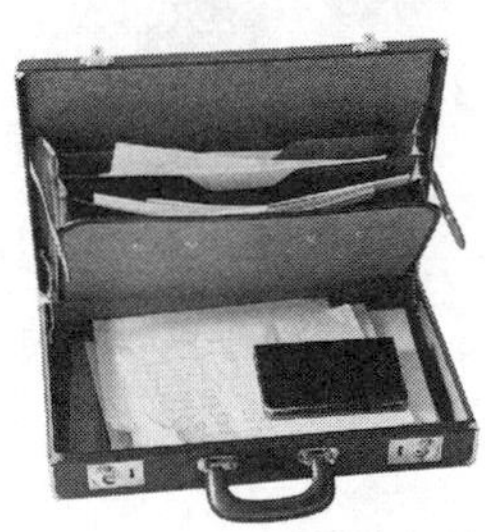

attaché case

a•top (ə tŏp′) *prep.* On top of: *The Supreme Court stands atop our judicial court system.*

ATP (ā′tē′pē′) *n.* A compound of carbon, hydrogen, nitrogen, oxygen, and phosphorus, in the proportions $C_{10}H_{16}N_5O_{13}P_3$, that acts as an energy source in metabolism, especially during muscular activity.

A•treus (ā′tro͞os′ *or* ā′trē əs) *n.* In Greek mythology, a king of Mycenae and the father of Agamemnon and Menelaus.

a•tri•um (ā′trē əm) *n., pl.* **a•tri•a** (ā′trē ə) or **a•tri•ums.** **1.** The open entrance court of an ancient Roman house. **2.** A cavity or chamber of the body, especially one of the chambers of the heart that receives blood from the veins and pumps it into a ventricle.

a•tro•cious (ə trō′shəs) *adj.* **1.** Extremely evil or cruel; wicked. **2.** Very bad; abominable: *atrocious weather.* [First written down in 1669 in Modern English, from Latin *atrōx*, cruel.] **—a•tro′cious•ly** *adv.* **—a•tro′cious•ness** *n.*

a•troc•i•ty (ə trŏs′ĭ tē) *n., pl.* **a•troc•i•ties.** **1.** The condition of being atrocious. **2.** An act of extreme cruelty and violence.

at•ro•phy (ăt′rə fē) *n., pl.* **at•ro•phies.** The wasting away of the body or of any of its organs or tissues, especially through imperfect nourishment or disuse. *—tr. & intr.v.* **at•ro•phied, at•ro•phy•ing, at•ro•phies.** To waste away or cause to waste away: *A month of inactivity had atrophied the patient's body.*

at•ro•pine (ăt′rə pēn′ *or* ăt′rə pĭn) also **at•ro•pin** (ăt′rə pĭn) *n.* A very poisonous bitter alkaloid composed of carbon, hydrogen, nitrogen, and oxygen in the proportions $C_{17}H_{23}NO_3$. It is obtained from belladonna and is used as a medicine to control muscle spasms and relax the pupils in examining the eye.

at•tach (ə tăch′) *v.* **at•tached, at•tach•ing, at•tach•es.** *—tr.* **1.** To fasten or join; connect: *attach the wires.* **2.** To bind by ties of affection or loyalty: *The brother and sister are very attached to each other.* **3.** To think of as belonging; ascribe: *I attach no importance to our different points of view.* **4.** To add (something) at the end; append: *The lawyer had all parties attach their signatures to the document.* **5.** To assign (military personnel) to a unit on a temporary basis: *attach soldiers to an expeditionary force.* **6.** To take or seize (property) by court order: *The bank attached the debtor's salary.* *—intr.* To adhere or belong: *Acclaim attaches to the hero.* [First written down in 1338 in Middle English and spelled *attachen*, from Old French *estachier*, from *estache*, stake, of Germanic origin.] **—at•tach′a•ble** *adj.*

at•ta•ché (ăt′ə shā′) *n.* A person assigned to the staff of a diplomatic mission to serve in some particular capacity: *a cultural attaché to the American Embassy.*

attaché case *n.* A briefcase resembling a small suitcase, with hinges and flat sides.

at•tach•ment (ə tăch′mənt) *n.* **1.** The act of attaching or condition of being attached: *attachment of a horse to a wagon.* **2.** Something that attaches as a supplementary part; an accessory: *This vacuum cleaner has several attachments.* **3.** A bond of affection or loyalty: *a strong attachment to a friend.*

at•tack (ə tăk′) *v.* **at•tacked, at•tack•ing, at•tacks.** *—tr.* **1.** To set upon with violent force: *Even large animals will not attack elephants.* **2.** To criticize strongly or in a hostile manner: *The candidates attacked each other in their debate.* **3.** To affect harmfully; afflict: *An epidemic of flu attacked thousands of people.* **4.** To start work on with purpose and vigor: *attack the problem of costly health care.* *—intr.* To launch an assault: *The troops attacked at dawn.* *—n.* **1.** The act of attacking; an assault. **2.** An expression of strong criticism. **3.** An occurrence or onset of a disease, especially when sudden: *an attack of asthma.* **4.** The manner in which a musical tone, phrase, or passage is begun: *a hard, cutting attack.* [First written down in 1600 in Modern English, from Old French *attaquer*, of Germanic origin.] **—at•tack′er** *n.*

at•tain (ə tān′) *tr.v.* **at•tained, at•tain•ing, at•tains.** **1.** To gain, accomplish, or achieve by effort: *attain a diploma by hard work.* See Synonyms at **reach.** **2.** To arrive at or reach, as through time, growth, or movement: *Today many people attain the age of 80.* [First written down before 1300 in Middle English and spelled *atteignen*, from Old French *ataindre*, to reach to : Latin *ad-*, to + Latin *tangere*, to touch.] **—at•tain′a•bil′i•ty** *n.* **—at•tain′a•ble** *adj.*

at•tain•der (ə tān′dər) *n.* In law, the loss of all civil rights of a person who has been sentenced for a serious crime.

at•tain•ment (ə tān′mənt) *n.* **1.** The act of attaining: *Despite attainment of independence, the United States remained closely associated with Great Britain.* **2.** Something attained; an acquirement, as a skill or an ability. Often used in the plural: *Eleanor Roosevelt is noted for her attainments in diplomacy.*

at•taint (ə tānt′) *tr.v.* **at•taint•ed, at•taint•ing, at•taints.** In law, to condemn by sentence of attainder.

at•tar (ăt′ər) *n.* A fragrant oil obtained from the petals of flowers, especially roses, and used in making perfume.

at•tempt (ə tĕmpt′) *tr.v.* **at•tempt•ed, at•tempt•ing, at•tempts.** To make an effort; try: *Inventors attempt to find new devices that help humans live more easily.* *—n.* **1.** An effort or a try: *an attempt to solve the mystery.* **2.** An attack; an assault: *an attempt on the king's life.* [First written down before 1393 in Middle English and spelled *attempten*, from Latin *attemptāre* : *ad-*, toward + *temptāre*, to test.] **—at•tempt′a•ble** *adj.*

at•tend (ə tĕnd′) *v.* **at•tend•ed, at•tend•ing, at•tends.** *—tr.* **1.** To be present at; go to: *Most pupils attend school all day.* **2.** To follow as a result or accompany as a circumstance: *Many risks attend mountain climbing.* **3.** To wait upon; serve: *The squire attended the knight during the joust.* **4.** To take care of: *Two nurses attended the sick boy.* *—intr.* **1.** To be present: *I wanted to go, but was ill and could not attend.* **2.** To apply oneself; give care and thought: *Please attend to the matter at hand.* **3.** To pay attention; heed: *The audience attended to the lecture with great interest.* **4.** To remain ready to serve: *Many courtiers attend upon the king.* [First written down before 1325 in Middle English and spelled *attenden*, from Latin *attendere*, to heed : *ad-*, toward + *tendere*, to stretch.]

at•ten•dance (ə tĕn′dəns) *n.* **1.** The act or practice of being present: *The child's attendance at school has been perfect.* **2.** The persons or number of persons present: *an attendance of 50,000 at the football game.* **3.** The act or state of taking care of someone or something, as at a hospital: *a physician in attendance.*

at•ten•dant (ə tĕn′dənt) *n.* A person who attends or waits on another: *a parking lot attendant.* *—adj.* Accompanying or following as a result: *attendant circumstances.*

at•ten•tion (ə tĕn′shən) *n.* **1.** Concentration of the mental powers upon something or someone: *Read the article carefully and pay attention to the details. The speaker held the listeners' attention for more than an hour.* **2.** Observant consideration; notice:

Your suggestion has come to our attention. **3. attentions.** Acts of courtesy or consideration, especially in trying to win a person's affection: *Do you think his attentions are sincere?* **4.** The posture taken by a soldier, with the body erect, eyes to the front, arms at the sides, and heels together: *Stand at attention.* —*interj.* An expression used as a command to assume an erect military posture.

at•ten•tive (ə tĕn′tĭv) *adj.* **1.** Giving attention to something; alert: *Only the most attentive students understood the explanation.* **2.** Marked by careful attention to the comfort of others; considerate: *an attentive host.* **—at•ten′tive•ly** *adv.* **—at•ten′tive•ness** *n.*

at•ten•u•ate (ə tĕn′yo͞o āt′) *v.* **at•ten•u•at•ed, at•ten•u•at•ing, at•ten•u•ates.** —*tr.* **1.** To make slender or thin: *The drought attenuated the river to a narrow channel.* **2.** To reduce, as in strength, force, or power; weaken: *Medicine attenuated the effect of the fever.* —*intr.* To become thin or slender. **—at•ten′u•a′tion** *n.*

at•test (ə tĕst′) *v.* **at•test•ed, at•test•ing, at•tests.** —*tr.* **1.** To declare or state to be true, correct, or genuine, especially by signing one's name as a witness: *attest a will.* **2.** To give evidence or proof of; prove: *Their rounded shapes attest the great age of the mountains.* —*intr.* To bear witness: *I can attest to his presence at the concert.*

at•test•ed (ə tĕs′tĭd) *adj.* Recorded in written form: *Use of the word* helicopter *is first attested in English in 1887.*

at•tic (ăt′ĭk) *n.* A story or room just below the roof of a building. [First written down in 1696 in Modern English, from *Attic story*, story of a building enclosed by one decorative structure placed above another, much taller decorative structure, usually involving the Attic order, an architectural order having square columns of any of the basic five orders, from Latin *Atticus*, of Attica, the region in Greece of which Athens was the capital.]

At•ti•la (ăt′l ə *or* ə tĭl′ə). A.D. 406?–453. King of the Huns (433?–453) and the most successful of the barbarian invaders of the Roman Empire.

at•tire (ə tīr′) *tr.v.* **at•tired, at•tir•ing, at•tires.** To dress, especially in fine or formal clothing: *an emperor attired in ceremonial robes.* —*n.* Clothing, costume, or apparel: *white tennis attire.*

at•ti•tude (ăt′ĭ to͞od′ *or* ăt′ĭ tyo͞od′) *n.* **1.** A state of mind with regard to someone or something; a point of view: *What is the mayor's attitude toward building a new city park?* **2.** A position of the body indicative of a mood or condition: *The kids sprawled on the couch in a relaxed attitude.* **3.** The position of a vehicle, such as an aircraft, in relation to its direction of motion or some other point of reference.

at•tor•ney (ə tûr′nē) *n., pl.* **at•tor•neys.** A person, especially a lawyer, legally appointed to act as agent for another.

attorney at law *n., pl.* **attorneys at law.** A lawyer.

attorney general *n., pl.* **attorneys general** or **attorney generals.** The chief law officer of a state or national government.

at•tract (ə trăkt′) *v.* **at•tract•ed, at•tract•ing, at•tracts.** —*tr.* To cause to draw near or adhere; direct to oneself or itself by some quality or action: *A magnet attracts nails by the physical force of magnetism. The fine beaches attract many tourists.* —*intr.* To have the power to draw to oneself or itself: *attract by magnetic force.* [First written down before 1425 in Middle English, from Latin *attrahere* : *ad-*, toward + *trahere*, to pull.] **—at•tract′er, at•trac′tor** *n.*

at•trac•tion (ə trăk′shən) *n.* **1.** The act or power of attracting: *the attraction of a magnet.* **2.** Something that attracts: *Its many theaters and museums are some of New York's greatest attractions.*

at•trac•tive (ə trăk′tĭv) *adj.* **1.** Having the power to attract: *the attractive forces of magnetism and gravity.* **2.** Pleasing to the eye or mind; appealing: *an attractive young couple; an attractive offer that should be profitable.* **—at•trac′tive•ly** *adv.* **—at•trac′tive•ness** *n.*

at•trib•ute (ə trĭb′yo͞ot) *tr.v.* **at•trib•ut•ed, at•trib•ut•ing, at•trib•utes.** To consider (something) as belonging to or resulting from someone or something; ascribe: *We attribute much air pollution to trucks and buses. This piece is attributed to Mozart.* —*n.* (ăt′rə byo͞ot′). A quality or characteristic belonging to a person or thing; a distinctive feature: *One of her best attributes is her quick wit.* See Synonyms at **quality.** **—at•trib′ut•a•ble** *adj.* **—at•trib′ut•er, at•trib′u•tor** *n.* **—at′tri•bu′tion** (ăt′rə byo͞o′shən) *n.*

at•trib•u•tive (ə trĭb′yə tĭv) *n.* A word or phrase placed next to the noun it modifies. In the phrase *city streets,* the word *city* is an attributive. —*adj.* Of or relating to an attributive. —See Note at **adjective.**

at•tri•tion (ə trĭsh′ən) *n.* **1.** A gradual loss of number or strength due to constant stress. **2.** A wearing away or rubbing down by friction: *The rocks became sand by attrition.* **3.** A gradual natural reduction in membership or personnel, as through retirement, resignation, or death.

At•tucks (ăt′əks), **Crispus.** 1723?–1770. American patriot who was among the five persons killed in the Boston Massacre.

at•tune (ə to͞on′ *or* ə tyo͞on′) *tr.v.* **at•tuned, at•tun•ing, at•tunes.** To bring into a harmonious relationship; adjust: *a person attuned to the times.* **—at•tune′ment** *n.*

atty. *abbr.* An abbreviation of attorney.

at wt *abbr.* An abbreviation of atomic weight.

a•typ•i•cal (ā tĭp′ĭ kəl) *adj.* Not typical; abnormal: *atypical behavior.* **—a•typ′i•cal•ly** *adv.*

Au The symbol for the element **gold** (sense 1).

au•burn (ô′bərn) *n.* A reddish brown. —*adj.* Reddish brown: *auburn hair.*

Auck•land (ôk′lənd). The largest city of New Zealand, on an isthmus of northwest North Island. Population, 860,000.

auc•tion (ôk′shən) *n.* A public sale in which goods or property is sold to the highest bidder. —*tr.v.* **auc•tioned, auc•tion•ing, auc•tions.** To sell at an auction: *auction a diamond ring.*

auc•tion•eer (ôk′shə nîr′) *n.* A person who conducts an auction.

au•da•cious (ô dā′shəs) *adj.* **1.** Fearlessly daring: *an audacious explorer.* **2.** Arrogant; impudent: *a show-off's audacious behavior.* **—au•da′cious•ly** *adv.* **—au•da′cious•ness** *n.*

au•dac•i•ty (ô dăs′ĭ tē) *n., pl.* **au•dac•i•ties. 1.** Courage and resolution; boldness. **2.** Insolence; impudence: *the unbecoming audacity of a smart aleck.*

au•di•ble (ô′də bəl) *adj.* Loud enough to be heard: *Speak in an audible voice so that others may hear you.* [First written down in 1529 in Modern English, from Late Latin *audībilis*, from Latin *audīre*, to hear.] **—au′di•bil′i•ty, au′di•ble•ness** *n.* **—au′di•bly** *adv.*

au•di•ence (ô′dē əns) *n.* **1.** The people gathered to see and hear a play, movie, concert, or other performance. **2.** The readers, hearers, or viewers reached by a book, radio broadcast, or television program: *The news reaches a wide audience over radio and television every day.* **3.** A formal hearing or conference: *an audience with the pope.* **4.** An opportunity to be heard; a hearing: *The planning*

Crispus Attucks

ă	pat	oi	**boy**
ā	**pay**	ou	**out**
âr	**care**	o͝o	**took**
ä	father	o͞o	**boot**
ĕ	pet	ŭ	cut
ē	be	ûr	**urge**
ĭ	pit	th	**thin**
ī	**pie**	*th*	**this**
îr	**pier**	hw	**whoop**
ŏ	pot	zh	vision
ō	**toe**	ə	about
ô	**paw**	N	*French* bon

John James Audubon
c. 1822 self-portrait

John James Audubon

When John James **Audubon** came to the United States in 1803, he started a small business in Kentucky. While there he began watching and sketching birds of the region. But it was only after his business failed that he made the drawings and paintings of American birds that he eventually published as *The Birds of America.* Although he was largely self-taught, Audubon's methods were by no means amateur; his paintings are based on careful observation (and in some cases dissection) and are considered true to nature.

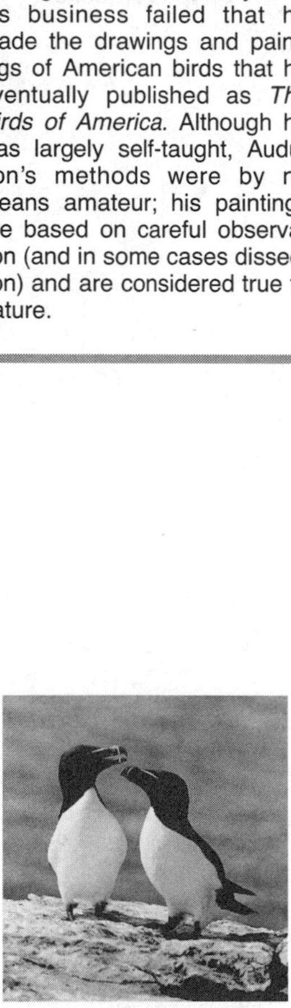

auk
Razor-billed auks

committee gave the builders an audience before voting on the project.

au•di•o (ô′dē ō′) *adj.* **1.** Of or relating to sound or hearing. **2.** Of or relating to the broadcasting, reception, or reproduction of sound: *a tape deck and other audio equipment.* —*n., pl.* **au•di•os. 1.** The broadcasting, reception, or reproduction of sound. **2.** Audible sound or an electric sound signal. [First written down in 1940 in Modern English, from Latin *audīre,* to hear.]

audio frequency *n.* A frequency corresponding to audible sound vibrations, usually between 15 hertz and 20,000 hertz for human beings.

au•di•om•e•ter (ô′dē ŏm′ĭ tər) *n.* An instrument used to measure how well a person can hear.

au•di•o-vis•u•al also **au•di•o•vis•u•al** (ô′dē ō vĭzh′o͞o əl) *adj.* **1.** Both audible and visible. **2.** Of or relating to materials, such as videotapes or compact disks, that use television and other electronic equipment to present information in both visible and audible form.

au•dit (ô′dĭt) *n.* An examination of financial records or accounts to check their accuracy. —*tr.v.* **au•dit•ed, au•dit•ing, au•dits. 1.** To examine and verify (financial records or accounts). **2.** To attend (a college course) without receiving academic credit.

au•di•tion (ô dĭsh′ən) *n.* A test or trial performance, as of a musician or actor who is applying for employment. —*v.* **au•di•tioned, au•di•tion•ing, au•di•tions.** —*intr.* To perform in an audition: *Several musicians auditioned for a place in the orchestra.* —*tr.* To give (a performer) an audition: *The director of the movie auditioned many actors.*

au•di•tor (ô′dĭ tər) *n.* **1.** A hearer or listener, especially of musical auditions. **2.** A person who examines financial records or accounts in order to check their accuracy. **3.** A person who audits courses in college.

au•di•to•ri•um (ô′dĭ tôr′ē əm) *n., pl.* **au•di•to•ri•ums** or **au•di•to•ri•a** (ô′dĭ tôr′ē ə). **1.** A room to seat a large audience in a building, such as a school. **2.** A large building used for public meetings, theatrical performances, or concerts. [First written down in 1384 in Middle English and spelled *auditorie,* from Latin *audītōrium,* from *audīre,* to hear.]

au•di•to•ry (ô′dĭ tôr′ē) *adj.* Of or relating to hearing or the organs of hearing: *the auditory canal of the ear.*

auditory nerve *n.* The nerve that carries impulses associated with hearing and balance from the inner ear to the brain.

Au•du•bon (ô′də bŏn′), **John James.** 1785–1851. Haitian-born American naturalist who wrote and illustrated *The Birds of America* (1827–1838). —See Note.

auf Wie•der•seh•en (ouf vē′dər zā′ən) *interj.* An expression used to say good-bye.

Aug. *abbr.* An abbreviation of August.

au•ger (ô′gər) *n.* A tool for boring holes. [First written down about 700 in Old English and spelled *nafogār,* altered to Middle English *(an) auger,* from the phrase *(a) nauger.*]

❑ *These sound alike:* **auger, augur** (predict).

aught[1] also **ought** (ôt) *pron.* Anything at all. Used especially in phrases such as *for aught I care* ("for all I care"), or *for aught I know* ("for all I know"). —*adv. Archaic.* At all. [First written down before 1000 in Old English and spelled *āuht.*]

❑ *These sound alike:* **aught**[1] (anything), **aught**[2] (zero), **ought** (be obliged).

aught[2] also **ought** (ôt) *n.* Zero; cipher. [First written down in 1872 in Modern English, from *(an) aught,* alteration of *(a) naught.*]

❑ *These sound alike:* **aught**[2] (zero), **aught**[1] (anything), **ought** (be obliged).

aug•ment (ôg mĕnt′) *v.* **aug•ment•ed, aug•ment•ing, aug•ments.** —*tr.* To make larger; increase: *The library's collection has been augmented by 5,000 new books.* —*intr.* To become greater; increase. **—aug•ment′a•ble** *adj.* **—aug′men•ta′tion** *n.* **—aug•ment′er** *n.*

au gra•tin (ō grät′n) *adj.* Topped with bread crumbs and often grated cheese and browned in an oven.

au•gur (ô′gər) *n.* A religious official of ancient Rome who foretold events by omens from the entrails of birds, thunder, and other natural signs. —*v.* **au•gured, au•gur•ing, au•gurs.** —*tr.* **1.** To predict (something), especially from signs or omens. **2.** To be a sign of; give promise of: *Early returns augured victory for the young candidate.* —*intr.* To make predictions from signs or omens. ***—idioms.*** **augur ill.** To indicate or promise an unfavorable outcome: *The quarterback's injury augurs ill for the game.* **augur well.** To indicate or promise a favorable outcome.

❑ *These sound alike:* **augur, auger** (drill).

au•gu•ry (ô′gyə rē) *n., pl.* **au•gu•ries. 1.** The art or practice of auguring. **2.** A sign or an omen.

au•gust (ô gŭst′) *adj.* Inspiring awe or reverence; majestic: *the august bearing of the king.* [First written down in 1664 in Modern English, from Latin *augustus.*] **—au•gust′ly** *adv.* **—au•gust′ness** *n.*

Au•gust (ô′gəst) *n.* The eighth month of the year in the Gregorian calendar, having 31 days. [First written down in 1097 in Old English, from Latin *(mēnsis) Augustus,* (month) of Augustus.]

Au•gus•ta (ô gŭs′tə). The capital of Maine, in the southwest part of the state north-northeast of Portland. A trading post was established here in 1628. Population, 21,325.

Au•gus•tine (ô′gə stēn′ *or* ô gŭs′tĭn), Saint. A.D. 354–430. Early Christian philosopher and bishop of Hippo (in present-day Algeria) from 396 until 430.

Au•gus•tus (ô gŭs′təs) Originally **Oc•ta•vi•an** (ŏk tā′vē ən). 63 B.C.–A.D. 14. First emperor of Rome (27 B.C.–A.D. 14). He defeated Mark Antony and Cleopatra in 31 and subsequently gained control over the empire.

au jus (ō zho͞os′ *or* ō zhü′) *adj.* Served in its own gravy or juice from cooking: *roast beef au jus.*

auk (ôk) *n.* Any of several black and white northern sea birds having a plump body and short wings. [First written down in 1674 in Modern English, from Old Norse *ālka.*]

auld (ôld) *adj. Scots.* Old.

auld lang syne (ôld′ lăng zīn′) *n.* The good old days.

aunt (ănt *or* änt) *n.* **1.** The sister of one's father or mother. **2.** The wife of one's uncle. [First written down about 1300 in Middle English and spelled *aunte,* from Latin *amita,* paternal aunt.]

❑ *These sound alike:* **aunt, ant** (insect).

au•ra (ôr′ə) *n., pl.* **au•ras** or **au•rae** (ôr′ē). A distinctive air or quality that characterizes a person or thing: *an aura of mystery about the old house.* [First written down before 1398 in Middle English and spelled *aura,* gentle breeze, from Latin, from Greek *aura,* breath.]

au•ral (ôr′əl) *adj.* Of, relating to, or perceived by the ear: *aural stimulation.* **—au′ral•ly** *adv.*

❑ *These sound alike:* **aural, oral** (of the mouth).

au•re•ole (ôr′ē ōl′) *n.* **1.** In art, a circle of light around the head of a sacred figure; a halo. **2.** A glow that surrounds the sun or the moon, especially when seen through a fog or haze.

Au•re•o•my•cin (ôr′ē ō mī′sĭn). A trademark for a powerful antibiotic drug obtained from soil bacteria.

au re•voir (ō′ rə **vwär′**) *interj.* An expression used to say good-bye.

au•ri•cle (**ôr′**ĭ kəl) *n.* **1.** The external part of the ear. **2.** An atrium of the heart.

❑ *These sound alike:* **auricle, oracle** (prophet).

au•ric•u•lar (ô **rĭk′**yə lər) *adj.* **1.** Of or relating to hearing or the organs of hearing. **2.** Of or relating to an auricle of the heart.

au•rochs (**ou′**rŏks′ *or* **ôr′**ŏks′) *n., pl.* **aurochs.** An extinct horned animal of the Old World, believed to be the ancestor of domestic cattle.

au•ro•ra (ô **rôr′**ə *or* ə **rôr′**ə) *n.* A brilliant display of bands or streamers of light visible in the night sky, chiefly in the polar regions. It is caused by electrically charged particles from the sun that are drawn into the atmosphere by the earth's magnetic field.

Au•ro•ra (ô **rôr′**ə *or* ə **rôr′**ə) *n.* In Roman mythology, the goddess of the dawn, identified with the Greek Eos.

aurora aus•tra•lis (ô **strā′**lĭs) *n.* The aurora of the Southern Hemisphere; the southern lights.

aurora bo•re•al•is (bôr′ē **ăl′**ĭs) *n.* The aurora of the Northern Hemisphere; the northern lights.

aus•pi•ces (**ô′**spĭ sĭz *or* **ô′**spĭ sēz′) *pl.n.* Protection and support; patronage: *The marathon was organized under the auspices of local athletic clubs.*

aus•pi•cious (ô **spĭsh′**əs) *adj.* Showing signs of a successful outcome or result; favorable: *Their first large orders were an auspicious beginning for the new business.* **—aus•pi′cious•ly** *adv.* **—aus•pi′cious•ness** *n.*

Aus•ten (**ô′**stən), **Jane.** 1775–1817. British writer whose novels include *Pride and Prejudice* (1813).

aus•tere (ô **stîr′**) *adj.* **aus•ter•er, aus•ter•est. 1.** Having a stern personality or appearance; somber: *an unsmiling, austere judge.* **2.** Living very simply, with few comforts: *a desert nomad's austere life.* **3.** Lacking decoration; plain or bare: *Their austere living quarters had no pictures on the walls.* **—aus•tere′ly** *adv.* **—aus•tere′ness** *n.*

aus•ter•i•ty (ô **stĕr′**ĭ tē) *n., pl.* **aus•ter•i•ties. 1.** The condition of being austere. **2.** Lack of luxury; extreme restraint in spending: *wartime austerity.*

Aus•tin (**ô′**stən *or* **ŏs′**tən). The capital of Texas, in the south-central part of the state northeast of San Antonio. It became the capital of the state of Texas in 1870. Population, 345,496.

Austin, Mary Hunter. 1868–1934. American writer known for her interest in the peoples and cultures of the Mojave Desert and for her support of women's rights.

Austin, Stephen Fuller. 1793–1836. American political leader who helped Texas settlers gain their independence (1836).

Aus•tra•lia (ô **strāl′**yə). **1.** The world's smallest continent, southeast of Asia between the Pacific and Indian oceans. **2.** A commonwealth made up of the continent of Australia and the island of Tasmania. The first Australian federation was formed in 1901. Canberra is the capital and Sydney is the largest city. Population, 15,544,500.

Aus•tra•lian (ô **strāl′**yən) *adj.* Of or relating to Australia or its peoples, languages, or cultures. *—n.* **1.** A native or inhabitant of Australia. **2.** A member of any of the aboriginal peoples of Australia. **3.** Any of the languages of the aboriginal peoples of Australia.

Australian ballot *n.* A ballot containing all names of candidates for election.

Aus•tri•a (**ô′**strē ə). A country of central Europe south of Germany and Czech Republic. Austria was annexed by Adolf Hitler in 1938, and full sovereignty was restored in 1955. Vienna is the capital and the largest city. Population, 7,555,338.

Aus•tri•a-Hun•ga•ry (ô′strē ə **hŭng′**gə rē). A former dual monarchy of central Europe formed in 1867 and lasting until 1918.

au•then•tic (ô **thĕn′**tĭk) *adj.* **1.** Worthy of belief; true; credible: *The characters were authentic and the situations realistic in the detective story.* **2.** Not counterfeit or copied; genuine: *an authentic medieval sword.* [First written down in 1369 in Middle English and spelled *autentik*, from Greek *authentikos*, from *authentēs*, author.] **—au•then′ti•cal•ly** *adv.*

Synonyms: authentic, genuine, real, true. These adjectives all mean not counterfeit or copied. *An expert assured us that the chair is an authentic antique, made in the 18th century. The recipe calls for genuine Italian olive oil, but the store sells only American brands. The bouquets were made with silk flowers instead of real ones. A true friend would be more understanding.*

au•then•ti•cate (ô **thĕn′**tĭ kāt′) *tr.v.* **au•then•ti•cat•ed, au•then•ti•cat•ing, au•then•ti•cates. 1.** To establish as being true; prove: *Witnesses will authenticate our account of the accident.* **2.** To establish (a painting, an antique, or another object) as being genuine: *I am sure that an expert can authenticate the old violin.* **—au•then′ti•ca′tion** *n.* **—au•then′ti•ca′tor** *n.*

au•then•tic•i•ty (ô′thĕn **tĭs′**ĭ tē) *n.* The condition or quality of being authentic: *The authenticity of our claim is established by these old records.*

au•thor (**ô′**thər) *n.* **1.** A person who writes a book, a story, an article, or another written work. **2.** The creator or originator of something: *the author of an idea.* *—tr.v.* **au•thored, au•thor•ing, au•thors.** To be the author of: *The professor has authored several books.* [First written down about 1384 in Middle English and spelled *auctour*, from Latin *auctor*, creator, from *augēre*, to create.]

au•thor•i•tar•i•an (ə thôr′ĭ **târ′**ē ən *or* ə thŏr′ĭ **târ′**ē ən) *adj.* Characterized by or favoring absolute obedience to authority: *the authoritarian government of a dictator.* *—n.* A person who believes in or practices authoritarian behavior. **—au•thor′i•tar′i•an•ism** *n.*

au•thor•i•ta•tive (ə **thôr′**ĭ tā′tĭv *or* ə **thŏr′**ĭ tā′tĭv) *adj.* **1.** Having or arising from proper authority; official: *the judge's authoritative manner.* **2.** Known to be accurate or excellent; reliable: *authoritative sources for the newspaper article.* **—au•thor′i•ta′tive•ly** *adv.* **—au•thor′i•ta′tive•ness** *n.*

au•thor•i•ty (ə **thôr′**ĭ tē *or* ə **thŏr′**ĭ tē) *n., pl.* **au•thor•i•ties. 1.a.** The power to enforce laws, command obedience, determine, or judge: *Our principal has the authority to close the school.* **b.** A person or an organization having this power: *government authorities.* **2.** An accepted source of expert information, as a book or person: *an authority on history.* **3.** Power to influence or affect resulting from knowledge or experience: *She writes about science with authority.*

au•thor•i•za•tion (ô′thər ĭ **zā′**shən) *n.* **1.** The act of authorizing. **2.** Legal or official power or right: *The President and Congress have authorization to govern from the Constitution.*

au•thor•ize (**ô′**thə rīz′) *tr.v.* **au•thor•ized, au•thor•iz•ing, au•thor•iz•es. 1.** To grant authority or power to: *President Jefferson authorized Lewis and Clark to explore the lands beyond the Mississippi River.* **2.** To approve or give permission for: *The state legislature authorized a highway project.* **—au′thor•iz′er** *n.*

Au•thor•ized Version (**ô′**thə rīzd′) *n.* The King James Bible.

au•thor•ship (**ô′**thər shĭp′) *n.* The origin, as of a book: *a book of unknown authorship.*

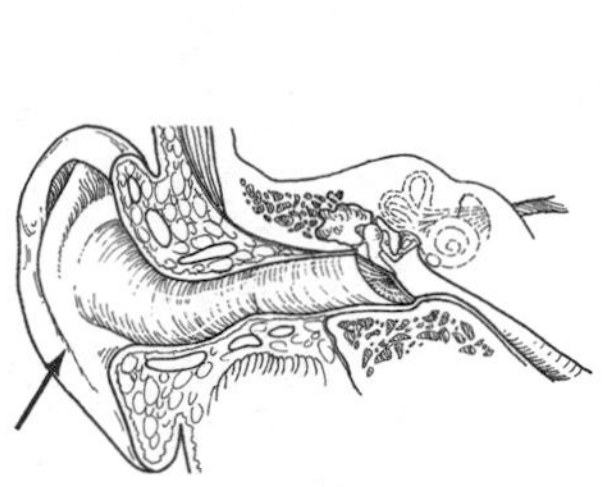

auricle

Jane Austen

ă	pat	oi	boy
ā	pay	ou	out
âr	care	ŏŏ	took
ä	father	ōō	boot
ĕ	pet	ŭ	cut
ē	be	ûr	urge
ĭ	pit	th	thin
ī	pie	*th*	this
îr	pier	hw	whoop
ŏ	pot	zh	vision
ō	toe	ə	about
ô	paw	N	*French* bon

au•tism (ô′tĭz′əm) *n.* A disorder in development characterized by an inability to relate socially to other people and a severe withdrawal from external reality.

au•to (ô′tō) *n., pl.* **au•tos.** An automobile.

auto– or **aut–** *pref.* A prefix that means: **1.** Self; same: *autobiography.* **2.** Automatic: *autopilot.*

au•to•bi•og•ra•phy (ô′tō bī ŏg′rə fē) *n., pl.* **au•to•bi•og•ra•phies.** The story of a person's life written by that person. **—au′to•bi•og′ra•pher** *n.* **—au′to•bi′o•graph′i•cal** (ô′tō bī′ə grăf′ĭ kəl), **au′to•bi′o•graph′ic** (ô′tō bī′ə grăf′ĭk) *adj.* **—au′to•bi′o•graph′i•cal•ly** *adv.*

au•to•clave (ô′tō klāv′) *n.* A tank used especially for antiseptic sterilizing under high-pressure steam.

au•toc•ra•cy (ô tŏk′rə sē) *n., pl.* **au•toc•ra•cies. 1.** Government by a person having absolute power. **2.** A country having this form of government.

au•to•crat (ô′tə krăt′) *n.* **1.** A ruler having unlimited power. **2.** An arrogant person with unlimited power: *The boss is an autocrat.*

au•to•crat•ic (ô′tə krăt′ĭk) *adj.* **1.** Of or relating to autocracy: *an autocratic government.* **2.** Like an autocrat; arrogant: *The professor has a very autocratic manner.* **—au′to•crat′i•cal•ly** *adv.*

au•to•graph (ô′tə grăf′) *n.* **1.** A signature, usually of a famous person, that is saved by an admirer or collector. **2.** A manuscript in the author's own handwriting. *—tr.v.* **au•to•graphed, au•to•graph•ing, au•to•graphs.** To write one's name or signature on. [First written down about 1640 in Modern English, from Late Latin *autographum*, from Greek *autographos*, written with one's own hand : *auto-*, self + *graphein*, to write.] **—au′to•graph′ic, au′to•graph′i•cal** *adj.*

Au•to•harp (ô′tō härp′). A trademark for a musical instrument that is somewhat like a zither and that is equipped with a device that damps all of its strings except those that form a desired chord.

au•to•im•mune (ô′tō ĭ myo͞on′) *adj.* Caused by the production of antibodies that attack the body's own cells and tissues.

au•to•im•mu•ni•ty (ô′tō ĭ myo͞o′nĭ tē) *n., pl.* **au•to•im•mu•ni•ties.** The condition in which antibodies produced by an organism attack the organism's own cells and tissues.

au•to•mak•er (ô′tō mā′kər) *n.* A manufacturer of automobiles.

au•tom•a•ta (ô tŏm′ə tə) *n.* A plural of **automaton.**

au•to•mate (ô′tə māt′) *v.* **au•to•mat•ed, au•to•mat•ing, au•to•mates.** *—tr.* To operate (a process, factory, or machine) with automatic machinery or processes: *automate an assembly line with robots.* *—intr.* To make use of automatic machinery and processes: *Costs of manufacturing were reduced after the factory automated.*

au•to•mat•ed teller machine (ô′tə mā′tĭd) *n.* An electronic machine that permits a bank customer to make deposits and withdrawals after inserting an identification card and recording the transaction by pressing numbered buttons.

automated teller machine

au•to•mat•ic (ô′tə măt′ĭk) *adj.* **1.** Acting or operating without the control of a human being; self-operating or self-regulating: *an automatic elevator.* **2.** Done or produced by the body without conscious control or awareness; involuntary: *the automatic shrinking of the pupils in bright light.* **3.** Capable of firing continuously until ammunition is gone or the trigger is released: *an automatic rifle.* *—n.* A device or machine, especially a firearm, that is wholly or partially automatic. [First written down in 1748 in Modern English, from Greek *automatos* : *auto-*, self + *-matos*, willing.] **—au′to•mat′i•cal•ly** *adv.*

automatic pilot *n.* A navigation device that automatically keeps to a preset course.

automatic teller machine *n.* An automated teller machine.

au•to•ma•tion (ô′tə mā′shən) *n.* **1.** The automatic operation or control of a process, machine, or system, often by electronic devices, such as computers or robots: *Automation has replaced many workers in manufacturing.* **2.** The engineering techniques and equipment needed to accomplish this.

au•tom•a•ton (ô tŏm′ə tən *or* ô tŏm′ə tŏn′) *n., pl.* **au•tom•a•tons** or **au•tom•a•ta** (ô tŏm′ə tə). **1.** An automatic machine, especially a robot. **2.** A person who behaves in a mechanical way.

au•to•mo•bile (ô′tə mō bēl′ *or* ô′tə mō′bēl′) *n.* A passenger vehicle generally moving on four wheels and propelled by a gasoline engine on land. *—adj.* Of or relating to automobiles; automotive.

au•to•mo•tive (ô′tə mō′tĭv) *adj.* **1.** Of or relating to self-propelled vehicles, such as automobiles and trucks. **2.** Self-propelled or self-propelling.

au•to•nom•ic (ô′tə nŏm′ĭk) *adj.* Of, relating to, or controlled by the autonomic nervous system.

autonomic nervous system *n.* The part of the nervous system of a vertebrate animal that regulates involuntary action, as of the intestines, heart, or glands.

au•ton•o•mous (ô tŏn′ə məs) *adj.* Self-governing; independent: *an autonomous organization; autonomous regions.* **—au•ton′o•mous•ly** *adv.*

au•ton•o•my (ô tŏn′ə mē) *n., pl.* **au•ton•o•mies.** Self-government.

au•to•pi•lot (ô′tō pī′lət) *n.* An automatic pilot.

au•top•sy (ô′tŏp′sē) *n., pl.* **au•top•sies.** A medical examination of a dead human body to determine the cause of death.

au•tumn (ô′təm) *n.* The season of the year between summer and winter, lasting from the autumnal equinox in late September to the winter solstice in late December. *—adj.* Of, occurring in, or appropriate to the season of autumn: *autumn colors.* [First written down about 1380 in Middle English and spelled *autumpne*, from Latin *autumnus.*]

au•tum•nal (ô tŭm′nəl) *adj.* Of, occurring in, or appropriate to the autumn. **—au•tum′nal•ly** *adv.*

autumnal equinox *n.* The equinox, occurring on or about September 23, in which the sun is moving from north to south, marking the beginning of autumn in the Northern Hemisphere.

aux•il•ia•ry (ôg zĭl′yə rē *or* ôg zĭl′ə rē) *adj.* **1.** Giving assistance or support: *a sailboat with an auxiliary engine.* **2.** Additional, subsidiary, or supplementary: *auxiliary branches of the fire department in outlying areas.* *—n., pl.* **aux•il•ia•ries. 1.** A person or thing that helps; an assistant. **2.** An auxiliary verb. **3.** An organization that is subsidiary to a larger one: *Members of the hospital auxiliary visit patients and run errands.* **4.** A member of a body of foreign troops serving a country in war.

auxiliary verb *n.* A verb that comes first in a verb phrase and helps form the tense, mood, or voice of the main verb. *Have, may, can, must* and *will* can act as auxiliary verbs.

aux•in (ôk′sĭn) *n.* Any of various hormones or similar synthetic substances that regulate the growth and development of plants.

aux. v. *abbr.* An abbreviation of auxiliary verb.

AV or **A.V.** *abbr.* An abbreviation of Authorized Version (of the Bible).

av. *abbr.* An abbreviation of: **1.** Average. **2.** Avoirdupois.

a•vail (ə vāl′) *v.* **a•vailed, a•vail•ing, a•vails.** *—tr.* To be of use or advantage to; help: *Nothing can avail us now.* *—intr.* To be of use or value; help: *A calculator avails little if you don't understand the* *problem.* —*n.* Use, benefit, or advantage: *Since all the doors were locked, the burglar's efforts were to no avail.* —*idiom.* **avail (oneself) of.** To make use of; take advantage of: *While visiting Paris you must avail yourself of the museums.* [First written down about 1300 in Middle English and spelled *availen* : Latin *ad-*, intensive prefix + Old French *valoir*, to be worth (from Latin *valēre*).]

a•vail•a•ble (ə **vā′**lə bəl) *adj.* **1.** Capable of being obtained: *Tickets are available at the box office.* **2.** At hand and ready for use: *Keep a calculator available during the test.* **3.** Willing to serve: *All available volunteers were asked to help.* —**a•vail′a•bil′i•ty, a•vail′a•ble•ness** *n.* —**a•vail′a•bly** *adv.*

av•a•lanche (**ăv′**ə lănch′) *n.* **1.** The fall or slide of a large mass, as of snow or rock, down the side of a mountain. **2.** A massive or overwhelming amount: *an avalanche of mail.* [First written down in 1771 in Modern English, from French; akin to Provençal *lavanca*, ravine, perhaps akin to Latin *lābī*, to slip.]

Av•a•lon (**ăv′**ə lŏn′) *n.* In Arthurian legend, an island paradise in the western seas where King Arthur goes at death.

a•vant-garde (ä′vänt **gärd′**) *n.* A group of people who are the leaders in promoting new or unconventional styles, ideas, or methods, especially in the arts. —*adj.* Exhibiting new or unconventional styles, ideas, or methods: *an avant-garde magazine.*

av•a•rice (**ăv′**ə rĭs) *n.* Extreme desire for getting money or wealth; greed.

av•a•ri•cious (ăv′ə **rĭsh′**əs) *adj.* Extremely desirous of money or wealth; greedy. —**av′a•ri′cious•ly** *adv.* —**av′a•ri′cious•ness** *n.*

a•vast (ə **văst′**) *interj.* An expression used as a command aboardship to stop an activity.

a•vaunt (ə **vônt′** *or* ə **vänt′**) *interj. Archaic.* An expression used as a command to get out or away.

ave. or **Ave.** *abbr.* An abbreviation of avenue.

A•ve Ma•ri•a (ä′vā mə **rē′**ə) *n.* A Hail Mary in Latin. [First written down about 1230 in Middle English and spelled *Ave marie*, from Medieval Latin, *Ave Maria*, Hail, Mary!]

a•venge (ə **vĕnj′**) *tr.v.* **a•venged, a•veng•ing, a•veng•es.** To take revenge or satisfaction for: *The hockey team vowed to avenge the loss to their rivals across town.* —**a•veng′er** *n.*

av•e•nue (**ăv′**ə no͞o′ *or* **ăv′**ə nyo͞o′) *n.* **1.** A wide street or thoroughfare. **2.** A means of reaching or achieving something: *We must seek many avenues for peace.*

a•ver (ə **vûr′**) *tr.v.* **a•verred, a•verr•ing, a•vers.** To state positively and firmly; assert; affirm.

av•er•age (**ăv′**ər ĭj *or* **ăv′**rĭj) *n.* **1.** A number, especially the arithmetic mean, that is derived from and considered typical or representative of a set of numbers. **2.** A typical kind or usual level or degree: *That musician's abilities are above average.* —*v.* **av•er•aged, av•er•ag•ing, av•er•ag•es.** —*tr.* **1.** To compute the average of (a set of numbers): *After the trip we averaged the number of miles we went each day.* **2.** To have or attain as an average: *The temperature averages about 75 degrees in the summer.* —*intr.* To be or amount to an average. —*adj.* **1.** Computed or determined as an average: *On our trip across the country our average speed was 50 miles per hour.* **2.a.** Typical, usual, or ordinary: *an average American family.* **b.** Not exceptional; undistinguished: *an average student.* —*idiom.* **on the average.** Using the average as a basis for judgment. [First written down in 1491 in Middle English and spelled *averay*, charge above the cost of freight, from Arabic *'awārīyah*, damaged goods.] —**av′er•age•ly** *adv.* —**av′er•age•ness** *n.*

a•verse (ə **vûrs′**) *adj.* Opposed; reluctant; unwilling: *Cats are extremely averse to getting wet.* —**a•verse′ly** *adv.* —**a•verse′ness** *n.*

a•ver•sion (ə **vûr′**zhən *or* ə **vûr′**shən) *n.* A strong dislike: *I have an aversion to crowds.*

a•vert (ə **vûrt′**) *tr.v.* **a•vert•ed, a•vert•ing, a•verts. 1.** To turn away or aside: *When we were stared at we averted our eyes.* **2.** To keep from happening; prevent: *She averted an accident by staying well behind the truck.* —**a•vert′a•ble, a•vert′i•ble** *adj.*

avg. *abbr.* An abbreviation of average.

a•vi•an (**ā′**vē ən) *adj.* Of or relating to birds.

a•vi•ar•y (**ā′**vē ĕr′ē) *n., pl.* **a•vi•ar•ies.** A large cage or enclosure for birds, as in a zoo.

a•vi•a•tion (ā′vē **ā′**shən *or* ăv′ē **ā′**shən) *n.* **1.** The art of operating and navigating aircraft. **2.** The design, development, and production of aircraft.

a•vi•a•tor (**ā′**vē ā′tər *or* **ăv′**ē ā′tər) *n.* A person who flies an aircraft; a pilot.

av•id (**ăv′**ĭd) *adj.* **1.** Eager: *avid for adventure.* **2.** Ardent; enthusiastic: *an avid reader of the editorial page; an avid baseball fan.* —**av′id•ly** *adv.* —**av′id•ness** *n.*

a•vid•i•ty (ə **vĭd′**ĭ tē) *n.* Eagerness or enthusiasm.

a•vi•on•ics (ā′vē **ŏn′**ĭks *or* ăv′ē **ŏn′**ĭks) *n.* *(used with a singular verb).* The science and technology of electronics as applied to aircraft and spacecraft.

av•o•ca•do (ăv′ə **kä′**dō *or* ä′və **kä′**dō) *n., pl.* **av•o•ca•dos. 1.** An edible, tropical American fruit having leathery green or blackish skin, mild-tasting yellow-green pulp, and a single large seed. **2.** The tree that bears such fruit. [First written down in 1763 in Modern English, from American Spanish, from Nahuatl *ahuacatl.*]

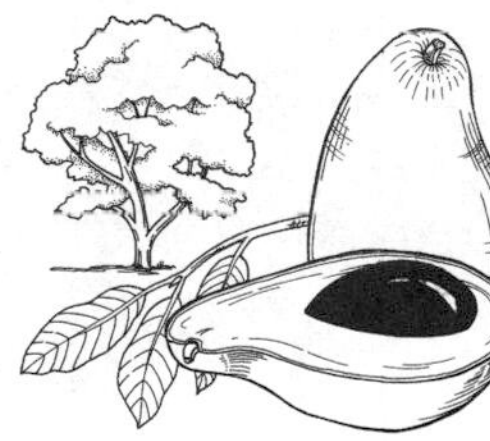

avocado

av•o•ca•tion (ăv′ō **kā′**shən) *n.* An interest or activity engaged in for pleasure or satisfaction, in addition to one's regular work.

a•void (ə **void′**) *tr.v.* **a•void•ed, a•void•ing, a•voids. 1.** To keep away from; stay clear of; shun: *avoid too many sweets; avoid the crowds at the mall.* **2.** To prevent; keep from happening: *avoid an accident.* —**a•void′a•ble** *adj.* —**a•void′a•bly** *adv.* —**a•void′ance** *n.*

av•oir•du•pois weight (ăv′ər də **poiz′**) *n.* A system of weights based on a pound of 16 ounces, traditionally used in English-speaking countries to weigh everything except gems, precious metals, and drugs.

a•vouch (ə **vouch′**) *tr.v.* **a•vouched, a•vouch•ing, a•vouch•es. 1.** To assert positively to be true; affirm. **2.** To take responsibility for; guarantee.

a•vow (ə **vou′**) *tr.v.* **a•vowed, a•vow•ing, a•vows.** To acknowledge openly; admit freely: *We avowed our support for the controversial law.* —**a•vow′a•ble** *adj.*

a•vow•al (ə **vou′**əl) *n.* An open admission or acknowledgment: *avowal of an unpopular opinion.*

a•vun•cu•lar (ə **vŭng′**kyə lər) *adj.* Of, relating to, or similar to an uncle.

aw (ô) *interj.* An expression used to show sympathy, doubt, or disgust.

❑ *These sound alike:* **aw, awe** (wonder).

a•wait (ə **wāt′**) *tr.v.* **a•wait•ed, a•wait•ing, a•waits. 1.** To wait for: *We sat up awaiting news of the election results.* See Synonyms at **expect. 2.** To be in store for: *The meeting with the principal awaits us at the end of the week.*

a•wake (ə **wāk′**) *v.* **a•woke** (ə **wōk′**) or **a•waked, a•waked** or **a•wok•en** (ə **wō′**kən), **a•wak•ing, a•wakes.** —*tr.* **1.** To rouse from sleep; waken: *The alarm clock awoke me at seven.* **2.** To stir the interest of; excite: *New evidence about heart disease awoke most of us to the benefits of exercise.* **3.** To produce (a feeling or memory, for example): *Seeing the old car awoke memories of my grandfather.* —*intr.* **1.** To wake up: *I awoke at dawn.* **2.** To

ă	pat	oi	boy
ā	pay	ou	out
âr	care	o͝o	took
ä	father	o͞o	boot
ĕ	pet	ŭ	cut
ē	be	ûr	urge
ĭ	pit	th	thin
ī	pie	*th*	this
îr	pier	hw	whoop
ŏ	pot	zh	vision
ō	toe	ə	about
ô	paw	N	*French* bon

become aware of: *Americans are awaking to the need for recycling.* —*adj.* **1.** Not asleep: *He was awake all night.* **2.** Alert, vigilant, or watchful: *awake to the dangers of an unhealthy diet.* [First written down before 1200 in Middle English and spelled *awaken*, from Old English *āwacan* : *ā-*, intensive prefix + *wacan*, wake.] —See Note at **wake**[1].

a•wak•en (ə wā′kən) *v.* **a•wak•ened, a•wak•en•ing, a•wak•ens.** —*intr.* To wake up: *I awakened early because of the noise.* —*tr.* **1.** To cause to wake up: *A barking dog awakened me during the night.* **2.** To stir up or produce (a feeling or memory, for example): *Becoming an aunt awakened in her a sense of responsibility.* —**a•wak′en•er** *n.* —See Note at **wake**[1].

a•ward (ə wôrd′) *tr.v.* **a•ward•ed, a•ward•ing, a•wards. 1.** To give or bestow (a prize, medal, or other honor) for outstanding performance or quality: *The committee awarded a ribbon to the best dog in the show.* **2.** To give or grant by legal or governmental decision: *award damages to the injured driver; award a contract to the lowest bidder.* —*n.* **1.** Something, such as a prize or medal, awarded for outstanding performance or quality: *an award for bravery.* **2.** Something judged as due by legal decision. —**a•ward′a•ble** *adj.* —**a•ward′er** *n.*

a•ware (ə wâr′) *adj.* Being mindful or conscious of; knowing; cognizant: *be aware of the abilities of each staff member.* —**a•ware′ness** *n.*

a•wash (ə wŏsh′ *or* ə wôsh′) *adj. & adv.* **1.** Level with or washed by waves: *The rocks were awash in the tide.* **2.** Floating on waves: *The wrecked ship's cargo was awash in the sea.*

a•way (ə wā′) *adv.* **1.** From a particular thing or place: *They got in the car and drove away.* **2.** At or to a distance: *We live two miles away from the beach.* **3.** In a different direction: *Don't look away now.* **4.** Into storage or a safe place: *Please put the toys away.* **5.** From one's presence or possession: *They gave away that old bicycle.* **6.** Out of existence: *The music faded away.* **7.** Continuously: *working away.* **8.** Freely; at will: *Fire away!* —*adj.* **1.** Absent: *My brother is away from home.* **2.** Distant, as in space or time: *Those mountains are miles away. The game is a week away.* **3.** Played on the opposing team's home grounds: *home games and away games.* **4.** In baseball, out: *two away in the ninth.* [First written down about 725 in Old English and spelled *aweg* : *a-*, on + *weg*, way.]

❑ *These sound alike:* **away, aweigh** (free of the bottom).

awe (ô) *n.* A feeling of wonder, fear, and respect inspired by something mighty or majestic: *gazing in awe at the mountains.* —*tr.v.* **awed, aw•ing, awes.** To fill with awe: *The size of the huge plane awed everyone.* [First written down about 1200 in Middle English and spelled *aghe*, from Old Norse *agi*.]

❑ *These sound alike:* **awe, aw** (interjection).

a•weigh (ə wā′) *adj.* Hanging clear of the bottom: *With the anchor aweigh, the boat began to drift.*

❑ *These sound alike:* **aweigh, away** (at a distance).

awe•some (ô′səm) *adj.* **1.** Inspiring awe: *an awesome sight.* **2.** Expressing or marked by awe: *We stood in awesome silence before the ruins.* —**awe′some•ly** *adv.* —**awe′some•ness** *n.*

awe•struck (ô′strŭk′) also **awe•strick•en** (ô′strĭk′ən) *adj.* Full of awe: *awestruck by the beauty of the mountains.*

aw•ful (ô′fəl) *adj.* **1.** Very bad or unpleasant; horrible: *awful weather; an awful book.* **2.** Inspiring awe or fear; fearsome: *the awful stillness before the tornado.* **3.** Great; considerable: *an awful lot of homework.* —*adv. Informal.* Very; extremely: *awful sick.* —**aw′ful•ness** *n.*

❑ *These sound alike:* **awful, offal** (rubbish).

aw•ful•ly (ô′fə lē) *adv.* **1.a.** In a manner that inspires awe; terribly: *The wind blew awfully.* **b.** *Informal.* Very badly: *She behaved awfully.* **2.** *Informal.* Very: *The tourists seemed awfully confused.*

a•while (ə wīl′) *adv.* For a short time: *We waited awhile until they returned.*

awk•ward (ôk′wərd) *adj.* **1.** Not graceful; clumsy: *an awkward dancer.* **2.** Causing embarrassment; trying: *An awkward silence fell over the shy students.* **3.** Difficult to handle or manage; cumbersome: *a large and awkward bundle to carry.* [First written down before 1400 in Middle English and spelled *awkeward*, in the wrong way : *awke*, wrong (from Old Norse *öfugr*, backward) + *-ward*, -ward.] —**awk′ward•ly** *adv.* —**awk′ward•ness** *n.*

awl (ôl) *n.* A pointed tool for making holes, as in wood or leather. [First written down about 700 in Old English and spelled *awel*.]

❑ *These sound alike:* **awl, all** (everything).

awn•ing (ô′nĭng) *n.* A protective structure set up over a window or door like a roof.

a•woke (ə wōk′) *v.* A past tense of **awake.**

a•wok•en (ə wō′kən) *v.* A past participle of **awake.**

AWOL or **awol** (ā′wôl′) *adj.* Absent without leave, as from an army base. —*n.* A person who is absent without leave.

a•wry (ə rī′) *adv.* **1.** Turned or twisted to one side or out of shape; askew: *The wind blew the curtains awry.* **2.** Wrong; amiss: *Our plans went awry.*

ax or **axe** (ăks) *n., pl.* **ax•es** (ăk′sĭz). A tool consisting of a head with a sharp blade on a long handle, used for cutting trees or chopping wood. —*tr.v.* **axed, ax•ing, ax•es.** To cut or chop (something) with an ax. —***idiom.* ax to grind.** A selfish or personal aim.

ax•es[1] (ăk′sēz′) *n.* Plural of **axis.**

ax•es[2] (ăk′sĭz) *n.* Plural of **ax.**

ax•i•al (ăk′sē əl) *adj.* Of, on, around, or forming an axis: *A wheel turns by axial motion.*

ax•il (ăk′sĭl) *n.* The angle between the upper side of a leaf or stem and the supporting stem or branch. A bud is usually found in the axil.

ax•i•om (ăk′sē əm) *n.* **1.** A statement that is accepted as true or assumed to be true without proof. "The whole is greater than any of its parts" is an example of an axiom. **2.** An established rule, principle, or law: *One of the axioms of driving is to stay to the right.* [First written down in 1485 in Middle English, from Greek *axiōma*, from *axios*, worthy.]

ax•i•o•mat•ic (ăk′sē ə măt′ĭk) *adj.* Of, relating to, or resembling an axiom; self-evident: *That all people are equal under the law is axiomatic.* —**ax′i•o•mat′i•cal•ly** *adv.*

ax•is (ăk′sĭs) *n., pl.* **ax•es** (ăk′sēz′). **1.** A straight line around which an object rotates or can be imagined to rotate: *The axis of the earth passes through both of its poles.* **2.** In geometry, a line, ray, or line segment with respect to which a figure or object is symmetrical: *the axis of a cone.* **3.** A reference line from which or along which distances or angles are measured in a system of coordinates: *the x-axis.* **4. Axis.** The alliance of Germany, Italy, Japan, and the other nations that opposed the Allies in World War II.

ax•le (ăk′səl) *n.* **1.** A shaft or spindle, on which one or more wheels revolve. **2.** The spindle of an axletree.

ax•le•tree (ăk′səl trē′) *n.* A crossbar or rod supporting a vehicle and having a spindle at each end on which a wheel turns.

awning

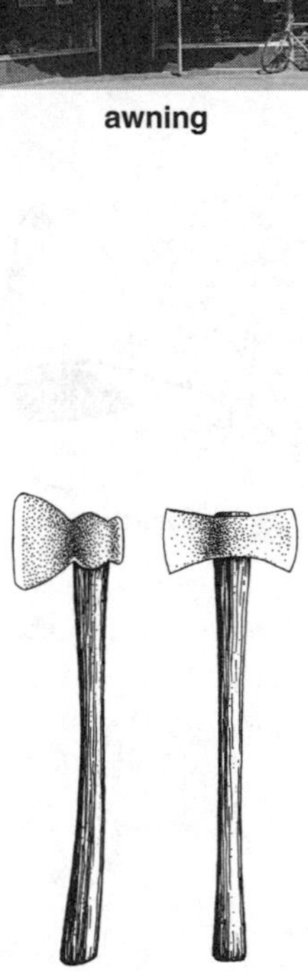

ax
Left: Broadax
Right: Full double-bitted ax

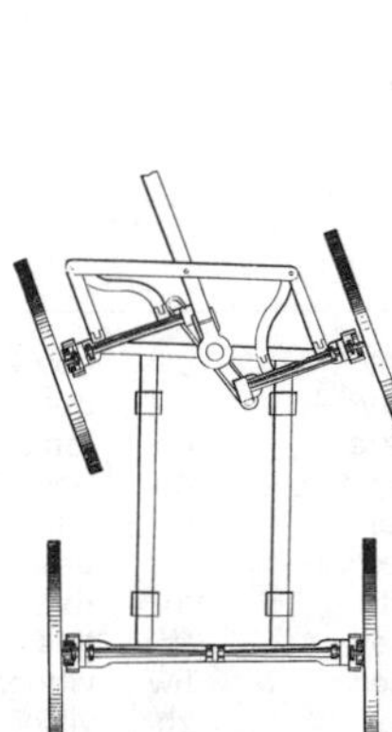

axle

ax•o•lotl (ăk′sə lŏt′l) *n.* Any of several salamanders of Mexico and the western United States that unlike most amphibians keep and continue to breathe with external gills when mature.

ax•on (ăk′sŏn′) *n.* The long extension of a nerve cell that carries impulses away from the body of the cell.

ay (ī) *n. & adv.* Variant of **aye.**

a•ya•tol•lah (ī′ə tō′lə *or* ī′ə tō lä′) *n.* A male Shiite religious teacher of the highest rank.

aye also **ay** (ī) *n.* **1.** A vote of yes. **2. ayes.** Those who vote yes: *The ayes have it; the motion is approved.* —*adv.* Yes; yea.

❑ *These sound alike:* **aye, eye** (organ of sight), **I**[1] (personal pronoun).

Ay•ma•ra (ī′mä rä′) *n., pl.* **Aymara** or **Ay•ma•ras. 1.** A member of a Native American people inhabiting Bolivia and Peru. **2.** The language of this people. **—Ay′ma•ran′** *adj.*

Ayr•shire (âr′shîr *or* âr′shər) *n.* One of a breed of brown and white dairy cattle originally raised in Scotland.

AZ *abbr.* An abbreviation of Arizona.

a•zal•ea (ə zāl′yə) *n.* Any of several evergreen shrubs related to the rhododendron and often cultivated for their funnel-shaped, variously colored flowers.

A•zer•bai•jan (ăz′ər bī jän′ *or* ä′zər bī jän′). A region and republic of Transcaucasia north of Iran. Formerly a kingdom that extended into northwest Iran, it was formed from territory ceded to Russia by Persia in 1813 and 1828. Baku is the capital. Population, 6,614,000.

az•i•muth (ăz′ə məth) *n.* An arc measured clockwise from a reference point, usually the northern point of the horizon, to the point where a vertical circle passing through a celestial body crosses the horizon. [First written down in 1388 in Middle English and spelled *azimut*, from Arabic *as-sumūt*, plural of *as-samt*, the way, compass bearing, from Latin *sēmita*, path.]

A•zores (ā′zôrz *or* ə zôrz′). A group of Portuguese islands in the northern Atlantic Ocean about 900 miles (1,448 kilometers) west of mainland Portugal.

AZT (ā′zē tē′) *n.* A drug used in the treatment of AIDS.

Az•tec (ăz′tĕk′) *n.* **1.** A member of a Native American people of Mexico whose civilization was at its height at the time of the Spanish conquest in the early 16th century. **2.** The Nahuatl language of the Aztecs. —*adj.* also **Az•tec•an** (ăz′tĕk′ən). Of or relating to the Aztecs or their language, culture, or empire.

az•ure (ăzh′ər) *n.* A light purplish blue.

Ayrshire
Ayrshire cow

ă	pat	oi	**boy**
ā	**pay**	ou	**out**
âr	**care**	ŏŏ	**took**
ä	father	ōō	**boot**
ĕ	pet	ŭ	cut
ē	**be**	ûr	**urge**
ĭ	pit	th	**thin**
ī	**pie**	*th*	**this**
îr	**pier**	hw	**whoop**
ŏ	**pot**	zh	vision
ō	**toe**	ə	about
ô	**paw**	N	*French* bon

Bb

b or **B** (bē) *n., pl.* **b's** or **B's. 1.** The second letter of the English alphabet. **2.** The second-best or second-highest grade: *get a B on a test.* **3.** In music, the seventh tone in the scale of C major. **4.** The second in a series or group: *row B in a theater.* **5.** One of the four types of blood in the ABO system.

B The symbol for the element **boron.**

Ba The symbol for the element **barium.**

B.A. *abbr.* An abbreviation of Bachelor of Arts.

baa (bă *or* bä) *intr.v.* **baaed, baa•ing, baas.** To bleat, as a sheep does. —*n.* The bleating sound made by a sheep.

bab•bitt metal (**băb′**ĭt) *n.* Any of several soft alloys of tin, copper, and antimony used in bearings to reduce friction in moving metal parts. [First written down in 1875 in Modern English and spelled *Babbitt's metal,* after Isaac *Babbitt* (1799–1862), American inventor.]

bab•ble (**băb′**əl) *v.* **bab•bled, bab•bling, bab•bles.** —*intr.* **1.** To utter indistinct or meaningless words or sounds: *Babies babble before they can talk.* **2.** To talk idly or foolishly; chatter: *babble on about neighborhood gossip.* **3.** To make a continuous low murmuring sound, as a brook. —*tr.* **1.** To utter indistinctly: *babble an answer to a teacher.* **2.** To disclose without consideration; blurt out. —*n.* **1.** Indistinct or meaningless words or sounds: *a babble of voices as we walked through the crowd.* **2.** Idle or foolish talk; chatter. **3.** A continous low murmuring sound, as of a brook. [First written down before 1250 in Middle English and spelled *babelen.*] —**bab′bler** *n.*

Johann Sebastian Bach

babe (bāb) *n.* A baby; an infant.

ba•bel also **Ba•bel** (**băb′**əl *or* **bā′**bəl) *n.* A confusion of sounds, voices, or languages: *a babel of voices in the street below.* [First written down in 1625 in Modern English, after the Tower of *Babel.*]

Ba•bel (**bā′**bəl *or* **băb′**əl). In the Bible, a city, now thought to be Babylon, where construction of a tower to heaven was interrupted when the builders became unable to understand one another's language.

ba•boon (bă **bo͞on′**) *n.* Any of several large monkeys of Africa and Asia having a face with a projecting muzzle like that of a dog and a short tail. [First written down about 1400 in Middle English and spelled *babewin,* from Old French *babuin,* gargoyle.]

ba•bush•ka (bə **bo͞osh′**kə) *n.* A woman's head scarf worn tied under the chin; a kerchief. [First written down in 1934 in Modern English, from Russian, grandmother.]

ba•by (**bā′**bē) *n., pl.* **ba•bies. 1.** A very young child; an infant: *Babies are not able to care for themselves.* **2.** The youngest member of a family: *My sister in second grade is the baby of the family.* **3.** A person who acts like a baby: *Don't be a baby and pout.* —*tr.v.* **ba•bied, ba•by•ing, ba•bies.** To treat like a baby; coddle: *baby a spoiled child.* See Synonyms at **pamper.** [First written down about 1378 in Middle English.]

ba•by•hood (**bā′**bē ho͝od′) *n.* The time or condition of being a baby.

ba•by•ish (**bā′**bē ĭsh) *adj.* **1.** Resembling a baby; childlike: *a little babyish whimper.* **2.** Childish; immature: *a babyish attitude about sharing.*

Bab•y•lon (**băb′**ə lən *or* **băb′**ə lŏn′). The capital of ancient Babylonia in Mesopotamia on the Euphrates River. Babylon was the site of the Hanging Gardens, one of the Seven Wonders of the World.

Bab•y•lo•ni•a (băb′ə **lō′**nē ə *or* băb′ə **lōn′**yə). An ancient empire of Mesopotamia in the Euphrates River valley in modern-day southern Iraq. It declined in importance after 562 B.C.

Bab•y•lo•ni•an (băb′ə **lō′**nē ən) *n.* **1.** A native or inhabitant of Babylonia or Babylon. **2.** The Semitic language of the Babylonians. —*adj.* Of or relating to Babylonia or Babylon or their people, language, or culture.

baby-sat (**bā′**bē săt′) *v.* Past tense of **baby-sit.**

ba•by's breath (**bā′**bēz) *n.* Any of several plants having branching clusters of small white flowers.

ba•by-sit (**bā′**bē sĭt′) *v.* **ba•by-sat** (**bā′**bē săt′), **ba•by-sit•ting, ba•by-sits.** —*intr.* To care for a child or children when the parents are not at home: *baby-sit for the parents in the apartment downstairs.* —*tr.* To take care of: *He babysat his younger brother.*

baby sitter *n.* A person hired to baby-sit.

baby tooth *n.* A milk tooth.

bac•ca•lau•re•ate (băk′ə **lôr′**ē ĭt) *n.* **1.** A bachelor's degree. **2.** A farewell address delivered to a graduating class at a college or university.

Bac•chus (**băk′**əs) *n.* Dionysus.

Bach (bäкн *or* bäk), **Johann Sebastian.** 1685–1750. German composer and organist. He wrote cantatas, orchestral works, numerous works for organ, harpsichord, other solo instruments, and chamber ensembles.

bach•e•lor (**băch′**ə lər *or* **băch′**lər) *n.* **1.** A man who has not married. **2.** A person who has a bachelor's degree. [First written down before 1300 in Middle English and spelled *bacheler,* from Medieval Latin *baccalārius,* tenant farmer.]

Bachelor of Arts *n.* A bachelor's degree in liberal arts.

Bachelor of Science *n.* A bachelor's degree in science or mathematics.

bach•e•lor's button (**băch′**ə lərz *or* **băch′**lərz) *n., pl.* **bachelor's buttons.** The cornflower.

bachelor's degree *n.* A degree given by a college or university to a person who has completed a four-year undergraduate program or its equivalent.

ba•cil•lus (bə **sĭl′**əs) *n., pl.* **ba•cil•li** (bə **sĭl′**ī′). **1.** Any of various rod-shaped bacteria. **2.** A bacterium. [First written down in 1883 in Modern English, from Late Latin, diminutive of Latin *baculum,* rod.]

back (băk) *n.* **1.** The rear part of the human body between the neck and the pelvis. **2.** The part of another animal that corresponds to this part in humans. **3.** The spine or backbone. **4.** The part or area farthest from the front: *the back of the theater* **5.** The part or side that is not usually seen or used; the reverse side: *the back of a photograph.* **6.** A part that supports the back of a person: *the back of a chair.* **7.** In football, any of the players in a team's backfield. —*v.* **backed, back•ing, backs.** —*tr.* **1.** To cause to move backward or in a reverse direction: *The police backed the crowd away from the fire.* **2.** To furnish or strengthen with a back or backing: *back a poster with cardboard.* **3.** To support: *A majority of voters backed the candidate who won.* —*intr.* **1.** To move backward: *We backed away from the barking dog.* **2.** To shift in a counterclockwise direction: *During the night the wind backed around to the northeast.* —*adj.* **1.** Located at the back or rear: *the back porch.* **2.** Distant from a center of activity; remote: *a back road.* **3.** Overdue: *trying to pay the back rent.* **4.** Of a past date; not current: *a back issue of the magazine.* **5.** Being in a backward direction: *a back flip.* —*adv.* **1.** At, to, or toward the rear: *Move back, please.* **2.** In, to, or toward a former place, time, or condition: *They went back to their old home.* **3.** In reserve or concealment: *It is dishonest to hold back the truth.* **4.** In reply or return: *If you send me a letter, I'll write back.* **5.** In check: *The fireman kept back the flames.* **—*idioms.* back down.** To withdraw from a stand that one has taken: *There was an argument because neither side was willing to back down.* **back off.** To retreat or retire, as from a dangerous position: *The senator backed off from his support of the bill.* **back out.** To retire or withdraw from something: *They accepted the invitation but backed out at the last minute.* **back up. 1.** To make a copy of (a computer program or file). **2.** To accumulate: *Traffic backed up at the intersection.* **behind (one's) back.** When one is not present: *Don't talk about me behind my back.* [First written down about 885 in Old English and spelled *bæc.*]

back•ache (băk′āk′) *n.* Pain or discomfort in the region of the spine or back.

back and forth *adv.* Backward and forward; to and fro.

back•bite (băk′bīt′) *v.* **back•bit** (băk′bĭt′), **back•bit•ten** (băk′bĭt′n), **back•bit•ing, back•bites.** —*tr.* To say mean or unpleasant things about (an absent person). —*intr.* To say mean or unpleasant things about an absent person. **—back′bit′er** *n.*

back•board (băk′bôrd′) *n.* **1.** In basketball, an elevated vertical sheet of wood or other material to which the basket is attached. **2.** A board placed under or behind something for support.

back•bone (băk′bōn′) *n.* **1.** The system of bones that forms the main support of a vertebrate; the spinal column. **2.** A principal support; a mainstay: *Manufacturing is the backbone of the economy.* **3.** Strength of character; courage; fortitude: *It takes backbone to refuse to go along with the crowd.*

back•break•ing (băk′brā′kĭng) *adj.* Requiring great physical exertion; exhausting: *backbreaking work.*

back•coun•try (băk′kŭn′trē) *n.* A rural region that has few people living in it.

back•drop (băk′drŏp′) *n.* **1.** A curtain, often painted to show a scene in the background, hung at the back of a stage. **2.** A background.

back•er (băk′ər) *n.* A person who supports or gives aid to a person, a group, or an enterprise.

back•field (băk′fēld′) *n.* **1.** In football, the group of a team's players stationed behind the linemen. **2.** The area behind the linemen.

back•fire (băk′fīr′) *n.* **1.** In a gasoline engine, an explosion of fuel that ignites too soon or an explosion of unburned fuel in the exhaust system. **2.** A controlled fire started in the path of an oncoming uncontrolled fire in order to deprive it of fuel and thereby extinguish it. —*intr.v.* **back•fired, back•fir•ing, back•fires. 1.** To explode in or make the sound of a backfire. **2.** To lead to a result opposite to that intended: *Their scheme to raise money backfired and everybody lost in the end.*

back-for•ma•tion or **back formation** (băk′-fôr mā′shən) *n.* **1.** A new word formed from an older word by dropping the ending or beginning of the older word, as *baby-sit* from *baby-sitter* or *diagnose* from *diagnosis.* **2.** The formation of words in this way.

back•gam•mon (băk′găm′ən) *n.* A game for two persons played on a specially marked board with pieces whose moves are determined by throws of dice.

back•ground (băk′ground′) *n.* **1.a.** The part of a picture, scene, or view that appears as if in the distance: *a river painted in the background.* **b.** The general scene or surface upon which designs, figures, or other forms are seen or represented: *blue background covered with white stars.* **2.** An inconspicuous position: *The police remained in the background during the demonstration.* **3.** Soft music played to accompany the dialogue or action in a play or motion picture. **4.** The circumstances or events surrounding or leading up to something: *The client filled in the lawyer on the background of the case.* **5.** A person's experience, training, and education: *a perfect background for the job.*

back•hand (băk′hănd′) *n.* **1.** In sports, a stroke, as of a racket, made with the back of the hand facing forward. **2.** Handwriting with letters that slant to the left. —*adj.* Backhanded. —*adv.* With a backhand stroke or motion: *hit the ball backhand.*

back•hand•ed (băk′hăn′dĭd) *adj.* **1.** With the motion or direction of a backhand: *a backhanded stroke in tennis.* **2.** Indirect or insincere: *a backhanded compliment.* **—back′hand′ed•ly** *adv.* **—back′hand′ed•ness** *n.*

back•hoe (băk′hō′) *n.* A machine used for digging, having a bucket attached to a hinged arm that is drawn back toward the machine when in use.

back•ing (băk′ĭng) *n.* **1.** Material that forms the back of something: *a table mat with a felt backing.* **2.a.** Support or aid: *financial backing for a new business.* **b.** Approval or endorsement: *a request with official backing from the mayor.*

back•lash (băk′lăsh′) *n.* **1.** A sudden or violent backward whipping motion. **2.** Strong and hostile reaction to an earlier action or event: *Lack of courtesy brought a backlash of complaints from the store's customers.*

back•log (băk′lŏg′ *or* băk′lôg′) *n.* **1.** An accumulation, especially of unfinished work: *a backlog of unfilled orders accumulated over vacation.* **2.** A large log placed at the back of a fire to support other logs and maintain heat.

back•pack (băk′păk′) *n.* **1.** A knapsack, sometimes mounted on a lightweight frame, that is worn on the back, as to carry books or camping supplies. **2.** A piece of equipment made to be carried on the back: *a firefighter's backpack.* —*intr.v.* **back•packed, back•pack•ing, back•packs.** To hike while carrying a backpack: *The children and their guide backpacked to the lake.* **—back′pack′er** *n.*

back•rest (băk′rĕst′) *n.* A rest for the back.

back-seat driver (băk′sēt′) *n.* **1.** A passenger in a car who frequently advises, corrects, or nags the driver. **2.** A person who persists in giving unwanted advice.

back•side (băk′sīd′) *n. Informal.* The buttocks.

back•slide (băk′slīd′) *intr.v.* **back•slid** (băk′slĭd′), **back•slid•ing, back•slides.** To lapse into improper habits or wrongdoing, especially in religious matters. **—back′slid′er** *n.*

back•spin (băk′spĭn′) *n.* In sports, a spin on a ball that tends to make it reverse the direction in which it is traveling.

back•stage (băk′stāj′) *adv.* **1.** In or toward the area of a theater that is behind the area where the per-

backboard

backpack

ă	**pat**	oi	**boy**
ā	**pay**	ou	**out**
âr	**care**	o͝o	**took**
ä	**father**	o͞o	**boot**
ĕ	**pet**	ŭ	**cut**
ē	**be**	ûr	**urge**
ĭ	**pit**	th	**thin**
ī	**pie**	*th*	**this**
îr	**pier**	hw	**whoop**
ŏ	**pot**	zh	**vision**
ō	**toe**	ə	**about**
ô	**paw**	N	*French* **bon**

backstop

Usage: bad

You should avoid using **bad** as an adverb in your writing. Instead of *We need water bad,* write *We need water badly.* Instead of *My tooth hurt bad,* write *My tooth hurt badly.*

formance takes place. **2.** In or toward a place closed to public view: *backstage at a political convention.* —*adj.* (băk′stāj′). **1.** Of, relating to, or situated behind the performing area of a theater: *a backstage orchestra.* **2.** Not open or known to the public: *backstage political dealings.*

back•stop (băk′stŏp′) *n.* **1.** A screen or fence in back of the playing area, as in tennis or baseball, used to stop a ball's movement. **2.** In baseball, a catcher.

back•stretch (băk′strĕch′) *n.* The part of an oval racecourse farthest from the spectators and opposite the homestretch.

back•stroke (băk′strōk′) *n.* A swimming stroke made while lying on the back and moving the arms alternately upward and backward.

back talk *n.* Rude and disrespectful remarks.

back•track (băk′trăk′) *intr.v.* **back•tracked, back•track•ing, back•tracks. 1.** To return over the route by which one has come: *We backtracked to find the side trail we had missed.* **2.** To reverse one's position or policy: *The President backtracked on his pledge not to raise taxes.*

back•up (băk′ŭp′) *n.* **1.** A reserve, as of provisions. **2.** A person standing by and ready to serve as a substitute: *The Assistant Fire Chief is the backup for the Chief.* **3.** A copy of a program, file, or other data in a computer memory or on a disk or tape, made to safeguard against loss of the original. **4.** An accumulation or overflow caused by the blockage or clogging of something: *a backup in the drain.* —*adj.* Ready and available as a substitute or in a case of emergency; extra; standby: *a backup pilot.*

back•ward (băk′wərd) *adj.* **1.** Directed or moving toward the rear: *a backward glance; a backward tumble.* **2.** Behind others, as in economic or social progress: *backward technology.* **3.** Unwilling to act; reluctant; shy. —*adv.* or **back•wards** (băk′wərdz). **1.** To or toward the back or rear. **2.** With the back or rear first: *With its hind legs a toad can dig its way into the ground backward.* **3.** In reverse order or direction: *count backward from 100.* **4.** Toward a worse condition: *As prices rise poor people slip backward.* **5.** To, toward, or into the past: *The study looks backward to discover the source of the problem.* —***idiom.*** **bend over backward** or **lean over backward.** To make an effort greater than is required: *They bent over backwards to be fair.* —**back′ward•ly** *adv.*

back•wash (băk′wŏsh′ *or* băk′wôsh′) *n.* **1.** The backward flow of water produced by the oars or propeller of a boat. **2.** The backward flow of air from a propeller of an aircraft. **3.** A result of an event: *the backwash of the storm's advance along the coast.*

back•wa•ter (băk′wô′tər *or* băk′wŏt′ər) *n.* **1.** Water held back by a dam. **2.** A place or situation regarded as stagnant or backward.

back•woods (băk′wŏŏdz′) *pl.n. (used with a singular or plural verb).* **1.** Heavily wooded, uncultivated, remote areas. **2.** An area that is far from population centers, often regarded as backward; a backwater.

back•woods•man (băk′wŏŏdz′mən) *n.* A person who lives in the backwoods.

back yard also **back•yard** (băk′yärd′) *n.* A yard at the back of a house.

ba•con (bā′kən) *n.* The salted and smoked meat from the back and sides of a pig.

Ba•con (bā′kən), **Francis.** First Baron Verulam and Viscount Saint Albans. 1561–1626. English philosopher, writer, and politician. His writings include *The Advancement of Learning* (1605).

bac•te•ri•a (băk tîr′ē ə) *n.* Plural of **bacterium.**

bac•te•ri•al (băk tîr′ē əl) *adj.* Of, relating to, or caused by bacteria: *a bacterial enzyme; a bacterial disease.*

bac•te•ri•o•log•i•cal (băk tîr′ē ə lŏj′ĭ kəl) *adj.* Of, relating to, or based on bacteriology: *bacteriological classification of diseases.* —**bac•te′ri•o•log′i•cal•ly** *adv.*

bac•te•ri•ol•o•gist (băk tîr′ē ŏl′ə jĭst) *n.* A scientist who specializes in bacteriology.

bac•te•ri•ol•o•gy (băk tîr′ē ŏl′ə jē) *n.* The scientific study of bacteria.

bac•te•ri•um (băk tîr′ē əm) *n., pl.* **bac•te•ri•a** (băk tîr′ē ə). Any of a large group of very small one-celled organisms that reproduce by fission or by forming spores. Some kinds can cause disease, while others are active in fermentation. [First written down about 1847 in Modern English, from Greek *baktērion,* diminutive of *baktron,* rod.]

Bac•tri•an camel (băk′trē ən) *n.* A two-humped camel of central and southwest Asia.

bad (băd) *adj.* **worse** (wûrs), **worst** (wûrst). **1.** Being below an acceptable standard; inferior; poor: *a bad book; a bad painter.* **2.** Evil or wicked; sinful. **3.** Disobedient; naughty: *bad behavior.* **4.** Unfavorable: *bad luck; bad weather.* **5.** Disagreeable, unpleasant, or disturbing: *a bad odor; bad news.* **6.** Faulty; incorrect; improper: *a bad choice of words.* **7.** Not working properly; defective: *a bad telephone connection.* **8.** Rotten; spoiled: *bad fish.* **9.** Harmful in effect; detrimental: *Candy is bad for your teeth.* **10.** Being in poor health or condition: *I feel bad today. The jogger has a bad knee.* **11.** Severe; violent; intense: *a bad cold; a bad snowstorm.* **12.** Sorry; regretful: *I feel very bad about what happened.* —*n.* Something bad: *You must learn to accept the bad with the good.* —***idioms.*** **not half bad** or **not so bad.** *Informal.* Reasonably good. **too bad.** Regrettable; unfortunate: *It's too bad you can't come along.* —**bad′ness** *n.* —See Note.

❑ *These sound alike:* **bad, bade** (commanded).

bad blood *n.* Bitterness or hostility between persons or groups.

bade (băd *or* bād) *v.* A past tense of **bid.**

❑ *These sound alike:* **bade, bad** (inferior).

badge (băj) *n.* **1.** An emblem worn to show rank, office, or membership. **2.** An emblem given as an award or honor.

badg•er (băj′ər) *n.* **1.** Any of several burrowing mammals having short legs, long claws on the front feet, and thick grayish fur. It has a heavy body and feeds mostly at night on insects and smaller animals. **2.** The fur of such a mammal. —*tr.v.* **badg•ered, badg•er•ing, badg•ers.** To trouble with many questions or protests; pester: *The speaker was badgered by the angry audience.* [First written down in 1523 in Modern English, perhaps from *badge.*]

bad•lands (băd′lăndz′) *pl.n.* An area of barren land with rough ridges and peaks.

bad•ly (băd′lē) *adv.* **1.** In a bad manner; poorly: *a job badly done.* **2.** Very much; greatly: *He misses his brother badly.* —See Note at **bad.**

bad•min•ton (băd′mĭn′tən) *n.* A game in which players use a light long-handled racket to hit a shuttlecock back and forth over a high net. [First written down in 1874 in Modern English, after *Badminton,* the Duke of Beaufort's country seat in western England.]

bad•mouth or **bad-mouth** (băd′mouth′ *or* băd′mouth′) *tr.v.* **bad•mouthed, bad•mouth•ing, bad•mouths.** *Slang.* To criticize or belittle, often unfairly or spitefully.

Baf•fin Island (băf′ĭn). An island of northeast Northwest Territories, Canada, west of Greenland. It is the fifth-largest island in the world.

baf•fle (băf′əl) *tr.v.* **baf•fled, baf•fling, baf•fles. 1.**

To confuse; puzzle: *Use the dictionary for any word that baffles you.* **2.** To interfere with or impede the force or movement of (a gas, sound, or liquid). *—n.* A partition or an enclosure that stops or regulates the movement of a gas, sound, or liquid: *A baffle partly over the opening prevents the air conditioner from blowing directly onto me.* [First written down in 1548 in Modern English, perhaps blend of Scottish Gaelic *bauchle*, to denounce, revile publicly, and French *bafouer*, to ridicule.] **—baf′fle•ment** *n.* **—baf′fler** *n.*

bag (băg) *n.* **1.** A container made of flexible material, such as paper, cloth, or plastic, used for carrying various articles. **2.a.** A bag with something in it: *buy a bag of onions.* **b.** The amount that a bag can hold: *eat a bag of peanuts.* **3.** A purse, handbag, or suitcase: *Many passengers carry their bags right onto the airplane.* **4.** The amount of game caught or killed in a hunting expedition. **5.** Something that is shaped like a bag or hangs loosely like a bag: *bags under one's eyes.* **6.** In baseball, a base. **7.** *Slang.* An area of interest or skill: *Cooking is not my bag.* *—v.* **bagged, bag•ging, bags.** *—tr.* **1.** To put into a bag: *I bag groceries at the supermarket.* **2.** To capture and kill, as game. *—intr.* To hang loosely like a bag. ***—idiom.* in the bag.** Assured of a successful outcome; virtually accomplished or won.

bag•a•telle (băg′ə tĕl′) *n.* An unimportant or insignificant thing; a trifle.

ba•gel (bā′gəl) *n.* A ring-shaped roll with a tough chewy texture. [First written down in 1919 in Modern English and spelled *beigel*, from Yiddish *beygl*, from Middle High German *bouc*, ring.]

bag•gage (băg′ĭj) *n.* **1.** The trunks, bags, suitcases, or boxes in which one carries one's belongings while traveling; luggage. **2.** The movable equipment and supplies of an army.

bag•gy (băg′ē) *adj.* **bag•gi•er, bag•gi•est.** Bulging or hanging loosely; loose-fitting: *baggy trousers.* **—bag′gi•ness** *n.*

Bagh•dad or **Bag•dad** (băg′dăd′). The capital and largest city of Iraq, in the center of the country on the Tigris River. It was founded in the eighth century. Population, 2,200,000.

Bag•nold (băg′nəld), **Enid.** 1889–1981. British writer whose works include the novel *National Velvet* (1935).

bag•pipe (băg′pīp′) *n.* A musical instrument that consists of a reed pipe for playing melodies and several other pipes that play continuous single tones, all being supplied with air from a large bag that is filled by the player's breath or by a bellows. Often used in the plural. **—bag′pip′er** *n.*

bah (bä *or* bă) *interj.* An expression used to show contempt or disgust.

Ba•ha•mas (bə hä′məz). An island country in the Atlantic Ocean east of Florida and Cuba made up of some 700 islands and islets. The country gained its independence from Great Britain in 1973. Nassau is the capital and the largest city. Population, 218,000.

Bah•rain or **Bah•rein** (bä rān′). A country made up of a group of low sandy islands in the Persian Gulf between Qatar and Saudi Arabia. Bahrain gained its independence from Great Britain in 1971. Manama, on **Bahrain Island**, is the capital. Population, 350,798.

baht (bät) *n., pl.* **bahts** or **baht.** The basic monetary unit of Thailand.

Bai•kal (bī kôl′ *or* bī kŏl′), **Lake.** A lake of south-central Russia. It is the world's deepest lake, with a maximum depth of 5,712 feet (1,742.2 meters).

bail[1] (bāl) *n.* **1.** Money supplied for the temporary release of an arrested person and guaranteeing a person's appearance for trial: *Friends posted bail of $500 for the accused thief.* **2.** The release so obtained: *The accused thief was out on bail until the trial.* **3.** A person who supplies the money for such a release. *—tr.v.* **bailed, bail•ing, bails. 1.** To secure the release of (an arrested person) by providing bail. **2.** To release or deliver from a difficult situation: *The bank loan bailed out her business when sales dropped.* [First written down before 1338 in Middle English and spelled *bail*, custody, from Old French *baillier*, to take charge of, from Latin *bāiulāre*, to carry a load.]

❑ *These sound alike:* **bail**[1] (money), **bail**[2] (remove water), **bail**[3] (handle), **bale** (bundle).

bail[2] (bāl) *tr.v.* **bailed, bail•ing, bails. 1.** To remove (water) from a boat by repeatedly filling a container and emptying it: *bail water with a coffee can.* **2.** To empty (a boat) of water by this means. ***—idiom.* bail out. 1.** To parachute from an aircraft; eject. **2.** To abandon a project or an enterprise. [First written down in 1613 in Modern English, from Middle English *baille*, bucket, from Latin *bāiulāre*, to carry a load.]

❑ *These sound alike:* **bail**[2] (remove water), **bail**[1] (money), **bail**[3] (handle), **bale** (bundle).

bail[3] (bāl) *n.* The arched handle of a pail, kettle, or similar container. [First written down in 1447 in Middle English and spelled *beil*, possibly of Scandinavian origin.]

❑ *These sound alike:* **bail**[3] (handle), **bail**[1] (money), **bail**[2] (remove water), **bale** (bundle).

bail•iff (bā′lĭf) *n.* An official who guards prisoners and maintains order in a courtroom. [First written down about 1242 in Middle English and spelled *baillif*, from Latin *bāiulus*, carrier.]

bail•i•wick (bā′lə wĭk′) *n.* **1.** The office or district of a bailiff. **2.** A person's specific area of interest, skill, or authority: *Repairing watches is the jeweler's particular bailiwick.*

bails•man (bālz′mən) *n.* A person who provides bail or security for another.

bairn (bârn) *n. Scots.* A child.

bait (bāt) *n.* **1.** Food placed on a hook or in a trap to lure fish, birds, or other animals: *I always use worms for bait.* **2.** Something used to lure or entice: *A free book was the bait to get people to attend the book fair.* *—tr.v.* **bait•ed, bait•ing, baits. 1.** To put bait on: *bait a fishhook.* **2.** To set dogs upon (a chained animal) for sport. **3.** To torment with repeated verbal attacks, insults, or ridicule. [First written down about 1300 in Middle English, from Old Norse *beita*, food, and *beita*, to hunt with dogs.]

baize (bāz) *n.* A thick, often green, woolen or cotton cloth that looks like felt, used chiefly on billiard tables.

Ba•ja Cal•i•for•nia (bä′hä kăl′ĭ fôr′nyə) also **Low•er California** (lō′ər). A mountainous peninsula of western Mexico bordering on the Pacific Ocean.

bake (bāk) *v.* **baked, bak•ing, bakes.** *—tr.* **1.** To cook in an oven with dry heat: *We baked several loaves of bread.* **2.** To harden or dry by heating in or as if in an oven: *bake bricks in the sun.* *—intr.* **1.** To cook food by dry heat: *He loves to bake bread.* **2.** To become hardened or dry by or as if by baking: *The ground baked in the hot sun.* [First written down before 893 in Old English and spelled *bacan*.]

bak•er (bā′kər) *n.* A person who bakes and sells bread, cakes, and pastries.

Ba•ker (bākər), **Ella.** 1903–1986. American social reformer who worked to organize the civil rights movement of the 1950's and 1960's.

bak•er's dozen (bā′kərz) *n.* A group of thirteen; one dozen plus one. [First written down in 1599 in Modern English, from the former custom among

bagpipe

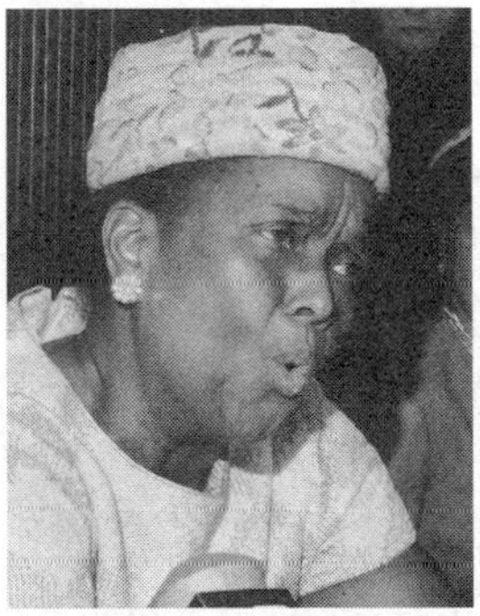

Ella Baker

ă	pat	oi	boy
ā	pay	ou	out
âr	care	o͝o	took
ä	father	o͞o	boot
ĕ	pet	ŭ	cut
ē	be	ûr	urge
ĭ	pit	th	thin
ī	pie	*th*	this
îr	pier	hw	whoop
ŏ	pot	zh	vision
ō	toe	ə	about
ô	paw	N	*French* bon

balalaika
20th-century Russian

bald eagle

baldric

bakers of adding an extra roll as a safeguard against the possibility of 12 weighing light.]

bak•er•y (bā′kə rē) *n., pl.* **bak•er•ies.** A place where products such as bread, cake, and pastries are baked or sold.

bak•ing powder (bā′kĭng) *n.* Any of several powdered mixtures of baking soda, starch, and a slightly acid compound such as cream of tartar, that are used as leavening in biscuits and other baked goods.

baking soda *n.* A white crystalline compound having the formula $NaHCO_3$, used especially in beverages and as leavening in baked goods; sodium bicarbonate.

Ba•ku (bä ko͞o′). The capital of Azerbaijan, in the eastern part of the republic on the Caspian Sea. Population, 1,104,000.

bal•a•lai•ka (băl′ə lī′kə) *n.* A Russian musical instrument that is somewhat like a guitar but has a triangular body and three strings.

bal•ance (băl′əns) *n.* **1.** A device in which the weight of an object is measured by putting it at one end of a rod that swings on a pivot at its center and adding known weights to the other side until the rod is level and motionless: *Chemists use a balance to weigh ingredients of a formula.* **2.** A condition in which all forces or influences are cancelled by equal and opposite forces or influences: *We keep a balance in our interests in science and music.* **3.** A state of bodily stability, as when standing erect: *I was thrown off balance by the gust of wind.* **4.** Mental or emotional stability; sanity. **5.** A condition in which an equation represents a correct statement in mathematics or chemistry: *The balance in the equation is maintained as equal quantities are added to each side.* **6.a.** An equality between the debit and credit sides of an account: *Our bookkeeper achieves a balance in books of account at the end of the month.* **b.** The difference between such sides: *There is a balance due of $50.00.* **7.** Something left over; a remainder: *After dinner the balance of the evening was spent playing cards.* **8.** A satisfying proportion or arrangement achieved between parts or elements; harmony: *The red curtains destroyed the balance of color in the room.* **9.** An action or influence that results in even, suitable, or fair distribution: *Part of the U.S. system of checks and balances is the division of power between the Congress and the President.* —*v.* **bal•anced, bal•anc•ing, bal•anc•es.** —*tr.* **1.** To bring into or keep in a condition of balance: *I balanced the book on my head.* **2.** To compare in the mind: *We tried to balance the pros and cons before deciding.* **3.** To act as an equalizing weight or factor to; offset: *Your skill in languages balances your lack of experience in foreign countries.* **4.** To equalize the sums of the debits and credits of (an account). **5.** In mathematics and chemistry, to bring (an equation) into balance. —*intr.* **1.** To be equal or equivalent, as in weight, force, or parts: *rewards that don't balance with the risks.* **2.** To be or come into a state of balance or stability: *He balanced on the top of the wall.* **3.** To be equal in accounts of debit and credit. —***idioms.*** **in the balance.** In an undetermined and often critical position. **on balance.** Taking everything into consideration; all in all. [First written down about 1200 in Middle English and spelled *balaunce*, from Latin *bilanx*, (scale) with two pans.]

balance beam *n.* A horizontal raised beam on which competitors in gymnastics perform balancing feats.

balance of payments *n.* The amount of a nation's total payments to foreign countries after calculating the total receipts from abroad.

balance of power *n.* A distribution of power whereby no one nation is able to dominate or interfere with others.

balance of trade *n.* The difference in value between the total exports and the total imports of a nation.

balance wheel *n.* A wheel that regulates the speed of a machine, as in a clock or watch.

bal•bo•a (băl bō′ə) *n.* The basic monetary unit of Panama. [First written down about 1909 in Modern English, after Vasco Núñez de *Balboa.*]

Bal•bo•a (băl bō′ə), **Vasco Núñez de.** 1475–1517. Spanish explorer who in 1513 discovered the Pacific Ocean and claimed it for Spain.

bal•brig•gan (băl brĭg′ən) *n.* A knitted cotton material used for underwear and hose. [First written down in 1859 in Modern English, after *Balbriggan*, a seaport of eastern Ireland.]

Balch (bôlch), **Emily Greene.** 1867–1961. American sociologist who helped found the Women's International League for Peace and Freedom (1919) and shared the 1946 Nobel Peace Prize.

bal•co•ny (băl′kə nē) *n., pl.* **bal•co•nies. 1.** A platform projecting from the wall of a building and surrounded by railing. **2.** An upper section of seats in a theater or an auditorium.

bald (bôld) *adj.* **bald•er, bald•est. 1.** Lacking hair on the head. **2.** Lacking a natural or usual covering: *a bald mountaintop without any vegetation.* **3.** Having a white spot or blaze on the head, as some birds or mammals. **4.** Plain; blunt: *a bald statement of unpleasant facts.* **—bald′ness** *n.*

bald eagle *n.* A North American eagle having a dark body and wings and a white head and tail.

bal•der•dash (bôl′dər dăsh′) *n.* Nonsense.

bald•pate (bôld′pāt′) *n.* A bald person.

bal•dric (bôl′drĭk) *n.* A belt worn over one shoulder across the chest to the opposite hip, used to support a sword or bugle.

Bald•win (bôld′wĭn), **James Arthur.** 1924–1987. American writer and critic of racism whose works include *Go Tell it on the Mountain* (1953) and *Notes of a Native Son* (1955).

bale (bāl) *n.* A large bound package or bundle of raw or finished material: *a bale of hay.* —*tr.v.* **baled, bal•ing, bales.** To wrap in bales: *bale cotton.* **—bal′er** *n.*

❑ *These sound alike:* **bale, bail**[1] (money), **bail**[2] (remove water), **bail**[3] (handle).

Bal•e•ar•ic Islands (băl′ē ăr′ĭk). A group of islands in the western Mediterranean Sea off the eastern coast of Spain. The islands are noted for their scenery and mild climate.

ba•leen (bə lēn′) *n.* Whalebone. [First written down about 1300 in Middle English and spelled *bleine*, from Greek *phalaina*, whale.]

bale•ful (bāl′fəl) *adj.* **1.** Threatening; menacing: *a baleful look.* **2.** Producing evil or harm; harmful: *a baleful influence.* **—bale′ful•ly** *adv.* **—bale′ful•ness** *n.*

Ba•li (bä′lē). An island of southern Indonesia just east of Java. It is largely mountainous with a tropical climate.

balk (bôk) *v.* **balked, balk•ing, balks.** —*intr.* **1.** To stop short and refuse to go on: *The horse balked and wouldn't jump the fence.* **2.** To refuse; recoil; shrink: *The workers balked at the low terms of the wage settlement.* **3.** In baseball, to make an illegal motion before pitching, allowing base runners to advance a base. —*tr.* To check or thwart: *The police balked the prisoners' plans to escape.* —*n.* **1.** A hindrance, check, or defeat. **2.** In baseball, the act of balking.

Bal•kan (bôl′kən) *adj.* Of or relating to the Balkan Peninsula or its inhabitants.

Balkan Peninsula. A peninsula of southeast Europe. The **Balkan States** include Albania, Bulgaria, continental Greece, southeast Romania, European Turkey, and most of the territories organized as Yugoslavia in 1918.

balk•y (bô′kē) *adj.* **balk•i•er, balk•i•est.** Given to stopping short and refusing to go on; stubborn: *a balky mule.*

ball[1] (bôl) *n.* **1.a.** Something that is spherical or nearly spherical; a round object: *The earth is a great round ball.* **b.** Such an object used in various sports and games: *a tennis ball.* **c.** Such an object moving, thrown, hit, or kicked in a certain way: *a fly ball; a curve ball.* **2.** A game, especially baseball, played with such an object. **3.** In baseball, a pitch that does not pass through the strike zone and is not swung at by the batter. **4.** A rounded part of the body: *the ball of the foot.* **5.** A solid projectile or shot for a firearm: *a cannon ball.* —*tr. & intr.v.* **balled, ball•ing, balls.** To form into a ball: *ball yarn for knitting.* —***idiom.* on the ball.** *Informal.* Alert, competent, or efficient. [First written down before 1200 in Middle English and spelled *bal.*]

❑ *These sound alike:* **ball**[1] (round object), **ball**[2] (dance), **bawl** (cry).

ball[2] (bôl) *n.* **1.** A formal social dance. **2.** *Slang.* A wonderful time: *had a ball at the beach.* [First written down in 1632 in Modern English, from French *bal,* from Greek *ballizein,* to dance.]

❑ *These sound alike:* **ball**[2] (dance), **ball**[1] (round object), **bawl** (cry).

bal•lad (băl′əd) *n.* **1.** A poem that tells a story in simple stanzas, often intended to be sung. **2.** The music for such a poem. **3.** A popular love song.

ball-and-sock•et joint (bôl′ən sŏk′ĭt) *n.* A flexible joint formed by a ball or knob fitting in a socket, permitting rotary motion, as in the shoulder and hip joint.

bal•last (băl′əst) *n.* **1.** Heavy material carried especially in the hold of a ship or the gondola of a balloon to provide weight and steadiness: *Submarines use water as ballast in order to submerge.* **2.** Gravel or small stones used to form a foundation for a roadway or for railroad tracks. —*tr.v.* **bal•last•ed, bal•last•ing, bal•lasts.** To provide with or stabilize with ballast: *They used heavy stones to ballast the ship.*

ball bearing *n.* **1.** A bearing, as for a turning shaft, in which the moving and stationary parts are held apart by small steel balls that turn in a collar around the moving parts and reduce friction. **2.** A small steel ball used in such a bearing.

bal•le•ri•na (băl′ə rē′nə) *n.* A female dancer in a ballet company.

bal•let (bă lā′ *or* băl′ā′) *n.* **1.** A form of artistic dancing based on a technique of jumps, turns, and poses requiring great precision and grace of movement. **2.** A theatrical performance of dancing to music, usually in costume, to convey a story or theme. **3.** Music written or used for ballet. **4.** A company or group that performs ballet. [First written down in 1667 in Modern English, from French, from Italian *balletto,* diminutive of *ballo,* dance, from *ballare,* to dance.]

bal•lis•tic (bə lĭs′tĭk) *adj.* Of or relating to ballistics or projectiles.

ballistic missile *n.* A projectile that is guided during the time that it is propelled and then allowed to fall or coast toward its target.

bal•lis•tics (bə lĭs′tĭks) *n.* (*used with a singular verb*). **1.** The scientific study of the characteristics of projectiles, such as bullets or missiles, and the way they move in flight. **2.** The study of firearms and ammunition.

bal•loon (bə lo͞on′) *n.* **1.** A large flexible bag filled with helium, hot air, or some other gas that is lighter than the surrounding air and designed to rise and float in the atmosphere, often with a gondola or instruments. **2.** A small brightly colored rubber or plastic bag that is inflated and used as a toy. —*intr. v.* **bal•looned, bal•loon•ing, bal•loons. 1.** To swell out like a balloon: *The tire ballooned as it was inflated with air.* **2.** To ride in a gondola suspended from a balloon.

bal•loon•ist (bə lo͞o′nĭst) *n.* A person who flies by means of a balloon.

bal•lot (băl′ət) *n.* **1.** A piece of paper used to cast a vote, especially a secret vote. **2.** The act, process, or method of voting: *In a democracy, many decisions are made by the ballot.* **3.** A list of candidates running for office in an election. **4.** The total of all votes cast in an election: *The ballot is especially heavy in the year of a presidential election.* **5.** The right to vote; franchise: *Many countries do not have the ballot.* —*intr.v.* **bal•lot•ed, bal•lot•ing, bal•lots.** To cast a ballot or ballots; vote. [First written down in 1549 in Modern English, from Italian *ballotta,* a small ball used to register a vote, diminutive of dialectal *balla,* ball.]

ball•park (bôl′pärk′) *n.* A stadium for playing baseball. —*adj. Slang.* Being approximately right or in the right range: *a ballpark figure; a ballpark estimate.* —***idiom.* in the ballpark.** *Slang.* Approximately right or within the right range.

ball•play•er (bôl′plā′ər) *n.* A baseball player.

ball•point pen (bôl′point′) *n.* A pen having a small ball bearing as its writing point that transfers ink from a cartridge onto a writing surface.

ball•room (bôl′ro͞om′ *or* bôl′ro͝om′) *n.* A large room for dancing.

bal•ly•hoo (băl′ē ho͞o′) *n., pl.* **bal•ly•hoos.** Sensational advertising, as for a product or political campaign. —*tr.v.* **bal•ly•hooed, bal•ly•hoo•ing, bal•ly•hoos.** To advertise in a sensational manner.

balm (bäm) *n.* **1.** Any of several plants related to the mint plant and having a pleasant spicy odor. **2.** Any of various fragrant resins obtained from several trees and shrubs. **3.** A fragrant ointment or oil. **4.** Something that soothes or comforts: *The teacher's tender words were balm to the child's hurt feelings.*

balm•y (bä′mē) *adj.* **balm•i•er, balm•i•est. 1.** Having the quality or fragrance of balm; soothing. **2.** Mild and pleasant: *balmy subtropical climates.* —**balm′i•ly** *adv.* —**balm′i•ness** *n.*

ba•lo•ney[1] (bə lō′nē) *n., pl.* **ba•lo•neys.** Variant of **bologna.**

ba•lo•ney[2] (bə lō′nē) *n. Slang.* Nonsense.

bal•sa (bôl′sə) *n.* **1.** A tropical American tree having wood that is unusually light in weight. **2.** The buoyant wood of this tree, used for rafts and floats and in making model airplanes. [First written down in 1593 in Modern English, from Spanish.]

bal•sam (bôl′səm) *n.* **1.** Any of several fragrant resins obtained from various trees and used in medicines and perfumes. **2.** A tree, especially the balsam fir tree, that yields such a resinous substance. **3.** Any of several plants having yellowish flowers.

balsam fir *n.* **1.** An evergreen tree of northeast North America, widely used for pulpwood. Turpentine and varnish are made from its resin. **2.** The wood of such a tree.

Balt (bôlt) *n.* A native or inhabitant of Estonia, Latvia, or Lithuania.

Bal•tic (bôl′tĭk) *adj.* **1.** Of or relating to the Baltic Sea or to the Baltic States. **2.** Of or relating to Baltic or a people that speaks Baltic. —*n.* A group of Indo-European languages that includes Lithuanian and Latvian.

Baltic Sea. An arm of the Atlantic Ocean in northern Europe bounded by Denmark, Sweden, Finland, Russia, Estonia, Latvia, Lithuania, Poland, and

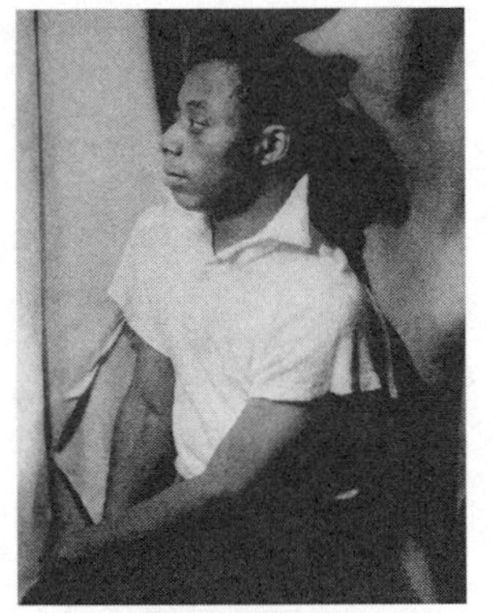

James Baldwin
Photographed in 1955 by Carl Van Vechten (1880–1964)

balloon
Hot-air balloons

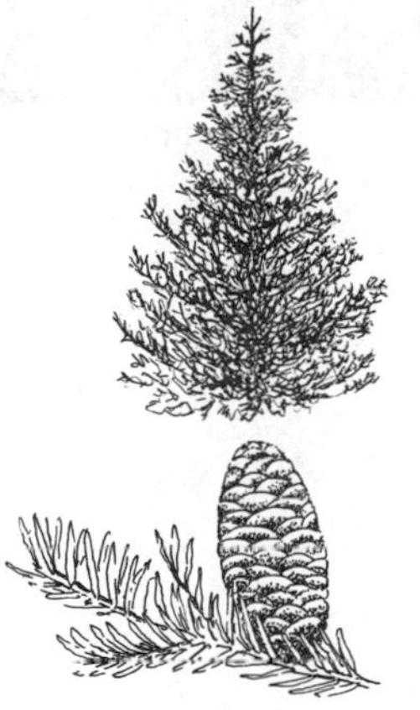

balsam fir

ă	pat	oi	boy
ā	pay	ou	out
âr	care	o͝o	took
ä	father	o͞o	boot
ĕ	pet	ŭ	cut
ē	be	ûr	urge
ĭ	pit	th	thin
ī	pie	*th*	this
îr	pier	hw	whoop
ŏ	pot	zh	vision
ō	toe	ə	about
ô	paw	N	*French* bon

balustrade

bamboo

Germany. It opens to the North Sea by way of channels and canals.

Baltic States. Estonia, Latvia, and Lithuania, on the eastern coast of the Baltic Sea. They were formerly Russian provinces and republics of the Soviet Union.

Bal•ti•more (bôl′tə môr′). A city of northern Maryland on an arm of Chesapeake Bay northeast of Washington, D.C. Population, 736,014.

bal•us•ter (băl′ə stər) *n.* One of the posts supporting a railing, as of a porch or banister.

bal•us•trade (băl′ə strād′) *n.* A handrail and the row of posts supporting it, as on a balcony or the edge of a staircase.

Ba•ma•ko (bä′mə kō′). The capital and largest city of Mali, in the southwest on the Niger River. Population, 502,000.

bam•bi•no (băm bē′nō *or* bäm bē′nō) *n., pl.* **bam•bi•nos** or **bam•bi•ni** (băm bē′nē *or* bäm bē′nē). **1.** A child; a baby. **2.** A representation of the infant Jesus.

bam•boo (băm bo͞o′) *n., pl.* **bam•boos. 1.** Any of various tall grasses having hollow jointed stems. Young shoots of some types are used as food. **2.** The strong woody stems of this plant, used for construction, fishing poles, walking sticks, and many other purposes. [First written down in 1598 in Modern English, from Malay *bambu.*]

bam•boo•zle (băm bo͞o′zəl) *tr.v.* **bam•boo•zled, bam•boo•zling, bam•boo•zles.** *Informal.* To deceive by elaborate trickery; hoodwink: *bamboozle a newcomer.* **—bam•boo′zler** *n.*

ban (băn) *tr.v.* **banned, ban•ning, bans.** To prohibit by law, decree, or rule; forbid: *The city council banned billboards on most streets.* —*n.* A prohibition made by law or official decree: *a ban on cigarette smoking on airplanes.*

ba•nal (bə năl′ *or* bā′nəl *or* bə näl′) *adj.* Commonplace; dull; trite: *Always remarking on the weather makes banal conversation.* **—ba•nal′ly** *adv.*

ba•nal•i•ty (bə năl′ĭ tē *or* bā năl′ĭ tē) *n.* **1.** The quality or condition of being banal; triteness: *The banality of the speaker's remarks put the audience to sleep.* **2.** Something that is banal: *Television commercials are full of banalities.*

ba•nan•a (bə năn′ə) *n.* **1.** A crescent-shaped fruit having sweet soft flesh and yellow to reddish skin that peels off easily. **2.** Any of several tropical plants that bear such fruit. [First written down in 1597 in Modern English, of African origin.]

band[1] (bănd) *n.* **1.a.** A strip of metal, cloth, or other flexible material, used to bind, trim, support, or hold things together: *A band of metal held the wooden barrel together.* **b.** A stripe, a mark, or an area suggestive of such a strip: *the band of colors forming the rainbow.* **2.** A specific range of wavelengths or frequencies in the electromagnetic spectrum, as those used in radio broadcasting: *the shortwave band.* —*tr.v.* **band•ed, band•ing, bands. 1.** To tie, bind, or encircle with or as if with a band: *band a skirt with a red ribbon.* **2.** To put a band on the leg of (a bird) for purposes of identification. [First written down in 1126 in Middle English, from Old Norse *band,* band, fetter and from Old French *bande,* band, strip, of Germanic origin.]

band[2] (bănd) *n.* **1.** A group of people or animals. **2.** A group of musicians who play together. —*tr. & intr.v.* **band•ed, band•ing, bands.** To form or gather in a group or an association: *The homesteaders banded together for protection.* [First written down in 1490 in Middle English, from Old French, probably of Germanic origin.]

band•age (băn′dĭj) *n.* A strip of cloth or other material used to bind, cover, or protect a wound or other injury. —*tr.v.* **band•aged, band•ag•ing, band•ag•es.** To cover or bind with a bandage: *bandage a wound.*

Band-Aid (bănd′ād′). A trademark for an adhesive bandage with a gauze pad in the center.

ban•dan•na or **ban•dan•a** (băn dăn′ə) *n.* A large brightly colored handkerchief, often having a printed pattern on a red or blue background. [First written down in 1752 in Modern English, from Hindi *bāndhnā,* to tie.]

Ban•dar Se•ri Be•ga•wan (bŭn′dər sĕr′ē bə gä′wən). The capital of Brunei, on the northwest coast of Borneo. Population, 63,868.

band•box (bănd′bŏks′) *n.* A light round box used to hold small articles of apparel.

ban•di•coot (băn′dĭ ko͞ot′) *n.* **1.** Any of several large rats of India that are often destructive to food crops. **2.** Any of several burrowing Australian mammals that are similar to a rat, have a long tapering snout, and feed on insects and plants.

ban•dit (băn′dĭt) *n.* **1.** A robber, often one who is a member of a gang of outlaws. **2.** An outlaw or a gangster. **—*idiom.* make out like a bandit.** *Slang.* To be highly successful in a given enterprise.

ban•di•try (băn′dĭ trē) *n.* The activity of a bandit.

band•mas•ter (bănd′măs′tər) *n.* The conductor of a musical band.

ban•do•leer or **ban•do•lier** (băn′də lîr′) *n.* A military belt that has small pockets or loops for carrying cartridges and is worn over the shoulder and across the chest. [First written down before 1577 in Modern English, from French *bandoulière.*]

band saw *n.* A power saw consisting of a toothed metal band driven around two wheels in a loop.

band•stand (bănd′stănd′) *n.* An outdoor platform, usually with a roof, for a musical band to give concerts.

band•wag•on (bănd′wăg′ən) *n.* **1.** A brightly decorated wagon for carrying musicians in a parade. **2.** *Informal.* A popular cause or party.

ban•dy (băn′dē) *tr.v.* **ban•died, ban•dy•ing, ban•dies. 1.** To toss, throw, or strike back and forth: *We bandied the ball over the net.* **2.** To give and take; exchange: *The opposing groups bandied insults at each other.* **3.** To say or discuss in a casual manner: *The movie star's name was bandied about in idle gossip.* —*adj.* Bent or curved outward; bowed: *bandy legs.*

ban•dy-leg•ged (băn′dē lĕg′ĭd *or* băn′dē lĕgd′) *adj.* Bowlegged.

bane (bān) *n.* A cause of great trouble, ruin, or death: *Fleas were the bane of the cat's existence.* [First written down about 725 in Old English and spelled *bana.*]

bane•ber•ry (bān′bĕr′ē) *n.* Any of several plants having clusters of white flowers and poisonous red, white, or blackish berries.

bane•ful (bān′fəl) *adj.* Harmful; destructive; evil: *a baneful infestation of aphids in the garden.*

bang[1] (băng) *n.* **1.** A loud, sharp, sudden noise: *The door slammed with a bang.* **2.** A sudden forceful blow; a thump: *a bang on the knee.* **3.** *Slang.* A feeling of excitement; thrill: *Most kids get a real bang out of the circus.* —*v.* **banged, bang•ing, bangs.** —*tr.* **1.** To strike or hit with a loud sharp noise: *The cook banged the pots and pans together.* **2.** To strike, hit, or move suddenly and with great force: *I banged my knee against the table.* **3.** To close suddenly and loudly; slam. —*intr.* **1.** To make a loud, sharp, sudden noise: *Firecrackers banged in the distance.* **2.** To crash noisily against or into something: *The toy car banged into the wall.* —*adv.* Directly; exactly: *The arrow hit bang on the target.* **—*idiom.* bang up.** To damage extensively. [First written down about 1550 in Modern English, probably from Old Norse *bang,* a hammering.]

bang[2] (băng) *n.* Hair cut straight across the forehead. Often used in the plural. [First written down in 1878 in Modern English, perhaps from *bangtail,* a racehorse.]

Bang•kok (**băng′**kŏk′ *or* băng **kŏk′**) also **Krung Thep** (gro͝ong **tĕp′**). The capital and largest city of Thailand, in the southwest near an arm of the South China Sea. Population, 5,174,682.

Bang•la•desh (bäng′glə **dĕsh′** *or* băng′glə **dĕsh′**). A country of southern Asia southeast of Nepal. It was formerly part of Bengal and became independent in 1971. Dacca is the capital and the largest city. Population, 87,052,000.

ban•gle (**băng′**gəl) *n.* **1.** A bracelet worn around the wrist or ankle. **2.** An ornament that hangs from a bracelet or necklace.

Ban•gui (bäng **gē′**). The capital and largest city of Central African Republic, in the southern part of the country near the borders of Congo and Zaire. Population, 340,000.

bang-up (**băng′**ŭp′) *adj. Informal.* Very good; great: *a bang-up party.*

ban•ish (**băn′**ĭsh) *tr.v.* **ban•ished, ban•ish•ing, ban•ish•es. 1.** To force to leave a country or place by official decree; exile: *The king banished the outlaw.* **2.** To drive away; cast out: *Banish all doubts from your mind.* **—ban′ish•ment** *n.*

ban•is•ter also **ban•nis•ter** (**băn′**ĭ stər) *n.* **1.** A handrail along with its supporting posts. **2.** One of the posts supporting a handrail on a staircase.

ban•jo (**băn′**jō) *n., pl.* **ban•jos** or **ban•joes.** A musical instrument having a narrow neck, a hollow circular body covered with a skin on one side, and four or sometimes five strings that are strummed or plucked. [First written down in 1764 in Modern English and spelled *banshaw;* akin to Jamaican English *banja,* fiddle, probably of African origin.]

Ban•jul (**bän′**jo͞ol′). The capital and largest city of Gambia, on an island in the Atlantic Ocean south of Dakar, Senegal. Population, 44,536.

bank[1] (băngk) *n.* **1.** The rising ground bordering a body of water, especially bordering a river. **2.** A hillside or slope: *the steep bank leading down to the valley.* **3.** A mound, pile, or ridge of earth or other material: *a snow bank.* **4.** A pile or mass, as of clouds or fog. **5.** An elevated area of a sea floor. Often used in the plural. **6.** The sideways tilt of an aircraft in making a turn. *—v.* **banked, bank•ing, banks.** *—tr.* **1.** To pile up (earth, snow, or other matter) in a ridge or sloping surface: *The plows banked snow along the edge of the road.* **2.** To pile ashes or fuel onto (a fire) to make it burn slowly: *bank a fire in the fireplace for the night.* **3.** To tilt (an aircraft) in making a turn. *—intr.* **1.** To rise in or take the form of a bank: *The snow banked along the fence.* **2.** To tilt an aircraft in making a turn: *The pilot banked to the left before descending.* [First written down about 1200 in Middle English, of Scandinavian origin.]

bank[2] (băngk) *n.* **1.** A place or an organization in which money is kept for saving or business purposes or is invested, supplied for loans, or exchanged. **2.** A small container in which money is saved: *She used a coffee can for a bank.* **3.** A supply or stock for future use: *the blood bank of a hospital.* **4.** A place of safekeeping or storage: *a computer's memory bank.* *—v.* **banked, bank•ing, banks.** *—tr.* To put (money) in a bank: *Many workers bank a part of their salary.* *—intr.* To have an account or savings at a particular bank. ***—idiom.*** **bank on.** To rely on; count on: *I'm banking on you to get the job done.* [First written down in 1474 in Middle English, from Old High German *banc,* bench, moneychanger's table.]

bank[3] (băngk) *n.* **1.** A set or group arranged in a row: *a bank of elevators.* **2.** A row of keys on a keyboard instrument, especially on an organ. **3.** A row of oars in a galley. [First written down before 1200 in Middle English and spelled *bank,* bench, from Late Latin *bancus,* of Germanic origin.]

bank•book (**băngk′**bo͝ok′) *n.* A book in which a bank enters the amounts deposited in or taken out of a savings or checking account; a passbook.

bank•card (**băngk′**kärd′) *n.* A card given by a bank to identify the holder, who can then use the card at an automated teller machine.

bank•er (**băng′**kər) *n.* A person who owns or is an executive of a bank.

bank•ing (**băng′**kĭng) *n.* The business or occupation of running a bank.

bank note *n.* A piece of paper acceptable as money and issued by a government-authorized bank rather than by the government itself.

bank•roll (**băngk′**rōl′) *n.* Available money; funds.

bank•rupt (**băngk′**rŭpt′) *adj.* **1.** Legally declared unable to pay one's debts because of lack of money and in turn having one's remaining property administered by or divided among the creditors. **2.** Completely without money; financially ruined. **3.** Lacking in or depleted of valuable qualities: *a book that is bankrupt of original ideas.* *—n.* A person who is bankrupt. *—tr.v.* **bank•rupt•ed, bank•rupt•ing, bank•rupts.** To cause to become bankrupt. [First written down in 1533 in Modern English and spelled *bank roupte,* from Italian *bancarotta,* bankruptcy: *banca,* moneychanger's table + *rotta,* broken.]

bank•rupt•cy (**băngk′**rəpt sē *or* **băngk′**rəp sē) *n.* The condition of being bankrupt.

Ban•ne•ker (**băn′**ĭ kər), **Benjamin.** 1731–1806. American mathematician and astronomer who helped survey the District of Columbia in 1791. Largely self-taught, Banneker published an astronomical almanac throughout the 1790's. —See Note.

ban•ner (**băn′**ər) *n.* **1.** A flag or piece of cloth, often having words or a special design on it: *Paraders marched with a banner for women's rights.* **2.** A headline spanning the width of a newspaper page. *—adj.* Unusually good; outstanding: *a banner year for our team.*

ban•nis•ter (**băn′**ĭ stər) *n.* Variant of **banister.**

banns also **bans** (bănz) *pl.n.* An announcement in a church that a particular couple intends to be married.

ban•quet (**băng′**kwĭt) *n.* A large elaborate meal; a feast. *—intr.v.* **ban•quet•ed, ban•quet•ing, ban•quets.** To eat such a meal; feast.

ban•shee (**băn′**shē) *n.* In Gaelic folklore, a female spirit supposed to warn of a death in a family by wailing loudly.

ban•tam (**băn′**təm) *n.* **1.** Any of various breeds of small chickens. **2.** A small person who is ready to fight.

ban•tam•weight (**băn′**təm wāt′) *n.* A professional boxer weighing between 112 and 118 pounds (approximately 51–53.5 kilograms).

ban•ter (**băn′**tər) *n.* Playful good-humored conversation. *—intr.v.* **ban•tered, ban•ter•ing, ban•ters.** To exchange joking or teasing remarks. **—ban′ter•er** *n.*

Ban•ting (**băn′**tĭng), Sir **Frederick Grant.** 1891–1941. Canadian physiologist who shared a 1932 Nobel Prize for the discovery of insulin.

Ban•tu (**băn′**to͞o) *n., pl.* **Bantu** or **Ban•tus. 1.** A member of a large group of people native to southern and central Africa. **2.** A family of languages spoken by these people, including Swahili and Zulu. **—Ban′tu** *adj.*

ban•yan (**băn′**yən) *n.* A tropical Indian fig tree hav-

banjo

Benjamin Banneker

Benjamin **Banneker,** the United States's first important Black scientist, taught himself math and astronomy when he was in his fifties. Working alone, Banneker soon learned enough calculus and trigonometry to produce an astronomical almanac containing tables of future positions of the planets. Published from 1791 to 1797, the almanac gained widespread recognition and earned Banneker national status as an astronomer. In 1792 Banneker sent Thomas Jefferson a copy of his almanac to disprove Jefferson's belief in Black intellectual inferiority, along with a letter that eloquently argued against slavery and for racial equality. Banneker is also known for helping to lay out the boundaries of the newly created District of Columbia.

ă	pat	oi	**boy**
ā	**pay**	ou	**out**
âr	**care**	o͝o	**took**
ä	father	o͞o	**boot**
ĕ	pet	ŭ	cut
ē	be	ûr	urge
ĭ	pit	th	**thin**
ī	**pie**	*th*	**this**
îr	**pier**	hw	**wh**oop
ŏ	pot	zh	vision
ō	**toe**	ə	about
ô	**paw**	N	*French* bon

baobab

Word History: barbarian

Our word **barbarian**, "a member of a savage people," comes from the ancient Greek word *barbaros*, "stammering, babbling," and "one who doesn't speak Greek." To these meanings the Greeks added "foreigner, foreign," then "outlandish, uncultured." The Romans, whom the Greeks considered to be barbarian, borrowed the Greek word and changed the meaning to "neither Greek nor Roman," then "outside the Roman Empire," then "uncivilized."

barbel
Barbels on a catfish

ing large oval leaves and spreading branches from which aerial roots grow to the ground to form new trunks.

ban•zai (bän **zī′**) *n.* A Japanese battle cry or patriotic cheer.

ba•o•bab (**bā′**ō băb′ *or* **bä′**ō băb′) *n.* A tree of tropical Africa, having a very thick trunk and large, hard-shelled, hanging fruit.

bap•tism (**băp′**tĭz′əm) *n.* **1.** A religious sacrament in which a person is sprinkled with or dipped in water as a sign of being cleansed of sin and admitted to membership in a Christian church. **2.** A first experience. **—bap•tis′mal** (băp **tĭz′**məl) *adj.*

Bap•tist (**băp′**tĭst) *n.* A member of a Protestant church that believes in baptism only for people old enough to understand its meaning. Baptists are usually baptized by placing the whole body in water. **—Bap′tist** *adj.*

bap•tis•ter•y also **bap•tis•try** (**băp′**tĭ strē) *n., pl.* **bap•tis•ter•ies** also **bap•tis•tries.** A part of a church or a separate building in which baptism is performed.

bap•tize (băp **tīz′** *or* **băp′**tīz′) *tr.v.* **bap•tized, bap•tiz•ing, bap•tiz•es. 1.** To admit into Christianity or a particular Christian church by baptism. **2.** To give a name to (a person who is being baptized). [First written down about 1280 in Middle English and spelled *baptizen*, from Greek *baptizein*, from *baptein*, to dip.]

bar (bär) *n.* **1.** A narrow, straight, rigid piece of solid material, often used to close an opening or as part of a machine or other device: *That long iron bar serves as an axle for the wagon.* **2.** A solid oblong piece of a substance: *a chocolate bar; a bar of soap.* **3.** A narrow marking, such as a stripe or band: *Some owls have bars of white on their feathers.* **4.** Something that prevents entry or progress; a barrier; an obstacle: *The fallen tree was a bar to our progress along the old dirt road.* **5.** A ridge of sand or gravel on a shore or stream bed, formed by the action of tides or currents. **6.a.** A high counter at which drinks, especially alcoholic drinks, and sometimes food, are served. **b.** A place having such a counter. **7.a.** The railing in a courtroom in front of which the judges, lawyers, and defendants sit. **b.** The occupation of a lawyer; the legal profession. **c.** Lawyers considered as a group. **d.** A place of judgment; a tribunal. **8.a.** A vertical line dividing a musical staff into equal measures. **b.** A measure of music: *Let's practice the final bars of this march.* *—tr.v.* **barred, bar•ring, bars. 1.** To close or fasten with a bar or bars: *slammed and barred the gate.* **2.** To block; close off; obstruct: *Fallen branches barred the way.* **3.** To keep out; exclude: *Hunters are barred from wildlife sanctuaries.* **4.** To rule out; except: *wrestling with no holds barred.* **5.** To mark with stripes or narrow bands. ***—idiom.*** **bar none.** With no exceptions: *This is the best pizza I've ever had, bar none.* [First written down before 1200 in Middle English and spelled *barre*, from Old French.]

barb (bärb) *n.* **1.** A sharp point projecting backward, as on a fishhook or an arrow. **2.** One of the hairlike branches on the shaft of a feather. **3.** A cutting or biting remark: *The author saved her best barbs for her critics.*

Bar•ba•dos (bär **bā′**dōs′ *or* bär **bā′**dōz′). A country on the easternmost island of the West Indies. The island gained its independence from Great Britain in 1966. Bridgetown is the capital and the largest city. Population, 248,983.

bar•bar•i•an (bär **bâr′**ē ən) *n.* **1.** A member of a people considered by those of another nation or group to be primitive, uncivilized, or savage. **2.** A crude, uncivilized, or brutal person: *The pirates were barbarians.* [First written down about 1350 in Middle English and spelled *barbariene*, from Latin *barbarus*, barbarous, from Greek *barbaros*, foreign.] —See Note.

bar•bar•ic (bär **băr′**ĭk) *adj.* **1.** Of, relating to, or characteristic of barbarians: *The native peoples considered the explorers barbaric.* **2.** Marked by crudeness or lack of restraint: *a barbaric custom.*

bar•ba•rism (**bär′**bə rĭz′əm) *n.* **1.** A barbarous uncivilized state. **2.** A barbarous act or custom: *Imprisoning debtors is now considered a barbarism.* **3.** A word or an expression regarded as being incorrect and showing lack of education or refinement.

bar•bar•i•ty (bär **băr′**ĭ tē) *n., pl.* **bar•bar•i•ties. 1.** Cruel or savage behavior. **2.** A cruel or savage act. **3.** Crudeness; coarseness: *The barbarity of the speaker's remarks disgusted the audience.*

bar•ba•rous (**bär′**bər əs) *adj.* **1.** Primitive in culture and customs; uncivilized: *The barbarous invaders burned the library.* **2.** Brutal; cruel: *barbarous acts of war.* **3.** Uncultured or unrefined, especially in the use of words: *barbarous writing.* **—bar′ba•rous•ly** *adv.* **—bar′ba•rous•ness** *n.*

Bar•ba•ry Coast (**băr′**bə rē *or* **băr′**brē). The Mediterranean coastal area of nothern Africa, including the coastlines of Egypt, Libya, Tunisia, Algeria, and Morocco.

bar•be•cue (**bär′**bĭ kyo͞o′) *n.* **1.** A social gathering at which food is cooked over an an open fire: *Everybody came to the neighborhood barbecue.* **2.** A whole animal or a piece of it roasted over an open fire. **3.** A grill, pit, or fireplace for roasting meat, often outdoors. *—tr.v.* **bar•be•cued, bar•be•cu•ing, bar•be•cues.** To cook (food) over an open fire, often with a spicy sauce: *barbecued ribs.* [First written down in 1697 in Modern English, from American Spanish *barbacoa*, of Taino origin.]

barbed (bärbd) *adj.* **1.** Having barbs: *the barbed head of a harpoon.* **2.** Cutting; stinging: *barbed criticism.*

barbed wire *n.* Twisted strands of wire with barbs at regular intervals, used in making fences.

bar•bel (**bär′**bəl) *n.* A slender feeler extending from the head of certain fishes, such as the catfish.

bar•bell (**bär′**bĕl′) *n.* A bar with adjustable weights at each end, lifted for sport or exercise.

bar•ber (**bär′**bər) *n.* A person whose work is cutting hair and shaving or trimming beards. *—v.* **bar•bered, bar•ber•ing, bar•bers.** *—tr.* To cut the hair of or shave or trim the beard of. *—intr.* To work as a barber.

bar•ber•ry (**bär′**bĕr′ē) *n.* Any of various shrubs having small leaves, yellowish flowers, and small red berries.

bar•ber•shop (**bär′**bər shŏp′) *n.* A barber's place of business. *—adj. Informal.* Of or relating to singing sentimental songs in four-part harmony: *a barbershop quartet.*

bar•bi•can (**bär′**bĭ kən) *n.* A tower at a gate or drawbridge at the entrance to a medieval castle or town.

bar•bi•tu•rate (bär **bĭch′**ər ĭt *or* bär **bĭch′**ə rāt′) *n.* Any of a group of related chemical compounds that are mainly used as sedatives or sleep-producing drugs.

bar•ca•role also **bar•ca•rolle** (**bär′**kə rōl′) *n.* **1.** A song of a Venetian gondolier with a rhythm that suggests rowing. **2.** A musical composition imitating such a song.

Bar•ce•lo•na (bär′sə **lō′**nə). A city of northeast Spain on the Mediterranean Sea north of Valencia. Population, 1,770,296.

bar code *n.* The Universal Product Code.

bard (bärd) *n.* **1.** A poet of ancient times who composed and recited verses about heroes and heroic deeds. **2.** A poet. [First written down in 1449 in Middle English and spelled *baird*, of Celtic origin.]

bare (bâr) *adj.* **bar•er, bar•est. 1.** Lacking clothing or covering; naked: *bare feet; a bare hillside.* **2.** Lacking the usual or expected furnishings, equipment, or supplies: *bare shelves; bare walls.* See Synonyms at **empty. 3.** Having no addition or restriction; simple or plain: *the bare facts.* **4.** Just sufficient or adequate; mere: *the bare necessities of life.* —*tr.v.* **bared, bar•ing, bares.** To uncover; expose to view: *The dog bared its teeth and growled.* [First written down about 725 in Old English and spelled *bær*.] **—bare′ness** *n.*

❑ *These sound alike:* **bare, bear[1]** (support), **bear[2]** (animal).

bare•back (bâr′băk′) also **bare•backed** (bâr′băkt′) *adv. & adj.* On a horse or pony without a saddle: *riding bareback; a bareback rider.*

bare•faced (bâr′fāst′) *adj.* Shameless; bold; brazen: *a barefaced lie.*

bare•foot (bâr′fo͝ot′) also **bare•foot•ed** (bâr′fo͝ot′-ĭd) *adv. & adj.* Without shoes or other covering on the feet: *running barefoot through the grass; a barefoot child.*

bare•hand•ed (bâr′hăn′dĭd) *adv. & adj.* With the hand or hands alone; without a glove, tool, weapon, or protection: *catching fish barehanded; a barehanded catch of a baseball.*

bare•head•ed (bâr′hĕd′ĭd) *adv. & adj.* Without a hat or other head covering: *walking bareheaded in the rain; bareheaded hikers.*

bare•leg•ged (bâr′lĕg′ĭd *or* bâr′lĕgd′) *adv. & adj.* With the legs uncovered: *ran barelegged through the surf; barelegged children at the beach.*

bare•ly (bâr′lē) *adv.* **1.** By very little; hardly; just: *We could barely see the shore in the dark.* **2.** In a bare or scanty manner; sparsely: *a barely furnished room.*

bar•gain (bär′gĭn) *n.* **1.** An arrangement or agreement between two sides, often involving payment or trade; a deal: *We made a bargain that I would cut the grass for ten dollars.* **2.** Something offered or bought at a low price: *The elegant dress that's now on sale is a bargain.* —*intr.v.* **bar•gained, bar•gain•ing, bar•gains.** To argue over or discuss the terms of an agreement, especially a price to be paid: *The hotel's cook bargained for vegetables in the market.* ***—idioms.*** **bargain for** or **bargain on.** To count on; expect: *That old car gave us more trouble than we bargained for.* **into the bargain** or **in the bargain.** Over and above what is expected; in addition.

barge (bärj) *n.* **1.** A large flat-bottomed boat used to carry loads on rivers, canals, and coastal waters. **2.** A large open boat used for parties and ceremonies. —*v.* **barged, barg•ing, barg•es.** —*intr.* To move, enter, or intrude clumsily: *The demonstrators barged into the room and interrupted the meeting.* —*tr.* To carry by barge. [First written down before 1300 in Middle English, from Latin *barca*, boat.]

bar graph *n.* A graph consisting of parallel bars or rectangles drawn at lengths that are in proportion to the quantities they represent.

bar•ite (bâr′īt *or* băr′īt) *n.* A white or colorless crystalline mineral of barium sulfate that is the chief source of barium.

bar•i•tone (băr′ĭ tōn′) *n.* **1.** A moderately low singing voice of a man, higher than a bass and lower than a tenor. **2.** A man having such a voice. **3.** A part written in the range of this voice. **4.** An instrument, especially a type of small tuba or saxaphone, having about the same range as this voice. [First written down in 1609 in Modern English, from Greek *barutonos*, deep-sounding.]

bar•i•um (bâr′ē əm *or* băr′ē əm) *n. Symbol* **Ba** A soft, silvery-white, metallic element that occurs only in combination with other elements, especially in barite. Barium compounds are used in making pigments and safety matches. See table at **element.**

barium sulfate *n.* A compound of barium, sulfur, and oxygen that occurs as a fine white powder and has the formula $BaSO_4$. It is used as a pigment, in making textiles, rubber, and plastic, and in taking x-ray photographs of the digestive tract.

bark[1] (bärk) *n.* **1.** The short gruff sound made by a dog and certain other animals such as seals and coyotes. **2.** A sound similar to this, such as a cough or the firing of a gun. —*v.* **barked, bark•ing, barks.** —*intr.* **1.** To make the sound of a bark: *The neighbor's dog barked all night.* **2.** To speak gruffly or sharply; snap: *The sergeant barked at the new recruits.* —*tr.* To say in a loud harsh voice: *The team captain barked commands.* ***—idiom.*** **bark up the wrong tree.** To misdirect one's energies or attention. [First written down about 1250 in Middle English, from Old English *beorcan*, to bark.]

bark[2] (bärk) *n.* The protective outer covering of the trunk, branches, and roots of trees and other woody plants. —*tr.v.* **barked, bark•ing, barks.** To bump or rub so as to scrape the skin from: *The climbers barked their shins on the rocks.* [First written down before 1325 in Middle English, from Old Norse *börkr*.]

bark[3] also **barque** (bärk) *n.* **1.** A sailing ship with three to five masts, all of them square-rigged except the after mast, which is fore-and-aft rigged. **2.** A light boat moved by a sail or oars. [First written down in 1420 in Middle English and spelled *barke*, boat, from Latin *barca*.]

bar•keep•er (bär′kē′pər) *n.* **1.** A person who owns or runs a bar for the sale of alcoholic beverages. **2.** A bartender.

bar•ken•tine (bär′kən tēn′) *n.* A sailing ship with three to five masts, of which only the foremast is square-rigged, the other masts being fore-and-aft rigged.

bark•er (bär′kər) *n.* **1.** A person or an animal that barks: *That dog is a loud barker.* **2.** A person who makes a loud colorful sales talk at the entrance to a show, carnival, or other attraction.

bar•ley (bär′lē) *n.* **1.** A grain-bearing grass having seeds used as food and for making beer and whiskey. **2.** The seeds of this plant.

bar•ley•corn (bär′lē kôrn′) *n.* The seed or grain of barley.

bar magnet *n.* A permanent magnet in the shape of a bar: *A bar magnet suspended from a string will serve as a simple compass by pointing north.*

bar•maid (bär′mād′) *n.* A woman who serves drinks in a bar.

bar•man (bär′mən) *n.* A man who serves drinks in a bar.

bar mitz•vah (bär mĭts′və) *n.* **1.** A ceremony in which a 13-year-old Jewish boy is admitted as an adult into the religious community. **2.** The boy for whom this ceremony is held. [First written down in 1861 in Modern English, from Hebrew *bar miṣwâ* : *bar*, son + *miṣwâ*, command, commandment.]

barn (bärn) *n.* A large farm building used for storing grain, hay, and other farm products and for sheltering livestock. [First written down about 950 in Old English and spelled *berærn* : *bere*, barley + *ærn*, house.]

bar•na•cle (bär′nə kəl) *n.* Any of various small hard-shelled sea animals that attach themselves to underwater objects, such as rocks, pilings, and the bottoms of ships.

barn dance *n.* A social gathering, often held in a barn, with music and square dancing.

barn•storm (bärn′stôrm′) *tr. & intr.v.* **barn•**

barbell
Kazushito Manabe at the 1984 Summer Olympics in Los Angeles

ă	pat	oi	boy
ā	pay	ou	out
âr	care	o͝o	took
ä	father	o͞o	boot
ĕ	pet	ŭ	cut
ē	be	ûr	urge
ĭ	pit	th	thin
ī	pie	*th*	this
îr	pier	hw	whoop
ŏ	pot	zh	vision
ō	toe	ə	about
ô	paw	N	*French* bon

P.T. Barnum

baroque

barrel organ

stormed, barn•storm•ing, barn•storms. To travel about the countryside appearing in shows or making political speeches: *During the campaign both candidates barnstormed the countryside.* —**barn′-storm′er** *n.*

barn swallow *n.* A widely distributed bird having a deeply forked tail, a dark-blue back, and tan underparts. It often builds its nest in the eaves of barns.

Bar•num (bär′nəm), **P(hineas) T(aylor).** 1810–1891. American circus manager who established The Greatest Show on Earth (1871), which later became the Barnum and Bailey Circus.

barn•yard (**bärn′**yärd′) *n.* The yard or area of ground around a barn.

bar•o•gram (**băr′**ə grăm′) *n.* A record made by a barograph.

bar•o•graph (**băr′**ə grăf′) *n.* A barometer that automatically records changes in air pressure.

ba•rom•e•ter (bə **rŏm′**ĭ tər) *n.* **1.** An instrument for measuring atmospheric pressure, used to determine height above sea level and in weather forecasting. **2.** Something that shows shifts and changes like those of the weather; an indicator: *Opinion polls are used as a barometer of public mood.* [First written down in 1665 in Modern English : Greek *baros*, weight + Greek *metron*, measure.]

bar•o•met•ric (băr′ə **mĕt′**rĭk) *adj.* Of, relating to, or measured by a barometer: *take a barometric reading.*

barometric pressure *n.* Atmospheric pressure.

bar•on (**băr′**ən) *n.* **1.a.** A British nobleman of the lowest rank. **b.** A nobleman of other parts of Europe, ranked differently in various countries. **2.** In feudal times, a man holding rights, lands, and a title directly from a king or another high-ranking nobleman. **3.** A businessman of great wealth and influence: *a baron of industry.*

❑ *These sound alike:* **baron, barren** (not productive).

bar•on•ess (**băr′**ə nĭs) *n.* **1.** The wife or widow of a baron. **2.** A woman holding the title to a barony.

bar•on•et (**băr′**ə nĭt *or* băr′ə **nĕt′**) *n.* In Great Britain, a man holding a hereditary title of honor reserved for commoners, ranking just below the barons.

bar•on•et•ess (**băr′**ə nĭ tĭs *or* băr′ə **nĕt′**ĭs) *n.* In Great Britain, a woman holding a hereditary title of honor reserved for commoners, ranking just below the barons.

ba•ro•ni•al (bə **rō′**nē əl) *adj.* **1.** Of or relating to a baron or a barony. **2.** Suitable for a baron; stately or splendid: *a large baronial home.*

bar•o•ny (**băr′**ə nē) *n., pl.* **bar•o•nies.** The rank or domain of a baron.

ba•roque (bə **rōk′**) *adj.* **1.** Also **Baroque.** Of, relating to, or characteristic of a style of art and architecture developed in Europe from about 1550 to 1700, characterized by elaborate and ornate forms. **2.** Also **Baroque.** Of, relating to, or characteristic of a style of musical composition that flourished in Europe from about 1600 to 1750 and was notable for strictness of form and elaborateness of ornamentation. **3.** Irregular in shape: *a baroque pearl.* **4.** Elaborate and fantastic; outlandish: *a strange, baroque novel.* —*n.* also **Baroque.** The baroque style or period in art, architecture, and music. [First written down in 1765 in Modern English, from Italian *barocco* and Portuguese *barroco*.]

ba•rouche (bə **rōōsh′**) *n.* A horse-drawn carriage with a folding top, passenger seats facing one another, and a driver's seat outside.

barque (bärk) *n.* Variant of **bark[3]**.

bar•rack (**băr′**ək) *n.* A building or group of buildings used to house soldiers, workers, or a large number of other people. Often used in the plural.

bar•ra•cu•da (băr′ə **kōō′**də) *n., pl.* **barracuda** or **bar•ra•cu•das.** Any of various ocean fishes having a long narrow body and a projecting jaw with very sharp teeth, found mostly in tropical waters.

bar•rage (bə **räzh′**) *n.* **1.** A concentrated firing of guns or missiles, often as a screen or protection for military troops. **2.** An overwhelming outpouring, as of words: —*tr.v.* **bar•raged, bar•rag•ing, bar•rag•es.** To direct a barrage at: *Reporters barraged the speaker with questions.*

barred (bärd) *adj.* **1.** Having secured with bars: *barred windows.* **2.** Having stripes: *the barred owl.*

bar•rel (**băr′**əl) *n.* **1.** A large container of wood, metal, plastic, or cardboard with round flat ends of equal size. Wooden barrels usually have sides that bulge out slightly and are held together by hoops. **2.** The amount that a barrel can hold: *spread a barrel of sawdust over the floor.* **3.** Any of various measures of volume or capacity ranging from 31 to 42 gallons (about 120 to about 159 liters). See table at **measurement. 4.a.** The long tube of a gun, through which a bullet or shell travels. **b.** A cylindrical machine part. **5.** *Informal.* A great amount: *a barrel of fun.* —*v.* **bar•reled, bar•rel•ing, bar•rels** or **bar•relled, bar•rel•ling, bar•rels.** —*tr.* To put or pack in a barrel or barrels: *barrel vinegar for shipping to market.* —*intr. Slang.* To move at great speed: *The express train barreled along the tracks.* [First written down before 1300 in Middle English and spelled *barel*, from Old French *baril*.]

barrel organ *n.* A portable musical instrument, similar to a small organ, in which the airflow to the pipes is controlled by valves that are operated by turning a barrel with a hand crank.

bar•ren (**băr′**ən) *adj.* **1.** Lacking plants or crops: *a barren desert; barren soil.* **2.** Unable to bear offspring or fruit: *an orchard of barren trees.* **3.** Not useful or productive: *barren efforts.* **4.** Empty; bare: *a life barren of pleasure.* —*n.* An area of barren or unproductive land. Often used in the plural. —**bar′ren•ness** *n.*

❑ *These sound alike:* **barren, baron** (nobleman).

bar•rette (bə **rĕt′**) *n.* A bar-shaped or oval clip used to hold the hair in place.

bar•ri•cade (**băr′**ĭ kād′ *or* băr′ĭ **kād′**) *n.* **1.** A structure set up hastily to obstruct the passage of an enemy. **2.** A barrier or an obstruction. —*tr.v.* **bar•ri•cad•ed, bar•ri•cad•ing, bar•ri•cades.** To close off, block, or protect with a barricade: *barricade streets to control the crowd at a parade.*

bar•ri•er (**băr′**ē ər) *n.* **1.** A structure, such as a fence or wall, built to obstruct passage: *Police set up a barrier at each end of the street the night before the fair began.* **2.** Something that obstructs; an obstacle: *Lack of education can be a barrier to success.*

barrier reef *n.* A long narrow ridge of coral deposits parallel to the mainland and separated from it by a deep lagoon.

bar•ring (**bär′**ĭng) *prep.* Apart from the occurrence of; excepting: *Barring a last-minute change, we'll be the first to arrive.*

bar•ri•o (**bä′**rē ō′ *or* **băr′**ē ō) *n., pl.* **bar•ri•os. 1.** A chiefly Spanish-speaking community or neighborhood in a U.S. city. **2.** A village or district in a Spanish-speaking country.

bar•ris•ter (**băr′**ĭ stər) *n. Chiefly British.* A lawyer who argues cases in a court of law.

bar•room (**bär′**rōōm′ *or* **bär′**rŏŏm′) *n.* A room or building in which alcoholic beverages are sold at a counter or bar.

bar•row[1] (**băr′**ō) *n.* **1.** A flat rectangular tray or cart with handles at each end, used for carrying loads. **2.** A wheelbarrow. [First written down about 1300 in Middle English and spelled *barowe*.]

bar•row² (băr′ō) *n.* A large mound of earth or stones placed over a grave in ancient times. [First written down about 725 in Old English and spelled *beorg*, hill.]

Bar•row (băr′ō), **Point.** The northernmost point of Alaska, in the northwest on the Arctic Ocean.

Bart. *abbr.* An abbreviation of baronet.

bar•tend•er (bär′tĕn′dər) *n.* A person who mixes and serves alcoholic drinks at a bar.

bar•ter (bär′tər) *v.* **bar•tered, bar•ter•ing, bar•ters.** —*intr.* To trade goods or services without using money. —*tr.* To trade (goods or services) without using money: *We bartered home-grown vegetables for firewood.* —*n.* The act or practice of bartering. —*adj.* Of, relating to, or being something based on bartering: *a barter economy.*

Bar•thol•o•mew (bär thŏl′ə myo͞o′), Saint. Sometimes called **Na•than•ael** (nə thăn′yəl). One of the 12 Apostles.

Bar•ton (bär′tn), **Clara.** 1821–1912. American administrator who did battlefield emergency care during the Civil War and organized the American Red Cross (1881).

bas•al (bā′səl *or* bā′zəl) *adj.* **1.** Of, located at, or forming a base: *a plant having a tuft of basal leaves.* **2.** Basic; fundamental; primary: *Most schools use basal readers in the early grades.*

basal metabolism *n.* The amount of energy used by an organism at complete rest.

ba•salt (bə sôlt′ *or* bā′sôlt′) *n.* A hard, dense, dark rock formed by volcanic action.

base¹ (bās) *n.* **1.** The lowest or bottom part: *the base of a cliff.* **2.a.** A part or layer on which something rests or is placed for support; a foundation: *a skyscraper built on a base of solid rock.* **b.** A fundamental part: *The theory of evolution forms the base of modern biology.* **3.** A chief ingredient or element of something; a basis: *a paint with an oil base.* **4.** A starting point or central place; a headquarters: *The explorers established a base on top of the glacier.* **5.** A center of supplies or operations for a military or naval force: *The Army has many bases around the country.* **6.a.** A starting point, safety area, or goal in certain games. **b.** In baseball, one of the four corners of the infield that must be touched by a runner to score a run. **7.** The side or face of a geometric figure to which an altitude is or is thought to be drawn. **8.a.** In a number system, the factor by which each place value of a number is multiplied to generate the next place value to the left. For example, 10 is the base of the decimal system and 100 represents $1 \times 10 \times 10$; 1000 represents $1 \times 10 \times 10 \times 10$. Two is the base of the binary system and 100 represents $1 \times 2 \times 2$; 1000 represents $1 \times 2 \times 2 \times 2$. **b.** A number that is raised to an exponent. For example, if $6^2 = 6 \times 6 = 36$, 6 is the base. **c.** The number to which the percent is applied in a percentage problem. For example, if 40 is the base, 20 percent of 40 is 8. **9.** A word or word part to which affixes or other word parts may be added. For example, in *filled, refill,* and *filling, fill* is the base. **10.** Any of a large class of substances that when dissolved in water react with an acid to form a salt, turn litmus dye blue, and have a slippery feel and bitter taste. **11.** The terminal of a transistor that acts somewhat like the grid of a vacuum tube. —*adj.* **1.** Forming or serving as a base: *a base layer of soil.* **2.** Situated at or near the bottom: *a base camp for the mountain climbers.* —*tr.v.* **based, bas•ing, bas•es. 1.** To find a basis for; establish: *base an opinion on facts.* **2.** To form or provide a base for: *The composer based this song on an old folk melody.* **3.** To locate; station: *The general based the troops in Europe.* —**idiom. off base.** Badly mistaken: *Your criticism of me is off base.* [First written down before 1300 in Middle English and spelled *bas*, from Greek *basis*.]

❑ *These sound alike:* **base¹** (lowest part), **base²** (mean), **bass²** (lowest tones in music).

base² (bās) *adj.* **bas•er, bas•est. 1.** Having or showing a lack of decency; mean; contemptible: *a base act.* **2.** Inferior in value or quality: *base metals such as iron and lead.* [First written down about 1390 in Middle English and spelled *bace*, from Medieval Latin *bassus*.] —**base′ly** *adv.* —**base′ness** *n.*

❑ *These sound alike:* **base²** (mean), **base¹** (lowest part), **bass²** (lowest tones in music).

base•ball (bās′bôl′) *n.* **1.** A game played with a bat and ball on a field with four bases laid out in a diamond pattern. Two teams of nine players take turns at bat and in the field, the members of the team at bat trying to score runs by touching all four bases. **2.** The ball used in this game.

base•board (bās′bôrd′) *n.* A molding along the lower edge of a wall, where it meets the floor of a room.

base hit *n.* In baseball, a hit by which the batter reaches base safely without an error or a force play being made.

base•less (bās′lĭs) *adj.* Having no basis or foundation in fact; unfounded: *The manufacturers were forced to withdraw the baseless claims for their product.*

base line *n.* **1.** A line serving as a base, as for measurement. **2.** In baseball, an area within which a base runner must stay when running between bases. **3.** A line bounding the back end of each side in a tennis court.

base•man (bās′mən) *n.* In baseball, the player who plays at or near first, second, or third base.

base•ment (bās′mənt) *n.* The lowest story of a building, often below ground level.

base on balls *n.* In baseball, an advance to first base awarded to a batter who takes four pitches that are balls.

base runner *n.* A baseball player on the team at bat who has safely reached or is trying to reach a base.

ba•ses (bā′sēz′) *n.* Plural of **basis.**

bash (băsh) *tr.v.* **bashed, bash•ing, bash•es. 1.** To strike with a heavy crushing blow: *The car skidded off the road and bashed the fence.* **2.** *Informal.* To criticize (a person or thing) harshly. —*n.* **1.** *Informal.* A heavy crushing blow. **2.** *Slang.* A party.

bash•ful (băsh′fəl) *adj.* Timid and embarrassed with other people; shy: *Some children are bashful around strangers.* —**bash′ful•ly** *adv.* —**bash′ful•ness** *n.*

ba•sic (bā′sĭk) *adj.* **1.** Of, relating to, or forming a base or basis; fundamental: *Basic changes in education do not occur very frequently.* **2.a.** Of, being, or containing a chemical base. **b.** Alkaline. —*n.* Something basic or fundamental. Often used in the plural: *learn the basics of arithmetic before studying algebra.* —**ba′si•cal•ly** *adv.*

BA•SIC or **Ba•sic** (bā′sĭk) *n.* A computer language using simple English and algebraic terms.

bas•il (băz′əl *or* bā′zəl) *n.* **1.** A fragrant plant related to mint, having leaves used as a seasoning. **2.** The leaves of such a plant.

ba•sil•i•ca (bə sĭl′ĭ kə) *n.* **1.** A type of ancient Roman building having two rows of columns dividing the interior into a central hall with two side aisles, and an arched semicircular part at one end. **2.** A Christian church built in this design.

bas•i•lisk (băs′ə lĭsk′ *or* băz′ə lĭsk′) *n.* **1.** A legendary serpent or dragon that could kill with its breath and glance. **2.** Any of various tropical American lizards having a crest on the head, back, and tail.

ba•sin (bā′sĭn) *n.* **1.** An open, usually round, shal-

Clara Barton

ă	pat	oi	boy
ā	pay	ou	out
âr	care	o͝o	took
ä	father	o͞o	boot
ĕ	pet	ŭ	cut
ē	be	ûr	urge
ĭ	pit	th	thin
ī	pie	*th*	this
îr	pier	hw	whoop
ŏ	pot	zh	vision
ō	toe	ə	about
ô	paw	N	*French* bon

bass clef

bass drum

basset hound

bassoon

low container used especially for holding liquids. **2.** The amount that a basin can hold: *drenched by a basin of water.* **3.** A sink, as in a bathroom: *Take the plug out of the basin.* **4.** An enclosed area filled with water: *a basin at the foot of the falls.* **5.** A region drained by a river and the streams that flow into it: *the Amazon basin.*

ba•sis (bā′sĭs) *n., pl.* **ba•ses** (bā′sēz′). **1.** A foundation on which something rests: *On what basis did you make this decision?* **2.** The main part or basic ingredient: *The basis for most liquids is water.* [First written down before 1398 in Middle English, base of a pyramid, from Greek.]

bask (băsk) *intr.v.* **basked, bask•ing, basks. 1.** To expose oneself to or enjoy a pleasant warmth: *turtles basking in the sun.* **2.** To take pleasure; live happily: *Many teachers bask in the glory of their students' achievements.*

bas•ket (**băs′**kĭt) *n.* **1.** A container made of interwoven twigs, strips of wood, or rushes. **2.** Something resembling such a container in shape or function: *a wastepaper basket.* **3.** The amount that a basket can hold: *a basket of peaches.* **4.a.** A metal hoop from which is hung a net that is open at the bottom, used as a goal in basketball. **b.** A score made by throwing the ball through this hoop.

bas•ket•ball (**băs′**kĭt bôl′) *n.* **1.** A game played by two teams of five players in which players try to throw a ball through an elevated basket on the opponent's end of a rectangular court. **2.** The ball used in this game.

bas•ket•ry (**băs′**kĭ trē) *n.* **1.** The craft or process of making baskets. **2.** Baskets considered as a group.

basket weave *n.* A method or pattern of weaving fabric in which double threads are interwoven to produce a plain latticework effect.

bas mitz•vah (bäs **mĭts′**və) *n. & v.* Variant of **bat mitzvah.**

Basque (băsk) *n.* **1.** A member of a people who live in the western Pyrenees of France and Spain. **2.** The language of the Basques, unrelated to any other known language. —**Basque** *adj.*

bas-re•lief (bä′rĭ **lēf′**) *n.* A sculpture in which figures are raised slightly from a flat background.

bass[1] (băs) *n., pl.* **bass** or **bass•es.** Any of several freshwater or saltwater fish of North America, often with prickly fins, caught for food or sport. [First written down about 700 in Old English and spelled *bærs.*]

bass[2] (bās) *n.* **1.** A male singing voice in the lowest range. **2.** A singer who has such a voice. **3.** The lowest part in four-part harmony. **4.** An instrument, especially a double bass, that produces tones in a low range. [First written down before 1500 in Middle English and spelled *bas,* from *bas,* low.]

❑ *These sound alike:* **bass**[2] (lowest tones in music), **base**[1] (lowest part), **base**[2] (mean).

bass clef (bās) *n.* A symbol used in writing music to indicate that the note on the fourth line from the bottom of the staff is F below middle C.

bass drum (bās) *n.* A large cylindrical drum that makes a deep booming sound when struck.

Basse•terre (băs **târ′** *or* bäs **târ′**). The capital of St. Christopher–Nevis, in the Leeward Islands of the West Indies. Population, 14,725.

Basse-Terre (băs **târ′** *or* bäs **târ′**). The capital of Guadeloupe, on **Basse-Terre Island** in the Leeward Islands of the West Indies. Population, 13,656.

basset hound (**băs′**ĭt) *n.* A dog having a long body, short legs, and drooping ears.

bas•si (bä′sē) *n.* Plural of **basso.**

bas•si•net (băs′ə **nĕt′** *or* **băs′**ə nĕt′) *n.* A bed for a small baby, resembling a basket and sometimes having a hood at one end.

bas•so (**băs′**ō *or* **bä′**sō) *n., pl.* **bas•sos** or **bas•si** (**bä′**sē). A bass singer, especially in opera.

bas•soon (bə **so͞on′**) *n.* A low-pitched woodwind instrument having a long wooden body connected to a double reed by a U-shaped metal tube. —**bas•soon′ist** *n.*

bass viol (bās) *n.* A double bass.

bass•wood (**băs′**wo͝od′) *n.* **1.** A linden tree. **2.** The soft light wood of such a tree.

bast (băst) *n.* The strong fibrous outer layer of certain plant stems, such as flax and hemp, used for making rope, cord, and some textiles.

bas•tard (**băs′**tərd) *n.* A child born of parents who are not married to each other.

baste[1] (bāst) *tr.v.* **bast•ed, bast•ing, bastes.** To sew with long loose stitches meant to be taken out when the final sewing is done: *baste a hem.* [First written down before 1400 in Middle English and spelled *basten,* from Old French *bastir.*]

baste[2] (bāst) *tr.v.* **bast•ed, bast•ing, bastes.** To moisten (meat) with liquid such as melted fat while roasting. [First written down before 1475 in Middle English and spelled *basten.*]

Bas•tille Day (bă **stēl′**) *n.* July 14, celebrated as a holiday in France in memory of the destruction of the Bastille, a fortress used as a prison, in 1789.

bas•tion (**băs′**chən *or* **băs′**tē ən) *n.* **1.** A part built out from the main body of a fort or rampart enabling defenders to aim at those attacking along a wall. **2.** A strongly protected or well-defended position; a stronghold: *That magazine is a bastion of freedom of speech.*

bat[1] (băt) *n.* **1.** A wooden stick or club, especially one used for hitting a ball, as in baseball or cricket. **2.** A blow, as with a stick. —*v.* **bat•ted, bat•ting, bats.** —*tr.* **1.** To hit with or as if with a bat: *The cat batted the toy mouse around the room.* **2.** In baseball, to have (a certain percentage) as a batting average: *He is batting .276 this season.* —*intr.* **1.** To use a bat: *She's batting well this season.* **2.** To be at bat: *Our team batted first.* —***idioms.*** **at bat.** Taking one's turn to bat, as in baseball. **go to bat for.** To give assistance to; defend: *The student went to bat for his friend who was wrongly accused.* **right off the bat.** Without hesitation; immediately: *We liked the new student right off the bat.* [First written down before 1200 in Middle English and spelled *batte.*]

bat[2] (băt) *n.* Any of various flying mammals that resemble the mice but have thin leathery wings that extend from long thin bones of the forelimbs to the hind legs and tail. Most species of bats eat insects or fruit. [First written down before 1325 in Middle English and spelled *bakke,* of Scandinavian origin.] —SEE NOTE.

bat[3] (băt) *tr.v.* **bat•ted, bat•ting, bats.** To move with a flapping motion; blink: *bat one's eyelashes.* —***idiom.*** **bat an eye.** To show surprise: *They didn't bat an eye when the firecracker exploded.* [First written down in 1615 in Modern English, from Old French *batre,* to beat.]

bat•boy (**băt′**boi′) *n.* A boy who takes care of a baseball team's bats and equipment.

batch (băch) *n.* **1.** An amount prepared at one time: *several loaves in a batch of homemade bread; mix a batch of cement.* **2.** A group or number of similar things: *recycle a batch of old newspapers.* **3.** In computer science, a set of data to be processed in a single run.

bate (bāt) *tr.v.* **bat•ed, bat•ing, bates.** To lessen the force or intensity of; moderate: *My parents bated their enthusiasm when they saw how much summer camp cost.* —***idiom.*** **with bated breath.** In a frightened or excited way, as if holding one's breath.

ba•teau (bă tō′) *n., pl.* **ba•teaux** (bă tōz′). A light flat-bottomed boat or rowboat.

Bates (bāts), **Katherine Lee.** 1859–1929. American educator and writer best known for her poem "America the Beautiful," written in 1893.

bat•girl (băt′gûrl′) *n.* A girl who takes care of a baseball team's bats and equipment.

bath (băth) *n., pl.* **baths** (băthz *or* băths). **1.a.** The act of washing or soaking the body, as in water or steam: *give the baby a bath.* **b.** The water used for a bath: *run a hot bath.* **2.** A bathtub or bathroom: *an apartment with three rooms and a bath.* **3.** A building equipped for bathing. **4.** A resort providing baths as a therapy for illness. Often used in the plural. **5.** A liquid or a liquid and its container in which an object is dipped or soaked in order to process it in some way: *a bath of dye.*

bathe (bā*th*) *v.* **bathed, bath•ing, bathes.** *—intr.* **1.** To take a bath: *bathe before breakfast.* **2.** To go into the water for swimming or recreation: *bathe in the surf.* *—tr.* **1.** To wash in water; give a bath to: *bathe the baby.* **2.** To soak in a liquid: *bathe a swollen leg.* **3.** To make wet; moisten: *Tears bathed the baby's cheeks.* **4.** To seem to wash or pour over; flood: *Moonlight bathed the side of the building.* **—bath′er** *n.*

ba•thet•ic (bə thĕt′ĭk) *adj.* Marked by bathos: *a bathetic passage in a novel.*

bath•house (băth′hous′) *n.* **1.** A building equipped for bathing. **2.** A building, as at a beach, used by swimmers for changing clothes.

bath•ing cap (bā′*th*ĭng) *n.* A tight elastic cap worn to keep the hair dry or away from the face while swimming.

bathing suit *n.* A swimsuit.

bath•mat (băth′măt′) *n.* A mat for use in a bathtub or on a bathroom floor, as to absorb water or prevent slipping.

bath•o•lith (băth′ə lĭth′) *n.* A large mass of igneous rock that has melted and flowed into surrounding rock layers below the surface.

ba•thos (bā′thŏs′ *or* bā′thôs′) *n.* A sudden and absurd change from a lofty or serious style to one that is very commonplace.

bath•robe (băth′rōb′) *n.* A loose robe worn before and after bathing and for lounging.

bath•room (băth′rŏŏm′ *or* băth′rōōm′) *n.* A room equipped for taking a bath or shower and usually also containing a sink and toilet.

bath•tub (băth′tŭb′) *n.* A tub for bathing, especially one installed in a bathroom.

bath•y•scaph (băth′ĭ skăf′) also **bath•y•scaphe** (băth′ĭ skăf′ *or* băth′ĭ skāf′) *n.* A deep-sea research vessel consisting of a large buoyant hull with an observation capsule secured to its bottom and capable of moving independently.

bath•y•sphere (băth′ĭ sfîr′) *n.* A strong spherical chamber in which a crew can be lowered by cable deep into the ocean to make underwater observations.

ba•tik (bə tēk′ *or* băt′ĭk) *n.* **1.** A method of dyeing a design on cloth by putting removable wax over the parts of the cloth not meant to be dyed. **2.** Cloth dyed by batik.

ba•tiste (bə tēst′) *n.* A fine light fabric, usually of cotton or linen. [First written down in 1697 in Modern English, from Old French, perhaps after *Baptiste* of Cambrai, 13th-century textile maker.]

bat mitz•vah (bät mĭts′ və) or **bas mitz•vah** (bäs mĭts′və) *n.* **1.** A ceremony for a Jewish girl of 12 to 14 years of age, in which she is admitted as an adult into the religious community. **2.** A girl for whom such a ceremony is celebrated. *—tr.v.* **bat mitz•vahed, bat mitz•vah•ing, bat mitz•vahs** or **bas mitz•vahed, bas mitz•vah•ing, bas mitz•vahs.** To recognize (a girl) in such a ceremony.

ba•ton (bə tŏn′ *or* băt′n) *n.* **1.** A thin tapered stick often used by a conductor in leading a band, a chorus, or an orchestra. **2.** A stick or staff such as that twirled by a drum major, passed in a relay race, or carried as a symbol of office.

Bat•on Rouge (băt′n rōōzh′). The capital of Louisiana, in the southeast-central part of the state on a bluff above the Mississippi River. It has notable pre–Civil War houses. Population, 219,531.

ba•tra•chi•an (bə trā′kē ən) *n.* An amphibian, such as a frog or toad, that has no tail.

bats•man (băts′mən) *n.* A batter in baseball or cricket.

bat•tal•ion (bə tăl′yən) *n.* **1.** A large group of soldiers organized as a unit, usually consisting of a headquarters and two or more companies of infantry or artillery. **2.** A large number: *a battalion of ants.*

bat•ten[1] (băt′n) *intr.v.* **bat•tened, bat•ten•ing, bat•tens.** To feed or thrive and grow fat. [First written down in 1591 in Modern English, ultimately from Old Norse *batna,* to improve.]

bat•ten[2] (băt′n) *n.* **1.** A narrow strip of wood or plastic, such as one used on a boat or ship to fasten a covering over a hatch or to stiffen the edge of a sail. **2.** A narrow strip of wood used as flooring or to hold other pieces of wood together. *—tr.v.* **bat•tened, bat•ten•ing, bat•tens.** To fasten or hold down with or as if with such strips: *batten down the hatches in preparation for a storm.* [First written down in 1427 in Middle English and spelled *bataunt,* from Old French, wooden strip, clapper.]

Bat•ten (băt′n), **Jean.** 1909–1982. New Zealand aviator who was the first woman to fly a solo round trip between England and Australia (1935).

bat•ter[1] (băt′ər) *v.* **bat•tered, bat•ter•ing, bat•ters.** *—tr.* **1.** To strike or pound repeatedly with heavy blows: *Heavy wind and rain battered the windows.* **2.** To injure or damage by rough treatment or hard wear: *The dented old car was badly battered.* *—intr.* To hit heavily and repeatedly; pound: *Waves battered against the pier.* [First written down about 1330 in Middle English and spelled *bateren,* from Latin *battuere.*]

bat•ter[2] (băt′ər) *n.* The player at bat in baseball or cricket. [First written down in 1773 in Modern English.]

bat•ter[3] (băt′ər) *n.* A beaten mixture, as of flour, milk, and eggs, used in cooking: *a bowl of cake batter.* [First written down in 1381 in Middle English and spelled *bater,* probably from Old French *bateure,* a beating, from *batre,* to beat.]

bat•ter•ing ram (băt′ər ĭng) *n.* **1.** A heavy wooden beam used in ancient warfare to batter down walls and gates. **2.** A heavy metal bar used by firefighters and law enforcement officers to break down walls and doors.

bat•ter•y (băt′ə rē) *n., pl.* **bat•ter•ies. 1.a.** Two or more connected electric cells that supply a direct current by converting chemical energy to electrical energy. **b.** A small dry cell designed to power a flashlight or other portable electric device. **2.a.** A group or set of large guns, as of artillery: *The fort had a battery of cannons.* **b.** A place where such guns are set up: *the old battery at the end of Manhattan Island.* **c.** A unit of soldiers in the artillery, corresponding to a company in the infantry. **3.** A group of things or people used or doing something together: *The celebrities faced a battery of cameras and reporters.* **4.** In baseball, the pitcher and catcher. **5.** The unlawful touching or beating of another person, with the intention of doing harm.

bat•ting (băt′ĭng) *n.* Cotton or wool fibers wadded

bat[2]

The well-known phrase "blind as a **bat**" is somewhat misleading. In fact, some bats have excellent eyesight, and bats on the whole are quite skilled in moving about and hunting prey in total darkness. Using a form of natural radar called *echolocation,* the bat emits a series of very high-pitched squeaks, inaudible to human ears, which reflect off objects in the bat's path. Relying on the pattern of echoes it hears, the bat can then avoid obstacles or home in on a specific target.

battering ram

ă	pat	oi	boy
ā	pay	ou	out
âr	care	ŏŏ	took
ä	father	ōō	boot
ĕ	pet	ŭ	cut
ē	be	ûr	urge
ĭ	pit	th	thin
ī	pie	*th*	this
îr	pier	hw	whoop
ŏ	pot	zh	vision
ō	toe	ə	about
ô	paw	N	*French* bon

battlement
Almansa Castle
in Almansa, Spain

bay window

into rolls or sheets, used to stuff mattresses or furniture or to line quilts.

batting average *n.* A measure of a baseball batter's performance obtained by dividing the number of base hits by the number of times at bat.

bat•tle (**băt′**l) *n.* **1.** A fight between two armed forces, usually on a large scale. **2.** Armed fighting; combat: *wounded in battle.* **3.** A struggle or sharp conflict: *a political battle; a battle of wits.* —*v.* **bat•tled, bat•tling, bat•tles.** —*intr.* To fight in or as if in battle; struggle: *The firefighters battled bravely against the flames.* —*tr.* To fight against: *The sailors battled the storm for hours.* **—bat′tler** *n.*

bat•tle-ax or **bat•tle-axe** (**băt′**l ăks′) *n.* A heavy ax with a broad head, used formerly as a weapon.

battle cry *n.* **1.** A shout to spur on fighting, uttered by troops in battle. **2.** A slogan used by the supporters of a cause: *The campaign's battle cry was "Lower Taxes."*

bat•tle•dore (**băt′**l dôr′) *n.* **1.** An early form of badminton played with a flat wooden paddle and a shuttlecock. **2.** The paddle used in this game.

bat•tle•field (**băt′**l fēld′) *n.* A field or an area where a battle is or was fought: *the battlefield at Gettysburg.*

bat•tle•front (**băt′**l frŭnt′) *n.* The line or area in which armed forces engage opponents in battle.

bat•tle•ground (**băt′**l ground′) *n.* A battlefield.

bat•tle•ment (**băt′**l mənt) *n.* A wall built with indented openings along the top edge of a tower, castle, or fort, used as protection and concealment for soldiers in warfare.

battle royal *n., pl.* **battles royal. 1.** A battle in which many people take part. **2.** A bitter or intense quarrel: *a battle royal over spending for public works.*

bat•tle•ship (**băt′**l shĭp′) *n.* Any of a class of warships of largest size, having the heaviest guns and armor.

bat•ty (**băt′**ē) *adj.* **bat•ti•er, bat•ti•est.** *Slang.* Crazy; insane.

bau•ble (**bô′**bəl) *n.* A showy ornament or trinket of little value.

baud (bôd) *n.* A unit of speed in data transmission usually equal to one bit per second. [First written down in 1932 in Modern English, after Jean Maurice Emile *Baudot* (1845–1903), French engineer.]

baux•ite (**bôk′**sīt′) *n.* A mixture of minerals, often resembling clay, that is the principal ore of aluminum.

Ba•var•i•a (bə **vâr′**ē ə). A region and former duchy of southern Germany. The region was one of the most important duchies of medieval Germany.

bawd•y (**bô′**dē) *adj.* **bawd•i•er, bawd•i•est.** Humorously coarse: *bawdy jokes.* **—bawd′i•ly** *adv.* **—bawd′i•ness** *n.*

bawl (bôl) *v.* **bawled, bawl•ing, bawls.** —*intr.* **1.** To cry or sob loudly; wail: *The unhappy baby kicked and bawled* **2.** To cry out loudly; shout. —*tr.* To utter or call in a loud strong voice: *The sentry bawled an order to halt.* —*n.* A loud wailing or bellowing cry: *the bawl of a stray calf.* **—*idiom.* bawl out.** *Informal.* To scold loudly or harshly.

❑ *These sound alike:* **bawl, ball**[1] (round object), **ball**[2] (dance).

bay[1] (bā) *n.* A body of water partially enclosed by land but having a wide outlet to the sea. A bay is usually smaller than a gulf and larger than a cove. [First written down before 1400 in Middle English, from Old French *baie.*]

❑ *These sound alike:* **bay**[1] (body of water), **bay**[2] (part of a room), **bay**[3] (reddish brown), **bay**[4] (bark), **bay**[5] (laurel), **bey** (Turkish governor).

bay[2] (bā) *n.* **1.** A part of a building divided by vertical supports such as columns or pillars: *an arcade with ten bays.* **2.** A bay window. **3.** A section or compartment, as of a building or an aircraft, set off for a specific purpose: *The cargo was stored in a loading bay.* **4.** A sickbay. [First written down about 1380 in Middle English, from Old French *baee,* an opening, from *baer,* to gape.]

❑ *These sound alike:* **bay**[2] (part of a room), **bay**[1] (body of water), **bay**[3] (reddish brown), **bay**[4] (bark), **bay**[5] (laurel), **bey** (Turkish governor).

bay[3] (bā) *adj.* Reddish brown: *a bay horse.* —*n.* **1.** A reddish brown. **2.** A reddish-brown horse. [First written down in 1341 in Middle English, from Latin *badius.*]

❑ *These sound alike:* **bay**[3] (reddish brown), **bay**[1] (body of water), **bay**[2] (part of a room), **bay**[4] (bark), **bay**[5] (laurel), **bey** (Turkish governor).

bay[4] (bā) *n.* **1.** A long howling bark. **2.** A position of or like that of an animal cornered by and facing its pursuers: *The barking hounds kept the stag at bay. The policeman chased the dog and brought it to bay.* **3.** The position of being kept at a distance: *Lights around the factory kept intruders at bay.* —*intr.v.* **bayed, bay•ing, bays.** To bark with loud howling cries. [First written down about 1300 in Middle English and spelled *abai,* cornering a hunted animal, from Old French *abaiier,* to bark.]

❑ *These sound alike:* **bay**[4] (bark), **bay**[1] (body of water), **bay**[2] (part of a room), **bay**[3] (reddish brown), **bay**[5] (laurel), **bey** (Turkish governor).

bay[5] (bā) *n.* **1.** A laurel having glossy fragrant leaves often used as a spice. **2.** Any of certain other trees or shrubs having fragrant leaves. [First written down in 1373 in Middle English, from Latin *bāca,* berry.]

❑ *These sound alike:* **bay**[5] (laurel), **bay**[1] (body of water), **bay**[2] (part of a room), **bay**[3] (reddish brown), **bay**[4] (bark), **bey** (Turkish governor).

bay•ber•ry (**bā′**bĕr′ē) *n.* **1.** The gray, waxy, pleasant-smelling berries of North American shrub, used to make candles. **2.** The shrub that bears such berries.

bay leaf *n.* The dried leaf of a kind of laurel, used as a seasoning in cooking.

bay•o•net (**bā′**ə nĭt *or* bā′ə **nĕt′**) *n.* A knife attached to the muzzle of a rifle for use in close combat. —*tr.v.* **bay•o•net•ed, bay•o•net•ing, bay•o•nets** or **bay•o•net•ted, bay•o•net•ting, bay•o•nets.** To stab or prod with a bayonet.

bay•ou (**bī′**o͞o *or* **bī′**ō) *n.* A sluggish marshy stream connected with a river, lake, or gulf, common in the southern United States.

bay rum *n.* A fragrant lotion made from the leaves of a tropical American tree.

bay window *n.* A window or group of windows projecting from the outer wall of a building and forming an alcove within.

ba•zaar (bə **zär′**) *n.* **1.** A market, usually consisting of a street lined with shops and stalls, especially in the Middle East. **2.** A store where various kinds of things are sold. **3.** A fair or sale, often to raise money for a charity: *a hospital bazaar.*

ba•zoo•ka (bə **zo͞o′**kə) *n.* A portable military weapon consisting of a tube from which antitank rockets are launched. [First written down in 1935 in American English, referring to a crude wind instrument made of pipes, invented and named by Bob Burns (1896–1956), American comedian.]

BB (**bē′**bē) *n.* A size of lead shot fired from a BB gun.

BBC (bē′bē **sē′**) *abbr.* An abbreviation of British Broadcasting Corporation.

BB gun *n.* A small air rifle that shoots BB's.

bbl. *abbr.* An abbreviation of barrel.

B.C. *abbr.* An abbreviation of before Christ (in a specified year before the birth of Jesus).

bd. *abbr.* An abbreviation of: **1.** Board. **2.** Bond. **3.** Bound.

bd. ft. *abbr.* An abbreviation of board foot.

be (bē) *v. Present tense*: first person singular **am** (ăm), second person singular **are** (är), third person singular **is** (ĭz), plural **are**, present participle **be•ing** (bē′ĭng). *Past tense*: first and third person singular **was** (wŭz *or* wŏz), second person singular **were** (wûr), plural **were**, past participle **been** (bĭn). —*intr.* **1.** To exist; have life or reality: *There are no longer any dinosaurs.* **2.** To occupy a position: *The food is on the table.* **3.** To take place; occur: *Where is the show?* **4.** To come or go: *Have you ever been to Alaska?* **5.a.** To equal in identity or meaning: *That experiment was a complete success.* **b.** To signify or stand for: *A is excellent; C is passing.* **c.** To belong to a specified class or group: *Snakes are reptiles.* **d.** To have or show a specified quality or characteristic: *Skyscrapers are tall.* **6.** To belong; befall: *Woe is me.* —*aux.* **1.** Used to form the passive voice in combination with the past participle of transitive verbs: *Elections are held once a year.* **2.** Used to express a continuing action in combination with the present participle of a verb: *We are working to improve housing conditions.* **3.** Used to indicate duty, possibility, or a future event with the infinitive of another verb: *I am to inform you that the package has arrived. How am I to know the answer? They are to be married Monday.* **4.** *Archaic.* Used to form the perfect tense with the past participle of certain verbs: *The guests are gone. Turn out the light when you are done.* [First written down before 830 in Old English and spelled *bēon.*]
❑ *These sound alike:* **be, bee[1]** (insect), **bee[2]** (gathering).

Be The symbol for the element **beryllium.**

be– *pref.* A prefix that means: **1.** Completely; thoroughly: *bemoan.* **2.** On; around; over: *bespatter.* **3.** Make; cause to become: *becloud.* **4.** About; to: *bespeak.* **5.** Affect or provide with: *befriend.*

beach (bēch) *n.* The area of accumulated sand, stone, or gravel deposited above the water line at a shore by the action of waves. —*tr.v.* **beached, beach•ing, beach•es.** To haul or run ashore: *The whale beached itself in shallow water.*
❑ *These sound alike:* **beach, beech** (tree).

Beach (bēch), **Sylvia Woodbridge.** 1887–1962. American bookseller. From 1919 to 1941 her shop in Paris was a gathering place for authors.

beach•head (bēch′hĕd′) *n.* A military position on an enemy shoreline captured by advance troops of an invading force.

bea•con (bē′kən) *n.* **1.** A guiding or warning signal, such as a lighthouse located on a coast. **2.** A radio transmitter that sends a guidance signal for aircraft. **3.** A source of guidance or inspiration: *Her achievements were a beacon to others.* **4.** A fire set as a signal or warning of an enemy's approach. [First written down about 725 in Old English and spelled *bēacen.*]

bead (bēd) *n.* **1.** A small, often round piece of glass, wood, plastic, or other material that is pierced for placing on a string or wire. **2. beads.** A necklace of beads on a string. **3. beads.** A rosary. **4.** A small round object, such as a drop of moisture: *beads of sweat on one's forehead.* **5.** A small knob of metal located at the muzzle of a rifle or pistol and used in taking aim. —*tr. & intr.v.* **bead•ed, bead•ing, beads.** To furnish with or collect into beads: *bead the collar around a sweater; water beading on the soda can.* —***idiom.*** **draw a bead on.** To take careful aim at. [First written down about 725 in Old English and spelled *gebed*, prayer.]

bead•ing (bē′dĭng) *n.* **1.** Beads or the material used for making them. **2.** Ornamentation using beads. **3.** A narrow piece of lace with openings through which ribbon may be run.

bea•dle (bēd′l) *n.* A minor official in an English church, whose duties include keeping order and ushering during services.

bead•work (bēd′wûrk′) *n.* Decorative work in beads.

bead•y (bē′dē) *adj.* **bead•i•er, bead•i•est.** Small, round, and shining: *beady eyes.*

bea•gle (bē′gəl) *n.* One of a breed of small hounds having drooping ears and a smooth coat with white, black, and tan markings.

beagle

beak (bēk) *n.* **1.** The hard, horny, projecting structure forming the mouth of a bird; a bill. **2.** A similar, often horny, part in other animals. Turtles and octopuses have beaks. **3.** A projecting part that resembles a bird's beak. [First written down before 1250 in Middle English and spelled *bec*, from Latin *beccus*, of Celtic origin.]

beak•er (bē′kər) *n.* **1.** A cylindrical glass container with a pouring lip, used especially in laboratories. **2.** A large drinking cup with a wide mouth. [First written down about 1380 in Middle English and spelled *bekir*, from Medieval Latin *bicārium.*]

beaker
Measuring liquid into a beaker

beam (bēm) *n.* **1.** A long rigid piece of wood or metal used especially as a horizontal support in construction. **2.** One of the main horizontal supports of a building or ship. **3.** The width of a ship at its widest part. **4.** In a balance, the bar from which the weights are hung. **5.** A stream of particles or waves, as of light, sound, or other radiation: *the beam of a flashlight; a laser beam.* **6.** A radio beam used to help ships or aircraft navigate. —*v.* **beamed, beam•ing, beams.** —*intr.* **1.** To give off light; shine: *The sun is beaming in the sky.* **2.** To smile broadly: *His face beamed with delight.* —*tr.* To emit or transmit: *beam a TV program to Europe by satellite.* [First written down about 725 in Old English and spelled *bēam.*]

bean (bēn) *n.* **1.a.** Any of various plants related to the pea, having seeds in pods that are usually long and narrow. **b.** The edible seed or pod of such a plant. **2.** A seed or pod similar to a bean: *a coffee bean; a vanilla bean.* —***idiom.*** **spill the beans.** To disclose a secret. [First written down about 1000 in Old English and spelled *bēan.*]

bean•bag (bēn′băg′) *n.* A small cloth bag filled with dried beans and used as a toy or for throwing in some games.

bean curd *n.* Tofu.

bean•ie (bē′nē) *n.* A small brimless cap.

beanie
Worn by a Brownie

bean sprouts *pl.n.* The tender shoots of certain bean plants, such as the soybean, used as food.

bean•stalk (bēn′stôk′) *n.* The stem of a bean plant.

bear[1] (bâr) *v.* **bore** (bôr), **borne** (bôrn) or **born** (bôrn), **bear•ing, bears.** —*tr.* **1.** To hold up; support: *a floor able to bear the weight of heavy machinery.* **2.** To carry on one's person; convey: *the right to bear arms.* **3.** To carry; transport: *The expedition used mules to bear their equipment.* **4.** To tell; transmit: *bear good news.* **5.** To be accountable for; assume: *We all shared in bearing the blame for our actions.* **6.** To carry (oneself) in a specified way: *Members of both teams bore themselves with pride.* **7.** To have in the heart or mind: *bear a grudge.* **8.** To have as a visible characteristic; show: *buildings bearing the scars of time; twins bearing a strong resemblance to each other.* **9.** To bring forth; produce: *Some trees bear fruit early in the spring. My savings account bears interest.* **10.** To give birth to: *That old dog has borne many pups.* **11.** To give or offer; provide: *bear witness in a written statement.* **12.** To put up with; endure: *I can't bear his smug attitude.* **13.** To call for; warrant: *This case bears investigation.* —*intr.* **1.** To yield fruit; produce: *fruit*

ă	pat	oi	boy
ā	pay	ou	out
âr	care	o͝o	took
ä	father	o͞o	boot
ĕ	pet	ŭ	cut
ē	be	ûr	urge
ĭ	pit	th	thin
ī	pie	*th*	this
îr	pier	hw	whoop
ŏ	pot	zh	vision
ō	toe	ə	about
ô	paw	N	*French* bon

bearskin

trees that bear well. **2.a.** To exert pressure: *She bore so hard on the pencil that it broke.* **b.** To exert influence: *bringing pressure to bear on reaching a settlement of the dispute.* **3.** To have relevance; apply: *Your remark does not bear upon the problem.* **4.** To proceed or turn in a given direction: *At the corner, bear right.* **—*idioms.*** **bear down. 1.** To exert pressure; press down: *Concern about water bears down heavily in times of drought.* **2.** To exert oneself; make a special effort: *By bearing down the staff was able to complete the job on time.* **bear down on. 1.** To affect in a harmful way: *The large amount of work was bearing down on the entire staff.* **2.** To move toward or approach rapidly: *The runners bore down on the finish line.* **bear in mind.** To hold in one's mind; remember: *Bear in mind that we're reporting, not taking sides.* **bear out.** To prove right; confirm: *The test results bear out our theory.* **bear up.** To withstand difficulty or stress: *The patient bore up well during a long illness.* **bear with.** To be patient or indulgent with: *Please bear with me while I find out where to go.* [First written down about 725 in Old English and spelled *beran.*]

❑ *These sound alike:* **bear[1]** (support), **bare** (uncovered), **bear[2]** (animal).

bear[2] (bâr) *n.* **1.** Any of various large mammals having a shaggy coat, a very short tail, and a flat-footed walk. Bears usually eat both plants and other animals, especially insects and small rodents. **2.** A rough clumsy person. **3.** *Slang.* Something that is difficult or unpleasant: *That exam was a bear!* **4.** A person who sells stocks or other securities expecting their price to fall. *—adj.* Characterized by falling prices: *a bear market in stocks.* [First written down before 893 in Old English and spelled *bera.*]

❑ *These sound alike:* **bear[2]** (animal), **bare** (uncovered), **bear[1]** (support).

bear•a•ble (bâr′ə bəl) *adj.* Capable of being borne; tolerable: *Resting from time to time made the long hike bearable.* **—bear′a•bly** *adv.*

beard (bîrd) *n.* **1.** The hair on a man's chin, cheeks, and throat. **2.** A hairy growth on the face of certain mammals, as the chin tuft of a goat. **3.** A tuft of hairs or bristles on certain plants, such as barley and wheat. *—tr.v.* **beard•ed, beard•ing, beards.** To face or defy boldly: *He was so sure of himself, he bearded his opponents at their own meeting.* [First written down before 830 in Old English.]

bear•er (bâr′ər) *n.* **1.** A person who carries or supports something: *a stretcher bearer; a message bearer.* **2.** A person who holds or presents a check, money order, bond, or other note for payment: *Checks direct a bank to pay the bearer a certain sum of money.*

bear•ing (bâr′ĭng) *n.* **1.** The manner or way in which one carries oneself: *The judge has a dignified bearing.* **2.** Relevance or relationship: *That issue has no bearing on my situation.* **3.** A supporting part of a structure. **4.** A mechanical part that supports a moving part, especially a turning shaft, and allows it to move with little friction: *a wheel bearing.* **5.** Direction, especially angular direction as used in navigation: *The ship took a bearing on the lighthouse.* **6.** The knowledge of one's position in relation to one's surroundings. Often used in the plural: *The hikers lost their bearings in the dark.*

bear•ish (bâr′ĭsh) *adj.* **1.** Rough, clumsy, or rude. **2.** Expecting or characterized by falling prices: *a bearish outlook on the bond market.* **—bear′ish•ly** *adv.*

bear•skin (bâr′skĭn′) *n.* **1.** The skin of a bear. **2.** A rug made from the skin of a bear. **3.** A tall military hat made of black fur.

beast (bēst) *n.* **1.** An animal other than a human being, especially a large four-footed animal: *the birds and the beasts of the jungle.* **2.** A cruel or brutal person. [First written down before 1200 in Middle English and spelled *beste,* from Latin *bēstia.*]

beast•ly (bēst′lē) *adj.* **beast•li•er, beast•li•est. 1.** Of or resembling a beast; bestial. **2.** Unpleasant; disagreeable: *a beastly drive through heavy rain.* *—adv. Chiefly British.* To an extreme degree; very: *a beastly hot day.* **—beast′li•ness** *n.*

beast of burden *n., pl.* **beasts of burden.** An animal, such as a horse, an ox, or a camel, used to carry loads or pull vehicles.

beat (bēt) *v.* **beat, beat•en** (bēt′n) or **beat, beat•ing, beats.** *—tr.* **1.** To strike or hit repeatedly: *The baby beat the table with a spoon.* **2.a.** To produce sound by striking, hitting, or tapping (something) repeatedly: *beat a drum.* **b.** To mark or count (a rhythm or pulse) by tapping, moving, or striking, as with a part of the body: *beat time with one's foot.* **3.** To shape or break by pounding: *Ancient artisans beat copper into spearheads.* **4.** To flap repeatedly: *Hummingbirds beat their wings very fast.* **5.** To mix rapidly with a utensil: *beat egg whites.* **6.a.** To defeat or overcome, as in a contest or battle. **b.** To surpass or be superior to: *Riding a bike beats walking.* **c.** To force to retreat; drive away: *The soldiers beat back the enemy.* **7.** To act ahead of or arrive before: *We beat you to the restaurant.* **8.** To forge or make by treading over: *The early settlers beat a path across the wilderness.* **9.** *Slang.* To baffle or perplex: *How the magician did that trick beats me.* **10.** *Informal.* To avoid or counter the effects of: *Let's leave early to beat the traffic.* *—intr.* **1.** To pound forcefully and repeatedly; dash: *Huge waves beat against the pier.* **2.** To fall in torrents: *The rain beat down on the field.* **3.** To shine or glare intensely: *The summer sun beat down on the thirsty bikers.* **4.** To make a sound when struck: *The drums beat loudly.* **5.** To throb; pulsate: *My heart beat faster with excitement.* **6.** To sail against the wind by tacking in a zigzag course. *—n.* **1.** A stroke or blow, especially one that makes a sound: *the beat of the drums in the parade.* **2.** A pulsation or throb: *the beat of your heart.* **3.a.** One of the succession of units that make up meter in music: *There are four beats in this measure.* **b.** A gesture with the hand, foot, or a baton that marks one of these units. **4.** An area regularly covered by a police officer, guard, or reporter. *—adj. Informal.* Tired; worn-out: *I'm really beat after a full day's work.* **—*idioms.*** **beat around the bush.** To avoid a subject; delay in coming to the point. **beat it.** *Slang.* To leave hurriedly. [First written down about 725 in Old English and spelled *bēaten.*]

❑ *These sound alike:* **beat, beet** (vegetable).

beat•en (bēt′n) *adj.* **1.** Thinned or formed by hammering: *a beaten copper bracelet.* **2.** Much traveled: *beaten paths.*

beat•er (bē′tər) *n.* **1.** A person or thing that beats, especially an instrument for beating: *Use an electric beater to mix bread dough.* **2.** A person who drives wild game from under cover in a hunt.

be•a•tif•ic (bē′ə tĭf′ĭk) *adj.* Showing extreme joy or bliss: *a beatific smile.* **—be′a•tif′i•cal•ly** *adv.*

be•at•i•fy (bē ăt′ə fī′) *tr.v.* **be•at•i•fied, be•at•i•fy•ing, be•at•i•fies. 1.** To make extremely happy. **2.** In the Roman Catholic Church, to declare (a deceased person) to be blessed and worthy of public veneration.

beat•ing (bē′tĭng) *n.* **1.** Punishment by whipping or flogging: *The car took a beating on the rough back roads.* **2.** A defeat: *The defending champions gave our team a beating.* **3.** A throbbing or pulsation, as of the heart.

be•at•i•tude (bē ăt′ĭ to͞od′ *or* bē ăt′ĭ tyo͞od′) *n.* **1.** Supreme blessedness. **2.** Any of the declarations made by Jesus in the Sermon on the Mount, beginning with the words "Blessed are."

beat•nik (bēt′nĭk) *n.* A person, originally a young person living in the 1950's, who acts and dresses unconventionally and is given to harsh criticism of society.

Be•a•trix (bā′ə trĭks′ *or* bē′ə trĭks′). Born 1938. Queen of the Netherlands (since 1980).

beat-up (bēt′ŭp′) *adj. Slang.* In bad condition; rundown: *a beat-up old car.*

beau (bō) *n., pl.* **beaus** or **beaux** (bōz). **1.** The boyfriend of a woman or girl. **2.** A man who is excessively interested in fine clothes and his appearance; a dandy.

❑ *These sound alike:* **beau, bow**[3] (weapon to shoot arrows).

Beau•fort (bō′fərt), **Margaret.** Countess of Richmond and Derby. 1441–1509. English patron who funded many educational facilities.

Beaufort scale *n.* A scale of wind velocities ranging from 0 (calm) to 12 (hurricane). [First written down in 1858 in Modern English, after Sir Francis *Beaufort* (1774–1857), British naval officer.]

beau•te•ous (byōō′tē əs) *adj.* Beautiful. **—beau′te•ous•ly** *adv.* **—beau′te•ous•ness** *n.*

beau•ti•cian (byōō tĭsh′ən) *n.* A person who is skilled in the cosmetic services offered by a beauty parlor.

beau•ti•ful (byōō′tə fəl) *adj.* Showing or having beauty; pleasing to the senses or the mind: *beautiful scenery; beautiful music.* **—beau′ti•ful•ly** *adv.* **—beau′ti•ful•ness** *n.*

beau•ti•fy (byōō′tə fī′) *tr. & intr.v.* **beau•ti•fied, beau•ti•fy•ing, beau•ti•fies.** To make or become beautiful: *Green parks and wide boulevards beautify the city.* **—beau′ti•fi•ca′tion** (byōō′tə fĭ kā′shən) *n.* **—beau′ti•fi′er** *n.*

beau•ty (byōō′tē) *n., pl.* **beau•ties. 1.** A pleasing quality, especially with regard to form, that delights the senses and appeals to the mind: *the beauty of the snowcapped mountains.* **2.** A person or thing that is beautiful: *Helen of Troy was a great beauty.* **3.** A feature that is most gratifying or effective: *The beauty of this scheme is that we come out ahead either way.* [First written down before 1325 in Middle English and spelled *bealte*, from Latin *bellus*, pretty.]

beauty parlor *n.* A business offering hair styling, manicures, facial treatments, and other cosmetic services, especially for women.

beauty salon *n.* A beauty parlor.

beauty shop *n.* A beauty parlor.

Beau•voir (bō vwär′), **Simone de.** 1908–1986. French writer and feminist whose works include *The Second Sex* (1949).

beaux (bōz) *n.* A plural of **beau.**

beaux-arts (bō zär′ *or* bō zärt′) *pl.n.* The fine arts.

bea•ver[1] (bē′vər) *n.* **1.a.** A mammal related to the rat, having thick fur, a flat broad tail, and large strong front teeth. Beavers live in and near lakes and streams and gnaw down trees to build dams and lodges in the water. **b.** The fur of a beaver. **2.** A top hat, originally made of beaver fur. *—adj.* Of or relating to a beaver or beavers: *a beaver dam.* [First written down about 1000 in Old English and spelled *beofor*.]

bea•ver[2] (bē′vər) *n.* A movable piece of metal armor worn on the front of a knight's helmet to protect his mouth and chin. [First written down before 1420 in Middle English and spelled *bavier*, from Old French *bave*, saliva.]

bea•ver•board (bē′vər bôrd′) *n.* A light building material of compressed wood pulp, used for walls, partitions, and bulletin boards.

be•calmed (bĭ kämd′) *adj.* Motionless for a lack of wind: *the limp and hanging sails of a becalmed ship.*

be•came (bĭ kām′) *v.* Past tense of **become.**

be•cause (bĭ kôz′ *or* bĭ kŭz′) *conj.* For the reason that; since: *The room is uncomfortable because it is too hot.*

because of *prep.* On account of; by reason of: *I stayed home because of illness.*

beck (bĕk) *n.* A gesture of beckoning. ***—idiom.* at (one's) beck and call.** Willingly obedient; ready to perform a service: *The staff of the hotel are generally at the beck and call of the guests.*

beck•on (bĕk′ən) *v.* **beck•oned, beck•on•ing, beck•ons.** *—tr.* **1.** To signal (a person) to come, as by nodding or waving: *The principal beckoned us to her office.* **2.** To attract because of an inviting appearance: *The lake beckoned me to dive in and cool off.* *—intr.* **1.** To signal to come: *The guide beckoned at the mouth of the cave.* **2.** To attract or entice: *Adventure beckoned down every road.*

be•cloud (bĭ kloud′) *tr.v.* **be•cloud•ed, be•cloud•ing, be•clouds.** To darken with or as if with clouds; obscure: *The debate was beclouded by passionate emotions.*

be•come (bĭ kŭm′) *v.* **be•came** (bĭ kām′), **be•come, be•com•ing, be•comes.** *—intr.* To grow or come to be: *As winter approaches the temperature becomes colder.* *—tr.* **1.** To be appropriate or suitable to: *It becomes a judge to act with dignity.* **2.** To look good with or cause to look good on: *The new coat becomes you.* ***—idiom.* become of.** To be the fate of; happen to: *What ever became of your friend that moved away?*

be•com•ing (bĭ kŭm′ĭng) *adj.* **1.** Appropriate; suitable: *a helpful and cheerful manner becoming to a nurse.* **2.** Pleasing or attractive to look at: *the baby's becoming smile.* **—be•com′ing•ly** *adv.*

bed (bĕd) *n.* **1.a.** A piece of furniture for resting and sleeping, consisting usually of a flat rectangular frame and a mattress resting on springs. **b.** A mattress: *a feather bed.* **c.** A mattress and bedclothes: *make up a bed on the floor.* **2.** A place where one may sleep; lodging: *I have a bed for the night at the inn.* **3.** The time at which one goes to sleep: *I drank a glass of water before bed.* **4.a.** A small plot for cultivating or growing things: *a bed of flowers.* **b.** A similar plot on the bottom of a body of water: *an oyster bed.* **5.** The bottom of a body of water: *a stream bed.* **6.** A supporting, underlying, or securing part: *Underneath the brick path is a bed of sand.* **7.** The part of a truck, trailer, or railroad car designed to carry loads. **8.** A mass of rock that extends under a large area and is bounded by different material: *a bed of coal.* *—tr.v.* **bed•ded, bed•ding, beds. 1.** To provide with a bed or sleeping quarters: *We bedded the guests in the living room.* **2.** To set or plant in a bed of soil: *bed tulip bulbs before the ground freezes.* [First written down about 700 in Old English.]

bed-and-break•fast (bĕd′n brĕk′fəst) *n.* A private residence that offers overnight lodging and breakfast as part of the charge.

be•daub (bĭ dôb′) *tr.v.* **be•daubed, be•daub•ing, be•daubs.** To smear; soil: *The chimneysweep was bedaubed with soot.*

be•daz•zle (bĭ dăz′əl) *tr.v.* **be•daz•zled, be•daz•zling, be•daz•zles.** To dazzle completely; confuse; bewilder: *The magician bedazzled the audience with tricks.* **—be•daz′zle•ment** *n.*

bed•bug (bĕd′bŭg′) *n.* A wingless insect that has a flat reddish body and lives in human dwellings and bedding and bites humans to feed on their blood.

bed•cham•ber (bĕd′chām′bər) *n.* A bedroom.

bed•clothes (bĕd′klōz′ *or* bĕd′klōthz′) *pl.n.* Coverings, such as sheets and blankets, used on a bed.

Simone de Beauvoir

beaver[1]

ă	pat	oi	boy
ā	pay	ou	out
âr	care	ŏŏ	took
ä	father	ōō	boot
ĕ	pet	ŭ	cut
ē	be	ûr	urge
ĭ	pit	th	thin
ī	pie	*th*	this
îr	pier	hw	whoop
ŏ	pot	zh	vision
ō	toe	ə	about
ô	paw	N	*French* bon

Ludwig van Beethoven

bed•ding (bĕd′ĭng) *n.* **1.** Sheets, blankets, and mattresses for beds. **2.** Material, such as straw or hay, for animals to sleep on. **3.** A foundation or bottom layer: *a bedding of gravel supporting the road.* **4.** The way in which layers of sedimentary rock are arranged.

be•deck (bĭ **dĕk′**) *tr.v.* **be•decked, be•deck•ing, be•decks.** To cover with decorations; adorn: *a hero bedecked with medals.*

be•dev•il (bĭ **dĕv′**əl) *tr.v.* **be•dev•iled, be•dev•il•ing, be•dev•ils** or **be•dev•illed, be•dev•il•ling, be•dev•ils. 1.** To plague; trouble; harass: *The project was bedeviled with accidents and injuries.* **2.** To possess with or as if with a devil; bewitch. **—be•dev′il•ment** *n.*

be•dew (bĭ **do͞o′** *or* bĭ **dyo͞o′**) *tr.v.* **be•dewed, be•dew•ing, be•dews.** To wet with or as if with dew: *cheeks bedewed with tears.*

bed•fel•low (**bĕd′**fĕl′ō) *n.* **1.** A person with whom one shares a bed. **2.** An associate or ally: *The opponents made strange bedfellows in their efforts to secure the agreement.*

be•di•zen (bĭ **dī′**zən *or* bĭ **dĭz′**ən) *tr.v.* **be•di•zened, be•di•zen•ing, be•di•zens.** To dress or ornament in a gaudy manner.

bed•lam (**bĕd′**ləm) *n.* **1.** A place or situation of confusion, disorder, or noisy uproar: *the bedlam of a one-day sale in the department store.* **2.** *Archaic.* An insane asylum. [First written down in 1663 in Modern English, from Middle English *Bedlem,* the Hospital of Saint Mary of *Bethlehem,* an institution in London for the mentally ill.]

Bed•ou•in (**bĕd′**o͞o ĭn *or* **bĕd′**wĭn) *n., pl.* **Bedouin** or **Bed•ou•ins.** A member of a nomadic people of North African, Arabian, and Syrian deserts.

bed•pan (**bĕd′**păn′) *n.* A container used as a toilet by a bedridden person.

be•drag•gled (bĭ **drăg′**əld) *adj.* **1.** Wet, drenched, or messy: *bedraggled clothes.* **2.** Run-down; deteriorated: *the bedraggled condition of the old buildings.*

bed•rid•den (**bĕd′**rĭd′n) *adj.* Confined to bed because of sickness or weakness.

bed•rock (**bĕd′**rŏk′) *n.* **1.** The solid rock that lies beneath the soil and other loose material on the surface of the earth. **2.** The lowest or bottom level: *Sales hit bedrock in the slow summer months.* **3.** The basis or foundation: *Making products of high quality is the bedrock of manufacturing.*

bed•roll (**bĕd′**rōl′) *n.* Blankets or a sleeping bag rolled up to be carried by a camper or a person who sleeps outdoors.

bed•room (**bĕd′**ro͞om′ *or* **bĕd′**ro͝om′) *n.* A room in which to sleep.

bed•side (**bĕd′**sīd′) *n.* The place alongside a bed: *The nurse stood at the patient's bedside.* —*adj.* Near a bed: *a bedside table; a bedside conversation.*

bed•sore (**bĕd′**sôr′) *n.* An ulcer of the skin caused by pressure, occurring in persons who are bedridden for long periods.

bed•spread (**bĕd′**sprĕd′) *n.* A covering for a bed.

bed•spring (**bĕd′**sprĭng′) *n.* One of the springs supporting the mattress of a bed.

bed•stead (**bĕd′**stĕd′) *n.* The frame supporting the springs and mattress of a bed.

bed•time (**bĕd′**tīm′) *n.* The time when a person usually goes to bed.

bee[1] (bē) *n.* Any of several winged, often stinging insects that have a hairy body and gather pollen and nectar from flowers. Some bees, such as the honeybee, live in colonies. **—*idiom.* a bee in (one's) bonnet.** An idea that persistently occupies one's mind; a notion: *My parents have a bee in their bonnet about redecorating the living room.* [First written down before 900 in Old English and spelled *bēo.*]

❑ *These sound alike:* **bee**[1] (insect), **be** (exist), **bee**[2] (gathering).

bee[2] (bē) *n.* A gathering where people work together or compete against one another: *a quilting bee; a spelling bee.* [First written down in 1769 in Modern English, probably from dialectal *bean,* neighborly help to a farmer, from Middle English *bene,* extra service by a tenant, from Old English *bēn,* prayer.]

❑ *These sound alike:* **bee**[2] (gathering), **be** (exist), **bee**[1] (insect).

bee•bread (**bē′**brĕd′) *n.* A brownish substance made by bees from pollen and nectar and fed to their young.

beech (bēch) *n.* **1.** A tree having smooth gray bark, small edible nuts, and strong heavy wood. **2.** The wood of such a tree.

❑ *These sound alike:* **beech, beach** (area of sand).

beech•nut (**bēch′**nŭt′) *n.* The edible nut of a beech tree, encased in a prickly husk.

beef (bēf) *n., pl.* **beeves** (bēvz) or **beef. 1.a.** The flesh of a full-grown steer, bull, ox, or cow, used as meat. **b.** A full-grown steer, bull, ox, or cow, especially one intended for use as meat. **2.** *Informal.* Human muscle; brawn: *football players with plenty of beef.* **3.** *pl.* **beefs.** *Slang.* A complaint. —*intr.v.* **beefed, beef•ing, beefs.** *Slang.* To complain. **—*idiom.* beef up.** *Informal.* To make greater or stronger: *beef up efforts to combat crime.*

beef•steak (**bēf′**stāk′) *n.* A slice of beef suitable for broiling or frying.

beef•y (**bē′**fē) *adj.* **beef•i•er, beef•i•est.** Heavy, strong, and muscular; brawny: *a beefy wrestler.* **—beef′i•ness** *n.*

bee•hive (**bē′**hīv′) *n.* **1.** A hive for bees. **2.** A very busy place: *The bus terminal is always a beehive of activity.*

bee•keep•er (**bē′**kē′pər) *n.* A person who keeps bees.

bee•line (**bē′**līn′) *n.* The fastest and most direct course, as one that might be taken by a bee going to its hive: *At noontime everybody made a beeline for the lunchroom.*

Be•el•ze•bub (bē **ĕl′**zə bŭb′) *n.* The Devil.

been (bĭn) *v.* Past participle of **be.**

❑ *These sound alike:* **been, bin** (container).

beep (bēp) *n.* A short sound, as from an automobile's horn or a radio transmitter. —*v.* **beeped, beep•ing, beeps.** —*intr.* To make a beep: *The transmitter beeped steadily.* —*tr.* To cause to make a beep: *The drivers beeped their horns in the traffic jam.*

beep•er (**bē′**pər) *n.* **1.** A person or thing that beeps. **2.** A small electronic device that emits a signal when the person carrying it is being paged.

beer (bîr) *n.* **1.** An alcoholic beverage brewed from malt and hops. **2.** A drink such as root beer or birch beer.

❑ *These sound alike:* **beer, bier** (stand for a coffin).

bees•wax (**bēz′**wăks′) *n.* **1.** The yellowish or brownish wax produced by honeybees for making their honeycombs. **2.** A processed and purified form of this wax used in making candles, crayons, and polishes.

beet (bēt) *n.* **1.a.** A leafy plant having a thick, rounded, dark-red root eaten as a vegetable. **b.** A form of this plant having a large whitish root from which sugar is made; the sugar beet. **2.** The root of either of these plants.

❑ *These sound alike:* **beet, beat** (strike).

Bee•tho•ven (**bā′**tō′vən), **Ludwig van.** 1770–1827. German composer whose music includes symphonies, sonatas, two Masses, an opera, and works for piano and violin. Many of his works were composed after he lost his hearing.

bee·tle[1] (bēt′l) *n.* **1.** Any of numerous insects that have biting mouthparts and hind wings folded and hidden under hard glossy front wings when not flying. Many beetles are harmful to plants. **2.** An insect resembling a beetle, as a ladybug. [First written down about 700 in Old English and spelled *bitula,* from *bītan,* to bite.]

❑ *These sound alike:* **beetle**[1] (insect), **beetle**[2] (overhang), **beetle**[3] (mallet), **betel** (plant).

bee·tle[2] (bēt′l) *intr.v.* **bee·tled, bee·tling, bee·tles.** To overhang; jut: *cliffs beetling over the valley below.* [First written down in 1602 in Modern English, from Middle English *bitel-brouwed,* grimbrowed.]

❑ *These sound alike:* **beetle**[2] (overhang), **beetle**[1] (insect), **beetle**[3] (mallet), **betel** (plant).

bee·tle[3] (bēt′l) *n.* A heavy wooden mallet. [First written down about 897 in Old English and spelled *bīetel.*]

❑ *These sound alike:* **beetle**[3] (mallet), **beetle**[1] (insect), **beetle**[2] (overhang), **betel** (plant).

bee·tle-browed (bēt′l broud′) *adj.* **1.** Having large overhanging brows: *the beetle-browed skull of a Neanderthal man.* **2.** Scowling.

beeves (bēvz) *n.* A plural of **beef.**

be·fall (bĭ fôl′) *v.* **be·fell** (bĭ fĕl′), **be·fall·en** (bĭ fô′lən), **be·fall·ing, be·falls.** —*intr.* To come to pass by chance; happen. —*tr.* To happen to: *Many serious mishaps befell the explorers.*

be·fit (bĭ fĭt′) *tr.v.* **be·fit·ted, be·fit·ting, be·fits.** To be suitable to or appropriate for: *He wore a tuxedo to befit the formal occasion.*

be·fog (bĭ fôg′ *or* bĭ fŏg′) *tr.v.* **be·fogged, be·fog·ging, be·fogs.** **1.** To cover or obscure with fog: *Clouds befogged the airport.* **2.** To cause confusion in; muddle: *Raising minor points is befogging the debate.*

be·fore (bĭ fôr′) *adv.* **1.** Earlier in time: *I told you about this before.* **2.** In front; ahead: *The people who went before were turned away.* —*prep.* **1.** Previous to; earlier than: *They got there before me.* **2.** In front of: *Eat what's set before you.* **3.** In store for; awaiting: *You've got a great future before you.* **4.a.** Under the consideration of: *The case is now before the court.* **b.** Into or in the presence of: *Each prisoner was brought before the judge.* **5.** In preference to or in higher esteem than: *I'd take a hamburger before a hot dog any day.* —*conj.* **1.** In advance of the time when: *See me before you leave.* **2.** Sooner than; rather than: *I'd die before I'd give in.* [First written down about 725 in Old English and spelled *beforan.*]

be·fore·hand (bĭ fôr′hănd′) *adv. & adj.* In advance; ahead of time: *The class starts at 9 o'clock, but I always get there beforehand.*

be·foul (bĭ foul′) *tr.v.* **be·fouled, be·foul·ing, be·fouls.** To make dirty; soil: *smokestacks befouling the air.*

be·friend (bĭ frĕnd′) *tr.v.* **be·friend·ed, be·friend·ing, be·friends.** To act as a friend to; assist: *A perfect stranger befriended the lost tourists.*

be·fud·dle (bĭ fŭd′l) *tr.v.* **be·fud·dled, be·fud·dling, be·fud·dles.** To confuse; perplex: *The problem befuddled even the experts.*

beg (bĕg) *v.* **begged, beg·ging, begs.** —*tr.* **1.** To ask for as charity: *begged money while sitting in a doorway.* **2.** To ask for humbly; plead for: *I beg your pardon.* **3.** To ask of; entreat: *We begged her for help.* —*intr.* **1.** To ask as help or charity. **2.** To ask earnestly; plead: *beg for another chance.* ***—idiom.*** **beg off.** To ask to be excused from something: *We had to beg off the invitation to the party.* [First written down before 1200 in Middle English and spelled *beggen.*]

be·gan (bĭ găn′) *v.* Past tense of **begin.**

be·gat (bĭ găt′) *v. Archaic.* A past tense of **beget.**

be·get (bĭ gĕt′) *tr.v.* **be·got** (bĭ gŏt′), **be·got·ten** (bĭ gŏt′n) or **be·got, be·get·ting, be·gets.** **1.** To father; sire. **2.** To cause to exist; produce: *Rudeness begets resentment.* **—be·get′ter** *n.*

beg·gar (bĕg′ər) *n.* **1.** A person who begs as a means of living. **2.** A person who is very poor; a pauper. —*tr.v.* **beg·gared, beg·gar·ing, beg·gars.** **1.** To make very poor; ruin. **2.** To outdo; go beyond: *The beauty of the Grand Canyon beggars description.*

beg·gar·ly (bĕg′ər lē) *adj.* **1.** Of, relating to, or befitting a beggar; poor. **2.** Mean; contemptible: *a beggarly remark of envy.* **—beg′gar·li·ness** *n.*

beg·gar·y (bĕg′ə rē) *n.* Extreme poverty.

be·gin (bĭ gĭn′) *v.* **be·gan** (bĭ găn′), **be·gun** (bĭ gŭn′), **be·gin·ning, be·gins.** —*intr.* **1.** To take the first step in doing something; start; commence: *We began with the kitchen and cleaned the whole house.* **2.** To come into being; originate: *Education begins at home.* **3.** To accomplish in the least way; come near: *The little bit of paint won't begin to cover the ceiling.* —*tr.* **1.** To start doing: *Most children begin their schooling in kindergarten.* **2.** To bring into being; originate: *The owner's grandfather began the newspaper many years ago.* **3.** To come first in: *The letter* A *begins the alphabet.* [First written down about 1000 in Old English and spelled *beginnan.*]

Synonyms: begin, commence, start, embark. These verbs mean to take the first step or to get working or moving. **Begin** is the most general word: *The play begins at eight o'clock.* **Commence** is a more formal word than **begin**: *Our meetings always commence with a call to order.* **Start** often means to begin from a standstill: *The train started as soon as we sat down.* **Embark** means to set out on a venture or journey: *After getting her teaching certificate, Barbara will embark on a new career.*
Antonym: end.

be·gin·ner (bĭ gĭn′ər) *n.* A person who is just starting to learn or do something; a novice: *A beginner at the piano plays simple pieces.*

be·gin·ning (bĭ gĭn′ĭng) *n.* **1.** The act or process of bringing or being brought into existence; a start: *The Founding Fathers assumed responsibility for the beginning of the nation.* **2.** The time or point when something begins or is begun: *the beginning of the world.* **3.** The place where something begins or is begun; an initial section, division, or part: *at the beginning of the play.* **4.a.** A source or an origin: *An early fort served as the beginning of the city of Chicago.* **b.** An early phase or rudimentary period. Often used in the plural: *the beginnings of life on Earth.*

be·gone (bĭ gôn′ *or* bĭ gŏn′) *v.* An expression used to order dismissal.

be·go·nia (bĭ gōn′yə) *n.* Any of various tropical plants often grown for their showy flowers or colorfully marked leaves. [First written down in 1751 in Modern English, after Michel *Bégon* (1638–1710), French governor in the West Indies.]

be·got (bĭ gŏt′) *v.* Past tense and a past participle of **beget.**

be·got·ten (bĭ gŏt′n) *v.* A past participle of **beget.**

be·grime (bĭ grīm′) *tr.v.* **be·grimed, be·grim·ing, be·grimes.** To soil with dirt or grime: *boots that were begrimed with mud.*

be·grudge (bĭ grŭj′) *tr.v.* **be·grudged, be·grudg·ing, be·grudg·es.** **1.** To envy (someone) for the possession or enjoyment of (something): *A generous person does not begrudge others their good for-*

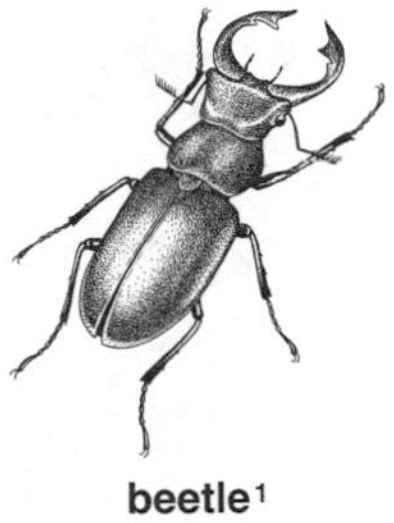

beetle[1]
Male stag beetle

ă	pat	oi	boy
ā	pay	ou	out
âr	care	ŏŏ	took
ä	father	ōō	boot
ĕ	pet	ŭ	cut
ē	be	ûr	urge
ĭ	pit	th	thin
ī	pie	*th*	this
îr	pier	hw	whoop
ŏ	pot	zh	vision
ō	toe	ə	about
ô	paw	N	*French* bon

tune. **2.** To give with reluctance: *He begrudged every penny spent on the repairs.* **—be•grudg′ing•ly** *adv.*

be•guile (bĭ **gīl′**) *tr.v.* **be•guiled, be•guil•ing, be•guiles. 1.** To deceive; trick: *The salesman beguiled me into buying more than I wanted.* **2.** To amuse; delight: *She beguiled us with song.* **3.** To pass pleasantly: *stories written to beguile the time during a journey.* **—be•guile′ment** *n.* **—be•guil′er** *n.*

be•gun (bĭ **gŭn′**) *v.* Past participle of **begin.**

be•half (bĭ **hăf′**) *n.* Interest; benefit: *On whose behalf did they act?* **—*idioms.* in behalf of.** For the benefit of; in the interest of: *We raised money in behalf of the Red Cross.* **on behalf of.** As the agent of; on the part of: *The principal thanked the parents for their help on behalf of the entire teaching staff.*

be•have (bĭ **hāv′**) *v.* **be•haved, be•hav•ing, be•haves.** *—intr.* **1.** To act, react, perform, or function in a certain way: *The car behaves well on rough roads.* **2.a.** To conduct oneself in a specified way: *behave badly.* **b.** To conduct oneself properly: *The babysitter told the child to behave.* *—tr.* **1.** To conduct (oneself) properly. **2.** To conduct (oneself) in a specified way: *She behaved herself with dignity at the wedding.* [First written down about 1410 in Middle English and spelled *behaven.*]

be•hav•ior (bĭ **hāv′**yər) *n.* **1.** The way in which a person behaves; conduct: *on one's best behavior.* **2.** The actions or reactions of persons or things under specified circumstances: *the behavior of matter at extremely low temperatures.*

behavioral (bĭ **hāv′**yər əl) *adj.* Of or relating to behavior: *Behavioral science seeks to understand the actions of animal life.* **—be•hav′ior•al•ly** *adv.*

be•hav•iour (bĭ **hāv′**yər) *n.* *Chiefly British.* Variant of **behavior.**

be•head (bĭ **hĕd′**) *tr.v.* **be•head•ed, be•head•ing, be•heads.** To cut off the head of; decapitate.

be•held (bĭ **hĕld′**) *v.* Past tense and past participle of **behold.**

be•he•moth (bĭ **hē′**məth *or* **bē′**ə məth) *n.* **1.** A huge animal, possibly the hippopotamus, mentioned in the Bible. **2.** Something enormous in size. [First written down before 1382 in Middle English and spelled *bemoth,* from Hebrew *bĕhēmôt,* intensive plural of *bĕhēmâ,* beast.]

be•hest (bĭ **hĕst′**) *n.* A command or an urgent request: *At the behest of the principal, no radios will be allowed in school.*

be•hind (bĭ **hīnd′**) *adv.* **1.** In a place or condition that has been passed or left: *I left my gloves behind.* **2.** In, to, or toward the rear: *They did not see me because I was walking behind.* **3.** In or into an inferior position; below the standard or acceptable level: *The sick student fell behind in the class.* *—prep.* **1.** At the back or in the rear of: *the shed behind the barn.* **2.** On the farther side of or on the other side of: *The broom is behind the door.* **3.** In a place or time that has been passed or left by: *Their worries are behind them.* **4.** In a state less advanced than: *Many nations are behind the United States in space technology.* **5.** In the background of; underlying: *Behind the theory there is much research and observation.* **6.** In support of: *Most of the people are behind the President.* **7.** In pursuit of: *The fox raced for the woods with the dogs fast behind it.* *—n.* *Informal.* The buttocks or backside. [First written down about 725 in Old English and spelled *behindan.*]

belfry

be•hind•hand (bĭ **hīnd′**hănd′) *adj.* Late; remiss or slow: *That tenant is always behindhand with the rent.*

be•hold (bĭ **hōld′**) *tr.v.* **be•held** (bĭ **hĕld′**), **be•hold•ing, be•holds.** To gaze upon; look at; see: *In a tomb the treasure hunters beheld a rich store of gold and jewels.* **—be•hold′er** *n.*

be•hold•en (bĭ **hōl′**dən) *adj.* Indebted: *We were beholden to our neighbors for shelter in the storm.*

be•hoove (bĭ **ho͞ov′**) *tr.v.* **be•hooved, be•hoov•ing, be•hooves.** To be necessary or proper for: *It behooves you to study for the test.*

beige (bāzh) *n.* A light grayish or yellowish brown. *—adj.* Light grayish or yellowish brown.

Bei•jing (**bā′jĭng′**) also **Pe•king** (**pē′kĭng′** *or* **pā′-kĭng′**). The capital of China, in the northeast part of the country. It was founded in about 700 B.C. Population, 5,860,000.

be•ing (**bē′**ĭng) *n.* **1.** The state or quality of existing; existence: *Rock 'n' roll music came into being in the 1950's.* **2.** A living organism, especially a person.

Bei•rut (bā **ro͞ot′**). The capital and largest city of Lebanon, in the western part of the country on the Mediterranean Sea. Population, 509,000.

be•jew•eled (bĭ **jo͞o′**əld) *adj.* Decorated with jewels.

bel (bĕl) *n.* A unit for measuring the difference in intensity of sounds, equal to ten decibels. [First written down in 1929 in Modern English, after Alexander Graham *Bell* (1847–1922), Scottish-born American inventor.]

be•la•bor (bĭ **lā′**bər) *tr.v.* **be•la•bored, be•la•bor•ing, be•la•bors. 1.** To attack with blows; beat. **2.** To attack verbally; assail: *The lawyer belabored the witness's testimony.* **3.** To go over repeatedly; harp on: *The audience got bored as the politician belabored the point.*

be•lat•ed (bĭ **lā′**tĭd) *adj.* Tardy; too late: *belated birthday wishes.* **—be•lat′ed•ly** *adv.* **—be•lat′ed•ness** *n.*

Be•lau (bə **lou′**) also **Pa•lau** (pə **lou′**) or **Pe•lew** (pə **lo͞o′**). A group of volcanic islands and islets in the Caroline Islands of the western Pacific Ocean. In 1978 Belau formed a republic administered by the United States.

be•lay (bĭ **lā′**) *v.* **be•layed, be•lay•ing, be•lays.** *—tr.* **1.** To secure (a rope) around a belaying pin. **2.** To secure (a mountain climber) with a rope. **3.** To cause to stop: *Belay that order, ensign!* *—intr.* Used in the imperative as an order to stop: *Belay there!*

be•lay•ing pin (bĭ **lā′**ĭng) *n.* A pin on the rail of a ship used to secure ropes.

belch (bĕlch) *v.* **belched, belch•ing, belch•es.** *—intr.* **1.** To expel gas noisily from the stomach through the mouth; burp. **2.** To gush forth; pour out: *smoke belching from the truck's exhaust.* *—tr.* To send out or eject (smoke or flames) violently: *The burning house belched smoke from its windows.* *—n.* The act or an instance of belching: *The old car stopped with a belch of smoke.* [First written down about 950 in Old English and spelled *bilkettan.*]

bel•dam or **bel•dame** (**bĕl′**dəm *or* **bĕl′**dăm) *n.* An old woman, especially one considered ugly.

be•lea•guer (bĭ **lē′**gər) *tr.v.* **be•lea•guered, be•lea•guer•ing, be•lea•guers. 1.** To surround with troops; besiege: *The king's troops beleaguered the city until the rebels surrendered.* **2.** To persecute constantly, as by threats or demands; harass: *During the power outage the electric company was beleaguered by its customers.* [First written down in 1589 in Modern English, probably from Dutch *belegeren* : *be-,* around + *leger,* camp.]

Bel•fast (**bĕl′**făst′ *or* bĕl **făst′**). The capital and largest city of Northern Ireland, in the eastern part of the country. Religious conflict has divided the city since the 19th century. Population, 318,600.

bel•fry (**bĕl′**frē) *n., pl.* **bel•fries. 1.** A tower or steeple in which one or more bells are hung. **2.** The part of a steeple in which the bells are hung.

Bel•gian (**bĕl′**jən) *adj.* Of or relating to Belgium or its people or culture. —*n.* A native or inhabitant of Belgium.

Bel•gium (**bĕl′**jəm). A country of northwest Europe on the North Sea north of France. It is culturally divided into the Dutch-speaking area north of Brussels and the French-speaking area to the south. Brussels is the capital and the largest city. Population, 9,858,017.

Bel•grade (**bĕl′**grăd′ *or* **bĕl′**gräd′). The capital and largest city of Serbia and of Yugoslavia, in the north-central part of Serbia on the Danube River. It was founded in the third century B.C. Population, 936,200.

Be•li•al (**bē′**lē əl *or* **bēl′**yəl) *n.* In the Bible, the personification of wickedness.

be•lie (bĭ **lī′**) *tr.v.* **be•lied, be•ly•ing, be•lies. 1.** To give a wrong or false idea of: *A cheerful greeting belied the clerk's grumpy mood.* **2.** To be inconsistent with; contradict: *The store's deceitful practices belied its good reputation.*

be•lief (bĭ **lēf′**) *n.* **1.** Mental acceptance or conviction of the truth or existence of something: *His explanation of what happens defies belief.* **2.** The mental act or condition of placing trust or confidence in a person: *My belief in you is as strong as ever.* **3.** Something believed or accepted as true, especially by a group of people: *We sometimes take our beliefs for granted until we meet someone who does not share them.*

be•lieve (bĭ **lēv′**) *v.* **be•lieved, be•liev•ing, be•lieves.** —*tr.* **1.** To accept as true or real: *Everyone believes matter is made of atoms.* **2.** To credit with trust; trust: *I believe you.* **3.** To expect or suppose; think: *I believe it will snow tomorrow.* —*intr.* **1.** To have faith, trust, or confidence: *believe in God; believe in getting plenty of sleep.* **2.** To have an opinion; think: *They have already left, I believe.* [First written down about 1000 in Old English and spelled *belȳfan.*] —**be•liev′a•ble** *adj.* —**be•liev′er** *adj.*

be•lit•tle (bĭ **lĭt′**l) *tr.v.* **be•lit•tled, be•lit•tling, be•lit•tles.** To represent or speak of as small or unimportant; disparage: *Don't belittle their efforts just because they are children.*

Be•lize (bə **lēz′**). Formerly **Brit•ish Hon•du•ras** (**brĭt′**ĭsh hŏn **do͝or′**əs *or* **brĭt′**ĭsh hŏn **dyo͝or′**əs). A country of Central America on the Caribbean Sea east of Guatemala. Belize gained its independence from Great Britain in 1981. Belmopan is the capital. Population, 145,353.

bell (bĕl) *n.* **1.** A hollow metal instrument, usually cup-shaped with a flared opening, that makes a metallic tone when struck. **2.** Something having a flared opening like that of a bell: *the bell of a trumpet.* **3. bells.** A musical instrument consisting of a set of metal tubes that emit tones when struck. **4.a.** A stroke of a bell to mark the half-hour aboard a ship. **b.** The time indicated by the striking of a bell. **5.** A diving bell. —*v.* **belled, bell•ing, bells.** —*tr.* To put a bell on: *bell a cat that lives outdoors.* —*intr.* To flare like a bell: *pants that bell below the knee.* [First written down before 900 in Old English and spelled *belle.*]

❑ *These sound alike:* **bell, belle** (girl or woman).

Bell (bĕl), **Alexander Graham.** 1847–1922. Scottish-born American inventor of the telephone. The first demonstration of the telephone took place in 1876.

bel•la•don•na (bĕl′ə **dŏn′**ə) *n.* **1.** A poisonous plant of Europe and Asia, having purplish bell-shaped flowers and small black berries; deadly nightshade. **2.** A medicinal substance containing the drug atropine and derived from this plant. [First written down in 1597 in Modern English, from Italian : *bella*, beautiful + *donna*, lady.]

bell-bot•tom (**bĕl′**bŏt′əm) *adj.* Having legs that flare out at the bottom: *bell-bottom trousers.*

bell-bot•toms (**bĕl′**bŏt′əmz) *pl.n.* Trousers that flare out at the bottom.

bell•boy (**bĕl′**boi′) *n.* A bellhop.

belle (bĕl) *n.* A very attractive and much-admired girl or woman, especially the most attractive one of a group: *the belle of the ball.*

❑ *These sound alike:* **belle, bell** (musical instrument).

belles-let•tres (bĕl **lĕt′**rə) *pl.n.* *(used with a singular verb).* Literature regarded for its artistic value rather than for its information or teaching content.

bell•flow•er (**bĕl′**flou′ər) *n.* Any of various plants having bell-shaped, usually purplish-blue flowers.

bell•hop (**bĕl′**hŏp′) *n.* A person employed by a hotel to carry luggage, run errands, and do other chores.

bel•li•cose (**bĕl′**ĭ kōs′) *adj.* Warlike in manner or disposition; belligerent: *a bellicose nation.* —**bel′li•cos′i•ty** (bĕl′ĭ **kŏs′**ĭ tē) *n.*

bel•lig•er•ence (bə **lĭj′**ər əns) *n.* A warlike or hostile attitude, nature, or disposition.

bel•lig•er•en•cy (bə **lĭj′**ər ən sē) *n.* **1.** The state of being at war or engaged in a conflict. **2.** Belligerence.

bel•lig•er•ent (bə **lĭj′**ər ənt) *adj.* **1.** Inclined to fight; hostile; aggressive: *a belligerent bully.* **2.** Of, relating to, or engaged in warfare: *a belligerent nation.* —*n.* A person, group, or nation engaged in war or a conflict. —**bel•lig′er•ent•ly** *adv.*

bell jar *n.* A large bell-shaped glass container with an open bottom, used to protect delicate instruments and in experiments to provide a space that is sealed off from the atmosphere.

bel•low (**bĕl′**ō) *v.* **bel•lowed, bel•low•ing, bel•lows.** —*intr.* **1.** To roar as a bull does. **2.** To shout in a deep loud voice. —*tr.* To utter in a loud voice: *The crowd bellowed its disapproval of the umpire's call.* —*n.* **1.** The loud roaring sound made by a bull or certain other large animals. **2.** A loud deep shout or cry.

bel•lows (**bĕl′**ōz *or* **bĕl′**əz) *pl.n.* *(used with a singular or plural verb).* A device for pumping air, consisting of a chamber with openings controlled by valves so that air enters at one opening and leaves at another as the chamber is forced to expand and contract.

bell•weth•er (**bĕl′**wĕ*th′*ər) *n.* A person or thing that leads or begins something else: *The fall of the Berlin wall was the bellwether of a new era.*

bel•ly (**bĕl′**ē) *n., pl.* **bel•lies. 1.** In human beings and other mammals, the front part of the body below the chest; the abdomen. **2.** The stomach. **3.** The underside of the body of certain vertebrates, such as snakes and fish. **4.** A part that bulges or protrudes: *the belly of a sail.* **5.** The deep hollow interior of something: *in the hold of a ship's belly.* —*intr. & tr.v.* **bel•lied, bel•ly•ing, bel•lies.** To swell; bulge: *The sails bellied in the breeze.* [First written down about 700 in Old English and spelled *bælg*, bag.]

bel•ly•ache (**bĕl′**ē āk′) *n.* Pain in the stomach or abdomen. —*intr.v.* **bel•ly•ached, bel•ly•ach•ing, bel•ly•aches.** *Slang.* To grumble or complain, especially in a whining way. —**bel′ly•ach′er** *n.*

bel•ly•band (**bĕl′**ē bănd′) *n.* A band passed around the belly of an animal to secure something, such as a saddle.

bel•ly•but•ton (**bĕl′**ē bŭt′n) *n.* *Informal.* The navel.

bel•ly-land (**bĕl′**ē lănd′) *intr.v.* **bel•ly-land•ed, bel•ly-land•ing, bel•ly-lands.** To land an airplane on its underside without the aid of landing gear. —**belly landing** *n.*

belly laugh *n.* A deep laugh.

Bel•mo•pan (bĕl′mō **păn′**). The capital of Belize, in

Alexander Graham Bell

Calling Chicago from New York, 1892

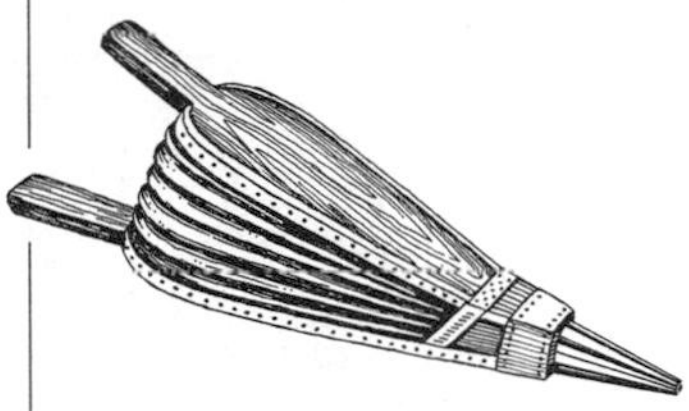

bellows

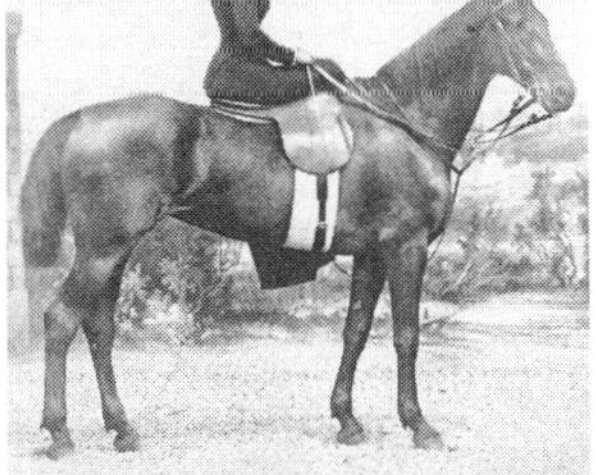

bellyband

ă	pat	oi	boy
ā	pay	ou	out
âr	care	o͝o	took
ä	father	o͞o	boot
ĕ	pet	ŭ	cut
ē	be	ûr	urge
ĭ	pit	th	thin
ī	pie	*th*	this
îr	pier	hw	whoop
ŏ	pot	zh	vision
ō	toe	ə	about
ô	paw	N	*French* bon

the north-central part of the country. It became the capital in 1970. Population, 2,935.

be•long (bĭ **lông′** *or* bĭ **lŏng′**) *intr.v.* **be•longed, be•long•ing, be•longs. 1.a.** To be proper or suitable: *A napkin belongs at every place setting.* **b.** To be in proper or suitable place: *The suit belongs in the closet.* **2.** To be owned as property: *This watch belonged to my grandmother.* **3.** To be a member of a group: *Many workers belong to this labor union.*

be•long•ings (bĭ **lông′**ĭngz *or* bĭ **lŏng′**ĭngz) *pl.n.* The things that belong to someone; possessions: *We took all of our belongings when we moved out of state.*

Be•lo•rus•sia (bĕl′ō **rŭsh′**ə) also **Bye•lo•rus•sia** (byĕl′ō **rŭsh′**ə). A region of Eastern Europe east of Poland, south of Lithuania and Latvia, and north of the Ukraine. It was a part of the Soviet Union from 1922 to 1991. Population, 9,942,000.

be•lov•ed (bĭ **lŭv′**ĭd *or* bĭ **lŭvd′**) *adj.* Dearly loved: *the parents' beloved children.* —*n.* A person who is dearly loved.

be•low (bĭ **lō′**) *adv.* **1.** In or to a lower place or level: *They paused on the bridge to admire the rapids below.* **2.** On or to a lower floor or deck: *The trunks were stowed in a compartment below.* **3.** Further down, as along a slope or stream: *There is a cabin in the valley below.* **4.** Following or farther down on a page: *A diagram is printed below with an explanation.* **5.** In a lower rank or class: *a decision of the courts below.* **6.** On earth: *all creatures here below.* —*prep.* **1.** Underneath; beneath: *We stood at the window watching the street below us.* **2.** Lower than, as in degree or rank: *temperatures below zero.* **3.** Unworthy of: *actions below contempt.* [First written down about 1325 in Middle English and spelled *biloghe* : *bi*, by + *loghe*, low.]

belt (bĕlt) *n.* **1.** A band of leather, cloth, or plastic worn around the waist to hold up trousers, weapons, or tools, or to serve as decoration. **2.** A broad strip or band: *a belt of trees along the highway.* **3.** A seat belt. **4.** A band that passes over two or more wheels or pulleys to transmit motion from one to another or to convey objects: *A belt connects the car motor to the fan.* **5.** A geographical region that is distinctive in some specific way: *the corn belt.* —*tr.v.* **belt•ed, belt•ing, belts. 1.** To encircle with or as if with a belt: *The equator belts the earth.* **2.** To fasten with a belt: *The hikers belted canteens around their waists.* **3.** To strike; hit: *He belted three homeruns in one game.* **4.** *Slang.* To sing loudly: *The audience belted out our school song.* ***—idioms.*** **below the belt.** Not according to the rules; unfairly: *The candidate's false accusations were below the belt.* **tighten (one's) belt.** To become thrifty and frugal: *We can save money if we tighten our belts.* [First written down about 1000 in Old English, ultimately from Latin *balteus.*]

belt•ing (**bĕl′**tĭng) *n.* Material used to make belts.

be•lu•ga (bə **lo͞o′**gə) *n.* **1.** A large white sturgeon of the Black and Caspian seas, whose roe is used for caviar. **2.** A small white or grayish whale living in northern waters. [First written down in 1591 in Modern English and spelled *bellougina*, from Russian *byelukha*, white whale, and *byeluga*, sturgeon, both from *byeliĭ*, white.]

be•moan (bĭ **mōn′**) *tr.v.* **be•moaned, be•moan•ing, be•moans.** To mourn over; lament; grieve for: *bemoan one's fate.*

be•mused (bĭ **myo͞ozd′**) *adj.* **1.** Confused; bewildered: *bemused by all the conflicting opinions.* **2.** Lost in thought; preoccupied: *bemused with a math problem.*

bench (bĕnch) *n.* **1.** A long seat, often without a back, for two or more persons. **2.** A sturdy table on which a carpenter, shoemaker, or other skilled person works. **3.** The seat for judges in a courtroom. **4.** The office or position of a judge: *appointed to the bench.* **5.** The judge or judges on a court. **6.a.** The place where the members of an athletic team sit when they are not playing. **b.** The reserve players on an athletic team. —*tr.v.* **benched, bench•ing, bench•es.** To remove or keep (a player) from a game. [First written down about 725 in Old English and spelled *benc.*]

bench•mark (**bĕnch′**märk′) *n.* A surveyor's mark made on some stationary object, such as a boulder, used as a reference point in reckoning differences in elevation.

bend (bĕnd) *v.* **bent** (bĕnt), **bend•ing, bends.** —*tr.* **1.** To make curved or crooked: *Bend the wire around the post.* **2.** To turn or direct: *bend one's steps toward home; bend their attention to the problem.* **3.** To force to yield; subdue: *He bent his employees to his will.* **4.** To change deceptively; distort: *You must not bend the facts to fit a conclusion.* —*intr.* **1.** To become curved or crooked: *The saplings bent in the wind.* **2.** To incline the body; stoop: *I bent over to pick up the ball.* **3.** To deviate from a straight line: *The road bends to the right at the bridge.* **4.** To submit; yield: *bend to someone's wishes.* —*n.* **1.** A turn, curve, or bent part: *a bend in the river.* **2. bends.** A form of decompression sickness that is caused by the formation of nitrogen bubbles in the blood and tissues after a rapid reduction in the surrounding pressure and is marked by pain in the joints and abdomen. [First written down about 1000 in Old English and spelled *bendan.*]

be•neath (bĭ **nēth′**) *adv.* In a lower place; below: *On the top of the hill we looked down at the valley beneath.* —*prep.* **1.** Lower than; below: *Beneath the tall date trees they planted flowers.* **2.** Covered or concealed by: *Most oil lies beneath the ground.* **3.** Under the force, control, or influence of: *The supervisor has six workers beneath her.* **4.** Unworthy of: *Lying is beneath me.* [First written down in 854 in Old English and spelled *beneothan* : *be*, by + *neothan*, below.]

Ben•e•dic•tine (bĕn′ĭ **dĭk′**tĭn *or* bĕn′ĭ **dĭk′**tēn′) *n.* A Roman Catholic monk or nun belonging to the order founded around 529 by Saint Benedict of Nursia (A.D. 480?–547?). —**Ben′e•dic′tine** *adj.*

ben•e•dic•tion (bĕn′ĭ **dĭk′**shən) *n.* A blessing, especially one recited at the close of a religious service by a member of the clergy.

ben•e•fac•tor (**bĕn′**ə făk′tər) *n.* A person who gives financial or other aid.

be•nef•i•cence (bə **nĕf′**ĭ səns) *n.* **1.** The quality or condition of being kind or charitable. **2.** A charitable act or gift: *The contributor's beneficence was large enough to complete the church building.*

be•nef•i•cent (bə **nĕf′**ĭ sənt) *adj.* Doing or bringing about good. —**be•nef′i•cent•ly** *adv.*

ben•e•fi•cial (bĕn′ə **fĭsh′**əl) *adj.* Bringing benefit; advantageous: *Many bacteria are beneficial to human life.* —**ben′e•fi′cial•ly** *adv.* —**ben′e•fi′cial•ness** *n.*

ben•e•fi•ci•ar•y (bĕn′ə **fĭsh′**ē ĕr′ē *or* bĕn′ə **fĭsh′**ə rē) *n., pl.* **ben•e•fi•ci•ar•ies. 1.** A person who derives benefit from something: *We are all beneficiaries of the large new library.* **2.** A person who is designated to receive funds or property from an insurance policy or a will.

ben•e•fit (**bĕn′**ə fĭt) *n.* **1.** Something that is of help; an advantage: *The field trip was of great benefit to the students.* **2.** A payment or favorable allowance made in accordance with a wage agreement, an insurance policy, or a public assistance program: *Her new job's benefits include three weeks of paid vacation.* **3.** A theatrical performance or social event held to raise money for a cause. —*v.* **ben•e•fit•ed, ben•e•fit•ing, ben•e•fits** also **ben•e•fit•ted, ben•e•fit•ting, ben•e•fits.** —*tr.* To be helpful or beneficial to: *The clean-air program will benefit the environment.* —*intr.* To receive help; profit: *You can benefit from the example put up on the board.* [First written down before 1376 in Middle English and spelled *benfet,* from Latin *benefactum,* good deed, from *benefacere,* to do a service.]

benefit of the doubt *n.* A favorable judgment made in the absence of more complete information.

be•nev•o•lence (bə **nĕv′**ə ləns) *n.* **1.** An inclination to do good; kindliness; good will. **2.** A kindly act.

be•nev•o•lent (bə **nĕv′**ə lənt) *adj.* **1.** Characterized by doing good; kindly: *a benevolent king; a benevolent attitude.* **2.** Of, relating to, or organized for charitable purposes: *a benevolent fund.* —**be•nev′o•lent•ly** *adv.*

Ben•gal (bĕn **gôl′** *or* bĕng **gôl′**). A region of eastern India and Bangladesh. It was a province of India until 1947.

Ben•ga•li (bĕn **gô′**lē *or* bĕng **gô′**lē) *adj.* Of or relating to Bengal or its people, language, or culture. —*n.* **1.** A native or inhabitant of Bengal. **2.** The language of west Bengal and Bangladesh.

Ben•gha•zi (bĕn **gä′**zē *or* bĕng **gä′**zē). A city of northeast Libya east of Tripoli. It was a capital of Libya from 1951 to 1972. Population, 367,600.

Ben Gur•i•on (bĕn **gŏŏr′**ē ən), **David.** 1886–1973. Polish-born Israeli prime minister (1948–1953 and 1955–1963) who organized the resistance against the British after World War II.

be•night•ed (bĭ **nī′**tĭd) *adj.* In a state of moral or intellectual backwardness; unenlightened: *benighted prejudice.*

be•nign (bĭ **nīn′**) *adj.* **1.** Kind; gentle: *a benign face with a warm smile.* **2.** Mild; favorable: *a benign climate of the tropics.* **3.** Not seriously harmful or malignant: *Warts are benign growths.* [First written down before 1325 in Middle English and spelled *benigne,* from Latin *benignus.*]

be•nig•nant (bĭ **nĭg′**nənt) *adj.* **1.** Favorable; beneficial: *the benignant effects of education.* **2.** Kind and gracious: *a benignant attitude.*

be•nig•ni•ty (bĭ **nĭg′**nĭ tē) *n., pl.* **be•nig•ni•ties. 1.** The quality or condition of being benign: *a dynasty noted for the benignity of its rulers.* **2.** A kindly or gracious act.

Be•nin (bə **nĭn′** *or* bĕ **nēn′**). **1.** A former kingdom of western Africa, now part of Nigeria. **2.** Formerly **Da•ho•mey** (də **hō′**mē *or* dä ô **mā′**). A country of western Africa west of Nigeria. It gained its independence from France in 1960. Port-Novo is the capital. Population, 3,567,000.

ben•i•son (**bĕn′**ĭ zən *or* **bĕn′**ĭ sən) *n.* A blessing; a benediction.

Ben•ja•min (**bĕn′**jə mən). In the Bible, the younger son of Jacob and Rachel and the ancestor of one of the tribes of Israel.

bent (bĕnt) *v.* Past tense and past participle of **bend.** —*adj.* **1.** Curved or crooked: *a bent nail.* **2.** Resolved; determined: *a runner bent on becoming a champion.* —*n.* A tendency or an inclination: *a strong bent for studying science.*

be•numb (bĭ **nŭm′**) *tr.v.* **be•numbed, be•numb•ing, be•numbs.** To make numb; deprive of feeling: *Cold benumbed our fingers.*

ben•zene (**bĕn′**zēn′ *or* bĕn **zēn′**) *n.* A clear colorless liquid that burns easily and has the formula C_6H_6. It is derived from petroleum and used to make detergents, insect poisons, motor fuels, and other chemical products.

ben•zine (**bĕn′**zēn′ *or* bĕn **zēn′**) *n.* A colorless flammable mixture of liquid hydrocarbons that is distilled from petroleum and used in cleaning and dyeing and as a motor fuel.

ben•zo•ate of soda (**bĕn′**zō āt′) *n.* Sodium benzoate.

ben•zo•ic acid (bĕn **zō′**ĭk) *n.* A white crystalline acid having the formula $C_7H_6O_2$. It is used as an antiseptic, as a food preservative, and in perfumes.

ben•zo•in (**bĕn′**zō ĭn *or* **bĕn′**zoin′) *n.* Any of various fragrant resins that contain benzoic acid and that are obtained from certain trees of Southeast Asia. They are used in making perfumes, ointments, and cough medicines.

ben•zol (**bĕn′**zôl′ *or* **bĕn′**zōl′) *n.* Benzene.

be•queath (bĭ **kwēth′** *or* bĭ **kwēth′**) *tr.v.* **be•queathed, be•queath•ing, be•queathes. 1.** To leave or give (property) by will. **2.** To pass on or hand down: *One generation bequeaths its knowledge to the next.* [First written down about 750 in Old English and spelled *becwethan* : *be-,* about + *cwethan,* to speak.]

be•quest (bĭ **kwĕst′**) *n.* **1.** The act of bequeathing: *From her bequest, he inherited great wealth.* **2.** Something that is bequeathed in a will.

be•rate (bĭ **rāt′**) *tr.v.* **be•rat•ed, be•rat•ing, be•rates.** To scold severely; upbraid.

Ber•ber (**bûr′**bər) *n.* **1.** A member of several Muslim peoples of North Africa. **2.** Any of the languages of the Berbers. —**Ber′ber** *adj.*

be•reave (bĭ **rēv′**) *tr.v.* **be•reaved** or **be•reft** (bĭ **rĕft′**), **be•reav•ing, be•reaves.** To leave alone or desolate, especially by death: *The woman was bereaved by the death of her husband.* [First written down about 725 in Old English and spelled *bereafian.*] —**be•reave′ment** *n.*

be•reft (bĭ **rĕft′**) *v.* A past tense and a past participle of **bereave.** —*adj.* Deprived of something: *an act that left him bereft of dignity.*

be•ret (bə **rā′**) *n.* A round, soft, brimless cap of wool or felt. [First written down in 1827 in Modern English, from French *béret,* from Late Latin *birrus,* hooded cloak.]

berg (bûrg) *n.* An iceberg.

Ber•gen (**bûr′**gən *or* **bĕr′**gən). A city of southwest Norway on inlets of the North Sea. It was founded in about 1070. Population, 207,232.

ber•i•ber•i (**bĕr′**ē **bĕr′**ē) *n.* A disease of the nervous system, caused by a lack of vitamin B_1 and accompanied by partial paralysis of the hands and feet, a general weakness, and loss of weight. [First written down in 1703 in Modern English, from Singhalese, from *beri,* weakness.]

Ber•ing Sea (**bîr′**ĭng *or* **bâr′**ĭng). A northward extension of the Pacific Ocean between Siberia and Alaska, lying north of the Aleutian Islands and connected with the Arctic Ocean by the Bering Strait.

Bering Strait. A narrow stretch of water separating Alaska from Siberia. It is believed that the strait once formed a land bridge by which the original inhabitants of North America arrived from Asia.

Berke•ley (**bûrk′**lē). A city of western California north of Oakland. It was founded in 1853. Population, 102,724.

ber•ke•li•um (bər **kē′**lē əm *or* **bûrk′**lē əm) *n. Symbol* **Bk** A radioactive metallic element produced artificially from americium, curium, or plutonium. It has 9 isotopes with mass numbers ranging from 243 to 250 and half-lives ranging from 3 hours to 1,380 years. Atomic number 97. See table at **element.** [First written down in 1950 in Modern English, after *Berkeley,* California.]

Ber•lin (bûr **lĭn′**). The capital and largest city of Germany, in the northeast part of the country. It was divided between 1945 and 1990 into **East Berlin** and **West Berlin.** Population, 3,034,118.

berm (bûrm) *n.* **1.** A terrace formed by waves de-

David Ben Gurion

beret

ă	pat	oi	boy
ā	pay	ou	out
âr	care	ŏŏ	took
ä	father	ōō	boot
ĕ	pet	ŭ	cut
ē	be	ûr	urge
ĭ	pit	th	thin
ī	pie	*th*	this
îr	pier	hw	whoop
ŏ	pot	zh	vision
ō	toe	ə	about
ô	paw	N	*French* bon

positing sand and small rocks along the top of a beach. **2.** A bank of earth placed against the wall of a building to provide protection or insulation.

Ber•mu•da (bər **myo͞o′**də). A self-governing British colony made up of about 300 coral islands in the Atlantic Ocean southeast of Cape Hatteras. Hamilton, on **Bermuda Island,** is the capital. Population, 56,000.

Bermuda shorts *pl.n.* Shorts that end slightly above the knees. [First written down in 1953 in Modern English, after *Bermuda.*]

Bern or **Berne** (bûrn *or* bĕrn). The capital of Switzerland, in the west-central part of the country. It was founded in 1191. Population, 140,600.

ber•ry (**bĕr′**ē) *n., pl.* **ber•ries. 1.** A usually small juicy fruit having many seeds in fleshy pulp. **2.** A seed or dried kernel of certain kinds of grain or other plants such as wheat, barley, or coffee. *—intr. v.* **ber•ried, ber•ry•ing, ber•ries.** To hunt for or gather berries. [First written down about 1000 in Old English and spelled *berie.*]

❑ *These sound alike:* **berry, bury** (cover with earth).

ber•serk (bər **sûrk′** *or* bər **zûrk′**) *adj. & adv.* In or into a crazed or violent frenzy.

berth (bûrth) *n.* **1.** A built-in bed or bunk in a ship or train. **2.** A space at a wharf for a ship to dock or anchor. **3.** A job or position: *have a berth on the U.S. Olympic Team.* *—v.* **berthed, berth•ing, berths.** *—tr.* **1.** To bring (a ship) to a berth. **2.** To provide with a berth. *—intr.* To come to a berth; dock: *berth at a pier along the river.*

❑ *These sound alike:* **berth, birth** (act of being born).

ber•yl (**bĕr′**əl) *n.* A transparent to translucent mineral of varied colors that is a silicate of beryllium and aluminum. It is the chief source of beryllium. Transparent varieties, such as emeralds and aquamarines, are valued as gems.

be•ryl•li•um (bə **rĭl′**ē əm) *n. Symbol* **Be** A grayish-white, hard, light, metallic element found in various minerals, having chemical properties similar to those of magnesium. Beryllium is used to make sturdy light alloys and to control the speed of neutrons in atomic reactors. Atomic number 4. See table at **element.**

be•seech (bĭ **sēch′**) *tr.v.* **be•sought** (bĭ **sôt′**) or **be•seeched, be•seech•ing, be•seech•es.** To ask earnestly; entreat; implore: *beseech the authorities for help.* **—be•seech′ing•ly** *adv.*

be•seem (bĭ **sēm′**) *tr.v.* **be•seemed, be•seem•ing, be•seems.** *Archaic.* To be appropriate for; befit.

be•set (bĭ **sĕt′**) *tr.v.* **be•set, be•set•ting, be•sets. 1.** To trouble persistently; harass: *beset by doubts about the right course to follow.* **2.** To attack from all sides: *Enemy troops beset the fort.* **3.** To hem in; surround: *Rising floodwaters beset the town.*

be•set•ting (bĭ **sĕt′**ĭng) *adj.* Constantly troubling: *besetting problems.*

be•side (bĭ **sīd′**) *prep.* **1.** At the side of; next to: *The cat sat down beside the radiator.* **2.** In comparison with: *The movie version is quite short beside the book.* **3.** Not relevant to: *a remark that was beside the point.* **4.** In addition to: *Three people beside me were waiting for the bus.* **—*idiom.* beside (oneself).** In a state of extreme excitement or emotion: *The winners were beside themselves with joy.*

be•sides (bĭ **sīdz′**) *adv.* **1.** In addition; also: *We had dinner and a late-night snack besides.* **2.** Moreover; furthermore: *It was time to go; besides, I was getting bored.* *—prep.* **1.** In addition to: *Dentists do other things besides drilling cavities.* **2.** Other than; except for: *There's nothing to eat here besides a little cheese.* —SEE NOTE at **together.**

Synonyms: **besides, too, also, likewise, furthermore.** These adverbs mean in addition to something else. **Besides** often introduces something that reinforces what has gone before it: *We don't feel like cooking; besides, there is no food in the house.* **Too** is the most casual, used in everyday speech: *If you're going to the library today, I'd like to go too.* **Also** is more formal than **too**: *Al is usually very friendly, but he is also capable of bearing a grudge.* **Likewise** is even more formal: *Their parents were likewise attending the ceremony.* **Furthermore** often stresses the clause following it as more important than the preceding clause: *I don't want you to go to that place; furthermore, I forbid it.*

---

be•siege (bĭ **sēj′**) *tr.v.* **be•sieged, be•sieg•ing, be•sieg•es. 1.** To surround and blockade in order to capture; lay siege to: *The king's troops besieged the city until it surrendered.* **2.** To crowd around and hem in: *A crowd of fans besieged the movie star.* **3.** To harass, as with requests: *The reporters besieged the police for information.* **—be•sieg′er** *n.*

be•smirch (bĭ **smûrch′**) *tr.v.* **be•smirched, be•smirch•ing, be•smirch•es.** To soil or tarnish; stain: *besmirch someone's good name by repeating slanderous remarks.*

be•sought (bĭ **sôt′**) *v.* A past tense and a past participle of **beseech.**

be•spat•ter (bĭ **spăt′**ər) *tr.v.* **be•spat•tered, be•spat•ter•ing, be•spat•ters.** To spatter with or as if with mud.

be•speak (bĭ **spēk′**) *tr.v.* **be•spoke** (bĭ **spōk′**), **be•spo•ken** (bĭ **spō′**kən) or **be•spoke, be•speak•ing, be•speaks.** To be or give a sign of; indicate: *a shake of the head that bespoke disbelief.*

be•spec•ta•cled (bĭ **spĕk′**tə kəld) *adj.* Wearing eyeglasses.

be•spoke (bĭ **spōk′**) *v.* Past tense and a past participle of **bespeak.**

be•spo•ken (bĭ **spō′**kən) *v.* A past participle of **bespeak.**

be•sprin•kle (bĭ **sprĭng′**kəl) *tr.v.* **be•sprin•kled, be•sprin•kling, be•sprin•kles.** To sprinkle.

Bes•se•mer converter (**bĕs′**ə mər) *n.* A large pear-shaped container in which molten iron is converted to steel by the Bessemer process.

Bessemer process *n.* A method for making steel by forcing compressed air through molten iron to burn out excess carbon and impurities. [First written down in 1856 in Modern English and spelled *Bessemer's process*, after Sir Henry *Bessemer* (1813–1898), British inventor.]

best (bĕst) *adj.* Superlative of **good, well**[2]. **1.** Surpassing all others in excellence, quality, or achievement: *the best singer in the choir.* **2.** Most satisfactory, suitable, or useful: *the best place to dig a well.* **3.** Largest or greatest: *We talked for the best part of the journey.* *—adv.* Superlative of **well**[2]. **1.** In the most excellent way; most properly or successfully: *Which of the three jackets fits best?* **2.** To the greatest degree or extent; most: *What do you like to eat best?* *—n.* **1.** A person or thing that surpasses all others: *That skier is surely the best in the race.* **2.** The best part or value: *The best is yet to come.* **3.** One's best effort or appearance: *do your best; look your best.* **4.** One's nicest clothing: *She put on her best and went to the dance.* **5.** One's warmest wishes or regards: *Give them my best.* *—tr.v.* **best•ed, best•ing, bests.** To get the better of; defeat: *besting their rivals in every game.* **—*idioms.* at best. 1.** Viewed most favorably; at the most: *There were 20 people in the theater at best.* **2.** Under the most favorable conditions: *This car has a top speed of 40 miles per hour at best.* **for the**

best. With an ultimately positive or preferable result. **get the best of** or **have the best of.** To outdo or outwit; defeat: *Nobody's ever gotten the best of me at checkers.* [First written down about 725 in Old English and spelled *betst.*]

Best (bĕst), **Charles Herbert.** 1899–1978. American-born Canadian physiologist noted for his work on the discovery and uses of insulin.

bes•tial (bĕs′chəl *or* bēs′chəl) *adj.* **1.** Characteristic of a beast. **2.** Lacking reason or intelligence. **3.** Brutal; cruel. **—bes′tial•ly** *adv.*

bes•ti•al•i•ty (bĕs′chē ăl′ĭ tē *or* bēs′chē ăl′ĭ tē) *n., pl.* **bes•ti•al•i•ties. 1.** The quality or condition of being an animal or like an animal. **2.** Cruel conduct or a brutal act.

be•stir (bĭ stûr′) *tr.v.* **be•stirred, be•stir•ring, be•stirs.** To stir to action; rouse: *People are now beginning to bestir themselves about protecting the water supply.*

best man *n.* The chief attendant of the bridegroom at a wedding.

be•stow (bĭ stō′) *tr.v.* **be•stowed, be•stow•ing, be•stows.** To give or present, especially as a gift or an honor; confer: *bestowed awards on the best actors and plays each season.* **—be•stow′al** *n.*

be•strew (bĭ stro͞o′) *tr.v.* **be•strewed, be•strewed** or **be•strewn** (bĭ stro͞on′), **be•strew•ing, be•strews. 1.** To scatter (a surface) with things so as to cover it: *The crowd bestrewed the street with confetti.* **2.** To lie or be scattered over: *Dead leaves bestrewed the yard.*

be•stride (bĭ strīd′) *tr.v.* **be•strode** (bĭ strōd′), **be•strid•den** (bĭ strĭd′n), **be•strid•ing, be•strides.** To sit or stand on with one leg on each side; straddle: *bestride a horse.*

best•sell•er (bĕst′sĕl′ər) *n.* A product, such as a book, that is among those sold in the largest numbers.

best-sell•ing (bĕst′sĕl′ĭng) *adj.* Selling in the largest numbers at a given time: *a best-selling novel.*

bet (bĕt) *n.* **1.** An agreement usually between two people or groups that the one who has made an incorrect prediction about an event will give something, such as a sum of money, to the other. **2.** An object or amount of money risked in a wager; a stake. **3.** A person, an animal, or an event on which a wager is or can be made: *That horse is a good bet to win the race.* **4.** Something that is likely to bring about a desired result: *The short route is probably your best bet home.* —*v.* **bet** or **bet•ted, bet•ting, bets.** —*tr.* **1.** To risk (something) in a bet. **2.** To make a bet with (a person or group). **3.** To state with confidence, as in a bet: *I bet you did well on the exam.* —*intr.* To make or place a bet. ***—idiom.*** **you bet.** *Informal.* Of course; surely. [First written down in 1597 in Modern English.]

be•ta (bā′tə *or* bē′tə) *n.* **1.** The second letter of the Greek alphabet, written Β, β. In English it is represented as *B, b.* **2.** The second item in a series.

be•take (bĭ tāk′) *tr.v.* **be•took** (bĭ to͝ok′), **be•tak•en** (bĭ tā′kən), **be•tak•ing, be•takes.** To cause (oneself) to go or move: *They betook themselves to the distant kingdom.*

beta particle *n.* A high-speed electron or positron, especially one emitted by an atomic nucleus undergoing radioactive decay.

beta ray *n.* A stream of beta particles.

be•ta•tron (bā′tə trŏn′ *or* bē′tə trŏn′) *n.* A machine that accelerates electrons to very high velocities by a changing magnetic field.

be•tel (bēt′l) *n.* A climbing Asian plant whose leaves are chewed together with the betel nut for the stimulating effect produced. [First written down in 1553 in Modern English, from Portuguese, from Malayalam *vettila,* from Tamil *verrilai.*]

❑ *These sound alike:* **betel, beetle**[1] (insect), **beetle**[2] (mallet), **beetle**[3] (overhang).

Be•tel•geuse (bēt′l jo͞oz′) *n.* A bright-red variable star in the constellation Orion. [First written down in 1796 in Modern English, probably from Arabic *yad al-jawzā′.*]

betel nut *n.* The seed of a tropical Asian palm.

bête noire (bĕt nwär′) *n.* A person or thing that is particularly disliked.

be•think (bĭ thĭngk′) *tr.v.* **be•thought** (bĭ thôt′), **be•think•ing, be•thinks.** To remind (oneself); remember: *bethink oneself of one's duties.*

Beth•le•hem (bĕth′lĭ hĕm′). A town in the West Bank south of Jerusalem. It is the traditional birthplace of Jesus. Population, 25,000.

be•thought (bĭ thôt′) *v.* Past tense and past participle of **bethink.**

Be•thune (bə tho͞on′ *or* bə thyo͞on′), **Mary McLeod.** 1875–1955. American educator and reformer. In 1935 she founded the National Council of Negro Women, serving as its president until 1949. —SEE NOTE.

be•tide (bĭ tīd′) *tr.v.* **be•tid•ed, be•tid•ing, be•tides.** To happen to: *Woe betide anyone who is late for class.*

be•times (bĭ tīmz′) *adv.* In good time; early: *awake betimes.*

be•to•ken (bĭ tō′kən) *tr.v.* **be•to•kened, be•to•ken•ing, be•to•kens.** To be a sign of; point to: *Public concern betokens a new attitude about our environment.*

be•took (bĭ to͝ok′) *v.* Past tense of **betake.**

be•tray (bĭ trā′) *tr.v.* **be•trayed, be•tray•ing, be•trays. 1.** To give aid or information to an enemy of (a country, for example). **2.** To be disloyal to: *betray a friend; a corrupt politician betraying the confidence of the voters.* **3.** To make known in a breach of trust; divulge: *betray a secret.* **4.** To give evidence of; indicate: *The redness of her face betrayed her embarrassment over the mistake.* [First written down about 1280 in Middle English and spelled *bitrayen.*] **—be•tray′er** *n.*

be•tray•al (bĭ trā′əl) *n.* The act of betraying, especially through disloyalty and deception.

be•troth (bĭ trōth′ *or* bĭ trôth′) *tr.v.* **be•trothed, be•troth•ing, be•troths. 1.** To promise to give in marriage: *The princess was betrothed by her parents to marry the duke.* **2.** To promise to marry.

be•troth•al (bĭ trō′*th*əl *or* bĭ trô′thəl) *n.* A promise to marry; an engagement.

be•trothed (bĭ trō*th*d′ *or* bĭ trôtht′) *adj.* Engaged to be married. —*n.* A person to whom one is engaged to be married.

bet•ter[1] (bĕt′ər) *adj.* Comparative of **good. 1.** Greater in excellence or higher in quality than another of the same kind: *Which of the twins is the better skater?* **2.** More useful, suitable, or desirable: *I know a better way to go.* **3.** Larger; greater: *It took the better part of an hour to get there.* **4.** Healthier than before: *Many days passed before I began to feel better.* —*adv.* Comparative of **well**[2]. **1.** In a more excellent way: *He sings better than his father.* **2.** To a greater extent or larger degree: *I like fish better when it's broiled.* **3.** More: *The play was first performed better than 20 years ago.* —*n.* **1.** The superior of two: *Both are good, but which is the better?* **2.** A superior: *I leave the delicate work to my betters.* —*v.* **bet•tered, bet•ter•ing, bet•ters.** —*tr.* **1.** To surpass or exceed: *The old record stood until another athlete bettered it.* **2.** To make better; improve: *The purpose of education is to better ourselves.* —*intr.* To become better: *Conditions bettered with time.* ***—idioms.*** **better off.** In a better

Mary McLeod Bethune

Mary McLeod Bethune

Mary McLeod **Bethune** devoted her life to creating educational opportunities for Black American children. In 1904 she founded a small girls' school in Florida. Under her leadership, the school quickly grew, merging in 1923 with a boys' school to become Bethune–Cookman College. Here Bethune promoted her own educational philosophy, which stressed practical skills and morals rather than academic subjects. In 1935 Bethune founded the National Council of Negro Women, a political and social organization whose goals included integrating African-American history into the public school classroom and training Black women for leadership roles. Bethune also served as director of the Division of Negro Affairs for the National Youth Administration from 1936 to 1945 and as a special adviser to President Franklin D. Roosevelt.

ă	**pat**	oi	**boy**
ā	**pay**	ou	**out**
âr	**care**	o͝o	**took**
ä	**father**	o͞o	**boot**
ĕ	**pet**	ŭ	**cut**
ē	**be**	ûr	**urge**
ĭ	**pit**	th	**thin**
ī	**pie**	*th*	**this**
îr	**pier**	hw	**whoop**
ŏ	**pot**	zh	**vision**
ō	**toe**	ə	**about**
ô	**paw**	N	*French* **bon**

Usage: better[1]

The phrase *had better,* meaning "must, ought," is acceptable only as long as the *had* or *'d,* the contraction of *had,* is present. You can say *You had better do it* or *You'd better do it* but not *You better do it.*

Usage: between

When two people or objects are discussed, **between** is correct and **among** is wrong: *the friendship between Jill and Jane.* When more than two people or objects are involved, however, or when the number is unspecified, use **between** to suggest distinct individuals and **among** for a group or mass. *Friendships between peers* refers to separate friendships between individuals, but *friendship among peers* suggests a single group of friends.

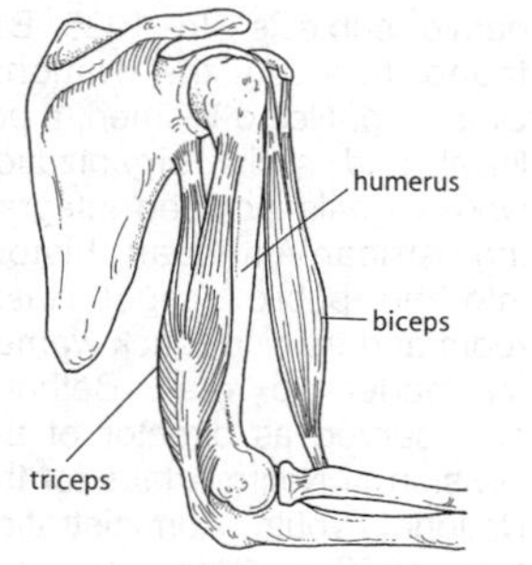

biceps

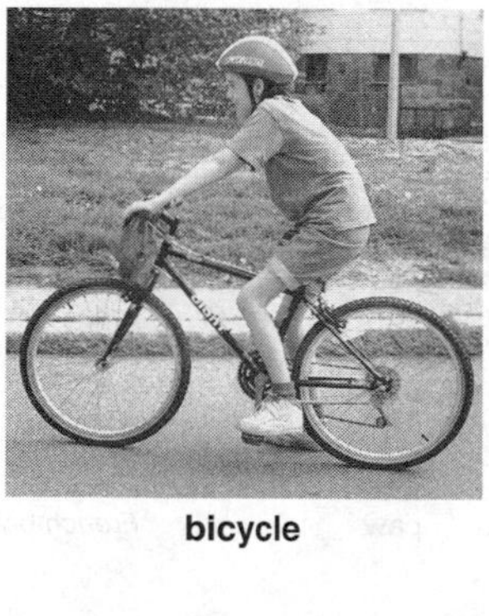
bicycle

condition: *With vaccines, people are better off than they were years ago.* **for the better.** Resulting in or aiming at an improvement. **had better.** Ought to; must: *We had better leave before dark.* [First written down about 725 in Old English and spelled *betera.*] —SEE NOTE.

❑ *These sound alike:* **better[1], bettor** (one who bets).

bet·ter[2] (bĕt′ər) *n.* Variant of **bettor.**

bet·ter·ment (bĕt′ər mənt) *n.* An improvement: *work for the betterment of our children.*

bet·tor also **bet·ter** (bĕt′ər) *n.* A person who bets.

❑ *These sound alike:* **bettor, better[1]** (greater).

be·tween (bĭ twēn′) *prep.* **1.a.** In or through the position or interval separating: *between the trees; between 11 and 12 o'clock; waters flowing between the banks.* **b.** Intermediate to, as in amount or degree: *costs between five and ten dollars.* **2.** Connecting over or through a space that is separating: *a long path between the cabin and the lake.* **3.** By the combined effect or effort of: *Between them, the friends finished the job.* **4.** In the combined ownership of: *We have ten dollars between us.* **5.** As measured against: *choose between milk and water; not much to choose between the two cars.* —*adv.* In an intermediate space, position, or time: *The plane went from New York to Los Angeles, and several cities between.* **—*idioms.* between you and me.** In the strictest confidence: *We can surprise the others if we keep the plans between you and me.* **in between.** In an intermediate situation: *There are two cities near each other, with a river running in between.* **in between times.** During an intervening period; in the meantime. [First written down about 750 in Old English and spelled *betwēonum.*] —SEE NOTE.

be·twixt (bĭ twĭkst′) *adv. & prep.* Between. **—*idiom.* betwixt and between.** In an intermediate position; neither wholly one thing nor another.

BeV *abbr.* An abbreviation of billion electron volts.

bev·el (bĕv′əl) *n.* **1.** A surface formed when two planes meet at a sloping edge. **2.** The angle at which these planes meet. **3.** A tool used to measure or mark such angles. —*tr.v.* **bev·eled, bev·el·ing, bev·els** or **bev·elled, bev·el·ling, bev·els.** To cut a bevel (on something): *bevel the edges of the picture frame.*

bev·er·age (bĕv′ər ĭj *or* bĕv′rĭj) *n.* A liquid for drinking, such as milk, tea, or juice, usually excluding water. [First written down about 1300 in Middle English, from Old French *bevrage,* from *beivre,* to drink, from Latin *bibere.*]

bev·y (bĕv′ē) *n., pl.* **bev·ies.** A group of animals or birds.

be·wail (bĭ wāl′) *tr.v.* **be·wailed, be·wail·ing, be·wails.** To express sorrow or regret over; bemoan: *bewail one's fate.*

be·ware (bĭ wâr′) *v.* **be·wared, be·war·ing, be·wares.** —*tr.* To watch out for; be on guard against: *Beware the smooth talk of the salesman.* —*intr.* To be cautious: *Beware of the dog.* [First written down about 1200 in Middle English and spelled *ben war,* to be on guard.]

be·wil·der (bĭ wĭl′dər) *tr.v.* **be·wil·dered, be·wil·der·ing, be·wil·ders.** To confuse greatly; puzzle. **—be·wil′dered·ly** *adv.* **—be·wil′der·ment** *n.*

be·witch (bĭ wĭch′) *tr.v.* **be·witched, be·witch·ing, be·witch·es. 1.** To cast a spell over: *The prince was bewitched by a fairy.* **2.** To captivate completely; fascinate; charm: *Her piano solo bewitched the audience.*

be·witch·ing (bĭ wĭch′ĭng) *adj.* Fascinating; enchanting: *a bewitching smile.* **—be·witch′ing·ly** *adv.*

bey (bā) *n.* **1.** A governor of a province in the former Ottoman Empire. **2.** A ruler of the former kingdom of Tunis.

❑ *These sound alike:* **bey, bay[1]** (body of water), **bay[2]** (part of a room), **bay[3]** (reddish brown), **bay[4]** (bark), **bay[5]** (laurel).

be·yond (bē ŏnd′ *or* bĭ yŏnd′) *prep.* **1.** On the far side of; past: *I planted carrots just beyond the fence.* **2.** To a degree or an amount greater than: *rich beyond his wildest dreams.* **3.** Later than: *Don't stay up beyond midnight.* **4.** Past the reach, scope, or understanding of: *beyond hope; beyond recall.* —*adv.* Farther along: *We walked under the trees into the bright sunlight beyond.* —*n.* The world beyond death; the hereafter. [First written down about 885 in Old English and spelled *begeondan.*]

Bho·pal (bō päl′). A city of central India south of Delhi. In 1984 a toxic gas leak at an insecticide plant here killed more than 2,000 people. Population, 671,018.

Bhu·tan (bo͞o tăn′ *or* bo͞o tän′). An isolated country of central Asia in the eastern Himalaya Mountains north of Bangladesh. Thimbu is the capital and the largest city. Population, 1,232,000.

Bi The symbol for the element **bismuth.**

bi–[1] or **bin–** *pref.* A prefix that means: **1.** Two: *bifocal.* **2.** Both sides, parts, or directions: *biconcave.* **3.** Occurring at intervals of two: *bicentennial.* **4.** Occurring twice during: *bimonthly.*

bi–[2] *pref.* Variant of **bio–.**

bi·a·ly (bē ä′lē) *n., pl.* **bia·lys.** A flat roll topped with onion flakes. [First written down in 1965 in Modern English, after *Bialystok,* in northeast Poland.]

bi·an·nu·al (bī ăn′yo͞o əl) *adj.* Happening twice each year; semiannual. **—bi·an′nu·al·ly** *adv.*

bi·as (bī′əs) *n.* **1.** The direction of a piece of fabric as it runs diagonal to the grain: *cut cloth on the bias.* **2.** A preference for or hostile feeling against a person or thing that interferes with impartial judgment; a prejudice. —*tr.v.* **bi·ased, bi·as·ing, bi·as·es** or **bi·assed, bi·as·sing, bi·as·ses.** To cause to have a bias: *His stubbornness biased the employer against him.*

bi·ased also **bi·assed** (bī′əst) *adj.* Marked by or showing bias; prejudiced.

bib (bĭb) *n.* **1.** A piece of cloth or plastic worn under the chin, especially by small children, to protect the clothes while eating. **2.** The part of an apron or a pair of overalls worn over the chest.

Bi·ble (bī′bəl) *n.* **1.** The sacred book of Christianity, a collection of ancient writings including the books of the Old Testament and the New Testament. **2.** The Hebrew Scriptures. **3.** The sacred writings of a religion: *The Koran is the Islamic Bible.* **4.** Often **bible.** A book considered authoritative in its field: *the bible of French cooking.* [First written down before 1325 in Middle English, from Greek *biblia,* plural of *biblion,* book.]

bib·li·cal also **Bib·li·cal** (bĭb′lĭ kəl) *adj.* Of, relating to, or in keeping with the nature of the Bible. **—bib′li·cal·ly** *adv.*

bib·li·o·graph·i·cal (bĭb′lē ə grăf′ĭ kəl) or **bib·li·o·graph·ic** (bĭb′lē ə grăf′ĭk) *adj.* Of or relating to bibliography: *the vast bibliographical resources of a great library.* **—bib′li·o·graph′i·cal·ly** *adv.*

bib·li·og·ra·phy (bĭb′lē ŏg′rə fē) *n., pl.* **bib·li·og·ra·phies. 1.** A list of the works of a specific author or publisher. **2.** A list of the writings on a specific subject: *a bibliography of Latin American history.* [First written down in 1678 in Modern English, from Greek *biblion,* book.]

bi·cam·er·al (bī kăm′ər əl) *adj.* Composed of two legislative branches or chambers: *The United States Congress is a bicameral legislature consisting of the*

Senate and the House of Representatives. [First written down before 1832 in Modern English : *bi-*, two + Latin *camera*, chamber.]

bi•car•bon•ate (bī kär′bə nāt′ *or* bī kär′bə nĭt) *n.* The radical HCO_3 or a compound, such as sodium bicarbonate, containing it.

bicarbonate of soda *n.* Sodium bicarbonate.

bi•cen•ten•ni•al (bī′sĕn tĕn′ē əl) *adj.* **1.** Relating to a 200th anniversary: *a bicentennial celebration.* **2.** Occurring once every 200 years. —*n.* A 200th anniversary or its celebration.

bi•ceps (bī′sĕps′) *n., pl.* **biceps** or **bi•ceps•es** (bī′-sĕp′sĭz). A muscle that has two points of attachment at one end, especially: **1.** The muscle at the front of the upper arm that bends the forearm. **2.** The muscle at the back of the thigh that bends the knee. [First written down in 1634 in Modern English, from Latin, *biceps*, two-headed : *bi-*, two + *caput*, head.]

bi•chlo•ride (bī klôr′īd) *n.* Dichloride.

bick•er (bĭk′ər) *intr.v.* **bick•ered, bick•er•ing, bick•ers.** To argue over an unimportant matter; squabble: *We bickered over whose turn it was to wash dishes.* —*n.* A petty quarrel; a squabble. **—bick′er•er** *n.*

bi•con•cave (bī′kŏn kāv′ *or* bī kŏn′kāv′) *adj.* Concave on both sides or surfaces: *a biconcave lens.*

bi•con•vex (bī′kŏn vĕks′ *or* bī kŏn′vĕks′) *adj.* Convex on both sides or surfaces: *a biconvex lens.*

bi•cus•pid (bī kŭs′pĭd) *adj.* Having two points or cusps, as a crescent moon. —*n.* A double-pointed premolar tooth that tears and grinds food. An adult human has eight bicuspids.

bi•cy•cle (bī′sĭk′əl *or* bī′sĭ kəl) *n.* A vehicle consisting of a light metal frame mounted on two wheels one behind the other and having a seat for the rider, who steers the front wheel by handlebars and pushes pedals that drive the rear wheel. —*intr.v.* **bi•cy•cled, bi•cy•cling, bi•cy•cles.** To ride on a bicycle: *I just bicycled down to the store.* **—bi′cy•cler, bi′cy•clist** *n.*

bid (bĭd) *v.* **bade** (băd *or* bād) or **bid, bid•den** (bĭd′-n) or **bid, bid•ding, bids.** —*tr.* **1.** To give a command to; direct: *The queen bid the courtiers to rise.* **2.** To request to come; invite: *The neighbors bid us to have tea with them.* **3.** To say or express (a greeting, wish, or farewell): *He bade us good night.* **4.** *past tense and past participle* **bid. a.** To offer (an amount of money) as a price for something: *The collector bid $5,000 for the antique desk.* **b.** To state one's intention to take (a certain number of tricks) in card games, as in bridge. —*intr.* **1.** *past tense and past participle* **bid.** To make an offer to pay a certain price: *We bid on the old lamp.* **2.** *past tense and past participle* **bid.** To try to win or achieve something: *Both candidates bid for election to Congress.* —*n.* **1.a.** An offer to pay a certain amount of money for something: *The auctioneer called for bids on the antique desk.* **b.** An amount bid: *He made a bid of $5,000.* **2.** A declaration of the number of tricks one expects to win in certain card games such as bridge: *My bid is three hearts.* **3.** An effort to win or attain something: *Several candidates made a bid for the Presidency.* [First written down about 725 in Old English and spelled *biddan.*] **—bid′der** *n.*

bid•ding (bĭd′ĭng) *n.* **1.** An order or a command: *Orchestras start to play at the conductor's bidding.* **2.** A request to appear; an invitation: *At my bidding, they accepted.* **3.** Bids considered as a group.

bid•dy (bĭd′ē) *n., pl.* **bid•dies.** A hen; a fowl.

bide (bīd) *tr. & intr.v.* **bid•ed** or **bode** (bōd), **bid•ed, bid•ing, bides.** To wait or wait for. —*idiom.* **bide (one's) time.** To wait for further developments: *If you bide your time, you too shall have a chance.*

bi•en•ni•al (bī ĕn′ē əl) *adj.* **1.** Lasting or living for two years: *biennial plants.* **2.** Occurring every second year: *biennial elections to Congress.* —*n.* A plant that grows and produces leaves in its first year and that flowers, produces seeds, and dies in its second year. Carrots are biennials. **—bi•en′ni•al•ly** *adv.*

bier (bîr) *n.* A stand on which a corpse or a coffin containing a corpse is placed before burial.

❑ *These sound alike:* **bier, beer** (alcoholic drink).

bi•fo•cal (bī fō′kəl *or* bī′fō′kəl) *adj.* **1.** Focusing light rays at two different points: *a bifocal lens.* **2.** Having one section that corrects for distant vision and another that corrects for near vision: *bifocal eyeglasses.* —*n.* **bi•fo•cals.** (bī fō′kəlz *or* bī′fō′-kəlz). A pair of eyeglasses having bifocal lenses to correct both near and distant vision.

big (bĭg) *adj.* **big•ger, big•gest. 1.** Of great size, number, quantity, or extent; large: *a big house; a big city; a big appetite.* See Synonyms at **large. 2.a.** Grown-up; adult: *Most big people are kind to young children.* **b.** Older: *Big brothers and sisters must look out for the little children in a family.* **3.** Prominent; influential: *a big banker.* **4.** Of great significance; momentous: *a big day in my life; practice for the big game.* **5.** Loud; resounding: *a big voice.* **6.** Full of self-importance; boastful: *a big talker.* —*adv.* With an air of self-importance; boastfully: *talk big about what one is going to do.* —*idiom.* **big on.** Enthusiastic about; partial to: *She's big on volleyball.* [First written down about 1300 in Middle English, perhaps of Scandinavian origin.] **—big′ness** *n.*

big•a•mist (bĭg′ə mĭst) *n.* A person who practices bigamy.

big•a•mous (bĭg′ə məs) *adj.* Guilty of bigamy.

big•a•my (bĭg′ə mē) *n., pl.* **big•a•mies.** The crime of marrying one person while still being legally married to another. [First written down about 1250 in Middle English and spelled *bigamie*, from Late Latin *bigamus*, twice married : Latin *bi-*, two + Greek *gamos*, marriage.]

big bang theory *n.* The theory that the universe originated in a cosmic explosion of an extremely hot dense mass of matter sometime between 10 and 20 billion years ago. —SEE NOTE.

big business *n.* Large businesses and industrial organizations considered as a group.

Big Dipper *n.* A group of seven stars in the constellation Ursa Major, four forming the bowl and three the handle in the shape of a dipper.

big-heart•ed (bĭg′här′tĭd) *adj.* Generous; kind. **—big′-heart′ed•ly** *adv.* **—big′-heart′ed•ness** *n.*

big•horn (bĭg′hôrn′) *n., pl.* **big•horn** or **big•horns.** A wild mountain sheep of western North America, having large curving horns in the male; the Rocky Mountain sheep.

bight (bīt) *n.* **1.a.** A loop in a rope. **b.** The middle or slack part of an extended rope. **2.a.** A long curve, especially in a shoreline. **b.** A wide bay formed by such a curve.

big league *n.* **1.** A major league in a professional sport, especially in baseball. **2.** *Informal.* The highest level of accomplishment in a field. Often used in the plural. **—big′-league′** *adj.*

big•ot (bĭg′ət) *n.* A person who is intolerant of people who are different, as in religion, race, or politics. [First written down in 1598 in Modern English, from Old French.]

big•ot•ed (bĭg′ə tĭd) *adj.* Characteristic of a bigot; intolerant; prejudiced.

big•ot•ry (bĭg′ə trē) *n.* The attitude or behavior of a bigot; intolerance.

big shot *n.* *Slang.* A very important person.

big time *n.* *Informal.* The highest level of attainment in a field, such as the arts, business, or sports.

big bang theory

For much of human history, most people believed that the universe was static and unchanging. But in the 1920's astronomers found that wherever we look in the sky, distant galaxies are moving rapidly away from us. In other words, the universe is expanding. At earlier times objects must have been closer together. By studying the speed of the galaxies' motion at various distances from the earth, astronomers learned that all galaxies began moving away from each other about 10 or 20 billion years ago. We can trace the expansion back to a time when the universe was infinitesimally small and infinitely dense. In the **big bang theory**, the universe began at that time as a big bang kicked off the expansion. The big bang was the origin of space and time.

bighorn

ă	pat	oi	boy
ā	pay	ou	out
âr	care	o͝o	took
ä	father	o͞o	boot
ĕ	pet	ŭ	cut
ē	be	ûr	urge
ĭ	pit	th	thin
ī	pie	*th*	this
îr	pier	hw	whoop
ŏ	pot	zh	vision
ō	toe	ə	about
ô	paw	N	*French* bon

big top

big top *n.* **1.** The main tent of a circus. **2.** The circus.
big tree *n.* The giant sequoia of the mountains of southern California.
big•wig (bĭg′wĭg′) *n. Slang.* An important person; a dignitary.
bike (bīk) *n.* **1.** A bicycle. **2.** A motorbike or motorcycle. —*intr.v.* **biked, bik•ing, bikes.** To ride a bike.
bik•er (bī′kər) *n.* A person who rides a bicycle, motorbike, or motorcycle.
bike•way (bīk′wā′) *n.* A lane or path for bicycles.
bi•ki•ni (bĭ kē′nē) *n.* **1.** A very brief two-piece bathing suit worn by women. **2.** A very brief bathing suit worn by men. [First written down in 1948 in Modern English, after *Bikini* Atoll in the Marshall Islands.]
bi•lat•er•al (bī lăt′ər əl) *adj.* **1.** Having two sides; two-sided. **2.** Affecting or undertaken by two sides: *a bilateral agreement.* **—bi•lat′er•al•ly** *adv.*
bilateral symmetry *n.* Arrangement along a central axis so that the body or body part is divided into two equivalent halves.
bile (bīl) *n.* **1.** A bitter, alkaline, greenish liquid that is produced by the liver and stored in the gallbladder. Bile aids digestion in the duodenum by neutralizing acids and emulsifying fats. **2.** Bitterness of temper; ill humor: *sarcastic remarks full of bile.*
bilge (bĭlj) *n.* **1.a.** The lowest inner part of a ship's hull. **b.** Bilgewater. **2.** The bulging part of a barrel. **3.** *Slang.* Stupid talk; nonsense. [First written down in 1513 in Modern English, possibly from *bulge.*]
bilge water *n.* Water that collects in the bilge of a ship.
bi•lin•gual (bī lĭng′gwəl) *adj.* **1.** Able to use two languages equally well: *Many diplomats are bilingual.* **2.** Of, relating to, or expressed in two languages: *a bilingual dictionary.* **—bi•lin′gual•ly** *adv.*
bil•ious (bĭl′yəs) *adj.* **1.** Of, relating to, or containing bile. **2.** Of, relating to, or characterized by an excess of bile. **3.** Relating to or suggestive of bilious distress or disease: *a bilious complexion.* **4.** Having a peevish disposition; ill-humored. **—bil′ious•ly** *adv.* **—bil′ious•ness** *n.*
bilk (bĭlk) *tr.v.* **bilked, bilk•ing, bilks.** To cheat, defraud, or swindle: *The art dealer bilked unsuspecting clients out of millions.*
bill[1] (bĭl) *n.* **1.** A statement of charges for goods supplied or work performed: *a telephone bill.* **2.** A piece of paper money worth a certain amount: *a ten-dollar bill.* **3.** The entertainment offered by a theater. **4.** An advertising poster: *Post no bills!* **5.** A draft of a law presented for approval to a legislature: *a conservation bill.* —*tr.v.* **billed, bill•ing, bills. 1.a.** To give or send a statement of charges to: *Bill me for the amount due.* **b.** To enter on a statement of charges; prepare a bill of: *Please bill these purchases to our account.* **2.** To advertise or schedule by public notice or as part of a program: *I see that the play is billed as a comedy.* [First written down in 1370 in Middle English and spelled *bille,* from Medieval Latin *bulla,* seal on a document.]

bill[2]
Of a pelican

bill[2] (bĭl) *n.* **1.** The horny projecting mouth parts of a bird; a beak. The bills of birds differ according to how they feed and what they eat. **2.** A part or projection resembling a bill. —*intr.v.* **billed, bill•ing, bills.** To touch beaks together. [First written down about 725 in Old English and spelled *bile.*]
bill•board (bĭl′bôrd′) *n.* A large upright board for the display of advertisements in public places or alongside highways.
bil•let (bĭl′ĭt) *n.* Lodging for soldiers in a civilian building such as a private house or hotel. —*v.* **bil•let•ed, bil•let•ing, bil•lets.** —*tr.* To house (soldiers), especially in civilian buildings: *The army billeted the soldiers in the village.* —*intr.* To be housed; lodge: *The soldiers billeted in an old farmhouse.*
bill•fold (bĭl′fōld′) *n.* A small case that folds flat, used for carrying paper money and personal documents, as in a pocket or handbag.
bil•liard (bĭl′yərd) *n.* A shot in billiards in which the cue ball strikes two balls; a carom.
bil•liards (bĭl′yərdz) *pl.n. (used with a singular verb).* **1.** A game played on a rectangular cloth-covered table with raised cushioned edges, in which a cue is used to hit three balls against one another or the side cushions of the table. **2.** One of several similar games, sometimes using a table with pockets, as in pool. [First written down in 1591 in Modern English, from French *billard,* from *bille,* log.]
bill•ing (bĭl′ĭng) *n.* The order in which performers' names are listed in programs, advertisements, and on theater marquees: *The two actors share top billing in the new play.*
bil•lion (bĭl′yən) *n.* **1.** The number, written as 10^9 or 1 followed by nine zeros, that is equal to one thousand times one million. **2.** *Chiefly British.* The number, written as 10^{12} or 1 followed by 12 zeros, that is equal to one million times one million. [First written down in 1690 in Modern English, from French, a million million : blend of *bi-,* two, twice, and *million,* million.] **—bil′lionth** *n.*
bil•lion•aire (bĭl′yə nâr′) *n.* A person whose wealth amounts to at least a billion dollars, pounds, or similar units in another currency.
bill of exchange *n., pl.* **bills of exchange.** A written order directing that a specified sum of money be paid to a particular person.
bill of fare *n., pl.* **bills of fare.** A menu.
bill of health *n., pl.* **bills of health.** A certificate stating whether there is infectious disease aboard a ship or in a port of departure, given to the ship's master for presentation at the next port of arrival. **—*idiom.* clean bill of health.** *Informal.* A good report based on a past record or condition.
bill of lading *n., pl.* **bills of lading.** A document listing and acknowledging receipt of goods for shipment.
bill of rights *n., pl.* **bills of rights. 1.** A formal statement of those rights and liberties considered essential to a people or group of people: *a consumer bill of rights.* **2.** Also **Bill of Rights.** The first ten amendments to the Constitution of the United States, guaranteeing certain rights and privileges to citizens, as freedom of speech.
bill of sale *n., pl.* **bills of sale.** A document that transfers ownership of something to a new owner.
bil•low (bĭl′ō) *n.* **1.** A great wave or surge of water. **2.** A great swell or mass of something: *billows of smoke.* —*v.* **bil•lowed, bil•low•ing, bil•lows.** —*intr.* **1.** To rise or surge in or as if in billows: *Flames and smoke billowed through the whole building.* **2.** To swell out; bulge: *At the open window there were curtains billowing in the wind.* —*tr.* To cause to swell out: *The wind billowed the ship's sails.* [First written down in 1552 in Modern English, from Old Norse *bylgja,* a wave.] **—bil′low•y** *adj.*
bil•ly (bĭl′ē) *n., pl.* **bil•lies.** A billy club.
billy club *n.* A short wooden club, especially one carried by a police officer on patrol.
billy goat *n. Informal.* A male goat.
bi•month•ly (bī mŭnth′lē) *adj.* **1.** Occurring once every two months: *There are six bimonthly meetings of the club each year.* **2.** Occurring twice a month. —*adv.* **1.** Once every two months. **2.** Twice a month: *Many businesses pay bimonthly, on the first and the fifteenth.* —*n., pl.* **bi•month•lies.** A publication issued bimonthly. —SEE NOTE at **bi-weekly.**

bin (bĭn) *n.* An enclosed space for storing food, grain, coal, or other dry substances.
❑ *These sound alike:* **bin, been** (existed).

bin– *pref.* Variant of **bi–**[1].

bi•na•ry (bī′nə rē) *adj.* **1.** Of, relating to, or based on the number 2 or the binary number system: *a binary numeral.* **2.** Consisting of or involving two different parts, kinds, or things: *a binary chemical compound.* —*n., pl.* **bi•na•ries.** A binary star. [First written down before 1464 in Middle English and spelled *binarie,* from Latin *bīnī,* two by two.]

binary digit *n.* Either of the digits 0 or 1, used in the binary number system; a bit. The binary digit is the basic unit of computer information.

binary number system *n.* A method of representing numbers as sums of powers of 2, in which all numbers can be written using only the two digits 0 and 1.

binary star *n.* A pair of stars that revolves around a common center of gravity, often appearing through a telescope as a single star.

bin•au•ral (bī nôr′əl *or* bĭn ôr′əl) *adj.* **1.** Of, having, or hearing with two ears. **2.** Of or relating to sound transmission or reception by two paths or channels; stereophonic.

bind (bīnd) *v.* **bound** (bound), **bind•ing, binds.** —*tr.* **1.** To fasten, tie, or secure by tying, as with a rope or cord: *bind a package with string; bind a prisoner in chains.* **2.** To bandage: *bound their wounds.* **3.** To cause to stick together in a mass: *Cement binds gravel to make concrete for paving roads.* **4.** To hold or restrain with or as if with bonds: *traditions that bind people to a way of life.* **5.** To compel, obligate, or unite: *Duty binds me to remain at my post.* **6.** To place under legal obligation: *The terms of the contract bind the author and the publisher.* **7.** To hold or employ as an apprentice or a servant; indenture: *The young man was bound out as a servant.* **8.** To cover with a border or edging for added protection or decoration: *bind a seam with tape.* **9.** To enclose and fasten between covers: *bind a book.* —*intr.* **1.** To be tight and uncomfortable: *Once a sweater shrinks it binds.* **2.** To become compact or solid; stick together: *Cement will not bind without water.* **3.** To stick or become stuck: *Will that glue bind to glass?* **4.** To be compelling or unifying: *We have family ties that bind.* —*n. Informal.* A difficult or confining situation: *He was in a bind when his car broke down.* [First written down about 725 in Old English and spelled *bindan.*]

bind•er (bīn′dər) *n.* **1.** A person who binds books. **2.** A notebook cover with rings for holding sheets of paper. **3.** Something used to tie or fasten, such as cord or rope. **4.** A material added to something to make it hold together: *Water is a binder in bread dough.* **5.** A farm machine that reaps and ties grain. **6.** A payment or written statement making an agreement legally binding until the completion of a contract, especially an insurance contract.

bind•er•y (bīn′də rē) *n., pl.* **bind•er•ies.** A place where books are bound.

bind•ing (bīn′dĭng) *n.* **1.** The cover that holds together the pages of a book. **2.** A strip of tape or fabric sewn over an edge or a seam to protect or decorate it. —*adj.* Imposing a firm obligation; obligatory: *a binding agreement.*

binding energy *n.* The net energy necessary to break a molecule, an atom, or a nucleus into its smaller component parts.

bind•weed (bīnd′wēd′) *n.* Any of various plants having twining stems and pink or white trumpet-shaped flowers.

binge (bĭnj) *n.* A period of unrestrained activity, such as drinking or spending; uncontrolled self-indulgence: *a shopping binge.*

bin•go (bĭng′gō) *n., pl.* **bin•goes.** A game of chance played by covering numbers on a printed card as they are called out. The winner is the player who covers the first five numbers in a row in any direction.

bin•na•cle (bĭn′ə kəl) *n.* The case that supports a ship's compass, usually near the helm.

bin•oc•u•lar (bə nŏk′yə lər *or* bī nŏk′yə lər) *adj.* Relating to or involving both eyes at once: *binocular vision.* —*n.* An optical device, such as a pair of field glasses, designed for use by both eyes at once and consisting of two small telescopes. Often used in the plural. [First written down in 1713 in Modern English : Latin *bīnī,* two at a time + English *ocular,* of the eyes.]

bi•no•mi•al (bī nō′mē əl) *adj.* Consisting of or relating to two names or terms: *a binomial expression in math.* —*n.* **1.** A mathematical expression that is written as a sum or difference of two terms, as, for example, $3a + 2b$. **2.** The scientific name of an organism consisting of two terms, the first indicating the genus and the second the species. *Passer domesticus,* the scientific name of the common house sparrow, is a binomial.

bio– or **bi–** *pref.* A prefix that means: **1.** Life or living organism: *biome.* **2.** Biology or biological: *biophysics.* —See Note.

bi•o•chem•i•cal (bī′ō kĕm′ĭ kəl) *adj.* Of or relating to biochemistry. —**bi′o•chem′i•cal•ly** *adv.*

bi•o•chem•ist (bī′ō kĕm′ĭst) *n.* A scientist who specializes in biochemistry.

bi•o•chem•is•try (bī′ō kĕm′ĭ strē) *n.* The study of the chemical composition of substances that form living matter and of chemical processes that go on in living matter.

bi•o•de•grad•a•ble (bī′ō dĭ grā′də bəl) *adj.* Capable of being decomposed by biological agents, especially bacteria: *a biodegradable detergent.*

bi•o•eth•ics (bī′ō ĕth′ĭks) *n. (used with a singular verb).* The study of the problems of behavior and conduct in biological and medical research.

bi•o•feed•back (bī′ō fēd′băk′) *n.* The use of monitoring devices in an attempt to gain some voluntary control over involuntary bodily functions, such as the heartbeat or blood pressure.

bi•og•ra•pher (bī ŏg′rə fər *or* bē ŏg′rə fər) *n.* A person who writes a biography.

bi•o•graph•i•cal (bī′ə grăf′ĭ kəl) also **bi•o•graph•ic** (bī′ə grăf′ĭk) *adj.* **1.** Of, relating to, or based on a person's life: *biographical information.* **2.** Of or relating to biography.

bi•og•ra•phy (bī ŏg′rə fē *or* bē ŏg′rə fē) *n., pl.* **bi•og•ra•phies.** An account of a person's life written by someone else.

bi•o•log•i•cal (bī′ə lŏj′ĭ kəl) also **bi•o•log•ic** (bī′ə lŏj′ĭk) *adj.* **1.** Of, relating to, or affecting living organisms: *biological processes such as growth and digestion.* **2.** Of or relating to biology: *the biological sciences.* —**bi′o•log′i•cal•ly** *adv.*

biological clock *n.* A part of the system in organisms that controls the cycle of various living functions and activities, such as photosynthesis in a plant.

biological warfare *n.* The use of disease-producing organisms, destructive insects, or specialized poisons to destroy crops, livestock, or human life.

bi•ol•o•gist (bī ŏl′ə jĭst) *n.* A scientist who specializes in biology.

bi•ol•o•gy (bī ŏl′ə jē) *n.* The scientific study of living organisms and life processes, including growth, structure, and reproduction. Among the branches of biology are botany, zoology, and ecology. [First written down in 1819 in Modern English, from German *Biologie* : Greek *bios,* life + Greek *-logia,* study.]

binocular

Word Building: bio–

The prefix **bio–** comes from the Greek word *bios,* meaning "life." When used to form words in English, **bio–** generally refers to living organisms or to biology, the science of living organisms. Many of the words that begin with **bio–**, such as **bioethics** and **biotechnology**, have only come into being in the twentieth century. Sometimes before an *o* **bio–** becomes **bi–: biopsy.**

ă	**pat**	oi	**boy**
ā	**pay**	ou	**out**
âr	**care**	ŏŏ	**took**
ä	**father**	ōō	**boot**
ĕ	**pet**	ŭ	**cut**
ē	**be**	ûr	**urge**
ĭ	**pit**	th	**thin**
ī	**pie**	*th*	**this**
îr	**pier**	hw	**whoop**
ŏ	**pot**	zh	**vision**
ō	**toe**	ə	**about**
ô	**paw**	N	*French* **bon**

biplane
World War I British fighter plane

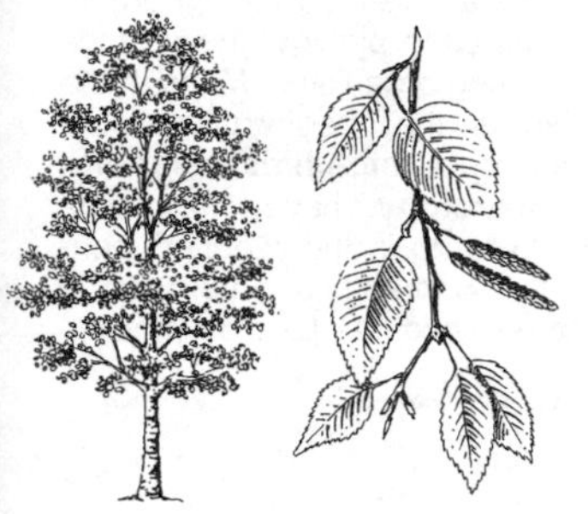
birch
Paper birch

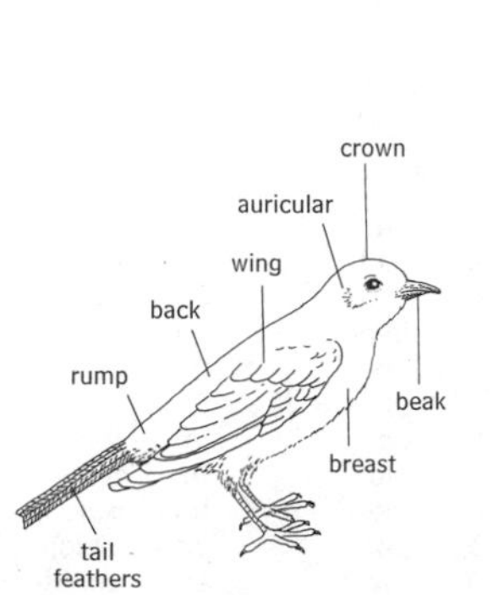

bird

bi•o•lu•mi•nes•cence (bī′ō lo͞o′mə **nĕs′**əns) *n.* Emission of light by living organisms, such as fireflies, jellyfish, and certain plants. **—bi′o•lu′mi•nes′cent** *adj.*

bi•o•mass (**bī′**ō măs′) *n.* **1.** The total amount of living material in a given habitat. **2.** Plant material, vegetation, or agricultural waste used as a fuel or an energy source.

bi•ome (**bī′**ōm′) *n.* A distinct natural community, such as a grassland or a desert, distinguished chiefly by its plant life and climate.

bi•o•met•rics (bī′ō **mĕt′**rĭks) *n.* *(used with a singular verb).* The statistical study of biological phenomena.

bi•on•ic (bī **ŏn′**ĭk) *adj.* **1.** Consisting of or assisted by electronic or mechanical devices that strengthen or replace a part of the body. **2.** Of or relating to bionics.

bi•on•ics (bī **ŏn′**ĭks) *n.* *(used with a singular verb).* The use of biological principles, as of the anatomy and physiology of animals, in industrial design or electronics.

bi•o•phys•ics (bī′ō **fĭz′**ĭks) *n.* *(used with a singular verb).* The branch of biology that applies the laws and methods of physics to biological problems and phenomena.

bi•op•sy (**bī′**ŏp′sē) *n., pl.* **bi•op•sies.** The surgical removal of a sample of tissue from a living body for examination and diagnosis.

bi•o•rhythm (**bī′**ō rĭ*th*′əm) *n.* An inborn, cyclical biological process or function.

bi•o•sphere (**bī′**ə sfîr′) *n.* **1.** The part of the earth and its atmosphere in which living organisms exist. **2.** The living organisms and their environment in the biosphere.

bi•o•tech•nol•o•gy (bī′ō tĕk **nŏl′**ə jē) *n.* **1.** The use of living organisms or biological substances to perform certain industrial or manufacturing processes. **2.** The engineering and biological study of relationships between humans and machines. **—bi′o•tech′no•log′i•cal** (bī′ō tĕk′nə **lŏj′**ĭ kəl) *adj.*

bi•ot•ic (bī **ŏt′**ĭk) *adj.* **1.** Of or relating to life or living organisms: *plants and animals forming a biotic community.* **2.** Produced or caused by living organisms.

bi•o•tin (**bī′**ə tĭn) *n.* A colorless crystalline vitamin composed of carbon, hydrogen, nitrogen, oxygen, and sulfur in the proportions $C_{10}H_{16}N_2O_3S$. It is often considered part of the vitamin B complex that promotes growth and is found in liver, egg yolk, milk, and yeast.

bi•par•ti•san (bī **pär′**tĭ zən *or* bī **pär′**tĭ sən) *adj.* Composed of or supported by two political parties, especially the Republican and Democratic parties: *a bipartisan bill to fight crime.*

bi•par•tite (bī **pär′**tīt′) *adj.* **1.** Having or consisting of two parts. **2.** Drawn up in two corresponding parts, one for each party: *a bipartite treaty.*

bi•ped (**bī′**pĕd′) *n.* An animal having two feet, such as a bird or human being.

bi•plane (**bī′**plān′) *n.* An airplane having two sets of wings, one above the other.

bi•ra•cial (bī **rā′**shəl) *adj.* Of, for, or consisting of members of two racial groups: *a biracial committee for cooperation between Black and white residents.*

birch (bûrch) *n.* **1.** Any of various trees of the Northern Hemisphere having toothed leaves and papery bark that peels easily. **2.** The hard wood of such a tree. **3.** A stick or switch from a birch tree, used for whipping. [First written down about 725 in Old English and spelled *birce.*]

bird (bûrd) *n.* **1.** Any of numerous warm-blooded, egg-laying animals that have two wings and a body covered with feathers. **2.** A shuttlecock. **3.** *Slang.* A person, especially one who is odd or unusual: *a strange bird.* **—*idiom.* birds of a feather.** People who are similar, as in character, personality, or tastes. [First written down about 750 in Old English and spelled *brid,* young bird.]

bird•bath (**bûrd′**băth′) *n.* A basin filled with water for birds to drink or bathe in.

bird•call (**bûrd′**kôl′) *n.* **1.** The song or cry of a bird. **2.a.** An imitation of the song or cry of a bird. **b.** A small device for producing this sound.

bird dog *n.* A dog trained to hunt game birds.

bird•er (**bûr′**dər) *n.* A bird watcher.

bird•house (**bûrd′**hous′) *n.* A box with one or more small holes, made as a nesting place for birds.

bird•ie (**bûr′**dē) *n.* **1.** *Informal.* A small bird. **2.** In golf, a score of one stroke under par for a hole.

bird•lime (**bûrd′**līm′) *n.* A sticky substance smeared on twigs to catch small birds.

bird of paradise *n., pl.* **birds of paradise.** Any of various birds of New Guinea and Australia, usually having brightly colored showy feathers in the male.

bird of passage *n., pl.* **birds of passage. 1.** A bird that migrates. **2.** A person who moves from place to place frequently.

bird of prey *n., pl.* **birds of prey.** Any of various birds, such as a hawk, an eagle, or an owl, that hunt and kill other animals for food.

bird•seed (**bûrd′**sēd′) *n.* A mixture of different kinds of seeds for feeding birds.

bird's-eye (**bûrdz′**ī′) *adj.* **1.** Marked with small rounded spots: *furniture made of bird's-eye maple; cotton cloth with a bird's-eye weave.* **2.** Seen from high above: *a bird's-eye view of the countryside.*

bird watcher *n.* A person who observes and identifies birds in their natural surroundings. **—bird watching** *n.*

bi•ret•ta (bə **rĕt′**ə) *n.* A stiff square cap worn by members of the Roman Catholic clergy. Birettas are black for priests, purple for bishops, and red for cardinals.

Bir•ming•ham (**bûr′**mĭng hăm′). **1.** (*also* **bûr′**mĭng əm). A city of central England northwest of London. Population, 1,022,300. **2.** The largest city of Alabama, in the north-central part of the state northwest of Montgomery. Population, 265,968.

birth (bûrth) *n.* **1.** The emergence and separation of offspring from the body of the mother: *At birth she weighed seven pounds.* **2.** The act or process of bearing young: *A second birth is usually easier than the first.* **3.** A beginning or an origin: *the birth of an idea.* **4.** Family background; ancestry: *an heir of noble birth.*

❑ *These sound alike:* **birth, berth** (bed).

birth control *n.* Control of the number of children born, especially by the planned use of contraceptive techniques.

birth•day (**bûrth′**dā′) *n.* **1.** The day of a person's birth. **2.** The anniversary of that day.

birth defect *n.* A defect or an imperfection present in the body from birth. Birth defects include physical abnormalities and chemical deficiencies.

birth•mark (**bûrth′**märk′) *n.* A mark or blemish present on the body from birth.

birth•place (**bûrth′**plās′) *n.* The place where someone is born or where something originates.

birth•rate (**bûrth′**rāt′) *n.* The ratio of total live births to total population in a specified area or community over a particular period of time, usually one year.

birth•right (**bûrth′**rīt′) *n.* A right to which a person is entitled because of birth or origin: *Freedom of speech is an American birthright.*

birth•stone (**bûrth′**stōn′) *n.* A jewel associated with the specific month of a person's birth.

Bis•cay (**bĭs′**kā), **Bay of.** An arm of the Atlantic

Ocean on the western coast of Europe from northwest France to northwest Spain.

bis•cuit (**bĭs′**kĭt) *n., pl.* **bis•cuits. 1.** A small flaky cake of bread leavened with baking powder or soda. **2.** *Chiefly British.* **a.** A cracker. **b.** A cookie. [First written down before 1338 in Middle English and spelled *besquite*, from Medieval Latin *bis coctus*, twice cooked.]

bi•sect (**bī′**sĕkt′ *or* bī **sĕkt′**) *tr.v.* **bi•sect•ed, bi•sect•ing, bi•sects.** To cut or divide into two equal parts: *bisect a triangle.* **—bi•sec′tion** *n.*

bi•sec•tor (**bī′**sĕk′tər *or* bī **sĕk′**tər) *n.* A straight line that bisects an angle or a line segment.

bi•sex•u•al (bī **sĕk′**sho͞o əl) *adj.* **1.** Of, relating to, or involving both sexes: *bisexual reproduction.* **2.** Having male and female reproductive organs in a single individual; hermaphroditic: *Earthworms are bisexual.* **3.** Sexual interest in or attraction to persons of both sexes. **—bi′sex•u•al′i•ty** (bī′ sĕk sho͞o **ăl′** ĭ tē) *n.* **—bi•sex′u•al•ly** *adv.*

Bish•kek (**bĭsh′**kĕk *or* **bēsh′**kĕk). Formerly **Frun•ze** (**fro͞on′**zə). The capital of Kirghiz, in the north-central part of the republic west of Alma-Ata, Kazakhstan. Population, 604,000.

bish•op (**bĭsh′**əp) *n.* **1.** A high-ranking Christian cleric, in modern churches usually in charge of a diocese. **2.** A chess piece that can move diagonally across any number of unoccupied spaces of the same color. [First written down before 830 in Old English and spelled *biscop*, from Greek *episkopos*, overseer.]

Bish•op (**bĭsh′**əp), **Elizabeth.** 1911–1979. American poet whose works include "Filling Station" (1965).

bish•op•ric (**bĭsh′**ə prĭk) *n.* The office, rank, or diocese of a bishop.

Bis•marck (**bĭz′**märk′). The capital of North Dakota, in the south-central part of the state on hills overlooking the Missouri River. Population, 49,256.

Bismarck, Prince **Otto Eduard Leopold von.** 1815–1898. First chancellor of the German Empire (1871–1890). He set in motion sweeping social reforms.

bis•muth (**bĭz′**məth) *n. Symbol* **Bi** A brittle, reddish-white, metallic element that occurs in nature as a free metal and in various ores and is used in medicine and in making low-melting alloys for fire-safety devices. Atomic number 83. See table at **element.** [First written down in 1668 in Modern English, from obsolete German *Bismut*, from Medieval Latin *wismutum*, from obsolete German *Wismut.*]

bi•son (**bī′**sən *or* **bī′**zən) *n.* **1.** A large mammal of western North America similar to an ox and having a massive head, a shaggy dark-brown mane, and short curved horns; a buffalo. **2.** A similar but smaller European animal. [First written down in 1611 in Modern English, from Latin *bisōn*, of Germanic origin.]

bisque (bĭsk) *n.* A thick cream soup: *lobster bisque.*

Bis•sau (bĭ **sou′**). The capital and largest city of Guinea-Bissau, on the Atlantic Ocean southeast of Banjul, Gambia. It was founded in 1687. Population, 109,486.

bis•tro (**bē′**strō *or* **bĭs′**trō) *n., pl.* **bis•tros.** A small bar, tavern, or nightclub.

bit¹ (bĭt) *n.* **1.** A small piece or amount: *a bit of lint; a bit of luck.* **2.** A brief amount of time; a moment: *Wait a bit.* **3.** A small role, as in a play or movie. **4.** *Informal.* An amount equal to ⅛ of a dollar: *two bits.* **—*idioms.* a bit.** To a small degree; somewhat: *The soup is a bit hot.* **bit by bit.** Little by little; gradually: *improved bit by bit.* [First written down before 1050 in Old English and spelled *bita.*]

bit² (bĭt) *n.* **1.** A pointed tool for drilling that fits into a brace or an electric drill. **2.** The sharp part of a tool, as the cutting edge of a knife. **3.** The metal mouthpiece of a bridle, used to control the horse. **4.** The part of a key that enters the lock and works the mechanism. [First written down about 725 in Old English and spelled *bite*, act of biting.]

bit³ (bĭt) *n.* **1.** In computer science: **a.** Either of the binary digits 0 or 1. **b.** Either of a pair of characters that are equivalent to 0 and 1, such as true and false or on and off. **2.** The smallest unit of information a computer can recognize; a binary digit. [First written down in 1948 in Modern English : from *b(inary) + (dig)it.*]

bit⁴ (bĭt) *v.* Past tense and a past participle of **bite.**

bitch (bĭch) *n.* A female dog or related animal, such as a coyote.

bite (bīt) *v.* **bit** (bĭt), **bit•ten** (**bĭt′**n) or **bit, bit•ing, bites.** *—tr.* **1.** To cut, grip, or tear with or as if with the teeth: *He bit the bread and tore off a piece.* **2.a.** To pierce the skin of (a person or an animal) with the teeth, fangs, or mouthparts: *A mosquito bit me in the leg.* **b.** To sting with a stinger. **3.** To cause to sting or smart: *The cold wind was biting my face.* **4.** To take strong hold of; grip or seize: *The wheels bit the gravel and the car departed.* *—intr.* **1.** To cut or tear something with or as if with the teeth: *The ax bit into the tree.* **2.** To have a stinging effect or sharp taste: *Hot food bites.* **3.** To grip or seize, as a surface: *The wheels have difficulty in biting when the road is icy.* **4.** To take or swallow bait: *Fish seem to bite more just before it starts to rain.* **5.** To be deceived by a trick or scheme: *She tried to pass off the old car as a bargain, but no one would bite.* *—n.* **1.** The act of biting: *The dog's bark is worse than his bite.* **2.** A wound or an injury resulting from biting: *a mosquito bite.* **3.** An amount of food taken into the mouth at one time; a mouthful: *Let me have a bite of your sandwich.* **4.** *Informal.* A light meal or snack: *We stopped for a bite.* **5.** A secure grip or hold by a tool or machine: *The pliers had a good bite on the nut.* **6.** The angle at which the upper and lower teeth meet: *He wore braces to correct his bite.* **—*idioms.* bite off more than one can chew.** To decide or agree to do more than one can accomplish. **bite the dust.** *Slang.* **1.** To fall dead. **2.** To come to an end. **bite the hand that feeds (one).** To repay generosity or kindness with ingratitude and injury. [First written down about 725 in Old English and spelled *bītan.*] **—bit′er** *n.*

❑ *These sound alike:* **bite, byte** (unit of computer measure).

bit•ing (**bī′**tĭng) *adj.* **1.** Tending to bite; sharp; stinging: *The snow was accompanied by a biting wind.* **2.** Causing an unpleasant feeling; sarcastic; cutting: *biting criticism.* **—bit′ing•ly** *adv.*

bit•ten (**bĭt′**n) *v.* A past participle of **bite.**

bit•ter (**bĭt′**ər) *adj.* **bit•ter•er, bit•ter•est. 1.** Having or being a taste that is sharp or unpleasant: *a bitter drink.* **2.** Causing sharp pain to the body; harsh: *a bitter wind.* **3.** Hard to accept, admit, or bear: *the bitter truth.* **4.** Showing or proceeding from strong dislike or animosity: *bitter foes; a bitter fight.* **5.** Resulting from severe grief, anguish, or disappointment: *cry bitter tears.* **6.** Having or showing a resentful feeling: *bitter about being cheated.* *—n.* **1.** *Chiefly British.* A sharp-tasting beer made with hops. **2. bitters.** A bitter, usually alcoholic liquid used in cocktails and as a tonic. [First written down about 725 in Old English and spelled *biter.*] **—bit′ter•ly** *adv.* **—bit′ter•ness** *n.*

bit•tern (**bĭt′**ərn) *n.* Any of several long-necked wading birds having mottled brownish plumage and a deep booming cry.

bit•ter•root (**bĭt′**ər ro͞ot′ *or* **bĭt′**ər ro͝ot′) *n.* A plant of the Rocky Mountain region of western North

Otto von Bismarck

bison
American Plains bison

ă	pat	oi	boy
ā	pay	ou	out
âr	care	o͝o	took
ä	father	o͞o	boot
ĕ	pet	ŭ	cut
ē	be	ûr	urge
ĭ	pit	th	thin
ī	pie	*th*	this
îr	pier	hw	whoop
ŏ	pot	zh	vision
ō	toe	ə	about
ô	paw	N	*French* bon

Usage: biweekly

The word **biweekly** means "once every two weeks" and **bimonthly** means "once every two months." **Semiweekly** means "twice a week" and **semimonthly** means "twice a month." Because many people mix up these **bi–** and **semi–** words, it is safest to use phrases like *every two weeks* or *twice a month.* A publication that comes out every two weeks, however, is always called a *biweekly.* One appearing every two months is a *bimonthly.*

black bear

blackberry

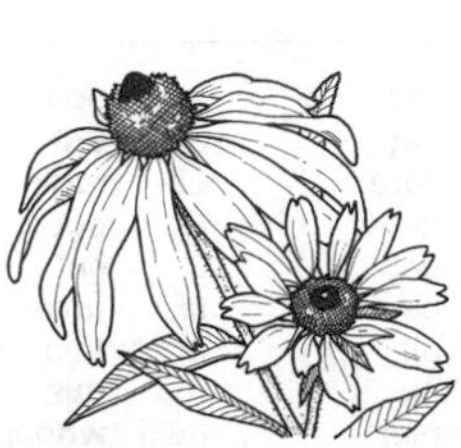

black-eyed Susan

America having showy pink or white flowers and an edible root.

bit•ter•sweet (bĭt′ər swēt′) *n.* **1.** A woody vine having orange or yellowish fruits that split open and expose seeds with fleshy red coverings. **2.** A plant native to Europe and Asia and widespread in North America, having purple flowers and poisonous red berries. *—adj.* **1.** Bitter and sweet at the same time: *bittersweet chocolate.* **2.** Pleasant and unpleasant at the same time: *was left with bittersweet memories of the event.*

bi•tu•men (bĭ to͞o′mən *or* bĭ tyo͞o′mən) *n.* Any of various flammable mixtures of hydrocarbons and other substances found in asphalt and tar. They occur naturally or are produced from petroleum and coal.

bi•tu•mi•nous (bĭ to͞o′mə nəs *or* bĭ tyo͞o′mə nəs) *adj.* **1.** Resembling or containing bitumen. **2.** Of or relating to bituminous coal.

bituminous coal *n.* A grade of coal that contains a high percentage of bitumen and burns with much smoke and a yellow flame; soft coal.

bi•va•lent (bī vā′lənt) *adj.* In chemistry, having a valence of +2 or −2.

bi•valve (bī′vălv′) *n.* A mollusk, such as a clam or an oyster, whose shell consists of two parts hinged together. *—adj.* **1.** Having a hinged shell: *a bivalve mollusk.* **2.** Consisting of two similar parts: *a bivalve shell.*

biv•ou•ac (bĭv′o͝o ăk′ *or* bĭv′wăk′) *n.* A temporary camp made by soldiers in the field. *—intr.v.* **biv•ou•acked, biv•ou•ack•ing, biv•ou•acs** also **biv•ou•acks.** To camp in a bivouac.

bi•week•ly (bī wēk′lē) *adj.* **1.** Occurring every two weeks. **2.** Occurring twice a week: *biweekly meetings on Tuesday and Thursday.* *—n., pl.* **bi•week•lies.** A publication issued biweekly. *—adv.* **1.** Once every two weeks: *The company gives out paychecks biweekly.* **2.** Twice a week. —SEE NOTE.

bi•zarre (bĭ zär′) *adj.* Very strange or odd: *a bizarre hat; a bizarre idea.*

Bk The symbol for the element **berkelium.**

blab (blăb) *v.* **blabbed, blab•bing, blabs.** *—tr.* To tell (a secret), especially through careless talk. *—intr.* **1.** To reveal secret matters: *The secret was out when I blabbed without thinking.* **2.** To chatter indiscreetly.

blab•ber (blăb′ər) *intr.v.* **blab•bered, blab•ber•ing, blab•bers.** To chatter. *—n.* **1.** Idle chatter. **2.** A person who blabs.

blab•ber•mouth (blăb′ər mouth′) *n. Informal.* A person who talks carelessly and at length.

black (blăk) *adj.* **black•er, black•est. 1.** Of or near the color black. **2.** Without light: *a black moonless night.* **3.** Often **Black. a.** Of, relating to, or belonging to a racial group having dark skin, especially a group of African origin. **b.** Of, relating to, or belonging to an American group of people descended from African peoples having dark skin; African-American. **4.** Gloomy; depressing: *a black day; black thoughts.* **5.** Often **Black.** Marked by disaster: *The stock market crashed on Black Friday.* **6.** Deserving of or indicating censure or dishonor: *the industry's blackest record as a polluter of the rivers.* **7.** Evil; wicked: *black deeds.* **8.** Angry; sullen: *He gave me a black look.* **9.** Served without cream or milk: *black coffee.* *—n.* **1.a.** The darkest extreme of the series of colors that runs through all the shades of gray to white, being the opposite of white. **b.** Clothing of this color, especially clothing worn for mourning: *At the funeral everyone was dressed in black.* **2.** A black paint, dye, or pigment. **3.** Often **Black. a.** A member of a racial group having dark skin, especially one of African origin. **b.** An American descended from peoples of African origin having dark skin; an African American. *—tr. & intr.v.* **blacked, black•ing, blacks.** To make or become black: *Black shoes to make them shine.* ***—idioms.*** **black out. 1.** To lose consciousness or memory temporarily: *He felt lightheaded and then blacked out.* **2.** To forbid or prevent the transmission of (a television program). **3.** To turn off or conceal all lights that might help enemy aircraft find a target during an air raid. **4.** To cause a failure of electrical power in: *The storm blacked out the street lights.* **in the black.** Making a profit; prosperous. [First written down about 700 in Old English and spelled *blæc.*] **—black′ly** *adv.* **—black′ness** *n.*

black-and-blue (blăk′ən blo͞o′) *adj.* Discolored by broken blood vessels under the skin; bruised.

black and white *n.* **1.** Writing or printing: *She did not believe it until she read it in black and white.* **2.** Photography or printmaking that uses only black and white: *a movie shot in black and white.*

black-and-white (blăk′ən wīt′) *adj.* **1.** Being done, drawn, or photographed in shades of black and white: *a black-and-white picture.* **2.** Partly black and partly white: *a black-and-white cow.* **3.** Making judgments based on two rigid categories, such as right and wrong: *black-and-white opinions.*

black art *n.* Black magic.

black•ball (blăk′bôl′) *n.* A negative vote. *—tr.v.* **black•balled, black•ball•ing, black•balls. 1.** To vote against and prevent (someone) from being admitted to an organization, as by placing a black ball in a ballot box. **2.** To shut out from participation: *an actor blackballed for her political views.*

black bear *n.* A North American bear that lives in forests and has thick black or dark-brown fur.

black belt *n.* The rank of expert in a system of self-defense, such as judo or karate.

black•ber•ry (blăk′bĕr′ē) *n.* **1.** The blackish, glossy, edible berry of any of various thorny plants related to the raspberry. **2.** A shrub that bears such berries.

black•bird (blăk′bûrd′) *n.* Any of various birds having black or mostly black feathers.

black•board (blăk′bôrd′) *n.* A hard, smooth, dark-colored panel for writing on with chalk; a chalkboard.

black•bod•y (blăk′bŏd′ē) *n.* A theoretical object that absorbs any radiation that strikes it.

black book *n.* A book containing names of people to blacklist.

black box *n.* **1.** A device, especially an electronic component, whose purpose or function are known, but whose inner workings or structure are unknown or irrelevant. **2.** A flight recorder.

black comedy *n.* Comedy that is morbid or bizarre in character.

black•damp (blăk′dămp′) *n.* A suffocating gas, mostly a mixture of carbon dioxide and nitrogen, found in mines after fires and explosions.

Black Death *n.* An extremely deadly form of bubonic plague that was widespread throughout Europe and much of Asia in the 14th century.

black•en (blăk′ən) *v.* **black•ened, black•en•ing, black•ens.** *—tr.* **1.** To make black: *Smoke blackened the sky.* **2.** To speak evil of; defame: *The scandal blackened the athlete's reputation.* *—intr.* To become dark or black: *The sky blackened before the storm.*

Black English *n.* The varieties of English spoken by American Black people.

black eye *n.* **1.** A black-and-blue discoloration of the skin around the eye, resulting from a blow. **2.** A bad name; a dishonored reputation: *Involvement in the scandal gave the politician a black eye.*

black-eyed pea (blăk′īd′) *n.* The cowpea.

black-eyed Su•san (so͞o′zən) *n.* Any of several North American plants having hairy stems and leaves and showy flowers that have orange-yellow petals surrounding a dark-brown center.

Black•foot (blăk′fo͝ot′) *n., pl.* **Blackfoot** or **Black•feet** (blăk′fēt′). **1.** A member of a Native American people of Montana, Alberta, and Saskatchewan. **2.** The Algonquian language of the Blackfoot.

black•guard (blăg′ərd *or* blăg′ärd′) *n.* A low unprincipled person; a scoundrel.

Black Hawk. Originally Makataimeshekiakiak. 1767–1838. Sauk leader who organized the resistance of the Fox and Sauk against white settlement of Native-held lands that ended in the Black Hawk War (1832).

black•head (blăk′hĕd′) *n.* A mass of fatty material and dirt that collects in and blocks one of the pores of the skin.

black hole *n.* An extremely compact celestial object that has such a strong gravitational pull that nothing can escape, not even light. A black hole is thought to be formed by collapse of matter in a supernova.

black humor *n.* Humor that is morbid or bizarre in character, especially in literature.

black•ing (blăk′ĭng) *n.* A black paste or liquid used as shoe polish.

black•ish (blăk′ĭsh) *adj.* Somewhat black in color.

black•jack (blăk′jăk′) *n.* **1.** A small leather-covered club with a flexible handle. **2.** A card game in which the object is to hold cards with a higher count than that of the dealer but not exceeding 21. **3.** The black flag of a pirate; the Jolly Roger. —*tr.v.* **black•jacked, black•jack•ing, black•jacks.** To strike or threaten with a blackjack.

black light *n.* An invisible form of light such as ultraviolet or infrared light.

black•list (blăk′lĭst′) *n.* A list of persons or organizations to be disapproved, boycotted, or penalized. —*tr.v.* **black•list•ed, black•list•ing, black•lists.** To place (a name) on a blacklist: *Many companies used to blacklist strikers.*

black lung *n.* A disease of the lungs caused by inhaling coal dust over a long period of time.

black magic *n.* Magic practiced for evil purposes, especially in league with evil spirits.

black•mail (blăk′māl′) *n.* **1.** The extortion of money or something of value from a person by the threat of exposing something criminal or discreditable about the person. **2.** Money or something of value paid or demanded as blackmail. —*tr.v.* **black•mailed, black•mail•ing, black•mails.** To subject (someone) to blackmail. —**black′mail′er** *n.*

black market *n.* **1.** The illegal business of buying or selling goods in violation of governmental restrictions, such as price controls or rationing. **2.** A place where this illegal business is carried on.

Black Muslim *n.* A member of a Black American group, the Nation of Islam, that professes Islamic beliefs.

black•out (blăk′out′) *n.* **1.** The act of putting out or concealing all lights that might help enemy aircraft find a target during a night raid. **2.** Lack of lighting caused by an electrical power failure. **3.** A temporary loss of consciousness or memory: *The driver's blackout caused the crash.* **4.** A suppression by censorship: *a news blackout.* **5.** The act of prohibiting the transmission of a television program in the area near its place of origin.

Black Power *n.* A movement among Black Americans emphasizing racial pride and social equality by creating Black political and cultural institutions rather than by seeking integration into the white community.

Black Sea. An inland sea between Europe and Asia. It is connected with the Aegean Sea by the Bosporus, the Sea of Marmara, and the Dardanelles.

black sheep *n.* A member of a family or group considered undesirable or disgraceful.

black•smith (blăk′smĭth′) *n.* A person who forges and shapes iron into horseshoes and other objects of metal. —SEE NOTE.

black•snake (blăk′snāk′) *n.* **1.** Any of various dark-colored, chiefly nonpoisonous snakes of eastern North America. **2.** A long tapering whip of braided leather.

black•thorn (blăk′thôrn′) *n.* A thorny shrub of Europe and Asia having white flowers and small bluish-black fruit.

black tie *n.* **1.** A black bow tie worn with a dinner jacket or tuxedo. **2.** Formal evening clothes for men: *He was dressed in black tie.* —**black′-tie′** *adj.*

black•top (blăk′tŏp′) *n.* A bituminous material, such as asphalt, used to pave roads. —*tr.v.* **black•topped, black•top•ping, black•tops.** To pave with blacktop.

Black•well (blăck′wĕl′), **Antoinette Louisa Brown.** 1825–1921. American social reformer who was the first formally appointed (1852) woman pastor in the United States.

Blackwell, Elizabeth. 1821–1910. British-born American physician who was the first woman in the United States or Europe to be awarded a medical degree (1849).

black widow *n.* A spider of Central and North America, the female of which has a black body with a red mark on the underside and produces poisonous venom.

blad•der (blăd′ər) *n.* **1.** Any of various sacs found in most animals and made of elastic membrane, especially the sac that stores urine secreted by the kidneys. **2.a.** A hollow structure or sac, as an air sac in certain seaweeds. **b.** Something resembling such a sac: *the bladder of a football.* [First written down about 700 in Old English and spelled *blǣdre.*]

blade (blād) *n.* **1.** The flat sharp-edged part of a cutting tool or weapon. **2.** A sword. **3.** The thin flat part of something: *the blade of an oar.* **4.** The broad flattened part of a leaf, extending from the stalk. **5.** The metal part of an ice skate. **6.** A dashing young man. [First written down about 725 in Old English and spelled *blæd*, leaf.]

blah (blä) *Informal. n.* Worthless nonsense. —*adj.* **1.** Dull and uninteresting. **2.** Low in spirits or health: *I'm feeling blah.*

Blake (blāk), **William.** 1757–1827. British poet and artist who printed many of his own volumes, including *Songs of Innocence* (1789).

blame (blām) *tr.v.* **blamed, blam•ing, blames. 1.** To hold (a person or thing) responsible or at fault: *The driver blamed the icy road for the accident.* **2.** To find fault with; censure: *You cannot blame them for wanting to live on a lake.* —*n.* **1.** The state of being responsible for a fault or an error: *I had to accept the blame for my mistake.* **2.** Condemnation or censure, as for a fault. —***idiom.*** **to blame.** Deserving censure; at fault. —**blam′a•ble** *adj.*

blame•less (blām′lĭs) *adj.* Free from blame or guilt; innocent: *a blameless case of mistaken identity.* —**blame′less•ly** *adv.* —**blame′less•ness** *n.*

blame•wor•thy (blām′wûr′thē) *adj.* **blame•wor•thi•er, blame•wor•thi•est.** Deserving blame: *All of us were blameworthy for leaving such a mess.* —**blame′wor′thi•ness** *n.*

Blanc (blăngk *or* bläɴ), **Mont.** The highest peak of the Alps, rising to 15,771 feet (4,810.2 meters) in southeast France on the Italian border.

blanch (blănch) *v.* **blanched, blanch•ing, blanch•es.** —*tr.* **1.** To make lighter in color; bleach or whiten. **2.** To place (almonds or tomatoes, for example) briefly in boiling water in order to remove the skins. **3.** To scald (vegetables) by plunging into boiling

Word History: blacksmith

Originally, a **smith** was a skilled worker in metal, wood, or cloth, but the meaning of *smith* has narrowed to "a worker in metal." A **blacksmith** is "a smith who works with iron," the black metal, especially with forging iron, which is at the beginning of the metalworking process. The opposite of the *blacksmith* is the *whitesmith*, who works with either white metal (iron plated with tin) or white iron (tin, because of its light, silvery color) or who polishes or otherwise finishes metal products.

Elizabeth Blackwell

black widow

ă	pat	oi	boy
ā	pay	ou	out
âr	care	o͝o	took
ä	father	o͞o	boot
ĕ	pet	ŭ	cut
ē	be	ûr	urge
ĭ	pit	th	thin
ī	pie	*th*	this
îr	pier	hw	whoop
ŏ	pot	zh	vision
ō	toe	ə	about
ô	paw	ɴ	*French* bon

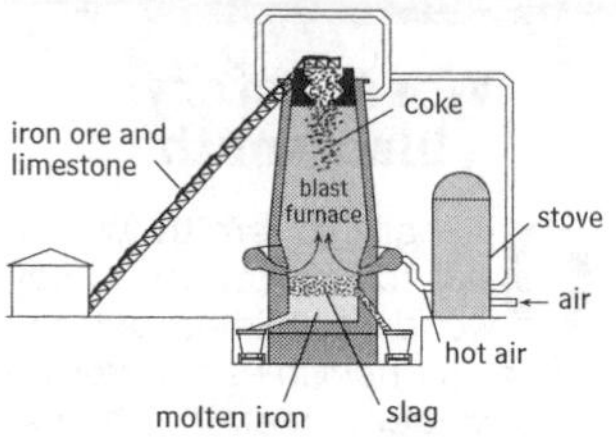

blast furnace

blastoff
Apollo 16 voyage to the moon, April 16, 1972

blazer

water, as before freezing. **4.** To cause to become pale: *Fear blanched the startled child's face.* —*intr.* To turn pale: *They blanched at the awful news.* [First written down before 1398 in Middle English and spelled *blaunchen*, from Old French *blanc*, white.]

bland (blănd) *adj.* **bland•er, bland•est. 1.** Pleasant or soothing in manner; gentle: *a bland smile.* **2.** Having a moderate, soft, or soothing quality; not irritating or stimulating: *a bland diet; a bland climate.* **3.** Lacking distinctive character; dull; flat: *a bland speech.* **—bland′ly** *adj.* **—bland′ness** *n.*

blan•dish (blăn′dĭsh) *tr.v.* **blan•dished, blan•dish•ing, blan•dish•es.** To coax by flattery or wheedling; cajole.

blan•dish•ment (blăn′dĭsh mənt) *n.* A word or an act meant to coax or flatter. Often used in the plural: *The advertisement's blandishments didn't persuade us to buy.*

blank (blăngk) *adj.* **blank•er, blank•est. 1.** Free of marks or writing: *a blank wall; a blank piece of paper.* **2.** Containing no information: *a blank tape.* See Synonyms at **empty. 3.** Having empty spaces to be filled in: *Fill in this blank application.* **4.** Showing no expression or interest: *a blank stare.* **5.** Lacking thought or attention: *a blank mind.* —*n.* **1.** An empty space or place; a void: *My mind was a complete blank on the subject.* **2.a.** An empty space on a document to be filled in with an answer or a comment. **b.** A document or form with empty spaces to be filled in: *a pad of order blanks.* **3.** A gun cartridge having a charge of powder but no bullet. —*tr.v.* **blanked, blank•ing, blanks.** To prevent (an opponent) from scoring in a game: *Our team blanked theirs 4–0.* [First written down in 1230 in Middle English, white, from Old French *blanc.*] **—blank′ly** *adv.* **—blank′ness** *n.*

blan•ket (blăng′kĭt) *n.* **1.** A large piece of cloth or other woven material used as a covering for warmth. **2.** A layer that covers: *a blanket of snow.* —*adj.* Covering a wide range of topics, conditions, or requirements: *They gave the proposals a blanket approval.* —*tr.v.* **blan•ket•ed, blan•ket•ing, blan•kets.** To cover with or as if with a blanket: *Snow blanketed the countryside.* [First written down about 1300 in Middle English and spelled *blaunket*, from Old French, an unbleached soft cloth, from *blanc*, white.]

blank verse *n.* Verse written in unrhymed lines, usually of iambic pentameter.

blare (blâr) *v.* **blared, blar•ing, blares.** —*intr.* To sound loudly and stridently: *horns blaring in the traffic jam.* —*tr.* To cause to sound loudly and stridently: *A brass band blared the national anthem.* —*n.* A loud strident noise.

blar•ney (blär′nē) *n.* Smooth flattering talk.

Blar•ney Stone (blär′nē). A famous stone located in the ruins of Blarney Castle, Ireland, supposed to impart great powers of eloquence and persuasion to anyone kissing it.

bla•sé (blä zā′) *adj.* Uninterested or unexcited because of constant exposure or indulgence: *People who live on the coast tend to be blasé about the ocean.*

blas•pheme (blăs fēm′ *or* blăs′fēm′) *v.* **blas•phemed, blas•phem•ing, blas•phemes.** —*tr.* To speak of (God or something sacred) in a disrespectful way. —*intr.* To speak blasphemy. **—blas•phem′er** *n.*

blas•phe•mous (blăs′fə məs) *adj.* Disrespectful and irreverent. **—blas′phe•mous•ly** *adv.*

blas•phe•my (blăs′fə mē) *n., pl.* **blas•phe•mies.** A remark or an act that is disrespectful of God or irreverent of something sacred.

blast (blăst) *n.* **1.** A strong gust of wind or air. **2.** A strong stream of air, gas, or steam from an opening. **3.** A loud sudden sound, especially one produced by forced air: *the blast of the steam whistle.* **4.a.** An explosion: *a blast of dynamite.* **b.** A quantity of explosive used at one time. —*v.* **blast•ed, blast•ing, blasts.** —*tr.* **1.a.** To knock down or tear apart with or as if with an explosive: *blasting rocks in a quarry.* **b.** To make or open by or as if by an explosion: *blast a road through the mountain.* **2.** To destroy or shatter as if by an explosion: *Defeat blasted our hopes.* **3.** To cause to shrivel or wither before flowering or bearing fruit or seeds. **4.** To cause to sound loudly; blare: *Buglers blasted their horns. The radio blasted music out the window.* **5.** To criticize severely: *The reviewer blasted the movie.* —*intr.* **1.** To emit a loud unpleasant sound: *Car horns blasted from the street below.* **2.** To criticize or attack: *The paper blasted away at the corrupt city government.* —***idioms.*** **blast off.** To take off, as a rocket. **full blast.** At full speed, volume, or capacity.

blast furnace *n.* A furnace in which combustion is made more intense by a forced stream of air.

blas•to•coel or **blas•to•coele** (blăs′tə sēl′) *n.* The central cavity of a blastula.

blas•to•derm (blăs′tə dûrm′) *n.* The layer of cells formed by the growth of a fertilized egg, later dividing into three layers, from which all parts of the animal are formed.

blast•off also **blast-off** (blăst′ôf′ *or* blăst′ŏf′) *n.* The launching of a rocket or spacecraft.

blas•tu•la (blăs′chə lə) *n., pl.* **blas•tu•las** or **blas•tu•lae** (blăs′chə lē′). An early form of an embryo, consisting of a hollow sphere bounded by a single layer of cells.

bla•tant (blāt′nt) *adj.* **1.** Unpleasantly loud: *blatant revelers.* **2.** Offensively conspicuous; obvious: *a blatant lie.* **—bla′tan•cy** (blāt′n sē) *n.* **—bla′tant•ly** *adv.*

blaze[1] (blāz) *n.* **1.a.** A brightly burning fire: *make a blaze out of a pile of twigs.* **b.** A destructive fire: *A blaze destroyed the building.* **2.** A bright or steady glare: *the blaze of the sun.* **3.** A brilliant or striking display: *The flowers were a blaze of color.* **4.** A sudden outburst, as of activity or emotion: *in a blaze of speed; a blaze of anger.* —*intr.v.* **blazed, blaz•ing, blaz•es. 1.** To burn brightly: *a fire blazing in the fireplace.* **2.** To shine brightly: *The hot noonday sun blazed down on the beach.* **3.** To be resplendent: *The garden blazed with colorful flowers.* **4.** To flare up suddenly: *My temper blazed at the insulting remark.* [First written down before 893 in Old English and spelled *blæse.*]

blaze[2] (blāz) *n.* **1.** A white spot on the face of an animal, such as a horse. **2.** A mark cut on a tree to indicate a trail. —*tr.v.* **blazed, blaz•ing, blaz•es. 1.** To indicate (a trail) by marking trees with cuts. **2.** To prepare or lead (something): *blaze the way in space exploration.* [First written down in 1639 in Modern English, of Germanic origin.]

blaze[3] (blāz) *tr.v.* **blazed, blaz•ing, blaz•es.** To make known publicly; proclaim. [First written down about 1380 in Middle English and spelled *blasen*, from Middle Dutch *blāsen*, to blow up, swell.]

blaz•er (blā′zər) *n.* A lightweight informal sport jacket, often striped or brightly colored.

bla•zon (blā′zən) *tr.v.* **bla•zoned, bla•zon•ing, bla•zons. 1.** To decorate or adorn with or as if with a coat of arms. **2.** To announce; proclaim: *Demonstrators marched with signs blazoning their protest.* —*n.* A coat of arms.

bldg. *abbr.* An abbreviation of building.

bleach (blēch) *v.* **bleached, bleach•ing, bleach•es.** —*tr.* **1.** To remove the color from (fibers or fabrics, for example) by means of sunlight or chemicals; whiten: *bleach a shirt or blouse.* **2.** To lighten the color of (hair). *—intr.* To turn white or lose color: *boards bleaching in the desert sun.* *—n.* A chemical agent used for bleaching. [First written down about 899 in Old English and spelled *blǣcan.*]

bleach•ers (blē′chərz) *pl.n.* Wooden planks set in tiers for spectators to sit on at a public event, especially an outdoor event such as a baseball or football game.

bleach•ing powder (blē′chĭng) *n.* A white powder made by treating slaked lime with chlorine and used as a bleach and disinfectant; chloride of lime.

bleak (blēk) *adj.* **bleak•er, bleak•est. 1.** Gloomy; dreary; depressing: *The prospects for success are bleak.* **2.** Exposed to the elements; barren and windswept: *bleak treeless moors.* **3.** Cold and harsh: *a damp bleak wind.* [First written down about 1300 in Middle English and spelled *bleik,* pale, from Old Norse *bleikr,* white.] **—bleak′ly** *adv.* **—bleak′ness** *n.*

blear (blîr) *tr.v.* **bleared, blear•ing, blears. 1.** To blur (the eyes) with or as if with tears. **2.** To blur; dim: *Smoke from the fire bleared my vision.*

blear•y (blîr′ē) *adj.* **blear•i•er, blear•i•est. 1.** Blurred by or as if by tears: *bleary eyes.* **2.** Vague or indistinct; blurred: *a bleary photograph.* **—blear′i•ness** *n.*

bleat (blēt) *n.* **1.** The hoarse broken cry of a goat, sheep, or calf. **2.** A sound resembling this. *—v.* **bleat•ed, bleat•ing, bleats.** *—intr.* **1.** To utter the cry of a goat, sheep, or calf. **2.** To make a similar sound. *—tr.* To utter with a bleat. **—bleat′er** *n.*

bleed (blēd) *v.* **bled** (blĕd), **bleed•ing, bleeds.** *—intr.* **1.** To lose blood: *My finger bled when I cut it on the glass.* **2.** To be wounded, especially in battle. **3.** To feel sympathetic grief: *My heart bleeds for you in your sorrow.* **4.** To lose sap or other fluid, as a plant does that has been cut. **5.** To become mixed and run, as dye in wet cloth: *When I washed my new jeans, the dye bled and ruined a white shirt.* **6.** To show through a layer of paint as a stain in wood. *—tr.* **1.a.** To take or remove blood from: *Long ago doctors bled patients as a cure.* **b.** To remove sap or juice from (a plant). **2.a.** To draw off (a liquid or gas) from a container or pipe: *bleed air from tires that are overly inflated.* **b.** To draw liquid or gas from; drain: *bleed radiators to stop them from knocking.*

bleed•er (blē′dər) *n.* A person who bleeds excessively from even small cuts; a hemophiliac.

bleed•ing heart (blē′dĭng) *n.* Any of various garden plants related to the poppy, having nodding pink, red, or white heart-shaped flowers.

bleep (blēp) *n.* A brief high-pitched sound, as from an electronic device. *—intr.v.* **bleeped, bleep•ing, bleeps.** To make a bleep.

blem•ish (blĕm′ĭsh) *tr.v.* **blem•ished, blem•ish•ing, blem•ish•es.** To impair or mar by a flaw; disfigure: *Scratches blemished the table.* *—n.* Something that impairs or mars; a flaw: *skin blemishes; a blemish on one's reputation.*

blench (blĕnch) *intr.v.* **blenched, blench•ing, blench•es.** To draw back or shy away, as from fear; flinch: *The deer blenched and fled from the onrushing cars.*

blend (blĕnd) *v.* **blend•ed** or **blent** (blĕnt), **blend•ing, blends.** *—tr.* **1.** To combine so that the parts are not distinct; mix thoroughly: *The cook blended milk and flour.* See Synonyms at **mix. 2.** To combine (varieties or grades of something) to make a mixture with unique qualities: *We blended the two coffees.* *—intr.* **1.** To form a mixture; be combined: *Oil does not blend with water.* **2.** To become merged into one; unite: *The blue blends into the green in this painting.* **3.** To be in harmony; go together: *Your tie blends with your jacket.* *—n.* **1.** Something blended; a harmonious mixture or combination: *a blend of colors; a blend of teas.* **2.** A word produced by combining parts of other words, as *smog* from *smoke* and *fog.* [First written down about 1325 in Middle English and spelled *blenden,* probably from Old Norse *blanda.*]

blend•er (blĕn′dər) *n.* **1.** An electrical appliance with whirling blades, used to blend or purée foods. **2.** A person or thing that blends.

bless (blĕs) *tr.v.* **blessed** or **blest** (blĕst), **bless•ing, bless•es. 1.** To make holy; consecrate: *The minister blessed the water for baptism.* **2.** To make the sign of the cross over: *The priest blessed the congregation.* **3.** To call divine favor upon. **4.** To praise as holy; glorify: *Bless the Lord.* **5.** To endow, favor, or enrich: *The artist was blessed with unusual talent.* [First written down about 725 in Old English and spelled *blētsian,* to consecrate.]

bless•ed (blĕs′ĭd) also **blest** (blĕst) *adj.* **1.** Worthy of worship; holy. **2.** Enjoying happiness; very fortunate. *I feel blessed.* **3.** Bringing happiness; pleasurable: *A new baby in a family is a blessed event.* **—bless′ed•ly** *adv.* **—bless′ed•ness** *n.*

Bless•ed Virgin Mary (blĕs′ĭd) *n.* The Virgin Mary.

bless•ing (blĕs′ĭng) *n.* **1.** A prayer calling for divine favor. **2.** A short prayer given at mealtime. **3.** Approval; sanction: *The expedition to explore the Northwest had the government's blessing.* **4.** Something that brings happiness or well-being. Often used in the plural: *the blessings of liberty.* **5.** A wish for happiness or success: *We gave our blessings to the bride and groom.*

blest (blĕst) *v.* A past tense and a past participle of **bless.** *—adj.* Variant of **blessed.**

blew[1] (blo͞o) *v.* Past tense of **blow**[1].

❑ *These sound alike:* **blew**[1] (expelled air), **blew**[2] (bloomed), **blue** (color).

blew[2] (blo͞o) *v.* Past tense of **blow**[3].

❑ *These sound alike:* **blew**[2] (bloomed), **blew**[1] (expelled air), **blue** (color).

blight (blīt) *n.* **1.** Any of numerous plant diseases that cause leaves, stems, fruits, and tissues to wither and die. Rust, mildew, and smut are blights. **2.** The bacterium, fungus, or virus that causes such a disease. **3.** Something that is harmful or destructive: *Corruption is a blight on government.* *—v.* **blight•ed, blight•ing, blights.** *—tr.* **1.** To cause to wither and die: *A dry summer blighted the wheat.* **2.** To ruin; destroy: *Several losses blighted the team's hopes of becoming county champions.* *—intr.* To suffer from blight.

blimp (blĭmp) *n.* An airship that does not have a rigid framework.

blind (blīnd) *adj.* **blind•er. 1.a.** Lacking the sense of sight; sightless. **b.** Having a visual acuity of one-tenth normal vision or less while wearing corrective lenses. **2.** Performed by instruments and without the use of sight: *blind navigation.* **3.** Unwilling or unable to perceive or understand: *Many people are blind to their own faults.* **4.** Not based on reason or evidence: *blind faith.* **5.** Performed without preparation or knowledge: *a blind attempt to fix the washing machine.* **6.** Hidden or screened from sight: *a blind driveway.* **7.** Closed at one end: *a blind alley.* *—n.* **1.** Something that shuts out light or hinders vision: *We pull the blinds over the windows at night.* **2.** A shelter for concealing hunters, photographers, or observers of wildlife. **3.** Something that conceals the true nature of an activity, especially of an illegal or improper one; a subterfuge: *The spies used the candy store as a blind for their operations.* *—adv.* Without being able to see: *The pilot had to fly blind in the fog.* *—tr.v.* **blind•ed,**

bleeding heart

blimp

The Goodyear blimp *Spirit of Akron*

ă	pat	oi	boy
ā	pay	ou	out
âr	care	o͝o	took
ä	father	o͞o	boot
ĕ	pet	ŭ	cut
ē	be	ûr	urge
ĭ	pit	th	thin
ī	pie	*th*	this
îr	pier	hw	whoop
ŏ	pot	zh	vision
ō	toe	ə	about
ô	paw	N	*French* bon

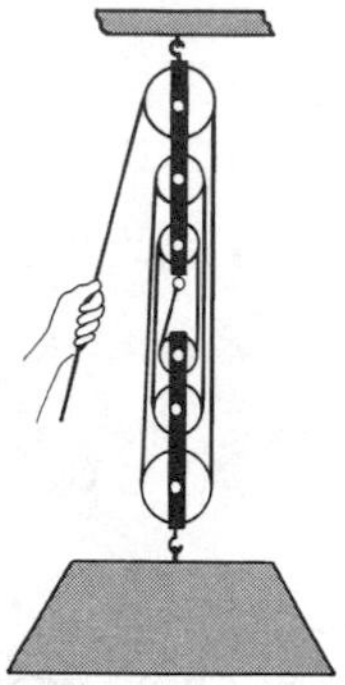
block and tackle
Multiple block and tackle

bloodhound

blind•ing, blinds. 1. To deprive of sight: *Lights from the oncoming cars blinded me.* **2.** To deprive (a person) of judgment or reason: *Prejudice blinds them to the advantages of the plan.* **—blind′ly** *adv.* **—blind′ness** *n.*

blind date *n.* A date between two people who have not previously met.

blind•ers (**blīn′**dərz) *pl.n.* A pair of leather flaps attached to a horse's bridle to prevent it from seeing things on either side.

blind•fold (**blīnd′**fōld′) *tr.v.* **blind•fold•ed, blind•fold•ing, blind•folds.** To cover the eyes of with or as if with a cloth: *blindfold a prisoner.* *—n.* A piece of cloth put over the eyes and tied around the head to keep someone from seeing. **—blind′fold′ed** *adj.*

blind•man's buff (**blīnd′**mănz′) *n.* A game in which a blindfolded person tries to catch and identify one of the other players.

blind spot *n.* **1.** The point on the retina, not sensitive to light, where the optic nerve leaves the eyeball. **2.** An area where radio or television reception is poor. **3.** A part of an area that cannot be observed directly: *a blind spot in the road.* **4.** A subject about which a person is noticeably ignorant or prejudiced: *Neatness is his blind spot; he just can't see its importance.*

blink (blĭngk) *v.* **blinked, blink•ing, blinks.** *—intr.* **1.** To close and open the eye or eyes rapidly: *blink at the bright light.* **2.** To flash off and on: *lights blinking on the horizon.* *—tr.* **1.** To close and open (the eye or eyes) rapidly; wink: *The cat blinked its eyes in the bright light.* **2.** To make flash off and on: *blink the lights of a car.* *—n.* **1.** A very brief closing of the eye or eyes. **2.** A brief flash of light. ***—idiom.*** **on the blink.** Out of working order.

blink•er (**blĭng′**kər) *n.* **1.** A light that blinks as a means of sending a message or warning. **2. blinkers.** Blinders.

blintz (blĭnts) also **blin•tze** (**blĭn′**tsə) *n.* A thin rolled pancake with a filling such as cream cheese or fruit. [First written down in 1903 in Modern English, from Yiddish *blintse*, of Russian origin.]

blip (blĭp) *n.* **1.** A spot of light on a radar or sonar screen indicating the position of a detected object, such as an aircraft. **2.** An interruption of sound in a television transmission or on a videotape. [First written down in 1894 in American English, of imitative origin.]

bliss (blĭs) *n.* Extreme happiness; joy.

bliss•ful (**blĭs′**fəl) *adj.* Full of or causing bliss: *a blissful silence; blissful ignorance of the problem.* **—bliss′ful•ly** *adv.* **—bliss′ful•ness** *n.*

blis•ter (**blĭs′**tər) *n.* **1.** A thin fluid-filled sac that forms on the skin as a result of a burn or an irritation. **2.** A raised bubble, as on a painted surface. *—intr. & tr.v.* **blis•tered, blis•ter•ing, blis•ters.** To form or cause to form blisters: *Her skin blistered from poison ivy. Tight shoes blistered the hiker's feet.* [First written down about 1325 in Middle English and spelled *blester*, probably from Old French *blestre*, of Germanic origin.] **—blis′ter•y** *adj.*

blis•ter•ing (**blĭs′**tər ĭng) *adj.* **1.** Extremely hot: *a blistering summer sun.* **2.** Very strong; intense: *blistering criticism.* **3.** Extremely rapid: *a blistering pace.*

blithe (blīth *or* blīth) *adj.* **blith•er, blith•est. 1.** Carefree and lighthearted: *the blithe atmosphere of the birthday party.* **2.** Showing a lack of concern: *a blithe disregard of danger.* **—blithe′ly** *adv.* **—blithe′ness** *n.*

blithe•some (**blīth′**səm *or* **blīth′**səm) *adj.* Cheerful; merry; lighthearted. **—blithe′some•ly** *adv.* **—blithe′some•ness** *n.*

blitz (blĭts) *n.* **1.** A blitzkrieg. **2.** An intense campaign: *an advertising blitz.* *—tr.v.* **blitzed, blitz•ing, blitz•es.** To subject to a blitz. [First written down in 1939 in Modern English, short for *blitzkrieg*.]

blitz•krieg (**blĭts′**krēg′) *n.* A swift, sudden military attack, usually by air and land forces. [First written down about 1939 in Modern English, from German : *Blitz*, lightning + *Krieg*, war.]

bliz•zard (**blĭz′**ərd) *n.* **1.** A very heavy snowstorm with strong winds. **2.** A great number or an unusually heavy flow: *a blizzard of phone calls congratulating the winning candidate.* [First written down in 1859 in Modern English.]

bloat (blōt) *intr. & tr.v.* **bloat•ed, bloat•ing, bloats.** To swell or cause to swell or puff up, as with liquid or gas: *a stomach bloated by overeating.* [First written down about 1300 in Middle English and spelled *blout*, soft, puffed, from Old Norse *blautr*, soft, soaked.]

blob (blŏb) *n.* A soft formless mass: *a blob of wax fell from the burning candle.*

bloc (blŏk) *n.* A group of nations, parties, or persons united by common interests or political aims: *representatives forming the farm bloc in Congress.* [First written down in 1903 in Modern English, from Old French *bloc*, block.]

❑ *These sound alike:* **bloc, block** (flat-sided object).

block (blŏk) *n.* **1.** A solid piece of wood or another hard substance having one or more flat sides: *Blocks of marble form the front of that building.* **2.** Such a piece on which chopping or cutting is done: *a butcher's block.* **3.** A stand from which articles are displayed at an auction. **4.** A mold or form upon which something is shaped or displayed: *a hat block.* **5.** A pulley or set of pulleys set in a casing. **6.** The metal casing that contains the cylinders of an engine. **7.** A set of like items sold or handled as a unit: *a block of tickets in the balcony.* **8.a.** An obstacle or a hindrance: *Road work caused a block in traffic.* **b.** In medicine, an obstruction of a bodily function: *an intestinal block.* **9.a.** A section of a city or town enclosed by connecting streets: *Walk the dog around the block.* **b.** The part of a street that lies between two successive cross streets: *Our home is in the middle of the block.* **10.** A large building divided into separate units, such as apartments. **11.** A length of railroad track controlled by one set of signals. **12.** In sports, an act of obstructing an opponent, especially in football, a legal act of using one's body to obstruct an opponent and thus protect the teammate who has the ball. *—v.* **blocked, block•ing, blocks.** *—tr.* **1.a.** To stop the movement of: *Road work was blocking traffic.* **b.** To stop movement through: *The stalled car blocked the intersection.* **2.** To be in the way of; obstruct visually: *You're blocking my view.* **3.** In medicine, to obstruct the functioning of (a nerve, for example). **4.** To shape or form with or on a block: *block a sweater after washing it.* **5.** In sports, to stop or hinder the movement of (an opponent or the ball) by physical interference. **6.** To indicate in a general way; sketch: *block out a plan of action.* *—intr.* In sports, to interfere with the movement of an opponent. [First written down in 1390 in Middle English, from Old French *bloc*, from Middle Dutch.]

❑ *These sound alike:* **block, bloc** (group).

block•ade (blŏ **kād′**) *n.* **1.** The closing off of a city, harbor, or country by troops or warships in order to prevent people and supplies from going in and out. **2.** The forces used in a blockade. **3.** Something that closes off or obstructs; an obstacle. *—tr.v.* **block•ad•ed, block•ad•ing, block•ades.** To set up a blockade against. **—block•ad′er** *n.*

block•ade-run•ner (blŏ **kād′**rŭn′ər) *n.* A ship or

person that attempts to go through or past an enemy blockade.

block•age (blŏk′ĭj) *n.* **1.** The act of obstructing. **2.** An obstruction: *an intestinal blockage.*

block and tackle *n.* An arrangement of pulleys and ropes used for lifting heavy objects.

block•bust•er (blŏk′bŭs′tər) *n. Informal.* **1.** Something, such as a movie or book, that is very popular or sells in large numbers. **2.** A large bomb capable of great destruction.

block•head (blŏk′hĕd′) *n.* A person who is considered stupid.

block•house (blŏk′hous′) *n.* **1.** A building made of heavy timbers, with a projecting upper story and loopholes for firing. **2.** A fortification made of concrete with slits for firing or observation. **3.** A heavily reinforced building from which the launching of rockets or space vehicles is observed and controlled.

bloke (blōk) *n. Chiefly British.* A fellow; a man.

blond also **blonde** (blŏnd) *adj.* **blond•er, blond•est. 1.** Having fair hair and skin: *a blond baby.* **2.** Having a pale yellow or golden color: *blond hair.* **3.** Light-colored: *blond furniture.* —*n.* A blond person. [First written down in 1481 in Middle English, from Old French *blonde,* of Germanic origin.] **—blond′ness** *n.*

blood (blŭd) *n.* **1.a.** The fluid circulated through the body by the action of the heart, distributing oxygen, nutrients, and hormones and carrying wastes to the excretory organs. **b.** A fluid that is similar in function in invertebrate animals. **2.** Temperament or disposition: *a person of hot blood and a fiery temper.* **3.** Family relationship; kinship: *related by blood.* **4.** Descent from a common ancestor; lineage. —***idiom.* in cold blood.** Deliberately, coldly, and dispassionately. [First written down about 725 in Old English and spelled *blōd.*]

blood bank *n.* **1.** A place where whole blood or blood plasma is classified according to blood groups for use in transfusions. **2.** Blood or plasma stored in such a place.

blood•bath (blŭd′băth′) *n.* Savage and widespread killing; a massacre.

blood count *n.* A count of the number of red and white blood cells and platelets in a sample of a person's blood.

blood•cur•dling (blŭd′kûrd′lĭng) *adj.* Causing great horror; terrifying.

blood•ed (blŭd′ĭd) *adj.* **1.** Having blood or a temperament of a specified kind: *a cold-blooded reptile.* **2.** Thoroughbred: *blooded racehorses.*

blood group *n.* A blood type.

blood•hound (blŭd′hound′) *n.* One of a breed of hounds having a smooth coat, drooping ears, loose folds of skin around the face, and a keen sense of smell.

blood•less (blŭd′lĭs) *adj.* **1.** Having no blood. **2.** Pale and anemic in color: *cold and bloodless hands.* **3.** Accomplished without killing: *a bloodless revolution.* **4.** Lacking spirit: *a dull bloodless tale.* **—blood′less•ly** *adv.* **—blood′less•ness** *n.*

blood•line (blŭd′līn′) *n.* A direct line of descent.

blood•mo•bile (blŭd′mə bēl′) *n.* A motor vehicle equipped for collecting blood from donors.

blood poisoning *n.* **1.** A disease in which the blood contains poisons; toxemia. **2.** A disease in which the blood contains bacteria or poisons produced by them; septicemia.

blood pressure *n.* The pressure that the blood exerts on the walls of the arteries or other blood vessels. Blood pressure varies with the strength of the heartbeat, the volume of the blood, the elasticity of the arteries, and the person's health, age, and physical condition.

blood•root (blŭd′ro͞ot′ *or* blŭd′ro͝ot′) *n.* A woodland plant of North America having a fleshy root, poisonous red sap, and a single white flower.

blood•shed (blŭd′shĕd′) *n.* The shedding of blood, especially the injuring or killing of human beings; slaughter.

blood•shot (blŭd′shŏt′) *adj.* Inflamed and overfilled with blood, often with the small blood vessels enlarged: *bloodshot eyes.*

blood•stained (blŭd′stānd′) *adj.* Stained or spotted with blood: *a bloodstained handkerchief.*

blood•stone (blŭd′stōn′) *n.* A deep-green, cloudy form of quartz that is flecked with red. It is used as a gem.

blood•stream (blŭd′strēm′) *n.* The blood as it flows through the body.

blood•suck•er (blŭd′sŭk′ər) *n.* An animal, such as a leech, that sucks blood.

blood test *n.* An examination of a sample of blood to determine its contents, as for ascertaining the blood group or diagnosing illness.

blood•thirst•y (blŭd′thûr′stē) *adj.* Eager to cause or see the shedding of blood; cruel. **—blood′thirst′i•ly** *adv.* **—blood′thirst′i•ness** *n.*

blood type *n.* Any of the four main types, A, B, AB, and O, into which human blood is divided on the basis of the presence or absence of certain proteins and antibodies; blood group. —SEE NOTE.

blood vessel *n.* An elastic tube or passage in the body through which blood circulates; an artery, a vein, or a capillary.

blood•y (blŭd′ē) *adj.* **blood•i•er, blood•i•est. 1.** Bleeding: *a bloody nose.* **2.** Stained with blood: *bloody bandages.* **3.** Causing or marked by bloodshed: *a bloody fight.* **4.** Bloodthirsty; cruel. —*adv.* Used as an intensive: *You're bloody right.* —*tr.v.* **blood•ied, blood•y•ing, blood•ies.** To make bloody: *My elbow was bloodied in the fall.* **—blood′i•ly** *adv.* **—blood′i•ness** *n.*

bloom (blo͞om) *n.* **1.** The flower or blossom of a plant. **2.** The condition or time of flowering: *a rosebush in bloom.* **3.** A condition or time of great development, vigor, or beauty: *a boy in the full bloom of youth.* **4.** A fresh rosy complexion: *a fine bloom to the cheeks.* **5.** A thin powdery coating sometimes occurring on fruits, leaves, or stems: *the bloom on a plum.* —*intr.v.* **bloomed, bloom•ing, blooms. 1.** To bear flowers; blossom: *Tulips bloom in the spring.* **2.** To grow or flourish: *Volunteer groups to teach reading are blooming.* **3.** To shine with health or vigor; glow. [First written down about 1200 in Middle English and spelled *blom,* from Old Norse *blōm.*]

bloom•ers (blo͞o′mərz) *pl.n.* **1.** Baggy trousers gathered at the knee, once worn by women and girls for sports, such as riding bicycles. **2.** Similar pants worn as underwear. [First written down in 1889 in Modern English, after Amelia Jenks *Bloomer* (1818–1894), American social reformer.]

bloom•ing (blo͞o′mĭng) *adv. & adj. Chiefly British.* Used as an intensive: *a blooming hot day; a blooming idiot.*

bloop•er (blo͞o′pər) *n.* **1.** A clumsy mistake, especially one made in public. **2.** In baseball, a weakly hit ball that carries just past the infield.

blos•som (blŏs′əm) *n.* **1.** A flower or cluster of flowers: *apple blossoms.* **2.** The condition or time of flowering: *spring flowers in blossom.* —*intr.v.* **blos•somed, blos•som•ing, blos•soms. 1.** To come into flower; bloom. **2.** To develop and do well; flourish: *The public's interest in science blossomed with space flight.* [First written down about 725 in Old English and spelled *blōstm.*]

blot (blŏt) *n.* **1.** A stain or spot: *an ink blot.* **2.** A stain on one's character or reputation; a disgrace. —*v.* **blot•ted, blot•ting, blots.** —*tr.* **1.** To spot or

blood type

Blood transfusions used to be a big problem—they often caused people to become sick and die. But in the 1890's, a scientist named Karl Landsteiner began to solve the transfusion puzzle. He found that all human blood cells belonged to one of four groups or **blood types**, which he named A, B, AB, and O. The types also describe the surface proteins, called *antigens*, that these cells have. These antigens tell the body to produce antibodies that cause blood cells of different blood types to clump. Thus the key to the transfusion puzzle is to give a person blood that has matching antigens—blood that matches his or her blood type.

bloomers

ă	pat	oi	**boy**
ā	**pay**	ou	**out**
âr	**care**	o͝o	**took**
ä	**father**	o͞o	**boot**
ĕ	**pet**	ŭ	**cut**
ē	**be**	ûr	**urge**
ĭ	**pit**	th	**thin**
ī	**pie**	*th*	**this**
îr	**pier**	hw	**whoop**
ŏ	**pot**	zh	**vision**
ō	**toe**	ə	**about**
ô	**paw**	N	*French* **bon**

blowhole
Of a dolphin

bluebell

stain: *Greasy fingerprints blotted the page.* **2.** To dry or soak up with absorbent material: *blot a spill with paper towels.* —*intr.* **1.** To spill or spread in a spot or stain. **2.** To become blotted or absorbed: *Water colors blot easily.* —***idiom.*** **blot out. 1.** To hide from view; obscure: *Storm clouds blotted out the sun.* **2.** To destroy completely; annihilate: *The frost blotted out the tomatoes.* [First written down in 1373 in Middle English.]

blotch (blŏch) *n.* **1.** A spot or blot; a splotch. **2.** A discoloration on the skin; a blemish. —*tr. & intr.v.* **blotched, blotch•ing, blotch•es.** To mark or become marked with blotches. —**blotch'y** *adv.*

blot•ter (blŏt'ər) *n.* **1.** A piece or pad of thick absorbent paper used to dry a surface by soaking up excess ink. **2.** A book containing daily records of occurrences or transactions: *A blotter kept at a police station records the arrests made.*

blouse (blous *or* blouz) *n.* **1.** A loosely fitting shirt that extends to the waist. **2.** A loose garment resembling a smock, worn by some workmen and peasants in Europe. **3.** The jacket of a military uniform.

blow[1] (blō) *v.* **blew** (blo͞o), **blown** (blōn), **blow•ing, blows.** —*intr.* **1.** To be in motion. Used of the air or of wind: *The wind blew hard all night.* **2.** To be moved by a current of air: *My hat blew off.* **3.** To send out a current of air: *Blow on your soup to cool it.* **4.** To sound: *The whistle blows at noon.* **5.** To burst suddenly: *The tire blew when we hit a rock.* **6.** To burn out or melt: *We were left in darkness when the fuse blew.* **7.** To spout water and air from the blowhole, as a whale does. —*tr.* **1.** To cause to move by a current of air: *The gale blew a tree across the power lines.* **2.** To expell (air) from the mouth. **3.a.** To cause (a wind instrument) to sound by forcing breath through it: *blow a trumpet.* **b.** To sound (a melody): *a bugle blowing taps.* **4.** To cause to explode: *To build the tunnel they blew rock out of the way with dynamite.* **5.** To clear by forcing air through: *blowing his nose noisily.* **6.** To shape (a pliable material, such as molten glass) by forcing air into it. **7.** To cause (an electrical fuse) to melt and open a circuit. **8.** To handle ineptly; mess up: *blow one's chance to go.* —*n.* **1.** A blast of air or wind. **2.** A storm. **3.** The act or an instance of blowing. —***idioms.*** **blow away.** *Slang.* **1.** To kill by shooting, especially with a firearm. **2.** To affect intensely; overwhelm: *That concert blew me away.* **blow in.** *Slang.* To arrive, especially when unexpected. **blow off.** To relieve or release (pressure); let off. **blow off steam.** To express pent-up emotion. **blow (one's) top** or **blow (one's) stack.** To lose one's temper. **blow out. 1.** To extinguish or be extinguished by a gust of air: *blow out the candles.* **2.** To fail, as an electrical apparatus: *The fuse blew out.* **blow over.** To subside or pass over with little lasting effect: *The storm will blow over soon.* **blow up. 1.** To come into being: *A storm blew up.* **2.** To fill with air; inflate: *blowing up balloons.* **3.** To enlarge (a photograph). **4.** To explode: *The gas tank blew up.* **5.** To lose one's temper. [First written down about 725 in Old English and spelled *blāwan.*]

blow[2] (blō) *n.* **1.** A sudden hard stroke or hit, as with the fist or a weapon. **2.** A sudden unexpected shock or great misfortune: *The closing of the museum was a blow to our weekend plans.* **3.** A sudden unexpected attack; an assault. [First written down about 1500 in Middle English and spelled *blaw.*]

blow[3] (blō) *intr. & tr.v.* **blew** (blo͞o), **blown** (blōn), **blow•ing, blows.** To bloom or cause to bloom. [First written down about 1000 in Old English and spelled *blōwan.*]

blow-dry (blō'drī') *tr.v.* **blow-dried, blow-dry•ing, blow-dries.** To dry and often style (hair) with a blow dryer.

blow dryer *n.* A portable electric blower for drying and styling hair.

blow•er (blō'ər) *n.* A device that produces a flow of air or other gas through a duct or an enclosed space.

blow•fly (blō'flī') *n.* Any of several flies that deposit their eggs on carcasses, on meat, or in wounds.

blow•gun (blō'gŭn') *n.* A long narrow pipe through which pellets or poison darts can be blown; a blowpipe.

blow•hole (blō'hōl') *n.* **1.** A nostril or hole for breathing in the top of the head of whales, porpoises, and dolphins. **2.** A hole in the ice through which seals, whales, and other water animals come up for air.

blown[1] (blōn) *v.* Past participle of **blow[1].**

blown[2] (blōn) *v.* Past participle of **blow[3].**

blow•out (blō'out') *n.* A sudden and violent loss of air pressure, as from an automobile tire.

blow•pipe (blō'pīp') *n.* **1.** A narrow tube for blowing air or gas into a flame to increase its heat, used especially in the identification of minerals. **2.** A long narrow iron pipe used to gather, work, and blow molten glass. **3.** A blowgun.

blow•sy (blou'zē) *adj.* Variant of **blowzy.**

blow•torch (blō'tôrch') *n.* A torch using air to produce a flame hot enough to melt soft metals and remove paint.

blow•up (blō'ŭp') *n.* **1.** An explosion. **2.** A photographic enlargement. **3.** An outburst of temper.

blow•zy also **blow•sy** (blou'zē) *adj.* **blow•zi•er, blow•zi•est** also **blow•si•er, blow•si•est. 1.** Ruddy and bloated in appearance. **2.** Not tidy; disheveled; messy.

blub•ber[1] (blŭb'ər) *v.* **blub•bered, blub•ber•ing, blub•bers.** —*intr.* To cry or sob in a noisy manner. See Synonyms at **cry.** —*tr.* To say while crying and sobbing: *The boy blubbered his name.* —*n.* A loud weeping and sobbing. [First written down about 1400 in Middle English and spelled *bluberen,* to bubble, from *bluber,* foam.] —**blub'ber•er** *n.*

blub•ber[2] (blŭb'ər) *n.* The fat of whales and some other sea animals, lying under the skin and over the muscles, from which oil is obtained. Blubber insulates the animal from heat loss and serves as a food reserve. [First written down about 1380 in Middle English and spelled *bluber,* foam.]

bludg•eon (blŭj'ən) *n.* A short heavy club with one end heavier or thicker than the other. —*tr.v.* **bludg•eoned, bludg•eon•ing, bludg•eons.** To beat or strike with or as if with a bludgeon.

blue (blo͞o) *n.* **1.** The color of the sky on a clear day; the color of the visible spectrum lying between green and violet. **2.** Often **Blue. a.** A Union soldier in the U.S. Civil War. **b.** The Union Army. **3.a.** The sea. **b.** The sky. —*adj.* **blu•er, blu•est. 1.** Of the color blue. **2.** Having a gray or purplish color, as from cold or a bruise: *lips blue from the chill.* **3.** Gloomy; depressed: *a sailor far from home, lonely and blue.* —*tr. & intr.v.* **blued, blu•ing, blues.** To make or become blue. —***idiom.*** **out of the blue. 1.** From an unexpected or unforeseen source: *a problem that came out of the blue.* **2.** At a completely unexpected time: *My friend showed up out of the blue last night.* [First written down about 1300 in Middle English and spelled *bleu,* from Old French, of Germanic origin.] —**blue'ly** *adv.* —**blue'ness** *n.*
❑ *These sound alike:* **blue, blew[1]** (expelled air), **blew[2]** (bloomed).

blue baby *n.* A newborn baby having a bluish tint to its skin because of a heart or lung defect, resulting in too little oxygen in its blood.

blue•bell (blo͞o'bĕl') also **blue•bells** (blo͞o'bĕlz') *n.*

Any of several plants having blue bell-shaped flowers.

blue•ber•ry (**blo͞o′**bĕr′ē) *n.* **1.** A round, juicy, edible blue or purplish berry. **2.** Any of numerous shrubs that bear such berries.

blue•bird (**blo͞o′**bûrd′) *n.* Any of several North American birds having blue feathers and usually a rust-colored breast in the male.

blue blood *n.* **1.** Noble or aristocratic descent. **2.** A member of the aristocracy or other high social group.

blue•bon•net (**blo͞o′**bŏn′ĭt) *n.* Either of two plants of western North America, having clusters of blue flowers.

blue•bot•tle (**blo͞o′**bŏt′l) *n.* Any of several large blowflies having a bright metallic-blue body.

blue cheese *n.* A tangy cheese streaked with bluish mold.

blue-col•lar (**blo͞o′**kŏl′ər) *adj.* Of or relating to wage earners whose jobs are performed in work clothes and often involve manual labor.

blue•fish (**blo͞o′**fĭsh′) *n.* Any of various bluish or greenish ocean fishes caught for food or sport.

blue flag *n.* Any of several irises having blue flowers.

blue•grass (**blo͞o′**grăs′) *n.* Any of various lawn and pasture grasses having bluish or grayish leaves and stems.

blue-green alga (**blo͞o′**grēn′) *n.* An alga of a bluish green color, from the pigment masking its chlorophyll, consisting of one or more cells that lack definite nuclei.

blue•ing (**blo͞o′**ĭng) *n.* A variant of **bluing.**

blue•ish (**blo͞o′**ĭsh) *adj.* Variant of **bluish.**

blue jay *n.* A North American bird having a crested head, blue feathers with white and black markings, and a harsh noisy cry.

blue jeans *pl.n.* Trousers of blue denim or similar cloth.

blue law *n.* **1.** A law passed in colonial New England to govern personal behavior and particularly to prohibit certain forms of recreation on Sunday. **2.** A law restricting Sunday activities, especially shopping.

blue•print (**blo͞o′**prĭnt′) *n.* **1.** A photographic copy of architectural plans or technical drawings appearing as white lines on a blue background. **2.** A carefully worked-out plan: *a blueprint for success.* —*tr. v.* **blue•print•ed, blue•print•ing, blue•prints.** To make a blueprint of.

blue ribbon *n.* The first prize or highest award.

Blue Ridge also **Blue Ridge Mountains.** A range of the Appalachian Mountains extending from southern Pennsylvania to northern Georgia. It rises to 6,684 feet (2,038.6 meters).

blues (blo͞oz) *pl.n.* *(used with a singular or plural verb).* **1.** A type of popular music that developed from southern Black American songs and has a slow tempo and flatted third and seventh tones. **2.** Lowness of spirit; melancholy: *The rainy weather is giving people the blues.*

blu•ets (**blo͞o′**ĭts) *pl.n.* *(used with a singular or plural verb).* Any of several low-growing plants of North America having small light-blue flowers.

blue whale *n.* A very large whale having a bluish-gray back and narrow grooves along the throat and belly. It can grow to over 95 feet in length.

bluff[1] (blŭf) *v.* **bluffed, bluff•ing, bluffs.** —*tr.* **1.** To deceive or mislead: *He bluffed the guard into thinking he worked for the bank.* **2.** To impress, hold back, or frighten by threats that are not meant to be carried out: *Management bluffed the union into signing the contract by announcing that the plant would be closed.* —*intr.* To engage in a false display of strength or confidence: *They were bluffing when the reporters said they knew the movie star.* —*n.* **1.** The act or an example of deceiving or misleading by a false display of strength or confidence. **2.** A person who bluffs. [First written down in 1674 in Modern English, probably from Dutch *bluffen,* from Low German.] —**bluff′er** *n.*

bluff[2] (blŭf) *n.* A steep headland, cliff, or riverbank. —*adj.* **bluff•er, bluff•est. 1.** Gruff or blunt in manner but not unkind: *bluff speech.* **2.** Having a broad steep front: *bluff cliffs along the riverbanks.* [First written down in 1687 in Modern English, probably from obsolete Dutch *blaf* or Middle Low German *blaff,* broad.] —**bluff′ly** *adv.* —**bluff′ness** *n.*

blu•ing also **blue•ing** (**blo͞o′**ĭng) *n.* A blue powder or liquid added to rinse water to prevent white fabrics from turning yellow during laundering.

blu•ish also **blue•ish** (**blo͞o′**ĭsh) *adj.* Somewhat blue.

blun•der (**blŭn′**dər) *n.* A foolish or careless mistake: *Using the wrong wax was a serious blunder.* —*intr. v.* **blun•dered, blun•der•ing, blun•ders. 1.** To make a foolish mistake: *We blundered in estimating the cost of the curtains.* **2.** To move clumsily or blindly; stumble: *blunder through the bushes into a stream.*

blun•der•buss (**blŭn′**dər bŭs′) *n.* An old type of gun with a wide muzzle for scattering shot at close range. [First written down in 1654 in Modern English, alteration of Dutch *donderbus* : *donder,* thunder + *bus,* gun.]

blunt (blŭnt) *adj.* **blunt•er, blunt•est. 1.** Having a thick dull edge or end; not sharp. **2.** Abrupt and frank in manner: *a blunt reprimand.* —*tr. & intr.v.* **blunt•ed, blunt•ing, blunts.** To make or become less sharp or keen; dull: *The knife was blunted from so much use.* —**blunt′ly** *adv.* —**blunt′ness** *n.*

blur (blûr) *v.* **blurred, blur•ring, blurs.** —*tr.* **1.** To make indistict or hazy in outline; obscure: *Clouds blurred the mountain.* **2.** To smear or stain; smudge: *My wet hands blurred the watercolors.* **3.** To reduce the ability to perceive; dim: *Dazzling lights blurred the driver's vision.* —*intr.* To become indistinct, vague, or hazy: *The mountain blurred in the snowstorm.* —*n.* **1.** Something that is indistinct and hazy: *The crowd was a blur of colors in the distance.* **2.** A smear or blot; a smudge.

blurb (blûrb) *n.* A brief favorable publicity notice, as on the jacket of a book.

blur•ry (**blûr′**ē) *adj.* Indistinct and hazy: *blurry sounds; a blurry picture.*

blurt (blûrt) *tr.v.* **blurt•ed, blurt•ing, blurts.** To say suddenly and without thought: *She blurted out the secret.*

blush (blŭsh) *intr.v.* **blushed, blush•ing, blush•es. 1.** To become suddenly red in the face from modesty, embarrassment, or shame. **2.** To feel ashamed: *I blushed at their rude remarks.* —*n.* **1.** A sudden reddening of the face caused by modesty, embarrassment, or shame. **2.** A reddish or rosy color: *The sun's last blushes tinted the hills.*

blush•er (**blŭsh′**ər) *n.* A cosmetic used to give the cheeks a rosy tint.

blus•ter (**blŭs′**tər) *intr.v.* **blus•tered, blus•ter•ing, blus•ters. 1.** To blow in loud violent gusts: *Winds blustered on the mountain top.* **2.** To utter noisy boasts or threats: *The angry customer blustered at the sales clerk.* —*n.* **1.** A violent gusty wind: *the bluster of a March storm.* **2.** Noisy confusion; commotion: *reporters amid the hustle and bluster of a political convention.* **3.** Loud, boastful, or threatening talk. —**blus′ter•er** *n.* —**blus′ter•ous** *adj.* —**blus′ter•y** *adj.*

blvd. or **Blvd.** *abbr.* An abbreviation of boulevard.

Bly (blī), **Nellie.** Elizabeth Cochrane Seaman.

bo•a (**bō′**ə) *n.* **1.** Any of several large non-poisonous snakes, such as the boa constrictor of tropical

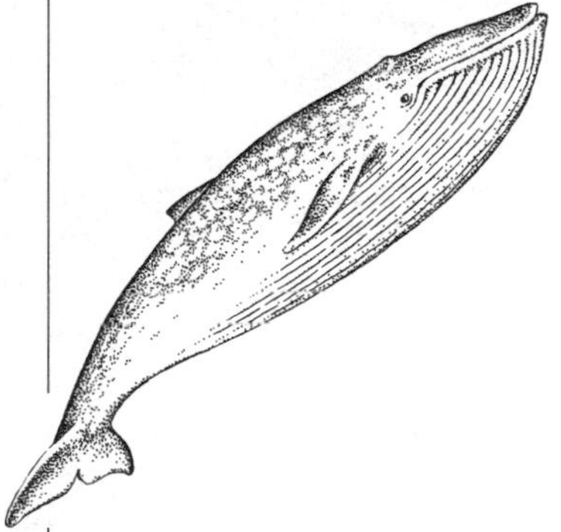

blue whale

ă	pat	oi	boy
ā	pay	ou	out
âr	care	o͝o	took
ä	father	o͞o	boot
ĕ	pet	ŭ	cut
ē	be	ûr	urge
ĭ	pit	th	thin
ī	pie	*th*	this
îr	pier	hw	whoop
ŏ	pot	zh	vision
ō	toe	ə	about
ô	paw	N	*French* bon

America, that coil around and crush their prey. **2.** A long fluffy scarf of fur or feathers.

Bo•ad•i•ce•a (bō′ăd ĭ sē′ə). Boudicca.

boar (bôr) *n.* **1.** A male pig. **2.** A wild pig of Europe, Asia, and North America having dark bristles and short tusks.

❑ *These sound alike:* **boar, bore**[1] (drill), **bore**[2] (make weary), **bore**[3] (tidal wave), **bore**[4] (supported).

board (bôrd) *n.* **1.** A flat thin length of sawed lumber; a plank: *The side of the hut was finished with old boards.* **2.** A flat piece of wood or similar material adapted for some special use: *a bulletin board; a chess board.* **3.a.** A table set for serving a meal: *a modest board.* **b.** Food served daily to paying guests: *room and board.* **4.** A group of persons organized to transact or administer some particular business: *the board of trustees.* **5.** A backboard in basketball. **6. boards.** The wooden structure enclosing an ice rink. —*v.* **board•ed, board•ing, boards.** —*tr.* **1.** To close with boards: *boarding up the windows.* **2.** To provide with food and lodging for a charge. **3.** To go aboard (a ship, train, or plane). —*intr.* To live as a paying guest: *board at the local hotel.* [First written down about 725 in Old English and spelled *board*, table, shield, side of a ship.]

❑ *These sound alike:* **board, bored** (wearied).

board•er (bôr′dər) *n.* A person who pays for and receives both meals and lodging at another person's home.

❑ *These sound alike:* **boarder, border** (edge).

board foot *n., pl.* **board feet.** A unit of measure for lumber, equal to the volume of an unplaned board one foot long, one foot wide, and one inch thick; 144 cubic inches of wood.

board•ing house (bôr′dĭng) *n.* A private home that provides meals and lodging for paying guests.

boarding school *n.* A school where pupils are provided with meals and lodging.

board•walk (bôrd′wôk′) *n.* A public walk or promenade along a beach, usually made of wooden planks.

boast (bōst) *v.* **boast•ed, boast•ing, boasts.** —*intr.* To speak with too much pride about oneself; brag. —*tr.* **1.** To speak about with too much pride: *The doctors boasted what their discovery meant.* **2.** To have as a desirable feature: *The area boasted great vineyards and gardens.* —*n.* **1.** A bragging or boastful statement: *a boast not supported by fact.* **2.** A source of pride: *The city's main boast is its beautiful park.* **—boast′er** *n.*

boast•ful (bōst′fəl) *adj.* Tending to boast or brag. **—boast′ful•ly** *adv.* **—boast′ful•ness** *n.*

boat (bōt) *n.* **1.** A small open craft for traveling on water. **2.** A large seagoing vessel; a ship or submarine. **3.** A dish shaped like a boat: *a gravy boat.* —*intr.* & *tr.v.* **boat•ed, boat•ing, boats.** To travel by boat; row or sail: *boat across the lake.* **—*idiom.* in the same boat.** In the same situation as someone else. [First written down about 725 in Old English and spelled *bāt.*]

boat•house (bōt′hous′) *n.* A house in which boats are kept, often near the water's edge.

boat•man (bōt′mən) *n.* A person who works on, deals with, or operates boats.

boat people *pl.n.* People who leave their country by boat seeking refuge in some country that will allow them to enter.

boat•swain also **bo's'n** or **bo•sun** (bō′sən) *n.* A warrant officer or petty officer in charge of a ship's deck crew, rigging, and anchors.

bob[1] (bŏb) *v.* **bobbed, bob•bing, bobs.** —*tr.* To cause to move up and down: *bobbed their heads.* —*intr.* **1.** To move or jerk up and down: *a cork bobbing on the water.* **2.** To grab at floating or hanging objects with the teeth: *bob for apples.* —*n.* A quick jerking movement of the head or body. **—*idiom.* bob up.** To appear or arise unexpectedly or suddenly. [First written down about 1390 in Middle English and spelled *bobben.*]

bob[2] (bŏb) *n.* **1.** A small hanging weight, such as a plumb bob. **2.** A fishing float or cork. **3.** A short haircut on a woman or child. —*v.* **bobbed, bob•bing, bobs.** —*intr.* To fish with a bob. —*tr.* To cut short: *She has bobbed her hair.* [First written down about 1390 in Middle English and spelled *bobbe*, cluster of fruit.]

bob[3] (bŏb) *n., pl.* **bob.** *Chiefly British.* A shilling. [First written down in 1789 in Modern English.]

bob•bin (bŏb′ĭn) *n.* A spool or reel that holds something, such as thread or yarn, for spinning, weaving, knitting, sewing, or making lace.

bob•ble (bŏb′əl) *v.* **bob•bled, bob•bling, bob•bles.** —*intr.* To bob up and down. —*tr.* To lose one's grip on (a ball) momentarily. —*n.* A mistake or blunder.

bob•by (bŏb′ē) *n., pl.* **bob•bies.** *Chiefly British.* A policeman. [First written down in 1844 in Modern English, after Sir Robert *Peel* (1788–1850), home secretary of England when the Metropolitan Police Force was created in 1829.]

bobby pin *n.* A small metal hairpin having springy ends pressed tightly together to hold the hair in place.

bobby socks also **bobby sox** *pl.n. Informal.* Short thick socks, usually worn by girls or women.

bob•cat (bŏb′kăt′) *n.* A North American wild cat having spotted reddish-brown fur and a short tail.

bob•o•link (bŏb′ə lĭngk′) *n.* A black, white, and tan American songbird related to the blackbird.

bob•sled (bŏb′slĕd′) *n.* **1.** A long racing sled with a steering device that controls the front runners. **2.a.** A long sled made of two shorter sleds joined one behind the other. **b.** Either of these two smaller sleds. —*intr.v.* **bob•sled•ded, bob•sled•ding, bob•sleds.** To ride or race in a bobsled.

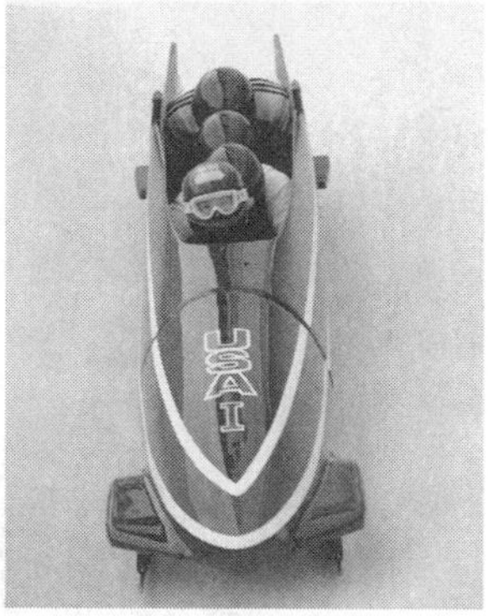

bobsled
U.S. bobsled team at the 1992 Winter Olympics in Albertville, France

bob•tail (bŏb′tāl′) *n.* **1.** A short tail or a tail that has been cut short. **2.** An animal, especially a horse, having such a tail.

bob•white (bŏb wīt′) *n.* A brown and white North American quail having a call that sounds like its name.

bode[1] (bōd) *tr.v.* **bod•ed, bod•ing, bodes.** To be a sign or an omen of (something to come): *A heavy sea boded trouble for the passengers on board.* **—*idioms.* bode ill.** To be a bad sign: *The coming hurricane bodes ill for many store owners along the beach.* **bode well.** To be a good sign: *A clear sky boded well for our trip to the mountains.* [First written down before 1200 and spelled *boden*, from Old English *bodian*, to announce.]

bode[2] (bōd) *v.* A past tense of **bide.**

bo•de•ga (bō dā′gə) *n.* A small grocery store in a Spanish-speaking community.

bod•ice (bŏd′ĭs) *n.* **1.** The fitted upper part of a dress. **2.** A woman's vest that laces in front, worn over a blouse.

bod•i•less (bŏd′ē lĭs) *adj.* Having no body, form, or substance: *a bodiless spirit.*

bod•i•ly (bŏd′l ē) *adj.* Of, relating to, or belonging to the body: *bodily ailments; food and other bodily needs.* —*adv.* **1.** In the flesh; in person: *a sleepy student that was present bodily but not mentally.* **2.** As a complete body; as a whole: *a rabbit lifted bodily by the eagle.*

bod•kin (bŏd′kĭn) *n.* **1.** A small pointed instrument for making holes in cloth or leather. **2.** A blunt needle for pulling tape or ribbon through loops or a hem. **3.** A small dagger or stiletto. **4.** A long ornamental hairpin.

bod•y (bŏd′ē) *n., pl.* **bod•ies. 1.a.** The entire physical structure and substance of a living thing, especially of a human being or an animal. **b.** A corpse or carcass. **2.** The main part of a person or an animal excluding the head and limbs; the trunk or torso. **3.** A mass or collection of material that is distinct from other masses: *a celestial body; a body of water.* **4.** A number of persons or things considered as a group: *the student body; a body of information.* **5.** The main or central part of something: *the body of a ship.* **6.** Consistency of substance; density: *a wine with fine body.* [First written down about 700 in Old English and spelled *bodeg.*]

bod•y•build•ing (bŏd′ē bĭl′dĭng) *n.* The process of building one's muscles through diet and exercise, such as weightlifting.

bod•y•guard (bŏd′ē gärd′) *n.* A person or group of persons that is responsible for protecting one or more specific persons against possible attack.

body language *n.* Gestures and postures of the body and facial expressions by which an individual communicates with others.

body politic *n.* The whole people of a nation or state, regarded as a political unit.

Boer (bōr *or* bôr) *n.* A Dutch colonist or a descendant of a Dutch colonist in South Africa. **—Boer** *adj.*

bog (bôg *or* bŏg) *n.* An area of wet spongy ground, consisting chiefly of decayed or decaying plant matter. *—v.* **bogged, bog•ging, bogs.** *—tr.* To cause to sink in or as if in a bog: *Rain bogged our car in a sea of mud.* *—intr.* To be hindered or slowed: *The plan to restore the building bogged down in government red tape.*

bo•gey also **bo•gy** or **bo•gie** (bō′gē) *n., pl.* **bo•geys** also **bo•gies. 1.** (*also* bo͝og′ē). An evil or mischievous spirit; a hobgoblin. **2.** In golf, a score of one stroke over par on a hole.

bog•ey•man (bo͝og′ē măn′ *or* bō′gē măn′) *n.* A terrifying spirit; a hobgoblin.

bog•gle (bŏg′əl) *v.* **bog•gled, bog•gling, bog•gles.** *—intr.* **1.** To hesitate or evade, as if in fear or doubt: *We boggled at telling where we had been.* **2.** To shy away with fright or astonishment: *My mind boggles at the thought of inheriting a fortune.* *—tr.* To cause to be overcome, as with fright or astonishment: *The amount of detail in checking a rocket for launch into space boggles the mind.*

bo•gie (bō′gē *or* bo͝og′ē) *n.* A variant of **bogey.**

Bo•go•tá (bō′gə tä′). The capital and largest city of Colombia, in the central part of the country on a high plain in the eastern Andes. It was a center of Chibcha culture before 1538. Population, 3,967,988.

bo•gus (bō′gəs) *adj.* Counterfeit; fake: *It is a crime to pass bogus money.*

bo•gy (bō′gē *or* bo͝og′ē) *n.* A variant of **bogey.**

Bo•he•mi•a (bō hē′mē ə). A historical region and former kingdom of present-day western Czech Republic. The Czechs settled in the area between the first and fifth centuries A.D. Bohemia became part of Czechoslovakia in 1918.

bo•he•mi•an (bō hē′mē ən) *n.* A person, especially an artist, who does not follow conventional standards of behavior. [First written down in 1848 in Modern English and spelled *Bohemian,* from French *bohémien,* from *Bohême,* Bohemia (from the unconventional lifestyle of its Gypsy inhabitants).]

boil[1] (boil) *v.* **boiled, boil•ing, boils.** *—intr.* **1.** To change from a liquid state to a gaseous state by being heated to the boiling point: *Water boils at 212°F.* **2.** To be cooked by boiling or putting into boiling water: *When the potatoes boil, turn off the gas.* **3.** To have the contents at a boil: *The kettle is boiling on the stove.* **4.** To be stirred up or greatly excited; *boil with anger at the insult.* **5.** To rush or churn: *The water boiled through the rapids.* *—tr.* **1.** To heat (a liquid) to a temperature at which it turns into a gaseous state, with bubbles breaking though the liquid's surface. **2.** To cook by boiling: *boil an egg; boil syrup.* *—n.* The condition or act of being boiled: *First you should bring the soup to a rapid boil.* **—*idioms.*** **boil down. 1.** To reduce in volume or amount by boiling: *boil down maple sap into maple syrup.* **2.** To reduce or be reduced to a simpler form: *Let's boil the problem down to its basic elements. The problem boils down to a lack of money.* **boil over. 1.** To overflow while boiling. **2.** To explode in rage; lose one's temper. [First written down about 1300 in Middle English and spelled *boillen,* from Latin *bullīre.*]

boil[2] (boil) *n.* A painful pus-filled swelling of the skin and the tissue beneath it, caused by a local bacterial infection. [First written down about 1000 in Old English and spelled *bȳle.*]

boil•er (boi′lər) *n.* **1.** A vessel in which a liquid, usually water, is heated and often vaporized for use in an engine, a turbine, or a heating system. **2.** A container, such as a kettle, for boiling liquids. **3.** A storage tank for hot water.

boil•ing point (boi′lĭng) *n.* **1.** The temperature at which a liquid boils, especially as measured at sea level. **2.** *Informal.* The point at which one loses one's temper: *The coach has a low boiling point.*

Boi•se (boi′sē *or* boi′zē). The capital and largest city of Idaho, in the southwest part of the state. The city was founded in 1863 after gold was discovered nearby. Population, 102,160.

bois•ter•ous (boi′stər əs *or* boi′strəs) *adj.* **1.** Rough and stormy; violent: *boisterous winds.* **2.** Noisy and lacking restraint or discipline: *boisterous cheers of an excited crowd.* **—bois′ter•ous•ly** *adv.* **—bois′ter•ous•ness** *n.*

bo•la (bō′lə) also **bo•las** (bō′ləs) *n.* A rope with weights attached, used in South America to catch cattle or game by entangling their legs. [First written down in 1826 in Modern English, from American Spanish *bolas,* plural of Spanish *bola,* ball, probably from Latin *bulla.*]

bold (bōld) *adj.* **bold•er, bold•est. 1.** Having no fear; brave; courageous: *bold explorers.* See Synonyms at **brave. 2.** Showing or requiring courage; daring; audacious: *a bold proposal.* **3.** Taking undue liberties; impudent; forward: *a bold glance; a bold reply.* **4.** Clear and distinct to the eye; vivid; clear: *bold colors; bold handwriting.* **—bold′ly** *adv.* **—bold′ness** *n.*

bold•face (bōld′fās′) *n.* Type that has thick heavy lines to make it immediately noticeable: *All entry words in this dictionary are in boldface.* **—bold′-face′** *adj.*

bold-faced (bōld′fāst′) *adj.* Printed or marked for printing in boldface.

bole (bōl) *n.* The trunk of a tree.
❑ *These sound alike:* **bole, boll** (seed pod), **bowl**[1] (dish), **bowl**[2] (roll a ball).

bo•le•ro (bō lâr′ō) *n., pl.* **bo•le•ros. 1.** A very short jacket of Spanish origin, worn open in the front. **2.a.** A Spanish dance. **b.** The music for this dance.

Bol•eyn (bo͝ol′ĭn *or* bo͞o lĭn′), **Anne.** 1507–1536. Queen of England (1533–1536) as the second wife of Henry VIII. She was the mother of Elizabeth I.

bo•li•var (bō lē′vär *or* bŏl′ə vər) *n., pl.* **bo•li•vars** or **bo•li•var•es** (bō lē′vä rĕs′). A basic monetary unit of Venezuela. [First written down about 1885 in Modern English, after Simón *Bolívar.*]

Bo•lí•var (bō′lə vär′ *or* bō lē′vär), **Simón.** Known as "the Liberator." 1783–1830. South American revolutionary leader who defeated the Spanish in

Simón Bolívar

ă	pat	oi	boy
ā	pay	ou	out
âr	care	o͝o	took
ä	father	o͞o	boot
ĕ	pet	ŭ	cut
ē	be	ûr	urge
ĭ	pit	th	thin
ī	pie	*th*	this
îr	pier	hw	whoop
ŏ	pot	zh	vision
ō	toe	ə	about
ô	paw	N	*French* bon

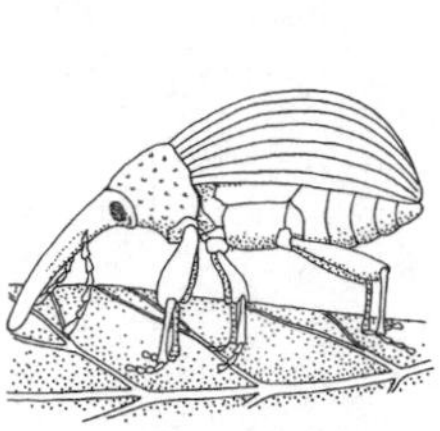

boll weevil

1819, was president of Greater Colombia (now Colombia, Venezuela, and Ecuador), and helped liberate (1823–1834) Peru and Bolivia.

Bo•liv•i•a (bə lĭv′ē ə *or* bō lĭv′ē ə). A landlocked country of western South America north of Argentina. Sucre is the legal capital. La Paz is the administrative center and the largest city. Population, 6,429,226.

boll (bōl) *n.* The rounded seed pod or capsule of a plant, especially that of cotton or flax.
❑ *These sound alike:* **boll, bole** (tree trunk), **bowl**[1] (dish), **bowl**[2] (roll a ball).

boll weevil *n.* A long-snouted beetle that lays its eggs in the buds and bolls of the cotton plant, where the larvae hatch and cause great damage.

bo•lo•gna (bə lō′nē *or* bə lō′nə) also **ba•lo•ney** or **bo•lo•ney** (bə lō′nē) *n.* A seasoned smoked sausage made of mixed meats such as pork and veal. [First written down in 1750 in Modern English and spelled *Bologna sausage*, after *Bologna*, Italy.]

Bo•lo•gna (bə lōn′yə). A city of north-central Italy at the foot of the Apennines north-northeast of Florence. It was originally an Etruscan town. Population, 455,853.

Bol•she•vik (bōl′shə vĭk′) *n., pl.* **Bol•she•viks** or **Bol•she•vi•ki** (bōl′shə vē′kē). **1.** A member of the Russian Social Democratic Workers' Party that adopted Lenin's ideas and seized control of the government in November 1917. **2.** A Communist. **3.** Often **bolshevik.** *Informal.* A radical, as in politics or art.

Bol•she•vism also **bol•she•vism** (bōl′shə vĭz′əm) *n.* **1.** The theories and practices developed by the Bolsheviks between 1903 and 1917 with a view to seizing governmental power and establishing the world's first Communist state. **2.** Soviet Communism, especially during the first generation following the Russian Revolution.

Bol•she•vist also **bol•she•vist** (bōl′shə vĭst) *n.* A Bolshevik. **—Bol′she•vik′** *adj.*

bol•ster (bōl′stər) *n.* A long narrow pillow or cushion. *—tr.v.* **bol•stered, bol•ster•ing, bol•sters.** To support or reinforce: *Visitors bolstered the patient's morale.*

bolt (bōlt) *n.* **1.** A rod or pin with a head at one end and threads onto which a nut is screwed at the other end, used to hold two parts together. **2.** A sliding bar of wood or metal for fastening a door or gate. **3.** A metal bar or rod in a lock that is pushed out or withdrawn at a turn of the key. **4.** A sliding bar that positions the cartridge in a rifle and closes the breech. **5.** A large roll of cloth, especially as it comes from the loom. **6.** A short heavy arrow used with a crossbow. **7.** A flash of lightning; a thunderbolt. **8.** A sudden movement toward or away from something: *Our cat made a bolt for the open door.* *—v.* **bolt•ed, bolt•ing, bolts.** *—tr.* **1.** To attach or fasten with a bolt or bolts: *bolted the rack to the wall.* **2.** To lock with a bolt: *Bolt the door.* **3.** To eat quickly and with little chewing; gulp. **4.** To break away from (a political party). *—intr.* **1.** To move or spring suddenly: *bolting from the room.* **2.** To break from a rider's control and run away: *a horse that shied and bolted.* **3.** To break away from a political party or its policies. ***—idioms.*** **bolt from the blue.** A sudden, usually shocking surprise: *The tearing down of the Berlin Wall came as a bolt from the blue.* **bolt upright.** Stiff and straight: *Realizing he was late, he sat bolt upright in bed.* [First written down about 950 in Old English and spelled *bolt*, heavy arrow.]

bomb (bŏm) *n.* **1.** An explosive weapon constructed to go off by striking something, by a timing mechanism, or by some other means. **2.** A weapon exploded to release gas or other destructive materials: *a smoke bomb.* **3.** A container for holding a substance under pressure, as a preparation for killing insects, that can be released as a spray or gas. **4.** *Slang.* A dismal failure: *That movie was a bomb.* *—tr.v.* **bombed, bomb•ing, bombs.** To attack, damage, or destroy with a bomb or bombs: *bomb a bridge.* [First written down in 1588 in Modern English and spelled *bome*, from Italian *bomba*, probably from Latin *bombus*, a booming sound, from Greek *bombos*.]

bom•bard (bŏm bärd′) *tr.v.* **bom•bard•ed, bom•bard•ing, bom•bards. 1.** To attack with bombs, shells, or other explosives: *bombard an enemy position.* **2.** To assail or shower (a person), as with questions or insults: *Reporters bombarded the police with questions.* **3.** To strike (the nucleus of an atom) with a stream of fast-moving subatomic particles in order to study the structure of the nucleus. **—bom•bard′ment** *n.*

bom•bar•dier (bŏm′bər dîr′) *n.* The member of a bomber crew who works the bombsight and releases the bombs.

bom•bast (bŏm′băst′) *n.* Extravagant or pompous speech or writing: *a politician full of bombast and bluster.*

bom•bas•tic (bŏm băs′tĭk) *adj.* Having an extravagant pompous style: *bombastic speech.* **—bom•bas′ti•cal•ly** *adv.*

Bom•bay (bŏm bā′). A city of west-central India on the Arabian Sea southwest of Delhi. It is India's main port. Population, 8,243,405.

bomb bay *n.* The compartment in a bomber from which bombs are dropped.

bomb•er (bŏm′ər) *n.* **1.** A military airplane that carries and drops bombs. **2.** A person who makes and sets off bombs.

bomb•shell (bŏm′shĕl′) *n.* **1.** A bomb. **2.** A great surprise or shock.

bomb•sight (bŏm′sīt′) *n.* A device in a military aircraft for aiming bombs.

bo•na fide (bō′nə fīd′ *or* bŏn′ə fīd′) *adj.* **1.** Done or made in good faith; sincere: *a bona fide offer to buy.* **2.** Genuine; authentic: *a bona fide painting by Rembrandt.* [First written down about 1542 in Modern English, from Latin *bonā fidē*, in good faith.]

bo•nan•za (bə năn′zə) *n.* **1.** A rich mine or vein of ore. **2.** A source of great wealth: *The rise in stock prices was a bonanza to shareholders.* [First written down in 1844 in Modern English, from Spanish, from Medieval Latin *bonacia*, calm sea.]

Bo•na•parte (bō′nə pärt′). Corsican family, all brothers of Napoleon I, including **Joseph** (1768–1844), who was king of Naples (1806–1808) and Spain (1808–1813), and **Louis** (1778–1846), who was king of Holland (1806–1810).

bon•bon (bŏn′bŏn′) *n.* A piece of candy, often with a creamy center and a chocolate coating. [First written down about 1786 in Modern English, from French, from *bon*, good, from Latin *bonus*.]

bond (bŏnd) *n.* **1.** Something that binds, ties, or fastens together, as a cord or rope: *bonds around the prisoner's wrists.* **2.** A force that unites; a tie; a link: *strong bonds between the newspaper and its loyal readers.* **3.** A force of attraction that holds atoms or groups of atoms together in a molecule, produced in general by a transfer or sharing of one or more electrons. **4.a.** Money paid as bail. **b.** A person who provides bail; a bondsman. **5.** A certificate of debt issued by a government or corporation that guarantees repayment of the original investment with interest by a specified date. **6.** An insurance contract that guarantees payment to an employer in the event of financial loss caused by the actions of an employee. *—v.* **bond•ed, bond•ing, bonds.** *—tr.* **1.**

To place (an employee) under bond so as to insure his or her employer against loss. **2.** To join securely, as with glue. **3.** To connect by strong emotional or social ties: *Love for our grandparents bonded us all.* —*intr.* To be joined together with a bond: *Oxygen bonds to hydrogen to form water.*

bond•age (**bŏn′**dĭj) *n.* The condition of being bound as a slave or serf; slavery or servitude.

bond•hold•er (**bŏnd′**hōl′dər) *n.* The owner of a bond or bonds.

bond•man (**bŏnd′**mən) *n.* A male bondservant.

bond•ser•vant (**bŏnd′**sûr′vənt) *n.* A person who is obligated to work for another without wages; a slave or serf.

bonds•man (**bŏndz′**mən) *n.* **1.** A male bondservant. **2.** A person who provides bail for another.

bond•wom•an (**bŏnd′**wo͝om′ən) *n.* A female bondservant.

bone (bōn) *n.* **1.a.** The hard, dense, calcified tissue that forms the skeleton of most vertebrates. **b.** One of the many distinct structures making up such a skeleton: *the bones of the foot.* **2. bones. a.** The skeleton. **b.** The body. **c.** Mortal remains: *May their bones rest in peace.* **3.** An animal material, such as ivory, resembling bone. —*tr.v.* **boned, bon•ing, bones.** *Informal.* In cooking, to remove the bones from: *bone fish.* —***idioms.* bone of contention.** The subject of a dispute: *Who goes first is often a bone of contention.* **bone to pick.** A reason for a complaint or dispute. **bone up on.** *Informal.* To study (a subject) intensively; review. [First written down about 700 in Old English and spelled *bān.*]

bone•black also **bone black** (**bōn′**blăk′) *n.* A black material made by roasting bones in an airtight container. It contains about 10 percent charcoal and is used as a pigment, as a filtering agent, and in removing the color from sugar.

bone-dry (**bōn′drī′**) *adj.* Without a trace of moisture; very dry.

bone•head (**bōn′**hĕd′) *n. Informal.* A stupid person.

bone meal *n.* Bones crushed and ground to a coarse powder, used as fertilizer and animal feed.

bon•er (**bō′**nər) *n. Informal.* A foolish mistake; a blunder.

bon•fire (**bŏn′**fīr′) *n.* A large outdoor fire. [First written down before 1415 in Middle English and spelled *bonnefire* : *bon,* bone + *fir,* fire.]

bon•go drums (**bŏng′**gō *or* **bông′**gō) *pl.n.* A pair of small drums, usually tuned to different pitches, that are held between the knees and beaten with the hands.

bon•gos (**bŏng′**gōz *or* **bông′**gōz) *pl.n.* Bongo drums. [First written down in 1920 in Modern English, of Bantu origin.]

bo•ni•to (bə **nē′**tō) *n., pl.* **bonito** or **bo•ni•tos.** Any of several ocean fishes related to the tuna, caught for food and sport.

Bonn (bŏn *or* bôn). The former capital of West Germany, in the western part of the country on the Rhine River. Since 1990 it has been the seat of the German government. Population, 291,291.

bon•net (**bŏn′**ĭt) *n.* **1.** A hat tied with ribbons under the chin and worn by a woman or child. **2.** A cap without a brim, worn by men in Scotland. **3.** *Chiefly British.* The hood of an automobile.

bon•ny also **bon•nie** (**bŏn′**ē) *adj.* **bon•ni•er, bon•ni•est.** *Scots.* Pleasing to the eye; pretty: *a bonny young lass.*

bon•sai (bŏn **sī′** *or* **bŏn′**sī′) *n., pl.* **bonsai. 1.** The art of growing miniature trees in small pots or dishes. **2.** A tree grown in this way. [First written down in 1950 in Modern English, from Japanese *bonsai,* potted plant : *bon,* basin + *sai,* to plant.]

bo•nus (**bō′**nəs) *n., pl.* **bo•nus•es.** Something given or paid in addition to what is usual or expected: *Each worker got a bonus of three extra days off for the holidays.*

bon voy•age (bŏn′ voi **äzh′**) *interj.* An expression used to wish a departing traveler a pleasant journey.

bon•y or **bon•ey** (**bō′**nē) *adj.* **bon•i•er, bon•i•est** or **bon•ey•er, bon•ey•est. 1.** Of, relating to, or resembling bone. **2.** Full of bones: *a bony piece of fish.* **3.** Having bones that stick out or show through; thin; gaunt: *bony cheeks.* —**bon′i•ness** *n.*

boo (bo͞o) *n., pl.* **boos.** A sound uttered to show dislike or disapproval. —*interj.* An expression used to show dislike or disapproval or to frighten or surprise. —*v.* **booed, boo•ing, boos.** —*intr.* To utter a boo: *The fans booed angrily.* —*tr.* To say "boo" to; jeer: *The spectators booed the umpire's decision.*

boob (bo͞ob) *n. Slang.* A stupid or foolish person; a dunce.

boo-boo also **boo•boo** (**bo͞o′**bo͞o) *n., pl.* **boo-boos** or **boo•boos.** *Informal.* **1.** A foolish or thoughtless mistake; a blunder. **2.** A slight physical injury, such as a scratch.

boo•by (**bo͞o′**bē) *n., pl.* **boo•bies. 1.** A stupid person; a dunce. **2.** Any of several large tropical sea birds having white or brown and white feathers and a long pointed bill.

booby prize *n.* An award given to the person who scores lowest in a game or contest.

booby trap *n.* **1.** A hidden bomb or mine set to go off when a harmless-looking object attached to it is moved or touched. **2.** A situation for catching a person off guard; a trap.

boog•ie-woog•ie (bo͝og′ē **wo͝og′**ē *or* bo͞o′gē **wo͞o′**-gē) *n.* A style of jazz piano playing in which a distinctive rhythmic and melodic pattern is repeated over and over in the bass.

book (bo͝ok) *n.* **1.** A set of printed, written, or blank pages fastened together along one edge and enclosed between covers. **2.a.** A printed or written literary work: *She's writing a new book about Mexico.* **b.** A main division of a larger written or printed work: *a book of the Old Testament.* **3. Book.** The Bible. **4.a.** A volume for recording financial transactions: *an account book.* **b. books.** Financial records in which an accounting is kept of money received, owed, and paid: *A bookkeeper keeps books.* **5.** A set of established rules: *She runs the company by the book.* **6.** A small packet of similar things bound together: *a book of matches.* **7.** The words or script of a play, a musical, or an opera. —*tr.v.* **booked, book•ing, books. 1.** To arrange for in advance; reserve or schedule: *We booked tickets to the show.* **2.** To write down charges against (a person) in a police record: *book a suspect.* —***idioms.* in (one's) book.** In one's opinion: *In my book she was one of the all-time greats.* **like a book.** Thoroughly; completely: *I know the town like a book.* **throw the book at. 1.** To make all possible charges against (an offender). **2.** To scold or punish severely. [First written down about 725 in Old English and spelled *bōc.*]

book•bind•er (**bo͝ok′**bīn′dər) *n.* A person whose business is binding books.

book•bind•er•y (**bo͝ok′**bīn′də rē) *n.* A business establishment where books are bound.

book•case (**bo͝ok′**kās′) *n.* A piece of furniture with shelves for holding books.

book club *n.* A business organization that sells books to its members at a discount from a selected list.

book•end (**bo͝ok′**ĕnd′) *n.* A prop placed at the end of a row of books to keep them upright.

book•ie (**bo͝ok′**ē) *n.* A person who accepts and pays off bets; a bookmaker.

book•ish (**bo͝ok′**ĭsh) *adj.* **1.** Fond of books and study; studious: *a bookish scholar.* **2.** Depending

bongo drums

bonsai

ă	pat	oi	boy
ā	pay	ou	out
âr	care	o͝o	took
ä	father	o͞o	boot
ĕ	pet	ŭ	cut
ē	be	ûr	urge
ĭ	pit	th	thin
ī	pie	*th*	this
îr	pier	hw	whoop
ŏ	pot	zh	vision
ō	toe	ə	about
ô	paw	N	*French* bon

boomerang

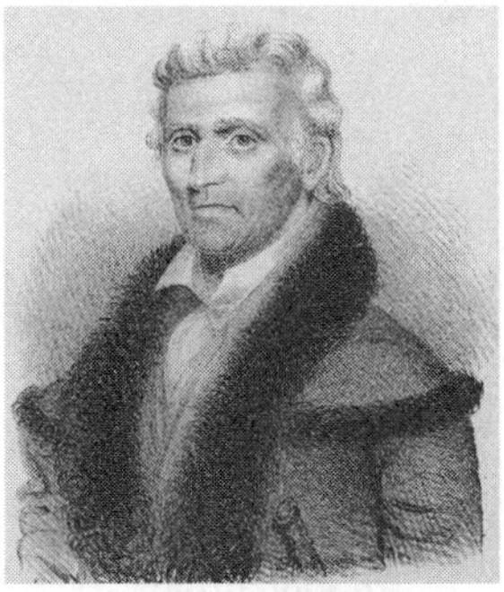
Daniel Boone

too much on books rather than experience: *a bookish notion of the world.* **3.** Scholarly or formal in a dull dry way: *bookish writing.*

book•keep•ing (bo͝ok′kē′pĭng) *n.* The work or skill of keeping records of money received, owed, or paid by a business. **—book′keep′er** *n.*

book•let (bo͝ok′lĭt) *n.* A small book or pamphlet, usually with paper covers.

book•mak•er (bo͝ok′mā′kər) *n.* **1.** A person or business that edits, prints, or publishes books. **2.** A person who accepts and pays off bets, especially on sporting events such as horse races. **—book′mak′ing** *n.*

book•mark (bo͝ok′märk′) *n.* An object, such as a ribbon or a strip of leather, placed between the pages of a book to mark the reader's place.

book•mo•bile (bo͝ok′mō bēl′) *n.* A truck with shelves of books in it, used as a traveling library.

Book of Common Prayer *n.* The book of services and prayers used in the Anglican Church.

Book of Mormon *n.* A sacred book of the Mormon Church, believed by Mormons to be a sacred history of the Americas revealed by the prophet Mormon to Joseph Smith.

Book of Revelation *n.* The last book of the New Testament containing prophetic visions of the end of the world and the last judgment of souls.

book•plate (bo͝ok′plāt′) *n.* A label pasted inside a book and bearing the owner's name.

book•sell•er (bo͝ok′sĕl′ər) *n.* A person or business that sells books.

book•shelf (bo͝ok′shĕlf′) *n.* A shelf or set of shelves for holding books.

book•shop (bo͝ok′shŏp′) *n.* A bookstore.

book•stand (bo͝ok′stănd′) *n.* **1.** A small counter where books are sold. **2.** A frame for holding an open book.

book•store (bo͝ok′stôr′) *n.* A store where books are sold.

book•worm (bo͝ok′wûrm′) *n.* **1.** The larva of various insects that infest books and feed on the paste in the bindings. **2.** A person who spends much time reading or studying.

Bool•e•an algebra (bo͞o′lē ən) *n.* A mathematical system dealing with the relationship between sets, used to solve problems in logic and engineering. Variables consist of 0 and 1 and operations are expressed as *and, or,* and *not.* Boolean algebra has been important in the development of modern computers and computer programs. [First written down in 1889 in Modern English, after George *Boole* (1815–1864), English mathematician.]

boom[1] (bo͞om) *v.* **boomed, boom•ing, booms.** *—intr.* **1.** To make a deep resonant sound: *The cannon boomed across the valley.* **2.** To grow or develop rapidly; thrive; flourish: *Business is booming.* *—tr.* To say or give forth with such a sound: *Rescuers boomed a message over their loudspeaker.* *—n.* **1.** A deep hollow sound, as from an explosion. **2.** A sudden increase, as in growth or production: *a boom in farm production filled the markets.* **3.** A time of economic prosperity: *California had a boom after gold was discovered.* [First written down before 1376 in Middle English and spelled *bomben*, imitative of a loud noise.]

boom[2] (bo͞om) *n.* **1.** A long pole extending from the mast of a boat to hold or stretch out the bottom of a sail. **2.a.** A long pole or similar structure that extends upward and outward from the mast of a derrick and supports the object being lifted. **b.** A similar support that holds a microphone. **3.** A chain, cable, or line of timbers that keeps logs from floating away. **4.** A floating barrier used to contain an oil spill. [First written down in 1543 in Modern English and spelled *boun*, from Dutch *boom*, tree, pole.]

boo•mer•ang (bo͞o′mə răng′) *n.* **1.** A flat curved piece of wood that can be thrown so that it returns to the thrower. It was originally used by the native people of Australia. **2.** Something that comes back to harm or surprise the originator. *—intr.v.* **boo•mer•anged, boo•mer•ang•ing, boo•mer•angs.** To have the opposite effect of that intended; backfire. [First written down in 1827 in Modern English, from Dharuk (Aboriginal language of southeast Australia) *bumariny.*]

boom•town (bo͞om′toun′) *n.* A town that experiences sudden growth and prosperity, as after a discovery or gold, silver, or oil.

boon[1] (bo͞on) *n.* **1.** A help or blessing: *Delay would be a blow to us and a boon to our competitors.* **2.** A favor, request, or service. [First written down before 1200 in Middle English and spelled *bone*, from Old Norse *bōn*, prayer.]

boon[2] (bo͞on) *adj.* Friendly and jolly; sociable: *a boon companion.* [First written down about 1380 in Middle English and spelled *bon*, good, from Latin *bonus.*]

boon•docks (bo͞on′dŏks′) *pl.n. Slang.* **1.** Rough uncleared country. **2.** Rural country; the backwoods.

Boone (bo͞on), **Daniel.** 1734–1820. American pioneer and folk hero who helped lead new settlers to what is now Kentucky.

boor (bo͝or) *n.* A crude person with rude or clumsy manners.

boor•ish (bo͝or′ĭsh) *adj.* Crude, rude, and offensive: *loud boorish behavior.* **—boor′ish•ly** *adv.* **—boor′ish•ness** *n.*

boost (bo͞ost) *tr.v.* **boost•ed, boost•ing, boosts. 1.** To lift by pushing up from below: *My friend boosted me into the tree.* **2.** To increase; raise: *Advertising often boosts sales.* **3.** To stir up enthusiasm for; promote; aid: *boost one's home town.* *—n.* **1.** A push upward or ahead: *Give me a boost up the pole.* **2.** An increase: *A boost in salary.*

boost•er (bo͞o′stər) *n.* **1.** Something that increases the power or effectiveness of a system or device: *a battery booster.* **2.** An amplifier for radio or televison signals: *a televison booster.* **3.** A rocket used to launch a missile or space vehicle. **4.** A booster shot. **5.** A person or thing that boosts: *The holiday was a morale booster.*

booster shot *n.* A dose of a vaccine or serum given to a person who is already immune in order to prolong or strengthen the immunity.

boot[1] (bo͞ot) *n.* **1.** A kind of shoe that covers the foot and ankle and usually part of the leg, often made of leather or rubber. **2.** Something shaped like a boot, as a peninsula: *the boot of Italy.* **3.** A kick: *give a ball a good boot.* **4.** *Chiefly British.* The trunk of an automobile. *—tr.v.* **boot•ed, boot•ing, boots. 1.** To kick: *The soccer player booted the ball down the field.* **2.** To put boots on. **3.** To start (a computer) by loading the operating system. [First written down about 1300 in Middle English and spelled *bote*, from Old French.]

boot[2] (bo͞ot) *intr.v.* **boot•ed, boot•ing, boots.** To benefit, help, or avail: *It boots you little to worry.* ***—idiom.* to boot.** In addition; besides: *He got a T-shirt and a baseball cap to boot.* [First written down before 1000 in Old English and spelled *bōtian*, from *bōt*, help.]

boot•black (bo͞ot′blăk′) *n.* A person who cleans and polishes shoes for a living.

boot camp *n.* A training camp for soldiers or sailors who have just joined the armed services.

boot•ed (bo͞o′tĭd) *adj.* Wearing boots: *The cowboys were booted and spurred.*

boo•tee also **boo•tie** (bo͞o'tē) *n.* A soft, usually knitted baby shoe.
❑ *These sound alike:* **bootee, booty** (loot).

Bo•ö•tes (bō ō'tēz) *n.* A constellation in the Northern Hemisphere near the handle of the Big Dipper.

booth (bo͞oth) *n., pl.* **booths** (bo͞o*th*z *or* bo͞oths). **1.** A small enclosed compartment: *a telephone booth.* **2.** A small stall or stand where things are sold or entertainment is provided: *a ticket booth.* **3.** A seating compartment consisting of a table enclosed by two facing benches with high backs: *We ate in a booth at the restaurant.*

Booth (bo͞oth), **John Wilkes.** 1838–1865. American actor who killed President Abraham Lincoln.

boot•jack (bo͞ot'jăk') *n.* A forked device that holds a boot while the foot is pulled out of it.

boot•leg (bo͞ot'lĕg') *v.* **boot•legged, boot•leg•ging, boot•legs.** —*tr.* To make, sell, or transport (alcoholic liquor) illegally. —*intr.* To engage in bootlegging alcoholic liquor. —*n.* A product, especially alcoholic liquor, that is illegally made, sold, or transported. —*adj.* Made, sold, or transported illegally: *bootleg music tapes.* **—boot'leg'ger** *n.*

boot•less (bo͞ot'lĭs) *adj.* Without advantage or benefit; useless; fruitless: *a bootless effort.*

boo•ty (bo͞o'tē) *n., pl.* **boo•ties. 1.** Plunder taken from an enemy in war: *Soldiers often carry off the booty of war.* **2.** Seized or stolen goods: *pirates' booty.* **3.** A valuable prize; a treasure: *Divers brought up booty from a sunken ship.*
❑ *These sound alike:* **booty, bootee** (baby shoe).

booze (bo͞oz) *Slang. n.* Alcoholic drink. —*intr.v.* **boozed, booz•ing, booz•es.** To drink alcoholic beverages to excess. **—booz'er** *n.*

bop (bŏp) *Informal. tr.v.* **bopped, bop•ping, bops.** To hit or strike. —*n.* A blow or punch.

bo•rate (bôr'āt') *n.* A salt of boric acid.

bo•rax (bôr'ăks') *n.* A white crystalline powder and mineral, used as an antiseptic, as a cleansing agent, in fusing metals, and in making heat-resistant glass. The mineral is an ore of boron.

Bor•deaux[1] (bôr dō'). A city of southwest France southwest of Paris. It is the trading center of a wine-producing region. Population, 208,159.

Bor•deaux[2] (bôr dō') *n., pl.* **Bor•deaux** (bôr dō' *or* bôr dōz'). A red or white wine made near the city of Bordeaux, France.

bor•der (bôr'dər) *n.* **1.** The line where one country, state, or region ends and another begins; a boundary: *the border between the United States and Canada.* **2.** A margin or an edge: *They picnicked on the border of the pond.* See Synonyms at **margin. 3.** A strip put on or around an edge, as for ornament: *a border of lace around the tablecloth.* —*tr.v.* **bor•dered, bor•der•ing, bor•ders. 1.** To lie along or next to: *Canada and Mexico border the United States.* **2.** To put a border or an edging on: *border a collar with lace.* **—*idiom.* border on** or **border upon. 1.** To be next to; touch: *France borders on Germany.* **2.** To come close to; approach: *This weather borders on the ideal.* [First written down about 1350 in Middle English and spelled *bordure,* from Old French *border,* to border, from *bort,* border, of Germanic origin.]
❑ *These sound alike:* **border, boarder** (lodger).

bor•der•land (bôr'dər lănd') *n.* **1.** Land on or near a border or frontier. **2.** An indefinite area or condition in which two different things seem to overlap: *the borderland between dreams and reality.*

bor•der•line (bôr'dər līn') *n.* **1.** A dividing line; a border or boundary. **2.** An indefinite line between two different conditions: *on the borderline between good and excellent.* —*adj.* Not clearly within a certain class or limit; uncertain: *a borderline condition, perhaps ready for surgery.*

Bor•der States (bôr'dər). The slave states of Delaware, Maryland, Virginia, Kentucky, and Missouri that bordered on the free states during the Civil War. Virginia joined the Confederacy in 1861, causing its western counties to form the new state of West Virginia. It and other Border States remained part of the Union despite strong Southern sympathies.

bore[1] (bôr) *v.* **bored, bor•ing, bores.** —*tr.* **1.** To make (a hole, tunnel, or well) by drilling or digging: *bore a tunnel through a mountain.* **2.** To make a hole in or through (something), as with a drill or an auger: *bore a mountain to make a tunnel.* —*intr.* To make a hole by drilling or digging: *The miners bored through the rock to get at the coal.* —*n.* **1.** The inside diameter of a hole, tube, cylinder, or other hollow object: *a pipe with a bore of three inches.* **2.** A bored hole, as in a pipe or the barrel of a firearm. [First written down about 1000 in Old English and spelled *borian.*]
❑ *These sound alike:* **bore**[1] (drill), **boar** (male pig), **bore**[2] (make weary), **bore**[3] (tidal wave), **bore**[4] (supported).

bore[2] (bôr) *tr.v.* **bored, bor•ing, bores.** To make weary by failing to interest or by being dull: *The speaker bored the audience by talking too long.* —*n.* An uninteresting or tiresome person or thing. [First written down in 1768 in Modern English.]
❑ *These sound alike:* **bore**[2] (make weary), **boar** (male pig), **bore**[1] (drill), **bore**[3] (tidal wave), **bore**[4] (supported).

bore[3] (bôr) *n.* A sudden high tidal wave that rushes upstream, with great force, at the mouth of a river. [First written down about 1320 in Middle English and spelled *bare,* wave, from Old Norse *bāra.*]
❑ *These sound alike:* **bore**[3] (tidal wave), **boar** (male pig), **bore**[1] (drill), **bore**[2] (make weary), **bore**[4] (supported).

bore[4] (bôr) *v.* Past tense of **bear**[1].
❑ *These sound alike:* **bore**[4] (supported), **boar** (male pig), **bore**[1] (drill), **bore**[2] (make weary), **bore**[3] (tidal wave).

bore•dom (bôr'dəm) *n.* The condition of being bored; weariness of mind.

bor•er (bôr'ər) *n.* **1.** A tool used for boring or drilling. **2.** An insect or insect larva that bores into plants or wood.

bo•ric acid (bôr'ĭk) *n.* A white or colorless crystalline compound occurring in nature or made from borax and composed of hydrogen, boron, and oxygen with the formula H_3BO_3. It is used as an antiseptic, as a preservative, and in cements and enamels.

bor•ing (bôr'ĭng) *adj.* Uninteresting; dull: *a long boring speech.* **—bor'ing•ly** *adv.* **—bor'ing•ness** *n.*

Synonyms: boring, dull, tedious, tiresome. These adjectives mean lacking in interest, liveliness, or imagination. **Boring** describes something that makes one feel tired and unhappy: *The movie was so boring that half the audience fell asleep or walked out before the end.* **Dull** means uninteresting and unsurprising: *The lecturer somehow managed to give an enthusiastic presentation on a dull topic.* **Tedious** describes something that is boring because of its slowness: *Wendy thinks train travel is romantic but we find it tedious.* **Tiresome** means tedious and repetitious: *I don't mind the tiresome job of returning bottles and cans because I want to help the environment.*
Antonyms: interesting, lively.

born (bôrn) *v.* A past participle of **bear**[1]. —*adj.* **1.** Brought into life or existence: *a political movement born in the last century.* **2.** Having a natural talent from birth: *a born artist.* **3.** Destined from birth: *She was born to sing.* **4.** Coming or resulting: *wisdom born of experience.*

John Wilkes Booth
Photographed c. 1862

ă	pat	oi	boy
ā	pay	ou	out
âr	care	o͝o	took
ä	father	o͞o	boot
ĕ	pet	ŭ	cut
ē	be	ûr	urge
ĭ	pit	th	thin
ī	pie	*th*	this
îr	pier	hw	whoop
ŏ	pot	zh	vision
ō	toe	ə	about
ô	paw	N	*French* bon

Usage: borrow

The word **borrow** means "to take (something) temporarily with the promise of returning it"; **lend** means "to give (something) temporarily on condition of having it returned." A library *lends* books; readers *borrow* them. Another verb very similar to "lend" is **loan**, meaning "to lend money or an object." *Lend* also has a figurative use, but *loan* does not: *The music lent spirit to the party; lend us your enthusiasm.*

borzoi

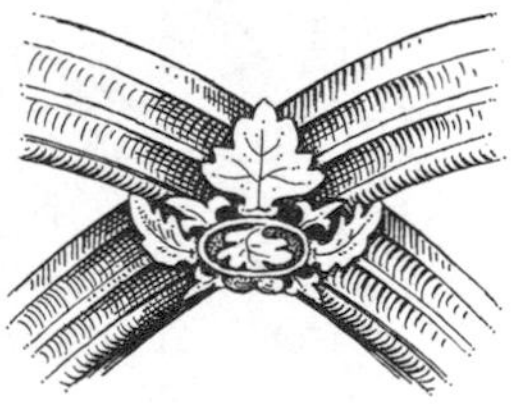

boss[2]

Boston terrier

born-a•gain (bôrn′ə gĕn′) *adj.* **1.** Of, relating to, or being a person who has made a conversion or renewed commitment to Jesus as his or her personal savior: *a born-again Christian.* **2.** Marked by renewed activity or revived interest or enthusiasm: *a born-again supporter of free speech.*

borne (bôrn) *v.* A past participle of **bear[1]**.

Bor•ne•o (**bôr′**nē ō′). An island of the western Pacific Ocean east of Sumatra and southwest of the Philippines. Brunei is on the northwest coast; the rest of the island is divided between Indonesia and Malaysia.

bo•ron (**bôr′**ŏn′) *n. Symbol* **B** A soft, brown, metalloid element extracted chiefly from borax and used in alloys, nuclear reactors, and abrasives. Atomic number 5. See table at **element.**

bor•ough (**bûr′**ō *or* **bŭr′**ō) *n.* **1.** A self-governing incorporated town, as in certain states of the United States. **2.** One of the five administrative units of New York City. **3.** A governmental district in Alaska, corresponding to a county. **4.** A town in Great Britain that sends one or more representatives to Parliament.

❑ *These sound alike:* **borough, burro** (donkey), **burrow** (hole).

bor•row (**bŏr′**ō) *v.* **bor•rowed, bor•row•ing, bor•rows.** —*tr.* **1.** To obtain or recover (something) with the promise of returning or replacing it later: *borrow a library book; borrow money.* **2.** To take (a word, idea, or method) from another source and use it as one's own: *We borrowed the word* kindergarten *from German in the 19th century.* **3.** In mathematics, to subtract (one) from a digit in a number in order to add ten to the value of the digit to the right. When subtracting 6 from 93, you borrow 1 from 9 to make 3 into 13, and then subtract 6, leaving 87. —*intr.* To obtain or receive something, especially money on loan: *I borrowed from the bank to buy a new car.* —**bor′row•er** *n.* —SEE NOTE.

bor•row•ing (**bŏr′**ō ĭng) *n.* Something that is borrowed, especially a word or phrase borrowed from another language: *The English word* plateau *is a borrowing from French.*

borscht (bôrsht) also **borsch** (bôrsh) *n.* A beet soup served hot or cold, often with sour cream. [First written down in 1884 in Modern English and spelled *borsch,* from Yiddish *borsht,* from Russian *borshch.*]

bor•zoi (**bôr′**zoi′) *n.* Any of a breed of large slender dog having a narrow pointed head and silky coat. It was developed in Russia to hunt game animals.

bosk•y (**bŏs′**kē) *adj.* **bosk•i•er, bosk•i•est. 1.** Wooded. **2.** Having many bushes and trees: *a bosky stretch of land along the river.*

bo's'n (**bō′**sən) *n.* Variant of **boatswain.**

Bos•ni•a-Her•ze•go•vi•na (**bŏz′**nē ə hĕrt′sə gō-**vē′**nə). A region of the northwest Balkan Peninsula west of Serbia. The region became a constituent republic of Yugoslavia in 1946 and declared its independence in March 1991. Capital, Sarajevo. Population, 3,710,965.

bos•om (**bo͝oz′**əm *or* **bo͞o′**zəm) *n.* **1.** The upper front part of the human body; the breast. **2.** The part of a garment that covers the breast: *the starched bosom of a shirt.* **3.** The human breast regarded as the center of emotion: *empty one's bosom of sorrow.* **4.** Emotional closeness and comfort: *We welcomed her into the bosom of our family.* —*adj.* Close; intimate: *bosom friends.*

Bos•po•rus (**bŏs′**pər əs). A narrow strait separating European and Asian Turkey and joining the Black Sea with the Sea of Marmara.

boss[1] (bôs *or* bŏs) *n.* **1.** A person who employs or directs workers. **2.** A person who is in charge or makes decisions: *Who is boss around here?* **3.** A powerful person who controls a political party or organization. —*tr.v.* **bossed, boss•ing, boss•es. 1.** To give orders to; order around: *Their older cousin tried to boss the children around.* **2.** To be in charge of; supervise: *A chief usually bosses a group of firefighters.* [First written down before 1649 in Modern English and spelled *base,* from Dutch *baas,* master.]

boss[2] (bôs *or* bŏs) *n.* A raised ornament projecting from a flat surface. —*tr.v.* **bossed, boss•ing, boss•es.** To decorate with bosses; emboss. [First written down before 1325 in Middle English and spelled *boce,* from Old French.]

boss•ism (**bô′**sĭz′əm *or* **bŏs′**ĭz′əm) *n.* The control of a political party or organization by a boss.

boss•y (**bô′**sē *or* **bŏs′**ē) *adj.* **boss•i•er, boss•i•est.** Inclined to order others around; domineering.

Bos•ton (**bô′**stən *or* **bŏs′**tən). The capital and largest city of Massachusetts, in the eastern part of the state on **Boston Bay.** It was founded in the 17th century. Population, 574,283.

Boston bull *n.* A Boston terrier.

Boston terrier *n.* Any of a breed of small short-haired dog having a smooth black or brindled coat with white markings.

bo•sun (**bō′**sən) *n.* Variant of **boatswain.**

bo•tan•i•cal (bə **tăn′**ĭ kəl) *adj.* Of or relating to plants or botany: *a collection of botanical specimens.* —**bo•tan′i•cal•ly** *adv.*

botanical garden *n.* A place for the study and exhibition of plants.

bot•a•nist (**bŏt′**n ĭst) *n.* A person who specializes in botany.

bot•a•ny (**bŏt′**n ē) *n., pl.* **bot•a•nies. 1.** The scientific study of plants. Botany deals with the structure, growth, and diseases of plant life. **2.** The plant life of a particular area: *the botany of Arizona.* [First written down in 1696 in Modern English, from *botanical,* from Greek *botanē,* fodder, plants.]

botch (bŏch) *tr.v.* **botched, botch•ing, botch•es.** To spoil by careless or clumsy work; bungle: *botch a repair job.* —*n.* A bad job or poor piece of work; a mess.

both (bōth) *adj.* One as well as the other; relating to or being two: *Both sides of the board are painted.* —*pron.* The one as well as the other: *Both of them skate well.* —*conj.* As well; equally: *The baby both walks and talks.* —SEE NOTE.

both•er (**bŏth′**ər) *v.* **both•ered, both•er•ing, both•ers.** —*tr.* **1.** To disturb or anger; annoy: *Noise in the hall bothered the teacher while she was teaching.* **2.a.** To make nervous or upset: *Being in high places bothers some people.* **b.** To puzzle: *A problem had been bothering them.* —*intr.* To take the trouble; concern oneself: *Don't bother to get up.* —*n.* An annoying thing; a nuisance: *Having to wait so long was a bother.* [First written down in 1718 in Modern English, probably from dialectal *bodder,* possibly of Celtic origin.]

both•er•some (**bŏth′**ər səm) *adj.* Causing trouble; troublesome: *He raised several bothersome questions about the details of the plan.*

Bot•swa•na (bŏt **swä′**nə). Formerly **Bech•u•a•na•land** (bĕch′**wän′**ə lănd′). A country of south-central Africa. It gained its independence from Great Britain in 1966. Gaborone is the capital. Population, 973,000.

bot•tle (**bŏt′**l) *n.* **1.** A container, usually made of glass or plastic, having a narrow neck and a mouth that can be corked or capped. **2.a.** A bottle with something in it: *buy a bottle of ketchup.* **b.** The amount that a bottle holds: *A whole bottle of perfume spilled on the table.* **3.** A bottle filled with milk or formula with a nipple for feeding a baby.

—*tr.v.* **bot•tled, bot•tling, bot•tles.** To put in a bottle or bottles: *a machine that bottles water.* **—*idiom.* bottle up.** To hold in or back; restrain: *bottle up one's anger; bottle up traffic for hours.* [First written down about 1380 in Middle English and spelled *botel*, from Medieval Latin *butticula*, diminutive of Late Latin *buttis*, cask.] **—bot'tler** *n.*

bot•tle•neck (bŏt'l nĕk') *n.* **1.** A narrow route or passage where movement is slowed down. **2.** A condition that slows or hinders progress: *Highway construction caused a bottleneck of traffic every morning.*

bot•tom (bŏt'əm) *n.* **1.** The lowest or deepest part of something: *the bottom of a page; the bottom of the hill.* **2.** The underside of something: *the bottom of a boot.* **3.** The solid surface under a body of water: *The diver went to the bottom of the lake.* **4.** The underlying truth or cause; the basis or heart: *get to the bottom of the mystery.* **5.** The low land that adjoins a river. Often used in the plural. **6.** The seat of a chair: *a cane bottom.* **7.** The part of a ship's hull below the water line: *barnacles growing on the bottom of a boat.* **8.** The second half of an inning in baseball. **9.** *Informal.* The buttocks. **—*idiom.* at bottom.** Basically: *Though gruff, at bottom the store owner was a kindly person.* [First written down about 725 in Old English and spelled *botm.*]

bot•tom•land (bŏt'əm lănd') *n.* Low lying land along a river. Often used in the plural: *Mississippi River bottomlands.*

bot•tom•less (bŏt'əm lĭs) *adj.* **1.** Having no bottom: *a bottomless barrel.* **2.** Too deep to be measured: *a bottomless lake.*

bottom line *n.* **1.** The last line in a financial statement that shows the amount of profit or loss for a business. **2.** The final result or statement; the upshot: *The bottom line of all our rehearsing was that the play was a success.* **3.** The main or essential point: *The bottom line is that he forgives you.*

bot•u•lism (bŏch'ə lĭz'əm) *n.* A serious, often fatal form of food poisoning usually caused by bacteria that grow in improperly canned or preserved foods and produce poisons that act on the nervous system. [First written down in 1887 in Modern English, from German *Botulismus*, from Latin *botulus*, sausage.]

Bou•dic•ca (bo͞o dĭk'ə) also **Bo•ad•i•ce•a** (bō'ăd ĭ sē'ə). First century A.D. Queen of ancient Britain who led a revolt against the Roman army.

bou•doir (bo͞o'dwär' *or* bo͞o'dwôr') *n.* A woman's private sitting room, dressing room, or bedroom.

bouf•fant (bo͞o fänt') *adj.* Full and puffed-out, as a hairdo, skirt, or sleeve.

bough (bou) *n.* A large or main branch of a tree.
❑ *These sound alike:* **bough, bow¹** (front of a ship), **bow²** (bend).

bought (bôt) *v.* Past tense and past participle of **buy.**

bouil•la•baisse (bo͞o'yə bās' *or* bo͝ol'yə bās') *n.* A highly seasoned thick soup made with several kinds of fish and shellfish.

bouil•lon (bo͝ol'yŏn' *or* bo͝ol'yən) *n.* A clear thin broth usually made by simmering meat in water with seasonings: *beef bouillon.*
❑ *These sound alike:* **bouillon, bullion** (gold).

boul•der (bōl'dər) *n.* A large rounded mass of rock lying on the ground or imbedded in the soil.

boul•e•vard (bo͝ol'ə värd') *n.* A broad city street, often lined with trees. [First written down in 1769 in Modern English, from Old French *bollevart*, rampart converted to a promenade, from Middle Dutch *bolwerc*, bulwark.]

bounce (bouns) *v.* **bounced, bounc•ing, bounc•es.** —*intr.* **1.** To hit a surface and spring back from it; rebound: *The ball bounced off the wall.* **2.** To move with a bobbing, jolting, or vibrating motion: *Cars bounced down the dirt road.* **3.** To jump, spring, or bound: *The excited children bounced out of the room.* **4.** To be reflected: *Sunlight bounced off the water into my eyes.* **5.** *Informal.* To be sent back by a bank as worthless: *Without enough money in their account their check bounced.* —*tr.* **1.** To cause to bounce: *Bounce the ball to me.* **2.** *Slang.* To throw (someone) out forcefully: *The disorderly group was bounced from the movie theater.* —*n.* **1.** An act of bouncing or a bouncing movement; a bound or rebound: *catch a ball of the first bounce.* **2.** Capacity to bounce; springiness: *a rubber ball with plenty of bounce.* **3.** Liveliness: *There is a certain bounce to march music.* **—*idiom.* bounce back.** To return to a normal condition; recover or begin anew: *bounce back after a serious illness.*

bounc•er (boun'sər) *n. Slang.* A person employed to remove disorderly persons from a nightclub, bar, or similar place of entertainment.

bounc•ing (boun'sĭng) *adj.* Big and strong; healthy; thriving: *a happy bouncing baby.*

bounc•y (boun'sē) *adj.* **bounc•i•er, bounc•i•est. 1.** Tending to bounce: *a bouncy ball.* **2.** Springy; elastic: *bouncy hair.* **3.** Lively; energetic: *bouncy tunes.* **—bounc'i•ly** *adv.*

bound¹ (bound) *intr.v.* **bound•ed, bound•ing, bounds. 1.** To leap, jump, or spring: *The dog bounded over the gate.* **2.** To move forward by leaps or springs: *The deer bounded into the woods.* —*n.* **1.** A leap or jump: *The deer was away in a single bound.* **2.** A rebound; a bounce. [First written down in 1586 in Modern English, from French *bondir*, to bounce, perhaps from Latin *bombitāre*, to hum, from *bombus*, a humming sound, from Greek *bombos.*]

bound² (bound) *n.* **1.** A limit. Often used in the plural: *Their enthusiasm knew no bounds.* **2.** A boundary. Often used in the plural: *within the bounds of the state.* —*v.* **bound•ed, bound•ing, bounds.** —*tr.* **1.** To be the bound or boundary of: *Water bounds the city on three sides.* **2.** To contain within limits; enclose: *The campfire was bounded by a circle of stones.* **3.** To name the boundaries of: *Can you bound California?* —*intr.* To border on another country, state, or place. [First written down before 1300 in Middle English, from Medieval Latin *bodina*, of Celtic origin.]

bound³ (bound) *v.* Past tense and past participle of **bind.** —*adj.* **1.** Being under obligation; obliged: *bound by a promise.* **2.** Certain: *If we leave after dark, we are bound to be late for dinner.* **3.** Confined by bonds; tied: *the bound hands of the prisoner.* **4.** Enclosed in a cover or binding: *a bound book.* **—*idiom.* bound up with.** Closely associated or connected with: *The migration of birds is bound up with change in the seasons.*

bound⁴ (bound) *adj.* Headed or intending to go in a certain direction: *We are bound for Quebec.* [First written down about 1200 in Middle English and spelled *boun*, ready, from Old Norse *būinn*, past participle of *būa*, to get ready.]

bound•a•ry (boun'də rē *or* boun'drē) *n., pl.* **bound•a•ries.** A border or limit: *the southern boundary of Montana; the boundary between right and wrong.*

bound•en (boun'dən) *adj.* Being an obligation; required: *a soldier's bounden duty.*

bound form *n.* A form or an element in a language that always occurs as part of another word and cannot stand alone, as *-ly* in *lovely.*

bound•less (bound'lĭs) *adj.* **1.** Without any known limits; infinite: *the boundless reaches of outer space.* **2.** Very great; enormous: *her boundless energy.* **—bound'less•ness** *n.*

boun•te•ous (boun'tē əs) *adj.* **1.** Giving generously: *a bounteous philanthropist.* **2.** Plentiful: *a bounte-*

Usage: both

The word **both** means "each of two, taken individually." *Both books weigh more than five pounds* means that each book weighs more than five pounds by itself, not that the two books weighed together come to more than five pounds. When *both* is used with *and* to link two words or phrases in a sentence, these words or phrases should be grammatically parallel. *In both India and China* or *both in India and in China* are acceptable. *Both in India and China* is not.

ă	pat	oi	boy
ā	pay	ou	out
âr	care	o͝o	took
ä	father	o͞o	boot
ĕ	pet	ŭ	cut
ē	be	ûr	urge
ĭ	pit	th	thin
ī	pie	*th*	this
îr	pier	hw	whoop
ŏ	pot	zh	vision
ō	toe	ə	about
ô	paw	N	*French* bon

Word History: boutique

The word **boutique**, "small, specialized retail shop," comes from French, as its spelling and pronunciation suggest. The French word *boutique* comes from Latin *apothēca*, "storehouse, warehouse." The same Latin word becomes *bodega* in Spanish and means "wine cellar, pantry, storeroom." In the United States the word **bodega** refers to a grocery store in a Spanish-speaking neighborhood.

boutonniere

ous harvest. —**boun′te•ous•ly** *adv.* —**boun′te•ous•ness** *n.*

boun•ti•ful (**boun′**tə fəl) *adj.* **1.** Plentiful; abundant: *bountiful crops.* **2.** Giving generously and kindly: *a bountiful friend.* —**boun′ti•ful•ly** *n.* —**boun′ti•ful•ness** *n.*

boun•ty (**boun′**tē) *n., pl.* **boun•ties. 1.** Generosity in giving: *an artist dependent on the bounty of patrons.* **2.** Plentiful gifts or provisions: *the bounty of the earth in a rich harvest.* **3.** A reward for performing a service for the government, as for capturing an outlaw or killing a destructive animal.

bou•quet (bō **kā′** *or* bo͞o **kā′**) *n.* **1.** A bunch of flowers. **2.** A pleasant odor, especially of a wine.

bour•bon (**bûr′**bən) *n.* A whiskey distilled mainly from fermented corn mash.

Bour•bon (**bo͝or′**bən *or* bo͝or **bôɴ′**). French royal family descended from Louis I, Duke of Bourbon (1270?–1342), whose members have ruled in France, Spain, and Naples and Sicily.

bour•geois (bo͝or **zhwä′** *or* **bo͝or′**zhwä′) *n., pl.* **bourgeois.** A member of the middle class or bourgeoisie. —*adj.* **1.** Of, relating to, or typical of the middle class: *bourgeois merchants and shopkeepers.* **2.** Caring too much about respectability and possessions: *bourgeois attitudes about social standing.*

bour•geoi•sie (bo͝or′zhwä **zē′**) *n.* **1.** The middle class in a society. **2.** In the political theory of Karl Marx, the social group opposed to the lower classes, consisting of landowners and other capitalists.

bourn[1] also **bourne** (bôrn *or* bo͝orn) *n.* A stream or brook. [First written down about 725 in Old English and spelled *burna.*]

bourn[2] also **bourne** (bôrn *or* bo͝orn) *n. Archaic.* **1.** A boundary or limit. **2.** A goal or destination. [First written down in 1523 in Modern English, from Old French *bodne*, from Medieval Latin *bodina*, of Celtic origin.]

bour•rée (bo͞o **rā′** *or* bo͞o **rā′**) *n.* **1.** A lively French dance of the 17th century, resembling the gavotte. **2.** Music written for this dance.

bout (bout) *n.* **1.** A contest, such as a boxing match. **2.** A period or spell: *a severe bout of the flu.*

bou•tique (bo͞o **tēk′**) *n.* A small retail shop that sells gifts, fashionable clothes, or other specialized merchandise. —See Note.

bou•ton•niere (bo͞o′tə **nîr′** *or* bo͞o′tən **yâr′**) *n.* A flower worn in a buttonhole, usually on a lapel.

bo•vine (**bō′**vīn′ *or* **bō′**vēn′) *adj.* **1.** Of, related to, or resembling a cow or cattle. **2.** Dull and placid: *He sat in front of the TV, wearing a bovine stare.* —*n.* A cow, an ox, or a related animal.

bow[1] (bou) *n.* The front section of a ship or boat. [First written down in 1342 in Middle English and spelled *boue*, probably of Low German origin.]

❑ *These sound alike:* **bow**[1] (front of a ship), **bough** (branch), **bow**[2] (bend).

bow[2] (bou) *v.* **bowed, bow•ing, bows.** —*intr.* **1.** To bend the body, head, or knee, as in greeting or agreement: *bow politely from the waist.* **2.** To bend downward; stoop: *The mover bowed beneath the heavy load.* **3.** To give in; yield: *They refused to bow to pressure.* —*tr.* **1.** The bend (the body, head, or knee), as in greeting, agreement, or respect: *bow the head in prayer.* **2.** To express by bowing: *They bowed their agreement.* —*n.* A bending of the body or head, as when showing respect or accepting applause. —***idioms.*** **bow out.** To remove oneself; withdraw: *The candidate bowed out of the race for mayor.* **take a bow.** To acknowledge or accept applause, as by standing up or coming out on stage: *The cast took a bow before the audience.* [First written down about 725 in Old English and spelled *būgan.*]

❑ *These sound alike:* **bow**[2] (bend), **bough** (branch), **bow**[1] (front of a ship).

bow[3] (bō) *n.* **1.** A weapon used to shoot arrows, consisting of a flexible curved strip, usually of wood or plastic, with a string stretched tightly from end to end. **2.** A slender rod having horsehair stretched between two raised ends, used in playing the violin, viola, and other stringed instruments. **3.** A knot usually having two loops and two ends: *tie shoes with a bow.* **4.** A curve or an arch, as of lips or eyebrows. **5.** A rainbow. —*v.* **bowed, bow•ing, bows.** —*tr.* **1.** To play with a bow: *bow a fiddle.* **2.** To bend into a curved shape: *The heavy snow bowed the branches until they broke.* —*intr.* **1.** To play a stringed instrument with a bow. **2.** To bend into a curved shape: *The branches bowed and snapped in the high wind.* [First written down about 700 in Old English and spelled *boga.*]

❑ *These sound alike:* **bow**[3] (weapon), **beau** (suitor).

bow•el (**bou′**əl) *n.* **1.** The intestine, especially of a human being. Often used in the plural. **2.** A part of the intestine: *the large bowel.* **3. bowels.** The interior part of something: *the bowels of a ship.*

bow•er (**bou′**ər) *n.* A leafy shaded nook or shelter; an arbor.

bow•ie knife (**bō′**ē *or* **bo͞o′**ē) *n.* A long heavy knife with a single-edged blade, carried in a sheath and used for hunting. [First written down in 1836 in Modern English, after James *Bowie* (1799–1836), American-born Mexican colonist.]

bowl[1] (bōl) *n.* **1.** A rounded hollow container or dish that can hold liquid or food: *a soup bowl; a mixing bowl.* **2.** The amount that a bowl holds: *Eat a bowl of cereal.* **3.** Something shaped like a bowl, such as the hollow part of a spoon or a valley. **4.a.** A stadium or an outdoor theater shaped like a bowl. **b.** One of several special football games played after the usual season ends. [First written down about 700 in Old English and spelled *bolla.*]

❑ *These sound alike:* **bowl**[1] (dish), **bole** (stem), **boll** (seed pod), **bowl**[2] (ball).

bowl[2] (bōl) *n.* **1.** A wooden or plastic ball shaped to roll in a curving line, used in the game of lawn bowling. **2.** A throwing or rolling of the ball in various bowling games. —*v.* **bowled, bowl•ing, bowls.** —*intr.* **1.** To play the game of bowling: *Do you like to bowl?* **2.** To roll or throw a ball in bowling: *You bowl first.* **3.** To move smoothly and rapidly: *Huge trucks bowled along the superhighway.* —*tr.* **1.** To play (a game) of bowling. **2.** To make (a score) in bowling: *The champion bowled a high score.* **3.** To knock down with or as if with a rolling ball: *The girl was bowled by the wave.* —***idiom.*** **bowl over.** To take by surprise or overwhelm: *The unexpected announcement bowled them over.* [First written down before 1400 in Middle English and spelled *boule*, from Latin *bulla*, round object.]

❑ *These sound alike:* **bowl**[2] (ball), **bole** (stem), **boll** (seed pod), **bowl**[1] (dish).

bow•leg (**bō′**lĕg′) *n.* A leg that curves outward at the knee.

bow•leg•ged (**bō′**lĕg′ĭd *or* **bō′**lĕgd′) *adj.* Having bowlegs: *a bowlegged horseman.*

bowl•er[1] (**bō′**lər) *n.* A person who bowls.

bowl•er[2] (**bō′**lər) *n.* A derby hat.

bow•line (**bō′**lĭn *or* **bō′**līn′) *n.* A knot forming a loop that does not slip.

bowl•ing (**bō′**lĭng) *n.* **1.** A game played by rolling a ball down a bowling alley to knock down ten wooden pins at the opposite end; tenpins. **2.** A similar game, such as ninepins or skittles. **3.** Lawn bowling.

bowling alley *n.* **1.** A smooth level wooden lane used in bowling. **2.** A building or room containing lanes for bowling.

bowling green *n.* A smooth grassy area on which the game of lawn bowling is played.

bowls (bōlz) *n.* Lawn bowling.

bow•man (**bō′**mən) *n.* A person who shoots with a bow and arrow; an archer.

bow•sprit (**bou′**sprĭt′ *or* **bō′**sprĭt′) *n.* A long pole sticking out of the front of a sailing ship, to which lines are attached for fastening sails.

bow•string (**bō′**strĭng′) *n.* The string of a bow that is pulled back to shoot an arrow.

bow tie (bō) *n.* A small necktie tied in a bow.

box[1] (bŏks) *n.* **1.a.** A stiff container having four sides, a bottom, and often a top or lid. **b.** The amount that a box can hold: *eat a box of crackers.* **2.** A rectangle or square: *Draw a box around the right answer.* **3.a.** A separated compartment holding seats in a theater or stadium. **b.** A small building serving as a shelter: *a sentry box.* **4.** A signaling device enclosed in a casing: *a fire-alarm box.* **5.** A compartment for mail: *a box in a post office.* **6.** An area on a baseball field marked by lines to show where the batter, catcher, or coach may stand. **7.** The driver's seat on a carriage, coach, or other horse-drawn vehicle. —*tr.v.* **boxed, box•ing, box•es. 1.** To put or pack in a box: *box fruit before shipping.* **2.** To enclose in something shaped like a box: *box the title of the story.* **3.** To hinder or impede, as by blocking or restricting: *The bus was boxed in by the traffic jam.* [First written down before 1000 in Old English, from Late Latin *buxis*, from Greek *puxis*, from *puxos*, box tree.]

box[2] (bŏks) *n.* A blow or slap with the hand: *a box on the ear.* —*v.* **boxed, box•ing, box•es.** —*tr.* **1.** To take part in a boxing match with (an opponent). **2.** To hit or slap with the hand. —*intr.* To fight with the fists in a boxing match. [First written down about 1300 in Middle English.]

box[3] (bŏks) *n., pl.* **box** or **box•es. 1.** Any of several shrubs or trees having small evergreen leaves and hard yellowish wood, used for hedges and ornamental borders. **2.** The wood of such a shrub. [First written down before 800 in Old English, from Latin *buxus*, from Greek *puxos*.]

box•car (**bŏks′**kär′) *n.* An enclosed railroad car used to carry freight that is loaded through a sliding door on each side.

box elder *n.* A maple tree of North America having coarsely toothed or lobed leaves.

box•er[1] (**bŏk′**sər) *n.* A person who fights with the fists, especially to earn money.

box•er[2] (**bŏk′**sər) *n.* A medium-sized dog having a short, smooth, brownish coat and a square-jawed face.

boxer shorts *pl.n.* Loose-fitting shorts worn especially as underwear or for sport.

box•ing (**bŏk′**sĭng) *n.* The sport of fighting with the fists, especially when boxing gloves are worn and special rules are followed.

boxing glove *n.* One of two heavily padded leather gloves worn by a boxer to protect the fists while fighting.

box office *n.* A booth where tickets are sold in a theater, an auditorium, or a stadium.

box score *n.* A printed summary of a game of baseball or another sport, in the form of a table recording each player's performance.

box seat *n.* A seat in a box at a theater or stadium.

box spring *n.* A bedspring consisting of a frame enclosed with cloth and containing rows of coiled springs.

box stall *n.* An enclosed stall for a single animal.

box turtle *n.* Any of several North American land turtles, having a high-domed shell into which it can withdraw entirely.

box•wood (**bŏks′**wo͝od′) *n.* **1.** The wood of the box shrub or tree, used to make rulers and musical instruments. **2.** The box shrub or tree.

box•y (**bŏk′**sē) *adj.* **box•i•er, box•i•est.** Resembling a box, as in shape: *Shoulder pads gave the actor a boxy look.*

boy (boi) *n.* **1.a.** A male child. **b.** A young man: *a college boy.* **2.a.** A son: *her youngest boy.* **b.** A brother or male cousin: *the Jones boys.* **c.** *Informal.* A fellow; a guy: *a night out with the boys.* **3.** *Offensive.* A male servant. —*interj.* An expression used to show astonishment, elation, or disgust: *Boy! What a great car!*

boy•cott (**boi′**kŏt′) *tr.v.* **boy•cott•ed, boy•cott•ing, boy•cotts. 1.** To act together in refusing to use, buy, or deal with, especially as an expression of protest: *boycott a store; boycott a meeting.* **2.** To refuse to use, buy, or deal with: *boycott foreign-made goods.* —*n.* **1.** A refusal to buy from or deal with a person, business, or nation, especially as a form of protest. **2.** A refusal to buy or use a product or service. [First written down in 1880 in Modern English, after Charles C. *Boycott* (1832–1897), English land agent in Ireland.]

boy•friend (**boi′**frĕnd′) *n.* *Informal.* **1.** A male sweetheart or favored companion. **2.** A male friend.

boy•hood (**boi′**ho͝od′) *n.* The time of being a boy: *spend one's boyhood on a farm.*

boy•ish (**boi′**ĭsh) *adj.* Of, resembling, or suitable for a boy. —**boy′ish•ly** *adv.* —**boy′ish•ness** *n.*

Boyle (boil), **Robert.** 1627–1691. Irish-born British physicist and chemist whose work began the separation of chemistry from alchemy.

Boyle's law (boilz) *n.* The physical principle that at a constant temperature the volume of a confined gas decreases as its pressure increases and increases as its pressure decreases. [First written down in 1660 in Modern English, after Robert *Boyle.*]

Boy Scout *n.* A member of the Boy Scouts.

Boy Scouts *n.* An organization for boys that attempts to develop self-reliance, good citizenship, and outdoor skills.

boy•sen•ber•ry (**boi′**zən bĕr′ē) *n.* **1.** A large dark-red or purplish berry related to the blackberry. **2.** The plant that bears such berries. [First written down in 1935 in Modern English, after Rudolph *Boysen* (died 1950), American botanist.]

Br The symbol for the element **bromine.**

bra (brä) *n.* A brassiere.

brace (brās) *n.* **1.** A device that holds parts together or in place; a clamp. **2.** A supporting beam in a building or a connecting wire that holds something steady. **3.** A medical device used to support a bodily part. **4.** A handle that holds a drill or bit and is turned to bore holes. **5.** Either of the symbols, { or }, used in printing and writing to connect several lines of text or staves of music and in mathematics to enclose members of a set. **6. braces.** Wires and bands attached to the teeth to straighten them. **7.** *Chiefly British.* Suspenders. **8.** A pair; a couple: *a brace of dogs.* —*tr.v.* **braced, brac•ing, brac•es. 1.** To give support to; make firm; strengthen: *brace a tent with poles.* **2.** To prepare for a shock or difficulty: *The candidates braced themselves for the coming election.* **3.** To fill with energy; invigorate: *The cold air of the mountains braced the hikers.*

brace•let (**brās′**lĭt) *n.* A band or chain worn around the wrist or arm as an ornament.

bra•chi•o•pod (**brā′**kē ə pŏd′ *or* **brăk′**ē ə pŏd′) *n.* Any of various sea animals resembling a clam but having paired upper and lower shells attached to a stalk, and hollow tentacles covered with cilia that sweep food into the mouth.

bow tie

box turtle

Eastern box turtle

ă	pat	oi	boy
ā	pay	ou	out
âr	care	o͝o	took
ä	father	o͞o	boot
ĕ	pet	ŭ	cut
ē	be	ûr	urge
ĭ	pit	th	thin
ī	pie	*th*	this
îr	pier	hw	whoop
ŏ	pot	zh	vision
ō	toe	ə	about
ô	paw	N	*French* bon

William Bradford

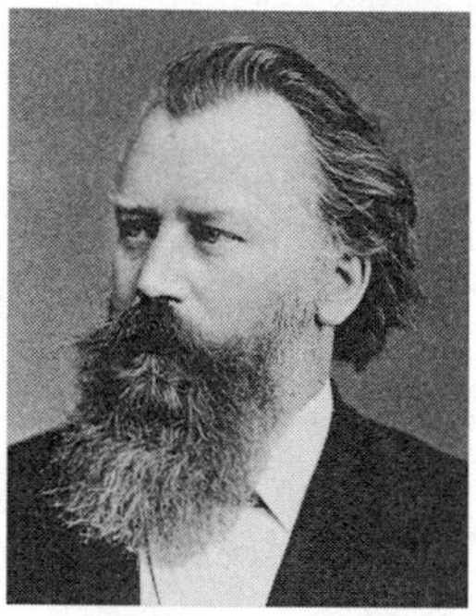

Johannes Brahms
Photographed c. 1880

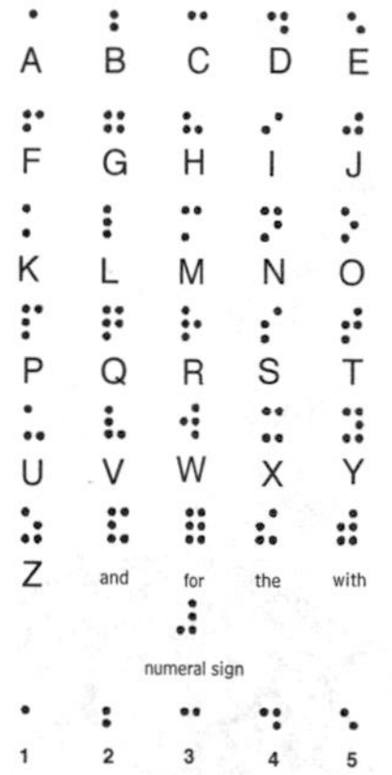

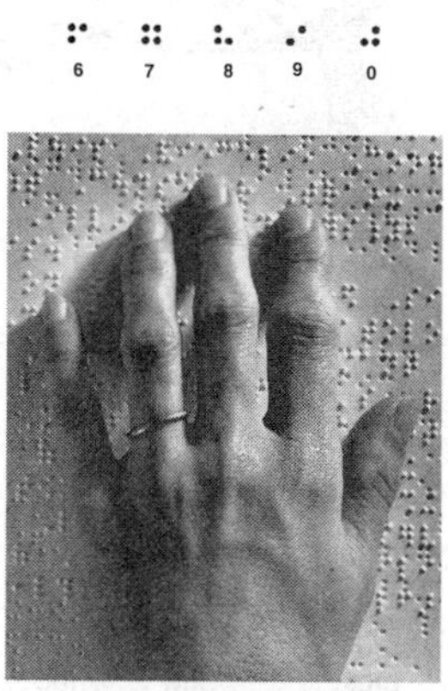

Braille
Top: Alphabet and numerals
Bottom: Printed material

brac•ing (brā′sĭng) *adj.* Giving strength and energy; refreshing: *a bracing wind.*

brack•en (brăk′ən) *n.* **1.** A large fern having triangular branching fronds. **2.** An area overgrown with such ferns.

brack•et (brăk′ĭt) *n.* **1.** A support or fixture fastened to a wall and sticking out to hold something, such as a shelf. **2.** A shelf supported by brackets. **3.** Either of the pair of symbols, [or], used to enclose printed or written material or to enclose a set of mathematical symbols that are to be considered a single expression. **4.** A group, class, or range within a numbered or graded series: *the 9-to-12 age bracket.* —*tr.v.* **brack•et•ed, brack•et•ing, brack•ets. 1.** To support with a bracket or brackets: *bracket shelves to strengthen them.* **2.** To place within brackets: *bracket words inserted in a quotation.* **3.** To classify or group together: *bracket taxpayers according to their earnings.*

brack•ish (brăk′ĭsh) *adj.* Slightly salty; briny: *brackish marsh waters near the ocean.*

bract (brăkt) *n.* A small plant part resembling a leaf and growing at the base of a flower or on a flower stalk. Most bracts are thin and inconspicuous, but some are showy or brightly colored and resemble petals.

brad (brăd) *n.* A thin nail with a small head. —*tr.v.* **brad•ded, brad•ding, brads.** To fasten with brads.

Brad•dock (brăd′ək), **Edward.** 1695–1755. British general in the American colonies during the French and Indian War.

Bradford (brăd′fərd), **William.** 1590–1657. English Puritan in the American colonies. He served as governor of Plymouth colony and led the settlement through its difficult early years.

Brad•street (brăd′strēt′), **Anne Dudley.** 1612–1672. English-born colonial American poet whose published works include *The Tenth Muse Lately Sprung Up in America* (1650).

brae (brā) *n. Scots.* A hillside; a slope.

brag (brăg) *v.* **bragged, brag•ging, brags.** —*intr.* To talk boastfully; boast: *brag about one's accomplishments.* —*tr.* To boast about: *brag of one's possessions.* —*n.* **1.** Boastful or conceited talk: *full of tiresome brag.* **2.** A boast. —**brag′ger** *n.*

brag•gart (brăg′ərt) *n.* A person who brags a lot. —*adj.* Very boastful.

Brahe (brä *or* brä′hē *or* brä′ə), **Tycho.** 1546–1601. Danish astronomer known for his accurate observations of the planets.

Brah•ma (brä′mə) *n.* **1.** In Hinduism, the god who created the world. **2.** Variant of **Brahman.**

Brah•man (brä′mən) also **Brah•ma** (brä′ma) *n.* **1.** Variant of **Brahmin. 2.** Also **Brahmin.** One of a breed of cattle native to India and having a hump between the shoulders and a fold of loose skin hanging below the neck.

Brah•man•ism (brä′mə nĭz′əm) *n.* **1.** The religion of ancient India. **2.** The religious and social system of the Brahmins of India.

Brah•ma•pu•tra (brä′mə po͞o′trə). A river of southern Asia rising in the Himalaya Mountains of southwest Tibet and flowing about 1,800 miles (2,896 kilometers) to join the Ganges River in central Bangladesh.

Brah•min (brä′mĭn) *n.* **1.** Also **Brah•man** (brä′-mən). A member of the highest Hindu class, responsible for officiating at religious rites. **2.** A member of the upper social class, especially a member of one of the old New England families. **3.** Variant of **Brahman** (sense 2).

Brahms (brämz), **Johannes.** 1833–1897. German composer. His works include concertos, four symphonies, chamber music, and choral compositions.

braid (brād) *tr.v.* **braid•ed, braid•ing, braids. 1.** To weave or twist together three or more strands of (hair, fiber, or fabric); plait: *She braided her long hair.* **2.** To make by weaving strands together: *braid a straw rug.* **3.** To decorate or edge with an ornamental trim. —*n.* **1.** A segment of braided hair, fabric, or other material. **2.** Ornamental cord or ribbon, used especially for trimming clothes. —**braid′er** *n.*

Braille or **braille** (brāl) *n.* A system of writing and printing for visually impaired or sightless people in which raised dots representing letters, numbers, and punctuation are read by touching them. [First written down in 1853 in Modern English, after Louis *Braille.*]

Braille, Louis. 1809–1852. French educator who invented a writing and printing system for visually impaired or sightless people (1829).

brain (brān) *n.* **1.** The large mass of gray and white nerve tissue enclosed in the skull of humans and other vertebrates. It interprets impulses from sense organs, coordinates and controls bodily activities and functions, and is the center of memory, thought, and feeling. **2.** The mind: *The plan took shape in his brain.* **3.** Intellectual power; intelligence. Often used in the plural: *It takes brains to be an economist.* **4.** *Informal.* **a.** A highly intelligent person: *That new student is a brain.* **b.** The main director or planner, as of an organization. Often used in the plural: *She is the brains of the business.* **5.** An electronic device, especially a computer, that is used to control a machine or vehicle, such as a ship. —*tr.v.* **brained, brain•ing, brains.** *Slang.* **1.** To smash the skull of. **2.** To hit hard on the head. —***idiom.*** **rack (one's) brain.** *Informal.* To think long and hard. [First written down about 1000 in Old English and spelled *brægen.*]

brain•child (brān′chīld′) *n. Informal.* The product of a person's mind; an original plan, idea, or invention: *The telephone was Bell's brainchild.*

brain-dead (brān′dĕd′) *adj.* Showing no electrical activity in the brain, indicating death of the cerebral cortex.

brain death *n.* Complete absence of electrical activity in the brain.

brain•less (brān′lĭs) *adj.* Without thought; stupid; foolish: *a brainless act of vandalism.* —**brain′less•ly** *adv.* —**brain′less•ness** *n.*

brain•pan (brān′păn′) *n.* The part of the skull that contains the brain; the cranium.

brain stem also **brain•stem** (brān′stĕm′) *n.* The part of the brain connecting the spinal cord to the forebrain.

brain•storm (brān′stôrm′) *n. Informal.* A sudden inspiration or clever idea.

brain•wash (brān′wŏsh′ *or* brān′wôsh′) *tr.v.* **brain•washed, brain•wash•ing, brain•wash•es. 1.** To indoctrinate (a person) forcibly so that his or her basic convictions are replaced with a different set of beliefs: *Several prisoners of war were brainwashed to confess to spying.* **2.** To persuade (a person) by intense means, such as repeated suggestions, to adopt a belief or behave in a certain way: *TV commercials brainwashed them into buying junk food.*

brain•wash•ing (brān′wŏsh′ĭng *or* brān′wô′shĭng) *n.* The act or process by which someone is brainwashed.

brain wave *n.* A rhythmic electric fluctuation arising from the brain and capable of being measured between points on the scalp. Brain waves are recorded by an electroencephalograph and are used to detect abnormalities in the brain.

brain•y (brā′nē) *adj.* **brain•i•er, brain•i•est.** *Informal.* Intelligent; smart.

braise (brāz) *tr.v.* **braised, brais•ing, brais•es.** To brown (meat or vegetables) in fat and then simmer in a little liquid in a covered container.

brake[1] (brāk) *n.* **1.** A device for slowing or stopping motion, as of a vehicle or machine: *The brakes failed and the car ran off the road.* **2.** Something that slows or stops an action or a process: *A bout of flu put a brake on my sightseeing.* —*v.* **braked, brak•ing, brakes.** —*tr.* To slow or stop with a brake or brakes: *brake a train.* —*intr.* To operate or apply a brake or brakes: *Slow down and brake before turning.* [First written down probably in 1552 in Modern English, bridle, curb, from Middle Dutch or Middle Low German, nose ring, curb.]

❑ *These sound alike:* **brake[1]** (device for stopping), **brake[2]** (fern), **brake[3]** (thicket), **break** (split).

brake[2] (brāk) *n.* Any of various ferns related to bracken, having compound leaves and popular as houseplants. [First written down before 1325 in Middle English, probably from *braken,* bracken.]

❑ *These sound alike:* **brake[2]** (fern), **brake[1]** (device for stopping), **brake[3]** (thicket), **break** (split).

brake[3] (brāk) *n.* An area overgrown with dense bushes or briers; a thicket. [First written down in 1440 in Middle English, from Middle Low German.]

❑ *These sound alike:* **brake[3]** (thicket), **brake[1]** (device for stopping), **brake[2]** (fern), **break** (split).

brake•man (brāk′mən) *n.* A member of a train crew who assists the conductor, as by uncoupling freight cars and checking on the operation of the train's brakes.

bram•ble (brăm′bəl) *n.* A prickly plant or shrub such as the blackberry or raspberry.

bram•bly (brăm′blē) *adj.* **1.** Full of brambles: *a brambly thicket.* **2.** Resembling brambles; prickly: *a brambly argument.*

bran (brăn) *n.* The outer husks of wheat, rye, and other grains, sifted out from the flour after milling. Bran is used in animal feed and in some cereals and bread as a source of dietary fiber.

branch (brănch) *n.* **1.a.** One of the woody parts growing out from the trunk, limb, or main stem of a tree or shrub. **b.** A part going out from a main part like a tree branch: *the branches of an antler; a stream that is a branch of this river.* **2.** A part or division of a larger whole: *Botany and zoology are branches of biology. Congress is the legislative branch of the U.S. government.* **3.** A division of a family of languages next below a subfamily. **4.** A local unit or office: *a bank branch.* —*intr.v.* **branched, branch•ing, branch•es. 1.** To put forth branches. **2.** To develop as a branch or division; diverge: *The road branches into two forks.* **3.** To expand one's interests, business, or activities: *The newspaper publisher branched out into radio and television.*

brand (brănd) *n.* **1.** A particular kind or make of product, especially as shown by a trademark: *a popular brand of soap; a good brand of coffee.* **2.** A name or symbol that identifies a product; a trademark: *This company owns several brands of breakfast cereal.* **3.** A distinctive category or kind: *That comedian is known for a rough brand of slapstick humor.* **4.a.** A mark indicating ownership burned into the hide of cattle with a hot iron. **b.** An iron used to make such a mark. **5.** A mark formerly burned into the flesh of criminals. **6.** A mark of disgrace; a stigma: *That store owner bears the brand of having defrauded customers.* **7.** A piece of burning or charred wood. —*tr.v.* **brand•ed, brand•ing, brands. 1.** To mark with a hot iron: *Cowhands branded the calves.* **2.** To mark with a label of disgrace; stigmatize: *The court branded the spies as traitors.* —**brand′er** *n.*

bran•dish (brăn′dĭsh) *tr.v.* **bran•dished, bran•dish•ing, bran•dish•es.** To wave or exhibit in a dramatic or threatening way: *brandish one's fist in defiance.*

brand-new (brănd′no͞o′ *or* brănd′nyo͞o′) *adj.* Completely new; not used.

bran•dy (brăn′dē) *n., pl.* **bran•dies.** An alcoholic liquor distilled from wine or fermented fruit juice. —*tr.v.* **bran•died, bran•dy•ing, bran•dies.** To mix, flavor, or preserve with brandy.

brant (brănt) *n., pl.* **brant** or **brants.** Any of several small wild geese that breed in arctic regions, having a black head and neck.

brash (brăsh) *adj.* **brash•er, brash•est. 1.** Shamelessly bold; impudent; saucy: *a brash young newcomer.* **2.** Hasty and unthinking; rash: *a brash move.* —**brash′ly** *adv.* —**brash′ness** *n.*

Bra•sí•lia (brə zĭl′yə). The capital of Brazil, in the central part of the country northwest of Rio de Janeiro. Population, 1,176,935.

brass (brăs) *n.* **1.** A yellow alloy of copper and zinc. **2.** Ornaments, objects, or utensils made of such metal: *Polish all the brass including the doorknobs.* **3.** Wind instruments made of brass or some other metal, including the French horn, trumpet, trombone, and tuba. Often used in the plural. **4.** *Informal.* Shameless boldness; impudence; nerve: *She had the brass to ask for another raise three months after her first one.* **5.** *Slang.* Military officers or civilian officials of high rank. [First written down about 1000 in Old English and spelled *bræs.*]

bras•siere (brə zîr′) *n.* A woman's undergarment worn to support the breasts.

brass instrument *n.* A wind instrument, such as a French horn or a trombone, made of brass or another metal.

brass tacks *pl.n. Informal.* Essential facts; basics: *Let's get down to brass tacks.*

brass•y (brăs′ē) *adj.* **brass•i•er, brass•i•est. 1.** Made of, decorated with, or having the color of brass. **2.** Resembling or featuring the sound of brass instruments: *a brassy voice.* **3.** *Informal.* Shamelessly bold; impudent; brazen: *the brassy behavior of a showoff.* —**brass′i•ly** *adv.* —**brass′i•ness** *n.*

brat (brăt) *n.* An ill-mannered or spoiled child.

bra•va•do (brə vä′dō) *n., pl.* **bra•va•dos** or **bra•va•does.** A show of pretended or defiant courage; false bravery: *The bravado of the coward before a fight.*

brave (brāv) *adj.* **brav•er, brav•est.** Having or showing courage: *a brave defiance of danger.* —*n.* A Native American warrior. —*tr.v.* **braved, brav•ing, braves.** To undergo or face with courage: *Firefighters brave many dangers in the line of duty.* [First written down in 1485 in Middle English, from Old French, probably from Latin *barbarus,* like a barbarian.] —**brave′ly** *adv.* —**brave′ness** *n.*

Synonyms: brave, courageous, fearless, bold, valiant. These adjectives mean having or showing courage in a difficult or dangerous situation. **Brave,** the most general, often refers to an inner quality: *I'm not brave enough to speak in front of such a large crowd.* **Courageous** means consciously drawing on one's inner strength to face peril: *The courageous captain guided the ship through the terrible storm.* **Fearless** emphasizes the absence of fear: *The fearless tightrope walker does not use a net.* **Bold** often means being brave and showing a tendency to seek out danger: *The bolder members of the search party went into the cave first.* **Valiant** means brave in a heroic way; it is usually used when describing a person: *The valiant firefighters had rescued everyone from the burning building.* **Antonym: cowardly.**

brav•er•y (brā′və rē *or* brāv′rē) *n., pl.* **brav•er•ies.** The quality or condition of being brave; courage.

bra•vo (brä′vō *or* brä vō′) *interj.* An expression used to show approval, as for a musical performance. —*n., pl.* **bra•vos.** A shout or cry of "bravo."

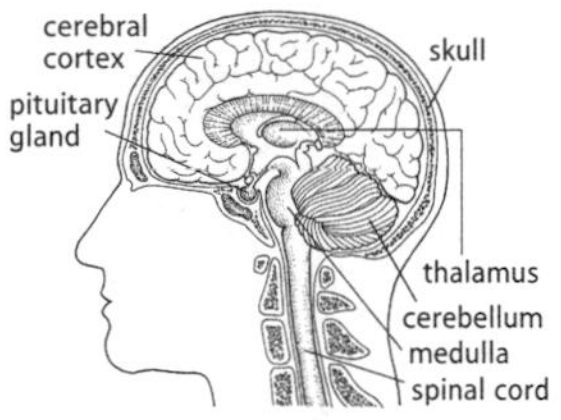

brain

brant

ă	pat	oi	boy
ā	pay	ou	out
âr	care	o͝o	took
ä	father	o͞o	boot
ĕ	pet	ŭ	cut
ē	be	ûr	urge
ĭ	pit	th	thin
ī	pie	*th*	this
îr	pier	hw	whoop
ŏ	pot	zh	vision
ō	toe	ə	about
ô	paw	ɴ	*French* bon

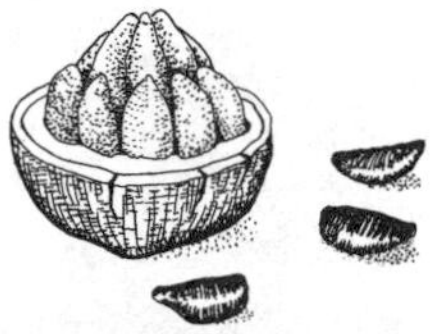
Brazil nut

bra•vu•ra (brə vo͝or′ə *or* brə vyo͝or′ə) *n.* **1.a.** Brilliant technique or style in a musical performance. **b.** A piece of music that requires great skill to play or sing. **2.** A showy display.

brawl (brôl) *n.* A noisy quarrel or fight. *—intr.v.* **brawled, brawl•ing, brawls.** To quarrel or fight noisily. [First written down in 1445 in Middle English and spelled *braul*, from *braullen*, to quarrel.]

brawn (brôn) *n.* Muscular strength and power.

brawn•y (brô′nē) *adj.* **brawn•i•er, brawn•i•est.** Strong and muscular. See Synonyms at **muscular.** **—brawn′i•ness** *n.*

bray (brā) *v.* **brayed, bray•ing, brays.** *—intr.* **1.** To utter the loud harsh cry of a donkey. **2.** To make a sound resembling this cry: *The foghorn brayed all night.* *—tr.* To utter loudly or harshly: *The car's horn brayed its warning.* *—n.* **1.** The loud harsh cry of a donkey. **2.** A sound resembling this cry: *the bray of trumpets.*

braze (brāz) *tr.v.* **brazed, braz•ing, braz•es.** To join (pieces of metal) together using a hard solder with a high melting point.

bra•zen (brā′zən) *adj.* **1.** Rudely bold; impudent; insolent: *a brazen remark.* **2.** Having a loud harsh sound: *the sound of a brazen bell.* **3.** Made of or resembling brass: *the brazen sky at sunset.* *—tr.v.* **bra•zened, bra•zen•ing, bra•zens.** To face or undergo with bold self-assurance: *The sailors brazened out the storm.* **—bra′zen•ly** *adv.* **—bra′zen•ness** *n.*

bra•zier (brā′zhər) *n.* A metal pan for holding burning coals or charcoal.

Bra•zil (brə zĭl′). A country of eastern South America on the Atlantic Ocean north of Uruguay. It is the largest country in the continent. Brasília is the capital and São Paulo the largest city. Population, 119,002,706.

Brazil nut *n.* The edible oily nut of a tropical South American tree, having a hard, three-sided, dark-brown shell.

Braz•za•ville (brăz′ə vĭl′ *or* brä zä vēl′). The capital and largest city of Congo, in the southern part of the country north of Kinshasa, Zaire. It is a major port. Population, 595,102.

breach (brēch) *n.* **1.** A gap or hole, especially in a solid structure: *The crowd poured through a breach in the barrier.* **2.** A violation or an infraction, as of a law, legal obligation, or promise: *a breach of contract.* **3.** A disruption of friendly relations; an estrangement: *An argument caused a breach between the friends.* *—tr.v.* **breached, breach•ing, breach•es.** To make a hole or gap in; break through: *Floodwaters breached the dike.* [First written down about 750 in Old English and spelled *brēc.*]

❑ *These sound alike:* **breach, breech** (rear of a gun barrel).

bread (brĕd) *n.* **1.** A food made from flour or meal mixed with water and other ingredients, usually combined with a leavening agent, and kneaded and baked in a loaf. **2.** Food in general, regarded as necessary to sustain life: *A farm family works long hours for its daily bread.* **3.** The necessities of life; livelihood: *earn one's bread as a writer.* **4.** *Slang.* Money. *—tr.v.* **bread•ed, bread•ing, breads.** To coat (food) with bread crumbs before cooking. [First written down about 950 in Old English and spelled *brēad.*]

❑ *These sound alike:* **bread, bred** (produced offspring).

bread-and-but•ter (brĕd′n bŭt′ər) *adj.* **1.** Relating to or undertaken out of necessity: *a bread-and-butter job.* **2.** Expressive of thanks for hospitality: *send a bread-and-butter note.*

bread•bas•ket (brĕd′băs′kĭt) *n.* **1.** A basket for serving bread. **2.** A region serving as a principal source of grain supply: *Iowa, Nebraska, and Kansas are part of America's breadbasket.* **3.** *Slang.* The stomach.

bread•fruit (brĕd′fro͞ot′) *n.* **1.** A large, round, edible fruit that has a rough skin and starchy flesh resembling bread when roasted. **2.** The tropical tree that bears such fruit.

bread line *n.* A line of people waiting to receive a free meal given out by a charitable organization or the government.

bread•stuff (brĕd′stŭf′) *n.* **1.** Bread. **2.** Flour, meal, or grain used in the baking of bread.

breadth (brĕdth) *n.* **1.a.** The distance from side to side of something; width: *The breadth of the road is several yards, while its thickness is only a few feet deep.* **b.** A piece of something having a regular width: *a breadth of cloth.* **2.** Freedom from narrowness, as of interests or attitudes: *a judge's great breadth and wisdom.* **3.** Wide extent or scope: *Her breadth of knowledge is impressive.*

bread•win•ner (brĕd′wĭn′ər) *n.* A person who earns money to support a household.

break (brāk) *v.* **broke** (brōk), **bro•ken** (brō′kən), **break•ing, breaks.** *—tr.* **1.a.** To cause to separate into two or more pieces as the result of force: *break a mirror.* **b.** To snap off; detach: *break a twig from a branch.* **2.** To fracture a bone of: *break an arm.* **3.** To make unusable; ruin: *I broke my watch when I sat on it.* **4.** To part or pierce the surface of: *break ground for a new building; fish breaking the water.* **5.** To force a way through: *The blade broke the skin.* **6.** To cause to burst: *I broke the balloon with a pin.* **7.** To escape from: *break jail.* **8.a.** To destroy the regularity, order, or completeness of: *break ranks and run; break a set of books.* **b.** To put an end to, as by force, opposition, or change: *One vote broke the tie.* **c.** To disrupt or end abruptly; interrupt: *A cry broke the silence.* **d.** To create a gap across which electricity cannot pass: *break a circuit.* **9.a.** To violate by failing to follow, conform, or observe; fail to keep: *break a law; break a promise.* **b.** To call off; cancel: *break a date.* **10.** To lessen or diminish in force or effect: *A big bush broke my fall.* **11.** To weaken or destroy; overwhelm: *Defeat broke the champion's spirit.* **12.** To reduce in rank; demote: *break a sergeant to a private.* **13.** *Informal.* To cause to be without money; bankrupt: *Big bills and few customers broke the new business.* **14.** To reduce to or exchange for smaller monetary units: *Break a dollar for change to pay the bus fare.* **15.** To surpass or outdo: *break a record.* **16.** To give up (a habit). **17.** To train to obey; tame: *break a wild mustang.* **18.** To find the solution or key to: *break a code.* **19.** To make known: *break sad news gently.* *—intr.* **1.** To become separated into pieces or fragments: *Glass breaks easily. The string broke with a snap.* **2.** To become unusable: *The radio broke.* **3.** To give way; collapse: *The bridge broke under the weight of the truck.* **4.** To burst: *The blister broke.* **5.** To scatter or disperse: *The clouds broke after the storm.* **6.** To move or escape suddenly: *The cattle broke out of their pen.* **7.** To change direction suddenly: *The fullback broke to the right.* **8.** To come into being or appear suddenly: *Crocuses broke from the soil.* **9.** To become known or noticed: *The story broke in the afternoon news.* **10.** To interrupt or cease an activity or association: *Let's break for five minutes.* **11.** To decrease rapidly: *Hot summer temperatures often break after a rainstorm.* **12.** To come to an end: *The cold spell finally broke.* **13.** To collapse or crash into surf or spray: *waves breaking on the beach.* **14.** To change suddenly in musical tone or pitch: *Her voice broke with emotion.* **15.** In baseball, to curve suddenly at or near home plate: *The pitch broke sharply.* *—n.* **1.** A result of breaking; a fracture or crack: *a break in a bone.* **2.a.** A gap or an opening: *a break in the clouds.* **b.** A beginning: *the break of day.* **3.** An interruption or disruption of regularity or continuity: *a break in the conversation; a break in an electrical circuit.* **4.** A pause or an interval, as from work: *Take a break for a few minutes.* **5.** A sudden run; a dash: *The rabbit made a break for cover.* **6.** An attempt to escape: *a jail break.* **7.** A sudden change: *a break in the weather.* **8.** A severing of ties: *a break between families.* **9.** An unexpected occurrence or chance: *a lucky break.* ***—idioms.*** **break down. 1.** To cause to collapse; destroy: *break down a wall.* **2.** To fail to function: *The truck broke down on the highway.* **3.a.** To decompose chemically: *Plastic takes years to break down.* **b.** To analyze or consider in parts: *Break the exercise down into several steps.* **4.** To become distressed or upset: *They broke down and cried when they got lost.* **break even.** To gain an amount equal to that invested, as in a business. **break in. 1.** To enter a building or property forcibly or illegally: *The burglars broke in but could not find the jewels.* **2.** To interrupt a conversation: *The operator broke in to tell us our time was up.* **3.** To train or instruct for some purpose: *break in a new worker.* **4.** To soften with use: *break in new shoes.* **break into. 1.** To enter forcibly and illegally: *The bear broke into the cabin.* **2.** To begin suddenly: *He broke into song.* **3.** To interrupt: *She broke into our discussion to tell us it was time to go.* **break off. 1.** To stop suddenly, as in speaking: *break off in the middle of a sentence.* **2.** To stop being friendly: *When the soldiers left the army they broke off with their old buddies.* **break out. 1.** To be affected with a skin irritation, such as a rash: *An allergy to wool makes me break out.* **2.** To begin suddenly: *Fire broke out during the night.* **3.** To ready for action or use: *Firefighters broke out the hoses.* **break (someone's) heart.** To disappoint or dispirit someone severely. **break up. 1.a.** To scatter; disperse: *The clouds are breaking up.* **b.** To separate into smaller parts: *break up a word into syllables.* **2.** To bring or come to an end: *The police broke up a fight. Their partnership broke up.* **3.** To interrupt: *broke up the long day by going swimming.* [First written down about 725 in Old English and spelled *brecan.*]

❑ *These sound alike:* **break, brake**[1] (device for stopping), **brake**[2] (fern), **brake**[3] (thicket).

Synonyms: break, crack, split, splinter, shatter. These verbs mean to separate into parts or pieces. **Break** is the most general: *Take care not to break anything while you're dusting.* **Crack** means to break, often with a sharp snapping sound, without dividing into parts: *We heard the ice cracking as we walked on it.* **Split** means to divide along something's length: *These pants have split along the seam.* **Splinter** means to split into long, thin, sharp pieces: *Lightning struck the tree and splintered it.* **Shatter** means to break into many loose scattered pieces: *The perfume bottle fell and shattered on the floor.*

---

break•a•ble (brā′kə bəl) *adj.* Capable of being broken; fragile.

break•age (brā′kĭj) *n.* **1.** The act of breaking. **2.** A quantity broken: *Breakage during shipping was extensive.* **3.** Loss or damage as a result of breaking: *The fire resulted in breakage of most of the store's windows.* **4.** Compensation, as in money, for such loss or damage.

break•down (brāk′doun′) *n.* **1.** The process of failing to function properly. **2.** The condition resulting from this process: *The breakdown of train service caused many to be delayed.* **3.** A collapse of physical or mental health: *Not getting enough sleep will eventually cause a breakdown in health.* **4.** Decomposition or disintegration into parts or elements: *Bacteria are used in the breakdown of sewage.* **5.** An analysis or a summary consisting of itemized data: *The sticker on the car window shows a breakdown of accessories.*

break•er (brā′kər) *n.* **1.** A person or thing that breaks: *a wave that breaks into foam on a shore.* **2.** A circuit breaker.

break•fast (brĕk′fəst) *n.* The first meal of the day. *—intr.v.* **break•fast•ed, break•fast•ing, break•fasts.** To eat breakfast. [First written down before 1393 in Middle English and spelled *breken fast* : *breken*, to break + *faste*, a fast (from Old Norse *fasta*, to fast).]

break•neck (brāk′nĕk′) *adj.* Dangerously fast: *The ambulance drove at breakneck speed.*

break•through (brāk′thro͞o′) *n.* A major achievement or success that permits further progress, as in technology: *Development of the transistor was a breakthrough in electronics.*

break•up (brāk′ŭp′) *n.* **1.** The act or an instance of breaking up; a separation or dispersal: *the breakup of an iceberg; the breakup of a large corporation.* **2.** The ending of a relationship, as of friends.

break•wa•ter (brāk′wô′tər *or* brāk′wŏt′ər) *n.* A barrier that protects a harbor or shore from the full impact of waves.

bream (brēm *or* brĭm) *n., pl.* **bream** or **breams. 1.** Any of several European freshwater fishes having a flattened body and silvery scales. **2.** Any of various freshwater sunfishes. [First written down about 1387 in Middle English and spelled *breem*, from Old French, of Germanic origin.]

breast (brĕst) *n.* **1.** In mammals, especially human beings, one of the glands in which a female produces milk to feed her young offspring. **2.** The upper part of the front surface of the human body, extending from the neck to the abdomen. **3.** The seat of affection or emotion: *Deep in his breast he felt an abiding sorrow.* *—tr.v.* **breast•ed, breast•ing, breasts.** To face or advance against boldy: *The rescuers breasted every danger to save the victims.*

breast•bone (brĕst′bōn′) *n.* The sternum.

breast-feed (brĕst′fēd′) *tr.v.* **breast-fed** (brĕst′fĕd′), **breast-feed•ing, breast-feeds.** To feed (a baby) mother's milk from the breast; nurse.

breast•plate (brĕst′plāt′) *n.* A piece of metal armor worn over the chest.

breast•stroke (brĕst′strōk′) *n.* A swimming stroke in which one lies face down and extends the arms in front of the head, sweeping them back to the sides while performing a frog kick.

breast•work (brĕst′wûrk′) *n.* A temporary, hastily constructed fortification, usually breast-high.

breath (brĕth) *n.* **1.** The air inhaled into and exhaled from the lungs. **2.** The ability to breathe, especially with ease: *I got short of breath as I ran up the hill.* **3.** The act or process of breathing. **4.** A single act of breathing, especially an inhalation: *The singer took a deep breath.* **5.** Exhaled air, as shown by vapor, odor, or heat: *You can see your breath in the cold winter air.* **6.** A slight breeze: *Not a breath of air stirred the leaves.* **7.** A trace or suggestion: *the first breath of spring.* ***—idioms.*** **out of breath.** Breathing with difficulty, as from exertion; gasping: *I was out of breath when I got to the top of the hill.* **under (one's) breath.** In a muted voice or whisper. [First written down before 900 in Old English and spelled *brǣth.*]

breathe (brēth) *v.* **breathed, breath•ing, breathes.** *—intr.* **1.** To inhale and exhale air: *As we climbed higher, it got harder to breathe.* **2.** To be alive; live: *As long as the dog breathed, it was loyal to its master.* **3.** To pause to rest or to regain breath, as after action: *Give me a moment to breathe.* *—tr.* **1.** To

breakwater

breastplate

ă	pat	oi	boy
ā	pay	ou	out
âr	care	o͝o	took
ä	father	o͞o	boot
ĕ	pet	ŭ	cut
ē	be	ûr	urge
ĭ	pit	th	thin
ī	pie	*th*	this
îr	pier	hw	whoop
ŏ	pot	zh	vision
ō	toe	ə	about
ô	paw	N	*French* bon

inhale and exhale (air, for example). **2.** To exhale; emit: *breathe a sigh of relief after the danger passed.* **3.** To impart (a quality) as if by breathing: *The artist breathed life into the painting of the children.* **4.** To utter, especially quietly; whisper: *Don't breathe a word of this.* **5.** To allow (a person or animal) to rest: *breathe a horse after a race.* —***idioms.*** **breathe down (someone's) neck.** To watch or monitor closely, often annoyingly. **breathe (one's) last.** To die.

breath•er (brē′*th*ər) *n. Informal.* A short period of rest.

breath•less (brĕth′lĭs) *adj.* **1.** Breathing with difficulty; gasping: *The runners were breathless after the race.* **2.** Holding the breath from excitement or suspense: *a breathless audience* **3.** Inspiring or marked by excitement that makes one hold the breath: *the breathless beauty of the mountains.* —**breath′less•ly** *adv.* —**breath′less•ness** *n.*

breath•tak•ing (brĕth′tā′kĭng) *adj.* Inspiring awe; very exciting: *The fireworks are always a breathtaking spectacle.*

bred (brĕd) *v.* Past tense and past participle of **breed.**

❑ *These sound alike:* **bred, bread** (food).

breech (brēch) *n.* **1.** The part of a firearm behind the barrel. **2.** The lower rear part of the human trunk; the buttocks. **3. breeches** (brĭch′ĭz *or* brē′chĭz). **a.** Pants extending to or just below the knees. **b.** *Informal.* Pants of any kind.

❑ *These sound alike:* **breech, breach** (gap).

breech•cloth (brēch′klôth′ *or* brēch′klŏth′) *n.* A cloth worn to cover the loins; a loincloth.

breeches buoy *n.* A device used for rescue at sea, made up of canvas pants attached to a life preserver that is suspended from a pulley running along a line from ship to ship or ship to shore.

breed (brēd) *v.* **bred** (brĕd), **breed•ing, breeds.** —*tr.* **1.** To produce (offspring): *Mice breed large litters.* **2.a.** To raise (animals or plants), often to produce new or improved types: *The researchers are trying to breed cattle with lean meat.* **b.** To arrange the mating of (animals) so as to produce offspring: *We hope to breed the dogs and sell the puppies.* **3.** To bring about; give rise to: *Poverty breeds crime.* **4.** To rear or train; bring up. —*intr.* **1.** To produce or reproduce by giving birth or hatching: *Mosquitoes breed rapidly.* **2.** To originate and grow: *Discontent breeds in hunger and injustice.* —*n.* **1.** A group of organisms having common ancestors and certain characteristics, often produced by mating selected parents: *a hardy breed of cattle; a breed of hybrid corn.* **2.** A type or kind: *a new breed of politician.* [First written down before 850 in Old English and spelled *brēdan.*]

breed•er (brē′dər) *n.* **1.** A person who breeds animals or plants: *a poultry breeder.* **2.** An animal or a plant kept for breeding.

breeder reactor *n.* A nuclear reactor that produces more fissionable material than it consumes.

breed•ing (brē′dĭng) *n.* **1.** Training in the proper forms of conduct: *Good manners are evidence of good breeding.* **2.** The producing of offspring or young. **3.** The reproduction of animals or plants, especially so as to produce new or improved varieties.

breeze (brēz) *n.* **1.** A light current of air; a gentle wind. **2.** *Informal.* Something that is easy to do. —*intr.v.* **breezed, breez•ing, breez•es.** *Informal.* To make rapid progress without effort: *We breezed through the homework.*

breeze•way (brēz′wā′) *n.* A roofed, open-sided passageway connecting two buildings, such as a house and a garage.

breez•y (brē′zē) *adj.* **breez•i•er, breez•i•est. 1.** Exposed to breezes; windy: *a breezy point along the shore.* **2.** Lively; sprightly: *a writer's breezy style.* —**breez′i•ly** *adv.* —**breez′i•ness** *n.*

breth•ren (brĕ*th*′rən) *n.* A plural of **brother** (sense 2).

Bret•on (brĕt′n) *adj.* Of or relating to Brittany, or its people, language, or culture. —*n.* **1.** A native or inhabitant of Brittany. **2.** The Celtic language of Brittany.

breve (brĕv *or* brēv) *n.* **1.** A mark (˘) placed over a vowel to show that it has a short sound, as the *ă* in *bat.* **2.** A similar mark used to indicate that a syllable is unstressed in a foot of verse.

bre•vi•ar•y (brē′vē ĕr′ē *or* brĕv′ē ĕr′ē) *n., pl.* **bre•vi•ar•ies.** In the Roman Catholic and Anglican churches, a book containing the daily prayers, hymns, and other readings of priests and members of certain religious orders.

brev•i•ty (brĕv′ĭ tē) *n.* Briefness, as of expression; shortness: *The brevity of the speaker's remarks prevented boredom.*

brew (bro͞o) *v.* **brewed, brew•ing, brews.** —*tr.* **1.** To make (beer or ale) from malt and hops. **2.** To make (a beverage) by boiling, steeping, or mixing ingredients: *brew tea.* **3.** To devise or plan; concoct: *Members of the opposing party brewed a plot to disgrace the President.* —*intr.* **1.** To be brewed: *The tea brewed quickly.* **2.** To be imminent; threaten to occur: *A storm brewed on the horizon.* —*n.* **1.** A beverage made by brewing. **2.** A serving of such a beverage. [First written down before 900 in Old English and spelled *brēowan.*] —**brew′er** *n.*

brew•er•y (bro͞o′ə rē *or* bro͝or′ē) *n., pl.* **brew•er•ies.** A place where malt liquors, such as beer and ale, are manufactured.

brew•ing (bro͞o′ĭng) *n.* The act, process, or business of making malt liquors, such as beer and ale.

Brezh•nev (brĕzh′nĕf), **Leonid Ilyich.** 1906–1982. Soviet politician who served terms as Communist Party secretary and president of the Soviet Union between 1960 and 1982.

bri•ar[1] also **bri•er** (brī′ər) *n.* **1.** A Mediterranean shrub having a hard woody root used to make tobacco pipes. **2.** A pipe made from the root of this shrub. [First written down in 1868 in Modern English, from French *bruyère,* heath, from Late Latin *brūcus,* heather, of Celtic origin.]

bri•ar[2] (brī′ər) *n.* Variant of **brier[1].**

bri•ar•wood (brī′ər wo͝od′) *n.* Wood from the root of the briar.

bribe (brīb) *n.* **1.** Something, such as money, property, or position, offered or given to someone in order to influence that person to act dishonestly: *Corrupt officials were dismissed for accepting bribes.* **2.** Something offered or serving to influence or persuade: *good behavior influenced by a bribe of staying up late.* —*tr.v.* **bribed, brib•ing, bribes.** To give or offer a bribe to: *It is a criminal act to bribe a judge.*

brib•er•y (brī′bə rē) *n., pl.* **brib•er•ies.** The act of giving, offering, or taking a bribe.

bric-a-brac (brĭk′ə brăk′) *n.* Small objects displayed in a room as ornaments.

brick (brĭk) *n., pl.* **bricks** or **brick. 1.** An oblong block of clay, baked by the sun or in a kiln until hard and used as a building and paving material. **2.** An object shaped like such a block: *a brick of cheese.* —*tr.v.* **bricked, brick•ing, bricks. 1.** To build, line, or pave with bricks. **2.** To close, wall, or fill with bricks: *The mason bricked up the window opening.* [First written down in 1416 in Middle English and spelled *brike,* from Middle Dutch *bricke.*]

brick•bat (brĭk′băt′) *n.* **1.** A piece of brick thrown as a weapon. **2.** An unfavorable remark; a criticism:

The candidates exchanged brickbats during the debate.

brick•lay•er (brĭk′lā′ər) *n.* A person who builds by laying bricks. —**brick′lay′ing** *n.*

brick•work (brĭk′wûrk′) *n.* A structure made of bricks.

brick•yard (brĭk′yärd′) *n.* A place where bricks are made or sold.

bri•dal (brīd′l) *adj.* Of or relating to a bride or a marriage ceremony: *a bridal veil; the bridal party.*
❑ *These sound alike:* **bridal, bridle** (straps for a horse's head).

bride (brīd) *n.* A woman who is about to be married or has been recently married.

bride•groom (brīd′gro͝om′ *or* brīd′gro͞om′) *n.* A man who is about to be married or has recently been married. [First written down in 1526 in Modern English and spelled *bridegrome*, alteration of Middle English *bridegome*, from Old English *brȳdguma* : *brȳd*, bride + *guma*, man.]

brides•maid (brīdz′mād′) *n.* A woman who attends the bride at a wedding.

bridge[1] (brĭj) *n.* **1.** A structure providing a way across a gap or an obstacle, such as a river, railroad, or gorge. **2.a.** The upper bony ridge of the human nose. **b.** The part of a pair of eyeglasses that rests against this ridge. **3.** A thin piece of wood that supports the strings above the sounding board in a violin, cello, and some other stringed instruments. **4.** A structure that replaces one or more missing teeth, usually anchored to teeth at both ends. **5.** A platform or an enclosed area above the main deck of a ship from which the ship is controlled. **6.** A musical passage that connects two sections of a song or composition. —*tr.v.* **bridged, bridg•ing, bridg•es. 1.** To build a bridge over: *bridge a river.* **2.** To cross by or as if by a bridge: *His career bridged two generations of technology.* [First written down about 1000 in Old English and spelled *brycg.*]

bridge[2] (brĭj) *n.* Any of several card games for four, derived from whist. [First written down possibly in 1843 in Modern English, alteration of *biritch*, from Russian *birich*, a call.]

bridge•head (brĭj′hĕd′) *n.* A military position seized by advancing troops in enemy territory as a place for launching further attacks.

Bridge•town (brĭj′toun′). The capital of Barbados, in the West Indies. It was founded in 1628. Population, 7,466.

bridge•work (brĭj′wûrk′) *n.* One or more dental bridges used to replace missing teeth.

bri•dle (brīd′l) *n.* **1.** A harness, consisting of straps, a bit, and reins, fitted about a horse's head and used to control the animal. **2.** A restraint or control: *The new rules put a bridle on rowdy behavior.* —*v.* **bri•dled, bri•dling, bri•dles.** —*tr.* **1.** To put a bridle on: *bridle a horse.* **2.** To control with or as if with a bridle: *Bridle your temper!* —*intr.* **1.** To lift the head and draw in the chin as an expression of scorn or resentment: *bridle with anger.* **2.** To show anger; take offense: *The author bridled at the criticism.*
❑ *These sound alike:* **bridle, bridal** (of a bride).

bridle path *n.* A trail for horseback riding.

brief (brēf) *adj.* **brief•er, brief•est. 1.** Short in time or duration: *I took a brief nap.* **2.** Short in length or extent: *a brief report taking only one page.* —*n.* **1.** A short statement or summary, especially a lawyer's summary of the facts relating to a case or argument. **2. briefs.** Short, tight-fitting underpants. —*tr.v.* **briefed, brief•ing, briefs.** To give instructions, information, or advice to: *The pilot was briefed on weather conditions before takeoff.* [First written down probably before 1300 in Middle English and spelled *bref*, from Latin *brevis.*] —**brief′ly** *adv.* —**brief′ness** *n.*

brief•case (brēf′kās′) *n.* A flat rectangular case for carrying books or papers.

brief•ing (brē′fĭng) *n.* **1.** The act or procedure of giving or receiving instructions, information, or advice: *give the President a briefing before a news conference.* **2.** The instructions, information, or advice given during a briefing.

bri•er[1] also **bri•ar** (brī′ər) *n.* A thorny shrub, especially a prickly-stemmed rosebush. [First written down about 1000 in Old English and spelled *brēr.*]

bri•er[2] (brī′ər) *n.* Variant of **briar**[1].

brig (brĭg) *n.* **1.** A two-masted sailing ship with two or more square headsails and a spanker behind the mizzenmast. **2.** A ship's prison. **3.** A guardhouse or jail on a military base. [First written down in 1720 in Modern English, short for *brigantine.*]

bri•gade (brĭ gād′) *n.* **1.** A large army unit, especially such a unit composed of two or more battalions. **2.** A group organized for a specific purpose: *a fire brigade.* [First written down in 1637 in Modern English, from Old Italian *brigata*, from *brigare*, to fight, from *briga*, strife, of Celtic origin.]

brig•a•dier (brĭg′ə dîr′) *n.* A brigadier general.

brigadier general *n., pl.* **brigadier generals.** A general ranking above a colonel and below a major general in the U.S. Army, Air Force, or Marine Corps.

brig•and (brĭg′ənd) *n.* A member of a roving band of robbers. [First written down before 1387 in Middle English and spelled *brigant*, from Old Italian *brigante*, skirmisher, from *brigare*, to fight.]

brig•an•tine (brĭg′ən tēn′) *n.* A two-masted sailing ship with square sails on the foremast only. [First written down in 1525 in Modern English and spelled *brigandyn*, from Old Italian *brigantino*, skirmishing ship, from *brigante*, skirmisher.]

bright (brīt) *adj.* **bright•er, bright•est. 1.** Emitting or reflecting light readily or in large amounts; shining: *the bright sun shining in a cloudless sky; a cat's bright glistening eyes.* **2.** Containing little or no black, white, or gray; vivid or intense: *bright green.* **3.** Full of light: *a bright day.* **4.** Intelligent; smart: *a bright attractive little child; a bright idea.* See Synonyms at **smart. 5.** Happy; cheerful: *a bright smiling face; a bright tune.* **6.** Full of promise and hope: *a bright future.* —*adv.* In a bright manner: *The moon shines bright on a clear night.* [First written down before 830 in Old English and spelled *berht.*] —**bright′ly** *adv.*

bright•en (brīt′n) *tr. & intr.v.* **bright•ened, bright•en•ing, bright•ens. 1.** To make or become bright or brighter: *Sunlight brightened the room. Stars brighten as the sun goes down.* **2.** To make or become happy or more cheerful: *Their faces brightened at the clown's approach.*

bright•ness (brīt′nĭs) *n.* **1.** The quality or condition of being bright: *Brightness in the sky announced the dawn.* **2.** The amount of light that appears to come from an object or a color.

bril•liance (brĭl′yəns) *n.* **1.** Extreme brightness: *the brilliance of the noonday sun.* **2.** Sharpness and clarity of musical tone: *Trumpets are noted for their brilliance.* **3.** Splendor; magnificence: *the brilliance of the palace.* **4.** Exceptional intelligence or inventiveness: *a discovery of great brilliance.*

bril•liant (brĭl′yənt) *adj.* **1.** Full of light; shining brightly: *A brilliant sun blazed in the sky.* **2.** Very vivid in color: *The sky was a brilliant blue.* **3.** Extremely intelligent or inventive: *A brilliant strategy won the chess match.* See Synonyms at **smart. 4.** Splendid; magnificent: *the brilliant court life of the kings of France.* **5.** Excellent; wonderful: *The musicians gave a brilliant performance.* **6.** Clear and

brickwork

bridge[1]
San Francisco–Oakland Bay suspension bridge

ă	pat	oi	boy
ā	pay	ou	out
âr	care	o͝o	took
ä	father	o͞o	boot
ĕ	pet	ŭ	cut
ē	be	ûr	urge
ĭ	pit	th	thin
ī	pie	*th*	this
îr	pier	hw	whoop
ŏ	pot	zh	vision
ō	toe	ə	about
ô	paw	N	*French* bon

penetrating, as a musical sound: *The trumpet has a firm brilliant tone.* —*n.* A precious gem, especially a diamond, cut so that it catches the light and sparkles. —**bril′liant•ly** *adv.*

brim (brĭm) *n.* **1.** The rim or uppermost edge of a hollow container, such as a cup or glass: *The pail was filled to the brim.* **2.** A projecting rim on a hat. **3.** A border or an edge, as of a canyon. —*intr.v.* **brimmed, brim•ming, brims.** To be full to the brim: *My cup is brimming with cider.* [First written down before 1200 in Middle English and spelled *brimme.*]

brim•ful (brĭm′fo͝ol′) *adj.* Full to the brim; completely full: *a glass brimful of milk.*

brim•stone (brĭm′stōn′) *n.* **1.** Sulfur. **2.** The torments of hell; hellfire. [First written down in 1125 in Middle English and spelled *brynstān.*]

brin•dle (brĭn′dl) *n.* A brindled color.

brin•dled (brĭn′dld) *adj.* Tan or gray with streaks or spots of a darker color.

brine (brīn) *n.* **1.** Water that contains a large amount of dissolved salt, especially sodium chloride. **2.** The water of a sea or an ocean. **3.** Salt water used for preserving or pickling foods.

bring (brĭng) *tr.v.* **brought** (brôt), **bring•ing, brings. 1.** To take with oneself to a place; carry along or convey: *I brought the books upstairs.* **2.** To cause to occur as a result: *The flood brought much property damage.* **3.** To persuade; convince: *People were having such a good time they could not bring themselves to leave.* **4.** To cause to come; attract: *Smoke from the barn brought the neighbors.* **5.** To call to mind; recall: *This song brings back memories.* **6.** To put or force into a particular situation, location, or condition: *His refusal brought the project to a halt. Bring the potatoes to a boil.* **7.** To put forward (a legal action or charge) against someone in court: *bring suit.* **8.** To sell for: *Diamonds always bring high prices.* **—*idioms.*** **bring about.** To cause to happen: *Hard work brought about the success of the play.* **bring around. 1.** To cause to adopt an opinion or take a certain course of action: *We tried to bring him around, but he did what he wanted anyway.* **2.** To cause to recover consciousness. **bring down. 1.** To cause to fall or collapse. *The revolution brought down the king.* **2.** To kill. **bring forth. 1.** To give rise to; produce: *The bulbs brought forth flowers in the spring.* **2.** To give birth to (young). **bring forward.** To present; produce: *bring forward proof.* **bring in. 1.** To give or submit (a verdict) to a court. **2.** To produce, yield, or earn (profits or income). **bring off.** To accomplish: *We brought off a successful play.* **bring on.** To cause to appear: *Working in the rain brought on a cold.* **bring out. 1.** To reveal or expose: *The article in the newspaper brought out the seriousness of the problem.* **2.** To produce or publish: *The company is bringing out a new book.* **3.** To nurture and develop (a quality, for example) to best advantage: *She brings out the best in us.* **bring to.** To cause to recover consciousness. *The patient was brought to after surgery.* **bring up. 1.** To take care of and educate (a child); rear. **2.** To introduce into discussion; mention: *I was surprised when they brought up the subject of my painting.* [First written down about 725 in Old English and spelled *bringan.*]

brink (brĭngk) *n.* **1.** The upper edge of a steep or vertical slope: *He stood at the brink of the crater.* **2.** The point at which something is likely to begin; the verge: *on the brink of extinction; at the brink of success.* See Synonyms at **margin.** [First written down about 1225 in Middle English, probably of Scandinavian origin.]

brin•y (brī′nē) *adj.* **brin•i•er, brin•i•est.** Of, relating to, or resembling brine; salty.

British Columbia

The province of **British Columbia** was originally a British colony. *Columbia* is a Latin word that comes from the family name of Christopher Columbus, the Italian explorer.

bri•quette also **bri•quet** (brĭ kĕt′) *n.* A block of compressed coal dust, charcoal, or sawdust, used for fuel.

brisk (brĭsk) *adj.* **brisk•er, brisk•est. 1.** Moving or acting quickly; lively; energetic: *a brisk walk to get to school on time.* **2.** Very active; not sluggish: *Business is brisk when the store has a sale.* **3.** Fresh and invigorating: *a brisk fall morning.* **4.** Sharp in speech or manner: *He gave us a friendly but brisk reply.* [First written down in 1560 in Modern English, probably of Scandinavian origin.] —**brisk′ly** *adv.* —**brisk′ness** *n.*

bris•ket (brĭs′kĭt) *n.* **1.** The chest of an animal. **2.** Meat from the chest of an animal: *a brisket of beef.*

bris•ling (brĭz′lĭng *or* brĭs′lng) *n.* The sprat.

bris•tle (brĭs′əl) *n.* **1.** A short stiff hair. **2.** A short, often synthetic piece resembling a hair: *the plastic bristles of a hairbrush.* —*v.* **bris•tled, bris•tling, bris•tles.** —*intr.* **1.** To raise the bristles, as in anger or fright: *The dog bristled and showed his teeth.* **2.** To stand out stiffly like bristles: *The hair on the dog's neck bristled.* **3.** To show sudden anger or annoyance: *The artist bristled at the criticism of his work.* **4.** To be thick with or as if with bristles: *The path bristled with thorns.* —*tr.* To cause to stand erect like bristles; stiffen: *A porcupine will bristle its quills if frightened.* [First written down probably about 700 in Old English and spelled *byrst.*]

bris•tly (brĭs′lē) *adj.* **bris•tli•er, bris•tli•est. 1.** Consisting of or similar to bristles: *a dog with a short bristly coat.* **2.** Easily angered or irritated: *a bristly disposition.*

Brit. *abbr.* An abbreviation of: **1.** Britain. **2.** British

Brit•ain (brĭt′n). The island of Great Britain during pre-Roman, Roman, and early Anglo-Saxon times before 871.

Bri•tan•nia (brĭ tăn′yə *or* brĭ tăn′ē ə) *n.* A female personification of Great Britain.

britch•es (brĭch′ĭz) *pl.n. Informal.* Breeches. —***idiom.*** **too big for (one's) britches.** Overconfident; cocky.

Brit•i•cism (brĭt′ĭ sĭz′əm) *n.* A word, a phrase, or an idiom characteristic of or peculiar to English as used in Great Britain.

Brit•ish (brĭt′ĭsh) *adj.* Of or relating to Great Britain or its people, language, or culture. —*n.* **1.** The people of Great Britain. **2.** British English. **3.** The Celtic language of the ancient Britons.

British Co•lum•bi•a (kə lŭm′bē ə). A province of western Canada on the Pacific Ocean south of Yukon Territory. It joined the Canadian confederation in 1871. Victoria is the capital and Vancouver the largest city. Population, 2,744,467. —See Note.

British Com•mon•wealth (kŏm′ən wĕlth′). Commonwealth of Nations.

British Empire. The countries and territories that were formerly ruled by Great Britain. It once included about one quarter of the world's land area and population.

British English *n.* The English language as used in Great Britain.

Brit•ish•er (brĭt′ĭ shər) *n. Informal.* A native or inhabitant of Great Britain.

British Hon•du•ras (hŏn do͝or′əs *or* hŏn dyo͝or′əs). Belize.

British Isles. A group of islands off the northwest coast of Europe made up of Great Britain, Ireland, and adjacent smaller islands.

British thermal unit *n.* The amount of heat that is needed to raise the temperature of one pound of water by one degree Fahrenheit. This unit is used mainly to measure heat, but it can be applied to other forms of energy.

British Vir•gin Islands (vûr′jĭn). A British colony in the eastern Caribbean east of Puerto Rico and the

U.S. Virgin Islands. Road Town is the capital. Population, 12,034.

British West In•dies (ĭn′dēz). The islands of the West Indies that were formerly ruled by Great Britain, including Jamaica, Barbados, Trinidad and Tobago, and the Bahamas.

Brit•on (brĭt′n) *n.* **1.** A native or inhabitant of Great Britain. **2.** A member of the Celtic people of ancient Britain.

Brit•ta•ny (brĭt′n ē). A region and former province of northwest France on a peninsula between the English Channel and the Bay of Biscay.

brit•tle (brĭt′l) *adj.* **brit•tler, brit•tlest.** Likely to break or snap: *a brittle porcelain plate.* [First written down before 1325 in Middle English and spelled *brotil*, from Old English *bryttian*, to shatter.] **—brit′tle•ness** *n.*

bro. *abbr.* An abbreviation of brother.

broach (brōch) *tr.v.* **broached, broach•ing, broach•es. 1.** To talk or write about for the first time; begin to discuss: *broach a subject tactfully.* **2.** To pierce in order to draw off liquid: *broach a keg of cider.* —*n.* A pointed tool used to shape or enlarge a hole.

❑ *These sound alike:* **broach, brooch** (pin).

broad (brôd) *adj.* **broad•er, broad•est. 1.** Wide from side to side: *a broad river.* **2.** Large in expanse; spacious: *broad fields of wheat.* **3.** Clear; bright: *broad daylight.* **4.** Covering a wide scope; general: *a broad rule; a broad topic.* **5.** Main or essential: *the broad sense of a word.* **6.** Plain and obvious: *a broad hint.* **7.** Liberal; tolerant: *a broad point of view.* **8.** Coarse; vulgar: *a broad joke.* **9.** Pronounced with the tongue low and flat and the mouth wide open, like the *a* in *father.* [First written down about 725 in Old English and spelled *brād.*] **—broad′ly** *adv.* **—broad′ness** *n.*

broad•ax or **broad•axe** (brôd′ăks′) *n.* An ax with a wide flat head and a short handle, used as a weapon or for cutting timber.

broad•cast (brôd′kăst′) *v.* **broad•cast** or **broad•cast•ed, broad•cast•ing, broad•casts.** —*tr.* **1.** To transmit by radio or television: *All the networks will broadcast the President's speech.* **2.** To make known over a wide area: *Rumors were broadcast all over town.* **3.** To sow (seed) over a wide area; scatter. —*intr.* **1.** To transmit a radio or television program: *Many stations broadcast from tall buildings.* **2.** To participate in a radio or television program: *The President will broadcast over a national network.* —*n.* **1.** A radio or television program or transmission. **2.** The act of scattering seed: *broadcast of seed by the wind.* —*adj.* **1.** Of or relating to transmission by radio or television: *Broadcast time for commercials is expensive.* **2.** Scattered over a wide area. —*adv.* In a scattered manner; far and wide. [First written down in 1767 in Modern English and spelled *broadcast*, scattered about.] **—broad′cast′er** *n.*

broad•cloth (brôd′klôth′ *or* brôd′klŏth′) *n.* **1.** A fine woolen cloth with a smooth glossy texture, used especially in making suits. **2.** A closely woven silk, cotton, or synthetic cloth with a narrow rib, used especially in making shirts.

broad•en (brôd′n) *tr. & intr.v.* **broad•ened, broad•en•ing, broad•ens.** To make or become broad or broader: *broaden a narrow street; a view of the world that broadened after a trip.*

broad jump *n.* The long jump.

broad•loom (brôd′lo͞om′) *adj.* Woven on a wide loom. —*n.* A carpet woven on a wide loom.

broad-mind•ed (brôd′mīn′dĭd) *adj.* Having liberal and tolerant views and opinions: *It's wise to keep a broad-minded attitude toward the politics of other people.* **—broad′mind′ed•ly** *adv.* **—broad′mind′ed•ness** *n.*

broad•side (brôd′sīd′) *n.* **1.** A ship's side above the water line. **2.** A firing of all the guns on one side of a warship. **3.** A forceful written or verbal attack, as in an editorial or a speech. —*adv.* With the side turned toward a specified object: *The wave caught them broadside and filled the canoe.*

broad•sword (brôd′sôrd′) *n.* A sword with a broad blade for cutting rather than thrusting.

Broad•way (brôd′wā′). **1.** A road in New York, the longest street in the world. It begins at the southern tip of Manhattan and extends about 150 miles (241 kilometers) north to Albany. **2.** The principal theater and amusement district of New York City, on the west side of midtown Manhattan centered on Broadway.

bro•cade (brō kād′) *n.* A heavy cloth with a rich raised design. —*tr.v.* **bro•cad•ed, bro•cad•ing, bro•cades.** To weave with a raised design.

broc•co•li (brŏk′ə lē) *n.* A plant closely related to the cauliflower and cabbage, having dense clusters of green flower buds that are eaten as a vegetable.

bro•chure (brō sho͝or′) *n.* A small pamphlet or booklet: *a travel brochure.*

bro•gan (brō′gən) *n.* A heavy work shoe extending to the ankle.

brogue[1] (brōg) *n.* **1.** A heavy oxford shoe decorated with rows of tiny holes on top. **2.** A heavy shoe of untanned leather, formerly worn in Scotland and Ireland. [First written down in 1586 in Modern English, from Irish and Scottish Gaelic *brōg*, from Old Irish *brōc*, shoe.]

brogue[2] (brōg) *n.* A strong dialectal accent, especially an Irish accent. [First written down in 1705 in Modern English, probably from the brogues worn by peasants.]

broil (broil) *v.* **broiled, broil•ing, broils.** —*tr.* **1.** To cook close to flame or direct heat: *broil the fish.* **2.** To expose to great heat: *The desert sun broiled everyone in the caravan.* —*intr.* **1.** To be cooked by direct heat: *The fish broiled for ten minutes.* **2.** To be exposed to great heat: *The tourists broiled under the tropical sun.* [First written down in 1350 in Middle English and spelled *brulen*, from Old French *brusler.*]

broil•er (broi′lər) *n.* **1.** A pan, grill, or part of a stove used for broiling. **2.** A young chicken suitable for broiling.

broke (brōk) *v.* **1.** Past tense of **break. 2.** *Nonstandard.* A past participle of **break.** —*adj. Informal.* Lacking money.

bro•ken (brō′kən) *v.* Past participle of **break.** —*adj.* **1.** Separated into pieces by force; fractured: *broken pieces of glass; a broken leg.* **2.** Out of order; not functioning: *a broken watch.* **3.** Not kept; violated: *a broken promise.* **4.** Spoken with gaps and errors: *broken English.* **5.** Overwhelmed, as by sadness or hardship: *a broken heart.* **6.** Stopping and starting at intervals having gaps; not continuous: *a broken line on a highway.* **7.** Lacking parts; not complete: *a broken set of books.* **8.** Rough; uneven: *patches of broken ground.* **9.** Tamed and trained: *a broken stallion.* **—bro′ken•ly** *adv.*

bro•ken-down (brō′kən doun′) *adj.* **1.** In poor condition, as from old age: *a broken-down cart horse.* **2.** Out of working order: *a broken-down car.*

bro•ken•heart•ed (brō′kən här′tĭd) *adj.* Overwhelmed with sadness; very sad. **—bro′ken•heart′ed•ly** *adv.*

bro•ker (brō′kər) *n.* A person who acts as an agent for others by negotiating contracts, purchases, or sales in return for a fee or commission: *a commodities broker.*

bro•ker•age (brō′kər ĭj) *n.* **1.** The business of a broker. **2.** A fee or commission paid to a broker.

bro•mide (brō′mīd′) *n.* **1.** A compound of bromine

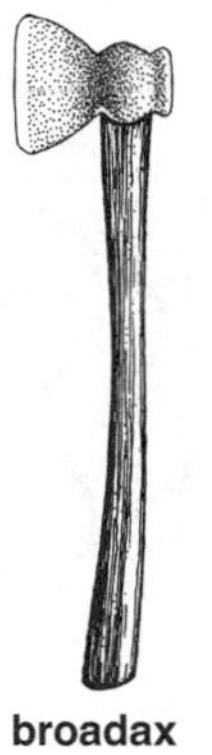

broadax

brocade

ă	pat	oi	boy
ā	pay	ou	out
âr	care	o͝o	took
ä	father	o͞o	boot
ĕ	pet	ŭ	cut
ē	be	ûr	urge
ĭ	pit	th	thin
ī	pie	*th*	this
îr	pier	hw	whoop
ŏ	pot	zh	vision
ō	toe	ə	about
ô	paw	N	*French* bon

Brontë
Detail of a portrait of Anne, Emily, and Charlotte by Patrick Branwell Brontë (1817–1848)

brontosaur

brontosaur

Take a little deception, add a little excitement, stir them with a century-long mistake, and you have the mystery of the **brontosaur**. Specifically, you have the mystery of its name. For 100 years these 70-foot-long, 30-ton vegetarian giants had two names. This case of double identity began in 1877, when bones of a large dinosaur were discovered. The creature was dubbed **apatosaur**, a name that meant "deceptive lizard." Two years later, bones of a larger dinosaur were found, and in all the excitement, scientists named it **brontosaur,** or "thunder lizard." This name stuck until scientists decided it was all a mistake—the two sets of bones actually belonged to the same type of dinosaur.

and another element or a radical, such as one with potassium, that is used as a sedative. **2.** A commonplace remark or notion; a platitude: *an editorial filled with the usual bromides about the importance of team spirit.*

bro•mine (**brō′**mēn) *n. Symbol* **Br** A dark brownish-red element that is a nonmetallic liquid somewhat like chlorine and iodine and gives off an irritating vapor. It is used in antiknock compounds for gasoline, in drugs, and in photography. Atomic number 35. See table at **element.** [First written down in 1827 in Modern English, from Greek *brōmos,* stench.]

bron•chi (**brŏng′**kī′) *n.* Plural of **bronchus.**

bron•chi•a (**brŏng′**kē ə) *pl.n.* The bronchial tubes that are smaller than the bronchi and larger than bronchioles.

bron•chi•al (**brŏng′**kē əl) *adj.* Of or relating to the bronchi, the bronchia, or the bronchioles.

bronchial tube *n.* A bronchus or any of the tubes branching from a bronchus.

bron•chi•ole (**brŏng′**kē ōl′) *n.* Any of the fine thin-walled tubes that extend from a bronchus.

bron•chi•tis (brŏn **kī′**tĭs *or* brŏng **kī′**tĭs) *n.* Inflammation of the mucous membrane of the bronchial tubes. **—bron•chit′ic** (brŏng **kĭt′**ĭk) *adj.*

bron•cho•scope (**brŏng′**kə skōp′) *n.* A slender tube with a small light on the end, used to examine the inside of the bronchi.

bron•chus (**brŏng′**kəs) *n., pl.* **bron•chi** (**brŏng′**kī′). Either of the two large main branches of the windpipe, leading directly to the lungs.

bron•co (**brŏng′**kō) *n., pl.* **bron•cos.** A small wild or half-wild horse of western North America.

Bron•të (**brŏn′**tē). Family of British writers including **Charlotte** (1816–1855), **Emily** (1818–1848), and **Anne** (1820–1849). In 1846 they issued *Poems by Currer, Ellis and Acton Bell.* In 1847 Charlotte published *Jane Eyre*; Emily published *Wuthering Heights*; and Anne published *Agnes Gray.*

bron•to•saur (**brŏn′**tə sôr′) or **bron•to•sau•rus** (brŏn′tə **sôr′**əs) *n.* A very large dinosaur that lived in swamps and streams and fed on plants during the Jurassic period. [First written down in 1879 in Modern English and spelled *brontosaurus* : Greek *brontē,* thunder + Greek *sauros,* lizard.] —See Note.

Bronx (brŏngks). A borough of New York City in southeast New York on the mainland north of Manhattan. It became part of New York in 1898. Population, 1,203,789.

bronze (brŏnz) *n.* **1.a.** An alloy of copper and tin, sometimes with traces of other metals. **b.** An alloy of copper and certain metals other than tin, such as aluminum. **2.** A work of art made of bronze. **3.** A yellowish or olive brown. *—adj.* **1.** Yellowish or olive brown. **2.** Made of or containing bronze: *bronze tools; a bronze statue.* *—tr.v.* **bronzed, bronz•ing, bronz•es.** To give the appearance of bronze to: *The sun had bronzed the faces of the lifeguards.* **—bronz′y** *adj.*

Bronze Age *n.* The period of human culture between the Stone Age and the Iron Age, characterized by the use of bronze implements and weapons. In Europe, it extended roughly from 3500 B.C. to 1000 B.C.

brooch (brōch *or* bro͞och) *n.* A large pin worn as an ornament, fastened to the clothing with a clasp.

❑ *These sound alike:* **brooch, broach** (begin to discuss).

brood (bro͞od) *n.* **1.** The young of certain animals, especially a group of young birds hatched at one time and cared for by the same mother. **2.** The children in one family: *The little house was too small for the Bensons' brood.* *—v.* **brood•ed, brood•ing, broods.** *—intr.* **1.** To sit on and hatch eggs. **2.** To think at length and unhappily; worry: *It seems pointless to brood about the past.* *—tr.* To sit on and hatch (eggs).

brood•er (**bro͞o′**dər) *n.* **1.** A person or an animal that broods. **2.** A heated enclosure in which young chickens are raised.

brook[1] (bro͝ok) *n.* A small natural stream of fresh water. [First written down about 847 in Old English and spelled *brōc.*] —See Note at **run.**

brook[2] (bro͝ok) *tr.v.* **brooked, brook•ing, brooks.** To put up with; tolerate: *We were late and scarcely in the mood to brook further delay.* [First written down about 725 in Old English and spelled *brūcan,* to use, enjoy.]

brook•let (**bro͝ok′**lĭt) *n.* A small brook.

Brook•lyn (**bro͝ok′**lĭn). A borough of New York City in southeast New York on western Long Island. The community became part of New York City in 1898. Population, 2,300,664.

Brooks (bro͝oks), **Gwendolyn Elizabeth.** Born 1917. American poet known for her verses relating the dreams and struggles of Black Americans.

brook trout *n.* A speckled freshwater food fish of eastern North America.

broom (bro͞om *or* bro͝om) *n.* **1.** An implement for sweeping, usually consisting of strands of straw or plastic bound together and attached to a long stick. **2.** Any of various Mediterranean shrubs having yellow flowers, small leaves, and many straight slender branches. [First written down about 700 in Old English and spelled *brōm.*]

❑ *These sound alike:* **broom, brougham** (carriage).

broom•corn (**bro͞om′**kôrn′ *or* **bro͝om′**kôrn′) *n.* A grass having stiff branching stalks that are used to make brooms and brushes.

broom•stick (**bro͞om′**stĭk′ *or* **bro͝om′**stĭk′) *n.* The long handle of a broom.

bros. *abbr.* An abbreviation of brothers.

broth (brôth *or* brŏth) *n., pl.* **broths** (brôths *or* brŏths *or* brô*th*z *or* brŏ*th*z). A clear soup made from the water in which meat, fish, or vegetables have been boiled.

broth•er (**brŭ*th*′**ər) *n., pl.* **broth•ers. 1.** A boy or man having the same mother and father as another person. **2.** Often **brethren** (**brĕ*th*′**rən). **a.** A person who shares common ancestors, a common allegiance to a country, or a common purpose with another or others. **b.** A fellow member of a group, such as a profession, fraternity, or labor union. **3.** A member of a men's Christian religious order who is not a priest. [First written down about 725 in Old English and spelled *brōthor.*]

broth•er•hood (**brŭ*th*′**ər ho͝od′) *n.* **1.** The relationship of being a brother or brothers. **2.** Brotherly feelings or friendship toward other human beings; fellowship. **3.** A group of people united for a common purpose such as those belonging to a fraternity, labor union, or a profession.

broth•er-in-law (**brŭ*th*′**ər ĭn lô′) *n., pl.* **broth•ers-in-law** (**brŭ*th*′**ərz ĭn lô′). **1.** The brother of one's husband or wife. **2.** The husband of one's sister. **3.** The husband of the sister of one's husband or wife.

broth•er•ly (**brŭ*th*′**ər lē) *adj.* Characteristic of or appropriate to brothers; affectionate: *a warm brotherly greeting.* **—broth′er•li•ness** *n.*

brougham (bro͞om *or* **bro͞o′**əm) *n.* **1.** A four-wheeled carriage with a closed compartment for passengers and an open driver's seat. **2.** An automobile with an open driver's seat. [First written down in 1851 in Modern English, after Henry Peter *Brougham,* First

Baron Brougham and Vaux (1778–1868), Scottish-born jurist.]

❑ *These sound alike:* **brougham, broom** (sweeping implement).

brought (brôt) *v.* Past tense and past participle of **bring.**

brow (brou) *n.* **1.** The forehead. **2.** An eyebrow. **3.** The upper edge of a steep place: *We stood on the brow of a hill overlooking the valley.*

brow•beat (**brou′**bēt′) *tr.v.* **brow•beat, brow•beat•en** (**brou′**bēt′n), **brow•beat•ing, brow•beats.** To bully or intimidate, as with frightening looks or harsh words.

brown (broun) *n.* The color of chocolate or coffee. *—adj.* **brown•er, brown•est. 1.** Of the color brown. **2.** Suntanned. *—tr. & intr.v.* **browned, brown•ing, browns. 1.** To make or become brown: *Silt browned the stream after the heavy rains.* **2.** To cook until brown on the outside: *The chef browned the meat.* **—brown′ness** *n.*

Brown (broun), **John.** 1800–1859. American abolitionist who was tried and hanged in 1859 after capturing the U.S. arsenal at Harper's Ferry as part of an effort to free Southern slaves.

brown bear *n.* Any of several large bears of North America, Europe, and Asia, having dark brown to yellowish fur.

brown Bet•ty (**bět′**ē) *n.* A baked pudding of apples, bread crumbs, brown sugar, butter, and spices.

brown coal *n.* Lignite.

brown•ie (**brou′**nē) *n.* **1.** In folklore, a small elf said to do helpful work such as household chores while people are asleep. **2.** A bar of moist chocolate cake with nuts. **3. Brownie.** A member of the Girl Scouts between six and eight years old.

Brown•ing (**brou′**nĭng), **Elizabeth Barrett.** 1806–1861. British poet. Her best-known work, *Sonnets from the Portuguese* (1850), is a series of love poems written to her husband, the poet **Robert Browning** (1812–1889), who published *Men and Women* in 1855.

brown•ish (**brou′**nĭsh) *adj.* Somewhat brown.

brown•out (**broun′**out′) *n.* A dimming or partial loss of electric lights and power in a city or other area, especially as the result of a shortage.

brown rice *n.* Rice that still has the outer layer of bran on the grain.

brown•stone (**broun′**stōn′) *n.* **1.** A brownish-red sandstone used as a building material. **2.** A house built or faced with such stone.

brown sugar *n.* Unrefined or partially refined sugar with a flavor similar to that of molasses.

browse (brouz) *v.* **browsed, brows•ing, brows•es.** *—intr.* **1.** To look at in a leisurely and casual way: *browse through a book; browse through a department store.* **2.** To feed on leaves, young shoots, twigs, and other plants. *—tr.* **1.** To look through (something) casually: *browse the evening paper.* **2.** To nibble at; graze on: *Cattle browsed the pasture.* *—n.* Vegetation, such as leaves, young shoots, and twigs, eaten by animals: *Very little browse is available after a heavy snowfall.* **—brows′er** *n.*

bru•in (**brōō′**ĭn) *n.* A bear. [First written down in 1481 in Middle English, name of the bear in *History of Reynard the Fox,* translated by the English printer William Caxton, from Middle Dutch *bruun, bruin,* brown, name of the bear in a Middle Dutch version of the fable.]

bruise (brōōz) *v.* **bruised, bruis•ing, bruis•es.** *—tr.* **1.** To injure (a part of the body) without breaking the skin, as by a blow: *When my bike tipped over I bruised my knees.* **2.** To hurt one's feelings; offend: *Criticism bruised the actor's pride.* *—intr.* To become bruised: *My skin bruises easily.* *—n.* **1.** An injury in which small blood vessels in the skin are broken by pressure or a blow, producing discoloration but leaving the skin itself unbroken: *get a bruise from a fall.* **2.** A similar injury to a fruit, vegetable, or plant.

bruis•er (**brōō′**zər) *n. Informal.* A large powerfully built man.

bruit (brōōt) *tr.v.* **bruit•ed, bruit•ing, bruits.** To spread news of; repeat: *The rumor was bruited about all over town.*

❑ *These sound alike:* **bruit, brute** (beast).

brunch (brŭnch) *n.* A meal eaten late in the morning that combines breakfast and lunch. [First written down in 1896 in Modern English : *br(eakfast)* + *(l)unch.*]

Bru•nei (brōō **nī′**). A sultanate of northwest Borneo on the South China Sea. It gained its independence from Great Britain in 1984. Bandar Seri Begawan is the capital. Population, 191,765.

bru•nette also **bru•net** (brōō **nĕt′**) *adj.* Having dark or brown hair, a dark complexion, and dark-colored eyes. *—n.* A person with dark brown hair.

brunt (brŭnt) *n.* The main impact, force, or burden: *Towns along the shore bore the brunt of the hurricane.*

brush¹ (brŭsh) *n.* **1.** An implement consisting of bristles, hairs, or wire fastened to a handle, used especially for scrubbing, applying paint, or grooming the hair. **2.** An application of a brush: *give one's hair a good brush.* **3.** A bushy tail, especially that of a fox. **4.** A light touch in passing; a graze: *the brush of a branch against my coat.* **5.** A sliding connection completing a circuit between a fixed and a moving conductor, as in a motor or generator. *—v.* **brushed, brush•ing, brush•es.** *—tr.* **1.** To clean, polish, or groom with a brush: *brush shoes until they shine.* **2.** To apply with a brush: *brush paint on evenly.* **3.** To remove with or as if with a brush: *brush dirt off one's jacket.* **4.** To pay no attention to; dismiss: *He brushed aside her objections and carried on.* **5.** To touch lightly in passing: *Their arms brushed in the crowded hall.* *—intr.* To move past something so as to touch it lightly: *The wet paint got on my clothes when I brushed against it.* ***—idiom.*** **brush up. 1.** To refresh one's memory. **2.** To renew a skill: *I'll have to brush up on my Spanish before going to Mexico.* [First written down in 1378 in Middle English and spelled *brusshe,* from Old French *brosse,* brushwood, brush.]

brush² (brŭsh) *n.* **1.a.** A dense growth of shrubs or bushes: *He got scratched running through the brush.* **b.** Land covered with such growth. **2.** Broken or cut branches; brushwood: *Pile the brush at the curb.* [First written down before 1338 in Middle English and spelled *brusshe,* from Old French *brosse,* brushwood.] **—brush′y** *adj.*

brush³ (brŭsh) *n.* A brief, often hostile or frightening encounter: *a brush with the law.* [First written down before 1400 in Middle English, from *brushen,* to rush.]

brush•land (**brŭsh′**lănd′) *n.* Land with a dense growth of shrubs or bushes; brush.

brush•off also **brush-off** (**brŭsh′**ôf′ *or* **brŭsh′**ŏf′) *n.* An abrupt dismissal; a snub: *She gave him the brushoff.*

brush•wood (**brŭsh′**wo͝od′) *n.* **1.** Cut or broken branches. **2.** A dense growth of shrubs or bushes; brush.

brush•work (**brŭsh′**wûrk′) *n.* **1.** Work done with a brush. **2.** The way in which a painter applies paint with a brush.

brusque (brŭsk) *adj.* Rudely abrupt in manner or speech; curt; blunt: *The busy shopkeeper gave a brusque reply to the curious children.* **—brusque′ly** *adv.* **—brusque′ness** *n.*

Brus•sels (**brŭs′**əlz). The capital and largest city of

Gwendolyn Brooks

John Brown

Elizabeth Barrett Browning

ă	pat	oi	**boy**
ā	pay	ou	**out**
âr	care	o͝o	took
ä	father	ōō	boot
ĕ	pet	ŭ	cut
ē	be	ûr	urge
ĭ	pit	th	**thin**
ī	pie	*th*	**this**
îr	pier	hw	**wh**oop
ŏ	pot	zh	vi**s**ion
ō	toe	ə	about
ô	paw	N	*French* bon

Marcus Junius Brutus
1539 study for a bust by Michelangelo

James Buchanan

Pearl Buck
Photographed in 1973

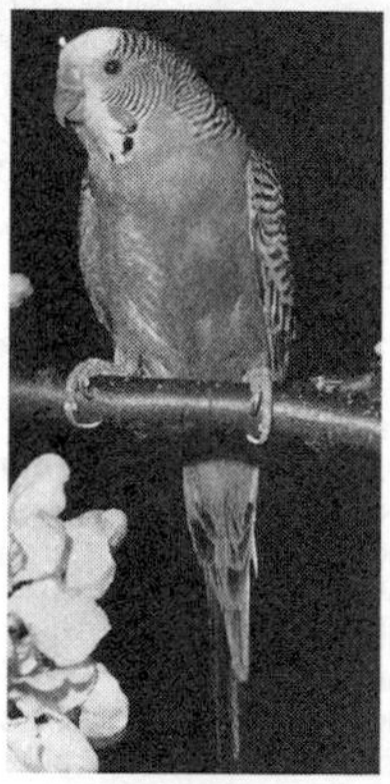

budgerigar

Belgium, in the central part of the country south of Antwerp. It is officially bilingual (Flemish and French). Metropolitan area population, 2,395,000.

Brussels sprouts *pl.n. (used with a singular or plural verb).* **1.** Small buds that resemble cabbages and grow from the thick stalk of a leafy plant, eaten as a vegetable. **2.** The plant that bears such buds.

bru•tal (**brōōt′**l) *adj.* **1.** Cruel; ruthless: *a brutal attack.* **2.** Harsh and forceful: *the brutal facts of the matter.* **—bru′tal•ly** *adv.*

bru•tal•i•ty (brōō **tăl′**ĭ tē) *n., pl.* **bru•tal•i•ties. 1.** The quality or condition of being brutal: *The brutality of boxing offends many people.* **2.** A ruthless, cruel, or harsh act.

bru•tal•ize (**brōōt′**l īz′) *tr.v.* **bru•tal•ized, bru•tal•iz•ing, bru•tal•iz•es. 1.** To make brutal. **2.** To treat cruelly or harshly: *The trucker refused to brutalize the animals by keeping them in narrow cages.*

brute (brōōt) *n.* **1.** An animal; a beast: *Man and brute struggle against the forces of nature.* **2.** A brutal person. *—adj.* **1.** Of or relating to beasts; animal. **2.** Lacking reason or intelligence: *a brute craving.* **3.** Entirely physical: *the brute force of the storm.* [First written down before 1425 in Middle English, senseless, stupid, from Latin *brūtus.*]
❑ *These sound alike:* **brute, bruit** (repeat).

brut•ish (**brōō′**tĭsh) *adj.* Resembling a brute; coarse, stupid, or cruel: *the brutish behavior of a gangster.* **—brut′ish•ly** *adv.* **—brut′ish•ness** *n.*

Bru•tus (**brōō′**təs), **Marcus Junius.** 85?–42 B.C. Roman politician and general who conspired to assassinate Julius Caesar. He later killed himself.

Bry•an (**brī′**ən), **William Jennings.** 1860–1925. American lawyer and politician who ran unsuccessfully for president in 1908.

Bry•ant (**brī′**ənt), **William Cullen.** 1794–1878. American poet, critic, and editor known especially for his early nature poems, such as "To a Waterfowl" (1821).

bry•o•phyte (**brī′**ə fīt′) *n.* A member of a large group of nonflowering plants that includes the mosses and liverworts.

B.S. *abbr.* An abbreviation of: **1.** Bachelor of Science. **2.** Bill of Sale.

B.S.A. *abbr.* An abbreviation of Boys Scouts of America.

B.Sc. *abbr.* An abbreviation of Bachelor of Science.

btry. *abbr.* An abbreviation of battery.

Btu *abbr.* An abbreviation of British thermal unit.

bu. *abbr.* An abbreviation of bushel.

bub•ble (**bŭb′**əl) *n.* **1.** A rounded thin film of liquid enclosing a pocket of air or other gas: *soap bubbles.* **2.** A small rounded pocket of gas that rises to the surface of a liquid or remains trapped in a solid or plastic material: *bubbles of air in ice cubes.* **3.** A glass or plastic dome: *a package of batteries enclosed under a plastic bubble.* *—intr.v.* **bub•bled, bub•bling, bub•bles. 1.** To form or give off bubbles: *Steam rose as water bubbled in the vat.* **2.** To move or flow with a gurgling sound: *a brook bubbling over the rocks.* **3.** To show lively activity or emotion: *As they entered the theater, the girls bubbled with excitement.* **—bub′bly** *adj.*

bubble chamber *n.* A device for detecting the paths of charged atomic particles by observation of the trails of gas bubbles that the particles leave in a superheated liquid.

bubble gum *n.* Chewing gum that can be blown into bubbles.

bu•bon•ic plague (bōō **bŏn′**ĭk *or* byōō **bŏn′**ĭk) *n.* A very contagious, often fatal disease caused by bacteria transmitted to human beings by fleas from infected rats or other rodents. Its symptoms include chills, fever, vomiting, diarrhea, and inflamed lymph nodes.

buc•ca•neer (bŭk′ə **nîr′**) *n.* A pirate.

Bu•chan•an (byōō **kăn′**ən *or* bə **kăn′**ən), **James.** 1791–1868. The 15th President of the United States (1857–1861). He was unable to prevent the secession of South Carolina in 1860.

Bu•cha•rest (**bōō′**kə rĕst′ *or* **byōō′**kə rĕst′). The capital and largest city of Romania, in the southeast part of the country on a tributary of the Danube River. It was founded in the 14th century. Population, 1,995,156.

buck[1] (bŭk) *n.* **1.** The adult male of certain animals, such as the deer, antelope, and rabbit. **2.** A sudden leap forward and upward, as by a horse or mule. *—v.* **bucked, buck•ing, bucks.** *—intr.* **1.** To leap upward arching the back: *The bronco bucked and kicked.* **2.** To resist; balk: *bucking against the trend in fashion.* *—tr.* **1.** To throw off (a rider) by bucking. **2.** To charge into: *The fullback bucked the opponents' line.* **3.** To struggle against; oppose: *The rebel only seems happy when he is bucking the rules.* *—adj.* ***—idiom.*** **buck up.** To summon one's courage or spirits; hearten. [First written down before 830 in Old English and spelled *bucca,* male goat.]

buck[2] (bŭk) *n. Informal.* A dollar. [First written down in 1856 in Modern English, short for *buckskin* (from its use in trade).]

Buck (bŭk), **Pearl Sydenstricker.** 1892–1973. American writer whose life as a missionary in China influenced her novels. She won the 1938 Nobel Prize for literature.

buck•a•roo (bŭk′ə **rōō′**) *n., pl.* **buck•a•roos.** A cowboy. [First written down in 1889 in American English, alteration of Spanish *vaquero,* from *vaca,* cow, from Latin *vacca.*]

buck•board (**bŭk′**bôrd′) *n.* An open four-wheeled carriage with the seat attached to a bed of flexible boards.

buck•et (**bŭk′**ĭt) *n.* **1.** A round open container with a curved handle, used for carrying liquids or solids; a pail. **2.a.** The amount that a bucket holds: *pour a bucket of sand on an icy sidewalk.* **b.** An unexpectedly great amount or quantity: *The rain came down in buckets.* **3.** Something resembling a bucket, such as the scoop on a steam shovel. ***—idiom.*** **a drop in the bucket.** An insufficient or trifling amount in comparison with what is needed.

buck•et•ful (**bŭk′**ĭt fōōl′) *n.* The amount that a bucket can hold.

bucket seat *n.* A seat with a rounded padded back, as in sports cars.

buck•eye (**bŭk′**ī′) *n.* **1.** Any of various North American trees or shrubs related to the horse chestnut, having large divided leaves, reddish or white flower clusters, and glossy brown nuts. **2.** The nut of such a tree.

buck•le (**bŭk′**əl) *n.* **1.** A clasp used to fasten one end of a strap or belt to the other: *the buckle on the strap of a watch.* **2.** An ornament that looks like such a clasp, as one on top of a shoe. **3.** A bend, bulge, warp, or other distortion: *A buckle in the dike showed it was soon going to break.* *—v.* **buck•led, buck•ling, buck•les.** *—tr.* **1.** To fasten with a buckle: *Buckle your seat belt before the car starts.* **2.** To cause to bend, warp, or crumple, as by pressure or heat: *Too much pressure buckled the sides of the box.* *—intr.* To sag, bend, or collapse: *Walls buckled in the heat of the fire.* ***—idiom.*** **buckle down.** To apply oneself with determination. [First written down in 1300 in Middle English and spelled *bukel,* from Latin *buccula,* cheek strap of a helmet, diminutive of *bucca,* cheek.]

buck•ler (**bŭk′**lər) *n.* A small round shield that is either carried or worn on the arm.

buck•ram (**bŭk′**rəm) *n.* A coarse cotton cloth stiff-

ened with glue, used especially for binding books.
buck•saw (bŭk′sô′) *n.* A saw usually set in an H-shaped frame, used for cutting wood.
buck•shot (bŭk′shŏt′) *n.* A large lead shot used in shotgun shells for hunting game.
buck•skin (bŭk′skĭn′) *n.* **1.** A soft, grayish-yellow leather, made from the skins of deer or sheep. **2.** **buckskins.** Breeches or shoes made of this leather.
buck•tooth (bŭk′to͝oth′) *n.* A prominent projecting upper front tooth. **—buck′toothed′** *adj.*
buck•wheat (bŭk′wēt′) *n.* **1.** A cereal plant of Asia having small triangular fruits resembling seeds that are often ground into flour. **2.** The fruits of this plant, often used as feed for livestock.
bu•col•ic (byo͞o kŏl′ĭk) *adj.* **1.** Of or characteristic of shepherds; pastoral: *bucolic poetry.* **2.** Of or characteristic of country life; rustic: *a bucolic scene.*
bud (bŭd) *n.* **1.a.** A small swelling on a branch or stem, containing an undeveloped flower, shoot, or leaf. **b.** A partly opened flower or leaf. **2.** A small outgrowth on a simple organism, such as a yeast or hydra, that grows into a complete new organism of the same species. **3.** A minute part or organ, such as a taste bud, that is shaped somewhat like a bud. **4.** A stage of early or incomplete development: *the bud of a new idea.* *—intr.v.* **bud•ded, bud•ding, buds. 1.** To form or produce a bud or buds: *Tulips bud in the very early spring.* **2.** To be in an early stage; begin to develop: *Businesses using new research are budding near the university.*
Bu•da•pest (bo͞o′də pĕst′ *or* bo͞o′də pĕsht′). The capital and largest city of Hungary, in the north-central part of the country on the Danube River. Population, 2,071,484.
Bud•dha (bo͞o′də *or* bo͝od′ə). 563?–483? B.C. Indian mystic and founder of Buddhism. He began preaching at the age of 35.
Bud•dhism (bo͞o′dĭz′əm *or* bo͝od′ĭz′əm) *n.* The religion, based on the teachings of Buddha, that holds that suffering is unavoidable in life and that extinguishing one's worldly desires leads to a state of understanding and compassion called nirvana. **—Bud′dhist** *n. & adj.*
bud•dy (bŭd′ē) *Informal. n., pl.* **bud•dies.** A close friend; a comrade.
buddy system *n.* An arrangement in which people pair up, as during a hike, swim, or similar activity, to look out for each other's safety.
budge (bŭj) *intr. & tr.v.* **budged, budg•ing, budg•es. 1.** To move or cause to move slightly: *The boulder did not budge. We cannot budge the boulder.* **2.** To alter or cause to alter a position or an attitude: *They won't budge once they have reached a decision. After the prime minister had made up her mind no one could budge her.*
budg•er•i•gar (bŭj′ə rē gär′) *n.* A small green, blue, or yellow parakeet often kept as a pet.
budg•et (bŭj′ĭt) *n.* A plan or an estimate of the amount of money that will be spent and received in a given period: *Congress must approve the government's budget each year.* *—tr.v.* **budg•et•ed, budg•et•ing, budg•ets. 1.** To plan in advance for the allocation of: *budget an allowance.* **2.** To enter or plan for in a budget: *budget repairs into the car expenses.* *—adj.* **1.** Of or relating to a budget: *Were these budget items approved by Congress?* **2.** Appropriate to a budget; inexpensive: *a budget car; budget meals.* **—bud′get•ar′y** (bŭj′ĭ tĕr′ē) *adj.*
budg•ie (bŭj′ē) *n. Informal.* A budgerigar.
Bue•nos Ai•res (bwā′nəs âr′ēz *or* bwā′nəs ī′rĭz). The capital and largest city of Argentina, in the eastern part of the country on the Río de la Plata. The city was founded in 1536. Population, 2,922,829.
buff[1] (bŭf) *n.* **1.** A soft, thick, yellowish leather made from the skins of buffalo, elk, or oxen. **2.** The color of this leather; a yellowish tan. **3.** A piece of soft material or an implement covered with such material used for polishing. *—tr.v.* **buffed, buff•ing, buffs.** To polish or shine with a piece of soft material: *buff shoes.* [First written down in 1552 in Modern English and spelled *buffalo*, from French *buffle*, from Late Latin *būfalus*, buffalo.]
buff[2] (bŭf) *n. Informal.* A person who has great interest in, and some knowledge of, a subject: *a train buff.* [First written down in 1903 in American English, from the buff-colored uniform once worn by New York City volunteer firemen, originally applied to an enthusiast of fires and fire fighting.]
buf•fa•lo (bŭf′ə lō′) *n., pl.* **buffalo** or **buf•fa•loes** or **buf•fa•los. 1.** The North American bison. **2.** Any of several African or Asian mammals similar to the ox, having large outward-curving horns, as the domesticated water buffalo. [First written down in 1588 in Modern English, from Late Latin *būfalus*, from Latin *būbalus*, from Greek *boubalos.*] —SEE NOTE.
Buf•fa•lo (bŭf′ə lō′). A city of western New York at the eastern end of Lake Erie on the Canadian border. Population, 328,123.
Buffalo Bill (bĭl). William Frederick Cody.
buff•er[1] (bŭf′ər) *n.* **1.** A soft pad or tool having a pad used to polish or shine objects. **2.** A person who polishes.
buff•er[2] (bŭf′ər) *n.* **1.** Something that reduces or absorbs the shock of a blow or collision: *a block of wood serving as a buffer when hammering.* **2.** A substance that minimizes change in the acidity of a solution when an acid or a base is added to the solution. **3.** Something located between two rivals or competitors and regarded as reducing the danger of conflict. **4.** A device or an area of a computer used to temporarily store data that is being transferred between two machines that process data at different rates, such as a computer and a printer. *—tr.v.* **buff•ered, buff•er•ing, buff•ers.** To treat (a solution) with a buffer. [First written down in 1835 in Modern English, perhaps from *buff*, blow, buffet, from Middle English *buffe.*]
buffer state *n.* A country that lies between two countries that are rivals or enemies.
buf•fet[1] (bə fā′ *or* bo͞o fā′) *n.* **1.** A large piece of furniture with drawers and cupboards for storing china, silverware, and table linens. **2.** A meal at which guests serve themselves from dishes arranged on a table or buffet. **3.** A counter from which food is served. *—adj.* Being a meal where diners serve themselves: *a buffet lunch.* [First written down in 1718 in Modern English, from French.]
buf•fet[2] (bŭf′ĭt) *n.* A blow or hit, especially made with or as if with the hand. *—tr.v.* **buf•fet•ed, buf•fet•ing, buf•fets.** To hit or strike against forcefully; batter: *The rough sea buffeted the small boat.* [First written down before 1200 in Middle English, from Old French *bufet*, diminutive of *buffe*, blow.]
buf•foon (bə fo͞on′) *n.* **1.** A clown or jester. **2.** A person given to making jokes. **3.** A bumbling or ridiculous person; a fool. **—buf•foon′er•y** *n.*
bug (bŭg) *n.* **1.** Any of a group of wingless or four-winged insects having sucking mouth parts. Bedbugs, lice, and chinch bugs are true bugs. **2.** An insect, a spider, or a similar organism: *Moths and other bugs flew around the light.* **3.a.** A microorganism that causes disease; a germ: *He caught a bug and got sick.* **b.** A disease caused by such a microorganism: *suffering from a bug.* **4.a.** A fault or defect in a system or device: *work the bugs out of a plan.* **b.** An error or a defect in a computer program. **5.** A hidden electronic device that allows private conversations to be overheard. **6.** *Slang.* An

Word History: buffalo

Many people know that what we call the North American **buffalo** is really a bison. Indeed *buffalo* and *bison* belong to two different genera or kinds of cattle and therefore are not very closely related. *Buffalo*, however, was the first word used for the North American animal, around 1635 in a description of Maryland. The correct identification of the animal as a *bison* appears in 1693 in a Latin description of the animals in the royal zoo at Westminster in London, England. The first definite correction of *buffalo* to *bison* occurs in 1844 in *North American Indians*, written by the artist George Catlin (1796–1872).

bug

The word **bug** is often informally used to refer to any insect and sometimes even to spiders, which are not insects. In strictest terms a bug is an insect having mouthparts that are adapted for piercing and sucking and are contained in a beak-shaped structure. By this definition, an aphid is classified as a bug, but a beetle is not. Furthermore, bugs are distinguished from spiders in that bugs, like other insects, have six legs and a body divided into three sections—head, thorax, and abdomen. Spiders, like other arachnids, have eight legs and only two body sections—**cephalothorax** (combined head and thorax) and **abdomen.**

ă	**p**a**t**	oi	**b**oy
ā	**p**ay	ou	out
âr	**c**are	o͝o	**t**oo**k**
ä	**f**a**th**er	o͞o	**b**oo**t**
ĕ	**p**e**t**	ŭ	**c**u**t**
ē	**b**e	ûr	urge
ĭ	**p**i**t**	th	**th**in
ī	**p**ie	*th*	**this**
îr	**p**ier	hw	**wh**oop
ŏ	**p**o**t**	zh	vi**s**ion
ō	**t**oe	ə	about
ô	**p**aw	N	*French* bon

bugle

bulldog

enthusiast; a buff. —*v.* **bugged, bug•ging, bugs.** —*intr.* To grow large; bulge: *Their eyes bugged out with surprise.* —*tr. Slang.* **1.** To annoy; trouble; pester: *TV commercials bug me.* **2.** To equip (a room or telephone circuit, for example) with a concealed electronic listening device. —***idiom.*** **bug off.** *Slang.* To leave someone alone; go away. [First written down in 1622 in Modern English.] —SEE NOTE on page 133.

bug•a•boo (bŭg′ə bo͞o′) *n., pl.* **bug•a•boos.** An imaginary or real object of fear.

bug•bear (bŭg′bâr′) *n.* **1.** A recurring or persistent problem: *Spelling has always been my bugbear in school.* **2.** A bugaboo.

bug•gy (bŭg′ē) *n., pl.* **bug•gies.** **1.** A small light carriage with a single seat and four wheels, drawn by a horse. **2.** A baby carriage.

bu•gle (byo͞o′gəl) *n.* A brass wind instrument similar to a trumpet but lacking valves. It is often used to sound signals in the military, such as reveille. —*intr. v.* **bu•gled, bu•gling, bu•gles.** To play a bugle. [First written down before 1300 in Middle English, from Latin *būculus*, steer, diminutive of *bōs*, ox.] —**bu′gler** *n.*

build (bĭld) *v.* **built** (bĭlt), **build•ing, builds.** —*tr.* **1.** To make or form by fitting together materials or parts; construct; erect: *It takes a long time to build a skyscraper. The body needs iron in the diet to build hemoglobin.* **2.** To make steadily and gradually; create and add to: *Reading helps build a rich vocabulary.* —*intr.* To progress toward a peak; grow steadily; develop: *A good mystery builds from the first chapters to its climax. Scientific discoveries build on the work of others.* —*n.* The physical make-up of a person or thing: *a muscular athletic build.* —***idioms.*** **build in** or **build into.** To construct as a permanent part of: *build in kitchen cabinets.* **build on** or **build onto.** To use as a basis or foundation: *We must build on our success.* **build up. 1.** To develop in stages or by degrees: *build up a business; build up a strong vocabulary.* **2.** To cover with buildings: *The downtown area is getting built up.* [First written down in 1016 in Old English and spelled *byldan.*]

build•er (bĭl′dər) *n.* **1.** A person or an animal that builds: *Beavers are great dam builders.* **2.** A person who constructs new buildings or develops land: *the architects and builders of a great city.*

build•ing (bĭl′dĭng) *n.* **1.** Something that is built; a structure. **2.** The act, process, or occupation of constructing.

build•up also **build-up** (bĭld′ŭp′) *n.* **1.** The act or process of building up: *the buildup of ashes in a fireplace.* **2.** Widely favorable publicity; high praise: *The newspaper gave the fund-raising committee a nice buildup.*

built (bĭlt) *v.* Past tense and past participle of **build.**

built-in (bĭlt′ĭn′) *adj.* Constructed as a permanent part of a larger unit: *a built-in cupboard.*

built-up (bĭlt′ŭp′) *adj.* **1.** Made by fastening layers or sections one on top of the other: *a built-up roof.* **2.** Filled with buildings; developed: *a built-up neighborhood.*

Bu•jum•bu•ra (bo͞o′jəm bo͝or′ə). The capital and largest city of Burundi, in the western part of the country south-southwest of Kigali, Rwanda. Population, 229,980.

bulb (bŭlb) *n.* **1.** A rounded plant bud that develops underground and contains the undeveloped shoots of a new plant that will grow from it: *an onion bulb; a tulip bulb.* **2.** An underground root or stem resembling a bulb, as a corm, rhizome, or tuber. **3.** A rounded part of something: *the bulb of a thermometer.* **4.** An incandescent lamp or its glass housing. **5.** Any of various rounded structures in the body, especially the medulla oblongata. [First written down in 1568 in Modern English, from Latin *bulbus*, from Greek *bolbos*, bulbous plant.]

bul•bous (bŭl′bəs) *adj.* **1.** Growing from or producing a bulb: *The tulip is a bulbous plant.* **2.** Bulb-shaped: *a bulbous nose.*

Bul•gar•i•a (bŭl gâr′ē ə *or* bo͝ol gâr′ē ə). A country of southeast Europe on the Black Sea south of Romania. It was settled in the sixth century A.D. Sofia is the capital and the largest city. Population, 8,960,679.

Bul•gar•i•an (bŭl gâr′ē ən *or* bo͝ol gâr′ē ən) *adj.* Of or relating to Bulgaria or its people, language, or culture. —*n.* **1.** A native or inhabitant of Bulgaria. **2.** The Slavic language of the Bulgarians.

bulge (bŭlj) *n.* A protruding part; an outward curve or a swelling: *A blister causes a bulge in the skin.* —*intr. & tr.v.* **bulged, bulg•ing, bulg•es.** To swell or cause to swell beyond the usual size: *eyes bulging with surprise; groceries bulging a bag.*

bulg•y (bŭl′jē) *adj.* **bulg•i•er, bulg•i•est.** Protruding or swelling outward; protuberant: *bulgy pockets.* —**bulg′i•ness** *n.*

bulk (bŭlk) *n.* **1.** Great size, mass, or volume: *the whale's enormous bulk.* **2.** The major portion of something; greater part: *The bulk of the dairy farm is pasture.* —***idiom.*** **in bulk. 1.** Unpackaged; loose: *That store sells apples in bulk.* **2.** In large numbers, amounts, or volume: *Flour mills buy wheat in bulk.* [First written down in 1350 in Middle English and spelled *bolke*, perhaps partly alteration of *bouk*, belly, trunk of the body (from Old English *būc*) and partly from Old Norse *bulki*, cargo, heap.]

bulk•head (bŭlk′hĕd′) *n.* **1.** One of the vertical walls that divide the inside of a ship or aircraft into compartments. **2.** A wall or an embankment, as in a mine or along a waterfront, built to protect against earth slides, fire, water, or gas.

bulk•y (bŭl′kē) *adj.* **bulk•i•er, bulk•i•est. 1.** Extremely large; massive: *Elephants and whales are bulky animals.* **2.** Taking up much space; clumsy; unwieldy: *The new lamp came in a bulky package.* —**bulk′i•ly** *adv.* —**bulk′i•ness** *n.*

bull[1] (bo͝ol) *n.* **1.a.** The full-grown male of cattle. **b.** The male of certain other large mammals, such as the elephant, moose, or seal. **2.** A person who buys stock or other securities expecting their price to rise. —*adj.* **1.** Male: *a bull seal.* **2.** Characterized by rising prices, especially in the stock market: *a bull market.* [First written down in 972 in Old English and spelled *bula*, probably from Old Norse *boli.*]

bull[2] (bo͝ol) *n.* An official document issued by the pope. [First written down about 1300 in Middle English and spelled *bulle*, from Medieval Latin *bulla*, blister, seal on a papal decree.]

bull•dog (bo͝ol′dôg′ *or* bo͝ol′dŏg′) *n.* Any of a breed of stocky short-haired dog having a large head and strong square jaws. —*adj.* Stubborn.

bull•doze (bo͝ol′dōz′) *tr.v.* **bull•dozed, bull•doz•ing, bull•doz•es. 1.** To clear, dig up, or move with a bulldozer: *bulldoze land for a new development.* **2.** To bully, intimidate, or coerce: *bulldoze a committee into action.*

bull•doz•er (bo͝ol′dō′zər) *n.* A large powerful tractor equipped with treads and a metal blade in front for moving earth and grading land.

bul•let (bo͝ol′ĭt) *n.* A small, rounded, usually pointed piece of metal to be fired from a firearm such as a rifle or pistol.

bul•le•tin (bo͝ol′ĭ tn) *n.* **1.** A statement on a matter of public interest, as in a newspaper, on television, or on radio: *a weather bulletin.* **2.** A newspaper, magazine, or pamphlet published regularly by an organization, such as a society or club: *Did you read the school bulletin this week?*

bulletin board *n.* **1.** A board on which notices are posted. **2.** A service for computer users that displays messages and other information and permits subscribers to communicate with each other through their computers.

bul•let•proof (**bo͝ol′**ĭt pro͞of′) *adj.* Designed to stop or repel bullets: *bulletproof glass.*

bull•fight (**bo͝ol′**fīt′) *n.* A spectacle, especially in Spain and Mexico, in which a bull is fought and usually killed with a sword. **—bull′fight′er** *n.* **—bull′fight′ing** *n.*

bull•finch (**bo͝ol′**fĭnch′) *n.* A European songbird related to the cardinal, having a short thick bill and a red breast.

bull•frog (**bo͝ol′**frôg′ *or* **bo͝ol′**frŏg′) *n.* Any of several large frogs of North America having a deep hollow croak.

bull•head (**bo͝ol′**hĕd′) *n.* **1.** Any of several North American freshwater catfishes having a large head. **2.** Any of several other large-headed fishes.

bull•head•ed (**bo͝ol′hĕd′**ĭd) *adj.* Very stubborn; headstrong. **—bull′head′ed•ness** *n.*

bull•horn (**bo͝ol′**hôrn′) *n.* A portable electric device resembling a megaphone and used to make the voice louder.

bul•lion (**bo͝ol′**yən) *n.* Gold or silver in the form of bars or ingots.
❑ *These sound alike:* **bullion, bouillon** (soup).

bull•ish (**bo͝ol′**ĭsh) *adj.* **1.** Aggressive or bullheaded. **2.a.** Causing, expecting, or characterized by rising stock market prices. **b.** Optimistic or confident: *bullish on the prospects for a negotiated settlement.* **—bull′ish•ly** *adv.* **—bull′ish•ness** *n.*

bul•lock (**bo͝ol′**ək) *n.* **1.** A castrated bull; a steer. **2.** A young ox or bull.

bull•pen (**bo͝ol′**pĕn′) *n.* **1.** An area in a baseball stadium for pitchers to warm up during a game. **2.** The relief pitchers of a baseball team considered as a group.

bull•ring (**bo͝ol′**rĭng′) *n.* A circular arena for bullfighting.

Bull Run (bo͝ol). A small stream of northeast Virginia southwest of Washington, D.C. It was the site of two Civil War battles (July 21, 1861, and August 29–30, 1862).

bull's-eye or **bull's eye** (**bo͝olz′**ī′) *n.* **1.a.** The small central circle on a target. **b.** A shot that hits this circle. **2.** A thick circular piece of glass set in the side or deck of a ship to admit light. **3.a.** A lens that is flat on one side and bulges outward on the other, used to concentrate light. **b.** A lantern or lamp having such a lens.

bull terrier *n.* Any of a breed of dog having a short coat and a tapering muzzle, developed from crossing a bulldog and a terrier.

bul•ly (**bo͝ol′**ē) *n., pl.* **bul•lies.** A person who habitually frightens or hurts smaller or weaker people. *—tr.v.* **bul•lied, bul•ly•ing, bul•lies.** To hurt or frighten as a bully does. [First written down in 1538 in Modern English, possibly from Middle Dutch *boele*, sweetheart, probably alteration of *broeder*, brother.]

bul•rush (**bo͝ol′**rŭsh′) *n.* Any of several tall plants similar to grass that grow in wet places, including the cattail.

bul•wark (**bo͝ol′**wərk *or* **bo͝ol′**wôrk′) *n.* **1.** A wall or barrier serving as a fortification: *The city's defenses lie in a bulwark of high walls.* **2.** Something that serves as a defense: *Freedom of speech is the citizen's bulwark against the power of government.* **3.** A breakwater. **4.** The part of a ship's side that is above the upper deck. Often used in the plural. [First written down about 1416 in Middle English and spelled *bulwerk*, from Middle Dutch *bolwerk*.]

bum (bŭm) *n.* **1.** A tramp; a hobo. **2.** A person who avoids work; a loafer. *—v.* **bummed, bum•ming, bums.** *—intr.* **1.** To wander about or live like a tramp. **2.** To live by begging. *—tr.* To obtain by begging; mooch: *bum a ride to the next town.* *—adj.* **bum•mer, bum•mest. 1.** Worthless: *bum directions.* **2.** Disabled: *a bum knee.* **3.** Unfavorable or unfair: *Breaking your leg before vacation was a bum deal.*

bum•ble•bee (**bŭm′**bəl bē′) *n.* Any of various large hairy bees related to the honeybee that fly with a humming sound.

bum•mer (**bŭm′**ər) *n. Slang.* **1.** A person who lives by begging or continuously wanders about. **2.** An unpleasant experience or situation: *Missing the bus home late at night was a real bummer.* **3.** A failure.

bump (bŭmp) *v.* **bumped, bump•ing, bumps.** *—tr.* **1.** To come up or knock against (a person or thing) forcefully: *They bumped heads as they both stooped to pick up the dime.* **2.** To cause (something) to knock against an obstacle: *I bumped the vacuum cleaner against the table.* *—intr.* **1.** To hit or knock against something forcefully: *My knee bumped against the wall.* **2.** To proceed with jerks and jolts: *an old car bumping down the road.* *—n.* **1.** A light blow, collision, or jolt: *fall and get a bump on the chin.* **2.** A small swelling, as from a blow or an insect sting. **3.** A small place that rises above the level of the surface surrounding it: *a bump in the road.* ***—idiom.*** **bump into.** To meet by chance: *We bumped into each other at the store.* [First written down in 1611 in Modern English and spelled *bumpe*, of imitative origin.]

bump•er¹ (**bŭm′**pər) *n.* A horizontal metal or rubber bar attached to the front or rear of an automobile to absorb the impact of a collision. [First written down in 1839 in Modern English, from *bump.*]

bump•er² (**bŭm′**pər) *n.* A drinking vessel filled to the top. *—adj.* Abundant: *a bumper crop.* [First written down in 1676 in Modern English, perhaps from *bump.*]

bumper sticker *n.* A sticker with a printed message to display on the bumper of a car or truck.

bump•kin (**bŭmp′**kĭn *or* **bŭm′**kĭn) *n.* An awkward or unsophisticated person: *a country bumpkin.*

bump•y (**bŭm′**pē) *adj.* **bump•i•er, bump•i•est. 1.** Full of bumps: *a bumpy road.* **2.** Marked by or causing jerks and jolts: *a bumpy ride.* **—bump′i•ly** *adv.* **—bump′i•ness** *n.*

bun (bŭn) *n.* **1.** A small bread roll: *a hamburger bun; a cinnamon bun.* **2.** A roll or coil of hair worn at the back of the head.

bunch (bŭnch) *n.* **1.** A group of things that are alike and growing, fastened, or placed together: *a bunch of fresh grapes; a bunch of keys.* **2.** *Informal.* A group of people having a common interest: *My brother and his bunch like video games.* **3.** *Informal.* A considerable number or amount: *a whole bunch of work.* *—v.* **bunched, bunch•ing, bunch•es.** *—tr.* To gather into a bunch: *bunch flowers into a bouquet.* *—intr.* To form a cluster or group: *Cold hikers bunched around a campfire.*

bun•dle (**bŭn′**dl) *n.* **1.** A number of objects bound, tied, or wrapped together: *a bundle of sticks.* **2.** Something tied up for carrying; a package. *—v.* **bun•dled, bun•dling, bun•dles.** *—tr.* **1.** To tie, wrap, or bind securely together: *bundle newspapers for recycling.* **2.** To send quickly; hustle: *bundle the children off to school.* **3.** To dress (a person) warmly: *She bundled up the baby and went outside.* *—intr.* To go hastily: *The children came bundling in from outside.*

bung (bŭng) *n.* **1.** A stopper for the hole in a cask. **2.** A bunghole.

bullhorn

ă	pat	oi	boy
ā	pay	ou	out
âr	care	o͝o	took
ä	father	o͞o	boot
ĕ	pet	ŭ	cut
ē	be	ûr	urge
ĭ	pit	th	thin
ī	pie	*th*	this
îr	pier	hw	whoop
ŏ	pot	zh	vision
ō	toe	ə	about
ô	paw	N	*French* bon

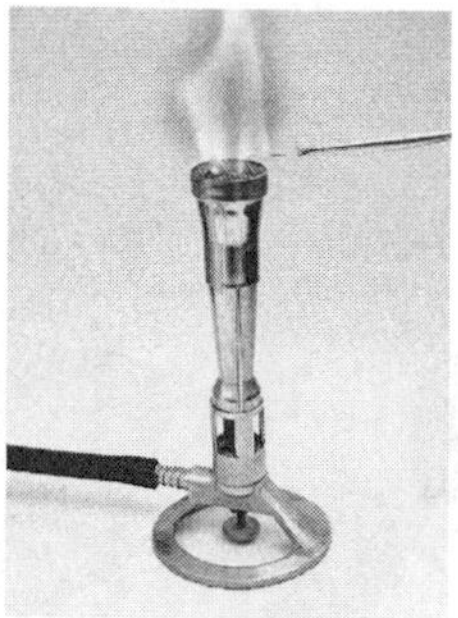

Bunsen burner

buoy

burnoose

bun•ga•low (bŭng′gə lō′) *n.* A small one-story house or cottage.

bung•hole (bŭng′hōl′) *n.* The hole in a cask through which liquid is poured in or drained out.

bun•gle (bŭng′gəl) *v.* **bun•gled, bun•gling, bun•gles.** —*intr.* To work or act in an inept or incompetent manner. —*tr.* To manage or handle poorly; botch: *He bungled the mixing of the ingredients and his pancakes were terrible.* —*n.* A clumsy inexpert performance of piece of work: *We made so many mistakes that the whole scene was an awful bungle.* **—bun′gler** *n.*

bun•ion (bŭn′yən) *n.* A painful inflamed swelling in the joint at the base of the big toe.

bunk[1] (bŭngk) *n.* **1.** A narrow bed built like a shelf against a wall. **2.** A narrow bed. —*intr.v.* **bunked, bunk•ing, bunks. 1.** To sleep in a bunk. **2.** To occupy makeshift sleeping quarters: *bunk on the sofa tonight.* [First written down in 1758 in Modern English, perhaps short for *bunker*.]

bunk[2] (bŭngk) *n.* Empty talk; nonsense. [First written down in 1900 in Modern English, short for *bunkum*, after *Buncombe* County, North Carolina, from a remark made around 1820 by its congressman, who felt obligated to give a dull speech "for Buncombe."]

bun•ker (bŭng′kər) *n.* **1.** An obstacle, usually sand in a shallow depression, on a golf course. **2.** A fortification or an earthwork, as a deep trench or tunnel. **3.** A bin for coal on a ship.

Bun•ker Hill (bŭng′kər). A low elevation, 107 feet (32.6 meters) high, in Boston, Massachusetts. The first major Revolutionary War battle took place nearby on June 17, 1775.

bunk•house (bŭngk′hous′) *n.* A crudely constructed building with sleeping quarters, usually having bunks, on a ranch or in a camp.

bun•ny (bŭn′ē) *n., pl.* **bun•nies.** A rabbit, especially a young one.

Bun•sen burner (bŭn′sən) *n.* A gas burner used in laboratories. It consists of a vertical tube with adjustable holes at its base that allow air to mix with the gas in order to make a very hot flame. [First written down in 1870 in Modern English, after Robert Wilhelm *Bunsen* (1811–1899), German chemist.]

bunt (bŭnt) *v.* **bunt•ed, bunt•ing, bunts.** —*tr.* **1.** In baseball, to bat or tap (a pitched ball) lightly so that the ball rolls in the infield. **2.** To push or strike with the horns or head; butt. —*intr.* In baseball, to bat a pitched ball by tapping it lightly. —*n.* **1.** An act of bunting. **2.** A ball that is bunted. **—bunt′er** *n.*

bunt•ing[1] (bŭn′tĭng) *n.* **1.** A light cotton or woolen cloth used for making flags. **2.** Flags considered as a group. **3.** Long strips of cloth with stripes or colors, used for holiday decoration. [First written down in 1742 in Modern English, perhaps from German *bunt*, colored.]

bunt•ing[2] (bŭn′tĭng) *n.* Any of various brightly colored birds having a short cone-shaped bill and related to the finches. [First written down before 1300 in Middle English.]

bunt•ing[3] (bŭn′tĭng) *n.* A hooded sleeping bag for an infant, usually made of heavy cloth. [First written down in 1922 in Modern English, perhaps from Scots *buntin*, plump, short.]

buoy (bo͞o′ē *or* boi) *n.* **1.** A float, often with a bell or light, used to warn ships of danger, such as a reef or bar, or to mark a channel or safe passage. **2.** A life buoy. —*tr.v.* **buoyed, buoy•ing, buoys. 1.** To keep afloat. **2.** To cheer; hearten: *The good news buoyed our spirits.*

buoy•an•cy (boi′ən sē *or* bo͞o′yən sē) *n.* **1.** The tendency or capacity to float in a liquid or to rise in air or other gas: *the buoyancy of wood in water.* **2.** The upward force that a fluid exerts on an object less dense than itself: *the buoyancy of salt water.* **3.** Lightness of spirit; cheerfulness: *The nurse's buoyancy cheered up the patient.*

buoy•ant (boi′ənt *or* bo͞o′yənt) *adj.* **1.** Having buoyancy; tending to float or floating: *a buoyant cork.* **2.** Lighthearted; cheerful: *a buoyant mood.* **—buoy′ant•ly** *adv.*

bur[1] also **burr** (bûr) *n.* **1.** A rough prickly covering enclosing a seed, fruit, nut, or flower head, as that of the chestnut or burdock. **2.** A plant or weed that bears burs. [First written down before 1300 in Middle English and spelled *burre*, of Scandinavian origin.]

bur[2] (bûr) *n. & v.* Variant of **burr**[2].

Bur•bank (bûr′băngk′), **Luther.** 1849–1926. American scientist who developed many new varieties of fruits, vegetables, and flowers.

bur•ble (bûr′bəl) *intr.v.* **bur•bled, bur•bling, bur•bles.** To bubble; gurgle: *The stream burbled over the mossy rocks.*

bur•den[1] (bûr′dn) *n.* **1.** Something that is carried; a load: *mules carrying their heavy burden uphill.* **2.** Something endured or assumed, especially as a duty or responsibility, and often carried with difficulty: *Citizens carry the burden of taxation. Having a sister who is so popular has been a burden to her.* **3.** The amount of cargo a ship can carry or that a ship is carrying. —*tr.v.* **bur•dened, bur•den•ing, bur•dens.** To load with or as if with something difficult to bear: *heavy snow burdening the branches of the tree; burdened with sad memories.* [First written down before 830 in Old English and spelled *byrthen.*]

bur•den[2] (bûr′dn) *n.* **1.a.** The chorus or refrain of a song or other musical composition. **b.** A bass accompaniment for a song. **2.** A main idea or recurring theme: *the burden of the argument rests on this central point.* [First written down about 1300 in Middle English, variant of *bourdon*, bass pipe of a bagpipe tuned to produce a single tone, from Old French.]

burden of proof *n.* The responsibility of proving a charge, an allegation, or another disputed point.

bur•den•some (bûr′dn səm) *adj.* Imposing a burden; hard to bear; heavy; arduous: *a burdensome task of cleaning out the basement.*

bur•dock (bûr′dŏk′) *n.* Any of several coarse weedy plants having large leaves and prickly purplish flowerheads.

bu•reau (byo͝or′ō) *n., pl.* **bu•reaus** or **bu•reaux** (byo͝or′ōz). **1.** A chest of drawers, especially for holding clothes. **2.** An office for a specific kind of business: *a travel bureau; a news bureau of a television station.* **3.** A department of a government.

bu•reauc•ra•cy (byo͝o rŏk′rə sē) *n., pl.* **bu•reauc•ra•cies. 1.** The administration of a government through bureaus and departments with appointed officials. **2.** The departments and their officials considered as a group. **3.** An administration, as of a business or government, in which the need to follow rules and regulations complicates and slows effective action: *Application for a refund was delayed in the bureaucracy of the accounting department.*

bu•reau•crat (byo͝or′ə krăt′) *n.* **1.** An official of a bureaucracy. **2.** An official who insists on rigid adherence to rules and routines. **—bu′reau•crat′ic** *adj.* **—bu′reau•crat′i•cal•ly** *adv.*

burg (bûrg) *n. Informal.* A city or town.

bur•geon (bûr′jən) *intr.v.* **bur•geoned, bur•geon•ing, bur•geons. 1.** To put forth new buds, leaves, or shoots; begin to sprout or grow. **2.** To develop as if by sprouting or growing; flourish: *New ideas burgeon when people are allowed to talk freely.*

burg•er (bûr′gər) *n.* A hamburger.

bur•gess (bûr′jĭs) *n.* A member of the lower house of colonial legislature of Virginia or Maryland.

burgh•er (bûr′gər) *n.* A citizen of a town, especially a merchant or trader in a medieval town.

bur•glar (bûr′glər) *n.* A person who commits burglary; a housebreaker.

bur•glar•ize (bûr′glə rīz′) *tr.v.* **bur•glar•ized, bur•glar•iz•ing, bur•glar•iz•es.** To enter and steal from (a building or home, for example).

bur•gla•ry (bûr′glə rē) *n., pl.* **bur•gla•ries.** The crime of breaking into a building, home, or some other place with the intention of stealing.

bur•go•mas•ter (bûr′gə măs′tər) *n.* The mayor of a town in Austria, Belgium, the Netherlands, or Germany.

Bur•goyne (bûr **goin′** *or* **bûr′**goin′), **John.** 1722–1792. British general. In the American Revolution he captured Fort Ticonderoga (July 6, 1777) but lost the Battle of Saratoga (October 17, 1777).

Bur•gun•dy[1] (bûr′gən dē). A region and former province of eastern France. It became a part of France in 1477. **—Bur•gun′di•an** (bər **gŭn′**dē ən) *adj. & n.*

Bur•gun•dy[2] (bûr′gən dē) *n., pl.* **Bur•gun•dies. 1.** A red or white wine made in Burgundy. **2.** A similar wine made in another place.

bur•i•al (bĕr′ē əl) *n.* The act of placing a dead body in a grave, a tomb, or the sea.

Bur•ki•na Fa•so (bər **kē′**nə **fä′**sō). Formerly **Up•per Vol•ta** (**ŭp′**ər **vŏl′**tə). A landlocked country of western Africa north of Ghana. It gained its independence from France in 1960. Ouagadougou is the capital and the largest city. Population, 6,965,886.

burl (bûrl) *n.* **1.** A large rounded outgrowth on a tree trunk or branch. **2.** Wood from such a growth, usually with a marked grain.

bur•lap (bûr′lăp′) *n.* A coarse cloth made of hemp, jute, or flax, used to make bags, sacks, curtains, and coverings.

bur•lesque (bər **lĕsk′**) *n.* **1.** An imitation of something, especially in a play, story, or song, that makes it seem ridiculous by treating it too seriously or too frivolously. **2.** A variety show with singing, dancing, and coarse comedy. *—adj.* **1.** Of or relating to burlesque entertainment: *a burlesque theater.* **2.** Mockingly imitative. *—tr.v.* **bur•lesqued, bur•les•quing, bur•lesques.** To imitate mockingly: *Many comedies burlesque traditional stories of success.*

bur•ly (bûr′lē) *adj.* **bur•li•er, bur•li•est.** Heavy and strong; muscular: *burly football players.* See Synonyms at **muscular. —bur′li•ness** *n.*

Bur•ma (bûr′mə). Officially (since 1989) **Myan•mar** (myän **mär′**). A country of southeast Asia northwest of Thailand. It gained its independence from Great Britain in 1948. Rangoon is the capital and the largest city. Population, 35,313,905.

Bur•mese (bər **mēz′** *or* bər **mēs′**) *n., pl.* **Burmese. 1.** A native or inhabitant of Burma. **2.** The language of Burma, related to Tibetan. *—adj.* Of or relating to Burma or its people, language, or culture.

burn[1] (bûrn) *v.* **burned** or **burnt** (bûrnt), **burn•ing, burns.** *—tr.* **1.** To cause to undergo combustion: *The body burns food for energy.* **2.** To set on fire: *We burned logs for warmth.* **3.** To destroy with fire: *Our town burns trash to generate electricity.* **4.** To damage or injure by fire, heat, a corrosive chemical such as acid, or some other means: *I burned my fingers with a match.* **5.** To use as fuel: *This furnace burns oil.* **6.** To produce by fire or heat: *The sparks burned holes in the rug.* **7.a.** To give a feeling of heat to: *Some highly seasoned food burns my mouth.* **b.** To make angry: *Their nasty remarks burned me up.* *—intr.* **1.** To undergo combustion or be consumed as fuel: *Wood and paper burn easily.* **2.** To be damaged, injured, or destroyed by or as if by fire: *The house burned to the ground.* **3.** To produce light and heat by or as if by fire: *The sun burned bright in the sky.* **4.** To feel or look hot: *burning with fever.* **5.** To be irritated or painful, as by inflammation: *My eyes are burning from the smoke.* **6.** To be consumed with strong emotion: *burn with anger; burning with a desire to win.* *—n.* **1.** An injury produced by fire, heat, a chemical, radiation, or electricity: *I got a blister from the burn.* **2.** A burned place or area: *a burn in the tablecloth.* **3.** In aerospace, a firing of a rocket: *The rocket made a good burn.* **4.** A sunburn. ***—idioms.*** **burn out. 1.** To stop burning from lack of fuel: *A campfire burns out if you don't keep putting wood on it.* **2.** To wear out or fail, especiallly because of heat: *The fan motor burned out from the short.* **3.** To make or become exhausted, especially as a result of long-term stress: *burned out from years of overwork.* **burn up.** To consume or be consumed by fire: *The books burned up in the fire.* [First written down about 830 in Old English and spelled *beornan.*] **—burn′a•ble** *adj.*

burn[2] (bûrn) *n. Scots.* A small stream or brook. [First written down about 1000 in Old English and spelled *burna.*]

burn•er (bûr′nər) *n.* **1.** A furnace or other device in which something is burned: *An oil burner heats the house.* **2.** The part of a stove, furnace, or lamp in which a flame is produced.

burn•ing (bûr′nĭng) *adj.* **1.** On fire; flaming; hot: *a burning candle.* **2.** Inflamed with strong emotion; heated: *a burning desire; a burning issue.*

bur•nish (bûr′nĭsh) *tr.v.* **bur•nished, bur•nish•ing, bur•nish•es.** To make smooth and glossy by or as if by rubbing; polish: *burnish a brass plate.* *—n.* A smooth glossy finish or appearance; luster.

bur•noose also **bur•nous** (bər **no͞os′**) *n.* A long, loose, flowing cloak with a hood, worn especially by Arabs.

burn•out (bûrn′out′) *n.* **1.** A failure of a device because of burning, heat, or friction. **2.** The end of a burn in a rocket engine, especially when the fuel has been exhausted or shut off. **3.** Exhaustion of physical or emotional strength.

Burns (bûrnz), **Robert.** 1759–1796. Scottish poet whose lyrics, written in dialect and full of humor, celebrate love, patriotism, and country life.

burnt (bûrnt) *v.* A past tense and a past participle of **burn**[1].

burp (bûrp) *n.* A belch. *—intr. & tr.v.* **burped, burp•ing, burps.** To belch or cause to belch: *He burped the baby after feeding.*

burr[1] (bûr) *n.* **1.** A rough edge or spot left on metal or other material after it has been cast, cut, or drilled. **2.** Variant of **bur**[1].

burr[2] also **bur** (bûr) *n.* **1.** The trilled "r" of Scottish pronunciation. **2.** A whirring sound. *—v.* **burred, burr•ing, burrs** also **burs.** *—tr.* To pronounce with a burr. *—intr.* **1.** To speak with a burr. **2.** To make a whirring sound. [First written down in 1760 in Modern English, of imitative origin.]

Burr (bûr), **Aaron.** 1756–1836. American politician who was Vice President of the United States (1801–1805) under Thomas Jefferson. In 1804 Burr mortally wounded his rival Alexander Hamilton in a duel.

bur•ri•to (bo͝o **rē′**tō) *n., pl.* **bur•ri•tos.** A flour tortilla wrapped around a filling, as of beef, beans, or cheese.

bur•ro (bûr′ō *or* bo͝or′ō *or* bŭr′ō) *n., pl.* **bur•ros.** A small donkey, usually used for carrying loads.

❑ *These sound alike:* **burro, borough** (town), **burrow** (animal hole).

bur•row (bûr′ō *or* bŭr′ō) *n.* A hole or tunnel dug in

Robert Burns

Aaron Burr

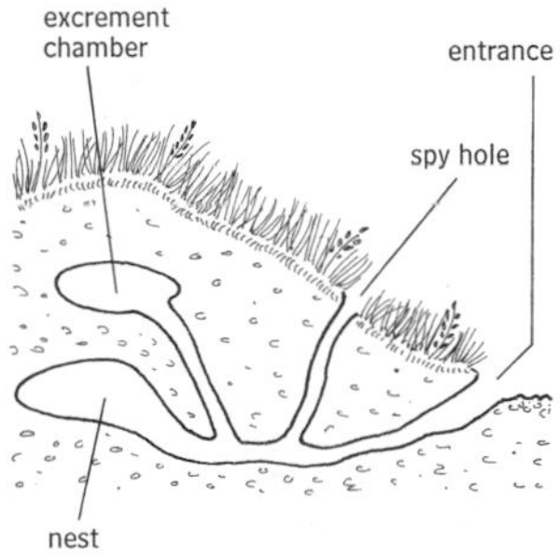

burrow

ă	pat	oi	boy
ā	pay	ou	out
âr	care	o͝o	took
ä	father	o͞o	boot
ĕ	pet	ŭ	cut
ē	be	ûr	urge
ĭ	pit	th	thin
ī	pie	*th*	this
îr	pier	hw	whoop
ŏ	pot	zh	vision
ō	toe	ə	about
ô	paw	N	*French* bon

the ground by a small animal, such as a rabbit or mole. —*v.* **bur•rowed, bur•row•ing, bur•rows.** —*intr.* **1.** To make a tunnel, hole, or shelter by or as if by digging or tunneling: *gophers burrowing in the fields.* **2.** To live or hide in or as if in a burrow: *Some animals burrow under the ground during the winter.* **3.** To search: *If you burrow in your desk, you will surely find a pencil.* —*tr.* To make (a tunnel or hole) by digging. —**bur′row•er** *n.*

❑ *These sound alike:* **burrow, borough** (town), **burro** (donkey).

bur•sa (bûr′sə) *n., pl.* **bur•sae** (bûr′sē) or **bur•sas.** A body cavity resembling a sac, especially one containing a lubricating fluid that reduces friction between a muscle or tendon and a bone.

bur•sar (bûr′sər *or* bûr′sär′) *n.* A treasurer, as at a college or university.

bur•si•tis (bər sī′tĭs) *n.* Inflammation of a bursa, especially in the shoulder, elbow, or knee.

burst (bûrst) *v.* **burst, burst•ing, bursts.** —*intr.* **1.** To break open suddenly and violently: *The balloon may burst.* **2.** To come forth, emerge, or arrive suddenly and in full force: *The police burst into the room.* **3.** To be or seem to be full to the point of breaking open; swell: *He's bursting with pride.* **4.** To give sudden utterance or expression: *burst out laughing; burst into tears.* —*tr.* To cause to break open suddenly and violently: *The heat of the lamp burst the balloon.* —*n.* **1.** A sudden outbreak or outburst; an explosion: *a burst of laughter.* **2.** A firing of bullets from an automatic weapon. **3.** A sudden and intense increase; a rush: *a burst of speed.*

Bu•run•di (bo͝o ro͞on′dē). A country of east-central Africa south of Rwanda. It gained its independence from Belgium in 1962. Bujumbura is the capital and the largest city. Population, 4,523,513.

bur•y (bĕr′ē) *tr.v.* **bur•ied, bur•y•ing, bur•ies. 1.** To place in the ground: *The dog buried a bone.* **2.** To place (a dead body) in a grave, a tomb, or the sea. **3.** To conceal; hide: *She buried her face in the pillow.* See Synonyms at **hide[1]**. **4.** To occupy (oneself) with deep concentration; absorb: *I buried myself in my homework.* **5.** To put an end to; abandon: *Let's shake hands and bury our quarrel.* [First written down about 1000 in Old English and spelled *byrgan.*]

❑ *These sound alike:* **bury, berry** (fruit).

bus (bŭs) *n., pl.* **bus•es** or **bus•ses. 1.** A long motor vehicle with rows of seats for carrying passengers. **2.** A circuit that connects the major components of a computer, allowing the transfer of electric signals from one component to another. —*v.* **bused, bus•ing, bus•es** or **bussed, bus•sing, bus•ses.** —*tr.* **1.** To carry or transport in a bus: *The club bussed us to the beach.* **2.** To transport (students) by bus to schools outside their neighborhoods, especially to achieve racial integration. —*intr.* To travel in a bus: *Many people bus to work and school.*

bus•boy also **bus boy** (bŭs′boi′) *n.* A waiter's helper who sets and clears the table in a restaurant.

bush (bo͝osh) *n.* **1.** A shrub, especially one having many separate branches starting from or near the ground. **2.** A thick growth of shrubs; a thicket. **3.** Land covered with dense shrubby growth. **4.** Land that is remote from human settlement: *a journey through the Australian bush.* —*intr.v.* **bushed, bush•ing, bushes.** To grow or branch out like a bush.

George Bush

Bush (bo͝osh), **George Herbert Walker.** Born 1924. The 41st President of the United States (1989–1993). He was Vice President (1981–1989) under Ronald Reagan.

bushed (bo͝osht) *adj. Informal.* Extremely tired.

bush•el (bo͝osh′əl) *n.* **1.** A unit of volume or capacity, used in dry measure in the United States and equal to 4 pecks (about 35.24 liters) or 2,150.42 cubic inches: *Many fruits and vegetables are measured by the bushel for market.* See table at **measurement. 2.** A container that holds this amount.

bush•ing (bo͝osh′ĭng) *n.* A metal tube that serves as a guide for or reduces wear on a moving part, as in machinery.

Bush•man (bo͝osh′mən) *n.* A San.

bush•mas•ter (bo͝osh′măs′tər) *n.* A large poisonous snake of Central and South America having brown and gray markings.

bush pilot *n.* A pilot who flies a small airplane to and from areas that are sparsely settled.

bush•whack (bo͝osh′wăk′) *v.* **bush•whacked, bush•whack•ing, bush•whacks.** —*tr.v.* To attack suddenly from a place of hiding; ambush. —*intr.v.* To cut one's way through thick undergrowth or forest. —**bush′whack′er** *n.*

bush•y (bo͝osh′ē) *adj.* **bush•i•er, bush•i•est. 1.** Overgrown with bushes: *bushy undergrowth.* **2.** Thick and shaggy: *a squirrel's bushy tail.* —**bush′i•ness** *n.*

bus•i•ly (bĭz′ə lē) *adv.* In a busy manner.

busi•ness (bĭz′nĭs) *n.* **1.** The occupation, trade, or work that provides a person with a means of living: *a group of salespersons in the automobile business.* **2.** Commercial, industrial, and professional dealings considered as a group: *Computers are now being used throughout business and industry.* **3.** A commercial establishment, such as a store or factory: *Will you go into the family business?* **4.** The volume or amount of trade: *Business falls off when summer begins.* **5.** One's rightful or proper concern: *What he does with his money is none of our business.* **6.** An affair; a matter: *The manager dealt with the business at hand.* **7.** Serious work: *Let's get down to business.*

Synonyms: business, industry, commerce, trade, traffic. These nouns mean activity that produces merchandise. **Business** means general commercial, financial, and industrial activity: *This article discusses why American business should invest more in research.* **Industry** means the manufacture of goods, especially on a large scale: *The automobile industry has experimented with robots on assembly lines.* **Commerce** and **trade** mean the exchange and distribution of goods: *The new economic treaties among European countries will have a profound effect on international commerce. Those rules don't apply to trade between those countries.* **Traffic** often means the business of transporting goods or people: *The city has renovated its harbor to attract shipping traffic.*

---

busi•ness•like (bĭz′nĭs līk′) *adj.* Systematic; efficient; orderly: *a friendly but businesslike manner.*

busi•ness•man (bĭz′nĭs măn′) *n.* A man engaged in business.

busi•ness•per•son (bĭz′nĭs pûr′sən) *n.* A businessman or businesswoman.

busi•ness•wom•an (bĭz′nĭs wo͝om′ən) *n.* A woman engaged in business.

bus•ing or **bus•sing** (bŭs′ĭng) *n.* The transportation of children by bus to schools outside their neighborhoods, especially as a means of achieving racial integration.

bus•ses (bŭs′ĭz) *n.* A plural of **bus.**

bust[1] (bŭst) *n.* **1.** A sculpture of a person's head, shoulders, and upper chest: *a marble bust of Lincoln.* **2.** A woman's bosom. [First written down in 1691 in Modern English, from Italian *busto*, possibly from Latin *bustum*, sepulchral monument.]

bust[2] (bŭst) *v.* **bust•ed, bust•ing, busts.** —*tr.* **1.** *Slang.* To smash or break: *I busted the ice with a hatchet.* **2.** *Slang.* To make unusable; break: *He busted the vending machine by putting in foreign* *coins.* **3.** To break or tame (a horse). **4.** To cause to become bankrupt or short of money: *The long drought busted many farmers.* **5.** *Slang.* To reduce the rank of; demote: *bust a sergeant to corporal.* **6.** To hit; punch. **7.** *Slang.* To place under arrest: *The cops busted the thief.* —*intr.* **1.** *Slang.* To become broken or unusable; break: *The bicycle chain busted as I went up the hill.* **2.** To become bankrupt or short of money. —*n.* **1.** A failure; a flop: *That movie is a real bust.* **2.** A financial depression: *times of boom and bust.* **3.** A punch or blow. **4.** *Slang.* An arrest: *a drug bust.* [First written down in 1806 in American English, variant of *burst.*]

bus•tard (bŭs′tərd) *n.* Any of various large brownish or grayish game birds having a long neck and legs and a heavy body, living in open grassy regions of Africa, Asia, and Australia.

bus•tle[1] (bŭs′əl) *intr.v.* **bus•tled, bus•tling, bus•tles.** To move busily and energetically: *The mechanics bustled about the airplane.* —*n.* Excited activity; commotion: *the hustle and bustle of city streets.* [First written down in 1350 in Middle English and spelled *bustelen,* possibly variant of obsolete *buskle,* from *busk,* to prepare oneself, from Old Norse *būask.*]

bus•tle[2] (bŭs′əl) *n.* A pad or frame worn by women in earlier times to puff out the back of a long skirt. [First written down in 1788 in Modern English.]

bus•y (bĭz′ē) *adj.* **bus•i•er, bus•i•est. 1.** Occupied with work; active: *The doctor was busy with a patient.* **2.** Crowded with activity: *the doctor's busy morning.* **3.** In use, as a telephone line: *The doctor's phone is busy.* —*tr.v.* **bus•ied, bus•y•ing, bus•ies.** To make (oneself) busy; occupy (oneself): *I busied myself with my chores.* —**bus′y•ness** *n.*

bus•y•bod•y (bĭz′ē bŏd′ē) *n.* A nosy or meddling person interested in the affairs of others.

bus•y•work (bĭz′ē wûrk′) *n.* An activity that takes up time but does not necessarily produce anything: *the busywork of sorting old newspapers.*

but (bŭt *or* bət *when unstressed*) *conj.* **1.a.** On the contrary; yet: *We organized our work but got very little done.* **b.** Nevertheless: *The plan may not work, but we must try.* **2.** *Informal.* Without the result that: *It never rains but it pours.* **3.** *Informal.* That: *There is no doubt but right will win out.* **4.** With the exception that; except that: *would have resisted but that they lacked courage.* —*prep.* Other than; except: *No one went but me.* —*adv.* **1.** Only; merely: *This is but one case in many.* **2.** No more than: *They had run but a few yards when the teacher called.* [First written down about 725 in Old English and spelled *būtan,* around the outside of.] —SEE NOTE at **not.**

❑ *These sound alike:* **but, butt**[1] (hit), **butt**[2] (object of scorn), **butt**[3] (end).

bu•ta•di•ene (byo͞o′tə **dī**′ēn′ *or* byo͞o′tə dī **ēn′**) *n.* A colorless flammable gas composed of carbon and hydrogen in the proportions C_4H_6. It is obtained from petroleum and is used in making synthetic rubber.

bu•tane (byo͞o′tān′) *n.* A gaseous hydrocarbon having the formula C_4H_{10}. It is produced from petroleum and is used as a fuel and in the making of synthetic rubber.

butch•er (bo͝och′ər) *n.* **1.** A person who kills animals and prepares their meat for food. **2.** A person who sells meat: *buy a steak from the local butcher.* **3.** A person who kills cruelly or without reason. —*tr.v.* **butch•ered, butch•er•ing, butch•ers. 1.** To slaughter or prepare (animals) for market. **2.** To kill brutally and without reason. **3.** To botch up; bungle: *The actor butchered the part by forgetting many lines.*

butch•er•y (bo͝och′ə rē) *n., pl.* **butch•er•ies.** Cruel or savage killing; slaughter.

but•ler (bŭt′lər) *n.* The chief male servant of a household.

butt[1] (bŭt) *tr.v.* **butt•ed, butt•ing, butts.** To hit or push with the head or horns: *The goat butted the farmer.* —*n.* A push or blow with the head or horns. —***idiom.*** **butt in** or **butt into.** *Informal.* To meddle; intrude: *Don't butt into other people's affairs.* [First written down about 1200 in Middle English and spelled *butten,* from Old French *bouter,* to strike, of Germanic origin.]

❑ *These sound alike:* **butt**[1] (hit), **but** (except), **butt**[2] (object of scorn), **butt**[3] (end).

butt[2] (bŭt) *n.* A person or thing that is an object of ridicule or scorn: *The clown was the butt of his own jokes.* [First written down about 1345 in Middle English and spelled *but,* target, from Old French.]

❑ *These sound alike:* **butt**[2] (object of scorn), **but** (except), **butt**[1] (hit), **butt**[3] (end).

butt[3] (bŭt) *n.* **1.** The thicker end of something: *the butt of a rifle.* **2.** An unused or unburned end, especially of a cigarette. [First written down about 1400 in Middle English, from Old French *but,* end, of Germanic origin.]

❑ *These sound alike:* **butt**[3] (end), **but** (except), **butt**[1] (hit), **butt**[2] (object of scorn).

butte (byo͞ot) *n.* A steep-sided hill with a flat top, often standing alone.

but•ter (bŭt′ər) *n.* **1.** A soft, yellowish, fatty food churned from milk or cream. **2.** A similar substance, such as a fruit spread: *There are many fruit butters such as apple butter.* —*tr.v.* **but•tered, but•ter•ing, but•ters.** To put butter in or on. —***idiom.*** **butter up.** To flatter: *He's always buttering up the boss.* [First written down about 1000 in Old English and spelled *butere,* from Latin *butyrum,* from Greek *bouturon* : *bous,* cow + *turos,* cheese.]

butter bean *n.* **1.** The wax bean. **2.** The lima bean, especially a variety grown in the southern United States.

but•ter•cup (bŭt′ər kŭp′) *n.* **1.** Any of numerous plants having usually yellow cup-shaped flowers. **2.** A flower of this plant.

but•ter•fat (bŭt′ər făt′) *n.* The fat that is contained in milk and from which butter is made.

but•ter•fin•gers (bŭt′ər fĭng′gərz) *pl.n. (used with a singular verb).* A clumsy or awkward person who is apt to drop things.

but•ter•fish (bŭt′ər fĭsh′) *n., pl.* **butterfish** or **but•ter•fish•es.** An ocean fish of North America having a silvery, flattened, very slippery body and a forked tail, often used for food.

but•ter•fly (bŭt′ər flī′) *n.* **1.** Any of various insects having four broad, often colorful wings, a narrow body, and slender antennae with knobs at the tips. **2.** A swimming stroke in which both arms are drawn upward out of the water and forward while the legs kick up and down.

but•ter•milk (bŭt′ər mĭlk′) *n.* The thick sour liquid that remains after butter has been churned from milk.

but•ter•nut (bŭt′ər nŭt′) *n.* **1.** The oily edible nut of a North American tree related to the walnuts. **2.** A tree that bears such nuts.

but•ter•scotch (bŭt′ər skŏch′) *n.* A candy or a flavoring made from brown sugar and butter. —*adj.* Made or flavored with butterscotch: *butterscotch ice cream.*

but•ter•y (bŭt′ə rē) *adj.* **1.** Resembling butter: *buttery soft leather.* **2.** Containing or spread with butter: *hot buttery muffins.*

but•tock (bŭt′ək) *n.* **1.** Either of the rounded fleshy

bustle[2]

ă	pat	oi	boy
ā	pay	ou	out
âr	care	o͝o	took
ä	father	o͞o	boot
ĕ	pet	ŭ	cut
ē	be	ûr	urge
ĭ	pit	th	thin
ī	pie	*th*	this
îr	pier	hw	whoop
ŏ	pot	zh	vision
ō	toe	ə	about
ô	paw	N	*French* bon

buttress

buzzard
Turkey vulture

Richard E. Byrd
Photographed c. 1933

parts of the rump. **2. buttocks.** The rump of the human body.

but•ton (bŭt′n) *n.* **1.** A disk or knob of plastic, metal, leather, or wood, sewn to cloth, usually fitting through a slit or loop to fasten edges together or to serve as decoration. **2.** A part that is pushed to work a switch, as to ring a bell, turn on a light, or start a machine: *Push the button to get the elevator.* **3.** Something resembling a button, as a round flat pin with words or a design on it: *a candidate's campaign button.* —*v.* **but•toned, but•ton•ing, but•tons.** —*tr.* To fasten with a button or buttons: *button up a coat.* —*intr.* To be or be capable of being fastened with buttons: *a coat that buttons down the front.* **—*idiom.* on the button.** Exactly; precisely: *We arrived at three o'clock on the button.* [First written down before 1300 in Middle English and spelled *bouton*, from Old French *bouter*, to thrust, of Germanic origin.]

but•ton•hole (bŭt′n hōl′) *n.* A slit in a garment or in cloth used to fasten a button. —*tr.v.* **but•ton•holed, but•ton•hol•ing, but•ton•holes.** **1.** To make a buttonhole in. **2.** To make (a person) stop and listen, as if grabbing the buttonhole in a garment.

but•ton•wood (bŭt′n wo͝od′) *n.* The sycamore tree of North America.

but•tress (bŭt′rĭs) *n.* **1.** A structure, often of brick or stone, built against a wall for support. **2.** Something that serves to support or reinforce: *Testimony of witnesses was a strong buttress to our side of the story.* —*tr.v.* **but•tressed, but•tress•ing, but•tress•es.** **1.** To brace or reinforce with a buttress: *buttress the roof of a tunnel with timbers.* **2.** To sustain or bolster: *buttress an argument with evidence.*

bux•om (bŭk′səm) *adj.* Healthily plump: *a buxom young woman.* **—bux′om•ness** *n.*

buy (bī) *v.* **bought** (bôt), **buy•ing, buys.** —*tr.* **1.** To get in exchange for money or something of equal value: *go to the store to buy groceries; buy land through a bank.* **2.** To be capable of purchasing: *Money can buy comfort but not happiness.* **3.** *Informal.* To bribe: *Money will not buy an honest judge.* —*intr.* To purchase goods: *buy on sale.* —*n.* *Informal.* Something cheaper than usual; a bargain: *The coats on sale are a good buy.* **—*idioms.* buy off.** To bribe: *It is illegal to try to buy off a government official.* **buy out.** To purchase the stock, rights, or interests of: *buy out a company.* **buy up.** To purchase all that is available: *The day after the elections, people bought up all the newspapers early in the morning.* [First written down about 1000 in Old English and spelled *bycgan*.]
❑ *These sound alike:* **buy, by** (near).

buy•er (bī′ər) *n.* **1.** A person who buys goods; a customer. **2.** A person who buys merchandise for a retail store.

buzz (bŭz) *v.* **buzzed, buzz•ing, buzz•es.** —*intr.* **1.** To make a low droning sound like that of a bee: *Flies buzzed near the cherries.* **2.** To talk in excited low tones: *The audience buzzed in anticipation of the show.* —*tr.* **1.** To signal, as with a buzzer: *The patient buzzed the nurse.* **2.** *Informal.* To fly a plane low over. —*n.* A low droning sound, such as the one made by a bee: *the buzz of a fly.* **—*idiom.* buzz off.** *Informal.* To leave quickly; go away. [First written down in 1530 in Middle English and spelled *bussen*, of imitative origin.]

buz•zard (bŭz′ərd) *n.* **1.** Any of various North American vultures, such as the turkey vulture. **2.** *Chiefly British.* Any of various hawks having broad wings and a broad tail. [First written down before 1300 in Middle English and spelled *busard*, hawk, from Latin *būteō*.]

buzz•er (bŭz′ər) *n.* An electrical device that makes a buzzing noise to give a signal or warning.

buzz saw *n.* A circular saw.

by (bī) *prep.* **1.** Close to; near: *the chair by the window; sitting by the wall.* **2.** Up to and beyond; past: *A car drove by us.* **3.** Through the agency or action of: *a building destroyed by fire; a novel by a young author.* **4.** With the help or use of; through: *come by the back road; crossing by ferry.* **5.** According to: *playing by the rules; by their own account.* **6.** In the course of; during: *sleeping by night and working by day.* **7.** In the amount of: *The President receives letters by the thousands.* **8.** Not later than: *finish by noon.* **9.** In the matter of; concerning: *They are storekeepers by trade.* **10.** After; following: *One by one they left.* **11.** Combined in multiplication, division, or measurement with: *Multiply 4 by 6. The room measures 12 by 20 feet. Divide 4 by 2.* **12.** With the difference of; to the extent of: *shorter by three inches.* —*adv.* **1.** Close at hand; nearby: *We just stood by watching.* **2.** Aside; away: *putting some money by for later.* **3.** Up to and beyond; past: *The car raced by.* **4.** Into the past: *as time goes by.* **—*idioms.* by and by.** Before long; later: *The weather always changes by and by.* **by and large.** On the whole; mostly: *By and large people are honest.* **by oneself. 1.** Alone: *I walked by myself in the woods.* **2.** Without help: *I repaired the car by myself.* **by the way.** Incidentally. [First written down about 725 in Old English and spelled *bī*.]
❑ *These sound alike:* **by, buy** (purchase).

by– or **bye–** *pref.* A prefix that means: **1.** Near; at hand: *bystander.* **2.** Out of the way; aside: *bypass.* **3.** Secondary: *byproduct.* **4.** Past: *bygone.*

bye-bye (bī′bī′ *or* bī bī′) *interj.* An expression used to say good-bye.

Bye•lo•rus•sia (byĕl′ō rŭsh′ə). Belorussia.

by•gone (bī′gôn′ *or* bī′gŏn′) *adj.* Gone by; past: *bygone days.* —*n.* A past occurrence. Often used in the plural.

by•law (bī′lô′) *n.* A law or rule made by a local government, corporation, club, or other organization governing its own affairs. [First written down in 1280 in Middle English and spelled *bilage*, body of local regulations; akin to Danish *by-lag*, township ordinance : Old Norse *bȳr*, settlement + Old Norse *lög*, laws.]

by•line (bī′līn′) *n.* A printed line at the head of a newspaper or magazine article giving the writer's name.

by•pass also **by-pass** (bī′păs′) *n.* **1.** A road that passes around a city or other congested area. **2.** A path that leads around some component of a system, as in an electric circuit or a system of pipes. **3.** A surgical operation to make a new passage for blood around old vessels that are blocked: *a coronary bypass around a blood vessel of the heart.* —*tr.v.* **by•passed, by•pass•ing, by•pass•es.** To go or send around by or as if by means of a bypass: *We can bypass all the salespeople if we see the manager directly.*

by-path (bī′păth′) *n.* An indirect or little-used path.

by-play (bī′plā′) *n.* Action taking place separately, while the main action is going on, as on a theater stage.

by•prod•uct or **by-prod•uct** (bī′prŏd′əkt) *n.* **1.** Something produced in the making of something else: *Asphalt and paraffin are byproducts of refining crude oil into gasoline.* **2.** A secondary result; a side effect: *Widespread illness and disease are a byproduct of unsanitary conditions.*

Byrd (bûrd), **Richard Evelyn.** 1888–1957. American naval officer and explorer who established a base for scientific discovery in Antarctica.

by•road (bī′rōd′) *n.* A side road; a back road.

By•ron (bī′rən), **George Gordon.** Sixth Baron Byron of Rochdale. 1788–1824. British romantic poet. Among his works are *Childe Harold* (1812–1818) and *Don Juan* (1819–1824).

by•stand•er (bī′stăn′dər) *n.* A person who is present at an event but does not take part: *Bystanders crowded around the scene of the accident.*

byte (bīt) *n.* **1.** A sequence of adjacent bits operated on as a unit by a computer. **2.** The amount of computer memory needed to store one character of a specified size, usually 8 or 16 bits. [First written down in 1964 in Modern English, alteration and blend of *bit*, single character, and *bite*.]

❑ *These sound alike:* **byte, bite** (grip with the teeth).

by•way (bī′wā′) *n.* A road not often used; a side road.

by•word (bī′wûrd′) *n.* **1.** A well-known saying; a proverb. **2.** A person or thing thought of as representing a type, class, or quality: *That newspaper is the byword for honest reporting.* **3.** An object of interest and notoriety.

Byz•an•tine (bĭz′ən tēn′ *or* bĭz′ən tīn′ *or* bĭ zăn′tĭn) *adj.* **1.** Of or relating to Byzantium, its inhabitants, or their culture. **2.** Of or relating to the Byzantine Empire. **3.** Of or belonging to the style of architecture developed in Byzantium, characterized by round arches, massive domes, and the extensive use of mosaic designs. —*n.* An inhabitant of Byzantium or the Byzantine Empire.

Byzantine Empire. The eastern part of the later Roman Empire, dating from A.D. 330 and focused around the Balkan Peninsula and Asia Minor. The empire collapsed in 1453.

By•zan•ti•um (bĭ zăn′shē əm *or* bĭ zăn′tē əm). A city of ancient Greece on the site of present-day Istanbul, Turkey. It was founded in the seventh century B.C.

ă	pat	oi	boy
ā	pay	ou	out
âr	care	ŏŏ	took
ä	father	ōō	boot
ĕ	pet	ŭ	cut
ē	be	ûr	urge
ĭ	pit	th	thin
ī	pie	*th*	this
îr	pier	hw	whoop
ŏ	pot	zh	vision
ō	toe	ə	about
ô	paw	N	*French* bon

Cc

cactus
Saguaro cactus

caduceus

c or **C** (sē) *n., pl.* **c's** or **C's.** **1.** The third letter of the English alphabet: *There are two c's in the word* clock. **2.** The third in a series or group: *row C in a theater.* **3.** The third best or third highest: *get a C on a test.* **4.** In music, the first tone in the scale of C major.

C[1] (sē) *n.* A computer programming language widely used on microcomputers.

C[2] **1.** The symbol for the element **carbon** (sense 1). **2.** Also **c** The symbol for the Roman numeral one hundred. **3. c** The symbol for the speed of light in a vacuum.

C[3] *abbr.* An abbreviation of: **1.** Celsius. **2.** Centigrade.

c. or **C.** *abbr.* An abbreviation of: **1.** Cent. **2.** Century. **3.** Chapter. **4.** Circa (approximately).

ca *abbr.* An abbreviation of circa (approximately).

Ca The symbol for the element **calcium.**

CA *abbr.* An abbreviation of California.

cab (kăb) *n.* **1.** A taxicab. **2.** A one-horse carriage for public hire. **3.** A covered compartment for the operator or driver of a heavy vehicle or machine, such as a locomotive, truck, or crane. [First written down in 1826 in Modern English, short for *cabriolet*, a two-wheeled carriage, from French *cabriole*, caper.]

ca•bal (kə **băl′**) *n.* **1.** A small group of people organized to carry out a secret plot or conspiracy. **2.** A plot organized by such a group.

cab•al•le•ro (kăb′ə **lâr′**ō *or* kä′bä **yĕ′**rō) *n., pl.* **cab•al•le•ros.** **1.** A Spanish gentleman; a cavalier. **2.** A skilled horseman.

ca•ban•a also **ca•ba•ña** (kə **băn′**ə *or* kə **băn′**yə) *n.* A shelter on a beach or near a swimming pool, used as a bathhouse.

cab•a•ret (kăb′ə **rā′**) *n.* **1.** A restaurant providing short programs of live entertainment. **2.** The entertainment presented in such a place.

cab•bage (**kăb′**ĭj) *n.* Any of several plants having a large rounded head of tightly overlapping green or reddish leaves eaten as a vegetable. [First written down in 1391 in Middle English and spelled *caboche*, from Old North French, head, possibly from Latin, *caput.*]

cab•by or **cab•bie** (**kăb′**ē) *n., pl.* **cab•bies.** A cabdriver.

cab•driv•er (**kăb′**drī′vər) *n.* A driver of a cab.

cab•in (**kăb′**ĭn) *n.* **1.** A small, simply built house; a cottage or hut. **2.** A room in a ship used as living quarters for a passenger or an officer. **3.** An enclosed compartment in a boat that serves as a shelter or as living quarters. **4.** The enclosed compartment in an airplane or a spacecraft for passengers, crew, or cargo.

cabin boy *n.* A male servant who serves the officers and passengers on a ship.

cabin cruiser *n.* A motorboat with a cabin.

cab•i•net (**kăb′**ə nĭt) *n.* **1.** A case or cupboard with shelves, drawers, or compartments for storing or displaying objects: *a kitchen cabinet; a filing cabinet.* **2.** Often **Cabinet.** A group of people appointed by a head of state or prime minister to act as official advisers and to head the various departments of state.

cab•i•net•mak•er (**kăb′**ə nĭt mā′kər) *n.* A person who makes fine articles of wooden furniture.

cab•i•net•work (**kăb′**ə nĭt wûrk′) *n.* Fine woodwork made by a cabinetmaker.

ca•ble (**kā′**bəl) *n.* **1.** A strong thick rope made of steel wires or fiber. **2.** A group of insulated electrical wires that are bound together. **3.** Cable television. **4.** A cablegram. —*v.* **ca•bled, ca•bling, ca•bles.** —*tr.* **1.** To send a cablegram to (a person, for example): *Several reporters cabled their newspapers about the earthquake.* **2.** To transmit (a message) by telegraph. —*intr.* To send a cablegram. [First written down before 1200 in Middle English, from Late Latin *capulum*, lasso.]

cable car *n.* A vehicle pulled by a cable that runs in an endless loop either overhead or beneath rails.

ca•ble•gram (**kā′**bəl grăm′) *n.* A telegraph message sent by submarine cable.

cable television *n.* A commercial television system in which the signals of the station are transmitted by cable to the receivers of subscribers who pay for the service.

ca•boose (kə **bo͞os′**) *n.* The last car of a freight train, having living facilities for the train crew. [First written down in 1747 in American English and spelled *caboose*, ship's galley, possibly from obsolete Dutch *cabūse.*]

Cab•ot (**kăb′**ət), **John.** 1450?–1498? Italian-born explorer who commanded an English expedition to the North American mainland in 1497.

cab•ri•o•let (kăb′rē ə **lā′**) *n.* A two-wheeled carriage pulled by one horse, having two seats and a folding top.

ca•ca•o (kə **kä′**ō *or* kə **kā′**ō) *n., pl.* **ca•ca•os.** **1.** The seeds from the pods of a tropical American evergreen tree, used to make chocolate, cocoa, and cocoa butter. **2.** The tree that bears such seeds. [First written down in 1555 in Modern English, from Spanish, from Nahuatl *cacahuatl.*]

cach•a•lot (**kăsh′**ə lŏt′ *or* **kăsh′**ə lō′) *n.* The sperm whale.

cache (kăsh) *n.* **1.** A hiding place, as for a supply of provisions or weapons. **2.** A supply of something hidden in such a place: *a cache of food.* —*tr.v.* **cached, cach•ing, cach•es.** To hide or store away in a cache: *squirrels caching nuts for winter.*

❑ *These sound alike:* **cache, cash** (money).

ca•chet (kă **shā′**) *n.* **1.** A mark or quality, as of distinction or individuality: *Doctors have a certain cachet in the United States.* **2.** A seal on a letter or document.

cack•le (**kăk′**əl) *v.* **cack•led, cack•ling, cack•les.** —*intr.* **1.** To make the shrill cry of a hen that has just laid an egg. **2.** To laugh or speak in a shrill manner. —*tr.* To utter in cackles: *cackled a reply.* —*n.* **1.** The act or sound of cackling. **2.** Shrill laughter or foolish chatter.

ca•coph•o•nous (kə **kŏf′**ə nəs) *adj.* Harsh and unpleasant in sound; dissonant.

ca•coph•o•ny (kə **kŏf′**ə nē) *n., pl.* **ca•coph•o•nies.**

Harsh unpleasant sound; dissonance: *the cacophony of horns in city traffic.*

cac•tus (kăk′təs) *n., pl.* **cac•ti** (kăk′tī′) or **cac•tus•es.** Any of various plants that have thick, leafless, often spiny stems and that grow in hot dry places, chiefly in North and South America. Some kinds have showy flowers and edible fruit. [First written down in 1607 in Modern English and spelled *cactus*, cardoon, a plant like an artichoke, from Greek *kaktos.*]

cad (kăd) *n.* An unprincipled, ungentlemanly man.

CAD *abbr.* An abbreviation of computer-aided design.

ca•dav•er (kə dăv′ər) *n.* A dead body, especially one that is to be dissected and studied.

ca•dav•er•ous (kə dăv′ər əs) *adj.* Resembling a corpse; pale and gaunt.

cad•dice fly (kăd′is) *n.* Variant of **caddis fly.**

cad•die also **cad•dy** (kăd′ē) *n., pl.* **cad•dies.** A person hired by a golfer to carry golf clubs. —*intr.v.* **cad•died, cad•dy•ing, cad•dies.** To serve as a caddie.

cad•dis fly also **cad•dice fly** (kăd′ĭs) *n.* Any of various insects that are similar to the moth and live near lakes and streams. The larva lives enclosed in a tubular case covered with grains of sand or tiny pieces of wood or shell.

Cad•do (kăd′ō) *n., pl.* **Caddo** or **Cad•dos. 1.** A member of a group of Native American peoples living in central Oklahoma. **2.** The Caddoan language of the Caddo.

Cad•do•an (kăd′ō ən) *n.* A family of Native American languages spoken in North Dakota and Oklahoma.

cad•dy¹ (kăd′ē) *n., pl.* **cad•dies.** A small container, such as a box, used especially for holding tea.

cad•dy² (căd′ē) *n. & v.* Variant of **caddie.**

ca•dence (kād′ns) *n.* **1.** Measured rhythmic flow, as of poetry or music: *poetry written in short quick cadences.* **2.** The measure or beat of movement, as in marching. **3.** A progression of chords that brings a phrase or other division of a musical composition to a close. **4.** The general rise and fall of the voice in speaking, as at the end of a question.

ca•den•za (kə dĕn′zə) *n.* An elaborate section for the soloist near the end of a musical composition.

ca•det (kə dĕt′) *n.* A student at a military or naval academy who is training to be an officer. [First written down in 1610 in Modern English, from French dialectal *capdet*, captain, from Late Latin *capitellum*, diminutive of Latin *caput*, head.]

cad•mi•um (kăd′mē əm) *n. Symbol* **Cd** A soft bluish-white element resembling tin that occurs only in combination with other elements and is used in plating metals to prevent corrosion, in making alloys, and in storage batteries. Atomic number 48. See table at **element.**

cad•re (kăd′rē *or* kä′drā) *n.* A group of persons trained to establish and teach new members in a larger organization.

ca•du•ce•us (kə do͞o′sē əs *or* kə dyo͞o′sē əs) *n., pl.* **ca•du•ce•i** (kə do͞o′sē ī′ *or* kə dyo͞o′sē ī′). **1.** In Greek mythology, a winged staff with two serpents coiled around it carried by Hermes. **2.** A similar staff used as a symbol of the medical profession.

cae•cum (sē′kəm) *n.* Variant of **cecum.**

cae•sar also **Cae•sar** (sē′zər) *n.* **1.** A title of Roman emperors after the reign of Augustus. **2.** A dictator or other ruler having absolute power. [First written down before 1200 in Middle English and spelled *kaisere*, from Latin *Caesar*, after Julius *Caesar.*]

Caesar, Julius. 100–44 B.C. Roman general and politician who was given a mandate by the people to rule as dictator for life (45). On March 15 of the following year he was murdered by a group who feared he intended to establish a monarchy.

cae•sar•e•an (sĭ zâr′ē ən) *adj. & n.* Variant of **cesarean.**

cae•si•um (sē′zē əm) *n.* Variant of **cesium.**

cae•su•ra (sĭ zho͝or′ə *or* sĭ zo͝or′ə) *n., pl.* **cae•su•ras** or **cae•su•rae** (sĭ zho͝or′ē *or* sĭ zo͝or′ē). A short pause in a line of verse or in a melody.

ca•fé also **ca•fe** (kă fā′) *n.* A coffeehouse, restaurant, or bar. [First written down in 1802 in Modern English, from French, *café*, coffee, café, from Italian *caffè*, coffee, from Ottoman Turkish *qahveh.*]

caf•e•te•ri•a (kăf′ĭ tîr′ē ə) *n.* A restaurant in which the customers are served at a counter and carry their meals on trays to tables.

caf•feine also **caf•fein** (kă fēn′ *or* kăf′ēn′) *n.* A bitter white alkaloid with the formula $C_8H_{10}N_4O_2$ that acts as a stimulant and is found in coffee, tea, and cola beverages.

caf•tan or **kaf•tan** (kăf′tăn′ *or* kăf tăn′) *n.* A full-length robe having long sleeves and worn in eastern Mediterranean countries.

cage (kāj) *n.* **1.** An enclosure for confining birds or other animals, having a grating of wires or bars on at least one side to let in air or light. **2.** Something similar to a cage: *a ticket seller's cage at the stadium.* **3.** An enclosure to confine prisoners. —*tr.v.* **caged, cag•ing, cag•es.** To put in a cage: *cage a wild animal.*

ca•gey also **ca•gy** (kā′jē) *adj.* **ca•gi•er, ca•gi•est.** Wary; shrewd; crafty: *a cagey lawyer with much experience.* —**cag′i•ly** *adv.* —**cag′i•ness** *n.*

ca•hoots (kə ho͞ots′) *pl.n. Informal.* Secret partnership: *a surprise party that she planned in cahoots with friends.*

CAI *abbr.* An abbreviation of computer-aided instruction.

cai•man also **cay•man** (kā′mən) *n., pl.* **cai•mans** also **cay•mans.** Any of various large tropical American reptiles related to and resembling the alligator.

Cain (kān). In the Bible, the eldest son of Adam and Eve, who murdered his brother Abel.

cairn (kârn) *n.* A mound of stones built as a landmark or memorial. [First written down in 1535 in Modern English, from Old Irish *carn.*]

Cai•ro (kī′rō). The capital and largest city of Egypt, in the northeast part of the country on the Nile River. Population, 6,205,000.

cais•son (kā′sŏn′ *or* kā′sən) *n.* **1.** A watertight structure inside of which construction work is done under water, as in the building of tunnels, bridges, or dams. **2.** A watertight container used to raise a sunken vessel by attaching it to the hull and filling it with air. **3.** A floating structure used to close the entrance of a dock or canal lock. **4.** A two-wheeled horse-drawn vehicle formerly used to carry military ammunition.

Ca•jan (kā′jən) *n. & adj.* Variant of **Cajun.**

ca•jole (kə jōl′) *tr.v.* **ca•joled, ca•jol•ing, ca•joles.** To persuade by flattery or insincere talk; coax: *Immigrants were cajoled into going west by promises of great wealth and land.*

ca•jol•er•y (kə jō′lə rē). *n., pl.* **ca•jol•er•ies.** Persuasion by flattery or insincere talk.

Ca•jun also **Ca•jan** (kā′jən) *n.* A member of a group of people living in Louisiana and descended from French colonists exiled from Acadia in the 18th century. —*adj.* Of or relating to the Cajuns: *Cajun life; Cajun cooking.*

cake (kāk) *n.* **1.** A sweet baked food made of flour, liquid, eggs, and other ingredients, often round or rectangular in shape and having icing on the top and sides. **2.** A flat rounded mass of dough or batter that is baked or fried: *a wheat cake.* **3.** A flat rounded mass of chopped food that is baked or

Julius Caesar

caftan

cairn

ă	pat	oi	boy
ā	pay	ou	out
âr	care	o͝o	took
ä	father	o͞o	boot
ĕ	pet	ŭ	cut
ē	be	ûr	urge
ĭ	pit	th	thin
ī	pie	*th*	this
îr	pier	hw	whoop
ŏ	pot	zh	vision
ō	toe	ə	about
ô	paw	N	*French* bon

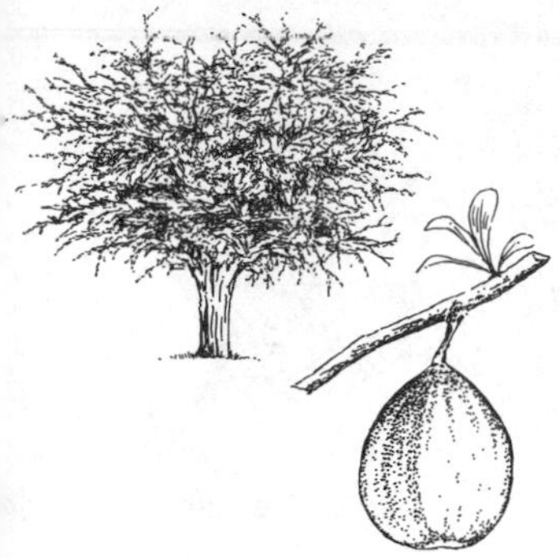

calabash

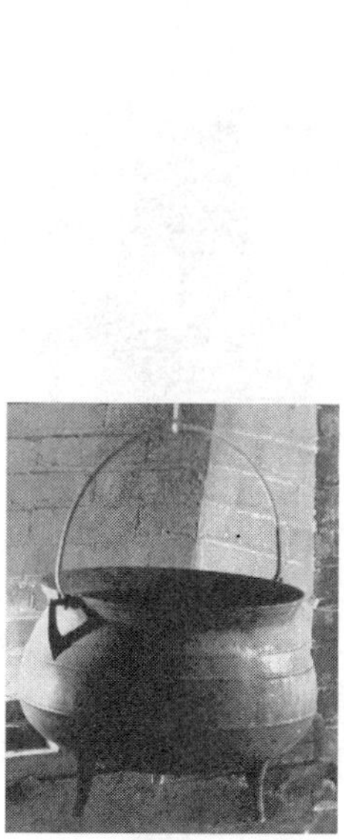

caldron

fried: *a fish cake.* **4.** A shaped or molded piece, as of soap. *—v.* **caked, cake•ing, cakes.** *—tr.* To cover or fill with a thick layer; encrust: *My shoes are caked with mud.* *—intr.* To form into a compact mass: *The melted cheese caked on the counter as it cooled.*

cake•walk (kāk′wôk′) *n.* **1.** Something that is easily accomplished. **2.** A public entertainment among American Black people in the 19th century in which walkers performing the most original steps won cakes as prizes. **3.a.** A strutting dance. **b.** The music for this dance. *—intr.v.* **cake•walked, cake•walk•ing, cake•walks.** To perform a strutting dance. **—cake′walk′er** *n.*

cal or **Cal** *abbr.* An abbreviation of calorie.

Cal. *abbr.* An abbreviation of California.

cal•a•bash (kăl′ə băsh′) *n.* **1.a.** A large gourd having a hard rind. **b.** The vine that bears such gourds. **2.a.** The similar fruit of a tropical American tree. **b.** The tree that bears such fruit. **3.** A bowl, ladle, or other article made from the hollowed-out shell of either of these fruits.

cal•a•boose (kăl′ə bo͞os′) *n.* A jail. [First written down in 1792 in Modern English, from Spanish *calabozo*, dungeon.]

Ca•lais (kă lā′ *or* kăl′ā). A city of northern France west of Brussels, Belgium, and southeast of Dover, England. Population, 76,527.

cal•a•mine (kăl′ə mīn′ *or* kăl′ə mĭn) *n.* A pink powder used in skin lotions and composed of zinc oxide mixed with a small amount of ferric oxide.

ca•lam•i•tous (kə lăm′ĭ təs) *adj.* Causing or resulting in a calamity; disastrous. **—ca•lam′i•tous•ly** *adv.*

ca•lam•i•ty (kə lăm′ĭ tē) *n., pl.* **ca•lam•i•ties. 1.** An event that causes great distress and suffering; a disaster: *The long summer drought was a calamity for farmers.* **2.** Distress or misfortune: *the calamity of unemployment.*

cal•car•e•ous (kăl kâr′ē əs) *adj.* Composed of or containing limestone, calcium, or calcium carbonate; chalky.

cal•ci•fi•ca•tion (kăl′sə fĭ kā′shən) *n.* **1.a.** The process of calcifying: *Calcification of cartilage often causes stiffness in the joints of the body.* **b.** A calcified part, such as tissue or an organ. **2.** The accumulation of calcium in certain soils, especially soils of cool temperate regions where leaching takes place very slowly.

cal•ci•fy (kăl′sə fī′) *tr. & intr.v.* **cal•ci•fied, cal•ci•fy•ing, cal•ci•fies.** To make or become stony or chalky by the deposit of calcium salts.

cal•ci•mine (kăl′sə mīn′) *n.* A white or tinted mixture of zinc oxide, water, and glue, formerly used to coat walls and ceilings. *—tr.v.* **cal•ci•mined, cal•ci•min•ing, cal•ci•mines.** To coat or wash (a surface) with calcimine.

cal•cine (kăl sīn′ *or* kăl′sīn′) *v.* **cal•cined, cal•cin•ing, cal•cines.** *—tr.* To dry, reduce, or oxidize (a substance) by heating it to a high temperature without causing it to melt: *a furnace to calcine limestone.* *—intr.* To be dried, reduced, or oxidized by intense heat. **—cal′ci•na′tion** (kăl′sə nā′shən) *n.*

cal•cite (kăl′sīt′) *n.* A crystalline mineral that is the main component of chalk, limestone, and marble. It is a natural form of calcium carbonate.

cal•ci•um (kăl′sē əm) *n. Symbol* **Ca** A soft, silvery-white metallic element found in limestone, chalk, milk, and bone. It is essential for the normal growth and development of most plants and animals. Calcium is used in alloys, plaster, and cement. Atomic number 20. See table at **element.** [First written down in 1808 in Modern English, from Latin *calx*, lime.]

calcium carbide *n.* A crystalline grayish-black compound of carbon and calcium that has the formula CaC_2 and reacts with water to form acetylene gas.

calcium carbonate *n.* A white or colorless crystalline compound of calcium, carbon, and oxygen that has the formula $CaCO_3$ and occurs naturally in chalk, limestone, and marble. It is used in the manufacture of toothpaste, white paint, and cleaning powder.

calcium chloride *n.* A white crystalline salt composed of calcium and chlorine and having the formula $CaCl_2$. It attracts water very strongly and is used in refrigeration and on roads to settle dust or melt ice.

calcium hydroxide *n.* A soft white powder composed of calcium, hydrogen, and oxygen and having the formula $Ca(OH)_2$. It is made by adding water to lime and used in making mortar, cement, and a variety of industrial products.

calcium oxide *n.* A white lumpy powder composed of calcium and oxygen and having the formula CaO; lime. It is obtained by heating limestone and used in making steel, glass, and insecticides and as an industrial alkali.

cal•cu•la•ble (kăl′kyə lə bəl) *adj.* Capable of being calculated or estimated. **—cal′cu•la•bil′i•ty** *n.*

cal•cu•late (kăl′kyə lāt′) *v.* **cal•cu•lat•ed, cal•cu•lat•ing, cal•cu•lates.** *—tr.* **1.** To find or determine (an answer or a result) by using mathematics; reckon: *calculate the total cost of the trip.* **2.** To make an estimate of; evaluate: *calculate the possibilties of succeeding.* **3.** To make for a specific purpose; design: *His remarks were calculated to please the stockholders.* *—intr.* **1.** To perform a mathematical process, such as addition; figure. **2.** *Informal.* To count, depend, or rely: *We are calculating on your help.* [First written down in 1570 in Modern English, from Latin *calculus*, small stone used for counting.]

cal•cu•lat•ed (kăl′kyə lā′tĭd) *adj.* **1.** Carefully estimated in advance: *a calculated risk.* **2.** Made or planned to accomplish a specific purpose: *a smile calculated to win favor.* **3.** Determined by mathematical calculation.

cal•cu•lat•ing (kăl′kyə lā′tĭng) *adj.* **1.** Used in or for performing calculation: *a calculating machine.* **2.** Shrewd; crafty: *the calculating defense of an experienced attorney.* **3.** Selfish; scheming: *a cold and calculating criminal.*

cal•cu•la•tion (kăl′kyə lā′shən) *n.* **1.** The act, process, or result of calculating: *All the calculations in my math homework turned out to be correct.* **2.** Careful thinking or planning: *They won the game by clever calculation.*

cal•cu•la•tor (kăl′kyə lā′tər) *n.* **1.** A person who calculates. **2.** A machine that automatically performs mathematical computations.

cal•cu•lus (kăl′kyə ləs) *n., pl.* **cal•cu•li** (kăl′kyə lī′) or **cal•cu•lus•es. 1.** An abnormal hard mass, usually of mineral salts, that forms in the body and is often found in the urinary bladder, gallbladder, or kidney. **2.** The branch of mathematics that extends the use of algebra to problems that involve rates of change in quantities. [First written down in 1666 in Modern English, from Latin *calculus*, small stone used for counting.]

Cal•cut•ta (kăl kŭt′ə). The largest city of India, in the eastern part of the country in the delta of the Ganges River. It was founded about 1690. Population, 3,305,006.

cal•dron also **caul•dron** (kôl′drən) *n.* A large kettle for boiling. [First written down about 1300 in Middle English and spelled *caudroun*, from Late Latin *caldāria*.]

cal•en•dar (kăl′ən dər) *n.* **1.** A chart showing the months, weeks, and days of a certain year. **2.** Any of various systems for reckoning time with regard to the beginning, length, and divisions of a year: *Many of the world's calendars divide the year into twelve months.* **3.** A list of dates, as of events or things to be done, arranged in order of time of occurrence: *a court calendar.* [First written down before 1200 in Middle English and spelled *calender*, from Latin *kalendārium*, account book.]

❑ *These sound alike:* **calendar, calender** (machine for treating paper).

cal•en•der (kăl′ən dər) *n.* A machine in which paper or cloth is given a smooth glossy finish by being pressed between rollers. —*tr.v.* **cal•en•dered, cal•en•der•ing, cal•en•ders.** To treat (paper or cloth) with a calender.

❑ *These sound alike:* **calender, calendar** (time chart).

calf[1] (kăf) *n., pl.* **calves** (kăvz). **1.** A young cow or bull. **2.** The young of certain other mammals, such as the elephant or whale. **3.** A type of leather made from the hide of a calf; calfskin. [First written down before 800 in Old English and spelled *cælf*.]

calf[2] (kăf) *n., pl.* **calves** (kăvz). The muscular back part of the human leg between the knee and ankle. [First written down before 1325 in Middle English, from Old Norse *kālfi*.]

calf•skin (kăf′skĭn′) *n.* The hide of a calf or leather made from it.

Cal•ga•ry (kăl′gə rē). A city of southern Alberta, Canada, south of Edmonton. The 1988 Winter Olympics were held here. Population, 592,743.

Cal•houn (kăl ho͞on′), **John Caldwell.** 1782–1850. Vice President of the United States (1825–1832) under John Quincy Adams and Andrew Jackson.

cal•i•ber (kăl′ə bər) *n.* **1.a.** The diameter of the inside of a tube. **b.** The inside diameter or bore of a firearm, usually expressed in decimal fractions. **2.** The diameter of a bullet or other projectile intended for a firearm: *a .45-caliber bullet.* **3.** Degree of worth; quality: *A judge should be a citizen of high caliber.*

cal•i•brate (kăl′ə brāt′) *tr.v.* **cal•i•brat•ed, cal•i•brat•ing, cal•i•brates. 1.** To check, adjust, or standardize (a measuring instrument), usually by comparing with an accepted model: *calibrate an oven thermometer.* **2.** To determine the caliber of (a tube). —**cal′i•bra′tion** *n.*

cal•i•co (kăl′ĭ kō′) *n., pl.* **cal•i•coes** or **cal•i•cos. 1.** A cotton cloth with a brightly colored or closely printed pattern. **2.** An animal, such as a cat, having a coat that has red, white, and black patches.

ca•lif (kā′lĭf *or* kăl′ĭf) *n.* Variant of **caliph.**

Cal•i•for•nia (kăl′ĭ fôr′nyə). A state of the western United States on the Pacific Ocean south of Oregon. It was admitted as the 31st state in 1850. Sacramento is the capital and Los Angeles the largest city. Population, 29,839,250. —SEE NOTE.

cal•i•for•ni•um (kăl′ə fôr′nē əm) *n. Symbol* **Cf** A radioactive metallic element produced artificially from curium. It has isotopes with mass numbers ranging from 244 to 254 and half-lives from 25 minutes to 800 years. Atomic number 98. See table at **element.**

cal•i•per also **cal•li•per** (kăl′ə pər) *n.* An instrument having two hinged legs that can be adjusted to measure diameter, thickness, or the distance between two points, as on a map or scale. Often used in the plural.

ca•liph also **ca•lif** (kā′lĭf *or* kăl′ĭf) *n.* A male leader of an Islamic nation.

ca•liph•ate (kā′lĭ fāt′ *or* kăl′ĭ fāt′) *n.* The office or reign of a caliph or the land under his rule.

cal•is•then•ics (kăl′ĭs thĕn′ĭks) *n.* **1.** *(used with a plural verb).* Gymnastic exercises usually done without special equipment to develop muscular strength and general health. **2.** *(used with a singular verb).* The practice of such exercises. [First written down in 1847 in Modern English : from Greek *kalli-*, beautiful + *sthenos*, strength.] —**cal′is•then′ic** *adj.*

calk[1] (kôk) *n.* A pointed piece of metal on the bottom of a horse's shoe, designed to prevent slipping. [First written down probably in 1447 in Middle English and spelled *kakun*, possibly from Latin *calcāneum*, heel bone.]

calk[2] (kôk) *v.* Variant of **caulk.**

call (kôl) *v.* **called, call•ing, calls.** —*tr.* **1.** To say in a loud voice; announce: *call the dog; call directions in a square dance.* **2.** To send for; summon: *call the fire department; call the guests in to dinner.* **3.** To summon to a particular career or pursuit: *felt he was called to the priesthood.* **4.** To order or invite to assemble; convoke: *call a meeting.* **5.** To bring into being, effect, or action, as by giving an order: *Either country could call an end to the trade agreements.* **6.a.** To give a name to; name: *What did they call the baby?* **b.** To describe as; designate: *We call her the athlete of the family.* **7.** To estimate as being; regard as; consider: *I would call him a great writer.* **8.** To telephone (someone): *call a friend and chat.* **9.** To halt or postpone; suspend: *call a game on account of rain.* **10.** To predict accurately: *The reporter called the outcome of the election.* **11.** To demand payment of: *The bank called the loan.* **12.** In baseball, to indicate a decision in regard to (a pitch, ball, or player): *The umpire called him safe.* **13.** To choose or select (plays to be made), as in football. **14.** In poker, to equal the bet of (the preceding bettor). —*intr.* **1.** To attract attention by shouting: *call until help comes.* **2.** To utter a characteristic cry: *pheasants calling to each other.* **3.** To telephone someone: *You've already called several times.* **4.** To pay a short visit: *We called to pay our respects.* —*n.* **1.** A shout or loud cry: *A frightened call came from the woods.* **2.a.** The typical cry of an animal, especially a bird: *the call of the blue jay.* **b.** An instrument or sound made to imitate such a cry, used as a lure: *a duck call used by hunters.* **c.** A word habitually used as a signal or direction: *Square dancing calls can be hard to follow.* **3.** A signal, such as one made by a horn or bell: *a bugle call to meals.* **4.** The act or an instance of communicating or trying to communicate by telephone: *an afternoon spent making calls to friends.* **5.** A short visit: *a friendly call on new neighbors.* **6.a.** A strong urge or feeling: *felt she had a call to become a teacher.* **b.** Attraction or appeal; fascination: *the call of camping in the wilderness.* **7.** Need, reason, or cause: *There was no call to be unpleasant.* **8.a.** Demand, as for a certain product: *There isn't much call for inkstands today.* **b.** A claim on one's time: *the call of duty.* **9.** In sports, a decision made by an official. —***idioms.*** **call back. 1.** To telephone in return. **2.** To summon (a person) to return: *The company called us back to work.* **call for. 1.** To go and get: *The taxi will call for you at eight.* **2.** To require; demand: *The recipe calls for half a cup of flour.* **call in. 1.** To summon for help or consultation: *call in a specialist.* **2.** To take out of circulation: *call in old dollar bills.* **call into question.** To raise doubt about: *The whole story is called into question by the lack of evidence.* **call off. 1.** To cancel: *call off a game.* **2.** To restrain or recall: *Call off your dogs!* **call on. 1.** To ask or order (someone) to speak: *The teacher called on the new student first.* **2.** To appeal to (someone) to do something: *The principal called on each of us to contribute something.* **call out. 1.** To say in a loud voice; yell: *The rescuers called out for more people to help.* **2.** To cause to assemble; summon: *The governor called out the National*

California

The name of the state of **California** was first used in a Spanish poem written around 1500. In the poem it was the name of a legendary island said to be located "near Paradise." Baja California was the first part of California reached by the Spaniards; it was thought to be an island and was so named after the poetic island. Since the author of the poem probably made up the name, its meaning is not known for certain.

ă	pat	oi	boy
ā	pay	ou	out
âr	care	o͝o	took
ä	father	o͞o	boot
ĕ	pet	ŭ	cut
ē	be	ûr	urge
ĭ	pit	th	thin
ī	pie	*th*	this
îr	pier	hw	whoop
ŏ	pot	zh	vision
ō	toe	ə	about
ô	paw	N	*French* bon

calliope

camcorder

Guard after the earthquake struck. **call to account.** To demand an explanation from: *The student was called to account for being late.* **call to mind.** To remind of: *The movie calls to mind other adventure stories.* **call up.** To summon into military service. **on call.** Available when summoned; ready: *a nurse on call.* [First written down about 1200 in Middle English and spelled *callen*, probably from Old Norse *kalla.*]

cal•la (kăl′ə) *n.* Any of several plants having a thick stalk of small white or yellow flowers surrounded by a long white leaf that resembles a petal.

call•er (kô′lər) *n.* **1.** A person who calls, especially by paying a short visit or making a telephone call: *Several callers came by to see the new baby.* **2.** A person who calls out numbers or directions, as in bingo or square dancing.

cal•lig•ra•phy (kə lĭg′rə fē) *n.* **1.** The art of fine handwriting. **2.** Handwriting. **—cal•lig′ra•pher** *n.*

call•ing (kô′lĭng) *n.* **1.** An inner urge or strong impulse; a call: *Some people feel a calling to travel.* **2.** An occupation, profession, or career: *Writing poetry is her calling.*

calling card *n.* An engraved card bearing one's full name, used for social or business purposes.

cal•li•o•pe (kə lī′ə pē′ *or* kăl′ē ōp′) *n.* A musical instrument consisting of a set of steam whistles controlled from a keyboard and used mostly at carnivals and circuses. [First written down in 1858 in Modern English, from *Calliope.*]

Cal•li•o•pe (kə lī′ə pē′) *n.* In Greek mythology, the Muse of epic poetry.

cal•li•per (kăl′ə pər) *n.* Variant of **caliper.**

call letters *pl.n.* The letters that identify a radio or television station.

call number *n.* A number used in libraries to classify a book and indicate its location on the shelves.

cal•los•i•ty (kə lŏs′ĭ tē) *n., pl.* **cal•los•i•ties. 1.** A hard growth or mass, such as a callus. **2.** Lack of feeling; hardheartedness.

cal•lous (kăl′əs) *adj.* **1.** Having calluses: *the callous hands of a logger.* **2.** Unfeeling; unsympathetic. [First written down before 1400 in Middle English, from Latin *callōsus*, from *callum*, hard skin.] **—cal′lous•ly** *adv.* **—cal′lous•ness** *n.*

❑ *These sound alike:* **callous, callus** (hard skin).

cal•low (kăl′ō) *adj.* Not completely developed; immature; inexperienced: *a callow youngster.* **—cal′low•ly** *adv.* **—cal′low•ness** *n.*

call-up (kôl′ŭp′) *n.* An order to report for military service.

cal•lus (kăl′əs) *n., pl.* **cal•lus•es.** An area of the skin that has become hardened and thick, usually because of prolonged pressure or rubbing.

❑ *These sound alike:* **callus, callous** (unfeeling).

calm (käm) *adj.* **calm•er, calm•est. 1.** Peacefully quiet; not excited; composed: *The children remained calm throughout the storm.* **2.** Nearly motionless; undisturbed; still: *Took a stroll along the calm lake waters.* —*n.* **1.** A condition of being peaceful; tranquillity; serenity: *Her calm was broken by the shouts in the street.* **2.** Lack of motion; stillness: *We felt a calm in the air just before the storm hit.* —*tr. & intr.v.* **calmed, calm•ing, calms.** To make or become calm or quiet: *calm a crying baby; calm down after an argument.* [First written down in 1380 in Middle English and spelled *calme*, from Late Latin *cauma*, resting place in the heat of the day, from Greek *kauma*, burning heat.] **—calm′ly** *adv.* **—calm′ness** *n.*

Synonyms: calm, peaceful, tranquil, placid, serene. These adjectives all describe the absence of any disturbance. **Calm** and **peaceful** mean emotionally untroubled: *The other children tried to annoy her but Charlotte remained calm. Which decade was the most peaceful in American history?* **Tranquil** describes a more lasting calm: *Howard wanted a tranquil life in the country.* **Placid** means calm in a pleasant, lazy way: *We spent an idle, placid weekend at the shore.* **Serene** means spiritually calm: *It took talent to capture her serene expression in the portrait.* **Antonyms: turbulent, upset.**

cal•o•mel (kăl′ə mĕl′ *or* kăl′ə məl) *n.* A white tasteless compound of mercury and chlorine, formerly used as a purgative and insecticide.

ca•lor•ic (kə lôr′ĭk *or* kə lŏr′ĭk) *adj.* Of or relating to heat or calories.

cal•o•rie (kăl′ə rē) *n.* **1.** A unit of heat equal to the amount of heat needed to raise the temperature of one gram of water one degree Celsius; a small calorie. **2.** A unit of heat equal to the amount of heat needed to raise the temperature of 1,000 grams of water one degree Celsius; a large calorie. **3.** A unit for measuring the amount of heat energy supplied by food. [First written down in 1866 in Modern English, from Latin *calor*, heat.]

cal•o•rif•ic (kăl′ə rĭf′ĭk) *adj.* Relating to or generating heat.

cal•o•rim•e•ter (kăl′ə rĭm′ĭ tər) *n.* An apparatus for measuring the quantity of heat given off by or present in a body, as the specific heat of different substances or the heat of chemical combination.

cal•u•met (kăl′yə mĕt′ *or* kăl′yə **mĕt′**) *n.* A sacred or ceremonial pipe used by certain Native American peoples. [First written down in 1665 in Modern English, from Latin *calamus*, reed.]

ca•lum•ni•ate (kə lŭm′nē āt′) *tr.v.* **ca•lum•ni•at•ed, ca•lum•ni•at•ing, ca•lum•ni•ates.** To make false statements about; slander. **—ca•lum′ni•a′tion** *n.* **—ca•lum′ni•a′tor** *n.*

ca•lum•ni•ous (kə lŭm′nē əs) *adj.* Containing or implying calumny; slanderous: *a calumnious attack.* **—ca•lum′ni•ous•ly** *adv.*

cal•um•ny (kăl′əm nē) *n., pl.* **cal•um•nies. 1.** A false statement made to injure another person's reputation: *calumnies springing from jealousy.* **2.** The making of such statements; slander.

Cal•va•ry (kăl′və rē *or* kăl′vrē) also **Gol•go•tha** (gŏl′gə thə). A hill outside ancient Jerusalem where Jesus was crucified.

calve (kăv) *intr.v.* **calved, calv•ing, calves. 1.** To give birth to a calf. **2.** To break and drop off a large mass of ice: *Glaciers calve.*

calves[1] (kăvz) *n.* Plural **calf**[1].

calves[2] (kăvz) *n.* Plural of **calf**[2].

Cal•vin (kăl′vĭn), **John.** 1509–1564. French-born Swiss Protestant whose theology is known today as Presbyterianism.

Cal•vin•ism (kăl′vĭ nĭz′əm) *n.* The Protestant doctrines of John Calvin, emphasizing God's omnipotence and predestination of souls to heaven and hell. [First written down in 1570 in Modern English, after John *Calvin.*] **—Cal′vin•ist** *n. & adj.* **—Cal′vin•is′tic** *adj.*

ca•ly•ces (kā′lĭ sēz′ *or* kăl′ĭ sēz′) *n.* A plural of **calyx.**

Ca•lyp•so or **ca•lyp•so** (kə lĭp′sō) *n.* A type of music that originated in the West Indies, characterized by improvised lyrics about humorous or timely subjects.

ca•lyx (kā′lĭks *or* kăl′ĭks) *n., pl.* **ca•lyx•es** or **ca•ly•ces** (kā′lĭ sēz′ *or* kăl′ĭ sēz′). The sepals of a flower considered as a group.

cam (kăm) *n.* An oddly shaped wheel or a projection on a wheel that is attached to a shaft and changes a regular circular motion into a back-and-forth motion in another part.

CAM *abbr.* An abbreviation of computer-aided manufacturing.

ca•ma•ra•der•ie (kä′mə rä′də rē *or* kăm′ə răd′ə rē) *n.* Goodwill and warm feeling between or among friends; comradeship.
cam•ber (kăm′bər) *n.* A slightly arched surface, as of a road or a ship's deck.
cam•bi•um (kăm′bē əm) *n.* A layer of tissue in the stems and roots of many seed-bearing plants, consisting of cells that divide rapidly and develop into tissues necessary for growth, support, and protection.
Cam•bo•di•a (kăm bō′dē ə) or **Kam•pu•che•a** (kăm′po͞o chē′ə). A country of southeast Asia southeast of Thailand. Cambodia gained its independence from France in 1953. Phnom Penh is the capital and the largest city. Population, 5,756,141.
Cam•bri•an (kăm′brē ən) *adj.* Of, belonging to, or being the geologic time of the earliest period of the Paleozoic Era. During the Cambrian there were large numbers of primitive invertebrate marine animals. See table at **geologic time.** —*n.* The Cambrian Period or its series of rocks.
cam•bric (kām′brĭk) *n.* A fine white linen or cotton cloth.
cambric tea *n.* A hot drink made from milk, sugar, water and usually a small amount of tea.
Cam•bridge (kām′brĭj). **1.** A borough of east-central England north-northeast of London. It is the site of Cambridge University. Population, 100,200. **2.** A city of eastern Massachusetts west of Boston. It was settled in 1630. Population, 95,802.
cam•cord•er (kăm′kôr′dər) *n.* A videotape recorder combined with a TV camera: *The portable camcorder allows on-the-scene news coverage.*
Cam•den (kăm′dən). A city of western New Jersey southwest of Trenton. The poet Walt Whitman lived here from 1873 to 1892. Population, 87,492.
came (kām) *v.* Past tense of **come.**
cam•el (kăm′əl) *n.* A long-necked humped mammal of northern Africa and western Asia that chews its cud and has the ability to go without water for long periods of time. It is widely used in desert regions for riding and carrying loads. [First written down about 950 in Old English, from Greek *kamēlos.*]
ca•mel•lia (kə mēl′yə) *n.* **1.** Any of several shrubs or trees having glossy evergreen leaves and showy flowers with waxy petals. **2.** The flower of such a shrub or tree, resembling a rose. [First written down in 1753 in Modern English, after George Josef *Kamel* (1661–1706), Jesuit missionary.]
Cam•e•lot (kăm′ə lŏt′) *n.* In Arthurian legend, the site of King Arthur's court.
cam•el's hair (kăm′əlz) *n.* **1.** The soft fine hair of a camel or a substitute for it. **2.** A soft, heavy, usually light tan cloth made chiefly of camel's hair.
Cam•em•bert (kăm′əm bâr′) *n.* A creamy rich cheese that softens on the inside as it matures.
cam•e•o (kăm′ē ō′) *n., pl.* **cam•e•os.** A gem, shell, or medallion usually having a carved design that projects from a background of a different color.
cam•er•a (kăm′ər ə *or* kăm′rə) *n.* **1.** A device for taking photographs, consisting of a lightproof box equipped with a lens through which light is focused to record an image on light-sensitive film. **2.** A similar device used in television that receives an image and changes it into electrical signals. [First written down in 1708 in Modern English, from Late Latin *camera,* chamber, from Greek *kamara,* vault.]
cam•er•a•man (kăm′ər ə măn′ *or* kăm′rə măn′) *n.* A man who operates a movie or television camera.
cam•er•a•wom•an (kăm′ər ə wo͝om′ən *or* kăm′rə wo͝om′ən) *n.* A woman who operates a movie or television camera.
Cam•e•roon (kăm′ə ro͞on′). A country of west-central Africa on the Atlantic Ocean southeast of Nigeria. It gained its independence from France and Great Britain in 1960. Capital, Yaoundé. Population, 9,542,400.
cam•i•sole (kăm′ĭ sōl′) *n.* A short sleeveless undergarment worn by a woman or girl.
cam•o•mile (kăm′ə mīl′ *or* kăm′ə mēl′) *n.* Variant of **chamomile.**
cam•ou•flage (kăm′ə fläzh′ *or* kăm′ə fläj′) *n.* **1.** A method of concealing military troops or equipment by making them appear to be part of the natural surroundings. **2.** Protective coloring or a disguise that conceals: *An alligator's camouflage makes it look like a log floating in the water.* **3.** Cloth or other material used for camouflage. —*tr.v.* **cam•ou•flaged, cam•ou•flag•ing, cam•ou•flag•es.** To conceal or hide by camouflage.
camp (kămp) *n.* **1.** A place where a group of people, such as vacationers, miners, or soldiers, live temporarily in tents, cabins, or other rough shelters. **2.** A cabin or shelter or group of such buildings: *They have a camp on a lake.* **3.** A place in the country that offers recreational activities or instruction, as for children on vacation. —*intr.v.* **camped, camp•ing, camps. 1.** To make or set up a camp: *We camped next to the river.* **2.** To live in or as if in a camp: *Our friends camped for a month in the Rocky Mountains.* [First written down in 1528 in Modern English, from Latin *campus,* field.]
cam•paign (kăm pān′) *n.* **1.** A series of military operations undertaken to achieve a specific purpose in a certain area: *Grant's campaign secured the Mississippi River for the Union.* **2.** Organized activity to attain a political, social, or commercial goal: *an advertising campaign.* —*intr.v.* **cam•paigned, cam•paign•ing, cam•paigns.** To engage in a campaign: *The candidates campaigned on television.* [First written down in 1647 in Modern English, from Late Latin *campānia,* battlefield, from *campus,* field.] —**cam•paign′er** *n.*
cam•pa•ni•le (kăm′pə nē′lē) *n., pl.* **cam•pa•ni•les** (kăm′pə nē′lēz) or **cam•pa•ni•li** (kăm′pə nē′lē). A bell tower, especially one near but not attached to a church or other building.
Camp•bell (kăm′bəl), **(Avril) Kim.** Born 1947. Canadian politician who was the first woman to serve as Canadian prime minister (1993).
camp•er (kăm′pər) *n.* **1.** A person who camps outdoors. **2.** A boy or girl who attends a summer camp. **3.** A motor vehicle having a space equipped as a dwelling place for camping on long trips.
camp•fire (kămp′fīr′) *n.* An outdoor fire in a camp, used for warmth or cooking.
Camp Fire Girl *n.* A member of an organization for girls that attempts to teach good values and develop practical skills.
camp•ground (kămp′ground′) *n.* An area used for setting up a camp or holding a camp meeting.
cam•phor (kăm′fər) *n.* A white crystalline compound of carbon, hydrogen, and oxygen in the proportions $C_{10}H_{16}O$, obtained from the aromatic wood of an evergreen tree of eastern Asia and used as an insect repellent, in making films, plastics, and explosives, and in medicine as a stimulant.
camp meeting *n.* An evangelistic gathering held in a tent or outdoors and often lasting a number of days.
camp•site (kămp′sīt′) *n.* An area used for camping.
cam•pus (kăm′pəs) *n., pl.* **cam•pus•es.** The grounds of a school, college, hospital, or university.
cam•shaft (kăm′shăft′) *n.* A shaft fitted with one or more cams, as in a gasoline engine.
can[1] (kăn; kən *when unstressed*) *aux.v.* Past tense **could** (ko͝od). **1.** To know how to: *My cousin can speak Arabic.* **2.** To be able to: *I can skate backward.* **3.** To possess the right or power to: *The President can veto bills passed by Congress.* **4.** To have

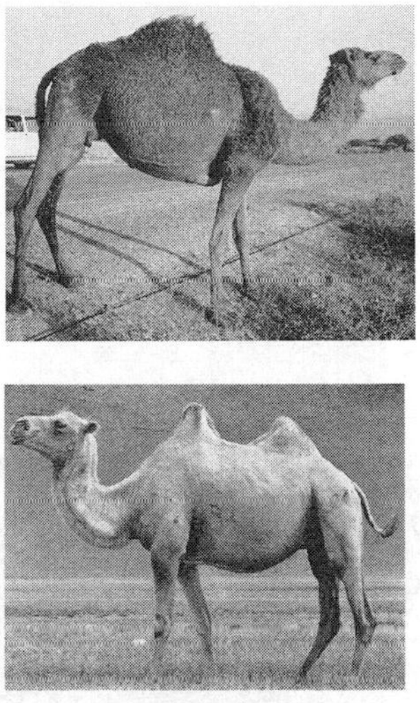

camel
Top: Dromedary
Bottom: Bactrian camel

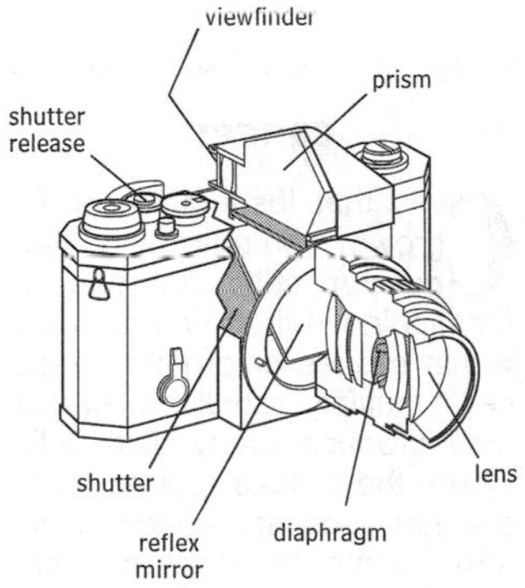

camera

ă	**pat**	oi	**boy**
ā	**pay**	ou	**out**
âr	**care**	o͝o	**took**
ä	**father**	o͞o	**boot**
ĕ	**pet**	ŭ	**cut**
ē	**be**	ûr	**urge**
ĭ	**pit**	th	**thin**
ī	**pie**	*th*	**this**
îr	**pier**	hw	**whoop**
ŏ	**pot**	zh	**vision**
ō	**toe**	ə	**about**
ô	**paw**	N	*French* **bon**

permission to; be allowed to: *You can borrow my pen if you like.* [First written down about 725 in Old English, from *cunnan*, to know, know how.]

can² (kăn) *n.* **1.a.** An airtight metal container in which food and beverages are preserved: *Put the empty cans in the trash.* **b.** The contents of such a container: *The baby ate a whole can of peaches.* **2.** A usually cylindrical metal container: *a garbage can.* —*tr.v.* **canned, can•ning, cans.** To preserve (food) in a sealed container: *spent the morning canning beans.* [First written down about 1000 in Old English and spelled *canne*, container.]

Can. *abbr.* An abbreviation of: **1.** Canada. **2.** Canadian.

Ca•naan (kā′nən). An ancient region of Palestine referred to in the Bible as the Promised Land.

Ca•naan•ite (kā′nə nīt′) *n.* A member of a Semitic people inhabiting Canaan before its conquest by the Israelites. —*adj.* Of or relating to Canaan or its people, language, or culture.

Can•a•da (kăn′ə də). A country of northern North America. The Dominion of Canada was formed in 1867. Ottawa, in Ontario, is the capital, and Montreal, in Quebec, is the largest city. Population, 23,343,181. —**Ca•na′di•an** (kə nā′dē ən) *adj. & n.*

Canada Day *n.* July 1, observed in Canada in commemoration of the formation of the Dominion in 1867.

Canada goose or **Canadian goose** *n.* A North American wild goose having gray, black, and white feathers and a white patch on its face.

Canadian bacon *n.* Cured, rolled, and very lean bacon from the loin of a pig.

Canadian French *n.* The French language as spoken in Canada.

ca•nal (kə năl′) *n.* **1.** A waterway that is built or artificially improved for irrigation, drainage, or navigation. **2.** A tube or duct in the body of an animal or plant, as for the passage of liquid, air, food, or other matter: *the alimentary canal; the ear canal.* **3.** One of the faint lines seen in early telescopic images of the surface of Mars.

Ca•nal Zone (kə năl′). A strip of land, about 10 miles (16 kilometers) wide, across the Isthmus of Panama.

ca•nard (kə närd′) *n.* An unfounded or false, deliberately misleading story.

ca•nar•y (kə nâr′ē) *n., pl.* **ca•nar•ies. 1.** A small greenish to yellow finch that is popular as a pet. **2.** A light to moderate or bright yellow. [First written down in 1576 in Modern English and spelled *canary bird*, from Spanish *canario*, of the Canary Islands, from Late Latin *Canăriae (Īnsulae)*, (islands) of dogs, from Latin *canis*, dog.]

Ca•nar•y Islands (kə nâr′ē). A group of Spanish islands in the Atlantic Ocean off the northwest coast of Africa.

Ca•nav•er•al (kə năv′ər əl *or* kə năv′rəl), **Cape.** Formerly (1963–1973) Cape **Ken•ne•dy** (kĕn′ĭ dē). A sandy promontory in the Atlantic Ocean off a barrier island on the east-central coast of Florida. It is the site of NASA's launching area for U.S. space missions.

Can•ber•ra (kăn′bər ə *or* kăn′bĕr′ə). The capital of Australia, in the southeast part of the country southwest of Sydney. It was settled in 1824. Population, 243,450.

can•cel (kăn′səl) *v.* **can•celed, can•cel•ing, can•cels** also **can•celled, can•cel•ling, can•cels.** —*tr.* **1.** To cross out with lines or other markings: *cancel items on a shopping list.* **2.** To make invalid; call off: *cancel an appointment.* **3.** To mark or perforate (a postage stamp, for example) to indicate that it may not be used again. **4.** To make up for; offset; balance: *Two opposing votes cancel each other out.* **5.a.** To remove (a common factor) from the numerator and denominator of a fraction. **b.** To remove (a common term or factor) from both sides of an equation. —*intr.* To balance or offset each other: *Spending and saving often cancel out.*

can•cel•la•tion (kăn′sə lā′shən) *n.* **1.** The act or process of canceling. **2.** A mark made, as on a stamp or check, to indicate that it has been canceled.

can•cer (kăn′sər) *n.* **1.** Any of various diseases in which cells of the body grow in an abnormal and unchecked way, often spreading throughout the body. **2.** A mass of cells that grows and spreads in this manner; a malignant tumor. **3.** A destructive spreading evil: *Poverty is a fearful social cancer.* [First written down about 1000 in Old English and spelled *cancer*, spreading sore, from Latin.] —**can′cer•ous** (kăn′sər əs) *adj.* —See Note.

Can•cer (kăn′sər) *n.* **1.** A constellation in the Northern Hemisphere. **2.** The fourth sign of the zodiac in astrology.

can•del•a (kăn dĕl′ə) *n.* A unit of luminous intensity, used to measure the brightness of a source of light.

can•de•la•bra (kăn′dl ä′brə *or* kăn′dl ăb′rə) *n.* A candelabrum.

can•de•la•brum (kăn′dl ä′brəm *or* kăn′dl ăb′rəm) *n., pl.* **can•de•la•bra** (kăn′dl ä′brə *or* kăn′dl ăb′rə) or **can•de•la•brums.** A large decorative candlestick with several arms or branches for holding candles.

can•did (kăn′dĭd) *adj.* **1.** Direct and frank; straightforward; open: *a candid opinion.* **2.** Free from prejudice; impartial: *a candid judgment.* **3.** Not posed or rehearsed: *a candid photograph.* [First written down in 1630 in Modern English, from Latin *candidus*, glowing, white, pure.] —**can′did•ly** *adv.* —**can′did•ness** *n.*

can•di•da•cy (kăn′dĭ də sē) *n., pl.* **can•di•da•cies.** The fact or condition of being a candidate.

can•di•date (kăn′dĭ dāt′ *or* kăn′dĭ dĭt) *n.* A person who seeks or is nominated for an office, a prize, or an honor. [First written down in 1600 in Modern English, from Latin *candidātus*, clothed in white (from the white togas worn by Romans seeking office), candidate, from *candidus*, white.]

can•died (kăn′dēd) *adj.* Cooked in or coated with a glaze of sugar: *candied sweet potatoes; candied fruit.*

can•dle (kăn′dl) *n.* **1.** A solid stick of wax, tallow, or other fatty substance with a wick inside that is lit and burned to provide light. **2.** An obsolete unit of luminous intensity, replaced by the candela. —*tr.v.* **can•dled, can•dling, can•dles.** To examine (an egg) for freshness by holding it in front of a bright light. [First written down about 725 in Old English and spelled *candel*, from Latin *candēla*.]

can•dle•light (kăn′dl līt′) *n.* **1.** The light given off by a candle. **2.** Dusk; twilight.

Can•dle•mas (kăn′dl məs) *n.* February 2, celebrated in some Christian churches in commemoration of the purification of the Virgin Mary and presentation of the infant Jesus in the temple.

can•dle•pow•er (kăn′dl pou′ər) *n.* The brightness or intensity of a source of light as expressed in candelas.

can•dle•snuff•er (kăn′dl snŭf′ər) *n.* An instrument with a small cup and often a long slender handle, used to extinguish the flame of a candle.

can•dle•stick (kăn′dl stĭk′) *n.* A holder with a cup or spike for a candle.

can•dle•wick (kăn′dl wĭk′) *n.* The wick of a candle.

can•dor (kăn′dər) *n.* **1.** The quality of saying freely what one thinks; openness; frankness: *criticize in all candor without regard to feelings.* **2.** Freedom

canal
The Corinth Canal in Greece

cancer

Cells that lose their normal growth controls are called **cancer** cells. Instead of functioning in their normal roles within tissues or organs, these cells multiply rapidly. Because they produce many new cells where the tissues around them are not growing, cancer cells form lumps of cancerous tissue. They also dissolve the material that would normally hold them in place. Thus freed, they can move around the body and form cancerous masses where they land. Changes to certain growth-control genes cause this uncontrolled increase. If these genes are altered by viruses, chemicals, or radiation, they become *oncogenes*. It is these oncogenes, scientists believe, that direct a cell to multiply abnormally.

from prejudice; fairness: *judge a matter in complete candor.*

can•dy (kăn′dē) *n., pl.* **can•dies. 1.** A sweet food made with sugar and often combined with fruit or nuts. **2.** A single piece of this food. —*v.* **can•died, can•dy•ing, can•dies.** —*tr.* To cook, preserve, or coat with sugar or syrup: *candy apples.* —*intr.* To turn into sugar: *The molasses candied along the edges of the jar.*

candy strip•er (strī′pər) *n.* A volunteer worker in a hospital.

can•dy•tuft (kăn′dē tŭft′) *n.* Any of several plants related to the mustard, having clusters of white, red, or light purple flowers.

cane (kān) *n.* **1.** A stick used as an aid in walking. **2.a.** A thin hollow or woody plant stem that usually has joints and is easily bent. **b.** A plant, such as bamboo or sugar cane, having such stems. **c.** Strips of such stems woven together to make chair seats or other objects. **3.** A rod used in flogging. —*tr.v.* **caned, can•ing, canes. 1.** To beat or flog with a cane. **2.** To make or repair (furniture, for example) with cane.

cane•brake (kān′brāk′) *n.* A dense growth of canes.

cane sugar *n.* A sugar obtained from the juice of sugar cane; sucrose.

ca•nine (kā′nīn) *adj.* **1.** Of, relating to, or characteristic of dogs or similar mammals. **2.** Of or belonging to a family of mammals that includes dogs and wolves. —*n.* **1.** An animal belonging to the canine family, especially a dog. **2.** One of the four pointed teeth next to the incisors; a cuspid. [First written down in 1607 in Modern English, from Latin *canis*, dog.]

can•is•ter (kăn′ĭ stər) *n.* A container, usually of metal, for holding coffee, tea, flour, spices, and other dry foods.

can•ker (kăng′kər) *n.* A sore similar to an ulcer on the lips or in the mouth. [First written down about 1000 in Old English and spelled *cancer*, from Latin *cancer*.]

can•ker•ous (kăng′kər əs) *adj.* **1.** Marked by or affected with a canker; ulcerous: *cankerous gums.* **2.** Tending to cause a canker: *a cankerous irritant.*

canker sore *n.* A canker.

can•ker•worm (kăng′kər wûrm′) *n.* The caterpillar of either of two moths that damages fruit trees and shade trees by feeding on the leaves.

can•na (kăn′ə) *n.* Any of various plants native to the tropics, having large leaves and showy red or yellow flowers.

can•na•bis (kăn′ə bĭs) *n.* **1.** The hemp plant; marijuana. **2.** The dried flowering parts of the hemp plant.

canned (kănd) *adj.* **1.** Preserved and sealed in an airtight can or jar: *canned vegetables.* **2.** *Informal.* Recorded or taped: *canned music.*

can•ner•y (kăn′ə rē) *n., pl.* **can•ner•ies.** A factory where fish, fruit, vegetables, or other foods are canned.

can•ni•bal (kăn′ə bəl) *n.* **1.** A person who eats the flesh of other human beings. **2.** An animal that feeds on others of its own kind.

can•ni•bal•ism (kăn′ə bə lĭz′əm) *n.* The practices of a cannibal. —**can′ni•bal•is′tic** *adj.*

can•ni•bal•ize (kăn′ə bə līz′) *tr.v.* **can•ni•bal•ized, can•ni•bal•iz•ing, can•ni•bal•iz•es.** To remove useful parts from (a machine or equipment) to use in the repair of other equipment: *cannibalize an old truck for its motor.*

can•non (kăn′ən) *n., pl.* **cannon** or **can•nons.** A large gun that is mounted on wheels or on a fixed base and fires heavy projectiles. [First written down in 1400 in Middle English and spelled *canon*, from Old Italian *cannone*, large tube, from Latin *canna*, reed, cane, from Greek *kanna*.]

❑ *These sound alike:* **cannon, canon[1]** (law), **canon[2]** (cleric).

can•non•ade (kăn′ə nād′) *tr. & intr.v.* **can•non•ad•ed, can•non•ad•ing, can•non•ades.** To assault or bombard with heavy artillery fire. —*n.* A long heavy artillery assault or bombardment.

can•non•ball also **cannon ball** (kăn′ən bôl′) *n.* An iron or steel ball fired from a cannon.

can•non•eer (kăn′ə nîr′) *n.* A soldier in the artillery.

can•not (kăn′ŏt *or* kə nŏt′ *or* kă nŏt′) *aux.v.* The negative form of **can[1]**.

can•ny (kăn′ē) *adj.* **can•ni•er, can•ni•est.** Careful and shrewd in one's actions and dealings; cautious. —**can′ni•ly** *adv.* —**can′ni•ness** *n.*

ca•noe (kə no͞o′) *n.* A light narrow boat that has pointed ends and is propelled by paddles. —*intr.v.* **ca•noed, ca•noe•ing, ca•noes.** To paddle or travel in a canoe. —**ca•noe′ist** *n.*

can•on[1] (kăn′ən) *n.* **1.** A law or code of laws enacted by a church. **2.** A principle or standard: *the canons of good behavior.* **3.** The books of the Bible accepted by a Christian church as authentic. **4.** A musical composition or passage in which a melody is repeated by different voices before the first part is finished. [First written down before 900 in Old English, from Latin *canōn*, rule, from Greek *kanōn*, measuring rod, rule.]

❑ *These sound alike:* **canon[1]** (law), **cannon** (gun), **canon[2]** (cleric).

can•on[2] (kăn′ən) *n.* **1.** A cleric serving in a cathedral or collegiate church. **2.** A member of certain religious communities living according to established rules. [First written down before 1200 in Middle English, from Late Latin *canōnicus*, one living under a rule, from *canōn*, rule, from Greek *kanōn*, measuring rod.]

❑ *These sound alike:* **canon[2]** (cleric), **cannon** (gun), **canon[1]** (law).

ca•ñon (kăn′yən) *n.* Variant of **canyon.**

ca•non•i•cal (kə nŏn′ĭ kəl) also **ca•non•ic** (kə nŏn′ĭk) *adj.* **1.** Of, relating to, or required by canon law. **2.** Of or appearing in the biblical canon. **3.** Conforming to established rules.

can•on•ize (kăn′ə nīz′) *tr.v.* **can•on•ized, can•on•iz•ing, can•on•iz•es.** To declare (a dead person) to be a saint. —**can′on•i•za′tion** (kăn′ə nĭ zā′shən) *n.*

canon law *n.* The official body of laws governing matters of faith and practice in a Christian church.

can•o•py (kăn′ə pē) *n., pl.* **can•o•pies. 1.** A covering, usually of cloth, hung above a bed or throne or supported by poles above an important person or a sacred object. **2.** A similar covering: *a canopy of leafy branches.* **3.** The transparent movable enclosure over an aircraft's cockpit. —*tr.v.* **can•o•pied, can•o•py•ing, can•o•pies.** To cover with or as if with a canopy.

canst (kănst) *aux.v. Archaic.* A second person singular present tense of **can[1]**.

cant[1] (kănt) *n.* **1.** A slant or slope: *The cant of the roof makes the rain run off.* **2.a.** A push or motion that causes something to tilt to one side. **b.** The tilt resulting from such a push or motion. —*v.* **cant•ed, cant•ing, cants.** —*tr.* **1.** To give a slanted edge to; bevel. **2.** To cause to slant or tilt to one side: *A gust of wind canted the sailboat so that it capsized.* —*intr.* **1.** To tilt or slant to one side or turn over. **2.** To swing around: *In a sudden turn the boat canted off to southward.* [First written down about 1375 in Middle English and spelled *cant*, side, from Latin *canthus*, rim of a wheel, tire, of Celtic origin.]

❑ *These sound alike:* **cant[1]** (slope), **cant[2]** (talk), **can't** (can not).

candytuft

canoe

canopy

ă	pat	oi	boy
ā	pay	ou	out
âr	care	o͝o	took
ä	father	o͞o	boot
ĕ	pet	ŭ	cut
ē	be	ûr	urge
ĭ	pit	th	thin
ī	pie	*th*	this
îr	pier	hw	whoop
ŏ	pot	zh	vision
ō	toe	ə	about
ô	paw	N	*French* bon

cant[2] (kănt) *n.* **1.** Insincere or trite talk, especially about moral or religious behavior: *hollow words that are mere cant.* **2.** The special vocabulary used by a certain group or class of people; jargon: Deadheading *is railroad cant for running without passengers or freight.* [First written down in 1567 in Modern English and spelled *cant*, to speak in a singsong, from Anglo-Norman *canter*, to sing, from Latin *cantāre*.]

❑ *These sound alike:* **cant[2]** (talk), **cant[1]** (slope), **can't** (can not).

can't (kănt) *v.* Contraction of *can not.*

❑ *These sound alike:* **can't, cant[1]** (slope), **cant[2]** (talk).

can•ta•loupe also **can•ta•loup** (**kăn′**tl ōp′) *n.* A variety of muskmelon having a ribbed rough rind and sweet orange flesh.

can•tan•ker•ous (kăn **tăng′**kər əs) *adj.* Quarrelsome and ill-tempered; disagreeable: *a cantankerous professor who is difficult to study with.* **—can•tan′ker•ous•ly** *adv.* **—can•tan′ker•ous•ness** *n.*

cantilever bridge

can•ta•ta (kən **tä′**tə) *n.* A musical composition centered around a story or poem that is sung by a chorus and soloists but not acted out.

can•teen (kăn **tēn′**) *n.* **1.** A container for carrying water or other liquid to drink. **2.** A store on or near a military base where supplies and refreshments are available. **3.** A place to get food or drinks in a school, factory, or camp.

can•ter (**kăn′**tər) *n.* A slow easy gallop. *—intr. & tr.v.* **can•tered, can•ter•ing, can•ters.** To move or cause to move at a canter: *The horse and rider cantered down the road. She cantered her horse across the field.*

❑ *These sound alike:* **canter, cantor** (singer).

Can•ter•bur•y (**kăn′**tər bĕr′ē). A borough of southeast England east-southeast of London. Canterbury was built on the site of an abbey founded in about 600. Population, 36,000.

cant hook *n.* A wooden pole with a hinged hook near the end, used for handling logs.

can•ti•cle (**kăn′**tĭ kəl) *n.* A song or chant, especially a hymn whose words are taken directly from the Bible.

can•ti•le•ver (**kăn′**tl ē′vər *or* **kăn′**tl ĕv′ər) *n.* A projecting structure, such as a beam, that is supported at only one end. *—tr.v.* **can•ti•le•vered, can•ti•le•ver•ing, can•ti•le•vers.** To build or extend outward as a cantilever.

cantilever bridge *n.* A bridge formed by two cantilevers each supported at one end by a pier and joined in the center by a connecting piece.

can•tle (**kăn′**tl) *n.* The raised part at the back of some saddles.

can•to (**kăn′**tō) *n., pl.* **can•tos.** A principal division of a long poem.

can•ton (**kăn′**tən *or* **kăn′**tŏn′) *n.* A small division of a country, especially one of the states of Switzerland.

Can•ton (**kăn′**tŏn′ *or* kăn′**tŏn′**). Guangzhou.

Can•ton•ese (kăn′tə **nēz′** *or* kăn′tə **nēs′**) *n.* The dialect of Chinese spoken in and around Guangzhou (formerly Canton). **—Can′ton•ese′** *adj.*

can•ton•ment (kăn **tōn′**mənt *or* kăn **tŏn′**mənt) *n.* A military installation in India.

can•tor (**kăn′**tər) *n.* **1.** The official who leads the congregation in the musical part of a Jewish religious service. **2.** The person who leads a church choir or congregation in singing.

❑ *These sound alike:* **cantor, canter** (gait of a horse).

can•vas (**kăn′**vəs) *n.* **1.** A heavy coarse cloth of cotton, hemp, or flax, used for making tents and sails. **2.a.** A piece of canvas used for painting. **b.** An oil painting on canvas: *That artist has several canvases hanging in this museum.*

❑ *These sound alike:* **canvas, canvass** (survey).

can•vas•back (**kăn′**vəs băk′) *n.* A North American wild duck having a reddish head and neck and a whitish back.

can•vass (**kăn′**vəs) *v.* **can•vassed, can•vass•ing, can•vass•es.** *—tr.* **1.** To visit (a person or region) asking for votes, opinions, sales, or contributions. **2.** To examine or discuss thoroughly: *canvass the newspapers for a job; canvass ideas in a meeting.* *—intr.* To go about a region asking for votes, sales, opinions, or contributions: *The candidate canvassed up and down the county for votes.* *—n.* **1.** The act of canvassing. **2.** A thorough examination or discussion. **—can′vass•er** *n.*

❑ *These sound alike:* **canvass, canvas** (cloth).

can•yon also **ca•ñon** (**kăn′**yən) *n.* A deep narrow valley with steep cliff walls, cut into the earth by running water; a gorge. [First written down in 1834 in Modern English and spelled *cañon*, from Spanish, from *caña*, tube, cane, from Latin *canna*, reed, from Greek *kanna*.]

caou•tchouc (**kou′**cho͝ok′ *or* **kou′**cho͞ok′) *n.* Crude natural rubber.

cap[1] (kăp) *n.* **1.a.** A usually soft, close-fitting head covering, either having no brim or with a visor. **b.** A special covering for the head worn to show rank, occupation, or membership in a group: *a soldier's cap.* **2.** A protective cover or seal: *a bottle cap; a cap on a tooth.* **3.a.** The top or highest part: *the polar cap.* **b.** A limit or restraint: *a cap on government spending.* **4.a.** A percussion cap. **b.** A small explosive charge enclosed in paper for use in a toy gun. *—tr.v.* **capped, cap•ping, caps. 1.** To cover, protect, or seal with a cap: *cap a bottle.* **2.** To outdo; excel: *Each joke capped the one before.*

cap[2] (kăp) *n.* A capital letter.

cap. *abbr.* An abbreviation of: **1.** Capacity. **2.** Capital. **3.** Capital letter.

ca•pa•bil•i•ty (kā′pə **bĭl′**ĭ tē) *n., pl.* **ca•pa•bil•i•ties. 1.** The quality of being capable; ability: *prove one's capability for the job.* **2.** Potential ability. Often used in the plural: *live up to one's capabilities.* **3.** The capacity to be used or developed for a specific purpose: *To become more energy-efficient we must make full use of our technological capability.*

ca•pa•ble (**kā′**pə bəl) *adj.* **1.** Having capacity or ability; able; competent: *a capable teacher.* **2.** Having the tendency or disposition: *She's just not capable of saying such a thing.* **3.** Having qualities permitting: *a statement capable of several interpretations.* **—ca′pa•bly** *adv.*

ca•pa•cious (kə **pā′**shəs) *adj.* Capable of containing a large quantity; roomy: *a capacious dining room.* **—ca•pa′cious•ly** *adv.* **—ca•pa′cious•ness** *n.*

ca•pac•i•tance (kə **păs′**ĭ təns) *n.* The capacity of a device to collect and store electric charge. Capacitance is equal to the amount of stored charge divided by the electrical potential of the device.

ca•pac•i•tor (kə **păs′**ĭ tər) *n.* A device used in an electric circuit to store charge temporarily.

ca•pac•i•ty (kə **păs′**ĭ tē) *n., pl.* **ca•pac•i•ties. 1.** The ability to hold, receive, or contain: *a can with a capacity of three quarts; a theater with a small seating capacity.* **2.** The maximum amount that can be contained: *a trunk filled to capacity.* **3.** The ability to perform or produce; capability. **4.** The maximum amount that can be produced: *a machine operating at full capacity.* **5.** Mental ability: *a person's capacity for learning.* **6.** The position in which a person functions; a role: *in your capacity as sales manager.*

ca•par•i•son (kə **păr′**ĭ sən) *n.* **1.** An ornamental covering for a horse or harness. **2.** Rich or fancy clothing; finery. —*tr.v.* **ca•par•i•soned, ca•par•i•son•ing, ca•par•i•sons. 1.** To put a caparison on: *caparison a horse.* **2.** To dress in splendid clothes.

cape[1] (kāp) *n.* A sleeveless outer garment fastened at the throat and worn hanging loose over the shoulders. [First written down before 1200 in Middle English, from Late Latin *cappa*, cloak.]

cape[2] (kāp) *n.* A point of land projecting into a body of water. [First written down about 1387 in Middle English and spelled *cap*, from Latin *caput*, head.]

Cape Bret•on Island (**brĕt′**n *or* **brĭt′**n). An island forming the northeast part of Nova Scotia, Canada.

ca•per[1] (**kā′**pər) *n.* **1.** A playful leap or hop: *the capers of a frisky pony.* **2.** A prank: *Halloween capers.* **3.** *Slang.* A criminal plot or act, especially one involving theft. —*intr.v.* **ca•pered, ca•per•ing, ca•pers.** To jump about playfully; gambol: *The lambs capered about the meadow.* [First written down in 1580 in Modern English, alteration of French *capriole*, a leap by a horse, from Italian *capriola*, somersault, from Latin *caper*, goat.]

ca•per[2] (**kā′**pər) *n.* **1.** A pickled flower bud of a spiny trailing shrub of the Mediterranean region, used to season food or eaten as a relish. **2.** The shrub that bears such buds. [First written down before 1382 in Middle English and spelled *caperis*, from Greek *kapparis*.]

Cape Town or **Cape•town** (**kāp′**toun′). The legislative capital of South Africa, in the extreme southwest part of the country on the Atlantic Ocean. It was founded in 1652. Population, 859,940.

Cape Verde (vûrd). An island country of the Atlantic Ocean west of Senegal. The islands gained independence from Portugal in 1975. Capital, Praia. Population, 296,093.

cap•il•lar•i•ty (kăp′ə **lăr′**ĭ tē) *n., pl.* **cap•il•lar•i•ties.** The tendency of the surface of a liquid to rise or fall where it is in contact with a solid, as in a capillary tube.

cap•il•lar•y (**kăp′**ə lĕr′ē) *adj.* **1.** Relating to or resembling a hair; fine; slender. **2.** Having a very small inside diameter. **3.** Of or relating to the capillaries in the body. —*n., pl.* **cap•il•lar•ies. 1.** One of the tiny blood vessels that connect the smallest arteries to the smallest veins. **2.** A tube that has a very small inside diameter.

capillary action *n.* Capillarity.

capillary attraction *n.* The force that causes a liquid to rise in a narrow tube or when in contact with a porous substance. It is the force that allows a paper towel to soak up a liquid or plants to draw up water from the ground.

capillary repulsion *n.* The force that causes a liquid, such as mercury, to be depressed when in contact with the sides of a narrow tube.

cap•i•tal[1] (**kăp′**ĭ tl) *n.* **1.** A city that is the seat of a state or national government: *Every state has a capital.* **2.** Wealth in the form of money or property that has accumulated in a business and is often used to create more wealth. **3.** A capital letter. —*adj.* **1.** First and foremost; principal: *a decision of capital importance.* **2.** Excellent; first-rate: *a capital idea.* **3.** Punishable by or involving death: *a capital offense.* **4.** Of or involving wealth and its use in investment: *capital improvements in the plant site.* **5.** Relating to a seat of government: *a capital city.* [First written down before 1200 in Middle English and spelled *capital*, principal, from Latin *capitālis*, from *caput*, head, money laid out.] —SEE NOTE.

❑ *These sound alike:* **capital[1]** (city), **capital[2]** (top of a column), **capitol** (building).

cap•i•tal[2] (**kăp′**ĭ tl) *n.* The top part of a pillar or column. [First written down before 1300 in Middle English, from Late Latin *capitellum*, diminutive of Latin *caput*, head.]

❑ *These sound alike:* **capital[2]** (top of a column), **capital[1]** (city), **capitol** (building).

capital gain *n.* The profit made by selling an investment, such as a stock or a piece of property.

cap•i•tal•ism (**kăp′**ĭ tl ĭz′əm) *n.* An economic system in which the means of production and distribution are privately owned by individuals or groups and competition for business establishes the price of goods and services. The means of production include labor, land, factories, and services. The means of distribution include trains, trucks, and airlines.

cap•i•tal•ist (**kăp′**ĭ tl ĭst) *n.* **1.a.** A person who invests capital in business, especially a large investor in an important business. **b.** A person of great wealth **2.** A person who supports capitalism. —*adj.* Of or relating to capitalism or capitalists: *a capitalist country.* —**cap′i•tal•is′tic** *adj.* —**cap′i•tal•is′ti•cal•ly** *adv.*

cap•i•tal•ize (**kăp′**ĭ tl īz′) *v.* **cap•i•tal•ized, cap•i•tal•iz•ing, cap•i•tal•iz•es.** —*tr.* **1.** To write or print with a capital letter or letters: *capitalize the title of a report.* **2.** To supply with capital or funds. —*intr.* To turn to advantage; profit by: *capitalize on an opponent's errors.* —**cap′i•tal•i•za′tion** (kăp′ĭ tl ĭ **zā′**shən) *n.*

capital letter *n.* A letter, such as A or B, written or printed in a size larger than and often in a form differing from its corresponding lowercase letter.

cap•i•tal•ly (**kăp′**ĭ tl ē) *adv.* In an excellent manner; admirably.

capital punishment *n.* The death penalty for certain crimes, such as murder or treason.

capital ship *n.* A warship of the largest class, such as a battleship.

capital stock *n.* The total amount of a company's stock, including both common and protected stock.

cap•i•tol (**kăp′**ĭ tl) *n.* **1. Capitol.** The building in Washington, D.C., where the Congress of the United States meets. **2.** A building in which a state legislature assembles. [First written down about 1375 in Middle English and spelled *capitolie*, Jupiter's temple in Rome, from Latin *Capitōlium*.] —SEE NOTE at **capital[1]**.

❑ *These sound alike:* **capitol, capital[1]** (city), **capital[2]** (top of a column).

ca•pit•u•late (kə **pĭch′**ə lāt′) *intr.v.* **ca•pit•u•lat•ed, ca•pit•u•lat•ing, ca•pit•u•lates.** To surrender under stated conditions; give in; yield: *The soldiers capitulated to the enemy after a long siege.*

ca•pit•u•la•tion (kə pĭch′ə **lā′**shən) *n.* **1.** The act of capitulating: *capitulation in the face of defeat.* **2.** A statement of the main points of a topic; an outline.

cap•let (**kăp′**lĭt) *n.* A tablet of medicine coated to make it easy to swallow.

ca•pon (**kā′**pŏn′ *or* **kā′**pən) *n.* A male chicken that has been castrated when young to improve the quality of its flesh for food.

cap•puc•ci•no (kăp′ə **chē′**nō) *n., pl.* **cap•puc•ci•nos.** A drink made with espresso coffee and steamed milk.

ca•price (kə **prēs′**) *n.* An impulsive change of mind; a whim: *the caprices of a vain and immature person.* [First written down in 1662 in Modern English, from Italian *capriccio*, from *caporiccio*, fright, sudden start : *capo*, head + *riccio*, curly.]

ca•pri•cious (kə **prĭsh′**əs *or* kə **prē′**shəs) *adj.* Subject to sudden unpredictable changes: *a capricious child; capricious weather.* —**ca•pri′cious•ly** *adv.* —**ca•pri′cious•ness** *n.*

Cap•ri•corn (**kăp′**rĭ kôrn′) *n.* **1.** A constellation in the Southern Hemisphere. **2.** The tenth sign of the zodiac in astrology. [First written down before

cape[1]

Usage: capital[1]

The word for a town or city that serves as a seat of government is **capital**: *Sacramento is the capital of California.* The term for the building in which a legislative assembly meets is **capitol**: *Daily tours of the capitol are offered.*

ă	pat	oi	boy
ā	pay	ou	out
âr	care	o͝o	took
ä	father	o͞o	boot
ĕ	pet	ŭ	cut
ē	be	ûr	urge
ĭ	pit	th	thin
ī	pie	*th*	this
îr	pier	hw	whoop
ŏ	pot	zh	vision
ō	toe	ə	about
ô	paw	N	*French* bon

capuchin
White-throated capuchin

capybara

Word History: car

Our word **car** comes from the Latin word *carrus*, "heavy two-wheeled wagon." Until the early 19th century *car* meant "chariot" and was associated with dignity, solemnity, and splendor: *the sun rides in a celestial car in his orbit; the heroes of myth ride to battle in horse-drawn cars.* In about 1826 in the United States, *car* was used for a carriage pulled by a railway locomotive. *Motor car* first appears around 1895 for a horseless carriage. *Car* later comes to mean any kind of wheeled vehicle and can be modified by words such as **passenger**, **freight**, and **street**.

1387 in Middle English and spelled *Capricorne*, from Latin *Capricornus* : *caper*, goat + *cornū*, horn.]

caps. *abbr.* An abbreviation of capsule.

cap•size (kăp′sīz′ *or* kăp sīz′) *intr. & tr.v.* **cap•sized, cap•siz•ing, cap•siz•es.** To overturn or cause to overturn: *Our boat did not capsize in the storm. A huge wave capsized the ship.*

cap•stan (kăp′stən *or* kăp′stăn′) *n.* A vertical cylinder that is rotated to wind in the anchor cable of a ship.

cap•su•lar (kăp′sə lər *or* kăp′syo͞o lər) *adj.* Of, relating to, or enclosed in a capsule: *a medicine in capsular form.*

cap•sule (kăp′səl *or* kăp′so͞ol) *n.* **1.** A small container, usually of gelatin or another soluble material, that contains a dose of a medicine to be taken by mouth. **2.** A membrane that encloses an organ or a part of the body. **3.** A compartment that can be separated from the rest of a spacecraft, especially one designed to accommodate a crew. **4.** A seed case that opens when ripe. *—adj.* Very brief; condensed: *a capsule description.* [First written down in 1652 in Modern English, from Latin *capsula*, diminutive of *capsa*, box.]

Capt. *abbr.* An abbreviation of captain.

cap•tain (kăp′tən) *n.* **1.** The leader of a group; chief: *the captain of the football team.* **2.** The person in command of a ship: *the captain of a tugboat.* **3.** An officer in the Army, Air Force, or Marine Corps ranking above a first lieutenant and below a major. **4.** An officer in the Navy or Coast Guard ranking above a commander and below a commodore. **5.** An officer in a police or fire department ranking above a lieutenant. **6.** One who is in the forefront of an enterprise; a leader: *a captain of industry. —tr.v.* **cap•tained, cap•tain•ing, cap•tains.** To command or direct; lead: *captain a soccer team; captain a ship.* [First written down about 1375 in Middle English and spelled *capitain*, from Late Latin *capitāneus*, chief, from Latin *caput*, head.]

cap•tain•cy (kăp′tən sē) *n., pl.* **cap•tain•cies.** The rank, authority, or skill of a captain.

cap•tion (kăp′shən) *n.* **1.a.** A short explanation accompanying an illustration or photograph. **b.** A subtitle in a motion picture. **2.** A heading, as of a legal document or a chapter of a book. *—tr.v.* **cap•tioned, cap•tion•ing, cap•tions.** To furnish a caption for.

cap•tious (kăp′shəs) *adj.* **1.** Inclined to criticize or find faults: *a captious movie critic.* **2.** Designed to confuse or ensnare, especially in an argument: *a captious question.* **—cap′tious•ly** *adv.* **—cap′tious•ness** *n.*

cap•ti•vate (kăp′tə vāt′) *tr.v.* **cap•ti•vat•ed, cap•ti•vat•ing, cap•ti•vates.** To fascinate or charm, as with wit, beauty, or intelligence: *The movie captivated audiences everywhere.* **—cap′ti•va′tion** *n.*

cap•tive (kăp′tĭv) *n.* A person or animal held under restraint or in bondage; a prisoner. *—adj.* **1.** Held as a prisoner. **2.** Kept under restraint or control; confined.

cap•tiv•i•ty (kăp tĭv′ĭ tē) *n., pl.* **cap•tiv•i•ties.** The condition or period of being held captive: *Few wild animals thrive in captivity.*

cap•tor (kăp′tər *or* kăp′tôr′) *n.* A person who takes or holds another as a captive.

cap•ture (kăp′chər) *tr.v.* **cap•tured, cap•tur•ing, cap•tures.** **1.** To get hold of, as by force or craft; seize: *Troops captured the rebel barricade.* **2.** To gain possession or control of: *The winner captured first prize.* **3.** To get or hold the interest of: *a mystery story that captures the imagination.* **4.** To hold or preserve in permanent form: *capture the sound of a howling wolf on tape. —n.* **1.** The act of capturing or the process of being captured: *The capture of first prize was a triumph for our side.* **2.** Someone or something that has been captured: *The British warship was a great capture for the Colonial Navy.* [First written down in 1541 in Modern English, from Latin *captūra*, a catching of animals, from *capere*, to seize.]

cap•u•chin (kăp′yə chĭn *or* kə pyo͞o′chĭn) *n.* **1.** Any of several long-tailed South and Central American monkeys having tufts of black hair on the head. **2.** A monk belonging to an order of Franciscan friars that wear long pointed hoods.

cap•y•ba•ra (kăp′ə bär′ə *or* kăp′ə băr′ə) *n.* A short-tailed South American rodent that lives in or near water and may grow to a length of 4 feet (1.2 meters). It is the largest living rodent.

car (kär) *n.* **1.** An automobile. **2.** A vehicle, such as a railroad car, that moves on rails. **3.** The part of an elevator or hot-air balloon that holds passengers or cargo. [First written down about 1350 in Middle English and spelled *carre*, cart, from Latin *carrus, carrum*, wagon, of Celtic origin.] —See Note.

car•a•bao (kä′rə bou′) *n., pl.* **car•a•baos.** A water buffalo of the Philippine Islands.

Ca•ra•cas (kə rä′kəs). The capital and largest city of Venezuela, in the northern part of the country near the coast of the Caribbean Sea. It was founded in 1567. Population, 3,041,000.

ca•rafe (kə răf′) *n.* A glass bottle for serving water or wine.

car•a•mel (kăr′ə məl *or* kär′məl) *n.* **1.** A smooth chewy candy made with sugar, butter, and cream or milk. **2.** Sugar heated to a brown syrup and used for coloring and sweetening foods.

car•a•pace (kăr′ə pās′) *n.* A shell or bony covering on the back of animals such as turtles, armadillos, lobsters, and crabs.

car•at (kăr′ət) *n.* **1.** A unit of weight for precious stones, equal to 200 milligrams or about 1/140 of an ounce. **2.** Variant of **karat.** [First written down in 1469 in Middle English, from Medieval Latin *quarātus*, from Arabic *qīrāṭ*, weight of four grains, from Greek *keration*, a measure of weight, diminutive of *keras*, horn.]

❑ *These sound alike:* **carat, caret** (proofreader's mark), **carrot** (plant), **karat** (measure of gold).

car•a•van (kăr′ə văn′) *n.* **1.** A group of travelers journeying together for safety in hostile regions such as the desert. **2.** A group of vehicles or pack animals traveling together in single file: *The caravan of trucks crossed over the mountains.* **3.** *Chiefly British.* A home on wheels, as a trailer or camper. [First written down in 1588 in Modern English, from Persian *kārvān*.]

car•a•van•sa•ry (kăr′ə văn′sə rē) also **car•a•van•se•rai** (kăr′ə văn′sə rī′) *n., pl.* **car•a•van•sa•ries** also **car•a•van•se•rais.** An inn with a large courtyard for the accommodation of caravans in the Near or Far East.

car•a•vel (kăr′ə vĕl′) *n.* A small light sailing ship with two or three masts used by the Spanish and Portugese in the 15th and 16th centuries.

car•a•way (kăr′ə wā′) *n.* **1.** A plant of Europe and Asia having strong-tasting crescent-shaped seeds used as flavoring in baking and cooking. **2.** The spicy aromatic seeds of this plant. [First written down in 1390 in Middle English and spelled *charuwe*, from Arabic *karāwiyā*, from Greek *karō*.]

Car•a•way (kăr′ə wā′), **Hattie Ophelia Wyatt.** 1878–1950. American legislator. She was the first woman elected to the U.S. Senate and served from 1932 until 1945.

car•bide (kär′bīd′) *n.* A chemical compound, especially calcium carbide, consisting of carbon and a metal.

car•bine (kär′bēn′ *or* kär′bīn′) *n.* A light rifle with a short barrel.

car•bo•hy•drate (kär′bō hī′drāt′) *n.* Any of a large class of compounds consisting of only carbon, hydrogen, and oxygen, produced in green plants by photosynthesis and composing a major type of food for animals. Sugars, starches, and cellulose are carbohydrates.

car•bo•lat•ed (kär′bə lā′tĭd) *adj.* Containing or treated with carbolic acid.

car•bol•ic acid (kär bŏl′ĭk) *n.* Phenol.

car•bon (kär′bən) *n.* **1.** *Symbol* **C** A nonmetallic element that occurs in all plants and animals and in all organic compounds. Diamonds and graphite are pure carbon in the form of crystals; coal and charcoal are mostly carbon in uncrystallized form. Atomic number 6. See table at **element. 2.a.** A sheet of carbon paper. **b.** A copy made by using carbon paper. [First written down in 1789 in Modern English and spelled *carbone*, from Latin *carbō*, a coal, charcoal.]

carbon 12 *n.* The most common isotope of carbon, adopted in place of oxygen as the standard for determining atomic weights.

carbon 14 *n.* A radioactive isotope of carbon that occurs in all objects that contain carbon, as animal and plant matter. Using the known rate of decay of carbon 14, it is possible to determine the age of archaeological materials and geologic formations that contain organic matter.

car•bo•na•ceous (kär′bə nā′shəs) *adj.* Of, containing, or yielding carbon: *coal fields and other carbonaceous deposits.*

car•bon•ate (kär′bə nāt′) *tr.v.* **car•bon•at•ed, car•bon•at•ing, car•bon•ates.** To charge with carbon dioxide gas, as a beverage: *Soda water is carbonated.* —*n.* (kär′bə nāt′ *or* kär′bə nĭt). A salt or ester of carbonic acid. —**car′bon•a′tion** *n.* —**car′bon•a′tor** *n.*

car•bon•at•ed water (kär′bə nā′tĭd) *n.* Soda water.

carbon copy *n.* **1.** A duplicate of something written or typed, made by using carbon paper. **2.** A person or thing that closely resembles another.

carbon cycle *n.* The circulation of carbon in nature, by which plants take in carbon dioxide from the atmosphere and convert it to carbohydrates by photosynthesis and animals in turn eat the plants and return the carbon to the atmosphere by respiration and by decay after death.

carbon dating *n.* A method of determining the age of geologic or archaeological specimens that contain organic matter by measuring the amount of carbon 14 in them; radiocarbon dating.

carbon dioxide *n.* A colorless odorless gas that does not burn, composed of carbon and oxygen in the proportion CO_2 and present in the atmosphere or formed when any fuel containing carbon is burned. It is exhaled from an animal's lungs during respiration and is used by plants in photosynthesis. Carbon dioxide is used in refrigeration, in fire extinguishers, and in carbonated drinks.

car•bon•ic (kär bŏn′ĭk) *adj.* Of, containing, or derived from carbon.

carbonic acid *n.* A weak acid having the formula H_2CO_3. It exists only in solution and decomposes readily into carbon dioxide and water.

Car•bon•if•er•ous (kär′bə nĭf′ər əs) *adj.* **1.** Of, belonging to, or being the geologic time of the period of the Paleozoic Era, following the Devonian and preceding the Permian. During the Carboniferous much of the earth was covered with dense plant growth that eventually sank into swamps and finally hardened into coal. See table at **geologic time. 2. carboniferous.** Producing or containing carbon or coal. —*n.* The Carboniferous Period or its series of rocks.

car•bon•ize (kär′bə nīz′) *tr.v.* **car•bon•ized, car•bon•iz•ing, car•bon•iz•es. 1.** To change an organic compound into carbon by heating. **2.** To treat, coat, or combine with carbon. —**car′bon•i•za′tion** (kär′bə nĭ zā′shən) *n.*

carbon monoxide *n.* A colorless odorless gas that is extremely poisonous and has the formula CO. Carbon monoxide is formed when carbon or a compound that contains carbon burns incompletely. It is present in the exhaust gases of automobile engines.

carbon paper *n.* A lightweight paper coated on one side with a dark coloring matter, placed between two sheets of blank paper so that the bottom sheet will receive a copy of what is typed or written on the top sheet.

carbon tet•ra•chlo•ride (tĕt′rə klôr′īd′) *n.* A colorless poisonous liquid that is composed of carbon and chlorine, has the formula CCL_4, and does not burn although it vaporizes easily. It is used in fire extinguishers and as a dry-cleaning fluid.

Car•bo•run•dum (kär′bə rŭn′dəm). A trademark for an abrasive made of silicon carbide, used to cut, grind, and polish.

car•bun•cle (kär′bŭng′kəl) *n.* **1.** A painful inflammation in the tissue under the skin that is somewhat like a boil but releases pus from several openings. **2.** A deep-red garnet.

car•bu•re•tor (kär′bə rā′tər *or* kär′byə rā′tər) *n.* A device in a gasoline engine that vaporizes the gasoline with air to form an explosive mixture. [First written down in 1866 in Modern English, from *carburet*, carbide, from Latin *carbō*, carbon.]

car•cass (kär′kəs) *n.* **1.** The dead body of an animal, especially one slaughtered for food. **2.** The remains of something: *the carcasses of old cars in a junkyard.* **3.** The body of a human being.

car•cin•o•gen (kär sĭn′ə jən *or* kär′sə nə jĕn′) *n.* A substance or agent that produces or tends to produce cancer. —**car′cin•o•gen′ic** (kär′sə nə jĕn′ĭk) *adj.*

car•ci•no•ma (kär′sə nō′mə) *n., pl.* **car•ci•no•mas** or **car•ci•no•ma•ta** (kär′sə nō′mə tə). A cancerous tumor of the skin, mucous membrane, or similar tissue of the body. [First written down in 1721 in Modern English, from Greek *karkinōma*, from *karkinos*, cancer.]

card¹ (kärd) *n.* **1.** A small, usually rectangular piece of stiff paper, cardboard, or plastic: *The address file is filled with cards.* **2.** One of a set of 52 pieces of stiff heavy paper bearing numbers or figures and divided into four suits, used for various games and for telling fortunes; a playing card. **3. cards.** *(used with a singular or plural verb).* **a.** A game played with one or more sets of 52 cards. **b.** The playing of such games. **4.a.** A piece of stiff paper, often printed with a picture or message, used to send a note or greeting **b.** A post card. **5.** A stiff piece of paper bearing a person's name, a book's title, or other information, used for indentification or classification: *a file card.* **6.** An amusing or eccentric person: *Our cousin is quite a card and entertains everyone with jokes.* —*idioms.* **in the cards.** Likely; probable. **put (one's) cards on the table** or **lay (one's) cards on the table.** To be frank and clear, as in one's intentions. [First written down before 1425 in Middle English and spelled *carde*, from Greek *khartēs*, paper made from papyrus.]

card² (kärd) *n.* A brush with teeth of wire, used to comb fibers of wool, flax, or cotton before spinning. —*tr.v.* **card•ed, card•ing, cards.** To comb with a card: *card wool.* [First written down in 1351 in Middle English, from Latin *carduus*, thistle.]

carafe

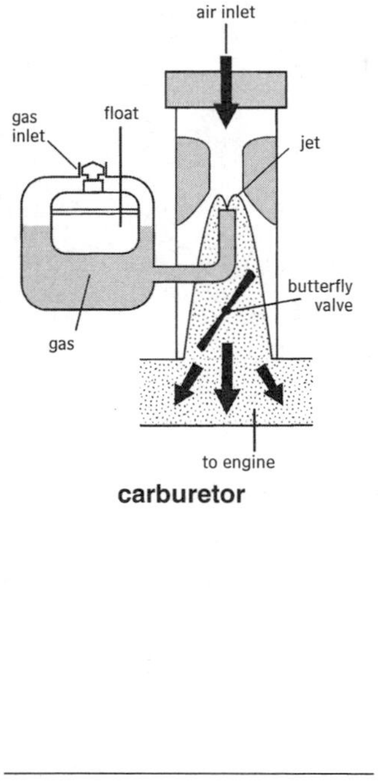

carburetor

ă	pat	oi	boy
ā	pay	ou	out
âr	care	ŏŏ	took
ä	father	ōō	boot
ĕ	pet	ŭ	cut
ē	be	ûr	urge
ĭ	pit	th	thin
ī	pie	*th*	this
îr	pier	hw	whoop
ŏ	pot	zh	vision
ō	toe	ə	about
ô	paw	N	*French* bon

card•board (kärd′bôrd′) *n.* A material similar to thick, stiff, heavy paper and made of pressed paper pulp or pasted sheets of paper.
card catalog *n.* An alphabetical listing, especially of books in a library, made with a separate card for each item.
car•di•ac (kär′dē ăk′) *adj.* Of or relating to the heart: *a cardiac disorder.* [First written down about 1440 in Middle English and spelled *cardiac*, vein associated with the heart, from Greek *kardiakos*, from *kardia*, heart.]
Car•diff (kär′dĭf). The capital and largest city of Wales, in the southeast part of the country west of London, England. Population, 281,300.
car•di•gan (kär′dĭ gən) *n.* A sweater or knitted jacket that opens down the front. [First written down in 1868 in Modern English, after the Seventh Earl of *Cardigan*, James Thomas Brudenell (1797–1868), British army officer.]

cardinal

car•di•nal (kär′dn əl *or* kärd′nəl) *adj.* **1.** Of primary importance; chief; foremost: *A good design is the cardinal element of a successful building.* **2.** Of a deep or vivid red color. —*n.* **1.** An official of the Roman Catholic Church who is appointed by a pope and whose rank is just below that of a pope. **2.** A deep or vivid red. **3.** A North American bird having a crested head and bright red feathers in the male. **4.** A cardinal number. [First written down before 1126 in Middle English, from Late Latin *cardinālis*, principal, pivotal, from Latin *cardō*, hinge.]
cardinal flower *n.* A plant of eastern North America that bears a cluster of brilliant scarlet flowers.
cardinal number *n.* A number, such as 3 or 11 or 412, used in counting to indicate quantity but not order.
cardinal point *n.* One of the four principal directions on a compass; north, south, east, or west.
car•di•o•gram (kär′dē ə grăm′) *n.* An electrocardiogram.
car•di•o•graph (kär′dē ə grăf′) *n.* An electrocardiograph.
car•di•ol•o•gist (kär′dē ŏl′ə jĭst) *n.* A physician who specializes in cardiology.
car•di•ol•o•gy (kär′dē ŏl′ə jē) *n.* The branch of medicine that deals with the heart, its diseases, and their treatment.
car•di•o•pul•mo•nar•y (kär′dē ō po͝ol′mə nĕr′ē *or* kär′dē ō pŭl′mə nĕr′ē) *adj.* Of or relating to the heart and lungs.
cardiopulmonary resuscitation *n.* A procedure used to restore normal breathing and circulation after a person's heart has stopped beating. It employs mouth-to-mouth resuscitation, pushing on the chest to force blood from the heart, and sometimes drugs.
car•di•o•vas•cu•lar (kär′dē ō văs′kyə lər) *adj.* Of, relating to, or involving the heart and blood vessels: *cardiovascular disease.*
care (kâr) *n.* **1.** A feeling of fear, doubt, or anxiety; worry: *on vacation and free from care.* **2.** An object or source of worry, attention, or concern: *The cares of running a business are many.* **3.a.** Serious attention or effort; painstaking application: *You should devote more care to your work.* **b.** Caution, as in avoiding harm or damage: *Glass should be handled with care.* **4.** Protection or supervision; charge; keeping: *The patient was left in the care of a nurse.* —*v.* **cared, car•ing, cares.** —*intr.* **1.** To be concerned or interested: *I don't care about going.* **2.** To object or mind: *Would you care if I turned on the radio?* **3.** To have a liking; like: *Do you really care for that person? Some people don't care for fish.* **4.** To have a wish; be inclined: *Would you care for another helping of peas?* **5.** To provide protection or help: *Who will care for the dog while we are away?* —*tr.* **1.** To be concerned or interested in: *I don't care what they think.* **2.** To wish; desire: *Would you care to go for a walk?* —*idiom.* **in care of.** At the address of or in the name of: *Address all letters for the club in care of the secretary.*

Synonyms: care, charge, keeping, trust. These nouns all refer to the function of watching, guarding, or overseeing something. *The neighbors left their dog in Gina's care when they went on vacation. Who has charge of collecting today's homework? I left the key in Dave's keeping. The Howells committed their important papers to the bank's trust.*

ca•reen (kə rēn′) *v.* **ca•reened, ca•reen•ing, ca•reens.** —*intr.* **1.** To lurch or swerve while in motion: *The car careened on the icy road.* **2.** To lean to one side, as a ship: *The ship careened wildly in the heavy winds.* —*tr.* **1.** To lean (a ship) onto its side for cleaning or repairing. **2.** To cause to lean to one side: *Strong winds will careen a small sailboat.*
ca•reer (kə rîr′) *n.* **1.** A profession or an occupation: *considering a career in medicine.* **2.** The general progress or course of one's life, especially in one's profession: *a police officer with a distinguished career.* —*intr.v.* **ca•reered, ca•reer•ing, ca•reers.** To move or run at full speed: *The startled horse went careering off through the meadow.*
care•free (kâr′frē′) *adj.* Free of worries or responsibilities: *a carefree vacation.*
care•ful (kâr′fəl) *adj.* **1.** Attentive to possible danger; cautious; prudent: *Be careful not to eat too much.* **2.** Done with care; thorough; conscientious: *a careful job on one's homework.* **3.** Showing concern; mindful; solicitous: *being careful of other people's feelings.* —**care′ful•ly** *adv.* —**care′ful•ness** *n.*
care•giv•er (kâr′gĭv′ər) *n.* A person who cares for older people, children, or the ill.
care•less (kâr′lĭs) *adj.* **1.** Taking insufficient care; negligent: *a careless worker; careless about one's appearance.* **2.** Done or made without care or attention: *a careless mistake.* **3.** Said or done without thought; inconsiderate: *a careless remark.* **4.** Free from cares; cheerful: *a careless smile.* —**care′less•ly** *adv.* —**care′less•ness** *n.*
ca•ress (kə rĕs′) *n.* A gentle touch or gesture of fondness, tenderness, or love: *The child's caresses reassured the frightened cat.* —*tr.v.* **ca•ressed, ca•ress•ing, ca•ress•es.** To touch or stroke affectionately.
car•et (kăr′ĭt) *n.* A proofreading symbol (^) used to indicate where something is to be inserted in a line of printed or written material.
❑ *These sound alike:* **caret, carat** (weight of gems), **carrot** (plant), **karat** (measure of gold).
care•tak•er (kâr′tā′kər) *n.* A person employed to look after and take care of a thing, place, or person: *the ever-watchful caretaker of a great estate.*
care•worn (kâr′wôrn′) *adj.* Showing signs of worry or anxiety; haggard: *the parent's careworn face.*
car•fare (kär′fâr′) *n.* The amount charged for a ride, as on a subway or bus.
car•go (kär′gō) *n., pl.* **car•goes** or **car•gos.** The freight carried by a ship, an airplane, or another vehicle: *The freighter delivered its cargo at the wharf.* [First written down in 1657 in Modern English, from Spanish, from *cargar*, to load, from Late Latin *carricāre*, from Latin *carrus*, Gaulish wagon.]
car•hop (kär′hŏp′) *n.* A person who waits on customers in their cars at a drive-in restaurant.
Car•ib (kăr′ĭb) *n., pl.* **Carib** or **Car•ibs. 1.** A member of a group of Native American peoples of northern South America and the Lesser Antilles in the Caribbean. **2.** A language of the Cariban family.
Car•i•ban (kăr′ə bən *or* kə rē′bən) *n., pl.* **Cariban**

or **Cari•bans.** A family of Native American languages spoken by the Carib. —**Car′i•ban** *adj.*

Car•ib•be•an (kăr′ə bē′ən *or* kə rĭb′ē ən) *n.* **1.** A Carib. **2.** The Caribbean Sea. —*adj.* **1.** Of or relating to the Caribbean Sea, its islands, or coastal lands. **2.** Of or relating to the peoples or cultures of this region. **3.** Of or relating to the Carib or their language or culture.

Caribbean Sea. An arm of the western Atlantic Ocean bounded by the coasts of Central and South America and the West Indies.

car•i•bou (kăr′ə bo͞o′) *n., pl.* **caribou** or **car•i•bous.** Any of several deer of arctic regions of North America, having large spreading antlers in both the males and females. [First written down about 1665 in Modern English, from Micmac *ĝalipu.*]

car•i•ca•ture (kăr′ĭ kə cho͝or′ *or* kăr′ĭ kə chər) *n.* **1.** A picture or description of a person or thing in which certain distinctive features are greatly exaggerated or distorted to produce a comic effect. **2.** The art of creating such pictures or descriptions: *The cartoonist is a master of caricature.* —*tr.v.* **car•i•ca•tured, car•i•ca•tur•ing, car•i•ca•tures.** To represent in caricature: *He caricatures political figures.* —**car′i•ca•tur′ist** *n.*

car•ies (kâr′ēz) *n., pl.* **caries. 1.** Decay of a bone or tooth. **2.** A cavity formed by decay in a tooth.

car•il•lon (kăr′ə lŏn′ *or* kăr′ə lən) *n.* A set of bells hung in a tower, usually played from a keyboard. [First written down in 1775 in Modern English, from French, alteration of Old French *quarregnon,* from Late Latin *quaterniō,* set of four.]

Car•mel•ite (kär′mə līt′) *n.* **1.** A monk or friar belonging to a religious order of Christians, founded in Syria in 1155. **2.** A member of a community of nuns in this order, founded in 1452. —**Car′mel•ite′** *adj.*

car•mine (kär′mĭn *or* kär′mīn′) *n.* A deep or purplish red.

car•nage (kär′nĭj) *n.* Great slaughter, especially in war; a massacre: *the carnage of battle.*

car•nal (kär′nəl) *adj.* **1.** Relating to the bodily appetites; sensual. **2.** Worldly or earthly. **3.** Of or relating to the body: *carnal remains.* —**car′nal•ly** *adv.*

car•na•tion (kär nā′shən) *n.* **1.** Any of numerous forms of a garden plant cultivated for its fragrant many-petaled white, pink, or red flowers. **2.** A flower of this plant. **3.** A pinkish red color.

car•nel•ian (kär nēl′yən) *n.* A pale to deep red type of clear quartz used as a gem.

car•ni•val (kär′nə vəl) *n.* **1.** A traveling amusement show that offers rides, games, and sideshows. **2.** A period of celebrating and feasting just before Lent. **3.** A time of merrymaking; a festival.

car•ni•vore (kär′nə vôr′) *n.* **1.** An animal that feeds chiefly on the flesh of other animals and generally has large sharp canine teeth. Carnivores include predators, such as dogs and cats, and scavengers, such as hyenas and raccoons. **2.** A plant that eats insects.

car•niv•o•rous (kär nĭv′ər əs) *adj.* **1.** Feeding on the flesh of other animals. **2.** Having leaves or other parts that trap insects, allowing the plant to feed on them. The pitcher plant and Venus's-flytrap are carnivorous. [First written down in 1646 in Modern English, from Latin *carnivorus* : *carō,* flesh + *-vorus,* eating.] —**car•niv′o•rous•ly** *adv.* —**car•niv′o•rous•ness** *n.*

car•ob (kăr′əb) *n.* An evergreen tree of the Mediterranean region that has compound leaves and bears long pods used as food.

car•ol (kăr′əl) *n.* A song of joy, especially for Christmas. —*v.* **car•oled, car•ol•ing, car•ols** also **car•olled, car•ol•ling, car•ols.** —*intr.* **1.** To sing joyously. **2.** To go from house to house singing Christmas carols. —*tr.* To sing (a song, for example) in a joyous manner. —**car′ol•er, car′ol•ler** *n.*

❑ *These sound alike:* **carol, carrel** (library nook).

Ca•ro•li•na. 1. (kăr′ə lī′nə). A colony of southeast North America, settled by the English in 1653 and divided into North Carolina and South Carolina in 1729. **2.** (kä′rô lē′nä). A city of northeast Puerto Rico east-southeast of San Juan. Population, 177,806.

Car•o•line Islands (kăr′ə līn′ *or* kăr′ə lĭn). A group of islands of the western Pacific Ocean east of the Philippines. The islands were included in the U.S. Trust Territory of the Pacific Islands in 1947.

car•om (kăr′əm) *n.* **1.** A shot in billiards or pool in which one ball strikes another or is bounced off a cushion in order to strike another or reach a pocket. **2.** A collision followed by a rebound, as of a ball bouncing off a wall. —*intr.v.* **car•omed, car•om•ing, car•oms.** To collide and rebound; make a carom: *The golf ball caromed off the tree.*

car•o•tene (kăr′ə tēn′) *n.* An orange to red hydrocarbon that occurs in many plants and in animal tissue. It is converted to vitamin A by the liver.

ca•rot•id (kə rŏt′ĭd) *n.* Either of the two large arteries in the neck that carry blood to the head. —*adj.* Of or relating to either of these arteries.

ca•rous•al (kə rou′zəl) *n.* A noisy riotous drinking party.

ca•rouse (kə rouz′) *n.* A carousal. —*intr.v.* **ca•roused, ca•rous•ing, ca•rous•es.** To drink a great deal of liquor, usually while having a noisy and merry time. —**ca•rous′er** *n.*

car•ou•sel or **car•rou•sel** (kăr′ə sĕl′) *n.* **1.** A merry-go-round. **2.** A circular conveyor, on which objects are displayed or presented: *the baggage carousel at the airport.*

carp[1] (kärp) *intr.v.* **carped, carp•ing, carps.** To find fault or complain in a petty or disagreeable way. [First written down about 1225 in Middle English and spelled *carpen,* from Old Norse *karpa,* to boast.]

carp[2] (kärp) *n., pl.* **carp** or **carps. 1.** A large freshwater fish of Europe and Asia, often bred in ponds and lakes and used as food. **2.** Any of various related fishes. [First written down in 1393 in Middle English and spelled *carpe,* from Medieval Latin *carpa,* of Germanic origin.]

car•pal (kär′pəl) *adj.* Of or relating to the carpus or wrist. —*n.* A bone of the carpus.

❑ *These sound alike:* **carpal, carpel** (flower pistil).

car•pel (kär′pəl) *n.* A part of the pistil of a seed-bearing plant in which the seeds develop.

❑ *These sound alike:* **carpel, carpal** (bone).

car•pen•ter (kär′pən tər) *n.* A person who builds or repairs wooden objects and structures such as cabinets, houses, and ships.

car•pen•try (kär′pən trē) *n.* The work or trade of a carpenter.

car•pet (kär′pĭt) *n.* **1.** A thick heavy covering for a floor, usually made of woven wool or synthetic fibers; a rug. **2.** The fabric used for floor covering: *a roll of carpet.* **3.** Something that covers a surface like a carpet: *a carpet of pine needles on the forest floor.* —*tr.v.* **car•pet•ed, car•pet•ing, car•pets.** To cover with or as with a carpet: *carpet the stairs.*

car•pet•bag (kär′pĭt băg′) *n.* A traveling bag made of carpet fabric, used chiefly in the United States during the 19th century.

car•pet•bag•ger (kär′pĭt băg′ər) *n.* A Northerner who went to the South after the Civil War to make money by taking advantage of the unsettled conditions there.

car•pet•ing (kär′pĭ tĭng) *n.* **1.** Material or fabric

caribou

Woodland caribou bull

carousel

ă	pat	oi	boy
ā	pay	ou	out
âr	care	o͝o	took
ä	father	o͞o	boot
ĕ	pet	ŭ	cut
ē	be	ûr	urge
ĭ	pit	th	thin
ī	pie	*th*	this
îr	pier	hw	whoop
ŏ	pot	zh	vision
ō	toe	ə	about
ô	paw	N	*French* bon

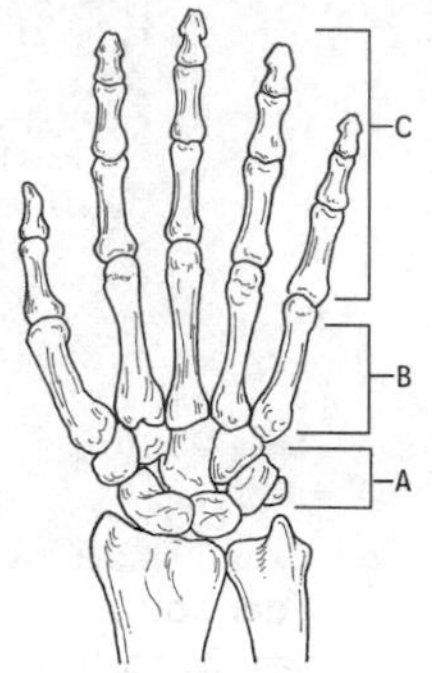

carpus
A. Carpus
B. Metacarpus
C. Phalanges

Regional Note: carry

When a Southerner offers to **carry** a non-Southerner somewhere, the non-Southerner might think this is an invitation to be picked up and bodily lugged to a destination. In fact, in the South the verb **carry** has the regional meaning of "to transport (someone) in a motor vehicle, such as an automobile."

Kit Carson
Photographed in 1864

Rachel Carson

used for carpets: *pretty red carpeting.* **2.** A carpet or carpets: *a room with wall-to-wall carpeting.*

car•pi (kär′pī′) *n.* Plural of **carpus.**

car pool *n.* **1.** An arrangement among a number of car owners who agree to take turns driving each other or their children to a regular destination, such as work or school. **2.** A group of people forming a car pool.

car-pool (kär′pōōl′) *v.* **car-pooled, car-pool•ing, car-pools.** *—intr.* To travel in a car pool: *Four of us car-pool to work every day.* *—tr.* To transport by means of a car pool: *Several families car-pool their children to school.* **—car′-pool′er** *n.*

car•port (kär′pôrt′) *n.* A shelter for a car under a roof projecting from the side of a building.

car•pus (kär′pəs) *n., pl.* **car•pi** (kär′pī′). **1.** The group of eight bones forming the joint between the hand and the forearm in humans; the wrist. **2.** The corresponding joint in four-footed animals.

car•rel (kăr′əl) *n.* A small enclosed area with a desk for study in a library.

❑ *These sound alike:* **carrel, carol** (song).

car•riage (kăr′ĭj) *n.* **1.** A wheeled passenger vehicle, usually drawn by horses. **2.** A small vehicle for a baby or a doll that is pushed by someone walking behind it. **3.** A wheeled structure on which a heavy object, such as a cannon, is moved. **4.** A movable part of a machine that often holds or shifts another part: *Many typewriters still have a carriage that holds the paper and moves it in front of the keys.* **5.** The manner in which one's head or body is held; posture. **6.** The act of transporting: *The explorers used porters for the carriage of supplies up the mountain.* **7.** The costs of transporting: *Carriage was added to the bill.*

car•ri•er (kăr′ē ər) *n.* **1.** A person or thing that transports or conveys: *a baggage carrier.* **2.** A person or business that deals in transporting passengers or goods: *Airlines, railroads, bus lines, and other carriers see an increase in business during holidays.* **3.** An aircraft carrier. **4.** A device or mechanism for moving or carrying something: *We attached our bikes to the carrier on top of the car.* **5.** A person or an animal that is infected with a disease, but shows none of its symptoms and is capable of transmitting it to others: *Mosquitoes are carriers of malaria.* **6.** An organism that carries a gene for a trait that is not expressed or manifested but that by mating with another carrier can produce offspring that express the gene's trait. **7.** A carrier wave.

carrier pigeon *n.* A homing pigeon.

carrier wave *n.* An electromagnetic wave whose amplitude or frequency is modulated to transmit a signal, as in radio broadcasting.

car•ri•on (kăr′ē ən) *n.* The decaying flesh of dead animals: *Vultures feed on carrion.* [First written down before 1325 in Middle English and spelled *caroine,* from Latin *carō,* flesh.]

Car•roll (kăr′əl), **Anna Ella.** 1815–1893. American activist who in 1862 published a pamphlet outlining what was to become President Abraham Lincoln's constitutional theory concerning the Confederacy.

Carroll, Lewis. Charles Lutwidge Dodgson.

car•rot (kăr′ət) *n.* **1.** A plant related to parsley having feathery leaves and a long, tapering, yellow-orange root. **2.** The root of this plant, eaten as a vegetable. [First written down in 1533 in Modern English, from Greek *karōton.*]

❑ *These sound alike:* **carrot, carat** (weight of gems), **caret** (proofreader's mark), **karat** (measure of gold).

car•rou•sel (kăr′ə sĕl′) *n.* Variant of **carousel.**

car•ry (kăr′ē) *v.* **car•ried, car•ry•ing, car•ries.** *—tr.* **1.** To hold or support while moving; bear: *carry the groceries into the house.* **2.** To take from one place to another; transport: *Airlines carry passengers and freight.* **3.** To serve as a means of conveying; transmit: *The pipes carry water from the reservoir.* **4.** To cause to move; propel: *The wind carried the ball over the fence.* **5.** To sustain the weight or responsibility of; bear: *She is carrying a heavy load of courses this semester.* **6.** To keep or have on one's person: *carry an umbrella.* **7.** To be pregnant with (a child). **8.** To hold and move (oneself, one's body or a part of it) in a certain way: *Dancers carry themselves very gracefully.* **9.** To have in stock; have for sale: *Drugstores carry many different health products.* **10.** To sing (a tune or melody) on key: *carry a tune.* **11.** To put (a digit) into the next column to the left, as in performing addition. **12.** To have as an attribute, a consequence, or an effect; involve: *The washing machine carries a guarantee for one year.* **13.** To express or contain: *The engineer's report carried a grim warning about unsafe bridges.* **14.a.** To win a majority of the votes in: *The President carried almost all the states.* **b.** To win support or acceptance for: *The proposition is carried by a large majority of votes.* **15.** To prolong, extend, or continue: *carry a joke too far.* **16.** To print or broadcast: *All the papers carried the story.* **17.** In football, to hold and run with (the ball). **18.** In basketball, to palm (the ball) in violation of the rules. *—intr.* **1.** To act as a bearer: *The dog could fetch and carry.* **2.** To be transmitted or conveyed: *a voice that carries well.* **3.** To be approved or accepted: *The proposal carried by a wide margin.* *—n., pl.* **car•ries. 1.** The range of a gun or a projectile: *The first cannons had a short carry of only a few hundred feet.* **2.** The distance covered by a ball or projectile. **3.** A portage, as between two bodies of water: *A short overland carry was necessary to canoe down the whole length of the river.* **4.** The act of carrying: *The halfback averages four yards per carry.* ***—idioms.*** **carry away.** To arouse great emotion or excitement in: *I was carried away by the music.* **carry off. 1.** To win: *He carried off first prize.* **2.** To handle successfully: *The debate was carried off without any difficulty.* **3.** To cause the death of; kill: *The epidemic carried off hundreds of sheep.* **carry on. 1.** To engage in or conduct: *carry on a conversation; carry on a correspondence.* **2.** To continue despite difficulties; persevere: *carry on even with a bad cold.* **3.** To behave in an excited or improper manner. *What are they carrying on about?* **carry out. 1.** To execute or accomplish: *carry out a plan.* **2.** To follow or obey: *carry out orders.* [First written down before 1338 in Middle English and spelled *carien,* from Old North French *carier,* from *carre,* cart.] —SEE NOTE.

car•ry•all (kăr′ē ôl′) *n.* A large bag, basket, or pocketbook.

car•ry•on (kăr′ē ŏn′) *adj.* Small or compact enough to be carried aboard an airplane, a train, or a bus by a passenger: *carryon luggage.* *—n.* A bag or other container small or compact enough to be carried aboard an airplane, a train, or a bus.

car•ry•out (kăr′ē out′) *adj.* Intended to be eaten away from the premises: *carryout pizza.*

car•sick (kär′sĭk′) *adj.* Nauseated by the motion of a car, bus, or other vehicle. **—car′sick′ness** *n.*

Car•son (kär′sən), **Christopher.** Known as "Kit." 1809–1868. American pioneer who was a guide for western expeditions, an agent for the Ute, and a Union general in the Civil War.

Carson, Rachel Louise. 1907–1964. American environmentalist and writer whose *Silent Spring* (1962) condemns the use of pesticides that are hazardous to wildlife.

Carson City. The capital of Nevada, in the western part of the state near the California border. It was named in honor of Kit Carson. Population, 40,443.

cart (kärt) *n.* **1.** A small wheeled vehicle, such as a grocery cart, pushed by hand. **2.** A two-wheeled wooden vehicle pulled by a horse or other animal and used to transport goods or people. **3.** A light motorized vehicle: *a golf cart.* —*tr.v.* **cart•ed, cart•ing, carts.** To transport in or as if in a cart:. *Trucks cart goods across the country.*

cart•age (kär′tĭj) *n.* **1.** The act or process of transporting or carting: *Many movers offer cartage overseas.* **2.** The cost of transporting or carting: *overseas cartage in the amount of $2,000.*

carte blanche (kärt blänsh′ *or* kärt blänch′) *n., pl.* **cartes blanches** (kärt blänsh′ *or* kärts blänch′). Complete freedom of action: *The teacher gave us carte blanche to organize the party.* [First written down in 1707 in Modern English and spelled *chart blanch*, from French *carte blanche* : *carte*, ticket + *blanche*, blank.]

car•tel (kär tĕl′) *n.* An association of independent business firms, often from different countries, organized to control prices, production, and sales by its members. [First written down in 1560 in Modern English, from Italian *cartello*, placard, from Medieval Latin *cartellus*, charter.]

Car•ter (kär′tər), **James Earl, Jr.** Known as "Jimmy." Born 1924. The 39th President of the United States (1977–1981), who established energy-conservation measures and negotiated peace talks between Egypt and Israel (1979).

Car•te•sian (kär tē′zhən) *adj.* Of or relating to the philosophy or methods of René Descartes. [First written down in 1656 in Modern English, after René *Descartes*.]

Cartesian coordinate system *n.* A system for locating any point in a plane by giving its distances from two perpendicular lines that intersect at an origin, the distance from each line being measured along a straight line parallel to the other.

Car•thage (kär′thĭj). An ancient city and state of northern Africa northeast of modern Tunis. It was founded in the ninth century B.C. —**Car′tha•gin′i•an** (kär′thə jĭn′ē ən) *adj. & n.*

Car•tier (kär tyā′), **Jacques.** 1491–1557. French explorer who navigated the St. Lawrence River (1535) and claimed the region for France.

car•ti•lage (kär′tl ĭj) *n.* A tough white connective tissue that forms a large part of the skeleton of humans and other vertebrates. It is more flexible than bone but not as hard.

car•ti•lag•i•nous (kär′tl ăj′ə nəs) *adj.* **1.** Of, relating to, or consisting of cartilage. **2.** Having a skeleton that consists mainly of cartilage: *The shark is a cartilaginous fish.*

car•tog•ra•phy (kär tŏg′rə fē) *n.* The art of making maps or charts. —**car•tog′ra•pher** *n.*

car•ton (kär′tn) *n.* **1.** A cardboard or plastic box made in various sizes: *an egg carton.* **2.** The contents of a carton: *drink a carton of milk.* [First written down in 1816 in Modern English, from Italian *cartone*, pasteboard.]

car•toon (kär to͞on′) *n.* **1.** A drawing showing a humorous situation or illustrating an opinion on a public issue. **2.** An animated cartoon. **3.** A comic strip. [First written down in 1671 in Modern English, from Italian *cartone*, pasteboard.]

car•toon•ist (kär to͞o′nĭst) *n.* A person who draws cartoons, as for a newspaper.

car•tridge (kär′trĭj) *n.* **1.a.** A cylindrical casing of metal or cardboard that holds the powder to propel a bullet or shot. **b.** Such a casing fitted with a bullet or containing shot. **2.** A small unit designed to be inserted into a larger piece of equipment: *an ink cartridge.* **3.** A removable case in a phonograph, containing the needle and electronic circuitry that transforms the movements of the needle into an electric current. **4.** A cassette containing magnetic tape. [First written down in 1579 in Modern English and spelled *cartage*, alteration of French *cartouche*, from Italian *cartuccio*.]

cart•wheel (kärt′wēl′) *n.* **1.** The wheel of a cart. **2.** A handspring in which the body turns over sideways with the arms and legs spread like the spokes of a wheel.

Cart•wright (kärt′rīt′), **Edmund.** 1743–1823. British cleric and inventor of the power loom (1785–1790).

carve (kärv) *v.* **carved, carv•ing, carves.** —*tr.* **1.** To make by or as if by cutting: *The settlers carved beams out of logs. France carved an empire in the New World.* **2.** To shape or decorate by cutting: *carve a block of marble into a statue.* **3.** To cut (meat or poultry) in pieces to be eaten: *carve a turkey.* —*intr.* To slice meat or poultry to eat. [First written down about 725 in Old English and spelled *ceorfan*.] —**carv′er** *n.*

Car•ver (kär′vər), **George Washington.** 1864?–1943. American botanist who sought to end the poverty of Southern Black sharecroppers by developing uses for the peanut, soybean, and sweet potato. —SEE NOTE.

carv•ing (kär′vĭng) *n.* **1.** The act or process of carving, especially of cutting wood or stone to form an object or design. **2.** An object or a design formed by cutting: *a wood carving.*

car wash *n.* An area or a building equipped for washing cars.

car•y•at•id (kăr′ē ăt′ĭd) *n., pl.* **car•y•at•ids** or **car•y•at•i•des** (kăr′ē ăt′ĭ dēz′). A supporting column, as of a building, sculptured in the shape of a draped woman.

ca•sa•ba also **cas•sa•ba** (kə sä′bə) *n.* A melon having a yellow rind and sweet whitish flesh.

Cas•a•blan•ca (kăs′ə blăng′kə *or* kä′sə bläng′kə). The largest city of Morocco, in the northwest on the Atlantic Ocean south-southwest of Tangier. It was founded in the 16th century. Population, 2,139,204.

cas•cade (kă skād′) *n.* **1.** A waterfall or a series of small waterfalls that flows over steep rocks. **2.** Something resembling a cascade: *a cascade of sparks from a grinding wheel.* —*intr.v.* **cas•cad•ed, cas•cad•ing, cas•cades.** To fall in or as if in a cascade: *The river cascades over a shelf of granite rock. The cards cascaded to the floor.*

Cas•cade Range (kă skād′). A mountain chain of western Canada and the United States extending about 700 miles (1,126 kilometers) south from British Columbia to northern California, where it joins the Sierra Nevada. It rises to 14,410 feet (4,395.1 meters).

cas•car•a (kă skăr′ə) *n.* **1.** A shrub or tree of northwest North America having reddish brown bark. **2.** The dried bark of this plant, used as a laxative.

case¹ (kās) *n.* **1.** An instance of something; an occurrence or example: *It was a case of mistaken identity.* **2.** A situation or state of affairs: *In that case there is nothing more we can do.* **3.** A situation that requires investigation: *the case of the missing diamonds.* **4.** An occurrence of a disease or disorder: *a case of chickenpox.* **5.** A person being assisted, treated, or studied, as by a doctor or a social worker. **6.a.** A legal action; a lawsuit: *The Supreme Court is the last court to consider a case.* **b.** A statement of facts by an attorney, for a court to consider: *The case was clearly presented by the defense.* **7.** A set of reasons or arguments offered in support of something: *There is a good case for changing the*

Jimmy Carter

George Washington Carver

George Washington Carver

Educator and agricultural scientist George Washington **Carver** helped Southern Black tenant farmers in the period following Reconstruction. He developed various uses for crops such as peanuts and sweet potatoes that would replenish the soil, making it more valuable and more fertile. Through lectures and how-to pamphlets, Carver encouraged farmers to grow these crops.

ă	**pat**	oi	**boy**
ā	**pay**	ou	**out**
âr	**care**	o͝o	**took**
ä	**father**	o͞o	**boot**
ĕ	**pet**	ŭ	**cut**
ē	**be**	ûr	**urge**
ĭ	**pit**	th	**thin**
ī	**pie**	*th*	**this**
îr	**pier**	hw	**whoop**
ŏ	**pot**	zh	**vision**
ō	**toe**	ə	**about**
ô	**paw**	N	*French* **bon**

law. **8.** In grammar, a set of forms of a noun, pronoun, or adjective that show relationships among words in a sentence. English has three cases: nominative, objective, and possessive. ***—idioms.*** **in any case.** No matter what happens; in any event: *In any case, we will have to leave soon.* **in case of.** If there should happen to be; in the event of: *In case of emergency, call the police.* [First written down before 1250 in Middle English and spelled *cas,* from Latin *cāsus,* from past participle of *cadere,* to fall.]

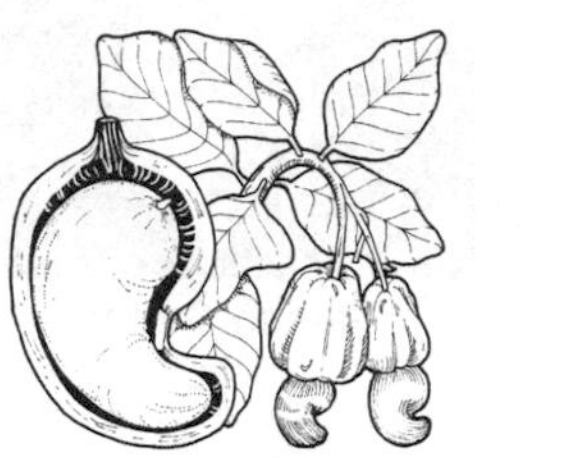

cashew

case² (kās) *n.* **1.** A container or receptacle: *a packing case.* **2.** A container and its contents: *We bought a case of soda.* **3.** A container or protective cover for holding or carrying jewelry, eyeglasses, or other delicate items: *a portable typewriter case.* [First written down before 1325 in Middle English, from Norman French *casse,* from Latin *capsa.*]

case history *n.* In fields such as medicine and psychology, a detailed list of the facts affecting the condition of a person or group under treatment or study.

ca•sein (**kā′**sēn′ *or* **kā′**sē ĭn) *n.* A white, tasteless, odorless protein derived from milk and cheese, used in making foods, plastics, adhesives, and paints.

case•load (**kās′**lōd′) *n.* The number of cases handled in a given period, as by a clinic or social services agency.

case•ment (**kās′**mənt) *n.* **1.** A window sash that opens outward on hinges. **2.** A window fitted with such sashes.

case•work (**kās′**wûrk′) *n.* Social work devoted to individual people or cases. **—case′work′er** *n.*

Mary Cassatt
1880 self-portrait

cash (kăsh) *n.* **1.** Money in the form of bills and coins: *I have five dollars in cash in my pocket.* **2.** Payment in the form of currency or a check: *We decided not to charge our purchases and paid cash.* *—tr.v.* **cashed, cash•ing, cash•es.** To exchange for or convert into ready money: *cash a check.* ***—idiom.*** **cash in on.** *Informal.* To take advantage of: *cash in on the sunshine and go to the beach.*

❑ *These sound alike:* **cash, cache** (hiding place).

cash crop *n.* A crop grown for direct sale rather than for livestock feed.

cash•ew (**kăsh′**o͞o *or* kə **sho͞o′**) *n.* **1.** The kidney-shaped edible nut of a tropical American tree. **2.** The evergreen tree that bears such nuts.

cash•ier¹ (kă **shîr′**) *n.* A person employed to receive and pay out money, as in a store, restaurant, hotel, or bank. [First written down in 1596 in Modern English, from French *caisse,* money box, from Latin *capsa,* case.]

ca•shier² (kă **shîr′**) *tr.v.* **ca•shiered, ca•shier•ing, ca•shiers.** To dismiss in disgrace from a position of command or responsibility: *cashier a soldier for neglect of duty.* [First written down in 1592 in Modern English, from Dutch *casseren,* from Old French *casser,* to annul, dismiss.]

ca•shier's check (kă **shîrz′**) *n.* A check drawn by a bank on its own funds and signed by the bank's cashier.

cash machine *n.* An automated teller machine.

cash•mere (**kăzh′**mîr′ *or* **kăsh′**mîr′) *n.* **1.** Fine soft wool growing beneath the outer hair of a goat native to the mountains of India and Tibet. **2.** Yarn or cloth made from this wool. [First written down in 1684 in Modern English, after *Kashmir.*] **—cash′mere′** *adj.*

cassowary
Southern cassowary

cash register *n.* A machine that records the amount of each cash sale and contains a drawer for holding money.

cas•ing (**kā′**sĭng) *n.* **1.** A protective case or covering, as for an automobile tire or a rocket. **2.** A case usually made of animal intestines and used as a wrapping for sausage meat. **3.** The frame or framework for a door or window.

ca•si•no (kə **sē′**nō) *n., pl.* **ca•si•nos. 1.** An establishment for gambling and other entertainment. **2.** Also **cassino.** A card game for two to four players in which cards on the table are matched with cards in the hand.

cask (kăsk) *n.* **1.** A barrel for holding liquids: *a cask of cider.* **2.** The amount that a cask can hold.

cas•ket (**kăs′**kĭt) *n.* **1.** A small case as for jewels or other valuables. **2.** A coffin.

Cas•pi•an Sea (**kăs′**pē ən). A saline lake between southeast Europe and western Asia. The lake is fed by the Volga River.

casque (kăsk) *n.* A helmet or other armor for the head.

cas•sa•ba (kə **sä′**bə) *n.* Variant of **casaba.**

Cas•san•dra (kə **săn′**drə) *n.* In Greek mythology, a daughter of Priam, King of Troy, endowed with the gift of prophecy but fated by Apollo never to be believed.

Cas•satt (kə **săt′**), **Mary Stevenson.** 1844?–1926. American artist whose paintings and prints are influenced by French impressionism and Japanese woodcuts.

cas•sa•va (kə **sä′**və) *n.* **1.** A tropical American plant having a large starchy root. **2.** Starch from this root, used in making tapioca and as food in tropical regions.

cas•se•role (**kăs′**ə rōl′) *n.* **1.** A dish, usually of pottery or glass, in which food is both baked and served. **2.** Food baked in such a dish.

cas•sette (kə **sĕt′**) *n.* **1.** A small case containing magnetic tape for use in a tape recorder. **2.** A lightproof case containing a roll of film that can be inserted directly into a camera. **3.** A videocassette. [First written down in 1793 in Modern English and spelled *cassette,* small box, from French, from Norman French *casse,* case.]

cas•sia (**kăsh′**ə) *n.* **1.a.** A tree of tropical Asia having aromatic bark used as a substitute for cinnamon. **b.** The bark of this tree. **2.** Any of various chiefly tropical trees and plants having long pods, some of which yield the medicine senna.

cas•si•no (kə **sē′**nō) *n.* Variant of **casino** (sense 2).

Cas•si•o•pe•ia (kăs′ē ə **pē′**ə) *n.* A constellation in the Northern Hemisphere.

cas•sock (**kăs′**ək) *n.* A robe reaching to the feet, worn by the clergy and others assisting in church services.

cas•so•war•y (**kăs′**ə wĕr′ē) *n., pl.* **cas•so•war•ies.** Any of several large flightless birds of New Guinea and northern Australia resembling the ostrich and having a bony projection on the top of the head.

cast (kăst) *v.* **cast, cast•ing, casts.** *—tr.* **1.** To throw or hurl: *Tourists cast coins into the fountain.* **2.** To throw off; shed: *The snake casts its skin as it grows.* **3.** To throw (a person) on the ground, as in wrestling. **4.** To cause to fall upon something, as if by throwing: *cast a shadow; cast doubt upon the report.* **5.** To turn or direct: *cast a glance in the mirror:* **6.** To deposit or indicate (a ballot or vote). **7.** To assign a role to: *The director cast the actor as a judge.* **8.a.** To form (an object) by pouring molten or soft material into a mold and allowing it to harden: *The artist cast the sculpture in bronze.* **b.** To pour (a liquid metal) in forming an object this way: *The factory casts molten iron into pipe.* *—intr.* **1.** To throw something, especially a fishing line: *The fisherman cast in the river all morning.* **2.** To be shaped in a mold: *Some metals, such as lead, cast easily.* *—n.* **1.** The act or an instance of throwing or casting: *a cast of the dice.* **2.** The distance thrown: *a winning cast of 40 meters.* **3.** The actors in a play or movie: *There were only four people in the cast.* **4.** A hard stiff bandage, usually of gauze and plaster, used to keep an injured bone or joint from moving. **5.a.** An object cast in or as if in a mold: *a cast of a statue.* **b.** An impression formed in a mold: *a plaster cast of a face.* **6.** A hue or shade: *The cloth has a slightly reddish cast.* **7.** Outward form, quality, or appearance: *New facts put a different cast on the matter.* **8.** A slight squint or turning of the eye in a certain direction: *a cast in the left eye.* —***idioms.*** **cast about.** To make a search; look around: *cast about for a way to escape.* **cast aside.** To discard or abandon: *cast aside a suggestion.* **cast lots.** To draw lots to determine something by chance. **cast off.** To release a ship from a dock. [First written down before 1200 in Middle English and spelled *casten*, from Old Norse *kasta.*]

❑ *These sound alike:* **cast, caste** (social class).

cas•ta•nets (kăs′tə **nĕts′**) *pl.n.* A rhythm instrument consisting of a pair of hollowed-out shells of wood or ivory, struck together with the fingers to make a sharp click. [First written down in 1647 in Modern English and spelled *castinettas*, from Spanish *castañeta*, from *castaña*, chestnut, from Latin *castanea.*]

cast•a•way (**kăst′**ə wā′) *adj.* **1.** Cast adrift or ashore; shipwrecked. **2.** Discarded; thrown away: *castaway clothes.* —*n.* **1.** A shipwrecked person. **2.** A person or thing that has been discarded.

caste (kăst) *n.* **1.** In India, one of the hereditary social classes in Hindu society. **2.** A social class as distinguished by rank, profession, or wealth: *the priestly caste of Aztec civilization.* **3.** A social system based on caste.

❑ *These sound alike:* **caste, cast** (throw).

cas•tel•lat•ed (**kăs′**tə lā′tĭd) *adj.* Having turrets and battlements like a castle.

cast•er (**kăs′**tər) *n.* **1.** A person or thing that casts: *a caster of fishing nets.* **2.** Also **castor.** A small roller or wheel attached under a piece of furniture or other heavy object to make it easier to move. **3.** Also **castor. a.** A small bottle, pot, or shaker for holding vinegar, mustard, salt, or a similar seasoning. **b.** A stand for a set of these containers.

❑ *These sound alike:* **caster, castor¹** (oil).

cas•ti•gate (**kăs′**tĭ găt′) *tr.v.* **cas•ti•gat•ed, cas•ti•gat•ing, cas•ti•gates.** To criticize severely; rebuke; berate: *be castigated for neglecting one's duty.* —**cas′ti•ga′tion** *n.* —**cas′ti•ga′tor** *n.*

Cas•tile (kăs **tēl′**). A region and former kingdom of central and northern Spain. It joined with Aragon in 1479, thus forming the core of modern Spain.

Castile soap *n.* A hard, white, odorless soap made with olive oil and sodium hydroxide.

Cas•til•ian (kă **stĭl′**yən) *n.* **1.a.** The Spanish dialect of Castile. **b.** The standard form of Spanish, based on this dialect. **2.** A native or inhabitant of Castile. —*adj.* Of or relating to Castile, its people, language, or culture.

cast•ing (**kăs′**tĭng) *n.* **1.** The act or process of making casts or molds. **2.** An object that has been formed in a mold. **3.** The selection of actors or performers, as for a play.

cast iron *n.* A hard brittle alloy of iron that contains carbon and small amounts of silicon, sulfur, manganese, and phosphorus.

cast-i•ron (**kăst′ī′**ərn) *adj.* **1.** Made of cast iron. **2.** Rigid or inflexible: *a cast-iron rule.* **3.** Hardy; strong: *With your cast-iron stomach you could eat anything!*

cas•tle (**kăs′**əl) *n.* **1.** A large building or group of buildings with high, thick walls, towers, and other defenses against attack, such as battlements or a moat. **2.** A building that resembles a castle in size or appearance. **3.** A rook in chess. —*intr. & tr.v.* **cas•tled, cas•tling, cas•tles.** In chess, to move the king two squares toward a rook and place the rook on the square next past the king. [First written down about 1000 in Old English and spelled *castel*, from Latin *castellum.*]

cast•off (**kăst′**ôf′ *or* **kăst′**ŏf′) *n.* A person or thing that has been discarded or thrown away. —**cast′-off′** *adj.*

cas•tor¹ (**kăs′**tər) *n.* An oily brown substance with a strong odor, obtained from glands in the skin of beavers and used in making various perfumes. [First written down before 1398 in Middle English, from Latin *castor*, beaver, from Greek *kastōr.*]

❑ *These sound alike:* **castor¹, caster** (wheel).

cas•tor² (**kăs′**tər) *n.* Variant of **caster** (senses 2, 3).

Cas•tor (**kăs′**tər) *n.* In Greek mythology, one of the twin sons of Leda, who along with his brother Pollux was transformed by Zeus into the constellation of Gemini.

castor oil *n.* An oil pressed from the seeds of a tropical plant, used as a light lubricant and in medicine as a laxative.

cas•trate (**kăs′**trāt′) *tr.v.* **cas•trat•ed, cas•trat•ing, cas•trates.** To remove the testicles of; geld or emasculate. —**cas•tra′tion** *n.*

Cas•tries (**kăs′**trēz′ *or* **kăs′**trēs′). The capital of St. Lucia, in the Windward Islands of the British West Indies. It was founded in 1650. Population, 50,798.

Cas•tro (**kăs′**trō *or* kä′strō), **Fidel.** Born 1927. Cuban revolutionary leader who overthrew a corrupt regime in 1959 and established a socialist state.

ca•su•al (**kăzh′**ōō əl) *adj.* **1.** Happening by chance; not planned; accidental: *a casual meeting of friends on a street corner.* **2.a.** Showing little interest; unconcerned; nonchalant: *a breezy casual manner.* **b.** Not thought about beforehand; passing: *a casual remark about the weather.* **3.** Suited for everyday wear or use; informal: *casual dress.* **4.** Not serious or thorough; superficial: *a casual inspection.* **5.** Not close or intimate: *a casual friendship.* —**cas′u•al•ly** *adv.* —**cas′u•al•ness** *n.*

ca•su•al•ty (**kăzh′**ōō əl tē) *n., pl.* **ca•su•al•ties. 1.a.** A person who is killed or injured in an accident. **b.** A person who is killed, wounded, captured, or missing during a military action. **2.** A serious accident, especially one in which someone is seriously injured or killed.

cat (kăt) *n.* **1.** A small carnivorous mammal having soft fur and sharp claws, kept as a pet or for catching mice and rats. **2.** Any of various related mammals, such as a lion, tiger, leopard, or lynx. —***idiom.*** **let the cat out of the bag.** To give away a secret; let a secret be known. [First written down before 800 in Old English and spelled *catt.*] —SEE NOTE.

ca•tab•o•lism (kə **tăb′**ə lĭz′əm) *n.* The phase of metabolism that yields energy by breaking down complex molecules into simpler ones. —**cat′a•bol′ic** (kăt′ə **bŏl′**ĭk) *adj.*

cat•a•clysm (**kăt′**ə klĭz′əm) *n.* **1.** A sudden and violent change in the earth's crust, as an earthquake or a volcanic eruption. **2.** A great upheaval or disaster, such as a revolution or war. —**cat′a•clys′mic** (kăt′ə **klĭz′**mĭk) *adj.*

cat•a•combs (**kăt′**əkōmz′) *pl.n.* An underground cemetery consisting of chambers or tunnels with recesses used as graves.

Cat•a•lan (**kăt′**l ăn′ *or* kăt′l **ăn′**) *adj.* Of or relating to Catalonia, its people, language, or culture. —*n.* **1.** A native or inhabitant of Catalonia. **2.** The Romance language of Catalonia and the surrounding region.

cat•a•lep•sy (**kăt′**l ĕp′sē) *n., pl.* **cat•a•lep•sies.** A condition in which the muscles of the body become rigid and a person is unaware of his or her surroundings and does not respond to stimuli. Catalepsy has been associated with epilepsy, schizo-

castle

Neuschwanstein Castle in Germany

Word History: cat

Cats are mysterious animals, and so is the word **cat**. We know the ancient Egyptians had domestic cats, but we don't know what they called them. The Romans used their native Latin word *fēlēs* (from which we get **feline**) for the Egyptian cat, but the Latin word refers to any small animal that caught mice, such as a ferret. *Catta*, which is related to our word, first appears in the works by the Roman poet Martial, who died about A.D. 100. There, the word may mean "bird" instead of "cat"—we just don't know. But by A.D. 250 the word is well established in the sense of our domestic cat. Unfortunately, the word is spelled *cattus*, *catus*, *cātus*, *gattus*, which are all indications of a word of uncertain origin and pronunciation.

ă	pat	oi	**boy**
ā	pay	ou	**out**
âr	care	ŏŏ	**took**
ä	father	ōō	**boot**
ĕ	pet	ŭ	**cut**
ē	be	ûr	**urge**
ĭ	pit	th	**thin**
ī	pie	*th*	**this**
îr	pier	hw	**whoop**
ŏ	pot	zh	**vision**
ō	toe	ə	**about**
ô	paw	N	*French* **bon**

catamaran

catapult

cathedral
Saint Basil's Cathedral in Moscow, Russia

Willa Cather

phrenia, and certain other mental disorders. —**cat′a•lep′tic** (kăt′l ĕp′tĭk) *adj.*

cat•a•log or **cat•a•logue** (kăt′l ôg′ *or* kăt′l ŏg′) *n.* **1.** A list of items, usually in alphabetical order, with a description of each item: *a library card catalog.* **2.** A book or pamphlet containing such a list: *a mail order catalog of merchandise.* —*tr.v.* **cat•a•loged, cat•a•log•ing, cat•a•logs** or **cat•a•logued, cat•a•logu•ing, cat•a•logues.** To list in a catalog; make a catalog of: *catalog the books in a library.* [First written down before 1425 in Middle English and spelled *cathaloge*, list, register, from Greek *katalogos* : *kata*, down, off + *legein*, to count.] —**cat′a•log′er, cat′a′logu′er** *n.*

Cat•a•lo•nia (kăt′l ōn′yə *or* kăt′l ō′nē ə). A region of northeast Spain bordering on France and the Mediterranean Sea.

ca•tal•pa (kə tăl′pə *or* kə tôl′pə) *n.* Any of various North American trees having large heart-shaped leaves, showy flower clusters, and long slender pods.

ca•tal•y•sis (kə tăl′ĭ sĭs) *n., pl.* **ca•tal•y•ses** (kə-tăl′ĭ sēz′). The speeding up of a chemical reaction by the action of a catalyst.

cat•a•lyst (kăt′l ĭst) *n.* **1.** A substance that increases the rate of a chemical reaction while undergoing no permanent change in composition itself. Enzymes are important catalysts in digestion. **2.** A person or thing that causes or speeds up a process or event.

cat•a•lyt•ic (kăt′l ĭt′ĭk) *adj.* Of, involving, or acting as a catalyst.

catalytic converter *n.* A device that changes harmful exhaust gases of an automotive engine from hydrocarbons and carbon monoxide into carbon dioxide and water vapor.

cat•a•lyze (kăt′l īz′) *tr.v.* **cat•a•lyzed, cat•a•lyz•ing, cat•a•lyz•es.** To bring out by catalysis.

cat•a•ma•ran (kăt′ə mə răn′) *n.* **1.** A boat with two parallel hulls. **2.** A long raft of logs tied together. [First written down in 1697 in Modern English, from Tamil *kaṭṭumaran* : *kaṭṭu*, to tie + *maram*, tree, log.]

cat•a•mount (kăt′ə mount′) *n.* A mountain lion.

cat•a•pult (kăt′ə pŭlt′ *or* kăt′ə po͝olt′) *n.* **1.** An ancient military machine for hurling stones, spears, arrows, or other missiles at an enemy. **2.** A mechanism for launching aircraft from the deck of a ship. **3.** A slingshot. —*v.* **cat•a•pult•ed, cat•a•pult•ing, cat•a•pults.** —*tr.* To hurl or launch from or as if from a catapult: *The volcano catapulted large boulders high into the air.* —*intr.* To move suddenly as if propelled from a catapult: *When the firefighters heard the alarm, they catapulted out of bed.* [First written down in 1577 in Modern English, from Greek *katapaltēs.*]

cat•a•ract (kăt′ə răkt′) *n.* **1.** A large steep waterfall. **2.** A great downpour. **3.** A condition in which the lens of an eye or the membrane that covers it turns cloudy, causing total or partial blindness.

ca•tarrh (kə tär′) *n.* Inflammation of mucous membranes, especially of the nose and throat, causing an abnormal discharge of mucus. —**ca•tarrh′al** *adj.*

ca•tas•tro•phe (kə tăs′trə fē) *n.* **1.** A great and sudden calamity, such as an earthquake or a flood. **2.** A complete failure: *The dry and crumbly cake was a catastrophe.*

cat•a•stroph•ic (kăt′ə strŏf′ĭk) *adj.* Of, relating to, or resulting in a catastrophe: *a catastrophic fire.* —**cat′a•stroph′i•cal•ly** *adv.*

cat•a•to•ni•a (kăt′ə tō′nē ə) *n.* An abnormal condition in which a person remains quiet, immobile, and dazed. It is associated with schizophrenia.

cat•a•ton•ic (kăt′ə tŏn′ĭk) *adj.* Of, relating to, or in a state of catatonia: *a catatonic trance.*

Ca•taw•ba (kə tô′bə) *n., pl.* **Catawba** or **Ca•taw•bas. 1.** A member of a Native American people of North and South Carolina. **2.** The Siouan language of the Catawba.

cat•bird (kăt′bûrd′) *n.* A dark-gray North American songbird having a call resembling the mewing of a cat.

cat•boat (kăt′bōt′) *n.* A small sailboat with a single sail on a mast set far forward in the bow.

cat•call (kăt′kôl′) *n.* A loud shrill call or whistle expressing disapproval or derision, usually directed from an audience toward a speaker or performer. —*intr.v.* **cat•called, cat•call•ing, cat•calls.** To make catcalls.

catch (kăch *or* kĕch) *v.* **caught** (kôt), **catch•ing, catch•es.** —*tr.* **1.** To get hold of or grasp: *catch a ball.* **2.** To capture or seize, especially after a chase: *The cat caught a mouse.* **3.** To come upon suddenly; take by surprise: *We caught the puppy stealing the cat's food.* **4.** To reach in time to board: *Can we still catch the 3:00 train?* **5.** To become infected with; contract: *catch a cold.* **6.** To cause to be hooked, entangled, or fastened: *I caught my shirt on a nail.* **7.** To hit; strike: *The falling tree caught a corner of the porch.* **8.** To attract: *They tried to catch our attention by yelling and waving their arms.* **9.** To take in or get momentarily: *catch sight of a deer; catch what was said over the noise.* **10.** To go to see (a play, motion picture, or other entertainment). **11.** To check or stop (oneself) during an action: *I caught myself before laughing.* **12.** In baseball, to play (a game) as catcher. —*intr.* **1.** To become hooked, entangled, or fastened: *My coat caught in the car door.* **2.** To burn; ignite: *The fire caught quickly.* **3.** In baseball, to play as catcher. —*n.* **1.** The act or an instance of catching: *The center fielder made a diving catch.* **2.** The amount of something caught, especially fish: *a huge catch of tuna.* **3.** A device, such as a hook or latch, for fastening or closing something: *a door catch.* **4.** A game in which two or more people throw a ball back and forth to each other: *They played catch until supper.* **5.** A choking or stoppage of the breath or voice. **6.** *Informal.* A hidden or tricky condition; a pitfall: *The offer is generous but there must be a catch.* ***—idioms.*** **catch fire. 1.** To begin to burn. **2.** To become popular: *a hobby that has caught fire around the country.* **catch on. 1.** *Informal.* To understand; get the idea: *The dancers caught on to the new steps quickly.* **2.** To become fashionable or popular. **catch (one's) breath.** To rest so as to be able to continue: *We caught our breath for a minute before climbing to the top of the mountain.* **catch up. 1.** To come up from behind; overtake: *We've almost caught up with them.* **2.** To become up to date: *We have to catch up on the latest news.* **3.** To absorb completely; captivate: *The scientist was caught up in challenging research.* [First written down before 1200 in Middle English and spelled *cacchen*, from Latin *captāre*, to grasp at.]

catch•all (kăch′ôl′ *or* kĕch′ôl′) *n.* **1.** A place for keeping odds and ends, as a box, shelf, or closet. **2.** Something that covers many different situations, as a phrase, word, or law.

catch•er (kăch′ər *or* kĕch′ər) *n.* A person or thing that catches, especially the baseball player stationed behind home plate who catches pitches.

catch•ing (kăch′ĭng *or* kĕch′ĭng) *adj.* **1.** Easily transmitted; contagious: *Flu is catching.* **2.** Attractive; catchy: *a catching tune; a catching idea.*

catch•up (kăch′əp *or* kĕch′əp) *n.* Variant of **ketchup.**

catch•word (kăch′wûrd′ *or* kĕch′wûrd′) *n.* A well-known word or phrase, especially one that sums up an idea or group.

catch•y (kăch′ē *or* kĕch′ē) *adj.* **catch•i•er, catch•i•**

est. 1. Attractive or appealing: *a catchy idea for a new book.* **2.** Easily remembered: *a catchy tune.* **3.** Tricky; deceptive: *a catchy question.*

cat•e•chism (**kăt′**ĭ kĭz′əm) *n.* **1.** A book giving a brief summary of the basic principles of Christianity in the form of questions and answers. **2.** A book giving basic instruction in a subject. **3.** A series of questions and answers used to examine something.

cat•e•chize (**kăt′**ĭ kīz′) *tr.v.* **cat•e•chized, cat•e•chiz•ing, cat•e•chiz•es. 1.** To teach Christian doctrine to (a person) by means of questions and answers. **2.** To question closely: *The coach catechized the team on the new plays until everyone knew them perfectly.*

cat•e•gor•i•cal (kăt′ĭ **gôr′**ĭ kəl *or* kăt′ĭ **gŏr′**ĭ kəl) *adj.* Being without exception or qualification; absolute: *a categorical rejection of an offer.* **—cat′e•gor′i•cal•ly** *adv.*

cat•e•go•rize (**kăt′**ĭ gə rīz′) *tr.v.* **cat•e•go•rized, cat•e•go•riz•ing, cat•e•go•riz•es.** To put into a category; classify: *categorize news reports into those about domestic matters and those about international affairs.* **—cat′e•go•ri•za′tion** (kăt′ĭ gər ĭ **zā′**shən) *n.*

cat•e•go•ry (**kăt′**ĭ gôr′ē) *n., pl.* **cat•e•go•ries.** A class or division in a system of classification.

ca•ter (**kā′**tər) *v.* **ca•tered, ca•ter•ing, ca•ters.** *—intr.* **1.** To provide and serve food and drinks: *His business caters for functions at the statehouse.* **2.** To act with special consideration: *The governor was accused of catering to big business.* *—tr.* To supply and serve food and drinks for: *cater a wedding.*

cat•er-cor•nered (**kăt′**ər kôr′nərd *or* **kăt′**ē kôr′nərd) also **cat•er-cor•ner** (**kăt′**ər kôr′nər *or* **kăt′**ē kôr′nər) or **cat•ty-cor•nered** (**kăt′**ē kôr′nərd) or **cat•ty-cor•ner** (**kăt′**ē kôr′nər) or **kit•ty-cor•nered** (**kĭt′**ē kôr′nərd) or **kit•ty-cor•ner** (**kĭt′**ē kôr′nər) *adj.* Diagonal. *—adv.* In a diagonal position.

ca•ter•er (**kā′**tər ər) *n.* A person or business that provides and serves food and drinks for weddings, banquets, and other special occasions.

cat•er•pil•lar (**kăt′**ər pĭl′ər *or* **kăt′**ə pĭl′ər) *n.* The larva of a butterfly or moth, often resembling a hairy worm.

cat•er•waul (**kăt′**ər wôl′) *intr.v.* **cat•er•wauled, cat•er•waul•ing, cat•er•wauls.** To utter a shrill cry or screech like that of a cat. *—n.* A shrill or howling cry.

cat•fish (**kăt′**fĭsh′) *n.* Any of numerous scaleless, mostly freshwater fishes having feelers that resemble whiskers near the mouth.

cat•gut (**kăt′**gŭt′) *n.* A tough thin cord made from the dried intestines of certain animals, especially sheep, used in making strings for musical instruments and tennis rackets and in sewing up surgical wounds.

ca•thar•tic (kə **thär′**tĭk) *adj.* Tending to stimulate the intestines as a laxative. *—n.* A cathartic drug or medicine.

Ca•thay (kă **thā′**). A medieval name for China, usually applied to the area north of the Yangtze River (Chang Jiang).

ca•the•dral (kə **thē′**drəl) *n.* **1.** The principal church of a bishop's diocese. **2.** A large or important church.

Cath•er (**kăth′**ər), **Willa Sibert.** 1873–1947. American author whose novels about frontier life include *My Ántonia* (1918).

Cath•e•rine II (**kăth′**ər ĭn *or* **kăth′**rĭn) Known as "Catherine the Great." 1729–1796. Empress of Russia (1762–1796) who greatly increased the territory of the empire.

Catherine of Ar•a•gon (**ăr′**ə gŏn′). 1485–1536. The first wife of Henry VIII of England (1508–1533). After Henry VIII was granted a divorce from her, she was forced to give up her title of queen.

cath•e•ter (**kăth′**ĭ tər) *n.* A thin flexible tube inserted into a duct of the body to remove a blockage or drain fluid.

cath•ode (**kăth′**ōd′) *n.* **1.** A negative electrode. **2.** The positive terminal in a battery or other device that is supplying current. [First written down in 1834 in Modern English, from Greek *kathados*, descent : *kata-*, down + *hodos*, way, path.]

cathode ray *n.* A stream of electrons from the cathode in a vacuum tube. When cathode rays strike a solid substance, they produce X rays.

cath•ode-ray tube (**kăth′**ōd rā′) *n.* A vacuum tube in which a stream of electrons is directed against a phosphorescent screen where, under the influence of electric or magnetic fields, it traces a picture or display. Cathode-ray tubes are used in producing images in television receivers, radar sets, and computer terminals.

cath•o•lic (**kăth′**ə lĭk *or* **kăth′**lĭk) *adj.* **1.** Broad in sympathies, interests, and understanding: *a person with catholic tastes.* **2. Catholic. a.** Of or relating to the Roman Catholic Church. **b.** Of or relating to the whole body of Christians or the universal Christian church. **c.** Of or relating to the ancient undivided Christian church or those churches claiming to descend directly from it, as the Eastern Orthodox Church and Anglican Church. *—n.* **Catholic.** A Roman Catholic. [First written down about 1350 in Middle English and spelled *catholik*, universally accepted, from Greek *katholikos*, from *katholou*, in general.]

Ca•thol•i•cism (kə **thŏl′**ĭ sĭz′əm) *n.* The faith, doctrine, practice, and organization of the Roman Catholic Church.

cat•i•on (**kăt′**ī′ən) *n.* A positively charged ion that moves toward the negative electrode in electrolysis.

cat•kin (**kăt′**kĭn) *n.* A dense, often drooping cluster of very small flowers, as those of a birch or willow. [First written down in 1578 in Modern English, from obsolete Dutch *katteken*, kitten.]

cat•nap (**kăt′**năp′) *n.* A short nap. *—intr.v.* **cat•napped, cat•nap•ping, cat•naps.** To take a short nap.

cat•nip (**kăt′**nĭp′) *n.* A plant related to the mint, having a strong spicy smell that is very attractive to cats. [First written down in 1796 in American English : *cat* + *nip*, catnip (from Old English *nepte*) (from Latin *nepeta*, aromatic herb).]

cat-o'-nine-tails (kăt′ə **nīn′**tālz′) *n., pl.* **cat-o'-nine-tails.** A whip consisting of nine knotted cords fastened to a handle, used for flogging.

CAT scan (kăt) *n.* An x-ray picture of a cross section of the body or some organ of the body, made by a computer that assembles views of a body taken at a series of different angles. [First written down in 1976 in Modern English, from *c(omputerized) a(xial) t(omography).*] **—CAT scan′ner** *n.*

cat's cradle (kăts) *n.* A child's game in which a loop of string is woven in patterns over the fingers of both hands and often transferred to the hands of another player who adds loops, the players transferring the string back and forth.

Cats•kill Mountains (**kăt′**skĭl′). A range of the Appalachian Mountains in southeast New York just west of the Hudson River. The mountains rise to 4,204 feet (1,282.2 meters).

cat's-paw also **cats•paw** (**kăts′**pô′) *n.* **1.** A person who is used by another to do something risky or illegal. **2.** A light breeze that ruffles small areas of water, as in a pool or pond. [First written down in 1785 in Modern English, from a fable about a monkey that used a cat's paw to pull chestnuts out of a fire.]

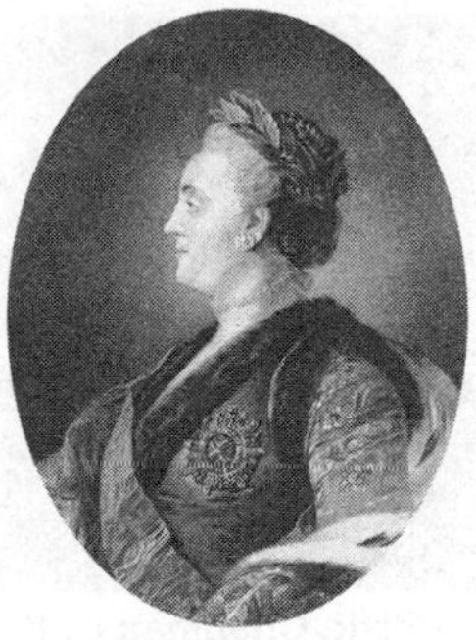

Catherine the Great

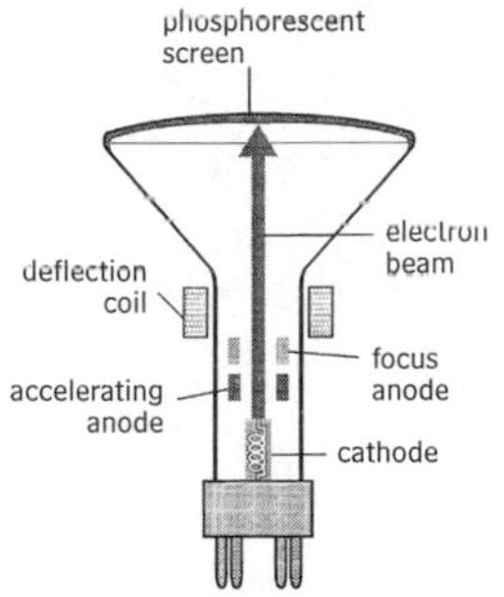

cathode-ray tube

cat's cradle

ă	pat	oi	boy
ā	pay	ou	out
âr	care	o͝o	took
ä	father	o͞o	boot
ĕ	pet	ŭ	cut
ē	be	ûr	urge
ĭ	pit	th	thin
ī	pie	*th*	this
îr	pier	hw	whoop
ŏ	pot	zh	vision
ō	toe	ə	about
ô	paw	N	*French* bon

Carrie Chapman Catt

cat•sup (**kăt′**səp *or* **kăch′**əp *or* **kĕch′**əp) *n.* Variant of **ketchup.**

Catt (kăt), **Carrie (Lane) Chapman.** 1859–1947. American suffragist who was an organizer and president of the National American Woman Suffrage Association. She organized the League of Women Voters in 1919.

cat•tail (**kăt′**tāl′) *n.* Any of various tall marsh plants having long leaves and a dense tube-shaped cluster of tiny flowers that turn brown in the fall.

cat•tle (**kăt′**l) *pl.n.* Any of various horned hoofed mammals bred and raised for beef and dairy products. Cows, bulls, and oxen are cattle. [First written down about 1250 in Middle English and spelled *catel*, property, livestock, from Medieval Latin *capitāle*, holdings, funds, from Latin *caput*, head.]

cat•tle•man (**kăt′**l mən) *n.* A man who tends or raises cattle.

cat•ty (**kăt′**ē) *adj.* **cat•ti•er, cat•ti•est. 1.** Spiteful; mean; malicious: *catty gossip.* **2.** Like a cat; stealthy. **—cat′ti•ly** *adv.* **—cat′ti•ness** *n.*

cat•ty-cor•nered (**kăt′**ē kôr′nərd) or **cat•ty-cor•ner** (**kăt′**ē kôr′nər) *adj. & adv.* Variants of **cater-cornered.**

cat•walk (**kăt′**wôk′) *n.* A narrow elevated platform or pathway, as on the sides of a bridge or above a stage.

Cau•ca•sian (kô **kā′**zhən) *adj.* **1.** Of or relating to a major division of human beings whose members characteristically have light or brown skin color and straight or wavy hair. This division includes the native inhabitants of Europe, northern Africa, southwest Asia, and the Indian subcontinent. In this sense, this word is no longer in scientific use. **2.** Of or relating to the Caucasus region or its peoples, languages, or cultures. *—n.* **1.** A native or inhabitant of the Caucasus. **2.** A Caucasian person.

Cau•ca•soid (**kô′**kə soid′) *adj.* Of or relating to the Caucasian racial division. *—n.* A Caucasian person. This word is no longer in scientific use.

Cau•ca•sus (**kô′**kə səs) also **Cau•ca•sia** (kô **kā′**zhə *or* kô **kā′**shə). A region between the Black and Caspian seas that includes Georgia, Azerbaijan, Armenia, and part of southwest Russia. The area was inhabited before 2000 B.C.

cau•cus (**kô′**kəs) *n., pl.* **cau•cus•es** or **cau•cus•ses.** A meeting of members of a political party to decide on a question of policy or to choose a candidate for office. *—intr.v.* **cau•cused, cau•cus•ing, cau•cus•es** or **cau•cussed, cau•cus•sing, cau•cus•ses.** To gather in or hold a caucus. [First written down in 1745 in American English and spelled *corcus*, after the *Caucus* Club of Boston (in the 1760's).]

cau•dal (**kôd′**l) *adj.* **1.** Of, at, or near the tail or hind parts of an animal: *a fish's caudal fin.* **2.** Resembling a tail.

caught (kôt) *v.* Past tense and past participle of **catch.**

caul•dron (**kôl′**drən) *n.* Variant of **caldron.**

cau•li•flow•er (**kô′**lĭ flou′ər *or* **kŏl′**ĭ flou′ər) *n.* **1.** The compact whitish flower head of a plant closely related to the cabbage and broccoli, eaten as a vegetable. **2.** The plant that bears such flower heads. [First written down in 1597 in Modern English and spelled *cole florie*, probably alteration (influenced by *flower*) of New Latin *cauliflora* : Latin *caulis*, stem + Latin *flōs*, flower.]

caulk also **calk** (kôk) *v.* **caulked, caulk•ing, caulks** also **calked, calk•ing, calks.** *—tr.* **1.** To make (a boat) watertight by packing the seams with caulking. **2.** To make watertight or airtight by filling or sealing with caulking: *caulk the cracks around the window.* *—intr.* To apply caulking. *—n.* Caulking. [First written down about 1378 in Middle English and spelled *cauken*, to press, from Latin *calcāre*, to tread, from *calx*, heel.] **—caulk′er** *n.*

caulk•ing (**kô′**kĭng) *n.* A material, such as oakum, tar, or a plastic compound, used to fill or seal spaces, such as the seams of a boat or joints of pipes.

caus•al (**kô′**zəl) *adj.* Being or constituting a cause: *the causal connection between a scarcity of goods and higher prices.* **—caus′al•ly** *adv.*

cause (kôz) *n.* **1.** A person or thing that makes something happen: *Scientists are investigating the cause of the extinction of the dinosaurs.* **2.** A basis for a certain feeling, action, or decision: *There is no cause for alarm.* **3.** An idea or a goal to which many people are dedicated: *the noble cause of peace.* *—tr. v.* **caused, caus•ing, caus•es.** To be the cause of; make happen; bring about: *Many bacteria cause disease.* [First written down before 1200 in Middle English, from Latin *causa*, reason, purpose.] **—cause′less** *adj.*

cause•way (**kôz′**wā′) *n.* A raised roadway, as across marshland or water.

caus•tic (**kô′**stĭk) *adj.* **1.** Capable of burning or destroying living tissue. **2.** Sarcastic; biting; cutting: *caustic remarks.* *—n.* A caustic material or substance. **—caus′ti•cal•ly** *adv.*

caustic soda *n.* Sodium hydroxide.

cau•ter•ize (**kô′**tə rīz′) *tr.v.* **cau•ter•ized, cau•ter•iz•ing, cau•ter•iz•es.** To burn or sear (a wound or dead tissue, for example), as with a caustic substance or a hot instrument, in order to stop bleeding or prevent infection. **—cau′ter•i•za′tion** (kô′tər ĭ **zā′**shən) *n.*

cau•tion (**kô′**shən) *n.* **1.** Care to avoid danger or trouble: *climb icy steps with caution.* **2.** A warning: *My doctor ended his advice with a caution about not getting enough sleep.* *—tr.v.* **cau•tioned, cau•tion•ing, cau•tions.** To warn against possible trouble or danger: *The sign cautioned drivers to go slowly.*

cau•tious (**kô′**shəs) *adj.* Showing or having caution; careful: *a slow and cautious driver.* **—cau′tious•ly** *adv.* **—cau′tious•ness** *n.*

cav•al•cade (kăv′əl **kād′** *or* **kăv′**əl kād′) *n.* **1.** A ceremonial procession of people on horseback, in carriages, or in automobiles: *The President and his cavalcade drove through town.* **2.** A succession of notable people, scenes, or events.

cav•a•lier (kăv′ə **lîr′**) *n.* **1.** An armed horseman; a knight. **2.** A gallant or chivalrous gentleman, especially one who escorts a lady. **3. Cavalier.** A supporter of King Charles I during the English civil war (1642-52). *—adj.* Casual and indifferent, often in an arrogant manner: *The official gave a cavalier answer to our demands for more information.* [First written down in 1589 in Modern English and spelled *cavaliero*, from Late Latin *caballārius*, from Latin *caballus*, horse.] **—cav′a•lier′ly** *adv.*

cav•al•ry (**kăv′**əl rē) *n., pl.* **cav•al•ries. 1.** A military unit using armored vehicles, such as tanks and helicopters. **2.** Troops trained to fight on horseback. [First written down in 1546 in Modern English and spelled *cavallery*, from Italian *cavalleria*, from *cavaliere*, cavalier.]

cave (kāv) *n.* A hollow or natural passage under the earth or in the side of a hill or mountain with an opening to the surface. *—tr. & intr.v.* **caved, cav•ing, caves.** To fall in or cause to fall in; collapse: *The ground above the old mine caved in. A surge of water caved in the banks of the river.* [First written down before 1250 in Middle English, from Latin *cava*, from *cavus*, hollow.]

ca•ve•at (**kăv′**ē ăt′ *or* **kä′**vē ät′) *n.* A warning.

cave dweller *n.* A person who lives in a cave, especially in prehistoric times.

cave-in (kāv′ĭn′) *n.* **1.** A collapse, as of a tunnel. **2.** A place where the ground has caved in.

cave•man also **cave man** (kāv′măn′) *n.* A prehistoric cave dweller.

cav•ern (kăv′ərn) *n.* A very large cave.

cav•ern•ous (kăv′ər nəs) *adj.* Resembling a cavern; huge, deep, and hollow: *the cavernous interior of a great cathedral.*

cav•i•ar also **cav•i•are** (kăv′ē är′ *or* kä′vē är′) *n.* The eggs of a sturgeon or other large fish, prepared with salt and eaten as a delicacy.

cav•il (kăv′əl) *intr.v.* **cav•iled, cav•il•ing, cav•ils** also **cav•illed, cav•il•ling, cav•ils.** To find fault unnecessarily; raise unimportant objections: *Let's not waste time caviling about the rules instead of getting on with the game.* —*n.* A trivial objection.

cav•i•ta•tion (kăv′ĭ tā′shən) *n.* The sudden formation and collapse of bubbles in a liquid caused by mechanical forces, such as the moving blades of a ship's propeller.

cav•i•ty (kăv′ĭ tē) *n., pl.* **cav•i•ties. 1.** A hollow or hole. **2.** A hollow area within the body: *the abdominal cavity.* **3.** A pocket of decay in a tooth.

ca•vort (kə vôrt′) *intr.v.* **ca•vort•ed, ca•vort•ing, ca•vorts. 1.** To leap about playfully; romp; frolic: *lambs cavorting in a pen.* **2.** To have lively or noisy fun: *The children cavorted in the pool.*

ca•vy (kā′vē) *n., pl.* **ca•vies.** Any of various tailless South American rodents, such as the guinea pig.

caw (kô) *n.* The hoarse harsh sound made by a crow or similar bird. —*intr.v.* **cawed, caw•ing, caws.** To make this sound.

cay (kē *or* kā) *n.* A small low island composed largely of coral or sand.

Cay•enne (kī ĕn′ *or* kā ĕn′). The capital of French Guiana, on **Cayenne Island.** It was founded in 1643. Population, 38,093.

cay•enne pepper (kī ĕn′ *or* kā ĕn′) *n.* A very strong sharp-tasting seasoning made from the ground pods of any of several red peppers. [First written down in 1576 in Middle English and spelled *cayan*, alteration of *kian*, from Tupi *quiínia*, hot pepper.]

cay•man (kā′mən) *n.* Variant of **caiman.**

Cay•man Islands (kā măn′ *or* kā′mən). A British-administered island group in the Caribbean Sea northwest of Jamaica. Georgetown, on **Grand Cayman,** is the capital. Population, 16,677.

Ca•yu•ga (kā yo͞o′gə *or* kī yo͞o′gə) *n., pl.* **Cayuga** or **Ca•yu•gas. 1.** A member of a Native American people of western New York State. **2.** The Iroquoian language of the Cayuga.

cay•use (kī yo͞os′ *or* kī′yo͞os′) *n.* A horse, especially a pony in the western United States.

Cay•use (kī yo͞os′ *or* kī′yo͞os′) *n., pl.* **Cayuse** or **Cay•us•es. 1.** A member of a Native American people of Oregon and Washington. **2.** The language of the Cayuse.

CB (sē bē′) *abbr.* An abbreviation of citizens band.

cc *abbr.* An abbreviation of cubic centimeter.

C clef *n.* A sign used to indicate which line of a musical staff represents middle C, used in forming the soprano clef, the alto clef, and the tenor clef.

Cd The symbol for the element **cadmium.**

CD *abbr.* An abbreviation of compact disk.

CD/ROM (sē′dē′rŏm′) *n.* A compact disk used for storing large amounts of computer data. CD/ROMs cannot be erased or filled with new data.

Ce The symbol for the element **cerium.**

cease (sēs) *intr. & tr.v.* **ceased, ceas•ing, ceas•es.** To come or bring to an end; stop: *The noise ceased. The factory ceased production.* See Synonyms at **stop.**

cease-fire or **cease•fire** (sēs′fīr′) *n.* A suspension of fighting in a war; a truce.

cease•less (sēs′lĭs) *adj.* Having no pause; constant or continual. —**cease′less•ly** *adv.* —**cease′less•ness** *n.*

ce•ca (sē′kə) *n.* A plural of **cecum.**

ce•cro•pi•a moth (sĭ krō′pē ə) *n.* A large North American moth having wings with red, white, and black markings.

ce•cum also **cae•cum** (sē′kəm) *n.* also **cae•ca,** *pl.* **ce•ca** (sē′kə). The first part of the large intestine, shaped like a pouch and closed at one end.

ce•dar (sē′dər) *n.* **1.** Any of several evergreen trees related to the pines and firs, having reddish pleasant-smelling wood. **2.** The wood of such a tree, used to make chests, pencils, and lining for closets. [First written down in 1325 in Middle English and spelled *cedre*, from Latin *cedrus*, from Greek *kedros*.]

Ce•dar Rapids (sē′dər). A city of east-central Iowa east-northeast of Des Moines. Population, 108,751.

cedar waxwing *n.* A North American bird having a crested head, brown feathers, and a tail with a yellow tip.

cede (sēd) *tr.v.* **ced•ed, ced•ing, cedes.** To surrender possession of, especially by treaty; yield; give up: *France ceded Canada to Great Britain at the end of the French and Indian War.* See Synonyms at **yield.**

❑ *These sound alike:* **cede, seed** (part that plants grow from).

ce•dil•la (sĭ dĭl′ə) *n.* A mark beneath the letter *c* in French and Portuguese and in certain words in English, such as *façade*, indicating that the letter is to be pronounced as *c* in *cent*. [First written down in 1599 in Modern English, from obsolete Spanish, diminutive of *ceda*, the letter *z* (so called because a small *z* was formerly written after a *c*, and later below it, to indicate that the normal hard *c* was to be pronounced as a sibilant, like *s* or *z*), from Late Latin *zeta*, zeta.]

ceil•ing (sē′lĭng) *n.* **1.** The inside upper surface of a room: *lights hung from the ceiling.* **2.** The maximum altitude at which an airplane can fly. **3.** The distance between the earth and the lowest clouds: *A ceiling of less than 500 feet gives poor visibility for an aircraft.* **4.** A maximum limit: *a ceiling on gasoline prices; a ceiling on crop production.*

Cel•e•bes (sĕl′ə bēz′ *or* sə lē′bēz′). An irregularly shaped island of central Indonesia on the equator east of Borneo. The island is noted for its rare species of animals.

cel•e•brant (sĕl′ə brənt) *n.* **1.** A person who officiates at a ceremony or rite. **2.** The priest who officiates at the celebration of Mass. **3.** A participant in a celebration.

cel•e•brate (sĕl′ə brāt′) *v.* **cel•e•brat•ed, cel•e•brat•ing, cel•e•brates.** —*tr.* **1.** To observe (a special occasion) with festive activity: *celebrate one's birthday.* **2.** To perform (a religious ceremony): *The priest celebrated Mass.* **3.** To praise publicly; honor; extol: *a poem that celebrates friendship.* —*intr.* **1.** To mark an occasion with proper ceremony or festivity. **2.** To engage in festivities: *celebrate after hearing the good news.* —**cel′e•bra′tion** *n.*

cel•e•brat•ed (sĕl′ə brā′tĭd) *adj.* Known and praised by many people: *a celebrated musician.* See Synonyms at **noted.**

ce•leb•ri•ty (sə lĕb′rĭ tē) *n., pl.* **ce•leb•ri•ties. 1.** A famous person: *The singer is a celebrity wherever he goes.* **2.** Fame; renown: *She achieved celebrity as an architect.*

ce•ler•i•ty (sə lĕr′ĭ tē) *n.* Quickness; speed: *move with celerity.*

cel•er•y (sĕl′ə rē) *n., pl.* **cel•er•ies. 1.** The crisp, juicy, green or white stems of a plant related to parsley, eaten raw or cooked. **2.** The plant that bears such stems.

ce•les•ta (sə lĕs′tə) also **ce•leste** (sə lĕst′) *n.* A mu-

C clef

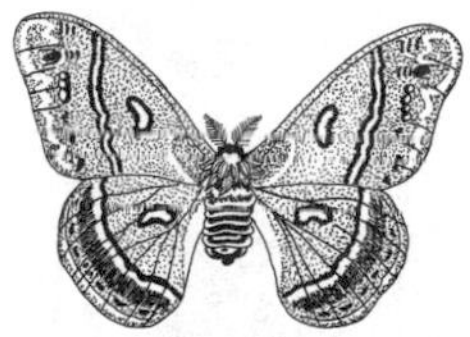

cecropia moth

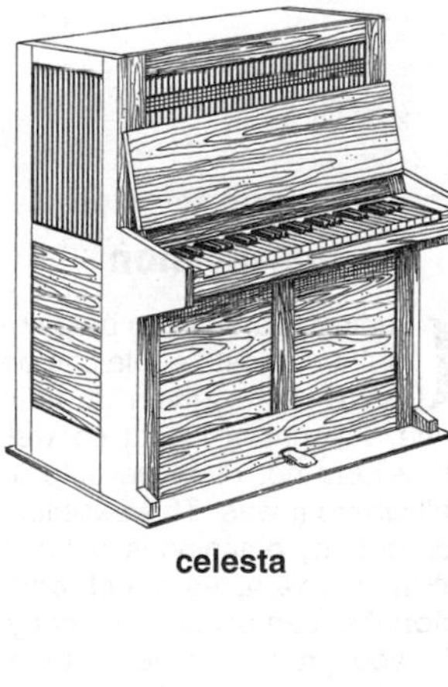

celesta

ă	pat	oi	boy
ā	pay	ou	out
âr	care	o͝o	took
ä	father	o͞o	boot
ĕ	pet	ŭ	cut
ē	be	ûr	urge
ĭ	pit	th	thin
ī	pie	*th*	this
îr	pier	hw	whoop
ŏ	pot	zh	vision
ō	toe	ə	about
ô	paw	N	*French* bon

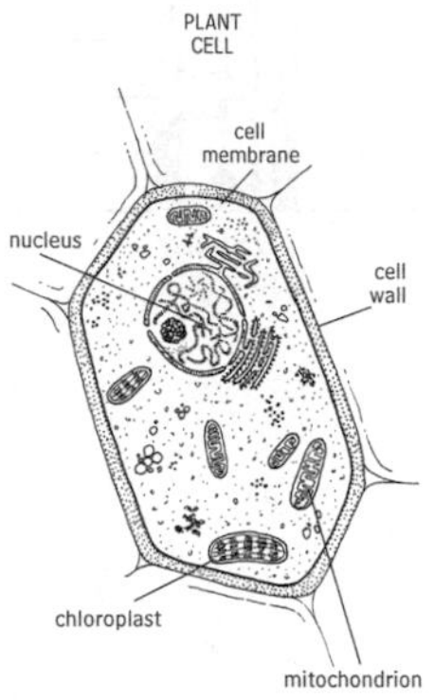

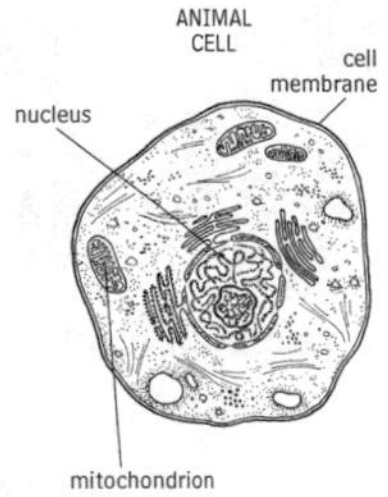

cell

cell division

Cutting yourself can be painful, but most people can be sure that, given a little time, the cut will heal so well they may not even be able to tell where it was. This excellent job of body-patching is just one of many examples of **cell division** that can occur in the body. As you grow, or when part of your body needs to be repaired or cells need to be replaced (for example, cells that die and peel off because of sunburn), cell division takes place. During division, one cell produces two cells that are just like it—they even contain the same genetic material. That's why your cut can be almost invisible when it heals—cells divided into new cells that perfectly match them.

sical instrument consisting of a set of metal bars that produce bell-like tones when struck by hammers controlled by a keyboard.

ce•les•tial (sə **lĕs′**chəl) *adj.* **1.** Of or related to the sky: *Stars and planets are celestial bodies.* **2.** Of heaven; divine: *Angels are celestial beings.* —**ce•les′tial•ly** *adv.*

celestial equator *n.* A great circle on the celestial sphere in the plane of the earth's equator.

celestial pole *n.* Either of the points at which the extensions of the earth's axis intersect the celestial sphere.

celestial sphere *n.* An imaginary sphere, having the earth as its center, on which the sun, moon, and stars appear to be located.

cel•i•ba•cy (**sĕl′**ə bə sē) *n.* The condition of being unmarried or of abstaining from sexual intercourse, especially for religious reasons.

cel•i•bate (**sĕl′**ə bĭt) *n.* A person who remains unmarried or abstains from sexual intercourse, especially for religious reasons. —*adj.* Unmarried or abstaining from sexual intercourse, especially for religious reasons.

cell (sĕl) *n.* **1.** A small confining room, as in a prison or convent. **2.** The basic unit of living matter in all organisms, consisting of protoplasm bound by a membrane and often containing a distinct nucleus that is also enclosed by a membrane. Some organisms consist of single cells, while others consist of vast numbers of cells. **3.** A single unit that is capable of changing some form of energy, such as chemical energy or radiant energy, into electricity. A flashlight battery is a single cell. **4.** A small enclosed cavity or space, such as a compartment in a honeycomb. [First written down before 1131 in Middle English and spelled *celle*, from Latin *cella*, chamber.]

❑ *These sound alike:* **cell, sell** (give for money).

cel•lar (**sĕl′**ər) *n.* **1.** A storage room beneath a house. **2.** A cool dark room for storing wines. [First written down before 1200 in Middle English and spelled *celer*, from Late Latin *cellārium*, pantry, from Latin *cella*, storeroom.]

❑ *These sound alike:* **cellar, seller** (one who gives something for money).

cell division *n.* The process by which a cell divides to form two identical cells with the same genetic material as the original cell. —See Note.

cel•list (**chĕl′**ĭst) *n.* A person who plays the cello.

cell membrane *n.* The thin membrane that forms the outer surface of the protoplasm of a cell and regulates the passage of materials in and out of the cell.

cel•lo (**chĕl′**ō) *n., pl.* **cel•los.** A large musical instrument of the violin family, having four strings and a pitch below that of the viola but higher than the double bass.

cel•lo•phane (**sĕl′**ə făn′) *n.* A thin, flexible, transparent material made from cellulose that is obtained from wood pulp, used as a moistureproof wrapping.

cel•lu•lar (**sĕl′**yə lər) *adj.* **1.** Of, relating to, or involving cells: *cellular division.* **2.** Made of or containing cells: *the cellular structure of the brain.*

cellular telephone *n.* A mobile telephone unit, especially in a motor vehicle, that extends communication over a particular geographical area by low-power radio transmitters.

cel•lu•lite (**sĕl′**yə līt′) *n.* A fatty deposit, as under the skin around the thighs.

cel•lu•loid (**sĕl′**yə loid′) *n.* A colorless flammable material made from cellulose and formerly used in making photographic film.

cel•lu•lose (**sĕl′**yə lōs′) *n.* A carbohydrate that is insoluble in water, forms the main component of plant tissues, and is used in making a variety of products, such as paper, cellophane, textiles, and explosives.

cellulose acetate *n.* A synthetic resin made from cellulose and used in making lacquers, photographic film, and magnetic tape.

cellulose nitrate *n.* Variant of **nitrocellulose.**

cell wall *n.* The rigid outer layer of a plant cell that surrounds the cell membrane and is composed mostly of cellulose.

Cel•si•us (**sĕl′**sē əs *or* **sĕl′**shəs) *adj.* Of or relating to a temperature scale on which the freezing point of water is 0° and the boiling point of water is 100° under normal atmospheric pressure. [First written down in 1797 in Modern English, after Anders *Celsius.*]

Celsius, Anders. 1701–1744. Swedish astronomer who invented (1742) the centigrade thermometer.

Celt (kĕlt *or* sĕlt) also **Kelt** (kĕlt) *n.* **1.** A member of an ancient Indo-European people, inhabiting central Europe and spreading to western Europe and the British Isles, especially a Briton or Gaul. **2.** A speaker of a modern Celtic language, such as Irish or Welsh, or a descendant of such a speaker. [First written down in 1607 in Modern English, from Latin *Celtae*, the Celts, from Greek *Keltoi.*]

Celt•ic (**kĕl′**tĭk *or* **sĕl′**tĭk) *adj.* Of or relating to the Celts and their languages. —*n.* A group of Indo-European languages including Welsh, Irish Gaelic, Scottish Gaelic, Manx, Breton, and Cornish.

ce•ment (sĭ **mĕnt′**) *n.* **1.** A building material made by grinding heated limestone with clay to form a powder that can be mixed with water and poured to harden as a solid mass. **2.** Concrete. **3.** A substance that hardens to hold things together; glue: *use cement to mend a broken cup.* **4.** Something that unites or joins: *Mutual respect for each other's opinions was the cement of their friendship.* —*tr.v.* **ce•ment•ed, ce•ment•ing, ce•ments. 1.** To join or cover with or as if with cement: *cement bricks in a wall.* **2.** To make binding; strengthen: *Signing the contract cemented the partners' agreement.* [First written down before 1300 in Middle English and spelled *ciment*, from Latin *caementum*, rough-cut stone, from *caedere*, to cut.]

cem•e•ter•y (**sĕm′**ĭ tĕr′ē) *n., pl.* **cem•e•ter•ies.** A place for burying the dead; a graveyard. [First written down in 1377 in Middle English and spelled *cimiterie*, from Greek *koimētērion*, from *koiman*, to put to sleep.]

Ce•no•zo•ic (sē′nə **zō′**ĭk *or* sĕn′ə **zō′**ĭk) *adj.* Of, belonging to, or being the geologic time of the latest era, which includes the Tertiary Period and the Quaternary Period. During the Cenozoic, birds and mammals and the continents developed into their present forms. See table at **geologic time.** —*n.* The Cenozoic Era.

cen•ser (**sĕn′**sər) *n.* A container for burning incense, especially in a religious ceremony.

❑ *These sound alike:* **censer, censor** (remover of material considered harmful).

cen•sor (**sĕn′**sər) *n.* **1.** A person who is authorized by a government or an organization to examine books, movies, or other materials and to remove or prevent from becoming available anything that is considered improper or harmful. **2.** One of two officials in ancient Rome responsible for taking the public census and supervising public behavior and morals. —*tr.v.* **cen•sored, cen•sor•ing, cen•sors.** To remove material from or prevent the publication of: *censor classified information in a letter.*

❑ *These sound alike:* **censor, censer** (incense container).

cen•so•ri•ous (sĕn **sôr′**ē əs) *adj.* Very critical: *The* *critic's censorious review seemed unfair.* —**cen•so′ri•ous•ly** *adv.* —**cen•so′ri•ous•ness** *n.*

cen•sor•ship (sĕn′sər shĭp′) *n.* **1.** The act or practice of censoring. **2.** The office or authority of a Roman censor.

cen•sure (sĕn′shər) *n.* An expression of strong disapproval or harsh criticism. —*tr.v.* **cen•sured, cen•sur•ing, cen•sures.** To express strong disapproval of; criticize: *The press censured the city government for corruption.* —**cen′sur•er** *n.*

cen•sus (sĕn′səs) *n.* An official counting of population, usually made at regular intervals and often including statistics on age, sex, occupation, and other information.

cent (sĕnt) *n.* **1.** A coin of the United States, Canada, Australia, New Zealand, and various other countries, that is 1/100 of a dollar. **2.** A coin of various other countries equal to 1/100 of the basic monetary unit. **3.** A small sum of money: *I haven't a cent to my name.* [First written down before 1375 in Middle English, from Latin *centum*, hundred.]

❑ *These sound alike:* **cent, scent** (smell), **sent** (transmitted).

cent. *abbr.* An abbreviation of: **1.** Centigrade. **2.** Central. **3.** Century.

cen•taur (sĕn′tôr′) *n.* In Greek mythology, a creature having the head, arms, and trunk of a human being and the body and legs of a horse.

cen•ta•vo (sĕn tä′vō) *n., pl.* **cen•ta•vos.** A unit of money equal to 1/100 of the peso of Argentina, Mexico, and certain other countries of Latin America and of the Philippines.

cen•te•nar•i•an (sĕn′tə nâr′ē ən) *n.* A person who is one hundred years old or older.

cen•ten•a•ry (sĕn tĕn′ə rē *or* sĕn′tə nĕr′ē) *n., pl.* **cen•ten•a•ries. 1.** A period of 100 years. **2.** A centennial. —*adj.* Centennial.

cen•ten•ni•al (sĕn tĕn′ē əl) *n.* A 100th anniversary or a celebration of it. —*adj.* **1.** Of or relating to a period of 100 years. **2.** Happening once every 100 years: *The United States has had two centennial celebrations of its founding.* —**cen•ten′ni•al•ly** *adv.*

cen•ter (sĕn′tər) *n.* **1.a.** A point within a circle or sphere that is equally distant from all points of the circumference or surface. **b.** A point that is equally distant from each vertex of a regular polygon. **2.** The middle position, part, or place of something: *the center of a table; chocolates with soft centers.* **3.** A place of concentrated activity: *a shopping center; a big city that is a trade center.* **4.** A person or thing that is the chief object of attention, interest, activity, or emotion: *Our guest was the center of the party.* **5.** Often **Center.** A political party or set of policies representing a moderate view between those of the right and left. **6.** A player on a team positioned in or near the middle of a playing area or forward line, as in football, basketball, and hockey. —*v.* **cen•tered, cen•ter•ing, cen•ters.** —*tr.* **1.** To place in or at the center: *center a picture on a page.* **2.** To concentrate on (something): *The moderator centered the discussion on the most urgent problems.* —*intr.* **1.** To be concentrated: *Support for the political opposition centered in the cities.* **2.** To have as a main theme, interest, or concern; focus: *The conversation centered on air pollution.*

cen•ter•board (sĕn′tər bôrd′) *n.* A flat board or metal plate that can be lowered through the bottom of a sailboat to prevent it from drifting.

center field *n.* **1.** In baseball, the middle part of the outfield, behind second base. **2.** The position of the center fielder.

center fielder *n.* In baseball, the player who defends center field.

center of gravity *n., pl.* **centers of gravity.** The point in a body around which its weight is evenly balanced.

cen•ter•piece (sĕn′tər pēs′) *n.* An ornamental object or bowl, as of flowers, placed at the center of a dining table.

cen•tes•i•mal (sĕn tĕs′ə məl) *adj.* **1.** Hundredth. **2.** Relating to or divided into hundredths. —**cen•tes′i•mal•ly** *adv.*

centi– *pref.* A prefix that means a hundredth: *centigram.*

cen•ti•grade (sĕn′tĭ grād′) *adj.* Celsius. [First written down in 1812 in Modern English, from French : Latin *centum*, hundred + Latin *gradus*, step, degree.]

cen•ti•gram (sĕn′tĭ grăm′) *n.* A unit of weight equal to one hundredth (10^{-2}) of a gram.

cen•ti•li•ter (sĕn′tə lē′tər) *n.* A unit of volume equal to one hundredth (10^{-2}) of a liter.

cen•time (sän′tēm′ *or* säɴ tēm′) *n.* **1.** A coin of Belgium, France, Ivory Coast, Switzerland, and various other countries, equal to 1/100 of a franc. **2.** A coin of Algeria, Haiti, Morocco, and other countries, equal to 1/100 of the basic monetary unit.

cen•ti•me•ter (sĕn′tə mē′tər) *n.* A unit of length equal to one hundredth (10^{-2}) of a meter. See table at **measurement.**

cen•ti•pede (sĕn′tə pēd′) *n.* Any of various small animals having a body divided into many segments, each with a pair of legs. The front legs have venom glands and are used as pincers that can give a painful wound. [First written down in 1646 in Modern English, from Latin *centipeda* : *centi-*, hundred + *pēs*, foot.]

cen•tral (sĕn′trəl) *adj.* **1.** Situated at, near, or in the center: *a central position from which to view the game.* **2.** Forming the center: *the central part of the state.* **3.a.** Having the dominant or controlling power: *the central office of the corporation.* **b.** Controlling all parts of a system from a particular place: *central air conditioning; central heating.* **4.** Essential or principal: *the central topic of a story.* —**cen′tral•ly** *adv.*

Cen•tral Af•ri•can Republic (sĕn′trəl ăf′rĭ kən). A country of central Africa east of Cameroon. It gained its independence from France in 1960. Bangui is the capital and the largest city. Population, 2,395,000.

Central A•mer•i•ca (ə mĕr′ĭ kə). A region of southern North America extending from the southern border of Mexico to the northern border of Colombia. It is linked to South America by the Isthmus of Panama.

central angle *n.* An angle formed by two rays from the center of a circle.

Central Intelligence Agency *n.* An agency of the U.S. government that gathers information on matters affecting national security.

cen•tral•ize (sĕn′trə līz′) *v.* **cen•tral•ized, cen•tral•iz•ing, cen•tral•iz•es.** —*tr.* **1.** To draw into or toward a center; consolidate: *centralize records in one office.* **2.** To bring under a central controlling authority: *The Constitution centralizes political power in the federal government.* —*intr.* To come together at a center; concentrate: *Their attention centralized on the essential problem.* —**cen′tral•i•za′tion** (sĕn′trə lĭ zā′shən) *n.*

central nervous system *n.* In a vertebrate animal, the part of the nervous system that consists of the brain and spinal cord.

Central Powers *n.* The nations that fought against the Allies in World War I; Germany, Austria-Hungary, Bulgaria, and Turkey.

central processing unit *n.* The part of a computer that interprets and carries out instructions.

Central Standard Time *n.* Standard time in the

cello

censer

ă	pat	oi	boy
ā	pay	ou	out
âr	care	o͝o	took
ä	father	o͞o	boot
ĕ	pet	ŭ	cut
ē	be	ûr	urge
ĭ	pit	th	thin
ī	pie	*th*	this
îr	pier	hw	whoop
ŏ	pot	zh	vision
ō	toe	ə	about
ô	paw	ɴ	*French* bon

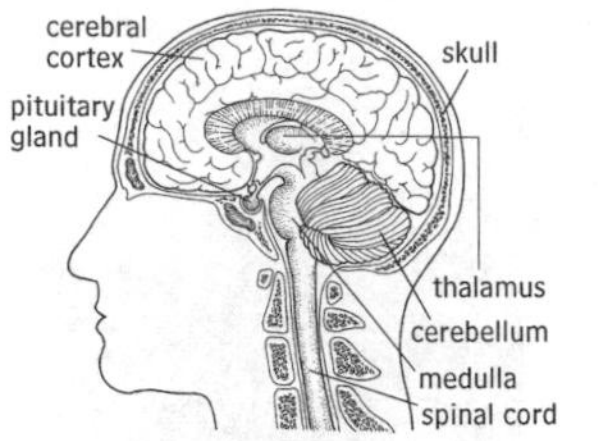

cerebellum

sixth time zone west of Greenwich, England, used in the central United States.

cen•tre (sĕn′tər) *n.* & *v. Chiefly British.* Variant of **center.**

cen•trif•u•gal (sĕn **trĭf′**yə gəl *or* sĕn **trĭf′**ə gəl) *adj.* Moving or directed away from a center: *the centrifugal action of a spinning top.* [First written down before 1721 in Modern English : Latin *centrum*, center + Latin *fugere*, to flee.] **—cen•trif′u•gal•ly** *adv.*

centrifugal force *n.* The force that appears to cause a body turning around a center to move away from the center. Centrifugal force is not a true force, but is actually an example of inertia.

cen•tri•fuge (**sĕn′**trə fyo͞oj′) *n.* A machine for separating substances varying in density, as cream from milk or bacteria from a fluid, by rotating them at high speeds. Centrifugal force throws the denser substance further outward. *—tr.v.* **cen•tri•fuged, cen•tri•fug•ing, cen•tri•fug•es.** To rotate (something) in a centrifuge.

cen•tri•ole (**sĕn′**trē ōl′) *n.* Either of a pair of rod-shaped bodies within the centrosome of a cell. Centrioles organize other materials in the cell and help determine the arrangement of chromosomes during cell division.

cen•trip•e•tal (sĕn **trĭp′**ĭ tl) *adj.* Directed or moving toward a center or axis. [First written down in 1709 in Modern English : Latin *centrum*, center + Latin *petere*, to seek.] **—cen•trip′e•tal•ly** *adv.*

centripetal force *n.* The force that tends to move things toward the center around which they are turning. Gravitation acts as a centripetal force.

cen•trist (**sĕn′**trĭst) *n.* A person whose political views fall midway between liberal and conservative. *—adj.* Marked by or adhering to moderate political views: *a centrist policy; a centrist representative.*

cen•tro•mere (**sĕn′**trə mîr) *n.* The condensed region of a chromosome that is attached to the spindle during cell division.

cen•tro•some (**sĕn′**trə sōm′) *n.* A small region of cytoplasm next to the nucleus of a cell that contains the centrioles.

cen•tu•ri•on (sĕn **to͝or′**ē ən *or* sĕn **tyo͝or′**ē ən) *n.* An officer commanding a unit of a hundred men in the army of ancient Rome.

cen•tu•ry (**sĕn′**chə rē) *n., pl.* **cen•tu•ries. 1.** A period of 100 years. **2.** Each of the 100-year periods counted forward or backward since the time of Jesus's birth: *the 20th century.* [First written down before 1398 in Middle English, from Latin *centuria*, a group of a hundred, from *centum*, hundred.]

century plant *n.* A tropical American plant having long thick stiff leaves and greenish flowers. It is a kind of agave that may grow more than 30 feet high, bears flowers only once after growing for 10 to 30 years, and then dies.

ce•phal•ic (sə **făl′**ĭk) *adj.* Relating to or located on or in the head. [First written down before 1425 in Middle English, from Greek *kephalē*, head.]

ceph•a•lo•pod (**sĕf′**ə lə pŏd′) *n.* Any of various ocean mollusks, such as the cuttlefish, squid, or nautilus, having long tentacles around the mouth, a large head, large eyes, and a sharp beak.

ceph•a•lo•tho•rax (sĕf′ə lə **thôr′**ăks′) *n.* The combined head and thorax of some animals, such as crabs and spiders.

Ce•phe•id (**sē′**fē ĭd *or* **sĕf′**ē ĭd) *n.* A type of star whose brightness varies in a regular periodic way.

ce•ram•ic (sə **răm′**ĭk) *n.* **1.** A hard brittle material that resists heat and corrosion and is made by treating clay or some other nonmetallic mineral with extreme heat. Ceramic is used in making pottery, electrical insulators, and other products. **2.** An object made of this material. **3. ceramics.** *(used with a singular verb).* The art or technique of making things from this material: *Ceramics is his hobby.* [First written down in 1850 in Modern English and spelled *keramic*, from Greek *keramos*, potter's clay.] **—ce•ram′ic** *adj.*

ce•re•al (**sîr′**ē əl) *n.* **1.** The seeds of certain grasses, such as wheat, rice, or corn, used as food. **2.** A grass bearing such seeds. **3.** A food, such as oatmeal or other breakfast food, prepared from such seeds. [First written down in 1818 in Modern English, from Latin *cereālis*, of grain, from *Cerēs*, Ceres.]
❑ *These sound alike:* **cereal, serial** (a series).

cer•e•bel•lum (sĕr′ə **bĕl′**əm) *n., pl.* **cer•e•bel•lums** or **cer•e•bel•la** (sĕr′ə **bĕl′**ə). A part of the brain, located at the rear of the skull, that regulates and coordinates complex muscular movements.

cer•e•bra (**sĕr′**ə brə *or* sə **rē′**brə) *n.* A plural of **cerebrum.**

cer•e•bral (**sĕr′**ə brəl *or* sə **rē′**brəl) *adj.* **1.** Of or relating to the brain or cerebrum: *a cerebral blood vessel.* **2.** Concerned with the intellect rather than the emotions.

cerebral cortex *n.* The outer layer of gray tissue that covers the two parts of the cerebrum, responsible for most of the higher functions of the nervous system, such as learning and memory.

cerebral palsy *n.* Weakness and lack of coordination of the muscles, resulting from damage to the brain, usually at or before birth. —See Note.

cer•e•bro•spi•nal (sĕr′ə brō **spī′**nəl *or* sə rē′brō **spī′**nəl) *adj.* Of or relating to the brain and spinal cord: *cerebrospinal fluid.*

cer•e•brum (**sĕr′**ə brəm *or* sə **rē′**brəm) *n., pl.* **cer•e•brums** or **cer•e•bra** (**sĕr′**ə brə *or* sə **rē′**brə). The large rounded structure of the brain that fills most of the skull, divided by a deep groove into two parts that are joined at the bottom. It controls thought and voluntary muscular movements.

cer•e•mo•ni•al (sĕr′ə **mō′**nē əl) *adj.* **1.** Of or appropriate to a ceremony: *ceremonial dances.* **2.** Characterized by or involved in ceremony: *ceremonial robes; ceremonial duties.* *—n.* A set of ceremonies established for a specific occasion; a ritual.

cer•e•mo•ni•ous (sĕr′ə **mō′**nē əs) *adj.* **1.** Careful about ceremony and formality; formally polite: *Diplomats are usually ceremonious people.* **2.** In accordance with a set of customary forms or rites; formal: *Inauguration of the President is a ceremonious occasion.* **—cer′e•mo′ni•ous•ly** *adv.* **—cer′e•mo′ni•ous•ness** *n.*

cer•e•mo•ny (**sĕr′**ə mō′nē) *n., pl.* **cer•e•mo•nies. 1.** A formal act or set of acts performed in honor or celebration of an occasion, such as a wedding, funeral, or national event. **2.** Proper or polite behavior; formality: *Mexico's president was welcomed with great ceremony.* [First written down before 1382 in Middle English and spelled *ceremoyn*, from Latin *caerimōnia*, religious rite.]

Ce•res (**sîr′**ēz) *n.* In Roman mythology, the goddess of agriculture, identified with the Greek Demeter.

ce•rise (sə **rēs′** *or* sə **rēz′**) *n.* A deep red.

ce•ri•um (**sîr′**ē əm) *n. Symbol* **Ce** A grayish metallic element that occurs only in combination with other elements. It is the most common of the rare-earth metals and is used in porcelain, glass, and alloys. Atomic number 58. See table at **element.**

cer•tain (**sûr′**tn) *adj.* **1.** Established or agreed upon; definite: *We save a certain amount each month.* **2.** Sure to come or happen; inevitable: *If the temperature keeps dropping, it is certain that the rain will turn to snow.* **3.** Established beyond doubt; indisputable: *It is certain that the planets revolve around the sun.* **4.** Reliable; dependable: *a certain remedy to the problem.* **5.** Confident; assured: *Are you certain that you left the book here?* **6.** Not named or

cerebral palsy

The condition known as **cerebral palsy** is not a disease; it is an incurable disorder that can happen to a baby before birth or in the first few years of its life. It is usually caused by a lack of oxygen to the brain, preventing the part of the brain that controls the body's muscles from developing correctly. The muscles stiffen and become difficult to coordinate, and speech and hearing may be impaired. Other brain functions, though, are not impaired. In fact, people with cerebral palsy usually have normal to high intelligence.

specified but assumed to be known: *There are certain laws for automobile safety.* **7.** Named but not familiar or known: *a certain Mr. Smith.* **8.** Some but not much; limited: *The report is accurate to a certain degree.* —*pron.* A certain number; some: *Certain of the watches are waterproof.* **—*idiom.* for certain.** Without doubt; definitely: *Winter will come for certain.* [First written down before 1300 in Middle English, from Latin *certus*.]

cer•tain•ly (sûr′tn lē) *adv.* Surely; definitely: *I am certainly going to the movies if I get a chance.*

cer•tain•ty (sûr′tn tē) *n., pl.* **cer•tain•ties. 1.** The condition or quality of being certain; freedom from doubt; sureness: *There is no certainty that the package will arrive today.* **2.** A clearly established fact: *It is a certainty that the moon affects the tides.*

cer•tif•i•cate (sər tĭf′ĭ kĭt) *n.* **1.** An official document that is proof of some fact, such as a date of birth. **2.** A document stating that a person has completed the requirements to practice a certain profession. **3.** A document that certifies ownership: *an automobile registration certificate; a stock certificate.*

cer•ti•fi•ca•tion (sûr′tə fĭ kā′shən) *n.* **1.** The act of certifying or the condition of being certified: *All states require the certification of doctors.* **2.** A certified document or statement; a certificate: *Our doctor's certification hung in a frame on the wall.*

cer•ti•fy (sûr′tə fī′) *v.* **cer•ti•fied, cer•ti•fy•ing, cer•ti•fies.** —*tr.* **1.** To guarantee to be true or valid by an official document: *Your license certifies that you know how to drive a car.* **2.** To guarantee the quality, value, or standard of: *The inspector certified the elevator as safe.* **3.** To issue a license or certificate to: *This document certifies that she can practice dentistry in this state.* —*intr.* To testify or declare: *Their fine work certifies to their ability.* [First written down before 1338 in Middle English and spelled *certifien*, from Late Latin *certificāre*, from Latin *certus*, certain.]

cer•ti•tude (sûr′tĭ to͞od′ *or* sûr′tĭ tyo͞od′) *n.* The condition of being certain; confidence; complete assurance: *the doctor's certitude about my good health.*

ce•ru•le•an (sə ro͞o′lē ən) *adj.* Sky-blue; azure.

Cer•van•tes (sər văn′tēz), **Miguel de.** 1547–1616. Spanish writer who is best known for his novel *Don Quixote* (1605–1615).

cer•vi•cal (sûr′vĭ kəl) *adj.* Of or relating to a neck or cervix: *the cervical vertebrae of the upper backbone.*

cer•vix (sûr′vĭks) *n., pl.* **cer•vix•es** or **cer•vi•ces** (sûr′vĭ sēz′ *or* sər vī′sēz). **1.** The neck. **2.** A neck-shaped part of the body, especially the narrow outer end of the uterus.

ce•sar•e•an also **cae•sar•e•an** (sĭ zâr′ē ən) *n.* A cesarean section. —*adj.* Of or relating to a cesarean section.

cesarean section *n.* A surgical procedure in which an incision is made through the abdominal wall and uterus in order to remove a fetus.

ce•si•um also **cae•si•um** (sē′zē əm) *n. Symbol* **Cs** A soft, silvery, metallic element that is liquid at room temperature and is used in photoelectric cells. The rate of vibration of cesium atoms is used as a standard for measuring time. Atomic number 55. See table at **element.**

ces•sa•tion (sĕ sā′shən) *n.* The act of ceasing or stopping; a halt: *A computer failure caused a cessation of stock trading.*

ces•sion (sĕsh′ən) *n.* A giving up or yielding to another: *the French cession of Acadia to Great Britain.*

cess•pool (sĕs′po͞ol′) *n.* A covered hole or pit in the ground for receiving drainage or sewage.

ce•ta•cean (sĭ tā′shən) *n.* Any of various marine mammals having an almost hairless body resembling that of a fish, a flat notched tail, and forelimbs modified into broad flippers. Whales, dolphins, and porpoises are cetaceans. —*adj.* Of or belonging to the cetaceans.

Cey•lon (sĭ lŏn′). Sri Lanka.

Cé•zanne (sā zăn′), **Paul.** 1839–1906. French artist. One of his most famous paintings is *The Card Players* (1890–1892).

Cf The symbol for the element **californium.**

cf. *abbr.* An abbreviation of compare.

cg *abbr.* An abbreviation of centigram.

C.G. *abbr.* An abbreviation of: **1.** Coast guard. **2.** Commanding general. **3.** Consul general.

cgm *abbr.* An abbreviation of centigram.

ch. *abbr.* An abbreviation of: **1.** Chapter. **2.** Church.

Chad (chăd). A country of north-central Africa west of Sudan. It gained its independence from France in 1960. Ndjamena is the capital and the largest city. Population, 4,405,000.

chafe (chāf) *v.* **chafed, chaf•ing, chafes.** —*tr.* **1.** To irritate by rubbing: *The starched collar chafed his neck.* **2.** To annoy; vex: *The fans' taunts chafed the pitcher.* **3.** To warm by rubbing: *The skaters chafed their cold hands.* —*intr.* **1.** To become irritated or sore from rubbing: *My hands chafed from washing them with harsh soap.* **2.** To feel irritation; be impatient: *chafe at the delay.* [First written down before 1382 in Middle English and spelled *chaufen*, to warm, from Latin *calefacere* : *calēre*, to be warm + *facere*, to make.]

chaff¹ (chăf) *n.* **1.** The husks of grain separated from the seeds by threshing. **2.** Finely cut straw or hay used as fodder. **3.** Trivial or worthless matter: *Their picky criticisms were just a lot of chaff.* [First written down about 1000 in Old English and spelled *ceaf*.]

chaff² (chăf) *tr.v.* **chaffed, chaff•ing, chaffs.** To make good-natured fun of; tease: *My classmates chaffed me about my picture in the newspaper.* —*n.* Good-natured teasing; banter. [First written down probably 1827 in Modern English, possibly alteration of *chafe* or *chaff*, husks.]

chaf•finch (chăf′ĭnch) *n.* A small European songbird often kept as a pet, the male of which has reddish-brown feathers.

chaf•ing dish (chā′fĭng) *n.* A pan set above a heating device, used to cook food or keep it warm at the table.

cha•grin (shə grĭn′) *n.* A strong feeling of unease or annoyance caused by disappointment, embarrassment, or humiliation, especially at a mistake or failure. —*tr.v.* **cha•grined, cha•grin•ing, cha•grins.** To cause to feel chagrin; annoy greatly: *I was chagrined at being corrected in front of my friends.*

chain (chān) *n.* **1.** A series of connected links, usually of metal, used especially to bind or hold something or to transmit mechanical power. **2.** A set of such links used as an ornament. **3.** A series of connected or related things: *a chain of events.* **4.** A number of stores, restaurants, theaters, or other establishments under common ownership or management: *a chain of supermarkets around the state.* **5. chains.** Something that restrains or confines: *They threw off the chains of slavery.* **6.** A unit of length used in land surveying, equal to 66 feet (20.1 meters). —*tr.v.* **chained, chain•ing, chains.** To bind or confine with or as if with a chain or chains: *chain an elephant to a stake; be chained to one's job.* [First written down before 1300 in Middle English and spelled *chaine*, from Latin *catēna*.]

chain gang *n.* A group of convicts chained together when doing heavy labor outside their prison.

chain letter *n.* A letter sent to a certain number of

Cervantes

Paul Cézanne
Self-portrait

ă	pat	oi	boy
ā	pay	ou	out
âr	care	o͝o	took
ä	father	o͞o	boot
ĕ	pet	ŭ	cut
ē	be	ûr	urge
ĭ	pit	th	thin
ī	pie	*th*	this
îr	pier	hw	whoop
ŏ	pot	zh	vision
ō	toe	ə	about
ô	paw	N	*French* bon

chain saw

chaise longue

people, asking each of them to copy and send it to the same number of people.

chain mail *n.* Flexible armor made of metal rings that are connected like links in a chain.

chain reaction *n.* **1.** A series of events each of which causes or influences the next: *The car crash caused a chain reaction on the highway that involved a number of other cars in accidents.* **2.** A continuous series of nuclear fissions in which neutrons released from the splitting of one atomic nucleus collide with nearby nuclei, which in turn release more neutrons to collide with more nuclei, thus keeping the reaction going.

chain saw *n.* A power saw with teeth set on a circular chain.

chain store *n.* One store in a number of retail stores under the same ownership or management.

chair (châr) *n.* **1.** A piece of furniture on which one may sit, consisting of a seat, back, legs, and sometimes arms at the sides. **2.** A position of authority, as that of a professor: *The head of the department has the chair of ancient history.* **3.** A chairperson: *address questions to the chair.* —*tr.v.* **chaired, chair•ing, chairs.** To preside over: *chair a meeting; chair a committee.* [First written down about 1225 in Middle English and spelled *chaiere*, from Latin *cathedra*.]

chair lift *n.* A series of chairs or bars suspended from an endless cable and used to carry skiers and others up or down a slope.

chair•man (**châr′**mən) *n.* A person who presides over a meeting or is the head of a committee, board, or similar group.

chair•man•ship (**châr′**mən shĭp′) *n.* The office of a chairperson or the period during which a chairperson is in office.

chair•per•son (**châr′**pûr′sən) *n.* A person who presides over a meeting or is the head of a committee, board, or similar group.

chair•wom•an (**châr′**wo͝om′ən) *n.* A woman who presides over a meeting or is the head of a committee, board, or similar group.

chaise (shāz) *n.* **1.** A light, usually two-wheeled carriage with a folding top, drawn by one horse. **2.** A chaise longue.

chaise longue (shāz **lông′**) *n., pl.* **chaise longues** or **chaises longues** (shāz **lông′**). A long chair on which one can sit and stretch out one's legs.

chaise lounge *n.* A chaise longue.

chal•ced•o•ny (kăl **sĕd′**n ē) *n., pl.* **chal•ced•o•nies.** A type of quartz that has a waxy luster and varies from transparent to translucent. It is used as a gemstone. Agate and onyx are forms of chalcedony.

Chal•de•a or **Chal•dae•a** (kăl **dē′**ə). An ancient region of southern Mesopotamia. It was settled in about 1000 B.C.

cha•let (shă **lā′** *or* **shăl′**ā) *n.* **1.** A wooden house with a gently sloping roof and overhanging eves. **2.** The hut of a herder in the Swiss Alps.

chal•ice (**chăl′**ĭs) *n.* **1.** A cup or goblet. **2.** A cup for the consecrated wine of the Eucharist.

chalk (chôk) *n.* **1.** A soft white, gray, or yellow limestone formed chiefly from fossil seashells. **2.** A piece of this material or a similar substance, used especially for making marks on a chalkboard or other surface: *make a picture using colored chalk.* —*tr.v.* **chalked, chalk•ing, chalks. 1.** To mark, draw, or write with chalk: *chalk math problems on the blackboard.* **2.** To treat or cover with chalk: *chalk a field in order to neutralize its acid soil.* —***idiom.*** **chalk up. 1.** To earn or score: *The team chalked up one victory after another.* **2.** To credit: *chalk up a success to pure luck.*

chalk•board (**chôk′**bôrd′) *n.* A panel, usually green or black, for writing on with chalk.

chalk•y (**chô′**kē) *adj.* **chalk•i•er, chalk•i•est. 1.** Of or containing chalk: *chalky water from washing the blackboards.* **2.** Resembling chalk: *chalky bits of dried paint.* —**chalk′i•ness** *n.*

chal•lah (**KHä′**lə *or* **hä′**lə) *n.* A white bread made with eggs and usually baked in the shape of a braid and traditionally eaten by Jews on the Sabbath.

chal•lenge (**chăl′**ənj) *n.* **1.** A call to take part in a contest or fight: *a challenge to a race.* **2.** A calling into question; a demand for an explanation: *The new evidence poses a challenge to their theory.* **3.** A sentry's call for identification: *"Who goes there?" was the challenge of the soldier.* **4.** Something that tests a person's skills, efforts, or resources: *the challenge of studying advanced mathematics.* **5.** A formal objection, especially to the qualifications of a juror or to certain evidence or rulings in a trial. —*tr.v.* **chal•lenged, chal•leng•ing, chal•leng•es. 1.** To call to engage in a contest or fight: *We challenged the other team to a game of basketball.* **2.** To question or dispute the truth or rightness of: *challenge a statement.* **3.** To order to halt and be identified: *The sentries challenged everybody who walked by.* **4.** To summon to action, effort, or use; stimulate: *a problem that challenges the imagination.* **5.** To make formal objection to a juror. [First written down before 1200 in Middle English and spelled *chalenge*, from Latin *calumnia*, trickery, false accusation.] —**chal′leng•er** *n.*

chal•leng•ing (**chăl′**ən jĭng) *adj.* **1.** Requiring the full use of one's abilities or skills: *a challenging job.* **2.** Arousing one's interest or curiosity; intriguing: *a challenging idea.*

chal•lis (**shăl′**ē) *n.* A lightweight fabric of wool, cotton, or rayon, usually having a printed pattern.

cham•ber (**chām′**bər) *n.* **1.** A private room, especially a bedroom. **2.** A room in which a person of high rank receives visitors: *the pope's audience chamber.* **3. chambers.** A judge's office in a courthouse: *Before the trial the lawyers met in the judge's chambers.* **4.a.** The hall used by a group of lawmakers or judges: *Inside the Capitol are the two chambers where the laws are made, the Senate and the House of Representatives.* **b.** A legislative or judicial body: *The Senate is called the upper chamber of the legislature.* **5.a.** An enclosed space or compartment in a machine or other device: *a bullet in the chamber of a rifle.* **b.** An enclosed space in the body of an organism, as in the brain or heart. —*tr.v.* **cham•bered, cham•ber•ing, cham•bers.** To put in or as if in a chamber; enclose; confine: *chamber oneself in order to get work done.* [First written down before 1200 in Middle English and spelled *chaumbre*, from Latin *camera*, vault, from Greek *kamara*.]

cham•ber•lain (**chām′**bər lən) *n.* **1.** An official who manages the household of a monarch or noble. **2.** A treasurer.

cham•ber•maid (**chām′**bər mād′) *n.* A woman who is employed to clean and take care of bedrooms, as in a hotel.

chamber music *n.* Music written for a small group of instruments and suitable for performance in a private home or small concert hall.

chamber of commerce *n., pl.* **chambers of commerce.** An association of businesspersons and merchants for the promotion of business interests in the community.

chamber pot *n.* A portable container used as a toilet, especially in a bedroom.

cham•bray (**shăm′**brā′) *n.* A fine lightweight gingham cloth woven with white threads crossing colored ones.

cha•me•leon (kə mēl′yən) *n.* **1.** Any of various small Old World lizards that can change color rapidly to blend in with their surroundings. **2.** Any of various small New World lizards that can also change their color. **3.** A changeable or inconstant person, especially one who changes mood or opinion quickly. [First written down before 1387 in Middle English and spelled *camelioun*, from Greek *khamaileōn* : *khamai*, on the ground + *leōn*, lion.]

cham•ois (shăm′ē) *n., pl.* **cham•ois** (shăm′ēz). **1.** An antelope of mountainous regions of Europe and western Asia that is similar to a goat. **2.** Soft yellowish leather originally made from the skin of this animal, used for washing and polishing.

cham•o•mile or **cam•o•mile** (kăm′ə mīl′ *or* kăm′ə mēl′) *n.* A strong-smelling plant having flowers similar to daisies and feathery leaves. The dried flowers can be steeped in hot water to make chamomile tea. [First written down about 1265 in Middle English and spelled *camemille*, from Greek *khamaimēlon* : *khamai*, on the ground + *mēlon*, apple.]

champ[1] (chămp) *tr. & intr.v.* **champed, champ•ing, champs.** To chew or bite upon noisily: *a horse champing its oats; a horse chewing and champing with great vigor.* —*idiom.* **champ at the bit.** To be impatient at being delayed: *The team was champing at the bit to start the game.* [First written down in 1530 in Modern English, probably of imitative origin.]

champ[2] (chămp) *n. Informal.* A champion. [First written down in 1868 in Modern English, from *champion.*]

cham•pagne (shăm pān′) *n.* **1.** A sparkling white wine produced in Champagne, a region of France. **2.** A similar wine made in another area.

cham•pi•on (chăm′pē ən) *n.* **1.** A person or thing that holds first place or wins first prize in a contest, especially in sports. **2.** A person who fights for or defends something, such as a cause or movement: *a champion of human rights.* —*tr.v.* **cham•pi•oned, cham•pi•on•ing, cham•pi•ons.** To fight for or defend; support actively: *champion the rights of poor people.* —*adj.* Holding first place or prize: *the champion team.* [First written down before 1200 in Middle English and spelled *championn*, combatant, athlete, from Medieval Latin *campiō*, from Latin *campus*, field.]

cham•pi•on•ship (chăm′pē ən shĭp′) *n.* **1.a.** The position or title of a champion: *hold the championship.* **b.** A contest held to determine a champion: *attend the championship.* **2.** Defense or support: *the championship of civil rights.*

Cham•plain (shăm plān′), **Lake.** A lake of northeast New York, northwest Vermont, and southern Quebec, Canada.

Cham•plain (shăm plān′), **Samuel de.** 1567?–1635. French explorer who founded a settlement on the site of present-day Quebec in 1608.

chance (chăns) *n.* **1.** The unknown or uncertain course of events that has no apparent cause: *Most card games are games of chance. By chance did you find your glasses?* **2.** The likelihood that something will happen; probability; possibility: *We still have a good chance of catching the train.* **3.** An opportunity: *We never miss a chance to go to the movies.* **4.** A risk or gamble: *You're taking a chance that the store will still be open.* **5.** A raffle or lottery ticket. —*adj.* Caused by chance; not planned: *a chance meeting.* —*v.* **chanced, chanc•ing, chanc•es.** —*intr.* To happen by accident: *I chanced to find a quarter on the sidewalk.* —*tr.* To take a chance with; risk: *They chanced crossing the river in a canoe.* —*idiom.* **chance on** or **chance upon.** To find or meet accidentally; happen upon: *I chanced on an old friend yesterday.*

chan•cel (chăn′səl) *n.* The space around the altar of a church for the clergy and choir, often set apart by a railing, lattice, or screen.

chan•cel•ler•y or **chan•cel•lor•y** (chăn′sə lə rē *or* chăn′slə rē) *n., pl.* **chan•cel•ler•ies. 1.** The rank or position of a chancellor. **2.** The office or building in which a chancellor is located. **3.** The office of an embassy or consulate; a chancery.

chan•cel•lor (chăn′sə lər *or* chăn′slər) *n.* **1.a.** The chief minister of state in some European countries. **b.** In the British government, any of various high officials, such as the Chancellor of the Exchequer. **2.** The president of certain American universities. **3.** The presiding judge of a court of equity in the United States.

Chancellor of the Exchequer *n.* The highest minister of finance in the British government and a member of the prime minister's cabinet.

chan•cel•lor•ship (chăn′sə lər shĭp′ *or* chăn′slər shĭp′) *n.* The position or term of office of a chancellor.

chan•cer•y (chăn′sə rē) *n., pl.* **chan•cer•ies. 1.** A court dealing with cases that are not covered by common law and that have to be tried according to a special body of laws; a court of equity. **2.** An office for the collection and safekeeping of official documents. **3.** A chancellery, especially of a country's embassy or consulate.

chan•cre (shăng′kər) *n.* A sore or an ulcer that forms on the skin, usually as an early indication of a diseased condition.

chanc•y (chăn′sē) *adj.* **chanc•i•er, chanc•i•est.** Uncertain as to outcome; risky: *a chancy undertaking.*

chan•de•lier (shăn′də lîr′) *n.* A lighting fixture that holds a number of bulbs or candles on branches and is suspended from a ceiling.

chan•dler (chănd′lər) *n.* **1.** A person who makes or sells candles. **2.** A person who sells goods or equipment for use on a ship.

Chang•chun (chăng′cho͞on′). A city of northeast China northeast of Beijing. Population, 1,480,000.

change (chānj) *v.* **changed, chang•ing, chang•es.** —*tr.* **1.** To cause to be different; alter: *change the rules; change the color of a room.* **2.** To take, put, or use (something) in place of another, usually of the same kind: *The company changed its name.* **3.a.** To give and receive (one thing for another); exchange; switch: *The twins changed places to fool everybody.* **b.** To exchange (a unit of money) for smaller units: *The machine changes a dollar bill into coins.* **4.** To put fresh clothes or coverings on: *It's your turn to change the baby. I'll show you how to change the bed.* —*intr.* **1.** To become different or altered: *The town grew and changed over the years.* **2.** To make an exchange; switch: *If you would rather sit in this seat, I'll change with you.* **3.** To put on other clothing: *They changed into work clothes.* **4.** To transfer from one vehicle to another: *We changed in Chicago on our way to the coast.* **5.** To become deeper in tone: *His voice began to change.* —*n.* **1.** The act, process, or result of changing: *a change in the schedule.* **2.a.** The money of smaller denomination exchanged for a unit of higher denomination: *Will you give me change of four quarters for a dollar?* **b.** The money returned when the amount given in paying for something is more than what is due: *The change was only a dime.* **c.** A number of coins: *a purse full of change.* **3.** Something different; a break in one's routine: *We finished dinner early for a change.* **4.** A fresh set of clothing. —*idioms.* **change hands.** To pass from one owner to another: *The store changed hands this year.* **change (one's) mind.** To alter a decision or an

chameleon
Horned chameleon

chandelier

ă	pat	oi	boy
ā	pay	ou	out
âr	care	o͝o	took
ä	father	o͞o	boot
ĕ	pet	ŭ	cut
ē	be	ûr	urge
ĭ	pit	th	thin
ī	pie	*th*	this
îr	pier	hw	whoop
ŏ	pot	zh	vision
ō	toe	ə	about
ô	paw	N	*French* bon

chaps

opinion. [First written down before 1200 in Middle English and spelled *changen*, from Latin *cambiāre*, to exchange.] **—chang′er** *n.*

change•a•ble (chān′jə bəl) *adj.* **1.** Likely to change; capricious: *changeable moods.* **2.** Capable of being altered: *changeable habits.* **3.** Changing color or appearance when seen from different angles: *the changeable iridescent plumage of a hummingbird.* **—change′a•bil′i•ty, change′a•ble•ness** *n.* **—change′a•bly** *adv.*

change•ful (chānj′fəl) *adj.* Having the tendency or ability to change; variable: *a changeful sky at sunset.* **—change′ful•ly** *adv.* **—change′ful•ness** *n.*

change•less (chānj′lĭs) *adj.* Never changing; constant: *He was changeless in his opposition to our proposal.* **—change′less•ly** *adv.* **—change′less•ness** *n.*

change•ling (chānj′lĭng) *n.* **1.** In folklore, a child of the fairies secretly exchanged for a human child. **2.** A human child secretly exchanged for another.

change•o•ver (chānj′ō′vər) *n.* A change from one way of doing something to another: *a changeover from typewriters to computers.*

Chang Jiang (chäng′ jyäng′). Yangtze River.

chan•nel (chăn′əl) *n.* **1.** The bed or deepest part of a stream or river. **2.** A part of a river or harbor deep enough to form a passage for ships and often maintained by dredging. **3.** A broad strait: *a channel between islands.* **4.** A passage or conduit for liquids: *Each side of the road had a channel for water to run off.* **5.** A course or way through which something, such as news, messages, or ideas, may travel: *opening new channels of information; a channel of thought.* **6.** A band of frequencies reserved for broadcasting or communication: *a television channel.* **7. channels.** Official routes of communication: *go through channels to get permission to enter the secluded forest.* **8.** The sound recorded by a separate microphone and played back through a single loudspeaker in a stereo system. *—tr.v.* **chan•neled, chan•nel•ing, chan•nels** also **chan•nelled, chan•nel•ling, chan•nels. 1.** To form a channel in or through: *The stream channeled the limestone.* **2.** To direct or guide along a desired route: *channel her thoughts towards making a movie.* [First written down before 1325 in Middle English and spelled *chanel*, from Latin *canālis*, canal.]

Chan•nel Islands (chăn′əl). A group of British islands in the English Channel off the coast of Normandy, France. The islands became part of England with the Norman Conquest of 1066.

chant (chănt) *n.* **1.** A simple melody in which many words or syllables are sung on the same note. **2.** A religious text sung to such a melody. **3.** A sustained rhythmic call or shout: *the chant of the crowd at a football game.* *—v.* **chant•ed, chant•ing, chants.** *—tr.* **1.** To sing to a chant: *The monks chanted psalms.* **2.** To call out in a sustained rhythmic way: *chant a slogan at a rally.* *—intr.* **1.** To call in a chant: *The crowd chanted for the President.* **2.** To sing a chant: *The monks chanted during the service.* **—chant′er** *n.*

chan•teuse (shän tœz′) *n.* A female singer, especially one who sings in small clubs.

chan•tey (shăn′tē *or* chăn′tē) *n., pl.* **chan•teys** also **chan•ties.** A work song sung by sailors in earlier times to the rhythm of their work.

❑ *These sound alike:* **chantey, shanty** (shack).

chan•ti•cleer (chăn′tĭ klîr′ *or* shăn′tĭ klîr′) *n.* A rooster. [First written down before 1300 in Middle English and spelled *chauntecler*, from Old French *chantecler*, the name of the rooster in the tale of Reynard the Fox : *chanter*, to sing + *cler*, clear.]

Chan•til•ly (shăn tĭl′ē). A village of northern France north of Paris noted for its porcelain and lace. Population, 10,065.

chan•ty (shăn′tē *or* chăn′tē) *n.* Variant of **chantey.**

Cha•nu•kah (KHä′nə kə *or* hä′nə kə) *n.* Variant of **Hanukkah.**

cha•os (kā′ŏs′) *n.* **1.** Great disorder or confusion: *The street was in chaos after the car accident.* **2.** Often **Chaos.** The shapeless and disordered state of unformed matter and infinite space supposed in some views to have existed before the creation of the universe.

cha•ot•ic (kā ŏt′ĭk) *adj.* In a state of chaos; in great disorder or confusion. **—cha•ot′i•cal•ly** *adv.*

chap¹ (chăp) *tr. & intr.v.* **chapped, chap•ping, chaps.** To make or become dry, scaly, and cracked: *Harsh soaps will chap your hands. My lips chap easily in the cold weather.* *—n.* A roughness and soreness of the skin, caused especially by cold. [First written down in 1440 in Middle English and spelled *chappen*.]

chap² (chăp) *n. Informal.* A man or boy; a fellow. [First written down in 1577 in Modern English, short for *chapman*, peddler.]

chap. *abbr.* An abbreviation of chapter.

chap•ar•ral (shăp′ə răl′) *n.* A dense growth of tangled, often thorny shrubs, especially in the southwest United States and Mexico. [First written down in 1845 in American English, from Spanish, from *chaparro*, evergreen oak, from Basque *txapar*.]

cha•peau (shă pō′) *n., pl.* **cha•peaus** or **cha•peaux** (shă pōz′). A hat.

chap•el (chăp′əl) *n.* **1.a.** A small church: *a little chapel in the hills.* **b.** A small place, with its own altar, within a church, reserved for special services: *The cathedral had a chapel dedicated to soldiers and sailors.* **2.** A place for religious services, as in a school, hospital, or military base. **3.** Religious services held at a chapel: *Students attended chapel before the holidays.*

chap•er•on or **chap•er•one** (shăp′ə rōn′) *n.* **1.** An older person who attends and supervises a dance or party for young unmarried people. **2.** A person, especially an older or married woman, who accompanies a young unmarried woman in public. *—tr.v.* **chaper•oned, chaper•on•ing, chaper•ones.** To act as a chaperon for: *chaperon a party.*

chap•lain (chăp′lĭn) *n.* A member of the clergy who conducts religious services and performs other duties for an institution, a military unit, or a school.

chap•let (chăp′lĭt) *n.* **1.** A wreath for the head. **2.** A short rosary. **3.** A string of beads.

chaps (chăps *or* shăps) *pl.n.* Heavy leather coverings worn over trousers by cowhands to protect their legs. Chaps buckle around the waist and have no seat. [First written down in 1844 in American English, short for Spanish *chaparreras*, from *chaparro*, chaparral.]

chap•ter (chăp′tər) *n.* **1.** A main division of a book. **2.** A series of related events or a part of a person's life: *That was an exciting chapter in my life.* **3.** A local branch of a club, fraternity, or other organization.

Cha•pul•te•pec (chə po͝ol′tə pĕk′). A rocky hill south of Mexico City, Mexico. It was the site of a major American victory (1847) during the Mexican War.

char (chär) *v.* **charred, char•ring, chars.** *—tr.* **1.** To reduce to charcoal by incomplete burning: *Most of the beams were charred and had to be replaced.* **2.** To burn the surface of; scorch: *The fire charred the papers.* *—intr.* **1.** To become reduced to charcoal. **2.** To become scorched.

char•ac•ter (kăr′ək tər) *n.* **1.** The combination of qualities or features that makes one person, group, or thing different from another: *The character of* *the town is calm and peaceful.* **2.** One's moral nature: *an honest and upstanding student of fine character.* **3.** Moral strength; integrity: *a respected citizen of character.* **4.** A person portrayed in a work of art, such as a novel, play, or movie: *The hero is the chief character in the play.* **5.** *Informal.* An odd or eccentric person. **6.** Status, capacity, or role: *She wrote the checks in her character as club treasurer.* **7.** A symbol, such as a letter or number, used in representing information, as in printing, writing, or a computer program. **8.** A physical trait or distinctive feature in the structure or function of an organism. **—*idioms.* in character.** Consistent with someone's general character or usual behavior. **out of character.** Not consistent with one's general character or usual behavior: *Teasing friends is quite out of character for him.* [First written down before 1333 in Middle English and spelled *caracter,* distinctive mark, imprint on the soul, from Greek *kharaktēr.*]

char•ac•ter•is•tic (kăr′ək tə **rĭs′**tĭk) *adj.* Being a feature or quality that distinguishes a person or thing: *the zebra's characteristic stripes; my friend's characteristic laugh.* —*n.* **1.** A feature or quality that distinguishes a person or thing: *A curved bill is a characteristic of parrots.* See Synonyms at **quality. 2.** The whole number in a logarithm. For example, if 2.713 is a logarithm, 2 is the characteristic. **—char′ac•ter•is′ti•cal•ly** *adv.*

char•ac•ter•i•za•tion (kăr′ək tər ĭ **zā′**shən) *n.* **1.** The act or an instance of characterizing. **2.** A description of qualities: *This book has characterizations of all the restaurants in town.* **3.** Representation of a character or characters in literature or drama: *The author uses very realistic characterization in the novel.*

char•ac•ter•ize (**kăr′**ək tə rīz′) *tr.v.* **character•ized, character•iz•ing, character•iz•es. 1.** To describe the character or qualities of; portray: *The supervisor's report characterized the nurse as very efficient.* **2.** To be a characteristic or quality of: *Spruce and birch forests characterize that region.*

cha•rade (shə **rād′**) *n.* *(used with a singular or plural verb).* **1. charades.** A game in which words or phrases are acted out in pantomime, often syllable by syllable, until guessed by the other players. **2.** Something done as a deception; a pretense: *Laughter is often a charade to cover up nervousness.*

char•coal (**chär′**kōl′) *n.* **1.** A black porous material composed chiefly of carbon, produced by heating wood or sometimes bone until the lighter materials in it are burned away. It is used as a fuel, a filtering material, and for drawing. **2.** A stick of this material, used for drawing.

chard (chärd) *n.* Swiss chard.

charge (chärj) *v.* **charged, charg•ing, charg•es.** —*tr.* **1.a.** To ask as a price: *The shop charges three dollars to sharpen skates.* **b.** To demand payment from: *The store will charge you for wrapping the gift.* **2.** To postpone payment on (a purchase) by recording the amount owed: *We can charge school supplies to our account at the bookstore.* **3.** To attack violently: *The soldiers charged the hill.* **4.** To accuse; blame: *The police charged the driver with reckless driving.* **5.** To command; order: *The judge charged the jury to consider all the evidence.* **6.** To entrust with a duty, task, or responsibility: *The editor charged the reporter to dig out all the facts.* **7.** To fill; load: *They charged the furnace with coal. The last scene of the movie was charged with excitement.* **8.** To fill with an amount of electrical energy; energize: *We can charge the car battery at the gas station.* —*intr.* **1.** To demand or ask payment: *They didn't charge for the repair.* **2.** To rush forward, as or as if in an attack; move quickly: *The children charged out of the room.* **3.** To postpone payment for a purchase. —*n.* **1.** An amount asked or made as payment: *There is no charge for this delivery.* **2.** Care; supervision; control: *the scientist in charge of the laboratory.* See Synonyms at **care. 3.** A person or thing for which one is responsible: *The camp counselors took their charges to the amusement park.* **4.** A duty or task; a responsibility: *My charge is to find out what happened and report back to the committee.* **5.** An order or a command: *received a written charge to attend the hearing.* **6.** An accusation, especially one made formally, as in a legal case: *The charge against the defendant was dismissed.* **7.** A rushing forceful attack: *the charge of a bull elephant.* **8.** The amount of electrical energy contained in an object, a particle, or a region of space. A charge is positive if the object or space contains fewer electrons than protons. A charge is negative if the object or space contains more electrons than protons. **9.** The quantity that an apparatus or container can hold: *They gave the battery a full charge.* **10.** An amount of explosive to be set off at one time: *a box of dynamite charges.* **11.** *Informal.* A feeling of excitement; a thrill: *They got a real charge from seeing the Grand Canyon.* **—*idioms.* in charge.** In a position of authority or management; in command: *The manager of the store is in charge.* **in charge of.** Having control over or responsibility for: *The recreation department is in charge of the annual fireworks display.* [First written down before 1250 in Middle English and spelled *chargen,* to load, from Late Latin *carricāre,* from Latin *carrus,* wagon, of Celtic origin.] —SEE NOTE.

charge account *n.* An arrangement of credit, as with a store, in which a customer receives goods or services before paying for them.

charge card *n.* A credit card.

char•gé d'af•faires (shär zhā′ dä **fâr′**) *n., pl.* **char•gés d'affaires** (shär zhā′ dä **fâr′** *or* shär **zhāz′** dä-**fâr′**). **1.** A government official who temporarily takes over the duties of an absent ambassador or minister. **2.** A diplomat of the lowest rank.

charg•er[1] (**chär′**jər) *n.* **1.** A horse ridden in battle. **2.** A device used to charge electric storage batteries. [First written down in 1762 in Modern English, from *charge.*]

charg•er[2] (**chär′**jər) *n.* A large shallow dish; a platter. [First written down about 1305 in Middle English and spelled *chargeour,* from Old French *chargier,* to load.]

char•i•ot (**chăr′**ē ət) *n.* A horse-drawn two-wheeled vehicle used in ancient times in battle, races, and processions.

char•i•o•teer (chăr′ē ə **tîr′**) *n.* A person who drives a chariot.

cha•ris•ma (kə **rĭz′**mə) *n., pl.* **cha•ris•ma•ta** (kə-**rĭz′**mə tə). A special quality of individuals who show an exceptional ability to lead and win the devotion of large numbers of people.

char•is•mat•ic (kăr′ĭz **măt′**ĭk) *adj.* Of or relating to charisma: *a charismatic leader.*

char•i•ta•ble (**chăr′**ĭ tə bəl) *adj.* **1.** Showing love or good will; full of kindness: *a warm charitable spirit.* **2.** Generous in giving money or help to the needy. **3.** Tolerant or lenient in judging others: *Most parents are charitable about their children's mistakes.* **4.** Of or for helping the needy: *made a donation to a charitable organization.* **—char′i•ta•ble•ness** *n.* **—char′i•ta•bly** *adv.*

char•i•ty (**chăr′**ĭ tē) *n., pl.* **chari•ties. 1.** Good will or kind feelings toward others. **2.** Tolerance and leniency in judging others: *Lincoln urged charity for all after the Civil War.* **3.** A kind or generous act. **4.** Help or relief to the needy: *raising money for*

charge

Electric **charge** is a basic property of elementary particles of matter. The protons in an atom have a positive charge, while its electrons have a negative charge. In an ordinary atom, the number of protons equals the number of electrons, so the atom is electrically neutral. If an atom gains some electrons, it becomes negatively charged. If it loses some electrons, it becomes positively charged. Atoms that become charged are called **ions**. Every charged particle is surrounded by an **electric field**, the region of space in which the charge exerts a force. Because of their electric fields, particles with unlike charges attract one another, and those with like charges repel one another. **Static electricity** consists of charged particles at rest. Electric **current** consists of moving charged particles, especially electrons or ions.

chariot

Late sixth-century B.C. bronze Etruscan ceremonial chariot

ă	**pat**	oi	**boy**
ā	**pay**	ou	**out**
âr	**care**	o͝o	**took**
ä	**father**	o͞o	**boot**
ĕ	**pet**	ŭ	**cut**
ē	**be**	ûr	**urge**
ĭ	**pit**	th	**thin**
ī	**pie**	*th*	**this**
îr	**pier**	hw	**whoop**
ŏ	**pot**	zh	**vision**
ō	**toe**	ə	**about**
ô	**paw**	N	*French* **bon**

Charlemagne
c. 1349 bust

Charybdis
Odysseus between the whirlpool Charybdis (*left*) and the sea monster Scylla (*right*)

charity. **5.** An institution or a fund established to help the needy: *a ten-dollar donation to a charity.* [First written down in 1137 in Middle English and spelled *carited*, from Latin *cāritās*.]

char•la•tan (shär′lə tən) *n.* A person who deceives others by falsely claiming to have expert knowledge or skill; a quack. [First written down in 1618 in Modern English, from Italian *ciarlatano*, probably alteration of *cerretano*, inhabitant of *Cerreto*, a city of Italy once famous for its quacks.]

Char•le•magne (shär′lə mān′). 742?–814. King of the Franks (768–814) whose court was the center of a cultural rebirth in Europe.

Charles I (chärlz). 1600–1649. King of England, Scotland, and Ireland (1625–1649) who was tried for treason and beheaded.

Charles II. 1630–1685. King of England, Scotland, and Ireland (1660–1685) who reigned during the Restoration.

Charles Mar•tel (mär tĕl′). 688?–741. Frankish ruler who was the grandfather of Charlemagne.

Charles•ton[1] (chärl′stən). **1.** A city of southeast South Carolina northeast of Savannah, Georgia. It was founded in colonial times. Population, 80,414. **2.** The capital and largest city of West Virginia, in the west-central part of the state. Population, 57,287.

Charles•ton[2] (chärl′stən) *n.* A quick lively dance popular in the 1920's.

char•ley horse (chär′lē) *n. Informal.* A muscle cramp or stiffness, especially in the arm or leg.

Char•lotte[1] (shär′lət). 1896–1985. Grand duchess of Luxembourg (1919–1984) who ruled in exile during the Nazi occupation of Luxembourg.

Char•lotte[2] (shär′lət). A city of southern North Carolina near the South Carolina border west-southwest of Raleigh. Settled in about 1750, it is the largest city in the state. Population, 395,934.

Charlotte A•ma•lie (ə mäl′yə). The capital of the U.S. Virgin Islands, on St. Thomas Island in the West Indies east of Puerto Rico. Population, 11,842.

Char•lotte•town (shär′lət toun′). The capital and largest city of Prince Edward Island, Canada, on the southern coast of the island. It was founded in about 1720. Population, 15,282.

charm (chärm) *n.* **1.** The power or ability to please or delight; appeal: *the charm of the peaceful countryside.* **2.** A quality or manner that pleases or attracts: *Her wit is one of her many charms.* **3.** A saying, action, or thing supposed to have magical power, as in warding off evil. **4.** A trinket or small ornament worn hanging on a bracelet or chain. *—tr.v.* **charmed, charm•ing, charms. 1.** To please greatly; delight; fascinate: *The audience was charmed by the young pianist.* **2.** To affect by or as if by magic; bewitch: *The children's laughter charmed us into playing the game again.* ***—idiom.*** **like a charm.** Exceedingly well. [First written down before 1300 in Middle English and spelled *charme*, magic spell, from Latin *carmen*, incantation.] **—charm′er** *n.*

charm•ing (chär′mĭng) *adj.* Delightful; attractive; very pleasing: *a charming person; charming manners.* **—charm′ing•ly** *adv.*

char•nel house (chär′nəl) *n.* A building, room, or vault in which the bodies or bones of the dead are placed.

Char•on (kâr′ən) *n.* In Greek mythology, the ferryman who carries the dead over the river Styx to Hades.

chart (chärt) *n.* **1.** Something written or drawn, as a table or graph, that presents information in an organized, easily viewed form: *a chart showing rainfall for the last ten years.* **2.** A map showing coastlines, water depths, or other information of use to navigators. *—tr.v.* **chart•ed, chart•ing, charts. 1.** To show or record on a chart; make a chart of: *chart the daily changes in temperature.* **2.** To plan in detail: *I hope to chart a course for success.* [First written down in 1571 in Modern English, from Latin *charta*, sheet of paper made from papyrus.]

char•ter (chär′tər) *n.* **1.** A written grant or document from a ruler, government, or other group, giving certain rights to a person, a corporation, or an entire people: *The Magna Carta is a famous charter granted by King John of England in 1215 to his nobles.* **2.** A document, such as a constitution, stating the principles, function, and form of a governing body or organization: *The United Nations is governed by a charter.* **3.** The hiring or renting of a bus, an aircraft, a boat, or another vehicle for a special use. *—tr.v.* **char•tered, char•ter•ing, char•ters. 1.** To grant a charter to; establish by charter: *Congress chartered the bank for twenty years.* **2.** To hire or rent by charter: *The travel club chartered a plane.* **—char′ter•er** *n.*

char•treuse (shär trooz′ *or* shär troos′) *n.* A light yellowish green.

char•wom•an (chär′wo͝om′ən) *n.* A woman hired to do cleaning, usually in an office or a large building.

char•y (châr′ē) *adj.* **char•i•er, char•i•est. 1.** Cautious; wary: *chary of walking on thin ice.* **2.** Not giving freely; sparing: *chary of compliments.* **—char′i•ly** *adv.* **—char′i•ness** *n.*

Cha•ryb•dis (kə rĭb′dĭs) *n.* In Greek mythology, a whirlpool opposite the cave of Scylla near Sicily, personified as a monster because of its ability to destroy ships.

chase (chās) *v.* **chased, chas•ing, chas•es.** *—tr.* **1.** To follow quickly and try to catch or overtake; pursue: *Our dog chased the cat.* **2.** To drive away: *chased the rabbits from the garden.* *—intr.* **1.** To go or follow in pursuit: *chase after a loose dog.* **2.** *Informal.* To hurry; rush: *chasing about town doing last-minute errands.* *—n.* **1.** The act of chasing; rapid pursuit: *The police arrested the driver after a wild chase.* **2.a.** The hunting of game. **b.** Something that is hunted; quarry: *The hunters drove their chase into the open.* [First written down before 1300 in Middle English and spelled *chasen*, to hunt, from Latin *captāre*, to capture.]

chas•er (chā′sər) *n.* **1.** A person or thing that chases or pursues. **2.** *Informal.* A drink of water, beer, or other liquid taken after a drink of hard liquor.

chasm (kăz′əm) *n.* **1.** A deep crack or opening in the surface of the earth; a gorge. **2.** A gap, such as that caused by a difference of opinion or attitude: *a chasm in communication.* [First written down in 1596 in Modern English, from Greek *khasma*.]

Chas•sid (KHä′sĭd *or* hä′sĭd) *n.* Variant of **Hasid.**

chas•sis (shăs′ē *or* chăs′ē) *n., pl.* **chas•sis** (shăs′ēz *or* chăs′ēz). **1.** The frame of an automotive vehicle that supports the body and includes the motor, gears, axles, and wheels. **2.** The landing gear of an aircraft. **3.** The structure that holds and supports the parts of a radio, television, or other piece of electronic equipment.

chaste (chāst) *adj.* **chast•er, chast•est. 1.** Morally pure in thought and conduct; decent; modest. **2.** Not ornate or extreme; pure in style or simple in design. **3.a.** Abstaining from sexual intercourse. **b.** Having never experienced sexual intercourse. **—chaste′ly** *adv.* **—chaste′ness** *n.*

chas•ten (chā′sən) *tr.v.* **chas•tened, chas•ten•ing, chas•tens. 1.** To discipline or correct by punishment. **2.** To cause to become subdued or meek; restrain; temper: *His spirit was chastened by hard experience.* —**chas′ten•er** *n.*

chas•tise (chăs tīz′ *or* chăs′tīz′) *tr.v.* **chas•tised, chas•tis•ing, chas•tis•es.** To punish or criticize severely for misbehavior or wrongdoing. —**chas•tise′ment** *n.* —**chas•tis′er** *n.*

chas•ti•ty (chăs′tĭ tē) *n.* The condition or quality of being chaste or pure.

chat (chăt) *intr.v.* **chat•ted, chat•ting, chats.** To converse in a relaxed, friendly, informal manner: *chat with friends.* —*n.* **1.** A relaxed, friendly, informal conversation. **2.** Any of several songbirds having a chattering call.

cha•teau also **châ•teau** (shă tō′) *n., pl.* **cha•teaus** or **cha•teaux** (shă tōz′). **1.** A French castle or manor house. **2.** A large country house. [First written down in 1739 in Modern English, from Old French *chastel*, from Latin *castellum*, castle.]

chat•e•laine (shăt′l ān′) *n.* **1.a.** The mistress of a castle. **b.** The mistress of a large fashionable household. **2.** A clasp or chain worn at the waist for holding keys, a watch, or a purse.

Chat•ta•noo•ga (chăt′ə no͞o′gə). A city of southeast Tennessee on the Georgia border southeast of Nashville. It was strategically important during the Civil War. Population, 152,466.

chat•tel (chăt′l) *n.* An article of personal property that can be moved from place to place, as a piece of furniture or an animal. [First written down about 1225 in Middle English and spelled *chatel*, from Old French, from Medieval Latin *capitāle*.]

chat•ter (chăt′ər) *v.* **chat•tered, chat•ter•ing, chat•ters.** —*intr.* **1.** To make short rapid sounds that resemble speech, as some animals and birds do: *Monkeys chattered in the trees.* **2.** To talk rapidly and at length about something unimportant; jabber. **3.** To make a rapid series of rattling or clicking noises: *My teeth chattered with cold.* —*tr.* To utter in a rapid and thoughtless way: *chatter nonsense.* —*n.* **1.** Idle talk about unimportant matters: *All of that gossip is just neighborhood chatter.* **2.** The sharp rapid sounds made by some birds and animals. **3.** A series of quick rattling or clicking sounds: *the chatter of typewriters.*

chat•ter•box (chăt′ər bŏks′) *n.* A person who seems to talk all the time.

chat•ty (chăt′ē) *adj.* **chat•ti•er, chat•ti•est. 1.** Given to informal conversation: *a chatty person full of gossip.* **2.** Having the tone or style of informal conversation: *a chatty newspaper column about current celebrities.* —**chat′ti•ly** *adv.* —**chat′ti•ness** *n.*

Chau•cer (chô′sər), **Geoffrey.** 1340?–1400. English poet regarded as the greatest literary figure of medieval England. His works include *The Canterbury Tales* (1387–1400).

chauf•feur (shō′fər *or* shō fûr′) *n.* A person who is hired to drive an automobile. —*tr.v.* **chauf•feured, chauf•feur•ing, chauf•feurs.** To serve as a driver for: *chauffering visiting relatives to see the local sights.* [First written down in 1899 in Modern English, from French *chauffeur*, stoker, from Old French *chaufer*, to heat, stoke.]

chau•vin•ism (shō′və nĭz′əm) *n.* **1.** Extreme devotion to one's country or a cause; fanatical patriotism. **2.** Unwarranted belief in the superiority of one's own group; prejudice. [First written down in 1870 in Modern English, from French *chauvinisme*, after Nicolas *Chauvin*, a legendary French soldier famous for his devotion to Napoleon.] —**chau′vin•ist** *n.* & *adj.*

Cha•vez (chä′vĕz′ *or* shä′vĕz′), **Cesar.** 1927–1993. American labor organizer who founded the National Farm Workers Association (1962).

cheap (chēp) *adj.* **cheap•er, cheap•est. 1.** Low in price; inexpensive or comparatively inexpensive: *Tomatoes are cheap and plentiful in the summer months.* **2.** Charging low prices: *a cheap restaurant.* **3.** Requiring little effort; easily gotten: *a cheap victory.* **4.** Of little value or poor quality; inferior: *cheap shoes that wear out quickly.* **5.** Worthy of no respect; contemptible: *cheap humor.* **6.** Not spending or giving money generously; stingy: *a miser's cheap ways.* —*adv.* **cheaper, cheapest.** At a low price: *an old car that we bought cheap.* [First written down about 1280 in Middle English and spelled *(god) chep*, (good) price, purchase, bargain, from Old English *cēap*, trade, from Latin *caupō*, shopkeeper.] —**cheap′ly** *adv.* —**cheap′ness** *n.*

❑ *These sound alike:* **cheap, cheep** (chirp).

cheap•en (chē′pən) *tr.* & *intr.v.* **cheap•ened, cheap•en•ing, cheap•ens.** To make or become cheap or cheaper: *Rude behavior tends to cheapen one's reputation.*

cheap shot *n.* An unfair statement directed especially at a defenseless person or group.

cheap•skate (chēp′skāt′) *n. Slang.* A stingy person; a miser.

cheat (chēt) *v.* **cheat•ed, cheat•ing, cheats.** —*tr.* **1.** To deceive by trickery: *The grocer cheated customers by selling old bread at full prices.* **2.** To deprive of something dishonestly or unfairly; swindle: *The grain dealer cheated farmers out of their profits.* **3.** To elude or escape as if by trickery or deception: *The daring mountain climbers cheated death.* —*intr.* To act dishonestly: *cheat to pass a test; cheat at cards.* —*n.* **1.** A person who cheats; a swindler. **2.** An act of cheating; a fraud or swindle: *a scheme that was nothing but a big cheat.* —**cheat′er** *n.*

check (chĕk) *v.* **checked, check•ing, checks.** —*tr.* **1.** To cause to stop suddenly; halt: *The farmers checked erosion by building terraces across their sloping fields.* **2.** To restrain or control: *The angry driver checked a sudden urge to shout.* **3.** To test, examine, or make sure of: *Check your answers after finishing the math problems. I will check the number in the telephone directory.* **4.** To mark with a check: *Check each item on the list that is missing on the shelf.* **5.** To place for temporary safekeeping or shipping: *They checked their baggage at the airport.* **6.** To mark with a pattern of squares: *A pattern of blue and white squares checked the floor.* **7.a.** In chess, to move a piece so as to place (an opponent's king) under direct attack. **b.** In hockey, to block or hinder (an opposing player with the puck). —*intr.* **1.** To make an examination; be sure something is true or correct: *check on departure times; check with the teacher before leaving.* **2.** To correspond item for item; agree: *Our two lists checked exactly.* —*n.* **1.** Something that stops motion or expression; a restraint: *The snowstorm was a check on all air travel.* **2.** The condition of being stopped or held back: *The dry weather kept the mosquitoes in check.* **3.** A careful examination or investigation to see that something is being done or working properly: *A check of the math homework revealed several errors.* **4.** A standard for testing or comparing: *a quality check.* **5.** A mark (√) made to show that something has been noted, selected, or is accurate. **6.** A written order to a bank to pay a certain amount from funds on deposit in an account: *write a check to pay a bill.* **7.** A ticket or slip for identifying and claiming something: *a baggage check.* **8.** A bill at a restaurant: *The waiter gave us our check at the end of the meal.* **9.a.** A pattern of squares resembling a checkerboard. **b.** A single square in such a pattern: *a floor made of black and white checks.* **c.** A fabric printed or woven with such a pattern. **10.** In chess, the situation of the king when under direct attack by an opponent's piece.

Chaucer

Cesar Chavez

ă	pat	oi	boy
ā	pay	ou	out
âr	care	o͝o	took
ä	father	o͞o	boot
ĕ	pet	ŭ	cut
ē	be	ûr	urge
ĭ	pit	th	thin
ī	pie	*th*	this
îr	pier	hw	whoop
ŏ	pot	zh	vision
ō	toe	ə	about
ô	paw	N	*French* bon

cheetah

11. In hockey, the action of blocking or hindering an opposing player who is in control of the puck. *—idioms.* **check in.** To register or sign in, as at a hotel: *check in before the flight.* **check out. 1.** To leave, as after paying a hotel bill. **2.a.** To take after having paid the amount owed: *check out groceries at a supermarket.* **b.** To take after having recorded what is being taken: *check out books from the library.* **3.** To be confirmed as true: *The suspect's story checks out.* [First written down about 1300 in Middle English and spelled *chek*, check in chess, from Old French *eschec*, from Arabic *shāh*, from Persian, king, king in chess.]

check•book (chĕk′bo͝ok′) *n.* A book containing blank checks, given by a bank to a depositor who has a checking account.

checked (chĕkt) *adj.* Having a pattern of squares; checkered: *a checked shirt.*

check•er (chĕk′ər) *n.* **1.** A person or thing that checks, as for accuracy: *Our word processor has a checker for spelling.* **2.** A person who receives items for safekeeping or shipping: *a baggage checker.* **3.** A cashier in a supermarket. **4.a. checkers.** *(used with a singular verb).* A game played on a checkerboard by two players, each using 12 round, flat pieces of a different color from those of the other. Each player tries to capture all of the opponent's pieces. **b.** One of the pieces used in this game. **5.a.** A pattern of many squares. **b.** One of the squares in such a pattern. *—tr.v.* **check•ered, check•er•ing, check•ers.** To mark with a pattern of squares. [First written down about 1250 in Middle English and spelled *cheker*, chessboard, from Old French *eschequier*, from *eschec*, check in chess.]

check•er•board (chĕk′ər bôrd′) *n.* A game board divided into 64 squares of alternating colors, on which the game of checkers is played.

check•ered (chĕk′ərd) *adj.* **1.** Marked with or divided into squares: *a checkered floor.* **2.** Full of many changes; varied: *a checkered career.*

check•ing account (chĕk′ĭng) *n.* A bank account from which payments may be made by writing checks against the amount on deposit.

check•list (chĕk′lĭst′) *n.* A list of items to be checked or remembered.

check•mate (chĕk′māt′) *tr.v.* **check•mat•ed, check•mat•ing, check•mates. 1.** In chess, to move so as to place (an opponent's king) under an attack from which there is no escape or defense, thus ending the game. **2.** To defeat completely. *—n.* **1.** In chess, a move or situation that places an opponent's king under attack from which there is no escape or defense. **2.** A situation in which one is completely defeated. [First written down before 1346 in Middle English and spelled *chekmat*, from Old French *eschec mat*, from Arabic *shāh māt*, the king is dead : *shāh*, king + *māt*, dead.]

check•out (chĕk′out′) *n.* **1.** The act or process of checking out, as at a supermarket, library, or hotel. **2.** A test or inspection, as of a machine, for working condition or accuracy.

check•point (chĕk′point′) *n.* A place where pedestrians or vehicles are stopped for inspection.

check•rein (chĕk′rān′) *n.* **1.** A short rein connected to a horse's bit to keep a horse from lowering its head. **2.** A rein joining the bit of one horse in a team to the driving rein of the other horse.

check•room (chĕk′ro͞om′ *or* chĕk′ro͝om′) *n.* A room where coats, packages, or baggage may be left temporarily.

check•up (chĕk′ŭp′) *n.* A thorough examination or inspection, as for health or general working condition: *regular medical checkups; an engine checkup.*

Ched•dar also **ched•dar** (chĕd′ər) *n.* A firm, smooth, usually yellowish cheese first made in Cheddar, a village of southwest England.

cheek (chēk) *n.* **1.** The part of either side of the face below the eye and between the nose and ear. **2.** Impudence; sauciness: *have the cheek to tell one's elders what to do.* [First written down before 830 in Old English and spelled *cēce*.]

cheek•bone (chēk′bōn′) *n.* A small bone on the side of the face just below the eye, forming the outermost point of the cheek.

cheek•y (chē′kē) *adj.* **cheek•i•er, cheek•i•est.** Impudent; impertinent: *a cheeky smart aleck.* **—cheek′i•ly** *adv.* **—cheek′i•ness** *n.*

cheep (chēp) *n.* A high-pitched chirp, like that of a young bird. *—intr.v.* **cheeped, cheep•ing, cheeps.** To make such a sound.

❑ *These sound alike:* **cheep, cheap** (inexpensive).

cheer (chîr) *v.* **cheered, cheer•ing, cheers.** *—intr.* **1.** To shout in happiness, approval, encouragement, or enthusiasm: *The audience cheered and clapped.* **2.** To become cheerful: *In spite of my disappointment, I soon cheered up.* *—tr.* **1.** To praise, encourage, or urge by or as if by shouting: *The fans cheered the runner on.* **2.** To make happier or more cheerful: *A warm fire soon cheered us up.* *—n.* **1.** A shout of happiness, approval, encouragement, or enthusiasm: *The crowd gave a loud cheer for the winning team.* **2.** A slogan or chant shouted in encourament or approval, as for a school's team at a game. **3.** Happiness; good spirits: *My grandparents are always full of cheer.* **4.** Something that gives joy or happiness: *Friends sent words of cheer and encouragement.* **5.** Food and drink: *came over for some holiday cheer.* [First written down before 1200 in Middle English and spelled *chere*, expression, mood, from Late Latin *cara*, face, from Greek *kara*, head.]

cheer•ful (chîr′fəl) *adj.* **1.** In good spirits; happy: *Everyone was cheerful at breakfast.* See Synonyms at **glad. 2.** Producing a feeling of cheer; pleasant and bright: *a cozy cheerful room.* **3.** Willing; good-humored: *cheerful acceptance of one's duty.* **—cheer′ful•ly** *adv.* **—cheer′ful•ness** *n.*

cheer•lead•er (chîr′lē′dər) *n.* A person who leads the cheering of spectators, as at a football game.

cheer•less (chîr′lĭs) *adj.* Lacking cheer; gloomy and depressing: *a cheerless rainy day.* **—cheer′less•ly** *adv.* **—cheer′less•ness** *n.*

cheer•y (chîr′ē) *adj.* **cheer•i•er, cheer•i•est.** Bright and cheerful: *a cheery smile; a cheery fire.* **—cheer′i•ly** *adv.* **—cheer′i•ness** *n.*

cheese (chēz) *n.* A food made from pressed curds of milk, often seasoned and aged. [First written down in 800 in Old English and spelled *cēse*, from Latin *cāseus*.]

cheese•burg•er (chēz′bûr′gər) *n.* A hamburger topped with melted cheese.

cheese•cake (chēz′kāk′) *n.* A cake made with sweetened cream cheese or cottage cheese and often with various flavorings.

cheese•cloth (chēz′klôth′ *or* chēz′klŏth′) *n.* A thin loosely woven cotton cloth resembling gauze, originally used for wrapping cheese.

chees•y (chē′zē) *adj.* **chees•i•er, chees•i•est. 1.** Containing or resembling cheese. **2.** *Informal.* Of poor quality; shoddy: *a cheap room with cheesy furniture.* **—chees′i•ness** *n.*

chee•tah (chē′tə) *n.* A long-legged swift-running wild cat of Africa and southwest Asia that has tawny fur with black spots. [First written down in 1781 in Modern English, from Hindustani *cītā*, from Sanskrit *citrakāyaḥ*, tiger, leopard.]

chef (shĕf) *n.* A cook, especially the chief cook of a large kitchen staff, as in a restaurant.

che•la (kē′lə) *n., pl.* **che•lae** (kē′lē). A pincerlike claw of a lobster, crab, or scorpion.

chem. *abbr.* An abbreviation of: **1.** Chemical. **2.** Chemist. **3.** Chemistry.

chem•i•cal (kĕm′ĭ kəl) *adj.* **1.** Of or relating to chemistry: *a chemical discovery.* **2.** Used in or produced by means of chemistry: *a chemical symbol; a chemical change.* —*n.* A substance obtained by or used in a chemical process. —**chem′i•cal•ly** *adv.*

chemical engineering *n.* The branch of engineering that deals with the industrial production of chemicals and chemical products and with the manufacture of products through chemical processes. —**chemical engineer** *n.*

chemical warfare *n.* Warfare that uses chemicals, such as poison gas, that kill or incapacitate human beings.

che•mise (shə mēz′) *n.* **1.** A woman's undergarment that resembles a short loose slip. **2.** A dress that hangs straight from the shoulders.

chem•ist (kĕm′ĭst) *n.* **1.** A scientist who specializes in chemistry. **2.** *Chiefly British.* A pharmacist. [First written down in 1562 in Modern English and spelled *chimist*, from Medieval Latin *alchymista*, alchemist, from *alchymia*, alchemy.]

chem•is•try (kĕm′ĭ strē) *n., pl.* **chem•is•tries. 1.** The science that deals with the structure, properties, and reactions of the elements and the compounds they form. **2.** The chemical properties of a substance or a system of substances: *the chemistry of the blood.*

che•mo•syn•the•sis (kē′mō sĭn′thĭ sĭs) *n.* The formation of carbohydrates from carbon dioxide and water with energy obtained from some cellular chemical reaction, rather than from light in photosynthesis. —**chem•o•syn•thet•ic** (kē′mo sĭn-thĕt′ĭk) *adj.*

che•mo•ther•a•py (kē′mō thĕr′ə pē) *n.* The treatment of disease and infection by chemicals that have a specific poisonous effect on the disease-producing organisms or malignant cells. Chemotherapy includes the treatment of bacterial infections with antibiotics and the treatment of cancer by chemicals. —**che′mo•ther′a•peu′tic** *adj.*

che•nille (shə nēl′) *n.* **1.** Cord or yarn of silk, cotton, wool, or rayon with a fuzzy velvety pile, used for making fringes, tassels, or embroidery. **2.** Fabric made with this cord, used for bedspreads, rugs, and curtains.

Che•ops (kē′ŏps). 2590–2567 B.C. A king of Egypt who is famous as the builder of the Great Pyramid.

cheque (chĕk) *n. Chiefly British.* Variant of **check.**

cher•ish (chĕr′ĭsh) *tr.v.* **cher•ished, cher•ish•ing, cher•ish•es. 1.** To care for tenderly and affectionately; hold dear: *The children cherished the little kittens.* **2.** To keep or regard fondly; value highly: *Peoples of democratic countries cherish freedom.* See Synonyms at **appreciate.**

Cher•o•kee (chĕr′ə kē′ *or* chĕr′ə kē′) *n., pl.* **Cherokee** or **Cher•o•kees. 1.** A member of a Native American people formerly living in the Appalachian Mountains of the western Carolinas, northern Georgia, and eastern Tennessee, now living mainly in Oklahoma and western North Carolina. **2.** The Iroquoian language of the Cherokee.

cher•ry (chĕr′ē) *n., pl.* **cher•ries. 1.** Any of various small, rounded, fleshy fruits having a hard pit or stone and a smooth skin. Cherries range in color from yellow and bright red to a dark purple. **2.** A tree that bears such fruit. **3.** The wood of such a tree. **4.** A deep or bright red. [First written down before 1300 in Middle English and spelled *chir*, from Greek *kerasia*, cherry tree.]

cher•ub (chĕr′əb) *n., pl.* **cher•u•bim** (chĕr′əbĭm). **1.** An angel of high rank. **2.** *pl.* **cher•ubs. a.** An angel, usually shown in pictures as a beautiful winged child with a chubby face. **b.** A sweet, pretty, or innocent-looking child. —**che•ru′bic** (chə ro͞o′bĭk) *adj.*

Ches•a•peake Bay (chĕs′ə pēk′). An inlet of the Atlantic Ocean bordering on mainland Maryland and Virginia.

chess (chĕs) *n.* A game played on a chessboard by two players, each starting with 16 pieces that are moved in various ways. The object of the game is to checkmate the opponent's king. [First written down before 1300 in Middle English and spelled *ches*, short for Old French *esches*, plural of *eschec*, check in chess.]

chess•board (chĕs′bôrd′) *n.* A board with 64 squares in alternating colors, used in playing chess.

chess•man (chĕs′măn′) *n.* One of the pieces used in the game of chess; a king, queen, bishop, knight, rook, or pawn.

chest (chĕst) *n.* **1.** The part of the body between the neck and the abdomen, enclosed by the ribs and breastbone. **2.** A sturdy box with a lid, used especially for holding or storing things: *a tool chest.* **3.** A chest of drawers.

ches•ter•field (chĕs′tər fēld′) *n.* **1.** An overcoat, usually with concealed buttons and a velvet collar. **2.** A large overstuffed sofa with rounded armrests.

chest•nut (chĕs′nŭt′) *n.* **1.** A smooth, reddish-brown, edible nut of any of several trees of northern regions that is enclosed in a prickly husk. **2.** A tree that bears such nuts. **3.** The wood of such a tree. **4.** A reddish brown. **5.** A reddish-brown horse. **6.** Something lacking freshness or originality, such as an old stale joke or story. —*adj.* Reddish brown.

chest of drawers *n., pl.* **chests of drawers.** A piece of furniture with several drawers, used chiefly for keeping clothes; a bureau or dresser.

chev•a•lier (shĕv′ə lîr′) *n.* **1.** A knight or nobleman. **2.** A member of certain male honorary groups or orders. [First written down about 1378 in Middle English and spelled *chivaler*, from Late Latin *caballārius*, horseman, from Latin *caballus*, horse.]

Chev•i•ot (shĕv′ē ət *or* chĕv′ē ət) *n.* **1.** A rough wool cloth with a coarse weave, used for suits and coats and originally made from the wool of Cheviot sheep. **2.** Any of a breed of hardy sheep having short thick wool.

chev•ron (shĕv′rən) *n.* A badge of stripes meeting at an angle, worn on the sleeve, as of a military, naval, or police uniform, to show rank, merit, or length of service.

chew (cho͞o) *v.* **chewed, chew•ing, chews.** —*tr.* To bite and grind with the teeth: *chew food thoroughly.* —*intr.* To crush or grind something with the teeth. —*n.* **1.** The act of chewing: *puppies having a good chew on a bone.* **2.** Something held in the mouth and chewed. [First written down before 1000 in Old English and spelled *cēowan.*] —**chew′er** *n.*

chew•ing gum (cho͞o′ĭng) *n.* A sweet flavored gum for chewing, usually made of chicle.

che•wink (chĭ wĭngk′) *n.* The towhee.

chew•y (cho͞o′ē) *adj.* **chew•i•er, chew•i•est.** Needing much chewing in order to swallow: *tough chewy steak.* —**chew′i•ness** *n.*

Chey•enne[1] (shī ĕn′ *or* shī ăn′) *n., pl.* **Cheyenne** or **Chey•ennes. 1.** A member of a Native American people formerly living in parts of the eastern Rocky Mountains and the western Great Plains, now living mainly in Oklahoma and Montana. **2.** The Algonquian language of the Cheyenne. —**Chey•enne′** *adj.*

Chey•enne[2] (shī ăn′ *or* shī ĕn′). The capital of Wyoming, in the southeast part of the state near the Nebraska and Colorado borders. It was founded in 1867. Population, 50,008.

chi (kī) *n.* The 22nd letter of the Greek alphabet,

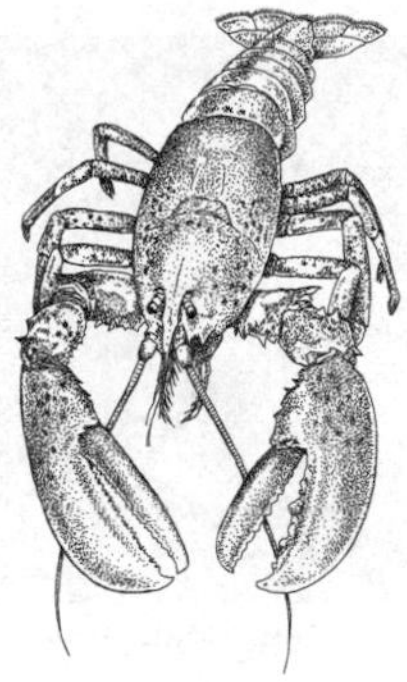

chela
Chelae of a lobster

chevron
On the uniform of a West Point graduate

ă	pat	oi	boy
ā	pay	ou	out
âr	care	o͝o	took
ä	father	o͞o	boot
ĕ	pet	ŭ	cut
ē	be	ûr	urge
ĭ	pit	th	thin
ī	pie	*th*	this
îr	pier	hw	whoop
ŏ	pot	zh	vision
ō	toe	ə	about
ô	paw	N	*French* bon

Chiang Kai-shek

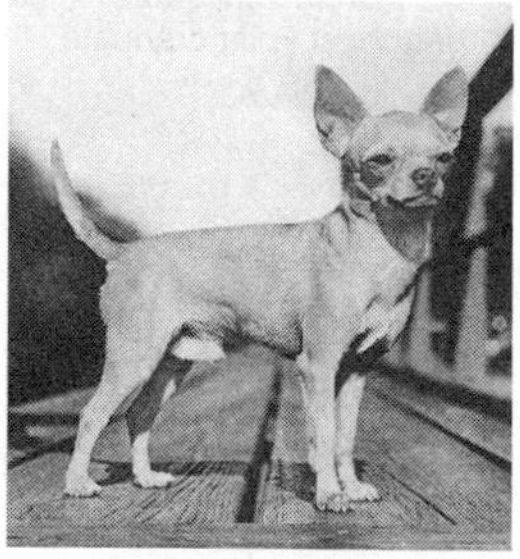

Chihuahua
Smooth-coat Chihuahua

written X, χ. In English, it is represented as *KH, kh* or *CH, ch*.

Chiang Kai-shek (chăng′ kī′shĕk′). 1887–1975. Chinese military and political figure who served as president of Taiwan from 1949 until 1975.

Chib•cha (chĭb′chə) *n., pl.* **Chibcha** or **Chib•chas. 1.** A member of an extinct Native American people who once inhabited Colombia. **2.** The language of the Chibcha.

chic (shēk) *adj.* **chic•er, chic•est.** Attractive and stylish; fashionable; smart: *a chic gown; a chic crowd.* —*n.* Style and elegance in dress or manner. [First written down in 1856 in Modern English, from French, probably from German *Schick*, skill, fitness, elegance.]

❑ *These sound alike:* **chic, sheik** (Arab leader).

Chi•ca•go (shĭ kä′gō *or* shĭ kô′gō). The largest city of Illinois, in the northeast part of the state on Lake Michigan. It is the commercial, financial, industrial, and cultural center of the Middle West. Population, 2,783,726.

Chi•ca•na (chĭ kä′nə *or* shĭ kä′nə) *n.* An American woman or girl who was born in Mexico or has Mexican ancestors. —**Chi•ca′na** *adj.*

chi•can•er•y (shĭ kā′nə rē *or* chĭ kā′nə rē) *n., pl.* **chi•can•er•ies.** Deception by trickery.

Chi•ca•no (chĭ kä′nō *or* shĭ kä′nō) *n., pl.* **Chi•ca•nos.** An American who was born in Mexico or has Mexican ancestors. —**Chi•ca′no** *adj.*

chick (chĭk) *n.* **1.** A young chicken. **2.** The young of any bird. **3.** A child.

chick•a•dee (chĭk′ə dē′) *n.* Any of several small plump birds that are mostly gray with a darker marking on the head.

Chick•a•mau•ga (chĭk′ə mô′gə). A city of extreme northwest Georgia south of Chattanooga, Tennessee. It is the site of a Confederate victory in the Civil War. Population, 2,232.

Chick•a•saw (chĭk′ə sô′) *n., pl.* **Chick•a•saw** or **Chick•a•saws. 1.** A member of a Native American people formerly living in Mississippi and Alabama and now living in Oklahoma. **2.** The Muskogean language of the Chickasaw.

chick•en (chĭk′ən) *n.* **1.** The common fowl raised for eggs or food; a hen or rooster. **2.** The meat of this fowl. **3.** Any of various similar birds. **4.** *Slang.* A person who is afraid or acts in a cowardly manner. —*adj. Slang.* Afraid; cowardly. —*intr.v.* **chick•ened, chick•en•ing, chick•ens.** *Slang.* To lose one's nerve; act in a cowardly manner: *chicken out at the last moment.* [First written down about 950 in Old English and spelled *cīcen.*]

chick•en-heart•ed (chĭk′ən här′tĭd) *adj.* Cowardly; timid.

chick•en•pox or **chicken pox** (chĭk′ən pŏks′) *n.* A contagious viral disease, mainly of young children, in which the skin breaks out in a rash and mild fever occurs.

chicken wire *n.* A wire mesh used as light fencing, especially where chickens are kept.

chick•pea (chĭk′pē′) *n.* **1.** The round edible seed of a bushy plant related to the pea; the garbanzo. **2.** The plant that bears such seeds.

chick•weed (chĭk′wēd′) *n.* Any of various low-growing weeds having small white flowers.

chic•le (chĭk′əl) *n.* The thickened milky juice of a tropical evergreen American tree, used as the main ingredient of chewing gum.

chic•o•ry (chĭk′ə rē) *n., pl.* **chic•o•ries. 1.** A plant related to lettuce, having blue flowers that resemble daisies and leaves used as salad greens. **2.** The root of this plant, dried, roasted, and ground and added to or used as a substitute for coffee.

chide (chīd) *tr. & intr.v.* **chid•ed** or **chid** (chĭd), **chid•ed** or **chid** or **chid•den** (chĭd′n), **chid•ing, chid•es.** To scold or reproach; reprove: *The director chided me for being late for rehearsal.*

chief (chēf) *n.* A person with the highest rank or authority; a leader: *the chief of a Scottish clan; the chief of the fire department.* —*adj.* **1.** Highest in rank or authority: *The chief engineer is in charge of the power station.* **2.** Most important; main; principal: *What is the country's chief crop?* —***idiom.*** **in chief.** With the highest rank or greatest authority: *Our editor-in-chief determines this newspaper's policies.* [First written down about 1300 in Middle English and spelled *chef*, from Latin *caput*, head.]

Chief Executive *n.* The President of the United States.

chief justice also **Chief Justice** *n.* A judge who presides over a court of several judges, as the United States Supreme Court.

chief•ly (chēf′lē) *adv.* **1.** Above all; especially: *They went home early, chiefly to avoid the storm.* **2.** For the most part; mostly; mainly: *grassy land used chiefly for grazing.*

chief of staff *n., pl.* **chiefs of staff. 1.** Often **Chief of Staff.** The highest ranking officer of the U.S. Army or Navy, responsible to the secretary of his or her branch of service and to the President. **2.** The senior military officer on the staff of a general or an admiral.

chief of state *n., pl.* **chiefs of state.** A person who is the formal head of a nation, but is not the head of the government: *In Great Britain the monarch is the chief of state.*

chief•tain (chēf′tən) *n.* The leader or head of a group, especially of a tribe or clan. [First written down before 1338 in Middle English and spelled *cheftain*, from Late Latin *capitāneus*, from Latin *caput*, head.]

chief•tain•cy (chēf′tən sē) *n., pl.* **chief•tain•cies.** The rank or position of a chieftain.

chif•fon (shĭ fŏn′ *or* shĭf′ŏn′) *n.* A soft, sheer, light fabric of silk, nylon, or rayon, used for scarfs, veils, dresses, and blouses. —*adj.* **1.** Of, relating to, or resembling chiffon. **2.** Made light and fluffy by the addition of beaten egg whites or gelatin: *lemon chiffon pie.*

chif•fo•nier (shĭf′ə nîr′) *n.* A narrow high chest of drawers, often with a mirror attached.

chig•ger (chĭg′ər) *n.* **1.** The tiny larva of any of various mites that clings to the skin of humans and animals, causing intense itching. **2.** The chigoe.

chi•gnon (shēn yŏn′ *or* shēn′yŏn′) *n.* A roll or knot of hair worn at the back of the head or nape of the neck.

chig•oe (chĭg′ō *or* chē′gō) *n.* **1.** A small tropical flea, the female of which burrows under the skin of humans and animals, causing intense itching and sores. **2.** Any of various mite larvae that cause itching; a chigger.

Chi•hua•hua (chĭ wä′wä) *n.* A tan or black dog having a smooth coat and pointed ears, belonging to an ancient breed that originated in Mexico. It is the smallest known dog.

chil•blain (chĭl′blān′) *n.* An itchy redness and soreness of the hands, feet, or ears, caused by exposure to damp cold.

child (chīld) *n., pl.* **chil•dren** (chĭl′drən). **1.** A person between birth and physical maturity. **2.a.** A son or daughter; an offspring: *There are several children in that big family.* **b.** An infant; a baby: *a newborn child.* **c.** An unborn baby; a fetus: *She is carrying a child in her womb.* **3.** An older person who behaves like a child; an immature person: *Most adults act the child now and then.* **4.** A descendant: *children of Abraham.* **5.** A person or thing considered as the offspring of some condition, agency, influence, or force: *a child of the 20th century.* —***idiom.*** **with**

child. Pregnant. [First written down about 750 in Old English and spelled *cild.*]
child•bear•ing (chīld′bâr′ĭng) *n.* Pregnancy and childbirth. —*adj.* Of or relating to childbirth: *The usual childbearing age of humans is between 15 and 45 years.*
child•birth (chīld′bûrth′) *n.* The act or process of giving birth to a child.
child•hood (chīld′ho͝od′) *n.* The time or condition of being a child: *Friends are easily made during childhood.*
child•ish (chīl′dĭsh) *adj.* **1.** Of, relating to, or suitable for a child: *a high childish voice; childish games.* **2.** Immature; foolish or silly: *childish behavior.* —**child′ish•ly** *adv.* —**child′ish•ness** *n.*
child•like (chīld′līk′) *adj.* Similar to or suitable for a child; innocent and simple: *childlike faith in others.*
child•proof (chīld′pro͞of′) *adj.* **1.** Designed to resist tampering by young children: *a childproof medicine bottle.* **2.** Made safe for young children: *Is the living room childproof?*
chil•dren (chĭl′drən) *n.* Plural of **child.**
child's play (chīldz) *n.* Something very easy to do: *These problems of addition are mere child's play.*
Chil•e (chĭl′ē *or* chē′lē). A country of southwest South America west of Argentina with a long Pacific coastline. Chile declared its independence from Spain in 1818. Capital, Santiago. Population, 11,329,736.
chil•i (chĭl′ē) *n., pl.* **chil•ies. 1.a.** The very sharp-tasting pod of any of several red peppers. **b.** A seasoning made from the dried or ground pods of such a pepper. **c.** A plant that bears such pods. **2.** Chili con carne. [First written down in 1846 in American English, from Spanish, from Nahuatl *chilli.*]
❑ *These sound alike:* **chili, chilly** (cold).
chili con car•ne (kŏn kär′nē) *n.* A spicy dish made with chili, tomatoes, meat, and often beans.
chili sauce *n.* A thick spicy sauce made with tomatoes, onions, and chili.
chill (chĭl) *n.* **1.** A moderate but penetrating coldness: *a chill in the fall air.* **2.** A feeling of coldness: *Chills and sneezing are signs of a cold.* **3.** A discouraging of enthusiasm or depressing of spirit: *The bad news put a chill on the celebration.* **4.** A feeling of fear: *We all felt a chill when the lights went out.* —*adj.* **1.** Moderately cold; chilly: *a chill north wind.* **2.** Not warm and friendly: *a chill greeting.* **3.** Discouraging: *My suggestions met with a chill response.* —*v.* **chilled, chill•ing, chills.** —*tr.* **1.** To make cold: *The icy wind chilled our faces.* **2.** To produce a feeling of cold, fear, or dismay in: *The eerie story chilled all who heard it.* **3.** To discourage; dampen: *Bad luck has chilled their enthusiasm.* —*intr.* **1.** To become cold: *Put the dessert in the refrigerator to chill.* **2.** To feel cold or be affected by a cold feeling: *The skaters chilled quickly in harsh wind.* [First written down before 830 in Old English and spelled *cele.*] —**chill′er** *n.*
chill•y (chĭl′ē) *adj.* **chill•i•er, chill•i•est. 1.** Cold enough to cause or feel discomfort: *Damp chilly weather is common along the seacoast.* See Synonyms at **cold. 2.** Feeling cold; shivering. **3.** Not enthusiastic: *a chilly reaction to the new plan.* **4.** Unfriendly: *a chilly greeting.* —**chill′i•ness** *n.*
❑ *These sound alike:* **chilly, chili** (seasoning).
chime (chīm) *n.* **1.** A set of bells tuned to different pitches and rung to make musical sounds. Often used in the plural. **2.** An orchestral instrument consisting of a set of metal tubes tuned to a musical scale and struck to make bell-like sounds. Often used in the plural. **3.** A single bell: *The chime in that clock strikes on the hour.* **4.** A musical sound produced by or as if by bells or chimes: *hear the chime of the church clock.* —*v.* **chimed, chim•ing, chimes.** —*intr.* To ring, as a bell or set of chimes. —*tr.* **1.** To strike (a bell) to produce music: *chime the church bells in celebration of peace.* **2.** To announce (the time of day) by ringing bells: *The clock chimed three o'clock.* —***idiom.*** **chime in.** To join in, as in song or conversation: *The audience chimed in on the chorus.* [First written down before 1300 in Middle English and spelled *chimbe*, from Latin *cymbalum*, cymbal.]
Chi•me•ra (kī mîr′ə *or* kĭ mîr′ə) *n.* **1.** In Greek mythology, a fire-breathing monster having the head of a lion, the body of a goat, and the tail of a serpent. **2.a.** A frightening monster or other creature of the imagination. **b.** A fantastic or impossible idea or fancy.
chi•mer•i•cal (kī mĕr′ĭ kəl *or* kĭ mĕr′ĭ kəl) *adj.* **1.** Like a Chimera; imaginary; fantastic: *chimerical theories about the end of the world.* **2.** Given to unrealistic fantasies; fanciful.
chim•ney (chĭm′nē) *n., pl.* **chim•neys. 1.** A hollow, usually vertical structure for the passage of smoke and gases rising from a fireplace, stove, or furnace. **2.** The part of such a structure that rises above a roof. **3.** The glass tube, often wide at the center and narrow at the top, placed around the flame of a lamp. **4.** Something resembling a chimney, as a narrow cleft in a cliff. [First written down about 1280 in Middle English and spelled *chimenai*, from Late Latin *camīnāta*, fireplace.]
chimney sweep *n.* A person employed to clean soot from chimneys.
chimney swift *n.* A small dark bird of North America, somewhat resembling a swallow, that often nests in unused chimneys.
chimp (chĭmp) *n. Informal.* A chimpanzee.
chim•pan•zee (chĭm′păn zē′ *or* chĭm păn′zē) *n.* A dark-haired African ape somewhat smaller than a gorilla, having a high degree of intelligence.
chin (chĭn) *n.* The front part of the face below the lips formed by the lower jaw and extending to the neck. —*tr.v.* **chinned, chin•ning, chins.** To grasp an overhead horizontal bar and pull (oneself) up with the arms until the chin clears the bar. [First written down about 725 in Old English and spelled *cin.*]
chi•na (chī′nə) *n.* **1.** A fine hard porcelain, originally made in China from a type of white clay, baked at high temperatures and often decorated with colored designs. **2.** Articles, such as dishes, vases, or figurines, made from this porcelain. **3.** Pottery of any kind.
Chi•na (chī′nə). A country of eastern Asia south of Mongolia and Russia. Its ancient civilization traditionally dates to around 2700 B.C. Beijing is the capital and Shanghai the largest city. Population, 1,008,175,288.
chi•na•ber•ry (chī′nə bĕr′ē) *n.* A spreading tree of Asia related to the mahogany and introduced to other southern climates for its shade and purplish flowers.
Chi•na•town (chī′nə toun′) *n.* A part of a city that is inhabited chiefly by Chinese people.
chi•na•ware (chī′nə wâr′) *n.* Dishes and other articles made of china or similar pottery.
chinch (chĭnch) *n.* **1.** A bedbug. **2.** The chinch bug.
chinch bug *n.* A small black-and-white insect that feeds on and damages wheat and other grains and grasses in dry weather.
chin•chil•la (chĭn chĭl′ə) *n.* **1.** A rodent native to the mountains of South America, resembling a squirrel and having soft pale-gray fur. **2.** The fur of this animal. **3.** A heavy cloth of wool and cotton with a nubby surface, often used for overcoats.
chine (chīn) *n.* **1.** The backbone; the spine. **2.** A cut of meat containing part of the backbone.
Chi•nese (chī nēz′ *or* chī nēs′) *adj.* Of or relating to

chimpanzee

ă	pat	oi	boy
ā	pay	ou	out
âr	care	o͝o	took
ä	father	o͞o	boot
ĕ	pet	ŭ	cut
ē	be	ûr	urge
ĭ	pit	th	thin
ī	pie	*th*	this
îr	pier	hw	whoop
ŏ	pot	zh	vision
ō	toe	ə	about
ô	paw	N	*French* bon

chipmunk
Eastern chipmunk

Shirley Chisholm

Word History: chivalry

The words **cavalry** and **cavalier** are first cousins to **chivalry** and **chevalier**. They all come from the Roman soldier's slang word *caballus*, "horse, pack horse, nag," and from a very late Latin noun *caballārius*, "horseman, rider." A *caballārius* becomes a *cavaliere* in Italian, and he rides in the *cavalleria*, "troop of horse soldiers, cavalry." Both *cavaliere* and *cavalleria* are taken into English as *cavalier* and *cavalry*. In French, however, *caballārius* becomes *chevalier*, "horseman, knight," who rides in a *chevalerie* or *chivalerie*, "troop of men-at-arms, knighthood." *Chevalier* and *chivalerie* come into English with knightly overtones as *chevalier* and *chivalry*.

China, the Chinese, or their languages and culture. —*n., pl.* **Chinese. 1.** A native or inhabitant of China. **2.** A person of Chinese ancestry. **3.** A group of languages and dialects spoken by the Chinese people.

Chinese checkers *pl.n. (used with a singular or plural verb).* A game for two to six players in which marbles are moved from holes of one point of the star-shaped board to a set of holes on the opposite side.

Chinese lantern *n.* A decorative lantern of thin brightly colored paper made in such a way that it can be collapsed.

Chinese puzzle *n.* A very complicated puzzle or difficult problem.

chink[1] (chĭngk) *n.* A narrow crack or opening. —*tr. v.* **chinked, chink•ing, chinks.** To seal or close narrow cracks or openings by filling: *They chinked the spaces between the logs of the cabin wall with mud.* [First written down probably about 888 in Old English and spelled *cine.*]

chink[2] (chĭngk) *n.* A short clinking sound, as of metal striking together: *the chink of coins.* —*intr. & tr.v.* **chinked, chink•ing, chinks.** To make or cause to make such a sound: *Coins chinked in my pocket. I chinked the coins in my pocket.* [First written down in 1573 in Modern English, of imitative origin.]

chi•no (**chē′**nō) *n., pl.* **chi•nos. 1.** A strong cotton cloth used chiefly for uniforms and sport clothes. **2. chinos.** Trousers made of this material.

Chi•nook (shĭ **no͝ok′** *or* chĭ **no͝ok′**) *n., pl.* **Chinook** or **Chi•nooks. 1.** A member of a Native American people living in the state of Washington. **2.** The language of this people. **3. chinook. a.** A moist warm wind that blows from the ocean onto the coasts of Washington and Oregon. **b.** A warm dry wind that comes down from the eastern slopes of the Rocky Mountains.

Chinook Jargon *n.* A blend of English, French, Chinook, and other Native American languages, formerly used by traders in the Pacific Northwest.

chintz (chĭnts) *n.* A printed and glazed cotton fabric, usually of bright colors.

chintz•y (**chĭnt′**sē) *adj.* **chintz•i•er, chintz•i•est. 1.** Of, relating to, or decorated with chintz. **2.** Gaudy; cheap: *chintzy trinkets.*

chin-up (**chĭn′**ŭp′) *n.* The act or exercise of chinning oneself on an overhead bar.

chip (chĭp) *n.* **1.** A small piece cut or broken off; a fragment: *a chip of wood.* **2.** A dent or mark left when a small piece is broken off: *A chip in the marble.* **3.a.** A thin slice of food: *a potato chip.* **b. chips.** French-fried potatoes: *fish and chips.* **4.** A minute square of semiconducting material, such as silicon, on which an electronic component or an integrated circuit is etched. **5.** A small disk that is used in poker and other games to represent money. —*v.* **chipped, chip•ping, chips.** —*tr.* **1.** To break off a small piece from (something), as by hitting, jarring, or scraping: *chip the edge of the glass.* **2.** To shape or carve by cutting or chopping: *chipped my name in stone.* —*intr.* To become broken off: *These dishes chip if you are not careful.* —***idioms.* a chip off the old block.** A child that closely resembles one parent or the other. **chip in.** To contribute money or labor: *How many people chipped in for the present?* **chip on (one's) shoulder.** An aggressive or hostile attitude: *My cousin has had a chip on his shoulder ever since our argument.*

Chip•e•wy•an (chĭp′ə **wī′**ən) *n., pl.* **Chipewyan** or **Chip•e•wy•ans. 1.** A member of a Native American people living in north-central Canada. **2.** The Athabascan language of the Chipewyan.

chip•munk (**chĭp′**mŭngk′) *n.* Any of several rodents of North America resembling a squirrel but smaller and having a striped back. Chipmunks burrow in the ground. [First written down in 1832 in American English and spelled *chitmunk*, perhaps from Ojibwa *ajidamoon?*, red squirrel.]

chipped beef (chĭpt) *n.* Dried beef, smoked and thinly sliced.

chipper (**chĭp′**ər) *adj.* Active; cheerful; sprightly.

Chip•pe•wa (**chĭp′**ə wô′ *or* **chĭp′**ə wä′) *n., pl.* **Chippewa** or **Chip•pe•was.** An Ojibwa.

chip•ping sparrow (**chĭp′**ĭng) *n.* A small North American sparrow having a reddish-brown crown.

Chi•ron (**kī′**rŏn′) *n.* In Greek mythology, the wise centaur who tutors Achilles, Hercules, and Asclepius.

chi•rop•o•dy (kĭ **rŏp′**ə dē *or* shĭ **rŏp′**ə dē) *n.* Podiatry. —**chi•rop′o•dist** *n.*

chi•ro•prac•tic (**kī′**rə prăk′tĭk) *n.* A method of treating diseases by manipulating the spine and certain other structures of the body, usually without the use of drugs or surgery.

chi•ro•prac•tor (**kī′**rə prăk′tər) *n.* A person who practices chiropractic.

chirp (chûrp) *n.* A short high-pitched sound, as that made by a small bird or a cricket. —*intr.v.* **chirped, chirp•ing, chirps.** To make such a sound: *The crickets chirped noisily.*

chir•rup (**chûr′**əp *or* **chĭr′**əp) *n.* The sound of repeated chirping; a series of chirps. —*intr.v.* **chir•ruped, chir•rup•ing, chir•rups.** To make or utter such a sound.

chis•el (**chĭz′**əl) *n.* A metal tool with a sharp beveled edge across the end of a thick blade, used to cut and shape stone, wood, or metal. —*v.* **chis•eled, chis•el•ing, chis•els** or **chis•elled, chis•el•ling, chis•els.** —*tr.* **1.** To cut into or shape with a chisel: *The sculptor chiseled the statue out of stone.* **2.** *Informal.* To cheat or obtain by deception. —*intr.* To use a chisel. —**chis′el•er** *n.*

Chis•holm (**chĭz′**əm), **Shirley Anita Saint Hill.** Born 1924. American politician who served as a U.S. representative from New York State and in 1972 was the first Black woman to seek the presidential nomination of a major party.

chit•chat (**chĭt′**chăt′) *n.* **1.** Casual conversation; small talk. **2.** Gossip: *listened to the neighborhood chitchat.* —*intr.v.* **chit•chat•ted, chit•chat•ting, chit•chats.** To engage in chitchat.

chi•tin (**kīt′**n) *n.* A horny substance that is the main component of the shells of crustaceans and of the outer coverings of insects. It is also found in the cell walls of certain fungi. —**chi′tin•ous** *adj.*

chit•lins or **chit•lings** (**chĭt′**lĭnz) *pl.n.* Variant of **chitterlings.**

chi•ton (**kīt′**n *or* **kī′**tŏn′) *n.* A loosely draped gown or tunic worn by men and women in ancient Greece.

Chit•ta•gong (**chĭt′**ə gông′ *or* **chĭt′**ə gŏng′). A city of southeast Bangladesh southeast of Dhaka. Population, 980,000.

chit•ter•lings also **chit•lins** or **chit•lings** (**chĭt′**lĭnz) *pl.n.* The small intestines of a pig, fried as food.

chiv•al•rous (**shĭv′**əl rəs) *adj.* **1.** Of or relating to the age of chivalry: *the chivalrous days of King Arthur.* **2.** Having or showing the qualities of the ideal knight; brave, honorable, and courteous: *a chivalrous act of self-sacrifice.* —**chiv′al•rous•ness** *n.*

chiv•al•ry (**shĭv′**əl rē) *n., pl.* **chiv•al•ries. 1.** The medieval institution of knighthood and its customs: *the code of chivalry.* **2.** The qualities of the ideal knight, such as bravery, courtesy, honor, and gallantry towards women: *the victorious general's chivalry toward the welfare of defeated enemy troops.* **3.** A group of knights or gallant gentlemen. [First written down before 1300 in Middle English and spelled *chevalrie*, from Old French *chevalier*, knight.] —SEE NOTE.

chive (chīv) *n.* **1.** A plant related to the onion, having long narrow leaves. **2. chives.** The onion-flavored leaves of this plant, used as seasoning. [First written down about 1390 in Middle English, from Latin *cēpa*, onion.]

chlo•ral hydrate (**klôr′**əl) *n.* A colorless crystalline compound of carbon, chlorine, hydrogen, and oxygen. It has the formula $C_2Cl_3H_3O_2$ and is used as a sedative.

chlo•ride (**klôr′**īd′) *n.* A chemical compound of chlorine and another element or radical.

chloride of lime *n.* Bleaching powder.

chlo•ri•nate (**klôr′**ə nāt′) *tr.v.* **chlo•ri•nat•ed, chlo•ri•nat•ing, chlo•ri•nates.** To treat or combine with chlorine or one of its compounds, especially in order to kill bacteria in water. **—chlo′ri•na′tion** *n.*

chlo•rine (**klôr′**ēn′ *or* **klôr′**ĭn) *n. Symbol* **Cl** A greenish-yellow gaseous halogen element found chiefly in combination with sodium as common salt. Chlorine is poisonous and very irritating to the nose, throat, and lungs. It is used in water purification, sewage treatment, manufacture of bleach, and refining of metal. Atomic number 17. See table at **element.** [First written down in 1810 in Modern English, from Greek *khlōros*, greenish-yellow.]

chlo•ro•form (**klôr′**ə fôrm′) *n.* A clear, colorless, heavy liquid composed of carbon, hydrogen, and chlorine and having the formula $CHCL_3$. It is used in refrigeration, in industrial chemicals, and sometimes as an anesthetic. *—tr.v.* **chlo•ro•formed, chlo•ro•form•ing, chlo•ro•forms.** To make unconscious or kill with chloroform.

Chlo•ro•my•ce•tin (klôr′ō mī **sēt′**n). A trademark for an antibiotic obtained from certain soil bacteria.

chlo•ro•phyll also **chlo•ro•phyl** (**klôr′**ə fĭl) *n.* A green pigment composed of carbon, hydrogen, magnesium, nitrogen, and oxygen, found in green plants and other living things. Chlorophyll is very complex in structure and absorbs light that provides the energy used in photosynthesis to change carbon dioxide and water into carbohydrates.

chlo•ro•plast (**klôr′**ə plăst′) also **chlo•ro•plas•tid** (klôr′ə **plăs′**tĭd) *n.* A very small green structure containing chlorophyll, found in plant cells and some microorganisms. Photosynthesis takes place in chloroplasts.

chm. *abbr.* An abbreviation of chairman.

chmn *abbr.* An abbreviation of chairman.

chock (chŏk) *n.* A block or wedge placed under something, such as a boat, barrel, or wheel, to keep it from moving. *—tr.v.* **chocked, chock•ing, chocks.** To hold in place with a chock or chocks: *chock the wheels of a truck parked on a hill.*

chock-full (**chŏk′fo͝ol′**) *adj.* Completely filled; stuffed: *a bus chock-full of people at rush hour.*

choc•o•late (**chô′**kə lĭt *or* **chôk′**lĭt *or* **chŏk′**lĭt) *n.* **1.** A food made from cacao seeds that have been roasted and ground. Chocolate for cooking is sold in powdered or block form. **2.a.** A sweetened drink made with a powdered form of this substance; cocoa. **b.** A candy made especially from a block of this substance. **3.** A grayish to deep reddish brown. *—adj.* **1.** Made of or flavored with chocolate: *a chocolate cake.* **2.** Of a deep grayish or reddish brown: *a chocolate dress.* [First written down in 1604 in Modern English, from Spanish, from Nahuatl *xocolatl* : *xococ*, bitter + *atl*, water.]

Choc•taw (**chŏk′**tô) *n., pl.* **Choctaw** or **Choc•taws. 1.** A member of a Native American people formerly living in parts of Mississippi and Alabama, now living mainly in Oklahoma and central Mississippi. **2.** The Muskogean language of the Choctaw.

choice (chois) *n.* **1.** The act of choosing; selection: *Did price influence your choice?* **2.** The power, right, or possibility to choose; option: *You leave me no choice in this matter.* **3.** Someone or something chosen: *The customer's choices were roast beef, mashed potatoes, and peas.* **4.** A variety from which to choose: *The cafeteria has a wide choice of sandwiches.* **5.** An alternative: *There is no choice but to obey the rules.* *—adj.* **choic•er, choic•est. 1.** Of fine quality; very good; select: *choice tidbits; choice vegetables.* **2.** Selected with care: *reply in a few choice words.* **3.** Graded by U.S. government standards as higher than good and lower than prime: *Hamburger is often made from choice beef.* **—choice′ly** *adv.*

Synonyms: choice, alternative, option, preference, selection. These nouns mean the act, power, or right of choosing. **Choice** suggests the freedom to choose from a set of things: *It is hard for me to make a choice of ice cream flavors at that store because they have so many.* **Alternative** means a choice between only two possibilities: *His alternative is to take a job he doesn't like or to keep looking for something better.* **Option** often means a power to choose that has been granted by someone else: *That school gives you the option of taking either art or music instead of study hall.* **Preference** means a choice based on one's values, bias, or tastes: *Sheila was offered her preference of colors.* **Selection** suggests a variety of things or persons to choose from: *The director of the play was very careful in her selection of actors during the audition.*

choir (kwīr) *n.* **1.** An organized group of singers, especially one that performs regularly in a church: *a children's choir; a cathedral choir.* **2.** The part of a church especially for the use of such singers. [First written down about 1300 in Middle English and spelled *queor*, from Old French *quer*, from Latin *chorus*, choral dance, from Greek *khoros.*] —SEE NOTE.

❑ *These sound alike:* **choir, quire** (unit of paper).

choir•boy (**kwīr′**boi′) *n.* A boy who is a member of a choir.

choir•girl (**kwīr′**gûrl′) *n.* A girl who is a member of a choir.

choke (chōk) *v.* **choked, chok•ing, chokes.** *—tr.* **1.** To interfere with the breathing of (a person or an animal) by squeezing or blocking the windpipe. **2.** To reduce the amount of air supplied to (a gasoline engine) so that it will start and warm up more easily. **3.** To check or slow down the movement, growth, or action of: *Weeds are choking the garden.* **4.** To stop or suppress by or as if by strangling: *Sobs choked her words.* **5.** To clog up; congest: *Traffic choked the highway.* *—intr.* **1.** To be unable to breathe, swallow, or speak normally, as when the throat is blocked: *choke on a piece of bread.* **2.** To be blocked up or obstructed: *The drain choked up with kitchen scraps.* *—n.* **1.** The act or sound of choking. **2.** A device that controls the amount of air taken in by a gasoline engine. ***—idioms.*** **choke back.** To hold back; control; suppress: *choke back tears.* **choke off.** To put an end to; stop: *Closing the train station would choke off business in the area.* **choke up.** To be unable to speak because of strong emotion.

choke•cher•ry (**chōk′**chĕr′ē) *n.* **1.** A shrub or tree having narrow clusters of small white flowers and bitter-tasting dark-red or black fruit. **2.** The fruit of such a shrub.

choke•damp (**chōk′**dămp′) *n.* Blackdamp.

choker (**chō′**kər) *n.* **1.** A person or thing that chokes: *Many dogs are trained on restraining collars that are chokers.* **2.** A short necklace that fits closely around the throat.

chock

Word History: choir

Why is the spelling of the word **choir** so much different from the pronunciation? *Choir* came from the Greek word *khoros*, "dance, musical composition, band of singers or dancers." Latin borrowed the Greek word as *chorus*, which became *quer* in Old French and *choeur* in Modern French. Middle English adopted the Old French word *quer* and spelled it *quer* or *quere* or *queere*, and perhaps pronounced it to rhyme with our word *square*. The word was later spelled *quyer* or *quire*, possibly rhyming with our word *queer*, and this spelling eventually took on our present pronunciation. Toward the end of the 17th century the written word *quire* was replaced by the word *choir* by people who knew the Greek and Modern French forms (with their *kh–* or *ch–* and *–o–*: Greek *khoros* or *choros* and French *choeur*).

ă	pat	oi	boy
ā	pay	ou	out
âr	care	o͝o	took
ä	father	o͞o	boot
ĕ	pet	ŭ	cut
ē	be	ûr	urge
ĭ	pit	th	thin
ī	pie	*th*	this
îr	pier	hw	whoop
ŏ	pot	zh	vision
ō	toe	ə	about
ô	paw	N	*French* bon

Frédéric Chopin

chol•er (kŏl′ər) *n.* Anger; irritability.
❑ *These sound alike:* **choler, collar** (neck band).

chol•er•a (kŏl′ər ə) *n.* A serious, often fatal disease of the intestines that is infectious and often epidemic. It is caused by bacteria and its symptoms include diarrhea, vomiting, and cramps.

chol•er•ic (kŏl′ə rĭk *or* kə lĕr′ĭk) *adj.* Easily made angry; bad-tempered.

cho•les•ter•ol (kə lĕs′tə rôl′) *n.* A white fatty substance that is important in metabolism and hormone production and is found in many animal and plant tissues, especially in bile, the blood, egg yolks, and seeds. In large amounts it is believed to cause heart and vascular disease by collecting on the inner walls of arteries and causing them to harden.

chomp (chŏmp) *v.* **chomped, chomp•ing, chomps.** —*tr.* To chew or bite on noisily: *a horse chomping oats.* —*intr.* To chew or bite on something: *chomping on a carrot.*

Chong•qing (chông′chĭng′) also **Chung•king** (chŏŏng′kĭng′). A city of south-central China on the Yangtze River (Chang Jiang). It was the capital of China from 1937 to 1946. Population, 2,080,000.

choose (cho͞oz) *v.* **chose** (chōz), **cho•sen** (chō′zən), **choos•ing, choos•es.** —*tr.* **1.** To select from a greater number; pick out: *choose a book in the library.* **2.** To see fit; prefer: *I chose potatoes over rice with chicken.* **3.** To decide: *We chose to walk to work.* —*intr.* To make a choice; select: *They had to choose for themselves.* —**choos′er** *n.*

choos•y also **choos•ey** (cho͞o′zē) *adj.* **choos•i•er, choos•i•est.** Very careful in choosing: *She's very choosy about the film she uses in her camera.*

chop[1] (chŏp) *v.* **chopped, chop•ping, chops.** —*tr.* **1.** To cut by striking with a heavy sharp tool, such as an ax: *chop wood.* **2.** To make by cutting in this way: *chop a path through the woods.* **3.** To cut up into small pieces; mince: *chop onions.* **4.** To cut short: reduce: *chop a report that is too long.* **5.** In sports, to hit or hit at with a short swift downward stroke: *The batter chopped a grounder through the infield.* —*intr.* To make heavy cutting strokes: *chop away at a block of ice.* —*n.* **1.** A quick short cutting stroke or blow: *A chop of the ax split the log.* **2.** A small cut of meat that usually contains a bone: *Ribs from lamb and pork make nice chops.* **3.** A short irregular movement of waves. [First written down before 1376 in Middle English and spelled *choppen*, probably variant of *chappen*, to split.]

chop[2] (chŏp) *intr.v.* **chopped, chop•ping, chops.** To change direction suddenly; swerve, as a ship in the wind. [First written down before 1200 in Middle English and spelled *chapen*, to barter, bargain, from Old English *ceāpian*.]

Cho•pin (shō ′păn′ *or* shō păn′), **Frédéric François.** 1810–1849. Polish-born French composer and pianist. His music is based on traditional Polish dance themes.

chop•per (chŏp′ər) *n.* **1.** *Informal.* A helicopter. **2.** A person or thing that chops: *a food chopper.*

chop•py[1] (chŏp′ē) *adj.* **chop•pi•er, chop•pi•est. 1.** Full of short irregular waves: *choppy seas.* **2.** Not smooth; jerky: *choppy prose.* [First written down in 1605 in Modern English, from *chop*, to cut.] —**chop′pi•ness** *n.*

chop•py[2] (chŏp′ē) *adj.* **chop•pi•er, chop•pi•est.** Shifting quickly; variable: *choppy winds.* [First written down in 1865 in Modern English, from *chop*, to shift.]

chops (chŏps) *pl.n.* The jaws, cheeks, or jowls.

chop•sticks (chŏp′stĭks′) *pl.n.* A pair of slender sticks usually made of wood or plastic and used as eating utensils in eastern Asia and in restaurants serving Asian food. [First written down in 1699 in Modern English, probably from Chinese (Cantonese) *kuài*, quick.]

chop su•ey (so͞o′ē) *n.* A Chinese-American dish made with bits of meat, bean sprouts, and other vegetables and served with rice.

cho•ral (kôr′əl) *adj.* Of, for, or sung by a chorus or choir: *a choral society; a choral passage.*

cho•rale also **cho•ral** (kə răl′) *n.* A hymn melody usually sung in unison or a harmonized version for organ.
❑ *These sound alike:* **chorale, corral** (fenced-in area).

chord[1] (kôrd) *n.* A combination of three or more musical tones sounded at the same time. [First written down in 1608 in Modern English, from Old French *acorde*, agreement, harmony.] —**chord′al** *adj.*
❑ *These sound alike:* **chord**[1] (musical tones), **chord**[2] (line segment), **cord** (string).

chord[2] (kôrd) *n.* A line segment whose end points lie on a curve or on the circumference of a circle. [First written down in 1543 in Modern English, alteration of *cord*, string.]
❑ *These sound alike:* **chord**[2] (line segment), **chord**[1] (musical tones), **cord** (string).

chor•date (kôr′dāt′ *or* kôr′dĭt) *n.* Any of a large group of animals having at some stage of development a spinal column or a strip of cartilage along the back and openings to allow water to pass over the gills. Chordates include all vertebrates and certain ocean animals.

chore (chôr) *n.* **1.** A routine or minor task: *Feeding the cat is a daily chore.* See Synonyms at **task. 2.** An unpleasant task: *Taking out the garbage is a chore I'd like to forget.*

cho•re•a (kô rē′ə) *n.* Any of various disorders of the nervous system that cause the arms, legs, and face to twitch and move uncontrollably.

cho•re•o•graph (kôr′ē ə grăf′) *v.* **cho•re•o•graphed, cho•re•o•graph•ing, cho•re•o•graphs.** —*tr.* To create the choreography of (a ballet or other stage work). —*intr.* To engage in choreography.

cho•re•o•graph•er (kôr′ē ŏg′rə fər) *n.* Someone who creates, arranges, and directs ballets or dances.

cho•re•og•ra•phy (kôr′ē ŏg′rə fē) *n., pl.* **cho•re•og•ra•phies.** The art of creating and arranging ballets or dances.

cho•ri•on (kôr′ē ŏn′) *n.* The outer membrane that encloses the embryo of a reptile, bird, or mammal. —**cho′ri•on′ic** (kôr′ē ŏn′ĭk) *adj.*

cho•ris•ter (kôr′ĭ stər *or* kŏr′ĭ stər) *n.* **1.** A person who sings in a choir. **2.** A choir leader.

cho•roid (kôr′oid′) *n.* A delicate membrane between the sclera and the retina of the eyeball.

choroid coat *n.* The choroid.

chor•tle (chôr′tl) *n.* A snorting chuckle. —*intr.v.* **chor•tled, chor•tling, chor•tles.** To laugh in a snorting joyful manner.

cho•rus (kôr′əs) *n., pl.* **cho•rus•es. 1.** An organized group of singers who perform together. **2.** A musical composition or a part of a musical composition written for such a group. **3.** A group of persons who speak or sing a part in a play all at the same time. **4.** A group of singers and dancers who play a supporting role in an opera, a musical comedy, or another stage production. **5.** A section of music that is repeated after each verse of a song; a refrain. **6.** Something uttered by many people at one time: *a chorus of laughter.* —*tr. & intr.v.* **cho•rused, cho•rus•ing, cho•rus•es** or **cho•russed, cho•rus•sing, cho•rus•ses.** To sing or utter at the same time. —***idiom.* in chorus.** All together: *The group responded to the suggestion in chorus.*

chose (chōz) *v.* Past tense of **choose.**

cho•sen (chō′zən) *v.* Past participle of **choose.**

—*adj.* **1.** Selected from or preferred above others: *the chosen few.* **2.** Selected by God; elect: *the chosen people.*

Chou En-lai (jō′ ĕn lī′). Zhou Enlai.

chow¹ (chou) *n.* Any of a breed of dog having a large head, a long, thick, reddish-brown or black coat and a blackish tongue. [First written down in 1889 in Modern English, possibly from Chinese (Cantonese) *gǒu*, dog.]

chow² (chou) *Slang. n.* Food. [First written down in 1856 in Modern English, possibly from Chinese (Cantonese) *zab*, food, miscellany, from Chinese (Mandarin) *zá*, mixed.]

chow•der (chou′dər) *n.* **1.** A thick soup or stew containing fish or shellfish, especially clams, and vegetables in a milk base. **2.** A thin soup of seafood with tomatoes in a meat broth. **3.** Either of these soups made with a vegetable, such as corn, as the main ingredient. [First written down in 1751 in Modern English, from Late Latin *caldāria*, stew pot, caldron.]

chow mein (chou′ mān′) *n.* A Chinese-American dish of bits of meat and cooked vegetables served over fried noodles. [First written down in 1903 in Modern English, from Chinese (Mandarin) *chǎo miàn* : *chǎo*, to stir-fry + *miàn*, noodles.]

Christ (krīst) *n.* **1.** The Messiah, as foretold by the prophets of the Bible. **2.** Jesus.

chris•ten (krĭs′ən) *tr.v.* **chris•tened, chris•ten•ing, chris•tens. 1.** To baptize into a Christian church. **2.** To give a name to at baptism: *They christened him "Joseph."* **3.** To name, especially at a ceremony: *christen a ship.* **4.** *Informal.* To use for the first time: *christen a new car with a ride around the block.*

Chris•ten•dom (krĭs′ən dəm) *n.* **1.** Christians considered as a group. **2.** The countries of the world where Christianity is the principal religion.

chris•ten•ing (krĭs′ə nĭng) *n.* The Christian ceremony of baptizing and naming a child.

Chris•tian (krĭs′chən) *adj.* **1.** Believing in Jesus as Christ or in the religion based on his teachings: *a Christian congregation.* **2.** Relating to or characteristic of Christianity or Christians: *Easter is a Christian holiday.* **3.** Showing qualities considered characteristic of Jesus, such as gentleness or humility: *a Christian act of forgivenenss.* —*n.* A person who believes in Jesus as Christ or follows a religion based on his teachings.

Chris•ti•a•ni•a (krĭs′tē ä′nē ə). Oslo.

Chris•ti•an•i•ty (krĭs′chē ăn′ĭ tē *or* krĭs′tē ăn′ĭ tē) *n., pl.* **Chris•ti•an•i•ties. 1.** The Christian religion, based on the life and teachings of Jesus. **2.** Christians considered as a group; Christendom: *Christianity celebrates Christmas.* **3.** The condition or fact of being a Christian.

Chris•tian•ize (krĭs′chə nīz′) *tr.v.* **Chris•tian•ized, Chris•tian•iz•ing, Chris•tian•iz•es.** To convert (another) to Christianity: *Missionaries tried to Christianize the native peoples of North America.* —**Chris′tian•i•za′tion** (krĭs′chə nĭ zā′shən) *n.* —**Chris′tian•iz′er** *n.*

Christian name *n.* **1.** A name given at baptism or confirmation. **2.** A name that precedes a person's family name, especially a first name.

Christian Science *n.* The religious system founded by Mary Baker Eddy that emphasizes healing through spiritual means. —**Christian Scientist** *n.*

Chris•tie (krĭs′tē), Dame **Agatha Mary Clarissa.** 1890–1976. British writer of more than 70 detective novels, including *And Then There Were None* (1940).

Christ•mas (krĭs′məs) *n.* **1.** December 25, celebrated by Christians in commemoration of the birth of Jesus. **2.** Christmastime.

Christmas Eve *n.* The evening before Christmas.

Christ•mas•tide (krĭs′məs tīd′) *n.* Christmastime.

Christ•mas•time (krĭs′məs tīm′) *n.* The season of Christmas.

Christmas tree *n.* An evergreen or artificial tree decorated with ornaments and lights at Christmastime.

chro•mat•ic (krō măt′ĭk) *adj.* **1.** Of or relating to color or colors. **2.** Of or based on the chromatic scale, as a melody or chord. —**chro•mat′i•cal•ly** *adv.*

chromatic aberration *n.* The failure of the different colors of light to meet in one focus when refracted through a lens.

chromatic scale *n.* A musical scale in which an octave is made up of twelve notes, each separated from the next by a semitone.

chro•ma•tin (krō′mə tĭn) *n.* The substance in the nucleus of a cell that condenses to form chromosomes during mitosis.

chro•ma•tog•ra•phy (krō′mə tŏg′rə fē) *n.* A technique that separates the components of a chemical mixture by moving the mixture along a stationary material such as gelatin. The components are taken up and held in the material at different rates, thus forming isolated bands that scientists can further separate and analyze.

chrome (krōm) *n.* **1.** Chromium. **2.** A material plated with chromium or one of its alloys.

chro•mic (krō′mĭk) *adj.* Of, relating to, or containing chromium.

chro•mi•um (krō′mē əm) *n. Symbol* **Cr** A grayish, hard, brittle metallic element that does not rust or become dull easily. Chromium is used in electroplating other metals, in making stainless steel and other alloys, in making dyes and paints, and in photography. Atomic number 24. See table at **element.**

chro•mo•some (krō′mə sōm′) *n.* A small body in all living cells, usually contained in a nucleus and composed mainly of DNA. It carries the genes that determine heredity. —**chro′mo•so′mal** (krō′mə sō′məl) *adj.*

chro•mo•sphere (krō′mə sfîr′) *n.* **1.** A glowing transparent layer of gas surrounding the photosphere of the sun. It is several thousand miles thick and is rich in hydrogen, helium, and calcium. **2.** A similar layer around a star.

chron•ic (krŏn′ĭk) *adj.* **1.** Lasting for a long time or recurring frequently: *chronic bronchitis.* **2.** Subject to a habit for a long time: *He is a chronic gossip.* —**chron′i•cal•ly** *adv.*

chron•i•cle (krŏn′ĭ kəl) *n.* **1.** A record of historical events arranged in order of occurrence. **2. Chronicles.** *(used with a singular verb).* One of two books of the Bible that tell the history of the Israelite kings. —*tr.v.* **chron•i•cled, chron•i•cling, chron•i•cles.** To record, as in a chronicle: *Medieval monks carefully chronicled the events of each year.* —**chron′i•cler** *n.*

chron•o•log•i•cal (krŏn′ə lŏj′ĭ kəl) *adj.* Arranged in order of time in which the events took place: *keep all historical facts in chronological order.* —**chron′o•log′i•cal•ly** *adv.*

chro•nol•o•gy (krə nŏl′ə jē) *n., pl.* **chro•nol•o•gies. 1.** The science that deals with determining the dates and order of events. **2.** A chronological list or table: *a detailed chronology of modern history.* **3.** The arrangement of events in time.

chro•nom•e•ter (krə nŏm′ĭ tər) *n.* A very accurate clock or other timepiece, especially as used in scientific experiments, navigation, or astronomical observations.

chrys•a•lid (krĭs′ə lĭd) *n.* A chrysalis.

chrys•a•lis (krĭs′ə lĭs) *n., pl.* **chrys•a•lis•es** or **chry•sal•i•des** (krĭ săl′ĭ dēz′). A butterfly or moth in the

chow¹

Agatha Christie

chrysalis
Of a mourning cloak butterfly

ă	pat	oi	boy
ā	pay	ou	out
âr	care	ŏŏ	took
ä	father	ōō	boot
ĕ	pet	ŭ	cut
ē	be	ûr	urge
ĭ	pit	th	thin
ī	pie	*th*	this
îr	pier	hw	whoop
ŏ	pot	zh	vision
ō	toe	ə	about
ô	paw	N	*French* bon

Winston Churchill

churn
Detail of a wood engraving by Alexander Anderson (1775–1870)

circadian

Why do you sometimes wake up on time even if your alarm clock fails to ring? In part, this happens because people have a form of internal clock that controls **circadian**, or daily, biological activities, such as sleep. In a process still not well understood, circadian patterns are controlled by certain hormones in the body. The release of these hormones is often influenced by external factors, such as the regular sequence of light and dark in each 24-hour day. Long-distance air travel, for example, can disrupt this schedule—the local time of day will no longer match the body's internal clock. This disruption upsets a person's circadian patterns for a short time, causing a condition known as **jet lag**.

inactive stage in its development, enclosed in a tough case from which the fully developed adult eventually emerges; a pupa. [First written down in 1601 in Modern English, from Greek *khrusallis*, gold-colored pupa of a butterfly, from *khrusos*, golden.]

chry•san•the•mum (krĭ **săn′**thə məm) *n.* **1.** Any of numerous plants having many cultivated forms with showy, round, variously colored flowers. **2.** The flower of such a plant.

chub (chŭb) *n., pl.* **chub** or **chubs. 1.** Any of various freshwater fishes of Europe related to the carp and minnow. **2.** Any of various small freshwater fishes of North America related to the whitefish.

chub•by (**chŭb′**ē) *adj.* **chub•bi•er, chub•bi•est.** Round and plump: *The baby has a chubby face.* **—chub′bi•ness** *n.*

chuck[1] (chŭk) *tr.v.* **chucked, chuck•ing, chucks. 1.** To pat affectionately, especially under the chin. **2.a.** To throw or toss: *chuck a stone in the pond.* **b.** *Informal.* To throw out; discard: *chuck an old shoe; chuck a poor plan.* *—n.* **1.** An affectionate pat, especially under the chin. **2.** A toss or throw. [First written down in 1583 in Modern English and spelled *chock*, possibly from French *choc*, knock, blow.]

chuck[2] (chŭk) *n.* **1.** A cut of beef extending from the neck to the ribs. **2.** In a machine such as a drill or lathe, a rotating clamp that holds either a tool or the work. [First written down in 1674 in Modern English, perhaps variant of *chock*, wedge, lump.]

chuck•le (**chŭk′**əl) *intr.v.* **chuck•led, chuck•ling, chuck•les.** To laugh quietly or to oneself. *—n.* A quiet laugh of amusement or satisfaction.

chuck wagon *n.* A wagon with food and cooking utensils for a group of workers, especially those moving from place to place, as on a cattle drive.

chuck•wal•la (**chŭk′**wŏl′ə) *n.* A large lizard of desert regions in the southwest United States that is related to the iguana.

chug (chŭg) *n.* A dull explosive sound made by or as if by an engine working hard. *—intr.v.* **chugged, chug•ging, chugs. 1.** To make such sounds: *The old truck's motor chugged under the hood.* **2.** To move making such sounds: *The little train chugged up the mountain.*

chum[1] (chŭm) *n.* A close friend or companion; a pal. *—intr.v.* **chummed, chum•ming, chums.** To be on terms of close friendship; keep company: *That group of kids chum around a lot after school.* [First written down in 1684 in Modern English, perhaps short for *chamber fellow*, roommate.]

chum[2] (chŭm) *n.* Bait consisting of cut-up fish scattered on the water. *—intr.v.* **chummed, chum•ming, chums.** To fish with chum. [First written down in 1857 in Modern English.]

chum•my (**chŭm′**ē) *adj.* **chum•mi•er, chum•mi•est.** Friendly; intimate: *a chummy bunch.*

chump (chŭmp) *n. Informal.* A foolish or stupid person.

Chung•king (**chŏŏng′kĭng′**). Chongqing.

chunk (chŭngk) *n.* **1.** A thick piece of something: *a chunk of ice.* **2.** A large portion or amount: *They spent a chunk of their free time making music.*

chunk•y (**chŭng′**kē) *adj.* **chunk•i•er, chunk•i•est. 1.** Short, strong, and somewhat fat; stocky: *a chunky horse.* **2.** Containing small thick pieces: *chunky soup.* **—chunk′i•ness** *n.*

church (chûrch) *n.* **1.** A building for public worship, especially Christian worship. **2.** A Christian congregation: *Her church holds a children's fair each spring.* **3.** Religious service in a church: *They go to church every week.* **4.** Often **Church.** A specified Christian denomination: *the Baptist Church.* **5.** Often **Church.** All Christians regarded as a single spiritual body: *the Church and its beliefs.* **6.** The clerical profession; clergy. **7.** Ecclesiastical power as distinguished from secular power: *The separation of church and state is firmly established by the First Amendment to the Constitution.* *—adj.* Of or relating to the church: *church music.*

church•go•er (**chûrch′**gō′ər) *n.* A person who attends church services regularly.

Chur•chill (**chûr′**chĭl′), Sir **Winston Leonard Spenser.** 1874–1965. British politician and writer who led Great Britain through World War II as prime minister. Churchill published several historical works and won the 1953 Nobel Prize for literature.

church•man (**chûrch′**mən) *n.* **1.** A man who is a cleric. **2.** A man who is a member of a church.

Church of Christ, Scientist *n.* Christian Science.

Church of England *n.* The national church of England, established in the 16th century under Henry VIII when it stopped recognizing the pope as its head.

Church of Jesus Christ of Latter-day Saints *n.* The Mormon Church.

church•war•den (**chûrch′**wôr′dn) *n.* A lay officer in an Anglican or Episcopal Church who helps manage parish business or legal affairs.

church•wom•an (**chûrch′**wŏŏm′ən) *n.* **1.** A woman who is a cleric. **2.** A woman who is a member of a church.

church•yard (**chûrch′**yärd′) *n.* A yard adjacent to a church, often used as a cemetery.

churl (chûrl) *n.* **1.** A rude surly person; a boor. **2.** A medieval English peasant.

churl•ish (**chûr′**lĭsh) *adj.* Rude; surly; boorish: *The criminal's churlish answer offended the judge.* **—churl′ish•ly** *adv.* **—churl′ish•ness** *n.*

churn (chûrn) *n.* A container in which milk or cream is stirred or beaten vigorously in order to make butter. *—v.* **churned, churn•ing, churns.** *—tr.* **1.** To stir or beat (milk or cream) in a churn to make butter. **2.** To move or swirl about violently: *Wind churned the leaves into piles.* *—intr.* **1.** To make butter in a churn. **2.** To stir or move violently: *waves churning in a storm.* [First written down about 1000 in Old English and spelled *cyrin.*]

chute (shōōt) *n.* **1.** A vertical or inclined trough or passage down which things can be dropped or slid: *a laundry chute; a chute for toboggans.* **2.** A waterfall or rapid. **3.** *Informal.* A parachute.
❑ *These sound alike:* **chute, shoot** (fire a weapon).

chut•ney (**chŭt′**nē) *n.* A spicy relish made of fruits and herbs.

chutz•pah (**KHŏŏt′**spə *or* **hŏŏt′**spə) *n.* Shameless boldness; impudence; gall.

chyle (kīl) *n.* A thick whitish liquid consisting of lymph and tiny fat globules, absorbed from the intestine during digestion.

chyme (kīm) *n.* The thick soft mass of partly digested food that is passed from the stomach to the small intestine.

CIA also **C.I.A.** *abbr.* An abbreviation of Central Intelligence Agency.

ci•ca•da (sĭ **kā′**də) *n., pl.* **ci•ca•das** or **ci•ca•dae** (sĭ-**kā′**dē′). Any of various insects having a broad head and two pairs of transparent wings. The males have specialized organs on the abdomen that when rubbed produce a high-pitched droning sound.

Cic•e•ro (**sĭs′**ə rō′), **Marcus Tullius.** 106–43 B.C. Roman politician and orator known for his superb prose.

–cide *suff.* A suffix that means: **1.** A killer of: *insecticide.* **2.** An act of killing: *suicide.*

ci•der (**sī′**dər) *n.* The juice pressed from apples, used as a beverage or to produce vinegar. [First written down about 1280 in Middle English and spelled *sider*, from Hebrew *šēkār*, intoxicating drink.]

ci•gar (sĭ gär′) *n.* A tight roll of tobacco leaves prepared for smoking. [First written down in 1730 in Modern English, from Spanish *cigarro*, possibly from Maya *sik*, tobacco.]

cig•a•rette (sĭg′ə rĕt′ *or* sĭg′ə rĕt′) *n.* A small roll of finely cut tobacco enclosed in a wrapper of thin paper for smoking.

cil•i•a (sĭl′ē ə) *n.* Plural of **cilium.**

cil•i•ar•y (sĭl′ē ĕr′ē) *adj.* **1.** Of, relating to, or resembling cilia. **2.** Of or relating to the ciliary body.

ciliary body *n.* A mass of tissue in the middle of the eyeball, containing a muscle that adjusts the lens and other related structures.

cil•i•ate (sĭl′ē ĭt *or* sĭl′ē āt′) *adj.* Having cilia. —*n.* A microorganism, such as a paramecium, having cilia.

cilium (sĭl′ē əm) *n., pl.* **cil•i•a** (sĭl′ē ə). **1.** A very small projection capable of a whipping motion and found in certain kinds of cells. Some microscopic organisms use cilia to move themselves. The respiratory tract in humans is lined with cilia that remove foreign matter from air before it reaches the lungs. **2.** An eyelash.

cinch (sĭnch) *n.* **1.** A strap that encircles a horse's body and is used for holding a saddle or pack. **2.** Something easy; a sure thing: *Riding a bike is a cinch when you know how.* —*tr.v.* **cinched, cinch•ing, cinch•es. 1.** To tighten the cinch on (a horse). **2.** *Informal.* To make certain of: *Several clues cinched the solution.*

cin•cho•na (sĭng kō′nə *or* sĭn chō′nə) *n.* Any of several evergreen trees and shrubs of South America whose bark is the source of quinine. [First written down in 1742 in Modern English and spelled *cinquona*, reputedly after Francisca Henríquez de Ribera (1576–1639), Countess of *Chinchón*.]

Cin•cin•na•ti (sĭn′sə năt′ē). A city of extreme southwest Ohio near the borders of Kentucky and Indiana. It was founded in 1788. Population, 364,040.

Cin•co de Ma•yo (sēng′kō də mä′yō) *n.* May 5, observed by Mexican communities in the Americas in celebration of the 1862 defeat of French troops at the Battle of Puebla.

cinc•ture (sĭngk′chər) *n.* A belt; a girdle.

cin•der (sĭn′dər) *n.* **1.a.** A burned or partly burned material, such as coal or wood, that cannot be burned further. **b.** A partly charred material that can burn further but without flame. **2. cinders.** Ashes.

cinder block or **cin•der•block** (sĭn′dər blŏk′) *n.* A hollow concrete block made with coal cinders and used in building.

cin•e•ma (sĭn′ə mə) *n.* **1.a.** A film or movie. **b.** A movie theater. **2.a.** The movie industry. **b.** The art of making movies or films. **—cin′e•mat′ic** (sĭn′ə măt′ĭk) *adj.*

cin•e•ma•tog•ra•pher (sĭn′ə mə tŏg′rə fər) *n.* A movie photographer.

cin•e•ma•tog•ra•phy (sĭn′ə mə tŏg′rə fē) *n.* The art or technique of movie photography.

cin•na•bar (sĭn′ə bär′) *n.* **1.** A red or brown mineral that is the chief source of mercury. **2.** Red mercuric sulfide used as a pigment. [First written down in 1440 in Middle English and spelled *cinabare*, from Greek *kinnabari*.]

cin•na•mon (sĭn′ə mən) *n.* **1.** A reddish brown spice made from the dried and often ground bark of certain tropical Asian trees. **2.** A tree from which this bark is obtained. **3.** A light reddish brown. —*adj.* Having a cinnamon color. [First written down about 1390 in Middle English and spelled *cinamome*, from Greek *kinnamōmon*, of Semitic origin.]

ci•on (sī′ən) *n.* Variant of **scion** (sense 2).

ci•pher (sī′fər) *n.* **1.** The numerical symbol O representing zero. **2.** A person or thing without influence or value. **3.a.** A system of writing in which letters are changed or substituted for other letters according to a code. **b.** A message in secret code. —*v.* **ci•phered, ci•pher•ing, ci•phers.** —*tr.* To put (a message) into a cipher. —*intr.* To do arithmetic. [First written down in 1399 in Middle English and spelled *siphre*, from Arabic *ṣifr*, from *ṣafira*, to be empty.]

cir•ca (sûr′kə) *prep.* About: *furniture made circa 1790.*

cir•ca•di•an (sər kā′dē ən) *adj.* Functioning or recurring in cycles of 24 hours: *sleep and wakeful periods in the human circadian rhythm.* —SEE NOTE.

Cir•ce (sûr′sē) *n.* In Greek mythology, a goddess who detains Odysseus on an island for a year and turns his men into swine.

cir•cle (sûr′kəl) *n.* **1.** A closed curve that has all of its points at the same distance from a fixed point called the center. **2.** A plane surface bounded by such a closed curve: *Draw a circle on the board.* **3.** Something having the shape of a circle: *sit in a circle around a campfire.* **4.** A group of people sharing common interests or activities: *an astronomer well known in scientific circles.* —*v.* **cir•cled, cir•cling, cir•cles.** —*tr.* **1.** To draw or form a circle around: *Circle the right answer.* **2.** To move or travel in a circle around: *A helicopter circled the city. Magellan's expedition circled the globe.* —*intr.* To move in a circle: *A hawk circled overhead.* [First written down about 1300 in Middle English and spelled *cercle*, from Latin *circulus*, from Greek *kirkos, krikos*.]

circle graph *n.* A pie chart.

cir•clet (sûr′klĭt) *n.* A small circle, especially a circular ornament.

cir•cuit (sûr′kĭt) *n.* **1.a.** A closed curve, such as a circle or an ellipse: *a circuit of stones around an ancient grave.* **b.** A path that forms a circle around something: *the moon's elliptical circuit around the earth.* **c.** The act of following such a route. **2.** A closed path through which an electric current flows or may flow: *Using too many appliances at once blew the circuit to the kitchen.* **3.** A system of electrically connected parts or devices: *A microchip contains all the circuits for this computer.* **4.a.** A regular route followed from place to place: *a salesperson on the West Coast circuit.* **b.** The district or area covered by such a route, especially the area under the jurisdiction of a judge who tries cases in various places. **5.** An association of theaters in which plays, shows, or films move from theater to theater for presentation: *The summer circuit brought good plays to many small towns.* **6.** An association of teams, clubs, or arenas of competition: *the professional tennis circuit.*

circuit board *n.* An insulated board on which circuits and electronic components are mounted.

circuit breaker *n.* A switch that automatically interrupts the flow of an electric current if the current becomes too strong.

circuit court *n.* In some states, a court holding sessions in various places in the area over which it has jurisdiction.

cir•cu•i•tous (sər kyōō′ĭ təs) *adj.* Not direct; roundabout: *take a circuitous route to the store; a confusing and circuitous argument.* **—cir•cu′i•tous•ly** *adv.* **—cir•cu′i•tous•ness** *n.*

circuit rider *n.* A preacher who travels from church to church in a rural district.

cir•cuit•ry (sûr′kĭ trē) *n., pl.* **cir•cuit•ries. 1.** The plan for an electric or electronic circuit. **2.** Electric

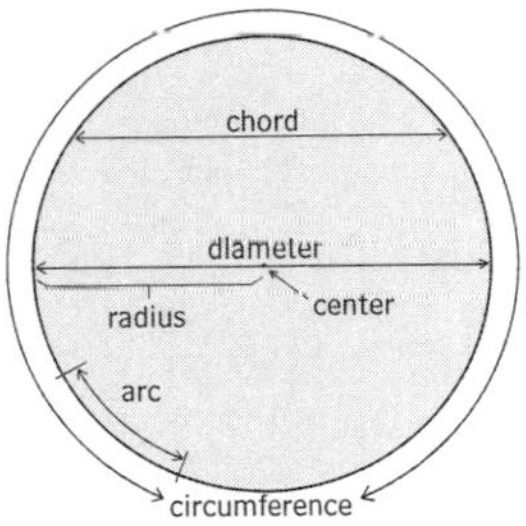

circle

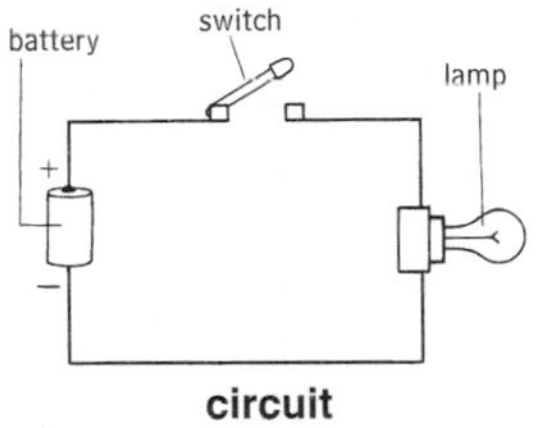

circuit

Electrical circuit

ă	pat	oi	boy
ā	pay	ou	out
âr	care	ŏŏ	took
ä	father	ōō	boot
ĕ	pet	ŭ	cut
ē	be	ûr	urge
ĭ	pit	th	thin
ī	pie	*th*	this
îr	pier	hw	whoop
ŏ	pot	zh	vision
ō	toe	ə	about
ô	paw	N	*French* bon

circular saw

circuits considered as a group: *The circuitry of television sets is complicated.*

cir•cu•lar (sûr′kyə lər) *adj.* **1.** Of, relating to, or shaped like a circle: *Most coins are circular pieces of metal.* **2.** Forming or moving in a circle: *circular motion.* —*n.* A printed advertisement, notice, or other statement intended for public distribution: *During the campaign, candidates sent out many circulars.* —**cir′cu•lar•ly** *adv.*

cir•cu•lar•ize (sûr′kyə lə rīz′) *tr.v.* **cir•cu•lar•ized, cir•cu•lar•iz•ing, cir•cu•lar•iz•es.** To send circulars to: *Candidates circularize their districts for votes.*

circular saw *n.* A power saw whose blade is a toothed metal disk that cuts as the blade rotates at a high speed.

cir•cu•late (sûr′kyə lāt′) *v.* **cir•cu•lat•ed, cir•cu•lat•ing, cir•cu•lates.** —*intr.* **1.** To move or flow in a closed path: *Blood circulates through the body.* **2.** To move or flow freely: *The fan helps the air circulate.* **3.** To spread widely among persons or places: *Rumors tend to circulate quickly.* —*tr.* **1.** To cause to move or flow: *The heart circulates blood throughout the body.* **2.** To spread or distribute among: *A topic that has been widely circulated in public discussion.*

cir•cu•lat•ing library (sûr′kyə lā′tĭng) *n.* A library from which books may be borrowed.

cir•cu•la•tion (sûr′kyə **lā′**shən) *n.* **1.a.** The act or process of circulating: *Opening the window will help the circulation of air.* **b.** The passage of something, such as money or news, from person to person or from place to place: *There aren't many two-dollar bills in circulation.* **2.** The flow of the blood from the heart through the arteries and veins back to the heart: *a person with poor circulation.* **3.a.** The distribution of printed matter, such as newspapers and magazines: *This popular magazine has a wide circulation.* **b.** The number of copies of a newspaper, magazine, book, or other printed matter, sold or distributed to the public: *a newspaper with a daily circulation of 400,000.*

cir•cu•la•tor•y (sûr′kyə lə tôr′ē) *adj.* **1.** Of or involving circulation. **2.** Of the circulatory system: *Hardening of the arteries is a circulatory disease.*

circulatory system *n.* The heart, blood vessels, and lymphatic system of the body.

circum– *pref.* A prefix that means around or about: *circumnavigate.*

cir•cum•cise (sûr′kəm sīz′) *tr.v.* **cir•cum•cised, cir•cum•cis•ing, cir•cum•cis•es.** To remove the foreskin of.

cir•cum•ci•sion (sûr′kəm **sĭzh′**ən) *n.* The act or process of circumcising.

cir•cum•fer•ence (sər **kŭm′**fər əns) *n.* **1.** The boundary of a circle. **2.** The boundary line of an area or object. **3.** The length of such a boundary: *The circumference of the moon is about 6,800 miles.* [First written down before 1393 in Middle English, from Latin *circumferre*, to carry around : *circum-*, around + *ferre*, to carry.]

cir•cum•flex (sûr′kəm flĕks′) *n.* The mark (ˆ) used over a vowel in certain languages or in a pronunciation key to indicate how the vowel is pronounced.

cir•cum•lo•cu•tion (sûr′kəm lō **kyo͞o′**shən) *n.* **1.** The use of wordy and indirect language: *The politician was a master of circumlocution.* **2.** A wordy or roundabout expression; for example, *the husband of my mother's sister* is a circumlocution for *my uncle.*

cir•cum•nav•i•gate (sûr′kəm **năv′**ĭ gāt′) *tr.v.* **cir•cum•nav•i•gat•ed, cir•cum•nav•i•gat•ing, cir•cum•nav•i•gates.** To sail completely around: *Sir Francis Drake was the first Englishman to circumnavigate the earth.* —**cir′cum•nav′i•ga′tion** *n.*

cir•cum•scribe (sûr′kəm skrīb′) *tr.v.* **cir•cum•scribed, cir•cum•scrib•ing, cir•cum•scribes. 1.a.** To draw (a figure) around another figure so as to touch as many points as possible: *A circle that is circumscribed around a triangle touches it at three points called the vertices of the triangle.* **b.** To enclose within a line or surface: *A circle will circumscribe a square but not a trapezoid.* **2.** To confine within or as if within bounds; limit: *Their plans for the future were circumscribed by their lack of money.* [First written down about 1385 in Middle English and spelled *circumscriben*, from Latin *circumscrībere* : *circum-*, around + *scrībere*, to write.]

cir•cum•spect (sûr′kəm spĕkt′) *adj.* Careful of circumstances or consequences; cautious; prudent: *The President must be circumspect about statements made to reporters.* —**cir′cum•spec′tion** *n.* —**cir′cum•spect′ly** *adv.*

cir•cum•stance (sûr′kəm stăns′) *n.* **1.** A condition, a fact, or an event connected with and usually affecting another event: *Snow and cold created circumstances that made the trip difficult.* **2.** A fact or an event. **3. circumstances.** Financial condition: *a wealthy family in comfortable circumstances.* **4.** Additional information; detail: *an explanation so full of circumstance that most never bothered to read it all.* **5.** Formal display; ceremony: *the pomp and circumstance of graduation.* —***idioms.*** **under no circumstances.** In no case; never: *Under no circumstances should you touch these two wires together.* **under the circumstances** or **in the circumstances.** Given these conditions; such being the case: *A storm was brewing, and under the circumstances we left for home.*

cir•cum•stan•tial (sûr′kəm **stăn′**shəl) *adj.* **1.** Of, relating to, or dependent on circumstances: *the flexibility to react to any circumstantial developments.* **2.** Not of primary importance; incidental: *circumstantial matters having little bearing on the main plan.* **3.** Full of detail; complete: *a circumstantial account of what happened last night.*

circumstantial evidence *n.* Evidence not directly relevant to the facts in a case but describing facts or events from which one might draw a conclusion about the facts in a case.

cir•cum•vent (sûr′kəm **vĕnt′**) *tr.v.* **cir•cum•vent•ed, cir•cum•vent•ing, cir•cum•vents. 1.** To avoid or get around by cleverness or ingenuity: *They tried to circumvent the building code when remodeling the garage.* **2.** To avoid by or as if by going around: *take side roads to circumvent construction.* —**cir′cum•ven′tion** *n.*

cir•cus (sûr′kəs) *n.* **1.a.** A public entertainment featuring acrobats, clowns, and trained animals. **b.** The traveling company of performers, animals, and workers that puts on the circus. **2.** A roofless arena used by the ancient Romans for athletic contests and public spectacles. **3.** *Informal.* Something suggestive of a circus, as in activity or disorder: *Holidays are a regular circus in our house.* [First written down about 1380 in Middle English, from Latin *circus*, circle, circus.]

cir•rho•sis (sĭ **rō′**sĭs) *n.* A chronic disease of the liver, in which normal tissue is gradually replaced by scar tissue so that its function is destroyed and the entire organ shrinks and hardens in the process.

cir•ri (sîr′ī′) *n.* Plural of **cirrus.**

cir•ro•cu•mu•lus (sîr′ō **kyo͞om′**yə ləs) *n.* A cloud composed of a series of small regularly arranged parts, found typically in the form of ripples or grains at high altitudes.

cir•ro•stra•tus (sîr′ō **strā′**təs *or* sîr′ō **străt′**əs) *n.* A thin hazy cloud composed of ice crystals, often covering the sky and producing a halo effect, found typically at high altitudes.

cir•rus (sîr′əs) *n., pl.* **cir•ri** (sîr′ī′). A cloud composed of white fleecy patches or bands of ice crystals, found typically at high altitudes. [First written down in 1803 in Modern English, from Latin *cirrus*, curl of hair.]

C.I.S. *abbr.* An abbreviation of Commonwealth of Independent States.

cis•tern (sĭs′tərn) *n.* A large tank or reservoir for holding liquid, especially for the collection and storage of rainwater.

cit•a•del (sĭt′ə dəl) *n.* **1.** A fortress overlooking a city. **2.** A stronghold or safe place: *The United States is often referred to as a citadel of democracy.*

ci•ta•tion (sī tā′shən) *n.* **1.** A reference or quotation: *a report full of citations from books and scholarly articles.* **2.** A summons to appear in court: *The police officer issued a citation to the speeding driver.* **3.** An official recommendation for bravery. **4.** The act of citing: *Citation of diaries and official documents made the book seem authoritative.*

cite (sīt) *tr.v.* **cit•ed, cit•ing, cites. 1.a.** To quote as an authority or example. **b.** To mention or bring forward as support, illustration, or proof: *Let me cite two cases of what I have in mind.* **2.** To summon before a court of law. **3.** To mention and commend for meritorious action: *The firefighter was cited for bravery beyond the call of duty.* —See Note at **quote.**

❑ *These sound alike:* **cite, sight** (vision), **site** (place).

cit•i•zen (sĭt′ĭ zən) *n.* **1.** A person owing loyalty to and entitled to the protection of a given country. **2.** A resident of a city or town, especially one entitled to vote and enjoy other privileges there. [First written down before 1300 in Middle English and spelled *citisein*, from Old French *cite*, city.]

cit•i•zen•ry (sĭt′ĭ zən rē) *n., pl.* **cit•i•zen•ries.** Citizens considered as a group.

cit•i•zens band (sĭt′ĭ zənz) *n.* A radio frequency band available for private use, as by truck drivers or motorists.

cit•i•zen•ship (sĭt′ĭ zən shĭp′) *n.* The status of a citizen with its duties, rights, and privileges.

cit•rate (sĭt′rāt′) *n.* A salt or ester of citric acid.

cit•ric acid (sĭt′rĭk) *n.* A white odorless acid with a sour taste that has the formula $C_6H_8O_7$. It is found in oranges, grapefruit, lemons, and other fruit and is used in medicine and as a flavoring.

cit•ron (sĭt′rən) *n.* **1.a.** A yellowish thick-skinned fruit similar to a lemon. **b.** A tree that bears such fruit. **2.** A melon having white flesh and a thick hard rind. **3.** The candied rind of either of these fruits, used especially in fruitcake, cookies, plum pudding, and other foods.

cit•ro•nel•la (sĭt′rə nĕl′ə) *n.* **1.** A pale yellow aromatic oil obtained from the leaves of a tropical grass and used in insect repellents and perfumes. **2.** The plant from which this oil is obtained.

cit•rus (sĭt′rəs) *n., pl.* **citrus** or **cit•rus•es. 1.** The fruit of any of various related evergreen trees or shrubs, having juicy flesh and a thick rind, as the orange, lemon, lime, or grapefruit. **2.** A tree or shrub that bears such fruit. —*adj.* Of or relating to such trees or their fruit. [First written down in 1882 in Modern English, from Latin *citrus*, citron tree.]

cit•y (sĭt′ē) *n., pl.* **cit•ies. 1.** A center of population, commerce, and culture; a large and important town: *Many people go into the city to work each day.* **2.** In the United States, a division of local government with stated boundaries of jurisdiction set forth in a charter granted by the state: *Our city is governed by the mayor and his council.* **3.** The people living in a city considered as a group. [First written down before 1200 in Middle English and spelled *cite*, from Latin *cīvitās*, from *cīvis*, citizen.]

city hall *n.* **1.** The building in which the offices of a city government are located. **2.** A city government, especially its officials considered as a group: *City hall released a statement about the new budget.*

city manager *n.* An administrator appointed by a city council to manage the affairs of city government.

cit•y-state (sĭt′ē stāt′) *n.* An independent state consisting of a city and its surrounding territory: *Sparta was a city-state of ancient Greece.*

civ•et (sĭv′ĭt) *n.* **1.** Any of various spotted mammals of Africa and Asia, similar to a cat, having scent glands that produce a fluid with a strong musky odor. **2.** This yellowish fluid, used in making perfumes. [First written down in 1532 in Modern English, from Medieval Latin *zibethus*, from Arabic *zabād*, civet perfume.]

civet
Otter civet

civ•ic (sĭv′ĭk) *adj.* **1.** Of, relating to, or belonging to a city: *The town's Fourth of July parade is our chief civic event.* **2.** Of, relating to, or belonging to a citizen or citizenship: *It is a civic duty to vote in elections.*

civ•ics (sĭv′ĭks) *n.* *(used with a singular verb).* The study of the purpose and function of local and national government and of the rights and duties of citizens.

civ•il (sĭv′əl) *adj.* **1.** Of or relating to a citizen or citizens: *voting and other civil responsibilities.* **2.** Of or relating to citizens and their relations to the government: *Most departments of the government are concerned with civil affairs.* **3.** Of or relating to the general public rather than to military or religious matters: *a couple married in a civil ceremony at city hall.* **4.** Polite; courteous: *a civil reply.* See Synonyms at **polite. 5.** Relating to the rights of private individuals and especially to legal affairs involving these rights, such as contracts, property, and injury: *The lawsuit for damages in the accident was a civil proceeding.* [First written down before 1387 in Middle English, from Latin *cīvīlis*, from *cīvis*, citizen.] —**civ′il•ly** *adv.*

civil defense *n.* The emergency measures to be taken for the protection of civilian life and property in the case of a natural disaster or enemy attack.

civil disobedience *n.* Nonviolent refusal by members of the public to obey laws, done in an effort to cause change in government policy or legislation.

civil engineer *n.* An engineer trained in the design and construction of projects such as bridges, roads, and dams. —**civil engineering** *n.*

ci•vil•ian (sĭ vĭl′yən) *n.* A person not serving in the armed forces. —*adj.* Of or relating to civilians: *civilian clothes; a civilian career.*

ci•vil•i•ty (sĭ vĭl′ĭ tē) *n., pl.* **ci•vil•i•ties. 1.** Courteous behavior; politeness: *Civility in daily affairs creates a harmonious atmosphere.* **2.** An act or expression of courtesy: *Saying 'good morning' is a pleasant civility.*

civ•i•li•za•tion (sĭv′ə lĭ zā′shən) *n.* **1.a.** A condition of human society in which there is a high level of development in the arts and sciences and political and social organizations. **b.** The act or process of civilizing or of reaching a civilized state. **2.** The kind of culture and society developed by a particular people or nation in some period of history: *Mayan civilization.* **3.** *Informal.* Modern society with its conveniences: *return to civilization after two weeks of camping.*

civ•i•lize (sĭv′ə līz′) *tr.v.* **civ•i•lized, civ•i•liz•ing, civ•i•liz•es. 1.** To bring to a higher level of development in the arts, sciences, culture, and political

ă	pat	oi	boy
ā	pay	ou	out
âr	care	ŏŏ	took
ä	father	ōō	boot
ĕ	pet	ŭ	cut
ē	be	ûr	urge
ĭ	pit	th	thin
ī	pie	*th*	this
îr	pier	hw	whoop
ŏ	pot	zh	vision
ō	toe	ə	about
ô	paw	N	*French* bon

organization. **2.** To refine by education and training: *civilize young minds.*

civ•i•lized (sĭv′ə līzd′) *adj.* **1.** Having or indicating a highly developed society and culture; not primitive: *civilized life.* **2.** Polite or cultured; refined: *a civilized person.*

civil law *n.* The body of law dealing with the rights of private citizens, as distinguished from military law and criminal law.

civil liberties *pl.n.* The legal guarantees of individual rights, such as freedom of speech and religion.

civil marriage *n.* A marriage ceremony performed by a civil official, such as a justice of the peace.

civil rights *pl.n.* The rights belonging to an individual as a citizen, especially of the United States, including civil liberties and freedom from discrimination.

civil servant *n.* A person employed in the civil service.

civil service *n.* **1.** All branches of government service that are not legislative, judicial, or military. **2.** Those persons employed by the civil branches of the government: *Most of the civil service in the United States government is appointed after competitive examination.*

civil war *n.* **1.** A war between opposing groups of the same country. **2. Civil War.** The war in the United States between the Union and the Confederacy from 1861 to 1865.

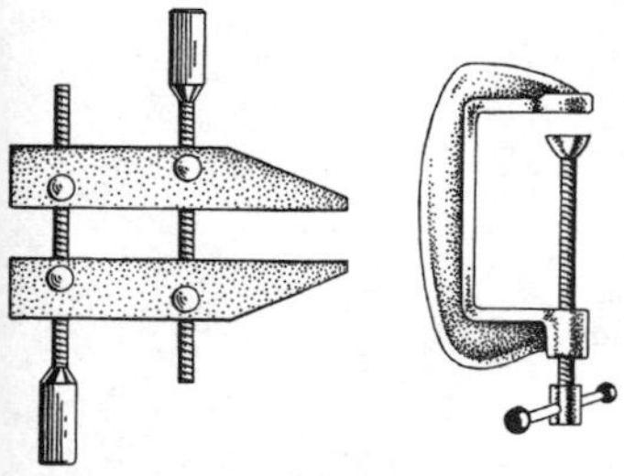

clamp
Left: Parallel clamp
Right: C-clamp

Cl The symbol for the element **chlorine.**

cl. *abbr.* An abbreviation of: **1.** Class. **2.** Classification.

clab•ber (klăb′ər) *n.* Sour curdled milk. —*tr. & intr. v.* **clab•bered, clab•ber•ing, clab•bers.** To curdle.

clack (klăk) *intr. & tr.v.* **clacked, clack•ing, clacks.** To make or cause to make a sudden sharp sound, as that of objects struck together. —*n.* A sudden sharp sound: *the clack of a typewriter.* [First written down before 1250 in Middle English and spelled *clacken*, from Old Norse *klaka*, of imitative origin.]
❑ *These sound alike:* **clack, claque** (applauding group).

clad (klăd) *v.* A past tense and a past participle of **clothe.**

claim (klām) *tr.v.* **claimed, claim•ing, claims. 1.** To demand or ask for (something) as one's own; assert one's right to: *claim luggage; claim a reward.* **2.** To declare to be true; assert: *The witnesses claim that they saw the accident.* **3.** To deserve or call for; require: *Studying for an exam should claim all your attention.* —*n.* **1.** A demand for something as one's rightful due: *file an insurance claim for losses from the fire.* **2.** A basis for demanding something; a right. **3.** A statement of something as fact; an assertion: *an advertisement that makes false claims concerning certain products.* **4.** Something claimed, especially a tract of land claimed by a miner or homesteader. —***idiom.*** **lay claim to.** To assert one's right to or ownership of: *laid claim to the land along the river.* [First written down before 1325 in Middle English and spelled *claimen*, from Latin *clāmāre*, to call.]

claim•ant (klā′mənt) *n.* A person making a claim.

clair•voy•ance (klâr voi′əns) *n.* The supposed power to see objects or events that cannot be perceived by the senses.

clair•voy•ant (klâr voi′ənt) *n.* A person said to have powers of clairvoyance. —*adj.* Of, relating to, or having the powers of clairvoyance. [First written down in 1671 in Modern English, from French : *clair*, clear (from Latin *clārus*) + *voir*, to see (from Latin *vidēre*).]

clam (klăm) *n.* Any of various mollusks having a soft body covered by a double hinged shell and burrowing into sand or mud under fresh or salt water. The soft body of many kinds of clam is used as food. —*intr.v.* **clammed, clam•ming, clams.** To dig or hunt for clams: *clamming along the seashore at low tide.* —***idiom.*** **clam up.** *Informal.* To refuse to talk; stop talking: *The suspect clammed up when the police started asking questions.* [First written down in 1500 in Modern English and spelled *clamshell*, shell that clamps, clam, from *clam*, clamp, vise, from Old English *clamm*, bond.]

clam•bake (klăm′bāk′) *n.* A picnic at which clams and other kinds of seafood are served.

clam•ber (klăm′bər *or* klăm′ər) *intr.v.* **clam•bered, clam•ber•ing, clam•bers.** To climb with difficulty, especially on all fours: *clamber up a rocky slope.*

clam•my (klăm′ē) *adj.* **clam•mi•er, clam•mi•est.** Unpleasantly damp, sticky, and usually cold: *clammy rain-soaked clothes; clammy feet in wet boots.* —**clam′mi•ness** *n.*

clam•or (klăm′ər) *n.* **1.** A loud, continuous, and usually confused noise: *the clamor of fans at a football game.* **2.** A strong or loud demand: *a public clamor for clean air.* —*intr.v.* **clam•ored, clam•or•ing, clam•ors.** To make a clamor: *The excited crowd clamored for an encore.* [First written down about 1385 in Middle English and spelled *clamour*, from Latin *clāmor*, shout, from *clāmāre*, to cry out.]

clam•or•ous (klăm′ər əs) *adj.* **1.** Loud and noisy: *a clamorous party.* **2.** Making or full of strong or loud demands: *a clamorous crowd of protesters.* —**clam′or•ous•ly** *adv.* —**clam′or•ous•ness** *n.*

clamp (klămp) *n.* A device for gripping or fastening things together, consisting of two parts that can be tightened together by pressure of a spring or by turning a screw. —*tr.v.* **clamped, clamp•ing, clamps.** To grip or fasten with or as if with a clamp: *glue and clamp two boards together.* —***idiom.*** **clamp down.** To become more strict or repressive; impose controls: *clamping down on polluters.*

clan (klăn) *n.* **1.** A group of families, as in the Scottish Highlands, claiming a common ancestor: *the MacIntyre clan.* **2.** A group of relatives, friends, or others having a common background or interest: *a clan of local politicians.* [First written down about 1425 in Middle English, from Scottish Gaelic *clann*, family, from Old Irish *cland*, offspring, from Latin *planta*, plant, sprout.]

clan•des•tine (klăn dĕs′tĭn) *adj.* Done secretly or kept secret, often for some unlawful purpose: *a clandestine meeting.* —**clan•des′tine•ly** *adv.*

clang (klăng) *tr. & intr.v.* **clanged, clang•ing, clangs.** To make or cause to make a loud, metallic ringing sound: *Bells clanged to announce the new year.* —*n.* A clanging sound: *the clang of an alarm.*

clan•gor (klăng′ər *or* klăng′gər) *n.* A clang or repeated clanging; a loud ringing; a din. —**clan′gor•ous** *adj.* —**clan′gor•ous•ly** *adv.*

clank (klăngk) *n.* A loud, metallic ringing sound: *The gate closed with a clank.* —*intr.v.* **clanked, clank•ing, clanks.** To make a clank: *The old car clanked and sputtered down the road.*

clan•nish (klăn′ĭsh) *adj.* **1.** Of, relating to, or characteristic of a clan. **2.** Inclined to cling together as a group and exclude outsiders. —**clan′nish•ly** *adv.*

clans•man (klănz′mən) *n.* A man belonging to a clan.

clans•wom•an (klănz′wo͝om′ən) *n.* A woman belonging to a clan.

clap (klăp) *v.* **clapped, clap•ping, claps.** —*intr.* **1.** To strike the hands together with a sudden loud sound: *The audience clapped at the end of the play.* **2.** To make a sudden sharp sound: *The door clapped shut.* —*tr.* **1.** To strike (the hands) together with an abrupt loud sound: *The crowd clapped their hands after she scored a goal.* **2.** To make (something) come together suddenly with a sharp noise: *The baby clapped the spoon on the table.* **3.** To tap with the open hand, as in hearty greeting: *clap a friend on the shoulder.* **4.** To put or place suddenly: *Clap the lid on the box before the cricket jumps out.* —*n.* **1.** The act or sound of clapping the hands. **2.** A loud, sharp, or explosive noise: *a clap of thunder.* **3.** A slap: *a friendly clap on the back.*

clap•board (klăb′ərd *or* klăp′bôrd′) *n.* A long narrow board with one edge thicker than the other, overlapped to cover the outside walls of a building. —*tr.v.* **clap•board•ed, clap•board•ing, clap•boards.** To cover with clapboards.

clap•per (klăp′ər) *n.* **1.** The tongue of a bell. **2.** A person or thing that claps. **3. clappers.** Two flat pieces of wood that are held between the fingers and struck together as a percussion instrument.

clap•trap (klăp′trăp′) *n.* Insincere, empty speech or writing.

claque (klăk) *n.* **1.** A group of persons hired to applaud at a performance. **2.** A group of fawning admirers.

❑ *These sound alike:* **claque, clack** (sharp sound).

clar•et (klăr′ĭt) *n.* **1.** A dry red wine. **2.** A dark purplish red.

clar•i•fy (klăr′ə fī′) *v.* **clar•i•fied, clar•i•fy•ing, clar•i•fies.** —*tr.* **1.** To make clear or easier to understand: *give a detailed explanation to clarify the instructions.* **2.** To make (a liquid, butter, or other substance) clear or pure by removing unwanted solid matter: *clarify butter by heating it; clarify vinegar by straining it.* —*intr.* To become clear. —**clar′i•fi•ca′tion** (klăr′ə fĭ kā′shən) *n.*

clar•i•net (klăr′ə nĕt′) *n.* A woodwind instrument having a cylindrical body, a flaring bell, and a mouthpiece with a single reed. It is played by covering holes in its body and pressing keys with the fingers. [First written down in 1796 in Modern English, from Old French *clarin*, clarion, from Latin *clārus*, clear.] —**clar′i•net′ist** *n.*

clar•i•on (klăr′ē ən) *adj.* Shrill and clear: *the clarion call of a trumpet.* —*n.* **1.** A medieval trumpet with a clear shrill tone. **2.** The sound made by this trumpet or a similar sound.

clar•i•ty (klăr′ĭ tē) *n.* The condition or quality of being clear: *clarity of speech; a writer with great clarity of style.*

Clark (klärk), **George Rogers.** 1752–1818. American military leader and pioneer who led numerous raids in the Northwest Territory during the Revolutionary War.

Clark, William. 1770–1838. American explorer who joined Meriwether Lewis in an expedition to the Pacific Ocean (1804–1806).

clash (klăsh) *v.* **clashed, clash•ing, clash•es.** —*intr.* **1.** To strike or collide with a loud harsh sound: *The cymbals clashed loudly.* **2.** To be strongly out of harmony; come into conflict: *That shirt clashes with your trousers.* —*tr.* To strike together or collide with a loud harsh noise: *At the end of the march I clashed the cymbals together.* —*n.* **1.** A conflict, an opposition, or a disagreement: *a clash of different personalities; a clash between political parties.* **2.** A loud, harsh, metallic sound: *a clash of cymbals.*

clasp (klăsp) *n.* **1.** A fastener, such as a hook or buckle, used to hold two objects or parts together. **2.** A firm grasp or embrace: *took my hand with a firm clasp.* —*tr.v.* **clasped, clasp•ing, clasps. 1.** To fasten with a clasp: *clasp a necklace.* **2.** To grasp or embrace tightly: *clasped each other after their long separation.* [First written down in 1307 in Middle English and spelled *claspe*, probably ultimately from Old English *clyppan*, to grasp, hold.]

class (klăs) *n.* **1.** A group of persons or things that are generally alike in some way; a kind or category: *the class of odd numbers; a class of ships.* **2.** A group of persons having approximately the same economic and social standing: *the working class.* **3.** A group of plants or animals having certain similar characteristics, ranking between an order and a phylum: *All mammals belong to the same class of animals.* See table at **taxonomy. 4.a.** A group of people graduated in the same year: *a reunion of the class of 1960.* **b.** A group of students who meet regularly to study the same subject: *Our biology class has 20 students.* **c.** The period during which such a group meets: *eat lunch before class; meet after class.* **5.a.** A grade of mail: *A letter is sent first class and a magazine third class.* **b.** The quality of accommodations on a public vehicle: *Going by business class on an airline costs more than tourist class.* **6.** *Informal.* Great style or quality: *This restaurant has a lot of class.* —*tr.v.* **classed, class•ing, class•es.** To assign to a class; classify: *class a novel as a murder mystery.* [First written down in 1602 in Modern English and spelled *classe*, from Latin *classis*, class of citizens.]

clas•sic (klăs′ĭk) *adj.* **1.** Long regarded as a model; serving as an outstanding example of its kind: *a classic example of colonial architecture.* **2.** Well-known and typical: *A runny nose and a cough are classic signs of a cold.* **3.** Simple and refined in form or in style: *the classic style of American furniture in the 1800's.* **4.** Of ancient Greece and Rome or their literature or art; classical: *classic oratory.* —*n.* **1.** A work of literature, music, or art generally considered to be of the highest rank: *Many early rock 'n' roll recordings are now classics.* **2. classics.** The languages and literature of ancient Greece and Rome. **3.** A traditional event held annually, as in sports: *The World Series is baseball's fall classic.* [First written down in 1613 in Modern English, from Latin *classicus*, belonging to the highest class of citizens, from *classis*, class.]

clas•si•cal (klăs′ĭ kəl) *adj.* **1.** Of or relating to the art, architecture, literature, and way of life of ancient Greece and Rome: *classical architecture of the Roman forum; a classical scholar.* **2.** Of or relating to music composed in forms that have developed over a long period of time in Europe. Classical music is distinguished from popular and folk music and includes symphonies, concertos, and chamber music. **3.** Standard or traditional rather than new or experimental; established: *The hand-held calculator has displaced the classical methods of arithmetic computation.* **4.** Well-known; typical; classic: *the classical defense by reason of insanity.* —**clas′si•cal•ly** *adv.*

clas•si•cism (klăs′ĭ sĭz′əm) *n.* **1.** The rules and ideals, as of form, simplicity, and proportion, that are the basis of the art and literature of ancient Greece and Rome. They include the use of regular order in design, simplicity in style, and restraint or proportion in form. **2.** The use of such rules or principles in artistic creation.

clas•si•cist (klăs′ĭ sĭst) *n.* A student of or an authority on the art, architecture, literature, languages, and cultures of ancient Greece and Rome.

clas•si•fi•ca•tion (klăs′ə fĭ kā′shən) *n.* **1.** The act or process of classifying; a grouping by categories: *The classification of books according to subject is the work of a librarian.* **2.a.** The result of classifying, as by category, name, or rating; a systematic arrangement: *chemical elements arranged in a classification by atomic weight.* **b.** In botany and zoology, the systematic grouping of plants and animals by evolutionary or structural relationships.

clas•si•fied (klăs′ə fīd′) *adj.* **1.** Arranged in classes;

clarinet

William Clark

ă	pat	oi	**boy**
ā	pay	ou	**out**
âr	care	o͝o	**took**
ä	father	o͞o	**boot**
ĕ	pet	ŭ	cut
ē	be	ûr	**urge**
ĭ	pit	th	**thin**
ī	pie	*th*	**this**
îr	pier	hw	**whoop**
ŏ	pot	zh	vision
ō	toe	ə	about
ô	paw	N	*French* bon

clavichord
Young Woman Playing a Clavichord, from the workshop of Jan Sanders Van Hemessen (1500?–1575?)

sorted; categorized: *the classified section of a newspaper.* **2.** Available only to authorized persons; secret: *classified information.*

classified advertisement *n.* An advertisement, usually brief and in small type, printed in a newspaper along with others of the same category.

clas•si•fy (klăs′ə fī′) *tr.v.* **clas•si•fied, clas•si•fy•ing, clas•si•fies. 1.** To arrange in classes or assign to a class; sort; categorize: *A librarian classifies books according to subject matter.* **2.** To designate (information) as available only to authorized persons. **—clas′si•fi′a•ble** *adj.* **—clas′si•fi′er** *n.*

class•mate (klăs′māt′) *n.* A member of the same class in a school or college.

class•room (klăs′ro͞om′ *or* klăs′ro͝om′) *n.* A room in which classes are held in a school or college.

class•y (klăs′ē) *adj.* **class•i•er, class•i•est.** *Informal.* Stylish; elegant: *a classy hat.*

clat•ter (klăt′ər) *v.* **clat•tered, clat•ter•ing, clat•ters.** *—intr.* **1.** To make a rattling sound: *The shutters clattered as the storm approached.* **2.** To move with a rattling sound: *A rickety old wagon clattered down the road.* **3.** To talk rapidly and noisily; chatter: *party guests clattering over lunch.* *—tr.* To cause to make a rattling sound: *The cook clattered pots and pans in the kitchen.* *—n.* **1.** A rattling sound: *the clatter of dishes falling to the floor.* **2.** Noisy talk: *the clatter of voices in the crowd.*

clause (klôz) *n.* **1.** In grammar, a group of words containing a subject and a verb phrase and forming part of a compound or complex sentence. In the complex sentence *The dog ran off before we caught it,* the phrase *The dog ran off* is an independent or main clause and the phrase *before we caught it* is a dependent or subordinate clause. **2.** A separate part of a document containing some distinct provision: *The contract had several clauses, each outlining the duties of the partners.* [First written down before 1200 in Middle English, from Medieval Latin *clausa,* close of a rhetorical period, from Latin, from *claudere,* to close.]

claus•tro•pho•bi•a (klô′strə fō′bē ə) *n.* An abnormal fear of being in small or confined spaces.

clav•i•chord (klăv′ĭ kôrd′) *n.* A keyboard musical instrument with a soft sound made by small metal hammers that strike the strings as keys are pushed. The modern piano was developed from it.

clav•i•cle (klăv′ĭ kəl) *n.* The collarbone.

cla•vier (klə vîr′ *or* klā′vē ər *or* klăv′ē ər) *n.* **1.** The keyboard of a musical instrument, such as a piano or an organ. **2.** A stringed keyboard instrument, such as a harpsichord.

claw (klô) *n.* **1.** A sharp curved nail on the toe of a mammal, reptile, or bird. **2.** A foot of an animal having sharp hooked nails. **3.** A pincer, as of a lobster or crab, used for grasping. **4.** Something resembling a claw: *I pulled out the bent nail with the claw of the hammer.* *—tr. & intr.v.* **clawed, claw•ing, claws.** To scratch, dig, tear, or seize with or as if with claws: *The dog clawed at the door to get in.* [First written down about 700 in Old English and spelled *clawu.*]

clay (klā) *n.* A stiff sticky earthy material that is soft and pliable when wet and consists mainly of various silicates of aluminum found in sedimentary rock and soils. It is widely used in making bricks, pottery, and tiles. [First written down about 1000 in Old English and spelled *clæg.*]

Clay, Henry. 1777–1852. American politician who pushed the Missouri Compromise through the U.S. House of Representatives (1820–1821).

clay pigeon *n.* A clay disk hurled as a flying target in skeet and trapshooting.

clean (klēn) *adj.* **clean•er, clean•est. 1.** Free from dirt, stain, or impurities; unsoiled: *clean clothing; drinking from a clean glass.* **2.a.** Free from pollution or contamination: *clean drinking water.* **b.** Producing little pollution: *The new law calls for clean fuels in all cars.* **3.** Free from wrongdoing; honorable: *a clean life of hard work; a clean record.* **4.** Having a smooth edge or surface; even; regular: *A clean break in the bone heals quickly.* **5.** Entire; thorough; complete: *They made a clean escape, leaving no clues as to where they went.* **6.** Blank: *a clean page.* **7.** Free from clumsiness; skillful; adroit: *a clean hit to center field.* *—adv.* **cleaner, cleanest. 1.a.** So as to be unsoiled: *We washed the wall clean.* **b.** In a fair manner: *They played the game clean.* **2.** *Informal.* Entirely; completely: *I clean forgot about the test.* *—v.* **cleaned, clean•ing, cleans.** *—tr.* **1.** To rid of dirt, stain, or disorder: *clean a room.* **2.** To get rid of (dirt, for example); remove: *Let's clean the dirt from the floor.* **3.** To prepare (fowl or other food) for cooking, as by removing entrails: *clean a fish.* **4.** To remove the contents from; empty: *I cleaned my plate.* *—intr.* To undergo or perform cleaning: *A wool rug cleans easily. A damp rag cleans well.* ***—idioms.*** **clean house.** *Slang.* To get rid of what is unwanted: *The new boss cleaned house and fired the unproductive workers.* **clean out. 1.** To rid of dirt, trash, or disorder: *clean out the garage.* **2.** *Slang.* To deprive completely, as of money; remove everything from: *Shopping cleaned out my savings.* **3.** To empty of contents: *cleaned out the refrigerator to make sandwiches.* **clean up. 1.** To rid of dirt or disorder: *clean up one's room; clean up the city government.* **2.** *Slang.* To make a large sum of money in a short period of time: *We cleaned up on the spring sale.* [First written down about 750 in Old English and spelled *clǣne.*] **—clean′ness** *n.*

Synonyms: clean, cleanly, immaculate, spotless. These adjectives all mean free from dirt. *Matt threw the clean pair of socks in the hamper by mistake. Cats are generally thought of as cleanly animals. The tablecloth was immaculate before you spilled mustard on it. The roommates made their apartment spotless before their guests arrived.* **Antonym: dirty.**

---

clean-cut (klēn′kŭt′) *adj.* **1.** Having a distinct sharp outline: *a racing car with clean-cut lines.* **2.** Neat and trim in appearance: *a clean-cut soldier.*

clean•er (klē′nər) *n.* **1.** A person whose job it is to clean: *Take these clothes to the cleaner.* **2.** A machine or substance used in cleaning: *Ammonia is a good household cleaner.*

clean•li•ness (klĕn′lē nĭs) *n.* The state of being clean: *Personal cleanliness is important for good health.*

clean•ly (klĕn′lē) *adj.* **clean•li•er, clean•li•est.** Habitually and carefully neat and clean: *Cats are thought of as cleanly animals.* See Synonyms at **clean.** *—adv.* (klēn′lē). In a clean manner: *The fruit stems had been severed cleanly by a knife.*

cleanse (klĕnz) *tr.v.* **cleansed, cleans•ing, cleans•es.** To make clean or pure: *cleanse a wound.* [First written down about 750 in Old English and spelled *clǣnsian,* from *clǣne,* pure, clean.]

cleans•er (klĕn′zər) *n.* A substance used for cleaning.

clean•up (klēn′ŭp′) *n.* **1.** The act or process of cleaning up: *a trash cleanup.* **2.** The fourth positon in a baseball batting order. **—clean′up′** *adj.*

clear (klîr) *adj.* **clear•er, clear•est. 1.** Free from clouds, mist, or haze: *a clear sky.* **2.** Free from anything that dims, darkens, or obscures; transparent: *a glass of cool clear water.* **3.** Free from obstruction or hindrance; open: *We had a clear view of the valley from the mountains. The road was clear of* *snow.* **4.a.** Easily perceived by the eye or ear; distinct: *a clear picture on the TV; the clear sound of church bells; a crisp clear voice.* **b.** Plain or evident to the mind; easily understood: *a clear explanation; clear directions.* **5.** Obvious; unmistakable: *a clear case of the flu.* **6.** Free from doubt or confusion; certain: *Are you clear about what has to be done?* **7.** Free from guilt; untroubled: *a clear conscience.* **8.** Free from flaw or blemish: *clear skin.* **9.** Free from charges or deductions; net: *After paying for expenses the shopkeeper earned a small but clear profit.* —*adv.* **1.** Out of the way: *The deer jumped clear of the oncoming car.* **2.** Distinctly; clearly: *spoke loud and clear before the audience.* **3.** *Informal.* All the way; entirely: *The baby cried clear through the night.* —*v.* **cleared, clear•ing, clears.** —*tr.* **1.** To make clear, light, or bright: *A fan will clear the smoke from the room.* **2.a.** To make free of objects or obstructions: *clear the table after dinner; clear the road of snow.* **b.** To remove (objects or obstructions): *clear the dishes from the table; clear snow from the sidewalk.* **3.** To pass by, under, or over without contact: *The runner cleared every hurdle.* **4.** To free from a legal charge; acquit: *The jury cleared the accused of all charges.* **5.** To rid of confusion or doubt: *Let's clear up the questions surrounding the lost book.* **6.** To win the approval of: *The bill cleared the Senate.* **7.** To pass (a check or bill of exchange) through a clearing-house: *Banks clear checks every day.* **8.** To earn (an amount of money) as net profit or earnings: *They cleared $45 selling baked goods.* —*intr.* **1.** To become clear, light, or bright: *The sky cleared in the afternoon.* **2.** To go away; disappear: *The fog cleared.* **3.** To pass through a clearing-house: *My check to pay the rent cleared today.* —***idioms.*** **clear out.** *Informal.* To leave a place, often quickly: *The raccoons cleared out before the campers returned.* **clear the air.** To dispel emotional tensions or differences: *A joke cleared the air.* **in the clear.** Free from burdens, dangers, guilt, or responsibility: *Once the facts were known the suspect was in the clear.* [First written down about 1280 in Middle English and spelled *cler*, bright, from Latin *clārus*, clear, bright.] —**clear′ly** *adv.* —**clear′ness** *n.*

clear•ance (klîr′əns) *n.* **1.** The act of clearing: *The city has begun land clearance where the abandoned buildings are.* **2.** A sale to dispose of old merchandise at reduced prices: *Department stores often have a clearance after the holidays.* **3.** The amount of distance or space by which a moving object clears something: *a small clearance for trucks passing under this bridge.* **4.** Permission for an airplane, ship, or other vehicle to proceed: *The control tower gave us clearance to take off.* **5.** Official certification of blamelessness, trustworthiness, or suitability: *You need clearance to handle classified material.*

clear-cut (klîr′kŭt′) *adj.* **1.** Outlined in sharp distinct form: *a face with clear-cut features.* **2.** Not vague or confused; obvious: *a clear-cut statement of fact.*

clear•ing (klîr′ĭng) *n.* An area of land from which trees and other obstructions have been removed: *a clearing in the forest.*

clear•ing-house or **clear•ing•house** (klîr′ĭng hous′) *n.* An office where banks exchange checks, drafts, and other notes and settle accounts.

cleat (klēt) *n.* **1.** A projecting piece of iron, rubber, or leather attached to the sole of a shoe to keep it from slipping. **2.** A piece of metal or wood with projecting arms or ends on which a rope can be wound.

cleav•age (klē′vĭj) *n.* **1.** The act of splitting or state of being split: *Earthquakes are often accompanied by cleavage of the ground.* **2.** The tendency of rocks, minerals, and crystals to split along definite planes, making smooth surfaces. **3.a.** The series of cell divisions by which a fertilized egg becomes a blastula. **b.** A stage in this series of divisions.

cleave[1] (klēv) *v.* **cleft** (klĕft) or **cleaved** or **clove** (klōv), **cleft** or **cleaved** or **clo•ven** (klō′vən), **cleav•ing, cleaves.** —*tr.* **1.** To split, as by a sudden blow: *The ax cleft the piece of wood.* **2.** To make or proceed through by or as if by cutting: *a ship cleaving its way through the ice.* —*intr.* **1.** To be capable of being split: *Certain brittle woods cleave easily.* **2.** To make one's way; pass: *cleave through the crowd.* [First written down in 910 in Old English and spelled *clēofan.*]

cleave[2] (klēv) *intr.v.* **cleaved, cleav•ing, cleaves.** **1.** To cling; adhere; stick fast: *Barnacles cleave to a hull.* **2.** To remain faithful: *cleave to old beliefs.* [First written down before 899 in Old English and spelled *cleofian.*]

cleav•er (klē′vər) *n.* A tool with a broad heavy blade and a short handle, used especially by butchers for cutting meat.

clef (klĕf) *n.* A symbol on a musical staff that tells which pitch each of the various lines and spaces represents. [First written down before 1577 in Modern English, from Latin *clāvis*, key.]

cleft (klĕft) *v.* A past tense and a past participle of **cleave[1]**. —*adj.* Divided; split: *a cleft chin.* —*n.* A crack or split: *My canteen fell into a cleft in the rock.*

cleft palate *n.* A split in the roof of the mouth, occurring when the two parts of the palate do not close before birth.

clem•a•tis (klĕm′ə tĭs *or* klĭ măt′ĭs) *n.* Any of various climbing vines having white, pink, or purplish flowers and feathery seeds. [First written down in 1551 in Modern English, from Greek *klēmatis.*]

clem•en•cy (klĕm′ən sē) *n., pl.* **clem•en•cies.** **1.** Mercy, as toward an offender or enemy; leniency: *The judge showed clemency in sentencing the defendant.* **2.** Mildness, especially of weather.

Clem•ens (klĕm′ənz), **Samuel Langhorne.** Pen name Mark Twain. 1835–1910. American writer who used his childhood along the Mississippi River as a source for his books, including *Tom Sawyer* (1876).

clem•ent (klĕm′ənt) *adj.* **1.** Inclined to be lenient or merciful: *a clement ruler.* **2.** Pleasant; mild: *clement spring weather.* —**clem′ent•ly** *adv.*

clench (klĕnch) *tr.v.* **clenched, clench•ing, clench•es.** **1.** To close (a hand or the teeth) tightly: *I clenched my fists in anger.* **2.** To grasp or grip tightly: *clenched the steering wheel.*

Cle•o•pat•ra (klē′ə păt′rə *or* klē′ə pä′trə). 69–30 B.C. Egyptian queen (51–49 and 48–30) noted for her political ambition.

cler•gy (klûr′jē) *n., pl.* **cler•gies.** The group of people ordained for religious service, as ministers, mullahs, or rabbis. —SEE NOTE at **collective noun.**

cler•gy•man (klûr′jē mən) *n.* A man who is a member of the clergy.

cler•gy•wom•an (klûr′jē wo͝om′ən) *n.* A woman who is a member of the clergy.

cler•ic (klĕr′ĭk) *n.* A member of the clergy. [First written down in 1621 in Modern English, from Late Latin *clēricus*, clerk.]

cler•i•cal (klĕr′ĭ kəl) *adj.* **1.** Of or relating to clerks or office workers: *typing and other clerical work.* **2.** Of or relating to the clergy: *dressed in clerical garb.* —**cler′i•cal•ly** *adv.*

clerk (klûrk) *n.* **1.** A person who works in an office doing such jobs as keeping records, filing, and typing. **2.** A person who keeps the records and performs the regular business of a court or legislative body. **3.** A person who sells merchandise in a store or works at a service desk, as in a hotel. —*intr.v.* **clerked, clerk•ing, clerks.** To work or serve as a

Samuel Clemens

"Mark Twain"

Cleopatra

Roman sculpture

ă	pat	oi	**boy**
ā	**pay**	ou	**out**
âr	**care**	o͝o	took
ä	father	o͞o	**boot**
ĕ	pet	ŭ	cut
ē	be	ûr	**urge**
ĭ	pit	th	**thin**
ī	**pie**	*th*	**this**
îr	**pier**	hw	**whoop**
ŏ	pot	zh	vision
ō	**toe**	ə	about
ô	**paw**	N	*French* bon

Grover Cleveland

Bill Clinton
Photographed in 1993

clerk: *clerk in a drugstore as a summer job.* [First written down about 975 in Old English and spelled *clēric*, clergyman, from Greek *klērikos*, belonging to the clergy.]

Cleve•land (klēv′lənd). A city of northeast Ohio on Lake Erie. The city was laid out in 1796. Population, 505,616.

Cleveland, (Stephen) Grover. 1837–1908. The 22nd and 24th President of the United States (1885–1889 and 1893–1897). He was known as an honest independent President.

clev•er (klĕv′ər) *adj.* **clev•er•er, clev•er•est. 1.** Having the capacity to learn and think quickly; bright; quick-witted: *A clever dog is easy to train.* **2.** Showing wit or ingenuity: *a clever plan; a clever trick.* **3.** Skilled at doing something, especially with the hands: *a clever magician.* **—clev′er•ly** *adv.* **—clev′er•ness** *n.*

clew (klo͞o) *Chiefly British.* *—n. & v.* Variant of **clue.**

cli•ché (klē shā′) *n.* An overused expression or idea that has lost its original quality or effect: *The expression* as fast as greased lightning *is a cliché.*

click (klĭk) *n.* A short sharp sound: *the click of train wheels over the tracks.* *—v.* **clicked, click•ing, clicks.** *—intr.* **1.** To produce a click or a series of clicks: *The wheels of the train clicked over the rails.* **2.** *Slang.* To be a success: *The new comedian clicked with the audience.* **3.** *Slang.* To work well together or be in harmony: *We clicked as soon as we met.* **4.** *Slang.* To become understandable; make sense: *The name clicked when I saw the actor's picture.* *—tr.* To cause to make such a sound: *clicked his ballpoint pen and started to write.*

cli•ent (klī′ənt) *n.* **1.** A person who uses the services of a professional person: *Lawyers have clients, but doctors are usually said to have patients.* **2.** A customer or patron: *That jewelry store has several wealthy clients.*

cli•en•tele (klī′ən tĕl′) *n.* The group of regular clients or customers, as of a store.

cliff (klĭf) *n.* A high, steep, or overhanging face of rock or earth: *stand on the cliffs overlooking the sea far below.*

cliff dweller *n.* A member of certain prehistoric peoples of the southwest United States who lived in caves in the sides of cliffs. The Pueblo are their descendants.

cliff•hang•er (klĭf′hăng′ər) *n.* **1.** A melodrama presented in episodes in which each one ends in suspense. **2.** A suspenseful situation at the end of a chapter, a scene, or an episode. **3.** A contest whose outcome is uncertain until the end: *The game was a cliffhanger—tied until the last minute.*

cli•mac•tic (klī măk′tĭk) *adj.* Relating to or forming a climax: *climactic events leading to the end of the mystery story.*

cli•mate (klī′mĭt) *n.* **1.** The general or average weather conditions of a certain region, including temperature, rainfall, and wind: *The coast of the Mediterranean has a summer climate of warm breezes and sunshine.* **2.** A region having certain weather conditions: *They live in tropical climate.* **3.** A general condition or attitude: *After the Berlin Wall came down, there was a climate of joy in Europe.* [First written down in 1375 in Middle English and spelled *climat*, from Greek *klima*, surface of the earth, region.]

cli•mat•ic (klī măt′ĭk) *adj.* Of or relating to climate: *climatic changes; climatic regions.* **—cli•mat′i•cal•ly** *adv.*

cli•ma•tol•o•gy (klī′mə tŏl′ə jē) *n.* The scientific study of climates.

cli•max (klī′măks′) *n.* **1.** The point in a series of events that is of greatest intensity or effect, usually occurring near the end: *The climax of the play comes in the last act when the hero wins out over the villain. Winning the Presidency was the climax of a long political career.* **2.** A climax community. *—tr. & intr.v.* **cli•maxed, cli•max•ing, cli•max•es.** To bring or come to a climax: *The appearance of a surprise guest climaxed the party.*

climax community *n.* A community in which populations of plants or animals remain stable and exist in balance with each other and their environment.

climb (klīm) *v.* **climbed, climb•ing, climbs.** *—intr.* **1.a.** To move upward, especially by using the hands and feet; ascend: *The hikers climbed all day to reach the top of the mountain.* **b.** To move in some direction, especially by means of the hands and feet: *The firefighter climbed across the roof and down the ladder.* **2.** To go higher; rise: *The morning sun climbed in the sky. The rocket climbed steadily. The patient's fever began to climb.* **3.** To slant or slope upward: *The trail climbs to the top of the cliff.* **4.** To grow upward by clinging to or twining around something: *The vine climbs around the tree.* *—tr.* **1.** To go up, over, or through (something), especially by using the hands and feet; ascend: *Leopards can climb trees. The hikers climbed the mountain.* **2.** To grow up on (something): *Roses climbed the trellis.* *—n.* **1.** The act of climbing: *a hard climb up the mountain; an executive's climb to power.* **2.** A place to be climbed: *That hill was a steep climb.* [First written down before 1000 in Old English and spelled *climban.*] **—climb′a•ble** *adj.*

❑ *These sound alike:* **climb, clime** (climate).

climb•er (klī′mər) *n.* **1.** A person or thing that climbs: *a mountain climber.* **2.** A plant, such as a vine, that climbs.

clime (klīm) *n.* Climate.

❑ *These sound alike:* **clime, climb** (move up).

clinch (klĭnch) *v.* **clinched, clinch•ing, clinch•es.** *—tr.* **1.** To fix or secure (a nail or bolt) by bending down or flattening the end that sticks out. **2.** To fasten securely, as with a nail or bolt: *clinch rafters in place.* **3.** To settle definitely: *clinch a deal; clinch a championship.* *—intr.* In boxing, to hold the opponent's body with one or both arms. *—n.* In boxing, the act or an instance of clinching: *The boxers went into a clinch at the end of the second round.*

clinch•er (klĭn′chər) *n.* **1.** Something that clinches, especially a nail or bolt. **2.** A final and decisive point, fact, or remark, as in an argument.

cling (klĭng) *intr.v.* **clung, cling•ing, clings. 1.** To hold tight or adhere to something: *The climbers must cling to the rope.* **2.** To stay near; remain close: *We clung together during the storm.* **3.** To remain attached emotionally; hold on: *cling to old beliefs; cling to a hope.* *—n.* A clingstone.

cling•stone (klĭng′stōn′) *adj.* Of or relating to a fruit whose flesh sticks to the stone: *a clingstone peach.* *—n.* A clingstone fruit, especially a peach.

clin•ic (klĭn′ĭk) *n.* **1.** A place that is connected with a hospital or medical school and provides treatment to patients who do not stay overnight. **2.** A place where medical specialists work together in research and treatment of particular illnesses: *an eye and ear clinic for the treatment of children.* **3.** A group offering special counseling or training: *an acting clinic; a tennis clinic.* **4.** A training session for medical students in which they observe while patients are examined and treated.

clin•i•cal (klĭn′ĭ kəl) *adj.* **1.** Of, relating to, or connected with a clinic: *a doctor on the clinical staff.* **2.** Involving or based on direct examination and treatment of patients: *a clinical diagnosis of disease.* **3.** Very objective; not emotional; analytical: *a clinical* *account of the state's economic problems.* **—clin′i•cal•ly** *adv.*

clink[1] (klĭngk) *tr. & intr.v.* **clinked, clink•ing, clinks.** To make or cause to make a light, sharp, ringing sound: *clink glasses after a toast. The ice clinked in the glass.* *—n.* A light, sharp, ringing sound: *the clink of glasses on a tray.* [First written down before 1325 in Middle English and spelled *clinken,* probably from Middle Dutch *klinken,* of imitative origin.]

clink[2] (klĭngk) *n. Slang.* A prison or prison cell. [First written down in 1515 in Modern English, after *Clink,* a district of London famous for its prison.]

clink•er (**klĭng′**kər) *n.* **1.** A lump of incombustible matter left over after coal has burned. **2.** *Slang.* A mistake; a blunder.

Clin•ton (**klĭn′**tən), **William Jefferson.** Known as "Bill." Born 1946. The 42nd President of the United States (since 1993).

clip[1] (klĭp) *v.* **clipped, clip•ping, clips.** *—tr.* **1.** To cut, cut off, or cut out with scissors or shears: *clip a picture out of the newspaper.* **2.** To cut short; trim: *clip a hedge.* **3.** To cut short; curtail: *Our discussion was clipped by our need to go home.* **4.** To shorten (a word or words) by leaving out letters or syllables: *clip one's words when speaking excitedly.* **5.** *Informal.* To hit or strike with a quick sharp blow: *Their car clipped ours in the front fender.* **6.** In football, to block (an opposing player) from behind. *—intr.* **1.** To cut or trim something. **2.** *Informal.* To move rapidly: *The sailboat clipped along in the strong wind.* *—n.* **1.** The act of clipping: *Just a few clips of the scissors will even your bangs.* **2.** The wool clipped from sheep at one shearing. **3.** Something clipped off, as a sequence clipped from a movie film. **4.** *Informal.* A quick sharp blow: *a clip on the chin.* **5.** *Informal.* A brisk pace: *The train sped along at a good clip.* **6.** In football, an act of clipping. [First written down about 1200 in Middle English and spelled *clippen,* from Old Norse *klippa.*]

clip[2] (klĭp) *n.* **1.** A device for gripping or holding things together: *A paper clip is fastening several pages together.* **2.** A holder for cartridges to be loaded into an automatic rifle or pistol. **3.** A piece of jewelry, such as a pin, that fastens with a clasp or clip. *—tr.v.* **clipped, clip•ping, clips.** To fasten with a clip: *clip the papers together.* [First written down in 1354 in Middle English, hook, from *clippen,* to clasp, embrace, from Old English *clyppan.*]

clip•board (**klĭp′**bôrd′) *n.* A small writing board with a spring clip at the top for holding papers or a writing pad.

clip•per (**klĭp′**ər) *n.* **1.** A person who clips, cuts, or shears. **2. clippers.** A tool for clipping, cutting, or shearing: *nail clippers; a barber's clippers.* **3.** A sailing vessel built for great speed, having tall masts and sharp lines. [First written down in 1830 in Modern English, from *clip,* to cut short, go fast.]

clip•ping (**klĭp′**ĭng) *n.* Something cut or trimmed off, especially an article or a photograph clipped from a newspaper or magazine.

clique (klēk *or* klĭk) *n.* A small group of people who stick together and remain aloof from others.

cliqu•ish (**klē′**kĭsh *or* **klĭk′**ĭsh) *adj.* Relating to or characteristic of a clique. **—cliqu′ish•ly** *adv.* **—cliqu′ish•ness** *n.*

clit•o•ris (**klĭt′**ər ĭs *or* **klī′**tər ĭs) *n.* A small organ that forms part of the external reproductive system in female mammals.

clo•a•ca (klō **ā′**kə) *n., pl.* **clo•a•cae** (klō **ā′**sē′). The cavity in the body of birds, reptiles, amphibians, and most fishes, into which the intestinal, urinary, and genital canals open.

cloak (klōk) *n.* **1.** A loose outer garment or wrap, usually having no sleeves. **2.** Something that covers or conceals: *a cloak of mystery surrounds their disappearance.* *—tr.v.* **cloaked, cloak•ing, cloaks.** To cover with or as if with a cloak: *The airport was cloaked in fog.* [First written down in 1293 in Middle English and spelled *cloke,* from Medieval Latin *clocca,* bell, cloak (from its shape).]

cloak•room (**klōk′**ro͞om′ *or* **klōk′**ro͝om′) *n.* A room where coats and other outdoor clothing may be left temporarily.

clob•ber (**klŏb′**ər) *tr.v.* **clob•bered, clob•ber•ing, clob•bers.** *Slang.* **1.** To hit or pound with great force. **2.** To defeat completely: *Our team was clobbered by theirs.*

clock (klŏk) *n.* An instrument other than a watch for measuring and indicating time, often having a digital display or a numbered dial with moving hands that point to the numbers. *—tr.v.* **clocked, clock•ing, clocks.** To record the time or speed of: *The bicyclist was clocked at 30 miles per hour.* [First written down about 1370 in Middle English and spelled *clokke,* from Old North French *cloque,* bell or from Middle Dutch *clocke,* bell, clock, both from Medieval Latin *clocca,* of imitative origin.]

clock radio *n.* A radio with a built-in clock that can be set to turn the radio on automatically.

clock•wise (**klŏk′**wīz′) *adv. & adj.* In the same direction as the rotating hands of a clock: *turn clockwise; a clockwise movement.*

clock•work (**klŏk′**wûrk′) *n.* A mechanism of gears driven by a spring, as in a mechanical clock. ***—idiom.*** **like clockwork.** With perfect regularity and precision: *The assembly line in the factory operates like clockwork.*

clod (klŏd) *n.* **1.** A lump of earth or clay. **2.** A dull or stupid person; a dolt.

clod•hop•per (**klŏd′**hŏp′ər) *n.* **1.** A clumsy country fellow; a bumpkin. **2. clodhoppers.** Big heavy shoes.

clog (klôg *or* klŏg) *n.* **1.** Something that obstructs or hinders: *a clog in the drain; a clog in the flow of traffic.* **2.** A heavy shoe, usually having a wooden sole. *—v.* **clogged, clog•ging, clogs.** *—tr.v.* To cause to become obstructed or blocked up: *Heavy traffic clogged the highway.* *—intr.* To become obstructed or blocked up: *The drain clogs easily.*

clois•ter (**kloi′**stər) *n.* **1.** A covered walk along the side of a building, such as a convent or church, with open arches facing into a courtyard. **2.** A place of religious seclusion, as a monastery or convent. **3.** A secluded quiet place. *—tr.v.* **clois•tered, clois•ter•ing, clois•ters.** To shut away or confine in or as if in a cloister; seclude: *The author was cloistered in the library all morning.*

clomp (klŏmp) *intr.v.* **clomped, clomp•ing, clomps.** To walk heavily and noisily.

clone (klōn) *n.* **1.** An organism or a group of organisms produced asexually from a single ancestor. A clone may be produced by grafting, as in plants; by fission, as in single-celled organisms; and by forming buds, as in hydras. **2.** A person or thing that copies or closely resembles another: *These computers are clones of a more expensive model.* *—v.* **cloned, clon•ing, clones.** *—tr.* To produce a copy of (a person or thing): *Many VCR's are cloned from an earlier American model.* *—intr.* To reproduce or breed asexually. [First written down in 1903 in Modern English, from Greek *klōn,* twig.]

clop (klŏp) *n.* The sound of horse's hoofs as they strike a pavement. *—intr.v.* **clopped, clop•ping, clops.** To make or move with such a sound.

close (klōs) *adj.* **clos•er, clos•est.** **1.** Near in space or time: *The airport is close to town.* **2.** Near in relationship: *They are close relatives.* **3.** Bound by

clipper
The *Agenor*

cloister
Palermo University in Italy

ă	**pat**	oi	**boy**
ā	**pay**	ou	**out**
âr	**care**	o͝o	**took**
ä	**father**	o͞o	**boot**
ĕ	**pet**	ŭ	**cut**
ē	**be**	ûr	**urge**
ĭ	**pit**	th	**thin**
ī	**pie**	*th*	**this**
îr	**pier**	hw	**whoop**
ŏ	**pot**	zh	**vision**
ō	**toe**	ə	**about**
ô	**paw**	N	*French* **bon**

clotheshorse

loyalties or affection; intimate: *close friends.* **4.** Having little space in between: *chairs arranged in close rows.* **5.** Very much like another or the original: *a close copy of an ancient statue.* **6.** Rigorous; thorough: *During the drought rangers kept a close watch for forest fires.* **7.** Fitting tightly: *a jacket with a close waist.* **8.** Confining; narrow; crowded: *The little cabin was close quarters for the three of us.* **9.** Very short or near to the surface: *a close haircut; a close shave.* **10.** Lacking fresh air; stuffy: *It's very close in this room with the window shut.* **11.** Almost even, as in a contest: *a close race; a close election.* **12.** Stingily; miserly: *close with one's money.* **13.** Secretive: *The accountant was very close about clients' affairs.* —*v.* (klōz). **closed, clos•ing, clos•es.** —*tr.* **1.** To move (a door, for example) so that an opening or a passage is blocked; shut. **2.** To prevent passage through; obstruct: *closed the bridge for repairs.* **3.** To stop the operations of: *Most shopkeepers close their stores around six o'clock.* **4.** To fill up or stop up: *Close the cracks in the wall with plaster.* **5.** To bring to an end; conclude: *close a letter; close a meeting.* See Synonyms at **complete. 6.** To draw together the edges of: *It took eight stitches to close the wound.* —*intr.* **1.** To become shut: *The window closed with a bang.* **2.** To come to an end: *The book closes with a reunion of friends.* **3.** To cease operation: *The museum closes on Wednesdays.* **4.** To draw near: *Our boat was closing fast on the one in front.* **5.** To come together: *The child's arms closed around the stuffed animal.* —*n.* (klōz). A conclusion; an end: *Sunset marks the close of day. The meeting came to a quick close.* —*adv.* (klōs). **closer, closest.** In a close position or manner: *Let's stick close together.* ***—idioms.*** **close down.** To stop operating: *The old factory finally closed down.* **close in.** To surround and advance upon: *The fog was quickly closing in on us.* **close out.** To sell at a reduced price in order to dispose of quickly: *The store closed out all winter clothes in March.* **close to.** On the brink of: *He was close to tears.* **—close′ly** *adv.* **—close′ness** *n.*

❑ *These sound alike:* **close, clothes** (garments).

close call (klōs) *n. Informal.* A narrow escape.

closed (klōzd) *adj.* **1.** Blocked to passage or entry: *a closed port.* **2.** Of or relating to a curve, such as a circle, having no endpoints. **3.** Producing only elements of the same set in a given mathematical operation. The set of whole numbers is closed under addition, but not under division because fractions may occur.

closed-cap•tioned (klōzd′**kăp′**shənd) *adj.* Having titles or captions that explain action or give dialogue on a television program but that can be seen only on a specially equipped receiver: *a closed-captioned news program for the hearing-impaired.*

closed circuit *n.* **1.** An electric circuit through which current can flow in an uninterrupted path. **2.** A television system in which the signal is usually sent by cable to a limited number of receivers.

closed shop *n.* A company or business in which only union members or people who agree to join the union within a certain time may be hired.

close-fist•ed (**klōs′fĭs′**tĭd) *adj.* Stingy: *a close-fisted business manager.*

close-knit (**klōs′**nĭt′) *adj.* Closely joined by a common bond, as a relationship or an interest: *a close-knit family.*

close-mouthed (**klōs′mou*th*d′** *or* **klōs′moutht′**) *adj.* Not talking much; giving away very little information.

close•out (**klōz′**out′) *n.* A sale in which goods are offered at greatly reduced prices in order to dispose of them.

clos•et (**klŏz′**ĭt *or* **klô′**zĭt) *n.* **1.** A small room or cabinet for hanging clothes, storing linens or supplies, or keeping food: *a clothes closet; a broom closet.* **2.** A small private room for study or prayer. —*tr.v.* **clos•et•ed, clos•et•ing, clos•ets.** To enclose in a private room, as for discussion: *The lawyers closeted themselves in conference for hours.*

close-up (**klōs′**ŭp′) *n.* **1.** A photograph taken at close range: *The portrait was a close-up of the President.* **2.** A close or intimate look or view: *The interview presented a close-up of the actor.*

clo•sure (**klō′**zhər) *n.* **1.** The act of closing: *Closure of the incision ended the operation.* **2.** Something that closes or shuts. **3.** In mathematics, the property of being closed.

clot (klŏt) *n.* A thickened or solid mass formed from a liquid: *a blood clot.* —*intr. & tr.v.* **clot•ted, clot•ting, clots.** To form or cause to form into clots: *Blood clots when exposed to air.*

cloth (klôth *or* klŏth) *n., pl.* **cloths** (klôths *or* klô*th*z *or* klŏths *or* klŏ*th*z). **1.** Fabric or material made by weaving, knitting, or matting fibers together. **2.** A piece of cloth used for a special purpose, as for a tablecloth. **3.** The clergy: *a man of the cloth.* [First written down before 800 in Old English and spelled *clāth.*]

clothe (klō*th*) *tr.v.* **clothed** or **clad** (klăd), **cloth•ing, clothes. 1.** To put clothes on or provide clothes for; dress: *feed and clothe a family.* **2.** To cover, as if with clothing: *trees clothed in their fall colors.*

clothes (klōz *or* klō*th*z) *pl.n.* **1.** Coverings worn on the body; garments, such as shirts, trousers, dresses, and coats. **2.** Bedclothes.

❑ *These sound alike:* **clothes, close** (shut).

clothes•horse (**klōz′**hôrs′ *or* **klō*th*z′**hôrs′) *n.* **1.** A frame on which clothes are hung to dry or air. **2.** A person who has an excessive interest in clothes and frequently wears new outfits.

clothes•line (**klōz′**līn′ *or* **klō*th*z′**līn′) *n.* A rope or wire on which clothes are hung to dry.

clothes moth *n.* A moth whose larvae feed on wool and fur.

clothes•pin (**klōz′**pĭn′ *or* **klō*th*z′**pĭn′) *n.* A clip of wood or plastic used to fasten clothes on a clothesline.

clothes tree *n.* An upright pole or stand having hooks or pegs on which to hang garments.

cloth•ier (**klō*th*′**yər *or* **klō′***th*ē ər) *n.* A person who makes or sells clothing or cloth.

cloth•ing (**klō′***th*ĭng) *n.* **1.** Clothes or garments considered as a group: *The model wore fashionable clothing.* **2.** A covering.

cloud (kloud) *n.* **1.a.** A visible mass of condensed water droplets or ice particles floating in the air at heights ranging up to several miles above sea level. **b.** A similar object formed of suspended particles or droplets, as of dust, steam, or smoke. **2.** A moving mass of things on the ground or in the air that is so large and dense that it appears to resemble a cloud: *A cloud of locusts swarmed above the field.* **3.** Something that depresses or makes gloomy: *The bad news cast a cloud over the celebration.* **4.** A charge or other cause of suspicion or disgrace: *A cloud of mistrust hung over the stockbroker until he resigned.* —*v.* **cloud•ed, cloud•ing, clouds.** —*tr.* **1.** To cover with or as if with clouds: *Heavy mist clouded the hills.* **2.** To make gloomy, obscure, or confused: *Superstition clouded their thinking.* **3.** To taint; tarnish; sully: *A charge of corruption clouded the mayor's reputation.* —*intr.* To become covered with or as if with clouds: *The sky clouded over.* [First written down before 1200 in Middle English and spelled *clude*, from Old English *clūd*, rock, hill.]

cloud•burst (**kloud′**bûrst′) *n.* A sudden heavy rainstorm; a downpour.

cloud chamber *n.* A device in which the paths of charged subatomic particles are made visible as trails of droplets. It contains a supersaturated vapor that condenses on the ions formed along the path of the charged particle.

cloud seed•ing (**sē′**dĭng) *n.* A method of making a cloud give up its moisture as rain, especially by releasing particles of solid carbon dioxide or silver iodide into the cloud.

cloud•y (**klou′**dē) *adj.* **cloud•i•er, cloud•i•est. 1.** Full of or covered with clouds; overcast: *a cloudy sky; a cloudy day.* **2.** Not clear; murky: *cloudy water.* **3.** Troubled, gloomy, or confused: *cloudy thinking.* **—cloud′i•ly** *adv.* **—cloud′i•ness** *n.*

clout (klout) *n.* **1.** A heavy blow, as with the fist: *a clout on the chin.* **2.** *Informal.* Power, prestige, or influence: *The president has great political clout.* —*tr.v.* **clout•ed, clout•ing, clouts.** To hit hard: *The batter clouted the ball over the fence.*

clove[1] (klōv) *n.* **1.** The dried aromatic flower bud of a tropical Asian tree, used whole or ground as a spice. **2.** The plant that bears this flower. [First written down before 1200 in Middle English and spelled *clow de gilofre,* from Old French *clou (de girofle),* nail (of the clove tree), from Latin *clāvus,* nail.]

clove[2] (klōv) *n.* One of the sections of a garlic bulb or a similar plant bulb. [First written down about 1000 in Old English and spelled *clufu.*]

clove[3] (klōv) *v.* **1.** A past tense of **cleave**[1]. **2.** *Archaic.* A past participle of **cleave**[1].

clove hitch *n.* A knot, often used to tie a rope to a post, consisting of two half hitches.

clo•ven (**klō′**vən) *v.* A past participle of **cleave**[1]. —*adj.* Split or divided into two parts: *the cloven hoofs of deer or cattle.*

clo•ver (**klō′**vər) *n.* Any of various plants having leaves divided into three leaflets and tightly clustered heads of small, often fragrant flowers. Many kinds of clover are grown to feed cattle and horses. [First written down about 1000 in Old English and spelled *clāfre.*]

clo•ver•leaf (**klō′**vər lēf′) *n.* A highway interchange whose exit and entrance ramps resemble a four-leaf clover and enable vehicles to go from one highway to the other in either direction.

clown (kloun) *n.* **1.** A performer, as in a circus or carnival, who jokes and does tricks or humorous stunts. **2.** A person who is always making jokes or acting foolishly: *the office clown.* —*intr.v.* **clowned, clown•ing, clowns. 1.** To perform as a clown in a circus or other show. **2.** To behave like a clown; act foolishly: *Practical jokers are always clowning around.* **—clown′ish** *adj.* **—clown′ish•ness** *n.*

cloy (kloi) *v.* **cloyed, cloy•ing, cloys.** —*tr.* To cause to feel overly full or disgusted, especially by supplying too much of something rich or sweet: —*intr.* To be too filling, rich, or sweet: *This dessert is cloying.*

club (klŭb) *n.* **1.** A heavy stick, usually thicker at one end than at the other, used as a weapon. **2.** A stick designed to drive a ball in certain games, especially golf. **3.a.** A black figure, shaped like a trefoil or the leaf of a clover, on a playing card. **b.** A card bearing this figure. **c. clubs.** The suit in a deck of cards having this figure as its symbol. **4.a.** A group of people organized for a common purpose: *a chess club.* **b.** The room, building, or other facility used by such a group. —*v.* **clubbed, club•bing, clubs.** —*tr.* To strike or beat with or as if with a club. —*intr.* To join together for a common purpose: *All the tenants clubbed together to clean up the apartment building.* [First written down before 1200 in Middle English and spelled *clubbe,* from Old Norse *klubba.*]

club•foot (**klŭb′**fo͝ot′) *n.* **1.** A deformity of the foot, usually marked by a curled or twisted shape, that arises as a birth defect. **2.** A foot having such a deformity. **—club′foot′ed** *adj.*

club•house (**klŭb′**hous′) *n.* **1.** A building occupied by a club. **2.** A locker room used by an athletic team.

club moss *n.* Any of various low-growing evergreen plants that do not bear flowers and have small leaves resembling needles.

club sandwich *n.* A sandwich made of two or three slices of bread with a filling of meat, tomato, lettuce, and mayonnaise.

club soda *n.* Soda water.

cluck (klŭk) *n.* The low short sound made by a hen sitting on eggs or calling for its chicks. —*intr.v.* **clucked, cluck•ing, clucks. 1.** To make such a sound. **2.** To make a sound similar to that of a hen, as when urging a horse to move.

clue (klo͞o) *n.* A fact or an object that helps to solve a problem or mystery: *Identifying the virus was a clue to the prevention of polio.* —*tr.v.* **clued, clue•ing** or **clu•ing, clues.** To give (someone) information: *Clue me in on what's happening.*

clump (klŭmp) *n.* **1.** A thick group or cluster, as of trees or bushes. **2.** A thick mass, as of dirt or sod. **3.** A heavy dull sound, as of footsteps. —*v.* **clumped, clump•ing, clumps.** —*intr.* **1.** To walk with a heavy dull sound. **2.** To form clumps: *Blood clumps as it forms a scab.* —*tr.* To gather into or form clumps of: *clump flowers together in bunches.* **—clump′y** *adj.*

clum•sy (**klŭm′**zē) *adj.* **clum•si•er, clum•si•est. 1.** Lacking grace or deftness; awkward: *a clumsy walk; clumsy animals.* **2.** Difficult to handle or maneuver: *clumsy wooden shoes.* **3.** Done without skill; inept: *a clumsy attempt to revise the newspaper story.* **—clum′si•ly** *adv.* **—clum′si•ness** *n.*

clung (klŭng) *v.* Past tense and past participle of **cling.**

clus•ter (**klŭs′**tər) *n.* A group of similar things growing or grouped close together: *a cluster of flowers; a cluster of stars.* —*intr.v.* **clus•tered, clus•ter•ing, clus•ters.** To gather or grow in clusters: *Everyone clustered around the fire.*

clutch[1] (klŭch) *v.* **clutched, clutch•ing, clutch•es.** —*tr.* To hold or grasp tightly: *I clutched the railing as I started down the stairs.* —*intr.* To try to grasp or seize something: *I clutched at the chair as I started to fall.* —*n.* **1.** A tight hold or grip. **2.** A hand, paw, or claw in the act of grasping. **3.** Control or power; possession. Often used in the plural: *fall into the clutches of the enemy.* **a.** A device used to connect and disconnect a shaft and a driving mechanism. **b.** The lever, pedal, or other control that operates such a device, as in an automobile or a truck. **4.** A critical situation: *our best hitter in the clutch.* [First written down about 1025 in Old English and spelled *clyccan.*]

clutch[2] (klŭch) *n.* **1.** The eggs produced at a single laying. **2.** A brood of chicks hatched from such eggs. [First written down in 1691 in Modern English and spelled *cletch,* from Middle English *clekken,* to hatch, from Old Norse *klekja.*]

clut•ter (**klŭt′**ər) *n.* A collection of things scattered about in a disorderly fashion; a jumble: *stumble over the clutter on the floor.* —*tr.v.* **clut•tered, clut•ter•ing, clut•ters.** To fill in such a way as to block movement or action: *On Sundays our living room floor is cluttered up with newspapers.*

Cly•tem•nes•tra (klī′təm **nĕs′**trə) *n.* In Greek mythology, the wife of Agamemnon, who murders him on his return from the Trojan War and is later murdered by her son, Orestes.

cm *abbr.* An abbreviation of centimeter.

cloverleaf

ă	pat	oi	boy
ā	pay	ou	out
âr	care	o͝o	took
ä	father	o͞o	boot
ĕ	pet	ŭ	cut
ē	be	ûr	urge
ĭ	pit	th	thin
ī	pie	*th*	this
îr	pier	hw	whoop
ŏ	pot	zh	vision
ō	toe	ə	about
ô	paw	N	*French* bon

Word Building: co–

We can trace the prefix **co–** back to the Latin prefix *co–*, a form of *com–*, meaning "with." In English, the prefix **co–** means "together, joint, jointly." In words such as *coheir* and *coedit*, **co–** has simply been affixed to words that already existed to create new words whose meanings are easy to guess.

coati

cobweb

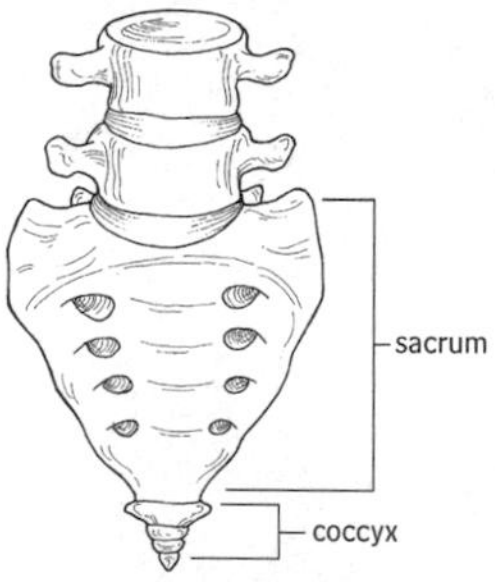

coccyx

Cochise

Cm The symbol for the element **curium.**
Co The symbol for the element **cobalt.**
CO *abbr.* An abbreviation of Colorado.
co. or **Co.** *abbr.* An abbreviation of: **1.** Company. **2.** County.
c/o *abbr.* An abbreviation of care of.
co– *pref.* A prefix that means: **1.** Together; jointly: *coexist.* **2.** Partner or associate: *coauthor.* **3.** To the same extent or degree: *coextensive.* —SEE NOTE.
coach (kōch) *n.* **coached, coach•ing, coach•es. 1.** A large closed carriage on four wheels, pulled by horses. **2.** A railroad passenger car. **3.** A bus. **4.** A low-priced class of passenger accommodations on a train, an airplane, or a bus. **5.** A person who trains or instructs athletes or athletic teams. **6.** A person who gives private instruction, as in singing or acting. —*v.* **coached, coach•ing, coach•es.** —*tr.* To train or teach: *coach a lacrosse team.* —*intr.* To act as a coach. [First written down in 1556 in Modern English, from Hungarian *kocsi*, after *Kocs*, a town of northwest Hungary (where such carriages were first made).]
coach•man (kōch′mən) *n.* A man who drives a coach.
co•ag•u•lant (kō ăg′yə lənt) *n.* A substance that causes coagulation.
co•ag•u•late (kō ăg′yə lāt′) *v.* **co•ag•u•lat•ed, co•ag•u•lat•ing, co•ag•u•lates.** —*tr.* To change (a liquid) into a solid or nearly solid mass; clot: *Exposure to air coagulates the blood.* —*intr.* To become solid or nearly solid: *Egg whites coagulate when heated.* [First written down before 1425 in Middle English and spelled *coagulaten*, from Latin *coāgulum*, something that coagulates, from *cōgere*, to condense : *co-*, together + *agere*, to drive.]
co•a•g•u•la•tion (kō ăg′yə lā′shən) *n.* **1.** The act or process of coagulating. **2.** A mass or clot that results from coagulation.
coal (kōl) *n.* **1.a.** A dark-brown to black natural solid substance formed from fossilized plants under conditions of great pressure, high humidity, and lack of air. Coal consists mainly of carbon and is widely used as a fuel and raw material. **b.** A piece of this substance. **2.** A glowing or charred piece of wood, coal, or other solid fuel; an ember: *Coals continue to give off heat long after the flame is out.* —*tr. & intr.v.* **coaled, coal•ing, coals.** To supply with or take on a supply of coal: *coal a ship.* [First written down about 700 in Old English and spelled *col.*]
co•a•lesce (kō′ə lĕs′) *intr.v.* **co•a•lesced, co•a•lesc•ing, co•a•lesc•es. 1.** To grow or blend into one; fuse: *Broken bones of young people usually coalesce quickly.* **2.** To come together so as to form one whole; unite: *two local groups that coalesced into a powerful national organization.* [First written down in 1541 in Modern English, from Latin *coalēscere* : *co-*, together + *alēscere*, to grow.] —**co′a•les′cense** *n.*
coal gas *n.* **1.** The mixture of gases given off when bituminous coal is heated without air, used as a fuel. **2.** The mixture of gases released when coal burns.
co•a•li•tion (kō′ə lĭsh′ən) *n.* An alliance of political parties or factions for some special purpose: *a coalition of small business owners to defeat a sales tax.*
coal oil *n.* Kerosene.
coal tar *n.* A thick sticky black liquid obtained by heating coal in the absence of air. It is used as a raw material for many dyes, drugs, and paints.
coarse (kôrs) *adj.* **coars•er, coars•est. 1.** Not smooth; rough: *coarse skin; coarse material.* **2.** Consisting of large particles: *coarse sand.* **3.** Not refined; crude; rude: *coarse and vulgar language.* **4.** Of low, common, or inferior quality: *coarse lumber fit only for planking.* —**coarse′ly** *adv.* —**coarse′ness** *n.*
❑ *These sound alike:* **coarse, course** (route).
coars•en (kôr′sən) *tr. & intr.v.* **coars•ened, coars•en•ing, coars•ens.** To make or become coarse.
coast (kōst) *n.* **1.** The edge of the land next to the sea; the seashore. **2.** A region next to or near the sea: *The western coast of South America includes large parts of Chile, Peru, Ecuador, and Colombia.* —*v.* **coast•ed, coast•ing, coasts.** —*intr.* **1.** To slide or continue to move without the use of power: *The car coasted to a stop.* See Synonyms at **slide. 2.** To move ahead or through with little effort: *Some students coast through math class.* **3.** To sail near or along a coast. —*tr.* To sail along or near the coast of: *The cruise ship coasted the islands of the Caribbean.*
coast•al (kō′stəl) *adj.* Relating to or being on or near a coast: *a coastal town.*
coast•er (kō′stər) *n.* **1.** A disk or plate placed under a bottle or glass to protect a surface, especially of a table. **2.** A ship engaged in coastal trade. **3.** A coasting sled or toboggan.
coast guard also **Coast Guard** *n.* A military organization whose job is to patrol the coast of a nation, carry out rescue operations of ships in trouble, and enforce immigration, navigation, and custom laws.
coast•line (kōst′līn′) *n.* The shape or outline of a coast.
coat (kōt) *n.* **1.a.** An outer garment with sleeves, usually worn for warmth or protection. **b.** A jacket usually forming the top part of a suit. **2.** The hair or fur of an animal. **3.** A layer of something spread over a surface: *a coat of paint.* —*tr.v.* **coat•ed, coat•ing, coats.** To cover with a layer: *Dust coated the table.*
❑ *These sound alike:* **coat, cote** (shed).
co•a•ti (kō ä′tē) *n.* Any of four kinds of mammals of the southwest United States and tropical America, related to and resembling the raccoon but having a longer tail and snout.
co•a•ti•mun•di (kō ä′tē mŭn′dē) *n.* The coati.
coat•ing (kō′tĭng) *n.* A layer of a substance spread over a surface, as for protection or decoration: *a sticky coating of varnish; a thin coating of ice on the streets.*
coat of arms *n., pl.* **coats of arms. 1.** An emblem on a shield that serves as the insignia of a nation, a family, an institution, or a group. **2.** A shield or drawing that represents such an emblem.
coat of mail *n., pl.* **coats of mail.** A coat made of chain mail or overlapping metal plates, worn as armor during the Middle Ages.
coat•room (kōt′ro͞om′ *or* kōt′ro͝om′) *n.* A cloakroom.
coat•tail (kōt′tāl′) *n.* The loose rear flap of a coat that hangs below the waist. —***idiom.* on (someone's) coattails.** As a result of the success of another: *Many local candidates win elections on the coattails of a popular governor.*
co•au•thor (kō ô′thər) *n.* One of two or more people who work together in writing a book, story, play, or other piece of writing. —*tr.v.* **co•au•thored, co•au•thor•ing, co•au•thors.** To be the coauthor of.
coax (kōks) *tr.v.* **coaxed, coax•ing, coax•es. 1.** To persuade or try to persuade by gently urging: *The trainer coaxed the lion into the cage.* **2.** To obtain by such persuasion: *My jokes coaxed a smile from the unhappy child.* —**coax′er** *n.*
co•ax•i•al cable (kō ăk′sē əl) *n.* A cable made of a conducting outer metal tube insulated from an inner conducting core. Coaxial cables are used to carry telephone, telegraph, and television signals.

cob (kŏb) *n.* **1.** The long hard central part of an ear of corn; a corncob. **2.** A male swan. **3.** A stocky short-legged horse.

co•balt (**kō′**bôlt′) *n. Symbol* **Co** A hard silver-white metallic element with a pinkish tint that occurs only in combination with other elements, especially nickel and iron. Cobalt is used in making alloys and pigments. Atomic number 27. See table at **element.**

cobalt 60 *n.* A radioactive isotope of cobalt having a mass number of 60. It is an intense source of gamma rays and is used in the treatment of cancer.

cobalt blue *n.* **1.** A blue to green pigment consisting of a mixture of cobalt oxide and aluminum oxide. **2.** A deep vivid blue.

cob•ble[1] (**kŏb′**əl) *n.* A cobblestone. —*tr.v.* **cob•bled, cob•bling, cob•bles.** To pave with cobblestones. [First written down about 1440 in Middle English and spelled *cobelstone*, from *cob*, round object.]

cob•ble[2] (**kŏb′**əl) *tr.v.* **cob•bled, cob•bling, cob•bles.** To make or mend (boots or shoes). [First written down in 1496 in Middle English and spelled *coblen*, probably from *cobeler*, shoemaker.]

cob•bler[1] (**kŏb′**lər) *n.* A shoemaker. [First written down in 1287 in Middle English and spelled *cobeler*.]

cob•bler[2] (**kŏb′**lər) *n.* A fruit pie topped with a biscuit crust and baked in a deep dish. [First written down in 1859 in American English.]

cob•ble•stone (**kŏb′**əl stōn′) *n.* A naturally rounded stone formerly used for paving streets.

CO•BOL (**kō′**bôl′) *n.* A language based on English words and phrases, used in programming computers for various business applications.

co•bra (**kō′**brə) *n.* Any of several poisonous Asian or African snakes capable of spreading out the skin of the neck to form a flattened hood.

cob•web (**kŏb′**wĕb′) *n.* **1.** A web spun by a spider. **2.** A single strand of such a web. **3.** Something resembling a cobweb in gauziness or flimsiness: *A cobweb of torn curtains hung at the window.* [First written down in 1323 in Middle English and spelled *coppeweb* : *coppe*, spider + *web*, web.]

co•ca (**kō′**kə) *n.* Any of certain South American trees or shrubs also found in parts of Asia whose leaves are chewed as a stimulant or processed for cocaine.

co•caine (kō **kān′** *or* **kō′**kān′) *n.* An alkaloid extracted from the leaves of the coca plant and composed of carbon, hydrogen, nitrogen, and oxygen in the proportions $C_{17}H_{21}NO_4$. Cocaine is an addictive drug and is sometimes used as a local anesthetic, especially for the eyes, nose, and throat.

coc•cus (**kŏk′**əs) *n., pl.* **coc•ci** (**kŏk′**sī *or* kŏk′ī). A bacterium with a spherical shape.

coc•cyx (**kŏk′**sĭks) *n., pl.* **coc•cy•ges** (kŏk **sī′**jēz *or* kŏk′sĭ-jēz′). A small triangular bone found at the base of the spinal column in human beings and in tailless apes.

coch•i•neal (kŏch′ə **nēl′** *or* **kŏch′**ə nēl′) *n.* A bright-red dye made from the dried bodies of a tropical American insect.

Co•chise (kō **chēs′** *or* kō **chēz′**). 1812?–1874. Apache leader who organized resistance to U.S. troops in Arizona (1861–1872).

coch•le•a (**kŏk′**lē ə) *n., pl.* **coch•le•ae** (**kŏk′**lē ē′) also **coch•le•as.** A spiral tube of the inner ear that resembles a snail shell and contains the nerve endings necessary for hearing.

cock[1] (kŏk) *n.* **1.** A full-grown male chicken; a rooster. **2.** An adult male of various other birds. **3.** A faucet or valve for regulating the flow of a liquid or gas. **4.a.** The hammer of a gun. **b.** The position of a gun hammer when ready for firing. **5.** A tilting or jaunty turning upward: *the cock of a sailor's cap.* —*tr.v.* **cocked, cock•ing, cocks. 1.** To set the hammer of (a gun) in position to fire. **2.** To set (a device) in a position ready for use: *cock the shutter on a camera.* **3.** To tilt or turn up to one side: *Birds often cock their heads to hear or see better.* [First written down before 900 in Old English and spelled *cocc*, probably from Late Latin *coccus*.]

cock[2] (kŏk) *n.* A cone-shaped pile of straw or hay. —*tr.v.* **cocked, cock•ing, cocks.** To arrange (straw or hay) in such piles. [First written down before 1398 in Middle English and spelled *cok*.]

cock•ade (kŏ **kād′**) *n.* A rosette or knot of ribbon usually worn on the hat as a badge.

cock•a•too (**kŏk′**ə to͞o′) *n., pl.* **cock•a•toos.** Any of various large brightly colored parrots of Australia and the East Indies, having feathers on the head that can be raised in a crest.

cock•a•trice (**kŏk′**ə trĭs *or* **kŏk′**ə trīs′) *n.* A mythical serpent hatched from a cock's egg, supposed to have the power of killing by its glance. It is depicted as half rooster, half serpent.

cocked hat (kŏkt) *n.* A hat with the brim turned up in two or three places.

cock•er•el (**kŏk′**ər əl) *n.* A young rooster.

cock•er spaniel (**kŏk′**ər) *n.* Any of a breed of dog having long drooping ears and a silky coat.

cock•eyed (**kŏk′**īd′) *adj. Informal.* **1.** Tilted or crooked; askew: *The picture hung cockeyed on the wall.* **2.** Ridiculous; absurd: *cockeyed schemes that are sure to fail.*

cock•fight (**kŏk′**fīt′) *n.* A fight between two gamecocks with metal spurs attached to their legs.

cock•horse (**kŏk′**hôrs′) *n.* A rocking horse.

cock•le (**kŏk′**əl) *n.* **1.** Any of various mollusks having a pair of heart-shaped shells with narrow ribbed markings. **2.** A cockleshell. —***idiom.*** **cockles of one's heart.** One's innermost feelings: *Their thoughtfulness warmed the cockles of my heart.*

cock•le•bur (**kŏk′**əl bûr′) *n.* **1.** Any of several coarse weedy plants having prickly burs. **2.** The bur of such a plant.

cock•le•shell (**kŏk′**əl shĕl′) *n.* **1.** A shell of a cockle. **2.** A small light boat used in shallow waters.

cock•ney (**kŏk′**nē) *n., pl.* **cock•neys. 1.** Often **Cockney.** A native of the eastern section of London. **2.** The distinctive dialect or accent of the cockneys. —*adj.* Of or relating to the cockneys or their dialect.

cock•pit (**kŏk′**pĭt′) *n.* **1.** The space in an airplane that has seats for the pilot and copilot and sometimes passengers. **2.** The space in a small boat from which the boat is steered. [First written down in 1587 in Modern English and spelled *cockpit*, a pit for holding cockfights.]

cock•roach (**kŏk′**rōch′) *n.* Any of numerous brownish or black insects having a flat body and usually long antennae that are common household pests.

cocks•comb (**kŏks′**kōm′) *n.* **1.** The fleshy red comb on the head of a rooster. **2.** A jester's cap, topped with a strip of red cloth notched like the comb of a rooster. **3.** A garden plant having dense fan-shaped clusters of red, purple, white, or yellow flowers.

cock•sure (**kŏk′shŏŏr′**) *adj.* Completely sure, especially too sure of oneself: *a cocksure young upstart.* —**cock′sure′ness** *n.*

cock•tail (**kŏk′**tāl′) *n.* **1.** An alcoholic drink consisting of a liquor mixed with fruit juice, soda, or another liquor, for example. **2.** An appetizer such as seafood, juice, or fruit: *a shrimp cocktail.*

cock•y (**kŏk′**ē) *adj.* **cock•i•er, cock•i•est.** Too sure of oneself; arrrogant; conceited: *a cocky showoff.* —**cock′i•ly** *adv.* —**cock′i•ness** *n.*

co•coa (**kō′**kō) *n.* **1.** A powder made of roasted ground cacao seeds from which much of the fat has been removed. **2.** A drink made with this powder,

cockatoo
Sulfur-crested cockatoo

cockpit
Airplane cockpit

cockscomb

ă	pat	oi	boy
ā	pay	ou	out
âr	care	o͝o	took
ä	father	o͞o	boot
ĕ	pet	ŭ	cut
ē	be	ûr	urge
ĭ	pit	th	thin
ī	pie	*th*	this
îr	pier	hw	whoop
ŏ	pot	zh	vision
ō	toe	ə	about
ô	paw	N	*French* bon

William F. Cody
"Buffalo Bill"

coffee
Detail of coffee shrub and seeds

sugar, and milk or water. **3.** A reddish brown. [First written down in 1707 in Modern English, alteration of *cacao*.] —**co′cao** *adj.*

cocoa butter *n.* A yellowish waxy solid obtained from cacao seeds and used in making soap, cosmetics, and confections.

co•co•nut also **co•coa•nut** (kō′kə nŭt′) *n.* **1.** The large hard-shelled nut of the coconut palm, having sweet white meat and a hollow center filled with a milky liquid. **2.** The edible white meat of this nut, often shredded and used as food and in confections. **3.** The coconut palm. [First written down before 1555 in Modern English and spelled *coco nut*, from Portuguese *côco*, grinning skull, goblin.]

coconut milk *n.* The cloudy sweet liquid of a coconut.

coconut oil *n.* An oil obtained from coconut meat and used for making sweets, soaps, and candles.

coconut palm *n.* A palm tree of tropical regions that bears coconuts as fruits.

co•coon (kə ko͞on′) *n.* **1.** A covering of silky strands spun by the larva of a moth or other insect as protection during its pupal stage. **2.** A similar protective covering or structure: *wrapped in a cocoon of blankets.*

cod (kŏd) *n., pl.* **cod** or **cods.** Any of various large food fishes of the northern Atlantic and Pacific Oceans; a codfish.

Cod (kŏd), **Cape.** A hook-shaped peninsula of southeast Massachusetts extending east and north into the Atlantic Ocean.

COD or **C.O.D.** *abbr.* An abbreviation of cash on delivery.

co•da (kō′də) *n.* A passage that ends a musical movement or composition. [First written down in 1753 in Modern English, from Italian, from Latin *cauda*, tail.]

cod•dle (kŏd′l) *tr.v.* **cod•dled, cod•dling, cod•dles. 1.** To cook in water just below the boiling point: *coddle eggs.* **2.** To treat tenderly; pamper; baby. See Synonyms at **pamper.**

code (kōd) *n.* **1.** A system of signals used to represent the letters and numerals in a message that is to be transmitted: *a telegraphic code.* **2.** A system of words, symbols, or letters given arbitrary meanings, usually used to keep messages secret. **3.** A system of symbols and rules used to represent instructions to a computer. **4.** A system of numbers used to represent a geographic area, as a Zip Code. **5.** A system or collection of laws or rules and regulations: *a building code; an honor code.* —*tr.v.* **cod•ed, cod•ing, codes.** To put (a text, numbers, or information) into a code: *code information to store in a computer.* [First written down about 1303 in Middle English, from Latin *cōdex*, book.]

co•deine (kō′dēn′) *n.* An alkaloid derived from opium or morphine and composed of carbon, hydrogen, nitrogen, and oxygen in the proportions $C_{18}H_{21}NO_3$. It is used to promote sleep and relieve coughing and pain.

cod•fish (kŏd′fĭsh′) *n.* **1.** A cod. **2.** The flesh of a cod, used as food.

codg•er (kŏj′ər) *n. Informal.* An odd or somewhat eccentric old man.

cod•i•cil (kŏd′ə sĭl) *n.* A supplement or an appendix to a will.

cod•i•fy (kŏd′ĭ fī′ *or* kō′də fī′) *tr.v.* **cod•i•fied, cod•i•fy•ing, cod•i•fies.** To arrange (laws, for example) in a systematic way. —**cod′i•fi•ca′tion** (kŏd′ĭ fĭ kā′shən) *n.* —**cod′i•fi′er** *n.*

cod•ling moth (kŏd′lĭng) *n.* A small moth whose caterpillars feed on and damage apples and other fruits.

cod-liv•er oil (kŏd′lĭv′ər) *n.* An oil rich in vitamins A and D, obtained from the livers of cod and certain other fish.

Co•dy (kō′dē), **William Frederick.** Known as "Buffalo Bill." 1846–1917. American frontier scout and performer who toured the United States and Europe with his Wild West Show.

co•ed or **co-ed** (kō′ĕd′) *Informal. n.* A woman who attends a coeducational college or university. —*adj.* Of or relating to coeducation: *a coed school.*

co•ed•u•ca•tion (kō ĕj′ə kā′shən) *n.* The system of education in which both male and female students take classes together at a school or college. —**co′ed•u•ca′tion•al** *adj.*

co•ef•fi•cient (kō′ə fĭsh′ənt) *n.* A number or symbol multiplying a variable or an unknown quantity in an algebraic term. In the term $4x$, 4 is the coefficient. In $x(a + b)$, x is the coefficient.

coe•la•canth (sē′lə kănth′) *n.* Any of various fishes having lobed fleshy fins, thought to be an ancestral type of vertebrate from which land vertebrates developed. They were known only from fossil remains until a living specimen was caught off the coast of southern Africa in 1938.

coe•len•ter•ate (sĭ lĕn′tə rāt′ *or* sĭ lĕn′tər ĭt) *n.* An animal that belongs to a large group of simple animals that live in fresh or salt water and have a hollow body with no backbone, as a hydra, jellyfish, sea anemone, or coral.

co•erce (kō ûrs′) *tr.v.* **co•erced, co•erc•ing, co•erc•es.** To force or compel into doing something by pressure, threats, or intimidation: *The committee coerced the president to resign by recommending his impeachment.* —**co•erc′er** *n.* —**co•er′cion** (kō ûr′zhən) *n.*

co•er•cive (kō ûr′sĭv) *adj.* Tending to coerce: *Public opinion has a coercive effect on elected officials.* —**co•er′cive•ly** *adv.* —**co•er′cive•ness** *n.*

co•ex•ist (kō′ĭg zĭst′) *intr.v.* **co•ex•ist•ed, co•ex•ist•ing, co•ex•ists.** To live or exist together, at the same time, or in the same place: *Bears and wolves coexist in the Alaskan wilderness. Many nations coexist on the European continent.* —**co′ex•is′tence** *n.* —**co′ex•is′tent** *adj.*

co•ex•ten•sive (kō′ĭk stĕn′sĭv) *adj.* Occupying the same space; having the same limits or boundaries: *The habitat of certain mammals is coextensive with the Great Plains.*

cof•fee (kô′fē *or* kŏf′ē) *n.* **1.** A drink made with hot water and the ground seeds of a tropical plant native to Africa. **2.** The dried whole or ground seeds of this tree. **3.** A tree or shrub that bears such seeds. **4.** A dark or yellowish brown. [First written down in 1598 in Modern English and spelled *chaoua*, from Arabic *qahwah*.]

coffee break *n.* A short period of relief from work during which coffee or other refreshments may be drunk.

cof•fee•cake (kô′fē kāk′ *or* kŏf′ē kāk′) *n.* A cake made of sweetened dough with yeast, often containing nuts and raisins and covered with sugar or icing.

cof•fee•house (kô′fē hous′ *or* kŏf′ē hous′) *n.* A restaurant where coffee and other refreshments are served.

cof•fee•pot (kô′fē pŏt′ *or* kŏf′ē pŏt′) *n.* A covered pot with a handle and spout, for making and pouring coffee.

coffee shop *n.* A small restaurant in which light meals are served.

coffee table *n.* A low table, often placed in front of a sofa.

cof•fer (kô′fər *or* kŏf′ər) *n.* **1.** A strongbox for holding money or other valuables. **2. coffers.** A treasury, as of a nation; financial resources: *The state coffers were opened to aid the poor.*

cof•fin (kô′fĭn *or* kŏf′ĭn) *n.* A box in which a dead person is buried. [First written down before 1338 in Middle English and spelled *coffin,* basket, from Greek *kophinos.*]

cog (kŏg *or* kôg) *n.* **1.** One of a series of teeth that fit between the teeth on another wheel so that one wheel can move the other. **2.** A cogwheel.

co•gent (kō′jənt) *adj.* Forceful and convincing: *a cogent argument based on facts.* —**co′gen•cy** (kō′-jən′sē) *n.* —**co′gent•ly** *adv.*

cog•i•tate (kŏj′ĭ tāt′) *intr.v.* **cog•i•tat•ed, cog•i•tat•ing, cog•i•tates.** To think carefully; reflect; ponder. —**cog′i•ta′tion** *n.*

co•gnac (kōn′yăk′) *n.* A brandy originally made from white wine near Cognac, a town in western France.

cog•nate (kŏg′nāt′) *adj.* **1.** Related in origin: *French and Spanish are cognate languages.* **2.** Related by blood; having a common ancestor: *cognate branches of the same family.* —*n.* A cognate person or thing, especially a word related to one in another language: *The English word* cup, *the Dutch word* kopje, *and the Italian word* coppa *are cognates from the Late Latin word* cuppa. [First written down about 1645 in Modern English, from Latin *cognātus* : *co-*, together + *gnātus*, born.]

cog•ni•tion (kŏg nĭsh′ən) *n.* The mental process or faculty by which knowledge is acquired, including perception, awareness, and reasoning.

cog•ni•tive (kŏg′nĭ tĭv) *adj.* Of or relating to cognition: *the cognitive development of young children.*

cog•ni•zance (kŏg′nĭ zəns) *n.* **1.** Knowledge or awareness: *We had no cognizance that a problem existed.* **2.** Ability to understand: *The origins of life are still beyond the cognizance of modern science.*

cog•ni•zant (kŏg′nĭ zənt) *adj.* Aware; conscious: *Until they heard a weather report, none of the sailors was cognizant of the approaching storm.*

cog•wheel (kŏg′wēl′ *or* kôg′wēl′) *n.* A wheel with cogs on its rim that mesh with those of another wheel so that one wheel can move the other.

co•hab•it (kō hăb′ĭt) *intr.v.* **co•hab•it•ed, co•hab•it•ing, co•hab•its.** To live together as or as if as spouses. —**co•hab′i•ta′tion** *n.*

co•here (kō hîr′) *intr.v.* **co•hered, co•her•ing, co•heres. 1.** To stick or hold together in a mass, as mud or wet sand. **2.** To be logically connected: *a careful argument in which one point coheres neatly with another.*

co•her•ence (kō hîr′əns *or* kō hĕr′əns) *n.* The quality or state of being coherent. —**co•her′en•cy** (kō hîr′ən sē) *n.*

co•her•ent (kō hîr′ənt *or* kō hĕr′ənt) *adj.* **1.** Sticking together: *coherent particles of wet sand.* **2.** Logically connected; easy to understand: *The editorial provides a coherent argument for a tax increase.* **3.** Composed of waves that oscillate together and travel in the same direction: *the coherent red light of a laser.* —**co•her′ent•ly** *adv.*

co•he•sion (kō hē′zhən) *n.* **1.** The attraction between molecules of the same kind: *The cohesion of molecules of H_2O produces drops of water.* **2.** The condition of cohering; a tendency to stick together; unity: *The cohesion of so many different groups is the result of a common belief in the freedom and equality of all citizens.*

co•he•sive (kō hē′sĭv) *adj.* **1.** Tending to cohere; sticking together: *the cohesive nature of water.* **2.** Producing cohesion: *the cohesive force of glue.* —**co•he′sive•ly** *adv.* —**co•he′sive•ness** *n.*

co•hort (kō′hôrt′) *n.* **1.** One of the divisions of a legion in the army of ancient Rome. **2.** A companion or an associate: *My cohorts on the newspaper staff agreed to publish the article.* **3.** A group or band: *A cohort of protesters assembled in front of city hall.*

coif (koif) *n.* **1.** A tight-fitting cap worn under a veil, as by nuns. **2.** A skullcap, such as one worn under a knight's helmet or an English lawyer's wig. **3.** (*also* kwäf). A coiffure. —*tr.v.* (*also* kwäf) **coifed, coif•ing, coifs.** To arrange or dress (the hair): *hair coiffed in an elaborate style.*

coif•fure (kwä fyo͝or′) *n.* A way of arranging the hair; a hairstyle.

coil (koil) *n.* **1.** A series of connected spirals or gathered loops: *a coil of rope.* **2.** A spiral or loop in such a series. **3.** An electrical device consisting of a number of turns of insulated wire, used as an electromagnet or to store energy in the form of a magnetic field. **4.** A spiral pipe or series of pipes, as in a radiator. —*v.* **coiled, coil•ing, coils.** —*tr.* To wind into a series of spirals or loops: *The snake coiled itself around a branch.* —*intr.* **1.** To form spirals or loops: *The hose that I was using coiled and knotted.* **2.** To move in a spiral course: *The smoke coiled up into the sky.* [First written down in 1611 in Middle English, probably from Latin *colligere*, gather together, collect.]

coin (koin) *n.* **1.** A piece of metal, usually flat and round, issued by a government for use as money. **2.** Pieces of metal money considered as a group: *Only the government can issue coin.* —*tr.v.* **coined, coin•ing, coins. 1.** To make (coins) from metal; mint: *The government coins dimes and quarters.* **2.** To make coins from (metal): *coin copper into pennies.* **3.** To invent (a word or phrase): *The computer industry has had to coin many new terms.* [First written down in 1304 in Middle English, from Latin *cuneus*, wedge.]

❑ *These sound alike:* **coin, quoin** (corner).

coin•age (koi′nĭj) *n.* **1.** The process of making coins: *the coinage of silver.* **2.** Coins considered as a group. **3.a.** A new word or phrase. **b.** The invention of new words: *Many words of recent coinage need to be explained.*

co•in•cide (kō′ĭn sīd′) *intr.v.* **co•in•cid•ed, co•in•cid•ing, co•in•cides. 1.** To be in the same position or occupy the same space: *The park coincides with the site of an old settlement.* **2.** To agree; be identical: *Our opinions of the movie coincided.* **3.** To occur at the same time or during the same period of time: *The date of your party coincides with my birthday.*

co•in•ci•dence (kō ĭn′sĭ dəns) *n.* **1.** A combination of events or circumstances that is accidental but seems to have been planned or arranged: *By a strange coincidence, John Adams and Thomas Jefferson both died on the 50th anniversary of the signing of the Declaration of Independence.* **2.** The state or fact of coinciding: *A curious coincidence of events brought the two nations together in agreement.*

co•in•ci•dent (kō ĭn′sĭ dənt) *adj.* **1.** Happening at the same time: *The girls had coincident concerts and could not see each other play.* **2.** Matching point for point; coinciding: *coincident circles.* **3.** Very similar; agreeing: *coincident opinions.* —**co•in′ci•dent•ly** *adv.*

co•in•ci•den•tal (kō ĭn′sĭ dĕn′tl) *adj.* Occurring as or resulting from coincidence: *a coincidental meeting of old friends.* —**co•in′ci•den′tal•ly** *adv.*

co•i•tus (kō′ĭ təs *or* kō ē′təs) *n.* Sexual union between a female and a male in which the penis enters the vagina.

coke (kōk) *n.* The solid material, chiefly carbon, that remains after the coal gas and coal tar have been removed from bituminous coal by heat. It is used as a fuel and in making steel.

col. *abbr.* An abbreviation of column.

cogwheel

ă	pat	oi	boy
ā	pay	ou	out
âr	care	o͝o	took
ä	father	o͞o	boot
ĕ	pet	ŭ	cut
ē	be	ûr	urge
ĭ	pit	th	thin
ī	pie	*th*	this
îr	pier	hw	whoop
ŏ	pot	zh	vision
ō	toe	ə	about
ô	paw	N	*French* bon

colander

coliseum
View of the Colosseum in Rome, Italy

Col. *abbr.* An abbreviation of **1.** Colonel. **2.** Colorado.

co•la[1] (kō′lə) *n.* A carbonated drink made with an extract from cola nuts. [First written down in 1887 in Modern English, of West African origin.]

co•la[2] (kō′lə) *n.* Plural of **colon**[2].

co•la[3] also **ko•la** (kō′lə) *n.* Either of two tropical African evergreen plants having reddish fragrant seeds that yield an extract used in beverages and medicine. [First written down in 1795 in Modern English, of West African origin.]

col•an•der (kŭl′ən dər *or* kŏl′ən dər) *n.* A bowl-shaped kitchen utensil with holes in the bottom, used for rinsing and draining off liquids from foods.

cold (kōld) *adj.* **cold•er, cold•est. 1.** Having a low temperature: *cold water; a cold day.* **2.a.** Having a temperature lower than normal or desirable: *cold hands and feet; cold oatmeal.* **b.** Feeling no warmth; chilled: *I am cold without a jacket.* **3.** Not friendly; aloof: *a cold and businesslike manner.* **4.** Showing no enthusiasm or interest: *a cold audience.* **5.** In games, still far from an object being sought. **6.** Unconscious: *was out cold after the anesthetic was given.* **7.** Having lost freshness; faint; weak: *The bear's trail was cold.* —*adv.* **1.** Completely; thoroughly; absolutely: *Our suggestion was turned down cold. The player was stopped cold on the 40-yard line.* **2.** Without preparation or prior notice: *We took the test cold.* —*n.* **1.** Lack of warmth: *Cold slows down chemical reactions.* **2.** The feeling resulting from lack of warmth; chill. **3.** Cold weather: *We were out in the cold all day.* **4.** A viral infection that causes a runny or stuffy nose, coughing, sneezing, and fever. —***idioms.*** **catch cold** or **take cold.** To become sick with a cold. **get cold feet** or **have cold feet.** To lack courage; be or become timid or fearful: *Their friends got cold feet and wouldn't go skiing with them.* **out in the cold.** Lacking benefits given to others; neglected: *Because she had just been hired, she was left out in the cold when raises were given.* [First written down about 725 in Old English and spelled *ceald.*] **—cold′ly** *adv.* **—cold′ness** *n.*

Synonyms: cold, chilly, frigid, frosty, icy. These adjectives all describe something at a very low temperature. *The cold wind made me wish I had worn a coat. They walked to the store even though the autumn day felt chilly. Gordon brought the heater into the frigid room. This frosty weather is perfect for sledding. The travelers warmed their icy hands by the fire.* **Antonym: hot.**

---

cold-blood•ed (kōld′blŭd′ĭd) *adj.* **1.** Having a body temperature that changes according to the temperature of the surroundings. Fish, frogs, and reptiles are cold-blooded. **2.a.** Having no feeling or emotion; cruel. **b.** Done without feeling or emotion: *a cold-blooded dismissal of an employee.* **—cold′-blood′ed•ly** *adv.* **—cold′-blood′ed•ness** *n.*

cold cream *n.* A creamy cosmetic for cleansing and softening the skin.

cold cuts *pl.n.* Slices of cold cooked meat.

cold front *n.* The forward edge of a mass of cold air in the atmosphere that replaces a mass of warm air, often accompanied by heavy showers.

cold-heart•ed (kōld′här′tĭd) *adj.* Lacking sympathy or feeling; callous: *a cold-hearted decision to sell the farm.* **—cold′-heart′ed•ly** *adv.* **—cold′-heart′ed•ness** *n.*

cold shoulder *n. Informal.* Deliberate coldness or disregard; a snub.

cold sore *n.* A small sore on the lips that often accompanies a fever or cold; a fever blister.

cold storage *n.* The storage of food, furs, or other perishable things in a refrigerated place.

cold war or **Cold War** *n.* **1.** Intense and hostile rivalry as that between nations, stopping just short of direct military conflict. **2.** The state of rivalry that existed between the United States and its allies and the Soviet Union and other Communist countries from the end of World War II until the collapse of the Soviet Union in 1991.

cole•slaw (kōl′slô′) *n.* A salad of shredded raw cabbage with a dressing; a slaw. [First written down in 1794 in Modern English and spelled *cold slaw*, from Dutch *koolsla* : *kool*, cabbage + *sla*, salad.]

co•le•us (kō′lē əs) *n.* Any of various plants grown for their colorful leaves that are often marked with red, purple, or yellow.

col•ic (kŏl′ĭk) *n.* Severe pain or cramping in the abdomen. [First written down about 1421 in Middle English and spelled *colik*, affecting the colon, from Greek *kōlikos*, from *kolon*, colon.] **—col′ick•y** *adj.*

col•i•se•um also **col•os•se•um** (kŏl′ĭ sē′əm) *n.* A large stadium or hall for sports events, exhibitions, or other public entertainment.

co•li•tis (kə lī′tĭs) *n.* Inflammation of the colon.

coll. *abbr.* An abbreviation of: **1.** College. **2.** Collegiate. **3.** Colloquial. **4.** Colloquialism.

col•lab•o•rate (kə lăb′ə rāt′) *intr.v.* **col•lab•o•rat•ed, col•lab•o•rat•ing, col•lab•o•rates. 1.** To work together on a project: *The scientists collaborated by sharing their discoveries and planning a new experiment.* **2.** To cooperate with an enemy that has invaded one's country: *Some Southerners collaborated with the Union during the Civil War.* **—col•lab′o•ra′tion** *n.* **—col•lab′o•ra′tor** *n.*

col•lage (kə läzh′) *n.* A work of art made by pasting materials or objects, such as pieces of cloth, metal, colored paper, string, and pictures, onto a surface. [First written down in 1919 in Modern English, from French, from *coller*, to glue.]

col•la•gen (kŏl′ə jən) *n.* The tough fibrous protein found in bone, cartilage, and connective tissue.

col•lapse (kə lăps′) *v.* **col•lapsed, col•laps•ing, col•laps•es.** —*intr.* **1.** To fall down or inward suddenly; cave in: *Part of the roof collapsed after the fire.* **2.** To break down or fail suddenly and completely: *collapse from overwork and fatigue; negotiatons collapsing in disagreement.* **3.** To fold together compactly: *This folding chair collapses very easily.* —*tr.* To cause to collapse: *The weight of the books collapsed the flimsy shelf.* —*n.* **1.** The act or an example of collapsing: *the collapse of the building; the collapse of a business deal.* **2.** A sudden and complete loss of strength or stamina; a breakdown. [First written down in 1732 in Modern English, from Latin *collābī*, to fall together : *com-*, together + *lābī*, to fall.]

col•laps•i•ble (kə lăp′sə bəl) *adj.* Capable of being collapsed or folded compactly: *a collapsible tent.*

col•lar (kŏl′ər) *n.* **1.** The part of a shirt, coat, or dress that encircles the neck. **2.** A separate band for the neck, as one of lace, linen, or jewels. **3.** A leather, metal, or plastic band put around the neck of an animal, such as a dog. **4.** The cushioned part of a harness that presses against the shoulders of a draft animal, such as a horse. **5.** A band or marking, as around the neck of an animal, resembling a collar: *The buzzard has a collar of white feathers.* **6.** A device shaped like a ring and used to guide or secure a machine part. —*tr.v.* **col•lared, col•lar•ing, col•lars. 1.** To put a collar on: *collar a sheep to attach a bell.* **2.** *Slang.* To seize, capture, or arrest: *The police collared the thief a few blocks away.* [First written down about 1300 in Middle English and spelled *coler*, from Latin *collāre*, from collum, neck.]

❑ *These sound alike:* **collar, choler** (anger).

col•lar•bone (kŏl′ər bōn′) *n.* A bone that connects

the breastbone and the shoulder blade; the clavicle.

col•lard (kŏl′ərd) *n.* **1.** Kale. **2.** **collards.** The leaves of kale, eaten as a vegetable.

col•late (kə lāt′ *or* kŏl′āt′ *or* kō′lāt′) *tr.v.* **col•lat•ed, col•lat•ing, col•lates. 1.** To examine and compare carefully (copies of texts or books, for example) in order to discover differences between them: *The scholar collated the early editions of the poem to determine which version was the original.* **2.** To arrange in proper sequence: *collate sections of the Sunday newspaper for delivery.* **—col•la′tion** *n.*

col•lat•er•al (kə lăt′ər əl) *adj.* **1.** Situated or running side by side; parallel: *collateral lines of a parallelogram.* **2.** Additional; supporting: *Further experiments provided collateral evidence for the theory.* **3.** Guaranteed by something pledged: *a collateral loan.* —*n.* Property, such as jewelry or bonds, pledged as security for a loan. **—col•lat′er•al•ly** *adv.*

col•league (kŏl′ēg′) *n.* A fellow member of a profession, staff, or organization; an associate.

col•lect (kə lĕkt′) *v.* **col•lect•ed, col•lect•ing, col•lects.** —*tr.* **1.** To bring together in a group; gather; assemble: *We collected firewood.* See Synonyms at **gather. 2.** To pick up and take away: *collect garbage; collect the laundry.* **3.** To accumulate as a hobby or for study: *collect stamps; collect specimens for a report about beetles.* **4.** To obtain payment of: *We collected a dollar from each student for the gift.* **5.** To recover control of; pull together: *They finally collected themselves after the accident.* —*intr.* **1.** To come together; congregate: *A group of bystanders collected on the sidewalk.* **2.** To build up; accumulate: *A pile of snow collected by the door.* **3.** To take in payments or donations: *The band collected for new uniforms.* —*adv.* & *adj.* With payment to be made by the receiver: *call home collect; a collect call.* [First written down before 1425 in Middle English and spelled *collecten,* from Latin *colligere* : *com-,* together + *legere,* to gather.] **—col•lect′a•ble, col•lect′i•ble** *adj.*

col•lect•ed (kə lĕk′tĭd) *adj.* **1.** In full control of oneself; composed; calm: *He did his best to remain cool and collected when speaking to a crowd.* **2.** Gathered together: *the collected works of Shakespeare.* **—col•lect′ed•ly** *adv.* **—col•lect′ed•ness** *n.*

col•lec•tion (kə lĕk′shən) *n.* **1.** The act or process of collecting: *Trash collection is on Tuesday.* **2.** A group of things brought or kept together for study or use or as a hobby: *a collection of folk songs; a coin collection.* **3.** An accumulation; a deposit: *the collection of dust on the piano.* **4.a.** The act of seeking and obtaining money, as during a church service. **b.** The amount of money so obtained.

col•lec•tive (kə lĕk′tĭv) *adj.* **1.** Formed by collecting; assembled or accumulated into a whole: *the collective accomplishments of the past.* **2.** Of or relating to a number of persons or nations acting as a group: *the collective opinion of the committee; our collective security.* **3.** Owned, managed, or operated by a group: *collective farming in the Soviet Union.* —*n.* **1.** A business or undertaking owned and controlled by its workers, usually under the supervision of a government. **2.** A collective noun. **—col•lec′tive•ly** *adv.*

collective bar•gain•ing (bär′gə nĭng) *n.* Negotiation between the representatives of organized workers and their employer or employers to determine wages and working conditions.

collective farm *n.* A farm or a group of farms managed and worked by a group of laborers, usually under the supervision of a government.

collective noun *n.* A noun that refers to a collection of persons or things regarded as a unit. —SEE NOTE.

col•lec•tiv•ism (kə lĕk′tə vĭz′əm) *n.* The theory or system in which the means of producing and distributing goods are owned and controlled by the people as a group or by the government. **—col•lec′tiv•ist** *adj.* & *n.*

col•lec•tiv•ize (kə lĕk′tə vīz′) *tr.v.* **col•lec•tiv•ized, col•lec•tiv•iz•ing, col•lec•tiv•iz•es.** To organize (an economy, an industry, or a business) on the basis of collectivism. **—col•lec′tiv•i•za′tion** (kə lĕk′tə vĭ zā′shən) *n.*

col•lec•tor (kə lĕk′tər) *n.* **1.** A person or thing that collects: *a garbage collector; a solar collector.* **2.** A person assigned to collect money: *a tax collector.* **3.** A person who assembles a collection: *a collector of autographs.*

col•leen (kŏ lēn′ *or* kŏl′ēn′) *n.* An Irish girl. [First written down in 1828 in Modern English, from Irish Gaelic *cailín,* diminutive of *caile,* girl.]

col•lege (kŏl′ĭj) *n.* **1.** A school of higher learning, entered after high school, that grants a bachelor's degree. **2.** An undergraduate division within a university. **3.** A school for special study, often connected with a university: *a teachers' college.* **4.** A body of persons having a common purpose or shared duties: *a college of surgeons.* [First written down about 1378 in Middle English, from Latin *collēgium,* association.]

col•le•gian (kə lē′jən *or* kə lē′jē ən) *n.* A college student.

col•le•giate (kə lē′jĭt *or* kə lē′jē ĭt) *adj.* Of, relating to, or suited to a college or college students: *collegiate activities.*

col•lide (kə līd′) *intr.v.* **col•lid•ed, col•lid•ing, col•lides. 1.** To strike or bump together with violent direct impact: *The car was badly damaged when it collided with the tree.* **2.** To meet in opposition; disagree strongly; clash: *The interests of the two nations collided over fishing rights in coastal waters.* [First written down in 1621 in Modern English, from Latin *collīdere* : *com-,* together + *laedere,* to strike.]

col•lie (kŏl′ē) *n.* A large dog having long white and tan hair and a narrow snout, originally used in Scotland to herd sheep. [First written down before 1651 in Modern English, perhaps variant of *colly,* like coal, from Middle English *col,* coal.]

col•lier (kŏl′yər) *n.* **1.** A coal miner. **2.** A ship for carrying coal.

col•lier•y (kŏl′yə rē) *n., pl.* **col•lier•ies.** A coal mine along with its equipment and buildings.

col•lin•e•ar (kə lĭn′ē ər) *adj.* Passing through or lying on the same straight line.

col•li•sion (kə lĭzh′ən) *n.* The act or process of colliding; a crash or conflict.

col•lo•ca•tion (kŏl′ō kā′shən) *n.* An arrangement or a juxtaposition, as of words.

col•loid (kŏl′oid′) *n.* A substance made up of a large number of tiny particles distributed throughout a gas, liquid, or solid. The particles in paints, gelatins, fogs, and many other colloids do not dissolve but remain suspended for long periods of time. —*adj.* Colloidal.

col•loi•dal (kə loid′l) *adj.* Of, relating to, or containing a colloid: *Foam rubber is a colloidal suspension of air in a rubber mixture.* **—col•loi′dal•ly** *adv.*

col•lo•qui•al (kə lō′kwē əl) *adj.* Characteristic of or suitable to spoken language or to writing that resembles speech; informal. **—col•lo′qui•al•ly** *adv.* **—col•lo′qui•al•ness** *n.*

col•lo•qui•al•ism (kə lō′kwē ə lĭz′əm) *n.* **1.** Colloquial style or quality. **2.** A colloquial expression: *Up a tree is a colloquialism meaning "in a difficult situation."*

col•lo•quy (kŏl′ə kwē) *n., pl.* **col•lo•quies.** A conversation or conference, especially a formal one.

Usage: collective noun

When referring to a collection considered as a whole, a collective noun takes a singular verb: *The family was united on this question.* A collective noun takes a plural verb when it refers to the members of the group as individuals, as in *My family are always fighting among themselves.* Among the common collective nouns are **committee**, **clergy**, **company**, **enemy**, **group**, **family**, **flock**, **public**, and **team**.

collie
Tricolor collie

ă	pat	oi	boy
ā	pay	ou	out
âr	care	ŏŏ	took
ä	father	ōō	boot
ĕ	pet	ŭ	cut
ē	be	ûr	urge
ĭ	pit	th	thin
ī	pie	*th*	this
îr	pier	hw	whoop
ŏ	pot	zh	vision
ō	toe	ə	about
ô	paw	N	*French* bon

Colorado

The name **Colorado** comes from a Spanish word meaning "colored, especially reddish colored." Spanish explorers first gave this name to the **Colorado River**, on account of its reddish waters. The state took its name from the river.

colossus
The Colossus of Rhodes, one of the Seven Wonders of the World

Christopher Columbus

[First written down in 1459 in Middle English and spelled *colloquy*, discourse, from Latin *colloquium*, conversation : *com-*, together + *loquī*, to speak.]

col•lu•sion (kə lo͞o′zhən) *n.* A secret agreement between persons seeking to deceive or cheat someone else. **—col•lu′sive** (kə lo͞o′sĭv) *adj.*

Colo. *abbr.* An abbreviation of Colorado.

co•logne (kə lōn′) *n.* A scented liquid made of alcohol and fragrant oils, used as light perfume.

Co•logne (kə lōn′). A city of western Germany on the Rhine River north of Bonn. It was a Roman settlement after A.D. 50. Population, 922,286.

Co•lom•bi•a (kə lŭm′bē ə). A country of northwest South America north of Ecuador and Peru with coastlines on the Pacific Ocean and the Caribbean Sea. It gained its independence from Spain in 1819. Bogotá is the capital and the largest city. Population, 26,525,670.

Co•lom•bo (kə lŭm′bō). The capital and largest city of Sri Lanka, on the western coast of the island on the Indian Ocean. Population, 587,647.

co•lon[1] (kō′lən) *n., pl.* **co•lons. 1.** A punctuation mark (:) used after a word introducing a quotation, an explanation, an example, or a series. **2.** The sign (:) used between numbers or groups of numbers in expressions of time (2:30 a.m., read as "two thirty") and ratios (1:2, read as "one to two"). [First written down in 1589 in Modern English, from Greek *kōlon*, limb, member, metrical unit.]

co•lon[2] (kō′lən) *n., pl.* **co•lons** or **co•la** (kō′lə). The lower part of the large intestine in which solid waste is accumulated and prepared for elimination from the body. The colon extends from the cecum to the rectum. [First written down before 1398 in Middle English, from Greek *kolon*, large intestine.]

co•lon[3] (kō lōn′) *n., pl.* **co•lons** or **co•lo•nes** (kō-lō′nās′). The basic monetary unit of Costa Rica and El Salvador. [First written down in 1892 in Modern English, from Spanish *colón*, after Cristóbal *Colón* Christopher Columbus.]

colo•nel (kûr′nəl) *n.* An officer in the U.S. Army, Air Force, or Marine Corps ranking below a brigadier general and above a major. [First written down in 1548 in Modern English and spelled *coronel*, from Old Italian *colonello*, from Latin *columna*, column.]

❑ *These sound alike:* **colonel, kernel** (seed).

co•lo•nes (kō lō′nās) *n.* A plural of **colon**[3].

co•lo•ni•al (kə lō′nē əl) *adj.* **1.** Of, relating to, or possessing a colony or colonies: *France and England were colonial powers in Africa and Asia.* **2.** Often **Colonial.** Of or relating to the 13 British colonies that became the United States of America: *the Colonial period of British rule before the Revolutionary War.* **3.** Often **Colonial.** Of or relating to the style of architecture and furniture often found in the British colonies in America. *—n.* A person who lives in a colony. **—co•lo′ni•al•ly** *adv.*

co•lo•ni•al•ism (kə lō′nē ə lĭz′əm) *n.* A governmental policy of acquiring or maintaining foreign territory as colonies.

col•o•nist (kŏl′ə nĭst) *n.* **1.** An original settler or founder of a colony. **2.** A person who lives in a colony.

col•o•nize (kŏl′ə nīz′) *tr. & intr.v.* **col•o•nized, col•o•niz•ing, col•o•niz•es.** To establish or settle a colony in: *Norwegian Vikings originally colonized Iceland.* **—col′o•ni•za′tion** (kŏl′ə nĭ zā′shən) *n.* **—col′o•niz′er** *n.*

col•on•nade (kŏl′ə nād′) *n.* A series of columns placed at regular intervals to support a roof or other structure of a building.

col•o•ny (kŏl′ə nē) *n., pl.* **col•o•nies. 1.** A group of people who settle in a distant land but remain subject to their native country: *The English Pilgrims founded a colony at Plymouth.* **2.** The area occupied by such a group. **3.** A territory ruled by a distant power: *The government built railroads in each of its colonies.* **4. Colonies.** The 13 British colonies that became the original United States of America and that included Connecticut, Delaware, Georgia, Maryland, Massachusetts, New Hampshire, New Jersey, New York, North Carolina, Pennsylvania, Rhode Island, South Carolina, and Virginia. **5.** A group of people of the same nationality, religion, or interests, living together in one area: *the American colony in Paris.* **6.** A group of the same kind of animals, plants, or one-celled organisms living or growing together: *a colony of ants; a colony of bacteria.* [First written down about 1384 in Middle English and spelled *colonie*, from Latin *colōnia*.]

col•or (kŭl′ər) *n.* **1.** The sensation produced by the effect of light waves striking the retina of the eye. The color of something depends mainly on which wavelengths of light it emits, reflects, or transmits. **2.** A color other than black, white, or gray. **3.** A dye, pigment, paint, or other coloring substance. **4.** The general appearance of the skin; complexion: *the rosy color of good health.* **5.** The skin of a person who is not classified as white: *laws against discrimination based on color.* **6. colors. a.** A flag or banner, as of a country or military unit: *At the beginning of the ceremony, they raised the colors.* **b.** A distinguishing symbol, badge, ribbon, color, or mark of something: *a tie with the college's colors on it.* **7.** Vivid and interesting detail, as of a scene or of an event in writing: *The author's description of the political campaign had a great deal of color.* **8.** Traits of personality or behavior that are appealing. *—v.* **col•ored, col•or•ing, col•ors.** *—tr.* **1.** To give color to or change the color of: *color a picture with crayons.* **2.** To give a distinctive character or quality to: *A sense of humor colored the author's writing.* **3.** To influence, especially by distortion or misrepresentation: *Anger colored the witness's account of the accident.* *—intr.* **1.** To take on or change color. **2.** To blush. [First written down about 1225 in Middle English and spelled *colur*, from Latin *color*.] **—col′or•er** *n.*

Col•o•ra•do (kŏl′ə răd′ō *or* kŏl′ə rä′dō). A state of the west-central United States north of New Mexico. It was admitted as the 38th state in 1876. The region was explored by the Spanish in the 16th and 17th centuries. Denver is the capital and the largest city. Population, 3,307,912. —SEE NOTE.

Colorado River. A river of the southwest United States rising in the Rocky Mountains and flowing about 1,450 miles (2,333 kilometers) southwest to the Pacific Ocean in northwest Mexico. The most spectacular of its gorges is the Grand Canyon.

col•or•a•tion (kŭl′ə rā′shən) *n.* Arrangement of colors: *Protective coloration helps some animals to hide from their enemies.*

col•or•blind or **col•or-blind** (kŭl′ər blīnd′) *adj.* Partly or totally unable to distinguish certain colors, such as red and green. **—col′or•blind′ness** *n.*

col•or-code (kŭl′ər kōd′) *tr.v.* **col•or-cod•ed, col•or-cod•ing, col•or-codes.** To color according to a code for easy identification: *color-code the sections of a telephone directory.*

col•ored (kŭl′ərd) *adj.* **1.** Having color. **2.** Often **Colored.** *Offensive.* Of or belonging to an ethnic group that is not considered white. **3.** Distorted by prejudice or biased by self-interest: *The drivers each gave a very colored version of the accident.*

col•or•fast (kŭl′ər făst′) *adj.* Having color that will not run or fade with washing or wear: *a colorfast fabric.*

col•or•ful (kŭl′ər fəl) *adj.* **1.** Full of color or colors:

Many butterflies have colorful wings. **2.** Rich in variety; vivid; distinctive: *a colorful description of a castle.* —**col′or•ful•ly** *adv.* —**col′or•ful•ness** *n.*

col•or•ing (kŭl′ər ĭng) *n.* **1.** The manner or process of applying color: *laws regulating the coloring of fruits and vegetables.* **2.** A substance used to color something: *hair coloring.* **3.** Appearance with regard to color: *animals protected by their coloring.* **4.** False or misleading appearance: *an excuse that had the coloring of truth.*

col•or•ize (kŭl′ə rīz′) *tr.v.* **col•or•ized, col•or•iz•ing, col•or•iz•es.** To color (a black and white film) by means of a computer process. —**col′or•i•za′tion** (kŭl′ər ĭ zā′shən) *n.*

col•or•less (kŭl′ər lĭs) *adj.* **1.** Lacking color: *Air is colorless.* **2.** Weak in color; pallid: *the colorless face of a sick patient.* **3.** Lacking in variety, interest, or distinction; dull: *a colorless account of the event.* —**col′or•less•ly** *adv.* —**col′or•less•ness** *n.*

co•los•sal (kə lŏs′əl) *adj.* Very great in size, extent, or degree; enormous; gigantic: *a city full of colossal buildings; a daring venture requiring colossal self-confidence.* —**co•los′sal•ly** *adv.*

col•os•se•um (kŏl′ĭ sē′əm) *n.* Variant of **coliseum.**

co•los•sus (kə lŏs′əs) *n., pl.* **co•los•si** (kə lŏs′ī′) or **co•los•sus•es. 1.** A huge statue. **2.** Something of enormous size or importance: *a colossus among clothing manufacturers.*

col•our (kŭl′ər) *n. & v. Chiefly British.* Variant of **color.**

colt (kōlt) *n.* A young male horse.

colt•ish (kōl′tĭsh) *adj.* **1.** Relating to a colt. **2.** Resembling a colt; lively; playful: *the coltish behavior of the children at the playground.*

Co•lum•bi•a (kə lŭm′bē ə). The capital and largest city of South Carolina, in the central part of the state. It was chosen as the capital in 1786. Population, 98,052.

Columbia River. A river rising in southeast British Columbia, Canada, and flowing about 1,210 miles (1,947 kilometers) south then west along the Washington-Oregon border to the Pacific Ocean.

col•um•bine (kŏl′əm bīn′) *n.* Any of various garden plants related to the buttercup, having colorful flowers with five narrow projecting parts. [First written down before 1310 in Middle English, from Latin *columba*, dove.]

Co•lum•bus (kə lŭm′bəs). **1.** A city of western Georgia south-southwest of Atlanta. It was settled in 1828 on the site of a Creek village. Population, 179,278. **2.** The capital of Ohio, in the central part of the state northeast of Cincinnatti. It was laid out in 1812. Population, 632,910.

Columbus, Christopher. 1451–1506. Italian explorer in the service of Spain who tried to reach Asia by sailing west from Europe but instead landed in America in 1492.

Columbus Day *n.* October 12, celebrated officially on the second Monday in October in honor of Christopher Columbus.

col•umn (kŏl′əm) *n.* **1.** A pillar, usually shaped like a cylinder, used in a building as a support or as a decoration. **2.** Something that resembles a pillar in shape or use: *a column of mercury in a thermometer.* **3.** One of two or more vertical sections of a page, lying side by side but separated from each other, in which lines of print are arranged: *Newspapers are often printed in six columns across the page.* **4.** A feature article that appears regularly in a newspaper or magazine: *a sports column.* **5.** A formation, as of soldiers or trucks, in which members or rows follow one behind the other. [First written down about 1440 in Middle English, from Latin *columna.*]

co•lum•nar (kə lŭm′nər) *adj.* **1.** Having the shape of a column. **2.** Having or constructed with columns: *a columnar design of a courtyard.*

col•um•nist (kŏl′əm nĭst *or* kŏl′ə mĭst) *n.* A person who writes a column for a newspaper or magazine.

com. *abbr.* An abbreviation of: **1.** Commerce. **2.** Common. **3.** Commonly. **4.** Commissioner. **5.** Committee.

Com. *abbr.* An abbreviation of: **1.** Commissioner. **2.** Committee.

com– *pref.* A prefix that means together or with: *commingle.* —SEE NOTE.

co•ma¹ (kō′mə) *n., pl.* **co•mas.** A state of deep unconsciousness resulting from disease, injury, or poisoning. [First written down in 1646 in Modern English, from Greek *kōma*, deep sleep.]

co•ma² (kō′mə) *n., pl.* **co•mae** (kō′mē). A luminous gaseous cloud around the nucleus of a comet. [First written down in 1669 in Modern English, from Greek *komē*, hair.]

Co•man•che (kə măn′chē) *n., pl.* **Comanche** or **Co•man•ches. 1.** A member of a Native American people formerly of the southern Great Plains and now living in Oklahoma. **2.** The language of the Comanche. —**Co•man′che** *adj.*

co•ma•tose (kō′mə tōs′ *or* kŏm′ə tōs′) *adj.* **1.** Being in a coma; deeply unconscious. **2.** Relating to or resembling a coma; *a comatose trance.*

comb (kōm) *n.* **1.** A thin strip of plastic, bone, metal, or hard rubber, having teeth and used to arrange or fasten the hair. **2.** Something resembling a comb in shape or use, as a card for arranging and cleaning wool. **3.** The brightly colored ridge of flesh on the top of the head of a rooster, hen, or certain other birds. **4.** A honeycomb. —*tr.v.* **combed, comb•ing, combs. 1.** To dress, arrange, or untangle with a comb. **2.** To search thoroughly: *combed many books for information.* [First written down about 700 in Old English and spelled *camb.*]

com•bat (kəm băt′ *or* kŏm′băt′) *tr.v.* **com•bat•ed, com•bat•ing, com•bats** or **com•bat•ted, com•bat•ting, com•bats. 1.** To oppose in battle. **2.** To fight or struggle against: *new drugs that combat infection.* See Synonyms at **oppose.** —*n.* (kŏm′-băt′). **1.** Armed conflict; battle: *soldiers wounded in combat.* **2.** A fight or struggle; a contest: *a combat between different schools of thought.* [First written down in 1564 in Modern English, from Late Latin *combattere* : Latin *com-*, with, against + Latin *battere*, to beat.]

com•bat•ant (kəm băt′nt *or* kŏm′bə tnt) *n.* A person engaged in fighting or combat.

com•bat•ive (kəm băt′ĭv) *adj.* Ready or disposed to fight; belligerent: *the lawyer's combative disposition.* —**com•bat′ive•ness** *n.*

comb•er (kō′mər) *n.* **1.** A person or thing that combs. **2.** A long wave that has reached its peak or broken into foam; a breaker.

com•bi•na•tion (kŏm′bə nā′shən) *n.* **1.** The act of combining or the condition of being combined: *The combination of fresh air and sunshine produced a beautiful day.* **2.** Something that results from combining two or more things: *An alloy is a combination of metals.* **3.** The series of numbers or letters used to open a combination lock. **4.** Any of the possible arrangements of numbers or letters in a set.

combination lock *n.* A lock that can be opened only by turning its dial through a particular sequence of numbers or letters.

com•bine (kəm bīn′) *v.* **com•bined, com•bin•ing, com•bines.** —*tr.* **1.** To bring together; make united; join: *a movie that combines an interesting story and a moral.* See Synonyms at **join. 2.** To join (two or more substances) to make a single substance; blend; mix: *combine water, gravel, and cement to make concrete.* —*intr.* **1.** To become united; come togeth-

Word Building: com–

The basic meaning of the prefix **com–** is "together, with." It comes from the Latin prefix *com–*. Before the consonants *l* and *r*, Latin *com–* became *col–* and *cor–*, respectively, as we see in our words **collaborate** and **correspond**. Before all other consonants except *p*, *b*, or *m*, *com–* became *con–*, as in **confirm**, **constitution**, and **contribute**.

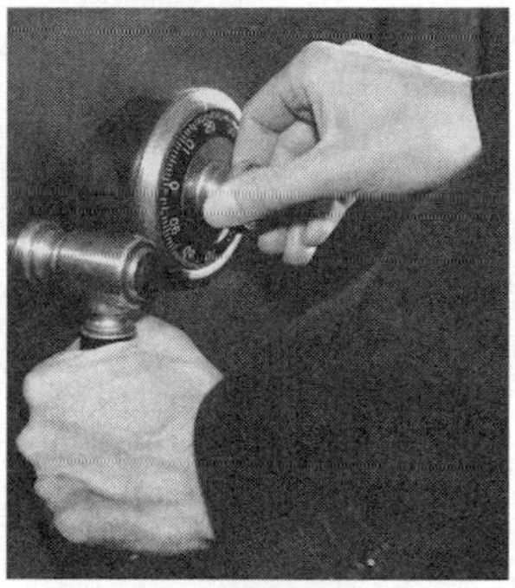

combination lock

combine
Harvesting wheat

ă	pat	oi	boy
ā	pay	ou	out
âr	care	o͝o	took
ä	father	o͞o	boot
ĕ	pet	ŭ	cut
ē	be	ûr	urge
ĭ	pit	th	thin
ī	pie	*th*	this
îr	pier	hw	whoop
ŏ	pot	zh	vision
ō	toe	ə	about
ô	paw	N	*French* bon

comet

er: *Friends combined to help the family after the fire.* **2.** To form a compound: *Two atoms of hydrogen combine with one of oxygen to form water.* —*n.* (**kŏm′**bīn′). **1.** A power-operated machine that cuts, threshes, and cleans grain. **2.** A group of persons or companies acting together in a business transaction. [First written down before 1420 in Middle English and spelled *combinen*, from Late Latin *combīnāre* : Latin *com-*, together + *bīnī*, two by two.]

com•bin•ing form (kəm **bī′**nĭng) *n.* A form of a word that combines with other word forms to create new words, as *electro-* (from *electric*) in *electromagnet.*

com•bo (**kŏm′**bō) *n., pl.* **com•bos. 1.** A small group of musicians: *a jazz combo.* **2.** *Informal.* A combination.

com•bus•ti•ble (kəm **bŭs′**tə bəl) *adj.* Capable of catching fire and burning. —*n.* A substance that catches fire and burns quickly. **—com•bus′ti•bil′i•ty** *n.* **—com•bus′ti•bly** *adv.*

com•bus•tion (kəm **bŭs′**chən) *n.* **1.** The process of burning. **2.** A chemical reaction, especially a rapid combination with oxygen, accompanied by heat and light.

Comdr. *abbr.* An abbreviation of commander.

Comdt. *abbr.* An abbreviation of commandant.

come (kŭm) *intr.v.* **came** (kām), **come, com•ing, comes. 1.** To advance toward the speaker or toward a specified place; approach: *Come over here.* **2.** To arrive at a particular result or end: *The rivals came to an agreement. Their arrangements finally came to nothing.* **3.** To move toward or arrive at a particular condition: *The new garden is coming along well.* **4.** To move or be brought to a particular position: *The bus came to a stop.* **5.** To extend; reach: *The snow came up to the window ledge.* **6.a.** To exist at a particular point or place: *The date of birth comes after the name in this listing.* **b.** To rank; have priority: *Work comes first. A comes before B.* **7.** To happen: *How did they come to be invited?* **8.** To happen as a result: *Difficulty often comes from stubborness.* **9.** To occur in the mind: *Sounds of the city come back to me.* **10.** To issue forth: *The giggle came from the back of the class.* **11.** To arise; originate: *Oaks come from acorns.* **12.** To be a native or resident of: *Her family comes from Chicago.* **13.** To become: *The knot came loose.* **14.** To be available or obtainable: *Shoes come in many styles.* **15.** To prove or turn out to be: *The dream came true.* ***—idioms.*** **come about. 1.** To occur; take place; happen: *It came about that we could go.* **2.** In sailing, to change tack or direction. **come across.** To meet or find by chance: *We came across some letters in the attic.* **come around. 1.** To recover; revive: *He fainted but came around quickly.* **2.** To change one's opinion or position: *The coach came around after hearing the whole story.* **come back. 1.** To remember; recall: *The author's name came back to me.* **2.** To return to past success after a period of misfortune: *The town came back after the flood.* **come by.** To acquire; get: *How did you come by that chair?* **come down. 1.** To lose wealth or position. **2.** To be handed down by tradition: *a custom that comes down from colonial times.* **come down with.** To become sick with (an illness): *came down with a cold.* **come in for.** *Informal.* To receive; get: *The reporter's work came in for criticism.* **come off.** To happen; occur: *The celebration came off on schedule.* **come out. 1.** To become known: *The whole story came out in the trial.* **2.** To be issued or brought out: *The author's new book just came out.* **3.** To declare oneself publicly: *The president has come out for the tax proposal.* **4.** To result; end up; turn out: *Everything came out fine, as we expected.* **5.** To make a formal social debut. **come through.** To do what is required or expected: *I asked for their help, and they came through.* **come to. 1.** To regain consciousness. **2.** To amount to: *The bill came to $15.* **come up. 1.** To show up; arise: *The question didn't come up at the meeting.* **2.** To rise: *The sun came up.* **come up with.** *Informal.* To propose; produce: *The committee came up with some interesting new ideas.* **come upon.** To discover or meet by accident. **how come?.** *Informal.* Why: *How come they left early?* [First written down before 830 in Old English and spelled *cuman.*]

come•back (**kŭm′**băk′) *n.* **1.** A return to prosperity or high rank: *The tennis star made a comeback.* **2.** A reply, especially a quick witty one; a retort.

co•me•di•an (kə **mē′**dē ən) *n.* **1.** A professional entertainer who tells jokes or does other things intended to make audiences laugh. **2.** A person who amuses or tries to be amusing; a clown: *the office comedian.* **3.** An actor in comedy.

co•me•di•enne (kə mē′dē **ĕn′**) *n.* A woman professional entertainer who tells jokes or does other things intended to make audiences laugh.

come•down (**kŭm′**doun′) *n.* A decline or drop in status or position: *Losing so badly was quite a comedown for the former champion.*

com•e•dy (**kŏm′**ĭ dē) *n., pl.* **com•e•dies. 1.** A play, a motion picture, an operetta, or another work that has a funny story with humorous characters and a happy ending. **2.** The branch of drama made up of such plays or other dramatic works: *The actor found comedy more difficult than tragedy.* **3.** Popular entertainment consisting of jokes, satire, and other things meant to be humorous. **4.** A funny incident. [First written down about 1385 in Middle English and spelled *comedie*, from Greek *kōmōidia* : *kōmos*, revel + *aeidein*, to sing.] **—co•me′dic** (kə **mē′**dĭk) *adj.*

come•ly (**kŭm′**lē) *adj.* **come•li•er, come•li•est.** Having a pleasing appearance; attractive: *a comely face.* **—come′li•ness** *n.*

come-on (**kŭm′**ŏn′ *or* **kŭm′**ôn′) *n.* Something offered to allure or attract; an inducement: *The come-on for renting cars was a free tank of gas.*

com•er (**kŭm′**ər) *n.* **1.** A person or thing that arrives or comes: *All comers were welcome.* **2.** A person or thing that shows promise of reaching success: *The critics think the young pianist may be a real comer.*

com•et (**kŏm′**ĭt) *n.* An object in the solar system consisting of a dense nucleus of frozen gases and dust, which develops a luminous halo and tail when near the sun. Comets travel around the sun in an immense elongated orbit. [First written down before 1200 in Middle English and spelled *comete*, from Greek *(astēr) komētēs*, long-haired (star).]

come•up•pance (kŭm′**ŭp′**əns) *n.* Punishment or retribution that one deserves: *The smart aleck finally got his comeuppance.*

com•fort (**kŭm′**fərt) *tr.v.* **com•fort•ed, com•fort•ing, com•forts. 1.** To soothe in time of grief or fear; console: *comfort a lost child.* **2.** To help relieve the pain and suffering of: *A nurse comforted the patient by putting a pillow behind her back.* —*n.* **1.** A condition of ease or well-being: *Pillows are available for the comfort of the passengers.* **2.** Relief in time of pain, grief, or fear: *The frightened child ran to its mother for comfort.* **3.** A person or thing that provides relief, ease, or well-being: *Pets are a comfort to their owners.* **4.** The capacity or ability to give ease or a sense of well-being: *Curtains and soft chairs added to the comfort of the room.* [First written down about 1280 in Middle English and spelled *comforten*, from Late Latin *cōnfortāre.*]

com•fort•a•ble (**kŭm′**fər tə bəl *or* **kŭmf′**tə bəl) *adj.*

1. Providing physical comfort: *a comfortable chair.* **2.** Free from worry or anxiety; at ease: *I felt very comfortable on stage.* **3.** Enough to meet a need; sufficient: *a comfortable income for a small family.* **—com′fort•a•ble•ness** *n.* **—com′fort•a•bly** *adv.*

com•fort•er (kŭm′fər tər) *n.* **1.** A person or thing that comforts: *a comforter of the sick.* **2.** A thick warm quilt used as a bed cover.

com•fy (kŭm′fē) *adj.* **com•fi•er, com•fi•est.** *Informal.* Comfortable.

com•ic (kŏm′ĭk) *adj.* **1.** Of or relating to comedy: *comic writing.* **2.** Humorous; amusing: *a comic situation:* —*n.* **1.** A person who is funny or amusing, especially a comedian: *A nightclub where comics tell jokes before an audience.* **2. comics.** *Informal.* Comic strips. [First written down before 1387 in Middle English and spelled *comice,* from Greek *kōmikos.*]

com•i•cal (kŏm′ĭ kəl) *adj.* Causing amusement or laughter; funny: *She looked comical in the large hat.* **—com′i•cal•ly** *adv.* **—com′i•cal•ness** *n.*

comic book *n.* A booklet of comic strips, usually telling only one or two stories.

comic opera *n.* An opera or operetta with a humorous story, some spoken dialogue, and usually a happy ending.

comic strip *n.* A series of cartoons that tells a joke or a story, usually printed in a newspaper.

com•ing (kŭm′ĭng) *adj.* **1.** Approaching; next: *The coastal towns prepared for the coming storm.* **2.** Showing promise of fame or success: *a young and coming political leader.* —*n.* Arrival: *With the coming of spring, the days become longer.*

com•ma (kŏm′ə) *n.* A punctuation mark (,) used to indicate a separation of elements within a sentence, such as a series of items or an independent clause. [First written down in 1586 in Modern English, from Greek *komma,* piece cut off, short clause, from *koptein,* to cut.]

comma fault *n.* The improper use of a comma to join two independent clauses.

com•mand (kə mănd′) *v.* **com•mand•ed, com•mand•ing, com•mands.** —*tr.* **1.** To direct with authority; give orders to: *The control tower commanded the pilot to land elsewhere.* **2.** To have control or authority over; rule: *The general commands thousands of troops.* **3.** To deserve and receive as due: *His bravery commands respect.* **4.** To have control over by position; overlook: *That mountain commands the valley below.* —*intr.* **1.** To give orders: *The coach commanded in a loud voice.* **2.** To exercise authority as a commander; be in control: *The general commanded through a staff of junior officers.* —*n.* **1.** An order or a direction: *Dogs can be trained to follow commands.* **2.** The possession or exercise of authority to command: *The admiral was in command of the navy.* **3.** Ability to control or use; mastery: *She has a command of French and Russian.* **4.a.** The extent or range of a commander: *He has command over three battalions.* **b.** A military unit or area under the control of one officer. —*adj.* **1.** Of, relating to, or being a command: *a command decision.* **2.** Done in response to a command: *a command performance.* [First written down before 1300 in Middle English and spelled *commanden,* from Late Latin *commandāre.*]

com•man•dant (kŏm′ən dănt′ *or* kŏm′ən dänt′) *n.* A commanding officer of a military organization.

com•man•deer (kŏm′ən dîr′) *tr.v.* **com•man•deered, com•man•deer•ing, com•man•deers.** To seize (property) for public use, especially for military use: *The police commandeered a taxi to chase the car thief.*

com•mand•er (kə măn′dər) *n.* **1.** A person who commands, especially a commanding military officer. **2.** An officer in the U.S. Navy or Coast Guard ranking below a captain and above a lieutenant commander.

commander in chief *n., pl.* **commanders in chief.** **1.** The commander of all the armed forces of a nation: *The President is commander in chief of the armed forces of the United States.* **2.** The officer commanding a major armed force: *the commander in chief of Pacific forces.*

com•mand•ing (kə măn′dĭng) *adj.* **1.** Having command; in charge: *The captain is the commanding officer of an ocean liner.* **2.** Dominating, as by reason of position or size: *a commanding lead over an opponent.*

com•mand•ment (kə mănd′mənt) *n.* **1. Commandment.** One of the Ten Commandments in the Bible. **2.** A command; an order.

com•man•do (kə măn′dō) *n., pl.* **com•man•dos** or **com•man•does.** A member of a small fighting force trained for making quick raids into enemy territory. [First written down in 1791 in Modern English, from Afrikaans *kommando,* from Spanish *comando,* from *comandar,* to command, from Late Latin *commandāre.*]

com•mem•o•rate (kə mĕm′ə rāt′) *tr.v.* **com•mem•o•rat•ed, com•mem•o•rat•ing, com•mem•o•rates.** **1.** To honor the memory of: *A large crowd gathered in the park to commemorate the sacrifice of all American soldiers.* **2.** To be a memorial to, as a holiday, ceremony, or statue: *Independence Day commemorates the adoption of the Declaration of Independence.* **—com•mem′o•ra′tion** *n.*

com•mem•o•ra•tive (kə mĕm′ər ə tĭv *or* kə-mĕm′ə rā′tĭv) *adj.* Serving to commemorate: *a commemorative service.*

com•mence (kə mĕns′) *intr. & tr.v.* **com•menced, com•menc•ing, com•menc•es.** To begin; start: *The festivities commenced with the singing of the national anthem. A lawsuit commences legal action.* See Synonyms at **begin.** [First written down about 1300 in Middle English and spelled *commencen,* from Old French *comencier* : Latin *com-,* intensive prefix + Late Latin *initiāre,* to begin.]

com•mence•ment (kə mĕns′mənt) *n.* **1.** A beginning; a start: *The commencement of the Olympic games is marked by a parade.* **2.** A graduation ceremony in which students receive their diplomas.

com•mend (kə mĕnd′) *tr.v.* **com•mend•ed, com•mend•ing, com•mends.** **1.** To speak highly of; praise: *The principal commended the students for their skill in algebra.* **2.** To recommend: *I commend the book without hesitation.* **3.** To put in the care of someone: *The sick patient was commended to the care of the doctor.* [First written down about 1350 in Middle English and spelled *commenden,* from Latin *commendāre.*]

com•mend•a•ble (kə mĕn′də bəl) *adj.* Praiseworthy: *a commendable performance of a difficult play.* **—com•mend′a•bly** *adv.*

com•men•da•tion (kŏm′ən dā′shən) *n.* **1.** Recommendation or praise: *commendation for advancement.* **2.** An official award or citation. **—com•men′da•to′ry** (kə mĕn′də tôr′ē) *adj.*

com•men•sal (kə mĕn′səl) *adj.* Of, relating to, or characterized by commensalism. —*n.* A plant or animal living in a commensal relationship with another. [First written down about 1400 in Middle English and spelled *commensall,* sharing a meal, from Medieval Latin *commēnsālis* : Latin *com-,* together + Latin *mēnsa,* table.]

com•men•sal•ism (kə mĕn′sə lĭz′əm) *n.* A relationship between two organisms of different species

commencement
College graduation ceremony

ă	pat	oi	boy
ā	pay	ou	out
âr	care	o͝o	took
ä	father	o͞o	boot
ĕ	pet	ŭ	cut
ē	be	ûr	urge
ĭ	pit	th	thin
ī	pie	*th*	this
îr	pier	hw	whoop
ŏ	pot	zh	vision
ō	toe	ə	about
ô	paw	N	*French* bon

in which one lives in or on the other, but not as a parasite, thus leaving the other unaffected.

com•men•su•ra•ble (kə mĕn′sər ə bəl *or* kə mĕn′shər ə bəl) *adj.* Properly proportioned; fitting; suitable: *The judge handed down a heavy sentence commensurable to the seriousness of the crime.* **—com•men′su•ra•bly** *adv.*

com•men•su•rate (kə mĕn′sər ĭt *or* kə mĕn′shər ĭt) *adj.* **1.** Of the same size, extent, or length of time as that of another: *Men and women should receive commensurate pay for the same job.* **2.** Corresponding in size or degree; proportionate: *I want a salary commensurate with my performance.* **—com•men′su•rate•ly** *adv.*

com•ment (kŏm′ĕnt) *n.* **1.** A written note or a remark that explains, interprets, or gives an opinion on something: *a critic's comment on a play; the newspaper's comments on the governor's speech.* **2.** Talk; gossip: *Their squabbling caused much comment among friends.* *—intr.v.* **com•ment•ed, com•ment•ing, com•ments.** To make a comment; remark: *He commented on my new red coat.* [First written down before 1387 in Middle English, from Late Latin *commentum*, interpretation.]

com•men•tar•y (kŏm′ən tĕr′ē) *n., pl.* **com•men•tar•ies. 1.** A series of explanations or interpretations: *Does your copy of the Bible contain a commentary?* **2.** An illustrating comment: *The scandal is a sad commentary on the state of our city government.*

com•men•ta•tor (kŏm′ən tā′tər) *n.* **1.** A person who writes commentaries: *Many social commentators criticize the state of our cities.* **2.** A writer or broadcaster who explains or gives opinions of events in the news: *The commentators gave opposing views at the end of the newscast.*

com•merce (kŏm′ərs) *n.* The buying and selling of goods, especially on a large scale; trade. See Synonyms at **business.** [First written down in 1537 in Modern English, from Latin *commercium* : *com-*, together + *merx*, merchandise.]

com•mer•cial (kə mûr′shəl) *adj.* **1.** Of or relating to commerce: *a commercial loan from the bank.* **2.** Done or created to make a profit: *The professor writes scholarly books, not commercial ones.* **3.** Sponsored by an advertiser or supported by advertising: *a commercial television station.* *—n.* An advertisement on radio or television. **—com•mer′cial•ly** *adv.*

com•mer•cial•ism (kə mûr′shə lĭz′əm) *n.* The practices of commerce or business, especially those that give chief importance to the making of profit. **—com•mer′cial•is′tic** *adj.*

com•mer•cial•ize (kə mûr′shə līz′) *tr.v.* **com•mer•cial•ized, com•mer•cial•iz•ing, com•mer•cial•iz•es. 1.** To apply business methods to (something) in order to make a profit: *commercialize agriculture.* **2.** To do, make, or exploit mainly for profit: *Many of the island's beaches have been heavily commercialized and spoiled.* **—com•mer′cial•i•za′tion** (kə mûr′shə lĭ zā′shən) *n.*

com•min•gle (kə mĭng′gəl) *tr. & intr.v.* **com•min•gled, com•min•gling, com•min•gles.** To blend or mix together; combine: *cities where people of many nationalities commingle.*

com•mis•er•ate (kə mĭz′ə rāt′) *v.* **com•mis•er•at•ed, com•mis•er•at•ing, com•mis•er•ates.** *—tr.* To feel or express sorrow or pity for; sympathize with: *defeated candidates commiserating with one another.* *—intr.* To feel or express sorrow or sympathy.

com•mis•er•a•tion (kə mĭz′ə rā′shən) *n.* A feeling or expression of sorrow or sympathy for the misfortune of another.

com•mis•sar (kŏm′ĭ sär′) *n.* The head of a commissariat in the Soviet Union.

com•mis•sar•i•at (kŏm′ĭ sâr′ē ĭt) *n.* **1.a.** A department of an army in charge of providing food and other supplies for the troops. **b.** The officers in charge of this department. **2.** A food supply. **3.** A major department in the government of the Soviet Union, known after 1946 as a ministry.

com•mis•sar•y (kŏm′ĭ sĕr′ē) *n., pl.* **com•mis•sar•ies. 1.** A store maintained by a company or an army post for the sale of food and supplies to its employees or personnel. **2.** A lunchroom or cafeteria that serves the employees of a company or the personnel of an institution, such as a university. **3.** A person to whom a special duty is given by a superior; a deputy.

com•mis•sion (kə mĭsh′ən) *n.* **1.a.** The act of granting authority to someone to carry out a certain job or duty: *The commission of ambassadors is one of the duties of the President.* **b.** The authority given by such a grant: *The commission of the Secretary of State is to direct the foreign policy of the United States.* **2.** A group of people who have been given authority by law to perform certain duties: *The President set up a commission to investigate ways of improving education.* **3.** The act of committing or doing something: *the commission of a crime.* **4.** Money in the form of a fee or a percentage of a price paid to a salesperson or agent for services: *The dealer's commission on the $500 sale was $50.* **5.a.** Appointment to the rank of a commissioned officer in the armed forces: *The pilot received a commission in the air force.* **b.** An official document issued by a government conferring such a rank. *—tr.v.* **com•mis•sioned, com•mis•sion•ing, com•mis•sions. 1.** To grant a commission to: *The king commissioned Columbus to find a western route to India. The Coast Guard commissioned new officers at graduation.* **2.** To place an order for: *The duke commissioned a new symphony from the composer.* **3.** To put (a ship) into active service. ***—idioms.*** **in commission. 1.** In active service, as a ship: *Several aircraft carriers are now in commission.* **2.** In use or in usable conditioned: *Only two computers are in commission.* **out of commission. 1.** Not in active service. Used of a ship. **2.** Not in working condition: *Three machines are out of commission and awaiting repair.* [First written down in 1344 in Middle English, from Latin *commissiō*, from *committere*, to entrust.]

com•mis•sioned officer (kə mĭsh′ənd) *n.* An officer who holds by a commission the rank of a second lieutenant or above in the U.S. Army, Air Force, or Marine Corps or the rank of an ensign or above in the U.S. Navy or Coast Guard.

com•mis•sion•er (kə mĭsh′ə nər) *n.* **1.** A member of a commission. **2.** An official in charge of a governmental department: *a police commissioner.* **3.** An official chosen by an athletic association or league as administrative head of an organized professional sport: *a baseball commissioner.*

com•mit (kə mĭt′) *tr.v.* **com•mit•ted, com•mit•ting, com•mits. 1.** To do, perform, or be guilty of: *commit a crime; commit a serious blunder.* **2.** To place in the charge or keeping of another; entrust: *commit oneself to the care of a doctor; commit responsibilities to an assistant.* **3.** To place in confinement or custody, as by an official act: *The judge committed the criminal to prison for two years.* **4.** To give over or entrust, as for future use or preservation: *committed the secret code to memory.* **5.** To bind or obligate, as by a pledge: *The heirs were committed to follow the terms of the will. New citizens commit themselves to obey the laws of the United States.* [First written down about 1390 in

Middle English and spelled *committen*, from Latin *committere* : *com-*, with + *mittere*, to send.] **—com•mit′ta•ble** *adj.*

com•mit•ment (kə mĭt′mənt) *n.* **1.** The act of committing; consignment: *the commitment of poems to memory.* **2.** A pledge or obligation, as to follow a certain course of action: *The President takes an oath that is a binding commitment to uphold the Constitution.* **3.** The state of being emotionally or mentally bound to another person or to a course of action: *We have a deep commitment to help clean up the environment.*

com•mit•tee (kə mĭt′ē) *n.* A group of people chosen to do a particular job or to fulfill specified duties: *A committee of five members will investigate the best ways of using computers to teach mathematics.* [First written down in 1495 in Middle English and spelled *committe*, trustee, from Anglo-Norman *comité*, past participle of *cometre*, to commit, entrust, from Latin *committere.*] —See Note at **collective noun.**

com•mit•tee•man (kə mĭt′ē mən) *n.* A man who is a member of a committee.

com•mit•tee•wom•an (kə mĭt′ē wo͝om′ən) *n.* A woman who is a member of a committee.

com•mode (kə mōd′) *n.* **1.** A low cabinet or chest of drawers. **2.** A movable stand containing a washbowl or a chamber pot.

com•mo•di•ous (kə mō′dē əs) *adj.* Having plenty of room; spacious: *an apartment with commodious closets.* **—com•mo′di•ous•ly** *adv.* **—com•mo′di•ous•ness** *n.*

com•mod•i•ty (kə mŏd′ĭ tē) *n., pl.* **com•mod•i•ties.** An article of trade or commerce, as an agricultural or mining product: *Wheat, oil, and aluminum are commodities of international trade.* [First written down in 1410 in Middle English and spelled *commoditee*, from Latin *commoditās*, convenience, from *commodus*, convenient.]

com•mo•dore (kŏm′ə dôr′) *n.* **1.** An officer in the U.S. Navy ranking above a captain and below a rear admiral. **2.** The presiding officer of a yacht club.

com•mon (kŏm′ən) *adj.* **com•mon•er, com•mon•est. 1.a.** Belonging to or shared equally by two or more: *common interests of the United States and Canada.* **b.** Of or relating to the community as a whole; public: *health regulations enforced for the common good.* **2.** Found or occurring often and in many places; widespread: *Gas stations became common as the use of cars grew.* **3.** Most widely known of its kind; ordinary: *the common field mouse.* **4.** Of no special quality; not costly or rare: *Common sneakers cost less than running shoes.* **5.** Unrefined or coarse in manner; vulgar: *thought her behavior was common.* —*n.* **1.** A tract of land belonging to or used by a community as a whole: *The early New England town had a common for citizens to graze their sheep.* **2. commons.** The common people. **3. commons.** *(used with a singular or plural verb).* A place for dining, especially at a college or university. **4. Commons.** *(used with a singular or plural verb).* The House of Commons. ***—idiom.*** **in common.** Equally with another or others; jointly: *The partners have interests in common.* [First written down before 1300 in Middle English and spelled *commune*, from Latin *commūnis.*] **—com′mon•ly** *adv.* **—com′mon•ness** *n.*

common cold *n.* A viral infection marked by discharge of mucus, sneezing, and watering of the eyes; a cold.

common denominator *n.* A number that is a multiple of the denominators of a group of fractions. For example, since $1/4 = 25/100$, $1/25 = 4/100$, $3/10 = 30/100$, and $4/5 = 80/100$, the fractions $1/4$, $1/25$, $3/10$, and $4/5$ can be expressed with the common denominator 100. By finding a common denominator it is possible to add and subtract fractions.

common divisor *n.* A common factor.

com•mon•er (kŏm′ə nər) *n.* A person without noble rank or title.

common factor *n.* A number that will divide each of a group of numbers without a remainder. For example, 3 is a common factor of 6, 9, 15, and 24.

common fraction *n.* A fraction whose numerator and denominator are both whole numbers. For example, $1/4$, $4/5$, and $7/8$ are common fractions.

common law *n.* The system of law based on court decisions and on customs and usages rather than on an organized body of written laws or statutes.

common logarithm *n.* A logarithm for which the number ten is used as the base.

Common Market. Officially **Eu•ro•pe•an Economic Community** (yo͝or′ə pē′ən). An economic union established in 1958 among the countries of western Europe. The original members—Belgium, Luxembourg, the Netherlands, France, Italy, and West Germany—were later joined by Ireland, Great Britain, Denmark, Greece, Spain, and Portugal.

common multiple *n.* A number divisable by two or more numbers without a remainder. For example, 12 is a common multiple of 2, 3, 4, and 6.

common noun *n.* A noun that is the name of a class or group of things or people. Common nouns refer to one or all members, as *teacher, car*, and *crowd* and are different from proper nouns that name a specific person, place, or thing, as *Iowa, Mozart*, and *Brooklyn Bridge.* —See Note at **noun.**

com•mon•place (kŏm′ən plās′) *adj.* Ordinary; common; uninteresting: *a commonplace plot of good guys against bad guys.* —*n.* A statement or remark that is dull or worn out through use.

common sense *n.* Good judgment gained from everyday experience.

common time *n.* In music, a meter in which each measure contains four quarter notes.

com•mon•weal (kŏm′ən wēl′) *n.* **1.** The public good or welfare. **2.** *Archaic.* A commonwealth.

com•mon•wealth (kŏm′ən wĕlth′) *n.* **1.** The people of a nation or state: *It is the duty of the commonwealth to defend the nation.* **2.** A nation or state governed by the people; a republic: *Canada and the United States are the two commonwealths of North America.* **3. Commonwealth. a.** The official title of some U.S. states, specifically Kentucky, Maryland, Massachusetts, Pennsylvania, and Virginia. **b.** The official title of Puerto Rico. **c.** The official title of some democratic countries, such as Australia. **4. Commonwealth.** The Commonwealth of Nations.

Commonwealth of Independent States. A federation of self-governing states in eastern Europe, Asia Minor, and central Asia including most of the republics of the former Soviet Union.

Commonwealth of Nations also **British Commonwealth.** An association made up of the United Kingdom, its dependencies, and many former British colonies.

com•mo•tion (kə mō′shən) *n.* **1.** A disturbance or tumult: *The argument created a commotion in the hall.* **2.** A condition of turbulent motion: *commotion of the water behind the propeller.*

com•mu•nal (kə myo͞o′nəl *or* kŏm′yə nəl) *adj.* **1.** Of or relating to a commune or a community: *the communal treasury.* **2.** Belonging to or serving the people of a community; public: *the communal dining room of a dormitory.* **—com•mu′nal•ly** *adv.*

com•mune[1] (kə myo͞on′) *intr.v.* **com•muned, com•mun•ing, com•munes. 1.** To feel a sense of closeness or intimacy: *a hiker communing with nature.*

ă	pat	oi	boy
ā	pay	ou	out
âr	care	o͝o	took
ä	father	o͞o	boot
ĕ	pet	ŭ	cut
ē	be	ûr	urge
ĭ	pit	th	thin
ī	pie	*th*	this
îr	pier	hw	whoop
ŏ	pot	zh	vision
ō	toe	ə	about
ô	paw	N	*French* bon

2. To receive the bread and wine of the Eucharist. [First written down about 1303 in Middle English and spelled *comonen*, from Old French *communier*, to communicate, and *communer*, to share.]

com•mune² (kŏm′yo͞on′ *or* kə **myo͞on′**) *n.* **1.** In some European countries, such as France and Italy, the smallest division of local government. **2.** A small community whose members have common interests and in which property is often shared or owned jointly. [First written down in 1792 in Modern English, from French, from Medieval Latin *commūnia*, community.]

com•mu•ni•ca•ble (kə **myo͞o′**nĭ kə bəl) *adj.* Capable of being communicated or transmitted from person to person: *Chicken pox and measles are communicable diseases.* **—com•mu′ni•ca•ble•ness** *n.* **—com•mu′ni•ca•bly** *adv.*

com•mu•ni•cant (kə **myo͞o′**nĭ kənt) *n.* **1.** A person who receives or is entitled to receive the Eucharist. **2.** A person who communicates something.

com•mu•ni•cate (kə **myo͞o′**nĭ kāt′) *v.* **com•mu•ni•cat•ed, com•mu•ni•cat•ing, com•mu•ni•cates.** *—tr.* **1.** To make known; impart: *A good speaker communicates thoughts and ideas clearly.* **2.** To transmit (a disease, for example); pass on. *—intr.* **1.** To have an exchange, as of ideas or information: *The telephone makes it possible to communicate over long distances.* **2.** To be connected: *a hallway that communicates with each bedroom.* [First written down in 1526 in Modern English, from Latin *commūnicāre*, from *commūnis*, common.] **—com•mu′ni•ca′tor** *n.*

com•mu•ni•ca•tion (kə myo͞o′nĭ **kā′**shən) *n.* **1.** The act of communicating; transmission: *Unsanitary conditions contribute to the communication of disease.* **2.** The exchange of thoughts, information, or messages, as by speech, signals, or writing: *Communication between people of different cultures is often difficult.* **3.** Something communicated; a message. **4. communications.** A system for sending and receiving messages, as by mail, telephone, or radio: *During the earthquake communications broke down with other towns.*

com•mu•ni•ca•tions satellite (kə myo͞o′nĭ **kā′**shənz) *n.* An artificial space satellite used to aid communications, as by reflecting or relaying a television or radio signal from one ground station to another.

com•mu•ni•ca•tive (kə **myo͞o′**nĭ kā′tĭv *or* kə**myo͞o′**nĭ kə tĭv) *adj.* Communicating thoughts or information readily; not secretive: *The frightened child was not very communicative.* **—com•mu′ni•ca′tive•ly** *adv.* **—com•mu′ni•ca′tive•ness** *n.*

com•mun•ion (kə **myo͞on′**yən) *n.* **1.** The act or an instance of sharing, as of thoughts, feelings, or interests: *a communion of purpose among the allied nations.* **2.** A body of Christians with the same religious faith; a denomination. **3. Communion. a.** The Christian sacrament of the Eucharist received by a congregation. **b.** The part of the Mass in which the Eucharist is received.

com•mu•ni•qué (kə myo͞o′nĭ **kā′** *or* kə **myo͞o′**nĭ kā′) *n.* An official announcement, such as one issued to the press after a meeting of world leaders.

com•mu•nism (**kŏm′**yə nĭz′əm) *n.* **1.** A theoretical economic system based on the writings of Karl Marx and Friedrich Engels and characterized by common ownership of property and by the organization of labor for the benefit of all of society. **2. Communism. a.** A system of government in which the state plans and controls the economy and a single party holds power, claiming to make progress toward a society in which all goods are shared equally by the people. **b.** The version of Communist theory advanced by Lenin that advocates the violent overthrow of capitalism by the proletariat.

Com•mu•nist (**kŏm′**yə nĭst) *n.* **1.** A member of a Communist Party. **2.** Often **communist.** A person who believes in or advocates communism. *—adj.* **1.** Of or relating to a Communist Party or its membership. **2.** Often **communist.** Relating to, characteristic of, or resembling communism or Communists.

com•mu•nis•tic (kŏm′yə **nĭs′**tĭk) *adj.* Based on or favoring the principles of communism. **—com′mu•nis′ti•cal•ly** *adv.*

com•mu•ni•ty (kə **myo͞o′**nĭ tē) *n., pl.* **com•mu•ni•ties. 1.a.** A group of people living in the same locality and under the same government: *The community decided to have a Fourth of July celebration.* **b.** The district or locality in which such a group lives: *a small community of only a few square miles.* **2.** A group of people who have close ties, as through common nationality or interests: *the American community in Rome.* **3.** Similarity or identity; closeness: *A community of interests united parents to work for a new playground.* **4.** Society as a whole; the public. **5.** A group of plants and animals living and interacting with one another in a specific environmental region. [First written down in 1375 in Middle English and spelled *comminite*, from Latin *commūnitās*, fellowship, from *commūnis*, common.]

community chest *n.* A fund raised by contributions from residents and businesses of an area and used for charity.

community college *n.* A junior college established to serve a certain community and often funded by the government.

com•mu•ta•tion (kŏm′yə **tā′**shən) *n.* **1.** The act of lessening or making something less severe, as a prison sentence: *a commutation of a jail sentence to community service.* **2.** The travel of a commuter, especially to and from work.

com•mu•ta•tive (**kŏm′**yə tā′tĭv *or* kə **myo͞o′**tə tĭv) *adj.* Of or relating to the property of addition and multiplication which states that the order in which numbers are added or multiplied will not change the result of the operation. For example, 2 + 3 gives the same sum as 3 + 2, and 2 × 3 gives the same product as 3 × 2.

com•mu•ta•tor (**kŏm′**yə tā′tər) *n.* A switching device in electric motors and generators that causes a current to reverse direction.

com•mute (kə **myo͞ot′**) *v.* **com•mut•ed, com•mut•ing, com•mutes.** *—intr.* To travel as a commuter. *—tr.* To reduce (a legal sentence) to a less severe one: *commute a sentence of imprisonment to home confinement.* *—n.* A trip made by a commuter: *a commute of 15 miles to work.* [First written down about 1450 in Middle English and spelled *commuten*, to transform, from Latin *commūtāre*.]

com•mut•er (kə **myo͞o′**tər) *n.* A person who travels regularly between a home in one community and work or an educational institution in another.

Com•o•ros (**kŏm′**ə rōz′). A country made up of the three main islands and numerous islets of the **Comoro Islands** in the Indian Ocean off southeast Africa between Mozambique and Madagascar. Moroni, on Grande Comoro Island, is the capital. Population, 346,992.

com•pact¹ (kəm **păkt′** *or* **kŏm′**păkt′) *adj.* **1.** Closely and firmly united or packed together; solid; dense: *flowers growing in tight compact clusters.* **2.** Occupying little space in comparison with others of the same kind: *a compact camera.* **3.** Brief and to the point; concise: *a compact weekly news summary.* *—tr.v.* (kəm **păkt′**). **com•pact•ed, com•pact•ing, com•pacts.** To press or join firmly together;

pack together: *The dirt was compacted by the heavy trucks running over it.* —*n.* (**kŏm′**păkt′). **1.** A small case containing face powder and sometimes blush. **2.** An automobile that is smaller than a standard model. [First written down before 1398 in Middle English, from Latin *compāctus*, past participle of *compingere*, to put together : *com-*, together + *pangere*, to fasten.] **—com•pact′ly** *adv.* **—com•pact′ness** *n.*

com•pact[2] (**kŏm′**păkt′) *n.* An agreement or a covenant: *a compact between nations to reduce tariffs.* [First written down in 1591 in Modern English, from Latin *compactum*, past participle of *compacīscī*, to make an agreement : *com-*, together + *pacīscī*, to agree.]

com•pact disk (**kŏm′**păkt′) or **compact disc** *n.* A small optical disk containing data or music in digital form.

com•pac•tor or **com•pact•er** (kəm **păk′**tər *or* **kŏm′**păk′tər) *n.* A machine that compresses trash into small packs for easy disposal.

com•pan•ion (kəm **păn′**yən) *n.* **1.** A person who accompanies or associates with another; a comrade. **2.** A person hired to assist, live with, or travel with another: *working as a companion to an elderly couple.* **3.** One of a pair or set of things; a mate: *I lost the companion to this sneaker.* [First written down before 1300 in Middle English and spelled *companioun*, from Old French *compaignon* : Latin *com-*, together + Latin *pānis*, bread.]

com•pan•ion•a•ble (kəm **păn′**yə nə bəl) *adj.* Suited to be a good companion; friendly: *Most dogs are companionable pets.* **—com•pan′ion•a•bil′i•ty** *n.* **—com•pan′ion•a•bly** *adv.*

com•pan•ion•ship (kəm **păn′**yən shĭp′) *n.* The relationship of companions; fellowship.

com•pan•ion•way (kəm **păn′**yən wā′) *n.* A staircase leading from a ship's deck to the area below.

com•pa•ny (**kŭm′**pə nē) *n., pl.* **com•pa•nies. 1.** A group of people; a gathering: *A great company of admirers crowded around the baseball player.* **2.** A guest or guests: *have company for dinner.* **3.a.** A companion or companions: *I find them very interesting company.* **b.** Companionship: *She went shopping with him, and he was grateful for the company.* **4.** A business enterprise; a firm: *That company makes many useful products.* **5.** A group of performers organized to present stage works, such as plays, operas, and ballets, or to produce motion pictures. **6.** A military unit consisting of two or more platoons. **7.** The officers and crew of a ship: *The ship's company went ashore.* **8.** A unit of firefighters. [First written down about 1150 in Middle English and spelled *companie*, from Old French *compaignie*.] —See Note at **collective noun.**

com•pa•ra•ble (**kŏm′**pər ə bəl) *adj.* **1.** Capable of being compared: *Buying a house is comparable to investing in a business.* **2.** Worthy of being compared; similar: *Some photographs are comparable to fine paintings.* **—com′pa•ra•bly** *adv.*

com•par•a•tive (kəm **păr′**ə tĭv) *adj.* **1.** Relating to, based on, or involving a comparison: *the comparative study of related languages.* **2.** Estimated by comparison; measured in relation to something else; relative: *He is a comparative beginner in computer skills.* **3.** In grammar, indicating an increase in quality, quantity, or some other relation expressed by an adjective or adverb: Bigger *is the comparative form of* big. —*n.* **1.** In grammar, the comparative degree of an adjective or adverb. **2.** An adjective or adverb expressing the comparative degree. **—com•par′a•tive•ly** *adv.*

com•pare (kəm **pâr′**) *v.* **com•pared, com•par•ing, com•pares.** —*tr.* **1.** To represent as similar; liken: *Shakespeare compared the world to a stage.* **2.** To examine so as to note the similarities and differences of: *Let's compare cooking over heat with cooking in a microwave oven.* **3.** In grammar, to form the positive, comparative, or superlative of (an adjective or adverb): *Some adjectives, such as* disastrous, *cannot be compared.* —*intr.* To be worthy of comparison: *His photographs do not compare with yours.* —*n.* Comparison: *Her singing ability is beyond compare.* [First written down in 1375 in Middle English and spelled *comparen*, from Latin *comparāre*, from *compār*, equal : *com-*, with + *pār*, equal.]

com•par•i•son (kəm **păr′**ĭ sən) *n.* **1.** The act of comparing: *My comparison of prices shows that you will save money if you shop downtown.* **2.** The quality of being similar; likeness: *There is no comparison between homemade bread and bread bought in a store.* **3.** In grammar, the changing of the form of the adjective or adverb to indicate the positive, comparative, and superlative degrees.

com•part•ment (kəm **pärt′**mənt) *n.* **1.** One of the parts or spaces into which something is subdivided: *My purse is divided into compartments for dollar bills and coins.* **2.** A separate room, section, or chamber: *a storage compartment.*

com•pass (**kŭm′**pəs *or* **kŏm′**pəs) *n.* **1.a.** A device used to determine geographical direction, usually consisting of a magnetic needle mounted so that it points to magnetic north. **b.** Any of several other devices, especially a gyrocompass or a radio compass, used to determine geographical direction. **2.** A device used for drawing circles and arcs and for measuring distances, consisting of two legs hinged together at one end. **3.** Range or scope; extent: *not within the compass of your authority.* **4.** An enclosing line or boundary; circumference: *within the compass of the garden.* —*tr.v.* **com•passed, com•pass•ing, com•pass•es. 1.** To go around; make a circuit of: *The sailboat compassed the island.* **2.** To surround or encircle: *A ring of hills compasses the valley.* **3.** To achieve or accomplish; obtain: *We finally compassed our goal.* **4.** To understand or comprehend: *Scientists tried to compass the implications of the discovery.* [First written down before 1325 in Middle English and spelled *compas*, from Old French, circle, from *compasser*, to measure : Latin *com-*, with + Latin *passus*, step.] —See Note.

com•pas•sion (kəm **păsh′**ən) *n.* The deep awareness of the suffering of another, together with a desire to relieve it. [First written down in 1340 in Middle English and spelled *compassioun*, from Late Latin *compassiō*, from *compatī*, to sympathize : Latin *com-*, with + Latin *patī*, to suffer.]

com•pas•sion•ate (kəm **păsh′**ə nĭt) *adj.* Feeling or showing compassion; sympathetic. **—com•pas′sion•ate•ly** *adv.*

com•pat•i•ble (kəm **păt′**ə bəl) *adj.* **1.** Capable of living or existing together in agreement or harmony: *They are very compatible with their cousins and enjoyed the trip together.* **2.** Capable of working together in the same system: *Is the printer compatible with the computer?* **3.** Capable of mixing or bonding together in a stable manner: *That glue is not compatible with wood.* [First written down in 1459 in Middle English, from Late Latin *compatī*, to sympathize.] **—com•pat′i•bil′i•ty** *n.* **—com•pat′i•bly** *adv.*

com•pa•tri•ot (kəm **pā′**trē ət) *n.* A person from one's own country.

com•pel (kəm **pĕl′**) *tr.v.* **com•pelled, com•pel•ling, com•pels. 1.** To make (a person) do something, as by force, necessity, or powerful influence: *The sudden storm compelled us to go indoors.* **2.** To make necessary; bring about by force; demand: *The*

compact disk

compass
Directional compass

Word History: compass

What is the connection between the **compass** we tell directions with and the *compass* we draw circles with? In the 14th century two of the meanings of the French *compas* and the related Italian *compasso* were "a circle" and a "pair of compasses for measuring or drawing a circle." Middle English already had the word *compass* with those meanings from French, but in English *compass* acquired the new meaning "mariner's compass." The most likely explanation is that the mariner's *compass*, which was round, was carried in a circular compass box, which in Italian is also *compasso*.

ă	**pat**	oi	**boy**
ā	**pay**	ou	**out**
âr	**care**	o͝o	**took**
ä	**father**	o͞o	**boot**
ĕ	**pet**	ŭ	**cut**
ē	**be**	ûr	**urge**
ĭ	**pit**	th	**thin**
ī	**pie**	*th*	**this**
îr	**pier**	hw	**whoop**
ŏ	**pot**	zh	**vision**
ō	**toe**	ə	**about**
ô	**paw**	N	*French* bon

Usage: complement

The word **complement** means "something that completes or brings to perfection": *The flowers were a perfect complement to the beautifully set table.* **Compliment** means "an expression of courtesy or praise": *They gave us a compliment on our beautiful table.*

teacher compelled obedience from the class. [First written down about 1350 in Middle English and spelled *compellen*, from Latin *compellere* : *com-*, together + *pellere*, to drive.]

com•pel•ling (kəm pĕl′ĭng) *adj.* Having a very strong influence or effect; powerful; forceful: *a compelling argument.* **—com•pel′ling•ly** *adv.*

com•pen•di•a (kəm pĕn′dē ə) *n.* Plural of **compendium.**

com•pen•di•ous (kəm pĕn′dē əs) *adj.* Giving facts or information about a subject in brief but complete form: *News broadcasts are supposed to be compendious reviews of the events of the day.*

com•pen•di•um (kəm pĕn′dē əm) *n., pl.* **com•pen•di•ums** or **com•pen•di•a** (kəm pĕn′dē ə). **1.** A short but complete summary of something: *a compendium of the committee's views.* **2.** A collection of various items: *a compendium of English poetry.*

com•pen•sate (kŏm′pən sāt′) *v.* **com•pen•sat•ed, com•pen•sat•ing, com•pen•sates.** *—tr.* To make satisfactory payment to; pay or reimburse: *The store compensates its clerks for extra time worked during the holiday season.* *—intr.* To act as or provide a balancing effect; make up: *We worked extra hard to compensate for the hour lost. In baseball speedy running can compensate for weak hitting.* [First written down in 1646 in Modern English, from Latin *compēnsāre* : *com-*, together + *pēnsāre*, to weigh.] **—com′pen•sa′tor** *n.* **—com•pen′sa•to′ry** (kəm pĕn′sə tôr′ē) *adj.*

com•pen•sa•tion (kŏm′pən sā′shən) *n.* **1.** Something given or received as payment or as a balance for a loss: *The committee investigated whether firefighters should get the same compensation as police officers.* **2.** The act of compensating: *The compensation of workers is handled by the payroll department.*

com•pete (kəm pēt′) *intr.v.* **com•pet•ed, com•pet•ing, com•petes.** To strive against another or others to attain something: *compete in a race; compete for someone's business.* [First written down in 1620 in Modern English, from Late Latin *competere*, to strive together : Latin *com-*, with + Latin *petere*, to seek.]

com•pe•tence (kŏm′pĭ təns) *n.* **1.** The ability to do what is required; adequate skill or knowledge. **2.** A range of ability, skill, or knowledge: *Is this task within his competence?*

com•pe•ten•cy (kŏm′pĭ tən sē) *n., pl.* **com•pe•ten•cies.** Competence.

com•pe•tent (kŏm′pĭ tənt) *adj.* **1.** Able to do something with adequate skill; capable: *a competent worker.* **2.** Legally qualified: *a competent physician registered to give medical treatment.* **—com′pe•tent•ly** *adv.*

com•pe•ti•tion (kŏm′pĭ tĭsh′ən) *n.* **1.** The act of competing, as for a prize; rivalry: *win the race in competition with ten contestants; competition in the jungle between predators for food.* **2.** A test of skill or ability; a contest: *a skating competition.* **3.** A competitor: *Is the competition as good as our team?* **4.** Rivalry between businesses for the same customers.

com•pet•i•tive (kəm pĕt′ĭ tĭv) *adj.* **1.** Of, involving, or decided by competition: *competitive games.* **2.** Liking competition or inclined to compete: *Most athletes are competitive people.* **—com•pet′i•tive•ly** *adv.* **—com•pet′i•tive•ness** *n.*

com•pet•i•tor (kəm pĕt′ĭ tər) *n.* A person, team, business organization, or other group that competes with another or others; an opponent or a rival.

com•pi•la•tion (kŏm′pə lā′shən) *n.* **1.** The act of compiling: *Computers are useful in the compilation of facts and figures.* **2.** Something that has been compiled, such as a collection of written works or a report.

com•pile (kəm pīl′) *tr.v.* **com•piled, com•pil•ing, com•piles. 1.** To put together (facts, information, or other matter from several sources) into a single collection, set, or record. **2.** To write or compose (a book) using material gathered from various sources: *compile a dictionary.* [First written down before 1325 in Middle English and spelled *compilen*, from Old French *compiler*, probably from Latin *compīlāre*, to plunder : *com-*, together + *pīla*, heap (of stone), pillar.] **—com•pil′er** *n.*

com•pla•cence (kəm plā′səns) *n.* Complacency.

com•pla•cen•cy (kəm plā′sən sē) *n.* A feeling of satisfaction with oneself or with what one has done: *The sudden drop in sales shook the business leaders out of their complacency.*

com•pla•cent (kəm plā′sənt) *adj.* Pleased or contented with oneself in an untroubled or uncritical manner; self-satisfied: *the complacent face of one who has won too often.* [First written down in 1660 in Modern English, from Latin *complacēre*, to please.] **—com•pla′cent•ly** *adv.*

❑ *These sound alike:* **complacent, complaisant** (willing).

com•plain (kəm plān′) *intr.v.* **com•plained, com•plain•ing, com•plains. 1.** To express feelings of pain, dissatisfaction, or resentment: *They worked hard all day and never complained.* **2.** To make an accusation about something one considers wrong or troublesome: *complain to the telephone company about a mistake in one's bill.* [First written down about 1370 in Middle English and spelled *complainen*, from Old French *complaindre.*]

com•plain•ant (kəm plā′nənt) *n.* A person who makes a formal complaint, as in a court of law.

com•plaint (kəm plānt′) *n.* **1.** An expression of pain, dissatisfaction, or resentment: *We should take his complaint about their carelessness seriously.* **2.** A cause or reason for complaining; a grievance: *The tenants sent a list of their complaints to the landlord.* **3.** A formal charge of the commission of a crime: *The storekeeper signed a complaint accusing the suspect of robbery.* **4.** Something, such as an illness, that causes pain or discomfort: *Colds are a common winter complaint.*

com•plai•sance (kəm plā′səns *or* kəm plā′zəns) *n.* The desire to comply willingly with the wishes of others.

com•plai•sant (kəm plā′sənt *or* kəm plā′zənt) *adj.* Showing a desire or willingness to please; cheerfully obliging: *offering to help with a complaisant tone of voice.* **—com•plai′sant•ly** *adv.*

❑ *These sound alike:* **complaisant, complacent** (self-satisfied).

com•ple•ment (kŏm′plə mənt) *n.* **1.** Something that completes, makes up a whole, or brings to perfection: *Attractive shrubs are a complement to a fine building.* **2.** The number or amount needed to make something complete: *library shelves with a full complement of books.* **3.** In grammar, a word or group of words that follows a transitive or linking verb and completes a predicate. For example, *worm* in *The robin ate the worm,* and *cold* in *The water feels cold* are complements. **4.** An angle related to another so that their sum is 90°. If an angle measures 30°, its complement is 60°. **5.** Either of two complementary colors. *—tr.v.* (kŏm′plə mĕnt′). **com•ple•ment•ed, com•ple•ment•ing, com•ple•ments.** To make complete; be a complement to: *That easy chair complements the furnishings of the room.* [First written down before 1398 in Middle

English, from Latin *complēmentum*, from *complēre*, to fill out.] —SEE NOTE.

❑ *These sound alike:* **complement, compliment** (praise).

com•ple•men•ta•ry (kŏm′plə **mĕn′**tə rē *or* kŏm′plə **mĕn′**trē) *adj.* Serving as a complement; supplying what is lacking or needed: *place settings and a complementary vase of flowers.*

❑ *These sound alike:* **complementary, complimentary** (praising).

complementary angles *pl.n.* Two angles whose sum is 90 degrees.

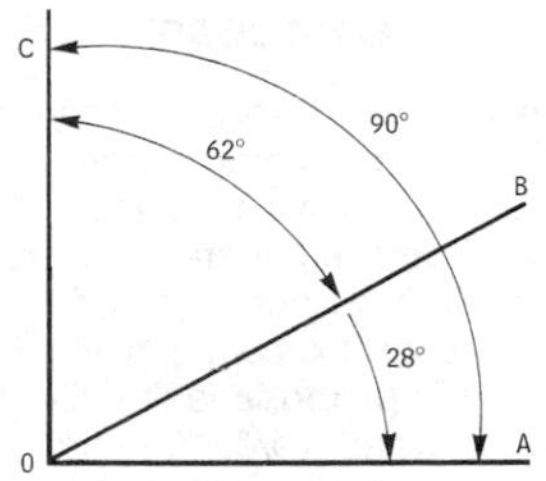

complementary angles

complementary color *n.* One of two colors, such as red and green, that form white or gray when mixed in the proper proportions.

com•plete (kəm **plēt′**) *adj.* **com•plet•er, com•plet•est. 1.** Having all necessary or normal parts; entire: *a complete encyclopedia.* **2.** Having come to an end; finished: *A job is complete when all the tools are put away.* **3.** Absolute; total: *a kitchen in a complete mess after a meal.* —*tr.v.* **com•plet•ed, com•plet•ing, com•pletes. 1.** To add what is missing; make whole: *complete one's education.* **2.** To bring to an end; finish: *The farmers completed the spring planting.* [First written down about 1384 in Middle English, from Latin *complētus*, past participle of *complēre*, to fill out.] —**com•plete′ly** *adv* —**com•plete′ness** *n.*

Synonyms: complete, close, end, conclude. These verbs mean to bring to a stopping point. **Complete** means to bring something to fulfillment: *The students will complete their science projects next week.* **Close** means to complete something that has been going on for some time: *The orchestra closed the concert with an encore.* **End** emphasizes a definite conclusion: *All of those television shows end the season with cliffhangers.* **Conclude** can mean to complete or close in a formal way: *The United Nations concluded the conference yesterday.*

com•ple•tion (kəm **plē′**shən) *n.* The act of completing something or the state of being completed: *Completion of the building took only three weeks.*

com•plex (kəm **plĕks′** *or* **kŏm′**plĕks′) *adj.* Consisting of many connected or interrelated parts or factors; intricate: *the complex wiring of a computer.* —*n.* (**kŏm′**plĕks′). **1.** A system or unit consisting of a large number of parts that are related in a complicated way: *a complex of businesses.* **2.** A group of related ideas, wishes, or emotions that influence a person's behavior and personality, often without the person being aware of them. [First written down before 1652 in Modern English, from Latin *complexus*, past participle of *complectī*, to entwine.] —**com•plex′ly** *adv.*

complex fraction *n.* A fraction having a fraction in the numerator, denominator, or both.

com•plex•ion (kəm **plĕk′**shən) *n.* **1.** The color, texture, and appearance of the skin, especially of the face: *The skier had a ruddy complexion from being outside.* **2.** General character, aspect, or nature: *The whole complexion of the situation brightened with the good news.*

com•plex•i•ty (kəm **plĕk′**sĭ tē) *n., pl.* **com•plex•i•ties. 1.** The condition of being complex: *the complexity of modern civilization.* **2.** Something complex: *the complexities of the immune system.*

complex number *n.* A number that can be expressed as $a + bi$, where a and b are real numbers and i is an imaginary number whose square equals -1.

complex sentence *n.* A sentence containing an independent clause and one or more dependent clauses. For example, *When the rain ends, we will go home* is a complex sentence.

com•pli•ance (kəm **plī′**əns) *n.* **1.** The act of complying: *Compliance with a country's laws is expected of all citizens.* **2.** A tendency to yield to others.

com•pli•an•cy (kəm **plī′**ən sē) *n.* Compliance.

com•pli•ant (kəm **plī′**ənt) *adj.* Inclined or willing to yield to the wishes or requests of others. —**com•pli′ant•ly** *adv.*

com•pli•cate (**kŏm′**plĭ kāt′) *tr.v.* **com•pli•cat•ed, com•pli•cat•ing, com•pli•cates.** To make more complex or confusing: *The new information only complicates a serious problem.* [First written down before 1425 in Middle English, from Latin *complicāre*, to fold together.]

com•pli•cat•ed (**kŏm′**plĭ kā′tĭd) *adj.* **1.** Containing intricately combined or involved parts: *a complicated computer program.* **2.** Not easy to understand or solve; perplexing: *a long complicated explanation.*

com•pli•ca•tion (kŏm′plĭ **kā′**shən) *n.* **1.** Something that complicates: *Your suggestions just add complications to an already difficult situation.* **2.** An intricate or confused state or condition: *The executive tried to simplify the complications of their methods for doing business.* **3.** The act of complicating.

com•plic•i•ty (kəm **plĭs′**ĭ tē) *n., pl.* **com•plic•i•ties.** Involvement as an accomplice in a crime or wrongdoing: *Complicity in the scheme cost the accountants their reputation.*

com•pli•ment (**kŏm′**plə mənt) *n.* **1.** An expression of praise, admiration, or congratulation: *The author received many compliments on the new book.* **2.** An act showing honor or courtesy: *The neighbors paid us the compliment of an invitation to dinner.* **3. compliments.** Good wishes; regards: *Please extend my compliments to your parents.* —*tr.v.* **com•pli•ment•ed, com•pli•ment•ing, com•pli•ments.** To pay a compliment to: *The critic complimented both artists on their work.* [First written down in 1578 in Modern English and spelled *complement*, from French, from Spanish *cumplimiento*, from Latin *complēre*, to fill up.] —SEE NOTE at **complement.**

❑ *These sound alike:* **compliment, complement** (something that completes).

com•pli•men•ta•ry (kŏm′plə **mĕn′**tə rē *or* kŏm′plə **mĕn′**trē) *adj.* **1.** Expressing, using, or resembling a compliment: *The reviewer was not very complimentary about the movie.* **2.** Given free: *a complimentary copy of a new book.*

❑ *These sound alike:* **complimentary, complementary** (completing).

com•ply (kəm **plī′**) *intr.v.* **com•plied, com•ply•ing, com•plies.** To act in accordance with a request, rule, or order: *The singer complied by giving several encores. Sick people should comply with their doctor's orders.* [First written down before 1333 in Middle English and spelled *complien*, to fulfill, from Latin *complēre*, to complete.]

com•po•nent (kəm **pō′**nənt) *n.* One of the parts that make up a whole: *Components such as batteries and resistors make up an electric circuit.* —*adj.* Being or functioning as a part or an ingredient: *The loudspeakers and amplifiers are component parts of our stereo system.* [First written down in 1563 in Modern English, from Latin *compōnere*, to put together : *com-*, together + *pōnere*, to put.]

com•port (kəm **pôrt′**) *v.* **com•port•ed, com•port•ing, com•ports.** —*tr.* To conduct or behave (oneself) in a certain way: *The students comported themselves very well in the teacher's absence.* —*intr.* To agree, correspond, or suit: *actions that comport with the dignity of a judge.*

com•port•ment (kəm **pôrt′**mənt) *n.* Behavior; conduct; manner: *the solemn comportment of the orchestra's conductor.*

ă	pat	oi	boy
ā	pay	ou	out
âr	care	o͝o	took
ä	father	o͞o	boot
ĕ	pet	ŭ	cut
ē	be	ûr	urge
ĭ	pit	th	thin
ī	pie	*th*	this
îr	pier	hw	whoop
ŏ	pot	zh	vision
ō	toe	ə	about
ô	paw	N	*French* bon

Word Building: compose

The word root *-pose-* in English comes from the French verb *poser,* "to put." **Compose** therefore literally means "to put together" (using the prefix *com-,* "with, together"); **propose** is literally "to put forward" (*prō,* "forward, in front"); **expose** means "to put out" (*ex-,* "out, out of"); **impose** is literally "to put upon" (*im-,* a form of *in-²,* "in, on"). French developed from Latin, and the French verb *poser* is a replacement of an earlier Latin verb *ponere.* The past participle of *ponere* is *positus,* from which is formed the Latin noun *positiō,* "position." It is from this Latin noun that we form the English noun forms that correspond to the verbs, that is, **composition**, **proposition**, **exposition**, **imposition**.

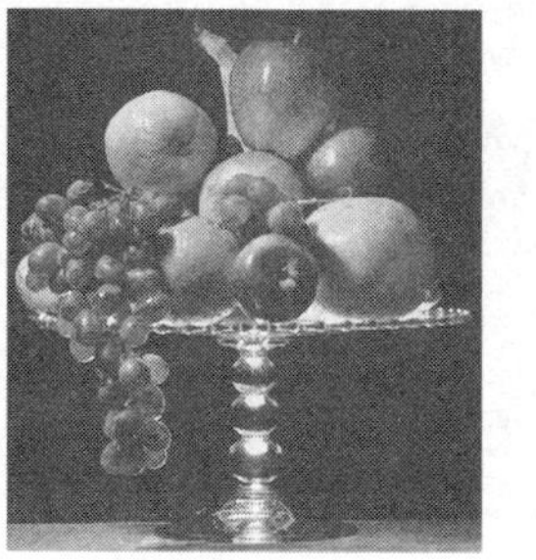

compote

ă	pat	oi	boy
ā	pay	ou	out
âr	care	o͝o	took
ä	father	o͞o	boot
ĕ	pet	ŭ	cut
ē	be	ûr	urge
ĭ	pit	th	thin
ī	pie	*th*	this
îr	pier	hw	whoop
ŏ	pot	zh	vision
ō	toe	ə	about
ô	paw	N	*French* bon

com•pose (kəm **pōz′**) *v.* **com•posed, com•pos•ing, com•pos•es.** *—tr.* **1.** To make up the parts of; form: *The heart, veins, arteries, and capillaries compose the circulatory system.* **2.** To make or create by putting parts or elements together: *She composed the speech from entries in her journal.* **3.** To create (a musical or literary work): *compose a symphony.* **4.** To make calm, controlled, or orderly: *compose oneself before making a speech.* **5.** To settle or adjust: *The two nations composed their differences and agreed to share the fishing grounds.* **6.** To arrange or set (type or matter to be printed): *compose type; compose a page.* *—intr.* To create literary or musical pieces: *Chopin composed mostly for the piano.* [First written down before 1402 in Middle English and spelled *compousen,* from Old French *composer,* from Latin *compōnere,* to put together.] —SEE NOTE.

com•posed (kəm **pōzd′**) *adj.* Being in control of one's emotions; calm; serene. **—com•pos′ed•ly** (kəm **pō′**zĭd lē) *adv.*

com•pos•er (kəm **pō′**zər) *n.* A person who composes, especially a creator of musical works.

com•pos•ite (kəm **pŏz′**ĭt) *adj.* **1.** Made up of distinctly different parts: *The photograph was a composite picture of several snapshots of family members.* **2.** Of or belonging to a plant family having flower heads made up of many small densely clustered flowers that give the impression of a single bloom. *—n.* **1.** Something made by combining different parts: *An almanac is a composite of many facts and tables from different sources.* **2.** A composite plant, such as the daisy or dandelion.

composite number *n.* A whole number divisible without a remainder by at least one whole number other than itself and 1.

com•po•si•tion (kŏm′pə **zĭsh′**ən) *n.* **1.** The act or process of putting together parts or elements to form a whole: *The composition of a symphony can take months.* **2.** A work created by such a process, as a musical work or a short essay: *My composition was six pages long.* **3.** The parts or constituents forming a whole; make-up: *the chemical composition of a mineral.* **4.** The arrangement of parts or elements forming a whole, as in an artistic work: *the orderly and colorful composition of a painting.* **5.** A mixture of substances: *Concrete is a composition of gravel and cement.* **6.** The setting of type for printing.

com•pos•i•tor (kəm **pŏz′**ĭ tər) *n.* A person who arranges or sets type for printing; a typesetter.

com•post (**kŏm′**pōst′) *n.* A mixture of decaying organic matter, such as leaves or manure, used to enrich the soil.

com•po•sure (kəm **pō′**zhər) *n.* Control over one's emotions; calmness: *Don't lose your composure over a mistake.*

com•pote (**kŏm′**pōt) *n.* **1.** Sweetened stewed fruit, served as a dessert. **2.** A long-stemmed dish for holding fruit, candy, or nuts.

com•pound¹ (kəm **pound′** *or* **kŏm′**pound′) *tr.v.* **com•pound•ed, com•pound•ing, com•pounds. 1.** To put together to form a whole; combine: *compound ingredients to make paint.* **2.** To produce or create by combining parts or ingredients: *The pharmacist compounded the medicine our doctor ordered.* **3.** To compute (interest) on the principal and on the accumulated interest. **4.** To add to; increase: *We compounded our difficulties by refusing to admit we had made a mistake.* *—adj.* (**kŏm′**pound′- *or* kəm **pound′**). Consisting of two or more parts, ingredients, elements, or substances. *—n.* (**kŏm′**-pound′). **1.** Something consisting of a combination of two or more parts or ingredients: *Cough syrup is usually a compound of alcohol, sweet flavoring, and some medicine.* **2.** A word consisting of a combination of two or more other words and forming a single unit with its own meaning. *Loudspeaker, baby-sit,* and *cell division* are compounds. **3.** A substance formed by chemical combination of two or more elements in definite proportions by weight: *Water is a compound of hydrogen and oxygen.* [First written down about 1380 in Middle English and spelled *compounen,* from Latin *compōnere,* to put together.] **—com•pound′a•ble** *adj.* **—com•pound′er** *n.*

com•pound² (**kŏm′**pound′) *n.* A group of houses or other buildings, enclosed by a wall, fence, or other barrier. [First written down in 1679 in Modern English, alteration of Malay *kampong,* village.]

compound eye *n.* An eye, as of an insect or crustacean, consisting of many small light-sensitive parts, each of which forms part of an image.

compound fraction *n.* A complex fraction.

compound fracture *n.* A bone fracture in which a sharp piece of bone cuts through nearby soft tissue and makes an open wound.

compound interest *n.* Interest computed on an amount of money constituting the principal plus all the unpaid interest already earned.

compound leaf *n.* A leaf, as of a clover or sumac, composed of several leaflets attached to a single stalk.

compound sentence *n.* A sentence of two or more independent clauses, usually joined by a conjunction such as *and, but,* or *or.* For example, *The problem was difficult, but I finally found the answer* is a compound sentence.

com•pre•hend (kŏm′prĭ **hĕnd′**) *tr.v.* **com•pre•hend•ed, com•pre•hend•ing, com•pre•hends. 1.** To grasp mentally; understand: *Many people do not comprehend the theory of relativity.* **2.** To take in as a part; include: *The factory comprehends the design, manufacture, and packaging of windows. The metropolitan area of a city comprehends the surrounding suburbs.* [First written down about 1340 in Middle English and spelled *comprehenden,* from Latin *comprehendere* : *com-,* intensive prefix + *prehendere,* to grasp.]

com•pre•hen•si•ble (kŏm′prĭ **hĕn′**sə bəl) *adj.* Readily understood; understandable: *I was able to make the menu comprehensible to our visitor from Japan.* **—com′pre•hen′si•bil′i•ty** *n.* **—com′pre•hen′si•bly** *adv.*

com•pre•hen•sion (kŏm′prĭ **hĕn′**shən) *n.* **1.** The act or fact of understanding: *Comprehension of basic chemistry is not as difficult as you think.* **2.** Knowledge gained by comprehending: *They have no comprehension of Russian.* **3.** The capacity to understand something: *Algebra is well within your comprehension.*

com•pre•hen•sive (kŏm′prĭ **hĕn′**sĭv) *adj.* Including much; broad in scope; thorough: *The last chapter is a comprehensive review of the book's contents.* **—com′pre•hen′sive•ly** *adv.* **—com′pre•hen′sive•ness** *n.*

com•press (kəm **prĕs′**) *tr.v.* **com•pressed, com•press•ing, com•press•es. 1.** To squeeze or press together: *He compressed his lips into a thin line.* **2.** To make more compact by or as if by squeezing or pressing: *Compress one's thoughts into a short statement.* *—n.* (**kŏm′**prĕs′). A soft pad of gauze, cotton, or other material, often moistened or medicated, applied to some part of the body, especially to a wound or injury. [First written down about 1380 in Middle English and spelled *compressen,* from Late Latin *compressāre,* from Latin *comprimere* : *com-,* together + *premere,* to press.]

com•pressed (kəm **prĕst′**) *adj.* Pressed together;

made smaller by pressure: *The tank contains compressed gas.*

compressed air *n.* Air that has been put under pressure greater than the pressure of the atmosphere, as in a storage tank. When released its force is often used to operate a mechanism, such as air brakes.

com•press•i•ble (kəm **prĕs′**ə bəl) *adj.* Capable of being compressed. **—com•press′i•bil′i•ty** *n.*

com•pres•sion (kəm **prĕsh′**ən) *n.* **1.** The act or process of compressing. **2.** The condition of being compressed.

com•pres•sor (kəm **prĕs′**ər) *n.* Something that compresses, especially a machine used to compress a gas, as in a refrigerator.

com•prise (kəm **prīz′**) *tr.v.* **com•prised, com•pris•ing, com•pris•es. 1.** To consist of; be composed of; include: *The United Nations comprises more than 130 countries.* **2.** To make up; form; constitute: *Milk, butter, and cheese comprise the bulk of dairy products.* [First written down about 1425 in Middle English and spelled *comprisen,* to be included, from Old French *compris,* included, past participle of *comprendre,* to include, from Latin *comprehendere.*]

com•pro•mise (**kŏm′**prə mīz′) *n.* **1.** A settlement of differences between opposing sides in which each side gives up some claims and agrees to some demands of the other: *By agreeing to share the cost, our neighbors reached a compromise over rebuilding the fence.* **2.** Something that combines qualities or elements of different things: *The design of the car is a compromise between style and safety.* *—v.* **com•pro•mised, com•pro•mis•ing, com•pro•mis•es.** *—tr.* **1.** To settle or adjust by compromise: *Those who often compromise their principles usually end up with none.* **2.** To expose to dishonor or suspicion: *The scandal will surely compromise his reputation.* *—intr.* To make a compromise: *We compromised and bought some of both kinds of tea.* [First written down in 1426 in Middle English, from Latin *comprōmissum,* mutual promise : *com-,* together + *prōmittere,* to promise.]

comp•trol•ler (kən **trō′**lər) *n.* Variant of **controller** (sense 2).

com•pul•sion (kəm **pŭl′**shən) *n.* **1.** The act of compelling or the state of being compelled. **2.** An irresistable urge or impulse: *a compulsion to stay up late.* [First written down before 1425 in Middle English, from Late Latin *compulsiō,* from Latin *compellere,* to compel.]

com•pul•sive (kəm **pŭl′**sĭv) *adj.* Of, having, or resulting from a strong irresistible impulse: *Some people have a compulsive desire to talk.* **—com•pul′sive•ly** *adv.* **—com•pul′sive•ness** *n.*

com•pul•so•ry (kəm **pŭl′**sə rē) *adj.* **1.** Required by law, regulations, or duty: *Education is compulsory for children in most countries.* **2.** Using or involving compulsion: *compulsory powers of the law.*

com•punc•tion (kəm **pŭngk′**shən) *n.* An uneasy feeling that one has done something wrong; remorse: *The children showed no compunction about eating all the cookies.*

com•pu•ta•tion (kŏm′pyŏŏ **tā′**shən) *n.* The act, process, method, or result of computing; mathematical calculation.

com•pute (kəm **pyōōt′**) *v.* **com•put•ed, com•put•ing, com•putes.** *—tr.* **1.** To work out (a result, an answer, or a solution) by mathematics; calculate: *The bank computes the interest on savings accounts.* **2.** To determine by use of a computer: *compute the most efficient design of a sailboat.* *—intr.* **1.** To determine an amount or a number. **2.** To use a computer. [First written down in 1631 in Modern English, from Latin *computāre* : *com-,* together + *putāre,* to reckon.]

com•put•er (kəm **pyōō′**tər) *n.* A device that computes, especially an electronic device capable of processing information according to a set of instructions stored within the device. —SEE NOTE.

computer graphics *n. (used with a singular or plural verb).* Graphic artwork, such as maps, diagrams, or pictures, produced with a computer.

com•put•er•ize (kəm **pyōō′**tə rīz′) *tr.v.* **com•put•er•ized, com•put•er•iz•ing, com•put•er•iz•es. 1.** To process or store (information) in an electronic computer: *computerize office files.* **2.** To furnish with a computer or a system of computers: *computerize an office.*

computer language *n.* A system of symbols, letters, and punctuation along with a set of rules that is used to tell a computer what to do and how to do it. BASIC and COBOL are examples of computer languages.

computer literacy *n.* The ability to operate a computer and to understand how a computer works.

computer science *n.* The study of the design and operation of computers and their application to science, business, and the arts.

com•rade (**kŏm′**răd′) *n.* **1.** A companion, especially a person who shares one's activities. **2.** Often **Comrade.** A fellow member of a group, especially a fellow member of the Communist Party. [First written down in 1591 in Modern English and spelled *camerade,* roommate, from Old Spanish *camarada,* from *camara,* room, from Late Latin *camera,* chamber.] **—com′rade•ship′** *n.*

con[1] (kŏn) *adv.* In opposition or disagreement; against: *arguing a question pro and con.* *—n.* An argument or a consideration against something: *discussing the pros and cons of the subject.* [First written down in 1572 in Modern English, from Latin *contrā,* against.]

con[2] (kŏn) *tr.v.* **conned, con•ning, cons.** To study or examine carefully, especially to learn or memorize something: *con one's books for an exam.* [First written down about 1425 in Middle English and spelled *connen,* to know, from Old English *cunnan.*]

con[3] (kŏn) *tr.v.* **conned, con•ning, cons.** *Slang.* To trick or coax (someone) into doing something by first winning the person's confidence: *con someone into buying a junky old car.* *—n.* A swindle. [First written down in 1896 in American English, from *confidence.*]

con[4] (kŏn) *n. Slang.* A convict. [First written down in 1893 in Modern English, from *convict.*]

Con•a•kry (**kŏn′**ə krē). The capital and largest city of Guinea, in the southwest part of the country on the Atlantic Ocean. Population, 600,000.

con•cave (kŏn **kāv′** *or* **kŏn′**kāv′) *adj.* Curved inward like the inside of a circle or sphere. *—n.* A concave surface or line. **—con•cave′ly** *adv.* **—con•cave′ness** *n.*

con•cav•i•ty (kŏn **kăv′**ĭ tē) *n., pl.* **con•cav•i•ties. 1.** The condition of being concave: *The concavity of the mirror allows it to focus the rays of the sun into a beam.* **2.** A concave surface or structure.

con•ceal (kən **sēl′**) *tr.v.* **con•cealed, con•ceal•ing, con•ceals. 1.** To keep from being seen; put out of sight: *A bank of clouds concealed the setting sun.* See Synonyms at **hide**[1]. **2.** To keep secret: *conceal hurt feelings.* [First written down before 1325 in Middle English and spelled *concelen,* from Latin *concēlāre* : *com-,* intensive prefix + *cēlāre,* to hide.] **—con•ceal′a•ble** *adj.* **—con•ceal′er** *n.* **—con•ceal′ment** *n.*

con•cede (kən **sēd′**) *v.* **con•ced•ed, con•ced•ing, con•cedes.** *—tr.* **1.** To admit as true or real, often unwillingly or hesitantly; acknowledge: *The losing candidate finally conceded defeat the morning after*

computer

Personal computer with monitor, disk drive, and keyboard

computer

Modern **computers** are essentially collections of extremely fast electronic switches. Each switch can be either off or on. The either/or nature of a switch fits perfectly with the **binary system** of numbers. OFF represents the value 0. ON represents the value 1. All data—words, symbols, sounds, pictures, and numbers—that a computer processes must be encoded as a series of 0's and 1's. The digits 0 and 1 are called **bits**. Each pattern of bits that represents a letter, symbol, or number is called a **byte**. Like decimal numbers, binary numbers can be added, subtracted, multiplied, and divided, so a computer can perform arithmetic operations. The bits can also stand for true (1) and false (0), which allows computers to perform logic operations such as comparing two numbers to see which is larger.

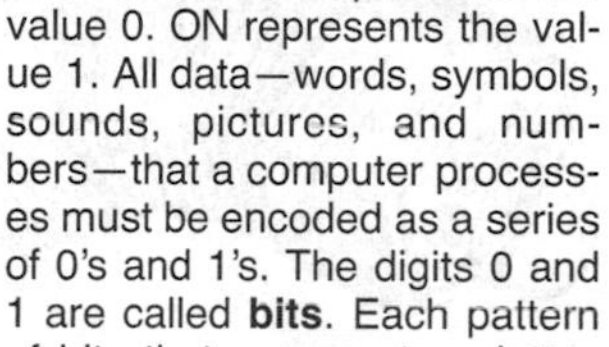

concave

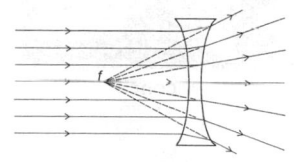

Light passing through a double-concave lens, with f indicating the focus

concertina
Double-action concertina

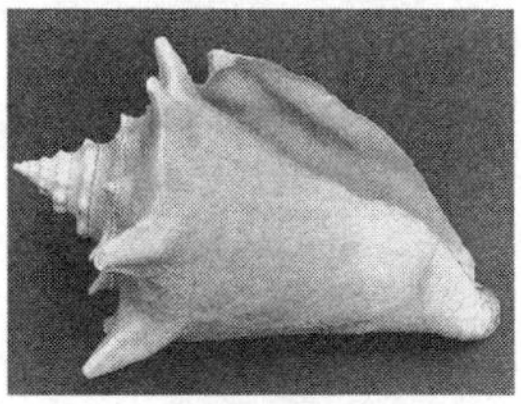

conch

election day. **2.** To give, yield, or grant: *After the uprising, the government conceded the right to vote to its citizens.* —*intr.* To make a concession; yield. [First written down in 1632 in Modern English, from Latin *concēdere.*]

con•ceit (kən sēt′) *n.* **1.** An overly high opinion of one's abilities or worth; vanity: *The famous author's conceit was unpleasant.* **2.** A witty expression or fanciful idea. [First written down about 1380 in Middle English and spelled *conceit*, conception, from Late Latin *conceptus*, concept.]

con•ceit•ed (kən sē′tĭd) *adj.* Holding or showing an overly high opinion of oneself: *a conceited braggart.* —**con•ceit′ed•ly** *adv.* —**con•ceit′ed•ness** *n.*

con•ceiv•a•ble (kən sē′və bəl) *adj.* Capable of being thought of; imaginable: *It is conceivable that life exists on other planets.*

con•ceive (kən sēv′) *v.* **con•ceived, con•ceiv•ing, con•ceives.** —*tr.* **1.** To form or develop in the mind: *James Watt conceived the idea of using steam to drive an engine.* **2.** To imagine or think of; consider: *We could not conceive such a strange place existed.* **3.** To become pregnant with: *conceive a child.* —*intr.* **1.** To have an idea or concept; think: *People in ancient times conceived of the earth as flat.* **2.** To become pregnant. —**con•ceiv′er** *n.*

con•cen•trate (kŏn′sən trāt′) *v.* **con•cen•trat•ed, con•cen•trat•ing, con•cen•trates.** —*intr.* **1.** To keep or direct one's thoughts, attention, or efforts: *It's hard to concentrate on writing a letter with the TV on.* **2.** To come toward or meet in a common center: *The migrating geese concentrate at ponds and streams.* —*tr.* **1.** To draw or gather toward one place or point; focus: *For centuries the population of Europe has been concentrated in large cities.* **2.** To make (a solution or mixture) stronger. —*n.* Something that has been concentrated: *orange juice concentrate.* [First written down in 1640 in Modern English, alteration of *concenter*, to meet in a common center : Latin *com-*, together + Latin *centrum*, center.]

con•cen•tra•tion (kŏn′sən trā′shən) *n.* **1.** The act or process of concentrating, especially the directing of close undivided attention: *The secret of doing your work in less time is complete concentration.* **2.** A close gathering or dense grouping: *Lights shown brightly from the concentration of houses in the new development.* **3.** The amount of a particular substance in a given amount of a solution or mixture: *the concentration of salt in sea water.*

concentration camp *n.* An area or a group of buildings where prisoners of war or political prisoners are confined, usually under harsh conditions.

con•cen•tric (kən sĕn′trĭk) *adj.* Having the same center: *a set of concentric circles.* —**con•cen′tri•cal•ly** *adv.*

con•cept (kŏn′sĕpt′) *n.* A general idea or understanding, especially one based on known facts or observation: *the concept that all matter is made up of atoms.* See Synonyms at **idea.** [First written down in 1556 in Modern English, from Late Latin *conceptus*, from Latin *concipere*, to conceive.]

con•cep•tion (kən sĕp′shən) *n.* **1.** A general idea or understanding; an idea: *The study of astronomy has given us some conception of the age of the universe.* **2.** A beginning or formation of an idea: *a history of the computer from its earliest conception to the most advanced integrated circuits.* **3.** The formation of a cell capable of developing into a new organism; fertilization.

con•cep•tu•al (kən sĕp′cho͞o əl) *adj.* Of, consisting of, or based on a concept or concepts: *The engineers came up with a conceptual proposal for a new electric car.* —**con•cep′tu•al•ly** *adv.*

con•cep•tu•al•ize (kən sĕp′cho͞o ə līz′) *tr. & intr. v.* **con•cep•tu•al•ized, con•cep•tu•al•iz•ing, con•cep•tu•al•iz•es.** To form a general idea or a concept about.

con•cern (kən sûrn′) *tr.v.* **con•cerned, con•cern•ing, con•cerns. 1.** To have to do with; relate to: *The story concerns the struggles of a group of rabbits who establish a new community.* **2.** To be of importance or interest to; involve: *Cleaning up the environment concerns all of us.* **3.** To fill with care or anxiety; worry; trouble: *The lack of rain deeply concerned the farmers.* —*n.* **1.** Something of interest or importance: *The author's chief concern is to write the history of the plastics industry.* **2.** Worry; anxiety: *the parents' concern for their sick child.* **3.** A business establishment; a firm: *Repair shops and banks are concerns that provide services rather than goods.* [First written down before 1420 in Middle English and spelled *concernen*, from Late Latin *concernere*, to mingle together.]

con•cerned (kən sûrnd′) *adj.* **1.** Interested or affected; involved: *Most concerned citizens recycle trash.* **2.** Worried; anxious; troubled: *a concerned expression on his face.*

con•cern•ing (kən sûr′nĭng) *prep.* In reference to; about: *science fiction stories concerning visitors from outer space.*

con•cert (kŏn′sərt) *n.* A musical performance usually given by one or more singers or instrumentalists or both. —***idiom.* in concert.** As a single unit or group; together: *Several nearby towns are working in concert to ease rush-hour traffic.* [First written down in 1665 in Modern English, from Old Italian *concerto*, agreement, harmony, from Latin *concernere*, to mingle together.]

con•cert•ed (kən sûr′tĭd) *adj.* Planned or accomplished together with others; combined: *a concerted fund-raising drive.*

con•cer•ti (kən chĕr′tē) *n.* A plural of **concerto.**

con•cer•ti•na (kŏn′sər tē′nə) *n.* A type of small accordion.

con•cer•to (kən chĕr′tō) *n., pl.* **con•cer•tos** or **con•cer•ti** (kən chĕr′tē). A musical composition written for one or more solo instruments and an orchestra.

con•ces•sion (kən sĕsh′ən) *n.* **1.** An act of yielding or conceding: *settle a dispute by mutual concession of right on both sides.* **2.** Something yielded or conceded: *More time off and other concessions were made by the company to solve the dispute with its workers.* **3.a.** A right to operate a business in a certain place: *The government gave land concessions to the railroads that encouraged their development across the United States.* **b.** A business that has such a right: *We got hot dogs at the food concession in the ball park.*

con•ces•sion•aire (kən sĕsh′ə nâr′) *n.* A person who holds or operates a business concession.

conch (kŏngk *or* kŏnch) *n., pl.* **conchs** (kŏngks) or **conch•es** (kŏn′chĭz). **1.** Any of various tropical sea animals related to the snails, having a large, often brightly colored spiral shell. **2.** The shell of this animal. [First written down in 1391 in Middle English, from Greek *konkhē*, mussel.]

❑ *These sound alike:* **conch, conk** (hit).

con•cil•i•ate (kən sĭl′ē āt′) *tr.v.* **con•cil•i•at•ed, con•cil•i•at•ing, con•cil•i•ates. 1.** To overcome the anger or distrust of; win over: *The baby sitter tried to conciliate the angry child by reading a story.* **2.** To gain (friendship, good will, or favor) by friendly behavior. **3.** To make harmonious; reconcile. [First written down in 1545 in Modern English, from Latin *conciliāre*, from *concilium*, meeting.] —**con•cil′i•a′tion** *n.* —**con•cil′i•a′tor** *n.*

con•cil•i•a•to•ry (kən sĭl′ē ə tôr′ē) *adj.* Intending to conciliate or having the effect of conciliating: *a conciliatory attitude.*

con•cise (kən **sīs′**) *adj.* Expressing much in a few words; brief and clear: *a concise summary of the main points of the meeting.* [First written down about 1590 in Modern English, from Latin *concīsus*, from *concīdere*, to cut up.] **—con•cise′ly** *adv.* **—con•cise′ness** *n.*

con•clave (**kŏn′**klāv′) *n.* A private or secret meeting.

con•clude (kən **klo͞od′**) *v.* **con•clud•ed, con•clud•ing, con•cludes.** *—tr.* **1.** To bring to an end; close; finish: *conclude a religious service with a prayer.* See Synonyms at **complete. 2.** To arrange or settle finally: *conclude an agreement on trade between two countries.* **3.** To form an opinion or judgment about; decide: *The scientist concluded that the bones were those of a dinosaur. —intr.* To come to an end; close: *The conference concluded with a call for action.* [First written down before 1325 in Middle English and spelled *concluden*, from Latin *conclūdere* : *com-*, intensive prefix + *claudere*, to close.] **—con•clud′er** *n.*

con•clu•sion (kən **klo͞o′**zhən) *n.* **1.** The close or last part of something; the end: *the exciting conclusion of a story.* **2.** A judgment or decision reached by reasoning: *Scientists check their observations thoroughly to arrive at accurate conclusions.* **3.** A final arrangement or settlement, as of a treaty. ***—idiom.* in conclusion.** As a last statement; finally.

con•clu•sive (kən **klo͞o′**sĭv) *adj.* Putting an end to doubt, question, or uncertainty; decisive: *The new piece of evidence was conclusive and proved that he was guilty.* **—con•clu′sive•ly** *adv.* **—con•clu′sive•ness** *n.*

con•coct (kən **kŏkt′**) *tr.v.* **con•coct•ed, con•coct•ing, con•cocts. 1.** To make by mixing or combining ingredients or parts: *concoct a stew from leftover meat and vegetables.* **2.** To make up; invent: *concoct an excuse to avoid going.* [First written down in 1533 in Modern English, from Latin *concoquere*, to boil together : *com-*, together + *coquere*, to cook.]

con•coc•tion (kən **kŏk′**shən) *n.* **1.** Something concocted, especially a mixture of ingredients: *She made a concoction of orange juice and soda.* **2.** The act or process of concocting something.

con•com•i•tant (kən **kŏm′**ĭ tənt) *adj.* Happening or existing along with something else; accompanying: *A fever and rash are concomitant symptoms of chicken pox. —n.* Something that happens or is found along with something else: *Poor health is often a concomitant of unsanitary living conditions.* **—con•com′i•tant•ly** *adv.*

con•cord (**kŏn′**kôrd′ *or* **kŏng′**kôrd′) *n.* **1.** A friendly or harmonious relationship: *The neighboring nations lived in peace and concord.* **2.** An agreement establishing such a relationship. [First written down before 1325 in Middle English, from Latin *concordia*, from *concors*, agreeing : *com-*, together + *cor*, heart.]

Con•cord (**kŏng′**kərd). **1.** A town of eastern Massachusetts on the **Concord River** west-northwest of Boston. An early battle of the Revolutionary War was fought here on April 19, 1775. Population, 17,076. **2.** The capital of New Hampshire, in the south-central part of the state. It became the capital in 1808. Population, 36,006.

con•cor•dance (kən **kôr′**dns) *n.* **1.** A state of agreement or harmony; concord. **2.** An alphabetical index of the words in a written work or collection of works, showing where they occur: *a concordance to the Bible.*

con•course (**kŏn′**kôrs′) *n.* **1.** A large open space in which crowds gather or pass through, as in an airport or a railroad station. **2.** A wide road or avenue. **3.** A large crowd. **4.** The act of coming, moving, or flowing together: *Pittsburg lies at the concourse of two rivers.*

con•crete (kŏn **krēt′** *or* **kŏn′**krēt′) *adj.* **1.** Made of concrete: *a concrete sidewalk.* **2.** Existing in reality as something that can be perceived by the senses: *concrete objects such as trees or rocks.* **3.** Of or relating to a material thing rather than an abstraction: *describing a scene in familiar concrete terms. —n.* (**kŏn′**krēt′ *or* kŏn **krēt′**). A building or paving material made of sand and pebbles or crushed stone, held together by cement. [First written down before 1398 in Middle English and spelled *concrete*, solid, real, from Latin *concrētus*, past participle of *concrēscere*, to grow together, harden : *com-*, together + *crēscere*, to grow.] **—con•crete′ly** *adv.* **—con•crete′ness** *n.* —See Note.

con•cu•bine (**kŏng′**kyə bīn′) *n.* A woman who lives with and has a sexual relationship with a man but is not married to him.

con•cur (kən **kûr′**) *intr.v.* **con•curred, con•cur•ring, con•curs. 1.** To have the same opinion; agree: *Most people concur on the need to stop pollution.* **2.** To occur at the same time: *When rain concurs with a cold snap, icy conditions usually follow.* [First written down in 1410 in Middle English and spelled *concurren*, from Latin *concurrere*, to meet, coincide : *com-*, together + *currere*, to run.]

con•cur•rence (kən **kûr′**əns *or* kən **kŭr′**əns) *n.* **1.** Agreement of opinion: *Concurrence among all of the partners led to a satisfactory business arrangement.* **2.** An occurrence, as of events, actions, or efforts, at the same time.

con•cur•rent (kən **kûr′**ənt *or* kən **kŭr′**ənt) *adj.* **1.** Happening at the same time: *concurrent events.* **2.** Being in accordance; harmonious: *concurrent opinions.* **3.** Meeting or tending to meet at the same point: *the intersection of concurrent lines.* **—con•cur′rent•ly** *adv.*

con•cus•sion (kən **kŭsh′**ən) *n.* **1.** A violent jarring; a shock: *A strong concussion from the blast shattered many windows.* **2.** An injury, especially to the brain, resulting from a hard blow.

con•demn (kən **dĕm′**) *tr.v.* **con•demned, con•demn•ing, con•demns. 1.** To express strong disapproval of; denounce: *The governor condemned the waste of taxpayers' money.* **2.a.** To judge to be guilty: *The suspect was condemned by the jury.* **b.** To sentence to a particular punishment: *He was condemned to 15 years in prison.* **3.** To declare unfit for use: *The city condemned the old warehouse after the fire.* **4.** To take over (private property) for public use: *The state condemned farms in the path of the new expressway.* [First written down before 1325 in Middle English and spelled *condempnen*, from Latin *condemnāre* : *com-*, intensive prefix + *damnāre*, to sentence (from *damnum*, penalty).]

con•dem•na•tion (kŏn′dĕm **nā′**shən) *n.* The act of condemning or state of being condemned: *The building was torn down after condemnation.*

con•den•sate (**kŏn′**dən sāt′ *or* kən **dĕn′**sāt′) *n.* A product of condensation.

con•den•sa•tion (kŏn′dən **sā′**shən) *n.* **1.** A changing of a gas or vapor to a liquid: *Cooling causes the condensation of steam to water.* **2.** A liquid or solid, especially water or ice, formed by this process: *condensation on the bathroom mirror.* **3.** The act or process of shortening something: *The author struggled in his condensation of the long story.*

con•dense (kən **dĕns′**) *v.* **con•densed, con•dens•ing, con•dens•es.** *—tr.* **1.** To cause (a gas or vapor) to change to a liquid or solid form: *A sudden drop in temperature may condense dew or even fog into ice crystals.* **2.** To make more concentrated or dense: *We boiled the soup to condense it.* **3.** To make shorter or more concise: *The author con-*

concrete

The ancient Romans used **cement** and **concrete** similar to the kinds used today. After the Roman Empire fell in the fifth century, people lost the art of making cement. It was not rediscovered until the mid 1700's. Cement is made from limestone and clay that is crushed, heated, and ground into a powder. It is mixed with water and materials such as sand, gravel, and broken stone to make concrete. Cement and water form a paste that binds the other materials together as the concrete hardens. *Reinforced concrete* is made by pouring concrete around steel bars. Without this added strength, the building of modern skyscrapers would be impossible. *Prestressed concrete* is made by pouring concrete around steel cables stretched by jacks. When the jacks are released, the cables compress the concrete and strengthen it.

ă	**p**a**t**	oi	**b**oy
ā	**p**ay	ou	out
âr	**c**are	o͝o	**t**oo**k**
ä	**f**a**th**er	o͞o	**b**oo**t**
ĕ	**p**e**t**	ŭ	**c**u**t**
ē	**b**e	ûr	**ur**ge
ĭ	**p**i**t**	th	**th**in
ī	**p**ie	*th*	**th**is
îr	**p**ier	hw	**wh**oop
ŏ	**p**o**t**	zh	vi**s**ion
ō	**t**oe	ə	**a**bout
ô	**p**aw	N	*French* bo**n**

condor
California condor

densed the book for use in a magazine. —*intr.* **1.** To become denser or more compact: *Stars may condense from matter scattered in space.* **2.** To change from a gas to a liquid: *Water vapor will often condense on window panes in the winter.* [First written down before 1425 in Middle English and spelled *condensen*, from Latin *condēnsāre* : *com-*, intensive prefix + *dēnsāre*, to thicken (from *dēnsus*, thick).] —**con•dens′a•ble** *adj.*

con•densed milk (kən **dĕnst′**) *n.* Sweetened cow's milk that has been made very thick by evaporation before canning.

con•dens•er (kən **dĕn′**sər) *n.* **1.** A person or thing that condenses. **2.** An apparatus used to condense a gas or vapor. **3.** A capacitor.

con•de•scend (kŏn′dĭ **sĕnd′**) *intr.v.* **con•de•scend•ed, con•de•scend•ing, con•de•scends. 1.** To agree to do something willingly that is regarded as beneath one's social rank or dignity: *The famous author condescended to autograph books at our used-book sale.* **2.** To act in a manner that shows one considers oneself superior to others: *The snobbish family in the big house condescends to all their neighbors.*

con•de•scend•ing (kŏn′dĭ **sĕn′**dĭng) *adj.* Showing that one considers oneself superior to others; patronizing: *a condescending manner.* —**con′de•scend′ing•ly** *adv.*

con•de•scen•sion (kŏn′dĭ **sĕn′**shən) *n.* **1.** The act of condescending. **2.** An attitude or a behavior that shows one considers oneself superior to others; haughtiness.

con•di•ment (**kŏn′**də mənt) *n.* A sauce, relish, or spice used as a seasoning for food. [First written down in 1440 in Middle English, from Latin *condīmentum*, from *condīre*, to season.]

con•di•tion (kən **dĭsh′**ən) *n.* **1.** A state of being or existence: *They worked hard to restore the old house to its original condition.* **2.a.** A state of health or fitness: *Exercise keeps you in good condition.* **b.** Readiness for use; working order: *A few repairs will put the car in condition.* **3.** A disease or physical ailment: *a heart condition.* **4. conditions.** The existing circumstances: *The committee investigated complaints about working conditions.* **5.** Something that is necessary to the occurrence of something else: *Practice is a condition of good performance.* **6.** Social rank or position: *In a democracy people of all conditions can vote.* —*tr.v.* **con•di•tioned, con•di•tion•ing, con•di•tions. 1.** To put into good or proper condition; make fit: *Running five miles a day will condition the track team.* **2.** To adapt; accustom to: *The visitors from Sweden were not conditioned to the hot weather here.* **3.** To train (an organism) by means of conditioning: *The researchers conditioned the chicken to go outside when a light was turned on.* —***idiom.*** **on condition that.** Provided that: *She gave us permission to use the computer on condition that we report any problems with it.* [First written down before 1333 in Middle English and spelled *condicioun*, from Latin *conditiō*, from *condīcere*, to agree : *com-*, together + *dīcere*, to talk.]

con•di•tion•al (kən **dĭsh′**ə nəl) *adj.* **1.** Depending on a condition or conditions: *While awaiting the response of parents, the committee gave conditional approval to the plan.* **2.** In grammar, expressing a condition on which an outcome or possibility depends. For example, *if it's sunny tomorrow* is a conditional clause in the sentence *We'll go swimming if it's sunny tomorrow.*

con•di•tioned (kən **dĭsh′**ənd) *adj.* **1.** Dependent on a condition or conditions. **2.** Physically fit. **3.a.** Determined or established by means of conditioning: *a conditioned reflex.* **b.** Trained by means of conditioning.

con•di•tion•er (kən **dĭsh′**ə nər) *n.* A device or substance used to improve something in some way: *a leather conditioner; a bottle of hair conditioner.*

con•di•tion•ing (kən **dĭsh′**ə nĭng) *n.* A process of behavior modification by which an experimental subject comes to associate a desired behavior with a previously unrelated stimulus.

con•do (**kŏn′**dō′) *n., pl.* **con•dos.** *Informal.* A condominium.

con•dole (kən **dōl′**) *intr.v.* **con•doled, con•dol•ing, con•doles.** To express sympathy or sorrow: *She condoled with the family over their loss.*

con•do•lence (kən **dō′**ləns) *n.* Sympathy or an expression of sympathy for a person who has experienced sorrow or misfortune.

con•dom (**kŏn′**dəm) *n.* A flexible cover for the penis to be worn during sexual intercourse to prevent pregnancy and sexually transmitted diseases. Condoms are usually made of thin rubber or latex.

con•do•min•i•um (kŏn′də **mĭn′**ē əm) *n.* **1.** An apartment building in which the individual apartments are owned by the tenants. **2.** An apartment in such a building. [First written down before 1714 in Modern English and spelled *condominium*, joint rule : Latin *con-*, together + Latin *dominium*, ownership, domain.]

con•done (kən **dōn′**) *tr.v.* **con•doned, con•don•ing, con•dones.** To forgive, overlook, or ignore: *a politician who condones corruption.* See Synonyms at **forgive.** [First written down in 1857 in Modern English, from Latin *condōnāre* : *com-*, intensive prefix + *dōnāre*, to give (from *dōnum*, gift).]

con•dor (**kŏn′**dôr′ *or* **kŏn′**dər) *n.* Either of two very large vultures, one living in the mountains of California and the other in the Andes, having a ruff of feathers on the neck and a bare head. [First written down in 1604 in Modern English, from Quechua *cuntur*.]

con•duce (kən **do͞os′** *or* kən **dyo͞os′**) *intr.v.* **con•duced, con•duc•ing, con•duc•es.** To contribute or lead to a specific result: *an atmosphere at home that was conducing to good study habits.*

con•du•cive (kən **do͞o′**sĭv *or* kən **dyo͞o′**sĭv) *adj.* Tending to cause, promote, or help bring about a specific result: *Noisy corridors in the school are not conducive to studying.* —**con•du′cive•ness** *n.*

con•duct (kən **dŭkt′**) *tr.v.* **con•duct•ed, con•duct•ing, con•ducts. 1.** To lead; guide: *The guide conducted us through the art museum.* **2.** To direct the course of; manage: *conduct an experiment; conduct negotiations.* **3.** To lead or direct (musicians or a musical work): *conduct an orchestra; conduct one of Mozart's symphonies.* **4.** To be a medium for; transmit: *Most metals conduct electricity well.* **5.** To behave (oneself) in a certain way: *In school most people conduct themselves in an orderly way.* —*n.* (**kŏn′**dŭkt′). **1.** The way a person acts; behavior: *rude and disorderly conduct.* **2.** The act of directing or controlling; management: *The President is responsible for the conduct of foreign affairs.* [First written down before 1422 in Middle English and spelled *conducten*, from Latin *condūcere* : *com-*, together + *dūcere*, to lead.] —**con•duct′i•bil′i•ty** *n.* —**con•duct′i•ble** *adj.*

con•duc•tance (kən **dŭk′**təns) *n.* A measure of the ability of a material to conduct electric charge.

con•duc•tion (kən **dŭk′**shən) *n.* The transmission or passage of something through a medium or along a path, especially the transmission of heat or electric charge through a substance.

con•duc•tive (kən **dŭk′**tĭv) *adj.* Of or showing conductivity.

con•duc•tiv•i•ty (kŏn′dŭk **tĭv′**ĭ tē) *n., pl.* **con•duc•**

tiv•i•ties. The ability or power to conduct heat, electricity, or sound.

con•duc•tor (kən **dŭk′**tər) *n.* **1.a.** A person who conducts; the leader, guide, or director of a group or organization. **b.** The person who conducts an orchestra or other group of musical performers. **2.** The person in charge of a train, bus, or streetcar. **3.** A material or an object that conducts heat, electricity, light, or sound: *Copper is a good conductor of heat and electricity.*

con•duit (**kŏn′**dōō ĭt *or* **kŏn′**dĭt) *n.* **1.** A channel or pipe for carrying fluids, such as water or natural gas. **2.** A tube or pipe through which electric wires or cables pass.

cone (kōn) *n.* **1.** A solid object in which the base is a circle and the sides narrow to form a point. **2.** Something having the shape of such a figure: *an ice-cream cone.* **3.** A rounded or long cluster of woody scales containing the seeds of a pine, fir, hemlock, or related tree. **4.** One of a group of cone-shaped cells of the retina of the eye that is sensitive to bright light and color. [First written down in 1562 in Modern English, from Greek *kōnos.*]

Con•es•to•ga wagon (kŏn′ĭ **stō′**gə) *n.* A heavy covered wagon first built at Conestoga, Pennsylvania, used by American pioneers in their westward travel.

co•ney also **co•ny** (**kō′**nē *or* **kŭn′**ē) *n., pl.* **co•neys** also **co•nies.** **1.** A rabbit, especially the common European rabbit. **2.** The fur of a rabbit.

con•fec•tion (kən **fĕk′**shən) *n.* A sweet food or preparation, such as candy. [First written down in 1345 in Middle English and spelled *confescioun,* from Latin *cōnfectiō,* a making, from *cōnficere,* to put together.]

con•fec•tion•er (kən **fĕk′**shə nər) *n.* A person who makes or sells candy and other confections.

con•fec•tion•ers' sugar (kən **fĕk′**shə nərz) *n.* A fine powdery sugar with cornstarch added.

con•fec•tion•er•y (kən **fĕk′**shə nĕr′ē) *n., pl.* **con•fec•tion•er•ies.** **1.** Candies and other confections. **2.** A confectioner's shop.

con•fed•er•a•cy (kən **fĕd′**ər ə sē) *n., pl.* **con•fed•er•a•cies.** **1.** A political union of peoples or states: *the powerful confederacy of Native American peoples called the Iroquois Nation.* **2. Confederacy.** The 11 Southern states that seceded from the United States in 1860 and 1861.

con•fed•er•ate (kən **fĕd′**ər ĭt) *n.* **1.** An associate in a plot or crime; an accomplice. **2.** A member of a confederacy. **3. Confederate.** A supporter of the American Confederacy. —*adj.* **1.** Belonging to a confederacy. **2. Confederate.** Of or relating to the American Confederacy. —*tr. & intr.v.* (kən **fĕd′**ə rāt′). **con•fed•er•at•ed, con•fed•er•at•ing, con•fed•er•ates.** To form into or become part of a confederacy.

con•fed•er•a•tion (kən fĕd′ə **rā′**shən) *n.* **1.** A group of confederates: *The teachers formed a national confederation to protect their interests.* **2.** The act of confederating or the state of being confederated.

con•fer (kən **fûr′**) *v.* **con•ferred, con•fer•ring, con•fers.** —*intr.* To meet in order to discuss something or compare opinions: *The President conferred with cabinet advisers.* —*tr.* To bestow or award: *The mayor conferred a medal on the two heroic firefighters.* [First written down in 1528 in Modern English, from Latin *cōnferre* : *com-,* together + *ferre,* to bring.]

con•fer•ence (**kŏn′**fər əns *or* **kŏn′**frəns) *n.* **1.** A meeting to discuss a subject or a number of subjects: *a peace conference.* **2.** A regional association of churches, athletic teams, or other groups. **3.** The act of conferring: *The principal and teachers were in conference for hours.*

conference call *n.* A conference by telephone in which three or more persons participate by means of a central switching unit.

con•fess (kən **fĕs′**) *v.* **con•fessed, con•fess•ing, con•fess•es.** —*tr.* **1.** To state openly or admit (something wrong or bad that one has done): *The children confessed that they ate all of the cookies.* **2.a.** To make known (one's sins) to a priest or to God. **b.** To hear the confession of (a person). —*intr.* **1.** To admit or acknowledge something wrong or bad that one has done: *The driver confessed to driving too fast.* **2.** To tell one's sins to a priest. [First written down about 1378 in Middle English and spelled *confessen,* from Latin *cōnfitērī.*]

con•fes•sion (kən **fĕsh′**ən) *n.* **1.** The act of confessing or admitting; acknowledgment: *The suspect's full confession of guilt cleared up the case.* **2.** The act of telling one's sins to a priest or to God. **3.** Something confessed: *Did the prisoner sign her confession?*

con•fes•sion•al (kən **fĕsh′**ə nəl) *n.* A small booth in which a priest hears confessions.

con•fes•sor (kən **fĕs′**ər) *n.* **1.** A priest who hears confession and gives absolution of sins. **2.** A person who accepts intimate confidences and consoles: *The counselor acted as confessor to the whole group.* **3.** A person who confesses.

con•fet•ti (kən **fĕt′**ē) *pl.n.* *(used with a singular verb).* Small pieces of colored paper that are scattered about on festive occasions. [First written down in 1895 in Modern English, from Italian, plural of *confetto,* candy, from Latin *cōnficere,* to prepare.]

con•fi•dant (**kŏn′**fĭ dănt′ *or* **kŏn′**fĭ dänt′) *n.* A person to whom a person confides personal matters or secrets.

con•fide (kən **fīd′**) *v.* **con•fid•ed, con•fid•ing, con•fides.** —*tr.* **1.** To tell confidentially: *confide a secret to a friend.* **2.** To put into another's keeping; entrust: *Before going on vacation, he confided the task of watering his plants to a friend.* —*intr.* To tell or share one's secrets with: *I know I can confide in you.* —**con•fid′er** *n.*

con•fi•dence (**kŏn′**fĭ dəns) *n.* **1.** A feeling of assurance, especially of self-assurance: *The lawyer argued the case with confidence. Most new drivers lack confidence in themselves for a while.* **2.** Trust or faith: *I am placing my confidence in your reliability.* **3.** A trusting relationship: *I have decided to take you into my confidence.* **4.** A feeling of assurance that someone will keep a secret: *I am telling you this in strict confidence.* **5.** Something confided; a secret: *the many confidences of close friends.*

con•fi•dent (**kŏn′**fĭ dənt) *adj.* Feeling or showing confidence, especially in being sure of oneself; certain: *The lawyer is confident of winning the case. The surgeon approached the operation with a confident air.* [First written down in 1576 in Modern English, from Latin *cōnfīdere,* to rely on : *com-,* intensive prefix + *fīdere,* to trust.] —**con′fi•dent•ly** *adv.*

con•fi•den•tial (kŏn′fĭ **dĕn′**shəl) *adj.* **1.** Told in confidence; secret: *A person's medical history is confidential information shared only with a doctor.* **2.** Entrusted with the confidence of someone else: *a confidential secretary.* **3.** Showing confidence or intimacy: *a confidential tone of voice.* —**con′fi•den′tial•ly** *adv.*

con•fid•ing (kən **fī′**dĭng) *adj.* Having a tendency to confide; trusting: *a confiding nature.*

con•fig•u•ra•tion (kən fĭg′yə **rā′**shən) *n.* The form or arrangement of the parts of something: *The gen-*

Conestoga wagon
c. 1837

ă	pat	oi	boy
ā	pay	ou	out
âr	care	ŏŏ	took
ä	father	ōō	boot
ĕ	pet	ŭ	cut
ē	be	ûr	urge
ĭ	pit	th	thin
ī	pie	*th*	this
îr	pier	hw	whoop
ŏ	pot	zh	vision
ō	toe	ə	about
ô	paw	N	*French* bon

Confucius

eral configuration of the earth and other planets is that of a ball.

con•fine (kən fīn′) *tr.v.* **con•fined, con•fin•ing, con•fines. 1.** To keep within bounds; restrict; limit: *Firefighters confined the fire to the roof.* **2.** To shut or keep inside, as in prison: *The dogs were confined to a backyard pen.* [First written down in 1523 in Modern English, from Latin *cōnfīnis*, adjoining : *com-*, together + *fīnis*, border.]

con•fine•ment (kən fīn′mənt) *n.* **1.** The act of confining or condition of being confined: *Confinement of the bear was for its own safety.* **2.** The period of childbirth.

con•fines (kŏn′fīnz′) *pl.n.* The limits of a space or area; the borders: *The dog wandered beyond the confines of the yard.*

con•firm (kən fûrm′) *tr.v.* **con•firmed, con•firm•ing, con•firms. 1.** To support or establish the certainty or validity of: *The results of the experiment confirmed the theory.* **2.** To make firmer; strengthen: *Reading about famous scientists confirmed her intention to study chemistry.* **3.** To make valid or binding by a formal or legal act; ratify: *The judge's appointment to the Supreme Court was confirmed by the Senate.* **4.** To admit to full membership in a church or synagogue by the rite of confirmation. [First written down before 1250 in Middle English and spelled *confirmien*, from Latin *cōnfirmāre* : *com-*, intensive prefix + *firmāre*, to strengthen (from *firmus*, strong).]

con•fir•ma•tion (kŏn′fər mā′shən) *n.* **1.** The act of confirming: *The President needs the Senate's confirmation to appoint an ambassador.* **2.** Something that confirms; proof: *The license was confirmation of the doctor's qualification to practice medicine.* **3.** A Christian ceremony in which a baptized person is made a full member of a church. **4.** A Jewish ceremony marking the completion of a young person's religious training.

con•firmed (kən fûrmd′) *adj.* **1.** Firmly established; proved: *a confirmed theory.* **2.** Settled in a habit or condition: *a confirmed gossip.* **—con•firm′ed•ly** (kən fûr′mĭd lē) *adv.*

con•fis•cate (kŏn′fĭ skāt′) *tr.v.* **con•fis•cat•ed, con•fis•cat•ing, con•fis•cates. 1.** To seize (private property) from someone for the public treasury: *The government confiscated the boat and its illegal goods.* **2.** To seize by authority; take away: *The teacher confiscated the pack of chewing gum.* **—con′fis•ca′tion** *n.*

con•fla•gra•tion (kŏn′flə grā′shən) *n.* A large fire.

con•flict (kŏn′flĭkt′) *n.* **1.** A state of fighting; a battle or war. **2.** A state of disagreement, as between persons, ideas, or interests. *—intr.v.* (kən flĭkt′). **con•flict•ed, con•flict•ing, con•flicts.** To be in opposition; differ; clash: *The meeting conflicts with my dental appointment.* [First written down before 1425 in Middle English, from Latin *cōnflīctus*, collision, from *cōnflīgere*, to strike together.]

con•flu•ence (kŏn′flo͞o əns) *n.* **1.** A flowing together: *A confluence of little streams form the headwaters of the river.* **2.** A gathering or meeting together, as of people. [First written down before 1425 in Middle English, from Latin *cōnfluere*, to flow together.]

con•flu•ent (kŏn′flo͞o ənt) *adj.* Flowing or running together; blending into one: *confluent rivers.*

con•form (kən fôrm′) *v.* **con•formed, con•form•ing, con•forms.** *—intr.* **1.** To act in agreement with established customs, rules, or styles: *Many young people do not like to conform to the way older people dress.* **2.** To correspond in form or character; be similar: *The computer conforms to the manufacturer's advertising claims.* *—tr.* To bring into agreement; make similar: *She doesn't often conform her thinking to the rest of the group.* See Synonyms at **adapt.** **—con•form′er** *n.*

con•for•ma•tion (kŏn′fər mā′shən) *n.* **1.** The way something is formed; shape or structure: *The conformation of a snake's skeleton is elongated.* **2.** The act of conforming or the state of being conformed.

con•form•ist (kən fôr′mĭst) *n.* A person who conforms to current customs, rules, or styles.

con•form•i•ty (kən fôr′mĭ tē) *n., pl.* **con•form•i•ties. 1.** Agreement; harmony: *act in conformity with established custom.* **2.** Action or behavior that is in agreement with current customs, rules, or styles.

con•found (kən found′ *or* kŏn found′) *tr.v.* **con•found•ed, con•found•ing, con•founds. 1.** To bewilder, puzzle, or perplex: *The dog's strange behavior confounded its master.* **2.** To mistake (one thing) for another; mix up: *The confused witness confounded fiction and fact.* [First written down about 1300 in Middle English and spelled *confounden*, from Latin *cōnfundere*, to mix together, confuse : *com-*, together + *fundere*, to pour.]

con•front (kən frŭnt′) *tr.v.* **con•front•ed, con•front•ing, con•fronts. 1.** To come face to face with, especially in opposition: *She finally confronted her rival on the tennis court.* **2.** To bring face to face with; cause to encounter: *The defendant was confronted with all the evidence and confessed.* [First written down about 1568 in Modern English, from Medieval Latin *cōnfrontāre*, to adjoin.]

con•fron•ta•tion (kŏn′frŭn tā′shən) *n.* **1.** The act of confronting or the state of being confronted: *The lawyer's confrontation of the witnesses proved their testimony was unreliable.* **2.** A direct encounter, especially a conflict or a clash, as of opponents: *The candidates met in several confrontations to debate issues.*

Con•fu•cian (kən fyo͞o′shən) *adj.* Of or relating to Confucius, his teachings, or his followers.

Con•fu•cian•ism (kən fyo͞o′shə nĭz′əm) *n.* A set of principles of conduct based on the teachings of Confucius and stressing social harmony, justice, and devotion to family ancestors.

Con•fu•cius (kən fyo͞o′shəs). c. 551–479 B.C. Chinese philosopher whose *Analects* contain a collection of his sayings and dialogues put together by disciples after his death.

con•fuse (kən fyo͞oz′) *tr.v.* **con•fused, con•fus•ing, con•fus•es. 1.** To cause to be unable to think clearly; throw off: *The poorly organized presentation only confused the audience.* **2.** To fail to distinguish between (one person or thing and another); mistake: *The coach confused me with my brother.* [First written down about 1330 in Middle English and spelled *confusen*, from Latin *cōnfūsus*, past participle of *cōnfundere*, to mix together.] **—con•fus′ing•ly** *adv.*

con•fused (kən fyo͞ozd′) *adj.* **1.** Bewildered; perplexed: *a confused look.* **2.** Mixed up; disordered: *a confused situation; a confused story.* **—con•fus′ed•ly** (kən fyo͞o′zĭd lē) *adv.*

con•fu•sion (kən fyo͞o′zhən) *n.* **1.** The act of confusing: *The confusion of the addresses meant the package was not delivered to the right place.* **2.** The state of being confused; bewilderment: *The unexpected news threw us all into confusion.*

con•fute (kən fyo͞ot′) *tr.v.* **con•fut•ed, con•fut•ing, con•futes.** To prove to be wrong or false; refute: *The facts confuted his testimony. An expert confuted the speaker.* **—con′fu•ta′tion** (kŏn′fyo͞o tā′shən) *n.* **—con•fut′er** *n.*

con•geal (kən jēl′) *v.* **con•gealed, con•geal•ing, con•geals.** *—intr.* **1.** To change from a liquid to a solid, as by freezing. **2.** To thicken or coagulate: *Blood congeals on exposure to air.* *—tr.* To cause to change from a liquid to a solid. [First written down about 1380 in Middle English and spelled *congelen,* from Latin *congelāre* : *com-*, together + *gelāre,* to freeze.] **—con•geal′ment** *n.*

con•gen•ial (kən **jēn′**yəl) *adj.* **1.** Having similar tastes, habits, or dispositions: *two congenial persons.* **2.** Of a pleasant disposition; friendly; amiable: *a congenial host.* **3.** Suited to one's nature; pleasant; agreeable: *The bright airy room provided congenial surroundings.* **—con•ge′ni•al′i•ty** (kən jē′nē **ăl′**ĭ tē) *n.* **—con•gen′ial•ly** *adv.*

con•gen•i•tal (kən **jĕn′**ĭ tl) *adj.* Existing before or from the time of birth: *Many congenital defects can now be corrected by surgery.* **—con•gen′i•tal•ly** *adv.*

con•ger (**kŏng′**gər) *n.* Any of various large ocean eels, often caught for food in Europe.

con•gest (kən **jĕst′**) *v.* **con•gest•ed, con•gest•ing, con•gests.** *—tr.* **1.** To overfill; overcrowd: *Heavy traffic congested the highway.* **2.** To cause an abnormally large amount of fluid to collect in (a vessel or an organ of the body). *—intr.* To become congested: *Pneumonia causes the lungs to congest with fluid.*

con•ges•tion (kən **jĕs′**chən) *n.* **1.** A condition of overcrowding: *traffic congestion during rush hour.* **2.** A condition in which fluid collects in an organ or tissue of the body: *Cough syrup can relieve bronchial congestion.*

con•ges•tive (kən **jĕs′**tĭv) *adj.* Of or involving congestion: *Congestive heart failure results from an inability of the heart to pump blood adequately.*

con•glom•er•ate (kən **glŏm′**ə rāt′) *intr. & tr.v.* **con•glom•er•at•ed, con•glom•er•at•ing, con•glom•er•ates.** To form or cause to form into a mass; cluster. *—n.* (kə **glŏm′**ər ĭt). **1.** A mass of material that clings together. **2.** A sedimentary rock that consists of pebbles, gravel, or seashells cemented together by hardened clay or a similar material. **3.** A business corporation made up of a number of different companies that operate in widely diversified fields. *—adj.* (kən **glŏm′**ər ĭt). **1.** Formed together into a mass: *conglomerate rock formed of sand and pebbles.* **2.** Made up of many parts: *The reformers were a conglomerate group from several political parties.*

con•glom•er•a•tion (kən glŏm′ə **rā′**shən) *n.* A collection or an accumulation of many different things or people.

Con•go (**kŏng′**gō). A country of west-central Africa west of Zaire with a short coastline on the Atlantic Ocean. It gained its independence from France in 1960. Capital, Brazzaville. Population, 1,912,429.

Con•go•lese (kŏng′gō **lēz′** *or* kŏng′gō **lēs′**) *n., pl.* **Con•go•lese.** A native or inhabitant of Congo. *—adj.* Of or relating to Congo or the Congolese.

Congo River also **Zaire River** (**zī′**îr *or* zä **îr′**). A river of central Africa flowing about 2,900 miles (4,666 kilometers) north, west, and southwest through Zaire to the Atlantic Ocean. The river forms part of the border between Zaire and Congo.

con•grat•u•late (kən **grăch′**ə lāt′ *or* kən **grăj′**ə lāt′) *tr.v.* **con•grat•u•lat•ed, con•grat•u•lat•ing, con•grat•u•lates.** To express joy or good wishes to (someone) for an achievement or good fortune: *Everyone crowded around to congratulate the newly elected mayor.* [First written down in 1548 in Modern English, from Latin *congrātulārī* : *com-*, with + *grātulārī,* to rejoice.]

con•grat•u•la•tion (kən grăch′ə **lā′**shən *or* kən-grăj′ə **lā′**shən) *n.* **1.** The act of congratulating: *a card of congratulation to the new parents.* **2.** An expression of joy or acknowledgement. Often used in the plural.

con•grat•u•la•to•ry (kən **grăch′**ə lə tôr′ē *or* kən-**grăj′**ə lə tôr′ē) *adj.* Expressing congratulations: *a congratulatory message.*

con•gre•gate (**kŏng′**grĭ gāt′) *intr.v.* **con•gre•gat•ed, con•gre•gat•ing, con•gre•gates.** To come together in a crowd or mass; assemble: *Salmon congregate at the falls in large numbers.* [First written down before 1425 in Middle English and spelled *congregaten,* from Latin *congregāre* : *com-*, together + *gregāre,* to assemble (from *grex,* herd).] **—con′gre•ga′tor** *n.*

con•gre•ga•tion (kŏng′grĭ **gā′**shən) *n.* **1.** A gathering of people or things: *The congregation of tourists crowded around the exhibit.* **2.a.** A group of people gathered for religious worship: *The congregation bowed their heads in prayer.* **b.** The members of a specific religious group who regularly worship at a church or synagogue. **3.** The act of assembling: *the congregation of swallows in the fall.*

con•gre•ga•tion•al (kŏng′grĭ **gā′**shə nəl) *adj.* **1.** Of or relating to a congregation: *congregational worship.* **2. Congregational.** Of or relating to Congregationalism or Congregationalists.

con•gre•ga•tion•al•ism (kŏng′grĭ **gā′**shə nə lĭz′-əm) *n.* **1.** Church government in which each local congregation governs itself. **2. Congregationalism.** The system of government and religious beliefs of a Protestant denomination in which each member church is self-governing. **—con′gre•ga′tion•al•ist, Con′gre•ga′tion•al•ist** *adj. & n.*

con•gress (**kŏng′**grĭs) *n.* **1.** A formal meeting of persons representing various nations, organizations, or professions to discuss problems: *a medical congress of heart specialists.* **2.** The lawmaking body of a republic. **3. Congress.** The national legislative body of the United States, consisting of the Senate and the House of Representatives. [First written down before 1400 in Middle English and spelled *congrece,* body of attendants, from Latin *congressus,* meeting, from past participle of *congredī,* to meet : *com-*, together + *gradī,* to go.] **—con•gres′sion•al** (kən **grĕsh′**ə nəl *or* kəng **grĕsh′**ə nəl) *adj.*

con•gress•man (**kŏng′**grĭs mən) *n.* A man who is a member of the United States Congress, especially of the House of Representatives.

con•gress•wom•an (**kŏng′**grĭs wo͝om′ən) *n.* A woman who is a member of the United States Congress, especially of the House of Representatives.

con•gru•ence (**kŏng′**gro͞o əns *or* kən **gro͞o′**əns) *n.* The condition of being congruent.

con•gru•en•cy (**kŏng′**gro͞o ən sē *or* kən **gro͞o′**ən sē) *n., pl.* **con•gru•en•cies.** Congruence.

con•gru•ent (**kŏng′**gro͞o ənt *or* kən **gro͞o′**ənt) *adj.* **1.** In geometry, matching exactly; having the same size and shape: *congruent triangles.* **2.** Corresponding or agreeing; harmonious: *congruent objectives of policy.* [First written down before 1425 in Middle English, from Latin *congruere,* to agree.] **—con′gru•ent•ly** *adv.*

con•gru•i•ty (kən **gro͞o′**ĭ tē) *n., pl.* **con•gru•i•ties.** **1.** Agreement; harmony: *The two leaders worked in congruity to achieve world peace.* **2.** The state or fact of being congruent: *congruity of triangles.*

con•ic (**kŏn′**ĭk) *adj.* Conical.

con•i•cal (**kŏn′**ĭ kəl) *adj.* Of, relating to, or shaped like a cone. **—con′i•cal•ly** *adv.*

conic section *n.* A curve, such as a circle, an ellipse, a hyperbola, or a parabola, formed by the intersection of a plane with a cone.

con•i•fer (**kŏn′**ə fər *or* **kō′**nə fər) *n.* Any of various trees or shrubs that bear cones. Conifers are usually evergreen and include the pine, fir, spruce, hemlock, and yew. [First written down in 1851 in Modern English, from Latin *cōnifer,* cone-bearing.]

co•nif•er•ous (kō **nĭf′**ər əs *or* kə **nĭf′**ər əs) *adj.* **1.** Bearing cones: *coniferous trees such as pines and*

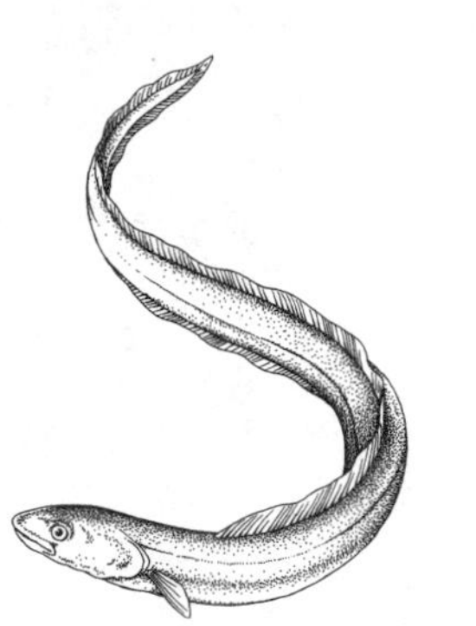

conger
American conger

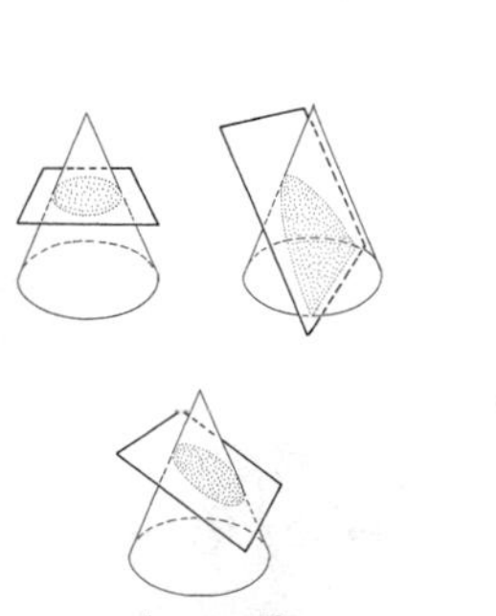

conic section
Top: Circle (*left*) and parabola (*right*)
Bottom: Ellipse

ă	pat	oi	boy
ā	pay	ou	out
âr	care	o͝o	took
ä	father	o͞o	boot
ĕ	pet	ŭ	cut
ē	be	ûr	urge
ĭ	pit	th	thin
ī	pie	*th*	this
îr	pier	hw	whoop
ŏ	pot	zh	vision
ō	toe	ə	about
ô	paw	N	*French* bon

hemlocks. **2.** Of or relating to conifers: *a coniferous forest.*

conj. *abbr.* An abbreviation of conjunction.

con•jec•tur•al (kən **jĕk′**chər əl) *adj.* Based on or inclined to conjecture: *a conjectural forecast of economic improvement.*

con•jec•ture (kən **jĕk′**chər) *n.* **1.** The formation of an opinion or a conclusion from incomplete or insufficient evidence; guesswork: *The origin of language is a matter of conjecture.* **2.** A statement, an opinion, or a conclusion based on guesswork; a guess: *make a conjecture about the outcome of the election.* —*intr.v.* **con•jec•tured, con•jec•tur•ing, con•jec•tures.** To make a conjecture; guess: *Several radio commentators were conjecturing on who would be the new mayor.*

con•join (kən **join′**) *tr. & intr.v.* **con•joined, con•join•ing, con•joins.** To join or become joined; connect; unite: *The two nations conjoined into one.* —**con•join′er** *n.*

con•joint (kən **joint′**) *adj.* Joined together; combined: *The houses of Congress made a conjoint resolution to support the President's policy.*

con•ju•gal (**kŏn′**jə gəl *or* kən **jo͞o′**gəl) *adj.* Of or relating to marriage or the relationship between husband and wife: *conjugal happiness.* —**con′ju•gal•ly** *adv.*

con•ju•gate (**kŏn′**jə gāt′) *v.* **con•ju•gat•ed, con•ju•gat•ing, con•ju•gates.** —*tr.* To give the inflected forms of a verb, usually in a set order. For example, the verb "to have" is conjugated *I have, you have, she has, we have, you have, they have.* —*intr.* In biology, to unite or fuse in conjugation. —*adj.* (**kŏn′**jə gĭt *or* **kŏn′**jə gāt′). Joined together, especially in pairs; coupled. [First written down in 1530 in Modern English, from Latin *coniugāre*, to join together : *com-*, together + *iugāre*, to join (from *iugum*, yoke).]

con•ju•ga•tion (kŏn′jə **gā′**shən) *n.* **1.a.** The inflection of a particular verb. **b.** A presentation of the complete set of inflected forms of a verb. **c.** A class of verbs having similar inflected forms. **2.a.** A type of sexual reproduction in which single-celled organisms of the same species join together and exchange nuclear material before each organism undergoes cell division. **b.** The union of sex cells to form a fertilized cell.

con•junc•tion (kən **jŭngk′**shən) *n.* **1.** The act of joining or state of being joined; combination: *A happy conjunction of circumstances strengthened the economy.* **2.** A word, such as *and, but, or,* or *yet,* that connects other words in a sentence. **3.** The position of two celestial bodies when they have the same longitude on the celestial sphere. [First written down in 1375 in Middle English, from Latin *coniūnctiō*, from *coniungere*, to join together.]

con•junc•ti•va (kŏn′jŭngk **tī′**və) *n., pl.* **con•junc•ti•vas** or **con•junc•ti•vae** (kŏn′jŭngk **tī′**vē). The mucous membrane that lines the inside of the eyelid and covers the surface of the eyeball.

con•junc•tive (kən **jŭngk′**tĭv) *adj.* **1.** Joined or serving to join together. **2.** In grammar, connecting or serving as a conjunction. Conjunctive adverbs, such as *however* and *therefore,* are used to connect sentences. —**con•junc′tive•ly** *adv.*

con•junc•ti•vi•tis (kən jŭngk′tə **vī′**tĭs) *n.* Inflammation of the conjunctiva, often in the form of pinkeye.

con•jure (**kŏn′**jər *or* kən **jo͝or′**) *v.* **con•jured, con•jur•ing, con•jures.** —*tr.* **1.** To summon (a devil or spirit) by a magic or supernatural power. **2.** To influence or bring about as if by magic: *In saving the patient our doctor conjured a miracle.* **3.** To call to mind: *The mention of Kansas conjures up images of fields of grain.* —*intr.* To practice magic; perform magic tricks. [First written down about 1280 in Middle English and spelled *conjuren*, to summon under oath, from Late Latin *coniūrāre*, to pray by something holy : Latin *com-*, together + Latin *iūrāre*, to swear.]

con•jur•er also **con•jur•or** (**kŏn′**jər ər *or* **kŭn′**-jər ər) *n.* A magician or sorcerer.

conk (kŏngk) *n.* A blow, especially on the head. —*tr. v.* **conked, conk•ing, conks.** *Slang.* To hit, especially on the head. —***idiom.*** **conk out. 1.** To fail suddenly; break down: *The engine conked out.* **2.** To fall asleep, especially suddenly: *He conked out while watching television.*

❑ *These sound alike:* **conk, conch** (mollusk).

Conn. *abbr.* An abbreviation of Connecticut.

con•nect (kə **nĕkt′**) *v.* **con•nect•ed, con•nect•ing, con•nects.** —*tr.* **1.** To join or fasten together; link: *A new road connects the two towns.* See Synonyms at **join. 2.** To consider as related; associate in the mind: *We connect summer with picnics and swimming.* **3.** To plug in (an electrical cord or device) to an outlet: *connect a television set.* **4.** To link by telephone: *The operator connected me with the order department.* —*intr.* **1.** To be or become joined: *The two streams connected to form a river.* **2.** To be scheduled so that passengers can transfer from one bus, train, or airplane to another: *The bus connected with the train at the station.* [First written down in 1440 in Middle English and spelled *connecten*, from Latin *cōnectere* : *cō-*, together + *nectere*, to bind.] —**con•nect′er, con•nec′tor** *n.* —**con•nect′i•ble** *adj.*

Con•nect•i•cut (kə **nĕt′**ĭ kət). A state of the northeast United States south of Massachusetts. It was admitted as one of the original Thirteen Colonies in 1788. In 1635 colonists from Massachusetts began to settle in the **Connecticut River** valley. Capital, Hartford. Population, 3,295,669. —See Note.

con•nec•tion (kə **nĕk′**shən) *n.* **1.** The act of connecting or the condition of being connected: *Connection of the telephone cables took several hours. That doctor's connection to the hospital has benefited many patients.* **2.** Something that connects or joins; a link: *a telephone connection; rail connections between the two cities.* **3.** An association or a relationship: *There is a connection between good health and eating well.* **4.** A person with whom one is associated, as by kinship, common interests, or marriage: *I heard about the job through family connections.* **5.** A means of continuing transportation: *I missed my connection in Chicago.*

con•nec•tive (kə **nĕk′**tĭv) *adj.* Connecting or serving to connect. —*n.* **1.** Something that connects. **2.** In grammar, a word such as a conjunction that connects words, phrases, clauses, or sentences.

connective tissue *n.* Tissue that forms the framework and supporting structures of the body, including bone, cartilage, mucous membrane, and fat.

con•ning tower (**kŏn′**ĭng) *n.* **1.** A raised enclosed structure on the deck of a submarine, used for observation and as an entrance or exit. **2.** The armored pilothouse of a warship.

con•nive (kə **nīv′**) *intr.v.* **con•nived, con•niv•ing, con•nives. 1.** To pretend not to notice or fail to deal with something that should be reported or condemned: *The mayor connived at the bribery of city officials.* **2.** To cooperate secretly in an illegal or wrongful action: *The traitor connived with the enemy.* —**con•niv′ance** (kə **nī′**vəns) *n.*

con•nois•seur (kŏn′ə **sûr′** *or* kŏn′ə **so͝or′**) *n.* A person who has expert knowledge or excellent judgment of something, such as art or fine food. [First written down in 1714 in Modern English, from Old French *connoisseor*, from *connoistre*, to know, from Latin *cognōscere*.]

Connecticut

The name for the state of **Connecticut** comes from a Mohegan word meaning "by the long river." The name was given to the **Connecticut River**, from which the state then took its name.

conning tower

con•no•ta•tion (kŏn′ə tā′shən) *n.* A meaning suggested by a certain word in addition to its literal or most exact meaning: *The word* lamb *has connotations of simplicity and innocence.*

con•note (kə nōt′) *tr.v.* **con•not•ed, con•not•ing, con•notes.** To suggest or imply in addition to literal or exact meaning: *In a political leader, hesitation is apt to connote weakness.*

con•nu•bi•al (kə nōō′bē əl *or* kə nyōō′bē əl) *adj.* Relating to marriage or the relationship between husband and wife; conjugal: *connubial bliss.*

con•quer (kŏng′kər) *v.* **con•quered, con•quer•ing, con•quers.** —*tr.* **1.** To defeat or subdue by force, especially by force of arms: *In 1066 the Norman French conquered England.* **2.** To gain control by overcoming ignorance, harsh conditions, or other difficulties: *Scientists have conquered many diseases by developing vaccines.* —*intr.* To be victorious; win: *American forces conquered against heavy odds in the Revolutionary War.* [First written down about 1300 in Middle English and spelled *conqueren*, from Latin *conquīrere*, to procure : *com-*, intensive prefix + *quaerere*, to seek.] **—con′quer•or, con′quer•er** *n.*

con•quest (kŏn′kwĕst′ *or* kŏng′kwĕst′) *n.* **1.** An act of conquering: *the Spanish conquest of Mexico.* **2.** Something conquered: *one of the empire's conquests.* [First written down before 1325 in Middle English, from Old French.]

con•quis•ta•dor (kŏn kwĭs′tə dôr′ *or* kŏng kē′stə dôr′) *n., pl.* **con•quis•ta•dors** or **con•quis•ta•dor•es** (kŏn kwĭs′tə dôr′ās *or* kŏng kē′stə dôr′ās). One of the Spanish conquerors of Mexico, Central America, and Peru in the 16th century.

con•science (kŏn′shəns) *n.* A sense of right and wrong that urges one to act morally: *Listen to your conscience and you'll be glad in the long run.*

con•sci•en•tious (kŏn′shē ĕn′shəs) *adj.* **1.** Guided by or done with a sense of what is right or proper: *a conscientious decision.* **2.** Careful and thorough: *a conscientious worker.* **—con′sci•en′tious•ly** *adv.* **—con′sci•en′tious•ness** *n.*

conscientious objector *n.* A person who on the basis of religious belief or moral principle refuses to serve in the armed forces or take up arms.

con•scious (kŏn′shəs) *adj.* **1.** Able to perceive what is happening around oneself; awake: *The patient was fully conscious throughout the operation.* **2.a.** Having an awareness of one's own existence, sensations, thoughts, and surroundings: *People are not always conscious of their talents.* **b.** Known to oneself or felt by oneself: *filled with conscious remorse.* **3.** Intentionally done; deliberate: *make a conscious effort to speak more distinctly.* [First written down in 1601 in Modern English, from Latin *cōnscius*.] **—con′scious•ly** *adv.*

con•scious•ness (kŏn′shəs nĭs) *n.* **1.** The condition of being conscious: *The doctor asked if the patient had lost consciousness.* **2.** All the ideas, opinions, feelings, and thoughts held by a person or group: *Love of freedom runs deep in the national consciousness.*

con•script (kŏn′skrĭpt′) *n.* A person who is drafted, especially into the armed forces. —*adj.* Conscripted; drafted. —*tr.v.* (kən skrĭpt′). **con•script•ed, con•script•ing, con•scripts.** To enroll by force into service in the armed forces; draft: *conscript civilians into the army.* **—con•scrip′tion** (kən skrĭp′shən) *n.*

con•se•crate (kŏn′sĭ krāt′) *tr.v.* **con•se•crat•ed, con•se•crat•ing, con•se•crates. 1.** To declare or set apart as sacred: *consecrate a new church.* **2.** To dedicate to a worthy purpose: *The nurse's life was consecrated to caring for the ill.* **3.** To sanctify (bread and wine) for use in Holy Communion. [First written down before 1387 in Middle English and spelled *consecraten*, from Latin *cōnsecrāre* : *com-*, intensive prefix + *sacrāre*, to make sacred.] **—con′se•cra′tion** *n.* **—con′se•cra′tor** *n.*

con•sec•u•tive (kən sĕk′yə tĭv) *adj.* Following in order, without a break or interruption; successive: *It rained this week for five consecutive days.* [First written down in 1611 in Modern English, from Medieval Latin *cōnsecūtīvus*, from Latin *cōnsequī*, to follow closely.] **—con•sec′u•tive•ly** *adv.* **—con•sec′u•tive•ness** *n.*

con•sen•sus (kən sĕn′səs) *n.* Collective opinion; general agreement: *The consensus among voters is for building the new school.*

con•sent (kən sĕnt′) *intr.v.* **con•sent•ed, con•sent•ing, con•sents.** To give permission; agree: *My parents finally consented to let me go skiing.* —*n.* Agreement and acceptance; permission: *Our teacher got the principal's consent to let us go early.* [First written down before 1200 in Middle English and spelled *consenten*, from Latin *cōnsentīre* : *com-*, together + *sentīre*, to feel.] —SEE NOTE.

con•se•quence (kŏn′sĭ kwĕns′) *n.* **1.** Something that follows from an action or a condition; an effect; a result: *Having a large vocabulary was a consequence of so much reading.* **2.** Importance; significance: *a minor matter of no consequence.* [First written down about 1380 in Middle English, from Latin *consequi*, to follow closely.]

con•se•quent (kŏn′sĭ kwĕnt′) *adj.* Following as an effect or result: *heavy rains and the consequent flooding of the farmlands.*

con•se•quen•tial (kŏn′sĭ kwĕn′shəl) *adj.* **1.** Consequent. **2.** Important; significant: *a consequential decision that affected us all.* **3.** Self-important; conceited; pompous. **—con′se•quen′tial•ly** *adv.*

con•se•quent•ly (kŏn′sĭ kwĕnt′lē) *adv.* As a result; therefore: *I forgot my wallet and consequently had to go back home for it.*

con•ser•va•tion (kŏn′sûr vā′shən) *n.* **1.** The act or process of conserving. **2.** Preservation from loss or damage, especially the controlled use and systematic protection of natural resources, such as forests, soil, and water.

con•ser•va•tion•ist (kŏn′sûr vā′shə nĭst) *n.* A person who advocates or practices conservation, especially of natural resources.

conservation of energy *n.* A principle of physics stating that the total energy in any closed system does not vary, although energy can be changed from one form into another.

conservation of mass *n.* A principle of physics stating that the total mass of a closed system remains constant regardless of reactions within the system. In a chemical reaction, matter is thought to be neither created nor destroyed but changed from one substance to another.

conservation of mass-en•er•gy (măs′ĕn′ər jē) *n.* A principle of physics stating that mass can be converted to energy and energy into mass and that the total mass plus the total energy in a closed system remains constant regardless of changes in the system. The relation between mass and energy is given by Einstein's equation $E = mc^2$, where E is energy, m mass, and c the speed of light.

con•ser•va•tism (kən sûr′və tĭz′əm) *n.* The tendency, especially in politics, to maintain customs, traditions, and existing arrangements as they are.

con•ser•va•tive (kən sûr′və tĭv) *adj.* **1.** Favoring things as they are; opposing change: *a conservative attitude toward manners.* **2.** Traditional in style; not showy: *a conservative dark suit.* **3.** Moderate; cautious; restrained: *a conservative estimate of expenses.* **4.** Of or belonging to a political party or group that emphasizes respect for traditional institutions, distrusts governmental solutions to prob-

Word Building: consent

The word roots *-sent-* and *-sens-* in English words come from the Latin verb *sentīre*, "to feel, sense, judge," which has the past participle *sēnsus*. **Consent** therefore means "to feel with, agree" (using the prefix *con-*, a form of *com-*, "with, together, all together"). **Dissent** is literally "to judge differently" (*dis-*, "apart"). A **consensus** is "a feeling all together, universal agreement"; **dissension** is the exact opposite—general disagreement.

ă	pat	oi	boy
ā	pay	ou	out
âr	care	ŏŏ	took
ä	father	ōō	boot
ĕ	pet	ŭ	cut
ē	be	ûr	urge
ĭ	pit	th	thin
ī	pie	*th*	this
îr	pier	hw	whoop
ŏ	pot	zh	vision
ō	toe	ə	about
ô	paw	N	*French* bon

conservatory

console²
Television console

Word History: consommé

The rich, thick, heavy broth we call **consommé** is soup that is all used up. *Consommé* in French means "finished, used up, completed," because the meat in the soup is slowly boiled to get all the nourishment out of it. *Consommé* is the past participle of the French verb *consommer*, "to finish, complete, end" and comes from the Latin word *consummāre*, "to finish up, finish off." From *consummāre* we also get the verb **consummate**, the adjective **consummate**, and the noun **consummation**.

lems, and opposes sudden change in the established arrangement of power. **5. Conservative.** Of or belonging to Conservative Judaism. *—n.* **1.** A person who is conservative. **2.** Often **Conservative.** A member of a conservative party. **—con•serv′a•tive•ly** *adv.*

Conservative Judaism *n.* The branch of Judaism that allows for changes in Jewish law that are authorized by rabbis.

con•ser•va•to•ry (kən **sûr′**və tôr′ē) *n., pl.* **con•ser•va•to•ries. 1.** A greenhouse in which plants are arranged for display. **2.** A school of music or dramatic art.

con•serve (kən **sûrv′**) *tr.v.* **con•served, con•serv•ing, con•serves. 1.** To protect from loss or harm; preserve: *conserve one's energy; conserve forests and other natural resources.* **2.** To use carefully; avoid wasting: *We turned down the thermostat to conserve energy.* **3.** To preserve (fruits) by cooking with sugar. *—n.* (**kŏn′**sûrv′). A jam made of fruits stewed in sugar. [First written down about 1380 in Middle English and spelled *conserven*, from Latin *cōnservāre.*]

con•sid•er (kən **sĭd′**ər) *v.* **con•sid•ered, con•sid•er•ing, con•sid•ers.** *—tr.* **1.** To think carefully about; reflect on; contemplate: *I will consider what you said and respond later.* **2.** To regard as; believe to be: *I consider this the most beautiful park in town.* **3.** To take into account; keep in mind: *She sings well if you consider the fact that she never had lessons.* **4.** To be thoughtful of; show consideration for: *Consider the feelings of other people.* *—intr.* To think carefully; reflect: *Give me time to consider.* [First written down in 1375 in Middle English and spelled *consideren*, from Latin *cōnsīderāre* : *com-*, intensive prefix + *sīdus*, star.]

con•sid•er•a•ble (kən **sĭd′**ər ə bəl) *adj.* **1.** Large or great in amount, extent, or degree: *They gave considerable thought to the matter.* **2.** Worth considering; important; significant: *a considerable issue.* **—con•sid′er•a•bly** *adv.*

con•sid•er•ate (kən **sĭd′**ər ĭt) *adj.* Taking into account other people's feelings; thoughtful: *quiet and considerate neighbors.* **—con•sid′er•ate•ly** *adv.* **—con•sid′er•ate•ness** *n.*

con•sid•er•a•tion (kən sĭd′ə **rā′**shən) *n.* **1.** Careful thought; deliberation: *The matter is complicated and needs consideration.* **2.** A factor to be considered in making a judgment or decision: *The health of the community should be an important consideration in voting for a new sewer system.* **3.** Thoughtful concern: *consideration for people's feelings.* **4.** A payment for a service rendered; a fee: *I agreed to take care of their dog for a small consideration.* *—**idiom.*** **in consideration of. 1.** In view of; on account of: *a medal awarded in consideration of bravery.* **2.** In return for: *payment in consideration of extra work.*

con•sid•ered (kən **sĭd′**ərd) *adj.* Reached after careful thought: *my considered opinion.*

con•sid•er•ing (kən **sĭd′**ər ĭng) *prep.* In view of; taking into consideration: *Considering the mistakes that were made, it is amazing that the job was completed.*

con•sign (kən **sīn′**) *tr.v.* **con•signed, con•sign•ing, con•signs. 1.** To give or hand over, especially to the care of another; entrust or commit: *The criminals have been consigned to prison.* **2.** To deliver (merchandise) for sale: *The manufacturer consigned the cars to the dealer.* **—con•sign′a•ble** *adj.*

con•sign•ment (kən **sīn′**mənt) *n.* **1.** The delivery of something, as for sale or safekeeping: *The governor requested consignment of food for the earthquake victims.* **2.** Something that is consigned, as for sale: *The store received a consignment of umbrellas.* *—**idiom.*** **on consignment.** With the agreement that payment is expected only after sales have been made and that unsold items may be returned: *The store owner accepted the shipment on consignment.*

con•sist (kən **sĭst′**) *intr.v.* **con•sist•ed, con•sist•ing, con•sists. 1.** To be made up or composed: *The United States consists of fifty states.* **2.** To have a basis; lie; rest: *The beauty of the author's style consists in its simplicity.* [First written down in 1526 in Modern English, from Latin *cōnsistere*, to stand still, to be composed of.]

con•sis•ten•cy (kən **sĭs′**tən sē) *n., pl.* **con•sis•ten•cies. 1.** Agreement or harmony among things or parts: *A polite greeting is in consistency with good manners.* **2.** Adherence to or agreement with the same principles or course of action: *They say they all believe in the same thing, but their statements lack consistency.* **3.** The degree or texture of firmness, density, or thickness: *mix water and clay to the consistency of thick cream.*

con•sis•tent (kən **sĭs′**tənt) *adj.* Continually adhering to the same principles or course of action: *a consistent supporter of women's rights.* **—con•sis′tent•ly** *adv.*

con•sis•to•ry (kən **sĭs′**tə rē) *n., pl.* **con•sis•to•ries. 1.** A council of the cardinals of the Roman Catholic Church, presided over by the pope. **2.** The governing assembly of certain Protestant churches.

con•so•la•tion (kŏn′sə **lā′**shən) *n.* **1.** The act or an instance of consoling or comforting. **2.** Something that consoles: *The one consolation in their leaving on a trip is that they will not be gone for long.*

consolation prize *n.* A prize given to someone who participates in but does not win a contest.

con•sole¹ (kən **sōl′**) *tr.v.* **con•soled, con•sol•ing, con•soles.** To comfort in time of disappointment or sorrow: *Friends consoled the widow at the funeral.* [First written down in 1693 in Modern English, from Latin *cōnsōlārī.*]

con•sole² (**kŏn′**sōl′) *n.* **1.** A cabinet for a radio, television set, or stereo system, designed to stand on the floor. **2.** The part of an organ facing the player, containing the keyboard, stops, and pedals. **3.** A panel housing the controls for a system of electronic or mechanical equipment. **4.** A decorative bracket for supporting a cornice or shelf. [First written down in 1706 in Modern English, from French, perhaps short for *consolider*, to strengthen, from Latin *cōnsolidāre.*]

con•sol•i•date (kən **sŏl′**ĭ dāt′) *v.* **con•sol•i•dat•ed, con•sol•i•dat•ing, con•sol•i•dates.** *—tr.* **1.** To combine into one; unite: *The ranch was formed when four small farms were consolidated.* **2.** To make secure and strong: *She consolidated her power during her first year in office.* *—intr.* To be united or combined: *The two businesses consolidated into one large firm.* [First written down in 1511 in Modern English, from Latin *cōnsolidāre* : *com-*, intensive prefix + *solidāre*, to make firm (from *solidus*, firm).] **—con•sol′i•da′tion** *n.*

con•som•mé (kŏn′sə **mā′** *or* **kŏn′**sə mā′) *n.* A clear soup made of meat or vegetable broth. —SEE NOTE.

con•so•nance (**kŏn′**sə nəns) *n.* **1.** Agreement; harmony; accord. **2.** A combination of musical tones that are regarded as pleasing.

con•so•nant (**kŏn′**sə nənt) *n.* **1.** A speech sound made by partially or completely blocking the flow of air through one's mouth. **2.** A letter of the alphabet representing such a sound, as *b, m, s,* and *t.* *—adj.* **1.** Consonantal: *a consonant sound.* **2.** Being in agreement or accord: *remarks consonant with one's beliefs.* **3.** Musically harmonious. [First written down before 1325 in Middle English, from Latin *cōnsonāre*, to agree : *com-*, together + *sonāre*, to sound.]

con•so•nan•tal (kŏn′sə **năn′**tl) *adj.* Of, relating to, or containing a consonant or consonants.

con•sort (**kŏn′**sôrt′) *n.* A husband or wife, especially of a monarch. —*intr.v.* (kən **sôrt′**). **con•sort•ed, con•sort•ing, con•sorts.** To keep company; associate: *a musician who consorts with movie stars.*

con•spic•u•ous (kən **spĭk′**yo͞o əs) *adj.* **1.** Easily seen; obvious: *a conspicuous spot on the front of my shirt.* **2.** Attracting attention; striking; remarkable: *a conspicuous achievement.* [First written down in 1545 in Modern English, from Latin *cōnspicuus*, from *cōnspicere*, to observe : *com-*, intensive prefix + *specere*, to look.] —**con•spic′u•ous•ly** *adv.* —**con•spic′u•ous•ness** *n.*

con•spir•a•cy (kən **spîr′**ə sē) *n., pl.* **con•spir•a•cies. 1.** The act of secretly planning together to commit something unlawful. **2.** A secret plan to commit an unlawful act; a plot: *A conspiracy to overthrow the government was uncovered.* **3.** A group planning such a secret act.

con•spir•a•tor (kən **spîr′**ə tər) *n.* A person who takes part in a conspiracy; a plotter.

con•spire (kən **spīr′**) *intr.v.* **con•spired, con•spir•ing, con•spires. 1.** To plan together secretly to commit an illegal or wrongful act: *Traitors conspired to assassinate the military leader.* **2.** To work together; combine: *Good weather and a reliable car conspired to make the trip a happy one.* [First written down before 1376 in Middle English and spelled *conspiren*, from Latin *cōnspīrāre* : *com-*, together + *spīrāre*, to breathe, whisper.] —**con•spir′er** *n.*

con•sta•ble (**kŏn′**stə bəl *or* **kŭn′**stə bəl) *n.* **1.** A public officer in a town or village having somewhat less authority than a sheriff. **2.** *Chiefly British.* A police officer. [First written down about 1200 in Middle English, from Late Latin *comes stabulī*, officer of the stable : Latin *comes*, officer, companion + Latin *stabulum*, stable.]

con•stab•u•lar•y (kən **stăb′**yə lĕr′ē) *n., pl.* **con•stab•u•lar•ies. 1.a.** The body of constables of a certain district. **b.** The district under the jurisdiction of a constable. **2.** An armed police force organized like a military unit.

con•stan•cy (**kŏn′**stən sē) *n.* **1.** The quality of remaining constant; changelessness: *the constancy of the stars.* **2.** Faithfulness; steadfastness: *constancy in friendship.*

con•stant (**kŏn′**stənt) *adj.* **1.** Not changing; remaining the same: *An electric motor maintains a constant speed.* **2.** Happening continually; persistent: *constant interruptions; constant reminders.* **3.** Steadfast in loyalty or affection; faithful: *a constant friend.* —*n.* **1.** Something that never changes. **2.** In mathematics: **a.** A number that has a fixed value in a specific situation: *In averaging final grades for the semester, the number of tests is a constant for each student.* **b.** A number that never varies: *The ratio of the circumference to the diameter of a circle is π, a constant.* [First written down about 1390 in Middle English and spelled *constaunt*, from Latin *cōnstāre*, to stand firm : *com-*, intensive prefix + *stāre*, to stand.] —**con′stant•ly** *adv.*

Con•stan•tine I (**kŏn′**stən tēn′ *or* **kŏn′**stən tīn′). A.D. 285?–337. Emperor of Rome (306–337) who adopted Christianity and suspended the persecution of Christians.

Con•stan•ti•no•ple (kŏn′stăn tə **nō′**pəl). Istanbul.

con•stel•la•tion (kŏn′stə **lā′**shən) *n.* **1.** A group of stars, especially one perceived as a design or mythological figure: *The Little Dipper and Orion are two well-known constellations.* **2.** A group or gathering of distinguished persons or things: *The Nobel Prize ceremony is usually attended by a constellaton of scientists and scholars.* [First written down about 1330 in Middle English, from Late Latin *cōnstellātiō* : *com-*, together + *stēlla*, star.]

con•ster•na•tion (kŏn′stər **nā′**shən) *n.* Great fear or dismay: *To our consternation the dog darted out into the road.*

con•sti•pate (**kŏn′**stə pāt′) *tr.v.* **con•sti•pat•ed, con•sti•pat•ing, con•sti•pates.** To cause constipation in.

con•sti•pa•tion (kŏn′stə **pā′**shən) *n.* Difficult or infrequent movement of the bowels.

con•stit•u•en•cy (kən **stĭch′**o͞o ən sē) *n., pl.* **con•stit•u•en•cies. 1.** A body of voters: *The constituency repeatedly returned the Senator to office.* **2.** A district represented by a delegate elected to a legislature: *a constituency of six counties.*

con•stit•u•ent (kən **stĭch′**o͞o ənt) *adj.* **1.** Making up part of a whole: *An atom is a constituent element of a molecule.* **2.** Authorized to draw up or change a constitution: *a constituent assembly.* —*n.* **1.** A constituent part; a component: *Flour is the main constituent of bread.* **2.** A person represented by an elected official.

con•sti•tute (**kŏn′**stĭ to͞ot′ *or* **kŏn′**stĭ tyo͞ot′) *tr.v.* **con•sti•tut•ed, con•sti•tut•ing, con•sti•tutes. 1.** To be the elements or parts of; compose: *Four quarters constitute a dollar.* **2.** To set up; establish: *Police departments are constituted to maintain law and order.* **3.** To appoint, elect, or designate: *The assembly was constituted to write a new city charter.* [First written down in 1442 in Middle English, from Latin *cōnstituere*, to set up.]

con•sti•tu•tion (kŏn′stĭ **to͞o′**shən *or* kŏn′stĭ **tyo͞o′**shən) *n.* **1.** The system of fundamental laws or principles by which a nation, government, or group is organized. **2.** A document in which such a system is written. **3.** The way in which something or someone is made up, especially the physical makeup of a person or organization; nature: *a healthy person with a strong constitution.* **4.** The act of setting up: *Many lawyers participated in the constitution of a new legal society.*

con•sti•tu•tion•al (kŏn′stĭ **to͞o′**shə nəl *or* kŏn′stĭ **tyo͞o′**shə nəl) *adj.* **1.** Of or relating to a constitution: *a constitutional amendment.* **2.** Consistent with or permissible according to a constitution: *The proposed law restricting the press is not constitutional.* **3.** Established by or operating under a constitution: *a constitutional government.* **4.** Basic or inherent in one's makeup: *a constitutional weakness in his health.* —*n.* A walk taken regularly for one's health. —**con′sti•tu′tion•al•ly** *adv.*

con•sti•tu•tion•al•i•ty (kŏn′stĭ to͞o′shə **năl′**ĭ tē *or* kŏn′stĭ tyo͞o′shə **năl′**ĭ tē) *n.* Accordance with a constitution: *The Supreme Court upheld the constitutionality of the law guaranteeing equal rights to all citizens.*

con•strain (kən **strān′**) *tr.v.* **con•strained, con•strain•ing, con•strains. 1.** To compel by physical or moral force; oblige: *Since I am against the plan, I feel constrained to voice my objections.* **2.** To hold back; restrain: *The dog was constrained by a leash.* —**con•strain′ed•ly** (kən **strā′**nĭd lē) *adv.* —**con•strain′er** *n.*

con•straint (kən **strānt′**) *n.* **1.** The threat or use of force to control the action of others: *a court order requiring appearance under constraint of the law.* **2.** Something that restricts or hampers: *Without moral constraints we would live in social chaos.* **3.** The holding back of one's natural feelings or behavior; awkwardness: *The new mayor showed constraint in the presence of television cameras.*

con•strict (kən **strĭkt′**) *tr. & intr.v.* **con•strict•ed, con•strict•ing, con•stricts.** To make or become smaller or narrower, as by contracting; compress: *This drug constricts blood vessels. I could feel the*

Constantine I

ă	**pat**	oi	**boy**
ā	**pay**	ou	**out**
âr	**care**	o͝o	**took**
ä	**father**	o͞o	**boot**
ĕ	**pet**	ŭ	**cut**
ē	**be**	ûr	**urge**
ĭ	**pit**	th	**thin**
ī	**pie**	*th*	**this**
îr	**pier**	hw	**whoop**
ŏ	**pot**	zh	**vision**
ō	**toe**	ə	**about**
ô	**paw**	N	*French* **bon**

muscles in my body constrict with fright. —**con•stric′tive** *adj.*

con•stric•tion (kən strĭk′shən) *n.* **1.** The act or process of constricting. **2.** A feeling of pressure or tightness: *a constriction in one's throat.* **3.** Something that constricts: *The narrowing of the road is a constriction on traffic.*

con•stric•tor (kən strĭk′tər) *n.* **1.** A muscle that contracts or compresses a part or organ of the body. **2.** Any of various snakes, such as the boa and python, that kill their prey by coiling around it and squeezing.

con•struct (kən strŭkt′) *tr.v.* **con•struct•ed, con•struct•ing, con•structs.** To build or put together; erect or compose: *construct new houses; construct an argument.* —**con•struc′tor** *n.*

con•struc•tion (kən strŭk′shən) *n.* **1.** The act or process of constructing: *Two new hotels are under construction.* **2.** A thing that is put together; a structure. **3.** The way in which something is put together; a design: *The new tool shed is a building of simple construction.* **4.** An interpretation or explanation given to a certain statement: *I put a favorable construction on his reply.* **5.a.** The arrangement of words to form a meaningful phrase, clause, or sentence. **b.** A group of words arranged in a meaningful way. —**con•struc′tion•al** *adj.* —**con•struc′tion•al•ly** *adv.*

con•struc•tive (kən strŭk′tĭv) *adj.* Serving a useful purpose or helping to improve something: *gave me constructive suggestions on my work.* —**con•struc′tive•ly** *adv.* —**con•struc′tive•ness** *n.*

con•strue (kən strōō′) *tr.v.* **con•strued, con•stru•ing, con•strues.** To determine or explain the meaning of; interpret: *construed her smile as approval.*

con•sul (kŏn′səl) *n.* **1.** An official appointed by a government to live in a foreign city, look after the government's interest, and give assistance to its citizens who live or travel there. **2.** Either of the two chief magistrates of the ancient Roman republic, elected for a term of one year. —**con′su•lar** (kŏn′sə lər) *adj.*

con•su•late (kŏn′sə lĭt) *n.* **1.** The building or offices occupied by a consul. **2.** The office or term of office of a consul.

con•sult (kən sŭlt′) *v.* **con•sult•ed, con•sult•ing, con•sults.** —*tr.* **1.** To seek information or advice from: *Consult your doctor.* **2.** To refer to: *We consulted the encyclopedia to settle the question.* **3.** To have regard for; consider: *Consult the feelings of others before going ahead.* —*intr.* To exchange views; confer: *The United States consulted with the Canadian government.* [First written down in 1527 in Modern English, from Latin *cōnsultāre*, from *cōnsulere*, to take counsel.]

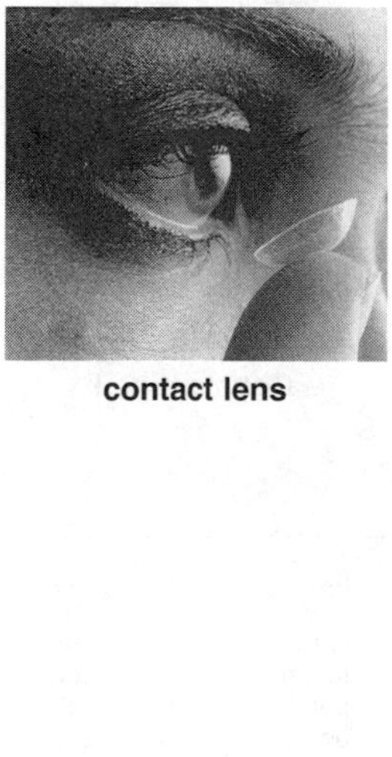

contact lens

con•sult•ant (kən sŭl′tənt) *n.* **1.** A person who gives expert or professional advice: *A lawyer is a consultant in legal matters.* **2.** A person who consults someone else.

con•sul•ta•tion (kŏn′səl tā′shən) *n.* **1.** An act of consulting: *Close consultation between the nurses and the doctor saved the patient.* **2.** A conference at which advice is given or views are exchanged: *Lawyers for the opposing sides in the case held a heated consultation.*

con•sul•ta•tive (kən sŭl′tə tĭv) *adj.* For consultation; advisory: *a consultative council.*

con•sume (kən sōōm′) *v.* **con•sumed, con•sum•ing, con•sumes.** —*tr.* **1.** To eat or drink up: *The guests consumed all the spaghetti, so we made more.* **2.** To use up; expend: *The experiment consumed her entire summer.* **3.** To destroy totally, as by fire: *Flames consumed the factory.* **4.** To occupy the attention of; engross: *The book consumed me for hours.* —*intr.* To be destroyed, expended, or wasted. [First written down about 1380 in Middle English and spelled *consumen*, from Latin *cōnsūmere.*] —**con•sum′a•ble** (kən sōō′mə bəl) *adj.*

con•sum•er (kən sōō′mər) *n.* **1.** A person or thing that consumes, especially a person who buys and uses goods and services: *The manufacturers passed on the price increase to consumers.* **2.** An organism that ingests other organisms or particles of organic matter.

con•sum•er•ism (kən sōō′mə rĭz′əm) *n.* **1.** A movement seeking to protect consumers by requiring honest advertising and packaging, fair prices, and improved safety standards of products. **2.** Attachment to materialistic values or possessions.

con•sum•mate (kŏn′sə māt′) *tr.v.* **con•sum•mat•ed, con•sum•mat•ing, con•sum•mates.** To bring to completion; conclude: *consummate a business deal.* —*adj.* (kən sŭm′ĭt *or* kŏn′sə mət). **1.** Complete or perfect in every respect: *consummate happiness.* **2.** Highly skilled; polished: *a consummate musician.* —**con•sum′mate•ly** *adv.* —**con′sum•ma′tion** *n.*

con•sump•tion (kən sŭmp′shən) *n.* **1.** The act or process of consuming: *Much manufacturing is based on the consumption of oil.* **2.** A quantity consumed: *The consumption of wood used for paper can be reduced by recycling.* **3.a.** A wasting away of the body, especially from tuberculosis of the lungs. **b.** Tuberculosis of the lungs. In this sense, this word is no longer in scientific use.

con•sump•tive (kən sŭmp′tĭv) *adj.* **1.** Tending to consume; destructive; wasteful: *She never developed the consumptive habits of a spendthrift.* **2.** Of, relating to, or suffering from tuberculosis of the lungs. —*n.* A person who is afflicted with tuberculosis of the lungs. —**con•sump′tive•ly** *adv.* —**con•sump′tive•ness** *n.*

cont. *abbr.* An abbreviation of continued.

con•tact (kŏn′tăkt′) *n.* **1.** The touching or coming together of persons or things. **2.** The condition of being in communication: *We lost contact with our former neighbors after they moved away.* **3.** *Informal.* A person who is in a position to be of help; a connection: *His uncle has numerous contacts in the government.* **4.a.** A connection between two conductors that allows an electric current to flow. **b.** A part or device that makes or breaks a connection in an electrical circuit: *the contacts of a switch.* **5.** A contact lens. —*v.* (kŏn′tăkt′ *or* kən tăkt′). **con•tact•ed, con•tact•ing, con•tacts.** —*tr.* **1.** To bring or put into contact with; touch: *If water contacts the paper it will leave a mark.* **2.** To get in touch with; communicate with: *The salesman contacted several customers by telephone.* —*intr.* To be or come into contact: *Bare wires that contact will cause a short circuit.* [First written down in 1626 in Modern English, from Latin *contāctus*, from past participle of *contingere*, to touch.]

contact lens *n.* A thin plastic or glass lens designed to correct a defect in vision, worn directly on the cornea of the eye.

con•ta•gion (kən tā′jən) *n.* **1.** The transmission of disease by direct or indirect contact between individuals: *Lack of sanitary conditions may lead to widespread contagion.* **2.** A disease that is or can be transmitted in this way: *Flu is a common contagion of the winter months.* **3.** The tendency to spread, as of an influence or emotional state: *the contagion of panic.*

con•ta•gious (kən tā′jəs) *adj.* **1.** Capable of being transmitted by direct or indirect contact: *Chicken pox is a highly contagious disease.* **2.** Capable of carrying disease: *He stayed home until he was no longer contagious.* **3.** Tending to spread from person to person: *contagious laughter.* [First written down about 1380 in Middle English, from Latin *contāgiō*, a touching, contagion, from *contingere*, to touch.] **—con•ta'gious•ly** *adv.* **—con•ta'gious•ness** *n.*

con•tain (kən tān') *tr.v.* **con•tained, con•tain•ing, con•tains. 1.** To have within; hold: *Orange juice contains vitamin C. The document contains important information.* **2.** To consist of; comprise; include: *A gallon contains four quarts.* **3.** To hold back; restrain: *I could scarcely contain my laughter.* [First written down before 1300 in Middle English and spelled *conteinen*, from Latin *continēre* : *com-*, together + *tenēre*, to hold.] **—con•tain'a•ble** *adj.*

con•tain•er (kən tā'nər) *n.* Something, such as a box, can, jar, or barrel, used to hold something; a receptacle.

con•tain•er•ize (kən tā'nə rīz') *tr.v.* **con•tain•er•ized, con•tain•er•iz•ing, con•tain•er•iz•es.** To package (something) in large containers: *A huge collection of books and paintings was containerized and shipped to the new museum.*

con•tain•ment (kən tān'mənt) *n.* **1.** The act or fact of containing something: *underground storage facilities for the containment of radioactive waste.* **2.** The policy of attempting to prevent the expansion of an opposing power or ideology.

con•tam•i•nant (kən tăm'ə nənt) *n.* Something that contaminates: *Contaminants polluted the nearby stream.*

con•tam•i•nate (kən tăm'ə nāt') *tr.v.* **con•tam•i•nated, con•tam•i•nat•ing, con•tam•i•nates.** To make impure or unclean by mixture or contact; pollute; foul: *The waters were contaminated with oil from a leaking tanker.* **—con•tam'i•na'tor** *n.*

con•tam•i•na•tion (kən tăm'ə nā'shən) *n.* **1.** The act of contaminating or the condition of being contaminated: *Dumping chemicals nearby caused contamination of the lake.* **2.** Something that contaminates; an impurity.

contd. *abbr.* An abbreviation of continued.

con•temn (kən tĕm') *tr.v.* **con•temned, con•temn•ing, con•temns.** To view or regard with contempt; despise.

con•tem•plate (kŏn'təm plāt') *v.* **con•tem•plat•ed, con•tem•plat•ing, con•tem•plates.** *—tr.* **1.** To look at carefully and thoughtfully: *contemplate the stars in wonder.* **2.** To think about (something) carefully; ponder: *I contemplated the offer of a job.* **3.** To think about doing (something); consider, intend, or expect: *We contemplated a trip to Africa.* *—intr.* To ponder; meditate: *He sat in the garden contemplating.* [First written down in 1592 in Modern English, from Latin *contemplārī* : *com-*, intensive prefix + *templum*, space for observing auguries.]

con•tem•pla•tion (kŏn'təm plā'shən) *n.* **1.** The act of looking at or thinking about something thoughtfully. **2.** Meditation on spiritual or religious matters. **3.** Intention or expectation: *We packed warm clothes in contemplation of our trip to the mountains.*

con•tem•pla•tive (kən tĕm'plə tĭv *or* kŏn'təm-plā'tĭv) *adj.* Characterized by or given to contemplation: *the contemplative life of a monk.* **—con•tem'pla•tive•ly** *adv.* **—con•tem'pla•tive•ness** *n.*

con•tem•po•ra•ne•ous (kən tĕm'pə rā'nē əs) *adj.* Originating, existing, or occurring at the same time. **—con•tem'po•ra'ne•ous•ly** *adv.* **—con•tem'po•ra'ne•ous•ness** *n.*

con•tem•po•rar•y (kən tĕm'pə rĕr'ē) *adj.* **1.** Living or occurring during the same period of time. **2.** Current; modern: *We wanted to buy contemporary computer equipment.* *—n., pl.* **con•tem•po•rar•ies. 1.** A person living at the same time as another: *Emily Dickinson and Walt Whitman were contemporaries.* **2.** A person of the present age.

con•tempt (kən tĕmpt') *n.* **1.a.** A feeling that a person or thing is low or worthless; scorn: *She has contempt for hypocrites.* **b.** The condition of being despised or dishonored. **2.** Open disobedience or disrespect to a court of law or to a legislative body: *Failure to appear before the judge put the witness in contempt.*

con•tempt•i•ble (kən tĕmp'tə bəl) *adj.* Deserving contempt; despicable. **—con•tempt'i•ble•ness** *n.* **—con•tempt'i•bly** *adv.*

con•temp•tu•ous (kən tĕmp'cho͞o əs) *adj.* Feeling or showing contempt: *a haughty and contemptuous refusal.* **—con•temp'tu•ous•ly** *adv.* **—con•temp'tu•ous•ness** *n.*

con•tend (kən tĕnd') *v.* **con•tend•ed, con•tend•ing, contends.** *—intr.* **1.** To struggle against difficulties: *Doctors contend with disease.* **2.** To compete; vie: *The two teams contended for the championship.* **3.** To strive in controversy or debate; dispute: *The lawyers contended for the innocence of their client.* *—tr.* To claim or maintain: *The witness contended the truth of his statement.* **—con•tend'er** *n.*

con•tent[1] (kŏn'tĕnt') *n.* **1.** Something that is contained in a receptacle. Often used in the plural: *empty a jar of its contents.* **2.** The subject matter of a written work, as a document or book. Often used in the plural: *The contents of the report were not revealed.* **3.** The substantive or meaningful part: *The content of the paper is fine, but the style needs work.* **4.** The amount of a substance contained in something: *the fat content of milk.* [First written down before 1425 in Middle English and spelled *contents*, from Medieval Latin *contentum*, from Latin *continēre*, to contain.]

con•tent[2] (kən tĕnt') *adj.* Desiring no more than what one has; satisfied: *He was content to live in the small apartment.* *—n.* A feeling of satisfied ease; contentment; satisfaction. *—tr.v.* **con•tent•ed, con•tent•ing, con•tents.** To make content or satisfied: *I contented myself with a cup of tea and a book.* [First written down before 1400 in Middle English, from Latin *contentus*, past participle of *continēre*, to restrain.]

con•tent•ed (kən tĕn'tĭd) *adj.* Satisfied with things as they are; content: *Few things are more peaceful than a contented look on a child's face.* **—con•tent'ed•ly** *adv.* **—con•tent'ed•ness** *n.*

con•ten•tion (kən tĕn'shən) *n.* **1.** The act of striving or contending: *The rival teams played in fierce but friendly contention.* **2.** A statement put forward in an argument: *The lawyer's contention was that the evidence was misleading.*

con•ten•tious (kən tĕn'shəs) *adj.* Inclined to argue; quarrelsome: *One of the newspaper editors was a contentious troublemaker.* **—con•ten'tious•ly** *adv.* **—con•ten'tious•ness** *n.*

con•tent•ment (kən tĕnt'mənt) *n.* The condition of being contented; satisfaction.

con•test (kŏn'tĕst') *n.* **1.** A struggle for victory or superiority between rivals: *The struggle for American independence was a long contest.* **2.** A competition, usually between entrants who perform separately and are rated by judges: *an essay contest; a skating contest.* *—v.* (kən tĕst' *or* kŏn'tĕst'). **con•test•ed, con•test•ing, con•tests.** *—tr.* **1.** To compete or strive for: *The two birds contested a nesting place.* **2.** To dispute; challenge: *contest a parking ticket; contest a will.* See Synonyms at **oppose.** *—intr.* To struggle or compete: *rival teams contesting for first place.* [First written down in 1603 in Modern English, from French *contester*, to dispute, from Latin *contestārī*, to call to witness : *com-*, to-

ă	pat	oi	boy
ā	pay	ou	out
âr	care	o͝o	took
ä	father	o͞o	boot
ĕ	pet	ŭ	cut
ē	be	ûr	urge
ĭ	pit	th	thin
ī	pie	*th*	this
îr	pier	hw	whoop
ŏ	pot	zh	vision
ō	toe	ə	about
ô	paw	N	*French* bon

gether + *testis,* witness.] —**con•test′a•ble** *adj.*

con•tes•tant (kən **tĕs′**tənt *or* **kŏn′**tĕs′tənt) *n.* A person who takes part in a contest.

con•text (**kŏn′**tĕkst′) *n.* **1.** The part of a statement or text that surrounds a particular word or passage and makes clear its meaning: *In some contexts* mad *means "insane"; in other contexts it means "angry."* **2.** A general setting or set of circumstances in which a particular event occurs; a situation: *Horses are out of place in the context of modern city life.* [First written down before 1425 in Middle English and spelled *context,* composition, from Latin *contextus,* from past participle of *contexere,* to join together : *com-,* together + *texere,* to weave.]

con•tex•tu•al (kən **tĕks′**cho͞o əl) *adj.* Of or depending on context. —**con•tex′tu•al•ly** *adv.*

con•tig•u•ous (kən **tĭg′**yo͞o əs) *adj.* **1.** Having a common boundary; adjoining: *New Hampshire is contiguous with Maine.* **2.a.** Connected without a break: *the 48 contiguous states.* **b.** Connected in time; uninterrupted: *served three contiguous terms.* —**con•tig′u•ous•ly** *adv.* —**con•tig′u•ous•ness** *n.*

con•ti•nence (**kŏn′**tə nəns) *n.* Self-restraint, especially with regard to passions and desires; moderation: *lived a life of continence.*

con•ti•nent[1] (**kŏn′**tə nənt) *n.* **1.** One of the seven great land masses of the earth, including Africa, Antarctica, Asia, Australia, Europe, North America, and South America. **2. Continent.** The mainland of Europe. [First written down about 1425 in Middle English, from Latin *(terra) continēns,* continuous (land), present participle of *continēre,* to hold together.]

con•ti•nent[2] (**kŏn′**tə nənt) *adj.* Self-restrained; moderate. [First written down before 1382 in Middle English, from Latin *continēns,* present participle of *continēre,* to restrain.]

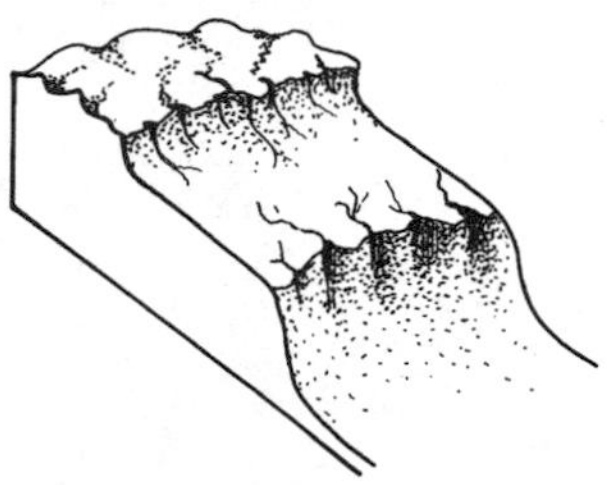
continental shelf

con•ti•nen•tal (kŏn′tə **nĕn′**tl) *adj.* **1.** Of, relating to, or characteristic of a continent: *the continental United States.* **2.** Often **Continental.** Of or relating to the mainland of Europe. **3. Continental.** Of or relating to the American colonies during and just after the Revolutionary War: *the Continental Army.* —*n.* **1.** Often **Continental.** An inhabitant of the mainland of Europe. **2. Continental.** A soldier in the Continental Army during the Revolutionary War. **3.** A piece of paper money issued by the Continental Congress during the Revolutionary War.

Con•ti•nen•tal Congress *n.* Either of two legislative assemblies of the American colonies and then of the United States. The first met in 1774; the second was the legislative and executive body of the government from 1775 until the Constitution took effect in 1789.

continental divide *n.* A region of high ground from each side of which the river systems of a continent flow in opposite directions.

Continental Divide. A series of mountain ridges extending from Alaska to Mexico that forms the watershed of North America. It is often called the **Great Divide** in the United States.

continental drift *n.* The gradual movement of sections of the earth's outer surface on which the continents rest, caused by pressure that makes the outer surface slip across the underlying molten mass of the earth.

continental shelf *n.* The part of the edge of a continent covered by shallow ocean waters and extending to the steep slopes that reach into the deep part of the ocean.

con•tin•gen•cy (kən **tĭn′**jən sē) *n., pl.* **con•tin•gen•cies. 1.** An event that may occur but is not likely or intended; a possibility: *People who work in emergency medical service must be prepared for any contingency.* **2.** The condition of being contingent: *Whether we will be able to drive through the mountain pass is a matter of contingency.*

con•tin•gent (kən **tĭn′**jənt) *adj.* **1.** Possible but not certain to occur; uncertain: *a contingent move of company offices.* **2.** Dependent on circumstances not yet known; conditional: *The success of our picnic is contingent on the weather.* **3.** Happening by chance; accidental; unexpected: *a quick contingent meeting in the hall.* —*n.* **1.** A representative group forming part of a gathering; a delegation: *the Maine contingent at the Democratic national convention.* **2.** A share, as of troops, contributed to a general effort: *The medical team at the earthquake site included a contingent of American doctors.* —**con•tin′gent•ly** *adv.*

con•tin•u•al (kən **tĭn′**yo͞o əl) *adj.* **1.** Repeated regularly and frequently: *the continual banging of the shutters in the wind.* **2.** Not broken or stopping; continuing over a long period of time; steady: *continual noise; a continual diet of rice and vegetables.* —**con•tin′u•al•ly** *adv.*

con•tin•u•ance (kən **tĭn′**yo͞o əns) *n.* **1.** The act, fact, or duration of continuing; lasting or staying: *a continuance of good feeling between two friends.* **2.** Adjournment of legal proceedings to a future date: *The judge gave the defense a continuance until witnesses could be found.*

con•tin•u•a•tion (kən tĭn′yo͞o **ā′**shən) *n.* **1.a.** The act or fact of going on or persisting: *Continuation of the heavy rain will cause flooding.* **b.** The act or fact of beginning again after stopping; resumption: *After a delay of several weeks there was a continuation of building.* **2.** Something by which another thing is continued; an extension to a further point; an added part: *Today's fair weather is a continuation of yesterday's sunny skies.*

con•tin•ue (kən **tĭn′**yo͞o) *v.* **con•tin•ued, con•tin•u•ing, con•tin•ues.** —*intr.* **1.** To keep on or persist: *We continue in our efforts to improve the quality of our products.* **2.** To go on after stopping; resume: *Our program continues after these commercials.* **3.** To remain in the same condition or place: *The rainy weather continued for weeks.* —*tr.* **1.** To carry on or persist in: *The police continued their investigation.* **2.** To begin with again after stopping; resume: *We will continue our discussion tomorrow.* **3.** To cause to remain or last; retain; maintain: *continue a family business.* **4.** In law, to postpone or adjourn: *The judge continued the beginning of the trial for another week.* [First written down about 1340 in Middle English and spelled *continuen,* from Latin *continuāre,* from *continuus,* continuous, from *continēre,* to hold together.]

con•ti•nu•i•ty (kŏn′tə **no͞o′**ĭ tē *or* kŏn′tə **nyo͞o′**ĭ tē) *n., pl.* **con•ti•nu•i•ties. 1.** An uninterrupted succession: *A telephone call broke the continuity of my thoughts.* **2.** The condition of being continuous: *His erratic thoughts lacked continuity.*

con•tin•u•ous (kən **tĭn′**yo͞o əs) *adj.* Continuing without interruption; unbroken: *Living cells must have a continuous supply of oxygen.* —**con•tin′u•ous•ly** *adv.* —**con•tin′u•ous•ness** *n.*

continuous spectrum *n.* A spectrum that covers a range of wavelengths without breaks or gaps.

con•tin•u•um (kən **tĭn′**yo͞o əm) *n., pl.* **con•tin•u•a** (kən **tĭn′**yo͞o ə) or **con•tin•u•ums.** Something that continues or extends without interruption.

con•tort (kən **tôrt′**) *tr.v.* **con•tort•ed, con•tort•ing, con•torts.** To twist or bend severely out of shape; wrench: *The pain of a toothache contorted his face.* —**con•tor′tion** *n.*

con•tor•tion•ist (kən **tôr′**shə nĭst) *n.* An acrobat who twists into contorted positions.

con•tour (**kŏn′**to͝or′) *n.* **1.** The outline of a figure, body, or mass: *the twisted contour of the coastline.*

2. A contour line. *—adj.* **1.** Following the contour lines of uneven terrain to limit erosion of topsoil: *contour plowing.* **2.** Shaped to fit the outline or form of something: *contour sheets on a bed.* [First written down in 1662 in Modern English, from French, from Italian *contornare,* to draw in outline.]

contour line *n.* A line on a map joining points of the same elevation.

contour map *n.* A map that shows elevations above sea level and surface features of the land by means of contour lines.

contra– *pref.* A prefix that means against or opposite: *contradistinction.* —SEE NOTE.

con•tra•band (kŏn′trə bănd′) *n.* **1.** Goods prohibited by law from being imported or exported. **2.** Smuggling. *—adj.* Prohibited from being imported or exported: *a contraband shipment.*

con•tra•bass (kŏn′trə bās′) *n.* A double bass. *—adj.* Pitched an octave below the normal bass range.

con•tra•bas•soon (kŏn′trə bə so͞on′) *n.* A large bassoon pitched about an octave below an ordinary bassoon.

con•tra•cep•tion (kŏn′trə sĕp′shən) *n.* The intentional prevention of conception and pregnancy, as by the use of drugs or a device such as a condom.

con•tra•cep•tive (kŏn′trə sĕp′tĭv) *adj.* Capable of preventing conception. *—n.* A contraceptive substance or device.

con•tract (kŏn′trăkt′) *n.* **1.** An agreement between two or more persons or groups, especially one that is written and enforceable by law. **2.** A document stating the terms of such an agreement: *a new labor contract.* *—v.* (kən trăkt′ *or* kŏn′trăkt′). **con•tract•ed, con•tract•ing, con•tracts.** *—tr.* **1.** To make smaller by drawing together: *Hot water contracted the wool fibers in my sweater and it shrank.* **2.** To arrange or settle by a formal agreement: *contract a business deal.* **3.** To get; acquire: *contract the mumps; contract a debt.* **4.** To shorten (a word or words) by omitting or combining some of the letters or sounds: *Most people contract "I am" to "I'm" when they speak.* *—intr.* **1.** To draw together; become smaller: *The pupils of the cat's eyes contracted.* **2.** To arrange by a formal agreement: *The developers contracted for construction of several new houses.* [First written down before 1333 in Middle English, from Latin *contrāctus,* past participle of *contrahere,* to draw together, make a contract : *com-,* together + *trahere,* to draw.]

con•trac•tile (kən trăk′təl *or* kən trăk′tīl′) *adj.* Capable of contracting or causing contraction: *contractile muscle fibers; contractile forces of cooling.*

contractile vacuole *n.* A vacuole in one-celled organisms that discharges a fluid by contracting.

con•trac•tion (kən trăk′shən) *n.* **1.** The act of contracting or the condition of being contracted: *Cold air causes the contraction of most substances.* **2.** A condensed word or phrase, formed by omitting or combining some of the letters or sounds. For example, *isn't* is a contraction of *is not.* **3.** The shortening and thickening of a muscle in action, especially of the uterus during labor.

con•trac•tor (kŏn′trăk′tər *or* kən trăk′tər) *n.* A person who contracts to do something, especially to provide materials and labor for a construction job.

con•trac•tu•al (kən trăk′cho͞o əl) *adj.* Of or relating to a contract: *a contractual arrangement between a carpenter and a house builder.* **—con•trac′tu•al•ly** *adv.*

con•tra•dict (kŏn′trə dĭkt′) *tr.v.* **con•tra•dict•ed, con•tra•dict•ing, con•tra•dicts. 1.** To assert or express the opposite of (a statement): *The witness gave information that contradicted previous testimony.* **2.** To deny the statement of: *The two scientists contradicted each other in heated debate.* **3.** To be contrary to or inconsistent with: *The results of the experiments contradicted his predictions.* [First written down about 1570 in Modern English, from Latin *contrādīcere* : *contrā-,* against + *dīcere,* to speak.]

con•tra•dic•tion (kŏn′trə dĭk′shən) *n.* **1.** The act of contradicting or the condition of being contradicted: *His persistent contradiction of the teacher embarrassed us.* **2.** An inconsistency; a discrepancy: *There's a contradiction between what you say and what your report states.* **3.** A statement that contradicts something.

con•tra•dic•to•ry (kŏn′trə dĭk′tə rē) *adj.* **1.** Involving or having the nature of a contradiction; opposing; contrary: *Contradictory reports about the vaccine's effectiveness perplexed the doctors.* **2.** Given to contradicting: *a quarrelsome and contradictory nature.* **—con′tra•dic′to•ri•ly** *adv.* **—con′tra•dic′tor•i•ness** *n.*

con•tra•dis•tinc•tion (kŏn′trə dĭ stĭngk′shən) *n.* Distinction by contrasting or by opposing qualities: *noise in contradistinction to music.*

con•tral•to (kən trăl′tō) *n., pl.* **con•tral•tos. 1.** The lowest female singing voice or voice part, lower than soprano and higher than tenor. **2.** A woman having such a voice.

con•trap•tion (kən trăp′shən) *n.* A mechanical device; a gadget.

con•trar•i•wise (kŏn′trĕr′ē wīz′ *or* kən trâr′ē wīz′) *adv.* **1.** In an opposite way or reverse order. **2.** On the contrary.

con•trar•y (kŏn′trĕr′ē) *adj.* **1.** Completely different; opposed: *The debaters held contrary points of view.* **2.** Adverse; unfavorable: *A contrary wind made sailing difficult.* **3.** (*also* kən trâr′ē). Stubbornly opposed to others; willful: *Little children often become contrary when they need a nap.* *—n., pl.* **con•trar•ies.** Something that is opposite: *Their theory made sense at first, but experimentation proved the contrary to be true.* *—idiom.* **on the contrary.** In opposition to the previous statement; conversely: *I'm not sick; on the contrary, I'm quite healthy.* **—con′trar′i•ly** *adv.* **—con′trar′i•ness** *n.*

con•trast (kən trăst′ *or* kŏn′trăst′) *v.* **con•trast•ed, con•trast•ing, con•trasts.** *—tr.* To compare in order to reveal differences: *The essay contrasts city and country life.* *—intr.* To show differences when compared: *light colors that contrast with a dark background.* *—n.* (kŏn′trăst′). **1.** Comparison, especially in order to reveal differences. **2.** A striking difference between things compared: *the startling contrast between modern life and that of pioneer times.* **3.** Something that is strikingly different from something else: *Driving a truck is quite a contrast to driving a compact car.* [First written down in 1695 in Modern English, from Medieval Latin *contrāstāre* : Latin *contrā-,* against + Latin *stāre,* to stand.]

con•trib•ute (kən trĭb′yo͞ot) *v.* **con•trib•ut•ed, con•trib•ut•ing, con•trib•utes.** *—tr.* **1.** To give or supply in common with others: *We contributed a lot of time to the project.* **2.** To submit (something written) for publication: *contribute an article to the school newspaper.* *—intr.* **1.** To give or supply something along with others: *contribute to the Red Cross.* **2.** To help in bringing about a result: *Exercise contributes to better health.* **3.** To submit material for publication. **—con•trib′u•tor** *n.*

con•tri•bu•tion (kŏn′trĭ byo͞o′shən) *n.* **1.** The act of contributing: *Contribution by several people is necessary to hold a good discussion.* **2.** Something contributed: *The clothes were a small contribution to the homeless.*

Word Building: contra–

The prefixes **contra–** and **counter–** both derive from the Latin word *contrā,* meaning "against." **Contra–** means primarily "against, opposite," and **counter–** means "contrary, opposite." Thus *contraposition* means "an opposite position," and *countercurrent* means "a current flowing in an opposite direction."

ă	pat	oi	boy
ā	pay	ou	out
âr	care	o͝o	took
ä	father	o͞o	boot
ĕ	pet	ŭ	cut
ē	be	ûr	urge
ĭ	pit	th	thin
ī	pie	*th*	this
îr	pier	hw	whoop
ŏ	pot	zh	vision
ō	toe	ə	about
ô	paw	N	*French* bon

control tower
La Guardia Airport
in New York City

convection

Heat is a form of energy that results in the motion of molecules. Heat travels by **conduction**, **convection**, or **radiation**. The molecules in solids move by vibrating back and forth within fixed limits. In conduction, heat spreads through a solid by making the molecules vibrate faster. As faster molecules bump slower ones, the slower ones are made to vibrate faster. The solid becomes hotter. The molecules in liquids and gases, on the other hand, are free to move about. When liquids and gases are heated, the molecules move farther apart. A heated gas or liquid expands, becomes less dense, and rises; a cooled gas or liquid contracts, becomes more dense, and sinks. The resulting circulation, called convection, spreads heat. Radiation carries heat in the form of waves through space. A hot object, like the hot wire in a heat lamp, gives off energy waves called **infrared** rays. When these rays strike the molecules of another object, the object absorbs the rays. Its molecules speed up, and it becomes hotter.

con•trib•u•to•ry (kən trĭb′yə tôr′ē) *adj.* Contributing toward a result; helping to bring about a result: *Carelessness was a contributory factor in the accident.*

con•trite (kən trīt′ *or* kŏn′trīt′) *adj.* **1.** Feeling deep regret and sorrow for one's wrongdoing: *a contrite sinner.* **2.** Arising from or showing deep regret or sorrow: *contrite tears.* [First written down before 1300 in Middle English and spelled *contrit*, from Latin *contrītus*, past participle of *conterere*, to crush : *com-*, intensive prefix + *terere*, to grind.] **—con•trite′ly** *adv.* **—con•trite′ness** *n.*

con•tri•tion (kən trĭsh′ən) *n.* Sincere remorse for wrongdoing; deep regret.

con•tri•vance (kən trī′vəns) *n.* **1.** The act of contriving: *the contrivance of friends to give a surprise party.* **2.** Something that is contrived, as a mechanical device or a clever plan: *Causing a commotion was only a contrivance to divert attention.*

con•trive (kən trīv′) *tr.v.* **con•trived, con•triv•ing, con•trives. 1.** To plan or devise cleverly: *contrive an excuse for being late.* **2.** To bring about, especially by scheming: *contrive a victory by surprise attack.* **3.** To make, especially by improvisation: *contrive a tent out of a blanket and rope.* [First written down before 1338 in Middle English and spelled *contreven*, from Medieval Latin *contropāre*, to compare.] **—con•triv′er** *n.*

con•trol (kən trōl′) *tr.v.* **con•trolled, con•trol•ling, con•trols. 1.** To exercise authority or influence over; direct: *The mayor controls the city government.* **2.** To adjust or regulate: *This valve controls the flow of water.* **3.** To hold in check; restrain: *control one's anger.* —*n.* **1.** Authority or power to regulate, direct, or dominate: *the coach's control over the team.* **2.** A means of restraint; a check: *A leash is a control over a dog.* **3.** A standard of comparison for testing the results of a scientific experiment. **4.** A device or set of devices used to operate, regulate, or guide a machine or vehicle. Often used in the plural: *The pilot was sitting at the controls of the airplane.* [First written down in 1422 in Middle English and spelled *controllen*, from Medieval Latin *contrārotulāre*, to check by duplicate register : Latin *contrā*, against, opposite + Latin *rotulus*, roll, diminutive of *rota*, wheel.] **—con•trol′la•ble** *adj.*

con•trol•ler (kən trō′lər) *n.* **1.** A person who controls or regulates something, such as air traffic. **2.** Also **comp•trol•ler** (kən trō′lər). An officer who supervises the financial affairs of a business or a governmental body.

control tower *n.* A tower at an airport from which the landing and takeoff of aircraft are controlled by radio and radar.

con•tro•ver•sial (kŏn′trə vûr′shəl *or* kŏn′trə vûr′sē əl) *adj.* Of, producing, or marked by argument or debate: *controversial writing; a controversial issue.* **—con′tro•ver′sial•ly** *adv.*

con•tro•ver•sy (kŏn′trə vûr′sē) *n., pl.* **con•tro•ver•sies. 1.** A dispute, especially a public one between sides holding opposite views: *A controversy arose over the size of the school budget.* **2.** The act of engaging in such disputes: *Their lawyers are skilled at controversy.* [First written down about 1384 in Middle English and spelled *controversie*, from Latin *contrōversus*, disputed : *contrā-*, against + *vertere*, to turn.]

con•tro•vert (kŏn′trə vûrt′ *or* kŏn′trə vûrt′) *tr.v.* **con•tro•vert•ed, con•tro•vert•ing, con•tro•verts.** To dispute or deny; contradict: *The facts controvert their weak argument.* **—con′tro•vert′i•ble** *adj.*

con•tu•sion (kən to͞o′zhən *or* kən tyo͞o′zhən) *n.* A bruise.

co•nun•drum (kə nŭn′drəm) *n.* **1.** A riddle in which a fanciful question is answered by a pun. **2.** A baffling problem.

con•va•lesce (kŏn′və lĕs′) *intr.v.* **con•va•lesced, con•va•lesc•ing, con•va•lesc•es.** To regain health and strength after illness or injury; recuperate. [First written down in 1483 in Middle English, from Latin *convalēscere* : *com*, intensive prefix + *valēscere*, to grow strong.]

con•va•les•cence (kŏn′və lĕs′əns) *n.* **1.** Gradual return to health and strength after illness or injury. **2.** The time needed for this: *a short convalescence in bed.*

con•va•les•cent (kŏn′və lĕs′ənt) *adj.* **1.** Relating to or for convalescence: *a convalescent home.* **2.** Recovering from illness or injury: *a convalescent patient.* —*n.* A patient who is convalescing.

con•vec•tion (kən vĕk′shən) *n.* The transfer of heat from one place to another by the circulation of heated currents within a gas or liquid. —See Note.

con•vene (kən vēn′) *intr. & tr.v.* **con•vened, con•ven•ing, con•venes.** To assemble or cause to assemble: *Members of the committee convene monthly to decide on club business. The governor convened the legislature.* [First written down about 1425 in Middle English and spelled *convenen*, from Latin *convenīre* : *com-*, together + *venīre*, to come.]

con•ven•ience (kən vēn′yəns) *n.* **1.** The quality of being convenient; suitablity: *the convenience of doing all of one's food shopping at a supermarket.* **2.** Personal comfort or advantage: *Each hotel room has a telephone for the convenience of the guests.* **3.** Something that provides comfort or saves effort, as a device or service: *A microwave oven is a modern convenience.*

con•ven•ient (kən vēn′yənt) *adj.* **1.** Suited or favorable to one's comfort, needs, or purpose: *An electric mixer is a convenient kitchen appliance.* **2.** Easy to reach or close by: *a bank with many convenient locations.* **—con•ven′ient•ly** *adv.*

con•vent (kŏn′vənt) *n.* **1.** A community of nuns. **2.** The building or buildings occupied by nuns; a nunnery.

con•ven•tion (kən vĕn′shən) *n.* **1.a.** A formal meeting of a group for a particular purpose: *a political convention for nominating candidates.* **b.** The group of persons attending such an assembly. **2.a.** General agreement on or acceptance of certain practices or attitudes: *Convention allows for much more casual dress today.* **b.** A widely accepted practice; a custom: *the convention of shaking hands.* **3.** A formal agreement or compact, as between nations.

con•ven•tion•al (kən vĕn′shə nəl) *adj.* **1.a.** Based on or approved by general usage; customary: *Saying "Hello" is a conventional way of answering the telephone.* **b.** Following accepted practice, customs, or taste: *a conventional wedding.* **2.** Following accepted practice so closely as to be dull or unimaginative: *a conventional plan for a house.* **3.** Using means other than nuclear weapons or energy: *conventional warfare; conventional power plants.* **—con•ven′tion•al′i•ty** (kən vĕn′shə năl′ĭ tē) *n.* **—con•ven′tion•al•ly** *adv.*

con•verge (kən vûrj′) *v.* **con•verged, con•verg•ing, con•verg•es.** —*intr.* **1.** To come together in one place; meet: *The three roads converge in the center of town.* **2.** To tend or move toward each other or toward the same conclusion or result: *Their minds converged on the same point.* —*tr.* To cause to converge: *A magnifying glass converges rays of light.* [First written down in 1691 in Modern English, from Late Latin *convergere*, to incline together.]

con•ver•gence (kən vûr′jəns) *n.* **1.** The act or process of converging; tendency to meet in one point.

2. The point of converging; a meeting place. —**con•ver′gent** *adj.*

con•ver•sant (kən vûr′sənt *or* kŏn′vər sənt) *adj.* Familiar, as by study: *She is conversant with medieval history.* —**con•ver′sant•ly** *adv.*

con•ver•sa•tion (kŏn′vər sā′shən) *n.* A spoken exchange of thoughts and feelings; a talk.

con•ver•sa•tion•al (kŏn′vər sā′shə nəl) *adj.* **1.** Of or relating to conversation: *in a normal conversational tone.* **2.** Adept at or given to conversation: *Friendly people are generally more conversational than others.* —**con′ver•sa′tion•al•ly** *adv.*

con•ver•sa•tion•al•ist (kŏn′vər sā′shə nə lĭst) *n.* A person who is fond of or skilled at conversation.

con•verse[1] (kən vûrs′) *intr.v.* **con•versed, con•vers•ing, con•vers•es.** To talk informally with others: *converse about family matters.* See Synonyms at **speak.** [First written down about 1380 in Middle English and spelled *conversen,* to associate with, from Latin *conversārī* : *com-,* with + *versārī,* to occupy oneself.]

con•verse[2] (kən vûrs′ *or* kŏn′vûrs′) *adj.* Reversed, as in order; contrary: *The converse order of the alphabet is hard to repeat.* —*n.* (kŏn′vûrs′). Something that has been reversed; an opposite: *Dark is the converse of light.* [First written down in 1570 in Modern English, from Latin *conversus,* past participle of *convertere,* to turn around.] —**con•verse′ly** *adv.*

con•ver•sion (kən vûr′zhən *or* kən vûr′shən) *n.* **1.** The act or process of changing one thing, use, or purpose into another: *A generator is used for the conversion of water power into electricity.* **2.** A change in which a person adopts a new belief, opinion, or religion.

con•vert (kən vûrt′) *v.* **con•vert•ed, con•vert•ing, con•verts.** —*tr.* **1.** To change into another form, substance, or condition: *convert water into ice.* **2.** To change from one use to another; adapt to a new purpose: *convert a bedroom into a study.* **3.** To persuade (a person) to adopt a particular religion or belief: *Spanish and French priests tried to convert the native peoples of the Americas to Christianity.* **4.a.** To exchange for something of equal value: *Since we are going to France, we need to convert our dollars into francs.* **b.** To express (a quantity) in alternative units: *convert 100 yards into meters.* —*intr.* **1.** To undergo a change; be converted: *This sofa converts easily into a bed.* **2.** To adopt a particular religion or belief: *Many pagans converted to Christianity in the Middle Ages.* —*n.* (kŏn′vûrt′). A person who has adopted a new religion or belief. [First written down about 1300 in Middle English and spelled *converten,* from Latin *convertere,* to turn around : *com-,* intensive prefix + *vertere,* to turn.]

con•vert•er (kən vûr′tər) *n.* **1.** A machine that changes alternating current to direct current or direct current to alternating current. **2.** An electronic device that changes the frequency of a radio or other electromagnetic signal. **3.** A furnace in which pig iron is changed into steel by the Bessemer process.

con•vert•i•ble (kən vûr′tə bəl) *adj.* **1.** Capable of being converted: *The convertible couch is also a bed.* **2.** Having a top that can be folded back or removed: *a convertible sports car.* —*n.* **1.** A convertible automobile. **2.** Something, such as a piece of furniture, that can be converted. —**con•vert′i•bil′i•ty** *n.* —**con•vert′i•bly** *adv.*

con•vex (kŏn′vĕks′ *or* kən vĕks′) *adj.* Curving outward like the outer boundary of a circle or sphere: *Rain rolled off the convex surface of the dome.* —**con•vex′ly** *adv.* —**con•vex′ness** *n.*

con•vex•i•ty (kən vĕk′sĭ tē) *n., pl.* **con•vex•i•ties.** **1.** The condition of being convex. **2.** A convex surface, line, or body.

con•vey (kən vā′) *tr.v.* **con•veyed, con•vey•ing, con•veys.** **1.** To take or carry from one place to another; transport: *A helicopter conveyed the skiers to the top of the glacier.* **2.** To serve as a means of transmission for; transmit: *Cables convey electrical power.* **3.** To make known; communicate: *His smile conveyed his pleasure.* **4.** To transfer ownership of: *The deed conveyed the land to a close relative.*

con•vey•ance (kən vā′əns) *n.* **1.** The act of conveying: *Airlines now serve as the chief means of conveyance for transatlantic passengers.* **2.** Something used to convey, especially a vehicle such as an automobile or a bus. **3.a.** The transfer of ownership from one person to another. **b.** A legal document that brings about such a transfer.

con•vey•er also **con•vey•or** (kən vā′ər) *n.* **1.** A person or thing that conveys: *a conveyer of good news.* **2.** A mechanical device, such as a continuous moving belt, that carries things from one place to another: *put the groceries on the conveyer.*

con•vict (kən vĭkt′) *tr.v.* **con•vict•ed, con•vict•ing, con•victs.** To find or prove guilty of an offense, especially in a court of law: *The judge convicted the polluter of endangering public health.* —*n.* (kŏn′vĭkt′). A person who has been found guilty of a crime and sentenced to prison. [First written down about 1340 in Middle English and spelled *convicten,* from Latin *convincere,* to convince.]

con•vic•tion (kən vĭk′shən) *n.* **1.** The judgment of a judge or jury that a person is guilty of a crime. **2.** The state of being found or proven guilty: *a trial ending in the swindler's conviction.* **3.** A strong opinion or belief: *act according to one's true convictions.*

con•vince (kən vĭns′) *tr.v.* **con•vinced, con•vinc•ing, con•vinc•es.** To cause (someone) to believe or feel certain; persuade: *More clues convinced us we were on the right track.* [First written down in 1530 in Modern English, from Latin *convincere,* to prove wrong : *com-,* intensive prefix + *vincere,* to conquer.]

con•vinc•ing (kən vĭn′sĭng) *adj.* Serving to convince; persuasive: *a convincing argument.* —**con•vinc′ing•ly** *adv.*

con•viv•i•al (kən vĭv′ē əl) *adj.* **1.** Fond of food, drink, and good company; sociable. **2.** Festive: *a convivial reunion of old friends.* —**con•viv′i•al′i•ty** (kən vĭv′ē ăl′ĭ tē) *n.* —**con•viv′i•al•ly** *adv.*

con•vo•ca•tion (kŏn′və kā′shən) *n.* **1.** The act of convoking: *the convocation of church leaders to enact new policy.* **2.** A summoned assembly, as of members of a college community.

con•voke (kən vōk′) *tr.v.* **con•voked, con•vok•ing, con•vokes.** To call together; cause to assemble: *the President convoked the new Congress.*

con•vo•lut•ed (kŏn′və lo͞o′tĭd) *adj.* **1.** Having many twists or coils: *a convoluted path winding around streams and boulders.* **2.** Complicated; intricate: *a convoluted argument that is difficult to understand.*

con•vo•lu•tion (kŏn′və lo͞o′shən) *n.* **1.** A winding or folding: *the convolutions of a coiled snake.* **2.** One of the folds on the surface of the brain.

con•voy (kŏn′voi′) *n.* **1.** A group, as of ships or motor vehicles, traveling with a protective military force or for safety or convenience. **2.** An accompanying and protecting force: *a convoy of warships protecting the supply ships.* —*tr.v.* (kŏn′voi′ *or* kən voi′). **con•voyed, con•voy•ing, con•voys.** To accompany as a protective escort: *A warship convoyed the merchant ship across the ocean.* [First written down about 1500 in Modern English, from

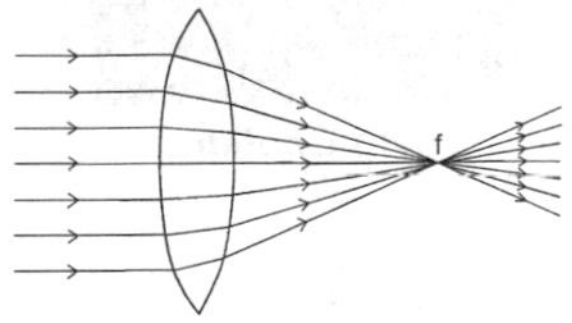

convex
Light passing through a double-convex lens, with f indicating the focus

conveyer

ă	pat	oi	boy
ā	pay	ou	out
âr	care	o͝o	took
ä	father	o͞o	boot
ĕ	pet	ŭ	cut
ē	be	ûr	urge
ĭ	pit	th	thin
ī	pie	*th*	this
îr	pier	hw	whoop
ŏ	pot	zh	vision
ō	toe	ə	about
ô	paw	N	*French* bon

Calvin Coolidge

Middle English *convoyen,* to escort, convey, from Old French *convoier.*]

con•vulse (kən vŭls′) *tr.v.* **con•vulsed, con•vuls•ing, con•vuls•es. 1.** To disturb violently; rock: *An explosion convulsed the area.* **2.** To cause to laugh uproariously: *Her impersonations convulsed the audience.* **3.** To cause (a person or animal) to have violent involuntary muscle contractions: *The patient was convulsed by high fever.* [First written down in 1643 in Modern English, from Latin *convellere,* to pull violently.]

con•vul•sion (kən vŭl′shən) *n.* **1.** A violent involuntary muscular contraction: *convulsions resulting from high fever.* **2.** An uncontrolled fit of laughter: *The audience went into convulsions watching the clown's antics.* **3.** A violent upheaval: *convulsions of the earth's crust.*

con•vul•sive (kən vŭl′sĭv) *adj.* **1.** Marked by or resembling convulsions: *convulsive movements.* **2.** Having or causing convulsions: *a convulsive disorder.* **—con•vul′sive•ly** *adv.*

co•ny (kō′nē *or* kŭn′ē) *n.* Variant of **coney.**

coo (ko͞o) *v.* **cooed, coo•ing, coos.** *—intr.* **1.** To make the murmuring sound of a pigeon or dove or a sound similar to it. **2.** To speak in murmurs. *—tr.* To express or utter by cooing: *coo words of affection.*

❑ *These sound alike:* **coo, coup** (strategem).

cook (ko͝ok) *v.* **cooked, cook•ing, cooks.** *—tr.* To prepare (food) for eating by using heat. *—intr.* **1.** To undergo cooking: *Fish cooks quickly.* **2.** To prepare food for eating by using heat: *A short-order chef must cook quickly.* *—n.* A person who prepares food for eating. ***—idiom.*** **cook up.** *Informal.* To concoct; invent: *cook up an excuse.* [First written down before 1387 in Middle English and spelled *coken,* from *coke,* a cook, from Old English *cōc,* from Latin *coquere,* to cook.]

Cook (ko͝ok), **James.** Known as "Captain Cook." 1728–1779. British navigator and explorer who commanded three major voyages, charting and naming many islands of the Pacific Ocean.

cook•book (ko͝ok′bo͝ok′) *n.* A book containing recipes and other information about cooking.

cook•er (ko͝ok′ər) *n.* A utensil or an appliance for cooking.

cook•er•y (ko͝ok′ə rē) *n., pl.* **cook•er•ies.** The preparation of food.

cook•ie also **cooky** (ko͝ok′ē) *n., pl.* **cook•ies.** A small, usually flat and crisp cake made from sweetened dough.

cook•out (ko͝ok′out′) *n.* A meal cooked and eaten outdoors.

cook•y (ko͝ok′ē) *n.* Variant of **cookie.**

cool (ko͞ol) *adj.* **cool•er, cool•est. 1.** Moderately cold; neither warm nor very cold: *cool fall weather.* **2.** Giving or allowing relief from heat: *a cool summer breeze; a cool light blouse.* **3.** Calm; unexcited: *a cool head in a crisis.* **4.** Indifferent or disdainful; unenthusiastic: *They were cool to the idea of hosting the party.* **5.** *Slang.* Excellent; first-rate: *It's a really cool movie.* **6.** *Informal.* Entire; full: *The deal brought the company a cool million in profit.* *—tr. & intr.v.* **cooled, cool•ing, cools. 1.** To make or become less warm: *cool a room by opening a window; let the pie cool.* **2.** To make or become less intense: *Having to wait cooled their enthusiasm. My anger cooled as time went by.* *—n.* **1.** A cool place, part, or time: *the cool of the evening.* **2.** *Slang.* Calmness of mind; composure: *When told there were no tickets left, several people lost their cool.* ***—idioms.*** *Slang.* To calm down; relax. **cool (one's) heels.** *Informal.* To wait or be kept waiting. [First written down about 725 in Old English and spelled *cōl.*] **—cool′ly** *adv.* **—cool′ness** *n.*

cool•ant (ko͞o′lənt) *n.* Something that cools, especially a fluid that circulates through a machine or over some of its parts in order to draw off heat.

cool•er (ko͞o′lər) *n.* A device or container for cooling something: *a water cooler.*

cool-head•ed (ko͞ol′hĕd′ĭd) *adj.* Not easily excited or flustered; calm. **—cool′-head′ed•ly** *adv.* **—cool′-head′ed•ness** *n.*

Coo•lidge (ko͞o′lĭj), **(John) Calvin.** 1872–1933. The 30th President of the United States (1923–1929), who encouraged business ventures that led to a stock market boom in the 1920's, followed by economic collapse.

coon (ko͞on) *n. Informal.* A raccoon.

coon•skin (ko͞on′skĭn′) *n.* The pelt of a raccoon.

coop (ko͞op) *n.* An enclosure or cage for poultry or small animals: *a chicken coop.* *—tr.v.* **cooped, coop•ing, coops.** To confine; shut in: *The author has been cooped up in that little room all day.*

❑ *These sound alike:* **coop, coupe** (two-door automobile).

co-op (kō′ŏp′ *or* kō ŏp′) *n.* A cooperative.

coop•er (ko͞o′pər) *n.* A person who makes or repairs wooden barrels, casks, and tubs.

Coo•per (ko͞o′pər *or* ko͝op′ər), **James Fenimore.** 1789–1851. American writer who is known for his novels of frontier life, such as *The Last of the Mohicans* (1826).

co•op•er•ate (kō ŏp′ə rāt′) *intr.v.* **co•op•er•at•ed, co•op•er•at•ing, co•op•er•ates.** To work or act with another or others for a common purpose: *Everyone cooperated in decorating the gym.*

co•op•er•a•tion (kō ŏp′ə rā′shən) *n.* The act of working together toward a common end or purpose: *international cooperation to reduce air pollution.*

co•op•er•a•tive (kō ŏp′ər ə tĭv *or* kō ŏp′ə rā′tĭv *or* kō ŏp′rə tĭv) *adj.* **1.** Done in cooperation with others: *a cooperative effort.* **2.** Willing to help or cooperate: *a cooperative and helpful assistant.* **3.** Of or relating to a cooperative: *a cooperative apartment.* *—n.* **1.** A business, farm, store, or residence owned jointly by those who use its facilities or services: *That apartment house is a cooperative in which the residents share the costs of operating the building.* **2.** An apartment in a building jointly owned by the residents: *a three-room cooperative on the first floor.* **—co•op′er•a•tive•ly** *adv.* **—co•op′er•a•tive•ness** *n.*

co-opt (kō ŏpt′ *or* kō′ŏpt′) *tr.v.* **co-opt•ed, co-opt•ing, co-opts. 1.** To appropriate or imitate for one's own purposes. **2.** To persuade or get (a person) to join a group or become part of a culture: *By promising pay raises, the company co-opted many strikers.*

co•or•di•nate (kō ôr′dn āt′ *or* kō ôr′dn ĭt) *n.* **1.** A person or thing that is equal in importance, rank, or degree. **2.** In mathematics, one of a set of numbers that determines the position of a point. If the point is on a line, only one coordinate is needed; if the point is in a plane, two are needed; and if the point is in space, three are required. *—adj.* (kō ôr′dn ĭt *or* kō ôr′dn āt′). **1.** Of equal importance, rank, or degree: *A compound sentence has two or more coordinate clauses.* **2.** Of or involving coordinates: *a coordinate system.* *—intr. & tr.v.* (kō ôr′dn āt′). **co•or•di•nat•ed, co•or•di•nat•ing, co•or•di•nates.** To work or cause to work together efficiently in a common cause or effort; harmonize: *The nursing staff of the hospital coordinates well. The nervous system coordinates activities of the body.* **—co•or′di•nate•ly** *adv.* **—co•or′di•na′tor** *n.*

co•or•di•nat•ing conjunction (kō ôr′dn ā′tĭng) *n.* A conjunction that connects two grammatical elements having identical construction. For example, *and* in *books and pencils, or* in *out of sight or out of mind,* and *yet* in *a man who tried hard, yet failed completely.*

co•or•di•na•tion (kō ôr′dn **ā′**shən) *n.* **1.** An act of coordinating or a condition or being coordinated: *Coordination among the rescue workers saved many of the earthquake victims.* **2.** The organized action of muscles or groups of muscles in the performance of complicated movements or tasks: *Gymnastics requires a great deal of coordination.*

coot (ko͞ot) *n.* **1.** Any of several water birds of North America and Europe having dark-gray feathers and a short bill and wings. **2.** *Informal.* A foolish or simple person. [First written down about 1300 in Middle English and spelled *coote,* possibly from Middle Dutch *coet.*]

coo•tie (**ko͞o′**tē) *n. Slang.* A body louse.

cop (kŏp) *n. Informal.* A police officer. [First written down in 1859 in Modern English, short for *copper,* probably from *cop,* to catch, capture, variant of *cap,* from Latin *capere.*]

cope[1] (kōp) *intr.v.* **coped, cop•ing, copes.** To contend or deal, especially successfully: *Computers help us cope with vast amounts of information.* [First written down before 1375 in Middle English and spelled *coupen,* to strike, fight against, from Old French, *couper,* from Late Latin *colpus,* a blow, from Greek *kolaphos.*]

cope[2] (kōp) *n.* A long cloak worn by priests or bishops during special ceremonies or processions. [First written down before 1121 in Middle English and spelled *-cāpe,* from Medieval Latin *cāpa,* cloak.]

Co•pen•ha•gen (**kō′**pən hā′gən *or* **kō′**pən hä′gən). The capital and largest city of Denmark, in the extreme eastern part of the country. It became the capital in 1443. Population, 482,937.

co•pe•pod (**kō′**pə pŏd′) *n.* Any of numerous very small water animals related to the shrimp. Copepods exist in huge numbers in all the oceans and seas and are a main source of food for many different kinds of water animals.

Co•per•ni•can (kō **pûr′**nĭ kən) *adj.* Of or relating to the theory, developed by Nicolaus Copernicus, that the earth rotates on its axis and, with the other planets of the solar system, revolves around the sun.

Co•per•ni•cus (kō **pûr′**nə kəs), **Nicolaus.** 1473–1543. Polish astronomer who put forth the theory that the earth and other planets revolve around the sun.

cop•i•er (**kŏp′**ē ər) *n.* **1.** A machine that makes photocopies; a photocopier. **2.** A person who makes written copies; a copyist.

co•pi•lot (**kō′**pī′lət) *n.* The second or relief pilot of an aircraft.

cop•ing (**kō′**pĭng) *n.* The top part of a wall or roof, usually slanted so as to shed rainwater or snow.

coping saw *n.* A saw with a narrow short blade stretched across a U-shaped frame, used for cutting designs in wood.

co•pi•ous (**kō′**pē əs) *adj.* Large in quantity; abundant: *Rainfall is copious in the tropics.* [First written down about 1350 in Middle English, from Latin *cōpiōsus,* from *cōpia,* abundance.] **—co′pi•ous•ly** *adv.* **—co′pi•ous•ness** *n.*

co•pla•nar (kō **plā′**nər) *adj.* Lying in the same plane: *coplanar points.*

Cop•land (**kōp′**lənd), **Aaron.** 1900–1990. American composer whose works include the ballet *Appalachian Spring* (1944).

Cop•ley (**kŏp′**lē), **John Singleton.** 1738–1815. American Loyalist painter who did many portraits of American colonists.

cop•per (**kŏp′**ər) *n.* **1.** *Symbol* **Cu** A tough reddish-brown metallic element that is an excellent conductor of heat and electricity and is widely used for electrical wiring, water piping, and corrosion-resistant parts, either pure or in alloys such as brass and bronze. Atomic number 29. See table at **element. 2.** A small coin made of copper or an alloy of copper. **3.** A reddish brown. *—tr.v.* **cop•pered, cop•per•ing, cop•pers.** To coat or finish with a layer of copper. [First written down about 1000 in Old English and spelled *coper,* from Late Latin *cuprum,* from Greek *Kupros,* Cyprus.] **—cop′per•y** *adj.*

cop•per•as (**kŏp′**ər əs) *n.* Ferrous sulfate.

cop•per•head (**kŏp′**ər hĕd′) *n.* **1.** A poisonous snake of the eastern United States, having reddish-brown markings. **2. Copperhead.** A Northerner who sympathized with the South during the Civil War.

cop•per•plate (**kŏp′**ər plāt′) *n.* **1.** A copper printing plate engraved or etched with a pattern of the picture or other design to be printed. **2.** A print or an engraving made with a copperplate.

cop•per•smith (**kŏp′**ər smĭth′) *n.* A worker or manufacturer of objects in copper.

cop•pice (**kŏp′**ĭs) *n.* A copse.

co•pra (**kō′**prə *or* **kŏp′**rə) *n.* Dried coconut meat from which coconut oil is extracted.

copse (kŏps) *n.* A thicket of small tress or bushes.

Copt (kŏpt) *n.* **1.** A native of Egypt descended from the ancient Egyptians. **2.** A member of the Coptic Church.

cop•ter (**kŏp′**tər) *n. Informal.* A helicopter.

Cop•tic (**kŏp′**tĭk) *n.* The language of the Copts, related to the Semitic languages and now used only in the Coptic Church. *—adj.* Of or relating to the Copts, the Coptic Church, or the Coptic language.

Coptic Church *n.* The Christian church of Egypt that believes that Jesus had a single divine nature and was not both God and man.

cop•u•la (**kŏp′**yə lə) *n.* A linking verb, such as a form of *be, feel,* or *seem,* that connects the subject of a sentence with a word or phrase that tells something about the subject. For example, in the sentence *The cats are frisky,* the copula is *are.*

cop•u•late (**kŏp′**yə lāt′) *intr.v.* **cop•u•lat•ed, cop•u•lat•ing, cop•u•lates.** To engage in sexual intercourse. **—cop′u•la′tion** *n.*

cop•y (**kŏp′**ē) *n., pl.* **cop•ies. 1.** An imitation or a reproduction of something original; a duplicate. **2.** One specimen or example of a printed text or picture: *a copy of the June issue of the magazine.* **3.** Written material to be set in type and printed: *Reporters hand in copy for newspaper articles.* *—v.* **cop•ied, cop•y•ing, cop•ies.** *—tr.* **1.** To make something that is exactly like an original; reproduce: *I copied my paper over again.* **2.** To follow as a model or pattern; imitate: *The builder copied the house next door.* See Synonyms at **imitate.** *—intr.* To make a copy or copies: *Good authors don't copy from others.* [First written down before 1338 in Middle English and spelled *copie,* from Medieval Latin *cōpia,* transcript, from Latin *cōpia,* profusion.]

cop•y•book (**kŏp′**ē bo͝ok′) *n.* A book with models of handwriting to imitate.

cop•y•cat (**kŏp′**ē kăt′) *n.* A person who mimics or imitates others, as in speech, dress, or action.

cop•y•ist (**kŏp′**ē ĭst) *n.* A person who makes written copies, as of a manuscript.

cop•y•right (**kŏp′**ē rīt′) *n.* The legal right to be the only one to publish, produce, sell, or distribute a literary, musical, dramatic, or artistic work. *—tr.v.* **cop•y•right•ed, cop•y•right•ing, cop•y•rights.** To secure a copyright for: *She copyrighted her new novel.*

Copernicus

ă	pat	oi	boy
ā	pay	ou	out
âr	care	o͝o	took
ä	father	o͞o	boot
ĕ	pet	ŭ	cut
ē	be	ûr	urge
ĭ	pit	th	thin
ī	pie	*th*	this
îr	pier	hw	whoop
ŏ	pot	zh	vision
ō	toe	ə	about
ô	paw	N	*French* bon

cop•y•writ•er (kŏp′ē rī′tər) *n.* A person who writes advertising copy.

co•quet•ry (kō′kĭ trē *or* kō kĕt′rē) *n., pl.* **co•quet•ries.** The behavior of a coquette; flirtation.

co•quette (kō kĕt′) *n.* A woman who flirts. —**co•quet′tish** *adj.* —**co•quet′tish•ly** *adv.* —**co•quet′tish•ness** *n.*

co•qui•na (kō kē′nə) *n.* **1.** Any of various small clams having brightly colored shells. **2.** A soft porous limestone containing shells and coral, used for building.

cor•a•cle (kôr′ə kəl *or* kŏr′ə kəl) *n.* A small rounded boat made of hide or other waterproof material stretched over a wicker or wooden frame.

coral

cor•al (kôr′əl *or* kŏr′əl) *n.* **1.** A hard stony substance formed by the skeletons of tiny, usually tropical sea animals massed together in great numbers. It is often white, pink, or reddish, and some kinds are used for making jewelry. **2.a.** Any of numerous tiny animals that form this substance. **b.** A mass of this substance, often branched or rounded in shape, as that forming a small island or reef. **3.** A yellowish pink or reddish orange. —*adj.* **1.** Made of coral: *a coral bracelet.* **2.** Yellowish-pink or reddish-orange. [First written down before 1300 in Middle English, from Greek *korallion.*]

coral reef *n.* A reef consisting mainly of coral and other organisms that deposit lime.

coral snake *n.* Any of various poisonous American snakes marked with red, black, and yellow bands.

Cor•bin (kôr′bĭn), **Margaret Cochran.** 1751–1800. American Revolutionary figure. She fought at the Battle of Fort Washington (1776) until she was seriously wounded.

cord (kôrd) *n.* **1.** A string or small rope of twisted strands. **2.** An insulated flexible electric wire fitted with a plug or plugs. **3.** A structure of the body, such as a nerve or tendon, that resembles a cord. **4.** A unit of measure for cut firewood, equal to a stack that measures four feet by four feet by eight feet or 128 cubic feet (3⅔ cubic meters). **5.a.** A raised ridge or rib on the surface of cloth. **b.** Cloth, such as corduroy, having raised ridges or ribs. **6. cords.** *Informal.* Corduroy pants. —*tr.v.* **cord•ed, cord•ing, cords. 1.** To fasten or bind with a cord: *Please cord the newspapers into bundles.* **2.** To cut and stack (firewood) in cords. [First written down in 1199 in Middle English, from Latin *chorda*, from Greek *khordē*.]

❑ *These sound alike:* **cord, chord**[1] (musical notes), **chord**[2] (line segment).

cord•age (kôr′dĭj) *n.* **1.** Cords or ropes, especially the ropes in a ship's rigging. **2.** An amount of wood measured in cords.

Charlotte Corday

Cor•day (kôr dā′), **Charlotte.** 1768–1798. French Revolutionary figure who was guillotined for the assassination of Jean Paul Marat in 1793.

cord•ed (kôr′dĭd) *adj.* **1.** Tied or bound with cords: *a corded bundle.* **2.** Ribbed or twilled, as corduroy. **3.** Stacked in cords, as firewood.

cor•dial (kôr′jəl) *adj.* Warm and sincere; hearty: *cordial relations with the neighbors.* —*n.* A liqueur. [First written down before 1400 in Middle English and spelled *cordial*, of the heart, from Medieval Latin *cordiālis*, from Latin *cor*, heart.] —**cor•dial′i•ty** (kôr jăl′ĭ tē *or* kôr′jē ăl′ĭ tē) *n.* —**cor′dial•ly** *adv.*

cor•dil•le•ra (kôr′dl yâr′ə) *n.* An extensive chain of mountains, especially the main mountain range of a large land mass.

cord•less (kôrd′lĭs) *adj.* Having no cord; using batteries: *a cordless telephone.*

cor•do•ba (kôr′də bə) *n.* The basic monetary unit of Nicaragua. [First written down in 1913 in Modern English, after Francisco Fernández de *Córdoba* (1475?–1526?), Spanish explorer.]

Cór•do•ba (kôr′də bə). A city of southern Spain east-northeast of Seville. Córdoba was renowned under the Moors as a cultural and intellectual center. Population, 291,370.

cordon

cor•don (kôr′dn) *n.* **1.** A line of military posts, people, or ships stationed around an area to enclose or guard it. **2.** A ribbon or cord worn as a decoration or badge of honor or rank. —*tr.v.* **cor•doned, cor•don•ing, cor•dons.** To form a cordon around: *The firefighters had cordoned off the burned-out building.*

cor•do•van (kôr′də vən) *n.* **1.** A soft fine leather used for shoes and other leather goods. **2.** A shoe made from this leather.

cor•du•roy (kôr′də roi′) *n.* **1.** A heavy cotton fabric with raised ribs or ridges. **2. corduroys.** Trousers made of this fabric.

corduroy road *n.* A road made of logs laid crosswise on the ground.

cord•wood (kôrd′wo͝od′) *n.* **1.** Wood cut and piled in cords. **2.** Wood sold by the cord.

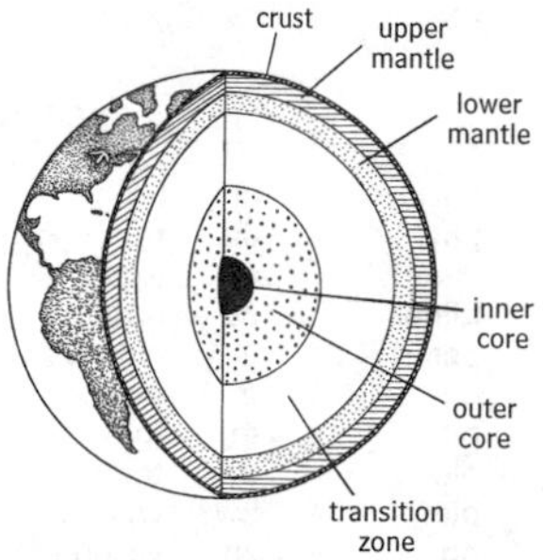

core
Cutaway view of Earth

core (kôr) *n.* **1.** The hard or stringy central part of certain fruits, such as an apple or a pear, containing the seeds. **2.** The innermost part of something; the heart: *the core of a golfball.* **3.** The basic or most important part of something; the essence: *The core of the problem was a lack of funds.* **4.** The central or innermost portion of Earth below the mantle, probably consisting of iron and nickel. **5.** A piece of magnetic material, such as a rod of soft iron, placed inside an electrical coil or transformer to intensify and provide a path for the magnetic field produced by the windings. **6.** A computer memory or one of the magnetic devices in a computer memory. —*tr.v.* **cored, cor•ing, cores.** To remove the core of: *core apples.* [First written down before 1400 in Middle English.] —**cor′er** *n.*

❑ *These sound alike:* **core, corps** (military unit).

co•ri•an•der (kôr′ē ăn′dər) *n.* **1.** A plant related to and resembling parsley, having spicy fruits similar to seeds. **2.** The young shoots of this plant, used in salads and as a garnish. **3.** The dried fruit of the coriander, used as a seasoning.

Cor•inth (kôr′ĭnth *or* kŏr′ĭnth). A city of southern Greece west of Athens. It is near the site of ancient Corinth, which was a maritime power in the seventh and sixth centuries B.C. Population, 22,658.

Co•rin•thi•an (kə rĭn′thē ən) *adj.* **1.** Of or relating to ancient Corinth or its people, language, or culture. **2.** Of or relating to an order of ancient Greek and Roman architecture characterized by a slender column with an ornate bell-shaped top decorated with a design of acanthus leaves: *a Corinthian column.* —*n.* **1.** A native or inhabitant of ancient Corinth. **2. Corinthians.** Either of two books of the New Testament, containing letters written by the Apostle Paul to the Christians on Corinth. Paul corrects the Corinthians on doctrine and morals and defends his status as an apostle.

cork (kôrk) *n.* **1.** The light spongy outer bark of the cork oak, used for bottle stoppers and in insulation, life rafts, and flooring. **2.a.** Something made of cork, especially a bottle stopper. **b.** A bottle stopper made of other material, such as rubber or plastic. **3.** A protective tissue of dead cells that forms the outermost layer of the bark of woody plants. —*tr.v.* **corked, cork•ing, corks.** To close up or stop with a cork: *cork a bottle.* [First written down in 1303 in Middle English, probably from Arabic dialectal *al-qūrq.*]

cork•er (kôr′kər) *n. Slang.* A remarkable or astounding person or thing.

cork oak *n.* An evergreen oak tree of the Mediterranean region, having thick bark that is the source of cork.

cork•screw (kôrk′skro͞o′) *n.* A device for drawing corks from bottles, consisting of a pointed metal spiral attached to a handle. —*adj.* Spiral in shape; twisted: *the corkscrew motion of a slowly spinning top.*

cork•y (kôr′kē) *adj.* **cork•i•er, cork•i•est.** Of or resembling cork.

corm (kôrm) *n.* A fleshy food-storing underground stem, as in the crocus or gladiolus.

cor•mo•rant (kôr′mər ənt) *n.* Any of several large water birds having blackish feathers, webbed feet, and a hooked bill with a pouch for holding fish.

corn[1] (kôrn) *n.* **1.a.** Any of numerous forms of a tall cereal grass bearing edible grains or kernels on large ears; maize. **b.** The ears or kernels of such a plant. **2.** *Chiefly British.* Any of various cereal plants or grains, such as wheat or rye. **3.** *Slang.* Something considered trite, outdated, or too melodramatic or sentimental. —*tr.v.* **corned, corn•ing, corns.** To preserve and season with salt or in brine: *corn beef.* [First written down about 700 in Old English and spelled *corn,* grain.] —See Note.

corn[2] (kôrn) *n.* A horny thickening of the skin, usually on or near a toe, resulting from pressure or rubbing. [First written down before 1425 in Middle English and spelled *corne,* from Latin *cornū,* horn.]

corn bread or **corn•bread** (kôrn′brĕd′) *n.* Bread made from cornmeal.

corn•cob (kôrn′kŏb′) *n.* The long hard central part of an ear of corn, bearing the kernels.

corn•crib (kôrn′krĭb′) *n.* A bin or building for storing and drying ears of corn.

cor•ne•a (kôr′nē ə) *n.* The tough transparent membrane of the outer coat of the eyeball that covers the iris and the pupil.

cor•ner (kôr′nər) *n.* **1.a.** The point at which two lines, edges, or surfaces meet: *the upper left-hand corner of the page; the corner of a table.* **b.** The area enclosed by the intersection of two lines, edges, or surfaces: *I sat in the corner.* **2.** The place where two roads or streets meet: *Meet me at the corner of Oak and Pine.* **3.** A remote or secluded place: *Americans have come from all corners of the world.* **4.** A threatening or difficult position: *I got myself in a corner by boasting I could outrun everybody.* **5.** A monopoly, as of a stock or commodity, that enables the supplier to control the price: *a corner on the wheat market.* —*tr.v.* **cor•nered, cor•ner•ing, cor•ners. 1.** To drive into a threatening or difficult position: *The dog cornered the cat in a closet.* **2.** To gain a monopoly over: *He attempted to corner the market in silver.* —*adj.* **1.** Located at a street corner: *the corner bookstore.* **2.** Designed for or used in a corner: *a corner cupboard for dishes.* [First written down about 1280 in Middle English, from Latin *cornua,* horns.]

cor•ner•stone (kôr′nər stōn′) *n.* **1.** A stone at one of the corners of a building's foundation, often inscribed and set in place with a special ceremony. **2.** The basis or foundation of something: *Good nutrition is the cornerstone of a healthy life.*

cor•net (kôr nĕt′) *n.* A brass instrument that is similar to the trumpet but has a mellower tone. [First written down before 1400 in Middle English and spelled *cornette,* from Old French, from Latin *cornū,* horn.]

cor•net•ist also **cor•net•tist** (kôr nĕt′ĭst) *n.* A person who plays a cornet.

corn•field (kôrn′fēld′) *n.* A field where corn is grown.

corn flakes *pl.n.* A crisp, flaky, cold cereal prepared from coarse cornmeal.

corn•flow•er (kôrn′flou′ər) *n.* A garden plant having flowers that are usually deep blue, but sometimes white or pink.

corn•husk (kôrn′hŭsk′) *n.* The leafy covering surrounding an ear of corn.

cor•nice (kôr′nĭs) *n.* **1.** The uppermost projection of stone or molding at the top of a wall or column. **2.** The molding at the top of the walls of a room, just below the ceiling. **3.** A horizontal frame used to conceal curtain rods.

Cor•nish (kôr′nĭsh) *adj.* Of or relating to Cornwall, its inhabitants, or the Cornish language. —*n.* A Celtic language spoken in Cornwall until about 1800.

corn•meal also **corn meal** (kôrn′mēl′) *n.* Coarse meal made from ground corn kernels.

corn•pone or **corn pone** (kôrn′ pōn′) *n.* Corn bread that is made without milk or eggs, baked in rounded patties.

corn•stalk (kôrn′stôk′) *n.* The stem of the corn plant.

corn•starch (kôrn′stärch′) *n.* A starchy flour made from corn, used as a thickener in cooking.

corn syrup *n.* A thick sweet syrup that is made from corn starch.

cor•nu•co•pi•a (kôr′nə kō′pē ə) *n.* **1.** A cone-shaped container overflowing with fruit, vegetables, and flowers, symbolizing prosperity; a horn of plenty. **2.** A cone-shaped ornament or container.

Corn•wall (kôrn′wôl′). A region of extreme southwest England. Its tin and copper mines were known in ancient times.

Corn•wal•lis (kôrn wŏl′ĭs *or* kôrn wô′lĭs), **Charles.** First Marquis and Second Earl Cornwallis. 1738–1805. British military leader who commanded forces during the American Revolution and surrendered to George Washington at Yorktown (1781).

corn•y (kôr′nē) *adj.* **corn•i•er, corn•i•est.** *Slang.* Trite, dated, melodramatic, or sentimental.

co•rol•la (kə rŏl′ə *or* kə rō′lə) *n.* The petals or floral leaves of a flower considered as a group.

cor•ol•lar•y (kôr′ə lĕr′ē *or* kŏr′ə lĕr′ē) *n., pl.* **cor•ol•lar•ies. 1.** A statement that follows with little or no proof required from an already proven statement: *If we know A equals B then the corollary is that B equals A.* **2.** A natural consequence or effect; a result: *Disease and suffering are the corollaries of unsanitary living conditions.*

co•ro•na (kə rō′nə) *n., pl.* **co•ro•nas** or **co•ro•nae** (kə rō′nē). **1.** The outer atmosphere of the sun, visible as a halo of light during a solar eclipse. **2.** A faintly colored shining ring seen around a celestial body, especially the moon or sun, when seen through a thin cloud or haze. **3.** A crown-shaped appendage on the inner side of the corolla in some flowers, such as the daffodil. [First written down in 1658 in Modern English, from Latin *corōna,* crown.]

cor•o•nar•y (kôr′ə nĕr′ē *or* kŏr′ə nĕr′ē) *adj.* **1.** Of or relating to either of the two arteries that branch from the aorta and supply blood directly to the heart. **2.** Of or relating to the heart: *Many hospitals have coronary care units.* —*n., pl.* **cor•o•nar•ies.** A coronary thrombosis.

coronary artery *n.* Either of the two arteries that supply blood directly to the heart.

coronary thrombosis *n.* The blockage of a coronary artery by a blood clot.

cor•o•na•tion (kôr′ə nā′shən *or* kŏr′ə nā′shən) *n.* The act or ceremony of crowning a sovereign, such as a king or queen.

cor•o•ner (kôr′ə nər *or* kŏr′ə nər) *n.* A public official who investigates any death not clearly due to natural causes.

cor•o•net (kôr′ə nĕt′ *or* kŏr′ə nĕt′) *n.* **1.** A small crown worn by princes, princesses, and other no-

Word History: corn[1]

Throughout the English-speaking world, people eat **corn**, but they don't eat the same thing. In Old English *corn* means "any small, hard particle or grain, as of sand or salt, or of a cereal, or a seed." The cereal grains include wheat, oats, barley, maize, and so forth, and *corn* is used for the cereal grain most commonly grown in a place. In most of England that crop is *wheat*, and *corn* usually means "wheat." In Ireland and Scotland that crop is *oats*, and *corn* means "oats" there. In the United States and Canada *corn* means "maize" because it is short for *Indian corn. Corn* in the sense of "grain of salt" appears in **corned beef**; in the sense of "seed," it appears in **peppercorn**.

cornet

c. 1840 brass valve cornet

cornucopia

ă	pat	oi	boy
ā	pay	ou	out
âr	care	o͝o	took
ä	father	o͞o	boot
ĕ	pet	ŭ	cut
ē	be	ûr	urge
ĭ	pit	th	thin
ī	pie	*th*	this
îr	pier	hw	whoop
ŏ	pot	zh	vision
ō	toe	ə	about
ô	paw	N	*French* bon

bles. **2.** A band for the head, decorated with gold or jewels. [First written down before 1400 in Middle English and spelled *crownette*, from Old French, diminutive of *corone*, crown.]

corp. *abbr.* An abbreviation of corporation.

cor•po•ra (kôr′pər ə) *n.* Plural of **corpus.**

cor•po•ral[1] (kôr′pər əl *or* kôr′prəl) *adj.* Of or relating to the body. [First written down about 1390 in Middle English and spelled *corporel*, from Latin *corporālis*, from *corpus*, body.]

cor•po•ral[2] (kôr′pər əl *or* kôr′prəl) *n.* A noncommissioned officer in the U.S. Army or Marine Corps ranking below a sergeant. [First written down in 1579 in Modern English, from Old Italian *caporale*, from *capo*, head, from Latin *caput*.]

cor•po•rate (kôr′pər ĭt *or* kôr′prĭt) *adj.* **1.** Of or relating to a corporation: *The government taxes corporate profits.* **2.** United or combined; collective: *a corporate effort of the citizens to clean up the parks.* **3.** Formed into a corporation; incorporated: *the corporate companies of industrial America.* **—cor′po•rate•ly** *adv.*

cor•po•ra•tion (kôr′pə rā′shən) *n.* A group of persons acting under a legal charter recognizing them as a separate unit with rights, privileges, and liabilities to act as if they were a single person.

cor•po•re•al (kôr pôr′ē əl) *adj.* **1.** Of or relating to the body: *corporeal needs of food and water.* **2.** Of a material nature; tangible: *buildings, land, and other corporeal property.* **—cor•po′re•al•ly** *adv.*

corps (kôr) *n., pl.* **corps** (kôrz). **1.** A section or branch of the armed forces having a special function: *The Medical Corps is trained to take care of the wounded.* **2.** A large military unit composed of two or more divisions along with supporting units and commanded by a lieutenant general. **3.** A group of people acting together: *the press corps.*

❑ *These sound alike:* **corps, core** (central part).

corps de bal•let (kôr′ də bă lā′) *n.* The dancers in a ballet troupe who perform as a group with no solo parts.

corpse (kôrps) *n.* A dead body, especially of a human being. [First written down before 1333 in Middle English and spelled *corps*, from Latin *corpus*, body.]

corps•man (kôr′mən *or* kôrz′mən) *n.* An enlisted person in the armed forces who is trained as a medical assistant.

cor•pu•lent (kôr′pyə lənt) *adj.* Overweight; fat. **—cor′pu•lence** *n.*

cor•pus (kôr′pəs) *n., pl.* **cor•po•ra** (kôr′pər ə). A large collection of writings of a specific kind or on a specific subject.

cor•pus•cle (kôr′pə səl *or* kôr′pŭs′əl) *n.* **1.** An unattached body cell, such as a blood or lymph cell. **2.** A very small particle.

cor•ral (kə răl′) *n.* **1.** An enclosed area for keeping cattle, horses, or sheep. **2.** An enclosed area within a circle of wagons for defense against attack: *The wagons formed a corral for protection at night.* *—tr.v.* **cor•ralled, cor•ral•ling, cor•rals. 1.** To drive into and hold in a corral: *corral cattle for shipment to market.* **2.** To arrange (wagons) in a corral. **3.** *Informal.* To surround or seize: *The soldiers corralled the revolutionaries.* [First written down in 1582 in Modern English, from Spanish, from Latin *currus*, cart, from *currere*, to run.]

❑ *These sound alike:* **corral, chorale** (hymn tune).

cor•rect (kə rĕkt′) *tr.v.* **cor•rect•ed, cor•rect•ing, cor•rects. 1.a.** To remove the mistakes from: *Correct your paper before you hand it in.* **b.** To indicate or mark the errors in: *The teacher corrected our tests.* **2.** To adjust so as to meet a standard. *Glasses will correct your vision. A kind word corrected a wrong impression.* **3.** To rebuke or punish for the purpose of improving: *Our teacher corrected us for running in the halls.* *—adj.* **1.** Free from error; accurate: *Your answers are absolutely correct.* **2.** Conforming to approved standards; proper: *the correct way to give artificial respiration.* [First written down in 1345 in Middle English and spelled *correcten*, from Latin *corrigere*.] **—cor•rect′ly** *adv.* **—cor•rect′ness** *n.*

cor•rec•tion (kə rĕk′shən) *n.* **1.** The act or process of correcting: *Correction of all my spelling mistakes did not take long.* **2.** Something that is offered or substituted for a mistake or fault; an improvement: *Several corrections are written in the margin.* **3.** Punishment intended to correct or improve.

cor•rec•tion•al facility (kə rĕk′shə nəl) *n.* A jail or prison.

correctional officer *n.* A prison guard.

cor•rec•tive (kə rĕk′tĭv) *adj.* Intended or tending to correct: *corrective lenses.* *—n.* Something that corrects: *Running laps around the track was a good corrective for our sloppy play in the game.* **—cor•rec′tive•ly** *adv.*

cor•re•late (kôr′ə lāt′ *or* kŏr′ə lāt′) *v.* **cor•re•lat•ed, cor•re•lat•ing, cor•re•lates.** *—tr.* To put or bring into a systematic relation: *We correlated the new data from our experiment with the old and revised our theory.* *—intr.* To have systematic connection; be related: *The new data correlates perfectly with earlier studies.*

cor•re•la•tion (kôr′ə lā′shən *or* kŏr′ə lā′shən) *n.* **1.** A relation or connection: *a correlation between smoking and lung disease.* **2.** An act of correlating or a condition of being correlated: *The navigator's correlation of speed and position kept the ship on course.*

cor•rel•a•tive (kə rĕl′ə tĭv) *adj.* **1.** Related; corresponding: *Reading and writing are correlative skills of language.* **2.** In grammar, indicating a relation and usually used in pairs. In the sentence, *Neither Jim nor Joe went along, neither* and *nor* are correlative conjunctions. **—cor•rel′a•tive•ly** *adv.*

cor•re•spond (kôr′ĭ spŏnd′ *or* kŏr′ĭ spŏnd′) *intr.v.* **cor•re•spond•ed, cor•re•spond•ing, cor•re•sponds. 1.** To be in agreement; match or compare closely: *This rainy weather hardly corresponds with yesterday's sunny forecast.* **2.** To be very similar or equivalent: *The eyelids correspond to the shutter of a camera.* **3.** To communicate by letter, often on a regular basis or over a period of time: *Even though you will be away we can still correspond over the summer.*

cor•re•spon•dence (kôr′ĭ spŏn′dəns *or* kŏr′ĭ spŏn′dəns) *n.* **1.** Agreement; conformity: *Correspondence in the wording of the documents shows one is a copy of the other.* **2.** Resemblance, as in function or structure; similarity: *Scientists classify animals and plants partly by the correspondences of their form.* **3.a.** Communication by the exchange of letters. **b.** The letters exchanged: *a drawer full of old correspondence.*

cor•re•spon•dent (kôr′ĭ spŏn′dənt *or* kŏr′ĭ spŏn′dənt) *n.* **1.** A person who communicates by letter, often on a regular basis. **2.** A person hired by a newspaper or radio or television station to report on news from a particular place: *the London correspondent for an American newspaper.* *—adj.* Corresponding.

cor•re•spond•ing (kôr′ĭ spŏn′dĭng *or* kŏr′ĭ spŏn′dĭng) *adj.* Matching closely; similar: *the corresponding function of feathers and fur.* **—cor′re•spond′ing•ly** *adv.*

cor•ri•dor (kôr′ĭ dər *or* kŏr′ĭ dər) *n.* **1.** A hall or passageway, often with rooms opening onto it. **2.** A tract of land forming a passageway: *a corridor for* *trains through the city.* [First written down in 1591 in Modern English, from Italian *corridore*, from *correre*, to run, from Latin *currere*.]

cor•rob•o•rate (kə rŏb′ə rāt′) *tr.v.* **cor•rob•o•rat•ed, cor•rob•o•rat•ing, cor•rob•o•rates.** To support or confirm by new evidence; make certain: *Similar results of several experiments corroborated the new scientific theory.* —**cor•rob′o•ra′tion** *n.* —**cor•rob′o•ra′tive** *adj.*

cor•rode (kə rōd′) *v.* **cor•rod•ed, cor•rod•ing, cor•rodes.** —*tr.* To dissolve or wear away (a metal or alloy), especially by chemical action. —*intr.* To be dissolved or worn away: *Most metals corrode in a solution of salt.* [First written down before 1400 in Middle English and spelled *corroden*, from Latin *corrōdere*, to gnaw away.]

cor•ro•sion (kə rō′zhən) *n.* **1.** The act or process of corroding: *Corrosion caused the pipe to leak.* **2.** The condition of being corroded. **3.** A substance, such as rust, produced by corroding.

cor•ro•sive (kə rō′sĭv) *adj.* Capable of producing or tending to produce corrosion: *The salt used to melt snow and ice on highways is corrosive to the metal rods in the concrete.* —*n.* A corrosive substance. —**cor•ro′sive•ly** *adv.* —**cor•ro′sive•ness** *n.*

cor•ru•gate (kôr′ə gāt′ *or* kŏr′ə gāt′) *v.* **cor•ru•gat•ed, cor•ru•gat•ing, cor•ru•gates.** —*tr.* To shape or fold into alternating and parallel ridges and grooves. —*intr.* To become corrugated.

cor•ru•ga•tion (kôr′ə gā′shən *or* kŏr′ə gā′shən) *n.* **1.** The act of corrugating or the condition of being corrugated. **2.** A groove or ridge in a corrugated surface.

cor•rupt (kə rŭpt′) *adj.* **1.** Immoral; wicked; depraved: *the corrupt life of a swindler.* **2.** Willing to accept bribes; dishonest: *a corrupt government.* **3.** Containing errors or changes, as in a text: *A corrupt translation of the poem made it incomprehensible.* —*v.* **cor•rupt•ed, cor•rupt•ing, cor•rupts.** —*tr.* **1.** To ruin morally; cause to behave wickedly: *Greed corrupts some people.* **2.** To destroy the honesty or integrity of, as by bribing: *They corrupted the Senator with offers of shares in their company.* **3.** To taint; infect; spoil: *Several chemical spills corrupted the water supply.* **4.** To change the original form of (a text, word, or language): *Careless copying corrupted later versions of the poem.* —*intr.* To become corrupt: *Absolute power corrupts absolutely.* [First written down in 1340 in Middle English and spelled *corupt*, from Latin *corruptus*, past participle of *corrumpere*, to destroy : *com-*, intensive prefix + *rumpere*, to break.] —**cor•rupt′er** *n.* —**cor•rupt′ly** *adv.* —**cor•rupt′ness** *n.*

cor•rupt•i•ble (kə rŭp′tə bəl) *adj.* Capable of being corrupted, as by bribery. —**cor•rupt′i•bil′i•ty** *n.* —**cor•rupt′i•bly** *adv.*

cor•rup•tion (kə rŭp′shən) *n.* **1.** The act or process of corrupting by making wicked or dishonest: *corruption of a powerful official.* **2.** Dishonesty or improper behavior, as by a person in a position of authority. **3.** A corrupted form, as of a word: *The word* lite *to describe some foods is a corruption of* light.

cor•sage (kôr säzh′ *or* kôr säj′) *n.* A flower or small bouquet worn by a woman, especially on the shoulder, waist, or wrist.

cor•sair (kôr′sâr′) *n.* **1.** A pirate, especially along the Barbary Coast. **2.** A pirate ship, often acting with the sanction of a government.

cor•se•let (kôr′slĭt) *n.* Metal armor worn to protect the body, especially the upper body.

cor•set (kôr′sĭt) *n.* A close-fitting undergarment, formerly worn by women to support or shape the waist and hips.

Cor•si•ca (kôr′sĭ kə). An island of France in the Mediterranean Sea north of Sardinia. Napoleon Bonaparte was born here. —**Cor′si•can** *adj. & n.*

cor•tege (kôr tĕzh′) *n.* **1.** A ceremonial procession, especially a funeral procession. **2.** A procession of attendants; a retinue.

Cor•tés (kôr tĕz′), **Hernando** or **Hernán.** 1485–1547. Spanish explorer who conquered Aztec Mexico for Spain.

cor•tex (kôr′tĕks′) *n., pl.* **cor•ti•ces** (kôr′tĭ sēz′) or **cor•tex•es. 1.** The outer layer of an organ or part of the body, as of the adrenal glands. **2.** The layer of gray matter that covers most of the surface of the brain. **3.** A layer of tissue under the outermost part of plant stems and roots. [First written down in 1653 in Modern English, from Latin *cortex*, bark.]

cor•ti•cal (kôr′tĭ kəl) *adj.* **1.** Of, relating to, or consisting of a cortex: *the rind and other cortical tissue of an orange.* **2.** Of, relating to, associated with, or depending on the cerebral cortex: *the cortical functions of the brain.* —**cor′ti•cal•ly** *adv.*

cor•ti•ces (kôr′tĭ sēz′) *n.* A plural of **cortex.**

cor•ti•sone (kôr′tĭ sōn′ *or* kôr′tĭ zōn′) *n.* A hormone produced by the adrenal cortex or produced synthetically, used in treating arthritis, allergies, and gout.

co•run•dum (kə rŭn′dəm) *n.* An extremely hard mineral composed mainly of aluminum oxide. It occurs in gem varieties such as ruby and sapphire and in a dark-colored variety that is used for polishing and scraping.

cor•vette (kôr vĕt′) *n.* **1.** A fast gunboat often used to protect convoys from submarines. **2.** A small sailing warship armed with one tier of guns.

cor•ymb (kôr′ĭmb *or* kŏr′ĭmb) *n.* A flower cluster whose outer flowers have longer stalks than the inner flowers, so that together they form a round, rather flat cluster on top.

cos *abbr.* An abbreviation of cosine.

co•se•cant (kō sē′kănt′) *n.* The ratio of the length of the hypotenuse in a right triangle to the length of the side opposite an acute angle.

co•sign (kō sīn′) *tr.v.* **co•signed, co•sign•ing, co•signs.** To sign (a legal document, such as a contract) with another or others.

co•sine (kō′sīn′) *n.* The ratio of the length of the side adjacent to an acute angle of a right triangle to the length of the hypotenuse.

cos•met•ic (kŏz mĕt′ĭk) *n.* A preparation, such as face powder or skin cream, designed to beautify the body. —*adj.* Done or used to improve the outward appearance, as of a person or building: *cosmetic surgery to remove a scar; a little paint and some other cosmetic repairs on a porch.*

cos•mic (kŏz′mĭk) *adj.* **1.** Of or relating to the universe. **2.** Infinitely extended; vast: *Overpopulation of the planet is an issue of cosmic importance.* —**cos′mi•cal•ly** *adv.*

cosmic dust *n.* Clouds of fine solid particles of matter in outer space.

cosmic ray *n.* A stream of radiation consisting chiefly of high-energy atomic nuclei and protons, that enters the atmosphere from outer space.

cos•mol•o•gy (kŏz mŏl′ə jē) *n., pl.* **cos•mol•o•gies.** The branch of astronomy that deals with the history and structure of the universe.

cos•mo•naut (kŏz′mə nôt′) *n.* An astronaut from Russia or the Soviet Union. [First written down in 1957 in Modern English, from Russian *kosmonaut* : Greek *kosmos*, universe + Greek *nautēs*, sailor.]

cos•mo•pol•i•tan (kŏz′mə pŏl′ĭ tn) *adj.* **1.** Composed of persons or elements from many different parts of the world: *Montreal is a cosmopolitan city.* **2.** Having broad interests or wide experience; sophisticated: *A cosmopolitan guest made the party interesting.* —*n.* A cosmopolitan person.

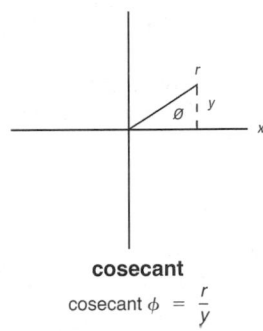

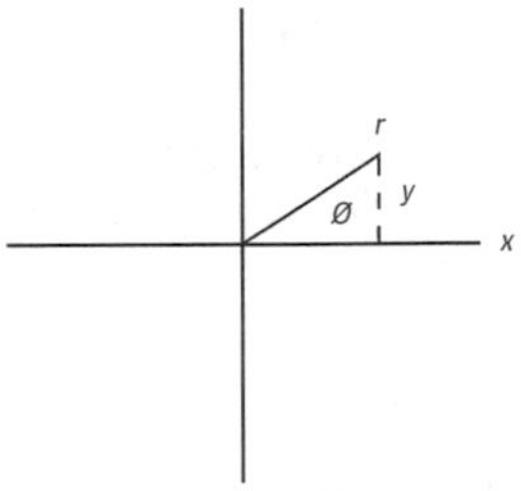

cosecant

cosecant $\phi = \frac{r}{y}$

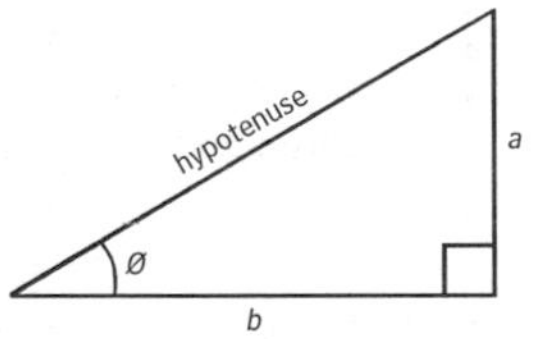

cosine

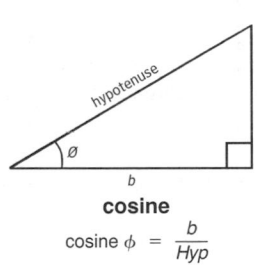

cosine $\phi = \frac{b}{Hyp}$

ă	**pat**	oi	**boy**
ā	**pay**	ou	**out**
âr	**care**	o͝o	**took**
ä	**father**	o͞o	**boot**
ĕ	**pet**	ŭ	**cut**
ē	**be**	ûr	**urge**
ĭ	**pit**	th	**thin**
ī	**pie**	*th*	**this**
îr	**pier**	hw	**whoop**
ŏ	**pot**	zh	**vision**
ō	**toe**	ə	**about**
ô	**paw**	N	*French* **bon**

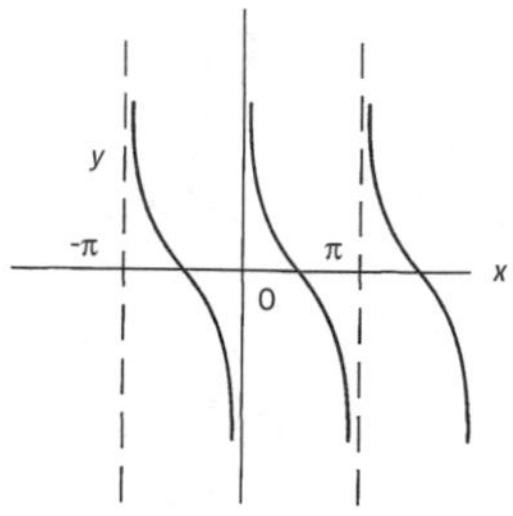

cotangent
Graph of a cotangent function: $y = \cot x$

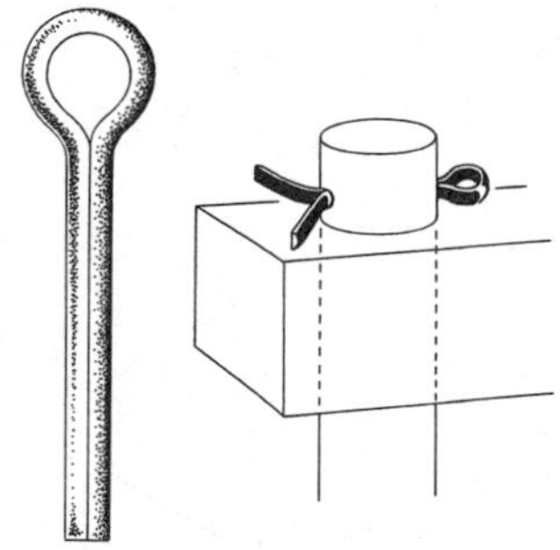

cotter pin

cottonwood
Eastern cottonwood

cos•mos (kŏz′məs *or* kŏz′mōs′) *n.* **1.** The universe regarded as an orderly and harmonious whole. **2.** An orderly and harmonious system. **3.** Any of various tall garden plants having pink, white, or red flowers that resemble daisies. [First written down about 1200 in Middle English, from Greek *kosmos.*]

Cos•sack (kŏs′ăk) *n.* A member of a people of southern Russia, whose men often served in the cavalry during the rule of the czars. —**Cos′sack′** *adj.*

cost (kôst) *n.* **1.** An amount paid or charged for a purchase; a price: *The cost of a fishing license is going up.* **2.** The loss or sacrifice necessary to attain a goal: *He worked day and night at the cost of his health.* **3. costs.** The expenses of a lawsuit. —*tr.v.* **cost, cost•ing, costs. 1.** To have or require as a price: *A subscription to the magazine costs $15.* **2.** To cause to lose or sacrifice: *Years of drought cost them their farm.*

cos•tal (kŏs′təl) *adj.* Of, relating to, or near the ribs.

Cos•ta Ri•ca (kŏs′tə rē′kə *or* kô′stə rē′kə). A country of Central America between Panama and Nicaragua. It gained its independence from Spain in 1821. Capital, San José. Population, 2,534,000.

cost•ly (kôst′lē) *adj.* **cost•li•er, cost•li•est. 1.** High-priced; expensive: *costly jewelry.* **2.** Involving great loss or sacrifice: *Going west was a costly decision for many pioneer families.* —**cost′li•ness** *n.*

cost of living *n.* The average cost of basic necessities, such as food, clothing, and shelter.

cos•tume (kŏs′to͞om′ *or* kŏs′tyo͞om′) *n.* **1.** An outfit or a disguise worn on special occasions such as Halloween. **2.** The style of clothing and hair typical of a certain time, place, or people: *The costume of the ancient Romans included togas and sandals.* **3.** A set of clothes suitable for a certain occsasion or season: *a skating costume.* —*tr.v.* (kŏ sto͞om′ *or* kŏ styo͞om′). **cos•tumed, cos•tum•ing, cos•tumes.** To dress in a costume: *Everyone was costumed for our Halloween party.* [First written down in 1715 in Modern English, from Italian, style, fashion, from Latin *cōnsuētūdō*, custom, habit.]

costume jewelry *n.* Jewelry made of inexpensive materials, such as colored glass, plated metals, and imitation stones.

cos•tum•er (kŏs′to͞o′mər *or* kŏs′tyo͞o′mər) *n.* A person who makes or supplies costumes, as for plays.

co•sy (kō′zē) *adj. & n.* Variant of **cozy.**

cot (kŏt) *n.* A narrow bed usually made of canvas stretched over a folding frame.

co•tan•gent (kō tăn′jənt) *n.* The ratio of the length of the adjacent side of an acute angle in a right triangle to the length of the opposite side.

cote (kōt) *n.* A small shed or coop for sheep or birds.
❑ *These sound alike:* **cote, coat** (garment).

co•ter•ie (kō′tə rē *or* kō′tə rē′) *n.* A group of people who share interests and associate frequently.

co•til•lion also **co•til•lon** (kō tĭl′yən) *n.* **1.** A dance for many partners with complicated steps. **2.** A large formal party with dancing.

cot•tage (kŏt′ĭj) *n.* **1.** A small house, usually in the country. **2.** A small house for summer use.

cottage cheese *n.* A soft white cheese made of curds of sour skim milk.

cot•tag•er (kŏt′ĭ jər) *n.* A person who lives in a cottage.

cot•ter pin (kŏt′ər) *n.* A split pin that fits through a hole in order to fasten parts together and is secured by bending back the ends.

cot•ton (kŏt′n) *n.* **1.** Any of various woody plants grown in warm regions for the downy white fibers that surround their seeds. **2.** The soft fine fibers of such a plant, used in making textiles and other products. **3.** Thread or cloth made of cotton fibers. —*intr.v.* **cot•toned, cot•ton•ing, cot•tons.** *Informal.* To take a liking; become friendly: *Our dog doesn't cotton to strangers.* [First written down in 1286 in Middle English and spelled *coton*, from Arabic *quṭn.*]

cotton candy *n.* A candy made of sugar spun into thin fibers that form a fluffy mass.

cotton gin *n.* A machine that separates the seeds, hulls, and other small objects from cotton fibers.

cot•ton•mouth (kŏt′n mouth′) *n.* The water moccasin.

cot•ton•seed (kŏt′n sēd′) *n.* The seed of the cotton plant, the source of cottonseed oil.

cottonseed oil *n.* An oil obtained by pressing cottonseed, used in cooking and in making shortening, margarine, paints, and soaps.

cot•ton•tail (kŏt′n tāl′) *n.* Any of several North American rabbits, having grayish or brownish fur and a short fluffy white tail.

cot•ton•wood (kŏt′n wo͝od′) *n.* Any of several American poplar trees having triangular leaves and seeds with cottony tufts.

cot•ton•y (kŏt′n ē) *adj.* **1.** Of or resembling cotton; fluffy or downy: *cottony foam.* **2.** Covered with fibers resembling cotton.

cot•y•le•don (kŏt′l ēd′n) *n.* A leaf of the embryo of a seed-bearing plant. A cotyledon is the first leaf or the first of a pair of leaves in a newly developing plant and contains stored food.

couch (kouch) *n.* A sofa. —*tr.v.* **couched, couch•ing, couch•es.** To word in a certain manner; phrase: *The negotiators couched their demands in tactful language.* [First written down in 1340 in Middle English, from Old French *couchier*, to lay down.]

cou•gar (ko͞o′gər) *n.* The mountain lion.

cough (kôf *or* kŏf) *v.* **coughed, cough•ing, coughs.** —*intr.* To force air from the lungs suddenly and noisily, usually to clear mucus or other matter from the throat or lungs: *cough from breathing smoke.* —*tr.* To clear from the respiratory tract by coughing: *cough up mucus.* —*n.* **1.** The act of coughing: *The student's cough disturbed the class.* **2.** An illness marked by coughing: *A deep cough kept me out of school.*

could (ko͝od) *aux.v.* Past tense of **can**[1]. **1.** Used to indicate possibility: *It could rain tomorrow.* **2.** Used to indicate ability: *I could run faster back then.* **3.** Used to indicated permission: *Only friends of the musicians could go backstage after the concert.* **4.** Used to indicate politeness: *Could I have some more juice?*

could•n't (ko͝od′nt). Contraction of *could not.*

couldst (ko͝odst) *v. Archaic.* A second person singular past tense of **can**[1].

cou•lee (ko͞o′lē) *n.* A deep gulch or ravine in the western United States, often dry in summer.

cou•lomb (ko͞o′lŏm′ *or* ko͞o′lōm′) *n.* A unit of electric charge equal to the quantity of charge transferred in one second by a steady current of one ampere, or equal to the charge carried by approximately six quintillion electrons. [First written down in 1881 in Modern English, after Charles Augustin de *Coulomb* (1736–1806), French physicist.]

coul•ter (kōl′tər) *n.* A blade or wheel attached to a plow to cut the soil in front of the plowshare.

coun•cil (koun′səl) *n.* **1.** A gathering of persons called together to discuss a problem or give advice. **2.** A body of people elected or appointed to make laws, policies, or decisions: *The President has a council of economic advisers.* [First written down in

1125 in Middle English and spelled *concilie*, from Latin *concilium*.] —SEE NOTE.

❑ *These sound alike:* **council, counsel** (advice).

coun•cil•man (koun′səl mən) *n.* A member of a council, especially of the group that makes the laws of a city.

coun•cil•or also **coun•cil•lor** (koun′sə lər *or* koun′slər) *n.* A member of a council. —SEE NOTE at **council.**

❑ *These sound alike:* **councilor, counselor** (adviser).

coun•cil•wom•an (koun′səl wo͝om′ən) *n.* A woman who is a member of a council, especially of the group that makes the laws of a city.

coun•sel (koun′səl) *n.* **1.** The act of exchanging opinions and ideas; consultation: *Frequent counsel among the members kept the committee informed.* **2.** Advice; guidance: *I will not make a decision without your counsel.* **3.** A lawyer or group of lawyers giving legal advice. —*tr.v.* **coun•seled, coun•sel•ing, coun•sels** or **coun•selled, coun•sel•ling, coun•sels. 1.** To give (a person) advice; advise: *The school counseled parents to keep children at home during the storm.* **2.** To recommend: *counsel swift action.* [First written down before 1200 in Middle English and spelled *cunsail*, from Latin *cōnsilium*.] —SEE NOTE at **council.**

❑ *These sound alike:* **counsel, council** (group).

coun•sel•or also **coun•sel•lor** (koun′sə lər *or* koun′slər) *n.* **1.** A person who advises or guides; an advisor: *a school counselor.* **2.** A lawyer. **3.** A person who supervises children at a summer camp. —SEE NOTE at **council.**

❑ *These sound alike:* **counselor, councilor** (member of a council).

count¹ (kount) *v.* **count•ed, count•ing, counts.** —*tr.* **1.** To find the total of; add up: *Count your change before leaving the store. Count the books before you return them to the library.* **2.** To name the numbers in order up to and including (a particular number): *Count three and jump.* **3.** To take account of; include: *There are seven in my family, counting me.* **4.** To regard; consider: *Count yourself lucky to have a bicycle.* —*intr.* **1.** To name numbers in order or list items: *count from 1 to 10.* **2.** To have importance or value: *It is not how much you write but how well you write that counts.* **3.** To keep time in music by counting. —*n.* **1.** The act of counting or calculating: *A count showed that most of the class came.* **2.** A number reached by counting: *The count of students on the bus was low.* **3.** In law, any of the separate charges listed in an indictment: *The thief was tried on five counts of robbery.* ***—idioms.*** **count in.** To include: *If you are going camping, count me in.* **count off.** To separate into groups by counting: *count off by twos.* **count on. 1.** To rely on: *You can count on me to help.* **2.** To be confident of; anticipate: *I am counting on an A in history.* **count out.** To exclude: *If there's going to be any roughness, you can count me out.* [First written down in 1341 in Middle English and spelled *counten*, from Latin *computāre*, to calculate.]

count² (kount) *n.* A nobleman in some European countries, corresponding to an English earl. [First written down about 1333 in Middle English and spelled *counte*, from Late Latin *comes*, occupant of any state office, from Latin *comes*, companion.]

count•down (kount′doun′) *n.* **1.** The counting backward from a starting number to indicate the time remaining before a scheduled event, such as the launching of a rocket. **2.** The checks and preparations carried out during this process.

coun•te•nance (koun′tə nəns) *n.* **1.** Appearance, especially the expression of the face: *The grim countenance of the building inspector meant bad news.* **2.** The face: *a long countenance with bushy eyebrows.* **3.** Approval; encouragement: *The committee gave countenance to the ambitious plans.* —*tr.v.* **coun•te•nanced, coun•te•nanc•ing, coun•te•nanc•es.** To give approval to; condone: *Most people won't countenance bad manners.*

coun•ter¹ (koun′tər) *adj.* Contrary; opposing: *views counter to public opinion.* —*n.* **1.** A person or thing that counters; an opposite. **2.** A blow given in return, as in boxing. **3.** A stiff piece of leather around the heel of a shoe. —*v.* **coun•tered, coun•ter•ing, coun•ters.** —*tr.* **1.** To move or act in opposition to; oppose: *They countered our plan with one of their own.* **2.** To return (a blow) with another blow. **3.** To offer or say in response: *She countered that she was too busy to write a long paper.* —*intr.* **1.** To move, act, or respond in opposition: *They countered with a weak argument.* **2.** To give a blow in return, as in boxing. —*adv.* In a contrary manner or direction: *a new method that runs counter to the regular way.* [First written down about 1450 in Middle English, from Latin *contrā*, against.]

count•er² (koun′tər) *n.* **1.** A flat surface on which goods are sold, money is counted, or food is prepared or served. **2.** A flat surface where food is prepared, usually on top of a low kitchen cabinet. **3.** A small object, such as a stone or bead, used for counting, as on an abacus, or for marking a place in a game. [First written down in 1345 in Middle English and spelled *contour*, from Medieval Latin *computātōrium*, counting house, from Latin *computāre*, to calculate.]

count•er³ (koun′tər) *n.* A person or thing that counts, especially a mechanical or electronic device that automatically counts.

counter– *pref.* A prefix that means: **1.** Contrary or opposite: *counteract; counterclockwise.* **2.** In return or opposing: *counterattack.* **3.** Complementary; corresponding: *countersign.*

coun•ter•act (koun′tər ăkt′) *tr.v.* **coun•ter•act•ed, coun•ter•act•ing, coun•ter•acts.** To oppose and lessen the effects of by contrary action; check: *Aspirin often counteracts a fever.*

coun•ter•at•tack (koun′tər ə tăk′) *n.* An attack made in return for another attack. —*intr. & tr.v.* (koun′tər ə tăk′). **coun•ter•at•tacked, coun•ter•at•tack•ing, coun•ter•at•tacks.** To attack in return.

coun•ter•bal•ance (koun′tər băl′əns) *n.* **1.** A force or an influence that counteracts another. **2.** A weight that balances another. —*tr.v.* (koun′tər băl′əns). **coun•ter•bal•anced, coun•ter•bal•anc•ing, coun•ter•bal•anc•es.** To act as a counterbalance to.

coun•ter•claim (koun′tər klām′) *n.* A claim made in opposition to another claim.

coun•ter•clock•wise (koun′tər klŏk′wīz′) *adv. & adj.* In a direction opposite to that of the movement of the hands of a clock: *move counterclockwise; counterclockwise motion.*

coun•ter•feit (koun′tər fĭt′) *v.* **coun•ter•feit•ed, coun•ter•feit•ing, coun•ter•feits.** —*tr.* **1.** To make a copy of (something) in order to deceive: *The defendant was found guilty of counterfeiting money.* **2.** To pretend; fake: *We counterfeited surprise to please the host.* —*intr.* **1.** To carry on a deception; pretend. **2.** To make fraudulent copies, especially of money. —*adj.* **1.** Made in imitation of what is genuine in order to deceive: *a counterfeit dollar bill.* **2.** Pretended; simulated: *counterfeit friendliness.* —*n.* Something counterfeited: *That $20 bill is a counterfeit.* [First written down about 1300 in Middle English and spelled *contrefeten*, from Old French *contrefait*, made in imitation : *contre-*, against +

Usage: council

The word **council** refers to a decision-making assembly, as in *city council* or *student council*; its members are known as **councilors**. The word **counsel**, on the other hand, means "advice and guidance"; a person who provides such counsel, as at a summer camp or in a legal dispute, is a **counselor**.

ă	pat	oi	boy
ā	pay	ou	out
âr	care	o͝o	took
ä	father	o͞o	boot
ĕ	pet	ŭ	cut
ē	be	ûr	urge
ĭ	pit	th	thin
ī	pie	*th*	this
îr	pier	hw	whoop
ŏ	pot	zh	vision
ō	toe	ə	about
ô	paw	N	*French* bon

faire, to make (from Latin *facere*).] —**coun′ter·feit′er** *n.*

coun·ter·in·tel·li·gence (koun′tər ĭn **tĕl′**ə jəns) *n.* The work of preventing enemy spies from gathering political and military information or carrying out sabotage.

coun·ter·mand (**koun′** tər mănd′ *or* koun′-tər **mănd′**) *tr.v.* **coun·ter·mand·ed, coun·ter·mand·ing, coun·ter·mands.** To cancel or reverse (a command or order).

coun·ter·march (**koun′**tər märch′) *n.* A march back or in the opposite direction.

coun·ter·mea·sure (**koun′**tər mĕzh′ər) *n.* A measure or an action taken to oppose or offset another.

coun·ter·move (**koun′**tər mo͞ov′) *n.* A move in opposition to another move: *countermoves in chess.*

coun·ter·of·fen·sive (**koun′**tər ə fĕn′sĭv) *n.* A large-scale attack by an army, intended to stop the offensive of an enemy force.

coun·ter·of·fer (**koun′**tər ô′fər *or* **koun′**tər ŏf′ər) *n.* An offer made in return by one who rejects an unsatisfactory offer.

coun·ter·pane (**koun′**tər pān′) *n.* A bedspread or quilt.

coun·ter·part (**koun′**tər pärt′) *n.* **1.** A person or thing that corresponds to another, as in function, relation, or position: *The ancient counterpart to the car was the chariot.* **2.** A person or thing that is a natural complement to another: *He has one sock but lost its counterpart.*

coun·ter·point (**koun′**tər point′) *n.* **1.** A musical technique in which two or more distinct melodies are combined in harmony while at the same time keeping their distinctness. **2.** A secondary melody designed to go along with a principal melody.

coun·ter·poise (**koun′**tər poiz′) *n.* **1.** A weight that balances another. **2.** A force or an influence that balances or equally counteracts another. —*tr.v.* **coun·ter·poised, coun·ter·pois·ing, coun·ter·pois·es.** To counterbalance or offset.

coun·ter·pro·duc·tive (koun′tər prə **dŭk′**tĭv) *adj.* Tending to hinder rather than help.

coun·ter·rev·o·lu·tion (koun′tər rĕv′ə **lo͞o′**shən) *n.* A movement arising in opposition to a revolution and aiming to restore the conditions before the revolution.

coun·ter·rev·o·lu·tion·ar·y (koun′tər rĕv′-ə **lo͞o′**shə nĕr′ē) *adj.* Of or tending to promote counterrevolution. —*n.* A person who is engaged in or supports counterrevolution.

coun·ter·sign (**koun′**tər sīn′) *tr.v.* **coun·ter·signed, coun·ter·sign·ing, coun·ter·signs.** To sign (a document previously signed by another), as to guarantee authenticity: *The property deed was signed by the new owner and countersigned by a notary public.* —*n.* **1.** A second or confirming signature. **2.** A secret sign or signal, especially one given in response to a military sentry, to obtain permission to pass: *The spies were caught when they failed to give the countersign.*

countersink

coun·ter·sink (**koun′**tər sĭngk′) *n.* **1.** A hole with the top part enlarged so that the head of a screw or bolt will lie flush with or below the surface. **2.** A tool for making such a hole. —*tr.v.* **coun·ter·sunk** (**koun′**tər sŭngk′), **coun·ter·sink·ing, coun·ter·sinks. 1.** To enlarge the top part of (a hole) so that the head of a screw or bolt will lie flush with or below the surface. **2.** To drive (a screw or bolt) into a hole so that the screw or bolt sits flush with or below the surface.

coun·ter·spy (**koun′**tər spī′) *n., pl.* **coun·ter·spies.** A spy working to uncover or oppose enemy espionage.

coun·ter·sunk (**koun′**tər sŭngk′) *v.* Past tense and past participle of **countersink.**

coun·ter·ten·or (**koun′**tər tĕn′ər) *n.* **1.** A man's voice higher than a tenor. **2.** A singer having such a voice. **3.** A musical part written in the range of this voice.

coun·ter·weight (**koun′**tər wāt′) *n.* A weight used as a counterbalance.

count·ess (**koun′**tĭs) *n.* **1.** A woman holding the title of count or earl. **2.** The wife or widow of a count or earl.

count·ing number (**koun′**tĭng) *n.* A number used to count objects; a whole number greater than zero. The numbers 1, 5, and 29 are counting numbers, but ¼ and −7 are not.

count·less (**kount′**lĭs) *adj.* Too many to be counted; innumerable: *the countless stars.*

count noun *n.* A noun, such as *chair* or *pen,* that refers to a single object and can form a plural or occur with the article *a* or *an.*

coun·tri·fied (**kŭn′**trĭ fīd′) *adj.* **1.** Resembling or having the characteristics of country life; rural; rustic: *a countrified look to a city apartment.* **2.** Lacking in sophistication: *countrified attitudes.*

coun·try (**kŭn′**trē) *n., pl.* **coun·tries. 1.a.** A nation or state: *Mexico and Canada are two countries in the Western Hemisphere.* **b.** The land of a nation or state: *Switzerland is a mostly mountainous country.* **2.** The land of one's birth or citizenship: *The sailors returned to their country at the end of the voyage.* **3.** The people of a nation or state: *The country will benefit from his invention.* **4.** A large area of land distinguished by certain physical, geographic, or cultural features: *hill country.* **5.** The region outside of cities or heavily populated districts; a rural area: *go to the country for a vacation.* —*adj.* Of, relating to, or typical of the country: *country life.* [First written down before 1250 in Middle English and spelled *contre,* from Latin *contrā,* opposite.]

country and western *n.* A type of popular music based on folk music of the southern rural United States or on the music of cowboys in the American West.

country club *n.* A suburban club with facilities for social and sports activities, usually having a golf course.

coun·try·man (**kŭn′**trē mən) *n.* **1.** A person from one's own country; a compatriot. **2.** A native or inhabitant of a particular country. **3.** A man who lives in the country.

country music *n.* **1.** Country and western. **2.** A type of music originating in the Appalachian Mountains and based on traditional folk melodies of the British Isles.

coun·try·side (**kŭn′**trē sīd′) *n.* **1.** A rural region. **2.** The inhabitants of the countryside: *The whole countryside resisted building the highway.*

coun·try·wom·an (**kŭn′**trē wo͝om′ən) *n.* **1.** A woman from one's own country; a compatriot. **2.** A woman who was born in or lives in a particular country. **3.** A woman who lives in the country.

coun·ty (**koun′**tē) *n., pl.* **coun·ties. 1.** In the United States, an administrative subdivision of a state. **2.** A major territorial division in Great Britain and Ireland. **3.** The people living in a county. [First written down about 1378 in Middle English and spelled *counte,* territorial division, from Old French *conte,* the territory of a count, from Late Latin *comitātus,* the office of count.]

county seat *n.* A town or city that is the center of government in its county.

coup (ko͞o) *n., pl.* **coups** (ko͞oz). **1.** A brilliantly executed move or action that achieves the desired results: *Quickly restoring peace between the enemy nations was a real coup for the ambassador.* **2.** A coup d'état. [First written down before 1400 in

Middle English and spelled *coupe*, a blow, from Late Latin *colpus*.]

❑ *These sound alike:* **coup, coo** (murmuring sound).

coup d'é•tat (dā tä′) *n., pl.* **coups d'état** or **coup d'é•tats** (dā tä′). The sudden overthrow of a government, bringing a new group into power: *The dictatorship started as a coup d'état.* [First written down in 1646 in Modern English, from French *coup d'état*, stroke of state.]

coupe (ko͞op) *n.* Variant of **coupé** (sense 1).

❑ *These sound alike:* **coupe, coop** (cage).

cou•pé (ko͞o pā′) *n.* **1.** Also **coupe** (ko͞op). A closed two-door automobile. **2.** A closed four-wheel carriage with two seats inside and one outside. [First written down in 1834 in Modern English, from French, from past participle of *couper*, to cut.]

cou•ple (kŭp′əl) *n.* **1.** Two things of the same kind; a pair: *a couple of shoes.* **2.** Two people united, as in marriage or interests: *a young couple just starting a family; a dance couple.* **3.** *Informal.* A few; several: *vacation for a couple of days; have only a couple of dollars.* —*v.* **cou•pled, cou•pling, cou•ples.** —*tr.* To link together; attach; join: *couple the cars of a train.* —*intr.* To form pairs; join: *Hard work coupled with good luck to make a successful business.* [First written down about 1280 in Middle English, from Latin *cōpula*, bond, pair.]

cou•pler (kŭp′lər) *n.* A person or thing that couples, especially a device that holds two railroad cars together.

cou•plet (kŭp′lĭt) *n.* A unit of verse consisting of two successive lines that usually rhyme and have the same meter.

cou•pling (kŭp′lĭng) *n.* A device that links or connects.

cou•pon (ko͞o′pŏn′ *or* kyo͞o′pŏn′) *n.* **1.a.** A detachable part of a ticket, card, or advertisement that entitles the person holding it to certain benefits, such as a cash refund or a gift. **b.** A printed form to be used to order something or to obtain a discount. **2.** One of a number of small certificates attached to a bond that represent sums of interest that can be collected at specified dates. [First written down in 1822 in Modern English, from Old French *colpon*, piece cut off.]

cour•age (kûr′ĭj *or* kŭr′ĭj) *n.* The quality of mind or spirit that enables one to face danger or hardship with confidence, resolution, and firm control of oneself; bravery: *It takes courage to defend people who hold unpopular beliefs.* [First written down before 1300 in Middle English and spelled *corage*, from Old French, from Latin *cor*, heart.]

cou•ra•geous (kə rā′jəs) *adj.* Having or displaying courage; brave. See Synonyms at **brave.** —**cou•ra′geous•ly** *adv.* —**cou•ra′geous•ness** *n.*

cou•ri•er (ko͝or′ē ər *or* kûr′ē ər) *n.* A messenger, expecially one on official diplomatic business: *Government requests for a truce were sent by courier.*

course (kôrs) *n.* **1.a.** Onward movement in a particular direction; progress; advance: *the course of events.* **b.** Onward movement in time; duration: *in the course of a week.* **2.** The route or direction taken by something or someone: *the course of a stream; strike a course due south.* **3.** An area of land or water on which a race is held or a sport is played: *the course of a marathon; a golf course.* **4.** A way of behaving or acting: *Your best course is to do what was asked.* **5.** A typical manner of proceeding; regular development: *The law took its steady course.* **6.** An orderly sequence: *a course of medical treatments.* **7.a.** A complete body of studies in a subject in a school, college, or university: *a four-year course in engineering.* **b.** A unit of such studies: *an algebra course.* **8.** A part of a meal served as a unit at one time: *Soup was our first course.* —*intr.v.* **coursed, cours•ing, cours•es.** To flow or move swiftly: *Blood courses through the veins.* —***idioms.*** **in due course.** At the proper or right time. **of course. 1.** In the natural of expected order of things; naturally. **2.** Without any doubt; certainly: *Of course we'll come to your party.* [First written down before 1300 in Middle English and spelled *cours*, from Latin *cursus*, from past participle of *currere*, to run.]

❑ *These sound alike:* **course, coarse** (rough).

cours•er (kôr′sər) *n.* A swift horse.

court (kôrt) *n.* **1.** An area of open ground partly or completely enclosed by walls or buildings; a courtyard. **2.** A short street, especially an alley enclosed by buildings on three sides. **3.a.** A person or body of officials who hear and make decisions on legal cases. **b.** The room or building in which such cases are heard; a courthouse or courtroom. **c.** The regular session of a judicial assembly: *Court is not held on a holiday.* **4.a.** A sovereign's governing body of ministers and state advisers: *The British monarchy is often called the Court of St. James.* **b.** An official meeting of this body, presided over by the sovereign: *hold court to try a traitor.* **5.a.** The people who attend a monarch, including family, servants, advisers, and friends: *In medieval days the court moved several times a year.* **b.** A royal mansion or palace. **6.** An open level area marked with lines for games such as tennis, handball, or basketball. —*v.* **court•ed, court•ing, courts.** —*tr.* **1.** To seek the affection of, especially with hopes of marrying: *The couple courted each other for a year before the wedding.* **2.** To seek the support or favor of; try to please: *Columbus courted the Queen and King of Spain to help pay for his expeditions.* **3.** To try to gain; seek, often foolishly or unwittingly: *court danger.* —*intr.* To pay loving attention; woo: *They courted in secret for a year.* [First written down before 1200 in Middle English and spelled *curt*, from Latin *cohors*, courtyard, retinue.]

cour•te•ous (kûr′tē əs) *adj.* Considerate toward others; gracious; polite: *a courteous manner.* See Synonyms at **polite.** —**cour′te•ous•ly** *adv.* —**cour′te•ous•ness** *n.*

cour•te•san (kôr′tĭ zən) *n.* A woman who is a prostitute, especially to men of high rank or great wealth.

cour•te•sy (kûr′tĭ sē) *n., pl.* **cour•te•sies. 1.** Polite behavior: *We try to treat all of our customers with courtesy.* **2.** An act or a gesture showing politeness: *Our host's many courtesies made the stay very enjoyable.*

court•house (kôrt′hous′) *n.* **1.** A building in which courts of law are held. **2.** A building that houses a county government.

court•i•er (kôr′tē ər) *n.* **1.** An attendant at the court of a king or other ruler. **2.** A person who seeks favor, especially by flattery.

court•ly (kôrt′lē) *adj.* **court•li•er, court•li•est.** Suitable for a royal court; dignified and elegant: *courtly manners.* —**court′li•ness** *n.*

court-mar•tial (kôrt′mär′shəl) *n., pl.* **courts-mar•tial** (kôrts′mär′shəl). **1.** A military court of officers appointed to try persons for offenses under military law. **2.** A trial by such a court. —*tr.v.* **court-mar•tialed** also **court-mar•tialled, court-mar•tial•ing** or **court-mar•tial•ling, court-mar•tials.** To try (someone) by court-martial.

court•room (kôrt′ro͞om′ *or* kôrt′ro͝om′) *n.* A room in which court proceedings of a court of law are carried on.

court•ship (kôrt′shĭp′) *n.* The act or period of courting.

coupler

ă	**pat**	oi	**boy**
ā	**pay**	ou	**out**
âr	**care**	o͝o	**took**
ä	**father**	o͞o	**boot**
ĕ	**pet**	ŭ	**cut**
ē	**be**	ûr	**urge**
ĭ	**pit**	th	**thin**
ī	**pie**	*th*	**this**
îr	**pier**	hw	**whoop**
ŏ	**pot**	zh	**vision**
ō	**toe**	ə	**about**
ô	**paw**	N	*French* **bon**

courtyard

covered wagon

cowcatcher

court•yard (kôrt′yärd′) *n.* An open space surrounded by walls or buildings.

cous•in (kŭz′ĭn) *n.* **1.** A child of one's aunt or uncle. **2.** A relative descended from a common ancestor, such as a grandparent. **3.** A member of a country or group having similar origins or interests: *our Canadian cousins.* [First written down about 1225 in Middle English and spelled *cosin*, a relative, from Latin *cōnsōbrīnus*, cousin.]

❑ *These sound alike:* **cousin, cozen** (deceive).

co•va•lent bond (kō vā′lənt) *n.* A chemical bond formed when electrons are shared between two atoms.

cove (kōv) *n.* **1.** A small sheltered bay or inlet. **2.a.** A recess or a small valley in the side of a mountain. **b.** A cave or cavern.

cov•en (kŭv′ən *or* kō′vən) *n.* A gathering or meeting of witches.

cov•e•nant (kŭv′ə nənt) *n.* A formal binding agreement made by two or more persons or parties: *a covenant between nations to reduce armaments.* —*intr.v.* **cov•e•nant•ed, cov•e•nant•ing, cov•e•nants.** To promise or pledge by a formal agreement.

cov•er (kŭv′ər) *v.* **cov•ered, cov•er•ing, cov•ers.** —*tr.* **1.** To place (something) upon or over, so as to protect or conceal: *cover a table; cover one's ears.* **2.** To spread over the surface of: *Dust covered the table.* **3.** To hide from view or knowledge: *He tried to cover up his mistakes.* **4.** To extend over; include: *a farm covering 100 acres.* **5.** To travel or journey over: *We covered 200 miles a day.* **6.** To be responsible for reporting the details of (an event or a situation), as for a newspaper: *The reporter covered the crisis in the Middle East.* **7.** To be enough for: *Will five dollars cover the cost of it?* **8.** To protect, as from loss: *We have fire insurance to cover our belongings.* **9.a.** To aim a firearm at: *The police officer covered the suspect.* **b.** To protect by having within range or by firing a gun at an enemy: *The entrance to the harbor is covered by the guns of the fort.* **10.** In sports: **a.** To guard the play of (an opponent). **b.** To defend (an area or a position): *The pitcher covers first base when the first baseman fields a grounder.* —*intr.* **1.** *Informal.* To act as a substitute for someone absent: *The stand-in covered for the ailing star of the play.* **2.** To hide something in order to save someone from punishment, embarrassment, or loss: *cover up for a friend's mistake.* —*n.* **1.** Something placed on or attached to something else, as for protection: *the covers on a bed; the cover of a book.* **2.** Vegetation covering an area. **3.** Shelter or protection: *seek cover in a cave during a storm.* **4.** Something that conceals or disguises: *The enemy retreated under the cover of darkness.* **5.** A table setting for one person. —***idioms.* take cover.** To seek a hiding place or protection, as from enemy fire. **under cover.** Secretly: *Spies work under cover.* [First written down about 1150 in Middle English and spelled *coveren*, from Latin *cooperīre*, to cover completely.]

cov•er•age (kŭv′ər ĭj) *n.* **1.** The extent to or way in which something is analyzed and reported: *television news coverage of local events.* **2.** The extent of protection given by an insurance policy: *We carry accident and theft coverage on our car.*

cov•er•alls (kŭv′ər ôlz′) *pl.n.* A one-piece garment of trousers and shirt, worn over other clothes to protect them.

cover crop *n.* A crop planted to prevent soil erosion in winter and to enrich the soil when plowed into the ground in the spring.

cov•ered wagon (kŭv′ərd) *n.* A large wagon covered with an arched canvas top, used by American pioneers for travel across the prairie.

cov•er•ing (kŭv′ər ĭng) *n.* Something that covers, protects, or hides: *a covering for a bed.*

cov•er•let (kŭv′ər lĭt) *n.* A bedspread.

cov•ert (kŭv′ərt *or* kō′vərt) *adj.* Concealed; secret: *a covert mission behind enemy lines.* —*n.* **1.** A covered or sheltered place; a hiding place. **2.** Thick underbrush that provides cover for game animals or birds. —**cov′ert•ly** *adv.* —**cov′ert•ness** *n.*

cov•er-up or **cov•er•up** (kŭv′ər ŭp′) *n.* An effort or a strategy designed to conceal something, such as a crime or scandal, that could be harmful or embarrassing if revealed.

cov•et (kŭv′ĭt) *tr.v.* **cov•et•ed, cov•et•ing, cov•ets.** **1.** To desire (something belonging to another). **2.** To wish for strongly; crave: *an ambitious person who coveted success.*

cov•et•ous (kŭv′ĭ təs) *adj.* Very desirous of something belonging to another. —**cov′et•ous•ly** *adv.* —**cov′et•ous•ness** *n.*

cov•ey (kŭv′ē) *n., pl.* **cov•eys.** A group or small flock of partridges, grouse, or similar birds.

cow[1] (kou) *n.* **1.** The mature female of domestic cattle. **2.** The mature female of certain other large mammals, such as elephants or moose. [First written down before 800 in Old English and spelled *cū*.]

cow[2] (kou) *tr.v.* **cowed, cow•ing, cows.** To frighten or subdue with threats or a show of force: *The approach of the troops cowed the rioting crowd.* [First written down in 1605 in Modern English, probably of Scandinavian origin.]

cow•ard (kou′ərd) *n.* A person who lacks courage to face danger or pain, or shows fear in a shameful way. [First written down before 1250 in Middle English and spelled *couard*, from Old French *coue*, tail, from Latin *cauda*.]

cow•ard•ice (kou′ər dĭs) *n.* Lack of courage or a shameful show of fear when facing danger or pain.

cow•ard•ly (kou′ərd lē) *adj.* **1.** Lacking courage: *a cowardly liar.* **2.** Characteristic of a coward: *cowardly behavior.* —*adv.* In the manner of a coward. —**cow′ard•li•ness** *n.*

cow•bell (kou′bĕl′) *n.* A bell hung from a collar around a cow's neck to indicate the cow's location, as in fog.

cow•bird (kou′bûrd′) *n.* Any of various blackbirds that lay their eggs in the nests of other birds and often live near cattle.

cow•boy (kou′boi′) *n.* A man or boy who tends cattle, especially in the western United States, performing many duties on horseback.

cowboy hat *n.* A felt hat having a tall crown and a very wide brim.

cow•catch•er (kou′kăch′ər *or* kou′kĕch′ər) *n.* An iron grille or a heavy metal plate on the front of a locomotive to clear away obstacles from the track.

cow•er (kou′ər) *intr.v.* **cow•ered, cow•er•ing, cow•ers.** To crouch or draw back, as from fear or pain; cringe: *The dog cowered under the table in the thunderstorm.*

cow•girl (kou′gûrl′) *n.* A woman or girl who tends cattle, especially in the western United States, performing many duties on horseback.

cow•hand (kou′hănd′) *n.* A cowboy or cowgirl.

cow•herd (kou′hûrd′) *n.* A person who herds or tends cattle.

cow•hide (kou′hīd′) *n.* **1.a.** The skin or hide of a cow. **b.** Leather made from this hide. **2.** A strong, heavy, flexible whip, usually made of braided leather.

cowl (koul) *n.* **1.** The hood worn especially by a monk. **2.** A robe or cloak having such a hood. **3.** The part of the front of an automobile body that supports the windshield and dashboard. **4.** The cowling on an aircraft.

cow•lick (**kou′**lĭk′) *n.* A tuft of hair that stands up from the head and will not lie flat.

cowl•ing (**kou′**lĭng) *n.* A removable metal cover for an engine, especially an engine of an aircraft.

cow•man (**kou′**mən) *n.* **1.** A man who owns cattle or a cattle ranch. **2.** A cowboy.

co•work•er (**kō′**wûr′kər) *n.* A person with whom one works; a fellow worker.

cow•poke (**kou′**pōk′) *n.* A cowboy.

cow•pox (**kou′**pŏks′) *n.* A contagious skin disease of cattle, caused by a virus that is used to vaccinate human beings against smallpox.

cow•punch•er (**kou′**pŭn′chər) *n. Informal.* A cowboy or cowgirl.

cow•rie or **cow•ry** (**kou′**rē) *n., pl.* **cow•ries.** Any of various tropical sea mollusks having glossy, often brightly marked shells that were formerly used as money in some parts of Africa and Asia.

cow•slip (**kou′**slĭp′) *n.* **1.** A primrose usually having fragrant yellow flowers and used in herbal medicine. **2.** The marsh marigold.

cox•comb (**kŏks′**kōm′) *n.* A vain and often foolish person; a conceited dandy; a fop.

cox•swain (**kŏk′**sən *or* **kŏk′**swān′) *n.* A person who steers a boat or racing shell or has charge of its crew.

coy (koi) *adj.* **coy•er, coy•est. 1.** Retiring in manner; shy; bashful. **2.** Pretending to be shy or modest, especially in a flirtatious way. **—coy′ly** *adv.* **—coy′ness** *n.*

coy•o•te (kī ō′tē *or* **kī′**ōt′) *n.* A mammal similar to the wolf, common in western North America and noted for its nighttime howling. [First written down in 1759 in Modern English, from Nahuatl *cóyotl.*]

coy•pu (**koi′**po͞o) *n., pl.* **coy•pus.** A large South American rodent that lives by rivers and has webbed feet and a long tail.

coz•en (**kŭz′**ən) *tr.v.* **coz•ened, coz•en•ing, coz•ens.** To deceive by means of a petty trick. **—coz′en•er** *n.*

❑ *These sound alike:* **cozen, cousin** (relative).

co•zy (**kō′**zē) *adj.* **co•zi•er, co•zi•est. 1.** Snug and comfortable; warm: *a cozy spot by the fire.* **2.** Friendly; intimate: *a cozy circle of friends.* **3.** *Informal.* Marked by close association for devious purposes: *a cozy deal between management and union leaders.* *—n., pl.* **co•zies.** A padded or knitted covering placed over a teapot to keep the tea hot. **—co′zi•ly** *adv.* **—co′zi•ness** *n.*

cp *abbr.* An abbreviation of candlepower.

cp. *abbr.* An abbreviation of compare.

C.P. *abbr.* An abbreviation of Communist Party.

CPA *abbr.* An abbreviation of certified public accountant.

Cpl. *abbr.* An abbreviation of corporal.

CPR *abbr.* An abbreviation of cardiopulmonary resuscitation.

cps *abbr.* An abbreviation of cycles per second.

CPU *abbr.* An abbreviation of central processing unit.

Cr The symbol for the element **chromium.**

crab[1] (krăb) *n.* **1.** Any of various primarily marine animals related to the lobster and shrimp, having a broad flattened body and five pairs of legs, of which the front pair are claws. **2.** Any of various similar related animals, such as the horseshoe crab or the hermit crab. *—intr.v.* **crabbed, crab•bing, crabs.** To hunt or catch crabs. [First written down about 1000 in Old English and spelled *crabba.*] **—crab′ber** *n.*

crab[2] (krăb) *n.* **1.** A crab apple tree or its fruit. **2.** *Informal.* A bad-tempered complaining person; a grouch. *—v.* **crabbed, crab•bing, crabs.** *Informal.* *—intr.* To complain irritably. *—tr.* To find fault with; complain about. [First written down about 1300 in Middle English and spelled *crabbe,* possibly from *crabbe,* crab (shellfish).]

crab apple *n.* **1.** A small sour fruit of any of various trees of North America and Europe, similar to an apple and used to make jelly. **2.** The tree that bears such fruit.

crab•bed (**krăb′**ĭd) *adj.* **1.** Crabby; ill-tempered. **2.** Difficult to read: *crabbed handwriting.* **—crab′bed•ly** *adv.* **—crab′bed•ness** *n.*

crab•by (**krăb′**ē) *adj.* **crab•bi•er, crab•bi•est.** *Informal.* Irritable and difficult to please; grouchy. **—crab′bi•ly** *adv.* **—crab′bi•ness** *n.*

crab•grass or **crab grass** (**krăb′**grăs′) *n.* Any of certain coarse grasses that spread rapidly and choke lawn grass.

crack (krăk) *v.* **cracked, crack•ing, cracks.** *—intr.v.* **1.** To break with a sharp sound: *The tree limb cracked in the storm.* See Synonyms at **break. 2.** To make a sharp snapping sound: *The pond ice cracked.* **3.** To break without dividing into parts: *The china cup cracked when the hot tea was poured.* **4.** To change sharply in pitch or timbre; break: *The reporter's voice cracked with emotion.* **5.** To break down; give out: *The young doctor cracked under the strain of long hours.* *—tr.* **1.** To break with a sharp sound: *We cracked walnuts.* **2.** To cause to make a sharp snapping sound: *The coach driver cracked a whip.* **3.** To cause to break without dividing into parts: *The hot tea cracked the cup.* **4.** To strike with a sudden sharp sound: *I cracked my head on the railing.* **5.** To break open or into: *Thieves cracked the safe.* **6.** To solve: *We cracked the spies' code.* **7.** *Informal.* To tell or say (a joke or something witty). **8.** To break down (a complex substance, especially petroleum) into simpler chemical compounds: *crack oil into gasoline.* *—n.* **1.** A sharp snapping sound: *a loud crack of thunder.* **2.** A partial split or break: *a crack in a plate.* **3.** A narrow space: *The door was opened just a crack.* **4.** A sharp blow: *a crack on the head.* **5.** A cracking tone or sound: *a crack in the singer's voice.* **6.** An attempt: *Take a crack at the job.* **7.** A witty or sarcastic remark. **8.** An instant; a moment: *the crack of dawn.* *—adj.* Excelling in skill; first-rate: *a crack shot.* ***—idioms.*** **crack down.** *Informal.* To become more severe or strict: *The principal cracked down on tardiness.* **crack up.** *Informal.* **1.** To damage or wreck: *cracked up the car.* **2.** To have a mental or physical breakdown: *crack up from overwork.* [First written down about 1000 in Old English and spelled *cracian.*]

crack•down (**krăk′**doun′) *n.* An action taken to stop an illegal or disapproved activity: *a crackdown on gambling.*

cracked (krăkt) *adj.* **1.** Having a crack or cracks: *a cracked dish.* **2.** Broken into pieces: *cracked ice.* **3.** Changing in pitch or timbre; uneven: *a cracked voice.* **4.** *Informal.* Crazy; insane.

crack•er (**krăk′**ər) *n.* **1.** A thin crisp wafer or biscuit: *have cheese and crackers.* **2.** A firecracker.

crack•er•jack (**krăk′**ər jăk′) *n. Slang.* A person or thing of excellent quality or ability. *—adj. Slang.* Of the highest quality or ability: *a crackerjack pilot.*

crack•ing (**krăk′**ĭng) *n.* The process of breaking down a complex substance, especially petroleum, into simpler compounds by means of heat and often various catalysts.

crack•le (**krăk′**əl) *intr.v.* **crack•led, crack•ling, crack•les.** To make slight sharp snapping sounds, as a small fire does: *The cellophane crackled as I crushed it.* *—n.* **1.** The act or sound of crackling: *the crackle of dry leaves underfoot.* **2.** A network of fine cracks on the surface of glazed pottery, china, or glassware.

crack•ling (**krăk′**lĭng) *n.* **1.** Sharp snapping sounds

coxswain
Coxswain and rower

coyote

crab apple
Sweet crab apple

ă	pat	oi	boy
ā	pay	ou	out
âr	care	o͝o	took
ä	father	o͞o	boot
ĕ	pet	ŭ	cut
ē	be	ûr	urge
ĭ	pit	th	thin
ī	pie	*th*	this
îr	pier	hw	whoop
ŏ	pot	zh	vision
ō	toe	ə	about
ô	paw	N	*French* bon

crampon

crane

Top: Black-crowned crane
Bottom: Mechanical crane

like those produced by a fire or by the crushing of paper. **2. cracklings.** Crisp bits remaining after fat from meat has been melted down, as in making lard.

crack•ly (**krăk′**lē) *adj.* Making or likely to make a crackling sound: *a crackly fire.*

crack•pot (**krăk′**pŏt′) *n.* A person with very strange ideas.

crack•up or **crack-up** (**krăk′**ŭp′) *n.* **1.** *Informal.* A collision, as of an aircraft or an automobile. **2.** A mental or physical breakdown.

cra•dle (**krād′**l) *n.* **1.** A small bed for a baby, usually mounted on rockers. **2.** A place of origin; a birthplace: *Boston was the cradle of the American Revolution.* **3.** Infancy: *The great pianist showed an interest in music almost from the cradle.* **4.** A framework of wood or metal used to support something, such as a ship, being built or repaired. **5.** The part of a telephone that holds the receiver. **6.** A frame attached to a scythe, used to catch stalks of grain as they are cut so they can be laid flat. **7.** A box on rockers, used for washing dirt that might contain gold. —*tr.v.* **cra•dled, cra•dling, cra•dles. 1.** To place or hold in or as if in a cradle: *cradle a baby in one's arms.* **2.** To hold or support in a construction cradle: *cradle a ship in drydock.* **3.** To wash (dirt believed to contain gold) in a cradle. **4.** To cut (grain) with a scythe having a cradle. [First written down about 1000 in Old English and spelled *cradol.*]

craft (krăft) *n.* **1.** Special skill or ability: *a table made with craft; the craft of fine needlework.* **2.** Skill in deception or evasion; cunning: *With great craft the spy escaped capture.* **3.a.** An occupation or a trade requiring special skill: *learning his craft as a printer.* **b.** The members of an occupation or a trade. **4.** *pl.* **craft.** A boat, ship, aircraft, or spacecraft. —*tr.v.* **craft•ed, craft•ing, crafts. 1.** To make by hand: *craft fine watches.* **2.** To make or devise with great care and skill: *craft an agreement between the warring nations.* [First written down before 899 in Old English and spelled *cræft.*]

crafts•man (**krăfts′**mən) *n.* A man who practices a craft with great skill. **—crafts′man•ship′** *n.*

crafts•wom•an (**krăfts′**wo͝om′ən) *n.* A woman who practices a craft with great skill.

craft union *n.* A labor union limited in membership to workers in the same craft.

craft•y (**krăf′**tē) *adj.* **craft•i•er, craft•i•est.** Skilled in underhanded dealing and deceit; cunning. **—craft′i•ly** *adv.* **—craft′i•ness** *n.*

crag (krăg) *n.* A steep projection of rock forming part of a cliff or mountain. [First written down before 1325 in Middle English, from Welsh *craig* or Scottish Gaelic *creagh.*]

crag•gy (**krăg′**ē) *adj.* **crag•gi•er, crag•gi•est. 1.** Having crags; steep and rugged: *a craggy mountain.* **2.** Rugged and uneven: *an old sailor's craggy face.* **—crag′gi•ness** *n.*

cram (krăm) *v.* **crammed, cram•ming, crams.** —*tr.* **1.** To force, press, or squeeze (persons or things) into too small a space: *I crammed my clothes into the suitcase.* **2.** To fill too tightly; crowd: *Cars crammed the street so that no traffic moved.* **3.** To stuff oneself with food; eat greedily. —*intr. Informal.* To study hastily for an examination. [First written down about 1000 in Old English and spelled *crammian.*]

cramp¹ (krămp) *n.* **1.** A sudden painful contraction of a muscle, often resulting from strain or chill: *A leg cramp forced the sprinter to drop out of the race.* **2.** A temporary partial paralysis of muscles that are used too much: *My fingers had writer's cramp after the test.* **3. cramps.** Sharp persistent pains in the abdomen: *An upset stomach and cramps made me feel sick.* —*intr. & tr.v.* **cramped, cramp•ing, cramps.** To have or cause to have a cramp or cramps: *The runner's leg cramped in the cold. Swimming so many laps eventually cramped her legs.* [First written down about 1378 in Middle English, from Old French, of Germanic origin.]

cramp² (krămp) *n.* **1.** An iron bar bent at both ends, used to hold together blocks of stone or timbers. **2.** A force or an influence that restrains: *The rain put a cramp in our picnic plans.* —*tr.v.* **cramped, cramp•ing, cramps. 1.** To hold together with a cramp. **2.** To confine or restrain: *were cramped on the crowded bus.* **3.** To jam (the wheels of a car) hard to the right or left: *cramp the wheels into the curb when parking on a hill.* [First written down in 1423 in Middle English, from Middle Dutch *crampe,* hook, cramp.]

cramped (krămpt) *adj.* **1.** Confined and limited in space: *a cramped little apartment.* **2.** Difficult to make out; crabbed: *cramped handwriting.*

cram•pon (**krăm′**pŏn′ *or* **krăm′**pən) *n.* An iron spike attached to the shoe to prevent slipping when walking or climbing on ice.

cran•ber•ry (**krăn′**bĕr′ē) *n.* **1.** The tart, shiny, red berry of an evergreen shrub that grows in damp places, used in making jelly and baked goods. **2.** The plant that bears such berries. [First written down in 1647 in American English, partial translation of Low German *Kraanbere* : *Kraan,* crane + *bere,* berry.]

crane (krān) *n.* **1.** Any of various large wading birds having a long neck, long legs, and a long bill. **2.** A machine for lifting heavy objects by means of cables attached to a movable boom. **3.** Any of various devices in which a swinging arm or rod is used to support a load: *Colonial fireplaces had a crane to swing heavy pots over the fire.* —*v.* **craned, cran•ing, cranes.** —*tr.* To strain and stretch (the neck) in order to see better. —*intr.* To stretch one's neck toward something for a better view.

cra•ni•a (**krā′**nē ə) *n.* A plural of **cranium.**

cra•ni•al (**krā′**nē əl) *adj.* Of or relating to the skull: *cranial nerves.*

cra•ni•um (**krā′**nē əm) *n., pl.* **cra•ni•ums** or **cra•ni•a** (**krā′**nē ə). **1.** The skull of a vertebrate animal. **2.** The part of the skull that encloses the brain. [First written down before 1425 in Middle English and spelled *craneum,* from Greek *kranion.*]

crank (krăngk) *n.* **1.** A rod and handle that can be attached to a shaft and turned to start a machine or run some device. **2.** *Informal.* **a.** An irritable person; a grouch. **b.** An eccentric person; a person with odd ideas. —*tr.v.* **cranked, crank•ing, cranks. 1.** To start or operate (an engine or a device) by means of a crank: *Electric starters replaced the need to crank early car motors.* **2.** To move or operate (a window, for example) by or as if by turning a handle. —*adj.* Of or produced by an irritable or eccentric person: *a crank letter.* **—*idiom.* crank out.** To produce, especially mechanically and rapidly: *The printing press is cranking out copies of the pamphlet.*

crank•case (**krăngk′**kās′) *n.* The bottom part of a gasoline engine that covers the crankshaft and holds the oil to lubricate it.

crank•shaft (**krăngk′**shăft′) *n.* A shaft that turns or is turned by a crank. In a gasoline engine it is connected to and rotated by the pistons.

crank•y (**krăng′**kē) *adj.* **crank•i•er, crank•i•est.** Easily annoyed; irritable; peevish. **—crank′i•ly** *adv.* **—crank′i•ness** *n.*

cran•ny (**krăn′**ē) *n., pl.* **cran•nies.** A small opening, as in a wall or rock face; a crevice.

crape (krāp) *n.* **1.** A light cloth with a crinkled surface; crepe. **2.** An armband of black crepe, worn as a sign of mourning.

crap•pie (krăp′ē *or* krŏp′ē) *n., pl.* **crap•pies.** Either of two edible North American freshwater fishes related to the sunfishes.

craps (krăps) *pl.n.* *(used with a singular or plural verb).* A gambling game played with a pair of dice.

crash (krăsh) *v.* **crashed, crash•ing, crash•es.** *—intr.* **1.** To break violently and noisily: *The dishes crashed to pieces on the floor.* **2.** To be damaged or destroyed by a collision or violent impact: *The car crashed into the tree.* **3.** To move noisily or violently: *The elephants crashed through the trees.* **4.** To fail suddenly: *The stock market crashed in 1929. The computer crashed as the lights went out.* **5.** To make a sudden loud noise: *Can you hear the cymbals crash?* *—tr.* **1.** To cause to fall, strike, or collide suddenly, violently, and noisily: *The boy crashed his bike into the garage door.* **2.** *Informal.* To join or enter without being invited: *crash a party.* *—n.* **1.** A loud noise, as of a sudden impact or collapse: *a crash of thunder.* **2.** A violent collision: *Their car was destroyed in a crash.* **3.** A sudden severe decline in business: *The Great Depression started with the crash of 1929.* **4.** The sudden failure of a computer or computer program. *—adj. Informal.* Marked by an intense effort to produce or accomplish something: *a crash diet to lose weight.* [First written down about 1390 in Middle English and spelled *crasschen.*]

crash dive *n.* A rapid dive by a submarine, especially in an emergency.

crash helmet *n.* A padded helmet, as one worn by a racing-car driver or pilot, to protect the head.

crash-land (krăsh′lănd′) *tr. & intr.v.* **crash-land•ed, crash-land•ing, crash-lands.** To land (an aircraft) under emergency conditions, often resulting in damage to it.

crass (krăs) *adj.* **crass•er, crass•est.** Crude or unfeeling; coarse: *a crass remark.* **—crass′ly** *adv.* **—crass′ness** *n.*

–crat *suff.* A suffix that means one who takes part in or supports a certain form of government: *bureaucrat.*

crate (krāt) *n.* A large packing case made of slats of wood. *—tr.v.* **crat•ed, crat•ing, crates.** To pack into a crate: *crate a painting to be sent to a museum; crate oranges for shipping.*

cra•ter (krā′tər) *n.* **1.** A bowl-shaped depression at the mouth of a volcano or geyser. **2.** A pit that resembles this, as one made by an explosion. **3.** A circular depression with steep jagged walls, found on the surface of the moon and formed by a meteorite impact. [First written down in 1613 in Modern English, from Greek *kratēr*, large mixing bowl.]

cra•vat (krə văt′) *n.* A necktie or a scarf worn as a tie.

crave (krāv) *tr.v.* **craved, crav•ing, craves. 1.** To have a very strong desire for; long for: *The thirsty runners craved water.* See Synonyms at **desire. 2.** To beg earnestly for; implore: *crave a favor of someone.*

cra•ven (krā′vən) *adj.* Very cowardly: *the traitor's craven behavior.* *—n.* A coward. **—cra′ven•ly** *adv.* **—cra′ven•ness** *n.*

crav•ing (krā′vĭng) *n.* A very strong desire; a yearning.

craw (krô) *n.* **1.** The crop of a bird or an insect. **2.** The stomach, especially of an animal. **—*idiom.*** **stick in (one's) craw.** To cause enduring discontent and resentment.

craw•fish (krô′fĭsh′) *n.* Variant of **crayfish.**

crawl (krôl) *intr.v.* **crawled, crawl•ing, crawls. 1.** To move slowly on the hands and knees or by dragging the body along the ground: *The baby crawled across the room.* **2.** To move or advance slowly or haltingly: *The bus crawled along in the heavy traffic.* **3.a.** To be covered with or as if with crawling things: *The scene was crawling with police.* **b.** To feel as if covered with crawling things: *The story made my skin crawl.* *—n.* **1.** A very slow pace: *Traffic moved at a crawl.* **2.** A rapid swimming stroke performed face down with alternating overarm strokes and a flutter kick. **—crawl′er** *n.*

cray•fish (krā′fĭsh′) also **craw•fish** (krô′fĭsh′) *n., pl.* **crayfish** or **cray•fish•es** also **crawfish** or **craw•fish•es.** Any of various freshwater shellfishes that resemble a small lobster, often used as food.

cray•on (krā′ŏn′ *or* krā′ən) *n.* **1.** A stick of colored wax used for drawing. **2.** A drawing made with crayons. *—tr.v.* **cray•oned, cray•on•ing, cray•ons.** To draw, color, or decorate with crayons. [First written down in 1644 in Modern English, from French, from Latin *crēta*, chalk.]

craze (krāz) *tr.v.* **crazed, craz•ing, craz•es. 1.** To make insane or seemingly insane: *The lost explorer was crazed by a lack of contact with other people.* **2.** To make fine cracks on the surface or glaze of a dish or glassware. *—n.* Something very popular for a brief time; a fad.

cra•zy (krā′zē) *adj.* **cra•zi•er, cra•zi•est. 1.a.** Mentally ill; insane. **b.** Very distressed or upset: *They were crazy with worry about the polluted lot nearby.* **2.** *Informal.* Not sensible; impractical or unwise: *a crazy idea for making money fast.* **3.** *Informal.* Full of enthusiasm or excitement: *The whole family is crazy about their new car.* **—*idiom.*** **like crazy.** *Informal.* To an exceeding degree: *They were running around like crazy, preparing for the holidays.* **—cra′zi•ly** *adv.* **—cra′zi•ness** *n.*

crazy bone *n. Informal.* The funny bone.

Cra•zy Horse (krā′zē hôrs′). 1849?–1877. Sioux leader who joined Sitting Bull in the defeat of Gen. George A. Custer at the Battle of Little Bighorn (1876).

crazy quilt *n.* A patchwork quilt made of oddly shaped pieces of cloth, usually of various colors, that are sewn together in an irregular pattern.

crazy quilt

creak (krēk) *intr.v.* **creaked, creak•ing, creaks.** To make or move with a grating or squeaking sound: *The rusty gate creaked as it swung open.* *—n.* A grating or squeaking sound: *creaks in the stairs.* **—creak′i•ly** *adv.* **—creak′i•ness** *n.*

❑ *These sound alike:* **creak, creek** (stream).

creak•y (krē′kē) *adj.* **creak•i•er, creak•i•est.** Likely to creak or giving off creaks: *a door on creaky hinges.* **—creak′i•ly** *adv.* **—creak′i•ness** *n.*

cream (krēm) *n.* **1.** The yellowish fatty part of milk that is not homogenized, used in cooking and making butter. **2.** A yellowish white. **3.** Any of various substances containing or resembling cream: *a pudding of lemon cream; hand cream.* **4.** The best part: *These juicy tomatoes are the cream of the crop.* *—v.* **creamed, cream•ing, creams.** *—intr.* To form cream or a layer of foam or froth on the top. *—tr.* **1.** To prepare (foods) in a cream sauce: *cream spinach.* **2.** To remove the cream from; skim: *creamed the milk before drinking it.* **3.** *Slang.* To defeat overwhelmingly: *We creamed them at the last basketball game.* [First written down in 1332 in Middle English and spelled *creyme*, from Late Latin *crāmum* (of Celtic origin) and from Greek *khrisma*, ointment.]

cream cheese *n.* A soft white cheese made of cream and milk.

cream•er (krē′mər) *n.* **1.** A small pitcher for cream. **2.** A powdered or liquid substitute for cream, used in coffee or tea.

cream•er•y (krē′mə rē) *n., pl.* **cream•er•ies.** A place where dairy products are prepared or sold.

ă	pat	oi	boy
ā	pay	ou	out
âr	care	o͝o	took
ä	father	o͞o	boot
ĕ	pet	ŭ	cut
ē	be	ûr	urge
ĭ	pit	th	thin
ī	pie	*th*	this
îr	pier	hw	whoop
ŏ	pot	zh	vision
ō	toe	ə	about
ô	paw	N	*French* bon

Usage: credible

The adjective **credible** is often used incorrectly where **credulous** properly fits the meaning. **Credible** means "believable," while **credulous** means "gullible": *The advertisement was just not credible, but the customer was credulous enough to believe it anyway.*

creel

cream of tartar *n.* A white crystalline powder, a salt of potassium and tartaric acid, that is used in baking powder; potassium bitartrate.

cream•y (krē′mē) *adj.* **cream•i•er, cream•i•est. 1.** Rich in cream: *a creamy filling.* **2.** Resembling cream, as in richness, texture, or color: *a creamy velvet.* **—cream′i•ly** *adv.* **—cream′i•ness** *n.*

crease (krēs) *n.* **1.** A line or mark made by pressing or folding: *a crease in his trousers.* **2.** A wrinkle: *creases on the old man's face.* *—tr. & intr.v.* **creased, creas•ing, creas•es.** To make or become creased, folded, or wrinkled: *crease a piece of paper; a face creased with age.* [First written down in 1665 in Modern English, alteration of *creaste*, perhaps from Middle English *creste*, ridge.]

cre•ate (krē āt′) *tr.v.* **cre•at•ed, cre•at•ing, cre•ates. 1.** To bring into being; cause to exist: *She created the school to teach practical skills to girls.* See Synonyms at **establish. 2.** To give rise to; produce: *The rumor created a panic among stockholders.* **3.** To produce through artistic effort: *create a poem.* [First written down about 1380 in Middle English and spelled *createn*, from Latin *creāre*.]

cre•a•tion (krē ā′shən) *n.* **1.** The act or process of creating: *the creation of a canyon by erosion.* **2.** Something produced by invention and imagination: *The x-ray machine and the computer are creations of modern science.* **3.** The universe, the world, and all created beings and things; the cosmos. **4. Creation.** In various religions, the act of God by which the world was brought into existence.

cre•a•tion•ism (krē ā′shə nĭz′əm) *n.* The belief that all living things were created by God in the form they now have and did not develop by evolution.

cre•a•tive (krē ā′tĭv) *adj.* **1.** Having the ability or power to create things; original: *a creative writer.* **2.** Showing imagination or originality: *creative work.* **—cre•a′tive•ly** *adv.* **—cre•a′tive•ness** *n.*

cre•a•tiv•i•ty (krē′ā tĭv′ĭ tē) *n.* The quality of being creative; originality and inventiveness.

cre•a•tor (krē ā′tər) *n.* **1.** A person who creates: *creators of sculpture.* **2. Creator.** God.

crea•ture (krē′chər) *n.* **1.** A living being, especially an animal: *birds, rabbits, and other creatures of the woods.* **2.** A human being; a person. **3.** A person who is totally dependent upon or subservient to another person or thing: *a creature of habit.* —See Note at **critter.**

crèche (krĕsh) *n.* A model of the Nativity with statues of the infant Jesus, Mary, Joseph, and others. [First written down in 1792 in Modern English, from Old French *cresche*, crib, of Germanic origin.]

cre•dence (krēd′ns) *n.* Acceptance as true; belief: *Don't put any credence in that rumor.*

cre•den•tial (krĭ dĕn′shəl) *n.* **1.** Something that entitles a person to confidence, credit, or authority: *An honest face was the borrower's only credential.* **2. credentials.** Letters or other written evidence of a person's qualifications or status: *The guard asked for credentials before letting the scholar into the library of rare books.*

cred•i•bil•i•ty (krĕd′ə bĭl′ĭ tē) *n.* The condition, quality, or power of being credible: *The leader lost his credibility by failing to back up his threats with action.*

cred•i•ble (krĕd′ə bəl) *adj.* Worthy of confidence or belief; believable: *a credible news report; a credible witness.* [First written down about 1380 in Middle English, from Latin *crēdibilis*, from *crēdere*, to believe.] **—cred′i•bly** *adv.* —See Note.

cred•it (krĕd′ĭt) *n.* **1.** Belief or confidence; trust: *We place full credit in our employees.* **2.** Reputation or standing: *It is to their credit that they worked so hard without complaining.* **3.** A source of honor or distinction: *This exceptional athlete is a credit to our team.* **4.** Approval or acclaim for some act or quality; praise: *The authors shared the credit for the book's success.* **5.a.** Certification that a student has fulfilled a requirement by completing a course of study. **b.** A unit of study certified as properly completed. **6.** An acknowledgment of work done, as in the production of a motion picture or play. Often used in the plural: *a long list of credits at the end of the movie.* **7.** Reputation for repaying debts and being financially honest that entitles a person to be trusted in buying and borrowing: *I have good credit at all the local stores.* **8.a.** A system of buying goods or services by requiring payment at a later time: *buy a car on credit.* **b.** The period of time allowed before a debt must be paid. **9.** The amount of money in the account of a person or group, as at a bank. **10.** In accounting: **a.** The amount paid on a debt. **b.** The right-hand side of an account, on which such payments are entered. *—tr.v.* **cred•it•ed, cred•it•ing, cred•its. 1.** To believe in; trust: *They credited my explanation of what happened.* **2.a.** To regard (a person) as having done something: *Two Canadian scientists are credited with the discovery of insulin.* **b.** To attribute (something) to a person: *Some credit the song to Haydn.* **3.** To give educational credits to (a student). **4.** In accounting: **a.** To give credit for (a payment) in an account: *The store credited $100 to my account.* **b.** To give credit to (a person's account). [First written down in 1542 in Modern English, from Latin *crēditum*, loan, from neuter past participle of *crēdere*, to entrust.]

cred•it•a•ble (krĕd′ĭ tə bəl) *adj.* Deserving praise or credit: *They made a creditable attempt to solve the problem.* **—cred′it•a•bil′i•ty, cred′it•a•ble•ness** *n.* **—cred′it•a•bly** *adv.*

credit card *n.* A card issued by a bank or business authorizing the holder to buy goods or services on credit.

cred•i•tor (krĕd′ĭ tər) *n.* A person or firm to whom money is owed.

cre•do (krē′dō *or* krā′dō) *n., pl.* **cre•dos.** A statement of belief; a creed: *The store owner's credo is "The customer always comes first."*

cre•du•li•ty (krĭ do͞o′lĭ tē *or* krĭ dyo͞o′lĭ tē) *n.* The tendency to believe too readily; gullibility: *The young boy's credulity led him to believe many stories that weren't true.*

cred•u•lous (krĕj′ə ləs) *adj.* Tending to believe too readily; gullible: *A credulous person is easily fooled.* **—cred′u•lous•ly** *adv.* **—cred′u•lous•ness** *n.* —See Note at **credible.**

Cree (krē) *n., pl.* **Cree** or **Crees. 1.** A member of a Native American people living across a large area of Canada. **2.** The Algonquian language of the Cree.

creed (krēd) *n.* **1.** A formal statement of religious belief. **2.** A system of belief or principles that guides a person's actions: *The creed of modern science dictates that a theory must be tested by experimentation.*

creek (krēk *or* krĭk) *n.* **1.** A small stream, often a shallow tributary to a river. **2.** *Chiefly British.* A small inlet in a shoreline. [First written down about 1220 in Middle English and spelled *kryk*, probably from Old Norse *kriki*, bend.] —See Note at **run.**

❑ *These sound alike:* **creek, creak** (squeak).

Creek (krēk) *n., pl.* **Creek** or **Creeks. 1.** A member of a Native American people formerly living in eastern Alabama, Georgia, and northern Florida and now located in Oklahoma and southern Alabama. **2.** The Muskogean language of these people. **3.** A member of a Native American confederacy made up of the Creek and various other southeast peoples.

creel (krēl) *n.* A wicker basket used for carrying fish. [First written down in 1323 in Middle English and spelled *crel*, from Latin *crāticula*, gridiron, diminutive of *crātis*, wickerwork.]

creep (krēp) *intr.v.* **crept** (krĕpt), **creep•ing, creeps. 1.** To move slowly or cautiously with the body close to the ground: *The cat crept cautiously toward the mouse.* **2.** To move in a timid, cautious, or stealthy way: *The embarrassed host crept out of the room.* **3.** To advance or spread slowly: *Traffic was creeping along during rush hour.* **4.** To have a tingling sensation, as if covered with crawling things: *Thinking of ghosts makes my flesh creep.* **5.** To grow or spread along the ground or by clinging to a surface: *The ivy was creeping up the wall.* —*n.* **1.** The act of creeping: *the silent creep of a tiger.* **2.** *Slang.* An unpleasant or annoying person. **3. creeps.** *Informal.* A sensation of fear and repugnance, as if things were crawling on one's skin: *This old house gives me the creeps.*

creep•er (**krē′**pər) *n.* **1.** A person or thing that creeps. **2.** A plant having stems that grow along the ground or cling to a surface for support.

creep•y (**krē′**pē) *adj.* **creep•i•er, creep•i•est.** *Informal.* Producing a tingling sensation of uneasiness or fear, as if things were creeping on one's skin. —**creep′i•ly** *adv.* —**creep′i•ness** *n.*

cre•mate (**krē′**māt′ *or* krĭ **māt′**) *tr.v.* **cre•mat•ed, cre•mat•ing, cre•mates.** To burn (a corpse) to ashes. [First written down in 1874 in Modern English, from Latin *cremāre*.] —**cre•ma′tion** *n.*

cre•ma•to•ri•um (krē′mə **tôr′**ē əm) *n., pl.* **cre•ma•to•ri•ums** or **cre•ma•to•ri•a** (krē′mə **tôr′**ē ə). A furnace or building with a furnace for burning corpses.

cre•ma•to•ry (**krē′**mə tôr′ē *or* **krĕm′**ə tôr′ē) *n., pl.* **cre•ma•to•ries.** A crematorium.

Cre•ole (**krē′**ōl′) *n.* **1.** A person of European descent born in the West Indies or Spanish America. **2.** A person of mixed Black and European ancestry who speaks a language that is a creole. **3.** A descendant of the original French settlers of the southern United States, especially Louisiana. **4.** The French dialect spoken by these people. **5.** A language formed when two or more groups of people speaking different languages have prolonged contact with one another: *Haitian Creole is a mixture of French and various West African languages.* —*adj.* **1.** Of or relating to the Creoles or their languages and cultures. **2. creole.** Cooked with a spicy sauce containing tomatoes, green peppers, and onions: *shrimp creole.*

cre•o•sol (**krē′**ə sôl′ *or* **krē′**ə sŏl′) *n.* An aromatic liquid obtained from wood tar, used formerly as an antiseptic and in making creosote.

cre•o•sote (**krē′**ə sōt′) *n.* A yellow to brown oily liquid obtained from coal tar and used as a wood preservative and disinfectant. —*tr.v.* **cre•o•sot•ed, cre•o•sot•ing, cre•o•sotes.** To treat with creosote.

crepe also **crêpe** (krāp) *n.* **1.** A light, soft, thin cloth with a crinkled surface, made of silk, cotton, or another fiber. **2.** A band of black crepe, worn or hung as a sign of mourning. **3.** A very thin pancake, usually served folded with a filling. **4.** Crepe rubber. [First written down in 1797 in Modern English, from Old French *crespe*, curly, from Latin *crispus*.]

crepe paper *n.* Paper like crepe with crinkles or puckers in it, made in various colors.

crepe rubber *n.* Rubber with a crinkled texture, used for shoe soles.

crept (krĕpt) *v.* Past tense and past participle of **creep.**

cres•cen•do (krə **shĕn′**dō) *n., pl.* **cres•cen•dos** or **cres•cen•di** (krə **shĕn′**dē). **1.** In music, a gradual increase in loudness. **2.** A musical passage performed with a gradual increase in loudness. —*adj.* Gradually increasing in loudness: *a crescendo passage.* —*adv.* With a crescendo.

cres•cent (**krĕs′**ənt) *n.* **1.** The figure of the moon as it appears in its first quarter, with concave and convex edges ending in points. **2.** Something shaped like such a figure: *The ancient Middle East is known as the Fertile Crescent.* —*adj.* **1.** Shaped like a crescent. **2.** Increasing; waxing: *the crescent phase of the moon.* [First written down in 1399 in Middle English and spelled *cressaunt*, from Anglo-Norman, from Old French *creistre*, to grow, from Latin *crēscere*.]

cress (krĕs) *n.* Any of several plants, such as watercress, having sharp-tasting leaves used in salads.

cres•set (**krĕs′**ĭt) *n.* A metal cup containing burning oil or pitch, mounted on the top of a pole or hung from a chain to give light.

crest (krĕst) *n.* **1.** A projecting tuft or outgrowth on the head of a bird or other animal. **2.** A plume worn as a decoration on top of a helmet. **3.a.** The top of something, such as a mountain or wave. **b.** The highest point, as of a process or action: *The novelist was at the crest of a long career.* **4.** A design placed above the shield on a coat of arms. —*v.* **crest•ed, crest•ing, crests.** —*tr.* **1.** To reach the top of: *The climbers crested the mountain.* **2.** To decorate or furnish with a crest. —*intr.* **1.** To form into a crest: *Waves crested over the sea wall.* **2.** To reach a crest: *The river crested after the heavy rain.*

crest•fall•en (**krĕst′**fô′lən) *adj.* Dejected; depressed: *Crestfallen over the loss, the team met to discuss what went wrong.* —**crest′fall′en•ly** *adv.*

Cre•ta•ceous (krĭ **tā′**shəs) *adj.* **1.** Of, belonging to, or being the geologic time of the third period of the Mesozoic Era. During the Cretaceous, flowering plants developed, chalk deposits formed, and dinosaurs died out. See table at **geologic time. 2. cretaceous.** Of, containing, or resembling chalk. —*n.* The Cretaceous Period or its series of rocks.

Cre•tan (**krēt′**n) *adj.* Of or relating to Crete or its people or culture. —*n.* A native or an inhabitant of Crete.

❑ *These sound alike:* **Cretan, cretin** (person with cretinism).

Crete (krēt). An island of southeast Greece in the eastern Mediterranean Sea. Its civilization was one of the earliest in the world and reached the height of its wealth and power in around 1600 B.C.

cre•tin (**krēt′**n) *n.* A person afflicted with cretinism.

❑ *These sound alike:* **cretin, Cretan** (person from Crete).

cre•tin•ism (**krēt′**n ĭz′əm) *n.* A condition marked by very short stature and mental retardation, caused by a lack of thyroid hormone during development before birth.

cre•tonne (krĭ **tŏn′** *or* **krē′**tŏn′) *n.* A heavy cotton, linen, or rayon cloth with colorful printed patterns, used for curtains and slipcovers.

cre•vasse (krĭ **văs′**) *n.* **1.** A deep crack, as in a glacier; a chasm. **2.** A crack in a dike or levee.

crev•ice (**krĕv′**ĭs) *n.* A narrow crack or opening; a fissure or cleft: *Snow seeped through the crevice under the door.*

crew[1] (kro͞o) *n.* **1.** A group of people who work together: *the stage crew for the new play.* **2.a.** The persons working together to operate a ship, an aircraft, a spacecraft, or a train. **b.** All the persons working together to operate a ship, an aircraft, or a spacecraft except the officers. **3.** A team of rowers. [First written down about 1437 in Middle English and spelled *creue*, military reinforcement, from Old French *creue*, increase, from *creistre*, to grow, from Latin *crēscere*.]

crew[2] (kro͞o) *v.* *Chiefly British.* A past tense of **crow[2].**

crescent
Of the moon

cresset
1877 woodcut

crew[1]
In a racing shell

ă	pat	oi	boy
ā	pay	ou	out
âr	care	o͝o	took
ä	father	o͞o	boot
ĕ	pet	ŭ	cut
ē	be	ûr	urge
ĭ	pit	th	thin
ī	pie	*th*	this
îr	pier	hw	whoop
ŏ	pot	zh	vision
ō	toe	ə	about
ô	paw	N	*French* bon

cricket[2]

Regional Note: critter

Difficult as it is to believe, the word **creature** is historically the same word as **critter**, a word that you may have heard in Westerns used for cows or horses. We now pronounce the *-ture* suffix with a (ch) sound (*-chər*), but people used to pronounce it with a (t) sound (*-tər*). This older pronunciation is still used in some parts of the United States. The most common meaning of **critter** is "a living creature," whether wild or domestic.

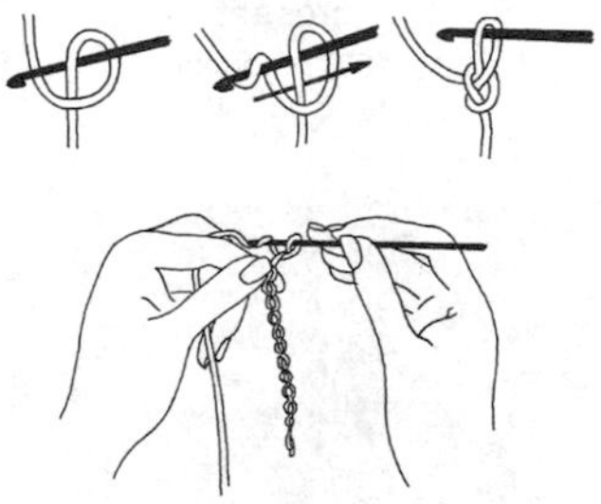

crochet

Davy Crockett

crew cut or **crew•cut** (kro͞o′kŭt′) *n.* A closely cropped haircut.

crew•el (kro͞o′əl) *n.* A loosely twisted worsted yarn used for a kind of embroidery.

crew•el•work (kro͞o′əl wûrk′) *n.* Needlework produced with crewel.

crib (krĭb) *n.* **1.** A small bed with high sides for a baby or young child. **2.** A small building for storing grain. **3.** A rack or trough from which cattle or horses eat. **4.** A framework to support or strengthen a mine or mine shaft. **5.** *Informal.* A list of answers or information consulted dishonestly during an examination. *—v.* **cribbed, crib•bing, cribs.** *—intr. Informal.* To use a list of answers or information in examinations; cheat. *—tr.* To copy dishonestly; plagiarize.

crib•bage (krĭb′ĭj) *n.* A card game in which the score is kept by inserting small pegs into holes arranged in rows on a small board.

crick (krĭk) *n.* A painful cramp or muscular spasm, especially in the back or the neck. *—tr.v.* **cricked, crick•ing, cricks.** To cause a crick in, as by turning or wrenching. [First written down about 1424 in Middle English and spelled *crike.*]

crick•et[1] (krĭk′ĭt) *n.* Any of various small black insects related to the grasshopper. The male produces a chirping sound by rubbing the front wings together. [First written down before 1325 in Middle English and spelled *criket*, from Old French *criquet*, from *criquer*, to click.]

crick•et[2] (krĭk′ĭt) *n.* **1.** An outdoor game played with bats, a ball, and wickets by two teams of 11 players each. It is popular in Great Britain, India, Australia, and other areas of the former British Commonwealth. **2.** *Informal.* Fair play. [First written down in 1598 in Modern English, from Old French *criquet*, stick for a bowling game.] **—crick′et•er** *n.*

cried (krīd) *v.* Past tense and past participle of **cry.**

cri•er (krī′ər) *n.* **1.** A person who cries. **2.** A person who shouts out public announcements, as in a court of law. **3.** A hawker of wares.

cries (krīz) *v.* Third person singular present tense of **cry.** *—n.* Plural of **cry.**

crime (krīm) *n.* **1.** A violation of the law in which a person either acts in a way the law forbids or fails to act as the law requires. **2.** Unlawful activity: *There is too much crime in our society.* **3.** A shameful or senseless act: *It's a crime to waste good food.* [First written down about 1250 in Middle English, from Latin *crīmen.*]

Cri•me•a (krī mē′ə *or* krĭ mē′ə). A region and peninsula of southern Ukraine on the Black Sea. The peninsula was the scene of the Crimean War (1853–1856).

crim•i•nal (krĭm′ə nəl) *adj.* **1.** Of or involving crime: *criminal behavior.* **2.** Relating to criminal law and the punishment of crime: *criminal court.* **3.** Guilty of crime: *a criminal offender.* **4.** *Informal.* Shameful; disgraceful: *a criminal waste of energy.* *—n.* A person who has committed or been convicted of a crime: *The judge sentenced the criminal to jail for burglary.* **—crim′i•nal•ly** *adv.*

criminal law *n.* Law involving crime and its punishment.

crim•i•nol•o•gist (krĭm′ə nŏl′ə jĭst) *n.* A person who specializes in criminology.

crim•i•nol•o•gy (krĭm′ə nŏl′ə jē) *n.* The scientific study of crime, criminals, criminal behavior, and corrections.

crimp (krĭmp) *tr.v.* **crimped, crimp•ing, crimps.** To press or bend into small regular folds or ridges: *crimp a pie crust.* *—n.* Something produced by crimping, as a fold or crease.

crimp•y (krĭm′pē) *adj.* Having crimps; wavy.

crim•son (krĭm′zən) *n.* A vivid purplish red. [First written down in 1416 in Middle English and spelled *cremesin*, from Arabic *qirmizīy*, from *qirmiz*, an insect used to make red dye.] **—crim′son** *adj.*

cringe (krĭnj) *intr.v.* **cringed, cring•ing, cring•es. 1.** To shrink back, as in fear; cower: *The puppy cringed when I tried to pet it.* **2.** To behave in a slavish manner; fawn: *The new secretary cringed before the boss.* *—n.* An act or an instance of cringing. **—cring′er** *n.*

crin•kle (krĭng′kəl) *v.* **crin•kled, crin•kling, crin•kles.** *—intr.* **1.** To form wrinkles or ripples: *Her face crinkles when she smiles.* **2.** To make a crackling sound; rustle: *The foil crinkled as I wrapped the leftovers.* *—tr.* **1.** To cause to form wrinkles or ripples: *I crinkled the wrapping paper when my hand slipped.* **2.** To cause to crackle. *—n.* A wrinkle or crease: *Crinkles form around the eyes from laughter.* **—crin′kly** *adj.*

cri•noid (krī′noid′) *n.* Any of various sea animals having a cup-shaped body, feathery arms, and a stalk by which they can attach themselves to a surface. Crinoids belong to the same group as the starfishes and sea urchins.

crin•o•line (krĭn′ə lĭn) *n.* **1.** A cloth used to stiffen collars, linings, hats, and petticoats. **2.** A stiff petticoat of this cloth, worn to make a skirt stand out. **3.** A hoop skirt.

crip•ple (krĭp′əl) *n.* A person or an animal that is partially disabled or unable to use a limb or limbs. *—tr.v.* **crip•pled, crip•pling, crip•ples. 1.** To cause to lose the use of a limb or limbs. **2.** To damage or disable: *The storm crippled the ship.* **—crip′pler** *n.*

cri•sis (krī′sĭs) *n., pl.* **cri•ses** (krī′sēz). **1.** A situation of great difficulty or danger, especially when political or economic conditions are unstable. **2.** A sudden change in the course of a serious illness: *Fever often marks the crisis of measles, mumps, and pneumonia.* **3.** A difficult or stressful event or change in a person's life. [First written down about 1425 in Middle English, from Greek *krisis*, decisive point, from *krinein*, to separate, decide.]

crisp (krĭsp) *adj.* **crisp•er, crisp•est. 1.** Firm but easily broken or crumbled; brittle: *crisp toast; crisp fried chicken.* **2.** Fresh and firm: *crisp lettuce.* **3.** Clean and new; not wrinkled: *a crisp dollar bill.* **4.** Refreshing; bracing: *a walk in the crisp autumn air.* **5.** Sharp, clear, and concise: *a crisp reply.* *—tr. & intr.v.* **crisped, crisp•ing, crisps.** To make or become crisp, as by heating or cooking. [First written down about 900 in Old English and spelled *crisp*, curly, from Latin *crispus.*] **—crisp′ly** *adv.* **—crisp′ness** *n.*

crisp•y (krĭs′pē) *adj.* **crisp•i•er, crisp•i•est.** Crisp. **—crisp′i•ness** *n.*

criss•cross (krĭs′krôs′ *or* krĭs′krŏs′) *v.* **criss•crossed, criss•cross•ing, criss•cross•es.** *—tr.* **1.** To mark with a pattern of crossing lines: *Animal trails crisscross the woods.* **2.** To move back and forth over or through: *Ships crisscrossed the sea.* *—intr.* To move back and forth: *Our paths crisscrossed throughout the day.* *—n.* A mark or pattern made of crossing lines. *—adj.* Crossing one another: *Criscross lines.* *—adv.* In crossing directions: *umbrellas leaning crisscross in the stand.* [First written down about 1475 in Middle English and spelled *Christcrosse*, Christ's cross.]

cri•te•ri•on (krī tîr′ē ən) *n., pl.* **cri•te•ri•a** (krī-tîr′ē ə) or **cri•te•ri•ons.** A rule or standard on which a judgment can be based: *Clarity of expression and organization of thought are two important criteria for judging the quality of an essay.*

crit•ic (krĭt′ĭk) *n.* **1.** A person who forms and expresses judgments about the qualities of something, especially in a report on an artistic work or performance: *a movie critic.* **2.** A person who tends to make harsh judgments. [First written down in 1588 in Modern English, from Greek *kritikos*, able to discern, from *kritēs*, judge, from *krinein*, to separate, judge.]

crit•i•cal (**krĭt′**ĭ kəl) *adj.* **1.** Inclined to judge severely; likely to find fault: *A critical person is seldom pleased with anything.* **2.** Marked by or exercising careful evaluation and judgment: *critical analysis of a poem.* **3.** Extremely important or decisive: *a critical point in the political campaign.* **4.a.** Of or being the crisis stage of a disease: *High fever is the critical point of pneumonia.* **b.** Extremely serious or dangerous: *a critical injury.* **5.** Being in a state of crisis or emergency: *a critical shortage of food.* **—crit′i•cal•ly** *adv.*

crit•i•cism (**krĭt′**ĭ sĭz′əm) *n.* **1.** The art or profession of forming and expressing judgments, especially about literary or artistic works. **2.** Unfavorable judgment; finding fault; disapproval: *constant criticism with no encouragement.* **3.** A comment, article, or review that expresses judgments: *Several reporters wrote criticisms of the new movie.*

crit•i•cize (**krĭt′**ĭ sīz′) *v.* **crit•i•cized, crit•i•ciz•ing, crit•i•ciz•es.** *—tr.* **1.** To judge the merits and faults of; evaluate: *The painter stepped back to criticize her last hour's work.* **2.** To judge severely; find fault with: *Newspapers criticized the library closing.* *—intr.* To express or utter criticism: *A judge must seldom criticize and never praise.* **—crit′i•ciz′er** *n.*

cri•tique (krĭ **tēk′**) *n.* A critical review or commentary, such as an evaluation of an artistic work.

crit•ter (**krĭt′**ər) *n.* A creature, especially an animal. —SEE NOTE.

croak (krōk) *n.* A low hoarse sound, such as that made by a frog or crow. *—v.* **croaked, croak•ing, croaks.** *—intr.* **1.** To make such a sound: *Bullfrogs croaked in the pond.* **2.** To speak with a low hoarse voice. *—tr.* To utter in a low hoarse voice: *croak an answer.*

Croat (krōt *or* **krō′**ăt′) *n.* **1.** A native or inhabitant of Croatia. **2.** Serbo-Croatian as used in Croatia, distinguished from Serbian by being written the Latin alphabet.

Cro•a•tia (krō **ā′**shə). A region of southern Europe along the northeast Adriatic coast. It was settled in the seventh century and was a part of Yugoslavia from 1946 until 1991, when it declared its independence. Capital, Zagreb. Population, 4,396,397.

Cro•a•tian (krō **ā′**shən) *n.* **1.** A Croat. **2.** The Croatian language; Croat. *—adj.* Of or relating to Croatia, or its people, language, or culture.

cro•chet (krō **shā′**) *v.* **cro•cheted** (krō **shād′**), **cro•chet•ing** (krō **shā′**ĭng), **cro•chets** (krō **shāz′**). *—tr.* To make by looping thread or yarn into connected links with a hooked needle: *crochet a sweater.* *—intr.* To crochet a piece of needlework. *—n.* Needlework made by crocheting. [First written down in 1846 in Modern English, from Old French *crochet*, hook, diminutive of *croche*, of Germanic origin.]

crock (krŏk) *n.* A pot or jar of earthenware.

crock•er•y (**krŏk′**ə rē) *n.* Earthenware.

Crock•ett (**krŏk′**ĭt), **David.** Known as "Davy." 1786–1836. American pioneer and politician who died at the siege of the Alamo.

croc•o•dile (**krŏk′**ə dīl′) *n.* **1.** Any of various large water reptiles having rough thick skin, sharp teeth, and long narrow jaws, living in the tropical regions of America, Africa, Asia, and Australia. **2.** Leather made from crocodile skin. [First written down before 1300 in Middle English and spelled *cokedrille*, from Latin *cocodrillus*, from Greek *krokodilos*.]

crocodile tears *pl.n.* A show of grief or tears that is not sincere.

cro•cus (**krō′**kəs) *n., pl.* **cro•cus•es.** Any of various small garden plants having purple, yellow, or white flowers that bloom early in spring.

Croe•sus (**krē′**səs). Died c. 546 B.C. The last king of Lydia in Asia Minor (560–546).

croft (krôft *or* krŏft) *n. Chiefly British.* **1.** A small enclosed field or pasture near a house. **2.** A small tenant farm.

croft•er (**krôf′**tər *or* **krŏf′**tər) *n. Chiefly British.* A person who rents and cultivates a croft.

crois•sant (krə **sänt′**) *n.* A rich crescent-shaped roll.

Cro-Mag•non (krō **măg′**nən *or* krō **măn′**yən) *n.* An early form of modern human being characterized by tall stature and known first from skeletal remains found in southern France. The Cro-Magnons made tools of stone and bone and are noted for extensive cave paintings. **—Cro-Mag′non** *adj.*

Crom•well (**krŏm′**wĕl′), **Oliver.** 1599–1658. English military, political, and religious figure who led the Parliamentarian victory in the English Civil War (1642–1649).

crone (krōn) *n.* An old woman.

Cro•nus (**krō′**nəs) *n.* In Greek mythology, a Titan who rules the universe until he is overthrown by his son Zeus.

cro•ny (**krō′**nē) *n., pl.* **cro•nies.** A close friend or companion.

crook (krŏŏk) *n.* **1.** An implement or a tool, such as a shepherd's staff, with a hook or hooked part. **2.** Something bent or curved: *a bag of groceries held in the crook of one's arm.* **3.** A curve or bend; a turn: *a crook in the road.* **4.** *Informal.* A person who makes a living dishonestly; a thief or swindler. *—tr. & intr.v.* **crooked, crook•ing, crooks.** To curve or become curved; bend: *crook one's arm around a package; a road that crooks sharply to the right.* [First written down before 1200 in Middle English and spelled *crok*, from Old Norse *krōkr*.]

crook•ed (**krŏŏk′**ĭd) *adj.* **1.** Not straight; bent or curved: *a crooked street.* **2.** *Informal.* Dishonest; underhanded: *a crooked merchant.* **—crook′ed•ly** *adv.* **—crook′ed•ness** *n.*

croon (krōōn) *v.* **crooned, croon•ing, croons.** *—tr.* To sing or hum softly: *croon a lullaby to the baby.* *—intr.* **1.** To sing or hum a melody softly. **2.** To sing popular songs in a sentimental manner. *—n.* A soft singing, humming, or murmuring. [First written down about 1400 in Middle English and spelled *crounen*, from Middle Dutch *krōnen*, to lament.] **—croon′er** *n.*

crop (krŏp) *n.* **1.a.** Cultivated plants or plant products such as grain, fruit, and vegetables: *Wheat is a common crop.* **b.** The amount of such a product grown or gathered in a single season or place: *Our orchard produced a huge crop of cherries last year.* **2.** A group or quantity appearing at one time: *candidates with a crop of new ideas; a promising crop of new students.* **3.** A short whip with a loop used in horseback riding. **4.** An enlargement of a bird's or insect's food passage where food is prepared for digestion. **5.** A short haircut. *—tr.v.* **cropped, crop•ping, crops.** **1.** To cut or bite off the tops or ends of: *Sheep cropped the grass very short.* **2.** To cut (hair, for example) short. **3.** To trim (a photograph, for example). **4.** To cause to grow or yield a crop or crops. ***—idiom.*** **crop up.** To appear unexpectedly: *Even when I'm careful, spelling errors crop up in my work.* [First written down about 700 in Old English and spelled *cropp*, ear of grain.]

crop-dust•ing (**krŏp′**dŭs′tĭng) *n.* The practice of spraying crops with powdered insecticide and fungicide from an airplane.

crop•land (**krŏp′**lănd′) *n.* Land for or suitable for growing crops.

crop•per[1] (**krŏp′**ər) *n.* A sharecropper.

crop•per[2] (**krŏp′**ər) *n.* **1.** A heavy fall: *As the horse*

crocodile

crocus

Oliver Cromwell

ă	pat	oi	boy
ā	pay	ou	out
âr	care	ŏŏ	took
ä	father	ōō	boot
ĕ	pet	ŭ	cut
ē	be	ûr	urge
ĭ	pit	th	thin
ī	pie	*th*	this
îr	pier	hw	whoop
ŏ	pot	zh	vision
ō	toe	ə	about
ô	paw	N	*French* bon

reared the rider took a cropper. **2.** A disastrous failure. *—idiom.* **come a cropper.** To fail suddenly or disastrously; come to grief. [First written down in 1858 in Modern English, perhaps from the phrase *neck and crop,* completely.]

crop rotation *n.* The practice of planting a sequence of different crops on the same land in order to prevent nutrients in the soil from being depleted and to control insects and disease.

cro•quet (krō **kā′**) *n.* A lawn game in which each player uses a mallet to hit a wooden ball through a course of wickets. [First written down in 1858 in Modern English, from Old North French, shepherd's crook.]

cro•quette (krō **kĕt′**) *n.* A small cake of minced food, often coated with bread crumbs and fried in deep fat: *chicken croquettes.*

cro•sier (**krō′**zhər) *n.* A staff with a crook or cross at the end, carried as a symbol of office by or before an abbot, a bishop, or an archbishop.

cross (krôs *or* krŏs) *n.* **1.a.** An upright post with a piece across it near the top, used in ancient times as an instrument of execution. **b.** Often **Cross.** The cross upon which Jesus was crucified. **c.** A representation of this cross; a crucifix. **2.** Any of various medals or emblems in the shape of a cross. **3.a.** A mark or pattern formed by the intersection of two lines. **b.** Such a mark (X) used as a signature by a person who cannot read or write. **4.** A trial or an affliction: *Feeling you always have to be right is a heavy cross to bear.* **5.a.** The process of crossbreeding. **b.** An animal or a plant produced by crossbreeding; a hybrid: *A mule is a cross between a horse and a donkey.* **6.** A combination of two different things: *The novel is a cross between a romance and a satire.* *—v.* **crossed, cross•ing, cross•es.** *—tr.* **1.** To go or extend across: *The chicken crossed the road. The bridge crosses the river.* **2.** To intersect: *at the corner where Elm crosses Main Street.* **3.** To place crosswise: *cross one'e legs.* **4.** To interfere with; thwart or obstruct: *Most people feel uncomfortable when they have been crossed.* **5.** To crossbreed: *cross a horse with a donkey.* **6.** To draw a line across: *Cross your T's.* **7.** To make the sign of the cross on or over: *They crossed themselves and entered the chapel.* **8.** To delete or eliminate by or as if by drawing a line through: *cross the names off the list.* **9.** To meet and pass: *We crossed each other on the way to the market.* *—intr.* **1.** To extend across; intersect: *The stream crosses through our yard.* **2.** To move across something; make a crossing: *We crossed into Mexico.* **3.** To meet in or as if in passing: *Our letters crossed in the mail.* **4.** To crossbreed. *—adj.* **1.** Lying crosswise; intersecting: *a cross street.* **2.** Showing anger or irritation; annoyed: *Teasing makes some people very cross.* **3.** Contrary or opposite: *opponents having cross interests.* [First written down about 963 in Old English and spelled *cros,* probably from Old Norse *kross,* from Old Irish *cros,* from Latin *crux.*] **—cross′ly** *adv.* **—cross′ness** *n.*

cross•bar (**krôs′**bär′ *or* **krŏs′**bär′) *n.* A horizontal bar, line, or stripe.

cross•beam (**krôs′**bēm′ *or* **krŏs′**bēm′) *n.* A horizontal beam or girder that crosses another or goes from one wall to another.

cross•bill (**krôs′**bĭl′ *or* **krŏs′**bĭl′) *n.* Any of various songbirds having a curved bill with narrow crossed tips.

cross•bones (**krôs′**bōnz′ *or* **krŏs′**bōnz′) *pl.n.* A representation of two bones placed crosswise, usually under a skull, used as a symbol of death or a warning of danger.

cross•bow (**krôs′**bō′ *or* **krŏs′**bō′) *n.* A weapon consisting of a bow fixed across a wooden stock, with grooves on the stock to direct an arrow or other projectile.

crossbow
Soldier, with foot in stirrup, resetting a crossbow

cross•breed (**krôs′**brēd′ *or* **krŏs′**brēd′) *v.* **cross•bred** (**krôs′**brĕd′ *or* **krŏs′**brĕd′), **cross•breed•ing, cross•breeds.** *—tr.* To produce (a hybrid animal or plant) by mating individuals of different breeds or varieties. *—intr.* To mate so as to produce hybrid offspring. *—n.* An animal or a plant produced by crossbreeding; a hybrid or cross.

cross-coun•try (**krôs′kŭn′**trē *or* **krŏs′kŭn′**trē) *adj.* **1.** Moving or directed across open countryside rather than following roads or tracks: *a cross-country race.* **2.** Going from one side of a country to the other: *a cross-country trip.* **—cross′-coun′try** *adv.*

cross•cut (**krôs′**kŭt′ *or* **krŏs′**kŭt′) *tr.v.* **cross•cut, cross•cut•ting, cross•cuts. 1.** To cut across (the grain of a piece of wood). **2.** To cut (a piece of wood) using a crosscut saw. *—adj.* Used for cutting crosswise: *crosscut teeth on a saw.* *—n.* **1.** A course or cut going crosswise. **2.** A shortcut.

crosscut saw *n.* A handsaw for cutting wood across the grain.

cross-ex•am•ine (krôs′ĭg **zăm′**ĭn *or* krŏs′ĭg **zăm′**ĭn) *tr.v.* **cross-ex•am•ined, cross-ex•am•in•ing, cross-ex•am•ines. 1.** To question (a witness already examined by the opposing side) in court. **2.** To question (someone) very closely, especially in order to check the answers against other answers given previously. **—cross′-ex•am′i•na′tion** *n.* **—cross′-ex•am′in•er** *n.*

cross-eyed (**krôs′**īd′ *or* **krŏs′**īd′) *adj.* Having one or both of the eyes turned inward toward the nose.

cross-fer•til•i•za•tion (krôs′fûr′tl ĭ **zā′**shən *or* krŏs′fûr′tl ĭ **zā′**shən) *n.* Fertilization of the ovum of one individual by the sperm of another, often of a different variety or species.

cross-fer•til•ize (**krôs′fûr′**tl īz′ *or* **krŏs′fûr′**tl īz′) *intr. & tr.v.* **cross-fer•til•ized, cross-fer•til•iz•ing, cross-fer•til•iz•es.** To undergo or cause to undergo cross-fertilization.

cross•fire (**krôs′**fīr′ *or* **krŏs′**fīr′) *n.* **1.** Lines of fire from two or more positions, crossing each other at a single point: *soldiers caught in a crossfire.* **2.** A rapid, often heated discussion: *The meeting erupted into a crossfire of threats and accusations.*

cross-grained (**krôs′grānd′** *or* **krŏs′grānd′**) *adj.* Having an irregular, transverse, or diagonal grain: *a piece of cross-grained wood.*

cross•hatch (**krôs′**hăch′ *or* **krŏs′**hăch′) *tr.v.* **cross•hatched, cross•hatch•ing, cross•hatch•es.** To mark or shade (part of a drawing or map) with two or more sets of intersecting parallel lines.

cross•ing (**krô′**sĭng *or* **krŏs′**ĭng) *n.* **1.** A place at which something, such as a street, railroad, or river, may be crossed: *a crossing for cattle along the highway.* **2.** A place where two or more things cross; an intersection: *a traffic light at the street crossing.* **3.** The act of crossing, especially a voyage or flight across an ocean.

cross-leg•ged (**krôs′lĕg′**ĭd *or* **krŏs′lĕg′**ĭd) *adv. & adj.* **1.** With legs or ankles crossed and knees spread wide, as when sitting on the ground: *sitting cross-legged around the fire.* **2.** With one leg lying across the other.

cross•o•ver (**krôs′**ō′vər *or* **krŏs′**ō′vər) *n.* Something, such as a bridge over a highway or a short stretch of connecting railroad track, that makes a crossing.

cross•piece (**krôs′**pēs′ *or* **krŏs′**pēs′) *n.* A crossing or horizontal piece, such as a crossbeam.

cross-pol•li•nate (**krôs′pŏl′**ə nāt′ *or* **krŏs′pŏl′**ə nāt′) *tr.v.* **cross-pol•li•nat•ed, cross-pol•li•nat•ing, cross-pol•li•nates.** To cause (a flower) to undergo cross-pollination.

cross-pol•li•na•tion (krôs′pŏl′ə **nā′**shən *or* krŏs′-

pŏl′ə nā′shən) *n.* The transfer of pollen from the anther of one flower to the stigma of another. Insects and wind are agents of cross-pollination.

cross-pur•pose (**krôs′pûr′**pəs *or* **krŏs′pûr′**pəs) *n.* A conflicting or contrary purpose. ***—idiom.* at cross-purposes.** Misinterpreting or failing to understand each other's purposes: *The two committees were at cross-purposes because of a lack of communication.*

cross-ref•er•ence (**krôs′rĕf′**ər əns *or* **krŏs′rĕf′**ər əns) *n.* A note directing the reader from one part of a book, catalogue, index, or file, to another part containing related information.

cross•road (**krôs′**rōd′ *or* **krŏs′**rōd′) *n.* **1.** A road that crosses another road. **2. crossroads.** *(used with a singular verb).* **a.** A place, often in the countryside, where two or more roads meet: *The bus for the city stops at the crossroads near our farm.* **b.** A crucial point or place, especially one where different courses of action may be taken: *I'm at a crossroads in my career.*

cross section *n.* **1.a.** A slice or section of an object made by cutting through it in a plane, usually at right angles to an axis: *the rings of growth in the cross section of a tree trunk.* **b.** A piece cut in this way or a picture or drawing of such a piece: *The picture is a cross section of the eye.* **2.** A sample of something meant to be representative of the whole. *A popular show usually appeals to a cross section of the people.*

cross-stitch (**krôs′**stĭch′ *or* **krŏs′**stĭch′) *n.* **1.** A stitch shaped like an X, used in sewing and embroidery. **2.** Needlework made with the cross-stitch. *—tr. & intr.v.* **cross-stitched, cross-stitch•ing, cross-stitch•es.** To make or embroider with cross-stitches.

cross-town or **cross•town** (**krôs′**toun′ *or* **krŏs′**toun′) *adj.* Running, extending, or going across a city or town: *a cross-town bus.* *—adv.* Across a city or town: *get snarled in traffic going cross-town.*

cross•walk (**krôs′**wôk′ *or* **krŏs′**wôk′) *n.* A path marked off for pedestrians crossing a street.

cross•way (**krôs′**wā′ *or* **krŏs′**wā′) *n.* A crossroad.

cross•wise (**krôs′**wīz′ *or* **krŏs′**wīz′) also **cross•ways** (**krôs′**wāz′ *or* **krŏs′**wāz′) *adv.* So as to be or lie in a cross direction; across: *logs laid crosswise on the fire.*

cross•word puzzle (**krôs′**wûrd′ *or* **krŏs′**wûrd′) *n.* A puzzle in which an arrangement of numbered squares, running down and across, are to be filled with letters of words that correspond to numbered clues. Some words cross each other by sharing letters.

crotch (krŏch) *n.* **1.** The place where a branch separates from a tree; a fork. **2.a.** The place where the human body branches into two legs. **b.** The place in a garment where the leg seams meet.

crotch•et (**krŏch′**ĭt) *n.* An odd, whimsical, or stubborn notion: *Many old-fashioned ways seem like crotchets today.*

crotch•et•y (**krŏch′**ĭ tē) *adj.* Full of contrary notions and whims; stubborn and eccentric. **—crotch′et•i•ness** *n.*

crouch (krouch) *intr.v.* **crouched, crouch•ing, crouch•es. 1.** To lower the body by bending or squatting: *The tiger crouched in the grass waiting for its prey.* **2.** To bend down or squat in fear; cringe: *The kittens crouched in the corner while the dog growled at them.* *—n.* The act or posture of crouching: *skiing in a crouch.* [First written down about 1395 in Middle English and spelled *crouchen*, from Old French *crochir*, to be bent, from *croche*, hook.]

croup (kro͞op) *n.* A diseased condition that affects the throat and windpipe, especially in children, producing difficult and noisy breathing and a hoarse cough. **—croup′y** *adj.*

crou•ton (**kro͞o′**tŏn′ *or* kro͞o **tŏn′**) *n.* A small piece of toasted or fried bread, used as a garnish in soups and salads. [First written down in 1806 in Modern English, from French *croûton*, from Old French *crouste*, crust, from Latin *crusta*.]

crow¹ (krō) *n.* Any of several large birds having glossy black feathers and a harsh hoarse call. ***—idiom.* as the crow flies.** In a straight line. [First written down before 700 in Old English and spelled *crāwe*.]

crow² (krō) *intr.v.* **crowed, crow•ing, crows. 1.** To utter the loud shrill cry of a rooster: *A rooster crowed at dawn.* **2.** To make a loud sound of pleasure or delight: *The happy baby kicked and crowed in its crib.* **3.** To boast, especially about someone else's defeat: *The winners crowed over their victory to all their friends.* *—n.* **1.** The loud high-pitched cry of a rooster. **2.** A loud sound expressing pleasure or delight. [First written down about 1000 in Old English and spelled *crāwan*.]

Crow (krō) *n., pl.* **Crow** or **Crows. 1.** A member of a Native American people formerly living on the northern Great Plains and now settled in Montana. **2.** The Siouan language of the Crow.

crow•bar (**krō′**bär′) *n.* A straight iron or steel bar, usually having one end bent or curved with a wedge-shaped edge, used as a lever for lifting or prying. [First written down before 1400 in Middle English and spelled *crow*, from the resemblance of its forked end to a crow's foot or beak.]

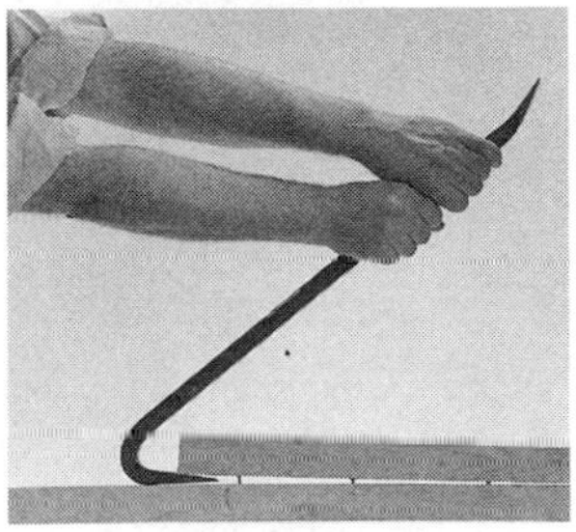

crowbar

crowd (kroud) *n.* **1.** A large number of people gathered together; a throng. **2.** The common people; the populace: *Do what you want to do and don't follow the crowd.* **3.** A particular group of people: *the college crowd; fall in with a bad crowd.* *—v.* **crowd•ed, crowd•ing, crowds.** *—tr.* **1.** To fill to overflowing: *Shoppers crowded the store.* **2.** To press tightly or cram together: *He crowded his old magazines in a cabinet.* **3.** To press or shove: *Subway riders crowd each other.* *—intr.* **1.** To gather together in a limited space: *Fans crowded around the rock star.* **2.** To move forward by shoving: *Everybody crowded into the cafeteria.* [First written down in 1567 in Modern English, from Middle English *crowden*, to crowd, from Old English *crūdan*, to hasten.]

crown (kroun) *n.* **1.** A head covering, often made of gold set with jewels, worn by a sovereign as a symbol of ruling power. **2.** Often **Crown. a.** The authority, power, or position of a sovereign: *the heir to the Crown.* **b.** The sovereign of a country. **3.** A wreath worn on the head: *a crown of laurel.* **4.** The top part of something, especially of the head. **5.** The head itself. **6.** The top part of a hat. **7.a.** The part of a tooth that projects beyond the gum. **b.** An artificial substitute for the natural crown of a tooth. **8.** A former British coin worth five shillings. **9.** A title, distinction, or reward: *win the heavyweight boxing crown.* *—tr.v.* **crowned, crown•ing, crowns. 1.** To place a crown or wreath on the head of: *crown the victor of the marathon.* **2.** To give regal power to; enthrone: *The king was crowned at the age of 15.* **3.** To give honor or recognition to: *The critics crowned her as the best pianist of all.* **4.** To cover or form the topmost part of: *Snow crowned the mountain peaks.* **5.** To be the highest achievement of: *The Nobel Prize crowned the scientist's career.* **6.** To put a crown on (a tooth). [First written down in 1111 in Middle English and spelled *coronan*, from Latin *corōna*, wreath, garland, crown.]

crown prince *n.* The male heir to a throne.

crown princess *n.* **1.** The female heir to a throne. **2.** The wife of a crown prince.

ă	**pat**	oi	**boy**
ā	**pay**	ou	**out**
âr	**care**	o͝o	**took**
ä	**father**	o͞o	**boot**
ĕ	**pet**	ŭ	**cut**
ē	**be**	ûr	**urge**
ĭ	**pit**	th	**thin**
ī	**pie**	*th*	**this**
îr	**pier**	hw	**whoop**
ŏ	**pot**	zh	**vision**
ō	**toe**	ə	**about**
ô	**paw**	N	*French* **bon**

crow's-nest

crow's-feet (krōz′fēt′) *pl.n.* Small wrinkles at the outer corner of the eye.

crow's-nest (krōz′nĕst′) *n.* A small lookout platform located near the top of a ship's mast.

CRT *abbr.* An abbreviation of cathode-ray tube.

cru•ces (kro͞o′sēz) *n.* A plural of **crux.**

cru•cial (kro͞o′shəl) *adj.* Of the utmost importance; decisive; critical: *The crucial moment in the trial came when the witness contradicted himself.* [First written down in 1830 in Modern English, from New Latin *(instantia) crucis*, crossroads (case), from Latin *crux*, cross.] **—cru′cial•ly** *adv.*

cru•ci•ble (kro͞o′sə bəl) *n.* **1.** A container that can withstand very high temperatures, used to melt ores, metals, and other materials. **2.** A severe test or trial.

cru•ci•fix (kro͞o′sə fĭks′) *n.* **1.** An image or a figure of Jesus on the cross. **2.** A cross viewed as a symbol of Jesus's crucifixion.

cru•ci•fix•ion (kro͞o′sə **fĭk′**shən) *n.* **1.** The act of executing a person on a cross. **2. Crucifixion. a.** The execution of Jesus on the cross. **b.** A representation of Jesus on the cross.

cru•ci•form (kro͞o′sə fôrm′) *adj.* Having the shape of a cross.

cru•ci•fy (kro͞o′sə fī′) *tr.v.* **cru•ci•fied, cru•ci•fy•ing, cru•ci•fies. 1.** To put (a person) to death by nailing or binding to a cross. **2.** To persecute or torment, as by harsh criticism: *The press crucified the senator for his moral failings.* **—cru′ci•fi′er** *n.*

crude (kro͞od) *adj.* **crud•er, crud•est. 1.** Being in an unrefined or natural state; raw: *crude oil.* **2.** Showing a lack of knowledge or skill; rough: *a quick crude sketch.* **3.** Lacking tact or refinement; not tasteful or finished: *a crude person with no manners; a crude remark made with little feeling.* [First written down about 1395 in Middle English, from Latin *crūdus.*] **—crude′ly** *adv.* **—crude′ness** *n.*

cru•di•ty (kro͞o′dĭ tē) *n.* The condition or quality of being crude; crudeness.

cru•el (kro͞o′əl) *adj.* **cru•el•er, cru•el•est** or **cru•el•ler, cru•el•lest. 1.** Given to causing pain or suffering: *a cruel dictator.* **2.** Causing suffering; painful: *a cruel act.* [First written down before 1200 in Middle English, from Latin *crūdēlis.*] **—cru′el•ly** *adv.* **—cru′el•ness** *n.*

cru•el•ty (kro͞o′əl tē) *n., pl.* **cru•el•ties. 1.** The condition or quality of being cruel: *cruelty to animals.* **2.** A cruel act or remark.

cru•et (kro͞o′ĭt) *n.* **1.** A small glass bottle for holding vinegar, oil, or other condiments at the table. **2.** A small vessel for water and wine used in the consecration of the Eucharist.

cruise (kro͞oz) *v.* **cruised, cruis•ing, cruis•es.** *—intr.* **1.** To sail or travel about in an unhurried way: *A patrol boat cruised along the coast.* **2.** To move or travel about with no special destination: *Taxis cruised through the business district looking for fares.* **3.** To travel at maximum efficient speed: *After takeoff the plane cruised at a high altitude.* *—tr.* To travel about or journey over: *A police car cruised the streets of the town.* *—n.* A sea voyage for pleasure: *We enjoyed our cruise to Bermuda.* [First written down in 1651 in Modern English, from Dutch *kruis*, cross, from Latin *crux.*]

❑ *These sound alike:* **cruise, cruse** (small bottle).

cruise missile *n.* An unmanned aircraft equipped with a bomb that uses radar or heat-sensitive devices to find its target.

cruis•er (kro͞o′zər) *n.* **1.** A medium-sized warship of high speed and a large cruising range, with less armor and firepower than a battleship. **2.** A large motorboat whose cabin is equipped with living facilities. **3.** A squad car.

crul•ler (krŭl′ər) *n.* A small, usually ringed-shaped or twisted cake of sweet dough fried in deep fat. [First written down in 1805 in Modern English, from obsolete Dutch *krulle-koken*, rolled-up cake, from Middle Dutch *crulle*, curly.]

crumb (krŭm) *n.* **1.** A tiny piece or particle of food: *We tossed crumbs of bread to the squirrels.* **2.** A little bit; a fragment; a scrap: *She has not a crumb of sympathy for him.*

crum•ble (krŭm′bəl) *v.* **crum•bled, crum•bling, crum•bles.** *—tr.* To break into small pieces or crumbs: *He always crumbles crackers into his soup.* *—intr.* **1.** To break up into small pieces: *The lump of dry dirt crumbled easily.* **2.** To fall apart; disintegrate: *The old barn finally crumbled in decay.*

crum•bly (krŭm′blē) *adj.* **crum•bli•er, crum•bli•est.** Easily crumbled: *crumbly old cake.* **—crum′bli•ness** *n.*

crum•my (krŭm′ē) *adj.* **crum•mi•er, crum•mi•est.** *Slang.* **1.** Of poor quality: *a crummy movie.* **2.** Miserable; wretched: *feeling crummy all afternoon.*

crum•pet (krŭm′pĭt) *n.* A light soft bread similar to a muffin, baked on a griddle and often toasted.

crum•ple (krŭm′pəl) *v.* **crum•pled, crum•pling, crum•ples.** *—tr.* To crush so as to form creases or wrinkles: *Don't crumple that freshly ironed shirt.* *—intr.* **1.** To become wrinkled or crushed: *Tissue paper crumples easily.* **2.** To collapse: *Stomach cramps caused the runner to crumple.*

crunch (krŭnch) *v.* **crunched, crunch•ing, crunch•es.** *—tr.* **1.** To chew with a noisy crackling sound: *crunch peanuts.* **2.** To crush, grind, or tread noisily: *crunch ice on a path.* *—intr.* **1.** To chew noisily: *crunch on celery.* **2.** To move with a crushing or cracking sound: *We crunched through the snow.* **3.** To make a crushing or cracking sound: *The snow crunched under my boots.* *—n.* **1.** The act of crunching. **2.** A crushing or cracking sound: *the crunch of gravel as the car drove up the driveway.* **3.** A critical situation, especially one resulting from a shortage of time, money, or resources: *an oil crunch.*

crunch•y (krŭn′chē) *adj.* **crunch•i•er, crunch•i•est.** Crisp; brittle: *crunchy potato chips.*

cru•sade (kro͞o **sād′**) *n.* **1.** Often **Crusade.** Any of a series of military expeditions undertaken by European Christians in the 11th, 12th, and 13th centuries to recover the Holy Land from the Muslims. **2.** A campaign or movement for a reform, cause, or ideal: *a crusade for women's rights.* *—intr.v.* **cru•sad•ed, cru•sad•ing, cru•sades.** To take part in a crusade: *The parents crusaded for better schools.* [First written down in 1577 in Modern English and spelled *croisade*, from Latin *crux*, cross.] **—cru•sad′er** *n.*

cruse (kro͞oz *or* kro͞os) *n.* A small jar or pot for holding oil, wine, or vinegar.

❑ *These sound alike:* **cruse, cruise** (travel).

crush (krŭsh) *v.* **crushed, crush•ing, crush•es.** *—tr.* **1.** To press or squeeze with enough force to break or injure: *The tree limb crushed the front of the car.* **2.** To break, grind, or pound into small pieces or powder: *crush rocks into gravel.* **3.** To crumple; wrinkle: *Packing the suitcase too tight will crush your clothes.* **4.** To shove, crowd, or press: *I was crushed against the wall of the crowded elevator.* **5.a.** To put down; subdue: *crush a rebellion.* **b.** To overwhelm; oppress: *The failure of the experiment did not crush the spirit of the researchers.* *—intr.* **1.** To be or become crushed: *The ice crushed under my feet.* **2.** To proceed or move by crowding or pressing: *The commuters crushed into the train.* *—n.* **1.** The act of crushing; extreme pressure: *The crush of the collision destroyed the car's engine.* **2.** A great crowd: *I was caught in the crush and couldn't get across the square.* **3.** A substance prepared by or as if by crushing: *orange crush.* **4.** *Informal.* A strong, often foolish and brief liking for someone. **—crush′er** *n.*

crust (krŭst) *n.* **1.a.** The hard outer layer of bread. **b.** A hard dry piece of bread: *had only a few crusts of bread for breakfast.* **2.** A pastry shell, as of a pie. **3.** A hard outer layer or covering: *Snow with a firm crust.* **4.** The solid outer layer of the earth. *—v.* **crust•ed, crust•ing, crusts.** *—tr.* **1.** To cover with a crust; encrust: *Snow and ice crusted the mountain trail.* **2.** To form into a crust: *Rust was crusted on the pipes.* *—intr.* To become covered with a crust: *The gravy cooled and crusted over.*

crus•ta•cean (krŭ **stā′**shən) *n.* Any of a group of animals, such as a lobster, crab, or shrimp, that live mostly in water and have a hard shell and jointed bodies and appendages. *—adj.* Of or belonging to this group of animals. [First written down in 1835 in Modern English, from New Latin *crustāceus,* hard-shelled, from Latin *crusta,* shell.]

crust•y (**krŭs′**tē) *adj.* **crust•i•er, crust•i•est.** **1.** Of or having a crust: *crusty bread.* **2.** Abrupt in speech or manner; gruff; harsh; curt: *The crusty old soldier was easy to provoke.* **—crust′i•ly** *adv.* **—crust′i•ness** *n.*

crutch (krŭch) *n.* A staff or support used by injured or disabled persons as an aid in walking, often having a padded crosspiece at the top that fits under the arm. [First written down about 900 in Old English and spelled *crycc.*]

crux (krŭks *or* kro͝oks) *n., pl.* **crux•es** or **cru•ces** (**kro͞o′**sēz). **1.** A basic or essential point: *Let's not lose sight of the crux of the problem.* **2.** A puzzling problem.

cru•zei•ro (kro͞o **zâr′**ō *or* kro͞o **zā′**ro͞o) *n., pl.* **cru•zei•ros.** The basic monetary unit of Brazil.

cry (krī) *v.* **cried** (krīd), **cry•ing, cries** (krīz). *—intr.* **1.** To shed tears and make sobbing sounds expressive of grief, sorrow, or pain; weep. **2.** To call loudly; shout: *We cried to our friends across the street.* **3.** To utter a characteristic sound or call: *The monkeys cried in the treetops.* *—tr.* **1.** To call out loudly; shout: *The umpire cried "Strike!"* **2.** To announce for sale; hawk: *The peddlers cry their wares in the streets.* **3.** To bring (oneself) into a particular condition by weeping: *She cried herself to sleep.* *—n., pl.* **cries** (krīz). **1.** A loud call; a shout: *a cry of warning.* **2.** A loud sound expressive of fear, grief, distress, or pain. **3.** A fit of weeping: *After a short cry the baby was fast asleep.* **4.** The characteristic sound or call of an animal: *the cry of an eagle swooping down on its prey.* **5.** A public or general demand or complaint; an outcry: *a cry for reform in city politics.* **6.** A call to action; a slogan: *a cry to arms.* **7.** A shout or call for help: *A neighbor heard their cries and called the police.* ***—idioms.*** **cry over spilled milk.** To regret what cannot be undone or fixed. **cry wolf.** To raise a false alarm. [First written down before 1200 in Middle English and spelled *crien,* from Latin *quirītāre,* to cry out.]

Synonyms: **cry, weep, blubber, sob, whimper.** These verbs mean to make sounds that show grief, unhappiness, or pain. **Cry** and **weep** both involve the shedding of tears: *Loud, sudden noises make the baby cry. No one wept at Scrooge's funeral.* **Blubber** refers to noisy crying mixed with speech that is broken or cannot be understood: *The child blubbered over the broken toy.* **Sob** refers to weeping and broken speech marked by gasps: *Stop sobbing for a minute and catch your breath!* **Whimper** means to make low, sorrowful, broken cries: *The poor dog came home limping and whimpering.* Antonym: **laugh.**

---

cry•ba•by (**krī′** bā′bē) *n.* A person who cries, whines, or complains frequently with little cause.

cry•ing (**krī′**ĭng) *adj.* Demanding immediate action or remedy: *a crying need for a new hospital.*

cry•o•gen•ics (krī′ə **jĕn′**ĭks) *n. (used with a singular or plural verb).* The branch of physics dealing with the production of low temperatures or the study of matter at low temperatures.

crypt (krĭpt) *n.* An underground vault or chamber, especially one that is used as a tomb beneath a church. [First written down in 1667 in Modern English, from Latin *crypta,* from Greek *kruptos,* hidden.]

cryp•tic (**krĭp′**tĭk) *adj.* Having a hidden meaning or secret nature; mysterious; puzzling: *a cryptic message.* See Synonyms at **vague.** **—cryp′ti•cal•ly** *adv.*

cryp•to•gram (**krĭp′**tə grăm′) *n.* Something written in a secret code or cipher.

cryp•to•graph (**krĭp′**tə grăf′) *n.* **1.** A cryptogram. **2.** A system or device using a secret code to encode and decode messages and documents.

cryp•tog•ra•pher (krĭp **tŏg′**rə fər) *n.* A person who specializes in cryptography.

cryp•tog•ra•phy (krĭp **tŏg′**rə fē) *n.* The study and use of secret codes and ciphers.

crys•tal (**krĭs′**təl) *n.* **1.a.** A solid composed of atoms, molecules, or ions arranged in regular patterns that are repeated throughout the structure to form a characteristic network: *Sugar crystals and salt crystals can be distinguished by the differences in their structure.* **b.** A transparent colorless mineral, especially a transparent form of pure quartz. **c.** A crystalline material with special electric properties, used in an electronic circuit. **2.a.** A clear colorless glass of high quality. **b.** An object made of this glass. **3.** A transparent cover that protects the face of a watch or clock. *—adj.* Clear; transparent: *I could see to the bottom in the crystal water of the lake.*

crystal ball *n.* A globe of crystal or glass in which images believed to predict the future are supposed to appear.

crys•tal•line (**krĭs′**tə lĭn *or* **krĭs′**tə līn′) *adj.* **1.** Composed of or resembling crystal. **2.** Made of crystals: *Snowflakes are crystalline.*

crystalline lens *n.* The lens of an eye.

crys•tal•lize (**krĭs′**tə līz′) *v.* **crys•tal•lized, crys•tal•liz•ing, crys•tal•liz•es.** *—tr.* **1.** To cause to form crystals or take on crystalline structure: *The researchers had to crystallize the protein before they could determine its structure.* **2.** To give a definite and permanent form to: *The scientists finally crystallized their ideas about the structure of the protein.* *—intr.* **1.** To take on crystalline form. **2.** To take on a definite and permanent form: *New political parties crystallized in eastern Europe after the Communist governments fell.* **—crys′tal•li•za′tion** (krĭs′tə lĭ **zā′**shən) *n.*

crys•tal•log•ra•phy (krĭs′tə **lŏg′**rə fē) *n.* The science that deals with the structure and properties of crystals.

Cs The symbol for the element **cesium.**

C.S.A. *abbr.* An abbreviation of Confederate States of America.

CST *abbr.* An abbreviation of Central Standard Time.

CT *abbr.* An abbreviation of Connecticut.

ct. *abbr.* An abbreviation of cent.

Ct. *abbr.* An abbreviation of Connecticut.

Cu The symbol for the element **copper** (sense 1).

cu. *abbr.* An abbreviation of cubic.

cub (kŭb) *n.* **1.** The young of certain animals, such as the bear, wolf, or lion. **2.** A beginner, especially in newspaper reporting. **3. Cub.** A Cub Scout.

Cu•ba (**kyo͞o′**bə). An island country in the Caribbean Sea south of Florida. It gained its independence from Spain in 1898. Capital, Havana. Population, 9,723,605.

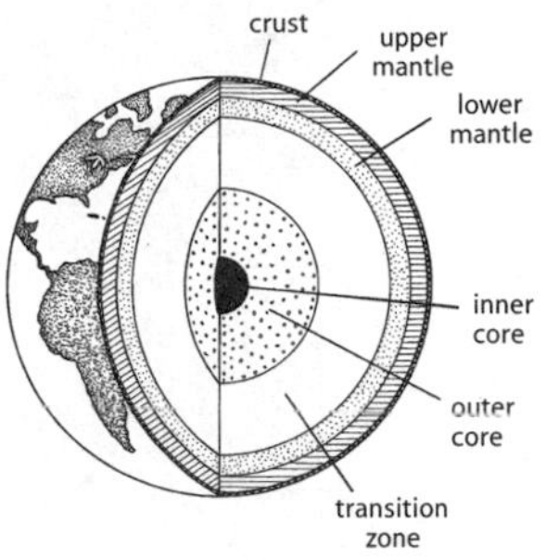

crust
Cutaway view of Earth

ă	**pat**	oi	**boy**
ā	**pay**	ou	**out**
âr	**care**	o͝o	**took**
ä	**father**	o͞o	**boot**
ĕ	**pet**	ŭ	**cut**
ē	**be**	ûr	**urge**
ĭ	**pit**	th	**thin**
ī	**pie**	*th*	**this**
îr	**pier**	hw	**whoop**
ŏ	**pot**	zh	**vision**
ō	**toe**	ə	**about**
ô	**paw**	N	*French* **bon**

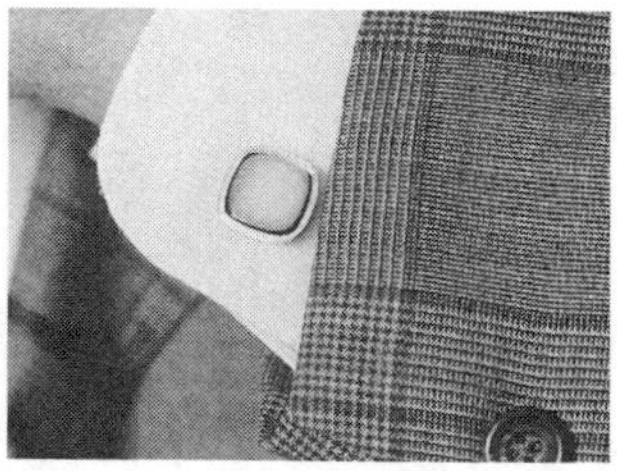
cuff link

culottes

cub•by•hole (kŭb′ē hōl′) *n.* A small and sometimes cramped space or room: *work in a cluttered cubbyhole of an office.*

cube (kyo͞ob) *n.* **1.** A solid having six equal square faces or sides. **2.** Something having this shape or almost this shape: *a bouillon cube.* **3.** The product that results when the same number is used three times as a factor. For example, the cube of 4, written 4^3, is equal to 4 × 4 × 4. *—tr.v.* **cubed, cub•ing, cubes. 1.** To form the cube of (a number). **2.** To express or measure the volume of (a container or space) in cubic units. **3.** To cut or form into a cube or cubes: *cube beets for a salad.* [First written down in 1551 in Modern English, from Greek *kubos.*]

cube root *n.* The number that produces a given number when cubed: *The cube root of 125 is 5.*

cu•bic (**kyo͞o′**bĭk) *adj.* **1.** Shaped like or nearly like a cube: *Dice have a cubic form.* **2.** Having length, breadth, and thickness; three-dimensional: *If you measure the volume of a room, you will express it in cubic feet and inches.* **3.** Of or involving a number or a variable that has been raised to the third power: *a cubic equation.*

cu•bi•cal (**kyo͞o′**bĭ kəl) *adj.* **1.** Cubic: *a room of cubical shape.* **2.** Of or involving volume: *cubical dimensions.*

❑ *These sound alike:* **cubical, cubicle** (small room).

cu•bi•cle (**kyo͞o′**bĭ kəl) *n.* A very small room or compartment.

❑ *These sound alike:* **cubicle, cubical** (cubic).

cubic measure *n.* A system for measuring volume using units, such as cubic inches and cubic centimeters, that are the cubes of linear units.

cub•ism also **Cub•ism** (**kyo͞o′**bĭz′əm) *n.* A style of 20th-century painting, drawing, and sculpture that portrays the subject matter as fragmented geometric forms. **—cub′ist** *adj. & n.*

cu•bit (**kyo͞o′**bĭt) *n.* An ancient unit of linear measure originally equal to the distance from the tip of the middle finger to the elbow, or about 17 to 22 inches (43 to 56 centimeters).

Cub Scout or **cub scout** *n.* A member of the junior division of the Boy Scouts, for boys of ages eight through ten.

cuck•oo (ko͞o′ko͞o *or* **ko͝ok′**o͞o) *n., pl.* **cuck•oos. 1.** A European bird having grayish feathers and a call of two notes that sounds like its name. It lays its eggs in the nests of birds of other species. **2.** The call or cry of a cuckoo. *—adj. Slang.* Crazy; foolish.

cuckoo clock *n.* A wall clock that marks the time by sounding a mechanical whistle imitating the cuckoo's call while a toy bird emerges from a small door.

cu•cum•ber (**kyo͞o′**kŭm′bər) *n.* **1.** The long cylindrical fruit of a climbing plant, having a green rind and white watery flesh, eaten in salads and used for making pickles. **2.** The vine that bears such fruit.

cud (kŭd) *n.* Food that has been partly digested and brought up from the first stomach to the mouth again for further chewing by mammals such as cattle and sheep.

cud•dle (**kŭd′**l) *v.* **cud•dled, cud•dling, cud•dles.** *—tr.* To hold tenderly and fondle: *cuddle a baby in one's arms.* *—intr.* To nestle; snuggle: *The two cats cuddled up near the fire.* *—n.* A hug or embrace.

cud•dly (**kŭd′**lē) *adj.* **1.** Fond of cuddling: *a couple of cuddly old cats.* **2.** Lovable; inviting cuddling: *The girl thought the kitten was so cuddly, she picked it up.*

cudg•el (**kŭj′**əl) *n.* A short, heavy club. *—tr.v.* **cudg•eled, cudg•el•ing, cudg•els** or **cudg•elled, cudg•el•ling, cudg•els.** To strike or beat with a cudgel.

cue[1] (kyo͞o) *n.* **1.** A long tapered stick used to strike the cue ball in billiards and pool. **2.** A line of waiting people or vehicles; a queue. [First written down in 1592 in Modern English and spelled *queue*, from Latin *cauda*, tail.]

❑ *These sound alike:* **cue[1]** (stick), **cue[2]** (signal), **queue** (line of people).

cue[2] (kyo͞o) *n.* **1.** A word or signal prompting an actor or singer to speak, sing, or do something during a performance. **2.** A signal for action. **3.** A hint or suggestion as to how to behave or what should be done: *Our host's yawn was a cue that it was time to go home.* *—tr.v.* **cued, cu•ing, cues.** To give (a person) a cue: *cue me when it's my turn.* [First written down in 1553 in Modern English and spelled *q*, perhaps from abbreviation of Latin *quandō*, when.]

❑ *These sound alike:* **cue[2]** (signal), **cue[1]** (stick), **queue** (line of people).

cue ball *n.* The white ball used to strike other balls in billiards and pool.

cuff[1] (kŭf) *n.* **1.** A band or fold of cloth at the bottom of a sleeve. **2.** The turned-up fold at the bottom of a trouser leg. **3.** A handcuff. ***—idiom.*** **off the cuff.** With little or no preparation; not rehearsed: *remarks made off the cuff.* [First written down before 1376 in Middle English and spelled *coffe*, mitten.]

cuff[2] (kŭf) *tr.v.* **cuffed, cuff•ing, cuffs.** To strike with or as if with the open hand; slap: *The bear cuffed her cubs.* *—n.* A blow or slap made with or as if with the open hand. [First written down in 1530 in Modern English and spelled *cuffe.*]

cuff link or **cuff•link** (**kŭf′**lĭngk′) *n.* One of a pair of fasteners for shirt cuffs, having a chain or shank that passes through the buttonholes.

cui•rass (kwĭ **răs′**) *n.* **1.** A piece of armor consisting of a breastplate and a piece for the back that are buckled together. **2.** The breastplate alone.

cui•sine (kwĭ **zēn′**) *n.* **1.** A style of cooking or preparing food: *French cuisine.* **2.** Food; fare: *a restaurant with excellent cuisine.*

cul-de-sac (**kŭl′**dĭ **săk′** *or* ko͝ol′dĭ **săk′**) *n., pl.* **culs-de-sac** (**kŭlz′**dĭ **săk′** *or* ko͝olz′ dĭ **săk′**) or **cul-de-sacs.** A blind alley or dead-end street.

cu•li•nar•y (**kyo͞o′**lə nĕr′ē *or* **kŭl′**ə nĕr′ē) *adj.* Of or relating to a kitchen or cookery: *a chef of great culinary skill.*

cull (kŭl) *tr.v.* **culled, cull•ing, culls. 1.** To pick out from others; gather selectively: *cull the prettiest flowers.* **2.** To remove undesirable members or parts from: *cull a herd of sheep.* *—n.* Something picked out from others as inferior: *Set the culls aside and freeze the rest of the strawberries.*

culm (kŭlm) *n.* The jointed, usually hollow stem characteristic of certain grasses.

cul•mi•nate (**kŭl′**mə nāt′) *intr.* **cul•mi•nat•ed, cul•mi•nat•ing, cul•mi•nates.** To reach the highest point or degree, often just before ending; climax: *The celebration culminated in a huge display of fireworks.* *—tr.* To bring to the highest point or degree, often just before completion: *An appearance by the President culminated the political convention.* [First written down in 1647 in Modern English, from Latin *culmen*, summit.] **—cul′mi•na′tion** *n.*

cu•lottes (ko͞o′lŏts′ *or* **kyo͞o′**lŏts′) *pl.n.* Women's trousers cut to resemble a skirt.

cul•pa•ble (**kŭl′**pə bəl) *adj.* Deserving blame: *Neglect of one's duty is culpable behavior.* [First written down about 1280 in Middle English and spelled *coupable*, from Latin *culpābilis*, from *culpa*, fault, blame.] **—cul′pa•bil′i•ty** *n.* **—cul′pa•bly** *adv.*

cul•prit (**kŭl′**prĭt) *n.* **1.** A person or thing guilty of a fault or crime: *The culprit who took the basketball net should put it back.* **2.** A person charged with a crime in a court of law.

cult (kŭlt) *n.* **1.a.** A system of religious worship and ritual: *the ancient cults of nature worship.* **b.** A religion or religious sect whose followers live in an unconventional manner under the guidance of a leader who demands strict obedience. **2.** A great or excessive attachment or devotion to a person, principle, or thing: *A cult of physical fitness has created large numbers of joggers and bikers nationwide.* **3.** A group of persons sharing a usually artistic or intellectual interest.

cul•ti•vate (kŭl′tə vāt′) *tr.v.* **cul•ti•vat•ed, cul•ti•vat•ing, cul•ti•vates. 1.a.** To prepare and improve (land), as by plowing or fertilizing, for raising crops; till. **b.** To loosen or dig soil around (growing plants). **2.** To grow or tend (plants or crops): *cultivate flowers.* **3.** To develop by study or teaching: *cultivate a love of music.* **4.** To seek the acquaintance or good will of (a person): *cultivate the new neighbors.* [First written down about 1620 in Modern English, from Medieval Latin *cultivāre*.]

cul•ti•vat•ed (kŭl′tə vā′tĭd) *adj.* **1.** Prepared and used to grow plants: *cultivated land ready for planting.* **2.** Grown by cultivation; not wild: *Many roses are cultivated flowers.* **3.** Improved by study or developed by training: *a cultivated appreciation of music.* **4.** Cultured; refined: *cultivated people with a love of opera.*

cul•ti•va•tion (kŭl′tə vā′shən) *n.* **1.** The process of tilling or growing: *the cultivation of fruits and vegetables.* **2.** Development or improvement by training: *cultivation of one's mind.* **3.** Culture; refinement: *a person of great cultivation.*

cul•ti•va•tor (kŭl′tə vā′tər) *n.* **1.** A person who cultivates. **2.** An implement or machine for loosening the earth and destroying weeds around growing plants: *A cultivator works faster than a hoe.*

cul•tur•al (kŭl′chər əl) *adj.* Of or relating to culture: *Paris is the cultural center of France.* **—cul′tur•al•ly** *adv.*

cul•ture (kŭl′chər) *n.* **1.** The arts, beliefs, customs, institutions, and all other products of human work and thought at a particular time: *the culture of Renaissance Italy.* **2.** The qualities of mind and the tastes that result from appreciation of the arts and sciences: *a writer of great culture.* **3.** Development of the mind through special training. **4.** The breeding of animals or growing of plants, especially to improve their development: *bee culture; silkworm culture.* **5.a.** The growing of microorganisms or tissues in a specially prepared nutrient substance for scientific study or medicinal use. **b.** Such a growth, as of bacteria or tissue: *a culture of penicillin-producing mold.* *—tr.v.* **cul•tured, cul•tur•ing, cul•tures.** To grow (microorganisms, tissues, or other living matter) in a specially prepared substance for scientific study. [First written down in 1440 in Middle English and spelled *culture*, cultivation, from Latin *cultūra*, from *cultus*, past participle of *colere*, to cultivate.]

cul•tured (kŭl′chərd) *adj.* **1.** Well-educated; refined: *a cultured supporter of the arts.* **2.** Grown or produced under artificial and controlled conditions: *cultured pearls.*

culture shock *n.* A condition of confusion and anxiety that can affect an individual suddenly exposed to an unfamiliar culture or environment.

cul•vert (kŭl′vərt) *n.* A water drain crossing under a road or an embankment.

cum•ber (kŭm′bər) *tr.v.* **cum•bered, cum•ber•ing, cum•bers.** To burden or trouble: *cumber a person with worries.*

Cum•ber•land Plateau or **Cumberland Mountains.** The southwest section of the Appalachian Mountains, extending from southern West Virginia into northern Alabama.

cum•ber•some (kŭm′bər səm) *adj.* Difficult to carry or manage: *cumbersome baggage.* **—cum′ber•some•ly** *adv.* **—cum′ber•some•ness** *n.*

cum•brous (kŭm′brəs) *adj.* Cumbersome. **—cum′brous•ly** *adv.* **—cum′brous•ness** *n.*

cum•in (kŭm′ĭn *or* ko͞o′mĭn *or* kyo͞o′mĭn) *n.* **1.** A plant of the Mediterranean region that is related to parsley and has spicy seeds. **2.** The seeds of this plant used for seasoning.

cum lau•de (ko͝om lou′də) *adv. & adj.* With honor: *She graduated cum laude. He is a cum laude graduate.*

cum•mer•bund (kŭm′ər bŭnd′) *n.* A broad sash worn around the waist, especially as part of a tuxedo.

cu•mu•la•tive (kyo͞om′yə lā′tĭv *or* kyo͞om′yə lə tĭv) *adj.* Increasing or growing by steady addition or in stages: *The cumulative efforts of many people helped control the epidemic.* **—cu′mu•la′tive•ly** *adv.* **—cu′mu•la′tive•ness** *n.*

cu•mu•lo•nim•bus (kyo͞om′yə lō nĭm′bəs) *n., pl.* **cu•mu•lo•nim•bus•es** or **cu•mu•lo•nim•bi** (kyo͞om′yə lō nĭm′bī). A very dense cloud with massive projections that billow upward to great heights, usually producing heavy rains, thunderstorms, or hailstorms.

cu•mu•lus (kyo͞om′yə ləs) *n., pl.* **cu•mu•li** (kyo͞om′yə lī′). A dense, white, fluffy cloud that billows upward from a flat base. [First written down in 1659 in Modern English, from Latin *cumulus*, heap.]

cu•ne•i•form (kyo͞o′nē ə fôrm′ *or* kyo͞o nē′ə fôrm′) *adj.* **1.** Of, relating to, or being the wedge-shaped characters used in writing by the Babylonians, Assyrians, Persians, and other peoples of ancient Mesopotamia. **2.** Written in or using such characters. *—n.* Cuneiform writing.

cun•ning (kŭn′ĭng) *adj.* **1.** Sly; crafty; clever: *a cunning scheme.* **2.** *Informal.* Charming; cute: *a cunning little child.* *—n.* **1.** Skill in deception; guile: *It takes great cunning to be a spy.* **2.** Skill in performance; expertness; cleverness: *a mystery writer of ingenious cunning.* **—cun′ning•ly** *adv.* **—cun′ning•ness** *n.*

cup (kŭp) *n.* **1.** A small open container, usually having a handle, from which to drink liquids: *The baby can now drink from a cup.* **2.** The contents of such a container: *drink a cup of cocoa.* **3.** In cooking, a measure equal to ½ pint, 8 ounces, or 16 tablespoons (237 milliliters). See table at **measurement. 4.** Something similar in shape to a cup: *the cup of a flower.* **5.** A cup-shaped vessel awarded as a prize or trophy: *We won the soccer cup.* **6.** In golf, a hole or the metal container inside a hole. *—tr.v.* **cupped, cup•ping, cups. 1.** To form in such a way as to resemble a cup: *cup one's hands to get a drink.* **2.** To place in or as if in a cup: *I cupped my ear with my hand to show I couldn't hear her.* [First written down about 1000 in Old English and spelled *cuppe*, from Late Latin *cuppa*, drinking vessel.]

cup•board (kŭb′ərd) *n.* A closet or cabinet, usually having shelves for storing food, dishes, or other small items: *a kitchen cupboard.*

cup•cake (kŭp′kāk′) *n.* A small cake baked in a cup-shaped container.

cup•ful (kŭp′fo͝ol′) *n., pl.* **cup•fuls.** The amount that a cup can hold.

Cu•pid (kyo͞o′pĭd) *n.* **1.** In Roman mythology, the god of love, identified with the Greek Eros. **2. cupid.** A figure of a winged boy used as a symbol of love.

cu•pid•i•ty (kyo͞o pĭd′ĭ tē) *n.* Extreme desire for something, especially wealth; greed.

cu•po•la (kyo͞o′pə lə) *n.* **1.** A small dome on top of a roof. **2.** A domed roof or ceiling.

cur (kûr) *n.* **1.** A dog considered to be undesirable;

culvert

cuneiform

ă	pat	oi	boy
ā	pay	ou	out
âr	care	o͝o	took
ä	father	o͞o	boot
ĕ	pet	ŭ	cut
ē	be	ûr	urge
ĭ	pit	th	thin
ī	pie	*th*	this
îr	pier	hw	whoop
ŏ	pot	zh	vision
ō	toe	ə	about
ô	paw	N	*French* bon

Marie Curie

Word History: curl

Everyone knows what a **curl** of hair is, and many of us know what a **cruller** is—a sweet, twisted cake or doughnut. What we may not know is how these two words are related. The connection lies in the twisted shape or twisting motion. *Curl* and *curly* come from a Middle English adjective *crulle*, "curly." The word *crulle* is related to the Dutch word *kruller*, "curl," and to the obsolete Dutch word *krulle-koken*, which meant "rolled-up cake." And it is from this word that we get our *cruller*.

a mongrel. **2.** A despicable or cowardly person.

cur•a•ble (**kyo͝or′**ə bəl) *adj.* Capable of being healed or cured: *a curable illness.* **—cur′a•bil′i•ty** *n.*

Cu•ra•çao (**ko͝or′**ə sou′ *or* **ko͝or′**ə sō′ *or* **kyo͝or′**-ə sou′). An island of the Netherlands Antilles in the southern Caribbean Sea off the northwest coast of Venezuela. It was settled in 1527.

cu•rate (**kyo͝or′**ĭt) *n.* A member of the clergy who assists the pastor, rector, or vicar of a church or parish.

cu•ra•tive (**kyo͝or′**ə tĭv) *adj.* Serving or tending to cure: *curative medicine.* —*n.* Something that cures; a remedy.

cu•ra•tor (kyo͞o **rā′**tər *or* **kyo͝or′**ə tər) *n.* A person who manages a museum, library, or zoo.

curb (kûrb) *n.* **1.** A concrete or stone border along the edge of a street: *Don't trip over the curb!* **2.** Something that checks or restrains: *a curb on spending.* **3.** A chain or strap used together with a bit to restrain a horse. —*tr.v.* **curbed, curb•ing, curbs.** To check, restrain, or control: *curb one's temper.*

curb•ing (**kûr′**bĭng) *n.* **1.** The material used to construct a curb. **2.** A curb.

curb•stone (**kûrb′**stōn′) *n.* A stone or row of stones used to make up a curb.

curd (kûrd) *n.* **1.** The thick part of milk that separates from the whey and is used to make cheese. **2.** A lumpy liquid that resembles curd.

cur•dle (**kûr′**dl) *v.* **cur•dled, cur•dling, cur•dles.** —*intr.* **1.** To form into curds: *The milk curdled overnight.* **2.** To seem to thicken and stop running, as because of fear or shock: *My blood curdled at the scream in the night.* —*tr.* To cause to form into curds: *Don't curdle the milk by leaving it out too long.*

cure (kyo͝or) *n.* **1.** Restoration of health; recovery from illness. **2.** A medical treatment or a series of such treatments used to restore health: *Penicillin is used as a cure for infections.* **3.** Something that restores health or improves a condition: *A trip was the perfect cure for overwork.* —*v.* **cured, cur•ing, cures.** —*tr.* **1.** To restore to health: *Strong medicine cured the patient quickly.* **2.** To bring about a recovery from: *cure a cold.* **3.** To remove (a harmful condition or influence): *cure a social problem.* **4.** To use a chemical, physical, or natural process in preparing, preserving, or finishing (a substance or material): *cure fish in a smokehouse.* —*intr.* **1.** To be or become restored to good health. **2.** To be prepared, preserved, or finished by a chemical or physical process: *The fish cured in the sun.* [First written down before 1300 in Middle English and spelled *coure*, from Latin *cūra*, medical treatment.]

cu•ré (kyo͞o **rā′** *or* **kyo͝or′**ā′) *n.* A parish priest.

cure-all (**kyo͝or′**ôl′) *n.* Something that cures diseases or evils; a panacea.

cur•few (**kûr′**fyo͞o) *n.* **1.** A regulation requiring certain people to be off the streets and indoors at a certain hour. **2.** The time at which such a regulation is in effect. **3.** The signal, such as the ringing of a bell, announcing the beginning of this regulation. [First written down about 1330 in Middle English and spelled *corfu*, from Old French *cuevrefeu* : *covrir*, to cover + *feu*, fire.]

cu•rie (**kyo͝or′**ē *or* kyo͞o **rē′**) *n.* A unit for measuring the intensity of radioactivity. [First written down in 1910 in Modern English, after Marie *Curie.*]

Cu•rie (**kyo͝or′**ē *or* kyo͞o **rē′**), **Marie.** 1867–1934. Polish-born French chemist who shared a 1903 Nobel Prize for research on radioactivity. In 1911 she won a second Nobel Prize for her discovery and study of radium and polonium.

cu•ri•o (**kyo͝or′**ē ō′) *n., pl.* **cu•ri•os.** A rare or unusual object: *a cupboard filled with tiny jars and other curios.*

cu•ri•os•i•ty (kyo͝or′ē **ŏs′**ĭ tē) *n., pl.* **cu•ri•os•i•ties. 1.** A desire to know or learn: *She was full of curiosity over who had sent the letter.* **2.** Something unusual or extraordinary.

cu•ri•ous (**kyo͝or′**ē əs) *adj.* **1.** Eager to learn more: *curious detectives.* **2.** Arousing interest because of strangeness: *We found a curious shell at the beach.* [First written down about 1340 in Middle English and spelled *curiouse*, from Latin *cūriōsus*, careful, inquisitive, from *cūra*, care.] **—cu′ri•ous•ly** *adv.* **—cu′ri•ous•ness** *n.*

Synonyms: curious, inquisitive, snoopy, nosy. These adjectives describe persons who show a marked desire for information or knowledge. **Curious** refers to a strong desire to know or learn: *If you are curious about a particular subject, the librarian can help you find a book about it.* **Inquisitive** often means too curious: *The inquisitive student asked a question every time the teacher paused for breath.* **Snoopy** means curious in a sneaky way: *The snoopy reporter searched through the movie star's garbage for evidence.* **Nosy** means rudely curious: *Lisa is so nosy she thinks nothing of reading other people's mail.* **Antonym: indifferent.**

cu•ri•um (**kyo͝or′**ē əm) *n. Symbol* **Cm** A radioactive metallic element produced artificially from plutonium or americium. It has 13 isotopes with mass numbers ranging from 238 to 250 and half-lives ranging from 64 minutes to 16.4 million years. Atomic number 96. See table at **element.** [First written down in 1946 in Modern English, after Marie *Curie* and Pierre *Curie* (1859–1906), French chemists.]

curl (kûrl) *v.* **curled, curl•ing, curls.** —*tr.* **1.** To twist or form into coils or ringlets: *curl one's hair.* **2.** To make curved or twisted: *I curled the string around a pencil.* —*intr.* **1.** To form ringlets or curls: *Her hair curls when it dries.* **2.** To move in a curve or spiral: *Smoke curled from the chimney.* —*n.* **1.** A coil or ringlet of hair. **2.** Something with a spiral or coiled shape: *a curl of smoke.* **3.** A weightlifing exercise in which a barbell is raised to the chest or shoulder and lowered without moving the upper arms, shoulders, or back. **—*idiom.* curl up.** To sit or lie down with the legs drawn up: *He curled up on the sofa to read.* —See Note.

curl•er (**kûr′**lər) *n.* A pin or roller on which strands of hair are wound for curling.

cur•lew (**kûrl′**yo͞o *or* **kûr′**lo͞o) *n.* Any of several shore birds related to the sandpiper and having brownish feathers, long legs, and a long downward-curving bill.

curl•i•cue (**kûr′**lĭ kyo͞o′) *n.* A fancy twist or curl, such as a flourish in a signature.

curl•ing (**kûr′**lĭng) *n.* A game originating in Scotland played on ice, in which two teams of four players slide heavy rounded stones toward a mark in the center of a circle.

curl•y (**kûr′**lē) *adj.* **curl•i•er, curl•i•est. 1.** Having curls or tending to curl: *curly hair.* **2.** Having a wavy grain or markings: *curly maple wood.* **—curl′i•ness** *n.*

cur•rant (**kûr′**ənt *or* **kŭr′**ənt) *n.* **1.a.** The small, sour, usually red or blackish fruit of any of various prickly shrubs, used especially for making jelly. **b.** A shrub that bears such fruit. **2.** A seedless raisin, used chiefly in baking. [First written down in 1391 in Middle English and spelled *(Raysyn of) Curans*, (raisin of) Corinth, currant.]

❑ *These sound alike:* **currant, current** (belonging to the present time).

cur•ren•cy (**kûr′**ən sē *or* **kŭr′**ən sē) *n., pl.* **cur•ren•cies. 1.** Money in any form when in actual use in a country: *U.S. currency is in dollars, and French currency is in francs.* **2.** General acceptance or use: *Many slang words and expressions have currency for only a short time.* **3.** A passing from one person to another; circulation: *By spreading gossip, people give currency to rumors.*

cur•rent (kûr′ənt *or* kŭr′ənt) *adj.* **1.** Belonging to the present time; present-day: *a person's current address.* **2.** Passing from one to another; circulating, as money or a rumor. **3.** Commonly accepted or used: *Use of hand calculators is current in schools today.* —*n.* **1.** A mass of liquid or gas that is in motion: *a current of cool air flowing through the room.* **2.** *Symbol* **I a.** A flow of electric charge. **b.** The amount of electric charge that passes a point in a unit of time, usually expressed in amperes. **3.** A general tendency or movement, as of events or opinions: *The current of voter opinion supports the President.* [First written down before 1300 in Middle English and spelled *curraunt*, from Old French *corant*, present participle of *courre*, to run, from Latin *currere*.] —**cur′rent•ly** *adv.*

❑ *These sound alike:* **current, currant** (fruit).

cur•ric•u•la (kə rĭk′yə lə) *n.* A plural of **curriculum.**

cur•ric•u•lar (kə rĭk′yə lər) *adj.* Of or relating to a curriculum.

cur•ric•u•lum (kə rĭk′yə ləm) *n., pl.* **cur•ric•u•la** (kə rĭk′yə lə) or **cur•ric•u•lums.** A set of courses of study offered at a particular educational institution or department: *the curriculum in engineering.* [First written down in 1824 in Modern English, from Latin *curriculum*, course, from *currere*, to run.]

cur•ry[1] (kûr′ē *or* kŭr′ē) *tr.v.* **cur•ried, cur•ry•ing, cur•ries.** To groom (a horse) with a currycomb. —***idiom.*** **curry favor.** To seek or gain favor by flattery: *The new worker tried to curry favor with the boss.* [First written down about 1300 in Middle English and spelled *coureyen*, from Anglo-Norman *curreier*.]

cur•ry[2] (kûr′ē *or* kŭr′ē) *n., pl.* **cur•ries. 1.** Curry powder. **2.** A pungent sauce or dish seasoned with curry powder: *We ate lamb curry for dinner.* —*tr.v.* **cur•ried, cur•ry•ing, cur•ries.** To season (food) with curry powder. [First written down in 1681 in Modern English, from Tamil *kaṟi*.]

cur•ry•comb (kûr′ē kōm′ *or* kŭr′ē kōm′) *n.* A comb with metal teeth used for grooming horses. —*tr.v.* **cur•ry•combed, cur•ry•comb•ing, cur•ry•combs.** To curry (a horse).

curry powder *n.* A mixture of sharp-flavored powdered spices including cumin and turmeric, used to prepare a pungent sauce or in seasoning food.

curse (kûrs) *n.* **1.a.** An appeal or a prayer for evil or harm to happen to a person or thing. **b.** The evil or harm that follows or seems to follow such an appeal. **2.** A word or group of words expressing great anger; an oath. **3.** Something that causes great evil or harm; a scourge: *Greed is a great curse of the human race.* —*v.* **cursed** or **curst** (kûrst), **curs•ing, curs•es.** —*tr.* **1.** To wish evil or harm on with a curse. **2.** To bring great harm to; afflict: *The farmers were cursed with bad weather at harvest time.* **3.** To swear at. —*intr.* To utter curses; swear. [First written down before 1050 in Old English and spelled *curs*.]

curs•ed (kûr′sĭd *or* kûrst) also **curst** (kûrst) *adj.* Deserving to be cursed; detestable. —**curs′ed•ly** *adv.*

cur•sive (kûr′sĭv) *adj.* Written or printed with connected letters; flowing: *cursive handwriting.* —*n.* A cursive character or letter. —SEE NOTE.

cur•sor (kûr′sər) *n.* A small square, dot, or bar of light on a computer screen that can be moved to indicate where the next operation takes place, such as taking out or inserting a letter.

cur•so•ry (kûr′sə rē) *adj.* Hasty and superficial; not thorough: *A cursory search of the file showed that many folders were out of order.* —**cur′so•ri•ly** *adv.*

curst (kûrst) *v.* A past tense and a past participle of **curse.** —*adj.* Variant of **cursed.**

curt (kûrt) *adj.* **curt•er, curt•est.** Rudely brief and abrupt in speech or manner; brusque: *They gave me only a curt greeting in their rush to catch the train.* —**curt′ly** *adv.* —**curt′ness** *n.*

cur•tail (kər tāl′) *tr.v.* **cur•tailed, cur•tail•ing, cur•tails.** To cut short; reduce: *We had to curtail our spending on the rest of the trip.* —**cur•tail′ment** *n.*

cur•tain (kûr′tn) *n.* **1.** Cloth or other material hanging in a window or door as a decoration, shade, or screen: *The wind was blowing the curtains at the open window.* **2.** Something that acts as a screen or cover: *mountains hidden by a thick curtain of fog.* **3.** The movable cloth or screen in a theater that separates the stage from the audience. **4.** The act of opening or closing a theater curtain for a performance. —*tr.v.* **cur•tained, cur•tain•ing, cur•tains.** To provide or shut off with or as if with a curtain. [First written down about 1303 in Middle English and spelled *curteyn*, from Late Latin *cōrtīna*.]

curt•sy or **curt•sey** (kûrt′sē) *n., pl.* **curt•sies** or **curt•seys.** A gesture of respect made chiefly by women by bending the knees with one foot forward and lowering the body. —*intr.v.* **curt•sied, curt•sy•ing, curt•sies** or **curt•seyed, curt•sey•ing, curt•seys.** To make a curtsy: *The singer curtsied before the audience.* [First written down in 1546 in Modern English, variant of *courtesy*.]

cur•va•ture (kûr′və cho͝or′ *or* kûr′və chər) *n.* **1.a.** The act of curving or the condition of being curved: *the curvature of the moon's orbit.* **b.** The degree to which something is curved: *a slight curvature in several warped boards.* **2.** A curving or bending of a body part, especially when abnormal: *curvature of the spine.*

curve (kûrv) *n.* **1.** A line or surface that bends in a smooth continuous way without sharp angles. **2.** Something that has the shape of a curve: *a curve in the road.* **3.** In mathematics, a line of a set of points defined by a function drawn on a surface or plane. **4.** In baseball, a curve ball. —*v.* **curved, curv•ing, curves.** —*intr.* To move in or take the shape of a curve: *The ball curved to the right. The road curves sharply just ahead.* —*tr.* To cause to curve: *curve a metal band.* [First written down in 1425 in Middle English and spelled *curve*, curved, from Latin *curvus*.]

curve ball or **curve•ball** (kûrv′bôl′) *n.* A pitched baseball that veers to one side as it nears the batter.

cush•ion (ko͝osh′ən) *n.* **1.** A pad or pillow with a soft filling, used to sit, lie, or rest on. **2.** Something used as a rest, support, or as a shock absorber. **3.** Something shaped like or used as a cushion: *He slept on a cushion of spruce boughs.* **4.** Something used to lessen a bad effect: *We have a savings account as a cushion against hard times.* —*tr.v.* **cush•ioned, cush•ion•ing, cush•ions. 1.** To place or seat on a cushion: *The cat cushioned itself on our pillows.* **2.** To furnish with a cushion or cushions: *Soft pillows cushioned the chair.* **3.** To lessen or soften the impact of: *My thick coat cushioned the fall.*

cusp (kŭsp) *n.* A point or pointed end, as on the new moon or a tooth.

cus•pid (kŭs′pĭd) *n.* A tooth having a single cusp; a canine.

cus•pi•dor (kŭs′pĭ dôr′) *n.* A spittoon.

cuss (kŭs) *Informal. intr. & tr.v.* **cussed, cuss•ing, cuss•es.** To curse. —*n.* **1.** An odd or perverse person: *an unpleasant cuss.* **2.** A curse.

cus•tard (kŭs′tərd) *n.* A pudding of milk, sugar, eggs, and flavoring that is baked or boiled.

currycomb

Word Building: cursive

The word roots *–cur–*, *–curr–*, and *–curs–* in English words come from the Latin verb *currere*, "to run," which has a past participle *cursus*. **Cursive** comes from the Latin adjective *cursīvus*, "running," and both the Latin and the English adjectives refer only to handwriting. The Latin noun *cursor* means "a runner, messenger, agent" and has been used in English for about 400 years to mean "a slide or runner on a measuring or surveying instrument." Since the mid 1960's **cursor** has been used for the flashing light on the monitor of a computer that shows where the next keystroke will fall.

ă	pat	oi	boy
ā	pay	ou	out
âr	care	o͝o	took
ä	father	o͞o	boot
ĕ	pet	ŭ	cut
ē	be	ûr	urge
ĭ	pit	th	thin
ī	pie	*th*	this
îr	pier	hw	whoop
ŏ	pot	zh	vision
ō	toe	ə	about
ô	paw	N	*French* bon

cutaway

Cus•ter (kŭs′tər), **George Armstrong.** 1839–1876. American soldier. He was killed by Sioux and Cheyenne led by Sitting Bull and Crazy Horse at the Battle of Little Bighorn in southern Montana.

cus•to•di•an (kŭ stō′dē ən) *n.* **1.** A person who has charge of something; a caretaker or guardian: *custodian of a museum collection.* **2.** A person who takes care of a building; a janitor.

cus•to•dy (kŭs′tə dē) *n., pl.* **cus•to•dies. 1.** Supervision; care: *The children were in the custody of their aunt and uncle while their parents were away.* **2.** The condition of being detained or held under guard, especially by the police: *The suspect was held in custody for questioning.*

cus•tom (kŭs′təm) *n.* **1.** An accepted practice or usual way followed by people of a particular group or region: *Shaking hands when meeting someone is a traditional custom.* **2.** A usual practice of an individual; a habit: *Their custom is to go to bed early.* See Synonyms at **habit. 3.** The usual or regular business a customer gives a store or other business: *The owners of the new store tried to obtain the custom of the wealthiest shoppers.* **4. customs.** *(used with a singular verb).* **a.** A duty or tax imposed on goods imported from another country. **b.** The government agency that collects these duties and inspects imported goods. *—adj.* **1.** Made to order: *custom suits made to the instructions of the buyer.* **2.** Making or selling things to order: *a custom tailor.* [First written down before 1200 in Middle English and spelled *custume,* from Latin *cōnsuētūdo.*]

cus•tom•ar•y (kŭs′tə mĕr′ē) *adj.* Established by custom; usual; habitual: *The customary place for a judge to sit is at the head of a courtroom.* **—cus′tom•ar′i•ly** (kŭs′tə mâr′ə lē) *adv.*

cus•tom-built (kŭs′təm bĭlt′) *adj.* Built according to the specifications of the buyer: *custom-built cabinets.*

cus•tom•er (kŭs′tə mər) *n.* **1.** A person who buys goods or services, especially on a regular basis. **2.** *Informal.* A person with whom one must deal: *a tough customer.*

cus•tom•house (kŭs′təm hous′) also **cus•toms•house** (kŭs′təmz hous′) *n.* A government building where customs duties are collected and ships are given permission to enter and leave a country.

cus•tom•ize (kŭs′tə mīz′) *tr.v.* **cus•tom•ized, cus•tom•iz•ing, cus•tom•iz•es.** To make or alter to suit an individual.

cus•tom-made (kŭs′təm mād′) *adj.* Made according to the specifications of the buyer: *custom-made draperies.*

cus•toms•house (kŭs′təmz hous′) *n.* Variant of **customhouse.**

cut (kŭt) *v.* **cut, cut•ting, cuts.** *—tr.* **1.** To make an opening in with a sharp edge or instrument: *I cut my finger on a piece of broken glass.* **2.** To separate or divide by using a sharp instrument: *cut paper with scissors.* **3.** To separate from the main body of something; detach: *cut a limb from a tree.* **4.** To pass through or across; cross: *The path cuts the neighbor's yard.* **5.** To shorten; trim: *cut hair; cut the lawn.* **6.** To form or shape by using a sharp instrument: *I cut a doll from the paper.* **7.** To reap; harvest: *cut wheat.* **8.** To cause to fall by sawing: *Each year loggers cut millions of trees.* **9.** To have (a new tooth) grow through the gums: *The baby cut two new teeth last week.* **10.** To interrupt or stop: *A bad storm cut our electric power for two hours.* **11.** To reduce the size or amount of: *The governor cut taxes.* **12.** To lessen the strength of; dilute: *The waiter cut the strong iced tea by adding water.* **13.** To eliminate; remove: *The director cut several scenes from the play.* **14.** To edit (film or audio tape). **15.** To hurt the feelings of: *Their unfriendly remarks cut me deeply.* **16.** *Informal.* To fail to attend purposely: *I cut my rehearsal today.* **17.** To divide (a deck of cards) in two, as before dealing. *—intr.* **1.** To make an opening or a separation: *The knife cut right through the rind. Swirling water cut under the rocks.* **2.** To allow an opening or severing: *Butter cuts easily.* **3.** To be like a sharp instrument: *The cold wind cut through my thin jacket.* **4.a.** To go by a short or direct route: *cut across the park to get home quickly.* **b.** To go across; cross: *This road cuts through the mountains.* **5.** To change direction abruptly: *The driver suddenly cut to the right.* **6.** To divide a deck of cards into two: *The dealer cuts first. —n.* **1.** The result of cutting; an opening or a wound. **2.** A blow or stroke, as with an ax: *The tree fell with a few cuts of the ax.* **3.** A part that has been cut from a main body: *an expensive cut of beef; a cut of cloth.* **4.** A passage made by excavating or drilling: *The highway runs through a cut in the mountain.* **5.** A removal of a part: *He made several cuts in the speech.* **6.** A reduction: *had to take a cut in pay.* **7.** The style in which a garment is cut: *The fine cut of my suit made it fit well.* **8.** *Informal.* A share of profits or earnings: *The salesman got a five percent cut at the end of the year.* **9.** A wounding remark; an insult: *That was an unkind cut you directed at me.* **10.a.** An engraved block or plate. **b.** A print made from such a block: *old cuts of life along the Mississippi River.* ***—idioms.*** **cut back. 1.** To shorten by cutting; prune: *cut back a tree limb.* **2.** To reduce or decrease: *cut back prices in a sale.* **cut down. 1.** To kill or strike down: *The cannon fire cut down the charging troops.* **2.** To reduce or curtail: *cut down one's spending.* **cut in. 1.** To move into a line of people or things out of turn: *The truck cut in at the head of the line for the tollbooth.* **2.** To interrupt: *cut in on our conversation.* **3.** To interrupt a dancing couple in order to dance with one of them. **cut off. 1.** To stop suddenly; shut off or discontinue: *cut off the electricity.* **2.** To disinherit: *The rich landowner will cut off most of the family without a cent.* **3.** To separate or isolate: *We were cut off from the mainland during the storm.* **cut out. 1.** To remove by cutting: *cut out a long sentence from the paragraph.* **2.** To form or shape by cutting: *cut out pieces for a coat.* **3.** To assign or determine as necessary: *I have my work cut out for me.* **4.** To be suited: *Many people are not cut out for city life.* **5.** To stop; cease: *Cut out the noise right now!* **6.** To deprive or disinherit: *cut a relative out of a will.* **cut up.** *Informal.* To behave in a playful or noisy way; clown. [First written down before 1300 in Middle English and spelled *cutten.*]

cut-and-dried (kŭt′n drīd′) also **cut-and-dry** (kŭt′n drī′) *adj.* **1.** Prepared and arranged in advance: *There are no cut-and-dried rules for good writing.* **2.** Lacking freshness or imagination; ordinary: *His advice was full of cut-and-dried old phrases.*

cu•ta•ne•ous (kyo͞o tā′nē əs) *adj.* Of, relating to, or affecting the skin: *cutaneous blood vessels.*

cut•a•way (kŭt′ə wā′) *n.* **1.** A man's formal daytime coat, cut so that the front edges slope away from the waist to form tails at the back. **2.** A model or diagram of an object with part of the outer layer removed so as to show the inside.

cut•back (kŭt′băk′) *n.* A decrease; a curtailment: *a cutback in government spending.*

cute (kyo͞ot) *adj.* **cut•er, cut•est. 1.** Delightfully pretty or dainty: *a cute puppy.* **2.** Obviously designed to charm; affected: *a cute remark.* **3.** Clever; shrewd: *a cute trick.* [First written down in 1731 in Modern English, short for *acute.*] **—cute′ly** *adv.* **—cute′ness** *n.*

cu•ti•cle (kyo͞o′tĭ kəl) *n.* **1.a.** The outer layer of skin; the epidermis. **b.** The outer layer or surface of a plant. **2.** The hard skin around the sides and base of a fingernail or toenail.

cut•lass also **cut•las** (kŭt′ləs) *n.* A heavy sword with a curved single-edged blade. [First written down in 1594 in Modern English and spelled *coutelace*, from Old French *coutelasse*, from Latin *cultellus*, small knife.]

cut•ler•y (kŭt′lə rē) *n.* **1.** Cutting instruments and tools, such as knives and scissors. **2.** Knives, forks, and spoons used as tableware.

cut•let (kŭt′lĭt) *n.* **1.** A thin slice of meat, as of veal, cut from the leg or ribs. **2.** A patty of chopped meat or fish. [First written down in 1706 in Modern English, from Old French *costelette*, diminutive of *coste*, rib, from Latin *costa*.]

cut•off (kŭt′ôf′ *or* kŭt′ŏf′) *n.* **1.** An indicated limit or stopping point: *Saturday is the cutoff for new job applications.* **2.** The act or an instance of cutting something off: *a cutoff of electricity.* **3.** A device used to stop a flow, as of a liquid or gas: *That valve is the cutoff for our water.* **4.** A short cut or bypass: *use the cutoff through the park.* **5. cutoffs.** Pants made into shorts by cutting off part of the legs. —*adj.* Indicating a limit or deadline: *a cutoff date.*

cut•out (kŭt′out′) *n.* **1.** Something cut out or intended to be cut out from something else: *cutouts of paper dolls.* **2.** A device that acts as a bypass or cutoff, especially in an electric circuit.

cut-rate (kŭt′rāt′) *adj.* Sold or on sale at a reduced price.

cut•ter (kŭt′ər) *n.* **1.** A worker whose job involves cutting some material, such as cloth, glass, or stone. **2.** A cutting device or machine: *a cookie cutter.* **3.** A small lightly armed boat used by the Coast Guard. **4.** A ship's boat, powered by a motor or pulled with oars, used for transporting stores or passengers. **5.** A fast single-masted sailing vessel. **6.** A light sleigh, usually drawn by a single horse.

cut•throat (kŭt′thrōt′) *n.* A murderer, especially one who cuts throats. —*adj.* **1.** Cruel; murderous: *a cutthroat band of thieves.* **2.** Ruthless or merciless in competition: *a cutthroat business.*

cut•ting (kŭt′ĭng) *adj.* **1.** Capable of or designed for cutting: *a cutting blade.* **2.** Injuring the feelings of others; insulting: *a cutting remark.* —*n.* **1.** A part cut off from a main body: *cuttings and scrapings.* **2.** A stem, twig, or leaf removed from a plant and placed in soil, sand, or water to form roots and develop into a new plant. **3.** *Chiefly British.* A clipping, as from a newspaper.

cut•tle•bone (kŭt′l bōn′) *n.* The chalky shell inside the body of the cuttlefish, used to supply calcium to caged birds or ground up to make a powder for polishing.

cut•tle•fish (kŭt′l fĭsh′) *n.* Any of various sea animals related to the squids and octopuses that have ten tentacles and a chalky internal shell and squirt a dark inky liquid when frightened.

cut•up (kŭt′ŭp′) *n.* *Informal.* A mischievous person.

cut•worm (kŭt′wûrm′) *n.* A moth caterpillar that is active at night and often destroys plants by eating through the stems at ground level.

cwt. or **cwt** *abbr.* An abbreviation of hundredweight.

–cy *suff.* A suffix that means: **1.** State; condition; quality: *bankruptcy.* **2.** Rank; office: *captaincy.*

cy•a•nide (sī′ə nīd′) *n.* Any of a large group of salts and esters containing the radical CN, especially the very poisonous salts sodium cyanide and potassium cyanide. Cyanides are used in making plastics and extracting and treating metals. [First written down in 1826 in Modern English, from Greek *kuanos*, dark blue.]

cy•ber•net•ics (sī′bər nĕt′ĭks) *n.* *(used with a singular verb).* The study of communication and control processes in biological, mechanical, and electronic systems.

cy•cad (sī′kăd′ *or* sī′kəd) *n.* Any of various large tropical evergreen plants that bear cones and resemble a palm tree.

cy•cla•men (sī′klə mən *or* sĭk′lə mən) *n.* Any of various plants having heart-shaped leaves and showy pink, red, or white flowers with petals that are turned outward.

cy•cle (sī′kəl) *n.* **1.a.** A series of events that is periodically repeated: *the moon's cycle from new moon to full moon.* **b.** The time during which such a series of events occurs. **2.** A long period of time; an age. **3.a.** The set of traditional poems or stories about a central theme or hero: *the Arthurian cycle.* **b.** A series of poems or songs that deal with the same theme: *a song cycle.* **4.** A bicycle, motorcycle, or similar vehicle. —*intr.v.* **cy•cled, cy•cling, cy•cles.** **1.** To occur in or pass through a cycle. **2.** To ride a bicycle, motorcycle, or similar vehicle. [First written down before 1387 in Middle English, from Greek *kuklos*, circle.]

cy•clic (sī′klĭk *or* sĭk′lĭk) or **cy•cli•cal** (sī′klĭ kəl *or* sĭk′lĭ kəl) *adj.* **1.** Of, relating to, or occurring in cycles: *the cyclic motion of the tides.* **2.** Of, relating to, or containing an arrangement of atoms in a ring or closed chain.

cy•clist (sī′klĭst) *n.* A person who rides a motorcycle, bicycle, or similar vehicle.

cy•clone (sī′klōn′) *n.* **1.** A storm or winds moving around and toward a calm center of low pressure, which also moves. In the Southern Hemisphere the direction of rotation is clockwise, while in the Northern Hemisphere the rotation is counterclockwise. **2.** A violent rotating windstorm, such as a hurricane or tornado. [First written down in 1848 in Modern English, from Greek *kuklōn*, moving in a circle, from *kuklos*, circle.]

cyclone cellar *n.* An underground shelter used for protection against violent windstorms.

cy•clon•ic (sī klŏn′ĭk) *adj.* Of or relating to a cyclone: *cyclonic winds.*

Cy•clops (sī′klŏps) *n., pl.* **Cy•clo•pes** (sī klō′pēz). In Greek mythology, any of a race of giants having one eye in the middle of the forehead.

cy•clo•tron (sī′klə trŏn′) *n.* A device that accelerates charged subatomic particles, such as protons and electrons, in an outwardly spiraling path, greatly increasing their energies.

cyg•net (sĭg′nĭt) *n.* A young swan.

❑ *These sound alike:* **cygnet, signet** (seal).

cyl•in•der (sĭl′ən dər) *n.* **1.** A solid figure bounded by a curved surface and two parallel circles of equal size at the ends. The curved surface is formed by all the line segments joining corresponding points of the two parallel circles. In a right circular cylinder the circles are perpendicular to the line segments; in an oblique circular cylinder they are not. **2.** An object or container having such a shape, as a can or a roller on a typewriter. **3.** The chamber in which a piston moves up and down, as in an engine or pump. **4.** The rotating chamber of a revolver that holds the cartridges. [First written down in 1570 in Modern English, from Greek *kulindros*.]

cy•lin•dri•cal (sə lĭn′drĭ kəl) also **cy•lin•dric** (sə lĭn′drĭk) *adj.* Of, relating to, or having the shape of a cylinder. —**cy•lin′dri•cal•ly** *adv.*

cym•bal (sĭm′bəl) *n.* One or a pair of musical instruments made into the shape of a dish from coils of brass fused together. Cymbals are sounded either by striking them together or by hitting them with a

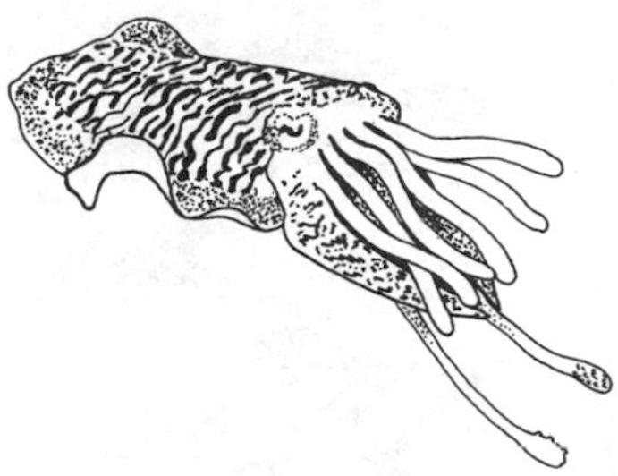

cuttlefish

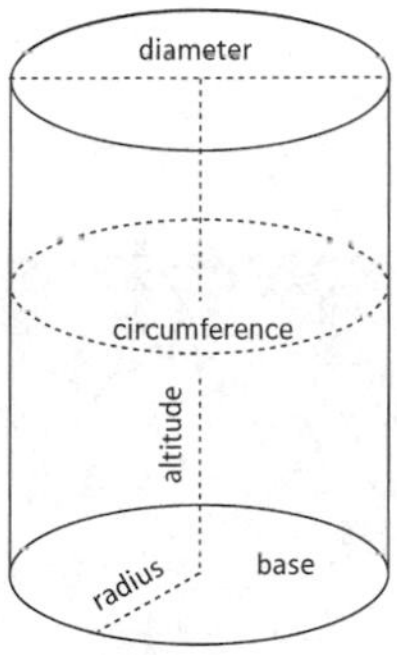

cylinder

cymbal

ă	pat	oi	boy
ā	pay	ou	out
âr	care	o͝o	took
ä	father	o͞o	boot
ĕ	pet	ŭ	cut
ē	be	ûr	urge
ĭ	pit	th	thin
ī	pie	*th*	this
îr	pier	hw	whoop
ŏ	pot	zh	vision
ō	toe	ə	about
ô	paw	N	*French* bon

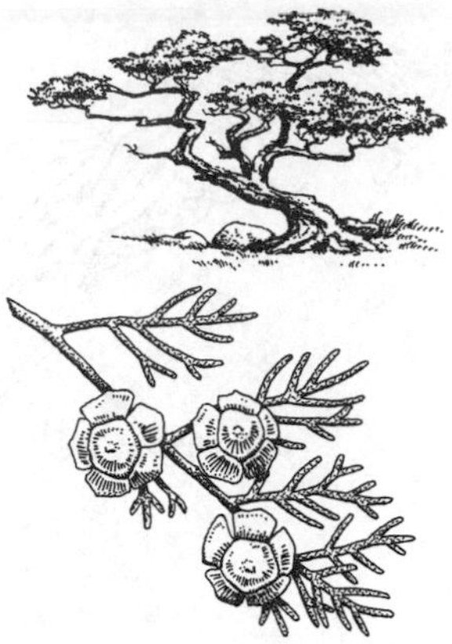

cypress

Cyrus the Great

drumstick or brush. [First written down about 825 in Old English, from Greek *kumbalon*, from *kumbē*, bowl.]

❑ *These sound alike:* **cymbal, symbol** (sign).

cyn•ic (sĭn′ĭk) *n.* A person who believes that people act mostly out of selfish interests. [First written down about 1547 in Modern English, from Greek *kunikos*, cynic philosopher, from *kuōn*, dog.]

cyn•i•cal (sĭn′ĭ kəl) *adj.* Scornful of the motives or virtues of others: *distrusting and cynical remarks about politics.* **—cyn′i•cal•ly** *adv.*

cyn•i•cism (sĭn′ĭ sĭz′əm) *n.* **1.** A scorning mocking attitude: *Recent scandals have increased cynicism about politics.* **2.** A scornful mocking comment or act.

cy•no•sure (sī′nə shŏŏr′ *or* sĭn′ə shŏŏr′) *n.* A center of attention or interest: *The early astronauts were the cynosure of the nation.*

cy•pher (sī′fər) *n.* *&* *v.* Variant of **cipher.**

cy•press (sī′prĭs) *n.* **1.a.** Any of various evergreen trees of warm regions of Asia, Europe, and North America, having hard wood and small leaves. **b.** The wood of any of these trees, used in making shingles and doors. **2.** Any of several similar or related trees that grow in swamps and shed their needles each year.

Cyp•ri•ot (sĭp′rē ət) also **Cyp•ri•ote** (sĭp′rē ōt′) *n.* **1.** A native or inhabitant of Cyprus. **2.** The ancient Greek or modern Greek dialect of Cyprus. *—adj.* Of or relating to Cyprus or its people, language, or culture.

Cy•prus (sī′prəs). An island country in the eastern Mediterranean Sea south of Turkey. It is the site of an ancient Neolithic culture. Cyprus gained its independence in 1960. Nicosia is the capital and the largest city. Population, 642,731.

Cy•ril•lic Alphabet (sə rĭl′ĭk) *n.* An old Slavic alphabet used in a modified form for Russian, Bulgarian, Serbian, and several other Slavic languages.

Cy•rus the Great (sī′rəs) Also Cyrus II 600?–529? B.C. King of Persia (550–529) and founder of the Persian Empire who conquered Lydia and Babylon.

cyst (sĭst) *n.* **1.** An abnormal sac or bladder in the body, composed of a membrane surrounding a gas, liquid, or soft solid material. **2.** A protective capsule in which certain organisms enclose themselves during inactive or reproductive periods.

cys•tic (sĭs′tĭk) *adj.* **1.** Of, relating to, or having the characteristics of a cyst: *a cystic growth.* **2.** Having, containing, or enclosed in a cyst. **3.** Of, relating to, or involving the gallbladder or urinary bladder.

cystic fi•bro•sis (fī brō′sĭs) *n.* An inherited disease of the glands of the body that discharge their fluids through ducts, such as the pancreas and sweat glands. It usually develops in childhood and affects the digestive and respiratory systems.

cys•ti•tis (sĭ stī′tĭs) *n.* Inflammation of the urinary bladder.

cy•tol•o•gist (sī tŏl′ə jĭst) *n.* A scientist who specializes in cytology.

cy•tol•o•gy (sī tŏl′ə jē) *n.* The branch of biology that deals with the formation, structure, and function of cells.

cy•to•plasm (sī′tə plăz′əm) *n.* The protoplasm of a cell outside the nucleus. **—cy′to•plas′mic** *adj.*

cy•to•sine (sī′tə sēn′) *n.* A base that is a component of DNA and RNA.

CZ or **C.Z.** *abbr.* An abbreviation of Canal Zone.

czar (zär *or* tsär) *n.* **1.** also **tsar** or **tzar** Any of the emperors who ruled Russia until the revolution of 1917. **2.** A person who has great authority or power. [First written down in 1555 in Modern English, from Russian *tsar′*, from Latin *Caesar*, emperor.]

cza•ri•na (zä rē′nə *or* tsä rē′nə) *n.* The wife of a Russian czar.

czar•ist (zär′ĭst) *adj.* Of, relating to, or in the time of the czars: *czarist Russia.*

cza•rit•za (zä rĭt′sə *or* tsä rēt′sə) *n.* Any of the empresses who ruled Russia until the revolution of 1917.

Czech (chĕk) *n.* **1.** A native or inhabitant of Czech Republic or of Czechoslovakia. **2.** The Slavic language of the Czechs. *—adj.* Of or relating to Czech Republic or to Czechoslovakia, the Czechs, their language, or culture.

Czech•o•slo•va•ki•a (chĕk′ə slə vä′kē ə). A former country of central Europe south of Poland. It was formed in 1918 and divided in January 1993 into Czech Republic and Slovakia. **—Czech′o•slo′vak, Czech′o•slo•va′ki•an** *adj.*

Czech Republic. A country of central Europe, part of Czechoslovakia until January 1993. Capital, Prague. Population, 10,291,927.

Dd

d or **D** (dē) *n., pl.* **d's** or **D's. 1.** The fourth letter of the English alphabet. **2.** The lowest passing grade in school. **3. D.** In music, the second tone in the scale of C major. **4.** The fourth in a series or group: *row D in a theater.*

D¹ also **d** The symbol for the Roman numeral 500.

D² *abbr.* An abbreviation of Democrat.

d. *abbr.* An abbreviation of: **1.** Date. **2.** Daughter. **3.** Dose. **4.** Died. **5.** Penny (1⁄12 of a shilling).

D. *abbr.* An abbreviation of department.

D.A. *abbr.* An abbreviation of district attorney.

dab (dăb) *v.* **dabbed, dab•bing, dabs.** *—tr.* **1.** To apply with short light strokes: *dab grease on a burn.* **2.** To pat quickly and lightly: *dab the face with cold cream.* *—intr.* To tap gently; pat. *—n.* **1.** A small amount, lump, or mass: *a dab of butter.* **2.** A light poking stroke or pat: *a kitten making dabs at a string.*

dab•ble (dăb′əl) *v.* **dab•bled, dab•bling, dab•bles.** *—tr.* To splash in and out of water: *The children dabbled their feet in the brook.* *—intr.* **1.** To splash or play in water: *The ducks dabbled in the shallow water.* **2.** To do or work on something casually or without serious intent: *I dabbled in photography for a time.* **—dab′bler** *n.*

da ca•po (dä kä′pō) *adv.* In music, from the beginning. Used as a direction to repeat a section of a composition.

Dac•ca also **Dha•ka** (dăk′ə *or* dä′kə). The capital and largest city of Bangladesh, in the east-central part of the country northwest of Chittagong. Population, 1,850,000.

dace (dās) *n., pl.* **dace** or **dac•es.** Any of various small freshwater fishes of Europe and North America, related to the minnows.

dachs•hund (däks′ho͝ont′ *or* däk′sənt) *n.* A small dog having a long body, a short-haired dark coat, drooping ears, and very short legs. [First written down in 1881 in Modern English, from German : *Dachs,* badger + *Hund,* dog.]

Da•cron (dā′krŏn′ *or* dăk′rŏn′). A trademark for a synthetic textile fiber or fabric that resists stretching and wrinkling.

dac•tyl (dăk′təl) *n.* In poetry, a metrical foot consisting of one accented syllable followed by two unaccented syllables, as in *flattery.*

dad (dăd) *n. Informal.* Father.

dad•dy (dăd′ē) *n., pl.* **dad•dies.** *Informal.* Father.

daddy long•legs (lông′lĕgz′ *or* lŏng′lĕgz′) *n., pl.* **daddy longlegs.** Any of various spiderlike arachnids having a small rounded body and long slender legs.

da•do (dā′dō) *n., pl.* **da•does. 1.** The section of a pedestal between the base and the crown or cap. **2.** The lower part of the wall of a room decorated with wooden panels or other material that is different from the rest of the wall.

Dae•da•lus (dĕd′l əs) *n.* In Greek mythology, the builder of the Labyrinth in Crete, who is later imprisoned in it with his son Icarus and makes wings for both of them to fly out.

daf•fo•dil (dăf′ə dĭl) *n.* A garden plant that grows from a bulb and has long slender leaves and showy, usually yellow flowers with a trumpet-shaped central part. [First written down before 1400 in Middle English and spelled *affodil,* from Latin *asphodelus,* asphodel.]

daf•fy (dăf′ē) *adj.* **daf•fi•er, daf•fi•est.** *Informal.* **1.** Silly; zany. **2.** Crazy; insane.

daft (dăft) *adj.* **daft•er, daft•est. 1.** Foolish; stupid: *a daft reply.* **2.** Crazy; insane. **—daft′ly** *adv.* **—daft′ness** *n.*

dag•ger (dăg′ər) *n.* **1.** A short pointed weapon, used for stabbing. **2.** A dagger-shaped symbol (†) often used as a reference to a footnote in a book or to some special category before a word in a list.

da•guerre•o•type (də gâr′ə tīp′) *n.* **1.** An early photographic process in which an image is formed on a silver-coated metal plate that is sensitive to light. **2.** A photograph made by this process. [First written down in 1839 in Modern English, after Louis *Daguerre* (1789–1851), French artist and inventor.]

dahl•ia (dăl′yə *or* däl′yə) *n.* Any of several garden plants having thick roots and showy flowers of various colors. [First written down in 1791 in Modern English, after Anders *Dahl* (1751–1787), Swedish botanist.]

Da•ho•mey (də hō′mē). Benin (sense 2).

dai•ly (dā′lē) *adj.* **1.** Done, happening, or appearing every day or weekday: *a daily walk.* **2.** Of or for each day: *a daily record.* *—adv.* Every day: *Exercise daily.* *—n., pl.* **dai•lies.** A newspaper published every day or every weekday.

dain•ty (dān′tē) *adj.* **dain•ti•er, dain•ti•est. 1.** Delicately beautiful: *dainty embroidery.* **2.** Very careful in choosing; fussy; finicky: *The cat is a dainty eater.* **3.** Delicious or choice; tasty: *She put together a dainty dish of fancy sandwiches.* *—n., pl.* **dain•ties.** A choice delicious food; a delicacy. **—dain′ti•ly** *adv.* **—dain′ti•ness** *n.*

dair•y (dâr′ē) *n., pl.* **dair•ies. 1.** A room or building where milk and cream are stored, prepared for use, or made into butter and cheese. **2.** A business or store that prepares or sells milk and milk products. **3.** A dairy farm. *—adj.* Of, for, or relating to milk or milk products. [First written down about 1300 in Middle English and spelled *deierie,* from *daie,* dairymaid, from Old English *dæge,* bread kneader.]

dairy cattle *pl.n.* Cows bred and raised for milk rather than meat.

dairy farm *n.* A farm for producing milk and milk products.

dair•y•ing (dâr′ē ĭng) *n.* The business of running a dairy or a dairy farm.

dair•y•maid (dâr′ē mād′) *n.* A woman or girl who works in a dairy.

dair•y•man (dâr′ē mən) *n.* A man who owns, manages, or works in a dairy.

dair•y•wom•an (dâr′ē wo͝om′ən) *n.* A woman who owns, manages, or works in a dairy.

da•is (dā′ĭs *or* dī′ĭs) *n.* A raised platform for a throne, a speaker, or a group of honored guests.

dai•sy (dā′zē) *n., pl.* **dai•sies.** Any of several plants having flowers with many narrow rays surrounding a flat round center, especially a Eurasian plant

dachshund

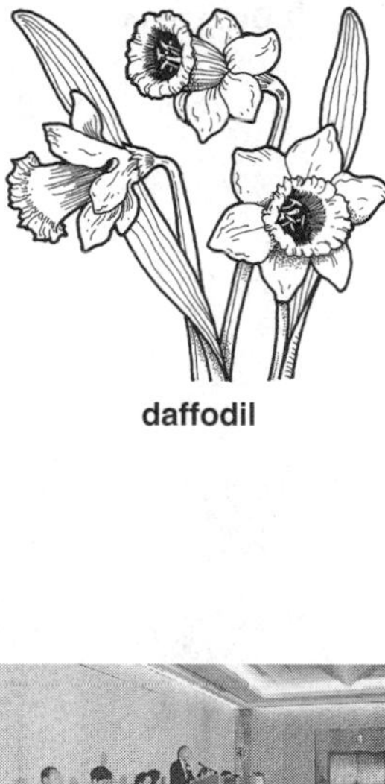

daffodil

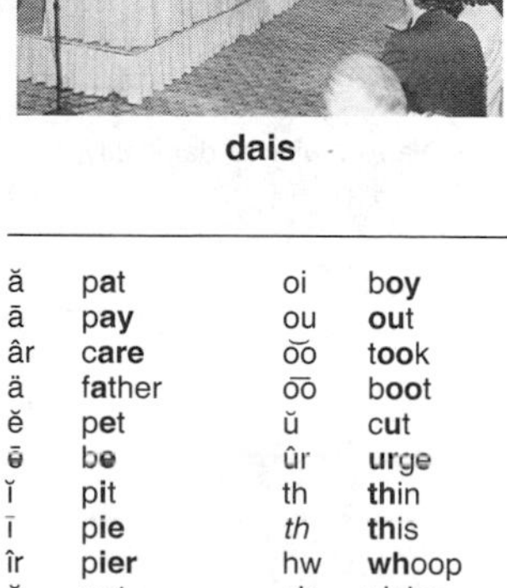

dais

ă	pat	oi	boy
ā	pay	ou	out
âr	care	o͝o	took
ä	father	o͞o	boot
ĕ	pet	ŭ	cut
ē	be	ûr	urge
ĭ	pit	th	thin
ī	pie	*th*	this
îr	pier	hw	whoop
ŏ	pot	zh	vision
ō	toe	ə	about
ô	paw	N	*French* bon

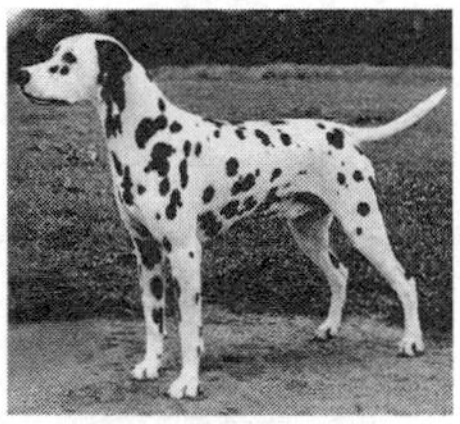
Dalmatian

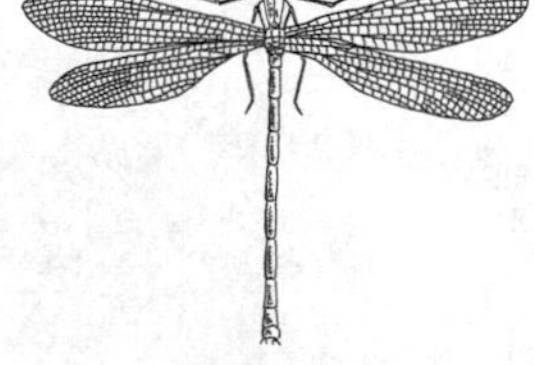
damselfly
Narrow-winged damselfly

whose flowers have a yellow center with white rays. [First written down about 1000 in Old English and spelled *dægesege* : *dæges*, of the day + *ēage*, eye.]

Da•kar (də **kär′** *or* **dăk′**är′). The capital and largest city of Senegal, in the western part of the country on the Atlantic Ocean. Population, 1,341,000.

Da•ko•ta (də **kō′**tə) *n., pl.* **Dakota** or **Da•ko•tas. 1.** A member of any of the Siouan peoples, especially of the Santee branch. **2.** The Siouan language of the Dakota. **—Da•ko′tan** *adj. & n.*

Da•ko•tas (də **kō′**təz). The states of North Dakota and South Dakota.

Da•lai La•ma (dä′lī **lä′**mə) *n.* The highest priest of Buddhism and the traditional ruler in Tibet and Mongolia. [First written down in 1698 in Modern English and spelled *Dalae-Lama*, from Tibetan : Mongolian *dalai*, ocean + Tibetan *bla-ma*, monk (so called because he is known as the ocean of compassion).]

dale (dāl) *n.* A valley.

Dal•las (**dăl′**əs). A city of northeast Texas north-northeast of Austin. It was founded in 1841. Population, 1,006,877.

dal•li•ance (**dăl′**ē əns) *n.* **1.** Playful flirting. **2.** Dawdling and wasting of time.

dal•ly (**dăl′**ē) *v.* **dal•lied, dal•ly•ing, dal•lies.** *—intr.* **1.** To flirt playfully; toy; trifle: *Don't dally with temptation.* **2.** To waste time; dawdle. *—tr.* To waste (time): *dally the morning away chatting.*

Dal•ma•tian (dăl **mā′**shən) *n.* A large dog having a short smooth white coat with many small black spots.

dam[1] (dăm) *n.* A barrier across a waterway to control the flow or raise the level of the water. *—tr.v.* **dammed, dam•ming, dams. 1.** To hold back by means of a dam: *Engineers dammed the river.* **2.** To hold back or restrain: *dam up emotions.* [First written down about 1340 in Middle English.]

❑ *These sound alike:* **dam**[1] (barrier), **dam**[2] (female animal), **damn** (condemn).

dam[2] (dăm) *n.* A female parent of a four-legged animal. [First written down before 1200 in Middle English, from Latin *domina*, lady.]

❑ *These sound alike:* **dam**[2] (female animal), **dam**[1] (barrier), **damn** (condemn).

dam•age (**dăm′**ĭj) *n.* **1.** Harm or injury that causes loss or makes a thing less valuable or useful: *damage done to a car in an accident.* **2. damages.** In law, money to be paid to make up for an injury or loss: *sue for damages.* *—tr.v.* **dam•aged, dam•ag•ing, dam•ag•es.** To harm, hurt, or injure: *Some insects damage plants.* See Synonyms at **hurt.** [First written down before 1300 in Middle English, from Latin *damnum*, financial loss.]

Da•mas•cus (də **măs′**kəs). The capital and largest city of Syria, in the southwest part of the country east-southeast of Beirut, Lebanon. It has been inhabited since prehistoric times. Population, 1,259,000.

Damascus steel *n.* An early form of steel having fine wavy markings, developed in the Near East and used mainly for making sword blades.

dam•ask (**dăm′**əsk) *n.* **1.** A rich glossy fabric woven with patterns that show on both sides, as a silk used for draperies or a linen used for tablecloths. **2.** Damascus steel.

dame (dām) *n.* **1.** Used formerly as a title for a woman in authority or a mistress of a household. **2.** A married woman; a matron. **3.** *Chiefly British.* **a.** A woman holding a nonhereditary title given by the queen or king to honor personal merit or service to the country. **b.** The wife or widow of a knight. **4.** *Slang.* A woman.

damn (dăm) *v.* **damned, damn•ing, damns.** *—tr.* **1.** To condemn (something) as being very bad: *Reviewers damned the new movie.* **2.a.** To condemn to failure or ruin: *Without money the project was damned.* **b.** To condemn to everlasting punishment in hell. **3.** To swear at or curse at. *—intr.* To swear; curse. *—interj.* An expression used to show anger, irritation, or disappointment. *—adj. & adv. Informal.* Very; damned: *a damn fool.* *—n. Informal.* The least bit; a jot: *not worth a damn.* [First written down about 1280 in Middle English and spelled *dampnen*, from Latin *damnāre*, to impose a fine on, pronounce guilty, from *damnum*, loss, fine.]

❑ *These sound alike:* **damn, dam**[1] (barrier), **dam**[2] (female animal).

dam•na•ble (**dăm′**nə bəl) *adj.* Deserving to be strongly condemned; hateful: *a damnable traitor.* **—dam′na•bly** *adv.*

dam•na•tion (dăm **nā′**shən) *n.* The act of damning or the condition of being damned to everlasting punishment in hell.

damned (dămd) *adj.* **damned•er** (**dăm′**dər), **damned•est** (**dăm′**dĭst). **1.** Condemned or doomed. **2.** *Informal.* Dreadful; awful: *this damned weather.* **3.** Used as an intensive: *a damned fool.* *—adv.* **damneder, damnedest.** *Informal.* Very; damn: *a damned good idea.*

Da•mon (**dā′**mən) *n.* A legendary Greek man who pledges his life as a guarantee that his condemned friend Pythias will return from arranging his affairs to face execution. Both Damon and Pythias are later pardoned.

damp (dămp) *adj.* **damp•er, damp•est.** Slightly wet; moist; humid: *a damp towel; damp air.* See Synonyms at **wet.** *—n.* **1.** Moisture in the air; humidity: *Don't go out in the damp.* **2.** A foul or poisonous gas that pollutes the air in a coal mine. **3.** A restraint or check; a discouragement. *—tr.v.* **damped, damp•ing, damps. 1.** To make damp; moisten. **2.** To extinguish (a fire, for example) by cutting off air. **3.** To discourage: *a cold mist that damped the hiker's spirits.* [First written down in 1316 in Middle English and spelled *damp*, poison gas, perhaps from Middle Dutch, vapor.] **—damp′ly** *adv.* **—damp′ness** *n.*

damp•en (**dăm′**pən) *v.* **damp•ened, damp•en•ing, damp•ens.** *—tr.* **1.** To moisten: *dampen a sponge.* **2.** To diminish or depress, as in strength or feeling: *The delay dampened their excitement.* *—intr.* To become damp. **—damp′en•er** *n.*

damp•er (**dăm′**pər) *n.* **1.** A movable plate in the flue of a furnace, stove, or fireplace for controlling the draft. **2.** A device for reducing or deadening vibrations, especially a pad that presses against the strings of a keyboard instrument. **3.** A depressing or restraining influence: *The rain put a damper on our vacation.*

dam•sel (**dăm′**zəl) *n.* A young woman or girl.

dam•sel•fly (**dăm′**zəl flī′) *n.* Any of various often brightly colored insects related to the dragonflies, having a slender body and wings that are folded together when at rest.

dam•son (**dăm′**zən *or* **dăm′**sən) *n.* **1.** A small, egg-shaped, dark-purple plum. **2.** A tree that bears such plums.

Dan (dăn). In the Bible, a son of Jacob and the ancestor of one of the tribes of Israel.

dance (dăns) *v.* **danced, danc•ing, danc•es.** *—intr.* **1.** To move with rhythmic steps and motions, especially in time to music. **2.** To leap, skip, or prance about: *excited children dancing about the room.* **3.** To bob up and down: *Moonlight danced on the water.* *—tr.* **1.** To engage in or perform (a dance): *dance a waltz.* **2.** To cause to dance: *He danced her across the room.* *—n.* **1.** A set of rhythmic steps and motions, usually performed to music. **2.** A party at which people dance: *Are you going to the dance?* **3.**

One round or turn of dancing: *May I have this dance?* **4.** The art of dancing: *study dance at a ballet school.* **5.** A piece of music composed as an accompaniment for dancing. [First written down before 1300 in Middle English and spelled *dauncen*, from Old French *danser*, perhaps of Germanic origin.] **—danc′er** *n.*

dan•de•li•on (dăn′dl ī′ən) *n.* A common weedy plant having bright yellow flowers and long notched leaves that are sometimes eaten in salads. After the flowers have bloomed, the ripe seeds form a fluffy rounded mass. [First written down in 1373 in Middle English and spelled *dent-de-lion*, from Old French *dentdelion*, from Medieval Latin *dēns leōnis*, lion's tooth (from its sharply indented leaves).]

dan•der[1] (dăn′dər) *n. Informal.* Temper or anger: *What got their dander up?* [First written down in 1832 in Modern English, perhaps alteration of *dunder*, fermented cane juice used in rum-making, fermentation.]

dan•der[2] (dăn′dər) *n.* Tiny particles from the coat or feathers of various animals, sometimes causing allergies in human beings. [First written down in 1591 in Modern English and spelled *dandro*, alteration of *dandruff*.]

dan•dle (dăn′dl) *tr.v.* **dan•dled, dan•dling, dan•dles.** To move (a small child) up and down on the knee or in the arms: *My grandparents dandled the baby on their knees.*

dan•druff (dăn′drəf) *n.* Small white scales of dead skin that are shed from the scalp.

dan•dy (dăn′dē) *n., pl.* **dan•dies. 1.** A man who prides himself on his elegant clothes and fine appearance; a fop. **2.** *Informal.* Something very good of its kind: *This horse is a dandy.* *—adj.* **dan•di•er, dan•di•est.** *Informal.* Very good; fine; first-rate: *That's a dandy idea!*

Dane (dān) *n.* A native or inhabitant of Denmark.

dan•ger (dān′jər) *n.* **1.** The chance or risk of harm or destruction: *a house in danger of being swept into the sea.* **2.** A possible cause or chance of harm; a threat or hazard: *Fog is a danger to pilots.* [First written down before 1250 in Middle English and spelled *daunger*, power, dominion, peril, from Latin *dominium*, dominion, from *dominus*, master.]

dan•ger•ous (dān′jər əs) *adj.* **1.** Involving danger; hazardous: *a dangerous job.* **2.** Able or likely to cause harm: *The crocodile is a dangerous animal.* **—dan′ger•ous•ly** *adv.* **—dan′ger•ous•ness** *n.*

dan•gle (dăng′gəl) *v.* **dan•gled, dan•gling, dan•gles.** *—intr.* To hang loosely and swing or sway: *A key dangled from the chain.* *—tr.* To cause to swing loosely: *The children sat dangling their feet in the water.* **—dan′gler** *n.*

dan•gling participle (dăng′glĭng) *n.* A participle that is not clearly connected with the subject of the sentence that it seems to modify. For example, in the sentence *Sitting at my desk, a loud noise startled me,* the word *sitting* is a dangling participle.

Dan•iel (dăn′yəl) *n.* **1.** A Hebrew prophet of the sixth century B.C. **2.** A book of the Bible, traditionally believed to have been written by Daniel, which tells of Daniel's adventures and prophetic dreams.

Dan•ish (dā′nĭsh) *n.* **1.** The Germanic language of the Danes. **2.** A Danish pastry. *—adj.* Of or relating to Denmark, the Danes, their language, or their culture.

Danish pastry *n.* A sweet buttery pastry made with raised dough.

dank (dăngk) *adj.* **dank•er, dank•est.** Uncomfortably damp; chilly and wet: *a dank and musty cellar.* **—dank′ly** *adv.* **—dank′ness** *n.*

Dan•te A•li•ghie•ri (dän′tā ä′lē gyĕ′rē). 1265–1321. Italian poet known for *The Divine Comedy* (completed 1321).

Dan•ube (dăn′yo͞ob). A river of south-central Europe rising in southwest Germany and flowing about 1,770 miles (2,848 kilometers) southeast to the Black Sea.

Dan•zig (dăn′sĭg). Gdańsk.

Daph•ne (dăf′nē) *n.* In Greek mythology, a nymph who turns into a laurel tree in order to escape from Apollo.

dap•per (dăp′ər) *adj.* **1.** Neatly dressed; trim; spruce: *dapper soldiers on parade.* **2.** Brisk and jaunty: *The horses trotted at a dapper pace.*

dap•ple (dăp′əl) *tr.v.* **dap•pled, dap•pling, dap•ples.** To mark with spots, streaks, or patches of a different color or shade: *Sunlight filtering through the leaves dappled the ground.* *—adj.* Dappled: *dapple horses.*

dap•pled (dăp′əld) *adj.* Marked with spots, streaks, or patches of a different color or shade: *a dappled fawn.*

Dar•da•nelles (där′dn ĕlz′). Formerly **Hel•les•pont** (hĕl′ĭ spŏnt′). A strait connecting the Aegean Sea with the Sea of Marmara.

dare (dâr) *v.* **dared, dar•ing, dares.** *—tr.* **1.** To have the courage necessary for; be bold enough to try: *She dared her most difficult dive. I didn't dare go into the cave.* **2.** To challenge (someone) to do something requiring courage: *They dared me to dive off the high board.* **3.** To confront or oppose boldly; defy: *The rescuers dared the freezing waters in their search.* *—intr.* To be courageous enough to do something. *—n.* A challenge: *I took their dare and swam across the pond.* [First written down about 725 in Old English and spelled *dearr*, from *durran*, to venture, dare.]

Dare (dâr), **Virginia.** 1587–1587? The first child of English parents born in America, who disappeared with the Lost Colony of Roanoke Island off the coast of North Carolina.

dare•dev•il (dâr′dĕv′əl) *n.* A person who takes risks with reckless boldness. *—adj.* Recklessly bold; fearless: *daredevil acrobatic feats.*

dare•say (dâr′sā′) *intr. & tr.v.* To think very likely or almost certain; suppose: *I daresay you're right.*

Dar es Sa•laam (där′ ĕs sə läm′). The unofficial capital and largest city of Tanzania, in the eastern part of the country on an arm of the Indian Ocean. Population, 757,346.

dar•ing (dâr′ĭng) *adj.* Willing to take risks; bold: *a daring test pilot.* *—n.* Fearless bravery; boldness; courage: *Climbing the mountain requires great daring.* **—dar′ing•ly** *adv.*

Da•ri•us I (də rī′əs). 550?–486 B.C. King of Persia (521–486) who expanded the empire and invaded Greece, and was defeated at the Battle of Marathon in 490.

dark (därk) *adj.* **dark•er, dark•est. 1.** Lacking light or having very little light: *a dark tunnel.* **2.** Of a shade closer to black than to white: *dark gray.* **3.** Gloomy; dismal: *a dark view of the future.* **4.** Evil; sinister: *a story full of dark deeds.* **5.** Secret; mysterious: *Keep our plans dark.* **6.** Lacking knowledge or learning; ignorant: *a dark age in the history of medicine.* *—n.* **1.** Absence of light; darkness: *groping around in the dark.* **2.** Night or nightfall: *Come home before dark.* **3.** A dark shade or color: *the darks and lights in a photograph.* ***—idiom.*** **in the dark. 1.** In secret: *The coach kept his game plan in the dark until yesterday.* **2.** In a state of ignorance; uninformed: *We were kept totally in the dark about the surprise.* [First written down about 725 in Old

Dante

Darius I

Fifth-century B.C. relief from Persepolis of a figure widely recognized as Darius

ă	**pat**	oi	**boy**
ā	**pay**	ou	**out**
âr	**care**	o͝o	**took**
ä	**father**	o͞o	**boot**
ĕ	**pet**	ŭ	**cut**
ē	**be**	ûr	**urge**
ĭ	**pit**	th	**thin**
ī	**pie**	*th*	**this**
îr	**pier**	hw	**wh**oop
ŏ	**pot**	zh	vi**s**ion
ō	**toe**	ə	**a**bout
ô	**paw**	N	*French* bo**n**

Charles Darwin
Portrait by John Collier
(1850–1934)

English and spelled *deorc.*] —**dark′ly** *adv.* —**dark′ness** *n.*

Synonyms: dark, dim, murky, dusky, obscure, shady, shadowy. These adjectives describe the absence of light. **Dark** means not lighted enough to see well: *The room was so dark I thought there had been a blackout.* **Dim** means so dark that the outlines of things cannot be seen clearly: *I stumbled down the dim hallway.* **Murky** means dark as in a smoky or foggy way: *The lighthouse beacon cut through the murky air.* **Dusky** describes decreasing light, as at twilight: *Will hurried down the dusky streets, trying to get home by dinnertime.* **Shady** describes something sheltered from light, especially sunlight: *We found a shady spot in the park for our picnic.* **Shadowy** often describes blocked light or shifting, mysterious shadows: *Sandra shone her flashlight into the shadowy well.* **Antonym: light.**

Dark Ages *pl.n.* The early part of the Middle Ages from about A.D. 476 to about the year 1000, thought of as a time when learning was neglected in Europe.

dark•en (**där′**kən) *tr. & intr.v.* **dark•ened, dark•en•ing, dark•ens. 1.** To make or become dark or darker: *Clouds darkened the sky. Twilight darkens into night.* **2.** To make or grow gloomy, sad, or somber: *News of the defeat darkened their faces.* —**dark′en•er** *n.*

dark horse *n.* **1.** A little-known entrant, as in a horse race. **2.** A person who receives unexpected support and success as a political candidate, especially during a convention.

dar•kling (**där′**klĭng) *adv.* In the dark. —*adj.* Dim; obscure; in the dark: *a darkling sky.*

dark•room (**därk′**ro͞om′ *or* **därk′**ro͝om′) *n.* A room in which photographs are developed, either in total darkness or in colored light to which they are not sensitive.

dar•ling (**där′**lĭng) *n.* **1.** A dearly loved person. **2.** A favorite: *That star was a darling of the theater for years.* —*adj.* **1.** Dearest; beloved: *my darling child.* **2.** *Informal.* Charming; adorable: *The little kittens are darling.* [First written down before 899 in Old English and spelled *dēorling*, from *dēore*, dear.]

Dar•ling River (**där′**lĭng). A river rising in southeast Australia and flowing about 1,702 miles (2,739 kilometers) generally southwest. It is the longest river in Australia.

darn[1] (därn) *v.* **darned, darn•ing, darns.** —*tr.* To mend (cloth) by weaving new thread across a hole: *darn socks.* —*intr.* To repair a hole, as in a garment, by weaving thread across it. —*n.* A place repaired by darning. [First written down about 1600 in Modern English, perhaps from Norman French *darne*, piece, from Breton *darn.*] —**darn′er** *n.*

darn[2] (därn) *interj.* An expression used to show displeasure or annoyance. —*adv. & adj.* Damn. —*tr. & intr.v.* **darned, darn•ing, darns.** To damn. [First written down in 1781 in Modern English, alteration of *damn.*]

darn•ing needle (**där′**nĭng) *n.* **1.** A long needle with a large eye, used in darning. **2.** A dragonfly. —See Note at **dragonfly.**

dart (därt) *v.* **dart•ed, dart•ing, darts.** —*intr.* To move suddenly and swiftly: *A squirrel darted across the path.* —*tr.* To shoot out or send forth with a swift sudden movement: *The bear darted a paw at the fish. They darted frightened glances behind them.* —*n.* **1.** A thin object with a sharp point, thrown at a target by hand or shot from a blowgun, crossbow, or other device. **2. darts.** *(used with a singular or plural verb).* A game in which darts are thrown at a board or other target. **3.** A quick rapid movement: *The cat made a sudden dart at the mouse.* **4.** A tapered tuck sewn to adjust the fit of a garment. [First written down about 1385 in Middle English and spelled *darten*, from *dart*, a dart, from Old French, of Germanic origin.]

date palm

Dar•win (**där′**wĭn), **Charles Robert.** 1809–1882. British naturalist who revolutionized the study of biology with his theory of evolution.

dash (dăsh) *v.* **dashed, dash•ing, dash•es.** —*intr.* **1.** To race or rush with sudden speed: *The children dashed down the stairs.* **2.** To strike, knock, or hurl with violent force: *Heavy rain dashed against the car windshield.* —*tr.* **1.** To hurl, knock, or thrust with sudden force: *The storm dashed the ship against the rocks.* **2.** To break or smash by striking violently: *dashed the bottle on the floor.* **3.** To splash: *A car passing through a puddle dashed water all over my clothes.* **4.** To destroy; wreck: *Illness dashed their hopes for a vacation.* **5.** To perform or complete hastily: *I dashed off a letter before leaving.* —*n.* **1.** A sudden movement; a rush: *a dash for shelter from a cloudburst.* **2.** A short footrace: *the 100-yard dash.* **3.** A small amount; a bit: *a dash of salt.* **4.** Lively spirit or style: *entertainers full of dash.* **5.** A swift forceful stroke: *the dash of oars against the water.* **6.** A punctuation mark (—) used to show a pause, break, or omission or to set off part of a sentence from the rest. **7.** A long sound or signal used in Morse code in combination with the dot and silent intervals to represent letters, numbers, or punctuation. **8.** A dashboard.

dash•board (**dăsh′**bôrd′) *n.* The panel beneath the windshield in an automobile, containing instruments, dials, and controls.

dash•ing (**dăsh′**ĭng) *adj.* **1.** Brave, bold, and daring: *a dashing hero.* **2.** Showy or stylish: *The band wore dashing uniforms.*

das•tard (**dăs′**tərd) *n.* A base sneaking coward.

das•tard•ly (**dăs′**tərd lē) *adj.* Cowardly, low, and mean: *dastardly deeds.* —**das′tard•li•ness** *n.*

da•ta (**dā′**tə *or* **dăt′**ə) *pl.n.* *(used with a singular or plural verb).* **1.** Information, especially when it is to be analyzed or used as the basis for a decision. **2.** Information, usually in numerical form, suitable for processing by computer. **3.** Plural of **datum** (sense 1). [First written down in 1646 in Modern English, from Latin, plural of *datum*, something given.]

da•ta•base also **data base** (**dā′**tə bās′ *or* **dăt′**ə bās′) *n.* A collection of data arranged for easy and speedy retrieval.

data processing *n.* Sorting, analysis, and other operations performed on data by computers.

date[1] (dāt) *n.* **1.a.** Time stated in terms of the day, month, and year: *What is the date of your birthday?* **b.** A statement of calendar time: *There is no date stamped on this coin.* **2.** A specified day of the month: *What is today's date?* **3.** A point or period of time in history: *At that date radio was unknown.* **4.** An agreement to meet someone or be somewhere at a particular time, especially as a social engagement: *We made a date to have lunch on Thursday.* **5.** A person with whom one has a social engagement. —*v.* **dat•ed, dat•ing, dates.** —*tr.* **1.** To mark with a date: *He dated the letter May 1.* **2.** To determine the age, time, or origin of: *They dated the rock by studying the fossils in it.* **3.** *Informal.* To go on dates with: *She's been dating him for two months.* —*intr.* **1.** To come from a particular time in the past: *This statue dates from about 500 B.C.* **2.** To go on dates: *They dated a lot during vacation.* —***idiom.* to date.** Up to the present time: *a new theory based on our observations to date.* [First written down about 1330 in Middle English, from Latin *data (Romae)*, issued (at Rome) (on a certain day).]

date[2] (dāt) *n.* **1.** The sweet, one-seeded, oval or oblong fruit of the date palm. **2.** The date palm. [First

written down about 1300 in Middle English, from Latin *dactylus*, from Greek *daktulos*, finger, date (from its shape).]
dat•ed (dā′tĭd) *adj.* **1.** Marked with a date: *a dated receipt.* **2.** Old fashioned: *a dated style.*
date•less (dāt′lĭs) *adj.* **1.** Having no date; lacking a date. **2.** Having no limits in time; endless.
date•line (dāt′līn′) *n.* A phrase at the beginning of a news story or report that gives its date and place of origin.
date line *n.* The International Date Line.
date palm *n.* A very tall tropical palm having a crown of feathery leaves and bearing clusters of dates.
da•tive (dā′tĭv) *adj.* Of or relating to the grammatical case that indicates the recipient of the action of a verb or the object of a preposition, and often corresponds to the words *to* and *for*. The dative case is used in Latin, Russian, and some other languages. —*n.* **1.** The dative case. **2.** A word or form in the dative case.
da•tum (dā′təm *or* dăt′əm) *n.* **1.** *pl.* **da•ta.** A fact used to draw a conclusion or make a decision. **2.** *pl.* **datums.** A point, line, or surface used as a reference, as in mapping or geology.
daub (dôb) *v.* **daubed, daub•ing, daubs.** —*tr.* **1.** To cover or smear with a soft sticky substance such as clay, plaster, or mud: *daub the cracks in the wall with mortar.* **2.** To spread or smear (a soft sticky substance): *daub mortar in the cracks.* **3.** To paint (something) with crude or careless strokes. —*intr.* To paint in a crude or amateurish fashion. —*n.* **1.** Something daubed on: *A daub of glue will mend the cup.* **2.** A spot or smear, as of paint. **3.** An amateurish painting.
daugh•ter (dô′tər) *n.* **1.** A person's female child. **2.** A female descendant. **3.** A woman considered as if in a relationship of child to parent: *She is a daughter of the Impressionist movement.* [First written down about 725 in Old English and spelled *dohtor*.]
daughter cell *n.* Either of two cells formed when a cell undergoes cell division.
daugh•ter-in-law (dô′tər ĭn lô′) *n., pl.* **daugh•ters-in-law** (dô′tərz ĭn lô′). The wife of one's son.
daunt (dônt *or* dänt) *tr.v.* **daunt•ed, daunt•ing, daunts.** To frighten, discourage, or dishearten: *The chance of failure did not daunt the inventor.*
daunt•less (dônt′lĭs *or* dänt′lĭs) *adj.* Not easily frightened or discouraged; fearless: *a dauntless explorer.* **—daunt′less•ly** *adv.* **—daunt′less•ness** *n.*
dau•phin (dô′fĭn) *n.* The eldest son of a king of France from 1349 to 1830.
dav•en•port (dăv′ən pôrt′) *n.* A large sofa, often convertible into a bed. [First written down in 1853 in Modern English and spelled *davenport*, a small writing desk, probably from the name of the manufacturer.]
Da•vid (dā′vĭd). Died about 962 B.C. The second king of Judah and Israel who is traditionally considered the author of many of the Psalms.
Da•vis (dā′vĭs), **Jefferson.** 1808–1889. American soldier and president of the Confederacy (1861–1865).
dav•it (dăv′ĭt *or* dā′vĭt) *n.* A small crane that projects over the side of a ship, used for lowering and hoisting boats and cargo.
Da•vy Jones (dā′vē jōnz′) *n.* The bottom of the sea, as personified in songs and stories.
Davy Jones's locker (jōn′zĭz *or* jōnz) *n.* The bottom of the sea, regarded as the grave of persons drowned or buried at sea.
daw (dô) *n.* A jackdaw.
daw•dle (dôd′l) *v.* **daw•dled, daw•dling, daw•dles.** —*intr.* To take more time than necessary: *If you dawdle over your work, it will take you all night to finish.* —*tr.* To waste (time): *dawdle away the morning.* **—daw′dler** *n.*
dawn (dôn) *n.* **1.** The time of the first appearance of daylight in the morning: *get up at dawn.* **2.** A first appearance of something; a beginning: *the dawn of recorded history.* —*intr.v.* **dawned, dawn•ing, dawns.** **1.** To begin to grow light in the morning: *We rose when the day dawned.* **2.** To come into existence; begin; start: *a new age dawned with the first flights into space.* **3.** To begin to be seen or understood; come as a realization: *As they stood there, it dawned on me they were waiting for an answer.* [First written down in 1599 in Modern English, from Middle English *daunen*, to dawn, from Old English *dagung*, daybreak, from *dagian*, to dawn.]
day (dā) *n.* **1.** The period of light between sunrise and sunset: *a clear sunny day.* **2.** The 24-hour period during which the earth makes one complete rotation on its axis: *It rained for three days without stopping.* **3.** The part of the day devoted to work or study: *work a seven-hour day; the school day.* **4.** A period filled with certain activity: *a day of rest.* **5.** A particular period of time: *before the days of automobiles.* **—*idioms.*** **day after day.** For many days in succession: *Day after day they marched across the desert.* **day in, day out.** Every day without a break: *Feeding a pet must be done day in, day out.* [First written down about 725 in Old English and spelled *dæg*.]
Day (dā), **Dorothy.** 1897–1980. American journalist and reformer who worked to promote peace and social justice.
day•break (dā′brāk′) *n.* The time each morning when light first appears; dawn: *Farmers often get up before daybreak.*
day•care or **day care** (dā′kâr′) *n.* Daytime care for children of preschool age or for the elderly or the disabled.
day•dream (dā′drēm′) *n.* The act of thinking in a dreamy way, often about things one wishes would come true. —*intr.v.* **day•dreamed** or **day•dreamt** (dā′drĕmt′), **day•dream•ing, day•dreams.** To have daydreams: *daydreaming of faraway places.* **—day′dream′er** *n.*
day•light (dā′līt′) *n.* **1.** The light of day; sunlight. **2.** Dawn: *at work before daylight.* **3.** Daytime. **4.** Knowledge or understanding of something that was formerly unknown: *They began to see daylight concerning the cause of the epidemic.*
day•light-sav•ing time (dā′līt sā′vĭng) *n.* Time during which clocks are set one hour ahead of standard time to provide extra daylight at the end of the working day during spring, summer, and fall.
Day of Atonement *n.* Yom Kippur.
day school *n.* **1.** A private school for pupils living at home. **2.** A school that holds classes during the day.
day•star (dā′stär′) *n.* **1.** The morning star. **2.** The sun.
day•time (dā′tīm′) *n.* The time between sunrise and sunset. —*adj.* Occurring in or appropriate to the daytime: *daytime activities; daytime TV.*
day-to-day (dā′tə dā′) *adj.* **1.** Happening every day; daily: *day-to-day routine.* **2.** Surviving one day at a time with little regard for the future: *The lost mountain climbers were existing on a day-to-day basis.*
Day•ton (dāt′n). A city of southwest Ohio north-northeast of Cincinnati. It was the home of Orville and Wilbur Wright. Population, 182,044.
daze (dāz) *tr.v.* **dazed, daz•ing, daz•es.** To stun or confuse, as with a blow, shock, or surprise: *The explosion dazed and deafened them.* —*n.* A stunned or confused condition: *The news left us all in a*

davit
Hoisting cargo

Dorothy Day

ă	pat	oi	boy
ā	pay	ou	out
âr	care	o͝o	took
ä	father	o͞o	boot
ĕ	pet	ŭ	cut
ē	be	ûr	urge
ĭ	pit	th	thin
ī	pie	*th*	this
îr	pier	hw	whoop
ŏ	pot	zh	vision
ō	toe	ə	about
ô	paw	N	*French* bon

Word Building: de–

The prefix **de–** can be traced back through Middle English and Old French to Latin *dē–*, meaning "from, off, apart, away, down, out." In English **de–** usually indicates reversal, removal, or reduction. Thus **deactivate** means "to make inactive," **decontaminate** means "to remove the contamination in," and **decompress** means "to remove or reduce pressure." **De–** is a prefix that occurs very frequently in English.

Usage: deaf

Some writers have lately introduced a distinction between the lowercase noun **deaf**, which is used to refer to people with extensive hearing disorders, and the capitalized noun **Deaf**, which refers to the culture and community that has grown up around the use of American Sign Language as a primary means of communication.

daze. [First written down about 1380 in Middle English and spelled *dasen*, of Scandinavian origin.] **—daz′ed•ly** (dā′zĭd lē) *adv.*

daz•zle (dăz′əl) *tr.v.* **daz•zled, daz•zling, daz•zles. 1.** To make nearly or momentarily blind with too much bright light: *The ranger's searchlight dazzled the eyes of the campers.* **2.** To amaze, impress, or astonish with a spectacular display: *The pianist dazzled us with his superb technique.* *—n.* Blinding brightness; glare: *the dazzle of sunlight on the water.* [First written down in 1481 in Middle English and spelled *dasel*, from *dasen*, to daze.] **—daz′zling•ly** *adv.*

dB *abbr.* An abbreviation of decibel.

dc or **DC** *abbr.* An abbreviation of direct current.

DC or **D.C.** *n.* An abbreviation of District of Columbia.

D.D. *abbr.* An abbreviation of Doctor of Divinity.

D.D.S. *abbr.* An abbreviation of Doctor of Dental Surgery.

DDT (dē′dē tē′) *n.* A powerful insecticide that is also poisonous to human beings and animals. It remains active in the environment for many years and has been banned in the United States for most uses since 1972.

DE *abbr.* An abbreviation of Delaware.

de– *pref.* A prefix that means: **1.** Reverse: *decode.* **2.** Remove: *defrost.* **3.** Reduce: *demote.* **4.** Out of: *deplane.* —SEE NOTE.

dea•con (dē′kən) *n.* **1.** A Protestant layperson who assists the minister by performing certain duties. **2.** In certain churches, a cleric ranking below a priest. [First written down before 899 in Old English and spelled *dīacon*, from Greek *diakonos*, attendant.]

dea•con•ess (dē′kə nĭs) *n.* A protestant laywoman who assists the minister by performing certain duties.

de•ac•ti•vate (dē ăk′tə vāt′) *tr.v.* **1.** To make inactive or ineffective: *deactivate a bomb.* **2.** To remove from active military duty: *deactivate soldiers in time of peace.*

dead (dĕd) *adj.* **dead•er, dead•est. 1.** No longer alive or living: *A dead tree cannot grow new leaves.* **2.** Having the appearance of death: *a dead color.* **3.** Having no life or living things; lifeless: *the dead cold moon.* **4.** Lacking feeling; numb: *My cold toes felt dead.* **5.** Not moving or circulating; motionless: *the dead air in a closed room.* **6.a.** No longer in existence, operation, or use: *a dead language.* **b.** No longer active: *a dead volcano.* **c.** Unexciting: *a dead party.* **7.** Out of operation; broken down: *The pump is dead.* **8.** Lacking electric power or charge: *a dead circuit; a dead battery.* **9.** Weary and worn-out; exhausted: *After finishing work I was dead on my feet.* **10.** Complete; absolute: *dead silence.* **11.** Sure; certain: *a dead shot who always hits the mark.* **12.** Sudden; abrupt: *a dead stop.* **13.** In sports, out of play: *When it crosses the sideline, the ball is dead.* *—n.* **1.** Those who have died; dead people: *The soldiers buried the dead.* **2.** The darkest, quietest, or coldest part: *the dead of night; the dead of winter.* *—adv.* **1.** Completely; absolutely: *You can be dead sure of that.* **2.** Straight; directly: *A huge boulder lay dead ahead.* **3.** Suddenly: *We stopped dead in our tracks.* [First written down about 725 in Old English and spelled *dēad*.]

dead•beat (dĕd′bēt′) *n. Slang.* **1.** A person who avoids paying debts. **2.** A lazy person; a loafer.

dead•en (dĕd′n) *tr.v.* **dead•ened, dead•en•ing, dead•ens. 1.** To make less sensitive, intense, or strong: *Anesthetics deaden pain.* **2.** To make soundproof: *Rugs helped deaden the room.*

dead end *n.* **1.** A street, alley, or other passage that is closed or blocked off at one end. **2.** A point beyond which no movement or progress can be made: *We reached a dead end in our argument.*

dead heat *n.* A race in which two or more contestants finish at the same time; a tie.

dead letter *n.* A letter that is not delivered or claimed, usually because the address is wrong or impossible to read.

dead•line (dĕd′līn′) *n.* A set time by which something must be done, finished, or settled; a time limit: *No one could enter the contest after the deadline.*

dead•lock (dĕd′lŏk′) *n.* A standstill that occurs when opposing forces are equally strong and neither will give way. *—tr. & intr.v.* **dead•locked, dead•lock•ing, dead•locks.** To bring or come to a deadlock: *The peace talks deadlocked over treaty terms.*

dead•ly (dĕd′lē) *adj.* **dead•li•er, dead•li•est. 1.** Causing or capable of causing death: *a deadly weapon.* **2.** Intending to kill or destroy; mortal: *deadly enemies.* **3.** Suggesting death: *a face with an ashen, deadly look.* **4.** Absolute; extreme; utter: *deadly earnestness.* **5.** Very accurate or effective: *The hunter is a deadly shot.* **6.** Very dull and boring: *a deadly play.* **7.** Causing or capable of causing spiritual death: *Envy is a deadly sin.* *—adv.* **1.** Extremely; utterly: *I'm deadly serious.* **2.** So as to suggest death: *turned deadly pale at the scream.* **—dead′li•ness** *n.*

deadly nightshade *n.* Belladonna.

dead•pan (dĕd′păn′) *adj.* Characterized by or showing no emotion or amusement: *a deadpan expression.* [First written down in 1928 in American English : *dead* + *pan*, face.]

dead reckoning *n.* A method of estimating the position of a ship or aircraft without astronomical observations, as by determination from its speed, time traveled, and winds and currents encountered.

Dead Sea (dĕd). A salt lake, about 1,300 feet (397 meters) below sea level, between Israel and Jordan. It is the lowest point on the earth.

Dead Sea Scrolls *pl.n.* A number of ancient parchment scrolls containing the earliest known version of several books of the Bible, found in caves near the Dead Sea.

dead•wood (dĕd′wo͝od′) *n.* **1.** Dead branches or wood on a tree. **2.** A person or thing that is burdensome or useless.

deaf (dĕf) *adj.* **deaf•er, deaf•est. 1.** Partially or completely lacking the ability to hear: *Many deaf people learn to use sign language.* **2. Deaf.** Of or relating to the Deaf or their culture. **3.** Unwilling to listen: *The principal was deaf to our complaints.* *—n. (used with a plural verb).* **1.** Deaf people considered as a group. **2. Deaf.** The community of deaf people who use American Sign Language as their main means of communication. [First written down about 750 in Old English and spelled *dēaf*.] **—deaf′ly** *adv.* **—deaf′ness** *n.* —SEE NOTE.

deaf•en (dĕf′ən) *tr.v.* **deaf•ened, deaf•en•ing, deaf•ens.** To make deaf: *The siren deafened us temporarily.*

deaf-mute also **deaf mute** (dĕf′myo͞ot′) *Offensive. n.* A person who can neither hear nor speak.

deal (dēl) *v.* **dealt** (dĕlt), **deal•ing, deals.** *—intr.* **1.** To be concerned or involved: *This book deals with the architecture of Los Angeles.* **2.** To behave toward another or others: *The counselor dealt fairly with the campers.* **3.** To take action regarding something: *deal with an emergency.* **4.** To do business; trade: *a merchant who deals in diamonds.* **5.** To distribute playing cards: *It's your turn to deal.* *—tr.* **1.** To give out as a share: *We dealt out crayons to the children.* See Synonyms at **distribute. 2.** To give or deliver: *The champion dealt the opponent a* *mighty blow.* **3.** To hand out (cards) to players in a card game: *Deal the cards.* —*n.* **1.** *Informal.* **a.** An agreement, as in business or politics: *We made a deal with our neighbors to buy their car.* **b.** A favorable sale; a bargain: *I got a real deal on a TV at sale prices.* **2.** A corrupt or secret arrangement: *The inspector made a deal with the builder to ignore inferior materials.* **3.** *Informal.* Treatment received: *a fair deal from the judge.* **4.a.** The distribution of playing cards. **b.** A player's turn to deal: *It's your deal.* **c.** A hand of cards dealt: *lose because of a bad deal.* ***—idiom.*** **a good deal** or **a great deal. 1.** A considerable amount; a lot: *We learned a great deal.* **2.** Much; considerably: *a good deal thinner.* [First written down about 725 in Old English and spelled *dǣlan*, to divide, share.]

deal•er (dē′lər) *n.* **1.** A person engaged in buying and selling: *a furniture dealer.* **2.** A person who distributes the playing cards in a game of cards.

deal•ing (dē′lĭng) *n.* **1. dealings.** Agreements or relations with others, especially when involving money or trade: *business dealings.* **2.** A way of acting or doing business; conduct toward others: *That store is known for its fair dealing.*

dealt (dĕlt) *v.* Past tense and past participle of **deal.**

dean (dēn) *n.* **1.** An official of a college or university in charge of a certain school or faculty: *dean of the medical school.* **2.** An official of a college or high school who counsels students and enforces rules. **3.** The head clergyman in charge of a cathedral. **4.** The oldest or most respected member of a group or profession: *the dean of American tennis.* [First written down about 1330 in Middle English and spelled *den*, from Late Latin *decānus*, chief of ten, from Greek *deka*, ten.]

dear (dîr) *adj.* **dear•er, dear•est. 1.** Loved and cherished: *my dear friend.* **2.** Greatly valued; precious: *Her dearest possessions are in the cabinet.* **3.** Highly esteemed or regarded, as in speaking to or writing letters: *my dear fellow.* **4.** High in price; expensive. —*adv.* **1.** At a high cost: *You will pay dear for that mistake.* **2.** Fondly or affectionately: *memories of old friends held dear to one's heart.* —*n.* A dearly loved person or animal: *the poor dear.* —*interj.* An expression used to show distress or surprise: *Oh dear!* [First written down about 725 in Old English and spelled *dēore.*] **—dear′ly** *adv.* **—dear′ness** *n.*
❑ *These sound alike:* **dear, deer** (animal).

dearth (dûrth) *n.* A lack or scarcity: *a dearth of knowledge about the ocean floor.*

death (dĕth) *n.* **1.** The act of dying; the end of life: *remained busy and active until death.* **2.** The condition of being dead. **3.** A cause of dying: *Such a fall is certain death.* **4.** The ending, destruction, or extinction of something: *the death of Communism.* ***—idioms.*** **put to death.** To kill; execute. **to death.** To an unbearable degree; extremely: *We were bored to death by the slide show.* [First written down about 725 in Old English and spelled *dēath.*]

death•bed (dĕth′bĕd′) *n.* **1.** The bed on which a person dies. **2.** A person's last hours of life.

death•blow (dĕth′blō′) *n.* **1.** A fatal blow. **2.** A destructive event: *The scandal was the deathblow for the previous government.*

death•less (dĕth′lĭs) *adj.* Enduring forever; undying; immortal: *His fame is deathless.* **—death′less•ness** *n.*

death•ly (dĕth′lē) *adj.* Of, resembling, or characteristic of death: *a deathly pallor.* —*adv.* **1.** So as to resemble death: *She was deathly pale.* **2.** Very; extremely: *deathly ill.*

death rate *n.* The ratio of total deaths to total population in a given community over a specified period of time.

death's-head (dĕths′hĕd′) *n.* The human skull as a symbol of death.

Death Valley (dĕth). An arid desert basin of eastern California and western Nevada. It includes the lowest point, 282 feet (86 meters) below sea level, in the Western Hemisphere.

de•ba•cle (dĭ bä′kəl *or* dĭ băk′əl) *n.* A sudden disastrous collapse, downfall, or defeat; a rout: *The party in power suffered a complete debacle in the election.*

de•bar (dē bär′) *tr.v.* **de•barred, de•bar•ring, de•bars.** To forbid, prohibit, exclude, or bar: *A person not born a U.S. citizen is debarred from running for the Presidency.*

de•bark (dĭ bärk′) *v.* **de•barked, de•bark•ing, de•barks.** —*tr.* To unload, as from a ship: *debark passengers.* —*intr.* To get off a ship; land: *American tourists debarked at the port.* **—de′bar•ka′tion** (dē′bär kā′shən) *n.*

de•base (dĭ bās′) *tr.v.* **de•based, de•bas•ing, de•bas•es.** To lower in character, quality, or worth: *Don't debase yourself by feeling envious.* **—de•base′ment** *n.*

de•bat•a•ble (dĭ bā′tə bəl) *adj.* Open to question, argument, or dispute: *an unproven and debatable theory.*

de•bate (dĭ bāt′) *v.* **de•bat•ed, de•bat•ing, de•bates.** —*intr.* **1.** To consider something; try to decide about something: *We debated about which trail to take.* **2.** To present or discuss arguments for and against something: *We debated about the fairness of the school's dress code.* —*tr.* **1.** To consider; try to decide: *I debated what to do next.* **2.** To discuss or argue about (something): *We debated whether the play was truly a tragedy.* —*n.* **1.** A discussion or consideration of the arguments for and against something: *the debate about reforming the health care system.* **2.** A formal contest in which opponents argue for opposite sides of an issue: *Two local schools held a debate on whether to register bicycles.* [First written down before 1380 in Middle English and spelled *debaten*, from *debat*, debate, from Old French *debatre*, to beat down, fight.] **—de•bat′er** *n.*

de•bauch (dĭ bôch′) *v.* **de•bauched, de•bauch•ing, de•bauch•es.** —*tr.* To lead away from good toward evil; corrupt morally. —*intr.* To indulge in too much eating, drinking, and other sensual pleasures. —*n.* An act or a period of debauchery.

de•bauch•er•y (dĭ bô′chə rē) *n., pl.* **de•bauch•er•ies.** Too much indulgence in eating, drinking, and other sensual pleasures.

de•bil•i•tate (dĭ bĭl′ĭ tāt′) *tr.v.* **de•bil•i•tat•ed, de•bil•i•tat•ing, de•bil•i•tates.** To make feeble; weaken: *A long illness usually debilitates the body.* [First written down in 1533 in Modern English, from Latin *dēbilis*, weak.] **—de•bil′i•ta′tion** *n.*

de•bil•i•ty (dĭ bĭl′ĭ tē) *n., pl.* **de•bil•i•ties.** The condition of abnormal bodily weakness; feebleness.

deb•it (dĕb′ĭt) *n.* **1.** A debt charged to and recorded in an account. **2.** The side of an account book showing such debt. **3.** The sum of such debt. —*tr.v.* **deb•it•ed, deb•it•ing, deb•its.** To charge with or as a debt: *The bank debited my account for the checks I wrote.*

deb•o•nair also **deb•o•naire** (dĕb′ə nâr′) *adj.* Gracious and charming in a cheerful carefree way: *The tall debonair professor won everybody's heart.* **—deb′o•nair′ly** *adv.* **—deb′o•nair′ness** *n.* —See Note.

de•brief (dē brēf′) *tr.v.* **de•briefed, de•brief•ing, de•briefs.** To question in order to obtain knowledge, especially knowledge gathered on a mission: *The astronauts were debriefed after returning from their mission.*

Word History: debonair

The word **debonair** comes from French, as its spelling and pronunciation suggest. In Old French *de bon aire* means "of good lineage or disposition." The *aire* in the phrase is not the air we breathe but comes from the Latin word *ārea*, "area, open space," and in Old French *aire* means "place, race, stock, disposition."

ă	pat	oi	boy
ā	pay	ou	out
âr	care	o͝o	took
ä	father	o͞o	boot
ĕ	pet	ŭ	cut
ē	be	ûr	urge
ĭ	pit	th	thin
ī	pie	*th*	this
îr	pier	hw	whoop
ŏ	pot	zh	vision
ō	toe	ə	about
ô	paw	N	*French* bon

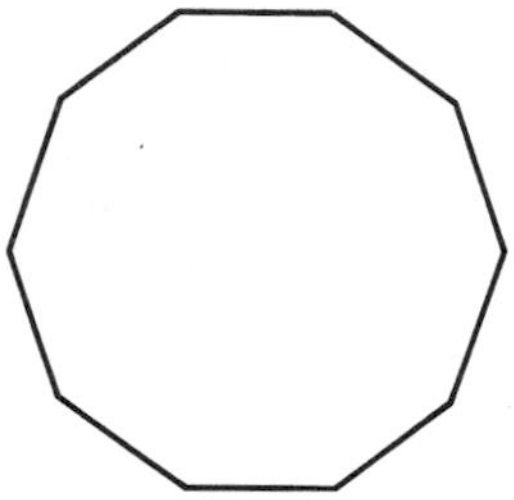

decagon

decal

de•bris also **dé•bris** (də brē′ *or* dā′brē′) *n.* The scattered remains of something broken, destroyed, or discarded; rubble or wreckage: *Debris from the storm was spread all over the beach.*

debt (dĕt) *n.* **1.** Something, such as money, owed by one person to another: *I will pay my debts as soon as I get paid. The people owe a great debt of thanks to soldiers of their country.* **2.** The condition of owing; indebtedness: *They are in debt to the bank for their loan.*

debt•or (dĕt′ər) *n.* A person who owes something to another.

de•bug (dē bŭg′) *tr.v.* **de•bugged, de•bug•ging, de•bugs.** To search for and fix errors in (a computer program).

de•bunk (dē bŭngk′) *tr.v.* **de•bunked, de•bunk•ing, de•bunks.** To expose or ridicule the falseness or exaggerated claims of: *It took centuries to debunk the theory that the planets revolve around the earth.*

De•bus•sy (dĕb′yo͞o sē′), **Claude Achille.** 1862–1918. French composer who is considered a leader in musical impressionism.

de•but also **dé•but** (dā byo͞o′ *or* dā′byo͞o′) *n.* **1.** The first public appearance: *a new actor's stage debut; the debut of a new line of computers.* **2.** The formal presentation of a young woman into society.

deb•u•tante (dĕb′yo͞o tänt′) *n.* A young woman making a debut into society.

Dec. or **Dec** *abbr.* An abbreviation of December.

deca– *pref.* A prefix that means ten: *decaliter.*

dec•ade (dĕk′ād′) *n.* A period of ten years. [First written down about 1451 in Middle English and spelled *decade*, a group of ten, from Greek *dekas*, from *deka*, ten.]

dec•a•dence (dĕk′ə dəns *or* dĭ kād′ns) *n.* A process, condition, or period of deterioration, decay, or decline, as in morals or art.

dec•a•dent (dĕk′ə dənt *or* dĭ kād′nt) *adj.* Marked by or in a condition of deterioration or decline; decaying: *a decadent society.* —*n.* A person who is in the process of mental or moral decay. **—dec′a•dent•ly** *adv.*

de•caf•fein•at•ed (dē kăf′ə nā′tĭd) *adj.* Having most of the caffeine removed: *decaffeinated coffee.*

dec•a•gon (dĕk′ə gŏn′) *n.* A plane geometric figure having ten sides and ten angles.

dec•a•he•dron (dĕk′ə hē′drən) *n., pl.* **dec•a•he•drons** or **dec•a•he•dra** (dĕk′ə hē′drə). A solid geometric figure having ten faces.

de•cal (dē′kăl′ *or* dĭ kăl′) *n.* A picture or design printed on specially treated paper to be transferred to another surface such as glass, metal, or plastic.

dec•a•li•ter (dĕk′ə lē′tər) *n.* A unit of volume equal to 10 liters.

Dec•a•logue or **Dec•a•log** (dĕk′ə lôg′ *or* dĕk′ə lŏg′) *n.* The Ten Commandments.

de•camp (dĭ kămp′) *intr.v.* **de•camped, de•camp•ing, de•camps. 1.** To pack up and leave a camping ground; break camp: *The battalion decamped at dawn.* **2.** To leave secretly or suddenly; run away: *The thief decamped under the cover of darkness.* **—de•camp′ment** *n.*

de•cant (dĭ kănt′) *tr.v.* **de•cant•ed, de•cant•ing, de•cants. 1.** To pour off (a liquid, especially wine) without disturbing the sediment at the bottom. **2.** To pour (a liquid) from one container into another.

de•cant•er (dĭ kăn′tər) *n.* A decorative glass bottle with a stopper, used for holding liquids such as wine.

de•cap•i•tate (dĭ kăp′ĭ tāt′) *tr.v.* **de•cap•i•tat•ed, de•cap•i•tat•ing, de•cap•i•tates.** To cut off the head of (a person or an animal); behead. [First written down in 1611 in Modern English, from Late Latin *dēcapitāre* : Latin *dē-*, off + Latin *caput*, head.] **—de•cap′i•ta′tion** *n.*

de•cath•lon (dĭ kăth′lən *or* dĭ kăth′lŏn′) *n.* An athletic contest in which each contestant participates in ten different track and field events. The contestant scoring the most total points for all events is the winner. [First written down in 1912 in Modern English : Greek *deka-*, ten + Greek *athlon*, contest.]

de•cay (dĭ kā′) *v.* **de•cayed, de•cay•ing, de•cays.** —*intr.* **1.** To rot or become rotten; decompose: *Dead trees gradually decay into pulp.* **2.** To undergo radioactive decay. **3.** To fall into ruin: *Why did this ancient civilization decay?* —*tr.* To cause to decay: *Fungus will decay wood.* —*n.* **1.** The act or process of rotting: *tooth decay; decay of old buildings through neglect.* **2.** The natural disintegration of a radioactive substance by the emission of particles and radiation from its nuclei. **3.** A gradual deterioration or decline, as in health or strength: *the decay of learning in the Middle Ages.* [First written down in 1475 in Middle English and spelled *decayen*, from Old French *decair* : Latin *dē-*, off, down + Latin *cadere*, to fall.]

de•cease (dĭ sēs′) *intr.v.* **de•ceased, de•ceas•ing, de•ceas•es.** To die. —*n.* The act or fact of dying; death.

de•ceased (dĭ sēst′) *adj.* No longer living; dead: *my deceased grandparents.* —*n., pl.* **deceased.** A dead person or persons: *spoke with members of the deceased's family.*

de•ce•dent (dĭ sēd′nt) *n.* In law, the deceased.

de•ceit (dĭ sēt′) *n.* **1.** The act or practice of deceiving; deception: *A successful spy is a expert in deceit.* **2.** A trick used to deceive someone else. **3.** The quality of being deceitful: *a swindler full of deceit.*

de•ceit•ful (dĭ sēt′fəl) *adj.* **1.** Practicing deceit: *a deceitful person.* **2.** Deliberately misleading; deceptive: *a deceitful excuse to avoid punishment.* **—de•ceit′ful•ly** *adv.* **—de•ceit′ful•ness** *n.*

de•ceive (dĭ sēv′) *v.* **de•ceived, de•ceiv•ing, de•ceives.** —*tr.* To make (a person) believe something that is not true; mislead; trick: *The fox ran back on its own trail to deceive the pursuing dogs.* —*intr.* To use deceit. **—de•ceiv′er** *n.*

de•cel•er•ate (dē sĕl′ə rāt′) *v.* **de•cel•er•at•ed, de•cel•er•at•ing, de•cel•er•ates.** —*tr.* To decrease the speed or rate of: *decelerated the car by jamming on the brakes.* —*intr.* To decrease in speed; slow down: *The spinning top decelerated slowly.* **—de•cel′er•a′tion** *n.* **—de•cel′er•a′tor** *n.*

De•cem•ber (dĭ sĕm′bər) *n.* The 12th month of the year in the Gregorian calendar, having 31 days. [First written down in 1122 in Middle English, from Latin *December*, the tenth month of the Roman year : *decem*, ten + *mēnsis*, month.]

de•cen•cy (dē′sən sē) *n., pl.* **de•cen•cies. 1.** The state or condition of being decent: *the decency to act in an honest and proper manner.* **2. decencies. a.** Decent or proper acts; proper observances: *the social decencies such as courtesy and good manners.* **b.** The things needed for a respectable and proper way of living: *A refrigerator is one of the decencies of life in a developed nation.*

de•cent (dē′sənt) *adj.* **1.** Conforming to the standards of proper behavior or to the rules and conventions of society: *Decent people abide by the law.* **2.** Kind; considerate: *It was very decent of you to help in time of trouble.* **3.** Adequate; passable: *a decent salary.* **4.** *Informal.* Properly or modestly dressed. **—de′cent•ly** *adv.*

de•cen•tral•ize (dē sĕn′trə līz′) *tr.v.* **de•cen•tral•ized, de•cen•tral•iz•ing, de•cen•tral•iz•es. 1.** To distribute the functions or powers of (a government or central authority) among several local authorities. **2.** To reorganize into smaller units of operation: *decentralize a school system.* **—de•cen'tral•i•za'tion** (dē sĕn'trə lĭ zā'shən) *n.*

de•cep•tion (dĭ sĕp'shən) *n.* **1.** The use of deceit: *fraudulent advertising and other forms of deception.* **2.** The condition of being deceived: *The magician achieved complete deception of the audience.* **3.** Something that deceives, as a trick or lie: *The scarecrow was a deception to frighten away the deer.*

de•cep•tive (dĭ sĕp'tĭv) *adj.* Deceiving or tending to deceive: *the deceptive calm before the storm.* **—de•cep'tive•ly** *adv.* **—de•cep'tive•ness** *n.*

deci– *pref.* A prefix that means one tenth: *deciliter.*

de•ci•bel (dĕs'ə bəl *or* dĕs'ə bĕl') *n.* A unit used in measuring the loudness of sounds: *The speaking voice of most people ranges from 45 to 75 decibels.*

de•cide (dĭ sīd') *v.* **de•cid•ed, de•cid•ing, de•cides.** *—tr.* **1.** To bring to a conclusion by removing uncertainty or resolving a conflict: *The court decided the case.* **2.** To influence or determine the outcome of: *a single goal decided the game.* **3.** To cause to reach or make a decision: *What decided you to leave so soon?* *—intr.* **1.** To give a judgment: *The judge decided against the defendant.* **2.** To make up one's mind: *We decided to go to the movies.* [First written down before 1393 in Middle English and spelled *deciden*, from Latin *dēcīdere*, to cut off, decide : *dē-*, off, away + *caedere*, to cut.]

de•cid•ed (dĭ sī'dĭd) *adj.* **1.** Clear-cut; definite; undoubted: *a decided advantage.* **2.** Free from hesitation; resolute: *The general has a decided manner of talking.* **—de•cid'ed•ly** *adv.* **—de•cid'ed•ness** *n.*

de•cid•u•ous (dĭ sĭj'o͞o əs) *adj.* **1.** Falling off at the end of a season or growing period: *deciduous antlers.* **2.** Shedding leaves at the end of the growing season: *deciduous trees.* [First written down in 1688 in Modern English, from Latin *dēciduus*, from *dēcidere*, to fall off : *dē-*, down, off + *cadere*, to fall.]

dec•i•li•ter (dĕs'ə lē'tər) *n.* A unit of volume equal to one tenth (10^{-1}) of a liter.

dec•i•mal (dĕs'ə məl) *n.* **1.** A number containing a decimal fraction, such as 66.03, 3.1415, or .099. **2.** A decimal fraction. *—adj.* Of or based on 10; proceeding by tens: *The system of decimal notation is an invention of mathematicians in India.* [First written down in 1608 in Modern English, from Latin *decima*, a tenth part, from *decem*, ten.]

decimal fraction *n.* A fraction in which the denominator is 10 or a power of 10. Expressed as decimal fractions, $^{29}/_{100}$ is .29, and $^{29}/_{1000}$ is .029.

decimal place *n.* The position of a digit in a decimal fraction. In .079, for example, 0 is in the first decimal place, 7 is in the second decimal place, and 9 is in the third decimal place.

decimal point *n.* A period placed to the left of a decimal fraction and used in decimals to separate whole numbers from fractions. For example, 1.3 represents 1 + $^{3}/_{10}$.

decimal system *n.* A number system based on units of 10.

dec•i•mate (dĕs'ə māt') *tr.v.* **dec•i•mat•ed, dec•i•mat•ing, dec•i•mates.** To destroy or kill a large part of: *The hurricane decimated the bird population of the small island.* [First written down in 1600 in Modern English, from Latin *decimāre*, to punish every tenth person, from *decimus*, tenth, from *decem*, ten.] **—dec'i•ma'tion** *n.*

dec•i•me•ter (dĕs'ə mē'tər) *n.* A unit of length equal to one tenth (10^{-1}) of a meter.

de•ci•pher (dĭ sī'fər) *tr.v.* **de•ci•phered, de•ci•pher•ing, de•ci•phers.** **1.** To change (a message) from a code or cipher to ordinary language; decode: *Telegraph operators must be able to decipher dots and dashes.* **2.** To read or interpret (something hard to understand or illegible). **—de•ci'pher•a•ble** *adj.*

de•ci•sion (dĭ sĭzh'ən) *n.* **1.** The act of deciding or making up one's mind: *Our friends have not come to a decision about going on the trip with us.* **2.** A conclusion or judgment: *The judge handed down a decision of not guilty.* **3.** Firmness of character or action; determination: *The President must be a person of great decision.*

de•ci•sive (dĭ sī'sĭv) *adj.* **1.a.** Having the power to settle something; conclusive: *a decisive argument.* **b.** Beyond doubt; unmistakable: *a decisive victory.* **2.** Characterized by decision and firmness; resolute: *A police officer should be a decisive person.* **—de•ci'sive•ly** *adv.* **—de•ci'sive•ness** *n.*

deck¹ (dĕk) *n.* **1.** A platform extending from one side of a ship to the other. **2.** A platform like the deck of a ship: *a parking deck on the roof of the building.* **3.** A pack of playing cards: *shuffle the deck and deal.* **4.** A tape deck. *—tr.v.* **decked, deck•ing, decks.** **1.** To provide with a deck: *deck a ship.* **2.** To knock down with force. ***—idiom.* on deck.** **1.** On hand; present. **2.** Waiting to take one's turn, especially as a batter in baseball. [First written down in 1466 in Middle English and spelled *dekke*, from Middle Dutch *dec*, roof, covering.]

deck² (dĕk) *tr.v.* **decked, deck•ing, decks.** **1.** To put fine clothes on: *She decked herself out for the party.* **2.** To decorate: *decked the halls for the holidays.* [First written down in 1513 in Modern English, from Dutch *dekken*, to cover.]

deck hand *n.* A member of a ship's crew assigned to work on deck.

de•claim (dĭ klām') *v.* **de•claimed, de•claim•ing, de•claims.** *—intr.* **1.** To deliver a speech, especially in a formal way. **2.** To speak loudly, pompously, or in a theatrical manner: *Everyone declaims against inefficient government, but few will do anything about it.* *—tr.* To recite formally: *declaim a poem.* **—de•claim'er** *n.*

dec•la•ma•tion (dĕk'lə mā'shən) *n.* **1.** The act of declaiming: *a sincere declamation of patriotism.* **2.** Something declaimed.

de•clam•a•to•ry (dĭ klăm'ə tôr'ē) *adj.* **1.** Of or suitable for declaiming: *a declamatory poem.* **2.** Pretentious and bombastic: *a long declamatory explanation.*

dec•la•ra•tion (dĕk'lə rā'shən) *n.* **1.** The act or process of declaring. **2.** A formal statement or announcement: *the declaration of one's candidacy for office.* **3.** A document listing goods that are taxable or subject to duty: *Travelers made out declarations before going through customs.*

Declaration of Independence *n.* A proclamation, adopted on July 4, 1776 by the Second Continental Congress, declaring the 13 American colonies independent of Great Britain.

de•clar•a•tive (dĭ klâr'ə tĭv *or* dĭ klăr'ə tĭv) *adj.* Making a statement, as opposed to a question or an order: *a declarative sentence such as "I'm going home."*

de•clare (dĭ klâr') *v.* **de•clared, de•clar•ing, de•clares.** *—tr.* **1.** To state with emphasis; affirm: *The teacher declared that cheating would be severely punished.* **2.** To state officially or formally: *Congress has the power to declare new national holidays.* **3.** To make a full statement of (dutiable goods) when entering a country at customs. *—intr.* To announce one's choice or opinion: *The senator declared against raising taxes.* [First written down before 1338 in Middle English and spelled *declaren*, from Latin *dēclārāre*, from *clārus*, clear.]

de•clen•sion (dĭ klĕn'shən) *n.* **1.** In some languages,

ă	pat	oi	boy
ā	pay	ou	out
âr	care	o͝o	took
ä	father	o͞o	boot
ĕ	pet	ŭ	cut
ē	be	ûr	urge
ĭ	pit	th	thin
ī	pie	*th*	this
îr	pier	hw	whoop
ŏ	pot	zh	vision
ō	toe	ə	about
ô	paw	N	*French* bon

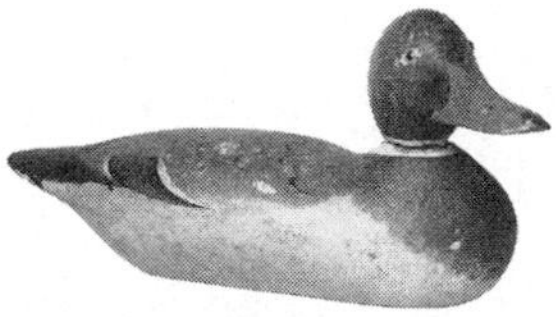

decoy
Wooden duck decoy

the inflection of nouns, pronouns, and adjectives in categories such as case, number, and gender. **2.** A class of words of one language with the same or a similar system of inflections, such as the first declension in Latin.

dec•li•na•tion (dĕk′lə **nā′**shən) *n.* **1.** Magnetic declination. **2.** The angular distance of a star or planet from the celestial equator.

de•cline (dĭ **klīn′**) *v.* **de•clined, de•clin•ing, de•clines.** —*tr.* **1.** To refuse politely: *They declined my offer to help. I have to decline the kitten, because we can't have pets.* See Synonyms at **refuse**[1]. **2.** In certain languages, to give the inflected forms of (a noun, a pronoun, or an adjective). —*intr.* **1.** To refuse politely to do or accept something: *I asked them home for a snack, but they declined.* **2.** To become less or decrease, as in strength, value, or importance: *Her health declined until she saw the doctor. Prices tend to decline when business is poor.* **3.** To slope or bend downward: *The hills decline into a hidden valley.* —*n.* **1.** The process or result of declining, as in strength or importance; deterioration: *The country was in a period of decline.* **2.** A change to a lower level or state, as in value: *a decline in prices.* **3.** The period when something is coming to an end: *Frost and bare trees marked the decline of fall.* **4.** A downward slope. [First written down before 1376 in Middle English and spelled *declinen*, from Latin *dēclīnāre*, to turn away : *dē-*, away + *-clīnāre*, to lean, bend.]

de•cliv•i•ty (dĭ **klĭv′**ĭ tē) *n., pl.* **de•cliv•i•ties.** A downward slope, as of a hill.

de•code (dē **kōd′**) *tr.v.* **de•cod•ed, de•cod•ing, de•codes.** To change (information) from a form that is in code into ordinary language; decipher: *decode Egyptian hieroglyphics.* —**de•cod′er** *n.*

de•com•pose (dē′kəm **pōz′**) *v.* **de•com•posed, de•com•pos•ing, de•com•pos•es.** —*tr.* **1.** To separate (a substance) into simpler substances or basic elements: *Heat decomposes chalk into lime and carbon dioxide.* **2.** To cause to rot; decay: *Microbes decomposed the dead plants on the forest floor.* —*intr.* **1.** To separate into component parts: *Sunlight decomposes into the colors of the spectrum as it passes through a prism.* **2.** To decay; rot.

de•com•pos•er (dē′kəm **pō′**zər) *n.* A fungus or bacterium that breaks down dead organic matter.

de•com•po•si•tion (dē kŏm′pə **zĭsh′**ən) *n.* The act or process of decomposing: *The decomposition of gasoline occurs during combustion.*

de•com•press (dē′kəm **prĕs′**) *tr.v.* **de•com•pressed, de•com•press•ing, de•com•press•es.** To bring (a person exposed to increased pressure) gradually to normal atmospheric pressure.

de•com•pres•sion (dē′kəm **prĕsh′**ən) *n.* The act or process of bringing a person exposed to increased pressure back to normal atmospheric pressure in gradual stages: *Divers and workers building deep tunnels must undergo decompression.*

decompression sickness *n.* A disorder, seen especially in deep-sea divers or tunnel workers, caused by the formation of nitrogen bubbles in the blood following a rapid drop in pressure and characterized by severe pain in the joints and chest, cramps, and paralysis.

de•con•ges•tant (dē′kən **jĕs′**tənt) *n.* A medication or treatment that eliminates or relieves congestion in the nose or bronchial passages.

de•con•tam•i•nate (dē′kən **tăm′**ə nāt′) *tr.v.* **de•con•tam•i•nat•ed, de•con•tam•i•nat•ing, de•con•tam•i•nates.** To free of contamination, especially by removing harmful substances, such as bacteria, poisonous chemicals, or radioactive materials. —**de′con•tam′i•na′tion** *n.*

de•con•trol (dē′kən **trōl′**) *tr.v.* **de•con•trolled, de•con•trol•ling, de•con•trols.** To free from control, especially from government control: *The government decontrolled the airlines, letting them set their own ticket prices.*

dé•cor or **de•cor** (dā′kôr′ *or* dā **kôr′**) *n.* **1.** The decorative style of a room, home, restaurant, or other area. **2.** Scenery in a theatrical or television show.

dec•o•rate (**dĕk′**ə rāt′) *tr.v.* **dec•o•rat•ed, dec•o•rat•ing, dec•o•rates.** **1.** To furnish with something attractive, beautiful, or striking; adorn: *The students decorated the auditorium with flowers for graduation.* **2.** To paint, paper, or select and organize the furnishings of (a room, house, or other area): *The painters decorated the hall in a soft green color.* **3.** To give a medal or other honor to: *The chief decorated the firefighter for bravery.*

dec•o•ra•tion (dĕk′ə **rā′**shən) *n.* **1.** The act or process of decorating: *Decoration of the auditorium for graduation took most of the morning.* **2.** Something that adorns or beautifies; an ornament: *We put up wreaths, streamers, and other decorations.* **3.** A medal, badge, or ribbon awarded as an honor: *The police officer received a decoration for bravery.*

Decoration Day *n.* Memorial Day.

dec•o•ra•tive (**dĕk′**ər ə tĭv *or* **dĕk′**ə rā′tĭv) *adj.* Serving to decorate; ornamental: *a decorative design in the ceiling.* —**dec′o•ra•tive•ly** *adv.*

dec•o•ra•tor (**dĕk′**ə rā′tər) *n.* A person who decorates, especially an interior decorator.

dec•o•rous (**dĕk′**ər əs *or* dĭ **kôr′**əs) *adj.* Characterized by decorum; proper: *decorous behavior.* —**dec′o•rous•ness** *n.*

de•co•rum (dĭ **kôr′**əm) *n.* Proper behavior or conduct; propriety.

de•coy (**dē′**koi′ *or* dĭ **koi′**) *n.* **1.** A model of a duck or other bird, used by hunters to attract wild birds or animals. **2.** A person or thing used to lead another into danger or a trap: *A false delivery of money was a decoy to catch the robbers.* —*tr.v.* (dĭ **koi′**). **de•coyed, de•coy•ing, de•coys.** **1.** To lure (wild animals such as birds) into a trap or position to be hunted: *decoy geese into a marsh.* **2.** To lure (a person) into danger or a trap by a trick or temptation. [First written down in 1625 in Modern English, possibly from Dutch *de kooi*, the cage : *de*, the + *kooi*, cage (from Latin *cavea*).]

de•crease (dĭ **krēs′**) *tr. & intr.v.* **de•creased, de•creas•ing, de•creas•es.** To make or become gradually less or smaller; diminish: *We must decrease spending to conserve our money. Oil supplies decreased during the winter.* —*n.* (**dē′**krēs′). **1.** The act or process of decreasing; a decline: *A decrease in sales forced the owners to close the store.* **2.** The amount by which something becomes less or smaller: *a decrease in the price of gasoline of five cents a gallon.*

Synonyms: decrease, lessen, reduce, diminish, dwindle. These verbs mean to become or cause to become smaller or less. **Decrease** and **lessen** both mean to become smaller or less at a steady, gradual rate: *City traffic decreases on holidays. My appetite lessens as the weather gets warmer.* **Reduce** means to bring down, as in size, degree, or strength: *Maybe you should reduce the amount of sugar in the cake recipe.* **Diminish** means to decrease by taking away something: *Each new scandal diminishes our respect for the senator.* **Dwindle** means to decrease bit by bit until no more is left: *Their savings dwindled over the years.* **Antonym: add.**

de•cree (dĭ **krē′**) *n.* An authoritative order; an edict: *The falsely accused prisoner was released by court decree.* —*tr.v.* **de•creed, de•cree•ing, de•crees.** To order or decide by decree: *The governor decreed a state holiday.*

dec•re•ment (**dĕk′**rə mənt) *n.* In mathematics, the

amount by which the value of a variable decreases.

de•crep•it (dĭ **krĕp′**ĭt) *adj.* Weakened, worn-out, or broken down because of old age or long use: *a decrepit old car.* **—de•crep′it•ly** *adv.*

de•crep•i•tude (dĭ **krĕp′**ĭ to͞od′ *or* dĭ **krĕp′**ĭ tyo͞od′) *n.* The condition of being decrepit; weakness: *The abandoned house was in a state of decrepitude.*

de•cre•scen•do (dā′krə **shĕn′**dō *or* dē′krə **shĕn′**-dō) *adv. & adj.* In music, with gradually diminishing force or loudness. *—n., pl.* **de•cre•scen•dos. 1.** A gradual decrease in musical force or loudness. **2.** A musical passage performed with a decrescendo.

de•crim•i•nal•ize (dē **krĭm′**ə nə līz′) *tr.v.* **de•crim•i•nal•ized, de•crim•i•nal•iz•ing, de•crim•i•nal•iz•es.** To reduce or abolish the legal penalties for doing or possessing (something): *Betting was decriminalized in many states.*

de•cry (dĭ **krī′**) *tr.v.* **de•cried, de•cry•ing, de•cries. 1.** To condemn as being wrong or bad; disapprove of strongly: *The judge decried the criminal's behavior.* **2.** To cause to seem unimportant or inferior; belittle: *decry watching television as a waste of time.*

ded•i•cate (**dĕd′**ĭ kāt′) *tr.v.* **ded•i•cat•ed, ded•i•cat•ing, ded•i•cates. 1.** To set apart for a special purpose: *This chapel is dedicated to the memory of sailors lost at sea.* **2.** To give or commit (oneself) fully to something, such as a course of action; devote: *Nurses dedicate their lives to the care of the sick.* **3.** To address or inscribe (a book, performance, or other creative work) to someone as a mark of respect or affection: *The composer dedicated the new symphony to an old friend.* [First written down before 1425 in Middle English and spelled *dedicaten*, from Latin *dēdicāre*, from *dicāre*, to proclaim.]

ded•i•ca•tion (dĕd′ĭ **kā′**shən) *n.* **1.** The act of dedicating or the state of being dedicated: *her dedication to helping others.* **2.** A ceremony dedicating something: *We went to the dedication of the new library.* **3.** A note in a book, musical composition, or other creative work dedicating it to someone. **—ded′i•ca•to′ry** (**dĕd′**ĭ kə tôr′ē) *adj.*

de•duce (dĭ **do͞os′** *or* dĭ **dyo͞os′**) *tr.v.* **de•duced, de•duc•ing, de•duc•es.** To reach (a conclusion) by reasoning, especially from a general principle: *The engineers deduced from the law of physics that the new airplane would fly.* [First written down in 1410 in Middle English and spelled *deducen*, from Latin *dēdūcere*, to lead away or down : *dē-*, down, away + *dūcere*, to lead.]

de•duct (dĭ **dŭkt′**) *tr.v.* **de•duct•ed, de•duct•ing, de•ducts.** To take away (a quantity from another); subtract: *The dealer deducted the amount of our earlier deposit from the final payment for the car.* [First written down in 1419 in Middle English and spelled *deducten*, from Latin *dēdūcere*, to lead away or down : *dē-*, down, away + *dūcere*, to lead.]

de•duct•i•ble (dĭ **dŭk′**tə bəl) *adj.* Capable of being deducted, especially from inclusion in one's taxable income.

de•duc•tion (dĭ **dŭk′**shən) *n.* **1.** The act of deducting; subtraction: *The salesman's deduction of the cost of installation persuaded us to buy the dishwasher.* **2.** An amount that is or may be deducted: *a deduction from one's taxable income for medical expenses.* **3.a.** The process of reaching a conclusion by reasoning, especially from general principles: *the judge's deduction that the law violated the Fourteenth Amendment.* **b.** A conclusion reached by this process.

de•duc•tive (dĭ **dŭk′**tĭv) *adj.* Of or involving logical deduction: *deductive reasoning.* **—de•duc′tive•ly** *adv.*

deed (dēd) *n.* **1.** An act or action: *Returning the lost money was a good deed.* **2.** A legal document showing ownership of property. *—tr.v.* **deed•ed, deed•ing, deeds.** To transfer or give (property) by means of a deed: *The government deeded land to the miners.* [First written down about 725 in Old English and spelled *dǣd.*]

dee•jay (**dē′**jā′) *Informal. n.* A disc jockey.

deem (dēm) *tr.v.* **deemed, deem•ing, deems.** To judge, consider, or believe: *The doctor deemed it essential for me to get more exercise.*

deep (dēp) *adj.* **deep•er, deep•est. 1.** Extending far down below a surface: *a deep hole in the river ice.* **2.** Extending from front to rear, or from the outside to the inside: *a deep closet.* **3.** Extending a specified distance in a given direction: *snow three feet deep.* **4.** Far distant down or in: *The hunters were deep in the woods.* **5.** Extreme; profound; intense: *a deep silence; a deep sleep.* **6.** Very much absorbed or involved: *She was deep in thought.* **7.** Showing much thought or feeling; strongly felt: *a deep understanding; a deep love of books.* **8.** Difficult to understand; mysterious: *a deep theory.* **9.** Rich and vivid in shade of color: *a deep red.* **10.** Low in pitch: *a deep voice.* *—adv.* **deeper, deepest. 1.** To a great depth: *dig deep into the earth.* **2.** Well along in time; late: *The researchers worked deep into the night.* *—n.* **1.** A deep place, such as the ocean or a place in the ocean: *We know little of life in the deep.* **2.** The most intense or extreme part: *the deep of night.* **—deep′ly** *adv.* **—deep′ness** *n.*

deep•en (**dē′**pən) *tr. & intr.v.* **deep•ened, deep•en•ing, deep•ens.** To make or become deep or deeper: *More digging slowly deepened the hole. Floodwaters deepened as the rain continued.*

deep-root•ed (**dēp′ro͞o′**tĭd *or* **dēp′ro͝ot′**ĭd) *adj.* **1.** Firmly implanted below the surface: *a deep-rooted oak.* **2.** Firmly fixed; deep-seated: *deep-rooted beliefs.*

deep-sea (**dēp′sē′**) *adj.* Of or relating to deep parts of the sea: *a deep-sea diver.*

deep-seat•ed (**dēp′sē′**tĭd) *adj.* **1.** Deeply implanted below the surface: *a deep-seated infection.* **2.** Firmly fixed; deeply rooted; strongly entrenched: *a deep-seated problem of long standing.*

deer (dîr) *n., pl.* **deer.** Any of various hoofed mammals, such as the elk and the white-tailed deer, that chew their cud and usually have antlers in the males. [First written down before 899 in Old English and spelled *dēor*, beast.]

❑ *These sound alike:* **deer, dear** (loved one).

deer
Mule deer buck

deer mouse *n.* A North American mouse having tan or brown fur, white feet, large ears, and a long tail.

deer•skin (**dîr′**skĭn′) *n.* **1.** The skin of a deer. **2.** Leather made from this skin. **3.** A garment made from such leather.

de-es•ca•late (dē **ĕs′**kə lāt′) *tr.v.* To reduce the scale, size, or intensity of: *Calm words de-escalated the crisis.* **—de-es′ca•la′tion** *n.*

def. *abbr.* An abbreviation of definition.

de•face (dĭ **fās′**) *tr.v.* **de•faced, de•fac•ing, de•fac•es.** To mar or spoil the surface or appearance of; disfigure: *deface a poster with a crayon.* **—de•face′ment** *n.*

de fac•to (dĭ **făk′**tō *or* dā **făk′**tō) *adj.* **1.** Existing in fact; actual; real: *de facto segregation.* **2.** Exercising power though not legally established: *a de facto government.*

def•a•ma•tion (dĕf′ə **mā′**shən) *n.* The act of making a statement that will damage a person's reputation; slander or libel: *defamation of a person's character.* **—de•fam′a•to′ry** (dĭ **făm′**ə tôr′ē) *adj.*

de•fame (dĭ **fām′**) *tr.v.* **de•famed, de•fam•ing, de•fames.** To attack or damage the reputation of by slander or libel: *He defamed her good name by spreading false rumors.*

de•fault (dĭ **fôlt′**) *n.* **1.** A failure to do what is re-

ă	pat	oi	boy
ā	pay	ou	out
âr	care	o͝o	took
ä	father	o͞o	boot
ĕ	pet	ŭ	cut
ē	be	ûr	urge
ĭ	pit	th	thin
ī	pie	*th*	this
îr	pier	hw	whoop
ŏ	pot	zh	vision
ō	toe	ə	about
ô	paw	N	*French* bon

quired, especially a failure to pay a debt: *The bankrupt company is guilty of default on its loans.* **2.** The failure of one or more competitors or teams to participate in or complete a contest: *win a contest by default.* **3.** A setting, such as the typeface for text, used by a computer unless and until the operator chooses a different setting. —*intr.v.* **de•fault•ed, de•fault•ing, de•faults. 1.** To fail to do what is required: *default on a business contract.* **2.** To fail to pay money when it is due: *default on a loan.* **3.** To lose a contest by failing to participate in or complete it: *Illness caused the tennis star to default in the match.* —**de•fault′er** *n.*

de•feat (dĭ fēt′) *tr.v.* **de•feat•ed, de•feat•ing, de•feats. 1.** To win victory over; beat: *The mayor defeated all opponents in the last election.* **2.** To prevent the success of; thwart: *A misunderstanding defeated our efforts at a compromise.* —*n.* **1.** The act of defeating or the state of being defeated: *The veto was a defeat of the new environmental measures.* **2.** Failure to win: *admit defeat.* [First written down about 1380 in Middle English and spelled *defeten*, from Medieval Latin *disfacere*, to undo, mutilate.]

de•feat•ism (dĭ fē′tĭz′əm) *n.* Acceptance of or resignation to the prospect of defeat: *Defeatism can prevent success.* —**de•feat′ist** *n.*

def•e•cate (dĕf′ĭ kāt′) *intr.v.* **def•e•cat•ed, def•e•cat•ing, def•e•cates.** To empty the bowels of waste matter. —**def′e•ca′tion** *n.*

de•fect (dē′fĕkt′ *or* dĭ fĕkt′) *n.* A lack of something necessary or desirable for completion or perfection; a deficiency: *A defect in the engine made it sputter and stall.* —*intr.v.* (dĭ fĕkt′). **de•fect•ed, de•fect•ing, de•fects. 1.** To disavow allegiance to one's country and take up residence in another: *a Chinese pilot who defected to Russia.* **2.** To abandon a position or an association, often to join an opposing group: *The American general Benedict Arnold defected to the British side.* [First written down before 1425 in Middle English, from Latin *dēficere*, to desert, be wanting.] —**de•fec′tion** *n.* —**de•fec′tor** *n.*

de•fec•tive (dĭ fĕk′tĭv) *adj.* Having a defect or flaw; faulty: *The defective clock never kept time well.* —**de•fec′tive•ly** *adv.*

de•fence (dĭ fĕns′) *n.* & *v.* *Chiefly British.* Variant of **defense.**

de•fend (dĭ fĕnd′) *tr.v.* **de•fend•ed, de•fend•ing, de•fends. 1.** To make or keep safe from attack, harm, or danger; guard: *The ants defended their colony against the invading predators.* **2.** To support or maintain, as by argument; justify: *The scientist defended the theory that germs cause disease.* **3.** To represent (a defendant) in a court of law: *the right to be defended by a lawyer.* —**de•fend′er** *n.*

Synonyms: defend, protect, guard, preserve, shield. These verbs mean to make or keep safe from danger, attack, or harm. **Defend** suggests taking measures to drive back an attack: *A small army was formed to defend the island against invasion.* **Protect** suggests the providing of some kind of cover for safety or comfort: *Wear goggles to protect your eyes from the chlorine in the swimming pool.* **Guard** means to keep watch over something: *The family bought three big dogs to guard the house.* **Preserve** means to act to keep something safe: *Ecologists work to preserve the balance of nature.* **Shield** means to protect the way armor would by standing in between the threat and the threatened: *The suspect's lawyers tried to shield him from the angry reporters.*

de•fen•dant (dĭ fĕn′dənt) *n.* The person or party against which a legal action or claim is brought.

de•fense (dĭ fĕns′) *n.* **1.** The act of defending against attack, harm, or danger: *The patriots fought in defense of their freedom.* **2.a.** A means or method of defending or protecting: *A heavy coat is a good defense against the cold.* **b.** An argument in support or justification of something: *The newspaper editorial is a strong defense for freedom of the press.* **3.a.** The reply or action of a defendant in opposition to a complaint. **b.** The defendant and his or her legal counsel. **4.** In sports, the team or those players on the team attempting to keep the opposition from scoring.

de•fense•less (dĭ fĕns′lĭs) *adj.* Having no defense; unprotected: *a defenseless infant.*

de•fen•si•ble (dĭ fĕn′sə bəl) *adj.* Capable of being defended, protected, or justified: *Blaming others for one's mistakes is not a defensible position.*

de•fen•sive (dĭ fĕn′sĭv) *adj.* **1.** Intended to or appropriate for defense: *a defensive moat surrounding the castle.* **2.** Intended to withstand or deter aggression or attack. **3.** Of or relating to defense: *a defensive attitude.* —*n.* A means of defense. —***idiom.*** **on the defensive.** Prepared to withstand or counter aggression or attack. —**de•fen′sive•ly** *adv.* —**de•fen′sive•ness** *n.*

de•fer¹ (dĭ fûr′) *tr.v.* **de•ferred, de•fer•ring, de•fers.** To put off; postpone: *defer going until we know what the weather will be.* [First written down about 1375 in Middle English and spelled *differren*, from Latin *differre* : *dis-*, off + *ferre*, to carry, put.] —**de•fer′ra•ble** *adj.*

de•fer² (dĭ fûr′) *intr.v.* **de•ferred, de•fer•ring, de•fers.** To submit to the wishes, opinion, or decision of another, as through recognition of authority or knowledge: *Let's defer to an expert on that matter.* [First written down before 1447 in Middle English and spelled *differren*, from Latin *dēferre*, to refer to : *dē-*, away + *ferre*, to carry.]

def•er•ence (dĕf′ər əns *or* dĕf′rəns) *n.* **1.** Submission or courteous yielding to the opinion, wishes, or judgment of another. **2.** Courteous respect: *The guests showed deference to their host by standing until he was seated.*

def•er•en•tial (dĕf′ə rĕn′shəl) *adj.* Marked by or showing deference; respectful: *deferential behavior.* —**def′er•en′tial•ly** *adv.*

de•fer•ment (dĭ fûr′mənt) *n.* The act or an example of delaying or putting off: *the deferment of payments on a loan.*

de•fi•ance (dĭ fī′əns) *n.* The act or an example of defying; open resistance to an opposing force or authority: *shook their fists in a gesture of defiance.* —***idiom.*** **in defiance of.** In spite of; contrary to: *We went on the picnic in defiance of bad weather forecasts.*

de•fi•ant (dĭ fī′ənt) *adj.* Marked by defiance; boldly resisting: *The rebels took a defiant stance.* —**de•fi′ant•ly** *adv.*

de•fi•cien•cy (dĭ fĭsh′ən sē) *n., pl.* **de•fi•cien•cies. 1.** The quality or condition of being deficient. **2.** A lack or shortage, especially of something essential to health: *A vitamin deficiency made the patient weak.*

deficiency disease *n.* A disease, such as pellagra or rickets, that results from a diet lacking in one or more vitamins or from an inability of the body to absorb or use certain essential nutrients.

de•fi•cient (dĭ fĭsh′ənt) *adj.* **1.** Lacking an essential quality or element: *a deficient diet.* **2.** Lacking in amount or degree; insufficient: *a deficient education.*

def•i•cit (dĕf′ĭ sĭt) *n.* **1.** Inadequacy or insufficiency. **2.** The amount by which a sum of money falls short of the required or expected amount; a shortage: *The deficit in the club's funds was caused by spending too much money on parties.*

de•file¹ (dĭ fīl′) *tr.v.* **de•filed, de•fil•ing, de•files. 1.** To make filthy or dirty; pollute: *Sewage seeping* *into the lake defiled the water.* **2.** To spoil the sacredness or purity of: *defile a temple.* [First written down before 1400 in Middle English and spelled *defilen*, alteration of *defoulen*, to trample on, abuse, pollute, from Old French *defouler*, to beat, trample down.] **—de•file′ment** *n.*

de•file[2] (dĭ **fīl′**) *intr.v.* **de•filed, de•fil•ing, de•files.** To march in single file or in columns. *—n.* A narrow gorge or pass that requires a group, as of soldiers, to move in file. [First written down in 1685 in Modern English, from French *défiler*, to march in rows : *dé-*, away, off + *file*, line, file.]

de•fine (dĭ **fīn′**) *tr.v.* **de•fined, de•fin•ing, de•fines. 1.** To state the precise meaning of (a word or phrase, for example): *Dictionaries define words.* **2.** To make distinct or clear in outline: *The hills were defined against the bright morning sky.* **3.** To describe; specify distinctly: *The Constitution defines the powers of the President. She defined the properties of the new drug.*

def•i•nite (**dĕf′**ə nĭt) *adj.* **1.** Having distinct limits; restricted: *definite restrictions on using the coupon.* **2.** Indisputable; certain: *It's still not definite whether they are going.* **3.** Clearly defined; precise and exact: *a definite plan; a definite time.* **—def′i•nite•ly** *adv.* **—def′i•nite•ness** *n.*

definite article *n.* A word used to introduce and refer to a particular noun or noun phrase. In English *the* is the definite article. —See Note at **article.**

def•i•ni•tion (dĕf′ə **nĭsh′**ən) *n.* **1.** A statement that explains the meaning of something, such as a word or phrase, as in a dictionary entry. **2.** The act of making clear and distinct: *a definition of one's purposes.* **3.** The state of being closely outlined or determined. **4.** The clarity of an image, as in photography or television: *The mountains in the snapshots had poor definition.*

de•fin•i•tive (dĭ **fĭn′**ĭ tĭv) *adj.* **1.** Serving to settle, decide, or put an end to; conclusive: *a definitive answer; a definitive victory.* **2.** Authoritative and complete: *a definitive biography based on diaries and personal papers.* **—de•fin′i•tive•ly** *adv.* **—de•fin′i•tive•ness** *n.*

de•flate (dĭ **flāt′**) *v.* **de•flat•ed, de•flat•ing, de•flates.** *—tr.* **1.** To release contained air or gas from: *A pin deflated the balloon.* **2.** To reduce or lessen the size or importance of: *The crowd's jeers soon deflated the speaker's confidence.* **3.** To reduce the amount or availability of (currency or credit), causing a decline in prices. *—intr.* To be or become deflated: *As the tire deflated, we pulled off to the side of the road.*

de•fla•tion (dĭ **flā′**shən) *n.* **1.** The act of deflating or the condition of being deflated: *Deflation made the balloon slowly sink toward the ground.* **2.** A general reduction in consumer prices or an increase in the purchasing power of money brought on by a reduction in available currency and credit.

de•flect (dĭ **flĕkt′**) *intr. & tr.v.* **de•flect•ed, de•flect•ing, de•flects.** To turn aside or cause to turn aside; bend or deviate: *Constant interruptions deflected the speaker's thoughts from his main purpose.* [First written down about 1555 in Modern English, from Latin *dēflectere* : *dē-*, away, from + *flectere*, to bend.] **—de•flec′tor** *n.*

de•flec•tion (dĭ **flĕk′**shən) *n.* **1.** The act of deflecting or the condition of being deflected. **2.a.** The movement of something from its normal or zero position. **b.** The amount of this movement.

de•fo•li•ant (dē **fō′**lē ənt) *n.* A chemical sprayed or dusted on plants to make their leaves fall off, used to control weeds in farming, for example.

de•fo•li•ate (dē **fō′**lē āt′) *tr.v.* **de•fo•li•at•ed, de•fo•li•at•ing, de•fo•li•ates.** To cause the leaves of (a plant or tree, for example) to fall off, especially by the use of a chemical dust or spray. **—de•fo′li•a′tion** *n.*

de•for•est (dē **fôr′**ĭst *or* dē **fŏr′**ĭst) *tr.v.* **de•for•est•ed, de•for•est•ing, de•for•ests.** To cut down and clear away the trees or forests from. **—de•for′es•ta′tion** *n.*

de•form (dĭ **fôrm′**) *v.* **de•formed, de•form•ing, de•forms.** *—tr.* **1.** To spoil the natural form of; misshape: *The heat of the fire deformed the candles.* **2.** To spoil the beauty or appearance of; disfigure. *—intr.* To become deformed.

de•for•ma•tion (dē′fôr **mā′**shən *or* dĕf′ər **mā′**shən) *n.* **1.** The act or process of deforming: *the deformation of plastic by heat.* **2.** The condition of being deformed. **3.** A change in form for the worse: *deformations in plants caused by poor growing weather.*

de•formed (dĭ **fôrmd′**) *adj.* Misshapen or distorted in form.

de•for•mi•ty (dĭ **fôr′**mĭ tē) *n., pl.* **de•for•mi•ties. 1.** A condition of being improperly formed. **2.** A deformed person or thing.

de•fraud (dĭ **frôd′**) *tr.v.* **de•fraud•ed, de•fraud•ing, de•frauds.** To take something from by fraud; swindle: *defrauded the prospectors by selling them worthless land claims.*

de•fray (dĭ **frā′**) *tr.v.* **de•frayed, de•fray•ing, de•frays.** To undertake the payment of (a cost or an expense): *Contributions will defray the cost of a political campaign.*

de•frost (dē **frôst′** *or* dē **frŏst′**) *v.* **de•frost•ed, de•frost•ing, de•frosts.** *—tr.* **1.** To remove ice or frost from: *defrost a windshield.* **2.** To cause to thaw. *—intr.* **1.** To become free of ice or frost: *a refrigerator that defrosts quickly.* **2.** To become thawed.

de•frost•er (dē **frô′**stər *or* dē **frŏs′**tər) *n.* A heating device that removes frost or prevents its formation, as on a car windshield.

deft (dĕft) *adj.* **deft•er, deft•est.** Quick and skillful; adroit: *the deft hands of a magician.* [First written down before 1250 in Middle English and spelled *deft*, gentle, humble, variant of *dafte*, foolish.] **—deft′ly** *adv.* **—deft′ness** *n.*

de•funct (dĭ **fŭngkt′**) *adj.* No longer in existence or use; dead: *a defunct business that failed years ago.*

de•fy (dĭ **fī′**) *tr.v.* **de•fied, de•fy•ing, de•fies. 1.** To oppose or resist openly or boldly: *defy the law; defy tradition.* **2.** To be beyond the power of: *That story defies belief.* **3.** To challenge or dare (someone) to do something: *I defy you to find an error in this report.* [First written down before 1300 in Middle English and spelled *defien*, from Old French *desfier* : Latin *dis-*, not + Latin *fīdus*, faithful.]

deg or **deg.** *abbr.* An abbreviation of degree.

de Gaulle (də **gōl′** *or* də **gôl′**), **Charles André Joseph Marie.** 1890–1970. French general and politician who gained popularity during World War II as the leader of Free French forces in exile. He served as president from 1959 to 1969.

de•gen•er•a•cy (dĭ **jĕn′**ər ə sē) *n., pl.* **de•gen•er•a•cies.** The process of degenerating or the state of being degenerate.

de•gen•er•ate (dĭ **jĕn′**ər ĭt) *adj.* **1.** Having declined, as in function or nature, from a former or original state: *a degenerate form of ancient toolmaking.* **2.** Having fallen into an inferior or undesirable state, especially in mental or moral qualities. *—n.* A corrupt, depraved, or vicious person. *—intr. v.* (dĭ **jĕn′**ə rāt′). **de•gen•er•at•ed, de•gen•er•at•ing, de•gen•er•ates. 1.** To sink into a much worse or lower condition, especially functionally or morally; deteriorate: *The discussion degenerated into a nasty argument.* **2.** To decline in quality: *The quality of her work degenerated during her illness.* **—de•gen′er•ate•ly** *adv.*

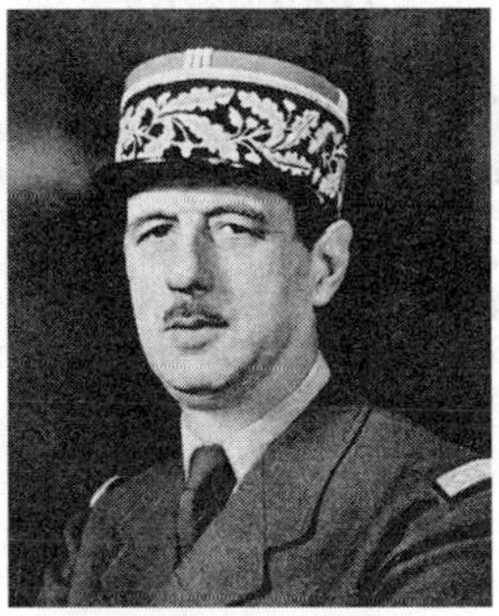

Charles de Gaulle

ă	pat	oi	boy
ā	pay	ou	out
âr	care	ŏŏ	took
ä	father	ōō	boot
ĕ	pet	ŭ	cut
ē	be	ûr	urge
ĭ	pit	th	thin
ī	pie	*th*	this
îr	pier	hw	whoop
ŏ	pot	zh	vision
ō	toe	ə	about
ô	paw	N	*French* bon

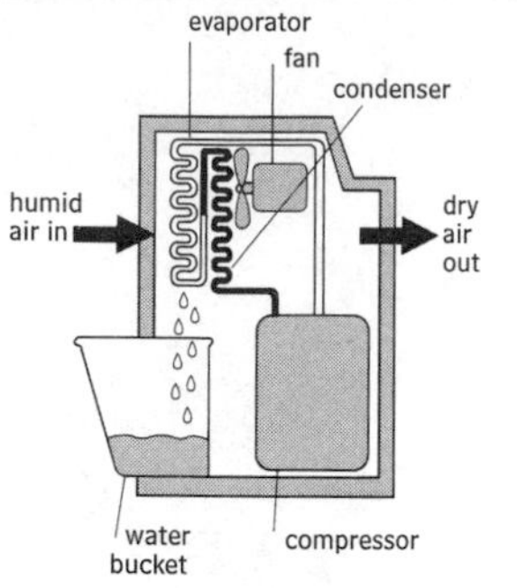

dehumidify

Delaware[2]

The state of **Delaware** takes its name from Delaware Bay and the Delaware River. The river and bay are named after Sir Thomas West, Lord de la Warre (1577–1618), who in 1610 became the first governor of Virginia.

de•gen•er•a•tion (dĭ jĕn′ə **rā′**shən) *n.* **1.** The process of degenerating. **2.** The condition of being degenerate.

de•grad•a•ble (dĭ **grā′**də bəl) *adj.* Capable of being degraded or decomposed by stages.

deg•ra•da•tion (dĕg′rə **dā′**shən) *n.* **1.** The act or process of degrading: *The erosion of rich soil causes the degradation of farmlands.* **2.** The state of being degraded: *the degradation of imprisonment.* **3.** A decline to a lower quality, condition, or level: *Pollution has caused the degradation of our air.*

de•grade (dĭ **grād′**) *tr.v.* **de•grad•ed, de•grad•ing, de•grades. 1.** To reduce in grade, rank, or status; demote: *The officer was degraded to private.* **2.** To lower in dignity; dishonor or disgrace: *I refuse to degrade myself by arguing over trivia.*

de•gree (dĭ **grē′**) *n.* **1.** One of a series of steps in a process, course, or progression. **2.** Relative social position or official rank: *An ambassador is a person of high degree.* **3.** Relative amount or extent: *a high degree of accuracy; various degrees of skill in acting.* **4.** A unit of measurement on a temperature scale: *The temperature of water at freezing is 32 degrees Fahrenheit.* **5.a.** A unit for measuring an angle or an arc of a circle. One degree is $1/360$ of the circumference of a circle. **b.** This unit used to measure latitude or longitude on the earth's surface. **6.a.** In a single algebraic term, the sum of the exponents of all the variables. For example, a^2b is a term of the third degree. **b.** In a polynomial, the degree of the term of highest degree. For example, $x^3 + 2xy + x$ is of the third degree. **7.a.** An academic title awarded by a college or university after completion of a required course of study: *a degree in chemistry.* **b.** A similar title granted as an honorary distinction: *an honorary degree awarded to the Senator.* **8.** In law, classification of a crime according to its seriousness: *Accidental murder is murder in the second degree.* **9.** One of the forms used in the comparison of an adjective or adverb: *The superlative degree of* new *is* newest. ***—idiom.* by degrees.** Little by little; gradually: *improved on the fiddle by degrees.* [First written down about 1200 in Middle English, from Old French : Latin *dē-*, down, off + Latin *gradus*, step.]

de•gree-day (dĭ **grē′**dā′) *n.* A unit used in estimating the amount of fuel or power required for heating buildings. It is equal to the number of degrees by which the average temperature on a given day falls below some standard temperature, usually 65°F (18°C).

de•hu•man•ize (dē **hyōō′**mə nīz′) *tr.v.* **de•hu•man•ized, de•hu•man•iz•ing, de•hu•man•iz•es.** To deprive of human qualities such as individuality or compassion: *Some people think that computers dehumanize our lives.* **—de•hu′man•i•za′tion** (dē hyōō′mə nĭ **zā′**shən) *n.*

de•hu•mid•i•fy (dē′hyōō **mĭd′**ə fī′) *tr.v.* **de•hu•mid•i•fied, de•hu•mid•i•fy•ing, de•hu•mid•i•fies.** To decrease the humidity of: *An air conditioner dehumidifies the air.* **—de′hu•mid′i•fi′er** *n.*

de•hy•drate (dē **hī′**drāt′) *v.* **de•hy•drat•ed, de•hy•drat•ing, de•hy•drates.** *—tr.* To cause to lose water or moisture; make dry: *dehydrate vegetables.* *—intr.* To lose water or moisture; become dry.

de•hy•dra•tion (dē′hī **drā′**shən) *n.* **1.** The act or process of dehydrating. **2.** A diseased condition in which the body or one of its organs or parts loses too much water.

de•ice (dē **īs′**) *tr.v.* **de•iced, de•ic•ing, de•ic•es.** To make or keep free of ice: *deice the wings of an airplane.* **—de•ic′er** *n.*

de•i•fi•ca•tion (dē′ə fĭ **kā′**shən) *n.* **1.** The act or process of deifying: *Deification of a great leader was common in early societies.* **2.** The condition of being deified: *After deification, the queen became the center of the religion.*

de•i•fy (**dē′**ə fī′) *tr.v.* **dei•fied, dei•fy•ing, dei•fies. 1.** To make a god of: *Some religions deify volcanoes and stars.* **2.** To worship or revere as a god: *deify a great leader.*

deign (dān) *v.* **deigned, deign•ing, deigns.** *—intr.* To think it appropriate to one's dignity; condescend to: *The speaker deigned to answer the hecklers' questions.* *—tr.* To condescend to give; vouchsafe: *They didn't deign so much as a nod in our direction.*

de•i•ty (**dē′**ĭ tē) *n., pl.* **de•i•ties. 1.** A god or goddess. **2.** The condition or nature of being a god; divinity: *The ancient Romans believed in the deity of Ceres, goddess of the harvest.* **3. Deity.** God. [First written down about 1300 in Middle English and spelled *deite*, from Late Latin *deitās*, divine nature, from Latin *deus*, god.]

de•ject•ed (dĭ **jĕk′**tĭd) *adj.* Being low in spirits; depressed: *The students felt dejected when the principal announced that the holiday was canceled.* **—de•ject′ed•ly** *adv.* **—de•ject′ed•ness** *n.*

de•jec•tion (dĭ **jĕk′**shən) *n.* The condition of being dejected; low spirits: *our dejection after we got the bad news.* [First written down about 1420 in Middle English and spelled *deieccion*, from Latin *dēicere*, to cast down : *dē-*, down + *iacere*, to throw.]

de ju•re (dē **jŏŏr′**ē) *adv. & adj.* According to law; by right.

Del. *abbr.* An abbreviation of Delaware.

Del•a•ware[1] (**dĕl′**ə wâr′) *n., pl.* **Delaware** or **Del•a•wares. 1.** A member of a Native American people formerly living in the Delaware and Hudson river valleys and now living in various midwestern states. **2.** The Algonquian language of the Delaware. **—Del′a•war′e•an** *adj.*

Del•a•ware[2] (**dĕl′**ə wâr′). A state of the eastern United States on the Atlantic Ocean east of Maryland. It was admitted as the first of the original Thirteen Colonies in 1787. Dover is the capital and Wilmington the largest city. Population, 668,696. —SEE NOTE.

de•lay (dĭ **lā′**) *v.* **de•layed, de•lay•ing, de•lays.** *—tr.* **1.** To put off until a later time; postpone: *We will have to delay dinner an hour.* **2.** To cause to be late or slower than expected or desired: *A traffic jam delayed me in getting home.* *—intr.* To act or move slowly: put off an action or a decision. *—n.* **1.** The act of delaying or the condition of being delayed: *Your order will be filled without delay.* **2.** A period of time during which one is delayed: *a delay of 15 minutes waiting for the bus to arrive.* [First written down before 1300 in Middle English and spelled *deleien*, from Old French *deslaier* : *des-*, off + *laier*, to leave.] **—de•lay′er** *n.*

de•lec•ta•ble (dĭ **lĕk′**tə bəl) *adj.* Greatly pleasing or delicious; enjoyable: *a delectable hot biscuit.*

del•e•gate (**dĕl′**ĭ gāt′ *or* **dĕl′**ĭ gĭt) *n.* **1.** A person chosen to speak and act for another; a representative or an agent: *Delegates to the convention were elected at the meeting.* **2.** A representative of a U.S. territory in the House of Representatives who is entitled to speak but not vote. *—tr.v.* (**dĕl′**ĭ gāt′). **del•e•gat•ed, del•e•gat•ing, del•e•gates. 1.** To authorize and send (another person) as one's representative: *The class delegated six students to serve on the committee.* **2.** To give or entrust to another: *delegate responsibility for feeding the animals.* [First written down before 1475 in Middle English and spelled *delegat*, from Medieval Latin *dēlēgāre*, to dispatch : *dē-*, away + *lēgāre*, to send.]

del•e•ga•tion (dĕl′ĭ **gā′**shən) *n.* **1.** The act of delegating: *delegation of power to an attorney.* **2.** The condition of being delegated; appointment. **3.** A person or persons chosen to represent another or others: *Each state sends a delegation to the convention.*

de•lete (dĭ lēt′) *tr.v.* **de•let•ed, de•let•ing, de•letes.** To remove by striking out or canceling: *delete the last sentence of a paragraph.* [First written down in 1534 in Modern English, from Latin *dēlēre*, to wipe out.]

del•e•te•ri•ous (dĕl′ĭ tîr′ē əs) *adj.* Harmful; injurious: *the deleterious effects of smoking.* **—del′e•te′ri•ous•ly** *adv.* **—del′e•te′ri•ous•ness** *n.*

de•le•tion (dĭ lē′shən) *n.* **1.** The act of deleting. **2.** A part that has been deleted, such as a word, sentence, or paragraph.

delft (dĕlft) *n.* Glazed earthenware of a usually blue-and-white style originally made in the city of Delft in the Netherlands.

Del•hi (dĕl′ē). A city of north-central India south-southeast of Islamabad, Pakistan. The new part of the city (New Delhi) became the capital of India in 1947. Population, 4,884,234.

del•i (dĕl′ē) *n., pl.* **del•is.** *Informal.* A delicatessen.

de•lib•er•ate (dĭ lĭb′ər ĭt) *adj.* **1.** Done or said on purpose; intentional: *a deliberate lie.* **2.** Arising from or marked by careful consideration: *a deliberate choice.* **3.** Not hasty or hurried; slow: *crossed the bridge with deliberate steps.* —*v.* (dĭ lĭb′ə rāt′). **de•lib•er•at•ed, de•lib•er•at•ing, de•lib•er•ates.** —*intr.* **1.** To think carefully and often slowly; reflect: *He deliberated over buying a new car.* **2.** To talk with others in an attempt to reach a decision: *The Senate deliberated throughout the night.* —*tr.* To consider (something) carefully and often slowly. [First written down before 1425 in Middle English, from Latin *dēlīberāre*, to consider, weigh : *dē-*, off + *lībrāre*, to balance (from *lībra*, a balance, scales).] **—de•lib′er•ate•ly** *adv.* **—de•lib′er•ate•ness** *n.*

de•lib•er•a•tion (dĭ lĭb′ə rā′shən) *n.* **1.** The act or process of deliberating. **2. deliberations.** Formal discussion and consideration on all sides of an issue: *The deliberations of Congress are printed in the* Congressional Record. **3.** Thoughtfulness in decision or action: *The mountain climber took each step with deliberation.*

de•lib•er•a•tive (dĭ lĭb′ə rā′tĭv *or* dĭ lĭb′ər ə tĭv) *adj.* Assembled or organized for deliberation or debate: *A legislature is a deliberative body.*

del•i•ca•cy (dĕl′ĭ kə sē) *n., pl.* **del•i•ca•cies. 1.** The quality of being delicate. **2.** A choice food: *Avocados are considered delicacies.* **3.** Fineness of quality, appearance, construction, or execution: *embroidery of great delicacy.* **4.** Frailty of body or health: *The delicacy of small children makes them subject to many diseases.* **5.** Sensitivity of perception, discrimination, or taste. **6.** Sensitivity to the feelings of others; tact: *phrased the apology with delicacy.* **7.** Sensitivity to or undue concern for what is offensive or improper.

del•i•cate (dĕl′ĭ kĭt) *adj.* **1.** Pleasing to the senses, especially in a subtle way: *a delicate pink; a delicate flavor.* **2.** Very fine in quality or appearance; dainty: *delicate lace.* **3.** Frail in health: *The patient is delicate and must get plenty of rest.* **4.** Easily broken or damaged; fragile: *a delicate china figurine.* **5.** Requiring consideration or tactful treatment: *a delicate matter that could embarrass one's friends.* **6.** Fine or soft in touch or skill: *a delicate surgeon.* **7.** Very responsive or sensitive: *a delicate thermometer to measure small variations.* **—del′i•cate•ly** *adv.* **—del′i•cate•ness** *n.*

del•i•ca•tes•sen (dĕl′ĭ kə tĕs′ən) *n.* A store that sells cooked or prepared foods ready for serving, such as cheeses, salads, and smoked meats. [First written down in 1889 in Modern English, from German *Delikatessen*, from French *délicatesse*, delicacy, from Latin *dēlicātus*, pleasing.]

de•li•cious (dĭ lĭsh′əs) *adj.* Very pleasing or agreeable, especially to the senses of taste or smell: *delicious fresh fruit; a delicious supper.* **—de•li′cious•ly** *adv.* **—de•li′cious•ness** *n.*

de•light (dĭ līt′) *n.* **1.** Great pleasure; joy: *The clown's face beamed with delight.* **2.** Something that gives great pleasure or enjoyment: *The birthday party was a delight to the whole family.* —*v.* **de•light•ed, de•light•ing, de•lights.** —*intr.* To take great pleasure or joy: *Most people delight in going to the circus.* —*intr.* To please greatly: *Paris cannot fail to delight the visitor.* [First written down before 1200 in Middle English and spelled *delit*, from Old French *delitier*, to please, charm, from Latin *dēlectāre*.]

de•light•ed (dĭ lī′tĭd) *adj.* Filled with delight: *The delighted winner waved to the crowd.* **—de•light′ed•ly** *adv.*

de•light•ful (dĭ līt′fəl) *adj.* Greatly pleasing: *We had a delightful time at the party.* **—de•light′ful•ly** *adv.* **—de•light′ful•ness** *n.*

De•li•lah (də lī′lə). In the Bible, the lover of Samson who betrayed him by having his hair, the source of his strength, cut off while he slept.

de•lim•it (dĭ lĭm′ĭt) *tr.v.* **de•lim•it•ed, de•lim•it•ing, de•lim•its.** To establish the limits or boundaries of: *delimited the line between our property and theirs.*

de•lin•e•ate (dĭ lĭn′ē āt′) *tr.v.* **de•lin•e•at•ed, de•lin•e•at•ing, de•lin•e•ates. 1.** To draw or trace the outline of: *delineate the state of California on a map.* **2.** To represent in a picture; depict. **3.** To state or describe in words or gestures: *The instructions delineate my duties carefully.*

de•lin•quen•cy (dĭ lĭng′kwən sē) *n., pl.* **de•lin•quen•cies. 1.** Juvenile delinquency. **2.** Failure to do what law or duty requires. **3.** An offense or a misdeed.

de•lin•quent (dĭ lĭng′kwənt) *adj.* **1.** Failing to do what law or duty requires: *The delinquent owners let their dog run free.* **2.** Overdue in payment: *a delinquent account.* —*n.* **1.** A juvenile delinquent. **2.** A person who fails to do what law or duty requires. **—de•lin′quent•ly** *adv.*

de•lir•i•a (dĭ lîr′ē ə) *n.* A plural of **delirium.**

de•lir•i•ous (dĭ lîr′ē əs) *adj.* **1.** Of, suffering from, or characteristic of delirium: *a delirious patient with a high fever.* **2.** Marked by uncontrolled excitement; ecstatic: *delirious happiness.* **—de•lir′i•ous•ly** *adv.* **—de•lir′i•ous•ness** *n.*

de•lir•i•um (dĭ lîr′ē əm) *n., pl.* **de•lir•i•ums** or **de•lir•i•a** (dĭ lîr′ē ə). **1.** A temporary state of mental confusion and clouded consciousness resulting from high fever, poisoning, or shock: *the delirium of patients suffering from malaria.* **2.** A state of uncontrolled excitement or emotion: *the delirium of great success.*

de•liv•er (dĭ lĭv′ər) *v.* **de•liv•ered, de•liv•er•ing, de•liv•ers.** —*tr.* **1.** To take or carry (something) to the proper place or person: *deliver the mail; deliver a package.* **2.** To surrender (a person or thing); hand over: *deliver a criminal to the authorities.* **3.** To throw or hurl; pitch: *Our pitcher delivers a good fastball.* **4.** To strike (a blow): *The logger delivered a blow of the ax that split the log completely.* **5.** To express in words; utter: *deliver a speech to an audience.* **6.a.** To give birth to: *She delivered a baby girl.* **b.** To assist in the birth of: *The midwife delivered the baby.* **7.** To set free, as from misery, peril, or evil: *deliver a hostage from captivity.* —*intr.* **1.** To make deliveries: *Only a few stores deliver nowadays.* **2.** To give birth. [First written down before

delft
Early 18th-century
Rosh Hashanah plate

delicatessen

ă	**pat**	oi	**boy**
ā	**pay**	ou	**out**
âr	**care**	ŏŏ	**took**
ä	**father**	ōō	**boot**
ĕ	**pet**	ŭ	**cut**
ē	**be**	ûr	**urge**
ĭ	**pit**	th	**thin**
ī	**pie**	*th*	**this**
îr	**pier**	hw	**whoop**
ŏ	**pot**	zh	**vision**
ō	**toe**	ə	**about**
ô	**paw**	N	*French* **bon**

delphinium

delta
United States Air Force delta wing aircraft

1200 in Middle English and spelled *deliuren*, from Late Latin *dēlīberāre* : Latin *dē-*, off, away + Latin *līberāre*, to free (from *līber*, free).] —**de•liv′er•er** *n.*

de•liv•er•ance (dĭ lĭv′ər əns *or* dĭ lĭv′rəns) *n.* **1.** The act of delivering or the condition of being delivered. **2.** Rescue from danger or slavery.

de•liv•er•y (dĭ lĭv′ə rē *or* dĭ lĭv′rē) *n., pl.* **de•liv•er•ies. 1.a.** The act of conveying or delivering: *The post office makes deliveries every day but Sunday.* **b.** Something that is delivered: *There is a delivery for you downstairs.* **2.** The act of giving up; surrender: *delivery of a ransom for the king.* **3.** The act or manner of throwing or discharging: *an overhand delivery.* **4.** The act of giving birth: *The woman had a natural delivery of a healthy baby.* **5.** The act or manner of speaking or singing: *The content of his speech was excellent, but his delivery was poor.* **6.** The act of releasing or rescuing: *delivery for all prisoners captured in war.*

dell (dĕl) *n.* A small secluded valley.

Del•phi (dĕl′fī′). An ancient town of central Greece northwest of Athens. It was the site of a famous oracle of Apollo.

Del•phic (dĕl′fĭk) *adj.* **1.** Of or relating to Delphi or the oracle of Apollo at Delphi: *a Delphic prophesy.* **2.** Obscurely prophetic: *ambiguous Delphic words.*

del•phin•i•um (dĕl fĭn′ē əm) *n.* A tall garden plant having long clusters of flowers that are usually blue, but sometimes white or pink.

del•ta (dĕl′tə) *n.* **1.** The fourth letter of the Greek alphabet, written Δ, δ. In English it is represented as *D, d.* **2.** An object resembling a triangle in shape. **3.** A mass of sand, mud, and earth that accumulates at the mouth of a river, usually shaped like a triangle.

de•lude (dĭ lo͞od′) *tr.v.* **de•lud•ed, de•lud•ing, de•ludes.** To deceive the mind or judgment of: *fraudulent ads that delude people into buying worthless products.*

del•uge (dĕl′yo͞oj) *n.* **1.** A great flood or heavy downpour: *The deluge from spring rains flooded fields and roads for miles around.* **2.** Something that overwhelms as if by a great flood: *a deluge of mail in response to the editorial.* **3. Deluge.** In the Bible, the great flood that occurred in the time of Noah. —*tr.v.* **del•uged, del•ug•ing, del•ug•es. 1.** To flood with water. **2.** To inundate with an overwhelming number or amount: *deluged with messages of congratulation.*

de•lu•sion (dĭ lo͞o′zhən) *n.* **1.** The act or process of deluding or the state of being deluded: *the delusion of a swindler's victim.* **2.** A false belief or opinion: *under the delusion that might makes right.*

de•lu•sive (dĭ lo͞o′sĭv) *adj.* Tending to delude; deceptive: *delusive claims about easy cures.* —**de•lu′sive•ly** *adv.*

de luxe also **de•luxe** (dĭ lŭks′ *or* dĭ lo͝oks′) *adj.* Of especially fine quality; elegant; luxurious: *stayed in a deluxe suite as part of the grand prize.* [First written down in 1819 in Modern English, from French : *de*, of + *luxe*, luxury.]

delve (dĕlv) *intr.v.* **delved, delv•ing, delves.** To search deeply and laboriously: *delved into the court records.* —**delv′er** *n.*

Dem. *abbr.* An abbreviation of: **1.** Democrat. **2.** Democratic.

de•mag•net•ize (dē măg′nĭ tīz′) *tr.v.* **de•mag•net•ized, de•mag•net•iz•ing, de•mag•net•iz•es. 1.** To remove magnetic properties from. **2.** To erase (a magnetic tape or disk).

dem•a•gog•ic (dĕm′ə gŏj′ĭk *or* dĕm′ə gŏg′ĭk) *adj.* Of, relating to, or characteristic of a demagogue: *a demagogic leader.*

dem•a•gogue (dĕm′ə gôg′ *or* dĕm′ə gŏg′) *n.* A leader who wins people's favor by appealing to their emotions and prejudices: *The demagogue's speech worked the crowd into a frenzy.* [First written down in 1648 in Modern English, from Greek *dēmagōgos*, popular leader : *dēmos*, people + *agōgos*, leading.]

dem•a•gogu•er•y (dĕm′ə gô′gə rē *or* dĕm′ə gŏg′ə rē) *n.* The practices or emotional style of speech of a demagogue.

dem•a•gog•y (dĕm′ə gŏj′ē *or* dĕm′ə gŏg′ē) *n.* The character or practices of a demagogue.

de•mand (dĭ mănd′) *tr.v.* **de•mand•ed, de•mand•ing, de•mands. 1.** To ask for urgently or insistently: *She demanded that they leave immediately.* **2.** To claim as just or due: *demand repayment of a loan.* **3.** To require as useful, just, proper, or necessary: *A lawyer's work demands skill and concentration.* —*n.* **1.** The act of demanding. **2.** Something demanded: *striking workers making new wage demands.* **3.** A requirement, need, or claim: *This project has made many demands on my time.* **4.** The state of being sought after: *Firewood is in great demand during winter months.* **5.** A desire or readiness to purchase a certain commodity or service: *a demand for heating oil in the winter.* —***idiom.* on demand.** When needed or asked for: *fed the baby on demand.* [First written down before 1382 in Middle English and spelled *demaunden*, from Latin *dēmandāre*, to entrust.] —**de•mand′a•ble** *adj.* —**de•mand′er** *n.*

de•mand•ing (dĭ măn′dĭng) *adj.* Requiring much effort or attention: *a very demanding task.* —**de•mand′ing•ly** *adv.*

de•mar•cate (dĭ mär′kāt′ *or* dē′mär kāt′) *tr.v.* **de•mar•cat•ed, de•mar•cat•ing, de•mar•cates. 1.** To set the boundaries of: *A river demarcates the border between the two states.* **2.** To separate clearly as if by boundaries; distinguish: *demarcate categories of art.*

de•mar•ca•tion (dē′mär kā′shən) *n.* **1.** The setting or marking of boundaries or limits: *the demarcation of fishing rights.* **2.** A separation; a distinction: *There is a fine demarcation between daring and foolishness.*

de•mean[1] (dĭ mēn′) *tr.v.* **de•meaned, de•mean•ing, de•means.** To conduct or behave (oneself) in a particular manner: *The students demeaned themselves calmly during the fire drill.* [First written down before 1300 in Middle English and spelled *demaynen*, from Old French *demener*.]

de•mean[2] (dĭ mēn′) *tr.v.* **de•meaned, de•mean•ing, de•means.** To lower, as in dignity or social standing: *demean oneself by continually asking for favors.* [First written down in 1601 in Modern English, from *mean*, humble.]

de•mean•or (dĭ mē′nər) *n.* The way in which a person behaves; deportment: *As head librarian, she has a demeanor of quiet authority.*

de•ment•ed (dĭ mĕn′tĭd) *adj.* Having a serious mental disorder; insane. —**de•ment′ed•ly** *adv.*

de•mer•it (dĭ mĕr′ĭt) *n.* **1.** A quality or characteristic deserving of blame; a fault: *work that has the demerits of sloppiness and inaccuracy.* **2.** A mark against one's record for a fault or misconduct.

de•mesne (dĭ mān′ *or* dĭ mēn′) *n.* **1.** In medieval times, the lands retained by a feudal lord for his own use. **2.** A realm; a domain.

De•me•ter (dĭ mē′tər) *n.* In Greek mythology, the goddess of the harvest, identified with the Roman Ceres.

demi– *pref.* A prefix that means partly: *demigod.*

dem•i•god (dĕm′ē gŏd′) *n.* A mythological male being, such as a minor god or the offspring of a god and a human being.

dem•i•god•dess (dĕm′ē gŏd′ĭs) *n.* A mythological female being, such as the offspring of a god and a human being.

dem•i•john (dĕm′ē jŏn′) *n.* A large bottle with a narrow neck, usually encased in wickerwork.

de•mil•i•ta•rize (dē mĭl′ĭ tə rīz′) *tr.v.* **de•mil•i•ta•rized, de•mil•i•ta•riz•ing, de•mil•i•ta•riz•es. 1.** To eliminate the military character of. **2.** To ban military forces in: *demilitarize an area.* **—de•mil′i•ta•ri•za′tion** (dē mĭl′ĭ tər ĭ zā′shən) *n.*

de•mise (dĭ mīz′) *n.* **1.** Death. **2.** The end of existence or activity; termination: *The invasion of the barbarians signaled the demise of the empire.*

dem•i•tasse (dĕm′ē tăs′ *or* dĕm′ē täs′) *n.* **1.** A small cup of strong black coffee. **2.** The small cup used to serve this drink.

dem•o (dĕm′ō) *n., pl.* **dem•os.** *Informal.* **1.** A demonstration, as of a product or service. **2.** Something used for demonstration, such as an automobile or a recording that shows a musician's qualities.

de•mo•bil•ize (dē mō′bə līz′) *tr.v.* **de•mo•bil•ized, de•mo•bil•iz•ing, de•mo•bil•iz•es.** To discharge from military service or use: *demobilize an artillery unit.* **—de•mo′bi•li•za′tion** (dē mō′bə lĭ zā′shən) *n.*

de•moc•ra•cy (dĭ mŏk′rə se) *n., pl.* **de•moc•ra•cies. 1.a.** Government by the people, exercised either directly or through representatives. **b.** A political or social unit that has such a government. **2.** The principles of social equality and respect for the individual in a community. [First written down in 1574 in Modern English, from Greek *dēmokratia* : *dēmos*, people + *kratos*, power.]

dem•o•crat (dĕm′ə krăt′) *n.* **1.** A person who advocates democracy. **2. Democrat.** A member of the Democratic Party.

dem•o•crat•ic (dĕm′ə krăt′ĭk) *adj.* **1.** Of, characteristic of, or advocating democracy. **2.** Of or for the people in general; popular: *a democratic movement.* **3. Democratic.** Of, relating to, or characteristic of the Democratic Party. **—dem′o•crat′i•cal•ly** *adv.*

Democratic Party *n.* One of the two major political parties of the United States, dating from 1828.

de•moc•ra•tize (dĭ mŏk′rə tīz′) *tr.v.* **de•moc•ra•tized, de•moc•ra•tiz•ing, de•moc•ra•tiz•es.** To make democratic. **—de•moc′ra•ti•za′tion** (dĭ mŏk′rə tĭ zā′shən) *n.*

dem•o•graph•ic (dĕm′ə grăf′ĭk *or* dē′mə grăf′ĭk) *adj.* Of or relating to demography.

dem•o•graph•ics (dĕm′ə grăf′ĭks *or* dē′mə grăf′ĭks) *n. (used with a plural verb).* The characteristics of human populations, especially when used to identify consumer markets.

de•mog•ra•phy (dĭ mŏg′rə fē) *n.* The study of the characteristics of human populations, such as growth, density, distribution, and birth and death rates.

de•mol•ish (dĭ mŏl′ĭsh) *tr.v.* **de•mol•ished, de•mol•ish•ing, de•mol•ish•es. 1.** To tear down completely; level: *demolish an old building.* **2.** To do away with completely; put an end to: *demolish an argument.* See Synonyms at **ruin.** [First written down about 1570 in Modern English, from Latin *dēmōlīrī* : *dē-*, away, off, un- + *mōlīrī*, to build (from *mōlēs*, mass).]

dem•o•li•tion (dĕm′ə lĭsh′ən *or* dē′mə lĭsh′ən) *n.* The act or process of wrecking or destroying, especially by means of explosives.

de•mon (dē′mən) *n.* **1.** An evil supernatural being; a devil. **2.** A tormenting person, force, or passion. **3.** A person who is very energetic, skillful, or diligent: *was working like a demon.* [First written down before 1200 in Middle English, from Greek *daimōn*, divine power, spirit.]

de•mo•ni•ac (dĭ mō′nē ăk′) *adj.* **1.** Possessed, produced, or influenced by a demon. **2.** Of, resembling, or suggestive of a demon. *—n.* A person who is or seems to be possessed by a demon. **—de′mo•ni′a•cal•ly** (dē′mə nī′ə kə lē) *adv.*

de•mon•ic (dĭ mŏn′ĭk) *adj.* **1.** Befitting a demon; fiendish. **2.** Driven by a spiritual force or genius; inspired.

de•mon•stra•ble (dĭ mŏn′strə bəl) *adj.* Capable of being demonstrated or proved: *a demonstrable truth.*

dem•on•strate (dĕm′ən strāt′) *v.* **dem•on•strat•ed, dem•on•strat•ing, dem•on•strates.** *—tr.* **1.** To show clearly and deliberately; manifest: *She demonstrated her skill as a gymnast.* **2.** To show to be true; prove: *demonstrate one's ability to do the job.* **3.a.** To describe or explain by experiment, practical application, or example: *demonstrate the effect of light on plants.* **b.** To show the use of (a product) to a prospective buyer: *demonstrate a washing machine.* *—intr.* To take part in a public display of opinion: *demonstrated against the new highway.* [First written down in 1552 in Modern English, from Latin *dēmōnstrāre* : *dē-*, completely + *mōnstrāre*, to show.]

dem•on•stra•tion (dĕm′ən strā′shən) *n.* **1.** The act of showing or making evident. **2.** Clear and conclusive proof; evidence. **3.** An explanation or a description, as of a theory or product, carried out by exemplification or practical application: *the demonstration of a theorem in geometry.* **4.** A display or an outward show, as of one's feelings: *a demonstration of solidarity among the workers.* **5.** A public display of group opinion, as by a rally or march.

de•mon•stra•tive (dĭ mŏn′strə tĭv) *adj.* **1.** Serving to manifest or prove. **2.** Openly expressing one's feelings, especially affection: *The demonstrative performer wept when she received the award.* **3.** In grammar, specifying or singling out the person or thing referred to; for example, the word *these* is a demonstrative pronoun in *These are my books* and a demonstrative adjective in *These books are mine.* *—n.* A demonstrative pronoun or adjective. **—de•mon′stra•tive•ly** *adv.* **—de•mon′stra•tive•ness** *n.*

dem•on•stra•tor (dĕm′ən strā′tər) *n.* **1.** A person who demonstrates, such as a participant in a public display of opinion. **2.** An article or a product used in a demonstration.

de•mor•al•ize (dĭ môr′ə līz′ *or* dĭ mŏr′ə līz′) *tr.v.* **de•mor•al•ized, de•mor•al•iz•ing, de•mor•al•iz•es. 1.** To weaken the confidence or morale of; dishearten: *Reading the negative reviews of the movie demoralized its director.* **2.** To weaken the morals of; corrupt: *Offers of favors have demoralized many politicians.* **—de•mor′al•i•za′tion** (dĭ môr′ə lĭ zā′shən *or* dĭ mŏr′ə lĭ zā′shən) *n.*

De•mos•the•nes (dĭ mŏs′thə nēz′). 384–322 B.C. Greek orator who urged the people of Athens to rebel against Philip II of Macedon.

de•mote (dĭ mōt′) *tr.v.* **de•mot•ed, de•mot•ing, de•motes.** To reduce in rank, grade, or status: *demoted from captain to lieutenant.* **—de•mo′tion** *n.*

de•mur (dĭ mûr′) *intr.v.* **de•murred, de•mur•ring, de•murs.** To raise objections; object: *demur at working such late hours.* *—n.* An objection; a demurral.

de•mure (ĭ myŏor′) *adj.* **de•mur•er, de•mur•est. 1.** Reserved and modest in manner or behavior: *a pleasant and demure person.* **2.** Affectedly shy, modest, or reserved: *demure behavior.* **—de•mure′ly** *adv.* **—de•mure′ness** *n.*

de•mur•ral (dĭ mûr′əl) *n.* The act of demurring, especially a mild or polite expression of opposition.

den (dĕn) *n.* **1.** The place where a wild animal lives; a lair: *The fox was safe in its den.* **2.** A hidden or squalid dwelling place: *a den of thieves.* **3.** A secluded room for study or relaxation. **4.** A unit of

demolition
Scollay Square in Boston being demolished in the 1960's

ă	pat	oi	boy
ā	pay	ou	out
âr	care	ŏŏ	took
ä	father	ōō	boot
ĕ	pet	ŭ	cut
ē	be	ûr	urge
ĭ	pit	th	thin
ī	pie	*th*	this
îr	pier	hw	whoop
ŏ	pot	zh	vision
ō	toe	ə	about
ô	paw	N	*French* bon

dendrite

Word History: denouement

The word **denouement**, "solution, resolution, outcome," is easy to remember and understand if you know how we get it. The word is obviously French since it still keeps its French pronunciation even in English. The modern French noun comes from the Old French noun *desnouement*, "an untying," which comes from the verb *desnouer*, "to untie a knot." The Old French prefix *des–* comes from the Latin prefix *dis–*, "apart, the reverse of." The Old French verb *nouer*, "to knot," comes from the Latin verb *nōdāre*, "to knot." *Nōdāre* comes from the noun *nodus*, "a knot," from which we also get **node**, **nodal**, and **nodule**.

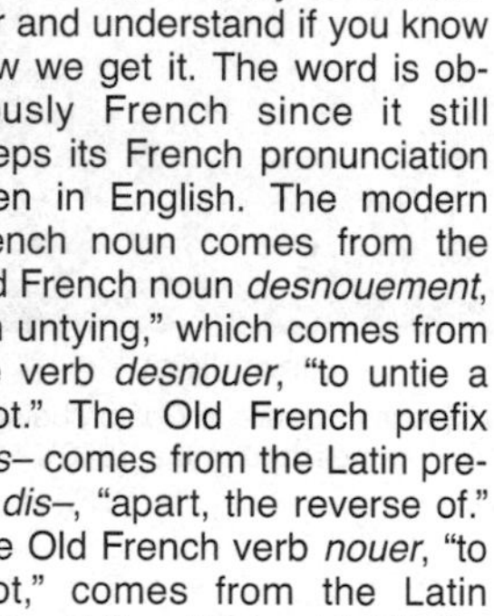

dentin

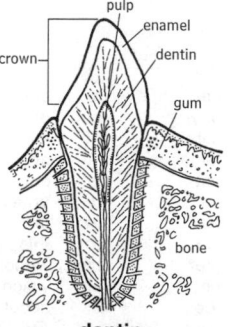

about eight to ten Cub Scouts. [First written down about 725 in Old English and spelled *denn*.]

De•na•li (də nä′lē). Mount McKinley.

de•na•ture (dē nā′chər) *tr.v.* **de•na•tured, de•na•tur•ing, de•na•tures. 1.** To change the nature or natural qualities of. **2.** To change (a substance) so that it is unfit for eating or drinking but is still useful for other purposes. **—de•na′tur•a′tion** *n.*

den•drite (dĕn′drīt′) *n.* **1.** A mineral that crystallizes in another mineral in the form of a branching mark. **2.** A branching part of a nerve cell that receives and transmits cell impulses. [First written down about 1727 in Modern English, from Greek *dendron*, tree.]

de•ni•al (dĭ nī′əl) *n.* **1.** A refusal to comply with or satisfy a request. **2.** A refusal to grant the truth of an accusation or allegation: *The charges of corruption prompted an immediate denial from the mayor.* **3.** A rejection of a doctrine or belief: *denial of a new theory of the origin of the universe.*

de•ni•er (dĭ nī′ər) *n.* A person who denies: *a denier of realities.*

den•i•grate (dĕn′ĭ grāt′) *tr.v.* **den•i•grat•ed, den•i•grat•ing, den•i•grates.** To attack the reputation or character of; speak ill of; defame. [First written down in 1526 in Modern English, from Latin *dēnigrāre*, to blacken, defame, from *niger*, black.] **—den′i•gra′tion** *n.*

den•im (dĕn′ĭm) *n.* **1.** A coarse, twilled, cotton cloth, usually used for jeans, overalls, and work uniforms. **2. denims.** Trousers or another garment made of this cloth. [First written down in 1695 in Modern English, from French *(serge) de Nîmes*, (serge) of Nîmes, after *Nîmes*, a city in France.]

den•i•zen (dĕn′ĭ zən) *n.* A person or an animal that lives in a particular place; an inhabitant: *Lions and jackals are denizens of the African plains.* [First written down in 1419 in Middle English and spelled *densin*, from Late Latin *dēintus*, from within.]

Den•mark (dĕn′märk′). A country of northern Europe north of Germany. It was unified in the 10th century under the Vikings. Copenhagen is the capital and the largest city. Population, 5,112,130.

de•nom•i•nate (dĭ nŏm′ə nāt′) *tr.v.* **de•nom•i•nat•ed, de•nom•i•nat•ing, de•nom•i•nates.** To give a name to; designate.

denominate number *n.* A number used with a unit of measure. In the measures 12 lb., 14¢, and 3 feet, 12, 14, and 3 are denominate numbers.

de•nom•i•na•tion (dĭ nŏm′ə nā′shən) *n.* **1.** An organized group of religious congregations under a common faith and name: *People of several denominations met to worship together.* **2.** One of a series of kinds, values, or sizes, as in a system of currency: *bills of different denominations.* **3.** A name, especially for a group or class of things; a designation.

de•nom•i•na•tion•al (dĭ nŏ′ə nā′shə nəl) *adj.* Related to or under the control of a religious denomination; sectarian.

de•nom•i•na•tor (dĭ nŏm′ə nā′tər) *n.* The number below the line in a fraction that indicates the number of equal parts into which one whole is divided. For example, in the fraction 2⁄7, 7 is the denominator.

de•no•ta•tion (dē′nō tā′shən) *n.* **1.** The act of denoting. **2.** The most specific or direct meaning of a word, in contrast to its figurative or associated meanings.

de•note (dĭ nōt′) *tr.v.* **de•not•ed, de•not•ing, de•notes. 1.** To be a sign of; mark: *The blue areas on the map denote water.* **2.** To signify directly; refer to specifically.

de•noue•ment also **dé•noue•ment** (dā′nōō män′) *n.* The outcome or resolution of the plot of a drama or novel. —See Note.

de•nounce (dĭ nouns′) *tr.v.* **de•nounced, de•nounc•ing, de•nounc•es. 1.** To condemn openly as being evil or reprehensible: *The Senator denounced the policy as wasteful and foolish.* **2.** To accuse formally; inform against: *denounced the swindler to the police.*

dense (dĕns) *adj.* **dens•er, dens•est. 1.** Having relatively high density. **2.** Crowded closely together; compact: *a dense population in the city.* **3.** Difficult to penetrate; thick: *a dense forest; a dense fog.* **4.** Difficult to understand because of complexity or obscurity: *a dense novel.* **5.** Slow to comprehend; thickheaded. [First written down before 1425 in Middle English, from Latin *dēnsus*.] **—dense′ly** *adv.* **—dense′ness** *n.*

den•si•ty (dĕn′sĭ tē) *n., pl.* **den•si•ties. 1.** In physics, the mass per unit of volume of a substance: *Lead has a greater density than water.* **2.** The amount of something in a unit or measure of length, volume, or area: *The population density in New York City is greater than in many other cities.* **3.** Thickness of consistency; impenetrability: *The density of the grass made the tiger invisible.* **4.** Stupidity; dullness.

dent (dĕnt) *n.* **1.** A hollow place in a surface, usually caused by pressure or a blow: *a dent in a garbage can.* **2.** *Informal.* Meaningful progress; headway: *If we work all day we will make a significant dent in this assignment.* —*v.* **dent•ed, dent•ing, dents.** —*tr.* To make a dent in: *When I bumped the guardrail, I dented the car's fender.* —*intr.* To become dented: *Aluminum cans dent easily.*

den•tal (dĕn′tl) *adj.* **1.** Of, relating to, or for the teeth: *a dental drill.* **2.** Of, relating to, or intended for dentistry: *a dental school.*

dental floss *n.* A thread used to remove food particles and plaque from the teeth.

dental hygienist *n.* A person trained to clean and examine the teeth.

den•ti•frice (dĕn′tə frĭs′) *n.* A powder, paste, or liquid used for cleaning the teeth.

den•tin (dĕn′tĭn) or **den•tine** (dĕn′tēn′) *n.* The hard bony part of a tooth that lies beneath the enamel and forms most of the tooth.

den•tist (dĕn′tĭst) *n.* A person who is trained and licensed to practice dentistry.

den•tist•ry (dĕn′tĭ strē) *n.* **1.** The scientific study and treatment of diseases and disorders of the mouth and teeth. **2.** The practice of this science as a profession.

den•ti•tion (dĕn tĭsh′ən) *n.* **1.** The type, number, and arrangement of teeth, as in an animal: *the different dentitions of cats and guinea pigs.* **2.** The process of cutting or growing teeth; teething.

den•ture (dĕn′chər) *n.* A set of artificial teeth.

de•nude (dĭ nōōd′ *or* dĭ nyōōd′) *tr.v.* **de•nud•ed, de•nud•ing, de•nudes.** To remove the covering from; make bare: *Cutting down the trees denuded the landscape.*

de•nun•ci•a•tion (dĭ nŭn′sē ā′shən) *n.* **1.** The act or an instance of denouncing, especially a public condemnation: *a denunciation of graft in government.* **2.** The act of accusing another of a crime before a public prosecutor: *the denunciation of the spy.*

Den•ver (dĕn′vər). The capital and largest city of Colorado, in the north-central part of the state on the South Platte River. It was settled in 1858. Population, 467,610.

de•ny (dĭ nī′) *tr.v.* **de•nied, de•ny•ing, de•nies. 1.** To declare to be untrue; contradict: *deny an accusation.* **2.** To refuse to believe; reject. **3.** To refuse to acknowledge; disavow: *deny a friendship.* **4.** To decline to grant or allow: *We could not deny seed to the hungry birds.* **5.** To restrain (oneself), especially from indulgence in pleasures: *I denied myself a rest and bicycled all the way home.* [First written down before 1325 in Middle English and spelled *denien,* from Latin *dēnegāre,* from *negāre,* to say no.]

de•o•dor•ant (dē ō′dər ənt) *n.* A preparation used to conceal or suppress odors: *a room deodorant; a body deodorant.*

de•o•dor•ize (dē ō′də rīz′) *tr.v.* **de•o•dor•ized, de•o•dor•iz•ing, de•o•dor•iz•es.** To conceal or neutralize the odor of. **—de•o′dor•i•za′tion** (dē ō′dər ĭ **zā′**shən) *n.* **—de•o′dor•iz′er** *n.*

de•ox•i•dize (dē **ŏk′**sĭ dīz′) *tr.v.* **de•ox•i•dized, de•ox•i•diz•ing, de•ox•i•diz•es.** To remove oxygen from (a chemical compound). **—de•ox′i•di•za′tion** (dē ŏk′sĭ dĭ **zā′**shən) *n.* **—de•ox′i•diz′er** *n.*

de•ox•y•ri•bo•nu•cle•ic acid (dē ŏk′sē rī′-bō nōō **klē′**ĭk *or* dē ŏk′sē rī′bō nyōō **klē′**ĭk) *n.* DNA.

de•part (dĭ **pärt′**) *intr.v.* **de•part•ed, de•part•ing, de•parts. 1.** To go away; leave: *depart for work early each morning.* **2.** To vary, as from a regular course; deviate: *depart from our custom of eating out on Saturdays.*

de•part•ed (dĭ **pär′**tĭd) *adj.* **1.** Bygone or past: *the departed days of vacation.* **2.** Dead; deceased. *—n.* **1.** A dead person. **2.** Dead people considered as a group; the dead.

de•part•ment (dĭ **pärt′**mənt) *n.* **1.** A distinct division of an organization, such as a government, company, or college: *the fire department; the personnel department; the English department.* **2.** A section of a department store selling a particular line of merchandise: *the shoe department.*

de•part•men•tal (dē′pärt **mĕn′**tl) *adj.* **1.** Of or relating to a department: *a departmental newsletter.* **2.** Separated into departments: *a departmental organization.*

department store *n.* A large store selling many kinds of goods and services and organized in separate departments.

de•par•ture (dĭ **pär′**chər) *n.* **1.** The act of going away: *Our departure was delayed by a flat tire.* **2.** A deviation or divergence, as from an established rule, plan, or procedure: *Going to bed early was a departure from our usual habit.* **3.** A starting out, as on a trip or a new course of action.

de•pend (dĭ **pĕnd′**) *intr.v.* **de•pend•ed, de•pend•ing, de•pends. 1.** To rely, especially for support or maintenance: *Many people depend on a pension when they retire.* **2.** To place trust or confidence: *You can depend on me to be on time.* **3.** To be determined by; hinge or rest on: *Our plans depend on the weather.* [First written down in 1410 in Middle English and spelled *dependen,* from Latin *dēpendēre* : *dē-,* down, from + *pendēre,* to hang.]

de•pend•a•ble (dĭ **pĕn′**də bəl) *adj.* Trustworthy: *The numbers in a telephone directory are fairly dependable.* **—de•pend′a•bil′i•ty** *n.* **—de•pend′a•bly** *adv.*

de•pend•ence (dĭ **pĕn′**dəns) *n.* **1.** The state of being dependent, as for support. **2.** Reliance; trust: *I place little dependence in the accuracy of this watch.* **3.** The state of being determined, influenced, or controlled by something else: *the dependence of a storekeeper on suppliers.* **4.** A compulsive or chronic need; an addiction.

de•pend•en•cy (dĭ **pĕn′**dən sē) *n., pl.* **de•pend•en•cies. 1.** Dependence. **2.** Something dependent or subordinate. **3.** A territory governed by a state of which it does not form an integral part.

de•pend•ent (dĭ **pĕn′**dənt) *adj.* **1.** Contingent on another: *The outcome is dependent on the voters.* **2.** Subordinate: *a clause dependent on the main clause.* **3.** Relying on or needing the help of another for support: *Plants are dependent upon sunlight.* *—n.* A person who relies on another especially for financial support: *My parents have three dependents including me.* **—de•pend′ent•ly** *adv.*

dependent clause *n.* A clause that cannot stand alone as a full sentence; a subordinate clause. For example, in the sentence *When I saw him he was feeling fine, when I saw him* is a dependent clause.

dependent variable *n.* A mathematical variable whose value is determined by one or more independent variables. For example, in $y = x^2 + 2x$, y is the dependent variable.

de•pict (dĭ **pĭkt′**) *tr.v.* **de•pict•ed, de•pict•ing, de•picts.** To represent in words or pictures; describe or show: *a book depicting life in ancient Rome; a painting that depicts a historical event.* **—de•pic′tion** *n.*

de•pil•a•to•ry (dĭ **pĭl′**ə tôr′ē) *adj.* Able to remove hair: *a depilatory lotion.* *—n., pl.* **de•pil•a•to•ries.** A preparation in the form of a liquid or cream used to remove unwanted body hair.

de•plane (dē **plān′**) *intr.v.* **de•planed, de•plan•ing, de•planes.** To disembark from an airplane.

de•plete (dĭ **plēt′**) *tr.v.* **de•plet•ed, de•plet•ing, de•pletes.** To decrease the fullness of; empty out or use up: *This cold snap has depleted our oil supplies.* [First written down in 1807 in Modern English, from Latin *dēplēre,* to empty : *dē-,* down, away + *plēre,* to fill.] **—de•ple′tion** *n.*

de•plor•a•ble (dĭ **plôr′**ə bəl) *adj.* **1.** Worthy of strong disapproval or reproach: *rude and deplorable behavior.* **2.** Lamentable; woeful: *The kitchen was in a deplorable state after we finished cooking.* **3.** Wretched; bad: *deplorable run-down housing.* **—de•plor′a•bly** *adv.*

de•plore (dĭ **plôr′**) *tr.v.* **de•plored, de•plor•ing, de•plores. 1.** To feel or express strong disapproval of; condemn: *We deplore cruelty to animals.* **2.** To express sorrow or grief over: *The world deplored the loss of the great actor.* [First written down in 1559 in Modern English, from Latin *dēplōrāre,* from *plōrāre,* to wail.]

de•ploy (dĭ **ploi′**) *tr. & intr.v.* **de•ployed, de•ploy•ing, de•ploys. 1.** To position or be in position in readiness for combat: *deploy troops for a battle.* **2.** To distribute or be distributed systematically or strategically: *The ships were deployed along the coast to intercept smugglers.* **—de•ploy′ment** *n.*

de•pop•u•late (dē **pŏp′**yə lāt′) *tr.v.* **de•pop•u•lat•ed, de•pop•u•lat•ing, de•pop•u•lates.** To sharply reduce the population of: *Severe flooding depopulated much of the lowland region.* **—de•pop′u•la′tion** *n.*

de•port (dĭ **pôrt′**) *tr.v.* **de•port•ed, de•port•ing, de•ports. 1.** To behave (oneself) in a certain manner: *Visitors usually deport themselves with quiet respect while in the cathedral.* **2.** To expel from a country; banish: *Government authorities deported the spy.* [First written down in 1474 in Middle English, from Latin *dēportāre,* to carry away : *dē-,* off, away + *portāre,* to carry.]

de•por•ta•tion (dē′pôr **tā′**shən) *n.* **1.** The act or an instance of deporting. **2.** Banishment from a country; expulsion: *The criminal's sentence was a long period of deportation.*

de•port•ment (dĭ **pôrt′**mənt) *n.* A manner of personal conduct; behavior: *She has a very dignified deportment.*

de•pose (dĭ **pōz′**) *tr.v.* **de•posed, de•pos•ing, de•pos•es. 1.** To remove from office or power. **2.** To state or affirm under oath, especially in writing.

de•pos•it (dĭ **pŏz′**ĭt) *tr.v.* **de•pos•it•ed, de•pos•it•ing, de•pos•its. 1.** To put or set down; place: *Please deposit books returned to the library at the front desk.* **2.** To lay down or leave behind by a natural process: *The flooding river deposited mud*

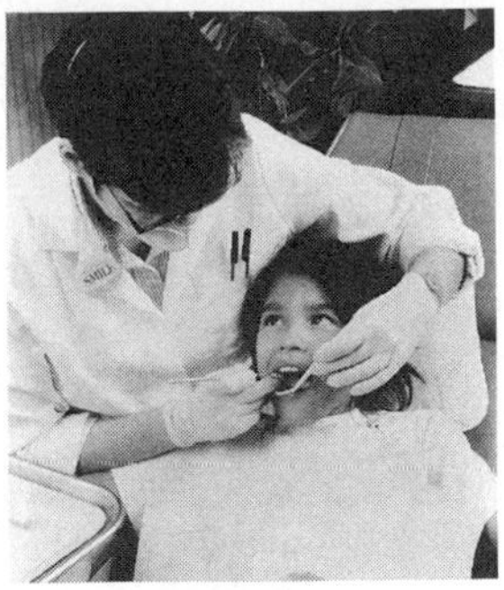

dentist

ă	pat	oi	boy
ā	pay	ou	out
âr	care	ŏŏ	took
ä	father	ōō	boot
ĕ	pet	ŭ	cut
ē	be	ûr	urge
ĭ	pit	th	thin
ī	pie	*th*	this
îr	pier	hw	whoop
ŏ	pot	zh	vision
ō	toe	ə	about
ô	paw	N	*French* bon

derby

and debris in the roads. **3.** To put (money) in a bank or financial account. **4.** To give as partial payment or security: *The store will hold the computer if we deposit half the cost now.* —*n.* **1.** Something, such as money, put in a place for safekeeping. **2.a.** A partial or initial payment of a cost or debt: *left a deposit on the coat.* **b.** An amount of money given as security for an item acquired for temporary use: *a deposit on a rented lawn mower.* **3.a.** Solid material left or laid down by a natural process: *Deposits of mud and sticks choked the stream.* **b.** A mass of naturally occurring mineral material: *deposits of coal in West Virginia.* **—*idiom.* on deposit.** Placed somewhere for safekeeping: *money on deposit in a bank account.* [First written down in 1624 in Modern English, from Latin *dēpositus*, past participle of *dēpōnere* : *dē-*, down + *pōnere*, to put.]

dep•o•si•tion (dĕp′ə **zĭsh′**ən) *n.* **1.** The act of deposing, as from high office. **2.** The act of depositing, especially the laying down of matter by a natural process: *deposition of rock by a retreating glacier.* **3.** Something deposited; a deposit. **4.** Testimony given under oath and usually in written form: *The expert's deposition was read to the court.*

de•pos•i•tor (dĭ **pŏz′**ĭ tər) *n.* A person who deposits money in a bank.

de•pos•i•to•ry (dĭ **pŏz′**ĭ tôr′ē) *n., pl.* **de•pos•i•to•ries.** A place where something is deposited, as for storage or safekeeping.

de•pot (**dē′**pō *or* **dĕp′**ō) *n.* **1.** A railroad or bus station. **2.** A warehouse or storehouse: *a trucking depot for freight.* **3.** A place where military equipment and supplies are stored: *an army depot.*

de•prave (dĭ **prāv′**) *tr.v.* **de•praved, de•prav•ing, de•praves.** To make morally bad; corrupt.

de•praved (dĭ **prāvd′**) *adj.* Morally corrupt; perverted.

de•prav•i•ty (dĭ **prăv′**ĭ tē) *n., pl.* **de•prav•i•ties. 1.** Moral corruption; degradation: *The depravity of the criminals knew no limits.* **2.** A depraved act or condition.

dep•re•cate (**dĕp′**rĭ kāt′) *tr.v.* **de•pre•cat•ed, de•pre•cat•ing, de•pre•cates. 1.** To express disapproval of: *Everyone deprecated the working conditions at the plant.* **2.** To speak of as having little value; belittle: *Don't deprecate the value of an education.* [First written down in 1624 in Modern English, from Latin *dēprecārī*, to ward off by prayer : *dē-*, away, off + *precārī*, to pray.] **—dep′re•ca′tion** *n.*

de•pre•ci•ate (dĭ **prē′**shē āt′) *v.* **de•pre•ci•at•ed, de•pre•ci•at•ing, de•pre•ci•ates.** —*tr.* **1.** To lessen the price or value of: *depreciate the value of an abandoned house.* **2.** To think or speak of as being of little worth; belittle. —*intr.* To go down in price or value: *The longer something is used the more it depreciates.* [First written down in 1464 in Middle English and spelled *depreciaten*, from Latin *dēpretiāre* : *dē-*, down + *pretium*, price.] **—de•pre′ci•a′tor** *n.* **—de•pre′ci•a•to′ry** (dĭ **prē′**shə tôr′ē) *adj.*

de•pre•ci•a•tion (dĭ prē′shē **ā′**shən) *n.* A decrease or loss in value, as because of wear, age, or market conditions.

dep•re•da•tion (dĕp′rĭ **dā′**shən) *n.* **1.** A predatory attack; a raid: *a bear's depredation of our campsite.* **2.** Damage or loss; ravage.

de•press (dĭ **prĕs′**) *tr.v.* **de•pressed, de•press•ing, de•press•es. 1.** To lower in spirits; deject: *The sad news depressed everyone.* **2.** To press down: *depress the brake pedal to stop the car.* **3.a.** To lessen the activity or force of; weaken: *Widespread layoffs have further depressed the economy.* **b.** To lower prices in (a stock market).

de•pres•sant (dĭ **prĕs′**ənt) *adj.* Tending to slow vital body processes; opposite in effect to a stimulant. —*n.* A depressant drug: *Sleeping pills are depressants.*

de•pressed (dĭ **prĕst′**) *adj.* **1.** Low in spirits; dejected: *The news of the accident left me feeling very depressed.* **2.** Sunk below the surrounding region: *the depressed center of a crater.* **3.** Suffering from social and economic hardship, as from poverty and unemployment: *a program of aid for depressed areas of the country.*

de•press•ing (dĭ **prĕs′**ĭng) *adj.* Causing especially emotional depression: *depressing news.*

de•pres•sion (dĭ **prĕsh′**ən) *n.* **1.** The act of depressing or the state of being depressed. **2.** An area that is sunk below its surroundings; a hollow: *Depressions in the sidewalk made it hard to walk on.* **3.** The condition of feeling sad and despondent: *a mood of depression and despair.* **4.** A lowering in amount, degree, or position: *a depression in the temperature.* **5.** A period of drastic decline in an economy: *A depression brings unemployment and hardship to many people.*

dep•ri•va•tion (dĕp′rə **vā′**shən) *n.* **1.** The act or an instance of depriving; loss. **2.** The condition of being deprived.

de•prive (dĭ **prīv′**) *tr.v.* **de•prived, de•priv•ing, de•prives. 1.** To take something away from; divest: *Revolution deprived the government of its power.* **2.** To prevent from having or enjoying; deny: *Heavy snow deprived the deer of food.*

dept. *abbr.* An abbreviation of department.

depth (dĕpth) *n.* **1.** The quality or condition of being deep. **2.** The measure or distance downward, backward, or inward: *Each lot reaches to a depth of about 300 feet from the street.* **3.** A deep part or place. Often used in the plural: *the ocean depths.* **4.** The severest or worst part: *in the depth of despair.* **5.** Intellectual complexity or penetration; profundity: *He wrote poetry and plays of unusual depth.* **6.** Lowness of pitch, as of a voice or a musical tone. **7.** Complete detail; thoroughness: *an interview conducted in great depth.*

depth charge *n.* An explosive charge designed for use underwater, especially one launched from a ship's deck for use against submarines.

depth perception *n.* The ability to see spatial relationships, especially distances, in three dimensions.

dep•u•ta•tion (dĕp′yə **tā′**shən) *n.* A person or group appointed to act for others; a delegation: *A deputation of staff members urged officials to improve conditions at the hospital.*

de•pute (dĭ **pyōōt′**) *tr.v.* **de•put•ed, de•put•ing, de•putes.** To appoint as an agent or a representative: *The President deputes ambassadors to foreign countries.*

dep•u•tize (**dĕp′**yə tīz′) *tr. & intr.v.* **dep•u•tized, dep•u•tiz•ing, dep•u•tiz•es.** To appoint or serve as a deputy.

dep•u•ty (**dĕp′**yə tē) *n., pl.* **dep•u•ties.** A person appointed or empowered to act in place of or for another: *The health officer has several deputies to help enforce environmental laws.* [First written down in 1406 in Middle English and spelled *depute*, from Old French *deputer*, to assign as an agent, from Latin *dēputāre*, to consider, from *putāre*, to ponder.]

de•rail (dē **rāl′**) *intr. & tr.v.* **de•railed, de•rail•ing, de•rails.** To go off or cause to go off the tracks: *The train derailed near Buffalo. A fallen tree on the tracks derailed the express.* **—de•rail′ment** *n.*

de•rail•leur (dĭ **rā′**lər) *n.* A mechanism on a bicycle that moves the pedal chain from one gearwheel to another.

de•range (dĭ **rānj′**) *tr.v.* **de•ranged, de•rang•ing,**

de•rang•es. 1. To upset the arrangement, functioning, or order of: *The flood completely deranged the furniture.* **2.** To unbalance mentally; make insane.

de•range•ment (dĭ **rānj′**mənt) *n.* **1.** Mental imbalance; insanity. **2.** A disturbance in arrangement, function, or order.

der•by (**dûr′**bē) *n., pl.* **der•bies. 1.** Any of various annual horse races, especially for three-year-olds. **2.** A formal race usually allowing anyone to enter: *a motorcycle derby.* **3.** A stiff felt hat with a round crown and a narrow curved brim. [First written down in 1870 in Modern English, after Edward Stanley, 12th Earl of *Derby* (1752–1834), founder of the English Derby.]

Der•by (**där′**bē). A city of central England west of Nottingham. It was settled by the Romans. Population, 216,500.

der•e•lict (**dĕr′**ə lĭkt′) *adj.* **1.** Deserted by an owner; abandoned: *a derelict building crumbling with the years.* **2.** Neglectful; remiss: *derelict in one's duty.* —*n.* **1.** Abandoned property, especially a ship abandoned at sea. **2.** A homeless or jobless person.

der•e•lic•tion (dĕr′ə **lĭk′**shən) *n.* Willful neglect, as of duty or principle.

de•ride (dĭ **rīd′**) *tr.v.* **de•rid•ed, de•rid•ing, de•rides.** To laugh at with contempt or scorn; scoff at; mock: *Many people deride customs they don't understand.*

de•ri•sion (dĭ **rĭzh′**ən) *n.* Contemptuous or jeering laughter; ridicule.

de•ri•sive (dĭ **rī′**sĭv *or* dĭ **rī′**zĭv) *adj.* Expressing ridicule; mocking: *Talk of the plan was silenced by derisive laughter.* **—de•ri′sive•ly** *adv.* **—de•ri′sive•ness** *n.*

der•i•va•tion (dĕr′ə **vā′**shən) *n.* **1.** The act or process of deriving. **2.** Something that is derived; a derivative. **3.** The source from which something is derived; origin: *The polka is a dance of eastern European derivation.* **4.** The historical origin and development of a word; an etymology: *Derivations are given for many of the words in this dictionary.* **5.** The process by which words are formed from existing words or bases, chiefly by the addition of prefixes or suffixes or by changing the form of the word or base.

de•riv•a•tive (dĭ **rĭv′**ə tĭv) *adj.* Resulting from or using derivation: *English has many derivative words.* —*n.* **1.** Something derived: *Gasoline is a derivative of oil.* **2.** A word formed from another by derivation, such as *electricity* from *electric.*

de•rive (dĭ **rīv′**) *v.* **de•rived, de•riv•ing, de•rives.** —*tr.* **1.** To obtain or receive from a source: *derive pleasure from music.* **2.** To trace the origin of (a word). —*intr.* To issue from a source; originate. [First written down about 1385 in Middle English and spelled *deriven,* from Latin *dērīvāre,* draw off, to derive : *dē-,* away, off + *rīvus,* stream.]

der•ma (**dûr′**mə) *n.* The dermis.

der•mal (**dûr′**məl) *adj.* Of or relating to the skin.

der•ma•tol•o•gist (dûr′mə **tŏl′**ə jĭst) *n.* A physician who specializes in dermatology.

der•ma•tol•o•gy (dûr′mə **tŏl′**ə jē) *n.* The medical study of the skin, its diseases, and their treatment.

der•mis (**dûr′**mĭs) *n.* The layer of skin, beneath the epidermis, that contains nerve endings, sweat glands, and blood and lymph vessels; the derma.

der•o•gate (**dĕr′**ə gāt′) *v.* **der•o•gat•ed, der•o•gat•ing, der•o•gates.** —*intr.* To detract; take away: *Cheating will derogate from one's reputation.* —*tr.* To belittle; disparage: *The critic derogated the book.* **—der′o•ga′tion** *n.*

de•rog•a•to•ry (dĭ **rŏg′**ə tôr′ē) *adj.* Tending to detract or make seem inferior; disparaging: *a derogatory remark.* **—de•rog′a•to′ri•ly** *adv.*

der•rick (**dĕr′**ĭk) *n.* **1.** A machine for lifting and moving heavy objects. It consists of a movable boom that is equipped with pulleys and cables and is connected to the base of a stationary vertical beam. **2.** A tall framework that supports the equipment used in drilling an oil well or a similar hole. [First written down in 1727 in Modern English, after *Derick,* 16th-century English hangman.]

der•ring-do (dĕr′ĭng **do͞o′**) *n.* Daring or reckless action: *an acrobat of derring-do.*

der•rin•ger (**dĕr′**ĭn jər) *n.* A small pistol with a short barrel and a large bore. [First written down in 1853 in American English, after Henry *Deringer* (1786–1868), American gunsmith.]

der•vish (**dûr′**vĭsh) *n.* A member of any of various Muslim religious orders that practice self-denial and poverty. Some engage in chanting and whirling dances as acts of ecstatic devotion.

de•sal•i•nize (dē **săl′**ə nīz′) *tr.v.* **de•sal•i•nized, de•sal•i•niz•ing, de•sal•i•niz•es.** To remove salt from (seawater or soil, for example).

des•cant (**dĕs′**kănt′) *n.* An ornamental melody played or sung above a theme. —*intr.v.* (**dĕs′**kănt′ *or* dĕ **skănt′**). **des•cant•ed, des•cant•ing, des•cants.** To talk at length; discourse: *descant on modern science.*

Des•cartes (dā **kärt′**), **René.** 1596–1650. French mathematician and philosopher who is considered the founder of analytic geometry.

de•scend (dĭ **sĕnd′**) *v.* **de•scend•ed, de•scend•ing, de•scends.** —*intr.* **1.** To move from a higher to a lower place; go or come down: *The airplane descended for a landing.* **2.** To slope or incline downward: *The path descended along the side of the cliff.* **3.** To come from an ancestor or ancestry: *Our neighbor descends from New England settlers.* **4.** To pass by inheritance: *The farm descended through several generations to its present owner.* **5.** To lower oneself; stoop: *Both candidates chose not to descend to the level of personal accusations.* **6.** To arrive or attack suddenly or with overwhelming effect: *Our relatives descended on us this weekend.* —*tr.* To move from a higher to a lower part of; go down: *We descended a fire escape.*

de•scen•dant (dĭ **sĕn′**dənt) *n.* A person or an animal descended from specified ancestors.

de•scent (dĭ **sĕnt′**) *n.* **1.** The act or an instance of descending: *the descent from the mountain.* **2.** A downward incline or slope: *Rocks and mud slid down the steep descent.* **3.** Hereditary derivation; lineage: *Many Americans are of a mixed descent.* **4.** A sudden visit or attack; an onslaught; *The descent of the children on the candy store sent the cashier running.*

❑ *These sound alike:* **descent, dissent** (disagreement).

de•scribe (dĭ **skrīb′**) *tr.v.* **de•scribed, de•scrib•ing, de•scribes. 1.** To give an account of in words; tell or write about: *a newspaper report describing the fire; an oral report describing one's experiences.* **2.** To convey an impression of; characterize: *described him as gentle and kind.* **3.** To trace or draw: *Describe a circle with your compass.* [First written down before 1425 in Middle English and spelled *describen,* from Latin *dēscrībere,* to write down : *dē-,* down + *scrībere,* to write.] **—de•scrib′a•ble** *adj.*

de•scrip•tion (dĭ **skrĭp′**shən) *n.* **1.** The act or process of describing: *The writer is so good at description that the characters seem real.* **2.** An account or a statement describing something: *The newspaper carried a description of the plane crash.* **3.** A kind or variety; a sort: *The zoo has animals of every description.*

de•scrip•tive (dĭ **skrĭp′**tĭv) *adj.* Involving or characterized by description; serving to describe:

derrick
For hole-boring equipment

dervish

René Descartes
Portrait by Frans Hals
(1581?–1666)

ă	**pat**	oi	**boy**
ā	**pay**	ou	**out**
âr	**care**	o͝o	**took**
ä	**father**	o͞o	**boot**
ĕ	**pet**	ŭ	**cut**
ē	**be**	ûr	**urge**
ĭ	**pit**	th	**thin**
ī	**pie**	*th*	**this**
îr	**pier**	hw	**whoop**
ŏ	**pot**	zh	**vision**
ō	**toe**	ə	**about**
ô	**paw**	N	*French* **bon**

descriptive words; a descriptive passage in a guidebook. **—de•scrip'tive•ly** *adv.* **—de•scrip'tive•ness** *n.*

de•scry (dĭ skrī') *tr.v.* **de•scried, de•scry•ing, de•scries.** To catch sight of (something difficult to see): *descry a ship through the mist.*

des•e•crate (dĕs'ĭ krāt') *tr.v.* **des•e•crat•ed, des•e•crat•ing, des•e•crates.** To violate the sacredness of; profane. **—des'e•crat'er** *n.* **—des'e•cra'tion** *n.*

de•seg•re•gate (dē sĕg'rĭ gāt') *tr.v.* **de•seg•re•gat•ed, de•seg•re•gat•ing, de•seg•re•gates.** To abolish racial segregation in (a school or workplace, for example). **—de•seg're•ga'tion** *n.*

des•ert[1] (dĕz'ərt) *n.* **1.** A dry barren region, often covered with sand, having little or no vegetation. **2.** An empty or forsaken place; a wasteland: *a cultural desert.* —*adj.* **1.** Of, relating to, characteristic of, or inhabiting a desert: *the desert life of a nomad; a desert animal.* **2.** Barren and uninhabited: *a desert island.* [First written down before 1200 in Middle English, from Late Latin *dēsertum,* from *dēserere,* to abandon.]

de•sert[2] (dĭ zûrt') *n.* Something deserved or merited, especially a punishment. Often used in the plural: *After conviction the thieves received their just deserts.* [First written down about 1300 in Middle English, from Old French *deserte,* from *deservir,* to deserve.]

❑ *These sound alike:* **desert**[2] (punishment), **desert**[3] (abandon), **dessert** (last course of a meal).

de•sert[3] (dĭ zûrt') *v.* **de•sert•ed, de•sert•ing, de•serts.** —*tr.* **1.** To leave empty or alone; abandon: *Miners deserted the valley after the ore ran out.* **2.** To abandon (a military post, for example) in violation of orders or an oath: *The soldiers deserted their posts just before the attack.* —*intr.* To forsake one's duty or post, especially without intending to return. [First written down in 1569 in Modern English, from Late Latin *dēsertāre,* from Latin *dēserere.*] **—de•sert'er** *n.*

❑ *These sound alike:* **desert**[3] (abandon), **desert**[2] (punishment), **dessert** (last course of a meal).

de•ser•tion (dĭ zûr'shən) *n.* **1.** The act or an instance of deserting: *Desertion from the military is considered a serious offense.* **2.** The state of being deserted.

de•serve (dĭ zûrv') *tr.v.* **de•served, de•serv•ing, de•serves.** To be worthy of; merit: *The rescuers deserved a reward for their courageous act.* [First written down about 1225 in Middle English and spelled *deserven,* from Latin *dēservīre,* to serve zealously.]

de•served (dĭ zûrvd) *adj.* Merited or earned: *a richly deserved reward.* **—de•serv'ed•ly** (dĭ zûr'vĭd lē) *adv.*

de•serv•ing (dĭ zûr'vĭng) *adj.* Worthy, as of aid, reward, or praise: *Scholarships are available for deserving students.*

des•ic•cate (dĕs'ĭ kāt') *tr.v.* **des•ic•cat•ed, des•ic•cat•ing, des•ic•cates.** To dry out thoroughly: *A long period of drought desiccated most of the farmland.*

de•sign (dĭ zīn') *v.* **de•signed, de•sign•ing, de•signs.** —*tr.* **1.** To form in the mind; invent: *designed an interesting story for the plot of the novel.* **2.** To draw up plans, sketches, or drawings for; plan or execute in outline: *design a building; design dresses.* **3.** To intend or set apart for a specific purpose: *This room was designed as a workshop.* **4.** To have as a goal or purpose; intend: *That chair was never designed to be used as a ladder.* —*intr.* To make or execute plans: *Engineers design for automobile manufacturers.* —*n.* **1.** A plan, drawing, or sketch, especially a detailed plan showing how something is to be made: *She drew up designs for the new gym.* **2.** The art of creating designs by making patterns, drawings, or sketches: *Engineers and architects are students of design.* **3.** An ornamental pattern: *a design on wallpaper.* **4.** A purpose or an intention: *We left early by design to meet the train.* **5.** A secretive plan or scheme. Often used in the plural: *My sister has designs on my new leather jacket.* [First written down before 1398 in Middle English and spelled *designen,* from Latin *dēsignāre,* to designate, from *signum,* sign.]

des•ig•nate (dĕz'ĭg nāt') *tr.v.* **des•ig•nat•ed, des•ig•nat•ing, des•ig•nates.** **1.** To indicate or specify; point out: *The fence designates the boundary of our property.* **2.** To give a name or title to; characterize: *a period of history designated as the Space Age.* **3.** To select and set aside for a duty, an office, or a purpose; appoint: *We designated two delegates to represent us at the meeting.*

des•ig•nat•ed hitter (dĕz'ĭg nā'tĭd) *n.* In baseball, a player designated at the start of a game to bat instead of the pitcher in the lineup.

des•ig•na•tion (dĕz'ĭg nā'shən) *n.* **1.** The act of designating; a marking or pointing out: *The designation of the trail is clearly shown on the map.* **2.** Appointment or selection, as for a duty or an office. **3.** An identifying name or title: *The designation of the head of a fire department is* Chief.

de•sign•er (dĭ zī'nər) *n.* A person who produces designs: *a book designer; a dress designer.*

de•sign•ing (dĭ zī'nĭng) *adj.* **1.** Conniving; crafty: *fooled by a designing partner.* **2.** Showing or using forethought.

de•sir•a•ble (dĭ zīr'ə bəl) *adj.* Worth wanting, seeking, or doing; good: *a desirable neighborhood; desirable changes in the law.* **—de•sir'a•bil'i•ty, de•sir'a•ble•ness** *n.* **—de•sir'a•bly** *adv.*

de•sire (dĭ zīr') *tr.v.* **de•sired, de•sir•ing, de•sires.** **1.** To wish or long for; want; crave: *The puppy seemed to desire only attention.* **2.** To express a wish for; request: *The customer desired information on the cost of a new stove.* —*n.* **1.** A wish or longing: *She had a lifelong desire to fly airplanes.* **2.** A request or petition: *The citizens made their desires known to the mayor.* **3.** The object of longing: *My desire is a trip to Mexico.* [First written down about 1200 in Middle English and spelled *desiren,* from Latin *dēsīderāre* : *dē-,* from + *sīdus,* star.]

Synonyms: desire, crave, want, wish. These verbs all mean to feel a strong longing for something. *After long years of fighting, both nations desire peace. Tom went to Hollywood craving fame and fortune. Do you want to come along? I wish summer vacation were here.*

---

de•sir•ous (dĭ zīr'əs) *adj.* Having or showing desire; desiring: *desirous of a vacation.*

de•sist (dĭ sĭst' *or* dĭ zĭst') *intr.v.* **de•sist•ed, de•sist•ing, de•sists.** To cease doing something: *Please desist from interrupting others.*

desk (dĕsk) *n.* **1.** A piece of furniture usually having a flat top for writing and often drawers or compartments. **2.** A table, counter, or booth at which a service is offered: *an information desk; a reservation desk.* **3.** A department of an organization in charge of a specific operation: *The shipping desk keeps track of all mail.*

desk•top (dĕsk'tŏp') *n.* The top of a desk. —*adj.* **1.** Designed for use on a desk or table. **2.** Small enough to fit on an individual desk: *a desktop computer.*

desktop publishing *n.* The design and production of publications, such as newsletters and brochures, using a microcomputer with graphics capability.

Des Moines (dĭ moin'). The capital and largest city

of Iowa, in the south-central part of the state west-southwest of Cedar Rapids. It was chosen as state capital in 1857. Population, 193,187.

des•o•late (**dĕs′**ə lĭt) *adj.* **1.** Having few or no inhabitants; deserted: *an abandoned shack on a desolate road.* **2.** Having little or no vegetation; barren: *a desolate stretch of desert land.* **3.** Dreary; dismal: *a desolate climate of rain and fog.* **4.** Bereft of friends or hope; sad and forlorn: *He was desolate when all of his friends went away on vacation.* See Synonyms at **sad.** —*tr.v.* (**dĕs′**ə lāt′). **des•o•lat•ed, des•o•lat•ing, des•o•lates. 1.** To rid or deprive of inhabitants. **2.** To lay waste to: *A fire desolated the forest.* **3.** To make lonely, forlorn, or wretched: *The loss of our old dog desolated us.* **—des′o•late•ly** *adv.*

des•o•la•tion (dĕs′ə **lā′**shən) *n.* **1.** The act or an instance of desolating: *desolation of a field by swarms of locusts.* **2.** The state of being desolate. **3.** Devastation; ruin: *The drought brought desolation to the region.* **4.** Loneliness or abandonment: *the desolation of being all alone in a foreign land.*

de So•to (dĭ **sō′**tō), **Hernando.** 1496?–1542. Spanish explorer who landed in Florida in 1539 and explored much of southern North America, including the Mississippi River.

de•spair (dĭ **spâr′**) *intr.v.* **de•spaired, de•spair•ing, de•spairs.** To lose all hope: *despaired of returning on the early train.* —*n.* **1.** Utter lack of hope: *gave up in despair as their supplies began to run out.* **2.** A person or thing despaired of or causing despair: *The leaky boat was the despair of the crew.* [First written down in 1340 in Middle English and spelled *despairen*, from Latin *dēspērāre* : *dē-*, away, off + *spērāre*, to hope.]

de•spair•ing (dĭ **spâr′**ĭng) *adj.* Marked by or resulting from despair: *despairing glances.* **—de•spair′ing•ly** *adv.*

des•patch (dĭ **spăch′**) *v. & n.* Variant of **dispatch.**

des•per•a•do (dĕs′pə **rä′**dō) *n., pl.* **des•per•a•does** or **des•per•a•dos.** A desperate or bold outlaw.

des•per•ate (**dĕs′**pər ĭt) *adj.* **1.** Having lost all hope; despairing. **2.** Willing to do or try anything as the result of an utter lack of hope: *desperate owners looking for their dog.* **3.** Marked by, arising from, or showing despair: *a desperate look.* **4.** Undertaken as a last resort: *desperate measures to save the business from failure.* **5.** Nearly hopeless; critical: *a desperate illness.* **6.** Suffering or driven by a great need for something: *desperate for medical attention.* **7.** Extremely intense: *in desperate need.* **—des′per•ate•ly** *adv.*

des•per•a•tion (dĕs′pə **rā′**shən) *n.* **1.** The condition of being desperate. **2.** Recklessness resulting from despair.

des•pi•ca•ble (**dĕs′**pĭ kə bəl *or* dĭ **spĭk′**ə bəl) *adj.* Deserving contempt or scorn; hateful. **—des′pi•ca•ble•ness** *n.* **—des′pi•ca•bly** *adv.*

de•spise (dĭ **spīz′**) *tr.v.* **de•spised, de•spis•ing, de•spis•es. 1.** To regard with contempt or scorn: *Everyone despises a traitor.* **2.** To dislike intensely; loathe. [First written down before 1300 in Middle English and spelled *despisen*, from Latin *dēspicere* : *dē-*, down + *specere*, to look.]

de•spite (dĭ **spīt′**) *prep.* In spite of; notwithstanding: *We took a hike despite the rainy skies.*

de•spoil (dĭ **spoil′**) *tr.v.* **de•spoiled, de•spoil•ing, de•spoils.** To rob of possessions; plunder: *The pirates despoiled the coastal town.* **—de•spoil′er** *n.* **—de•spo′li•a′tion** (dĭ spō′lē **ā′**shən) *n.*

de•spon•dent (dĭ **spŏn′**dənt) *adj.* Feeling or expressing despondency; dejected: *became despondent during his long absence from home.* **—de•spon′dence, de•spon′den•cy** *n.* **—de•spon′dent•ly** *adv.*

des•pot (**dĕs′**pət) *n.* **1.** A ruler with absolute power. **2.** A person who wields power oppressively; a tyrant.

des•pot•ic (dĭ **spŏt′**ĭk) *adj.* Ruling with absolute power; tyrannical: *a despotic government.* **—des•pot′i•cal•ly** *adv.*

des•pot•ism (**dĕs′**pə tĭz′əm) *n.* **1.** Rule by or as if by a despot. **2.** The actions of a despot; tyranny: *the despotism of a dictator.* **3.** A government in which a ruler holds absolute power.

des•sert (dĭ **zûrt′**) *n.* The last course of a meal, usually consisting of a sweet dish such as fruit, ice cream, or pastry. [First written down in 1600 in Modern English and spelled *desert*, from Old French *desservir*, to clear the table : *des-*, off, away + *servir*, to serve.]

❑ *These sound alike:* **dessert, desert**[2] (punishment), **desert**[3] (abandon).

des•ti•na•tion (dĕs′tə **nā′**shən) *n.* The place to which a person or thing is going or is sent: *The destination of that package is written on the label.*

des•tine (**dĕs′**tĭn) *tr.v.* **des•tined, des•tin•ing, des•tines. 1.** To determine beforehand; preordain: *a movie destined to become a classic.* **2.** To set aside for a specific use or purpose: *land destined to be a park.*

des•ti•ny (**dĕs′**tə nē) *n., pl.* **des•ti•nies. 1.** The fortune, fate, or lot of a particular person or thing, considered as something inevitable or necessary: *Her destiny was to become a playwright.* **2.** The power believed to determine events in advance: *events shaped by destiny.*

des•ti•tute (**dĕs′**tĭ to͞ot′ *or* **dĕs′**tĭ tyo͞ot′) *adj.* **1.** Having none; void: *a barren land destitute of trees.* **2.** Being without food, shelter, or other means of subsistence; completely impoverished.

des•ti•tu•tion (dĕs′tĭ **to͞o′**shən *or* dĕs′tĭ **tyo͞o′**shən) *n.* A state of being in extreme want of resources or means of subsistence; complete poverty.

de•stroy (dĭ **stroi′**) *tr.v.* **de•stroyed, de•stroy•ing, de•stroys. 1.** To ruin completely; spoil: *The explosion destroyed several homes.* **2.** To put an end to; eliminate: *Hostile action destroyed all hope of a peaceful settlement.* **3.** To put to death; kill: *The rabid raccoon had to be destroyed.* See Synonyms at **ruin.** [First written down before 1200 in Middle English and spelled *destruen*, from Latin *dēstruere* : *dē-*, off, down + *struere*, to pile up.]

de•stroy•er (dĭ **stroi′**ər) *n.* **1.** A person or thing that destroys. **2.** A small, fast, highly maneuverable warship armed with missiles, guns, torpedoes, and depth charges.

de•struct (dĭ **strŭkt′** *or* **dē′**strŭkt′) *n.* The intentional destruction of a rocket or missile after launching. —*v.* **de•struct•ed, de•struct•ing, de•structs.** —*tr.* To destroy (a rocket or missile) after launching. —*intr.* To be destroyed. Used of a rocket or missile.

de•struc•ti•ble (dĭ **strŭk′**tə bəl) *adj.* Breakable or easily destroyed.

de•struc•tion (dĭ **strŭk′**shən) *n.* **1.** The act of destroying: *Destruction of the old house was completed in two days.* **2.** The condition of having been destroyed; ruin: *The tornado caused great destruction.* **3.** The cause or means of destroying: *An unwillingness to discuss problems is the destruction of many a good friendship.*

de•struc•tive (dĭ **strŭk′**tĭv) *adj.* **1.** Causing destruction; ruinous: *a destructive storm.* **2.** Designed or intending to disprove or discredit: *Destructive criticism does not offer helpful recommendations.* **—de•struc′tive•ly** *adv.* **—de•struc′tive•ness** *n.*

destructive distillation *n.* A process by which sub-

Hernando de Soto

destroyer

ă	pat	oi	boy
ā	pay	ou	out
âr	care	o͝o	took
ä	father	o͞o	boot
ĕ	pet	ŭ	cut
ē	be	ûr	urge
ĭ	pit	th	thin
ī	pie	*th*	this
îr	pier	hw	whoop
ŏ	pot	zh	vision
ō	toe	ə	about
ô	paw	N	*French* bon

detector
Metal detector

stances such as wood and coal are heated in the absence of air and broken down to produce useful products such as coke, charcoal, and gases.

des•ul•to•ry (**dĕs′**əl tôr′ē) *adj.* Moving or jumping from one thing to another; disconnected: *The speaker talked in a desultory manner, skipping from one topic to another.* **—des′ul•to′ri•ly** *adv.* **—des′ul•to′ri•ness** *n.*

de•tach (dĭ **tăch′**) *tr.v.* **de•tached, de•tach•ing, de•tach•es. 1.** To separate or unfasten; disconnect: *detach the trailer from the car; detach a plug from a wall socket.* **2.** To send (troops or ships, for example) on a special mission; assign: *detach a ship to take up patrol.*

de•tach•a•ble (dĭ **tăch′**ə bəl) *adj.* Capable of being detached: *The raincoat has a detachable hood.* **—de•tach′a•bil′i•ty** *n.* **—de•tach′a•bly** *adv.*

de•tached (dĭ **tăcht′**) *adj.* **1.** Standing apart; disconnected; separate: *a house with a detached garage.* **2.** Marked by an absence of emotional involvement; impartial: *a detached view of this problem.*

de•tach•ment (dĭ **tăch′**mənt) *n.* **1.** The act or process of separating or disconnecting. **2.** Indifference to or remoteness from the concerns of others; aloofness: *attended to various duties with a bored detachment.* **3.** Absence of prejudice or bias: *A judge must consider legal matters with detachment.* **4.** The dispatch of a military unit for a special duty or mission.

de•tail (dĭ **tāl′** *or* **dē′**tāl′) *n.* **1.** An individual part or item; a particular: *The story has many details about life on a schooner.* **2.** Particulars considered individually and in relation to a whole: *Scientific investigation is concerned with detail.* **3.** A minor or unimportant item or aspect: *Several lawyers are studying the details of the case.* **4.a.** A small group assigned to a special duty, usually a fatigue duty. **b.** The duty assigned: *We have clean-up detail all week.* *—tr.v.* (dĭ **tāl′**). **de•tailed, de•tail•ing, de•tails. 1.** To report or relate minutely or in particulars: *The chief detailed the fire to the reporters.* **2.** To assign to a special duty: *The highway department detailed extra plows to clear the snow.* ***—idiom.*** **in detail.** With attention to particulars; minutely: *The planning board examined the design of the new park in detail.* [First written down in 1603 in Modern English, from Old French *detail,* a piece cut off, from *detaillir,* to cut up : *de-,* off, apart + *tailler,* to cut.]

de•tailed (dĭ **tāld′** *or* **dē′**tāld′) *adj.* Marked by abundant use of detail or thoroughness of treatment: *a detailed drawing; a detailed study of the evidence in the case.*

de•tain (dĭ **tān′**) *tr.v.* **de•tained, de•tain•ing, de•tains. 1.** To keep from going on; delay: *Friends detained me awhile at lunch.* **2.** To keep in custody; confine temporarily: *Police detained several suspects overnight.* [First written down about 1425 in Middle English and spelled *deteinen,* from Latin *dētinēre* : *dē-,* off, back + *tenēre,* to hold.] **—de•tain′ment** *n.*

de•tect (dĭ **tĕkt′**) *tr.v.* **de•tect•ed, de•tect•ing, de•tects.** To discover or determine the existence, presence, or fact of: *detect the smell of smoke; detect errors in a report.* [First written down before 1425 in Middle English and spelled *detecten,* from Latin *dētegere,* to uncover : *dē-,* off, away + *tegere,* to cover.] **—de•tect′a•ble, de•tect′i•ble** *adj.*

de•tec•tion (dĭ **tĕk′**shən) *n.* The act or process of detecting; discovery: *the detection of cracks in a vase.*

de•tec•tive (dĭ **tĕk′**tĭv) *n.* A police officer or private investigator who investigates crimes and obtains evidence or information. *—adj.* **1.** Of or relating to detectives or their work: *a detective story.* **2.** Suited for or used in detection: *detective methods.*

de•tec•tor (dĭ **tĕk′**tər) *n.* A person or thing that detects, especially a mechanical, chemical, or electrical device that indicates the presence of a particular substance or agent: *a metal detector in an airport; a smoke detector on the ceiling.*

dé•tente (dā **tänt′**) *n.* A relaxation or lessening of tensions between nations: *A policy of détente has increased trade.*

de•ten•tion (dĭ **tĕn′**shən) *n.* **1.a.** The act of detaining or holding back. **b.** The state of being detained, especially a period of custody: *The prisoners were held in detention.* **2.** *A forced or punitive delay.*

de•ter (dĭ **tûr′**) *tr.v.* **de•terred, de•ter•ring, de•ters.** To prevent or discourage from doing something, as by means of fear: *The threat of rain deterred us from picnicking.* [First written down in 1579 in Modern English, from Latin *dēterrēre* : *dē-,* away, off + *terrēre,* to frighten.] **—de•ter′ment** *n.*

de•ter•gent (dĭ **tûr′**jənt) *n.* A cleaning agent that increases the ability of water to penetrate fabric and to break down oils and fats. *—adj.* Having cleansing power: *a detergent soap.*

de•te•ri•o•rate (dĭ **tîr′**ē ə rāt′) *tr. & intr.v.* **de•te•ri•o•rat•ed, de•te•ri•o•rat•ing, de•te•ri•o•rates.** To make or become inferior in quality, character, or value; worsen: *Moisture deteriorated the cover of the old book. The railroads deteriorated as air travel grew.* **—de•te′ri•o•ra′tion** *n.*

de•ter•mi•nant (dĭ **tûr′**mə nənt) *adj.* Tending, able, or serving to determine: *a determinant factor in one's thinking.* *—n.* An influencing or determining factor: *A vote is the basic determinant of a democratic government.*

de•ter•mi•na•tion (dĭ tûr′mə **nā′**shən) *n.* **1.** The act of making a decision: *The determination of the judges is final.* **2.** Firmness of purpose; resolve: *The determination of the team helped them to win.* **3.** The act of finding out the quality, quantity, position, or character of something: *the determination of the ship's longitude.*

de•ter•mine (dĭ **tûr′**mĭn) *tr.v.* **de•ter•mined, de•ter•min•ing, de•ter•mines. 1.** To settle or decide firmly and conclusively: *determine whether a statement is true or false.* **2.** To establish definitely, as after consideration, calculation, or investigation: *determine the answer to a math problem.* **3.** To cause (someone) to come to a conclusion or resolution: *The rain determined us to take the bus.* **4.** To be the cause of; regulate: *Climate determines how people in different parts of the world live.* **5.** To limit in scope or extent: *Time will determine how much we can do.* [First written down about 1350 in Middle English and spelled *determinen,* from Latin *dētermināre,* to limit, from *terminus,* boundary.]

de•ter•mined (dĭ **tûr′**mĭnd) *adj.* Marked by or showing determination: *a determined leader; a determined effort.* **—de•ter′mined•ly** *adv.* **—de•ter′mined•ness** *n.*

de•ter•min•er (dĭ **tûr′**mə nər) *n.* A word belonging to a class of noun modifiers that includes articles, demonstrative pronouns, possessive adjectives, and other words such as *any, both,* and *whose.*

de•ter•rence (dĭ **tûr′**əns *or* dĭ **tŭr′**əns) *n.* The act or a means of deterring: *The fence around the yard served as a deterrence to dogs.*

de•ter•rent (dĭ **tûr′**ənt *or* dĭ **tŭr′**ənt) *adj.* Tending to deter. *—n.* A person or thing that deters: *The supervisor's lack of interest was a deterrent to the rest of us to work hard.*

de•test (dĭ **tĕst′**) *tr.v.* **de•test•ed, de•test•ing, de•tests.** To dislike strongly; abhor: *Many people detest snakes.*

de•test•a•ble (dĭ tĕs′tə bəl) *adj.* Inspiring or deserving hatred or scorn: *Lying is a detestable habit.* **—de•test′a•ble•ness** *n.* **—de•test′a•bly** *adv.*

de•tes•ta•tion (dē′tĕ stā′shən) *n.* **1.** Strong dislike or hatred: *detestation of prejudice.* **2.** A person or thing that is detested.

de•throne (dē thrōn′) *tr.v.* **de•throned, de•thron•ing, de•thrones. 1.** To remove from the throne; depose. **2.** To remove from a position of power or prominence. **—de•throne′ment** *n.*

det•o•nate (dĕt′n āt′) *intr. & tr.v.* **det•o•nat•ed, det•o•nat•ing, det•o•nates.** To explode or cause to explode: *The explosives detonated in sequence. The miners detonated a charge of explosives.* **—det′o•na′tion** *n.*

det•o•na•tor (dĕt′n ā′tər) *n.* A device used to set off an explosive charge.

de•tour (dē′to͝or′ *or* dĭ to͝or′) *n.* **1.** A road used temporarily instead of a main route. **2.** A roundabout way or course. *—intr. & tr.v.* **de•toured, de•tour•ing, de•tours.** To go or cause to go by a roundabout way: *Police detoured traffic because of heavy flooding.* [First written down in 1738 in Modern English, from Old French *destor*, from *destorner*, to turn away : *des-*, away + *torner*, to turn.]

de•tox•i•fi•ca•tion (dē tŏk′sə fĭ kā′shən) *n.* The act or process of counteracting or removing poison or other harmful substances: *Some dumps need detoxification.*

de•tox•i•fy (dē tŏk′sə fī′) *tr.v.* **de•tox•i•fied, de•tox•i•fy•ing, de•tox•i•fies. 1.** To counteract or destroy the toxic properties of. **2.** To remove poison or other harmful substances from.

de•tract (dĭ trăkt′) *v.* **de•tract•ed, de•tract•ing, de•tracts.** *—tr.* To draw or take away; divert. *—intr.* To undergo reduction in value, importance, or quality: *Drab curtains detract from the beauty of the room.* **—de•trac′tion** *n.* **—de•trac′tor** *n.* —See Note.

det•ri•ment (dĕt′rə mənt) *n.* **1.** Damage, harm, or loss: *was out sick a week without detriment to his grades.* **2.** Something that causes damage, harm, or loss: *Oil spills are a serious detriment to coastal wildlife.*

det•ri•men•tal (dĕt′rə mĕn′tl) *adj.* Causing damage or harm; injurious: *Being overweight is detrimental to one's health.* **—det′ri•men′tal•ly** *adv.*

de•tri•tus (dĭ trī′təs) *n., pl.* **detritus.** Loose fragments, such as sand or gravel, that have been worn away from rock.

De•troit (dĭ troit′). A city of southeast Michigan opposite Windsor, Ontario, on the **Detroit River,** about 32 miles (51 kilometers) long. It was founded in 1701. Population, 1,027,974.

deuce[1] (do͞os *or* dyo͞os) *n.* **1.** A playing card or side of a die bearing two spots; a two. **2.** In tennis, a tied score when a game can be won by winning two successive points. [First written down in 1475 in Middle English and spelled *deus*, from Latin *duōs*, two.]

deuce[2] (do͞os *or* dyo͞os) *Informal. n.* The devil. [First written down in 1651 in Modern English, probably from Low German *duus*, a throw of two in dice games, bad luck, ultimately from Latin *duōs*, two.]

deu•te•ri•um (do͞o tîr′ē əm *or* dyo͞o tîr′ē əm) *n.* An isotope of hydrogen whose atoms have about twice the mass of ordinary hydrogen. Deuterium occurs in heavy water.

Deu•ter•on•o•my (do͞o′tə rŏn′ə mē *or* dyo͞o′tə rŏn′ə mē) *n.* The fifth book of the Bible, which includes many Jewish laws.

deut•sche mark (doi′chə) *n.* The basic monetary unit of Germany.

De Va•le•ra (dĕv′ə lĕr′ə *or* dĕv′ə lîr′ə), **Eamon.** 1882–1975. American-born Irish political leader who was the first president of the Republic of Ireland (1959–1973).

de•val•ue (dē văl′yo͞o) *tr.v.* **de•val•ued, de•val•u•ing, de•val•ues. 1.** To lessen or cancel the value of: *The scientist never devalued the contributions of his assistants.* **2.** To lower the exchange value of (a currency). **—de•val′u•a′tion** *n.*

dev•as•tate (dĕv′ə stāt′) *tr.v.* **dev•as•tat•ed, dev•as•tat•ing, dev•as•tates. 1.** To lay waste; destroy: *The storms devastated much of the countryside.* **2.** To overwhelm; confound: *Layoffs devastated the old mill towns.* **—dev′as•tat′ing•ly** *adv.* **—dev′as•ta′tor** *n.*

dev•as•ta•tion (dĕv′ə stā′shən) *n.* The act of devastating or the condition of being devastated; ruin; destruction: *Dikes saved the land from devastation by flooding.*

de•vel•op (dĭ vĕl′əp) *v.* **de•vel•oped, de•vel•op•ing, de•vel•ops.** *—tr.* **1.** To aid in the growth of; strengthen: *develop muscle by exercising.* **2.** To increase the intricacy, complexity, or quality of: *develop one's vocabulary from reading.* **3.a.** To bring into being gradually: *develop a new industry.* **b.** To set forth or clarify by degrees: *develop a plan; develop a story.* **4.a.** To come to have gradually: *develop a taste for citrus fruits.* **b.** To become affected with; contract: *She developed a rash.* **5.** To cause (a tract of land) to serve a particular purpose. **6.** To treat (photographic film) with chemicals to make images recorded on it appear. *—intr.* **1.** To grow by degrees into a more advanced or mature state: *A student's mind develops with education and time.* **2.** To increase or expand: *The town developed into a city over the years.* **3.** To come gradually into existence or activity: *A friendship soon developed between the two.* **4.** To come gradually to light; be disclosed: *I'll give you the details as they develop.* [First written down in 1656 in Modern English, from Old French *desveloper* : *des-*, off, away + *voloper*, to wrap, roll.]

de•vel•op•er (dĭ vĕl′ə pər) *n.* **1.** A person or thing that develops, especially a person who develops real estate by preparing a site for residential or commercial use. **2.** A chemical used in developing a photographic film or similar material.

de•vel•op•ing (dĭ vĕl′ə pĭng) *adj.* Having a relatively low level of economic and industrial development: *a developing nation.*

de•vel•op•ment (dĭ vĕl′əp mənt) *n.* **1.** The act of developing: *The development of a vaccine requires much research.* **2.** The state of being developed: *The plans for the project are in development.* **3.** A significant event, happening, or change: *The newspaper related the latest developments in the peace talks.* **4.** A group of dwellings built by the same contractor: *The development includes homes and a shopping center.* **—de•vel′op•men′tal** *adj.*

de•vi•ant (dē′vē ənt) *adj.* Differing from a norm or from accepted social standards: *deviant behavior.* *—n.* A person whose attitude, character, or behavior differ from accepted social standards.

de•vi•ate (dē′vē āt′) *intr.v.* **de•vi•at•ed, de•vi•at•ing, de•vi•ates.** To depart, as from a norm or purpose; stray: *Their plans deviated from what we originally agreed to do.* *—n.* (dē′vē ĭt). A deviant. [First written down before 1633 in Modern English, from Late Latin *dēviāre* : Latin *dē-*, away, off + Latin *via*, road, track.]

de•vi•a•tion (dē′vē ā′shən) *n.* **1.** The act of deviating or turning aside. **2.** An abnormality; a departure: *Staying up late is a deviation from our routine.*

de•vice (dĭ vīs′) *n.* **1.** A contrivance or an invention designed or used for a particular purpose; a mechanism: *An eggbeater is a handy device.* **2.** A plan,

Word Building: detract

The word root *–tract–* in English words comes from the past participle *tractus* of the Latin verb *trahere,* "to pull, drag, draw." Thus **detract** means "to drag down" (using the prefix *dē–*, "down"); **extract** is literally "to pull out" (*ex–*, "out, out of"); **protract** means "to drag forward" (*prō–*, "forward, in front"); **attract** is literally "to draw toward" (*at–*, a form of *ad–*, "to, toward"); and **retract** means "to draw back" (*re–*, "back"). **Tractor** and **traction** come from Latin words meaning "puller" and "pulling."

Eamon De Valera

ă	pat	oi	boy
ā	pay	ou	out
âr	care	o͝o	took
ä	father	o͞o	boot
ĕ	pet	ŭ	cut
ē	be	ûr	urge
ĭ	pit	th	thin
ī	pie	*th*	this
îr	pier	hw	whoop
ŏ	pot	zh	vision
ō	toe	ə	about
ô	paw	N	*French* bon

dew

diadem

Worn by Queen Victoria

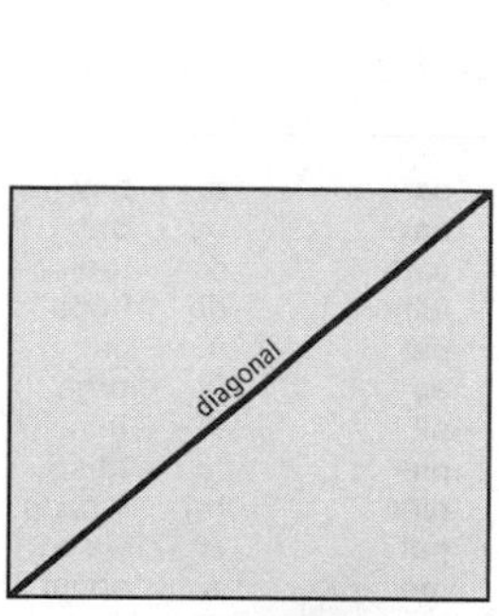

diagonal

scheme, or trick: *used crying and other devices to get his way.* **3.** A decorative design, figure, or pattern, as one used in embroidery. —***idiom.*** **leave to (one's) own devices.** To allow to do as one pleases: *left the child to her own devices for an hour.*

dev•il (dĕv′əl) *n.* **1.** Often **Devil.** In many religions, the personified spirit of evil who is often also the ruler of Hell and the enemy of God. **2.** An evil spirit; a demon. **3.** A wicked or bad-tempered person. **4.** A person: *The baby is a handsome devil.* **5.** A person who is daring, clever, or full of mischief. **6.** A severe reproach or an expression of anger: *gave me the devil for being late.* —*tr.v.* **dev•iled, dev•il•ing, dev•ils** or **dev•illed, dev•il•ling, dev•ils. 1.** To season (food) heavily, as with mustard: *devil eggs.* **2.** To annoy, torment, or harass: *deviled me about my clothes.* [First written down about 725 in Old English and spelled *dēofol,* from Greek *diabolos,* slanderer, from *diaballein,* to slander.]

dev•il•fish (dĕv′əl fĭsh′) *n.* **1.** The manta. **2.** The octopus.

dev•il•ish (dĕv′ə lĭsh) *adj.* **1.** Of, resembling, or characteristic of a devil; evil: **2.** Mischievous, teasing, or annoying: *That devilish kitten unrolled a ball of string.* **—dev′il•ish•ly** *adv.* **—dev′il•ish•ness** *n.*

dev•il-may-care (dĕv′əl mā kâr′) *adj.* Very careless; reckless.

dev•il•ment (dĕv′əl mənt) *n.* Devilish behavior; mischief.

dev•il•ry *n.* (dĕv′əl rē). Variant of **deviltry.**

dev•il's advocate (dĕv′əlz) *n.* A person who argues against a position simply for the sake of argument or to test the validity of the position.

dev•il's food cake *n.* A rich chocolate cake.

dev•il•try (dĕv′əl trē) or **dev•il•ry** (dĕv′əl rē) *n., pl.* **dev•il•tries** or **dev•il•ries. 1.** Reckless mischief: *dangerous deviltry.* **2.** Extreme cruelty; wickedness.

de•vi•ous (dē′vē əs) *adj.* **1.** Not straightforward; shifty: *a devious character.* **2.** Veering from the correct or accepted way: *They achieved success by devious means.* **3.** Away from the main or direct road or course: *We took a devious route to avoid the traffic.* **—de′vi•ous•ly** *adv.* **—de′vi•ous•ness** *n.*

de•vise (dĭ vīz′) *tr.v.* **de•vised, de•vis•ing, de•vis•es.** To form or arrange in the mind; plan: *devise a way to keep the window open with a stick.* **—de•vis′er** *n.*

de•void (dĭ void′) *adj.* Completely lacking; destitute or empty: *a person devoid of humor.*

de•volve (dĭ vŏlv′) *intr. & tr.v.* **de•volved, de•volv•ing, de•volves.** To pass or be passed on to another who acts as a substitute or delegate; transfer: *During his illness various duties devolved upon me.*

De•vo•ni•an (dĭ vō′nē ən) *adj.* Of, belonging to, or being the geologic time of the fourth period of the Paleozoic Era, following the Silurian and preceding the Carboniferous. During the Devonian, the first forests and amphibians appeared. See table at **geologic time.** —*n.* The Devonian Period or its series of rocks.

de•vote (dĭ vōt′) *tr.v.* **de•vot•ed, de•vot•ing, de•votes. 1.** To give or apply (one's time, attention, or self) entirely to a specified activity, cause, or person: *a musician who devotes time to helping students.* **2.** To set apart for a specific purpose; dedicate: *devote a few hours to working on the vegetable garden.* [First written down in 1586 in Modern English, from Latin *dēvovēre,* to vow.]

de•vot•ed (dĭ vō′tĭd) *adj.* **1.** Feeling or expressing strong affection or attachment: *a devoted friend.* **2.** Dedicated: *a devoted scientist.* **—de•vot′ed•ly** *adv.* **—de•vot′ed•ness** *n.*

dev•o•tee (dĕv′ə tē′) *n.* A person who is ardently devoted to something; a fan: *A devotee of fishing will be out in all kinds of weather.*

de•vo•tion (dĭ vō′shən) *n.* **1.** Ardent affection and dedication, as to a person: *the devotion of a parent.* **2.** An act of religious observance or prayer, especially when private. Often used in the plural. **3.** The act of devoting or the state of being devoted: *devotion of time to teaching English to immigrants.*

de•vo•tion•al (dĭ vō′shə nəl) *adj.* Of, relating to, or used in devotion, especially religious devotion. **—de•vo′tion•al•ly** *adv.*

de•vour (dĭ vour′) *tr.v.* **de•voured, de•vour•ing, de•vours. 1.** To eat up greedily: *The hungry campers devoured their dinner.* **2.** To destroy or consume: *Flames devoured the building.* **3.** To take in greedily: *devour an exciting mystery story.* [First written down before 1333 in Middle English and spelled *devouren,* from Latin *dēvorāre* : *dē-,* completely + *vorāre,* to swallow.] **—de•vour′ing•ly** *adv.*

de•vout (dĭ vout′) *adj.* **de•vout•er, de•vout•est. 1.** Devoted to religion or to religious obligations: *a devout monk.* **2.** Sincere; earnest: *a devout wish for peace.* **—de•vout′ly** *adv.* **—de•vout′ness** *n.*

dew (do͞o *or* dyo͞o) *n.* **1.** Water droplets condensed from the air, mostly at night, onto cool surfaces. **2.** Something moist, fresh, renewing, or pure. **3.** Moisture appearing in small drops, as tears or perspiration. —*tr.v.* **dewed, dew•ing, dews.** To wet with or as if with dew.

❑ *These sound alike:* **dew, do**[1] (perform), **due** (owing).

dew•ber•ry (do͞o′bĕr′ē *or* dyo͞o′bĕr′ē) *n.* **1.** A black berry from any of several low-growing shrubs related to the blackberry. **2.** A shrub that bears such fruit.

dew•claw (do͞o′klô′ *or* dyo͞o′klô′) *n.* **1.** A small useless inner claw or toe in some dogs and other animals, that does not reach the ground in walking. **2.** The false hoof of deer, hogs, and other hoofed mammals, consisting of two toes.

dew•drop (do͞o′drŏp′ *or* dyo͞o′drŏp′) *n.* A drop of dew.

Dew•ey decimal system (do͞o′ē *or* dyo͞o′ē) *n.* A system for classifying library books and magazines into subject categories corresponding to three-digit numerals. Each category is subdivided by the addition of decimals to the number. [First written down in 1879 in Modern English, after Melvil *Dewey* (1851–1931), American librarian.]

dew•lap (do͞o′lăp′ *or* dyo͞o′lăp′) *n.* A loose fold of skin hanging from the neck of certain animals, such as some dogs or cattle.

dew point *n.* The temperature at which air becomes saturated with water vapor and dew forms.

dew•y (do͞o′ē *or* dyo͞o′ē) *adj.* **dew•i•er, dew•i•est. 1.** Moist with or as if with dew: *dewy fields of early morning.* **2.** Suggesting dew, as in freshness or purity. **—dew′i•ness** *n.*

dex•ter•i•ty (dĕk stĕr′ĭ tē) *n.* Skill or grace in using the hands, body, or mind.

dex•ter•ous (dĕk′stər əs *or* dĕk′strəs) also **dex•trous** (dĕk′strəs) *adj.* Skillful in the use of the hands or mind: *a dexterous carpenter.* [First written down in 1597 in Modern English, from Latin *dexter,* on the right, skillful.] **—dex′ter•ous•ly** *adv.* **—dex′ter•ous•ness** *n.*

dex•trose (dĕk′strōs′) *n.* A sugar found in plant and animal tissues and also derived from starch. It is the most common form of glucose and has the chemical formula $C_6H_{12}O_6$.

Dha•ka (dăk′ə *or* dä′kə). Dacca.

di– *pref.* A prefix that means two, twice, or double: *dicotyledon; dioxide.*

dia– or **di–** *pref.* A prefix that means through or across: *diaphanous; diagonal.*

di•a•be•tes (dī′ə **bē′**tĭs *or* dī′ə **bē′**tēz) *n.* A metabolic disorder in which too little insulin is produced by the pancreas, resulting in an inability of the body to control the level of sugar in the blood, causing excessive passage of urine and persistent thirst. It is fatal unless treated.

di•a•bet•ic (dī′ə **bĕt′**ĭk) *adj.* Of, relating to, having, or resulting from diabetes. —*n.* A person having diabetes.

di•a•bol•i•cal (dī′ə **bŏl′**ĭ kəl) also **di•a•bol•ic** (dī′ə **bŏl′**ĭ k) *adj.* Of, concerning, or characteristic of the devil; satanic. **—di′a•bol′i•cal•ly** *adv.* **—di′a•bol′i•cal•ness** *n.*

di•a•crit•ic (dī′ə **krĭt′**ĭk) *n.* A diacritical mark.

di•a•crit•i•cal mark (dī′ə **krĭt′**ĭ kəl) *n.* A mark, such as a cedilla or an acute accent, added to a letter to indicate a certain pronunciation or stress.

di•a•dem (**dī′**ə dĕm′) *n.* A crown worn as a sign of royalty.

di•aer•e•sis (dī **ĕr′**ĭ sĭs) *n.* Variant of **dieresis.**

di•ag•nose (**dī′**əg nōs′ *or* **dī′**əg nōz′) *tr.v.* **di•ag•nosed, di•ag•nos•ing, di•ag•nos•es.** To make a careful examination of; identify and study: *Doctors diagnose disease, and mechanics diagnose car trouble.*

di•ag•no•sis (dī′əg **nō′**sĭs) *n., pl.* **di•ag•no•ses** (dī′əg **nō′**sēz). **1.** The act or process of identifying or determining the nature and cause of a disease or injury by examining a patient, analyzing a patient's medical history, and reviewing the results of laboratory tests. **2.a.** A close analysis of the nature of something. **b.** The conclusions reached by such an analysis: *When the computer broke down, the diagnosis was a short circuit.* [First written down in 1681 in Modern English, from Greek *diagnōsis*, discernment, from *diagignōskein*, to distinguish : *dia-*, apart + *gignōskein*, to come to know, discern.]

di•ag•nos•tic (dī′əg **nŏs′**tĭk) *adj.* Of, relating to, or used in diagnosis: *X-ray machines and stethoscopes are diagnostic tools of medicine.* **—di′ag•nos′ti•cal•ly** *adv.*

di•ag•nos•ti•cian (dī′əg nŏ **stĭsh′**ən) *n.* A person, especially a physician, who specializes in making medical diagnoses.

di•ag•o•nal (dī **ăg′**ə nəl) *adj.* **1.a.** Connecting two nonadjacent corners in a polygon: *a diagonal line sloping down across a square.* **b.** Connecting two nonadjacent corners in a polyhedron that do not lie in the same face. **2.** Slanting or oblique: *the diagonal stripes on a tie.* —*n.* **1.** A diagonal line segment. **2.** Something having a sloping or slanting direction, as a row, course, or part: *The path across the field was a diagonal.* [First written down in 1563 in Modern English, from Greek *diagōnios*, from angle to angle : *dia-*, across, through + *gōnia*, angle, corner.] **—di•ag′o•nal•ly** *adv.*

di•a•gram (**dī′**ə grăm′) *n.* A plan, drawing, or sketch that shows how something works or indicates how parts are put together: *A diagram of the apartment shows where each room is.* —*tr.v.* **di•a•grammed, di•a•gram•ming, di•a•grams** or **di•a•gramed, di•a•gram•ing, di•a•grams.** To show or represent by or as if by a diagram: *diagram a floor plan.*

di•a•gram•mat•ic (dī′ə grə **măt′**ĭk) *adj.* **1.** In the form of a diagram: *A diagrammatic plan of the tunnel explains how it will be built.* **2.** In outline form only; sketchy: *an essay in diagrammatic form.* **—di′a•gram•mat′i•cal•ly** *adv.*

di•al (**dī′**əl) *n.* **1.** A graduated surface or face on which a measurement, such as speed, is indicated by a moving needle or pointer. **2.** A sundial. **3.** The control that selects the station to which a radio or television is tuned. **4.** A movable disk on a telephone with numbers and letters, used to signal the number to which a call is made. —*v.* **di•aled, di•al•ing, di•als** or **di•alled, di•al•ling, di•als.** —*tr.* **1.** To operate by using a dial, as in a combination lock: *We dialed the combination and the lock opened.* **2.** To control or select by means of a dial. **3.** To call (a party) on a telephone. —*intr.* To use a dial, as on a telephone: *dial until you get an answer.* [First written down before 1420 in Middle English, sundial, clock, from Medieval Latin *diālis*, daily from *diēs*, day.]

di•a•lect (**dī′**ə lĕkt′) *n.* A variety of a language spoken in a particular region or by a particular group of people: *Cockney is a dialect of English.* —See Note.

di•a•lec•tal (dī′ə **lĕk′**təl) *adj.* Of or relating to a dialect: *dialectal speech.*

di•a•logue or **di•a•log** (**dī′**ə lôg′ *or* **dī′**ə lŏg′) *n.* **1.** A conversation between two or more people: *a friendly dialogue.* **2.** The words spoken by the characters of a play or story: *The dialogue of the comedy was very witty.* **3.** A literary work written in the form of a conversation: *Many students of philosophy have read the dialogues of Plato.* **4.** An exchange of ideas or opinions: *a dialogue among members of the club.*

dial tone *n.* A low steady tone in a telephone receiver, telling the user that a number may be dialed.

di•al•y•sis (dī **ăl′**ĭ sĭs) *n., pl.* **di•al•y•ses** (dī **ăl′**ĭ sēz′). **1.** The process of separating dissolved substances by diffusion through a membrane that blocks the passage of large molecules, but allows smaller molecules to penetrate the membrane. **2.** The removal of wastes from the bloodstream by a machine that performs dialysis when the kidneys do not function properly.

diam. *abbr.* An abbreviation of diameter.

di•am•e•ter (dī **ăm′**ĭ tər) *n.* **1.** A straight line segment that passes through the center of a circle or sphere from one side to the other. **2.** The length of such a line segment. [First written down before 1387 in Middle English, from Greek *diametros* : *dia-*, across, through + *metron*, measure.]

di•a•met•ri•cal (dī′ə **mĕt′**rĭ kəl) also **di•a•met•ric** (dī′ə **mĕt′**rĭk) *adj.* **1.** Of or along a diameter: *a diametrical measurement.* **2.** Exactly opposite; contrary: *debaters with diametrical points of view.* **—di•a•met′ri•cal•ly** *adv.*

di•a•mond (**dī′**ə mənd *or* **dī′**mənd) *n.* **1.** A form of pure carbon that occurs as a clear crystal and is the hardest of all known minerals. It is used as a gemstone in its finer varieties and as an abrasive and an edge on cutting tools. **2.a.** A figure with four equal sides forming two inner obtuse angles and two inner acute angles. **b.** A playing card bearing a red figure shaped like this. **c.** The suit in a deck of cards having this figure as its symbol. Often used in the plural. **3.a.** A baseball infield. **b.** The whole playing field in baseball. [First written down about 1325 in Middle English and spelled *diamaund*, from Medieval Latin *diamas*, alteration of Latin *adamas*, from Greek *adamas*, steel.]

diamondback rattlesnake (**dī′**ə mənd băk′ *or* **dī′**mənd băk′) *n.* Either of two large rattlesnakes of the United States and Mexico, having diamond-shaped markings on the back.

diamondback terrapin *n.* Any of several turtles of the southeast coast of the United States, having knobby or ridged markings on the upper shell.

Di•an•a (dī **ăn′**ə) *n.* In Roman mythology, the goddess of the moon and of hunting, identified with the Greek Artemis.

di•a•per (**dī′**ə pər *or* **dī′**pər) *n.* A folded piece of absorbent material, such as paper or cloth, used as

Usage: dialect

One language may have several dialects that differ from each other in such things as pronunciation or choice of words. The dialect of English that is taught in your school and used by newspapers, magazines, radio, and television is called Standard English. Depending on which part of the country you live in, you probably pronounce words in a certain way and even use certain words because of the dialect spoken. For example, if you live in the northeast United States, you probably call a carbonated soft drink a **soda**. If you live in the Midwest or farther west, you probably call it **pop**. People in Boston call it **tonic**.

diamondback rattlesnake
Red diamond rattlesnake

ă	pat	oi	boy
ā	pay	ou	out
âr	care	o͝o	took
ä	father	o͞o	boot
ĕ	pet	ŭ	cut
ē	be	ûr	urge
ĭ	pit	th	thin
ī	pie	*th*	this
îr	pier	hw	whoop
ŏ	pot	zh	vision
ō	toe	ə	about
ô	paw	N	*French* bon

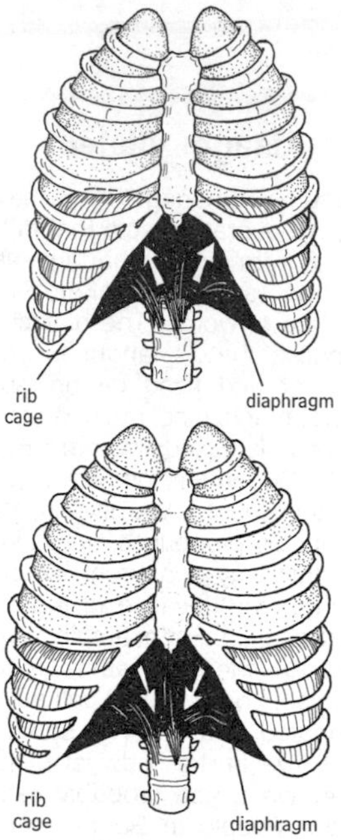

diaphragm
Top: Exhalation
Bottom: Inhalation

Charles Dickens

Emily Dickinson
Only known extant photograph, taken at age 16

underpants for a baby. —*tr.v.* **di•a•pered, di•a•per•ing, di•a•pers.** To put a diaper on (a baby). [First written down about 1300 in Middle English and spelled *diapre*, a patterned fabric, from Medieval Greek *diaspros*, pure white.]

di•aph•a•nous (dī **ăf′**ə nəs) *adj.* Of such fine texture as to allow light to show through: *a diaphanous curtain.* —**di•aph′a•nous•ly** *adv.* —**di•aph′a•nous•ness** *n.*

di•a•phragm (**dī′**ə frăm′) *n.* **1.** A membrane of muscle that separates the chest cavity from the abdominal cavity. As the diaphragm contracts and expands it forces air into and out of the lungs. **2.** A membrane that divides or separates. **3.** A thin disk, especially in a microphone or telephone receiver, that vibrates in response to sound waves to produce electrical signals or vibrates in response to electrical signals to produce sound waves. **4.** A disk with an opening in the center to regulate the amount of light entering a camera or microscope.

di•ar•rhe•a (dī′ə **rē′**ə) *n.* A condition in which bowel movements are too frequent and watery.

di•a•ry (**dī′**ə rē) *n., pl.* **di•a•ries. 1.** A daily record, especially a personal record of experiences, observations, and events. **2.** A book of blank pages for keeping such a record. [First written down in 1581 in Modern English, from Latin *diārium*, daily allowance, daily journal, from *diēs*, day.]

di•as•to•le (dī **ăs′**tə lē) *n.* The normal rhythmical period of relaxation and expansion of the heart when its cavities fill with blood.

di•a•stol•ic (dī′ə **stŏl′**ĭk) *adj.* Of, relating to, or during diastole: *diastolic pressure of the arteries.*

di•a•tom (**dī′**ə tŏm′) *n.* Any of various tiny one-celled water algae having hard shells composed mostly of silica.

di•a•tom•ic (dī′ə **tŏm′**ĭk) *adj.* Made up of two atoms: *a diatomic molecule.*

di•a•ton•ic scale (dī′ə **tŏn′**ĭk) *n.* A standard major or minor musical scale in which an octave is made up of eight tones.

di•a•tribe (**dī′**ə trīb′) *n.* A bitter and abusive denunciation: *attack one's enemy in a fierce diatribe.*

dibs (dĭbz) *pl.n. Slang.* A claim; rights: *I have dibs on the last waffle.*

dice (dīs) *n.* Plural of **die[2]** (sense 2). —*v.* **diced, dic•ing, dic•es.** —*intr.* To play or gamble with dice. —*tr.* To cut (food) into small cubes: *dice vegetables for soup.*

dick•ens (**dĭk′**ənz) *n. Informal.* **1.** A severe reprimand or an expression of anger: *gave me the dickens for being late.* **2.** Used as an intensive: *Where in the dickens did you get that?*

Dick•ens (**dĭk′**ĭnz), **Charles John Huffam.** 1812–1870. British writer known for his tales of Victorian life and times, including *Oliver Twist* (1837–1838).

dick•er (**dĭk′**ər) *intr.v.* **dick•ered, dick•er•ing, dick•ers.** To bargain; barter: *dickered over the price of the chair.* —*n.* The act or process of bargaining.

dick•ey (**dĭk′**ē) *n., pl.* **dick•eys. 1.a.** A woman's blouse front worn under a suit jacket or sweater. **b.** A man's detachable shirt front. **2.** A shirt collar. **3.** A small bird.

Dick•in•son (**dĭk′**ĭn sən), **Emily Elizabeth.** 1830–1886. American poet who wrote more than a thousand verses full of emotional depth and subtlety.

di•cot (**dī′**kŏt′) *n.* A dicotyledon.

di•cot•y•le•don (dī′kŏt′l **ēd′**n) *n.* A flowering plant having two cotyledons. Most cultivated plants and many trees are dicotyledons, while the grasses are monocotyledons. —**di′cot′y•le′don•ous** *adj.*

dict. *abbr.* An abbreviation of dictionary.

dic•ta (**dĭk′**tə) *n.* A plural of **dictum.**

dic•tate (**dĭk′**tāt′ *or* dĭk **tāt′**) *v.* **dic•tat•ed, dic•tat•ing, dic•tates.** —*tr.* **1.** To say or read aloud to be recorded or written by another: *dictate an order over the phone; dictate a letter.* **2.** To establish with authority; impose: *Hospital rules dictate visiting hours.* —*intr.* **1.** To say or read aloud material to be recorded or written by another: *The reporter dictated into the tape recorder.* **2.** To issue orders or commands. —*n.* (**dĭk′**tāt′). An order; a command. [First written down in 1592 in Modern English, from Latin *dictāre*, from *dīcere*, to say.]

dic•ta•tion (dĭk **tā′**shən) *n.* **1.a.** The act or process of dictating material to another to be written down or recorded: *dictation of a letter over the telephone.* **b.** The material so dictated. **2.** An authoritative command or order.

dic•ta•tor (**dĭk′**tā′tər *or* dĭk **tā′**tər) *n.* **1.** An absolute ruler. **2.** A tyrant; a despot.

dic•ta•to•ri•al (dĭk′tə **tôr′**ē əl) *adj.* **1.** Tending to dictate; domineering: *the chef's dictatorial manner in the kitchen.* **2.** Of, relating to, or characteristic of a dictator or dictatorship: *dictatorial power of an occupying army.* —**dic′ta•to′ri•al•ly** *adv.*

dic•ta•tor•ship (dĭk **tā′**tər shĭp′ *or* **dĭk′**tā′tər shĭp′) *n.* **1.** The office or tenure of a dictator. **2.** A state or government under the rule of a dictator. **3.** Absolute or despotic control or power.

dic•tion (**dĭk′**shən) *n.* **1.** Choice and use of words in speaking or writing: *A mystery writer's diction must be convincing to be successful.* **2.** Degree of clearness and distinctness in pronouncing words; enunciation: *The singer had good diction and so we could enjoy both words and music.*

dic•tion•ar•y (**dĭk′**shə nĕr′ē) *n., pl.* **dic•tion•ar•ies. 1.** A reference book containing an alphabetical list of words with information given for each word. Such information usually includes meaning, pronunciation, and etymology. **2.** A book containing a list of words in one language translated into another language: *a Russian-English dictionary.* **3.** A book listing words in a particular subject or category with information about each word: *a medical dictionary.*

dic•tum (**dĭk′**təm) *n., pl.* **dic•ta** (**dĭk′**tə) or **dic•tums.** An authoritative, often formal pronouncement: *Nutrition experts issued a new dictum about junk food.*

did (dĭd) *v.* Past tense of **do[1].**

di•dac•tic (dī **dăk′**tĭk) *adj.* **1.** Intended to instruct: *Many legends have a didactic purpose.* **2.** Inclined to teach or moralize too much. —**di•dac′ti•cal•ly** *adv.*

did•n't (**dĭd′**nt). Contraction of *did not.*

Di•do (**dī′**dō) *n.* In Roman mythology, the founder and queen of Carthage who falls in love with Aeneas and kills herself when he abandons her.

didst (dĭdst) *v. Archaic.* Second person singular past tense of **do[1].**

die[1] (dī) *intr.v.* **died, dy•ing** (**dī′**ĭng), **dies. 1.** To stop living; become dead: *The sunflowers died in the first frost.* **2.** To cease existing; become extinct: *We don't know why the dinosaurs died.* **3.** To experience an agony; suffer: *He nearly died of embarrassment.* **4.** To want something very much: *I'm dying to see that movie.* **5.** To stop working or operating: *The motor died when we ran out of gas.* —***idioms.*** **die down.** To lose strength; subside: *The winds died down.* **die off.** To undergo a sudden sharp decline in population. **die out.** To cease living completely; become extinct: *Some customs survive and others just die out.* [First written down about 1200 in Middle English and spelled *deien*, probably from Old Norse *deyja*.]

❑ *These sound alike:* **die[1]** (stop living), **die[2]** (device for shaping material), **dye** (color).

die[2] (dī) *n.* **1.** *pl.* **dies.** A tool or device that shapes materials by stamping, cutting, or punching: *Dies are used to make coins.* **2.** *pl.* **dice** (dīs). A small cube marked on each side with one to six dots and usually used in pairs in games. [First written down before 1300 in Middle English and spelled *di*, gaming die, from Latin *datum*, given, from *dare*, to give.]

❑ *These sound alike:* **die**[2] (device for shaping material), **die**[1] (stop living), **dye** (color).

Die•fen•ba•ker (dē′fən bā′kər), **John George.** 1895–1979. Canadian politician who served as prime minister (1957–1963).

die-hard also **die•hard** (dī′härd′) *adj.* Stubbornly resisting change or clinging to a seemingly hopeless cause: *a die-hard supporter.* —*n.* A person who stubbornly refuses to give up a cause or resists change.

di•er•e•sis or **di•aer•e•sis** (dī ĕr′ĭ sĭs) *n., pl.* **di•er•e•ses** or **di•aer•e•ses** (dī ĕr′ĭ sēz′). **1.** A mark (¨) placed over the second of two adjacent vowels to show that the second vowel is to be pronounced as a separate sound, as in *naïve.* **2.** A mark (¨) placed over a vowel, such as the final vowel in *Brontë*, to indicate that the vowel is not silent.

die•sel (dē′zəl *or* dē′səl) *n.* **1.** A diesel engine. **2.** A vehicle powered by a diesel engine.

diesel engine *n.* An internal-combustion engine in which the fuel oil is ignited by the heat of air that has been highly compressed in the cylinder. [First written down in 1894 in Modern English, after Rudolph *Diesel* (1858–1913), German engineer.]

di•et[1] (dī′ĭt) *n.* **1.** The usual food and drink eaten by a person or an animal. **2.** A regulated selection of foods, especially as prescribed for medical reasons: *The diet of a diabetic excludes most sugar.* —*intr.v.* **di•et•ed, di•et•ing, di•ets.** To eat and drink according to a regulated system, especially so as to control a medical condition or lose weight. [First written down before 1200 in Middle English and spelled *diete*, from Greek *diaita*, way of living.] —**di′et•er** *n.*

di•et[2] (dī′ĭt) *n.* A national or local legislative assembly in certain countries, such as Japan. [First written down about 1450 in Middle English, from Medieval Latin *diēta*, day's journey, meeting day, from Latin *diaeta*, daily routine.]

di•e•tar•y (dī′ĭ tĕr′ē) *adj.* Of or relating to diet: *a good dietary plan.*

di•e•tet•ic (dī′ĭ tĕt′ĭk) *adj.* **1.** Of or relating to diet or its regulation. **2.** Made or processed for restricted diets: *dietetic foods prepared with less salt and sugar.*

di•e•tet•ics (dī′ĭ tĕt′ĭks) *n.* *(used with a singular verb).* The study of nutrition as it relates to health.

di•e•ti•tian or **di•e•ti•cian** (dī′ĭ tĭsh′ən) *n.* A person who specializes in dietetics: *The hospital dietitian plans the meals for each patient.*

dif•fer (dĭf′ər) *intr.v.* **dif•fered, dif•fer•ing, dif•fers. 1.** To be unlike, as in nature or amount: *The weather often differs from one part of a state to another.* **2.** To be of a different opinion; disagree: *Members of the committee differed over what plan to accept.* [First written down about 1375 in Middle English and spelled *differren*, from Latin *differre*, to delay, differ : *dis-*, apart + *ferre*, to carry.]

dif•fer•ence (dĭf′ər əns *or* dĭf′rəns) *n.* **1.** The quality or condition of being unlike or dissimilar: *the difference between summer and winter.* **2.** An instance of being unlike or different. **3.** A noticeable change or effect: *Exercise has made a big difference in her health.* **4.a.** A disagreement or controversy: *We settled our differences amicably.* **b.** A cause of a disagreement or controversy. **5.** The amount by which one quantity is greater or less than another; what is left when one number is subtracted from another: *The difference between 10 and 4 is 6.*

dif•fer•ent (dĭf′ər ənt *or* dĭf′rənt) *adj.* **1.** Unlike in form, quality, amount, or nature: *The two breeds of dog are very different.* **2.** Distinct or separate: *We ran into each other on three different occasions today.* **3.** Differing from all others; unusual: *The seahorse is a very different fish.* —**dif′fer•ent•ly** *adv.* —See Note.

dif•fer•en•tial (dĭf′ə rĕn′shəl) *adj.* Of, relating to, or showing a difference: *differential rates in air fares.* —*n.* **1.** A differential gear. **2.** A difference in wage rate or in price: *There is a substantial differential between flying to Florida in the winter and in the summer.* —**dif′fer•en′tial•ly** *adv.*

differential gear *n.* An arrangement of gears used in an automobile or a truck that permits the drive shaft to turn the two rear-wheel or front-wheel axle shafts at different speeds, so that the wheels can rotate at different speeds when the vehicle is turning.

dif•fer•en•ti•ate (dĭf′ə rĕn′shē āt′) *v.* **dif•fer•en•ti•at•ed, dif•fer•en•ti•at•ing, dif•fer•en•ti•ates.** —*tr.* **1.** To be the difference between: *Red shirts and blue shirts differentiate the teams.* **2.** To understand or show the differences between: *Differentiate the various wildflowers.* —*intr.* **1.** To become distinct or specialized: *Cells differentiating into red blood cells accumulate hemoglobin.* **2.** To make distinctions; discriminate: *A doctor can differentiate between a rash and chicken pox.* —**dif′fer•en′ti•a′tion** *n.*

dif•fi•cult (dĭf′ĭ kŭlt′) *adj.* **1.** Hard to do or perform: *a difficult task.* **2.** Hard to understand or solve: *a difficult math problem.* **3.** Hard to please, satisfy, or manage: *A perfectionist can be difficult.* [First written down before 1400 in Middle English, from Latin *difficilis*.]

dif•fi•cul•ty (dĭf′ĭ kŭl′tē *or* dĭf′ĭ kəl tē) *n., pl.* **dif•fi•cul•ties. 1.** The quality or condition of being difficult: *The difficulty of the subject made the book on botany hard to understand.* **2.** A troublesome or embarrassing state of affairs. Often used in the plural: *The store was in financial difficulties and had to close.* **3.** A laborious effort; a struggle: *I finished the exam with difficulty.* **4.** A disagreement or dispute: *There was a small difficulty over the boundary line.*

dif•fi•dence (dĭf′ĭ dəns) *n.* A quality or state of being timid or shy: *Diffidence held him back from calling out the answer.*

dif•fi•dent (dĭf′ĭ dənt) *adj.* Lacking or marked by a lack of self-confidence; timid and shy. —**dif′fi•dent•ly** *adv.*

dif•fract (dĭ frăkt′) *intr. & tr.v.* **dif•fract•ed, dif•fract•ing, dif•fracts.** To undergo or cause to undergo diffraction.

dif•frac•tion (dĭ frăk′shən) *n.* **1.** The spreading or bending of light waves as they pass the edge of an obstacle or through a hole or slit. The colors of the spectrum can be produced by the diffraction of light. **2.** A similar spreading and bending of sound or other kinds of waves. [First written down in 1671 in Modern English, from Latin *diffrāctus*, past participle of *diffringere* : *dis-*, apart + *frangere*, to break.]

dif•fuse (dĭ fyōōz′) *v.* **dif•fused, dif•fus•ing, dif•fus•es.** —*tr.* **1.** To cause to spread out freely: *The lamp diffuses light over the table.* **2.** To scatter; disseminate: *diffuse ideas; diffuse knowledge.* —*intr.* **1.** To become spread out or scattered: *A lighthouse beam diffuses far out over the ocean.* **2.** To become mixed together: *Water and air diffuse to create fog.* —*adj.* (dĭ fyōōs′). **1.** Widely spread or scattered: *Diffuse light is often hard to read by.* **2.** Wordy; long-winded: *a diffuse description.* [First written

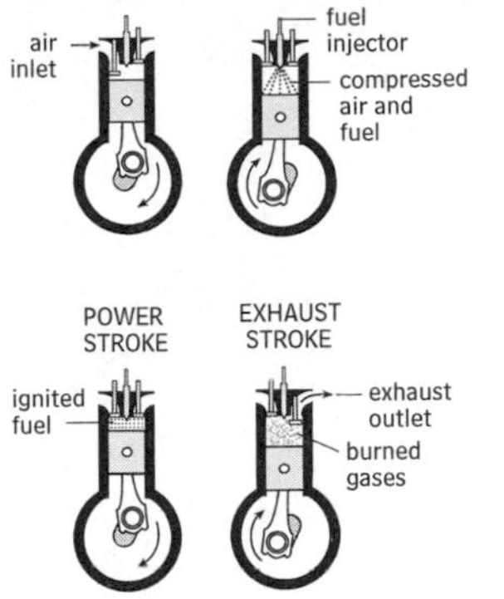

diesel engine

Usage: different

When you are making a comparison between two persons or things, **different** should be followed by **from** instead of **than**: *My book is different from* (not *than*) *yours.*

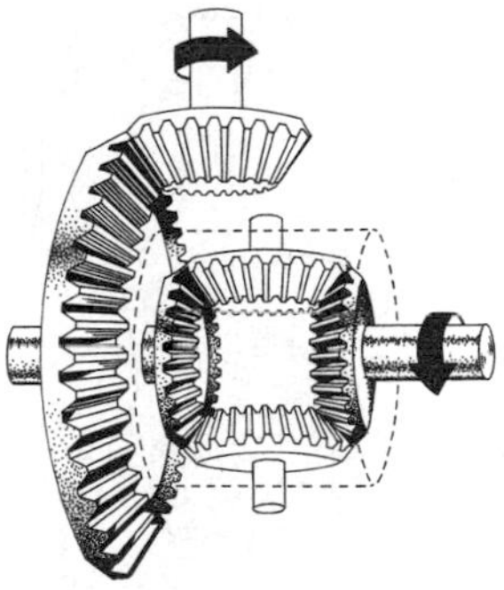

differential gear

ă	pat	oi	boy
ā	pay	ou	out
âr	care	ŏŏ	took
ä	father	ōō	boot
ĕ	pet	ŭ	cut
ē	be	ûr	urge
ĭ	pit	th	thin
ī	pie	*th*	this
îr	pier	hw	whoop
ŏ	pot	zh	vision
ō	toe	ə	about
ô	paw	N	*French* bon

down before 1400 in Middle English, from Latin *diffūsus*, spread out, from *diffundere*, to spread out : *dis-*, apart, out + *fundere*, to pour.]

dif•fu•sion (dĭ fyo͞o′zhən) *n.* **1.** The process of diffusing or the condition of being diffused: *the diffusion of knowledge.* **2.** The use of too many words; wordiness. **3.** The spreading out of light or other radiation through a space so that its intensity becomes more or less uniform. **4.** The gradual mixing together of different gases or liquids as a result of the random motions of their atoms or molecules.

dig (dĭg) *v.* **dug** (dŭg), **dig•ging, digs.** —*tr.* **1.** To break, turn over, or remove (earth, for example), as with a shovel, a spade, or the hands: *The dog was digging the dirt to crawl under the fence.* **2.** To make or form by removing earth or other material: *A woodchuck dug a hole in the garden.* **3.** To get by digging: *dig clams.* **4.** To learn or discover by investigation or research: *dig up information in a library.* **5.** To poke, prod, or thrust: *The cat dug its claws into a tree.* **6.** *Slang.* **a.** To understand fully: *Do you dig what I mean?* **b.** To take notice of: *Dig that fantastic car!* —*intr.* **1.** To loosen, turn over, or remove earth or other material: *I'm going out to the garden to dig.* **2.** To make one's way by or as if by pushing aside or removing material: *dig through the trash to find a lost earring.* **3.** *Slang.* To have an understanding: *Do you dig?* —*n.* **1.** A poke or thrust: *a dig in the ribs.* **2.** A sarcastic taunting remark: *a nasty dig about my accent.* **3.** An archaeological excavation. ***—idiom.*** **dig in. 1.** To dig trenches for protection: *The army dug in for battle.* **2.** To begin to eat heartily: *We were hungry and quickly dug in.* [First written down before 1220 in Middle English and spelled *diggen*; perhaps akin to Old French *digue*, dike, trench.] **—dig′ger** *n.*

di•gest (dī jĕst′ *or* dĭ jĕst′) *v.* **di•gest•ed, di•gest•ing, di•gests.** —*tr.* **1.** To change (food) chemically into materials that the cells of the body can assimilate, store, or oxidize and use as nourishment: *As carbohydrates are digested, the body turns them into sugar and starch.* **2.** To absorb mentally; comprehend: *Reporters must digest facts quickly in order to write their stories.* —*intr.* To be taken in as food or as if food; be assimilated by the body or mind: *Some foods do not digest easily.* —*n.* (dī′jĕst′). A collection of previously published materials, such as essays or reports, usually in condensed form: *Many scientific groups publish digests of their members' work.* [First written down before 1387 in Middle English and spelled *digesten*, from Latin *dīgerere*, to separate, arrange : *dī-*, *dis-*, apart + *gerere*, to carry.]

di•gest•i•ble (dī jĕs′tə bəl *or* dĭ jĕs′tə bəl) *adj.* Capable of being digested easily or readily. **—di•gest′i•bil′i•ty** *n.*

di•ges•tion (dī jĕs′chən *or* dĭ jĕs′chən) *n.* **1.a.** The process of digesting food. **b.** The ability to carry on this process: *poor digestion.* **2.** The decomposition of organic matter in sewage by bacteria.

di•ges•tive (dī jĕs′tĭv *or* dĭ jĕs′tĭv) *adj.* Relating to, aiding, or active in digestion: *digestive juices.* **—di•ges′tive•ly** *adv.*

digestive system *n.* The system of organs of the body that breaks down and absorbs food as nourishment. It consists of the esophagus, stomach, intestines, and other organs of the alimentary canal together with the glands, such as the liver, salivary glands, and pancreas, that produce substances necessary for digestion.

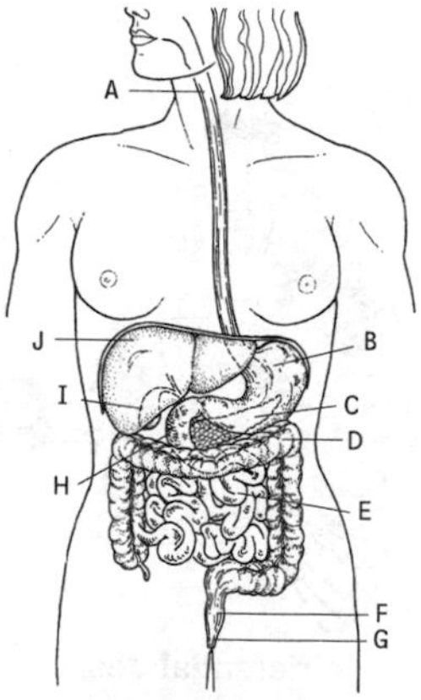

digestive system

A. Esophagus
B. Stomach
C. Pancreas
D. Large Intestine
E. Small Intestine
F. Rectum
G. Anus
H. Duodenum
I. Gallbladder
J. Liver

dig•gings (dĭg′ĭngz) *pl.n.* An excavation site: *The old diggings were once a tin mine.*

dig•it (dĭj′ĭt) *n.* **1.** A human finger or toe. **2.** A corresponding part in other vertebrate animals. **3.** One of the ten Arabic numerals, 0 through 9. [First written down before 1400 in Middle English, from Latin *digitus*.]

dig•i•tal (dĭj′ĭ tl) *adj.* **1.** Of, relating to, or resembling a digit, especially a finger. **2.** Having digits. **3.** Expressed in digits, especially for use by a computer: *digital information.* **4.** Using or giving a reading in digits: *a digital clock; a digital speedometer.* —*n.* A key operated by a finger, as on a piano. **—dig′i•tal•ly** *adv.*

digital computer *n.* A computer that performs operations on data that are represented as series of digits, especially the binary digits 0 and 1.

dig•i•tal•is (dĭj′ĭ tăl′ĭs) *n.* **1.** The foxglove. **2.** A drug prepared from the seeds and dried leaves of the foxglove, used as a powerful heart stimulant.

digital recording *n.* **1.** A way of recording in which sound waves are represented by numbers and stored for later reproduction. **2.** A record, tape, or disk that is recorded this way.

dig•ni•fied (dĭg′nə fīd′) *adj.* Having or expressing dignity: *the careful and dignified manner of an ambassador.*

dig•ni•fy (dĭg′nə fī′) *tr.v.* **dig•ni•fied, dig•ni•fy•ing, dig•ni•fies. 1.** To give dignity or honor to: *The mayor's presence dignified our school ceremony.* **2.** To raise the status of (something unworthy and lowly): *My parents would not dignify the gossip by responding to it.*

dig•ni•tar•y (dĭg′nĭ tĕr′ē) *n., pl.* **dig•ni•tar•ies.** A person of high rank or position.

dig•ni•ty (dĭg′nĭ tē) *n., pl.* **dig•ni•ties. 1.** The quality or state of being worthy of esteem or respect. **2.** A stately or poised manner: *The judge maintained his dignity in the court at all times.* **3.** The respect and honor that go with an important position or station. **4.** A high office or rank. [First written down before 1200 in Middle English and spelled *dignite*, from Latin *dignitās*, from *dignus*, worthy.]

di•gress (dī grĕs′ *or* dĭ grĕs′) *intr.v.* **di•gressed, di•gress•ing, di•gress•es.** To turn aside, especially from the main subject in writing or speaking: *digressed from the sermon to tell a personal story.*

di•gres•sion (dī grĕsh′ən *or* dĭ grĕsh′ən) *n.* **1.** The act of digressing. **2.** An instance of digressing, especially in speech or writing: *tiresome digressions in an otherwise interesting article.*

di•he•dral (dī hē′drəl) *adj.* Formed by a pair of planes or sections of planes that intersect: *An open door forms a dihedral angle with the wall.* —*n.* An angle formed by two geometric planes that intersect.

dike (dīk) *n.* **1.** A wall or an embankment built to hold back water and prevent flooding, as by a river or the sea. **2.** A long mass of igneous rock that cuts across the structure of adjoining rock. —*tr.v.* **diked, dik•ing, dikes.** To protect or provide with a dike.

di•lap•i•dat•ed (dĭ lăp′ĭ dā′tĭd) *adj.* In a condition of deterioration or disrepair, as through neglect: *The dilapidated building was beyond repair.*

di•lap•i•da•tion (dĭ lăp′ĭ dā′shən) *n.* A condition of deterioration or disrepair: *The run-down house showed signs of dilapidation.*

di•late (dī lāt′ *or* dī′lāt′) *tr. & intr.v.* **di•lat•ed, di•lat•ing, di•lates.** To make or become larger or wider; expand: *When the horse whinnied its nostrils dilated.* **—di•la′tion** *n.*

dil•a•to•ry (dĭl′ə tôr′ē) *adj.* **1.** Intended to delay: *hold up legislation with dilatory tactics such as the filibuster.* **2.** Tending to postpone or delay: *a dilatory student who always hands her homework in late.*

di•lem•ma (dĭ lĕm′ə) *n.* A situation that requires a person to choose between options that are or seem equally unfavorable: *faced the dilemma of taking a cut in pay or losing her job.*

dil•et•tante (dĭl′ĭ tänt′ *or* dĭl′ĭ tänt′ *or* dĭl′ĭ tän′tē) *n., pl.* **dil•et•tantes** also **dil•et•tan•ti** (dĭl′ĭ tän′-tē). A person who dabbles in an art or a branch of knowledge.
dil•i•gence (dĭl′ə jəns) *n.* Earnest and persistent application or effort: *It took a lot of diligence to stick with such an unrewarding project.*
dil•i•gent (dĭl′ə jənt) *adj.* Marked by persevering painstaking effort: *A diligent search of the records revealed new evidence.* **—dil′i•gent•ly** *adv.*
dill (dĭl) *n.* **1.** The very fine leaves or spicy seeds of a plant related to parsley, dried and used as seasoning. **2.** The plant bearing such leaves and seeds.
dill pickle *n.* A pickled cucumber flavored with dill.
dil•ly-dal•ly (dĭl′ē dăl′ē) *intr.v.* **dil•ly-dal•lied, dil•ly-dal•ly•ing, dil•ly-dal•lies.** To waste time, especially in indecision; dawdle.
di•lute (dī lo͞ot′ *or* dĭ lo͞ot′) *tr.v.* **di•lut•ed, di•lut•ing, di•lutes. 1.** To make thinner or less concentrated by adding a liquid such as water: *dilute thick soup.* **2.** To weaken the force, intensity, purity, or condition of: *A lack of facts diluted the argument.* *—adj.* Weakened; diluted: *a dilute solution of acid.* [First written down about 1555 in Modern English, from Latin *dīluere* : *dī-, dis-*, apart, away + *-luere*, to wash.]
di•lu•tion (dī lo͞o′shən *or* dĭ lo͞o′shən) *n.* **1.** The act of diluting or the condition of being diluted. **2.** A diluted substance: *a 50 percent dilution of a concentrated solution.*
dim (dĭm) *adj.* **dim•mer, dim•mest. 1.** Lacking in brightness: *a dim corner of the big room.* See Synonyms at **dark. 2.** Giving off only a small amount of light: *a dim star.* **3.** Lacking luster; dull and subdued: *dim colors faded by the sun.* **4.** Faintly outlined; indistinct: *could just make out the dim shape of a ship in the mist.* **5.** Not sharp or clear; lacking keenness of understanding or perception: *dim eyesight; a dim idea for a story.* **6.** Not favorable: *took a dim view of my excuses.* *—tr. & intr.v.* **dimmed, dim•ming, dims.** To make or become dim: *Drivers must dim their headlights in traffic. The lights dimmed as the play began.* [First written down before 1000 in Old English and spelled *dimm.*] **—dim′ly** *adv.* **—dim′ness** *n.*
dime (dīm) *n.* A coin of the United States or Canada worth ten cents. ***—idioms.*** **a dime a dozen.** Overly abundant; commonplace: *Personal computers are a dime a dozen these days.* **on a dime.** At a precise point; within a narrowly defined area: *This car stops on a dime.* [First written down about 1378 in Middle English and spelled *dime*, tenth part, from Latin *decima (pars)*, tenth (part), from *decem*, ten.]
di•men•sion (dĭ mĕn′shən *or* dī mĕn′shən) *n.* **1.** The measurement of a length, width, or thickness: *The dimensions of the window are 2 feet by 4 feet.* **2.** Extent or magnitude; scope. Often used in the plural: *a problem of huge dimensions.* **3.** A physical quantity, such as mass, length, or time, on which other measurements are based. [First written down before 1398 in Middle English and spelled *dimencioun*, from Latin *dīmēnsiō*, extent, from *dīmētīrī*, to measure out : *dī-, dis-*, off, out + *mētīrī*, to measure.]
di•men•sion•al (dĭ mĕn′shə nəl) *adj.* **1.** Of or relating to a dimension or dimensions. **2.** Having a specified number of dimensions: *a two-dimensional picture.*
di•min•ish (dĭ mĭn′ĭsh) *tr. & intr.v.* **di•min•ished, di•min•ish•ing, di•min•ish•es.** To make or become smaller or less; reduce or decrease: *A drought diminished their water supply. Light diminished steadily as the sun went down.* See Synonyms at **decrease. —di•min′ish•ing** *adj.*
di•min•u•en•do (dĭ mĭn′yo͞o ĕn′dō) *n., adj., & adv.* Decrescendo.
dim•i•nu•tion (dĭm′ə no͞o′shən *or* dĭm′ə nyo͞o′-shən) *n.* The act or process of diminishing; a lessening or reduction: *Lack of exercise contributes to the diminution of strength.*
di•min•u•tive (dĭ mĭn′yə tĭv) *adj.* **1.** Extremely small in size; tiny: *diminutive figures in a collection of miniatures.* **2.** Of or relating to a suffix that expresses smallness, youth, or affection, as *-let* in *booklet*, *-ette* in *dinette*, and *-ie* in *dearie*. *—n.* A diminutive suffix, word, or name. For example, *droplet* is a diminutive of *drop*. **—di•min′u•tive•ly** *adv.* **—di•min′u•tive•ness** *n.*
dim•i•ty (dĭm′ĭ tē) *n., pl.* **dim•i•ties.** A sheer crisp cotton cloth with raised woven checks or stripes, used chiefly for curtains and dresses.
dim•mer (dĭm′ər) *n.* A device used to vary the brightness of an electric light.
dim•ple (dĭm′pəl) *n.* A small indentation in the flesh on a part of the human body, especially in the chin or on the cheek. *—intr.v.* **dim•pled, dim•pling, dim•ples.** To form dimples by smiling.
din (dĭn) *n.* A jumble of loud, usually discordant sounds: *We couldn't hear them over the din of the traffic.* See Synonyms at **uproar.** *—v.* **dinned, din•ning, dins.** *—tr.* **1.** To stun with deafening noise: *The horns dinned our ears.* **2.** To impart by wearying repetition: *My teacher dinned the verb forms into my head.* *—intr.* To make a loud noise.
di•nar (dĭ när′ *or* dē′när′) *n.* The basic monetary unit of numerous countries, including Algeria, Iraq, Libya, and Yemen.
dine (dīn) *v.* **dined, din•ing, dines.** *—intr.* To have dinner: *We dined early.* *—tr.* To give dinner to; entertain at dinner. [First written down about 1300 in Middle English and spelled *dinen*, from Old French *disner* : Latin *dis-*, away, off + Latin *iēiūnium*, fast.]
❑ *These sound alike:* **dine, dyne** (unit of force).
din•er (dī′nər) *n.* **1.** A person who dines. **2.** A dining car. **3.** A restaurant that has a long counter and booths, housed in a building designed to resemble a railroad car.
di•nette (dī nĕt′) *n.* A small dining room or alcove for informal meals.
ding (dĭng) *intr. & tr.v.* **dinged, ding•ing, dings.** To ring or cause to ring with a clanging sound. *—n.* A ringing sound.
ding-dong (dĭng′dông′ *or* dĭng′dŏng′) *n.* The peal of a bell.
din•ghy (dĭng′ē) *n., pl.* **din•ghies.** A small open boat, especially a rowboat carried by a larger boat. [First written down in 1810 in Modern English, from Hindi *ḍiṅgī*, diminutive of *ḍeṅgā*, boat.]
din•gle (dĭng′gəl) *n.* A small wooded valley; a dell.
din•go (dĭng′gō) *n., pl.* **din•goes.** A wild dog of Australia, having a yellowish-brown coat and resembling a wolf.
din•gy (dĭn′jē) *adj.* **din•gi•er, din•gi•est.** Darkened with grime or soot; dirty or discolored: *a dark and dingy room in need of paint.* **—din′gi•ly** *adv.* **—din′gi•ness** *n.*
din•ing car (dī′nĭng) *n.* A railroad car in which meals are served; a diner.
dining room *n.* A room, as in a house or hotel, in which meals are eaten.
din•ky (dĭng′kē) *adj.* **din•ki•er, din•ki•est.** *Informal.* Of small size or consequence; insignificant: *a dinky shack in the woods.*
din•ner (dĭn′ər) *n.* **1.** The main meal of the day, eaten at midday or in the evening. **2.** A banquet or formal meal in honor of a person or an event: *hold a dinner to celebrate someone's birthday.*

dimple

dingo

ă	pat	oi	boy
ā	pay	ou	out
âr	care	o͝o	took
ä	father	o͞o	boot
ĕ	pet	ŭ	cut
ē	be	ûr	urge
ĭ	pit	th	thin
ī	pie	*th*	this
îr	pier	hw	whoop
ŏ	pot	zh	vision
ō	toe	ə	about
ô	paw	N	*French* bon

diploma
High-school graduate

din•ner•time (dĭn′ər tīm′) *n.* The time when dinner is usually eaten.

di•no•flag•el•late (dī′nō **flăj′**ə lĭt *or* dī′nō **flăj′**-ə lāt′) *n.* Any of numerous tiny flagellates found in the ocean, some kinds of which produce a red substance poisonous to fish.

di•no•saur (**dī′**nə sôr′) *n.* One of a large group of extinct carnivorous or herbivorous reptiles that lived mostly on land many millions of years ago. The fossil remains of their bones show that though the dinosaurs included the largest land animals ever known to exist, some kinds were no larger than dogs. [First written down in 1841 in Modern English : Greek *deinos*, monstrous + Greek *sauros*, lizard.]

dint (dĭnt) *n.* Force or effort; power: *By dint of practice, she became an accomplished musician.*

di•o•cese (**dī′**ə sĭs *or* **dī′**ə sēs′) *n.* The district or churches under the authority of a bishop.

di•ode (**dī′**ōd′) *n.* An electron tube or a semiconductor that allows current to flow in one direction only.

Di•o•ny•sus (dī′ə **nī′**səs *or* dī′ə **nē′**səs) *n.* In Greek and Roman mythology, the god of wine and of the power and fertility of nature.

di•o•ram•a (dī′ə **răm′**ə) *n.* A miniature or life-size scene with lifelike figures and objects set against a painted background.

di•ox•ide (dī **ŏk′**sīd) *n.* A compound with two atoms of oxygen per molecule.

dip (dĭp) *v.* **dipped, dip•ping, dips.** *—tr.* **1.** To plunge briefly in or into a liquid: *dip a cracker into soup.* **2.** To color or dye by putting into a liquid: *dip eggs in dye.* **3.** To immerse (a sheep or other animal) in a disinfecting bath. **4.** To make (a candle) by repeatedly immersing a wick in melted wax or tallow. **5.** To scoop up by plunging the hand or a receptacle below the surface, as of a liquid: *dip water from a stream to get a drink.* **6.** To lower and raise (a flag) in salute. *—intr.* **1.** To plunge briefly into water or other liquid: *The oars dipped in and out of the water.* **2.** To plunge the hand or a receptacle into liquid or a container, especially so as to take something out: *dip into a pickle jar.* **3.** To drop down or sink out of sight suddenly: *The temperature dipped below freezing.* **4.** To slope downward; decline: *The path dips to the river.* *—n.* **1.** A brief plunge, especially a quick swim: *a dip in the pool.* **2.** A liquid into which something is dipped, as for dyeing or disinfecting: *a flea dip for dogs.* **3.** A creamy food mixture into which crackers or other foods may be dipped: *a vegetable dip.* **4.** An amount taken up by dipping; a scoop: *a double dip of ice cream.* **5.** A downward slope; a decline: *a dip in the road.* [First written down about 975 in Old English and spelled *dyppan*.]

diph•the•ri•a (dĭf **thîr′**ē ə *or* dĭp **thîr′**ē ə) *n.* A serious contagious disease caused by certain bacilli. Its symptoms include high fever and the formation of false membranes in the throat that cause difficulty in breathing. [First written down in 1857 in Modern English, from Greek *diphthera*, piece of hide, leather.]

diph•thong (**dĭf′**thông′ *or* **dĭp′**thông′) *n.* A speech sound blending two vowels in the same syllable. For example, the speech sounds represented by *oy* in *boy* and *i* in *nice* are diphthongs. [First written down in 1483 in Middle English and spelled *diptonge*, from Greek *diphthongos* : *di-*, two + *phthongos*, sound.]

dip•loid (**dĭp′**loid′) *adj.* Having two sets of each chromosome except for those that determine sex. *—n.* A diploid cell or individual.

di•plo•ma (dĭ **plō′**mə) *n.* A document or certificate issued by an educational institution showing that a person has earned a degree or completed a course of study. [First written down about 1645 in Modern English, from Greek *diplōma*, folded paper, document, from *diploos*, double.]

di•plo•ma•cy (dĭ **plō′**mə sē) *n.* **1.** The art or practice of handling international relations. It includes negotiating alliances, treaties, and trade agreements. **2.** Skill in dealing with others; tact: *The lawyer was known for her diplomacy.*

dip•lo•mat (**dĭp′**lə măt′) *n.* **1.** A person, such as an ambassador, who has been appointed to represent a government in its dealings with other governments. **2.** A person who uses tact and skill in dealing with others.

dip•lo•mat•ic (dĭp′lə **măt′**ĭk) *adj.* **1.** Of, relating to, or involving diplomacy or diplomats. **2.** Using or marked by skill and tact in dealing with others: *a diplomatic handling of unpleasant matters.* [First written down in 1711 in Modern English, from Latin *diplōma*, letter of introduction.] **—dip′lo•mat′-i•cal•ly** *adv.*

dip•per (**dĭp′**ər) *n.* **1.** A person or thing that dips. **2.** A container for scooping up liquids.

Dip•per (**dĭp′**ər) *n.* **1.** The Big Dipper. **2.** The Little Dipper.

dip•ter•ous (**dĭp′**tər əs) *adj.* Of, relating to, or belonging to an order of insects that have one pair of wings and a pair of small club-shaped organs for balance. Mosquitoes, gnats, and houseflies belong to this group.

dire (dīr) *adj.* **dir•er, dir•est. 1.** Warning of or having dreadful or terrible consequences; calamitous: *a dire accident.* **2.** Urgent; desperate: *in dire want.* [First written down in 1567 in Modern English, from Latin *dīrus*.]

di•rect (dĭ **rĕkt′** *or* dī **rĕkt′**) *v.* **di•rect•ed, di•rect•ing, di•rects.** *—tr.* **1.** To manage or conduct the affairs of; regulate: *direct a business.* **2.** To instruct, order, or command: *The general directed the soldiers to free all prisoners.* **3.** To cause to move toward a goal; aim. **4.** To show or indicate the way for: *I directed them to the post office.* **5.** To indicate the intended recipient of (a letter, for example): *direct a note to the benefits department.* **6.** To make (remarks, for example) to someone in particular or to an audience: *The principal directed a few words of welcome to the new students.* **7.** To give guidance and instruction to (actors or musicians, for example) in the rehearsal and performance of a work. *—intr.* **1.** To give commands or directions: *police officers directing at an intersection.* **2.** To conduct a performance or rehearsal: *The conductor is directing in front of the orchestra.* *—adj.* **1.** Proceeding in a straight course or line; not roundabout: *The dancers moved in a direct line across the stage.* **2.** Straightforward and candid; frank: *They gave direct answers to my questions.* **3.** Having no intervening persons, agencies, or conditions; immediate: *direct sunlight; a direct line to the president.* **4.** Effected by action of the voters rather than through representatives or delegates: *direct election.* **5.** Being of unbroken descent; lineal: *the direct descendant of early settlers.* **6.** Consisting of the exact words of a writer or speaker: *a direct quote from the article.* **7.** Absolute: *direct opposites.* **8.** Varying in the same manner as another quantity; increasing if another quantity increases or decreasing if it decreases. *—adv.* Straight; directly: *We flew direct from California to New York.* [First written down about 1385 in Middle English and spelled *directen*, from Latin *dīrigere*, to give direction to : *dī-*, *dis-*, apart + *regere*, to guide.] **—di•rect′ness** *n.*

direct current *n.* An electric current flowing in one direction only, as that of a battery.

di•rec•tion (dĭ **rĕk′**shən *or* dī **rĕk′**shən) *n.* **1.** Management, control, or guidance of an action or operation: *The fire department is under the direction of the chief.* **2.** An instruction or a series of instructions for doing or finding something. Often used in the plural: *directions for starting the car; directions for getting to the ballpark.* **3.** An order or a command: *My whistle was a direction for my dog to come.* **4.** The line or course along which a person or thing moves or lies: *The ship headed in a northerly direction. The old farmhouse is in the direction of the peach orchard.* **5.** A course or an area of development: *The orchestra took a different direction by performing contemporary compositions.* [First written down about 1385 in Middle English, from Latin *dīrēctiō*, from *dīrigere*, to direct.]

di•rec•tion•al (dĭ **rĕk′**shə nəl *or* dī **rĕk′**shə nəl) *adj.* **1.** Of or indicating direction: *a car's directional signals.* **2.** Capable of receiving or sending signals in one direction only: *a directional radar antenna.* **—di•rec′tion•al•ly** *adv.*

direction finder *n.* A device for finding the direction from which a radio signal is transmitted. It consists of a radio receiver and a compass attached to a coiled antenna that can turn in any direction.

di•rec•tive (dĭ **rĕk′**tĭv *or* dī **rĕk′**tĭv) *n.* An order or instruction, especially one issued by a central authority: *a directive from the coach about attendance at practice.*

di•rect•ly (dĭ **rĕkt′**lē *or* dī **rĕkt′**lē) *adv.* **1.** In a direct line or manner; straight: *The cat headed directly for its food.* **2.** Without anything intervening: *The students spoke directly to the superintendent about the issue.* **3.** Exactly or totally: *His views on this issue are directly opposite to mine.* **4.** Without delay; at once: *I'll meet you there directly after work.*

direct mail *n.* Advertising circulars or other printed matter sent directly through the mail to possible customers or contributors.

direct object *n.* The word or words in a sentence that indicate the person or thing receiving the action of a transitive verb. For example, in the sentence *I wrote a poem,* the direct object is *poem.*

di•rec•tor (dĭ **rĕk′**tər *or* dī **rĕk′**tər) *n.* **1.** A person who supervises, controls, or manages: *The magazine has a new art director.* **2.** A member of a group of persons chosen to control or govern the affairs of a company or an institution: *a meeting of the board of directors.* **3.** A person who supervises and guides the performers and others involved in a dramatic production, film, or other performance.

di•rec•tor•ate (dĭ **rĕk′**tər ĭt *or* dī **rĕk′**tər ĭt) *n.* **1.** The office or position of a director. **2.** A board of directors, as of a corporation.

di•rec•to•ri•al (dĭ rĕk′**tôr′**ē əl) or (dī rĕk′**tôr′**ē əl) *adj.* **1.** Of or relating to a director or directorate: *directorial responsibilities.* **2.** Serving to direct: *a directorial report.*

di•rec•to•ry (dĭ **rĕk′**tə rē *or* dī **rĕk′**tə rē) *n., pl.* **di•rec•to•ries. 1.** A book containing a list of names, addresses, or other facts, such as telephone numbers, in alphabetical or other order: *a building directory to the offices of different companies.* **2.** A listing of the data files stored in a computer memory.

dire•ful (**dīr′**fəl) *adj.* Inspiring dread; terrible: *a direful tale of misery and starvation.* **—dire′ful•ly** *adv.* **—dire′ful•ness** *n.*

dirge (dûrj) *n.* A sad solemn piece of music, such as a funeral hymn or lament.

dir•ham (də **răm′**) *n.* The basic monetary unit of Morocco and United Arab Emirates.

dir•i•gi•ble (**dĭr′**ə jə bəl *or* də **rĭj′**ə bəl) *n.* A self-propelled aircraft that can be steered and has a rigid frame covered with fabric. It is filled with gas to make it lighter than air; an airship. [First written down in 1885 in Modern English, from Latin *dīrigere*, to direct.]

dirk (dûrk) *n.* A dagger.

dirn•dl (**dûrn′**dl) *n.* **1.** A dress with a full gathered skirt and a fitted bodice. **2.** A full skirt with a gathered waistband. [First written down in 1937 in Modern English, from German *Dirndlkleid* : German dialectal *Dirndl*, little girl + *Kleid*, dress.]

dirt (dûrt) *n.* **1.** Earth or soil: *Rock and dirt came tumbling down the mountain.* **2.** A substance that soils, such as mud, dust, or grease: *A detergent removes dirt from clothes.* **3.** A person or thing that is mean, contemptible, or vile. **4.** Malicious or scandalous gossip: *This magazine publishes all the dirt about movie stars.* [First written down before 1300 in Middle English and spelled *drit*, filth, mud, from Old Norse.]

dirt bike *n.* A motorcycle or bicycle for use on dirt roads and rough terrain.

dirt-cheap (**dûrt′chēp′**) *adv. & adj.* Very cheap: *buy a truck dirt-cheap; a dirt-cheap hotel.*

dirt•y (**dûr′**tē) *adj.* **dirt•i•er, dirt•i•est. 1.a.** Soiled, as with dirt; unclean: *dirty water; dirty clothes; a dirty floor.* **b.** Apt to soil with dirt or grime: *Planting a garden is a dirty job.* **2.** Mean, contemptible, or obscene: *a dirty trick; a dirty joke.* **3.** Not playing fair: *a dirty card player.* **4.** Expressing disapproval or hostility: *a dirty look.* —*tr. & intr.v.* **dirt•ied, dirt•y•ing, dirt•ies.** To make or become soiled: *I dirtied the tablecloth. White clothes dirty easily.*

dis– *pref.* A prefix that means: **1.** Not: *dissimilar.* **2.** Absence: *disfavor.* **3.** Opposite of: *distrust.* **4.** Do the opposite of: *disapprove.* **5.** Deprive of: *disarm.* —See Note.

dis•a•bil•i•ty (dĭs′ə **bĭl′**ĭ tē) *n., pl.* **dis•a•bil•i•ties. 1.** The condition of being disabled. **2.** Something that disables.

dis•a•ble (dĭs **ā′**bəl) *tr.v.* **dis•a•bled, dis•a•bling, dis•a•bles.** To weaken or impair the capacity or abilities of; incapacitate: *The storm disabled the steamer's engine.* **—dis•a′ble•ment** *n.*

dis•a•bled (dĭs **ā′**bəld) *adj.* **1.** Inoperative: *a disabled car.* **2.** Impaired, as in physical functioning: *a disabled veteran.* —*n.* Physically impaired people considered as a group: *The new building has access for the disabled.*

dis•a•buse (dĭs′ə **byōōz′**) *tr.v.* **dis•a•bused, dis•a•bus•ing, dis•a•bus•es.** To free from a falsehood or misconception: *disabuse someone of preconceived notions.*

dis•ad•van•tage (dĭs′əd **văn′**tĭj) *n.* **1.** An unfavorable condition or circumstance: *A disadvantage of river transportation is its slowness.* **2.** Damage or harm; loss: *The shorter library hours worked to the disadvantage of the public.*

dis•ad•van•taged (dĭs′əd **văn′**tĭjd) *adj.* Deprived of some of the basic necessities or advantages of life, such as housing, health care, or education.

dis•ad•van•ta•geous (dĭs ăd′vən **tā′**jəs *or* dĭs′ăd vən **tā′**jəs) *adj.* Detrimental; unfavorable: *disadvantageous living conditions.* **—dis•ad′van•ta′geous•ly** *adv.* **—dis•ad′van•ta′geous•ness** *n.*

dis•af•fect (dĭs′ə **fĕkt′**) *tr.v.* **dis•af•fect•ed, dis•af•fect•ing, dis•af•fects.** To cause to lose affection or loyalty. **—dis′af•fec′tion** *n.*

dis•af•fect•ed (dĭs′ə **fĕk′**tĭd) *adj.* Resentful and rebellious, especially against authority: *The disaffected workers voted to go on strike.*

dis•a•gree (dĭs′ə **grē′**) *intr.v.* **dis•a•greed, dis•a•gree•ing, dis•a•grees. 1.** To fail to correspond; differ: *Your answer disagrees with mine.* **2.** To have a differing opinion: *Scientists disagree on why dinosaurs died out.* **3.** To dispute or quarrel: *Rival countries often disagree about trade regulations.* **4.**

dirigible
United States Navy airship

dirt bike

Word Building: dis–

The prefix **dis–** has several senses, but its basic meaning is "not, not any." Thus **disbelieve** means "to refuse to believe" and **discomfort** means "a lack of comfort." **Dis–** came into English from the Old French prefix *des–*, which in turn came from the Latin prefix *dis–*, which came from the adverb *dis*, meaning "apart, asunder." **Dis–** is an important prefix that occurs very frequently in English in words such as **discredit**, **disrepair**, and **disrespect**.

ă	pat	oi	**boy**
ā	pay	ou	**out**
âr	care	ŏŏ	**took**
ä	father	ōō	boot
ĕ	pet	ŭ	cut
ē	be	ûr	**urge**
ĭ	pit	th	**thin**
ī	pie	*th*	**this**
îr	**pier**	hw	**whoop**
ŏ	pot	zh	vision
ō	**toe**	ə	about
ô	**paw**	N	*French* bon

To cause bad effects: *Fried food disagrees with me.*

dis•a•gree•a•ble (dĭs′ə grē′ə bəl) *adj.* **1.** Not to one's liking; unpleasant or offensive: *a strong and disagreeable odor.* **2.** Having a quarrelsome bad-tempered manner: *Many people are disagreeable when they first awaken.* **—dis′a•gree′a•ble•ness** *n.* **—dis′a•gree′a•bly** *adv.*

dis•a•gree•ment (dĭs′ə grē′mənt) *n.* **1.** A failure or refusal to agree. **2.** A conflict or difference of opinion: *Their disagreement ended in loud words.*

dis•al•low (dĭs′ə lou′) *tr.v.* **dis•al•lowed, dis•al•low•ing, dis•al•lows. 1.** To refuse to allow: *disallow eating in one's room.* **2.** To reject as invalid, untrue, or improper: *disallow an unsigned will as evidence.*

dis•ap•pear (dĭs′ə pîr′) *intr.v.* **dis•ap•peared, dis•ap•pear•ing, dis•ap•pears. 1.** To pass out of sight; vanish: *The ship disappeared over the horizon.* **2.** To cease to exist: *Warm weather disappears in the fall.*

Synonyms: **disappear, evaporate, fade, vanish.** These verbs mean to pass out of sight or existence. *The small plane disappeared in the fog. Alvin's courage evaporated when the time came to go to the dentist. As I watched Sally break the record time, my hopes of winning the race faded away. No one could figure out how the magician made the coin vanish.*

dis•ap•pear•ance (dĭs′ə pîr′əns) *n.* The act or an example of disappearing: *Disappearance of the ship during the storm led most to believe it sank.*

dis•ap•point (dĭs′ə point′) *tr.v.* **dis•ap•point•ed, dis•ap•point•ing, dis•ap•points. 1.** To fail to satisfy the hope, desire, or expectation of: *The ads were exciting, but the movie disappointed me.* **2.** To frustrate or thwart: *So far our efforts to get payment have been disappointed.*

dis•ap•point•ed (dĭs′ə poin′tĭd) *adj.* Thwarted in hope, desire, or expectation.

dis•ap•point•ing (dĭs′ə poin′tĭng) *adj.* Not up to expectations: *He finished the marathon in a disappointing 12th place.*

dis•ap•point•ment (dĭs′ə point′mənt) *n.* **1.** The act of disappointing. **2.** The condition or feeling of being disappointed: *couldn't hide their disappointment.* **3.** A person or thing that disappoints: *The picnic was a disappointment.*

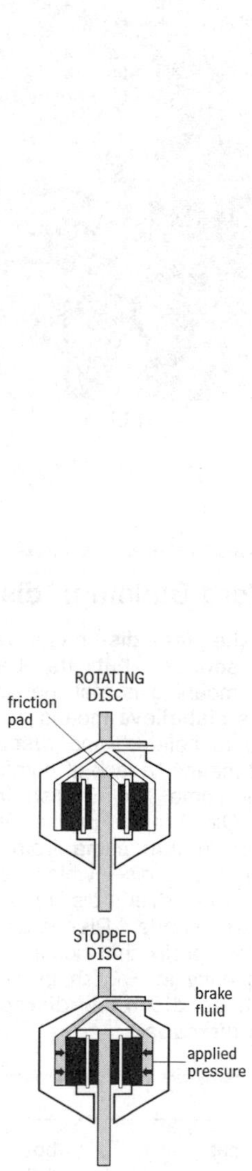

disc brake

dis•ap•prov•al (dĭs′ə pro͞o′vəl) *n.* The act of disapproving; censure or condemnation.

dis•ap•prove (dĭs′ə pro͞ov′) *v.* **dis•ap•proved, dis•ap•prov•ing, dis•ap•proves.** *—tr.* **1.** To have an unfavorable opinion of; condemn. **2.** To refuse to approve: *The state disapproved the new zoning proposal.* *—intr.* To have an unfavorable opinion: *disapprove of shouting.*

dis•arm (dĭs ärm′) *v.* **dis•armed, dis•arm•ing, dis•arms.** *—tr.* **1.** To take a weapon or weapons from: *The police officer disarmed the robber.* **2.** To make harmless: *disarm a charge of dynamite.* **3.** To overcome the suspicion or unfriendliness of; win the confidence of: *Her kind words disarmed us right away.* *—intr.* **1.** To lay down arms. **2.** To reduce or get rid of armed forces: *The countries voted to disarm.*

dis•ar•ma•ment (dĭs är′mə mənt) *n.* The reduction of a country's armed forces or weapons of destruction.

dis•arm•ing (dĭs är′mĭng) *adj.* Serving to remove suspicion or unfriendliness; winning favor or confidence: *a disarming smile.* **—dis•arm′ing•ly** *adv.*

dis•ar•range (dĭs′ə rānj′) *tr.v.* **dis•ar•ranged, dis•ar•rang•ing, dis•ar•rang•es.** To upset the proper order or arrangement of: *The wind disarranged my hair.* **—dis′ar•range′ment** *n.*

dis•ar•ray (dĭs′ə rā′) *n.* **1.** A state of disorder; confusion: *The mail lay in disarray on the desk.* **2.** Disorderly dress. *—tr.v.* **dis•ar•rayed, dis•ar•ray•ing, dis•ar•rays.** To throw into confusion; upset.

dis•as•sem•ble (dĭs′ə sĕm′bəl) *v.* **dis•as•sem•bled, dis•as•sem•bling, dis•as•sem•bles.** *—tr.* To take apart: *We have to disassemble the engine to repair it.* *—intr.* To come apart: *This telephone disassembles easily.*

dis•as•ter (dĭ zăs′tər) *n.* **1.** Something that causes widespread destruction and distress; a calamity: *Tornadoes, earthquakes, and floods are natural disasters.* **2.** *Informal.* A total failure. [First written down in 1591 in Modern English, from Italian *disastro* : *dis-*, bad + *astro*, star (from Greek *astron*).]

dis•as•trous (dĭ zăs′trəs) *adj.* Accompanied by or causing disaster; calamitous: *a disastrous earthquake; a disastrous error in judgment.* **—dis•as′trous•ly** *adv.*

dis•a•vow (dĭs′ə vou′) *tr.v.* **dis•a•vowed, dis•a•vow•ing, dis•a•vows.** To disclaim knowledge of, responsibility for, or association with.

dis•a•vow•al (dĭs′ə vou′əl) *n.* The act or an example of disavowing; a denial or repudiation.

dis•band (dĭs bănd′) *v.* **dis•band•ed, dis•band•ing, dis•bands.** *—tr.* To dissolve the organization of (a corporation, for example): *disband an orchestra.* *—intr.* To stop functioning as an organization; disperse: *The glee club disbanded last year.*

dis•bar (dĭs bär′) *tr.v.* **dis•barred, dis•bar•ring, dis•bars.** To expel (a lawyer) from the practice of law by official action or procedure. **—dis•bar′ment** *n.*

dis•be•lief (dĭs′bĭ lēf′) *n.* Refusal or reluctance to believe: *express disbelief at a fantastic story.*

dis•be•lieve (dĭs′bĭ lēv′) *v.* **dis•be•lieved, dis•be•liev•ing, dis•be•lieves.** *—tr.* To refuse to believe in; reject: *disbelieve stories of fabulous wealth.* *—intr.* To withhold or reject belief.

dis•bur•den (dĭs bûr′dn) *tr.v.* **dis•bur•dened, dis•bur•den•ing, dis•bur•dens. 1.** To relieve (a pack animal, for example) of a burden. **2.** To free of a trouble or worry: *He disburdened his mind by telling the truth.*

dis•burse (dĭs bûrs′) *tr.v.* **dis•bursed, dis•burs•ing, dis•burs•es.** To pay out, as from a fund; expend: *disburse large sums to advertise a product.* [First written down in 1530 in Modern English and spelled *disbourse*, from Old French *desborser* : *des-*, out + *borse*, purse (from Late Latin *bursa*).]

dis•burse•ment (dĭs bûrs′mənt) *n.* **1.** The act or process of disbursing. **2.** Money paid out; expenditure: *small disbursements.*

disc (dĭsk) *n. & v.* Variant of **disk.**

dis•card (dĭ skärd′) *v.* **dis•card•ed, dis•card•ing, dis•cards.** *—tr.* **1.** To throw away; reject: *discard old shoes; discard a childish habit.* **2.** In card games, to throw out (a playing card) from one's hand. *—intr.* To throw out a playing card. *—n.* (dĭs′kärd′). **1.** The act of discarding in a card game. **2.** A discarded playing card. **3.** Something that is discarded: *Charities will usually accept discards.*

disc brake also **disk brake** *n.* A brake that works by pressing pads against each side of a disk attached to the wheel of a car or truck.

dis•cern (dĭ sûrn′ *or* dĭ zûrn′) *v.* **dis•cerned, dis•cern•ing, dis•cerns.** *—tr.* To perceive with the eyes or intellect; detect: *discern a figure in the shadows.* *—intr.* To perceive differences; discriminate: *discern between right and wrong.* [First written down about 1380 in Middle English and spelled *discernen*, from Latin *discernere*, to separate : *dis-*, apart + *cernere*, to perceive.]

dis•cern•i•ble (dĭ sûr′nə bəl *or* dĭ zûr′nə bəl) *adj.*

Perceptible, as by the faculty of vision or the intellect: *few discernible differences between the two theories.* **—dis•cern′i•bly** *adv.*

dis•cern•ing (dĭ sûr′nĭng *or* dĭ zûr′nĭng) *adj.* Showing keen observation and good judgment; perceptive: *a discerning mind.* **—dis•cern′ing•ly** *adv.*

dis•cern•ment (dĭ sûrn′mənt *or* dĭ zûrn′mənt) *n.* **1.** The act or process of using or showing keen insight and good judgment. **2.** Keenness of insight or judgment: *having great discernment for new art.*

dis•charge (dĭs chärj′) *v.* **dis•charged, dis•charg•ing, dis•charg•es.** *—tr.* **1.a.** To relieve of a burden or of contents; unload. **b.** To unload or empty (contents). **2.** To let go or dismiss; release: *The steel plant closed and discharged its workers.* **3.** To send or pour forth: *Pipes discharge water into the lake.* **4.** To shoot: *discharged a volley of arrows.* **5.** To perform the obligations or requirements of (an office, a duty, or a task): *discharge the duties of mayor.* **6.** To comply with the terms of (a debt or promise, for example): *discharged the loan by making regular payments.* **7.** To take an electric charge from: *We discharged the battery while trying to start the car.* *—intr.* **1.** To get rid of a burden, load, or weight. **2.** To go off; fire. **3.** To pour forth contents: *Several streams discharge into the river.* **4.** To give off or lose an electric charge: *Flashlight batteries discharge when the light is on.* *—n.* (dĭs′chärj′ *or* dĭs chärj′). **1.** The act of removing a load or burden: *a discharge of freight from the ship.* **2.** The act of firing or shooting: *We could hear the discharges of a distant cannon.* **3.** A pouring out or flowing forth; an emission: *a discharge of pus from an infection.* **4.** Something poured or flowing forth: *a gummy discharge from a tree trunk.* **5.** Fulfillment of the terms of something, such as a debt or promise: *the discharge of the loan.* **6.a.** Dismissal or release: *a discharge from the hospital.* **b.** A certificate showing such release. **7.a.** A release of electric charge from a capacitor in a circuit or from a conducting body, such as a cloud in a thunderstorm. **b.** The conversion of chemical energy to electric energy in a battery. **c.** The passage of an electric current through a gas.

disc harrow *n.* Variant of **disk harrow.**

dis•ci•ple (dĭ sī′pəl) *n.* **1.** A person who accepts and assists in spreading the teachings of a leader. **2.** Often **Disciple.** In the Bible, one of the 12 original followers of Jesus. [First written down about 900 in Old English and spelled *discipul*, from Latin *discipulus*, pupil, from *discere*, to learn.]

dis•ci•pli•nar•i•an (dĭs′ə plə nâr′ē ən) *n.* A person who enforces or believes in strict discipline.

dis•ci•pli•nar•y (dĭs′ə plə nĕr′ē) *adj.* Of, relating to, or used for discipline: *disciplinary measures.*

dis•ci•pline (dĭs′ə plĭn) *n.* **1.a.** Training expected to produce a specific skill, behavior, or character. **b.** Controlled behavior resulting from such training. **c.** A systematic method to regulate behavior: *military discipline.* **2.** Punishment intended to correct or train. **3.** A branch of knowledge or of teaching: *Mathematics and computer science are related disciplines.* *—tr.v.* **dis•ci•plined, dis•ci•plin•ing, dis•ci•plines.** **1.** To train by instruction and practice. **2.** To punish in order to gain control or enforce obedience: *discipline a dog with a quick swat.* [First written down before 1200 in Middle English, from Latin *disciplīna*, from *discipulus*, pupil.]

disc jockey *n.* An announcer who presents and comments on popular recorded music, especially on the radio.

dis•claim (dĭs klām′) *v.* **dis•claimed, dis•claim•ing, dis•claims.** *—tr.* To deny or give up any claim to or connection with; disown. *—intr.* **1.** To deny the validity of; repudiate. **2.** To give up one's legal right or claim to: *disclaimed any part of the inheritance.*

dis•claim•er (dĭs klā′mər) *n.* A repudiation or denial of a responsibility or connection: *issue a disclaimer of involvement in an investment scheme.*

dis•close (dĭ sklōz′) *tr.v.* **dis•closed, dis•clos•ing, dis•clos•es.** **1.** To expose to view; uncover: *The excavation disclosed remains of an ancient city.* **2.** To make known (something previously kept secret). [First written down before 1393 in Middle English and spelled *disclosen*, from Old French *desclore* : *des-*, away, off + *clore*, to close (from Latin *claudere*).]

dis•clo•sure (dĭ sklō′zhər) *n.* **1.** The act or process of revealing or uncovering: *The company withheld disclosure of information about its new car.* **2.** Something uncovered; a revelation.

dis•co (dĭs′kō) *n., pl.* **dis•cos.** **1.** A discotheque. **2.** Popular dance music having strong repetitive bass rhythms. *—intr.v.* **dis•coed, dis•co•ing, dis•cos.** To dance to disco music: *They discoed until they were worn out.* [First written down in 1964 in American English, short for *discotheque*.]

dis•col•or (dĭs kŭl′ər) *tr. & intr.v.* **dis•col•ored, dis•col•or•ing, dis•col•ors.** To alter or become altered in color; stain: *Flood waters discolored the painting. Metal discolors with rust.*

dis•col•or•a•tion (dĭs kŭl′ə rā′shən) *n.* **1.** The act of discoloring or the condition of being discolored: *the discoloration of curtains washed in rusty water.* **2.** A stain: *Water damage left several large discolorations on the carpet.*

dis•com•fit (dĭs kŭm′fĭt) *tr.v.* **dis•com•fit•ed, dis•com•fit•ing, dis•com•fits.** **1.** To make uneasy or confused; embarrass: *Trying to speak a foreign language discomfits many people.* **2.** To prevent the fulfillment of; frustrate the plans of; thwart: *The robbers were discomfited by an alert guard.*

dis•com•fi•ture (dĭs kŭm′fĭ cho͝or′) *n.* **1.** Frustration; disappointment: *quit a project in total discomfiture.* **2.** Discomfort; embarrassment: *the discomfiture of a public scolding.*

dis•com•fort (dĭs kŭm′fərt) *n.* **1.** A lack of comfort; uneasiness: *a patient in discomfort.* **2.** Something that disturbs comfort: *A lumpy mattress is a discomfort when sleeping.*

dis•com•pose (dĭs′kəm pōz′) *tr.v.* **dis•com•posed, dis•com•pos•ing, dis•com•pos•es.** To disturb the composure or calm of; perturb: *The shouts of a few protesters discomposed the speaker.*

dis•com•po•sure (dĭs′kəm pō′zhər) *n.* The absence of composure; confusion or uneasiness: *The pianist's discomposure was evident from the mistakes made during the performance.*

dis•con•cert (dĭs′kən sûrt′) *tr.v.* **dis•con•cert•ed, dis•con•cert•ing, dis•con•certs.** To upset the self-possession of; embarrass or confuse: *All of the horns honking disconcerted the student driver.* [First written down in 1687 in Modern English, from Old French *desconcerter*.] **—dis′con•cert′ing•ly** *adv.*

dis•con•nect (dĭs′kə nĕkt′) *tr.v.* **dis•con•nect•ed, dis•con•nect•ing, dis•con•nects.** To break or interrupt the connection of or between; separate: *Disconnect the TV before you move it. Our telephone call was disconnected during the storm.* **—dis′con•nec′tion** *n.*

dis•con•nect•ed (dĭs′kə nĕk′tĭd) *adj.* **1.** Not connected; separate: *disconnected buildings.* **2.** Not clear or logical; disorderly: *a disconnected account of the accident; disconnected bits.* **—dis′con•nect′ed•ly** *adv.* **—dis′con•nect′ed•ness** *n.*

dis•con•so•late (dĭs kŏn′sə lĭt) *adj.* Very sad; hopeless: *We were left disconsolate when our cat disappeared.* **—dis•con′so•late•ly** *adv.* **—dis•con′so•late•ness** *n.*

disc jockey

ă	pat	oi	boy
ā	pay	ou	out
âr	care	o͝o	took
ä	father	o͞o	boot
ĕ	pet	ŭ	cut
ē	be	ûr	urge
ĭ	pit	th	thin
ī	pie	*th*	this
îr	pier	hw	whoop
ŏ	pot	zh	vision
ō	toe	ə	about
ô	paw	N	*French* bon

dis•con•tent (dĭs′kən **tĕnt′**) *n.* Lack of contentment; dissatisfaction: *Not getting a raise caused discontent among the workers.* —*tr.v.* **dis•con•tent•ed, dis•con•tent•ing, dis•con•tents.** To make discontented: *No electricity for three days discontented everyone.* —**dis′con•tent′ment** *n.*

dis•con•tent•ed (dĭs′kən **tĕn′**tĭd) *adj.* Not contented; unhappy: *Discontented tenants refused to pay rent until they got heat.* —**dis′con•tent′ed•ly** *adv.* —**dis′con•tent′ed•ness** *n.*

dis•con•tin•u•a•tion (dĭs′kən tĭn′yo͞o **ā′**shən) *n.* A termination; an ending: *discontinuation of bus service during the storm.* —**dis′con•tin′u•ance** (dĭs′kən **tĭn′**yo͞o əns) *n.*

dis•con•tin•ue (dĭs′kən **tĭn′**yo͞o) *v.* **dis•con•tin•ued, dis•con•tin•u•ing, dis•con•tin•ues.** —*tr.* To put a stop or end to; stop: *discontinue publication of a magazine.* —*intr.* To come to an end: *Bus service discontinued after midnight.*

dis•con•tin•u•ous (dĭs′kən **tĭn′**yo͞o əs) *adj.* Not continuous; broken up; interrupted: *a discontinuous supply of natural gas.* —**dis′con•tin′u•ous•ly** *adv.* —**dis′con•tin′u•ous•ness** *n.*

dis•cord (**dĭs′**kôrd′) *n.* **1.** Lack of agreement or harmony: *an angry meeting filled with discord.* **2.** A combination of musical tones that sounds harsh or unpleasant; a lack of harmony. **3.** A confused or harsh mingling of sounds: *the early morning discord of rush-hour traffic.* [First written down about 1230 in Middle English and spelled *descorde*, from Latin *discors*, disagreeing : *dis-*, apart + *cor*, heart.]

dis•cor•dant (dĭ **skôr′**dnt) *adj.* **1.** Not in agreement; conflicting: *a discordant meeting.* **2.** Disagreeable in sound; harsh: *discordant sounds of the city streets.* —**dis•cor′dance** *n.* —**dis•cor′dant•ly** *adv.*

dis•co•theque (**dĭs′**kə tĕk′ *or* dĭs′kə **tĕk′**) *n.* A nightclub that offers dancing to recorded music. [First written down in 1954 in Modern English, from Italian *discoteca*, record library : *disco*, disk, record (from Latin *discus*, quoit) + *biblioteca*, library (from Latin *bibliothēca*).]

dis•count (**dĭs′**kount′ *or* dĭs **kount′**) *tr.v.* **dis•count•ed, dis•count•ing, dis•counts. 1.** To deduct or subtract (an amount or a percentage) from a cost or price of an item, as in a sale: *The dealer discounted 25 percent off the original price of the rug.* **2.** To sell or offer for sale at a reduced price: *The store discounts its coats each spring.* **3.** To disregard or doubt (something) as an exaggeration or not trustworthy: *The scientist discounted the rumors of a new energy source.* —*n.* (**dĭs′**kount′). A reduction from the full amount of a price or debt. [First written down in 1629 in Modern English and spelled *discompt*, from Old French *desconter* : *des-*, away, down + *conter*, to count.]

dis•cour•age (dĭ **skûr′**ĭj *or* dĭ **skŭr′**ĭj) *tr.v.* **dis•cour•aged, dis•cour•ag•ing, dis•cour•ag•es. 1.** To make less hopeful or confident; dishearten: *The size of the job discouraged me.* **2.** To try to prevent by expressing disapproval or raising objections; dissuade: *Friends discouraged them from going.* **3.** To hinder or deter: *Severe penalties are supposed to discourage tax evasion.*

dis•cour•age•ment (dĭ **skûr′**ĭj mənt *or* dĭ **skŭr′**ĭj mənt) *n.* **1.** A condition of being or feeling discouraged: *Discouragement and hardship destroyed the hopes of many pioneers.* **2.** Something that discourages: *Harsh winters are a discouragement to living in the far north.* **3.** The act of discouraging: *The discouragement of my family made me more determined to be an actor.*

dis•course (**dĭs′**kôrs′) *n.* **1.** Talking; conversation: *cheerful discourse among friends.* **2.** A formal discussion, either spoken or written: *The minister gave a long discourse on morality. The book is a discourse on politics.* —*intr.v.* (dĭ **skôrs′**). **dis•coursed, dis•cours•ing, dis•cours•es.** To speak or write formally and often at length: *The mayor discoursed on the role of the government in improving city life.* [First written down about 1380 in Middle English and spelled *discours*, process of reasoning, from Medieval Latin *discursus* : Latin *dis-*, apart + Latin *currere*, to run.]

dis•cour•te•ous (dĭs **kûr′**tē əs) *adj.* Lacking courtesy; not polite; rude. —**dis•cour′te•ous•ly** *adv.* —**dis•cour′te•ous•ness** *n.*

dis•cour•te•sy (dĭs **kûr′**tĭ sē) *n., pl.* **dis•cour•te•sies. 1.** Lack of courtesy; rudeness. **2.** A rude or impolite act: *the discourtesy of interrupting others.*

dis•cov•er (dĭ **skŭv′**ər) *tr.v.* **dis•cov•ered, dis•cov•er•ing, dis•cov•ers. 1.** To find or see for the first time: *The explorers discovered the source of the river.* **2.** To learn of; gain knowledge of: *discover errors by checking.* [First written down before 1325 in Middle English and spelled *discoveren*, to reveal, from Late Latin *discooperīre* : *dis-*, away + *cooperīre*, to cover.] —**dis•cov′er•er** *n.*

dis•cov•er•y (dĭ **skŭv′**ə rē) *n., pl.* **dis•cov•er•ies. 1.** The act of discovering: *Discovery of a polio vaccine ended fear of the disease.* **2.** Something discovered: *Atomic energy is one of the greatest discoveries of science.*

dis•cred•it (dĭs **krĕd′**ĭt) *tr.v.* **dis•cred•it•ed, dis•cred•it•ing, dis•cred•its. 1.** To damage in reputation; disgrace: *The report of corruption discredits our politicians.* **2.** To cast doubt on; cause to be distrusted: *new scientific evidence that discredits earlier theories.* **3.** To refuse to believe in: *discredit a story as mere gossip.* —*n.* **1.** Loss or damage to one's reputation: *Dishonest officials brought discredit to the city government.* **2.** Lack or loss of trust or belief; doubt: *An eyewitness account that brings earlier testimony into discredit.* **3.** Something that brings disgrace or distrust: *He is a discredit to his family.*

dis•cred•it•a•ble (dĭs **krĕd′**ĭ tə bəl) *adj.* Deserving or bringing discredit; disgraceful: *Lying in court is a discreditable act.* —**dis•cred′it•a•bly** *adv.*

dis•creet (dĭ **skrēt′**) *adj.* Having or showing caution or self-restraint in one's speech or behavior; prudent: *The teacher was discreet in discussing the student's mistake. Keep a discreet distance from any wild animal.* [First written down about 1385 in Middle English and spelled *discret*, from Medieval Latin *discrētus*, from Latin *discernere*, to separate, discern.] —**dis•creet′ly** *adv.* —**dis•creet′ness** *n.*

❑ *These sound alike:* **discreet, discrete** (distinct).

dis•crep•an•cy (dĭ **skrĕp′**ən sē) *n., pl.* **dis•crep•an•cies.** Lack of agreement; inconsistency: *There was a large discrepancy between their statement and the facts.*

dis•crep•ant (dĭ **skrĕp′**ənt) *adj.* Showing discrepancy; disagreeing. [First written down in 1450 in Middle English and spelled *discrepaunt*, from Latin *discrepāre*, to disagree : *dis-*, apart + *crepāre*, to rattle.]

dis•crete (dĭ **skrēt′**) *adj.* Separate from others; distinct: *The police commissioner oversees several discrete departments. I have only a few discrete memories of my early childhood.* [First written down about 1385 in Middle English, from Latin *discrētus*, past participle of *discernere*, to separate.] —**dis•crete′ly** *adv.*

❑ *These sound alike:* **discrete, discreet** (prudent).

dis•cre•tion (dĭ **skrĕsh′**ən) *n.* **1.** The quality of being discreet; prudence: *Diplomats must use great discretion in negotiating treaties.* **2.** Freedom of action or judgment: *Choosing numbers for their jerseys was left to the players' discretion.*

dis•cre•tion•ar•y (dĭ skrĕsh′ə nĕr′ē) *adj.* Left to or determined by one's own discretion or judgment: *The governor has a discretionary fund for emergencies.*

dis•crim•i•nate (dĭ skrĭm′ə nāt′) *v.* **dis•crim•i•nat•ed, dis•crim•i•nat•ing, dis•crim•i•nates.** —*intr.* **1.** To make a clear distinction; distinguish: *discriminate shades of meaning for similar words.* **2.** To show preference or prejudice: *Some employers discriminate against older workers.* —*tr.* To make or see a clear distinction between: *A critic discriminates good books from poor ones.* [First written down in 1628 in Modern English, from Latin *discrīmen*, distinction.] **—dis•crim′i•na′tor** *n.*

dis•crim•i•nat•ing (dĭ skrĭm′ə nā′tĭng) *adj.* **1.** Showing careful judgment or fine taste: *a discriminating critic of modern music.* **2.** Serving to distinguish or set apart from others; distinctive: *a discriminating characteristic.* **3.** Marked by or showing bias; discriminatory. **—dis•crim′i•nat′ing•ly** *adv.*

dis•crim•i•na•tion (dĭ skrĭm′ə nā′shən) *n.* **1.** The ability to recognize or make fine distinctions: *clothes bought without care or discrimination; discrimination of color essential to the work of an artist.* **2.** Treatment of people based on their belonging to a class or category rather than on individual merit; partiality or prejudice: *The Constitution protects citizens from racial and religious discrimination.*

dis•crim•i•na•to•ry (dĭ skrĭm′ə nə tôr′ē) *adj.* Showing prejudice; biased. **—dis•crim′i•na•to′ri•ly** *adv.*

dis•cur•sive (dĭ skûr′sĭv) *adj.* Wandering from one subject to another; rambling: *discursive talk without much point to it.* **—dis•cur′sive•ly** *adv.* **—dis•cur′sive•ness** *n.*

dis•cus (dĭs′kəs) *n., pl.* **dis•cus•es.** A heavy disk of wood and metal that is hurled for distance in athletic contests.

dis•cuss (dĭ skŭs′) *tr.v.* **dis•cussed, dis•cuss•ing, dis•cuss•es.** To talk over or write about: *We met to discuss plans for a new park.* [First written down about 1380 in Middle English and spelled *discussen*, to examine, from Latin *discussus*, past participle of *discutere*, to break apart : *dis-*, apart + *quatere*, to shake.]

dis•cus•sion (dĭ skŭsh′ən) *n.* A consideration of a subject by different people; a conversation or an exchange of views.

dis•dain (dĭs dān′) *tr.v.* **dis•dained, dis•dain•ing, dis•dains.** To consider or treat with contempt; despise: *The composer disdained the judgments of critics in the press.* —*n.* A show of contempt and aloofness; scorn: *She responded with disdain to his offers of a bribe.* [First written down about 1380 in Middle English and spelled *disdaignen*, from Latin *dēdignārī* : *dē-*, away, off + *dignārī*, to deem worthy (from *dignus*, worthy).]

dis•dain•ful (dĭs dān′fəl) *adj.* Feeling or showing disdain; scornful. **—dis•dain′ful•ly** *adv.*

dis•ease (dĭ zēz′) *n.* A condition of an organism that makes it unable to function in the normal or proper way; sickness: *Malaria is one of the most widespread diseases in the world.*

dis•eased (dĭ zēzd′) *adj.* Affected with or suffering from disease: *a diseased heart.*

dis•em•bark (dĭs′ĕm bärk′) *v.* **dis•em•barked, dis•em•bark•ing, dis•em•barks.** —*intr.* To get off a ship or an airplane: *We disembark at Montreal's airport.* —*tr.* To put or let off a ship or an airplane: *The captain disembarked passengers for the day.* **—dis•em′bar•ka′tion** *n.*

dis•em•bod•ied (dĭs′ĕm bŏd′ēd) *adj.* Freed or separated from the body: *disembodied spirits.*

dis•em•bow•el (dĭs′ĕm bou′əl) *tr.v.* **dis•em•bow•eled, dis•em•bow•el•ing, dis•em•bow•els** or **dis•em•bow•elled, dis•em•bow•el•ling, dis•em•bow•els.** To remove the bowels from: *The elephant disemboweled the lion with its tusks.* **—dis′em•bow′el•ment** *n.*

dis•en•chant (dĭs′ĕn chănt′) *tr.v.* **dis•en•chant•ed, dis•en•chant•ing, dis•en•chants.** To free from enchantment or false belief; disillusion: *One look at the crumbling house was enough to disenchant any buyer.* **—dis′en•chant′ment** *n.*

dis•en•cum•ber (dĭs′ĕn kŭm′bər) *tr.v.* **dis•en•cum•bered, dis•en•cum•ber•ing, dis•en•cum•bers.** To free from something that burdens, hinders, or troubles: *disencumber oneself of worry.*

dis•en•fran•chise (dĭs′ĕn frăn′chīz′) *tr.v.* **dis•en•fran•chised, dis•en•fran•chis•ing, dis•en•fran•chis•es.** To disfranchise. **—dis′en•fran′chise′ment** (dĭs′ĕn frăn′chīz′mənt *or* dĭs′ĕn frăn′chĭz mənt) *n.*

dis•en•gage (dĭs′ĕn gāj′) *v.* **dis•en•gaged, dis•en•gag•ing, dis•en•gag•es.** —*tr.* **1.** To make free from something that holds fast, entangles, or connects: *disengage the car's clutch.* **2.** To free or release (oneself) from an engagement, a promise, or an obligation. —*intr.* To become free or detach oneself: *As the brakes disengaged, the car rolled backwards.* **—dis′en•gage′ment** *n.*

dis•en•tan•gle (dĭs′ĕn tăng′gəl) *tr.v.* **dis•en•tan•gled, dis•en•tan•gling, dis•en•tan•gles.** To free from tangles or confusion: *disentangle a knotted clothesline; disentangle fact from a web of accusations.* **—dis′en•tan′gle•ment** *n.*

dis•fa•vor (dĭs fā′vər) *n.* **1.** Unfavorable regard; disapproval. **2.** The condition of being regarded with dislike or disapproval: *The governor was in disfavor with voters.* —*tr.v.* **dis•fa•vored, dis•fa•vor•ing, dis•fa•vors.** To view or treat with dislike or disapproval: *The company disfavored any expenditure to clean up the environment.*

dis•fig•ure (dĭs fĭg′yər) *tr.v.* **dis•fig•ured, dis•fig•ur•ing, dis•fig•ures.** To spoil the appearance of; mar the beauty of: *Vandals disfigured the statue with paint.*

dis•fran•chise (dĭs frăn′chīz′) *tr.v.* **dis•fran•chised, dis•fran•chis•ing, dis•fran•chis•es.** To deprive of a privilege or a right, especially the right to vote. **—dis•fran′chise′ment** (dĭs frăn′chīz′mənt *or* dĭs frăn′chĭz mənt) *n.*

dis•gorge (dĭs gôrj′) *tr.v.* **dis•gorged, dis•gorg•ing, dis•gorg•es.** **1.** To bring up and discharge from the throat or stomach; vomit. **2.** To pour forth violently; spew: *The volcano disgorged lava into the ocean.* **3.** To give up (stolen goods, for example) unwillingly. [First written down about 1477 in Middle English and spelled *disgorgen*, from Old French *desgorger*, from *gorge*, throat.]

dis•grace (dĭs grās′) *n.* **1.** Loss of honor, respect, or reputation; shame: *The scandal brought disgrace on the politician's family.* **2.** The condition of being strongly disapproved: *in disgrace for telling a secret.* **3.** A person or thing that brings dishonor or disfavor: *The dirty streets are a disgrace to the city.* —*tr.v.* **dis•graced, dis•grac•ing, dis•grac•es.** **1.** To bring shame or dishonor upon: *The thief's conviction disgraced family and friends.* **2.** To put (someone) out of favor: *The mayor disgraced the aide for failing to investigate the problem.*

dis•grace•ful (dĭs grās′fəl) *adj.* Causing or deserving disgrace; shameful. **—dis•grace′ful•ly** *adv.* **—dis•grace′ful•ness** *n.*

dis•grun•tle (dĭs grŭn′tl) *tr.v.* **dis•grun•tled, dis•grun•tling, dis•grun•tles.** To make discontented; displease or disgust: *Loss of two vacation days dis-*

discus
Preparing to throw a discus

ă	pat	oi	boy
ā	pay	ou	out
âr	care	o͝o	took
ä	father	o͞o	boot
ĕ	pet	ŭ	cut
ē	be	ûr	urge
ĭ	pit	th	thin
ī	pie	*th*	this
îr	pier	hw	whoop
ŏ	pot	zh	vision
ō	toe	ə	about
ô	paw	N	*French* bon

gruntled all the employees. [First written down in 1682 in Modern English, from *gruntle*, to grumble.] **—dis•grun′tle•ment** *n.*

dis•guise (dĭs gīz′) *tr.v.* **dis•guised, dis•guis•ing, dis•guis•es. 1.** To hide the identity of by changing the appearance: *The princess disguised herself as a shepherd boy.* **2.** To hide or cause to appear different: *She disguised her embarrassment with a smile.* —*n.* **1.** Clothes or other effects used to conceal one's true identity: *The two spies wore the disguise of repairmen.* **2.** An act or a manner of behaving that is designed to hide something: *Their laughter was a disguise for nervousness.*

dis•gust (dĭs gŭst′) *tr.v.* **dis•gust•ed, dis•gust•ing, dis•gusts.** To cause feelings of sickening dislike, distaste, or annoyance: *We are disgusted by your refusal to cooperate.* —*n.* A feeling of extreme dislike, distaste, or annoyance: *The fans showed their disgust by booing the umpire.* [First written down in 1601 in Modern English, from Old French *desgouster*, to lose one's appetite : *des-*, away, not + *gouster*, to eat, taste (from Latin *gustāre*).]

dis•gust•ed (dĭs gŭs′tĭd) *adj.* Filled with disgust: *a disgusted look.* **—dis•gust′ed•ly** *adv.*

dis•gust•ing (dĭs gŭs′tĭng) *adj.* Causing disgust: *disgusting food; a disgusting remark.* **—dis•gust′ing•ly** *adv.*

dish (dĭsh) *n.* **1.a.** A shallow container for holding or serving food. **b.** The amount that a dish can hold: *I ate two dishes of fruit.* **2.** A particular kind or preparation of food: *Chow mein is our favorite dish.* **3.** A radio, television, or radar antenna having the shape of a dish. —*tr.v.* **dished, dish•ing, dish•es.** To serve (food) in a dish or dishes: *dish out the vegetables.* [First written down about 700 in Old English and spelled *disc*, from Latin *discus*.]

dish
Radar dish antenna

dis•heart•en (dĭs här′tn) *tr.v.* **dis•heart•ened, dis•heart•en•ing, dis•heart•ens.** To cause to lose courage and hope: *Lack of interest in their new battery disheartened the inventors.* **—dis•heart′en•ing•ly** *adv.*

di•shev•eled or **di•shev•elled** (dĭ shĕv′əld) *adj.* Untidy; disorderly: *disheveled clothes; a disheveled look.* [First written down about 1410 in Middle English and spelled *discheveled*, from Old French *descheveler*, to disarrange the hair : *des-*, apart + *chevel*, hair (from Latin *capillus*).]

dis•hon•est (dĭs ŏn′ĭst) *adj.* **1.** Inclined to lie, cheat, or deceive: *a dishonest art dealer.* **2.** Showing or resulting from falseness or fraud: *a dishonest answer; dishonest dealings.* **—dis•hon′est•ly** *adv.*

dis•hon•es•ty (dĭs ŏn′ĭ stē) *n., pl.* **dis•hon•es•ties. 1.** Lack of honesty or integrity. **2.** A dishonest act or statement.

dis•hon•or (dĭs ŏn′ər) *n.* **1.** Loss of honor, respect, or reputation; shame. **2.** A person or thing that causes loss of honor: *a dishonor to the whole team.* —*tr.v.* **dis•hon•ored, dis•hon•or•ing, dis•hon•ors.** To bring shame or disgrace on: *His rude behavior dishonors the reputation of his company.*

dis•hon•or•a•ble (dĭs ŏn′ər ə bəl) *adj.* Characterized by or causing dishonor: *the dishonorable acts of a swindler.* **—dis•hon′or•a•ble•ness** *n.* **—dis•hon′or•a•bly** *adv.*

dish•tow•el (dĭsh′tou′əl) *n.* A towel for drying dishes.

dish•wash•er (dĭsh′wŏsh′ər *or* dĭsh′wô′shər) *n.* **1.** A machine that washes dishes. **2.** A person who washes dishes, especially in a restaurant.

dish•wa•ter (dĭsh′wô′tər *or* dĭsh′wŏt′ər) *n.* Water in which dishes are or have been washed.

dis•il•lu•sion (dĭs′ĭ lo͞o′zhən) *tr.v.* **dis•il•lu•sioned, dis•il•lu•sion•ing, dis•il•lu•sions.** To free from a false idea or belief: *Many newcomers to the country were disillusioned by the high cost of living.* **—dis′il•lu′sion•ment** *n.*

dis•in•cli•na•tion (dĭs ĭn′klə nā′shən) *n.* Unwillingness, reluctance, or aversion: *a disinclination to try new foods.*

dis•in•clined (dĭs′ĭn klīnd′) *adj.* Unwilling; reluctant: *I am disinclined to take a job with such long hours.*

dis•in•fect (dĭs′ĭn fĕkt′) *tr.v.* **dis•in•fect•ed, dis•in•fect•ing, dis•in•fects.** To cleanse so as to destroy microorganisms that cause disease: *disinfect a cut.* **—dis′in•fec′tion** *n.*

dis•in•fec•tant (dĭs′ĭn fĕk′tənt) *n.* A substance that kills microorganisms that cause disease: *wash a wound with disinfectant.* —*adj.* Destroying or slowing the growth of microorganisms that cause disease: *disinfectant soap.*

dis•in•her•it (dĭs′ĭn hĕr′ĭt) *tr.v.* **dis•in•her•it•ed, dis•in•her•it•ing, dis•in•her•its.** To take from (a person) an inheritance or the right to inherit: *The eccentric millionaire disinherited his entire family.*

dis•in•te•grate (dĭs ĭn′tĭ grāt′) *v.* **dis•in•te•grat•ed, dis•in•te•grat•ing, dis•in•te•grates.** —*intr.* **1.** To break into small pieces; separate into bits: *rock disintegrating into sand.* **2.** In nuclear physics, to undergo disintegration. —*tr.* To cause to break into separate pieces or bits: *Water disintegrated the cement to pebble-sized pieces.*

dis•in•te•gra•tion (dĭs ĭn′tĭ grā′shən) *n.* **1.a.** The act or process of disintegrating: *Freezing and thawing caused disintegration of the concrete.* **b.** The condition of being disintegrated: *Disintegration will continue until repairs are made.* **2.** In nuclear physics, a process in which an atomic nucleus is transformed as it throws off particles or rays.

dis•in•ter (dĭs′ĭn tûr′) *tr.v.* **dis•in•terred, dis•in•ter•ring, dis•in•ters. 1.** To dig up or remove (a body) from a grave. **2.** To make public; disclose: *disinter old documents from the library.* **—dis′in•ter′ment** *n.*

dis•in•ter•est•ed (dĭs ĭn′trĭ stĭd *or* dĭs ĭn′tə rĕs′-tĭd) *adj.* **1.** Free of bias and self-interest; impartial: *the disinterested decision of an umpire.* **2.** Uninterested or unconcerned: *My friends are totally disinterested in the movie.* **—dis•in′ter•est•ed•ly** *adv.*

dis•joint (dĭs joint′) *tr.v.* **dis•joint•ed, dis•joint•ing, dis•joints. 1.** To take apart at the joints: *The butcher quickly disjointed the chicken for frying.* **2.** To pull out of joint; dislocate: *That tackle disjointed the football player's shoulder.* **3.** To break up; put out of order: *The flooding disjointed the business section of town.* —*adj.* In mathematics, having no common members. {0, 1, 2} and {3, 4, 5} are disjoint sets.

dis•joint•ed (dĭs join′tĭd) *adj.* **1.** Separated at the joints: *a disjointed leg of lamb.* **2.** Lacking order or coherence; disconnected: *a disjointed paragraph.* **—dis•joint′ed•ly** *adv.*

disk also **disc** (dĭsk) *n.* **1.** A thin, flat, circular object, such as a plate or coin. **2.** Something that resembles such an object: *the moon's disk reflected in the pond.* **3.** Often **disc. a.** A phonograph record. **b.** A round flat plate coated with a magnetic substance on which computer data is stored. **c.** An optical disk, especially a compact disk. [First written down in 1664 in Modern English, from Greek *diskos*, quoit, from *dikein*, to throw.]

disk brake *n.* **disc brake.**

disk drive *n.* A device in a computer that stores or retrieves data from a rotating disk.

disk•ette (dĭ skĕt′) *n.* A floppy disk.

disk harrow or **disc harrow** *n.* A harrow consisting of a series of rotating disks on one or more axles, used to break up soil for seeding or planting.

disk jockey *n.* Variant of **disc jockey.**

dis•like (dĭs līk′) *tr.v.* **dis•liked, dis•lik•ing, dis•likes.** To regard with distaste: *I dislike his idea.* —*n.* A feeling of distaste: *I have a strong dislike of board games.*

dis•lo•cate (dĭs′lō kāt′ *or* dĭs lō′kāt) *tr.v.* **dis•lo•cat•ed, dis•lo•cat•ing, dis•lo•cates. 1.** To put out of joint: *I dislocated my thumb catching the ball barehanded.* **2.** To throw into confusion or disorder; upset: *The drought dislocated the state's economy. The snowstorm dislocated rail and air traffic.* **—dis′lo•ca′tion** *n.*

dis•lodge (dĭs lŏj′) *tr.v.* **dis•lodged, dis•lodg•ing, dis•lodg•es.** To move or force out of position: *Heavy rains dislodged boulders from the hillside.*

dis•loy•al (dĭs loi′əl) *adj.* Lacking loyalty; unfaithful. **—dis•loy′al•ly** *adv.*

dis•loy•al•ty (dĭs loi′əl tē) *n., pl.* **dis•loy•al•ties. 1.** Lack of loyalty; unfaithfulness. **2.** A disloyal act: *Taking all the credit for the discovery was a disloyalty to fellow researchers.*

dis•mal (dĭz′məl) *adj.* **1.** Causing gloom or depression; dreary: *a dismal fog.* **2.** Feeling gloomy; depressed; miserable: *feeling dismal from a bad cold.* **—dis′mal•ly** *adv.* **—dis′mal•ness** *n.* —SEE NOTE.

dis•man•tle (dĭs măn′tl) *tr.v.* **dis•man•tled, dis•man•tling, dis•man•tles. 1.** To pull down; take apart: *We dismantled the table to get it through the door.* **2.** To strip of furnishings or equipment: *Movers dismantled the apartment.* [First written down in 1579 in Modern English and spelled *dismantle*, to tear down fortifications, from Old French *desmanteler* : *des-*, off, down + *emmanteler*, to cover with a coat, shelter (from *mantel*, cloak).] **—dis•man′tle•ment** *n.*

dis•may (dĭs mā′) *tr.v.* **dis•mayed, dis•may•ing, dis•mays. 1.** To fill with dread; make anxious or afraid: *The fear of an epidemic dismayed the whole city.* **2.** To discourage or dishearten: *A low grade on the exam dismayed the student.* —*n.* A sudden loss of courage or confidence in the face of danger or trouble: *Being lost in the woods filled the hikers with dismay.* [First written down before 1300 in Middle English and spelled *dismaien*, from Old French *esmaier*, to frighten.]

dis•mem•ber (dĭs mĕm′bər) *tr.v.* **dis•mem•bered, dis•mem•ber•ing, dis•mem•bers. 1.** To cut, tear, or pull off the limbs of: *The fox dismembered the chicken.* **2.** To divide into pieces: *The Roman Empire has been dismembered into numerous states.* **—dis•mem′ber•ment** *n.*

dis•miss (dĭs mĭs′) *tr.v.* **dis•missed, dis•miss•ing, dis•miss•es. 1.** To end the employment or service of; discharge: *Several workers were dismissed for loafing on the job.* **2.** To direct or allow to leave: *The students were dismissed for the holidays.* **3.** To put out of one's mind or consider as unimportant: *We dismissed the story as gossip.* **4.** To put (a claim or an action) out of court without further hearing: *The judge dismissed the case because there was not enough evidence.* [First written down about 1432 in Middle English and spelled *dismissen*, from Latin *dīmittere* : *dī-*, *dis-*, away + *mittere*, to send.]

dis•miss•al (dĭs mĭs′əl) *n.* **1.** The act of dismissing: *the principal's dismissal of students because of the coming snowstorm.* **2.** The condition of being dismissed. **3.** An order or a notice of discharge: *Two workers found to be stealing received their dismissals by mail.*

dis•mount (dĭs mount′) *v.* **dis•mount•ed, dis•mount•ing, dis•mounts.** —*intr.* To get off or down, as from a horse or bicycle; alight. —*tr.* **1.** To unseat from a horse: *The frightened horse dismounted its rider.* **2.** To remove (a thing) from its support or mounting: *dismounted the old cannon for storage.* **3.** To take apart (a mechanism).

dis•o•be•di•ence (dĭs′ə bē′dē əns) *n.* Refusal or failure to obey.

dis•o•be•di•ent (dĭs′ə bē′dē ənt) *adj.* Refusing or failing to obey: *a disobedient child.* **—dis′o•be′di•ent•ly** *adv.*

dis•o•bey (dĭs′ə bā′) *tr. & intr.v.* **dis•o•beyed, dis•o•bey•ing, dis•o•beys.** To refuse or fail to obey: *Pedestrians sometimes disobey traffic signals. A trained horse seldom disobeys.*

dis•or•der (dĭs ôr′dər) *n.* **1.** Lack of order or regular arrangement; confusion: *Your desk is always in a state of disorder.* **2.** A public disturbance: *Police responded to a disorder in our neighborhood.* **3.** A sickness of the body or mind: *a nervous disorder.* —*tr.v.* **dis•or•dered, dis•or•der•ing, dis•or•ders. 1.** To throw into disorder; muddle: *Early arrival of our guests disordered all our arrangements.* **2.** To upset the mental or physical health of: *Rich foods thoroughly disorder my digestion.*

dis•or•der•ly (dĭs ôr′dər lē) *adj.* **1.** Lacking regular or orderly arrangement; messy: *a disorderly room.* **2.** Lacking discipline; unruly: *a noisy disorderly crowd.* **—dis•or′der•li•ness** *n.*

dis•or•gan•ize (dĭs ôr′gə nīz′) *tr.v.* **dis•or•gan•ized, dis•or•gan•iz•ing, dis•or•gan•iz•es.** To destroy the organization or orderly arrangement of; throw into confusion or disorder: *The airline strike disorganized air schedules.* **—dis•or′gan•i•za′tion** (dĭs ôr′gə nĭ zā′shən) *n.*

dis•o•ri•ent (dĭs ôr′ē ĕnt′) *tr.v.* **dis•o•ri•ent•ed, dis•o•ri•ent•ing, dis•o•ri•ents.** To cause to lose one's sense of direction or bearings; confuse: *Walking around in an unfamiliar part of the city disoriented us.* **—dis•o′ri•en•ta′tion** *n.*

dis•own (dĭs ōn′) *tr.v.* **dis•owned, dis•own•ing, dis•owns.** To refuse to claim or accept as one's own; repudiate; reject: *The father disowned his son for refusing to join the family business.*

dis•par•age (dĭ spăr′ĭj) *tr.v.* **dis•par•aged, dis•par•ag•ing, dis•par•ag•es. 1.** To speak of as unimportant or inferior; belittle: *He disparages the accomplishments of others.* **2.** To lower in regard or position; discredit: *The article disparages environmentalists as busybodies.* [First written down before 1375 in Middle English and spelled *desparagen*, from Old French *desparager* : *des-*, away, down + *parage*, high birth (from *per*, peer).] **—dis•par′age•ment** *n.* **—dis•par′ag•ing•ly** *adv.*

dis•pa•rate (dĭs′pər ĭt *or* dĭ spăr′ĭt) *adj.* Completely distinct or different in kind; entirely dissimilar. [First written down in 1608 in Modern English, from Latin *disparāre*, to separate : *dis-*, apart + *parāre*, to prepare.] **—dis′pa•rate•ly** *adv.*

dis•par•i•ty (dĭ spăr′ĭ tē) *n., pl.* **dis•par•i•ties. 1.** Inequality; difference: *the disparity in population between one city and another.* **2.** Lack of similarity; unlikeness: *a great disparity in the accounts of what happened.* [First written down about 1555 in Modern English, from Late Latin *disparitās* : Latin *dis-*, not + Late Latin *paritās*, equality.]

dis•pas•sion•ate (dĭs păsh′ə nĭt) *adj.* Not influenced by strong feelings or emotions: *the dispassionate judgment of a judge.* **—dis•pas′sion•ate•ly** *adv.* **—dis•pas′sion•ate•ness** *n.*

dis•patch also **des•patch** (dĭ spăch′) *tr.v.* **dis•patched, dis•patch•ing, dis•patch•es** also **des•patched, des•patch•ing, des•patch•es. 1.** To send off to a specific destination or on specific business: *dispatch a letter; dispatch a police car to the scene of a disturbance.* **2.** To complete or dispose of promptly: *The police dispatched their duty and left.* **3.** To put to death quickly and without ceremony: *The ranger dispatched the injured deer.* —*n.* **1.** The act of sending off: *the dispatch of a representative to the conference.* **2.** Quickness and efficiency in

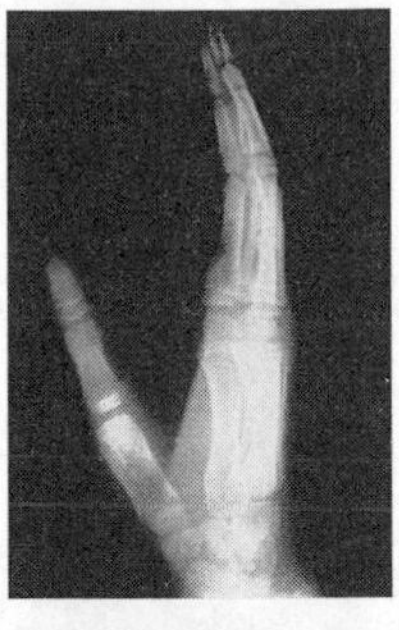

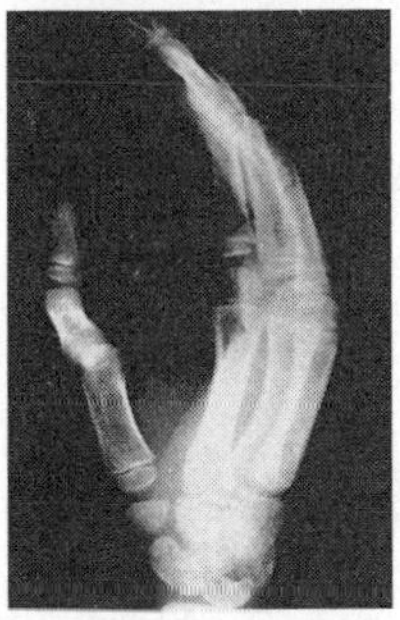

dislocate

Top: X-ray of a normal hand
Bottom: X-ray showing a dislocated thumb

Word History: **dismal**

For many of us Monday is **dismal**, a bad day. Our English word *dismal* comes from the medieval French phrase *dis mal*, literally "bad days." The *dis mal* were the two unlucky days of each month, and they also meant unlucky days in general. Those English who didn't understand French added "days" to *dismal*, which therefore meant "bad days days," and eventually *dismal* was felt to be an adjective meaning "bad, unlucky" and not a phrase meaning "unlucky days."

ă	pat	oi	boy
ā	pay	ou	out
âr	care	o͝o	took
ä	father	o͞o	boot
ĕ	pet	ŭ	cut
ē	be	ûr	urge
ĭ	pit	th	thin
ī	pie	*th*	this
îr	pier	hw	whoop
ŏ	pot	zh	vision
ō	toe	ə	about
ô	paw	N	*French* bon

performance: *The owl killed its prey with dispatch.* **3.** A written message, especially an official communication, sent with speed: *The messenger carried a dispatch from headquarters.* **4.** A news report sent to a newspaper or broadcasting station. [First written down in 1517 in Modern English, probably from Old Provençal *empachar*, to impede, from Latin *impingere*, dash against.]

dis•patch•er (dĭs **păch′**ər) *n.* A person who dispatches or controls the departure and movements of trains, taxicabs, or delivery trucks.

dis•pel (dĭ **spĕl′**) *tr.v.* **dis•pelled, dis•pel•ling, dis•pels.** To cause to disappear by or as if by scattering; drive away; disperse: *Light dispelled the fog.* [First written down before 1400 in Middle English and spelled *dispelen*, from Latin *dispellere* : *dis-*, apart, away + *pellere*, to drive.]

dis•pen•sa•ble (dĭ **spĕn′**sə bəl) *adj.* Not essential; unimportant: *To shorten the report, I removed all of the dispensable comments.* **—dis•pen′sa•bil′i•ty** *n.*

dis•pen•sa•ry (dĭ **spĕn′**sə rē) *n., pl.* **dis•pen•sa•ries. 1.** An office in a hospital, school, or other institution where medicines and medical supplies are given out. **2.** A place where medicines and medical treatment are provided, usually at little or no cost.

dis•pen•sa•tion (dĭs′pən **sā′**shən) *n.* **1.** The act or process of dispensing or giving out; distribution: *dispensation of medicine by the local clinic.* **2.** Something given out or distributed: *There were no red pens in this month's dispensation of supplies.* **3.** Freedom or a release from an obligation or a rule, granted in a particular case: *a dispensation allowing new businesses relief from taxes.*

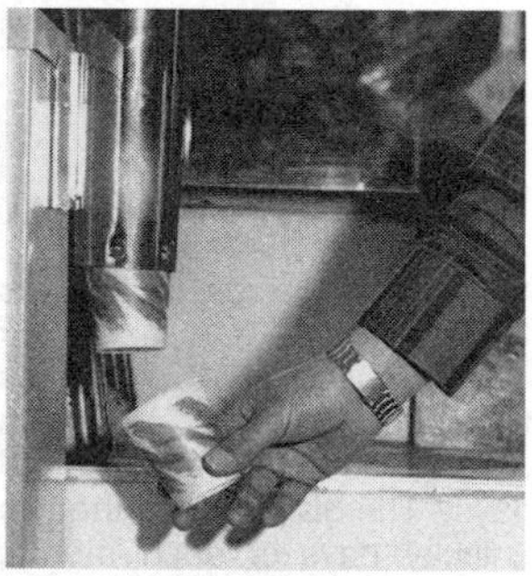

dispenser
Paper cup dispenser

dis•pense (dĭ **spĕns′**) *tr.v.* **dis•pensed, dis•pens•ing, dis•pens•es. 1.** To deal out or distribute in parts or portions: *The relief worker dispensed food to the refugees.* **2.** To prepare and give out (medicines). **3.** To carry out; administer: *The judge dispensed justice in an even-handed way.* ***—idiom.*** **dispense with.** To manage without; forgo: *Let's dispense with the formalities and get down to business.* [First written down about 1350 in Middle English and spelled *dispencen*, from Latin *dispēnsāre* : *dis-*, out + *pendere*, to weigh.]

dis•pens•er (dĭ **spĕn′**sər) *n.* A person or thing that dispenses: *a paper cup dispenser.*

dis•per•sal (dĭ **spûr′**səl) *n.* The act of dispersing or the condition of being dispersed: *the dispersal of a crowd; dispersal of aid among the needy.*

dis•perse (dĭ **spûrs′**) *v.* **dis•persed, dis•pers•ing, dis•pers•es.** *—tr.* **1.** To drive off or scatter in different directions: *The rain dispersed the crowd.* **2.** To cause to vanish or disappear; dispel: *Winds dispersed the clouds.* **3.** To separate (light or other radiation) into its different wavelengths. *—intr.* **1.** To move or scatter in different directions: *The protesters dispersed when the police arrived.* **2.** To vanish or disappear: *The mist dispersed with the morning sun.* [First written down before 1425 in Middle English and spelled *dispersen*, from Latin *dispergere* : *dis-*, apart + *spargere*, to scatter.]

dis•per•sion (dĭ **spûr′**zhən *or* dĭ **spûr′**shən) *n.* **1.** The separation of light or other radiation into components, usually according to wavelength. **2.** The act of dispersing or the state of being dispersed: *Bright sunlight caused dispersion of the fog.*

dis•pir•it (dĭ **spĭr′**ĭt) *tr.v.* **dis•pir•it•ed, dis•pir•it•ing, dis•pir•its.** To lower in spirit; discourage; dishearten.

dis•pir•it•ed (dĭ **spĭr′**ĭ tĭd) *adj.* Depressed; disheartened; discouraged: *feeling tired and dispirited.* **—dis•pir′it•ed•ly** *adv.* **—dis•pir′it•ed•ness** *n.*

dis•place (dĭs **plās′**) *tr.v.* **dis•placed, dis•plac•ing, dis•plac•es. 1.** To change the place or position of: *The refugees were displaced by the war.* **2.** To take the place of; replace: *Many workers have been displaced in their jobs by robots.* **3.** To take the space of (a quantity of liquid or gas): *An equal amount of oxygen displaced the carbon dioxide.* **4.** To dismiss from an office or a position: *In the election, the voters displaced their representative.*

dis•placed person (dĭs **plāst′**) *n.* A person who has been driven from his or her home country by war or other calamity.

dis•place•ment (dĭs **plās′**mənt) *n.* **1.a.** The weight or volume of fluid displaced by a body floating in it. The weight of the body is equal to the weight of the fluid it displaces. **b.** The measure of the distance that a body has been moved from one point to another through space. **2.** The act of displacing or the condition of being displaced: *Flooding caused the displacement of many people.*

dis•play (dĭ **splā′**) *tr.v.* **dis•played, dis•play•ing, dis•plays. 1.** To put in view; exhibit: *The library displays its new books in a case.* **2.** To make noticeable; show evidence of: *display good humor.* **3.** To show off; flaunt: *Displaying wealth is unseemly.* *—n.* **1.** The act of displaying: *a display of kindness.* **2.** A public exhibition: *a display of Native American pottery.* **3.** A show designed to impress or to attract attention: *The lavish party was just a display of wealth.* **4.** A device, such as a computer screen, that gives information in visual form. [First written down before 1300 in Middle English and spelled *displayen*, from Medieval Latin *displicāre*, to unfold : Latin *dis-*, apart + Latin *plicāre*, to fold.]

dis•please (dĭs **plēz′**) *v.* **dis•pleased, dis•pleas•ing, dis•pleas•es.** *—tr.* To cause annoyance or irritation to: *Bad manners displease me.* *—intr.* To cause annoyance or irritation.

dis•pleas•ure (dĭs **plĕzh′**ər) *n.* The condition of being displeased; dissatisfaction: *The coach showed great displeasure over our performance in the first half.*

dis•port (dĭ **spôrt′**) *v.* **dis•port•ed, dis•port•ing, dis•ports.** *—intr.* To frolic; play. *—tr.* To entertain (oneself) by sport or play.

dis•pos•a•ble (dĭ **spō′**zə bəl) *adj.* Designed to be thrown away after use: *disposable razors.*

dis•pos•al (dĭ **spō′**zəl) *n.* **1.** The act of getting rid of something: *The disposal of garbage is a serious problem for cities.* **2.** The act of attending to or settling a matter: *The mayor's decision led to a prompt disposal of the problem.* **3.** The act of transferring something, as by giving or selling: *the disposal of property to his children.* ***—idiom.*** **at (one's) disposal.** Available for one's use: *All of the library books are at the disposal of patrons.*

dis•pose (dĭ **spōz′**) *tr.v.* **dis•posed, dis•pos•ing, dis•pos•es. 1.** To place or set in a particular order; arrange: *The gardeners disposed the tulips in beds throughout the park.* **2.a.** To make willing or ready; incline: *a friend disposed to forgive a mistake.* **b.** To make susceptible or liable: *My brother is disposed to ear infections.* ***—idiom.*** **dispose of. 1.** To get rid of: *We disposed of the leftovers in the garbage.* **2.** To sell or give away: *The dealer quickly disposed of the cars.* **3.** To settle or decide: *We disposed of the problem quickly.* [First written down in 1373 in Middle English and spelled *disposen*, from Latin *dispōnere*, to arrange.]

dis•po•si•tion (dĭs′pə **zĭsh′**ən) *n.* **1.** The usual mood or attitude of a person or an animal; temperament; nature: *a young child's affectionate disposition.* **2.** A tendency or an inclination: *She has a disposition to argue about minor points.* **3.** Arrangement or distribution: *the disposition of books by subject on library shelves.* **4.** An act of settling;

settlement: *disposition of legal matters at the lawyer's office.* **5.** An act of transferring: *the disposition of her property to her heirs.*

dis•pos•sess (dĭs′pə **zĕs′**) *tr.v.* **dis•pos•sessed, dis•pos•sess•ing, dis•pos•sess•es.** To deprive (a person) of the possession of something, such as land or a house: *The bank may dispossess a person of land for failure to make payment on a loan.* **—dis′pos•ses′sion** (dĭs′pə **zĕsh′**ən) *n.*

dis•proof (dĭs **pro͞of′**) *n.* **1.** An act of disproving. **2.** Evidence that disproves.

dis•pro•por•tion (dĭs′prə **pôr′**shən) *n.* A lack of proportion; imbalance: *the disproportion between the size of a piece of balsa wood and its very light weight.*

dis•pro•por•tion•ate (dĭs′prə **pôr′**shə nĭt) *adj.* Out of proportion to something else, as in size or shape; not suitably proportioned. **—dis′pro•por′tion•ate•ly** *adv.* **—dis′pro•por′tion•ate•ness** *n.*

dis•prove (dĭs **pro͞ov′**) *tr.v.* **dis•proved, dis•prov•ing, dis•proves.** To prove to be false or in error; refute: *Shadows of buildings in the photograph disprove the witness's testimony that it was a stormy day.*

dis•put•a•ble (dĭ **spyo͞o′**tə bəl *or* **dĭs′**pyə tə bəl) *adj.* Open to dispute; debatable: *The facts are well known, but your interpretation of them is disputable.* **—dis•put′a•bil′i•ty** *n.*

dis•pu•tant (dĭ **spyo͞ot′**nt *or* **dĭs′**pyə tənt) *n.* A person taking part in an argument, a debate, or a quarrel.

dis•pu•ta•tion (dĭs′pyə **tā′**shən) *n.* The act of disputing; debate.

dis•pute (dĭ **spyo͞ot′**) *v.* **dis•put•ed, dis•put•ing, dis•putes.** *—tr.* **1.** To argue about; debate: *The editors disputed the literary merit of the manuscript.* **2.** To question the truth or validity of; doubt: *We disputed her account of what happened.* **3.** To quarrel or fight over: *The nations disputed the territory.* *—intr.* **1.** To engage in discussion; argue: *The candidates disputed over where city expenses should be cut.* **2.** To quarrel angrily. *—n.* **1.** A debate; an argument: *Each scientist in the dispute had a different theory.* **2.** A quarrel. [First written down about 1300 in Middle English and spelled *desputen*, from Latin *disputāre*, to examine : *dis-*, apart + *putāre*, to reckon.]

dis•qual•i•fi•ca•tion (dĭs kwŏl′ə fĭ **kā′**shən) *n.* **1.** The act of disqualifying or the condition of being disqualified. **2.** Something that disqualifies: *Very poor vision is a disqualification for getting a driver's license.*

dis•qual•i•fy (dĭs **kwŏl′**ə fī′) *tr.v.* **dis•qual•i•fied, dis•qual•i•fy•ing, dis•qual•i•fies.** **1.** To make unqualified or unfit: *Poor eyesight disqualifies many people who wish to become pilots.* **2.** To declare to be unqualified or ineligible: *The judges disqualified the swimmer from the race.*

dis•qui•et (dĭs **kwī′**ĭt) *tr.v.* **dis•qui•et•ed, dis•qui•et•ing, dis•qui•ets.** To make uneasy; trouble; worry: *Strange noises disquieted the guard.* *—n.* Worry, uneasiness, or anxiety: *Rumors of engine trouble caused disquiet among the airplane passengers.*

dis•qui•e•tude (dĭs **kwī′**ĭ to͞od′ *or* dĭs **kwī′**ĭ tyo͞od′) *n.* Worry; uneasiness; anxiety.

Dis•rae•li (dĭz **rā′**lē), **Benjamin.** First Earl of Beaconsfield. 1804–1881. British politician who served as prime minister in 1868 and from 1874 to 1880.

dis•re•gard (dĭs′rĭ **gärd′**) *tr.v.* **dis•re•gard•ed, dis•re•gard•ing, dis•re•gards.** To pay little or no attention to; ignore: *They disregarded the warnings not to hike in stormy weather.* *—n.* Lack of attention or regard: *a disregard for safety.*

dis•re•pair (dĭs′rĭ **pâr′**) *n.* The condition of being in need of repair: *an abandoned house in disrepair.*

dis•rep•u•ta•ble (dĭs **rĕp′**yə tə bəl) *adj.* Having a bad reputation; not respectable: *a disreputable building contractor.* **—dis•rep′u•ta•ble•ness** *n.* **—dis•rep′u•ta•bly** *adv.*

dis•re•pute (dĭs′rĭ **pyo͞ot′**) *n.* Damage to or loss of reputation; disgrace.

dis•re•spect (dĭs′rĭ **spĕkt′**) *n.* Lack of respect or courtesy; rudeness: *His behavior showed disrespect for the law.*

dis•re•spect•ful (dĭs′rĭ **spĕkt′**fəl) *adj.* Having or showing a lack of respect; rude: *disrespectful behavior.* **—dis′re•spect′ful•ly** *adv.* **—dis′re•spect′ful•ness** *n.*

dis•robe (dĭs **rōb′**) *tr. & intr.v.* **dis•robed, dis•rob•ing, dis•robes.** To undress: *disrobe a doll; disrobe for an x-ray.*

dis•rupt (dĭs **rŭpt′**) *tr.v.* **dis•rupt•ed, dis•rupt•ing, dis•rupts.** To throw into confusion or disorder: *The noise from the jackhammer disrupted the class.* [First written down in 1657 in Modern English, from Latin *disrumpere*, to break apart.] **—dis•rupt′er** *n.*

dis•rup•tion (dĭs **rŭp′**shən) *n.* The act of disrupting or the state of being disrupted: *the storm's disruption of electric power.*

dis•rup•tive (dĭs **rŭp′**tĭv) *adj.* Causing disruption: *The street repairs were disruptive to city traffic.* **—dis•rup′tive•ly** *adv.* **—dis•rup′tive•ness** *n.*

dis•sat•is•fac•tion (dĭs săt′ĭs **făk′**shən) *n.* The feeling of being displeased or dissatisfied; discontent: *dissatisfaction among teachers and parents over the closing of the library.*

dis•sat•is•fied (dĭs **săt′**ĭs fīd′) *adj.* Feeling or showing a lack of contentment or satisfaction: *The dissatisfied customer returned his purchase.*

dis•sat•is•fy (dĭs **săt′**ĭs fī′) *tr.v.* **dis•sat•is•fied, dis•sat•is•fy•ing, dis•sat•is•fies.** To fail to satisfy; displease: *Your careless work dissatisfies me.*

dis•sect (dĭ **sĕkt′** *or* dī **sĕkt′** *or* **dī′**sĕkt′) *tr.v.* **dis•sect•ed, dis•sect•ing, dis•sects.** **1.** To cut apart or separate (tissue) for study or examination: *dissect an animal in a lab.* **2.** To examine, analyze, or criticize in detail: *We dissected the plan to see where it might go wrong.* [First written down in 1607 in Modern English, from Latin *dissecāre*, to cut apart : *dis-*, apart + *secāre*, to cut up.]

dis•sec•tion (dĭ **sĕk′**shən *or* dī **sĕk′**shən) *n.* **1.** The act or process of dissecting: *the complicated dissection of a frog.* **2.** Something that has been dissected, as a tissue being studied. **3.** A thoroughly conducted examination or analysis: *the lawyer's dissection of the evidence.*

dis•sem•ble (dĭ **sĕm′**bəl) *v.* **dis•sem•bled, dis•sem•bling, dis•sem•bles.** *—tr.* **1.** To conceal or hide behind a false appearance or manner: *dissemble one's disappointment by making a joke.* **2.** To make a false show of; pretend; feign: *I dissembled sympathy I didn't really feel.* *—intr.* To hide one's real character, feelings, or motives under a false appearance. [First written down before 1420 in Middle English and spelled *dissemblen*, from Old French *dessembler*, to be different : *des-*, apart + *sembler*, to appear, seem (from Latin *simulāre*, to pretend, seem).] **—dis•sem′bler** *n.*

dis•sem•i•nate (dĭ **sĕm′**ə nāt′) *tr.v.* **dis•sem•i•nat•ed, dis•sem•i•nat•ing, dis•sem•i•nates.** To make known widely; spread abroad: *The TV newscast disseminated the report instantly.* **—dis•sem′i•na′tion** *n*

dis•sen•sion (dĭ **sĕn′**shən) *n.* Difference of opinion; disagreement.

dis•sent (dĭ **sĕnt′**) *intr.v.* **dis•sent•ed, dis•sent•ing, dis•sents.** To think or feel differently; disagree: *Many angry citizens dissented from the government action of raising taxes.* *—n.* **1.** Differ-

Benjamin Disraeli

ă	pat	oi	boy
ā	pay	ou	out
âr	care	o͝o	took
ä	father	o͞o	boot
ĕ	pet	ŭ	cut
ē	be	ûr	urge
ĭ	pit	th	thin
ī	pie	*th*	this
îr	pier	hw	whoop
ŏ	pot	zh	vision
ō	toe	ə	about
ô	paw	N	*French* bon

ence of opinion or feeling; disagreement: *dissent over the British right to tax the American colonists.* **2.** The refusal to conform to the authority or rules of a government or church: *The Puritans' dissent from the Church of England led to their migration to the New World.* [First written down about 1425 in Middle English and spelled *dissenten,* from Latin *dissentīre* : *dis-,* apart + *sentīre,* to feel.]

❑ *These sound alike:* **dissent, descent** (ancestry).

dis•sent•er (dĭ sĕn′tər) *n.* **1.** A person who dissents. **2.** Often **Dissenter.** A person who refuses to accept the beliefs and practices of an established or national church, especially a Protestant who dissents from the Church of England.

dis•ser•ta•tion (dĭs′ər tā′shən) *n.* A lengthy and formal discussion of a subject, especially one written at a university.

dis•serv•ice (dĭs sûr′vĭs) *n.* A harmful action; an injury: *He did us a disservice by telling everyone that our play is boring.*

dis•sev•er (dĭ sĕv′ər) *tr. & intr.v.* **dis•sev•ered, dis•sev•er•ing, dis•sev•ers.** To separate or divide into parts.

dis•si•dence (dĭs′ĭ dəns) *n.* Disagreement as in opinion or belief; dissent.

dis•si•dent (dĭs′ĭ dənt) *adj.* Disagreeing, as in opinion or belief; dissenting: *Dissident opinions were voiced before the final vote was taken.* —*n.* A person who disagrees; a dissenter.

dis•sim•i•lar (dĭ sĭm′ə lər) *adj.* Unlike; different: *We have dissimilar views.* **—dis•sim′i•lar•ly** *adv.*

dis•sim•i•lar•i•ty (dĭ sĭm′ə lăr′ĭ tē) *n., pl.* **dis•sim•i•lar•i•ties. 1.** The quality or condition of being unlike; difference: *There is marked dissimilarity of climate between the wet coastal regions and the arid inland plains.* **2.** A point of distinction or difference: *Even identical twins have little dissimilarities.*

dis•sim•u•late (dĭ sĭm′yə lāt′) *v.* **dis•sim•u•lat•ed, dis•sim•u•lat•ing, dis•sim•u•lates.** —*tr.* To hide (one's true feelings or intentions) under a false appearance. —*intr.* To conceal one's true feelings or intentions. [First written down before 1425 in Middle English and spelled *dissimulaten,* from Latin *dissimulāre* : *dis-,* apart + *simulāre,* to simulate, pretend.] **—dis•sim′u•la′tion** *n.*

dis•si•pate (dĭs′ə pāt′) *v.* **dis•si•pat•ed, dis•si•pat•ing, dis•si•pates.** —*tr.* **1.** To drive away by or as if by dispersing; scatter: *A strong wind dissipated the clouds.* **2.** To use up unwisely; waste; squander: *They dissipated their wealth on needless luxuries.* —*intr.* **1.** To vanish by dispersion; disappear: *The fog dissipated shortly after sunrise.* **2.** To indulge excessively in the pursuit of pleasure.

dis•si•pat•ed (dĭs′ə pā′tĭd) *adj.* **1.** Indulging in harmful or destructive pleasures; dissolute: *a dissipated life.* **2.** Wasted; squandered: *a dissipated fortune.*

dis•si•pa•tion (dĭs′ə pā′shən) *n.* **1.** The act of scattering or the condition of being scattered; dispersion: *the dissipation of storm clouds.* **2.** Wasteful use or expenditure, as of money, energy, or time. **3.** Overindulgence in pleasure.

dis•so•ci•ate (dĭ sō′shē āt′ *or* dĭ sō′sē āt′) *v.* **dis•so•ci•at•ed, dis•so•ci•at•ing, dis•so•ci•ates.** —*tr.* To break association with; part: *We dissociated ourselves from the committee because we disagree with its report.* —*intr.* In chemistry, to undergo dissociation.

dis•so•ci•a•tion (dĭ sō′sē ā′shən *or* dĭ sō′shē ā′shən) *n.* **1.** The separation of a substance into two or more simpler substances or of a molecule into atoms or ions by the action of heat, solvent, or some chemical process. **2.** The act of breaking away or separating.

dis•sol•u•ble (dĭ sŏl′yə bəl) *adj.* Capable of being dissolved.

dis•so•lute (dĭs′ə lo͞ot′) *adj.* Lacking moral restraint; immoral. **—dis′so•lute′ly** *adv.* **—dis′so•lute′ness** *n.*

dis•so•lu•tion (dĭs′ə lo͞o′shən) *n.* **1.a.** The act or process of breaking up into parts; disintegration: *Failure to take in new members caused the gradual dissolution of the garden club.* **b.** The ending of a formal or legal bond; termination: *dissolution of a business partnership.* **2.** The act or process of changing from a solid to a liquid. **3.** Excessive indulgence in pleasures.

dis•solve (dĭ zŏlv′) *v.* **dis•solved, dis•solv•ing, dis•solves.** —*tr.* **1.** To cause to pass into solution: *dissolve salt in water.* **2.** To change a (solid matter) to a liquid: *Warm weather dissolved the ice on the lake.* **3.** To bring to an end; terminate: *dissolve a partnership; dissolve a meeting.* **4.** To cause to disappear; dispel: *Growing older dissolves fear of the dark for most children.* —*intr.* **1.** To be taken up into solution: *Alcohol dissolves in water, but oil does not.* **2.** To change from a solid into a liquid: *The ice cubes dissolved in the warm tea.* **3.** To break up; disperse: *The mist dissolved in the wind.* **4.** To fade away; disappear: *Once beaten, the team's confidence dissolved quickly.* **5.** To be overcome emotionally: *The lost child dissolved into tears.* [First written down about 1380 in Middle English and spelled *dissolven,* from Latin *dissolvere.*] **—dis•solv′a•ble** *adj.*

dis•so•nance (dĭs′ə nəns) *n.* **1.** A harsh combination of sounds; discord: *the dissonance of horns in heavy traffic.* **2.** Lack of agreement or consistency; conflict: *Dissonance among committee members brought their plans to a halt.*

dis•so•nant (dĭs′ə nənt) *adj.* **1.** Being or having a harsh combination of sounds: *a dissonant passage in the symphony.* **2.** Lacking agreement: *a dissonant meeting.* [First written down before 1425 in Middle English and spelled *dissonaunt,* from Latin *dissonāre,* to be dissonant : *dis-,* apart + *sonāre,* to sound.] **—dis′so•nant•ly** *adv.*

dis•suade (dĭ swād′) *tr.v.* **dis•suad•ed, dis•suad•ing, dis•suades.** To discourage or keep (a person) from a purpose or course of action by persuasion or advice: *Friends dissuaded me from leaving early.* **—dis•sua′sion** (dĭ swā′zhən) *n.*

dist. *abbr.* An abbreviation of: **1.** Distance. **2.** District.

dis•taff (dĭs′tăf′) *n.* A stick holding flax or wool that is pulled off to be spun by hand into yarn or thread. [First written down about 1000 in Old English and spelled *distæf* : *dis-,* bunch of flax + *stæf,* staff.]

distaff side *n.* The female side or branch of a family.

dis•tance (dĭs′təns) *n.* **1.** The extent of space between two points or things: *The distance between my house and the post office is half a mile.* **2.** A stretch of space without definite limits: *We could see a whale swimming in the distance.*

dis•tant (dĭs′tənt) *adj.* **1.** Far away; remote: *a distant peak on the horizon.* **2.** Separate or apart in space: *Our house is two miles distant from the station.* **3.** Far away or apart in time: *the distant past.* **4.** Far apart in relationship: *a distant cousin.* **5.** Unfriendly in manner; aloof: *The new neighbors appeared cold and distant until we got to know them.* [First written down about 1391 in Middle English, from Latin *distāns,* present participle of *distāre,* to be remote : *dis-,* apart + *stāre,* to stand.] **—dis′tant•ly** *adv.*

dis•taste (dĭs tāst′) *n.* A dislike or strong objection: *a distaste for modern music.*

dis•taste•ful (dĭs tāst′fəl) *adj.* Unpleasant; disagreeable; offensive: *Cleaning the basement is a distasteful job.* **—dis•taste′ful•ly** *adv.* **—dis•taste′ful•ness** *n.*

dis•tem•per (dĭs tĕm′pər) *n.* Any of various infectious, often fatal diseases of dogs, cats, and other animals, caused by a virus and characterized by fever and vomiting.

dis•tend (dĭ stĕnd′) *v.* **dis•tend•ed, dis•tend•ing, dis•tends.** *—intr.* To swell or expand from or as if from internal pressure: *The puppies ate until their stomachs distended.* *—tr.* To cause to expand by or as if by internal pressure: *Fluid distends a blister.* [First written down before 1400 in Middle English and spelled *distenden*, from Latin *distendere* : *dis-*, out, apart + *tendere*, to stretch.]

dis•till also **dis•til** (dĭ stĭl′) *v.* **dis•tilled, dis•till•ing, dis•tills** also **dis•tilled, dis•til•ling, dis•tils.** *—tr.* **1.** To treat (a substance) by the process of distillation. **2.** To separate (a substance) from a mixture by distillation. **3.** To separate or extract the core or essential part of: *distill the important points of a book in a report.* *—intr.* **1.** To undergo or be produced by distillation. **2.** To fall in drops or small quantities.

dis•til•late (dĭs′tə lāt′ *or* dĭ stĭl′ĭt) *n.* A liquid condensed from vapor and collected in distillation.

dis•til•la•tion (dĭs′tə lā′shən) *n.* **1.** The process of boiling a liquid and condensing and collecting the vapor. Distillation is used to purify liquids, such as sea water, or to separate liquid mixtures, such as petroleum. **2.** Something distilled from another substance or from a more complex form; a distillate.

dis•till•er (dĭ stĭl′ər) *n.* **1.** A person or thing that distills, especially a condenser. **2.** A person or company that produces alcoholic liquors.

dis•till•er•y (dĭ stĭl′ə rē) *n., pl.* **dis•till•er•ies.** An establishment for distilling, especially for distilling alcoholic liquors.

dis•tinct (dĭ stĭngkt′) *adj.* **1.** Different from all others; separate: *We discussed the issue on two distinct occasions.* **2.** Easily perceived by the senses or mind; definite: *Onions have a distinct odor.* **3.** Clear; unquestionable: *Doctors have distinct limitations on their time.* [First written down about 1390 in Middle English, from Latin *distīnctus*, past participle of *distinguere*, to distinguish.] **—dis•tinct′ly** *adv.* **—dis•tinct′ness** *n.*

dis•tinc•tion (dĭ stĭngk′shən) *n.* **1.** The act of distinguishing; discrimination: *Employers must hire without distinction of age or race.* **2.** The condition or fact of being distinct; difference: *a distinction between studying and casual reading.* **3.** Something that sets one apart; a distinguishing mark or characteristic: *the distinction of being the best singer in the choir.* **4.** Excellence, as of performance, character, or reputation: *a composer of great distinction.* **5.** Recognition of achievement or superiority; honor: *She graduated with distinction.*

dis•tinc•tive (dĭ stĭngk′tĭv) *adj.* Serving to identify, characterize, or set apart from others: *Your team wears a distinctive uniform.* **—dis•tinc′tive•ly** *adv.* **—dis•tinc′tive•ness** *n.*

dis•tin•guish (dĭ stĭng′gwĭsh) *v.* **dis•tin•guished, dis•tin•guish•ing, dis•tin•guish•es.** *—tr.* **1.** To recognize as being different or distinct: *Counting the number of legs is one way to distinguish spiders from ants.* **2.** To see or hear clearly; make out; discern: *the ear's ability to distinguish musical notes.* **3.** To make noticeable or different; set apart: *The beaver is distinguished by its broad flat tail.* **4.** To cause (oneself) to gain fame, esteem, or honor: *Some artists distinguished themselves as great portrait painters.* *—intr.* To recognize differences; discriminate: *distinguish between right and wrong.* **—dis•tin′guish•a•ble** *adj.*

dis•tin•guished (dĭ stĭng′gwĭsht) *adj.* **1.** Recognized as excellent; eminent; renowned: *a distinguished composer.* **2.** Dignified in conduct or appearance: *the distinguished air of a great dancer.*

dis•tort (dĭ stôrt′) *tr.v.* **dis•tort•ed, dis•tort•ing, dis•torts.** **1.** To twist (something) out of the usual shape; contort: *a grin that distorted the clown's face.* **2.** To give a false account of; misrepresent: *distort the facts.* **3.** To change (an electronic signal) so as to result in poor quality reception or reproduction, as of radio or recorded music. [First written down about 1586 in Modern English, from Latin *distorquēre* : *dis-*, apart + *torquēre*, to twist.]

dis•tor•tion (dĭ stôr′shən) *n.* **1.a.** The act of distorting: *Distortion of the facts gave a false impression of what actually happened.* **b.** The condition of being distorted: *The distortion in the photograph is due to the camera being out of focus.* **2.** Something distorted: *Their vague idea of what happened was full of distortions.*

dis•tract (dĭ străkt′) *tr.v.* **dis•tract•ed, dis•tract•ing, dis•tracts.** **1.** To draw (the attention, for example) away from something: *The noise distracted the students in the library.* **2.** To pull in opposite emotional directions; unsettle: *Worries about moving to a new city distracted the whole family.* [First written down about 1340 in Middle English and spelled *distracten*, from Latin *distrahere*, to pull away : *dis-*, apart, away + *trahere*, to draw.]

dis•trac•tion (dĭ străk′shən) *n.* **1.** Something that distracts: *The new kittens were a continuous distraction from homework.* **2.** Great mental agitation: *Worry over paying the bills nearly drove the shopkeeper to distraction.* **3.** The act of drawing away the attention: *the distraction of watching TV.* **4.** Relief from care or work; amusement: *A good book brings distraction to the reader.*

dis•traught (dĭ strôt′) *adj.* **1.** Anxious or agitated; worried: *distraught with fear.* **2.** Insane; mad.

dis•tress (dĭ strĕs′) *tr.v.* **dis•tressed, dis•tress•ing, dis•tress•es.** To cause (a person) to suffer in mind or body. *—n.* **1.** Pain or suffering of mind or body: *Injuries from the accident caused the victim severe distress.* **2.** The condition of being in need of immediate assistance: *a motorist in distress.* **3.** Something that causes discomfort: *Seeing an animal suffering is a great distress to me.*

dis•tress•ful (dĭ strĕs′fəl) *adj.* Causing or experiencing distress; painful. **—dis•tress′ful•ly** *adv.*

dis•trib•ute (dĭ strĭb′yo͞ot) *tr.v.* **dis•trib•ut•ed, dis•trib•ut•ing, dis•trib•utes.** **1.** To divide and give out in portions; parcel out: *distribute newspapers to the door of each apartment.* **2.** To supply or send out; deliver: *distribute fresh vegetables to other parts of the country.* **3.** To spread or scatter over an area: *The storm distributed heavy snow throughout the region.* **4.** To separate into categories; classify: *Biologists distribute new plant specimens by their various characteristics.* [First written down before 1425 in Middle English and spelled *distributen*, from Latin *distribuere* : *dis-*, apart, away + *tribuere*, to give.]

Synonyms: distribute, divide, dispense[1], deal, ration. These verbs mean to give out in portions or shares. **Distribute** is the most general: *In the 19th century the United States government distributed land to settlers.* **Divide** means to give out portions on the basis of a plan or a purpose: *The estate will be divided among the heirs.* **Dispense** often means to give carefully measured or weighed portions: *The clerk dispensed the spices carefully.* **Deal** means to distribute in a fair orderly way: *Each guest was dealt a party hat.* **Ration** means to deal out

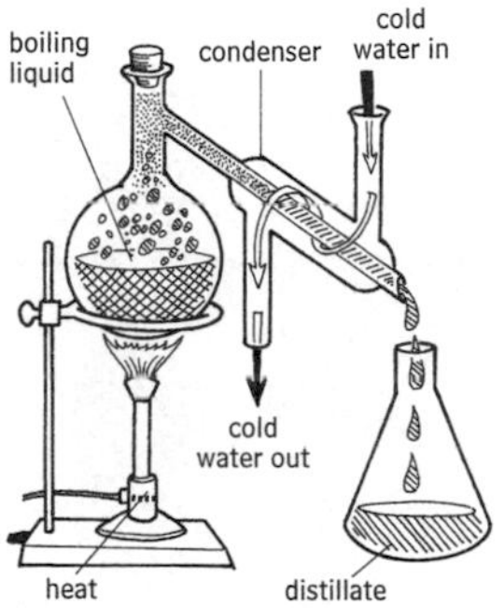

distillation
Simple distillation

ă	pat	oi	boy
ā	pay	ou	out
âr	care	o͝o	took
ä	father	o͞o	boot
ĕ	pet	ŭ	cut
ē	be	ûr	urge
ĭ	pit	th	thin
ī	pie	*th*	this
îr	pier	hw	whoop
ŏ	pot	zh	vision
ō	toe	ə	about
ô	paw	N	*French* bon

scarce items: *Every household should ration water during the drought.* **Antonym: gather.**

dis•tri•bu•tion (dĭs′trə **byōō′**shən) *n.* **1.** The act of distributing: *the distribution of gifts at the holidays.* **2.** The way in which something is distributed: *a map showing the distribution of population in America.* **3.** The process of marketing and supplying goods, especially to retailers. **4.** Something distributed; a portion: *Water distribution is carefully controlled in California.*

dis•trib•u•tive (dĭ **strĭb′**yə tĭv) *adj.* **1.** Of or relating to distribution: *the distributive function of the blood stream.* **2.** In mathematics, of or relating to a property stating that the product of a factor and a sum is equal to the sum of the products. For example, $5 \times (6 + 7) = (5 \times 6) + (5 \times 7)$ and $a \times (b + c) = (a \times b) + (a \times c)$. **3.** In grammar, referring to each part or member of a group separately. *Each* and *every* are distributive words. **—dis•trib′u•tive•ly** *adv.*

dis•trib•u•tor (dĭ **strĭb′**yə tər) *n.* **1.** A person or thing that distributes, especially a device that applies electric current at the proper time to each spark plug in an engine. **2.** A person or company that markets or sells merchandise, especially a wholesaler.

dis•trict (**dĭs′**trĭkt) *n.* **1.** A part of an area marked out by law for a particular purpose: *our school district.* **2.** An area, especially one having a particular characteristic or function: *a shopping district.* *—tr. v.* **dis•trict•ed, dis•trict•ing, dis•tricts.** To mark off or divide into districts. [First written down in 1611 in Modern English, from Medieval Latin *districtus*, from Latin *distringere*, to hinder.]

district attorney *n.* The attorney who conducts the government's side of a case in a judicial district, especially the attorney who prosecutes people accused of a crime.

Dis•trict of Co•lum•bi•a (**dĭs′**trĭkt′ əv kə **lŭm′**bē ə). A federal district of the eastern United States on the Potomac River between Virginia and Maryland. It was established by congressional acts of 1790 and 1791 on a site chosen by George Washington.

dis•trust (dĭs **trŭst′**) *n.* Lack of confidence or trust; suspicion. *—tr.v.* **dis•trust•ed, dis•trust•ing, dis•trusts.** To lack confidence or trust in; doubt; suspect: *I distrust TV commercials that sound too good.*

dis•trust•ful (dĭs **trŭst′**fəl) *adj.* Feeling or showing doubt; suspicious. **—dis•trust′ful•ly** *adv.* **—dis•trust′ful•ness** *n.*

dis•turb (dĭ **stûrb′**) *tr.v.* **dis•turbed, dis•turb•ing, dis•turbs. 1.** To break up or destroy the peace, order, or settled state of: *a breeze that disturbed the papers on my desk.* **2.** To make uneasy or anxious; trouble; upset: *I was disturbed when I didn't know where you were.* **3.** To intrude upon; bother: *The visitors disturbed the musician's practice.* [First written down before 1200 in Middle English and spelled *disturben*, from Latin *disturbāre* : Latin *dis-*, apart + Latin *turbāre*, to agitate (from *turba*, confusion).]

diver
Scuba diver

dis•tur•bance (dĭ **stûr′**bəns) *n.* **1.** The act of disturbing or the condition of being disturbed: *a disturbance in the TV signal.* **2.** Something that disturbs; an interruption or intrusion: *The coughing of a few was a disturbance to the rest of the audience.* **3.** A commotion or scuffle: *Angry fans created a disturbance at the game.*

di•sul•fide (dī **sŭl′**fīd′) *n.* A chemical compound that contains two atoms of sulfur combined with another element or radical.

dis•un•ion (dĭs **yōōn′**yən) *n.* **1.** The condition of being divided or broken up into parts; separation. **2.** Lack of unity or agreement; discord.

dis•u•nite (dĭs′yōō **nīt′**) *tr. & intr.v.* **dis•u•nit•ed, dis•u•nit•ing, dis•u•nites.** To make or become separate or divided: *differences of opinion that disunited our club.*

dis•u•ni•ty (dĭs **yōō′**nĭ tē) *n., pl.* **dis•u•ni•ties.** Lack of unity or agreement; discord; dissension.

dis•use (dĭs **yōōs′**) *n.* The condition of not being used or of being no longer in use.

ditch (dĭch) *n.* A long narrow trench dug in the ground. *—v.* **ditched, ditch•ing, ditch•es.** *—tr.* **1.** To dig or make a ditch in or around: *ditch swampy land to drain it.* **2.** To drive (a vehicle) into a ditch. **3.** *Slang.* To throw aside; get rid of. **4.** To bring (an aircraft) to a forced landing on water. *—intr.* To be forced to land an aircraft on water: *The helicopter pilot ditched in the harbor.*

dith•er (**dĭth′**ər) *n.* A condition of nervous excitement or indecision: *in a dither about getting ready for the party.* *—intr.v.* **dith•ered, dith•er•ing, dith•ers.** To be nervously unable to make a decision or act on something.

dit•to (**dĭt′**ō) *n., pl.* **dit•tos. 1.** The same as stated above or before. **2.** A duplicate or copy. **3.** A ditto mark.

ditto mark *n.* A pair of marks (") used directly below a word that would otherwise be repeated, as on long lists, bills, and tables. Often used in the plural.

dit•ty (**dĭt′**ē) *n., pl.* **dit•ties.** A short simple song.

di•ur•nal (dī **ûr′**nəl) *adj.* **1.** Occurring in a 24-hour period; daily: *The diurnal rise of the sun.* **2.** Occurring or active during the daytime rather than at night: *diurnal birds of prey.* **3.** Opening by day and closing by night, as certain flowers do. **—di•ur′nal•ly** *adv.*

di•van (dĭ **văn′**) *n.* A long couch, usually without a back or arms. [First written down in 1586 in Modern English, from Turkish, from Persian *dīvān*, place of assembly, roster.]

dive (dīv) *v.* **dived** or **dove** (dōv), **dived, div•ing, dives.** *—intr.* **1.** To plunge into water, especially headfirst. **2.** To go toward the bottom of a body of water; submerge: *The submarine dived.* **3.** To descend rapidly at a steep angle: *The airplane turned and dived.* **4.** To rush headlong and vanish into: *dive into the crowd.* **5.** To engage in something vigorously: *She dove into the project with great enthusiasm.* *—tr.* To cause to dive: *dive a plane.* *—n.* **1.** A plunge into water, especially headfirst. **2.** A sharp downward descent or plunge, as of an airplane or a submarine. **3.** *Informal.* A run-down bar or nightclub. [First written down before 1200 in Middle English and spelled *duven*, from Old English *dӯfan*, to dip, and *dūfan*, to sink.] —SEE NOTE at **wake**[1].

div•er (**dī′**vər) *n.* **1.** A person who dives into water: *a champion diver.* **2.** A person who works underwater, as in gathering pearl oysters or performing salvage operations. **3.** Any of several diving birds, especially the loon.

di•verge (dĭ **vûrj′** *or* dī **vûrj′**) *v.* **di•verged, di•verg•ing, di•verg•es.** *—intr.* **1.** To go or extend in different directions from a common point; branch out: *a small dirt road that diverged into two tracks.* **2.** To depart from a set course, standard, or norm; deviate: *Today's class diverged from the usual because we had a debate.* **3.** To differ, as in opinion or manner: *The twins diverged in their interests as they grew older.* *—tr.* To cause to diverge. [First written down in 1665 in Modern English, from Latin *dīvergere* : Latin *dī-*, *dis-*, apart, away + Latin *vergere*, to bend.]

di•ver•gence (dĭ **vûr′**jəns *or* dī **vûr′**jəns) *n.* **1.** The act of diverging. **2.** Departure from an established course, pattern, or standard: *divergence from the regular schedule.* **3.** Difference, as of opinion: *Divergence among members of the board prevented it from coming to a decision.*

di•ver•gent (dĭ vûr′jənt *or* dī vûr′jənt) *adj.* **1.** Drawing apart from a common point; diverging. **2.** Differing: *widely divergent views of the problem.* **—di•ver′gent•ly** *adv.*

di•vers (dī′vərz) *adj.* Various; several; diverse: *the many and divers foods available in a market.* [First written down about 1275 in Middle English, from Latin *dīversus*, past participle of *dīvertere*, to divert.]

di•verse (dĭ vûrs′ *or* dī vûrs′ *or* dī′vûrs′) *adj.* **1.** Distinct in kind; different: *Members of the same family can have very diverse personalities.* **2.** Made up of several or many kinds: *America is a land of diverse people.* [First written down about 1300 in Middle English, from Latin *dīversus*, past participle of *dīvertere*, to divert.] **—di•verse′ly** *adv.* **—di•verse′ness** *n.*

di•ver•si•fy (dĭ vûr′sə fī′ *or* dī vûr′sə fī′) *v.* **di•ver•si•fied, di•ver•si•fy•ing, di•ver•si•fies.** *—tr.* To give diversity or variety to; make diverse: *After becoming successful as a portrait photographer, she diversified the kinds of pictures she took.* *—intr.* To become diversified, especially by making or dealing in different products: *The soap company diversified into producing a line of perfumes.* **—di•ver′si•fi•ca′tion** (dĭ vûr′sə fĭ kā′shən) *n.*

di•ver•sion (dĭ vûr′zhən *or* dī vûr′zhən) *n.* **1.** The act of diverting: *the diversion of a stream for irrigation.* **2.** Something that relaxes or entertains; recreation: *Playing music has been a wonderful diversion for me.* **3.** Something that draws the attention to a different course, direction, or action: *We started yelling to create a diversion from the game.*

di•ver•si•ty (dĭ vûr′sĭ tē *or* dī vûr′sĭ tē) *n., pl.* **di•ver•si•ties. 1.** The quality of being diverse; difference. **2.** Variety: *a diversity of foods on a menu.*

di•vert (dĭ vûrt′ *or* dī vûrt′) *v.* **di•vert•ed, di•vert•ing, di•verts.** *—tr.* **1.** To turn aside from a course or direction; deflect: *divert traffic around a fallen tree on the road.* **2.** To draw (the mind or attention) to another direction: *A passing fire truck diverted our attention from the game.* **3.** To amuse or entertain: *divert little children by singing songs on a rainy afternoon.* *—intr.* To turn aside: *The pilot had to divert from the airport closed in by fog.* [First written down before 1420 in Middle English and spelled *diverten*, from Latin *dīvertere* : *dī-*, *dis-*, away, aside + *vertere*, to turn.] —SEE NOTE.

di•ver•ti•men•to (dĭ vĕr′tə mĕn′tō) *n., pl.* **di•ver•ti•men•tos** or **di•ver•ti•men•ti** (dĭ vĕr′tə mĕn′tē). A chamber music form, usually in several movements, commonly written during the 18th century.

di•vest (dĭ vĕst′ *or* dī vĕst′) *tr.v.* **di•vest•ed, di•vest•ing, di•vests. 1.** To strip, as of clothes: *They divested themselves of their heavy winter coats before sitting down by the fire.* **2.** To deprive, as of rights or property: *A person convicted of a felony is divested of the right to vote.* **3.** To free of, as by selling: *He divested himself of several properties.*

di•vide (dĭ vīd′) *v.* **di•vid•ed, di•vid•ing, di•vides.** *—tr.* **1.** To separate into parts, groups, or branches: *The teacher divided the class into four groups.* **2.** To separate into opposing factions: *Different opinions divided Congress over the issue of air pollution.* **3.** To separate from; cut off; keep apart: *A mountain chain divides France and Spain.* **4.** To separate and group according to kind; classify: *divide books into fiction and nonfiction.* **5.** To apportion or distribute among a number: *Volunteers divided the different jobs among themselves.* **6.** To determine how many times (one number) contains another: *I divided 24 by 4 and got 6.* *—intr.* **1.** To become separated into parts, groups, or factions: *The country divided on the issue of how to improve the economy.* **2.** To perform the mathematical operation of division. *—n.* A ridge separating two areas of land each drained by a different river system: *hills that form a divide between rivers flowing eastward and westward.* [First written down before 1325 in Middle English and spelled *dividen*, from Latin *dīvidere* : *dī-*, *dis-*, apart + *-videre*, to separate.]

div•i•dend (dĭv′ĭ dĕnd′) *n.* **1.** A number or quantity that is to be divided. **2.a.** Profits earned by a company during a particular period and divided among the stockholders or owners. **b.** A share of profits paid to a stockholder of a company. **3.** *Informal.* A share of a surplus, especially as a benefit or an advantage; a bonus: *Cleaning up our environment will provide dividends for us all.*

di•vid•er (dĭ vī′dər) *n.* **1.** A person or thing that divides, especially a screen or other partition: *a room divider.* **2.** A device that is like a compass, used for dividing lines and transferring measurements.

div•i•na•tion (dĭv′ə nā′shən) *n.* **1.** The art of foretelling the future by interpreting omens or using magic powers. **2.** Something that has been predicted by this art: *There have been numerous divinations about the end of the world.* **3.** A clever guess.

di•vine (dĭ vīn′) *adj.* **di•vin•er, di•vin•est. 1.** Of or relating to God or a god: *divine wisdom.* **2.** Coming from or given by God or a god: *divine guidance.* **3.** Directed to God or a god; sacred: *divine worship.* *—n.* **1.** A cleric. **2.** A person learned in theology. *—tr.v.* **di•vined, di•vin•ing, di•vines. 1.** To foretell or prophesy by divination: *Ancients seers divined disasters from the flights of birds.* **2.** To guess: *The mechanic divined my car's problem after looking at the tires.* [First written down about 1380 in Middle English, from Latin *dīvīnus*, from *dīvus*, god.] **—di•vine′ly** *adv.* **—di•vine′ness** *n.* **—di•vin′er** *n.*

div•ing bell (dī′vĭng) *n.* A large chamber for persons working underwater that is raised and lowered by a cable and supplied with air under pressure to keep water from coming in its open bottom.

diving board *n.* A flexible board from which a person can dive, secured at one end and sticking out over the water at the other.

diving suit *n.* A heavy waterproof garment for work underwater with a helmet into which air is pumped from the surface.

di•vin•ing rod (dĭ vī′nĭng) *n.* A forked stick held in the hand and believed to indicate the presence of underground water or minerals by bending downward when over a source.

di•vin•i•ty (dĭ vĭn′ĭ tē) *n., pl.* **di•vin•i•ties. 1.** The quality or condition of being divine. **2. Divinity. a.** God. **b.** A god or goddess. **3.** The study of God and religion; theology: *Ministers study at a school of divinity.*

di•vis•i•ble (dĭ vĭz′ə bəl) *adj.* Capable of being divided, especially with no remainder. **—di•vis′i•bil′i•ty** *n.* **—di•vis′i•bly** *adv.*

di•vi•sion (dĭ vĭzh′ən) *n.* **1.** The act of dividing or the condition of being divided; separation into parts: *the division of a book into chapters.* **2.** One of the parts or groups into which something is divided: *a division in a company.* **3.** Something, such as a partition or boundary, that divides or keeps separate: *The wall marked the division between east and west Berlin.* **4.** Disagreement; disunity: *The meeting was marked by deep division among delegates from different sections of the country.* **5.** An army unit that is smaller than a corps and is composed of several regiments. **6.** The highest tax-

Word Building: divert

The word root *-vert-* in English words comes from the Latin verb *vertere*, "to turn." Thus **divert** is literally "to turn aside" (using the prefix *dī-*, a form of *dis-*, "apart, aside"); **revert** means "to turn back" (*re-*, "back"); and **advert** is literally "to turn to, call attention to, as by an advertisement" (*ad-*, "to, toward"). The past participle of *vertere* is *versus*, from which we form the words **reverse**, "turned around or backward" (*re-*, "back"); **obverse**, "turned to the front" (*ob-*, "in front of, in the way of"); and **transverse**, "turned sideways" (*trans-*, "across").

ă	**pat**	oi	**boy**
ā	**pay**	ou	**out**
âr	**care**	o͝o	**took**
ä	**father**	o͞o	**boot**
ĕ	**pet**	ŭ	**cut**
ē	**be**	ûr	**urge**
ĭ	**pit**	th	**thin**
ī	**pie**	*th*	**this**
îr	**pier**	hw	**whoop**
ŏ	**pot**	zh	**vision**
ō	**toe**	ə	**about**
ô	**paw**	N	*French* **bon**

Dorothea Dix

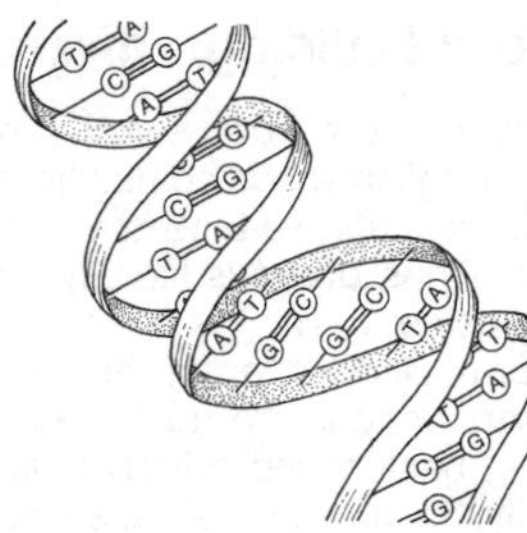

DNA

DNA

One of the wonders of nature is that the complexity and diversity of life can be contained in a relatively simple molecule with a rather long name—**deoxyribonucleic acid**, commonly called **DNA**. In most organisms DNA exists in the nucleus of each cell. It usually consists of two long strands that spiral around each other, forming a structure resembling a twisted ladder. Each rung is made up of two chemical bases (there are just four kinds in DNA) that are bonded together. The sequence of these bases along the strands forms a code that contains an organism's genetic information. When certain components in the cell read this code, they produce proteins, the building blocks of life.

onomic category of plants, made up of one or more related classes and roughly corresponding to a phylum in animal classification. See table at **taxonomy.** **7.** The operation of dividing one number or quantity by another; the process of finding out how many times one number or quantity is contained in another.

division sign *n.* A symbol (÷) placed between two numbers to indicate that the first is to be divided by the second.

di•vi•sive (dĭ **vī′**sĭv) *adj.* Creating or tending to create disagreement or disunity: *a divisive political issue.* **—di•vi′sive•ly** *adv.* **—di•vi′sive•ness** *n.*

di•vi•sor (dĭ **vī′**zər) *n.* The number or quantity by which another is to be divided.

di•vorce (dĭ **vôrs′**) *n.* **1.** The legal ending of a marriage. **2.** A complete separation: *His view of the economy is noteworthy chiefly for its divorce from reality.* —*v.* **di•vorced, di•vorc•ing, di•vorc•es.** —*tr.* **1.** To end the marriage of (persons): *The judge divorced husband and wife.* **2.** To end marriage with (one's spouse) by legal divorce: *She divorced her husband.* **3.** To separate or remove: *We cannot divorce a good diet from fitness.* —*intr.* To obtain a divorce. [First written down about 1378 in Middle English and spelled *devorse,* from Latin *dīvortere,* to divert, variant of *dīvertere.*]

di•vor•cé (dĭ vôr **sā′**) *n.* A man who is divorced.

di•vor•cée (dĭ vôr **sā′**) *n.* A woman who is divorced.

div•ot (**dĭv′**ət) *n.* A piece of turf torn up by a golf club in hitting the ball.

di•vulge (dĭ **vŭlj′**) *tr.v.* **di•vulged, di•vulg•ing, di•vulg•es.** To make known; reveal; tell: *divulge a secret.* **—di•vulg′er** *n.*

div•vy (**dĭv′**ē) *tr.v.* **div•vied, div•vy•ing, div•vies.** To divide; share: *We divvied up the pizza so that each of us got a piece.*

Dix (dĭks), **Dorothea Lynde.** 1802–1887. American reformer who was a pioneer in the movement for better treatment of the mentally ill.

Dix•ie (**dĭk′**sē). A region of the southern and eastern United States, usually made up of the states that joined the Confederacy during the Civil War.

Dix•ie•land (**dĭk′**sē lănd′) *n.* A style of jazz associated with New Orleans and characterized by a fast two-beat rhythm.

diz•zy (**dĭz′**ē) *adj.* **diz•zi•er, diz•zi•est. 1.** Having a sensation of whirling or feeling a tendency to fall; giddy: *A ride on the roller coaster made me feel dizzy.* **2.** Producing or tending to produce giddiness: *a dizzy height.* **3.** Bewildered or confused: *dizzy with excitement.* —*tr.v.* **diz•zied, diz•zy•ing, diz•zies.** To make dizzy: *So many facts and figures dizzied my brain.* [First written down before 830 in Old English and spelled *dysig,* foolish.] **—diz′zi•ly** *adv.* **—diz′zi•ness** *n.*

Dja•kar•ta (jə **kär′**tə). Jakarta.

Dji•bou•ti (jĭ **bo͞o′**tē). **1.** A country of eastern Africa northwest of Somalia. It gained its independence from France in 1977. Population 226,000. **2.** The capital and largest city of Djibouti, in the southeast part of the country northeast of Addis Ababa, Ethiopia. Population, 120,000.

DMZ *abbr.* An abbreviation of demilitarized zone.

DNA (dē′ĕn **ā′**) *n.* An acid found in all living cells, usually in the nucleus, having a structure resembling a twisted ladder and forming the main component of chromosomes. It is the genetic material determining the makeup of all cells and many viruses. [First written down in 1944 in Modern English, from *d(eoxyribo)n(ucleic) a(cid).*] —SEE NOTE.

do[1] (do͞o) *v.* **did** (dĭd), **done** (dŭn), **do•ing, does** (dŭz). —*tr.* **1.** To perform, carry out, or accomplish: *Do a good job. Do your duty.* **2.a.** To create, produce, or make: *do a painting; do a report.* **b.** To create or produce for an audience: *The actors did a new play.* **3.** To bring about; effect: *Crying won't do any good.* **4.** To put into action; exert: *I'll do everything in my power to help you.* **5.** To put into order or take care of: *do one's hair; do the dishes.* **6.** To render or give: *do a favor.* **7.** To work at for a living: *What work do you do?* **8.** To work out the details of (a problem); solve: *I did this equation.* **9.a.** To travel (a specified distance): *do a mile in 7 minutes.* **b.** To travel at a speed of: *He was only doing 50 on the highway.* **10.** To be sufficient or convenient for; suffice: *This room will do us very nicely.* **11.** *Informal.* To serve (a prison term): *Both did time for theft.* —*intr.* **1.** To behave or conduct oneself; act: *You did well on the test.* **2.** To get along; manage; get on: *The new student is doing well.* **3.** To serve a purpose: *That old coat will do for now.* **4.** Used instead of a preceding verb: *She reads as much as I do.* —*aux.* **1.** Used to ask questions: *Do you want to go? Did you understand?* **2.** Used to make negative statements: *I did not sleep at all. We do not understand.* **3.** Used to form inverted phrases: *Little did I suspect.* **4.** Used to emphasize or make stronger: *We do want to go. I do want to be sure.* —*n., pl.* **do's** or **dos.** A statement of what should be done: *a long list of do's and don'ts.* **—idioms. do away with. 1.** To get rid of; dispose of: *doing away with outmoded laws.* **2.** To kill or destroy: *do away with rats and other vermin.* **do in. 1.** *Slang.* To exhaust: *That hike really did me in.* **2.** To kill: *Nobody really knows who did him in.* **do over.** *Informal.* To redecorate: *Professionals are doing over the room.* **do up. 1.** To dress lavishly: *all done up for the party.* **2.** To wrap and tie (a package). **do without.** To manage without (something): *We can do without that kind of help.* [First written down about 725 in Old English and spelled *dōn.*]

❑ *These sound alike:* **do[1], dew** (water droplets), **due** (owed).

do[2] (dō) *n.* In music, the first tone of a major scale. [First written down about 1670 in Modern English, from Italian.]

❑ *These sound alike:* **do[2]** (musical tone), **doe** (deer), **dough** (flour mixture).

do. *abbr.* An abbreviation of ditto.

dob•bin (**dŏb′**ĭn) *n.* A horse, especially an old or plodding workhorse.

Do•ber•man pin•scher (**dō′**bər mən **pĭn′**shər) *n.* A large dog of a breed originally developed in Germany, having a short, smooth, usually black coat. [First written down in 1917 in Modern English : after Ludwig *Dobermann,* 19th-century German dog breeder + German *Pinscher,* terrier.]

doc (dŏk) *n. Informal.* A doctor.

❑ *These sound alike:* **doc, dock[1]** (platform), **dock[2]** (clip), **dock[3]** (place in court), **dock[4]** (sorrel).

doc•ile (**dŏs′**əl *or* **dŏs′**īl′) *adj.* Easy to train or handle; tractable; submissive: *a docile horse with a good disposition.* **—doc′ile•ly** *adv.* **—do•cil′i•ty** (dŏ **sĭl′**ĭ tē *or* dō **sĭl′**ĭ tē) *n.*

dock[1] (dŏk) *n.* **1.a.** A structure extending from a shore over water and supported by piles or pillars, used for loading and unloading ships. **b.** A loading platform for loading and unloading trucks or trains. **2.** A group of piers that serve as the landing area of a harbor. Often used in the plural. **3.** The area of water between or alongside piers for ships. —*v.* **docked, dock•ing, docks.** —*tr.* **1.** To maneuver or come into a dock: *dock a big liner.* **2.** To join together (two or more spacecraft) while in space. —*intr.* To come into dock: *The ferry docked in the evening.* [First written down in 1513 in Modern English from Middle Dutch *doc.*]

❑ *These sound alike:* **dock[1]** (platform), **doc** (doctor), **dock[2]** (clip), **dock[3]** (place in court), **dock[4]** (sorrel).

dock[2] (dŏk) *tr.v.* **docked, dock•ing, docks. 1.** To clip or cut off (an animal's tail, for example). **2.a.** To withhold a part of (a salary): *The restaurant docked the waiter's pay to make up for broken dishes.* **b.** To penalize (a worker) by such deduction: *Printers are docked if they make too many mistakes.* [First written down about 1378 in Middle English and spelled *dokken.*]

❑ *These sound alike:* **dock[2]** (clip), **doc** (doctor), **dock[1]** (platform), **dock[3]** (place in court), **dock[4]** (sorrel).

dock[3] (dŏk) *n.* An enclosed place where the defendant stands or sits in a criminal court. [First written down in 1586 in Modern English, from obsolete Flemish *docke,* cage.]

❑ *These sound alike:* **dock[3]** (place in court), **doc** (doctor), **dock[1]** (platform), **dock[2]** (clip), **dock[4]** (sorrel).

dock[4] (dŏk) *n.* Sorrel. [First written down about 1000 in Old English and spelled *docce.*]

❑ *These sound alike:* **dock[4]** (sorrel), **doc** (doctor), **dock[1]** (platform), **dock[2]** (clip), **dock[3]** (place in court).

dock•et (**dŏk′**ĭt) *n.* **1.** A calender or list of cases awaiting court action. **2.** A list of things to be done; an agenda: *several jobs on the docket for today.* **3.** A label or ticket attached to a package and listing its contents. *—tr.v.* **dock•et•ed, dock•et•ing, dock•ets. 1.** To enter in a docket; schedule. **2.** To label or ticket (a parcel).

dock•yard (**dŏk′**yärd′) *n.* A shipyard.

doc•tor (**dŏk′**tər) *n.* **1.** A person who is trained and licensed to practice any of the healing arts, such as medicine or dentistry. **2.** A person who holds the highest degree given by a college or university. *—tr. v.* **doc•tored, doc•tor•ing, doc•tors. 1.** *Informal.* To give medical treatment to. **2.** To tamper with or falsify: *doctor the results of an experiment.* [First written down about 1303 in Middle English and spelled *doctour,* an expert, authority, from Latin *doctor,* teacher, from *docēre,* to teach.]

doc•tor•al (**dŏk′**tər əl) *adj.* Of or relating to a doctor or doctorate: *a doctoral dissertation.*

doc•tor•ate (**dŏk′**tər ĭt) *n.* The degree or status of a doctor as awarded by a university: *a doctorate in English literature.*

doc•trine (**dŏk′**trĭn) *n.* **1.** A principle or set of principles held and put forward by a religious or philosophical group; dogma. **2.** A statement of government policy, especially in foreign affairs. **—doc′tri•nal** *adj.*

doc•u•ment (**dŏk′**yə mənt) *n.* A written or printed paper that can be used to give evidence or information: *A birth certificate is usually one's first document.* *—tr.v.* (**dŏk′**yə mĕnt′). To prove or support with evidence: *document a report with photographs and letters.*

doc•u•men•ta•ry (dŏk′yə **mĕn′**tə rē) *adj.* **1.** Consisting of, relating to, or based on documents: *documentary evidence.* **2.** Presenting facts objectively and without adding fictional material, as in a motion picture or television program. *—n., pl.* **doc•u•men•ta•ries.** A motion picture or television program giving a factual account of some subject and often showing actual events.

doc•u•men•ta•tion (dŏk′yə mĕn **tā′**shən) *n.* **1.** The act of supplying documents or supporting references: *Documentation of the scandal took many months to complete.* **2.** The documents or references provided: *Documentation for the trial was stored in several large boxes.* **3.** The charts, data, background materials, and instructions that serve as the basis for a computer program and explain its makeup.

dod•der (**dŏd′**ər) *intr.v.* **dod•dered, dod•der•ing, dod•ders.** To tremble or move shakily, as from old age; totter. **—dod′der•ing** *adj.*

dodge (dŏj) *v.* **dodged, dodg•ing, dodg•es.** *—tr.* **1.** To avoid by moving quickly aside or out of the way: *The dog dodged the cars as it ran across the street.* **2.** To evade by cunning, trickery, or other means: *The candidate dodged the reporter's questions.* *—intr.* To move by jumping aside suddenly: *The boy dodged through the crowd.* *—n.* **1.** The act of dodging. **2.** A trick to cheat or avoid: *the dodges of a spy.*

dodg•er (**dŏj′**ər) *n.* A person who dodges or evades.

Dodg•son (**dŏj′**sən), **Charles Lutwidge.** Pen name Lewis Carroll. 1832–1898. British writer whose stories about Alice appear in *Alice's Adventures in Wonderland* (1865) and *Through the Looking-Glass* (1872).

do•do (**dō′**dō) *n., pl.* **do•does** or **do•dos.** A large flightless bird that formerly lived on an island in the Indian Ocean but has been extinct for about 300 years. It had a hooked bill and very short wings.

Do•do•ma (**dō′**də mä). The official capital of Tanzania, in the central part of the country. Population, 46,000.

doe (dō) *n., pl.* **doe** or **does. 1.** A female deer. **2.** The female of certain other animals, such as the hare or kangaroo. [First written down about 1000 in Old English and spelled *dā.*]

❑ *These sound alike:* **doe, do[2]** (musical tone), **dough** (flour mixture).

do•er (**do͞o′**ər) *n.* A person who does something, especially an active and energetic person: *She is a doer and does not hesitate to act.*

does (dŭz) *v.* Third person singular present tense of **do[1]**.

doe•skin (**dō′**skĭn′) *n.* **1.** The skin of a female deer or of a sheep or lamb. **2.** Soft leather made from such skin, used especially for gloves. **3.** A soft smooth woolen fabric with a nap on it.

does•n't (**dŭz′**ənt). Contraction of *does not.*

doff (dôf *or* dŏf) *tr.v.* **doffed, doff•ing, doffs.** To take off; remove: *They doffed their hats in salute to the passing flag.* [First written down before 1375 in Middle English and spelled *doffen,* from *don off,* to do off.]

dog (dôg *or* dŏg) *n.* **1.** A four-legged mammal that eats meat and is bred in many varieties, some of which resemble the related wolf and fox. For thousands of years dogs have been kept as pets and trained to hunt or guard. **2.a.** Any of various mammals related to the dogs, as the fox, wolf, or coyote. **b.** The male of any of these animals. *—tr.v.* **dogged, dog•ging, dogs.** To trail persistently: *The detective dogged the suspect's every move.*

dog•cart (**dôg′**kärt′ *or* **dŏg′**kärt′) *n.* **1.** A vehicle drawn by one horse and accommodating two persons seated back to back. **2.** A small cart pulled by dogs.

dog•catch•er (**dôg′**kăch′ər *or* **dŏg′**kăch′ər) *n.* A person hired to catch stray dogs.

dog days *pl.n.* The hot sultry period between mid-July and September.

doge (dōj) *n.* The elected chief magistrate of the former republic of Venice or Genoa.

dog-ear (**dôg′**îr′ *or* **dŏg′**îr′) *n.* A turned-down corner of a page in a book. *—tr.v.* **dog-eared, dog-ear•ing, dog-ears.** To turn down the corner of (a page in a book). **—dog′-eared′** *adj.*

dog•fight (**dôg′**fīt′ *or* **dŏg′**fīt′) *n.* **1.** A violent fight between or as if between dogs. **2.** A battle between fighter planes.

dog•fish (**dôg′**fĭsh′ *or* **dŏg′**fĭsh′) *n.* Any of various

Doberman pinscher

Charles Dodgson
"Lewis Carroll"

dodo

ă	pat	oi	boy
ā	pay	ou	out
âr	care	o͝o	took
ä	father	o͞o	boot
ĕ	pet	ŭ	cut
ē	be	ûr	urge
ĭ	pit	th	thin
ī	pie	*th*	this
îr	pier	hw	whoop
ŏ	pot	zh	vision
ō	toe	ə	about
ô	paw	N	*French* bon

small sharks having a slender grayish body and a forked tail.

dog•ged (dô′gĭd *or* dŏg′ĭd) *adj.* Not giving up easily; persevering; stubborn: *The doctor's dogged efforts succeeded in discovering a cure for the disease.* **—dog′ged•ly** *adv.* **—dog′ged•ness** *n.*

dog•ger•el (dô′gər əl *or* dŏg′ər əl) *n.* Crudely made verse, often intended to be funny.

dog•gy or **dog•gie** (dô′gē *or* dŏg′ē) *n., pl.* **dog•gies.** A dog, especially a small or a young dog.

doggy bag *n.* A bag for leftover food taken home from a restaurant.

dog•house (dôg′hous′ *or* dŏg′hous′) *n.* A small house or shelter for a dog. ***—idiom.* in the doghouse.** *Slang.* In disfavor; in trouble: *You'll be in the doghouse for forgetting his birthday.*

dog•ma (dôg′mə *or* dŏg′mə) *n., pl.* **dog•mas. 1.** A doctrine or system of doctrines proclaimed true by a religion. **2.** A belief, an opinion, or an idea considered to be true: *Political dogmas of the past often seem barbaric today.*

dog•mat•ic (dôg măt′ĭk *or* dŏg măt′ĭk) *adj.* **1.** Of or relating to dogma; doctrinal: *a dogmatic idea.* **2.** Characterized by the expression of principles, beliefs, or opinions in an authoritative, often arrogant way: *a dogmatic person.* **—dog•mat′i•cal•ly** *adv.*

dog•ma•tism (dôg′mə tĭz′əm *or* dŏg′mə tĭz′əm) *n.* Dogmatic assertion of an opinion or a belief.

do-good•er (do͞o′go͝od′ər) *n. Informal.* A person who is eager to make reforms and help people.

dog paddle *n.* A simple swimming stroke in which the arms and legs remain below the surface paddling in short kicks and strokes.

dog•sled (dôg′slĕd′ *or* dŏg′slĕd′) *n.* A sled pulled by one or more dogs.

Dog Star *n.* Sirius.

dog•tooth violet (dôg′to͞oth′ *or* dŏg′to͞oth′) *n.* Any of several North American plants having leaves with reddish blotches and colorful nodding flowers.

dog•trot (dôg′trŏt′ *or* dŏg′trŏt′) *n.* A steady trot like that of a dog.

dog•watch (dôg′wŏch′ *or* dŏg′wŏch′) *n.* Either of two periods of watch aboard a ship, from 4 to 6 P.M. or from 6 to 8 P.M.

dog•wood (dôg′wo͝od′ *or* dŏg′wo͝od′) *n.* A tree having showy white or pink leaves surrounding small greenish flowers that develop into red berries in the fall.

Do•ha (dō′hə). The capital of Qatar, on the Persian Gulf. Population, 190,000.

doi•ly (doi′lē) *n., pl.* **doi•lies.** A small fancy mat, as of lace, linen, or paper, often used to protect or decorate a table top. [First written down in 1678 in Modern English, after *Doily* or *Doyly*, 18th-century London draper.]

do•ings (do͞o′ĭngz) *n.* Activities, especially social activities: *doings at the club.*

do-it-your•self (do͞o′ĭt yər sĕlf′) *adj.* Of, relating to, or designed to be done or assembled by an amateur: *do-it-yourself home repairs.*

dol•drums (dōl′drəmz′ *or* dŏl′drəmz′) *pl.n. (used with a singular or plural verb).* **1.** A period or condition of depression or inactivity: *in the doldrums over some bad luck.* **2.** A region of the ocean near the equator where there is little or no wind: *Several sailing ships were delayed by being caught in the doldrums.* [First written down in 1811 in Modern English, from Middle English *dold*, past participle of *dullen*, to dull.]

dole (dōl) *n.* **1.** The charitable distribution of goods, especially of money, food, or clothing. **2.** A share of money, food, or clothing distributed as charity. *—tr.v.* **doled, dol•ing, doles. 1.** To distribute as charity: *The organization doles out food and medicine.* **2.** To distribute in small portions; give out sparingly. [First written down about 725 in Old English and spelled *gedāl.*]

dole•ful (dōl′fəl) *adj.* Filled with or expressing grief; mournful: *the cat's doleful cry in the rain.* [First written down before 1300 in Middle English and spelled *diolful*, from *dol*, grief, from Latin *dolēre*, to suffer.] **—dole′ful•ly** *adv.*

doll (dŏl) *n.* **1.** A child's usually small toy representing a human being. **2.** *Slang.* A sweetheart or darling. ***—idiom.* doll up.** To dress up smartly, as for a special occasion: *The guests were dolled up for the party.*

dol•lar (dŏl′ər) *n.* The basic monetary unit in the United States and many other countries, including Australia, Canada, Fiji, New Zealand, Taiwan, and Zimbabwe.

dol•lop (dŏl′əp) *n.* **1.** A large lump or portion: *a dollop of ice cream.* **2.** A small amount; a bit: *not a dollop of truth in those rumors.*

dol•ly (dŏl′ē) *n., pl.* **dol•lies. 1.** *Informal.* A child's doll. **2.** A hand truck or low mobile platform that rolls on small wheels, used for moving heavy loads.

dol•men (dōl′mən *or* dŏl′mən) *n.* A prehistoric structure made up of two or more massive upright stones supporting a horizontal stone, typically forming a chamber.

dol•o•mite (dō′lə mīt′ *or* dŏl′ə mīt′) *n.* **1.** A gray, pink, or white mineral consisting mainly of a carbonate of calcium and magnesium. **2.** A rock containing dolomite and resembling limestone, used as a building stone. [First written down in 1794 in Modern English, after Déodat de *Dolomieu* (1750–1801), French geologist.]

do•lor (dō′lər) *n.* Sorrow; grief.

do•lor•ous (dō′lər əs *or* dŏl′ər əs) *adj.* Marked by or showing sorrow, grief, or pain. **—do′lor•ous•ly** *adv.*

dol•phin (dŏl′fĭn *or* dôl′fĭn) *n.* **1.** Any of various marine mammals related to the whales but smaller and having a snout shaped like a beak. Dolphins are noted for their remarkable intelligence. **2.** Either of two edible marine fishes of warm waters, having iridescent coloring when removed from the water.

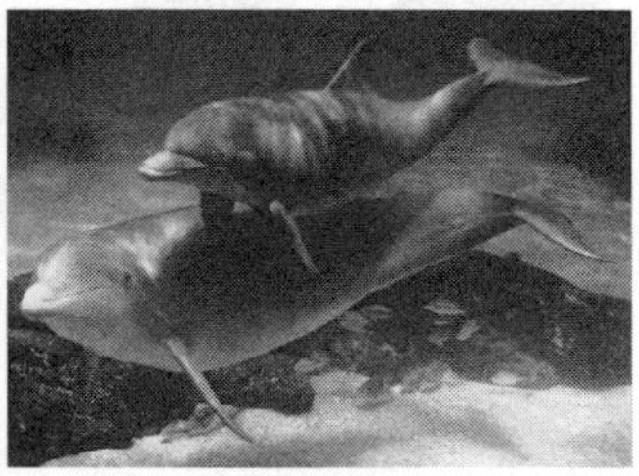

dolphin

Calf (*top*) and adult female (*bottom*)

dolt (dōlt) *n.* A person regarded as stupid.

–dom *suff.* A suffix that means: **1.** Condition; state: *stardom.* **2.** Position; rank: *dukedom.*

do•main (dō măn′) *n.* **1.** A territory or range of rule or control; a realm: *the duke's domain.* **2.** A sphere of interest or activity; a field: *The new teacher's domain is math.* **3.** In mathematics, the set of all values that an independent variable can have. [First written down about 1425 in Middle English, from Latin *dominium*, property, from *dominus*, lord.]

dome (dōm) *n.* **1.** A rounded roof or vault built in the shape of a hemisphere. **2.** A structure or other object resembling such a roof or vault: *the dome of the sky.* *—tr.v.* **domed, dom•ing, domes. 1.** To cover with or as if with a roof or vault in the shape of a hemisphere. **2.** To shape like such a roof or vault.

do•mes•tic (də mĕs′tĭk) *adj.* **1.** Of or relating to the family or household: *domestic chores.* **2.** Enjoying or interested in home life and household affairs. **3.** Tame or domesticated. Used of animals: *cats and other domestic animals.* **4.** Produced in or native to a particular country; not foreign or imported: *domestic cars.* *—n.* A household servant. **—do•mes′ti•cal•ly** *adv.*

do•mes•ti•cate (də mĕs′tĭ kāt′) *tr.v.* **do•mes•ti•cat•ed, do•mes•ti•cat•ing, do•mes•ti•cates. 1.** To cause to feel comfortable at home. **2.** To train to live with or be of use to human beings; tame: *Human beings domesticated cattle long ago.* **—do•mes′ti•ca′tion** *n.*

do•mes•tic•i•ty (dō′mĕ stĭs′ĭ tē) *n., pl.* **do•mes•**

tic•i•ties. **1.** The quality or condition of being domestic. **2.** Home life or devotion to it: *the intimate domesticity of a small family.* **3. domesticities.** The affairs of a household.

dom•i•cile (dŏm′ĭ sĭl′ *or* dō′mĭ sĭl′) *n.* **1.** A residence; a home. **2.** A person's legal residence. —*v.* **dom•i•ciled, dom•i•cil•ing, dom•i•ciles.** —*tr.* To establish (oneself or another person) in a residence. —*intr.* To dwell; reside: *domicile with relatives.*

dom•i•nance (dŏm′ə nəns) *n.* The condition or fact of being dominant.

dom•i•nant (dŏm′ə nənt) *adj.* **1.** Having the most influence or control: *the dominant dog in a pack.* **2.** Most prominent, as in position: *The tallest buildings are dominant in a city's skyline.* **3.** Of, relating to, or indicating the gene in any pair of differing genes in an organism that masks or dominates the other. **4.** Of or based on the fifth tone of a musical scale: *the dominant chord in the scale of C major.* —*n.* **1.** The fifth tone of a musical scale: *In the key of C major, G is the dominant.* **2.** A dominant gene. —**dom′i•nant•ly** *adv.*

dom•i•nate (dŏm′ə nāt′) *v.* **dom•i•nat•ed, dom•i•nat•ing, dom•i•nates.** —*tr.* **1.** To rule, control, or govern by superior power or authority: *Great Britain dominated about one-fourth of the world in the 19th century.* **2.** To occupy a commanding controlling position in or over: *The mountain dominates the countryside for miles around.* —*intr.* **1.** To have or exert strong authority or influence. **2.** To have the most prominent or superior position: *Tall people dominate in a crowd.*

dom•i•na•tion (dŏm′ə nā′shən) *n.* Supremacy over another or others: *British domination of its colonies.*

dom•i•neer (dŏm′ə nîr′) *intr. & tr.v.* **dom•i•neered, dom•i•neer•ing, dom•i•neers.** To rule over or control arbitrarily or arrogantly; tyrannize.

dom•i•neer•ing (dŏm′ə nîr′ĭng) *adj.* Tending to domineer; overbearing: *His domineering manner offended many people.* —**dom′i•neer′ing•ly** *adv.*

Dom•i•nic (dŏm′ə nĭk), Saint. 1170?–1221. Spanish-born priest who founded the Dominican order of friars (1216).

Dom•i•ni•ca (dŏm′ə nē′kə *or* də mĭn′ĭ kə). An island country of the eastern Caribbean north-northwest of Martinique. The island gained its independence from Great Britain in 1978. Capital, Roseau. Population, 77,000. —**Dom′i•ni′can** *adj. & n.*

Do•min•i•can¹ (də mĭn′ĭ kən) *adj.* Of or relating to the Dominican Republic or its people or culture. —*n.* A native or inhabitant of the Dominican Republic.

Do•min•i•can² (də mĭn′ĭ kən) *n.* A member of a Roman Catholic order of preaching friars established in 1216 by Saint Dominic.

Dominican Republic. A country of the West Indies on the eastern part of the island of Hispaniola. The country achieved its independence from Haiti in 1844. Santo Domingo is the capital and the largest city. Population, 5,674,977.

dom•i•nie (dŏm′ə nē′ *or* dō′mə nē′) *n. Scots.* A schoolteacher.

do•min•ion (də mĭn′yən) *n.* **1.** Control or exercise of control; sovereignty. **2.** A territory or sphere of influence or control; a realm: *The dominion of the British monarchy once included part of France.* **3. Dominion.** One of the self-governing nations within the British Commonwealth.

dom•i•no¹ (dŏm′ə nō′) *n., pl.* **dom•i•noes** or **dom•i•nos. 1.** A small rectangular block divided into halves, each half of which is blank or marked by one to six dots. **2. dominoes.** *(used with a singular or plural verb).* A game played with a set of these small blocks. [First written down in 1801 in Modern English, probably from *domino,* mask, perhaps because of the resemblance between the eyeholes and the spots on some of the tiles.]

dom•i•no² (dŏm′ə nō′) *n., pl.* **dom•i•noes** or **dom•i•nos. 1.** A masquerade costume made up of a hooded robe worn with an eye mask. **2.** The mask so worn. [First written down in 1694 in Modern English, probably from Latin *(benedīcāmus) dominō,* (let us praise) the Lord.]

domino theory *n.* A theory that one event will set off a chain of similar events.

don¹ (dŏn) *n.* **1. Don.** Used as a courtesy title before the name of a man in a Spanish-speaking area. **2.** *Chiefly British.* A college or university professor. [First written down in 1523 in Modern English, from Latin *dominus,* lord.]

don² (dŏn) *tr.v.* **donned, don•ning, dons.** To put on (clothing): *don a coat.* [First written down before 1350 in Middle English, contraction of *do on,* to put on.]

Do•ña (dō′nyä) *n.* Used as a courtesy title before the name of a woman in a Spanish-speaking area.

do•nate (dō′nāt′ *or* dō nāt′) *tr.v.* **do•nat•ed, do•nat•ing, do•nates.** To present as a gift to a fund or cause; contribute: *donate clothing to the Red Cross.*

do•na•tion (dō nā′shən) *n.* **1.** The act of giving to a fund or cause. **2.** A gift or grant; a contribution: *make a small donation to charity.*

done (dŭn) *v.* Past participle of **do¹**. —*adj.* **1.** Having been completely accomplished or finished: *a done deed.* **2.** Cooked adequately: *Is the fish done?* **3.** Socially acceptable: *Eating with the fingers is not done in certain cultures.* —***idiom.* done for.** Doomed to death or destruction.

❑ *These sound alike:* **done, dun¹** (ask for payment), **dun²** (grayish-brown).

don•jon (dŏn′jən *or* dŭn′jən) *n.* The main tower of a castle; a keep.

❑ *These sound alike:* **donjon, dungeon** (prison).

don•key (dŏng′kē *or* dông′kē) *n., pl.* **don•keys. 1.** A mammal related to the horse but smaller and having longer ears, used as a pack animal; an ass. **2.** A stubborn or stupid person.

Don•na (dŏn′ə *or* dôn′nä) *n.* Used as a courtesy title before the name of a woman in an Italian-speaking area.

don•nish (dŏn′ĭsh) *adj.* Of, relating to, or typical of a university don; bookish.

don•ny•brook (dŏn′ē bro͝ok′) *n.* A brawl or an uproar.

do•nor (dō′nər) *n.* **1.** A person who contributes something, such as money, to a cause or fund. **2.** A person or animal from whom blood, tissue, or an organ is taken for use in grafting or in a transfusion or transplant.

do-no•thing (do͞o′nŭth′ĭng) *Informal. adj.* Making no effort for change, especially in politics: *a do-nothing mayor.* —*n.* An idle or lazy person.

Don Qui•xo•te (dŏn′ kē hō′tē) *n.* An impractical idealist who tries to right wrongs. [First written down in 1648 in Modern English and spelled *Quixot,* after *Don Quixote,* hero of a satirical chivalric romance by Miguel de Cervantes.]

don't (dōnt). Contraction of *do not.*

do•nut (dō′nŭt′ *or* do′nət) *n.* Variant of **doughnut.**

doo•dle (do͞od′l) *v.* **doo•dled, doo•dling, doo•dles.** —*intr.v.* To scribble aimlessly: *doodle on a pad during a phone call.* —*tr.v.* To scribble (a design or figure) while preoccupied. —*n.* A design or figure drawn while preoccupied. —**doo′dler** *n.*

doo•dle•bug (do͞od′l bŭg′) *n.* The larva of the ant lion.

doom (do͞om) *n.* **1.** Fate, especially a tragic or ruinous one: *events that doomed the revolution to fail-*

domino¹

donkey

ă	pat	oi	boy
ā	pay	ou	out
âr	care	o͝o	took
ä	father	o͞o	boot
ĕ	pet	ŭ	cut
ē	be	ûr	urge
ĭ	pit	th	thin
ī	pie	*th*	this
îr	pier	hw	whoop
ŏ	pot	zh	vision
ō	toe	ə	about
ô	paw	N	*French* bon

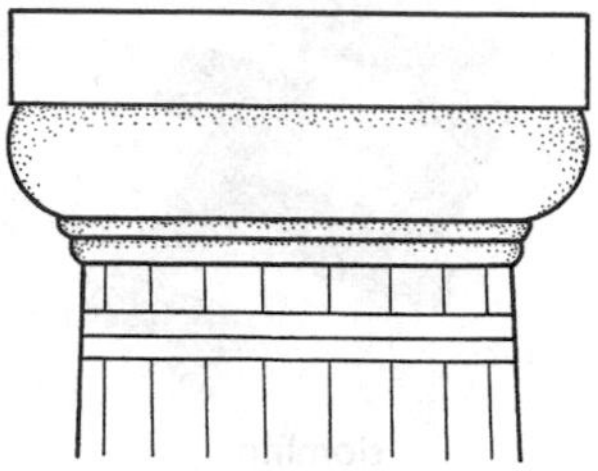

Doric
Doric style column

dormer

double bass

ure. **2.** A decision or judgment, especially an official condemnation: *the justice of the prisoner's doom.* —*tr.v.* **doomed, doom•ing, dooms. 1.** To pronounce a severe judgment against; condemn. **2.** To destine to an unhappy end: *The injury doomed the patient to several weeks in bed.*

dooms•day (do͞omz′dā′) *n.* Judgment Day.

door (dôr) *n.* **1.** A moveable structure used to close off an entrance, typically made of a panel that swings on hinges or slides on a track. **2.** A doorway: *The neighbors stood in the door and talked.* **3.** The room or building to which a door belongs: *The deli is several doors down the street.* **4.** A means of approach or access: *An education can be a door to success.* [First written down about 725 in Old English and spelled *duru.*]

door•bell (dôr′bĕl′) *n.* A buzzer or bell outside a door that is rung to announce the presence of a visitor.

door•jamb (dôr′jăm′) *n.* Either of the two vertical pieces framing a doorway.

door•knob (dôr′nŏb′) *n.* A knob-shaped handle for opening and closing a door.

door•man (dôr′mən) *n.* A man employed to attend the entrance of a hotel, an apartment house, or other building.

door•mat (dôr′măt′) *n.* A mat placed before a doorway for wiping the shoes.

door•nail (dôr′nāl′) *n.* A large-headed nail. —***idiom.*** **dead as a doornail.** Undoubtedly dead.

door•sill (dôr′sĭl′) *n.* The threshold of a doorway.

door•step (dôr′stĕp′) *n.* A step leading to a door.

door•stop (dôr′stŏp′) *n.* **1.** A wedge inserted beneath a door to hold it open. **2.** A weight or spring that prevents a door from slamming. **3.** A rubber-tipped projection on a wall to protect it from the impact of an opening door.

door•way (dôr′wā′) *n.* The entrance to a room or building.

door•yard (dôr′yärd′) *n.* A yard in front of the door of a house.

do•pa•mine (dō′pə mēn′) *n.* A hormone formed in the brain that is necessary for normal nerve activity in the central nervous system.

dop•ant (dō′pənt) *n.* A substance added in small amounts to a semiconductor material to change how it conducts electricity.

dope (dōp) *n.* **1.** *Informal.* A narcotic, stimulant, or other drug, especially an addictive drug sold and used illegally. **2.** *Informal.* A person regarded as stupid. **3.** A sticky paste applied to seal pipe joints. **4.** *Informal.* Information, especially from a person: *He gave me the dope on the new teacher.* —*tr.v.* **doped, dop•ing, dopes. 1.** *Informal.* To give a narcotic drug to. **2.** To treat (a semiconductor) with a dopant. [First written down in 1807 in Modern English, from Dutch *doop*, sauce, from *doopen*, to dip.]

dop•ey (dō′pē) *adj.* **dop•i•er, dop•i•est.** *Slang.* Mentally dull; stupid.

Dop•pler effect (dŏp′lər) *n.* The apparent change in the frequency of waves, as of sound or light, when the source of the waves is approaching or receding from an observer. For example, as the source of sound waves and an observer approach each other, the sound rises in pitch. As the source and an observer move apart, the sound falls in pitch. [First written down in 1871 in Modern English and spelled *Doppler's principle*, after Christian Johann *Doppler* (1803–1853), Austrian physicist.]

Dor•ic (dôr′ĭk *or* dŏr′ĭk) *adj.* In the style of an order of classical Greek architecture characterized by heavy fluted columns with plain saucer-shaped capitals: *a Doric column.*

dorm (dôrm) *n. Informal.* A dormitory.

dor•man•cy (dôr′mən sē) *n.* The condition of being dormant: *Winter is a time of dormancy for many animals.*

dor•mant (dôr′mənt) *adj.* **1.** In an inactive state in which growth and development stop, only to start again when conditions are favorable: *seeds are dormant during winter.* **2.** Not active but capable of renewed activity: *a dormant volcano.* [First written down about 1387 in Middle English and spelled *dormaunt*, from Old French, from Latin *dormīre*, to sleep.]

dor•mer (dôr′mər) *n.* **1.** A window set in a small gable projecting from a sloping roof. **2.** The gable holding such a window.

dor•mi•to•ry (dôr′mĭ tôr′ē) *n., pl.* **dor•mi•to•ries. 1.** A room providing sleeping quarters for a number of people. **2.** A building for housing a number of persons, as at a school. [First written down in 1440 in Middle English and spelled *dormitorie*, from Latin *dormītōrium*, from *dormīre*, to sleep.]

dor•mouse (dôr′mous′) *n.* Any of various small rodents of Europe, Asia, and northern Africa that resemble the squirrels. Dormice sleep most of the winter. [First written down about 1425 in Middle English, probably from Anglo-Norman *dormeus*, sleepy, hibernating, from Old French *dormir*, to sleep.]

dor•sal (dôr′səl) *adj.* Of, on, or near the back or upper surface of an organ, part, or body of an animal: *the dorsal fin of a fish.* —**dor′sal•ly** *adv.*

do•ry (dôr′ē) *n., pl.* **do•ries.** A small flat-bottomed fishing boat with high flaring sides.

dos•age (dō′sĭj) *n.* **1.** The administration or application of medicine or some treatment in regulated amounts: *the dosage of a drug three times a day.* **2.** The amount administered or applied at one time: *The doctor reduced my dosage of antihistamine.*

dose (dōs) *n.* **1.** The amount of medicine or other substance or treatment given or taken at one time: *a dose of medicine every four hours.* **2.** *Informal.* An amount, especially of something unpleasant, to which one is subjected: *a dose of hard luck.* —*tr.v.* **dosed, dos•ing, dos•es.** To give or prescribe (medicine) in specified amounts. [First written down about 1425, from Greek *dosis*, something given, from *didonai*, to give.]

dos•si•er (dŏs′ē ā′ *or* dô′sē ā′) *n.* A collection of papers giving detailed information about a particular person or subject: *Army records included a dossier on each soldier.* [First written down in 1880 in Modern English, from Old French, bundle of papers labeled on the back, from *dos*, back, from Latin *dorsum.*]

dost (dŭst) *v. Archaic.* A second person singular present tense of **do**[1].

❑ *These sound alike:* **dost, dust** (particles).

Dos•to•yev•sky or **Dos•to•ev•ski** (dŏs′tə **yĕf′**skē *or* dŏs′toi **yĕf′**skē), **Feodor Mikhailovich.** 1821–1881. Russian writer whose novels include *Crime and Punishment* (1866).

dot (dŏt) *n.* **1.** A small round mark; a spot: *a dot over the small letter i.* **2.** The short sound or signal used in Morse code in combination with the dash and silent intervals to represent letters, numbers, or punctuation. —*tr.v.* **dot•ted, dot•ting, dots. 1.** To mark with dots. **2.** To cover with or as if with dots: *Dandelions dotted the green field.* —***idiom.*** **on the dot.** Exactly at the appointed time; punctual or punctually: *I arrived at nine o'clock on the dot.*

dot•age (dō′tĭj) *n.* A deterioration of mental faculties; senility.

dote (dōt) *intr.v.* **dot•ed, dot•ing, dotes.** To show excessive love or fondness: *They doted on their only grandchild.*

doth (dŭth) *v. Archaic.* A third person singular present tense of **do**[1].

dot•ty (dŏt′ē) *adj.* **dot•ti•er, dot•ti•est. 1.** Mentally unbalanced; crazy. **2.** Amusingly eccentric or unconventional.

dou•ble (dŭb′əl) *adj.* **1.** Twice as much in size, strength, number, or amount: *a double dose.* **2.** Composed of two like parts: *double doors.* **3.** Composed of two unlike parts; dual: *a double meaning.* **4.** Accomodating or designed for two: *a double hotel room.* **5.** Having more than the usual number of petals, usually in a crowded or overlapping arrangement: *a double chrysanthemum.* —*n.* **1.** Something increased twofold. **2.** A person or thing that closely resembles another; a duplicate: *She's her sister's double.* **3. doubles.** A form of a game, such as tennis or handball, having two players on each side. **4.** In baseball, a hit that enables the batter to reach second base safely. —*v.* **dou•bled, dou•bling, dou•bles.** —*tr.* **1.** To make twice as great: *Double the amount of food if both of you go hiking.* **2.** To be twice as much as: *doubled the score of her opponent.* **3.** To fold in two: *double the blanket to get more warmth.* **4.** To clench (one's fist). **5.** To duplicate; repeat: *Double the* t *in* hit *when you spell* hitting. **6.** To sail around: *double a cape.* —*intr.* **1.** To be increased twofold: *Our rent has doubled in 10 years' time.* **2.** To turn sharply backward; reverse: *The bear doubled back on its trail.* **3.** To serve in an additional capacity: *My bed doubles as a couch.* **4.** To be a substitute: *The assistant doubled for the coach today.* **5.** In baseball, to hit a double. —*adv.* **1.** To twice the amount or extent; doubly: *paid double for the customized car.* **2.** Two together; in pairs: *ride double on a horse.* **3.** In two: *bent double with laughter.* —***idioms.*** **double up. 1.** To bend suddenly, as in pain or laughter: *The joke made us double up.* **2.** To share accomodations meant for one person. **on the double.** Immediately or quickly: *We need help on the double!* [First written down before 1200 in Middle English and spelled *duble,* from Latin *duplus.*]

double bar *n.* A pair of vertical lines or a heavy black line drawn through a musical staff to indicate the end of a large section of a composition.

dou•ble-bar•reled (dŭb′əl băr′əld) *adj.* **1.** Having two barrels mounted side by side: *a double-barreled shotgun.* **2.** Serving two purposes; twofold: *a double-barreled question.*

double bass (bās) *n.* The largest and lowest pitched of the stringed instruments that are normally played with a bow.

double bassoon *n.* A contrabassoon.

double boiler *n.* A cooking utensil consisting of an upper pot fitted into a lower pot. Water boiling in the lower pot allows the slow even cooking or heating of food in the upper pot.

dou•ble-breast•ed (dŭb′əl brĕs′tĭd) *adj.* Having two rows of buttons and fastened by lapping one edge of the front of a garment well over the other: *a double-breasted jacket.*

dou•ble-check (dŭb′əl chĕk′) *v.* To inspect or examine again; verify: *double-check one's subtraction.*

double chin *n.* A fold of fatty flesh beneath the chin.

dou•ble-cross (dŭb′əl krôs′ *or* dŭb′əl krŏs′) *tr.v.* **dou•ble-crossed, dou•ble-cross•ing, dou•ble-cross•es.** To betray by acting contrary to a prior agreement. —*n.* An act of betrayal. —**dou′ble-cross′er** *n.*

double-deal•er (dŭb′əl dē′lər) *n.* A person who engages in deceitful or treacherous behavior; a double-crosser.

dou•ble-deal•ing (dŭb′əl dē′lĭng) *adj.* Duplicitous or deceitful; treacherous. —*n.* Duplicity or deceit; treachery.

dou•ble-deck•er (dŭb′əl dĕk′ər) *n.* **1.** A vehicle, such as a bus or railway car, having two decks or tiers for passengers. **2.** *Informal.* A large sandwich having three slices of bread and two layers of filling.

dou•ble-dig•it (dŭb′əl dĭj′ĭt) *adj.* Being between 10 and 99 percent: *double-digit inflation.*

double dribble *n.* In basketball, an illegal dribble in which a player uses both hands at the same time to dribble the ball or begins to dribble the ball a second time after a complete stop.

dou•ble-edged (dŭb′əl ĕjd′) *adj.* **1.** Having two cutting edges: *a double-edged knife.* **2.** Effective or capable of being interpreted in two ways: *a double-edged compliment.*

dou•ble-en•ten•dre (dŭb′əl än tän′drə) *n.* A word or phrase having a double meaning, especially when the second meaning is indecent or improper.

dou•ble-head•er also **dou•ble•head•er** (dŭb′əl hĕd′ər) *n.* Two games played one after the other on the same day, especially in baseball.

double jeopardy *n.* The conditon of being tried a second time for the same offense. It is prohibited by the U.S. Constitution.

dou•ble-joint•ed (dŭb′əl join′tĭd) *adj.* Having unusually flexible joints, especially of the limbs or fingers.

double knit *n.* A fabric somewhat like jersey, knitted so that a double thickness of fabric is produced in which the two sides of the fabric are interlocked.

double negative *n.* A construction in which two negatives are used, especially to express one negative thought. —See Note.

dou•ble-park (dŭb′əl pärk′) *tr. & intr.v.* **dou•ble-parked, dou•ble-park•ing, dou•ble-parks.** To park alongside another vehicle already parked parallel to the curb.

double play *n.* In baseball, a play in which two players are put out.

double pneumonia *n.* Pneumonia in which both lungs are affected.

dou•ble-quick (dŭb′əl kwĭk′) *adj.* Very quick; rapid. —*n.* A marching cadence; double time.

double reed *n.* A pair of joined reeds that vibrate together to produce sound in certain wind instruments such as the bassoon and oboe.

double standard *n.* A set of standards that allows greater freedom to one group than another, especially one granting more freedom to men than to women.

double star *n.* A binary star.

dou•blet (dŭb′lĭt) *n.* **1.** A close-fitting jacket, with or without sleeves, worn by European men between the 15th and 17th centuries. **2.** One of two words derived from the same source but not through the same route.

double take *n.* A delayed reaction to something unusual: *He did a double take when he saw her strange costume.*

double talk *n.* **1.** Meaningless speech that consists of nonsense syllables mixed with real words. **2.** Talk that is purposefully ambiguous or evasive: *campaign double talk.*

double time *n.* **1.** A rapid marching pace of 180 three-foot steps per minute. **2.** A wage rate that is double the normal rate: *get double time for Saturday work.*

dou•ble-time (dŭb′əl tīm′) *intr. & tr.v.* To move or cause to move in double time.

dou•bloon (dŭ blo͞on′) *n.* A gold coin formerly used in Spain and Spanish America. [First written down in 1622 in Modern English, from Spanish *doblón,* from Latin *duplus,* double.]

double-decker

Tour bus in Vancouver, Canada

Usage: double negative

The use of a **double negative,** such as *He didn't say nothing,* should be avoided. Instead write *I said nothing* or *I didn't say anything.* A double negative can be used to say something affirmative, as in *I cannot just do nothing,* but such expressions can be confusing.

doublet

c. 1565 portrait of Robert Dudley, First Earl of Leicester, by Steven van der Meulen (fl. 1543–1563)

ă	pat	oi	boy
ā	pay	ou	out
âr	care	o͝o	took
ä	father	o͞o	boot
ĕ	pet	ŭ	cut
ē	be	ûr	urge
ĭ	pit	th	thin
ī	pie	*th*	this
îr	pier	hw	whoop
ŏ	pot	zh	vision
ō	toe	ə	about
ô	paw	N	*French* bon

Frederick Douglass

Frederick Douglass

Born a slave on a Maryland plantation, at the age of 21 Frederick **Douglass** disguised himself as a sailor and escaped to the North. Douglass soon became known as a powerful orator, lecturing throughout the North as the agent of the Massachusetts Anti-Slavery Society. In 1845 Douglass published his *Narrative of the Life of Frederick Douglass, an American Slave*, and then traveled to England to avoid capture as a fugitive slave in the United States. While abroad, Douglass went on a lecture circuit, earning enough money to buy his freedom on his return home. In Rochester, New York, in 1847, Douglass founded the *North Star* (named for the star that guided escaping slaves to freedom in the North), a weekly antislavery newspaper. The newspaper continued under Douglass for many years and established him as the most important Black abolition leader. Douglass's autobiography is widely read today and remains an outstanding example of the American slave narrative.

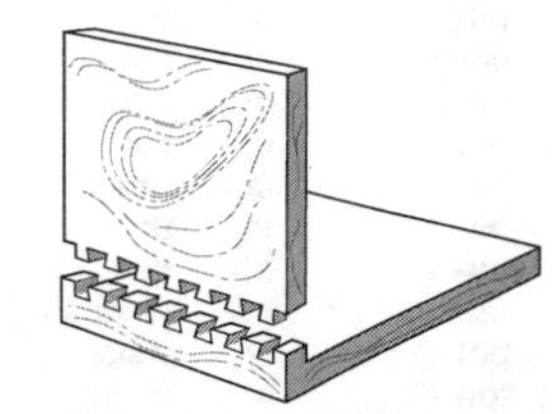

dovetail

dou•bly (**dŭb′**lē) *adv.* To a double degree; twice: *Make doubly sure the totals are right.*

doubt (dout) *v.* **doubt•ed, doubt•ing, doubts.** *—tr.* **1.** To be undecided or skeptical about: *At first many people doubted the rumor.* **2.** To be uncertain of; question or distrust: *I should have never doubted such a good friend.* **3.** To regard as unlikely: *I doubt that we'll arrive on time.* *—intr.* To be undecided or skeptical. *—n.* **1.** A lack of certainty. Often used in the plural. **2.** A lack of trust. **3.** The condition of being unsettled or unresolved: *The outcome of the horse race is still in doubt.* ***—idioms.*** **beyond doubt** or **without doubt.** Without question; certainly; definitely. **no doubt.** Certainly or probably. [First written down before 1200 in Middle English and spelled *duten*, from Latin *dubitāre*, to waver.]

doubt•ful (**dout′**fəl) *adj.* **1.** Subject to or causing doubt: *a doubtful claim.* **2.** Having or showing doubt; questioning: *We were doubtful about the proposed plan.* **3.** Questionable; suspicious: *a shady person with a doubtful past.* **—doubt′ful•ly** *adv.*

doubt•less (**dout′**lĭs) *adv.* **1.** Certainly; assuredly: *The bad weather was doubtless a factor in the delay.* **2.** Presumably; probably: *They will doubtless reject our proposal.* **—doubt′less•ly** *adv.*

douche (do͞osh) *n.* **1.** A stream of liquid or air applied to a part or cavity of the body in order to cleanse or apply medication. **2.** An instrument for applying a douche. *—tr. & intr.v.* **douched, douch•ing, douch•es.** To cleanse or treat by means of a douche.

dough (dō) *n.* **1.** A soft thick mixture of dry ingredients, such as flour or meal, and liquid, such as water, that is kneaded, shaped, and baked, especially as bread or pastry. **2.** *Slang.* Money. [First written down about 1000 in Old English and spelled *dāg*.]

❑ *These sound alike:* **dough, do²** (musical tone), **doe** (deer).

dough•nut also **do•nut** (**dō′**nŭt′ *or* **dō′**nət) *n.* A small ring-shaped cake made of rich dough that is fried in deep fat.

dough•ty (**dou′**tē) *adj.* **dough•ti•er, dough•ti•est.** Marked by stouthearted courage; very brave. **—dough′ti•ness** *n.*

dough•y (**dō′**ē) *adj.* **dough•i•er, dough•i•est.** Having the appearance or consistency of dough: *a doughy face.* **—dough′i•ness** *n.*

Doug•las (**dŭg′**ləs), **Stephen Arnold.** 1813–1861. American politician who in 1858 took part in a famous series of debates with Abraham Lincoln.

Douglas fir *n.* A tall evergreen tree of western North America having short needles, egg-shaped cones, and strong heavy wood valuable as lumber. [First written down in 1856 in Modern English and spelled *Douglass spruce*, after David *Douglas* (1798–1834), Scottish botanist.]

Doug•lass (**dŭg′**ləs), **Frederick.** 1817–1895. American abolitionist who escaped from slavery (1838) and edited the *North Star* (1847–1860), an abolitionist newspaper. —SEE NOTE.

dour (do͝or *or* dour) *adj.* **dour•er, dour•est. 1.** Marked by sternness or harshness; forbidding. **2.** Silently ill-humored; gloomy: *had a dour temperament that won him few friends.* **—dour′ly** *adv.* **—dour′ness** *n.*

douse (dous) *v.* **doused, dous•ing, dous•es.** *—tr.* **1.** To plunge into liquid; immerse: *douse the shirts in clean water.* **2.** To wet thoroughly; drench. **3.** To put out (a light or fire); extinguish. *—intr.* To become thoroughly wet.

dove¹ (dŭv) *n.* **1.** Any of various birds, including the pigeons, having a small head and a characteristic cooing call. **2.** A person who advocates peace, negotiation, or conciliation as methods of solving international problems. [First written down probably before 1200 in Old English and spelled *duve*.]

dove² (dōv) *v.* A past tense of **dive.**

dove•cote (**dŭv′**kōt′ *or* **dŭv′**kŏt′) also **dove•cot** (**dŭv′**kŏt′) *n.* A small structure, often raised on a pole, for housing domesticated pigeons.

Do•ver (**dō′**vər). **1.** A municipal borough of southeast England on the English Channel opposite Calais, France. Site of a Roman lighthouse, it is a strategic port. Population, 33,700. **2.** The capital of Delaware, in the central part of the state. It became capital in 1777. Population, 27,630.

dove•tail (**dŭv′**tāl′) *n.* **1.** One of a series of pieces cut into the end of a board so as to fit into corresponding indentations cut into another board. Both boards together form an interlocking joint. **2.** A joint formed by interlocking such pieces. *—v.* **dove•tailed, dove•tail•ing, dove•tails.** *—tr.* **1.** To join or fit together by means of dovetails. **2.** To connect, fit together, or combine harmoniously: *Let's try to dovetail our travel plans so we see each other.* *—intr.* **1.** To be joined or fitted together by means of dovetails. **2.** To be combined or fitted together harmoniously: *Our travel plans dovetail for one weekend.*

dow•a•ger (**dou′**ə jər) *n.* **1.** A widow who holds a title or property derived from her dead husband: *a dowager princess.* **2.** An elderly woman of high social station.

dow•dy (**dou′**dē) *adj.* **dow•di•er, dow•di•est.** Lacking stylishness or neatness; shabby: *dowdy old clothes.* **—dow′di•ly** *adv.* **—dow′di•ness** *n.*

dow•el (**dou′**əl) *n.* A round wooden pin that fits into a corresponding hole to fasten or align two adjacent pieces: *Dowels hold the leaves of the tabletop in place.* *—tr.v.* **dow•eled, dow•el•ing, dow•els** also **dow•elled, dow•el•ling, dow•els.** To fasten or align with dowels.

dow•er (**dou′**ər) *n.* The part of a deceased man's real estate allotted by law to his widow for her lifetime.

down¹ (doun) *adv.* **1.a.** From a higher to a lower place: *hiked down from the summit.* **b.** To, on, or toward the ground, floor, or bottom: *tripped and fell down.* **2.** In or to a sitting or reclining position: *sat down; lay down on the grass.* **3.** Toward or in the south: *going down to Florida.* **4.** Away from a central place: *down on the farm.* **5.** Toward or at a lower point on a scale: *body temperature coming down after a fever.* **6.** To or into an inferior condition: *The mayor went down in defeat.* **7.** From an earlier to a later time: *traditions handed down through the ages.* **8.** In partial payment at the time of purchase: *put fifty dollars down on the T.V. set.* **9.** In writing: *The reporter took the statement down.* **10.** To the source: *tracking a rumor down.* **11.** Seriously, intensely, or diligently: *Let's get down to work.* **12.** Into a secure position: *nail down the boards.* *—adj.* **1.a.** Moving or directed downward: *a down elevator.* **b.** Low or lower: *The room is dark because the blinds are down.* **2.** Sick; not feeling well: *He is down with a bad cold.* **3.** In low spirits; depressed. **4.** Not functioning or operating, especially temporarily: *They can't issue report cards because the school's computers are down.* *—prep.* **1.** In a descending direction upon, along, through, or into: *ran down the stairs.* **2.** Along the course of: *walking down the road.* *—n.* **1.** A downward movement; descent. **2.** In football, any of a series of four plays during which a team must advance at least ten yards to retain possession of the ball. *—v.* **downed, down•ing, downs.** *—tr.* **1.** To bring, strike, or throw down. **2.** To swallow hastily; gulp: *downed a lot of water before the race.* *—intr.* To go or come down; descend. *—**idioms.*** **down in the mouth** or **down at the mouth.** Discouraged; sad. **down on.** *Informal.* Hostile or negative toward: *she was down on jogging after her injury.* [First written down before 830 in Old English and spelled *dūne*, from *dūn*, hill.]

down[2] (doun) *n.* **1.** The soft feathers of a bird: *the down of a chick.* **2.** Fine soft hair, as on some plants and fruits. [First written down about 1345 in Middle English and spelled *doun*, from Old Norse *dūnn.*]

down[3] (doun) *n.* An expanse of rolling grassy treeless land used for grazing. Often used in the plural. [First written down in 661 in Old English and spelled *dūn*, hill.]

down•beat (**doun′**bēt′) *n.* The downward stroke made by a conductor to indicate the first beat of a musical measure.

down•cast (**doun′**kăst′) *adj.* **1.** Directed downward: *downcast eyes.* **2.** Low in spirits; depressed: *feeling downcast after repeated failure.*

down•er (**dou′**nər) *n. Slang.* A depressing experience or situation: *Not getting to see the movie was a real downer.*

down•fall (**doun′**fôl′) *n.* **1.** A sudden loss of wealth, reputation, happiness, or status; ruin: *An investigation resulted in the downfall of the corrupt banker.* **2.** A cause of sudden ruin: *Careless spending was the treasurer's downfall.* **3.** A fall of rain or snow, especially one that is heavy or unexpected.

down•grade (**doun′**grād′) *n.* A descending slope, as in a road; a downward course: *The truck sped up on the downgrade.* *—tr.v.* **down•grad•ed, down•grad•ing, down•grades. 1.** To lower the status or salary of: *downgrade an employee for constant carelessness.* **2.** To minimize the importance, value, or reputation of.

down•heart•ed (**doun′här′**tĭd) *adj.* Low in spirits; depressed. **—down′heart′ed•ly** *adv.* **—down′heart′ed•ness** *n.*

down•hill (**doun′hĭl′**) *adv.* **1.** Down the slope of a hill: *We raced downhill.* **2.** Toward a lower or worse position. *—adj.* (**doun′**hĭl′). Sloping downward; descending: *a downhill direction.*

Down•ing Street[1] (**dou′**nĭng). A thoroughfare of London, England. Nearly all prime ministers have lived at No. 10 Downing Street since the early 1700's.

Down•ing Street[2] (**dou′**nĭng) *n.* The British government.

down•load (**doun′**lōd′) *tr.v.* To transfer (data) from a central computer to another computer or to a terminal.

down payment *n.* A partial payment made at the time of purchase, with the balance to be paid later.

down•play (**doun′**plā′) *tr.v.* **down•played, down•play•ing, down•plays.** To minimize the importance of: *downplayed the severity of the earthquake.*

down•pour (**doun′**pôr′) *n.* A heavy fall of rain.

down•right (**doun′**rīt′) *adj.* **1.** Thoroughgoing; unequivocal: *a downright scoundrel.* **2.** Straightforward; candid. *—adv.* Thoroughly; absolutely: *They acted downright unpleasant.*

Down's syndrome (dounz) *n.* Variant of **Down syndrome.**

down•stairs (**doun′stârz′**) *adv.* **1.** Down the stairs: *I slipped going downstairs.* **2.** To or on a lower floor: *I ran downstairs to answer the phone.* *—adj.* (**doun′**stârz′). Located on a lower floor: *a downstairs bedroom.* *—n.* (**doun′stârz′**). *(used with a singular verb).* The lower or main floor of a building: *The whole downstairs was a mess after the party.*

down•stream (**doun′**strēm′) *adj.* In the direction of a stream's current: *a downstream boat race.* *—adv.* (**doun′strēm′**). Down a stream: *The raft floated downstream.*

Down syndrome (doun) or **Down's syndrome** (dounz) *n.* A disorder present from birth, characterized by mental retardation, short stature, and a flattened facial profile. It is caused by the presence of an extra chromosome. [First written down in 1961 in Modern English and spelled *Down's syndrome*, after J.L.H. *Down* (1828–1896), English physician.]

down•time (**doun′**tīm′) *n.* The period of time when something, such as a factory or a piece of machinery, is not in operation.

down-to-earth (**doun′**tə **ûrth′**) *adj.* Realistic; sensible.

down•town (**doun′**toun′) *n.* The lower part or the business center of a city or town. *—adv.* (**doun′toun′**). Toward or in the lower part or business center of a city or town: *Let's walk downtown.* *—adj.* (**doun′**toun′). Being in or going toward the business center of a city or town: *a downtown restaurant; a downtown bus.*

down•trod•den (**doun′**trŏd′n) *adj.* Harshly treated; oppressed.

down•turn (**doun′**tûrn′) *n.* A tendency downward, especially in business or economic activity: *In a recession there is a marked downturn in business.*

down•ward (**doun′**wərd) *adv. & adj.* **1.** From a higher to a lower place, level, or condition: *floating downward; a downward trend.* **2.** From a prior source or an earlier time: *traditions passed downward through the ages.*

down•wind (**doun′**wĭnd**′**) *adv.* In the direction toward which the wind blows.

down•y (**dou′**nē) *adj.* **down•i•er, down•i•est. 1.** Covered with or made of down: *a downy chick.* **2.** Resembling down: *downy white clouds.*

dow•ry (**dou′**rē) *n., pl.* **dow•ries.** Money or property brought by a bride to her husband at marriage.

dowse (douz) *intr.v.* **dowsed, dows•ing, dows•es.** To use a divining rod to search for underground water or minerals. **—dows′er** *n.*

dox•ol•o•gy (dŏk **sŏl′**ə jē) *n., pl.* **dox•ol•o•gies.** A hymn or verse in praise of God.

Doyle (doil), Sir **Arthur Conan.** 1859–1930. British writer known for his stories featuring the brilliant detective Sherlock Holmes.

Arthur Conan Doyle

doz. *abbr.* An abbreviation of dozen.

doze (dōz) *v.* **dozed, doz•ing, doz•es.** *—intr.* To sleep lightly; nap: *doze on the porch in the sun.* *—tr.* To spend (time) dozing or as if dozing: *doze the afternoon hours away.* *—n.* A short light sleep; a nap. *—**idiom.*** **doze off.** To fall into a light sleep: *I dozed off during the play's first act.*

doz•en (**dŭz′**ən) *n., pl* **dozen. 1.** A set of 12: *Two dozen eggs are 24 eggs.* **2.** *pl.* **dozens.** A large undetermined number: *Dozens of salmon swam below.* *—adj.* Twelve: *a dozen eggs.* [First written down before 1300 in Middle English and spelled *dosein*, from Latin *duodecim*, twelve : *duo*, two + *decem*, ten.]

doz•enth (**dŭz′**ənth) *adj.* Twelfth.

DP *abbr.* An abbreviation of displaced person.

dpt. *abbr.* An abbreviation of department.

Dr. *abbr.* An abbreviation of: **1.** Doctor. **2.** Drive (street).

drab (drăb) *adj.* **drab•ber, drab•best. 1.a.** Of a light dull brown. **b.** Of a light olive brown or khaki color: *a drab uniform.* **2.** Faded and dull in appearance. **3.** Dull or commonplace in character; dreary: *a drab cheerless house.* *—n.* **1.** A light dull brown or grayish brown. **2.** A light olive brown; khaki color. **3.** Cloth of a light dull brown or grayish brown, especially a heavy woolen or cotton fabric. **—drab′ly** *adv.* **—drab′ness** *n.*

ă	**pat**	oi	**boy**
ā	**pay**	ou	**out**
âr	**care**	ŏŏ	**took**
ä	**father**	ōō	**boot**
ĕ	**pet**	ŭ	**cut**
ē	**be**	ûr	**urge**
ĭ	**pit**	th	**thin**
ī	**pie**	*th*	**this**
îr	**pier**	hw	**whoop**
ŏ	**pot**	zh	**vision**
ō	**toe**	ə	**about**
ô	**paw**	N	*French* **bon**

dragonfly

Regional Note: dragonfly

People have different names for the same thing depending on where they live. What most people in the United States call a **dragonfly** is known by other names in various parts of the country. In the southern states the most common term is *snake doctor* because of the folk belief that dragonflies care for snakes. In the middle part of the United States we find the name *snake feeder.* In some parts of the South some people call it a *mosquito hawk* or a *skeeter hawk.* People in some parts of the northern states call it a *darning needle* or a *devil's darning needle.* Those in coastal New Jersey call it a *spindle*, and in Northern California they say *ear sewer* (from the belief that it could sew up ears).

Sir Francis Drake

drach•ma (**drăk′**mə) *n., pl.* **drach•mas** or **drach•mae** (**drăk′**mē). **1.** The basic monetary unit of Greece. **2.** A silver coin of ancient Greece. **3.** One of several modern units of weight, especially the dram.

draft (drăft) *n.* **1.** A current of air in an enclosed area: *feel a cold draft on one's feet.* **2.** A device that controls the flow or circulation of air. **3.** The act of pulling loads; traction: *a pair of large horses used for draft.* **4.** The depth of a vessel's keel below the water line. **5.** A document for directing the payment of money from an account or fund. **6.a.** A gulp, a swallow, or an inhalation. **b.** The amount taken in by a single act of drinking or inhaling. **7.a.** The drawing of a liquid, as from a cask or keg. **b.** An amount of liquid so drawn. **8.a.** The process of selecting one or more individuals from a group, as for a service or duty. **b.** Compulsory enrollment in the armed forces; conscription. **c.** A body of people selected or conscripted. **9.a.** The act of drawing in a fishnet. **b.** The amount of fish caught. **10.a.** A preliminary outline of a plan, document, or picture. **b.** A representation of something to be constructed: *The architect showed us a draft of the building.* —*tr.v.* **draft•ed, draft•ing, drafts. 1.** To select from a group for some usually compulsory service: *draft citizens for military service* **2.** To draw up a preliminary plan, sketch, or version of: *drafted several versions of a speech.* —*adj.* Suited for or used for drawing heavy loads: *a team of draft horses.* [First written down about 1200 in Middle English and spelled *draht*, act of drawing or pulling.]

draft•ee (drăf **tē′**) *n.* A person who is drafted, especially into the armed forces.

drafts•man (**drăfts′**mən) *n.* A man who draws plans or designs, as of structures to be built. **—drafts′-man•ship′** *n.*

drafts•per•son (**drăfts′**pûr′sən) *n.* A person who drafts plans or designs.

drafts•wom•an (**drăfts′**wo͝om′ən) *n.* A woman who draws plans or designs, as of structures to be built.

draft•y (**drăf′**tē) *adj.* **draft•i•er, draft•i•est.** Having or exposed to drafts of air: *a drafty old house.* **—draft′i•ly** *adv.* **—draft′i•ness** *n.*

drag (drăg) *v.* **dragged, drag•ging, drags.** —*tr.* **1.** To draw along with difficulty or effort; haul: *dragged the heavy box out of the way.* **2.** To cause to trail along the ground: *Don't drag your coat in the mud.* **3.** To search the bottom of (a body of water), as with a hook or net: *They dragged the river looking for the suitcase that was thrown from the bridge.* **4.** To prolong tediously: *They dragged the discussion out.* —*intr.* **1.** To trail along the ground: *The chain dragged along behind the tractor.* **2.** To move slowly or with difficulty: *The exhausted hikers dragged back to camp.* **3.** To pass or proceed slowly or tediously: *The long speech dragged on and on.* —*n.* **1.** Something that is pulled along the ground, especially something for carrying loads: *The horse was harnessed to the drag.* **2.** A device for dragging under water, such as a grappling hook. **3.** A person or thing that slows or stops motion or progress: *High interest rates can act as a drag on the economy.* **4.** The force produced by friction that hinders motion through a fluid, such as air or water. **5.** *Slang.* A person or thing that is obnoxiously tiresome. **—*idiom.* drag (one's) feet.** To act or work with intentional slowness: *drag one's feet about completing a chore.* [First written down in 1440 in Middle English and spelled *draggen*, from Old Norse *draga.*]

drag•gle (**drăg′**əl) *tr. & intr.v.* **drag•gled, drag•gling, drag•gles.** To make or become wet and muddy by dragging along the ground.

drag•net (**drăg′**nĕt′) *n.* **1.** A coordinated system of search used by the police to find criminal suspects. **2.** A net for trawling; a trawl.

drag•on (**drăg′**ən) *n.* A mythical giant reptile often represented as a winged fire-breathing monster. [First written down before 1250 in Middle English and spelled *dragun*, from Greek *drakōn*, large serpent.]

drag•on•fly (**drăg′**ən flī′) *n.* Any of various large insects having a long body and four narrow clear wings with fine networks of veins. They feed on various insects including mosquitoes. —SEE NOTE.

dra•goon (drə **go͞on′**) *n.* A heavily armed mounted soldier in some European armies of the 17th and 18th centuries. —*tr.v.* **dra•gooned, dra•goon•ing, dra•goons.** To compel or force by violent measures: *dragooned the townspeople into supplying the troops with food.* [First written down in 1622 in Modern English, from French *dragon*, carbine, from Old French *dragon*, dragon.]

drag race *n.* A short race between cars to determine which can accelerate faster from a standstill.

drain (drān) *v.* **drained, drain•ing, drains.** —*tr.* **1.** To draw off (a liquid) gradually: *drain water from a sink.* **2.** To make dry or empty by drawing off liquid: *drain the pond.* **3.** To drink all the contents of: *The child drained the cup.* **4.** To deplete gradually, especially to the point of complete exhaustion: *The performance drained the cast and crew.* —*intr.* **1.** To flow off or out: *Melted snow drained off the roof.* **2.** To become empty by the draining off of liquid: *The tub drained slowly.* **3.** To discharge surface or excess water: *Most large rivers drain into the sea.* —*n.* **1.** A pipe or channel by which liquid is drained off: *clog up the drain.* **2.** Something that causes a gradual loss: *Building a new library is a drain on the resources for buying more books.* **—*idiom.* down the drain.** To or into the condition of being wasted or lost: *When our first plan went down the drain, we quickly came up with another.* [First written down about 1000 in Old English and spelled *drēahnian.*]

drain•age (**drā′**nĭj) *n.* **1.** The action or a method of draining: *Drainage in swampland is very poor.* **2.** A natural or artificial system of drains. **3.** Material that is drained off: *Storm sewers carried the drainage away.*

drain•pipe (**drān′**pīp′) *n.* A pipe for carrying off water or sewage.

drake (drāk) *n.* A male duck.

Drake (drāk), Sir **Francis.** 1540?–1596. English explorer who was the first Englishman to sail around the world.

dram (drăm) *n.* **1.a.** A unit of weight in the U.S. Customary System equal to 1/16 of an ounce or 27.34 grains (about 1.77 grams). See table at **measurement. b.** A unit of apothecary weight equal to 1/8 of an ounce or 60 grains (3.89 grams). **2.** A small drink. [First written down about 1373 in Middle English and spelled *dram*, a drachma, a unit of weight, from Greek *drakhmē*, drachma.]

dra•ma (**drä′**mə *or* **drăm′**ə) *n.* **1.** A literary work that tells a story in prose or verse and is meant to be performed by actors. **2.a.** Theatrical plays of a particular kind or period: *modern drama.* **b.** The art and practice of writing and producing works for the stage. **3.** A situation or a series of events in real life that resemble a play: *the day by day drama within Congress.* **4.** The quality or condition of being dramatic: *The cellist's solo was filled with emotion and drama.*

dra•mat•ic (drə **măt′**ĭk) *adj.* **1.** Of or relating to drama or the theater: *dramatic performances.* **2.** Resembling a drama in action or emotion: *the dramatic events that led to Lincoln's election.* **3.** Arresting or forceful in appearance or effect: *a* *dramatic mountain range.* [First written down in 1589 in Modern English and spelled *drammatick*, from Greek *dramatikos*, from *drama*.] **—dra•mat′i•cal•ly** *adv.*

dra•mat•ics (drə măt′ĭks) *n.* **1.** *(used with a singular or plural verb).* The art or practice of acting in or staging plays: *Dramatics is the actor's great interest.* **2.** *(used with a plural verb).* Dramatic or exaggerated behavior: *Dramatics are a tiresome way to get attention.*

dram•a•tis per•so•nae (drăm′ə tĭs pər sō′nē *or* drä′mə tĭs pər sō′nī′) *pl.n.* The characters in a play or story.

dram•a•tist (drăm′ə tĭst *or* drä′mə tĭst) *n.* A person who writes plays; a playwright.

dram•a•tize (drăm′ə tīz′ *or* drä′mə tīz′) *v.* **dram•a•tized, dram•a•tiz•ing, dram•a•tiz•es.** *—tr.* **1.** To adapt (a literary work) into a play or screenplay. **2.** To present or view in a dramatic or melodramatic way: *The report dramatizes the plight of the flood victims.* *—intr.* To be adaptable to dramatic form: *a biography that dramatizes well.* **—dram′a•ti•za′tion** (drăm′ə tĭ zā′shən *or* drä′mə tĭ zā′shən) *n.*

drank (drăngk) *v.* Past tense of **drink.**

drape (drāp) *v.* **draped, drap•ing, drapes.** *—tr.* **1.** To cover or hang with or as if with cloth in loose folds: *The artist draped the painting with a cloth.* **2.** To arrange or let fall in loose folds: *draped a long cape over one shoulder.* **3.** To hang or rest limply: *I draped my legs over the back of the chair.* *—intr.* To fall or hang in loose folds: *Silk drapes easily.* *—n.* **1.** A drapery; a curtain: *pull the drapes over the window.* **2.** The way in which cloth falls or hangs: *the drape of fine suit material.* [First written down before 1400 in Middle English and spelled *draperen*, from Old French *draper*, to weave, from *drap*, cloth, from Late Latin *drappus*.]

drap•er (drā′pər) *n.* *Chiefly British.* A dealer in cloth or dry goods.

drap•er•y (drā′pə rē) *n., pl.* **drap•er•ies. 1.** Cloth or clothing arranged in loose folds. **2.** A piece or pieces of heavy fabric hanging straight in loose folds, used as a curtain.

dras•tic (drăs′tĭk) *adj.* Severe or radical in nature; extreme: *Calling out troops was a drastic measure to restore order.* [First written down before 1691 in Modern English, from Greek *drastikos*, active, from *drastos*, to be done, from *dran*, to do.] **—dras′ti•cal•ly** *adv.*

drat (drăt) *interj.* An expression used to show annoyance.

draught (drăft) *n., v., & adj.* *Chiefly British.* Variant of **draft.**

draughts (drăfts *or* dräfts) *n.* *(used with a singular or plural verb).* *Chiefly British.* The game of checkers.

Dra•vid•i•an (drə vĭd′ē ən) *n.* **1.** A large family of languages spoken in southern India and northern Sri Lanka. **2.** A member of a people that speaks one of these languages. **—Dra•vid′i•an, Dra•vid′ic** (drə vĭd′ĭk) *adj.*

draw (drô) *v.* **drew** (dro͞o), **drawn** (drôn), **drawing, draws.** *—tr.* **1.a.** To pull or move (something) after or toward one by applying force; drag: *a team of horses drawing a load.* **b.** To cause to move, as by leading: *She drew us into the room to show us her presents.* **c.** To cause to move in a given direction or to a given position: *drew the curtain.* **2.** To cause to flow forth: *a deep scratch that drew blood; draw water for a bath.* **3.** To suck or take in (air, for example): *The singer drew a deep breath.* **4.** To require (a specified depth of water) for floating: *A boat drawing 18 inches.* **5.a.** To pull or take out: *draw a sword from a sheath.* **b.** To extract or take from for one's own use: *drew strength from her example.* **6.** To attract; entice: *Our beaches draw many tourists.* **7.** To get as a response; elicit: *The comic drew laughter from the audience.* **8.** To earn; gain: *draw interest on a savings account.* **9.** To withdraw (money) from an account. **10.** To take or receive by chance: *I drew the lucky number.* **11.** To stretch tight: *draw a string around the package.* **12.a.** To inscribe (a line or lines) with a pencil or other marking implement. **b.** To make a picture of, using mostly lines; sketch: *drawing illustrations for a new book.* **c.** To represent in words: *The poet drew scenes of far-off places with words.* **13.** To deduce from evidence at hand; formulate: *We can draw a conclusion from the facts already gathered.* *—intr.* **1.** To proceed or move steadily: *The boat drew near shore.* **2.** To take in a draft of air: *The fireplace chimney doesn't draw well.* **3.** To contract or tighten: *The smile drew into a frown.* **4.** To tie in a contest: *The chess players drew after 32 moves.* **5.** To make a likeness with lines on a surface: *Several students draw especially well.* *—n.* **1.** An act of drawing. **2.** Something that attracts interest, customers, or spectators: *a good draw at the box office.* **3.** A contest ending in a tie. **4.** A ravine or gully that water drains into. ***—idioms.*** **draw out.** To prolong; protract: *drew out the meeting until we were quite bored.* **draw the line.** To set a limit, as on behavior. **draw up. 1.** To write up in a set form; compose: *draw up a list; draw up an agreement.* **2.** To bring (oneself) into an erect posture. **3.** To bring (troops, for example) into order. **4.** To bring or come to a halt: *The truck drew up at the gate.* [First written down before 900 in Old English and spelled *dragan*.]

draw•back (drô′băk′) *n.* A disadvantage or inconvenience: *The pay was good but the long hours were a drawback.*

draw•bridge (drô′brĭj′) *n.* A bridge that can be raised or drawn aside either to prevent access or to permit passage beneath it.

drawbridge

draw•er (drô′ər) *n.* **1.** A person who draws. **2.** A compartment that can be pulled in and out of a piece of furniture by a handle. **3. drawers** (drôrz). Underpants.

draw•ing (drô′ĭng) *n.* **1.** The act or an instance of drawing. **2.** The art of representing forms and figures on a surface by means of lines. **3.** A work produced by this art: *There are several fine drawings of horses on the wall.*

drawing room *n.* A large room in which guests are entertained.

draw•knife (drô′nīf′) *n.* A woodworking tool having an adjustable blade and two handles, used for shaving wood surfaces.

drawl (drôl) *intr. & tr.v.* **drawled, drawl•ing, drawls.** To speak or utter with lengthened or drawn-out vowels. *—n.* The speech or manner of speaking of one who drawls: *spoke with a pronounced drawl.*

drawn (drôn) *v.* Past participle of **draw.** *—adj.* Haggard, as from fatigue or ill health: *The survivors looked drawn after their rescue.*

drawn butter *n.* Melted butter that has been clarified to separate out the milk solids.

draw•string (drô′strĭng′) *n.* A cord or ribbon run through a hem or casing and pulled to tighten or close an opening.

dray (drā) *n.* A low heavy cart without sides, used for hauling. *—tr.v.* **drayed, dray•ing, drays.** To haul by means of a dray.

dread (drĕd) *v.* **dread•ed, dread•ing, dreads.** *—tr.* **1.** To be in terror of: *Many people dread snakes.* **2.** To anticipate with alarm, distaste, or reluctance: *We were dreading the long drive home.* *—intr.* To be very afraid. *—n.* **1.** Profound fear; terror. **2.**

ă	pat	oi	boy
ā	pay	ou	out
âr	care	o͝o	took
ä	father	o͞o	boot
ĕ	pet	ŭ	cut
ē	be	ûr	urge
ĭ	pit	th	thin
ī	pie	*th*	this
îr	pier	hw	whoop
ŏ	pot	zh	vision
ō	toe	ə	about
ô	paw	N	*French* bon

Fearful or distasteful anticipation: *They lived in dread of an earthquake.* —*adj.* Inspiring fear, terror, or awe: *a dread disease.* [First written down probably before 1200 in Middle English and spelled *dreden*, from Old English *adrædan*, to fear.]

dread•ful (drĕd′fəl) *adj.* **1.** Inspiring dread; terrible: *a dreadful epidemic.* **2.** Extremely unpleasant; distasteful or shocking: *dreadful furniture; dreadful behavior.* —**dread′ful•ly** *adv.* —**dread′ful•ness** *n.*

dread•locks (drĕd′lŏks′) *pl.n.* Thin dense long braids or natural locks of hair worn in a style popularized by Rastafarians.

dread•nought (drĕd′nôt′) *n.* A heavily armed battleship.

dream (drēm) *n.* **1.** A series of mental images, ideas, and emotions occurring during sleep. **2.** A daydream. **3.** A state of abstraction; a trance: *wandering about in a dream.* **4.** A hope or an aspiration: *dreams of world peace.* **5.** Something especially gratifying, excellent, or useful: *The new car runs like a dream.* —*v.* **dreamed** or **dreamt** (drĕmt), **dream•ing, dreams.** —*intr.* **1.** To have a dream while sleeping. **2.** To daydream: *dreaming of far-off places.* **3.** To consider as feasible or practical: *I wouldn't even dream of going.* —*tr.* **1.** To have a dream of during sleep: *Did it storm last night, or did I dream it?* **2.** To conceive of; imagine: *We never dreamed it might snow so hard.* **3.** To pass (time) idly or in daydreaming. —***idiom.*** **dream up.** To invent; concoct: *dreamed up a plan to get rich quick.* [First written down about 670 in Old English and spelled *drēam*, joy, music.] —**dream′er** *n.*

dream•land (drēm′lănd′) *n.* An ideal or imaginary place.

dreamt (drĕmt) *v.* A past tense and a past participle of **dream.**

dream•y (drē′mē) *adj.* **dream•i•er, dream•i•est. 1.** Like a dream; vague; hazy: *a dreamy memory of early childhood.* **2.** Given to daydreams: *a dreamy person who seldom pays attention.* **3.** Soothing and serene: *soft dreamy music.* **4.** *Informal.* Inspiring delight; wonderful. —**dream′i•ly** *adv.* —**dream′i•ness** *n.*

drear (drîr) *adj.* Dreary.

drea•ry (drîr′ē) *adj.* **drea•ri•er, drea•ri•est. 1.** Dismal; bleak: *a dreary January rain.* **2.** Boring; dull: *the dreary tasks of housekeeping.* [First written down about 725 in Old English and spelled *drēorig*, bloody, sad, from *drēor*, gore.] —**drear′i•ly** *adv.* —**drear′i•ness** *n.*

dredge[1] (drĕj) *n.* **1.** A machine equipped with an underwater scooping or suction device, used especially to deepen a harbor or waterway. **2.** A ship or barge equipped with such a machine. —*v.* **dredged, dredg•ing, dredg•es.** —*tr.* **1.** To clean, deepen, or widen with a dredge. **2.** To bring up with a dredge: *dredge dirt and rock out of the river to make a channel.* **3.** To come up with; unearth. —*intr.* To use a dredge. [First written down in 1471 in Middle English and spelled *dreg*; akin to Old English *dragan*, to draw.]

dredge[2] (drĕj) *tr.v.* **dredged, dredg•ing, dredg•es.** To coat (food) by sprinklng with a powder, such as flour or bread crumbs. [First written down in 1596 in Modern English, from Middle English *dragge*, a sweetmeat, from Greek *tragēma*.]

dregs (drĕgz) *pl.n.* **1.** The sediment in a liquid: *rinse the dregs out of the coffeepot.* **2.** The basest or least desirable portion.

Drei•ser (drī′sər *or* drī′zər), **Theodore Herman Albert.** 1871–1945. American writer whose novels, such as *Sister Carrie* (1900), show life as a struggle against ungovernable forces.

drench (drĕnch) *tr.v.* **drenched, drench•ing, drench•es.** To wet through and through; soak: *A thunderstorm drenched everyone outside.* [First written down about 1000 in Old English and spelled *drencan*, to give to drink, drown.]

drenched (drĕncht) *adj.* Thoroughly wet; soaked: *The dog was drenched from the rain.*

Dres•den (drĕz′dən). A city of east-central Germany on the Elbe River east-southeast of Leipzig. Population, 522,532.

Dresden china *n.* A fine, heavily decorated china.

dress (drĕs) *v.* **dressed, dress•ing, dress•es.** —*tr.* **1.** To put clothes on: *Dress the baby warmly.* **2.a.** To decorate or adorn: *dress a Christmas tree.* **b.** To arrange a display in: *dress a store window.* **3.** To apply medicine or bandages to (a wound): *After the operation the nurse dressed the incision.* **4.** To arrange or style (the hair). **5.** To groom (an animal); curry. **6.** To clean (fish or fowl) for cooking or sale: *dress a turkey.* **7.** To arrange (troops) in ranks; align: *dress soldiers for a parade.* —*intr.* **1.** To put on clothes: *I got up late and dressed in a hurry.* **2.** To wear clothes of a certain kind or style: *She dresses casually.* **3.** To wear formal clothes: *We don't need to dress for dinner.* —*n.* **1.** Clothing; apparel: *wore formal dress to the reception.* **2.** A style of clothing: *Bankers often wear conservative dress.* **3.** A one-piece outer garment worn by women and girls. —*adj.* **1.** Suitable for formal occasions: *wear a tie with a dress shirt.* **2.** Calling for formal clothes: *a dress reception.* —***idioms.*** **dress down.** To scold; reprimand. **dress up.** To wear formal or fancy clothes: *They dressed up for the party.* [First written down probably before 1300 in Middle English and spelled *dressen*, to arrange, put on clothing, from Old French *drecier*, to arrange, from Latin *dīrigere*, to direct.]

dres•sage (drə säzh′) *n.* The guiding of a horse through a series of complex maneuvers by a rider using very slight movements of the hands, legs, and weight.

dress•er[1] (drĕs′ər) *n.* **1.** A person who dresses: *She is a careful dresser.* **2.** A wardrobe assistant, as for an actor.

dress•er[2] (drĕs′ər) *n.* **1.** A chest of drawers, often having a mirror above it and typically used for holding clothing and personal items. **2.** A cupboard or set of shelves for dishes or kitchen utensils. [First written down in 1393 in Middle English and spelled *dresser*, from Old French *dresser*, to get ready.]

dress•ing (drĕs′ĭng) *n.* **1.** Medicine or bandages applied to a wound. **2.** A sauce for certain dishes, such as salads. **3.** A stuffing, as for poultry or fish.

dressing gown *n.* A robe worn for lounging or before dressing.

dressing room *n.* A room, as in a theater, for changing costumes or clothes and applying makeup.

dressing table *n.* A low table with a mirror at which one sits while applying makeup.

dress•mak•er (drĕs′mā′kər) *n.* A person who makes women's clothing, especially dresses.

dress•mak•ing (drĕs′mā′kĭng) *n.* The act or occupation of making women's clothing, especially dresses.

dress rehearsal *n.* A full uninterrupted rehearsal of a play with costumes and stage properties.

dress•y (drĕs′ē) *adj.* **dress•i•er, dress•i•est. 1.** Showy or elegant in dress or appearance. **2.** Smart; stylish. —**dress′i•ly** *adv.* —**dress′i•ness** *n.*

drew (dro͞o) *v.* Past tense of **draw.**

drib•ble (drĭb′əl) *v.* **drib•bled, drib•bling, drib•bles.** —*intr.* **1.** To flow or fall in drops or an unsteady stream; trickle: *Water dribbled out of the leaky faucet.* **2.** To let saliva drip from the mouth; drool: *Most babies dribble when they are teething.* **3.** To move a ball or puck with repeated light bounces or kicks: *The player dribbled around an opponent.* —*tr.* **1.** To let flow or fall in drops or an unsteady stream: *I dribbled gravy on the potatoes.* **2.** To move (a ball or puck) by repeated light bounces or kicks, as in basketball or soccer: *The forward dribbled the ball right past the defender.* —*n.* **1.** A small quantity; a drop: *a dribble of milk.* **2.** The act of dribbling a ball: *a fast dribble across the court.* **—drib′bler** *n.*

drib•let (drĭb′lĭt) *n.* A small amount or portion: *pay off a loan in driblets.*

dried (drīd) *v.* Past tense and past participle of **dry.**

dri•er[1] also **dry•er** (drī′ər) *n.* **1.** A person or thing that dries: *We did the dishes, and I was the drier.* **2.** A substance added, as to paint or varnish, to speed drying.

dri•er[2] (drī′ər) *adj.* A comparative of **dry.**

dries (drīz) *v.* Third person singular present tense of **dry.**

dri•est (drī′ĭst) *adj.* A superlative of **dry.**

drift (drĭft) *v.* **drift•ed, drift•ing, drifts.** —*intr.* **1.** To be carried along by a current of water or air: *The boat drifted slowly toward shore.* **2.a.** To proceed or move unhurriedly and smoothly: *drifted among the guests at the party.* **b.** To move leisurely or sporadically from place to place, especially without purpose or regular employment: *drift through the summer.* **3.** To wander from a course or point of attention; stray: *My attention drifted from my assignment.* **4.** To be piled up in banks or heaps by the force of a current: *snow drifting against a stone wall.* —*tr.* **1.** To cause to be carried in a current: *Waves drifted debris all along the shore.* **2.** To pile up in heaps or banks: *The winds drifted the snow.* —*n.* **1.** The act or condition of drifting: *a continuous drift of sand.* **2.** Something moving along in a current of air or water. **3.** The mass of material, such as sand or snow, deposited by a current of air or water: *snow drifts six feet high.* **4.** Fragments of rock that are carried and deposited by a glacier: *These drifts appeared at the end of the last ice age.* **5.** A general meaning or direction of thought: *The drift of their conversation was hard to follow.* **6.** A gradual deviation from an original course, model, method, or intention. [First written down in 1584 in Modern English, from Middle English *drift,* drove, herd, act of driving.]

drift•er (drĭf′tər) *n.* A person who moves aimlessly from place to place or from job to job.

drift•wood (drĭft′wo͝od′) *n.* Wood floating in or washed up by the water.

drill[1] (drĭl) *n.* **1.** A tool used to bore holes in materials, usually by a rotating action or by repeated blows. **2.** Disciplined repetitious exercise as a means of teaching and perfecting a skill or procedure. **3.** A task or an exercise for teaching a skill or procedure by repetition: *a fire drill.* —*v.* **drilled, drill•ing, drills.** —*tr.* **1.** To make a hole with a drill in (a hard material): *drilling wood.* **2.** To make (a hole) with or as if with a drill. **3.** To teach or train by continuous repetition: *drill a company of soldiers.* —*intr.* **1.** To make a hole with or as if with a drill: *drill into a board.* **2.** To perform a training exercise: *The astronauts drill before attempting repairs in space.* [First written down in 1611 in Modern English, from Middle Dutch *drillen,* to bore a hole.]

drill[2] (drĭl) *n.* **1.** A shallow trench or furrow in which seeds are planted. **2.** A machine or an implement for planting seeds in furrows. [First written down in 1727 in Modern English, perhaps from *drill,* rill.]

drill[3] (drĭl) *n.* A strong cotton or linen twilled cloth, generally used for work clothes. [First written down in 1743 in Modern English, from Middle High German *drilich,* threefold, from Latin *trilīx,* triple-threaded.]

drink (drĭngk) *v.* **drank** (drăngk), **drunk** (drŭngk), **drink•ing, drinks.** —*tr.* **1.** To take into the mouth and swallow (a liquid): *drink water every day.* **2.** To swallow the liquid contents of (a vessel): *I drank a mug of hot cocoa.* **3.** To take in or soak up; absorb: *The parched earth drank up the rain.* **4.** To take in eagerly through the senses or intellect: *The tourists drank in the grandeur of the mountains.* **5.** To give or make (a toast): *We drank a toast to happiness.* —*intr.* **1.** To swallow liquid: *The thirsty hikers drank from a clear stream.* **2.** To salute a person or an occasion with a toast: *We'll drink to your health.* **3.** To drink alcoholic beverages. —*n.* **1.** A liquid for drinking; a beverage: *Orange juice is a satisfying drink.* **2.** An amount of liquid swallowed: *took a drink of water.* **3.** An alcoholic beverage. [First written down about 725 in Old English and spelled *drincan.*] **—drink′a•ble** *adj.* **—drink′er** *n.*

drip (drĭp) *intr. & tr.v.* **dripped, drip•ping, drips.** To fall or let fall in drops: *Water dripped from the faucet. I dripped paint on the floor.* —*n.* **1.** The process of forming and falling in drops: *the drip of water from leaky gutters.* **2.** Liquid or moisture that falls in drops: *Drips of paint spattered the floor.* **3.** The sound made by liquid falling in drops: *The constant drip of the faucet was annoying.* [First written down about 1300 in Middle English and spelled *drippen.*]

drip-dry (drĭp′drī′) *adj.* Made of a fabric that will not wrinkle when hung dripping wet for drying: *a drip-dry suit.* —*intr.v.* **drip-dried, drip-dry•ing, drip-dries.** To dry with no wrinkles when hung dripping wet: *let a shirt drip-dry.*

drip•pings (drĭp′ĭngz) *pl.n.* The fat and juices from roasting meat, often used in making gravy.

drive (drīv) *v.* **drove** (drōv), **driv•en** (drĭv′ən), **driv•ing, drives.** —*tr.* **1.a.** To push, propel, or press onward forcibly: *drove the horses into the corral.* **b.** To repulse forcefully; put to flight: *The dog drove off the raccoon.* **2.a.** To guide, control, or direct (a vehicle): *They drive their car to work every day.* **b.** To convey or transport in a vehicle: *The neighbors drove me to the store.* **3.a.** To supply the motive force or power to and cause to function: *Electricity drives many motors.* **b.** To compel or force to work, often excessively: *The need for recognition drives him.* **c.** To force into or from a particular state or act: *Constant interruptions drove me to despair.* **4.** To force to penetrate: *drive a nail into wood.* **5.** To carry through vigorously to a conclusion: *drive home one's point in an argument.* **6.** To hit (a ball) hard: *The golfer drove the ball right down the fairway.* —*intr.* **1.** To move along or advance quickly as if pushed by a force: *The car drove into the ditch.* **2.** To guide or control a vehicle or an animal: *Many people drive too fast on this road.* **3.** To go or be carried in a vehicle: *We drove to the supermarket.* **4.** To make an effort to reach or achieve an objective; aim: *The author drove hard to complete the book on time.* **5.** In basketball, to move directly toward the basket with the ball. —*n.* **1.** A trip or journey in a vehicle: *go for a quiet drive in the country.* **2.a.** A road for automobiles and other vehicles: *Cars may use the drive in the park.* **b.** A driveway. **3.a.** The means for transmitting motion to a machine: *Lathes often have a belt drive between the motor and the part that holds the piece being shaped.* **b.** The means by which automotive power is applied to a roadway: *Vehicles used by forest rangers often have four-wheel drive.* **4.a.** An organized effort to accomplish something: *a charity drive.* **b.** A massive and sustained military offensive. **5.a.** Energy, push, or aggressiveness: *People who*

drill[1]
Drill press

ă	pat	oi	boy
ā	pay	ou	out
âr	care	o͝o	took
ä	father	o͞o	boot
ĕ	pet	ŭ	cut
ē	be	ûr	urge
ĭ	pit	th	thin
ī	pie	*th*	this
îr	pier	hw	whoop
ŏ	pot	zh	vision
ō	toe	ə	about
ô	paw	N	*French* bon

dromedary

drop leaf
Mid to late 18th-century American drop leaf table

have drive and ambition often achieve their goals. **b.** A strong motivating instinct: *the basic drive to satisfy one's hunger and thirst.* **6.** The act of hitting a ball very swiftly. **7.a.** The act of rounding up and driving cattle, as to new pastures. **b.** A gathering and driving of logs down a river. —***idioms.*** **drive at.** To mean to do or say: *I'm not sure what you are driving at.* **drive in.** In baseball, to cause (a run) to be scored when batting. [First written down about 725 in Old English and spelled *drīfan.*]

drive-in (**drīv′ĭn′**) *n.* An establishment, such as an outdoor movie theater or a restaurant, designed to allow customers to remain in their vehicles while being accommodated.

driv•el (**drĭv′**əl) *v.* **driv•eled, driv•el•ing, driv•els** or **driv•elled, driv•el•ling, driv•els.** —*intr.* **1.** To slobber; drool. **2.** To talk stupidly or childishly: *drivel on about nothing.* —*tr.* To say (something) stupidly: *driveled their usual empty promises.* —*n.* **1.** Saliva flowing from the mouth. **2.** Stupid or senseless talk. [First written down about 1000 in Old English and spelled *dreflian.*] —**driv′el•er, driv′el•ler** *n.*

driv•en (**drĭv′**ən) *v.* Past participle of **drive.**

driv•er (**drī′**vər) *n.* **1.** A person who drives a motor vehicle. **2.** A tool, such as a screwdriver or hammer, that is used to give forceful pressure to another object. **3.** A golf club with a wide head, used for making long shots from the tee. **4.** A machine part that transmits motion or power to something else.

drive shaft *n.* A rotating shaft that transmits mechanical power from a motor or engine to the place where power is applied.

drive•way (**drīv′**wā′) *n.* A private road connecting a house, a garage, or another building with the street.

driz•zle (**drĭz′**əl) *intr.v.* **driz•zled, driz•zling, driz•zles.** To rain gently in a fine mist. —*n.* A fine gentle misty rain. —**driz′zly** *adj.*

droll (drōl) *adj.* **droll•er, droll•est.** Amusingly odd; comical. —**droll′ness** *n.*

drom•e•dar•y (**drŏm′**ĭ dĕr′ē *or* **drŭm′**ĭ dĕr′ē) *n., pl.* **drom•e•dar•ies.** The one-humped camel, widely used for riding and carrying loads in northern Africa and southwest Asia. [First written down about 1280 in Middle English and spelled *dromedarie,* from Late Latin *dromedārius,* from Latin *dromas,* from Greek *dromas,* running.]

drone[1] (drōn) *n.* **1.** A male bee, especially a honeybee that fertilizes the queen. Drones have no stings, do no work, and do not produce honey. **2.** An idle person who lives off others; a loafer. **3.** An aircraft that has no crew on board and is operated by remote control. [First written down about 1000 in Old English and spelled *drān.*]

drone[2] (drōn) *v.* **droned, dron•ing, drones.** —*intr.* **1.** To make a continuous low dull humming sound: *An airplane droned far overhead.* **2.** To speak in a monotonous tone. —*tr.* To utter in a dull monotone. —*n.* A continuous low humming or buzzing sound: *the drone of the bumblebee.* [First written down about 1500 in Modern English, probably from *drone,* male bee.]

drool (dro͞ol) *intr.v.* **drooled, drool•ing, drools. 1.** To let saliva dribble from the mouth; drivel. **2.** To show great appreciation or desire: *They drooled over the expensive bicycles in the window.* —*n.* Saliva: *wipe the drool from the baby's chin.* [First written down in 1802 in Modern English and spelled *drule,* perhaps alteration of *drivel.*]

droop (dro͞op) *v.* **drooped, droop•ing, droops.** —*intr.* **1.** To bend or hang downward; sag: *The flowers are beginning to droop.* **2.** To sag in dejection or exhaustion: *The sightseers began to droop toward the end of the day.* —*tr.* To let bend or hang down: *The dog drooped its ears.* —*n.* The act or condition of drooping. [First written down before 1300 in Middle English and spelled *drupen,* from Old Norse *drūpa.*]

❑ *These sound alike:* **droop, drupe** (fruit).

droop•y (**dro͞o′**pē) *adj.* Bending or hanging downward; sagging: *droopy eyelids.* —**droop′i•ly** *adv.* —**droop′i•ness** *n.*

drop (drŏp) *n.* **1.** A small mass of liquid in a rounded shape: *drops of paint.* **2.** A small quantity of a substance: *There isn't a drop of juice left.* **3. drops.** Liquid medicine administered in drops: *eye drops.* **4.** A trace or hint: *not a drop of pity.* **5.** Something resembling a drop in shape or size, especially a small globular piece of candy: *a lemon drop.* **6.** The act of falling; descent. **7.** A sudden fall or decrease, as in quality, quantity, or intensity: *a drop in temperature; a drop in prices.* **8.** The vertical distance from a higher to a lower level: *a drop of 200 feet.* **9.** A sheer incline, such as the face of a cliff: *The hikers avoided the drop.* **10.** Something that is arranged to fall or be lowered, as a curtain on a stage. —*v.* **dropped, drop•ping, drops.** —*intr.* **1.** To fall in drops. **2.** To fall from a higher to a lower place or position: *I heard the plate drop on the floor.* **3.** To become less, as in intensity or number; decrease: *The temperature dropped as the sun went down.* **4.** To descend from one level to another: *The sun dropped toward the western hills.* **5.** To fall or sink into a state of exhaustion or death: *drop from overexertion.* **6.** To pass or sink into a specified state or condition: *dropped into a doze.* —*tr.* **1.** To let fall by releasing hold of: *I dropped the hot frying pan.* **2.** To let fall in drops: *drop medicine in a baby's ear.* **3.** To say or offer casually: *drop a hint.* **4.** To write at one's leisure: *drop a postcard to a friend.* **5.** To cease consideration or treatment of: *Let's drop the matter.* **6.** To terminate an association or a relationship with: *drop one's friends.* **7.** To leave out (a letter, for example) in speaking or writing. **8.** To set down at a particular place; deliver or unload: *drop passengers at their destination; dropped a package off.* —***idioms.*** **drop behind.** To fall behind: *I have to work hard to keep from dropping behind.* **drop by.** To stop in for a short visit. **drop off. 1.** To fall asleep. **2.** To decrease: *Temperatures usually drop off in the evening.* **drop out.** To withdraw from participation, as in a game, club, or school. [First written down about 725 in Old English and spelled *dropa.*]

drop cloth *n.* A large cloth or sheet of plastic used to cover and protect furniture and floors while a room is being painted.

drop kick *n.* A kick made by dropping a football to the ground and kicking it just as it starts to rebound.

drop leaf *n.* A hinged wing on a table that can be folded down when not in use.

drop•let (**drŏp′**lĭt) *n.* A tiny drop.

drop•out (**drŏp′**out′) *n.* **1.** A person who quits school. **2.** A person who withdraws from a given social group.

drop•per (**drŏp′**ər) *n.* A small glass or plastic tube with a suction bulb at one end for drawing in a liquid and releasing it in drops.

drop•pings (**drŏp′**ĭngz) *pl.n.* The excrement of animals.

drop•sy (**drŏp′**sē) *n.* Edema.

dro•soph•i•la (drō **sŏf′**ə lə *or* drə **sŏf′**ə lə) *n.* Any of various small fruit flies, especially a kind used extensively in genetic research.

dross (drŏs *or* drôs) *n.* **1.** The waste material that rises to the surface of a molten metal as it is being smelted or refined. **2.** Worthless, commonplace, or trivial matter.

drought (drout) *n.* A long period of little or no rainfall.

drove[1] (drōv) *v.* Past tense of **drive.**

drove[2] (drōv) *n.* **1.** A flock or herd being driven in a group. **2.** A large mass of people moving or acting as a body: *droves of visitors on their way to the White House.* [First written down in 971 in Old English and spelled *drāf*, from *drīfan*, drive.]

drov•er (drō′vər) *n.* A person who drives cattle or sheep.

drown (droun) *v.* **drowned, drown•ing, drowns.** —*tr.* **1.** To kill by submerging and suffocating in water or another liquid. **2.** To drench thoroughly or cover with or as if with a liquid: *They drowned their meat in gravy.* **3.** To deaden one's awareness of; blot out: *drown disappointment in the company of friends.* **4.** To muffle or mask (a sound) with a louder sound: *Their laughter drowned out the speaker's voice.* —*intr.* To die by suffocating in water or other liquid: *Many animals drowned on the flooded farmland.* [First written down about 1325 in Middle English and spelled *drounen*, probably of Scandinavian origin.]

drowse (drouz) *intr.v.* **drowsed, drows•ing, drows•es.** To be half-asleep: *The cat drowsed in the sun.* —*n.* The condition of being sleepy.

drows•y (drou′zē) *adj.* **drows•i•er, drows•i•est. 1.** Dull with sleepiness; sluggish: *feeling drowsy after dinner.* **2.** Causing sleepiness: *a drowsy lullaby.* —**drows′i•ly** *adv.* —**drows′i•ness** *n.*

drub (drŭb) *tr.v.* **drubbed, drub•bing, drubs. 1.** To beat with a stick. **2.** To instill forcefully. **3.** To defeat throughly: *drub an opposing team.*

drudge (drŭj) *n.* A person who does tedious, unpleasant, or menial work. —*intr.v.* **drudged, drudg•ing, drudg•es.** To do tedious, unpleasant, or menial work.

drudg•er•y (drŭj′ə rē) *n., pl.* **drudg•er•ies.** Tedious, unpleasant, or menial work: *Keeping records is often drudgery.*

drug (drŭg) *n.* **1.** A substance that affects the life processes of an organism, especially a substance used in medicine, as for curing disease or relieving symptoms. **2.** A narcotic or other substance whose main effect is on the nervous system, especially one whose use tends to become habitual. —*tr.v.* **drugged, drug•ging, drugs. 1.** To administer a drug to: *drug a patient with an anesthetic before an operation.* **2.** To mix a drug into (food or drink). **3.** To make dull or sleepy with or as if with a drug. [First written down about 1387 in Middle English and spelled *drogge*, perhaps from Middle Dutch *droge (vate)*, dry (cases).]

drug•gist (drŭg′ĭst) *n.* **1.** A pharmacist. **2.** A person who sells drugs.

drug•store (drŭg′stôr′) *n.* A store where prescriptions are filled and medical supplies and other items are sold.

dru•id also **Dru•id** (dro͞o′ĭd) *n.* A member of an order of pagan priests in ancient Britain and Gaul. [First written down in 1509 in Modern English and spelled *Druydan*, from Latin *druidēs*, druids, of Celtic origin.]

drum (drŭm) *n.* **1.** A musical instrument consisting of a hollow container shaped like a cylinder or bowl with a head made of animal skin or plastic stretched across it. Drums are played by beating on the head, either with sticks or the hands. **2.** A sound produced by this instrument. **3.** Something having a shape or structure like a drum: *an oil drum; a cable drum.* —*v.* **drummed, drum•ming, drums.** —*intr.* **1.** To play a drum or drums. **2.** To thump or tap rhythmically or continually: *I drummed on the table with my pencil.* —*tr.* **1.** To perform (a musical part or piece) on or as if on a drum. **2.** To make known to or force upon (a person) by constant repetition: *I drummed the facts into my head to pass the test.* **3.** To expel or dismiss in disgrace: *drummed the private out of the corps.* —***idiom.*** **drum up.** To bring about by continuous persistent effort: *Students drummed up support for their trip.* [First written down about 1427 in Middle English and spelled *drom*, from Middle Dutch *tromme*, probably of imitative origin.]

drum•beat (drŭm′bēt′) *n.* The sound produced by beating a drum.

drum•lin (drŭm′lĭn) *n.* A ridge or an elongated hill having a smooth summit, formed from glacial deposits.

drum major *n.* A man who leads a marching band or drum corps, often twirling a baton.

drum majorette *n.* A woman who leads a marching band or drum corps, often twirling a baton.

drum•mer (drŭm′ər) *n.* A person who plays a drum, as in a band.

drum•stick (drŭm′stĭk′) *n.* **1.** A stick for beating a drum. **2.** The lower part of the leg of a cooked chicken or turkey.

drunk (drŭngk) *v.* Past participle of **drink.** —*adj.* **1.** Intoxicated with alcoholic liquor. **2.** Overcome by strong feeling or emotion: *The dictator is drunk with power.* —*n.* A drunken spree.

drunk•ard (drŭng′kərd) *n.* A person who is habitually drunk.

drunk•en (drŭng′kən) *adj.* **1.** Drunk; intoxicated. **2.** Of, involving, or occurring during intoxication: *a drunken brawl.* —**drunk′en•ly** *adv.* —**drunk′en•ness** *n.*

drupe (dro͞op) *n.* A fleshy fruit, such as a cherry, plum, or peach, whose seed is contained in a hard pit or stone surrounded by soft pulpy flesh.
❑ *These sound alike:* **drupe, droop** (sag).

druth•ers (drŭ*th*′ərz) *pl.n. Informal.* A choice or preference.

dry (drī) *adj.* **dri•er** (drī′ər), **dri•est** (drī′ĭst) or **dry•er, dry•est. 1.** Free from liquid or moisture: *dry clothes; dry air.* **2.** Having little or no rainfall; arid: *the dry season; a dry area.* **3.** Not under water: *We stepped ashore on dry land.* **4.** Having all or almost all of the liquid or water drained away or used up: *a dry stream; a dry well.* **5.** No longer yielding milk: *a dry cow.* **6.** Not shedding tears: *dry sobs.* **7.** Needing or desiring drink: *My throat is dry.* **8.** Not sweet. Used of wines. **9.** Eaten or served without butter or other spread: *dry toast.* **10.** Having no adornment; plain: *a dry speaker; dry facts.* **11.** Quietly humorous; ironic: *a dry wit.* **12.** Not permitting the sale or consumption of alcoholic beverages: *a dry county.* —*v.* **dried** (drīd), **dry•ing, dries** (drīz). —*tr.* To remove the moisture from; make dry: *We dried the dishes after supper.* —*intr.* To become dry: *The laundry dried quickly in the sun.* —***idiom.*** **dry up.** To make or become unproductive, especially to do so gradually: *The stream dried up over the hot arid summer.* [First written down before 900 in Old English and spelled *drȳge*.] —**dry′ly** *adv.* —**dry′ness** *n.*

dry•ad (drī′əd *or* drī′ăd′) *n.* In Greek mythology, a wood nymph.

dry cell *n.* An electric cell in which the chemical producing the current is made into a paste so that its contents cannot spill.

dry-clean (drī′klēn′) *tr.v.* **dry-cleaned, dry-clean•ing, dry-cleans.** To clean (clothing or fabrics) with chemical solvents that have little or no water.

dry cleaner *n.* A person or business that dry-cleans clothes.

dry cleaning *n.* The cleaning of fabrics with chemical solvents.

dry dock *n.* A large dock in the form of a basin from which the water can be emptied, used for building or repairing a ship below its waterline.

dry dock
Launching of U.S.S.
Samuel Adams

ă	**pat**	oi	**boy**
ā	**pay**	ou	**out**
âr	**care**	ŏŏ	**took**
ä	**father**	o͞o	**boot**
ĕ	**pet**	ŭ	**cut**
ē	**be**	ûr	**urge**
ĭ	**pit**	th	**thin**
ī	**pie**	*th*	**this**
îr	**pier**	hw	**whoop**
ŏ	**pot**	zh	**vision**
ō	**toe**	ə	**about**
ô	**paw**	N	*French* **bon**

dry-dock (drī′dŏk′) *tr. & intr.v.* **dry-docked, dry-dock•ing, dry-docks.** To place in or go into a dry dock.

dry•er (drī′ər) *n.* **1.** A appliance that removes moisture by heating or another process: *a clothes dryer.* **2.** Variant of **drier**[1].

dry farming *n.* A type of farming practiced in arid regions without irrigation by maintaining a mulch on the surface that protects the natural moisture of the soil from evaporation.

dry goods *pl.n.* Cloth, clothing, and related articles of trade.

dry ice *n.* Carbon dioxide compressed and chilled into a solid and used as a cooling agent.

dry•ing oil (drī′ĭng) *n.* An organic oil, such as linseed oil, used in paints and varnishes. It dries into a tough elastic layer when exposed to air.

dry•ly (drī′lē) *adv.* In a dry way; unemotionally: *speak dryly of political affairs.*

dry measure *n.* A system of units for measuring dry commodities, such as grains, fruits, and vegetables.

dry rot *n.* A fungous disease that causes timber to become brittle and crumble.

dry run *n.* A trial exercise; a rehearsal.

dry wall *n.* **1.a.** Plasterboard. **b.** A wall or ceiling constructed of a prefabricated material, such as plasterboard. **2.** A stone wall constructed without mortar.

DST or **D.S.T.** *abbr.* An abbreviation of daylight-saving time.

du•al (dōō′əl *or* dyōō′əl) *adj.* **1.** Composed of two parts; double: *dual controls for pilot and copilot.* **2.** Having a double character or purpose. **—du′al•ly** *adv.*

❑ *These sound alike:* **dual, duel** (combat).

du•al•i•ty (dōō ăl′ĭ tē *or* dyōō ăl′ĭ tē) *n.* The quality or condition of being twofold.

dub[1] (dŭb) *tr.v.* **dubbed, dub•bing, dubs. 1.** To confer knighthood on (a man) by tapping him on the shoulder with a sword. **2.** To give a nickname to: *The cat was named Cleo, but the children dubbed it "Mittens."* [First written down in 1085 in Old English and spelled *dubbian*, perhaps from Old French *aduber*.]

dub[2] (dŭb) *tr.v.* **1.** To insert (new sounds) into an existing recording, as on magnetic tape or the sound track of a film. **2.** To provide (a film) with a new sound track, often with the dialogue in a different language: *The Russian film was dubbed in English for American audiences.* [First written down in 1929 in Modern English, short for *double.*]

Du•bai (dōō bī′). A city of eastern United Arab Emirates on the Persian Gulf. Population, 265,702.

du•bi•ous (dōō′bē əs *or* dyōō′bē əs) *adj.* **1.** Feeling or showing doubt or uncertainty; uncertain: *I am dubious of the outcome.* **2.** Questionable in character; shady; suspicious: *His schemes to get rich quickly sounded dubious.* **—du′bi•ous•ly** *adv.* **—du′bi•ous•ness** *n.*

Dub•lin (dŭb′lĭn). The capital and largest city of Ireland, in the east-central part of the country on the Irish Sea. Population, 525,882.

Du Bois (dōō bois′), **William Edward Burghardt.** 1868–1963. American civil rights leader who cofounded the NAACP and worked to promote the concerns of Black Americans and Africans.

W.E.B. Du Bois

du•cal (dōō′kəl *or* dyōō′kəl) *adj.* Of or relating to dukedom.

duc•at (dŭk′ət) *n.* Any of various gold or silver coins formerly used in Europe.

duch•ess (dŭch′ĭs) *n.* **1.** The wife or widow of a duke. **2.** A woman holding a duchy.

duch•y (dŭch′ē) *n., pl.* **duch•ies.** The territory ruled by a duke or duchess.

duck[1] (dŭk) *n.* **1.** Any of various wild or domesticated water birds having a broad flat bill, short neck and legs, and webbed feet. **2.** A female duck, as distinguished from a drake. **3.** The meat of a duck used as food. [First written down in 967 in Old English and spelled *dūce.*]

duck[2] (dŭk) *v.* **ducked, duck•ing, ducks.** *—tr.* **1.** To lower (the head and body) quickly: *She ducked her head getting into the car.* **2.** To evade; dodge: *duck a responsibility.* **3.** To push suddenly under water: *duck someone in the pool.* *—intr.* **1.** To lower the head or body quickly: *The boy ducked under the table.* **2.** To push or dip suddenly under water. **3.** *Informal.* To enter or leave quickly or temporarily: *duck out of a meeting.* [First written down before 1325 in Middle English and spelled *duken*, to dive.]

duck[3] (dŭk) *n.* **1.** A strong cotton or linen cloth that is lighter than canvas. **2. ducks.** Trousers, especially white ones, made of this fabric. [First written down in 1640 in Modern English, from Dutch *doek*, cloth.]

duck•bill (dŭk′bĭl′) *n.* The platypus.

duck•ling (dŭk′lĭng) *n.* A young duck.

duck•weed (dŭk′wēd′) *n.* Any of various small stemless water plants that form floating masses on the surface of ponds and other quiet waters.

duct (dŭkt) *n.* **1.** A tube through which something flows: *Ducts carry heat from the furnace to the rest of the house.* **2.** A tube in the body for carrying a bodily fluid, especially a fluid secreted by a gland. **3.** A tube or pipe that carries electric cables or wires. [First written down in 1650 in Modern English, from Latin *ductus*, act of leading, from *dūcere*, to lead.]

duc•tile (dŭk′təl *or* dŭk′tīl′) *adj.* **1.** Easily drawn out into a fine strand or wire: *Silver is a ductile metal.* **2.** Easily molded or shaped: *Plastic pipe is ductile if heated.* **3.** Readily persuaded or influenced; tractable. **—duc•til′i•ty** (dŭk tĭl′ĭ tē) *n.*

duct•less gland (dŭkt′lĭs) *n.* An endocrine gland.

dud (dŭd) *n.* **1.** A bomb or shell that fails to explode. **2.** A person or thing that turns out to be ineffective or unsuccessful: *Our hasty plan was a real dud.*

dude (dōōd *or* dyōōd) *n.* **1.** A city person who vacations on a ranch in the American West. **2.** *Informal.* A man who is overly concerned with clothes; a dandy. **3.** *Slang.* A fellow; a chap.

dude ranch *n.* A resort patterned after a Western ranch, featuring horseback riding and other outdoor activities.

dudg•eon (dŭj′ən) *n.* A sullen, angry, or indignant state of mind: *The insulted customer walked out of the shop in high dudgeon.*

due (dōō *or* dyōō) *adj.* **1.** Owed or owing as a debt: *We must pay the amount still due.* **2.** Fitting or appropriate; suitable: *Every citizen is required to show due respect for the law.* **3.** As much as needed; sufficient; adequate: *We left early, taking due care to be on time.* **4.** Expected or scheduled: *When is the train due to arrive?* **5.** Expecting or ready for something as part of a normal course or sequence: *We're due for some rain.* *—n.* **1.** Something that is owed or deserved: *a dedicated scholar who finally got his due.* **2. dues.** A charge or fee for membership, as in a club. *—adv.* Straight; directly: *The settlers traveled due west.* [First written down about 1350 in Middle English and spelled *dewe*, from Old French *deu*, from *devoir*, to owe, from Latin *dēbēre.*]

❑ *These sound alike:* **due, dew** (water droplets), **do**[1] (perform).

du•el (dōō′əl *or* dyōō′əl) *n.* **1.** A combat arranged in advance between two people, usually fought to settle an argument or a point of honor. **2.** A struggle between two opponents: *a duel of wits between* *lawyers in the courtroom.* —*tr. & intr.v.* **du•eled, du•el•ing, du•els** or **du•elled, du•el•ling, du•els.** To fight in a duel. [First written down about 1475 in Middle English and spelled *duelle,* from Latin *duellum,* war, variant of *bellum.*] —**du′el•er, du′el•ler, du′el•ist, du′el•list** *n.*

❑ *These sound alike:* **duel, dual** (twofold).

due process *n.* An established course of proceeding in judicial or other governmental activity that is designed to protect the legal rights of the individual.

du•et (do͞o ĕt′ *or* dyo͞o ĕt′) *n.* **1.** A musical composition for two voices or two instruments. **2.** The two performers of such a composition.

due to *prep.* Because of: *The cancellation of the concert was due to bad weather.*

duf•fel or **duf•fle** (dŭf′əl) *n.* **1.** A coarse woolen cloth with a nap on both sides. **2.** Clothing and other personal gear carried when camping. [First written down in 1917 in Modern English, after *Duffel,* a town of northern Belgium.]

duffle bag or **duffel bag** *n.* A large cylindrical cloth bag of canvas or duck for carrying personal belongings.

dug (dŭg) *v.* Past tense and past participle of **dig.**

du•gong (do͞o′gŏng′ *or* do͞o′gông′) *n.* A plant-eating tropical sea mammal having a broad snout, a pair of front flippers, and a flat broad tail.

dug•out (dŭg′out′) *n.* **1.** A boat or canoe made by hollowing out a log. **2.** A rough shelter dug into the ground or on a hillside and used especially in battle for protection from artillery. **3.** Either of two low shelters at the side of a baseball field where the players stay while not on the field.

duke (do͞ok *or* dyo͞ok) *n.* **1.** A nobleman of the highest rank, especially a man of the highest level of the British peerage. **2.** A man who rules an independent duchy.

duke•dom (do͞ok′dəm *or* dyo͞ok′dəm) *n.* **1.** A duchy. **2.** The rank, office, or title of a duke.

dul•cet (dŭl′sĭt) *adj.* Soothing and agreeable, especially to the ear: *sweet dulcet tones.*

dul•ci•mer (dŭl′sə mər) *n.* **1.** A musical instrument having three or four strings stretched over a sound box and a fretted neck and played by plucking or strumming. **2.** A musical instrument consisting of a set of strings stretched across a trapezoidal sound box and played with two small hammers.

dull (dŭl) *adj.* **dull•er, dull•est. 1.** Not sharp or pointed; blunt: *a dull knife; a dull pencil.* **2.** Not interesting; boring: *a dull book; dull work.* See Synonyms at **boring. 3.** Mentally weak; stupid. **4.** Not keenly or intensely felt: *a dull ache in my throat.* **5.** Not bright or vivid; dim: *a dull red.* **6.** Not loud or clear; muffled: *the dull rumble of distant thunder.* —*tr. & intr.v.* **dulled, dull•ing, dulls.** To make or become dull: *The saw blade dulled as it cut more wood.* —**dull′ness** *n.* —**dull′y** *adv.*

dull•ard (dŭl′ərd) *n.* A dull or stupid person.

du•ly (do͞o′lē *or* dyo͞o′lē) *adv.* **1.** In a proper manner; rightfully: *a duly elected candidate.* **2.** At the expected time; punctually: *The loan was duly repaid.*

dumb (dŭm) *adj.* **dumb•er, dumb•est. 1.** *Offensive.* Incapable of using speech; mute. **2.** Unwilling to speak; silent: *The witness remained dumb under questioning.* **3.** Temporarily speechless, as with shock or fear: *I was dumb with disbelief.* **4.** Conspicuously unintelligent; stupid. —**dumb′ly** *adv.* —**dumb′ness** *n.*

dumb•bell (dŭm′bĕl′) *n.* **1.** A weight lifted for exercise, consisting of a short bar with a metal ball at each end. **2.** *Slang.* A person regarded as stupid or ignorant.

dumb•found also **dum•found** (dŭm′found′) *tr.v.* **dumb•found•ed, dumb•found•ing, dumb•founds** or **dum•found•ed, dum•found•ing, dum•founds.** To make speechless with astonishment; amaze or bewilder: *The sophistication of the young man's answers dumbfounded the experts.*

dumb show *n.* Communication or acting by means of gestures; pantomime.

dumb•wait•er (dŭm′wā′tər) *n.* A small elevator used to carry food, dishes, or other articles from one floor to another.

dum•found (dŭm′found′) *v.* Variant of **dumbfound.**

dum•my (dŭm′ē) *n., pl.* **dum•mies. 1.** A model of the human body, used as a substitute for a person: *A dummy was used to test the seat belt.* **2.** Something made to look like a real object; an imitation or counterfeit: *The drawer in the cabinet is a dummy.* **3.** A person or organization secretly working for another. **4.** A stupid of foolish person. **5.** A model of a book or a page to show how the final copy will look. **6.** The player in a card game whose hand is shown and played by a partner. —*adj.* **1.** Made to work like or resemble a real object; imitation; fake: *Dummy cannons fooled the enemy.* **2.** Secretly in the service of another: *a dummy corporation covering up their criminal activities.*

dump (dŭmp) *tr.v.* **dumped, dump•ing, dumps. 1.** To release or throw down in a mass: *The factory dumped waste into the river. Don't dump your books on the table.* **2.** To empty out (a container or vehicle): *dump a wastebasket.* **3.** To get rid of or reject: *The President dumped several controversial candidates for the position.* **4.** To sell (goods) in large quantities and at a low price: *The company dumped its old stock of air conditioners in several countries.* **5.** To print out or transfer (information stored in computer memory) without processing it. —*n.* **1.** A place where garbage or trash is discarded: *The town dump is nearly full.* **2.** An untidy accumulation of things; a pile: *That messy storage closet is a dump.* **3.** A military storage place: *an ammunition dump.* **4.** A shabby rundown place: *The old house is a dump.*

dump•ling (dŭmp′lĭng) *n.* **1.** A small ball of dough cooked in stew or soup or steamed and served with meat. **2.** Sweetened dough wrapped around fruit, such as an apple, baked and served as dessert.

dumps (dŭmps) *pl.n.* Low gloomy spirits; depression: *down in the dumps.*

Dump•ster (dŭmp′stər). A trademark used for containers designed for receiving, transporting, and dumping waste materials.

dump truck *n.* A heavy-duty truck having a bed that tilts backward to dump loose material.

dump•y (dŭm′pē) *adj.* **dump•i•er, dump•i•est.** Being short and plump; squat. —**dump′i•ly** *adv.* —**dump′i•ness** *n.*

dun[1] (dŭn) *tr.v.* **dunned, dun•ning, duns.** To ask (a debtor) persistently for payment. —*n.* **1.** A demand for payment of a debt. **2.** A person who persistently demands payment. [First written down before 1626 in Modern English.]

❑ *These sound alike:* **dun**[1] (ask for payment), **done** (finished), **dun**[2] (grayish-brown).

dun[2] (dŭn) *n.* **1.** A dull grayish brown. **2.** A horse of this color. [First written down in 953 in Old English and spelled *dunn,* perhaps of Celtic origin.]

❑ *These sound alike:* **dun**[2] (grayish-brown), **done** (finished), **dun**[1] (ask for payment).

dunce (dŭns) *n.* A person regarded as stupid. [First written down in 1577 in Modern English and spelled *Duns,* After John *Duns Scotus* (1265?–1308), Scottish scholastic theologian whose writings and philosophy were ridiculed in the 16th century.]

dune (do͞on *or* dyo͞on) *n.* A hill or ridge of wind-blown sand. [First written down in 1790 in Modern English, from French, from Middle Dutch *dūne.*]

dugout

dulcimer

Appalachian dulcimer

ă	pat	oi	boy
ā	pay	ou	out
âr	care	o͝o	took
ä	father	o͞o	boot
ĕ	pet	ŭ	cut
ē	be	ûr	urge
ĭ	pit	th	thin
ī	pie	*th*	this
îr	pier	hw	whoop
ŏ	pot	zh	vision
ō	toe	ə	about
ô	paw	N	*French* bon

dune buggy

Word Building: duplex

The word root *–plex* in English words comes from the Latin word root *–plex*, where it means "–fold." **Duplex** means "twofold, double" (using the word *duo*, "two"); **triplex** is literally "threefold" (*tri–*, "three"); **multiplex** means "manifold, multiple" (*multi–*, "many"). The Latin verb formed from *–plex* is *plicāre*, "to fold," which has the past participle *plicātus*, from which we form the verb **duplicate**.

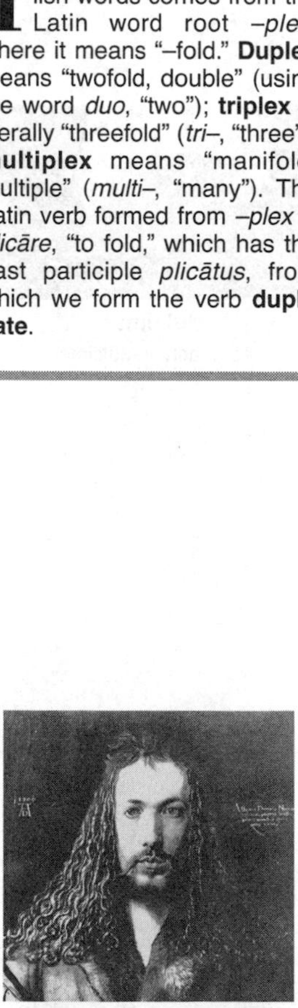

Albrecht Dürer
1500 self-portrait

dune buggy *n.* A small light automobile, usually equipped with oversize tires for driving on sand dunes.

dung (dŭng) *n.* **1.** The excrement of animals. **2.** Manure.

dun•ga•ree (dŭng′gə **rē′**) *n.* **1.** A sturdy, often blue denim fabric. **2. dungarees.** Overalls or trousers made from this fabric. [First written down in 1613 in Modern English and spelled *dongerijns*, from Hindi *dungrī*.]

dun•geon (**dŭn′**jən) *n.* A dark, often underground chamber or cell used to confine prisoners.

❑ *These sound alike:* **dungeon, donjon** (tower).

dunk (dŭngk) *tr.v.* **dunked, dunk•ing, dunks. 1.** To dip or briefly submerge (something) in a liquid: *dunk a doughnut in tea.* **2.** To submerge (someone) playfully, as in a swimming pool.

Dun•kirk (**dŭn′**kûrk′). A city of northern France on the North Sea. In World War II more than 330,000 Allied troops were evacuated from its beaches (May–June 1940). Population, 73,120.

du•o (**do͞o′**ō *or* **dyo͞o′**ō) *n., pl.* **du•os. 1.** A duet, as of musical performers. **2.** A couple; a pair.

du•o•dec•i•mal (do͞o′ə **dĕs′**ə məl *or* dyo͞o′ə **dĕs′**ə məl) *adj.* Relating to or based on twelfths or the number 12: *a duodecimal digit.* —*n.* A number in the duodecimal system. [First written down in 1714 in Modern English, from Latin *duodecim*, twelve : *duo*, two + *decem*, ten.]

duodecimal system *n.* A number system with a base of 12. It uses twelve digits instead of the more familiar ten digits of the decimal system.

du•o•de•num (do͞o′ə **dē′**nəm *or* dyo͞o′ə **dē′**nəm) *n., pl.* **du•od•e•na** (do͞o′ə **dē′**nə *or* dyo͞o′ə **dē′**nə) or **du•o•de•nums.** The portion of the small intestine below the stomach and extending to the jejunum. —**du′o•de′nal** *adj.*

dupe (do͞op *or* dyo͞op) *n.* A person who is used or taken advantage of through deception and trickery. —*tr.v.* **duped, dup•ing, dupes.** To deceive; trick; fool: *The advertisement duped us into believing the bicycles were on sale.*

du•ple (**do͞o′**pəl *or* **dyo͞o′**pəl) *adj.* **1.** Consisting of two parts or units; double. **2.** Consisting of two beats or some multiple of two beats to a musical measure.

du•plex (**do͞o′**plĕks′ *or* **dyo͞o′**plĕks′) *adj.* Having two parts; twofold; double: *Both plugs will fit in a duplex electrical outlet.* —*n.* **1.** A house divided into two living units, usually with separate entrances. **2.** A duplex apartment. —SEE NOTE.

duplex apartment *n.* An apartment that has rooms on two floors.

du•pli•cate (**do͞o′**plĭ kĭt *or* **dyo͞o′**plĭ kĭt) *adj.* **1.** Having two exactly corresponding parts; double: *the duplicate wings of many insects.* **2.** Copied from an original: *a duplicate key.* —*n.* **1.** An exact copy; a double: *That letter is a duplicate of the original.* **2.** Something that corresponds exactly to another: *Your bike is a duplicate of mine.* —*tr.v.* (**do͞o′**plĭ kāt′ *or* **dyo͞o′**plĭ kāt′). **du•pli•cat•ed, du•pli•cat•ing, du•pli•cates. 1.** To make an exact copy of: *duplicate a key.* **2.** To do or perform again; repeat: *duplicate an experiment.* [First written down before 1425 in Middle English, from Latin *duplicātus*, from *duplicāre*, to double, from *duplex*, twofold.]

du•pli•ca•tion (do͞o′plĭ **kā′**shən *or* dyo͞o′plĭ **kā′**shən) *n.* **1.** The act or condition of being duplicated: *Duplication of the experiment confirmed its original results.* **2.** A duplicate; a replica: *This statue is a duplication of a Roman statue of Caesar.*

du•pli•ca•tor (**do͞o′**plĭ kā′tər *or* **dyo͞o′**plĭ kā′tər) *n.* A machine that makes exact copies of something printed or written.

du•plic•i•ty (do͞o **plĭs′**ĭ tē *or* dyo͞o **plĭs′**ĭ tē) *n., pl.* **du•plic•i•ties.** Deliberate deceptiveness in behavior or speech; deceit.

du•ra•ble (**do͝or′**ə bəl *or* **dyo͝or′**ə bəl) *adj.* **1.** Capable of withstanding wear and tear; sturdy: *Denim is a durable fabric used for work clothes.* **2.** Lasting or enduring; stable: *a durable friendship.* [First written down about 1390 in Middle English, from Latin *dūrāre*, to last.] —**du′ra•bil′i•ty, du′ra•ble•ness** *n.* —**du′ra•bly** *adv.*

durable goods *pl.n.* Manufactured products that can be used for a long time. Furniture, refrigerators, and automobiles are durable goods.

du•rance (**do͝or′**əns *or* **dyo͝or′**əns) *n.* Forced confinement; imprisonment.

du•ra•tion (do͞o **rā′**shən *or* dyo͞o **rā′**shən) *n.* The period of time during which something exists or persists: *the duration of a storm.*

Dü•rer (**do͝or′**ər *or* **dyo͝or′**ər), **Albrecht.** 1471–1528. German painter and engraver who incorporated Italian Renaissance classicism into northern European art.

du•ress (do͞o **rĕs′** *or* dyo͞o **rĕs′**) *n.* **1.** The use of force or threat to compel someone to do something: *The prisoner confessed under duress.* **2.** Unlawful imprisonment.

dur•ing (**do͝or′**ĭng *or* **dyo͝or′**ĭng) *prep.* **1.** Throughout the course or duration of: *We talked during the entire evening.* **2.** Within the time of; at some time in: *He was born during the last half of the 19th century.*

durst (dûrst) *v. Archaic.* A past tense and a past participle of **dare.**

du•rum (**do͝or′**əm *or* **dyo͝or′**əm) *n.* A kind of wheat having hard grains, used chiefly in making pasta.

Du•shan•be (do͞o **shăm′**bə *or* do͞o shäm bə). The capital of Tadzhikistan, in the western part of the republic. Population, 552,000.

dusk (dŭsk) *n.* The time of evening just before darkness; the darker stage of twilight: *Only a few stars shine at dusk.*

dusk•y (**dŭs′**kē) *adj.* **dusk•i•er, dusk•i•est. 1.** Rather dark in color: *Beavers have dusky fur of deep brown.* **2.** Having little light; dim: *a dusky room.* See Synonyms at **dark.** —**dusk′i•ly** *adv.* —**dusk′i•ness** *n.*

dust (dŭst) *n.* **1.** Fine dry particles of matter: *clouds of dust raised by a herd of cattle; the dust gathering on old books.* **2.** Earth, especially when regarded as the remains of a decayed body. —*v.* **dust•ed, dust•ing, dusts.** —*tr.* **1.** To remove dust from by wiping or brushing: *We dusted the shelves.* **2.** To sprinkle with a powdery substance: *She dusted the rose bushes with insecticide.* —*intr.* To clean by removing dust: *The cleaning staff must dust every day.* ***—idiom.*** **dust off.** To restore or revise for current use: *dust off an old essay for publication.* [First written down about 725 in Old English and spelled *dūst*.]

❑ *These sound alike:* **dust, dost** (do).

dust bowl *n.* A region in which dry weather and dust storms have produced conditions like those of a desert.

dust•er (**dŭs′**tər) *n.* **1.** A person or thing that dusts. **2.** A cloth or brush used to remove dust. **3.** A device for spreading powder on plants. **4.** A coat or smock worn to protect the clothing from dust.

dust jacket *n.* **1.** A paper cover used to protect the outside of a book. **2.** A cardboard sleeve used to protect a phonograph record.

dust•pan (**dŭst′**păn′) *n.* A short-handled pan, shaped like a shovel, into which dust is swept.

dust storm *n.* A windstorm that sweeps clouds of dust across a large area, especially in a dry region.

dust•y (**dŭs′**tē) *adj.* **dust•i•er, dust•i•est. 1.** Covered or filled with dust: *a dusty road; a dusty room.* **2.** Tinged with gray: *a dusty beard.* **3.** Consisting of or resembling dust; powdery: *dusty soil.* **—dust′i•ness** *n.*

Dutch (dŭch) *n.* **1.** *(used with a plural verb).* The people of the Netherlands. **2.** The Germanic language of the Netherlands. *—adj.* Of or relating to the Netherlands or its people, language, or culture. ***—idioms.*** **go Dutch.** To pay one's own expenses, as on a date. **in Dutch.** In trouble or disfavor: *in Dutch for being late.* [First written down in 1333 in Middle English and spelled *Duch*, Germanic, from Middle Dutch *Duutsch*.]

Dutch door *n.* A door divided in two horizontally so that one part may be left open or closed.

Dutch East In•dies (ĭn′dēz). Indonesia.

Dutch Gui•a•na (gē ăn′ə *or* gē ä′nə). Suriname.

Dutch•man (dŭch′mən) *n.* A man who is a native or inhabitant of the Netherlands.

Dutch oven *n.* **1.** A large heavy pot or kettle with a tight lid, used for slow cooking. **2.** A wall oven in which food is baked by means of preheated brick walls. **3.** An open metal box equipped with shelves and set before a fire for baking or roasting food.

Dutch treat *n. Informal.* An outing, as for dinner or a movie, for which each person pays his or her own share of the cost.

Dutch West In•dies (ĭn′dēz). Netherlands Antilles.

Dutch•wom•an (dŭch′wo͝om′ən) *n.* A woman who is a native or inhabitant of the Netherlands.

du•te•ous (do͞o′tē əs *or* dyo͞o′tē əs) *adj.* Obedient; dutiful: *a duteous and attentive assistant.* **—du′te•ous•ly** *adv.*

du•ti•a•ble (do͞o′tē ə bəl *or* dyo͞o′tē ə bəl) *adj.* Subject to a tax or duty: *Dutiable goods, such as perfume and shoes, must be paid for before they can be imported.*

du•ti•ful (do͞o′tĭ fəl *or* dyo͞o′tĭ fəl) *adj.* **1.** Careful to perform one's duty; obedient. **2.** Expressing or coming from a sense of duty: *dutiful words.* **—du′ti•ful•ly** *adv.* **—du′ti•ful•ness** *n.*

du•ty (do͞o′tē *or* dyo͞o′tē) *n., pl.* **du•ties. 1.** Something that a person ought to or must do; an obligation: *In a democracy one of the chief duties of a citizen is to vote.* **2.** Moral obligation: *We went to the ceremony out of duty.* **3.** A task, assignment, or function that is part of one's work: *household duties.* **4.** A tax charged by a government on imported or exported goods. [First written down in 1333 in Middle English and spelled *dewete*, from Anglo-Norman, from Old French *deu*, duc.]

Dvoř•ák (dvôr′zhäk), **Anton** or **Antonín.** 1841–1904. Czech composer whose works are often based on folk music.

dwarf (dwôrf) *n., pl.* **dwarfs** or **dwarves** (dwôrvz). **1.a.** A person who is much smaller than normal and whose limbs and features are often improperly proportioned or formed. **b.** An atypically small plant or animal. **2.** In fairy tales and legends, a tiny, often ugly creature resembling a human who has magical powers. **3.** A dwarf star. *—tr.v.* **dwarfed, dwarf•ing, dwarfs. 1.** To check the natural growth of; stunt: *Lack of water dwarfed the trees.* **2.** To make seem small by comparison: *The skyscraper dwarfed the old church.* [First written down about 700 in Old English and spelled *duerg*.]

dwarf star *n.* A star of relatively small size and mass that emits an average or below average amount of light. The sun is a dwarf star.

dwarves (dwôrvz) *n.* A plural of **dwarf.**

dwell (dwĕl) *intr.v.* **dwelt** (dwĕlt) or **dwelled, dwell•ing, dwells. 1.** To live as a resident; reside: *dwell in a city.* **2.** To speak or write about at length: *Then article dwells on the need for better health care.* **3.** To focus one's attention on; brood about: *Don't dwell on past mistakes.* [First written down about 725 in Old English and spelled *dwellan*, to mislead, delay.] **—dwell′er** *n.*

dwell•ing (dwĕl′ĭng) *n.* A place to live in; a residence: *Our house is a two-story dwelling.*

dwelt (dwĕlt) *v.* A past tense and a past participle of **dwell.**

DWI *abbr.* An abbreviation of driving while intoxicated.

dwin•dle (dwĭn′dl) *intr.v.* **dwin•dled, dwin•dling, dwin•dles.** To become gradually less until little is left: *Their savings dwindled away to nothing over the year.* See Synonyms at **decrease.**

Dy The symbol for the element **dysprosium.**

dye (dī) *n.* **1.** A substance used to color food, hair, cloth, or other materials. **2.** A color produced by dyeing: *The dye in the curtains faded in sunlight.* *—v.* **dyed, dye•ing, dyes.** *—tr.* To color with a dye: *dye a fabric red.* *—intr.* To become colored by a dye: *Some fabrics dye more easily than others.* [First written down about 1000 in Old English and spelled *dēah*.] **—dy′er** *n.*

❑ *These sound alike:* **dye, die**[1] (stop living), **die**[2] (device for shaping material).

dyed-in-the-wool (dīd′ĭn *thə* wo͝ol′) *adj.* Thoroughgoing; outright: *A dyed-in-the-wool conservative is always suspicious of governmental solutions to economic problems.*

Dy•er (dī′ər), **Mary.** Died 1660. English-born American Quaker martyr who was hanged for her beliefs.

dye•stuff (dī′stŭf′) *n.* A substance used as a dye: *Indigo is a deep blue dyestuff.*

dy•ing (dī′ĭng) *v.* Present participle of **die**[1]. *—adj.* **1.** About to die: *the shriveled leaves of the dying plant.* **2.** Drawing to an end: *a dying day.* **3.** Done or uttered just before death: *dying words.*

dy•nam•ic (dī năm′ĭk) *adj.* **1.** Marked by intensity and vigor; forceful: *the dynamic personality of a political leader.* **2.** Changing; active: *a dynamic stock market.* **3.** Of or relating to energy or to objects in motion. **4.** Of or relating to the science of dynamics. [First written down in 1817 in Modern English, from Greek *dunamis*, power, from *dunasthai*, to be able.] **—dy•nam′i•cal•ly** *adv.*

dy•nam•ics (dī năm′ĭks) *n.* **1.** *(used with a singular verb).* The branch of physics that deals with the effects of forces on the motions of bodies. **2.** *(used with a plural verb).* The forces that produce activity and change in a particular area: *the dynamics that have increased international trade.*

dy•na•mism (dī′nə mĭz′əm) *n.* Continuous change or activity; vigor; energy: *the dynamism of a new government administration.*

dy•na•mite (dī′nə mīt′) *n.* **1.** A powerful explosive composed of nitroglycerin and ammonium nitrate combined with an absorbent material and used in blasting and mining. **2.** *Slang.* Something that is especially exciting or wonderful: *These new video games are dynamite!* *—tr.v.* **dy•na•mit•ed, dy•na•mit•ing, dy•na•mites.** To blow up or destroy with dynamite: *The old office building was dynamited to make space for new construction.* [First written down in 1867 in Modern English, from Swedish *dynamit*, from Greek *dunamis*, power.] **—dy′na•mit′er** *n.*

dy•na•mo (dī′nə mō′) *n., pl.* **dy•na•mos. 1.** An electric generator, especially one that produces direct current. **2.** *Informal.* An extremely energetic and forceful person.

dy•nas•tic (dī năs′tĭk) *adj.* Of or relating to a dynasty: *a long tradition of dynastic rule.*

dy•nas•ty (dī′nə stē) *n., pl.* **dy•nas•ties. 1.** A succession of rulers from the same family: *the Hapsburg dynasty.* **2.** A family or group that maintains

Anton Dvořák

Mary Dyer

Bronze statue by
Sylvia Shaw Judson
(1897–1978)

ă	pat	oi	boy
ā	pay	ou	out
âr	care	o͝o	took
ä	father	o͞o	boot
ĕ	pet	ŭ	cut
ē	be	ûr	urge
ĭ	pit	th	thin
ī	pie	*th*	this
îr	pier	hw	whoop
ŏ	pot	zh	vision
ō	toe	ə	about
ô	paw	N	*French* bon

ă	pat	oi	boy
ā	pay	ou	out
âr	care	o͝o	took
ä	father	o͞o	boot
ĕ	pet	ŭ	cut
ē	be	ûr	urge
ĭ	pit	th	thin
ī	pie	*th*	this
îr	pier	hw	whoop
ŏ	pot	zh	vision
ō	toe	ə	about
ô	paw	N	*French* bon

great power, wealth, or success for a sustained period.

dyne (dīn) *n.* A unit of force equal to the amount of force required to give a mass of one gram an acceleration of one centimeter per second for each second the force is applied.

❑ *These sound alike:* **dyne, dine** (eat).

dys•en•ter•y (**dĭs′**ən tĕr′ē) *n.* An infection of the lower intestines that produces pain, fever, and severe diarrhea, often accompanied by discharges of blood or mucus.

dys•func•tion (dĭs **fŭngk′**shən) *n.* Abnormal functioning of a system or an organ of the body.

dys•gen•ic (dĭs **jĕn′**ĭk) *adj.* Relating to or causing the deterioration of inherited characteristics: *Dysgenic mutations can cause weak or deformed offspring.*

dys•lex•i•a (dĭs **lĕk′**sē ə) *n.* A learning disorder that interferes with the ability to recognize and comprehend written words.

dys•lex•ic (dĭs **lĕk′**sĭk) *adj.* Of, relating to, or affected with dyslexia. —*n.* A person affected with dyslexia.

dys•pep•sia (dĭs **pĕp′**shə *or* dĭs **pĕp′**sē ə) *n.* Poor digestion; indigestion.

dys•pep•tic (dĭs **pĕp′**tĭk) *adj.* **1.** Of, relating to, or suffering from dyspepsia. **2.** Gloomy; depressed: *a dyspeptic outlook on life.* —*n.* A person who often suffers from dyspepsia. **—dys•pep′ti•cal•ly** *adv.*

dys•pro•si•um (dĭs **prō′**zē əm *or* dĭs **prō′**zhē əm) *n.* *Symbol* **Dy** A soft rare-earth metallic element that forms highly magnetic compounds and is used in nuclear research. Atomic number 66. See table at **element.**

dz. *abbr.* An abbreviation of dozen.

Ee

e or **E** (ē) *n., pl.* **e's** or **E's. 1.** The fifth letter of the English alphabet. **2.** In music, the third tone in the scale of C major. **3.** The fifth in a series or group: *row E in a theater.*

E *abbr.* An abbreviation of: **1.** East. **2.** Eastern. **3.** Energy. **4.** English.

ea. *abbr.* An abbreviation of each.

each (ēch) *adj.* Being one of two or more persons or things considered individually; every: *The teacher talked to each student for ten minutes.* —*pron.* Every one of a group of persons, objects, or things: *Each of us took a turn looking in the telescope.* —*adv.* For or to each one; apiece: *The apples cost 25¢ each.* [First written down before 830 in Old English and spelled *ǣlce.*] —SEE NOTE.

each other *pron.* Each the other. Used to show that each person or thing does the same as the other: *The girls greeted each other.*

ea•ger (ē′gər) *adj.* **ea•ger•er, ea•ger•est.** Having or showing keen interest or desire: *Thousands of eager sports fans cheered the players.* —**ea′ger•ly** *adv.* —**ea′ger•ness** *n.*

ea•gle (ē′gəl) *n.* Any of various large birds of prey having a hooked bill, keen vision, and broad wings. [First written down before 1338 in Middle English and spelled *egle,* from Latin *aquila.*]

ea•gle-eyed (ē′gəl īd′) *adj.* Having very keen eyesight: *an eagle-eyed watchdog.*

ea•glet (ē′glĭt) *n.* A young eagle.

ear[1] (îr) *n.* **1.a.** The organ of hearing in human beings and other animals. The ear is made up of the inner ear, middle ear, and external ear. **b.** The part of this organ that shows on the outside of the body: *Some dogs' ears stick up and some flop over.* **2.** The sense of hearing: *Most singing sounds pleasant to the ear.* **3.** The ability to distinguish tones or sounds very accurately or acutely: *the sensitive ear of a musician.* **4.** Attention; heed: *Give me your ear until I finish the explanation.* **5.** Something shaped like an ear, as the handle of a pitcher. —***idioms.*** **all ears.** Listening eagerly; paying careful attention: *Some people are all ears when they hear gossip.* **give an ear** or **lend an ear.** To pay attention; listen carefully. **in one ear and out the other.** Without any influence or effect: *I could tell that my directions went in one ear and out the other.* **play it by ear. 1.** To perform music or play a musical instrument without using written music. **2.** To act according to the circumstances; improvise. [First written down before 1000 in Old English and spelled *ēare.*]

ear[2] (îr) *n.* The part of a cereal plant, such as corn, wheat, oats, barley, or rye, that bears flowers from which grains develop. [First written down before 800 in Old English and spelled *ēar.*]

ear•ache (îr′āk′) *n.* A pain in the ear.

ear•drum (îr′drŭm′) *n.* The membrane that separates the middle ear from the external ear and vibrates when sound waves strike it; the tympanic membrane.

eared (îrd) *adj.* **1.** Having an ear or ears: *an eared seal.* **2.** Having a certain kind or number of ears: *a long-eared puppy.*

ear•ful (îr′fo͝ol′) *n.* **1.** A flow of gossip or information: *I got an earful about the scandal from a neighbor.* **2.** A scolding or strong criticism: *The gardener gave me an earful for walking across the newly seeded grass.*

Ear•hart (âr′härt′), **Amelia.** 1897?–1937. American aviator who was the first woman to fly solo across the Atlantic Ocean (1932) and from Hawaii to California (1935). —SEE NOTE.

earl (ûrl) *n.* A British nobleman holding a title and rank below that of a marquis and above that of a viscount. [First written down before 616 in Old English and spelled *eorl,* nobleman.]

earl•dom (ûrl′dəm) *n.* **1.** The rank of an earl. **2.** The territory of an earl.

ear•lobe (îr′lōb′) *n.* The soft fleshy part at the bottom of the external ear of humans.

ear•ly (ûr′lē) *adj.* **ear•li•er, ear•li•est. 1.** Of or happening near the beginning of a time period, series, or course of development: *the early morning; people in their early twenties; the early stages of an animal's growth.* **2.** Of or belonging to a previous or distant period of time: *Early humans made simple tools.* **3.** Appearing or happening before the usual or expected time: *We had an early spring this year.* **4.** Happening in the near future: *Lawyers predict an early end to the trial.* —*adv.* **ear•lier, ear•liest. 1.** Near the beginning of a period of time or course of events: *The hikers set out early in the morning.* **2.** Before the usual or expected time: *arrive early.* **3.** Far back in time; long ago: *The Greek islands were settled as early as 5000* B.C. [First written down about 950 in Old English and spelled *ǣrlīce.*] —**ear′li•ness** *n.*

early bird *n. Informal.* A person who wakes up, arrives, or starts being active before most others.

ear•mark (îr′märk′) *n.* **1.** A notch or mark made on the ear of an animal to show that it belongs to a particular person: *The ranchers find their cattle by their earmarks.* **2.** A special quality or mark that sets a person or thing apart: *Careful observation is one of the earmarks of a good scientist.* —*tr.v.* **ear•marked, ear•mark•ing, ear•marks. 1.** To mark the ear of (an animal) for identification: *The ranchers earmarked their sheep.* **2.** To set aside for some purpose: *We earmarked part of the prize money for a new car.*

ear•muff (îr′mŭf′) *n.* One of a pair of protective coverings for the ears, often attached to an adjustable headband.

earn (ûrn) *tr.v.* **earned, earn•ing, earns. 1.** To get by working or by supplying a product or service: *earn money by mowing lawns.* **2.** To deserve or win by one's efforts or actions: *earn a reputation for being very thoughtful.* **3.** To produce as income or profit: *A savings account earns interest on your money.* [First written down before 899 in Old English and spelled *earnian.*] —**earn′er** *n.*

❑ *These sound alike:* **earn, urn** (container).

ear•nest[1] (ûr′nĭst) *adj.* Showing or expressing sincerity or seriousness: *an earnest offer to help.* —***idiom.*** **in earnest.** With serious purpose or intent: *After a slow start, we began working on the play in earnest.* [First written down about 1000 in Old

Usage: each

When the subject of a sentence begins with **each**, the verb and following pronouns must be singular: *Each of the suites has its own bath.* When **each** follows a plural subject, however, the verb and pronouns remain in the plural: *The suites each have their own baths.*

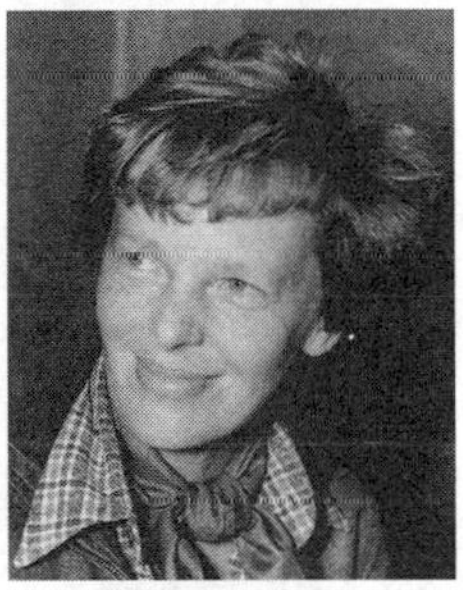
Amelia Earhart

Amelia Earhart

Amelia **Earhart** advanced early aviation greatly, and she also served as a role model for women, encouraging them to become leaders and to have careers of their own. In 1932 Earhart became the first woman to cross the Atlantic Ocean in a solo flight, setting a record for time. She went on in 1935 to pilot the first solo flight from Honolulu, Hawaii, to California, and the first nonstop flight from Mexico City, Mexico, to Newark, New Jersey. In an attempted round-the-world flight in 1937, Amelia Earhart's airplane disappeared over the Pacific Ocean and was never found.

earphone

easel

Easter Island
Massive carved figures on Easter Island

eaves

English and spelled *eornoste.*] **—ear′nest•ly** *adv.* **—ear′nest•ness** *n.*

ear•nest² (ûr′nĭst) *n.* Something, especially money, given or offered as a pledge for the rest to come. [First written down about 1200 in Middle English and spelled *ernesse,* from Old French *erres,* pledges, from Latin *arra,* pledge, from Greek *arrabōn,* earnest-money, from Hebrew *'ērābôn.*]

earn•ings (ûr′nĭngz) *pl.n.* **1.** Money earned for work; wages. **2.** Profits, as from a business or an investment.

ear•phone (îr′fōn′) *n.* A receiver for a radio, television, or telephone that is worn over or in the ear.

ear•ring (îr′rĭng *or* îr′ĭng) *n.* A piece of jewelry worn on or hanging from the earlobe.

ear•shot (îr′shŏt′) *n.* The range or distance within which sound can be heard: *Their shouts were not within earshot and went unnoticed.*

ear•split•ting (îr′splĭt′ĭng) *adj.* Loud enough to hurt the ears; deafening.

earth (ûrth) *n.* **1.** Often **Earth.** The planet on which human beings live, the third planet from the sun at a mean distance of 93 million miles (149 million kilometers), and the fifth largest in the solar system with a mean radius of 3,959 miles (6,374 kilometers). **2.** Dry land; the ground: *snowflakes falling to the earth.* **3.** Dirt; soil: *seeds sprouting in the moist earth.* **4.** All of the human inhabitants of the world: *The earth rejoiced at the news of peace.* [First written down about 725 in Old English and spelled *eorthe.*]

earth•en (ûr′thən) *adj.* Made of earth or clay: *the earthen floor of a cabin; an earthen pot.*

earth•en•ware (ûr′thən wâr′) *n.* Pottery made from a porous clay that is fired at relatively low temperatures. Delft is an example of earthenware.

earth•ling (ûrth′lĭng) *n.* A person who lives on the earth; a human being.

earth•ly (ûrth′lē) *adj.* **1.** Of or relating to the earth rather than heaven: *the everyday earthly business of earning a living.* **2.** Possible; imaginable: *a remark with no earthly meaning.* **—earth′li•ness** *n.*

earth•quake (ûrth′kwāk′) *n.* A sudden movement of the earth's crust, followed by a series of shocks. Earthquakes are caused by volcanic action or by the release of built-up stress within the rocks along geologic faults.

earth science *n.* Any of several sciences, such as geology or meteorology, concerned with the origin, composition, and physical features of the earth.

earth•ward (ûrth′wərd) *adv.* & *adj.* To or toward the earth: *snowflakes drifting earthward.* **—earth′wards** *adv.*

earth•work (ûrth′wûrk′) *n.* An earthen bank or wall used as a fortification.

earth•worm (ûrth′wûrm′) *n.* Any of various common worms that have a segmented body and burrow in soil; an angleworm.

earth•y (ûr′thē) *adj.* **earth•i•er, earth•i•est. 1.** Of or resembling earth or soil: *the earthy smell of the woods after rain.* **2.** Hearty; natural: *an earthy enjoyment of life.* **3.** Crude; indecent: *earthy humor.* **—earth′i•ness** *n.*

ear•wig (îr′wĭg′) *n.* Any of various insects having a pair of movable pincers protruding from the rear of the body.

ease (ēz) *n.* **1.** Freedom from difficulty, strain, or great effort: *I solved the problem with ease.* **2.** Freedom from pain or worry: *Her mind was at ease, knowing the children had returned safely.* **3.** Freedom from awkwardness or embarrassment; naturalness: *She spoke before the crowd with ease.* —*v.* **eased, eas•ing, eas•es.** —*tr.* **1.** To free from pain, worry, or agitation: *Knowing she was not offended eased his conscience.* **2.** To make less troublesome or difficult: *The school eased its entrance requirements.* **3.** To lessen the discomfort or pain of; relieve: *The medicine eased the earache.* **4.** To cause to move slowly and carefully: *The captain eased the ship alongside the dock.* **5.** To reduce the pressure or strain of; loosen: *ease the dog's collar.* —*intr.* To relax; let up: *The tension eased when the angry customer left the store.* [First written down before 1200 in Middle English and spelled *eise,* from Old French *aise,* perhaps from Latin *adiacēns,* lying near.]

ea•sel (ē′zəl) *n.* An upright stand or rack used to display or support something, such as an artist's canvas. [First written down in 1634 in Modern English, from Dutch *ezel,* ass, from Latin *asellus,* diminutive of *asinus.*]

eas•i•ly (ē′zə lē) *adv.* **1.** In an easy manner; with ease: *Libraries are arranged so that you can find books easily.* **2.** Without doubt; surely: *That is easily the best book I have ever read.* **3.** Very likely: *If we beat their team, we could easily win the championship.*

east (ēst) *n.* **1.** The direction from which the sun is seen to rise, directly opposite west. **2.** Often **East.** A region or part of a country lying in the east. **3.** Often **East. a.** The eastern part of the earth, especially eastern Asia. **b.** The part of the United States along the Atlantic coast especially from Maine to Maryland. —*adj.* **1.** Of, in, or toward the east: *the east bank of the river; the east road to town.* **2.** From the east: *An east wind is blowing.* —*adv.* In, from, or toward the east: *a river flowing east.* [First written down about 725 in Old English and spelled *ēast.*]

east•bound (ēst′bound′) *adj.* Going toward the east: *an eastbound train.*

East Chi•na Sea (chī′nə). An arm of the western Pacific Ocean bounded by China, South Korea, Taiwan, and parts of Japan.

Eas•ter (ē′stər) *n.* A Christian feast commemorating the Resurrection of Jesus. In the Western Church it is held on the first Sunday following the full moon that occurs on or after March 21.

Easter Island. An island of Chile in the southern Pacific Ocean about 2,300 miles (3,701 kilometers) west of the mainland. Discovered by Dutch explorers on Easter Day, 1722, the island is famous for ancient ruins.

east•er•ly (ē′stər lē) *adj.* **1.** Situated toward the east: *the most easterly point of land; flying in an easterly direction.* **2.** Coming from the east: *easterly wind.* —*n., pl.* **east•er•lies.** A storm or wind from the east. **—east′er•ly** *adv.*

east•ern (ē′stərn) *adj.* **1.** Of, in, or toward the east: *eastern Europe; the eastern slope of a mountain.* **2.** From the east: *an eastern wind.* **3.** Often **Eastern. a.** Of, relating to, or characteristic of eastern regions or the East. **b.** Of, relating to, or characteristic of the part of the United States along the Atlantic coast: *the Eastern vote for President.*

Eastern Church *n.* The Eastern Orthodox Church.

east•ern•er also **East•ern•er** (ē′stər nər) *n.* A person who lives in or comes from the east, especially the eastern United States.

Eastern Hemisphere. The half of the earth including Europe, Africa, Asia, and Australia.

east•ern•most (ē′stərn mōst′) *adj.* Farthest east: *Maine is the easternmost state.*

Eastern Orthodox Church *n.* A group of churches, including the Greek Orthodox and the Russian Orthodox, that trace their origin to the early Christian Church established during the Byzantine Empire.

Eastern Standard Time *n.* Standard time in the fifth time zone west of Greenwich, England, used, for example, in the eastern United States.

Eas•ter•tide (ē′stər tīd′) *n.* The Easter season.

East Ger•ma•ny (jûr′mə nē). A former country of northern Europe on the Baltic Sea. It was formed in 1949 from part of Germany and unified with West Germany in October 1990.

East In•dies (ĭn′dēz). Indonesia. The term sometimes means all of Southeast Asia.

east•ward (ēst′wərd) *adv.* To or toward the east: *a river flowing eastward; the eastward flow of the current.* —*n.* A direction or region to the east: *the fields are located to the eastward.* —**east′wards** *adv.*

eas•y (ē′zē) *adj.* **eas•i•er, eas•i•est. 1.** Requiring little or no effort or trouble: *an easy task; handwriting that is easy to read.* **2.** Free from worry, strain, or pain: *an easy life.* **3.** Not forced, hurried, or strenuous: *within easy walking distance; an easy drive.* **4.** Relaxed; comfortable: *a natural easy manner; an easy smile.* **5.** Not strict or demanding; lenient: *Most teachers are easy on new students.* —*adv.* **1.** Without haste or worry: *Take it easy and you'll do a better job.* **2.** With little effort; easily: *Playing the banjo came easy to her.* **3.** Without much hardship: *He got off easy with only a small fine.* [First written down before 1200 in Middle English and spelled *aisie*, from Old French *aaisier*, to put at ease.] —**eas′i•ness** *n.*

Synonyms: easy, simple, effortless, smooth. These adjectives mean requiring little effort. **Easy** describes tasks that are not difficult: *It's easy to take care of a pet hamster.* **Simple** describes something that is easy because it is not complex: *The best party games have simple rules.* **Effortless** means seemingly easy because of the strength or skill applied: *The skater performed an effortless jump.* **Smooth** means free from difficulties or obstacles: *The road to success is hardly ever smooth.*

easy chair *n.* A large comfortable upholstered chair.

eas•y•go•ing (ē′zē gō′ĭng) *adj.* **1.** Relaxed; carefree: *an artist's easygoing life; an easygoing manner of speech.* **2.** Not hurried; leisurely: *an easygoing pace.*

eat (ēt) *v.* **ate** (āt), **eat•en** (ēt′n), **eat•ing, eats.** —*tr.* **1.** To take (solid food) into the body through the mouth: *Owls eat mice.* **2.** To wear away, corrode, or destroy by or as if by eating: *Rust has eaten away the iron pipes.* **3.** To make by eating: *Moths ate holes in the blanket.* —*intr.* **1.** To take food; have a meal: *They usually eat about seven o'clock.* **2.** To wear away; corrode: *Home improvements ate into their savings.* —***idiom.* eat up.** *Slang.* To enjoy greatly; be greedy for: *The actor eats up compliments.* [First written down about 725 in Old English and spelled *etan*.] —**eat′er** *n.*

eat•a•ble (ē′tə bəl) *adj.* Fit for eating; edible. —*n.* **eatables.** Food.

eat•en (ēt′n) *v.* Past participle of **eat.**

eat•er•y (ē′tə rē) *n., pl.* **eat•er•ies.** *Informal.* A lunchroom; a diner.

eats (ēts) *pl.n. Slang.* Food, especially snacks.

eau de co•logne (ō′ də kə lōn′) *n., pl.* **eaux de co•logne** (ō′ də kə lōn′). A lightly perfumed cologne.

eaves (ēvz) *pl.n.* The part of a roof that forms the lower edge and projects beyond the walls. [First written down before 1000 in Old English and spelled *efes*.]

eaves•drop (ēvz′drŏp′) *intr.v.* **eaves•dropped, eaves•drop•ping, eaves•drops.** To listen secretly to the private conversation of others: *hid behind the door to eavesdrop.* —**eaves′drop′per** *n.* —SEE NOTE.

ebb (ĕb) *n.* **1.** Ebb tide. **2.** A period of decline: *The king's fortunes were at their lowest ebb.* —*intr.v.* **ebbed, ebb•ing, ebbs. 1.** To flow back; recede: *The flood waters began to ebb after the storm passed.* **2.** To fade or fall away; decline: *The hooked fish struggled less as its strength ebbed.* [First written down before 1000 in Old English and spelled *ebba*.]

ebb tide *n.* **1.** The tide flowing away from the shore. **2.** The period between high tide and low tide.

eb•on•ite (ĕb′ə nīt′) *n.* A hard black rubber made by heating rubber in the presence of large amounts of sulfur and used as an electrical insulator.

eb•on•y (ĕb′ə nē) *n., pl.* **eb•on•ies. 1.** The hard black or blackish wood of a tropical tree native to southern Asia, used especially for piano keys. **2.** The tree that yields such wood. —*adj.* **1.** Made of ebony: *an ebony cabinet.* **2.** Black: *ebony hair.* [First written down probably in 1384 in Middle English and spelled *hebenyf*, from Greek *ebenos*, ebony tree, of Egyptian origin.]

e•bul•lient (ĭ bo͝ol′yənt *or* ĭ bŭl′yənt) *adj.* Full of excitement, enthusiasm, or high spirits: *the ebullient feeling of victory.* —**e•bul′lient•ly** *adv.*

ec•cen•tric (ĭk sĕn′trĭk) *adj.* **1.** Odd or unusual in appearance, behavior, or manner; strange; peculiar: *an eccentric hat; an eccentric person; an eccentric habit.* **2.** Not perfectly circular; elliptical: *an eccentric orbit.* —*n.* A person who is odd or unusual in behavior. [First written down before 1430 in Middle English and spelled *eccentrik*, planetary orbit of which the earth is not at the center, from Greek *ekkentros*, not having the same center : *ek-*, out of, away + *kentron*, center.] —**ec•cen′tri•cal•ly** *adv.*

ec•cen•tric•i•ty (ĕk′sĕn trĭs′ĭ tē) *n., pl.* **ec•cen•tric•i•ties. 1.** The quality or condition of being eccentric: *the eccentricity of the moon's orbit.* **2.** An act or a habit that is odd or strange; a peculiarity. **3.** The amount or degree by which something is eccentric.

Ec•cle•si•as•tes (ĭ klē′zē ăs′tēz′) *n. (used with a singular verb).* A book of the Bible, traditionally believed to have been written by Solomon, that stresses the vanity of human wishes and achievements.

ec•cle•si•as•tic (ĭ klē′zē ăs′tĭk) *adj.* Ecclesiastical. —*n.* A member of the Christian clergy; a minister or priest.

ec•cle•si•as•ti•cal (ĭ klē′zē ăs′tĭ kəl) *adj.* Of or relating to a church: *ecclesiastical robes.* —**ec•cle′si•as′ti•cal•ly** *adv.*

ech•e•lon (ĕsh′ə lŏn′) *n.* **1.** A formation of military aircraft, naval vessels, or soldiers resembling a series of steps. **2.** A level of command or authority: *The President and Cabinet officers are among the highest echelons of government.* [First written down in 1796 in Modern English, from Old French *eschelon*, rung of a ladder, from Latin *scālae*, steps.]

e•chid•na (ĭ kĭd′nə) *n.* Any of several burrowing egg-laying mammals of Australia, Tasmania, and New Guinea, having a spiny coat, a slender snout, and a sticky tongue for catching insects.

e•chi•no•derm (ĭ kī′nə dûrm′) *n.* Any of numerous sea animals, such as a starfish or sea urchin, that have a spiny hard outer covering and parts that radiate from a center.

ech•o (ĕk′ō) *n., pl.* **ech•oes. 1.** A repeated sound that is caused by the reflection of sound waves from a surface. **2.** A repetition or imitation of something: *New fashions in dress usually have echoes of earlier styles.* **3.** A reflected radio wave. Echoes of radio waves are the basis for radar. —*v.* **ech•oed, ech•o•ing, ech•oes.** —*tr.* **1.** To repeat (a sound) by an echo: *The canyon echoed their shouts.* **2.** To repeat or imitate: *She echoed our feelings in her statement to the board.* —*intr.* **1.** To be repeated by an echo: *The shouts echoed from the mountainside.* **2.** To resound with an echo; reverberate: *The long hallway echoed with many footsteps.* [First written

Word History: eavesdrop

The edge of the roof of a building that overhangs the side of the building is the **eaves**, and an **eavesdrop** is the space on the ground below the eaves where the rainwater falls from the eaves. The verb *eavesdrop* originally meant "to stand in the *eavesdrop* next to the side of a building by a window to listen secretly to a conversation inside." Now we can *eavesdrop* anywhere.

echelon

echidna

ă	**pat**	oi	**boy**
ā	**pay**	ou	**out**
âr	**care**	o͝o	**took**
ä	**father**	o͞o	**boot**
ĕ	**pet**	ŭ	**cut**
ē	**be**	ûr	**urge**
ĭ	**pit**	th	**thin**
ī	**pie**	*th*	**this**
îr	**pier**	hw	**whoop**
ŏ	**pot**	zh	**vision**
ō	**toe**	ə	**about**
ô	**paw**	N	*French* **bon**

eclipse
Solar eclipse

edelweiss

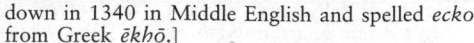

down in 1340 in Middle English and spelled *ecko*, from Greek *ēkhō*.]

Ech•o (ĕk′ō) *n.* In Greek mythology, a nymph whose love for Narcissus is not returned by him, causing her to pine away until nothing but her voice remains.

e•cho•ic (ĕ kō′ĭk) *adj.* Of or resembling an echo.

é•clair (ā klâr′ *or* ā′klâr′) *n.* An oblong pastry filled with custard or whipped cream and usually iced with chocolate.

e•clec•tic (ĭ klĕk′tĭk) *adj.* Choosing or taking what appears to be the best from various sources: *an eclectic painter blending elements of realism and abstract art.* —*n.* A person whose opinions and beliefs are drawn from several sources. [First written down in 1683 in Modern English, from Greek *eklektikos*, selective, from *eklegein*, to select : *ek-*, out + *legein*, to gather.] **—e•clec′ti•cal•ly** *adv.*

e•clipse (ĭ klĭps′) *n.* **1.** The partial or total blocking of light from one celestial body as it passes behind or through the shadow of another celestial body. In a solar eclipse the moon comes between the sun and the earth. In a lunar eclipse the moon enters the earth's shadow. **2.** A decline in importance, use, or fame: *The singer's popularity has suffered an eclipse since her retirement.* —*tr.v.* **e•clipsed, e•clips•ing, e•clips•es. 1.** To cause an eclipse of: *When the moon eclipsed the sun it caused partial darkness.* **2.** To obscure or overshadow in importance, fame, or reputation; surpass: *The war eclipsed all other news for a while.* [First written down about 1280 in Middle English, from Greek *ekleipsis*, from *ekleipein*, to fail to appear : *ek-*, out + *leipein*, to leave.]

e•clip•tic (ĭ klĭp′tĭk) *n.* The apparent path of the sun among the stars in one year. The ecliptic is the great circle of the celestial sphere which is cut by the plane containing the orbit of the earth.

e•col•o•gist (ĭ kŏl′ə jĭst) *n.* A scientist who specializes in ecology.

e•col•o•gy (ĭ kŏl′ə jē) *n., pl.* **e•col•o•gies. 1.** The branch of biology that studies the relationships between living things and their environments. **2.** The relationship between living things and their environments. [First written down in 1858 in Modern English, from German *Ökologie* : Greek *oikos*, house + Greek *-logia*, study, science.] **—ec′o•log′i•cal** (ĕk′ə lŏj′ĭ kəl *or* ē′kə lŏj′ĭ kəl) *adj.* **—ec′o•log′i•cal•ly** *adv.*

ec•o•nom•ic (ĕk′ə nŏm′ĭk *or* ē′kə nŏm′ĭk) *adj.* **1.** Of or relating to the production, development, and management of wealth, as of a country, household, or business: *A government's economic policy is supposed to foster new businesses.* **2.** Of or relating to the science of economics: *economic theories of how money works in society.*

ec•o•nom•i•cal (ĕk′ə nŏm′ĭ kəl *or* ē′kə nŏm′ĭ kəl) *adj.* Not wasteful or extravagant; prudent and thrifty: *an economical use of time; an economical way to produce better crops.* **—ec′o•nom′i•cal•ly** *adv.*

ec•o•nom•ics (ĕk′ə nŏm′ĭks *or* ē′kə nŏm′ĭks) *n.* **1.** *(used with a singular verb).* The science that deals with the ways in which goods and services are produced, transported, sold, and used. Economics also deals with the effects of taxes and the distribution of money within an economy. **2.** *(used with a singular or plural verb).* Economic matters, especially those relating to cost and profit: *the economics of running a store.*

e•con•o•mist (ĭ kŏn′ə mĭst) *n.* A person who specializes in economics.

e•con•o•mize (ĭ kŏn′ə mīz′) *v.* **e•con•o•mized, e•con•o•miz•ing, e•con•o•miz•es.** —*intr.* To be thrifty; reduce expenses or avoid waste: *economize by bringing your own lunch to work.* —*tr.* To use or manage with thrift: *economize your time to get more done.*

e•con•o•my (ĭ kŏn′ə mē) *n., pl.* **e•con•o•mies. 1.** The careful use or management of resources, such as money, materials, or labor: *practice economy in running the household.* **2.** An example or a result of this; a saving: *the economy of using public transportation.* **3.** The economic system of a country, region, or state: *The rise in housing prices boosted the city's economy.* **4.** A specific kind of economic system: *an industrial economy.* [First written down in 1440 in Middle English and spelled *yconomye*, management of a household, from Greek *oikonomia* : *oikos*, house + *nemein*, to allot, manage.]

ec•o•sys•tem (ĕk′ō sĭs′təm *or* ē′kō sĭs′təm) *n.* An ecological community, including plants, animals, and microorganisms, considered together with their environment: *A pond is an example of a complex ecosystem.*

ec•ru (ĕk′rōō *or* ā′krōō) *n.* A pale yellowish-brown color.

ec•sta•sy (ĕk′stə sē) *n., pl.* **ec•sta•sies.** Intense joy or delight: *After years of practice the runner was in ecstasy over winning an Olympic medal.*

ec•stat•ic (ĕk stăt′ĭk) *adj.* **1.** Marked by or expressing intense joy or delight: *the ecstatic final movement of the symphony.* **2.** In a state of ecstasy; enraptured: *I was ecstatic over the chance to go to Europe.* **—ec•stat′i•cal•ly** *adv.*

ecto– *pref.* A prefix that means outer or external: *ectoderm.*

ec•to•derm (ĕk′tə dûrm′) *n.* The outer cell layer of an early embryo that develops into the outer skin, hair, nails, and parts of the nervous system.

ec•to•plasm (ĕk′tə plăz′əm) *n.* The outer portion of the cytoplasm of a cell.

Ec•ua•dor (ĕk′wə dôr′). A country of northwest South America on the Pacific Ocean south of Colombia. The area was liberated from Spain in 1822 and formally separated from Colombia in 1830. Quito is the capital and Guayaquil the largest city. Population, 8,050,630.

ec•u•men•i•cal (ĕk′yə mĕn′ĭ kəl) *adj.* **1.** Of or relating to the worldwide Christian church: *an ecumenical council.* **2.** Worldwide in range or relevance; universal: *an ecumenical view of environmental planning.* **—ec′u•men′i•cal•ly** *adv.*

ec•ze•ma (ĕk′sə mə *or* ĕg′zə mə) *n.* An inflammation of the skin, marked by redness, itching, and the formation of sores that discharge fluid and become crusted and scaly.

ed. *abbr.* An abbreviation of: **1.** Edition. **2.** Editor. **3.** Edited. **4.** Education.

–ed[1] *suff.* A suffix that forms the past tense of regular verbs: *cared; carried.*

–ed[2] *suff.* A suffix that forms the past participle of regular verbs: *ended; expected.*

–ed[3] *suff.* A suffix that means having, characterized by, or resembling: *hardhearted; wretched.*

E•dam (ē′dəm *or* ē′dăm′) *n.* A mild yellow Dutch cheese, pressed into balls and usually covered with red paraffin.

ed•dy (ĕd′ē) *n., pl.* **ed•dies.** A current, as of water or air, that moves opposite to the direction of a main current, especially in a circular motion. —*intr. v.* **ed•died, ed•dy•ing, ed•dies.** To move in or as if in an eddy: *wisps of mist eddying through the valley.*

Ed•dy (ĕd′ē), **Mary (Morse) Baker.** 1821–1910. American religious leader who founded Christian Science (1879) and the *Christian Science Monitor* (1908), a daily newspaper.

e•del•weiss (ā′dəl vīs′ *or* ā′dəl wīs′) *n.* A small plant native to high mountain areas of Europe, having small yellow flowers surrounded by whitish downy leaves.

e•de•ma (ĭ dē′mə) *n.* A diseased condition in which an excess of fluid collects in bodily tissue and causes swelling.

E•den (ēd′n) *n.* **1.** In the Bible, the garden that was the first home of Adam and Eve. **2.** A delightful place; a paradise.

edge (ĕj) *n.* **1.** The thin sharpened side of a blade: *the edge of a knife.* **2.** The line or point where two surfaces meet: *the edge of a table.* **3.a.** A dividing line; a border: *a house on the edge of town.* See Synonyms at **margin. b.** The area or part farthest from the middle: *the edge of the carpet.* **4.** An advantage: *We had a slight edge over the other team.* —*v.* **edged, edg•ing, edg•es.** —*tr.* **1.** To give an edge to; sharpen. **2.** To be the edge of: *Flowers edged the lawn.* **3.** To put a border or an edge on: *edge a sleeve with lace.* **4.** To advance or move gradually; push: *The photographers edged their way through the crowd.* —*intr.* To move gradually: *The child edged slowly toward the door.* ***—idioms.*** **edge out.** To surpass or beat by a small margin. **on edge.** Tense or nervous; irritable: *He was on edge from listening to the baby cry.* [First written down about 725 in Old English and spelled *ecg.*]

edge•wise (ĕj′wīz′) also **edge•ways** (ĕj′wāz′) *adv.* **1.** With the edge forward: *Turn the table edgewise to get it through the door.* **2.** On, by, with, or toward the edge: *The cricket moved edgewise along the side of the box.* ***—idiom.*** **get a word in edgewise.** To manage to say something in a conversation dominated by another person: *The others talked so much I couldn't get a word in edgewise.*

edg•ing (ĕj′ĭng) *n.* Something that forms an edge or a border: *an edging of bricks along the path.*

edg•y (ĕj′ē) *adj.* **edg•i•er, edg•i•est.** Nervous or irritable: *We got edgy waiting for the concert to begin.* —**edg′i•ness** *n.*

ed•i•ble (ĕd′ə bəl) *adj.* Fit to be eaten: *The spoiled cheese was no longer edible.* —*n.* Something to be eaten; food. [First written down in 1611 in Modern English, from Late Latin *edibilis,* from Latin *edere,* to eat.]

e•dict (ē′dĭkt′) *n.* An order or a decree issued by a person in authority. [First written down in 1483 in Middle English, from Latin *ēdictum,* from past participle of *ēdīcere,* to declare : *ē-, ex-,* out + *dīcere,* to speak.]

ed•i•fi•ca•tion (ĕd′ə fĭ kā′shən) *n.* Intellectual, moral, or spiritual improvement; enlightenment: *She wrote the book for the edification of the people.*

ed•i•fice (ĕd′ə fĭs) *n.* A building, especially one that is very imposing in size or appearance.

ed•i•fy (ĕd′ə fī′) *tr.v.* **ed•i•fied, ed•i•fy•ing, ed•i•fies.** To instruct so as to encourage intellectual, moral, or spiritual improvement: *His poems are intended to edify young readers.*

Ed•in•burgh (ĕd′n bûr′ə *or* ĕd′n bŭr′ə). The capital of Scotland, in the eastern part of the country on an inlet of the North Sea. The city is the site of a yearly international festival of the arts. Population, 446,361.

Ed•i•son (ĕd′ĭ sən), **Thomas Alva.** 1847–1931. American inventor who patented many inventions, including the microphone (1877) and a light bulb (1879).

ed•it (ĕd′ĭt) *tr.v.* **ed•it•ed, ed•it•ing, ed•its. 1.** To make (written material) ready for publication by correcting, revising, or marking directions for a printer: *The staff edited reporters' stories for publication in the newspaper.* **2.** To supervise and be responsible for the publication of (a newspaper or magazine): *That scholar edits a literary magazine.* **3.** To put together or cut out parts of (a motion picture, videotape, or musical recording): *We edited our videotape of the wedding down to a 30-minute show.*

edit. *abbr.* An abbreviation of: **1.** Edition. **2.** Editor.

e•di•tion (ĭ dĭsh′ən) *n.* **1.a.** The entire number of copies of a book or newspaper printed at one time and having the same content: *today's edition of the newspaper.* **b.** A single copy from such a number: *I bought this month's edition of the magazine.* **2.** Any of the various forms in which a publication is issued: *a paperback edition of a novel.*

ed•i•tor (ĕd′ĭ tər) *n.* **1.** A person who edits written material for publication. **2.** A person who prepares a motion picture, videotape, or musical recording for viewing or hearing by assembling its parts. **3.** A person who directs the writing and layout of a newspaper or magazine or supervises one of its departments. [First written down in 1649 in Modern English, from Late Latin *ēditor,* publisher, from *ēdere,* to publish : *ē-, ex-,* out + *dare,* to give.]

ed•i•to•ri•al (ĕd′ĭ tôr′ē əl) *n.* **1.** An article in a newspaper or magazine expressing the opinions of its editors or publisher. **2.** A commentary on television or radio expressing the opinion of the owners. —*adj.* **1.** Of or relating to an editor or editing: *an editorial position in a publishing company.* **2.** Expressing opinion rather than reporting news: *the editorial page of the newspaper.* —**ed′i•to′ri•al•ly** *adv.*

ed•i•to•ri•al•ize (ĕd′ĭ tôr′ē ə līz′) *intr.v.* **ed•i•to•ri•al•ized, ed•i•to•ri•al•iz•ing, ed•i•to•ri•al•iz•es. 1.** To express an opinion in or as if in an editorial: *Most newspapers editorialize in each issue.* **2.** To express an opinion or opinions in what is supposed to be a report of facts: *The author feels so strongly about the issue, he cannot keep himself from editorializing.*

ed•i•tor•ship (ĕd′ĭ tər shĭp′) *n.* The position, duties, or guidance of an editor.

Ed•mon•ton (ĕd′mən tən). The capital and largest city of Alberta, Canada, in the central part of the province north of Calgary. It was founded in 1795. Population, 532,246.

ed•u•ca•ble (ĕj′ə kə bəl) *adj.* Capable of being educated.

ed•u•cate (ĕj′ə kāt′) *v.* **ed•u•cat•ed, ed•u•cat•ing, ed•u•cates.** —*tr.* To provide with knowledge or training, especially through formal schooling; teach. See Synonyms at **teach.** —*intr.* To provide instructions and training: *Their purpose is to educate through the use of visual aids.* [First written down in 1447 in Middle English and spelled *educaten,* from Latin *ēducāre* : *ē-, ex-,* out + *dūcere,* to lead.]

ed•u•cat•ed (ĕj′ə kā′tĭd) *adj.* **1.** Having an education, especially one above the average: *Librarians are educated people.* **2.** Showing evidence of schooling; cultured; refined: *an educated taste for books and learning.* **3.** Based on experience or factual knowledge: *an educated guess.*

ed•u•ca•tion (ĕj′ə kā′shən) *n.* **1.a.** The process of imparting or obtaining knowledge or skill: *Many people want to continue their education after high school.* **b.** The knowledge or skill obtained by such a process; learning: *It takes a lot of education to be an engineer.* **2.** A program of instruction of a specified kind or level: *a college education.* **3.** The field of study that is concerned with teaching and learning: *Many teachers are graduates of schools of education.*

ed•u•ca•tion•al (ĕj′ə kā′shə nəl) *adj.* **1.** Of or relating to education: *educational standards.* **2.** Serving to give knowledge or skill; instructive: *educational television.* —**ed′u•ca′tion•al•ly** *adv.*

ed•u•ca•tor (ĕj′ə kā′tər) *n.* **1.** A person who is

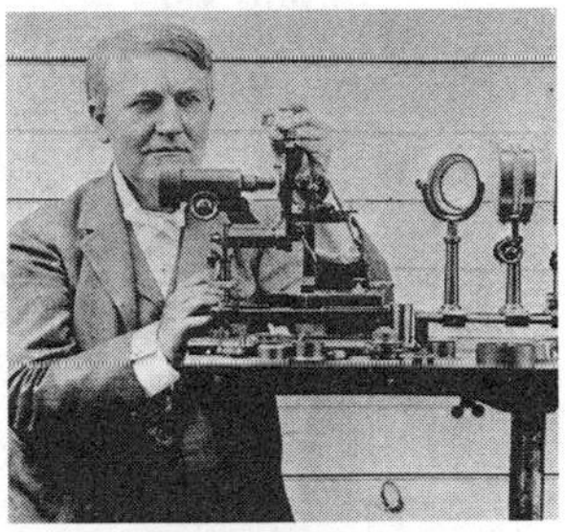

Thomas Edison
Photographed in 1893

ă	pat	oi	boy
ā	pay	ou	out
âr	care	ŏŏ	took
ä	father	ōō	boot
ĕ	pet	ŭ	cut
ē	be	ûr	urge
ĭ	pit	th	thin
ī	pie	*th*	this
îr	pier	hw	whoop
ŏ	pot	zh	vision
ō	toe	ə	about
ô	paw	N	*French* bon

Edward VIII
Photographed while Duke of Windsor

eggplant

trained in teaching; a teacher. **2.** A specialist in the theory and practice of education.

e•duce (ĭ **do͞os′** *or* ĭ **dyo͞os′**) *tr.v.* **e•duced, e•duc•ing, e•duc•es.** To draw or bring out; elicit: *By clever questions the judge educed the facts of the case from the witnesses.* **—e•duc′i•ble** *adj.*

Ed•ward VII (**ĕd′**wərd). 1841–1910. King of Great Britain and Ireland (1901–1910) who improved Britain's international relations.

Edward VIII. Later known as Duke of Windsor. 1894–1972. King of Great Britain and Ireland (1936) who gave up the throne in order to marry Wallis Simpson, an American divorcée.

–ee *suff.* A suffix that means: **1.** A person who receives or benefits from an action: *appointee; trainee.* **2.** A person or an animal that performs an action: *absentee; escapee.* **3.** A person who possesses something: *grantee.*

eel (ēl) *n., pl.* **eel** or **eels.** Any of various long slippery fishes that lack scales and resemble snakes. [First written down about 1000 in Old English and spelled *ǣl.*]

e'en¹ (ēn) *n.* Evening.

e'en² (ēn) *adv.* Even.

–eer *suff.* A suffix that means a person who is associated with or involved in: *auctioneer; racketeer.*

e'er (âr) *adv.* Ever.

❑ *These sound alike:* **e'er, air** (gas), **ere** (before), **heir** (inheritor).

ee•rie or **ee•ry** (**îr′**ē) *adj.* **ee•ri•er, ee•ri•est.** Inspiring fear without a clear reason; strange and frightening: *The eerie old house made us feel uneasy.* [First written down before 1325 in Middle English and spelled *eri*, fearful, from Old English *earg*, cowardly.] **—ee′ri•ly** *adv.* **—ee′ri•ness** *n.*

ef•face (ĭ **fās′**) *tr.v.* **ef•faced, ef•fac•ing, ef•fac•es.** To remove by or as if by rubbing out; erase: *The name on the gravestone had been effaced by time.* **—ef•face′ment** *n.* **—ef•fac′er** *n.*

ef•fect (ĭ **fĕkt′**) *n.* **1.** Something brought about by a cause or an agent; a result: *The effect of advertising should be an increase in sales.* **2.** The power to bring about a result; influence: *The new regulation had no effect on improving air quality.* **3.a.** An artistic technique that produces a specific impression: *Thunder and lightning and other special effects can be used in making a movie.* **b.** The impression produced by some artistic technique: *A light and lively musical passage was meant to create the effect of spring.* **4. effects.** Movable belongings; goods. *—tr.v.* **ef•fect•ed, ef•fect•ing, ef•fects.** To produce as a result; cause to occur: *New technologies have effected many changes in the way people live.* ***—idiom.*** **in effect. 1.** In essence; actually: *By turning off the lights they were in effect telling us to go home.* **2.** In active force: *The new law is now in effect.* [First written down about 1350 in Middle English, from Latin *effectus*, past participle of *efficere*, to accomplish : *ex-*, out + *facere*, to make.] —See Note at **affect¹.**

ef•fec•tive (ĭ **fĕk′**tĭv) *adj.* **1.** Having an intended or expected effect: *a vaccine effective against polio.* **2.** Operative; in effect: *The law will be effective as soon as the governor signs it.* **3.** Producing a strong impression or response: *The President made an effective speech that united the country behind him.* **—ef•fec′tive•ly** *adv.* **—ef•fec′tive•ness** *n.*

ef•fec•tu•al (ĭ **fĕk′**cho͞o əl) *adj.* Producing or sufficient to produce a desired effect; fully adequate: *Practice is the only effectual method of learning to play a musical instrument.* **—ef•fec′tu•al•ly** *adv.* **—ef•fec′tu•al•ness** *n.*

ef•fec•tu•ate (ĭ **fĕk′**cho͞o āt′) *tr.v.* **ef•fec•tu•at•ed, ef•fec•tu•at•ing, ef•fec•tu•ates.** To bring about; effect: *effectuate a change in the rule.*

ef•fem•i•nate (ĭ **fĕm′**ə nĭt) *adj.* Having qualities associated with women rather than men. **—ef•fem′i•na•cy** (ĭ **fĕm′**ə nə sē), **ef•fem′i•nate•ness** *n.* **—ef•fem′i•nate•ly** *adv.*

ef•fer•ent (**ĕf′**ər ənt) *adj.* Directed away from a central organ or point: *Efferent nerves carry impulses from the brain to the muscles.*

ef•fer•vesce (ĕf′ər **vĕs′**) *intr.v.* **ef•fer•vesced, ef•fer•vesc•ing, ef•fer•vesc•es. 1.** To give off bubbles of gas, as a carbonated liquid. **2.** To show high spirits; be lively. [First written down in 1702 in Modern English, from Latin *effervēscere* : *ex-*, up, out + *fervēscere*, to start boiling.] **—ef′fer•ves′cent** *adj.*

ef•fer•ves•cence (ĕf′ər **vĕs′**əns) *n.* **1.** The process of giving off small bubbles of gas: *the effervescence of soda water.* **2.** Sparkling high spirits; vivacity.

ef•fete (ĭ **fēt′**) *adj.* Having lost vitality, strength, or effectiveness: *an effete period of a once great civilization.* **—ef•fete′ly** *adv.* **—ef•fete′ness** *n.*

ef•fi•ca•cious (ĕf′ĭ **kā′**shəs) *adj.* Producing or capable of producing the desired effect; effective: *an efficacious treatment of a disease.* **—ef′fi•ca′cious•ly** *adv.* **—ef′fi•ca′cious•ness** *n.*

ef•fi•ca•cy (**ĕf′**ĭ kə sē) *n.* Power or capacity to produce a desired effect; effectiveness: *The efficacy of most medicines declines over time.*

ef•fi•cien•cy (ĭ **fĭsh′**ən sē) *n., pl.* **ef•fi•cien•cies. 1.** The condition or quality of being efficient: *Tired people can't work with efficiency.* **2.** The ratio of the useful work a machine does to the energy required to operate it.

efficiency apartment *n.* A small apartment, usually with cooking facilities and room for one or two persons.

ef•fi•cient (ĭ **fĭsh′**ənt) *adj.* Acting or producing effectively with a minimum of waste, expense, or effort: *an efficient worker; an efficient motor.* [First written down about 1380 in Middle English, from Latin *efficere*, to effect.] **—ef•fi′cient•ly** *adv.*

ef•fi•gy (**ĕf′**ə jē) *n., pl.* **ef•fi•gies. 1.** A crude figure or dummy of a hated person. **2.** A likeness or sculpture of a person: *a stone effigy on a tomb.* ***—idiom.*** **in effigy.** In the form of an effigy: *The colonists burned King George in effigy.*

ef•flo•res•cence (ĕf′lə **rĕs′**əns) *n.* **1.** The state or period of a blossoming or flowering. **2.** A growth of salt crystals on a surface caused by the evaporation of salt water. **3.** A rash or sore on the skin. **—ef′flo•res′cent** *adj.*

ef•flu•ent (**ĕf′**lo͞o ənt) *adj.* Flowing out or forth. *—n.* **1.** Something that flows out or forth, such as a stream that flows from a lake. **2.** The liquid waste or sewage that flows from a factory, water purification plant, or other system: *Effluent from the mill flowed directly into the stream, polluting it.* [First written down in 1440 in Middle English, from Latin *effluere*, to flow out : *ex-*, out + *fluere*, to flow.]

ef•fort (**ĕf′**ərt) *n.* **1.** The use of physical or mental energy to do something; exertion: *It took a lot of effort to edit this book.* **2.** An attempt, especially an earnest attempt: *We made an effort to arrive on time.* **3.** Something done or produced through exertion; an achievement: *This painting is the artist's best and latest effort.* [First written down about 1480 in Middle English, from Old French *esfort*, from Medieval Latin *exfortiāre*, to force, exert : Latin *ex-*, out + Latin *fortis*, strong.]

ef•fort•less (**ĕf′**ərt lĭs) *adj.* Requiring or showing little or no effort: *Watching TV is an effortless activity. The skater glided in effortless turns around the ice.* See Synonyms at **easy. —ef′fort•less•ly** *adv.* **—ef′fort•less•ness** *n.*

ef•front•er•y (ĭ **frŭn′**tə rē) *n., pl.* **ef•front•er•ies.** Shameless or insulting boldness; audacity: *In spite* *of making several rude remarks they had the effrontery to ask for our help.*

ef•ful•gent (ĭ fo͝ol′jənt *or* ĭ fŭl′jənt) *adj.* Shining brilliantly; radiant. **—ef•ful′gence** *n.* **—ef•ful′gent•ly** *adv.*

ef•fu•sion (ĭ fyo͞o′zhən) *n.* **1.** An outpouring, as of fluid: *The effusion of blood was stopped by a compress.* **2.** An unrestrained outpouring of feeling, as in speech or writing: *Such an effusion of praise embarrassed me.*

ef•fu•sive (ĭ fyo͞o′sĭv) *adj.* Unrestrained or excessive in emotional expression; gushy: *an effusive display of gratitude.* **—ef•fu′sive•ly** *adv.* **—ef•fu′sive•ness** *n.*

eft (ĕft) *n.* A newt, especially one in an immature stage that lives on land.

e.g. *abbr.* An abbreviation of exempli gratia (for the sake of example).

egg[1] (ĕg) *n.* **1.** A female sex cell of humans and many kinds of animals from which an embryo develops. In animals such as birds, turtles, frogs, fish, and insects, an egg contains nourishment for the developing embryo and may have a protective shell or covering. **2.** A hard-shelled egg, the contents of which are used for food, especially a chicken egg: *Scrambled eggs are a favorite of mine.* **3.** *Informal.* A person: *What a good egg!* [First written down about 1340 in Middle English and spelled *eg*, bird's egg, from Old Norse *egg*.]

egg[2] (ĕg) *tr.v.* **egged, egg•ing, eggs.** To encourage or urge: *If my best friend hadn't egged me on, I never would have tried to ski down that hill.* [First written down before 1200 in Middle English and spelled *eggen*, from Old Norse *eggja*.]

egg•beat•er (ĕg′bē′tər) *n.* A kitchen utensil with rotating blades for beating eggs, whipping cream, or mixing ingredients together.

egg cell *n.* A female reproductive cell; an ovum.

egg•head (ĕg′hĕd′) *n.* *Informal.* An intellectual.

egg•nog (ĕg′nŏg′) *n.* A drink of milk and beaten eggs, often mixed with an alcoholic liquor such as rum or brandy.

egg•plant (ĕg′plănt′) *n.* **1.** The large egg-shaped fruit of a bushy plant, usually having a purple skin and eaten as a vegetable. **2.** The plant that bears such fruit.

egg roll *n.* A casing of egg dough filled with minced vegetables, sometimes with seafood or meat, and fried.

egg•shell (ĕg′shĕl′) *n.* **1.** The thin hard outer covering of the egg of a bird or reptile. **2.** A light yellowish white.

egg white *n.* The albumen of an egg.

e•gis (ē′jĭs) *n.* Variant of **aegis.**

eg•lan•tine (ĕg′lən tīn′ *or* ĕg′lən tēn′) *n.* The sweetbrier.

e•go (ē′gō) *n., pl.* **e•gos. 1.** The awareness of oneself as separate and different from other things; the self. **2.** Egotism; conceit: *Self-important people are often full of ego.* **3.** Self-confidence; self-esteem: *A leader needs enough ego to take a lot of criticism.* [First written down in 1789 in Modern English, from Latin *ego*, I.]

e•go•cen•tric (ē′gō sĕn′trĭk) *adj.* Concerned only with oneself; self-centered: *An egocentric person usually does not work well in a group.*

e•go•ism (ē′gō ĭz′əm) *n.* **1.** The tendency to think or act with only one's own interests in mind; selfishness. **2.** Conceit; egotism. **—e′go•ist** *n.*

e•go•tism (ē′gə tĭz′əm) *n.* **1.** The tendency to talk about oneself too much. **2.** An exaggerated sense of one's own importance; conceit.

e•go•tist (ē′gə tĭst) *n.* **1.** A conceited boastful person. **2.** A selfish self-centered person.

e•go•tis•ti•cal (ē′gə tĭs′tĭ kəl) *adj.* Conceited, boastful, or self-centered. **—e′go•tis′ti•cal•ly** *adv.*

e•gre•gious (ĭ grē′jəs) *adj.* Outstandingly bad or offensive; outrageous; flagrant: *An egregious error in the computer program caused the spacecraft to fall out of orbit.* **—e•gre′gious•ly** *adv.* **—e•gre′gious•ness** *n.*

e•gress (ē′grĕs′) *n.* **1.** A path or means of going out; an exit: *When fire blocked the doorway there was no egress from the building.* **2.** The right to go out: *The guard denied them egress.* **3.** The act of going out.

e•gret (ē′grĭt *or* ĕg′rĭt) *n.* Any of several wading birds having a long neck, a pointed bill, and usually white feathers. Many egrets have long drooping plumes during the breeding season. [First written down about 1353 in Middle English, from Old French *aigrette*, from Old Provençal *aigron*, heron, of Germanic origin.]

E•gypt (ē′jĭpt). A country of northeast Africa north of Sudan on the Mediterranean Sea. Ancient Egypt was the site of one of the earliest known civilizations. The country gained its independence from Great Britain in 1922. Cairo is the capital and the largest city. Population, 48,503,000.

E•gyp•tian (ĭ jĭp′shən) *n.* **1.** A native or inhabitant of Egypt. **2.** The extinct language of the ancient Egyptians. *—adj.* **1.** Of or relating to Egypt, the Egyptians, or their culture. **2.** Of or relating to the language of the ancient Egyptians.

eh (ā *or* ĕ) *interj.* An expression used in asking for agreement or confirmation: *That's not a bad looking car, eh?*

ei•der (ī′dər) *n.* **1.** Any of several large ducks of northern regions of the Atlantic and Pacific Oceans, having very soft downy feathers. **2.** Eiderdown.

ei•der•down (ī′dər doun′) *n.* **1.** The soft light down of the eider, used for stuffing coats, quilts, pillows, and sleeping bags. **2.** A quilt stuffed with this down.

eight (āt) *n.* **1.** The number, written 8, that is equal to 7 + 1. **2.** The eighth in a set or sequence. [First written down about 725 in Old English and spelled *eahta*.]

❑ *These sound alike:* **eight, ate** (eat).

eight•een (ā tēn′) *n.* **1.** The number, written 18, that is equal to 17 + 1. **2.** The 18th in a set or sequence.

eight•eenth (ā tēnth′) *n.* **1.** The ordinal number matching the number 18 in a series. **2.** One of 18 equal parts.

eighth (ātth *or* āth) *n.* **1.** The ordinal number matching the number eight in a series. **2.** One of eight equal parts.

eighth note *n.* A musical note having one eighth the time value of a whole note.

eight•i•eth (ā′tē ĭth) *n.* **1.** The ordinal number matching the number 80 in a series. **2.** One of 80 equal parts.

eight•y (ā′tē) *n., pl.* **eight•ies.** The number, written 80, that is equal to 8 × 10.

Ein•stein (īn′stīn′), **Albert.** 1879–1955. German-born American scientist whose theories revolutionized modern thought on the nature of space and time. He won a 1921 Nobel Prize.

ein•stein•i•um (īn stī′nē əm) *n.* *Symbol* **Es** An unstable radioactive element, first discovered in the debris of a hydrogen bomb explosion and later produced by nuclear bombardment. It has 12 isotopes with mass numbers ranging from 245 to 256 and half-lives ranging from 1.2 minutes to 276 days. Atomic number 99. See table at **element.** [First written down in 1955 in Modern English, after Albert *Einstein*.]

Ei•sen•how•er (ī′zən hou′ər), **Dwight David.** Known as "Ike." 1890–1969. American general

egret
Snowy egret

Albert Einstein

Dwight D. Eisenhower
Photographed in 1956

ă	**pat**	oi	**boy**
ā	**pay**	ou	**out**
âr	**care**	o͝o	**took**
ä	**father**	o͞o	**boot**
ĕ	**pet**	ŭ	**cut**
ē	**be**	ûr	**urge**
ĭ	**pit**	th	**thin**
ī	**pie**	*th*	**this**
îr	**pier**	hw	**whoop**
ŏ	**pot**	zh	**vision**
ō	**toe**	ə	**about**
ô	**paw**	N	*French* **bon**

Usage: either

When used as a pronoun, **either** is singular and takes a singular verb: *You can take French or Spanish; either is a good choice.* This rule holds even when *either* is followed by *of* and a plural noun: *Either of the two languages is a good one to study.* In an *either . . . or* construction, you use the singular when the words used as the subject of a sentence are singular: *Either Jennifer or June chairs the meeting.* When the words are plural, the verb is plural: *Either the Montoyas or the Smiths throw a party every year.* It is best to avoid sentences in which *either* is followed by one singular and one plural.

eland

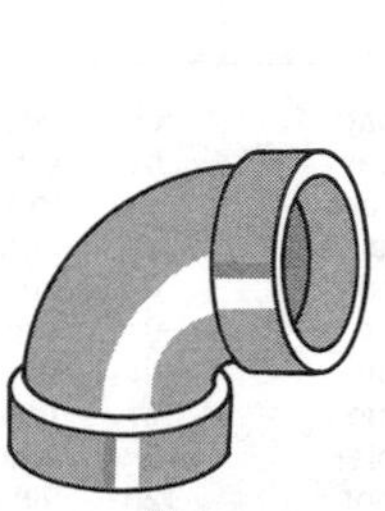
elbow
Pipe elbow

and the 34th President of the United States (1953–1961).

ei•ther (ē′thər *or* ī′thər) *pron.* One or the other of two: *It was a while before either of them spoke.* —*conj.* Used before the first of two or more words or groups of words linked by *or: Either we go now or we forget about going.* —*adj.* **1.** One or the other; any one of two: *Wear either coat.* **2.** One and the other; each of the two: *Candles stood on either end of the mantelpiece.* —*adv.* Any more than the other; likewise; also: *I didn't go to the movies, and my friends didn't either.* [First written down before 900 in Old English and spelled *ǣther*.] —SEE NOTE.

e•jac•u•late (ĭ jăk′yə lāt′) *tr.v.* **e•jac•u•lat•ed, e•jac•u•lat•ing, e•jac•u•lates. 1.** To discharge (semen). **2.** To utter suddenly and passionately; exclaim.

e•jac•u•la•tion (ĭ jăk′yə lā′shən) *n.* **1.** The act or process of ejaculating. **2.** A sudden utterance; an exclamation.

e•ject (ĭ jĕkt′) *tr.v.* **e•ject•ed, e•ject•ing, e•jects. 1.** To throw out; expel: *Active volcanoes eject hot ash and lava.* **2.** To drive out; force out: *The noisy people were ejected from the theater.* [First written down before 1425 in Middle English and spelled *ejecten*, from Latin *ēicere* : *ē-*, *ex-*, out + *iacere*, to throw.]

e•jec•tion (ĭ jĕk′shən) *n.* **1.** The act of ejecting or the condition of being ejected: *The ejection of the pilot from the stalled plane saved her.* **2.** Something ejected: *Heavy metal nets were laid over the rock to catch ejections from blasting.*

e•jec•tor (ĭ jĕk′tər) *n.* A person or thing that ejects.

eke (ēk) *tr.v.* **eked, ek•ing, ekes. 1.** To get with great effort or strain: *The farmers managed to eke out an existence during the drought.* **2.** To add to with great effort; strain to fill out: *eked out an income by working two jobs.*

EKG *abbr.* An abbreviation of: **1.** Electrocardiogram. **2.** Electrocardiograph.

el. *abbr.* An abbreviation of elevation.

e•lab•o•rate (ĭ lăb′ər ĭt) *adj.* Planned or made with great attention to numerous parts or details; intricate: *We made elaborate preparations for the festivities.* —*v.* (ĭ lăb′ə rāt′). **e•lab•o•rat•ed, e•lab•o•rat•ing, e•lab•o•rates.** —*tr.* To work out with care and detail; develop thoroughly: *It may take scientists many years to elaborate a theory.* —*intr.* To express oneself at greater length or in greater detail; provide further information: *The author elaborated on the difficulty of writing the book.* [First written down in 1581 in Modern English and spelled *elaborate*, worked out, from Latin *ēlabōrātus*, past participle of *ēlabōrāre*, to work out : *ē-*, *ex-*, out + *labōrāre*, to work (from *labor*, work).] —**e•lab′o•rate•ly** *adv.* —**e•lab′o•rate•ness** *n.* —**e•lab′o•ra′tion** *n.*

e•land (ē′lənd) *n., pl.* **eland** also **e•lands.** Either of two large African antelopes having long twisted horns. [First written down in 1786 in Modern English, from Afrikaans, from Dutch *eland*, elk, from obsolete German *Elend*, of Baltic origin.]

e•lapse (ĭ lăps′) *intr.v.* **e•lapsed, e•laps•ing, e•laps•es.** To pass; go by: *Months elapsed before I heard from my friend again.* [First written down in 1644 in Modern English, from Latin *ēlapsus*, past participle of *ēlābī* : *ē*, *ex-*, out, away + *lābī*, to slip.]

e•las•tic (ĭ lăs′tĭk) *adj.* **1.** Capable of returning to its original shape or arrangement after being stretched, compressed, or otherwise deformed. **2.** Capable of adapting or being adapted to change or a variety of circumstances; flexible: *An elastic interpretation of the rules allows some children to come to school early.* **3.** Quick to recover or revive: *He has an elastic spirit.* —*n.* **1.** A fabric woven with strands of rubber or a similar synthetic fiber to make it stretch: *Elastic held the sleeves of my jacket around my wrists.* **2.** A rubber band. —**e•las′ti•cal•ly** *adv.*

e•las•tic•i•ty (ĭ lă **stĭs′**ĭ tē *or* ē′lă **stĭs′**ĭ tē) *n.* The condition or property of being elastic: *The rubber band broke when it lost its elasticity.*

e•late (ĭ lāt′) *tr.v.* **e•lat•ed, e•lat•ing, e•lates.** To raise the spirits of; make very happy or joyful: *The news of victory elated the candidate's supporters.*

e•lat•ed (ĭ lā′tĭd) *adj.* Joyful; happy; in high spirits: *the elated feeling of winning a race.* —**e•lat′ed•ly** *adv.*

e•la•tion (ĭ lā′shən) *n.* An intense feeling of happiness or joy: *the elation of succeeding after much effort.*

El•ba (ĕl′bə). An island of Italy between Corsica and the mainland. Napoleon Bonaparte spent his first period of exile here (May 1814–February 1815).

El•be (ĕl′bə *or* ĕlb). A river of Czech Republic and Germany flowing about 725 miles (1,167 kilometers) to the North Sea.

el•bow (ĕl′bō′) *n.* **1.** The joint or bend between the forearm and the upper arm. **2.** Something having a bend or sharp angle, especially a length of pipe that has a sharp bend in it. —*tr.v.* **el•bowed, el•bow•ing, el•bows. 1.** To push, jostle, or shove with or as if with the elbows: *She elbowed me in the ribs to get me to stop laughing.* **2.** To make (one's way) by pushing with the elbows: *The detectives elbowed their way through the crowd.* [First written down about 1000 in Old English and spelled *elnboga*.]

elbow grease *n. Informal.* Strenuous physical effort: *Polishing a car requires elbow grease.*

el•bow•room (ĕl′bō ro͝om′ *or* ĕl′bō ro͞om′) *n.* Room to move around or function in; ample space: *Their cramped cubicles didn't give the artists enough elbowroom to lay out their work.*

eld•er[1] (ĕl′dər) *adj.* Born before another; older; senior: *my elder sister; an elder statesman.* —*n.* **1.** An older person: *The children rely on their elders for guidance and support.* **2.** An older influential person of a family, tribe, or community: *In colonial times, a council of elders governed the affairs of many settlements.* **3.** One of the officers of certain churches. [First written down about 725 in Old English and spelled *eldra*.]

el•der[2] (ĕl′dər) *n.* Any of various shrubs having clusters of small white flowers and blackish or red berries; the elderberry. [First written down before 800 in Old English and spelled *ellærn*.]

el•der•ber•ry (ĕl′dər bĕr′ē) *n.* **1.** The small round fruit of the elder, used to make wine or preserves. **2.** The elder.

eld•er•ly (ĕl′dər lē) *adj.* Approaching old age; rather old: *an elderly person.* —*n. (used with a plural verb).* Older people considered as a group. —**eld′er•li•ness** *n.*

eld•est (ĕl′dĭst) *adj.* Oldest: *The king's eldest child became the new ruler.*

El Do•ra•do[1] (ĕl də rä′dō). A legendary city of South America, fabled for its great wealth of gold and precious jewels.

El Do•ra•do[2] (ĕl də rä′dō) *n.* A place of fabulous wealth.

e•lect (ĭ lĕkt′) *tr.v.* **e•lect•ed, e•lect•ing, e•lects. 1.** To choose by vote for an office or for membership: *The citizens of each state vote to elect two senators.* **2.** To choose or decide: *I elected an art course. I elected to take geology, too.* —*adj.* Elected but not yet installed in office: *The governor-elect will take office in January.* —*n. (used with a plural verb).* A chosen or privileged group: *one of the elect* *who have power in the state government.* [First written down before 1425 in Middle English and spelled *electen*, from Latin *ēligere*, to select : *ē-*, *ex-*, out + *legere*, to choose.]

e•lec•tion (ĭ **lĕk′**shən) *n.* **1.** The act or power of choosing by vote among candidates to fill an office or a position: *The election of representatives takes place every two years.* **2.** The fact of being so chosen. **3.** Selection; choice: *The election of contest winners was announced by the judges.*

e•lec•tion•eer (ĭ lĕk′shə **nîr′**) *intr.v.* **e•lec•tion•eered, e•lec•tion•eer•ing, e•lec•tion•eers.** To work actively for a particular candidate or party in an election.

e•lec•tive (ĭ **lĕk′**tĭv) *adj.* **1.** Filled or obtained by election: *The Presidency is an elective office.* **2.** Chosen by election: *The President is the highest elective official.* **3.** Permitting a choice; not required; optional: *Italian is an elective course in my school.* —*n.* An optional course in school: *My electives are music and French.*

e•lec•tor (ĭ **lĕk′**tər) *n.* **1.** A person who has the right to vote in an election. **2.** A member of the Electoral College of the United States.

e•lec•tor•al (ĭ **lĕk′**tər əl) *adj.* **1.** Of or relating to electors, especially the members of the Electoral College: *The President had a majority of the electoral vote.* **2.** Of or relating to election: *electoral reforms that will make it easier to vote.*

Electoral College *n.* A group of electors chosen by the voters to elect the President and Vice President of the United States. The number of electors allotted to each state is based on population.

e•lec•tor•ate (ĭ **lĕk′**tər ĭt) *n.* All those persons qualified to vote in an election: *The United States has a huge electorate, but not all voters vote.*

e•lec•tric (ĭ **lĕk′**trĭk) *adj.* **1.** Also **e•lec•tri•cal** (ĭ **lĕk′**trĭ kəl). Of, relating to, or operated by electricity: *electric power; an electrical appliance.* **2.** Charged with emotion; exciting; thrilling: *the electric feeling of watching a very close race.* [First written down in 1646 in Modern English, from New Latin *ēlectricus*, deriving from amber, as by rubbing, from Greek *ēlektron*, amber.] —**e•lec′tri•cal•ly** *adv.*

electrical engineering *n.* The branch of engineering that deals with the practical uses of electricity and their effects. —**electrical engineer** *n.*

electric chair *n.* **1.** A chair used to electrocute a person sentenced to death. **2.** Execution by electrocution.

electric eel *n.* A South American freshwater fish that resembles an eel and can produce a strong electric shock.

electric eye *n.* A photoelectric cell.

e•lec•tri•cian (ĭ lĕk **trĭsh′**ən *or* ē′lĕk **trĭsh′**ən) *n.* A person who installs, maintains, repairs, or operates electric equipment and electrical circuits.

e•lec•tric•i•ty (ĭ lĕk **trĭs′**ĭ tē *or* ē′lĕk **trĭs′**ĭ tē) *n.* **1.** The collection of physical effects resulting from the existence of charged particles, especially electrons and protons, and their interactions. Particles with like charge repel each other. Particles with opposite charges attract each other. **2.** Electric current used as a source of power: *Electricity lights our homes.* **3.** Emotional excitement: *Electricity filled the air during the last period of the game.*

e•lec•tri•fy (ĭ **lĕk′**trə fī′) *tr.v.* **e•lec•tri•fied, e•lec•tri•fy•ing, e•lec•tri•fies. 1.** To charge with electricity: *throw the switch to electrify a circuit.* **2.a.** To wire or equip for the use of electric power: *electrify a building.* **b.** To supply with electric power: *The new power station made it possible to electrify the whole valley.* **3.** To thrill, startle, or shock: *The goalie's play electrified the audience.* —**e•lec′tri•fi•ca′tion** (ĭ lĕk′trə fĭ **kā′**shən) *n.*

electro– or **electr–** *pref.* A prefix that means: **1.** Electric: *electromagnet.* **2.** Electric or electrically: *electrocute.*

e•lec•tro•car•di•o•gram (ĭ lĕk′trō **kär′**dē ə grăm′) *n.* The curve traced by an electrocardiograph, used to determine how well a heart is working or what is wrong with it.

e•lec•tro•car•di•o•graph (ĭ lĕk′trō **kär′**dē ə grăf′) *n.* An instrument that records the electrical activity of the heart, usually in the form of a curve traced on a chart.

e•lec•tro•chem•is•try (ĭ lĕk′trō **kĕm′**ĭ strē) *n.* The study of chemical reactions that involve electricity, especially reactions that occur when an electric current flows through a solution. —**e•lec′tro•chem′i•cal** *adj.* —**e•lec′tro•chem′i•cal•ly** *adv.*

e•lec•tro•cute (ĭ **lĕk′**trə kyo͞ot′) *tr.v.* **e•lec•tro•cut•ed, e•lec•tro•cut•ing, e•lec•tro•cutes.** To kill or execute with electricity: *The workers shut off the power to avoid any danger of being electrocuted.* [First written down in 1889 in American English : *electro-* + *(exe)cute*.]

e•lec•tro•cu•tion (ĭ lĕk′trə **kyo͞o′**shən) *n.* Death or execution caused by electric current.

e•lec•trode (ĭ **lĕk′**trōd′) *n.* A conductor through which an electric current enters or leaves a liquid or gas.

e•lec•tro•en•ceph•a•lo•gram (ĭ lĕk′trō ĕn **sĕf′**ə lə grăm′) *n.* The curve traced by an electroencephalograph, used to determine how the brain is working and to diagnose diseases.

e•lec•tro•en•ceph•a•lo•graph (ĭ lĕk′trō ĕn **sĕf′**ə lə grăf′) *n.* An instrument that records the electrical activity of the brain, usually in the form of a curve on a graph.

e•lec•trol•y•sis (ĭ lĕk **trŏl′**ĭ sĭs *or* ē′lĕk **trŏl′**ĭ sĭs) *n.* **1.** Chemical change, especially decomposition, produced in a chemical compound that breaks apart into ions when an electric current is passed through it. **2.** Destruction of living tissue, such as the roots of hairs, by an electric current. [First written down in 1834 in Modern English : *electro-* + Greek *lusis*, a loosening.]

e•lec•tro•lyte (ĭ **lĕk′**trə līt′) *n.* **1.** A substance that when dissolved or melted becomes electrically conductive by breaking apart into ions. **2.** Any of various ions, such as sodium, potassium, magnesium, or chloride, required by cells to regulate the electric charge and flow of water molecules across the cell membrane.

e•lec•tro•lyt•ic (ĭ lĕk′trə **lĭt′**ĭk) *adj.* **1.** Of or relating to electrolysis. **2.** Of or using electrolytes. —**e•lec′tro•lyt′i•cal•ly** *adv.*

e•lec•tro•lyze (ĭ **lĕk′**trə līz′) *tr.v.* **e•lec•tro•lyzed, e•lec•tro•lyz•ing, e•lec•tro•lyz•es.** To cause to decompose by electrolysis.

e•lec•tro•mag•net (ĭ lĕk′trō **măg′**nĭt) *n.* A magnet that consists of a coil of insulated wire wrapped around an iron core that becomes magnetized only when an electric current flows through the wire.

e•lec•tro•mag•net•ic (ĭ lĕk′trō măg **nĕt′**ĭk) *adj.* Of or relating to electromagnetism.

electromagnetic wave *n.* A wave of energy from an accelerating electric charge that spreads through space as a disturbance of electric and magnetic fields. Radio waves, light waves, and x-rays are electromagnetic waves.

e•lec•tro•mag•net•ism (ĭ lĕk′trō **măg′**nĭ tĭz′əm) *n.* **1.** Magnetism produced by electric charge in motion. **2.** The scientific study of electricity and magnetism and the relationships between them.

e•lec•tro•mo•tive (ĭ lĕk′trō **mō′**tĭv) *adj.* **1.** Of or producing an electric current. **2.** Of or relating to electromotive force.

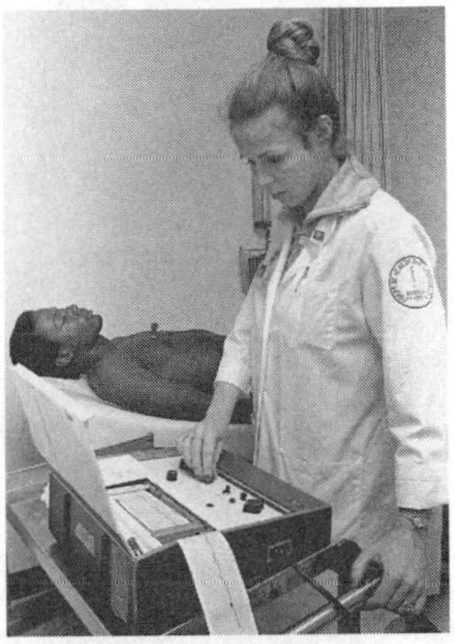

electrocardiograph
Monitoring an electrocardiograph

ă	pat	oi	boy
ā	pay	ou	out
âr	care	o͝o	took
ä	father	o͞o	boot
ĕ	pet	ŭ	cut
ē	be	ûr	urge
ĭ	pit	th	thin
ī	pie	*th*	this
îr	pier	hw	whoop
ŏ	pot	zh	vision
ō	toe	ə	about
ô	paw	N	*French* bon

elephant
Top: African elephant
Bottom: Indian elephant

George Eliot

electromotive force *n.* **1.** A force that produces electric current. **2.** The energy, usually measured in volts, that is converted into electrical form by a battery, generator, or similar device.

e•lec•tron (ĭ **lĕk′**trŏn′) *n.* A subatomic particle having the smallest unit of negative charge, which is equal in strength but opposite in sign to that of a proton. All atoms have electrons grouped around the nucleus. [First written down in 1891 in Modern English : *electr(ic)* + *-on*, particle.]

electron gun *n.* A device that generates a beam of high-speed electrons. In the cathode-ray tube of a television set, the electron gun focuses an electron beam on the screen to create a picture.

e•lec•tron•ic (ĭ lĕk **trŏn′**ĭk *or* ē′lĕk **trŏn′**ĭk) *adj.* Of or relating to electrons or electronics: *an electronic calculator.* **—e•lec•tron′i•cal•ly** *adv.*

electronic mail *n.* **1.** A system for sending messages by computer or other electronic means instead of through the post office. **2.** Messages sent or received by this system.

electronic music *n.* Music produced by electronic devices, such as a tape recorder or synthesizer.

e•lec•tron•ics (ĭ lĕk′**trŏn′**ĭks *or* ē′lĕk **trŏn′**ĭks) *n.* *(used with a singular verb).* The science and technology concerned with the study of electrons in motion and the development of devices operated by a controlled flow of electrons: *Electronics has made the computer possible.*

electron microscope *n.* An instrument in which a beam of electrons is focused by magnetic fields on objects that are too small to be seen or studied with an ordinary microscope.

electron tube *n.* A sealed glass tube containing either a vacuum or a small amount of gas, in which electrons act as the main carriers of current between two or more electrodes. Electron tubes have been largely replaced by transistors in radios and amplifiers.

electron volt *n.* A unit of energy used in physics to measure the energies of subatomic particles. It is equal to the energy gained by an electron that is accelerated to a position at which the electric potential is one volt greater.

e•lec•tro•plate (ĭ **lĕk′**trə plāt′) *tr.v.* **e•lec•tro•plat•ed, e•lec•tro•plat•ing, e•lec•tro•plates.** To cover or coat with a thin layer of metal by means of electrolysis.

e•lec•tro•scope (ĭ **lĕk′**trə skōp′) *n.* An instrument used to detect electric charges and to determine whether they are positive or negative.

e•lec•tro•stat•ic (ĭ lĕk′trō **stăt′**ĭk) *adj.* Of, produced by, or caused by stationary electric charges.

electrostatic generator *n.* A machine that generates high voltages by accumulating large quantities of static electric charges.

el•e•gance (**ĕl′**ĭ gəns) *n.* **1.** Refinement, grace, and beauty in appearance or behavior: *The old castle still had signs of past elegance in its great staircase.* **2.** Something that is elegant: *Expensive jewelry is an elegance few can afford.*

el•e•gant (**ĕl′**ĭ gənt) *adj.* Marked by or showing elegance: *elegant clothes; an elegant restaurant.* [First written down about 1485 in Middle English, from Latin *ēlegāns*, choosing, from *ēligere*, to select.] **—el′e•gant•ly** *adv.*

el•e•gi•ac (ĕl′ə **jī′**ək) *adj.* Of or relating to elegy.

el•e•gize (**ĕl′**ə jīz′) *v.* **el•e•gized, el•e•giz•ing, el•e•giz•es.** *—intr.* To compose an elegy. *—tr.* To compose an elegy about.

el•e•gy (**ĕl′**ə jē) *n., pl.* **el•e•gies.** A poem or song that expresses sorrow, especially one composed to lament a person who has died. [First written down in 1514 in Modern English, from Greek *elegeia*.]

el•e•ment (**ĕl′**ə mənt) *n.* **1.** A part of a whole, especially a fundamental or essential part: *The story contains elements of a detective novel and a romance.* **2. elements.** The basic principles: *Composers must learn the elements of music.* **3.** A substance that cannot be broken down into simpler substances by chemical means. An element is composed of atoms that have the same number of protons in their nuclei: *Oxygen, carbon, and sulfur are chemical elements.* **4.** In mathematics, a member of a set. **5. elements.** The forces of the weather, especially the cold, wind, and rain: *The rescuers braved the elements to hunt for the lost children.* **6.** An environment to which a person or thing is suited or adapted: *The sea was as much the sailors' element as the land.* [First written down about 1300 in Middle English, from Latin *elementum*.]

element 104 *n.* A synthetic radioactive element, having isotopes with mass numbers ranging from 257 to 261 and half-lives ranging from 0.1 to 70 seconds. Atomic number 104. See table at **element.**

element 105 *n.* A synthetic radioactive element, having isotopes with mass numbers ranging from 260 to 262 and half-lives ranging from 1.6 to 40 seconds. Atomic number 105. See table at **element.**

el•e•men•tal (ĕl′ə **mĕn′**tl) *adj.* **1.** Of or relating to an element. **2.** Of or resembling a force of nature in power or effect: *the elemental fury of the hurricane.* **3.** Fundamental; basic: *Most students are familiar with the elemental concepts of physics.*

el•e•men•ta•ry (ĕl′ə **mĕn′**tə rē *or* ĕl′ə **mĕn′**trē) *adj.* Of, relating to, or involving the fundamental or simplest aspects of a subject: *an elementary textbook in math.*

elementary particle *n.* A subatomic particle.

elementary school *n.* A school attended for the first six to eight years of a child's formal classroom instruction; a grammar school.

el•e•phant (**ĕl′**ə fənt) *n.* Either of two mammals of Asia and Africa having thick, almost hairless skin, a long flexible trunk, and long tusks. Elephants are the largest living land animals. [First written down before 1300 in Middle English and spelled *olifaunt*, from Greek *elephas*.]

el•e•phan•tine (ĕl′ə **făn′**tēn′ *or* ĕl′ə **făn′**tīn′) *adj.* **1.** Of or relating to an elephant. **2.** Enormous in size or strength: *elephantine warehouses near the airport.* **3.** Slow and clumsy.

el•e•vate (**ĕl′**ə vāt′) *tr.v.* **ele•vat•ed, ele•vat•ing, ele•vates. 1.** To raise to a higher place or position; lift up: *A nurse elevated the head of the bed so the patient could sit up to read.* **2.** To promote to a higher rank: *The publisher elevated him to editor-in-chief.* **3.** To bring to a higher moral, cultural, or intellectual level: *By using its melody in a symphony the composer elevated the folk song to heights of great beauty.* [First written down before 1410 in Middle English and spelled *elevaten*, from Latin *ēlevāre* : *ē-*, *ex-*, out, up + *levāre*, to raise.]

el•e•vat•ed (**ĕl′**ə vā′tĭd) *adj.* **1.** Raised or placed above a given level: *the elevated speaker's platform.* **2.** Exalted; lofty; dignified: *elevated thought.* *—n.* An elevated railway.

elevated railway *n.* A railway that operates on a track raised high enough so that vehicles and pedestrians can pass beneath.

el•e•va•tion (ĕl′ə **vā′**shən) *n.* **1.** An elevated place or position: *That hill is the highest elevation for miles around.* **2.** The height to which something is elevated, especially the height above sea level: *The ridge rises to an elevation of 3,300 feet.* **3.** The act of elevating or the condition of being elevated: *Elevation to high position in government is a great honor.*

el•e•va•tor (**ĕl′**ə vā′tər) *n.* **1.** A car, platform, or cage raised or lowered in a vertical shaft to carry freight or people, as from floor to floor in a building. **2.** A grain elevator. **3.** A movable piece attached to a horizontal part of an airplane tail used to turn the nose of the craft upward or downward.

e•lev•en (ĭ **lĕv′**ən) *n.* **1.** A number, written 11, that is equal to 10 + 1. **2.** The 11th in a set or sequence. [First written down before 900 in Old English and spelled *endleofan.*]

e•lev•enth (ĭ **lĕv′**ənth) *n.* **1.** The ordinal number matching the number 11 in a series. **2.** One of 11 equal parts.

eleventh hour *n.* The latest possible time: *They waited until the eleventh hour to buy tickets for the concert.*

elf (ĕlf) *n., pl.* **elves** (ĕlvz). A tiny, often mischievous creature supposed to have magical powers. [First written down about 725 in Old English and spelled *ælf.*]

elf•in (**ĕl′**fĭn) *adj.* Relating to or suggestive of an elf or elves: *an elfin smile.*

elf•ish (**ĕl′**fĭsh) *adj.* Elfin. **—elf′ish•ly** *adv.* **—elf′ish•ness** *n.*

El Grec•o (**grĕk′**ō). See **El Greco.**

e•lic•it (ĭ **lĭs′**ĭt) *tr.v.* **e•lic•it•ed, e•lic•it•ing, e•lic•its.** To bring out; draw forth; evoke: *By clever questioning the lawyer elicited the truth from the witness.* [First written down in 1641 in Modern English, from Latin *ēlicere* : *ē-, ex-*, out + *lacere*, to entice.]

❑ *These sound alike:* **elicit, illicit** (illegal).

el•i•gi•ble (**ĕl′**ĭ jə bəl) *adj.* Fit or worthy to be chosen; qualified or suited: *Eligible voters may go to the polls to vote on election day.* [First written down before 1425 in Middle English, from Latin *ēligere*, to select.] **—el′i•gi•bil′i•ty** *n.*

E•li•jah (ĭ **lī′**jə). Ninth century B.C. A Hebrew prophet who according to the Bible did not die but was carried into the sky in a chariot of fire.

e•lim•i•nate (ĭ **lĭm′**ə nāt′) *tr.v.* **e•lim•i•nat•ed, e•lim•i•nat•ing, e•lim•i•nates. 1.** To get rid of; remove: *We must make greater efforts to eliminate illiteracy.* **2.** To leave out or omit from consideration; reject: *The police eliminated two of the four suspects in the case.* **3.** To rid the body of (waste products); excrete. [First written down in 1568 in Modern English, from Latin *ēlīmināre*, to banish : *ē-, ex-*, out, off + *līmen*, threshold.]

e•lim•i•na•tion (ĭ lĭm′ə **nā′**shən) *n.* The act of eliminating or the state of being eliminated: *elimination of language barriers; elimination from the contest.*

El•i•ot (**ĕl′**ē ət), **George.** Pen name of Mary Ann Evans. 1819–1880. British writer whose novels include *Silas Marner* (1861).

Eliot, T(homas) S(tearns). 1888–1965. American-born British writer known for his poems, including *The Wasteland* (1922). He won a 1948 Nobel Prize.

E•li•sha (ĭ **lī′**shə). Ninth century B.C. In the Bible, a Hebrew prophet.

e•lite or **é•lite** (ĭ **lēt′** *or* ā **lēt′**) *n. (used with a plural verb).* **1.** Those considered as the best, superior, or wealthiest members of a society or group: *the elite of the sports world.* **2.** A small and privileged group. **—e•lite′** *adj.*

e•lit•ism or **é•lit•ism** (ĭ **lē′**tĭz′əm *or* ā **lē′**tĭz′əm) *n.* **1.** The belief that certain persons of a group deserve special treatment because they are superior to others. **2.** Rule or domination by an elite. **—e•lit′ist** *adj.* & *n.*

e•lix•ir (ĭ **lĭk′**sər) *n.* **1.** A sweetened and flavored solution of alcohol and water containing one or more medicinal substances. **2.** In medieval alchemy, a substance believed to have the power to change base metals into gold. **3.** A substance believed to have the power to cure all ills. **4.** A substance believed to maintain life indefinitely.

E•liz•a•beth I (ĭ **lĭz′**ə bəth). 1533–1603. Queen of England and Ireland (1558–1603) who reestablished Protestantism in England. She had Mary Queen of Scots executed (1587).

Elizabeth II. Born 1926. Queen of Great Britain and Northern Ireland since 1952.

E•liz•a•be•than (ĭ lĭz′ə **bē′**thən *or* ĭ **lĭz′**ə **bĕth′**ən) *adj.* Of or characteristic of the reign of Elizabeth I: *Elizabethan style of dress; Elizabethan drama.* —*n.* An English person living during the reign of Elizabeth I.

Elizabeth Pe•trov•na (pə **trôv′**nə). 1709–1762. Empress of Russia who ruled from 1741 to 1762.

elk (ĕlk) *n., pl.* **elk** or **elks. 1.** The wapiti. **2.** The moose. [First written down before 1437 in Middle English, probably alteration of Old English *eolh.*]

ell[1] (ĕl) *n.* A wing of a building at right angles to the main structure. [First written down in 1688 in Modern English, from its resemblance to the shape of the capital letter L, or short for *elbow.*]

ell[2] (ĕl) *n.* An English measure of length equal to 45 inches (114 centimeters). [First written down about 1000 in Old English and spelled *eln*, the length from the elbow to the middle finger's tip, ell.]

El•ling•ton (**ĕl′**ĭng tən), **Edward Kennedy.** Known as "Duke." 1899–1974. American jazz composer and pianist whose compositions include "Mood Indigo" (1930).

el•lipse (ĭ **lĭps′**) *n.* A figure that forms a closed curve shaped like an oval with both ends alike. The sum of the distances of any point on an ellipse from two fixed points remains constant.

el•lip•sis (ĭ **lĭp′**sĭs) *n., pl.* **el•lip•ses** (ĭ **lĭp′**sēz). **1.** The omission of a word or phrase needed to make a sentence grammatically complete but not necessary to understanding. **2.** A mark or series of marks (. . .) used in writing or printing to show the omission of a word or phrase.

el•lip•tic (ĭ **lĭp′**tĭk) or **el•lip•ti•cal** (ĭ **lĭp′**tĭ kəl) *adj.* **1.** Of, relating to, or shaped like an ellipse: *an elliptic window over a door.* **2.** Containing or characterized by ellipsis: *an elliptic sentence.* **—el•lip′ti•cal•ly** *adv.*

elm (ĕlm) *n.* **1.** Any of various tall shade trees having arching or curving branches. **2.** The hard strong wood of such a tree. [First written down about 1000 in Old English.]

El Ni•ño (**nēn′**yō) *n.* A current of warm water flowing southward along the coast of Ecuador. Periodically it extends as far south as the coast of Peru, killing fish and plankton and affecting weather over much of the Pacific Ocean.

el•o•cu•tion (ĕl′ə **kyōō′**shən) *n.* The art of public speaking that emphasizes gestures and vocal delivery. [First written down before 1439 in Middle English and spelled *ellocucioun*, from Latin *ēlocūtus*, past participle of *ēloquī*, to speak out : *ē-, ex-*, out + *loquī*, to speak.]

e•lon•gate (ĭ **lông′**gāt′ *or* ĭ **lŏng′**gāt′) *tr. & intr.v.* **e•lon•gat•ed, e•lon•gat•ing, e•lon•gates.** To make or grow longer; lengthen: *The artist often elongates faces and figures in cartoons.* —*adj.* or **elongated.** Long and thin; lengthened; extended.

e•lon•ga•tion (ĭ lông′**gā′**shən *or* ĭ lŏng′**gā′**shən) *n.* Something that elongates; an extension.

e•lope (ĭ **lōp′**) *intr.v.* **e•loped, e•lop•ing, e•lopes.** To run away with a lover, especially with the intention of getting married. **—e•lope′ment** *n.*

el•o•quence (**ĕl′**ə kwəns) *n.* **1.** Persuasive powerful discourse. **2.** The skill or power of using such discourse: *The lawyer's eloquence influenced the jury.*

el•o•quent (**ĕl′**ə kwənt) *adj.* **1.** Marked by persuasive powerful discourse: *an eloquent appeal for jus-*

T.S. Eliot

Elizabeth II
Photographed in 1986 by her son Prince Andrew

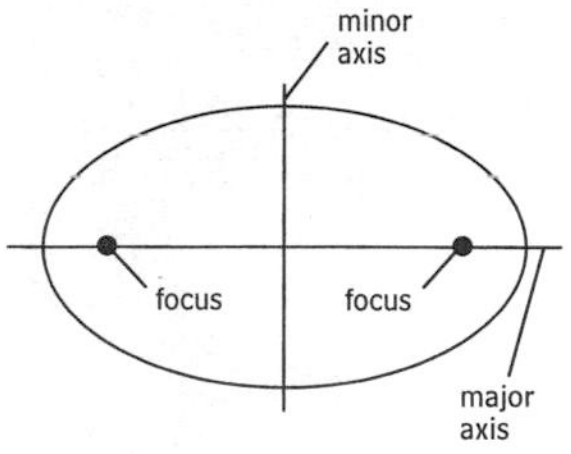

ellipse

ă	pat	oi	boy
ā	pay	ou	out
âr	care	ŏŏ	took
ä	father	ōō	boot
ĕ	pet	ŭ	cut
ē	be	ûr	urge
ĭ	pit	th	thin
ī	pie	*th*	this
îr	pier	hw	whoop
ŏ	pot	zh	vision
ō	toe	ə	about
ô	paw	N	*French* bon

PERIODIC TABLE OF THE ELEMENTS

The periodic table arranges the chemical elements in two ways. The first is by atomic number, the number of protons in each element's nucleus. The elements are arranged so that their atomic numbers increase as you read across each row, or period, from left to right. The second is by chemical families. Each column, or group, contains elements with similar chemical properties.

The first periodic table was devised by Dmitri Mendeleev in 1869. At that time, only 63 elements were known. Mendeleev left empty spaces in his table to make the known elements fit in the correct columns. He correctly predicted that the spaces would later be filled in as more elements were discovered. The modern periodic table is basically the same as Mendeleev's chart, with some improvements.

In the table as shown here, elements that are nonmetals have light shading. Darker shading indicates the metalloids. Elements with no shading are metals. The lanthanide series (elements 57–71) and the actinide series (elements 89–103) do not match the way the other elements fit into the table. They are placed below the main body of the table to make it easier to read.

1	1 **H** Hydrogen								
2	3 **Li** Lithium	4 **Be** Beryllium							
3	11 **Na** Sodium	12 **Mg** Magnesium							
4	19 **K** Potassium	20 **Ca** Calcium	21 **Sc** Scandium	22 **Ti** Titanium	23 **V** Vanadium	24 **Cr** Chromium	25 **Mn** Manganese	26 **Fe** Iron	27 **Co** Cobalt
5	37 **Rb** Rubidium	38 **Sr** Strontium	39 **Y** Yttrium	40 **Zr** Zirconium	41 **Nb** Niobium	42 **Mo** Molybdenum	43 **Tc** Technetium	44 **Ru** Ruthenium	45 **Rh** Rhodium
6	55 **Cs** Cesium	56 **Ba** Barium	57–71* Lanthan-ides	72 **Hf** Hafnium	73 **Ta** Tantalum	74 **W** Tungsten	75 **Re** Rhenium	76 **Os** Osmium	77 **Ir** Iridium
7	87 **Fr** Francium	88 **Ra** Radium	89–103** Actinides	104	105				

*** LANTHANIDES**	57 **La** Lanthanum	58 **Ce** Cerium	59 **Pr** Praseo-dymium	60 **Nd** Neodymium	61 **Pm** Promethium	62 **Sm** Samarium	63 **Eu** Europium
**** ACTINIDES**	89 **Ac** Actinium	90 **Th** Thorium	91 **Pa** Protactinium	92 **U** Uranium	93 **Np** Neptunium	94 **Pu** Plutonium	95 **Am** Americium

TABLE OF THE ELEMENTS

ELEMENT	SYMBOL	ATOMIC NUMBER	ELEMENT	SYMBOL	ATOMIC NUMBER	ELEMENT	SYMBOL	ATOMIC NUMBER	ELEMENT	SYMBOL	ATOMIC NUMBER
Actinium	Ac	**89**	Cadmium	Cd	**48**	Element 104	–	**104**	Holmium	Ho	**67**
Aluminum	Al	**13**	Calcium	Ca	**20**	Element 105	–	**105**	Hydrogen	H	**1**
Americium	Am	**95**	Californium	Cf	**98**	Erbium	Er	**68**	Indium	In	**49**
Antimony	Sb	**51**	Carbon	C	**6**	Europium	Eu	**63**	Iodine	I	**53**
Argon	Ar	**18**	Cerium	Ce	**58**	Fermium	Fm	**100**	Iridium	Ir	**77**
Arsenic	As	**33**	Cesium	Cs	**55**	Fluorine	F	**9**	Iron	Fe	**26**
Astatine	At	**85**	Chlorine	Cl	**17**	Francium	Fr	**87**	Krypton	Kr	**36**
Barium	Ba	**56**	Chromium	Cr	**24**	Gadolinium	Gd	**64**	Lanthanum	La	**57**
Berkelium	Bk	**97**	Cobalt	Co	**27**	Gallium	Ga	**31**	Lawrencium	Lr	**103**
Beryllium	Be	**4**	Copper	Cu	**29**	Germanium	Ge	**32**	Lead	Pb	**82**
Bismuth	Bi	**83**	Curium	Cm	**96**	Gold	Au	**79**	Lithium	Li	**3**
Boron	B	**5**	Dysprosium	Dy	**66**	Hafnium	Hf	**72**	Lutetium	Lu	**71**
Bromine	Br	**35**	Einsteinium	Es	**99**	Helium	He	**2**	Magnesium	Mg	**12**

			BORON GROUP	CARBON GROUP	NITROGEN GROUP	OXYGEN GROUP	HALOGENS	INERT GASES
								2 **He** Helium
			5 **B** Boron	6 **C** Carbon	7 **N** Nitrogen	8 **O** Oxygen	9 **F** Fluorine	10 **Ne** Neon
			13 **Al** Aluminum	14 **Si** Silicon	15 **P** Phosphorus	16 **S** Sulfur	17 **Cl** Chlorine	18 **Ar** Argon
28 **Ni** Nickel	29 **Cu** Copper	30 **Zn** Zinc	31 **Ga** Gallium	32 **Ge** Germanium	33 **As** Arsenic	34 **Se** Selenium	35 **Br** Bromine	36 **Kr** Krypton
46 **Pd** Palladium	47 **Ag** Silver	48 **Cd** Cadmium	49 **In** Indium	50 **Sn** Tin	51 **Sb** Antimony	52 **Te** Tellurium	53 **I** Iodine	54 **Xe** Xenon
78 **Pt** Platinum	79 **Au** Gold	80 **Hg** Mercury	81 **Tl** Thallium	82 **Pb** Lead	83 **Bi** Bismuth	84 **Po** Polonium	85 **At** Astatine	86 **Rn** Radon

64 **Gd** Gadolinium	65 **Tb** Terbium	66 **Dy** Dysprosium	67 **Ho** Holmium	68 **Er** Erbium	69 **Tm** Thulium	70 **Yb** Ytterbium	71 **Lu** Lutetium
96 **Cm** Curium	97 **Bk** Berkelium	98 **Cf** Californium	99 **Es** Einsteinium	100 **Fm** Fermium	101 **Md** Mendelevium	102 **No** Nobelium	103 **Lr** Lawrencium

ELEMENT	*SYMBOL*	*ATOMIC NUMBER*
Manganese	Mn	**25**
Mendelevium	Md	**101**
Mercury	Hg	**80**
Molybdenum	Mo	**42**
Neodymium	Nd	**60**
Neon	Ne	**10**
Neptunium	Np	**93**
Nickel	Ni	**28**
Niobium	Nb	**41**
Nitrogen	N	**7**
Nobelium	No	**102**
Osmium	Os	**76**
Oxygen	O	**8**
Palladium	Pd	**46**
Phosphorus	P	**15**
Platinum	Pt	**78**
Plutonium	Pu	**94**
Polonium	Po	**84**
Potassium	K	**19**
Praseodymium	Pr	**59**
Promethium	Pm	**61**
Protactinium	Pa	**91**
Radium	Ra	**88**
Radon	Rn	**86**
Rhenium	Re	**75**
Rhodium	Rh	**45**
Rubidium	Rb	**37**
Ruthenium	Ru	**44**
Samarium	Sm	**62**
Scandium	Sc	**21**
Selenium	Se	**34**
Silicon	Si	**14**
Silver	Ag	**47**
Sodium	Na	**11**
Strontium	Sr	**38**
Sulfur	S	**16**
Tantalum	Ta	**73**
Technetium	Tc	**43**
Tellurium	Te	**52**
Terbium	Tb	**65**
Thallium	Tl	**81**
Thorium	Th	**90**
Thulium	Tm	**69**
Tin	Sn	**50**
Titanium	Ti	**22**
Tungsten	W	**74**
Uranium	U	**92**
Vanadium	V	**23**
Xenon	Xe	**54**
Ytterbium	Yb	**70**
Yttrium	Y	**39**
Zinc	Zn	**30**
Zirconium	Zr	**40**

Word Building: elucidate

The word root *–luc–* in English words comes from the Latin verb *lūcēre,* "to shine." *Lūcidus* is a Latin adjective meaning "bright, shining, clear," and is the source of the English word **lucid**. The Latin verb *ēlūcidāre,* "to make lucid, shine out on" (using the prefix *ē–,* a form of *ex–,* "out, out of"), is formed from *lucidus.* The past participle of *ēlūcidāre* is *ēlūcidātus,* the source of **elucidate**.

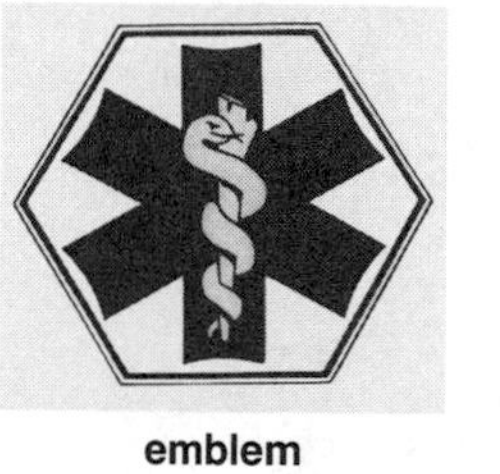

emblem
International medical alert emblem

embroidery
Cross-stitch needlework

tice. **2.** Vividly or movingly expressive: *an eloquent smile.* [First written down before 1393 in Middle English, from Old French, from Latin *ēloquī,* to speak out.] **—el′o•quent•ly** *adv.*

El Sal•va•dor (săl′və dôr′). A country of Central America bordering on the Pacific Ocean northwest of Nicaragua. It gained its independence from Spain in 1821. San Salvador is the capital and the largest city. Population, 4,949,000.

else (ĕls) *adj.* **1.** Other; different: *Somebody else will see you today.* **2.** Additional; more: *Would you like something else to eat?* —*adv.* **1.** Differently: *How else could it have been done?* **2.** If not; otherwise: *Run, or else you will be caught in the rain.*

else•where (ĕls′wâr′) *adv.* In or to a different or another place: *We decided to go elsewhere.*

e•lu•ci•date (ĭ lo͞o′sĭ dāt′) *tr.v.* **e•lu•ci•dat•ed, e•lu•ci•dat•ing, e•lu•ci•dates.** To make clear or plain; explain: *She elucidated the meaning of the poem so that everyone could understand it.* **—e•lu′ci•da′tion** *n.* —See Note.

e•lude (ĭ lo͞od′) *tr.v.* **e•lud•ed, e•lud•ing, e•ludes. 1.** To avoid or escape from, as by skill, cunning, or daring: *The fox eluded the hunters.* **2.** To escape the understanding or grasp of: *Very small details often elude us.* [First written down in 1538 in Modern English, from Latin *ēlūdere* : *ē-, ex-,* out + *lūdere,* to play (from *lūdus,* play).]

e•lu•sive (ĭ lo͞o′sĭv *or* ĭ lo͞o′zĭv) *adj.* **1.** Tending to elude: *an elusive butterfly; an elusive metaphor.* **2.** Difficult to define or describe. **—e•lu′sive•ly** *adv.* **—e•lu′sive•ness** *n.*

❑ *These sound alike:* **elusive, illusive** (unreal).

el•ver (ĕl′vər) *n.* A young eel.

elves (ĕlvz) *n.* Plural of **elf.**

el•y•tron (ĕl′ĭ trŏn′) *n., pl.* **el•y•tra** (ĕl′ĭ trə). Either of the modified forewings of a beetle or a related insect that encase the thin hind wings used in flight.

em– *pref.* Variant of **en–.**

'em (əm) *pron. Informal.* Them.

e•ma•ci•ate (ĭ mā′shē āt′) *tr. & intr.v.* **e•ma•ci•at•ed, e•ma•ci•at•ing, e•ma•ci•ates.** To make or become extremely thin, especially by starvation. **—e•ma′ci•a′tion** *n.*

em•a•nate (ĕm′ə nāt′) *intr. & tr.v.* **em•a•nat•ed, em•a•nat•ing, em•a•nates.** To come or send forth, as from a source: *The sound of a piano emanated from the house.* [First written down in 1756 in Modern English, from Latin *ēmānāre* : *ē-, ex-,* out + *mānāre,* to flow.]

em•a•na•tion (ĕm′ə nā′shən) *n.* **1.** The act or an instance of emanating: *the emanation of heat from a fire.* **2.** Something that emanates from a source: *steamy emanations from a kettle of boiling water.*

e•man•ci•pate (ĭ măn′sə pāt′) *tr.v.* **e•man•ci•pat•ed, e•man•ci•pat•ing, e•man•ci•pates.** To free from bondage, oppression, or restraint; liberate. **—e•man′ci•pa′tor** *n.*

e•man•ci•pa•tion (ĭ măn′sə pā′shən) *n.* The act or an instance of emancipating or the condition of being emancipated: *The emancipation of the slaves happened during the Civil War.*

Emancipation Proclamation *n.* A proclamation issued by President Abraham Lincoln on January 1, 1863, freeing slaves in those areas of the Confederacy still at war against the United States.

e•mas•cu•late (ĭ măs′kyə lāt′) *tr.v.* **e•mas•cu•lat•ed, e•mas•cu•lat•ing, e•mas•cu•lates. 1.** To castrate. **2.** To deprive of strength; weaken. **—e•mas′cu•la′tion** *n.*

em•balm (ĕm bäm′) *tr.v.* **em•balmed, em•balm•ing, em•balms.** To treat (a corpse) with preservatives in order to prevent or slow decay; preserve. **—em•balm′er** *n.*

em•bank•ment (ĕm băngk′mənt) *n.* A mound of earth or stone built up to hold back water or to support a roadway.

em•bar•go (ĕm bär′gō) *n., pl.* **em•bar•goes. 1.** An order by a government prohibiting merchant ships from entering or leaving its ports. **2.** A prohibition by a government on certain or all trade with a foreign nation: *an embargo on trade with South Africa.* **3.** A prohibition; a ban. —*tr.v.* **em•bar•goed, em•bar•go•ing, em•bar•goes.** To place an embargo on. [First written down about 1593 in Modern English, from Spanish *embargar,* to impede, barricade.]

em•bark (ĕm bärk′) *v.* **em•barked, em•bark•ing, em•barks.** —*tr.v.* To cause to board an aircraft or a ship. —*intr.* **1.** To go aboard an aircraft or a ship. **2.** To set out on a venture; begin: *embark on a campaign to clean up the environment.* See Synonyms at **begin. —em′bar•ka′tion** (ĕm′băr kā′shən) *n.*

em•bar•rass (ĕm băr′əs) *tr.v.* **em•bar•rassed, em•bar•rass•ing, em•bar•rass•es. 1.** To cause to feel self-conscious or ill at ease; disconcert: *Not knowing the answer to the question embarrassed me.* **2.** To involve in or hamper with financial difficulties. **3.** To hinder with obstacles or difficulties. [First written down in 1672 in Modern English, from Italian *imbarazzo,* obstacle, obstruction, from *imbarrare,* to block, bar.]

em•bar•rass•ing (ĕm băr′ə sĭng) *adj.* Causing embarrassment: *an embarrassing remark.* **—em•bar′rass•ing•ly** *adv.*

em•bar•rass•ment (ĕm băr′əs mənt) *n.* **1.** The condition of being embarrassed: *My face turned red with embarrassment.* **2.** Something that embarrasses: *Their argument in public was an embarrassment.*

em•bas•sy (ĕm′bə sē) *n., pl.* **em•bas•sies. 1.** A building containing the offices of an ambassador and staff. **2.** The position, function, or assignment of an ambassador. **3.** A staff of diplomatic representatives headed by an ambassador.

em•bat•tled (ĕm băt′ld) *adj.* **1.** Prepared or fortified for battle or engaged in battle: *the embattled countries of Europe during World War II.* **2.** Beset with attackers, criticism, or controversy: *an embattled candidate fighting to win election.*

em•bed (ĕm bĕd′) also **im•bed** (ĭm bĕd′) *tr.v.* **em•bed•ded, em•bed•ding, em•beds** also **im•bed•ded, im•bed•ding, im•beds.** To fix firmly in a surrounding mass: *The splinter was deeply embedded in my finger.*

em•bel•lish (ĕm bĕl′ĭsh) *tr.v.* **em•bel•lished, em•bel•lish•ing, em•bel•lish•es. 1.** To make beautiful, as by ornamentation; decorate: *embellish a tablecloth with fine embroidery.* **2.** To add fanciful or fictitious details to: *embellish a story with some invented characters.* [First written down about 1380 in Middle English and spelled *embelisen,* from Old French *embellir,* from *bel,* beautiful (from Latin *bellus*).] **—em•bel′lish•ment** *n.*

em•ber (ĕm′bər) *n.* **1.** A piece of glowing coal or wood, as in a dying fire. **2. embers.** The smoldering coal or ash of a dying fire: *Embers still glowed in the fireplace.*

em•bez•zle (ĕm bĕz′əl) *tr.v.* **em•bez•zled, em•bez•zling, em•bez•zles.** To take (money, for example) for one's own use in violation of a trust: *The bank president was caught embezzling funds.* **—em•bez′zle•ment** *n.* **—em•bez′zler** *n.*

em•bit•ter (ĕm bĭt′ər) *tr.v.* **em•bit•tered, em•bit•ter•ing, em•bit•ters.** To arouse bitter feelings in.

em•bla•zon (ĕm blā′zən) *tr.v.* **em•bla•zoned, em•bla•zon•ing, em•bla•zons. 1.** To ornament (a surface) richly with prominent markings: *An embroidered coat of arms emblazoned the tapestry.*

2. To make brilliant with colors: *Fireworks emblazoned the sky.* **3.** To celebrate; make illustrious.

em•blem (ĕm′bləm) *n.* An object or a representation that functions as a symbol: *The bald eagle is the emblem of the United States.*

em•blem•at•ic (ĕm′blə **măt′**ĭk) or **em•blem•at•i•cal** (ĕm′blə **măt′**ĭ kəl) *adj.* Of, relating to, or serving as an emblem; symbolic: *The dove is emblematic of peace.*

em•bod•i•ment (ĕm **bŏd′**ē mənt) *n.* **1.** The act of embodying or the state of being embodied. **2.** A person or thing that embodies.

em•bod•y (ĕm **bŏd′**ē) *tr.v.* **em•bod•ied, em•bod•y•ing, em•bod•ies. 1.** To give a bodily form to; personify: *A hero embodies our ideal of bravery.* **2.** To make part of a system or whole; incorporate: *Our constitution embodies a plan for democratic government.*

em•bold•en (ĕm **bōl′**dən) *tr.v.* **em•bold•ened, em•bold•en•ing, em•bold•ens.** To foster boldness or courage in; encourage: *Our many supporters emboldened us to present a list of demands.*

em•bo•li (**ĕm′**bə lī′) *n.* Plural of **embolus.**

em•bo•lism (**ĕm′**bə lĭz′əm) *n.* The obstruction of a blood vessel by an embolus.

em•bo•lus (**ĕm′**bə ləs) *n., pl.* **em•bo•li** (**ĕm′**bə lī′). An air bubble, blood clot, globule of fat, or other substance that is carried in the bloodstream and can block a blood vessel.

em•boss (ĕm **bôs′** *or* ĕm **bŏs′**) *tr.v.* **em•bossed, em•boss•ing, em•boss•es. 1.** To mold or carve in relief: *emboss a head and lettering on a coin.* **2.** To decorate with or as if with a raised design: *emboss a leather belt.*

em•brace (ĕm **brās′**) *v.* **em•braced, em•brac•ing, em•brac•es.** —*tr.* **1.** To clasp or hold close with the arms, usually as a sign of affection; hug: *embrace a child.* **2.** To enclose or surround: *The warm water of the pool embraced us.* **3.** To take up willingly; adopt eagerly: *embraced the hectic life of the big city.* **4.** To include as part of something broader: *Her education embraced all the sciences.* —*intr.* To join in an embrace: *The twins embraced at their reunion.* —*n.* The act of holding close with the arms; a hug: *the cordial embrace of old friends.* [First written down about 1350 in Middle English and spelled *embracen,* from Old French *embracer* : *en-,* in + *brace,* the two arms.]

em•bra•sure (ĕm **brā′**zhər) *n.* **1.** An opening in a thick wall for a window or door. **2.** A flared opening for a gun in a wall or parapet.

em•broi•der (ĕm **broi′**dər) *v.* **em•broi•dered, em•broi•der•ing, em•broi•ders.** —*tr.* **1.** To ornament with needlework: *embroider a pillowcase.* **2.** To make by means of needlework: *embroider a design on a handkerchief.* **3.** To add imaginary or fanciful details to: *The author embroidered the general's biography.* —*intr.* **1.** To make needlework. **2.** To add embellishments or fanciful details. [First written down about 1380 in Middle English and spelled *embrouderen,* from Old English *brogden,* woven, and from Old French *embroder,* to embroider.]

em•broi•der•y (ĕm **broi′**də rē) *n., pl.* **em•broi•der•ies. 1.** The act or art of embroidering. **2.** A piece of embroidered fabric.

em•broil (ĕm **broil′**) *tr.v.* **em•broiled, em•broil•ing, em•broils. 1.** To involve in argument or contention: *embroiled the candidate in a debate.* **2.** To throw into confusion or disorder; entangle.

em•bry•o (**ĕm′**brē ō′) *n., pl.* **em•bry•os. 1.** An organism in its earliest stages of development, especially before it has reached a distinctively recognizable form. **2.** An undeveloped plant within a seed. **3.** An early or beginning stage.

em•bry•ol•o•gist (ĕm′brē **ŏl′**ə jĭst) *n.* A scientist who specializes in embryology.

em•bry•ol•o•gy (ĕm′brē **ŏl′**ə jē) *n.* The branch of biology that deals with embryos and their development. —**em′bry•o•log′i•cal** (ĕm′brē ə **lŏj′**ĭ kəl), **em′bry•o•log′ic** (ĕm′brē ə **lŏj′**ĭk) *adj.*

em•bry•on•ic (ĕm′brē **ŏn′**ĭk) *adj.* **1.** Of or relating to an embryo: *the stages of embryonic development.* **2.** In an early undeveloped state: *an embryonic outline.*

em•cee (**ĕm′sē′**) *n.* A master of ceremonies. —*tr. & intr.v.* **em•ceed, em•cee•ing, em•cees.** To serve as master of ceremonies of: *That announcer emcees a quiz program.*

e•mend (ĭ **mĕnd′**) *tr.v.* **e•mend•ed, e•mend•ing, e•mends.** To improve by critical editing: *emended the preface so that it reads more easily.*

e•men•da•tion (ĭ mĕn′**dā′**shən *or* ē′mĕn **dā′**shən) *n.* **1.** The act of emending. **2.** A change made with the purpose of improving: *I made emendations to the text.*

em•er•ald (**ĕm′**ər əld *or* **ĕm′**rəld) *n.* **1.** A brilliant green transparent form of beryl that is used as a gem. **2.** A strong yellowish green color. —*adj.* Of a strong yellowish green color. [First written down before 1300 in Middle English and spelled *emeraude,* from Medieval Latin *esmeralda,* from Greek *smaragdos.*]

e•merge (ĭ **mûrj′**) *intr.v.* **e•merged, e•merg•ing, e•merg•es. 1.** To rise from or as if from immersion: *Sea mammals must emerge to breathe.* **2.** To come forth from obscurity: *The new nation soon emerged as an important power.* **3.** To become evident: *The truth emerged at the hearing.* [First written down about 1563 in Modern English, from Latin *ēmergere* : *ē-, ex-,* out + *mergere,* to sink.]

e•mer•gence (ĭ **mûr′**jəns) *n.* The act or process of emerging: *the emergence of a butterfly from a cocoon; emergence of the truth under questioning.*

e•mer•gen•cy (ĭ **mûr′**jən sē) *n., pl.* **e•mer•gen•cies.** A serious situation or occurrence that happens suddenly and calls for immediate action: *A fire extinguisher is kept in the hall for use in case of an emergency.*

e•mer•gent (ĭ **mûr′**jənt) *adj.* Coming into existence, view, or attention: *an emergent political leadership.*

e•mer•i•tus (ĭ **mĕr′**ĭ təs) *adj.* Retired but retaining an honorary title corresponding to that held immediately before retirement: *a professor emeritus.*

Em•er•son (**ĕm′**ər sən), **Ralph Waldo.** 1803–1882. American writer and philosopher whose essays include *Nature* (1836).

em•er•y (**ĕm′**ə rē *or* **ĕm′**rē) *n.* A dark mineral that is very hard and is used in a crushed or powdered form for grinding and polishing.

e•met•ic (ĭ **mĕt′**ĭk) *adj.* Causing vomiting. —*n.* An emetic drug or medicine.

emf or **EMF** *abbr.* An abbreviation of electromotive force.

em•i•grant (**ĕm′**ĭ grənt) *n.* A person who emigrates: *The United States accepts emigrants.*

em•i•grate (**ĕm′**ĭ grāt′) *intr.v.* **em•i•grat•ed, em•i•grat•ing, em•i•grates.** To leave one country or region to settle in another: *My parents emigrated from Germany.* —See Note.

em•i•gra•tion (ĕm′ĭ **grā′**shən) *n.* The act of emigrating: *Emigration has brought many people to the United States.*

é•mi•gré (**ĕm′**ĭ grā′) *n.* A person who has left a native country, especially for political reasons.

em•i•nence (**ĕm′**ə nəns) *n.* **1.** A position of great distinction or superiority: *She rose to eminence as a scientist.* **2.** A rise of ground; a hill. **3.** Also **Eminence.** A title and form of address for a cardinal in

Ralph Waldo Emerson

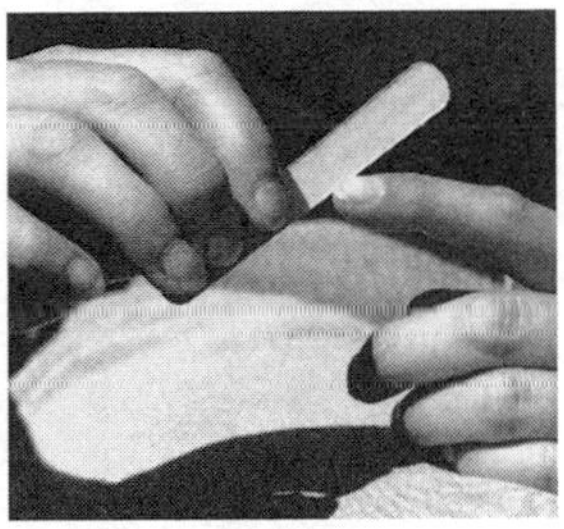

emery

Emery board for filing fingernails

Usage: emigrate

The words **emigrate** and **immigrate** are both used of people involved in a permanent move, generally across a political boundary. **Emigrate** refers to the point of departure: *He emigrated from Germany* (that is, left Germany). By contrast, **immigrate** refers to the new location: *The promise of prosperity in the United States encouraged many people to immigrate* (that is, move to the United States).

ă	pat	oi	boy
ā	pay	ou	out
âr	care	o͝o	took
ä	father	o͞o	boot
ĕ	pet	ŭ	cut
ē	be	ûr	urge
ĭ	pit	th	thin
ī	pie	*th*	this
îr	pier	hw	whoop
ŏ	pot	zh	vision
ō	toe	ə	about
ô	paw	N	*French* bon

the Roman Catholic Church: *Your Eminence.*

em•i•nent (ĕm′ə nənt) *adj.* Standing out above others, as in performance, character, or rank: *an eminent surgeon.* [First written down about 1425 in Middle English, from Latin *ēminēre*, to stand out : *ē-*, *ex-*, out + *-minēre*, to jut out.] **—em′i•nent•ly** *adv.*

e•mir (ĭ mîr′ *or* ā mîr′) *n.* A prince, chieftain, or governor, especially in the Middle East. [First written down in 1612 in Modern English and spelled *emeer*, from Arabic *'amīr*, commander.]

e•mir•ate (ĭ mîr′ĭt *or* ĭ mîr′āt′) *n.* **1.** The office of an emir. **2.** The nation or territory ruled by an emir.

em•is•sar•y (ĕm′ĭ sĕr′ē) *n., pl.* **em•is•sar•ies.** A person sent on a mission as the representative of another: *sent an emissary to discuss the terms of a new trade agreement.*

e•mis•sion (ĭ mĭsh′ən) *n.* **1.** The act or process of emitting: *For environmental safety we must seek to reduce the factory's emission of fumes and smoke.* **2.** Something that is emitted: *harmful emissions from automobiles.*

e•mis•sive (ĭ mĭs′ĭv) *adj.* Emitting or tending to emit; radiating: *radio signals from a highly emissive star.*

e•mit (ĭ mĭt′) *tr.v.* **e•mit•ted, e•mit•ting, e•mits. 1.** To release or send out (matter or energy): *Volcanoes emit lava and hot gases.* **2.** To utter; express: *The baby emitted a cry.* [First written down in 1626 in Modern English, from Latin *ēmittere* : *ē-*, *ex-*, out + *mittere*, to send.] **—e•mit′ter** *n.*

e•mol•lient (ĭ mŏl′yənt) *adj.* Softening and soothing, especially to the skin: *an emollient cream.* —*n.* Something that softens and soothes the skin: *Various oils act as emollients.*

e•mo•tion (ĭ mō′shən) *n.* A strong and complex feeling that arises subjectively rather than through conscious effort, as love, sorrow, happiness, or anger: *He read the lines of the poem with great emotion.* See Synonyms at **feeling.** [First written down in 1579 in Modern English, from French *émotion*, from Old French *esmovoir*, to excite : Latin *ex-*, out + Latin *movēre*, to move.]

e•mo•tion•al (ĭ mō′shə nəl) *adj.* **1.** Of or relating to emotion: *an emotional conflict.* **2.** Easily affected with or stirred by emotion: *an emotional person who is easily upset.* **3.** Arousing or intended to arouse the emotions: *an emotional piece of music.* **4.** Marked by or showing emotion: *their emotional reaction.* **—e•mo′tion•al•ly** *adv.*

e•mo•tion•al•ism (ĭ mō′shə nə lĭz′əm) *n.* **1.** A tendency to rely on or place too much value on emotion: *the emotionalism of young children.* **2.** Undue display of emotion.

em•pan•el (ĕm păn′əl) *v.* Variant of **impanel.**

em•pa•thy (ĕm′pə thē) *n.* Identification with and understanding of another's situation, feelings, and motives: *empathy between parent and child.*

em•per•or (ĕm′pər ər) *n.* A man who is the ruler of an empire. [First written down before 1200 in Middle English and spelled *empereur*, from Latin *imperātor*, from *imperāre*, to command.]

em•pha•sis (ĕm′fə sĭs) *n., pl.* **em•pha•ses** (ĕm′fə sēz′). **1.** Special forcefulness of expression that gives importance or significance: *a lecture on computers with emphasis on developing technologies.* **2.** Prominence given to a syllable, word, or phrase. [First written down in 1573 in Modern English, from Greek, from *emphainein*, to exhibit, display : *en-*, in, on + *phainein*, to show.]

em•pha•size (ĕm′fə sīz′) *tr.v.* **em•pha•sized, em•pha•siz•ing, em•pha•siz•es.** To give emphasis to; stress: *emphasize an idea by repeating it in several different ways.*

em•phat•ic (ĕm făt′ĭk) *adj.* **1.** Expressed or performed with emphasis: *an emphatic shake of the head.* **2.** Forceful and definite in expression or action: *an emphatic person.* **3.** Standing out in a striking way: *The party was an emphatic success.* **—em•phat′i•cal•ly** *adv.*

em•phy•se•ma (ĕm′fĭ sē′mə *or* ĕm′fĭ zē′mə) *n.* A disease in which the small air sacs of the lungs become stretched and lose their elasticity, resulting in an often severe loss of breathing ability.

em•pire (ĕm′pīr′) *n.* **1.** A group of territories or nations headed by a single supreme authority: *the empire of Alexander the Great.* **2.** The territories included in such a group. **3.** Imperial or imperialistic power and authority. **4.** An extensive enterprise under a unified authority: *a publishing empire of newspapers and magazines.* [First written down before 1338 in Middle English, from Latin *imperium*, from *imperāre*, to command.]

em•pir•i•cal (ĕm pîr′ĭ kəl) *adj.* Relying on or derived from observation or experiment rather than theory: *empirical results that support the hypothesis.* [First written down in 1569 in Modern English, from Greek *empeirikos*, experienced.] **—em•pir′i•cal•ly** *adv.*

em•pir•i•cism (ĕm pîr′ĭ sĭz′əm) *n.* **1.** The view that experience, especially of the senses, is the only source of knowledge. **2.** The employment of methods based on experience, experiment, and observation. **—em•pir′i•cist** *n.*

em•place•ment (ĕm plās′mənt) *n.* A prepared position for heavy guns, as a mounting or platform, for example.

em•ploy (ĕm ploi′) *tr.v.* **em•ployed, em•ploy•ing, em•ploys. 1.** To engage the services of; put to work: *The store employs many salespeople.* **2.** To put to use or service: *They employed all their skills to build the bridge.* **3.** To devote (time, for example) to an activity or purpose: *I employ my free time with bicycling and reading.* —*n.* The condition of being employed: *in the employ of the government.* **—em•ploy′a•ble** *adj.*

em•ploy•ee also **em•ploy•e** (ĕm ploi′ē *or* ĕm′ploi ē′) *n.* A person who works for another in return for financial or other compensation.

em•ploy•er (ĕm ploi′ər) *n.* A person or business that employs people for financial or other compensation.

em•ploy•ment (ĕm ploi′mənt) *n.* **1.** The act of employing or the condition of being employed: *the employment of new technology in industry.* **2.** The work in which a person is engaged; an occupation: *employment as a carpenter.*

em•po•ri•um (ĕm pôr′ē əm) *n., pl.* **em•po•ri•ums** or **em•po•ri•a** (ĕm pôr′ē ə). **1.** A place where various goods are bought and sold; a marketplace. **2.** A large retail store or place of business.

em•pow•er (ĕm pou′ər) *tr.v.* **em•pow•ered, em•pow•er•ing, em•pow•ers.** To invest with power, especially legal power or official authority: *The state legislature empowered the governor to levy new taxes.*

em•press (ĕm′prĭs) *n.* **1.** A woman who is the ruler of an empire. **2.** The wife or widow of an emperor.

emp•ty (ĕmp′tē) *adj.* **emp•ti•er, emp•ti•est. 1.** Holding or containing nothing: *an empty box; an empty gas tank.* **2.** Having no occupants or inhabitants; vacant; unoccupied: *an empty house; an empty lot.* **3.** Lacking force or power: *an empty threat.* **4.** Lacking purpose or substance; meaningless: *Everything you said was empty talk.* **5.** Not put to use; idle: *empty hours of daydreaming.* **6.** Needing food; hungry: *went to bed with an empty stomach.* —*v.* **emp•tied, emp•ty•ing, emp•ties.** —*tr.* **1.** To remove the contents of: *I emptied the dishwasher.* **2.** To transfer or pour off: *Please empty* *the garbage from the wastebasket.* —*intr.* **1.** To become empty: *The sink emptied when the plumber opened the drain.* **2.** To discharge or flow out: *The river empties into a bay.* —*n., pl.* **emp•ties.** *Informal.* An empty container: *we recycled the empties.* [First written down before 899 in Old English and spelled *æmettig*, unoccupied, from *æmetta*, leisure.] —**emp′ti•ly** *adv.* —**emp′ti•ness** *n.*

Synonyms: empty, vacant, blank, void, bare. These adjectives describe what contains nothing and therefore lacks what it could have or should have. **Empty** means having no contents or substance: *I thought there were some cherries left, but the bowl was empty.* **Vacant** can mean not occupied: *There are many vacant seats left in the auditorium.* **Blank** means missing something meaningful or important, especially on a surface: *Every poem starts out as a blank piece of paper.* **Void** means absolutely empty: *The guard's face was void of all expression.* **Bare** means lacking surface covering or detail; it also means stripped of contents: *I need to go to the supermarket; the kitchen shelves are all bare.*

emp•ty-hand•ed (ĕmp′tē **hăn′**dĭd) *adj.* **1.** Bearing nothing: *They arrived at the birthday party empty-handed.* **2.** Having received or gained nothing.

empty set *n.* The set that has no members; the null set.

em•py•re•al (ĕm′pī **rē′**əl *or* ĕm **pîr′**ē əl) *adj.* Of the sky; celestial.

em•py•re•an (ĕm′pī **rē′**ən *or* ĕm **pîr′**ē ən) *n.* **1.** The highest reaches of heaven. **2.** The sky. —*adj.* Heavenly; celestial.

e•mu (**ē′**myo͞o) *n.* A large flightless Australian bird related to and resembling the ostrich. [First written down in 1613 in Modern English and spelled *eme*, cassowary, from Portuguese *ema*, rhea.]

em•u•late (**ĕm′**yə lāt′) *tr.v.* **em•u•lat•ed, em•u•lat•ing, em•u•lates.** To strive to equal or excel, especially through imitation: *an experienced pianist whose style I tried to emulate.*

em•u•la•tion (ĕm′yə **lā′**shən) *n.* **1.** Effort or ambition to equal or surpass another: *the young writer's emulation of the famous novelist.* **2.** Imitation of another.

e•mul•si•fy (ĭ **mŭl′**sə fī′) *tr.v.* **e•mul•si•fied, e•mul•si•fy•ing, e•mul•si•fies.** To make into an emulsion: *Soap emulsifies fats in warm water.* —**e•mul′si•fi•ca′tion** (ĭ mŭl′sə fĭ **kā′**shən)

e•mul•sion (ĭ **mŭl′**shən) *n.* **1.** A suspension of small droplets of one liquid in a second liquid with which the first does not mix, as the suspension of cream in homogenized milk. **2.** The coating of a photographic film or paper that is sensitive to light. [First written down in 1612 in Modern English, from Latin *ēmulsus*, past participle of *ēmulgēre*, to milk out : *ē-*, *ex-*, out + *mulgēre*, to milk.]

en– or **em–** or **in–** *pref.* A prefix that means: **1.** To put into or onto: *encapsulate.* **2.** To cover or provide with: *encircle.* **3.** To cause to be: *endear.* **4.** Thoroughly: *entangle.*

–en¹ *suff.* A suffix that means: **1.** To cause to be: *cheapen.* **2.** To become: *redden.* **3.** To cause to have: *hearten.* **4.** To come to have: *lengthen.* —SEE NOTE.

–en² *suff.* A suffix that means made of or resembling: *earthen; wooden.*

en•a•ble (ĕ **nā′**bəl) *tr.v.* **en•a•bled, en•a•bling, en•a•bles.** To give the means, ability, or opportunity to do something: *The new computer system enables the store owners to keep close track of inventory.*

en•act (ĕn **ăkt′**) *tr.v.* **en•act•ed, en•act•ing, en•acts.** **1.** To make into law: *The Senate enacted legislation to help schools throughout the country.* **2.** To act (something) out, as on a stage: *They enacted the final scene without any mistakes.*

en•act•ment (ĕn **ăkt′**mənt) *n.* **1.** The act of enacting or the state of being enacted: *the enactment of laws by Congress.* **2.** Something that has been enacted.

e•nam•el (ĭ **năm′**əl) *n.* **1.** A glassy coating baked onto the surface of metal, porcelain, or pottery for decoration or protection. **2.** A paint that dries to a hard glossy surface. **3.** The hard substance that covers the exposed part of a tooth. —*tr.v.* **e•nam•eled, e•nam•el•ing, e•nam•els** or **e•nam•elled, e•nam•el•ling, e•nam•els.** To coat, inlay, or decorate with enamel. [First written down in 1421 in Middle English and spelled *anamell*, from Anglo-Norman *enamailler*, to put on enamel : *en-*, on + Old French *esmail*, enamel (of Germanic origin).]

e•nam•el•ware (ĭ **năm′**əl wâr′) *n.* Objects of metal, porcelain, or pottery coated with enamel.

en•am•or (ĭ **năm′**ər) *tr.v.* **en•am•ored, en•am•or•ing, en•am•ors.** To inspire with love; captivate: *We were enamored with the beautiful landscape.*

en•camp (ĕn **kămp′**) *v.* **en•camped, en•camp•ing, en•camps.** —*intr.* To set up camp or live in a camp: *encamp in the woods.* —*tr.* To provide quarters for in a camp.

en•camp•ment (ĕn **kămp′**mənt) *n.* **1.** The act of encamping. **2.** The state of being encamped. **3.** A camp or campsite: *The encampment is just down the road.*

en•cap•su•late (ĕn **kăp′**sə lāt′) *tr.v.* **en•cap•su•lat•ed, en•cap•su•lat•ing, en•cap•su•lates.** **1.** To enclose in or as if in a capsule. **2.** To express in a brief summary: *The statement encapsulated the long committee report.* —**en•cap′su•la′tion** *n.*

en•case (ĕn **kās′**) *tr.v.* **en•cased, en•cas•ing, en•cas•es.** To enclose in or as if in a case: *The skull encases the brain.*

–ence *suff.* A suffix that means: **1.** State or condition: *dependence.* **2.** Action: *emergence.*

en•ceph•a•li•tis (ĕn sĕf′ə **lī′**tĭs) *n.* Inflammation of the brain.

en•chant (ĕn **chănt′**) *tr.v.* **en•chant•ed, en•chant•ing, en•chants.** **1.** To cast a spell; bewitch. **2.** To attract and delight; entrance: *The play enchanted everyone who saw it.* [First written down about 1378 in Middle English and spelled *enchaunten*, from Latin *incantāre*, to utter an incantation, cast a spell : *in-*, against + *cantāre*, to sing.] —**en•chant′er** *n.*

en•chant•ing (ĕn **chăn′**tĭng) *adj.* Having the power to enchant; charming: *an enchanting melody.*

en•chant•ment (ĕn **chănt′**mənt) *n.* **1.** The act of enchanting. **2.** The state of being enchanted. **3.** Something that enchants; a magic spell.

en•chi•la•da (ĕn′chə **lä′**də) *n.* A rolled tortilla having a cheese or meat filling and served with a spicy sauce. [First written down in 1887 in American English, from American Spanish : *en-*, in + *chile*, chili pepper.]

en•cir•cle (ĕn **sûr′**kəl) *tr.v.* **en•cir•cled, en•cir•cling, en•cir•cles.** **1.** To form a circle around; surround: *Trees encircled the house.* **2.** To move or go around completely: *It takes the earth one year to encircle the sun.* —**en•cir′cle•ment** *n.*

en•clave (**ĕn′**klāv′ *or* **ŏn′**klāv′) *n.* **1.** A country or part of a country that lies completely within the boundaries of another. **2.** A distinctly separated area enclosed within a larger unit: *ethnic enclaves in a large city.*

en•close (ĕn **klōz′**) also **in•close** (ĭn **klōz′**) *tr.v.* **en•closed, en•clos•ing, en•clos•es** also **in•closed, in•clos•ing, in•clos•es.** **1.** To surround on all sides; close in: *A high fence encloses the yard.* **2.** To contain, especially so as to envelop or shelter. **3.** To insert in the same envelope or package: *I enclosed a check for twenty-five dollars with the order.*

emu

Word Building: –en¹

The basic meaning of the suffix **–en¹** is "to cause to be" or "to become." When added to nouns and adjectives, **–en¹** forms verbs: **lengthen, soften.** The suffix **–en²**, meaning "made of; resembling," is an adjective suffix. That is, **–en²** changes nouns into adjectives: **wooden, golden.** The suffix **–en¹** comes from Old English *–nian*, and **–en²** is from Old English *–en.*

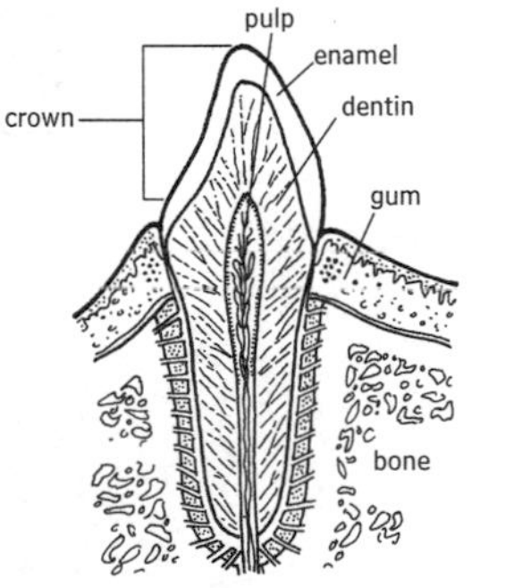

enamel

Cross section of an incisor

ă	pat	oi	boy
ā	pay	ou	out
âr	care	o͝o	took
ä	father	o͞o	boot
ĕ	pet	ŭ	cut
ē	be	ûr	urge
ĭ	pit	th	thin
ī	pie	*th*	this
îr	pier	hw	whoop
ŏ	pot	zh	vision
ō	toe	ə	about
ô	paw	N	*French* bon

en•clo•sure (ĕn klō′zhər) *n.* **1.** The act of enclosing or the state of being enclosed: *enclosure of a payment.* **2.** Something enclosed: *a garden in the middle of the enclosure; a business letter with enclosures.* **3.** Something that encloses, as a wall or fence: *The zoo had a high enclosure to keep the antelopes in.*

en•code (ĕn kōd′) *tr.v.* **en•cod•ed, en•cod•ing, en•codes.** To put (a message, for example) into code: *encoded the note.* **—en•cod′er** *n.*

en•co•mi•um (ĕn kō′mē əm) *n., pl.* **en•co•mi•ums** or **en•co•mi•a** (ĕn kō′mē ə). A formal expression of praise; a tribute.

en•com•pass (ĕn kŭm′pəs) *tr.v.* **en•com•passed, en•com•pass•ing, en•com•pass•es. 1.** To form a circle or ring about; surround. **2.** To constitute or include: *The report encompassed a number of different subjects.*

en•core (ŏn′kôr′) *n.* **1.** A demand by an audience for an additional performance, usually expressed by applause. **2.** An additional performance in response to such a demand: *Three short songs made the perfect encore.* —*interj.* An expression used to demand an additional performance. [First written down in 1712 in Modern English, from French *encore*, still, yet, again.]

en•coun•ter (ĕn koun′tər) *n.* **1.** A chance or unexpected meeting: *a frightening encounter with a bear.* **2.** A hostile or adversarial confrontation: *an encounter between British and Colonial troops.* —*tr.v.* **en•coun•tered, en•coun•ter•ing, en•coun•ters. 1.** To meet, especially unexpectedly: *encounter a snake on the path.* **2.** To confront in battle or contention. **3.** To come up against: *encounter many problems.* [First written down about 1300 in Middle English and spelled *encontre*, from Old French *encontrer*, to meet, from Late Latin *incontrāre*.]

en•cour•age (ĕn kûr′ĭj *or* ĕn kŭr′ĭj) *tr.v.* **en•cour•aged, en•cour•ag•ing, en•cour•ag•es. 1.** To give hope, courage, or confidence to; hearten: *The favorable report encouraged me somewhat.* **2.** To give support to; foster. **3.** To stimulate; spur: *Fertilizer encourages the growth of plants.*

en•cour•age•ment (ĕn kûr′ĭj mənt *or* ĕn kŭr′ĭj mənt) *n.* **1.** The act of encouraging: *the encouragement of friends to enter a contest.* **2.** A person or thing that encourages: *Kind words are an encouragement.*

en•cour•ag•ing (ĕn kûr′ə jĭng *or* ĕn kŭr′ə jĭng) *adj.* Giving courage, hope, or confidence: *We were heartened to hear the encouraging news.*

en•croach (ĕn krōch′) *intr.v.* **en•croached, en•croach•ing, en•croach•es. 1.** To take another's possessions or rights gradually or stealthily: *encroach on a neighbor's land.* **2.** To advance beyond proper or former limits: *the ocean encroaching on the shore.* **—en•croach′ment** *n.*

en•crust (ĕn krŭst′) *tr.v.* **en•crust•ed, en•crust•ing, en•crusts.** To cover with or as if with a crust or hard layer: *Ice encrusted the windowpanes. The crown was encrusted with jewels.* **—en′crus•ta′tion** *n.*

en•cum•ber (ĕn kŭm′bər) *tr.v.* **en•cum•bered, en•cum•ber•ing, en•cum•bers. 1.** To put a heavy load on; burden: *The heavy pack encumbered the hiker.* **2.** To hinder or impede the action or performance of: *restrictions that encumber police work.* **3.** To burden with legal or financial obligations.

en•cum•brance (ĕn kŭm′brəns) *n.* A person or thing that encumbers; a burden or an obstacle.

–ency *suff.* A suffix that means quality or condition: *dependency; emergency.*

en•cyc•li•cal (ĕn sĭk′lĭ kəl) *n.* A letter from the pope addressed to the bishops of the Roman Catholic Church or to the hierarchy of a particular country.

en•cy•clo•pe•di•a (ĕn sī′klə pē′dē ə) *n.* A book or set of books containing articles, usually arranged in alphabetical order and covering one particular field or a wide variety of subjects. [First written down in 1531 in Modern English, from Greek *enkuklios paideia*, general education : *enkuklios*, circular, general + *paideia*, education (from *pais*, child).]

en•cy•clo•pe•dic (ĕn sī′klə pē′dĭk) *adj.* **1.** Of, relating to, or characteristic of an encyclopedia. **2.** Having or covering many subjects; comprehensive: *a scholar with encyclopedic knowledge.*

end (ĕnd) *n.* **1.a.** Either point where something that has length begins or stops: *They sat at opposite ends of the table.* **b.** The extreme edge or limit of a space or area; a boundary: *Buffalo lies at the eastern end of Lake Erie.* **2.** The finish or conclusion of something: *Summer vacation is coming to an end. I'll get paid at the end of the month.* **3.** Something toward which one strives; a goal. **4.** Death or ruin. **5.** The ultimate extent of something; the final limit: *at the end of one's savings; at the end of one's patience.* **6.** A share of a responsibility: *your end of the bargain; the financial end of a business.* **7.** In football, either of two players stationed at the outermost position of a team's line. —*v.* **end•ed, end•ing, ends.** —*tr.* **1.** To bring to a conclusion; finish: *a nice way to end a trip.* See Synonyms at **complete. 2.** To form the last or concluding part of: *A chase ends the story.* —*intr.* To come to a finish; cease: *The game ended in a tie.* **—*idioms.* in the end.** Eventually; ultimately: *There were many problems, but it worked out in the end.* **no end.** A great deal: *We have no end of stories to tell after all our adventures.* [First written down about 725 in Old English and spelled *ende*.]

en•dan•ger (ĕn dān′jər) *tr.v.* **en•dan•gered, en•dan•ger•ing, en•dan•gers.** To put in danger; imperil: *Forest fires endanger wildlife.*

en•dan•gered (ĕn dān′jərd) *adj.* In danger of extinction: *The rhinoceros is an endangered species.*

en•dear (ĕn dîr′) *tr.v.* **en•deared, en•dear•ing, en•dears.** To make beloved or very sympathetic: *The kitten quickly endeared itself to the whole family.* **—en•dear′ing•ly** *adv.*

en•dear•ment (ĕn dîr′mənt) *n.* **1.** The act of endearing. **2.** An expression of affection.

en•deav•or (ĕn dĕv′ər) *n.* An earnest effort toward an end; a serious attempt. —*tr.v.* **en•deav•ored, en•deav•or•ing, en•deav•ors.** To make an effort (to do or accomplish something); try: *endeavored to improve their quality of life.* [First written down in 1417 in Middle English and spelled *endevour*, from *endeveren*, to make an effort, from *(putten) in dever*, (to put oneself) in duty, make it one's duty, from Old French *deveir*, duty.]

en•dem•ic (ĕn dĕm′ĭk) *adj.* Common in or restricted to a particular region, area, country, or group of people: *a disease endemic in a certain country.* —*n.* An endemic disease.

end•ing (ĕn′dĭng) *n.* **1.** The concluding part, especially of a book, play, or film: *The comedy has a happy ending.* **2.** A letter or letters added to the end of a word to change the meaning or show some relationship of grammar, as in adding *-ed* to *walk* to make the past tense *walked.*

en•dive (ĕn′dīv′ *or* ŏn′dēv′) *n.* **1.** A plant having crisp, curly, or wavy leaves used in salads. **2.** A related plant having a narrow pointed cluster of whitish leaves used in salads. [First written down in 1373 in Middle English, from Greek *entubon*.]

endive
Top: Curly endive
Bottom: Belgian endive

end•less (ĕnd′lĭs) *adj.* **1.** Being or seeming to be without an end; infinite: *endless stretches of sandy* *beaches.* **2.** Formed with the ends joined; continuous: *an endless chain.* —**end′less•ly** *adv.* —**end′less•ness** *n.*

end•most (ĕnd′mōst′) *adj.* Being at or closest to the end; last: *the endmost rooms on a hall.*

endo– or **end–** *pref.* A prefix that means inside or within: *endoderm; endosperm.*

en•do•car•di•um (ĕn′dō kär′dē əm) *n., pl.* **en•do•car•di•a** (ĕn′dō kär′dē ə). The smooth membrane that lines the cavities of the heart.

en•do•crine (ĕn′də krĭn *or* ĕn′də krēn′) *adj.* **1.** Secreting internally rather than through a duct; secreting hormones directly into the blood or lymph. **2.** Of or relating to endocrine glands or the hormones they secrete: *endocrine secretions; an endocrine disease.* —*n.* **1.** An endocrine gland. **2.** The secretion of an endocrine gland.

endocrine gland *n.* Any of various ductless glands, such as the thyroid gland or adrenal gland, that produce hormones that pass directly into the bloodstream or lymphatic system.

en•do•cri•nol•o•gy (ĕn′də krə nŏl′ə jē) *n.* The branch of biology or medicine that deals with endocrine glands, their functions, and their diseases.

en•do•derm (ĕn′də dûrm′) *n.* The innermost of the three layers of cells found in an early embryo, developing into the lining of the digestive system and lungs and certain organs such as the liver and pancreas.

en•do•plasm (ĕn′də plăz′əm) *n.* The inner portion of the cytoplasm of a cell.

en•dor•phin (ĕn dôr′fĭn) *n.* Any of a group of chemicals present in the brain that affect various bodily responses, such as pain or emotion.

en•dorse (ĕn dôrs′) *tr.v.* **en•dorsed, en•dors•ing, en•dors•es. 1.** To write one's signature on the back of (a check, for example) as evidence of the legal transfer of its ownership: *endorse a check in order to receive payment.* **2.** To give approval of; support: *Many have already endorsed the idea of national health care.* [First written down before 1400 in Middle English and spelled *endossen*, from Medieval Latin *indorsāre* : Latin *in-*, in, on + Latin *dorsum*, back.] —**en•dors′er** *n.*

en•dorse•ment (ĕn dôrs′mənt) *n.* **1.** Something, such as a signature, that endorses or validates. **2.** Approval; support: *The plan has the endorsement of the mayor.*

en•do•scope (ĕn′də skōp′) *n.* An optical instrument for examining the inside of a hollow organ or tube, such as the urethra or rectum.

en•do•skel•e•ton (ĕn′dō skĕl′ĭ tn) *n.* A supporting structure or framework within the body, as the skeleton in humans and other vertebrates.

en•do•sperm (ĕn′də spûrm′) *n.* A part of a plant seed that contains stored food and supplies nourishment for the developing embryo.

en•do•ther•mic (ĕn′dō thûr′mĭk) *adj.* Causing or characterized by absorption of heat: *an endothermic chemical reaction.*

en•dow (ĕn dou′) *tr.v.* **en•dowed, en•dow•ing, en•dows. 1.** To provide with property, income, or a source of income: *endow a school.* **2.** To provide with a talent or quality: *Nature endowed him with a good singing voice.* [First written down in 1375 in Middle English and spelled *indowen*, from Anglo-Norman *endouer*, from Latin *dōtāre*, to provide with a dowry.]

en•dow•ment (ĕn dou′mənt) *n.* **1.** Money or property donated to an institution or person as a source of income: *An endowment pays for new library books.* **2.** A natural gift, ability, or quality.

end•point or **end point** (ĕnd′point′) *n.* **1.** Either of two points that mark the ends of a line segment. **2.** A tip or point of termination.

end table *n.* A small table, usually placed beside a chair or couch.

en•dur•a•ble (ĕn do͝or′ə bəl *or* ĕn dyo͝or′ə bəl) *adj.* Capable of being endured; tolerable: *an endurable pain.* —**en•dur′a•bly** *adv.*

en•dur•ance (ĕn do͝or′əns *or* ĕn dyo͝or′əns) *n.* **1.** The act, quality, or power to withstand stress or hardship: *Climbing a high mountain is a test of endurance.* **2.** The state or fact of persevering. **3.** Continuing existence; duration.

en•dure (ĕn do͝or′ *or* ĕn dyo͝or′) *v.* **en•dured, en•dur•ing, en•dures.** —*tr.* **1.** To carry on through, despite hardships: *The early settlers of America endured long cold winters.* **2.** To bear with tolerance; put up with: *I could no longer endure such rudeness.* —*intr.* **1.** To continue to exist; last: *a name that will endure forever.* **2.** To suffer patiently without yielding: *The prisoners endured in spite of terrible conditions.* [First written down about 1380 in Middle English and spelled *enduren*, from Latin *indūrāre*, to make hard, from *dūrus*, hard.]

en•dur•ing (ĕn do͝or′ĭng *or* ĕn dyo͝or′ĭng) *adj.* Lasting; durable: *the enduring friendship of the old schoolmates.*

end•wise (ĕnd′wīz′) also **end•ways** (ĕnd′wāz′) *adv.* **1.** On end; upright: *Stand the books endwise on the shelf.* **2.** With the end forward: *a bookcase standing endwise out into the room.* **3.** Lengthwise: *a couch placed endwise along a wall.* **4.** End to end: *Lay the bricks endwise to make the wall.*

end zone *n.* In football, the area between the goal line and the end line at each end of the playing field.

en•e•ma (ĕn′ə mə) *n., pl.* **en•e•mas. 1.** The injection of a liquid into the rectum through the anus for cleansing, as a laxative, or for other therapeutic purposes. **2.** The liquid used in this way.

en•e•my (ĕn′ə mē) *n., pl.* **en•e•mies. 1.** A person who feels hatred toward, intends injury to, or opposes the interests of another; a foe. **2.a.** A hostile power or force, such as a nation: *During a war, neighboring nations may be enemies.* **b.** A unit or member of such a force: *The enemy sailed into battle with guns blazing.* **3.** Something harmful or destructive: *Disease is an enemy of plant and animal life.* —*adj.* Of, relating to, or being a hostile power or force: *enemy soldiers.* [First written down about 1225 in Middle English and spelled *enemi*, from Latin *inimīcus* : *in-*, not + *amīcus*, friend.] —SEE NOTE at **collective noun.**

en•er•get•ic (ĕn′ər jĕt′ĭk) *adj.* Possessing, exerting, or displaying energy: *The energetic efforts of the crew helped us meet our building deadline.* —**en′er•get′i•cal•ly** *adv.*

en•er•gize (ĕn′ər jīz′) *tr.v.* **en•er•gized, en•er•giz•ing, en•er•giz•es.** To give energy to; activate or invigorate: *This switch energizes the electric circuit.* —**en′er•giz′er** *n.*

en•er•gy (ĕn′ər jē) *n., pl.* **en•er•gies. 1.** The capacity for work or vigorous activity; vigor; power: *lacked the energy to finish the job.* **2.** Exertion of power or vigor: *a project requiring a lot of energy.* **3.** Usable heat or power. **4.** The capacity for doing work, as turning, pushing, or raising something. Energy can be electrical, mechanical, chemical, thermal, or nuclear. It is measured by the work done. [First written down in 1599 in Modern English, from Greek *energeia*, from *energos*, active : *en-*, in, at + *ergon*, work.]

en•er•vate (ĕn′ər vāt′) *tr.v.* **en•er•vat•ed, en•er•vat•ing, en•er•vates.** To weaken or destroy the strength or vitality of: *The prolonged hot weather enervated everyone.* —**en′er•va′tion** *n.*

en•fee•ble (ĕn fē′bəl) *tr.v.* **en•fee•bled, en•fee•bling, en•fee•bles.** To deprive of strength; make feeble. —**en•fee′ble•ment** *n.*

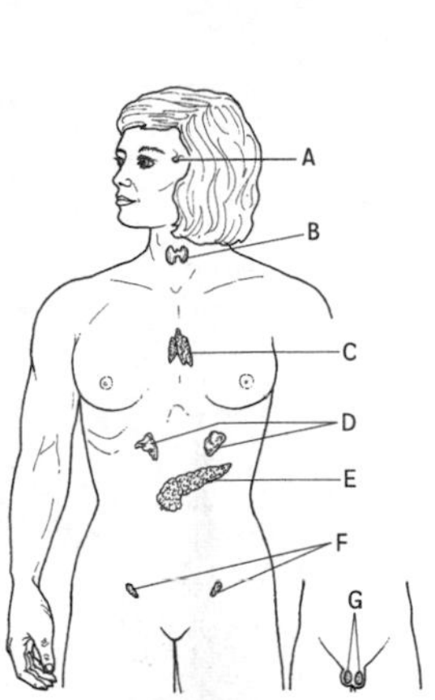

endocrine gland
A. Pituitary gland
B. Thyroid
C. Thymus
D. Adrenal glands
E. Pancreas
F. Ovaries
G. Testes

ă	pat	oi	boy
ā	pay	ou	out
âr	care	o͝o	took
ä	father	o͞o	boot
ĕ	pet	ŭ	cut
ē	be	ûr	urge
ĭ	pit	th	thin
ī	pie	*th*	this
îr	pier	hw	whoop
ŏ	pot	zh	vision
ō	toe	ə	about
ô	paw	N	*French* bon

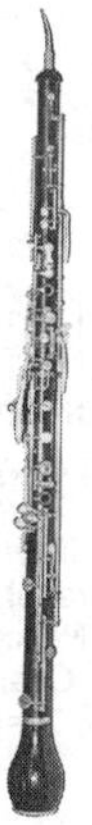

English horn

engraving
Pattern on a knife blade

en•fold (ĕn fōld′) *tr.v.* **en•fold•ed, en•fold•ing, en•folds. 1.** To cover with or as if with folds; envelop: *enfold a baby in a blanket.* **2.** To embrace.

en•force (ĕn fôrs′) *tr.v.* **en•forced, en•forc•ing, en•forc•es. 1.** To compel observance of or obedience to: *enforce parking regulations.* **2.** To compel; force: *Librarians enforce silence in the library.* **3.** To give force to; reinforce: *a documentary film that enforced our opinions.* **—en•force′a•ble** *adj.* **—en•force′ment** *n.*

en•fran•chise (ĕn frăn′chīz′) *tr.v.* **en•fran•chised, en•fran•chis•ing, en•fran•chis•es.** To endow with the rights of citizenship, especially the right to vote: *An amendment to the Constitution enfranchised women.* **—en•fran′chise•ment** *n.*

eng. *abbr.* An abbreviation of: **1.** Engine. **2.** Engineer. **3.** Engineering.

Eng. *abbr.* An abbreviation of: **1.** England. **2.** English.

en•gage (ĕn gāj′) *v.* **en•gaged, en•gag•ing, en•gag•es.** *—tr.* **1.** To obtain or contract for the services of; employ: *engage a carpenter to build a porch.* **2.** To arrange for the use of; reserve: *engage a room for a meeting.* **3.** To pledge or promise, especially to marry. **4.** To attract and hold the attention of: *The parade of fire trucks engaged us for an hour.* **5.** To require the use of; occupy: *Studying engages much of my time.* **6.** To enter or bring into conflict with: *planes that engaged the enemy over the bay.* **7.** To interlock or cause to interlock; mesh: *A lever engages the gears.* *—intr.* **1.** To involve oneself or become occupied; participate: *They engaged in a lively conversation.* **2.** To assume an obligation; agree: *They engaged to finish the project on schedule.* **3.** To enter into conflict or battle: *The armies engaged at dawn.* **4.** To become meshed or interlock: *The gears engaged.* [First written down in 1430 in Middle English and spelled *engagen*, to pledge something as security for repayment of debt, from Old French *engagier* : *en-*, in + *gage*, pledge, of Germanic origin.]

en•gaged (ĕn gājd′) *adj.* **1.** Employed, occupied, or busy. **2.** Pledged to marry; betrothed: *an engaged couple.* **3.** Being in gear; meshed.

en•gage•ment (ĕn gāj′mənt) *n.* **1.** An act of engaging or the state of being engaged. **2.a.** Betrothal. **b.** Something that serves to engage; a pledge. **3.** A promise to be at a particular place at a certain time: *a dinner engagement.* **4.** Employment, especially for a set length of time: *an actor's two-week engagement.* **5.** A battle; a military encounter.

en•gag•ing (ĕn gā′jĭng) *adj.* Charming; attractive: *an engaging smile.* See Synonyms at **interesting.** **—en•gag′ing•ly** *adv.*

En•gels (ĕng′əlz *or* ĕng′əls), **Friedrich.** 1820–1895. German socialist theorist who collaborated with Karl Marx on *The Communist Manifesto* (1848).

en•gen•der (ĕn jĕn′dər) *tr.v.* **en•gen•dered, en•gen•der•ing, en•gen•ders.** To give rise to; bring into existence: *A candid manner engenders trust.*

en•gine (ĕn′jĭn) *n.* **1.** A machine that turns energy into mechanical force or motion, especially one that gets its energy from a source of heat, as the burning of a fuel. **2.** A mechanical appliance, instrument, or tool: *The battering ram is an ancient engine of warfare.* **3.** A railroad locomotive: *The freight train was drawn by a diesel engine.* [First written down before 1300 in Middle English, from Latin *ingenium*, innate ability.]

en•gi•neer (ĕn′jə nîr′) *n.* **1.** A person who is specially trained or works in a branch of engineering. **2.** A person who operates an engine: *a locomotive engineer.* **3.** A person who skillfully or shrewdly manages a project: *The head of our advertising department was the engineer of this sales campaign.* *—tr.v.* **en•gi•neered, en•gi•neer•ing, en•gi•neers. 1.** To plan, construct, or manage as an engineer: *engineer a new bridge.* **2.** To plan, manage, and accomplish by skill or shrewdness; maneuver: *engineered the entire party.*

en•gi•neer•ing (ĕn′jə nîr′ĭng) *n.* The use of scientific and mathematical principles to design and build structures, machines, and systems. Bridges, automobiles, and electronic circuits are products of engineering.

Eng•land (ĭng′glənd). A division of the United Kingdom in the southern part of the island of Great Britain east and south of Wales. England is joined with Wales, Scotland, and Northern Ireland in forming the United Kingdom. London is the capital and the largest city of both England and the United Kingdom. Population, 46,220,955.

Eng•lish (ĭng′glĭsh) *adj.* Of, relating to, or characteristic of England or its people or culture. *—n.* **1.** The people of England. **2.** The West Germanic language of England, the United States, and other countries that are or have been under English influence or control. **3.** Often **english.** The spin given to a ball by striking it on one side or releasing it with a sharp twist.

English Channel. An arm of the Atlantic Ocean between western France and southern England. It opens into the North Sea.

English horn *n.* A woodwind instrument similar to but larger than the oboe and pitched below it.

Eng•lish•man (ĭng′glĭsh mən) *n.* **1.** A man who is a native or inhabitant of England. **2.** A man of English descent.

English muffin *n.* A flat round muffin made of yeast dough, usually split and served toasted.

English sparrow *n.* The house sparrow.

Eng•lish•wom•an (ĭng′glĭsh wo͝om′ən) *n.* **1.** A woman who is a native or inhabitant of England. **2.** A woman of English descent.

en•gorge (ĕn gôrj′) *tr.v.* **en•gorged, en•gorg•ing, en•gorg•es. 1.** To devour greedily: *engorged a meal in just minutes.* **2.** To congest or overfill with blood or other fluid: *The tick was engorged with blood.* **—en•gorge′ment** *n.*

en•graft (ĕn grăft′) *tr.v.* **en•graft•ed, en•graft•ing, en•grafts.** To graft (a shoot) onto a tree or plant.

en•grave (ĕn grāv′) *tr.v.* **en•graved, en•grav•ing, en•graves. 1.** To carve, cut, or etch into a material: *engrave a name on a plaque.* **2.** To carve, cut, or etch a design or letters into: *engrave a marble stone with a coat of arms.* **3.a.** To carve, cut, or etch into a block or surface used for printing: *engrave a poem into a copper plate using fine tools.* **b.** To print from a block or plate made by such a process. **4.** To impress deeply as if by carving or etching: *engrave rules of safety in a child's mind.* [First written down before 1475 in Middle English and spelled *ingraven*, from *graven*, to carve, from Old English *grafan*.] **—en•grav′er** *n.*

en•grav•ing (ĕn grā′vĭng) *n.* **1.** The art or technique of one that engraves. **2.** A design or text engraved on a surface. **3.** An engraved surface for printing. **4.** A print made from an engraved plate or block.

en•gross (ĕn grōs′) *tr.v.* **en•grossed, en•gross•ing, en•gross•es.** To occupy the complete attention of; absorb: *The interesting new book engrossed him.* [First written down before 1400 in Middle English and spelled *engrosen*, to collect in large quantity, monopolize, from Old French *en gros*, in large quantity.]

en•gross•ing (ĕn grō′sĭng) *adj.* Wholly absorbing; occupying one's complete attention: *an engrossing movie.*

en•gulf (ĕn gŭlf′) *tr.v.* **en•gulfed, en•gulf•ing, en•**

gulfs. To swallow up or overwhelm by or as if by overflowing and enclosing: *Flood waters engulfed the land near the river.*

en•hance (ĕn hăns′) *tr.v.* **en•hanced, en•hanc•ing, en•hanc•es.** To make greater, as in value, beauty, or reputation: *The gardens enhanced the grounds.* [First written down about 1280 in Middle English and spelled *anhaunsen*, from Late Latin *inaltāre*, from Latin *altus*, high.] **—en•hance′ment** *n.*

e•nig•ma (ĭ nĭg′mə) *n.* A person or thing that is puzzling, ambiguous, or hard to explain: *The disappearance of the dinosaurs remains an enigma.* [First written down before 1449 in Middle English and spelled *enigmate*, from Greek *ainigma*, from *ainissesthai*, to speak in riddles.]

en•ig•mat•ic (ĕn′ĭg măt′ĭk) or **en•ig•mat•i•cal** (ĕn′ĭg măt′ĭ kəl) *adj.* Of or resembling an enigma; puzzling: *the enigmatic behavior of an eccentric person.* **—en′ig•mat′i•cal•ly** *adv.*

en•join (ĕn join′) *tr.v.* **en•joined, en•join•ing, en•joins. 1.** To direct or impose with authority and emphasis: *The doctor enjoined the patient to walk one mile each day.* **2.** To prohibit or forbid: *The court enjoined the company from merging with its competitor.*

en•joy (ĕn joi′) *v.* **en•joyed, en•joy•ing, en•joys.** *tr.v.* **1.** To receive pleasure or satisfaction from: *I enjoy living in the country.* See Synonyms at **love. 2.** To have the use or benefit of: *You seem to enjoy good health.* *—intr.* To have a pleasurable or satisfactory time. **—*idiom.* enjoy (oneself).** To have a good time: *I enjoyed myself at the ball game.* [First written down about 1384 in Middle English and spelled *enjoien*, from Old French *enjoir*, from Latin *gaudēre*.]

en•joy•ment (ĕn joi′mənt) *n.* **1.** The act or state of enjoying. **2.** Use or possession of something beneficial or pleasurable: *the enjoyment of good health.* **3.** Something that gives pleasure: *My grandparents' garden is their chief enjoyment.*

en•large (ĕn lärj′) *v.* **en•larged, en•larg•ing, en•larg•es.** *—tr.* To make larger; add to: *enlarge a house.* *—intr.* To become larger; grow: *The town enlarged as new businesses moved in.* See Synonyms at **increase. —*idiom.* enlarge on** or **enlarge upon.** To speak or write about more thoroughly: *The second article enlarged on the subject of the first.*

en•large•ment (ĕn lärj′mənt) *n.* **1.** An act of enlarging or the state of being enlarged: *Enlargement of the library will permit the school to buy more books.* **2.** Something that has been enlarged, especially a photograph that is larger than the original print.

en•larg•er (ĕn lär′jər) *n.* A person or thing that enlarges, especially an optical device used to make enlargements of photographic negatives.

en•light•en (ĕn līt′n) *tr.v.* **en•light•ened, en•light•en•ing, en•light•ens.** To give spiritual or intellectual insight to: *The movie enlightened us about the difficulties of improving health care in underdeveloped countries.*

en•light•en•ment (ĕn līt′n mənt) *n.* **1.** The act or means of enlightening or the state of being enlightened. **2. Enlightenment.** A movement of the 18th century that called for critical examination of previously unchallenged doctrines and beliefs.

en•list (ĕn lĭst′) *v.* **en•list•ed, en•list•ing, en•lists.** *—tr.* **1.** To engage (persons or a person) for service in the armed forces: *The army enlisted three people from the same neighborhood.* **2.** To engage the support or cooperation of: *The minister enlisted our help in giving food to the homeless.* *—intr.* **1.** To enter the armed forces: *enlist in the army after high school.* **2.** To participate actively in a cause or an enterprise: *Many volunteers enlisted as drivers.*

en•list•ed man (ĕn lĭs′tĭd) *n.* A man in the armed forces ranking below a commissioned officer or warrant officer.

enlisted woman *n.* A woman in the armed forces ranking below a commissioned officer or warrant officer.

en•liv•en (ĕn lī′vən) *tr.v.* **en•liv•ened, en•liv•en•ing, en•liv•ens.** To make lively or spirited; animate: *Music enlivened the party.*

en masse (ŏn măs′) *adv.* In a group or body; all together: *Our guests arrived en masse by taxi.*

en•mesh (ĕn mĕsh′) *tr.v.* **en•meshed, en•mesh•ing, en•mesh•es.** To entangle or catch in or as if in a net: *enmeshed in local politics.*

en•mi•ty (ĕn′mĭ tē) *n., pl.* **en•mi•ties.** Deep-seated, often mutual hatred. [First written down before 1382 in Middle English and spelled *enemite*, from Old French *enemistie*, from Latin *inimīcus*, enemy.]

en•no•ble (ĕn nō′bəl) *tr.v.* **en•no•bled, en•no•bling, en•no•bles. 1.** To make noble: *Working for a good cause ennobles a person's life.* **2.** To confer nobility upon: *ennoble a person for distinguished service.* **—en•no′ble•ment** *n.*

en•nui (ŏn wē′) *n.* Dissatisfaction resulting from lack of interest; boredom.

e•nor•mi•ty (ĭ nôr′mĭ tē) *n., pl.* **e•nor•mi•ties. 1.** The quality of passing all moral bounds; excessive wickedness or outrageousness. **2.** A monstrous offense or evil; an outrage.

e•nor•mous (ĭ nôr′məs) *adj.* Very great in size, extent, number, or degree: *an enormous elephant; the enormous cost of building a sports arena.* See Synonyms at **large.** [First written down in 1531 in Modern English, from Latin *enormis*, unusual, huge : *ē-*, *ex-*, out of + *norma*, norm.] **—e•nor′mous•ly** *adv.* **—e•nor′mous•ness** *n.*

e•nough (ĭ nŭf′) *adj.* Sufficient to meet a need or satisfy a desire: *There is enough food for everybody.* *—pron.* An adequate amount or quantity: *The hungry hiker ate enough for two.* *—adv.* **1.** To a satisfactory amount or degree; sufficiently: *Are you warm enough?* **2.** Very; fully; quite: *We were glad enough to leave after waiting so long.* **3.** Tolerably; rather: *The songs were good enough, but the show didn't draw a big audience.* [First written down before 899 in Old English and spelled *genōg*.]

en•quire (ĕn kwīr′) *v.* Variant of **inquire.**

en•quir•y (ĕn kwīr′ē *or* ĕn′kwə rē) *n., pl.* **en•quir•ies.** Variant of **inquiry.**

en•rage (ĕn rāj′) *tr.v.* **en•raged, en•rag•ing, en•rag•es.** To put into a rage; infuriate: *The plan to put a highway right through town enraged the residents.*

en•rap•ture (ĕn răp′chər) *tr.v.* **en•rap•tured, en•rap•tur•ing, en•rap•tures.** To fill with rapture or delight: *The music enraptured the audience.*

en•rich (ĕn rĭch′) *tr.v.* **en•riched, en•rich•ing, en•rich•es. 1.** To make rich or richer: *Foreign words have enriched the English language.* **2.** To add fertilizer to (soil). **3.** To add nutrients, such as vitamins and minerals, to (food). **4.** To increase the amount of a radioactive isotope in (a material): *enrich nuclear fuel.* **—en•rich′ment** *n.*

en•roll also **en•rol** (ĕn rōl′) *v.* **en•rolled, en•roll•ing, en•rolls** also **en•rols.** *—tr.* To enter or register in a list, record, or roll: *enrolled the child in kindergarten; enroll new students for an art class.* *—intr.* To place one's name on a roll or register: *enroll as a voter before the elections; enroll in the advanced Spanish class.*

en•roll•ment also **en•rol•ment** (ĕn rōl′mənt) *n.* **1.** The act or process of enrolling. **2.** The number enrolled: *The school has an enrollment of 600.*

en route (ŏn ro͞ot′ *or* ĕn ro͞ot′) *adv. & adj.* On or

ă	**pat**	oi	**boy**
ā	**pay**	ou	**out**
âr	**care**	o͝o	**took**
ä	**father**	o͞o	**boot**
ĕ	**pet**	ŭ	**cut**
ē	**be**	ûr	**urge**
ĭ	**pit**	th	**thin**
ī	**pie**	*th*	**this**
îr	**pier**	hw	**whoop**
ŏ	**pot**	zh	**vision**
ō	**toe**	ə	**about**
ô	**paw**	N	*French* **bon**

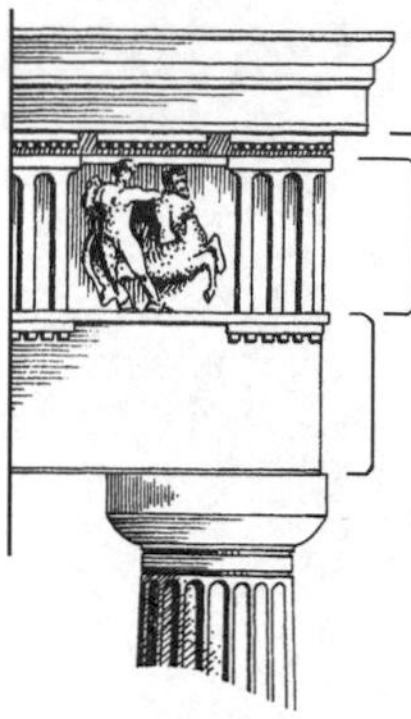

entablature

Word History: enthuse

The verb **enthuse** is a **back-formation**, which is a word formed by dropping a suffix from another word that already exists. *Enthuse* was made from **enthusiasm**. Many back-formations sound strange at first and are not fully accepted, and *enthuse* is one of these. Another such unwelcome intruder is the verb *burgle*, which is a back-formation from **burglar** and means "to burglarize." Other back-formations may enter respectable society, such as the verbs **donate**, from **donation**, and **diagnose**, from **diagnosis**.

along the way: *We'll pick you up en route to the theater.*

en•sconce (ĕn **skŏns′**) *tr.v.* **en•sconced, en•sconc•ing, en•sconc•es. 1.** To settle (oneself) comfortably or snugly: *Our visitors ensconced themselves on the couch.* **2.** To put or hide in a safe place.

en•sem•ble (ŏn **sŏm′**bəl) *n.* **1.** A coordinated outfit or costume: *a colorful ensemble of dress, shoes, and bag.* **2.** A group of musicians, singers, dancers, or actors who perform together. **3.** A musical work for two or more vocalists or instrumentalists. [First written down before 1500 in Middle English, from Late Latin *īnsimul*, at the same time.]

en•shrine (ĕn **shrīn′**) *tr.v.* **en•shrined, en•shrin•ing, en•shrines. 1.** To enclose in or as if in a shrine. **2.** To cherish as sacred. **—en•shrine′ment** *n.*

en•shroud (ĕn **shroud′**) *tr.v.* **en•shroud•ed, en•shroud•ing, en•shrouds.** To cover with or as if with a shroud: *Fog enshrouded the city.*

en•sign (**ĕn′**sən *or* **ĕn′**sīn′) *n.* **1.** A national flag displayed on ships and aircraft: *the naval ensign of the United States.* **2.** A badge of office or power; a token. **3.** (**ĕn′**sən). An officer in the U.S. Navy or Coast Guard ranking below lieutenant junior grade. [First written down in 1375 in Middle English and spelled *ensigne*, from Latin *īnsignia*, signal, sign.]

en•si•lage (**ĕn′**sə lĭj) *n.* **1.** The process of storing and fermenting green fodder in a silo. **2.** Silage.

en•slave (ĕn **slāv′**) *tr.v.* **en•slaved, en•slav•ing, en•slaves.** To make into or as if into a slave. **—en•slave′ment** *n.*

en•snare (ĕn **snâr′**) *tr.v.* **en•snared, en•snar•ing, en•snares.** To catch in or as if in a trap or snare: *ensnare customers into buying something they don't need.*

en•snarl (ĕn **snärl′**) *tr.v.* **en•snarled, en•snarl•ing, en•snarls.** To entangle in or as if in a snare: *The net ensnarled the ship's propeller.*

en•sue (ĕn **so͞o′**) *intr.v.* **en•sued, en•su•ing, en•sues. 1.** To follow as a consequence or result: *After their angry words a real fight ensued.* **2.** To follow immediately afterward. See Synonyms at **follow.** [First written down before 1400 in Middle English and spelled *insuyen*, from Latin *īnsequī*, to follow closely.]

en•sure (ĕn **sho͝or′**) *tr.v.* **en•sured, en•sur•ing, en•sures.** To make sure or certain; guarantee: *measures to ensure good health.* —SEE NOTE at **assure.**

–ent *suff.* A suffix that means: **1.** Performing, promoting, or causing a specified action: *absorbent.* **2.** Being in a specified state or condition: *independent.* **3.** A person or thing that performs, promotes, or causes a specified action: *superintendent; correspondent.*

en•tab•la•ture (ĕn **tăb′**lə cho͝or′) *n.* The upper section of a classical structure, resting on the columns and made up of the architrave, frieze, and cornice.

en•tail (ĕn **tāl′**) *tr.v.* **en•tailed, en•tail•ing, en•tails.** To impose or require as a necessary accompaniment or consequence: *Building a new tunnel will entail great expense.*

en•tan•gle (ĕn **tăng′**gəl) *tr.v.* **en•tan•gled, en•tan•gling, en•tan•gles. 1.** To make tangled; snarl: *The bushes entangled the fishing line.* **2.** To complicate or confuse: *Their explanation was entangled by many angry outbursts.* **3.** To involve in or as if in a tangle: *become entangled in a neighborhood quarrel.* **—en•tan′gle•ment** *n.*

en•ter (**ĕn′**tər) *v.* **en•tered, en•ter•ing, en•ters.** *—tr.* **1.** To come or go into: *The train entered the tunnel.* **2.** To become a part of or participant in: *enter a discussion; enter a contest.* **3.** To cause to become a participant, member, or part of; enroll: *enter a child in kindergarten; enter a collie in a dog show.* **4.** To take up; make a beginning in; start: *enter a business as a clerk; enter a medical profession.* **5.a.** To write or put in: *enter names in a guest book; enter data into a computer.* **b.** To place formally upon the records; record: *enter a plea of not guilty.* *—intr.* To come or go in: *We entered at the side of the building. Trucks enter from both sides of the road.* ***—idioms.*** **enter into. 1.** To participate in: *enter into a conversation; enter into an agreement.* **2.** To be a factor: *Many considerations entered into the decision to move.* **enter on** or **enter upon.** To begin; start: *The doctor entered on a career after graduating from medical school.* [First written down about 1275 in Middle English and spelled *entren*, from Latin *intrāre*, from *intrā*, inside.]

en•ter•i•tis (ĕn′tə **rī′**tĭs) *n.* Inflammation of the intestinal tract.

en•ter•prise (**ĕn′**tər prīz′) *n.* **1.** An undertaking, especially one of some importance, complication, and risk: *a new business enterprise.* **2.** Readiness to undertake new ventures; initiative.

en•ter•pris•ing (**ĕn′**tər prī′zĭng) *adj.* Showing initiative and willingness to undertake new projects: *An inventor must be an enterprising person.* **—en′ter•pris′ing•ly** *adv.*

en•ter•tain (ĕn′tər **tān′**) *v.* **en•ter•tained, en•ter•tain•ing, en•ter•tains.** *—tr.* **1.** To hold the attention of with something amusing or diverting: *A country music band entertained us.* **2.** To extend hospitality toward: *entertain friends at dinner.* **3.** To consider or keep in mind: *We entertained the idea of holding a fair.* *—intr.* To show hospitality to guests.

en•ter•tain•er (ĕn′tər **tā′**nər) *n.* A person, such as a singer or comic, who performs for an audience.

en•ter•tain•ing (ĕn′tər **tā′**nĭng) *adj.* Amusing; agreeably diverting: *The clown told many entertaining stories.* **—en′ter•tain′ing•ly** *adv.*

en•ter•tain•ment (ĕn′tər **tān′**mənt) *n.* **1.** The act of entertaining: *After a while the expenses of entertainment add up.* **2.** Something intended to amuse or divert, especially a performance or show. **3.** The pleasure that comes from being entertained; amusement: *offered to play the piano for our entertainment.*

en•thrall (ĕn **thrôl′**) *tr.v.* **en•thralled, en•thrall•ing, en•thralls. 1.** To hold spellbound; captivate: *The magic show enthralled everyone.* **2.** To enslave. **—en•thrall′ment** *n.*

en•throne (ĕn **thrōn′**) *tr.v.* **en•throned, en•thron•ing, en•thrones. 1.** To place on a throne. **2.** To invest with sovereign power or with the authority of high office. **3.** To raise to a lofty position; exalt. **—en•throne′ment** *n.*

en•thuse (ĕn **tho͞oz′**) *tr. & intr.v.* **en•thused, en•thus•ing, en•thus•es.** To cause to become enthusiastic or to show enthusiasm. —SEE NOTE.

en•thu•si•asm (ĕn **tho͞o′**zē ăz′əm) *n.* Great interest in or excitement for a subject or cause: *The audience applauded with enthusiasm.* [First written down in 1603 in Modern English and spelled *enthusiasme*, possession by a god, from Greek *enthousiasmos*, from *entheos*, possessed : *en-*, in + *theos*, god.]

en•thu•si•ast (ĕn **tho͞o′**zē ăst′) *n.* A person who is ardently absorbed in an interest or a pursuit: *a tennis enthusiast.*

en•thu•si•as•tic (ĕn tho͞o′zē **ăs′**tĭk) *adj.* Having or showing enthusiasm: *an enthusiastic welcome; enthusiastic support of a team.* **—en•thu′si•as′ti•cal•ly** *adv.*

en•tice (ĕn **tīs′**) *tr.v.* **en•ticed, en•tic•ing, en•tic•es.** To attract by arousing hope or desire; lure: *Advertising entices people to buy things.* **—en•tice′ment** *n.* **—en•tic′ing•ly** *adv.*

en•tire (ĕn **tīr′**) *adj.* **1.a.** Having no part missing or excepted; whole: *the entire country; his entire savings.* **b.** Without reservation or limitation; complete: *The plan has my entire approval.* **2.** All in one piece; intact. [First written down about 1390 in Middle English and spelled *entere*, from Latin *integer*.]

en•tire•ly (ĕn tīr′lē) *adv.* **1.** Wholly; completely: *an argument entirely forgotten.* **2.** Solely or exclusively: *He was entirely to blame.*

en•tire•ty (ĕn tī′rĭ tē *or* ĕn tīr′tē) *n., pl.* **en•tire•ties. 1.** The condition of being entire; completeness: *I'd like to see the plan in its entirety.* **2.** The entire amount or extent; the whole: *They wasted the entirety of their evening watching TV.*

en•ti•tle (ĕn tīt′l) *tr.v.* **en•ti•tled, en•ti•tling, en•ti•tles. 1.** To give a name or title to. **2.** To give a right or privilege to something: *This coupon entitles you to a discount.*

en•ti•ty (ĕn′tĭ tē) *n., pl.* **en•ti•ties.** Something that exists and may be distinguished from other things: *American English and British English are distinct entities.*

en•tomb (ĕn toom′) *tr.v.* **en•tombed, en•tomb•ing, en•tombs.** To place in or as if in a tomb or grave; bury: *The eruption of the volcano entombed whole buildings.* **—en•tomb′ment** *n.*

en•to•mol•o•gist (ĕn′tə mŏl′ə jĭst) *n.* A scientist who specializes in entomology.

en•to•mol•o•gy (ĕn′tə mŏl′ə jē) *n.* The branch of zoology that deals with insects. [First written down in 1766 in Modern English, from Greek *entomon*, insect.]

en•tou•rage (ŏn′tōō räzh′) *n.* A group of associates or attendants who accompany an important person: *arrived with an entourage of staff members.*

en•trails (ĕn′trālz′ *or* ĕn′trəlz) *pl.n.* The internal organs of the body, especially the intestines.

en•train (ĕn trān′) *intr. & tr.v.* To go or put aboard a train.

en•trance[1] (ĕn′trəns) *n.* **1.** The act or an instance of entering: *an actor's entrance onstage.* **2.** A means or point by which to enter: *Use the back entrance of the building for deliveries.* **3.** The permission or power to enter; admission: *Entrance to the meeting was free.* [First written down in 1473 in Middle English and spelled *entraunce*, right to enter, from Old French, from *entrer*, to enter.]

en•trance[2] (ĕn trăns′) *tr.v.* **en•tranced, en•tranc•ing, en•tranc•es. 1.** To put into a trance. **2.** To fill with delight, enchantment, or wonder; fascinate: *The exciting movie entranced us all.* [First written down in 1593 in Modern English, from *trance*.] **—en•tranc′ing** *adj.*

en•trant (ĕn′trənt) *n.* A person or an animal that enters a competition, such as a race or contest.

en•trap (ĕn trăp′) *tr.v.* **en•trapped, en•trap•ping, en•traps. 1.** To catch in or as if in a trap: *A net entrapped the fish.* **2.** To lure into danger or difficulty. **—en•trap′ment** *n.*

en•treat (ĕn trēt′) *tr.v.* **en•treat•ed, en•treat•ing, en•treats.** To ask earnestly; beg; implore.

en•treat•y (ĕn trē′tē) *n., pl.* **en•treat•ies.** An earnest request; a plea.

en•trée or **en•tree** (ŏn′trā *or* ŏn trā′) *n.* **1.** The main course of a meal. **2.** The power, permission, or liberty to enter; admittance: *gained entrée to the meeting.*

en•trench (ĕn trĕnch′) *tr.v.* **en•trenched, en•trench•ing, en•trench•es. 1.** To provide with a trench, especially to fortify or defend: *The general entrenched the forces and waited for an attack.* **2.** To fix firmly or securely: *Their opinions are so entrenched they cannot change.* **—en•trench′ment** *n.*

en•tre•pre•neur (ŏn′trə prə nûr′ *or* ŏn′trə prə nŏŏr′) *n.* A person who organizes and operates a business enterprise and assumes the risks involved.

en•trust (ĕn trŭst′) *tr.v.* **en•trust•ed, en•trust•ing, en•trusts. 1.** To turn over (something) to another for safekeeping, care, or action: *Our neighbors entrusted the care of their dog to me.* **2.** To give as a trust to (someone): *entrusted an aide with an important message.*

en•try (ĕn′trē) *n., pl.* **en•tries. 1.** The act or right of entering; entrance: *A visa is needed for entry into the country.* **2.** A means or place by which to enter: *The entry is a narrow hall.* **3.** An item written in a diary, register, list, or other record: *Each sale is an entry in this account book.* **4.** A word, phrase, or term entered and defined, as in a dictionary or an encyclopedia. **5.** A person or thing entered in a contest: *That horse was a late entry in the race.*

en•try•way (ĕn′trē wā′) *n.* A passage or an opening by which to enter.

en•twine (ĕn twīn′) *tr.v.* **en•twined, en•twin•ing, en•twines.** To twine around or together: *Ivy entwined the pillars of the porch.*

e•nu•mer•ate (ĭ nōō′mə rāt′ *or* ĭ nyōō′mə rāt′) *tr.v.* **e•nu•mer•at•ed, e•nu•mer•at•ing, e•nu•mer•ates. 1.** To count off or name one by one; list: *My list of objectives is too long to enumerate.* **2.** To determine the number of; count. **—e•nu′mer•a′tion** *n.* **—e•nu′mer•a′tor** *n.*

e•nun•ci•ate (ĭ nŭn′sē āt′) *v.* **e•nun•ci•at•ed, e•nun•ci•at•ing, e•nun•ci•ates.** *—tr.* **1.** To pronounce; articulate: *The speaker enunciated every word clearly.* **2.** To state or set forth precisely or systematically: *The speech enunciated a new program of education reforms.* *—intr.* To make articulate sounds: *The actors enunciated so poorly that we could hardly understand the play.* **—e•nun′ci•a′tor** *n.*

e•nun•ci•a•tion (ĭ nŭn′sē ā′shən) *n.* **1.** The way in which a person articulates words: *the enunciation of a preacher.* **2.** An official statement.

en•vel•op (ĕn vĕl′əp) *tr.v.* **en•vel•oped, en•vel•op•ing, en•vel•ops.** To enclose or encase completely with or as if with a covering: *Fog enveloped the tallest buildings.* [First written down in 1390 in Middle English and spelled *envolupen*, to be involved in, from Old French *envoluper* : *en-*, in + *voloper*, to wrap up.] **—en•vel′op•ment** *n.*

en•ve•lope (ĕn′və lōp′ *or* ŏn′və lōp′) *n.* **1.** A flat folded paper container, especially one used for mailing a letter. **2.** Something that envelops; a wrapping. **3.** The section of an airship or a balloon that is filled with gas. [First written down in 1705 in Modern English, from French *enveloppe*, from *envelopper*, to envelop.]

en•vi•a•ble (ĕn′vē ə bəl) *adj.* Admirable or desirable enough to be envied: *an enviable achievement.* **—en′vi•a•ble•ness** *n.* **—en′vi•a•bly** *adv.*

en•vi•ous (ĕn′vē əs) *adj.* Feeling, expressing, or characterized by envy: *Other contestants were envious of the winner.* **—en′vi•ous•ly** *adv.* **—en′vi•ous•ness** *n.*

en•vi•ron•ment (ĕn vī′rən mənt *or* ĕn vī′ərn mənt) *n.* **1.a.** All of the surroundings and conditions that affect the growth and development of living things: *Fish and birds, like all living things, must adapt to their environments.* **b.** The condition of the surroundings, such as water, soil, and air in which living things exist: *a clean environment without industrial pollution.* **2.** The social and cultural conditions affecting the nature of a person or community. [First written down in 1603 in Modern English, from Old French *environ*, round about.]

en•vi•ron•men•tal (ĕn vī′rən mĕn′tl *or* ĕn vī′ərn mĕn′tl) *adj.* Of, relating to, or associated with the environment: *Climate is an important environ-*

ă	pat	oi	boy
ā	pay	ou	out
âr	care	ŏŏ	took
ä	father	ōō	boot
ĕ	pet	ŭ	cut
ē	be	ûr	urge
ĭ	pit	th	thin
ī	pie	*th*	this
îr	pier	hw	whoop
ŏ	pot	zh	vision
ō	toe	ə	about
ô	paw	N	*French* bon

eohippus

epaulet

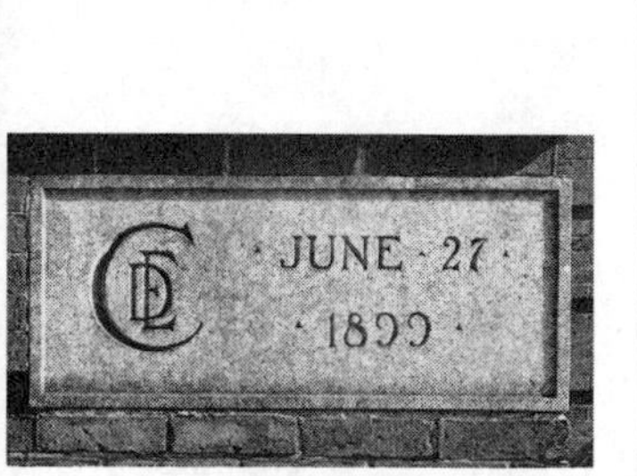
epigraph
Inscription on the Dimock Community Health Center building in Roxbury, Massachusetts

mental factor that affects plant and animal life. **—en•vi′ron•men′tal•ly** *adv.*

en•vi•rons (ĕn vī′rənz *or* ĕn vī′ərnz) *pl.n.* A surrounding area, especially of a city: *The historical environs of Boston include Lexington and Concord.*

en•vis•age (ĕn vĭz′ĭj) *tr.v.* **en•vis•aged, en•vis•ag•ing, en•vis•ag•es.** To form a picture of in the mind; conceive of: *envisage world peace.*

en•vi•sion (ĕn vĭzh′ən) *tr.v.* **en•vi•sioned, en•vi•sion•ing, en•vi•sions.** To picture in the mind; imagine.

en•voy (ĕn′voi′ *or* ŏn′voi′) *n.* **1.** A representative of a government who is sent on a special diplomatic mission. **2.** A diplomat who represents a government and ranks next below an ambassador. **3.** A messenger; an agent.

en•vy (ĕn′vē) *n., pl.* **en•vies. 1.** A feeling of discontent and resentment caused by wanting something that is possessed by or is achieved by someone else: *felt envy for her friend's new baseball glove.* **2.** The object of such a feeling: *The racing bike was the envy of everyone who saw it.* —*tr.v.* **en•vied, en•vy•ing, en•vies. 1.** To feel envy toward: *I envy you for the chance to travel to Mexico.* **2.** To regard with envy: *envy the talent of a great musician.* [First written down about 1280 in Middle English and spelled *envie*, from Latin *invidia*, from *invidēre*, to look at enviously : *in-*, on, at + *vidēre*, to see.]

en•wrap (ĕn răp′) *tr.v.* **en•wrapped, en•wrap•ping, en•wraps.** To wrap up or enclose: *presents enwrapped in beautiful paper.*

en•zyme (ĕn′zīm) *n.* Any of numerous proteins produced in living cells and acting as catalysts in the chemical processes of living organisms. Enzymes such as the lipases, for example, help break down food so that it can be digested. [First written down in 1881 in Modern English, from Medieval Greek *enzumos*, leavened : Greek *en-*, in + Greek *zumē*, yeast.]

E•o•cene (ē′ə sēn′) *adj.* Of, belonging to, or being the geologic time of the second epoch of the Tertiary Period. During the Eocene, the ancestors of many modern mammals appeared. See table at **geologic time.** —*n.* The Eocene Epoch or its series of rocks.

e•o•hip•pus (ē′ō hĭp′əs) *n.* A small extinct mammal that lived about 65 million years ago in North America and Europe. It was an ancestor of the modern horse and had several toes on each hoof.

E•o•lith•ic (ē′ə lĭth′ĭk) *adj.* Of or relating to a very early period of human culture characterized by use of roughly shaped stone tools; the earliest part of the Stone Age.

e•on (ē′ŏn′ *or* ē′ən) *n.* **1.** An extremely long period of time; an age; eternity. **2.** A division of geologic time that contains two or more eras. [First written down in 1647 in Modern English and spelled *aeon*, from Greek *aiōn*, age, lifetime.]

E•os (ē′ŏs′) *n.* In Greek mythology, the goddess of the dawn, identified with the Roman Aurora.

ep•au•let also **ep•au•lette** (ĕp′ə lĕt′ *or* ĕp′ə lĕt′) *n.* An ornamental strap worn on the shoulder of an officer's uniform.

e•phed•rine (ĭ fĕd′rĭn *or* ĕf′ĭ drēn′) *n.* A drug used to treat allergies, asthma, and hay fever.

e•phem•er•al (ĭ fĕm′ər əl) *adj.* **1.** Lasting only a brief time; short-lived: *Fame is often ephemeral, lasting only so long as the public remembers.* **2.** Living or lasting for one day, as certain plants or insects do. **—e•phem′er•al•ly** *adv.*

E•phe•sian (ĭ fē′zhən) *n.* **1.** A native or inhabitant of ancient Ephesus. **2. Ephesians.** *(used with a singular verb).* A book of the New Testament in which the Apostle Paul, in a letter to the Christians of Ephesus, discusses the nature of salvation and the moral duties of Christians. —*adj.* Of or relating to ancient Ephesus or its people, language, or culture.

Eph•e•sus (ĕf′ĭ səs). An ancient city of Greek Asia Minor in present-day western Turkey.

epi– or **ep–** *pref.* A prefix that means: **1.** On; upon: *epiphyte.* **2.** Over; above: *epicenter.*

ep•ic (ĕp′ĭk) *n.* **1.** A long poem about the deeds of heroic characters. **2.** A literary or other artistic work that has the qualities of an epic. —*adj.* **1.** Of or resembling an epic: *an epic film.* **2.** Resembling something described in an epic; grand; tremendous: *an epic achievement.* [First written down in 1589 in Modern English, from Greek *epikos*, of an epic, from *epos*, song.] **—ep′i•cal•ly** *adv.*

ep•i•cen•ter (ĕp′ĭ sĕn′tər) *n.* The part of the earth's surface that is directly above the point where an earthquake begins.

ep•i•cure (ĕp′ĭ kyo͝or′) *n.* A person with refined tastes, especially in food and wine; a gourmet. [First written down about 1384 in Middle English, after *Epicurus* (341?–270 B.C.), Greek philosopher.]

ep•i•cu•re•an (ĕp′ĭ kyo͝o rē′ən *or* ĕp′ĭ kyo͝or′ē ən) *adj.* **1.** Fond of fine food, luxurious things, and comfort: *an epicurean taste for good food.* **2.** Suited to the tastes of an epicure: *an epicurean meal of exotic foods.* —*n.* An epicure.

ep•i•dem•ic (ĕp′ĭ dĕm′ĭk) *adj.* Spreading rapidly and widely among the inhabitants of an area: *Measles is a dangerous epidemic disease.* —*n.* **1.** An outbreak of a contagious disease that spreads rapidly. **2.** A rapid spread or development: *There were so many strikes the country was in an epidemic of labor troubles.* [First written down in 1603 in Modern English, from Greek *epidēmos*, prevalent : *epi-*, upon + *dēmos*, people.]

ep•i•der•mis (ĕp′ĭ dûr′mĭs) *n.* **1.** The outer protective layer of the skin of vertebrates. **2.** The outer protective layer of cells of the stems, roots, and leaves of plants.

ep•i•glot•tis (ĕp′ĭ glŏt′ĭs) *n.* A thin triangular plate of cartilage at the base of the tongue that covers the glottis during swallowing to keep food from entering the windpipe.

ep•i•gram (ĕp′ĭ grăm′) *n.* **1.** A short witty poem expressing a single thought. **2.** A short witty saying.

ep•i•gram•mat•ic (ĕp′ĭ grə măt′ĭk) *adj.* **1.** Of or resembling an epigram; terse; witty. **2.** Containing or inclined to use epigrams. **—ep′i•gram•mat′i•cal•ly** *adv.*

ep•i•graph (ĕp′ĭ grăf′) *n.* **1.** An inscription, as on a building or statue. **2.** A quotation at the beginning of a book or a chapter of a book that suggests its theme.

ep•i•lep•sy (ĕp′ə lĕp′sē) *n.* A disorder of the nervous system marked by seizures that sometimes involve loss of consciousness or convulsions. [First written down in 1578 in Modern English, from Greek *epilēpsis*, from *epilambanein*, to lay hold of : *epi-*, upon + *lambanein*, to seize.]

ep•i•lep•tic (ĕp′ə lĕp′tĭk) *adj.* Of or suffering from epilepsy: *an epileptic attack.* —*n.* A person who has epilepsy.

ep•i•logue also **ep•i•log** (ĕp′ə lôg′ *or* ĕp′ə lŏg′) *n.* **1.** A short poem or speech spoken directly to the audience at the end of a play. **2.** A short section at the end of a literary work, often discussing what happens to the characters after the main story. [First written down about 1425 in Middle English and spelled *epilog*, from Greek *epilogos*, conclusion of a speech : *epi-*, after + *logos*, word, speech.]

ep•i•neph•rine also **ep•i•neph•rin** (ĕp′ə nĕf′rĭn) *n.* Adrenaline.

e•piph•a•ny (ĭ pĭf′ə nē) *n., pl.* **e•piph•a•nies. 1. Epiphany.** A Christian feast that in the Western

Church celebrates the visit of the Magi to the infant Jesus and in the Eastern Churh celebrates the baptism of Jesus. **2.** A revelatory manifestation of a divine being. **3.** A sudden understanding or perception by means of intuition.

ep•i•phyte (ĕp′ə fīt′) *n.* A plant growing on another plant or object that provides support but not food; an air plant. Spanish moss and many orchids are epiphytes. **—ep′i•phyt′ic** (ĕp′ə **fĭt′**ĭk) *adj.*

e•pis•co•pal (ĭ **pĭs′**kə pəl) *adj.* **1.** Of, relating to, or governed by bishops. **2. Episcopal.** Of or relating to the Episcopal Church. [First written down about 1460 in Middle English, from Late Latin *episcopus*, bishop, from Greek *episkopos*, overseer.]

Episcopal Church *n.* The church in the United States that agrees with the Church of England in doctrine and most practices.

E•pis•co•pa•lian (ĭ pĭs′kə **pā′**lē ən *or* ĭ pĭs′kə **pāl′**yən) *adj.* Of or relating to the Episcopal Church. *—n.* A member of the Episcopal Church.

ep•i•sode (**ĕp′**ĭ sōd′) *n.* **1.a.** An event or incident in the course of a larger series: *Living in India was an exciting episode in her life.* **b.** An incident that forms a distinct part of a story. **2.** A part of a novel or radio or television program presented as a series: *The story was divided into six episodes for TV.* **—ep•i•sod′ic** (ĕp′ĭ **sŏd′**ĭk) *adj.*

e•pis•tle (ĭ **pĭs′**əl) *n.* **1.** A letter, especially a formal one. **2. Epistle.** One of the letters written by the Apostles to guide and instruct the members of the early Christian churches and included as books in the New Testament.

ep•i•taph (**ĕp′**ĭ tăf′) *n.* An inscription on a tombstone or monument in memory of the person buried there.

ep•i•the•li•um (ĕp′ə **thē′**lē əm) *n., pl.* **ep•i•the•li•ums** or **ep•i•the•li•a** (ĕp′ə **thē′**lē ə). The thin tissue that covers most of the inner and outer surfaces of an animal body and lines the inside of certain organs. **—ep′i•the′li•al** *adj.*

ep•i•thet (**ĕp′**ə thĕt′) *n.* A term used to describe the nature of a person or thing; for example, *The Big Apple* is an epithet for New York City.

e•pit•o•me (ĭ **pĭt′**ə mē) *n.* **1.** A person or thing that is a typical example of an entire class or type: *Her remark was the epitome of good judgment.* **2.** A summary of a book, article, or other literary work; an abstract.

e•pit•o•mize (ĭ **pĭt′**ə mīz′) *tr.v.* **e•pit•o•mized, e•pit•o•miz•ing, e•pit•o•miz•es.** To be a typical example of: *Daniel Boone epitomizes the independent frontiersman.*

e plu•ri•bus u•num (ē′ **plo͝or′**ə bəs **yo͞o′**nəm). Out of many, one (the official motto of the seal of the United States).

ep•och (**ĕp′**ək *or* **ē′**pŏk′) *n.* **1.** A period, especially one in history marked by certain important events or developments; an era: *the epoch of space exploration.* **2.** A unit of time that is a division of a geologic period. [First written down in 1614 in Modern English and spelled *epocha*, from Greek *epokhē*, a point in time.]

ep•och•al (**ĕp′**ə kəl) *adj.* **1.** Of or characteristic of an epoch. **2.** Highly important or significant; momentous: *epochal decisions made by Lincoln during the Civil War.*

ep•ox•y (ĭ **pŏk′**sē) *n., pl.* **ep•ox•ies.** Any of various synthetic resins that are tough, strongly adhesive, and resistant to chemicals, used in making protective coatings and glues.

ep•si•lon (**ĕp′**sə lŏn′) *n.* The fifth letter of the Greek alphabet, written Ε, ε. In English it is represented as *E, e.*

Ep•som salts (**ĕp′**səm) *pl.n. (used with a singular verb).* A colorless crystalline compound of magnesium, sulfur, and oxygen, used as a laxative and for bathing inflamed or sore parts of the body.

eq. *abbr.* An abbreviation of: **1.** Equal. **2.** Equation. **3.** Equivalent.

eq•ua•ble (**ĕk′**wə bəl *or* **ē′**kwə bəl) *adj.* **1.** Not varying; steady; even: *the equable climate of the Caribbean.* **2.** Even-tempered; not easily upset; serene: *Our teacher has an equable disposition.* **—eq′ua•bil′i•ty** *n.* **—eq′ua•bly** *adv.*

e•qual (**ē′**kwəl) *adj.* **1.a.** Having the same quantity, measure, or extent as another: *equal strength; equal size.* **b.** Having the same value: *3 + 2 and 6 − 1 are equal.* **2.** Having the same privileges, status, or rights: *All citizens are equal before the law.* **3.** Being the same for all members of a group; even: *Every player had an equal chance to win.* *—n.* A person or thing that is equal to another: *Most people want to be treated as equals.* *—tr.v.* **e•qualed, e•qual•ing, e•quals** or **e•qualled, e•qual•ling, e•quals. 1.** To be equal to: *Two pints equal a quart. My ability equals theirs.* **2.** To do, make, or produce something equal to: *The athlete equaled the world's record in the mile run.* [First written down about 1390 in Middle English, from Latin *aequālis*, from *aequus*, even, level.] **—e′qual•ly** *adv.*

e•qual•i•ty (ĭ **kwŏl′**ĭ tē) *n., pl.* **e•qual•i•ties.** The condition of being equal, especially the condition of enjoying equal rights: *equality under the law.*

e•qual•ize (**ē′**kwə līz′) *tr.v.* **e•qual•ized, e•qual•iz•ing, e•qual•iz•es. 1.** To make equal: *Opening the bottle equalizes the pressure with the outside air.* **2.** To make uniform: *Move this box to equalize the weight on both sides of the car.* **—e′qual•i•za′tion** (ē′kwə lĭ **zā′**shən) *n.* **—e′qual•iz′er** *n.*

equal sign *n.* The symbol (=) used in mathematics to show that something is equal to something else, as in $a = b$ and $2 + 2 = 4$.

e•qua•nim•i•ty (ē′kwə **nĭm′**ĭ tē *or* ĕk′wə **nĭm′**ĭ tē) *n.* The condition or quality of being calm and even-tempered; composure: *Judges are expected to show equanimity in court.*

e•quate (ĭ **kwāt′**) *tr.v.* **e•quat•ed, e•quat•ing, e•quates.** To make equal or consider as equal or equivalent: *Many people equate fame with success.*

e•qua•tion (ĭ **kwā′**zhən *or* ĭ **kwā′**shən) *n.* **1.** A mathematical statement asserting the equality of two expressions. For example, $3 \times 2 = 6$, $y = 2 + 8$, and $x + y = 18$ are all equations. **2.** An expression using chemical formulas and symbols to show the quantities and substances in a chemical reaction. For example, two hydrogen molecules reacting with an oxygen molecule to form two molecules of water is expressed by the equation $2H_2 + O_2 = 2H_2O$.

e•qua•tor (ĭ **kwā′**tər) *n.* **1.** The imaginary line that circles the earth halfway between the North and South poles. It divides the earth into the Northern Hemisphere and the Southern Hemisphere. **2.** A similar circle on any celestial body: *the sun's equator.* **3.** The celestial equator. [First written down in 1391 in Middle English, from Medieval Latin *aequator (diei et noctis)*, equalizer (of day and night), from *aequare*, to equalize.]

e•qua•to•ri•al (ē′kwə **tôr′**ē əl *or* ĕk′wə **tôr′**ē əl) *adj.* **1.** Of or near the equator: *an equatorial region of Brazil.* **2.** Characteristic of conditions at the earth's equator: *equatorial heat.*

E•qua•to•ri•al Guin•ea (ē′kwə **tôr′**ē əl **gĭn′**ē *or* **ĕk′**wə **tôr′**ē əl **gĭn′**ē). A country of west-central Africa north of Gabon including islands in the Atlantic Ocean. It gained its independence from Spain in 1968. Malabo is the capital and the largest city. Population, 300,000.

eq•uer•ry (**ĕk′**wə rē) *n., pl.* **eq•uer•ries. 1.** An officer in charge of the horses in a royal or noble

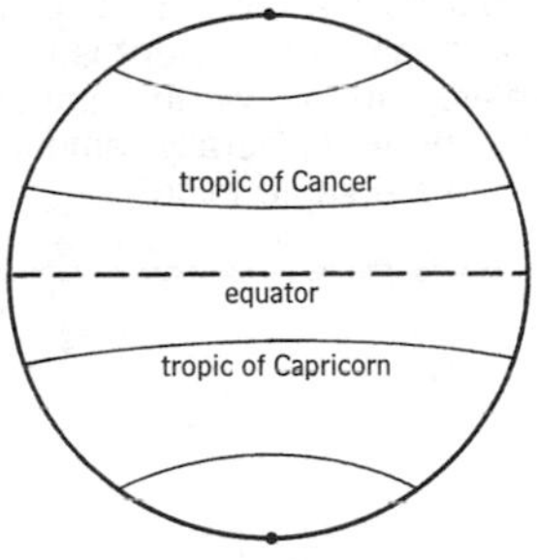

equator

ă	pat	oi	boy
ā	pay	ou	out
âr	care	o͝o	took
ä	father	o͞o	boot
ĕ	pet	ŭ	cut
ē	be	ûr	urge
ĭ	pit	th	thin
ī	pie	*th*	this
îr	pier	hw	whoop
ŏ	pot	zh	vision
ō	toe	ə	about
ô	paw	ɴ	*French* bon

equestrian

Word Building: equi–

The prefix **equi–** means "equal" or "equally." **Equi–** is from the Latin prefix *aequi–*, which came from the Latin word *aequus*, meaning "equal." Thus **equidistant** means "equally distant." **Equi–** often occurs in words with Latin elements. For example, **equinox** means "having the night equal (to the day)," from Latin *nox*, "night." **Equivalent** is from *valēre*, "to be worth, amount to," and so is literally "amounting to the same thing."

Erasmus

household. **2.** In England, a personal attendant to a member of the royal family.

e•ques•tri•an (ĭ **kwĕs′**trē ən) *adj.* **1.** Of or relating to horseback riders or horseback riding: *equestrian ability.* **2.** Mounted or represented as mounted on horseback: *an equestrian statue of the king.* —*n.* A person who rides a horse or performs on horseback. [First written down about 1656 in Modern English, from Latin *equester*, from *eques*, horseman, from *equus*, horse.]

e•ques•tri•enne (ĭ kwĕs′trē **ĕn′**) *n.* A woman who rides a horse or performs on horseback.

equi– *pref.* A prefix that means equal or equally: *equidistant.* —SEE NOTE.

e•qui•an•gu•lar (ē′kwē **ăng′**gyə lər) *adj.* Having all angles equal: *Rectangles are equiangular.*

e•qui•dis•tant (ē′kwĭ **dĭs′**tənt) *adj.* Equally distant. —**e′qui•dis′tant•ly** *adv.*

e•qui•lat•er•al (ē′kwə **lăt′**ər əl) *adj.* Having all sides equal: *an equilateral triangle.* —**e′qui•lat′er•al•ly** *adv.*

e•qui•lib•ri•um (ē′kwə **lĭb′**rē əm) *n.* **1.** A condition of balance or stability: *Ideally, the supply of a product should be in equilibrium with the demand for it.* **2.** Mental or emotional balance; poise: *The unpleasant quarrel upset their equilibrium for the whole morning.*

e•quine (**ē′**kwīn′ *or* **ĕk′**wīn′) *adj.* Of, relating to, or characteristic of a horse.

e•qui•noc•tial (ē′kwə **nŏk′**shəl *or* ĕk′wə **nŏk′**shəl) *adj.* **1.** Relating to an equinox. **2.** Occurring at or near the time of an equinox: *an equinoctial storm.*

e•qui•nox (**ē′**kwə nŏks′ *or* **ĕk′**wə nŏks′) *n.* Either of the times of year when the sun crosses the celestial equator and day and night are about equal in length. In the Northern Hemisphere, the vernal equinox occurs about March 21 and the autumnal equinox occurs about September 23. [First written down in 1391 in Middle English, from Latin *aequinoctium* : *aequi-*, equal + *nox*, night.]

e•quip (ĭ **kwĭp′**) *tr.v.* **e•quipped, e•quip•ping, e•quips.** To supply with what is needed; provide: *The expedition was equipped with oxygen tanks for climbing at high altitudes.* [First written down in 1523 in Modern English, from Old French *esquiper*, of Germanic origin; akin to Old Norse *skipa* (from *skip*, ship).]

eq•ui•page (**ĕk′**wə pĭj) *n.* **1.** Equipment, as of an army. **2.** An elegantly equipped horse-drawn carriage, usually attended by footmen.

e•quip•ment (ĭ **kwĭp′**mənt) *n.* **1.** The things needed or used for a particular purpose: *a tent, sleeping bag, and other camping equipment.* **2.** The act of equipping or state of being equipped: *The equipment of the expedition took over a month to complete.*

e•qui•poise (**ē′**kwə poiz′ *or* **ĕk′**wə poiz′) *n.* **1.** Equality in distribution, as of weight or force; balance; equilibrium. **2.** A weight or force that balances another; a counterbalance.

eq•ui•ta•ble (**ĕk′**wĭ tə bəl) *adj.* Just and impartial: *Judges are expected to make equitable decisions.* —**eq′ui•ta•bly** *adv.*

eq•ui•ty (**ĕk′**wĭ tē) *n., pl.* **eq•ui•ties. 1.** Justice; fairness; impartiality: *The law relies on the equity of a jury.* **2.a.** Something that is fair and just. **b.** A system of justice that concerns matters not covered under common law or statute law and is designed to find fair settlement of claims. **3.** The value of a business or property after debts and mortgages on it are subtracted.

e•quiv•a•lence (ĭ **kwĭv′**ə ləns) *n.* The condition or property of being equivalent.

e•quiv•a•lent (ĭ **kwĭv′**ə lənt) *adj.* **1.** Equal, as in value, meaning, or force: *The wish of the king is equivalent to a command.* **2.** Having a one-to-one correspondence, as between parts: *equivalent geometric figures.* —*n.* Something that is equivalent: *A dime is the equivalent of two nickels.* [First written down about 1425 in Middle English, from Late Latin *aequivalēre*, to have equal force : *aequi-*, equal + *valēre*, to be strong, to be worth.]

e•quiv•o•cal (ĭ **kwĭv′**ə kəl) *adj.* **1.** Capable of being interpreted in more than one way; ambiguous or misleading: *The politician gave an equivocal answer to the reporter's question.* **2.** Of uncertain significance: *The experiment gave equivocal results that we could not interpret with certainty.* **3.** Suspicious or questionable in nature: *an equivocal glance.* —**e•quiv′o•cal•ly** *adv.* —**e•quiv′o•cal•ness** *n.*

e•quiv•o•cate (ĭ **kwĭv′**ə kāt′) *intr.v.* **e•quiv•o•cat•ed, e•quiv•o•cat•ing, e•quiv•o•cates.** To use language that can be interpreted in more than one way, especially in order to mislead: *Stop equivocating and tell us what you really think.* —**e•quiv′o•ca′tor** *n.*

e•quiv•o•ca•tion (ĭ kwĭv′ə **kā′**shən) *n.* **1.** The use of language that is ambiguous or misleading. **2.** A misleading or ambiguous statement: *The facts prove the report is an equivocation.*

Er The symbol for the element **erbium.**

–er¹ *suff.* A suffix that means: **1.** A person or thing that does a specified action: *swimmer; blender.* **2.** A person who is born in or lives in a place: *islander; New Yorker.* **3.** A person or thing that is: *foreigner; six-footer.* **4.** A person or thing that is associated or involved with: *banker; gardener.*

–er² *suff.* A suffix used to form the comparative degree of adjectives and adverbs: *neater; slower.*

e•ra (**îr′**ə *or* **ĕr′**ə) *n.* **1.** A period of time as marked from a specific date or event: *The atomic era and the postwar era began with the conclusion of World War II in 1945.* **2.** A period of time characterized by particular circumstances, events, or persons: *took place during the Colonial era of American history.* **3.** The longest division of geologic time, containing one or more periods. [First written down in 1615 in Modern English and spelled *æra*, from Latin *aera*, counters, plural of *aes*, bronze coin.]

e•rad•i•cate (ĭ **răd′**ĭ kāt′) *tr.v.* **e•rad•i•cat•ed, e•rad•i•cat•ing, e•rad•i•cates. 1.** To get rid of; destroy: *Vaccination has eradicated smallpox.* **2.** To tear up by the roots. [First written down before 1425 in Middle English and spelled *eradicaten*, from Latin *ērādīcāre* : *ē-*, *ex-*, out + *rādīx*, root.] —**e•rad′i•ca′tion** *n.*

e•rase (ĭ **rās′**) *tr.v.* **e•rased, e•ras•ing, e•ras•es. 1.** To remove (something written or drawn) by rubbing, scraping, or wiping: *erase a mistake.* **2.** To remove writing or a recording from: *erase a tape.* **3.** To remove or destroy as if by wiping out: *Time will erase hurt feelings.* [First written down in 1605 in Modern English, from Latin *ērāsus*, past participle of *ērādere*, to scratch out : *ē-*, *ex-*, out + *rādere*, to scrape.]

e•ras•er (ĭ **rā′**sər) *n.* An implement that erases marks made with pencil, ink, or chalk.

E•ras•mus (ĭ **răz′**məs), **Desiderius.** 1466?–1536. Dutch scholar and theologian whose works include *The Manual of the Christian Knight* (1503).

e•ra•sure (ĭ **rā′**shər) *n.* **1.** The act of erasing. **2.** Something erased, as a word or number: *The paper had numerous erasures.*

er•bi•um (**ûr′**bē əm) *n. Symbol* **Er** A soft rare-earth element used in nuclear research and to color glass. Atomic number 68. See table at **element.**

ere (âr) *prep.* Previous to; before. —*conj.* Sooner

than; rather than. [First written down about 725 in Old English and spelled *ǣr*.]

❑ *These sound alike:* **ere, air** (gas), **e'er** (ever), **heir** (inheritor).

e•rect (ĭ **rĕkt′**) *adj.* In a vertical or upright position: *a soldier's erect posture.* —*tr.v.* **e•rect•ed, e•rect•ing, e•rects. 1.** To build; put up; construct: *erect a skyscraper.* **2.** To raise upright; set on end: *erect a new telephone pole.* **3.** To set up; establish: *The country erected a model legal system.* —**e•rect′ly** *adv.* —**e•rect′ness** *n.*

e•rec•tion (ĭ **rĕk′**shən) *n.* **1.** The act of erecting, building, or raising upright: *The erection of the new temple took nearly two years.* **2.** Something erected, as a building. **3.** The stiffening of certain tissues of the body when they fill with blood.

erg (ûrg) *n.* A unit of energy or work equal to the work done by a force of one dyne acting through a distance of one centimeter.

er•go (**ûr′**gō *or* **âr′**gō) *conj. & adv.* Consequently; therefore.

er•got (**ûr′**gət *or* **ûr′**gŏt′) *n.* A fungus that infects rye, wheat, and other grain plants, forming black masses among the seeds. Grain infected with ergot is poisonous and can cause serious illness.

er•got•ism (**ûr′**gə tĭz′əm) *n.* Poisoning that results from eating grain that is infected with ergot.

Er•ic•son (**ĕr′**ĭk sən), **Leif.** Flourished about 1000. Norwegian navigator who, according to legend, was blown off course during a voyage and landed on the eastern coast of North America.

E•rie (**îr′**ē) *n., pl.* **Erie** or **E•ries. 1.** A member of a Native American people formerly living in the region south of Lake Erie. **2.** The Iroquoian language of the Erie.

Erie, Lake. One of the Great Lakes, southwest of Lake Ontario and surrounded by southern Ontario, western New York, northwest Pennsylvania, northern Ohio, and southeast Michigan.

Erie Canal. An artificial waterway extending about 360 miles (579 kilometers) across central New York from Albany to Buffalo. It was constructed from 1817 to 1825.

Er•in (**ĕr′**ĭn). A poetic name for Ireland.

er•mine (**ûr′**mĭn) *n.* **1.** A weasel of northern regions having brownish fur that turns white in winter. **2.** The valuable white fur of this animal.

e•rode (ĭ **rōd′**) *v.* **e•rod•ed, e•rod•ing, e•rodes.** —*tr.* **1.** To wear away by or as if by rubbing or scraping: *Wind eroded the hillside.* **2.** To eat into; corrode: *The acidity of the water eroded the pipes.* **3.** To form by wearing away: *The river eroded a deep gorge through the rock.* **4.** To cause to diminish or disappear: *The bookkeeper's mistakes eroded their trust in his work.* —*intr.* To become worn away gradually: *Dust storms are caused by soil that erodes in a strong wind.* [First written down in 1612 in Modern English, from Latin *ērōdere*, to gnaw off, eat away : *ē-*, *ex*, off, away + *rōdere*, to gnaw.]

Er•os (**ĕr′**ŏs′ *or* **îr′**ŏs′) *n.* In Greek mythology, the god of love, son of Aphrodite, identified with the Roman Cupid.

e•ro•sion (ĭ **rō′**zhən) *n.* The gradual wearing away by the action of water, wind, or a glacier: *farmland lost by soil erosion.*

e•ro•sive (ĭ **rō′**sĭv) *adj.* Acting or tending to erode: *erosive winds.*

e•rot•ic (ĭ **rŏt′**ĭk) *adj.* Of or arousing sexual desire. —**e•rot′i•cal•ly** *adv.*

err (ûr *or* ĕr) *intr.v.* **erred, err•ing, errs. 1.** To make a mistake or an error; be incorrect: *We erred in thinking the bus would be on time.* **2.** To commit an act that is wrong; sin.

er•rand (**ĕr′**ənd) *n.* **1.** A short trip taken to do something, usually for someone else: *Our neighbor asked me to run an errand to the store downtown.* **2.** The purpose or object of such a trip: *My errand was to mail a letter.* [First written down about 725 in Old English and spelled *ǣrend*; akin to *ār*, messenger.]

er•rant (**ĕr′**ənt) *adj.* **1.** Roving or wandering: *errant knights seeking adventure.* **2.** Straying from the proper course or correct behavior: *an errant youth.*

er•rat•ic (ĭ **răt′**ĭk) *adj.* **1.** Lacking a fixed course; wandering. **2.** Irregular or uneven, as in quality or progress: *erratic work.* **3.** Straying from the usual course in conduct or opinion; eccentric: *erratic behavior.* —**er•rat′i•cal•ly** *adv.*

er•ro•ne•ous (ĭ **rō′**nē əs) *adj.* Containing or derived from error; mistaken: *an erroneous belief.* —**er•ro′ne•ous•ly** *adv.*

er•ror (**ĕr′**ər) *n.* **1.** Something that is incorrect, wrong, or false: *The waiter made an error in adding up our bill.* **2.** The condition of being incorrect or wrong: *The statement is in error.* **3.** The difference between the measured value of a quantity and its exact or true value: *The error in the thermostat was 10 degrees.* **4.** In baseball, a fielding or throwing play in which a player misses the ball or throws it inaccurately, allowing a runner to reach first base or advance one or more bases. [First written down before 1300 in Middle English and spelled *errour*, from Latin *error*, from *errāre*, to err.]

er•satz (**ĕr′**zäts′) *adj.* Being a substitute or an imitation; artificial: *ersatz leather.*

erst•while (**ûrst′**wīl′) *adv.* In times past; formerly. —*adj.* Former: *an erstwhile foe.*

er•u•dite (**ĕr′**yə dīt′ *or* **ĕr′**ə dīt′) *adj.* Having or marked by great knowledge or learning; learned: *an erudite book; an erudite person.* —**er′u•dite′ly** *adv.* —**er′u•dite′ness** *n.*

er•u•di•tion (ĕr′yə **dĭsh′**ən *or* ĕr′ə **dĭsh′**ən) *n.* Extensive learning.

e•rupt (ĭ **rŭpt′**) *v.* **e•rupt•ed, e•rupt•ing, e•rupts.** —*intr.* **1.** To become violently active: *War erupted between the two nations.* **2.** To appear or develop suddenly and violently: *Their conversation erupted into a fierce argument.* **3.** To force out or release something with violence and suddenness: *The water heater erupted in a burst of steam.* **4.** To appear on the skin: *A rash erupted on the child's back.* —*tr.* To shoot forth violently: *The volcano erupted clouds of ash high into the sky.* [First written down in 1657 in Modern English, from Latin *ēruptus*, past participle of *ērumpere* : *ē-*, *ex-*, out + *rumpere*, to break.] —**e•rup′tive** *adj.*

e•rup•tion (ĭ **rŭp′**shən) *n.* **1.** The fact or an instance of erupting: *the eruption of a geyser.* **2.** A sudden, almost violent outburst: *an eruption of anger.* **3.** A rash or blemish on the skin: *an eruption caused by a virus.*

–ery or **–ry** *suff.* A suffix that means: **1.** A place for: *bakery.* **2.** A collection or class: *greenery.* **3.** A state or condition: *slavery.* **4.** Act or practice: *bribery.*

e•ryth•ro•cyte (ĭ **rĭth′**rə sīt′) *n.* A red blood cell.

Es The symbol for the element **einsteinium.**

–es[1] *suff.* Variant of **–s**[1].

–es[2] *suff.* Variant of **–s**[2].

E•sau (**ē′**sô). In the Bible, the eldest son of Isaac and Rebecca, who sold his birthright to his twin brother, Jacob, for a dish of stew.

es•ca•late (**ĕs′**kə lāt′) *tr. & intr.v.* **es•ca•lat•ed, es•ca•lat•ing, es•ca•lates.** To increase or cause to increase by stages, as in value, scope, or intensity: *Congress has escalated the fight against pollution over the last ten years. Rents escalated during the 1980's.* [First written down in 1922 in Modern English, back-formation from *escalator*.] —**es′ca•la′tion** *n.*

Leif Ericson
Bronze statue by Alexander Stirling Calder (1870–1945)

ermine

eruption
Paricutin volcano in Mexico erupting in 1943

ă	**pat**	oi	**boy**
ā	**pay**	ou	**out**
âr	**care**	ŏŏ	**took**
ä	**father**	ōō	**boot**
ĕ	**pet**	ŭ	**cut**
ē	**be**	ûr	**urge**
ĭ	**pit**	th	**thin**
ī	**pie**	*th*	**this**
îr	**pier**	hw	**whoop**
ŏ	**pot**	zh	**vision**
ō	**toe**	ə	**about**
ô	**paw**	N	*French* **bon**

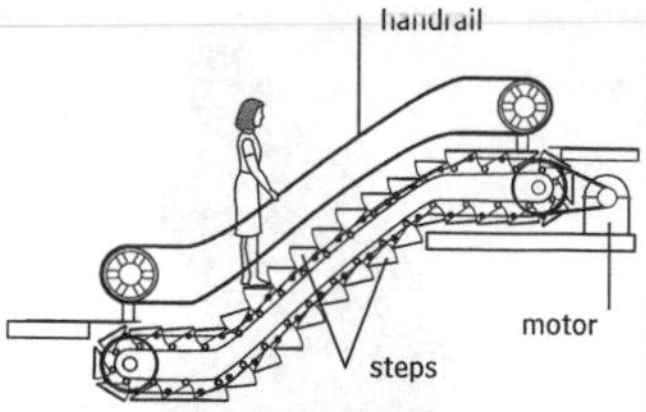

escalator
Cutaway view

escapement

espadrille

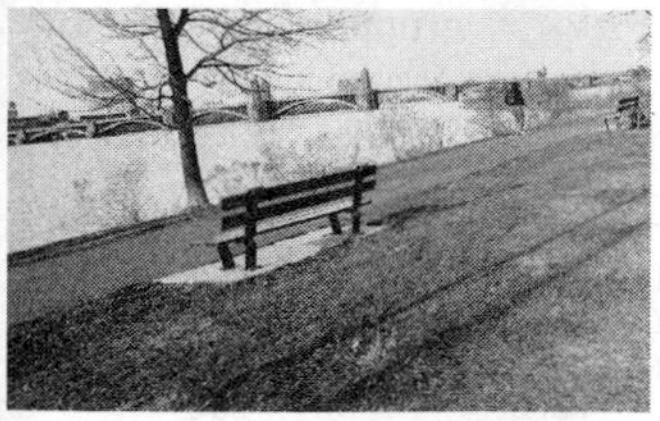
esplanade
The Esplanade in Boston

es•ca•la•tor (ĕs′kə lā′tər) *n.* A moving stairway consisting of steps attached to a continuously circulating belt.

es•cal•lop (ĭ skŏl′əp *or* ĭ skăl′əp) *n. & v.* Variant of **scallop.**

es•ca•pade (ĕs′kə pād′) *n.* A carefree or reckless undertaking.

es•cape (ĭ skāp′) *v.* **es•caped, es•cap•ing, es•capes.** —*intr.* **1.** To break loose from confinement; get free: *The prisoners escaped by climbing the wall.* **2.** To avoid capture, danger, or harm: *The thieves escaped every time the police tried to catch them.* **3.** To leak or seep out: *All the air escaped from the balloon.* —*tr.* **1.** To get free of; break loose from: *A vacation will allow me to escape the noise of the city.* **2.** To succeed in avoiding (capture, danger, or harm): *I barely escaped injury when the ladder fell.* **3.** To fail to be noticed or remembered by: *The name of the new worker escapes me.* **4.** To issue from involuntarily: *A cry of delight escaped the child's lips.* —*n.* **1.** The act or means of escaping: *prisoners planning an escape.* **2.** A means of escaping: *An open gate provided the dog's escape.* **3.** A means of obtaining temporary freedom from worry, care, or unpleasantness: *For her, running provides an escape from everyday problems.* [First written down about 1300 in Middle English and spelled *ascapien*, from Old North French *escaper* : Latin *ex-*, out + Medieval Latin *cappa*, cloak.]

es•cap•ee (ĭ skā′pē′) *n.* A person who has escaped, especially an escaped prisoner.

es•cape•ment (ĭ skāp′mənt) *n.* **1.** A device in watches and clocks that controls the speed at which the movement runs. It consists of a gearwheel controlled by a ratchet having teeth that fit into the wheel as the ratchet swings, allowing the wheel to escape or move one tooth at a time. **2.** A mechanism that controls the back-and-forth movement of a typewriter carriage.

escape velocity *n.* The velocity that a body, such as a rocket, must achieve to overcome the gravitational pull of the earth or another celestial body.

es•cap•ism (ĭ skā′pĭz′əm) *n.* The tendency to escape from daily routine or responsibilities by engaging in daydreams, entertainment, or other forms of distraction. —**es•cap′ist** *adj. & n.*

es•ca•role (ĕs′kə rōl′) *n.* A kind of endive having densely clustered ruffled leaves used in salads.

es•carp•ment (ĭ skärp′mənt) *n.* **1.** A steep slope or long cliff formed by erosion or by vertical movement of the earth's crust along a fault. **2.** A steep slope or embankment in front of a fortification.

–escence *suff.* A suffix that means the state or process: *convalescence; luminescence.*

–escent *suff.* A suffix that means beginning to be or becoming: *convalescent; luminescent.*

es•chew (ĕs chōō′) *tr.v.* **es•chewed, es•chew•ing, es•chews.** To take care to avoid; shun: *eschew bad company.*

es•cort (ĕs′kôrt′) *n.* **1.** One or more persons accompanying another to give protection or guidance or to pay honor: *The visiting foreign leader was given a police escort.* **2.** One or more airplanes, warships, or other vehicles accompanying another or others to provide protection. **3.** A man who is the companion of a woman, especially on a social occasion. —*tr.v.* (ĭ skôrt′ *or* ĕs′kôrt′). **es•cort•ed, es•cort•ing, es•corts.** To accompany as an escort: *An honor guard escorted the President during the parade.* [First written down in 1579 in Modern English, from Italian *scorta*, from *scorgere*, to guide : Latin *ex-*, intensive prefix + Latin *corrigere*, to set right.]

es•crow (ĕs′krō′ *or* ĕ skrō′) *n.* Money, property, a deed, or a bond put into the custody of a third party until certain conditions are fulfilled. —*idiom.* **in escrow.** In the care of another until various conditions are met: *The bank is holding the savings account in escrow until the heirs reach their twenty-first birthday.*

es•cu•do (ĭ skōō′dō) *n., pl.* **es•cu•dos.** The basic monetary unit of Portugal and Cape Verde.

es•cutch•eon (ĭ skŭch′ən) *n.* A shield or an emblem in the shape of a shield bearing a coat of arms.

–ese *suff.* A suffix that means: **1.** Of or relating to a certain place: *Japanese.* **2.** Native or inhabitant of: *Chinese.* **3.** A language or dialect of: *Portuguese.*

es•ker (ĕs′kər) *n.* A ridge of coarse gravel deposited by a stream flowing in or under a melting sheet of glacial ice.

Es•ki•mo (ĕs′kə mō′) *n., pl.* **Eskimo** or **Es•ki•mos.** **1.** A member of a group of peoples inhabiting the Arctic coastal regions of North America and parts of Greenland and northeast Siberia. **2.** Any of the languages of the Eskimo peoples. —**Es′ki•mo′** *adj.*

Eskimo dog *n.* A large dog of a breed used in Arctic regions to pull sleds, having a thick coat and a plumed tail.

e•soph•a•gus (ĭ sŏf′ə gəs) *n., pl.* **e•soph•a•gi** (ĭ sŏf′ə jī′). The tube of the alimentary canal that connects the throat and the stomach for the passage of food.

es•o•ter•ic (ĕs′ə tĕr′ĭk) *adj.* **1.** Intended for or understood by only a small group: *an esoteric book.* **2.** Not publicly disclosed; confidential. —**es′o•ter′i•cal•ly** *adv.*

ESP (ē′ĕs pē′) *n.* Communication or perception by means other than the physical senses.

esp. *abbr.* An abbreviation of especially.

es•pa•drille (ĕs′pə drĭl′) *n.* A sandal having a rope sole and a canvas upper part.

es•pe•cial (ĭ spĕsh′əl) *adj.* Of special note; exceptional: *a portrait painted with especial skill.*

es•pe•cial•ly (ĭ spĕsh′ə lē) *adv.* To an extent or degree deserving of special emphasis; particularly: *We came by especially to visit our friend.*

Es•pe•ran•to (ĕs′pə răn′tō *or* ĕs′pə rän′tō) *n.* An artificial language for international use, based on word roots common to many European languages. [First written down in 1892 in Modern English, after Dr. *Esperanto*, "one who hopes," pseudonym of Ludwik Lejzer Zamenhof (1859–1917), Polish philologist.]

es•pi•o•nage (ĕs′pē ə näzh′ *or* ĕs′pē ə nĭj) *n.* **1.** The act or practice of spying. **2.** The use of spies to gain secret information about another government or business: *Many countries engage in espionage in time of war.* [First written down in 1793 in Modern English, from Old Italian *spione*, spy.]

es•pla•nade (ĕs′plə näd′ *or* ĕs′plə nād′) *n.* A flat open stretch of pavement or grass used as a promenade, especially along a shore.

es•pous•al (ĭ spou′zəl *or* ĭ spou′səl) *n.* **1.** Adoption of an idea or cause: *espousal of equal rights.* **2.a.** A betrothal. **b.** A wedding ceremony.

es•pouse (ĭ spouz′) *tr.v.* **es•poused, es•pous•ing, es•pous•es.** **1.** To give loyalty or support to (an idea or a cause); adopt: *Their government espouses free elections.* **2.** To take in marriage; marry. **3.** To promise or present (a woman) in marriage.

es•pres•so (ĕ sprĕs′ō) *n., pl.* **es•pres•sos.** A strong coffee brewed by forcing steam through long-roasted, powdered coffee beans. [First written down in 1945 in Modern English, from Italian *(caffè) espresso*, espresso (coffee), from *esprimere*, to press out, from Latin *exprimere* : *ex-*, out + *premere*, to press.]

es•prit (ĕ sprē′) *n.* Liveliness of mind and expression; wit.

esprit de corps (də kôr′) *n.* A spirit of devotion and

enthusiasm among members of a group for one another, their group, and its cause.

es•py (ĭ spī′) *tr.v.* **es•pied, es•py•ing, es•pies.** To catch sight of; glimpse: *The lookout espied a sail on the horizon.*

Esq. *abbr.* An abbreviation of Esquire.

–esque *suff.* A suffix that means in the manner of or resembling: *statuesque.*

es•quire (ĕs′kwīr′ *or* ĭ skwīr′) *n.* **1.** In medieval times, a man or boy who wished to be a knight and served as a knight's attendant and shield bearer. **2.** A man belonging to the English gentry ranking just below a knight. **3. Esquire.** In the United States, a title of courtesy used especially after the name of a lawyer. [First written down in 1374 in Middle English and spelled *esquier*, from Late Latin *scūtārius*, shield bearer, from Latin *scūtum*, shield.]

–ess *suff.* A suffix that means female: *heiress; lioness.*

es•say (ĕs′ā′ *or* ĕ sā′) *n.* **1.** A short literary composition on a single subject, usually presenting the personal views of the author. **2.** An attempt; a try: *He made a brief essay at politics before settling on a teaching career.* —*tr.v.* (ĕ sā′ *or* ĕs′ā′). **es•sayed, es•say•ing, es•says.** To make an attempt at; try: *The actor essayed a new role on television.*

es•say•ist (ĕs′ā ĭst) *n.* A writer of essays.

es•sence (ĕs′əns) *n.* **1.** The quality or qualities of a thing that give it its identity or character: *The essence of democray is freedom to choose.* **2.** A concentrated form or extract of a substance that keeps the basic or most desirable properties: *Turpentine is an essence of pine tar.* **3.** A perfume or scent. [First written down before 1398 in Middle English and spelled *essencia*, from Latin *essentia*, being, from *esse*, to be.]

es•sen•tial (ĭ sĕn′shəl) *adj.* **1.** Of the greatest importance; indispensable; necessary: *The essential requirements for combustion are heat, oxygen, and fuel.* **2.** Of or being the essence of something: *The essential work of the police is to protect the citizens from harm.* —*n.* Something fundamental, necessary, or indispensable: *Take along only the essentials when traveling.* **—es•sen′tial•ly** *adv.*

EST or **E.S.T.** *abbr.* An abbreviation of Eastern Standard Time.

–est¹ *suff.* A suffix used to form the superlative degree of adjectives and adverbs: *greatest; earliest.*

–est² *suff.* A suffix used to form the archaic second person singular of verbs: *wherever thou goest.*

es•tab•lish (ĭ stăb′lĭsh) *tr.v.* **es•tab•lished, es•tab•lish•ing, es•tab•lish•es. 1.** To settle securely in a position or condition; install: *It took several years for the new family to establish itself in this town.* **2.** To begin or set up; found: *Their ancestors established the company in 1789.* **3.** To show to be true; prove: *Several witnesses established the suspect's innocence.* **4.** To cause to be recognized and accepted without question: *The flight established Lindbergh as a national hero.* [First written down about 1380 in Middle English and spelled *establishen*, from Latin *stabilīre*, from *stabilis*, firm.]

Synonyms: establish, create, found, institute. These verbs all mean to bring something into existence and set it in operation. *The first public high school for girls in the United States was established in 1824. Our class created a scale model of a feudal manor. Scientists hope to found a colony on Mars someday. The library instituted an annual book sale.*

es•tab•lish•ment (ĭ stăb′lĭsh mənt) *n.* **1.** The act of establishing or the condition of being established: *The new government's first priority was the establishment of peace.* **2.** An organization or institution, such as a business, hospital, or school: *Most of the town's commercial establishments contributed to the fund for the new playground.* **3.** Often **Establishment.** A group of people holding most of the power and influence in a government, society, or field of endeavor.

es•tate (ĭ stāt′) *n.* **1.** A large piece of land, usually with a large house. **2.** Everything one owns, especially all of the property and debts left by a deceased person: *When the shopkeeper died, the family inherited a small estate.* **3.** The circumstances of one's life: *a farmer's estate in life.* **4.** A class of citizens, such as the nobility, the commons, or the clergy, formerly possessing distinct political rights.

es•teem (ĭ stēm′) *tr.v.* **es•teemed, es•teem•ing, es•teems. 1.** To regard with respect; value: *Judges are esteemed for their fairness and honesty.* **2.** To judge to be; regard as; consider: *Improving public transportation was esteemed the best way to deal with the parking problem.* —*n.* Favorable regard; respect: *The doctor is held in high esteem.*

es•ter (ĕs′tər) *n.* Any of a large group of organic chemical compounds formed when an acid and an alcohol interact. Animal and vegetable fats and oils are esters.

Es•ther (ĕs′tər) *n.* **1.** In the Bible, the Jewish queen of Persia who saved her people from massacre. **2.** A book of the Bible that tells the story of Esther.

es•thete (ĕs′thēt) *n.* Variant of **aesthete.**

es•thet•ic (ĕs thĕt′ĭk) *adj.* Variant of **aesthetic.**

es•thet•ics (ĕs thĕt′ĭks) *n.* Variant of **aesthetics.**

es•ti•ma•ble (ĕs′tə mə bəl) *adj.* Worthy of or deserving high regard; admirable: *Patience, honesty, and fairness are estimable characteristics.* **—es′ti•ma•bly** *adv.*

es•ti•mate (ĕs′tə māt′) *tr.v.* **es•ti•mat•ed, es•ti•mat•ing, es•ti•mates. 1.** To make a judgment about the approximate cost, quantity, or extent of; calculate roughly: *I estimate that 25 people will come to the party.* **2.** To form an opinion about; evaluate: *We estimated her singing ability and decided to give her the lead role in the show.* —*n.* (ĕs′tə mĭt). **1.** A rough calculation: *Our estimate is that we will arrive in about an hour.* **2.** A preliminary calculation of the cost of work to be undertaken: *The plumber's estimate to fix the pipe was reasonable.* **3.** An opinion; an evaluation: *The critic's estimate of the play was that it needed work.* [First written down about 1532 in Modern English, from Latin *aestimāre*.]

es•ti•ma•tion (ĕs′tə mā′shən) *n.* **1.** The act or an instance of estimating: *Estimation of the storm damage took several weeks.* **2.** An opinion; a judgment: *In my estimation that is a good painting.* **3.** High regard; esteem: *a teacher held in high estimation by all the students.*

es•ti•vate (ĕs′tə vāt′) *intr.v.* **es•ti•vat•ed, es•ti•vat•ing, es•ti•vates.** To spend the summer in a dormant or inactive condition, as some snakes do.

Es•to•ni•a (ĕ stō′nē ə). A country of northeast Europe, the northernmost of the Baltic States. It was settled before the first century A.D. Estonia was a part of the Soviet Union from 1940 to 1991. Capital, Tallinn. Population, 1,530,000.

Es•to•ni•an (ĕ stō′nē ən) *adj.* Of or relating to Estonia or its people, language, or culture. —*n.* **1.** A native or inhabitant of Estonia. **2.** The language of Estonia, related to Finnish.

es•trange (ĭ strānj′) *tr.v.* **es•tranged, es•trang•ing, es•trang•es.** To cause (a person) to change from friendly or affectionate to unfriendly or indifferent: *The neighbors were estranged over differences about who was responsible for repairing the fence.* **—es•trange′ment** *n.*

es•tro•gen (ĕs′trə jən) *n.* Any of several hormones

ă	**pat**	oi	**boy**
ā	**pay**	ou	**out**
âr	**care**	ŏŏ	**took**
ä	**father**	ōō	**boot**
ĕ	**pet**	ŭ	**cut**
ē	**be**	ûr	**urge**
ĭ	**pit**	th	**thin**
ī	**pie**	*th*	**this**
îr	**pier**	hw	**whoop**
ŏ	**pot**	zh	**vision**
ō	**toe**	ə	**about**
ô	**paw**	N	*French* **bon**

that cause the development of female characteristics and regulate the female reproductive cycle.

es•trous (ĕs′trəs) *adj.* Of or relating to estrus.

estrous cycle *n.* The recurring bodily changes in the female of most mammals occurring from one period of estrus to another.

es•trus (ĕs′trəs) *n.* A regularly recurring period during which most female mammals are ready to mate; heat.

es•tu•ar•y (ĕs′cho͞o ĕr′ē) *n., pl.* **es•tu•ar•ies. 1.** The wide lower course of a river where its current is met by the tides. **2.** An arm of the sea that extends inland to meet the mouth of a river.

–et *suff.* A suffix that means small: *eaglet.*

e•ta (ā′tə *or* ē′tə) *n.* The seventh letter of the Greek alphabet, written H, η. In English it is represented as *ē*.

et al. *abbr.* An abbreviation of et alii (and others).

etc. *abbr.* An abbreviation of et cetera.

et cet•er•a (ĕt sĕt′ər ə *or* ĕt sĕt′rə). And other things of the same type; and so forth. [First written down about 1150 in Middle English and spelled *& cetera*, from Latin *et cētera* : *et*, and + *cētera*, the rest.]

etch (ĕch) *v.* **etched, etch•ing, etch•es.** *—tr.* **1.** To cut into (metal, glass, or other material) by using acid. **2.** To make (a picture or pattern) by using acid to cut into a material. **3.** To impress or imprint clearly: *The sight of that waterfall is etched in my memory.* *—intr.* To practice the art of etching. [First written down in 1634 in Modern English, from Dutch *etsen*, from Old High German *ezzen*, to eat.]

etch•ing (ĕch′ĭng) *n.* **1.** The art or technique of making etched metal plates and printing pictures and designs from them. **2.** A design or picture etched on such a plate: *The artist finished the etching.* **3.** A print made from such a plate: *Several etchings hung on the wall.*

e•ter•nal (ĭ tûr′nəl) *adj.* **1.** Having no beginning or end; existing outside of time. **2.** Continuing without interruption: *the eternal tides.* **3.** Forever true or changeless: *eternal truths.* **4.** Seemingly endless; incessant: *eternal complaining.* *—n.* **Eternal.** God. [First written down about 1380 in Middle English, from Latin *aeternus*.] **—e•ter′nal•ly** *adv.*

e•ter•ni•ty (ĭ tûr′nĭ tē) *n., pl.* **e•ter•ni•ties. 1.** All of time without beginning or end; infinite time: *We cannot measure eternity.* **2.a.** The timeless state following death. **b.** The afterlife; immortality. **3.** A very long or seemingly very long time: *It was an eternity before they opened the doors of the theater.*

–eth[1] or **–th** *suff.* A suffix used to form the archaic third person singular of the present tense of verbs: *He leadeth.*

–eth[2] *suff.* Variant of **–th.**

eth•ane (ĕth′ān′) *n.* A colorless odorless gas composed of carbon and hydrogen and having the formula C_2H_6. It occurs in natural gas and is used as a fuel and in refrigeration.

eth•a•nol (ĕth′ə nôl′ *or* ĕth′ə nŏl′) *n.* An alcohol obtained from the fermentation of sugars and starches and also made artificially. It is found in beer, wine, and liquor and is also used as a solvent.

e•ther (ē′thər) *n.* **1.** An organic compound in which two hydrocarbon groups are linked by an oxygen atom. **2.** A colorless flammable liquid that is formed from ethanol and used as a solvent and an anesthetic. **3.** The region of space beyond the earth's atmosphere; the heavens.

e•the•re•al (ĭ thîr′ē əl) *adj.* **1.** Delicate; light and airy: *ethereal music.* **2.** Of heaven; heavenly: *Angels are ethereal beings.* **—e•the′re•al•ly** *adv.*

eth•ic (ĕth′ĭk) *n.* **1.** A set of principles of right conduct; a system of moral values. **2. ethics.** *(used with a singular verb).* The branch of philosophy that deals with the general nature of morals and specific moral choices. **3. ethics.** *(used with a singular or plural verb).* Standards of right behavior or conduct; moral principles: *The code of ethics in the medical profession prohibits doctors from discussing individual patients by name.* [First written down about 1386 in Middle English and spelled *ethik*, from Greek *ēthikos*, ethical, from *ēthos*, character.]

eth•i•cal (ĕth′ĭ kəl) *adj.* **1.** Conforming to accepted standards of right behavior or conduct: *It is not considered ethical for a lawyer to represent both sides in a dispute.* **2.** Of or dealing with ethics: *ethical standards of right and wrong.* **—eth′i•cal•ly** *adv.*

E•thi•o•pi•a (ē′thē ō′pē ə). Formerly **Ab•ys•sin•i•a** (ăb′ĭ sĭn′ē ə). A country of northeast Africa on the Red Sea east of Sudan. It gained its independence from Italy in 1896. Addis Ababa is the capital and the largest city. Population, 32,775,000.

eth•nic (ĕth′nĭk) *adj.* Of or relating to a group of people that have the same racial, national, religious, linguistic, or cultural background. *—n.* A member of a particular ethnic group. [First written down about 1375 in Middle English and spelled *ethnic*, heathen, from Greek *ethnikos*, from *ethnos*, people, nation.] **—eth′ni•cal•ly** *adv.*

eth•nic•i•ty (ĕth nĭs′ĭ tē) *n.* The condition of belonging to a particular ethnic group.

eth•nol•o•gy (ĕth nŏl′ə jē) *n.* The study and comparison of the characteristics, history, and development of human cultures and of the origins of ethnic groups and the relations among them. **—eth′no•log′i•cal** (ĕth′nə lŏj′ĭ kəl) *adj.*

eth•yl (ĕth′əl) *n.* The radical that has the formula C_2H_5. It is present in many organic compounds, such as ethanol and ether.

ethyl alcohol *n.* Ethanol.

eth•yl•ene (ĕth′ə lēn′) *n.* A colorless flammable gas having the formula C_2H_4. It is obtained from petroleum and natural gas and used as a fuel and in ripening and coloring citrus fruits.

ethylene gly•col (glī′côl′ *or* glī′cŏl′) *n.* A poisonous, syrupy, colorless alcohol composed of carbon, hydrogen, and oxygen and having the formula $C_2H_6O_2$. It is used as an antifreeze in heating and cooling systems that use water.

e•ti•ol•o•gy (ē′tē ŏl′ə jē) *n., pl.* **e•ti•ol•o•gies. 1.** The branch of medicine that deals with the causes of diseases. **2.** The cause or origin of a disease.

et•i•quette (ĕt′ĭ kĕt′ *or* ĕt′ĭ kĭt) *n.* The forms and rules of proper behavior required by custom among people: *Good etiquette requires a person to thank another for a gift or favor.*

Et•na also **Aet•na** (ĕt′nə), **Mount.** An active volcano, 10,902 feet (3,325.1 meters) high, of eastern Sicily. Its first known eruption was in 475 B.C.

E•trus•can (ĭ trŭs′kən) *n.* **1.** A member of of an ancient people who lived in what is now west-central Italy. **2.** The extinct language of the Etruscans. **—E•trus′can** *adj.*

–ette *suff.* A suffix that means: **1.** Small: *kitchenette.* **2.** Female: *majorette.* **3.** Imitation or substitute: *leatherette.*

e•tude (ā′to͞od′ *or* ā′tyo͞od′) *n.* A piece of music, usually written for a solo instrument, meant to develop some point of playing technique. [First written down before 1837 in Modern English, from Old French *estudie*, study.]

et•y•mo•log•i•cal (ĕt′ə mə lŏj′ĭ kəl) *adj.* Of or relating to etymology. **—et′y•mo•log′i•cal•ly** *adv.*

et•y•mol•o•gist (ĕt′ə mŏl′ə jĭst) *n.* A person who specializes in etymology.

et•y•mol•o•gy (ĕt′ə mŏl′ə jē) *n., pl.* **et•y•mol•o•gies. 1.** The origin and development of a word as shown by its earliest use and changes in form and meaning: *Many medical terms have etymologies that go back to ancient Greek.* **2.** An account of the development of a specific word: *Many dictionaries include etymologies of words.* **3.** The study of the origin and history of words: *Etymology requires a knowledge of many languages.* [First written down before 1398 in Middle English and spelled *ethymologye*, from Greek *etumologia* : *etumon*, true sense of a word + *-logia*, study.]

Eu The symbol for the element **europium.**

eu•ca•lyp•tus (yo͞o′kə **lĭp′**təs) *n., pl.* **eu•ca•lyp•tus•es** or **eu•ca•lyp•ti** (yo͞o′kə **lĭp′**tī′). Any of numerous tall Australian evergreen trees having aromatic leaves that yield an oil used in medicine and wood that is used as timber. [First written down in 1809 in Modern English, from New Latin : Greek *eu-*, well + Greek *kaluptos*, covered (from *kaluptein*, to cover).]

Eu•cha•rist (**yo͞o′**kər ĭst) *n.* **1.** The Christian rite commemorating Jesus's Last Supper in which bread and wine are consecrated and consumed in remembrance of Jesus's death; Communion. **2.** The consecrated bread and wine used in this rite.

Eu•clid (**yo͞o′**klĭd). Third century B.C. Greek mathematician who applied principles of logic to geometry.

eu•gen•ic (yo͞o **jĕn′**ĭk) *adj.* **1.** Of or relating to eugenics. **2.** Relating to the production of improved offspring.

eu•gen•ics (yo͞o **jĕn′**ĭks) *n. (used with a singular verb).* The study of improving human beings by the controlled selection of parents.

eu•gle•na (yo͞o **glē′**nə) *n.* Any of various tiny one-celled water organisms that move with a long tail and are usually green in color.

eu•lo•gize (**yo͞o′**lə jīz′) *tr.v.* **eu•lo•gized, eu•lo•giz•ing, eu•lo•giz•es.** To praise highly in speech or writing. **—eu′lo•gist** (**yo͞o′**lə jĭst) *n.*

eu•lo•gy (**yo͞o′**lə jē) *n., pl.* **eu•lo•gies.** A speech or piece of writing praising a person or thing, especially a person who has just died: *A lifelong friend delivered the eulogy at the memorial service.* [First written down before 1475 in Middle English and spelled *euloge*, from Greek *eulogia*, praise : *eu-*, well + *-logia*, speaking.]

eu•nuch (**yo͞o′**nək) *n.* A castrated man employed as a household attendant or the guard of a harem in certain Asian courts.

eu•phe•mism (**yo͞o′**fə mĭz′əm) *n.* **1.** An inoffensive or indirect word or expression substituted for one considered offensive or too direct; for example, *pass away* is a euphemism for *die.* **2.** The use of such words or expressions. **—eu′phe•mis′tic** (yo͞o′fə **mĭs′**tĭk) *adj.*

eu•pho•ni•ous (yo͞o **fō′**nē əs) *adj.* Pleasing in sound; agreeable to the ear. **—eu•pho′ni•ous•ly** *adv.*

eu•pho•ni•um (yo͞o **fō′**nē əm) *n.* A brass musical instrument that looks like a tuba but has a mellower and higher sound.

eu•pho•ny (**yo͞o′**fə nē) *n., pl.* **eu•pho•nies.** Agreeable sound, especially in the use of words.

eu•pho•ri•a (yo͞o **fôr′**ē ə) *n.* A feeling of happiness and well-being: *After peace was declared, the whole country was in a state of euphoria.*

Eu•phra•tes (yo͞o **frā′**tēz). A river of southwest Asia flowing about 1,700 miles (2,735 kilometers) from central Turkey through Syria and into Iraq. It was a major source of water for ancient Mesopotamia.

Eur•a•sia (yo͞o **rā′**zhə). The land mass made up of the continents of Europe and Asia.

Eur•a•sian (yo͞o **rā′**zhən) *adj.* Of or relating to Eurasia. *—n.* A person of mixed European and Asian descent.

eu•re•ka (yo͞o **rē′**kə) *interj.* An expression used to express triumph upon discovering something or finding a solution to a problem. [First written down in 1570 in Modern English and spelled EYPHKA, from Greek *heurēka*, I have found (it) (supposedly exclaimed by Archimedes upon discovering how to measure the volume of an irregular solid and thereby determine the purity of a gold object), from *heuriskein*, to find.]

Eu•rope (**yo͝or′**əp). The sixth-largest continent, extending west from Asia to the Atlantic Ocean.

Eu•ro•pe•an (yo͝or′ə **pē′**ən) *n.* **1.** A native or inhabitant of Europe. **2.** A person of European descent. *—adj.* Of or relating to Europe or its peoples, languages, or cultures.

European Economic Community. Common Market.

eu•ro•pi•um (yo͞o **rō′**pē əm) *n. Symbol* **Eu** A soft, gray, rare-earth element used in the control rods of nuclear reactors. Atomic number 63. See table at **element.**

Eu•ryd•i•ce (yo͞o **rĭd′**ĭ sē) *n.* In Greek mythology, the wife of Orpheus.

eu•sta•chian tube or **Eu•sta•chian tube** (yo͞o **stā′**-shən *or* yo͞o **stā′**shē ən) *n.* The narrow passage that connects the middle ear and the pharynx and allows the pressure on both sides of the eardrum to equalize. [First written down in 1741 in Modern English, after Bartolommeo *Eustachio* (1524–1574), Italian anatomist.]

eu•tha•na•sia (yo͞o′thə **nā′**zhə *or* yo͞o′thə **nā′**-zhē ə) *n.* The act or practice of ending the life of a person suffering from an incurable illness or injury; mercy killing.

e•vac•u•ate (ĭ **văk′**yo͞o āt′) *tr.v.* **e•vac•u•at•ed, e•vac•u•at•ing, e•vac•u•ates. 1.** To send away or withdraw (inhabitants or troops) from an area: *evacuate a neighborhood threatened by toxic fumes.* **2.** To withdraw or depart from; vacate: *The fire-fighters quickly evacuated the burning building.* **3.** To expel or discharge (waste matter), especially from the bowels. [First written down in 1542 in Modern English, from Latin *ēvacuāre* : *ē-*, *ex-*, out + *vacuus*, empty.]

e•vac•u•a•tion (ĭ văk′yo͞o **ā′**shən) *n.* **1.** The act of evacuating or the condition of being evacuated: *The evacuation of children was begun at the first sign of danger.* **2.** Discharge of waste materials from the body, especially from the bowels.

e•vac•u•ee (ĭ văk′yo͞o **ē′**) *n.* A person evacuated from a dangerous area.

e•vade (ĭ **vād′**) *tr.v.* **e•vad•ed, e•vad•ing, e•vades. 1.** To escape or avoid, as by cleverness or deceit: *evade arrest.* **2.** To avoid the fulfillment or performance of: *By blaming the source of the information, the reporter evaded responsibility for the mistake.* **3.** To avoid giving a direct answer to: *The mayor evaded the question by talking about something else.* [First written down in 1513 in Modern English, from Latin *ēvādere* : *ē-*, *ex-*, out, away + *vādere*, to go.]

e•val•u•ate (ĭ **văl′**yo͞o āt′) *tr.v.* **e•val•u•at•ed, e•val•u•at•ing, e•val•u•ates. 1.** To find out or estimate the value or worth of; examine and appraise: *evaluate a course of action; evaluate paintings for sale.* **2.** To find the numerical value of (an algebraic expression). **—e•val′u•a′tion** *n.*

ev•a•nes•cent (ĕv′ə **nĕs′**ənt) *adj.* Tending to vanish or last only a short time; fleeting: *the rainbow's evanescent beauty.* **—ev′a•nes′cence** *n.* **—ev′a•nes′cent•ly** *adv.*

e•van•gel•i•cal (ē′văn **jĕl′**ĭ kəl) also **e•van•gel•ic** (ē′văn **jĕl′**ĭk) *adj.* **1.** Of or in accordance with the Christian gospel, especially the four Gospels of the New Testament. **2. Evangelical.** Of or being a Protestant group that stresses belief solely in the author-

eucalyptus

euphonium

ă	pat	oi	boy
ā	pay	ou	out
âr	care	o͝o	took
ä	father	o͞o	boot
ĕ	pet	ŭ	cut
ē	be	ûr	urge
ĭ	pit	th	thin
ī	pie	*th*	this
îr	pier	hw	whoop
ŏ	pot	zh	vision
ō	toe	ə	about
ô	paw	N	*French* bon

Mount Everest

ity of the Bible and salvation through faith in Jesus. —*n.* **Evangelical.** A member of an evangelical church. —**e′van•gel′i•cal•ly** *adv.*

e•van•gel•ism (ĭ văn′jə lĭz′əm) *n.* The practice of preaching and spreading the gospel, as through missionary work. —**e•van′gel•is′tic** (ĭ văn′jə lĭs′tĭk) *adj.*

e•van•gel•ist (ĭ văn′jə lĭst) *n.* **1.** Often **Evangelist.** Any of the authors of the New Testament Gospels: Matthew, Mark, Luke, or John. **2.** A person who practices evangelism, especially a Protestant preacher or missionary. [First written down about 1200 in Middle English and spelled *ewangeliste*, from Greek *euangelion*, good news : *eu-*, good + *angelos*, messenger.]

e•van•gel•ize (ĭ văn′jə līz′) *tr. & intr.v.* **e•van•gel•ized, e•van•gel•iz•ing, e•van•gel•iz•es.** To preach and spread the gospel.

Ev•ans (ĕv′ənz), **Mary Ann.** See George **Eliot.**

e•vap•o•rate (ĭ văp′ə rāt′) *v.* **e•vap•o•rat•ed, e•vap•o•rat•ing, e•vap•o•rates.** —*tr.* **1.** To cause to change from a liquid into a vapor, especially without boiling: *The sun evaporates water from the ocean.* **2.** To extract water or other liquid from: *evaporate milk.* —*intr.* **1.** To change from a liquid into a vapor: *The dew evaporated as the sun came up.* **2.** To disappear; vanish; fade: *My fear evaporated as the airplane took off.* See Synonyms at **disappear.** —**e•vap′o•ra′tion** *n.*

e•vap•o•rat•ed milk (ĭ văp′ə rā′tĭd) *n.* Unsweetened milk that has been slightly thickened by evaporation of some of the water in it.

e•va•sion (ĭ vā′zhən) *n.* **1.** The act or an instance of evading: *His evasion of paying taxes led to his imprisonment.* **2.** A means of evading; an excuse: *His father saw through his evasions and insisted that he go to church.*

e•va•sive (ĭ vā′sĭv) *adj.* **1.** Tending or intended to evade: *The submarine took evasive action to elude its pursuers.* **2.** Intentionally misleading or ambiguous: *the candidate's evasive answers to her questions.* —**e•va′sive•ly** *adv.* —**e•va′sive•ness** *n.*

eve (ēv) *n.* **1.** The evening or day preceding a special day, such as a holiday. **2.** The period immediately preceding a certain event: *the eve of war.* **3.** Evening. Used chiefly in poetry.

Eve (ēv). In the Bible, the first woman and the wife of Adam.

e•ven[1] (ē′vən) *adj.* **1.a.** Having a horizontal surface; flat: *The even lawn is good for playing croquet.* **b.** Having no roughness, dents, or bumps; smooth: *an even board.* **c.** Being in the same plane or line; parallel: *Is your writing even with the top of the page?* **2.** Having no variation; uniform: *an even speed.* **3.** Calm; peaceful: *an even temper.* **4.a.** Equally matched: *an even fight.* **b.** Equal in degree, extent or amount: *even portions of a meal.* **5.** Containing 2 as a factor; exactly divisible by 2: *8 is an even number.* **6.** Having equal probability: *Our team has an even chance of winning.* **7.a.** Having an equal score: *The teams are even.* **b.** Being equal for each opponent: *an even score.* **8.** Having nothing due: *Pay me one dollar, and we are even.* **9.** Having an exact amount, extent, or number: *an even pound.* —*adv.* **1.** To a higher or greater degree; yet; still: *an even better idea.* **2.** At the same time as; just: *Even as we watched, the tree fell.* **3.** Indeed; moreover: *She was relieved, even happy, to see us.* **4.** Used to emphasize something that is unexpected: *He refused even to consider our idea.* —*tr.v.* **e•vened, e•ven•ing, e•vens.** To make even: *even out a garden with a rake.* —***idiom.*** **on an even keel.** In a stable or unimpaired state: *The new contract put the relationship between the company and its workers on an even keel.* [First written down about 725 in Old English and spelled *efen.*] —**e′ven•ly** *adv.* —**e′ven•ness** *n.*

e•ven[2] (ē′vən) *n. Archaic.* Evening. [First written down about 725 in Old English and spelled *ǣfen.*]

e•ven•hand•ed (ē′vən hăn′dĭd) *adj.* Dealing fairly with all; impartial.

eve•ning (ēv′nĭng) *n.* **1.** The period of decreasing daylight between afternoon and night: *At evening the moon rose over the lake.* **2.** The period between sunset and bedtime: *We spent a quiet evening at home.* **3.** A later period or time: *in the evening of life.*

evening dress *n.* **1.** Clothing worn for evening social events. **2.** An evening gown.

evening gown *n.* A woman's formal dress, usually reaching to the floor or close to it.

evening star *n.* A planet, especially Venus, that shines brightly in the western sky shortly after sunset.

e•ven•song (ē′vən sông′ *or* ē′vən sŏng′) *n.* **1.** A church service held in the late afternoon or early evening; vespers. **2.** A song sung in the evening.

e•vent (ĭ vĕnt′) *n.* **1.** An occurrence, incident, or experience, especially one of significance: *A trip to Brazil was the great event of her adolescence.* **2.** An item in a program of sports: *I like to watch the jumping events at a horse show.* —***idioms.*** **in any event.** In any case; anyhow. **in the event.** If it should happen; in case: *In the event of the President's death, the Vice President takes over.* [First written down about 1570 in Modern English, from Latin *ēventus*, from past participle of *ēvenīre*, to happen : *ē-*, *ex-*, out + *venīre*, to come.]

e•vent•ful (ĭ vĕnt′fəl) *adj.* **1.** Full of events: *an eventful afternoon.* **2.** Important; momentous: *an eventful decision to change jobs.* —**e•vent′ful•ly** *adv.* —**e•vent′ful•ness** *n.*

e•ven•tide (ē′vən tīd′) *n.* Evening. Used chiefly in poetry.

e•ven•tu•al (ĭ vĕn′cho͞o əl) *adj.* Occurring at an unspecified future time; ultimate: *We never lost hope of eventual victory.* —**e•ven′tu•al•ly** *adv.*

e•ven•tu•al•i•ty (ĭ vĕn′cho͞o ăl′ĭ tē) *n., pl.* **e•ven•tu•al•i•ties.** Something that may occur; a possibility: *One prepares for the worst eventuality and hopes for the best outcome.*

ev•er (ĕv′ər) *adv.* **1.** At all times; always: *They lived happily ever after.* **2.** At any time: *Have you ever visited Pittsburgh?* **3.** By any chance; in any possible case or way: *How could they ever have thought they would get away with that?* **4.** To a great extent or degree. Used for emphasis often with *so: She's ever so sorry.*

Ev•er•est (ĕv′ər ĭst *or* ĕv′rĭst), **Mount.** A mountain, 29,028 feet (8,853.5 meters) high, of the central Himalaya Mountains on the border of Tibet and Nepal. It is the highest elevation in the world.

ev•er•glade (ĕv′ər glād′) *n.* A large area of marshland covered in places with tall grass.

Ev•er•glades (ĕv′ər glādz′). A swamp area of southern Florida including **Everglades National Park.** It is noted for its wildlife.

ev•er•green (ĕv′ər grēn′) *adj.* Having green leaves or needles all year: *evergreen trees.* —*n.* An evergreen tree, shrub, or plant: *Pine, holly, and rhododendron are evergreens.*

ev•er•last•ing (ĕv′ər lăs′tĭng) *adj.* **1.** Lasting forever; eternal. **2.** Continuing for a long time: *everlasting happiness.* **3.** Lasting too long; wearisome: *everlasting work.* —*n.* **Everlasting.** God. —**ev′er•last′ing•ly** *adv.*

ev•er•more (ĕv′ər môr′) *adv.* Forever; always.

eve•ry (ĕv′rē) *adj.* **1.** Each member of a group without exception: *every student in the class.* **2.** Each in a specified series or at specific intervals: *every third* *seat; every two hours.* **3.** The highest degree of; the utmost: *I have every confidence they will succeed.* **—*idioms.* every bit.** *Informal.* In all ways; equally: *every bit as clever as we thought.* **every now and then** or **every now and again.** From time to time; occasionally: *The whole family goes camping every now and then.* **every other.** Each alternate: *every other seat.* **every so often.** At intervals; occasionally: *We exchange letters every so often.* [First written down about 1200 in Middle English and spelled *eauer-euch*, from Old English *æfre ælc*, ever each.] —See Note at **he.**

eve•ry•bod•y (ĕv**′**rē bŏd′ē *or* ĕv**′**rē bŭd′ē) *pron.* Every person; everyone.

eve•ry•day (ĕv**′**rē dā**′**) *adj.* **1.** Suitable for ordinary days or occasions: *everyday clothes.* **2.** Ordinary; usual: *an everyday event.*

eve•ry•one (ĕv**′**rē wŭn′) *pron.* Every person; everybody: *Everyone has bought a ticket.*

eve•ry•thing (ĕv**′**rē thĭng′) *pron.* **1.** All things or all of a group of things: *Everything in this room must be packed.* **2.** The most important fact or consideration: *When telling a joke, timing is everything.*

eve•ry•where (ĕv**′**rē wâr′) *adv.* In any or every place; in all places: *People were celebrating the news everywhere in town.*

e•vict (ĭ vĭkt**′**) *tr.v.* **e•vict•ed, e•vict•ing, e•victs.** To put out (a tenant) by legal process: *The landlord evicted the man who was living in that apartment for failure to pay rent.* [First written down in 1447 in Middle English and spelled *evicten*, from Latin *ēvincere*, to vanquish : *ē-, ex-*, intensive prefix + *vincere*, to defeat.] **—e•vic′tion** *n.*

ev•i•dence (ĕv**′**ĭ dəns) *n.* **1.** A thing or things helpful in making a judgment or coming to a conclusion: *The fossils of seashells were evidence that the region had once been covered by water.* **2.** The statements, objects, and facts accepted for consideration in a court of law: *The evidence was not clear enough to convince the jury that the defendant was guilty.* **3.** Something that indicates; a sign: *Constant laughter was evidence that the show was very funny.* *—tr.v.* **ev•i•denced, ev•i•denc•ing, ev•i•denc•es.** To indicate clearly; prove: *Cheers and applause evidenced the audience's approval.* **—*idiom.* in evidence.** Plainly visible; to be seen: *The welcome signs were much in evidence among the crowd at the airport.*

ev•i•dent (ĕv**′**ĭ dənt) *adj.* Easily seen or understood; clear; plain: *From the warm temperature and abundant flowers, it is evident that spring is here.* [First written down before 1382 in Middle English, from Latin *ēvidēns* : *ē-, ex-*, out + *vidēns*, present participle of *vidēre*, to see.]

ev•i•dent•ly (ĕv**′**ĭ dənt lē *or* ĕv′ĭ **dĕnt′**lē) *adv.* Plainly; clearly: *They evidently did not practice enough and played poorly.*

e•vil (ē**′**vəl) *adj.* **e•vil•er, e•vil•est. 1.** Morally bad or wrong; wicked: *evil deeds.* **2.** Causing pain or injury; harmful: *an evil temper; an evil tongue.* **3.** Indicating misfortune: *evil signs.* *—n.* **1.** Wickedness: *a story about good and evil.* **2.** Something that causes harm: *the social evil of poverty.* [First written down about 725 in Old English and spelled *yfel.*] **—e′vil•ly** *adv.* **—e′vil•ness** *n.*

e•vil•do•er (ē**′**vəl do͞o′ər) *n.* A person who does evil things.

e•vince (ĭ vĭns**′**) *tr.v.* **e•vinced, e•vinc•ing, e•vinc•es.** To show or demonstrate clearly; exhibit: *The lawyer evinced surprise at the witness's statement.*

e•vis•cer•ate (ĭ vĭs**′**ə rāt′) *tr.v.* **e•vis•cer•at•ed, e•vis•cer•at•ing, e•vis•cer•ates. 1.** To remove the intestines or other internal organs of. **2.** To take away a vital or essential part of: *Leaving out the facts and figures eviscerated the report.* **—e•vis′cer•a′tion** *n.*

ev•o•ca•tion (ĕv′ə **kā′**shən *or* ē′və **kā′**shən) *n.* The act of calling forth: *the evocation of a pleasant memory.*

e•voc•a•tive (ĭ **vŏk′**ə tĭv) *adj.* Tending to evoke: *The walk in the woods was evocative of the hikes I took in my childhood.*

e•voke (ĭ **vōk′**) *tr.v.* **e•voked, e•vok•ing, e•vokes. 1.** To summon or call forth; inspire: *The question evoked a long and complicated reply.* **2.** To call to mind by naming or suggesting: *a song that evokes memories.* [First written down about 1623 in Modern English, from Latin *ēvocāre* : *ē-, ex-*, out, forth + *vocāre*, to call.]

ev•o•lu•tion (ĕv′ə **lo͞o′**shən) *n.* **1.** A gradual process by which something changes into a different form: *the evolution of jazz.* **2.** The process by which groups of organisms, such as species, change over a long period of time through natural selection, so that descendants are different from their ancestors. **3.** The historical development of a related group of organisms: *plant evolution.* **4.** The mathematical process of finding a square root, cube root, or other root of a number. [First written down in 1622 in Modern English, from Latin *ēvolūtiō*, from *ēvolvere*, to unroll, evolve.] **—ev′o•lu′tion•ar′y** (ĕv′ə **lo͞o′**shə nĕr′ē) *adj.*

e•volve (ĭ **vŏlv′**) *v.* **e•volved, e•volv•ing, e•volves.** *—tr.* **1.** To develop or achieve gradually: *Several bankers evolved a plan to save the city from bankruptcy.* **2.** To develop (a characteristic) by biological evolution: *Cats have evolved an extraordinary sense of balance.* *—intr.* **1.** To undergo biological evolution: *Scientists think that birds may have evolved from reptiles.* **2.** To undergo change or development: *Butterflies evolve from larvae.* [First written down in 1664 in Modern English, from Latin *ēvolvere*, to unroll : *ē-, ex-*, out + *volvere*, to roll.]

ewe (yo͞o) *n.* A full-grown female sheep. [First written down about 1000 in Old English and spelled *eōwu.*]

❑ *These sound alike:* **ewe, yew** (shrub), **you** (pronoun).

ew•er (**yo͞o′**ər) *n.* A large, wide-mouthed pitcher or jug.

ewer

ex. *abbr.* An abbreviation of example.

ex– *pref.* A prefix that means former: *ex-President.* —See Note.

ex•ac•er•bate (ĭg **zăs′**ər bāt′) *tr.v.* **ex•ac•er•bat•ed, ex•ac•er•bat•ing, ex•ac•er•bates.** To make worse or more severe; aggravate: *The rumor exacerbated tensions between groups.* **—ex•ac′er•ba′tion** *n.*

ex•act (ĭg **zăkt′**) *adj.* **1.** Fully in agreement with fact or an original: *a person's exact words; an exact duplicate.* **2.** Characterized by accurate measurement: *An exact reading of these instruments is necessary in this experiment.* *—tr.v.* **ex•act•ed, ex•act•ing, ex•acts. 1.** To force the payment of: *The king exacted new taxes from the people.* **2.** To require or demand, especially by force or authority: *The teacher exacts strict discipline in class.* [First written down in 1533 in Modern English, from Latin *exāctus*, past participle of *exigere*, to weigh out, demand : *ex-*, out + *agere*, to weigh.] **—ex•act′ness** *n.*

ex•act•ing (ĭg **zăk′**tĭng) *adj.* **1.** Making great demands: *I learn the most from an exacting teacher.* **2.** Requiring great effort, attention, or care: *A medical operation is an exacting procedure.* **—ex•act′ing•ly** *adv.*

ex•ac•tion (ĭg **zăk′**shən) *n.* **1.** The act of exacting or demanding. **2.** Something exacted or demanded, as a tax considered to be excessive.

Word Building: ex–

The prefix **ex–** comes from Latin *ex–*, *ē–*, meaning "out of, from." It usually occurs with word roots that come from Latin verbs. Thus combining *ex–* with the Latin verb *tendere*, "to stretch," gives us **extend**, "to stretch out." Similarly, in **express**, *ex–* combines with the root *press–*, which comes from the verb *premere*, "to squeeze." So when we express ourselves, we "sqeeze out" our thoughts. When followed by *f*, **ex–** becomes **ef–**, as in **efface**. Sometimes **ex–** takes the form of **e–**, as in **emit** (from Latin *mittere*, "to send").

ă	pat	oi	boy
ā	pay	ou	out
âr	care	o͝o	took
ä	father	o͞o	boot
ĕ	pet	ŭ	cut
ē	be	ûr	urge
ĭ	pit	th	thin
ī	pie	*th*	this
îr	pier	hw	whoop
ŏ	pot	zh	vision
ō	toe	ə	about
ô	paw	N	*French* bon

excavation

ex•ac•ti•tude (ĭg **zăk′**tĭ to͞od *or* ĭg **zăk′**tĭ tyo͞od′) *n.* The quality or condition of being exact; exactness.

ex•act•ly (ĭg **zăkt′**lē) *adv.* **1.** In an exact manner; precisely: *The cake did not rise because I failed to follow the recipe exactly.* **2.** In all respects; just: *Do exactly as you see fit.* **3.** Quite so; as you say: *"Exactly," he replied, "I feel the same way."*

ex•ag•ger•ate (ĭg **zăj′**ə rāt′) *v.* **ex•ag•ger•at•ed, ex•ag•ger•at•ing, ex•ag•ger•ates.** —*tr.* **1.** To speak or write about (something) as if greater or more important than is actually the case: *He exaggerated his accomplishments in an attempt to get the job.* **2.** To enlarge or increase to an abnormal degree: *The unusually high tides exaggerated the destructive force of the hurricane.* —*intr.* To make overstatements: *It's important not to exaggerate when writing stories for a newspaper.* **—ex•ag′ger•a′tion** *n.*

ex•alt (ĭg **zôlt′**) *tr.v.* **ex•alt•ed, ex•alt•ing, ex•alts.** **1.** To raise in position, status, rank, or regard; elevate: *The emperor exalted the faithful servant to a place among his most trusted advisors.* **2.** To praise; honor; glorify. **—ex′al•ta′tion** (ĕg′zôl **tā′**shən) *n.*

ex•alt•ed (ĭg **zôl′**tĭd) *adj.* **1.** Having high rank or status; dignified: *The emperor is an exalted personage.* **2.** Elevated as in style or condition; lofty; noble: *the exalted style of epic poetry.*

ex•am (ĭg **zăm′**) *n.* An examination.

ex•am•i•na•tion (ĭg zăm′ə **nā′**shən) *n.* **1.** The act of examining or the state of being examined: *Close examination of the diamond showed it was a fake.* **2.** A set of questions or exercises testing knowledge or skill; a test. **3.** A formal interrogation: *the lawyer's examination of the witness in a trial.*

ex•am•ine (ĭg **zăm′**ĭn) *tr.v.* **ex•am•ined, ex•am•in•ing, ex•am•ines.** **1.** To observe carefully; inspect or study: *Examine the plant cells under a microscope.* **2.** To inspect or test for evidence of disease, abnormality, or defects: *The inspector examined the boiler for leaks.* **3.** To interrogate or question formally to obtain information or facts: *The prosecutor examined the witness.* **4.** To present questions to in order to test knowledge: *State boards examine teachers before giving them a license.* See Synonyms at **ask.** [First written down about 1303 in Middle English and spelled *examinen*, from Latin *exāmināre*, from *exāmen*, a weighing out, from *exigere*, to weigh out.] **—ex•am′in•er** *n.*

ex•am•ple (ĭg **zăm′**pəl) *n.* **1.** A person or thing that is typical of a whole class or group; a sample or specimen: *The Empire State Building is an example of a graceful skyscraper.* **2.** A person or thing that is worthy of imitation; a model: *This article is an example of good writing.* **3.** A person or thing that is intended to serve as a warning to others: *The court made an example of the fraudulent dealer by imposing heavy fines on him.* **4.** A problem or an exercise worked out to illustrate a principle or method: *an example of multiplication; an example of the form of a composition.* **—*idiom.* for example.** As an illustration; for instance: *We have several team sports, for example, baseball and soccer.*

ex•as•per•ate (ĭg **zăs′**pə rāt′) *tr.v.* **ex•as•per•at•ed, ex•as•per•at•ing, ex•as•per•ates.** To make angry or impatient; irritate greatly: *The dog's constant barking exasperated the neighbors.*

ex•as•per•a•tion (ĭg zăs′pə **rā′**shən) *n.* The condition of being exasperated; extreme irritation: *The baby's whining had me in exasperation by the end of the day.*

Ex•cal•i•bur (ĕk **skăl′**ə bər) *n.* In Arthurian legend, the sword of King Arthur.

ex•ca•vate (**ĕk′**skə vāt′) *tr.v.* **ex•ca•vat•ed, ex•ca•vat•ing, ex•ca•vates.** **1.** To make a hole in; hollow out: *excavate a hillside to build a tunnel.* **2.** To form by digging out: *excavate the foundation for a house.* **3.** To remove by digging or scooping out: *The bulldozer excavated ten truckloads of earth.* **4.** To expose or uncover by or as if by digging: *excavated the remains of an ancient settlement.* [First written down in 1571 in Modern English, from Latin *excavāre*, to hollow out : *ex-*, out + *cavus*, hollow.]

ex•ca•va•tion (ĕk′skə **vā′**shən) *n.* **1.** The act or process of excavating: *Excavation of the basement is to begin soon.* **2.** A hole formed by excavation: *a deep excavation for the new skyscraper.*

ex•ca•va•tor (**ĕk′**skə vā′tər) *n.* A person or thing that excavates, especially a backhoe.

ex•ceed (ĭk **sēd′**) *tr.v.* **ex•ceed•ed, ex•ceed•ing, ex•ceeds.** **1.** To be greater than; surpass: *The play's tremendous success exceeded everyone's hopes.* **2.** To go beyond the limits of: *Do not exceed the speed limit.*

ex•ceed•ing (ĭk **sē′**dĭng) *adj.* Extreme; extraordinary: *a night of exceeding darkness.*

ex•ceed•ing•ly (ĭk **sē′**dĭng lē) *adv.* To an advanced or unusual degree; extremely: *exceedingly hot weather; exceedingly delicate work.*

ex•cel (ĭk **sĕl′**) *v.* **ex•celled, ex•cel•ling, ex•cels.** —*tr.* To do or be better than; surpass: *Their performance excelled all the others.* —*intr.* To be better than others: *Few people excel at every sport.*

ex•cel•lence (**ĕk′**sə ləns) *n.* The condition or quality of excelling; superiority: *artistic excellence; a prize given for excellence in writing.*

Ex•cel•len•cy (**ĕk′**sə lən sē) *n., pl.* **Ex•cel•len•cies.** Used as a title and form of address for certain high officials, such as ambassadors, viceroys, or bishops: *Your Excellency.*

ex•cel•lent (**ĕk′**sə lənt) *adj.* Of the highest or finest quality; superb: *an excellent report; an excellent book.* **—ex′cel•lent•ly** *adv.*

ex•cept (ĭk **sĕpt′**) *prep.* With the exclusion of; but: *All the rooms except one are clean. Everybody went to the movies except for me.* —*conj.* **1.** If it were not for the fact that; only: *I could baby-sit except that I have to study.* **2.** Otherwise than: *He would not open his mouth except to argue.* —*tr.v.* **ex•cept•ed, ex•cept•ing, ex•cepts.** To leave out; exclude: *I had helped earlier and was excepted from staying to clean up.* [First written down about 1378 in Middle English and spelled *excepte*, from Latin *exceptus*, past participle of *excipere*, to exclude : *ex-*, out + *capere*, to hold.]

ex•cept•ing (ĭk **sĕp′**tĭng) *prep.* With the exception of: *No one excepting our father wanted to go fishing in the rain.*

ex•cep•tion (ĭk **sĕp′**shən) *n.* **1.** The act of excepting or the condition of being excepted: *All our guests have arrived with the exception of two.* **2.** A person or thing that is excepted: *I like all my classes with one exception. Certain exceptions to the rule will be considered.* **3.** An objection or a criticism: *opinions that are open to exception.*

ex•cep•tion•a•ble (ĭk **sĕp′**shə nə bəl) *adj.* Open or liable to objection or debate: *an exceptionable description of their opponents.*

ex•cep•tion•al (ĭk **sĕp′**shə nəl) *adj.* **1.** Being an exception; uncommon: *The speaker discussed the topic with exceptional frankness.* **2.** Well above average; extraordinary: *an exceptional memory.* **—ex•cep′tion•al•ly** *adv.*

ex•cerpt (**ĕk′**sûrpt′) *n.* A passage or scene selected from a longer work, such as a book, film, or piece of music. —*tr.v.* (ĭk **sûrpt′**). **ex•cerpt•ed, ex•cerpt•ing, ex•cerpts.** To select or use (a passage or segment from a longer work): *The author excerpted parts of several famous speeches.*

ex•cess (ĭk **sĕs′** *or* **ĕk′**sĕs′) *n.* **1.** The state of exceeding what is normal or sufficient: *filled my glass to excess.* **2.** An amount or a quantity beyond what is normal or sufficient; a surplus. **3.** The amount or degree by which one quantity exceeds another: *an excess of four pounds.* —*adj.* Being more than what is usual, permitted, or required: *Skim off the excess fat.* —***idiom.*** **in excess of.** Greater than; more than: *a package weighing in excess of 40 pounds.*

ex•ces•sive (ĭk **sĕs′**ĭv) *adj.* Exceeding a normal, usual, reasonable, or proper limit: *Excessive rains cause flooding.* —**ex•ces′sive•ly** *adv.* —**ex•ces′sive•ness** *n.*

ex•change (ĭks **chānj′**) *v.* **ex•changed, ex•chang•ing, ex•chang•es.** —*tr.* **1.** To give in return for something received: *I exchanged my pesos for dollars.* **2.** To give and receive mutually; interchange: *exchange glances; exchange letters.* **3.** To give up for a substitute: *exchanged knives and blankets for food and canoes.* **4.** To turn in for replacement: *exchanged the tie for a belt at the store.* —*intr.* To make an exchange. —*n.* **1.** An act or an instance of exchanging: *an exchange of gifts; an exchange of ideas.* **2.** A person or thing that is exchanged: *The watch seemed a fair exchange for the compass.* **3.** A place where things, especially stocks or commodities, are exchanged or traded: *a stock exchange.* **4.** A telephone exchange. —**ex•change′a•ble** *adj.* —**ex•chang′er** *n.*

exchange rate *n.* A rate of exchange.

exchange student *n.* A high school or college student taking part in a program of arranged exchanges between students of different countries.

ex•cheq•uer (**ĕks′**chĕk′ər *or* ĭks **chĕk′**ər) *n.* **1. Exchequer.** The department of the British government in charge of the national revenue. **2.** A treasury, as of a nation or an organization.

ex•cise[1] (**ĕk′**sīz′) *n.* An excise tax. [First written down in 1494 in Middle English, from Middle Dutch *accijs*, tax.]

ex•cise[2] (ĭk **sīz′**) *tr.v.* **ex•cised, ex•cis•ing, ex•cis•es.** To remove by or as if by cutting: *excise two scenes from a movie.* [First written down in 1578 in Modern English, from Latin *excīdere* : *ex-*, out + *caedere*, to cut.] —**ex•ci′sion** (ĭk **sĭzh′**ən) *n.*

ex•cise tax (**ĕk′**sīz′) *n.* A tax on production, sale, or use of certain items or services within a country.

ex•cit•a•ble (ĭk **sī′**tə bəl) *adj.* Easily excited: *a jumpy and excitable cat.* —**ex•cit′a•bil′i•ty, ex•cit′a•ble•ness** *n.* —**ex•cit′a•bly** *adv.*

ex•cite (ĭk **sīt′**) *tr.v.* **ex•cit•ed, ex•cit•ing, ex•cites. 1.** To stir to activity: *The vaccine excites the immune system to produce antibodies against the disease.* **2.** To call forth (a reaction or an emotion, for example); elicit: *The news report excited our curiosity.* **3.** To arouse strong feeling in: *The charismatic speaker excited the audience.* **4.** To increase the energy of (an electron, atom, or molecule). [First written down about 1340 in Middle English and spelled *exciten*, from Latin *excitāre*.]

ex•cit•ed (ĭk **sī′**tĭd) *adj.* Emotionally aroused; stirred: *The astronomers were very excited about their discovery of a new star.* —**ex•cit′ed•ly** *adv.*

ex•cite•ment (ĭk **sīt′**mənt) *n.* **1.** The act or an instance of exciting or the state of being excited. **2.** Activity; agitation: *There was excitement in the air before the performance.*

ex•cit•ing (ĭk **sī′**tĭng) *adj.* Creating or producing excitement: *an exciting rafting trip down the river.* —**ex•cit′ing•ly** *adv.*

ex•claim (ĭk **sklām′**) *tr. & intr.v.* **ex•claimed, ex•claim•ing, ex•claims.** To express (something) or cry out suddenly, as from surprise: *"How nice of you to stop by!" he exclaimed. She exclaimed with pleasure when she saw the new bike.* [First written down in 1570 in Modern English and spelled *exclame*, from Latin *exclāmāre* : *ex-*, out + *clāmāre*, to call.]

ex•cla•ma•tion (ĕk′sklə **mā′**shən) *n.* **1.** Something said suddenly or forcefully: *exclamations of surprise.* **2.** An outcry, as of protest.

exclamation mark *n.* An exclamation point.

exclamation point *n.* A punctuation mark (!) used after an exclamation.

ex•clam•a•tory (ĭk **sklăm′**ə tôr′ē) *adj.* Of, containing, using, or being an exclamation: *a sudden exclamatory remark; an exclamatory sentence.*

ex•clude (ĭk **skl**o͞o**d′**) *tr.v.* **ex•clud•ed, ex•clud•ing, ex•cludes. 1.** To prevent from entering; keep out: *a rule that excludes young children from the big swimming pool.* **2.** To prevent from being included, considered, or accepted: *Let's not exclude the possibility of rain in making our plans.* [First written down about 1384 in Middle English and spelled *excluden*, from Latin *exclūdere* : *ex-*, out + *claudere*, to shut.]

ex•clu•sion (ĭk **skl**o͞o**′**zhən) *n.* **1.** The act or practice of excluding: *The exclusion of large trucks from some streets eases traffic congestion.* **2.** The condition or fact of being excluded.

ex•clu•sive (ĭk **skl**o͞o**′**sĭv) *adj.* **1.** Not divided or shared with others: *the exclusive owner of the estate.* **2.** Undivided; complete: *The spectators gave the diver their exclusive attention.* **3.** Excluding some or most, as from membership or participation; restricted: *an exclusive school.* —**ex•clu′sive•ly** *adv.* —**ex•clu′sive•ness** *n.*

exclusive of *prep.* Not including; besides: *Exclusive of last-minute changes, this book is finished.*

ex•com•mu•ni•cate (ĕks′kə **my**o͞o**′**nĭ kāt′) *tr.v.* **ex•com•mu•ni•cat•ed, ex•com•mu•ni•cat•ing, ex•com•mu•ni•cates.** To deprive of the right of church membership by official authority: *In 1533 the Pope excommunicated Henry VIII.*

ex•com•mu•ni•ca•tion (ĕks′kə myo͞o′nĭ **kā′**shən) *n.* **1.** The act of excommunicating. **2.** The state of being excommunicated.

ex•cre•ment (**ĕk′**skrə mənt) *n.* Waste matter that passes from the body after digestion, especially from the intestinal tract.

ex•cres•cence (ĭk **skrĕs′**əns) *n.* An abnormal growth on the body, as a wart.

ex•crete (ĭk **skrēt′**) *tr.v.* **ex•cret•ed, ex•cret•ing, ex•cretes.** To eliminate (waste matter) from the body: *Sweat and urine are excreted from the body.*

ex•cre•tion (ĭk **skrē′**shən) *n.* **1.** The act or process of excreting. **2.** The waste matter, such as urine and sweat, that is excreted.

ex•cre•to•ry (**ĕk′**skrĭ tôr′ē) *adj.* Of, involving, or used in excretion: *excretory organs.*

ex•cru•ci•at•ing (ĭk **skr**o͞o**′**shē ā′tĭng) *adj.* Intensely painful; agonizing: *the excruciating pain of a toothache.* —**ex•cru′ci•at′ing•ly** *adv.*

ex•cur•sion (ĭk **skûr′**zhən) *n.* **1.** A usually short journey made for pleasure; an outing: *an excursion to the park.* **2.** A round trip on a passenger vehicle at a special reduced fare: *Excursions are a cheap way to travel abroad.*

ex•cuse (ĭk **sky**o͞o**z′**) *tr.v.* **ex•cused, ex•cus•ing, ex•cus•es. 1.** To seek to remove the blame from: *She excused herself for being late.* **2.** To pardon; forgive: *Excuse me for taking your chair.* See Synonyms at **forgive. 3.** To serve as an apology for; justify: *Nothing excuses such rudeness.* **4.** To free or release, as from a duty, an activity, or an obligation: *All seniors will be excused from school early today.* —*n.* (ĭk **sky**o͞o**s′**). **1.** An explanation offered to justify or obtain forgiveness. **2.** Something that serves to excuse; a justification: *There is no excuse for such thoughtless behavior.* **3.** An act of excusing. **4.** A note explaining an absence: *You'll need an*

ă	**pat**	oi	**boy**
ā	**pay**	ou	**out**
âr	**care**	o͝o	**took**
ä	**father**	o͞o	**boot**
ĕ	**pet**	ŭ	**cut**
ē	**be**	ûr	**urge**
ĭ	**pit**	th	**thin**
ī	**pie**	*th*	**this**
îr	**pier**	hw	**whoop**
ŏ	**pot**	zh	**vision**
ō	**toe**	ə	**about**
ô	**paw**	N	*French* **bon**

excuse to miss a day of school. **5.** *Informal.* An inferior example: *Their old station wagon is a poor excuse for a car.* [First written down about 1225 in Middle English and spelled *escusen*, from Latin *excūsāre* : *ex-*, off, away + *causa*, accusation.] —**ex•cus′a•ble** *adj.* —**ex•cus′a•ble•ness** *n.* —**ex•cus′a•bly** *adv.* —**ex•cus′er** *n.*

exec. *abbr.* An abbreviation of executive.

ex•e•crate (ĕk′sĭ krāt′) *tr.v.* **ex•e•crat•ed, ex•e•crat•ing, ex•e•crates. 1.** To declare to be hateful; denounce. **2.** To loathe; hate; detest. —**ex′e•cra′tion** *n.*

ex•e•cute (ĕk′sĭ kyo͞ot′) *tr.v.* **ex•e•cut•ed, ex•e•cut•ing, ex•e•cutes. 1.** To put into effect; carry out: *The government must execute the law fairly.* **2.** To perform; do: *execute a U-turn.* **3.** To create (a work of art, for example) according to a design. **4.** To make valid, as by signing: *execute a deed.* **5.** To put to death, especially by carrying out a legal sentence: *execute a convicted criminal.* [First written down about 1385 in Middle English and spelled *executen*, from Latin *execūtus*, past participle of *exsequī*, to carry out : *ex-*, out + *sequī*, to follow.]

ex•e•cu•tion (ĕk′sĭ **kyo͞o′**shən) *n.* **1.** The act of executing something: *administrators responsible for the execution of a new school policy; the execution of a piece of pottery.* **2.** The manner, style, or result of carrying out: *cleverness in the design and execution of a plan.* **3.a.** The act of putting a person to death as a lawful penalty. **b.** An instance of a person being put to death as a lawful penalty. **4.** The validation of a legal document by the performance of all necessary formalities: *the execution of a will.*

ex•e•cu•tion•er (ĕk′sĭ **kyo͞o′**shə nər) *n.* A person who executes, especially one who puts a condemned person to death.

ex•ec•u•tive (ĭg **zĕk′**yə tĭv) *n.* **1.** A person or group that manages the affairs of an organization, especially a corporation: *an executive responsible for the running of a company.* **2.** The chief officer of a government, state, or political division. **3.** The branch of government responsible for putting laws into effect or managing the affairs of a country. —*adj.* **1.** Of, relating to, or capable of carrying out plans, duties, or other tasks: *a committee having executive powers.* **2.** Having, marked by, or relating to administrative or managerial authority. **3.** Of or relating to the branch of government concerned with putting laws into effect or managing the affairs of a country: *an executive department.*

ex•ec•u•tor (ĭg **zĕk′**yə tər *or* **ĕk′**sĭ kyo͞o′tər) *n.* A person who is responsible for carrying out the terms of a will.

ex•em•pla•ry (ĭg **zĕm′**plə rē) *adj.* **1.** Worthy of imitation; commendable: *exemplary behavior.* **2.** Serving as an illustration; typical: *an exemplary Supreme Court case.* **3.** Serving as a warning: *an exemplary glance.* —**ex•em′pla•ri•ly** *adv.*

ex•em•pli•fy (ĭg **zĕm′**plə fī′) *tr.v.* **ex•em•pli•fied, ex•em•pli•fy•ing, ex•em•pli•fies.** To serve as an example of; illustrate: *a movie that exemplifies a director's style.* —**ex•em′pli•fi•ca′tion** (ĭg zĕm′plə fĭ **kā′**shən) *n.*

ex•empt (ĭg **zĕmpt′**) *tr.v.* **ex•empt•ed, ex•empt•ing, ex•empts.** To free from a duty or an obligation; excuse: *Regulations exempt certain people from serving on juries.* —*adj.* Freed from a duty or an obligation required of others; excused: *Church property is exempt from taxes.* [First written down in 1402 in Middle English and spelled *exempten*, from Latin *exemptus*, past participle of *eximere*, to take out.] —**ex•empt′i•ble** *adj.*

ex•emp•tion (ĭg **zĕmp′**shən) *n.* The act of exempting or the condition of being exempt: *the exemption of food from the sales tax.*

ex•er•cise (**ĕk′**sər sīz′) *n.* **1.** The active use or performance of something: *the exercise of good judgment; the exercise of official duties.* **2.** An activity that requires strenuous mental or physical effort, especially when performed to maintain or develop fitness: *Dancers must do exercises daily.* **3.** A lesson, problem, or task performed to develop or maintain fitness or increase skill: *a book with vocabulary exercises at the end of each chapter.* **4. exercises.** A program that includes speeches and other ceremonial activities performed before an audience: *high school graduation exercises.* —*v.* **ex•er•cised, ex•er•cis•ing, ex•er•cis•es.** —*tr.* **1.** To make active use of; employ: *By voting we exercise our rights as citizens.* **2.** To subject to practice or exertion in order to train, strengthen, or develop: *exercise a horse; exercise your stiff muscles.* —*intr.* To take exercise: *We exercise for an hour daily.* [First written down about 1340 in Middle English, from Latin *exercitium*, from *exercēre*, to exercise : *ex-*, away + *arcēre*, to restrain.]

ex•ert (ĭg **zûrt′**) *tr.v.* **ex•ert•ed, ex•ert•ing, ex•erts. 1.** To put to use or effect; put forth: *exerted all my strength to move the box.* **2.** To put (oneself) to strenuous effort: *The hikers exerted themselves to climb the mountain by noon.* [First written down in 1660 in Modern English, from Latin *exserere*, to put forth, stretch out : *ex-*, out + *serere*, to join.]

ex•er•tion (ĭg **zûr′**shən) *n.* The act or an instance of exerting, especially a strenuous effort: *the tremendous exertion of running a marathon.*

ex•ha•la•tion (ĕks′hə **lā′**shən *or* ĕk′sə **lā′**shən) *n.* **1.** The act or process of exhaling: *exhalation of air from the lungs.* **2.** Something, such as air or vapor, that is exhaled.

ex•hale (ĕks **hāl′** *or* ĕk **sāl′**) *v.* **ex•haled, ex•hal•ing, ex•hales.** —*intr.* To breathe out. —*tr.* To breathe (something) out or blow (something) forth: *The dragon exhaled fire and smoke. The spring flowers exhaled a delicate perfume.* [First written down before 1400 in Middle English and spelled *exalen*, from Latin *exhālāre* : *ex-*, out + *hālāre*, to breathe.]

ex•haust (ĭg **zôst′**) *tr.v.* **ex•haust•ed, ex•haust•ing, ex•hausts. 1.** To wear out completely; tire: *Moving the heavy furniture exhausted us all.* **2.** To use up completely: *Tickets and snacks exhausted our money.* **3.** To drain the contents of; empty: *exhaust the fuel tank.* **4.** To let out or draw off: *exhaust vaporous wastes through a pipe.* **5.** To treat completely; cover thoroughly: *exhaust a topic of conversation.* —*n.* **1.** The escape or release of waste gases or vapors, as from an engine: *The fan is too small to ensure quick exhaust of the fumes.* **2.** The vapors or gases so released: *A cloud of exhaust came from the bus.* **3.** A device or system that allows vapors or gases to escape: *replaced the exhaust on the truck.* [First written down in 1533 in Modern English, from Latin *exhaustus*, past participle of *exhaurīre* : *ex-*, out + *haurīre*, to draw.] —**ex•haust′ed•ly** *adv.*

ex•haus•tion (ĭg **zôs′**chən) *n.* **1.** An act or an instance of exhausting: *exhaustion of the water supply.* **2.** The state of being exhausted; extreme fatigue: *The runner collapsed from exhaustion.*

ex•haus•tive (ĭg **zô′**stĭv) *adj.* Complete; thorough: *an exhaustive search for a solution.* —**ex•haus′tive•ly** *adv.* —**ex•haus′tive•ness** *n.*

ex•hib•it (ĭg **zĭb′**ĭt) *tr.v.* **ex•hib•it•ed, ex•hib•it•ing, ex•hib•its. 1.** To present for the public to view; display: *exhibit new artworks at a gallery.* **2.** To give evidence of; show; demonstrate: *The doctors exhibited great skill in repairing the patient's knee.* —*n.* **1.** Something exhibited; a display: *She studied the museum's fossil exhibits for her new* *book.* **2.** A public showing; an exhibition: *The art exhibit will open next month.* **3.** Something formally introduced as evidence in a court of law. [First written down in 1447 in Middle English and spelled *exhibiten,* from Latin *exhibēre* : *ex-,* out + *habēre,* to hold.] —**ex•hib′i•tor, ex•hib′it•er** *n.*

ex•hi•bi•tion (ĕk′sə **bĭsh′**ən) *n.* **1.** The act or an instance of exhibiting. **2.** Something exhibited; an exhibit. **3.** A large-scale public showing: *attended an exhibition of boating equipment.*

ex•hi•bi•tion•ism (ĕk′sə **bĭsh′**ə nĭz′əm) *n.* The act or practice of deliberately behaving so as to attract attention. —**ex′hi•bi′tion•ist** *n.*

ex•hil•a•rate (ĭg **zĭl′**ə rāt′) *tr.v.* **ex•hil•a•rat•ed, ex•hil•a•rat•ing, ex•hil•a•rates. 1.** To cause to feel happy; elate: *The victory exhilarated the whole school.* **2.** To invigorate; stimulate: *A walk in the cold will exhilarate us.* [First written down in 1540 in Modern English, from Latin *exhilarāre,* from *hilaris,* cheerful, from Greek *hilaros.*] —**ex•hil′a•ra′tion** *n.*

ex•hort (ĭg **zôrt′**) *tr.v.* **ex•hort•ed, ex•hort•ing, ex•horts.** To urge by strong argument or earnest appeal: *The candidate exhorted the crowd to vote.*

ex•hor•ta•tion (ĕg′zôr **tā′**shən *or* ĕk′sôr **tā′**shən) *n.* **1.** The act or an instance of exhorting: *No amount of exhortation could persuade them to give up.* **2.** A speech intended to advise or encourage: *delivered a fiery exhortation to her team.*

ex•hume (ĭg **zo͞om′** *or* ĭg **zyo͞om′**) *tr.v.* **ex•humed, ex•hum•ing, ex•humes. 1.** To dig up or remove from a grave: *an order to exhume the body.* **2.** To bring to light; uncover. [First written down in 1783 in Modern English, from Medieval Latin *exhumāre* : Latin *ex-,* out + Latin *humus,* ground.]

ex•i•gen•cy (**ĕk′**sə jən sē) *n., pl.* **ex•i•gen•cies. 1.** A situation demanding swift attention; an emergency. **2.** Urgent requirements; pressing needs. Often used in the plural: *The exigencies of the schedule meant no holiday.*

ex•i•gent (**ĕk′**sə jənt) *adj.* Requiring immediate action or remedy; urgent.

ex•ile (**ĕg′**zīl′ *or* **ĕk′**sīl′) *n.* **1.a.** Enforced removal from one's native country: *Exile was the punishment for opposing political activities.* **b.** Voluntary absence from one's country: *The author chose exile over living in a country he found oppressive.* **2.** The condition or a period of living away from one's native country. **3.** A person who lives away from his or her native country. —*tr.v.* **ex•iled, ex•il•ing, ex•iles.** To send into exile; banish: *The dictator exiled members of the opposition party.* [First written down before 1300 in Middle English, from Latin *exilium,* from *exsul,* exiled person, wanderer.]

ex•ist (ĭg **zĭst′**) *intr.v.* **ex•ist•ed, ex•ist•ing, ex•ists. 1.** To have actual being; be real: *How many chemical elements have been shown to exist?* **2.a.** To have life; live: *Dinosaurs existed millions of years ago.* **b.** To live at a minimal level; subsist: *Animals cannot exist without food and water.* **3.** To continue to be; persist: *old traditions that still exist in parts of the country.* **4.** To be present; occur: *A new spirit of cooperation existed on both sides.*

ex•is•tence (ĭg **zĭs′**təns) *n.* **1.** The fact or condition of existing; being. **2.** The fact or condition of continued being; life: *our existence on Earth.* **3.** A manner of existing: *lived an ordinary existence.* **4.** Occurrence; presence: *The existence of oil deposits in the rocks brought many people to the region.* [First written down about 1380 in Middle English, from Latin *existere,* to exist : *ex-,* out + *sistere,* to stand.]

ex•is•tent (ĭg **zĭs′**tənt) *adj.* **1.** Having life or being; existing: *existent creatures.* **2.** Occurring or present at the moment; current: *existent customs.*

ex•it (**ĕg′**zĭt *or* **ĕk′**sĭt) *n.* **1.** The act of going away or out: *I made a hasty exit from the snake house at the zoo.* **2.** A passage or way out: *Exits must be clearly marked.* **3.** A performer's departure from the stage. —*v.* **ex•it•ed, ex•it•ing, ex•its.** —*intr.* To make one's exit; depart: *Please exit to the left.* —*tr.* To go out of; leave: *exited the plane through a rear door.* [First written down in 1538 in Modern English and spelled *exit,* a direction to leave the stage, from Latin, third person singular of *exīre,* to go out : *ex-,* out + *īre,* to go.]

exit poll *n.* A poll of voters taken as they leave a polling place.

exo– *pref.* A prefix that means outside or external: *exoskeleton.*

ex•o•bi•ol•o•gy (ĕk′sō bī **ŏl′**ə jē) *n.* The study of extraterrestrial organisms. —**ex′o•bi•ol′o•gist** *n.*

ex•o•crine gland (**ĕk′**sə krĭn *or* **ĕk′**sə krēn) *n.* A gland of external secretion that discharges its product through a duct or into a cavity, including those that secrete saliva, tears, sweat, and milk.

ex•o•dus (**ĕk′**sə dəs) *n.* **1.** A departure of a large number of people: *an exodus from the cities to the suburbs.* **2. Exodus. a.** In the Bible, the departure of the Israelites from Egypt. **b.** The book of the Bible that tells of this departure and of God's giving of the Ten Commandments to Moses. [First written down about 1000 in Old English and spelled *exodus,* from Greek *exodos* : *ex-,* out + *hodos,* way, journey.]

ex of•fi•ci•o (ĕks′ ə **fĭsh′**ē ō′) *adv. & adj.* By virtue of the office or position one holds: *The mayor is ex officio a member of the city council.*

ex•on•er•ate (ĭg **zŏn′**ə rāt′) *tr.v.* **ex•on•er•at•ed, ex•on•er•at•ing, ex•on•er•ates.** To free from blame: *The jury's decision exonerated the defendant.* —**ex•on′er•a′tion** *n.*

ex•or•bi•tant (ĭg **zôr′**bĭ tənt) *adj.* Going beyond all bounds, as of custom or fairness: *an exorbitant price on an imported car.* —**ex•or′bi•tance** *n.* —**ex•or′bi•tant•ly** *adv.*

ex•or•cise (**ĕk′**sôr sīz′) *tr.v.* **ex•or•cised, ex•or•cis•ing, ex•or•cis•es. 1.** To drive away (an evil spirit) by or as if by incantation, prayer, or command. **2.** To free from evil spirits: *the exorcising of an old house.* —**ex′or•cis′er** *n.*

ex•or•cism (**ĕk′**sôr sĭz′əm) *n.* **1.** The act or practice of exorcising. **2.** A formula used in exorcising. —**ex′or•cist** *n.*

ex•o•skel•e•ton (ĕk′sō **skĕl′**ĭ tn) *n.* A hard protective outer body covering, as the shell of a crab; an external skeleton. [First written down in 1847 in Modern English : Greek *exō,* outside + *skeleton.*]

ex•o•sphere (**ĕk′**sō sfîr′) *n.* The outermost layer of the earth's atmosphere lying beyond the ionosphere and extending thousands of miles into space. —**ex′o•spher′ic** (ĕk′sō **sfîr′**ĭk *or* ĕk′sō **sfĕr′**ĭk) *adj.*

ex•o•ther•mic (ĕk′sō **thûr′**mĭk) also **ex•o•ther•mal** (ĕk′sō **thûr′**məl) *adj.* Releasing or giving off heat: *an exothermic chemical reaction.*

ex•ot•ic (ĭg **zŏt′**ĭk) *adj.* **1.** From another part of the world; foreign: *exotic imported birds.* **2.** Strikingly unfamiliar or unusual; excitingly strange: *the exotic beauty of the Galápagos Islands.* —*n.* A person or thing that is exotic: *many exotics exhibited at the flower show.* [First written down in 1599 in Modern English, from Greek *exōtikos,* from *exō,* outside.] —**ex•ot′i•cal•ly** *adv.* —**ex•ot′ic•ness** *n.*

ex•pand (ĭk **spănd′**) *v.* **ex•pand•ed, ex•pand•ing, ex•pands.** —*tr.* **1.** To increase the size, number, volume, or scope of; enlarge: *expand a balloon with air; expanded the business into new areas.* **2.** To express at length or in detail; enlarge upon: *She promised to expand her ideas in her next presentation.* **3.** To open (something) up or out: *The owl*

Exodus
Moses leading the Israelites out of Egypt

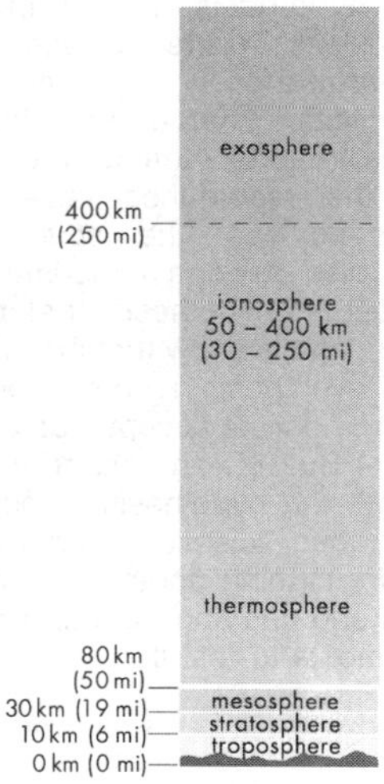

exosphere

ă	**pat**	oi	**boy**
ā	**pay**	ou	**out**
âr	**care**	o͝o	**took**
ä	**father**	o͞o	**boot**
ĕ	**pet**	ŭ	**cut**
ē	**be**	ûr	**urge**
ĭ	**pit**	th	**thin**
ī	**pie**	*th*	**this**
îr	**pier**	hw	**whoop**
ŏ	**pot**	zh	**vision**
ō	**toe**	ə	**about**
ô	**paw**	N	*French* bon

experiment

The job of a scientist involves being a careful observer of nature. The observations that scientists make often give rise to questions such as how or why a certain thing happens. Scientists try to answer these questions by creating a **hypothesis**, a statement that explains what happens. Scientists next must test the hypothesis in controlled conditions. This test is called an **experiment**. In experiments, scientists observe what happens, make measurements, and then record these observations so that other scientists can also perform experiments to test the hypothesis. If all the experiments show that the original hypothesis is not wrong, then scientists accept it as correct. But if an experiment shows the hypothesis is incorrect, then scientists start over again, forming another hypothesis and carrying out more experiments to test it.

expanded its wings and flew away. The article expanded the author's ideas. **4.** To express or write (a number or mathematical expression) in an extended form, as by writing 3,452 as 3,000 + 400 + 50 + 2. *—intr.* **1.** To become greater in size, volume, quantity, or scope: *Gases expand when heated.* See Synonyms at **increase. 2.** To open up or out; unfold: *The sofa expands into a bed.* **3.** To speak or write at length or in detail: *expanded on the issues at the meeting.* [First written down in 1422 in Middle English and spelled *expaunden,* from Latin *expandere* : ex- *out* + *pandere,* to spread.] **—ex•pand'a•ble** *adj.*

ex•panse (ĭk **spăns'**) *n.* A wide and open extent, as of surface, land, or sky: *a vast expanse of desert.*

ex•pan•sion (ĭk **spăn'**shən) *n.* **1.** The act or process of expanding: *the growth and expansion of industry.* **2.** Something formed or produced by expansion: *These suburbs are an expansion of the city.* **3.** The extent or amount by which something has expanded: *a 40 percent expansion in sales.* **4.** A number or other mathematical expression written in an extended form; for example, $a^2 + 2ab + b^2$ is the expansion of $(a + b)^2$.

ex•pan•sion•ism (ĭk **spăn'**shə nĭz'əm) *n.* A nation's practice or policy of territorial or economic expansion. **—ex•pan'sion•ist** *adj. & n.*

ex•pan•sive (ĭk **spăn'**sĭv) *adj.* **1.** Capable of expanding or tending to expand: *Balloons are made of expansive material.* **2.** Broad in size or extent; comprehensive: *an expansive view of world affairs.* **3.** Disposed to be open, communicative, and generous. **4.** Grand in scale: *the calm expansive lake.* **—ex•pan'sive•ly** *adv.* **—ex•pan'sive•ness** *n.*

ex•pa•ti•ate (ĭk **spā'**shē āt') *intr.v.* **ex•pa•ti•at•ed, ex•pa•ti•at•ing, ex•pa•ti•ates.** To speak or write at length; elaborate: *Our guide expatiated on the history and wildlife of the area.* **—ex•pa'ti•a'tion** *n.*

ex•pa•tri•ate (ĕk **spā'**trē āt') *tr.v.* **ex•pa•tri•at•ed, ex•pa•tri•at•ing, ex•pa•tri•ates. 1.** To send into exile. **2.** To remove (oneself) from residence in one's native land: *Many writers expatriated themselves to France in the 1920's.* *—n.* (ĕk **spā'**trē ĭt). A person who has taken up residence in a foreign country. **—ex•pa'tri•a'tion** *n.*

ex•pect (ĭk **spĕkt'**) *tr.v.* **ex•pect•ed, ex•pect•ing, ex•pects. 1.** To look forward to the probable occurrence or appearance of: *expecting a telephone call.* **2.** To consider reasonable or due: *The host will expect an apology for breaking the dish.* **3.** *Informal.* To presume; suppose: *I expect you're right.* [First written down in 1560 in Modern English, from Latin *exspectāre* : *ex-,* off, away + *spectāre,* to look at.]

Synonyms: expect, anticipate, hope, await. These verbs have to do with looking ahead to something in the future. **Expect** means to look forward to something that is likely to happen: *Tony expects to get his braces removed next week.* **Anticipate** often means to take advance action, such as to prevent the occurrence of something expected: *Ellen anticipated trouble and put the pot roast out of the dog's reach.* **Hope** means to look forward to something with desire and usually to trust that it will actually happen: *We hope to see you at the annual meeting.* **Await** means to wait expectantly for something: *I am eagerly awaiting your letter.*

ex•pec•tan•cy (ĭk **spĕk'**tən sē) *n., pl.* **ex•pec•tan•cies. 1.** The act or state of expecting; anticipation: *I was filled with expectancy as I waited for my flight.* **2.** Something that is expected.

ex•pec•tant (ĭk **spĕk'**tənt) *adj.* **1.** Having or marked by expectation: *an expectant audience; an expectant look.* **2.** Awaiting the birth of a child: *expectant parents.* **—ex•pec'tant•ly** *adv.*

ex•pec•ta•tion (ĕk'spĕk **tā'**shən) *n.* **1.** The act of expecting. **2.** Anticipation: *eyes shining with expectation.* **3. expectations.** Prospects, especially of success or gain.

ex•pec•to•rant (ĭk **spĕk'**tər ənt) *adj.* Helping to discharge phlegm or mucus from the respiratory tract. *—n.* An expectorant medicine or drug.

ex•pec•to•rate (ĭk **spĕk'**tə rāt') *v.* **ex•pec•to•rat•ed, ex•pec•to•rat•ing, ex•pec•to•rates.** *—tr.* **1.** To force from the mouth; spit. **2.** To cough up and spit (phlegm, for example). *—intr.* To spit. **—ex•pec'to•ra'tion** *n.*

ex•pe•di•ence (ĭk **spē'**dē əns) *n.* Expediency.

ex•pe•di•en•cy (ĭk **spē'**dē ən sē) *n., pl.* **ex•pe•di•en•cies. 1.** Appropriateness to the purpose at hand; fitness. **2.** Adherence to self-serving means: *Their plans seem to be nothing but expediency.* **3.** A means; an expedient.

ex•pe•di•ent (ĭk **spē'**dē ənt) *adj.* **1.** Suited to a particular purpose; appropriate: *It was expedient to replace the old building with a park.* **2.** Promoting one's own interests; self-serving: *We try to do what is right, not what is merely expedient.* *—n.* Something that is a means to an end: *Shopping by mail is a useful expedient for people in remote areas.* **—ex•pe'di•ent•ly** *adv.*

ex•pe•dite (**ĕk'**spĭ dīt') *tr.v.* **ex•pe•dit•ed, ex•pe•dit•ing, ex•pe•dites. 1.** To speed up the progress of; facilitate: *My telephone call expedited delivery of the package.* **2.** To perform quickly and efficiently: *expedite a job.* **—ex'pe•dit'er, ex'pe•di'tor** *n.*

ex•pe•di•tion (ĕk'spĭ **dĭsh'**ən) *n.* **1.** A trip made by a group of people with a definite purpose: *a geological expedition through the canyon.* **2.** The group making such a trip: *The expedition set off at dawn.* **3.** Speed in performance; promptness: *The cleanup was done well and with expedition.* [First written down before 1425 in Middle English and spelled *expedicion,* military campaign, from Latin *expeditiō,* from *expedīre,* to make ready.]

ex•pe•di•tion•ar•y (ĕk'spĭ **dĭsh'**ə nĕr'ē) *adj.* Relating to or being an expedition.

ex•pe•di•tious (ĕk'spĭ **dĭsh'**əs) *adj.* Acting or done with speed and efficiency: *The most expeditious transportation over long distances is by airplane.* **—ex'pe•di'tious•ly** *adv.* **—ex'pe•di'tious•ness** *n.*

ex•pel (ĭk **spĕl'**) *tr.v.* **ex•pelled, ex•pel•ling, ex•pels. 1.** To force or drive out; eject forcefully: *expel air from the lungs.* **2.** To force to leave; deprive of membership: *The principal expelled several students for cheating.* [First written down about 1385 in Middle English, from Latin *expellere* : *ex-,* out + *pellere,* to drive.]

ex•pend (ĭk **spĕnd'**) *tr.v.* **ex•pend•ed, ex•pend•ing, ex•pends. 1.** To lay out; spend: *expend tax money on health care.* **2.** To use up; consume: *expend energy.*

ex•pend•a•ble (ĭk **spĕn'**də bəl) *adj.* **1.** Subject to use or consumption: *an expendable source of energy.* **2.** Not worth salvaging or reusing. **3.** Subject to being sacrificed, usually to gain an objective: *In peacetime, some army bases are expendable.*

ex•pen•di•ture (ĭk **spĕn'**də chər) *n.* **1.** The act or process of expending; outlay: *the expenditure of city funds for a recycling plant.* **2.** An amount expended.

ex•pense (ĭk **spĕns'**) *n.* **1.** Something spent to attain a goal or achieve a purpose: *an expense of time and effort on the project.* **2.** A loss for the sake of something gained; a sacrifice: *outlaw demonstrations at the expense of free speech.* **3.** An expenditure of money; a cost: *With so many visitors, food is our biggest expense.* **4. expenses.** Charges brought about by an employee in doing a job or in carrying out an assignment: *My expenses include food and lodging.* **5.** Something requiring the expenditure of money: *Owning a car can be a big expense.* [First written down before 1382 in Middle English, from Latin *(pecunia) expēnsa,* (money) paid out, from past participle of *expendere,* to pay out : *ex-,* out + *pendere,* to weigh.]

ex•pen•sive (ĭk **spĕn′**sĭv) *adj.* **1.** Requiring a large expenditure; costly: *an expensive limousine.* **2.** Marked by high prices: *an expensive store.* **—ex•pen′sive•ly** *adv.* **—ex•pen′sive•ness** *n.*

ex•pe•ri•ence (ĭk **spîr′**ē əns) *n.* **1.a.** Active participation in events or activities, leading to the accumulation of knowledge or skill: *learned more from experience than from reading books.* **b.** The knowledge or skill so derived: *a carpenter with a lot of experience.* **2.** An event or series of events participated in or lived through: *the experience of traveling in space.* *—tr.v.* **ex•per•i•enced, ex•per•i•enc•ing, ex•per•i•enc•es.** To participate in personally; undergo: *experience a great adventure; experience the excitement of winning a race.* [First written down about 1378 in Middle English, from Latin *experientia,* from *experiēns,* present participle of *experīrī,* to try.]

ex•pe•ri•enced (ĭk **spîr′**ē ənst) *adj.* Skilled or knowledgeable through active participation or practice: *an experienced teacher.*

ex•per•i•ment (ĭk **spĕr′**ə mənt) *n.* **1.** A test to find out about or demonstrate something: *experiments in the use of color for road signs; medical experiments with new drugs to fight infection.* **2.** The process of conducting such a test; experimentation. *—intr.v.* (ĭk **spĕr′**ə mĕnt′). **ex•per•i•ment•ed, ex•per•i•ment•ing, ex•per•i•ments. 1.** To conduct an experiment; make tests or trials. **2.** To try something new, especially in order to gain experience: *We experimented with different kinds of paint.* [First written down about 1348 in Middle English, from Latin *experīmentum,* from *experīrī,* to try.] **—ex•per′i•ment′er** *n.* —See Note.

ex•per•i•men•tal (ĭk spĕr′ə **mĕn′**tl) *adj.* **1.** Relating to or based on experiments: *Physics and chemistry are experimental sciences.* **2.** Of the nature of an experiment; being or undergoing a test: *an experimental treatment for tooth decay.* **—ex•per′i•men′tal•ly** *adv.*

ex•per•i•men•ta•tion (ĭk spĕr′ə mĕn **tā′**shən) *n.* The act, process, or practice of experimenting: *I discovered how to make good biscuits after much experimentation.*

ex•pert (**ĕk′**spûrt′) *n.* A person with great knowledge of or skill in a particular field: *Doctors are experts in medicine.* *—adj.* (**ĕk′**spûrt *or* ĭk **spûrt′**). Having or showing great knowledge or skill as the result of experience or training: *The forest ranger was an expert guide.* See Synonyms at **proficient.** [First written down about 1384 in Middle English, from Latin *expertus,* past participle of *experīrī,* to try.] **—ex′pert′ly** *adv.* **—ex′pert′ness** *n.*

ex•per•tise (ĕk′spûr **tēz′**) *n.* Expert advice, opinion, skill, or knowledge: *the expertise of a fine jeweler.*

ex•pi•ate (**ĕk′**spē āt′) *tr.v.* **ex•pi•at•ed, ex•pi•at•ing, ex•pi•ates.** To atone or make amends for: *expiate sins by acts of penance.* **—ex′pi•a′tion** *n.*

ex•pi•ra•tion (ĕk′spə **rā′**shən) *n.* **1.** The act of coming to a close; termination. **2.** The act or process of breathing out; exhalation.

ex•pire (ĭk **spīr′**) *intr.v.* **ex•pired, ex•pir•ing, ex•pires. 1.** To come to an end; terminate: *When our dog's license expires, we have to renew it.* **2.** To die: *The injured bird expired before we could get help for it.* **3.** To breathe out; exhale. [First written down in 1419 in Middle English and spelled *expiren,* from Latin *exspīrāre* : *ex-,* out + *spīrāre,* to breathe.]

ex•plain (ĭk **splān′**) *v.* **ex•plained, ex•plain•ing, ex•plains.** *—tr.* **1.** To make plain or comprehensible: *explain the rules of a game; explain a job to a substitute.* **2.** To define or interpret: *The professor explained the meaning of the poem.* **3.** To offer reasons for or a cause of; justify: *We were asked to explain our noisy behavior during class.* *—intr.* To make something plain or comprehensible. ***—idiom.*** **explain away.** To dismiss or get rid of by or as if by explaining: *There is no way to explain away my carelessness.* **—ex•plain′a•ble** *adj.* **—ex•plain′er** *n.* —See Note.

ex•pla•na•tion (ĕk′splə **nā′**shən) *n.* **1.** The act or process of explaining. **2.** Something that explains: *Give a simple explanation of how to make a kite. The police looked for an explanation for the crime.*

ex•plan•a•to•ry (ĭk **splăn′**ə tôr′ē) *adj.* Serving or intended to explain: *The math book has explanatory notes to go along with some problems.*

ex•ple•tive (**ĕk′**splĭ tĭv) *n.* **1.** An exclamation or oath, especially one that is profane, vulgar, or obscene. **2.** A word or phrase added to a sentence or line of verse that does not give any meaning but fills out the sentence or line.

ex•pli•ca•ble (**ĕk′**splĭ kə bəl) *adj.* Possible to explain: *explicable phenomena.*

ex•pli•cate (**ĕk′**splĭ kāt′) *tr.v.* **ex•pli•cat•ed, ex•pli•cat•ing, ex•pli•cates.** To make clear the meaning of; explain: *explicate a scientific theory.* **—ex′pli•ca′tion** *n.*

ex•plic•it (ĭk **splĭs′**ĭt) *adj.* **1.** Fully and clearly expressed or defined; having nothing left out: *an explicit statement of their plans for a new school.* **2.** Clear and outspoken: *We were explicit in demanding that the marsh should be preserved.* **—ex•plic′it•ly** *adv.* **—ex•plic′it•ness** *n.*

ex•plode (ĭk **splōd′**) *v.* **ex•plod•ed, ex•plod•ing, ex•plodes.** *—intr.* **1.** To release energy in an explosion; blow up: *Fireworks exploded all around.* **2.** To burst violently as a result of internal pressure: *Suddenly the bottle of soda water exploded.* **3.** To burst forth or break out suddenly: *exploded with anger at the trespassers.* **4.** To increase suddenly and sharply: *The population has exploded in the past decade.* *—tr.* **1.** To cause to undergo an explosion; detonate: *The engineers exploded the dynamite to open a passage through the rock.* **2.** To show to be false or unreliable: *explode a hypothesis.* [First written down in 1538 in Modern English, from Latin *explōdere,* to drive out by clapping : *ex-,* out + *plaudere,* to clap.] **—ex•plod′er** *n.*

ex•ploit (**ĕk′**sploit′) *n.* An act or a deed, especially a brilliant or heroic one: *the exploits of legendary figures such as Robin Hood.* *—tr.v.* (ĭk **sploit′**). **ex•ploit•ed, ex•ploit•ing, ex•ploits. 1.** To use to the greatest possible advantage: *exploit an idea to make a profit.* **2.** To make use of selfishly or unethically: *exploit unskilled workers.* [First written down about 1300 in Middle English and spelled *espleit,* from Latin *explicitum,* past participle of *explicāre,* to unfold.] **—ex•ploit′a•ble** *adj.* **—ex•ploit′er** *n.*

ex•ploi•ta•tion (ĕk′sploi **tā′**shən) *n.* **1.** The act of using to the greatest possible advantage: *the exploitation of oil fields.* **2.** The use of a person or group for selfish purposes: *the exploitation of immigrant labor.*

ex•plo•ra•tion (ĕk′splə **rā′**shən) *n.* The act or an instance of exploring: *Arctic exploration; an exploration of new medical treatments.* **—ex•plor′a•to′ry** (ĭk **splôr′**ə tôr′ē) *adj.*

ex•plore (ĭk **splôr′**) *v.* **ex•plored, ex•plor•ing, ex•**

Word History: **explain**

The verbs **explain** and **explicate** are synonyms; they mean pretty much the same thing. *Explain* comes from the Latin verb *explānāre,* "to open out, make flat or smooth." *Ex–* means "out," and *plānāre,* "to make level," comes from the adjective *plānus,* "level, plain." *Explicate* comes from the Latin verb *explicāre,* "to fold out, unfold." There are two past participles of *explicāre.* The first one is *explicātus,* from which we get *explicate,* "to make clear, explain." The second past participle is *explicitus,* "made plain, made clear," from which we get **explicit.**

ă	pat	oi	boy
ā	pay	ou	out
âr	care	ŏŏ	took
ä	father	ōō	boot
ĕ	pet	ŭ	cut
ē	be	ûr	urge
ĭ	pit	th	thin
ī	pie	*th*	this
îr	pier	hw	whoop
ŏ	pot	zh	vision
ō	toe	ə	about
ô	paw	N	*French* bon

plores. —*tr.* **1.** To investigate systematically; examine: *explored the possibilities of a new trade agreement.* **2.** To travel in or search into for the purpose of discovery: *explore a vast region of rain forest.* —*intr.* To make a careful examination or search: *Geologists were hired to explore for oil.* [First written down in 1585 in Modern English, from Latin *explōrāre.*]

ex•plor•er (ĭk splôr′ər) *n.* A person or thing that explores, especially a person who explores a geographic area.

ex•plo•sion (ĭk splō′zhən) *n.* **1.** The act of bursting apart or blowing up with a sudden violent release of energy: *an explosion of fireworks.* **2.** The loud sharp sound made by bursting apart or blowing up: *an explosion heard for miles.* **3.** A sudden, often vehement outbreak: *an explosion of laughter.* **4.** A sudden great increase: *a population explosion.*

ex•plo•sive (ĭk splō′sĭv) *adj.* **1.** Of or having the nature of an explosion: *an explosive laugh; an explosive fit of temper.* **2.** Tending to explode: *an explosive powder.* —*n.* A substance that tends to explode or is capable of exploding: *Explosives were used to make the tunnel through the mountain.* **—ex•plo′sive•ly** *adv.* **—ex•plo′sive•ness** *n.*

ex•po•nent (ĭk spō′nənt *or* ĕk′spō′nənt) *n.* **1.** A person who explains or interprets something. **2.** A person who speaks for, represents, or advocates something: *exponents of sanitary measures in surgery.* **3.** A number or symbol, placed to the right of and above the expression to which it applies, that indicates the number of times a mathematical expression is used as a factor. For example, the exponent 3 in 5^3 indicates $5 \times 5 \times 5$; the exponent 2 in $(x + y)^2$ indicates $(x + y) \times (x + y)$. [First written down in 1706 in Modern English, from Latin *expōnere,* to expound : *ex-,* out, away + *pōnere,* to place.]

ex•po•nen•tial (ĕk′spə nĕn′shəl) *adj.* Of, containing, or involving one or more exponents in a mathematical expression: *an exponential increase.*

ex•port (ĭk spôrt′ *or* ĕk′spôrt′) *tr.v.* **ex•port•ed, ex•port•ing, ex•ports.** To send or transport (goods or products) to another country, especially for trade or sale: *export fruit to England.* —*n.* (ĕk′spôrt′). Exportation. [First written down about 1485 in Middle English and spelled *exsporten,* from Latin *exportāre* : *ex-,* out, away + *portāre,* to carry.] **—ex•port′a•ble** *adj.* **—ex•port′er** *n.*

ex•por•ta•tion (ĕk′spôr tā′shən) *n.* The act or an instance of exporting: *The exportation of automobiles is an important element of the Japanese economy.*

ex•pose (ĭk spōz′) *tr.v.* **ex•posed, ex•pos•ing, ex•pos•es.** **1.** To lay open or subject to an action or an influence: *expose young children to literature; expose a visitor to a cold.* **2.** To subject (a photographic film, for example) to the action of light. **3.** To make visible; reveal: *Paint remover exposed the old wood underneath.* **4.** To make known (something discreditable) or reveal the guilt of: *expose a dishonest official.* [First written down before 1422 in Middle English and spelled *exposen,* from Old French *exposer,* from Latin *expōnere,* to set forth.] **—ex•pos′er** *n.*

ex•po•sé (ĕk′spō zā′) *n.* An exposure or a revelation of something discreditable: *a magazine exposé of corruption in government.*

ex•po•si•tion (ĕk′spə zĭsh′ən) *n.* **1.** An exact and detailed explanation of difficult material: *The astronomer gave a long exposition on the nature of the eclipse.* **2.** The first part of a musical composition in sonata form that introduces the themes. **3.** A large public exhibition or fair: *an international computer exposition.* **—ex•pos′i•to′ry** (ĭk spŏz′ĭ tôr′ē) *adj.* **—ex•pos′i•tor** *n.*

ex post fac•to (ĕks′ pōst făk′tō) *adj.* Enacted after an event but applying to it nonetheless. Used especially of a law.

ex•pos•tu•late (ĭk spŏs′chə lāt′) *intr.v.* **ex•pos•tu•lat•ed, ex•pos•tu•lat•ing, ex•pos•tu•lates.** To reason earnestly with someone, especially in an effort to dissuade or correct: *The parent expostulated with the committee on the need for new computers in school.* **—ex•pos′tu•la′tion** *n.*

ex•po•sure (ĭk spō′zhər) *n.* **1.** The act or an instance of exposing, as: **a.** An act or an instance of subjecting or being subjected to an action or influence: *a child's exposure to measles; her exposure to city living.* **b.** Appearance in public or in the mass media. **c.** Revelation, especially of crime or guilt. **2.** A position in relation to climatic or weather conditions or points of the compass: *Our house has a southern exposure.* **3.a.** The act of exposing a photographic film or plate. **b.** The amount of light needed to expose a photographic film: *This exposure will not produce a clear image.* **c.** An exposed section of a roll of film: *We took several exposures.*

ex•pound (ĭk spound′) *v.* **ex•pound•ed, ex•pound•ing, ex•pounds.** —*tr.* To set forth or give a detailed statement of: *Debaters must always expound their views clearly.* —*intr.* To make a detailed statement: *The candidate expounded on the need for good government.* **—ex•pound′er** *n.*

ex•press (ĭk sprĕs′) *tr.v.* **ex•pressed, ex•press•ing, ex•press•es.** **1.** To put into words; state: *A good speaker expresses ideas clearly.* **2.a.** To manifest or communicate, as by a gesture; show: *The winner's face expressed great joy.* **b.** To make known the opinions or feelings of (oneself): *She expressed herself in a letter to the editor.* **3.** To represent by a sign or symbol: *In arithmetic, the minus sign expresses subtraction.* **4.** To squeeze or press out, as juice from an orange: *a machine that expresses juice from berries and fruits.* **5.** To send by special messenger or rapid transport: *express a letter to the office in Atlanta.* —*adj.* **1.** Clearly stated; explicit: *my express wish to go home.* **2.** Particular; specific: *The express object of the exercise was to teach cooperation.* **3.a.** Direct, rapid, and usually making few or no stops: *an express train.* **b.** Of or sent by rapid transportation: *an express package; an express service.* **c.** Of, relating to, or appropriate for rapid travel: *an express lane on the highway.* —*adv.* By express transport or delivery: *send a package express.* —*n.* **1.** A system or company that provides rapid and direct delivery of goods and mail: *Call the local express to handle that box of fruit.* **2.** A means of transportation, such as a train, that travels rapidly and makes few or no stops before its destination: *Take an express to the airport.* [First written down about 1384 in Middle English and spelled *expressen,* from Medieval Latin *expressāre,* from Latin *exprimere* : Latin *ex-,* out + Latin *premere,* to press.] **—ex•press′i•ble** *adj.*

ex•pres•sion (ĭk sprĕsh′ən) *n.* **1.** The act of expressing, as in words, art, action, or movement: *the expression of one's opinion by means of voting.* **2.a.** Something that expresses or communicates: *These flowers are an expression of my gratitude.* **b.** A facial aspect or look that indicates a certain mood or feeling: *an expression of joy in his eyes.* **3.** A symbol or arrangement of symbols that indicates a mathematical operation or quantity. For example, $x + y$ is an algebraic expression. **4.** A manner of speaking, depicting, or performing that expresses particular feeling or meaning: *The poet read several poems with great expression.* **5.** A particular word or phrase: Burnt to a crisp *is a familiar expression.*

ex•pres•sion•ism (ĭk **sprĕsh′**ə nĭz′əm) *n.* A movement in the fine arts during the late 19th and early 20th centuries that emphasized the expression of artists' feelings and experiences.
ex•pres•sion•less (ĭk **sprĕsh′**ən lĭs) *adj.* Lacking expression: *a dull expressionless voice.*
ex•pres•sive (ĭk **sprĕs′**ĭv) *adj.* **1.** Serving to express or indicate: *The kitten's crying was expressive of its hunger.* **2.** Full of meaning; significant: *an expressive smile.* **—ex•pres′sive•ly** *adv.* **—ex•pres′sive•ness** *n.*
ex•press•ly (ĭk **sprĕs′**lē) *adv.* **1.** In an express or a definite manner; explicitly: *The rules expressly say that only four can play at a time.* **2.** Especially; particularly: *scissors made expressly for left-handed people.*
ex•press•way (ĭk **sprĕs′**wā′) *n.* A major divided highway designed for high-speed travel.
ex•pro•pri•ate (ĕk **sprō′**prē āt′) *tr.v.* **ex•pro•pri•at•ed, ex•pro•pri•at•ing, ex•pro•pri•ates.** To transfer (property) to oneself: *The government expropriated the home of the tax evaders.* **—ex•pro′pri•a′tion** *n.*
ex•pul•sion (ĭk **spŭl′**shən) *n.* The act of expelling or the state of being expelled: *the expulsion of gases from a jet engine; a representative faced with expulsion from the legislature.* [First written down before 1400 in Middle English and spelled *expulcioun*, from Old French *expulsion*, from Latin *expulsus*, past participle of *expellere*, to expel.]
ex•punge (ĭk **spŭnj′**) *tr.v.* **ex•punged, ex•pung•ing, ex•pung•es.** To remove completely; delete; erase: *expunge a statement from the records of a trial.* [First written down in 1602 in Modern English, from Latin *expungere* : *ex-*, out, away + *pungere*, to prick.]
ex•pur•gate (**ĕk′**spər gāt′) *tr.v.* **ex•pur•gat•ed, ex•pur•gat•ing, ex•pur•gates.** To remove objectionable passages from (a book, for example) before publication: *References to several living people were expurgated from the play.* [First written down in 1621 in Modern English, from Latin *expūrgāre*, to purify, from *pūrgāre*, to cleanse.] **—ex′pur•ga′tion** *n.*
ex•qui•site (**ĕk′**skwĭ zĭt *or* ĭk **skwĭz′**ĭt) *adj.* **1.** Characterized by intricate and beautiful design or execution: *an exquisite vase.* **2.** Acutely perceptive or discriminating: *exquisite taste in art.* **3.** Intense; keen: *took exquisite pleasure in the success of their children.* [First written down before 1425 in Middle English and spelled *exquisit*, carefully chosen, from Latin *exquīsītus*, past participle of *exquīrere*, to search out : *ex-*, out + *quaerere*, to seek.] **—ex′qui•site•ly** *adv.*
ex•tant (**ĕk′**stənt *or* ĕk **stănt′**) *adj.* Still in existence; not destroyed, lost, or extinct: *extant diaries of early settlers.*
ex•tem•po•ra•ne•ous (ĭk stĕm′pə **rā′**nē əs) *adj.* Done or made with little or no preparation; impromptu: *The scientist stood up and gave an extemporaneous speech. The reporter interviewed people asking for extemporaneous remarks about the proposed park.* **—ex•tem′po•ra′ne•ous•ly** *adv.* **—ex•tem′po•ra′ne•ous•ness** *n.*
ex•tem•po•rar•y (ĭk **stĕm′**pə rĕr′ē) *adj.* Extemporaneous. **—ex•tem′po•rar′i•ly** (ĭk stĕm′pə **râr′**ə lē) *adv.*
ex•tend (ĭk **stĕnd′**) *v.* **ex•tend•ed, ex•tend•ing, ex•tends.** —*tr.* **1.** To open or straighten (something) out: *Extend your left arm.* **2.** To stretch or spread (something) out to greater or fuller length: *Better living conditions have extended the average life span.* **3.** To enlarge the area, scope, or range of: *extend the boundaries of the park.* See Synonyms at **increase. 4.** To offer or provide: *extend congratulations to the graduates; extend aid to an underdeveloped country.* **5.** To prolong the time allowed for payment of: *The bank extended our loan for a few more months.* —*intr.* To be or become long, large, or comprehensive: *The beach extends for miles. The influence of our democracy extends around the world.* [First written down before 1338 in Middle English and spelled *extenden*, from Latin *extendere* : *ex-*, out + *tendere*, to stretch.]
ex•tend•ed (ĭk **stĕn′**dĭd) *adj.* **1.** Stretched or pulled out: *extended arms.* **2.** Continued for a long period of time; prolonged: *an extended vacation in the Caribbean.* **3.** Enlarged or broad in meaning, scope, or influence: *extended television coverage of the Congressional hearings.* **—ex•tend′ed•ly** *adv.*
extended family *n.* A family that includes parents, children, and other close relatives, often living near to each other.
ex•ten•sion (ĭk **stĕn′**shən) *n.* **1.** The act of extending of the condition of being extended: *Extension of the highway has snarled traffic.* **2.a.** The act of straightening or extending a part of the body by a muscle: *extension of the leg to relieve muscle cramps.* **b.** The position assumed by an extended limb. **3.** Something that extends from a main part; an addition: *An extension was added to the back of the building.* **4.** An additional telephone connected to a main line: *We have two extensions to our telephone.*
extension cord *n.* A long electric cord with a socket and plug, used to connect an electric device to a wall socket.
ex•ten•sive (ĭk **stĕn′**sĭv) *adj.* Large in extent, range, or amount: *An extensive park runs along the ocean. We made extensive renovations to the old building.* **—ex•ten′sive•ly** *adv.* **—ex•ten′sive•ness** *n.*
ex•ten•sor (ĭk **stĕn′**sər) *n.* A muscle that extends or stretches a limb of the body.
ex•tent (ĭk **stĕnt′**) *n.* **1.** The area, magnitude, or distance over which something extends; size: *increased the extent of their lands; underestimated the extent of the damage.* **2.** The degree to which something extends: *prosecuted to the fullest extent of the law.* **3.** An extensive space or area: *an extent of pine forest.*
ex•ten•u•ate (ĭk **stĕn′**yo͞o āt′) *tr.v.* **ex•ten•u•at•ed, ex•ten•u•at•ing, ex•ten•u•ates.** To lessen or attempt to lessen the magnitude of, especially by providing a partial excuse: *Lack of experience extenuated the fault of the goalie in the team's loss.* **—ex•ten′u•a′tor** *n.* **—ex•ten′u•a•to′ry** (ĭk **stĕn′**yo͞o ə tôr′ē) *adj.*
ex•ten•u•a•tion (ĭk stĕn′yo͞o **ā′**shən) *n.* The act of extenuating or the condition of being extenuated; partial justification.
ex•te•ri•or (ĭk **stîr′**ē ər) *adj.* **1.** Outer; external: *the exterior walls of a castle.* **2.** Originating or acting from the outside: *exterior pressures.* **3.** Suitable for use outside: *an exterior paint able to withstand sun and rain.* —*n.* **1.** A part or surface that is outside: *the exterior of the house.* **2.** An outward appearance: *The town had a cheerful exterior.* [First written down in 1528 in Modern English and spelled *exterieur*, from Latin *exterior*, comparative of *exter*, outward.]
exterior angle *n.* The angle formed between a side of a polygon and an extended adjacent side.
ex•ter•mi•nate (ĭk **stûr′**mə nāt′) *tr.v.* **ex•ter•mi•nat•ed, ex•ter•mi•nat•ing, ex•ter•mi•nates.** To get rid of by destroying completely; wipe out: *exterminate a colony of termites.* [First written down in 1541 in Modern English, from Latin *exterminare*, to drive out : *ex-*, out + *terminus*, boundary.] **—ex•ter′mi•na′tion** *n.*
ex•ter•mi•na•tor (ĭk **stûr′**mə nā′tər) *n.* A person

expressionism
No More War! by Käthe Kollwitz

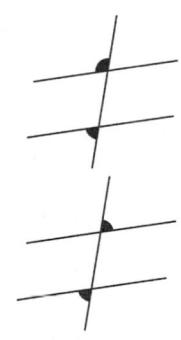

exterior angle
Top: Exterior angles on the same side
Bottom: Exterior opposite angles

ă	pat	oi	boy
ā	pay	ou	out
âr	care	o͝o	took
ä	father	o͞o	boot
ĕ	pet	ŭ	cut
ē	be	ûr	urge
ĭ	pit	th	thin
ī	pie	*th*	this
îr	pier	hw	whoop
ŏ	pot	zh	vision
ō	toe	ə	about
ô	paw	N	*French* bon

extinguisher
Fire extinguisher

whose occupation is exterminating insects, rodents, or other pests.

ex•ter•nal (ĭk stûr′nəl) *adj.* **1.** Relating to, existing on, or connected with the outside or an outer part; exterior: *external repairs on a house.* **2.** Suitable for application to an outer surface: *a salve for external use only.* **3.** Acting or coming from the outside: *an external force.* **4.** Of or relating chiefly to outward appearance; superficial: *an external display of pleasure.* **5.** Of or relating to foreign affairs or foreign countries. [First written down before 1425 in Middle English, from Latin *externus*, outward.] **—ex•ter′nal•ly** *adv.*

external ear *n.* The parts of the ear that collect sound waves and pass them inward, including the eardrum; the outer ear.

ex•tinct (ĭk stĭngkt′) *adj.* **1.** No longer existing or living: *an extinct species.* **2.** No longer burning or active: *an extinct volcano.* [First written down before 1425 in Middle English, from Latin *exstīnctus*, past participle of *extinguere*, to extinguish.]

ex•tinc•tion (ĭk stĭngk′shən) *n.* **1.** The act of extinguishing. **2.** The fact of being extinct or the process of becoming extinct: *Early trappers hunted the beaver almost to extinction.*

ex•tin•guish (ĭk stĭng′gwĭsh) *tr.v.* **ex•tin•guished, ex•tin•guish•ing, ex•tin•guish•es. 1.** To put out (a fire, for example); quench: *extinguish a candle; extinguish the lights.* **2.** To put an end to (hopes, for example); destroy: *Missing the bus extinguished our hope of arriving on time.* [First written down before 1503 in Modern English, from Latin *exstinguere* : *ex-*, out + *stinguere*, to quench.] **—ex•tin′guish•a•ble** *adj.*

ex•tin•guish•er (ĭk stĭng′gwĭ shər) *n.* A portable device for spraying and extinguishing a fire with chemicals.

ex•tir•pate (ĕk′stər pāt′) *tr.v.* **ex•tir•pat•ed, ex•tir•pat•ing, ex•tir•pates.** To destroy totally; exterminate: *extirpate the evils of prejudice and ignorance.* **—ex′tir•pa′tion** *n.*

ex•tol also **ex•toll** (ĭk stōl′) *tr.v.* **ex•tolled, ex•tol•ling, ex•tols** or **ex•tolls.** To praise highly; laud: *extol the achievements of a great humanitarian.* **—ex•tol′ler** *n.*

ex•tort (ĭk stôrt′) *tr.v.* **ex•tort•ed, ex•tort•ing, ex•torts.** To obtain from another by threats or force: *The blackmailer extorted money from a man who had lied about his past.* [First written down before 1420 in Middle English, from Latin *extortus*, past participle of *extorquēre*, to wrench out, extort : *ex-*, out + *torquēre*, to twist.] **—ex•tort′er** *n.*

ex•tor•tion (ĭk stôr′shən) *n.* **1.** The act or an instance of extorting. **2.** Illegal use of one's official position or powers to obtain property or funds. **—ex•tor′tion•ist** *n.*

ex•tor•tion•ate (ĭk stôr′shə nĭt) *adj.* **1.** Characterized by extortion: *the extortionate demands of the rebel forces.* **2.** Exorbitant; immoderate: *extortionate prices for gasoline.* **—ex•tor′tion•ate•ly** *adv.*

ex•tra (ĕk′strə) *adj.* More than what is usual, normal, expected, or necessary; additional: *earn extra money by working part-time.* *—n.* **1.** Something additional, for which one pays an added charge: *We bought a new car with all the extras such as a stereo.* **2.** A special edition of a newspaper: *The extra gave the latest news of the crisis.* **3.** A performer hired to play a minor part as in a crowd scene. *—adv.* To an exceptional extent or degree; unusually: *The audience was extra quiet during the vocalist's solo.* [First written down in 1654 in Modern English, probably short for *extraordinary.*]

extra– or **extro–** *pref.* A prefix that means outside or beyond: *extracurricular.*

ex•tract (ĭk străkt′) *tr.v.* **ex•tract•ed, ex•tract•ing, ex•tracts. 1.** To draw out forcibly or with effort; pull out: *extract a tooth; extract ore from a mine.* **2.** To obtain despite resistance: *extract a confession.* **3.** To obtain from a substance by a chemical or physical process: *extract aluminum from bauxite; extract the juice of berries.* **4.** To remove for separate consideration or publication; excerpt. **5.** To derive or gain from an experience or a source: *extract pleasure from listening to music.* *—n.* (**ĕk′**străkt′). **1.** A passage from a literary work; an excerpt: *The book is made up of extracts from other works.* **2.** A concentrated substance from a food or flavoring: *vanilla extract; an extract of coffee.* [First written down before 1425 in Middle English and spelled *extracten*, from Latin *extrāctus*, past participle of *extrahere* : *ex-*, out + *trahere*, to draw.] **—ex•trac′tor** *n.*

ex•trac•tion (ĭk străk′shən) *n.* **1.** The act of extracting or the condition of being extracted: *The extraction of impacted wisdom teeth is quite common.* **2.** Something obtained by extraction; an extract. **3.** Descent; origin: *of French-Canadian extraction.*

ex•tra•cur•ric•u•lar (ĕk′strə kə rĭk′yə lər) *adj.* Being outside the regular course of study of a school or college: *Debating is an extracurricular activity.*

ex•tra•dite (ĕk′strə dīt′) *tr.v.* **ex•tra•dit•ed, ex•tra•dit•ing, ex•tra•dites. 1.** To give up or deliver (a prisoner or fugitive, for example) to the jurisdiction of another government or authority for trial. **2.** To obtain the extradition of.

ex•tra•di•tion (ĕk′strə dĭsh′ən) *n.* Legal surrender of a fugitive to the jurisdiction of another state, country, or government for trial.

ex•tra•ne•ous (ĭk strā′nē əs) *adj.* **1.** Not essential; irrelevant: *These minor points are extraneous to my report.* **2.** Coming from the outside; foreign. **—ex•tra′ne•ous•ly** *adv.* **—ex•tra′ne•ous•ness** *n.*

ex•traor•di•nar•y (ĭk strôr′dn ĕr′ē *or* ĕk′strə ôr′dn ĕr′ē) *adj.* Very unusual; exceptional; remarkable: *Landing on the moon was an extraordinary accomplishment. Great intelligence is an extraordinary gift.* [First written down in 1431 in Middle English and spelled *extraordinaire*, from Latin *extraordinārius* : *extrā*, outside + *ōrdō*, order, rule.] **—ex•traor′di•nar′i•ly** (ĭk strôr′dn âr′ə lē *or* ĕk′strə ôr′dn âr′ə lē) *adv.*

ex•trap•o•late (ĭk străp′ə lāt′) *v.* **ex•trap•o•lat•ed, ex•trap•o•lat•ing, ex•trap•o•lates.** *—tr.* **1.** To infer or estimate (something unknown) on the basis of known information: *We extrapolated next year's expenses from a review of this year's bills.* **2.** In mathematics, to estimate the value of a quantity that falls outside the range in which its values are known. *—intr.* To make an estimate or prediction of something not known on the basis of known information. **—ex•trap′o•la′tion** *n.*

ex•tra•sen•so•ry (ĕk′strə sĕn′sə rē) *adj.* Outside the normal range of the senses: *Extrasensory powers are said to enable some people to predict the future.*

extrasensory perception *n.* Perception by means other than the usual senses: *People who seem to know what others are thinking sometimes claim they have extrasensory perception.*

ex•tra•ter•res•tri•al (ĕk′strə tə rĕs′trē əl) *adj.* Beyond the earth or outside its atmosphere: *extraterrestrial bodies such as stars and comets.* *—n.* A creature from outer space.

ex•trav•a•gance (ĭk străv′ə gəns) *n.* **1.** The quality of being extravagant. **2.** Immoderate expense or display: *Such extravagance can lead to debt.* **3.** Something that is excessively costly: *Their latest extravagance is an expensive race car.*

ex•trav•a•gant (ĭk străv′ə gənt) *adj.* **1.** Given to lavish or imprudent spending: *an extravagant ex-*

ecutive. **2.** Unreasonably high; excessive: *extravagant fees for the service.* **—ex•trav′a•gant•ly** *adv.*

ex•trav•a•gan•za (ĭk străv′ə **găn′**zə) *n.* An elaborate spectacular display or entertainment: *The circus is one huge extravaganza.*

ex•treme (ĭk **strēm′**) *adj.* **1.** The farthest possible; outermost: *the extreme end of the room.* **2.** Very great or intense: *exercise extreme caution; suffer from the extreme cold.* **3.** Extending far beyond the norm: *hold extreme opinions in politics.* **4.** Drastic; severe: *The doctors took extreme measures to control the baby's temperature.* —*n.* **1.** The greatest or utmost degree or point: *eager to the extreme.* **2.** Either of two things set at opposite ends of a range: *His opinions go from one extreme to another.* **3.** A drastic measure: *resort to extremes in an emergency.* **4.** In mathematics, the first or last term of a proportion. [First written down before 1425 in Middle English, from Latin *extrēmus.*] **—ex•treme′ly** *adv.* **—ex•treme′ness** *n.*

extremely high frequency *n.* A radio frequency between 30,000 and 300,000 megahertz.

extremely low frequency *n.* A radio frequency below 300 hertz.

ex•trem•ist (ĭk **strē′**mĭst) *n.* A person with views extending far beyond the norm, especially in politics. **—ex•trem′ism** *n.*

ex•trem•i•ty (ĭk **strĕm′**ĭ tē) *n., pl.* **ex•trem•i•ties. 1.** The outermost or farthest point: *Patagonia is at the southern extremity of South America.* **2.** The greatest or utmost degree. **3.** Very great danger, distress, or need. **4.** An extreme or severe measure: *resort to extremities in a crisis.* **5.a.** A bodily limb or appendage. **b.** A hand or foot: *Frostbite often affects the extremities first.*

ex•tri•cate (**ĕk′**strĭ kāt′) *tr.v.* **ex•tri•cat•ed, ex•tri•cat•ing, ex•tri•cates.** To set free from an entanglement or a difficulty; disengage: *extricate oneself from an embarrassing situation.* [First written down in 1614 in Modern English, from Latin *extricāre* : *ex-*, out + *tricae*, hindrances, perplexities.] **—ex′tri•ca′tion** *n.*

ex•trin•sic (ĭk **strĭn′**sĭk *or* ĭk **strĭn′**zĭk) *adj.* **1.** Not essential or basic; extraneous: *Your arguments are extrinsic to the discussion.* **2.** Originating from the outside; external: *extrinsic forces on the environment.* **—ex•trin′si•cal•ly** *adv.*

ex•tro•vert (**ĕk′**strə vûrt′) *n.* A person interested mainly in other people or external circumstances rather than his or her own thoughts and feelings.

ex•trude (ĭk **strōōd′**) *v.* **ex•trud•ed, ex•trud•ing, ex•trudes.** —*tr.* **1.** To push or thrust out. **2.** To shape (plastic, for example) by forcing it through a die. —*intr.* To protrude or project: *Lava extruded from a crack in the mountainside.*

ex•tru•sion (ĭk **strōō′**zhən) *n.* **1.** The act or process of extruding: *Pieces for plastic furniture are often made by extrusion.* **2.** Something that has been extruded.

ex•u•ber•ance (ĭg **zōō′**bər əns) *n.* The condition or quality of being exuberant: *The crowd cheered in wild exuberance.*

ex•u•ber•ant (ĭg **zōō′**bər ənt) *adj.* **1.** Full of unrestrained enthusiasm or joy: *Spectators of the parade were in an exuberant mood.* **2.** Lavish or extravagant; overflowing: *exuberant praise of the hero.* [First written down in 1459 in Middle English, from Latin *exūberāre*, to be exuberant.] **—ex•u′ber•ant•ly** *adv.*

ex•u•da•tion (ĕks′yōō **dā′**shən) *n.* **1.** The act or an instance of oozing forth: *a slight exudation of blood from a cut.* **2.** Something that has oozed forth.

ex•ude (ĭg **zōōd′** *or* ĭk **sōōd′**) *tr. & intr.v.* **ex•ud•ed, ex•ud•ing, ex•udes.** To give or come forth by or as if by oozing: *The body exudes sweat through the pores. Sap exuded from the cuts in the plant's stem. Confidence exuded in their cocky manner.* [First written down in 1574 in Modern English, from Latin *exsūdāre* : *ex-*, out + *sūdāre*, to sweat.]

ex•ult (ĭg **zŭlt′**) *intr.v.* **ex•ult•ed, ex•ult•ing, ex•ults.** To rejoice greatly; be jubilant or triumphant: *The entire town exulted in the team's victory.* [First written down in 1570 in Modern English, from Latin *exsultāre* : *ex-*, out, up + *saltāre*, to dance, leap.]

ex•ul•tant (ĭg **zŭl′**tənt) *adj.* Marked by great joy or jubilation: *an exultant victor.* **—ex•ult′ant•ly** *adv.*

ex•ul•ta•tion (ĕk′səl **tā′**shən *or* ĕg′zəl **tā′**shən) *n.* The act or condition of rejoicing greatly.

-ey *suff.* Variant of **–y**[1].

eye (ī) *n.* **1.a.** An organ of the body by means of which an animal is able to see or sense light. In vertebrates the eye consists of a hollow structure that contains a photosensitive retina on which a lens focuses incoming light. **b.** The outer visible part of this organ, especially the colored iris: *People may have blue, green, or brown eyes.* **c.** The area and the structures around the eye, including the eyelids, eyelashes, and eyebrows. **2.** Sight; vision: *A lifeguard must have a sharp eye.* **3.** The ability to estimate, judge, or note: *The coach had an eye for new talent.* **4.** A way of regarding something; a point of view or an opinion: *saw the world with a critical eye.* **5.** Something that resembles an eye, as a bud on a potato or a spot on a peacock's tail feather. **6.** The hole in a needle through which the thread goes. **7.** A loop, as of metal, rope, or thread. **8.** The relatively calm area at the center of a hurricane or similar storm. —*tr.v.* **eyed, eye•ing** or **ey•ing** (ī′ĭng), **eyes.** To look at; watch; regard: *The child eyed the big dog suspiciously.* **—*idioms.* an eye for an eye.** Punishment in which an offender suffers what the victim has suffered: *Execution of the murderer was defended as an eye for an eye.* **eye to eye.** In agreement: *see eye to eye on most issues.* **in the public eye.** Frequently seen in public or in the media: *It is impossible to relax when one is always in the public eye.* **lay (one's) eyes on** or **set (one's) eyes on.** To see: *Have you laid eyes on my lost glasses?* **with an eye to.** With a view to: *We left early with an eye to getting home before dark.* [First written down about 700 in Old English and spelled *ēge.*]

❑ *These sound alike:* **eye, aye** (yes), **I**[1] (pronoun).

eye•ball (**ī′**bôl′) *n.* The part of the eye shaped like a ball and enclosed by the socket behind eyelids. It is connected at the rear to the optic nerve.

eye•brow (**ī′**brou′) *n.* **1.** The bony ridge of the skull that extends over the eye. **2.** The line of short hairs covering this ridge.

eye•cup (**ī′**kŭp′) *n.* A small cup with a rim shaped to fit over the eye, used for washing the eye or applying liquid medicine to it.

eye•drop•per (**ī′**drŏp′ər) *n.* A dropper for applying liquid medicine to the eye.

eye•ful (**ī′**fo͝ol′) *n.* **1.** An amount of something that gets into the eye: *The wind was blowing and I got an eyeful of dust.* **2.** A complete view; a good look: *We got a real eyeful during the tour of the auto plant.*

eye•glass (**ī′**glăs′) *n.* **1. eyeglasses. a.** A pair of lenses worn in front of the eyes to correct vision; glasses. **b.** A lens worn or held in front of the eye to correct vision; a monocle. **2.** An eyepiece, as of a microscope or telescope.

eye•lash (**ī′**lăsh′) *n.* **1.** A row of hairs that forms a fringe on the edge of the eyelid. **2.** One of the hairs in this row.

eye•let (**ī′**lĭt) *n.* **1.a.** A small hole for a lace, cord, or hook to fit through: *Shoelaces are threaded through eyelets.* **b.** A metal ring used as a rim to strengthen such a hole: *The eyelets on the flag protected it*

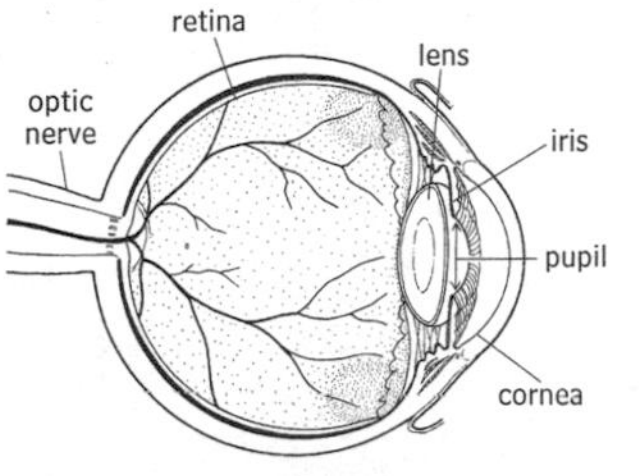

eye

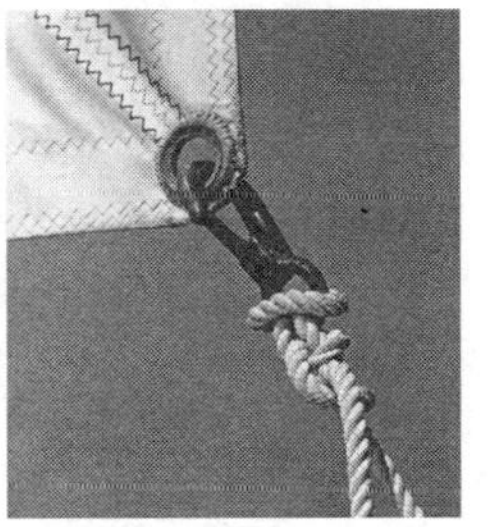
eyelet

ă	pat	oi	boy
ā	pay	ou	out
âr	care	o͝o	took
ä	father	o͞o	boot
ĕ	pet	ŭ	cut
ē	be	ûr	urge
ĭ	pit	th	thin
ī	pie	*th*	this
îr	pier	hw	whoop
ŏ	pot	zh	vision
ō	toe	ə	about
ô	paw	N	*French* bon

eyestalk
On a crab

from tearing. **2.** A small hole edged with embroidered stitches as part of a design.

❑ *These sound alike:* **eyelet, islet** (small island).

eye•lid (ī′lĭd′) *n.* Either one of a pair of folds of skin and muscle that can be brought together to cover the eye.

eye•lin•er (ī′lī′nər) *n.* Makeup used to outline the eyes.

eye opener *n. Informal.* A startling or shocking revelation: *The article about the water shortage was a real eye opener.*

eye•piece (ī′pēs′) *n.* The lens or group of lenses closest to the eye in a telescope, microscope, or similar optical instrument.

eye shadow *n.* A cosmetic applied to the eyelids to enhance the eyes.

eye•sight (ī′sīt′) *n.* **1.** The ability to see; vision; sight: *People wear glasses to correct poor eyesight.* **2.** Range of vision; view: *a stream within eyesight of the house.*

eye socket *n.* The bony cavity in the skull that holds the eyeball.

eye•sore (ī′sôr′) *n.* An ugly or unpleasant sight: *That junkyard is an eyesore.*

eye•spot (ī′spŏt′) *n.* **1.** An area that is sensitive to light and functions somewhat like an eye, found in certain lower animals such as flatworms. **2.** A round marking resembling an eye, as on the tail feather of a peacock.

eye•stalk (ī′stôk′) *n.* A movable stalk having an eye on its tip, found on crabs, lobsters, and other crustaceans.

eye•strain (ī′strān′) *n.* Pain and fatigue of the eyes, often resulting from prolonged use of the eyes or uncorrected defects of vision.

eye•tooth (ī′to͞oth′) *n.* Either of the two canine teeth of the upper jaw.

eye•wash (ī′wŏsh′ *or* ī′wôsh′) *n.* **1.** A solution used to wash or medicate the eyes. **2.** *Informal.* Actions or remarks intended to conceal the facts of a situation.

eye•wit•ness (ī′wĭt′nĭs) *n.* A person who has seen something or someone and can bear witness to the fact, as in a trial or other proceeding.

ey•rie also **eyry** (âr′ē *or* îr′ē) *n.* Variants of **aerie.**

E•ze•ki•el (ĭ zē′kē əl) *n.* **1.** A Hebrew prophet of the 6th century B.C., author of the Book of Ezekiel. **2.** A book of the Bible containing Ezekiel's teaching on individual responsibility and his prophecies on the destruction of Israel.

Ez•ra (ĕz′rə) *n.* **1.** A Hebrew priest, scribe, and reformer of the 5th century B.C. **2.** A book of the Bible describing the return of the Hebrew people from exile in Babylon and their efforts to build a temple in Jerusalem.

Ff

f or **F** (ĕf) *n., pl.* **f's** or **F's.** **1.** The sixth letter of the English alphabet: *There are two f's in off.* **2. F.** A failing grade in school. **3.** In music, the fourth tone in the scale of C major. **4.** The sixth in a series or group: *row F in the stadium.*

F[1] The symbol for the element **fluorine.**

F[2] *abbr.* An abbreviation of Fahrenheit.

f. *abbr.* An abbreviation of: **1.** Female. **2.** Feminine. **3.** Forte. **4.** Franc.

F. *abbr.* An abbreviation of: **1.** French. **2.** Friday.

fa (fä) *n.* In music, the fourth tone of a major scale.

fa•ble (**fā′**bəl) *n.* **1.** A tale or story that teaches a useful lesson about human nature, often with animal characters that speak and act like human beings. **2.** A legend or myth. **3.** A falsehood; a lie. [First written down before 1300 in Middle English, from Latin *fābula,* from *fārī,* to speak.]

fa•bled (**fā′**bəld) *adj.* **1.** Made known or famous by fables; legendary: *the fabled city of El Dorado.* **2.** Existing only in fables; fictitious.

fab•ric (**făb′**rĭk) *n.* **1.** A cloth produced usually by knitting, weaving, or pressing fibers together: *Lace, felt, and jersey are different types of fabric.* **2.** An underlying structure or framework: *Crime is threatening the very fabric of American society.* [First written down in 1483 in Middle English and spelled *fabryke,* something constructed, from Latin *fabrica,* craft, workshop, from *faber,* artificer.]

fab•ri•cate (**făb′**rĭ kāt′) *tr.v.* **fab•ri•cat•ed, fab•ri•cat•ing, fab•ri•cates. 1.** To make, build, or manufacture, especially by assembling parts: *fabricate refrigerators on an assembly line.* **2.** To make up; invent: *fabricate an excuse for being late.* **—fab′ri•ca′tion** *n.*

fab•u•list (**făb′**yə lĭst) *n.* A person who composes fables.

fab•u•lous (**făb′**yə ləs) *adj.* **1.** Barely believable; astonishing: *a fabulous rise to fame.* **2.** Of a fable; legendary or mythical: *the fabulous phoenix who rises from its ashes every 500 years.* **3.** Famous in old stories; legendary; fabled: *the fabulous lands of the New World.* **4.** *Informal.* Extremely pleasing or successful; wonderful: *a fabulous vacation.* [First written down before 1425 in Middle English, from Latin *fābulōsus,* from *fābula,* fable.] **—fab′u•lous•ly** *adv.* **—fab′u•lous•ness** *n.*

fa•çade also **fa•cade** (fə **säd′**) *n.* **1.** The face or front of a building: *the decorated façade of a great cathedral.* **2.** An artificial or false front: *The salesman's friendly manner was only a façade to gain our confidence.* [First written down about 1656 in Modern English, from Italian *facciata,* from *faccia,* face.]

face (fās) *n.* **1.** The front of the head: *had a mask over her face.* **2.a.** The expression of the face; countenance: *a friendly face.* **b.** A twisted facial expression: *The baby learned to make faces.* **3.** The surface presented to view; the front: *the face of a building.* **4.** An outer surface: *the face of the earth.* **5.** The upper or marked side: *the face of a playing card.* **6.** A plane surface that bounds a geometric solid: *the face of a cube.* **7.** The outward appearance; look: *With so many new buildings, the face of the city has changed.* **8.** Value or standing in the eyes of others; dignity; prestige: *They saved face by saying they were misled.* **9.** Boldness; impudence: *Where did they get the face to say such things?* **10.** In printing, typeface. *—v.* **faced, fac•ing, fac•es.** *—tr.* **1.** To have or turn the face toward: *The actor faced the audience.* **2.** To have the front toward; look out on: *The cathedral faces the square.* **3.** To meet or deal with boldly or bravely: *Police officers face danger every day.* **4.** To recognize and be ready to deal with: *You've got to face the facts.* **5.** To cover a surface with a different material: *face the front of the fireplace with marble.* **6.** To line or trim the edge of: *face a cloth collar with satin.* *—intr.* **1.** To be turned or placed with the front in a certain direction: *The house faces toward the west.* **2.** To turn the face in a certain direction: *I faced into the wind.* ***—idioms.*** **face off.** To start play in ice hockey, lacrosse, and other games by releasing the puck or ball between two opposing players. **face up.** To confront an unpleasant situation boldly: *finally faced up to the problem.* **in the face of.** In spite of; despite: *The team won in the face of strong competition.* [First written down before 1300 in Middle English and spelled *fas,* from Old French, from Latin *faciēs.*]

face card *n.* A king, queen, or jack in a deck of playing cards.

face•less (**fās′**lĭs) *adj.* **1.** Having no face. **2.** Unidentified or unidentifiable; anonymous.

face-lift (**fās′**lĭft′) *n.* **1.** An operation to tighten wrinkles or sagging skin of the face. **2.** A change or renovation to improve the appearance: *Even with the face-lift, it's the same old building.*

fac•et (**făs′**ĭt) *n.* **1.** One of the flat polished surfaces cut on a gem or occurring naturally on a crystal. **2.** One of the ways of considering something; an aspect: *a complex problem with many facets to consider.* **3.** One of the individual outer visual units or lenses of a compound eye. [First written down in 1625 in Modern English, from Old French *facette,* diminutive of *face.*]

fa•ce•tious (fə **sē′**shəs) *adj.* Meant to be funny; humorous: *a facetious remark.* [First written down in 1592 in Modern English, from Latin *facētia,* a jest.] **—fa•ce′tious•ly** *adv.* **—fa•ce′tious•ness** *n.*

face value *n.* **1.** The value indicated on postage stamps, money, checks, bonds, or other paper securities: *an old coin worth 10 times its face value.* **2.** The apparent value or meaning: *Take such compliments at face value.*

fa•cial (**fā′**shəl) *adj.* Of or relating to the face: *facial expressions.* *—n.* A treatment for the face, usually including a massage.

fac•ile (**făs′**əl) *adj.* **1.** Done with little effort or difficulty; easy: *a facile task.* **2.** Working, acting, or speaking effortlessly or quickly: *a facile speaker; a facile writer.* **3.** Arrived at or presented without proper care or effort; superficial: *We don't need another facile solution to the problem.*

fa•cil•i•tate (fə **sĭl′**ĭ tāt′) *tr.v.* **fa•cil•i•tat•ed, fa•cil•i•tat•ing, fa•cil•i•tates.** To make easier; assist:

ă	**pat**	oi	**boy**
ā	**pay**	ou	**out**
âr	**care**	o͝o	**took**
ä	**father**	o͞o	**boot**
ĕ	**pet**	ŭ	**cut**
ē	**be**	ûr	**urge**
ĭ	**pit**	th	**thin**
ī	**pie**	*th*	**this**
îr	**pier**	hw	**whoop**
ŏ	**pot**	zh	**vision**
ō	**toe**	ə	**about**
ô	**paw**	N	*French* **bon**

factory
Automobile assembly line

Word History: **fair**[1]

The adjective **fair** comes from the Old English adjective *fæger,* "lovely, pleasant, agreeable, beautiful," and the original meanings survive in expressions like "fair weather" and "fair price." *Fair* in the sense "neither very bad nor very good" probably came from people using the word *fair* to avoid hurting other people's feelings about something that was not very well done.

The bank loans will facilitate the building of a new sports arena. **—fa•cil′i•ta′tion** *n.*

fa•cil•i•ty (fə sĭl′ĭ tē) *n., pl.* **fa•cil•i•ties. 1.** Ease in moving, acting, or doing; aptitude: *She has a real facility for learning foreign languages.* **2.** Something built or designed to provide a service or convenience. Often used in the plural: *The building has ample storage facilities.*

fac•ing (fā′sĭng) *n.* **1.** A piece of material sewn to the edge of a garment as a lining or decoration. **2.** An outer covering of different material applied to a surface for decoration or protection: *a wood house with a stone facing.*

fac•sim•i•le (făk sĭm′ə lē) *n.* An exact copy or reproduction: *The exhibit contained facsimiles of medieval manuscripts.* [First written down in 1662 in Modern English and spelled *fac simile,* from Latin *fac simile,* make similar.]

facsimile machine *n.* A fax machine.

fact (făkt) *n.* **1.** Something known to be true or to have actually happened: *The fact is that the bridge collapsed.* **2.** The quality of being actual: *This movie mixes fact and fiction.* **3.** A piece of information about something actual or real: *a book full of facts.* **4.** A thing that has been done, especially a crime: *an accessory after the fact.* ***—idiom.*** **in fact.** In reality; in truth. [First written down in 1539 in Modern English, from Latin *factum,* deed, from past participle of *facere,* to do.]

fac•tion (făk′shən) *n.* **1.** A group of people who have certain interests that are not shared with others in a larger group: *Factions form in organizations when members feel discontented with things as they are.* **2.** Internal discord; conflict within a nation, an organization, or another group: *The town government was torn by faction.* **—fac′tion•al** *adj.* **—fac′tion•al•ism** *n.*

fac•tious (făk′shəs) *adj.* Tending to cause conflict or discord; divisive: *factious members of a group.* **—fac′tious•ly** *adv.* **—fac′tious•ness** *n.*

fac•tor (făk′tər) *n.* **1.** Something that helps bring about a certain result; an element or ingredient: *Many factors contributed to the success of the celebration.* **2.** One of two or more numbers or expressions that are multiplied to obtain a given product. For example, 2 and 3 are factors of 6, and $a + b$ and $a - b$ are factors of $a^2 - b^2$. *—tr.v.* **fac•tored, fac•tor•ing, fac•tors.** To find the factors of (a number or an expression). ***—idiom.*** **factor in.** To figure in: *We factored in the possibility of getting stuck in traffic when we scheduled the meeting.* [First written down in 1432 in Middle English and spelled *factour,* perpetrator, agent, from Latin *factor,* maker, from *facere,* to make.]

fac•tor•a•ble (făk′tər ə bəl) *adj.* In arithmetic, being an integer having prime factors other than 1 and itself: *The number 4 is factorable; 5 is not.*

fac•to•ri•al (făk tôr′ē əl) *n.* The product of all of the positive integers from 1 to a given positive integer. For example, the factorial of 4, written 4!, is $1 \times 2 \times 3 \times 4 = 24$. *—adj.* Of or relating to a factorial: *a factorial symbol.*

fac•to•ry (făk′tə rē) *n., pl.* **fac•to•ries.** A building or group of buildings in which goods are manufactured; a plant: *The new automobile factory is filled with automated machines.*

fac•to•tum (făk tō′təm) *n.* An assistant who does many kinds of work. [First written down in 1618 in Modern English, from Medieval Latin *factōtum,* do everything.]

fac•tu•al (făk′cho͞o əl) *adj.* Based on or containing facts: *a factual account of what happened.* **—fac′tu•al•ly** *adv.*

fac•ul•ty (făk′əl tē) *n., pl.* **fac•ul•ties. 1.** One of the powers of the mind or body: *the faculty of speech.* **2.** A special ability or skill: *He has a faculty for doing impersonations.* **3.a.** The teaching staff of a school, college, or university: *The faculty voted to change the curriculum.* **b.** One of the divisions or departments of learning at a college or university: *the science faculty.*

fad (făd) *n.* Something that is done or adopted with great enthusiasm by many people for a brief period of time; a craze.

fade (fād) *v.* **fad•ed, fad•ing, fades.** *—intr.* **1.** To lose brightness; dim: *The colors faded in the wash.* **2.** To lose freshness; wither: *The flowers are beginning to fade.* **3.** To disappear slowly; vanish: *The sound of footsteps gradually faded away.* See Synonyms at **disappear.** *—tr.* To cause to lose brightness: *The sun faded the colors in the quilt.* ***—idioms.*** **fade in.** To become visible or audible gradually: *The movie fades in to the next scene, 20 years later.* **fade out.** To become invisible or inaudible gradually. [First written down before 1325 in Middle English and spelled *faden,* from Old French *fade,* faded, from Latin *fatuus,* insipid.]

fade-in or **fade•in** (fād′ĭn′) *n.* The gradual brightening of an image or the increasing of sound, as in film, radio, or television.

fade-out or **fade•out** (fād′out′) *n.* The gradual dimming of an image or decreasing of sound, as in film, radio, or television.

fa•er•ie also **fa•er•y** (fā′ə rē *or* fâr′ē) *n., pl.* **fa•er•ies.** A fairy.

fag (făg) *v.* **fagged, fag•ging, fags.** *—intr.* To become exhausted, as from work. *—tr.* To exhaust from long work; fatigue: *Three hours on the tennis court fagged us out.*

fag end *n.* **1.** The frayed, worn, or untwisted end of a piece of cloth or rope. **2.** The last and least useful part of something: *the fag end of an exhausting day.*

fag•ot also **fag•got** (făg′ət) *n.* A bundle of twigs, sticks, or branches bound together, especially for firewood.

Fahr•en•heit (făr′ən hīt′) *adj.* Of, relating to, or based on a temperature scale that indicates the freezing point of water as 32° and the boiling point of water as 212° under standard atmospheric pressure. [First written down in 1753 in Modern English, after G.D. *Fahrenheit* (1686–1736), German physicist.]

fail (fāl) *v.* **failed, fail•ing, fails.** *—intr.* **1.** To be unsuccessful in attempting to do something, especially something wanted or expected: *Their first attempt at climbing the mountain failed.* **2.** To be lacking or not enough; fall short: *After months of drought the water supply failed.* **3.** To receive a grade that is less than acceptable in school. **4.** To stop functioning correctly; break down: *The brakes on the car failed.* **5.** To decline, as in strength or effectiveness. **6.** To become bankrupt: *A number of downtown stores failed in the recession.* *—tr.* **1.** To leave (something) undone; neglect: *The defendant failed to appear in court.* **2.** To disappoint or prove undependable to: *I won't fail you this time.* **3.** To abandon; forsake: *His strength failed him on the homestretch.* **4.a.** To receive an academic grade that is below the acceptable minimum in (a course, for example): *Did any students fail geometry?* **b.** To give an academic grade indicating unacceptability to: *The professor failed several students in the class.* ***—idiom.*** **without fail.** Definitely; certainly: *The job will be finished tomorrow without fail.* [First written down before 1200 in Middle English and spelled *failen,* from Latin *fallere,* to deceive.]

fail•ing (fā′lĭng) *n.* **1.** A fault or weakness; a shortcoming: *One of my failings is being late with library books.* **2.** The act of a person or thing that fails; a failure: *a failing of the water supply.* —*prep.* In the absence of; without: *Failing directions, we will have to find the office on our own.*

faille (fīl) *n.* A ribbed woven fabric of silk, cotton, or rayon: *curtains of blue faille.*

❑ *These sound alike:* **faille, file**[1] (folder), **file**[2] (tool).

fail-safe (fāl′sāf′) *adj.* **1.** Capable of stopping or changing operation in case of a failure, as in a mechanism: *Fail-safe switches on machinery have saved many workers from injury.* **2.** Guaranteed not to fail: *a fail-safe plan.*

fail•ure (fāl′yər) *n.* **1.** The condition of not achieving something desired; lack of success: *Early airplane experiments ended in failure.* **2.** The neglect or inability to do something: *My failure to return library books meant a large fine.* **3.** The condition of being insufficient or falling short: *a crop failure during a drought.* **4.** A stopping of function or performance: *an electric power failure.* **5.** Bankruptcy: *The failure of the shop put several people out of work.* **6.** A person or thing that has failed: *I'm a failure as a trombone player.*

fain (fān) *adv.* Willingly or gladly. —*adj. Archaic.* Willing or glad.

❑ *These sound alike:* **fain, feign** (pretend).

faint (fānt) *adj.* **faint•er, faint•est. 1.** Lacking brightness or clarity; dim; indistinct: *a faint light.* **2.** Lacking strength; weak; slight: *a faint odor; a faint resemblance.* **3.** Likely to fall unconscious; dizzy and weak: *Extreme hunger made the hiker feel faint.* **4.** Lacking boldness or courage; faint-hearted. —*n.* A sudden, usually short loss of consciousness, often caused by too little blood flowing to the brain. —*intr.v.* **faint•ed, faint•ing, faints.** To lose consciousness for a short time; swoon: *The dancer fainted in the heat.* —**faint′ly** *adv.* —**faint′ness** *n.*

❑ *These sound alike:* **faint, feint** (pretend).

faint-heart•ed (fānt′här′tĭd) *adj.* Lacking conviction or courage; cowardly; timid. —**faint′-heart′ed•ly** *adv.* —**faint′-heart′ed•ness** *n.*

fair[1] (fâr) *adj.* **fair•er, fair•est. 1.** Free of favoritism; impartial or just: *a fair price; a fair trial.* **2.** Conforming to the rules or moral standards: *fair play.* **3.** Pleasing to look at; beautiful; lovely: *a fair face.* **4.** Light in color: *fair hair.* **5.** Clear and sunny; free of clouds or storms: *fair weather.* **6.** Somewhat good; acceptable: *The movie was only fair.* **7.** Free from stain, error, or corrections: *a fair copy of a document.* **8.** In baseball, lying or falling within the foul lines: *a fair ball.* —*adv.* In a fair manner; properly: *I believe in playing fair.* —***idioms.*** **fair and square.** Just and honest. **no fair.** Something contrary to the rules. [First written down before 900 in Old English and spelled *fæger*, lovely, pleasant.] —**fair′ness** *n.* —SEE NOTE.

❑ *These sound alike:* **fair**[1] (just), **fair**[2] (market), **fare** (travel cost).

fair[2] (fâr) *n.* **1.** A gathering for the buying and selling of goods, often held at a particular time and place; a market: *We went to the annual book fair.* **2.** A display, as of agricultural and home products, often together with entertainment: *a county fair.* **3.** A social event held for charity and usually including the sale of articles; a bazaar: *the hospital fair.* [First written down about 1250 in Middle English and spelled *feire*, from Late Latin *fēria*, holiday.]

❑ *These sound alike:* **fair**[2] (market), **fair**[1] (just), **fare** (travel cost).

fair game *n.* **1.** Animals that can be legally hunted: *Deer are fair game in many states in the fall.* **2.** A person or thing that seems suitable for pursuit or attack: *Politicians are fair game for reporters, especially during a campaign.*

fair•ground (fâr′ground′) *n.* An outdoor space where fairs, exhibitions, or other public events are held.

fair-haired (fâr′hârd′) *adj.* **1.** Having blond hair. **2.** Favorite: *the fair-haired member of the family.*

fair•ly (fâr′lē) *adv.* **1.** In a fair or just manner: *treating everyone fairly.* **2.** Moderately; rather: *I am feeling fairly well today.* **3.** Actually; positively: *The walls fairly shook from the wind.*

fair-mind•ed (fâr′mīn′dĭd) *adj.* Just and impartial; not prejudiced: *a fair-minded judge.* —**fair′-mind′ed•ness** *n.*

fair•way (fâr′wā′) *n.* The part of a golf course covered with short grass and extending from the tee to the putting green.

fair•y (fâr′ē) *n., pl.* **fair•ies.** A tiny imaginary being in human form, supposed to have magical powers.

fair•y•land (fâr′ē lănd′) *n.* **1.** An imaginary place where fairies are supposed to live. **2.** An enchanting place; a wonderland: *Snow turned the woods into a fairyland.*

fairy tale *n.* **1.** A story about fairies, magical creatures, or legendary deeds, usually intended for children. **2.** An explanation that is not true; a very fanciful story.

fait ac•com•pli (fā′tä kôN plē′) *n., pl.* **faits ac•com•plis** (fā′tä kôN plē′ *or* fā′tä kôN plēz′). An accomplished fact; something done that cannot be undone.

faith (fāth) *n.* **1.** Confidence or trust in a person or thing: *You must have faith in yourself.* **2.** Belief in God: *a person of great faith.* **3.** The set of teachings of a religion: *the Muslim faith.* **4.** Loyalty to a person or thing: *keeping faith with one's supporters.* **5.** A set of principles or beliefs: *A democratic faith guides this country.* —***idioms.*** **bad faith.** Deceit; insincerity: *The striking union said that management had negotiated in bad faith.* **good faith.** Sincerity; honesty: *A signature is a token of one's good faith.* **on faith.** With trust; confidently: *You'll have to accept my promise on faith.* [First written down about 1250 in Middle English and spelled *feith*, from Latin *fidēs*.]

faith•ful (fāth′fəl) *adj.* **1.** Loyal and dutiful; trustworthy: *a faithful friend; faithful performance of duty.* **2.** Accurate; exact: *a faithful copy of the manuscript.* —*n., pl.* **faithful** or **faith•fuls. 1.** The practicing members of a religion. **2.** A loyal follower or supporter: *The faithful journeyed to the huge rock concert in the park.* —**faith′ful•ly** *adv.* —**faith′ful•ness** *n.*

faith•less (fāth′lĭs) *adj.* **1.** Not trustworthy; disloyal: *The candidate was betrayed by a faithless friend.* **2.** Having no religious faith. —**faith′less•ly** *adv.* —**faith′less•ness** *n.*

fake (fāk) *adj.* False; counterfeit: *a fake document; a fake diamond.* —*n.* **1.** A person who deceives by pretending and making false claims; a faker: *The doctor turned out to be a fake.* **2.** Something that looks authentic but is not; a forgery: *Experts discovered a fake in the museum's art collection.* —*tr. v.* **faked, fak•ing, fakes. 1.** To simulate; pretend; feign: *fake illness.* **2.** To make in order to deceive; counterfeit: *fake an identification card.* —**fak′er** *n.*

fak•er•y (fā′kə rē) *n.* **1.** The act or process of faking: *An artist was responsible for the fakery of many famous paintings.* **2.** Something faked: *The Roman statue proved to be a complete fakery.*

fa•kir (fə kîr′ *or* fä kîr′) *n.* A Muslim or Hindu holy person who lives by begging and may perform unusual feats of endurance or magic. [First written down in 1609 in Modern English, from Arabic *faqīr*.]

fal•con (făl′kən *or* fôl′kən *or* fô′kən) *n.* Any of various swift, small to medium-sized hawks having long pointed wings and long tails. Certain falcons

fair[2]
Fairground

falcon
Peregrine falcon

ă	pat	oi	boy
ā	pay	ou	out
âr	care	o͝o	took
ä	father	o͞o	boot
ĕ	pet	ŭ	cut
ē	be	ûr	urge
ĭ	pit	th	thin
ī	pie	*th*	this
îr	pier	hw	whoop
ŏ	pot	zh	vision
ō	toe	ə	about
ô	paw	N	*French* bon

fallow deer

have been trained to hunt small animals and birds for sport. [First written down about 1250 in Middle English and spelled *faucun*, from Late Latin *falcō*.]

fal•con•er (făl′kə nər *or* fôl′kə nər *or* fô′kə nər) *n.* A person who raises, trains, or hunts with falcons.

fal•con•ry (făl′kən rē *or* fôl′kən rē *or* fô′kən rē) *n.* **1.** The sport of hunting with falcons. **2.** The art of training falcons for hunting.

Falk•land Islands (fôk′lənd *or* fôlk′lənd). A group of islands in the southern Atlantic Ocean east of the Strait of Magellan. The islands are controlled by Great Britain but are also claimed by Argentina.

fall (fôl) *intr.v.* **fell** (fĕl), **fall•en** (fô′lən), **fall•ing, falls. 1.** To drop or come down without restraint: *The snow fell silently to the ground.* **2.a.** To come down from an upright position suddenly: *Several people slipped on the ice and fell.* **b.** To drop oneself to a lower or less upright position: *She fell into a chair.* **3.** To be wounded or killed, especially in battle. **4.** To come as if by descending suddenly: *Darkness fell and all was silent. A hush fell over the crowd.* **5.** To slope downward: *The fields fall steeply toward the river.* **6.** To hang down: *The horse's mane fell smoothly on its neck.* **7.** To assume a downcast look: *The child's face fell upon seeing the injured puppy.* **8.** To become lower or less, as in value, intensity, or amount: *The temperature fell below freezing.* **9.** To decline, as in moral standing; err or sin. **10.** To suffer defeat, destruction, capture, or overthrow: *The monarchy fell in the revolution.* **11.** To come to rest; settle: *Light fell on the book.* **12.** To occur at a specific place: *The accent of "control" falls on the last syllable.* **13.** To happen; occur: *Thanksgiving always falls on a Thursday in November.* **14.** To pass from one state or condition into another: *fall asleep; fall ill.* **15.** To be given, as a task, a right, an assignment, or a duty: *The task of cleaning the room fell to us.* **16.** To come by chance: *The papers fell into the enemy's hands.* **17.** To be divided or put into categories: *The books fall into three categories: novels, biographies, and scholarly works.* **18.** To be uttered; come out: *Angry words fell from my lips.* —*n.* **1.** A dropping or coming down from a higher place without restraint: *the fall of leaves from trees; a heavy fall of snow.* **2.** A sudden drop from an upright position: *a bad fall on the ice.* **3.** The distance that something falls: *a fall of ten feet.* **4.** An amount of something that has fallen: *We expect a fall of two inches of snow.* **5.** A downward movement or slope: *the gentle fall of fields toward the river.* **6.** Often **Fall.** The season of the year occurring between summer and winter. In the Northern Hemisphere, it lasts from the autumnal equinox until the winter solstice or, in common usage, from September until December. **7. falls.** *(used with a singular or plural verb).* A waterfall; a cascade. **8.** A reduction in amount, intensity, or value: *a fall in water pressure.* **9.** A capture, an overthrow, or a collapse: *the fall of a corrupt government.* **10.** A specific place or position: *the fall of an accent on the last syllable.* **11.** A decline in standing, rank, or importance: *a story of one family's fall from wealth to poverty.* **12.** A woman's hair piece having long hair that hangs down loose. **13.** In wrestling, the act of pinning one's opponent to the ground. **14.** A moral decline; a lapse: *the politician's fall was caused by greed.* **15. Fall.** In the Bible, Adam's sin of disobeying God and yielding to temptation by eating the forbidden fruit. —*adj.* Of, occurring in, or appropriate to the season of Fall: *fall fashions.* —***idioms.*** **fall back.** To give ground; retreat. **fall back on.** To rely on or resort to: *fall back on savings.* **fall behind.** To fail to keep up with: *We fell behind the group we were traveling with. They fell behind in paying their bills.* **fall flat.** To produce no result; fail: *Their hasty plans fell flat.* **fall for.** *Informal.* **1.** To become infatuated with; fall in love with. **2.** To be taken in by: *They fell for the swindler's scheme.* **fall in.** To take one's place in a military formation. **fall in with. 1.** To associate or begin to associate with: *She fell in with a new crowd at school.* **2.** To agree to: *They immediately fell in with my suggestions.* **fall off.** To become smaller or fewer; decline: *Attendance fell off in the spring.* **fall on** or **fall upon. 1.** To attack suddenly: *The cat fell on the mice.* **2.** To find; come across: *They fell upon the ruins of an ancient city in the desert.* **fall out. 1.** To quarrel; become estranged: *The cousins fell out over an inheritance.* **2.** To leave one's place in a military formation. **fall short. 1.** To fail to reach a specified amount or degree: *Our donations fell short of expectations.* **2.** To be inadequate: *Food supplies fell short.* **fall through.** To fail; collapse: *Their plans for a vacation fell through.* **fall to.** To begin an activity; start: *The shoppers fell to as soon as the doors were opened.* **fall under.** To come under the influence of: *The student fell under the spell of his teacher and became a great cellist.* [First written down before 900 in Old English and spelled *feallan*.]

fal•la•cious (fə lā′shəs) *adj.* **1.** Based on a fallacy: *fallacious arguments based on a misunderstanding of the facts.* **2.** Tending to mislead; deceptive: *The dealer made fallacious claims about the car's gas mileage.* —**fal•la′cious•ly** *adv.*

fal•la•cy (făl′ə sē) *n., pl.* **fal•la•cies. 1.** A false notion or mistaken belief: *It is a fallacy that money can buy happiness.* **2.** False reasoning, belief, or argument. [First written down about 1303 in Middle English and spelled *fallace*, from Latin *fallāx*, deceitful.]

fall•en (fô′lən) *v.* Past participle of **fall.**

fal•li•ble (făl′ə bəl) *adj.* Capable of making mistakes; tending to err: *Each of us is a fallible human being.* —**fal′li•bil′i•ty** *n.* —**fal′li•bly** *adv.*

fall•ing-out (fô′lĭng out′) *n., pl.* **fall•ings-out** or **fall•ing-outs.** A disagreement; a quarrel.

fall•ing star (fô′lĭng) *n.* A meteor.

fall line *n.* **1.** The boundary between a plateau and a plain, marking the end of layers of hard rock and the beginning of softer rock layers. Usually many waterfalls and rapids in rivers occur along a fall line. **2.** The natural line of descent between two points on a slope.

fal•lo•pi•an tube also **Fal•lo•pi•an tube** (fə lō′pē ən) *n.* Either of a pair of tubes found in female mammals that carry egg cells from the ovaries to the uterus. [First written down in 1860 in Modern English, after Gabriele *Fallopio* (1523–1562), Italian anatomist.]

fall•out (fôl′out′) *n.* **1.** The tiny particles of debris discharged into the atmosphere by an explosion, especially radioactive debris from a nuclear explosion. **2.** The fall of such particles back to earth.

fal•low (făl′ō) *adj.* Plowed and tilled but left unseeded during a growing season: *The soil in a fallow field will be more fertile when next planted.*

fallow deer *n.* A small deer of Europe and Asia having broad flattened antlers and a brownish coat spotted with white in the summer.

false (fôls) *adj.* **fals•er, fals•est. 1.** Not true; incorrect: *The information she gave you is false.* **2.** Deliberately untrue: *false testimony.* **3.** Meant to mislead; deceitful: *false promises.* **4.** Based on mistaken ideas or information: *The early news report raised false hopes.* **5.** Unfaithful; disloyal: *a false friend.* **6.** Not natural or genuine; not real: *a false signature.* **7.** In music, of a pitch that is not correct or within a specific range: *False notes spoiled the singer's performance.* [First written down about

1000 in Old English and spelled *fals*, from Latin *falsus*, from past participle of *fallere*, to deceive.] **—false′ly** *adv.* **—false′ness** *n.*

false•hood (fôls′ho͝od′) *n.* **1.** An untrue statement; a lie: *a report filled with falsehoods.* **2.** The quality of being false; untruthfulness: *the falsehood of the accusation.* **3.** The practice of making false statements; lying.

fal•set•to (fôl sĕt′ō) *n., pl.* **fal•set•tos.** An unnaturally high-pitched man's singing voice.

fal•si•fy (fôl′sə fī′) *v.* **fal•si•fied, fal•si•fy•ing, fal•si•fies.** *—tr.* **1.** To state untruthfully; misrepresent: *It is a crime to falsify the facts when testifying under oath.* **2.** To change (a document, for example) in order to deceive; counterfeit: *falsify a driver's license.* *—intr.* To make an untrue statement; lie. **—fal′si•fi•ca′tion** (fôl′sə fĭ kā′shən) *n.* **—fal′si•fi′er** *n.*

fal•si•ty (fôl′sĭ tē) *n., pl.* **fal•si•ties. 1.** The condition of being false; falseness: *Experiment proved the falsity of that theory.* **2.** Something false; a lie.

fal•ter (fôl′tər) *intr.v.* **fal•tered, fal•ter•ing, fal•ters. 1.** To lose confidence or purpose; hesitate: *My determination faltered as the work became more difficult.* **2.** To speak hesitatingly; stammer: *Several times the speaker faltered from embarrassment.* **3.** To move haltingly; stumble: *We faltered along the slippery path.* [First written down about 1390 in Middle English and spelled *faltren*, to stagger, possibly from Old Norse *faltrask*, to be puzzled, hesitate.] **—fal′ter•er** *n.* **—fal′ter•ing•ly** *adv.*

fame (fām) *n.* Great reputation; public esteem; renown. [First written down before 1200 in Middle English, from Latin *fāma*.]

famed (fāmd) *adj.* Having great fame; famous; renowned.

fa•mil•ial (fə mĭl′yəl) *adj.* **1.** Of or relating to family. **2.** Occurring among the members of a family, especially several members of the same generation; hereditary: *the familial tendency for diabetes.*

fa•mil•iar (fə mĭl′yər) *adj.* **1.** Well-known; often encountered; common: *a familiar sight.* **2.** Having some knowledge; acquainted: *I am familiar with those streets in your neighborhood.* **3.** Of established friendship; close: *We are on familiar terms with the neighbors.* **4.** Unduly forward; presumptuous: *It is a mistake to be too familiar with one's boss.* [First written down about 1380 in Middle English and spelled *familier*, from Latin *familiāris*, domestic, from *familia*, family.] **—fa•mil′iar•ly** *adv.*

fa•mil•iar•i•ty (fə mĭl′yăr′ĭ tē *or* fə mĭl′ē ăr′ĭ tē) *n., pl.* **fa•mil•iar•i•ties. 1.** Acquaintance with or knowledge of something: *Familiarity with the city's streets is a necessity for a cab driver.* **2.** Friendship or informality: *the familiarity of close associates.* **3.** Improper friendliness; forwardness: *I was offended by the salesperson's familiarity on the telephone.*

fa•mil•iar•ize (fə mĭl′yə rīz′) *tr.v.* **fa•mil•iar•ized, fa•mil•iar•iz•ing, fa•mil•iar•iz•es. 1.** To make acquainted with: *They familiarized themselves with the new library.* **2.** To make (something) known or recognized: *TV familiarized the special vocabulary of the space program.*

fam•i•ly (făm′ə lē *or* făm′lē) *n., pl.* **fam•i•lies. 1.** A social group typically consisting of parents and their offspring: *Most of my family lives in Arizona.* **2.** All the members of a household living under one roof: *His family includes his grandmother and his uncle, who live on the first floor.* **3.** The children of the same father and mother: *They raised a large family.* **4.** A group of persons sharing common ancestors; relatives: *Each year our whole family gets together.* **5.** Line of descent; ancestry: *I come from an old Virginia family.* **6.** A group of things that are alike; a class: *The family of brass instruments includes the trumpet and trombone.* **7.** A group of related plants or animals ranking above a genus and below an order: *Dogs, wolves, coyotes, and foxes belong to the same family.* See table at **taxonomy. 8.** A group of languages derived from the same parent language: *French, Spanish, and Italian are of the same family.* [First written down before 1425 in Middle English and spelled *familie*, from Latin *familia*, household, servants of a household, from *famulus*, servant.] —See Note at **collective noun.**

family name *n.* A surname.

family planning *n.* The planning of the number and timing of children in a family through birth control.

family tree *n.* A diagram showing the relationships among the ancestors of a family.

fam•ine (făm′ĭn) *n.* A drastic, widespread shortage of food: *Famine may strike after a prolonged drought.* [First written down before 1376 in Middle English and spelled *famin*, from Old French, from Latin *famēs*, hunger.]

fam•ished (făm′ĭsht) *adj.* Extremely hungry; starving.

fa•mous (fā′məs) *adj.* Widely known; famed; renowned: *a country famous for its beautiful mountains.* See Synonyms at **noted.**

fan[1] (făn) *n.* **1.** A collapsible flat implement, usually shaped like a half-circle, waved in the hand to create a cooling breeze. **2.** Something that resembles an open fan: *The turkey's tail feathers spread into a fan.* **3.** An electrical device that moves air, especially for cooling, by means of rotating metal or plastic blades. *—v.* **fanned, fan•ning, fans.** *—tr.* **1.** To direct a current of air to blow upon (a person or thing), especially in order to cool: *We sat fanning ourselves under a tree.* **2.** To move or create a current of (air) with or as if with a fan. **3.** To stir up by or as if by fanning: *Rumors fanned smoldering anger in the crowd.* **4.** To open (something) out into the shape of a fan: *The peacock fanned its tail.* **5.** In baseball, to strike out (a batter): *The pitcher fanned three batters in succession.* *—intr.* **1.** To spread like a fan: *The search parties fanned out in different directions.* **2.** In baseball, to strike out. [First written down before 800 in Old English and spelled *fon*, winnowing device, from Latin *vannus*.]

fan[1]
Top: Hand-held fan
Bottom: Peacock's fan

fan[2] (făn) *n. Informal.* An enthusiastic devotee or admirer: *a baseball fan.* [First written down 1682 in Modern English and spelled *fann*, short for *fanatic*.]

fa•nat•ic (fə năt′ĭk) *n.* A person who is excessively or unreasonably devoted to a cause or belief. *—adj.* Fanatical. [First written down about 1525 in Modern English, from Latin *fānāticus*, relating to a temple, from *fānum*, temple.]

fa•nat•i•cal (fə năt′ĭ kəl) *adj.* Unreasonably enthusiastic or zealous. **—fa•nat′i•cal•ly** *adv.*

fa•nat•i•cism (fə năt′ĭ sĭz′əm) *n.* Unreasonable or excessive enthusiasm or devotion.

fan•ci•er (făn′sē ər) *n.* A person with a special interest in something: *a cat fancier.*

fan•ci•ful (făn′sĭ fəl) *adj.* **1.** Created in the mind; imaginary; unreal: *fanciful tales.* **2.** Using or tending to use the imagination: *a fanciful mind.* **3.** Original in design; imaginative: *fanciful figures made with odds and ends of cloth.* **—fan′ci•ful•ly** *adv.* **—fan′ci•ful•ness** *n.*

fan•cy (făn′sē) *n., pl.* **fan•cies. 1.** Imagination, especially of a playful or whimsical sort: *The characters are all creations of the author's fancy.* **2.** An impulsive idea or thought; a whim: *We had a sudden fancy to go to the diner.* **3.** A liking, a fondness, or an inclination: *The stray dog took a fancy to our family.* *—adj.* **fan•ci•er, fan•ci•est. 1.** Highly decorated; elaborate: *fancy carvings around the door.* **2.** Requiring or done with great skill; complex; in-

ă	pat	oi	boy
ā	pay	ou	out
âr	care	o͝o	took
ä	father	o͞o	boot
ĕ	pet	ŭ	cut
ē	be	ûr	urge
ĭ	pit	th	thin
ī	pie	*th*	this
îr	pier	hw	whoop
ŏ	pot	zh	vision
ō	toe	ə	about
ô	paw	N	*French* bon

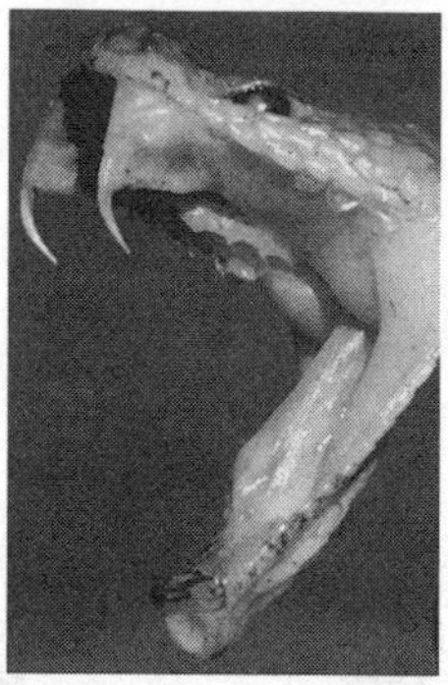
fang

farm

tricate: *a tap dancer's fancy footwork.* **3.** Of superior grade; fine: *fancy fruits and vegetables.* **4.** Exorbitant; excessive: *That store charges very fancy prices.* —*tr.v.* **fan•cied, fan•cy•ing, fan•cies. 1.** To picture in the mind; imagine: *I tried to fancy myself as an actor.* **2.** To have a liking for; enjoy: *Would you fancy a movie tonight?* See Synonyms at **love. 3.** To suppose; guess; surmise: *I fancy the meeting will end soon.* [First written down about 1462 in Middle English and spelled *fantsy*, imagination, fantasy, from *fantasie*.] **—fan′ci•ly** *adv.* **—fan′ci•ness** *n.*

fan•fare (făn′fâr′) *n.* **1.** A short melody played by one or more brass instruments; a flourish. **2.** A spectacular public display or ceremony: *The astronauts were welcomed home with great fanfare.*

fang (făng) *n.* **1.** A long pointed tooth, especially one used by a poisonous snake to inject venom into its prey. **2.** Something thin and tapering that is shaped like a fang.

fan•tail (făn′tāl′) *n.* **1.** A pigeon, goldfish, or other animal having a fan-shaped tail. **2.** A tail or end resembling a fan. **3.** The stern overhang of a ship.

fan•tas•tic (făn tăs′tĭk) *adj.* **1.** Based on or existing only in fantasy; unreal: *a fantastic story of life in another galaxy.* **2.** Weird; bizarre: *dancers dressed in fantastic costumes.* **3.** Remarkable; outstanding; superb: *The carpenter did a fantastic job of restoring the old house.* **—fan•tas′ti•cal•ly** *adv.*

fan•ta•sy (făn′tə sē *or* făn′tə zē) *n., pl.* **fan•ta•sies. 1.** The creative imagination: *Her fantasy is vigorously at work in her latest science fiction novel.* **2.** Something that is a creation of the imagination, as a fanciful work of fiction. **3.** An imagined event or situation, especially one that fulfills a wish: *He has this fantasy about becoming a movie star.* [First written down before 1350 in Middle English and spelled *fantasie*, from Greek *phantasia*, appearance, imagination.]

far (fär) *adv.* **far•ther** (fär′*th*ər), **far•thest** (fär′*th*ĭst) or **fur•ther** (fûr′*th*ər), **fur•thest** (fûr′*th*ĭst). **1.** To, from, or at a distance: *My home is situated far from town.* **2.** To or at a specific distance, degree, or position: *How far do you intend to take this argument?* **3.** To a great degree; much: *I feel far better today than I did yesterday.* —*adj.* **farther, farthest** or **further, furthest. 1.** Being at great distance in space or time: *a far country halfway around the world; the far past.* **2.** More distant than another; opposite: *the far side of the mountain.* **3.** Extensive or long: *a far trek into the jungle.* **4.** Politically extreme: *the far right.* **—*idioms.* as far as.** To the distance, extent, or degree that: *As far as I know they left an hour ago.* **by far.** To a great degree: *Their grades are better than mine by far.* **far and away.** By a wide margin: *This is far and away the best movie we've seen.* **far and wide.** Everywhere. **so far. 1.** Up to the present moment: *We haven't heard from anyone so far.* **2.** To a limited extent: *You can only go so far on $10.*

far•ad (făr′əd *or* făr′ăd′) *n.* A unit of electric capacitance. A capacitor that is raised to an electric potential of one volt when it is charged with one coulomb has a capacitance of one farad. [First written down in 1881 in Modern English, after Michael *Faraday* (1791–1867), British physicist.]

far•a•day (făr′ə dā′) *n.* A unit of electric charge, equal to about 96,494 coulombs, used in electrolysis to measure the electricity required to break down a compound. [First written down in 1904 in Modern English, after Michael *Faraday* (1791–1867), British physicist.]

far•a•way (fär′ə wā′) *adj.* **1.** Very distant; remote: *The explorer spent years traveling in faraway places.* **2.** Dreamy; preoccupied: *a faraway look in his eyes.*

farce (färs) *n.* **1.** A comic play with an unlikely story and characters exaggerated for humorous effect. **2.** Something ridiculous or laughable; a mockery: *Baseball practice turned into a farce after the coach left.* [First written down before 1399 in Middle English and spelled *fars*, stuffing, from Latin *farsa*, past participle of *farcīre*, to stuff.]

far•ci•cal (fär′sĭ kəl) *adj.* Of or resembling a farce; absurd; foolish: *farcical errors.* **—far′ci•cal•ly** *adv.*

fare (fâr) *intr.v.* **fared, far•ing, fares. 1.** To get along; progress: *How are you faring with your project?* **2.** To travel; go. —*n.* **1.** The money charged for transportation from one place to another: *The subway fare has gone up.* **2.** A passenger who pays a fare: *The taxi stopped to pick up a fare.* **3.** Food and drink: *The fare at this inn is superb.* [First written down about 725 in Old English and spelled *faran*.]

❑ *These sound alike:* **fare, fair**[1] (just), **fair**[2] (market).

Far East (fär). The countries and regions of eastern and southeast Asia, especially China, Japan, North Korea, South Korea, and Mongolia.

fare•well (fâr wĕl′) *interj.* An expression used to say good-bye. —*n.* **1.** The act of saying good-bye, usually with good wishes: *a nod of farewell.* **2.** An expression at parting; good-bye: *It was hard to say our farewells.*

far-fetched (fär′fĕcht′) *adj.* Hard to believe; strained and improbable: *a far-fetched story.*

far-flung (fär′flŭng′) *adj.* Extending over a large area: *the far-flung operations of an international airline.*

Far•go (fär′gō). A city of eastern North Dakota east of Bismarck. It was founded in 1871 and is the largest city in the state. Population, 74,111.

fa•ri•na (fə rē′nə) *n.* A fine meal used as a cooked cereal or in puddings.

farm (färm) *n.* **1.** An area of land on which crops or animals are raised. **2.** An area of water devoted to raising aquatic animals: *a trout farm.* **3.** A farm team. —*v.* **farmed, farm•ing, farms.** —*tr.* To cultivate or produce a crop on: *We farm 1,000 acres.* —*intr.* To engage in farming; grow crops or raise livestock. **—*idiom.* farm out.** To send (work) out to be done by another business: *All the sewing done by hand is farmed out by the manufacturer.*

farm•er (fär′mər) *n.* A person who owns or operates a farm.

farm•ers' market (fär′mərz) *n.* A market at which farmers sell their produce directly to customers.

farm hand *n.* A person who works on a farm.

farm•house (färm′hous′) *n.* A house on a farm.

farm•land (färm′lănd′) *n.* Land suitable or used for farming.

farm•stead (färm′stĕd′) *n.* A farm, including its land and buildings.

farm team *n.* In baseball, a minor-league team affiliated with a major-league team for the training of young players.

farm•yard (färm′yärd′) *n.* An area surrounded by or next to farm buildings: *Chickens and geese wandered freely in the farmyard.*

far-off (fär′ôf′ *or* fär′ŏf′) *adj.* Faraway; distant: *Home seemed very far-off.*

far-out (fär′out′) *adj. Slang.* Extremely unconventional; very unusual: *a far-out movie.*

far-reach•ing (fär′rē′chĭng) *adj.* Having a wide influence or effect: *A tax on energy will have far-reaching effects in the economy.*

far•ri•er (făr′ē ər) *n.* A person who shoes horses; a blacksmith.

far•row (făr′ō) *n.* A litter of pigs. —*intr.v.* **far•**

rowed, far•row•ing, far•rows. To give birth to a litter of pigs.

far•see•ing (fär′sē′ĭng) *adj.* **1.** Able to see far; keen-sighted. **2.** Planning wisely for the future; foresighted.

Far•si (fär′sē) *n.* The Indo-European language of Iran; Persian.

far•sight•ed or **far-sight•ed** (fär′sī′tĭd) *adj.* **1.** Able to see distant objects better than objects at close range: *I am farsighted and wear glasses to read.* **2.** Planning wisely for the future; foresighted. —**far′sight′ed•ly** *adv.* —**far′sight′ed•ness** *n.*

far•ther (fär′*th*ər) *adv.* A comparative of **far. 1.** To or at a greater distance: *We walked farther than we had expected.* **2.** To a greater extent or degree: *I've read farther in the book and I like it now.* **3.** In addition; also; further. —*adj.* A comparative of **far.** More distant; remoter: *at the farther end of the street.* —See Note.

far•ther•most (fär′*th*ər mōst′) *adj.* Farthest; most remote: *explore the farthermost corners of the earth.*

far•thest (fär′*th*ĭst) *adj.* A superlative of **far.** Most remote or distant: *the farthest regions of the Arctic.* —*adv.* A superlative of **far. 1.** To or at the greatest distance in space or time: *The Chinese had come farthest to this meeting.* **2.** By the greatest extent or degree; most: *Their research had progressed farthest of all.*

far•thing (fär′*th*ĭng) *n.* **1.** A coin formerly used in Great Britain worth one-fourth of a penny. **2.** Something of very little value. [First written down about 950 in Old English and spelled *fēorthung*, a fourth.]

far•thin•gale (fär′*th*ĭn gāl′ *or* fär′*th*ĭng gāl′) *n.* A framework worn under a skirt or petticoat to make it stand out around the waist, worn by women in the 16th and 17th centuries.

fas•ci•nate (făs′ə nāt′) *tr.v.* To capture and hold the interest and attention of; captivate: *This book fascinates me so much I cannot put it down.* [First written down in 1598 in Modern English, from Latin *fascināre*, from *fascinum*, an evil spell, amulet.]

fas•ci•nat•ing (făs′ə nā′tĭng) *adj.* Arousing great interest and attention; captivating: *a fascinating story.* See Synonyms at **interesting.** —**fas′ci•nat′ing•ly** *adv.*

fas•ci•na•tion (făs′ə nā′shən) *n.* **1.** The condition of being fascinated: *Everyone watched in fascination as the rocket took off.* **2.** The power of fascinating; charm; attraction: *All the stories are about the fascination of the sea.*

fas•cism or **Fascism** (făsh′ĭz′əm) *n.* **1.** A system of government marked by dictatorship, government control of the economy, zealous nationalism, and suppression of all opposition. **2.** A political movement advocating such a system of government.

fas•cist or **Fascist** (făsh′ĭst) *n.* A person who advocates or believes in fascism. —*adj.* Of or relating to fascism or fascists: *a fascist regime.*

fash•ion (făsh′ən) *n.* **1.** The current style or custom, as in dress or behavior: *an idea now in fashion.* **2.** Something, such as a garment, that is in the current style: *a store carrying the latest fashions.* **3.** A manner of doing something; a way: *She works in an organized fashion.* —*tr.v.* **fash•ioned, fash•ion•ing, fash•ions.** To shape or form into: *fashion figures from clay.* —*idiom.* **after a fashion** or **in a fashion.** In some way or other; to some extent: *We sing after a fashion but have little training.* [First written down about 1300 in Middle English and spelled *fasoun*, form, appearance, from Latin *factiō*, a making, from *facere*, to make, do.]

fash•ion•a•ble (făsh′ə nə bəl) *adj.* **1.** Conforming to the current style; stylish: *a fashionable wardrobe.* **2.** Associated with or used by stylish people: *a fashionable hotel.* —**fash′ion•a•bly** *adv.*

fast[1] (făst) *adj.* **fast•er, fast•est. 1.** Moving, acting, or capable of moving or acting quickly; swift: *a fast train; a fast computer.* **2.** Accomplished in very little time: *We ate a fast lunch.* **3.** Suitable or made for rapid movement: *a fast racetrack.* **4.** Ahead of the correct time: *My watch is fast.* **5.** Firmly fixed or fastened: *Keep a fast grip on the rope.* **6.** Permanent; not likely to fade: *Fast colors will not run in the wash.* **7.** Loyal; firm: *fast friends.* **8.** Disregarding moral standards; wild: *He hangs out with a fast crowd.* —*adv.* **faster, fastest. 1.** Quickly; rapidly: *You are driving too fast.* **2.** Firmly; securely: *Hold fast to the railing.* **3.** Deeply; soundly: *The child is fast asleep.* **4.** So as to run ahead of the correct time: *My watch runs fast.* [First written down before 900 in Old English and spelled *fæst*, firm, fixed.]

Synonyms: fast, rapid, swift, quick, hasty. These adjectives describe something marked by great speed. **Fast** often describes the person or thing in motion: *You would become a fast runner if you stayed in shape.* **Rapid** often describes the activity or movement involved: *Rapid advances in technology have changed daily life in a short period of time.* **Swift** describes smoothness and sureness of movement: *Be careful of the swift current while you're swimming.* **Quick** usually describes what takes little time: *Her quick reaction prevented the accident.* **Hasty** describes hurried action and often a lack of care or thought: *The contest judges came to regret their hasty decision.*

---

fast[2] (făst) *intr.v.* **fast•ed, fast•ing, fasts.** To eat little or no food or only certain foods, especially for religious reasons or as a form of protest. —*n.* The act or a period of fasting. [First written down in 971 in Old English and spelled *fæstan.*]

fas•ten (făs′ən) *v.* **fas•tened, fas•ten•ing, fas•tens.** —*tr.* **1.** To attach firmly to; join; connect: *fasten a button to a shirt; unable to fasten blame on anyone.* **2.** To make fast or secure: *Fasten your seat belts.* **3.** To fix or direct steadily: *She fastened her gaze on the stranger.* —*intr.* **1.** To become attached, fixed, or joined: *The helmet fastens under your chin.* **2.** To fix or focus steadily: *My eyes fastened on the approaching plane.* —**fas′ten•er** *n.*

fas•ten•ing (făs′ə nĭng) *n.* Something, such as a hook, used to fasten things together.

fast food *n.* Restaurant food prepared and served quickly.

fast-food (făst′fo͞od′) *adj.* Specializing in foods prepared and served quickly: *a fast-food restaurant.*

fas•tid•i•ous (fă stĭd′ē əs *or* fə stĭd′ē əs) *adj.* **1.** Careful in all details: *Reporters must pay fastidious attention to the facts.* **2.** Difficult to please; choosy or finicky: *a fastidious eater.* —**fas•tid′i•ous•ly** *adv.* —**fas•tid′i•ous•ness** *n.*

fast•ness (făst′nĭs) *n.* **1.** A remote or secure place, as a stronghold or fortress: *a mountain fastness.* **2.** The condition or quality of being secure or firmly fixed: *Check the locks for fastness.* **3.** Rapidity; swiftness: *Sport cars are known for their elegance and fastness.*

fat (făt) *n.* **1.** Any of a large number of oily white or yellow compounds that are widely found in plant and animal tissues and serve as reserve sources of energy. **2.** Animal tissue containing such compounds: *cut the fat off the steak.* **3.** A solidified animal or vegetable oil: *french fries cooked in fat.* **4.** Plumpness or obesity: *Exercise will take off the fat.* **5.** The best part of something: *live off the fat of the land.* —*adj.* **fat•ter, fat•test. 1.** Having much or too much body fat; obese. **2.** Full of fat or oil; greasy: *Fat foods are not good for you.* **3.** Big; ample; generous: *a fat paycheck.* —*tr. & intr.v.* **fat•**

Usage: farther

The word **farther** should be used when you refer to physical distance and the word **further** when you refer to distances that are not physical: *If you are planning to drive any farther, you'd better stop at a filling station. We won't be able to answer these questions until we are further along in our research.*

farthingale
Mid 18th-century English

ă	pat	oi	boy
ā	pay	ou	out
âr	care	o͝o	took
ä	father	o͞o	boot
ĕ	pet	ŭ	cut
ē	be	ûr	urge
ĭ	pit	th	thin
ī	pie	*th*	this
îr	pier	hw	whoop
ŏ	pot	zh	vision
ō	toe	ə	about
ô	paw	N	*French* bon

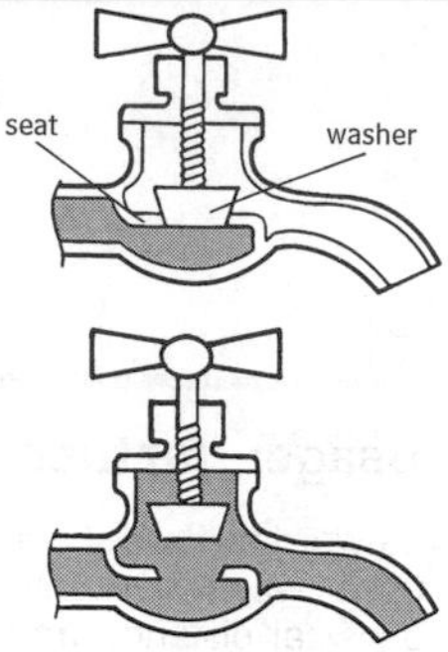

faucet
Top: Closed
Bottom: Open

William Faulkner
Photographed in 1950

fawn²
White-tailed deer fawn

Word History: fawn²

The noun **fawn**, "a baby deer," comes from the Middle English and Old French word *faon*, "a young animal." The Old French word comes from a Latin word root *fētōn–*. *Fētōn–* comes from the Latin noun *fētus*, "offspring," which we have also borrowed into English directly from Latin.

ted, fat•ting, fats. To fatten. *—idiom.* **fat chance.** *Slang.* Very little or no chance. [First written down before 900 in Old English and spelled *fǣtt*, stuffed.] **—fat′ness** *n.*

fa•tal (**fāt′**l) *adj.* **1.** Causing or capable of causing death: *a fatal disease.* **2.** Causing ruin or destruction; disastrous: *The investment was a blunder that proved fatal to the business.* **3.** Most decisive; fateful: *the fatal moment of going onstage to perform.* **—fa′tal•ly** *adv.*

fa•tal•ism (**fāt′**l ĭz′əm) *n.* **1.** The belief that all events are determined in advance by fate and cannot be altered. **2.** Acceptance of this belief; submission to fate: *His fatalism prevented him from acting to improve the situation.* **—fa′tal•ist** *n.* **—fa′tal•is′tic** *adj.*

fa•tal•i•ty (fā **tăl′**ĭ tē *or* fə **tăl′**ĭ tē) *n., pl.* **fa•tal•i•ties. 1.** A death resulting from an accident or a disaster: *Three fatalities occurred in the fire.* **2.** The ability to cause death: *a disease known for its fatality.*

fat•back (**făt′**băk′) *n.* Salt-cured fat from the upper part of a side of pork.

fate (fāt) *n.* **1.** A force or power that is supposed to determine the course of events. **2.** Something supposed to be caused by fate, especially an unfavorable destiny: *It was his fate never to defeat his rival.* **3.** A final result; an outcome: *The fate of the plane remains unknown.* **4. Fates.** In Greek and Roman Mythology, the three goddesses who govern human destiny.

❑ *These sound alike:* **fate, fete** (festival).

fate•ful (**fāt′**fəl) *adj.* **1.** Decisively important; momentous: *the colonists' fateful decision to go to war against Great Britain.* **2.** Indicating approaching trouble or disaster; unfavorably prophetic: *The fever was a fateful sign that the patient was getting worse.* **3.** Bringing death or disaster; fatal: *a fateful battle in which thousands died.* **4.** Controlled by or as if by fate: *a fateful journey.* **—fate′ful•ly** *adv.* **—fate′ful•ness** *n.*

fa•ther (**fä′**thər) *n.* **1.** A male parent or guardian of a child. **2.** A man who acts as a father, especially an older responsible person: *My older brother became a father to me when Dad got sick.* **3.** A male ancestor; a forefather: *the land of our fathers.* **4.** A male leader or official: *the city fathers.* **5.** A man who creates, starts, or founds something: *Chaucer is considered the father of English poetry.* **6. Father.** God. **7. Father.** Used as a title and form of address for a priest or other clergyman. *—tr.v.* **fa•thered, fa•ther•ing, fa•thers. 1.** To be the male parent of; beget: *father two children.* **2.** To act or serve as a father to: *He willingly undertook the duties of fathering his new stepchildren.* **3.** To create, start, or found: *an organization fathered by a group of scientists.*

fa•ther•hood (**fä′**thər ho͝od′) *n.* The condition of being a father.

fa•ther-in-law (**fä′**thər ĭn lô′) *n., pl.* **fa•thers-in-law** (**fä′**thərz ĭn lô′). The father of one's husband or wife.

fa•ther•land (**fä′**thər lănd′) *n.* **1.** A person's native land; the country of one's birth. **2.** The land of one's ancestors.

fa•ther•less (**fä′**thər lĭs) *adj.* Having no living or known father.

fa•ther•ly (**fä′**thər lē) *adj.* Of, resembling, or appropriate to a father: *a fatherly interest in my progress in school.* **—fa′ther•li•ness** *n.*

Fa•ther's Day (**fä′**thərz) *n.* The third Sunday in June, observed in the United States in honor of fathers.

fath•om (**făth′**əm) *n., pl.* **fathom** or **fath•oms.** A unit of length equal to six feet (1.8 meters), used for measurements of the depth of water. *—tr.v.* **fath•omed, fath•om•ing, fath•oms. 1.** To measure the depth of; sound: *fathom a channel in a river.* **2.** To understand; comprehend: *Motives are very often difficult to fathom.* [First written down about 725 in Old English and spelled *fæthm*, outstretched arms.] **—fath′om•a•ble** *adj.*

fath•om•less (**făth′**əm lĭs) *adj.* **1.** Too deep to be measured: *the fathomless oceans.* **2.** Impossible to understand: *His motivation for leaving seemed fathomless.*

fa•tigue (fə **tēg′**) *n.* **1.** Weariness or exhaustion resulting from hard work or great effort. **2.** Manual nonmilitary work, such as barracks cleaning, assigned to soldiers. **3. fatigues.** Clothing worn by soldiers for heavy work or field duty. *—tr.v.* **fa•tigued, fa•tigu•ing, fa•tigues.** To tire out; exhaust: *The long hike fatigued us.*

fat•ten (**făt′**n) *tr. & intr.v.* **fat•tened, fat•ten•ing, fat•tens.** To make or become fat: *fatten cattle; fatten on a rich diet.*

fat•ty (**făt′**ē) *adj.* **fat•ti•er, fat•ti•est. 1.** Composed of or containing fat: *fatty food.* **2.** Characteristic of fat; greasy. **—fat′ti•ness** *n.*

fatty acid *n.* Any of a large group of organic acids, especially those found in animal and vegetable fats and oils.

fat•u•ous (**făch′**o͞o əs) *adj.* Foolish and self-satisfied; silly: *a fatuous smile.* **—fat′u•ous•ly** *adv.* **—fat′u•ous•ness** *n.*

fau•cet (**fô′**sĭt) *n.* A device with an adjustable valve that regulates the flow of liquid from a pipe; a tap.

Faulk•ner (**fôk′**nər), **William.** 1897–1962. American writer who set many of his works in the post–Civil War South. He won a 1949 Nobel Prize.

fault (fôlt) *n.* **1.** A defect or shortcoming: *A fault in the book is its small type.* **2.** A mistake; an error: *a fault in addition.* **3.** Responsibility for a mistake or an error: *The mix-up was all my fault.* **4.** A break in a rock mass caused by a shifting of the earth's crust. The rock surface along one side of the break is shifted up, down, or sideways relative to the other rock surface. **5.** In tennis and other racquet games, a serve that falls outside a boundary. *—tr.v.* **fault•ed, fault•ing, faults.** To find fault in; criticize: *No one can fault such a fine performance.* *—idiom.* **at fault.** Deserving of blame; guilty: *He admitted to being at fault.* [First written down about 1280 in Middle English and spelled *faute*, from Old French, from Latin *fallere*, to deceive, fail.]

fault•find•er (**fôlt′**fīn′dər) *n.* A person who habitually finds fault with and freely criticizes others. **—fault′find′ing** *n. & adj.*

fault•ing (**fôl′**tĭng) *n.* The process of fracturing and movement that produces a geological fault.

fault•less (**fôlt′**lĭs) *adj.* Being without fault or flaw: *faultless manners.* See Synonyms at **perfect. —fault′less•ly** *adv.* **—fault′less•ness** *n.*

fault•y (**fôl′**tē) *adj.* **fault•i•er, fault•i•est.** Having a fault or faults; imperfect or defective: *faulty electric wiring; a faulty argument.* **—fault′i•ly** *adv.* **—fault′i•ness** *n.*

faun (fôn) *n.* In Roman mythology, a god of the woods and fields having the body of a man and the ears, horns, tail, and sometimes the legs of a goat. [First written down about 1385 in Middle English and spelled *fawn*, from Latin *Faunus*, Roman god of nature.]

❑ *These sound alike:* **faun, fawn¹** (flatter), **fawn²** (young deer).

fau•na (**fô′**nə) *n., pl.* **fau•nas** or **fau•nae** (**fô′**nē′). The animals of a particular region or time period: *tropical fauna; prehistoric fauna.*

Faust (foust) also **Faus•tus** (**fou′**stəs *or* **fô′**stəs) *n.* A magician in German legend who sells his soul to the Devil in exchange for power and knowledge.

fa•vor (fā′vər) *n.* **1.** A kind or helpful act: *My friend agreed to go with me as a favor.* **2.** Approval or support; liking: *The plan is fast gaining favor.* **3.** A small gift given to each guest at a party or ball. **4.** Friendly regard; partiality: *A judge cannot show favor in the court.* **5.** Behalf; interest: *The cashier made an error in our favor.* —*tr.v.* **fa•vored, fa•vor•ing, fa•vors. 1.** To perform a kindness or service for; oblige: *The singer favored us with two more songs.* **2.** To approve or support: *I favor longer vacations.* **3.** To be partial to; indulge: *favor the youngest child.* **4.** To make easier or more likely; aid; promote: *The climate there favors fruit farming.* **5.** To be gentle with; treat with care: *The lineman favored his left leg while walking off the field.* **6.** To resemble; look like: *She favors her father.* —***idiom.* in favor of. 1.** In support of: *All those in favor of the motion say "aye."* **2.** To the advantage of: *The judge decided in favor of the defendant.* [First written down before 1300 in Middle English and spelled *favour*, from Latin *favor*, from *favēre*, to be favorable.]

fa•vor•a•ble (fā′vər ə bəl *or* fāv′rə bəl) *adj.* **1.** Helpful; advantageous: *a sailboat running swiftly before favorable winds.* **2.** Pleasing or promising: *The new student made a favorable impression on us.* **3.** Approving or praising: *favorable reviews of a movie.* **4.** Granting what has been desired or requested: *a favorable reply.* **—fa′vor•a•ble•ness** *n.* **—fa′vor•a•bly** *adv.*

fa•vor•ite (fā′vər ĭt *or* fāv′rĭt) *n.* **1.** A person or thing viewed or treated with special regard, especially one preferred to all others: *That song is my favorite.* **2.** A contestant believed most likely to win: *Our team is the favorite in today's game.* —*adj.* Liked or preferred above all others: *Green is my favorite color.*

fa•vor•it•ism (fā′vər ĭ tĭz′əm *or* fāv′rĭ tĭz′əm) *n.* Better treatment given to one person or group over another; partiality: *gain promotion by favoritism rather than by skill.*

fawn[1] (fôn) *intr.v.* **fawned, fawn•ing, fawns. 1.** To show affection or attempt to please, as a dog does by wagging its tail or whining. **2.** To seek favor by flattery or by acting slavishly: *The clerk fawned on the customer hoping to make a sale.* [First written down about 888 in Old English and spelled *fægnian*, to rejoice, from *fagen, fægen*, glad.]

❑ *These sound alike:* **fawn**[1] (flatter), **faun** (woodland god), **fawn**[2] (young deer).

fawn[2] (fôn) *n.* **1.** A young deer, especially one less than a year old. **2.** A yellowish or reddish brown. [First written down before 1338 in Middle English and spelled *fowen*, from Old French *faon*, young animal, from Latin *fētus*, offspring.] —SEE NOTE.

❑ *These sound alike:* **fawn**[2] (young deer), **faun** (woodland god), **fawn**[1] (flatter).

fax (făks) *n.* **1.** A fax machine. **2.** A copy of material sent or received by a fax: *a fax of a birth certificate.* —*tr.v.* **faxed, fax•ing, fax•es.** To send by a fax: *Businesses fax new information in minutes to their sales staff.*

fax machine *n.* An electronic device that sends and receives exact copies of letters, drawings, or other documents over telephone lines.

fay (fā) *n.* A fairy or an elf.

faze (fāz) *tr.v.* **fazed, faz•ing, faz•es.** To upset; bother: *Some people do not let anything faze them.*

❑ *These sound alike:* **faze, phase** (aspect).

FBI also **F.B.I.** *abbr.* An abbreviation of Federal Bureau of Investigation.

FCC *abbr.* An abbreviation of Federal Communications Commission.

F clef *n.* In music, a bass clef.

Fe The symbol for the element **iron** (sense 1).

fe•al•ty (fē′əl tē) *n., pl.* **fe•al•ties. 1.** In feudal times, the loyalty owed by a vassal to his lord. **2.** Loyalty; faithfulness: *the fealty of friends.* [First written down before 1300 in Middle English and spelled *feute*, from Latin *fidēlitās*, faithfulness, from *fidēlis*, faithful.]

fear (fîr) *n.* **1.** A feeling of alarm or fright caused by the expectation of danger. **2.** A state or condition marked by this feeling: *The citizens of the beseiged town lived in fear.* **3.** An anxious feeling; concern: *a fear of looking foolish.* **4.** A cause for fear; dread: *My greatest fear is having to finish the job by myself.* —*v.* **feared, fear•ing, fears.** —*tr.* **1.** To be afraid of; be frightened of: *The boy does not fear spiders.* **2.** To feel anxious or concerned about; worry about: *We fear mistakes will show up.* —*intr.* **1.** To be afraid; feel fear. **2.** To feel anxious or worried: *The captain feared for the ship near the rocks.*

fear•ful (fîr′fəl) *adj.* **1.** Feeling fear; afraid: *I was fearful of losing my way in the forest.* **2.** Causing fear; terrible: *We heard a fearful explosion.* **3.** Showing anxiety, fear, or terror: *a fearful glance.* **4.** *Informal.* Very bad; dreadful: *a fearful blunder.* **—fear′ful•ly** *adv.* **—fear′ful•ness** *n.*

fear•less (fîr′lĭs) *adj.* Having no fear; brave: *a fearless explorer.* See Synonyms at **brave. —fear′less•ly** *adv.* **—fear′less•ness** *n.*

fear•some (fîr′səm) *adj.* **1.** Causing or capable of causing fear; frightening; awesome: *A tornado is a fearsome sight.* **2.** Fearful; afraid. **—fear′some•ly** *adv.* **—fear′some•ness** *n.*

fea•si•ble (fē′zə bəl) *adj.* **1.** Capable of being done or carried out; possible: *Development of rockets made space exploration feasible.* **2.** Likely; logical: *That answer seems feasible enough.* **—fea′si•bil′i•ty** *n.* **—fea′si•bly** *adv.*

feast (fēst) *n.* **1.** A large elaborate meal, especially one prepared for a special occasion; a banquet. **2.** A religious festival. —*v.* **feast•ed, feast•ing, feasts.** —*tr.* **1.** To give a feast for; entertain lavishly: *feasted all their friends with an elaborate dinner party.* **2.** To give pleasure to; delight: *feast one's eyes on the beautiful landscape.* —*intr.* To eat heartily: *feast on the first corn of summer.* [First written down before 1200 in Middle English and spelled *feste*, from Latin *fēstus*, festive.]

Feast of Lights *n.* Hanukkah.

feat (fēt) *n.* An outstanding deed or accomplishment; an exploit that requires much skill or daring: *The dam is a remarkable feat of engineering.* [First written down before 1376 in Middle English and spelled *fet*, action, deed, from Latin *factum*, from past participle of *facere*, to make, do.]

❑ *These sound alike:* **feat, feet** (plural of foot).

feath•er (fĕ*th*′ər) *n.* **1.** One of the light flat growths that cover the skin of birds. A feather has a narrow hollow shaft bearing flat vanes formed of many parallel barbs. **2.** A fringe or tuft of long hair, as on the legs or tail of various dogs. —*tr.v.* **feath•ered, feath•er•ing, feath•ers. 1.** To cover or fit with a feather or feathers: *feather an arrow.* **2.** To turn (an oar) so that its blade is parallel to the surface of the water between strokes. —***idioms.* a feather in (one's) cap.** Something to be proud of; a great achievement. **feather (one's) nest.** To get rich by taking advantage of circumstances. [First written down about 725 in Old English and spelled *fether*.]

feather bed *n.* A soft mattress or quilt stuffed with feathers or down.

feath•er•bed•ding (fĕ*th*′ər bĕd′ĭng) *n.* The practice of requiring an employer to hire more workers than are needed or to refrain from laying off workers whose jobs have become obsolete, usually as the

fax

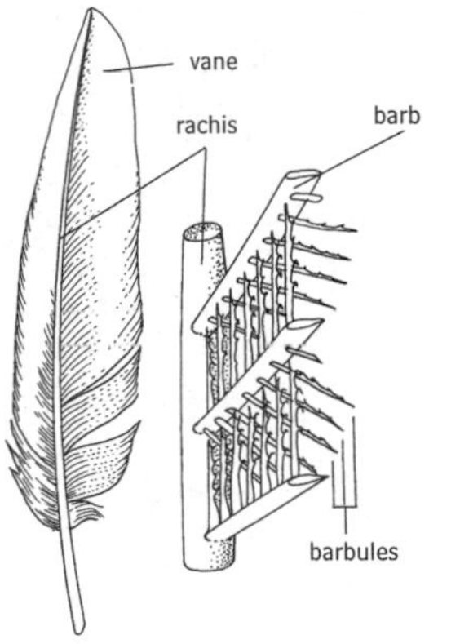

feather

ă	pat	oi	boy
ā	pay	ou	out
âr	care	ŏŏ	took
ä	father	ōō	boot
ĕ	pet	ŭ	cut
ē	be	ûr	urge
ĭ	pit	th	thin
ī	pie	*th*	this
îr	pier	hw	whoop
ŏ	pot	zh	vision
ō	toe	ə	about
ô	paw	N	*French* bon

fedora

result of safety regulations or labor union rules.

feath•ered (fĕth′ərd) *adj.* Covered or trimmed with feathers: *a feathered headdress.*

feath•er•weight (fĕth′ər wāt′) *n.* **1.** A boxer weighing more than 118 pounds (54 kilograms) and not more than 126 pounds (57 kilograms). **2.** A very small or unimportant person or thing.

feath•er•y (fĕth′ə rē) *adj.* **1.** Made of or covered with feathers. **2.** Resembling or suggestive of a feather or feathers, as in form or lightness: *the feathery leaves of the hemlock.*

fea•ture (fē′chər) *n.* **1.** A prominent part, quality, or characteristic: *Dust and craters are features of the moon's surface. Several features of the plan caught our attention.* **2.a.** Any of the distinct parts of the face: *couldn't make out his features from a distance.* **b.** The appearance of the face or its parts: *our friend's cheerful features.* **3.** The main film of a motion-picture program. **4.** A special article or column in a newspaper or magazine. —*tr.v.* **fea•tured, fea•tur•ing, fea•tures. 1.** To give special attention to; offer prominently: *an exhibit that features Native American pottery.* **2.** To have or include as a prominent part or characteristic: *The play featured a famous actor.*

Feb. also **Feb** *abbr.* An abbreviation of February.

Feb•ru•ar•y (fĕb′ro͞o ĕr′ē *or* fĕb′yo͞o ĕr′ē) *n., pl.* **Feb•ru•ar•ies.** The second month of the year in the Gregorian calendar, having 28 days, or in leap years, 29 days. [First written down before 1150 in Middle English and spelled *Februarius*, from Latin *Februārius (mēnsis)*, (month) of purification, from *februa*, offerings of expiation.]

fe•cal (fē′kəl) *adj.* Of or relating to feces.

fe•ces (fē′sēz) *pl.n.* Waste matter excreted from the bowels; excrement.

feck•less (fĕk′lĭs) *adj.* **1.** Lacking purpose or vitality; weak or ineffective. **2.** Careless and irresponsible: *an idle feckless youth.* **—feck′less•ness** *n.*

fe•cund (fē′kənd *or* fĕk′ənd) *adj.* Productive; fertile; fruitful: *the artist's fecund imagination.*

fe•cun•di•ty (fĭ kŭn′dĭ tē) *n.* **1.** The ability to produce offspring or vegetation, especially in abundance; fertility. **2.** Productive or creative power.

fed (fĕd) *v.* Past tense and past participle of **feed.**

Fed (fĕd) *n. Informal.* **1.** The Federal Reserve System. **2.** A federal agent or official.

fed•er•al (fĕd′ər əl *or* fĕd′rəl) *adj.* **1.a.** Of, relating to, or being a form of government in which separate states retain control over local affairs but are united under a central government that manages affairs of common concern to all the states. **b.** Of or relating to the central government of such a union rather than a government of its member states: *federal courts; federal laws applying to all the states.* **2.a.** Often **Federal.** Of or relating to the central government of the United States: *a Federal Court of Appeals; Federal income tax.* **b. Federal.** Of or supporting the Union during the American Civil War: *a Federal soldier.* **c. Federal.** Of or relating to Federalism or the Federalist Party. —*n.* **Federal.** A supporter of the Union during the American Civil War. [First written down in 1645 in Modern English and spelled *foederal*, from Latin *foedus*, league, treaty.] **—fed′er•al•ly** *adv.*

fed•er•al•ism (fĕd′ər ə lĭz′əm *or* fĕd′rə lĭz′əm) *n.* **1.** A system of government in which power is divided between a central government and member states. **2.** Advocacy of or belief in such a system of government. **3. Federalism.** The principles of the Federalist Party.

fed•er•al•ist (fĕd′ər ə lĭst *or* fĕd′rə lĭst) *n.* **1.** A person who supports federalism. **2. Federalist.** A supporter or member of the Federalist Party.

Federalist Party *n.* An American political party that flourished in the 1790's under the leadership of Alexander Hamilton and advocated a strong central government.

Federal Reserve System *n.* The centralized U.S. banking system that regulates banking throughout the country, consisting of 12 Federal Reserve Banks responsible for the banks located within their districts.

fed•er•ate (fĕd′ə rāt′) *tr. & intr.v.* **fed•er•at•ed, fed•er•at•ing, fed•er•ates.** To bring or join together in a league, federal union, or other association: *The unions voted to federate under one national organization.*

fed•er•a•tion (fĕd′ə rā′shən) *n.* **1.** The act of joining together in a league, federal union, or other association. **2.** A league or an association formed by federating: *a federation of independent small business owners.*

fe•do•ra (fĭ dôr′ə) *n.* A soft felt hat with a crown creased lengthwise and a brim that can be turned up or down.

fed up *adj.* Unable or unwilling to put up with something any longer: *The manager got fed up with his excuses for being late.*

fee (fē) *n.* **1.** A charge or payment for a service or privilege: *an admission fee to the movies; fee for advice from our lawyer; a tuition fee for school.* **2.** In feudal times, an estate of land granted by a lord to a vassal; a fief. [First written down before 1300 in Middle English and spelled *fe*, from Old French *fief, fie*, of Germanic origin.]

fee•ble (fē′bəl) *adj.* **fee•bler, fee•blest. 1.** Lacking strength; weak: *a very old and feeble person recovering from surgery.* **2.** Without adequate force, power, or intensity; inadequate: *a feeble attempt; a feeble voice.* [First written down before 1200 in Middle English and spelled *feble*, from Latin *flēbilis*, lamentable, from *flēre*, to weep.] **—fee′ble•ness** *n.* **—fee′bly** *adv.*

feed (fēd) *v.* **fed** (fĕd), **feed•ing, feeds.** —*tr.* **1.** To give food to; supply with nourishment: *People feed the birds in the park.* **2.** To provide as food or nourishment: *We fed the leftover turkey to the cat.* **3.a.** To serve as food for: *a turkey large enough to feed a dozen.* **b.** To produce food for: *This valley feeds an entire country.* **4.** To supply material needed for growth, maintenance, or operation: *We fed more wood to the fire. Scientists fed data into a computer.* —*intr.* To use as food; eat: *Young turtles feed on insects.* —*n.* **1.** Food for animals or birds; fodder. **2.** *Informal.* A meal, especially a large one. [First written down about 725 in Old English and spelled *fēdan*.]

feed•back (fēd′băk′) *n.* **1.** The return of a part of the output of a system or process to the input, especially when used to regulate an electrical system or an electronic process. Computers use feedback to regulate their operations. **2.** A response or reaction: *We asked the employees for feedback on the new cafeteria.*

feed•er (fē′dər) *n.* **1.** A person or thing that supplies feed: *a bird feeder on a window ledge.* **2.** A person or thing that eats: *Caterpillars are greedy feeders that damage trees.* **3.** Something that feeds materials into a machine to be processed. **4.** A branch or tributary, as of a river, railroad, or corporation.

feel (fēl) *v.* **felt** (fĕlt), **feel•ing, feels.** —*tr.* **1.** To be aware of through the sense of touch: *feel the softness of velvet.* **2.** To be aware of as a physical sensation: *feel a sharp pain; feel the cold.* **3.** To touch or examine by touching in order to find something out: *The nurse felt the patient's forehead for fever.* **4.** To find (one's way) by touching; grope: *In the dark we felt our way up the steps.* **5.** To sense or experience: *They felt my annoyance over their loud* *music.* **6.** To be affected by: *She still feels the loss of her cat.* **7.** To believe; consider: *We feel the idea is worth trying.* *—intr.* **1.** To experience sensations of touch: *The doctor poked my finger to see if it could feel.* **2.** To produce a particular sensation or feeling: *The sheets felt cool and smooth. It feels good to be home.* **3.** To be aware of a quality or an emotional state: *We all felt satisfied with the results of our work.* **4.** To try to find something by touching: *We felt around for the light switch.* **5.** To have compassion or sympathy: *I feel for him.* *—n.* **1.** Awareness or sensation caused by physical touch: *the feel of raindrops.* **2.** A quality that can be sensed by touching: *the smooth and slippery feel of satin.* ***—idioms.*** **feel in (one's) bones.** To have an intuition about: *I feel in my bones that this project will succeed.* **feel like.** *Informal.* To be in the mood for: *I did not feel like going for a walk.* **feel like (oneself).** To be aware of oneself as being in the usual state of health or spirits: *I don't feel quite myself this morning.* **feel out.** To try cautiously to find out the viewpoint of (a person): *We felt them out about playing a football game.* [First written down before 900 in Old English and spelled *fēlan.*]

feel•er (fē′lər) *n.* **1.** A slender body part, such as the antenna of an insect, used for touching or feeling. **2.** A remark, question, or suggestion used to find out the attitude or intention of others: *The letter was a feeler sent to see if there was any interest in our project.*

feel•ing (fē′lĭng) *n.* **1.** The sense of touch: *I had no feeling in my cut finger.* **2.** A physical sensation, especially one produced by touch: *the feeling of ice.* **3.** An emotion, such as joy or sorrow: *a feeling of excitement.* **4.** An awareness; an impression: *a feeling of danger nearby.* **5.** A tender emotion; a fondness: *She has a feeling for all her students.* **6.** **feelings.** The sensitive nature of one's emotions: *His lack of concern hurt my feelings.* **7.** An opinion; a sentiment: *The engineer's feeling is that the bridge is still strong.*

Synonyms: feeling, emotion, passion, sentiment. These nouns refer to an intense, complicated mental state such as love or hate. **Feeling** is the most general and neutral: *A feeling of relief washed over the audience when the tightrope walker regained her balance.* **Emotion** is a stronger term; it often means an excited or agitated feeling: *The thought of returning home after so many years filled them with emotions.* **Passion** means an intense, compelling emotion: *Getting carried away by passions can lead to serious harm.* **Sentiment** often refers to delicate, sensitive, refined feelings: *Don't let your sentiments get the better of you.*

---

feel•ing•ly (fē′lĭng lē) *adv.* With much emotion or sensitivity: *The poet writes feelingly about his home town.*

feet (fēt) *n.* Plural of **foot.**

❑ *These sound alike:* **feet, feat** (accomplishment).

feign (fān) *v.* **feigned, feign•ing, feigns.** *—tr.* To give a false appearance of; pretend: *feign illness.* *—intr.* To make a false appearance; pretend: *The opossum isn't really dead; it's only feigning to fool the dog.*

❑ *These sound alike:* **feign, fain** (willingly).

feint (fānt) *n.* **1.** A movement or an attack that is meant to deceive by diverting attention from the real target or objective: *With a feint to the left, she fooled the goalie and scored.* **2.** A deceptive action meant to mislead: *The robbers made a feint of repairing the window they were going to break into.* *—intr.v.* **feint•ed, feint•ing, feints.** To make a feint: *My opponent feinted as if to take a shot at the basket.*

❑ *These sound alike:* **feint, faint** (pass out).

feist•y (fī′stē) *adj.* **feist•i•er, feist•i•est.** Scrappy or frisky: *a feisty little terrier.*

feld•spar (fĕld′spär′ *or* fĕl′spär′) also **fel•spar** (fĕl′spär′) *n.* Any of a group of crystalline minerals that occur widely in various rocks and are composed largely of silicates combined with sodium and either potassium or calcium. Feldspars are used in the manufacture of glass.

fe•lic•i•tate (fĭ lĭs′ĭ tāt′) *tr.v.* **fe•lic•i•tat•ed, fe•lic•i•tat•ing, fe•lic•i•tates.** To wish happiness to; congratulate: *Guests felicitated the newlyweds.*

fe•lic•i•ta•tion (fĭ lĭs′ĭ tā′shən) *n.* Congratulation. Often used in the plural: *Family and friends offered their felicitations to the graduating senior.*

fe•lic•i•tous (fĭ lĭs′ĭ təs) *adj.* **1.** Well-chosen; apt; appropriate: *a felicitous choice of words.* **2.** Having an agreeable manner or style: *the mayor's felicitous greeting to the guests.* **—fe•lic′i•tous•ly** *adv.*

fe•lic•i•ty (fĭ lĭs′ĭ tē) *n., pl.* **fe•lic•i•ties. 1.** Great happiness; bliss: *the felicity of the moment of victory.* **2.** A source of great happiness: *the felicity of a generous heart.* **3.** An appropriate and pleasing manner or style: *She writes with felicity of expression.* **4.** A pleasing and appropriate expression; a well-chosen phrase: *The felicities of their greeting touched everyone.*

fe•line (fē′līn′) *adj.* **1.** Of or belonging to the family of carnivorous mammals that includes the cats, lions, tigers, and leopards. **2.** Suggestive of a cat: *walking with feline grace.* *—n.* An animal belonging to the feline family. [First written down in 1681 in Modern English, from Latin *fēlīnus*, from *fēlēs*, cat.]

fell[1] (fĕl) *tr.v.* **felled, fell•ing, fells. 1.** To cause to fall; cut or knock down: *They felled trees to build a cabin.* **2.** To sew or finish (a seam) by turning under and stitching down the edges. [First written down before 800 in Old English and spelled *fellan.*]

fell[2] (fĕl) *adj.* **1.** Of a cruel nature; fierce and ruthless: *a fell crew of pirates.* **2.** Capable of destroying; lethal: *a fell potion.* ***—idiom.*** **at one fell swoop** or **in one fell swoop.** All at once. [First written down about 1300 in Middle English and spelled *fel*, from Old French, from *felon*, evil.]

fell[3] (fĕl) *n.* The hide of an animal; a skin. [First written down about 725 in Old English.]

fell[4] (fĕl) *v. Past tense of* **fall.**

fel•lah (fĕl′ə *or* fə lä′) *n., pl.* **fel•la•hin** or **fel•la•heen** (fĕl′ə hēn′, fə-lä-hēn′). A peasant or an agricultural laborer in an Arab country.

fel•low (fĕl′ō) *n.* **1.** A man or boy: *The little fellow was afraid of the thunder.* **2.** A comrade or an associate: *Robin Hood and his fellows hid in the forest.* **3.** A member of a learned society. **4.** A graduate student who receives a grant of money for further study. **5.** One of a matched pair; a counterpart: *Here's the fellow of your sneaker.* *—adj.* Being of the same kind, group or class; sharing certain characteristics or interests: *our fellow workers.* [First written down in 1016 in Old English and spelled *fēolaga*, from Old Norse *fēlagi*, business partner, from *fēlag*, partnership : *fē*, property, money + *lag*, a laying down.]

fel•low•ship (fĕl′ō shĭp′) *n.* **1.** Friendly association of people; companionship: *We enjoyed the fellowship of the other workers.* **2.a.** A group of people sharing common interests. **b.** Membership in such a group: *admitted to fellowship.* **3.** A grant of money awarded a graduate student in a college or university.

fel•on (fĕl′ən) *n.* A person who has committed a felony. [First written down about 1300 in Middle

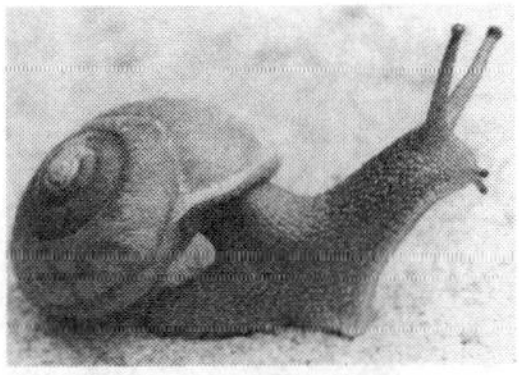

feeler
Feelers of a snail

ă	**pat**	oi	**boy**
ā	**pay**	ou	**out**
âr	**care**	ŏŏ	**took**
ä	**father**	ōō	**boot**
ĕ	**pet**	ŭ	**cut**
ē	**be**	ûr	**urge**
ĭ	**pit**	th	**thin**
ī	**pie**	*th*	**this**
îr	**pier**	hw	**whoop**
ŏ	**pot**	zh	**vision**
ō	**toe**	ə	**about**
ô	**paw**	N	*French* **bon**

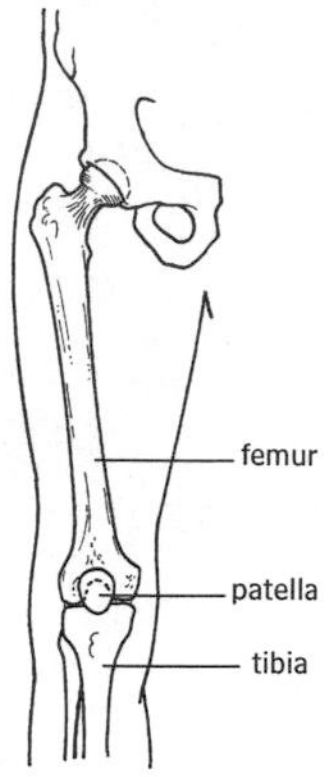

femur

Ferdinand V

Enrico Fermi

English and spelled *feloun*, from Medieval Latin *fellō*.]

fe•lo•ni•ous (fə lō′nē əs) *adj.* Of or having the nature of a felony: *carrying a gun with felonious intent.*

fel•o•ny (fĕl′ə nē) *n., pl.* **fel•o•nies.** A serious crime, such as murder, rape, or burglary, for which the law demands more severe punishment than for a misdemeanor.

felt[1] (fĕlt) *n.* A smooth firm cloth made by pressing and matting wool, fur, or other fibers together instead of weaving them. *—adj.* Made of or resembling felt: *a felt hat.* [First written down in 1000 in Old English.]

felt[2] (fĕlt) *v.* Past tense and past participle of **feel.**

Fel•ton (fĕl′tən), **Rebecca Ann Latimer.** 1835–1930. American politician who in 1922 became the first woman senator.

fem. *abbr.* An abbreviation of: **1.** Female. **2.** Feminine.

fe•male (fē′māl′) *adj.* **1.** Of, relating to, or characteristic of the sex that produces eggs or gives birth to offspring. **2.** Composed of women or girls: *a female choir.* **3.** Having a part into which a corresponding male part fits: *a female plug.* **4.** Having flowers that contain pistils but not stamens. *—n.* **1.** A female animal or plant. **2.** A woman or girl. [First written down before 1333 in Middle English and spelled *femele*, from Latin *fēmella*, diminutive of *fēmina*, woman.]

fem•i•nine (fĕm′ə nĭn) *adj.* **1.** Of or relating to women or girls: *Requirements for feminine nutrition are somewhat different from those for men.* **2.** Marked by or possessing qualities traditionally attributed to a woman: *The lace curtains gave the house a feminine feeling.* **3.** In grammar, relating to or belonging to the gender of nouns that refer to females or to things classified as female: *In German, the word for "world" is feminine.* **—fem′i•nine•ly** *adv.*

fem•i•nin•i•ty (fĕm′ə nĭn′ĭ tē) *n., pl.* **fem•i•nin•i•ties.** The quality or condition of being feminine.

fem•i•nism (fĕm′ə nĭz′əm) *n.* **1.** Belief in the same rights for women and men in all aspects of public and private life. **2.** The movement organized around this belief. **—fem′i•nist** *n. & adj.*

fe•mur (fē′mər) *n., pl.* **fe•murs** or **fem•o•ra** (fĕm′ər ə). **1.** The long bone of the leg between the knee and pelvis in human beings; the thighbone. **2.** A corresponding bone in other animals.

fen (fĕn) *n.* Low swampy land; a marsh or bog.

fence (fĕns) *n.* **1.** A structure usually made of posts or stakes joined together by wire, boards, or rails, that serves as an enclosure, a boundary, or a barrier. **2.** A person who receives and sells stolen goods. *—v.* **fenced, fenc•ing, fenc•es.** *—tr.* To surround or separate with a fence: *fence a pasture to keep cows in; fence in the dog for the night.* *—intr.* To practice the sport of fencing: *Both actors fenced with skill.* ***—idiom.* on the fence.** *Informal.* Undecided as to which of two sides to support; uncommitted. **—fenc′er** *n.*

fenc•ing (fĕn′sĭng) *n.* **1.** The art or sport of using a sword, especially a foil, in attack and defense. **2.** Material, such as wire, stakes, and rails, used to construct fences: *That lumber yard sells fencing.* **3.** A barrier or an enclosure of fences: *Low stone fencing surrounds the park.*

fend (fĕnd) *v.* **fend•ed, fend•ing, fends.** *—tr.* To ward off: *fend off an attack.* *—intr.* To attempt to manage without assistance: *I'll have to fend for myself until my parents get home from work.*

fend•er (fĕn′dər) *n.* **1.** A guard over each wheel of an automobile or other vehicle that is shaped and positioned so as to keep mud or water from splashing up. **2.** A device at the front end of a locomotive or streetcar designed to push aside obstructions. **3.** A cushion made of fiber, rubber, or wood and hung over the side of a dock or vessel to absorb friction or impact. **4.** A screen or metal frame placed in front of a fireplace to keep hot coals and debris from falling out.

fend•er-bend•er or **fender bender** (fĕn′dər bĕn′dər) *n. Informal.* A collision between two or more automobiles that results in only minor damage.

fen•nel (fĕn′əl) *n.* **1.** The edible seeds, stalks, or leaves of a plant that tastes like licorice. The seeds are used as flavoring and in medicine, and the stalks and leaves are eaten in salads. **2.** The plant that bears such seeds, stalks, and leaves, having clusters of small yellow flowers.

fer-de-lance (fĕr′dl ăns′ *or* fĕr′dl äns′) *n., pl.* **fer-de-lance.** A large poisonous snake of tropical America that has brown and grayish markings and is related to the rattlesnake.

Fer•di•nand V (fûr′dn ănd′) Known as "Ferdinand the Catholic." 1452–1516. King of Spain (1474–1504) who ruled jointly with his wife, Isabella I. Their marriage (1469) marked the beginning of the modern Spanish state.

fer•ment (fûr′mĕnt′) *n.* **1.** A substance that causes fermentation, such as a yeast, a mold, or an enzyme. **2.** Fermentation. **3.** A state of agitation; unrest. *—v.* (fər mĕnt′). **fer•ment•ed, fer•ment•ing, fer•ments.** *—tr.* **1.** To cause to undergo fermentation: *Yeast ferments starch and sugar.* **2.** To agitate or excite. *—intr.* **1.** To undergo fermentation: *Our apple cider had fermented overnight.* **2.** To be in an agitated or excited state.

fer•men•ta•tion (fûr′mĕn tā′shən) *n.* **1.** A chemical reaction in which enzymes break down complex organic compounds into simpler compounds. Yeasts convert sugar to alcohol and carbon dioxide by fermentation. **2.** Unrest; agitation.

Fer•mi (fĕr′mē), **Enrico.** 1901–1954. Italian-born American scientist who won a 1938 Nobel Prize for his work on radioactivity.

fer•mi•um (fûr′mē əm *or* fĕr′mē əm) *n. Symbol* **Fm** A radioactive metallic element that is artificially produced from plutonium or uranium. Atomic number 100. See table at **element.** [First written down in 1955 in Modern English, after Enrico *Fermi.*]

fern (fûrn) *n.* Any of numerous plants having feathery fronds divided into many leaflets. Ferns do not have flowers or seeds but reproduce by means of spores.

fe•ro•cious (fə rō′shəs) *adj.* **1.** Extremely savage; fierce: *the tiger's ferocious attack.* **2.** Extreme; intense: *ferocious heat.* **—fe•ro′cious•ly** *adv.* **—fe•ro′cious•ness** *n.*

fe•roc•i•ty (fə rŏs′ĭ tē) *n.* The state or quality of being ferocious; fierceness.

fer•ret (fĕr′ĭt) *n.* **1.** A North American mammal similar to the weasel and having yellowish or brown fur and dark feet. **2.** The domesticated European polecat, having white or yellowish-white fur and often trained to hunt rats or rabbits. *—v.* **fer•ret•ed, fer•ret•ing, fer•rets.** *—tr.* **1.** To hunt (rabbits, for example) with ferrets. **2.** To bring to light by searching; uncover: *ferreted out the solution to the mystery.* *—intr.* **1.** To engage in hunting with ferrets. **2.** To search intensively: *ferreting among old records.*

fer•ric (fĕr′ĭk) *adj.* Of, relating to, or containing iron.

ferric oxide *n.* A reddish-brown to black, iron-containing compound that is often used as a pigment.

Fer•ris wheel (fĕr′ĭs) *n.* An amusement ride consisting of an upright wheel having seats suspended from its rim that remain horizontal as the wheel revolves. [First written down in 1893 in Modern English, after George Washington Gale *Ferris* (1859–1896), American engineer.]

fer•rous (fĕr′əs) *adj.* Of, relating to, or containing iron.

fer•ry (fĕr′ē) *v.* **fer•ried, fer•ry•ing, fer•ries.** —*tr.* **1.** To transport (people, vehicles, or goods) by boat across a body of water. **2.** To cross (a body of water) by a ferry: *We ferried the river before a bridge was built.* **3.** To deliver (a vehicle) under its own power to its eventual user. **4.** To transport (people or things), especially by aircraft: *Volunteers ferried everyone from the disaster area to the hospital.* —*intr.* To cross a body of water on or as if on a ferry: *We ferried across the bay.* —*n., pl.* **fer•ries. 1.** A boat used to transport passengers, vehicles, or goods across a body of water; a ferryboat. **2.** A place where passengers or goods are transported across a body of water by a ferry: *There was a crowd waiting at the ferry.* [First written down about 725 in Old English and spelled *ferian.*]

fer•ry•boat (fĕr′ē bōt′) *n.* A boat used to transport passengers, vehicles, or goods across a body of water.

fer•tile (fûr′tl) *adj.* **1.** Capable of producing offspring, seeds, or fruit; able to reproduce: *a fertile cow; a fertile plant.* **2.** Capable of developing into a complete organism; fertilized: *A fertile egg from a hen will produce a chick.* **3.** Capable of supporting plant life; favorable to the growth of crops and plants: *fertile soil; a fertile valley.* **4.** Highly productive or active; inventive: *the writer's fertile imagination.*

Fertile Crescent. A region of the Middle East extending from the Nile River valley in Egypt to the Tigris and Euphrates rivers in Iraq.

fer•til•i•ty (fər tĭl′ĭ tē) *n.* The quality or condition of being fertile: *the fertility of good soil.*

fer•til•i•za•tion (fûr′tl ĭ zā′shən) *n.* **1.** The act or process of fertilizing. **2.** The union of a male reproductive cell and a female reproductive cell to form a cell that is capable of developing into a new organism.

fer•til•ize (fûr′tl īz′) *tr.v.* **fer•til•ized, fer•til•iz•ing, fer•til•iz•es. 1.** To cause (an egg cell) to become fertile, especially by a union with sperm. **2.** To make (soil, for example) fertile: *last fall's leaves will fertilize the ground.* **3.** To spread fertilizer on: *fertilize the garden.*

fer•til•iz•er (fûr′tl ī′zər) *n.* A material, such as manure, compost, or a chemical compound, added to soil to increase its productivity or fertility.

fer•ule (fĕr′əl) *n.* A cane or flat stick formerly used in punishing children.

fer•ven•cy (fûr′vən sē) *n., pl.* **fer•ven•cies.** The quality or condition of being fervent.

fer•vent (fûr′vənt) *adj.* Having or showing great emotion or zeal; ardent: *the fervent leaders of the reform movement; a fervent plea for help.* —**fer′vent•ly** *adv.*

fer•vid (fûr′vĭd) *adj.* Marked by great passion or zeal: *a fervid desire to play baseball.* —**fer′vid•ly** *adv.* —**fer′vid•ness** *n.*

fer•vor (fûr′vər) *n.* Intensity of emotion; ardor.

fes•tal (fĕs′təl) *adj.* Of or related to a feast or festival; festive: *Flags gave a festal appearance to the village.*

fes•ter (fĕs′tər) *intr.v.* **fes•tered, fes•ter•ing, fes•ters. 1.** To form pus, as an infected wound does: *An unclean cut will fester and become painful.* **2.** To be or become a source of irritation; rankle: *bitterness that festered and grew.*

fes•ti•val (fĕs′tə vəl) *n.* **1.** An occasion for feasting or celebration, especially a day or time of religious significance. **2.** An often regularly recurring series of cultural performances, exhibitions, or competitions: *an international film festival.* [First written down in 1589 in Modern English, from Middle English *festival*, festive, from Latin *fēstus.*]

fes•tive (fĕs′tĭv) *adj.* **1.** Of or relating to a feast or festival. **2.** Merry; joyous: *a festive party; festive decorations.* —**fes′tive•ly** *adv.* —**fes′tive•ness** *n.*

fes•tiv•i•ty (fĕ stĭv′ĭ tē) *n., pl.* **fes•tiv•i•ties. 1.** The joy and gaiety of a celebration or festival: *a holiday full of festivity.* **2.** The proceedings or events of a festival. Often used in the plural: *Mardi gras festivities included parades, banquets, and balls.*

fes•toon (fĕ sto͞on′) *n.* **1.** A string or garland, as of leaves or flowers, suspended in a curve between two points. **2.** A representation of such a string or garland, as in painting or sculpture. —*tr.v.* **fes•tooned, fes•toon•ing, fes•toons. 1.** To decorate with or as if with festoons. **2.** To form or make into festoons.

fet•a (fĕt′ə *or* fē′tə) *n.* A white Greek cheese made usually of goat's or ewe's milk and preserved in brine.

fe•tal (fēt′l) *adj.* Of, relating to, or characteristic of a fetus: *a fetal heartbeat.*

fetch (fĕch) *v.* **fetched, fetch•ing, fetch•es.** —*tr.* **1.** To go after and bring or take back; get: *Shall I fetch your bags for you?* **2.** To cause to come; succeed in bringing: *My phone call fetched them home quickly.* **3.** To bring in as a price: *The painting fetched $200 at the auction.* —*intr.* To go after something and return with it: *If you throw the ball, the dog will fetch.* [First written down about 1000 in Old English and spelled *feccan.*]

fetch•ing (fĕch′ĭng) *adj.* Very attractive; charming: *a fetching smile.* —**fetch′ing•ly** *adv.*

fete also **fête** (fāt *or* fĕt) *n.* **1.** A festival or feast **2.** An elaborate party. —*tr.v.* **fet•ed, fet•ing, fetes** also **fêt•ed, fêt•ing, fêtes.** To honor with a festival, a feast, or an elaborate entertainment: *They feted the veterans on Memorial Day.*

❑ *These sound alike:* **fete, fate** (destiny).

fet•id (fĕt′ĭd *or* fē′tĭd) *adj.* Having an offensive odor. —**fet′id•ly** *adv.* —**fet′id•ness** *n.*

fet•ish (fĕt′ĭsh *or* fē′tĭsh) *n.* **1.** An object that is believed to have magical or spiritual powers. **2.** An object of too much attention or reverence.

fet•ish•ism (fĕt′ĭ shĭz′əm *or* fē′tĭ shĭz′əm) *n.* **1.** Worship of or belief in magical fetishes. **2.** Too much attention to or attachment for something. —**fet′ish•ist** *n.*

fet•lock (fĕt′lŏk′) *n.* **1.** A projection on the back of the leg of a horse or related animal, just above the hoof. **2.** A tuft of hair on this projection.

fet•ter (fĕt′ər) *n.* **1.** A chain or shackle for the ankles or feet. **2.** Something that restricts or restrains. —*tr.v.* **fet•tered, fet•ter•ing, fet•ters. 1.** To put fetters on; shackle. **2.** To restrict the freedom of: *Bad weather fettered our travel plans.*

fet•tle (fĕt′l) *n.* Proper or sound mental or physical condition or state: *The horse is in fine fettle for today's race.*

fet•tuc•ci•ne (fĕt′ə chē′nē) *n.* **1.** Pasta in narrow flat strips. **2.** A dish made with such strips of pasta.

fe•tus (fē′təs) *n., pl.* **fe•tus•es.** The unborn young of a mammal at the later stages of its development, especially a human embryo from its eighth week of development to its birth.

feud (fyo͞od) *n.* A bitter quarrel or state of enmity between two people, families, or groups, often continuing for generations: *An ancient feud came between the families.* —*intr.v.* **feud•ed, feud•ing, feuds.** To carry on a bitter quarrel or state of en-

ferret
Black-footed ferret

Ferris wheel
Detail of photograph showing Ferris wheel at 1893 World's Columbian Exposition in Chicago

festoon

ă	pat	oi	boy
ā	pay	ou	out
âr	care	o͝o	took
ä	father	o͞o	boot
ĕ	pet	ŭ	cut
ē	be	ûr	urge
ĭ	pit	th	thin
ī	pie	*th*	this
îr	pier	hw	whoop
ŏ	pot	zh	vision
ō	toe	ə	about
ô	paw	N	*French* bon

Usage: few

You use the word **fewer** with expressions denoting things that can be counted: *fewer than four players*; while you use **less** with mass terms denoting things of measurable extent: *less paper*; *less water*. **Less**, however, is the correct word in the expression *less than* when it is used before a plural noun denoting a measure of time, amount, or distance, as *less than 50 miles*.

fez

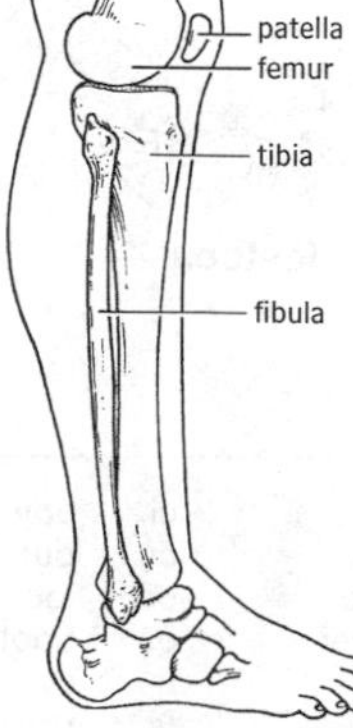

fibula

mity. [First written down before 1325 in Middle English and spelled *fede*, from Old French *faide*, of Germanic origin.]

feu•dal (fyo͞od′l) *adj.* Of, relating to, or characteristic of feudalism. [First written down in 1614 in Modern English, from Medieval Latin *feudum*, fee, fief.]

feu•dal•ism (fyo͞od′l ĭz′əm) *n.* A political and economic system in Europe during the Middle Ages, in which a landowner granted the use of land to a vassal in exchange for military service and various other duties. **—feu′dal•is′tic** *adj.*

fe•ver (fē′vər) *n.* **1.** A body temperature higher than normal. **2.** A disease in which a high body temperature is one of the main symptoms. **3.** A condition of great activity or excitement: *a fever of enthusiasm during the game.* [First written down about 1000 in Old English and spelled *fefor*, from Latin *febris*.]

fever blister *n.* A cold sore.

fe•ver•ish (fē′vər ĭsh) *adj.* **1.a.** Of, relating to, or resembling a fever. **b.** Having a fever or symptoms characteristic of a fever: *The sick child was feverish.* **c.** Causing or tending to cause fever. **2.** Marked by intense agitation, emotion, or activity: *a feverish worker.* **3.** Intensely excited or active: *The team was struck with a feverish desire to win.* **—fe′ver•ish•ly** *adv.* **—fe′ver•ish•ness** *n.*

few (fyo͞o) *adj.* **few•er, few•est.** Amounting to a small number; not many: *Few people like to swim in cold water.* —*n. (used with a plural verb).* **1.** A small number of persons or things: *I invited only a few to my party.* **2.** A limited group; a minority: *the happy few.* —*pron. (used with a plural verb).* A small number of persons or things: *Many felt it was an interesting idea, but few seemed willing to do anything about it.* —See Note.

fez (fĕz) *n., pl.* **fez•zes.** A man's felt cap in the shape of a flat-topped cone, usually red with a black tassel, worn chiefly in the eastern Mediterranean region. [First written down in 1802 in Modern English, from Turkish *fes*, from *Fez*, Morocco.]

ff *abbr.* An abbreviation of fortissimo.

ff. *abbr.* An abbreviation of: **1.** Folios. **2.** Following.

fi•an•cé (fē′än sā′ *or* fē än′sā′) *n.* A man engaged to be married.

fi•an•cée (fē′än sā′ *or* fē än′sā′) *n.* A woman engaged to be married.

fi•as•co (fē ăs′kō) *n., pl.* **fi•as•coes** or **fi•as•cos.** A complete failure: *Without enough rehearsal, the play was a fiasco.*

fi•at (fē′ăt′ *or* fē′ät′) *n.* An arbitrary order or decree.

fib (fĭb) *n.* A lie about something unimportant or small: *Their excuse is just a fib.* —*intr.v.* **fibbed, fib•bing, fibs.** To tell an insignificant or childish lie. **—fib′ber** *n.*

fi•ber (fī′bər) *n.* **1.** A slender strand; a thread: *Cotton, wool, and nylon fibers may be spun into yarn.* **2.** Any of various elongated cells in the body, especially those of muscle or nerve tissue. **3.** Essential character or structure. **4.** Basic strength or toughness: *a person of moral fiber.* **5.** The part of grains, fruits, and vegetables not absorbed or digested by the human body, containing cellulose and stimulating the muscles of the intestinal walls. [First written down in 1540 in Modern English and spelled *fibre*, from Latin *fibra*.]

fi•ber•board (fī′bər bôrd′) *n.* A building material made from wood chips or plant fibers bonded together and compressed into rigid sheets.

fi•ber•glass (fī′bər glăs′) *n.* A material made up of very fine glass fibers, used in making various products, such as building insulation and boat hulls.

fiber optics *n. (used with a singular verb).* The technology based on the use of fine glass or plastic fibers that are capable of transmitting light around curves. Fiber optics is used in medicine and for long-distance telephone and computer lines.

fi•bre (fī′bər) *n. Chiefly British.* Variant of **fiber.**

fib•ril•la•tion (fĭb′rə lā′shən *or* fī′brə lā′shən) *n.* A tremor in a muscle, especially one of the muscles of the heart.

fi•brin (fī′brĭn) *n.* A fibrous elastic and insoluble protein that is formed when blood clots.

fi•brin•o•gen (fī brĭn′ə jən) *n.* A soluble protein that is normally present in the plasma of the blood and forms fibrin.

fi•broid (fī′broid′) *adj.* Made up of or resembling fibers or fibrous tissue: *a fibroid tumor.*

fi•brous (fī′brəs) *adj.* Made up of, resembling, or having fibers: *fibrous tissue.*

fib•u•la (fĭb′yə lə) *n., pl.* **fib•u•lae** (fĭb′yə lē′) or **fib•u•las. 1.** The outer and smaller of the two bones of the leg in human beings. It extends from the knee to the ankle. **2.** A similar bone in the hind leg of vertebrate animals.

–fic *suff.* A suffix that means making or causing: *soporific.*

fick•le (fĭk′əl) *adj.* Changeable; not stable or constant, especially with regard to affections: *a fickle friend.* **—fick′le•ness** *n.*

fic•tion (fĭk′shən) *n.* **1.** An invention of the imagination; something made up: *The story seems real but is complete fiction.* **2.** A lie: *told a small fiction to get out of going to the party.* **3.** A literary work whose content is based on the imagination and not on fact. **4.** The category of literature made up of works of this kind, including novels and short stories. [First written down about 1412 in Middle English and spelled *ficcioun*, from Latin *fictiō*, from *fictus*, past participle of *fingere*, to form.] **—fic′tion•al** *adj.*

fic•tion•al•ize (fĭk′shə nə līz′) *tr.v.* **fic•tion•al•ized, fic•tion•al•iz•ing, fic•tion•al•iz•es.** To treat as fiction or make into fiction: *A writer may fictionalize real-life stories.*

fic•ti•tious (fĭk tĭsh′əs) *adj.* Of, relating to, or characterized by fiction; imaginary: *a fictitious character.* **—fic•ti′tious•ly** *adv.* **—fic•ti′tious•ness** *n.*

fid•dle (fĭd′l) *n.* A violin, especially as used to play country music. —*v.* **fid•dled, fid•dling, fid•dles.** —*intr.* **1.** To play the fiddle: *We sang while they fiddled.* **2.** To move one's fingers or hands nervously: *I was fiddling with my hat.* **3.** To tinker with something in an attempt to fix or adjust it: *Don't fiddle with the television!* —*tr.* To play (a tune) on a violin: *The musicians fiddled a reel.* **—*idiom.* fiddle away.** To waste or squander: *We fiddled away the last week of summer vacation.* **—fid′dler** *n.*

fiddler crab *n.* Any of various burrowing crabs of warm coastal areas, the male of which has one front claw much larger than the other.

fid•dle•sticks (fĭd′l stĭks′) *interj.* An expression used to show mild annoyance or impatience.

fi•del•i•ty (fĭ dĕl′ĭ tē *or* fī dĕl′ĭ tē) *n., pl.* **fi•del•i•ties. 1.** Faithfulness to obligations, duties, or observances: *the soldier's fidelity to duty.* **2.** Exact correspondence with the facts; accuracy: *the fidelity of the witness's account of the accident.* **3.** The degree to which an electronic system, such as a radio or tape recorder, reproduces sound without distortion. [First written down before 1425 in Middle English and spelled *fidelite*, from Latin *fidēlitās*, from *fidēlis*, faithful, from *fidēs*, faith.]

fidg•et (fĭj′ĭt) *intr.v.* **fidg•et•ed, fidg•et•ing, fidg•ets.** To behave or move nervously or restlessly: *I fidgeted while waiting for the play to start.* —*n.* **1.** A condition of nervousness or restlessness. Often used in the plural: *a case of the fidgets.* **2.** A person who fidgets: *Don't be an annoying fidget!* **—fidg′·et·y** *adj.*

fie (fī) *interj.* An expression used to show distaste or shock.

fief (fēf) *n.* **1.** A fee. **2.** A fiefdom. [First written down in 1611 in Modern English, from Old French, of Germanic origin.]

fief·dom (fēf′dəm) *n.* The estate or domain of a feudal lord.

field (fēld) *n.* **1.** A broad, level, open expanse of land. **2.** A meadow: *a field of wildflowers.* **3.** A cultivated area of land, especially one devoted to a particular crop: *cotton fields; a field ready for spring planting.* **4.** A portion of land or a geologic formation containing a natural resource: *oil fields; a gold field.* **5.** A wide unbroken expanse, as of ice. **6.** A battleground. **7.** A battle. **8.** A background area, as on a flag or painting: *white stars on a field of blue.* **9.** An area in which an athletic event takes place. **10.** All the contestants or participants in an event: *a large field of horses in the Kentucky Derby.* **11.** An area of human activity or interest: *the field of American history.* **12.** Profession, employment, or business: *What field are you in?* **13.** A scene of practical work or observation outside an office, a school, a factory, or a laboratory. **14.** The region of space throughout which a physical force operates: *An electric field surrounds a charged body. The moon is within the earth's gravitational field.* **15.** The area in which an image is visible to the eye or an optical instrument: *the field of a microscope; the field of vision.* —*adj.* **1.** Growing, living, or cultivated in fields or open land. **2.** Made, used, or carried on in the field: *field operations.* —*v.* **field·ed, field·ing, fields.** —*tr.* **1.** In sports, especially baseball, to stop or catch (a ball): *fielded several fly balls.* **2.** In sports, to place in the field to play: *field a team.* —*intr.* To play as a fielder: *The team fielded well.* [First written down about 725 in Old English and spelled *feld.*]

field day *n.* **1.** A day set aside for sports or athletic competition. **2.** *Informal.* A time of great activity, pleasure, or opportunity: *The campers had a field day splashing in the stream.*

field·er (fēl′dər) *n.* In baseball, a player stationed in the field who attempts to put out the team at bat.

field glasses *pl.n.* Portable binoculars used especially outdoors for viewing distant objects.

field goal *n.* **1.** In football, a score worth three points made by a place kick that makes a goal. **2.** In basketball, a score of two or three points made by throwing the ball through the basket.

field hockey *n.* A game played on a field in which two opposing teams of players using wooden sticks try to drive a ball into the opponents' goal.

field house *n.* A building at an athletic field having storage and training facilities and locker rooms.

field magnet *n.* A magnet used to produce a magnetic field for the operation of an electrical device such as a motor or generator.

field marshal *n.* An officer in some European armies, usually ranking just below the commander in chief.

field mouse *n.* Any of various small mice that live in meadows and fields, often causing damage to crops.

field test *n.* A test of a new product under actual operating conditions.

field-test (fēld′tĕst′) *n.* To test (a technique or product, for example) under conditions of actual operation or use: *field-test a new kind of lawnmower.*

field trip *n.* A group excursion for the purpose of firsthand observation, as to a museum, the woods, or a historic place.

fiend (fēnd) *n.* **1.** An evil spirit; a demon. **2.** An evil or wicked person. **3.** *Informal.* A person absorbed in or obsessed with a certain thing: *a baseball fiend; a fresh-air fiend.* [First written down about 725 in Old English and spelled *fēond.*]

fiend·ish (fēn′dĭsh) *adj.* **1.** Of, relating to, or suggestive of a fiend; evil, wicked, or cruel: *a fiendish weapon.* **2.** Extremely bad, disagreeable, or difficult: *a fiendish problem.* **—fiend′ish·ly** *adv.* **—fiend′ish·ness** *n.*

fierce (fîrs) *adj.* **fierc·er, fierc·est. 1.** Having a violent and savage nature; ferocious: *a fierce beast.* **2.** Extremely severe or violent; terrible: *a fierce snowstorm.* **3.** Extremely intense or ardent: *fierce loyalty.* [First written down in 1240 in Middle English and spelled *fiers,* from Latin *ferus.*] **—fierce′ly** *adv.* **—fierce′ness** *n.*

fier·y (fīr′ē *or* fī′ə rē) *adj.* **fier·i·er, fier·i·est. 1.** Consisting of or containing fire: *the fiery crater of the volcano.* **2.** Having the color of fire: *a fiery sunset.* **3.** Very hot: *the fiery pavements of the city in summer.* **4.** Burning or glowing: *fiery coals.* **5.** Easily excited up or provoked; tempestuous: *a fiery temper.* **6.** Charged with emotion; high-spirited: *a fiery speech.* **—fier′i·ly** *adv.* **—fier′i·ness** *n.*

fi·es·ta (fē ĕs′tə) *n.* A festival or religious holiday, especially a saint's day celebrated in Spanish-speaking countries. [First written down in 1844 in American English, from Spanish, from Latin *fēstus,* festive.]

fife (fīf) *n.* A small high-pitched musical instrument similar to a flute, often used with drums to accompany military music. [First written down in 1555 in Modern English, probably from German *Pfeife,* from Latin *pīpāre,* to chirp.]

fif·teen (fĭf tēn′) *n.* **1.** A number, written 15, that is equal to 14 + 1. **2.** The 15th in a set or sequence.

fif·teenth (fĭf tēnth′) *n.* **1.** The ordinal number matching the number 15 in a series. **2.** One of 15 equal parts.

fifth (fĭfth) *n.* **1.** The ordinal number matching the number five in a series. **2.** One of five equal parts. **3.** One fifth of a gallon or four fifths of a quart of liquor. **4.a.** The interval covering five tones in a musical scale, as C, D, E, F, and G. **b.** The fifth tone of a musical scale; the dominant. **5.** The transmission gear used to produce speeds next highest to those of fourth in a motor vehicle. **—fifth** *adv. & adj.*

fifth column *n.* A secret organization working within a country to further the political and military aims of that country's enemies.

fif·ti·eth (fĭf′tē ĭth) *n.* **1.** The ordinal number matching the number 50 in a series. **2.** One of 50 equal parts.

fif·ty (fĭf′tē) *n.* A number, written 50, that is equal to 5 × 10. [First written down about 725 in Old English and spelled *fiftig.*]

fif·ty-fif·ty (fĭf′tē fĭf′tē) *adj.* **1.** Divided or shared in two equal portions: *The partners agreed on a fifty-fifty split of the money.* **2.** Being equally balanced between favorable and unfavorable: *had a fifty-fifty chance to win the game.* **—fif′ty-fif′ty** *adv.*

fig (fĭg) *n.* **1.** A sweet pear-shaped fruit of any of several trees or shrubs, having many seeds. Figs may be eaten fresh, dried, or canned. **2.** A tree that bears such fruit, growing in warm regions. **3.** A very small or trivial amount: *I don't care a fig about bad weather.* [First written down before 1200 in Middle English, from Latin *fīcus.*]

fig. *abbr.* An abbreviation of figure.

fight (fīt) *v.* **fought** (fôt), **fight·ing, fights.** —*intr.* **1.** To take part in combat or battle: *fought bravely against the invaders.* **2.** To participate in boxing or

field hockey

field mouse
Common field mouse

fife

ă	pat	oi	boy
ā	pay	ou	out
âr	care	ŏŏ	took
ä	father	ōō	boot
ĕ	pet	ŭ	cut
ē	be	ûr	urge
ĭ	pit	th	thin
ī	pie	*th*	this
îr	pier	hw	whoop
ŏ	pot	zh	vision
ō	toe	ə	about
ô	paw	N	*French* bon

figurehead

Word History: file¹

The **file** in which we keep things in alphabetical order comes from the Old French word *fil,* "a thread," and refers to the traditional system of running a string or thread through a pile of papers to keep them in order. The file we use to roughen or smooth metal comes from the Old English *fīl,* "a file, a cutting tool."

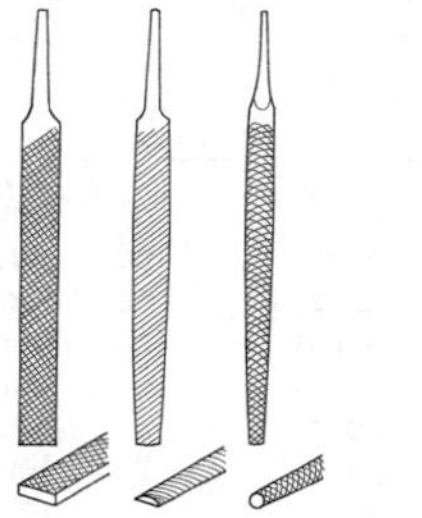

file²
Left to right: Flat, half-rounded, and round tipped files

wrestling: *They fought for the gold medal.* **3.** To engage in a quarrel; argue: *The neighbors fought for years over the boundary.* **4.** To strive vigorously and resolutely: *fought for freedom.* —*tr.* **1.** To contend with physically or in battle: *The Union troops fought the Confederates at Gettysburg.* **2.** To carry on or engage in (a battle). **3.** To box or wrestle against in a ring: *fight a contender in the Olympics.* **4.** To contend with or struggle against: *fight illiteracy; fight rising floodwaters.* See Synonyms at **oppose. 5.** To gain by struggle or striving: *We fought our way through the dense undergrowth.* —*n.* **1.a.** A physical conflict between two or more individuals. **b.** A quarrel or conflict: *a fight over who would empty the trash.* **2.** A battle waged between opposing forces. **3.** A boxing or wrestling match. **4.** A struggle to achieve a goal: *the fight for freedom.* **5.** The power or will to battle or struggle. ***—idioms.*** **fight fire with fire.** To combat one evil or one set of negative circumstances by reacting in kind. **fight off.** To defend against or drive back (a hostile force, for example): *A fever is one way in which the body fights off germs.* [First written down about 900 in Old English and spelled *feohtan.*]

fight•er (fīʹtər) *n.* **1.** A soldier; a warrior: *Many colonists were brave fighters against the British troops.* **2.** A boxer or wrestler. **3.** A fast maneuverable airplane used in combat.

fig•ment (fĭgʹmənt) *n.* Something invented, made up, or imagined: *a mere figment of the imagination.*

fig•u•ra•tive (fĭgʹyər ə tĭv) *adj.* **1.** Based on or using figures of speech; metaphorical: *figurative language.* **2.** Containing many figures of speech; ornate. **3.** Represented by a likeness or figure; emblematic: *An oil lamp is a figurative representation of knowledge.* **—figʹur•a•tive•ly** *adv.* **—figʹur•a•tive•ness** *n.*

fig•ure (fĭgʹyər) *n.* **1.** A written or printed symbol, especially a numeral, representing something that is not a letter. **2. figures.** Mathematical calculations: *Accountants need to have a good head for figures.* **3.** An amount represented in numbers: *priced at a high figure.* **4.** In geometry, any combination of points, lines, or surfaces: *Circles and triangles are plane figures.* **5.** The shape or form of a human body: *People buy clothes to suit their figures.* **6.** An indistinct object or shape: *saw a tall figure standing in the doorway.* **7.** A person, especially a well-known one: *The President is an important public figure.* **8.** Impression or appearance made: *cuts an impressive figure in uniform.* **9.** A pictorial or sculptural representation, especially of the human body: *lifelike figures in wax.* **10.a.** A diagram: *On that page the figure shows a bird in flight.* **b.** A design or pattern, as on cloth: *figures in a tapestry.* **11.** A group of movements in dancing or ice skating: *the lovely figures of the minuet.* **12.** A brief or melodic harmonic unit, often expanded into a larger musical phrase or structure; a motif: *the opening figure of a symphony.* —*v.* **fig•ured, fig•ur•ing, fig•ures.** —*tr.* **1.** To calculate with numbers: *figured the cost of something.* **2.** *Informal.* To conclude, believe, or predict: *I figured that you'd want to go swimming.* —*intr.* **1.** To calculate; compute: *Most store clerks can figure quickly and accurately.* **2.** To be or seem important: *The opening of the store figured in the local news.* **3.** *Informal.* To seem reasonable or expected: *It figures that they decided to work as a team because they work well together.* ***—idioms.*** **figure on.** *Informal.* To depend on: *You can always figure on some guests to be late.* **figure out.** *Informal.* To solve, decipher, or discover: *figure out a puzzle.* [First written down before 1200 in Middle English, from Latin *figūra.*]

fig•ured (fĭgʹyərd) *adj.* Decorated with a design; patterned: *figured wallpaper.*

fig•ure•head (fĭgʹyər hĕdʹ) *n.* **1.** A person given a position of leadership in name only and having no actual authority. **2.** A carved figure on the prow of a ship.

figure of speech *n., pl.* **figures of speech.** An expression in which words are used in unusual or nonliteral ways to create vivid or dramatic effects. Metaphor, simile, hyperbole, and personification are figures of speech.

figure skating *n.* Ice skating in which the skater traces prescribed, often elaborate figures. **—figure skater** *n.*

fig•u•rine (fĭgʹyə rēnʹ) *n.* A small molded or sculpted figure; a statuette.

Fi•ji (fēʹjē). An island country of the southwest Pacific Ocean located southwest of Samoa and made up of about 320 islands. The country gained its independence from Great Britain in 1970. Suva is the capital. Population, 686,000.

fil•a•ment (fĭlʹə mənt) *n.* **1.** A fine or slender thread, wire, or fiber. **2.** A slender part of a plant that supports the anther of a flower, as the stalk of a stamen. **3.a.** A fine wire that is enclosed in the bulb of an electric lamp and that is heated by the passage of current until it gives off light. **b.** An electrically heated wire that acts as the cathode of some electron tubes. [First written down in 1594 in Modern English, from Late Latin *filāre,* to spin, from Latin *fīlum,* thread.]

fil•bert (fĭlʹbərt) *n.* A hazelnut. [First written down about 1390 in Middle English, after Saint *Philibert* (died 684), whose feast day in late August coincides with the ripening of the nut.]

filch (fĭlch) *tr.v.* **filched, filch•ing, filch•es.** To steal (something, especially something of little value) in a sly manner; pilfer. **—filchʹer** *n.*

file¹ (fīl) *n.* **1.** A container, such as a cabinet or folder, for keeping papers in order: *drawings stored in large files.* **2.a.** A collection of papers or published materials kept or arranged in convenient order. **b.** A collection of related data for a computer: *How many files are there now on your floppy disk?* **3.** A row or single line of people or things arranged one behind the other: *The ducks waddled across the road in a file.* —*v.* **filed, fil•ing, files.** —*tr.* **1.** To put or keep (papers, for example) in useful order for storage or reference. **2.** To submit or send (copy) to a newspaper: *Reporters file stories daily.* **3.** To enter (a legal document) on public official record: *file a claim in court for payment of damages.* —*intr.* **1.** To march or walk in a line: *The nine justices solemnly filed in.* **2.** To make application; apply: *Candidates for election must file with the county clerk.* [First written down in 1525 in Modern English, from Middle English *filen,* to put documents on file, from Old French *filer,* to put documents on a thread, from Latin *fīlum,* thread.] **—filʹer** *n.* —See Note.

❑ *These sound alike:* **file¹** (folder), **faille** (silk), **file²** (tool).

file² (fīl) *n.* Any of several steel tools having a series of sharp ridges, used in smoothing, shaping, or grinding down. —*tr.v.* **filed, fil•ing, files.** To smooth, reduce, or remove with or as if with a file: *If you file the edge of the blade it will cut better.* [First written down before 800 in Old English and spelled *fīl.*]

❑ *These sound alike:* **file²** (tool), **faille** (silk), **file¹** (folder).

fi•let¹ (fĭ lāʹ *or* fĭlʹāʹ) *n.* A net or lace with a simple pattern of squares. [First written down in 1881 in Modern English, from Old French, diminutive of *fil,* thread, from Latin *fīlum.*]

fi•let[2] (fĭ **lā′** *or* **fĭl′**ā′) *n.* Variant of **fillet** (sense 2). —*v.* Variant of **fillet.**

fi•let mi•gnon (fĭ lā′ mēn **yôɴ′**) *n., pl.* **fi•lets mi•gnons** (fĭ lā′ mēn **yôɴ′**). A round, very choice cut of beef from the loin.

fil•i•al (**fĭl′**ē əl) *adj.* Of, relating to, or befitting a son or daughter: *filial duty; filial love.* **—fil′i•al•ly** *adv.*

fil•i•bus•ter (**fĭl′**ə bŭs′tər) *n.* **1.** The use of delaying tactics, such as making a long speech and introducing an irrelevant issue, in an attempt to prevent the passage of a piece of legislation. **2.** An instance of this, especially a long speech made by a legislator. —*v.* **fil•i•bus•tered, fil•i•bus•ter•ing, fil•i•bus•ters.** —*intr.* To delay or obstruct the passage of a legislative bill by filibuster. —*tr.* To delay or obstruct the passage of (a legislative bill) by filibuster. **—fil′i•bus′ter•er** *n.*

fil•i•gree (**fĭl′**ĭ grē′) *n.* **1.** Delicate and intricate ornamental work of twisted gold or silver wire. **2.** A lacy delicate design or pattern. —*tr.v.* **fil•i•greed, fil•i•gree•ing, fil•i•grees.** To decorate with or as if with filigree: *Frost filigreed the windowpanes.* [First written down in 1668 in Modern English and spelled *filigrane,* from Italian *filigrana* : Latin *fīlum,* thread + Latin *grānum,* grain.]

fil•ing (**fī′**lĭng) *n.* A particle or shaving removed by a file: *metal filings.*

Fil•i•pi•no (fĭl′ə **pē′**nō) *n., pl.* **Fil•i•pi•nos.** A native or inhabitant of the Philippines. —*adj.* Of or relating to the Philippines or its peoples, languages, or cultures.

fill (fĭl) *v.* **filled, fill•ing, fills.** —*tr.* **1.** To put as much into as can be held: *fill a glass; fill an album with pictures.* **2.a.** To stop or plug up (an opening, for example): *fill a hole in the road.* **b.** To repair a cavity in (a tooth). **3.** To satisfy or meet; fulfill: *fill the requirements for a job.* **4.** To supply as required: *fill a prescription; fill an order for 20 books.* **5.** To place a person in: *We filled the job with an experienced worker.* **6.** To take up the whole of; occupy: *Music filled the room. A dense fog filled the valley.* **7.** To engage or occupy completely: *Memories of the summer filled my mind.* —*intr.* To become full: *The boat quickly filled with water.* —*n.* **1.** An amount that is needed to make full, complete, or satisfied: *We ate our fill of the blueberries.* **2.** Earth, gravel, or other material used to build up or fill in land. ***—idioms.*** **fill in. 1.** *Informal.* To provide with information that is essential or newly acquired: *We filled in the police chief on the details of the theft.* **2.** To act as a substitute; stand in: *an understudy who filled in at the last minute.* **fill out. 1.** To complete (a form, for example) by providing required information: *Did you fill out the job application?* **2.** To become or make more fleshy: *The pup filled out to become a full-grown dog.* **fill (someone's) shoes.** To take someone's position or duties: *It will be hard to fill the manager's shoes.* [First written down before 1000 in Old English and spelled *fyllan.*]

fill•er (**fĭl′**ər) *n.* **1.** Something added to increase weight or size or to fill space: *They use cartoons and advertisements as filler in the newspaper.* **2.** A stack of loose papers used to fill a notebook or binder.

fil•let (**fĭl′**ĭt) *n.* **1.** A narrow band or ribbon, often worn as a headband. **2.** Also **fi•let** (fĭ **lā′** *or* **fĭl′**ā′). A boneless piece of meat or fish, especially the beef tenderloin. —*tr.v.* Also **filet** (fĭ **lā′** *or* **fĭ′**lā′). **fil•let•ed, fil•let•ing, fil•lets** also **fi•let•ed, fil•et•ing, fi•lets.** To slice, bone, or make into fillets: *I watched the fisherman fillet a trout.* [First written down before 1325 in Middle English and spelled *filet,* from Old French, diminutive of *fil,* thread, from Latin *fīlum.*]

fill-in (**fĭl′**ĭn′) *n. Informal.* A person or thing that serves as a substitute: *The understudy was a fill-in for the star.*

fill•ing (**fĭl′**ĭng) *n.* **1.** Something used to fill a space, cavity, or container: *a gold filling in a tooth.* **2.** An edible mixture used to fill pastries, sandwiches, or cakes: *a pie with a rhubarb filling.*

filling station *n.* A service station.

fil•lip (**fĭl′**əp) *n.* **1.** A snap made by pressing a finger against the thumb and suddenly releasing it. **2.** A mild incentive; a small stimulus.

Fill•more (**fĭl′**môr′), **Millard.** 1800–1874. The 13th President of the United States (1850–1853).

fil•ly (**fĭl′**ē) *n., pl.* **fil•lies.** A young female horse. [First written down in 1404 in Middle English and spelled *fyly,* from Old Norse *fylja.*]

film (fĭlm) *n.* **1.** A thin coating, layer, skin, or sheet: *a film of oil over the puddle; a film of dust on a tabletop.* **2.** A thin, flexible, transparent sheet, as of plastic, used in wrapping or packaging. **3.** A thin flexible roll or sheet of material coated with a substance that is sensitive to light, used to make photographs. **4.** A motion picture; a movie. —*v.* **filmed, film•ing, films.** —*tr.* **1.** To cover with or as if with a film. **2.** To make a movie of or based on: *We filmed porpoises swimming alongside our boat.* —*intr.* **1.** To become coated or obscured with or as if with a film: *My glasses filmed over when I came in from the cold.* **2.** To make or shoot scenes for a movie. [First written down about 1000 in Old English and spelled *filmen,* membrane, skin.]

film•strip (**fĭlm′**strĭp′) *n.* A strip of photographic film that is shown one frame at a time.

film•y (**fĭl′**mē) *adj.* **film•i•er, film•i•est. 1.** Of, resembling, or made of film; gauzy: *filmy curtains.* **2.** Covered by or as if by a film; hazy: *a filmy sky.* **—film′i•ly** *adv.* **—film′i•ness** *n.*

fil•ter (**fĭl′**tər) *n.* **1.** A device that strains solid particles from a liquid or gas passing through it: *A filter on the faucet collects particles of dirt from the water.* **2.** Paper, sand, screening, charcoal, felt, or other porous material used in such a device. **3.** A device that allows certain frequencies of waves to pass and blocks the passage of others. For example, filters on photographic lenses allow only certain colors of light to enter the camera. —*v.* **fil•tered, fil•ter•ing, fil•ters.** —*tr.* **1.** To pass (a liquid or gas) through a filter: *filter water for drinking.* **2.** To remove by passing through a filter: *The screen filters leaves from the water.* —*intr.* To flow through or as if through a filter: *Light filtered through the blinds.* [First written down before 1425 in Middle English and spelled *filtre,* from Medieval Latin *filtrum,* of Germanic origin.]

❑ *These sound alike:* **filter, philter** (love potion).

fil•ter•a•ble (**fĭl′**tər ə bəl *or* **fĭl′**trə bəl) also **fil•tra•ble** (**fĭl′**trə bəl) *adj.* **1.** Capable of being filtered or separated by filtering. **2.** Small enough to pass through a given pore size: *a filterable virus.*

filth (fĭlth) *n.* **1.** Foul or dirty matter or refuse. **2.** Something, such as language, considered obscene or immoral.

filth•y (**fĭl′**thē) *adj.* **filth•i•er, filth•i•est. 1.** Covered or smeared with filth; disgustingly dirty: *filthy streets strewn with litter.* **2.** Obscene: *filthy language.* **—filth′i•ly** *adv.* **—filth′i•ness** *n.*

fil•tra•ble (**fĭl′**trə bəl) *adj.* Variant of **filterable.**

fil•trate (**fĭl′**trāt′) *tr. & intr.v.* **fil•trat•ed, fil•trat•ing, fil•trates.** To put or go through a filter. —*n.* A liquid or another material that has passed through a filter.

fil•tra•tion (fĭl **trā′**shən) *n.* The act or process of filtering.

fin (fĭn) *n.* **1.** One of the movable parts of the body of a fish or other aquatic animal that is somewhat

Millard Fillmore

fin

Of a killer whale

ă	pat	oi	boy
ā	pay	ou	out
âr	care	o͝o	took
ä	father	o͞o	boot
ĕ	pet	ŭ	cut
ē	be	ûr	urge
ĭ	pit	th	thin
ī	pie	*th*	this
îr	pier	hw	whoop
ŏ	pot	zh	vision
ō	toe	ə	about
ô	paw	ɴ	*French* bon

finch
American goldfinch

finger painting

fir
Douglas fir

like a wing or fan and is used for propelling, steering, and balancing the body in water. **2.** Something shaped or used like a fin, as the tail of an aircraft. **3.** A rubber covering for the foot having a flat flexible extension, used in swimming and diving; a flipper. [First written down about 1000 in Old English and spelled *finn.*]

fi•na•gle (fə nā′gəl) *v.* **fi•na•gled, fi•na•gling, fi•na•gles.** *Informal.* —*tr.* **1.** To get or achieve by indirect, usually deceitful methods: *finagle free tickets to the museum.* **2.** To cheat or swindle: *The dishonest stockbrokers finagled their clients out of millions.* —*intr.* To use crafty or deceitful methods. **—fi•na′gler** *n.*

fi•nal (fī′nəl) *adj.* **1.** Forming or occurring at the end; last: *final preparations before leaving on a trip; the exciting final moments of a game.* **2.** Not to be reconsidered or changed; conclusive: *The judge's decision is final.* —*n.* **1.** The last or one of the last in a series of contests: *the finals of a spelling bee.* **2.** The last examination of an academic course: *Our final covered a whole year's work.* [First written down before 1338 in Middle English, from Latin *fīnālis,* from *fīnis,* end.]

fi•nal•e (fə năl′ē *or* fə nä′lē) *n.* The concluding part, especially of a musical composition.

fi•nal•ist (fī′nə lĭst) *n.* A contestant in the final session of a competition.

fi•nal•i•ty (fī năl′ĭ tē *or* fə năl′ĭ tē) *n., pl.* **fi•nal•i•ties.** The fact or condition of being final: *a decision given with finality; the finality of leaving.*

fi•nal•ize (fī′nə līz′) *tr.v.* **fi•nal•ized, fi•nal•iz•ing, fi•nal•iz•es.** To put into final form; complete or conclude: *finalize travel plans; finalize an agreement.* **—fi′nal•i•za′tion** (fī′nə lĭ zā′shən) *n.* **—fi′nal•iz′er** *n.*

fi•nal•ly (fī′nə lē) *adv.* **1.** At last; at the end: *After much delay, the taxi finally arrived.* **2.** Decisively; with finality: *That problem has been disposed of finally.*

fi•nance (fə năns′ *or* fī′năns′) *n.* **1.** The science of the management of money and other financial assets. **2.** The management of money, banking, investments, and credits: *A banker is a specialist in matters of finance.* **3. finances.** Monetary resources; funds: *My finances were getting low.* —*tr.v.* **fi•nanced, fi•nanc•ing, fi•nanc•es.** To provide or raise funds or capital for: *We financed our new car with a bank loan.*

finance company *n.* A company that makes loans to clients.

fi•nan•cial (fə năn′shəl *or* fī năn′shəl) *adj.* Of, relating to, or involving finance, finances, or financiers: *The treasurer is responsible for the financial affairs of our club.* **—fi•nan′cial•ly** *adv.*

fin•an•cier (fĭn′ən sîr′ *or* fə năn′sîr′) *n.* A person who is engaged in or an expert in large-scale financial affairs.

finch (fĭnch) *n.* Any of various songbirds having a short thick bill used for cracking seeds. The cardinal, canary, and house sparrow are finches.

find (fīnd) *tr.v.* **found** (found), **find•ing, finds. 1.** To come upon, often by accident: *I found a quarter on the sidewalk.* **2.a.** To come upon after a search: *At last I found my glasses.* **b.** To discover or ascertain through observation, experience, or study: *Can you find the solution to these problems?* **3.** To perceive to be after observation or experience: *found the book entertaining.* **4.** To recover the use of; regain: *I found my voice and shouted for help.* **5.** To succeed in reaching; arrive at: *The arrow found its mark.* **6.** To obtain or acquire by effort: *find the money to make the trip.* **7.** To decide on and make a declaration about: *The jury found the accused innocent of all charges.* **8.** To furnish; supply: *We can find a bed for you in the house tonight.* **9.** To perceive (oneself) to be in a specific location or condition: *The lost hikers found themselves in difficulty.* —*n.* Something that is found, especially an unexpectedly valuable discovery: *news of oil finds in Alaska.* ***—idiom.*** **find out. 1.** To discover (something), as through examination or inquiry: *I found out when she's arriving.* **2.** To detect the true nature or character of: *The impostor was soon found out.* [First written down about 725 in Old English and spelled *findan.*]

find•er (fīn′dər) *n.* **1.** A person who finds something. **2.** A device, usually an extra lens or telescope, used to help locate an object or area for a camera or large telescope.

find•ing (fīn′dĭng) *n.* **1.** Something that has been found: *The tomb was a great finding for the archaeologist.* **2.** A conclusion reached after an examination or investigation: *one of the findings in the cause of the plane crash.*

fine[1] (fīn) *adj.* **fin•er, fin•est. 1.** Of superior quality, skill, or appearance: *a fine day; a fine performance.* **2.** Very small in size, weight, or thickness: *fine paper.* **3.** Free from impurities: *a fine metal.* **4.** Very sharp; keen: *a fine point on a pencil.* **5.** Very thin; slender: *fine hair.* **6.** Showing delicate and careful artistry: *a fine painting; fine china.* **7.** Consisting of small particles; not coarse: *fine dust; the fine spray of a garden hose.* **8.** Subtle or precise: *the fine differences between a rabbit and a hare.* **9.** Characterized by refinement or elegance: *fine manners.* **10.** Being in a state of good health; quite well; *I'm fine, thank you.* —*adv.* **finer, finest.** *Informal.* **1.** In small pieces or parts: *Chop the onions fine.* **2.** Very well; splendidly: *The two dogs are getting along fine.* [First written down about 1250 in Middle English and spelled *fin,* from Old French, from Latin *fīnis,* end.] **—fine′ness** *n.*

fine[2] (fīn) *n.* A sum of money imposed as a penalty for an offense: *a $15 fine for overtime parking.* —*tr.v.* **fined, fin•ing, fines.** To impose a fine on: *fine a borrower who doesn't return library books.* [First written down before 1250 in Middle English and spelled *fin,* from Old French *fin,* end of legal case, settlement, compensation, from Latin *fīnis,* end.]

fine art *n.* Any of the art forms, such as painting, sculpture, and music, that are used to create works intended for beauty rather than utility. Often used in the plural.

fine-drawn (fīn′drôn′) *adj.* **1.** Drawn out to a slender threadlike state: *fine-drawn wire.* **2.** Subtly or precisely fashioned: *a fine-drawn analysis.*

fine•ly (fīn′lē) *adv.* **1.** In a fine manner; splendidly: *a finely groomed horse.* **2.** To a small point; discriminatingly. **3.** In small pieces or parts; minutely: *The recipe calls for finely chopped parsley.*

fin•er•y (fī′nə rē) *n., pl.* **fin•er•ies.** Elaborate adornment, especially fine clothing and accessories: *a portrait of the captain in naval finery.*

fi•nesse (fə nĕs′) *n.* **1.** Refinement and delicacy of performance, execution, or artisanship: *the finesse of an experienced glass blower.* **2.** Subtle handling of a situation; tact and skill: *the lawyer's finesse in forging an agreement between the partners.* —*tr.v.* **fi•nessed, fi•ness•ing, fi•ness•es.** To accomplish or handle with finesse. [First written down in 1528 in Modern English, from French, from *fin,* fine.]

fin•ger (fĭng′gər) *n.* **1.** One of the five parts that extend outward from the palm of the hand, especially one other than the thumb. **2.** The part of a glove that covers a finger. **3.** Something, such as an oblong peninsula, that resembles a finger: *a finger of land extending into the ocean.* **4.** The length or width of a finger: *Add about two fingers of juice.* —*tr.v.* **fin•gered, fin•ger•ing, fin•gers. 1.** To handle or feel with the fingers; touch: *stooped to finger the dry soil.* **2.** To play (a musical instrument) by using the fingers in a particular way. **3.** *Slang.* To inform on; point out as responsible: *finger a thief for the police.* —***idiom.*** **have one's fingers crossed** or **keep one's fingers crossed.** To hope for a successful or advantageous outcome: *I'm keeping my fingers crossed until our team has won the game.* [First written down about 825 in Old English.]

fin•ger•board (fĭng′gər bôrd′) *n.* A strip of wood on the neck of a stringed instrument against which the strings are pressed in playing.

finger hole *n.* **1.** Any of the holes on a wind instrument that cause a change in pitch when covered by a finger. **2.** A hole for a finger, as on a bowling ball.

fin•ger•ing (fĭng′gər ĭng) *n.* **1.** The technique used in playing a musical instrument with the fingers: *The fingering for the flute is different from that for the clarinet.* **2.** The symbols on a musical score that show which fingers are to be used in playing.

fin•ger•nail (fĭng′gər nāl′) *n.* The thin layer of horny transparent material that covers the back of the tip of each finger.

finger painting *n.* **1.** The technique of painting by applying color to moistened paper with the fingers. **2.** A painting made with this technique.

fin•ger•print (fĭng′gər prĭnt′) *n.* An impression of the curves formed by the ridges in the skin that cover the tips of the fingers, especially such an impression made in ink and used as a means of identification. —*tr.v.* **fin•ger•print•ed, fin•ger•print•ing, fin•ger•prints.** To take the fingerprints of.

fin•ger•tip (fĭng′gər tĭp′) *n.* The extreme tip or end of a finger.

fin•i•cal (fĭn′ĭ kəl) *adj.* Finicky. —**fin′i•cal•ly** *adv.*

fin•ick•y (fĭn′ĭ kē) *adj.* Very fussy; fastidious: *finicky about certain food.*

fin•is (fĭn′ĭs *or* fē nē′) *n.* The end; the conclusion.

fin•ish (fĭn′ĭsh) *v.* **fin•ished, fin•ish•ing, fin•ish•es.** —*tr.* **1.** To arrive at or attain the end of: *finish a race.* **2.** To bring to an end; complete: *Finish your homework before going outside.* **3.** To consume all of; use up: *finish a bottle of ketchup.* **4.** To bring to a desired or required state: *correct the spelling to finish a book report.* **5.** To give (a surface) a desired texture: *finish a floor with clear varnish.* —*intr.* **1.** To come to an end; stop: *Call me when the washing machine finishes.* **2.** To reach the end of a task, course, or relationship: *The runner finished well ahead of the pack.* —*n.* **1.** The conclusion of something; the end: *The finish of the play was exciting.* **2.a.** The surface or texture produced by preparing or coating something: *a shiny finish to the waxed floor.* **b.** The material used in surfacing or finishing something: *Paint is a good finish for wood.* **3.** Completeness, refinement, or smoothness of execution; polish: *The musicians lacked finish.* [First written down before 1375 in Middle English and spelled *finischen,* from Latin *fīnīre,* from *fīnis,* end.] —**fin′ish•er** *n.*

fin•ished (fĭn′ĭsht) *adj.* **1.** High skilled or accomplished: *a finished actor.* **2.** Showing a high degree of skill or polish: *a finished essay.*

fi•nite (fī′nīt′) *adj.* **1.** Having bounds; limited: *a finite list of choices.* **2.a.** That can be reached by counting: *The number of whole numbers between 1 and 100 is finite.* **b.** Not infinite or infinitesimal: *a finite sum; a finite line segment.* **3.** In grammar, limited by person, number, and tense; for example, *am, is,* and *are* are finite verb forms as distinguished from *being* or *been.* [First written down in 1410 in Middle English and spelled *finit,* from Latin *fīnītus,* past participle of *fīnīre,* to limit, from *fīnis,* end.] —**fi′nite•ly** *adv.* —**fi′nite•ness** *n.*

Fin•land (fĭn′lənd). A country of northern Europe on the **Gulf of Finland,** an arm of the Baltic Sea east of Sweden. It declared its independence from Russia in 1917. Helsinki is the capital and the largest city. Population, 4,893,748.

Finn (fĭn) *n.* A native or inhabitant of Finland.

fin•nan had•die (fĭn′ən hăd′ē) *n.* Smoked haddock.

finned (fĭnd) *adj.* Having a fin or fins: *a finned whale.*

Finn•ish (fĭn′ĭsh) *adj.* Of or relating to Finland or its people, language, or culture. —*n.* The language of the Finns.

fin•ny (fĭn′ē) *adj.* **fin•ni•er, fin•ni•est. 1.** Having a fin or fins: *a finny creature.* **2.** Resembling a fin. **3.** Of, relating to, or full of fish.

fiord (fyôrd) *n.* Variant of **fjord.**

fir (fûr) *n.* **1.** Any of various evergreen trees having flat needles and bearing cones. **2.** The wood of such a tree. [First written down about 1300 in Middle English, probably of Scandinavian origin.]
❑ *These sound alike:* **fir, fur** (pelt).

fire (fīr) *n.* **1.** The flame, light, and heat given off when something is burning: *The fire was bright enough to read by.* **2.** Something that is burning, especially a pile of burning fuel, such as wood: *We started a fire in the fireplace.* **3.** Burning intensity of feeling; ardor: *The veterans played with the fire of rookies.* **4.** The discharge of firearms: *heard the fire of cannon.* —*v.* **fired, fir•ing, fires.** —*tr.* **1.** To cause to burn; ignite: *A match fired this pile of leaves.* **2.** To maintain or fuel a fire in: *fire a furnace with oil.* **3.** To bake in a kiln: *fire clay pots to harden them.* **4.** To arouse; stimulate: *The book fired my interest in science.* **5.** To discharge (a firearm) or launch (a missile): *fire a cannon; fire a rocket.* **6.** *Informal.* To hurl with force and speed: *fire a fast ball across the plate.* **7.** *Informal.* To discharge from a job; dismiss: *The company fired several workers today.* —*intr.* **1.** To shoot a weapon: *The soldiers fired into the air as a warning.* **2.** To ignite fuel, as in an engine: *The car motor will not fire properly when it's wet.* —***idioms.*** **on fire. 1.** Burning; ablaze. **2.** Filled with enthusiasm or excitement: *The team was on fire after tying the game.* **under fire.** Under attack: *The new regulation came under fire.* [First written down about 725 in Old English and spelled *fȳr.*]

fire alarm *n.* **1.** The signal, especially a loud noise, that warns of fire. **2.** A device, such as a siren, that sets off such a warning.

fire ant *n.* Any of several ants originally of South America that build large mounds and can give a painful burning sting.

fire•arm (fīr′ärm′) *n.* A weapon, especially a pistol or rifle, that uses an explosive charge to propel a projectile.

fire•ball (fīr′bôl′) *n.* **1.** The hot, brightly glowing cloud of dust and gases formed by a nuclear explosion. **2.** A very bright meteor. **3.** Something that resembles a burning ball, such as a ball of lightning.

fire•boat (fīr′bōt′) *n.* A boat equipped to put out fires in harbors and on ships.

fire•brand (fīr′brănd′) *n.* **1.** A person who stirs up trouble or kindles a revolt. **2.** A piece of burning wood.

fire•bug (fīr′bŭg′) *n.* *Informal.* A person who commits arson; an arsonist.

fire•crack•er (fīr′krăk′ər) *n.* A small explosive charge and a fuse in a heavy paper casing, exploded to make noise, as at celebrations.

fire•damp (fīr′dămp′) *n.* A gas that occurs naturally in coal mines and forms a dangerously explosive mixture with air.

fire•dog (fīr′dôg′ *or* fīr′dŏg′) *n.* An andiron.

fire drill *n.* An exercise in the use of firefighting

fireboat

ă	pat	oi	boy
ā	pay	ou	out
âr	care	ŏŏ	took
ä	father	ōō	boot
ĕ	pet	ŭ	cut
ē	be	ûr	urge
ĭ	pit	th	thin
ī	pie	*th*	this
îr	pier	hw	whoop
ŏ	pot	zh	vision
ō	toe	ə	about
ô	paw	N	*French* bon

fire escape

equipment or the evacuation of a building in case of a fire.

fire engine *n.* Any of various large motor vehicles that carry firefighters and equipment to a fire.

fire escape *n.* A metal stairway or ladder attached to the outside of a building and used as an emergency exit in case of a fire.

fire extinguisher *n.* A portable container filled with chemicals to spray on a small fire to put it out.

fire•fight•er also **fire fighter** (fīr′fī′tər) *n.* A member of a fire department who fights fires. —**fire′fight′ing** *n.*

fire•fly (fīr′flī′) *n.* Any of various beetles that fly at night and give off a flashing light from the rear part of the body; a lightning bug.

fire•house (fīr′hous′) *n.* A fire station.

fire hydrant *n.* A large upright pipe with a nozzle for drawing water from a water main.

fire•light (fīr′līt′) *n.* The light from a fire, as in a fireplace.

fire•man (fīr′mən) *n.* **1.** A firefighter. **2.** A man who tends fires, as in a steam engine; a stoker. **3.** An enlisted man in the U.S. Navy engaged in the operation of engineering machinery.

Fi•ren•ze (fē rĕn′dzĕ). Florence.

fire•place (fīr′plās′) *n.* **1.** An open recess in a room for holding a fire at the base of a chimney; a hearth. **2.** A structure, usually of stone or brick, for holding a fire outdoors.

fire•plug (fīr′plŭg′) *n.* A fire hydrant.

fire•pow•er (fīr′pou′ər) *n.* **1.** The capacity, as of a weapon, military unit, or position, for delivering fire. **2.** The ability to deliver fire against an enemy in combat.

fire•proof (fīr′pro͞of′) *adj.* Made of material that is impervious or resistant to fire: *Many fireproof buildings are made of concrete.* —*tr.v.* **fire•proofed, fire•proof•ing, fire•proofs.** To make fireproof.

fire screen *n.* A metal screen placed in front of an open fireplace to catch sparks.

fire•side (fīr′sīd′) *n.* **1.** The area surrounding a fireplace or hearth: *We sat about the fireside and chatted.* **2.** A home.

fire station *n.* A building for firefighters and firefighting equipment.

fire tower *n.* A tower from which a lookout watches for fires, especially forest fires.

fire•trap (fīr′trăp′) *n.* A building that can catch fire easily or is difficult to escape from in the event of fire.

fire truck *n.* A fire engine.

fire•wall *n.* A fireproof wall used as a barrier to prevent the spread of fire.

fire•wood (fīr′wo͝od′) *n.* Wood used as fuel.

fire•work (fīr′wûrk′) *n.* **1.** An explosive device, often attached to a small rocket, set off to create bright lights and loud noises for amusement. **2. fireworks.** A display of such devices.

fir•ing line (fīr′ĭng) *n.* **1.** The line of positions from which gunfire is directed against a target. **2.** The foremost position in a pursuit or an activity.

firing pin *n.* The part of the bolt of a firearm that strikes the primer and causes the charge of a projectile to explode.

firm[1] (fûrm) *adj.* **firm•er, firm•est. 1.** Resistant to externally applied pressure: *a firm mattress; an athlete's firm muscles.* **2.** Securely fixed in place; not easily moved: *a firm fence post set in concrete.* **3.** Showing or having resolution or determination: *a firm voice; a firm belief.* **4.** Constant; steadfast: *a firm friendship; a firm partnership.* **5.** Not subject to change; fixed and definite: *a firm price on the car.* **6.** Strong and sure: *a firm grip on the handlebars.* —*tr. & intr.v.* **firmed, firm•ing, firms.** To make or become firm: *One must firm the dirt around newly potted plants. The jello firmed quickly.* —*adv.* **firm•er, firm•est.** Without wavering; resolutely: *stood firm.* [First written down about 1378 in Middle English and spelled *ferm,* from Latin *firmus.*] —**firm′ly** *adv.* —**firm′ness** *n.*

firm[2] (fûrm) *n.* A business partnership of two or more persons. [First written down in 1744 in Modern English, from Italian *firma,* from *firmare,* to ratify by signature, from Latin *firmāre,* to confirm, from *firmus,* firm.]

fir•ma•ment (fûr′mə mənt) *n.* The heavens; the sky. [First written down about 1250 in Middle English, from Latin *firmāmentum,* support, from *firmāre,* to strengthen.]

first (fûrst) *n.* **1.** The ordinal number matching the number one in a series. **2.** A person or thing coming, occurring, or ranking before or above all others. **3.** The beginning; the outset: *At first he was afraid of the water, but now he enjoys swimming.* **4.** The transmission gear used to produce the lowest range of speeds in a motor vehicle. —*adj.* **1.** Corresponding in order to the number one. **2.** Coming before all others in order or location: *January, the first month of the year; the first chapter of the book.* **3.** Ranking above all others, as in importance or quality: *first in her class.* **4.** Being highest in pitch or carrying the principal part: *first soprano; first trumpet.* **5.** Of or relating to the transmission gear used to produce the lowest range of speeds in a motor vehicle. —*adv.* **1.** Before or above all others: *Who will speak first?* **2.** For the first time: *When did you first meet the new neighbors?* **3.** Rather; preferably: *The musicians said they would quit first and not accept lower pay.* [First written down in 963 in Old English and spelled *fyrst.*]

first aid *n.* Emergency care given to an injured or sick person before professional medical care is available. —**first′-aid′** *adj.*

first base *n.* **1.** In baseball, the base that must be touched first by a batter who has hit a fair ball, located to the right as one looks toward the pitcher from home plate. **2.** The position played by the first baseman. **3.** *Slang.* The first step or stage toward completion or success: *The reform bill never got to first base.*

first baseman *n.* The baseball player defending the area near first base.

first-born (fûrst′bôrn′) *adj.* First in order of birth; born first. —*n.* The child in a family who is born first.

first class *n.* **1.** The first, highest, or best group in a system of classification. **2.** The best and most expensive class of accommodations on a train, a ship, or an airplane. **3.** A class of mail including letters, postcards, and packages sealed against inspection. —**first class** *adv.*

first-class (fûrst′klăs′) *adj.* **1.** Of the first, highest, or best group in a system of classification: *first-class mail; a first-class restaurant.* **2.** Of the foremost excellence or highest quality; first-rate: *a first-class author.*

first-de•gree burn (fûrst′dĭ grē′) *n.* A mild burn that produces redness of the skin.

first•hand (fûrst′hănd′) *adj.* Received from the original source: *firsthand information.* —**first′hand′** *adv.*

first lady *n.* **1.** Often **First Lady.** The wife or hostess of the chief executive of a country, state, or city. **2.** The foremost woman of a profession or an art: *the first lady of modern dance.*

first lieutenant *n.* An officer in the U.S. Army, Air Force, or Marine Corps ranking above a second lieutenant and below a captain.

first•ly (fûrst′lē) *adv.* In the first place; to begin with.

first person *n.* **1.** A group of words or word forms, such as verbs and pronouns, indicating the speaker or writer of the sentence in which they appear. *I* and *we* are pronouns in the first person. **2.** The style of writing in which forms in the first person are used: *a novel written in the first person.*

first-rate (fûrst′rāt′) *adj.* Foremost in quality, rank, or importance: *a first-rate hotel; a first-rate mechanic.* —*adv. Informal.* Excellently; very well.

first-string (fûrst′strĭng′) *adj.* In sports, of, relating to, or being a regular member of a team rather than a substitute: *the first-string quarterback.*

firth (fûrth) *n.* A long narrow inlet of the sea. [First written down about 1425 in Middle English, from Old Norse *fjördhr.*]

fis•cal (fĭs′kəl) *adj.* **1.** Of or relating to the treasury or finances of a government: *Carefully controlled spending is the fiscal policy during a slowdown of business.* **2.** Of or relating to finance or finances: *The accountant is our fiscal agent.* —**fis′cal•ly** *adv.*

fiscal year *n.* A period of twelve months for which organization plans the use of its funds.

fish (fĭsh) *n., pl.* **fish** or **fish•es. 1.a.** Any of numerous cold-blooded animals that live in water and have a backbone, gills for breathing, and a vertical tail. Most fish have scales and a skeleton of hard bone, but sharks and some others have an elastic skeleton of cartilage. **b.** An animal that looks like a fish and swims in water, such as the porpoise or the whale. **c.** A jellyfish, starfish, or shellfish. **2.** The flesh of a fish used as food. —*v.* **fished, fish•ing, fish•es.** —*intr.* **1.** To catch or try to catch fish. **2.** To look for something by feeling one's way: *I fished in my pocket for a quarter.* **3.** To seek something in a sly or indirect way: *was always fishing for compliments.* —*tr.* **1.a.** To catch or try to catch (fish). **b.** To catch or try to catch fish in: *We fished the lake for several hours.* **2.** To catch or pull as if fishing: *fish the keys out of the drawer.* —***idiom.*** **like a fish out of water.** Completely unfamiliar with one's surroundings or activity: *was like a fish out of water in her new profession.*

fish and chips *pl.n.* Fried fillets of fish and French-fried potatoes.

fish•er (fĭsh′ər) *n.* **1.** A person or ship that fishes. **2.a.** A North American meat-eating mammal related to the mink and weasel, having thick dark-brown fur. **b.** The fur of this mammal.

❑ *These sound alike:* **fisher, fissure** (crack).

fish•er•man (fĭsh′ər mən) *n.* A person who fishes as an occupation or for sport.

fish•er•y (fĭsh′ə rē) *n., pl.* **fish•er•ies. 1.** The industry or occupation of catching, processing, and selling fish or other aquatic animals. **2.** A place where fish or other aquatic animals are caught: *the cod and haddock fisheries of the northwest Atlantic.* **3.** A hatchery for fish.

fish farm *n.* A commercial facility having tanks or ponds where fish are raised for food.

fish hawk *n.* The osprey.

fish•hook (fĭsh′ho͝ok′) *n.* A barbed hook for catching fish.

fish•ing (fĭsh′ĭng) *n.* The act, occupation, or sport of catching fish.

fishing rod *n.* A rod of wood, steel, or fiberglass used with a line for catching fish.

fish•mon•ger (fĭsh′mŭng′gər *or* fĭsh′mŏng′gər) *n. Chiefly British.* A person who sells fish.

fish•net (fĭsh′nĕt′) *n.* **1.** Netting used to catch fish. **2.** A mesh fabric resembling such netting.

fish•pond (fĭsh′pŏnd′) *n.* A pond containing or stocked with edible fish.

fish stick *n.* An oblong piece of breaded fish fillet.

fish story *n. Informal.* A boastful story that is probably not true.

fish•wife (fĭsh′wīf′) *n.* **1.** A woman who sells fish. **2.** A woman regarded as coarse or abusive.

fish•y (fĭsh′ē) *adj.* **fish•i•er, fish•i•est. 1.** Tasting, resembling, or smelling of fish. **2.** Cold or expressionless: *a fishy stare.* **3.** *Informal.* Inspiring doubt or suspicion: *something fishy about that excuse.* —**fish′i•ness** *n.*

fis•sion (fĭsh′ən) *n.* **1.** The act or process of splitting into parts. **2.** A reaction in which an atomic nucleus collides with a neutron and splits into two fragments, releasing tremendous energy; nuclear fission. **3.** A reproductive process in which a single cell splits to form two independent cells that later grow to full size. [First written down in 1841 in Modern English, from Latin *fissiō*, a cleaving, from *fissus*, past participle of *findere*, to split.]

fis•sion•a•ble (fĭsh′ə nə bəl) *adj.* Capable of undergoing fission: *Uranium and plutonium are fissionable elements.*

fis•sure (fĭsh′ər) *n.* A long narrow crack or opening, as in the face of a rock. [First written down before 1400 in Middle English, from Latin *fissūra*, from *fissus*, past participle of *findere*, to split.]

❑ *These sound alike:* **fissure, fisher** (one that fishes).

fist (fĭst) *n.* The hand closed tightly with the fingers bent against the palm. [First written down before 900 in Old English and spelled *fȳst.*]

fist•fight (fĭst′fīt′) *n.* A fight with the bare fists.

fist•ful (fĭst′fo͝ol′) *n., pl.* **fist•fuls.** The amount a fist can hold.

fist•i•cuffs (fĭs′tĭ kŭfs′) *pl.n.* **1.** A fistfight. **2.** Boxing.

fis•tu•la (fĭs′chə lə) *n., pl.* **fis•tu•las** or **fis•tu•lae** (fĭs′chə lē′). An abnormal passage from an abscess, a cavity, or an organ to the surface of the body or to another hollow organ, caused by a disease or wound.

fit¹ (fĭt) *v.* **fit•ted** or **fit, fit•ted, fit•ting, fits.** —*tr.* **1.** To be the proper size and shape for: *Do the shoes fit you?* **2.** To cause to be the proper size and shape: *The tailor fitted the new pants perfectly.* **3.** To be appropriate for or suitable to: *A dignified appearance fitted the judge's high office.* **4.** To equip or provide: *We fitted the car with new tires.* **5.** To provide a place or time for: *Can you fit all of your books in one bag?* —*intr.* **1.** To be the proper size and shape: *If the key fits, open the door.* **2.** To be suited; agree; belong: *Their jolly mood fit in with the joyous occasion.* —*adj.* **fit•ter, fit•test. 1.** Suited, adapted, or acceptable for a given purpose or circumstance: *Late at night is hardly a fit time for a meeting. The dinner was not fit to eat.* **2.** Appropriate; proper: *Do as you see fit.* **3.** Physically sound; healthy: *Fresh air and exercise help keep people fit.* —*n.* **1.** The state, quality, or way of being fitted: *a perfect fit.* **2.** The way something fits: *The fit of the sweater was too tight.* [First written down before 1400 in Middle English and spelled *fitten.*]

fit² (fĭt) *n.* **1.** A seizure or convulsion, especially one caused by epilepsy. **2.** A sudden appearance of a disease or a symptom of a disease: *a fit of coughing.* **3.** A sudden outburst of emotion: *a fit of jealousy.* **4.** A sudden period of vigorous activity: *a fit of housekeeping.* —***idiom.*** **by fits and starts** or **in fits and starts.** With irregular intervals of action and inaction; intermittently: *practice the piano by fits and starts.* [First written down before 1376 in Middle English and spelled *fitte*, hardship, probably from Old English *fitt*, struggle.]

fitch (fĭch) *n.* **1.** The polecat of Europe. **2.** The fur of this mammal.

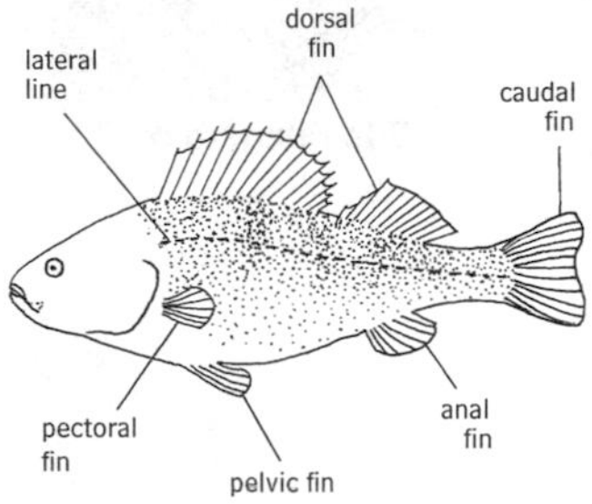

fish

fisher

ă	**pat**	oi	**boy**
ā	**pay**	ou	**out**
âr	**care**	o͝o	**took**
ä	**father**	o͞o	**boot**
ĕ	**pet**	ŭ	**cut**
ē	**be**	ûr	**urge**
ĭ	**pit**	th	**thin**
ī	**pie**	*th*	**this**
îr	**pier**	hw	**whoop**
ŏ	**pot**	zh	**vision**
ō	**toe**	ə	**about**
ô	**paw**	N	*French* **bon**

Ella Fitzgerald

Regional Note: fix

The phrase *fixing to* is used in the South to mean "on the verge of or in preparation for (doing a given thing)." The phrase can refer only to events that immediately follow the point in time that the speaker is referring to. You cannot say *I'm fixing to go to college in a few years*, but you would say *I'm fixing to leave in a few minutes*.

flag[1]
Flag of the Olympic games

fit•ful (fĭt′fəl) *adj.* Occurring in or marked by intermittent bursts, as of activity; irregular: *fitful coughing; fitful sleep.* **—fit′ful•ly** *adv.* **—fit′ful•ness** *n.*

fit•ness (fĭt′nĭs) *n.* The state or condition of being physically fit, especially as the result of exercise and proper nutrition.

fit•ting (fĭt′ĭng) *adj.* Being in keeping with a situation; appropriate: *a fitting remark.* *—n.* **1.** The act of trying on clothes whose fit is being adjusted. **2.** A small part for a machine or mechanical device: *a box of nuts, washers, joints, and other fittings.*

Fitz•ger•ald (fĭts jĕr′əld), **Ella.** Born 1918. American jazz singer known for her interpretation of ballads.

five (fīv) *n.* **1.** The number, written 5, that is equal to 4 + 1. **2.** The fifth in a set or sequence. [First written down about 1000 in Old English and spelled *fīf*.]

five-and-dime (fīv′ən dīm′) *n.* A five-and-ten.

five-and-ten (fīv′ən tĕn′) *n.* A store selling a wide variety of inexpensive articles.

Five Nations *pl.n.* The Iroquois confederacy as it originally existed, consisting of the Cayuga, Mohawk, Oneida, Onondaga, and Seneca peoples.

fix (fĭks) *v.* **fixed, fix•ing, fix•es.** *—tr.* **1.** To place securely; make stable or firm: *fix a post in the ground.* **2.** To treat (a photographic image) with a chemical that prevents it from fading or changing color. **3.** To direct steadily: *We fixed our eyes on the screen.* **4.** To establish definitely; specify: *fix a time for the meeting; fix a price on a house.* **5.** To attribute; assign: *A witness fixed the blame on the careless driver.* **6.** To set right; repair: *fix a car; fix a misspelling.* **7.** To make ready; prepare: *We are fixing dinner for ourselves.* **8.** *Informal.* To get even with; take revenge upon. **9.** *Informal.* To influence the outcome of by unlawful means: *fix a horse race.* *—intr.* **1.** To direct one's attention or concentration: *Let's fix on finding a solution to the problem.* **2.** To become rigid or firm: *The plaster will fix in a few hours.* *—n.* **1.** The act of adjusting, correcting, or repairing. **2.** The position, as of a ship or an aircraft, determined by visual observations or by radio signals: *get a fix on a disabled ship.* **3.** A difficult or embarrassing situation; a predicament: *We lost our oars and were in a fix out in the middle of the lake.* **4.** *Slang.* An intravenous injection of a narcotic. ***—idiom.* fix up. 1.** To improve the appearance or condition of: *They fixed up the old house with a fresh coat of paint.* **2.** To supply; provide: *We fixed up a bed for our guests.* [First written down about 1370 in Middle English and spelled *fixen*, from Latin *fīxus*, past participle of *fīgere*, to fasten.] **—fix′a•ble** *adj.* **—fix•er** *n.* —SEE NOTE.

fix•a•tion (fĭk sā′shən) *n.* **1.** The act or process of fixing. **2.** An obsessive preoccupation: *The child had a fixation on a particular blanket.*

fix•a•tive (fĭk′sə tĭv) *n.* A substance used to treat something and make it permanent or resistant to change: *Fixative keeps chalk drawings from smudging.*

fixed (fĭkst) *adj.* **1.** Firmly in position; stationary: *a row of fixed desks.* **2.** Not subject to change or variation; constant: *living on a fixed income.* **3.** Firmly held; steady: *a fixed stare; old and fixed ideas.* **4.** Illegally prearranged as to outcome: *a fixed election.*

fixed star *n.* A star so distant from Earth that it appears not to change position in relation to other stars. Its movements can be measured only by careful observations over long periods of time.

fix•ings (fĭk′sĭngz) *pl.n.* *Informal.* Accessories; trimmings: *a Thanksgiving dinner with all the fixings.*

fix•ture (fĭks′chər) *n.* **1.** Something that is installed in a permanent location: *a plumbing fixture; a lighting fixture.* **2.** A person or thing that stays or seems to stay in one place: *After 30 years of teaching, he seems like a fixture at the middle school.*

fizz (fĭz) *intr.v.* **fizzed, fizz•ing, fizz•es.** To make a hissing or bubbling sound: *Baking soda will fizz if you pour water on it.* *—n.* **1.** A hissing or bubbling sound: *the fizz of soda.* **2.** Effervescence. **—fizz′y** *adj.*

fiz•zle (fĭz′əl) *intr.v.* **fiz•zled, fiz•zling, fiz•zles. 1.** To make a hissing or sputtering sound: *The hot coals of our campfire fizzled in the rain.* **2.** *Informal.* To fail or end weakly, especially after a hopeful beginning. *—n.* *Informal.* A failure; a fiasco.

fjord or **fiord** (fyôrd) *n.* A long narrow inlet from the sea between steep slopes. [First written down in 1674 in Modern English, from Old Norse *fjördhr*.]

fl or **fl.** *abbr.* An abbreviation of: **1.** Fluid. **2.** Flourished.

FL *abbr.* An abbreviation of Florida.

Fla. *abbr.* An abbreviation of Florida.

flab (flăb) *n.* Soft fatty body tissue.

flab•ber•gast (flăb′ər găst′) *tr.v.* **flab•ber•gast•ed, flab•ber•gast•ing, flab•ber•gasts.** To cause to be overcome with astonishment; astound: *The news flabbergasted us.*

flab•by (flăb′ē) *adj.* **flab•bi•er, flab•bi•est.** Lacking firmness; flaccid: *getting flabby around the waist.* **—flab′bi•ly** *adv.* **—flab′bi•ness** *n.*

flac•cid (flăk′sĭd *or* flăs′ĭd) *adj.* Lacking firmness, resilience, or muscle tone. **—flac•cid′i•ty, flac′cid•ness** *n.* **—flac′cid•ly** *adv.*

flac•on (flăk′ən *or* flăk′ŏn′) *n.* A small, often decorative bottle with a stopper.

flag[1] (flăg) *n.* A piece of cloth of a particular color or design, used as a symbol for a nation, a signal, or an emblem for a monarch or an organization: *flags of member nations flying at the United Nations.* *—tr.v.* **flagged, flag•ging, flags. 1.** To signal with or as if with a flag: *flagged a motorist to get help.* **2.** To signal to stop: *flag down a passing car.* [First written down in 1530 in Modern English.]

flag[2] (flăg) *n.* An iris or a similar plant. [First written down before 1387 in Middle English and spelled *flagge*, reed, of Scandinavian origin.]

flag[3] (flăg) *intr.v.* **flagged, flag•ging, flags.** To lose vigor or strength; weaken: *Our spirits flagged when we saw how much we had to do.* [First written down in 1545 in Modern English and spelled *flag*, to flop about weakly, possibly of Scandinavian origin; akin to Old Norse *flögra*.]

flag[4] (flăg) *n.* A flagstone. [First written down about 1415 in Middle English, of Scandinavian origin.]

Flag Day *n.* June 14, observed in commemoration of the adoption in 1777 of the official U.S. flag.

fla•gel•la (flə jĕl′ə) *n.* Plural of **flagellum.**

flag•el•late (flăj′ə lāt′) *tr.v.* **flag•el•lat•ed, flag•el•lat•ing, flag•el•lates.** To whip or flog. *—adj.* (flăj′ə lĭt *or* flăj′ə lāt′). **1.** Having a flagellum, as certain one-celled organisms. **2.** Resembling a flagellum. *—n.* (flăj′ə lĭt *or* flăj′ə lāt′). A single-celled organism, such as a euglena, having one or more flagella used for moving through the water and for obtaining food. **—flag′el•la′tion** *n.*

fla•gel•lum (flə jĕl′əm) *n., pl.* **fla•gel•la** (flə jĕl′ə). A slender tail or part that extends from some one-celled organisms, such as bacteria and protozoa, usually whipped back and forth as a means of moving.

flag•eo•let (flăj′ə lĕt′ *or* flăj′ə lā′) *n.* A musical instrument similar to a recorder, having a mouthpiece at one end and six finger holes.

flag•man (flăg′mən) *n.* A person who signals with or carries a flag: *a flagman on road construction.*

flag•on (flăg′ən) *n.* **1.** A large container for liquids, usually of metal or pottery, having a handle, a spout, and often a lid. **2.** The amount of liquid that such a container can hold. [First written down in 1459 in Middle English, from Late Latin *flascō*, bottle.]
flag•pole (flăg′pōl′) *n.* A pole on which a flag is raised.
fla•grant (flā′grənt) *adj.* Conspicuously offensive; notorious or scandalous: *a flagrant misuse of public funds.* **—fla′grant•ly** *adv.*
flag•ship (flăg′shĭp′) *n.* A ship that carries a fleet or squadron commander and bears the commander's flag.
flag•staff (flăg′stăf′) *n.* A flagpole.
flag•stone (flăg′stōn′) *n.* A flat stone slab used as a paving material.
flail (flāl) *n.* A tool for threshing grain by hand, having a long wooden handle and a shorter and heavier free-swinging stick attached to its end. *—tr. & intr. v.* **flailed, flail•ing, flails. 1.** To beat or strike with or as if with a flail: *He flailed the horse with the reins.* **2.** To wave or swing vigorously: *I flailed my arms to get their attention.*
flair (flâr) *n.* A natural talent or aptitude; a knack: *a flair for imitating voices.*
❑ *These sound alike:* **flair, flare** (blaze).
flak (flăk) *n.* **1.a.** Antiaircraft artillery. **b.** The bursting shells fired from such artillery: *many planes hit by flak.* **2.** *Informal.* Criticism; opposition: *Our plan got a lot of flak.* [First written down in 1938 in Modern English, from German, from *Fl(ieger)a(bwehr)k(anone)*, aircraft-defense gun.]
flake (flāk) *n.* **1.** A small thin piece of something: *Large flakes of paint had fallen on the floor.* **2.** A snowflake. **3.** *Slang.* A person who is somewhat eccentric. *—intr.v.* **flaked, flak•ing, flakes.** To come off in flakes; chip off: *The paint is flaking off the fence.*
flak•y (flā′kē) *adj.* **flak•i•er, flak•i•est. 1.** Forming or tending to form flakes or thin crisp fragments: *flaky crackers.* **2.** *Slang.* Eccentric; odd. **—flak′i•ly** *adv.* **—flak′i•ness** *n.*
flam•boy•ant (flăm boi′ənt) *adj.* **1.** Very elaborate; ornate: *a flamboyant style of writing.* **2.** Exaggerated or showy in style or manner: *With many large gestures, the actor gave a flamboyant performance.* **3.** Brilliant; vivid: *flamboyant colors.* **—flam•boy′ance, flam•boy′an•cy** *n.* **—flam•boy′ant•ly** *adv.*
flame (flām) *n.* **1.** A hot glowing mass of burning gas or vapor. **2.** The condition of active blazing combustion: *burst into flame.* **3.** A burning or intense feeling; a passion: *a flame of enthusiasm.* **4.** *Informal.* A sweetheart. *—intr.v.* **flamed, flam•ing, flames. 1.** To burn brightly; blaze: *The logs flamed as I fanned them.* **2.** To flush; acquire color: *My cheeks flamed with embarrassment.*
fla•men•co (flə mĕng′kō) *n., pl.* **fla•men•cos. 1.** A dance style of the Spanish Gypsies that is characterized by forceful rhythms and the clicking of castanets. **2.** The guitar music for this dance style.
flame•throw•er (flām′thrō′ər) *n.* A weapon that shoots out a steady stream of burning fuel.
flam•ing (flā′mĭng) *adj.* **1.** On fire; blazing: *flaming logs.* **2.** Resembling a flame in brilliance, color, or form: *flaming red and yellow autumn leaves.*
fla•min•go (flə mĭng′gō) *n., pl.* **fla•min•gos** or **fla•min•goes.** Any of several long-legged, long-necked tropical wading birds having reddish or pinkish feathers. [First written down in 1565 in Modern English, probably from Old Provençal *flamenc*, from Latin *flamma*, flame.]
flam•ma•ble (flăm′ə bəl) *adj.* Easily ignited and capable of burning rapidly: *Kerosene is flammable.*
Flan•ders (flăn′dərz). A historical region of northwest Europe including parts of northern France, western Belgium, and southwest Netherlands along the North Sea. The region suffered heavy damage during both World Wars.
flange (flănj) *n.* A projecting rim or edge, as on a wheel or a pipe, used to strengthen an object, hold it in place, or attach it to something.
flank (flăngk) *n.* **1.a.** The side of the body between the ribs and the hip. **b.** A cut of meat from this part of an animal. **2.** A side part: *The flank of the mountain rose steeply from the valley.* **3.** The right or left side of a military formation or a fort. *—tr.v.* **flanked, flank•ing, flanks. 1.** To attack or maneuver around the flank of: *flank an opposing force.* **2.** To occupy a place at the side of: *Two chairs flanked the fireplace.* [First written down before 1100 in Old English and spelled *flanc*, from Old French, of Germanic origin.]
flank•er (flăng′kər) *n.* **1.** A person or thing that protects a flank. **2.** In football, a halfback stationed to the side of the linemen, used chiefly as a pass receiver.
flan•nel (flăn′əl) *n.* **1.** A soft cotton cloth woven with a nap, used for sheets, light blankets, and baby clothes; flannelette. **2.** A soft woolen cloth woven with a nap, used especially in making coats, jackets, and trousers. **3. flannels.** Trousers and other clothes made out of flannel.
flan•nel•ette (flăn′ə lĕt′) *n.* Soft cotton flannel.
flap (flăp) *n.* **1.** A flat piece attached along one side only: *the flap of a pocket.* **2.** A section of the rear edge of an aircraft wing that moves up and down in order to control the lift and drag. **3.** The sound or action of waving or fluttering: *the flap of a bird's wings.* **4.** *Slang.* A state of agitation or nervous excitement. *We all got into a flap when no one could find the car keys.* *—v.* **flapped, flap•ping, flaps.** *—tr.* **1.** To move (the wings or arms) up and down; beat. **2.** To cause to move with a waving or fluttering motion: *A brisk wind flapped the clothes on the line.* *—intr.* **1.** To wave about while attached to something stationary; flutter: *A flag flapped softly in the breeze.* **2.** To wave the arms or wings up and down. [First written down before 1300 in Middle English and spelled *flappe*, slap.]
flap•jack (flăp′jăk′) *n.* A pancake.
flap•per (flăp′ər) *n.* **1.** A broad part that flaps: *the flapper on an exhaust pipe.* **2.** A young woman of the 1920's who did not follow conventional dress or behavior.
flare (flâr) *intr.v.* **flared, flar•ing, flares. 1.** To burn with a sudden or unsteady flame: *The candle flared briefly and went out.* **2.** To burst out or erupt: *Tempers flared during the tense meeting.* **3.** To spread outward in a shape: *A horn flares at the end.* *—n.* **1.** A brief wavering blaze of light. **2.** A device that produces a bright light for signaling or lighting. **3.** An outbreak, as of emotion or activity: *a flare of anger.* **4.** A shape or form that spreads out: *the flare of a trumpet.*
❑ *These sound alike:* **flare, flair** (talent).
flare-up (flâr′ŭp′) *n.* **1.** A sudden outbreak of flame or light. **2.** An outburst or eruption: *a flare-up of anger.*
flash (flăsh) *v.* **flashed, flash•ing, flash•es.** *—intr.* **1.** To give off a sudden bright light: *Bursts of fireworks flashed in the sky.* **2.** To be lighted on and off: *A lighthouse flashed in the distance.* **3.** To appear or occur suddenly: *an idea for a story flashed through my mind.* **4.** To move rapidly: *A shooting star flashed across the sky.* *—tr.* **1.** To send forth suddenly or for an instant: *flash a light into a cave.* **2.** To make known or signal by flashing lights: *The yellow light flashed its warning.* **3.** To send (a message) at great speed: *flash a news bulletin to the*

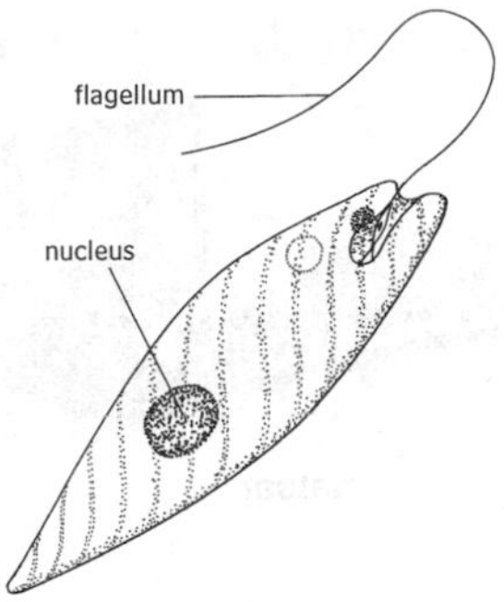

flagellum

flamingo

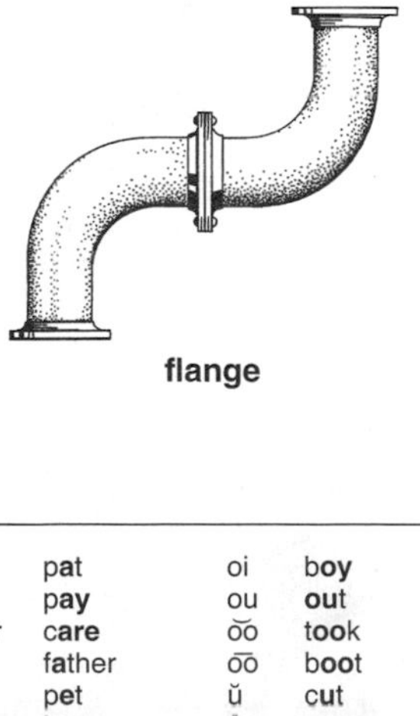

flange

ă	pat	oi	boy
ā	pay	ou	out
âr	care	o͝o	took
ä	father	o͞o	boot
ĕ	pet	ŭ	cut
ē	be	ûr	urge
ĭ	pit	th	thin
ī	pie	*th*	this
îr	pier	hw	whoop
ŏ	pot	zh	vision
ō	toe	ə	about
ô	paw	N	*French* bon

flatcar

world capitals. —*n.* **1.** A short sudden display of light: *a flash of lightning.* **2.** A sudden brief burst: *a flash of insight.* **3.** A split second; an instant: *I ran to the phone in a flash.* **4.** A brief important news item broadcast over radio or television: *Stations broadcast flashes about the election all day.* —*idiom.* **flash in the pan.** A person or thing that promises great success but fails: *Their latest idea was just another flash in the pan.* [First written down before 1200 in Middle English and spelled *flasken*, to splash, of imitative origin.] —**flash′er** *n.*

flash•back (**flăsh′**băk′) *n.* **1.** The insertion of an earlier event into a story, play, or movie. **2.** A scene or an episode showing an earlier event that is inserted in a story, play, or movie. **3.** A recurring, vivid mental image of a past experience.

flash•bulb or **flash bulb** (**flăsh′**bŭlb′) *n.* An electric bulb that produces a flash of light for taking photographs.

flash card *n.* One of a set of cards marked with words, numbers, or other symbols to be learned through drill.

flash flood *n.* A sudden violent flood after a heavy rain.

flash•light (**flăsh′**līt′) *n.* A portable electric light that is powered by batteries.

flash point *n.* **1.** The lowest temperature at which the vapor of a flammable liquid can be made to catch fire in air. **2.** The point at which something, such as a disagreement or quarrel, becomes an open conflict: *Disputes over their boundaries became the flash point for war between the two countries.*

flash•y (**flăsh′**ē) *adj.* **flash•i•er, flash•i•est. 1.** Creating a brief impression of brilliance; eye-catching: *the acrobat's flashy performance.* **2.** Cheap and showy; gaudy: *a flashy tie.* —**flash′i•ly** *adv.* —**flash′i•ness** *n.*

flask (flăsk) *n.* **1.** A small bottle with a flattened shape, made to be fit in one's pocket. **2.** A rounded container with a long neck, used in laboratories. [First written down about 1355 in Middle English and spelled *flask*, cask, keg, from Late Latin *flascō*, of Germanic origin.]

flat[1] (flăt) *adj.* **flat•ter, flat•test. 1.** Having a smooth even surface; level: *flat land.* **2.** Having a broad surface and little thickness or depth: *a flat dish.* **3.** Extending or lying full length; horizontal: *flat on my back in bed.* **4.** Having lost air; deflated: *a flat tire.* **5.** Lacking interest or excitement; dull: *a flat performance.* **6.** Having lost effervescence or sparkle: *flat soda.* **7.** Complete; absolute: *a flat refusal to help.* **8.** Not changing; fixed: *The taxi charges a flat rate.* **9.** Not glossy; dull: *finished with a flat paint.* **10.a.** Lower in musical pitch than is correct. **b.** Lower in pitch by a half step than a corresponding natural tone or key: *D flat.* —*adv.* **1.** On or against a flat surface: *press dough flat.* **2.** Exactly: *He ran the race in 50 seconds flat.* **3.** Completely: *I bought a CD player, and now I'm flat broke.* **4.** Below the correct pitch: *Don't sing flat.* —*n.* **1.** A flat surface or part: *the flat of my hand.* **2.** An area of level low-lying ground. Often used in the plural: *dig clams in the mud flats.* **3.** A deflated tire: *The car has a flat.* **4.** A shoe with a flat heel. **5.** A shallow box or frame for growing seeds. **6.a.** A musical note or tone that is a half step lower than a corresponding natural tone or key. **b.** The symbol (♭) attached to a note or tone to indicate that it is flat. —*tr. & intr.v.* **flat•ted, flat•ting, flats.** To sing or play flat. [First written down about 1300 in Middle English, from Old Norse *flatr.*] —**flat′ly** *adv.* —**flat′ness** *n.*

flat[2] (flăt) *n.* An apartment usually on one floor of a building. [First written down about 725 in Old English and spelled *flet*, floor, dwelling.]

flat•boat (**flăt′**bōt′) *n.* A flat-bottomed barge for transporting freight in shallow rivers or canals.

flat•car (**flăt′**kär′) *n.* A railroad car without sides or a roof, used for carrying bulky freight.

flat•fish (**flăt′**fĭsh′) *n.* Any of numerous fishes, such as the flounder, halibut, or sole, that have a flattened body and both eyes on one side.

flat•foot (**flăt′**fo͝ot′) *n.* **1.** *pl* **flat•feet** (**flăt′**fēt′). A condition in which the arch of the foot is very low and most or all of the sole touches the ground. **2.** *pl.* **flat•foots.** *Slang.* A police officer.

flat-foot•ed (**flăt′**fo͝ot′ĭd) *adj.* **1.** Of or suffering from flatfoot. **2.** Unable to react quickly; unprepared: *The question caught me flat-footed.* —**flat′-foot′ed•ly** *adv.* —**flat′-foot′ed•ness** *n.*

Flat•head (**flăt′**hĕd′) *n., pl.* **Flathead** or **Flat•heads. 1.** A member of a Native American people living in western Montana and northern Idaho. **2.** The Salishan language of the Flathead.

flat•i•ron (**flăt′**ī′ərn) *n.* An iron for pressing clothes.

flat•land (**flăt′**lănd′) *n.* **1.** Land that has almost no hills or valleys. **2. flatlands.** A geographic area made up chiefly of flatland.

flat•ten (**flăt′**n) *v.* **flat•tened, flat•ten•ing, flat•tens.** —*tr.* **1.** To make flat or flatter: *A rolling pin flattens dough.* **2.** To knock down; lay low: *The wind flattened the old shed.* —*intr.* To become flat or flatter: *All the wrinkles flattened out when the shirt was ironed.* —**flat′ten•er** *n.*

flat•ter (**flăt′**ər) *v.* **flat•tered, flat•ter•ing, flat•ters.** —*tr.* **1.** To compliment too much or praise insincerely, especially in order to win favor. **2.** To please or gratify: *The award flattered me.* **3.** To portray or show favorably: *This photograph flatters her.* —*intr.* To use flattery. [First written down before 1200 in Middle English and spelled *flatren*, from Old French *flater*, of Germanic origin.] —**flat′ter•er** *n.*

flat•ter•y (**flăt′**ə rē) *n., pl.* **flat•ter•ies.** Excessive or insincere praise.

flat•top (**flăt′**tŏp′) *n.* *Informal.* **1.** An aircraft carrier. **2.** A short haircut in which the hair is cut flat across the top of the head.

flat•u•lent (**flăch′**ə lənt) *adj.* Afflicted with excessive gas in the digestive tract. —**flat′u•lence** *n.*

flat•ware (**flăt′**wâr′) *n.* **1.** Tableware that is fairly flat, as plates. **2.** Table utensils such as knives, forks, and spoons.

flat•worm (**flăt′**wûrm′) *n.* Any of various worms, such as a tapeworm or planarian, having a flattened body and living in water or in an animal or human body as a parasite.

flaunt (flônt) *v.* **flaunt•ed, flaunt•ing, flaunts.** —*tr.* To show off: *flaunt one's knowledge.* —*intr.* **1.** To show oneself off; make a display of oneself. **2.** To wave proudly: *banners flaunting in the wind.* [First written down in 1566 in Modern English.] —**flaunt′ing•ly** *adv.*

flau•tist (**flô′**tĭst *or* **flou′**tĭst) *n.* A flutist.

fla•vor (**flā′**vər) *n.* **1.** Distinctive taste of something; savor: *the spicy flavor of applesauce.* **2.** A seasoning or flavoring: *Vanilla is a common flavor.* **3.** A quality felt to be characteristic of a thing: *a story full of the flavor of India.* —*tr.v.* **fla•vored, fla•vor•ing, fla•vors.** To give flavor to: *Vinegar flavored the salad.* [First written down about 1380 in Middle English and spelled *flavour*, aroma, from Old French *flaor*, from Latin *flāre*, to blow.] —**fla′vor•ful, fla′vor•some** *adj.*

fla•vor•ing (**flā′**vər ĭng) *n.* A substance, such as an extract or a spice, used to flavor food: *raspberry flavoring.*

flaw (flô) *n.* A defect, a shortcoming, or an imperfection: *The dish broke where there was a flaw in* *it. Their argument had many flaws and failed to convince anyone.* —*tr.v.* **flawed, flaw•ing, flaws.** To make defective: *The report was flawed with several errors.*

flaw•less (flô′lĭs) *adj.* Being without a flaw; perfect: *a flawless performance.* See Synonyms at **perfect.** —**flaw′less•ly** *adv.* —**flaw′less•ness** *n.*

flax (flăks) *n.* **1.** A light-colored fiber from which linen is made, obtained from the stems of the flax plant. **2.** The plant that yields such fibers, having blue flowers and seeds from which linseed oil is obtained. [First written down before 899 in Old English and spelled *fleax.*]

flax•en (flăk′sən) *adj.* **1.** Made of flax: *flaxen thread.* **2.** Having the pale-yellow color of flax fiber: *flaxen hair.*

flax•seed (flăks′sēd′) *n.* The seed of flax, from which linseed oil is pressed.

flay (flā) *tr.v.* **flayed, flay•ing, flays. 1.** To strip off the skin of: *flay a deer.* **2.** To criticize or scold harshly.

flea (flē) *n.* Any of various small, wingless, jumping insects that live on the bodies of human beings and other animals and suck their blood. [First written down about 700 in Old English and spelled *flēah.*]
❑ *These sound alike:* **flea, flee** (run away).

flea collar *n.* A collar, especially for a cat or dog, that contains a substance for killing fleas.

fleck (flĕk) *n.* **1.** A small mark or spot: *flecks of grey paint on the floor.* **2.** A small bit or flake: *a fleck of paper.* —*tr.v.* **flecked, fleck•ing, flecks.** To mark with flecks; spot: *Spots of paint flecked the floor.*

fled (flĕd) *v.* Past tense and past participle of **flee.**

fledge (flĕj) *v.* **fledged, fledg•ing, fledg•es.** —*tr.* **1.** To take care of (a young bird) until it is ready to fly: *We fledged an orphan wren.* **2.** To provide or cover with or as if with feathers: *fledge an arrow.* —*intr.* To grow the feathers needed to fly: *Robins fledge in just a few weeks.*

fledg•ling also **fledge•ling** (flĕj′lĭng) *n.* **1.** A young bird that has just grown the feathers needed to fly. **2.** A young or inexperienced person. —*adj.* New and inexperienced: *a fledgling skier.*

flee (flē) *v.* **fled** (flĕd), **flee•ing, flees.** —*intr.* **1.** To run away, as from trouble or danger: *The thieves fled when they heard the police siren.* **2.** To pass swiftly away; vanish: *The night fled and the sky brightened.* —*tr.* To run away from; escape from: *flee the burning house.* [First written down about 825 in Old English and spelled *flēon.*]
❑ *These sound alike:* **flee, flea** (insect).

fleece (flēs) *n.* **1.** The coat of wool of a sheep or similar animal. **2.** The amount of wool sheared from a sheep or similar animal at one time. **3.** Soft wooly fabric used to line coats, boots, and other outer clothing. —*tr.v.* **fleeced, fleec•ing, fleec•es. 1.** To shear the fleece from. **2.** To swindle or cheat (a person) of money or belongings: *a dishonest dealer fleeced the car buyer.*

fleec•y (flē′sē) *adj.* **fleec•i•er, fleec•i•est.** Of or resembling fleece: *fleecy blankets; fleecy clouds.* —**fleec′i•ness** *n.*

fleet[1] (flēt) *n.* **1.** A group of warships under one commander. **2.** A number of boats or vehicles owned or operated as a group: *a fishing fleet; a fleet of taxis.* [First written down before 1000 in Old English and spelled *flēot,* from *flēotan,* to float.]

fleet[2] (flēt) *adj.* **fleet•er, fleet•est.** Moving swiftly; nimble: *fleet as a deer.* —*intr.v.* **fleet•ed, fleet•ing, fleets.** To move or pass swiftly: *clouds fleeting across the sky.* [First written down before 1529 in Modern English and spelled *flete,* probably from Old Norse *fljōtr.*] —**fleet′ly** *adv.* —**fleet′ness** *n.*

Fleet Admiral *n.* Admiral of the Fleet.

fleet•ing (flē′tĭng) *adj.* Passing quickly; very brief: *a fleeting glimpse of the eclipse.* —**fleet′ing•ly** *adv.*

Flem•ing (flĕm′ĭng) *n.* **1.** A native or inhabitant of Flanders. **2.** A Belgian whose native language is Flemish.

Fleming, Sir **Alexander.** 1881–1955. British scientist who discovered penicillin in 1928 and shared a 1945 Nobel Prize.

Flem•ish (flĕm′ĭsh) *n.* **1.** *(used with a plural verb).* The people of Flanders. **2.** The West Germanic language of these people, related to Dutch. —*adj.* Of or relating to Flanders, the Flemish, or their language or culture.

flense (flĕns) *tr.v.* **flensed, flens•ing, flens•es.** To strip the blubber or skin from: *flense a whale.*

flesh (flĕsh) *n.* **1.** The soft tissue of the body composed mostly of muscles and fat and covering the bones. **2.** The meat of animals used as food. **3.** The pulpy part of a fruit or vegetable used as food: *the sweet flesh of a ripe melon.* **4.** The body as distinguished from the mind or soul. —***idioms.*** **flesh and blood.** A blood relative or relatives; kin. **in the flesh.** In person; actually present: *I have never seen the President in the flesh, only on TV.*

flesh•ly (flĕsh′lē) *adj.* **flesh•li•er, flesh•li•est. 1.** Of or relating to the body; physical: *fleshly need of nourishment.* **2.** Not spiritual; sensual or worldly: *fleshly pleasures.*

flesh•y (flĕsh′ē) *adj.* **flesh•i•er, flesh•i•est. 1.** Relating to, consisting of, or having flesh. **2.** Having much flesh; plump: *fleshy cheeks.*

fleur-de-lis or **fleur-de-lys** (flûr′də lē′) *n., pl.* **fleurs-de-lis** or **fleurs-de-lys** (flûr′də lēz′). **1.** A design in heraldry that has a three-petaled iris flower, used to symbolize the royal family of France. **2.** An iris, especially a white one.

flew (flo͞o) *v.* Past tense of **fly[1].**
❑ *These sound alike:* **flew, flu** (influenza), **flue** (pipe).

flex (flĕks) *tr.v.* **flexed, flex•ing, flex•es. 1.** To bend: *Flex your elbow.* **2.** To cause (a muscle) to contract.

flex•i•ble (flĕk′sə bəl) *adj.* **1.** Capable of bending or being bent; supple; pliable: *a flexible hose.* **2.** Capable of or responsive to change; adaptable: *Our plans are flexible.* —**flex′i•bil′i•ty** *n.* —**flex′i•bly** *adv.*

flex•ion (flĕk′shən) *n.* A bending of a joint in the body by the action of flexors.

flex•or (flĕk′sər) *n.* A muscle that bends a joint in the body.

flick (flĭk) *n.* **1.** A light quick blow, jerk, or touch: *turn on a light with a flick of the finger.* **2.** The sound made by such a blow or stroke: *We heard the flick of the switch.* —*tr.v.* **flicked, flick•ing, flicks. 1.** To touch or hit with a light quick blow: *The horse flicked flies with its tail.* **2.** To cause to move with a light blow; snap: *flick a switch.* **3.** To remove with a light quick blow: *flick a bug off the table.* [First written down in 1591 in Modern English and spelled *flicke,* of imitative origin.]

flick•er[1] (flĭk′ər) *intr.v.* **flick•ered, flick•er•ing, flick•ers. 1.** To burn or shine waveringly: *The candles flickered in the breeze.* **2.** To move unevenly; flutter: *Shadows flickered on the wall.* —*n.* **1.** An uneven or wavering light: *only the flicker of a candle to light our way.* **2.** A brief or slight indication or sensation: *a flicker of disappointment.* **3.** A short quick movement; a tremor: *the flicker of a butterfly's wings.* [First written down about 1000 in Old English and spelled *flicorian.*]

flick•er[2] (flĭk′ər) *n.* Any of various large North American woodpeckers having a brown back and a spotted breast. [First written down in 1808 in American English, perhaps from *flick.*]

Sir Alexander Fleming

fleur-de-lis

ă	pat	oi	boy
ā	pay	ou	out
âr	care	o͝o	took
ä	father	o͞o	boot
ĕ	pet	ŭ	cut
ē	be	ûr	urge
ĭ	pit	th	thin
ī	pie	*th*	this
îr	pier	hw	whoop
ŏ	pot	zh	vision
ō	toe	ə	about
ô	paw	N	*French* bon

flied (flīd) *intr.v.* Past tense and past participle of **fly**[1] (sense 7).

fli•er also **fly•er** (flī′ər) *n.* **1.** A person or thing that flies, especially a pilot or an aviator. **2.** *Informal.* A pamphlet or circular; a handbill: *We distributed fliers for the candidate.*

flies[1] (flīz) *v.* Third person singular present tense of **fly**[1]. —*n.* Plural of **fly**[1].

flies[2] (flīz) *n.* Plural of **fly**[2].

flight[1] (flīt) *n.* **1.** The act or process of flying: *a bird's flight.* **2.** A scheduled airline trip: *My flight to Milwaukee is set for Friday.* **3.** The distance covered in such a trip: *The flight was 3,000 miles.* **4.** A group, especially of birds or aircraft, flying together. **5.** An effort that soars above the ordinary: *a brilliant flight of the imagination.* **6.** A series of stairs, as between floors: *We climbed three flights to get to the top floor.* [First written down before 900 in Old English and spelled *flyht.*]

flight[2] (flīt) *n.* An act of running away; an escape. [First written down before 1200 in Middle English and spelled *fluht.*]

flight attendant *n.* An attendant who looks after passengers in an airplane.

flight•less (flīt′lĭs) *adj.* Incapable of flying: *Ostriches and penguins are flightless birds.*

flight recorder *n.* An electronic device that records information about the operation of each flight of an aircraft and is kept in a sealed box for recovery after a crash.

flight•y (flī′tē) *adj.* **flight•i•er, flight•i•est.** Given to unsteady or fickle behavior. **—flight′i•ness** *n.*

flim•sy (flĭm′zē) *adj.* **flim•si•er, flim•si•est. 1.** Thin or light: *flimsy cloth.* **2.** Not solid or strong; likely to fall apart: *a flimsy table.* **3.** Not believable; unconvincing: *a flimsy excuse.* **—flim′si•ly** *adv.* **—flim′si•ness** *n.*

flinch (flĭnch) *intr.v.* **flinched, flinch•ing, flinch•es.** To shrink or wince, as from pain or fear; draw back: *The patient flinched when the doctor put medicine on the cut.*

fling (flĭng) *v.* **flung** (flŭng), **fling•ing, flings.** —*tr.* **1.** To throw forcefully: *We were flinging acorns at a tree.* See Synonyms at **throw. 2.** To put or send suddenly or unexpectedly: *fling troops into battle.* —*intr.* To go quickly or angrily; rush: *The insulted guest flung out of the room without saying goodbye.* —*n.* **1.** The act of flinging; a throw. **2.** A lively dance of the Scottish Highlands. **3.** A brief period of doing whatever one wants; a spree or binge. **4.** *Informal.* A brief attempt or try: *take a fling at skiing.*

flint (flĭnt) *n.* **1.** A very hard, gray to black quartz that makes sparks when struck with steel. **2.** A piece of flint used to produce sparks, as in a musket. [First written down about 700 in Old English.]

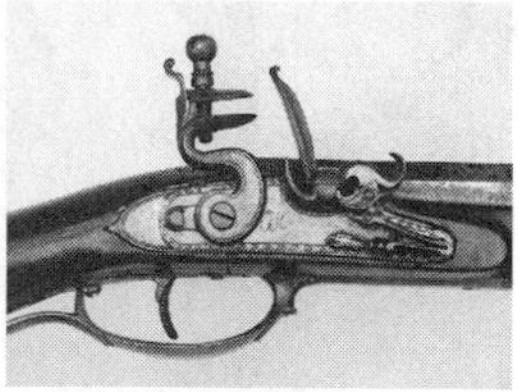

flintlock
Late 18th-century American Kentucky rifle

flint•lock (flĭnt′lŏk′) *n.* **1.** A gunlock in which a flint strikes a metal plate and produces sparks that ignite the gunpowder. **2.** A firearm having such a gunlock.

flint•y (flĭn′tē) *adj.* **flint•i•er, flint•i•est. 1.** Composed of or containing flint: *gray flinty hills.* **2.** Unyielding; stony: *a cold flinty look.* **—flint′i•ness** *n.*

flip (flĭp) *v.* **flipped, flip•ping, flips.** —*tr.* **1.** To toss with a light quick motion, especially with a spin or turn: *flip a coin.* **2.** To turn over with a light quick motion: *flip the pages of a magazine.* —*intr.* **1.** To turn over: *The canoe flipped in the rapids.* **2.** To move in twists and turns: *The fish flipped in the net.* **3.** To turn a somersault in the air: *This dog flips for treats.* —*n.* **1.** An act of flipping, especially a quick turning movement: *give the pancake a flip.* **2.** A somersault. —*adj.* **flip•per, flip•pest.** *Informal.* Flippant: *a flip attitude.*

flip-flop (flĭp′flŏp′) *n.* **1.** The movement or sound of repeated flapping: *the flip-flop of a shade against a window.* **2.** A backward somersault or handspring. **3.** *Informal.* A reversal of opinion or direction: *The mayor's flip-flop on the important issue left everyone wondering.* **4.** A rubber sandal or thong. **5.** An electronic circuit that can be either on or off, especially a computer circuit used to store a single bit of information.

flip•pant (flĭp′ənt) *adj.* Casually or humorously disrespectful: *flippant remarks.* **—flip′pan•cy** *n.* **—flip′pant•ly** *adv.*

flip•per (flĭp′ər) *n.* **1.** A wide flat limb, as of a seal or walrus, adapted for swimming. **2.** A rubber covering for the foot with a wide flat part extending from the toes, used for swimming.

flirt (flûrt) *v.* **flirt•ed, flirt•ing, flirts.** —*intr.* **1.** To act romantically, especially in a playful or teasing way. **2.** To deal with in a playful way as being of little importance; trifle: *Bullfighters flirt with danger.* —*tr.* To toss or move abruptly or jerkily; flick: *The bird flirted its tail.* —*n.* **1.** A person given to romantic flirting. **2.** An abrupt jerking movement: *The squirrel gave a flirt of its tail and ran off.*

flir•ta•tion (flûr tā′shən) *n.* **1.** The act or practice of flirting. **2.** A casual or brief romance.

flir•ta•tious (flûr tā′shəs) *adj.* **1.** Given to flirting: *a flirtatious person.* **2.** Lightheartedly romantic: *a flirtatious look.* **—flir•ta′tious•ly** *adv.* **—flir•ta′tious•ness** *n.*

flit (flĭt) *intr.v.* **flit•ted, flit•ting, flits. 1.** To move quickly and nimbly: *Birds flitted about in the thicket.* **2.** To pass quickly: *A smile flitted across the child's face.*

float (flōt) *v.* **float•ed, float•ing, floats.** —*intr.* **1.** To rest on the surface of a fluid: *The raft floated until we all got on.* **2.** To move or drift supported by or as if by a fluid: *The spacecraft floated toward the distant planet.* —*tr.* **1.** To cause to float or move on the surface of a fluid: *float logs down the river.* **2.** To offer for sale: *float a new company.* **3.** To arrange for (a loan). —*n.* **1.** An object designed to float, especially a buoy or a raft fixed in place. **2.** A cork or ball on a fishing line that keeps the line up in the water and bobs when a fish bites. **3.** A hollow ball attached to a lever to regulate the water level in a tank, as in a toilet tank. **4.** A decorated exhibit displayed on a large flat vehicle in a parade. **5.** A soft drink with ice cream in it. [First written down in 1031 in Old English and spelled *flotian.*] **—float′er** *n.*

float•ing rib (flō′tĭng) *n.* One of the four lower ribs that are not connected to the breastbone.

flock (flŏk) *n.* **1.** A group of animals, such as birds or sheep, that live, travel, or feed together. **2.** The members of a church. **3.** A large crowd or number: *A flock of weekend visitors crowded into the museum.* —*intr.v.* **flocked, flock•ing, flocks.** To gather or travel in a flock or crowd: *People flocked to the cities for jobs.* —See Note at **collective noun.**

floe (flō) *n.* A mass or sheet of floating ice.
❑ *These sound alike:* **floe, flow** (run freely).

flog (flŏg *or* flôg) *tr.v.* **flogged, flog•ging, flogs.** To beat harshly with a whip or rod. **—flog′ger** *n.*

flood (flŭd) *n.* **1.a.** An overflowing of water onto land that is normally dry. **b. Flood.** In the Bible, the flood covering the earth in the days of Noah. **2.** A large flow or outpouring: *a flood of job applications.* **3.** The flood tide. —*v.* **flood•ed, flood•ing, floods.** —*tr.* **1.** To cover with or as if with a flood: *The heavy rain flooded the cellar.* **2.** To fill or overwhelm with too much of something: *Telephone calls flooded the electric company during the power outage.* —*intr.* To overflow; pour forth: *The stream floods every spring.* [First written down about 725 in Old English and spelled *flōd.*]

flood•gate (flŭd′gāt′) *n.* A gate used to control the flow of water, as from a lake or a river.

flood•light (flŭd′līt′) *n.* **1.** An electric lamp that produces a broad, intensely bright beam of light. **2.** The beam of light produced by such a lamp: *The fountain sparkled in the floodlight.* —*tr.v.* **flood•light•ed** or **flood•lit** (flŭd′lĭt′), **flood•light•ing, flood•lights.** To light with a floodlight.

flood•plain (flŭd′plān′) *n.* Flatland bordering a river and made up of soil deposited during floods.

flood tide *n.* The incoming or rising tide.

floodwater (flŭd′wô′tər *or* flŭd′wŏ′ər) *n.* The water of a flood. Often used in the plural.

floor (flôr) *n.* **1.** The surface of a room on which one stands. **2.** The ground or bottom surface, as of a forest or an ocean. **3.** A story or level of a building: *Our apartment is on the fifth floor.* **4.** The part of a building where the members of a legislature meet and carry on their business. **5.** The right to address an assembly: *The representative from Hawaii has the floor.* —*tr.v.* **floored, floor•ing, floors. 1.** To provide with a floor: *floor a deck with planks.* **2.** To knock down: *The boxer was floored twice.* **3.** To stun; overwhelm: *The thrilling news floored me.*

floor•board (flôr′bôrd′) *n.* **1.** A board in a floor. **2.** The floor of a motor vehicle.

floor•ing (flôr′ĭng) *n.* **1.** Material, such as lumber, used to make floors. **2.** A floor: *The house had flooring of fine wood.*

floor•show (flôr′shō′) *n.* A series of entertainments, such as singing or comedy acts, presented in a nightclub.

floor•walk•er (flôr′wô′kər) *n.* An employee of a large store who supervises sales people and helps customers.

flop (flŏp) *v.* **flopped, flop•ping, flops.** —*intr.* **1.** To fall heavily and noisily; plop: *I flopped on my bed.* **2.** To move about loosely or limply: *The dog's ears flopped as it ran along.* **3.** *Informal.* To fail: *The musical comedy totally flopped in New York.* —*tr.* To cause to fall down heavily or drop noisily: *I flopped the heavy package on the table.* —*n.* **1.** The action or sound of flopping. **2.** *Informal.* A failure: *The play was a complete flop.*

flop•py (flŏp′ē) *adj.* **flop•pi•er, flop•pi•est.** Tending to flop: *floppy ears; big floppy sleeves.* —*n., pl.* **flop•pies.** A floppy disk. —**flop′pi•ness** *n.*

floppy disk *n.* A flexible plastic disk coated with magnetic material and covered by a protective jacket, used to store computer data.

flo•ra (flôr′ə) *n., pl.* **flo•ras** or **flo•rae** (flôr′ē′). The plants of a particular region or time period considered as a group: *desert flora.*

flo•ral (flôr′əl) *adj.* Of, relating to, or suggestive of flowers: *a floral arrangement; floral perfume.*

Flor•ence (flôr′əns *or* flŏr′əns). Also **Fi•ren•ze** (fē rĕn′dzĕ). A city of central Italy east of Pisa. Florence was an important artistic center during the Renaissance. Population, 453,293.

flo•ret (flôr′ĭt) *n.* A small flower that forms part of the flower head of a composite plant, such as the daisy or dandelion.

flor•id (flôr′ĭd *or* flŏr′ĭd) *adj.* **1.** Flushed with rosy color; ruddy: *a florid complexion.* **2.** Elaborate; flowery: *a florid style of writing.*

Flor•i•da (flôr′ĭ də *or* flŏr′ĭ də). A state of the southeast United States south of Georgia bordering on the Atlantic Ocean and the Gulf of Mexico. It was admitted as the 27th state in 1845. Tallahassee is the capital and Jacksonville the largest city. Population, 13,003,362. —See Note.

flor•in (flôr′ĭn *or* flŏr′ĭn) *n.* **1.** A guilder. **2.** Any of several former European gold or silver coins.

flo•rist (flôr′ĭst *or* flŏr′ĭst) *n.* A person who raises or sells ornamental plants and flowers.

floss (flôs *or* flŏs) *n.* **1.** A soft, loosely twisted silk or cotton thread used in embroidery. **2.** Dental floss. **3.** A mass of soft silky fibers, such as the fluff in milkweed pods or corn silk. —*v.* **flossed, floss•ing, floss•es.** —*tr.* To clean with dental floss: *Floss your teeth carefully.* —*intr.* To clean the teeth with dental floss. —**floss′y** *adj.*

flo•til•la (flō tĭl′ə) *n.* **1.** A small fleet. **2.** A fleet of boats or other small vessels: *a flotilla of canoes.*

flot•sam (flŏt′səm) *n.* Floating wreckage or cargo from a shipwreck.

flounce[1] (flouns) *n.* A strip of decorative cloth gathered or pleated along one edge and sewn to a curtain or clothing as a trimming. —*tr.v.* **flounced, flounc•ing, flounc•es.** To trim with a flounce or flounces. [First written down about 1378 in Middle English and spelled *frounce*, pleat, from Old French *fronce*, of Germanic origin.]

flounce[2] (flouns) *intr.v.* **flounced, flounc•ing, flounc•es. 1.** To move in a lively or bouncy manner: *The children flounced about the room.* **2.** To walk with a show of anger or impatience: *flounce out of the room in a huff.* [First written down in 1542 in Modern English, possibly of Scandinavian origin.]

floun•der[1] (floun′dər) *intr.v.* **floun•dered, floun•der•ing, floun•ders. 1.** To move clumsily or with difficulty: *floundering through deep snow.* **2.** To struggle clumsily and in confusion or embarrassment: *flounder through a speech.* [First written down in 1592 in Modern English, probably alteration of *founder*, to sink.]

floun•der[2] (floun′dər) *n., pl.* **flounder** or **floun•ders.** Any of various flatfishes used as food. [First written down in 1304 in Middle English and spelled *flundr*, from Anglo-Norman *floundre*, of Scandinavian origin.]

flour (flour) *n.* **1.** A fine powdery meal made by grinding and sifting grain, especially wheat. **2.** Any of various similar powdery foods, as that made from cassavas or potatoes. —*tr.v.* **floured, flour•ing, flours.** To cover or coat with flour: *flour chicken before frying.*

flour•ish (flûr′ĭsh *or* flŭr′ĭsh) *v.* **flour•ished, flour•ish•ing, flour•ish•es.** —*intr.* **1.** To grow or develop well or luxuriantly; thrive: *Most flowers flourish in full sunlight.* **2.** To do well; prosper: *The lawyer's practice flourished.* **3.** To be in a period of highest accomplishment or vitality: *The writer flourished late in life.* —*tr.* To wave vigorously or dramatically: *Marchers flourished their hats in front of the reviewing stand.* —*n.* **1.** A dramatic action or gesture: *the flourish of a sword.* **2.** An added decorative touch; an embellishment: *handwriting with many flourishes.* **3.** In music, a showy passage or a fanfare: *Trumpets played a flourish.*

flout (flout) *tr.v.* **flout•ed, flout•ing, flouts.** To show contempt for; scorn: *flout convention.* [First written down in 1551 in Modern English, possibly from Middle English *flouten*, to play the flute, from Old French *flauter*, from *flaute*, flute.] —**flout′er** *n.*

flow (flō) *intr.v.* **flowed, flow•ing, flows. 1.** To move or run smoothly in a stream: *Oil flowed from the well.* **2.** To proceed steadily and easily: *The preparations for the party flowed smoothly.* **3.** To be plentiful: *a river flowing with fish.* **4.** To be full or overflow: *Their hearts flowed with warm feelings.* **5.** To hang loosely and gracefully: *The judges' robes flowed behind them.* **6.** To rise: *The tide flows in and out.* —*n.* **1.** A stream or current: *a lava flow.* **2.** A continuous movement: *the flow of traffic.* **3.** The act of flowing: *Downstream the flow is much slower.* **4.** The rising of the tide: *the ocean's flow towards shore.*

❑ *These sound alike:* **flow, floe** (ice mass).

floppy disk

Top: 3.5-inch floppy disk
Bottom: 5.25-inch floppy disk

Florida

The Spanish explorer Juan Ponce de León gave **Florida** its name when he landed there in 1513 during the Easter season. He was thinking of the Spanish expression for Easter, *Pascua Florida*, which means "flowery feast." The state of Florida is still a "flowery" place today.

ă	pat	oi	boy
ā	pay	ou	out
âr	care	o͝o	took
ä	father	o͞o	boot
ĕ	pet	ŭ	cut
ē	be	ûr	urge
ĭ	pit	th	thin
ī	pie	*th*	this
îr	pier	hw	whoop
ŏ	pot	zh	vision
ō	toe	ə	about
ô	paw	N	*French* bon

Word Building: fluent

The word roots *–flu–*, *–flux–*, and *–fluc–* in English words come from the Latin verb *fluere*, "to flow." The Latin present participle of *fluere* has the form *fluent–* and therefore means "flowing." It is the source of **fluent**, "flowing, graceful, smooth." The Latin noun *influentia*, meaning "an inflow" (using the prefix *in–*[2], "in, into"), is the source of our **influence**. The past participle of *fluere* is *fluxus*, from which we form the word **influx**, "an inflow." The Latin noun *fluctus* means "wave"; the verb *fluctuāre* means "to make waves" and is the source of the word **fluctuate**.

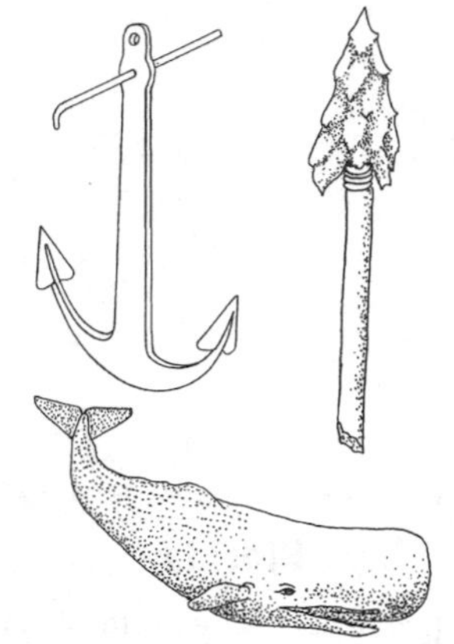

fluke[2]
Of an admiralty anchor (*top left*), an arrowhead (*top right*), and a sperm whale (*bottom*)

flute

flow chart also **flow•chart** (flō′chärt′) *n.* A diagram that shows the order of operations or sequence of tasks for solving a problem or managing a complex project.

flow•er (flou′ər) *n.* **1.** The part of a plant that produces seeds, usually surrounded by brightly colored petals; a blossom. **2.** A plant that is grown mainly for its flowers: *The pansies, marigolds, and other flowers made a colorful garden bed.* **3.** Time or period of coming into bloom: *a meadow in full flower.* **4.** The best example or representative of something: *Shakespeare and other writers who were the flower of Elizabethan England.* —*intr.v.* **flow•ered, flow•er•ing, flow•ers. 1.** To produce flowers; bloom: *Shrubs usually flower in spring.* **2.** To develop fully; reach a peak: *His artistic talents flowered early in life.* [First written down before 1200 in Middle English and spelled *flur*, flower, best of anything, flour, from Latin *flōs*.]

flow•er•ing plant (flou′ər ĭng) *n.* A plant that produces flowers and fruit.

flow•er•y (flou′ə rē) *adj.* **flow•er•i•er, flow•er•i•est. 1.** Full of or suggestive of flowers: *flowery meadows; a flowery fragrance.* **2.** Full of fancy words or expressions: *a flowery speech.* **—flow′er•i•ness** *n.*

flown (flōn) *v.* Past participle of **fly[1]**.

fl oz or **fl. oz.** *abbr.* An abbreviation of fluid ounce.

flu (flo͞o) *n. Informal.* Influenza.
❑ *These sound alike:* **flu, flew** (moved through the air), **flue** (pipe).

flub (flŭb) *tr.v.* **flubbed, flub•bing, flubs.** To botch or bungle: *He flubbed the pass and dropped the ball.* —*n.* A blunder; an error.

fluc•tu•ate (flŭk′cho͞o āt′) *intr.v.* **fluc•tu•at•ed, fluc•tu•at•ing, fluc•tu•ates.** To change or vary irregularly; waver: *In summer the temperature fluctuates a great deal.* **—fluc′tu•a′tion** *n.*

flue (flo͞o) *n.* A pipe, tube, or other channel for carrying smoke, steam, or waste gases, as from a fireplace to a chimney.
❑ *These sound alike:* **flue, flew** (moved through the air), **flu** (influenza).

flu•en•cy (flo͞o′ən sē) *n.* Smoothness and ease, especially in speaking or writing.

flu•ent (flo͞o′ənt) *adj.* **1.** Capable of expressing oneself smoothly and effortlessly: *a fluent speaker; fluent in German and French.* **2.** Flowing or moving smoothly; graceful: *a yacht with fluent lines.* **—flu′ent•ly** *adv.* —See Note.

fluff (flŭf) *n.* **1.** Light down or fuzz: *the fluff from a woolen sweater.* **2.** Something having a very light or downy appearance: *The ducklings were little balls of fluff.* **3.** *Informal.* An error; a flub. —*tr.v.* **fluffed, fluff•ing, fluffs. 1.** To make light and puffy by patting or shaking: *fluff a pillow.* **2.** *Informal.* To make an error in; spoil: *fluff an exam; fluff a speech.*

fluff•y (flŭf′ē) *adj.* **fluff•i•er, fluff•i•est. 1.** Of, resembling, or covered with fluff or down: *a fluffy blanket.* **2.** Light and airy; soft: *fluffy whipped potatoes; fluffy curls.* **—fluff′i•ness** *n.*

flu•id (flo͞o′ĭd) *n.* A substance, such as air or water, that flows easily and takes on the shape of its container. All liquids and gases are fluids. —*adj.* **1.** Capable of flowing; liquid or gaseous: *The waters of this lake remain fluid all winter.* **2.** Easily changed or tending to change: *Our vacation plans remained fluid until we knew how much time we had.*

fluid dram *n.* A unit equal to ⅛ of a fluid ounce (3.70 milliliters).

flu•id•i•ty (flo͞o ĭd′ĭ tē) *n.* The quality or condition of being fluid.

fluid ounce *n.* A liquid measure equal to 1/16 of a pint (29.57 milliliters). See table at **measurement**.

fluke[1] (flo͞ok) *n.* **1.** Any of various flatfishes, especially the flounder. **2.** A trematode. [First written down before 700 in Old English and spelled *flōc*.]

fluke[2] (flo͞ok) *n.* **1.** The triangular blade at the end of either arm of an anchor, designed to dig into the ocean bottom to hold the anchor in place. **2.** The barbed head of a harpoon, a lance, or an arrow. **3.** Either of the two flattened fins of a whale's tail. [First written down in 1561 in Modern English, possibly from *fluke*, flatfish.]

fluke[3] (flo͞ok) *n.* Something happening by chance, especially a stroke of good luck: *It was a fluke that we all arrived at the same time.* [First written down in 1857 in Modern English.]

flume (flo͞om) *n.* **1.** A narrow gorge with a stream flowing through it. **2.** An artificial channel or chute for flowing water, as for floating logs or furnishing waterpower.

flum•mox (flŭm′əks) *tr.v.* **flum•moxed, flum•mox•ing, flum•mox•es.** *Informal.* To confuse; perplex: *I was flummoxed by a question I could not answer.*

flung (flŭng) *v.* Past tense and past participle of **fling.**

flunk (flŭngk) *Informal. v.* **flunked, flunk•ing, flunks.** —*intr.* To fail, especially in an examination or a course. —*tr.* **1.** To fail (a test or subject in school). **2.** To give (a person) a failing grade.

flun•ky also **flun•key** (flŭng′kē) *n., pl.* **flun•kies** also **flun•keys. 1.** A person who slavishly obeys and fawns on another to win favor. **2.** A person who does a servant's work. **3.** A uniformed servant.

fluo•resce (flo͞o rĕs′ *or* flô rĕs′) *intr.v.* **fluo•resced, fluo•resc•ing, fluo•resc•es.** To produce or show fluorescence.

fluo•res•cence (flo͞o rĕs′əns *or* flô rĕs′əns) *n.* **1.** The giving off of light by a substance when it is exposed to electromagnetic radiation, such as ultraviolet rays or x-rays. Light is emitted only as long as the electromagnetic radiation continues to bombard the substance. **2.** The light produced in this way.

fluo•res•cent (flo͞o rĕs′ənt *or* flô rĕs′ənt) *adj.* Relating to, showing, or produced by fluorescence: *fluorescent light.*

fluorescent lamp *n.* A lamp that produces visible light by fluorescence, especially a glass tube coated on the inside with a fluorescent material and filled with an ionized gas that emits ultraviolet rays.

fluor•i•date (flo͝or′ĭ dāt′ *or* flôr′ĭ dāt′) *tr.v.* **fluor•i•dat•ed, fluor•i•dat•ing, fluor•i•dates.** To add a compound of fluorine to (drinking water) in order to prevent tooth decay. **—fluor′i•da′tion** *n.*

fluor•ide (flo͝or′īd′ *or* flôr′īd′) *n.* A chemical compound of fluorine and another element or radical.

fluor•ine (flo͝or′ēn′ *or* flôr′ēn′) *n. Symbol* **F** A pale-yellow, poisonous chemical element that is a highly corrosive gas. It is added to the water supply in small amounts to prevent tooth decay. Atomic number 9. See table at **element**.

fluor•o•scope (flo͝or′ə skōp′ *or* flôr′ə skōp′) *n.* An x-ray machine that projects shadows of internal parts of objects, such as machinery or the human body, onto a fluorescent screen for viewing.

flur•ry (flûr′ē *or* flŭr′ē) *n., pl.* **flur•ries. 1.** A brief light fall of snow. **2.** A sudden gust of wind. **3.** A sudden burst of confusion, excitement, or activity; a stir: *a flurry of interest in the new product.* —*tr.v.* **flur•ried, flur•ry•ing, flur•ries.** To confuse, excite, or agitate; fluster: *Unexpected questions flurried the speaker.*

flush[1] (flŭsh) *v.* **flushed, flush•ing, flush•es.** —*intr.* **1.** To turn red in the face; blush. **2.** To flow and spread out suddenly and abundantly: *Blood flushed to the angry driver's face.* **3.** To be emptied or cleaned by a rapid gush of water. *—tr.* **1.** To clause to redden or glow: *The disappointed customer was flushed with annoyance.* **2.** To excite or elate, as with a feeling of pride or accomplishment: *The winning team was flushed with victory.* **3.** To wash, empty, or purify with a sudden rapid flow of water: *We flushed the pipe of debris with a hose.* *—n.* **1.** A flow or rush of water. **2.** A blush or rosy glow. **3.** A rush of strong feeling or excitement; exhilaration: *a flush of enthusiasm.* **4.** A state of freshness or vigor: *the first flush of youth.* *—adj.* **flush•er, flush•est. 1.** Having an abundant supply of money: *The company was flush with cash from sales of its latest product.* **2.** Marked by abundance; plentiful: *rivers flush with spring rains.* **3.** Having surfaces that are even, level, or close together: *sections of the sidewalk that are flush.* *—adv.* So as to be even or aligned: *The figures are written flush down the column.* [First written down in 1548 in Modern English, probably from *flush*, to dart out.]

flush² (flŭsh) *n.* In card games, a hand in which all of the cards are of the same suit. [First written down before 1529 in Modern English, from Latin *flŭxus*, flux.]

flush³ (flŭsh) *v.* **flushed, flush•ing, flush•es.** *—tr.* To cause (a bird or an animal) to dart or fly from a hiding place: *Our noise flushed several ducks from the tall grass.* *—intr.* To dart out or fly from a hiding place: *The dog barked and the two grouse flushed from the thicket.* [First written down about 1250 in Middle English and spelled *flusen*.]

flus•ter (flŭs′tər) *tr.v.* **flus•tered, flus•ter•ing, flus•ters.** To make nervous, excited, or confused: *Shouts from the protesters flustered the speaker.* *—n.* A state of excitement, confusion, or agitation: *The heavy city traffic put the driver in a fluster.*

flute (flo͞ot) *n.* **1.** A woodwind instrument consisting of a tube with finger holes and keys on the side, sounded by blowing across a hole near one end. **2.** A rounded groove, especially one carved on the shaft of a column. **3.** A groove in cloth, as in a pleated ruffle. *—v.* **flut•ed, flut•ing, flutes.** *—tr.* **1.** To play (a tune) on a flute. **2.** To produce with a tone like that of a flute. **3.** To make grooves in: *A carpenter fluted the tops of the new columns.* *—intr.* **1.** To play a flute. **2.** To sing or whistle with a tone like that of a flute.

flut•ing (**flo͞o′**tĭng) *n.* A series of rounded grooves, as on a column.

flut•ist (**flo͞o′**tĭst) *n.* A person who plays the flute.

flut•ter (**flŭt′**ər) *v.* **flut•tered, flut•ter•ing, flut•ters.** *—intr.* **1.** To wave or flap rapidly and lightly: *curtains fluttered in the breeze.* **2.a.** To fly with a quick light flapping of the wings. **b.** To flap the wings while making short hops: *The chicken fluttered across the yard.* **3.** To beat rapidly or in an irregular way: *When I was scared my heart fluttered wildly.* **4.** To move quickly in a nervous, restless, or excited fashion; flit: *Clerks fluttered about trying to look busy.* **5.** To fall or move lightly with an irregular motion: *Hundreds of feathers fluttered to the floor after the pillow fight.* *—tr.* To cause to flutter: *A light breeze fluttered the curtain.* *—n.* **1.** An act of fluttering: *the flutter of a butterfly.* **2.** A condition of nervous excitement or agitation: *We were in a flutter getting ready for the party.* **—flut′ter•er** *n.*

flutter kick *n.* A swimming kick in which the legs are moved rapidly up and down without bending the knees.

flux (flŭks) *n.* **1.** Continual change: *The price of gold is in flux.* **2.** A flowing or flow: *the flux of the outgoing tide.* **3.** A substance applied to a metal surface that is to be soldered or welded. Flux cleans the surface, improves the flow of solder, and prevents the formation of oxides that would weaken the joint. **4.** A substance used in a smelting furnace to make metals melt more easily. **5.a.** The rate of flow of fluids, particles, or energy across a given surface or area. **b.** Magnetic flux. **6.** A heavy discharge of fluid from the body, especially the discharge of watery waste material from the intestines.

fly¹ (flī) *v.* **flew** (flo͞o), **flown** (flōn), **fly•ing, flies** (flīz). *—intr.* **1.** To move through the air by means of wings: *Birds fly south in winter.* **2.a.** To move or travel by air: *We flew to Seattle for vacation.* **b.** To pilot an aircraft or a spacecraft: *The crew flew from New York to Mexico City.* **3.a.** To rise in or be carried through the air by the wind: *Dust and pollen flew through the air.* **b.** To float or flutter in the air: *pennants flying from buildings.* **4.** To be sent or driven through the air with great speed or force: *The plate flew from my hands when I tripped.* **5.** To rush or flee: *flew down the hall; fly from danger.* **6.** To pass by swiftly: *a vacation flying by.* **7.** *past tense and past participle* **flied.** In baseball, to hit a fly ball. **8.** To react explosively; burst: *fly into a rage.* *—tr.* **1.** To cause to float or flutter in the air: *fly a kite.* **2.a.** To pilot (an aircraft or a spacecraft). **b.** To carry or transport in an aircraft or a spacecraft: *fly supplies to a remote area.* **c.** To pass over in flight: *fly the ocean.* **3.** To flee from: *Many people flew the country.* *—n.***1.** A fly ball in baseball. **2.** A cloth flap covering a zipper or set of buttons, especially one on the front of trousers. **3.** A cloth flap that covers the door or extends the roof of a tent or wagon. ***—idioms.*** **fly at.** To attack fiercely; assault. **let fly. 1.** To shoot, hurl, or release (a weapon). **2.** To lash out; criticize harshly: *The mayor let fly with an attack on her critics.* **on the fly. 1.** On the run; in a hurry: *I got a sandwich on the fly.* **2.** While in the air; in flight: *The bird was singing on the fly.* [First written down about 725 in Old English and spelled *flēogan*.]

fly² (flī) *n.***1.** Any of numerous two-winged insects, especially one of a group that includes the common housefly, gnat, and mosquito. **2.** A fishhook made to look like such an insect, as by attaching bits of feathers. [First written down before 800 in Old English and spelled *flȳge*.]

fly ball *n.* In baseball, a ball that is batted high in the air, usually to the outfield.

fly•catch•er (**flī′**kăch′ər *or* **flī′**kĕch′ər) *n.* Any of various birds that catch insects while flying, as the phoebe.

fly•er (**flī′**ər) *n.* Variant of **flier.**

fly-fish•ing (**flī′**fĭsh′ĭng) *n.* The art or sport of fishing using artificial flies for bait.

fly•ing (**flī′**ĭng) *adj.* **1.** Capable of or engaged in flight: *a flying insect.* **2.** Swiftly moving: *the pianist's flying fingers.* **3.** Brief; hurried: *a flying visit.* **4.** Of or relating to aviation: *flying lessons.* *—n.* **1.** Flight, as in an aircraft: *Flying is an exciting way to travel.* **2.** The operation of an aircraft: *A pilot is an expert in flying.*

flying buttress *n.* A support consisting of a pier or column connected to the wall of a building by an arch, used to prevent the wall from collapsing under the weight of the roof.

flying fish *n.* Any of various marine fishes having large side fins that spread out like wings as they leap and glide above the water.

flying jib *n.* A light triangular sail that extends beyond the jib.

flying saucer *n.* An unidentified flying object, usually said to be shaped like a disk.

flying squirrel *n.* Any of various squirrels that make long gliding leaps between trees with the aid of broad folds of skin that stretch along each side of the body between the front and hind legs.

flying buttress
Amiens Cathedral, France

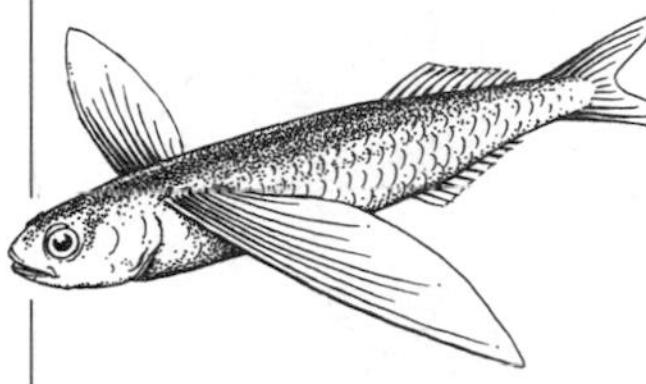

flying fish

flying squirrel

ă	pat	oi	**boy**
ā	pay	ou	**out**
âr	care	o͝o	**took**
ä	father	o͞o	**boot**
ĕ	pet	ŭ	**cut**
ē	be	ûr	**urge**
ĭ	pit	th	**thin**
ī	pie	*th*	**this**
îr	pier	hw	**whoop**
ŏ	pot	zh	vision
ō	toe	ə	about
ô	paw	N	*French* bon

Elizabeth Gurley Flynn

fly•leaf (flī′lēf′) *n.* A blank page at the beginning or end of a book.

Flynn (flĭn), **Elizabeth Gurley.** 1890–1964. American labor organizer who was a founder of the American Civil Liberties Union.

fly•pa•per (flī′pā′pər) *n.* Paper coated with a sticky, sometimes poisonous substance, used to catch flies.

fly•speck (flī′spĕk′) *n.* **1.** A small stain or spot of dirt left by a fly. **2.** A small spot.

fly swatter *n.* An implement used to kill flies or other insects, usually consisting of a piece of plastic or wire mesh attached to a long handle.

fly•way (flī′wā′) *n.* A route followed by migrating birds.

fly•weight (flī′wāt′) *n.* A boxer of the lightest weight class, weighing not more than 112 pounds.

fly•wheel (flī′wēl′) *n.* A wheel with a heavy rim, attached to a shaft of a machine to keep it turning at a steady speed.

Fm The symbol for the element **fermium.**

FM or **fm** *abbr.* An abbreviation of frequency modulation.

f-num•ber (ĕf′nŭm′bər) *n.* A number that is the focal length of a lens divided by its diameter, used in photography as a measure of the amount of light let in through the lens. The lower the f-number the wider the opening.

foal (fōl) *n.* The young offspring of a horse, zebra, or similar animal, especially one less than a year old. —*intr.v.* **foaled, foal•ing, foals.** To give birth to a foal: *a mare ready to foal.* [First written down about 950 in Old English and spelled *fola.*]

foam (fōm) *n.* **1.** A mass of bubbles formed in a liquid, as in surf or liquid soap, from shaking, boiling, or fermenting; froth. **2.** A spongy plastic or rubber formed with many tiny airholes in it. —*intr. v.* **foamed, foam•ing, foams.** To form foam or come forth in foam; froth: *The soap foamed as I sprayed water on it.*

foam rubber *n.* A light spongy rubber used for cushioning, packaging, and insulation.

foam•y (fō′mē) *adj.* **foam•i•er, foam•i•est.** Full of, covered with, or resembling foam: *foamy suds.* **—foam′i•ly** *adv.* **—foam′i•ness** *n.*

fob[1] (fŏb) *n.* **1.** A small pocket in a man's trousers or a vest, used to hold a watch, change, or other small items. **2.** A short chain or ribbon attached to a watch carried in a pocket. **3.** An ornament attached to a chain or ribbon. [First written down in 1653 in Modern English, probably of Germanic origin.]

fob[2] (fŏb) *tr.v.* **fobbed, fob•bing, fobs.** *Archaic.* To cheat someone. ***—idiom.* fob off. 1.** To get rid of by some trick or dishonest scheme: *fob off a copy as an original.* **2.** To put (a person) off by trickery: *He fobbed off the bill collector with a phony excuse.* [First written down about 1375 in Middle English and spelled *fobben,* probably from *fob,* trickster.]

f.o.b. also **F.O.B.** *abbr.* An abbreviation of free on board.

fo•cal (fō′kəl) *adj.* Of or relating to a focus: *The focal point of the discussion was rights for minority groups.* **—fo′cal•ly** *adv.*

focal length *n.* The distance from the surface of a mirror or lens to its point of focus.

fo•ci (fō′sī′ *or* fō′kī′) *n.* A plural of **focus.**

fo'c's'le (fōk′səl) *n.* Variant of **forecastle.**

fo•cus (fō′kəs) *n., pl.* **fo•cus•es** or **fo•ci** (fō′sī′ *or* fō′kī′). **1.a.** A point at which rays of light come together or from which they appear to spread apart, as after passing through a lens. **b.** Focal length. **2.a.** The degree of clarity with which an eye or optical instrument produces an image: *a telescope with excellent focus.* **b.** The condition or adjustment in which an eye or optical instrument gives its best image: *The camera is out of focus.* **3.** A center of interest, attention, or activity: *The senator was the focus of attention at the assembly.* **4.** Concentration or emphasis: *The narrator's focus is on the characters in the story rather than the action.* **5.** A central point or region, such as the point at which an earthquake starts or a region of the body in which an infection is largely confined. **6.** A fixed point or one of a pair of fixed points used in constructing a curve such as an ellipse, a parabola, or a hyperbola. —*v.* **fo•cused, fo•cus•ing, fo•cus•es** or **fo•cussed, fo•cus•sing, fo•cus•ses.** —*tr.* **1.a.** To bring (an object or image) into focus by adjusting the eyes or an optical instrument. **b.** To adjust (the eyes or an optical instrument) to produce a clear image: *Focus the telescope on the moon.* **2.** To concentrate or center; fix: *Focus your attention on the lesson. Public attention focused on the Olympics.* —*intr.* **1.** To adjust one's eyes or an optical instrument to produce a clear image. **2.** To concentrate attention or energy: *Let's focus on the problem at hand.*

fod•der (fŏd′ər) *n.* Food, such as chopped corn stalks or hay, for livestock.

foe (fō) *n.* An enemy, opponent, or adversary: *Foes of the new city dump met to fight the plan.* [First written down about 1000 in Old English and spelled *gefā,* from *fāh,* hostile.]

fog (fôg *or* fŏg) *n.* **1.** Condensed water vapor in cloudy masses lying close to the surface of the ground or water. **2.** A cloud of material, such as dust or smoke, that floats in the air: *a fog of insect spray.* **3.** A confused or unthinking condition: *All reason vanished in the fog of anger.* —*v.* **fogged, fog•ging, fogs.** —*tr.* **1.** To cover with or as if with fog: *Steam fogged the bathroom mirror.* **2.** To make uncertain or unclear; confuse: *The strong medicine fogged the patient's mind.* —*intr.* To become covered with or as if with fog: *The car windows fogged up in the rain.*

fo•gey (fō′gē) *n.* Variant of **fogy.**

fog•gy (fô′gē *or* fŏg′ē) *adj.* **fog•gi•er, fog•gi•est. 1.** Full of or surrounded by fog: *a foggy valley.* **2.** Confused or vague; clouded: *I have only a foggy memory of what happened.* **—fog′gi•ly** *adv.* **—fog′gi•ness** *n.*

fog•horn (fôg′hôrn′ *or* fŏg′hôrn′) *n.* A horn, usually having a deep tone, blown to warn ships of danger in foggy weather.

fo•gy also **fo•gey** (fō′gē) *n., pl.* **fo•gies** also **fo•geys.** A person with old-fashioned or narrow-minded notions.

foi•ble (foi′bəl) *n.* A minor personal fault or failing: *Laughing too loudly is an annoying foible.*

foil[1] (foil) *tr.v.* **foiled, foil•ing, foils.** To prevent from being successful; frustrate; thwart: *an alarm system to foil thieves.* [First written down before 1300 in Middle English and spelled *foilen,* to trample, defile, variant of *filen,* to defile.]

foil[2] (foil) *n.* **1.** A thin flexible sheet of metal: *aluminum foil.* **2.** A person or thing that makes another stand out by contrast: *The serious official was a perfect foil for the comedian.* [First written down about 1325 in Middle English, from Latin *folia,* plural of *folium,* leaf.]

foil[3] (foil) *n.* A long thin sword used in fencing, having a blunt point to prevent injury. [First written down in 1594 in Modern English.]

foist (foist) *tr.v.* **foist•ed, foist•ing, foists.** To pass off as genuine, valuable, or worthy; palm off: *The dishonest merchant tried to foist damaged goods on his customers.*

fold[1] (fōld) *v.* **fold•ed, fold•ing, folds.** —*tr.* **1.** To bend over or double up so that one part lies over another: *Fold your paper in half.* **2.** To close or flatten by bending, pressing, or doubling jointed or connected parts: *The bird folded its wings. The sunbathers folded their chairs and left.* **3.** To bring to an extended position; unfold: *I folded out the map to see where we were.* **4.a.** To clasp or embrace: *I folded the infant in my arms.* **b.** To enclose or wrap: *fold the garbage in a newspaper.* **5.** To blend (an ingredient) into a mixture by gently turning one part over another: *Fold the beaten egg whites into the batter.* —*intr.* **1.** To be folded or be capable of being folded: *My wallet folds in the middle.* **2.** *Informal.* To fail and close: *The business folded during the recession.* —*n.* **1.** A line or crease formed by folding: *Tear the paper along the fold.* **2.** A folded edge or part: *The little child hid in the folds of the curtain.* **3.** A bend in a layer of rock. [First written down before 899 in Old English and spelled *fealdan*.]

fold² (fōld) *n.* **1.** A pen for sheep. **2.** An established group, such as a church or political party, whose members share the same beliefs, aims, or interests. [First written down before 700 in Old English and spelled *fald*.]

-fold *suff.* A suffix that means: **1.** Multiplied by a specified number: *a fivefold increase in sales.* **2.** Divided into a specified number of parts: *a threefold problem.*

fold•er (fōl′dər) *n.* **1.** A folded sheet of cardboard or heavy paper used as a holder for loose papers: *a file folder.* **2.** A booklet or pamphlet made of one or more folded sheets of paper: *travel folders.* **3.** A person or machine that folds things.

fo•li•age (fō′lē ĭj *or* fō′lĭj) *n.* Plant leaves, especially tree leaves, considered as a group. [First written down in 1447 in Middle English and spelled *foilage*, from Old French *foillage*, from *foille*, leaf.]

fo•lic acid (fō′lĭk *or* fŏl′ĭk) *n.* A member of the vitamin B complex that occurs in green plants, fresh fruit, liver, and yeast, and is used to treat certain forms of anemia.

fo•li•o (fō′lē ō′) *n., pl.* **fo•li•os. 1.a.** A large sheet of paper folded once, making two leaves or four pages of a book. **b.** A book of the largest common size, consisting of such folded sheets, usually about 15 inches high. **2.** A page number in a book. [First written down in 1447 in Middle English, from Late Latin *folium*, leaf of paper, from Latin *folium*, leaf.]

folk (fōk) *n., pl.* **folk** or **folks. 1.** A people or nation. **2.** People: *city folk; honest folk.* **3. folks.** *Informal.* **a.** People considered as a group: *The warning sign scared folks away.* **b.** One's family or relatives: *My folks are coming to visit.* —*adj.* Of, occurring in, or coming from the common people or their culture: *a folk hero; a folk tune.* [First written down about 725 in Old English and spelled *folc*.]

folk dance *n.* **1.** A traditional dance originating among the common people of a country or region: *The mazurka is a Polish folk dance.* **2.** The music for such a dance. —**folk dancing** *n.*

folk etymology *n.* A change in the form of a word by influence of another word or words mistakenly believed to be related to it. For example, a crayfish is a crab and not a fish, but the word *crayfish* comes from Old French *crevise*. People mistakenly pronounced the last part of *crevise* as "fish," and so by folk etymology, a crab became a crayfish.

folk•lore (fōk′lôr′) *n.* The traditional beliefs, legends, and customs, handed down by a people from generation to generation.

folk music *n.* Music that is traditional among the common people of a country or region, usually passed from person to person.

folk-rock (fōk′rŏk′) *n.* A variety of popular music that combines elements of rock 'n' roll and folk music.

folk•sing•er (fōk′sĭng′ər) *n.* A person who specializes in singing folksongs. —**folk sing′ing** *n.*

folk•song (fōk′sông′ *or* fōk′sŏng′) *n.* **1.** A song that is part of the folk music of a people. **2.** A song composed in the style of such a song.

folk•sy (fōk′sē) *adj.* **folk•si•er, folk•si•est.** *Informal.* Simple and informal: *folksy people.*

folk•tale (fōk′tāl′) *n.* A traditional story or legend handed down by the common people of a country or region from one generation to the next.

fol•li•cle (fŏl′ĭ kəl) *n.* **1.** A small cavity, sac, or gland in the body. Hairs grow from follicles. **2.** A dry one-celled fruit that splits open along one seam only, as the fruit of the milkweed.

fol•low (fŏl′ō) *v.* **fol•lowed, fol•low•ing, fol•lows.** —*tr.* **1.** To go or come after: *Follow the usher to your seats.* **2.** To chase or trail: *The detectives followed the suspect at a distance.* **3.** To move along the same course as: *We followed a path to the beach.* **4.** To come after in order, time, or position: *Night follows day.* **5.** To occur as a result of: *General agreement followed the discussion.* **6.a.** To act in agreement with; obey: *follow the rules of the game.* **b.** To use as a guide or model: *Follow my example. Follow the recipe carefully.* **7.** To accept, believe in, or support: *follow a religion.* **8.** To work at (a trade or an occupation): *follow a trade such as carpentry.* **9.** To listen to or watch closely: *Weather forecasters followed the progress of the storm on their radar screens.* **10.** To keep up with; stay informed about: *Scientists follow new developments in genetics.* **11.** To grasp the meaning of; understand: *Do you follow what I'm saying?* —*intr.* **1.** To come, move, or take place after another person or thing in order or time: *A picnic followed after the baseball game.* **2.** To occur as a result: *Success will follow if you keep practicing.* —***idioms.*** **follow through. 1.** To carry something to completion: *She followed through on her promise.* **2.** In sports, to continue a stroke beyond the point of hitting the ball: *The batter followed through with a full swing.* **follow up. 1.** To make (a previous action) more effective by doing something else: *He followed up his interview with a thank-you letter.* **2.** To carry to completion: *We followed up their recommendation with a plan.* [First written down about 725 in Old English and spelled *folgian*.]

Synonyms: follow, succeed, ensue, result. These verbs mean to come after something or someone in time or order. **Follow** is the most general: *I followed Brian to the restaurant because I didn't know the way.* **Succeed** means to follow, especially in a planned order determined by rank, inheritance, or election: *His daughter succeeded him as publisher of the local newspaper.* **Ensue** means to follow as an effect or logical development: *If you do not cleanse the wound, an infection may ensue.* **Result** means to follow as a direct effect: *Failure to return a library book on time will result in a fine.*

fol•low•er (fŏl′ō ər) *n.* **1.** A person or thing that follows. **2.** A person who follows the beliefs or ideas of another. **3.** A close observer, a fan, or an enthusiast: *a follower of new developments in computers.*

fol•low•ing (fŏl′ō ĭng) *adj.* Coming next in order or time: *the following afternoon.* —*n.* **1.** A group of admirers, supporters, or disciples: *a popular politician with a large following.* **2.** The items or ones to be mentioned next: *Please buy the following: milk, bread, and eggs.* —*prep.* After: *Following dinner, we watched a movie.*

fol•low-up or **fol•low•up** (fŏl′ō ŭp′) *n.* Something that reinforces or enhances a previous action or

folk dance

ă	pat	oi	boy
ā	pay	ou	out
âr	care	o͝o	took
ä	father	o͞o	boot
ĕ	pet	ŭ	cut
ē	be	ûr	urge
ĭ	pit	th	thin
ī	pie	*th*	this
îr	pier	hw	whoop
ŏ	pot	zh	vision
ō	toe	ə	about
ô	paw	N	*French* bon

font¹
Baptismal font

Word History: fool

Apparently **fools** have been around for quite a while. Our word comes from the Old French *fol*, "an ignorant person." The Old French word comes from the Latin noun *follis*, "a bag or sack, an inflated ball, a bellows." In later Latin *follis* means "a silly, ignorant, or unintelligent person," and Saint Augustine of Hippo uses *follis inflātus* "inflated sack," in the sense of "puffed-up windbag."

footbridge
McMinnville's Airport Park in Oregon

event: *The software was a successful follow-up to the original product.*

fol•ly (fŏl′ē) *n., pl.* **fol•lies. 1.** Lack of good sense or judgment; foolishness. **2.** A foolish act or idea. [First written down before 1200 in Middle English and spelled *folie*, from Old French, from *fol*, foolish, from Late Latin *follis*, windbag, fool.]

fo•ment (fō mĕnt′) *tr.v.* **fo•ment•ed, fo•ment•ing, fo•ments.** To stir up; arouse; provoke: *The protesters were charged with fomenting a riot.* [First written down about 1425 in Middle English and spelled *fomenten*, to apply warm liquids to the skin, from Latin *fōmentum*, poultice, from *fovēre*, to warm.]

fond (fŏnd) *adj.* **fond•er, fond•est. 1.** Having a strong liking: *Are you fond of gardening?* **2.** Loving or affectionate: *a fond embrace.* **3.** Foolishly affectionate: *fond and doting pet owners.* **4.** Cherished; dear: *my fondest hopes.* **—fond′ly** *adv.*

fon•dle (fŏn′dl) *tr. & intr.v.* **fon•dled, fon•dling, fon•dles.** To touch or stroke lovingly; caress.

fond•ness (fŏnd′nĭs) *n.* **1.** Liking or inclination: *a fondness for the outdoors.* **2.** Warm affection.

fon•due (fŏn do͞o′ *or* fŏn dyo͞o′) *n.* **1.** A hot dish made of melted cheese and wine, eaten with bread. **2.** A hot dish of cooking oil or rich sauce in which small pieces of meat or other food are dipped or cooked and then eaten. [First written down in 1878 in Modern English, from French *fondue*, melted.]

Fon•ga•fa•le (fŏn′gə fä′lē). The capital of Tuvalu, in the southern Pacific Ocean north of Fiji. Population, 2,191.

font¹ (fŏnt) *n.* **1.** A basin that holds holy water or water used in baptism. **2.** A source or an origin: *The professor is a font of knowledge.* [First written down about 1000 in Old English, from Latin *fōns*, fountain.]

font² (fŏnt) *n.* A complete set of printing type of one size and style. [First written down in 1578 in Modern English, from French *fonte*, casting, from Latin *fundere*, to pour out.]

food (fo͞od) *n.* **1.** Material that a plant or an animal can take in and use for energy and to maintain life and growth. **2.** A supply of things to eat: *He brought them food and medicine.* **3.** A particular kind of nourishment: *plant food; dog food.* **4.** Something that stimulates or encourages some activity or growth: *The movie gave them food for thought.* [First written down about 1000 in Old English and spelled *fōda*.]

food chain *n.* A series of organisms within an environment, in which each kind of organism in the series is eaten by another kind higher up in the chain. A common food chain begins with grass eaten by cattle, which supply food for human beings.

food cycle *n.* A food web.

food poisoning *n.* Poisoning that results from eating food that has become contaminated with bacteria.

food proc•es•sor (prŏs′ĕs′ər *or* prō′sĕs′ər) *n.* An appliance with interchangeable blades that processes food, as by slicing or shredding, at high speeds.

food stamp *n.* A stamp, issued by the government to people with low incomes, that can be used to buy food at stores.

food•stuff (fo͞od′stŭf′) *n.* A substance that can be used or prepared for use as food.

food web *n.* A group of interrelated food chains in a particular ecological community.

fool (fo͞ol) *n.* **1.** A person who lacks judgment or good sense. **2.** A member of a royal or noble household who provided entertainment, as by telling jokes and clowning; a jester. *—v.* **fooled, fool•ing, fools.** *—tr.* **1.** To deceive or trick; mislead: *They fooled me into thinking they had left.* **2.** To take unawares; surprise: *We were sure their plan would fail, but they fooled us.* *—intr.* **1.** *Informal.* To act frivolously or idly: *If you continue fooling, you'll never finish your homework.* **2.** To act or speak in jest; joke: *My friend thought I was serious, but I was only fooling.* **3.** To play or meddle foolishly: *Don't fool with the knobs on the oven.* ***—idiom.*** **fool around.** *Informal.* To act frivolously or idly; waste time: *fooling around with friends on a summer afternoon.* [First written down about 1200 in Middle English and spelled *fol*, from Old French *fol*, from Late Latin *follis*, windbag, fool, from Latin *follis*, bellows.] —See Note.

fool•har•dy (fo͞ol′här′dē) *adj.* **fool•har•di•er, fool•har•di•est.** Foolishly bold; rash; reckless: *a foolhardy beginner trying to ski down the steepest slopes.* **—fool′har′di•ness** *n.*

fool•ish (fo͞o′lĭsh) *adj.* **1.** Lacking in good sense or judgment; unwise: *a foolish choice.* **2.** Absurd; ridiculous: *I looked foolish dressed as a clown.* **—fool′ish•ly** *adv.* **—fool′ish•ness** *n.*

fool•proof (fo͞ol′pro͞of′) *adj.* So safe, simple, and reliable that error or misuse is impossible: *a foolproof toaster; a foolproof plan.*

fools•cap (fo͞olz′kăp′) *n.* Writing paper in large sheets about 13 inches (32 centimeters) wide and 16 inches (40.5 centimeters) long.

fool's gold (fo͞olz) *n.* Any of several minerals, especially pyrite, sometimes mistaken for gold.

foot (fo͝ot) *n., pl.* **feet** (fēt). **1.** The part of the leg that rests on or touches the ground or floor in standing or walking. **2.** A similar part used for moving or attachment, as the muscular organ extending from the shell of a snail or clam. **3.** A part or base resembling a foot, as the end of a table leg. **4.** The lowest part of something high or long; the bottom: *the foot of the stairs; the foot of the page.* **5.** The end opposite the head in position or rank: *the foot of the bed; the foot of the class.* **6.** The part of a boot or stocking that covers the foot. **7.** A unit of length equal to ⅓ of a yard or 12 inches (about 30.5 centimeters). See table at **measurement. 8.** A unit of poetry, such as an iamb or a dactyl, consisting of a combination of stressed and unstressed syllables. *—tr.v.* **foot•ed, foot•ing, foots.** *Informal.* To pay: *I'll foot the bill.* ***—idiom.*** **on foot.** Walking or running: *We're going to the restaurant on foot.*

foot•age (fo͝ot′ĭj) *n.* A length or an amount of something as measured in feet: *film footage.*

foot-and-mouth disease (fo͝ot′n mouth′) *n.* A highly contagious disease of cattle and other hoofed animals, marked by fever and blisters around the mouth and hoofs.

foot•ball (fo͝ot′bôl′) *n.* **1.a.** A game played by two teams of 11 players each on a rectangular field with goals at either end, the object being to carry the ball across the opponent's goal line or to kick it between the opponent's goal posts. **b.** The inflated oval ball used in this game. **2.** *Chiefly British.* **a.** Soccer or Rugby. **b.** The ball used in soccer or Rugby.

foot•board (fo͝ot′bôrd′) *n.* **1.** A board or small platform on which to support or rest the feet. **2.** An upright board across the foot of a bedstead.

foot•bridge (fo͝ot′brĭj′) *n.* A bridge used only by people on foot.

foot-can•dle (fo͝ot′kăn′dl) *n.* A unit of light intensity equal to the illumination of a surface that has each of its points one foot away from a candle.

foot•ed (fo͝ot′ĭd) *adj.* Having a foot or feet: *a footed sofa; a four-footed animal.*

foot•fall (fo͝ot′fôl′) *n.* The sound made by a footstep.

foot•hill (fo͝ot′hĭl′) *n.* A low hill located near the base of a mountain or mountain range.

foot•hold (fo͝ot′hōld′) *n.* **1.** A place to put the foot so that it won't slip, especially when climbing. **2.** A firm secure position from which it is possible to advance: *He got a foothold in business by first working as an assistant.*

foot•ing (fo͝ot′ĭng) *n.* **1.** A firm placing of the feet allowing one to stand or move without falling: *lose one's footing.* **2.** A secure place to put the foot; a foothold. **3.** The condition of a surface for walking or running: *The road was icy and the footing treacherous.* **4.** A basis or standing: *You'll be on an equal footing with the others.*

foot•lights (fo͝ot′līts′) *pl.n.* Lights placed in a row along the front of a stage floor.

foot•loose (fo͝ot′lo͞os′) *adj.* Having no attachments or responsibilities; free to do as one pleases.

foot•man (fo͝ot′mən) *n.* A male servant, usually in uniform, who opens doors, serves at the table, and does various other domestic jobs.

foot•note (fo͝ot′nōt′) *n.* A note at the bottom of a page explaining something in the text or giving the source of a quotation, a fact, or an idea.

foot•path (fo͝ot′păth′) *n.* A narrow path for people to walk on.

foot-pound (fo͝ot′pound′) *n.* A unit of work equal to the work or energy needed to lift a one-pound weight a distance of one foot against the force of Earth's gravity.

foot•print (fo͝ot′prĭnt′) *n.* A mark left by a foot or shoe, as in sand or snow.

foot•race or **foot race** (fo͝ot′rās′) *n.* A race run by people on foot.

foot•rest (fo͝ot′rĕst′) *n.* A low stool, metal bar, or other support on which to rest the feet.

foot soldier *n.* A soldier in the infantry.

foot•sore (fo͝ot′sôr′) *adj.* Having sore or tired feet from much walking.

foot•step (fo͝ot′stĕp′) *n.* **1.** A step taken by a foot. **2.** The sound of a foot stepping: *I heard their footsteps on the stairs.* **3.** A footprint. ***—idiom.*** **follow in (someone's) footsteps.** To carry on the behavior, work, or tradition of.

foot•stool (fo͝ot′sto͞ol′) *n.* A low stool on which to rest the feet while sitting.

foot•wear (fo͝ot′wâr′) *n.* Coverings for the feet, such as shoes or boots.

foot•work (fo͝ot′wûrk′) *n.* The movement of the feet, as in boxing or dancing.

fop (fŏp) *n.* A man who is vain about his clothes and appearance; a dandy. **—fop′pish** *adj.* **—fop′pish•ly** *adv.* **—fop′pish•ness** *n.*

fop•per•y (fŏp′ə rē) *n., pl.* **fop•per•ies.** The dress or manner of a fop.

for (fôr; fər *when unstressed*) *prep.* **1.a.** With the purpose, goal, or object of: *swimming for exercise; studying for the exam; eager for fame.* **b.** Directed or addressed to: *a letter for Jim.* **2.** In order to go toward or arrive at: *Let's head for home.* **3.** As a result of: *They were rewarded for their hard work.* **4.** On behalf of: *She spoke for all of us.* **5.** In favor or support of: *Are you for the idea or not?* **6.** In place of: *She used her coat for a blanket.* **7.** In the amount of; at the price of: *a bill for five dollars; a radio bought for ten dollars.* **8.** To the extent of or through the duration of: *We drove for miles. We talked for an hour.* **9.** At the stated time of: *I have an appointment for 2 o'clock.* **10.a.** As regards; concerning: *He's a stickler for neatness.* **b.** Considering the usual character of. *It's a warm day for October.* **c.** In honor of: *She was named for her aunt.* **11.** Suitable to: *It's really for her to decide.* **12.** In spite of: *For all his complaining, he seems to like his job.* *—conj.* Because; since: *We must be careful measuring the windows, for it's easy to make mistakes.* [First written down about 725 in Old English and spelled *for,* on account of.]

❑ *These sound alike:* **for, fore** (at the front), **four** (number).

for•age (fôr′ĭj *or* fŏr′ĭj) *n.* **1.** Food for horses, cattle, or other animals; fodder. **2.** A search to find available food or supplies. *—v.* **for•aged, for•ag•ing, for•ag•es.** *—intr.* **1.** To search for food: *Raccoons forage in garbage dumps.* **2.** To search or hunt about, as for something needed or desired: *foraging in a drawer for a sock.* *—tr.* **1.** To get by searching about: *We foraged cookies from the pantry.* **2.** To obtain food, supplies, or other goods from, often by force; plunder: *Pirates foraged the coastal towns.* [First written down before 1333 in Middle English, from Old French *fourrage,* from *forrer,* to forage, from *feurre,* fodder, of Germanic origin.] **—for′ag•er** *n.*

for•as•much as (fôr′əz mŭch′) *conj.* Inasmuch as.

for•ay (fôr′ā′ *or* fŏr′ā′) *n.* A sudden raid or military expedition. *—intr.v.* **for•ayed, for•ay•ing, for•ays.** To make a raid: *foray into enemy territory.* [First written down about 1375 in Middle English, from Old French *forrer,* to forage.]

for•bad (fôr băd′) *v.* A past tense of **forbid.**

for•bade (fôr băd′ *or* fôr bād′) *v.* A past tense of **forbid.**

for•bear[1] (fôr bâr′) *v.* **for•bore** (fôr bôr′), **for•borne** (fôr bôrn′), **for•bear•ing, for•bears.** *—tr.* To keep from; refrain from; resist: *I could not forbear telling him the truth.* *—intr.* **1.** To hold back; refrain: *forbear from replying.* **2.** To be patient or tolerant: *Forbear with my misunderstanding.* [First written down about 725 in Old English and spelled *forberan,* to endure.]

for•bear[2] (fôr′bâr′) *n.* Variant of **forebear.**

for•bear•ance (fôr bâr′əns) *n.* Patience, tolerance, or restraint: *He showed forbearance in disciplining the unruly children.*

for•bid (fôr bĭd′) *tr.v.* **for•bade** (fôr băd′ *or* fôr bād′) or **for•bad** (fôr băd′), **for•bid•den** (fôr bĭd′n) or **for•bid, for•bid•ding, for•bids. 1.** To refuse to allow; prohibit or deny: *The law forbids robbery.* **2.** To order (a person) not to do something: *I forbid you to go.* [First written down about 725 in Old English and spelled *forbēodan.*]

for•bid•ding (fôr bĭd′ĭng) *adj.* Looking threatening, dangerous, or unfriendly: *a forbidding desert.*

for•bore (fôr bôr′) *v.* Past tense of **forbear**[1].

for•borne (fôr bôrn′) *v.* Past participle of **forbear**[1].

force (fôrs) *n.* **1.** Strength; power; energy: *the force of an explosion.* See Synonyms at **strength. 2.** Power, pressure, or violence used on a person or thing that resists: *use force in driving a nail; a promise obtained by force.* **3.** Something that causes a change in the speed or direction of a body's motion, or a quantity that measures this change in motion: *the attractive force between two opposite electric charges.* **4.a.** A group of people organized or available for a certain purpose: *a large labor force; a police force.* **b. forces.** Military units, as of an army: *Napoleon's forces.* **5.** A strong influence acting as an urge or a restraint: *forces affecting modern life.* **6.** The power to influence or persuade; effectiveness: *the force of a reasonable appeal.* *—tr. v.* **forced, forc•ing, forc•es. 1.** To make (a person) do something, as through pressure or necessity: *The storm forced us to postpone our meeting.* **2.** To get by the use of force: *I forced the ball from his hand.* **3.** To impose or inflict. *The invaders forced their laws on the peoples they conquered.* **4.** To move, push, or drive by pressure: *The pump forces water through the pipe.* **5.** To bring on or bring about through effort or pressure: *I forced a smile on my face.* **6.** To make (one's way) by pushing, thrusting, or breaking: *They forced their way through the*

ă	**pat**	oi	**boy**
ā	**pay**	ou	**out**
âr	**care**	o͝o	**took**
ä	**father**	o͞o	**boot**
ĕ	**pet**	ŭ	**cut**
ē	**be**	ûr	**urge**
ĭ	**pit**	th	**thin**
ī	**pie**	*th*	**this**
îr	**pier**	hw	**whoop**
ŏ	**pot**	zh	**vision**
ō	**toe**	ə	**about**
ô	**paw**	N	*French* **bon**

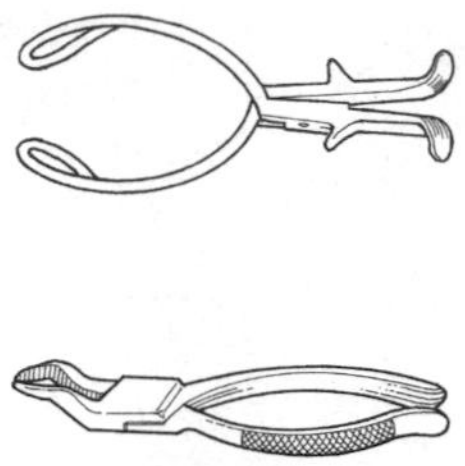

forceps
Top: Obstetrical
Bottom: Dental

Gerald Ford

Word Building: fore–

The prefix **fore–** means "before, in front." A **forerunner** is "one that goes before," and a **foreleg** is "a front leg of an animal." It is important not to confuse **fore–** with the prefix *for–* (sometimes spelled *fore–*), which appears in many English words but is no longer used to form words in English. This prefix bears the meaning of exclusion or rejection and survives in words like **forbid** and **forswear**.

thorn hedge. **7.** To break open or pry open by using violence: *force the door; force a lock.* **8.** To cause to grow or bloom rapidly by artificial means: *force flowers in a greenhouse.* **—*idiom.* in force. 1.** In effect; in operation; valid: *a rule no longer in force.* **2.** In full strength: *The protesters turned out in force.* [First written down before 1300 in Middle English, from Medieval Latin *fortia*, from Latin *fortis*, strong.] **—forc′er** *n.*

forced (fôrst) *adj.* **1.** Done under force, not by free choice; compulsory: *forced labor* **2.** Not natural; strained: *forced laughter.*

force•ful (**fôrs′**fəl) *adj.* Full of force; effective: *The winning candidate is a forceful speaker.* **—force′ful•ly** *adv.* **—force′ful•ness** *n.*

force play *n.* In baseball, a play in which a runner is put out when forced by the batter to move to the next base.

for•ceps (**fôr′**səps) *n., pl.* **forceps.** A pair of special pincers or tongs used especially by surgeons or dentists for grasping, holding, or pulling. [First written down in 1563 in Modern English, from Latin *forceps*, fire tongs, pincers.]

forc•i•ble (**fôr′**sə bəl) *adj.* **1.** Accomplished through the use of force: *The firefighters broke in by forcible entry.* **2.** Having force; forceful: *a forcible personality.* **—for′ci•bly** *adv.*

ford (fôrd) *n.* A shallow place in a stream or river where one can walk, ride, or drive across. *—tr.v.* **ford•ed, ford•ing, fords.** To cross (a stream or river) by wading, riding, or driving through a ford. [First written down before 899 in Old English.] **—ford′a•ble** *adj.*

Ford (fôrd), **Gerald Rudolph.** Born 1913. The 38th President of the United States (1974–1977), who became President after Richard Nixon's resignation over the Watergate scandal.

Ford, Henry. 1863–1947. American automobile manufacturer who founded the Ford Motor Company (1903) and produced the Model T (1908–1927), the first widely available and affordable car.

fore (fôr) *adj.* In, at, or toward the front; forward: *The fore part of the new building faces the avenue.* *—n.* **1.** Something that is located at or toward the front. **2.** The front part: *checked the ropes at the fore.* *—adv.* At, toward, or near the front; forward: *ran fore to check the damage.* *—interj.* An expression used by golfers to warn others on the course that the ball is about to be hit in their direction. **—*idiom.* to the fore.** In, into, or toward a position of prominence: *New issues bring new leaders to the fore.* [First written down about 725 in Old English.]

❑ *These sound alike:* **fore, for** (with the purpose of), **four** (number).

fore– *pref.* A prefix that means: **1.** Before; earlier: *foresight; forefather.* **2.** Front; in front of: *forepaw; foremast.* —See Note.

fore and aft *adv.* **1.** From the bow of a ship to the stern; lengthwise: *sails rigged fore and aft.* **2.** In, at, or toward both ends of a ship.

fore-and-aft (fôr′ən **ăft′**) *adj.* Extending lengthwise along a structure, such as a ship; from bow to stern: *the fore-and-aft sails of a sloop.*

fore•arm¹ (fôr **ärm′**) *tr.v.* **fore•armed, fore•arm•ing, fore•arms.** To arm or prepare in advance of a conflict. [First written down in 1592 in Modern English : *fore-*, before + *arm*, to arm.]

fore•arm² (**fôr′**ärm′) *n.* The part of the arm between the wrist and elbow. [First written down in 1741 in Modern English : *fore-*, before + *arm*, body part.]

fore•bear also **for•bear** (**fôr′**bâr′) *n.* An ancestor. [First written down in 1470 in Middle English : *fore-*, before + *beer*, one who is (from *been*, to be).]

fore•bode (fôr **bōd′**) *v.* **fore•bod•ed, fore•bod•ing, fore•bodes.** *—tr.* **1.** To indicate the likelihood of; portend: *A dark sky sometimes forebodes a storm.* **2.** To have a sense or feeling of (something bad to come): *The scowls on their faces foreboded a fight.* *—intr.* To prophesy or predict. **—fore•bod′er** *n.*

fore•bod•ing (fôr **bō′**dĭng) *n.* A sense of impending evil.

fore•brain (**fôr′**brān′) *n.* The part of the brain that includes the thalamus, the hypothalamus, the cerebrum, and the ends of the olfactory nerves.

fore•cast (**fôr′**kăst′) *tr.v.* **fore•cast** or **fore•cast•ed, fore•cast•ing, fore•casts.** To tell in advance what might or will happen, especially to predict weather conditions: *forecast snow for the weekend.* *—n.* A prediction, as of coming events or conditions: *the weather forecast.* [First written down in 1400 in Middle English and spelled *forecasten*, to plan beforehand : *fore-*, before + *casten*, to throw, calculate, prepare.] **—fore′cast′er** *n.*

fore•cas•tle (**fōk′**səl *or* **fôr′**kăs′əl) also **fo'c's'le** (**fōk′**səl) *n.* **1.** The section of a ship's upper deck located forward of the foremast. **2.** The crew's quarters at the bow of a merchant ship.

fore•close (fôr **klōz′**) *v.* **fore•closed, fore•clos•ing, fore•clos•es.** *—tr.* **1.** To take away the right to pay off (a mortgage), as when payments have not been made: *The bank foreclosed the mortgage and took away the property.* **2.** To shut out or rule out; bar. *—intr.* To bar a right to redeem a mortgage.

fore•clo•sure (fôr **klō′**zhər) *n.* The act of foreclosing, especially a legal proceeding by which a mortgage is foreclosed.

fore•doom (fôr **do͞om′**) *tr.v.* **fore•doomed, fore•doom•ing, fore•dooms.** To doom or condemn beforehand.

fore•fa•ther (**fôr′**fä′*th*ər) *n.* An ancestor.

fore•fin•ger (**fôr′**fĭng′gər) *n.* The finger next to the thumb; the index finger.

fore•foot (**fôr′**fo͝ot′) *n.* One of the front feet of a four-legged animal.

fore•front (**fôr′**frŭnt′) *n.* **1.** The part or area at the very front. **2.** The most important or most advanced position: *at the forefront in the fight against crime.*

fore•gath•er (fôr **găth′**ər) *v.* Variant of **forgather.**

fore•go¹ (fôr **gō′**) *tr.v.* **fore•went** (fôr **wĕnt′**), **fore•gone** (fôr **gôn′** *or* fôr **gŏn′**), **fore•go•ing, fore•goes** (fôr **gōz′**). To precede, as in time or place.

fore•go² (fôr **gō′**) *v.* Variant of **forgo.**

fore•go•ing (fôr **gō′**ĭng *or* **fôr′**gō′ĭng) *adj.* Said, written, or encountered just before; previous: *Refer to the foregoing figures.*

fore•gone *v.* (fôr **gôn′** *or* fôr **gŏn′**). Past participle of **forego¹.** *—adj.* (**fôr′**gôn′ *or* **fôr′**gŏn′). Having gone before; previous.

fore•ground (**fôr′**ground′) *n.* The part of a scene or picture that is nearest to and in front of the viewer.

fore•hand (**fôr′**hănd′) *n.* In sports, a stroke, as of a racket, made or done with the palm of the hand turned forward. **—fore′hand′** *adj.*

fore•head (**fôr′**hĕd′ *or* **fôr′**hĕd′) *n.* The part of the face above the eyebrows.

for•eign (**fôr′**ĭn *or* **fŏr′**ĭn) *adj.* **1.** Located away from one's own country: *a foreign country.* **2.** Of, relating to, or from another country or place: *a foreign language; foreign customs.* **3.** Conducted or involved with other nations or governments: *foreign trade.* **4.** Not naturally or normally belonging; alien: *Jealousy is foreign to her nature.* [First written down about 1250 in Middle English and spelled *ferren*, from Late Latin *forānus*, on the outside.]

for•eign•er (**fôr′**ə nər *or* **fŏr′**ə nər) *n.* **1.** A person from a foreign country or place: *Millions of foreigners have immigrated to the United States.* **2.** An outsider.

fore•know (fôr nō′) *tr.v.* **fore•knew** (fôr no͞o′ *or* fôr-nyo͞o′), **fore•known** (fôr nōn′), **fore•know•ing, fore•knows.** To have knowledge of something before its existence or occurrence.

fore•knowl•edge (fôr nŏl′ĭj *or* fôr′nŏl′ĭj) *n.* Knowledge of something before its occurrence or existence.

fore•leg (fôr′lĕg′) *n.* One of the front legs of a four-legged animal.

fore•limb (fôr′lĭm′) *n.* A front limb such as an arm, a wing, a foreleg, or a flipper.

fore•lock (fôr′lŏk′) *n.* A lock of hair that grows from or falls on the forehead.

fore•man (fôr′mən) *n.* **1.** A man who has charge of a group of workers, as in a factory. **2.** A man who chairs and speaks for a jury.

fore•mast (fôr′məst *or* fôr′măst′) *n.* The forward mast on a sailing ship.

fore•most (fôr′mōst′) *adj.* First in time, place, rank, or position; most important or leading: *the world's foremost authority on the subject.* —*adv.* In the first or front position.

fore•noon (fôr′no͞on′ *or* fôr no͞on′) *n.* The period of time between sunrise and noon; morning.

fo•ren•sic (fə rĕn′sĭk *or* fə rĕn′zĭk) *adj.* Relating to, used in, or appropriate for courts of law or for public discussion.

fore•or•dain (fôr′ôr dān′) *tr.v.* **fore•or•dained, fore•or•dain•ing, fore•or•dains.** To determine or appoint beforehand; predestine: *They believed their fate was foreordained.*

fore•part (fôr′pärt′) *n.* The first, early, or front part.

fore•paw (fôr′pô′) *n.* The paw of an animal's foreleg.

fore•quar•ter (fôr′kwôr′tər) *n.* The front legs, shoulders, and sometimes the near ribs of a four-footed animal, especially of a cow, sheep, or pig.

fore•run•ner (fôr′rŭn′ər) *n.* **1.** A person or thing that precedes, as in time; a predecessor: *Roller skates were the forerunners of skateboards.* **2.** A person who announces the coming of another; a herald. **3.** A warning sign or symptom: *A sore throat is often the forerunner of a cold.*

fore•sail (fôr′səl *or* fôr′sāl′) *n.* **1.** The principal sail on the foremast of a square-rigged ship. **2.** The principal fore-and-aft sail on the foremast of a fore-and-aft rigged vessel.

fore•see (fôr sē′) *tr.v.* **fore•saw** (fôr sô′), **fore•seen** (fôr sēn′), **fore•see•ing, fore•sees.** To see or know beforehand: *As the mountain got steeper, the hikers foresaw a difficult climb.* **—fore•see′a•ble** *adj.* **—fore•se′er** *n.*

fore•shad•ow (fôr shăd′ō) *tr.v.* **fore•shad•owed, fore•shad•ow•ing, fore•shad•ows.** To present an indication or a suggestion of beforehand: *Everyone hoped that the border dispute did not foreshadow a wider war.*

fore•short•en (fôr shôr′tn) *tr.v.* **fore•short•ened, fore•short•en•ing, fore•short•ens.** To shorten the lines of (an object) in a drawing or painting so as to give the illusion of depth or distance.

fore•sight (fôr′sīt′) *n.* **1.** Perception of the importance and nature of events before they occur. **2.** Care in providing for the future: *Spending all of your money at once shows little foresight.* **—fore′sight′ed** *adj.*

fore•skin (fôr′skĭn′) *n.* The loose fold of skin that covers the end of the penis; the prepuce.

for•est (fôr′ĭst *or* fŏr′ĭst) *n.* A dense growth of trees, plants, and underbrush covering a large area. [First written down before 1300 in Middle English, from Medieval Latin *forestis (silva)*, outside (forest), from Latin *forīs*, outside.] **—for′es•ta′tion** *n.*

fore•stall (fôr stôl′) *tr.v.* **fore•stalled, fore•stall•ing, fore•stalls. 1.** To prevent, delay, or hinder by acting in advance: *ended the news conference to forestall any more questions.* **2.** To deal with or think of beforehand; anticipate. **—fore•stall′er** *n.*

for•est•er (fôr′ĭ stər *or* fŏr′ĭ stər) *n.* A person trained in forestry.

for•est•ry (fôr′ĭ strē *or* fŏr′ĭ strē) *n.* The science or work of cultivating, developing, and maintaining forests.

fore•taste (fôr′tāst′) *n.* A slight taste or sample of something to come: *Her first published story was a foretaste of later successful novels.*

fore•tell (fôr tĕl′) *tr.v.* **fore•told** (fôr tōld′), **fore•tell•ing, fore•tells.** To tell or indicate beforehand; predict: *Can you foretell what will happen?*

fore•thought (fôr′thôt′) *n.* Thought, planning, or consideration for the future; foresight.

fore•told (fôr tōld′) *v.* Past tense and past participle of **foretell.**

for•ev•er (fər ĕv′ər) *adv.* **1.** For everlasting time; eternally: *No one can live forever.* **2.** At all times; incessantly: *The baby is forever fussing.* —*n.* A seemingly very long time: *The bus is taking forever to come.*

for•ev•er•more (fər ĕv′ər môr′) *adv.* Forever.

fore•warn (fôr wôrn′) *tr.v.* **fore•warned, fore•warn•ing, fore•warns.** To warn in advance: *Dark clouds forewarned them of an approaching storm.*

fore•went (fôr wĕnt′) *v.* Past tense of **forego**[1].

fore•wing (fôr′wĭng′) *n.* Either of a pair of front wings of certain insects, such as the moth, butterfly, or dragonfly.

fore•wom•an (fôr′wo͝om′ən) *n.* **1.** A woman who has charge of a group of workers, as in a factory. **2.** The woman who chairs and speaks for a jury.

fore•word (fôr′wərd) *n.* A preface or an introductory note, as for a book.

for•feit (fôr′fĭt) *n.* Something surrendered or paid as a punishment or a penalty. —*tr.v.* **for•feit•ed, for•feit•ing, for•feits.** To surrender or give up the right to (something) as a penalty or punishment for a crime, an error, or an offense: *By failing to appear, the opposing team forfeited the game.* [First written down before 1376 in Middle English and spelled *forfet*, crime, penalty, from Old French *forfaire*, to commit a crime, act outside the law.]

for•fei•ture (fôr′fĭ cho͝or′ *or* fôr′fĭ chər) *n.* **1.** The act of surrendering something as a forfeit. **2.** Something that is forfeited; a penalty.

for•gath•er also **fore•gath•er** (fôr găth′ər) *intr.v.* **for•gath•ered, for•gath•er•ing, for•gath•ers.** To gather together; assemble.

for•gave (fər gāv′ *or* fôr gāv′) *v.* Past tense of **forgive.**

forge[1] (fôrj) *n.* A furnace or hearth where metal is heated so that it can be hammered into shape; a smithy. —*v.* **forged, forg•ing, forg•es.** —*tr.* **1.** To form (metal, for example) by heating in a forge and hammering into shape. **2.** To give form or shape to, especially by means of careful effort: *The coach forged a close relationship with his players.* **3.** To reproduce or copy for fraudulent purposes; counterfeit: *forge a signature on a document.* —*intr.* **1.** To work at a forge or smithy. **2.** To make a forgery or counterfeit. [First written down in 1279 in Middle English, from Latin *fabrica*, from *faber*, worker.] **—forg′er** *n.*

forge[2] (fôrj) *intr.v.* **forged, forg•ing, forg•es. 1.** To move forward gradually but steadily: *The explorers forged through the swamp.* **2.** To advance with an abrupt increase in speed: *forged into first place.* [First written down in 1611 in Modern English, probably from *forge*, furnace.]

for•ger•y (fôr′jə rē) *n., pl.* **for•ger•ies. 1.** The act of forging, especially the illegal production of some-

forehand

ă	**pat**	oi	**boy**
ā	**pay**	ou	**out**
âr	**care**	o͝o	**took**
ä	**father**	o͞o	**boot**
ĕ	**pet**	ŭ	**cut**
ē	**be**	ûr	**urge**
ĭ	**pit**	th	**thin**
ī	**pie**	*th*	**this**
îr	**pier**	hw	**whoop**
ŏ	**pot**	zh	**vision**
ō	**toe**	ə	**about**
ô	**paw**	N	*French* **bon**

forget-me-not

forked
Forked tongue
of a timber rattlesnake

forklift

thing counterfeit: *the forgery of a painting.* **2.** Something counterfeit, forged, or fraudulent.

for•get (fər gĕt′ *or* fôr gĕt′) *tr.v.* **for•got** (fər gŏt′ *or* fôr gŏt′), **for•got•ten** (fər gŏt′n *or* fôr gŏt′n) or **for•got, for•get•ting, for•gets. 1.** To be unable to remember (something): *We forgot the telephone number. I completely forgot my lines in the play.* **2.** To disregard or neglect; fail to do or mention: *I forgot to give you the message.* **3.** To leave behind unintentionally: *I forgot my toothbrush.* ***—idiom.*** **forget oneself.** To lose one's reserve, temper, or self-restraint: *The bystanders forgot themselves and ran to shake the President's hand.* [First written down about 725 in Old English and spelled *forgytan.*] **—for•get′ta•ble** *adj.* **—for•get′ter** *n.*

for•get•ful (fər gĕt′fəl *or* fôr gĕt′fəl) *adj.* **1.** Tending or likely to forget: *When I am sleepy I can be forgetful.* **2.** Neglectful; thoughtless: *forgetful of one's responsibilities.* **—for•get′ful•ly** *adv.* **—for•get′ful•ness** *n.*

for•get-me-not (fər gĕt′mē nŏt′ *or* fôr gĕt′mē nŏt′) *n.* Any of various low-growing garden plants having clusters of small blue flowers.

for•give (fər gĭv′ *or* fôr gĭv′) *v.* **for•gave** (fər gāv′ *or* fôr gāv′), **for•giv•en** (fər gĭv′ən *or* fôr gĭv′ən), **for•giv•ing, for•gives.** *—tr.* **1.** To excuse for a fault or an offense; pardon: *Our friends forgave us for making them late.* **2.** To absolve from payment of (a debt, for example). *—intr.* To grant forgiveness: *A parent usually forgives easily.* [First written down about 900 in Old English and spelled *forgiefan.*] **—for•giv′a•ble** *adj.* **—for•giv′er** *n.*

Synonyms: forgive, pardon, excuse, condone. These verbs mean to decide not to punish an offender. **Forgive** means to grant pardon without resentment: *He forgave you because he knew you didn't mean what you said.* **Pardon** means to free from a penalty: *After the revolution all political prisoners were pardoned.* **Excuse** means to forgive in effect by overlooking a mistake or fault: *Please excuse the child for her bad manners.* **Condone** means to excuse an offense, usually a serious one: *I cannot condone such horrible behavior by ignoring it.*

for•give•ness (fər gĭv′nĭs *or* fôr gĭv′nĭs) *n.* The act of forgiving; pardon.

for•giv•ing (fər gĭv′ĭng *or* fôr gĭv′ĭng) *adj.* Inclined or able to forgive: *a kind, forgiving person.*

for•go also **fore•go** (fôr gō′) *tr.v.* **for•went** (fôr-wĕnt′) or **for•gone** (fôr gôn′ *or* fôr gŏn′), **for•go•ing, for•goes.** To give up; do without: *I will forgo the day at the beach and finish my work instead.*

for•got (fər gŏt′ *or* fôr gŏt′) *v.* Past tense and a past participle of **forget.**

for•got•ten (fər gŏt′n *or* fôr gŏt′n) *v.* A past participle of **forget.**

fo•rint (fôr′ĭnt′) *n.* The basic monetary unit of Hungary.

fork (fôrk) *n.* **1.** A utensil with two or more prongs, used to serve or eat food. **2.** A large farm tool of similar shape, used to pick up hay or turn up ground. **3.a.** A separation into two or more branches, as of a stream or road. **b.** One of the branches of such a separation: *the right fork of the road.* *—v.* **forked, fork•ing, forks.** *—tr.* **1.** To raise, carry, pitch, or pierce with a fork. **2.** *Informal.* To pay: *forked over the money to cover the dinner expenses.* *—intr.* To divide into two or more branches: *The road forks beyond the hill.* [First written down about 1000 in Old English and spelled *forca,* from Latin *furca.*]

forked (fôrkt *or* fôr′kĭd) *adj.* Having a fork or forks; divided: *a forked river; a snake's forked tongue.*

fork•lift (fôrk′lĭft′) *n.* A small vehicle having a pair of prongs in front that can be slid under a load to be lifted and moved.

for•lorn (fər lôrn′ *or* fôr lôrn′) *adj.* **1.** Appearing sad or lonely because deserted or abandoned: *a forlorn puppy.* **2.** Wretched or pitiful in appearance or condition: *a forlorn shack.* [First written down in 1137 in Middle English and spelled *forloren,* past participle of *forlesen,* to abandon, from Old English *forlēosan.*] **—for•lorn′ly** *adv.* **—for•lorn′ness** *n.*

form (fôrm) *n.* **1.** The shape and structure of an object: *the form of a snowflake.* **2.** The body or outward appearance of a person or an animal; the figure: *a statue of the human form.* **3.** The manner in which a thing exists, acts, or manifests itself; kind: *Our negotiations took the form of private talks.* **4.** A customary way of doing something; a procedure. **5.** A document with blanks that are to be filled in: *The patient's condition is recorded on a medical form.* **6.** Behavior according to a fixed or accepted standard: *It is not good form to talk during a movie.* **7.** Fitness or good condition of mind or body: *The athlete is in top form this season.* **8.** The manner in which an artistic, musical, or literary work is arranged or put together: *in sonata form; arranged my ideas in outline form.* **9.** A mold for the setting of concrete. **10.** A grade in a British school or in some American private schools. **11.** One of the ways a word may be spelled or pronounced: Feet *is the plural form of* foot. *—v.* **formed, form•ing, forms.** *—tr.* **1.** To give form to; shape: *form clay into figures.* **2.** To develop in the mind; conceive: *form an opinion.* **3.** To organize or arrange: *form a students' committee.* **4.** To come to have; develop or acquire: *form a bad habit.* **5.a.** To produce (a tense, for example) by adding certain elements: *form a plural by adding an* s *to the singular.* **b.** To make (a word) by combining different word elements: *form a word by adding* -tion *to the root.* *—intr.* To come into being by taking form; arise: *Buds form in the spring.* [First written down before 1200 in Middle English and spelled *furme,* from Latin *fōrma.*]

for•mal (fôr′məl) *adj.* **1.** Of or relating to outward form rather than structure. **2.** Structured according to forms or conventions: *a formal meeting.* **3.** Executed, carried out, or done in proper or regular form: *a formal document.* **4.** Stiffly ceremonious: *a formal manner.* *—n.* Something, such as a gown or a social affair, that is formal in nature. [First written down about 1390 in Middle English, from Latin *fōrma,* shape.] **—for′mal•ly** *adv.*

for•mal•de•hyde (fôr măl′də hīd′) *n.* A colorless gas with the formula CH_2O. It has a sharp suffocating odor and is used in making plastics and in solution as a preservative for biological specimens and a disinfectant.

for•mal•ism (fôr′mə lĭz′əm) *n.* Strict observance of accepted or recognized forms, as in religion or art.

for•mal•i•ty (fôr măl′ĭ tē) *n., pl.* **for•mal•i•ties. 1.** Strict observance of accepted rules, forms, or customs: *There was no formality at our dinner table.* **2.** An established rule, form, or custom, especially one followed merely for the sake of procedure: *the legal formalities of a trial.*

for•mal•ize (fôr′mə līz′) *tr.v.* **for•mal•ized, for•mal•iz•ing, for•mal•iz•es. 1.** To give a definite form or shape to: *formalize the style of a book report.* **2.** To make formal or official: *They formalized the treaty by signing it.* **—for′mal•iz′er** *n.*

for•mat (fôr′măt′) *n.* **1.** A plan for the organization or arrangement of something: *The format of the new television program was a series of interiews.* **2.** The form or layout of a publication: *the format of a newspaper.* *—tr.v.* **for•mat•ted, for•mat•ting, for•mats. 1.** To plan or arrange in a specified form:

format a conference. **2.** To divide (a computer disk) into sectors so that it may store data.

for•ma•tion (fôr **mā′**shən) *n.* **1.** The act or process of forming something or of taking form: *the formation of political parties.* **2.** Something formed: *a cloud formation.* **3.** A specified arrangement: *The geese flew overhead in a V formation.*

form•a•tive (**fôr′**mə tĭv) *adj.* **1.** Forming or capable of forming: *Childhood experiences often have a formative influence on writers.* **2.** Of or relating to growth or development: *The growth of industry marked a formative period in the history of the United States.*

for•mer (**fôr′**mər) *adj.* **1.** Of, relating to, or taking place in the past: *the tools of former civilizations; our former president.* **2.** Coming before in place or order: *the former part of the book.* **3.** Being the first of two mentioned.

for•mer•ly (**fôr′**mər lē) *adv.* At an earlier time; once: *Machines do work formerly done by people.*

For•mi•ca (fôr **mī′**kə). A trademark for several types of plastic sheets that are used especially to cover surfaces on tables and counters.

for•mi•da•ble (**fôr′**mĭ də bəl) *adj.* **1.** Arousing fear, dread, or alarm: *the formidable prospect of major surgery.* **2.** Admirable; awe-inspiring: *a formidable musical talent.* **3.** Difficult to surmount, defeat, or undertake: *a formidable challenge.* [First written down about 1450 in Middle English, from Latin *formidāre*, to fear.] **—for′mi•da•bil′i•ty** *n.* **—for′mi•da•bly** *adv.*

form•less (**fôrm′**lĭs) *adj.* Having no definite form; shapeless: *a formless mist.* **—form′less•ly** *adv.* **—form′less•ness** *n.*

For•mo•sa (fôr **mō′**sə). Taiwan.

for•mu•la (**fôr′**myə lə) *n., pl.* **for•mu•las** or **for•mu•lae** (**fôr′**myə lē′). **1.** An established set of words or symbols used in a ceremony or procedure. **2.** A set of symbols showing the composition of a chemical compound; for example, H_2O is the formula for water. **3.** A set of symbols in mathematics that expresses a rule or principle; for example, the formula for the area of a rectangle is $a = lw$, where *a* is the area, *l* the length, and *w* the width. **4.** A list of the ingredients and processes used in making something; a recipe: *the formula for making toothpaste.* **5.** A liquid food for infants, containing many of the nutrients in human milk. **—for′mu•la′ic** (fôr′myə **lā′**ĭk) *adj.*

for•mu•late (**fôr′**myə lāt′) *tr.v.* **for•mu•lat•ed, for•mu•lat•ing, for•mu•lates.** To express in or as if in a formula; plan in an orderly way: *formulate a process; formulate an idea.* **—for′mu•la′tion** *n.*

for•sake (fôr **sāk′**) *tr.v.* **for•sook** (fôr **so͝ok′**), **for•sak•en** (fôr **sā′**kən), **for•sak•ing, for•sakes. 1.** To give up (something formerly held dear); renounce. **2.** To leave altogether; abandon: *Do not forsake us when we need help.* [First written down about 700 in Old English and spelled *forsacan*.]

for•sooth (fôr **so͞oth′** *or* fər **so͞oth′**) *adv.* In truth; indeed.

for•swear (fôr **swâr′**) *v.* **for•swore** (fôr **swôr′**), **for•sworn** (fôr **swôrn′**), **for•swear•ing, for•swears.** *—tr.* **1.** To renounce seriously: *We forswore all junk food.* **2.** To disavow under oath; deny. *—intr.* To swear falsely; commit perjury.

for•syth•i•a (fôr **sĭth′**ē ə *or* fər **sĭth′**ē ə) *n.* Any of several shrubs having yellow flowers that bloom early in spring. [First written down in 1814 in Modern English, after William *Forsyth* (1737–1804), Scottish horticulturist.]

fort (fôrt) *n.* A fortified place or position stationed with troops; a fortification. [First written down before 1375 in Middle English and spelled *forte*, strength, stronghold, from Latin *fortis*, strong.]

❑ *These sound alike:* **fort, forte**[1] (strong point).

forte[1] (fôrt *or* **fôr′**tā′) *n.* Something in which a person excels; a strong point: *Jazz was the trumpet player's forte.* [First written down in 1648 in Modern English, from Old French *fort*, strong, from Latin *fortis*.]

❑ *These sound alike:* **forte**[1]**, fort** (stronghold).

for•te[2] (**fôr′**tā′) *adv. & adj.* In music, in a loud forceful manner. [First written down in 1724 in Modern English, from Italian *forte*, strong, from Latin *fortis*.]

forth (fôrth) *adv.* **1.** Forward in time, place, or order: *From this time forth.* **2.** Out into view: *After the movie the audience poured forth from the theater.*

❑ *These sound alike:* **forth, fourth** (number).

forth•com•ing (fôrth **kŭm′**ĭng) *adj.* **1.** About to appear or take place; approaching: *The authors gave an interview about their forthcoming book.* **2.** Available when required or as promised: *More funds were not forthcoming.*

forth•right (**fôrth′**rīt′) *adj.* Direct and without evasion; straightforward: *gave a forthright answer to my question.*

forth•with (fôrth **wĭth′** *or* fôrth **wĭth′**) *adv.* At once; immediately.

for•ti•eth (**fôr′**tē ĭth) *n.* **1.** The ordinal number matching the number 40 in a series. **2.** One of 40 equal parts.

for•ti•fi•ca•tion (fôr′tə fĭ **kā′**shən) *n.* **1.** The act or process of fortifying: *the fortification of the city against enemy invaders.* **2.** Something that fortifies or defends, especially military works erected to fortify a position or place.

for•ti•fy (**fôr′**tə fī′) *v.* **for•ti•fied, for•ti•fy•ing, for•ti•fies.** *—tr.* **1.** To strengthen and secure (a position) with fortifications: *They fortified the castle with a deep moat.* **2.** To strengthen physically; invigorate: *The hikers fortified themselves with a hearty breakfast.* **3.** To strengthen or improve (food, for example), as by adding vitamins; enrich. *—intr.* To build fortifications. [First written down before 1425 in Middle English and spelled *fortifien*, from Late Latin *fortificāre*, from Latin *fortis*, strong.] **—for′ti•fi′er** *n.*

for•tis•si•mo (fôr **tĭs′**ə mō′) *adv. & adj.* In music, in a very loud manner.

for•ti•tude (**fôr′**tĭ to͞od′ *or* **fôr′**tĭ tyo͞od′) *n.* Strength of mind that allows one to deal with pain or adversity with courage.

fort•night (**fôrt′**nīt′) *n.* A period of two weeks.

fort•night•ly (**fôrt′**nīt′lē) *adj.* Appearing or happening once in or every two weeks. *—adv.* Once every two weeks.

FOR•TRAN (**fôr′**trăn′) *n.* A computer programming language that uses algebraic expressions to solve problems in science and engineering.

for•tress (**fôr′**trĭs) *n.* A fortified place, especially a large military stronghold.

for•tu•i•tous (fôr **to͞o′**ĭ təs *or* fôr **tyo͞o′**ĭ təs) *adj.* **1.** Happening by accident or chance; unplanned. **2.** Lucky; fortunate: *A fortuitous change in the weather made the picnic possible.* [First written down before 1652 in Modern English, from Latin *fortuītus*, from *forte*, by chance.] **—for•tu′i•tous•ly** *adv.* **—for•tu′i•tous•ness** *n.*

for•tu•nate (**fôr′**chə nĭt) *adj.* **1.** Bringing something good and unforeseen. **2.** Having good fortune; lucky: *I am fortunate in having good friends.* [First written down before 1387 in Modern English, from Latin *fortūnātus*, from *fortūna*, chance.] **—for′tu•nate•ly** *adv.*

for•tune (**fôr′**chən) *n.* **1.** The chance happening of fortunate or adverse events; chance: *I had the good*

ă	pat	oi	boy
ā	pay	ou	out
âr	care	o͝o	took
ä	father	o͞o	boot
ĕ	pet	ŭ	cut
ē	be	ûr	urge
ĭ	pit	th	thin
ī	pie	*th*	this
îr	pier	hw	whoop
ŏ	pot	zh	vision
ō	toe	ə	about
ô	paw	N	*French* bon

fortune cookie

fossil

Stephen Foster
c. 1850 portrait attributed to Thomas Hicks (1823–1890)

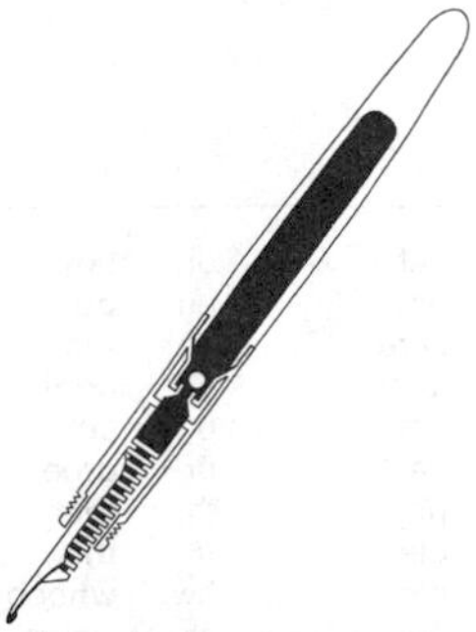
fountain pen
Cutaway view

fortune to meet interesting people during my visit. **2.** Extensive amounts of material possessions or wealth; riches. **3.** Destiny; fate: *told fortunes at the fair.* [First written down before 1325 in Middle English, from Latin *fortūna.*]

fortune cookie *n.* A cookie made of a thin layer of dough folded and baked around a slip of paper on which a prediction of fortune or a clever saying is written.

for•tune•tell•er (fôr′chən tĕl′ər) *n.* A person who professes to predict future events. **—for′tune•tell′ing** *n.*

Fort Wayne (fôrt wān). A city of northeast Indiana northeast of Indianapolis. A trading post and fort were built here in the late 17th century. Population, 173,072.

Fort Worth (wûrth). A city of northeast Texas west of Dallas. It was built on the site of a military post established in the 1840's. Population, 447,619.

for•ty (fôr′tē) *n., pl.* **for•ties.** The number, written 40, that is equal to 4 × 10.

for•ty-nin•er (fôr′tē nī′nər) *n.* A person who took part in the California gold rush of 1849.

fo•rum (fôr′əm) *n., pl.* **fo•rums. 1.** The public square of an ancient Roman city, especially the public square of ancient Rome. **2.** A public meeting place for open discussion: *a forum on the environment.* **3.** A court of law. [First written down before 1464 in Middle English, from Latin.]

for•ward (fôr′wərd) *adj.* **1.** At, near, or belonging to the front of something: *the forward section of an airplane.* **2.** Going or moving toward the front: *a bad forward fall.* **3.a.** Prompt; eager: *a forward student wanting to answer every question.* **b.** Presumptuous; bold: *I resented the clerk's forward manner in suggesting a choice.* **4.** Being ahead of current economic, political, or technological trends; progressive: *forward ideas about recycling.* **5.** Advanced in mental, physical, or social development: *a forward child.* —*adv.* **1.** Toward or tending to the front; frontward: *All volunteers please step forward.* **2.** In or toward the future: *I look forward to my vacation.* —*n.* **1.** A player in certain sports, such as basketball or soccer, who is part of the front line of offense. **2.** The position played by such a person. —*tr.v.* **for•ward•ed, for•ward•ing, for•wards. 1.** To send on to a further destination or address: *forward letters to a new address.* **2.** To promote or advance: *forward one's own interests.* **—for′ward•ly** *adv.* **—for′ward•ness** *n.*

for•wards (fôr′wərdz) *adv.* To or tending to the front; forward.

for•went (fôr wĕnt′) *v.* Past tense of **forgo.**

fos•sil (fŏs′əl) *n.* **1.** A remnant or trace of a plant or an animal that lived long ago. Fossils are often found in layers of rock and in old streams or river beds. **2.** A person or thing that is regarded as old-fashioned or outdated. [First written down in 1619 in Modern English, from Latin *fossilis,* dug up, from *fossus,* past participle of *fodere,* to dig.]

fossil fuel *n.* A fossil material that burns, such as coal, petroleum, or natural gas.

fos•sil•ize (fŏs′ə līz′) *tr. & intr.v.* **fos•sil•ized, fos•sil•iz•ing, fos•sil•iz•es.** To change into or become a fossil: *The shells of many prehistoric sea animals have fossilized in layers of rock.* **—fos′sil•i•za′tion** (fŏs′ə lĭ zā′shən) *n.*

fos•ter (fô′stər *or* fŏs′tər) *tr.v.* **fos•tered, fos•ter•ing, fos•ters. 1.** To bring up; nurture: *foster a child.* **2.** To promote the development or growth of; cultivate: *The teacher fostered the students' interest in writing.* —*adj.* Giving or receiving parental care or nurture to or from those not legally related: *a foster child; a foster parent.*

Fos•ter (fô′stər *or* fŏs′tər), **Abigail Kelley.** 1810–1887. American suffragist who refused to pay taxes on her farm because she did not have the right to vote.

Foster, Stephen Collins. 1826–1864. American songwriter known for his popular works, such as "Oh! Susannah" (1848).

fought (fôt) *v.* Past tense and past participle of **fight.**

foul (foul) *adj.* **foul•er, foul•est. 1.** Offensive or unpleasant to the taste or smell: *the foul flavor of spoiled food; a foul smell of automobile exhaust.* **2.** Full of dirt or mud; dirty: *the foul fur of the stray dog.* **3.** Morally offensive; wicked: *foul rumors.* **4.** Bad or unfavorable: *foul weather.* **5.** Of a vulgar or obscene nature: *foul language.* **6.** In sports, contrary to the rules of a game: *A foul blow in boxing is one below the waist.* **7.** In baseball, outside the foul lines: *a foul fly ball.* —*n.* **1.** In sports, a violation of the rules of play: *a foul in a game of basketball.* **2.** In baseball, a foul ball. —*adv.* In a foul manner. —*v.* **fouled, foul•ing, fouls.** —*tr.* **1.** To make dirty or foul: *Factory smoke fouls the air.* **2.** To clog or obstruct: *Leaves fouled the drainpipe.* **3.** To entangle or catch (a rope, for example): *The dog fouled its leash in trying to get at the cat.* **4.** In sports, to commit a foul against. **5.** In baseball, to hit (a ball) outside the foul lines. —*intr.* **1.** To become foul. **2.** In sports, to commit a foul. **3.** In baseball, to hit a ball outside the foul lines. **4.** To become entangled or twisted: *The anchor line fouled on a rock.* **—*idioms.* foul out.** In sports, to be put out of a game for exceeding the number of permissible fouls. **foul up.** To blunder or cause to blunder because of mistakes or poor judgment; botch: *I fouled up the recipe by adding too much milk.* [First written down before 800 in Old English and spelled *fūl.*]

❑ *These sound alike:* **foul, fowl** (bird).

fou•lard (fo͞o lärd′) *n.* **1.** A lightweight fabric of silk or silk and cotton, usually having a small printed pattern: *a bathrobe of foulard.* **2.** A necktie, a scarf, or another article made of this material.

foul ball *n.* In baseball, a batted ball that lands or is caught outside a foul line.

foul line *n.* **1.** In baseball, one of two lines extending from home plate to the outfield barriers to indicate the area in which a fair ball can be hit. **2.** In basketball, a line 15 feet in front of the backboard from which a fouled player shoots a free throw. **3.** In sports, a boundary limiting the playing area, as in tennis or soccer.

foul play *n.* Unfair or treacherous action, especially when involving violence.

foul-up (foul′ŭp′) *n.* **1.** A condition of confusion caused by mistakes or poor judgment. **2.** A mechanical failure.

found[1] (found) *tr.v.* **found•ed, found•ing, founds. 1.** To originate or establish (something); create; set up: *founded the college in 1871.* See Synonyms at **establish. 2.** To establish the foundation or basis of: *found a report on concrete facts.* [First written down about 1290 in Middle English and spelled *founden,* from Latin *fundāre,* from *fundus,* bottom.]

found[2] (found) *tr.v.* **found•ed, found•ing, founds. 1.** To melt (metal) and pour into a mold. **2.** To make (objects) by pouring molten material into a mold; cast. [First written down before 1399 in Middle English and spelled *founden,* from Latin *fundere.*]

found[3] (found) *v.* Past tense and past participle of **find.**

foun•da•tion (foun dā′shən) *n.* **1.** The act of founding or establishing. **2.** The basis on which something stands, is founded, or is supported: *the* *foundations of modern science; the foundation of a building.* **3.** Funds for the support of an institution; an endowment. **4.** An institution that is founded and supported by an endowment.

foun•der[1] (**foun′**dər) *v.* **foun•dered, foun•der•ing, foun•ders.** *—intr.* **1.** To sink below the water: *several ships foundered in the gale.* **2.** To collapse or cave in: *The building foundered in the tremor.* **3.** To fail: *Their business foundered.* **4.** To stumble, especially to stumble and go lame: *The horse foundered on the muddy ground.* *—tr.* To cause to founder. [First written down before 1338 in Middle English and spelled *fondren,* to sink to the ground, from Old French *fondrer,* from Latin *fundus,* bottom.]

found•er[2] (**foun′**dər) *n.* A person who founds or helps to establish the basis of something: *the founders of the school.*

Found•ing Father (**foun′**dĭng) *n.* **1.** A member of the convention that drafted the U.S. Constitution in 1787. **2. founding father.** A man who founds or establishes something.

found•ling (**found′**lĭng) *n.* A deserted or abandoned child of unknown parentage.

foun•dry (**foun′**drē) *n., pl.* **foun•dries.** A place in which metals are cast and molded. [First written down in 1601 in Modern English and spelled *founderie,* business of casting metal, from French *fonderie,* from *fondre,* to found.]

fount (fount) *n.* **1.** A fountain. **2.** A person or thing that initiates or dispenses; a source.

foun•tain (**foun′**tən) *n.* **1.a.** An artificially created jet or stream of water. **b.** A structure, often decorative, from which such a jet or stream rises and flows: *the beautiful fountains of Rome; a drinking fountain.* **2.** A spring, especially the source of a stream. **3.** A soda fountain. **4.** A point of origin; a source: *The zookeeper was a fountain of knowledge about animals.* [First written down about 1410 in Middle English and spelled *fownteyne,* from Latin *fontānus,* of a spring, from *fōns,* spring.]

foun•tain•head (**foun′**tən hĕd′) *n.* **1.** A spring that is the source of a stream. **2.** A chief source or an originator: *The old philosopher was a fountainhead of wisdom.*

fountain pen *n.* A pen containing a reservoir of ink that automatically feeds the writing point.

four (fôr) *n.* **1.** The number, written 4, that is equal to 3 + 1. **2.** The fourth in a set or sequence. **3.** Something having four parts or units, such as a musical quartet. ***—idiom.*** **all fours.** All four limbs of an animal or a person: *Babies crawl around on all fours.* [First written down about 725 in Old English and spelled *fēower.*]

❑ *These sound alike:* **four, for** (with the purpose of), **fore** (front part).

Four-H Club (**fôr′ăch′**) *n.* An organization for young people that offers instruction in agriculture and home economics.

four-leaf clover (**fôr′**lēf′) *n.* A clover leaf that has four leaflets instead of the usual three, considered a sign of good luck.

four-o'clock (**fôr′**ə klŏk′) *n.* Any of several garden plants having variously colored flowers that have a funnel shape and open in the late afternoon.

four-post•er (**fôr′pō′**stər) *n.* A bed with tall corner posts originally intended to support curtains or a canopy.

four•score (**fôr′skôr′**) *adj.* Four times twenty; eighty.

four•some (**fôr′**səm) *n.* **1.** A group of four persons or things. **2.a.** A game, especially a golf match, played by four persons, two on each side. **b.** The players in such a game.

four•square (**fôr′skwâr′**) *adj.* **1.** Having four equal sides and four right angles; square. **2.** Firm and unwavering; forthright: *a foursquare refusal to yield.* *—adv.* In a forthright manner; squarely.

four•teen (fôr **tēn′**) *n.* **1.** The number, written 14, that is equal to 13 + 1. **2.** The 14th in a set or sequence.

four•teenth (fôr **tēnth′**) *n.* **1.** The ordinal number matching the number 14 in a series. **2.** One of 14 equal parts.

fourth (fôrth) *n.* **1.** The ordinal number matching the number four in a series. **2.** One of four equal parts. **3.a.** The interval covering four tones in a musical scale, as C, D, E, and F. **b.** The fourth tone in a musical scale; the subdominant. **4.** The transmission gear used to produce speeds next highest to those of third in a motor vehicle. **5. Fourth.** The Fourth of July; Independence Day. **—fourth** *adv. & adj.*

❑ *These sound alike:* **fourth, forth** (forward).

fourth estate *n.* Journalists considered as a group.

Fourth of July *n.* Independence Day.

four-wheel drive *n.* An automotive drive system in which mechanical power is transmitted from the drive shaft to all four wheels.

fowl (foul) *n., pl.* **fowl** or **fowls. 1.** A bird, such as a chicken, duck, turkey, or pheasant, that is raised or hunted for food. **2.** The meat of any of these birds used as food. [First written down about 725 in Old English and spelled *fugel.*]

❑ *These sound alike:* **fowl, foul** (rotten).

fox (fŏks) *n., pl.* **fox•es** also **fox. 1.** Any of various meat-eating mammals related to the dog and the wolf, having a pointed snout, upright ears, and a long bushy tail. **2.** The fur of this mammal. **3.** A crafty, clever, or sly person: *The old fox outwitted everyone.*

Fox (fŏks) *n.* **1.** A member of a Native American people formerly inhabiting parts of Michigan, Wisconsin, Illinois, and Iowa, now living in Iowa and Oklahoma. **2.** The Algonquian language of the Fox.

fox•glove (**fŏks′**glŭv′) *n.* Any of several plants having a long cluster of tubular purplish, yellow, or white flowers, used as a source of digitalis.

fox•hole (**fŏks′**hōl′) *n.* A shallow pit dug by a soldier for protection in combat.

fox•hound (**fŏks′**hound′) *n.* Any of various usually smooth-coated dogs trained for fox hunting.

fox terrier *n.* Any of various small terriers having a smooth or wiry white coat with dark markings, originally used to hunt foxes in their burrows.

fox•trot (**fŏks′**trŏt′) *intr.v.* To dance the fox trot.

fox trot *n.* **1.** A ballroom dance in 2/4 or 4/4 time, composed of a combination of fast and slow steps. **2.** The music for this dance.

fox•y (**fŏk′**sē) *adj.* **fox•i•er, fox•i•est.** Slyly clever; crafty. **—fox′i•ly** *adv.* **—fox′i•ness** *n.*

foy•er (**foi′**ər *or* **foi′**ā′) *n.* **1.** A lobby or an anteroom, as of a theater or hotel. **2.** An entrance hall, as of a private house or an apartment.

Fr The symbol for the element **francium.**

fr. *abbr.* An abbreviation of: **1.** Fragment. **2.** Franc. **3.** From.

Fr. *abbr.* An abbreviation of: **1.** Father. **2.** France. **3.** French. **4.** Friday.

fra•cas (**frā′**kəs *or* **frăk′**əs) *n. Informal.* A disorderly uproar.

frac•tion (**frăk′**shən) *n.* **1.** A number that compares part of an object or a set with the whole, especially the quotient of two whole numbers written in the form a/b: *The fraction $1/2$ can represent 10 pencils out of a box of 20, or 50 cents out of a dollar.* **2.** A part or bit of something: *A fraction of the people voted.*

frac•tion•al (**frăk′**shə nəl) *adj.* **1.** Of, relating to, or composed of a fraction or fractions. **2.** Very small;

fox
Red fox

foxhound
American foxhound

ă	**pat**	oi	**boy**
ā	**pay**	ou	**out**
âr	**care**	o͝o	**took**
ä	**father**	o͞o	**boot**
ĕ	**pet**	ŭ	**cut**
ē	**be**	ûr	**urge**
ĭ	**pit**	th	**thin**
ī	**pie**	*th*	**this**
îr	**pier**	hw	**whoop**
ŏ	**pot**	zh	**vision**
ō	**toe**	ə	**about**
ô	**paw**	N	*French* **bon**

Word Building: fragile

The word root *–frag–* in English words comes from a form of the Latin verb *frangere*, "to break." The Latin adjective *fragilis*, "breakable," is the source of our **fragile.** The same Latin adjective becomes *frele* in Old French, which is the source of our **frail**. The Latin noun *fragmentum*, "something broken," is the source of **fragment**. The past participle of *frangere* is *fractus*, from which the Latin nouns *fractiō*, "a breaking," and *fractūra*, "a break," are formed. From these words we get **fraction** and **fracture**.

Anne Frank
Photographed in the early 1940's

insignificant: *a fractional share of the vote.* **—frac′tion•al•ly** *adv.*

frac•tious (frăk′shəs) *adj.* **1.** Likely to make trouble; unruly. **2.** Cross; peevish; cranky. **—frac′tious•ly** *adv.* **—frac′tious•ness** *n.*

frac•ture (frăk′chər) *n.* **1.** The act or process of breaking: *enough pressure to cause the fracture of solid rock.* **2.** A break, rupture, or crack, as in bone. *—tr. & intr.v.* **frac•tured, frac•tur•ing, frac•tures.** To break or cause to break: *I fractured my arm in the fall. The foundation of the building fractured in the earthquake.*

frag•ile (frăj′əl *or* frăj′īl′) *adj.* **1.** Easily damaged or broken; frail: *a fragile glass vase.* **2.** Lacking physical or emotional strength; delicate. **3.** Lacking substance; flimsy: *a fragile claim.* [First written down in 1513 in Modern English and spelled *fragyll*, from Latin *fragilis*, from *frangere*, to break.] **—fra′gile•ly** *adv.* **—fra•gil′i•ty** (frə jĭl′ĭ tē) *n.* —See Note.

frag•ment (frăg′mənt) *n.* **1.** A small part broken off or detached from a whole: *a fragment of a shattered china plate.* **2.** An incomplete or isolated portion; a bit: *We could overhear fragments of their conversation.* *—tr. & intr.v.* (frăg′mĕnt′). **frag•ment•ed, frag•ment•ing, frag•ments.** To break or become broken into fragments: *An explosion had fragmented the sinking ship. After the election, the committee fragmented.*

frag•men•tar•y (frăg′mən tĕr′ē) *adj.* Consisting of small disconnected parts: *Only fragmentary sentences of the damaged document were legible.*

frag•men•ta•tion (frăg′mən tā′shən) *n.* The act or process of fragmenting or breaking into pieces: *A tremendous volcanic explosion caused the fragmentation of enormous rocks.*

fra•grance (frā′grəns) *n.* A sweet or pleasant odor; a scent: *the fresh fragrance of pine.*

fra•grant (frā′grənt) *adj.* Having a pleasant odor; sweet-smelling: *a fragrant flower garden.* **—fra′grant•ly** *adv.*

frail (frāl) *adj.* **frail•er, frail•est. 1.** Physically weak; not robust. **2.** Not strong or substantial: *a frail and delicate flower.* **3.** Easily led astray; morally weak. [First written down about 1350 in Middle English and spelled *frele*, from Old French, from Latin *fragilis*, from *frangere*, to break.] **—frail′ness** *n.*

frail•ty (frāl′tē) *n., pl.* **frail•ties. 1.** The quality or condition of being frail; weakness. **2.** A fault arising from human weakness; a failing: *Envy and greed are common human frailties.*

frame (frām) *tr.v.* **framed, fram•ing, frames. 1.** To build by putting together the structural parts of: *frame an agreement; frame a house.* **2.** To enclose in or as if in a frame: *frame a picture.* **3.** *Informal.* To make up evidence so as to incriminate (someone) falsely: *The witness was paid to frame an innocent bystander.* *—n.* **1.a.** A structure that shapes or supports: *the frame of a car.* **b.** An open structure or rim used to encase, hold, or border: *a door frame; a picture frame.* **c.** The structure of a human or animal body: *a lanky frame.* **2.** The general structure of something; a system: *the frame of government.* **3.** A round of play in some games, such as bowling. **4.** A single picture on a roll of movie film. **—fram′er** *n.*

frame-up (frām′ŭp′) *n. Informal.* A plot to incriminate an innocent person.

frame•work (frām′wûrk′) *n.* **1.** A structure that shapes or supports; a frame: *The building was constructed on a framework of steel girders.* **2.** A fundamental structure, as for a written work or a system of ideas: *Education is the framework on which to build a productive life.*

franc (frăngk) *n.* The basic monetary unit of Belgium, France, Mali, Niger, Switzerland, and many other countries. [First written down about 1390 in Middle English and spelled *frank*, from Old French *franc*, from Medieval Latin *Francōrum rēx*, king of the Franks (from the legend on the first of these coins).]

❑ *These sound alike:* **franc, frank¹** (sincere), **frank²** (frankfurter).

France (frăns). A country of western Europe on the Atlantic Ocean and the English Channel north-northeast of Spain. It was settled by a Frankish people after the retreat of the Romans. Widespread poverty and discontent led to the French Revolution in 1789. Paris is the capital and the largest city. Population, 54,334,871.

fran•chise (frăn′chīz′) *n.* **1.** The right to vote; suffrage: *In earlier times only landowners had the franchise.* **2.a.** An authorization, a right, or a privilege granted to a person or group, as for selling a product within a district or for administering a territory: *The franchise for collecting trash in the town was awarded to a private company.* **b.** The limits or district within which such authorization, right, or privilege may be exercised.

Fran•cis•can (frăn sĭs′kən) *n.* A member of a religious order of the Roman Catholic Church founded by Saint Francis of Assisi in 1209. *—adj.* Of or relating to Saint Francis or to the order he founded.

Fran•cis of As•si•si (frăn′sĭs əv ə sē′zē), Saint. 1182?–1226. Italian monk who founded the Franciscan order (1209).

fran•ci•um (frăn′sē əm) *n. Symbol* **Fr** A radioactive metallic element that has several isotopes, the most stable of which is Fr 223 with a half-life of 21 minutes. Atomic number 87. See table at **element.**

Fran•co (frăng′kō *or* frăng′kō), **Francisco.** 1892–1975. Spanish political leader who directed the rebel armed forces in the Spanish Civil War (1936–1939) and ruled the country as dictator from 1939 to 1975.

frank¹ (frăngk) *adj.* **frank•er, frank•est.** Open and sincere in expression; straightforward: *made several frank remarks about the quality of their work.* *—tr. v.* **franked, frank•ing, franks. 1.** To put an official mark on (mail) so that it can be sent free of charge. **2.** To send (mail) free of charge. *—n.* **1.** A mark placed on a piece of mail to indicate the right to send it free of charge. **2.** The right to send mail free of charge. [First written down before 1300 in Middle English and spelled *franc*, free, open, from Late Latin *Francus*, a Frank.] **—frank′ness** *n.*

❑ *These sound alike:* **frank¹** (sincere), **franc** (money), **frank²** (frankfurter).

frank² (frăngk) *n. Informal.* A frankfurter. [First written down in 1936 in American English, from *frankfurter*.]

❑ *These sound alike:* **frank²** (frankfurter), **franc** (money), **frank¹** (sincere).

Frank (frăngk) *n.* A member of a Germanic tribe that conquered Gaul around A.D. 500 and established a large empire. [First written down about 725 in Old English and spelled *Franca*, from Late Latin *Francus*, of Germanic origin.]

Frank (frăngk *or* frängk), **Anne.** 1929–1945. German Jewish diarist whose account of her years of hiding in Amsterdam (1942–1944) was published in 1947. She died in a concentration camp.

Frank•fort (frăngk′fərt). The capital of Kentucky, in the north-central part of the state northwest of Lexington. It was chosen as capital in 1792. Population, 25,968.

Frank•furt (frănk′fərt *or* frängk′fŏŏrt′). Also **Frankfurt am Main** (äm mīn′). A city of west-central Germany on the Main River. It was founded in the first century B.C. by the Romans. Population, 599,634.

frank•furt•er (frăngk′fər tər) *n.* A smoked sausage of beef or beef and pork made in long reddish links. [First written down in 1894 in American English, after *Frankfurt* Germany.]

frank•in•cense (frăng′kĭn sĕns′) *n.* A gum having a pleasant spicy odor, obtained from certain African and Asian trees and burned as incense.

Frank•ish (frăng′kĭsh) *adj.* Of or relating to the Franks or their language. —*n.* The West Germanic language of the Franks.

Frank•lin (frăngk′lĭn), **Benjamin.** 1706–1790. American public official, inventor, and writer who published *Poor Richard's Almanac* (1732–1757) and helped draft the Constitution (1787–1789).

frank•ly (frăngk′lē) *adv.* **1.** In a frank manner; candidly: *Speaking frankly, the principal warned the students about their bad behavior.* **2.** Honestly; in truth: *Frankly, I don't know.*

fran•tic (frăn′tĭk) *adj.* Very excited with fear or anxiety; desperate; frenzied: *frantic with worry.* [First written down about 1378 in Middle English, from Latin *phrenēticus*, frenetic, from Greek *phrenitis*, inflammation of the brain.] **—fran′ti•cal•ly** *adv.* **—fran′tic•ness** *n.*

frap•pé (fră pā′) *n.* **1.** A fruit drink served almost frozen or poured over crushed ice. **2.** Often **frappe** (frăp). A drink made with ice cream; a milk shake. —SEE NOTE at **milk shake.**

fra•ter•nal (frə tûr′nəl) *adj.* **1.a.** Of or relating to brothers: *a close fraternal tie.* **b.** Showing comradeship: *a fraternal greeting.* **2.** Of or consisting of a fraternity: *The Masons are a fraternal society.* **3.** Of or relating to twins that develop from separately fertilized egg cells, have distinct hereditary characteristics, and can be of different sexes: *fraternal twins.* **—fra•ter′nal•ly** *adv.*

fra•ter•ni•ty (frə tûr′nĭ tē) *n., pl.* **fra•ter•ni•ties. 1.** A group of people associated or linked by similar interests, backgrounds, or occupations: *the local business fraternity; the medical fraternity.* **2.** A social organization of male college or university students. **3.** The quality or condition of being brothers.

frat•er•nize (frăt′ər nīz′) *intr.v.* **frat•er•nized, frat•er•niz•ing, frat•er•niz•es. 1.** To associate with others in a brotherly or friendly way: *Teachers and students fraternize in the cafeteria.* **2.** To associate on friendly terms with the people of an enemy or opposing group. **—frat′er•ni•za′tion** (frăt′ər nĭ zā′shən) *n.*

frat•ri•cide (frăt′rĭ sīd′) *n.* The killing of one's brother or sister. **—frat′ri•cid′al** (frăt′rĭ sīd′l)

Frau (frou) *n., pl.* **Frau•en** (frou′ən). Used as a title for a woman in a German-speaking area.

fraud (frôd) *n.* **1.** A deliberate deception practiced in order to gain unfair or unlawful gain: *A government agency protects consumers against fraud.* **2.** An incidence of trickery; a trick. **3.** A person who practices deception and trickery; an impostor or a swindler. [First written down in 1345 in Middle English, from Latin *fraus.*]

fraud•u•lent (frô′jə lənt) *adj.* Of, gained by, or engaging in fraud: *a fraudulent scheme; a fraudulent merchant.* **—fraud′u•lence** *n.* **—fraud′u•lent•ly** *adv.*

fraught (frôt) *adj.* Filled with a specified element; charged: *Every moment is fraught with significance.*

Fräu•lein (froi′līn′ *or* frou′līn′) *n., pl.* **Fräulein.** Used as a title for an unmarried woman or a girl in a German-speaking area.

fray[1] (frā) *n.* A scuffle; a brawl: *Several bystanders were caught up in the fray.* [First written down about 1350 in Middle English, alteration of *affrai*, from Old French *esfraier*, to disturb.]

fray[2] (frā) *v.* **frayed, fray•ing, frays.** —*tr.* **1.** To wear away (the edges of fabric, for example) by rubbing. **2.** To strain; chafe: *The constant noise of traffic frayed the driver's nerves.* —*intr.* To become worn away or tattered along the edges. [First written down about 1405 in Middle English and spelled *fraien*, to wear, bruise, from Latin *fricāre*, to rub.]

fraz•zle (frăz′əl) *Informal. v.* **fraz•zled, fraz•zling, fraz•zles.** —*tr.* **1.** To wear away along the edges; fray. **2.** To exhaust physically or emotionally: *frazzled by hard work and pressure.* —*intr.* To become frazzled. —*n.* **1.** A frayed or tattered condition. **2.** A condition of exhaustion: *The long perilous climb wore us to a frazzle.*

freak (frēk) *n.* **1.** A thing or an occurrence that is markedly unusual or irregular: *The summer snowstorm was a freak of nature.* **2.** An organism, especially a person or an animal, that develops in an abnormal way. **3.** *Slang.* An enthusiast: *a movie freak; a running freak.*

freak•ish (frē′kĭsh) *adj.* Markedly abnormal or unusual; strange: *freakish warm weather in winter.* **—freak′ish•ly** *adv.* **—freak′ish•ness** *n.*

freck•le (frĕk′əl) *n.* A small spot of dark pigment in the skin, often caused by exposure to the sun. —*tr. & intr.v.* **freck•led, freck•ling, freck•les.** To mark or become marked with freckles or spots of color. [First written down before 1400 in Middle English and spelled *fraclis*, freckles, alteration of *fraknes*, probably of Scandinavian origin.]

Fred•er•ick II (frĕd′rĭk *or* frĕd′ər ĭk) Known as "Frederick the Great." 1712–1786. King of Prussia (1740–1786) who was successful in the Seven Years' War (1756–1763) and brought Prussia great military prestige in Europe.

Fred•er•ic•ton (frĕd′rĭk tən *or* frĕd′ər ĭk tən). The capital of New Brunswick, Canada, in the south-central part of the province northwest of Halifax, Nova Scotia. It was made capital in 1785. Population, 43,723.

free (frē) *adj.* **fre•er, fre•est. 1.** At liberty; not imprisoned or enslaved. **2.** Not controlled by duty or the will of another: *You're free to go.* **3.a.** Having political independence: *a free country.* **b.** Not subject to arbitrary interference by a government: *a free press.* **4.a.** Not affected by a given condition or circumstance: *free of germs; free from worry.* **b.** Not subject to taxes or other charges; exempt: *Medicine is free of sales tax.* **5.** Not literal or exact: *a free translation.* **6.** Costing nothing; gratuitous: *a free meal.* **7.a.** Not occupied or used: *free space.* **b.** Not taken up by scheduled activities: *a free hour at lunchtime.* **8.** Unobstructed; clear: *a free lane.* **9.** Unguarded in expression or manner; frank. **10.** Liberal or lavish: *very free with the inherited money.* **11.** In chemistry, not combined with something else: *Oxygen exists free in air.* —*adv.* **1.** In a free manner; without restraint: *The rope swung free.* **2.** Without charge: *We were admitted free.* —*tr.v.* **freed, free•ing, frees. 1.** To set at liberty: *The convict was freed from prison.* **2.** To relieve of a burden, an obligation, or a restraint: *Vacation frees us from daily jobs for a short time.* **3.** To unfasten or untangle; detach: *We freed the rope caught on a nail.* **—*idiom.* for free.** *Informal.* Without charge: *I used a special coupon to get tickets for free.* [First written down about 725 in Old English and spelled *frēo.*] **—free′ly** *adv.* **—free′ness** *n.* —SEE NOTE.

free•boot•er (frē′bo͞o′tər) *n.* A person who plunders, especially a pirate. [First written down in 1570 in Modern English and spelled *frebetter*, from Dutch *vrijbuiter* : *vrij*, free + *buit*, booty.]

freed•man (frēd′mən) *n.* A man who has been freed from slavery.

free•dom (frē′dəm) *n.* **1.** The condition of being free from restraints: *freedom of speech.* **2.** Liberty of the person from slavery, detention, or oppres-

Benjamin Franklin
c. 1785 portrait by
Joseph Siffred Duplessis
(1725–1802)

Frederick the Great

Word History: free

The word **free** has a wonderful history. The Old English adjective is *frēo*, with the same meaning as *free*, and it is applied especially to members of a family or clan who are related to the head of the family or the clan and who therefore are not slaves or hired hands. The bond that exists among all these family members is love, and the Old English verb *frēon* means both "to free" and "to love." The word **friend** is also related to *free*.

ă	**pat**	oi	**boy**
ā	**pay**	ou	**out**
âr	**care**	o͝o	**took**
ä	**father**	o͞o	**boot**
ĕ	**pet**	ŭ	**cut**
ē	**be**	ûr	**urge**
ĭ	**pit**	th	**thin**
ī	**pie**	*th*	**this**
îr	**pier**	hw	**whoop**
ŏ	**pot**	zh	**vision**
ō	**toe**	ə	**about**
ô	**paw**	N	*French* **bon**

John C. Frémont

Word History: French

French is probably the foreign language that has had the most influence on English. Perhaps 60 percent of our common, everyday vocabulary comes from French. French, like Spanish and Italian, is a descendant of ancient Latin; so you can think of Latin as the "parent" or "mother" language. French, then, is a "daughter" language of Latin, and French, Spanish, and Italian are "sister" languages. Spanish and Italian resemble their "mother" (and therefore each other) very closely, much more than French does. For instance, the Spanish word for "chain," *cadena*, and the Italian word, *catena*, look a lot more like the Latin word for "chain," *catēna*, than the French word *chaîne* does. Most French words look very different from the Latin originals, but once the French words come into English like **chain** from Old French *chaine*, we usually make little further change in them.

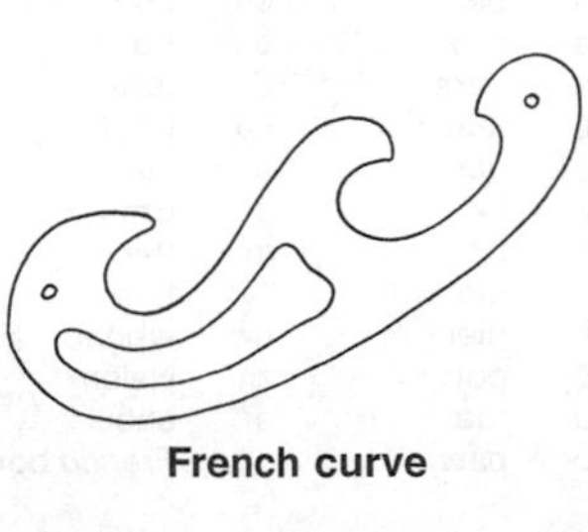

French curve

sion. **3.** The capacity to exercise choice; free will: *the freedom to do what we want.* **4.** Frankness or boldness; lack of reserve: *a casual freedom in their manner.* **5.** Ease or facility of movement. **6.** The use of or access to something: *Investigators were given the freedom of the files.*

freed•wom•an (frēd′wo͝om′ən) *n.* A woman who has been freed from slavery.

free enterprise *n.* The freedom of private businesses to operate competitively for profit with minimal government regulation.

free fall *n.* The fall of a body toward the earth without any force restraining it other than the drag produced by the atmosphere.

free-for-all (frē′fər ôl′) *n.* A disorderly quarrel, fight, or competition in which anyone may take part.

free•hand (frē′hănd′) *adj.* Drawn by hand without the aid of tracing or drafting tools. **—free′hand′** *adv.*

free•lance (frē′lăns′) *n.* An artist, a writer, an editor, or another trained person who sells his or her services to different employers as the work is needed. *—intr.v.* **free•lanced, free•lanc•ing, free•lanc•es.** To work as a freelance. *—adj.* Of, relating to, or working as a freelance: *a freelance editor.* **—free′lanc′er** *n.*

free•man (frē′mən) *n.* **1.** A person not in slavery or serfdom. **2.** A person who possesses the rights and privileges of a citizen.

Free•ma•son (frē′mā′sən) *n.* A member of the Free and Accepted Masons, an international fraternal and charitable organization.

Free•ma•son•ry (frē′mā′sən rē) *n.* The institutions, precepts, and rites of the Freemasons.

free-soil (frē′soil′) *adj.* **1.** Prohibiting slavery: *free-soil states.* **2. Free-Soil.** Of or being a U.S. political party founded in 1848 to oppose the spread of slavery into U.S. Territories and the admission of slave states into the Union.

free•stand•ing (frē′stăn′dĭng) *adj.* Standing without support or attachment; able to stand alone: *a freestanding garage.*

free•stone (frē′stōn′) *n.* **1.** A fruit, especially a peach or plum, having pulp that separates easily from the stone. **2.** A stone, such as sandstone or limestone, soft enough to be cut easily without breaking.

free•style (frē′stīl′) *n.* **1.** A competitive sports event, especially a swimming race, in which any style, maneuver, or movement may be used by the competitor. **2.** A rapid swimming stroke consisting of alternating overarm strokes and a flutter kick. **—free′style′** *adv. & adj.*

free•think•er (frē′thĭng′kər) *n.* A person who forms opinions independently and does not follow traditional dogma, especially in matters of politics and religion. **—free′think′ing** *adj. & n.*

free throw *n.* In basketball, a shot worth one point, made from the foul line and awarded to a fouled player.

Free•town (frē′toun′). The capital and largest city of Sierra Leone, in the western part of the country on the Atlantic Ocean. It was settled in 1787 by freed slaves from England. Population, 300,000.

free verse *n.* Poetry that does not have a regular meter or rhyme scheme.

free•way (frē′wā′) *n.* A highway for high-speed travel, having several lanes.

free•wheel•ing (frē′wē′lĭng) *adj.* Free of restraints or limits; acting freely: *freewheeling television advertising campaigns.*

free•will (frē′wĭl′) *adj.* Done of one's own will; voluntary.

free will *n.* **1.** The power or opportunity to choose; free choice: *I decided of my own free will to join the navy.* **2.** The power to make free choices that are unconstrained by persons or things beyond one's control.

freeze (frēz) *v.* **froze** (frōz), **fro•zen** (frō′zən), **freez•ing, freez•es.** *—intr.* **1.** To change from a liquid to a solid by loss of heat: *Pure water freezes at a higher temperature than salt water.* **2.** To have ice form in or on: *The pond freezes early in winter. The pipes froze.* **3.** To be harmed or killed by cold or frost: *Many fruits freeze in very cold weather.* **4.** To be or feel very cold: *We froze without sweaters.* **5.** To become motionless or unable to move: *The climber froze with fear on the slippery rocks.* **6.** To become icily silent in manner: *We froze after the harsh words.* *—tr.* **1.** To convert into ice. **2.** To cause ice to form upon: *The cold snap froze the river.* **3.** To preserve (food, for example) by subjecting to a freezing temperature: *freeze vegetables.* **4.** To harm or kill by cold: *The deep cold froze the oranges.* **5.** To make very cold: *The winter wind froze my fingers.* **6.** To make motionless or unable to move: *Fear froze the deer in the beam of our lights.* **7.** To set (prices or wages) at a certain amount: *The company froze wages at last year's levels.* *—n.* **1.a.** The act of freezing: *a freeze on hiring.* **b.** The state of being frozen: *a price freeze.* **2.** A period of cold weather; a frost: *crops ruined by the early freeze.* **—*idiom.* freeze out.** To shut out or exclude, as by cold or unfriendly treatment: *Chain stores that freeze out small merchants.* [First written down before 971 in Old English and spelled *frēosan*.]

❑ *These sound alike:* **freeze, frieze** (horizontal band).

freeze-dry (frēz′drī′) *tr.v.* **freeze-dried, freeze-dry•ing, freeze-dries.** To preserve (food, for example) by rapid freezing and drying in a vacuum.

freez•er (frē′zər) *n.* A refrigerated compartment that is kept at a very low temperature for freezing and storing food.

freez•ing point (frē′zĭng) *n.* The temperature at which a liquid freezes.

freight (frāt) *n.* **1.a.** Goods carried as cargo by truck, train, ship, or aircraft. **b.** The charge for transporting such goods. **2.** Commercial transportation of goods. **3.** A railway train carrying goods only. *—tr.v.* **freight•ed, freight•ing, freights. 1.** To transport commercially as cargo. **2.** To load or fill with cargo: *ships waiting to be freighted.* [First written down in 1228 in Middle English and spelled *fraght*, from Middle Dutch or Middle Low German *vracht, vrecht*.]

freight car *n.* A railroad car designed to carry freight.

freight•er (frā′tər) *n.* **1.** A vehicle, especially a ship, for carrying freight. **2.** A shipper of cargo.

freight train *n.* A railroad train made up of freight cars.

Fré•mont (frē′mŏnt′), **John Charles.** 1813–1890. American explorer and politician who mapped much of the American West and Northwest.

French (frĕnch) *adj.* **1.** Of, relating to, or characteristic of France or its people or culture. **2.** Of or relating to the French language. *—n.* The Romance language of France and parts of Switzerland, Belgium, Canada, and certain other countries. [First written down about 1000 in Old English and spelled *frencisc*, Frankish, from *Franca*, Frank.] —SEE NOTE.

French and Indian War *n.* A war (1754–1763) fought in North America between England and France and involving some Native Americans as allies of the French.

French-Ca•na•di•an also **French Ca•na•di•an**

(frĕnch′kə nä′dē ən) *n.* A Canadian of French descent.

French curve *n.* A flat drafting instrument with curved edges and scroll-shaped cutouts, used as a guide in drawing curves.

French door *n.* A door, usually one of a pair, with glass panes extending for most of its length.

French fry *n.* A thin strip of potato fried in deep fat. Often used in the plural.

French-fry (**frĕnch′**frī′) *tr.v.* To fry (potato strips, for example) in deep fat.

French Gui•a•na (gē ăn′ə *or* gē ä′nə). A French territory of northeast South America on the Atlantic Ocean east of Suriname. Cayenne is the capital and the largest city. Population, 72,012.

French horn *n.* A brass musical instrument having a long coiled tube ending in a wide bell.

French•man (**frĕnch′**mən) *n.* A man who is a native or inhabitant of France.

French Revolution *n.* A revolution in France, lasting from 1789 to 1799, in which the monarchy was overthrown and a republic established.

French toast *n.* Sliced bread soaked in a batter of milk and egg and lightly fried.

French•wom•an (**frĕnch′**wo͝om′ən) *n.* A woman who is a native or inhabitant of France.

fre•net•ic (frə **nĕt′**ĭk) *adj.* Wildly active or excited; frantic; frenzied: *worked at a frenetic pace to get the project done.* **—fre•net′i•cal•ly** *adv.*

fren•zied (**frĕn′**zēd) *adj.* Affected with or maked by frenzy; frantic: *a frenzied rush for the exit.* **—fren′zied•ly** *adv.*

fren•zy (**frĕn′**zē) *n., pl.* **fren•zies.** A state of violent agitation or wild excitement: *The frightened horses dashed about in a frenzy.*

fre•quen•cy (**frē′**kwən sē) *n., pl.* **fre•quen•cies. 1.** The condition of occurring repeatedly at short intervals: *The frequency of the buyers' calls is proof of their interest in the property.* **2.** The number of times some event occurs within a given period; rate of occurrence. **3.** The number of complete cycles of a wave, such as a radio wave, that occur per second. **4.** The ratio of the number of occurrences of some event to the number of opportunities for its occurrence.

frequency modulation *n.* A method of broadcasting in which the frequency of the carrier wave is varied according to the signal being transmitted. Frequency modulation reduces static in radio transmission.

fre•quent (**frē′**kwənt) *adj.* Occurring or appearing quite often or at close intervals: *While my teeth were being straightened, I made frequent visits to the dentist.* *—tr.v.* (*also* frē **kwĕnt′**). **fre•quent•ed, fre•quent•ing, fre•quents.** To pay frequent visits to; be in or at often: *They frequented the museum on weekends.* **—fre′quent•ly** *adv.*

fres•co (**frĕs′**kō) *n., pl.* **fres•coes** or **fres•cos. 1.** The art of painting on fresh moist plaster. **2.** A painting done in this manner.

fresh (frĕsh) *adj.* **fresh•er, fresh•est. 1.** New to one's experience; not known before: *fresh reports from the scene of the earthquake.* **2.** Being unusual or different; novel: *a fresh approach to old problems.* **3.** Recently made, produced, or gathered; not stale or spoiled: *fresh bread; fresh fruit.* **4.** Not preserved, as by canning, smoking, or freezing: *fresh vegetables.* **5.** Not saline or salty: *fresh water.* **6.** Not yet used or soiled; clean: *fresh paper towels.* **7.** New or additional; further: *a fresh coat of paint.* **8.** Bright and clear; not dull or faded: *recent experiences that are fresh in one's memory.* **9.** Having the glowing unspoiled appearance of youth: *a bright fresh face.* **10.** Not tired; refreshed; rested: *felt fresh after a short nap.* **11.** Fairly strong; brisk: *a fresh morning breeze.* **12.** *Informal.* Bold; impudent. **—fresh′ly** *adv.* **—fresh′ness** *n.*

fresh•en (**frĕsh′**ən) *v.* **fresh•ened, fresh•en•ing, fresh•ens.** *—intr.* To become fresh, as in vigor or appearance. *—tr.* To make fresh: *Rain freshened the air.*

fresh•et (**frĕsh′**ĭt) *n.* **1.** A sudden overflow of a stream as a result of a heavy rain or a thaw. **2.** A stream of fresh water that runs into a body of salt water.

fresh•man (**frĕsh′**mən) *n.* A student in the first-year class of a high school, university, or college.

fresh•wa•ter (**frĕsh′**wô′tər *or* **frĕsh′**wŏt′ər) *adj.* Of, relating to, living in, or consisting of water that is not salty: *freshwater fish; a freshwater pond.*

fret[1] (frĕt) *v.* **fret•ted, fret•ting, frets.** *—tr.* **1.** To cause to be uneasy; vex: *I tried not to fret my parents unnecessarily.* **2.** To gnaw or wear away; erode. *—intr.* To be uneasy, troubled, or worried: *fretted over each detail.* *—n.* The act or an instance of fretting. [First written down about 725 in Old English and spelled *fretan*, to eat up.]

fret[2] (frĕt) *n.* One of several ridges set across the fingerboard of a stringed instrument, such as a guitar. [First written down about 1500 in Modern English.] **—fret′ted** *adj.*

fret[3] (frĕt) *n.* An ornamental design within a band or border, consisting of repeated and symmetrical designs. *—tr.v.* **fret•ted, fret•ting, frets.** To provide with such a design. [First written down about 1386 in Middle English and spelled *fret*, interlaced work, from Old French *frete*.]

fret•ful (**frĕt′**fəl) *adj.* Feeling or showing worry and distress; troubled. **—fret′ful•ly** *adv.* **—fret′ful•ness** *n.*

fret saw *n.* A saw with a narrow, fine-toothed blade, used for cutting thin wood or metal.

fret•work (**frĕt′**wûrk′) *n.* Ornamental work consisting of three-dimensional frets; geometric openwork.

Freud (froid), **Sigmund.** 1856–1939. Austrian founder of psychoanalysis whose theories influenced modern thought.

Freud•i•an (**froi′**dē ən) *adj.* Relating to or being in accordance with the psychoanalytic theories of Sigmund Freud. *—n.* A person who accepts and applies the psychoanalytic theories of Freud.

Fri. *abbr.* An abbreviation of Friday.

fri•a•ble (**frī′**ə bəl) *adj.* Easily crumbled; brittle: *friable stone.* **—fri′a•bil′i•ty, fri′a•ble•ness** *n.*

fri•ar (**frī′**ər) *n.* A man who is a member of certain Roman Catholic orders. [First written down before 1200 in Middle English and spelled *frere*, from Old French, from Latin *frāter*, brother.]

❑ *These sound alike:* **friar, fryer** (young chicken).

fric•as•see (frĭk′ə **sē′** *or* **frĭk′**ə sē′) *n.* Poultry or meat cut up and stewed in a thick gravy. *—tr.v.* **fric•as•seed, fric•as•see•ing, fric•as•sees.** To prepare as a fricassee.

fric•tion (**frĭk′**shən) *n.* **1.** The rubbing of one object or surface against another: *Friction of flint and steel can produce sparks.* **2.** The force that resists motion between two objects in contact: *By oiling the wheels, we reduced the friction.* **3.** The conflict or irritation that occurs between people who have different opinions or beliefs: *The debate caused friction between the two Senators.* **—fric′tion•al** *adj.* **—fric′tion•al•ly** *adv.*

Fri•day (**frī′**dē *or* **frī′**dā′) *n.* The sixth day of the week.

fried (frīd) *v.* Past tense and past participle of **fry[1]**.

friend (frĕnd) *n.* **1.** A person who is known and liked by another: *My friends came to my birthday party.* **2.** A person who supports a group, cause, or movement; a person on the same side: *Their support of conservation made them friends of the en-*

French horn

fret[2]

Frets on a guitar

Sigmund Freud

ă	**pat**	oi	**boy**
ā	**pay**	ou	**out**
âr	**care**	o͝o	**took**
ä	**father**	o͞o	**boot**
ĕ	**pet**	ŭ	**cut**
ē	**be**	ûr	**urge**
ĭ	**pit**	th	**thin**
ī	**pie**	*th*	**this**
îr	**pier**	hw	**whoop**
ŏ	**pot**	zh	**vision**
ō	**toe**	ə	**about**
ô	**paw**	N	*French* **bon**

vironmental agency. **3. Friend.** A member of the Society of Friends; a Quaker. [First written down about 725 in Old English and spelled *frēond.*]

friend•ly (frĕnd′lē) *adj.* **friend•li•er, friend•li•est. 1.** Of, relating to, or suitable to a friend or friends: *friendly cooperation.* **2.** Not feeling or showing enmity or hostility: *a friendly handshake.* **3.** Giving support; comforting: *friendly words.* **—friend′li•ness** *n.*

friend•ship (frĕnd′shĭp′) *n.* **1.** The condition or fact of being friends: *a friendship from childhood.* **2.** A feeling of warmth toward another; friendliness: *friendship between people who like the same things.*

fri•er (frī′ər) *n.* Variant of **fryer.**

fries (frīz) *v.* Third person singular present tense of **fry**[1]. *—n.* Plural of **fry**[1].

frieze (frēz) *n.* **1.** In classical architecture, a plain or decorated horizontal band that is above the columns and below the roof. **2.** A decorative horizontal band, as along the upper part of a wall in a room. [First written down in 1563 in Modern English, from Medieval Latin *frisium*, embroidery, from Latin *Phrygium (opus)*, (work) of Phrygia (ancient region of Asia Minor).]

❑ *These sound alike:* **frieze, freeze** (form ice).

frigate bird
Male frigate bird

frig•ate (frĭg′ĭt) *n.* **1.** A warship used as an escort and to destroy submarines. **2.** A fast square-rigged warship built in the 17th, 18th, and 19th centuries.

frigate bird *n.* Any of various tropical sea birds having long powerful wings, dark feathers, and a forked tail. Frigate birds snatch food from other birds in flight.

Frigg (frĭg) also **Frig•ga** (frĭg′ə) *n.* In Norse mythology, the goddess of the heavens and the wife of Odin.

fright (frīt) *n.* **1.** Sudden intense fear, as of something immediately threatening; alarm: *Fright caused the flock of birds to take flight.* **2.** *Informal.* Something very unsightly or alarming: *Their dirty windblown hair looked a fright.* [First written down before 830 in Old English and spelled *fyrhtu.*]

fright•en (frīt′n) *v.* **fright•ened, fright•en•ing, fright•ens.** *—tr.* **1.** To fill with fear; alarm or startle: *A loud noise frightened me.* **2.** To drive or force by arousing fear: *frightened him into making a confession.* *—intr.* To become afraid.

Synonyms: **frighten, scare, alarm, terrify, panic.** These verbs mean to cause fear in a person or thing. **Frighten** is the most general: *It's hard to believe that elephants are frightened of mice.* **Scare** is also general, but less formal: *Don't let the amount of homework scare you.* **Alarm** means to frighten suddenly: *Her loss of ten pounds in a month alarmed her doctor.* **Terrify** means to overwhelm with fear: *We were terrified that the footbridge would collapse as we walked on it.* **Panic** means to alarm a person to the point of losing self-control: *False reports of an invasion panicked the whole city.*

fright•en•ing (frīt′n ĭng) *adj.* Causing fright or sudden alarm: *a frightening thunderstorm.* **—fright′en•ing•ly** *adv.*

fright•ful (frīt′fəl) *adj.* **1.** Causing disgust or shock; horrifying: *The number of hungry refugees is frightful.* **2.** Causing fright; terrifying: *frightful Halloween masks.* **3.** *Informal.* Extreme; excessive: *frightful traffic at rush hour.* **—fright′ful•ly** *adv.* **—fright′ful•ness** *n.*

frig•id (frĭj′ĭd) *adj.* **1.** Extremely cold: *a frigid room.* See Synonyms at **cold. 2.** Stiff and formal in manner: *the frigid manner of a judge.* **—fri•gid′i•ty** (frĭ jĭd′ĭ tē), **frig′id•ness** *n.* **—frig′id•ly** *adv.*

Frigid Zone (frĭj′ĭd). Either of two extreme latitude zones of the earth, the **North Frigid Zone,** extending north of the Arctic Circle, or the **South Frigid Zone,** south of the Antarctic Circle.

fri•jol (frē hōl′ *or* frē′hōl′) also **fri•jo•le** (frē hō′lē) *n., pl.* **fri•jo•les** (frē hō′lēz). A bean cultivated and used for food.

frill (frĭl) *n.* **1.** A ruffled, gathered, or pleated piece of fancy trimming, as on a fabric edge: *frills on a doll's dress.* **2.** *Informal.* Something desirable but unnecessary added on as an extra: *a straightforward speech without any frills.* *—tr.v.* **frilled, frill•ing, frills.** To put a ruffle or frill on: *frill a skirt.* **—frill′y** *adj.*

fringe (frĭnj) *n.* **1.** A decorative border or edging of hanging threads or cords, often attached to a separate band. **2.** Something that resembles such a border or edging: *a fringe of eyelashes.* **3.** An outer part; a margin; an edge: *stand on the fringe of the crowd.* *—tr.v.* **fringed, fring•ing, fring•es. 1.** To decorate with or as if with a fringe: *fringe curtains.* **2.** To form a fringe along the edge of: *Sunlight fringed the horizon.*

fringe benefit *n.* An employment benefit, such as medical care, given in addition to wages or salary.

frip•per•y (frĭp′ə rē) *n., pl.* **frip•per•ies. 1.** Pretentious showy finery. **2.** Pretentious elegance; ostentation.

Fris•bee (frĭz′bē). A trademark used for a disk-shaped object that players throw and catch.

Fri•sian (frĭzh′ən *or* frē′zhən) *n.* **1.** A native or inhabitant of the Frisian Islands or Friesland, a northern province of the Netherlands. **2.** The Germanic language of the Frisians. **—Fri′sian** *adj.*

frisk (frĭsk) *v.* **frisked, frisk•ing, frisks.** *—intr.* To move about briskly and playfully; frolic: *Squirrels frisked in the trees.* *—tr.* To search (a person) for something concealed, especially a weapon.

frisk•y (frĭs′kē) *adj.* **frisk•i•er, frisk•i•est.** Energetic, lively, and playful: *a frisky kitten.* **—frisk′i•ly** *adv.* **—frisk′i•ness** *n.*

frit•ter[1] (frĭt′ər) *tr.v.* **frit•tered, frit•ter•ing, frit•ters.** To reduce or squander little by little; waste: *frittered the day away watching TV and playing solitaire.* [First written down in 1728 in Modern English, probably from *fritter*, fragment, probably from *fitter*, to break into small pieces.] **—frit′ter•er** *n.*

frit•ter[2] (frĭt′ər) *n.* A small fried cake of batter that often contains fruit, vegetables, or seafood. [First written down in 1381 in Middle English and spelled *frutur*, from Late Latin *frīctūra*, from Latin *frīctus*, roasted, fried.]

fri•vol•i•ty (frĭ vŏl′ĭ tē) *n., pl.* **fri•vol•i•ties. 1.** The quality or condition of being frivolous. **2.** A frivolous act or thing.

friv•o•lous (frĭv′ə ləs) *adj.* **1.** Not worthy of serious attention; trivial: *wasting time on frivolous ideas.* **2.** Inappropriately silly: *a frivolous purchase.* **—friv′o•lous•ly** *adv.* **—friv′o•lous•ness** *n.*

frizz (frĭz) *tr. & intr.v.* **frizzed, frizz•ing, frizz•es.** To form or be formed into small tight tufts or curls. *—n.* A small tight curl or tuft. [First written down in 1660 in Modern English, from Old French *friser*, possibly from *frire*, to fry.]

friz•zle[1] (frĭz′əl) *v.* **friz•zled, friz•zling, friz•zles.** *—tr.* To fry (something) until crisp or curled. *—intr.* To fry with a sizzling noise. [First written down in 1839 in Modern English, possibly blend of *fry* and *sizzle.*]

friz•zle[2] (frĭz′əl) *tr. & intr.v.* **friz•zled, friz•zling, friz•zles.** To form or cause to be formed into small tight curls. *—n.* A small tight curl. [First written down about 1565 in Modern English.]

friz•zly (frĭz′lē) *adj.* **friz•zli•er, friz•zli•est.** Frizzy.

friz•zy (frĭz′ē) *adj.* **friz•zi•er, friz•zi•est.** Tightly curled: *frizzy hair.*

fro (frō) *adv.* Away; back: *A pendulum swings to and fro.*

frock (frŏk) *n.* **1.** A woman's dress. **2.** A long loose outer garment, such as a priest's robe or an artist's smock.

frock coat *n.* A man's double-breasted dress coat coming to the knees.

frog (frôg *or* frŏg) *n.* **1.** Any of numerous animals having smooth moist skin, webbed feet, long hind legs used for leaping, and no tail when fully grown. Frogs are amphibians, and many kinds live chiefly in water. **2.** An ornamental fastener made of braid or cord with a looped piece that fits around a button. **3.** A device that allows the wheels of railway cars to roll smoothly over the junction. **4.** *Informal.* Hoarseness in the throat.

frog kick *n.* A swimming kick in which the legs are drawn up close to the hips and then thrust outward and drawn together when straight.

frog•man (**frôg′**măn′ *or* **frŏg′**măn′) *n.* A swimmer provided with breathing apparatus and other equipment to perform underwater maneuvers, especially military maneuvers.

frol•ic (**frŏl′**ĭk) *n.* **1.** Gaiety; merriment. **2.** A gay carefree time. —*intr.v.* **frol•icked, frol•ick•ing, frol•ics.** To behave playfully; romp: *The rabbits frolicked in the grass.*

frol•ic•some (**frŏl′**ĭk səm) *adj.* Full of fun; frisky and playful: *a frolicsome puppy.*

from (frŭm *or* frŏm; frəm *when unstressed*) *prep.* **1.** Used to indicate a specified place or time as a starting point: *walked home from the station; from midnight until dawn.* **2.** Used to indicate a source, a cause, or an instrument: *a gift from a friend; a note from the teacher.* **3.** Because of: *faint from hunger.* **4.** Out of or off of: *taking a book from the shelf.* **5.** Out of the control or possession of: *They took the ball from us.* **6.** So as not to be engaged in: *kept from playing.* **7.** As opposed to: *knowing right from wrong.*

frond (frŏnd) *n.* **1.** The leaf of a fern or palm tree, usually divided into smaller leaflets. **2.** A part that resembles a leaf, as of seaweed.

front (frŭnt) *n.* **1.** The forward part or surface, as of a building: *a shirt with buttons down the front; a desk at the front of the room.* **2.** The area, location, or position directly before or ahead: *A crowd gathered in front of the building.* **3.** A person's outward manner, behavior, or appearance: *keeping up a brave front despite misfortune.* **4.** Land bordering a lake, river, or street: *a lake front.* **5.** In warfare, an area where a battle is taking place. **6.** The boundary between two air masses having different temperatures: *a cold front.* **7.** A field of activity: *Conditions on the economic front are poor.* **8.** A group or movement uniting persons or organizations that seek a common goal; a coalition: *Unions and workers formed a labor front.* **9.** An outwardly respectable person or business that serves as a cover for secret or illegal activity. —*adj.* Of, relating to, aimed at, or located in the front: *the front door; the front pages; the front view.* —*v.* **front•ed, front•ing, fronts.** —*tr.* **1.** To face or look out upon: *The building fronts the main street.* **2.** To meet in opposition; directly confront. —*intr.* To have a front; face onto something else: *The motel fronts on the highway.* [First written down about 1300 in Middle English, from Latin *frōns*, forehead, front.]

front•age (**frŭn′**tĭj) *n.* **1.** The front part of a piece of property. **2.** The land between a building and the street. **3.** The land adjacent to something, such as a building, street, or body of water.

fron•tal (**frŭn′**tl) *adj.* **1.** Of, at, or concerning the front: *a frontal assault.* **2.** Of or relating to the forehead. —**fron′tal•ly** *adv.*

frontal bone *n.* A bone of the skull, consisting of a part that corresponds to the forehead and a part that forms the roof of the eye sockets and cavities of the nose.

fron•tier (frŭn **tîr′** *or* **frŭn′**tîr′) *n.* **1.** A boundary between countries or the land along such a boundary; a border. **2.** A region just beyond or at the edge of a settled area. **3.** An undeveloped area or field of research or interest: *exploring new frontiers in space.* [First written down in 1392 in Middle English and spelled *frountres*, altar cloths, from Old French *frontier*, from *front*, forehead, front.]

fron•tiers•man (frŭn **tîrz′**mən) *n.* A man who lives on the frontier.

fron•tiers•wom•an (frŭn **tîrz′**wo͝om′ən) *n.* A woman who lives on the frontier.

fron•tis•piece (**frŭn′**tĭ spēs′) *n.* An illustration that faces or comes just before the title page of a book.

front•line (**frŭnt′līn′**) *n.* A front or boundary, especially one between political or military positions. —*adj.* **1.** Located or used at a military front. **2.** Of or relating to the most advanced position in a field or an undertaking: *frontline research.*

front-run•ner also **front•run•ner** (**frŭnt′**rŭn′ər) *n.* A person who leads in a race or other competition.

frost (frôst *or* frŏst) *n.* **1.** A deposit of small ice crystals, formed from frozen water vapor, covering a surface: *The frost on the car windshield is frozen dew.* **2.** A temperature low enough to cause frost. —*v.* **frost•ed, frost•ing, frosts.** —*tr.* **1.** To cover with or as if with frost. **2.** To damage or kill by frost. **3.** To cover or decorate (a cake, cupcake, or other baked goods) with icing. —*intr.* To become covered with frost: *The windows frosted up.* [First written down about 725 in Old English and spelled *forst.*]

Frost (frôst *or* frŏst), **Robert Lee.** 1874–1963. American poet whose works, such as "Stopping by Woods on a Snowy Evening" (1923), are often set in rural New England.

frost•bite (**frôst′**bīt′ *or* **frŏst′**bīt′) *n.* Injury to a part of the body as a result of exposure to freezing temperatures. —*tr.v.* **frost•bit** (**frôst′**bĭt′ *or* **frŏst′**-bĭt′), or **frost•bit•ten** (**frôst′**bĭt′n *or* **frŏst′**bĭt′n), **frost•bit•ing, frost•bites.** To injure (a part of the body) by freezing.

frost•ing (**frô′**stĭng *or* **frŏs′**tĭng) *n.* **1.** A sweet mixture of sugar and other ingredients, used to cover and decorate cakes or cookies; icing. **2.** A roughened or speckled surface on glass or metal.

frost•y (**frô′**stē *or* **frŏs′**tē) *adj.* **frost•i•er, frost•i•est.** **1.** Producing or characterized by frost: *A sudden chill made the night frosty and cold.* See Synonyms at **cold.** **2.** Covered with frost or having a surface resembling frost: *the frosty bedroom window; a frosty texture.* **3.** Cold in manner; unfriendly: *The hostility between the neighbors was noticeable in their frosty greeting.* —**frost′i•ly** *adv.* —**frost′i•ness** *n.*

froth (frôth *or* frŏth) *n.* **1.** A mass of bubbles in or on a liquid; foam. **2.** Something lacking in substance or depth: *Most gossip is mere froth.* —*v.* (*also* frôth *or* frŏth). **frothed, froth•ing, froths.** —*tr.* **1.** To cover with foam. **2.** To cause to foam. —*intr.* To give off or form foam: *The sick dog frothed at the mouth.* —**froth′i•ly** *adv.* —**froth′i•ness** *n.* —**froth′y** *adj.*

frown (froun) *v.* **frowned, frown•ing, frowns.** —*intr.* **1.** To wrinkle the brow, as in thought or displeasure; scowl. **2.** To regard something with disapproval or distaste: *Most people frown on rudeness.* —*tr.* To show by a frown: *He frowned his displeasure at being interrupted.* —*n.* The act of wrinkling the brow in thought or displeasure; a scowl. [First written down about 1395 in Middle English and spelled *frounen*, from Old French *frogne*, grimace, of Celtic origin.]

frog
Bullfrog

frond

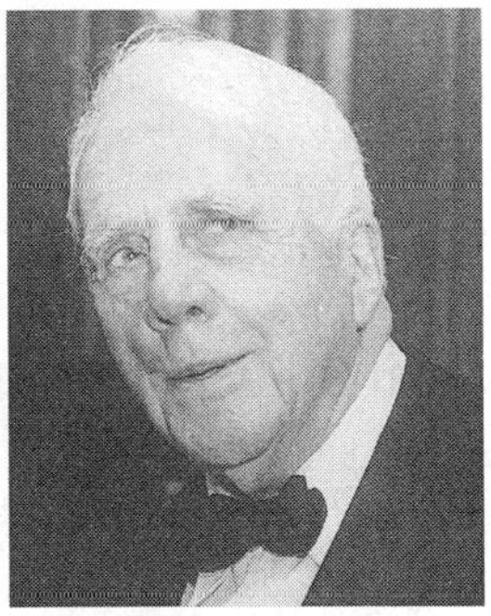

Robert Frost

ă	pat	oi	boy
ā	pay	ou	out
âr	care	o͝o	took
ä	father	o͞o	boot
ĕ	pet	ŭ	cut
ē	be	ûr	urge
ĭ	pit	th	thin
ī	pie	*th*	this
îr	pier	hw	whoop
ŏ	pot	zh	vision
ō	toe	ə	about
ô	paw	N	*French* bon

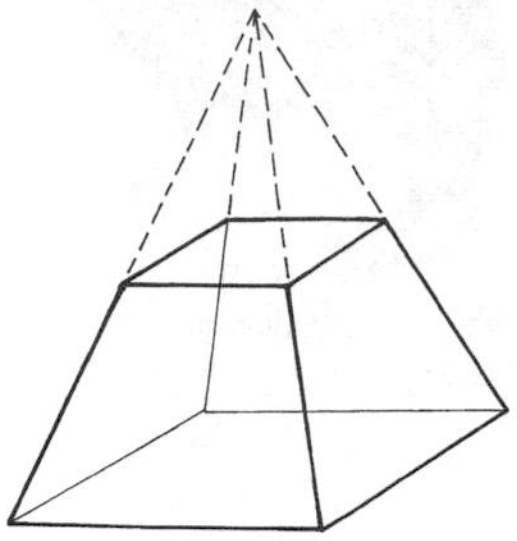

frustum

Regional Note: frying pan

The words **frying pan** and **skillet** can now be used virtually interchangeably. At one time, however, **frying pan** was a New England term. **Skillet** seems to have been used in the middle part of the country.

Word Building: –ful

The suffix **–ful** comes from the Old English adjective *full*, meaning "full." *Full* was commonly added to a noun in order to form adjectives meaning "full of" or "characterized by" whatever quality was denoted by the noun: **playful, careful**. The use of **–ful** to form nouns meaning "a quantity that would fill" a particular receptacle (**cupful, mouthful**) also goes back to Old English. In modern usage the correct way to form the plural of these nouns is to add an *s* to the end of the suffix: **cupfuls**.

frow•zy (frou′zē) *adj.* **frow•zi•er, frow•zi•est. 1.** Untidy; slovenly; unkempt: *frowzy wind-blown hair.* **2.** Having an unpleasant smell; musty: *frowzy odors from the old clothes.* **—frow′zi•ness** *n.*

froze (frōz) *v.* Past tense of **freeze.**

fro•zen (frō′zən) *v.* Past participle of **freeze.** *—adj.* **1.a.** Made into ice: *frozen orange juice.* **b.** Covered with or surrounded by ice: *a frozen pool.* **2.** Very cold: *the frozen North.* **3.** Preserved by freezing: *frozen strawberries.* **4.** Incapable of moving, as from fright: *frozen with fear.* **5.** Damaged or killed by frost: *frozen crops.* **6.** Unfriendly; cold: *a frozen stare.*

fruc•tose (frŭk′tōs′ *or* frŏŏk′tōs′) *n.* A very sweet sugar found in honey and in many fruits, having the chemical formula $C_6H_{12}O_6$; fruit sugar.

fru•gal (frōō′gəl) *adj.* **1.** Careful in spending or in using resources; thrifty: *Frugal use of energy saves natural resources.* **2.** Costing little; inexpensive: *a frugal lunch.* **—fru•gal′i•ty** (frōō găl′ĭ tē) *n.* **—fru′gal•ly** *adv.*

fruit (frōōt) *n., pl.* **fruit** or **fruits. 1.a.** The ripened part of a flowering plant that contains the seeds. Berries and pods are fruits. **b.** A fleshy, often sweet plant part of this kind, eaten as food, as an apple or orange. **2.** A plant crop or product: *the fruit of this year's planting.* **3.** A result or outcome: *at last enjoying the fruit of our labor.* *—intr. & tr.v.* **fruit•ed, fruit•ing, fruits.** To produce or cause to produce fruit: *Apple trees fruit in the fall.* [First written down before 1200 in Middle English and spelled *frut*, from Latin *frūctus*, enjoyment, fruit.]

fruit•cake (frōōt′kāk′) *n.* A rich spiced cake containing various dried and preserved fruits and nuts.

fruit fly *n.* Any of various small flies whose larvae hatch in and feed on ripening or decaying fruit and vegetables.

fruit•ful (frōōt′fəl) *adj.* **1.** Producing or bearing fruit. **2.** Producing something in abundance; productive: *Thomas Edison was a fruitful inventor.* **3.** Producing good results; beneficial or profitable: *Going into business for themselves proved to be a fruitful idea.* **—fruit′ful•ly** *adv.* **—fruit′ful•ness** *n.*

fru•i•tion (frōō ĭsh′ən) *n.* **1.** The achievement of something desired or worked for; accomplishment: *Our idea for a student newspaper finally reached fruition.* **2.** The condition of bearing fruit.

fruit•less (frōōt′lĭs) *adj.* **1.** Having little or no result; unproductive: *Only after many fruitless attempts did explorers reach the South Pole.* **2.** Producing no fruit. **—fruit′less•ly** *adv.* **—fruit′less•ness** *n.*

fruit sugar *n.* Fructose.

fruit•y (frōō′tē) *adj.* **fruit•i•er, fruit•i•est.** Tasting or smelling of fruit: *the fruity smell of ripe peaches.* **—fruit′i•ness** *n.*

Frun•ze (frōōn′zə). Bishkek.

frus•ta (frŭs′tə) *n.* A plural of **frustum.**

frus•trate (frŭs′trāt′) *tr.v.* **frus•trat•ed, frus•trat•ing, frus•trates. 1.** To prevent from accomplishing something; thwart: *Lack of money frustrated my efforts to continue studying the piano.* **2.** To cause feelings of discouragement or bafflement in: *The scientists were frustrated by the negative results of the experiment.* **3.** To bring to nothing; defeat: *Bad weather frustrated our plans to go fishing.* [First written down in 1445 in Middle English and spelled *frustraten*, from Latin *frūstrā*, in vain.] **—frus•tra′tion** *n.*

frus•tum (frŭs′təm) *n., pl.* **frus•tums** or **frus•ta** (frŭs′tə). The section of a solid, such as a cone or pyramid, between the base and a plane through the solid parallel to the base.

fry¹ (frī) *v.* **fried** (frīd), **fry•ing, fries** (frīz). *—tr.v.* To cook (food) over direct heat in hot oil or fat: *We fried potatoes in a pan.* *—intr.v.* To be cooked over direct heat in hot oil or fat: *Eggs fry quickly.* *—n., pl.* **fries** (frīz). **1.** A French fry. **2.** An informal gathering where food is fried and eaten: *a fish fry.* [First written down about 1300 in Middle English and spelled *frien*, from Latin *frīgere*.]

fry² (frī) *pl.n.* Small fish, especially young, recently hatched fish. [First written down in 1293 in Middle English and spelled *fri*, probably from Anglo-Norman *frie*, from *frier*, to rub, from Latin *fricāre*.]

fry•er also **fri•er** (frī′ər) *n.* **1.** A small young chicken suitable for frying. **2.** A pot or pan having a basket for frying foods.

❑ *These sound alike:* **fryer, friar** (member of a religious order).

fry•ing pan (frī′ĭng) *n.* A shallow pan with a long handle, used for frying food. —SEE NOTE.

ft. *abbr.* An abbreviation of foot.

fuch•sia (fyōō′shə) *n.* **1.** Any of various tropical plants grown for their drooping, often red, purple, or pink flowers. **2.** A bright purplish red. [First written down in 1753 in Modern English, after Leonhard *Fuchs* (1501–1566), German botanist.]

fud•dle (fŭd′l) *tr.v.* **fud•dled, fud•dling, fud•dles.** To muddle or confuse, as with liquor; intoxicate.

fudge (fŭj) *n.* **1.** A soft rich candy, often flavored with chocolate. **2.** Nonsense; humbug.

fu•el (fyōō′əl) *n.* **1.** A substance, such as coal, wood, oil, or gas, that is burned to produce useful heat or energy. **2.** A substance that can be made to undergo a nuclear reaction and produce energy. **3.** Something that feeds or encourages a feeling: *Being insulted added fuel to his anger.* *—v.* **fu•eled, fu•el•ing, fu•els** also **fu•elled, fu•el•ling, fu•els.** *—tr.* To provide with fuel: *A tank truck fueled the plane.* *—intr.* To take in fuel: *The freighter fueled at the nearest port.* [First written down before 1200 in Middle English and spelled *feoile*, from Old French *fouaille*, from Latin *focus*, hearth, fireplace.]

fuel cell *n.* A device that produces electricity by the chemical reaction between a fuel and an oxidizer.

fu•gi•tive (fyōō′jĭ tĭv) *adj.* **1.** Running or having run away, as from the law or justice. **2.** Passing quickly; fleeting: *relaxing for a few fugitive hours.* *—n.* A person who flees: *The escaped criminal was a fugitive from the law.* [First written down about 1380 in Middle English and spelled *fugitif*, from Latin *fugitīvus*, from *fugere*, to flee.]

fugue (fyōōg) *n.* A musical composition in which one or more themes are repeated by different voices or instruments with variations on the themes.

–ful *suff.* A suffix that means: **1.** Full of: *eventful; playful.* **2.** Characterized by: *boastful.* **3.** Tending or able to: *helpful; useful.* **4.** A quantity that fills: *armful; cupful.* —SEE NOTE.

ful•crum (fŏŏl′krəm *or* fŭl′krəm) *n., pl.* **ful•crums** or **ful•cra** (fŏŏl′krə *or* fŭl′krə). The point or support on which a lever turns.

ful•fill also **ful•fil** (fŏŏl fĭl′) *tr.v.* **ful•filled, ful•fill•ing, ful•fills** also **ful•fils. 1.** To make come true; make real: *After many years they fulfilled their lifelong dream.* **2.** To carry out (a duty or order): *Citizens should fulfill their duty as voters.* **3.** To measure up to; satisfy: *fulfilling all requirements.* **—ful•fill′ment** *n.*

full (fŏŏl) *adj.* **full•er, full•est. 1.** Containing all that is normal or possible; filled: *a full bucket.* **2.** Not deficient; complete: *I need your full attention.* **3.** Of highest degree or development: *at full speed; in full bloom.* **4.** Having a great many or a great deal of: *shelves full of books.* **5.** Rounded in shape; plump: *a full face and figure.* **6.** Have or made with a generous amount of fabric: *a full skirt.* **7.** Filled with food; abundantly fed: *The guests were full after the huge banquet.* **8.** Having depth and body; rich: *a full flavor.* *—adv.* **1.** To a complete extent;

entirely: *Fill the pitcher full.* **2.** Exactly; directly: *The tree fell full across the middle of the road.* —*n.* The maximum or complete size, amount, or degree: *a bill paid in full.* [First written down in 917 in Old English.] **—full′ness** *n.*

full•back (fŏŏl′băk′) *n.* **1.** In football, the player who, along with the halfbacks and quarterback, is in a team's offensive backfield. **2.** In soccer, Rugby, and field hockey, either of two defensive players stationed near their team's goal.

full-blood•ed (fŏŏl′blŭd′ĭd) *adj.* **1.** Of unmixed ancestry; purebred: *a full-blooded Arabian horse.* **2.** Full of vigor; energetic.

full-blown (fŏŏl′blōn′) *adj.* **1.** Having blossomed or opened fully: *a full-blown tulip.* **2.** Fully matured or developed: *a full-blown case of chickenpox.*

full dress *n.* Clothing appropriate or required for formal occasions or ceremonies.

Ful•ler (fŏŏlər), **(Sarah) Margaret.** 1810–1850. American writer known for *Woman in the Nineteenth Century* (1845).

full-fledged (fŏŏl′flĕjd′) *adj.* **1.** Having reached full development; mature. **2.** Having full standing or rank: *The teacher is also a full-fledged lawyer.*

full-length (fŏŏl′lĕngkth′ *or* fŏŏl′lĕngth′) *adj.* **1.** Covering the entire length of a person or thing: *a full-length mirror; a full-length coat.* **2.** Of normal or standard length: *a full-length motion picture.*

full moon *n.* **1.** The moon when it is visible as a fully illuminated disk. **2.** The time of the month when this occurs.

full-scale (fŏŏl′skāl′) *adj.* **1.** Of the actual or full size; not reduced: *The design for the new car was produced in a full-scale model.* **2.** Not limited; complete; all-out: *Everyone turned out for a full-scale demonstration against local water pollution.*

full-size (fŏŏl′sīz′) *adj.* Of the standard or normal size: *a full-size poodle.*

full-time (fŏŏl′tīm′) *adj.* Employed for or involving a standard number of hours of working time: *a full-time editor; a full-time job.* **—full′-time′** *adv.*

ful•ly (fŏŏl′ē) *adv.* **1.** Totally or completely: *The deer was fully aware of our presence.* **2.** At least; no less than: *Fully half the students had to take the test over.*

ful•mi•nate (fŏŏl′mə nāt′ *or* fŭl′mə nāt′) *intr.v.* **ful•mi•nat•ed, ful•mi•nat•ing, ful•mi•nates. 1.** To make a loud strong verbal attack or denunciation: *The speaker fulminated against the waste of resources.* **2.** To explode with sudden violence or force. —*n.* Any of a number of salts that explode violently at the slightest shock and are used as detonators. [First written down before 1425 in Middle English and spelled *fulminaten*, from Latin *fulmināre*, to strike with lightning, from *fulmen*, lightning that strikes.] **—ful′mi•na′tion** *n.*

ful•some (fŏŏl′səm) *adj.* Excessive or insincere: *received fulsome praise for her efforts.* **—ful′some•ly** *adv.* **—ful′some•ness** *n.*

Ful•ton (fŏŏl′tən), **Robert.** 1765–1815. American engineer who produced the first practical steamboat, the *Clermont* (1807).

fum•ble (fŭm′bəl) *v.* **fum•bled, fum•bling, fum•bles.** —*intr.* **1.** To touch or handle something nervously or idly: *The driver fumbled with the car keys.* **2.** To feel around awkwardly while searching; grope: *The child fumbled for the light switch in the dark.* **3.** In sports, to mishandle or drop a ball. —*tr.* **1.** To handle clumsily or idly: *She fumbled the glass and it broke.* **2.** To make a botch of; bungle: *The bank robber fumbled the job.* **3.** In sports, to mishandle or drop (a ball). —*n.* **1.** An act of fumbling. **2.** A ball that has been fumbled.

fume (fyōōm) *n.* Smoke, vapor, or gas, especially if irritating, harmful, or smelly: *the choking fumes from a smokestack.* —*v.* **fumed, fum•ing, fumes.** —*tr.* To subject to or treat (something) by exposure to fumes. —*intr.* **1.** To produce or give off fumes. **2.** To feel or show anger or agitation; seethe: *After being put off for the third time, he was fuming.* [First written down about 1390 in Middle English, from Latin *fūmus.*]

fu•mi•gant (fyōō′mĭ gənt) *n.* A poisonous compound used in fumigating.

fu•mi•gate (fyōō′mĭ gāt′) *tr.v.* **fu•mi•gat•ed, fu•mi•gat•ing, fu•mi•gates.** To expose (a room or an object) to fumes in order to kill insects, rats, or other pests. **—fu′mi•ga′tion** *n.* **—fu′mi•ga′tor** *n.*

fun (fŭn) *n.* **1.** Enjoyment; amusement: *We had fun at the picnic.* **2.** A source of enjoyment or amusement: *The trampoline was fun.* ***—idiom.*** **for fun** or **in fun.** As a joke; playfully.

func•tion (fŭngk′shən) *n.* **1.** The normal or proper activity of a person or thing; purpose: *The function of the heart is to pump blood.* **2.** An assigned duty or activity: *Creating a menu is part of her function as head chef.* **3.a.** A quantity whose value depends on the value given to one or more related quantities: *The area of a square is a function of the length of its side.* **b.** A relationship between two sets that matches each member of the first set with a unique member of the second set. **4.** A formal social gathering or official ceremony. —*intr.* **func•tioned, func•tion•ing, func•tions.** To have or perform a function; serve: *Posts function as a support for the deck.* [First written down in 1533 in Modern English and spelled *funccion*, from Latin *fūnctiō*, performance, execution, from *fungī*, to perform, execute.]

func•tion•al (fŭngk′shə nəl) *adj.* **1.** Of or relating to a function or functions: *the functional responsibilities of a manager.* **2.** Having or carrying out a function; working: *Is this clock functional?* **3.** Designed for or adapted to a particular purpose or use: *The log cabin is an example of functional architecture.* **—func′tion•al•ly** *adv.*

func•tion•ar•y (fŭngk′shə nĕr′ē) *n., pl.* **func•tion•ar•ies.** A person who holds a position of authority or trust; an official: *The tax collector is a functionary in the local government.*

function word *n.* A word, such as a preposition, an auxiliary verb, or a conjunction, that expresses relationships between words, clauses, and sentences. In the sentence *It rained and we did not go until later, and* and *until* are function words.

fund (fŭnd) *n.* **1.** A sum of money raised or set aside for a certain purpose: *Our library has a new book fund each year.* **2. funds.** Available money; ready cash: *I'm a little short of funds.* **3.** A source of supply; a stock: *An encyclopedia is a fund of knowledge.* —*tr.v.* **fund•ed, fund•ing, funds.** To provide money for: *Several citizens of the town funded our sports program.* [First written down in 1677 in Modern English, from Latin *fundus*, bottom, piece of land.]

fun•da•men•tal (fŭn′də mĕn′tl) *adj.* Of, relating to, or forming a foundation; elemental; basic; primary: *A fundamental knowledge of mathematics should be part of everyone's education.* —*n.* **1.** Something that is an elemental or basic part; an essential: *the fundamentals of good cooking.* **2.** The component of a wave that has the lowest frequency. **—fun′da•men′tal•ly** *adv.*

fun•da•men•tal•ism (fŭn′də mĕn′tl ĭz′əm) *n.* **1.** Belief in the Bible as a complete and accurate historical record and statement of prophecy. **2.** Strict observance of the basic principles of a religion. **—fun′da•men′tal•ist** *n. & adj.*

fu•ner•al (fyōō′nər əl) *n.* **1.** The ceremonies that accompany burial or cremation of the dead. **2.** The

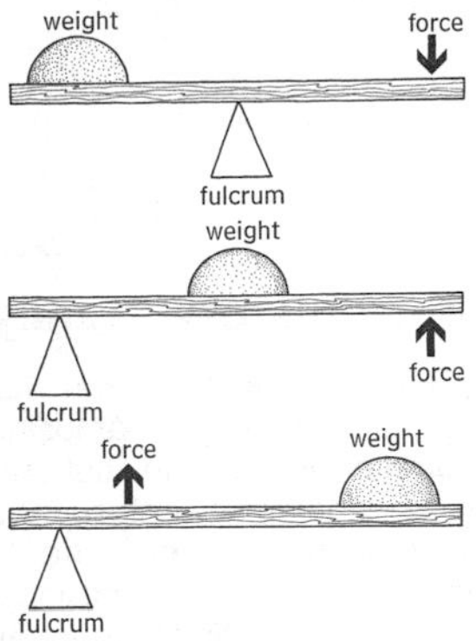

fulcrum

Margaret Fuller

Robert Fulton

ă	pat	oi	boy
ā	pay	ou	out
âr	care	ŏŏ	took
ä	father	ōō	boot
ĕ	pet	ŭ	cut
ē	be	ûr	urge
ĭ	pit	th	thin
ī	pie	*th*	this
îr	pier	hw	whoop
ŏ	pot	zh	vision
ō	toe	ə	about
ô	paw	N	*French* bon

Word History: funny

Everyone knows that **fun** means having an amusing, entertaining time, but **funny** now has us so confused that we sometimes are not sure if it means "amusing" or "strange." The noun *fun* is first recorded in 1700 and means "a trick, hoax, practical joke." It soon acquired the sense "amusement, diversion." *Funny*, "amusing," is first recorded in 1756; *funny*, "strange," first appears in 1806. Modern German has the same confusion of meanings in its adjective *komisch* [kō′mĭsh], "comic, amusing, funny, strange." If you go up to a clerk in a store to return something you just bought, say, a book with pages missing, he or she will look at the book and say "*das ist komisch*," meaning not "that's amusing," but "that's strange."

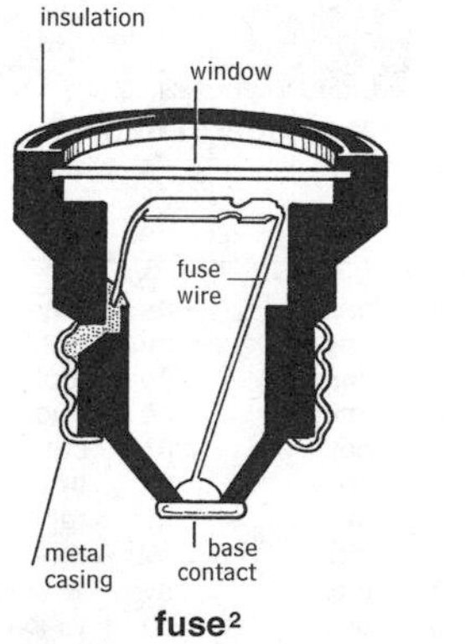

fuse[2]
Cutaway view

procession accompanying a body to the grave. [First written down in 1437 in Middle English and spelled *funerelles*, funeral rites, from Medieval Latin *fūnerālia*, from Latin *fūnus*, death rites.]

funeral director *n.* A person whose business is to prepare the dead for burial or cremation and to assist at funerals.

funeral home *n.* A building in which the dead are prepared for burial and cremation, and in which wakes and funerals are held.

fu•ne•re•al (fyo͞o nîr′ē əl) *adj.* Of, suitable for, or suggestive of a funeral: *funereal gloom.* **—fu•ne′re•al•ly** *adv.*

fun•gal (fŭng′gəl) also **fun•gous** (fŭng′gəs) *adj.* **1.** Of, relating to, or typical of a fungus or fungi. **2.** Caused by a fungus.

fun•gi (fŭn′jī *or* fŭng′gī) *n.* A plural of **fungus.**

fun•gi•cide (fŭn′jĭ sīd′ *or* fŭng′gĭ sīd′) *n.* A chemical substance that destroys or prevents the growth of fungi.

fun•gous (fŭng′gəs) *adj.* Variant of **fungal.**

❑ *These sound alike:* **fungous, fungus** (mold).

fun•gus (fŭng′gəs) *n., pl.* **fun•gi** (fŭn′jī *or* fŭng′gī) or **fun•gus•es.** Any of a kingdom of organisms, including the mushrooms, molds, yeasts, and mildews, that have no green coloring and obtain their nourishment from living or dead plant or animal matter. [First written down in 1527 in Modern English, from Latin; perhaps akin to Greek *sphongos*, sponge.]

❑ *These sound alike:* **fungus, fungous** (of a fungus).

funk (fŭngk) *n.* **1.** A state of fear; panic. **2.** A state of depression: *They were in a funk because their trip was canceled.*

funk•y[1] (fŭng′kē) *adj.* **funk•i•er, funk•i•est.** Frightened; panicky. [First written down in 1845 in Modern English, from *funk*, panic.]

funk•y[2] (fŭng′kē) *adj.* **1.** *Slang.* Having qualities of music similar to the blues; earthy: *funky jazz.* **2.** *Slang.* Original; unconventional; offbeat: *a funky shirt.* **3.** Having a moldy or musty smell. **—funk′i•ness** *n.* [First written down in 1784 in Modern English and spelled *funkey*, from *funk*, strong smell, perhaps ultimately from Latin *fūmus*, smoke.]

fun•nel (fŭn′əl) *n.* **1.** A utensil with a wide opening at one end and a tube at the other, used to pour liquids or other substances into a container with a small mouth. **2.** The smokestack of a ship or steam engine. **3.** Something shaped like a funnel: *the funnel of a tornado.* *—v.* **fun•neled, fun•nel•ing, fun•nels** or **fun•nelled, fun•nel•ling, fun•nels.** *—intr.* To move through or as if through a funnel: *Tourists funneled through the museum exhibit.* *—tr.* To cause to move through or as if through a funnel: *funnel juice into a pitcher.* [First written down in 1402 in Middle English and spelled *fonel*, from Latin *īnfundibulum*, from *īnfundere*, to pour in.]

fun•nies (fŭn′ēz) *pl.n.* **1.** Comic strips. **2.** A newspaper section containing comic strips.

fun•ny (fŭn′ē) *adj.* **fun•ni•er, fun•ni•est. 1.** Causing laughter or amusement: *a funny cartoon.* **2.** Strange; odd; curious: *It's funny that I can't remember where I left my shoes.* **—fun′ni•ly** *adv.* **—fun′ni•ness** *n.* —See Note.

funny bone *n. Informal.* A point near the elbow where a nerve can be pressed against the bone, producing a numb or tingling feeling in the arm.

fur (fûr) *n.* **1.** The thick soft hair covering the body of a mammal, such as a rabbit, cat, or fox. **2.** The skin and hair of such a mammal, treated and used for clothing, trimming, or lining. **3.** A coat, cape, or hat made of fur. **4.** A coating similar to the fur of an animal. [First written down about 1375 in Middle English and spelled *furre*, from Old French *fuerre*, lining, of Germanic origin.]

❑ *These sound alike:* **fur, fir** (evergreen).

fur•bish (fûr′bĭsh) *tr.v.* **fur•bished, fur•bish•ing, fur•bish•es. 1.** To brighten by cleaning or rubbing; polish: *The jeweler furbished the old silver bracelet.* **2.** To restore to a usable condition; renovate. **—fur′bish•er** *n.*

fu•ri•ous (fyo͝or′ē əs) *adj.* **1.** Full of or marked by extreme anger; raging. **2.** Suggestive of extreme anger in action or appearance; fierce; violent: *The horse ran at a furious pace.* **—fu′ri•ous•ly** *adv.* **—fu′ri•ous•ness** *n.*

furl (fûrl) *v.* **furled, furl•ing, furls.** *—tr.* To roll up and fasten (a flag or sail) to a pole, yard, or mast. *—intr.* To become rolled up: *The flag furled around the pole in the wind.* *—n.* **1.** The act of furling. **2.** A rolled section of something furled.

fur•long (fûr′lông′ *or* fûr′lŏng′) *n.* A unit for measuring distance, equal to ⅛ mile or 220 yards (201 meters).

fur•lough (fûr′lō) *n.* A vacation or leave of absence, especially one granted to a member of the armed forces. *—tr.v.* **fur•loughed, fur•lough•ing, fur•loughs.** To grant a leave to.

fur•nace (fûr′nĭs) *n.* An enclosed chamber in which fuel is burned to produce heat. Furnaces are used to heat buildings and to manufacture metal and glass. [First written down about 1200 in Middle English and spelled *furneise*, from Latin *fornāx*, oven.]

fur•nish (fûr′nĭsh) *tr.v.* **fur•nished, fur•nish•ing, fur•nish•es. 1.** To outfit with furniture and other necessities: *furnish each room of an apartment.* **2.** To supply; give: *The lamp furnished enough light to read.* **—fur′nish•er** *n.*

fur•nish•ing (fûr′nĭ shĭng) *n.* **1.** A piece of equipment necessary or useful for comfort or convenience. **2. furnishings.** The furniture, appliances, and other movable articles in a house or other building. **3. furnishings.** Clothes and accessories: *This store specializes in children's furnishings.*

fur•ni•ture (fûr′nĭ chər) *n.* The movable articles, such as chairs, tables, or appliances, that make a room fit for living or an office suitable for working.

fu•ror (fyo͝or′ôr′ *or* **fyo͝or′**ər) *n.* **1.** A noisy outburst; a commotion or an uproar: *Rumors of the President's arrival caused a furor of excitement.* **2.** Violent anger; frenzy: *the furor of the mob.*

fur•ri•er (fûr′ē ər) *n.* A person who deals in fur or makes and repairs fur garments.

fur•row (fûr′ō *or* fŭr′ō) *n.* **1.** A long narrow groove made in the ground by a plow or other tool: *furrows cut in the field for planting.* **2.** A rut, groove, or depression: *The car's tires made deep furrows in the dirt road.* *—tr.v.* **fur•rowed, fur•row•ing, fur•rows. 1.** To make furrows in; plow: *furrowed the cornfield into neat rows.* **2.** To form deep wrinkles in: *Months of worry had furrowed the banker's brow.*

fur•ry (fûr′ē *or* fŭr′ē) *adj.* **fur•ri•er, fur•ri•est. 1.** Consisting of or resembling fur: *a furry coat.* **2.** Covered with fur: *a furry kitten.* **—fur′ri•ness** *n.*

fur•ther (fûr′*th*ər) *adj.* A comparative of **far. 1.** More distant in space, time, or degree: *You couldn't be further from the truth.* **2.** Additional; more: *Stay tuned for further bulletins.* *—adv.* A comparative of **far. 1.** To a greater extent; more: *We will explore the matter further at a later time.* **2.** In addition; furthermore; also: *He stated further that he thought the mayor's remarks were unfair.* **3.** At or to a more distant or advanced point: *I read five pages further.* *—tr.v.* **fur•thered, fur•ther•ing, fur•thers.** To help the progress of; forward; advance: *The dedicated teacher furthered the careers* *of many students with sound advice.* —SEE NOTE at **farther.**

fur•ther•ance (fûr′*th*ər əns) *n.* The act of advancing or helping forward; advancement.

fur•ther•more (fûr′*th*ər môr′) *adv.* Moreover; in addition; besides.

fur•ther•most (fûr′*th*ər mōst′) *adj.* Most distant or remote.

fur•thest (fûr′*th*ĭst) *adj.* A superlative of **far.** Most distant in space, time, or degree: *Radio can transmit to the furthest corners of the earth.* —*adv.* A superlative of **far. 1.** To the greatest extent or degree: *The scientist's explanation went furthest toward providing a solution.* **2.** At or to the most distant or advanced point: *The champion threw the javelin furthest.*

fur•tive (fûr′tĭv) *adj.* Done or acting in a stealthy manner: *He cast a furtive glance at the clock.* [First written down in 1490 in Middle English, from Latin *furtum*, theft, from *fūr*, thief.] **—fur′tive•ly** *adv.* **—fur′tive•ness** *n.*

fu•ry (fyŏŏr′ē) *n., pl.* **fu•ries. 1.** Violent anger; rage. See Synonyms at **anger. 2.** Violent and uncontrolled action; turbulence; agitation: *the blizzard's fury.* **3. Furies.** In Greek and Roman mythology, the three terrible winged goddesses who pursue and punish those who commit unavenged crimes.

furze (fûrz) *n.* The gorse.

fuse[1] also **fuze** (fyōōz) *n.* **1.** A cord of easily burned material that is lighted at one end to carry a flame that detonates an explosive charge at the other end. **2.** Often **fuze.** A mechanical or electronic device used to set off an explosive charge or device, such as a bomb or grenade. [First written down in 1644 in Modern English, from Italian *fuso*, spindle (originally from its shape), from Latin *fūsus*.]

fuse[2] (fyōōz) *v.* **fused, fus•ing, fus•es.** —*tr.* **1.** To melt by heating. **2.** To blend by or as if by melting: *The music fuses African and Caribbean rhythms.* See Synonyms at **mix.** —*intr.* **1.** To become liquid from heat; melt. **2.** To become mixed or united by or as if by melting together: *The two cultures fused over the years to produce a new civilization.* —*n.* A safety device that protects an electric circuit, containing a length of wire that melts and breaks the circuit when the current reaches an unsafe level. [First written down in 1681 in Modern English, from Latin *fūsus*, past participle of *fundere*, to melt.]

fu•se•lage (fyōō′sə läzh′ *or* fyōō′zə läzh′) *n.* The main body of an airplane that holds cargo, passengers, and crew. [First written down in 1909 in Modern English, from Old French *fusel*, spindle, from Latin *fūsus*.]

fu•si•ble (fyōō′zə bəl) *adj.* Capable of being fused or melted. **—fu′si•bil′i•ty** *n.*

fu•sil•lade (fyōō′sə läd′ *or* fyōō′sə läd′) *n.* **1.** The discharge of many guns at the same time or in rapid succession. **2.** A rapid outburst: *a fusillade of complaints.*

fu•sion (fyōō′zhən) *n.* **1.** The act or process of melting or mixing different things into one by heat: *the fusion of copper and zinc to produce brass.* **2.** A mixture or blend formed by fusing two or more things: *An alloy is a fusion of two or more metals.* **3.** A nuclear reaction in which light nuclei combine to form heavier nuclei, releasing large amounts of energy. Fusion reactions power the sun and stars. **4.** A union formed by merging different things or groups: *The building is a fusion of different styles of architecture.*

fuss (fŭs) *n.* **1.** Needlessly nervous or useless activity; commotion: *There was a lot of fuss in the confusion of moving to a new office.* **2.** A display of concern or worry, especially over an unimportant matter: *Why make a fuss about a harmless remark?* **3.** A protest; a complaint: *The cancellation of the party provoked a fuss from the workers.* —*intr.v.* **fussed, fuss•ing, fuss•es. 1.** To be overly careful or concerned: *The caterer fussed over dinner.* **2.** To protest, complain, or act in an upset manner: *The baby was fussing all night.* **—fuss′er** *n.*

fuss•y (fŭs′ē) *adj.* **fuss•i•er, fuss•i•est. 1.** Easily upset; given to bouts of fussing: *a fussy baby.* **2.** Paying great or too much attention to small details: *She is very fussy about the arrangement of her room.* **3.** Requiring attention to small details: *Organizing a big wedding is a fussy job.* **—fuss′i•ly** *adv.* **—fuss′i•ness** *n.*

fus•ty (fŭs′tē) *adj.* **fus•ti•er, fus•ti•est. 1.** Smelling of mildew or decay; musty; moldy: *a fusty smell in the damp basement.* **2.** Old-fashioned; antique. **—fus′ti•ly** *adv.* **—fus′ti•ness** *n.*

fu•tile (fyōōt′l *or* fyōō′tīl′) *adj.* **1.** Having no useful result; hopeless; vain: *It is futile to argue that the earth is flat.* **2.** Of no importance; frivolous. [First written down about 1555 in Modern English, from Latin *fūtilis*.] **—fu′tile•ly** *adv.*

fu•til•i•ty (fyōō tĭl′ĭ tē) *n., pl.* **fu•til•i•ties. 1.** The condition or quality of being futile; uselessness; ineffectiveness: *The attempt to turn iron into gold was an exercise in futility.* **2.** Lack of importance or purpose.

fu•ton (fōō′tŏn) *n., pl.* **futon** or **fu•tons.** A pad of cotton batting or similar material used on a floor or on a raised platform as a mattress or comforter. [First written down in 1876 in Modern English, from Japanese *futon*, bedclothes, bedding.]

futon

fu•ture (fyōō′chər) *n.* **1.** The period of time yet to come: *Let's try to do better in the future.* **2.** Something that will happen in time to come: *The business's future is in the hands of new management.* **3.** Chance of success or advancement; outlook: *The young doctor faced a bright future.* **4.** The future tense. —*adj.* That will be or occur in time to come: *Let's review our progress at some future date.* [First written down in 1380 in Middle English, from Latin *futūrus*, about to be.]

future perfect tense *n.* A verb tense expressing action or a state completed by a specified time in the future. It is formed in English by combining *will have* or *shall have* with a past participle, as in the sentence *By noon tomorrow the train will have arrived there.*

future tense *n.* A verb tense used to express action or a state in the future. It is formed in English with the auxiliary verbs *shall* and *will*, as in the sentences *I shall be back tonight* and *They will leave in half an hour.*

fu•tur•is•tic (fyōō′chə rĭs′tĭk) *adj.* Of or relating to the future. **—fu′tur•is′ti•cal•ly** *adv.*

fu•tu•ri•ty (fyōō tŏŏr′ĭ tē *or* fyōō tyŏŏr′ĭ tē *or* fyōō chŏŏr′ĭ tē) *n., pl.* **fu•tu•ri•ties. 1.** The time yet to come; the future. **2.** The condition or quality of being in or of the future: *the futurity of experimental car design.* **3.** A future event or possibility.

fuze (fyōōz) *n.* Variant of **fuse[1].**

fuzz (fŭz) *n.* Soft short fibers or hairs; down: *the fuzz on a peach.*

fuzz•y (fŭz′ē) *adj.* **fuzz•i•er, fuzz•i•est. 1.** Covered with fuzz: *a fuzzy peach.* **2.** Of or resembling fuzz: *fuzzy hair of a little kitten.* **3.** Not clear; blurred: *a fuzzy memory.* **—fuzz′i•ly** *adv.* **—fuzz′i•ness** *n.*

–fy or **–ify** *suff.* A suffix that means to make or cause to become: *beautify; solidify.* —SEE NOTE.

Word Building: –fy

The verb suffix **–fy**, which means "to make or cause to become," derives from Latin *–ficāre* or *–ficārī*, from *facere*, meaning "to do or make." Thus **purify** means "to make pure, cleanse" (coming from Latin *pūrificāre*, from *pūrus* "clean" + *–ficāre*). In English the suffix **–fy** now normally takes the form **–ify**: **acidify, humidify.** Verbs ending in **–fy** often have related nouns ending in *–fication* or *–faction*: **magnify, magnification; satisfy, satisfaction.**

ă	pat	oi	boy
ā	pay	ou	out
âr	care	ŏŏ	took
ä	father	ōō	boot
ĕ	pet	ŭ	cut
ē	be	ûr	urge
ĭ	pit	th	thin
ī	pie	*th*	this
îr	pier	hw	whoop
ŏ	pot	zh	vision
ō	toe	ə	about
ô	paw	N	*French* bon

Gg

gable roof
Gables on the House of the Seven Gables in Salem, Massachusetts

Yuri Gagarin

g[1] or **G** (jē) *n., pl.* **g's** or **G's. 1.** The seventh letter of the English alphabet. **2.** In music, the fifth tone in the scale of C major. **3.** The seventh in a series or group: *row G in a theater.*

g[2] *abbr.* An abbreviation of: **1.** Gravity. **2.** Gram.

G (jē) *n.* A movie rating that recommends admission to persons of all ages.

Ga The symbol for the element **gallium.**

GA also **Ga.** *abbr.* An abbreviation of Georgia.

gab (găb) *Slang. intr.v.* **gabbed, gab•bing, gabs.** To talk idly and often too much; chatter: *The neighbors gabbed over the fence.* —*n.* Idle talk. [First written down in 1369 in Middle English and spelled *gabben,* to speak foolishly, from Old Norse *gabba,* to scoff.]

gab•ar•dine (găb′ər dēn′ *or* găb′ər **dēn′**) *n.* A firm woven cloth of cotton, rayon, or wool, having a smooth surface and slanting ribs and used for coats or suits.

gab•by (**găb′**ē) *adj.* **gab•bi•er, gab•bi•est.** *Slang.* Tending to talk too much. **—gab′bi•ness** *n.*

gab•er•dine (**găb′**ər dēn′ *or* găb′ər **dēn′**) *n.* Gabardine.

ga•ble (**gā′**bəl) *n.* **1.** The triangular section of wall between the two slopes of a roof. **2.** An end wall of a building having a gable roof. **3.** A triangular, usually ornamental section over a window or door. [First written down in 1347 in Middle English and spelled *gabell,* from Norman French *gable* (perhaps of Celtic origin) and from Old Norse *gafl.*] **—ga′bled** *adj.*

gable roof *n.* A pitched roof having a gable at each end.

Ga•bon (gă **bōn′**). A country of west-central Africa on the Atlantic Ocean south of Cameroon. Gabon gained its independence from France in 1960. Libreville is the capital and the largest city. Population, 1,312,000.

Ga•bo•ro•ne (gä′bə **rō′**nē). The capital of Botswana, in the southeast part of the country near the South African border. It was founded in about 1890. Population, 72,000.

Ga•bri•el (**gā′**brē əl) *n.* In the Bible, the archangel acting as the messenger of God.

gad (găd) *intr.v.* **gad•ded, gad•ding, gads.** To roam about relentlessly and with little purpose.

gad•a•bout (**găd′**ə bout′) *n.* A person who goes about relentlessly seeking amusement or excitement.

gad•fly (**găd′**flī′) *n.* **1.** Any of various flies that bite and annoy cattle, horses, and other animals. **2.** A person who annoys or provokes others: *The critic is the gadfly of the artist.*

gadg•et (**găj′**ĭt) *n.* A small mechanical device; a contrivance: *can openers, whisks, and other kitchen gadgets.*

gad•o•lin•i•um (găd′l **ĭn′**ē əm) *n. Symbol* **Gd** A white rare-earth element used in making heat-resistant alloys. Atomic number 64. See table at **element.** [First written down in 1886 in Modern English, after Johan *Gadolin* (1760–1852), Finnish chemist.]

Gae•a (**gā′**ə) *n.* In Greek mythology, the goddess of the earth, who gives birth to and marries Uranus and becomes the mother of the Titans.

Gael (gāl) *n.* **1.** A Gaelic-speaking Celt who is a native of Scotland, Ireland, or the Isle of Man. **2.** A Scottish Highlander.

Gael•ic (**gā′**lĭk) *adj.* Of or relating to the Gaels or their culture or languages. —*n.* Any of the Celtic languages of Ireland, Scotland, and the Isle of Man.

gaff (găf) *n.* **1.** An iron hook attached to a pole or handle and used to land large fish. **2.** A spar used to support the top edge of a fore-and-aft sail. —*tr.v.* **gaffed, gaf•fing, gaffs.** To hook or land (a fish) with a gaff. [First written down before 1325 in Middle English and spelled *gaffe,* from Old Provençal *gaf,* from *gafar,* to seize, of Germanic origin.]

gaf•fer (**găf′**ər) *n.* **1.** An electrician in charge of the lighting on a movie or television set. **2.** *Chiefly British.* An old man.

gag (găg) *n.* **1.** Something put into or over a person's mouth to prevent speaking or crying out. **2.** Something, such as a law or ruling, that limits or censors free speech: *The judge put a gag on press reporting while the trial was in progress.* **3.a.** A humorous remark intended to make people laugh; a joke. **b.** A practical joke; a hoax. —*v.* **gagged, gag•ging, gags.** —*tr.* **1.** To prevent from speaking or crying out by using a gag. **2.** To prevent from exercising free speech. **3.** To cause to choke or retch: *The strong gas fumes gagged several passers-by.* —*intr.* To choke; retch. [First written down in 1553 in Modern English, from Middle English *gaggen,* to suffocate, perhaps of imitative origin.]

Ga•ga•rin (gə **gär′**ĭn), **Yuri Alekseyevich.** 1934–1968. Soviet cosmonaut who in 1961 became the first person to travel in space.

gage[1] (gāj) *n.* Something deposited or given as a pledge that an obligation will be met: *The landlord required a month's rent as a gage for use of the house.* [First written down before 1300 in Middle English, from Old French, of Germanic origin.]

❑ *These sound alike:* **gage**[1], **gauge** (measurement).

gage[2] (gāj) *n. & v.* Variant of **gauge.**

Gage (gāj), **Thomas.** 1721–1787. British general whose efforts to suppress colonial resistance in Massachusetts led to the start of the American Revolution.

gag•gle (**găg′**əl) *n.* **1.** A flock of geese. **2.** A cluster or group: *a gaggle of fans.* [First written down before 1450 in Middle English and spelled *gagalle,* from *gagelen,* to cackle, probably of imitative origin.]

gai•e•ty also **gay•e•ty** (**gā′**ĭ tē) *n., pl.* **gai•e•ties** also **gay•e•ties. 1.** The condition of being gay or merry; cheerfulness: *the gaiety of the laughing children.* **2.** Merrymaking; celebration: *Mardi gras is a season of gaiety.* **3.** Showiness or brightness in dress or appearance; finery: *The gaiety of the colorful flowers brightened the room.*

gai•ly also **gay•ly** (**gā′**lē) *adv.* **1.** In a joyful, cheerful, or happy manner; merrily. **2.** Brightly; colorfully; showily: *The parade moved down the gaily decorated streets.*

gain (gān) *v.* **gained, gain•ing, gains.** *—tr.* **1.** To obtain; acquire: *We gained experience by working during the summer.* **2.** To acquire in competition; win: *The general gained a decisive victory over the enemy.* **3.** To get an increase of; build up: *Students gain knowledge by reading.* **4.** To come to; reach: *gained the top of the mountain.* See Synonyms at **reach.** *—intr.* **1.** To increase; grow: *Has your house gained in value?* **2.** To become better; improve: *The recovering patient is gaining in strength.* **3.** To come nearer; get closer: *The hounds gained on the fleeing fox.* *—n.* **1.a.** Something gained or acquired: *territorial gains.* **b.** Progress; advancement: *We have made great social gains since the early 1900's.* **2.** An increase, as in wealth: *the financial gains made from careful investment.* **3.** The act of acquiring something; attainment. [First written down in 1530 in Modern English and spelled *gaine*, from Old French *gaaignier*, of Germanic origin.]

gain•er (gā′nər) *n.* **1.** A person or thing that gains. **2.** A dive in which the diver leaves the board facing forward, does a back somersault, and enters the water feet first.

gain•ful (gān′fəl) *adj.* Providing an income or advantage; profitable: *gainful employment.* **—gain′ful•ly** *adv.*

gain•say (gān sā′ *or* gān′sā′) *tr.v.* **gain•said** (gān sād′ *or* gān sĕd′), **gain•say•ing, gain•says** (gān sāz′ *or* gān sĕz′). To declare false; deny or contradict: *While disagreeing with the ruling, the lawyer would not gainsay the judge in court.*

gait (gāt) *n.* **1.** A way of walking or running: *a shuffling gait.* **2.** The way in which a horse moves, as a walk, trot, or gallop. [First written down before 1200 in Middle English and spelled *gate*, path, gait, from Old Norse *gata*, path.]
❑ *These sound alike:* **gait, gate** (entrance).

gai•ter (gā′tər) *n.* **1.** A leather or cloth covering for the lower leg or ankle, worn over the top of a shoe. **2.** An ankle-high shoe with elastic sides. **3.** An overshoe with a cloth top.

gal (găl) *n. Informal.* A girl.

gal. *abbr.* An abbreviation of gallon.

ga•la (gā′lə *or* găl′ə *or* gä′lə) *n.* A festive occasion or celebration. *—adj.* Festive: *The city greeted the home team's victory with a gala celebration.*

ga•lac•tic (gə lăk′tĭk) *adj.* Of or relating to a galaxy, especially the Milky Way.

Gal•a•had (găl′ə hăd′) *n.* In Arthurian legend, the most virtuous of King Arthur's knights, who finds the Holy Grail.

Ga•lá•pa•gos Islands (gə lä′pə gəs *or* gə lăp′ə gəs). A group of islands of Ecuador in the Pacific Ocean west of the mainland. The islands are famous for their rare wildlife, including the giant tortoises for which they are named.

Ga•la•tians (gə lā′shənz) *pl.n. (used with a singular verb).* A book of the New Testament, written as a letter by Saint Paul to Christians living in Galatia, a country in Asia Minor, in which Paul defends his authority to instruct others.

gal•ax•y (găl′ək sē) *n., pl.* **gal•ax•ies. 1.a.** A vast grouping of stars, gas, and dust held together by the force of gravity. A galaxy has billions of stars. **b.** Often **Galaxy.** The galaxy that contains our solar system; the Milky Way. **2.** An assembly of brilliant, beautiful, or distinguished persons or things: *a galaxy of television stars.* [First written down about 1380 in Middle English and spelled *galaxie*, the Milky Way, from Greek *galaxias*, milky, from *gala*, milk.]

gale (gāl) *n.* **1.** A very strong wind, especially one having a speed between 32 and 63 miles (50-102 kilometers) per hour. **2.** A noisy outburst: *gales of laughter.*

Ga•len (gā′lən). A.D. 130?–200?. Greek physician whose theories formed an early basis of European medicine.

ga•le•na (gə lē′nə) *n.* A gray mineral, composed of lead and sulfur, that is the main ore of lead.

Gal•i•le•an (găl′ə lē′ən) *n.* **1.** A native or inhabitant of Galilee. **2.** A Christian. **3.** Jesus. *—adj.* Of or relating to Galilee or the Galileans.

Gal•i•lee (găl′ə lē′). A region of northern Israel that was the center of Jesus's ministry.

Galilee, Sea of. Formerly Lake **Ti•be•ri•as** (tī bîr′ē əs). A freshwater lake of northeast Israel. It is about 700 feet (214 meters) below sea level.

Ga•li•le•o Ga•li•lei (găl′ə lē′ō găl′ə lā′). 1564–1642. Italian physicist and astronomer who was the first to use a telescope to study the stars (1610).

gall[1] (gôl) *n.* **1.** A bitter yellow or green liquid secreted by the liver to aid digestion; bile. **2.** Bitter feeling; spite: *The feuding neighbors were full of gall.* **3.** Insulting boldness; impudence; nerve: *They had the gall to barge into the party uninvited.* [First written down before 830 in Old English and spelled *gealla, galla.*]

gall[2] (gôl) *n.* A sore on the skin caused by rubbing: *a saddle gall on a horse.* *—v.* **galled, gall•ing, galls.** *—tr.* **1.** To annoy. **2.** To make sore or chafed. *—intr.* To become sore by rubbing. [First written down about 1000 in Old English and spelled *gealla*, possibly from Latin *galla*, nutlike swelling on a tree.]

gall[3] (gôl) *n.* An abnormal swelling on a plant, caused by insects or disease organisms. [First written down before 1398 in Middle English and spelled *galle*, from Latin *galla*, nutlike swelling on a tree.]

gal•lant (găl′ənt) *adj.* **1.** Stylish in appearance; dashing: *He was very gallant at the ball.* **2.** Brave and noble; courageous; valorous: *a gallant resistance to the invasion.* **3.** Stately or majestic; grand: *a gallant ship.* **4.** (gə lănt′ *or* gə länt′). Polite and attentive to women; chivalrous: *our host's gallant manner.* *—n.* (gə lănt′ *or* gə länt′ *or* găl′ənt). **1.** A fashionable young man. **2.** A man who is polite and attentive to women. **—gal′lant•ly** *adv.*

gal•lant•ry (găl′ən trē) *n., pl.* **gal•lant•ries. 1.** Heroic courage or brave and noble conduct. **2.** Considerate attention to women; courtliness. **3.** A gallant act or action.

gall•blad•der also **gall bladder** (gôl′blăd′ər) *n.* A small, pear-shaped muscular sac, located near the right lobe of the liver, in which bile is stored.

gal•le•on (găl′ē ən *or* găl′yən) *n.* A large sailing ship of the 15th to 17th centuries, used especially by the Spanish.

gal•ler•y (găl′ə rē) *n., pl.* **gal•ler•ies. 1.** A long narrow walk or passage, often with a roof and windows along one side. **2.** An enclosed passageway, such as a hall or corridor: *a shooting gallery.* **3.** A narrow balcony, usually with railing, along the outside of a building. **4.a.** The balcony in a theater or church: *The gallery in the concert hall has the cheapest seats.* **b.** The seats in such a balcony. **c.** The people occupying these seats: *The gallery applauded and whistled.* **5.** A large audience, as at a sports event: *The golfer tipped his hat toward the gallery.* **6.** A building or hall for displaying works of art. **7.** An underground tunnel or other passageway, as in a mine.

gal•ley (găl′ē) *n., pl.* **gal•leys. 1.** A long narrow ship driven by sails and oars and used primarily in the Mediterranean until the 17th century. **2.** The kitchen on a ship or an airliner. **3.a.** A long tray for holding metal type that has been set to print a publication. **b.** A galley proof.

galley proof *n.* A proof of printed material taken

galaxy
Andromeda galaxy

Galileo

galleon

ă	pat	oi	boy
ā	pay	ou	out
âr	care	o͝o	took
ä	father	o͞o	boot
ĕ	pet	ŭ	cut
ē	be	ûr	urge
ĭ	pit	th	thin
ī	pie	*th*	this
îr	pier	hw	whoop
ŏ	pot	zh	vision
ō	toe	ə	about
ô	paw	N	*French* bon

Vasco da Gama

Indira Gandhi
Photographed in 1982

Mahatma Gandhi

from composed type, used to detect and correct errors before final composition into pages.

gall•fly (gôl′flī′) *n.* Any of various small insects that deposit their eggs on plant stems or in the bark of trees, causing galls to form.

Gal•lic (găl′ĭk) *adj.* Of or relating to ancient Gaul or modern France.

gall•ing (gô′lĭng) *adj.* Very irritating or exasperating: *A mechanical problem caused another galling delay in our flight.* **—gall′ing•ly** *adv.*

gal•li•um (găl′ē əm) *n. Symbol* **Ga** A rare, silvery metallic element used in thermometers and in compounds as a semiconductor. Atomic number 31. See table at **element.** [First written down in 1875 in Modern English, from Latin *gallus*, rooster, translation of surname of Paul Émile *Lecoq* de Boisbaudran (1838–1912), French chemist.]

gal•li•vant (găl′ə vănt′) *intr.v.* **gal•li•vant•ed, gal•li•vant•ing, gal•li•vants.** To travel or roam about in search of pleasure or amusement.

gal•lon (găl′ən) *n.* **1.** A unit of volume or capacity used for measuring liquids, equal to 4 quarts (3.785 liters). See table at **measurement. 2.a.** A container having a capacity of one gallon. **b.** The amount of a substance that can be held in such a container: *a gallon of milk.*

gal•lop (găl′əp) *n.* **1.** A fast gait of a horse or other four-footed animal, in which all four feet are off the ground at the same time during each stride. **2.** A ride on a horse going at a gallop. *—v.* **gal•loped, gal•lop•ing, gal•lops.** *—tr.* To cause to gallop: *The rider galloped the horse around the track.* *—intr.* **1.** To ride at a gallop: *gallop around the field.* **2.** To move or progress swiftly: *Summer is galloping by.* **—gal′lop•er** *n.*

gal•lows (găl′ōz) *n., pl.* **gallows** or **gal•lows•es. 1.** An upright framework from which a noose is suspended, used for execution by hanging. **2.** Execution on a gallows or by hanging.

gall•stone (gôl′stōn′) *n.* A small hard mass that forms in the gallbladder or in a bile duct.

ga•lore (gə lôr′) *adj.* In great numbers; in abundance: *The streets were filled with shoppers galore during the holiday season.*

ga•losh (gə lŏsh′) *n.* A waterproof overshoe.

gal•van•ic (găl văn′ĭk) *adj.* **1.** Of or relating to electricity that is produced by chemical action. **2.** Producing electricity by chemical action.

gal•va•nism (găl′və nĭz′əm) *n.* Direct-current electricity produced by chemical action. [First written down in 1797 in Modern English, after Luigi *Galvani* (1737–1798), Italian physiologist.]

gal•va•nize (găl′və nīz′) *tr.v.* **gal•va•nized, gal•va•niz•ing, gal•va•niz•es. 1.** To coat (iron or steel) with zinc as protection against rust. **2.** To stir to action or awareness; spur: *Destruction of important habitats in our state galvanized us to support the conservation law.* **—gal′va•ni•za′tion** (găl′və nĭ zā′shən) *n.*

gal•va•nom•e•ter (găl′və nŏm′ĭ tər) *n.* An instrument that detects, measures, and determines the direction of small electric currents.

Ga•ma (găm′ə *or* gä′mə), **Vasco da.** 1460?–1524. Portuguese explorer who sailed to India (1497–1498) and opened the area to Portuguese trade and colonization.

Gam•bi•a (găm′bē ə). A country of western Africa on the Atlantic Ocean surrounded by Senegal. It gained its independence from Great Britain in 1965. Banjul is the capital and the largest city. Population, 696,000.

gam•bit (găm′bĭt) *n.* **1.** An opening move in chess in which a pawn or piece is sacrificed in order to gain a favorable position. **2.** An action or a remark designed to bring about a desired result.

gam•ble (găm′bəl) *v.* **gam•bled, gam•bling, gam•bles.** *—intr.* **1.** To bet money on the outcome of a game, contest, or other event. **2.** To take a risk in the hope of gaining an advantage: *The builder is gambling on the need for more houses soon.* *—tr.* **1.** To risk (something) in gambling; wager. **2.** To expose to hazard; risk: *The soldier gambled a promising career in refusing to obey an order.* *—n.* **1.** A bet or wager. **2.** An act of undertaking something uncertain; a risk. [First written down in 1726 in Modern English, perhaps from obsolete *gamel*, to play games, from Old English *gamenian*, from *gamen*, fun.] **—gam′bler** *n.*

❑ *These sound alike:* **gamble, gambol** (frolic).

gam•bol (găm′bəl) *intr.v.* **gam•boled, gam•bol•ing, gam•bols** or **gam•bolled, gam•bol•ling, gam•bols.** To skip or run about playfully; frolic. *—n.* The act of skipping or frolicking about.

❑ *These sound alike:* **gambol, gamble** (bet).

gam•brel roof (găm′brəl) *n.* A ridged roof with two slopes on each side, the lower slope having a steeper pitch.

game¹ (gām) *n.* **1.** An activity that provides entertainment or amusement: *The children made a game of counting cars that passed.* **2.** A sport or contest governed by specific rules: *Tennis is my favorite game.* **3.** A single contest between two opponents or teams: *a football game on Saturday.* **4.** The number of points needed to win a game. **5.** The equipment, such as a board and pieces, needed for playing certain games: *The game came with its own box.* **6.** A particular style or ability at a certain game: *A few of the golfers seemed off their game today.* **7.a.** Wild animals, birds, or fish hunted for food or sport. **b.** The flesh of these animals, used as food. **8.** *Informal.* A plan or scheme: *Anyone can see through that old game.* **9.** *Informal.* An occupation, profession, or activity: *the game of politics.* *—tr. & intr.v.* **gamed, gam•ing, games.** To gamble. *—adj.* **gam•er, gam•est. 1.** Courageous; plucky: *They put up a game fight.* **2.** Ready and willing: *I'm game for climbing the mountain.* [First written down about 725 in Old English and spelled *gamen.*] **—game′ly** *adv.* **—game′ness** *n.*

game² (gām) *adj.* **gam•er, gam•est.** Lame or injured: *a game leg.* [First written down in 1787 in Modern English.]

game•cock (gām′kŏk′) *n.* A rooster bred and trained for fighting.

game•keep•er (gām′kē′pər) *n.* A person employed to protect and maintain wildlife, especially on an estate or a preserve.

game show *n.* A television show in which contestants compete for prizes by playing a game, such as a quiz.

game•ster (gām′stər) *n.* A person who plays games, especially a gambler.

gam•ete (găm′ēt′ *or* gə mēt′) *n.* A germ cell that unites with another to form a fertilized cell that develops into a new organism; an egg cell or a sperm cell of an animal, or a grain of pollen or an ovule of a plant.

ga•me•to•phyte (gə mē′tə fīt′) *n.* The individual plant or generation of a plant that produces gametes.

game warden *n.* An official who enforces hunting and fishing regulations.

gam•in (găm′ĭn) *n.* A homeless boy who roams about the streets; an urchin.

gam•ing (gā′mĭng) *n.* The playing of games of chance; gambling.

gam•ma (găm′ə) *n.* The third letter of the Greek alphabet, written Γ, γ. In English it is represented as G, *g* except before *g*, *k*, or *kh*, when it is represented as N, *n.*

gamma globulin *n.* A globulin in human blood plasma known to contain antibodies against certain infectious diseases, such as measles and hepatitis, and sometimes used in their treatment.

gamma ray *n.* Electromagnetic radiation with wavelengths shorter than those of x-rays and having greater energy and penetrating power. Gamma rays are given off by unstable nuclei during radioactive decay.

gam•ut (găm′ət) *n.* **1.** The entire range of musical tones. **2.** The complete range of something: *the gamut of feelings from high hope to utter despair.*

gam•y (gā′mē) *adj.* **gam•i•er, gam•i•est. 1.** Having the flavor or odor of game, especially game that is slightly spoiled. **2.** Showing great spirit; plucky: *a gamy horse that loves to run.* **—gam′i•ly** *adv.* **—gam′i•ness** *n.*

gan•der (găn′dər) *n.* **1.** A male goose. **2.** *Informal.* A look or glance.

Gan•dhi (gän′dē), **Indira Nehru.** 1917–1984. Indian politician who served as prime minister from 1966 to 1977 and from 1980 to 1984.

Gandhi, Mohandas Karamchand. Known as "Mahatma." 1869–1948. Indian leader who developed the practice of nonviolent disobedience that gained independence for India (1947).

gang (găng) *n.* **1.** An organized group of criminals. **2.** A group of young people who band together, especially a group of delinquents. **3.** *Informal.* A group of friends: *The whole gang went to see a movie.* **4.** A group of laborers who work together under a single supervisor: *a road gang filling potholes.* *—intr.v.* **ganged, gang•ing, gangs.** To band together in a group or gang: *The reporters ganged around the governor.* ***—idiom.*** **gang up.** To act together as a group: *Researchers ganged up to fight the disease.*

Gan•ges (găn′jēz′) also **Gan•ga** (gŭng′gə). A river of northern India and Bangladesh rising in the Himalaya Mountains and flowing about 1,560 miles (2,510 kilometers) generally east to the Bay of Bengal.

gan•gli•a (găng′glē ə) *n.* A plural of **ganglion.**

gan•gling (găng′glĭng) *adj.* Tall and awkward; lanky.

gan•gli•on (găng′glē ən) *n., pl.* **gan•gli•a** (găng′glē ə) or **gan•gli•ons.** A compact group of nerve cells forming a nerve center, especially one located outside the brain or spinal cord.

gang•plank (găng′plăngk′) *n.* A board or ramp used as a bridge between a ship and a pier.

gan•grene (găng′grēn′ *or* găng grēn′) *n.* Decay of tissue in a living body, caused by a stoppage of the blood supply from injury or disease. *—tr. & intr.v.* **gan•grened, gan•gren•ing, gan•grenes.** To affect or become affected with gangrene. **—gan′gre•nous** (găng′grə nəs) *adj.*

gang•ster (găng′stər) *n.* A member of an organized group of criminals.

gang•way (găng′wā′) *n.* **1.a.** A gangplank. **b.** An opening in the side of a ship through which passengers may board. **2.** A passage along either side of a ship's upper deck.

gan•net (găn′ĭt) *n.* Any of several large, mostly white sea birds that nest in large colonies on rocky coasts. Gannets have long bills for catching fish and can fly over a long distance. [First written down about 725 in Old English and spelled *ganot.*]

gant•let[1] (gônt′lĭt *or* gänt′lĭt) *n.* Variant of **gauntlet[1].**

gant•let[2] (gônt′lĭt *or* gänt′lĭt) *n.* Variant of **gauntlet[2].**

gan•try (găn′trē) *n., pl.* **gan•tries. 1.a.** A framework that supports a traveling crane and resembles a bridge mounted on towers that move along railroad tracks. **b.** A similar structure on which signals are mounted over several railroad tracks. **2.** A large vertical structure somewhat like a scaffold, used in assembling or servicing a rocket, especially on a launching pad.

Gan•y•mede (găn′ə mēd′) *n.* In Greek mythology, a Trojan boy of great beauty whom Zeus carries away to be cupbearer to the gods.

gaol (jāl) *n. Chiefly British.* Variant of **jail.**

gap (găp) *n.* **1.** An opening or a break, as in a wall or fence. **2.** A break in something continuous: *There are many gaps in our knowledge of the universe.* **3.** A pass through mountains. **4.** A wide difference or imbalance: *There is a gap between what he says and what he does.* *—v.* **gapped, gap•ping, gaps.** *—tr.* To make a gap in. *—intr.* To have a gap. [First written down about 1250 in Middle English, from Old Norse *gap,* chasm.]

gape (gāp *or* găp) *intr.v.* **gaped, gap•ing, gapes. 1.** To open the mouth wide, as if to bite or swallow. **2.** To stare in amazement, often with the mouth open: *The fans gaped as the ball went soaring towards the stands in right field.* **3.** To open wide; form a gap: *Cracks gaped in the ground after the earthquake.* *—n.* The act or an instance of gaping: *The gape of the lion's yawn made us cringe.*

gar (gär) *n.* Any of several freshwater fishes of North and Central America having long narrow bodies, sharp teeth, and long narrow jaws.

ga•rage (gə räzh′ *or* gə räj′) *n.* **1.** A building or an indoor space in which to park a motor vehicle. **2.** A business where cars are repaired, serviced, or parked. *—tr.v.* **ga•raged, ga•rag•ing, ga•rag•es.** To put or keep in a garage. [First written down in 1902 in Modern English, from French, from Old French *guerrer, garer,* to shelter, of Germanic origin.]

garage sale *n.* A sale of used household items or clothing held at the home of the seller.

garb (gärb) *n.* A style or form of clothing: *the informal garb of most tourists.* *—tr.v.* **garbed, garb•ing, garbs.** To clothe or dress: *The judge was garbed in robes of court.*

gar•bage (gär′bĭj) *n.* **1.** Food wastes, as from a kitchen. **2.** Worthless or inferior material; trash: *That novel is nothing but garbage.*

gar•ban•zo (gär bän′zō) *n., pl.* **gar•ban•zos.** The chickpea.

gar•ble (gär′bəl) *tr.v.* **gar•bled, gar•bling, gar•bles.** To distort or mix up: *The report sounded great, but she garbled the facts.* *—n.* The act or an instance of garbling: *a confused garble of voices.*

gar•den (gär′dn) *n.* **1.** A piece of land used for growing flowers, vegetables, herbs, or fruit. **2.** A park or other public place ornamented with flowers and other plants: *a botanical garden.* *—v.* **gar•dened, gar•den•ing, gar•dens.** *—tr.* To make (a plot of ground) into a garden. *—intr.* To plant or tend a garden.

gar•den•er (gärd′nər *or* gär′dn ər) *n.* A person who works in or takes care of a garden.

gar•de•nia (gär dēn′yə) *n.* **1.** Any of various shrubs having glossy evergreen leaves and large, fragrant, usually white flowers. **2.** The flower of this shrub. [First written down in 1757 in Modern English, after Alexander *Garden* (1730?–1791), Scottish-born American naturalist.]

Garden of Eden *n.* In the Bible, the garden that was the first home of Adam and Eve.

Gard•ner (gärd′nər), **Isabella Stewart.** 1840–1924. American art collector and patron who opened her villa and gallery in Boston to the public in 1903.

Gar•field (gär′fēld′), **James Abram.** 1831–1881. The 20th President of the United States (1881).

gar•fish (gär′fĭsh′) *n.* A gar.

gangplank

Isabella Stewart Gardner

1888 portrait by John Singer Sargent (1856–1925)

James A. Garfield

ă	pat	oi	boy
ā	pay	ou	out
âr	care	ŏŏ	took
ä	father	ōō	boot
ĕ	pet	ŭ	cut
ē	be	ûr	urge
ĭ	pit	th	thin
ī	pie	*th*	this
îr	pier	hw	whoop
ŏ	pot	zh	vision
ō	toe	ə	about
ô	paw	N	*French* bon

gargoyle
On the cathedral of
Notre Dame de Paris, France

Giuseppe Garibaldi

William Lloyd Garrison

gar•gan•tu•an (gär **găn′**cho͞o ən) *adj.* Of immense size; enormous; huge: *a stadium of gargantuan proportions.*

gar•gle (**gär′**gəl) *v.* **gar•gled, gar•gling, gar•gles.** *—intr.* To wash or rinse the mouth or throat by exhaling air through a liquid held there. *—tr.* To circulate (a liquid) in the mouth or throat by gargling. *—n.* A liquid used for gargling. [First written down in 1527 in Modern English, from Old French *gargouiller.*]

gar•goyle (**gär′**goil′) *n.* A waterspout or an ornamental figure in the form of a grotesque animal or person projecting from the gutter of a building. [First written down in 1286 in Middle English and spelled *gargurl,* from Old French *gargole, gargouille,* throat, waterspout.]

Gar•i•bal•di (găr′ə **bôl′**dē), **Giuseppe.** 1807–1882. Italian general who led a group of volunteers in the capture of Sicily and Naples (1860).

gar•ish (**gâr′**ĭsh *or* **găr′**ĭsh) *adj.* Too bright or ornamented; gaudy: *The clown wore a suit of garish colors.* **—gar′ish•ly** *adv.* **—gar′ish•ness** *n.*

gar•land (**gär′**lənd) *n.* A wreath or chain, as of flowers or leaves, worn as a crown or used for ornament. *—tr.v.* **gar•land•ed, gar•land•ing, gar•lands.** To decorate with a garland.

gar•lic (**gär′**lĭk) *n.* **1.** The bulb of a plant related to the onion, divided into cloves and having a strong taste and odor and used as seasoning. **2.** The plant that bears this bulb.

gar•ment (**gär′**mənt) *n.* An article of clothing.

garment bag *n.* A long zippered bag used to carry and protect clothes when traveling.

gar•ner (**gär′**nər) *tr.v.* **gar•nered, gar•ner•ing, gar•ners.** To gather and store: *The bird garnered sticks for its nest.*

gar•net (**gär′**nĭt) *n.* **1.** A common crystalline silicate mineral of aluminum or calcium. It is usually red and is used as a gem and as an abrasive. **2.** A dark red color.

gar•nish (**gär′**nĭsh) *tr.v.* **gar•nished, gar•nish•ing, gar•nish•es. 1.** To adorn; decorate: *The plain coat was garnished with a fur collar.* **2.** To decorate (a food or drink) with colorful or tasty items: *garnish mashed potatoes with parsley.* **3.** To garnishee. *—n.* **1.** Ornamentation; decoration: *a garnish of roses on the table.* **2.** Something added to a food or drink to give it extra color or flavor.

gar•nish•ee (gär′nĭ **shē′**) *tr.v.* **gar•nish•eed, gar•nish•ee•ing, gar•nish•ees.** To take and hold (someone's pay or property) by a legal proceeding in order to pay off a debt.

gar•ret (**găr′**ĭt) *n.* A room on the top floor of a house, typically under a pitched roof; an attic.

gar•ri•son (**găr′**ĭ sən) *n.* **1.** A military post. **2.** The troops stationed at such a post. *—tr.v.* **gar•ri•soned, gar•ri•son•ing, gar•ri•sons. 1.** To assign (troops) to a military post. **2.** To supply (a post or other place) with troops for defense.

Gar•ri•son (**găr′**ĭ sən), **William Lloyd.** 1805–1879. American abolitionist who founded and published *The Liberator* (1831–1865), an antislavery journal.

gar•ru•li•ty (gə **ro͞o′**lĭ tē) *n.* The quality of being overly talkative.

gar•ru•lous (**găr′**ə ləs *or* **găr′**yə ləs) *adj.* Excessively talkative, especially about unimportant matters: *a garrulous person.* **—gar′ru•lous•ness** *n.*

gar•ter (**gär′**tər) *n.* An elastic band or strap worn on the leg to hold up a stocking or sock. *—tr.v.* **gar•tered, gar•ter•ing, gar•ters.** To fasten and hold with a garter.

garter snake *n.* Any of various small, harmless North American snakes that are brownish or greenish in color and have stripes along their backs.

Gar•vey (**gär′**vē), **Marcus (Moziah) Aurelius.** 1887–1940. Jamaican Black nationalist who worked in the United States urging Black Americans to establish a country in Africa.

Gar•y (**gâr′**ē *or* **găr′**ē). A city of northwest Indiana on Lake Michigan near the Illinois border. It was founded in 1905. Population, 116,646.

gas (găs) *n., pl.* **gas•es** or **gas•ses. 1.** One of the three basic forms of matter, composed of molecules in constant random motion. Unlike a solid, a gas has no fixed shape and will take on the shape of the space available. Unlike a liquid, it has no fixed volume and will expand to fill the space available. **2.** A gas or mixture of gases burned as fuel for cooking or heating. **3.** Gasoline. **4.** A chemical gas that chokes, irritates, or poisons, used as a weapon. **5.** An anesthetic that is in the form of gas. *—tr.v.* **gassed, gas•sing, gas•es** or **gas•ses. 1.** To treat chemically with gas. **2.** To injure or poison with gas. ***—idiom.*** **gas up.** To supply a vehicle with gas or gasoline: *We gassed the car up before going on our trip.* [First written down in 1658 in Modern English, from Dutch *gas,* an occult physical principle supposed to be present in all bodies, alteration of Greek *khaos,* chaos, empty space.]

gas•e•ous (**găs′**ē əs *or* **găsh′**əs) *adj.* Of, relating to, or existing as a gas: *The sun is in a gaseous state.*

gas-guz•zler (**găs′**gŭz′lər) *n. Informal.* An automobile that gets low gas mileage.

gash (găsh) *tr.v.* **gashed, gash•ing, gash•es.** To make a long deep cut or wound in. *—n.* A long deep cut or wound.

gas•ket (**găs′**kĭt) *n.* Any of a wide variety of seals or packings placed between machine parts or around pipe joints to prevent the escape of gas or fluid.

gas•light (**găs′**līt′) *n.* **1.** Light made by burning gas in a lamp. **2.** A lamp that uses gas as fuel.

gas mask *n.* A mask that covers the face or the face and head and is equipped with an air filter as protection against poisonous gases.

gas•o•hol (**găs′**ə hôl′) *n.* A fuel for cars that is a blend of ethyl alcohol and unleaded gasoline.

gas•o•line (**găs′**ə lēn′ *or* găs′ə **lēn′**) *n.* A highly flammable mixture of liquid hydrocarbons that evaporates very easily and is used chiefly as a fuel for internal-combustion engines in automobiles, motorcycles, and small trucks.

gasp (găsp) *v.* **gasped, gasp•ing, gasps.** *—intr.* To inhale in a sudden, sharp, and usually fitful way, as from shock, surprise, or great exertion. *—tr.* To say in a breathless manner. *—n.* A sudden, violent, or fitful intake of the breath.

gas station *n.* A service station.

gas•sy (**găs′**ē) *adj.* **gas•si•er, gas•si•est.** Of, resembling, containing, or filled with gas.

gas•tric (**găs′**trĭk) *adj.* Of, relating to, or concerning the stomach: *a gastric disorder.*

gastric juice *n.* The digestive fluid secreted by the glands that line the inside of the stomach. It contains pepsin and other enzymes and hydrochloric acid.

gas•tro•in•tes•ti•nal (găs′trō ĭn **tĕs′**tə nəl) *adj.* Of or relating to the stomach and intestines.

gas•tro•nom•ic (găs′trə **nŏm′**ĭk) also **gas•tro•nom•i•cal** (găs′trə **nŏm′**ĭ kəl) *adj.* Of or relating to gastronomy. **—gas′tro•nom′i•cal•ly** *adv.*

gas•tron•o•my (gă **strŏn′**ə mē) *n.* The art or science of good eating. [First written down in 1814 in Modern English, from Greek *gastronomia* : *gastēr,* belly, stomach + *nomos,* rule.]

gas•tro•pod (**găs′**trə pŏd′) *n.* Any of various mollusks, such as the snail, slug, cowrie, or whelk, having a head with eyes and feelers, a usually coiled shell, and a muscular foot on the underside of its body with which it moves. *—adj.* Of or relating to such mollusks. [First written down in 1826 in Modern English and spelled *gasteropod* : Greek *gastēr*, belly, stomach + Greek *pous*, foot.]

gas•tru•la (găs′trə lə) *n., pl.* **gas•tru•las** or **gas•tru•lae** (găs′trə lē′). An embryo at the stage when it forms a hollow structure open at one end, consisting of two layers of cells, the ectoderm and the endoderm.

gat (găt) *v. Archaic.* A past tense of **get**.

gate (gāt) *n.* **1.a.** A hinged or sliding barrier that serves as a door in a wall or fence. **b.** An opening in a wall or fence; a gateway. **2.** A device for controlling the flow of water or gas through a pipe, dam, or similar system. **3.** The number of people attending an event or a performance: *a gate of 500 people.* **4.** The total amount of money paid for people attending an event or a performance: *The gate for the game was $750.*

❑ *These sound alike:* **gate, gait** (way of walking).

gate•crash•er (gāt′krăsh′ər) *n. Slang.* A person who attends a gathering, performance, private party, or sports event without being invited or without paying.

gate•house (gāt′hous′) *n.* A house built over or near a gate, usually lived in by a gatekeeper.

gate•keep•er (gāt′kē′pər) *n.* A person in charge of a gate.

gate•post (gāt′pōst′) *n.* An upright post on which a gate is hung or against which a gate closes.

Gates (gāts), **Horatio.** 1728?–1806. American general in the Revolutionary War.

gate•way (gāt′wā′) *n.* **1.** An opening, as in a wall or fence, that may be closed with a gate. **2.** Something that serves as a means of access or an entrance: *Denver is thought of as the gateway to the Rockies.*

gath•er (găth′ər) *v.* **gath•ered, gath•er•ing, gath•ers.** *—tr.* **1.** To bring together in a group; convene; assemble: *The teacher gathered the students around the exhibit.* **2.** To pick; collect: *Squirrels gather nuts.* **3.** To summon up; muster (mental or physical powers). **4.** To gain or increase gradually: *The avalanche gathered speed and size as it slid down the mountain.* **5.** To conclude; infer: *I gather that you didn't like the movie.* **6.** To run a thread through (cloth) so as to draw it up into small folds or pleats: *gather material at the waist of a full skirt.* **7.** To draw or bring closer: *gather a frightened kitten in one's arms.* *—intr.* **1.** To come together in a group; assemble: *The children gathered to wait for the school bus.* **2.** To grow or increase bit by bit; accumulate: *Dust gathered under the couch.* *—n.* One of the small folds or pleats made in cloth by gathering it. **—gath′er•er** *n.*

Synonyms: gather, collect, assemble, accumulate. These verbs mean to bring together in a group or mass. **Gather** is the most general: *I gathered sticks to build a fire.* **Collect** often means to select like or related things that then become part of an organized whole: *Many people like to collect stamps and coins from around the world.* **Assemble** means to gather persons or things that have a definite and usually close relationship: *The curator is assembling Stone Age artifacts to make an interesting exhibit.* **Accumulate** describes the increase of like or related things over an extended period of time: *We accumulated piles of old newspapers in the basement.*

gath•er•ing (găth′ər ĭng) *n.* **1.** An assembly of persons; a meeting: *a family gathering.* **2.** The act of a person or thing that gathers.

Gat•ling gun (găt′lĭng) *n.* A machine gun having a cluster of barrels that are fired as the cluster is turned. [First written down in 1867 in American English, after Richard Jordan *Gatling* (1818–1903), American inventor.]

gauche (gōsh) *adj.* Lacking social grace; tactless; clumsy: *Talking about people within their hearing is gauche.*

gau•cho (gou′chō) *n., pl.* **gau•chos.** A cowhand of the South American pampas.

gaud•y (gô′dē) *adj.* **gaud•i•er, gaud•i•est.** Too brightly colored and showy to be in good taste. **—gaud′i•ly** *adv.* **—gaud′i•ness** *n.*

gauge also **gage** (gāj) *n.* **1.** A standard or scale of measurement. **2.** An instrument for measuring or testing: *The motorist measured the air pressure with a tire gauge.* **3.** A means of estimating or evaluating; a test: *How a person handles a difficult situation is a good gauge of character.* **4.** The distance between the two rails of a railroad. **5.** The diameter of a shotgun barrel as determined by the number of lead balls of a size fitting the barrel that make one pound. **6.** Thickness or diameter, as of sheet metal or wire. *—tr.v.* **gauged, gaug•ing, gaug•es** also **gaged, gag•ing, gag•es. 1.** To measure precisely: *gauge the depth of the ocean.* **2.** To evaluate or judge: *gauge a person's ability.* [First written down in 1332 in Middle English and spelled *gage*, from Old North French *gauge*, rod for measuring, of Germanic origin.] **—gauge′a•ble** *adj.*

❑ *These sound alike:* **gauge, gage[1]** (pledge).

Gaul[1] (gôl) *n.* **1.** A Celt of ancient Gaul. **2.** A French person.

Gaul[2] (gôl). An ancient region of western Europe south and west of the Rhine River, west of the Alps, and north of the Pyrenees, corresponding roughly to modern-day France and Belgium.

Gaul•ish (gô′lĭsh) *n.* The Celtic language of ancient Gaul.

gaunt (gônt) *adj.* **gaunt•er, gaunt•est. 1.** Thin and bony; haggard; emaciated. **2.** Bleak and desolate; stark: *the gaunt forbidding mountains around the valley.* **—gaunt′ly** *adv.* **—gaunt′ness** *n.*

gaunt•let[1] also **gant•let** (gônt′lĭt *or* gänt′lĭt) *n.* **1.** A heavy leather glove, usually covered with chain mail, worn with medieval armor. **2.** A heavy glove with a wide flaring cuff that covers the wrist and part of the arm. [First written down before 1425 in Middle English and spelled *gantelet*, from Old French, diminutive of *gant*, glove, of Germanic origin.]

gaunt•let[2] also **gant•let** (gônt′lĭt *or* gänt′lĭt) *n.* **1.** A form of punishment in which a person is forced to run between two lines of people and is beaten with clubs, sticks, or other weapons. **2.** An attack from all sides. **3.** A severe trial; an ordeal. [First written down in 1646 in Modern English and spelled *gantlope*, from Swedish *gatlopp* : *gata*, lane + *lopp*, course, running.]

gauze (gôz) *n.* A loosely woven, somewhat transparent cloth used especially for bandaging.

gauz•y (gô′zē) *adj.* **gauz•i•er, gauz•i•est.** Resembling gauze in thinness or transparency. **—gauz′i•ness** *n.*

gave (gāv) *v.* Past tense of **give**.

gav•el (găv′əl) *n.* A small wooden mallet used by a presiding officer or an auctioneer to signal for attention or order or to mark the conclusion of a transaction.

ga•votte (gə vŏt′) *n.* **1.** A French peasant dance somewhat resembling a minuet. **2.** Music written for this dance.

Ga•wain (gə wān′ *or* gä′wān′ *or* gou′ən) *n.* In Arthurian legend, a nephew of King Arthur and a Knight of the Round Table.

gawk (gôk) *intr.v.* **gawked, gawk•ing, gawks.** To stare stupidly; gape.

gas mask

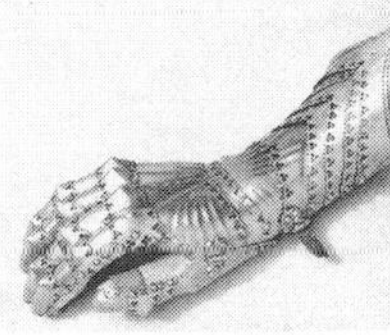

gauntlet[1]

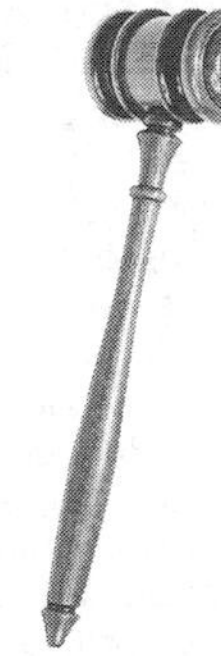

gavel

ă	pat	oi	boy
ā	pay	ou	out
âr	care	ŏŏ	took
ä	father	ōō	boot
ĕ	pet	ŭ	cut
ē	be	ûr	urge
ĭ	pit	th	thin
ī	pie	*th*	this
îr	pier	hw	whoop
ŏ	pot	zh	vision
ō	toe	ə	about
ô	paw	N	*French* bon

gazelle

gene

With 100,000 or more pieces, it is an enormous puzzle. And like many puzzles, it is being worked on by a lot of people. But it will not be easy to solve. No one knows what the final picture will look like. This is a biological puzzle, called the Human Genome Project, and its pieces are the tiny, complex units of chemical information known as **genes**. Researchers on this project aim to make a blueprint of the hereditary information within human beings. They plan to map the human **genome**, to pinpoint the location of each gene in a cell's 23 tiny pairs of gene strings called **chromosomes**. Scientists will be able to use the finished map for many things, like finding genes that cause disorders such as Down syndrome and muscular dystrophy.

gawk•y (gô′kē) *adj.* **gawk•i•er, gawk•i•est.** Awkward; clumsy: *a gawky colt.* —**gawk′i•ly** *adv.* —**gawk′i•ness** *n.*

gay (gā) *adj.* **gay•er, gay•est. 1.** Merry; lighthearted: *a gay mood; gay music.* **2.** Bright or lively, especially in color: *The package was tied with gay ribbons.* **3.** Homosexual. —*n.* A homosexual person, especially a man.

gay•e•ty (gā′ĭ tē) *n.* Variant of **gaiety.**

gay•ly (gā′lē) *adv.* Variant of **gaily.**

gaze (gāz) *intr.v.* **gazed, gaz•ing, gaz•es.** To look intently, as with wonder or curiosity; stare: *The visitors gazed in awe at the wild beauty of the Grand Canyon.* —*n.* An intent steady look: *The crowd fixed their gaze on the speaker.*

ga•ze•bo (gə zā′bō *or* gə zē′bō) *n., pl.* **ga•ze•bos** or **ga•ze•boes.** An outdoor structure that provides a shady resting place.

ga•zelle (gə zĕl′) *n.* Any of various slender swift-running antelopes of Africa and Asia. [First written down in 1600 in Modern English, from Arabic *ġazāl.*]

ga•zette (gə zĕt′) *n.* **1.** A newspaper. **2.** An official journal or periodical.

gaz•et•teer (găz′ĭ tîr′) *n.* A book with an alphabetical list of geographic names, as of countries, cities, mountains, and bodies of water, often accompanied by a brief description of each name.

gaz•pa•cho (gə spä′chō) *n.* A chilled soup made with tomatoes, onions, peppers, and herbs.

G.B. *abbr.* An abbreviation of Great Britain.

G clef *n.* A treble clef.

Gd The symbol for the element **gadolinium.**

Gdańsk (gə dänsk′ *or* gə dănsk′) also **Dan•zig** (dăn′sĭg *or* dän′sĭg). A city of northern Poland northwest of Warsaw on the **Gulf of Gdańsk,** an inlet of the Baltic Sea. Adolf Hitler's demand that Gdańsk be turned over to Germany led to the beginning of World War II (September 1939). Population, 467,200.

Ge The symbol for the element **germanium.**

gear (gîr) *n.* **1.a.** A wheel with teeth around its rim that mesh with the teeth of another wheel to transmit motion. **b.** An arrangement of such interlocking wheels, as in a watch, a sewing machine, or an automobile, used to transmit power or change the direction of motion in a mechanism. Speed in various parts of a machine is usually determined by the arrangement of gears. **c.** An assembly of gears or moving parts that serves a particular function in a larger machine: *the landing gear of an aircraft.* **2.** Equipment, such as tools or clothing, needed for a particular activity: *fishing gear.* —*v.* **geared, gear•ing, gears.** —*tr.* **1.** To provide with or connect by gears: *gear a motor to a propeller.* **2.** To adjust or adapt: *The scientists geared their remarks to a youthful audience.* —*intr.* To be or become in gear; mesh: *The cogs of an automobile transmission gear into each other.* —***idiom.*** **gear up.** To get ready for a coming action or event: *We are geared up for our family's upcoming camping trip.* [First written down before 1200 in Middle English and spelled *gære,* equipment, from Old Norse *gervi;* akin to *gera,* to do, make ready.]

gear•ing (gîr′ĭng) *n.* A system of gears and related parts that work to transfer motion or power from one part of a machine to another.

gear•shift (gîr′shĭft′) *n.* A device for changing from one gear to another in a transmission, as in an automobile.

gear•wheel also **gear wheel** (gîr′wēl′) *n.* A wheel having teeth around its rim; a cogwheel.

geck•o (gĕk′ō) *n., pl.* **geck•os** or **geck•oes.** Any of various small tropical lizards that eat insects and have adhesive toe tips that allow them to cling to walls. [First written down in 1711 in Modern English and spelled *chacco,* from Malay *ge'kok.*]

gee[1] (jē) *interj.* An expression used to command a horse or an ox to turn to the right or to go forward.

gee[2] (jē) *interj.* An expression used as a mild oath or as an exclamation of surprise.

geese (gēs) *n.* Plural of **goose.**

ge•fil•te fish (gə fĭl′tə) *n.* Seasoned chopped fish mixed with bread or cracker crumbs and eggs, formed into balls and cooked in a broth.

Gei•ger counter (gī′gər) *n.* An electronic instrument that detects and measures ionizing radiation, such as x-rays, gamma rays, or cosmic rays, by counting the ions produced as the radiation passes through a gas-filled tube. [First written down in 1924 in Modern English, after Hans Wilhelm *Geiger* (1882–1945), German physicist.]

gei•sha (gā′shə *or* gē′shə) *n., pl.* **geisha** or **gei•shas.** A Japanese woman trained as a professional entertainer to provide singing, dancing, or amusing talk, especially in the company of men.

gel (jĕl) *n.* A semisolid mixture formed when particles suspended in a liquid become relatively large, as when boiled fruit juices thicken and cool to form a jelly or colloid. —*intr.v.* **gelled, gel•ling, gels.** To form a gel.

❑ *These sound alike:* **gel, jell** (congeal).

gel•a•tin also **gel•a•tine** (jĕl′ə tn) *n.* **1.** An odorless colorless protein substance obtained by boiling the prepared skin, bones, and connective tissue of animals. The preparation forms a gel when mixed with hot water and allowed to cool. It is used in foods, drugs, glue, and photographic film. **2.** A flavored jelly made with gelatin, often used as a dessert or in salads. [First written down in 1713 in Modern English, from Italian *gelatina,* from Latin *gelāre,* to freeze.]

ge•lat•i•nous (jə lăt′n əs) *adj.* **1.** Similar in texture to gelatin; thick and viscous. **2.** Of, relating to, or containing gelatin.

geld (gĕld) *tr.v.* **geld•ed** or **gelt** (gĕlt), **geld•ing, gelds.** To remove the testicles of (a horse or another animal).

geld•ing (gĕl′dĭng) *n.* A gelded animal, especially a horse.

gelt (gĕlt) *v.* A past tense and a past participle of **geld.**

gem (jĕm) *n.* **1.** A precious or semiprecious stone cut and polished as a jewel: *a ring of precious gems set in gold.* **2.** Something that is much admired or appreciated: *This painting is the gem of the museum's collection.* —*tr.v.* **gemmed, gem•ming, gems.** To set or adorn with gems: *The artisan gemmed a gold box with stones of different colors.* [First written down before 1300 in Middle English and spelled *gemme,* from Latin *gemma.*]

Gem•i•ni (jĕm′ə nī′ *or* jĕm′ə nē′) *pl.n.* *(used with a singular verb).* **1.** A constellation in the Northern Hemisphere. **2.** The third sign of the zodiac in astrology.

gem•stone (jĕm′stōn′) *n.* A precious or semiprecious stone used as a jewel when cut and polished.

gen. *abbr.* An abbreviation of: **1.** Genus. **2.** Gender. **3.** Genitive. **4.** General.

Gen. *abbr.* An abbreviation of: **1.** General. **2.** Genesis.

gen•darme (zhän′därm′) *n.* **1.** A police officer in France and in some other parts of Europe. **2.** A police officer.

gen•der (jĕn′dər) *n.* **1.** In grammar, one of the categories used to classify nouns, pronouns, adjectives, and in some languages verbs. Gender includes the categories feminine, masculine, and neuter, and the gender of many words corresponds to their sexual classification. **2.** Sexual identity: *the male gender.*

gene (jēn) *n.* A segment of DNA, located at a particular point on a chromosome, that determines hereditary characteristics. Hair and eye color in human beings are characteristics controlled by genes. [First written down in 1911 in Modern English, from Greek *genos,* race, offspring.] —See Note.

ge•ne•al•o•gist (jē′nē ŏl′ə jĭst *or* jē′nē ăl′ə jĭst) *n.* A person who studies and traces genealogies.

ge•ne•al•o•gy (jē′nē ŏl′ə jē *or* jē′nē ăl′ə jē) *n., pl.* **ge•ne•al•o•gies. 1.** A record of the descent of a family or person from an ancestor or ancestors. **2.** Direct descent from an ancestor or ancestors; lineage. **3.** The study of ancestry and family histories. [First written down before 1325 in Middle English and spelled *genealogi,* from Greek *genealogia* : *genea,* family + *-logia,* study.] **—ge′ne•a•log′i•cal** (jē′nē ə lŏj′ĭkəl) *adj.*

gen•er•a (jĕn′ər ə) *n.* Plural of **genus.**

gen•er•al (jĕn′ər əl) *adj.* **1.** Concerned with, applying to, or affecting all members of a category: *An election is supposed to express the general will.* **2.** Affecting a majority of those involved; prevalent; widespread: *general satisfaction.* **3.** Not limited in scope, area, or application: *as a general rule; general studies.* **4.** Involving only the main features of something rather than details or particulars: *The witness could only give a general account of what happened.* **5.** Highest or superior in rank: *the general manager.* —*n.* **1.** An officer holding the rank above lieutenant general in the U.S. Army, Air Force, or Marine Corps. **2.** A person who holds this rank or a similar rank in another military organization. ***—idiom.* in general.** Generally; for the most part. [First written down before 1200 in Middle English, from Latin *generālis,* from *genus,* kind.]

general assembly *n.* **1.** A legislative body, especially a U.S. state legislature. **2. General Assembly.** The main body of the United Nations, in which each member nation is represented and has one vote.

gen•er•al•ist (jĕn′ər ə lĭst) *n.* A person with general knowledge and skills in several fields.

gen•er•al•i•ty (jĕn′ə răl′ĭ tē) *n., pl.* **gen•er•al•i•ties. 1.** The state or quality of being general. **2.** A statement or principle that has general application. **3.** A statement or an idea that is vague or imprecise: *a speech full of generalities and empty phrases.*

gen•er•al•i•za•tion (jĕn′ər ə lĭ zā′shən) *n.* **1.** The act of generalizing: *A reporter must be careful of generalization and should stick to the facts.* **2.** A general statement or principle; a generality.

gen•er•al•ize (jĕn′ər ə līz′) *v.* **gen•er•al•ized, gen•er•al•iz•ing, gen•er•al•iz•es.** —*tr.* **1.** To consider or state in terms of a general form or principle. **2.** To draw (a general conclusion) from particular facts. —*intr.* To draw a general conclusion from particular facts: *Scientists generalize about dinosaurs from their fossilized bones.*

gen•er•al•ly (jĕn′ər ə lē) *adv.* **1.** Usually; as a rule: *I generally go for a walk before breakfast.* **2.** Widely; commonly: *The fact is not generally known.* **3.** In general terms: *Generally speaking, there are two ways to handle the problem.*

General of the Air Force *n.* An officer having the highest rank in the U.S. Air Force.

General of the Army *n.* An officer having the highest rank in the U.S. Army.

general practitioner *n.* A doctor who does not specialize in one field but treats a variety of medical problems.

gen•er•al•ship (jĕn′ər əl shĭp′) *n.* **1.** The rank of general. **2.** Leadership or skill in the command of an army. **3.** Skillful leadership or management.

gen•er•ate (jĕn′ə rāt′) *tr.v.* **gen•er•at•ed, gen•er•at•ing, gen•er•ates.** To bring into being; produce: *generate heat; generate interest among voters; generate a computer program.* [First written down in 1509 in Modern English, from Latin *generāre,* to produce, from *genus,* birth.]

gen•er•a•tion (jĕn′ə rā′shən) *n.* **1.** A group of people who grow up at about the same time, often thought to have similar social and cultural attitudes: *the younger generation.* **2.** A group of organisms that are at the same age and have the same parent or parents: *My grandmother and mother are of different generations.* **3.** The average length of time between the birth of parents and the birth of their offspring: *Many generations have passed since this land was cleared for a farm.* **4.** A class of things derived from an earlier class, usually by making improvements and refinements: *the new generation of computers.* **5.** The act or process of generating: *the generation of electric power; the generation of new ideas.*

generation gap *n.* The difference in values and attitudes between one generation and the next, especially between young people and their parents.

gen•er•a•tive (jĕn′ər ə tĭv *or* jĕn′ə rā′tĭv) *adj.* **1.** Having the ability to generate. **2.** Of or relating to the production of offspring.

gen•er•a•tor (jĕn′ə rā′tər) *n.* **1.** A person or thing that generates, especially a machine that converts mechanical energy into electrical energy. **2.** An apparatus used to generate a gas or vapor.

ge•ner•ic (jə nĕr′ĭk) *adj.* **1.** Of or relating to an entire group or class; general. **2.** Of or relating to a genus: *Cats and dogs show generic differences.* **3.** Not protected by a trademark and therefore applicable to an entire class of products: Aspirin *is the generic name for a certain kind of drug.* **—ge•ner′i•cal•ly** *adv.* —See Note.

gen•er•os•i•ty (jĕn′ə rŏs′ĭ tē) *n., pl.* **gen•er•os•i•ties. 1.** The quality or condition of being generous: *Teachers are known for their generosity in giving help to students.* **2.** Nobility of thought or behavior: *The coach speaks of our rivals with generosity.* **3.** A generous act.

gen•er•ous (jĕn′ər əs) *adj.* **1.** Willing to give or share; unselfish: *a generous contributor to worthy causes.* **2.** Large; abundant; ample: *This restaurant serves very generous portions.* **3.** Having or showing high moral character; gracious; kind: *The critic gave a generous review of the inexperienced actor's performance.* [First written down in 1588 in Modern English and spelled *generous,* of noble birth, magnanimous, from Latin *generōsus,* from *genus,* birth.] **—gen′er•ous•ly** *adv.*

gen•e•sis (jĕn′ĭ sĭs) *n., pl.* **gen•e•ses** (jĕn′ĭ sēz′). **1.** The coming into being of something; the origin: *the genesis of an idea.* **2. Genesis.** The first book of the Bible, describing the creation of the world, the banishment of Adam and Eve from the Garden of Eden, and the early history of the Jewish people.

gene-splic•ing (jēn′splī′sĭng) *n.* The process in which genetic material from one or more organisms is combined to form recombinant DNA.

ge•net•ic (jə nĕt′ĭk) *adj.* **1.** Of or relating to genetics: *genetic research.* **2.** Of or relating to genes: *genetic disease.* **—ge•net′i•cal•ly** *adv.*

genetic code *n.* The various combinations of nucleotides that occur in the DNA of a chromosome. The genetic code determines the sequence of amino acids in a protein.

genetic engineering *n.* The scientific alteration of genes or genetic material, especially by gene-splicing, to produce desirable new traits in organisms or to eliminate undesirable traits.

ge•net•i•cist (jə nĕt′ĭ sĭst) *n.* A scientist who specializes in genetics.

Word Building: generic

The word root *–gen–* in English words comes both from Latin and from Greek. In Latin the noun *genus* means "type, kind, class, origin, race." A form of *genus,* which occurs for example in the plural *genera,* gives us **general, generic,** and **generation**. From French, which is derived from Latin, we have **genre**. From the Greek noun *genesis,* "creation, origin," we have **genesis**. From the Greek noun *genos,* which has the same meanings as the Latin *genus,* we have the word **gene** (the unit in heredity, as in "the gene for blue eyes.") The Greek adjective *genetikos,* "relating to the origin," is the source of our **genetic**.

ă	pat	oi	boy
ā	pay	ou	out
âr	care	o͝o	took
ä	father	o͞o	boot
ĕ	pet	ŭ	cut
ē	be	ûr	urge
ĭ	pit	th	thin
ī	pie	*th*	this
îr	pier	hw	whoop
ŏ	pot	zh	vision
ō	toe	ə	about
ô	paw	N	*French* bon

Genghis Khan
Portrait from a 16th-century Persian manuscript

Word Building: geo–

The basic meaning of the prefix **geo–** is "earth." It comes from the Greek prefix *geō–*, from the Greek word *gē*, meaning "earth." Thus **geography** (from Greek *geō–* + *–graphia*, "writing") is "the study of the earth and its surface features." When used to form words in English, **geo–** can mean either "earth" or "geography." For example, **geomagnetism** refers to the magnetism of the earth, and **geopolitics** refers to the relationship between politics and geography.

geodesic dome

ge•net•ics (jə **nĕt′**ĭks) *n.* **1.** *(used with a singular verb).* The branch of biology that deals with the principles of heredity and the variation of inherited characteristics among similar or related organisms. **2.** *(used with a plural verb).* The genetic makeup of an individual or a group.

Ge•ne•va (jə **nē′**və). A city of southwest Switzerland located on **Lake Geneva** and bisected by the Rhone River. It was originally an ancient Celtic settlement. Population, 159,500.

Gen•ghis Khan (**jĕng′**gĭs **kän′** *or* **gĕng′**gĭs **kän′**). 1162?–1227. Mongol conqueror who united the Mongol tribes and annexed northern China, central Asia, Iran, and southern Russia.

gen•ial (**jēn′**yəl) *adj.* **1.** Cheerful, friendly, and good-humored: *an enthusiatic and genial personality.* **2.** Favorable to health or growth; warm and pleasant: *the genial sunshine of springtime.* **—ge′ni•al′i•ty** (jē′nē **ăl′**ĭ tē) *n.* **—gen′ial•ly** *adv.*

ge•nie (**jē′**nē) *n.* **1.** A spirit that appears in human form and fulfills wishes with magic powers. **2.** A jinni. [First written down in 1655 in Modern English and spelled *geny*, from Latin *genius*, guardian spirit.]

ge•ni•i (**jē′**nē ī′) *n.* Plural of **genius** (sense 7).

gen•i•tal (**jĕn′**ĭ tl) *adj.* **1.** Of or relating to biological reproduction: *the genital organs.* **2.** Of or relating to the genitals.

gen•i•ta•li•a (jĕn′ĭ **tā′**lē ə *or* jĕn′ĭ **tāl′**yə) *pl.n.* The genitals.

genitals (**jĕn′**ĭ tlz) *pl.n.* The external sex organs that function in biological reproduction.

gen•i•tive (**jĕn′**ĭ tĭv) *adj.* Of or relating to the grammatical case that expresses possession or source. *—n.* The genitive case.

gen•ius (**jēn′**yəs) *n., pl.* **gen•ius•es. 1.** Extraordinary mental ability or creative power: *Artists of genius are remembered centuries after their deaths.* **2.** A person of extraordinary mental ability or creative power: *The great inventor was a genius.* **3.** A strong natural talent or ability: *a genius for leadership.* **4.** A person who has a natural talent or ability: *My cousin is a mechanical genius.* **5.** The special spirit or character of a person, place, time, or group: *the genius of ancient Rome.* **6.** A person who has great influence over another: *My genius was my science teacher.* **7.** *pl.* **ge•ni•i** (**jē′**nē ī′). In Roman mythology, the guardian spirit of a person or place. [First written down before 1393 in Middle English and spelled *genius*, guardian spirit, from Latin.]

Gen•o•a (**jĕn′**ō ə). A city of northwest Italy on the **Gulf of Genoa**, an arm of the Ligurian Sea. It is Italy's chief port. Population, 760,300.

gen•o•cide (**jĕn′**ə sīd′) *n.* The deliberate destruction or killing off of a racial, religious, political, or cultural group. **—gen′o•cid′al** (jĕn′ə **sīd′**l) *adj.*

Gen•o•ese (jĕn′ō **ēz′** *or* jĕn′ō **ēs′**) *adj.* Of or relating to Genoa or its people. *—n.* A native or inhabitant of Genoa.

ge•nome (**jē′**nōm) *n.* The complete genetic information of an organism. In a cell with a nucleus, the genome includes one member from each pair of chromosomes. In a cell without a nucleus, the genome is the single chromosome.

gen•o•type (**jĕn′**ə tīp′ *or* **jē′**nə tīp′) *n.* The genetic makeup of an organism or a group as distinguished from its physical characteristics or phenotype.

gen•re (**zhän′**rə) *n.* A particular type or class of literary, musical, or artistic composition: *Novels and plays are of different literary genres.*

gent (jĕnt) *n. Informal.* A man or gentleman.

gen•teel (jĕn **tēl′**) *adj.* **1.** Refined in manner; well bred and polite: *a genteel young man.* **2.** Elegantly stylish: *She had a genteel appearance.* **—gen•teel′ly** *adv.* **—gen•teel′ness** *n.*

gen•tian (**jĕn′**shən) *n.* Any of numerous plants having stemless leaves and usually deep-blue flowers. [First written down in 1373 in Middle English and spelled *gencian*, from Latin *gentiāna*, perhaps after *Gentius*, second-century B.C. king of Illyria, a region on the Balkan Peninsula.]

gen•tile (**jĕn′**tīl′) *n.* **1.** Often **Gentile.** A person who is not a Jew, especially a Christian. **2.** A pagan or heathen. **3.** Often **Gentile.** A person who is not a Mormon. *—adj.* Of or relating to a Gentile. [First written down before 1382 in Middle English, from Late Latin *gentīlis*, pagan.]

gen•til•i•ty (jĕn **tĭl′**ĭ tē) *n.* **1.** Good manners; politeness; refinement. **2.** The condition of coming from a family of high social standing. **3.** Persons of high social standing considered as a group.

gen•tle (**jĕn′**tl) *adj.* **gen•tler, gen•tlest. 1.** Considerate or kindly in manner; thoughtful and good-natured. **2.** Not harsh or severe; mild and soft: *a gentle tap on the shoulder.* **3.** Not steep or sudden; gradual: *a gentle slope.* **4.** Easily managed or handled; docile: *a gentle horse.* **5.** Of good family; well-born: *a child of gentle birth.* **6.** Polite; refined; well-mannered: *a gentle greeting to a stranger.* [First written down before 1200 in Middle English and spelled *gentil*, courteous, noble, from Latin *gentīlis*, of the same clan, from *gēns*, clan.] **—gen′tle•ness** *n.* **—gen′tly** *adv.*

gen•tle•folk (**jĕn′**tl fōk′) *pl.n.* People of good family and usually high social standing.

gen•tle•man (**jĕn′**tl mən) *n.* **1.** A man born to a family of high social standing. **2.** A man with very good manners and behavior. **3.** A man: *The gentleman sitting at their table would like spaghetti.* **4. gentlemen.** Used as a form of address for a group of men: *Good evening, ladies and gentlemen.*

gen•tle•man's agreement or **gen•tle•men's agreement** (**jĕn′**tl mənz) *n.* An informal agreement guaranteed only by the promise of the people involved to honor it.

gen•tle•wom•an (**jĕn′**tl wo͝om′ən) *n.* **1.** A woman born to a family of high social standing. **2.** A woman with very good manners and behavior. **3.** A woman acting as a personal attendant to a noblewoman.

gen•tri•fi•ca•tion (jĕn′trə fĭ **kā′**shən) *n.* The restoration of rundown urban property by the middle classes, often resulting in the displacement of people with low incomes.

gen•tri•fy (**jĕn′**trə fī′) *tr.v.* **gen•tri•fied, gen•tri•fy•ing, gen•tri•fies.** To restore (rundown urban property) by gentrification.

gen•try (**jĕn′**trē) *n., pl.* **gen•tries. 1.** People of good family and high social standing. **2.** In England, a social class ranking next below the nobility.

gen•u•flect (**jĕn′**yə flĕkt′) *intr.v.* **gen•u•flect•ed, gen•u•flect•ing, gen•u•flects.** To bend one knee to or toward the ground, as a gesture of respect and worship. **—gen′u•flec′tion** *n.*

gen•u•ine (**jĕn′**yo͞o ĭn) *adj.* **1.** Not false; real or pure: *a necklace of genuine gold.* See Synonyms at **authentic. 2.** Free of pretense; sincere; honest: *genuine affection.* **—gen′u•ine•ly** *adv.* **—gen′u•ine•ness** *n.*

ge•nus (**jē′**nəs) *n., pl.* **gen•er•a** (**jĕn′**ər ə). **1.** A group of related plants or animals ranking below a family and above a species: *Dogs, wolves, and coyotes belong to the same genus.* See table at **taxonomy. 2.** A class, group, or kind with common characteristics: *the genus of boats known as pleasure crafts.*

geo– or **ge–** *pref.* A prefix that means: **1.** Earth: *geocentric.* **2.** Geography: *geopolitical.* —SEE NOTE.

ge•o•cen•tric (jē′ō **sĕn′**trĭk) *adj.* **1.** Relating to or measured from the earth's center. **2.** Having the earth as the center: *Belief in a geocentric universe was prevalent until Copernicus.*

ge•o•chem•is•try (jē′ō **kĕm′**ĭ strē) *n.* The study of the chemistry of the earth, including its crust, waters, and atmosphere.

ge•ode (**jē′**ōd′) *n.* A small, hollow, usually rounded rock lined on the inside with crystals.

ge•o•des•ic (jē′ə **dĕs′**ĭk *or* jē′ə **dē′**sĭk) *adj.* Of or relating to a geodesic or geodesy. —*n.* The shortest line between two points on a surface, especially a curved surface.

geodesic dome *n.* A structure having the shape of a hemisphere, assembled of straight pieces that form triangles or polygons that fit rigidly together.

ge•od•e•sy (jē **ŏd′**ĭ sē) *n.* The scientific study of the size and shape of the earth.

ge•o•det•ic (jē′ə **dĕt′**ĭk) *adj.* Geodesic.

geog. *abbr.* An abbreviation of: **1.** Geographer. **2.** Geographic. **3.** Geography.

ge•og•ra•pher (jē **ŏg′**rə fər) *n.* A person who specializes in geography.

ge•o•graph•ic (jē′ə **grăf′**ĭk) also **ge•o•graph•i•cal** (jē′ə **grăf′**ĭ kəl) *adj.* Of or relating to geography: *geographic boundaries; geographical names.* —**ge′o•graph′i•cal•ly** *adv.*

geographic mile *n.* A nautical mile.

ge•og•ra•phy (jē **ŏg′**rə fē) *n., pl.* **ge•og•ra•phies. 1.** The study of the earth's surface and its various climates, continents, countries, peoples, resources, industries, and products. **2.** The physical features of a region or place: *We studied the geography of Hawaii.* **3.** A book on geography. [First written down in 1542 in Modern English, from Greek *geōgraphia* : *gē*, earth + *-graphia*, writing.]

ge•o•log•ic (jē′ə **lŏj′**ĭk) or **ge•o•log•i•cal** (jē′ə **lŏj′**ĭ kəl) *adj.* Of or relating to geology: *a geologic study of Alaska.* —**ge′o•log′i•cal•ly** *adv.*

geologic time *n.* The period of time covering the formation and development of the earth. See Table on page 424.

ge•ol•o•gist (jē **ŏl′**ə jĭst) *n.* A scientist who specializes in geology.

ge•ol•o•gy (jē **ŏl′**ə jē) *n., pl.* **ge•ol•o•gies. 1.** The science that studies the origin, history, and structure of the earth. **2.** The structure of a specific region, including its rocks, soils, mountains, and other features. [First written down in 1735 in Modern English, from Medieval Latin *geōlogia*, study of earthly things : Greek *gē*, earth + Greek *-logia*, study.]

geom. *abbr.* An abbreviation of: **1.** Geometric. **2.** Geometry.

ge•o•mag•ne•tism (jē′ō **măg′**nĭ tĭz′əm) *n.* The magnetism of the earth. —**ge′o•mag•net′ic** (jē′ō măg **nĕt′**ĭk) *adj.*

ge•o•met•ric (jē′ə **mĕt′**rĭk) also **ge•o•met•ri•cal** (jē′ə **mĕt′**rĭ kəl) *adj.* **1.** Of or relating to geometry and its methods and principles: *a geometric problem.* **2.** Consisting of or using simple shapes formed from straight lines or curves: *geometric figures; a geometric design.* —**ge′o•met′ri•cal•ly** *adv.*

geometric progression *n.* A sequence of numbers in which each number is multiplied by the same factor to obtain the next number in the sequence. In the geometric progression 5, 25, 125, 625, each number is multiplied by the factor of 5 to obtain the following number.

ge•om•e•try (jē **ŏm′**ĭ trē) *n., pl.* **ge•om•e•tries. 1.** The mathematical study of the properties, measurement, and relationships of points, lines, planes, surfaces, angles, and solids. **2.** A shape or an arrangement of parts, as in a design: *the geometry of a building.* [First written down about 1330 in Middle English and spelled *geometrie*, from Greek *geōmetria* : *gē*, earth, land + *metrein*, to measure.]

ge•o•mor•phol•o•gy (jē′ō môr **fŏl′**ə jē) *n.* The scientific study of the arrangement and evolution of surface features of the earth, such as mountains and valleys.

ge•o•phys•i•cal (jē′ō **fĭz′**ĭ kəl) *adj.* Of or relating to geophysics: *geophysical research.*

ge•o•phys•ics (jē′ō **fĭz′**ĭks) *n.* *(used with a singular verb).* The applicaton of physics to the study of the earth and its environment.

ge•o•pol•i•tics (jē′ō **pŏl′**ĭ tĭks) *n.* *(used with a singular verb)* The study of the relationship among politics and geography, demographics, and economics. —**ge′o•po•lit′i•cal** (jē′ō pə **lĭt′**i kəl) *adj.*

George (jôrj), Saint. Died c. A.D. 303. Christian martyr who, according to legend, killed a fearsome dragon.

George II. 1683–1760. King of Great Britain and Ireland (1727–1760) who was the last British monarch to lead troops in battle.

George III. 1738–1820. King of Great Britain and Ireland (1760–1820) whose policies fed American discontent, leading to revolution in 1776.

George V. 1865–1936. King of Great Britain and Northern Ireland and emperor of India (1910–1936).

George VI. 1895–1952. King of Great Britain and Northern Ireland (1936–1952) and emperor of India (1936–1947) who won popularity during World War II.

George•town (**jôrj′**toun′). **1.** The capital of the Cayman Islands, in the West Indies west of Jamaica. Population, 7,617. **2.** The capital and largest city of Guyana, in the northern part of the country on the Atlantic Ocean. It was founded in 1781. Population, 78,500.

Geor•gia (**jôr′**jə). **1.** A region of Asia Minor in the Caucasus on the Black Sea south of Russia. It developed as a kingdom from about the 4th century B.C. and reached its height in the 12th and 13th centuries. Georgia was part of the Soviet Union from 1922 to 1991. Capital, Tbilisi. Population, 5,201,000. **2.** A state of the southeast United States on the Atlantic Ocean north of Florida. It was admitted as one of the original Thirteen Colonies in 1788. Atlanta is the capital and the largest city. Population, 6,508,419. —SEE NOTE.

Geor•gian (**jôr′**jən) *adj.* **1.** Of, relating to, or characteristic of the reigns of the four kings of England named George who ruled from 1714 to 1830: *Georgian architecture.* **2.** Of or relating to the U.S. state of Georgia or its inhabitants. **3.** Of or relating to the Georgian Republic or its people, language, or culture. —*n.* **1.** A native or inhabitant of the U.S. state of Georgia. **2.** A native or inhabitant of the Georgian Republic. **3.** The language of the Georgians.

ge•o•ther•mal (jē′ō **thûr′**məl) *adj.* Of or relating to the internal heat of the earth.

ge•ot•ro•pism (jē **ŏt′**rə pĭz′əm) *n.* The movement or growth of a living organism in response to the earth's gravity. Examples of geotropism include the downward growth of plant roots and the upward growth of new shoots on a plant.

Ger. *abbr.* An abbreviation of: **1.** German. **2.** Germany.

ge•ra•ni•um (jə **rā′**nē əm) *n.* **1.** Any of various plants having rounded leaves and showy clusters of red, pink, or white flowers, often grown as potted plants. **2.** Any of various related plants having pink or purplish flowers. [First written down in 1548 in Modern English, from Latin *geranium*, crane's bill.]

ger•bil (**jûr′**bəl) *n.* Any of various small rodents somewhat like a mouse, having long hind legs and a long tail and native to desert regions of Africa and Asia. Gerbils are often kept as pets or laboratory animals.

Saint George

Early 15th-century Italian painting by an unknown artist

George III

Georgia

The state of **Georgia** is named for King George II of England, who first gave James Oglethorpe permission to establish a colony there in 1732. A Latin ending was added to the king's name to create the name for the colony, and the state took its name from the colony.

ă	pat	oi	boy
ā	pay	ou	out
âr	care	o͝o	took
ä	father	o͞o	boot
ĕ	pet	ŭ	cut
ē	be	ûr	urge
ĭ	pit	th	thin
ī	pie	*th*	this
îr	pier	hw	whoop
ŏ	pot	zh	vision
ō	toe	ə	about
ô	paw	N	*French* bon

GEOLOGIC TIME

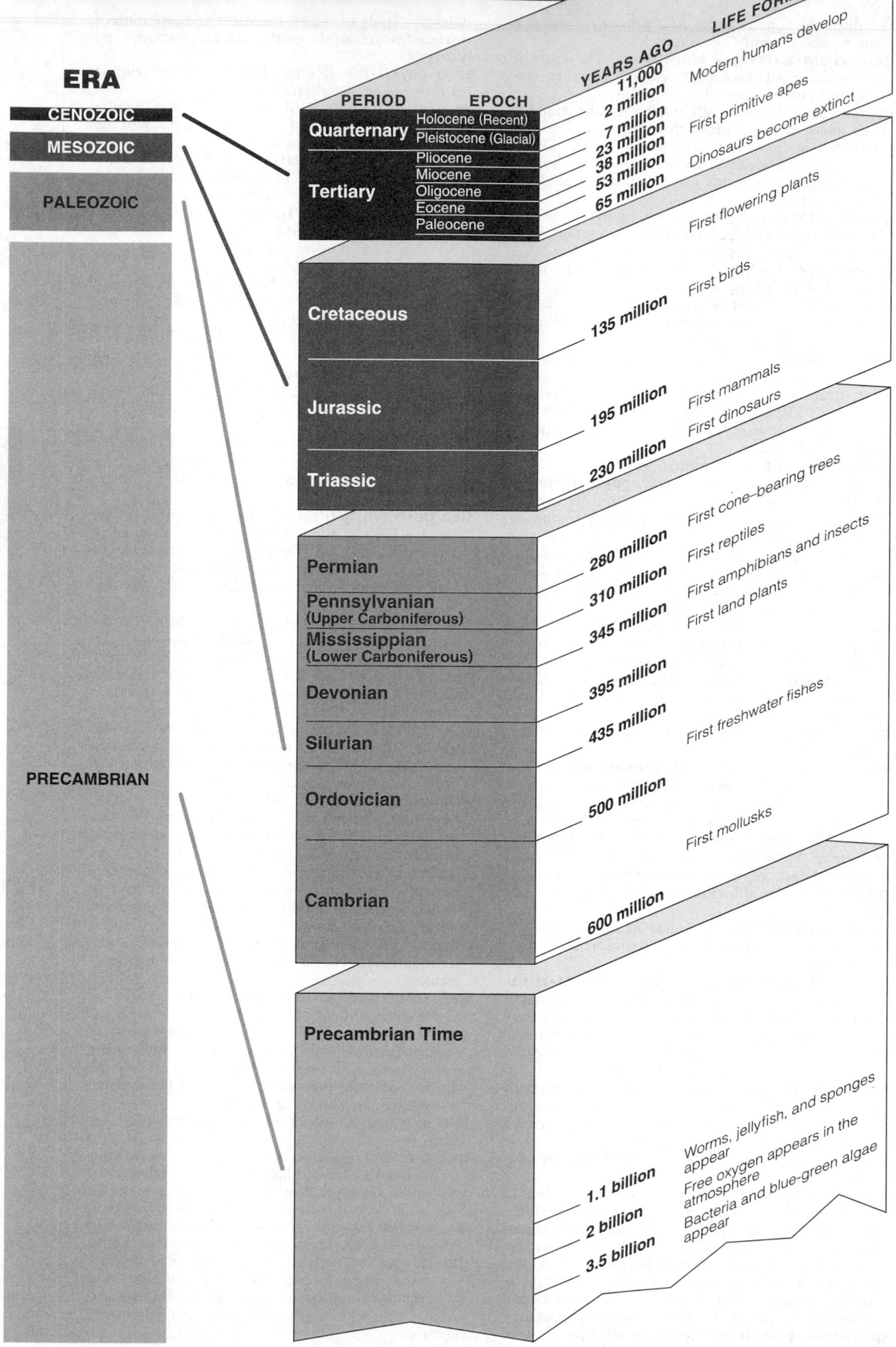
ERA
CENOZOIC
MESOZOIC
PALEOZOIC
PRECAMBRIAN
PERIOD
EPOCH
YEARS AGO
LIFE FORMS
Quarternary
Holocene (Recent)
Pleistocene (Glacial)
Tertiary
Pliocene
Miocene
Oligocene
Eocene
Paleocene
11,000
2 million
7 million
23 million
38 million
53 million
65 million
Modern humans develop
First primitive apes
Dinosaurs become extinct
First flowering plants
Cretaceous
First birds
135 million
Jurassic
First mammals
195 million
First dinosaurs
Triassic
230 million
First cone-bearing trees
Permian
280 million
First reptiles
Pennsylvanian
(Upper Carboniferous)
310 million
First amphibians and insects
Mississippian
(Lower Carboniferous)
345 million
First land plants
Devonian
395 million
Silurian
435 million
First freshwater fishes
Ordovician
500 million
First mollusks
Cambrian
600 million
Precambrian Time
Worms, jellyfish, and sponges appear
1.1 billion
Free oxygen appears in the atmosphere
2 billion
Bacteria and blue-green algae appear
3.5 billion

ger•fal•con (jûr′făl′kən *or* jôr′fôl′kən *or* jûr′fô′kən) *n.* Variant of **gyrfalcon.**

ger•i•at•rics (jĕr′ē **ăt′**rĭks) *n. (used with a singular verb).* The medical study of the biological process of aging and the treatment of diseases of old age.

germ (jûrm) *n.* **1.** A microscopic organism, especially one that causes disease. Certain bacteria and viruses are considered to be germs. **2.** The earliest form of a living thing; a seed, spore, or bud: *wheat germ.* **3.** The earliest form of something; the basis: *The discovery that the earth orbits the sun was the germ of a revolution in astronomy.* [First written down about 1450 in Middle English and spelled *germ*, bud, sprout, from Latin *germen.*]

Ger•man (**jûr′**mən) *n.* **1.** A native or inhabitant of Germany. **2.** The Germanic language of Germany, Austria, and part of Switzerland. *—adj.* Of or relating to Germany or its people, language, or culture.

ger•mane (jər **mān′**) *adj.* Closely or naturally related; appropriate; pertinent: *Their comments were not germane to the discussion.* [First written down in 1340 in Middle English and spelled *germain*, closely related, from Latin *germānus.*]

Ger•man•ic (jər **măn′**ĭk) *adj.* **1.** Of or relating to Germany or its people, language, or culture. **2.** Of or relating to the branch of the Indo-European language family that includes English, German, Dutch, and the Scandinavian languages. **3.** Teutonic. *—n.* The Germanic branch of the Indo-European language family.

ger•ma•ni•um (jər **mā′**nē əm) *n. Symbol* **Ge** A brittle, gray metalloid element found in zinc ores. It is used as a semiconductor in transistors. Atomic number 32. See table at **element.**

German measles *n. (used with a singular or plural verb).* Rubella.

German shepherd *n.* Any of a breed of large dog developed in Germany, having a thick black or brownish coat and often trained to help police officers or guide the blind; a police dog.

German silver *n.* Nickel silver.

Ger•ma•ny (**jûr′**mə nē). A country of north-central Europe west of Poland and bordered on the north by the Baltic and North seas. From 1949 to 1990 the territory was divided between **West Germany** and **East Germany.** Berlin is the capital and largest city and Bonn the seat of government. Population, 77,750,743.

germ cell *n.* A reproductive cell of a plant or an animal, as an egg or a sperm.

ger•mi•cide (**jûr′**mĭ sīd′) *n.* A substance that kills germs, especially disease germs. **—ger′mi•cid′al** (gûr′mĭ **sīd′**l) *adj.*

ger•mi•nal (**jûr′**mə nəl) *adj.* **1.** Of, relating to, or having the nature of a germ cell. **2.** Of, relating to, or occurring in an early stage of development: *a germinal sprout.*

ger•mi•nate (**jûr′**mə nāt′) *intr. & tr.v.* **ger•mi•nat•ed, ger•mi•nat•ing, ger•mi•nates.** To begin or cause to begin to grow; sprout: *Seeds need water and warmth to germinate.* [First written down in 1610 in Modern English, from Latin *germināre*, to sprout, from *germen*, seed.] **—ger′mi•na′tion** *n.* **—ger′mi•na′tor** *n.*

germ plasm (**plăz′**əm) *n.* The hereditary substance in germ cells, now known to consist of the chromosomes, that is transmitted to the offspring.

germ warfare *n.* Biological warfare.

Ge•ron•i•mo (jə **rŏn′**ə mō′). 1829–1909. Apache leader who resisted the U.S. government and led raids against Mexican and American settlements in the Southwest (1876–1886).

ger•ry•man•der (**jĕr′**ē măn′dər *or* **gĕr′**ē măn′dər) *tr.v.* **ger•ry•man•dered, ger•ry•man•der•ing, ger•ry•man•ders.** To divide (voting districts of a state or county) in such a way as to give unfair advantage to one political party. *—n.* An act or example of gerrymandering. [First written down in 1812 in American English : after Elbridge *Gerry* (1744–1814), American politician + *(sala)mander* (from the shape of an election district created while Gerry was governor of Massachusetts).]

ger•und (**jĕr′**ənd) *n.* A noun formed from a verb. In English the gerund ends in *-ing.* In the sentence *Hitting a ball hard requires strength,* the word *hitting* is a gerund. Like a noun, a gerund may be the subject of a sentence, but like a verb it may have a direct object and be modified by an adverb.

Ge•sta•po (gə **stä′**pō) *n.* The secret police force of Nazi Germany, notorious for its ruthlessness against people thought to be disloyal.

ges•ta•tion (jĕ **stā′**shən) *n.* **1.** The carrying and development of young in the uterus from conception to birth; pregnancy. **2.** The period of gestation. **3.** The conception or development of a plan or an idea.

ges•tic•u•late (jĕ **stĭk′**yə lāt′) *intr.v.* **ges•tic•u•lat•ed, ges•tic•u•lat•ing, ges•tic•u•lates.** To make gestures in order to emphasize meaning or express one's feelings: *The angry speaker gesticulated wildly by flailing the air with his hands.* **—ges•tic′u•la′tion** *n.*

ges•ture (**jĕs′**chər) *n.* **1.** Movement of the limbs, head, or body to help express meaning: *A mime must rely on gestures to tell a story.* **2.** Something done or said for its effect on the feelings or opinions of others: *Sending someone a birthday card is a thoughtful gesture.* *—v.* **ges•tured, ges•tur•ing, ges•tures.** *—intr.* To make a gesture or gestures: *The police officer gestured for the car to proceed.* *—tr.* To express or signal by gesture: *With a nod the judge gestured a willingness to listen.* [First written down about 1400 in Middle English, from Medieval Latin *gestūra*, bearing.]

get (gĕt) *v.* **got** (gŏt), **got•ten** (**gŏt′**n) or **got, get•ting, gets.** *—tr.* **1.** To come to have or use; receive: *She got skates for her birthday.* **2.** To go after and obtain; acquire: *I got some food at the supermarket.* **3.** To gain; earn: *The student got a prize for high achievement.* **4.** To go after and bring; fetch: *Please get me a pencil.* **5.a.** To become affected with; catch: *I've got the flu.* **b.** To be subjected to; experience: *He got a broken ankle.* **6.** To have; possess: *I've already got that record.* **7.** To cause to be or become: *The long journey got the children tired and cross.* **8.** To make ready; prepare: *get lunch for a crowd.* **9.** To cause (someone to do something): *got the guide to give us the complete tour.* **10.** To be obligated; need: *We have got to leave early.* **11.** To hit; strike: *The snowball got me on the arm.* **12.** To understand or comprehend: *I don't get the connection between those ideas.* **13.** To make contact with: *We got the manager on the telephone.* *—intr.* **1.** To reach; come to: *get to the airport; get to shore.* **2.** To be or become: *get well; get stuck in traffic.* **3.** To come or go: *get going; get up the icy steps.* **4.** To be allowed or permitted: *I never got to see the movie.* ***—idioms.*** **get along. 1.** To be or remain friendly with: *The two little children got along well.* **2.** To manage with reasonable success: *We're not rich, but we're getting along.* **3.** To advance; make progress: *How's your project getting along?* **4.** To move on; leave: *I think I'll be getting along now.* **get around. 1.** To evade; overcome: *Many lazy people try to get around rules.* **2.** To trick: *You can't get around me with that story.* **3.** To travel from place to place. **4.** To become widely known; spread: *The rumor got around quickly.* **get at. 1.** To reach: *The sponge fell behind the sink where I can't get at it.*

German shepherd

Geronimo
1907 photogravure
by Edward Sheriff Curtis
(1868–1952)

Usage: get

When writing you should avoid using **get** in the passive, as in *Our choir got written up in the paper for giving the fall concert.* Instead you could say *Our choir was written up in the paper for giving the fall concert.*

ă	pat	oi	boy
ā	pay	ou	out
âr	care	ŏŏ	took
ä	father	ōō	boot
ĕ	pet	ŭ	cut
ē	be	ûr	urge
ĭ	pit	th	thin
ī	pie	*th*	this
îr	pier	hw	whoop
ŏ	pot	zh	vision
ō	toe	ə	about
ô	paw	N	*French* bon

geyser
Old Faithful,
Yellowstone National Park

gibbon
Lar gibbon

Gila monster

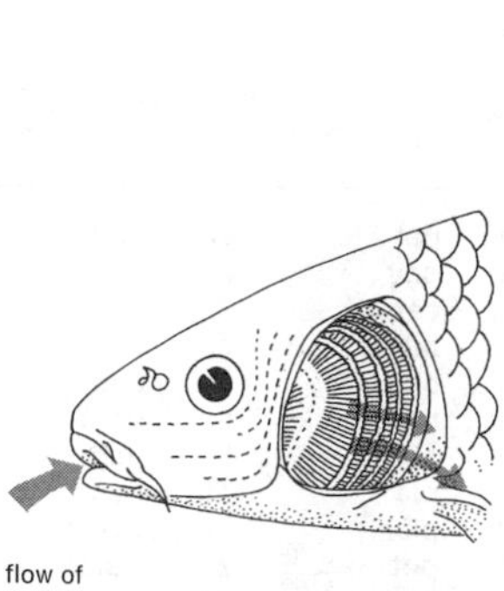

flow of water

gill[1]

2. To express or mean: *Do you understand what I am getting at?* **get away. 1.** To go away: *We want to get away on a trip to the country.* **2.** To escape: *The lion got away from the zoo.* **get away with.** To do something without being punished or found out: *get away with a crime.* **get back.** To return to a person, place, or condition: *Let's get back to work.* **get by. 1.** To manage; survive: *They were unprepared for rain but got by somehow.* **2.** To pass without being noticed: *The prisoners got by the guards.* **get in. 1.** To enter or be allowed to enter: *Can we get in without a ticket?* **2.** To arrive: *The plane gets in at midnight.* **3.** To put in: *I couldn't get in a word during the conversation.* **get it. 1.** To understand; comprehend: *I just don't get it.* **2.** *Informal.* To be punished or scolded: *You're really going to get it when your mother comes home.* **get off. 1.** To get down from or out of: *get off the train.* **2.** To leave; depart: *Tomorrow we get off early.* **3.** To escape punishment or obligation: *The student got off from detention.* **get on. 1.** To climb up onto or into; enter: *Get on the boat before it leaves.* **2.** To be on friendly terms: *The neighbors got on for years and then suddenly had a fight.* **3.** To advance in years: *The old dog is getting on in years.* **4.** To continue, proceed, or progress: *I got on with the work.* **get out. 1.** To leave or escape: *Our canary got out.* **2.** To become known: *The secret finally got out.* **3.** To publish: *That author gets out a new book every year.* **get out of.** To escape from or be released from: *The cows somehow got out of the pasture.* **get over.** To recover from: *get over a cold.* **get through. 1.** To finish; complete: *trying to get through a big job.* **2.** To succeed in making contact: *I telephoned twice, but couldn't get through.* **get together. 1.** To meet; assemble: *getting together for supper tonight.* **2.** To come to an agreement: *The feuding parties finally got together.* **get up. 1.** To arise: *They got up early to see the sunrise.* **2.** To sit or stand up: *He got up out of the chair.* [First written down about 1200 in Middle English and spelled *geten,* from Old Norse *geta.*] —See Note on page 425.

get•a•way (gĕt′ə wā′) *n.* **1.** The act of getting away; an escape. **2.** The start, as of a race.

get-to•geth•er (gĕt′tə gĕth′ər) *n. Informal.* A small party or gathering.

Get•tys•burg (gĕt′ēz bûrg′). A town of southern Pennsylvania west-southwest of Philadelphia. It was the site of a major Union victory in the Civil War (July 1–3, 1863) and Abraham Lincoln's famous Gettysburg Address. Population, 7,194.

get•up (gĕt′ŭp′) *n.* **1.** *Informal.* An outfit or a costume, especially one that is odd or different. **2.** The way a thing is put together; arrangement.

get-up-and-go (gĕt′ŭp′ən gō′) *n. Informal.* Ambition and energy.

gew•gaw (gyōō′gô′ *or* gōō′gô′) *n.* A showy trinket of little value; a bauble.

gey•ser (gī′zər) *n.* A natural hot spring that regularly ejects a spray of steam and boiling water into the air.

Gha•na (gä′nə *or* găn′ə). A country of western Africa east of Ivory Coast. Ghana was inhabited by a number of ancient kingdoms, including that of the Ashanti people, and gained independence from Great Britain in 1957. Accra is the capital and the largest city. Population, 12,205,574.

ghast•ly (găst′lē) *adj.* **ghast•li•er, ghast•li•est. 1.** Terrifying; horrible: *a ghastly crime.* **2.** Resembling a ghost; extremely pale: *The patient had a ghastly complexion.* **3.** Extremely unpleasant or bad: *His cooking is ghastly.* [First written down before 1300 in Middle English and spelled *gastlich,* from *gasten,* to terrify, from Old English *gāst,* spirit.] **—ghast′li•ness** *n.*

Ghent (gĕnt). A city of western Belgium west-northwest of Brussels. It was founded in the seventh century. Population, 236,540.

gher•kin (gûr′kĭn) *n.* A small cucumber used for making pickles.

ghet•to (gĕt′ō) *n., pl.* **ghet•tos** or **ghet•toes. 1.** A section of a city inhabited by a minority group because of economic necessity or social pressure. **2.** A section or quarter in a European city where Jews were formerly restricted.

ghost (gōst) *n.* **1.** The spirit of a dead person, supposed to haunt or appear to living persons. **2.** A slight trace; a bit: *a ghost of a smile; a ghost of a chance.* [First written down before 800 in Old English and spelled *gāst,* breath, spirit.]

ghost•ly (gōst′lē) *adj.* **ghost•li•er, ghost•li•est.** Of or resembling a ghost: *Dressed in a white cape, she took on a ghostly appearance in the moonlight.* **—ghost′li•ness** *n.*

ghost town *n.* A town, especially one of the Western frontier in the United States, that has been abandoned.

ghost•write (gōst′rīt′) *tr.v.* **ghost•wrote** (gōst′rōt′), **ghost•writ•ten** (gōst′rĭt′n), **ghost•writ•ing, ghost•writes.** To write (something, such as an article or a speech) for another person who is credited as the author. **—ghost•writ′er** *n.*

ghoul (gōōl) *n.* **1.** A person who robs graves. **2.** A person who delights in brutal or horrible things. **3.** In Islamic folklore, an evil spirit believed to plunder graves and feast on corpses. [First written down in 1786 in Modern English, from Arabic *ġūl.*] **—ghoul′ish** *adj.* **—ghoul′ish•ly** *adv.* **—ghoul′ish•ness** *n.*

GI[1] (jē′ī′) *n., pl.* **GIs** or **GI's.** An enlisted person in or a veteran of any of the U.S. armed forces. —*adj.* Relating to or characteristic of a GI: *a GI uniform.*

GI[2] *abbr.* An abbreviation of: **1.** Gastrointestinal. **2.** Government issue.

gi•ant (jī′ənt) *n.* **1.** A person or thing of great size, ability, or importance: *a musical giant.* **2.** A being of great size and strength having human form and found in myth or folklore. —*adj.* Gigantic; huge: *a giant airport.*

giant star *n.* A very large, bright star of low density.

gib•ber (jĭb′ər) *intr.v.* **gib•bered, gib•ber•ing, gib•bers.** To speak rapidly and in a nonsensical way; chatter. —*n.* Gibberish.

gib•ber•ish (jĭb′ər ĭsh) *n.* Meaningless or nonsensical talk or writing.

gib•bet (jĭb′ĭt) *n.* **1.** A gallows. **2.** A wooden arm that projects from an upright post where the bodies of executed criminals were hung for public viewing. —*tr.v.* **gib•bet•ed, gib•bet•ing, gib•bets** or **gib•bet•ted, gib•bet•ting, gib•bets. 1.** To execute by hanging. **2.** To hang on a gibbet for public viewing.

gib•bon (gĭb′ən) *n.* Any of several small tree-dwelling apes of tropical Asia, having a slender body, long arms, and no tail.

gib•bous (gĭb′əs) *adj.* **1.** More than half but not fully illuminated: *a gibbous moon.* **2.** Curved out; convex.

gibe also **jibe** (jīb) *n.* A scornful remark; a jeer. —*intr.v.* **gibed, gib•ing, gibes** also **jibed, jib•ing, jibes.** To make scornful or jeering remarks: *They gibed at my first efforts to waterski.*

❑ *These sound alike:* **gibe, jibe**[1] (shift a sail), **jibe**[2] (agree).

gib•lets (jĭb′lĭts) *pl.n.* The edible heart, liver, and gizzard of a fowl.

Gi•bral•tar (jə brôl′tər). A British colony at the northwest end of the **Rock of Gibraltar,** a peninsula on the south-central coast of Spain in the **Strait of Gibraltar,** connecting the Mediterranean Sea and the Atlantic Ocean. The population of the colony is 29,648.

gid•dy (gĭd′ē) *adj.* **gid•di•er, gid•di•est. 1.a.** Having a whirling sensation in the head; dizzy: *The climber became giddy at the top of the mountain.* **b.** Causing or capable of causing dizziness: *The roller coaster moved at a giddy speed.* **2.** Frivolous; not serious: *The good news put everyone in a giddy mood.* **—gid′di•ly** *adv.* **—gid′di•ness** *n.*

gift (gĭft) *n.* **1.** Something given; a present. **2.** A special talent, aptitude, or ability: *a gift for mathematics.* **3.** The act of giving: *Ownership of the car was transferred by gift.*

gift•ed (gĭf′tĭd) *adj.* Endowed with great natural ability, intelligence, or talent: *a gifted athlete.*

gift-wrap (gĭft′răp′) *tr.v.* **gift-wrapped, gift-wrap•ping, gift-wraps.** To wrap (something intended as a gift) with fancy paper, ribbon, or other trimmings.

gig¹ (gĭg) *n.* **1.** A light two-wheeled carriage drawn by one horse. **2.** A long light ship's boat, usually used only by the ship's captain. [First written down in 1790 in Modern English, perhaps from obsolete *gig*, spinning top.]

gig² (gĭg) *n.* **1.** A set of fish hooks usually dragged through a school of fish to hook them in their bodies. **2.** A pronged fishing spear. *—tr. & intr.v.* **gigged, gig•ging, gigs.** To fish with a gig. [First written down in 1722 in Modern English, from *fishgig*, from Spanish *fisga*.]

gig³ (gĭg) *n. Slang.* A job for a musician, especially at a club. [First written down in 1926 in Modern English.]

gig•a•hertz (jĭg′ə hûrtz′ *or* gĭg′ə hûrtz′) *n.* A unit of frequency equal to one billion hertz.

gi•gan•tic (jī găn′tĭk) *adj.* Suggestive of a giant; huge; enormous: *a gigantic basketball player; a gigantic factory.* **—gi•gan′ti•cal•ly** *adv.*

gig•gle (gĭg′əl) *intr.v.* **gig•gled, gig•gling, gig•gles.** To laugh in a silly or nervous way; titter or chuckle. *—n.* A short silly laugh. **—gig′gler** *n.* **—gig′gly** *adj.*

Gi•la monster (hē′lə) *n.* A poisonous lizard of the southwest United States and northern Mexico, having a thick body with black and orange or yellow markings.

gild (gĭld) *tr.v.* **gild•ed** or **gilt** (gĭlt), **gild•ing, gilds. 1.** To cover with a thin layer of gold: *gild the frame of a mirror.* **2.** To give a deceptively attractive or improved appearance to (something): *In gilding the facts the author made the commander seem less cruel.*

❑ *These sound alike:* **gild, guild** (association).

gill¹ (gĭl) *n.* **1.** The organ that enables fish and certain other water animals to take oxygen from the water. It consists of a series of membranes that have many small blood vessels. Oxygen passes into and carbon dioxide passes out of the bloodstream through the thin walls of the gills. **2.** One of the thin plates on the underside of a mushroom cap. ***—idiom.*** **to the gills.** *Informal.* As full as possible; completely. [First written down before 1325 in Middle English, of Scandinavian origin.]

gill² (jĭl) *n.* A unit of volume or capacity used mainly for liquids. It is equal to 4 ounces or 7.216 cubic inches (118.3 milliters). [First written down in 1310 in Middle English and spelled *gille*, from Late Latin *gillō*, vessel for cooling liquids.]

gill net (gĭl) *n.* A fishnet set vertically in the water so that fish swimming into it are caught by the gills.

gil•ly•flow•er (gĭl′ē flou′ər) *n.* A carnation or similar plant having fragrant flowers.

Gil•man (gĭl′mən), **Charlotte Anna Perkins.** 1860–1935. American feminist and writer whose works include "The Yellow Wall Paper" (1892).

gilt (gĭlt) *v.* A past tense and a past participle of **gild.** *—n.* A thin layer of gold or something similar to gold, like gold-colored paint, applied to a surface. *—adj.* Covered with gold or something resembling gold; gilded: *a picture in a gilt frame.*

❑ *These sound alike:* **gilt, guilt** (remorse).

gim•crack (jĭm′krăk′) *n.* A cheap and showy object of little or no use.

gim•let (gĭm′lĭt) *n.* A small hand tool with a screw tip, used to bore holes.

gim•mick (gĭm′ĭk) *n. Slang.* **1.** A clever idea, scheme, or device, often used to promote something: *an advertising gimmick.* **2.** A gadget.

gin¹ (jĭn) *n.* A strong alcoholic liquor distilled from grain and flavored with juniper berries. [First written down in 1706 in Modern English and spelled *geneva*, from Dutch *jenever*, from Latin *iūniperus*, juniper.]

gin² (jĭn) *n.* A cotton gin. *—tr.v.* **ginned, gin•ning, gins.** To remove the seeds from (cotton) with a gin. [First written down in 1740 in American English, from Middle English *gin*, device, from Old French *engin*, skill.] **—gin′ner** *n.*

gin³ (jĭn) *n.* Gin rummy. [First written down in 1956 in Modern English, from *gin rummy*.]

gin•ger (jĭn′jər) *n.* **1.a.** A tropical plant having a root with a sharp spicy flavor. **b.** The root of this plant, often preserved and used for flavoring or candied. **2.** *Informal.* Liveliness; vigor: *a kitten full of ginger.* **3.** A reddish brown. [First written down about 1000 in Old English and spelled *gingifer*, from Greek *zingiberis*.]

ginger ale *n.* A soft drink flavored with ginger.

ginger beer *n.* A soft drink similar to ginger ale but flavored with fermented ginger.

gin•ger•bread (jĭn′jər brĕd′) *n.* **1.** A cake or cookie flavored with ginger and molasses. **2.** Elaborate and tasteless ornamentation, especially in architecture or furniture.

gin•ger•ly (jĭn′jər lē) *adv.* Cautiously; carefully; warily: *The cat rubbed herself gingerly against the horse's legs.* *—adj.* Cautious; careful: *It is best to offer advice in a gingerly fashion.*

gin•ger•snap (jĭn′jər snăp′) *n.* A flat crisp cookie made with molasses and ginger.

ging•ham (gĭng′əm) *n.* A light cotton cloth woven with colored thread in checks, stripes, plaids, or solid colors. [First written down in 1615 in Modern English, from Malay *genggang*, at intervals.]

gink•go also **ging•ko** (gĭng′kō) *n., pl.* **gink•goes** also **ging•koes.** An ornamental tree native to China, having leaves shaped like fans. [First written down in 1773 in Modern English, from Japanese *ginkyō*.]

gin rummy *n.* A kind of rummy, usually for two players.

Gins•burg (gĭnz′bərg), **Ruth Bader.** Born 1933. American jurist who was appointed an associate justice of the U.S. Supreme Court in 1993.

gin•seng (jĭn′sĕng′) *n.* **1.** Any of several plants of Asia and North America having small greenish flowers and a forked root. **2.** The root of this plant, used especially in traditional Chinese medicine. [First written down in 1654 in Modern English and spelled *gimsem*, from Chinese (Mandarin) *rén shēn*.]

Giot•to (jô′tō). 1267?–1337. Italian artist who was considered the greatest painter of his period in Italy.

Gip•sy (jĭp′sē) *n.* Variant of **Gypsy.**

gi•raffe (jə răf′) *n., pl.* **gi•raffes** or **giraffe.** An African mammal having a very long neck and legs, a tan coat with brown patches, and short horns. It is the tallest living mammal. [First written down in 1594 in Modern English and spelled *gyraffa*, from Arabic dialectal *zirāfah*.]

gird (gûrd) *tr.v.* **gird•ed** or **girt** (gûrt), **gird•ing,**

Charlotte Perkins Gilman

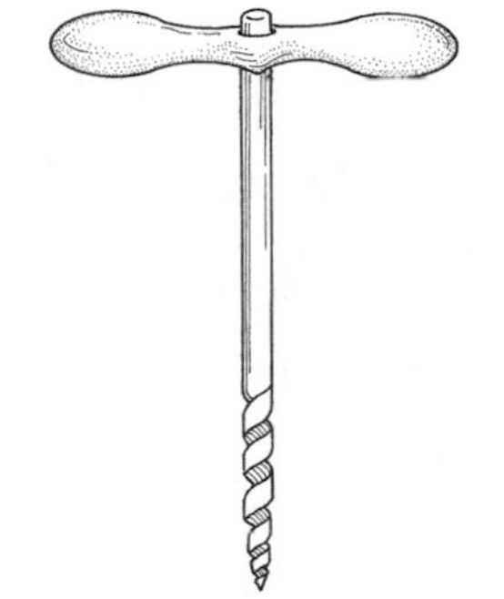

gimlet

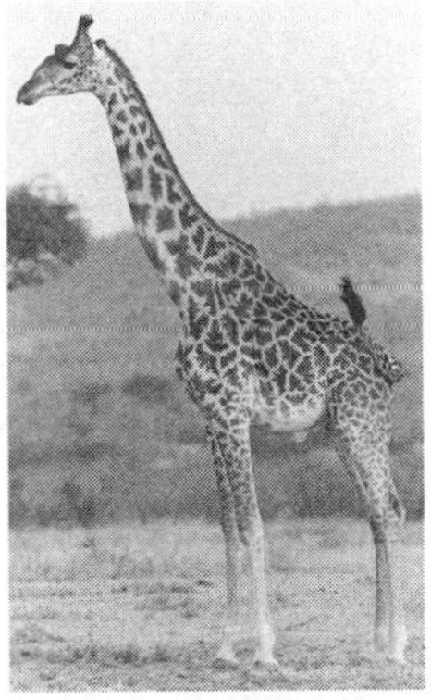

giraffe
Masai giraffe

ă	pat	oi	boy
ā	pay	ou	out
âr	care	ŏŏ	took
ä	father	ōō	boot
ĕ	pet	ŭ	cut
ē	be	ûr	urge
ĭ	pit	th	thin
ī	pie	*th*	this
îr	pier	hw	whoop
ŏ	pot	zh	vision
ō	toe	ə	about
ô	paw	N	*French* bon

girds. **1.** To encircle or attach with a belt or band: *The monks girded their robes with a long cord.* **2.** To prepare (oneself) for action: *The employees girded themselves to ask for a raise in pay.* **3.** To encircle or surround: *Bushes and flowers girded the cottage.*

gird•er (gûr′dər) *n.* A horizontal beam, as of steel or wood, that acts as one of the main supports of a building, bridge, or other structure.

gir•dle (gûr′dl) *n.* **1.** A belt, sash, or band worn around the waist. **2.** A woman's elastic undergarment, worn over the waist and hips. **3.** Something that surrounds like a belt: *a girdle of mountains around the valley.* —*tr.v.* **gir•dled, gir•dling, gir•dles. 1.** To encircle with or as if with a belt: *Embroidery girdled the waist of the dress.* **2.** To remove a strip of bark from around the trunk of (a tree), usually as a means of killing.

girl (gûrl) *n.* **1.a.** A female child. **b.** A young woman, especially one who is unmarried. **2.** A daughter: *our youngest girl.* **3.** *Informal.* A woman: *an evening out with the girls.* **4.** *Offensive.* A female servant, such as a maid. **5.** *Informal.* A female sweetheart; a girlfriend. [First written down before 1300 in Middle English and spelled *girle*, child, girl.] **—girl′hood′** *n.*

girl•friend also **girl friend** (gûrl′frĕnd′) *n.* **1.** A favored female companion or sweetheart. **2.** A female friend.

Girl Guide *n.* A member of the Girl Guides, a British youth organization founded in 1910.

girl•ish (gûr′lĭsh) *adj.* Characteristic of or suitable for a girl. **—girl′ish•ly** *adv.* **—girl′ish•ness** *n.*

Girl Scout *n.* A member of the Girl Scouts.

Girl Scouts *pl.n.* An organization for girls whose goals include helping girls develop self-reliance, good citizenship, and outdoor skills.

girt (gûrt) *v.* A past tense and past participle of **gird.**

girth (gûrth) *n.* **1.** The distance around something; the circumference. **2.** A strap encircling the body of a horse or pack animal in order to hold a load or saddle on its back.

gist (jĭst) *n.* The central idea; main point: *the gist of a message.*

give (gĭv) *v.* **gave** (gāv), **giv•en** (gĭv′ən), **giv•ing, gives.** —*tr.* **1.** To make a present of: *My sister gave me a new watch.* **2.** To place in the hands of; hand over; pass: *Please give me the salt.* **3.** To hand over or deliver in exchange or in payment; sell or pay: *We gave them the bike for $25. They gave us $25 for the bike.* **4.a.** To bestow; confer; award: *They gave first prize to the best speller.* **b.** To administer: *The doctor gave me a vaccine.* **c.** To convey or deliver by physical action: *She gave me a hug.* **5.** To provide; furnish; supply: *Green vegetables give us vitamins and minerals.* **6.** To grant; let have: *The principal gave us permission to go on the field trip.* **7.** To allot; assign: *The teacher gave me the task of cleaning the blackboard.* **8.a.** To offer or present: *Could you give us your ideas on the state of the economy?* **b.** To offer as entertainment: *We gave a party in his honor.* **9.** To emit or issue; put forth; utter: *give an order.* **10.** To be a source of; afford: *Music gives me great pleasure.* **11.** To produce; yield: *Their cows gave milk and cream.* **12.** To yield, as to pressure: *give ground to the enemy.* —*intr.* **1.** To make a gift or donation: *They give generously to local charities.* **2.** To yield to force or pressure: *The door gave when I ran against it.* —*n.* Elasticity; flexibility: *The diving board has a lot of give.* ***—idioms.*** **give away. 1.** To make a gift of: *We gave away many of the vegetables from our garden.* **2.** To present (a bride) to the bridegroom at a wedding ceremony. **3.** To reveal or make known, often by accident: *I gave away the surprise party when I mentioned buying balloons and streamers.* **give back.** To return: *Give me back my book.* **give birth to.** To bear as offspring. **give in.** To surrender; yield: *The babysitter gave in and let the children watch TV.* **give it to.** *Informal.* To punish or scold severely. **give off.** To send forth; emit: *The moon gave off an eerie light.* **give out. 1.** To let (something) be known: *gave out the bad news.* **2.** To distribute: *give out paychecks to employees.* **3.** To stop working; fail: *The water pump gave out.* **4.** To become used up; run out: *The runner's energy gave out after five miles.* **give over. 1.** To hand over. **2.** make available for a purpose; devote: *The last part of the program is given over to questions from the audience.* **give rise to.** To be the cause or origin of; bring about. **give up. 1.** To surrender: *The thieves gave themselves up to the police.* **2.** To stop: *My uncle has given up smoking.* **3.** To admit defeat and stop trying: *They finally gave up and stopped looking for the ring.* **4.** To abandon hope for: *We gave the cat up as lost.* **give way. 1.** To withdraw; retreat: *The animals gave way before the advancing fire.* **2.** To abandon oneself: *Don't give way to panic.* **3.** To collapse; break: *The old flooring might give way.* [First written down about 725 in Old English and spelled *giefan*.] **—giv′er** *n.*

give-and-take also **give and take** (gĭv′ən tāk′) *n.* **1.** Willingness on both sides to make concessions; compromise: *the give-and-take necessary to reach an agreement.* **2.** A lively exchange of talk: *The give-and-take of our student debates.*

give•a•way (gĭv′ə wā′) *n.* *Informal.* **1.** Something given away or sold at a very low price. **2.** Something revealed or exposed, often by accident: *His refusal to answer the question was a giveaway that he knew more about what happened.*

giv•en (gĭv′ən) *v.* Past participle of **give.** —*adj.* **1.** Specified; stated: *obtain all the facts on one given country.* **2.** Assumed; acknowledged; granted: *Given the condition of the car, it's a wonder it runs at all.* **3.** Having a tendency; inclined: *given to talking too much.*

given name *n.* The name given to a person at birth or at baptism: *Elizabeth is her given name; Morrison is her family name.*

giz•mo (gĭz′mō) *n., pl.* **giz•mos.** A gadget whose name is forgotten or not yet known.

giz•zard (gĭz′ərd) *n.* The second stomach of a bird, often containing sand or gravel, that assists in the breakdown of food before digestion.

gla•cial (glā′shəl) *adj.* **1.** Of, relating to, or produced by a glacier: *Glacial lakes are scattered around the area.* **2.** Suggesting the extreme slowness of a glacier. **3.** Extremely cold; icy. **4.** Lacking warmth or friendliness: *a glacial stare.* **—gla′cial•ly** *adv.*

glacial epoch *n.* **1.** Any of several geological times when much of the earth was covered with glaciers; an ice age. **2.** The most recent ice age in the Northern Hemisphere; the Ice Age or Pleistocene Epoch. See table on page 424.

gla•cier (glā′shər) *n.* A large mass of ice slowly moving over a mountain or through a valley, formed over many years from packed snow in areas where snow accumulates faster than it melts. [First written down in 1744 in Modern English, from Latin *glaciēs*, ice.]

glad (glăd) *adj.* **glad•der, glad•dest. 1.** Experiencing or showing joy and pleasure: *We were so glad to get your letter.* **2.** Providing joy and pleasure: *The wedding was a glad occasion.* **3.** Pleased; willing: *I would be glad to help.* **—glad′ly** *adv.* **—glad′ness** *n.*

Synonyms: glad, happy, cheerful, lighthearted, joyful. These adjectives mean being in or showing good spirits. **Glad** often means satisfied with immediate circumstances: *I am so glad we finally met.* **Happy** can mean feeling pleasurable contentment, as from a sense of fulfillment: *Jane is happy with her new job.* **Cheerful** means having good spirits, as from being pleased: *Leroy tried to remain cheerful while he was in the hospital.* **Lighthearted** means free of cares and worries: *Summertime always puts you in a lighthearted mood.* **Joyful** means having great happiness and liveliness: *Their wedding was a joyful occasion.*

glad•den (glăd′n) *tr.v.* **glad•dened, glad•den•ing, glad•dens.** To make glad: *The good news gladdened our hearts.*

glade (glād) *n.* An open space in a forest.

glad•i•a•tor (glăd′ē ā′tər) *n.* In ancient Rome, a person, especially a slave, captive, or criminal, who engaged in mortal combat in an arena to entertain the public. [First written down before 1439 in Middle English, from Latin *gladiātor*, from *gladius*, sword.]

glad•i•o•lus (glăd′ē ō′ləs) also **glad•i•o•la** (glăd′ē ō′lə) *n., pl.* **glad•i•o•li** (glăd′ē ō′lī) or **glad•i•o•lus•es** also **glad•i•o•las.** Any of numerous plants having leaves shaped like swords and a long cluster of showy, variously colored flowers. [First written down in 1440 in Middle English and spelled *gladiol*, from Latin *gladiolus*, wild iris, diminutive of *gladius*, sword.]

glad•some (glăd′səm) *adj.* **1.** Glad; joyful. **2.** Causing gladness; pleasant: *gladsome tidings.* **—glad′some•ly** *adv.* **—glad′some•ness** *n.*

glam•or (glăm′ər) *n.* Variant of **glamour.**

glam•or•ize also **glam•our•ize** (glăm′ə rīz′) *tr.v.* **glam•or•ized, glam•or•iz•ing, glam•or•iz•es** also **glam•our•ized, glam•our•iz•ing, glam•our•iz•es.** To make glamorous: *Motion pictures have glamorized the life of gangsters.*

glam•or•ous also **glam•our•ous** (glăm′ər əs) *adj.* Having or showing glamour; fascinating; alluring: *a glamorous life of wealth and adventure.* **—glam′or•ous•ly** *adv.* **—glam′or•ous•ness** *n.*

glam•our also **glam•or** (glăm′ər) *n.* An air of romantic charm or excitement surrounding a person or thing; allure: *the glamour of being a movie star.* [First written down in 1720 in Modern English and spelled *glamour*, magic spell, from *grammar* (from the association of learning with magic).]

glance (glăns) *intr.v.* **glanced, glanc•ing, glanc•es. 1.** To look briefly or hastily: *They didn't even glance at my new outfit.* **2.** To strike a surface at such an angle as to fly off to one side: *The ax glanced off the log and struck the ground.* —*n.* **1.** A brief or hasty look: *a quick glance over the shoulder.* **2.** A glancing off; a deflection. **—*idiom.* at first glance.** On initial consideration: *At first glance it seemed impossible, but then I saw how we could make it work.*

gland (glănd) *n.* **1.** An organ in the body that produces some special substance, such as a hormone or an enzyme. The liver, the kidneys, the pancreas, and the thyroid are glands. **2.** A lymph node or other organ of the body that resembles a gland.

glan•du•lar (glăn′jə lər) *adj.* **1.** Of, relating to, affecting, or resembling a gland or its secretion. **2.** Having glands.

glare (glâr) *v.* **glared, glar•ing, glares.** —*intr.* **1.** To stare fiercely or angrily: *The angry customer glared at the sales clerk.* **2.** To shine intensely; dazzle: *The sun glared off the windshield.* —*tr.* To express with a fierce or angry stare: *The prisoners glared defiance at their captors.* —*n.* **1.** A fixed angry stare. **2.** A very strong and blinding light: *the sun's glare.* [First written down in 1275 in Middle English and spelled *glaren*, to glitter.]

glar•ing (glâr′ĭng) *adj.* **1.** Staring fiercely or angrily: *glaring eyes.* **2.** Shining intensely: *a glaring summer sun.* **3.** Too showy; gaudy: *The clown wore a suit of glaring colors.* **4.** Obvious; conspicuous: *a glaring error.* **—glar′ing•ly** *adv.*

glar•y (glâr′ē) *adj.* **glar•i•er, glar•i•est.** Dazzlingly bright; glaring.

Glas•gow (glăs′kō *or* glăs′gō *or* glăz′gō). The largest city of Scotland, in the southwest part of the country west of Edinburgh. It was founded in the late sixth century. Population, 767,456.

glass (glăs) *n.* **1.** A hard material made by melting sand with soda and lime. Glass is generally transparent or translucent and usually breaks or shatters easily. **2.** Something made of glass, as a mirror or a windowpane: *When I threw the ball it broke the glass.* **3.** A container used for drinking, especially one made of glass. **4.** The amount contained in a drinking container; a glassful: *spill a whole glass of milk.* **5. glasses.** A pair of lenses mounted in a light frame, used to correct faulty vision or protect the eyes. —*tr.v.* **glassed, glass•ing, glass•es. 1.** To cover with glass: *We glassed in the breezeway.* **2.** To put into a glass container: *The professor glassed the butterfly collection.* [First written down about 750 in Old English and spelled *glæs*.]

glass blowing *n.* The art or process of shaping an object from a mass of molten glass by blowing air into it through a tube. **—glass blower** *n.*

glass•ful (glăs′fo͝ol′) *n.* The quantity that a glass can hold.

glass snake *n.* Any of several legless lizards that look like a snake and have a tail that breaks off very easily.

glass•ware (glăs′wâr′) *n.* Objects, especially containers, made of glass.

glass•y (glăs′ē) *adj.* **glass•i•er, glass•i•est. 1.** Resembling glass; smooth: *the glassy surface of a highly polished table.* **2.** Having no expression; lifeless; blank: *a glassy stare.* **—glass′i•ly** *adv.* **—glass′i•ness** *n.*

glau•co•ma (glou kō′mə *or* glô kō′mə) *n.* An eye disease in which the pressure of fluid inside the eyeball becomes abnormally high, often damaging the optic nerve and leading eventually to blindness.

glaze (glāz) *n.* **1.** A thin, smooth, shiny coating: *A glaze of ice covered the roads.* **2.** A coating, as of colored material, applied to ceramics before firing in a kiln. —*v.* **glazed, glaz•ing, glaz•es.** —*tr.* **1.** To fit or furnish with glass: *glaze a window.* **2.** To apply a glaze to: *The baker glazed the buns with egg white. The potter glazed the mugs and bowls.* —*intr.* To become glazed or glassy: *His eyes glazed over from boredom.*

gla•zier (glā′zhər) *n.* A person who cuts and fits glass for windows, doors, and picture frames.

gleam (glēm) *n.* **1.** A brief beam or flash of light: *occasional gleams of sunshine through the clouds.* **2.** A steady glow: *the soft pale gleam of moonlight.* **3.** A brief or faint indication; a trace: *a gleam of hope.* —*intr.v.* **gleamed, gleam•ing, gleams.** To give off a gleam; shine: *The frost gleamed like diamonds.*

glean (glēn) *tr.v.* **gleaned, glean•ing, gleans. 1.** To gather (grain) left behind by reapers. **2.** To gather bit by bit: *After weeks of investigation, the reporter gleaned enough information for the article.* **—glean′er** *n.*

glee (glē) *n.* **1.** A feeling of delight; joy. **2.** An un-

gladiolus

glass blowing

ă	pat	oi	boy
ā	pay	ou	out
âr	care	o͝o	took
ä	father	o͞o	boot
ĕ	pet	ŭ	cut
ē	be	ûr	urge
ĭ	pit	th	thin
ī	pie	*th*	this
îr	pier	hw	whoop
ŏ	pot	zh	vision
ō	toe	ə	about
ô	paw	N	*French* bon

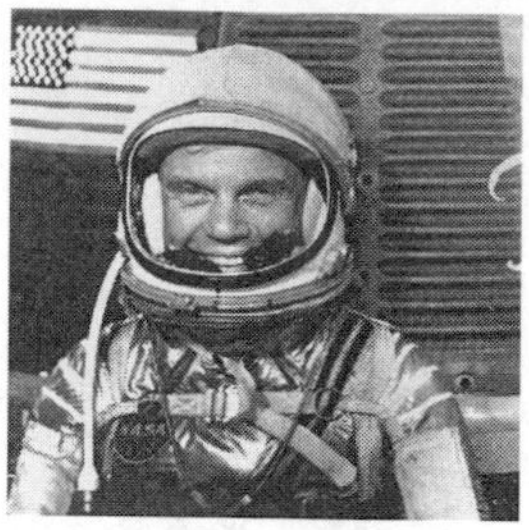

John Glenn

glider
Glider towed by larger aircraft

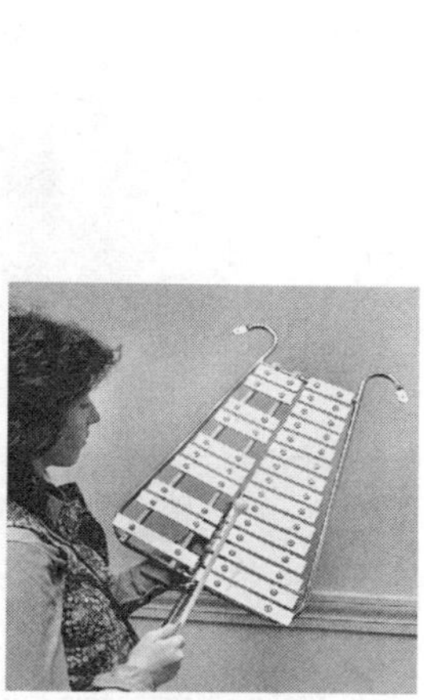

glockenspiel

accompanied song for three or more male voices, popular in the 18th century.

glee club *n.* A group of singers who perform usually short pieces of choral music.

glee•ful (**glē′**fəl) *adj.* Full of glee; merry. —**glee′ful•ly** *adv.* —**glee′ful•ness** *n.*

glen (glĕn) *n.* A valley.

Glenn (glĕn), **John Herschel, Jr.** Born 1921. American astronaut who in 1962 was the first American to orbit the earth.

glib (glĭb) *adj.* **glib•ber, glib•best.** Speaking or writing smoothly but suggesting lack of thought or sincerity: *a glib reply to a serious question.* —**glib′ly** *adv.* —**glib′ness** *n.*

glide (glīd) *v.* **glid•ed, glid•ing, glides.** —*intr.* **1.** To move smoothly and with little effort: *The skaters glided over the ice.* See Synonyms at **slide. 2.** To pass or occur without notice: *The weekend had glided by.* **3.** To fly without using propelling power. —*tr.* To cause to move smoothly and with little effort. —*n.* **1.** The act or process of gliding. **2.** A smooth effortless movement.

glid•er (**glī′**dər) *n.* **1.** An aircraft that has no engine and is designed to glide after being towed aloft by an airplane or launched from a catapult. **2.** A long swinging seat that hangs in a vertical frame.

glim•mer (**glĭm′**ər) *n.* **1.** A dim or unsteady light; a flicker: *the glimmer of candles in the breeze.* **2.** A faint indication; a trace: *a glimmer of understanding.* —*intr.v.* **glim•mered, glim•mer•ing, glim•mers.** To give off a dim or flickering light: *A single lamp glimmered in the window.*

glimpse (glĭmps) *n.* A brief incomplete view or look: *caught just a glimpse of the sun on the cloudy day.* —*v.* **glimpsed, glimps•ing, glimps•es.** —*tr.* To obtain a brief incomplete view of: *glimpsed a speeding car.* —*intr.* To look for a moment: *glimpse at the news on TV.*

glint (glĭnt) *n.* A brief flash of light; a sparkle: *a glint in her eyes.* —*intr.v.* **glint•ed, glint•ing, glints.** To gleam or flash; sparkle: *The creek glinted in the moonlight.*

glis•san•do (glĭ **sän′**dō) *n., pl.* **glis•san•di** (glĭ-**sän′**dē) or **glis•san•dos.** In music, a rapid glide from one tone to another.

glis•ten (**glĭs′**ən) *intr.v.* **glis•tened, glis•ten•ing, glis•tens.** To shine with a sparkling reflected light: *The snow glistened in the sunlight.* —*n.* A shine or sparkle.

glitch (glĭch) *n.* A mishap, malfunction, or problem: *a glitch in the computer program.*

glit•ter (**glĭt′**ər) *n.* **1.** A sparkling light or brightness: *the glitter of polished silver.* **2.** Striking attractiveness or showiness: *the glitter of the queen's coronation.* —*intr.v.* **glit•tered, glit•ter•ing, glit•ters. 1.** To sparkle brilliantly: *The stars glittered in the night sky.* **2.** To be brilliantly, often deceptively attractive: *The chance of making a fortune glittered in front of them.* —**glit′ter•y** *adj.*

gloat (glōt) *intr.v.* **gloat•ed, gloat•ing, gloats.** To feel or express great, often spiteful pleasure: *The rival team gloated over their victory.*

glob (glŏb) *n.* A drop or rounded mass or lump: *a glob of mashed potatoes.*

glob•al (**glō′**bəl) *adj.* **1.** Shaped like a globe; spherical. **2.** Of the entire earth; worldwide: *a global population figure.* —**glob′al•ly** *adv.*

globe (glōb) *n.* **1.** An object having the general shape of a ball or sphere, especially a representation of the earth or the celestial sphere. **2.** The earth: *The space station is designed to circle the globe constantly.* **3.** A spherical container, especially a glass sphere covering a light bulb. [First written down about 1450 in Middle English, from Latin *globus.*]

glob•u•lar (**glŏb′**yə lər) *adj.* **1.** Having the shape of a globe or globule. **2.** Made up of globules.

glob•ule (**glŏb′**yo͞ol) *n.* A very small rounded mass, especially a small drop of liquid.

glob•u•lin (**glŏb′**yə lĭn) *n.* Any of a class of simple proteins found in blood, milk, muscle tissue, and plant seeds, that are insoluble in water and coagulate when heated.

glock•en•spiel (**glŏk′**ən spēl′ *or* **glŏk′**ən shpēl′) *n.* A musical instrument consisting of a series of tuned metal bars and played with two light hammers. [First written down in 1825 in Modern English, from German : *Glocken,* bells + *Spiel,* play.]

gloom (glo͞om) *n.* **1.** Partial or total darkness; dimness: *He peered into the gloom of the night.* **2.** Lowness of spirit; sadness; depression.

gloom•y (**glo͞o′**mē) *adj.* **gloom•i•er, gloom•i•est. 1.** Partially or totally dark; dismal: *a gloomy deserted castle.* **2.** Showing or filled with gloom; dejected; sad: *His gloomy face indicated the news was not good.* **3.** Causing low spirits; depressing. —**gloom′i•ly** *adv.* —**gloom′i•ness** *n.*

Glo•ri•a (**glôr′**ē ə) *n.* **1.** A Christian hymn of praise to God, beginning with the Latin word *Gloria.* **2.** The music for one of these hymns.

glo•ri•fy (**glôr′**ə fī′) *tr.v.* **glo•ri•fied, glo•ri•fy•ing, glo•ri•fies. 1.** To give honor or high praise to; exalt: *The Egyptians glorified their king by building a pyramid.* **2.** To give glory or honor to, especially through worship: *prayers that glorify God.* **3.** To make seem more glorious or excellent than is actually the case: *Their description glorified the old house as a mansion.* —**glo′ri•fi•ca′tion** (glôr′ə fĭ **kā′**shən) *n.* —**glo′ri•fi′er** *n.*

glo•ri•ous (**glôr′**ē əs) *adj.* **1.** Having or deserving glory; famous: *The glorious achievements of the Renaissance.* **2.** Giving or advancing glory: *a glorious victory.* **3.** Having great beauty or splendor; magnificent: *a glorious sunset.* —**glo′ri•ous•ly** *adv.*

glo•ry (**glôr′**ē) *n., pl.* **glo•ries. 1.** Great honor or praise given by others; fame; renown: *The swimmer won glory by breaking the world record.* **2.** Something that brings honor, praise, or renown: *a symphony that is one of the glories of 18th-century music.* **3.** Adoration or praise offered in worship. **4.** Great beauty: *The sun was setting in a blaze of glory.* **5.** A period of highest achievement or prosperity: *Rome in its greatest glory.* —*intr.v.* **glo•ried, glo•ry•ing, glo•ries.** To rejoice: *The team gloried in its victory.* [First written down before 1200 in Middle English and spelled *gloire,* from Latin *glōria.*]

gloss[1] (glôs *or* glŏs) *n.* **1.** A shine on a surface; a sheen: *the gloss of a polished table.* **2.** A superficially attractive appearance intended to hide the real nature of something. —*tr.v.* **glossed, gloss•ing, gloss•es. 1.** To give a bright shine or luster to. **2.** To make attractive or acceptable by concealing or misrepresenting: *The committee glossed over serious problems in its report.* [First written down in 1538 in Modern English, perhaps of Scandinavian origin; akin to Icelandic *glossi,* a spark.]

gloss[2] (glôs *or* glŏs) *n.* **1.** A brief note that explains or translates a difficult word, phrase, or section of a text or manuscript. **2.** A glossary. —*tr.v.* **glossed, gloss•ing, gloss•es.** To provide (a text) with glosses: *This science textbook glosses all technical terms.* [First written down about 1300 in Middle English and spelled *glose,* from Late Latin *glōssa,* foreign word requiring explanation, from Greek *glōssa,* tongue, language.]

glos•sa•ry (**glô′**sə rē *or* **glŏs′**ə rē) *n., pl.* **glos•sa•ries.** A list of specialized words with their definitions: *a glossary of computer terms.*

gloss•y (**glô′**sē *or* **glŏs′**ē) *adj.* **gloss•i•er, gloss•i•**

est. Smooth and shiny: *Satin is a glossy fabric.* **—gloss′i•ly** *adv.* **—gloss′i•ness** *n.*

glot•tal (glŏt′l) *adj.* Relating to the glottis.

glot•tis (glŏt′ĭs) *n., pl.* **glot•tis•es** or **glot•ti•des** (glŏt′ĭ dēz′). The space between the vocal cords at the upper part of the larynx.

glove (glŭv) *n.* **1.** A covering for the hand, with a separate section for each finger and the thumb. **2.a.** A special covering for the hand, often of padded leather, used in playing baseball, handball, or some other sport. **b.** A boxing glove. *—tr.v.* **gloved, glov•ing, gloves. 1.** To cover or provide with a glove. **2.** To catch in a baseball glove: *The outfielder gloved a long fly ball.* [First written down about 725 in Old English and spelled *glōf*.]

glow (glō) *intr.v.* **glowed, glow•ing, glows. 1.** To shine brightly and steadily with heat: *The embers glowed in the fireplace.* **2.** To have a bright warm color: *The skier's cheeks glowed in the cold.* **3.** To be radiant with emotion: *glow with happiness. —n.* **1.** A light given off by something that is hot. **2.** A brilliance or warmth of color: *the glow of buildings facing the setting sun.* **3.** A feeling of warmth, especially when caused by emotion: *the glow on a child's happy face.* [First written down about 1000 in Old English and spelled *glōwan*.]

glow•er (glou′ər) *intr.v.* **glow•ered, glow•er•ing, glow•ers.** To look or stare angrily: *The unfriendly neighbors glowered at us. —n.* An angry or threatening stare.

glow•ing (glō′ĭng) *adj.* **1.** Giving or reflecting brilliant light: *glowing coals.* **2.** Having a rich warm color, as from health or strong emotion: *a glowing complexion.* **3.** Enthusiastic; highly favorable: *we received glowing reports of their success.* **—glow′ing•ly** *adv.*

glow•worm (glō′wûrm′) *n.* Any of various female beetles or beetle larvae that give off a glowing light, especially the larva or wingless female of the firefly.

glu•cose (glo͞o′kōs′) *n.* **1.** A common kind of sugar found in plant and animal tissue. In animals, carbohydrates carried in the blood are mainly in the form of glucose. Plants make cellulose and starch from glucose. **2.** A thick mixture of different sugars and water, used in commercial baking, tanning, and in treating tobacco.

glue (glo͞o) *n.* **1.** A thick sticky substance used to join things together, made by boiling animal skins, bones, and hooves with water. **2.** A similar adhesive substance made of resins, silicons, polyethylene, or other material. *—tr.v.* **glued, glu•ing, glues. 1.** To stick or fasten together with glue: *glue the broken leg of a chair.* **2.** To fix or hold firmly as if with glue: *The dog glued its eyes on the stranger.*

glum (glŭm) *adj.* **glum•mer, glum•mest.** Feeling or appearing sad or dejected; gloomy: *a glum look on his face.* **—glum′ly** *adv.* **—glum′ness** *n.*

glut (glŭt) *tr.v.* **glut•ted, glut•ting, gluts. 1.** To fill beyond capacity, especially with food: *The lions slept after glutting themselves on their kill.* **2.** To provide (a market) with too many goods so that the supply is much greater than the demand. *—n.* An excess amount; an oversupply: *A glut of gasoline caused lower prices.*

glu•ten (glo͞ot′n) *n.* A tough sticky plant protein found in grains such as corn and wheat, used as an adhesive and as a flour substitute.

glu•ti•nous (glo͞ot′n əs) *adj.* Resembling glue; thick and sticky: *a glutinous mixture of flour and water.*

glut•ton (glŭt′n) *n.* **1.** A person who eats to excess. **2.** A person with an unusually great capacity to receive or withstand something: *a glutton for work.* **—glut′ton•ous** *adj.* **—glut′ton•ous•ly** *adv.* **—glut′ton•ous•ness** *n.*

glut•ton•y (glŭt′n ē) *n., pl.* **glut•ton•ies.** Excess in eating.

glyc•er•in also **glyc•er•ine** (glĭs′ər ĭn) *n.* Glycerol.

glyc•er•ol (glĭs′ə rôl′ *or* glĭs′ə rōl′ *or* glĭs′ə rŏl′) *n.* A sweet syrupy liquid obtained from animal fats and oils and having the formula $C_3H_8O_3$. It is used as a solvent, a sweetener, and an antifreeze, and in the manufacture of explosives and soaps.

gly•co•gen (glī′kə jən) *n.* A carbohydrate having the formula $(C_6H_{10}O_5)_n$. It is stored in the muscles and the liver of animals and is converted to glucose for energy.

gm. *abbr.* An abbreviation of gram.

G-man (jē′măn′) *n.* An agent of the Federal Bureau of Investigation.

gnarl (närl) *n.* A knot in wood: *a smooth board without gnarls. —tr.v.* **gnarled, gnarl•ing, gnarls.** To make knotted or deformed; twist: *Disease gnarled the patient's fingers.* [First written down in 1824 in Modern English, from *gnarled*, probably from Middle English *knarre*, knot in wood.]

gnarled (närld) *adj.* Having gnarls; knotty and misshapen: *the gnarled boards on the side of an old barn.*

gnash (năsh) *tr.v.* **gnashed, gnash•ing, gnash•es.** To grind (the teeth) together. [First written down about 1300 in Middle English and spelled *gnaisten*, possibly of Scandinavian origin; akin to Old Norse *gnastan*, a gnashing.]

gnat (năt) *n.* Any of various very small winged insects that give itching bites. Gnats suck blood or plant juices. [First written down before 830 in Old English and spelled *gneat*.]

gnaw (nô) *v.* **gnawed, gnaw•ing, gnaws.** *—tr.* **1.** To bite, chew, or erode with the teeth: *animals gnawing the bark of trees.* **2.** To produce by gnawing: *Rats gnawed a hole in the wall.* **3.** To reduce gradually as if by gnawing: *The waves gnawed at the base of the cliff during high tide.* **4.** To cause distress or pain to. *—intr.* **1.** To bite or chew on: *The dog gnawed on the rope.* **2.** To trouble or distress: *The lack of success gnawed at the scientist for weeks.* [First written down before 1000 in Old English and spelled *gnagan*.]

gneiss (nīs) *n.* A type of metamorphic rock consisting of light-colored layers, usually of quartz and feldspar, alternating with dark-colored layers of other minerals. [First written down in 1757 in Modern English, from German *Gneis*.]

❑ *These sound alike:* **gneiss, nice** (pleasant).

gnome (nōm) *n.* In folklore, a dwarf that dwells underground and guards treasure. [First written down in 1712 in Modern English, from New Latin *gnomus*.]

gnu (no͞o *or* nyo͞o) *n.* Either of two large African antelopes having a beard and mane, a long tufted tail, and curved horns. [First written down in 1777 in Modern English, from Xhosa *i-ngu*, white-tailed gnu.]

❑ *These sound alike:* **gnu, knew** (had knowledge), **new** (not used).

go (gō) *v.* **went** (wĕnt), **gone** (gôn *or* gŏn), **go•ing, goes** (gōz). *—intr.* **1.** To move along or forward; proceed: *The bus went along steadily in the rain.* **2.** To move or proceed to a specified place; advance: *I am going to New York.* **3.** To move from a place; depart: *We must go at once.* **4.** To function, operate, move, or work: *A battery makes the watch go.* **5.** To take part or continue in an activity of: *go study; go skating.* **6.** To pursue a course: *go to a lot of trouble; go too far.* **7.a.** To belong in a definite place or position: *This book goes on that shelf.* **b.** To be suitable as an accessory: *Does this tie go with my shirt?* **8.** To extend between two points or in a certain direction: *The windows go from the ceiling*

gnu
White-tailed gnu

Usage: go

Some people use **go** when they report speech, as in *Then he goes, "You think you're on time, don't you?"* You should avoid using **go** in this way in your school writing and speaking.

ă	pat	oi	boy
ā	pay	ou	out
âr	care	o͝o	took
ä	father	o͞o	boot
ĕ	pet	ŭ	cut
ē	be	ûr	urge
ĭ	pit	th	thin
ī	pie	*th*	this
îr	pier	hw	whoop
ŏ	pot	zh	vision
ō	toe	ə	about
ô	paw	N	*French* bon

goatee

goblet

Early 19th-century German silver goblet

Goethe

1791 engraving by Johann Heinrich Lips (1758–1817)

goggles

Ski goggles

to the floor. The road goes north. **9.** To pass; elapse: *Time goes quickly when you are busy.* **10.** To be allotted or awarded: *First prize went to my friend. This money goes for food.* **11.** To proceed or end in a particular way; turn out: *How did your day go? How does the rest of the story go?* **12.** To be expressed or phrased: *How does that nursery rhyme go?* **13.a.** To become weak; fail: *My eyes are going.* **b.** To come apart; break up: *The pier looks about ready to go.* **14.** To be sold or auctioned off: *Most of the old books went for high prices.* **15.** To come to be in a certain state or condition: *go mad; go to sleep; a tire going flat.* **16.** Used to indicate future intention or expectation: *I am going to climb that mountain.* —*tr.* To proceed or move along: *We went separate ways.* —*n., pl.* **goes. 1.** *Informal.* An attempt; an effort: *Let's have a go at the puzzle.* **2.** *Informal.* Something successful; a success: *They tried to make a go of their store.* **3.** *Informal.* Energy; vitality: *That athlete has got a lot of go and will be a winner.* —*adj. Informal.* Ready for action or working correctly: *Everything is go for the parade.* ***—idioms.*** **go about.** To set about to do; undertake: *How does one go about building a house?* **go along.** To cooperate: *Why don't you stop criticizing the project and go along?* **go around. 1.** To satisfy a demand or requirement: *We have enough food to go around.* **2.** To go here and there; move from place to place. **3.** To circulate: *rumors going around.* **go at. 1.** To attack, especially with energy. **2.** To approach; undertake: *He went at the assignment diligently.* **go back on.** To fail to honor or keep: *Don't go back on your word!* **go by.** To elapse; pass: *Time goes by fast sometimes.* **go down. 1.a.** To drop below the horizon; set: *The sun went down.* **b.** To fall to the ground. **c.** To sink. **2.** To be easy to swallow: *This cough syrup goes right down.* **3.** To come to be remembered in posterity: *He went down in history as a famous inventor.* **go for. 1.** *Informal.* To have a special liking for: *I really go for jazz.* **2.** To attack. **go in for.** To have an interest or take part in: *She goes in for water skiing.* **go off. 1.** To explode: *fireworks going off.* **2.** To make a noise; sound: *The alarm went off, but it was just a test.* **3.** To leave: *They went off for a hike.* **go on. 1.** To take place; happen: *What's going on?* **2.a.** To continue: *How long has this discussion been going on?* **b.** To keep on (doing something): *They went on talking.* **c.** To proceed: *She went on to be a famous scientist.* **3.** *Informal.* To talk volubly: *He does go on.* **go out. 1.** To become extinguished. **2.a.** To go outdoors; leave one's residence. **b.** To take part in social life outside the home: *Let's go out for ice cream.* **3.** To become unfashionable: *That dance went out years ago.* **go out of (one's) way.** To inconvenience oneself in doing something beyond what is required. **go over. 1.** To gain acceptance or approval: *My idea went over well.* **2.** To examine: *Did you go over my paper yet?* **go steady.** To date someone exclusively. **go through. 1.** To examine carefully: *I've gone through your paper and it's great!* **2.** To experience: *We all go through some sad times.* **go under.** To fail: *The business went under.* **go with.** To date regularly. **go without saying.** To be self-evident: *Some rules go without saying.* **on the go.** Constantly busy or active. **to go.** To be taken out, as restaurant food or drink: *He ordered a pizza to go.* —SEE NOTE on page 431.

goad (gōd) *n.* **1.** A long stick with a pointed end used for prodding animals, especially cattle. **2.** Something that prods or urges: *Competition is often a goad to hard work.* —*tr.v.* **goad•ed, goad•ing, goads.** To prod with or as if with a goad: *The bad grade goaded us to study harder.* [First written down about 725 in Old English and spelled *gād.*]

go-a•head (gō'ə hĕd') *Informal. n.* Permission to go ahead or proceed.

goal (gōl) *n.* **1.** The purpose toward which one is working; an objective: *The student's goal was to become a doctor.* **2.** The finish of a race. **3.a.** In certain sports, a structure or an area into which players must propel the ball or puck in order to score. **b.** The score awarded for doing this. [First written down before 1333 in Middle English and spelled *gol,* boundary.]

goal•ie (gō'lē) *n.* A goalkeeper.

goal•keep•er (gōl'kē'pər) *n.* The player who defends the goal in sports such as hockey and soccer.

goal line *n.* A line at either end of a playing area, on which a goal or goal post is positioned.

goal post *n.* One of a pair of posts often joined with a crossbar and set at each end of a playing field to form a goal.

goat (gōt) *n.* **1.** Any of various hoofed mammals having hollow horns and a beard, related to the sheep and raised in many parts of the world for wool, milk, and meat. **2.** *Informal.* A scapegoat. [First written down about 700 in Old English and spelled *gāt.*]

goat•ee (gō tē') *n.* A small beard ending in a point just below a man's chin.

goat•skin (gōt'skĭn') *n.* **1.** The skin of a goat. **2.** Leather made from the skin of a goat. **3.** A container, as for water, made out of this leather.

gob (gŏb) *n.* **1.** A small piece or lump: *a gob of wax.* **2.** *Informal.* A large quantity, as of money. Often used in the plural. [First written down about 1382 in Middle English and spelled *gobbe,* probably from Old French *gobe,* mouthful.]

gob•ble[1] (gŏb'əl) *tr.v.* **gob•bled, gob•bling, gob•bles.** To devour in big greedy gulps. [First written down in 1601 in Modern English, from Middle English *gobben,* to drink greedily, probably from *gobbe,* lump, mouthful.]

gob•ble[2] (gŏb'əl) *n.* The throaty chortling sound made by a male turkey. —*intr.v.* **gob•bled, gob•bling, gob•bles.** To make this sound. [First written down in 1680 in Modern English, of imitative origin.]

gob•ble•dy•gook also **gob•ble•de•gook** (gŏb'-əl dē go͝ok') *n.* Unclear, often wordy speech or writing. [First written down in 1944 in American English, imitative of the gobbling of a turkey.]

gob•bler (gŏb'lər) *n.* A male turkey.

go-be•tween (gō'bĭ twēn') *n.* A person who acts as an intermediary or a messenger between two sides.

Go•bi (gō'bē). A desert of southeast Mongolia and northern China.

gob•let (gŏb'lĭt) *n.* A drinking glass with a stem and base.

gob•lin (gŏb'lĭn) *n.* An ugly elfin creature of folklore, thought to cause mischief or evil. [First written down before 1320 in Middle English and spelled *gobilin,* from the Norman French name of a ghost that supposedly haunted the town of Évreux in the 12th century.]

god (gŏd) *n.* **1. God.** A being regarded as the creator and ruler of the universe, forming the object of worship in many religions. **2.** A being of supernatural powers, worshiped by a people, especially a male being thought to control some part of nature. **3.** An image or idol of a god. **4.** Something considered to be of great value or high importance: *Absolute power was his god.* [First written down about 725 in Old English.]

god•child (gŏd'chīld') *n.* A child for whom a person serves as sponsor at baptism.

god•daugh•ter (gŏd'dô'tər) *n.* A female godchild.

god•dess (gŏd'ĭs) *n.* **1.** A female being of supernatural powers, worshiped by a people. **2.** An image or idol of a goddess.

god•fa•ther (gŏd′fä′*th*ər) *n.* A man who serves as sponsor at one's baptism.

god•head (gŏd′hĕd′) *n.* **1.** The essential and divine nature of God; divinity. **2. Godhead.** God, especially the Christian Trinity.

god•less (gŏd′lĭs) *adj.* **1.** Not believing in God or a god. **2.** Immoral; wicked. **—god′less•ly** *adv.* **—god′less•ness** *n.*

god•like (gŏd′līk′) *adj.* Resembling or of the nature of God or a god; divine.

god•ly (gŏd′lē) *adj.* **god•li•er, god•li•est.** Having great reverence for God; pious. **—god′li•ness** *n.*

god•moth•er (gŏd′mŭ*th*′ər) *n.* A woman who serves as sponsor at one's baptism.

god•par•ent (gŏd′pâr′ənt *or* gŏd′păr′ənt) *n.* A godfather or godmother.

god•send (gŏd′sĕnd′) *n.* Something wanted or needed that comes or happens unexpectedly: *Her brother's volunteering to watch the baby was a godsend when she needed to study.*

god•son (gŏd′sŭn′) *n.* A male godchild.

God•speed (gŏd′spēd′) *n.* Success or good fortune: *With a wish of Godspeed they bid me farewell.*

Godt•håb (gôt′hôp′). The capital of Greenland, on the southwest coast of the island on **Godthåb Fjord.** It was founded in 1721. Population, 10,559.

Goe•the (gœ′tə), **Johann Wolfgang von.** 1749–1832. German writer and scientist who spent 50 years on his two-part dramatic poem *Faust* (published 1808 and 1832).

go-get•ter (gō′gĕt′ər *or* gō′gĕt′ər) *n. Informal.* An energetic person with much determination and ambition.

gog•gle (gŏg′əl) *intr.v.* **gog•gled, gog•gling, gog•gles.** To stare with wide and bulging eyes.

gog•gle-eyed (gŏg′əl īd′) *adj.* Having prominent or rolling eyes.

gog•gles (gŏg′əlz) *pl.n.* A pair of eyeglasses worn tight against the head to protect the eyes.

Gogh (gō), **Vincent van.** See Vincent **van Gogh.**

go•ing (gō′ĭng) *n.* **1.** The act of leaving or moving away; departure: *comings and goings of passengers in the terminal.* **2.** The condition of the ground or road in as it affects how one walks or rides: *It was rough going over the icy roads, but we made it.* **3.** *Informal.* Progress toward a goal: *Learning this new computer program has been easy going.* —*adj.* **1.** Working; running: *The clock is in going order.* **2.** In full operation; flourishing: *Our business is at last a going operation.* **3.** Available or now in existence: *We make the best bikes going.* **4.** Current; prevailing: *The going rates for bank loans will soon increase.*

goi•ter (goi′tər) *n.* An enlargement of the thyroid gland, visible as a swelling at the front of the neck and often associated with a diet that contains too little iodine. [First written down in 1625 in Modern English, from Latin *guttur*, throat.]

gold (gōld) *n.* **1.** *Symbol* **Au** A soft, shiny, yellow element that resists chemical change. It is much used in making fine jewelry and coins. Atomic number 79. See table at **element. 2.** A deep, strong, or metallic yellow: *when fall leaves turn to red and gold.* **3.** Gold coins. **4.** Money; riches. **5.** Something thought of as having great value or goodness: *a heart of gold.* —*adj.* **1.** Relating to or containing gold: *a gold ring; a gold coin.* **2.** Having a deep, strong, or metallic yellow color. [First written down about 725 in Old English.]

gold•brick (gōld′brĭk′) *Slang. n.* A person, especially a soldier, who avoids duties or work. —*intr.v.* **gold•bricked, gold•brick•ing, gold•bricks.** To avoid one's duties or work. **—gold′brick′er** *n.*

Gold Coast (gōld). A section of coastal western Africa along the southeast shore of Ghana. It was named for the large quantities of gold found in the area.

gold•en (gōl′dən) *adj.* **1.** Relating to, made of, or containing gold: *golden earrings.* **2.** Having the color of gold or a yellow color suggestive of gold: *a golden wheat field.* **3.a.** Of great value or importance; precious: *golden memories of a happy childhood.* **b.** Very favorable; excellent: *a golden opportunity.* **4.** Marked by peace, prosperity, and often creativeness: *a golden era in our past.*

golden age *n.* A period usually of peace and prosperity when a nation and its culture are at their height: *Spain's golden age of art and exploration was founded on the riches of the New World.*

Golden Fleece *n.* In Greek mythology, the fleece of the golden ram, stolen by Jason and the Argonauts.

golden mean *n.* The course between extremes; moderation.

gold•en•rod (gōl′dən rŏd′) *n.* Any of numerous plants having clusters of small yellow flowers that bloom on the ends of tall stalks in late summer or fall.

golden rule *n.* The rule of conduct that one should behave toward others as one would have others behave toward oneself.

gold-filled (gōld′fĭld′) *adj.* Made of hard metal with an outer layer of gold: *a gold-filled case for a watch.*

gold•finch (gōld′fĭnch′) *n.* **1.** Any of several small North American finches, of which the male has yellow feathers with a black forehead, wings, and tail. **2.** A European finch having black, yellow, and red markings.

gold•fish (gōld′fĭsh′) *n.* A small freshwater fish, usually orange or reddish, often kept in outdoor ponds and home aquariums.

gold leaf *n.* Gold beaten into extremely thin sheets used for gilding.

Gold•man (gōld′mən), **Emma.** 1869–1940. Russian-born American anarchist who was deported to the Soviet Union in 1919. Her writings include *Living My Life* (1931).

gold rush *n.* A rush of people to an area where gold has been discovered.

gold•smith (gōld′smĭth′) *n.* A person who makes or deals in objects of gold.

Gold•smith (gōld′smĭth′), **Oliver.** 1730?–1774. British writer whose works include the novel *The Vicar of Wakefield* (1766).

gold standard *n.* A monetary standard for which the basic unit of money is equal in value to a specified amount of gold.

golf (gŏlf *or* gôlf) *n.* A game played over a large outdoor course having a series of 9 or 18 holes spaced far apart. A player, using various clubs, tries to take as few strokes as possible in hitting a ball into one hole after another. —*intr.v.* **golfed, golf•ing, golfs.** To play golf. [First written down in 1457 in Middle English.] **—golf′er** *n.*

golf club *n.* **1.** One of a set of clubs, having a slender shaft and a head usually made of wood or iron, used in golf. **2.** An association of golfers.

golf course *n.* A large tract of land laid out for golf.

Gol•go•tha (gŏl′gə thə). Calvary.

Go•li•ath (gə lī′əth). In the Bible, a giant who was killed by David with a stone and sling.

Go•mor•rah (gə môr′ə *or* gə mŏr′ə). An ancient city of Palestine near Sodom that according to the Bible was destroyed by fire because of its wickedness.

–gon *suff.* A suffix that means a specified number of angles: *octagon.*

go•nad (gō′năd′) *n.* An organ in which egg cells or sperm cells are produced; an ovary or a testis.

goldenrod

Emma Goldman

golf

ă	pat	oi	boy
ā	pay	ou	out
âr	care	o͝o	took
ä	father	o͞o	boot
ĕ	pet	ŭ	cut
ē	be	ûr	urge
ĭ	pit	th	thin
ī	pie	*th*	this
îr	pier	hw	whoop
ŏ	pot	zh	vision
ō	toe	ə	about
ô	paw	N	*French* bon

Maud Gonne

Regional Note: goober

Most Southerners know that a **goober** is a peanut. The word *goober* is related to *n-guba*, "peanut," in a Bantu language of west-central Africa. *Goober* is one of a small group of words in English that come from African languages and were brought over by slaves. **Gumbo** is also of Bantu origin, and **okra** and **yam** are of West African origin.

Usage: good

The adjective **good** is often used with linking verbs such as **be**, **seem**, or **appear**: *The future looks good. He seems very good as an actor.* **Good** should not be used as an adverb with other verbs: *The car runs well* (not *good*).

Mikhail Gorbachev
Photographed in 1987

gon•do•la (gŏn′dl ə *or* gŏn **dō′**lə) *n.* **1.** A long narrow boat with a high pointed prow and stern, propelled from the stern by a single oar and used on the canals of Venice. **2.** An open railroad freight car with low sides. **3.** A basket or a cabin attached to the underside of a balloon. **4.** An enclosed car suspended from a cable used for transporting passengers, as up and down a ski slope. [First written down in 1549 in Modern English, from Old Italian *gondula.*]

gon•do•lier (gŏn′dl îr′) *n.* The person who rows a gondola.

gone (gôn *or* gŏn) *v.* Past participle of **go.** —*adj.* **1.** Away from a place; absent: *I'll be gone for a few days.* **2.** Dead. **3.** Used up or consumed: *When natural resources are gone they cannot be replaced. Their strength was gone.*

gon•er (gô′nər *or* **gŏn′**ər) *n. Slang.* A person or thing that is ruined or doomed: *A car with a bent frame is usually a goner.*

gong (gông *or* gŏng) *n.* A saucer-shaped metal disk that produces a loud ringing tone when struck. [First written down about 1600 in Modern English, from Malay *gōng.*]

Gonne (gŏn *or* gŭn), **Maud.** 1865–1953. Irish patriot who was a leader of the Irish independence movement.

gon•or•rhe•a (gŏn′ə **rē′**ə) *n.* A sexually transmitted bacterial disease that causes inflammation of the genitals and urinary tract.

goo (go͞o) *n. Informal.* A sticky wet substance.

goo•ber (**go͞o′**bər) *n. Informal.* A peanut. [First written down in 1933 in American English, of Bantu origin.] —See Note.

good (go͝od) *adj.* **bet•ter** (**bĕt′**ər), **best** (bĕst). **1.** Having positive or desirable qualities; not bad or poor: *a good book; good food.* **2.** Providing a benefit; helpful: *Earthworms are good for our soil.* **3.** Superior to average; skilled: *a good painter.* **4.** Not spoiled; usable: *The milk is still good.* **5.** Genuine; real: *a good dollar bill.* **6.** Valid; true: *a good reason.* **7.** In effect; valid: *The warranty on that car is still good.* **8.** Providing pleasure; enjoyable: *a good time.* **9.** Attractive; handsome: *good looks.* **10.a.** Morally upright: *a good honest person.* **b.** Honorable: *a good name.* **11.a.** Well-behaved; obedient: *a good dog.* **b.** Loyal; devoted: *a good friend.* **12.** Proper; correct: *good manners.* **13.** Substantial; ample: *a good income.* **14.** Not less than; full: *It is a good mile to the station.* **15.** Thorough; complete: *a good housecleaning.* **16.** More than a little likely: *Our team has a good chance of winning the competition.* —*n.* **1.** Something good: *You must learn to accept the bad with the good.* **2.** Benefit; welfare: *for the good of the country.* **3.** Value; use: *What good is a bicycle without a chain?* **4. goods. a.** Things that can be bought and sold; merchandise. **b.** Personal belongings: *They lost all their household goods in the fire.* **c.** *(Used with a singular or plural verb).* Cloth; fabric. ***—idioms.*** **as good as.** Nearly; almost: *This car is as good as new.* **for good.** Permanently; forever: *They left town for good.* **good and.** *Informal.* Very; entirely: *We are good and mad at them.* **no good.** Useless; worthless: *It's no good arguing with them.* **to the good.** Advantageous; in one's favor. [First written down about 725 in Old English and spelled *gōd.*] —See Note.

good-bye or **good•bye** also **good-by** (go͝od **bī′**) *interj.* An expression used to say farewell. —*n., pl.* **good-byes** also **good-bys.** An expression of farewell. [First written down about 1573 in Modern English and spelled *godbwye*, from *God be with you.*]

good-for-noth•ing (**go͝od′**fər **nŭth′**ĭng) *n.* A person considered worthless or useless. —*adj.* Having little worth; useless.

Good Friday *n.* The Friday before Easter, observed by Christians in commemoration of the Crucifixion of Jesus.

good•heart•ed (**go͝od′här′**tĭd) *adj.* Kind and generous: *a goodhearted person.* **—good′heart′ed•ly** *adv.* **—good′heart′ed•ness** *n.*

Good Hope (go͝od′ **hōp′**), **Cape of.** A high ridge on the southwest coast of South Africa jutting into the Atlantic Ocean south of Cape Town.

good-hu•mored (**go͝od′hyo͞o′**mərd) *adj.* Cheerful; amiable: *a good-humored remark.* **—good′-hu′mored•ly** *adv.*

good-look•ing (**go͝od′lo͝ok′**ĭng) *adj.* Having a pleasing appearance; attractive; handsome: *was dressed in good-looking clothes.*

good•ly (**go͝od′**lē) *adj.* **good•li•er, good•li•est. 1.** Rather large; considerable: *a goodly number of people.* **2.** Pleasing in appearance or character: *a goodly house.*

good-na•tured (**go͝od′nā′**chərd) *adj.* Having a pleasant disposition; cheerful. **—good′-na′tured•ly** *adv.* **—good′-na′tured•ness** *n.*

good•ness (**go͝od′**nĭs) *n.* **1.** The quality or condition of being good; excellence. **2.** The best or nutritious part. —*interj.* An expression used to show surprise.

Good Samaritan *n.* **1.** In one of Jesus' parables in the New Testament, the only passerby who helped a man who had been beaten and robbed. **2.** A person who unselfishly helps others; a good neighbor.

good-sized (**go͝od′sīzd′**) *adj.* Of a fairly large size: *a good-sized rabbit.*

good•will also **good will** (**go͝od′wĭl′**) *n.* **1.** An attitude of kindliness or friendliness: *Her goodwill made us feel welcome in the neighborhood.* **2.** Cheerful consent or willingness: *The lender accepted the risk with goodwill.* **3.** A good relationship of a nation with other nations or a business with its customers.

good•y (**go͝od′**ē) *Informal. interj.* An expression used to show delight. —*n.* also **good•ie,** *pl.* **good•ies.** Something attractive or delectable, especially something good to eat.

goo•ey (**go͞o′**ē) *adj.* **goo•i•er, goo•i•est.** Thick and sticky: *gooey tar.*

goof (go͞of) *Slang. n.* **1.** A careless mistake; a slip. **2.** An incompetent or stupid person. —*v.* **goofed, goof•ing, goofs.** —*intr.* **1.** To make a careless mistake; blunder. **2.** To waste or kill time: *We goofed off all afternoon.* —*tr.* To do (something) wrong: *He goofed up his lines in the play.*

goof•y (**go͞o′**fē) *adj.* **goof•i•er, goof•i•est.** *Slang.* Silly; ridiculous: *a goofy mistake.* **—goof′i•ness** *n.*

goo•gol (**go͞o′**gôl′) *n.* The number 10 raised to the 100th power, written as 10^{100} or as 1 followed by 100 zeros. [First written down in 1940 in Modern English, coined at the age of nine by Milton Sirotta, nephew of Edward Kasner (1878–1955), American mathematician.]

goon (go͞on) *n. Slang.* **1.** A thug hired to intimidate or harm people, especially workers on strike. **2.** A stupid or oafish person. [First written down in 1921 in American English, probably from *gooney*, albatross, simpleton.]

goose (go͞os) *n., pl.* **geese** (gēs). **1.a.** Any of various water birds related to the ducks but larger and having a longer neck and a shorter, more pointed bill. **b.** The female of such a bird: *The goose and her gander made a nest by the lake.* **c.** The meat of such a bird, used as food. **2.** *Informal.* A silly person. [First written down about 700 in Old English and spelled *gōs.*]

goose•ber•ry (**go͞os′**bĕr′ē *or* **go͞os′**bə rē) *n.* **1.** A juicy greenish berry of a European shrub, used chiefly for making jam or tarts. **2.** The shrub that bears such berries.

goose bumps *pl.n.* Momentary roughness of the skin caused by tiny bumps that form in the areas surrounding the hairs on the skin as a reaction to cold or fear.

goose flesh *n.* Goose bumps.

goose•neck (go͞os′nĕk′) *n.* A slender curved object or part, such as the flexible shaft of a type of desk lamp.

goose step *n.* A marching step made by swinging the legs from the hips and keeping the knees unbent.

GOP or **G.O.P.** *abbr.* An abbreviation of Grand Old Party (the Republican Party).

go•pher (gō′fər) *n.* **1.** Any of various burrowing North American rodents having large cheek pouches. **2.** A ground squirrel. [First written down in 1814 in American English.]

Gor•ba•chev (gôr′bə chôf′ *or* gôr′bə chŏf′), **Mikhail Sergeyevich.** Born 1931. Soviet politician who served as general secretary of the Communist Party (1985–1991) and president of the U.S.S.R. (1989–1991). He won the 1990 Nobel Peace Prize.

gore[1] (gôr) *tr.v.* **gored, gor•ing, gores.** To pierce or stab with a horn or tusk. [First written down before 1400 in Middle English and spelled *goren*, probably from *gore*, spear, from Old English *gār*.]

gore[2] (gôr) *n.* A triangular piece of cloth forming a part of something, as in a skirt or sail. [First written down before 899 in Old English and spelled *gāra*, triangular piece of land.]

gore[3] (gôr) *n.* Blood, especially dried blood from a wound. [First written down about 725 in Old English and spelled *gor*.]

gorge (gôrj) *n.* A deep narrow passage with steep rocky sides, often with a stream flowing through it: *The gorge was the only pass through the mountains.* —*v.* **gorged, gorg•ing, gorg•es.** —*tr.* **1.** To stuff with food; satiate: *gorged themselves with spaghetti.* **2.** To devour greedily: *gorged my dinner.* —*intr.* To eat greedily.

gor•geous (gôr′jəs) *adj.* Dazzlingly beautiful or magnificent: *The snowcapped mountains were gorgeous in the sunset.* —**gor′geous•ly** *adv.* —**gor′geous•ness** *n.*

Gor•gon (gôr′gən) *n.* In Greek mythology, one of three sisters who have snakes for hair and eyes that if looked into turn the beholder into stone.

go•ril•la (gə rĭl′ə) *n.* An ape of the central African forests and mountains having a heavy stocky body and dark hair. It is the largest and most powerful of the apes.
❑ *These sound alike:* **gorilla, guerrilla** (fighter).

gorse (gôrs) *n.* Any of several spiny shrubs having fragrant yellow flowers.

go•ry (gôr′ē) *adj.* **go•ri•er, go•ri•est. 1.** Covered or stained with gore; bloody. **2.** Full of or marked by bloodshed and violence: *a gory movie.* —**gor′i•ly** *adv.* —**gor′i•ness** *n.*

gosh (gŏsh) *interj.* An expression used to show mild surprise or delight.

gos•hawk (gŏs′hôk′) *n.* A large powerful hawk having broad rounded wings.

gos•ling (gŏz′lĭng) *n.* A young goose.

gos•pel (gŏs′pəl) *n.* **1.** Often **Gospel.** The teachings of Jesus and the Apostles. **2. Gospel. a.** One of the first four books of the New Testament, describing the life and teachings of Jesus. **b.** A reading from any of the Gospels included as part of a religious service. **3.** Something, such as an idea or a principle, believed to be unquestionably true: *They took her explanation as gospel.* [First written down about 750 in Old English and spelled *gōdspel* : *gōd*, good + *spel*, news.]

gospel music *n.* A kind of religious music that combines elements of folk music, jazz, and spirituals and was developed by Southern Black Americans.

gos•sa•mer (gŏs′ə mər) *n.* **1.** A soft, sheer, gauzy cloth. **2.** Something delicate, light, or flimsy. **3.** Fine silky film of cobwebs often seen caught on bushes or grass. —*adj.* Light, sheer, or delicate.

gos•sip (gŏs′əp) *n.* **1.** Trivial talk, often involving rumors of people and their personal affairs. **2.** A person who habitually engages in such talk. —*intr.v.* **gos•siped, gos•sip•ing, gos•sips.** To engage in or spread gossip: *gossip about one's neighbors.* —**gos′sip•er** *n.*

got (gŏt) *v.* Past tense and a past participle of **get.**

Goth (gŏth) *n.* A member of a Germanic people who invaded the Roman Empire in the third, fourth and fifth centuries A.D.

Goth•ic (gŏth′ĭk) *adj.* **1.** Of or relating to the Goths or their language. **2.** Of or relating to a style of architecture used in western Europe from the 12th through the 15th century and characterized by pointed arches and flying buttresses. **3.** Of or relating to a style of fiction that emphasizes the grotesque and mysterious: *a Gothic novel.* —*n.* **1.** The extinct Germanic language of the Goths. **2.** Gothic art or architecture.

got•ten (gŏt′n) *v.* A past participle of **get.**

gouge (gouj) *n.* **1.** A chisel with a rounded grooved blade. **2.** A groove or hole made with or as if with such a chisel: *The bump left a deep gouge in the wood.* —*tr.v.* **gouged, goug•ing, goug•es. 1.** To cut or scoop out with or as if with a gouge: *gouge out watermelon seeds.* **2.** *Slang.* To cheat, especially out of money. —**goug′er** *n.*

gou•lash (go͞o′läsh′ *or* go͞o′lăsh′) *n.* A meat and vegetable stew seasoned with paprika. [First written down in 1866 in Modern English, from Hungarian *gulyás (hús)*, herdsman's (meat), goulash, from *gulya*, herdsman.]

gourd (gôrd *or* go͝ord) *n.* **1.** The fruit of a vine related to the pumpkin, squash, and cucumber, having a hard rind and often an irregular shape. **2.** The dried hollowed-out shell of such a fruit, used as a ladle, bowl, or cup. **3.** The vine that bears such fruit. [First written down about 1303 in Middle English and spelled *gourde*, ultimately from Latin *cucurbita*.]

gour•mand (go͝or mänd′ *or* go͝or′mənd) *n.* A lover of good food.

gour•met (go͝or mā′ *or* go͝or′mā′) *n.* A person who enjoys and is knowledgeable about fine food and drink.

gout (gout) *n.* A painful disease in which hard deposits of salts from urine form in the joints, especially of the legs, feet, and hands.

gout•y (gou′tē) *adj.* **1.** Of, resembling, or relating to gout. **2.** Suffering from or affected by gout. —**gout′i•ness** *n.*

gov. or **Gov.** *abbr.* An abbreviation of governor.

gov•ern (gŭv′ərn) *v.* **gov•erned, gov•ern•ing, gov•erns.** —*tr.* **1.** To make and administer the public policy and affairs of: *In elections the voters decide who will govern the country.* **2.** To exercise a determining influence on: *The weather governs the success or failure of crops.* **3.** To keep under control; restrain: *a child who could not be governed.* —*intr.* To exercise political authority. [First written down about 1280 in Middle English and spelled *governen*, from Latin *gubernāre*, from Greek *kubernan*.] —**gov′ern•a•ble** *adj.*

gov•er•ness (gŭv′ər nĭs) *n.* A woman employed to teach and train the children of a household.

gov•ern•ment (gŭv′ərn mənt) *n.* **1.** The act or process of governing, especially the control and administration of a political unit. **2.** A system by which a

gorilla
Mountain gorilla

gourd

Usage: government

The word **government** always takes a singular verb: *The government is divided over how much to raise taxes. The government of the United States is divided into the executive, legislative, and judicial branches.*

ă	pat	oi	boy
ā	pay	ou	out
âr	care	o͝o	took
ä	father	o͞o	boot
ĕ	pet	ŭ	cut
ē	be	ûr	urge
ĭ	pit	th	thin
ī	pie	*th*	this
îr	pier	hw	whoop
ŏ	pot	zh	vision
ō	toe	ə	about
ô	paw	N	*French* bon

Martha Graham
Performing in *Letter to the World*

political unit is governed: *democratic government.* **3.** The people who make up a governing body. **—gov′ern•men′tal** (gŭv′ərn **mĕn′**tl) *adj.* —See Note on page 435.

gov•er•nor (**gŭv′**ər nər) *n.* **1.** The chief executive of a state in the United States. **2.** An official appointed to govern a colony or territory. **3.** A person who directs the operation of a business or an organization: *There are several governors on the board of the club.* **4.** A device that automatically regulates the speed, pressure, or temperature of a machine.

gov•er•nor•ship (**gŭv′**ər nər shĭp′) *n.* The office or duties of a governor or the period during which a governor is in office.

govt. or **Govt.** *abbr.* An abbreviation of government.

gown (goun) *n.* **1.** A long, loose, flowing garment, such as a nightgown. **2.** A woman's dress, especially a long formal one. **3.** An outer robe for official ceremonies, worn by scholars and clerics, for example.

Go•ya y Lu•ci•en•tes (**goi′**ə ē lo͞o **syĕn′**tĕs), **Francisco José de.** 1746–1828. Spanish artist whose works include portraits of Spanish nobility.

G.P. or **GP** *abbr.* An abbreviation of general practitioner.

gr. *abbr.* An abbreviation of: **1.** Gram. **2.** Gross. **3.** Grain (measurement).

Gr. *abbr.* An abbreviation of: **1.** Grecian. **2.** Greece. **3.** Greek.

grab (grăb) *v.* **grabbed, grab•bing, grabs.** *—tr.* **1.** To take suddenly; snatch: *The monkey grabbed the peanut out of my hand.* **2.** To obtain forcibly: *The dictator grabbed power.* *—intr.* To make a snatch: *She grabbed for the dog's leash.* *—n.* **1.** The act of grabbing; a snatch: *I made a grab at the frog.* **2.** Something that is grabbed.

grab bag *n.* A container filled with articles, such as party gifts, to be drawn out unseen.

grace (grās) *n.* **1.** Seemingly effortless beauty of movement, form, or manner: *the grace of a swan swimming across a lake.* **2.** A charming or pleasing quality or characteristic. **3.** The state of being protected or sanctified by the favor and love of God. **4.** A short prayer of blessing or thanks said before or after a meal. **5.** A temporary immunity or exemption; a reprieve. **6. Grace.** A title and form of address for a duke, a duchess, or an archbishop: *Your Grace.* **7. Graces.** In Greek mythology, three sister goddesses who dispense charm and beauty. *—tr.v.* **graced, grac•ing, grac•es. 1.** To honor; favor: *The governor's presence graced the meeting.* **2.** To give beauty, elegance, or charm to: *A bouquet of fresh flowers graced the mantelpiece.* ***—idioms.*** **in the bad graces of.** Out of favor with. **in the good graces of.** In favor with. [First written down before 1200 in Middle English, from Latin *grātia*, from *grātus*, pleasing.]

grace•ful (**grās′**fəl) *adj.* Showing grace of movement, form, or proportion: *a graceful dance.* **—grace′ful•ly** *adv.* **—grace′ful•ness** *n.*

grace•less (**grās′**lĭs) *adj.* **1.** Lacking grace; clumsy: *a graceless fall.* **2.** Without a sense of propriety or decency: *a rude and graceless remark.* **—grace′less•ly** *adv.* **—grace′less•ness** *n.*

grace note *n.* A very short musical note added to a melody as an ornament, usually independent of the harmony.

gra•cious (**grā′**shəs) *adj.* **1.** Characterized by kindness and courtesy: *a gracious and thoughtful host.* **2.** Characterized by tact and propriety: *responded to the insult with gracious good humor.* **3.** Of a merciful or sympathetic nature. *—interj.* An expression used to show surprise or mild emotion: *Goodness gracious! My gracious!* **—gra′cious•ly** *adv.* **—gra′cious•ness** *n.*

grack•le (**grăk′**əl) *n.* Any of several American blackbirds having shiny blackish feathers and a harsh husky call.

grad (grăd) *n. Informal.* A graduate of a school or college.

gra•da•tion (grā **dā′**shən) *n.* **1.** A series of gradual successive stages or steps: *the gradation in shading from light to dark.* **2.** Any of the stages or steps in such a series.

grade (grād) *n.* **1.a.** A position in a scale of size, quality, or intensity: *a poor grade of lumber.* **b.** A group of persons or things within the same quality, rank, or value; a class: *several sheets of the finest grade sandpaper.* **2.a.** A slope or an incline, as of a road: *The truck couldn't stop on the grade.* **b.** The degree to which something, such as a road or railroad track, slopes: *the steep grade of a mountain road.* **3.** A division or section of the course of study in elementary and high school, usually determined as a year's work: *the ninth grade.* **4.** A mark showing the quality of a student's work: *I always get good grades in science.* *—v.* **grad•ed, grad•ing, grades.** *—tr.* **1.** To arrange in a series or according to a scale. **2.** To give a grade to (a student or an assignment, for example): *grade book reports.* **3.** To level or smooth to a desired or horizontal gradient: *bulldozers grading a road.* *—intr.* To change or progress gradually: *The various piles of gravel grade from coarse to fine.* [First written down in 1796 in Modern English, from Latin *gradus*.]

grade crossing *n.* An intersection of roads, railroad tracks, or a combination of these at the same level.

grad•er (**grā′**dər) *n.* **1.** A student in a specific grade at school: *a fifth grader; a seventh grader.* **2.** A piece of heavy equipment used to level or smooth road or other surfaces.

grade school *n.* Elementary school.

gra•di•ent (**grā′**dē ənt) *n.* **1.** The degree to which something inclines; a slope: *the steep gradient of the hillside.* **2.** A part that slopes upward or downward; an incline: *skidded on the icy gradient.* **3.** The rate of change of a variable, such as temperature or pressure, with distance.

grad•u•al (**grăj′**o͞o əl) *adj.* Occurring in small stages or degrees or by even continuous change: *the gradual increase in prices.* **—grad′u•al•ly** *adv.*

grad•u•ate (**grăj′**o͞o āt′) *v.* **grad•u•at•ed, grad•u•at•ing, grad•u•ates.** *—intr.* To receive an academic degree or diploma: *graduate from high school.* *—tr.* **1.** To grant an academic degree or diploma to: *Our high school graduated 100 students.* **2.** To divide or mark into intervals indicating measures, as of length or volume: *A thermometer is graduated into degrees.* *—n.* (**grăj′**o͞o ĭt). A person who has received an academic degree or diploma. *—adj.* (**grăj′**o͞o ĭt). **1.** Possessing an academic degree or diploma. **2.** Of, for, or relating to studying beyond the bachelor's degree: *graduate courses.* [First written down in 1421 in Middle English and spelled *graduaten*, to confer a degree, from Medieval Latin *graduārī*, to take a degree, from Latin *gradus*, step.]

grad•u•a•tion (grăj′o͞o **ā′**shən) *n.* **1.a.** The conferral or receipt of an academic degree or a diploma. **b.** A ceremony for giving out academic degrees or diplomas. **2.** Any of the marks made on a container or an instrument to show amounts or measures: *This thermometer is marked with such fine graduations that they are hard to read.*

graf•fi•ti (grə **fē′**tē) *n.* A drawing or an inscription made on a wall or other surface, usually so as to be seen by the public.

graft¹ (grăft) *tr.v.* **graft•ed, graft•ing, grafts. 1.** To join (a plant shoot or bud) to another living plant so that the two grow together as a single plant. **2.** To transplant (tissue or an organ) by means of surgery from one part of the body to another or from one person to another. *—n.* **1.** A shoot or bud that has been grafted onto another plant. **2.** An organ or a piece of tissue transplanted by surgery. [First written down about 1378 in Middle English and spelled *graffen*, from Old French *graffe*, stylus, graft (from its shape).]

graft[2] (grăft) *n.* **1.** The dishonest use of one's position to derive profit or advantage; extortion. **2.** Money or an advantage gained by such use. [First written down in 1865 in American English.]

gra•ham (**grā′**əm) *n.* Whole-wheat flour. [First written down in 1834 in American English, after Sylvester *Graham* (1794–1851), American cleric and social reformer.]

Gra•ham (**grā′**əm), **Martha.** 1894–1991. American dancer and choreographer who founded the Dance Repertory Theatre in New York City in 1930.

Grail (grāl) *n.* In medieval legend, the cup used by Jesus at the Last Supper and the object of many quests by Knights of the Round Table.

grain (grān) *n.* **1.a.** A small hard seed, especially of wheat, corn, rice, or other cereal plants. **b.** The seeds of such plants considered as a group: *a harvest of grain.* **2.** Cereal plants, such as wheat or rye, considered as a group: *a field of grain.* **3.a.** A small particle similar to a seed: *a grain of salt.* **b.** A small amount or the smallest possible amount: *not a grain of sense in what they say.* **4.** A unit of weight equal to 0.002285 ounce (0.065 gram). See table at **measurement. 5.a.** The markings, pattern, or texture in wood: *the fine grain of hard woods.* **b.** The direction of such markings: *cut a board with the grain.* **6.** The direction or texture of fibers in a woven fabric. ***—idiom.* with a grain of salt.** With reservations; skeptically: *Take everything he says with a grain of salt.*

grain alcohol *n.* Ethanol.

grain elevator *n.* A building equipped with lifting machines and used for storing grain.

grain•y (**grā′**nē) *adj.* **grain•i•er, grain•i•est. 1.** Consisting of or resembling grains; granular: *grainy flour.* **2.** Resembling the grain of wood: *a grainy surface.*

gram (grăm) *n.* A unit of mass or weight in the metric system, equal to about 1/28 ounce. See table at **measurement.**

-gram *suff.* A suffix that means something written or drawn: *cardiogram; telegram.*

gram atom *n.* The quantity of an element whose weight in grams is numerically equal to its atomic weight. For example, carbon has an atomic weight of 12, so 1 gram atom of carbon weighs 12 grams.

gram•mar (**grăm′**ər) *n.* **1.** The study of the structure of words, the relationships between words, and the arrangement of words to make sentences. **2.** The system of rules that allow sentences to be made in a given language: *Latin grammar relies heavily on inflections.* **3.** A book containing the rules for making sentences in a given language: *The library has several grammars of French.* **4.** The use of words with reference to an accepted standard among educated speakers of a language: *The teacher criticized my paper for bad grammar.* [First written down in 1176 in Middle English and spelled *gramaire*, from Greek *grammatikos*, of letters, from *gramma*, letter.]

gram•mar•ian (grə **mâr′**ē ən) *n.* A specialist in grammar.

grammar school *n.* **1.** An elementary school. **2.** *Chiefly British.* A secondary or preparatory school.

gram•mat•i•cal (grə **măt′**ĭ kəl) *adj.* **1.** Of or relating to grammar: *grammatical principles.* **2.** Conforming to the rules of grammar: *a grammatical sentence.* **—gram•mat′i•cal•ly** *adv.*

gramme (grăm) *n. Chiefly British.* Variant of **gram.**

gram•pus (**grăm′**pəs) *n.* A sea mammal related to and resembling the dolphins but having a blunt snout.

Gra•na•da (grə **nä′**də). A city of southern Spain southeast of Córdoba. It was founded in the eighth century. Population, 256,191.

gran•a•ry (**grăn′**ə rē *or* **grā′**nə rē) *n., pl.* **gran•a•ries.** A building for storing grain.

grand (grănd) *adj.* **grand•er, grand•est. 1.** Large and impressive in size, scope, or extent; magnificent: *The bridge that crosses the bay is a grand structure.* See Synonyms at **magnificent. 2.** Very pleasing or wonderful: *had a grand time.* **3.a.** Having higher rank than others of the same category: *the grand admiral of the fleet.* **b.** Being the most important of a category; principal: *the grand prize.* **4.** Noble or dignified; lofty: *The United Nations has a grand purpose.* **5.** Including or covering all units or aspects: *the grand total.* *—n.* **1.** A grand piano. **2.** *Slang.* A thousand dollars. [First written down in 1125 in Middle English, from Latin *grandis.*] **—grand′ly** *adv.* **—grand′ness** *n.*

grand•aunt (**grănd′ănt′** *or* **grănd′änt′**) *n.* A great-aunt.

Grand Banks (grănd). An area of sandy banks in the western Atlantic Ocean off southeast Newfoundland, Canada. The area is a major source of food fish, especially cod.

Grand Canyon. A gorge of the Colorado River in northwest Arizona. It is up to 1 mile (1.6 kilometers) deep, from 4 to 18 miles (6.4 to 24 kilometers) wide, and more than 200 miles (321.8 kilometers) long.

grand•child (**grănd′**chīld′ *or* **grăn′**chīd′) *n.* A child of one's daughter or son.

Grand Cou•lee (**ko͞o′**lē). A gorge, about 30 miles (48 kilometers) long, of north-central Washington. It is fed by water from **Grand Coulee Dam.**

grand•dad (**grăn′**dăd′) *n. Informal.* A grandfather.

grand•dad•dy (**grăn′**dăd′ē) *n. Informal.* A grandfather.

grand•daugh•ter (**grăn′**dô′tər) *n.* A daughter of one's daughter or son.

gran•dee (grăn **dē′**) *n.* **1.** A nobleman of the highest rank in Spain or Portugal. **2.** A person of high rank or great importance.

Grande-Terre (**grăn′târ′**). An island of eastern Guadeloupe in the Leeward Islands of the West Indies.

gran•deur (**grăn′**jər *or* **grăn′**jo͝or′) *n.* The quality or condition of being grand; magnificence: *the grandeur of the pyramids in Egypt.*

grand•fa•ther (**grănd′**fä′*th*ər *or* **grăn′**fä′*th*ər) *n.* The father of one's mother or father.

grandfather clock *n.* A pendulum clock enclosed in a tall narrow cabinet.

grand•fa•ther•ly (**grănd′**fä′*th*ər lē *or* **grăn′**fä′*th*ər lē) *adj.* Typical of or befitting a grandfather.

gran•dil•o•quence (grăn **dĭl′**ə kwəns) *n.* Pompous expression or lofty speech.

gran•dil•o•quent (grăn **dĭl′**ə kwənt) *adj.* Using lofty words or having a pompous style or manner. **—gran•dil′o•quent•ly** *adv.*

gran•di•ose (**grăn′**dē ōs′ *or* grăn′dē **ōs′**) *adj.* **1.** Characterized by greatness of scope or intent; grand: *a grandiose style of writing.* See Synonyms at **magnificent. 2.** Characterized by pretended or affected grandeur; pompous: *a grandiose apology.* **—gran′di•ose′ly** *adv.* **—gran′di•os′i•ty** (grăn′dē **ŏs′**ĭ tē), **gran′di•ose′ness** *n.*

grand jury *n.* A jury of 12 to 23 persons that meets in private to evaluate accusations against a person charged with a crime and determines whether an indictment should be made.

Grand Canyon

grandfather clock

ă	pat	oi	boy
ā	pay	ou	out
âr	care	o͝o	took
ä	father	o͞o	boot
ĕ	pet	ŭ	cut
e	be	ûr	urge
ĭ	pit	th	thin
ī	pie	*th*	this
îr	pier	hw	whoop
ŏ	pot	zh	vision
ō	toe	ə	about
ô	paw	N	*French* bon

grand piano

Ulysses S. Grant

grape

grapeshot

grand•ma (grănd′mä′ *or* grăn′mä′ *or* grăm′mä′) *n. Informal.* A grandmother.

Grand•ma Mo•ses (grănd′mä mō′zĭz). Anna Mary Robertson Moses.

grand•moth•er (grănd′mŭ*th*′ər *or* grăn′mŭ*th*′ər) *n.* The mother of one's father or mother.

grand•moth•er•ly (grănd′mŭ*th*′ər lē *or* grăn′-mŭ*th*′ər lē) *adj.* Typical of or befitting a grandmother.

grand•neph•ew (grănd′nĕf′yo͞o *or* grăn′nĕf′yo͞o) *n.* A son of one's nephew or niece.

grand•niece (grănd′nēs′ *or* grăn′nēs′) *n.* A daughter of one's nephew or niece.

grand opera *n.* A serious or melodramatic drama having the entire text set to music.

grand•pa (grănd′pä′ *or* grăn′pä′ *or* grăm′pä′) *n. Informal.* A grandfather.

grand•par•ent (grănd′pâr′ənt *or* grănd′păr′ənt) *n.* A parent of one's mother or father.

grand piano *n.* A piano whose strings are stretched in a harp-shaped frame supported usually on three legs.

Grand Rapids. A city of west-central Michigan west-northwest of Lansing. It was built on the site of an Ottawa village. Population, 189,126.

grand slam *n.* **1.** In baseball, a home run hit when three runners are on base. **2.** In bridge, the winning of all the tricks in one hand.

grand•son (grănd′sŭn′ *or* grăn′sŭn′) *n.* A son of one's daughter or son.

grand•stand (grănd′stănd′ *or* grăn′stănd′) *n.* **1.** A roofed stand for spectators at a stadium or racetrack. **2.** The spectators or audience at an event. —*intr.v.* **grand•stand•ed, grand•stand•ing, grand•stands.** To perform for effect, especially so as to impress an audience.

grand•un•cle (grănd′ŭng′kəl) *n.* A great-uncle.

Grange (grānj) *n.* **1.** An association of farmers founded in the United States in 1867. **2.** One of the branch lodges of this association.

gran•ite (grăn′ĭt) *n.* A common, coarse-grained, hard rock composed mostly of quartz, feldspar, and mica. It is an igneous rock and is used in buildings and monuments. [First written down in 1646 in Modern English, from Italian *granito*, grainy, from *grano*, grain, from Latin *grānum.*]

gran•ny or **gran•nie** (grăn′ē) *n., pl.* **gran•nies.** *Informal.* A grandmother.

granny knot *n.* A knot resembling a square knot but with the second tie crossed incorrectly.

gra•no•la (grə nō′lə) *n.* Rolled oats mixed with various ingredients, such as dried fruit, brown sugar, and nuts, and used especially as a breakfast cereal.

grant (grănt) *tr.v.* **grant•ed, grant•ing, grants. 1.** To give or allow (something asked for): *grant a request.* **2.** To confer or bestow as a favor, prerogative, or privilege: *The Constitution grants certain powers to the Supreme Court.* **3.** To concede; acknowledge: *I'll grant that it's not the best car, but it still is reliable.* —*n.* **1.** The act of or an example of granting. **2.** Something granted: *The student received a grant of $3000 for college tuition.* [First written down about 1225 in Middle English and spelled *granten*, from Old French *creanter*, from Latin *crēdēns*, believing.]

Grant (grănt), **Ulysses Simpson.** Originally Hiram Ulysses Grant. 1822–1885. The 18th President of the United States (1869–1877) and a general of the Union Army in the Civil War. His presidency was marked by graft and corruption.

grant•ee (grăn tē′) *n.* A person to whom a grant is made.

gran•tor (grăn′tər *or* grăn′tôr′) *n.* A person who makes a grant.

gran•u•lar (grăn′yə lər) *adj.* Made of or appearing to be made of grains or granules: *the granular surface of a rock; the granular consistency of rice.*

gran•u•late (grăn′yə lāt′) *v.* **gran•u•lat•ed, gran•u•lat•ing, gran•u•lates.** —*tr.* **1.** To form into grains or granules. **2.** To roughen the surface of. —*intr.* To become granular or grainy. —**gran′u•la′tion** *n.*

gran•ule (grăn′yo͞ol) *n.* A small grain or pellet. [First written down in 1652 in Modern English, from Late Latin *grānulum*, diminutive of Latin *grānum*, grain.]

grape (grāp) *n.* **1.** A small, rounded, juicy fruit of any of numerous vines, having smooth, usually purple or green skin and growing in clusters. Grapes are eaten fresh and are used for making wine, raisins, and jelly or jam. **2.** A vine that bears such fruit. [First written down about 1250 in Middle English, from Old French *grape*, bunch of grapes, hook, of Germanic origin.]

grape•fruit (grāp′fro͞ot′) *n.* **1.** A large round fruit of an evergreen tree related to the orange, having a yellow skin and a somewhat sour taste. **2.** The tree that bears such fruit, found in warm climates.

grape•shot (grāp′shŏt′) *n.* A cluster of small iron balls formerly used as a cannon charge.

grape sugar *n.* Dextrose obtained from grapes.

grape•vine (grāp′vīn′) *n.* **1.** A vine on which grapes grow. **2.** The informal transmission of gossip, rumor, or information from person to person: *I heard through the grapevine that school will be closed tomorrow.*

graph (grăf) *n.* **1.** A diagram showing the relationship of quantities, especially such a diagram in which lines, bars, or proportional areas represent how one quantity depends on or changes with another. **2.** A curve or line showing a mathematical function or equation. —*tr.v.* **graphed, graph•ing, graphs.** To make a graph of.

–graph *suff.* A suffix that means: **1.** Something that writes or records: *seismograph; telegraph.* **2.** Something written or drawn: *homograph.*

graph•eme (grăf′ēm′) *n.* A letter of an alphabet or combination of letters that represents a phoneme.

–grapher *suff.* A suffix that means someone who writes or records: *stenographer.*

graph•ic (grăf′ĭk) *adj.* **1.a.** Of or relating to written or drawn representations: *A pronunciation key in a dictionary has graphic symbols of speech.* **b.** Of or relating to graphics. **c.** Of or relating to the graphic arts. **2.** Of, relating to, or represented by or as if by a graph: *the graphic scale of a map.* **3.** Described in vivid detail: *The witness gave a graphic description of the incident.* [First written down before 1637 in Modern English, from Greek *graphein*, to write.] —**graph′i•cal•ly** *adv.*

graphic arts *pl.n.* **1.** The visual arts that involve the application of lines and strokes to a flat surface. **2.** The visual arts that involve producing images from blocks, plates, or type.

graph•ics (grăf′ĭks) *n. (used with a singular verb).* **1.** The making of drawings in accordance with the rules of mathematics, as in engineering and architecture. **2.** The process by which a computer produces and displays information as pictures, diagrams, and charts, rather than as letters and numerals.

graph•ite (grăf′īt′) *n.* A crystalline form of carbon that is steel-gray to black in color and rather soft. It is used in making lubricants, paints, electrodes, and as the writing substance in pencils.

–graphy *suff.* A suffix that means: **1.** A writing or representation produced in a certain way: *photography.* **2.** A writing about a specific subject: *oceanography.*

grap•nel (grăp′nəl) *n.* **1.** A small anchor with three or more claws. **2.** A grappling iron.

grap•ple (grăp′əl) *n.* **1.** A grappling iron. **2.** A grapnel. **3.** The act of grappling. —*v.* **grap•pled, grap•pling, grap•ples.** —*tr.* To grasp with or as if with a grappling iron. —*intr.* **1.** To hold onto something with or as if with a grappling iron. **2.** To struggle in or as if in wrestling: *grapple with a difficult problem.*

grap•pling iron (grăp′lĭng) *n.* An iron bar with several claws at one end for grasping or holding something.

grasp (grăsp) *v.* **grasped, grasp•ing, grasps.** —*tr.* **1.** To seize and hold firmly with or as if with the hands: *Grasp the rope and pull.* **2.** To take hold of in the mind; understand: *You fail to grasp the problem.* —*intr.* **1.** To make a motion of seizing, snatching, or clutching: *The sailor grasped at the dangling line.* **2.** To show eager acceptance: *grasped at the opportunity to go to college.* —*n.* **1.** A firm hold or grip: *The puppy wriggled out of my grasp.* **2.** The ability to attain; reach: *Victory was within the team's grasp.* **3.** Understanding; comprehension: *The teacher has a thorough grasp of the subject.* [First written down about 1350 in Middle English and spelled *graspen.*]

grasp•ing (grăs′pĭng) *adj.* Eager for material gain; greedy. —**grasp′ing•ly** *adv.* —**grasp′ing•ness** *n.*

grass (grăs) *n.* **1.** Any of various plants having narrow leaves, hollow stems, and clusters of very small flowers, as wheat, corn, sugar cane, or bamboo. **2.** Ground, such as a lawn or pasture, covered with such plants. **3.** Grazing land; pasture. [First written down about 725 in Old English and spelled *græs.*]

grass•hop•per (grăs′hŏp′ər) *n.* Any of numerous insects having two pairs of wings and long hind legs used for jumping. Grasshoppers, such as the locust, feed on plants, often causing great destruction to crops.

grass•land (grăs′lănd′) *n.* An area, such as a prairie or meadow, covered with grass.

Gras•so (grăs′ō *or* grä′sō), **Ella Tambussi.** 1919–1981. American public official who as governor of Connecticut (1975–1981), was the first woman to hold the office of governor in her own right.

grass•roots (grăs′ro͞ots′ *or* grăs′ro͝ots′) *pl.n.* *(used with a singular or plural verb).* People or society at a local level rather than at the center of major political activity.

grass•y (grăs′ē) *adj.* **grass•i•er, grass•i•est. 1.** Covered with or abounding in grass: *a grassy plain.* **2.** Resembling or suggestive of grass, as in color or odor: *a grassy green.*

grate[1] (grāt) *v.* **grat•ed, grat•ing, grates.** —*tr.* **1.** To reduce to fragments, shreds, or powder by rubbing against a rough surface: *Grate the cabbage for coleslaw.* **2.** To cause to make a harsh grinding or rasping sound by rubbing: *She grated her teeth in anger.* —*intr.* **1.** To make a harsh grinding or rasping sound by rubbing: *The wagon grated on its rusty wheels.* **2.** To cause irritation or annoyance: *Your sarcasm grates on my nerves.* [First written down before 1399 in Middle English and spelled *graten,* from Old French *grater,* to scrape, of Germanic origin.]

❑ *These sound alike:* **grate[1]** (shred), **grate[2]** (framework), **great** (large).

grate[2] (grāt) *n.* **1.** A framework of parallel or interwoven bars for blocking an opening. **2.** A similar framework used to hold fuel or food in a stove, furnace, or fireplace. [First written down in 1348 in Middle English, from Latin *crātis,* wickerwork.]

❑ *These sound alike:* **grate[2]** (framework), **grate[1]** (shred), **great** (large).

grate•ful (grāt′fəl) *adj.* **1.a.** Appreciative of benefits received: *grateful for needed help.* **b.** Expressing gratitude: *a grateful look.* **2.** Affording pleasure; agreeable: *grateful relief from the rays of the sun.* [First written down in 1552 in Modern English, from obsolete *grate,* pleasing, from Latin *grātus.*] —**grate′ful•ly** *adv.* —**grate′ful•ness** *n.*

grat•er (grā′tər) *n.* A kitchen utensil with slits and perforations on which to grate food.

grat•i•fi•ca•tion (grăt′ə fĭ kā′shən) *n.* **1.** The act of gratifying or the condition of being gratified. **2.** An instance or a cause of being gratified: *The student's success in mathematics was a great gratification to the teacher.*

grat•i•fy (grăt′ə fī′) *tr.v.* **grat•i•fied, grat•i•fy•ing, grat•i•fies. 1.** To please or satisfy: *The test results gratified the patient.* **2.** To give what is desired to; indulge: *gratify one's curiosity.* —**grat′i•fi′er** *n.*

grat•ing (grā′tĭng) *n.* A grill or network of bars set across an opening, such as a window or a street drain; a grate.

grat•is (grăt′ĭs *or* grä′tĭs *or* grā′tĭs) *adv. & adj.* Without charge: *We went to the show gratis. The tickets are gratis.*

grat•i•tude (grăt′ĭ to͞od′ *or* grăt′ĭ tyo͞od′) *n.* The state of being grateful; thankfulness: *The family was full of gratitude for their neighbor's help during the fire.*

gra•tu•i•tous (grə to͞o′ĭ təs *or* grə tyo͞o′ĭ təs) *adj.* **1.** Given without cost or obligation; free: *gratuitous help.* **2.** Unnecessary or unwarranted: *a gratuitous criticism.* —**gra•tu′i•tous•ly** *adv.* —**gra•tu′i•tous•ness** *n.*

gra•tu•i•ty (grə to͞o′ĭ tē *or* grə tyo͞o′ĭ tē) *n., pl.* **gra•tu•i•ties.** A favor or gift, usually of money, given in return for service; a tip.

grave[1] (grāv) *n.* **1.** A hole dug in the ground for the burial of a corpse. **2.** A place of burial: *The sea is the grave of many sailors.* **3.** Death or extinction. [First written down before 1000 in Old English and spelled *græf.*]

grave[2] (grāv) *adj.* **grav•er, grav•est. 1.** Requiring serious thought; momentous: *a grave decision.* **2.** Fraught with danger or harm: *a grave illness.* **3.** Dignified and somber in conduct or character: *The judge looked grave.* [First written down in 1541 in Modern English, from Latin *gravis.*] —**grave′ly** *adv.* —**grave′ness** *n.*

grave[3] (grāv) *tr.v.* **graved, grav•en** (grā′vən) or **graved, grav•ing, graves.** To sculpt or carve; engrave. [First written down before 1000 in Old English and spelled *grafan.*]

grave accent (grāv *or* gräv) *n.* A mark (`) indicating that an additional syllable is pronounced, as *burnèd.*

grav•el (grăv′əl) *n.* A loose mixture of pebbles or small pieces of rock, often used for roads and walks. —*tr.v.* **grav•eled, grav•el•ing, grav•els** or **grav•elled, grav•el•ling, grav•els.** To cover with gravel: *gravel a driveway.*

grav•el•ly (grăv′ə lē) *adj.* **1.** Of, covered with, or containing gravel: *gravelly soil.* **2.** Having a harsh rasping sound: *a low gravelly voice.*

grav•en (grā′vən) *v.* A past participle of **grave[3]**.

graven image *n.* An idol carved in wood or stone.

grave•stone (grāv′stōn′) *n.* A stone placed over a grave as a marker; a tombstone.

grave•yard (grāv′yärd′) *n.* A cemetery.

grav•i•tate (grăv′ĭ tāt′) *intr.v.* **grav•i•tat•ed, grav•i•tat•ing, grav•i•tates. 1.** To move under or as if under the influence of gravity. **2.** To move downward: *Dead leaves gravitated to the bottom of the pond.* **3.** To be attracted by or as if by an irresistible force: *The grazing sheep gravitated toward the greener parts of the hillside.*

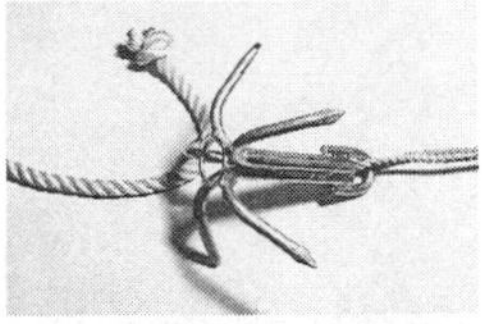

grappling iron

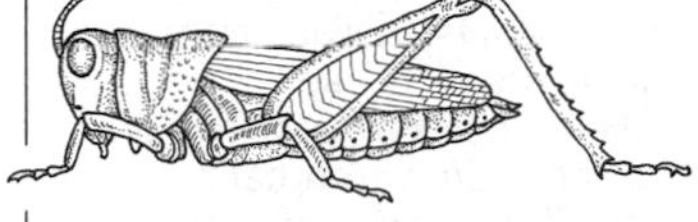

grasshopper
Spur-throated grasshopper

ă	pat	oi	boy
ā	pay	ou	out
âr	care	o͝o	took
ä	father	o͞o	boot
ĕ	pet	ŭ	cut
ē	be	ûr	urge
ĭ	pit	th	thin
ī	pie	*th*	this
îr	pier	hw	whoop
ŏ	pot	zh	vision
ō	toe	ə	about
ô	paw	N	*French* bon

Great Wall of China
Section at Gubeikou, northeast of Beijing

greenhouse effect

Every greenhouse stays warm because its glass roof lets in light from the sun to heat the soil. The soil radiates out longer-wave infrared radiation, which cannot escape back out through the glass and therefore heats the air inside. The same process takes place on Earth as a whole. Some of the radiation from the sun that reaches Earth's atmosphere is absorbed by the surface. Energy is radiated back from the surface in the form of infrared waves, which warm the atmosphere because the water vapor, carbon dioxide, and other gases in the air act like the glass roof of a greenhouse. Scientists call this process the **greenhouse effect**. Although the greenhouse effect is necessary for life on Earth, some scientists are concerned that it may be increasing. According to their theory, carbon dioxide gas is constantly being added to the atmosphere by the burning of fossil fuels—coal, oil, and natural gas. As the amount of carbon dioxide in the atmosphere increases, more of the energy radiated from Earth is trapped, and the atmosphere could become warmer. The changes that could result include higher sea levels and altered patterns of rainfall.

grav•i•ta•tion (grăv′ĭ tā′shən) *n.* **1.** The force of attraction that tends to draw together any two objects in the universe. **2.** The act or process of gravitating. **3.** A movement toward a source of attraction: *the gravitation of the middle class to the suburbs.* **—grav′i•ta′tion•al** *adj.* **—grav′i•ta′tion•al•ly** *adv.*

grav•i•ty (grăv′ĭ tē) *n.* **1.a.** The natural force that causes objects to move or tend to move toward the center of the earth as a result of gravitation. **b.** The force of attraction that makes objects move or tend to move toward each other; gravitation. **2.** Grave consequence; seriousness or importance: *The students realized the gravity of the test and its effect on their grades.* [First written down in 1509 in Modern English, from Latin *gravitās*, heaviness, from *gravis*, heavy.]

gra•vy (grā′vē) *n., pl.* **gra•vies. 1.** The juices that drip from cooking meat. **2.** A sauce made from these juices and thickened, as with flour.

gray also **grey** (grā) *adj.* **gray•er, gray•est** also **grey•er, grey•est. 1.** Having the color gray. **2.** Having gray hair. **3.** Lacking in cheer; gloomy: *a gray mood.* *—n.* **1.** A color made by mixing black and white. **2.** Often **Gray. a.** A Confederate soldier in the U.S. Civil War. **b.** The Confederate Army. *—tr. & intr.v.* **grayed, gray•ing, grays** also **greyed, grey•ing, greys.** To make or become gray: *Age grays the hair. The driftwood grayed in the sun.* **—gray′ly** *adv.* **—gray′ness** *n.*

gray•beard (grā′bîrd′) *n.* An old man.

gray•ish (grā′ĭsh) *adj.* Somewhat gray.

gray•ling (grā′lĭng) *n., pl.* **grayling** or **gray•lings.** Any of several freshwater fishes related to the trout and salmon, having a large back fin and valued for food.

gray matter *n.* **1.** The brownish-gray tissue of the brain and spinal cord, made up of nerve cells and fibers and some supporting tissue. **2.** *Informal.* Brains; intellect.

gray wolf *n.* A grayish or whitish wolf of northern forest regions.

graze[1] (grāz) *v.* **grazed, graz•ing, graz•es.** *—intr.* To feed on growing grasses and herbage: *Cattle grazed in the field.* *—tr.* **1.** To feed on the grass of (a piece of land): *The goats grazed the mountain pasture.* **2.** To put (livestock) out to feed: *grazed their cattle on the plains.* [First written down about 1000 in Old English and spelled *grasian*, from *græs*, grass.]

graze[2] (grāz) *v.* **grazed, graz•ing, graz•es.** *—tr.* **1.** To touch lightly in passing: *The suitcase just grazed my leg.* **2.** To scrape or scratch slightly: *I fell off my bike and grazed my knees and elbows.* *—intr.* To scrape or touch something lightly in passing. *—n.* **1.** The act of brushing or scraping along a surface. **2.** A minor scratch or scrape. [First written down in 1604 in Modern English, perhaps from *graze*, eat grass.]

grease (grēs) *n.* **1.** Animal fat when melted or soft, often used in cooking. **2.** A thick sticky oil or similar material, used to lubricate moving parts, as of a machine. *—tr.v.* (grēs *or* grēz). **greased, greas•ing, greas•es.** To apply grease to: *grease the pan before cooking; grease the track of a sliding door.* [First written down about 1300 in Middle English and spelled *grece*, from Latin *crassus*, fat, thick.]

grease•paint also **grease paint** (grēs′pānt′) *n.* Makeup worn by actors, clowns, and other performers.

greas•y (grē′sē *or* grē′zē) *adj.* **greas•i•er, greas•i•est. 1.** Coated or soiled with grease: *greasy pots and pans.* **2.** Containing grease; oily: *a greasy hamburger.* **3.** Slippery. **—greas′i•ly** *adv.* **—greas′i•ness** *n.*

great (grāt) *adj.* **great•er, great•est. 1.** Very large in size, number, amount, or extent: *a great crowd of fans.* See Synonyms at **large. 2.** Remarkable or outstanding in magnitude or degree: *a great crisis.* **3.** Important; significant: *The signing of the treaty was a great moment in history.* **4.** Prominent; distinguished: *a great athlete.* **5.** *Informal.* Enthusiastic: *a great tennis fan.* **6.** *Informal.* Very good; first-rate: *a great party; a great time.* [First written down before 899 in Old English and spelled *grēat*, thick, coarse.] **—great′ness** *n.*

❑ *These sound alike:* **great, grate**[1] (shred), **grate**[2] (framework).

great-aunt or **great aunt** (grāt′ănt′ *or* grāt′änt′) *n.* A sister of one's grandparent.

Great Barrier Reef. The largest coral reef in the world, about 1,250 miles (2,011 kilometers) long, off the northeast coast of Australia. It is known for its exotic fish and crustaceans.

Great Basin (grāt). A desert region of the western United States made up of most of Nevada and parts of Utah, California, Idaho, Wyoming, and Oregon.

Great Brit•ain (brĭt′n). **1.** An island off the western coast of Europe east of Ireland and made up of England, Scotland, and Wales. It is separated from the mainland by the English Channel. **2.** United Kingdom.

great circle *n.* A circle on a sphere that has its plane passing through the center of the sphere, as the great circle of the earth's equator does.

great•coat (grāt′kōt′) *n.* A heavy overcoat.

Great Dane *n.* Any of a breed of large powerful dog having a muscular body, a smooth short coat, and a narrow head.

Great Di•vide (dĭ vīd′). Continental Divide.

great-grand•child (grāt′grănd′chīld′ *or* grāt′grăn′-chīld′) *n.* A child of one's grandchild.

great-grand•daughter (grāt′grăn′dô′tər) *n.* A daughter of one's grandchild.

great-grand•father (grāt′grănd′fä′*th*ər *or* grāt′-grăn′fä′*th*ər) *n.* The father of one's grandparent.

great-grand•mother (grāt′grănd′mŭ*th*′ər *or* grāt′-grăn′mŭ*th*′ər) *n.* The mother of one's grandparent.

great-grand•parent (grāt′grănd′pâr′ənt *or* grāt′-grănd′păr′ənt) *n.* The parent of one's grandparent.

great-grand•son (grāt′grănd′sŭn′ *or* grāt′grăn′-sŭn′) *n.* A son of one's grandchild.

great•heart•ed (grāt′här′tĭd) *adj.* **1.** Courageous or noble in spirit. **2.** Generous; magnanimous: *The great-hearted landowner donated land for a park.* **—great′-heart′ed•ness** *n.*

Great Lakes. A group of five freshwater lakes of central North America between the United States and Canada, including Lakes Superior, Huron, Erie, Ontario, and Michigan. The Great Lakes connect Midwestern ports with the Atlantic Ocean by way of the St. Lawrence Seaway.

great•ly (grāt′lē) *adv.* To a great degree; very much: *Families vary greatly in size.*

great•neph•ew (grāt′nĕf′yo͞o) *n.* A grandnephew.

great•niece (grāt′nēs′) *n.* A grandniece.

Great Plains. A vast grassland region of central North America extending from south-central Canada southward to Texas. Much of the area is used for cattle and wheat ranching.

Great Salt Lake (sôlt). A shallow body of salt water of northwest Utah northwest of Salt Lake City. The lake is a remnant of a prehistoric lake that covered a large area of the Great Basin. **Great Salt Lake Desert,** to the west of the lake, is barren and uncultivated.

Great Spirit *n.* The principal god in the religion of many Native American peoples.

great-un•cle or **great uncle** (grāt′ŭng′kəl) *n.* A brother of one's grandparent.

Great Wall of Chi•na (chī′nə). A wall extending approximately 1,500 miles (2,414 kilometers) across northern China. It was built in the third century B.C. by about 300,000 laborers.

greave (grēv) *n.* Leg armor worn below the knee. Often used in the plural.

grebe (grēb) *n.* Any of various diving birds having a pointed bill and fleshy flaps along each toe.

Gre•cian (grē′shən) *adj.* Greek. —*n.* A native or inhabitant of Greece.

Gre•co (grĕk′ō), **El.** 1541–1614. Greek-born Spanish painter of religious works.

Greece (grēs). A country of southeast Europe on the southern Balkan Peninsula and including numerous islands in the surrounding seas. Greece was an important center of early civilization. Athens is the capital and largest city. Population, 9,740,417.

greed (grēd) *n.* A selfish desire for more than one needs or deserves.

greed•y (grē′dē) *adj.* **greed•i•er, greed•i•est. 1.** Filled with greed; wanting more than one needs or deserves: *The greedy prospector refused to share with his partners.* **2.** Wanting to eat or drink more than is reasonable; gluttonous. [First written down about 725 in Old English and spelled *grǣdig.*] —**greed′i•ly** *adv.* —**greed′i•ness** *n.*

Greek (grēk) *n.* **1.** The ancient or modern language of Greece. **2.** A native or inhabitant of Greece. **3.** Something that is unintelligible: *Robotics is Greek to me.* —*adj.* Of or relating to Greece or its people, language, or culture.

Greek Orthodox Church *n.* The state church of Greece, an autonomous part of the Eastern Orthodox Church.

Gree•ley (grē′lē), **Horace.** 1811–1872. American journalist who founded and edited the *New York Tribune* (1841–1872).

green (grēn) *n.* **1.** The color of most plant leaves and growing grass. In the spectrum it is between yellow and blue. **2. greens. a.** The branches and leaves of green plants used for decoration: *Christmas greens.* **b.** Leafy plants or plant parts eaten as vegetables: *salad greens.* **3.** A grassy area located usually at the center of a town or city; a common: *the village green.* **4.** A putting green. **5.** Often **Green.** A person or movement that supports environmental protection. —*adj.* **green•er, green•est. 1.** Of the color green: *a green sweater.* **2.** Covered with growing plants, grass, or foliage: *green meadows.* **3.** Not mature or ripe: *a green banana.* **4.** Lacking training or experience: *green musicians.* **5.** Not aged, cured, dried, seasoned, or otherwise prepared for use: *green wood.* **6.** Pale and sickly in appearance; wan: *After riding the roller coaster we had green faces.* [First written down about 700 in Old English and spelled *grœ̄ni.*]

green•back (grēn′băk′) *n.* A piece of paper money of U.S. currency.

green bean *n.* A string bean.

Greene (grēn), **Nathanael.** 1742–1786. American Revolutionary general who worked to weaken British strength in the South.

green•er•y (grē′nə rē) *n., pl.* **green•er•ies.** Green plants or leaves.

green•gage (grēn′gāj′) *n.* A large sweet plum having yellowish-green skin and pulp. [First written down in 1724 in Modern English, after Sir William *Gage*, 18th-century English botanist.]

green•gro•cer (grēn′grō′sər) *n. Chiefly British.* A person who sells fresh fruit and vegetables.

green•horn (grēn′hôrn′) *n.* An inexperienced or immature person, especially one who is easily fooled.

green•house (grēn′hous′) *n.* A room or building with a glass roof and sides, used for growing plants that need an even, usually warm temperature; a hothouse.

greenhouse effect *n.* The trapping of the sun's radiation in the earth's atmosphere. It is caused by the buildup of carbon dioxide and water vapor in the atmosphere, which allows incoming sunlight to pass through but absorbs heat radiated back from the earth's surface. —SEE NOTE.

green•ish (grē′nĭsh) *adj.* Somewhat green.

Green•land (grēn′lənd *or* grēn′lănd′). An island of Denmark in the northern Atlantic Ocean off northeast Canada. The largest island in the world, most of Greenland lies within the Arctic Circle.

green pepper *n.* The unripened green fruit of any of various varieties of the pepper plant.

green•sward (grēn′swôrd′) *n.* Ground that is green with grass; turf.

green thumb *n.* An ability for making plants grow well.

Green•wich (grĕn′ĭch *or* grĭn′ĭj). A borough of Greater London in southeast England on the Thames River. The prime meridian passes through Greenwich.

Greenwich time *n.* Universal time.

green•wood (grēn′wo͝od′) *n.* A wood or forest in spring and summer when the leaves are green.

greet (grēt) *tr.v.* **greet•ed, greet•ing, greets. 1.** To address in a friendly way, as upon meeting or in opening a letter: *The hosts greeted their guests.* **2.** To receive with a specified reaction: *Our parents greeted the news with great joy.* **3.** To be perceived by: *A cry of "Surprise!" greeted our ears.*

greet•ing (grē′tĭng) *n.* A gesture or word of welcome or salutation.

gre•gar•i•ous (grĭ gâr′ē əs) *adj.* **1.** Seeking out and enjoying the company of others; sociable: *a gregarious person.* **2.** Living in flocks, herds, colonies, or similar groups with others of the same kind: *Zebras are gregarious.* [First written down in 1668 in Modern English, from Latin *gregārius*, belonging to a flock, from *grex*, flock.] —**gre•gar′i•ous•ly** *adv.* —**gre•gar′i•ous•ness** *n.*

Gre•go•ri•an calendar (grĭ gôr′ē ən) *n.* The calendar in use throughout most of the world, sponsored by Pope Gregory XIII (1502–1585) in 1582 as a corrected version of the Julian calendar.

Gregorian chant *n.* A liturgical chant that is sung without accompaniment.

Greg•o•ry I (grĕg′ə rē), **Saint.** 540?–604. Pope (590–604) who sponsored many missionary expeditions, including that of Saint Augustine to Britain (596).

grem•lin (grĕm′lĭn) *n.* An imaginary creature whose mischief is said to cause mechanical failures.

Gre•na•da (grə nā′də). An island country in the Windward Islands of the West Indies. The country gained its independence from Great Britain in 1974. St. George's is the capital and the largest city. Population, 110,100.

gre•nade (grə nād′) *n.* **1.** A small bomb detonated by a fuse and thrown by hand or fired from a launcher. **2.** A glass bottle filled with a chemical that is scattered when the bottle is thrown and smashed. [First written down about 1532 in Modern English, from Old French *(pome) grenate*, pomegranate.]

gren•a•dier (grĕn′ə dîr′) *n.* **1.** A soldier equipped with grenades. **2.** A member of the British Grenadier Guards, the first regiment of the royal household infantry.

grew (gro͞o) *v.* Past tense of **grow.**

grey (grā) *n., adj., & v.* Variant of **gray.**

grey•hound (grā′hound′) *n.* Any of a breed of slender dog having long legs, a smooth coat, and a narrow head and bred to hunt and race.

greyhound

ă	pat	oi	boy
ā	pay	ou	out
âr	care	o͝o	took
ä	father	o͞o	boot
ĕ	pet	ŭ	cut
ē	be	ûr	urge
ĭ	pit	th	thin
ī	pie	*th*	this
îr	pier	hw	whoop
ŏ	pot	zh	vision
ō	toe	ə	about
ô	paw	N	*French* bon

Edvard Grieg

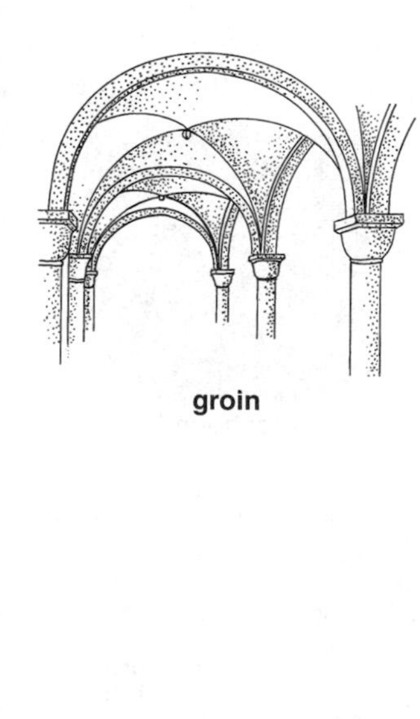

groin

grid (grĭd) *n.* **1.** A framework of parallel or crisscrossed bars; a grating. **2.** A pattern of regularly spaced horizontal and vertical lines forming squares of equal size, such as those used on a map or graph as a reference for locating points: *city streets arranged as a grid.* **3.** An electrode consisting of parallel wires or a screen, used to control the flow of electrons from cathode to anode in an electron tube. **4.** A metal conducting plate in a storage battery.

grid•dle (grĭd′l) *n.* A heavy flat metal surface, such as a pan, that is used for cooking by dry heat. [First written down before 1200 in Middle English and spelled *gridil*, gridiron, from Latin *crātīcula*, diminutive of *crātis*, wickerwork hurdle, lattice.]

grid•dle•cake (grĭd′l kāk′) *n.* A pancake.

grid•i•ron (grĭd′ī′ərn) *n.* **1.** A flat framework of parallel metal bars used to broil meat or fish; a grill. **2.** A football field.

grid•lock (grĭd′lŏk′) *n.* **1.** A complete halt in the movement of motor vehicle traffic, especially at an intersection of major streets. **2.** A complete halt in an activity resulting in a backup.

grief (grēf) *n.* **1.** Deep mental anguish, such as that arising from bereavement. **2.** A cause of deep mental anguish.

Grieg (grēg), **Edvard Hagerup.** 1843–1907. Norwegian composer whose works are based on traditional folk music.

griev•ance (grē′vəns) *n.* **1.** A real or imagined wrong regarded as just cause for protest: *Lack of affordable housing is a legitimate grievance.* **2.** A complaint based on such a circumstance: *delivered a list of grievances to the mayor.*

grieve (grēv) *v.* **grieved, griev•ing, grieves.** *—tr.* To cause to be sorrowful; distress: *The news grieved us deeply.* *—intr.* To experience or express grief.

griev•ous (grē′vəs) *adj.* **1.** Causing grief, pain, or sorrow: *a grievous loss.* **2.** Serious or grave; dire: *a grievous crime.* **—griev′ous•ly** *adv.* **—griev′ous•ness** *n.*

grif•fin (grĭf′ən) *n.* A fabled beast with the head and wings of an eagle and the body of a lion.

grill (grĭl) *tr.v.* **grilled, grill•ing, grills. 1.** To cook on a grill: *grill fish in the back yard.* **2.** *Informal.* To question closely and relentlessly; cross-examine: *The lawyer grilled a witness on the stand.* *—n.* **1.** A cooking utensil of parallel metal bars; a gridiron. **2.** Food cooked by broiling or grilling. **3.** An informal restaurant where grilled foods are served. [First written down in 1685 in Modern English, from Latin *crātīcula*, diminutive of *crātis*, wickerwork, lattice.]

grille also **grill** (grĭl) *n.* A metal or wood grating, often of decorative design, that covers a door, window, or other opening, or the front end of a motor vehicle.

grill•work (grĭl′wûrk′) *n.* Material formed into a grille or grilles: *Fancy grillwork formed the iron gate.*

grim (grĭm) *adj.* **grim•mer, grim•mest. 1.** Unrelenting; rigid: *worked with grim determination.* **2.** Uninviting or unnerving in appearance; forbidding: *The judge was grim when passing the severe sentence.* **3.** Dismal; gloomy: *We started out on a cold, dark, and grim morning.* **4.** Ghastly; sinister: *grim reminders of war.* [First written down about 725 in Old English and spelled *grimm*, fierce, severe.] **—grim′ly** *adv.* **—grim′ness** *n.*

grim•ace (grĭm′ĭs *or* grĭ mās′) *n.* A sharp contortion of the face, expressing pain, disgust, or contempt: *His face contracted in a grimace.* *—intr.v.* **grim•aced, grim•ac•ing, grim•ac•es.** To make a sharp contortion of the face: *Most people grimace when tasting a lemon.*

grime (grīm) *n.* Black dirt or soot clinging to or ground into a surface.

Grim•ké (grĭm′kē), **Sarah Moore.** 1792–1873. American feminist and abolitionist who with her sister **Angelina Emily Grimké** (1805–1879) lectured widely against slavery and the repression of women.

Grimm (grĭm), **Jakob Ludwig Karl.** 1785–1863. German storyteller who with his brother **Wilhelm Karl Grimm** (1786–1859) collected folk tales and published them as *Grimm's Fairy Tales* (1812–1815).

grim•y (grī′mē) *adj.* **grim•i•er, grim•i•est.** Covered with grime: *The window was so grimy it was impossible to see through it.* **—grim′i•ly** *adv.* **—grim′i•ness** *n.*

grin (grĭn) *v.* **grinned, grin•ning, grins.** *—intr.* To smile broadly: *grin with delight.* *—tr.* To express with a grin: *Our host grinned a warm welcome.* *—n.* A broad smile: *a happy grin.*

grind (grīnd) *v.* **ground** (ground), **grind•ing, grinds.** *—tr.* **1.** To crush into small bits or a fine powder: *grind wheat into flour; grind coffee.* **2.** To shape, smooth, or sharpen by rubbing on something rough: *grind scissors to a fine edge; grind lenses for eyeglasses.* **3.** To rub (two surfaces) together; gnash: *grind the teeth.* **4.** To bear down on harshly; crush: *The team's spirit was ground down by a string of losses.* **5.a.** To operate by turning a crank: *grind a pepper mill.* **b.** To produce or process by turning a crank: *grinding a pound of beef.* **6.** To produce mechanically or without inspiration. *—intr.* **1.** To become crushed, pulverized, or powdered by friction. **2.** To move with noisy friction; grate: *The train ground to a halt.* **3.** *Informal.* To devote oneself to study or work: *grind away at a long report.* *—n.* **1.** The act of grinding: *a grind of the brakes.* **2.** A specific grade or degree of pulverization: *a fine grind of coffee.* **3.** *Informal.* A laborious task, routine, or study: *the daily grind of homework.* **4.** *Informal.* A student who works or studies all the time. [First written down about 725 in Old English and spelled *forgrindan*.] **—grind′ing•ly** *adv.*

grind•er (grīn′dər) *n.* **1.** A person who grinds, especially a person who sharpens scissors, knives, or other tools. **2.** A mechanical device for grinding: *a meat grinder.* **3.** One of the back teeth used for grinding food; a molar.

grind•stone (grīnd′stōn′) *n.* A revolving stone disk, used for grinding, polishing, or sharpening tools. ***—idiom.*** **put (one's) nose to the grindstone.** *Informal.* To work hard and steadily.

grip (grĭp) *n.* **1.** A tight hold; a firm grasp: *a good grip on the rope.* **2.** A manner of grasping and holding: *The grip for holding a baseball bat is different from the grip for swinging a golf club.* **3.** A part designed to be grasped and held; a handle: *the grips on the handlebars of a bicycle.* **4.** Ability to function well or properly; competence: *have a good grip on the new technique.* **5.** Understanding; mastery: *He now has a good grip on Spanish.* **6.** A suitcase or valise. *—tr.v.* **gripped, grip•ping, grips. 1.** To grasp and hold tightly; seize firmly. **2.** To hold the interest and attention of: *a real-life drama that gripped the nation.* [First written down about 725 in Old English and spelled *gripe*, grasp.]

❑ *These sound alike:* **grip, grippe** (influenza).

gripe (grīp) *v.* **griped, grip•ing, gripes.** *—intr.* **1.** *Informal.* To complain; grumble: *Everyone griped about the new regulations.* **2.** To have sharp pains in the bowels. *—tr.* **1.** *Informal.* To irritate; annoy: *The criticisms really griped me.* **2.** To cause sharp pains in the bowels of. *—n.* **1.** *Informal.* A complaint: *Everyone has some gripe about winter weather.* **2. gripes.** Sharp repeated pains in the bowels. [First written down about 725 in Old English and spelled *grīpan*, to seize.]

grippe (grĭp) *n.* Influenza. [First written down in 1776 in Modern English, from Old French *grippe*, claw, quarrel, from *gripper*, to seize, grasp, of Germanic origin.]

❑ *These sound alike:* **grippe, grip** (firm grasp).

gris•ly (grĭz′lē) *adj.* **gris•li•er, gris•li•est.** Inspiring repugnance; gruesome. —**gris′li•ness** *n.*

❑ *These sound alike:* **grisly, grizzly** (grayish).

grist (grĭst) *n.* **1.** Grain or a quantity of grain for grinding. **2.** Ground grain.

gris•tle (grĭs′əl) *n.* Tough tissue or cartilage, especially when found in meat.

gris•tly (grĭs′lē) *adj.* **gris•tli•er, gris•tli•est.** Composed of, resembling, or containing gristle: *a gristly piece of steak.*

grist•mill (grĭst′mĭl′) *n.* A mill for grinding grain.

grit (grĭt) *n.* **1.** Tiny rough particles, as of sand or stone: *Grit had collected on the chain of my bicycle.* **2.** A coarse sandstone used for grindstones and millstones. **3.** *Informal.* Indomitable spirit; great courage and determination: *To be a good athlete one needs plenty of grit.* —*v.* **grit•ted, grit•ting, grits.** —*tr.* To clamp or grind (the teeth) together. —*intr.* To make a grinding noise: *Wagon wheels gritted over the lane.*

grits (grĭts) *pl.n.* *(used with a singular or plural verb).* **1.** Coarsely ground hominy or corn kernels cooked and served for breakfast or as a side dish. **2.** Coarsely ground grain, especially corn.

grit•ty (grĭt′ē) *adj.* **grit•ti•er, grit•ti•est. 1.** Containing, covered with, or resembling grit. **2.** Showing determination and strength; plucky. —**grit′ti•ness** *n.*

griz•zled (grĭz′əld) *adj.* **1.** Streaked with or partly gray: *a grizzled beard.* **2.** Having brownish fur or hair tipped with gray.

griz•zly (grĭz′lē) *adj.* **griz•zli•er, griz•zli•est.** Grayish or flecked with gray. —*n., pl.* **griz•zlies.** A grizzly bear.

❑ *These sound alike:* **grizzly, grisly** (horrifying).

grizzly bear *n.* A large brown or grayish bear of the mountainous regions of western North America. Its fur is tipped with white and looks grizzled.

groan (grōn) *v.* **groaned, groan•ing, groans.** —*intr.* **1.** To utter a deep and prolonged sound, as of pain, grief, or displeasure: *groan over a toothache.* **2.** To make a low creaking sound resembling this: *The floorboards groaned.* —*tr.* To utter or communicate by groaning: *The audience groaned their dissatisfaction at the play's ending.* —*n.* The sound made in groaning. —**groan′er** *n.*

❑ *These sound alike:* **groan, grown** (past tense of grow).

groats (grōts) *pl.n.* *(used with a singular or plural verb).* Hulled, usually crushed grain, especially oats.

gro•cer (grō′sər) *n.* A storekeeper who sells food and household supplies. [First written down in 1418 in Middle English and spelled *grocer*, wholesaler, from Late Latin *grossus*, thick, large.]

gro•cer•y (grō′sə rē) *n., pl.* **gro•cer•ies. 1.** A store selling food and household supplies. **2. groceries.** The goods sold by a grocer.

grog (grŏg) *n.* Rum or another liquor diluted with water. [First written down in 1770 in Modern English and spelled *grogg*, after Old *Grog*, nickname of Edward Vernon (1684–1757), British admiral who ordered that diluted rum be served to his sailors. He got this name from his habit of wearing a cloak made of grogram, a kind of coarse fabric.]

grog•gy (grŏg′ē) *adj.* **grog•gi•er, grog•gi•est.** Unsteady and dazed; shaky: *still groggy from a bout with the flu.* —**grog′gi•ly** *adv.* —**grog′gi•ness** *n.*

groin (groin) *n.* **1.** The fold or crease where the thigh joins the body, including the area nearby. **2.** In architecture, the curved line where two ceiling vaults come together.

grom•met (grŏm′ĭt) *n.* **1.** A reinforced eyelet, as in cloth or leather. **2.** A small metal or plastic ring used to reinforce an eyelet.

groom (gro͞om *or* gro͝om) *n.* **1.** A person employed to take care of horses. **2.** A bridegroom. —*tr.v.* **groomed, groom•ing, grooms. 1.** To make neat and trim, especially in personal appearance: *groomed themselves in front of the mirror before going to the party.* **2.** To clean and brush (an animal). **3.** To train (a person), as for a certain job or position: *groom a successor to the manager.*

grooms•man (gro͞omz′mən *or* gro͝omz′mən) *n.* A man who attends the bridegroom at a wedding.

groove (gro͞ov) *n.* **1.** A long narrow furrow or channel: *The drawer moves in and out on grooves.* **2.** *Slang.* A settled routine: *We got out of the groove over vacation.* **3.** *Slang.* A very pleasurable experience. —*tr.v.* **grooved, groov•ing, grooves.** To cut a groove or grooves in: *groove the surface of a highway.*

groov•y (gro͞o′vē) *adj.* **groov•i•er, groov•i•est.** *Slang.* Very pleasing; wonderful: *a groovy song.* —**groov′i•ly** *adv.* —**groov′i•ness** *n.*

grope (grōp) *v.* **groped, grop•ing, gropes.** —*intr.* To reach about or search blindly or uncertainly: *grope for the light switch; grope for an answer.* —*tr.* To make (one's way) by reaching about uncertainly: *grope one's way down a long dark hall.* —**grop′ing•ly** *adv.*

gros•beak (grōs′bēk′) *n.* Any of various finches having a thick rounded bill and colorful plumage.

gros•grain (grō′grān′) *n.* **1.** A heavy woven silk or rayon fabric having narrow horizontal ribs. **2.** A ribbon made of this fabric.

gross (grōs) *adj.* **gross•er, gross•est. 1.** Having nothing subtracted; total: *gross pay of $6.00 an hour.* **2.** Very easy to see; glaring: *a gross error.* **3.** Vulgar; coarse: *a gross remark.* **4.** Offensive; disgusting. **5.** Overweight. —*n., pl.* **gross. 1.** The entire body or amount, as of income, before the necessary deductions have been made: *The company's gross was impressive, but once expenses were figured in, it didn't seem so great.* **2.** A group of 144 items; 12 dozen: *This box holds a gross of oranges.* —*tr.v.* **grossed, gross•ing, gross•es.** To earn as a total income or profit before deductions. —***idiom.*** **gross out.** To fill with disgust; nauseate: *The violent scene in the movie grossed me out.* [First written down in 1347 in Middle English and spelled *gross*, large, from Late Latin *grossus*, thick.] —**gross′ly** *adv.* —**gross′ness** *n.*

gross national product *n.* The total market value of all goods and services produced by a nation during a specified period.

gro•tesque (grō tĕsk′) *adj.* **1.** Characterized by ludicrous distortion, as of appearance or manner. **2.** Outlandish or bizarre, as in character or appearance: *The grotesque clown made us laugh.* —**gro•tesque′ly** *adv.* —**gro•tesque′ness** *n.*

grot•to (grŏt′ō) *n., pl.* **grot•toes** or **grot•tos. 1.** A small cave or cavern. **2.** A structure or an excavation built to look like a cave or cavern. —SEE NOTE.

grouch (grouch) *n.* **1.** A person who habitually complains or grumbles. **2.** A grumbling or sulky mood: *in a grouch for no good reason.* —*intr.v.* **grouched, grouch•ing, grouch•es.** To complain; grumble: *Why grouch about the weather?*

grouch•y (grou′chē) *adj.* **grouch•i•er, grouch•i•est.** Tending to complain or grumble; peevish: *Don't be so grouchy!* —**grouch′i•ly** *adv.* —**grouch′i•ness** *n.*

ground[1] (ground) *n.* **1.** The solid surface of the earth; land; soil: *The ground is still frozen.* **2.** An

grommet

Word History: grotto

You may not be so eager to go back into that picturesque **grotto** next time. Our word comes from the Italian, as the spelling and pronunciation suggest. The actual Italian form is *grotta*, and it comes from an earlier word *grupta* or *crupta*. *Crupta* comes from the Latin word *crypta*, "an underground vault, chamber, or pit," the source of our **crypt**.

ă	pat	oi	boy
ā	pay	ou	out
âr	care	o͝o	took
ä	father	o͞o	boot
ĕ	pet	ŭ	cut
ē	be	ûr	urge
ĭ	pit	th	thin
ī	pie	*th*	this
îr	pier	hw	whoop
ŏ	pot	zh	vision
ō	toe	ə	about
ô	paw	N	*French* bon

Usage: group

The word **group** as a **collective noun** can be followed by a singular or plural verb. It takes a singular verb when those making up the group are considered as a body: *The group is all here for the party.* **Group** takes a plural verb when those making up the group are considered individually: *The group are divided about where to go for pizza.*

grouse¹
Male ruffed grouse

area or plot of land set aside for a special purpose. Often used in the plural: *camp grounds; a burial ground.* **3.** The land surrounding a house or other building. Often used in the plural: *the school grounds.* **4.** The basis or reason for a belief or an action. Often used in the plural: *grounds for making an accusation.* **5.** An area of reference or discussion; a subject: *covered new ground in today's talk.* **6.** A surrouding area; a background: *The flag has white stars on a blue ground.* **7. grounds.** The sediment that settles at the bottom of a liquid, such as coffee. **8.** A connection between an electrical conductor and the earth. —*v.* **ground•ed, ground•ing, grounds.** —*tr.* **1.** To place on or cause to touch the ground. **2.** To run (a vessel) aground: *We grounded our boat by accident.* **3.** To instruct in fundamentals or basics: *This class grounds students in basic science.* **4.** To provide a basis for (a theory, for example); justify: *grounded his argument on facts.* **5.** To connect (an electric circuit or conductor) with the earth. **6.** To prevent (an aircraft or a pilot) from flying: *Bad weather grounded all flights.* **7.** In baseball, to hit (a ball) onto the ground. —*intr.* **1.** To touch or reach the ground. **2.** To run aground: *The ship grounded in the storm.* **3.** In baseball, to hit a ground ball. ***—idiom.* ground out.** In baseball, to be put out by hitting a ground ball that is fielded and thrown to first base. [First written down about 725 in Old English and spelled *grund.*]

ground² (ground) *v.* Past tense and past participle of **grind.**

ground ball *n.* In baseball, a batted ball that rolls or bounces along the ground.

ground•break•ing (**ground′**brā′kĭng) *n.* The act or ceremony of turning up ground to start construction: *Groundbreaking for the new hospital is to begin today.* —*adj.* Characterized by originality and innovation: *groundbreaking technology.*

ground crew *n.* A team of mechanics and technicians responsible for the maintenance and service of aircraft on the ground.

ground•er (**groun′**dər) *n.* A ground ball.

ground floor *n.* **1.** The floor of a building at or nearest ground level. **2.** *Informal.* The start of something, as a project or business: *I started in this business on the ground floor as a messenger.*

ground•hog (**ground′**hôg′ *or* **ground′**hŏg′) *n.* The woodchuck. —See Note at **woodchuck.**

Groundhog Day *n.* February 2, which predicts that there will be an early spring if the groundhog does not see its shadow when coming out of its burrow or that there will be six weeks more of winter weather if the groundhog does see its shadow.

ground•less (**ground′**lĭs) *adj.* Having no ground or foundation; unsupported by the facts: *groundless worries.* **—ground′less•ly** *adv.* **—ground′less•ness** *n.*

ground•nut (**ground′**nŭt′) *n.* **1.** Any of several plants, such as the peanut, having edible underground tubers that resemble nuts. **2.** The seed or tuber of any of these plants.

ground pine *n.* A low creeping club moss having evergreen stalks often used for decoration.

ground rule *n.* A basic rule. Often used in the plural: *ground rules for tennis; set ground rules for a club.*

ground squirrel *n.* Any of several small burrowing rodents related to and resembling the chipmunk.

ground•swell (**ground′**swĕl′) *n.* **1.** Deep rolling waves in the ocean, often the result of a distant storm or earthquake. **2.** A sudden gathering of force, as of public opinion: *a groundswell of support for the proposed law.*

ground water also **ground•wa•ter** (**ground′**wô′tər *or* **ground′**wŏt′ər) *n.* Water that flows or seeps beneath the surface of the earth, soaking soil or porous rock, and supplying wells and springs.

ground•work (**ground′**wûrk′) *n.* Work that lays the basis for something; a foundation.

group (gro͞op) *n.* **1.** A number of persons or things gathered or located together: *a group of students in a museum; a group of islands off the coast of Alaska.* **2.** A number of persons or things classed together because of similarities: *a small group of supporters across the country.* **3.** Two or more atoms bound together that act as a unit in a number of chemical compounds: *a hydroxyl group.* **4.** In the periodic table, a vertical column that contains elements having similar properties. —*v.* **grouped, group•ing, groups.** —*tr.* To place or arrange in a group: *group books on the same topic together.* —*intr.* To belong to or form a group: *The class grouped on the steps for their picture.* [First written down in 1695 in Modern English, from Italian *gruppo*, probably of Germanic origin.] —See Note.

grou•per (**gro͞o′**pər) *n., pl.* **grouper** or **grou•pers.** Any of various large, mostly tropical ocean fishes that often group around rocks and coral reefs.

group•ing (**gro͞o′**pĭng) *n.* **1.** The act or process of uniting in groups: *The grouping of the children into teams took several minutes.* **2.** A collection of things or persons united in a group: *There is a large grouping of reference books in the library.*

grouse¹ (grous) *n., pl.* **grouse** or **grous•es.** Any of various plump birds having mottled brown or grayish feathers on the body and legs, often hunted as game. [First written down before 1547 in Modern English.]

grouse² (grous) *Informal. intr.v.* **groused, grous•ing, grous•es.** To complain; grumble: *groused about the poor hotel service.* [First written down in 1887 in Modern English, possibly from Old French *grouchier.*]

grove (grōv) *n.* A group of trees with open ground between them, as in an orchard: *an orange grove.*

grov•el (**grŏv′**əl *or* **grŭv′**əl) *intr.v.* **grov•eled, grov•el•ing, grov•els** also **grov•elled, grov•el•ling, grov•els. 1.** To behave in a servile or demeaning manner; cringe: *Be proud of yourself and do not grovel.* **2.** To lie flat or crawl on one's belly, as in humility or submission: *The dog began to grovel at its owner's feet.* **—grov′el•er, grov′el•ler** *n.*

grow (grō) *v.* **grew** (gro͞o), **grown** (grōn), **grow•ing, grows.** —*intr.* **1.** To become bigger by a natural process of development; mature: *The seedlings grew into plants.* **2.** To be capable of growth; thrive; flourish: *Banana trees grow well in tropical climates.* **3.** To increase or spread; expand: *The business grew rapidly.* **4.** To come to be by a gradual process or by degrees: *grow rich; grow dark outside.* —*tr.* **1.** To cause to grow; produce; cultivate: *grow vegetables in a garden.* **2.** To allow (something) to develop or increase by a natural process: *grow a beard.* ***—idioms.* grow out of.** To develop or come into existence from: *The book grew out of our scribbled notes.* **grow up.** To become an adult. [First written down about 725 in Old English and spelled *grōwan.*]

grow•er (**grō′**ər) *n.* **1.** A person who grows something, especially a person who grows a particular crop for sale: *a fruit grower.* **2.** A plant that grows in a particular way: *Most weeds are fast growers.*

growl (groul) *n.* **1.** A low, throaty, menacing sound made by a animal: *the growl of a dog.* **2.** A gruff surly utterance: *answered me with a growl.* —*v.* **growled, growl•ing, growls.** —*intr.* **1.** To make a low throaty sound or utterance. **2.** To speak in a surly or angry manner. —*tr.* To utter by growling: *The dog growled a warning.*

grown (grōn) *v.* Past participle of **grow.** *—adj.* **1.** Having full growth; mature: *act like a grown person.* **2.** Produced or cultivated: *locally grown produce.*
❑ *These sound alike:* **grown, groan** (moan).

grown•up also **grown-up** (**grōn′**ŭp′) *n.* An adult.

grown-up (**grōn′**ŭp′) *adj.* Of or intended for adults; mature: *a grown-up movie.*

growth (grōth) *n.* **1.** The process of growing; development: *the growth of a child.* **2.** Something that grows or has grown: *A thick growth of weeds covered the yard.* **3.** An amount grown; an increase or expansion: *measure the growth of a country's population.* **4.** An abnormal mass of tissue growing in or on a living organism: *A wart is a growth on the body.*

grub (grŭb) *v.* **grubbed, grub•bing, grubs.** *—tr.* **1.** To dig up by or as if by the roots: *grub turnips.* **2.** To clear of roots and stumps by digging: *grubbed a small plot.* *—intr.* **1.** To dig in the ground: *grub for potatoes.* **2.** To work hard; drudge: *grub for a living.* *—n.* **1.** The thick wormlike larva of certain beetles and other insects. **2.** *Slang.* Food: *buy the grub for a camping trip.*

grub•by (**grŭb′**ē) *adj.* **grub•bi•er, grub•bi•est.** Dirty; grimy: *grubby work clothes.* **—grub′bi•ly** *adv.* **—grub′bi•ness** *n.*

grub•stake (**grŭb′**stāk′) *n.* Supplies or funds advanced to a mining prospector or a person starting a business in return for a promised share of the profits. *—tr.v.* **grub•staked, grub•stak•ing, grub•stakes.** To supply with a grubstake.

grudge (grŭj) *tr.v.* **grudged, grudg•ing, grudg•es.** To be reluctant to give or admit: *grudged me a small discount for paying in cash.* *—n.* A deep-seated feeling of resentment: *holds a grudge about the accident.* [First written down in 1459 in Middle English, from *grucchen,* to grumble, complain, from Old French *grouchier,* probably of Germanic origin.]

grudg•ing•ly (**grŭj′**ĭng lē) *adv.* In a reluctant manner: *The children grudgingly went to bed.*

gru•el (**grōō′**əl) *n.* A thin watery porridge. [First written down about 1330 in Middle English, from Old French, of Germanic origin.]

gru•el•ing also **gru•el•ling** (**grōō′**ə lĭng *or* **grōō′**lĭng) *adj.* Physically or mentally exhausting: *Working in a coal mine is a grueling job.*

grue•some (**grōō′**səm) *adj.* Causing horror and shock; frightful: *a gruesome accident.* **—grue′some•ly** *adv.* **—grue′some•ness** *n.*

gruff (grŭf) *adj.* **gruff•er, gruff•est. 1.** Brusque or stern in manner or appearance: *a gruff reply.* **2.** Harsh-sounding; hoarse: *a gruff voice.* **—gruff′ly** *adv.* **—gruff′ness** *n.*

grum•ble (**grŭm′**bəl) *v.* **grum•bled, grum•bling, grum•bles.** *—intr.* **1.** To complain in a surly manner; mutter in discontent: *They grumbled about the store's prices.* **2.** To rumble or growl. *—tr.* To express in a grumbling or discontented manner: *grumbled a response.* *—n.* **1.** A muttered complaint. **2.** A rumble; a growl: *the grumble of distant thunder.* **—grum′bler** *n.*

grump•y (**grŭm′**pē) *adj.* **grump•i•er, grump•i•est.** Surly and peevish; cranky: *a grumpy mood.* **—grump′i•ly** *adv.* **—grump′i•ness** *n.*

grunt (grŭnt) *v.* **grunt•ed, grunt•ing, grunts.** *—intr.* **1.** To make a deep throaty sound, as a hog does. **2.** To make a sound similar to a grunt, as in disgust. *—tr.* To utter or express with a deep throaty sound: *The irritated clerk grunted a reply.* *—n.* **1.** A deep throaty sound, as that made by a hog. **2.** Any of the various chiefly tropical ocean fishes that make grunting sounds when removed from the water.

Gt. Brit. *abbr.* An abbreviation of Great Britain.

Gua•da•la•ja•ra (gwŏd′l ə **hä′**rə). A city of west-central Mexico west-northwest of Mexico City. The city is at an altitude of more than 5,000 feet (1,525 meters). Population, 1,626,152.

Gua•de•loupe (**gwŏd′**l ōōp′ *or* gwŏd′l **ōōp′**). An overseas department of France made up of the islands of Grande-Terre and Basse-Terre and smaller islands in the Leeward Islands of the West Indies. Capital, Basse-Terre. Population, 328,400.

Guam (gwäm). A territory of the United States, the largest and southernmost of the Mariana Islands in the western Pacific Ocean. Captial, Agana. Population, 105,979.

gua•na•co (gwə **nä′**kō) *n., pl.* **gua•na•cos** or **guanaco.** A brownish South American animal related to and resembling the llama. [First written down in 1604 in Modern English, from Quechua *huanaco.*]

guanaco

Guang•zhou (**gwäng′**jō′). Formerly **Can•ton** (**kăn′**tŏn′ *or* kăn′**tŏn′**). A city of southern China on a delta near the South China Sea. Its port was opened to foreign trade in the middle 1800's. Population, 2,570,000.

gua•nine (**gwä′**nēn′) *n.* A base that is a component of DNA and RNA.

gua•no (**gwä′**nō) *n., pl.* **gua•nos. 1.** The dung of certain sea birds or bats, used as fertilizer. **2.** A similar fertilizer, such as one made from ground fish parts.

gua•ra•ni (gwä′rə **nē′**) *n., pl.* **guarani** or **gua•ra•nis.** The basic monetary unit of Paraguay.

Gua•ra•ni (gwä′rə **nē′**) *n., pl.* **Guarani** or **Gua•ra•nis. 1.** A member of a South American Indian people of Paraguay, Argentina, and Brazil. **2.** The language of this people.

guar•an•tee (găr′ən **tē′**) *n.* **1.** Something that assures a particular condition or outcome: *Money is not a guarantee of happiness.* **2.** A promise or an assurance that attests to a product's quality or durability. **3.** A guaranty. *—tr.v.* **guar•an•teed, guar•an•tee•ing, guar•an•tees. 1.** To render certain; make sure: *The rains guarantee a good crop.* **2.** To undertake to accomplish (something) for another: *Jefferson wanted to guarantee freedom of speech for future generations.* **3.** To assume responsibility for the quality or performance of: *The manufacturer guarantees these microwave ovens for five years.* **4.** To provide security for: *Insurance guarantees a car owner against costs of injury or of repairs.* [First written down about 1436 in Middle English and spelled *garant,* warranty, from Old French, of Germanic origin.]

guar•an•tor (găr′ən **tôr′** *or* **găr′**ən tər) *n.* A person who makes or gives a promise, an assurance, or a pledge.

guar•an•ty (**găr′**ən tē) *n., pl.* **guar•an•ties. 1.** An agreement to assume the responsibility of payment or fulfillment of another's debts or obligations: *My cousin signed a guaranty for my bank loan.* **2.** Something given as security for the fulfillment of an obligation or the payment of a debt. **3.** A guarantee, as for a product or service. *—tr.v.* **guar•an•tied, guar•an•ty•ing, guar•an•ties.** To guarantee: *Employers may guaranty loans for trusted employees.*

guard (gärd) *v.* **guard•ed, guard•ing, guards.** *—tr.* **1.** To protect from harm by or as if by watching over: *guard a building after dark.* See Synonyms at **defend. 2.** To watch over so as to prevent escape or violence: *guard a prisoner.* **3.** To keep (an opposing player) from scoring or playing efficiently in certain sports, such as basketball and hockey. **4.** To furnish (a device or an object) with a protective piece. *—intr.* To take precautions: *guard against illness by getting plenty of rest and taking vitamins.* *—n.* **1.** Something that gives protection; a safeguard: *a*

ă	pat	oi	boy
ā	pay	ou	out
âr	care	ŏŏ	took
ä	father	ōō	boot
ĕ	pet	ŭ	cut
ē	be	ûr	urge
ĭ	pit	th	thin
ī	pie	*th*	this
îr	pier	hw	whoop
ŏ	pot	zh	vision
ō	toe	ə	about
ô	paw	N	*French* bon

guava

Guernsey
Guernsey cow

guide dog

guard against tooth decay. **2.** A person who keeps watch, protects, or acts as a sentinel: *a prison guard.* **3.** Protection or watch: *The sheepdog kept guard over the herd.* **4.** A device or an attachment that protects or shields the user: *Bicycle fenders are a guard against water and dirt.* **5.** In football, either of the two players on a team's offensive line on each side of the center. **6.** In basketball, either of two players stationed near their team's basket. ***—idioms.*** **off guard** or **off (one's) guard.** Unprepared; not alert: *The thunderclap caught me off guard, and I jumped.* **on guard** or **on (one's) guard.** Alert and watchful; cautious: *Be on guard for patches of ice on the sidewalk.* [First written down in 1448 in Middle English and spelled *garden,* from Old French *garder,* of Germanic origin.]

guard cell *n.* Either of a pair of crescent-shaped cells that control the opening and closing of one of the tiny pores on the outer surface of a leaf.

guard•ed (gär′dĭd) *adj.* **1.** Defended; protected: *a heavily guarded border.* **2.** Cautious; restrained: *give a guarded answer.* **—guard′ed•ly** *adv.*

guard•house (gärd′hous′) *n.* **1.** A building that accommodates soldiers on guard. **2.** A military jail for personnel guilty of minor offenses or awaiting court-martial.

guard•i•an (gär′dē ən) *n.* **1.** A person or thing that guards, protects, or watches over: *The courts act as a guardian of the law.* **2.** A person who is legally responsible for the care and management of the person or property of someone who cannot manage his or her own affairs.

guard•rail (gärd′rāl′) *n.* A protective railing, as on a highway or stairway.

guard•room (gärd′ro͞om′ *or* gärd′ro͝om′) *n.* A room used by guards on duty.

guards•man (gärdz′mən) *n.* **1.** A person who acts as a guard. **2.** A member of the U.S. National Guard.

Gua•te•ma•la (gwä′tə mä′lə). **1.** A country of northern Central America west of Honduras. Inhabited by Mayans for more than a thousand years, Guatemala was colonized by Spain in 1524 and achieved its independence in 1839. Capital, Guatemala. Population, 6,054,227. **2.** Also **Guatemala City.** The capital and largest city of Guatemala, in the south-central part of the country. It was founded in 1776. Population, 754,243.

gua•va (gwä′və) *n.* **1.** The sweet yellow fruit of any of various tropical American trees, used to make jelly and preserves. **2.** A tree that bears such fruit. [First written down in 1555 in Modern English, from Spanish *guayaba,* of Caribbean Indian origin.]

gu•ber•na•to•ri•al (go͞o′bər nə tôr′ē əl *or* gyo͞o′-bər nə tôr′ē əl) *adj.* Of or relating to a governor. [First written down in 1734 in American English, from Latin *gubernātor,* governor.]

gudg•eon (gŭj′ən) *n.* A small freshwater fish of Europe and Asia, related to the carp and often used for bait.

Guern•sey (gûrn′zē) *n., pl.* **Guern•seys.** Any of a breed of brown and white cattle raised for milk.

guer•ril•la or **gue•ril•la** (gə rĭl′ə) *n.* A member of a usually indigenous military force operating in small bands in occupied territory to harass the enemy, as by surprise raids. [First written down in 1809 in Modern English, from Spanish, from *guerra,* war.]
❑ *These sound alike:* **guerrilla, gorilla** (ape).

guess (gĕs) *v.* **guessed, guess•ing, guess•es.** *—tr.* **1.** To assume, presume, or assert (a fact) without sufficient information: *The reporter guessed that 6,000 people were at the concert.* **2.** To form a correct estimate or conjecture of: *I guessed the answer to the math problem.* **3.** To suppose; think: *I guess you're right.* *—intr.* To make an estimate or a conjecture: *We can only guess at their reason for staying home.* *—n.* A conjecture arrived at by guessing: *If you're not sure of the answer, at least make a guess.* [First written down about 1303 in Middle English and spelled *gessen,* probably of Scandinavian origin.] **—guess′er** *n.*

guess•ti•mate (gĕs′tə mĭt) *n. Informal.* An estimate based on conjecture.

guess•work (gĕs′wûrk′) *n.* **1.** The process of making guesses: *There is a lot of guesswork involved in predicting sales of a new product.* **2.** An estimate or a judgment made by guessing.

guest (gĕst) *n.* **1.a.** A person who is a recipient of hospitality at the home or table of another: *We invited several guests for dinner.* **b.** A person who is a recipient of hospitality or entertainment by a host or hostess, as at a party. **2.** A person who pays for meals or accommodations at a restaurant, hotel, or other establishment. **3.** A visiting performer, speaker, or contestant, as on a television program. [First written down before 1200 in Middle English and spelled *gest,* from Old Norse *gestr.*]

guf•faw (gə fô′) *n.* A hearty boisterous burst of laughter. *—intr.v.* **guf•fawed, guf•faw•ing, guf•faws.** To laugh heartily and boisterously: *The audience guffawed at the jokes.*

Gui•an•a (gē ăn′ə *or* gē ä′nə). A region of northeast South America including southeast Venezuela, part of northern Brazil, and French Guiana, Suriname, and Guyana.

guid•ance (gīd′ns) *n.* **1.** The act or process of guiding: *Success of the expedition depended on the guidance of their scouts.* **2.** Counseling, as on vocational, educational, or personal problems. **3.** A process by which the course of a missile can be controlled or corrected in flight.

guide (gīd) *n.* **1.** A person or thing that shows the way, directs, leads, or advises: *a tour guide; a guide to good manners.* **2.** A person employed to conduct others, as through a museum, and give information. **3.** A guidebook. **4.** A device, such as a ruler, tab, or bar, that acts to regulate operation or direct motion. *—tr.v.* **guid•ed, guid•ing, guides. 1.** To serve as a guide for; conduct: *The ranger guided the tourists through the park.* **2.** To direct the course of; steer: *guide a car down a narrow street.* **3.** To exert control or influence over: *Lincoln guided our nation through the Civil War.* [First written down before 1376 in Middle English and spelled *gide,* from Old French *guide,* from Old Provençal *guidar,* to guide, of Germanic origin.] **—guid′a•ble** *adj.* **—guid′er** *n.*

Synonyms: **guide, lead, shepherd, steer, usher.** These verbs all mean to conduct on the way or direct to the way. *We were guided to our seats. The teacher led the students in a discussion of the novel's themes. The tourists were shepherded to the chartered bus. The secretary steered the applicant to the proper department. The host will now usher the contestants into a soundproof booth.*

---

guide•book (gīd′bo͝ok′) *n.* A handbook of directions and information, especially for travelers and tourists.

guid•ed missile (gī′dĭd) *n.* A missile whose course can be controlled while it is in flight.

guide dog *n.* A dog trained to lead a person who is visually impaired.

guide•line (gīd′līn′) *n.* A statement or other indication of policy or procedure, intended to give practical guidance: *The President presented guidelines for economic development and aid to other countries.*

guide•post (gīd′pōst′) *n.* A post with a sign to give directions for travelers, often placed at a crossroads.

guide•word (gīd′wûrd′) *n.* A word or term placed at the top of a column or page in a reference book to indicate the first or last entry on the page.

guild (gĭld) *n.* **1.** An association of persons who share a trade or pursuit, formed to protect mutual interests and maintain standards. **2.** A similar association, as of merchants or artisans, in medieval times.

❑ *These sound alike:* **guild, gild** (cover with gold).

guil•der (gĭl′dər) *n.* The basic monetary unit of the Netherlands, Suriname, and the Netherlands Antilles.

guild•hall (gĭld′hôl′) *n.* **1.** The meeting hall of a guild. **2.** A town hall.

guile (gīl) *n.* Treacherous cunning; skillful deceit.

guile•ful (gīl′fəl) *adj.* Full of guile; crafty; deceitful.

guile•less (gīl′lĭs) *adj.* Free of guile; artless.

guil•lo•tine (gĭl′ə tēn′ *or* gē′ə tēn′) *n.* A device consisting of a heavy blade held aloft between two upright guides and dropped to behead the person below. —*tr.v.* **guil•lo•tined, guil•lo•tin•ing, guil•lo•tines.** To behead with a guillotine. [First written down in 1793 in Modern English, after Joseph Ignace *Guillotin* (1738–1814), French physician.]

guilt (gĭlt) *n.* **1.** The fact of being responsible for the committing of an offense: *Thorough investigation uncovered the suspect's guilt.* **2.** Remorseful awareness of having done something wrong. **3.** Guilty behavior; sin.

❑ *These sound alike:* **guilt, gilt** (layer of gold).

guilt•less (gĭlt′lĭs) *adj.* Free of guilt; innocent.

guilt•y (gĭl′tē) *adj.* **guilt•i•er, guilt•i•est. 1.** Having done wrong; deserving of blame; culpable: *The thief was found guilty.* **2.** Burdened with or prompted by a sense of guilt: *a guilty conscience.* **—guilt′i•ly** *adv.* **—guilt′i•ness** *n.*

guin•ea (gĭn′ē) *n.* **1.** A gold coin formerly used in England and worth one pound and one shilling. **2.** The sum of one pound and one shilling.

Guin•ea (gĭn′ē). A country of western Africa on the Atlantic Ocean north of Sierra Leone. It gained its independence from France in 1958. Conakry is the capital and the largest city. Population, 4,830,000.

Guinea, Gulf of. A broad inlet of the Atlantic Ocean formed by the great bend in the west-central coast of Africa.

Guin•ea-Bis•sau (gĭn′ē bĭ sou′). A country of western Africa on the Atlantic Ocean south of Senegal. It gained its independence from Portugal in 1974. Bissau is the capital and the largest city. Population, 777,214.

guinea fowl *n.* Any of several birds resembling the pheasant, having blackish feathers with many small white spots and raised for food.

guinea pig *n.* **1.** Any of various rodents related to the woodchucks, mice, and squirrels, having short ears, short legs, and little or no tail. They are often kept as pets or used as laboratory animals. **2.** A person who is used as a subject for experimentation.

Guin•e•vere (gwĭn′ə vîr′) also **Guen•e•vere** (gwĕn′ə vîr′) *n.* In Arthurian legend, King Arthur's wife, who is loved by Lancelot.

guise (gīz) *n.* **1.** Outward appearance; aspect. **2.** False appearance; pretense: *spoke to me under the guise of friendship.* **3.** Mode of dress; garb: *The spy entered the enemy castle in the guise of a beggar.*

gui•tar (gĭ tär′) *n.* A stringed musical instrument having a long fretted neck and a large, pear-shaped sound box with a flat back.

gui•tar•ist (gĭ tär′ĭst) *n.* A person who plays the guitar.

gulch (gŭlch) *n.* A deep narrow ravine, especially one cut by the course of a stream or sudden water flow.

gulf (gŭlf) *n.* **1.** A large body of ocean or sea water that is partly surrounded by land. **2.** A deep wide chasm in the earth; an abyss: *Eruption of the volcano blew a gulf in the side of the mountain.* **3.** A wide gap, as in understanding: *the gulf between one generation and the next.*

Gulf Stream (gŭlf). A warm ocean current of the northern Atlantic Ocean off eastern North America. It flows from the Gulf of Mexico up the eastern coast of the United States and then northeast toward Europe.

gull[1] (gŭl) *n.* Any of various chiefly coastal water birds having a strong curved beak, webbed feet, long wings, and usually gray and white feathers. [First written down before 1450 in Middle English and spelled *gulle.*]

gull[2] (gŭl) *n.* A person who is easily tricked or cheated; a dupe. —*tr.v.* **gulled, gull•ing, gulls.** To deceive or cheat. [First written down before 1550 in Modern English, probably from Middle English *golen,* to make swallowing motions.]

gul•let (gŭl′ĭt) *n.* **1.** The tube that connects the throat and stomach; the esophagus. **2.** The throat.

gul•li•ble (gŭl′ə bəl) *adj.* Easily deceived or duped: *Ignorance often makes people gullible.* **—gul′li•bil′i•ty** *n.*

gul•ly (gŭl′ē) *n., pl.* **gul•lies.** A ditch or channel cut in the earth by running water, especially after heavy rain.

gulp (gŭlp) *v.* **gulped, gulp•ing, gulps.** —*tr.* **1.** To swallow greedily or rapidly in large amounts: *We were late and had to gulp our lunch.* **2.** To choke back by or as if by swallowing. —*intr.* **1.** To choke or gasp, as in swallowing large amounts of liquid. **2.** To swallow air, as in nervousness. —*n.* **1.** The act of gulping: *His bag of peanuts disappeared in just a few gulps.* **2.** An amount swallowed at one time: *a large gulp of water.*

gum[1] (gŭm) *n.* **1.a.** Any of various thick sticky substances produced by certain plants and trees that dries into a brittle solid and dissolves in water. **b.** A tree that is a source of gum, especially a eucalyptus tree. **2.** Rubber made from a plant substance. **3.** A sticky substance often made from the natural gum of plants; mucilage: *Gum on the flap of an envelope gets sticky after you lick it.* **4.** Chewing gum. —*v.* **gummed, gum•ming, gums.** —*tr.* To cover, smear, seal, fill, or fasten in place with or as if with gum: *Grease has gummed the drain.* —*intr.* To become sticky or clogged. [First written down before 1325 in Middle English, from Late Latin *gumma,* from Greek *kommi.*]

gum[2] (gŭm) *n.* The firm connective tissue that surrounds and supports the bases of the teeth. [First written down before 830 in Old English and spelled *gōma,* palate, jaw.]

gum arabic *n.* A gum produced by certain African trees, including acacias, and used in making pills, emulsions, and various foods, and in mucilage.

gum•bo (gŭm′bō) *n., pl.* **gum•bos. 1.** The okra plant and its pods. **2.** A soup or stew thickened with okra pods. **3.** A fine soil that contains much clay and becomes sticky when wet. [First written down in 1805 in American English, from Louisiana French *gombo,* of Bantu origin.] —SEE NOTE at **goober.**

gum•drop (gŭm′drŏp′) *n.* A small sugar-coated candy made of sweetened gum arabic or gelatin.

gum•my (gŭm′ē) *adj.* **gum•mi•er, gum•mi•est. 1.** Consisting of or containing gum. **2.** Covered or clogged with or as if with gum: *the gummy branches of a pine tree.* **3.** Thick and sticky: *gummy tar all over my shoes.* **—gum′mi•ness** *n.*

guinea pig

guitar

ă	pat	oi	boy
ā	pay	ou	out
âr	care	o͝o	took
ä	father	o͞o	boot
ĕ	pet	ŭ	cut
ē	be	ûr	urge
ĭ	pit	th	thin
ī	pie	*th*	this
îr	pier	hw	whoop
ŏ	pot	zh	vision
ō	toe	ə	about
ô	paw	N	*French* bon

Regional Note: gunnysack

Large sacks made from loosely woven coarse material such as burlap have a number of names in different parts of the United States. From the Ohio Valley westward to California the usual term is **gunnysack**. This goes back to the Sanskrit word *goṇī,* meaning "jute or hemp fiber." In parts of the South such a sack is called a *tow sack,* and in Eastern North Carolina, a *tow bag.* The word *tow* probably comes from an Old English word meaning "spinning." In other parts of the South the same type of bag is called a *crocus sack* or a *croker sack. Crocus* is a material like burlap that was once used to make clothes for slaves and laborers. Its name probably comes from sacks used to ship crocus or saffron.

Johann Gutenberg

gump•tion (gŭmp′shən) *n. Informal.* Boldness, initiative, or spunk.

gum resin *n.* A mixture of gum and resin produced by various plants or trees.

gun (gŭn) *n.* **1.** A weapon that shoots bullets or shells through a heavy metal tube, usually by the explosion of gunpowder. Pistols, rifles, and cannons are guns. **2.** A device that resembles a gun, as in its ability to project something under pressure: *Painting with a spray gun is quick.* **3.** A discharge of a gun as a signal or salute. —*v.* **gunned, gun•ning, guns.** —*tr.* **1.** To shoot (a person). **2.** To open the throttle of (an engine) so as to accelerate: *gunned the engine and sped away.* —*intr.* To hunt with a gun.

gun•boat (gŭn′bōt′) *n.* A small armed vessel.

gun•cot•ton (gŭn′kŏt′n) *n.* An explosive made from nitrocellulose.

gun•fire (gŭn′fīr′) *n.* The firing of guns.

gung ho (gŭng′ hō′) *adj. Slang.* Extremely dedicated or enthusiastic: *a gung ho baseball fan.* [First written down in 1959 in American English, from Chinese (Mandarin) *gōnghé,* to work together.]

gun•lock (gŭn′lŏk′) *n.* The mechanism in a gun that explodes the charge of gunpowder.

gun•man (gŭn′mən) *n.* A man armed with a gun, especially a killer or criminal.

gun•ner (gŭn′ər) *n.* **1.** A member of the armed forces who operates a gun. **2.** In the U.S. Marine Corps, a warrant officer in charge of a ship's guns. **3.** A person who hunts with a gun.

gun•ner•y (gŭn′ə rē) *n.* **1.** The science that deals with the techniques and procedures of operating guns. **2.** The use of guns; shooting.

gun•ny (gŭn′ē) *n., pl.* **gun•nies. 1.** A strong coarse cloth made of jute or hemp, used especially for sacks. **2.** Burlap. [First written down in 1711 in Modern English and spelled *goney,* from Hindi *gonī,* from Sanskrit *goṇī,* sack.]

gun•ny•sack (gŭn′ē săk′) *n.* A bag or sack made of gunny. —See Note.

gun•pow•der (gŭn′pou′dər) *n.* An explosive powder used in guns, fireworks, and blasting, especially a mixture of potassium nitrate, charcoal, and sulfur.

gun•shot (gŭn′shŏt′) *n.* **1.** Shot fired from a gun. **2.** The range of a gun: *within gunshot.* **3.** The shooting of a gun.

gun•smith (gŭn′smĭth′) *n.* A person who makes or repairs firearms.

gun•wale also **gun•nel** (gŭn′əl) *n.* The upper edge of the side of a ship or boat.

gup•py (gŭp′ē) *n., pl.* **gup•pies.** A small tropical freshwater fish that is brightly colored in the male and is often kept in home aquariums. The female does not lay eggs but bears live offspring. [First written down in 1925 in Modern English, after R.J. Lechmere *Guppy* (1836–1916), clergyman of Trinidad who first supplied specimens to the British Museum.]

gur•gle (gûr′gəl) *v.* **gur•gled, gur•gling, gur•gles.** —*intr.* **1.** To flow in an irregular current, making a bubbling sound: *A stream gurgled over the rocks.* **2.** To make such a bubbling sound: *The baby gurgled with contentment.* —*tr.* To express with an irregular bubbling sound: *The baby gurgled its delight.* [First written down before 1425 in Middle English and spelled *gurgulen,* from Latin *gurguliō,* gullet.]

gu•ru (gŏŏr′ōō *or* gōō rōō′) *n., pl.* **gu•rus. 1.** A Hindu spiritual teacher. **2.** A person who is followed as a leader or teacher. [First written down in 1800 in Modern English and spelled *gooroo,* from Sanskrit *guruḥ,* from *guru-,* heavy, venerable.]

gush (gŭsh) *v.* **gushed, gush•ing, gush•es.** —*intr.* **1.** To flow forth suddenly in great volume: *Water gushed from the broken pipe.* **2.** To make an excessive display of enthusiasm or sentiment: *Be sincere when thanking someone, but don't gush.* —*tr.* To emit abundantly; pour forth: *The new well gushed oil.* —*n.* **1.** A sudden outpouring: *a gush of tears.* **2.** A display of too much enthusiasm or sentiment.

gush•er (gŭsh′ər) *n.* An oil or gas well that pours out a steady flow without pumping.

gush•y (gŭsh′ē) *adj.* **gush•i•er, gush•i•est.** Showing excessive enthusiasm or sentiment. **—gush′i•ly** *adv.* **—gush′i•ness** *n.*

gus•set (gŭs′ĭt) *n.* A triangular insert, as in the seam of a garment, for added strength or expansion.

gust (gŭst) *n.* **1.** A sudden strong rush of wind. **2.** A sudden burst, as of rain or smoke. **3.** An outburst of feeling: *a gust of anger.*

gus•ta•to•ry (gŭs′tə tôr′ē) *adj.* Of or relating to the sense of taste.

gus•to (gŭs′tō) *n., pl.* **gus•toes.** Great enjoyment; zest: *We were hungry and ate lunch with gusto.* [First written down in 1629 in Modern English, from Latin *gustus,* taste.]

gust•y (gŭs′tē) *adj.* **gust•i•er, gust•i•est.** Blowing in or marked by gusts: *gusty March weather.* **—gust′i•ly** *adv.* **—gust′i•ness** *n.*

gut (gŭt) *n.* **1.** The alimentary canal or any of its parts, especially the stomach or intestines. **2. guts.** The intestines; bowels. **3.** Catgut. **4. guts.** *Slang.* Courage, fortitude, or nerve: *had guts to stand up to such a powerful foe.* —*tr.v.* **gut•ted, gut•ting, guts. 1.** To remove the intestines of; eviscerate. **2.** To destroy the contents or interior of: *The fire gutted their apartment.* —*adj. Slang.* Arousing or involving basic emotions: *The student's gut reaction was to protest.*

Gu•ten•berg (gōōt′n bûrg′), **Johann** or **Johannes.** 1400?–1468?. German printer who is traditionally considered the inventor of movable type.

gut•less (gŭt′lĭs) *adj. Slang.* Lacking courage, drive, or fortitude. **—gut′less•ness** *n.*

gut•ter (gŭt′ər) *n.* **1.a.** A channel near a curb for draining off water at the edge of a street. **b.** A trough fixed under or along the eaves for draining water off a roof. **2.** A groove or trough, as the one on either side of a bowling alley. —*v.* **gut•tered, gut•ter•ing, gut•ters.** —*tr.* To form gutters or channels in: *Heavy rain guttered the hillside.* —*intr.* **1.** To flow in channels. **2.** To melt away rapidly in streams, as the wax of a lighted candle does in a breeze. **3.** To burn low and unsteadily; flicker. [First written down in 1280 in Middle English, from Old French *gotier,* from Latin *gutta,* drop.]

gut•tur•al (gŭt′ər əl) *adj.* **1.** Of or relating to the throat. **2.** Having a harsh sound, as those produced in the back of the mouth: *a deep guttural voice.* **3.** Formed with the back of the tongue on or near the soft palate, as the *g* in *good.* [First written down in 1594 in Modern English, from Latin *guttur,* throat.] **—gut′tur•al•ly** *adv.*

guy[1] (gī) *n.* A rope, cord, or cable used to steady, guide, or secure something. —*tr.v.* **guyed, guy•ing, guys.** To fasten, guide, or secure with a rope, cord, or cable: *Telephone poles are sometimes guyed by steel cables.* [First written down before 1375 in Middle English and spelled *gie,* guide, guy, from Old French *guie,* from *guier,* to guide.]

guy[2] (gī) *n.* **1.** *Informal.* A man or boy; a fellow. **2. guys.** Persons of either sex. [First written down in 1836 in Modern English, after *Guy* Fawkes (1570–1606), English conspirator.]

Guy•a•na (gī ăn′ə *or* gī ä′nə). A country of northeast South America on the Atlantic Ocean west of Suriname. It gained its independence from Great

Britain in 1966. Georgetown is the capital and the largest city. Population, 918,000.

guz•zle (gŭz′əl) *tr. & intr.v.* **guz•zled, guz•zling, guz•zles.** To drink greedily or habitually: *guzzle a can of soda.* —**guz′zler** *n.*

gym (jĭm) *n.* **1.** A gymnasium. **2.** A class in physical education: *I have gym at 10:15.*

gym•na•si•um (jĭm **nā′**zē əm) *n., pl.* **gym•na•si•ums** or **gym•na•si•a** (jĭm **nā′**zē ə). **1.** A room or building equipped for indoor sports: *play basketball in the gymnasium.* **2.** (gĭm **nä′**zē ŏŏm′). A high school in some European countries, especially Germany.

gym•nast (**jĭm′**năst′ *or* **jĭm′**nəst) *n.* A person skilled in gymnastics.

gym•nas•tic (jĭm **năs′**tĭk) *adj.* Of or relating to gymnastics: *gymnastic exercise.*

gym•nas•tics (jĭm **năs′**tĭks) *n.* Physical exercises designed to develop and display strength, balance, and agility, especially those performed on or with special apparatus.

gym•no•sperm (**jĭm′**nə spûrm′) *n.* Any of a group of plants, including the pines and other cone-bearing trees that produce seeds that are not enclosed in a fruit or an ovary.

gy•ne•col•o•gist (gī′nĭ **kŏl′**ə jĭst *or* jĭn′ĭ **kŏl′**ə jĭst) *n.* A physician who specializes in gynecology.

gy•ne•col•o•gy (gī′nĭ **kŏl′**ə jē *or* jĭn′ĭ **kŏl′**ə jē) *n.* The branch of medicine that deals with the diagnosis and treatment of disorders of the female reproductive system.

gyp (jĭp) *Slang. tr.v.* **gypped, gyp•ping, gyps.** To deprive (another person) of something by fraud; cheat or swindle. —*n.* A fraud or swindle.

gyp•sum (**jĭp′**səm) *n.* A white mineral containing calcium, used in manufacturing plaster of Paris, plasterboard, Portland cement, and fertilizers.

Gyp•sy also **Gip•sy** (**jĭp′**sē) *n., pl.* **Gyp•sies** also **Gip•sies. 1.** A member of a nomadic people that originally migrated to Europe from India around the 14th century. **2.** Romany.

gypsy moth *n.* A small moth having hairy caterpillars that feed on leaves and do great damage to trees.

gy•rate (**jī′**rāt′) *intr.v.* **gy•rat•ed, gy•rat•ing, gy•rates. 1.** To revolve around a fixed point or axis: *The earth gyrates about its axis.* **2.** To move in a spiral or circular path: *The dancers gyrated around the room.* —**gy•ra′tion** *n.*

gyr•fal•con also **ger•fal•con** (**jûr′**făl′kən *or* **jûr′**-fôl′kən *or* **jûr′**fô′kən) *n.* A large falcon of northern regions having white or grayish feathers.

gy•ro (**jī′**rō) *n., pl.* **gy•ros.** A gyroscope.

gy•ro•com•pass (**jī′**rō kŭm′pəs *or* **jī′**rō kŏm′pəs) *n.* A compass using a gyroscope instead of a magnetic needle. It points to true north instead of magnetic north.

gy•ro•scope (**jī′**rə skōp′) *n.* An instrument consisting of a disk or wheel that spins rapidly about an axis like a top. The spinning motion keeps the axis fixed, though its base may be turned in any direction, making the gyroscope an accurate navigational instrument and an effective stabilizing device in ships and airplanes. [First written down in 1856 in Modern English, from Greek *guros*, circle.]

gy•ro•scop•ic (jī′rə **skŏp′**ĭk) *adj.* **1.** Of or relating to a gyroscope or its physical action. **2.** Operating by means of a gyroscope: *a gyroscopic stabilizer.* —**gy′ro•scop′i•cal•ly** *adv.*

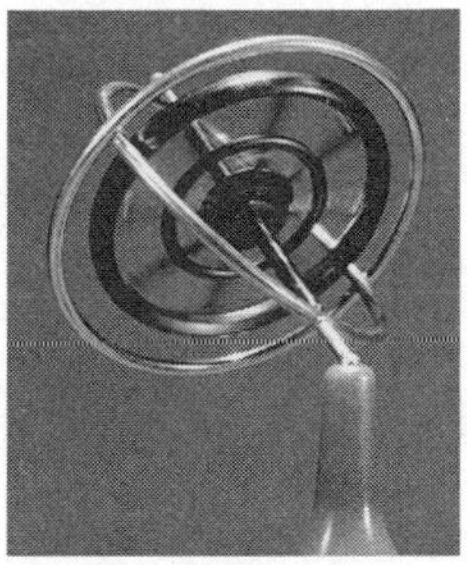

gyroscope

ă	pat	oi	boy
ā	pay	ou	out
âr	care	ŏŏ	took
ä	father	ōō	boot
ĕ	pet	ŭ	cut
ē	be	ûr	urge
ĭ	pit	th	thin
ī	pie	*th*	this
îr	pier	hw	whoop
ŏ	pot	zh	vision
ō	toe	ə	about
ô	paw	N	*French* bon

Hh

h¹ or **H** (āch) *n., pl.* **h's** or **H's. 1.** The eighth letter of the English alphabet. **2.** The eighth in a series or group: *row H in a theater.*

h² *abbr.* An abbreviation of: **1.** Hit. **2.** Hour.

H The symbol for the element **hydrogen.**

h. also **H.** *abbr.* An abbreviation of: **1.** Height. **2.** Hundred.

ha also **hah** (hä) *interj.* An expression used to show surprise, wonder, triumph, or puzzlement.

Ha•bak•kuk (hăb′ə ko͝ok′ *or* hə băk′ək) *n.* **1.** A Hebrew prophet of the seventh century B.C. **2.** A book of the Bible in which Habakkuk prophesies that the oppressors of the Jews will be punished by God and that God will sustain the innocent.

ha•be•as corpus (hā′bē əs) *n.* Any of various court orders issued to bring a person before a court in order to determine if the person has been lawfully imprisoned.

hab•er•dash•er (hăb′ər dăsh′ər) *n.* A dealer in articles of clothing for men.

hab•er•dash•er•y (hăb′ər dăsh′ə rē) *n., pl.* **hab•er•dash•er•ies. 1.** A haberdasher's shop: *get a belt and cuff links at the haberdashery.* **2.** The goods a haberdasher sells.

ha•bil•i•ment (hə bĭl′ə mənt) *n.* Clothes or garb, especially that associated with an office or a profession. Often used in the plural: *the habiliments of the theater.*

hab•it (hăb′ĭt) *n.* **1.** A recurrent pattern of behavior that is acquired through repetition and is often done without thinking: *Many people have a habit of fidgeting when they are nervous.* **2.** Customary practice or manner: *in the habit of taking an early-morning walk.* **3.** An addiction. **4.a.** The distinctive clothing or costume worn by members of a religious order: *a nun's habit.* **b.** A riding habit. *—tr.v.* **hab•it•ed, hab•it•ing, hab•its.** To clothe; dress. [First written down before 1200 in Middle English, from Latin *habitus*, behavior, custom.]

Synonyms: habit, practice, custom. These nouns refer to a pattern of behavior established by repetition. **Habit** means a way of acting that has been repeated so many times it no longer involves conscious thought: *Paula has a habit of covering her mouth when she laughs.* **Practice** means a routine, often chosen way of acting: *It is their practice to eat dinner early.* **Custom** means a usually longstanding practice in line with social conventions: *It is a Japanese custom not to wear shoes in the house.*

hab•it•a•ble (hăb′ĭ tə bəl) *adj.* Suitable or fit to live in or on: *Is the old house still habitable?* **—hab′it•a•bil′i•ty** *n.*

hab•i•tat (hăb′ĭ tăt′) *n.* The area or natural environment in which an animal or a plant normally lives or grows: *Bears are used to cooler northern habitats.*

hab•i•ta•tion (hăb′ĭ tā′shən) *n.* **1.** A place in which to live; a residence. **2.** The act of inhabiting or the condition of being inhabited: *The Antarctic climate is not suitable for human habitation.*

hab•it-form•ing (hăb′ĭt fôr′mĭng) *adj.* Leading to or causing addiction: *a habit-forming drug.*

ha•bit•u•al (hə bĭch′o͞o əl) *adj.* **1.a.** Of the nature of habit; done constantly or repeatedly: *Their habitual lateness annoyed everyone.* **b.** Behaving or performing in a certain manner by habit: *a habitual early riser.* **2.** Established by long use; usual: *his habitual confusion.* **—ha•bit′u•al•ly** *adv.*

ha•bit•u•ate (hə bĭch′o͞o āt′) *tr.v.* **ha•bit•u•at•ed, ha•bit•u•at•ing, ha•bit•u•ates.** To familiarize by repetition or constant exposure; accustom: *He is habituated to commuting to work every day.* **—ha•bit′u•a′tion** *n.*

ha•bit•u•é (hə bĭch′o͞o ā′ *or* hə bĭch′o͞o ā′) *n.* A person who visits a particular place of entertainment frequently.

ha•ci•en•da (hä′sē ĕn′də) *n.* **1.** A large estate or plantation in Spanish-speaking countries. **2.** The house of the owner of such an estate. [First written down in 1758 in Modern English, from Spanish, from Latin *facienda*, things to be done.]

hack¹ (hăk) *v.* **hacked, hack•ing, hacks.** *—tr.* **1.** To cut or chop with repeated and irregular blows: *hacked down the saplings.* **2.** *Slang.* To cut or mutilate as if by hacking: *hacked a large amount off the budget.* **3.** *Slang.* To cope with successfully; manage: *Do you think you can hack such responsibilities?* *—intr.* **1.** To chop or cut by hacking: *hack at a tree stump.* **2.** To work or perform as a hacker. **3.** To cough roughly or harshly: *hacking with a bad cold.* *—n.* **1.** A rough irregular cut or notch made by hacking. **2.** A rough dry cough. [First written down before 1200 in Middle English and spelled *hacken*, from Old English *haccian.*]

hack² (hăk) *n.* **1.** A horse used for riding or driving; a hackney. **2.** A worn-out horse for hire. **3.** A person, especially a writer, who does routine work for hire. **4.** A carriage or hackney for hire. **5.** *Informal.* A taxicab. [First written down before 1700 in Modern English, short for *hackney.*]

hack•er (hăk′ər) *n.* A person skilled in the use of a computer, especially one who gains access to computer systems to steal information or money.

hack•le (hăk′əl) *n.* **1.** One of the long, slender, often glossy feathers on the neck of a rooster or other bird. **2. hackles.** Hairs on the back of an animal's neck that can rise and bristle out with anger or fear.

hack•ney (hăk′nē) *n., pl.* **hack•neys. 1.** A horse suited for routine riding or driving. **2.** A couch or carriage for hire.

hack•neyed (hăk′nēd) *adj.* Overfamiliar through overuse; trite: *writing full of hackneyed phrases.*

hack•saw (hăk′sô′) *n.* A saw with a tough, fine-toothed blade stretched taut in a frame, used especially for cutting metal.

had (hăd) *v.* Past tense and past participle of **have.**

had•dock (hăd′ək) *n., pl.* **haddock** or **had•docks.** A food fish of the northern Atlantic Ocean, related to and resembling the cod but smaller, and having a black stripe from head to tail.

Ha•des (hā′dēz) *n.* **1.** In Greek mythology, the god of the underworld and the dispenser of earthly riches. **2.** In Greek mythology, the underworld kingdom. **3.** also **hades.** Hell.

had•n't (hăd′nt) *v.* Contraction of *had not.*

hadst (hădst) *v. Archaic.* A second person singular past tense of **have.**

haf•ni•um (hăf′nē əm) *n. Symbol* **Hf** A silvery metallic element found in zirconium ores. Hafnium is used in making the control rods of nuclear reactors. Atomic number 72. See table at **element.** [First written down in 1923 in Modern English, after *Hafnia*, Medieval Latin name for Copenhagen, Denmark.]

haft (hăft) *n.* A handle or hilt, especially the handle of a tool or weapon.

hag (hăg) *n.* **1.** An old woman considered ugly or frightful. **2.** A witch; a sorceress.

Hag•ga•i (hăg′ē ī′ *or* hăg′ī′) *n.* **1.** A Hebrew prophet of the sixth century B.C. **2.** A book of the Bible that urges the rebuilding of the Temple of Jerusalem.

hag•gard (hăg′ərd) *adj.* Appearing worn and exhausted; gaunt: *a haggard face.* **—hag′gard•ly** *adv.* **—hag′gard•ness** *n.*

hag•gle (hăg′əl) *intr.v.* **hag•gled, hag•gling, hag•gles. 1.** To bargain, as over the price of something: *a shopper haggling with a fruit seller.* **2.** To argue in an attempt to come to terms: *The countries haggled over their boundary.* **—hag′gler** *n.*

Hag•i•og•ra•pha (hăg′ē ŏg′rə fə *or* hā′jē ŏg′rə fə) *n.* The third division of the Hebrew Scriptures; the Writings.

Hague (hāg), **The.** The capital of the Netherlands, in the western part of the country near the North Sea. The Hague is the seat of the country's legislature and supreme court and of the International Court of Justice. Population, 445,213.

hah (hä) *interj.* Variant of **ha.**

hah•ni•um (hä′nē əm) *n.* Element 105. [First written down in 1970 in Modern English, after Otto *Hahn* (1879–1968), German chemist.]

Hai•da (hī′də) *n., pl.* **Haida** or **Hai•das. 1.** A member of a Native American people of several islands off the coasts of Alaska and British Columbia. **2.** Any of the languages of the Haida. **—Hai′dan** *adj.*

hai•ku (hī′ko͞o) *n., pl.* **haiku** also **hai•kus.** A form of Japanese poetry consisting of three unrhymed lines of five, seven, and five syllables. [First written down in 1899 in Modern English and spelled *haikai*, from Japanese *haiku*, haiku.]

hail[1] (hāl) *n.* **1.** Precipitation in the form of rounded pellets of ice and hard snow that usually falls during thunderstorms. **2.** Something that falls with the force of a shower of ice and hard snow: *a hail of pebbles; a hail of criticism.* *—v.* **hailed, hail•ing, hails.** *—intr.* To fall as hail: *It hailed this afternoon.* *—tr.* To pour (something) down or forth: *The two drivers hailed insults at each other.* [First written down about 750 in Old English and spelled *hægl.*]

❑ *These sound alike:* **hail**[1] (ice pellets), **hail**[2] (greeting), **hale**[1] (healthy), **hale**[2] (force).

hail[2] (hāl) *tr.v.* **hailed, hail•ing, hails. 1.** To salute or greet: *hail a friend across the street.* **2.** To signal or call loudly in order to catch the attention of: *hail a cab.* *—interj.* An expression used to show a greeting or tribute. ***—idiom.*** **hail from.** To come or originate from: *They hail from Ohio.* [First written down about 1200 in Middle English and spelled *heilen*, from *(wæs) hæil*, (be) healthy.] **—hail′er** *n.*

❑ *These sound alike:* **hail**[2] (greeting), **hail**[1] (ice pellets), **hale**[1] (healthy), **hale**[2] (force).

Hai•le Se•las•sie (hī′lē sə lăs′ē *or* hī′lē sə lä′sē) Title of Ras Taffari Makonnen. 1892–1975. Emperor of Ethiopia (1930–1974) who was deposed in a military coup (1974).

Hail Mar•y (hāl′ mâr′ē) *n., pl.* **Hail Mar•ys.** A Roman Catholic prayer addressed to the Virgin Mary.

hail•stone (hāl′stōn′) *n.* A pellet of hail.

hail•storm (hāl′stôrm′) *n.* A storm in which hail falls.

hair (hâr) *n.* **1.** One of the fine strands that grow from the skin of human beings and other mammals. **2.** A mass of such fine strands: *My cat has soft hair.* **3.** A fine growth from the outer layer of plants. **4.** A tiny distance or narrow margin: *We won by a hair.* [First written down about 800 in Old English and spelled *hēr.*] **—hair′like′** *adj.*

❑ *These sound alike:* **hair, hare** (rabbit).

hair•breadth (hâr′brĕdth′) *adj. & n.* Variant of **hairsbreadth.**

hair•brush (hâr′brŭsh′) *n.* A brush for the hair.

hair•cloth (hâr′klôth′ *or* hâr′klŏth′) *n.* A wiry fabric with horsehair or camel's hair woven into it, used in upholstery or to stiffen clothing.

hair•cut (hâr′kŭt′) *n.* **1.** The act or an instance of cutting the hair: *You need a haircut.* **2.** A style in which hair is cut: *a short haircut.*

hair•do (hâr′do͞o′) *n., pl.* **hair•dos.** A style in which hair is arranged.

hair•dress•er (hâr′drĕs′ər) *n.* A person who cuts or arranges hair.

hair•less (hâr′lĭs) *adj.* Having little or no hair.

hair•line (hâr′līn′) *n.* **1.** The edge of hair growing above the forehead or around the head. **2.** A very thin line.

hair•piece (hâr′pēs′) *n.* A covering or bunch of human or artificial hair worn to cover a bald spot or as part of a hairdo.

hair•pin (hâr′pĭn′) *n.* A thin, U-shaped cylindrical strip of metal used to secure a hairdo.

hair-rais•ing (hâr′rā′zĭng) *adj.* Causing excitement, terror, or thrills: *a hair-raising ride on a roller coaster.*

hairs•breadth or **hair's-breadth** (hârz′brĕdth′) also **hair•breadth** (hâr′brĕdth′) *n.* A small space, distance, or margin: *win by a hairsbreadth.*

hair•split•ting (hâr′splĭt′ĭng) *n.* The making of distinctions that are too fine to be important: *The hairsplitting between the lawyers annoyed the judge.* **—hair′split′ter** *n.*

hair spray *n.* A preparation sprayed on the hair to keep it in place.

hair•spring (hâr′sprĭng′) *n.* A fine spring that regulates the movement of the balance wheel of a watch or clock.

hair•style (hâr′stīl′) *n.* A style of cutting or arranging the hair.

hair trigger *n.* A gun trigger that responds to a very slight pressure.

hair•y (hâr′ē) *adj.* **hair•i•er, hair•i•est. 1.** Covered with hair or projections resembling hair: *a hairy caterpillar.* **2.** Consisting of or resembling hair: *a hairy blanket.* **3.** *Slang.* Fraught with difficulties; hazardous: *a hairy escape.* **—hair′i•ness** *n.*

Hai•ti (hā′tē). **1.** A country of the West Indies made up of the western part of the island of Hispaniola and two offshore islands. The country gained its independence from France in 1804 following a slave revolt. Capital, Port-au-Prince. Population, 5,053,791. **2.** Hispaniola.

Hai•tian (hā′shən *or* hā′tē ən) *adj.* Of or relating to Haiti or its people or culture. *—n.* **1.** A native or inhabitant of Haiti. **2.** Haitian Creole.

Haitian Creole *n.* A language spoken by the majority of Haitians, based on French and a variety of African languages.

hake (hāk) *n., pl.* **hake** or **hakes.** Any of various ocean fishes used for food, related to and resembling the cod but thinner.

hal•berd (hăl′bərd *or* hôl′bərd) *n.* A weapon used in the 15th and 16th centuries, having an ax blade and a spike mounted on a long pole.

hal•cy•on (hăl′sē ən) *n.* A fabled bird identified

Haile Selassie

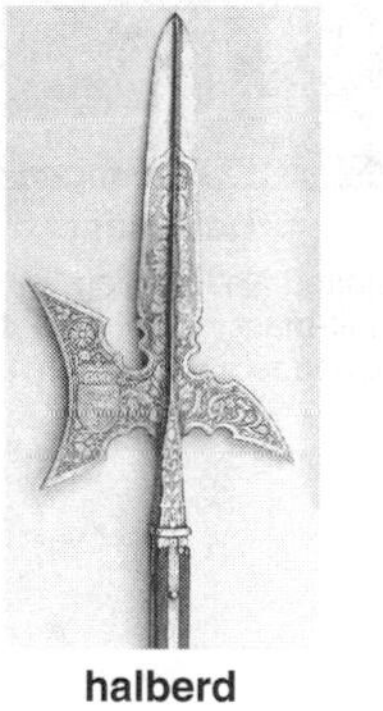

halberd
Austrian

ă	pat	oi	boy
ā	pay	ou	out
âr	care	o͝o	took
ä	father	o͞o	boot
ĕ	pet	ŭ	cut
ē	be	ûr	urge
ĭ	pit	th	thin
ī	pie	*th*	this
îr	pier	hw	whoop
ŏ	pot	zh	vision
ō	toe	ə	about
ô	paw	N	*French* bon

Usage: half

The phrases *a half, half of,* and *half a* or *half an* are all correct. They may differ slightly in meaning. For example, we say *a half day* when *day* has the special sense "a working day," and the phrase then means "4 hours." *Half of a day* and *half a day* are not restricted in this way and can mean either 4 or 12 hours.

half-mast
United Nations flag flying at half-mast after the death of Charles de Gaulle in 1970

Halley's comet
In 1986

with the kingfisher that is supposed to have the power to calm the wind and the waves while it nests on the sea during the winter solstice. —*adj.* Calm and peaceful; tranquil: *halcyon days.*

hale¹ (hāl) *adj.* **hal•er, hal•est.** Free from infirmity or illness; sound. [First written down about 725 in Old English and spelled *hāl.*]

❑ *These sound alike:* **hale¹** (healthy), **hail¹** (ice pellets), **hail²** (greeting), **hale²** (force).

hale² (hāl) *tr.v.* **haled, hal•ing, hales. 1.** To force to go: *hale an offender into court.* **2.** *Archaic.* To pull, drag, or hoist. [First written down before 1200 in Middle English and spelled *halen,* to pull, drag, from Old French *haler,* of Germanic origin.]

❑ *These sound alike:* **hale²** (force), **hail¹** (ice pellets), **hail²** (greeting), **hale¹** (healthy).

Hale (hāl), **Nathan.** 1755–1776. American Revolutionary soldier who was hanged by the British as a spy.

half (hăf) *n., pl.* **halves** (hăvz). **1.a.** One of two equal parts that together make up a whole: *Fifty cents is one half of a dollar.* **b.** One of two approximately equal parts: *the smaller half of a sandwich.* **2.** In football and other sports, either of the two equal time periods that make up a game. **3.** Half an hour: *at half past one.* —*adj.* **1.a.** Being one of two equal parts. **b.** Being approximately a half: *a half glass of milk.* **2.** Partial or incomplete: *a half truth.* —*adv.* **1.** To the extent of exactly or nearly 50 percent: *a half empty tank.* **2.** Not completely; partly: *I was still half asleep.* —***idioms.*** **in half.** Into halves. **not half.** Not at all: *not half bad.* [First written down about 700 in Old English.] —SEE NOTE.

half•back (hăf′băk′) *n.* **1.** In football, one of two players positioned near the flanks behind the line of scrimmage. **2.** In various sports, one of several players positioned behind the forward line.

half-baked (hăf′bākt′) *adj.* **1.** Only partly baked. **2.** *Informal.* Not fully thought out; poorly conceived: *a half-baked idea.*

half brother *n.* A brother related through one parent only.

half-dol•lar (hăf′dŏl′ər) *n.* A U.S. silver coin worth 50 cents.

half gainer *n.* A dive in which the diver springs from the board facing forward and rotates backward to enter the water headfirst.

half•heart•ed (hăf′här′tĭd) *adj.* Showing or feeling little enthusiasm, interest, or heart; uninspired: *With so much work left, I made only a halfhearted attempt to finish it.* —**half′heart′ed•ly** *adv.*

half hitch *n.* A knot made by looping a rope around an object and then back around itself, bringing the end of the rope through the loop.

half-hour (hăf′our′) *n.* **1.** A period of 30 minutes. **2.** The middle point of an hour: *News bulletins are broadcast on the half-hour.*

half-life (hăf′līf′) *n.* The time needed for half the nuclei in a sample of radioactive material to undergo decay.

half-mast (hăf′măst′) *n.* The position about halfway up a mast or pole at which a flag is flown as a symbol of mourning for the dead or as a signal of distress.

half-moon (hăf′mo͞on′) *n.* The moon when just half of its disk appears lighted.

half nelson *n.* A wrestling hold in which one arm is passed under an opponent's arm from behind to the back of the neck.

half note *n.* A musical note having one half the time value of a whole note.

half•pen•ny (hā′pə nē *or* hāp′nē) *n., pl.* **half•pence** (hā′pəns) or **half•pen•nies.** A British coin worth one half of a new penny.

half sister *n.* A sister related through one parent only.

half-slip (hăf′slĭp′) *n.* A woman's slip that hangs from the waist.

half-staff (hăf′stăf′) *n.* Half-mast.

half step *n.* A musical interval equal to one half the interval between full tones in a scale. Half steps separate C, C-sharp, and D.

half•time (hăf′tīm′) *n.* In sports, the intermission between halves in certain games.

half•tone (hăf′tōn′) *n.* **1.** A tone or color between very light and very dark. **2.** A picture in which the shades of light and dark are produced by tiny dots either closely or more widely spaced.

half tone *n.* A half step; a semitone.

half-track (hăf′trăk′) *n.* A lightly armored military vehicle having caterpillar treads in place of wheels.

half•way (hăf′wā′) *adj.* **1.** Midway between two points or conditions: *the halfway point on the trail to the summit.* **2.** Reaching or including only half or a portion; partial: *halfway measures to control pollution.* —*adv.* **1.** To or at half the distance: *I'll meet you halfway between your house and mine.* **2.** Partially: *I halfway gave in to their demands.*

hal•i•but (hăl′ə bət *or* hŏl′ə bət) *n., pl.* **halibut** or **hal•i•buts.** Any of several large flatfishes of northern ocean waters, used for food and often weighing several hundred pounds.

Hal•i•fax (hăl′ə făks′). The capital and largest city of Nova Scotia, Canada, in the south-central part of the province on the Atlantic Ocean. It was founded in 1749. Population, 114,594.

hal•ite (hăl′īt′ *or* hā′līt′) *n.* Rock salt. [First written down in 1868 in Modern English, from Greek *hals,* salt.]

hal•i•to•sis (hăl′ĭ tō′sĭs) *n.* The condition of having breath that smells unpleasant; bad breath.

hall (hôl) *n.* **1.** A corridor or passageway in a building: *The hall had several classrooms off it.* **2.** An entrance room or vestibule in a building; a lobby: *We waited in the hall at the elevators.* **3.** A building where meetings, parties, concerts, or other gatherings are held: *a lecture hall.* **4.** A building used for the meetings, entertainments, or living quarters of a social or religious organization. **5.** A school, college, or university building: *Students live in three halls at the back of campus.* **6.** The main house of an English landowner. [First written down about 725 in Old English and spelled *heall,* place covered with a roof.]

❑ *These sound alike:* **hall, haul** (drag).

hal•lah (KHä′lə *or* hä′lə) *n.* Variant of **challah.**

hal•le•lu•jah (hăl′ə lo͞o′yə) *interj.* An expression used to show praise or joy. —*n.* **1.** An exclamation of "hallelujah." **2.** A song or hymn of praise based on the word *hallelujah.* [First written down in 1535 in Modern English and spelled *halleluya,* from Hebrew *hallĕlûyāh,* praise the Lord.]

Hal•ley's comet (hăl′ēz *or* hā′lēz) *n.* A comet that appears about every 76 years. It last appeared in 1986. [First written down after 1758 in Modern English, after Edmond *Halley* (1656–1742), English astronomer.]

hall•mark (hôl′märk′) *n.* **1.** A mark that indicates excellence or quality. **2.** A mark indicating a certain level of purity, stamped in England on articles made of gold and silver. **3.** A distinguishing characteristic, feature, or trait: *Good design and quality materials are hallmarks of fine automobiles.* —*tr.v.* **hall•marked, hall•mark•ing, hall•marks.** To stamp (gold and silver articles) with a mark indicating a standard of purity.

hal•loo (hə lo͞o′) *interj.* **1.** An expression used to get someone's attention. **2.** An expression used to urge on hounds in a hunt. —*n., pl.* **hal•loos.** A shout or call of "halloo." —*intr.v.* **hal•looed, hal•loo•ing, hal•loos.** To shout "halloo."

hal•low (**hăl′**ō) *tr.v.* **hal•lowed, hal•low•ing, hal•lows. 1.** To make or set apart as holy: *An ancient burial mound hallows this ground.* **2.** To respect or honor greatly: *hallow the memory of one's ancestors.*

hal•lowed (**hăl′**ōd) *adj.* **1.** Sanctified; consecrated: *hallowed ground.* **2.** Honored; revered: *a hallowed name.*

Hal•low•een also **Hal•low•e'en** (hăl′ə **wēn′** *or* hŏl′ə **wēn′**) *n.* October 31, celebrated by children going door to door in costumes and begging treats and playing pranks. [First written down in 1556 in Modern English and spelled *All Hallow Even.*]

hal•lu•ci•nate (hə **lo͞o′**sə nāt′) *intr.v.* **hal•lu•ci•nat•ed, hal•lu•ci•nat•ing, hal•lu•ci•nates.** To have hallucinations.

hal•lu•ci•na•tion (hə lo͞o′sə **nā′**shən) *n.* **1.** An illusion of seeing, hearing, or otherwise being aware of something that does not really exist. **2.** A vision, an image, or a sound that is seen or heard as such an illusion: *People with high fevers may see hallucinations.*

hal•lu•ci•na•to•ry (hə **lo͞o′**sə nə tôr′ē) *adj.* **1.** Of or marked by hallucination: *a hallucinatory experience.* **2.** Hallucinogenic.

hal•lu•cin•o•gen (hə **lo͞o′**sə nə jən) *n.* A drug that produces or tends to produce hallucinations.

hal•lu•ci•no•gen•ic (hə lo͞o′sə nə **jĕn′**ĭk) *adj.* Producing or tending to produce hallucinations: *a hallucinogenic drug.*

hall•way (**hôl′**wā′) *n.* **1.** A corridor in a building. **2.** An entrance hall: *The mail is left in the hallway of our apartment building.*

ha•lo (**hā′**lō) *n., pl.* **ha•los** or **ha•loes. 1.** A circular band of light that surrounds the sun, the moon, a star, or another light source, resulting from effects such as reflection and refraction of light through ice crystals suspended in air. **2.** A ring or disk of light surrounding the heads or bodies of sacred figures in religious paintings. [First written down in 1563 in Modern English, from Greek *halōs.*]

hal•o•gen (**hăl′**ə jən) *n.* A group of elements with similar properties, including fluorine, chlorine, bromine, iodine, and astatine. Halogens combine directly with most metals to form salts.

halt¹ (hôlt) *n.* A temporary stop of movement or progress: *The car rolled to a halt when it stalled.* —*intr. & tr.v.* **halt•ed, halt•ing, halts.** To stop or cause to stop: *The hikers halted for lunch and some rest. The government hopes to halt air pollution.* See Synonyms at **stop.** [First written down about 1591 in Modern English and spelled *alt,* from German *Halt,* from Old High German *haltan,* to hold back.]

halt² (hôlt) *intr.v.* **halt•ed, halt•ing, halts. 1.** To proceed or act with uncertainty or indecision; waver: *We halted in our decision to go to the beach on such a windy day.* **2.** To limp or hobble. —*adj. Archaic.* Limping; lame. [First written down about 830 in Old English and spelled *haltian,* to be lame.]

hal•ter (**hôl′**tər) *n.* **1.** A device of rope or leather straps that fits around the head or neck of an animal and is used to lead or secure the animal. **2.** A rope with a noose used for execution by hanging. **3.** A blouse that ties behind or loops around the neck and across the back, leaving the back, arms, and shoulders bare. [First written down before 830 in Old English and spelled *hælftre.*]

halt•ing (**hôl′**tĭng) *adj.* Hesitant or wavering: *a low and halting voice.*

halve (hăv) *tr.v.* **halved, halv•ing, halves. 1.** To divide (something) into two equal portions or parts: *A friend and I halved the remaining apple.* **2.** To reduce or lessen by half: *The storekeeper halved the prices for the sale.* [First written down before 1200 in Middle English and spelled *halfen,* from *half,* half.]

❑ *These sound alike:* **halve, have** (possess).

halves (hăvz) *n.* Plural of **half.**

hal•yard (**hăl′**yərd) *n.* A rope used on a ship to raise or lower a sail or flag.

ham (hăm) *n.* **1.** The hind leg of certain animals, especially of a hog. **2.** A cut of meat from the thigh of a hog. **3. hams.** The buttocks and backs of the thighs. **4.** An actor who overacts or a performer who exaggerates. **5.** A licensed amateur radio operator. —*intr.v.* **hammed, ham•ming, hams.** To exaggerate or overdo a dramatic role, for example; overact. [First written down about 1000 in Old English and spelled *hamm.*]

Ham•burg (**hăm′**bûrg′ *or* **häm′**bo͝org′). A city of northern Germany on the Elbe River northwest of Berlin. It was founded in the early ninth century. Population, 1,592,447.

ham•burg•er (**hăm′**bûr′gər) also **ham•burg** (**hăm′**bûrg′) *n.* **1.** Ground meat, usually beef. **2.** A patty of such meat. **3.** A sandwich made with a patty of ground meat usually in a roll or bun. [First written down in 1889 in American English and spelled *Hamburger steak* after *Hamburg,* Germany.]

Ham•il•ton (**hăm′**əl tən). **1.** The capital of Bermuda, on Bermuda Island. It was founded in 1790. Population, 1,676. **2.** A city of southeast Ontario, Canada, at the western end of Lake Ontario southwest of Toronto. Population, 306,434.

Hamilton, Alexander. 1755?–1804. American politician who served as the first U.S. secretary of the treasury (1789–1795).

Alexander Hamilton

Hamilton, Edith. 1867–1963. German-born American classicist noted for her studies of ancient life, including *The Greek Way* (1930).

ham•let (**hăm′**lĭt) *n.* A small village.

ham•mer (**hăm′**ər) *n.* **1.** A hand tool usually consisting of an iron head attached to a handle, used chiefly for driving in nails or for pounding and shaping metals. **2.** Something used or shaped like a hammer, as one of the padded wooden pieces that strikes the strings of a piano or the device used to strike a gong or bell. **3.** The part of a gun that strikes the firing pin or percussion cap, causing the gun to fire. **4.** A metal ball weighing 16 pounds and having a long wire or wooden handle by which athletes throw it for distance. **5.** The largest of three small bones in the middle ear that transmit vibrations to the inner ear; the malleus. **6.** A small mallet used by auctioneers. —*v.* **ham•mered, ham•mer•ing, ham•mers.** —*tr.* **1.** To hit, especially repeatedly, with or as if with a hammer: *hammer a nail.* **2.** To beat into shape with or as if with a hammer: *hammer a dent out of a fender.* **3.** To force upon by constant repetition: *hammer grammar into their heads.* —*intr.* **1.** To deal repeated blows with or as if with a hammer; pummel: *hammer on a door.* **2.** *Informal.* To keep at something continuously: *We hammered away at our homework.* [First written down about 725 in Old English and spelled *hamor.*] —**ham′mer•er** *n.*

ham•mer•head (**hăm′**ər hĕd′) *n.* Any of several large sharks having a long sideways projection with an eye at the end on each side of the head.

ham•mer•lock (**hăm′**ər lŏk′) *n.* A wrestling hold in which the opponent's arm is pulled behind the back and twisted upward.

ham•mock (**hăm′**ək) *n.* A hanging bed or couch made of strong fabric suspended by cords between

ă	pat	oi	boy
ā	pay	ou	out
âr	care	o͝o	took
ä	father	o͞o	boot
ĕ	pet	ŭ	cut
ē	be	ûr	urge
ĭ	pit	th	thin
ī	pie	*th*	this
îr	pier	hw	whoop
ŏ	pot	zh	vision
ō	toe	ə	about
ô	paw	N	*French* bon

two trees or other supports. [First written down in 1555 in Modern English, from Taino.]

Ham•mu•ra•bi (hăm′ə rä′bē *or* hä′mə rä′bē). Died 1750 B.C. Babylonian king (1792–1750) who made Babylon the chief Mesopotamian kingdom.

ham•per[1] (hăm′pər) *tr.v.* **ham•pered, ham•per•ing, ham•pers.** To prevent the progress, free movement, or action of: *The snowstorm hampered our plane's flight.* [First written down before 1375 in Middle English and spelled *hampren.*]

ham•per[2] (hăm′pər) *n.* A large basket, usually with a cover. [First written down in 1316 in Middle English and spelled *hampir,* from Old French *hanepier,* a case for holding goblets, from *hanap,* goblet.]

ham•ster (hăm′stər) *n.* A small rodent having soft fur, large cheek pouches, and a short tail, often kept as a pet or used as a laboratory animal. Hamsters are native to many parts of Europe and Asia.

ham•string (hăm′strĭng′) *n.* **1.** Either of two large tendons at the back of the human knee. **2.** A large tendon at the back of the hind leg of a horse or other four-footed animal. —*tr.v.* **ham•strung** (hăm′strŭng′), **ham•string•ing, ham•strings. 1.** To cripple (a person or an animal) by cutting a hamstring. **2.** To destroy or hinder the efficiency of; frustrate: *Poor education and lack of resources have hamstrung the development of many nations.*

Han•cock (hăn′kŏk′), **John.** 1737–1793. American politician and Revolutionary leader who was the first to sign the Declaration of Independence.

hand (hănd) *n.* **1.a.** The part of the human arm that is below the wrist. It consists of a palm to which four fingers and a thumb are attached, and is used for holding or grasping. **b.** A similar part in other animals, such as monkeys or raccoons, that grasp with their forefeet. **2.** Something like a hand in shape or use, especially a pointer on a dial, as that of a clock or gauge. **3.** A style of handwriting: *The message was written in a good clear hand.* **4.** Side or direction indicated according to the way in which one is facing: *At my right hand you see a box.* **5.** Physical assistance; help: *Give me a hand with this heavy carton.* **6.** A person who does manual labor; a laborer: *Many a hired hand worked in the field.* **7.** A member of a group or crew: *All hands on deck!* **8.** An aptitude or ability: *decided to try my hand at painting.* **9.** A manner or way of performing something: *The surgeon works with a delicate hand.* **10.** An influence or effect: *She had a hand in the decision.* **11.** A round of applause: *The audience gave us a tremendous hand.* **12.** A pledge of marriage or permission to marry: *ask for someone's hand.* **13.a.** A player in card games: *We need four hands for bridge.* **b.** The cards dealt to and held by such a player: *Don't look at my hand.* **c.** One round of a card game: *I'll play one more hand.* **14.** Possession, ownership, or keeping. Often used in the plural: *The books should be in your hands by noon.* **15.** Participation or involvement: *One can see the hand of the teacher in their class play.* **16.** A unit of length equal to four inches (10.2 cm), used especially to indicate the height of horses. —*tr.v.* **hand•ed, hand•ing, hands. 1.** To give or pass with or as if with the hands; transmit: *Hand the flashlight to me.* **2.** To lead or help with the hand: *The usher handed the guests to their seats.* **—idioms. at hand. 1.** Close by; near: *remain close at hand.* **2.** About to occur; imminent: *Spring is at hand.* **at the hand of** or **at the hands of.** By the action of: *He died at the hands of an assassin.* **by hand.** Performed manually: *These dresses have been sewn by hand.* **hand and foot.** With concerted, never-ending effort: *We waited on them hand and foot.* **hand down. 1.** To give or pass on, as an inheritance to one's heirs: *The family handed down the painting from generation to generation.* **2.** To make and pronounce an official decision, especially a court verdict. **hand in.** To turn in; submit: *Hand in your term papers by May 1.* **hand in glove.** In close association or on intimate terms: *The partners worked together hand in glove.* **hand in hand.** In cooperation; jointly: *Proper diet and good health go hand in hand.* **hand out.** To give out; distribute: *handed out leaflets to passers-by.* **hand over.** To release or relinquish to another: *Hand over the goods.* **hand over fist.** *Informal.* At a tremendous rate: *making money hand over fist.* **hands down.** With no trouble; easily: *win the award hands down.* **in hand. 1.** Under control: *We succeeded in keeping the situation in hand.* **2.** Ready; within reach: *I arrived at my exam room with pencil in hand.* **on the one hand.** From one standpoint. **on the other hand.** From another standpoint. **out of hand.** Out of control: *We can't let our expenses get out of hand.* [First written down about 700 in Old English.]

hand•bag (hănd′băg′) *n.* **1.** A woman's purse used to hold money, keys, or other personal items. **2.** A piece of small hand luggage.

hand•ball (hănd′bôl′) *n.* **1.** A game in which two or more players hit a ball against a wall with the hand usually while wearing a special glove. **2.** The small rubber ball used in this game.

hand•bill (hănd′bĭl′) *n.* A printed sheet or pamphlet distributed by hand; a leaflet.

hand•book (hănd′bo͝ok′) *n.* A small reference book or manual providing specific information on a certain subject.

hand•cart (hănd′kärt′) *n.* A small, usually two-wheeled cart pushed or pulled by hand.

hand•craft (hănd′krăft′) *n.* Variant of **handicraft.** —*tr.v.* (hănd krăft′). **hand•craft•ed, hand•craft•ing, hand•crafts.** To fashion or make by hand: *handcraft wooden toys.*

hand•cuff (hănd′kŭf′) *n.* A restraining device consisting of a pair of metal hoops that are chained together and that can be tightened and locked around the wrists; a manacle. Often used in the plural. —*tr.v.* **hand•cuffed, hand•cuff•ing, hand•cuffs.** To restrain with or as if with handcuffs: *The sheriff handcuffed the prisoner.*

hand•ed (hăn′dĭd) *adj.* **1.** Of or relating to dexterity, preference, or size with respect to a hand or hands: *left-handed; large-handed.* **2.** Relating to a specified number of people: *a four-handed card game.*

Han•del (hăn′dl), **George Frederick.** 1685–1759. German-born composer whose works include *Messiah* (1742).

George Frederick Handel

hand•ful (hănd′fo͝ol′) *n., pl.* **hand•fuls. 1.** The amount that a hand can hold: *a handful of coins.* **2.** A small but unspecified quantity or number: *a handful of people.* **3.** A person or thing that is difficult to control or handle easily: *The fussy baby is a real handful.*

hand•gun (hănd′gŭn′) *n.* A firearm that can be used with one hand.

hand•i•cap (hăn′dē kăp′) *n.* **1.** A race or contest in which advantage or compensations are given to different contestants to equalize the chances of winning. **2.** Such an advantage or disadvantage. **3.** A physical or mental disability. **4.** A hindrance: *Disorganization is my chief handicap.* —*tr.v.* **hand•i•capped, hand•i•cap•ping, hand•i•caps. 1.** To cause to be at a disadvantage; impede: *A sore throat handicapped the singer.* **2.** To give a handicap or handicaps to (a contestant): *handicap a contestant in a golf match.*

hand•i•capped (hăn′dē kăpt′) *adj.* Physically or mentally disabled.

hand•i•craft (hăn′dē krăft′) also **hand•craft**

(hănd′krăft′) *n.* **1.** Skill and facility with the hands. **2.** A craft or an occupation requiring skilled use of the hands, as weaving or basketry. **3.** Work produced by skilled hands: *The shop sells handicrafts from many countries.*

hand•i•ly (hăn′dĭ lē *or* hăn′dl ē) *adv.* **1.** In an easy manner: *The student answered the test questions handily.* **2.** In a convenient manner.

hand•i•work (hăn′dē wûrk′) *n.* **1.** Work performed by hand: *Knitting is a handiwork that requires dexterity.* **2.** The product of a person's efforts and actions.

hand•ker•chief (hăng′kər chĭf *or* hăng′kər chēf′) *n., pl.* **hand•ker•chiefs** also **hand•ker•chieves** (hăng′kər chĭvz *or* hăng′kər chēvz′). **1.** A small square of cloth used especially to wipe the nose and mouth. **2.** A kerchief or scarf.

han•dle (hăn′dl) *v.* **han•dled, han•dling, han•dles.** —*tr.* **1.** To touch, hold, or lift with the hands: *Please do not handle the merchandise.* **2.** To operate with the hands; manipulate: *know how to handle chopsticks.* **3.** To deal with or treat in a specified way: *handles problems well.* **4.** To manage, direct, or train: *handle a tennis player.* **5.** To deal with, perform, or manage successfully: *I couldn't handle the melody of the song.* **6.** To deal in; buy and sell: *Drugstores handle a wide variety of goods.* —*intr.* To act or function in a given way while in operation: *This new car handles well on the highway.* —*n.* A part that is designed to be held or operated with the hand: *carry a pail by its handle.* ***—idiom.*** **get a handle on** or **have a handle on.** To reach an understanding of: *I finally got a handle on the problem.*

han•dle•bar (hăn′dl bär′) *n.* **1.** A curved metal steering bar, as on a bicycle. Often used in the plural. **2.** A long curved mustache resembling a handlebar in shape.

han•dler (hănd′lər) *n.* **1.** A person who handles a person or thing: *a handler of office supplies.* **2.** A person who trains an animal and exhibits it in shows: *a dog handler.* **3.** A person who acts as the trainer or second of a boxer.

hand•made (hănd′mād′) *adj.* Made or prepared by hand rather than by machine: *a handmade quilt.*

hand•maid (hănd′mād′) also **hand•maid•en** (hănd′mād′n) *n.* A woman attendant or servant.

hand-me-down (hănd′mē doun′) *n.* Something, such as an article of clothing, passed on from one person to another: *The sweater is a hand-me-down from my sister.*

hand organ *n.* A barrel organ operated by turning a crank with the hand.

hand•out (hănd′out′) *n.* **1.** Food, clothing, or money given to the needy. **2.** A folder or leaflet given out free of charge. **3.** A prepared news or publicity release.

hand•pick (hănd′pĭk′) *tr.v.* **hand•picked, hand•pick•ing, hand•picks. 1.** To gather or pick by hand. **2.** To select personally: *hand-pick members of a committee.*

hand•rail (hănd′rāl′) *n.* A narrow railing to be grasped with the hand for support.

hand•saw (hănd′sô′) *n.* A saw operated with one hand.

hand•shake (hănd′shāk′) *n.* The grasping of hands by two people, as in greeting or leave-taking.

hand•some (hăn′səm) *adj.* **hand•som•er, hand•som•est. 1.** Pleasing and dignified in form and appearance: *a handsome couple.* **2.** Generous or liberal: *a handsome reward.* **3.** Large: *Lawyers often earn a handsome salary.* **—hand′some•ly** *adv.* **—hand′some•ness** *n.*

❑ *These sound alike:* **handsome, hansom** (carriage).

hands-on (hăndz′ŏn′ *or* hăndz′ôn′) *adj.* Involving active participation; applied, as opposed to theoretical: *We use computers in the classroom in hands-on job training.*

hand•spike (hănd′spīk′) *n.* A bar used as a lever.

hand•spring (hănd′sprĭng′) *n.* A gymnastic feat in which the body is flipped completely forward or backward from an upright position, landing first on the hands and then on the feet.

hand•stand (hănd′stănd′) *n.* The act of balancing on the hands with one's feet in the air.

hand-to-hand (hănd′tə hănd′) *adj.* Being at close quarters: *hand-to-hand combat.*

hand-to-mouth (hănd′tə mouth′) *adj.* Having or providing only the bare essentials: *a hand-to-mouth existence.*

hand•work (hănd′wûrk′) *n.* Work done by hand rather than by machine: *Sewing buttons on is handwork.*

hand•writ•ing (hănd′rī′tĭng) *n.* **1.** Writing done with the hand. **2.** The writing characteristic of a particular person.

hand•y (hăn′dē) *adj.* **hand•i•er, hand•i•est. 1.** Skillful in using one's hands: *A carpenter must be handy with tools.* **2.** Readily accessible: *a handy supply of wood for the fireplace; a handy place for the telephone directory.* **3.** Useful; convenient: *A can opener is a handy gadget.* **4.** Easy to use or handle: *a handy reference book.*

Han•dy (hăn′dē), **William Christopher.** 1873–1958. American musician and composer who was the first person to publish a blues composition, "The Memphis Blues" (1911).

hand•y•man also **handy man** (hăn′dē măn′) *n.* A man hired to perform various odd jobs.

hang (hăng) *v.* **hung** (hŭng), **hang•ing, hangs.** —*tr.* **1.** To fasten from above with no support from below; suspend: *hang a clothesline.* **2.** To fasten so as to allow free movement at or about the point of suspension: *hang a door.* **3.** *Past tense and past participle* **hanged** (hăngd). To execute by suspending by the neck. **4.** To hold or bend downward; let droop: *hang one's head in sorrow.* **5.** To attach to a wall: *hang wallpaper.* **6.** To furnish or decorate by suspending objects around or about: *We've decided to hang the walls with pictures.* **7.** To exhibit: *The city hangs the flag on all national holidays.* **8.** To deadlock (a jury) by failing to come to a unanimous verdict. —*intr.* **1.** To be attached from above with no support from below: *A sign hung over the door.* **2.** To be fastened so as to allow free movement from a hinge or hook: *The gate hangs on its hinges.* **3.** To die as a result of hanging. **4.** To remain unresolved or uncertain: *His future hangs in the balance.* **5.** To be dependent; depend: *A great deal hangs on your decision.* **6.** To incline downward; droop: *The spectators hung over the rail.* **7.** To remain suspended over a place or an object; hover: *A rain cloud hangs over the field.* **8.** To be exhibited: *Many famous paintings hang in this museum.* **9.** To pay strict attention: *The student hung on the teacher's every word.* —*n.* **1.** The way in which something hangs. **2.** *Informal.* The proper way of doing, handling, or using something: *I can't get the hang of this new camera.* **3.** Particular meaning or significance: *None of us understood the hang of the story.* ***—idioms.*** **hang around.** *Informal.* **1.** To spend time idly; loiter: *hang around the beach all day.* **2.** To keep company: *hang around with old friends.* **hang back.** To be averse; hold back: *When the teacher asked a question, several students hung back.* **hang on. 1.** To cling tightly to something: *Hang onto the rope and pull yourself up.* **2.** To remain on the telephone; hold the line. **3.** To continue persistently; persevere: *This fever keeps hang-*

handstand

W.C. Handy

ă	pat	oi	boy
ā	pay	ou	out
âr	care	o͝o	took
ä	father	o͞o	boot
ĕ	pet	ŭ	cut
ē	be	ûr	urge
ĭ	pit	th	thin
ī	pie	*th*	this
îr	pier	hw	whoop
ŏ	pot	zh	vision
ō	toe	ə	about
ô	paw	N	*French* bon

hang glider

Lorraine Hansberry

hardhat

ing on. **hang out.** *Slang.* **1.** To spend one's free time in a certain place. **2.** To keep company: *hanging out with her classmates.* **hang together. 1.** To stand united; stick together: *hang together as a group.* **2.** To make sense as a whole; be understandable: *The sentences hang together to form a good paragraph.* **hang up. 1.** To end a telephone conversation. **2.** To suspend on a hook or hanger: *Before class begins, the children hang up their coats.* **3.** To delay or impede; hinder. [First written down in 1137 in Middle English and spelled *hongen*, from Old English *hangian*, to be suspended, and from Old English *hōn*, to hang.]

han•gar (**hăng′**ər *or* **hăng′**gər) *n.* A building used for housing or repairing aircraft. [First written down in 1852 in Modern English, from Old French *hangard*, shed, of Germanic origin.]

❑ *These sound alike:* **hangar, hanger** (hook).

hang•dog (**hăng′**dôg′ *or* **hăng′**dŏg′) *adj.* Shamefaced or guilty: *a hangdog look on the criminal's face.*

hanged (hăngd) *v.* Past tense and past participle of **hang** (sense 3).

hang•er (**hăng′**ər) *n.* **1.** A frame or hook on which an article of clothing can be hung. **2.** A person who hangs something: *a wallpaper hanger.*

❑ *These sound alike:* **hanger, hangar** (aircraft building).

hang•er-on (**hăng′**ər **ŏn′** *or* **hăng′**ər **ôn′**) *n., pl.* **hang•ers-on** (**hăng′**ərz **ŏn′** *or* **hăng′**ərz **ôn′**). A person who cultivates the friendship of an influential person in the hope of achieving personal gain; a parasite.

hang glider *n.* A device resembling a kite from which a rider hangs in a harness while gliding from a height.

hang gliding *n.* The sport of riding a hang glider.

hang•ing (**hăng′**ĭng) *n.* **1.** Execution on a gallows: *death by hanging.* **2.** Something, such as a tapestry, that is hung: *a wall hanging.* —*adj.* **1.** Projecting downward; overhanging: *a hanging lamp; hanging moss.* **2.** Situated on a steep slope or on top of a high place.

hang•man (**hăng′**mən) *n.* A man who is employed to execute convicted criminals by hanging.

hang•nail (**hăng′**nāl′) *n.* A small flap of dead skin that hangs from the side or base of a fingernail.

hang•out (**hăng′**out′) *n. Slang.* A frequently visited place: *The mall is a favorite hangout of teenagers.*

hang•o•ver (**hăng′**ō′vər) *n.* **1.** A condition, often characterized by nausea and a headache, that results from drinking more alcohol than the body can tolerate. **2.** Something left from an earlier time; a holdover.

hang-up (**hăng′**ŭp′) *n. Informal.* **1.** An inhibition or emotional difficulty with something. **2.** An obstacle or inconvenience.

hank (hăngk) *n.* **1.** A coil or loop: *a hank of rope.* **2.** A looped bundle, as of yarn. [First written down in 1294 in Middle English, from Old Norse *hönk*.]

han•ker (**hăng′**kər) *intr.v.* **han•kered, han•ker•ing, han•kers.** To have a longing or yearning; crave: *hanker to travel abroad.* [First written down in 1601 in Modern English, perhaps from Dutch dialectal *hankeren*.]

Han•ni•bal (**hăn′**ə bəl). 247–183? B.C. Carthaginian general who crossed the Alps in 218 with his troops and defeated Roman armies in 217 and 216.

Ha•noi (hă **noi′** *or* hə **noi′**). The capital of Vietnam, in the northern part of the country near an arm of the South China Sea. It was founded before the seventh century. Population, 819,913.

Hans•ber•ry (**hănz′**bĕr ē), **Lorraine.** 1930–1965. American playwright known for her play *A Raisin in the Sun* (1959).

han•som (**hăn′**səm) *n.* A two-wheeled carriage drawn by one horse with the driver's seat high up at the rear. [First written down in 1847, after Joseph Aloysius *Hansom* (1803–1882), British architect.]

❑ *These sound alike:* **hansom, handsome** (attractive).

Ha•nuk•kah or **Ha•nu•kah** also **Cha•nu•kah** (**KHä′**nə kə *or* **hä′**nə kə) *n.* A Jewish festival lasting eight days and celebrating the victory in 165 B.C. of the Maccabees over the king of Syria and the rededication of the Temple at Jerusalem.

hap (hăp) *n.* Fortune; chance. —*intr.v.* **happed, hap•ping, haps.** To happen. [First written down about 1205 in Middle English, from Old Norse *happ*.]

hap•haz•ard (hăp **hăz′**ərd) *adj.* Dependent on or characterized by mere chance; random: *He had left the papers in a haphazard arrangement on the desk.* —**hap•haz′ard•ly** *adv.* —**hap•haz′ard•ness** *n.*

hap•less (**hăp′**lĭs) *adj.* Unfortunate; unlucky: *a hapless business scheme.* [First written down in 1568 in Modern English, from *hap*, chance, luck.] —**hap′less•ly** *adv.* —**hap′less•ness** *n.*

hap•loid (**hăp′**loid′) *adj.* Having half the number of chromosomes found in a given species: *Reproductive cells in animals are usually haploid.* —*n.* A haploid cell or individual.

hap•ly (**hăp′**lē) *adv.* By chance or accident.

hap•pen (**hăp′**ən) *intr.v.* **hap•pened, hap•pen•ing, hap•pens. 1.** To occur or take place by chance. **2.** To come to pass. **3.** To come upon something by chance: *I happened upon an interesting article in the newspaper last week.* [First written down about 1380 in Middle English and spelled *happenen*, from *hap*, chance.]

hap•pen•ing (**hăp′**ə nĭng) *n.* Something that happens; an event or occurrence: *an interesting recent happening.*

hap•pen•stance (**hăp′**ən stăns′) *n.* A chance circumstance: *By happenstance I met an old friend on the street.*

hap•pi•ly (**hăp′**ə lē) *adv.* **1.** In a happy way; with pleasure, joy, and gladness: *The children go happily to the fair this weekend.* **2.** By luck; with good fortune: *Happily, the parts I needed were all in stock at the hardware store.*

hap•pi•ness (**hăp′**ē nĭs) *n.* The state or quality of being happy.

hap•py (**hăp′**ē) *adj.* **hap•pi•er, hap•pi•est. 1.** Having, showing, or marked by a feeling of joy or pleasure: *a happy child; the happiest day of my life.* See Synonyms at **glad. 2.** Characterized by good luck; fortunate: *a happy sequence of events.* **3.** Being especially well adapted or suited: *Their greeting was a happy choice of words.* **4.** Cheerful; willing: *We'll be happy to help.* [First written down about 1380 in Middle English, from *hap*, luck.]

hap•py-go-luck•y (hăp′ē gō **lŭk′**ē) *adj.* Taking things easily; carefree: *a happy-go-lucky attitude.*

Haps•burg (**hăps′**bûrg′). A royal German family whose members ruled many European states from the late Middle Ages until the 20th century.

ha•ra-ki•ri (**hăr′**ĭ **kîr′**ē *or* **hä′**rē **kîr′**ē) *n., pl.* **ha•ra-ki•ris.** Suicide by cutting open the abdomen with a dagger or knife, formerly practiced by Japanese samurai. [First written down in 1856 in Modern English and spelled *hara-kari*, from Japanese *hara-kiri*.]

ha•rangue (hə **răng′**) *n.* A long loud speech, often one in which the speaker denounces a person or thing: *The dictator delivered a harangue against enemies of the government.* —*v.* **ha•rangued, ha•rangu•ing, ha•rangues.** —*tr.* To deliver a harangue to: *harangue one's followers for their shortcomings.* —*intr.* To deliver a harangue.

Ha•ra•re (hə **rär′**ā). The capital and largest city of

Zimbabwe, in the northeast part of the country. It was founded in 1890. Population, 656,011.

har•ass (hăr′əs *or* hə răs′) *tr.v.* **ha•rassed, ha•rass•ing, ha•rass•es. 1.** To irritate or torment persistently: *harass a speaker with whistles and shouts.* **2.** To carry out repeated attacks and raids against. [First written down before 1618 in Modern English, from French *harasser.*] **—ha•rass′ment** *n.*

har•bin•ger (här′bĭn jər) *n.* Something that indicates or foreshadows what is to come; a forerunner: *The robin is a harbinger of spring.*

har•bor (här′bər) *n.* **1.** A sheltered part of a body of water deep enough to serve as a port for ships. **2.** A place of shelter; a refuge: *Home is always a safe harbor.* —*tr.v.* **har•bored, har•bor•ing, har•bors. 1.** To give shelter to: *harbor a fugitive.* **2.** To have (a specified thought or feeling): *harboring a grudge against an old enemy.* [First written down about 1125 in Middle English and spelled *herbirge*, probably from Old English *herebeorg*, lodging.]

hard (härd) *adj.* **hard•er, hard•est. 1.** Resistant to pressure; not readily penetrated: *a hard surface; hard as a rock.* **2.** Difficult to understand, express, or convey: *a hard question; a hard concept to explain.* **3.** Requiring great effort; arduous: *A cross-country race is a hard run.* **4.** Bad; adverse: *hard luck.* **5.** Intense; forceful: *a hard blow; a hard twist of the knob.* **6.** Difficult to endure; trying; harsh: *a hard life.* **7.** Strict and demanding; stern: *My music teacher is a hard taskmaster.* **8.** Making few concessions: *The opposing lawyer drove a hard bargain.* **9.** Close; penetrating: *take a hard look at the facts.* **10.** Definite or real; true and unchangeable: *hard facts of the evidence.* **11.** Causing damage to; tending to wear down quickly: *Freezing weather is hard on a car.* **12.** Bitter; rancorous; resentful: *There is much hard feeling between those old enemies.* **13.a.** Designating currency as opposed to checks or notes: *pay in hard cash.* **b.** Readily exchanged for gold or other currency: *hard currency.* **14.** Designating the sound represented by the letters *c* and *g* as they are pronounced in *cat* and *go.* **15.a.** Having high alcoholic content; intoxicating: *hard liquor.* **b.** Rendered alcoholic by fermentation: *hard cider.* **16.** In printed rather than electronic form: *The typist made a hard copy of the manuscript.* **17.** Containing dissolved salts that interfere with the action of soap: *hard water of high mineral content.* —*adv.* **hard•er, hard•est. 1.** With much effort; intently; earnestly: *work hard.* **2.** With great force, vigor, or energy: *Press hard on the lever.* **3.** In such a way as to cause great damage or hardship: *A number of towns were hard hit by the storm.* **4.** With great distress, grief, pain, or resentment: *took the news hard.* **5.** Toward or into a solid condition: *The little pond is frozen hard all winter.* **6.** Near in space or time; close: *The trees stand hard by the edge of the road.* ***—idioms.*** **hard and fast.** Defined, fixed, and invariable: *a hard and fast rule.* **hard of hearing.** Having a partial loss of hearing. **hard put.** Undergoing great difficulty: *I'm hard put to explain what he meant.* **hard up.** *Informal.* In need; poor. [First written down about 725 in Old English and spelled *heard.*] **—hard′ness** *n.*

hard•back (härd′băk′) *adj.* Bound in cloth, cardboard, or leather rather than paper. Used of books. —*n.* A book bound in cloth, cardboard, or leather.

hard•ball (härd′bôl′) *n.* **1.** Baseball. **2.** *Informal.* The use of tough and aggressive means to obtain an objective: *The negotiator played hardball to get the opposition to cave in.*

hard-bit•ten (härd′bĭt′n) *adj.* Made tough through experience: *a hard-bitten criminal lawyer.*

hard-boiled (härd′boild′) *adj.* **1.** Boiled in the shell to a solid consistency. Used of eggs. **2.** Unsentimental and practical; tough: *a hard-boiled newspaper reporter.*

hard•bound (härd′bound′) *adj. & n.* Hardback.

hard coal *n.* Anthracite.

hard-core (härd′kôr′) *adj.* **1.** Intensely loyal: *a hard-core golfer.* **2.** Resistant to improvement or change: *a hard-core criminal.*

hard•cov•er (härd′kŭv′ər) *adj.* Hardback. —*n.* A hardback book.

hard disk *n.* A computer disk that cannot be removed. Hard disks hold more data and are faster than floppy disks.

hard•en (här′dn) *v.* **hard•ened, hard•en•ing, hard•ens.** —*tr.* **1.** To make hard or harder: *harden steel.* **2.** To toughen; make rugged: *harden young athletes by long periods of exercise.* **3.** To make unfeeling, unsympathetic, or callous: *Seeing so much poverty and disease hardened the young doctor's heart.* —*intr.* **1.** To become hard or harder: *Allow the mixture to cool until it hardens.* **2.** To rise and become stable. Used of prices.

hard•hat or **hard-hat** (härd′hăt′) *n.* **1.** A lightweight protective helmet worn by workers in industrial settings. **2.** *Informal.* A construction worker.

hard•head•ed (härd′hĕd′ĭd) *adj.* **1.** Stubborn; willful: *a hardheaded mule.* **2.** Pragmatic; realistic: *a hardheaded business manager.* **—hard′head′ed•ly** *adv.* **—hard′head′ed•ness** *n.*

hard•heart•ed (härd′här′tĭd) *adj.* Lacking in feeling or compassion; pitiless. **—hard′heart′ed•ly** *adv.* **—hard′heart′ed•ness** *n.*

har•di•hood (här′dē ho͝od′) *n.* Boldness and daring.

Har•ding (här′dĭng), **Warren Gamaliel.** 1865–1923. The 29th President of the United States (1921–1923).

hard line *n.* A firm uncompromising policy, position, or stance: *Our teacher took a hard line on turning in homework late.*

hard-line (härd′līn′) *adj.* Firm and uncompromising, as in policy, position, or stance: *a hard-line foreign policy.*

hard•ly (härd′lē) *adv.* **1.** Barely; only just: *We hardly noticed it was getting late.* **2.** Probably or almost surely not: *I would hardly expect visitors on such a snowy day.* **3.** With severity; harshly. —See Note.

hard palate *n.* The hard bony forward part of the roof of the mouth.

hard•pan (härd′păn′) *n.* **1.** A layer of hard, often clayey subsoil. Plant roots do not usually grow through hardpan. **2.** Hard unbroken ground.

hard•ship (härd′shĭp′) *n.* A cause of suffering or difficulty: *The settlers suffered great hardships.*

hard•tack (härd′tăk′) *n.* A hard biscuit or bread made of flour and water.

hard•ware (härd′wâr′) *n.* **1.** Articles made of metal, as tools, locks, and cutlery. **2.** A computer and its equipment, such as the keyboard, monitor, disk drive, and printer. **3.** Machinery used in industry and by the military.

hard•wood (härd′wo͝od′) *n.* **1.** Any of various flowering trees having broad leaves that are usually shed each year. **2.** The compact wood of such a tree, including maple, oak, cherry, and mahogany.

har•dy (här′dē) *adj.* **har•di•er, har•di•est. 1.** Being in robust and sturdy good health. **2.** Capable of withstanding harsh or difficult conditions, such as cold weather or poor food: *A hardy rosebush can withstand freezing temperatures.* [First written down before 1200 in Middle English, from Old French *hardi*, hardened.]

Har•dy (här′dē), **Thomas.** 1840–1928. British writer noted for his novels, including *Tess of the d'Urbervilles* (1891).

hare (hâr) *n.* Any of various mammals similar to rabbits but having longer ears and legs. [First writ-

Warren G. Harding

Usage: hardly

The words **hardly**, **rarely**, and **scarcely** have the force of negatives and so should not be used with other negatives. You should write *I could hardly believe it* rather than *I couldn't hardly believe it.*

Thomas Hardy

ă	pat	oi	boy
ā	pay	ou	out
âr	care	o͝o	took
ä	father	o͞o	boot
ĕ	pet	ŭ	cut
ē	be	ûr	urge
ĭ	pit	th	thin
ī	pie	*th*	this
îr	pier	hw	whoop
ŏ	pot	zh	vision
ō	toe	ə	about
ô	paw	N	*French* bon

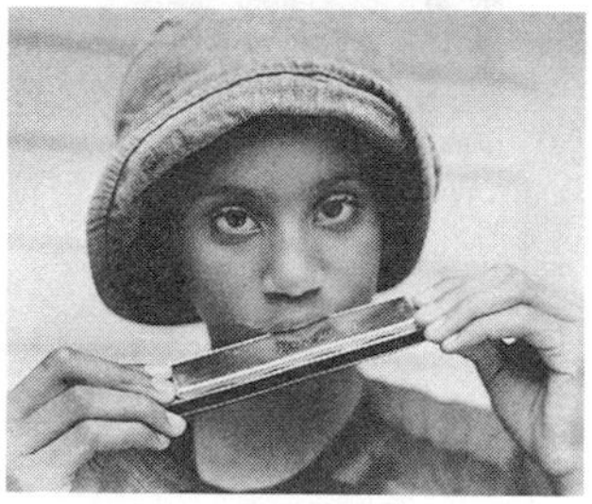

harmonica

harp

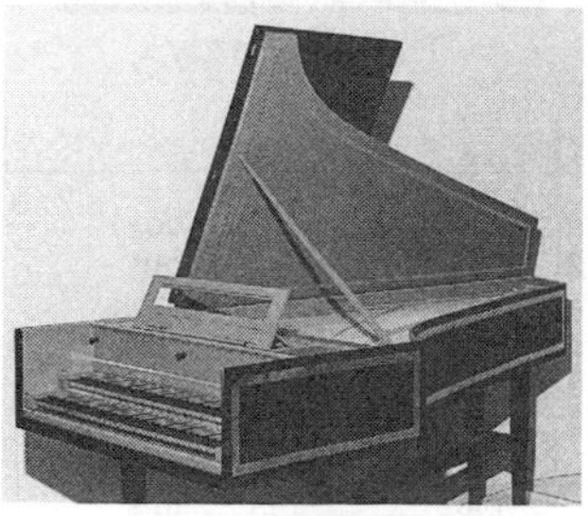

harpsichord

ten down about 700 in Old English and spelled *hara.*]

❑ *These sound alike:* **hare, hair** (strands).

hare•bell (hâr′bĕl′) *n.* A plant having slender stems, narrow leaves, and blue flowers shaped like bells.

hare•brained (hâr′brānd′) *adj.* Foolish; flighty: *a hare-brained idea.*

hare•lip (hâr′lĭp′) *n.* An abnormal condition existing from birth in which the upper lip is divided into two or more parts. **—hare′lipped′** *adj.*

har•em (hâr′əm *or* hăr′əm) *n.* **1.** The part of a Muslim house in which the women live. **2.** The women who live in a Muslim household. [First written down in 1634 in Modern English and spelled *haram,* from Arabic *ḥarīm,* forbidden place.]

Har•greaves (här′grēvz′), **James.** Died 1778. British inventor of a power-operated spinning machine, the spinning jenny (about 1764).

hark (härk) *intr.v.* **harked, hark•ing, harks.** To listen carefully. **—*idiom.* hark back.** To return to a previous point, as in a narrative.

har•ken (här′kən) *v.* Variant of **hearken.**

Har•lem (här′ləm). A section of New York City in northern Manhattan that is one of the largest Black communities in the United States. In the 1920's a flowering of Black art and literature was known as the Harlem Renaissance.

har•le•quin (här′lĭ kwĭn *or* här′lĭ kĭn) *n.* **1. Harlequin.** A comic pantomime character, usually appearing in a mask and a costume of many colors. **2.** A clown; a buffoon.

har•lot (här′lət) *n.* A prostitute.

harm (härm) *n.* **1.** Injury or damage: *Locusts often cause great harm to crops.* **2.** Wrong; evil: *There was no harm meant in their careless mistake.* *—tr.v.* **harmed, harm•ing, harms.** To do harm to. [First written down about 725 in Old English and spelled *hearm.*]

harm•ful (härm′fəl) *adj.* Causing or capable of causing harm; injurious: *Insects can be harmful to plants.* **—harm′ful•ly** *adv.* **—harm′ful•ness** *n.*

harm•less (härm′lĭs) *adj.* Incapable of causing harm: *a harmless kitten.* **—harm′less•ly** *adv.* **—harm′less•ness** *n.*

har•mon•ic (här mŏn′ĭk) *n.* A tone that occurs with a fundamental tone and has a frequency of vibration that is an exact multiple of the fundamental tone. *—adj.* **1.** Of or relating to musical harmony. **2.** Of or relating to overtones produced when a lower tone occurs or is played. **—har•mon′i•cal•ly** *adv.*

har•mon•i•ca (här mŏn′ĭ kə) *n.* A small, rectangular musical instrument consisting of a series of tuned metal reeds set back in air holes, played by exhaling or inhaling.

har•mo•ni•ous (här mō′nē əs) *adj.* **1.** Showing accord in feeling or action: *a harmonious gathering of friends.* **2.** Having elements pleasingly or appropriately combined: *a harmonious arrangement of colors.* **3.** Characterized by harmony of sound; melodious. **—har•mo′ni•ous•ly** *adv.*

har•mo•nize (här′mə nīz′) *v.* **har•mo•nized, har•mo•niz•ing, har•mo•niz•es.** *—tr.* **1.** To bring into agreement; make harmonious: *harmonize different ideas into a plan.* **2.** To provide harmony for (a melody). *—intr.* **1.** To be in agreement; be harmonious. **2.** To sing or play in harmony: *The choir harmonized in song.* **—har′mo•ni•za′tion** (här′mə nĭ zā′shən) *n.*

har•mo•ny (här′mə nē) *n., pl.* **har•mo•nies. 1.a.** The combination of notes forming a chord: *The piano fills in the harmony for the voice part of the singer.* **b.** The study of the structure, succession, and relationships of chords. **2.** A combination of musical sounds considered to be pleasing. **3.** A pleasing combination of elements that form a whole: *The developers destroyed the harmony of the beautiful mountain scenery.* **4.** Agreement in feeling or opinion; accord: *a family that lives in harmony.* [First written down about 1380 in Middle English and spelled *armonie,* from Greek *harmonia,* articulation, agreement, from *harmos,* joint.]

har•ness (här′nĭs) *n.* **1.** A set of leather straps and metal pieces by which an animal is attached to and pulls a vehicle or plow. **2.** Something resembling a harness, as the arrangement of straps used to hold a parachute to the body. *—tr.v.* **har•nessed, har•ness•ing, har•ness•es. 1.** To put a harness on (a draft animal): *harness a horse to a wagon.* **2.** To bring under control and direct the force of: *Solar panels harness the sun's energy.* **—*idiom.* in harness.** At one's work; on duty: *get back in harness after a vacation.* [First written down before 1300 in Middle English and spelled *harnais,* from Old French *harneis,* of Germanic origin.]

harp (härp) *n.* A musical instrument consisting of an upright triangular frame on which a series of strings are played by plucking with the fingers. *—intr.v.* **harped, harp•ing, harps.** To play a harp. **—*idiom.* harp on.** To write or talk about to an excessive or tedious degree: *harping on how much it costs to go to the movies.* [First written down about 725 in Old English and spelled *hearpe.*]

Har•pers Ferry (här′pərz). A locality of extreme northeast West Virginia. It was the scene of John Brown's rebellion (1859), in which he briefly seized the U.S. arsenal here.

harp•ist (här′pĭst) *n.* A person who plays the harp.

har•poon (här po͞on′) *n.* A weapon like a spear with a barbed head that is used in hunting whales and large fish. *—tr.v.* **har•pooned, har•poon•ing, har•poons.** To strike, kill, or catch with or as if with a harpoon. [First written down in 1625 in Modern English and spelled *harpon,* from Old French, possibly from Greek *harpē,* sickle.] **—har•poon′er** *n.*

harp seal *n.* A seal of the North Atlantic and Arctic oceans whose pups are hunted for their fur.

harp•si•chord (härp′sĭ kôrd′) *n.* A keyboard instrument that resembles a piano, having strings that are plucked by means of quills or plectrums.

Har•py (här′pē) *n., pl.* **Har•pies. 1.** In Greek mythology, a hideous monster with the head and trunk of a woman and the tail, wings, and claws of a bird. **2. harpy.** A predatory person.

har•que•bus (här′kə bəs *or* här′kwə bəs) also **ar•que•bus** (är′kə bəs *or* är′kwə bəs) *n.* A heavy portable gun invented during the 15th century.

har•ri•dan (hăr′ĭ dn) *n.* A woman regarded as vicious and scoldiing.

har•ri•er[1] (hăr′ē ər) *n.* **1.** A person or thing that harries. **2.** Any of various slender hawks having narrow wings and preying on small animals.

har•ri•er[2] (hăr′ē ər) *n.* Any of a breed of small hound originally bred to hunt hares. [First written down in 1408 in Middle English and spelled *hayrer,* possibly from Old French *errier,* wanderer, from *errer,* to wander, rove.]

Har•ris•burg (hăr′ĭs bûrg′). The capital of Pennsylvania, in the southeast-central part of the state west-northwest of Philadelphia. It was settled in the early 1700's and became the capital in 1812. Population, 52,376.

Har•ri•son (hăr′ĭ sən), **Benjamin**[1]. 1726–1791. American Revolutionary leader who served as a member of the Continental Congress (1774–1778).

Harrison, Benjamin[2]. 1833–1901. The 23rd President of the United States (1889–1893).

Harrison, William Henry. 1773–1841. The ninth President of the United States (1841).

har•row (hăr′ō) *n.* A farm implement consisting of a heavy frame with sharp teeth or upright disks, used to break up and even off plowed land. —*tr.v.* **har•rowed, har•row•ing, har•rows. 1.** To break up and level (soil or land) with a harrow. **2.** To cause great worry or anguish to (someone). [First written down about 1300 in Middle English and spelled *harewe*.] **—har′row•er** *n.*

har•row•ing (hăr′ō ĭng) *adj.* Extremely distressing; agonizing: *a harrowing experience.*

har•ry (hăr′ē) *tr.v.* **har•ried, har•ry•ing, har•ries. 1.** To disturb or distress by or as if by repeated attacks; harass: *harried me with constant phone calls.* **2.** To raid, as in war; sack or pillage: *The invading army harried the countryside.*

harsh (härsh) *adj.* **harsh•er, harsh•est. 1.** Unpleasantly coarse and rough to the touch. **2.** Unpleasant to the senses: *a harsh angry voice.* **3.** Extremely severe or cruel; stern: *harsh words of criticism.* **—harsh′ly** *adv.* **—harsh′ness** *n.*

hart (härt) *n., pl.* **harts** or **hart.** A male deer, especially a male red deer over five years old.
❑ *These sound alike:* **hart, heart** (organ).

har•te•beest (här′tə bēst′ *or* härt′bēst′) *n., pl.* **har•te•beests** or **hartebeest.** Any of various African antelopes having a brownish coat and outward-curving horns that bend backward.

Hart•ford (härt′fərd). The capital of Connecticut, in the north-central part of the state on the Connecticut River. Settled 1635–1636 by Massachusetts colonists, it became the core of the Connecticut Colony in 1639. Population, 139,739.

har•um-scar•um (hâr′əm skâr′əm *or* hăr′əm skăr′əm) *adj.* Lacking a sense of responsibility; reckless. —*adv.* With abandon; recklessly: *ran harum-scarum around the yard.*

har•vest (här′vĭst) *n.* **1.** The act or process of gathering a crop. **2.** The crop that ripens or is gathered in a season: *a large corn harvest.* **3.** The time or season of such gathering: *Harvest lasts about six weeks.* **4.** The result or consequence of an action: *Our trip to the Grand Canyon yielded a rich harvest of memories.* —*v.* **har•vest•ed, har•vest•ing, har•vests.** —*tr.* **1.** To gather (a crop): *harvest wheat.* **2.** To gather a crop from: *harvest an apple orchard.* **3.** To receive (the benefits or consequences of an action): *harvest the rewards of hard work.* —*intr.* To gather a crop. [First written down about 750 in Old English and spelled *hærfest*.]

har•vest•er (här′vĭ stər) *n.* **1.** A person who gathers a crop. **2.** A machine for harvesting crops; a reaper.

harvest moon *n.* The full moon that occurs nearest the beginning of autumn.

Har•vey (här′vē), **William.** 1578–1657. English physician who discovered the circulation of blood in the human body in 1628.

has (hăz) *v.* Third person singular present tense of **have.**

has-been (hăz′bĭn′) *n., pl.* **has-beens.** *Informal.* A person whose fame, popularity, or success has passed: *The actor is a has-been.*

hash (hăsh) *n.* **1.** A dish of chopped meat, potatoes, and onions or other vegetables browned and cooked together. **2.** A jumble or hodgepodge: *a hash of disconnected sentences.* —*tr.v.* **hashed, hash•ing, hash•es. 1.** To chop into pieces; mince: *hash potatoes.* **2.** *Informal.* To discuss carefully; review: *hash over a problem.*

hash•ish also **hash•eesh** (hăsh′ēsh′ *or* hă shēsh′) *n.* A dry resinous extract prepared from the hemp plant, used as a narcotic.

Ha•sid or **Has•sid** also **Chas•sid** (ᴋʜä′sĭd *or* hä′sĭd) *n., pl.* **Ha•si•dim** or **Has•si•dim** also **Chas•si•dim** (ᴋʜä sē′dĭm *or* hä sē′dĭm). A member of a Jewish movement of popular mysticism founded in Eastern Europe in the 18th century.

has•n't (hăz′ənt). Contraction of *has not.*

hasp (hăsp) *n.* A metal fastener with a hinged slotted part that is passed over a staple and secured by a pin, bolt, or padlock.

has•sle (hăs′əl) *Informal. n.* **1.** An argument or a fight. **2.** Trouble or bother: *Driving in the snow is a real hassle.* —*v.* **has•sled, has•sling, has•sles.** —*intr.* To argue or fight. —*tr.* To bother or harass: *The bully hassled me on my way to school.*

has•sock (hăs′ək) *n.* **1.** A thick cushion used as a footstool or for kneeling. **2.** A dense clump of grass.

hast (hăst) *v. Archaic.* Second person singular present tense of **have.**

haste (hāst) *n.* **1.** Swiftness of motion or action; rapidity. **2.** Overeagerness to act: *In their haste they forgot to lock the front door.* **—*idiom.* make haste.** To move or act swiftly; hurry: *Make haste to get there on time.*

has•ten (hā′sən) *v.* **has•tened, has•ten•ing, has•tens.** —*intr.* To move or act swiftly; hurry: *I hastened to tell them the good news.* —*tr.* **1.** To cause to hurry. **2.** To cause (something) to happen faster or sooner: *The medicine hastened my recovery.*

Has•tings (hā′stĭngz). A borough of southeast England on the English Channel. Hastings is near the site of William the Conqueror's victory over the Saxons (October 14, 1066). Population, 75,900.

hast•y (hā′stē) *adj.* **hast•i•er, hast•i•est. 1.** Marked by speed; swift; rapid: *a hasty departure.* See Synonyms at **fast[1]. 2.** Done or made too quickly to be accurate or wise; rash: *hasty judgments.* **—hast′i•ly** *adv.* **—hast′i•ness** *n.*

hasty pudding *n.* **1.** Cornmeal mush served with a sweetener such as maple syrup or brown sugar. **2.** *Chiefly British.* A flour or oatmeal porridge.

hat (hăt) *n.* A covering for the head, especially one with a crown and brim. —*tr.v.* **hat•ted, hat•ting, hats.** To supply or cover with a hat. **—*idioms.* at the drop of a hat.** At the slightest pretext or provocation. **pass the hat.** To take up a collection of money: *passed the hat to collect donations.* **take (one's) hat off to.** To respect, admire, or congratulate: *I take my hat off to anyone who can get a high mark on that test.*

hat•band (hăt′bănd′) *n.* A band of ribbon or cloth worn just above the brim on a hat.

hat•box (hăt′bŏks′) *n.* A box or case for a hat.

hatch[1] (hăch) *n.* **1.** An opening, as in the deck of a ship, in the roof or floor of a building, or in an airplane. **2.** A trap door or cover for such an opening. [First written down in 1015 in Old English and spelled *hæc*.]

hatch[2] (hăch) *v.* **hatched, hatch•ing, hatch•es.** —*intr.* To come out of an egg or eggs: *Ten chicks hatched today.* —*tr.* **1.** To cause to come out of an egg or eggs: *The hen hatched a brood of ten chicks.* **2.** To cause (an egg or eggs) to produce young: *The warmth of the sun hatches the eggs of most turtles.* **3.** To devise or plot, especially in secret: *hatching a plan of escape.* —*n.* The young hatched at one time; a brood. [First written down before 1250 in Middle English and spelled *hacchen*.]

hatch•back (hăch′băk′) *n.* An automobile having a sloping back with a hatch that opens upward.

hatch•er•y (hăch′ə rē) *n., pl.* **hatch•er•ies.** A place where eggs, especially those of fish or chickens, are hatched.

hatch•et (hăch′ĭt) *n.* A small ax with a short handle used with one hand. [First written down in 1307 in Middle English and spelled *hachet*, from Old French *hachete*, small ax.]

hatch•way (hăch′wā′) *n.* A passage or an opening leading to a hold, compartment, or cellar.

Benjamin Harrison[2]

William Henry Harrison

hatchback

ă	pat	oi	boy
ā	pay	ou	out
âr	care	o͝o	took
ä	father	o͞o	boot
ĕ	pet	ŭ	cut
ē	be	ûr	urge
ĭ	pit	th	thin
ī	pie	*th*	this
îr	pier	hw	whoop
ŏ	pot	zh	vision
ō	toe	ə	about
ô	paw	ɴ	*French* bon

Hatshepsut

hauberk

Hawaii

The name for the state of **Hawaii** comes from the name the original Polynesian inhabitants gave their island. This name probably comes from an earlier Polynesian term, *Sawaiki,* meaning "the underworld" or "ancestral home." Although the English explorer Captain James Cook had named the island group the Sandwich Islands, after the Earl of Sandwich (1718–1792), it joined the United States in 1959 as Hawaii.

hawk[1]
Red-tailed hawk

hate (hāt) *v.* **hat•ed, hat•ing, hates.** *—tr.* **1.** To have a great dislike for; detest. **2.** To feel dislike or distaste for: *We hate washing dishes.* *—intr.* To feel hatred. *—n.* Intense animosity or dislike; hatred. **—hat′er** *n.*

hate•ful (hāt′fəl) *adj.* **1.** Arousing or deserving hatred. **2.** Feeling or showing hatred; full of hate: *They stared at me in a hateful manner.* **—hate′ful•ly** *adv.* **—hate′ful•ness** *n.*

hath (hăth) *v. Archaic.* Third person singular present tense of **have.**

hat•pin (hăt′pĭn′) *n.* A long straight pin used to fasten a hat to the hair.

ha•tred (hā′trĭd) *n.* Intense animosity or hostility.

Hat•shep•sut (hăt shĕp′so͞ot′). Died about 1482 B.C. Queen of Egypt (1503–1482) who as regent for her son took the title of pharaoh.

hat•ter (hăt′ər) *n.* A person who makes, sells, or repairs hats.

Hat•ter•as Island (hăt′ər əs). A long barrier island off the eastern coast of North Carolina in the Atlantic Ocean, with **Cape Hatteras** on the southeast part.

hau•berk (hô′bərk) *n.* A long tunic made of chain mail.

haugh•ty (hô′tē) *adj.* **haugh•ti•er, haugh•ti•est.** Scornfully and condescendingly proud: *The haughty waiter offended many customers.* See Synonyms at **proud.** **—haugh′ti•ly** *adv.* **—haugh′ti•ness** *n.*

haul (hôl) *v.* **hauled, haul•ing, hauls.** *—tr.* **1.** To pull or drag forcibly; tug: *We hauled the wood into the shed.* **2.** To transport, as with a truck or cart: *used trucks to haul away the dirt and debris.* *—intr.* To pull or tug. *—n.* **1.** The act of pulling or dragging. **2.** A distance, especially the distance over which something is transported or pulled: *a long haul across country.* **3.** Everything collected or acquired by a single effort; the take: *a big haul of fish.* [First written down before 1200 in Middle English and spelled *halen*, from Old French *haler*, of Germanic origin.] **—haul′er** *n.*

❑ *These sound alike:* **haul, hall** (corridor).

haunch (hônch *or* hŏnch) *n.* **1.** The hip, buttock, and upper thigh of a person or an animal: *The dog settled back on its haunches.* **2.** The loin and leg of an animal, especially as used for food: *a haunch of beef.*

haunt (hônt *or* hŏnt) *tr.v.* **haunt•ed, haunt•ing, haunts. 1.** To visit, appear to, or inhabit in the form of a ghost or other supernatural being: *spirits haunting the woods.* **2.** To visit often; frequent: *haunts the local bookstores.* **3.** To come to mind continually; obsess: *That bad experience has haunted me ever since.* *—n.* A place that is visited often: *This café is a favorite haunt of artists.* [First written down about 1200 in Middle English and spelled *hanten*, to do habitually, to frequent, from Old French *hanter*.]

haunt•ing (hôn′tĭng *or* hŏn′tĭng) *adj.* Continually recurring to the mind; unforgettable: *a haunting melody.* **—haunt′ing•ly** *adv.*

Hau•sa (hou′sə *or* hou′zə) *n., pl.* **Hausa** or **Hau•sas. 1.** A member of a chiefly Muslim people living in Nigeria and Niger. **2.** The language of the Hausa.

haut•boy (hō′boi′ *or* ō′boi′) *n., pl.* **haut•boys.** An oboe.

hau•teur (hō tûr′) *n.* Haughtiness in bearing and attitude; arrogance: *Their hauteur made them unbearable.*

Ha•van•a (hə văn′ə). The capital and largest city of Cuba, in the northwest part of the country on the Gulf of Mexico. It was founded in 1519. Population, 1,961,674.

have (hăv) *v.* **had** (hăd), **hav•ing, has** (hăz). *—tr.* **1.** To be in possession of; own: *My family has an old car.* **2.** To possess as a characteristic, function, or quality: *That singer has a good voice.* **3.** To possess or contain as a part: *This typewriter has a correction key.* **4.** To be in a certain relationship to: *I have a brother and a sister.* **5.** To possess knowledge of or experience in: *This class has had no Spanish at all.* **6.** To hold in the mind: *I have many doubts about this trip. She has a good idea.* **7.** To receive or get: *I had more than a dozen cards on my birthday.* **8.** To accept; take: *Will you have an orange?* **9.** To go through; experience: *I had a good summer.* **10.** To allow; permit: *Our teacher won't have sloppy writing.* **11.a.** To cause (someone to do something): *The coach had the students rake the infield.* **b.** To cause (something to be done): *We had the house cleaned for the party.* **12.** To carry on; engage in: *We have arguments but are still good friends.* **13.** To be forced or obliged; must: *We have to leave now.* **14.** To get the better of; cheat or deceive: *I've been had.* **15.** To give birth to; bear: *Our cat is having kittens soon.* **16.** To partake of: *I'd like to have a snack.* *—aux.* Used with a past participle to form the perfect tenses indicating completed action: *They have already had their lunch. We had just finished lunch when they arrived. We will have finished lunch by the time they arrive.* *—n.* A person or country enjoying especially material wealth: *the gap between haves and have-nots.* ***—idioms.*** **have at.** To attack: *We watched two birds have at each other over some seeds.* **have done with.** To stop; cease: *Let's have done with this nonsense once and for all.* **have had it.** To have endured all that one can: *I've had it with this traffic.* **have it in for (someone).** To intend to harm, especially because of a grudge. **have it out.** To settle decisively, especially through discussion or argument: *We had it out and decided we would share all our chores.* **have on.** To wear: *The band members have on their dress uniforms.* **have to do with.** To be concerned or associated with: *The book has to do with the U.S. Civil War.*

❑ *These sound alike:* **have, halve** (divide).

haven (hā′vən) *n.* **1.** A harbor or an anchorage; a port. **2.** A place of refuge or safety; a sanctuary: *The library is a haven from noise.*

have-not (hăv′nŏt′) *n.* A person or country enjoying little or no material wealth.

have•n't (hăv′ənt). Contraction of *have not.*

hav•er•sack (hăv′ər săk′) *n.* A bag worn over one shoulder to carry supplies, as on a hike.

hav•oc (hăv′ək) *n.* Very great destruction; devastation: *The hurricane created havoc throughout the coastal area.*

haw[1] (hô) *n.* A sound made by a speaker who is trying to think of what to say. *—intr.v.* **hawed, haw•ing, haws.** To make this sound during a pause in speaking: *The manager hawed before deciding to close early.* [First written down in 1632 in Modern English, of imitative origin.]

haw[2] (hô) *n.* **1.** The fruit of a hawthorn. **2.** A hawthorn or similar tree or shrub. [First written down before 1000 in Old English and spelled *haga*.]

haw[3] (hô) *interj.* An expression used to command a horse or an ox to turn to the left. [First written down in 1843 in Modern English.]

Ha•wai•i (hə wä′ē *or* hə wī′ē). A state of the United States in the central Pacific Ocean made up of the Hawaiian Islands. Hawaii was admitted as the 50th state in 1959. Honolulu is the capital and the largest city. Population, 1,115,274. —SEE NOTE.

Ha•wai•ian (hə wä′yən) *n.* **1.** A native or inhabitant of Hawaii. **2.** A member or descendant of the native Polynesian people of the Hawaiian Islands. **3.** The Polynesian language of the Hawaiians. *—adj.* Of or relating to Hawaii or the Hawaiian Islands or their people, language, or culture.

Hawaiian Islands. A group of islands in the central Pacific Ocean making up the state of Hawaii. There are eight major islands and more than a hundred minor ones. The islands were settled by Polynesians in the sixth century A.D.

hawk[1] (hôk) *n.* **1.** Any of various birds having a short hooked bill, keen eyesight, and strong claws with which they catch small birds and animals for food. **2.** *Informal.* A person who favors aggressive action or policy: *The Senator is a hawk on U.S. trade policy.* —*intr.v.* **hawked, hawk•ing, hawks.** To hunt with a trained hawk. [First written down about 700 in Old English and spelled *habuc.*]

hawk[2] (hôk) *tr.v.* **hawked, hawk•ing, hawks.** To sell (goods) in the street by calling out; peddle. [First written down in 1390 in Middle English and spelled *hauken,* from Middle Low German *höker,* street peddler.]

hawk[3] (hôk) *intr.v.* **hawked, hawk•ing, hawks.** To clear or try to clear the throat by coughing up phlegm. [First written down in 1581 in Modern English, of imitative origin.]

hawk•er (**hô′**kər) *n.* A person who peddles goods in the street, especially by calling out.

hawk-eyed (**hôk′**īd′) *adj.* Having very sharp eyesight.

hawk moth *n.* Any of various moths having a long body and narrow wings and feeding on the nectar of flowers.

haw•ser (**hô′**zər) *n.* A heavy line or cable used to moor or tow a ship.

haw•thorn (**hô′**thôrn′) *n.* Any of various usually thorny shrubs or trees having white, red, or pinkish flowers and red berries.

Haw•thorne (**hô′**thôrn′), **Nathaniel.** 1804–1864. American writer whose works, such as *The Scarlet Letter* (1850), are marked by moral and spiritual themes.

hay (hā) *n.* Grass, clover, alfalfa, and other plants cut and dried for use as food for horses and cattle. —*v.* **hayed, hay•ing, hays.** —*intr.* To cut and dry grass or other plants so as to make them into hay. —*tr.* To feed with hay.

❑ *These sound alike:* **hay, hey** (expression used to attract attention).

hay•cock (**hā′**kŏk′) *n. Chiefly British.* A cone-shaped mound of hay in a field.

Haydn (**hīd′**n), **Franz Joseph.** 1732–1809. Austrian composer who wrote numerous symphonies, string quartets, operas, and concertos.

Hayes (hāz), **Rutherford Birchard.** 1822–1893. The 19th President of the United States (1877–1881), who won the election of 1876 by one electoral vote and removed federal troops from the South (1877).

hay fever *n.* A severe irritation of the eyes, nose, and breathing passages, caused by an allergy to various pollens that are blown about in the air.

hay•fork (**hā′**fôrk′) *n.* **1.** A pitchfork. **2.** A machine for moving or loading hay.

hay•loft (**hā′**lôft′ *or* **hā′**lŏft′) *n.* A loft in a barn or stable for storing hay.

hay•mow (**hā′**mou′) *n.* **1.** A hayloft. **2.** The hay stored in a hayloft.

hay•rack (**hā′**răk′) *n.* **1.** A rack from which livestock feed. **2.** A rack mounted on a wagon for carrying hay. **3.** A wagon fitted with such a rack.

hay•rick (**hā′**rĭk′) *n.* A haystack.

hay•ride (**hā′**rīd′) *n.* A ride taken for pleasure in a wagon partly filled with hay.

hay•seed (**hā′**sēd′) *n.* **1.** Grass seed that is shaken out of hay. **2.** *Slang.* A person from the country who is considered unsophisticated.

hay•stack (**hā′**stăk′) *n.* A large stack of hay that stands out in the open in the winter.

hay•wire (**hā′**wīr′) *n.* Wire used for tying up bales of hay. —*adj. Informal.* **1.** Not functioning properly; broken: *The ship went haywire when the rudder broke.* **2.** Mentally confused; upset: *The writer went haywire when told he would have to revise the article again.*

haz•ard (**hăz′**ərd) *n.* **1.a.** A chance of being injured or harmed; danger: *the hazards of sailing.* **b.** A possible source of danger: *The stacks of old newspapers were a fire hazard.* **2.** A sandtrap, pond, or other obstacle on a golf course. —*tr.v.* **haz•ard•ed, haz•ard•ing, haz•ards. 1.** To expose to danger; risk: *Firefighters hazard their lives for the safety of others.* **2.** To dare; venture: *hazard a guess.*

haz•ard•ous (**hăz′**ər dəs) *adj.* Full of danger; risky; perilous: *a hazardous voyage.*

hazardous waste *n.* A material, such as nuclear waste or an industrial byproduct, that can damage the environment and harm the health of human beings and other living organisms.

haze[1] (hāz) *n.* **1.** Fine dust, smoke, or water vapor suspended in the air: *The skyscrapers were shrouded in haze.* **2.** A vague or confused state of mind: *Many people are in a haze just after waking up.* [First written down about 1674 in Modern English, from *hazy.*]

haze[2] (hāz) *tr.v.* **hazed, haz•ing, haz•es.** To play rough or humiliating jokes on or force to perform humiliating or unpleasant tasks: *haze new members of the club.* [First written down in 1850 in Modern English, perhaps from Old French *haser,* to annoy.]

ha•zel (**hā′**zəl) *n.* **1.** Any of various shrubs or small trees related to the birch and having edible nuts enclosed in a leafy husk. **2.** A light yellowish brown. [First written down about 700 in Old English and spelled *hæsel.*]

ha•zel•nut (**hā′**zəl nŭt′) *n.* The edible nut of a hazel, having a hard brown shell.

haz•y (**hā′**zē) *adj.* **haz•i•er, haz•i•est. 1.** Marked by the presence of haze; misty: *a hazy sun.* **2.** Not clear; vague: *a hazy recollection of an incident long past.* —**haz′i•ly** *adv.* —**haz′i•ness** *n.*

H-bomb (**āch′**bŏm′) *n.* A hydrogen bomb.

he (hē) *pron.* **1.** The man or boy previously mentioned: *Tom worked here last summer, but now he is back in school.* **2.** The male animal previously mentioned: *Our dog usually sleeps outside, but he slept in my room last night.* **3.** A person whose gender is not specified or known: *He who laughs last laughs best.* —*n.* A male animal or person: *If the puppy is a he, we'll call him Shep.* [First written down about 725 in Old English and spelled *hē.*] —SEE NOTE at **she.**

He The symbol for the element **helium.**

head (hĕd) *n.* **1.** The uppermost or forwardmost part of the body of a vertebrate, containing the brain or principal nerve centers and the eyes, ears, nose, mouth, and jaws. **2.** A similar part in other organisms: *the head of an ant.* **3.** The seat of reason; intelligence, intellect, or mind: *I can do all the figuring in my head.* **4.** A mental ability or aptitude: *Our teacher has a good head for mathematics.* **5.** A weight, fixture, or part that sticks out at the end of an object: *the head of a pin.* **6.** The part of a tool used to cut or strike: *the head of a hammer.* **7.** A rounded tightly clustered mass of leaves, buds, or flowers growing from the main stem: *a head of cabbage.* **8.** A person who leads, rules, or is in charge of something; a leader or director: *the head of the corporation.* **9.** The most important part or leading position: *The girl marched at the head of the parade.* **10.** The uppermost part of something; the top: *Place the appropriate name at the head of each column.* **11.** A distinct topic or category; a heading: *a lengthy report divided into several heads.* **12.** A point when something decisive happens; a turning

Nathaniel Hawthorne

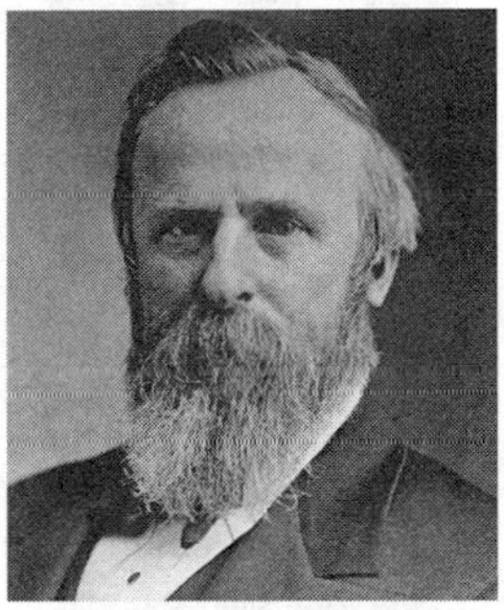

Rutherford B. Hayes
Photographed by Mathew Brady

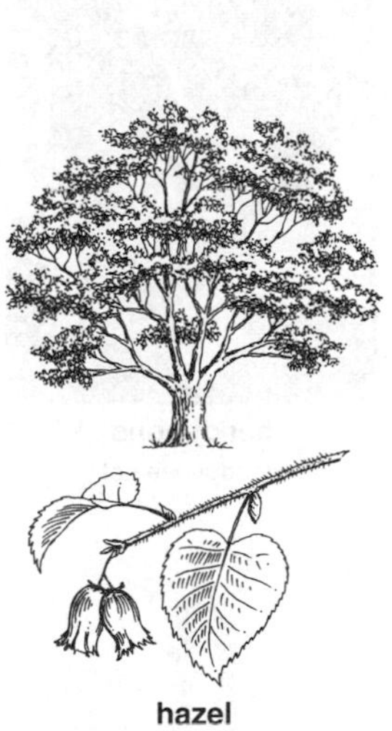

hazel

ă	pat	oi	boy
ā	pay	ou	out
âr	care	o͝o	took
ä	father	o͞o	boot
ĕ	pet	ŭ	cut
ē	be	ûr	urge
ĭ	pit	th	thin
ī	pie	*th*	this
îr	pier	hw	whoop
ŏ	pot	zh	vision
ō	toe	ə	about
ô	paw	N	*French* bon

headdress
Top: Chinese
Bottom: Native American

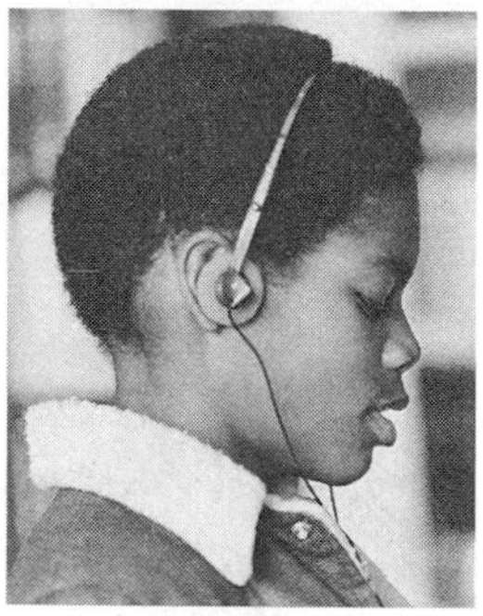

headphone
Headphone set

headstand

point: *Continual smog over the city brought the matter of air pollution to a head.* **13.** *pl.* **head.** A single animal or person: *seven head of cattle.* **14.** The side of a coin having the principal design and the date. Often used in the plural with a singular verb. **15.** The tip of a boil, a pimple, or an abscess, in which pus forms. **16.** Water that forms the source of a river or stream: *the little stream that forms the head of a great river.* **17.** The pressure exerted by a liquid or gas: *a head of steam.* **18.** The membrane or skin stretched across an instrument, such as a drum or banjo. **19.** A device for recording, playing, or erasing a magnetic tape or electronic disk: *a tape recorder with three heads.* —*adj.* **1.** Most important; ranking first; chief: *the head coach.* **2.** Placed on top or in the front: *the head name on a list; the head truck of a convoy.* —*v.* **head•ed, head•ing, heads.** —*tr.* **1.** To aim, point, or turn in a certain direction: *They headed the team of horses up the hill.* **2.** To be in charge of; lead: *The mayor headed the delegation.* **3.** To be in the first or foremost position of: *Collins heads the list of candidates for the job.* **4.** To place a heading on: *head each column with a number.* **5.** In soccer, to hit (a ball) into the air with one's head. —*intr.* To proceed or go in a certain direction: *head for home.* ***—idioms.*** **head off.** To block the progress or completion of; intercept: *They tried to head him off before he went home.* **head over heels. 1.** Rolling, as in a somersault: *He tripped and fell head over heels.* **2.** Completely; hopelessly: *Those two are head over heels in love.* **off (one's) head** or **out of (one's) head.** Insane; crazy. **over (one's) head.** Beyond one's understanding: *At first he thought physics was over his head.*

head•ache (hĕd′āk′) *n.* **1.** A pain in the head. **2.** *Informal.* Something that causes trouble: *Their continual interruptions are a real headache.*

head•band (hĕd′bănd′) *n.* A band worn around the head to absorb sweat or hold hair in place.

head•board (hĕd′bôrd′) *n.* A board, frame, or panel that stands at the head of a bed.

head•dress (hĕd′drĕs′) *n.* A covering or decoration for the head.

head•ed (hĕd′ĭd) *adj.* **1.** Growing or grown into a head. **2.** Having hair of a certain kind or color. Often used in combination: *the red-headed twins.* **3.** Having a specified kind or number of heads. Often used in combination: *a three-headed monster.* **4.** Having a specified kind of disposition. Often used in combination: *a cool-headed surgeon.*

head•first (hĕd′fûrst′) *adv.* **1.** With the head leading; headlong: *dove headfirst into the water.* **2.** Hastily and with little thought; rashly: *rushing headfirst into a complicated project.*

head•gear (hĕd′gîr′) *n.* **1.** A covering for the head, as a hat or helmet. **2.** The part of a harness that fits about a horse's head.

head•ing (hĕd′ĭng) *n.* **1.** A title, subtitle, or topic put at the head of a page, chapter, or section of a printed or written work: *Each chapter has a heading on the first page.* **2.** The course or direction in which a ship or an aircraft is moving: *The ship's heading was due south.*

head•land (hĕd′lənd *or* hĕd′lănd′) *n.* A point of land, usually high and with a sheer drop, extending out into a body of water; a promontory.

head•less (hĕd′lĭs) *adj.* **1.** Having no head. **2.** Lacking a leader or director.

head•light (hĕd′līt′) *n.* A bright light mounted on the front of an automobile, a train, or another vehicle.

head•line (hĕd′līn′) *n.* The title of a newspaper article, usually printed in large type. —*tr.v.* **head•lined, head•lin•ing, head•lines. 1.** To give a headline to (a page or an article). **2.** To publicize: *headline a new product.* **3.** To publicize as the main attraction: *headline several stars in the film.*

head•lock (hĕd′lŏk′) *n.* A wrestling hold in which the head of an opponent is encircled and held tightly between the arm and chest.

head•long (hĕd′lông′ *or* hĕd′lŏng′) *adv.* **1.** With the head leading; headfirst: *He slid headlong into third base.* **2.** At reckless speed or with uncontrolled force: *The wolf ran headlong in pursuit.* **3.** Hastily and without thinking; rashly. —*adj.* (hĕd′lông′ *or* hĕd′lŏng′). **1.** Done with the head leading: *a headlong fall down the steps.* **2.** Recklessly fast or uncontrollably forceful: *a headlong race to the finish.* **3.** Done in a rush; caused by or characterized by little thought: *a headlong decision to go.*

head•man (hĕd′mən *or* hĕd′măn′) *n.* The male leader or chief of a small village or community.

head•mas•ter (hĕd′măs′tər) *n.* A man who is a school principal, usually of a private school.

head•mis•tress (hĕd′mĭs′trĭs) *n.* A woman who is a school principal, usually of a private school.

head-on (hĕd′ŏn′ *or* hĕd′ôn′) *adj.* **1.** Having the front end receiving the impact: *a head-on crash of two cars.* **2.** Facing forward; direct: *the head-on fury of the storm.* —*adv.* **1.** With the head or front first: *The truck ran head-on into the fence.* **2.** In open conflict; directly: *Their opponent attacked the idea head-on.*

head•phone (hĕd′fōn′) *n.* A receiver, as for a radio, held to the ear by a headband.

head•piece (hĕd′pēs′) *n.* A helmet or cap worn to protect the head.

head•quar•ters (hĕd′kwôr′tərz) *pl.n.* *(used with a singular or plural verb).* **1.** The building or offices from which a commander, as of a military unit or police force, issues orders. **2.** A center of operations: *the headquarters of the company.*

head•set (hĕd′sĕt′) *n.* A pair of headphones.

head•stand (hĕd′stănd′) *n.* A position in which one balances oneself vertically on one's head, placing the hands on the floor for support.

head start *n.* **1.** A start before other competitors in a race. **2.** An early start that provides some advantage.

head•stone (hĕd′stōn′) *n.* A memorial stone set at the head of a grave.

head•strong (hĕd′strông′ *or* hĕd′strŏng′) *adj.* **1.** Inclined to insist on having one's own way; stubbornly and recklessly willful: *a proud and headstrong person.* See Synonyms at **obstinate. 2.** Resulting from willfulness or stubbornness: *a headstrong decision.*

head•wait•er (hĕd′wā′tər) *n.* A waiter who is in charge of other waiters and is often responsible for taking reservations and seating guests.

head•wa•ters (hĕd′wô′tərz *or* hĕd′wŏt′ərz) *pl.n.* The water that forms the source of a river.

head•way (hĕd′wā′) *n.* **1.** Movement forward; advance: *The canoe barely made headway against the strong current.* **2.** Progress toward a goal: *We made a great deal of headway in planning our experiment.* **3.** The distance that separates a bridge, an archway, or another overhead structure from the surface beneath it; clearance.

head•wind (hĕd′wĭnd′) *n.* A wind blowing in the direction directly opposite the course of a ship or an aircraft.

head•word (hĕd′wûrd′) *n.* A word, phrase, or name usually set in large type and serving as the heading of an entry in a dictionary or an encyclopedia.

head•y (hĕd′ē) *adj.* **head•i•er, head•i•est. 1.** Tending to make one dizzy or foolish: *the heady effects of high altitude.* **2.** Characterized by hasty action or willfully rash behavior; headstrong: *a heady outburst of resentment.* **—head′i•ly** *adv.* **—head′i•ness** *n.*

heal (hēl) *v.* **healed, heal•ing, heals.** *—tr.* **1.** To make healthy and sound; cure: *heal the sick.* **2.** To set right; amend: *The two friends apologized and healed the rift between them.* *—intr.* To become healthy and sound: *Most small cuts heal in a short time.* [First written down about 725 in Old English and spelled *hǣlan*, to make whole.] **—heal′er** *n.* —SEE NOTE.

❑ *These sound alike:* **heal, heel**[1] (foot part), **heel**[2] (tilt), **he'll** (he will).

health (hĕlth) *n.* **1.** The overall condition of an organism or a thing at a particular time. **2.** Freedom from disease, injury, or defect; soundness of body and mind: *Rest is important to your health.* **3.** A wish for a person's well-being, often expressed as a toast. [First written down about 1000 in Old English and spelled *hǣlth*.]

health care *n.* The treatment of illness and the preservation of health through the services of medical professionals.

health food *n.* Food considered to be especially beneficial to health and usually grown organically and free of chemical additives.

health•ful (hĕlth′fəl) *adj.* **1.** Tending to promote good health; beneficial: *a healthful diet.* **2.** Healthy: *a healthful athlete.* **—health′ful•ly** *adv.* **—health′ful•ness** *n.*

health maintenance organization *n.* An HMO.

health•y (hĕl′thē) *adj.* **health•i•er, health•i•est.** **1.** In a state of good health: *a healthy student.* **2.** Promoting good health; healthful: *a healthy climate.* **3.** Indicating or characteristic of good health: *a healthy appearance.* **4.** Great or sizable: *a healthy portion of squash.* **—health′i•ly** *adv.* **—health′i•ness** *n.*

heap (hēp) *n.* **1.** A group of things thrown together; a pile: *a rubbish heap.* **2.** *Informal.* A great amount; a lot. Often used in the plural: *The game was heaps of fun.* *—tr.v.* **heaped, heap•ing, heaps.** **1.** To put or throw in a heap; pile up: *They heaped wood by the fireplace.* **2.** To fill to overflowing; pile high: *They heaped the cart with groceries.* **3.** To give or bestow in abundance: *The critics heaped compliments on the popular author.* [First written down about 725 in Old English and spelled *hēap*.]

hear (hîr) *v.* **heard** (hûrd), **hear•ing, hears.** *—tr.* **1.** To be aware of or receive (sound) by the ears: *Did you hear the pheasant calling?* **2.** To learn by hearing; be told by others: *We heard the news from a friend.* **3.** To listen to attentively: *They loved to hear their grandmother's stories.* **4.** To listen to officially or formally: *The judge will hear the case in court.* *—intr.* To be capable of perceiving or receiving by the ear: *I don't hear well.* ***—idiom.*** **hear from.** To get a letter, telephone call, or message from: *I haven't heard from her in years.* [First written down before 800 in Old English and spelled *hēran*.] **—hear′er** *n.*

❑ *These sound alike:* **hear, here** (at this place).

heard (hûrd) *v.* Past tense and past participle of **hear.**

❑ *These sound alike:* **heard, herd** (cattle).

hear•ing (hîr′ĭng) *n.* **1.** The sense by which sound is perceived; the capacity to hear: *Dogs have excellent hearing.* **2.** The region within which sounds from a particular source can be heard; earshot: *They were talking within my hearing.* **3.** An opportunity to be heard: *The protesters deserve a hearing on their concerns.* **4.** A formal session for listening to testimony or arguments: *Congress holds hearings before passing new laws.*

hearing aid *n.* A small electronic device used to amplify sound for persons who are hard of hearing.

hear•ing-im•paired (hîr′ĭng ĭm pârd′) *adj.* **1.** Having a weakened sense of hearing; hard of hearing. **2.** Completely unable to hear; deaf. *—n. (used with a plural verb).* People who are hard of hearing or are deaf considered as a group.

hear•ken (här′kən) *intr.v.* **hear•kened, hear•ken•ing, hear•kens.** To listen attentively; pay close attention. [First written down about 1000 in Old English and spelled *hercnian*.]

hear•say (hîr′sā′) *n.* Information or news heard from another person.

hearse (hûrs) *n.* A vehicle for carrying a dead person to a cemetery. [First written down before 1300 in Middle English and spelled *herse*, a harrow-shaped structure for holding candles over a coffin, from Latin *hirpex*, harrow.]

heart (härt) *n.* **1.a.** The hollow muscular organ that pumps blood throughout the body of a vertebrate by contracting and relaxing. **b.** A similar organ in invertebrate animals. **2.** The general area of the chest containing this organ; the breast. **3.** The vital center and source of one's being, emotions, and sensibilities: *I could feel joy welling up in my heart.* **4.a.** Emotional state, disposition, or mood: *I walked to the park with a light heart.* **b.** Love; affection. *The children won their teacher's heart.* **c.** The capacity to feel sympathy, kindness, or concern; compassion: *Have you no heart for these people?* **5.** Courage; determination: *The captain's stirring talk gave the crew heart.* **6.a.** The central part; the center: *the heart of the city.* **b.** The essential part; the basis: *the heart of the matter.* **7.** A two-lobed representation of the heart, often colored red or pink. **8.a.** A red heart-shaped figure on certain playing cards. **b.** A playing card bearing this figure. **c. hearts.** The suit of such playing cards. **9. hearts.** A card game in which the object is to avoid hearts in taking tricks or to take all the hearts. ***—idioms.*** **by heart.** Learned by rote; memorized word for word: *He knows that poem by heart.* **from the bottom of (one's) heart** or **from the depths of (one's) heart.** With the deepest appreciation; most sincerely. **have (one's) heart in the right place.** To be well-intentioned. **in (one's) heart of hearts.** In the seat of one's truest feelings. **near (one's) heart** or **close to (one's) heart.** Loved by or important to one. **take to heart.** To take seriously and be affected or troubled by: *Don't take my criticism too much to heart.* **to (one's) heart's content.** To one's entire satisfaction; without limitation. **with all (one's) heart.** With the deepest feeling or devotion. [First written down about 725 in Old English and spelled *heorte*.]

❑ *These sound alike:* **heart, hart** (male deer).

heart•ache (härt′āk′) *n.* Emotional anguish; deep sorrow.

heart attack *n.* A sudden interruption in the normal functioning of the heart, usually accompanied by severe pain, caused by an insufficient supply of blood to the tissues of the heart.

heart•beat (härt′bēt′) *n.* **1.** A single cycle of contraction and relaxation of the heart. **2.** The general nature of the heart's contractions or the rate at which they occur: *a weak and rapid heartbeat.*

heart•break (härt′brāk′) *n.* Great sorrow, grief, or disappointment.

heart•break•ing (härt′brā′kĭng) *adj.* Causing great sorrow, grief, or disappointment: *heartbreaking news.* **—heart′break′ing•ly** *adv.*

heart•bro•ken (härt′brō′kən) *adj.* Suffering from great sorrow, grief, or disappointment; overcome by grief or despair. **—heart′bro′ken•ly** *adv.*

heart•burn (härt′bûrn′) *n.* A burning feeling in the

Word History: heal

Most of us would be able to figure out the relationship between **heal** and **health** even if we had never thought of it before, like **steal** and **stealth.** We would not likely be able to make the leap from *heal* and *health* to *whole*; nevertheless, the connection is there. *Heal, health,* and *whole* are formed from the Germanic word root *hail–*, "whole, uninjured." To *heal* means "to make whole," and *health* is "a state of being whole or of wholeness." The *w* in *whole* is a leftover from a dialect pronunciation common in the 16th century.

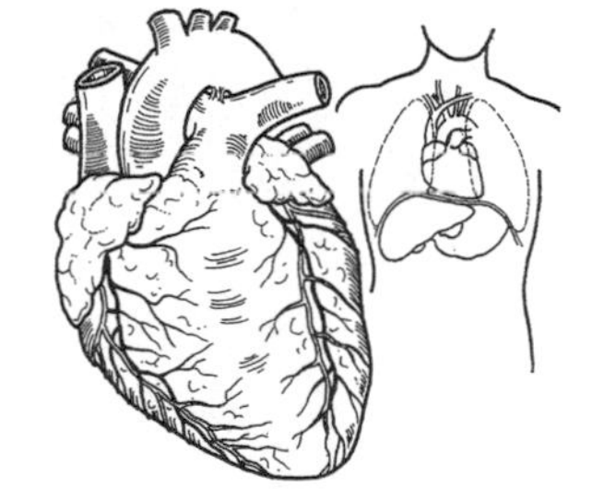

heart

ă	pat	oi	boy
ā	pay	ou	out
âr	care	ŏŏ	took
ä	father	ōō	boot
ĕ	pet	ŭ	cut
ē	be	ûr	urge
ĭ	pit	th	thin
ī	pie	*th*	this
îr	pier	hw	whoop
ŏ	pot	zh	vision
ō	toe	ə	about
ô	paw	N	*French* bon

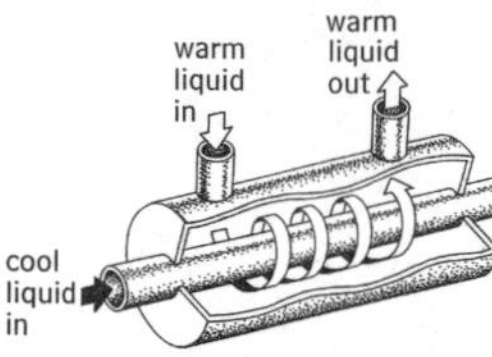

heat exchanger

chest area, usually caused by excess acid in the stomach.

heart•en (här′tn) *tr.v.* **heart•ened, heart•en•ing, heart•ens.** To give strength or courage to; encourage: *The break in the clouds heartened the mountain climbers.*

heart failure *n.* A condition in which the heart loses its ability to pump an adequate supply of blood to body tissues.

heart•felt (härt′fĕlt′) *adj.* Deeply felt; sincere: *my heartfelt good wishes.*

hearth (härth) *n.* **1.** The floor of a fireplace, often extending into a room. **2.** Family life; the home: *The weary travelers longed for their own hearth.* **3.** The lower part of a blast furnace, from which the molten metal flows. [First written down about 725 in Old English and spelled *heorth.*]

hearth•stone (härth′stōn′) *n.* **1.** Stone used in the construction of a hearth. **2.** Family life; the home.

heart•i•ly (här′tl ē) *adv.* **1.** In a warm and friendly manner; sincerely: *They welcomed their old friends heartily.* **2.** With vigor or enthusiasm: *Everyone plunged heartily into the game.* **3.** Thoroughly; completely: *The mayor heartily disapproved of the plan.* **4.** With much appetite or enjoyment: *After a long day the workers ate heartily.*

heart•land (härt′lănd′) *n.* An important central geographical region considered vital to a nation's well-being.

heart•less (härt′lĭs) *adj.* Lacking sympathy or compassion; pitiless. **—heart′less•ly** *adv.* **—heart′less•ness** *n.*

heart-rend•ing or **heart•rend•ing** (härt′rĕn′dĭng) *adj.* Causing grief, anguish, or suffering: *The U.S. Civil War was a heart-rending conflict for many families.* **—heart′-rend′ing•ly** *adv.*

hearts•ease also **heart's-ease** (härts′ēz′) *n.* Peace of mind.

heart•sick (härt′sĭk′) *adj.* Profoundly disappointed; very unhappy.

heart•strings (härt′strĭngz′) *pl.n.* A person's deepest feelings: *The actor's lines of grief tugged at the audience's heartstrings.*

heart-to-heart (härt′tə härt′) *adj.* Personal and sincere; frank: *a heart-to-heart talk.*

heart•wood (härt′wo͝od′) *n.* The central nonliving wood in the trunk of a tree, usually harder than the sapwood that surrounds it.

heart•y (här′tē) *adj.* **heart•i•er, heart•i•est. 1.** Showing warm feelings; cheerful and friendly: *a hearty greeting.* **2.a.** Complete; thorough: *We gave the team our hearty support.* **b.** Vigorous; robust: *a hearty appearance of health.* **3.a.** Giving much nourishment; substantial: *a hearty soup.* **b.** Enjoying or requiring much food: *a hearty appetite.* *—n., pl.* **heart•ies.** A good comrade, especially a sailor. **—heart′i•ness** *n.*

heat (hēt) *n.* **1.** A form of energy produced by the motion of molecules that make up a substance. **2.** The condition of being hot; warmth: *feel the heat of the sun.* **3.** A period of hot weather: *We left for the mountains to escape the summer heat.* **4.** A furnace or other source of warmth: *Is the heat on?* **5.** The most intense or active stage: *In the heat of their debate both candidates were shouting.* **6.** A single contest in a competition, such as a race: *The competition was reduced to six runners after the first heat.* **7.** A time in which a female mammal, other than a human, is ready to mate; estrus. *—tr. & intr.v.* **heat•ed, heat•ing, heats. 1.** To make or become warm or hot: *The sun heats the earth.* **2.** To fill or become filled with intensity of emotion: *The controversial speaker heated the crowd more than ever.* ***—idiom.*** **heat up.** *Informal.* To become acute or intense: *Their quarrel heated up rapidly.* [First written down about 725 in Old English and spelled *hǣtu.*]

heat•ed (hē′tĭd) *adj.* Excited or angry: *a heated debate.* **—heat′ed•ly** *adv.* **—heat′ed•ness** *n.*

heat•er (hē′tər) *n.* An apparatus, such as a furnace or stove, that supplies heat.

heat exchanger *n.* A device used to transfer heat between two fluids, as a radiator in which the heat from the hot fluid inside is dispersed when the metal walls come in contact with cold air.

heat exhaustion *n.* A condition caused by exposure to heat, resulting in the loss of bodily fluids through excessive sweating and causing weakness, dizziness, and nausea.

heath (hēth) *n.* **1.** Any of various usually low-growing shrubs having small evergreen leaves and small, colorful, urn-shaped flowers. **2.** An open uncultivated stretch of land covered with low shrubs or plants; a moor. [First written down about 700 in Old English and spelled *hǣth.*]

hea•then (hē′*th*ən) *n., pl.* **hea•thens** or **heathen. 1.** A person who does not believe in the God of Judaism, Christianity, or Islam. **2.** Such persons considered as a group: *The missionary had a strong desire to convert the heathen.* **3.** A person regarded as uncivilized or uncultured. [First written down about 725 in Old English and spelled *hǣthen.*]

heath•er (hĕ*th*′ər) *n.* A low Eurasian shrub having tiny evergreen leaves and small bell-shaped purple or pink flowers. [First written down in 1335 in Middle English and spelled *hathir.*]

heat lightning *n.* Distant flashes of light seen especially on hot summer evenings.

heat shield *n.* A barrier that prevents the heating of an object, as a layer of tiles or other coating on a spacecraft to protect it against the tremendous heat of friction caused by reentry into the earth's atmosphere.

heat stroke *n.* A severe illness caused by prolonged exposure to too much heat. Its symptoms include headache, fever, hot and dry skin, rapid heartbeat, and sometimes collapse.

heat wave *n.* A period of unusually hot weather.

heave (hēv) *v.* **heaved, heav•ing, heaves.** *—tr.* **1.a.** To raise or lift with effort or force; hoist: *heaved the pack onto the mule's back.* **b.** *past tense and past participle* **hove.** To raise or haul by means of a rope, line, or cable: *They hove anchor and set sail.* **2.** To throw with force or effort; hurl: *heave rocks down the hill.* **3.** To utter painfully or with effort: *heaved a sigh of relief.* *—intr.* **1.** To pull with force or effort; haul: *We heaved on the rope to raise the flag.* **2.** To rise and fall repeatedly: *Seaweed heaved on the gentle waves.* **3.** To be forced upward; bulge: *Parts of the sidewalk heaved after the ground froze.* **4.** To vomit. **5.** *past tense and past participle* **hove.** To move to a specified position: *A tugboat hove alongside the huge tanker.* *—n.* **1.** An act or effort of heaving; a throw: *Each heave on the line loosened the anchor a bit more.* **2. heaves.** *(used with a singular or plural verb).* A disease of horses affecting the lungs and characterized by coughing and difficulty in breathing. ***—idioms.*** **heave into sight** or **heave into view.** To rise over the horizon into view, as land or a ship. **heave to.** To bring a ship at sea to a standstill. [First written down about 725 in Old English and spelled *hebban.*]

heave-ho (hēv′hō′) *n. Slang.* Dismissal from one's job or from one's position: *gave him the old heave-ho last week.*

heav•en (hĕv′ən) *n.* **1.** The sky or universe as seen from the earth. Often used in the plural: *a star shooting across the heavens.* **2.** Often **Heaven.** In certain religions, the place where God resides with other holy beings. **3. Heaven.** God: *Thank Heaven* *you're safe.* **4. heavens.** Used in exclamations to express surprise: *Good heavens! Look at that crowd!* **5.** A place or condition of great happiness; bliss: *It'll be heaven to vacation in the quiet of the country.* [First written down about 1000 in Old English and spelled *heofon.*]

heav•en•ly (**hĕv′**ən lē) *adj.* **1.** Of or relating to heaven; celestial: *the planets and other heavenly bodies.* **2.** Relating or belonging to the dwelling place of God; divine. **3.** Very pleasing; delightful; lovely: *a heavenly summer's day.* **—heav′en•li•ness** *n.*

heav•en•ward (**hĕv′**ən wərd) *adv. & adj.* Toward, to, or in heaven.

heav•y (**hĕv′**ē) *adj.* **heav•i•er, heav•i•est. 1.** Having great or unusually great weight: *a heavy package; a heavy skillet.* **2.** Large in amount or intensity: *a heavy rain; heavy traffic.* **3.** Having great power or force; violent: *a heavy blow; heavy seas.* **4.a.** Having considerable thickness, density, body, or strength: *a heavy winter coat; drew a heavy line.* **b.** Thick or dense; slow to disperse: *a heavy mist.* **5.** Weighed down, as from weight: *branches heavy with apples; eyelids heavy with sleep.* **6.** Gloomy or sad, as from grief or depression: *a heavy heart.* **7.** Deserving careful consideration; grave; serious: *a heavy issue.* **8.a.** Requiring much effort to accomplish; arduous: *heavy reading.* **b.** Hard to endure; severe or burdensome: *a heavy penalty.* **9.** Not easily digested; too rich: *a heavy dessert.* **10.** Moving with or as if with difficulty: *the heavy steps of the movers.* **11.** Involving large-scale manufacturing of basic products, such as steel: *heavy industry.* **12.** Indulging or participating to a great degree: *a heavy eater; a heavy investor.* *—adv.* **heavier, heaviest.** Heavily: *These thoughts weigh heavy on his mind.* *—n., pl.* **heav•ies. 1.** A serious or tragic role in a play. **2.** A villain in a story or play. [First written down about 725 in Old English and spelled *hefig.*] **—heav′i•ly** *adv.* **—heav′i•ness** *n.*

heav•y-dut•y (hĕv′ē **dōō′**tē *or* hĕv′ē **dyōō′**tē) *adj.* Made to withstand hard use or wear.

heav•y-hand•ed (**hĕv′**ē **hăn′**dĭd) *adj.* **1.** Awkward or clumsy: *a heavy-handed performance on the piano.* **2.** Harsh in treating others; oppressive: *heavy-handed discipline.* **—heav′y-hand′ed•ness** *n.*

heav•y-heart•ed (**hĕv′**ē **här′**tĭd) *adj.* Melancholy; sad; depressed. **—heav′y-heart′ed•ness** *n.*

heavy hydrogen *n.* An isotope of hydrogen with a mass greater than that of ordinary hydrogen; deuterium or tritium.

heav•y•set (**hĕv′**ē **sĕt′**) *adj.* Having a heavy build; stocky: *The wrestler was heavyset and muscular.*

heavy water *n.* Water formed of oxygen and deuterium. Heavy water is much like ordinary water, but has higher freezing and boiling points and is used in certain nuclear reactors for cooling.

heav•y•weight (**hĕv′**ē wāt′) *n.* **1.** A person or thing of more than average weight. **2.** A boxer, wrestler, or weightlifter in the heaviest weight class, often weighing more than 175 pounds.

He•bra•ic (hĭ **brā′**ĭk) *adj.* Of or relating to the Hebrews or their language or culture.

He•brew (**hē′**brōō) *n.* **1.** A member of the Semitic people claiming descent from Sarah and Abraham; an Israelite; a Jew. **2.a.** The Semitic language of the ancient Hebrews. **b.** The modern form of this language, especially the language of the Israelis. **3. Hebrews.** *(used with a singular verb).* A book of the New Testament traditionally thought to be an epistle to a group of converted Hebrews, asserting the fulfillment of the Old Testament in Jesus's teaching. **—He′brew** *adj.*

Hebrew Scriptures *pl.n.* The sacred book of Judaism, consisting of the Pentateuch, the Prophets, and the Writings, and corresponding to the Old Testament in Christianity.

Heb•ri•des (**hĕb′**rĭ dēz′). An island group of western and northwest Scotland in the Atlantic Ocean, divided into the **Inner Hebrides,** closer to the Scottish mainland, and the **Outer Hebrides,** to the northwest.

Hec•a•te (**hĕk′**ə tē *or* **hĕk′**ĭt) *n.* In Greek mythology, an ancient fertility goddess who later became identified with Persephone as queen of Hades and protector of witches.

heck•le (**hĕk′**əl) *tr.v.* **heck•led, heck•ling, heck•les.** To harass or bother with questions, annoying remarks, or mocking yells: *The crowd heckled the speaker at the rally.* **—heck′ler** *n.*

hec•tare (**hĕk′**târ′) *n.* A unit of area in the metric system, equal to 2.471 acres. See table at **measurement.**

hec•tic (**hĕk′**tĭk) *adj.* Marked by intense activity, confusion, or excitement: *Constantly changing plans resulted in a hectic departure.* [First written down before 1398 in Middle English and spelled *etik*, feverish, from Greek *hektikos*, habitual.] **—hec′ti•cal•ly** *adv.*

hecto– or **hect–** *pref.* A prefix that means hundred: *hectometer.*

hec•to•me•ter (**hĕk′**tə mē′tər *or* hĕk **tŏm′**ĭ tər) *n.* A unit of length in the metric system, equal to 100 meters.

hec•tor (**hĕk′**tər) *n.* A bully. *—tr.v.* **hec•tored, hec•tor•ing, hec•tors.** To try to frighten or control by bullying.

Hec•tor (**hĕk′**tər) *n.* In Greek mythology, the bravest Trojan warrior and eldest son of Hecuba and Priam, killed by Achilles.

Hec•u•ba (**hĕk′**yə bə) *n.* In Greek mythology, the wife of Priam and mother of Cassandra, Hector, and Paris.

he'd (hēd). **1.** Contraction of *he had.* **2.** Contraction of *he would.*

❑ *These sound alike:* **he'd, heed** (listen).

hedge (hĕj) *n.* **1.** A row of closely planted shrubs or small trees forming a fence or boundary. **2.** A means of protection or defense: *They put some of their savings in stocks as a hedge against inflation.* *—v.* **hedged, hedg•ing, hedg•es.** *—tr.* **1.** To enclose or separate with a hedge or hedges: *hedge a yard.* **2.** To restrict or confine; hem in: *The flooded river hedged us in on one side.* **3.** To protect against possible losses on (a bet, an investment, or another risk) by balancing one risk against another: *She hedged her investment in stocks by investing in bonds.* *—intr.* To avoid giving a clear or direct answer or statement. [First written down in 785 in Old English and spelled *hecg.*]

hedge•hog (**hĕj′**hôg′ *or* **hĕj′**hŏg′) *n.* Any of several small mammals of Europe, Asia, and Africa that feed on insects and are covered with short stiff spines. The hedgehog rolls up into a ball for protection when frightened.

hedgehog
European hedgehog

hedge•row (**hĕj′**rō′) *n.* A row of bushes or small trees forming a hedge.

heed (hēd) *v.* **heed•ed, heed•ing, heeds.** *—tr.* To pay attention to; listen to and consider: *I did not heed his warning.* *—intr.* To pay attention. *—n.* Close attention or consideration; notice: *They gave no heed to my greeting. Take heed while crossing the highway.* [First written down about 725 in Old English and spelled *hēdan.*]

❑ *These sound alike:* **heed, he'd** (he would).

heed•ful (**hēd′**fəl) *adj.* Paying close attention; mindful: *The builders were heedful of the architect's advice.*

heed•less (**hēd′**lĭs) *adj.* Paying little or no attention;

ă	pat	oi	boy
ā	pay	ou	out
âr	care	ŏŏ	took
ä	father	ōō	boot
ĕ	pet	ŭ	cut
ē	be	ûr	urge
ĭ	pit	th	thin
ī	pie	*th*	this
îr	pier	hw	whoop
ŏ	pot	zh	vision
ō	toe	ə	about
ô	paw	N	*French* bon

helicon

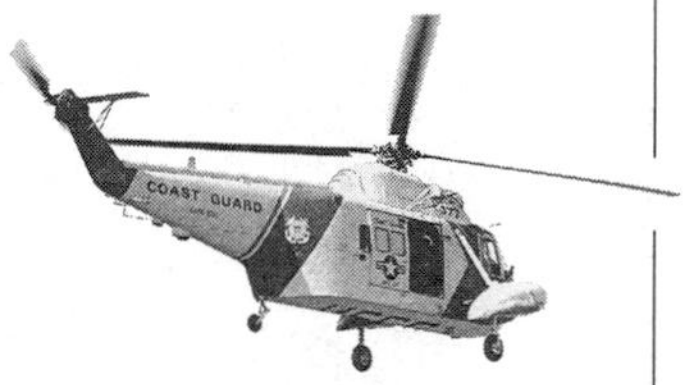
helicopter

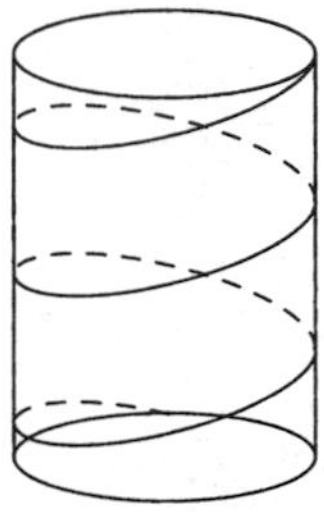
helix
Cylindrical model

hellebore
White hellebore

unmindful: *heedless of danger.* —**heed′less•ly** *adv.* —**heed′less•ness** *n.*

hee•haw (hē′hô′) *n.* **1.** The loud harsh sound made by a braying donkey. **2.** *Informal.* A noisy laugh; a guffaw. —*intr.v.* **hee•hawed, hee•haw•ing, hee•haws.** To make such a sound.

heel[1] (hēl) *n.* **1.a.** The rounded rear part of the human foot below the ankle. **b.** A similar part of the hind leg of some other vertebrates. **2.** The rounded fleshy base on the palm of the human hand. **3.** The part of a sock, shoe, or stocking that covers the heel of the foot. **4.** The part of a shoe or boot that supports the heel of the foot. **5.** A lower or back part, such as the crusty end of a loaf of bread or the end of a tool next to the handle. **6.** *Informal.* A dishonest person; a cad. —*v.* **heeled, heel•ing, heels.** —*tr.* To put a heel or heels on: *The cobbler heeled the old shoes.* —*intr.* To follow at one's heels: *I taught the dog to heel.* —***idioms.*** **on the heels of** or **upon the heels of.** Directly behind or immediately following: *The first spring birds come on the heels of winter.* **take to (one's) heels.** To run away; flee. [First written down about 800 in Old English and spelled *hēla.*]

❑ *These sound alike:* **heel**[1] (part of a foot), **heel**[2] (tilt), **heal** (make healthy), **he'll** (he will).

heel[2] (hēl) *intr. & tr.v.* **heeled, heel•ing, heels.** To tilt or cause to tilt to one side: *Gale winds dangerously heeled the ship. The cargo shifted, and the ship heeled over.* [First written down about 725 in Old English and spelled *hyldan.*]

❑ *These sound alike:* **heel**[2] (tilt), **heel**[1] (part of a foot), **heal** (make healthy), **he'll** (he will).

heft (hĕft) *n.* Weight; heaviness; bulk. —*tr.v.* **heft•ed, heft•ing, hefts. 1.** To lift or hoist up: *Hefting picks and axes, they went to work.* **2.** To lift (something) in order to estimate or test its weight: *I hefted the heavy package to determine whether I could carry it.*

heft•y (hĕf′tē) *adj.* **heft•i•er, heft•i•est. 1.** Weighty; heavy: *a truck carrying a hefty load.* **2.** Big and strong; muscular: *a hefty sailor.* **3.** *Informal.* Substantial or considerable: *The cowhand ate a hefty meal.*

He•gel (hā′gəl), **Georg Wilhelm Friedrich.** 1770–1831. German philosopher whose works include *Encyclopedia of the Philosophical Sciences* (1817).

he•gem•o•ny (hĭ jĕm′ə nē *or* hĕj′ə mō′nē) *n., pl.* **he•gem•o•nies.** Dominance, especially great influence of one nation over another.

he•gi•ra also **he•ji•ra** (hĭ jī′rə *or* hĕj′ər ə) *n.* **1.** Also **Hegira.** The flight of Muhammad from Mecca to Median in 622. **2.** A flight, as from danger or hardship.

heif•er (hĕf′ər) *n.* A young cow that has not given birth to a calf. [First written down about 900 in Old English and spelled *hēahfore.*]

heigh-ho (hī′hō′ *or* hā′hō′) *interj.* An expression used to show fatigue, mild surprise, boredom, or disappointment.

height (hīt) *n.* **1.** The distance from the top to the bottom of something: *The height of that tree is more than 60 feet.* **2.** Elevation above a given level; altitude: *What is the height of that mountain?* **3.** The condition of being relatively high or tall: *Height is an advantage in basketball.* **4.** A high place, such as a hill or mountain. **5.** The highest point or most advanced degree. *Late summer is the height of the tourist season. Many believe that nation has passed the height of its power.* [First written down before 900 in Old English and spelled *hēhthu, hēahthu.*]

height•en (hīt′n) *tr. & intr.v.* **height•ened, height•en•ing, height•ens. 1.** To increase or rise in degree or quantity; intensify: *His angry glare heightened the tension.* **2.** To make or become high or higher; raise or be raised: *The barber heightened the chair for the little boy.*

Hei•long Jiang (hā′lông′ jyäng′). Amur River.

Heim•lich maneuver (hīm′lĭk′) *n.* A method of discharging something lodged in a person's throat in order to prevent choking. It consists of an upward push just below the rib cage to force air out of the victim's lungs and up through the windpipe.

hei•nous (hā′nəs) *adj.* Very wicked or evil; abominable: *a heinous crime.* [First written down about 1385 in Middle English, from Old French *haine,* hatred.] —**hei′nous•ly** *adv.* —**hei′nous•ness** *n.*

heir (âr) *n.* A person who inherits or is legally entitled to inherit the property or title of another. [First written down about 1225 in Middle English, from Latin *hērēs.*]

❑ *These sound alike:* **heir, air** (gas), **e'er** (ever), **ere** (before).

heir apparent *n., pl.* **heirs apparent.** A person who will inherit property or a title if the owner or ancestor dies first.

heir•ess (âr′ĭs) *n.* A woman who inherits or is legally entitled to inherit the property or title of another.

heir•loom (âr′lo͞om′) *n.* A possession passed down through succeeding generations of a family. [First written down in 1421 in Middle English and spelled *aire lome* : *aire,* heir + *lome,* implement.]

heir presumptive *n., pl.* **heirs presumptive.** A person who will inherit property or a title unless a relative with a stronger legal claim to the inheritance is born.

he•ji•ra (hĭ jī′rə *or* hĕj′ər ə) *n.* Variant of **hegira.**

held (hĕld) *v.* Past tense and past participle of **hold**[1].

Hel•e•na (hĕl′ə nə). The capital of Montana, in the west-central part of the state. It was founded in 1864 and became the state capital in 1889. Population, 24,569.

Hel•en of Troy (hĕl′ən əv troi) *n.* In Greek mythology, the wife of Menelaus. Her abduction by Paris caused the Trojan War.

hel•i•cal (hĕl′ĭ kəl *or* hē′lĭ kəl) *adj.* Of or having the shape of a helix. —**hel′i•cal•ly** *adv.*

hel•i•ces (hĕl′ĭ sēz′ *or* hē′lĭ sēz′) *n.* A plural of **helix.**

hel•i•con (hĕl′ĭ kŏn′ *or* hĕl′ĭ kən) *n.* A large circular tuba that fits around the player's shoulder.

hel•i•cop•ter (hĕl′ĭ kŏp′tər) *n.* A wingless aircraft that is lifted by blades that rotate horizontally above the aircraft. [First written down in 1887 in Modern English : Greek *helix,* spiral + Greek *pteron,* wing.]

he•li•o•cen•tric (hē′lē ō sĕn′trĭk) *adj.* **1.** In relation to the sun as seen from the sun's center: *the heliocentric position of a planet.* **2.** Having the sun as center: *a heliocentric alignment of the planets.*

He•li•os (hē′lē ŏs′) *n.* In Greek mythology, the god of the sun, who drives his chariot across the sky from east to west each day.

he•lio•trope (hēl′yə trōp′ *or* hē′lē ə trōp′) *n.* **1.** Any of several garden plants having clusters of small, fragrant, purplish flowers. **2.** A light reddish purple.

he•li•ot•ro•pism (hē′lē ŏt′rə pĭz′əm) *n.* A tendency of plants and some other organisms to turn or bend toward or away from sunlight.

hel•i•port (hĕl′ə pôrt′) *n.* A place for helicopters to take off and land.

he•li•um (hē′lē əm) *n. Symbol* **He** A very light, colorless, odorless, gaseous element. It has the lowest boiling point of any substance and is the second most abundant element in the universe. Atomic number 2. See table at **element.** [First written down in 1868 in Modern English, from Greek *hēlios*, sun.]

he•lix (hē′lĭks) *n., pl.* **he•lix•es** or **hel•i•ces** (hĕl′ĭ-sēz′ *or* hē′lĭ sēz′). **1.** A three-dimensional curve that lies on a cone or cylinder, so that its angle to a plane perpendicular to the axis is constant. **2.** A spiral form or structure, such as the thread of a screw.

hell (hĕl) *n.* **1.** A place, such as Hades, where the spirits of the dead remain for eternity; the underworld. **2.** Often **Hell.** In certain religions, the place where devils and the souls of the wicked reside after death. **3.a.** Misery, torment, or anguish: *the hell of battle.* **b.** A place of misery, torment, or anguish: *City streets are a real hell when choked with traffic.* [First written down about 725 in Old English and spelled *hel.*]

he'll (hēl). **1.** Contraction of *he will.* **2.** Contraction of *he shall.*

❑ *These sound alike:* **he'll, heal** (make healthy), **heel**[1] (part of a foot), **heel**[2] (tilt).

hell•bend•er (hĕl′bĕn′dər) *n.* A large salamander of rivers and streams of the eastern and central United States.

hel•le•bore (hĕl′ə bôr′) *n.* **1.** Any of various plants of Europe and Asia that are related to the buttercup and have large showy flowers and thick roots used in medicine. **2.** Any of various plants that are related to the lily and have purple, white, or greenish flowers and a root used in medicines.

Hel•lene (hĕl′ēn′) *n.* A Greek.

Hel•len•ic (hĕ lĕn′ĭk) *adj.* Of or relating to the ancient Greeks or their language or history. —*n.* The Greek branch of the Indo-European family.

Hel•le•nis•tic (hĕl′ə nĭs′tĭk) *adj.* Of or relating to Greek history and culture from the death of Alexander the Great in 323 B.C. until the time that Augustus became Emperor of Rome in 27 B.C.

Hel•les•pont (hĕl′ĭ spŏnt′). Dardanelles.

hell•ish (hĕl′ĭsh) *adj.* Of, resembling, or worthy of hell; terrible: *hellish confusion and noise.* **—hell′ish•ly** *adv.* **—hell′ish•ness** *n.*

hel•lo (hĕ lō′ *or* hə lō′) also **hul•lo** (hə lō′) *interj.* An expression used to greet someone, answer the telephone, or express surprise. —*n., pl.* **hel•los.** A call or greeting of "hello."

helm[1] (hĕlm) *n.* **1.** The steering apparatus of a ship, especially the wheel or tiller. **2.** A position of leadership or control: *a new president at the helm.* [First written down before 830 in Old English and spelled *helma.*]

helm[2] (hĕlm) *Archaic. n.* A helmet. [First written down about 725 in Old English.]

hel•met (hĕl′mĭt) *n.* A covering of metal, plastic, or other hard material worn to protect the head from injury, as in battle, work, or sports.

helms•man (hĕlmz′mən) *n.* A person who steers a ship.

hel•ot (hĕl′ət) *n.* **1. Helot.** A member of a class of serfs in ancient Sparta. **2.** A serf; a slave.

help (hĕlp) *v.* **helped, help•ing, helps.** —*tr.* **1.** To give assistance or support to; aid: *The salesperson helped the customer.* **2.** To contribute to; further the progress or advancement of: *His cheerful attitude helped heal the rift between them.* **3.** To relieve; ease: *This medicine will help your cold.* **4.** To be able to prevent or change: *I cannot help it if the train is late.* **5.** To refrain from; avoid: *We couldn't help laughing.* —*intr.* To be of service; give assistance: *Do what you can to help.* —*n.* **1.** The act of helping; assistance; aid: *With the help of a dictionary, you can find out what words mean.* **2.** A person or thing that helps: *A vacuum cleaner is a help in doing housework.* **3.** A person or a group of people hired to work as a helper or helpers: *The restaurant needs kitchen help.* **4.** Relief; remedy: *There is no help for certain diseases.* ***—idioms.*** **cannot help but.** To be compelled to; be unable to avoid or resist: *I cannot help but admire their efforts to assist those in need.* **help (oneself) to.** To take what one wants, sometimes without permission: *The guests were told to help themselves to the punch.* [First written down about 725 in Old English and spelled *helpan.*] **—help′er** *n.*

Synonyms: help, aid, assist. These verbs mean to contribute to fulfilling a need, furthering an effort, or achieving a purpose. **Help** and **aid** are the most general: *A new medicine has been developed to help* (or *aid*) *digestion.* **Help** often means to aid in an active way: *I'll help you move the sofa.* **Assist** often means to play a secondary role in aiding: *A few of the students assisted the professor in researching the data.*

help•ful (hĕlp′fəl) *adj.* Providing assistance; useful: *gave me some helpful advice.* **—help′ful•ly** *adv.* **—help′ful•ness** *n.*

help•ing (hĕl′pĭng) *n.* A portion of food for one person.

helping verb *n.* An auxiliary verb.

help•less (hĕlp′lĭs) *adj.* **1.** Unable to manage by oneself; powerless: *as helpless as a baby.* **2.** Lacking protection; defenseless: *The townspeople were helpless in the violent storm.* **3.** Bewildered; confused: *a helpless glance.* **—help′less•ly** *adv.* **—help′less•ness** *n.*

help•mate (hĕlp′māt′) *n.* A helper or helpful companion, especially a husband or wife.

Hel•sin•ki (hĕl′sĭng′kē *or* hĕl sĭng′kē). The capital and largest city of Finland, in the southern part of the country. It was founded in 1550 and became capital of Finland in 1812. Population, 484,263.

hel•ter-skel•ter (hĕl′tər skĕl′tər) *adv.* In disorderly haste: *The toys were strewn helter-skelter in the living room.* —*adj.* Hurried and confused: *a helter-skelter retreat from the sudden shower.*

helve (hĕlv) *n.* A handle of a tool, such as an ax or a hammer.

hem[1] (hĕm) *n.* An edge or a border of a garment or piece of cloth, made by folding the raw edge under and sewing it down. —*tr.v.* **hemmed, hem•ming, hems. 1.** To fold back and sew down the edge of: *The tailor hems skirts and pants.* **2.** To surround and shut in; enclose: *a valley hemmed in by high mountains.* [First written down about 1000 in Old English.]

hem[2] (hĕm) *n.* A short cough or clearing of the throat made especially to gain attention, hide embarrassment, or fill in a pause when speaking. —*intr.v.* **hemmed, hem•ming, hems.** To make this sound. ***—idiom.*** **hem and haw.** To be hesitant and indecisive: *I hemmed and hawed before making a decision.* [First written down in 1526 in Modern English, of imitative origin.]

he•ma•tite (hē′mə tīt′) *n.* A mineral that is the most abundant iron ore. It is reddish-brown when crushed to powder. [First written down before 1398 in Middle English and spelled *emachites*, from Greek *haima*, blood.]

hemi– *pref.* A prefix that means half: *hemisphere.*

Hem•ing•way (hĕm′ĭng wā′), **Ernest Miller.** 1899–1961. American writer of short stories and novels who won the 1954 Nobel Prize for literature.

hem•i•sphere (hĕm′ĭ sfîr′) *n.* **1.** One half of a sphere formed by a plane that passes through the center of the sphere. **2.** A half of the human brain. **3.** One half of the earth's surface. The Northern and Southern Hemispheres are divided by the equator. The Eastern and Western Hemispheres are divided by a meridian.

helmet

Cycling helmet

Ernest Hemingway

ă	pat	oi	boy
ā	pay	ou	out
âr	care	o͝o	took
ä	father	o͞o	boot
ĕ	pet	ŭ	cut
ē	be	ûr	urge
ĭ	pit	th	thin
ī	pie	*th*	this
îr	pier	hw	whoop
ŏ	pot	zh	vision
ō	toe	ə	about
ô	paw	N	*French* bon

Henry VIII

Katharine Hepburn

hem•i•spher•ic (hĕm′ĭ sfîr′ĭk *or* hĕm′ĭ sfĕr′ĭk) or **hem•i•spher•i•cal** (hĕm′ĭ sfîr′ĭ kəl *or* hĕm′ĭ sfĕr′ĭ kəl) *adj.* Of, relating to, or shaped like a hemisphere.

hem•lock (hĕm′lŏk′) *n.* **1.a.** Any of various evergreen trees having short flat needles and small cones. The reddish bark of the hemlock is used in tanning leather. **b.** The wood of any of these trees. **2.a.** Any of several poisonous plants having feathery leaves and clusters of small white flowers. **b.** A poison made from any of these plants. [First written down about 700 in Old English and spelled *hymlice.*]

hemo– or **hema–** or **hem–** *pref.* A prefix that means blood: *hemophilia.*

he•mo•glo•bin (hē′mə glō′bĭn) *n.* The substance, made up of protein and iron, that gives the red blood cells of vertebrates their characteristic color. Hemoglobin carries oxygen from the lungs to other body tissues and carries carbon dioxide from the tissues to the lungs.

he•mo•phil•i•a (hē′mə fĭl′ē ə *or* hē′mə fēl′yə) *n.* An inherited blood disease, affecting principally males, in which the blood does not clot properly, making it very difficult to stop bleeding.

he•mo•phil•i•ac (hē′mə fĭl′ē ăk′ *or* hē′mə fē′lē ăk′) *n.* A person who has hemophilia.

hem•or•rhage (hĕm′ər ĭj) *n.* A great amount of bleeding. *—intr.v.* **hem•or•rhaged, hem•or•rhag•ing, hem•or•rhag•es.** To have a hemorrhage; bleed heavily.

hem•or•rhoids (hĕm′ə roidz′) *pl.n.* Itching or painful swollen tissue and enlarged veins near the anus.

hemp (hĕmp) *n.* **1.** A tough fiber obtained from the stems of a tall plant and used for making rope, cord, and coarse cloth. **2.** The plant that yields such fibers. [First written down before 1000 in Old English and spelled *hænep.*]

hemp•en (hĕm′pən) *adj.* Made of or resembling hemp.

hem•stitch (hĕm′stĭch′) *n.* **1.** A fancy stitch that leaves an open design in cloth, made by pulling out several parallel threads and drawing the remaining threads together in even bunches. **2.** Decorative needlework made with hemstitching. *—tr.v.* **hem•stitched, hem•stitch•ing, hem•stitch•es.** To hem or decorate with this stitch.

hen (hĕn) *n.* **1.** An adult female chicken: *Our hens lay eggs daily.* **2.** The female of various other birds. [First written down about 700 in Old English.]

hence (hĕns) *adv.* **1.** For this reason; therefore: *These dolls are handmade and hence expensive.* **2.** From this time; from now: *30 years hence.* **3.** From this place; away from here: *Get thee hence!*

hence•forth (hĕns′fôrth′) *adv.* From this time on; from now on.

hence•for•ward (hĕns fôr′wərd) *adv.* Henceforth.

hench•man (hĕnch′mən) *n.* **1.** A loyal and trusted follower, as of a politician. **2.** A member of a criminal gang.

hen•na (hĕn′ə) *n.* **1.a.** A brownish-red dye obtained from the leaves of an Asian or African shrub, used to color the hair. **b.** The shrub that yields such dye. **2.** A brownish red color. *—tr.v.* **hen•naed, hen•na•ing, hen•nas.** To dye or color with henna. [First written down in 1600 in Modern English, from Arabic *ḥinnā'.*]

hen•ry (hĕn′rē) *n., pl.* **hen•ries** or **hen•rys.** A unit of inductance. When a current varies at the rate of one ampere per second and induces an electromotive force of one volt, the circuit has an inductance of one henry. [First written down in 1893 in Modern English, after Joseph *Henry* (1797–1878), American physicist.]

Hen•ry I (hĕn′rē). 1068–1135. King of England (1100–1135) who conquered Normandy (1106).

Henry VII. 1457–1509. King of England (1485–1509) who united the houses of York and Lancaster and founded the Tudor line.

Henry VIII. 1491–1547. King of England (1509–1547) whose divorce from Catherine of Aragon caused him to break away from the Catholic Church.

Henry the Navigator. 1394–1460. Prince of Portugal who directed voyages that enlarged Portugal's empire.

he•pat•i•ca (hĭ păt′ĭ kə) *n.* Any of several low woodland plants having lavender, white, or pink flowers and leaves with three lobes.

hep•a•ti•tis (hĕp′ə tī′tĭs) *n., pl.* **hep•a•tit•i•des** (hĕp′ə tĭt′ĭ dēz′). Inflammation of the liver, caused by infection and characterized by jaundice and fever. [First written down in 1727 in Modern English, from Greek *hēpatos*, of the liver.]

Hep•burn (hĕp′bûrn′), **Katharine Houghton.** Born 1909. American actress known for her motion pictures, including *The African Queen* (1951).

He•phaes•tus (hĭ fĕs′təs) *n.* In Greek mythology, the god of fire and metalworking, identified with the Roman Vulcan.

hepta– or **hept–** *pref.* A prefix that means seven: *heptagon.*

hep•ta•gon (hĕp′tə gŏn′) *n.* A plane figure having seven angles and seven sides.

her (hər *or* ər; hûr *when stressed*) *adj.* The possessive form of **she.** Of or belonging to her: *She picked up her package.* *—pron.* The objective form of **she.** **1.** Used as the direct object of a verb: *We brought her to the train station.* **2.** Used as the indirect object of a verb: *I wrote her a letter.* **3.** Used as the object of a preposition: *I gave all the popcorn to her.* —SEE NOTE at **me.**

He•ra (hîr′ə) *n.* In Greek mythology, the sister and wife of Zeus.

Her•a•cles or **Her•a•kles** (hĕr′ə klēz′) *n.* Variants of **Hercules.**

her•ald (hĕr′əld) *n.* **1.** A person who carries messages or makes announcements. **2.** A person or thing that gives an indication of something to come; a harbinger: *The crocus is a herald of spring.* *—tr.v.* **her•ald•ed, her•ald•ing, her•alds.** To indicate the coming of; foretell; announce: *The evening star heralds the arrival of nightfall.* [First written down about 1300 in Middle English and spelled *heraud*, from Anglo-Norman *heralt*, of Germanic origin.]

he•ral•dic (hə răl′dĭk) *adj.* Of or relating to heralds or heraldry.

her•ald•ry (hĕr′əl drē) *n., pl.* **her•ald•ries.** The study or art concerned with coats of arms and the history of families. Heraldry confers the privilege of using a coat of arms, determines the order of descent among families, and designs new coats of arms.

herb (ûrb *or* hûrb) *n.* **1.** Any of various often aromatic plants used especially in medicine or as a seasoning. **2.** A plant having fleshy or soft stems that do not become woody. [First written down before 1300 in Middle English and spelled *herbe*, from Latin *herba.*]

her•ba•ceous (hûr bā′shəs *or* ûr bā′shəs) *adj.* Relating to, characteristic of, or consisting of an herb: *a herbaceous plant.*

herb•age (ûr′bĭj *or* hûr′bĭj) *n.* Grass or other leafy plants having soft stems, especially when grown to be eaten by grazing animals.

herb•al (ûr′bəl *or* hûr′bəl) *adj.* Of, relating to, or containing herbs: *herbal medicine.* *—n.* A book that describes the kinds and uses of herbs.

herb•al•ist (ûr′bə lĭst *or* hûr′bə lĭst) *n.* A person

who grows, collects, or specializes in the use of herbs, especially medicinal herbs.

her•bar•i•um (hûr bâr′ē əm *or* ûr bâr′ē əm) *n., pl.* **her•bar•i•ums** or **her•bar•i•a** (hûr bâr′ē ə *or* ûr-bâr′ē ə). **1.** A collection of dried plants mounted and labeled for use in scientific study. **2.** A special place or building where such a collection is kept.

her•bi•cide (hûr′bĭ sīd′ *or* ûr′bĭ sīd′) *n.* A chemical substance used to destroy or reduce the growth of plants.

her•bi•vore (hûr′bə vôr′ *or* ûr′bə vôr′) *n.* An animal that feeds mainly on plants.

her•biv•o•rous (hûr bĭv′ər əs *or* ûr bĭv′ər əs) *adj.* Feeding mainly on plants: *Cattle, deer, and rabbits are herbivorous animals.*

Her•cu•la•ne•um (hûr′kyə lā′nē əm). An ancient city of south-central Italy that was completely destroyed by the eruption of Mount Vesuvius in A.D. 79.

Her•cu•le•an (hûr′kyə lē′ən *or* hûr kyo͞o′lē ən) *adj.* **1.** Often **herculean.** Demanding great strength or courage; tremendously difficult: *Moving the whole library was a herculean task.* **2.** Of or resembling Hercules: *It took Herculean strength to move the fallen tree trunk.*

Her•cu•les (hûr′kyə lēz′) **Her•a•cles** or **Her•a•kles** (hĕr′ə klēz′) *n.* In Greek mythology, a mortal son of Zeus known for his great strength and courage.

herd (hûrd) *n.* **1.a.** A group of cattle or other domestic animals of a single kind kept together for a specific purpose. **b.** A number of wild animals of one kind that stay together as a group: *a herd of elephants.* **2.** A large number of people; a crowd. —*v.* **herd•ed, herd•ing, herds.** —*tr.* **1.** To gather, keep, or flock together: *Dogs herded the sheep into the pen.* **2.** To tend or watch over (sheep or cattle): *herd sheep in the mountains.* —*intr.* To come together in a herd: *Buffalo herded together on the plains.* [First written down before 1000 in Old English and spelled *heord.*]

❑ *These sound alike:* **herd, heard** (past tense of hear).

herd•er (hûr′dər) *n.* A person who takes care of or drives a herd, as of sheep or cattle.

herds•man (hûrdz′mən) *n.* A person who owns or breeds livestock.

here (hîr) *adv.* **1.** At or in this place: *Put the package here.* **2.** At this time; now: *Let's stop practicing here and break for lunch.* **3.** To this place; hither: *Come here and sit beside me.* —*interj.* An expression used to answer to one's name in a roll call, to call to an animal, or to get someone's attention. —*n.* **1.** This place: *I went from here to the store.* **2.** This life or this time: *We should think more about the here and now than about what might happen.* —*idiom.* **neither here nor there.** Not to the point; off the subject; unimportant: *Their vague remarks were neither here nor there.* [First written down about 725 in Old English and spelled *hēr.*]

❑ *These sound alike:* **here, hear** (listen).

here•a•bout (hîr′ə bout′) also **here•a•bouts** (hîr′ə bouts′) *adv.* In this area; around here: *The ball rolled hereabouts.*

here•af•ter (hîr ăf′tər) *adv.* From now on; after this: *Hereafter, when you write use my full address.* —*n.* Life after death.

here•by (hîr bī′) *adv.* By virtue of this; by this means: *All drivers are hereby required to have an eye test.*

he•red•i•tar•y (hə rĕd′ĭ tĕr′ē) *adj.* **1.** Passed or capable of being passed from parent to offspring by means of genes: *a hereditary trait.* **2.** Passed down by inheritance to a legal heir: *a hereditary title.* **3.** Traditional; ancestral: *a hereditary home.* **4.** Encouraged by or coming from one's parents or ancestors: *a hereditary belief.*

he•red•i•ty (hə rĕd′ĭ tē) *n., pl.* **he•red•i•ties. 1.** The passage of traits or characteristics from parents to offspring by biological inheritance through genes. **2.** The traits or characteristics passed to an offspring in this way. [First written down about 1540 in Modern English and spelled *heredity*, inheritance, from Latin *hērēditās*, from *hērēs*, heir.]

Here•ford (hûr′fərd *or* hĕr′ə fərd) *n.* Any of a breed of cattle originally developed in England and having a reddish-brown coat, white face, and white markings on the body.

here•in (hîr ĭn′) *adv.* In this thing, matter, fact, or place: *She likes to read, and herein lies the source of her large vocabulary.*

here•of (hîr ŭv′ *or* hîr ŏv′) *adv.* Of this: *We will speak no more hereof.*

here•on (hîr ŏn′ *or* hîr ôn′) *adv.* On this: *This is the Constitution, and our Bill of Rights was founded hereon.*

her•e•sy (hĕr′ĭ sē) *n., pl.* **her•e•sies. 1.** An opinion or belief that is different from the established beliefs of a religion. **2.** An opinion that is contrary to prevailing views, as in politics or science. **3.** The holding of such a belief or opinion.

her•e•tic (hĕr′ĭ tĭk) *n.* A person who holds beliefs or opinions that are different from accepted beliefs or opinions, as of a church or a political party.

he•ret•i•cal (hə rĕt′ĭ kəl) *adj.* **1.** Of or relating to heresy or heretics. **2.** Characterized by or revealing heresy: *The speaker's heretical statements made the audience uneasy.*

here•to (hîr to͞o′) *adv.* To this document or matter: *Attached hereto is my signature.*

here•to•fore (hîr′tə fôr′) *adv.* Before this; previously: *Such a huge ship had not been seen heretofore.*

here•un•to (hîr ŭn′to͞o) *adv.* Hereto.

here•up•on (hîr′ə pŏn′ *or* hîr′ə pôn′) *adv.* **1.** Immediately after this: *A few bystanders shouted taunts and hereupon began an argument.* **2.** Upon this point; upon this: *We believe in free speech and hereupon the court has remained firm.*

here•with (hîr wĭth′ *or* hîr wĭth′) *adv.* **1.** Along with this: *I am sending herewith a snapshot of the baby.* **2.** By means of this; hereby: *I herewith renounce all claim to the estate.*

her•i•ta•ble (hĕr′ĭ tə bəl) *adj.* **1.** Capable of being inherited: *heritable property.* **2.** Capable of inheriting: *She has many heritable relatives.* **—her′i•ta•bil′i•ty** *n.*

her•i•tage (hĕr′ĭ tĭj) *n.* **1.** Property that is or can be inherited. **2.** Something other than property passed down from preceding generations; a tradition: *Our country has a great heritage of folk music.*

her•maph•ro•dite (hər măf′rə dīt′) *n.* An organism, such as an earthworm, having both male and female sex organs in a single individual.

Her•mes (hûr′mēz) *n.* In Greek mythology, the messenger of the gods and patron of travelers, thieves, and commerce, identified with the Roman Mercury.

her•met•ic (hər mĕt′ĭk) also **her•met•i•cal** (hər mĕt′ĭ kəl) *adj.* Sealed so that air cannot enter or escape; airtight. **—her•met′i•cal•ly** *adv.*

her•mit (hûr′mĭt) *n.* A person who has withdrawn from society and lives a solitary existence. [First written down in 1196 in Middle English and spelled *heremite*, from Greek *erēmitēs*, from *erēmos*, solitary.]

her•mit•age (hûr′mĭ tĭj) *n.* **1.** The home of a hermit. **2.** A monastery.

hermit crab *n.* Any of various crabs that use an empty snail shell or a similar shell to protect their soft unarmored bodies.

hermit thrush *n.* A North American bird having a

Hereford
Hereford bull

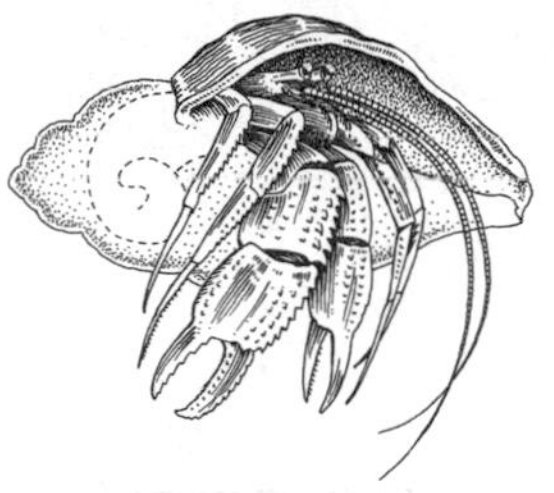

hermit crab

ă	pat	oi	boy
ā	pay	ou	out
âr	care	o͝o	took
ä	father	o͞o	boot
ĕ	pet	ŭ	cut
ē	be	ûr	urge
ĭ	pit	th	thin
ī	pie	*th*	this
îr	pier	hw	whoop
ŏ	pot	zh	vision
ō	toe	ə	about
ô	paw	N	*French* bon

heron
Great egret

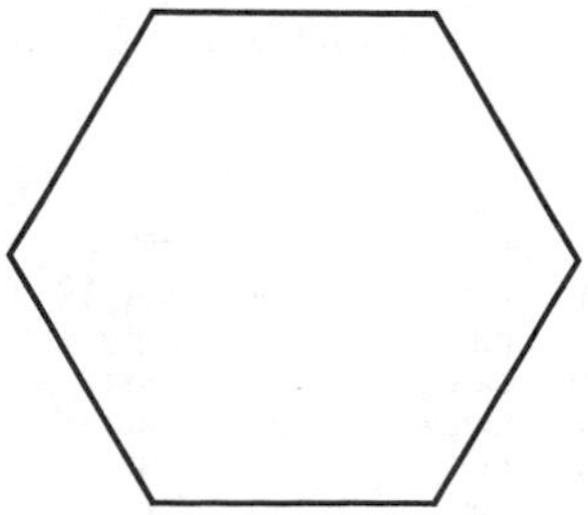
hexagon

brownish back, a spotted breast, and a melodious song.

her•ni•a (hûr′nē ə) *n., pl.* **her•ni•as** or **her•ni•ae** (hûr′nē ē′). A condition in which an organ or other structure of the body protrudes through an abnormal opening in the wall that normally contains it; a rupture.

he•ro (hîr′ō) *n., pl.* **he•roes. 1.** In mythology and legend, a man of great courage and strength who is celebrated for his bold deeds. **2.** A person noted for courageous acts or significant achievements: *a sports hero.* **3.** The protagonist in a novel, poem, play, or movie. **4.** A submarine sandwich. [First written down in 1555 in Modern English, from Greek *hērōs.*] —See Note at **submarine.**

Her•od An•ti•pas (hĕr′əd ăn′tĭ păs′). Died about A.D. 40. Ruler of Judea and tetrarch in Galilee (4 B.C.–A.D. 40) to whom Jesus was sent for judgment.

he•ro•ic (hĭ rō′ĭk) also **he•ro•i•cal** (hĭ rō′ĭ kəl) *adj.* **1.** Having or showing the qualities of a hero; courageous; noble: *heroic deeds; the heroic voyage of Magellan's crew.* **2.** Of, relating to, or resembling the heroes of literature, legend, or myth. **—he•ro′i•cal•ly** *adv.*

her•o•in (hĕr′ō ĭn) *n.* A bitter white crystalline chemical compound derived from morphine. It is a powerful and highly addictive narcotic drug.
❑ *These sound alike:* **heroin, heroine** (courageous woman).

her•o•ine (hĕr′ō ĭn) *n.* **1.** A woman noted for courageous acts or significant achievements. **2.** The female protagonist in a novel, poem, play, or movie.
❑ *These sound alike:* **heroine, heroin** (drug).

her•o•ism (hĕr′ō ĭz′əm) *n.* Heroic conduct or action; courage; bravery.

her•on (hĕr′ən) *n.* Any of various wading birds having a long neck, long legs, and a long pointed bill.

her•pes (hûr′pēz) *n.* Any of several diseases caused by viruses in which there is an eruption of blisters on the skin or a mucous membrane.

her•pe•tol•o•gy (hûr′pĭ tŏl′ə jē) *n.* The scientific study of reptiles and amphibians.

her•ring (hĕr′ĭng) *n., pl.* **herring** or **her•rings.** Any of various fishes of Atlantic and Pacific waters, caught in large numbers and used as a fresh or preserved food.

her•ring•bone (hĕr′ĭng bōn′) *n.* **1.** A zigzag pattern made up of short parallel lines arranged in rows that slant first one way, then another. **2.** Cloth woven in this pattern.

hers (hûrz) *pron. (used with a singular or plural verb).* The one or ones belonging to her: *If his desk is occupied, use hers.*

her•self (hûr sĕlf′) *pron.* **1.** That one that is the same as her: **a.** Used as the direct object or indirect object of a verb or as the object of a preposition to show that the action of the verb refers back to the subject: *She pulled herself up by the rope. She bought herself a new pen. She had a photograph of herself.* **b.** Used to give emphasis: *Mother herself is going. She herself saw it.* **2.** Her normal or healthy self: *She has not been herself since her friend left town.*

hertz (hûrts) *n., pl.* **hertz.** A unit of frequency of vibrations and waves equal to one cycle per second. [First written down in 1928 in Modern English, after Heinrich Rudolf *Hertz* (1857–1894), German physicist.]

Her•ze•go•vi•na (hĕrt′sə gō vē′nə *or* hûrt′sə gō vē′nə). The southern region of Bosnia-Herzegovina. It has been joined with Bosnia since the 15th century.

he's (hēz). **1.** Contraction of *he is.* **2.** Contraction of *he has.*

hes•i•tan•cy (hĕz′ĭ tən sē) *n., pl.* **hes•i•tan•cies.** The condition or quality of being hesitant; indecision: *a hesitancy in speaking one's mind.*

hes•i•tant (hĕz′ĭ tənt) *adj.* Inclined or tending to hesitate; doubtful, uncertain, or reluctant: *We were hesitant to fly in such bad weather.* **—hes′i•tant•ly** *adv.*

hes•i•tate (hĕz′ĭ tāt′) *intr.v.* **hes•i•tat•ed, hes•i•tat•ing, hes•i•tates. 1.a.** To be slow to act, speak, or decide: *We hesitated about whether to go over the rickety bridge.* **b.** To pause or wait in uncertainty: *I hesitated before answering since I was not sure how he would react.* **2.** To be reluctant or unwilling: *They hesitated to ask for help when they saw how busy I was.* **3.** To speak haltingly; stammer. [First written down before 1622 in Modern English, from Latin *haesitāre,* from *haerēre,* to hold fast.]

hes•i•ta•tion (hĕz′ĭ tā′shən) *n.* **1.** The act or an instance of hesitating: *After a short hesitation, we decided to continue the game.* **2.** A pause in speech.

Hesse (hĕs). A region and former grand duchy of west-central Germany.

Hes•sian (hĕsh′ən) *n.* **1.** A native or inhabitant of Hesse. **2.** A German soldier hired to fight in the British army in America during the Revolutionary War. —*adj.* Of or relating to Hesse or its people.

hetero– or **heter–** *pref.* A prefix that means other or different: *heterogeneous.*

het•er•o•dox (hĕt′ər ə dŏks′) *adj.* Not in agreement with generally accepted beliefs, especially in religion.

het•er•o•dox•y (hĕt′ər ə dŏk′sē) *n., pl.* **het•er•o•dox•ies. 1.** The condition of being heterodox. **2.** A heterodox belief.

het•er•o•ge•ne•ous (hĕt′ər ə jē′nē əs *or* hĕt′ər ə jēn′yəs) *adj.* **1.** Consisting of parts that are not alike; having unlike elements: *the museum's vast heterogeneous collection of insects.* **2.** Different in kind; not alike: *the heterogeneous insects in the museum's collection.* **—het′er•o•ge′ne•ous•ly** *adv.* **—het′er•o•ge′ne•ous•ness** *n.*

het•er•o•sex•u•al (hĕt′ə rō sĕk′shōō əl) *adj.* **1.** Relating to or having sexual feelings for members of the opposite sex. **2.** Of or relating to different sexes. —*n.* A heterosexual person. **—het′er•o•sex′u•al′i•ty** (hĕt′ə rō sĕk′shōō ăl′ĭ tē) *n.*

het•er•o•zy•gous (hĕt′ər ə zī′gəs) *adj.* Having a contrasting pair of genes, as for tallness and shortness, at corresponding positions on the chromosomes of an organism.

hew (hyōō) *v.* **hewed, hewn** (hyōōn) or **hewed, hew•ing, hews.** —*tr.* **1.** To make or shape with or as if with an ax: *We hewed our way through the thicket.* **2.** To cut down with an ax; fell: *hew down an oak.* **3.** To strike or cut: *hew a log into pieces.* —*intr.* To adhere; keep; hold: *Hew closely to the regulations.*
❑ *These sound alike:* **hew, hue** (color).

hex (hĕks) *n.* **1.** An evil spell; a curse. **2.** A person or thing that brings bad luck: *The new player seemed to be a hex on the team, for we lost four games in a row.* —*tr.v.* **hexed, hex•ing, hex•es. 1.** To work evil on; bewitch. **2.** To wish or bring bad luck to.

hexa– or **hex–** *pref.* A prefix that means six: *hexagon.*

hex•a•dec•i•mal (hĕk′sə dĕs′ə məl) *adj.* Of, relating to, or using 16 as the base of a number system.

hex•a•gon (hĕk′sə gŏn′) *n.* A plane figure having six angles and six sides.

hex•ag•o•nal (hĕk săg′ə nəl) *adj.* Of, relating to, or shaped like a hexagon; six-sided.

hex•a•he•dron (hĕk′sə hē′drən) *n., pl.* **hex•a•he•drons** or **hex•a•he•dra** (hĕk′sə hē′drə). A solid figure having six faces, as a cube.

hex•am•e•ter (hĕk săm′ĭ tər) *n.* A line of poetry composed of six metrical feet.

hey (hā) *interj.* **1.** An expression used to show surprise, appreciation, or wonder: *Hey, that's nice!* **2.** An expression used to attract attention: *Hey, you!*
❑ *These sound alike:* **hey, hay** (dried grass).

hey•day (hā′dā′) *n.* The period of greatest popularity, success, or power; prime: *The heyday of very large cars seems to have passed.*

Hf The symbol for the element **hafnium.**

HF or **hf** *abbr.* An abbreviation of high frequency.

hf. *abbr.* An abbreviation of half.

Hg The symbol for the element **mercury** (sense 1).

H.H. *abbr.* **1.** An abbreviation of: **a.** Her Highness. **b.** His Highness. **2.** His Holiness.

hi (hī) *interj. Informal.* An expression used as a greeting.
❑ *These sound alike:* **hi, hie** (hurry), **high** (elevated).

HI *abbr.* An abbreviation of Hawaii.

H.I. *abbr.* An abbreviation of Hawaiian Islands.

hi•a•tus (hī ā′təs) *n., pl.* **hi•a•tus•es** or **hiatus.** A gap, especially one caused by a missing part or section; a break or an interruption: *There was a long hiatus in the ancient manuscript where whole pages had been lost.*

Hi•a•wa•tha (hī′ə wŏth′ə *or* hī′ə wô′thə). Flourished about 1570. Onondagan leader who is credited with organizing the Iroquois confederacy.

hi•ba•chi (hĭ bä′chē) *n., pl.* **hi•ba•chis.** A small charcoal-burning stove of Japanese origin used for cooking. [First written down in 1863 in Modern English, from Japanese : *hi*, fire + *bachi*, bowl.]

hi•ber•nate (hī′bər nāt′) *intr.v.* **hi•ber•nat•ed, hi•ber•nat•ing, hi•ber•nates.** To spend the winter in an inactive state resembling deep sleep. Bears and some other wild animals hibernate. [First written down before 1802 in Modern English, from Latin *hībernus*, relating to winter.] **—hi′ber•na′tion** *n.*

Hi•ber•ni•a (hī bûr′nē ə). The Latin and poetic name for Ireland.

hi•bis•cus (hī bĭs′kəs) *n.* Any of various tropical plants, shrubs, or trees having large red, white, or pink flowers shaped like bells.

hic•cup also **hic•cough** (hĭk′əp) *n.* **1.** A sudden and uncontrolled contraction of the muscles of the diaphragm and throat causing the breath to be quickly cut off with a short sharp sound. **2. hiccups.** An attack in which spasms of this kind occur repeatedly. *—intr.v.* **hic•cupped, hic•cup•ping, hic•cups** also **hic•coughed, hic•cough•ing, hic•coughs. 1.** To make the sound of a hiccup. **2.** To have the hiccups. [First written down in 1538 in Modern English and spelled *hycock*, of imitative origin.]

hick (hĭk) *Informal. n.* A usually rural person held to be unsophisticated, gullible, or ignorant. *—adj.* Considered rural and unsophisticated.

hick•o•ry (hĭk′ə rē) *n., pl.* **hick•o•ries. 1.** Any of several mostly North American trees that are related to the walnut and bear edible nuts. **2.** The hard, tough, heavy wood of such a tree. [First written down in 1671 in American English, from Virginia Algonquian *pocohiquara*, drink made of pressed hickory nuts.]

hide¹ (hīd) *v.* **hid** (hĭd), **hid•den** (hĭd′n) or **hid, hid•ing, hides.** *—tr.* **1.** To put or keep out of sight; conceal: *I hid his birthday present in my closet.* **2.** To prevent from being known; keep secret: *The disguise was a perfect way to hide her true identity.* **3.** To cut off from sight; cover up: *Clouds hid the stars.* *—intr.* To keep oneself out of sight: *The lion hid in the tall grass.* ***—idiom.*** **hide out.** To be in hiding, as from a pursuer: *The gangsters hid out in a remote cabin until it was safe to return to the city.* [First written down before 899 in Old English and spelled *hȳdan.*]

Synonyms: hide, conceal, secrete, screen, bury. These verbs mean to keep from the sight or knowledge of others. **Hide** and **conceal** are the most general: *She smiled to hide her hurt feelings. A throw rug concealed the stain on the carpet.* **Secrete** means to hide in a place unknown to others: *The lioness secreted her cubs in the tall grass.* **Screen** means to shield or block from the view of others: *Tall shrubs screen the actor's home from inquisitive tourists.* **Bury** means to conceal something by covering it over: *He buried his hands in his pockets so the teacher couldn't see his dirty fingernails.*

hide² (hīd) *n.* The skin of an animal, especially the thick tough skin or pelt of a large animal. [First written down in 891 in Old English and spelled *hȳd.*]

hide-and-seek (hīd′n sēk′) *n.* A children's game in which one player tries to find and catch the other players who are hiding.

hide•a•way (hīd′ə wā′) *n.* **1.** A hideout. **2.** A secluded or isolated place: *Spend a vacation at a hideaway in the mountains.*

hide•bound (hīd′bound′) *adj.* Adhering stubbornly to one's own opinions or prejudices; narrow-minded: *The hidebound conservative refused to stay for the speech of the opposing party.*

hid•e•ous (hĭd′ē əs) *adj.* Horribly revolting; disgusting: *a hideous monster; a hideous murder.* **—hid′e•ous•ly** *adv.* **—hid′e•ous•ness** *n.*

hide•out (hīd′out′) *n.* A place of shelter or concealment.

hie (hī) *intr. & tr.v.* **hied, hie•ing** or **hy•ing** (hī′ĭng), **hies.** To hasten; hurry. [First written down before 899 in Old English and spelled *hīgian.*]
❑ *These sound alike:* **hie, hi** (greeting), **high** (elevated).

hi•er•ar•chi•cal (hī′ə rär′kĭ kəl *or* hī rär′kĭ kəl) or **hi•er•ar•chic** (hī′ə rär′kĭk *or* hī′rär′kĭk) *adj.* Of or relating to a hierarchy. **—hi′er•ar′chi•cal•ly** *adv.*

hi•er•ar•chy (hī′ə rär′kē *or* hī′rär′kē) *n., pl.* **hi•er•ar•chies. 1.** A group of persons or things classified according to rank or grade: *We made a chart to show the hierarchy of positions in the corporation.* **2.** A body of church officials organized by rank. [First written down about 1343 in Middle English and spelled *ierarchie*, from Greek *hierarkhēs*, high priest.]

hi•er•o•glyph (hī′ər ə glĭf′ *or* hī′rə glĭf′) *n.* A picture or symbol used in hieroglyphic writing.

hi•er•o•glyph•ic (hī′ər ə glĭf′ĭk *or* hī′rə glĭf′ĭk) *adj.* Of or related to a system of writing in which pictures or symbols are used to represent words or sounds: *The ancient Egyptians used hieroglyphic writing.* *—n.* **1.** A hieroglyph. **2. hieroglyphics.** Hieroglyphic writing. [First written down in 1585 in Modern English : Greek *hieros*, holy + Greek *gluphē*, carving.] **—hi′er•o•glyph′i•cal•ly** *adv.*

hi•fa•lu•tin (hī′fə lo͞ot′n) *adj. Informal.* Variant of **highfalutin.**

hi-fi (hī′fī′) *n., pl.* **hi-fis.** *Informal.* **1.** High fidelity. **2.** Electronic equipment that reproduces realistic sound from records, tapes, compact disks, or radio transmission.

hig•gle•dy-pig•gle•dy (hĭg′əl dē pĭg′əl dē) *adv.* In complete disorder or confusion. *—adj.* Disordered; jumbled.

high (hī) *adj.* **high•er, high•est. 1.a.** Being a relatively great distance above a certain level, as above sea level or the surface of the earth: *These high mountains are over 15,000 feet.* **b.** Extending a specified distance upward: *The cabinet is 3 feet high.* **2.** Greater than usual in degree, amount, qual-

hibiscus
Rose of Sharon

hieroglyphics

ă	pat	oi	boy
ā	pay	ou	out
âr	care	o͝o	took
ä	father	o͞o	boot
ĕ	pet	ŭ	cut
ē	be	ûr	urge
ĭ	pit	th	thin
ī	pie	*th*	this
îr	pier	hw	whoop
ŏ	pot	zh	vision
ō	toe	ə	about
ô	paw	N	*French* bon

high jump
Fosbury flop technique

ity, force, or intensity: *high temperature; a high standard of living; high winds.* **3.** Above the middle range of musical pitch; shrill; sharp: *the high tones of a flute; a high shriek.* **4.** Being at or near the peak: *Election to the Presidency was the high point of a long career in politics.* **5.** Advanced in development or complexity: *higher forms of animal life.* **6.** Greater than others in rank, status, or importance: *a high official; a high priority.* **7.** Serious; grave: *Treason is a high crime.* **8.** Showing joy or excitement: *high spirits.* **9.** Favorable: *The students held their teacher in high regard.* **10.** Expensive; extravagant: *accustomed to high living.* **11.** Situated far from the equator: *high latitudes.* —*adv.* **higher, highest.** At, in, or to a high position, level, or degree: *Hawks fly high in the sky. A general ranks high above a private.* —*n.* **1.** A high degree or level: *Gold prices reached a new high.* **2.** A mass of atmospheric air that exerts greater pressure than the air in the regions surrounding it: *This clear dry weather is the result of a high from the West.* **3.** *Informal.* An elevated state of good feeling or well-being: *The runner was on a high after winning the race.* **4.** The gear in a transmission that produces the fastest speeds. —***idioms.*** **high and dry.** Helpless and alone: *When our car broke down in the wilderness, we were left high and dry.* **high and low.** Everywhere: *I looked high and low for the keys.* [First written down about 825 in Old English and spelled *hēh.*]

❑ *These sound alike:* **high, hi** (greeting), **hie** (hurry).

high blood pressure *n.* Hypertension.

high•born (hī′bôrn′) *adj.* Of noble birth.

high•boy (hī′boi′) *n.* A tall chest of drawers divided into two sections and supported on four legs.

high•brow (hī′brou′) *adj.* Highly cultured or intellectual: *highbrow literature.* —*n.* A person who has or seems to have a high degree of learning or culture.

high•fa•lu•tin or **hi•fa•lu•tin** (hī′fə lo͞ot′n) *adj. Informal.* Pompous or making a showy pretense: *highfalutin words.*

high fidelity *n.* The electronic reproduction of sounds, as on records or magnetic tape, with very little distortion.

high-flown (hī′flōn′) *adj.* **1.** Lofty; exalted: *high-flown ideals.* **2.** Full of showy pretense; inflated: *high-flown language.*

high frequency *n.* A radio wave frequency in the range between 3 and 30 megahertz.

high-grade (hī′grād′) *adj.* Of superior quality.

high•hand•ed (hī′hăn′dĭd) *adj.* Arrogant; overbearing: *The manager's highhanded rejection of my application annoyed me.* —**high′hand′ed•ly** *adv.* —**high′hand′ed•ness** *n.*

high-hat (hī′hăt′) *Informal. tr.v.* **high•-hat•ted, high•-hat•ting, high•-hats.** To be condescending or snobbish toward. —*adj.* Snobbish.

High Holy Days *pl.n.* The period from Rosh Hashanah until the end of Yom Kippur.

high jump *n.* **1.** A jump for height made over a raised horizontal bar in an athletic contest. **2.** A contest in which such jumps are made.

high•land (hī′lənd) *n.* **1.** Elevated land. **2. highlands.** A mountainous or hilly part of a country, or a region at a high elevation. —*adj.* Of or relating to a highland.

high•land•er (hī′lən dər) *n.* A person who lives in the highlands.

Highland fling *n.* A lively folk dance of the Scottish Highlands.

High•lands (hī′ləndz). A mountainous region of central and northern Scotland. The area maintained a separate culture until well into the 19th century.

high•light (hī′līt′) *n.* **1.** An area in a painting or photograph where light is represented as most intense. **2.** The most outstanding event or part: *The highlight of the trip was visiting the botanical gardens.* —*tr.v.* **high•light•ed, high•light•ing, high•lights. 1.** To cast light on or make brighter with the use of lighter colors. **2.** To emphasize; make prominent. **3.** To mark important passages of (text) with a usually fluorescent marker for later reference: *highlight chapter headings in a book.*

high•ly (hī′lē) *adv.* **1.** To a great degree; extremely; very: *highly developed; highly amusing.* **2.** In a good or favorable way: *I think highly of the candidate.* **3.** In a high position or rank: *a highly placed official of our state.* **4.** At a high price, cost, or rate: *a highly paid executive.*

high-mind•ed (hī′mīn′dĭd) *adj.* Having lofty ideals; noble. —**high′-mind′ed•ness** *n.*

high•ness (hī′nĭs) *n.* **1.** The quality or condition of being tall or high; height. **2. Highness.** Used as a title and form of address for a prince or princess: *Her Royal Highness the Princess Margaret.*

high noon *n.* **1.** Exactly noon; the very middle of the day. **2.** The highest stage or most advanced period: *The judge was at the high noon of his career.*

high-pitched (hī′pĭcht′) *adj.* **1.** High in pitch; shrill: *a high-pitched flute.* **2.** Steeply sloped: *a high-pitched roof.*

high-pres•sure (hī′prĕsh′ər) *adj.* **1.** Having, using, or withstanding pressures higher than normal: *a high-pressure tire.* **2.** Having a high atmospheric pressure: *a high-pressure area.* **3.** *Informal.* Using vigorous and persistent methods of persuasion: *a high-pressure sales pitch.*

high-rise (hī′rīz′) *adj.* Very tall and having many stories: *high-rise apartment building.* —*n.* or **high rise.** A high-rise building.

high•road (hī′rōd′) *n. Chiefly British.* A main road; a highway.

high school *n.* A secondary school including grades 9 or 10 through 12. —**high′-school′** *adj.*

high seas *pl.n.* The open waters of an ocean or sea beyond the limits of any nation's jurisdiction.

high-speed (hī′spēd′) *adj.* **1.** Designed for use at high speed: *a high-speed blender.* **2.** Taking place at high speed: *a high-speed chase.*

high-spir•it•ed (hī′spĭr′ĭ tĭd) *adj.* Having a proud or fiery disposition: *a high-spirited horse.*

high-strung (hī′strŭng′) *adj.* Very nervous and easily excited; tense.

high technology *n.* Technology involving highly advanced scientific methods or newly developed and specialized devices, such as electronic equipment.

high-ten•sion (hī′tĕn′shən) *adj.* Having a high voltage: *high-tension wires.*

high tide *n.* **1.** The tide when the water reaches its highest level. **2.** The time at which this occurs.

high time *n.* The time just before it is too late; fully time: *If you want to catch the train, it's high time we go.*

high treason *n.* Treason against one's country or sovereign.

high-wa•ter mark (hī′wô′tər *or* hī′wŏt′ər) *n.* **1.** A mark showing the highest level reached by a body of water. **2.** The highest point of something; the apex: *The band reached a high-water mark with its third album.*

high•way (hī′wā′) *n.* A main public road: *A highway connects the cities.*

high•way•man (hī′wā′mən) *n.* A man who robs travelers on a road.

high wire *n.* A tightrope on which acrobats perform, stretched tightly above the ground.

hi•jack (hī′jăk′) *Informal. tr.v.* **hi•jacked, hi•jack•ing, hi•jacks. 1.** To stop and rob (a vehicle in transit). **2.** To steal (goods) from a vehicle in transit: *The rebels hijacked medical supplies.* **3.** To seize or take control of (a moving vehicle) by use of force, especially in order to reach a different destination. **—hi'jack'er** *n.*

hike (hīk) *v.* **hiked, hik•ing, hikes.** *—intr.* To go on an extended walk, especially for pleasure: *hike through the woods.* *—tr.* **1.** To pull or raise, especially with a sudden motion; hitch: *I hiked up my socks.* **2.** To increase or raise: *The new sales tax will hike up prices.* *—n.* **1.** A long walk or trip on foot. **2.** A hitch or tug upward: *Give your socks a hike.* **3.** A rise; an increase: *a hike in gasoline prices.* [First written down in 1809 in Modern English.] **—hik'er** *n.*

hi•la (hī'lə) *n.* Plural of **hilum.**

hi•lar•i•ous (hĭ lâr'ē əs *or* hĭ lăr'ē əs) *adj.* Very funny; provoking much laughter: *a hilarious story.* [First written down in 1823 in Modern English, from Latin *hilaris,* cheerful.] **—hi•lar'i•ous•ly** *adv.* **—hi•lar'i•ous•ness** *n.*

hi•lar•i•ty (hĭ lăr'ĭ tē *or* hĭ lâr'ĭ tē) *n.* Great merriment or fun.

hill (hĭl) *n.* **1.** A part of the earth's surface rising above the level of the land, but not as high as a mountain. **2.** A small heap, mound, or pile: *an ant hill.* **3.** A mound of earth that covers seeds or a plant: *corn hills.* *—idiom.* **over the hill.** *Informal.* Past one's prime. [First written down about 1000 in Old English and spelled *hyll.*]

hill•bil•ly (hĭl'bĭl'ē) *n., pl.* **hill•bil•lies.** *Informal.* A person who lives in the backwoods or a remote mountain area.

hill•ock (hĭl'ək) *n.* A small hill.

hill•side (hĭl'sīd') *n.* The side of a hill.

hill•top (hĭl'tŏp') *n.* The top or crest of a hill.

hill•y (hĭl'ē) *adj.* **hill•i•er, hill•i•est.** **1.** Having many hills: *Northern Missouri is hilly.* **2.** Similar to a hill; steep: *a hilly path.* **—hill'i•ness** *n.*

hilt (hĭlt) *n.* The handle of a sword or dagger. *—idiom.* **to the hilt.** To the limit; completely: *They played their roles to the hilt.* [First written down about 725 in Old English.]

hi•lum (hī'ləm) *n., pl.* **hi•la** (hī'lə). A mark or scar on a seed, such as a bean, showing the point of attachment to the plant.

him (hĭm) *pron.* The objective form of **he. 1.** Used as the direct object of a verb: *We helped him.* **2.** Used as the indirect object of a verb: *She gave him a ride.* **3.** Used as the object of a preposition: *This package is for him.* —See Note at **me.**

❑ *These sound alike:* **him, hymn** (song).

Him•a•la•ya Mountains (hĭm'ə lā'ə *or* hĭ mäl'yə). A mountain system of south-central Asia extending about 1,500 miles (2,414 kilometers) through Kashmir, northern India, southern Tibet, Nepal, and Bhutan. —See Note.

him•self (hĭm sĕlf') *pron.* **1.** That one that is the same as him: **a.** Used as the direct object or indirect object of a verb or as the object of a preposition to show that the action of the verb refers back to the subject: *He dressed himself. He gave himself plenty of time. He saved some popcorn for himself.* **b.** Used to give emphasis: *He took care of his problem himself.* **2.** His real, normal, or healthy self: *He looks more like himself after the vacation.*

hind¹ (hīnd) *adj.* Located at or forming the rear or back, especially of an animal: *a horse's hind legs.* [First written down about 725 in Old English and spelled *bihindan.*]

hind² (hīnd) *n.* A female red deer. [First written down before 970 in Old English.]

hin•der (hĭn'dər) *tr.v.* **hin•dered, hin•der•ing, hin•ders.** To prevent the action or progress of; hamper: *Heavy rains hindered traffic on the highway.* [First written down about 1000 in Old English and spelled *hindrian.*]

Hin•di (hĭn'dē) *n.* An Indo-European language widely spoken in northern India. **—Hin'di** *adj.*

hind•most (hīnd'mōst') *adj.* Farthest to the rear.

hind•quar•ter (hīnd'kwôr'tər) *n.* **1. hindquarters.** The rump or haunches of a four-footed animal. **2.** The rear part of a side of beef, lamb, or other meat, including the leg and rump.

hin•drance (hĭn'drəns) *n.* **1.** A person or thing that hinders; an obstacle: *The heavy backpack was a hindrance to the hiker.* **2.** The act of hindering or the condition of being hindered: *Because of the weather's hindrance, we waited another day to go hiking.*

hind•sight (hīnd'sīt') *n.* The understanding of the significance of a past event: *In hindsight I know I should have ignored their rude remarks.*

Hin•du (hĭn'do͞o) *n.* **1.** A native or inhabitant of India, especially of northern India. **2.** A believer in Hinduism. *—adj.* **1.** Of or relating to the Hindus or their culture. **2.** Of or relating to Hinduism.

Hin•du•ism (hĭn'do͞o ĭz'əm) *n.* A body of religion, philosophy, and cultural practices predominant in India and characterized by belief in reincarnation and in a supreme being who has many forms and natures.

Hindu Kush (ko͞osh *or* kŭsh). A mountain range of southwest Asia extending more than 500 miles (805 kilometers) westward from northern Pakistan to northeast Afghanistan. It rises to 25,230 feet (7,695.2 meters).

Hin•du•sta•ni (hĭn'do͞o stä'nē *or* hĭn'do͞o stăn'ē) *n.* A group of languages used in India and including Urdu and Hindi. *—adj.* Of or relating to northern India, its people, or the Hindustani language.

hinge (hĭnj) *n.* **1.** A joint on which a door, gate, lid, or cover turns or swings. **2.** A structure in a human or an animal that allows similar movement: *the hinge of the elbow; the hinge of a clam shell.* *—v.* **hinged, hing•ing, hing•es.** *—tr.* To attach by a hinge or hinges: *The carpenter hinged the door.* *—intr.* To depend: *Their grades hinge on this exam.* [First written down in 1356 in Middle English and spelled *heyngge.*]

hint (hĭnt) *n.* **1.** A slight indication or an indirect suggestion; a clue: *Can't you give me a hint about the answer to this math problem?* **2.** A small amount; a trace: *There is just a hint of vanilla in these cookies.* *—v.* **hint•ed, hint•ing, hints.** *—tr.* To make known or indicate in an indirect manner: *Our host hinted that it was time to leave.* *—intr.* To give a hint: *She refused to hint at what really happened.* [First written down in 1604 in Modern English, probably from Old English *hentan,* to grasp.] **—hint'er** *n.*

hin•ter•land (hĭn'tər lănd') *n.* **1.** Land away from a seacoast; an inland area. **2.** An area far from cities or towns; backcountry.

hip¹ (hĭp) *n.* **1.** The projecting part of the human body between the waist and thigh. **2.** A similar part in animals, where the hind leg joins the body. **3.** The hipbone or the hip joint. [First written down before 800 in Old English and spelled *hype.*]

hip² (hĭp) *adj.* **hip•per, hip•pest.** *Slang.* Knowledgeable about or aware of what is new. [First written down in 1904 in Modern English, perhaps from Wolof *hipi, hepi,* to open one's eyes, be aware.]

hip³ (hĭp) *n.* The fruit of a rose, resembling a smooth berry or a tiny apple. [First written down about 800 in Old English and spelled *hēope.*]

hip•bone (hĭp'bōn') *n.* Either of the large, flat, irregularly shaped bones that with the lower backbone form the pelvis.

Himalaya Mountains

The **Himalaya Mountains** are snowy. *hima–* means "snow" in Sanskrit, the classical language of ancient India, and *himalaya* means "abode of snow." The Latin noun *hiems* and the ancient Greek noun *kheima,* both meaning "winter," are related to the Sanskrit *hima–.*

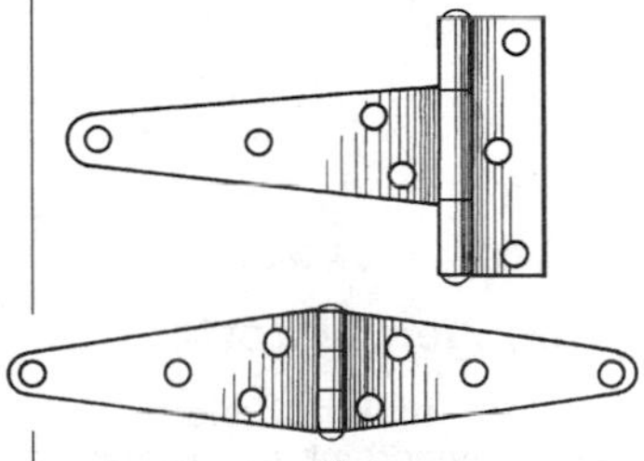

hinge

Top: T hinge
Bottom: Strap hinge

ă	pat	oi	boy
ā	pay	ou	out
âr	care	o͝o	took
ä	father	o͞o	boot
ĕ	pet	ŭ	cut
ē	be	ûr	urge
ĭ	pit	th	thin
ī	pie	*th*	this
îr	pier	hw	whoop
ŏ	pot	zh	vision
ō	toe	ə	about
ô	paw	N	*French* bon

hippopotamus

Hirohito
Photographed in 1984

Usage: historic

The word **historic** refers to what is important in history: *The Revolutionary War was a historic event.* **Historical** refers to whatever existed in the past, whether regarded as important or not: *The author used many historical characters in her novels.* There is overlap in the meanings of these two words, but if you use them as described here, your meaning will be clear.

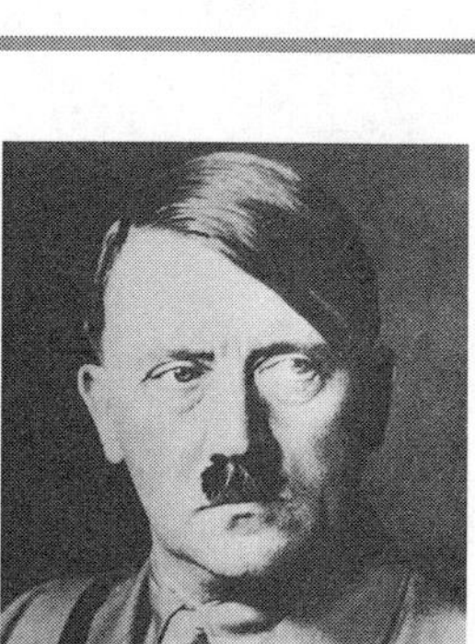

Adolf Hitler

hip joint *n.* The ball-and-socket joint between the hipbone and the femur.

hip•pie (hĭp′ē) *n., pl.* **hip•pies.** *Slang.* A person who opposes conventional standards and customs, as of behavior and dress.

hip•po (hĭp′ō) *n., pl.* **hip•pos.** A hippopotamus.

Hip•poc•ra•tes (hĭ pŏk′rə tēz′) Called "the Father of Medicine." 460?–377? B.C. Greek physician who is traditionally considered the author of the Hippocratic oath.

Hip•po•crat•ic oath (hĭp′ə krăt′ĭk) *n.* A statement dating from ancient times that sets forth the duties and obligations of a physician. Today many physicians still swear to abide by its principles.

hip•po•drome (hĭp′ə drōm′) *n.* **1.** A stadium with an oval racetrack, used for horse and chariot races in ancient Greece and Rome. **2.** An arena used for horse shows.

Hip•pol•y•ta (hĭ pŏl′ĭ tə) *n.* In Greek mythology, a queen of the Amazons.

hip•po•pot•a•mus (hĭp′ə pŏt′ə məs) *n., pl.* **hip•po•pot•a•mus•es** or **hip•po•pot•a•mi** (hĭp′ə pŏt′ə mī′). A large, very heavy African mammal having dark, almost hairless thick skin, short legs, a broad snout, and a wide mouth. It lives in and near rivers and lakes, eating large amounts of plants and staying under water for long periods of time. [First written down in 1563 in Modern English and spelled *hippopotame*, from Greek *hippopotamos* : *hippos*, horse + *potamos*, river.]

hire (hīr) *tr.v.* **hired, hir•ing, hires. 1.** To pay (a person) for working or performing a service; employ: *hire teachers for the new school.* **2.** To pay for the use of (something) for a limited time; rent: *hire a car.* —*n.* **1.** Payment for doing work or for the use of something: *The day's hire for the car is ten dollars.* **2.** The act or fact of hiring; employment: *The hire of the two assistants made the work easier.*

hire•ling (hīr′lĭng) *n.* A person who works only for money, especially a person willing to do tedious or unpleasant tasks for a fee.

Hi•ro•hi•to (hîr′ō hē′tō). 1901–1989. Emperor of Japan (1926–1989) whose unconditional surrender ended World War II (1945).

Hi•ro•shi•ma (hîr′ə shē′mə *or* hĭ rō′shə mə). A city of southwest Honshu, Japan, west of Osaka. Founded in the 16th century, it was destroyed in World War II by an atomic bomb. Population, 1,044,129.

hir•sute (hûr′so͞ot′ *or* hîr′so͞ot′) *adj.* Hairy. —**hir′sute′ness** *n.*

his (hĭz) *adj.* The possessive form of **he.** Of or belonging to him: *His house was not far from ours. The boy was careful to see that his studies came first.* —*pron. (used with a singular or plural verb).* The one or ones belonging to him: *The book is his. I am a friend of his. If you can't find your hat, take his.*

His•pan•ic (hĭ spăn′ĭk) *adj.* **1.** Of or relating to Spain or Spanish-speaking Latin America. **2.** Of or relating to a Spanish-speaking people or culture. —*n.* A person of Spanish or Latin-American descent, especially one living in the United States.

His•pan•io•la (hĭs′pən yō′lə). Formerly **Hai•ti** (hā′tē). An island of the West Indies east of Cuba, divided between Haiti and the Dominican Republic. It was visited by Columbus in 1492.

hiss (hĭs) *n.* A sound like that made by pronouncing the letter *s*: *the hiss of air escaping from a tire.* —*v.* **hissed, hiss•ing, hiss•es.** —*intr.* **1.** To make a sound like that of the letter *s*: *A cat will hiss when frightened.* **2.** To express dislike or disapproval with such a sound: *"You are making too much noise," someone hissed from behind.* —*tr.* To say or express by hissing: *The audience hissed its displeasure with the comedian.*

hist. *abbr.* An abbreviation of: **1.** Historian. **2.** History.

his•ta•mine (hĭs′tə mēn′ *or* hĭs′tə mĭn) *n.* A chemical compound, $C_5H_9N_3$, found in plant and animal tissue. It is released in allergic reactions in humans, causing enlargement of blood vessels.

his•tol•o•gy (hĭ stŏl′ə jē) *n., pl.* **his•tol•o•gies.** The scientific study of the structure of plant and animal tissues.

his•to•ri•an (hĭ stôr′ē ən *or* hĭ stŏr′ē ən) *n.* A person who writes about or studies history.

his•tor•ic (hĭ stôr′ĭk *or* hĭ stŏr′ĭk) *adj.* **1.** Important or famous in history: *the historic city of Williamsburg.* **2.** Historical. —SEE NOTE.

his•tor•i•cal (hĭ stôr′ĭ kəl *or* hĭ stŏr′ĭ kəl) *adj.* **1.** Of or relating to history: *historical events.* **2.** Based on or concerned with events in history: *a historical novel.* **3.** Historic. —**his•tor′i•cal•ly** *adv.* —SEE NOTE at **historic.**

historical linguistics *n. (used with a singular verb).* The study of how a language or a group of languages changes over time.

his•to•ry (hĭs′tə rē) *n., pl.* **his•to•ries. 1.** A written account or record of past events. **2.** The study of past events as a special field of knowledge: *History is a favorite subject among students.* **3.** The events that form the subject matter of a historical account: *printing and other important inventions in history.* **4.** A past that is known and sometimes recorded: *an old building with an interesting history.* [First written down before 1393 in Middle English and spelled *histoire*, from Greek *historein*, to inquire, from *histōr*, learned man.]

his•tri•on•ic (hĭs′trē ŏn′ĭk) *adj.* **1.** Excessively dramatic or emotional. **2.** Of or relating to actors or acting.

his•tri•on•ics (hĭs′trē ŏn′ĭks) *n. (used with a singular or plural verb).* Showy exaggerated emotional behavior.

hit (hĭt) *v.* **hit, hit•ting, hits.** —*tr.* **1.** To give a blow to; strike with a blow or stroke: *I hit the tennis ball with the racket.* **2.** To strike against with force; crash into: *The car hit the fence.* **3.** To cause (something) to come against a person or thing: *He hit his fist against the table.* **4.** To get to; reach: *hit a high note; going smoothly until we hit a bumpy road.* **5.** To strike with a bullet, arrow, or other missile: *She hit the center of the target.* **6.** In baseball, to make (a base hit): *The batter hit a home run.* **7.** To affect painfully or severely, as if by a blow: *A period of bad business hit the store hard.* —*intr.* **1.** To give or strike a blow: *The post went in deeper every time I hit.* **2.** To come against a person or thing; collide: *The two boats hit in the fog.* **3.** To happen or occur: *The blizzard hit during the night.* **4.** To make an attack: *The enemy hit at midnight.* **5.** To achieve or find something desired or sought: *We hit on the right answer.* —*n.* **1.** A blow that strikes something: *Two or three hits of the hammer will drive the nail in.* **2.** A person or thing that is a popular success: *The new musical is the hit of the season.* **3.** A base hit in baseball. —***idioms.*** **hit it off.** To get along well together. **hit the nail on the head.** To be absolutely right. [First written down before 1075 in Old English and spelled *hyttan*, from Old Norse *hitta*.] —**hit′ter** *n.*

hit-and-run (hĭt′n rŭn′) *adj.* Involving a driver of a vehicle who hits someone or damages something and flees to avoid responsibility.

hitch (hĭch) *v.* **hitched, hitch•ing, hitch•es.** —*tr.* **1.** To tie or fasten something with a rope, strap, or loop: *The trapper hitched a dog team to the sled.* **2.**

To raise or pull with a tug or jerk: *The driver hitched the heavy branch out of the way.* **3.** *Informal.* To get (a ride) by hitchhiking: *We hitched a lift to the gas station.* —*intr.* **1.** To become entangled or fastened: *The hose hitched around the bush.* **2.** To move slowly and in a jerky manner: *The weary climber hitched along the narrow rocky ledge.* **3.** *Informal.* To hitchhike. —*n.* **1.** A short pull or jerk; a tug. **2.** A delay or difficulty; a snag: *a hitch in our plans.* **3.** Any of various knots used for temporary fastening, as the timber hitch. **4.** A device used to connect one thing to another; a fastening. **5.** A time period, especially of military service. **6.** *Informal.* A ride obtained by hitchhiking. [First written down about 1200 in Middle English and spelled *icchen*, to move, jerk.]

hitch•hike (**hĭch′**hīk′) *intr.v.* **hitch•hiked, hitch•hik•ing, hitch•hikes.** To travel by getting a free ride from drivers of passing cars or trucks. —**hitch′hik′er** *n.*

hith•er (**hĭ*th*′**ər) *adv.* To or toward this place: *Come hither.* —***idiom.*** **hither and thither** or **hither and yon.** In or to many places; here and there: *running hither and thither all day.*

hith•er•to (**hĭ*th*′**ər to͞o′) *adv.* Until this time; up to now: *hitherto unobserved stars.*

Hit•ler (**hĭt′**lər), **Adolf.** Known as "Der Führer." 1889–1945. Austrian-born founder of the German Nazi Party who ruled Germany as an absolute dictator after 1934. His regime was marked by the killing of millions of people, especially European Jews. He killed himself in 1945.

hit-or-miss (**hĭt′** ər **mĭs′**) *adj.* Careless or unplanned; random.

Hit•tite (**hĭt′**īt′) *n.* **1.** A member of a people who lived in Asia Minor and northern Syria from 2000 B.C. to 1200 A.D. **2.** The Indo-European language of this people. —*adj.* Of or relating to the Hittites or their language or culture.

HIV (āch′ī **vē′**) *n.* The virus that causes AIDS by destroying the body's immune system.

hive (hīv) *n.* **1.a.** A structure for housing bees, especially honeybees. **b.** A colony of bees living in such a structure. **2.** A crowded place full of activity: *The supermarket was a hive of frantic last-minute shopping.* —*tr.v.* **hived, hiv•ing, hives.** To gather (bees) in a hive. [First written down about 725 in Old English and spelled *hȳf*.]

hives (hīvz) *pl.n.* *(used with a singular or plural verb).* A condition of the skin characterized by red welts that itch severely and resulting from an allergic reaction, a local infection, or some psychological cause.

HMO (āch′ĕm **ō′**) *n.* An organization for providing health care to members who pay insurance premiums to cover costs and agree to certain limits in treatment, as in the choosing of physicians.

HMS or **H.M.S.** *abbr.* An abbreviation of Her or His Majesty's Ship.

ho (hō) *interj.* An expression used to show surprise or to attract attention: *Land ho!*

❑ *These sound alike:* **ho, hoe** (tool).

Ho The symbol for the element **holmium.**

hoar (hôr) *adj.* White or gray; hoary.

❑ *These sound alike:* **hoar, whore** (prostitute).

hoard (hôrd) *n.* A hidden supply that is stored for future use: *the squirrel's hoard of nuts for winter.* —*tr.v.* **hoard•ed, hoard•ing, hoards.** To save and store away; accumulate: *The squirrel hoarded nuts for winter.* —**hoard′er** *n.*

❑ *These sound alike:* **hoard, horde** (crowd).

hoar•frost (**hôr′**frôst′ *or* **hôr′**frŏst′) *n.* A white coating of ice crystals that forms when dew freezes on an exposed object.

hoarse (hôrs) *adj.* **hoars•er, hoars•est. 1.** Low and gruff in sound; husky: *The cold reduced my voice to a hoarse whisper.* **2.** Having a low gruff voice: *The football fans were hoarse with shouting.* [First written down about 1000 in Old English and spelled *hās*.] —**hoarse′ly** *adv.* —**hoarse′ness** *n.*

❑ *These sound alike:* **hoarse, horse** (animal).

hoar•y (**hôr′**ē) *adj.* **hoar•i•er, hoar•i•est. 1.** White or grayish: *a hoary beard.* **2.** Very old; aged: *hoary ruins of the ancient city.* —**hoar′i•ness** *n.*

hoax (hōks) *n.* A trick or an act intended to deceive others, often in the form of a practical joke or false report: *The report that the store was going out of business proved to be a hoax.* —*tr.v.* **hoaxed, hoax•ing, hoax•es.** To deceive or cheat by using a hoax. —**hoax′er** *n.*

hob[1] (hŏb) *n.* A shelf at the back or side of a fireplace for keeping food warm. [First written down in 1511 in Modern English and spelled *hubbe*.]

hob[2] (hŏb) *n.* *Chiefly British.* **1.** A hobgoblin; an elf. **2.** Mischievous behavior. [First written down about 1460 in Middle English and spelled *Hob*, a nickname for Robert.]

hob•ble (**hŏb′**əl) *v.* **hob•bled, hob•bling, hob•bles.** —*intr.* To walk with difficulty; limp: *The patient hobbled along with one leg in a cast.* —*tr.* **1.** To put a rope or strap around the legs of (an animal) to hamper but not prevent movement. **2.** To impede or hinder: *Quarreling hobbled the efforts of the committee to reach a decision.* —*n.* **1.** An awkward walk or a limp. **2.** A rope or strap used to hobble an animal.

hob•by (**hŏb′**ē) *n., pl.* **hob•bies.** An activity, such as collecting stamps or gardening, that is outside one's regular occupation and is engaged in for pleasure. —**hob′by•ist** *n.*

hob•by•horse (**hŏb′**ē hôrs′) *n.* **1.** A toy made of a stick with an imitation of a horse's head on one end. **2.** A rocking horse.

hob•gob•lin (**hŏb′**gŏb′lĭn) *n.* **1.** A mischievous or troublesome elf; a goblin. **2.** A source of fear or dread.

hob•nail (**hŏb′**nāl′) *n.* A short nail with a thick head that is used to protect the soles of shoes or boots.

hob•nob (**hŏb′**nŏb′) *intr.v.* **hob•nobbed, hob•nob•bing, hob•nobs.** To meet, talk, or spend time together in a friendly familiar manner: *hobnobbing with friends in the park.*

ho•bo (**hō′**bō) *n., pl.* **ho•boes** or **ho•bos.** A person who wanders from place to place and does odd jobs or begs for a living.

Ho Chi Minh (**hō′ chē′ mĭn′**). 1890–1969. Vietnamese leader and first president of North Vietnam (1954–1969).

Ho Chi Minh City (**hō′ chē′ mĭn′**). Formerly **Sai•gon** (sī **gŏn′**). The largest city of Vietnam, in the southern part of the country near the South China Sea. It is built on the site of an ancient Khmer settlement. Population, 2,441,185.

hock[1] (hŏk) *n.* The joint of the hind leg of a horse or other animal having hoofs, corresponding to the human ankle. [First written down about 1410 in Middle English and spelled *hokke*, from Old English *hōh*, heel.]

hock[2] (hŏk) *tr.v.* **hocked, hock•ing, hocks.** *Slang.* To pawn: *I hocked my ring for some cash.* [First written down in 1859 in Modern English, probably from Dutch *hok*, prison.]

hock•ey (**hŏk′**ē) *n.* **1.** Ice hockey. **2.** Field hockey.

ho•cus-po•cus (hō′kəs **pō′**kəs) *n.* **1.** Meaningless syllables or words used in performing magic tricks. **2.** Meaningless speech or behavior used to deceive: *the hocus-pocus of a swindler.*

hod (hŏd) *n.* **1.** A trough fastened to a long handle and carried over the shoulder for moving bricks, cement, or mortar. **2.** A coal scuttle.

hive

Beehive

hobbyhorse

hockey

Ice hockey

ă	pat	oi	boy
ā	pay	ou	out
âr	care	o͝o	took
ä	father	o͞o	boot
ĕ	pet	ŭ	cut
ē	be	ûr	urge
ĭ	pit	th	thin
ī	pie	*th*	this
îr	pier	hw	whoop
ŏ	pot	zh	vision
ō	toe	ə	about
ô	paw	N	*French* bon

Dorothy Hodgkin

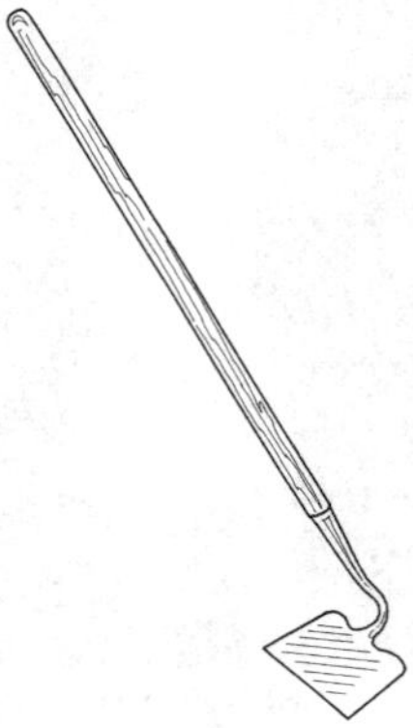

hoe
Garden hoe

Billie Holiday

Regional Note: hollow

One feature of English spoken in parts of the South is its pronunciation of the final syllable in words such as *hollow*, *window*, and *potato* as [-ər]. The spellings *holler*, *winder*, and *tater* reflect this kind of pronunciation.

hodge•podge (hŏj′pŏj′) *n.* A mixture of various things; a jumble: *a hodge-podge of items in a desk drawer.* [First written down in 1381 in Middle English and spelled *ochepot*, from Old French *hochepot*, stew.]

Hodg•kin (hŏj′kĭn), **Dorothy Mary Crowfoot.** Born 1910. Egyptian-born British chemist who won a 1964 Nobel Prize for her work in combating anemia.

hoe (hō) *n.* A tool with a flat blade on a long handle, used to loosen the soil and weed around plants. —*v.* **hoed, hoe•ing, hoes.** —*tr.* To weed or dig up with a hoe: *We hoed the garden.* —*intr.* To use a hoe: *We hoed for an hour.* **—ho′er** *n.*

❑ *These sound alike:* **hoe, ho** (expression of surprise).

hoe•cake (hō′kāk′) *n.* A bread made of cornmeal.

hoe•down (hō′doun′) *n.* **1.** A square dance. **2.** A party where there is square-dancing. **3.** The music for a square dance.

hog (hôg *or* hŏg) *n.* **1.** Any of various pigs, especially a full-grown pig raised for meat. **2.** A greedy, selfish, or filthy person. —*tr.v.* **hogged, hog•ging, hogs.** *Informal.* To take more than one's fair share of: *Some thoughtless drivers hog the road.*

ho•gan (hō′gän′ *or* hō′gən) *n.* A Navajo dwelling usually built of logs and covered with earth. [First written down in 1871 in American English, from Navajo *hooghan.*]

hog•gish (hô′gĭsh *or* hŏg′ĭsh) *adj.* **1.** Very greedy or selfish. **2.** Very dirty; filthy. **—hog′gish•ly** *adv.* **—hog′gish•ness** *n.*

hog•nose snake (hôg′nōz′ *or* hŏg′nōz′) *n.* Any of several nonpoisonous North American snakes having a thick body and an upturned snout.

hogs•head (hôgz′hĕd′ *or* hŏgz′hĕd′) *n.* **1.** A large barrel or cask. In the United States, a hoghead holds from 62 to 140 gallons (238 to 530 liters). **2.** A liquid measure equal to 63 gallons (238 liters).

hog-tie (hôg′tī′ *or* hŏg′tī′) *tr.v.* **hog-tied, hog-tie•ing** or **hog-ty•ing, hog-ties. 1.** To tie together the legs or feet of: *Cowhands usually hog-tie cattle to brand them.* **2.** To restrain in movement or disrupt in action; hamper: *The legislature was hog-tied in lengthy debate.*

hog•wash (hôg′wŏsh′ *or* hôg′wôsh′ *or* hŏg′wŏsh′ *or* hŏg′wôsh′) *n.* **1.** Worthless or ridiculous speech or writing; nonsense. **2.** Garbage fed to hogs.

hoi pol•loi (hoi′ pə loi′) *n.* The common people; the masses.

hoist (hoist) *tr.v.* **hoist•ed, hoist•ing, hoists.** To raise or haul up usually with the help of a pulley or machinery: *A tall crane hoisted bricks to the top of the new building.* —*n.* **1.** A device for hoisting, as a crane, winch, or rope and pulley. **2.** A pull or lift: *Let's give the log a hoist onto the wagon.*

Hok•kai•do (hŏ kī′dō). An island of Japan north of Honshu. Hokkaido became part of Japan about 1600.

hold¹ (hōld) *v.* **held** (hĕld), **hold•ing, holds.** —*tr.* **1.** To hold and keep in one's grasp: *The baby can hold a rattle now.* **2.** To keep from moving or getting away: *He held the dog by a leash.* **3.** To restrain, stop, or control: *Hold your tongue!* **4.** To keep in prison or custody: *The suspect is being held in the county jail.* **5.** To occupy by force: *The army held the town for a month.* **6.** To have or take as contents; contain: *This box holds a dozen eggs.* **7.** To support; bear: *Will that bridge hold such a heavy load?* **8.** To have in one's possession: *That family holds hundreds of acres of land.* **9.** To have as a position or privilege: *Thomas Jefferson held the office of President for two terms.* **10.** To have as an achievement: *She holds the school record for diving.* **11.** To carry on; engage in: *Hold elections; hold a conversation.* **12.** To keep or capture the attention or interest of: *The speaker held the audience spellbound.* **13.** To keep in the mind: *The teacher holds a high opinion of this class.* **14.** To consider; judge: *That painting was held to be the best.* **15.** To state or affirm: *The court holds that the law is not constitutional.* —*intr.* **1.** To continue in a state or condition; last: *The good weather held for two weeks.* **2.** To remain firm or secure: *The knot held against the strain.* **3.** To continue in the same direction: *The ship held to a southerly course.* **4.** To be true or correct: *The theory holds in all cases.* —*n.* **1.** The act or a means of grasping: *keep a firm hold on the handle.* **2.** Something that may be grasped or used for support: *The rocks had many holds for climbers.* **3.** A very strong influence or power: *England's hold over the American colonies ended with the Revolution.* **4.** In music, a symbol over or under a note or a rest to show that it should be held for a longer time. ***—idioms.*** **get hold of. 1.** To get possession of; find: *Where can I get hold of that magazine?* **2.** To communicate with, especially by telephone: *I tried to get hold of you.* **3.** To gain control of: *Get hold of yourself.* **hold down.** To work at and keep: *hold down a job.* **hold forth.** To talk at great length; make a long speech. **hold off.** To delay or wait: *I hope the rain holds off until after the picnic.* **hold on. 1.** To keep a grip; cling. **2.** To continue to do something: *He held on arguing until we were angry.* **3.** To stop or wait for a person or thing: *Hold on a minute.* **hold (one's) own.** To do well despite difficulty. **hold out. 1.** To last: *How long will our water supply hold out?* **2.** To continue to resist: *The strikers held out against the management.* **hold over. 1.** To delay or postpone. **2.** To keep for an additional period of time: *The play was held over for another week.* **hold up. 1.** To stop or delay. **2.** To remain in good condition; function well: *This car should hold up for many years.* **3.** To show as an example: *The essay was held up as an example of good writing.* **4.** To rob by threatening with harm or force. [First written down before 855 in Old English and spelled *haldan.*]

hold² (hōld) *n.* The lower inside part of a ship or an aircraft, where cargo is stored. [First written down in 1591 in Modern English, from Middle English *hole*, husk, hull of a ship, from Old English *hulu.*]

hold•er (hōl′dər) *n.* **1.** A person who holds, owns, or possesses something: *a ticket holder; a job holder.* **2.** A device for holding something: *a napkin holder.*

hold•ing (hōl′dĭng) *n.* **1.** Legally owned property, such as land, stocks, or bonds. Often used in the plural: *has huge holdings in the oil industry.* **2.** In sports, an illegal hampering of an opponent's movements with the hands or arms.

holding company *n.* A company that is formed to own stocks and bonds in other companies, usually for the purpose of controlling them.

hold•up (hōld′ŭp′) *n.* **1.** A stopping of progress or activity; a delay: *a holdup in production.* **2.** A robbery committed by an armed person.

hole (hōl) *n.* **1.** An opening or open place; a gap or space: *wear a hole in the elbow of a sweater; a hole in a fence.* **2.** A hollowed place in something solid; a cavity or pit: *dig a hole to plant the tree.* **3.** An animal's hollowed-out shelter, such as a burrow: *a mouse's hole in the wall.* **4.** An ugly, dirty, or depressing dwelling; a hovel. **5.** A bad or troublesome situation; a difficulty: *help a friend out of a hole.* **6.** A fault or defect: *Let's find the holes in that argument.* **7.a.** In golf, one of the small cups into which the ball must be hit. **b.** One of the 9 or 18 divisions of a golf course. —*tr.v.* **holed, hol•ing, holes. 1.** To put or punch a hole or holes in: *hole paper for a*

notebook. **2.** To hit (a golf ball) into the hole. ***—idiom.* hole up.** To sleep, hide, or take shelter in or as if in a burrow or other shelter: *The bear has holed up for the winter.* [First written down about 700 in Old English and spelled *hol.*]
❑ *These sound alike:* **hole, whole** (complete).

hol•i•day (hŏl′ĭ dā′) *n.* **1.** A day on which general business activity is stopped to commemorate or celebrate a particular event. **2.** *Chiefly British.* A period of time for relaxing away from work; a vacation. **3.** A religious feast day; a holy day. [First written down about 950 in Old English and spelled *hālig dæg,* holy day.]

Hol•i•day (hŏl′ĭ dā′), **Eleanora.** Known as "Billie." 1915–1959. American singer who was the leading female jazz vocalist of her time.

ho•li•ness (hō′lē nĭs) *n.* **1.** The condition or quality of being holy. **2. Holiness.** Used as a title for the pope.

ho•lis•tic (hō lĭs′tĭk) *adj.* Emphasizing the importance of the whole of something over any one of its parts: *holistic medicine.*

Hol•land (hŏl′ənd). The Netherlands.

hol•ler (hŏl′ər) *tr. & intr.v.* **hol•lered, hol•ler•ing, hol•lers.** To yell or shout: *Don't holler at me. She hollered a greeting to friends across the street.* See Synonyms at **shout.** *—n.* A shout or yell.

hol•low (hŏl′ō) *adj.* **hol•low•er, hol•low•est. 1.** Having a space or opening inside: *a hollow log.* **2.** Shaped like a bowl or cup; concave or indented: *A puddle always forms in the hollow spot in the back yard.* **3.** Echoing as if coming from an empty place: *the hollow sound of far-off thunder.* **4.** Not true or sincere; empty: *a hollow promise.* *—n.* **1.** An opening or a space; a hole: *The rabbits made a hollow at the foot of the tree.* **2.** A small valley. *—tr.v.* **hol•lowed, hol•low•ing, hol•lows. 1.** To make hollow: *hollow out a pumpkin.* **2.** To scoop or form by making into the shape of a bowl or cup: *The turtle hollowed out a nest in the sand.* [First written down before 1300 in Middle English and spelled *holeh,* from Old English *holh,* hole, burrow.] **—hol′low•ly** *adv.* **—hol′low•ness** *n.* —See Note.

hol•ly (hŏl′ē) *n., pl.* **hol•lies. 1.** Any of numerous shrubs or trees having evergreen leaves with prickly edges and bright-red berries. **2.** Sprigs or branches of such a shrub or tree, traditionally used as Christmas decorations. [First written down about 958 in Old English and spelled *holegn.*]

hol•ly•hock (hŏl′ē hŏk′) *n.* A tall garden plant having showy, variously colored flowers that grow along a hairy stem.

Hol•ly•wood (hŏl′ē wo͝od′). A district of Los Angeles, California. It has long been a film and entertainment center.

Holmes (hōmz *or* hōlmz), **Oliver Wendell.** 1809–1894. American physician and writer whose works include *The Autocrat of the Breakfast Table* (1858).

Holmes, Oliver Wendell, Jr. 1841–1935. American jurist who served as an associate justice of the U.S. Supreme Court (1902–1932).

hol•mi•um (hŏl′mē əm) *n. Symbol* **Ho** A soft, metallic, rare-earth element found in certain minerals. Atomic number 67. See table at **element.** [First written down in 1879 in Modern English, after *Holmia* (Stockholm), Sweden.]

hol•o•caust (hŏl′ə kôst′ *or* hō′lə kôst′) *n.* **1.** Great or total destruction by fire. **2.** Widespread destruction. **3.** A sacrificial offering that is entirely consumed by flames. **4. Holocaust.** The mass killing of European Jews and others by the Nazis during World War II.

Hol•o•cene (hŏl′ə sēn′ *or* hō′lə sēn′) *adj.* Of, belonging to, or being the geologic time epoch of the second Quaternary Period, extending from the end of the Pleistocene epoch to the present. See table at **geologic time.** *—n.* The Holocene Epoch or its series of rocks.

hol•o•gram (hŏl′ə grăm′ *or* hō′lə grăm′) *n.* The photographic record of an image produced by holography.

hol•o•graph (hŏl′ə grăf′ *or* hō′lə grăf′) *n.* A document, as a letter, will, or manuscript, for example, written entirely in the handwriting of the person who signs it.

ho•log•raph•y (hō lŏg′rə fē) *n.* A method of producing a three-dimensional image of an object by using a divided beam of light from a laser. The laser light is directed by mirrors so that one beam reflects off the object onto a photographic plate or film and the other beam illuminates the plate or film at the same time.

Hol•stein (hōl′stīn′ *or* hōl′stēn′) *n.* Any of a breed of black-and-white cattle raised for milk and milk products.

hol•ster (hōl′stər) *n.* A case to hold a pistol or tools, usually made of leather and worn on a belt.

ho•ly (hō′lē) *adj.* **ho•li•er, ho•li•est. 1.** Belonging to, coming from, or associated with a divine power; sacred: *The Bible and the Koran are holy books.* **2.** Living according to highly moral or religious principles; saintly: *a holy person.* **3.** Regarded with special respect or awe; revered: *To music lovers this concert hall is a holy place.* [First written down about 725 in Old English and spelled *hālig.*]
❑ *These sound alike:* **holy, wholly** (completely).

Holy Ark *n.* The cabinet in a synagogue in which the scrolls of the Torah are kept.

Holy Communion *n.* The Christian rite commemorating Jesus's last supper, in which bread and wine or juice are blessed and eaten in remembrance of Jesus's death.

holy day *n.* A day of a special religious observance.

Holy Father *n.* Used as a title and form of address for the pope.

Holy Ghost *n.* The Holy Spirit.

Holy Grail (grāl) *n.* The Grail.

Holy Land. The biblical region of Palestine.

holy of ho•lies (hō′lēz) *n.* **1.** The innermost sanctuary of the ancient Temple in Jerusalem, in which the Ark of the Covenant was kept. **2.** A sacred or revered place.

Holy Ro•man Empire (rō′mən). A European empire that began in 962 and lasted until 1806. By 1273 the empire consisted primarily of regions in Austria and Spain.

Holy See *n.* The official position, authority, or court of the pope.

Holy Spirit *n.* The third person of the Christian Trinity.

ho•ly•stone (hō′lē stōn′) *n.* A piece of soft sandstone used for scouring the wooden decks of a ship. *—tr.v.* **ho•ly•stoned, ho•ly•ston•ing, ho•ly•stones.** To scrub or scour with a holystone.

Holy Thursday *n.* Maundy Thursday.

holy water *n.* Water blessed by a priest and used for baptism and in other religious services.

Holy Week *n.* The week before Easter.

Holy Writ *n.* The Bible.

hom•age (hŏm′ĭj *or* ŏm′ĭj) *n.* **1.** Special honor or respect; reverence: *The President paid homage to the poet by quoting her in his speech.* **2.** The acknowledgment of allegiance made by a vassal to a lord in a ceremony under feudal law. [First written down about 1225 in Middle English, from Old French, probably from Latin *homō,* person, man.]

hom•bre (ŏm′brā′ *or* ŏm′brē) *n. Slang.* A man; a fellow. [First written down in 1846 in American English, from Spanish, from Latin *homō.*]

home (hōm) *n.* **1.** A place in which a person lives:

hollyhock

Oliver Wendell Holmes

holster
Tool holster

ă	pat	oi	boy
ā	pay	ou	out
âr	care	o͝o	took
ä	father	o͞o	boot
ĕ	pet	ŭ	cut
ē	be	ûr	urge
ĭ	pit	th	thin
ī	pie	*th*	this
îr	pier	hw	whoop
ŏ	pot	zh	vision
ō	toe	ə	about
ô	paw	N	*French* bon

Our home is in that apartment building. **2.** A group of people, especially a family, that lives together in a dwelling place; a household: *Those happy children come from a loving home.* **3.** The place in which one was born, grew up, or has lived a long time: *No matter where I live, I will always think of Montana as my home.* **4.** The region or place in which an animal, a plant, or a thing is commonly found; a native habitat: *The forest is the home of many plants and animals.* **5.** A place where people are cared for: *a home for the elderly.* **6.** The place, such as a city or stadium, where a sports team originates or plays most of its games. **7.** In certain games, a goal or place of safety that the players try to reach. **8.** In baseball, home plate. *—adj.* **1.** Of, relating to, or taking place in a home: *home life; home cooking.* **2.** Played on the grounds where a team originates or plays most of its games: *a home game.* *—adv.* **1.** At, to, or toward one's home: *The children raced home from school.* **2.** On or into the point or mark at which something is directed: *The arrow struck home.* **3.** To the center or heart of something; deeply: *Their arguments struck home.* *—intr.v.* **homed, hom•ing, homes. 1.** To return home. **2.** To be guided to a destination or target: *These birds home in on their nesting grounds each spring.* ***—idiom.* at home. 1.** In one's home or country: *While abroad, we read about problems at home.* **2.** Comfortable and relaxed; at ease: *felt at home with strangers.* [First written down about 725 in Old English and spelled *hām*.]

home base *n.* **1.** A goal toward which players of certain games try to make progress. **2.** Home plate. **3.** A center of operations; a headquarters.

home•bod•y (**hōm′**bŏd′ē) *n.* A person whose interests and pleasures lie in the home.

home•com•ing (**hōm′**kŭm′ĭng) *n.* **1.** A return to one's home: *The soldier's homecoming was a joyous occasion.* **2.** In some high schools and colleges, a yearly celebration held for returning graduates.

home economics *n. (used with a singular or plural verb).* The science and art of managing a household. **—home economist** *n.*

home•grown (**hōm′grōn′**) *adj.* **1.** Made or grown at home: *homegrown tomatoes from our garden.* **2.** Coming from or characteristic of a particular place: *homegrown country music.*

home•land (**hōm′**lănd′) *n.* **1.** The country in which one was born or has lived for a long time. **2.** A country that one regards as one's true home.

home•less (**hōm′**lĭs) *adj.* Having no home or haven. *—n. (used with a plural verb).* People who have no home considered as a group.

home•ly (**hōm′**lē) *adj.* **home•li•er, home•li•est. 1.** Not attractive or good-looking. **2.** Simple and plain: *a homely manner.* **—home′li•ness** *n.*

home•made (**hōm′mād′**) *adj.* **1.** Made at home: *delicious homemade bread.* **2.** Crudely or simply made, as if made at home: *rough homemade furniture.*

home•mak•er (**hōm′**mā′kər) *n.* A person who manages a household. **—home′mak′ing** *n.*

ho•me•o•sta•sis (hō′mē ō **stā′**sĭs) *n.* The ability or tendency of an organism or a cell to maintain the internal balance of its functions, such as steady temperature, regardless of outside conditions.

home plate *n.* In baseball, the base at which the batter stands, which must be touched by a runner in order to score a run.

hom•er (**hō′**mər) *n.* A home run. *—intr.v.* **ho•mer•ed, ho•mer•ing, ho•mers.** To hit a home run.

Ho•mer (**hō′**mər). Flourished about 850 B.C. Greek epic poet. The *Iliad* and the *Odyssey* are attributed to him.

Homer

home•room (**hōm′**ro͞om′ *or* **hōm′**ro͝om′) *n.* A classroom in which a group of pupils are required to gather each day, as for attendance.

home run *n.* In baseball, a hit that allows the batter to touch all the bases and score a run.

home•sick (**hōm′**sĭk′) *adj.* Longing for home. **—home′sick′ness** *n.*

home•spun (**hōm′**spŭn′) *adj.* **1.** Spun or woven at home: *homespun cloth.* **2.** Made of homespun cloth: *a homespun shirt.* **3.** Plain and simple; folksy: *homespun humor.* *—n.* **1.** A plain coarse cloth woven from yarn that is spun at home. **2.** A similar cloth.

home•stead (**hōm′**stĕd′) *n.* **1.** A house, especially a farmhouse or similar dwelling, together with the land and buildings belonging to it. **2.** A piece of land given to a settler by the U.S. government, usually with conditions such as clearing and working the land for five years. *—intr.v.* **home•stead•ed, home•stead•ing, home•steads.** To settle on land claimed as a homestead. **—home′stead′er** *n.*

home•stretch (**hōm′**strĕch′) *n.* **1.** The part of a racetrack from the last turn to the finish line. **2.** The last stage of something: *I am in the homestretch of writing this report.*

home•ward (**hōm′**wərd) *adv. & adj.* Toward or at home: *They turned their canoe and paddled homeward; the homeward journey.* **—home′wards** *adv.*

home•work (**hōm′**wûrk′) *n.* **1.** Work that is done at home. **2.** School assignments that are done at home or outside the classroom.

hom•ey (**hō′**mē) *adj.* **hom•i•er, hom•i•est.** *Informal.* Suggesting a home; pleasant, cheerful, and comfortable: *a restaurant with a homey atmosphere.*

hom•i•cide (**hŏm′**ĭ sīd′ *or* **hō′**mĭ sīd′) *n.* **1.** The killing of one person by another. **2.** A person who kills another person. [First written down about 1230 in Middle English, from Latin *homicīdium*.] **—hom′i•cid′al** *adj.*

hom•i•ly (**hŏm′**ə lē) *n., pl.* **hom•i•lies. 1.** A sermon, especially one on practical matters, delivered to a congregation. **2.** A tiresome lecture or article that urges virtuous behavior.

hom•ing pigeon (**hō′**mĭng) *n.* A pigeon trained to fly back to its home roost.

hom•i•nid (**hŏm′**ə nĭd) *n.* A member of the family of primates that includes human beings. Human beings are the only living hominids today. *—adj.* Being a hominid.

hom•i•ny (**hŏm′**ə nē) *n.* Hulled and dried kernels of corn, ground into a coarse white meal and cooked by boiling. [First written down in 1629 in American English, from Virginia Algonquian *uskatahomen*.]

homo– or **hom–** *pref.* A prefix that means same or similar: *homogeneous.*

ho•mo•ge•ne•i•ty (hō′mə jə **nē′**ĭ tē *or* hō′mə jə **nā′**ĭ tē) *n., pl.* **ho•mo•ge•ne•i•ties.** The state or quality of being homogeneous.

ho•mo•ge•ne•ous (hō′mə **jē′**nē əs *or* hō′mə **jēn′**yəs) *adj.* **1.** Of the same or similar kind; uniform throughout: *a homogeneous class of students having about the same ability.* **2.** Made up of similar parts; having similar elements: *a housing development of homogeneous architecture.* **—ho′mo•ge′ne•ous•ly** *adv.* **—ho′mo•ge′ne•ous•ness** *n.*

ho•mog•e•nize (hə **mŏj′**ə nīz′) *tr.v.* **ho•mog•e•nized, ho•mog•e•niz•ing, ho•mog•e•niz•es. 1.** To make homogeneous or uniform throughout. **2.** To reduce to particles and disperse throughout a fluid: *homogenize paint.* **3.** To make (milk) uniform in consistency by reducing the fat to small globules. **—ho•mog′e•ni•za′tion** (hə mŏj′ə nĭ **zā′**shən) *n.*

hom•o•graph (**hŏm′**ə grăf′ *or* **hō′**mə grăf′) *n.* A word that has the same spelling as another word but differs in meaning, origin, and sometimes in pronunciation; for example, *ring* (circle) and *ring* (sound), and *bass* (fish) and *bass* (deep tone) are homographs. [First written down in 1810 in Modern English : Greek *homos*, same + Greek *graphein*, to write.]

ho•mol•o•gous (hə mŏl′ə gəs) *adj.* **1.** Similar in structure and evolutionary origin, as the arm of a human being and the flipper of a seal. **2.** Of or indicating either of a pair of chromosomes whose genes are arranged in the same way. Homologous chromosomes contain genes for the same traits.

hom•o•nym (hŏm′ə nĭm′ *or* hō′mə nĭm′) *n.* A word that has the same sound and sometimes the same spelling as another word but a different meaning and origin; for example, *die* (stop living), *die* (stamping), and *dye* (color) are all homonyms. [First written down in 1697 in Modern English : Greek *homos*, same + Greek *onuma*, name.] —**ho•mon′y•mous** (hō mŏn′ə məs *or* hə mŏn′ə məs) *adj.*

hom•o•phone (hŏm′ə fōn′ *or* hō′mə fōn′) *n.* A word that has the same sound as another word but differs in spelling, meaning, and origin; for example, *for, fore,* and *four* are homophones. [First written down in 1843 in Modern English : Greek *homos*, same + Greek *phōnē*, sound.] —**ho•moph′o•nous** (hō mŏf′ə nəs *or* hə mŏf′ə nəs) *adj.*

ho•mop•ter•ous (hō mŏp′tər əs) *adj.* Of or related to insects having mouths adapted for piercing and sucking, as cicadas.

Ho•mo sa•pi•ens (hō′mō sā′pē ənz) *n.* The modern species of human beings. [First written down in 1802 in Modern English : Latin *homō*, person, man + Latin *sapiēns*, discerning.]

ho•mo•sex•u•al (hō′mə sĕk′sho͞o əl) *adj.* Relating to or having sexual feelings for members of the same sex. —*n.* A homosexual person.

ho•mo•sex•u•al•i•ty (hō′mə sĕk′sho͞o ăl′ĭ tē) *n.* **1.** Sexual interest in or attraction to persons of the same sex. **2.** Sexual relations with a person of the same sex.

ho•mo•zy•gous (hō′mō zī′gəs *or* hŏm′ə zī′gəs) *adj.* Having two like genes for a hereditary trait such as tallness.

Hon. *abbr.* An abbreviation of: **1.** Honorable. **2.** Honorary.

Hon•du•ras (hŏn do͝or′əs *or* hŏn dyo͝or′əs). A country of northern Central America east of Guatemala. It was originally inhabited by a Mayan civilization and gained its independence from Spain in 1821. Tegucigalpa is the capital and the largest city. Population, 4,092,000.

hone (hōn) *n.* A fine-grained stone used to sharpen knives or other sharp tools. —*tr.v.* **honed, hon•ing, hones. 1.** To sharpen (a knife or other sharp tool) on a fine-grained stone. **2.** To make more effective: *Authors must hone their skills by writing a great deal.* [First written down in 939 in Old English and spelled *hān*, stone.]

hon•est (ŏn′ĭst) *adj.* **1.** Not lying, stealing, or cheating; trustworthy: *The bank teller is an honest worker.* **2.** Done or obtained without lying, cheating, or stealing: *an honest profit.* **3.** Not hiding anything; frank; straightforward; sincere: *an honest opinion.* **4.** Being just what it appears to be; not false; true; genuine: *a scale certified to give honest weight.* [First written down before 1300 in Middle English, from Latin *honestus*, honorable.] —**hon′est•ly** *adv.*

hon•es•ty (ŏn′ĭ stē) *n., pl.* **hon•es•ties.** The quality of being honest; truthfulness, sincerity, or genuineness: *No one questioned the honesty of the judge's statement.*

hon•ey (hŭn′ē) *n., pl.* **hon•eys. 1.** A sweet, thick, syrupy substance made by bees from the nectar of flowers and used as food. **2.** Sweetness; pleasantness. **3.** *Informal.* Sweetheart; dear. —*tr.v.* **hon•eyed** or **hon•ied** (hŭn′ēd), **hon•ey•ing, hon•eys. 1.** To sweeten with or as if with honey: *The baker honeyed the buns on top.* **2.** To coax or flatter with sweet talk: *You can't honey me into believing such a tall tale.* [First written down about 700 in Old English and spelled *hunig.*]

hon•ey•bee (hŭn′ē bē′) *n.* Any of several bees that produce honey, especially a domesticated bee raised commercially for its honey and beeswax.

hon•ey•comb (hŭn′ē kōm′) *n.* **1.** A wax structure having many small six-sided compartments, used by honeybees to hold honey, pollen, and eggs. **2.** Something full of openings or spaces like those in a honeycomb: *The building was a honeycomb of small rooms and passages.* —*tr.v.* **hon•ey•combed, hon•ey•comb•ing, hon•ey•combs.** To fill with openings or spaces like those in a honeycomb: *Tiny shops and stalls honeycombed the village.*

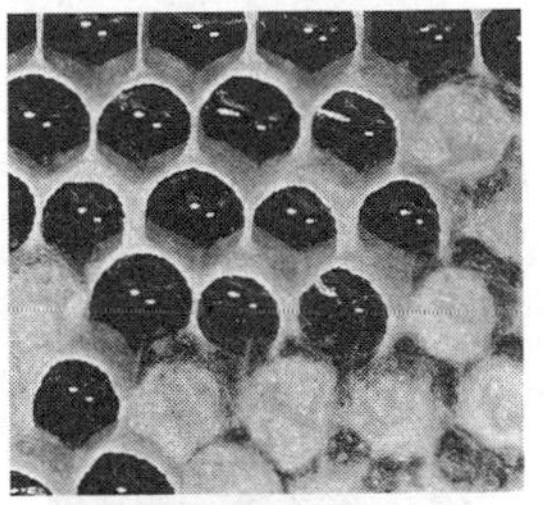

honeycomb
Close-up of hexagon-shaped cells

hon•ey•dew (hŭn′ē do͞o′ *or* hŭn′ē dyo͞o′) *n.* **1.** A sweet sticky substance given off by aphids and certain other insects. **2.** A sweet sticky substance sometimes given off by the leaves of certain plants in hot weather. **3.** A honeydew melon.

honeydew melon *n.* A melon having a smooth whitish rind and sweet green flesh.

hon•eyed also **hon•ied** (hŭn′ēd) *adj.* **1.** Containing or sweetened with honey. **2.** Intended to coax or please: *honeyed words.*

hon•ey•moon (hŭn′ē mo͞on′) *n.* **1.** A trip or vacation taken by a newly married couple. **2.** A period of harmony early in a relationship: *the honeymoon between the new President and Congress.* —*intr.v.* **hon•ey•mooned, hon•ey•moon•ing, hon•ey•moons.** To have or spend a honeymoon. —**hon′ey•moon′er** *n.*

hon•ey•suck•le (hŭn′ē sŭk′əl) *n.* Any of various vines or shrubs having tubular, often fragrant yellowish, white, or pink flowers.

Hong Kong (hŏng′kŏng′ *or* hông′kông′). A British colony on the southeast coast of China southeast of Guangzhou, including **Hong Kong Island** and adjacent areas. The colony will pass to China in 1997. Capital, Victoria. Population, 5,021,066.

Ho•ni•a•ra (hō′nē är′ə). The capital of the Solomon Islands, in the Pacific Ocean east of the island of New Guinea. Population, 16,125.

hon•ied (hŭn′ēd) *v.* A past tense and a past participle of **honey.** —*adj.* Variant of **honeyed.**

honk (hôngk *or* hŏngk) *n.* A loud harsh sound such as that made by a goose or an automobile horn. —*intr. & tr.v.* **honked, honk•ing, honks.** To make or cause to make a honk: *A flock of geese honked overhead. The impatient driver honked the car horn.* —**honk′er** *n.*

Hon•o•lu•lu (hŏn′ə lo͞o′lo͞o). The capital and largest city of Hawaii, on the southeast coast of Oahu. Settlement of the area began in 1816. Population, 365,272.

hon•or (ŏn′ər) *n.* **1.** Special respect or high regard: *The award is given to show honor to great film directors.* **2.** A source of credit or mark of distinction: *a great writer who is an honor to the profession.* **3.** An act that shows respect or high regard: *a hero's funeral with full honors.* **4.** A sense of what is right; high principles; integrity: *A person of honor does not lie, cheat, or steal.* **5.** Good name or reputation: *I must defend my honor.* **6.** Often **Honor.** Used as a title and form of address for certain officials, such as judges and mayors: *Her honor the mayor.* **7. honors.** Special recognition of a student for unusual achievement: *graduated from high school with honors.* —*tr.v.* **hon•ored, hon•or•ing, hon•ors. 1.** To show special respect or recognition to; treat with honor: *We honored the volunteers with a party.* **2.** To think highly of; esteem: *a doctor*

ă	pat	oi	boy
ā	pay	ou	out
âr	care	o͝o	took
ä	father	o͞o	boot
ĕ	pet	ŭ	cut
ē	be	ûr	urge
ĭ	pit	th	thin
ī	pie	*th*	this
îr	pier	hw	whoop
ŏ	pot	zh	vision
ō	toe	ə	about
ô	paw	N	*French* bon

hoop skirt

Herbert Hoover

Usage: **hopefully**

Many people use **hopefully** as an adverb modifying a sentence, as in *Hopefully we will get to leave early today*. People who are sensitive about how language is used did not like this way of using the word when it first came to their attention, and many still do not like it. In any case it is wise to avoid using **hopefully** too much.

who was honored everywhere for achievements in medicine. **3.** To accept as payment: *honor a check.* ***—idiom.* on (one's) honor.** Under a solemn pledge to be truthful and do what is right. [First written down before 1200 in Middle English and spelled *onur*, from Latin *honor*.]

hon•or•a•ble (ŏn′ər ə bəl) *adj.* **1.** Deserving honor and respect: *Teaching is an honorable profession.* **2.** Bringing distinction or recognition: *honorable efforts to achieve peace.* **3.** Having or showing a sense of what is right or just: *an honorable person; an honorable solution to a difficult problem.* **4.** Done with or accompanied by marks of honor: *an honorable burial.* **5.** Distinguished; illustrious; great: *an honorable family.* **6.** Often **Honorable.** Used as a title for certain high officials or people of importance. **—hon′or•a•ble•ness** *n.* **—hon′or•a•bly** *adv.*

hon•o•rar•i•um (ŏn′ə râr′ē əm) *n., pl.* **hon•o•rar•i•ums** or **hon•o•rar•i•a** (ŏn′ə râr′ē ə). A payment made to a professional person for services, such as advice or a lecture.

hon•or•ar•y (ŏn′ə rĕr′ē) *adj.* Given or holding as an honor: *an honorary degree from a university.*

honor system *n.* A set of rules by which students are trusted to act properly or honestly without being closely supervised.

hon•our (ŏn′ər) *n. & v. Chiefly British.* Variant of **honor.**

Hon•shu (hŏn′sho͞o). The largest island of Japan, in the central part of the country south-southwest of Hokkaido.

hood[1] (ho͝od) *n.* **1.** A soft covering for the head and neck, often attached to a coat, cape, or robe: *The Inuits wear heavy parkas with hoods attached.* **2.** The hinged metal lid over the engine of an automobile. **3.** The raised metal cover of a ventilator over a stove. **4.** An expanded part or marking on or near an animal's head, as the flaring skin around a cobra's neck. *—tr.v.* **hood•ed, hood•ing, hoods.** To supply or cover with a hood. [First written down about 700 in Old English and spelled *hōd*.] **—hood′like′** *adj.*

hood[2] (ho͝od) *n. Slang.* A hoodlum. [First written down in 1930 in American English, short for *hoodlum*.]

–hood *suff.* A suffix that means: **1.** Condition or quality: *manhood; falsehood.* **2.** A group sharing a certain condition or quality: *sisterhood; priesthood.*

hood•ed (ho͝od′ĭd) *adj.* Covered with or having a hood: *a hooded rider; a hooded cape.*

hood•lum (ho͞od′ləm *or* ho͝od′ləm) *n.* **1.** A gangster or thug. **2.** A tough and aggressive young man. [First written down in 1871 in American English.]

hood•wink (ho͝od′wĭngk′) *tr.v.* **hood•winked, hood•wink•ing, hood•winks.** To deceive or mislead; trick.

hoof (ho͝of *or* ho͞of) *n., pl.* **hoofs** or **hooves** (ho͞ovz, ho͝ovz). **1.** The tough horny covering on the lower part of the foot of certain mammals, such as horses, cattle, deer, and pigs. **2.** The whole foot of such an animal. *—intr.v.* **hoofed, hoof•ing, hoofs.** *Slang.* **1.** To dance, especially to tap-dance. **2.** To go on foot; walk. ***—idiom.* hoof it.** To walk: *We hoofed it into town.* [First written down about 1000 in Old English and spelled *hōf*.]

hoofed (ho͝oft *or* ho͞oft) *adj.* Having hoofs.

hook (ho͝ok) *n.* **1.** A curved or sharply bent piece of metal or other stiff material, used to catch, hold, fasten, or pull something: *Coats hung on hooks in the hall.* **2.** A fishhook. **3.** Something shaped or used like a hook. **4.** A sharp curve or bend, as in a river. **5.** A spit of land with a curved end. **6.** In sports, the flight of a ball that goes to the left when hit by a right-handed player or to the right when hit by a left-handed player. **7.** In boxing, a short swinging blow delivered with a crooked arm. *—v.* **hooked, hook•ing, hooks.** *—tr.* **1.** To catch, hang, or connect with a hook: *hook a tuna while fishing.* **2.** To fasten by means of a hook: *hook a picture on the wall.* **3.** To make (a rug, for example) by looping yarn through a loosely woven material with a hook. **4.** In sports, to hit (a ball) with a hook: *hook a shot in golf.* **5.** To hit with a hook in boxing. *—intr.* **1.** To move, throw, or extend in a curve: *The road hooks toward the river.* **2.** To be fastened by means of a hook: *The gate hooks on the post.* ***—idioms.* by hook or by crook.** By whatever means possible, fair or unfair. **hook up.** To connect or make a connection between: *The electricity was hooked up to the house.* **off the hook.** *Informal.* Free of blame or obligation. [First written down before 700 in Old English and spelled *hōc*.]

hook•ah (ho͝ok′ə) *n.* A smoking pipe used chiefly in countries of the eastern Mediterranean. It has a long tube attached to a container of water that cools the smoke as it is drawn through.

hook and eye *n.* **1.** A fastener for clothes consisting of a small hook and loop which can be linked together. **2.** A latch consisting of a hook that is inserted in a screw eye.

hooked (ho͝okt) *adj.* **1.** Curved or bent like a hook: *the owl's hooked beak.* **2.** Having a hook or hooks: *a hooked spear.* **3.** Made with a hook: *a hooked rug.* **4.** *Slang.* Addicted or devoted to something: *She's hooked on canoeing.*

hook•up (ho͝ok′ŭp′) *n.* **1.** An arrangement of interconnected parts in an electrical or electronic system: *a nationwide radio and television hookup.* **2.** A connection or an arrangement: *a hookup between buyer and seller.*

hook•worm (ho͝ok′wûrm′) *n.* Any of numerous parasitic worms that fasten themselves to the inside wall of the intestines of various animals, including humans.

hook•y (ho͝ok′ē) *n. Informal.* Absence without permission: *play hooky from school.*

hoo•li•gan (ho͞o′lĭ gən) *n. Informal.* A hoodlum.

hoop (ho͞op *or* ho͝op) *n.* **1.** A circular band or ring of wood, metal, bone, or plastic used to hold something together, as the staves of a barrel, or to spread something out, as a piece of embroidery or a fancy skirt. **2.** A ring of wood, plastic, or metal used as a toy. *—tr.v.* **hooped, hoop•ing, hoops.** To bind or fasten together with a hoop or hoops.

❑ *These sound alike:* **hoop, whoop** (shout).

hoop•la (ho͞op′lä′ *or* ho͝op′lä′) *n. Slang.* **1.** Noisy or confusing commotion. **2.** Extravagant publicity.

hoop skirt *n.* A woman's long skirt worn over a framework of connected flexible hoops that keep it spread out.

hoo•ray (ho͞o rā′ *or* hə rā′) *interj., n., & v.* Variant of **hurrah.**

hoot (ho͞ot) *v.* **hoot•ed, hoot•ing, hoots.** *—intr.* **1.** To make the cry of an owl. **2.** To make a shout or loud cry of contempt or disapproval: *Demonstrators hooted at the speaker.* *—tr.* **1.** To shout at or drive away with scornful cries or jeers: *The hecklers hooted the candidate off the platform.* **2.** To express by hooting: *The fans hooted their disappointment.* *—n.* **1.** The cry of an owl. **2.** A sound similar to this, especially the sound of a horn. **3.** A shout of scorn or disapproval. ***—idiom.* give a hoot** or **care a hoot.** To be completely indifferent to: *I don't give a hoot if it rains.*

hoot•en•an•ny (ho͞ot′n ăn′ē) *n., pl.* **hoot•en•an•nies.** An informal performance by folk singers, usually with the audience joining in.

Hoo•ver (ho͞o′vər), **Herbert Clark.** 1874–1964. The

31st President of the United States (1929–1933).

hooves (ho͝ovz *or* ho͞ovz) *n.* A plural of **hoof.**

hop[1] (hŏp) *v.* **hopped, hop•ping, hops.** —*intr.* **1.** To move with light springing leaps or skips: *The frightened rabbit hopped away.* **2.** To jump on one foot. —*tr.* **1.** To jump over: *hopped the fence in a single bound.* **2.** *Informal.* To jump aboard: *hop a freight train.* —*n.* **1.** A hopping motion; a springy jump: *The squirrel crossed the lawn in short hops.* **2.** A trip, especially by air: *It is a short hop between Boston and New York.* **3.** A rebound; a bounce: *The ball took a bad hop.* [First written down about 1000 in Old English and spelled *hoppian.*]

hop[2] (hŏp) *n.* **1.** A twining vine having green flower clusters that resemble small pine cones. **2. hops.** The dried flowers of this plant, used in making beer. [First written down about 1440 in Middle English and spelled *hoppe*, from Middle Dutch.]

hope (hōp) *v.* **hoped, hop•ing, hopes.** —*intr.* To trust in or wish for a favorable outcome: *I think I can win the race; at least I hope so.* —*tr.* **1.** To look forward to with a feeling of expectation or confidence: *I hope to be there by five o'clock.* See Synonyms at **expect. 2.** To desire very much; wish earnestly: *I hope that I have not misspelled any of the words on the test.* —*n.* **1.** A feeling of confident expectation: *The young composer is full of hope for success.* **2.** A reason for or cause of such a feeling: *A home run is the team's only hope for victory.* **3.** Something that is hoped for or desired: *My hopes of becoming a doctor are unchanged.* [First written down in 971 in Old English and spelled *hopian.*]

hope•ful (**hōp′**fəl) *adj.* **1.** Feeling or showing hope; expectant: *The immigrants arrived hopeful of a better life.* **2.** Inspiring hope; encouraging: *We were gladdened by hopeful signs of peace.* —*n.* A person who wishes to succeed or shows promise of succeeding in something: *Several hopefuls tried out for the lead in the play.* **—hope′ful•ness** *n.*

hope•ful•ly (**hōp′**fə lē) *adv.* **1.** In a hopeful manner. **2.** *Informal.* It is to be hoped. —SEE NOTE.

hope•less (**hōp′**lĭs) *adj.* **1.** Having no hope; despairing: *After many hours of wandering in the forest the lost hikers felt hopeless.* **2.** Offering no hope; bleak: *A long search for my wallet proved hopeless.* **3.** Having no hope of improvement: *My room is a hopeless mess.* **—hope′less•ly** *adv.* **—hope′less•ness** *n.*

Ho•pi (hō′pē) *n., pl.* **Hopi** or **Ho•pis. 1.** A member of a Native American people of northeast Arizona. **2.** The Uto-Aztecan language of this people.

hop•per (**hŏp′**ər) *n.* **1.** A person or thing that hops. **2.** A container having a wide open top and a narrow opening at the bottom through which the contents, such as coal or grain, can be fed into a machine or container.

hop•scotch (**hŏp′**skŏch′) *n.* A children's game in which players toss a small object into the numbered spaces of a pattern of rectangles marked on the ground or pavement and then hop through the spaces to pick up the object and return.

ho•ra (**hôr′**ə) *n.* A traditional dance of Romania and Israel performed by dancers moving around in a circle.

horde (hôrd) *n.* **1.** A large group, crowd, or swarm: *hordes of people at the fair.* **2.** A wandering tribe or group of people: *In 1264 the Mongol hordes invaded China.*

❑ *These sound alike:* **horde, hoard** (store away).

hore•hound (**hôr′**hound′) *n.* **1.** An aromatic plant having woolly whitish leaves that yield a bitter substance used in cough medicine and in flavoring. **2.** An extract, a medicine, or a candy prepared using this plant.

ho•ri•zon (hə **rī′**zən) *n.* **1.** The line along which the earth and sky appear to meet. **2.** The limit of one's experience, knowledge, or interests: *Lack of education often narrows a person's horizons.* [First written down about 1385 in Middle English and spelled *orisonte*, from Greek *horizōn (kuklos)*, limiting (circle).]

hor•i•zon•tal (hôr′ĭ **zŏn′**tl *or* hŏr′ĭ **zŏn′**tl) *adj.* **1.** Parallel to or in the plane of the horizon; level. **2.** Of, relating to, or near the horizon. —*n.* A horizontal line or plane. **—hor′i•zon′tal•ly** *adv.*

hor•mon•al (hôr **mō′**nəl) *adj.* Of, relating to, or caused by a hormone or hormones: *a hormonal imbalance.*

hor•mone (**hôr′**mōn′) *n.* A substance produced by an endocrine gland and carried in the bloodstream to tissues and other organs that it stimulates by chemical action. Hormones control basic bodily processes and functions such as growth and metabolism. [First written down in 1905 in Modern English, from Greek *hormōn*, present participle of *horman*, to urge on.]

horn (hôrn) *n.* **1.** One of the hard bony growths on the heads of cattle, sheep, goats, and other hoofed mammals. **2.** A hard growth, such as an antler or a growth on the head of a giraffe, that resembles a horn. **3.** The hard durable substance that forms the outer covering of the horns of cattle and related animals. **4.** A container made from an animal's horn: *a powder horn.* **5.** Something shaped like a horn, as either end of a new moon or the pommel of a saddle. **6.a.** A wind instrument made of animal horn. **b.** A brass wind instrument, such as a trombone or tuba. **7.** A warning device that produces a loud sound: *an automobile horn.* —*intr.v.* **horned, horn•ing, horns.** *Slang.* To join in without being invited; intrude: *The older children horned in on the game of tag.* [First written down about 725 in Old English.] **—horn′less** *adj.* **—horn′like′** *adj.*

horn
Left: American bighorn
Right: Mountain goat

Horn (hôrn), **Cape.** The southernmost point of South America, in the Tierra del Fuego islands of southern Chile.

horn•bill (**hôrn′**bĭl′) *n.* Any of various birds of Africa and tropical Asia, having a large curved bill often with a horny lump on top.

horn•blende (**hôrn′**blĕnd′) *n.* A common green to black mineral found in many metamorphic and igneous rocks. Iron, calcium, magnesium, and other metals occur in hornblende.

horn•book (**hôrn′**bo͝ok′) *n.* An early primer consisting of a single page, usually with the alphabet on it and protected by a transparent sheet of horn.

horned toad
Texas horned toad

horned (hôrnd) *adj.* Having a horn, horns, or a hornlike growth: *a horned snail.*

horned toad *n.* Any of several small lizards of southwest North America, having spiny projections on the head and body and a short tail.

hor•net (**hôr′**nĭt) *n.* Any of various large stinging wasps that live in colonies and build large papery nests.

horn of plenty *n., pl.* **horns of plenty.** A cornucopia.

horn•pipe (**hôrn′**pīp′) *n.* **1.** A wind instrument made of horn and having a bell. **2.** A lively dance, usually performed by one person and originally popular among sailors. **3.** Music for this dance.

horn•y (**hôr′**nē) *adj.* **horn•i•er, horn•i•est. 1.** Having horns or hornlike projections. **2.** Made of horn or a similar substance: *the horny shell of a lobster.* **3.** Tough and callous: *the horny hands of a mason.*

hor•o•scope (**hôr′**ə skōp′ *or* **hŏr′**ə skōp′) *n.* **1.** The relative position of the planets and stars at a given moment, as the hour of a person's birth, for example. **2.** A prediction, especially of a person's future, based on the position of the planets and stars. [First written down in 1568 in Modern English, from

ă	pat	oi	boy
ā	pay	ou	out
âr	care	o͝o	took
ä	father	o͞o	boot
ĕ	pet	ŭ	cut
ē	be	ûr	urge
ĭ	pit	th	thin
ī	pie	*th*	this
îr	pier	hw	whoop
ŏ	pot	zh	vision
ō	toe	ə	about
ô	paw	N	*French* bon

Greek *hōroskopos* : *hōra*, hour, season + *skopos*, observer.]

hor•ren•dous (hô rĕn′dəs *or* hə rĕn′dəs) *adj.* Terrible; dreadful. **—hor•ren′dous•ly** *adv.*

hor•ri•ble (hôr′ə bəl *or* hŏr′ə bəl) *adj.* **1.** Causing horror; dreadful: *a horrible crime.* **2.** Extremely unpleasant: *a horrible noise.* **—hor′ri•ble•ness** *n.* **—hor′ri•bly** *adv.*

hor•rid (hôr′ĭd *or* hŏr′ĭd) *adj.* **1.** Causing horror; horrible. **2.** Extremely disagreeable; offensive. **—hor′rid•ly** *adv.* **—hor′rid•ness** *n.*

hor•ri•fy (hôr′ə fī′ *or* hŏr′ə fī′) *tr.v.* **hor•ri•fied, hor•ri•fy•ing, hor•ri•fies. 1.** To cause to feel horror: *The possibility of a violent earthquake horrified people.* **2.** To surprise unpleasantly; shock: *The class's poor performance on the test horrified the teacher.*

hor•ror (hôr′ər *or* hŏr′ər) *n.* **1.** A feeling of fear and disgust; terror. **2.** Something that causes horror: *the horrors of war.* **3.** Intense dislike; loathing: *Winston has a horror of rats.*

hors d'oeuvre (ôr dûrv′) *n., pl.* **hors d'oeuvres** (ôr dûrvz′) or **hors d'oeuvre.** An appetizer served before a meal.

horse (hôrs) *n.* **1.** A large four-legged mammal having solid hoofs and a long coarse mane and tail. The horse is used for riding, pulling vehicles, and carrying loads. **2.** An adult male horse. **3.** A frame consisting of a crossbar and four legs, used for supporting or holding. **4.** A piece of gymnasium equipment having an upholstered body, used especially for vaulting. *—tr.v.* **horsed, hors•ing, hors•es.** To provide with a horse. ***—idioms.*** **beat a dead horse** or **flog a dead horse. 1.** To continue to pursue a cause that has no hope of success. **2.** To dwell tiresomely on a matter that has already been decided. **horse around.** *Informal.* To indulge in horseplay or frivolous activity. [First written down about 700 in Old English and spelled *hors.*]

❑ *These sound alike:* **horse, hoarse** (husky).

horse•back (hôrs′băk′) *n.* The back of a horse: *police officers on horseback. —adv. & adj.* On the back of a horse: *ride horseback; horseback riding.*

horse chestnut *n.* **1.** Any of several large shade trees having upright clusters of white flowers and nuts enclosed in a spiny bur. **2.** The brown, shiny, inedible nut of such a tree.

horse•fly (hôrs′flī′) *n.* Any of numerous large flies, the female of which bites and sucks blood from horses, cattle, and other animals.

horse•hair (hôrs′hâr′) *n.* **1.** The coarse hair from a horse's mane or tail. **2.** Stiff cloth made of the hair of horses.

horse latitudes *pl.n.* Either of two regions notable for high barometric pressure and calm or light variable wind. They are found over the oceans at about 30 degrees north and south latitudes.

horse•man (hôrs′mən) *n.* **1.** A man who rides a horse. **2.** A man skilled at riding horses.

horse•man•ship (hôrs′mən shĭp′) *n.* The skill of riding horses: *Rodeo riders must have superior horsemanship.*

horse•play (hôrs′plā′) *n.* Rough or rowdy play.

horse•pow•er (hôrs′pou′ər) *n.* A unit for measuring the power of engines and motors, equal to the power needed to lift 550 pounds one foot in one second.

horse•rad•ish (hôrs′răd′ĭsh) *n.* **1.** A tall plant having long leaves, white flowers, and a large whitish root with a sharp taste. **2.** The grated root of this plant, often used as a condiment.

horse sense *n. Informal.* Common sense.

horse•shoe (hôrs′sho͞o′ *or* hôrsh′sho͞o′) *n.* **1.** A flat U-shaped metal plate fitted and nailed to a horse's hoof for protection. **2.** Something shaped like a horseshoe. **3. horseshoes.** *(used with a singular verb).* A game in which the players try to toss horseshoes around or near a stake.

horseshoe crab *n.* Any of various sea animals similar to the crabs, having a large oval shell and a stiff pointed tail.

horse•whip (hôrs′wĭp′) *n.* A whip used to drive or control a horse. *—tr.v.* **horse•whipped, horse•whip•ping, horse•whips.** To beat with or as if with a horsewhip.

horse•wom•an (hôrs′wo͝om′ən) *n.* **1.** A woman who rides a horse. **2.** A woman skilled at riding horses.

hors•y also **hors•ey** (hôr′sē) *adj.* **hors•i•er, hors•i•est. 1.** Of, relating to, or resembling a horse or horses: *run with a lumbering horsy trot.* **2.** Devoted to horses and horsemanship: *the horsy set.*

hor•ti•cul•ture (hôr′tĭ kŭl′chər) *n.* **1.** The science or art of raising and caring for plants, especially flowers, fruits, and vegetables. **2.** The cultivation of a garden. **—hor′ti•cul′tur•al** *adj.*

hor•ti•cul•tur•ist (hôr′tĭ kŭl′chər ĭst) *n.* A person who specializes in horticulture.

ho•san•na (hō zăn′ə) *interj.* An expression used to show praise or adoration of God. *—n.* A cry of "hosanna."

hose (hōz) *n.* **1.** *pl.* **hose.** Stockings; socks. Used only in the plural. **2.** *pl.* **hose.** Tights once worn by men as trousers. Used only in the plural. **3.** *pl.* **hos•es.** A flexible tube for carrying liquids or gases under pressure: *use an air hose to fill the car tires. —tr.v.* **hosed, hos•ing, hos•es.** To wash or spray with water from a hose: *hose down a car while washing it.* [First written down before 1100 in Old English and spelled *hosa*, leg covering.]

Ho•se•a (hō zē′ə *or* hō zā′ə) *n.* **1.** A Hebrew prophet of the eighth century B.C. **2.** A book of the Bible in which Hosea rebukes the Israelites for unfaithfulness and urges repentance.

ho•sier•y (hō′zhə rē) *n.* Stockings and socks; hose.

hos•pice (hŏs′pĭs) *n.* **1.** A shelter or lodging for travelers or those who are very poor, often maintained by a religious order. **2.** A program providing care and support for people who are suffering from terminal illness.

hos•pi•ta•ble (hŏs′pĭ tə bəl *or* hŏ spĭt′ə bəl) *adj.* **1.** Disposed to treat guests with warmth and generosity: *The hotel staff is extremely hospitable.* **2.** Having an open mind; receptive: *The new manager is hospitable to new ideas.* **—hos′pi•ta•bly** *adv.*

hos•pi•tal (hŏs′pĭ tl *or* hŏs′pĭt′l) *n.* An institution providing medical, surgical, or psychiatric care and treatment for those who are sick and injured. [First written down about 1300 in Middle English, from Latin *hospitālis*, of a guest.]

hos•pi•tal•i•ty (hŏs′pĭ tăl′ĭ tē) *n., pl.* **hos•pi•tal•i•ties.** Welcoming or generous treatment of guests.

hos•pi•tal•i•za•tion (hŏs′pĭ tl ĭ zā′shən) *n.* **1.** The act of placing a person in a hospital as a patient. **2.** The condition of being hospitalized: *Hospitalization may increase the chances of recovery from serious illness.* **3.** Insurance that fully or partially covers a patient's hospital expenses.

hos•pi•tal•ize (hŏs′pĭt l īz′) *tr.v.* **hos•pi•tal•ized, hos•pi•tal•iz•ing, hos•pi•tal•iz•es.** To place in a hospital, as for treatment or care: *I was hospitalized for two days with appendicitis.*

host¹ (hōst) *n.* **1.a.** A person who receives or entertains guests in a social or an official capacity: *The new neighbors were our hosts for the evening.* **b.** The keeper of an inn or a hotel. **c.** The emcee or interviewer on a radio or television program. **2.** A living plant or animal on or in which a parasite lives and feeds. *—tr.v.* **host•ed, host•ing, hosts.** To serve as host to or at: *host a party; host an inter-*

view on TV. [First written down about 1250 in Middle English and spelled *oste,* from Late Latin *hospes.*]

host[2] (hōst) *n.* **1.** An army. **2.** A great number; a multitude. [First written down in 1265 in Middle English, from Latin *hostis,* enemy.]

host[3] also **Host** (hōst) *n.* The consecrated bread or wafer of the Eucharist. [First written down about 1303 in Middle English and spelled *oste,* from Latin *hostia,* sacrifice.]

hos•tage (**hŏs′**tĭj) *n.* **1.** A person who is held by another or by a group in a conflict as security that a specified demand will be met. **2.** A person or thing that serves as security against an implied threat. [First written down about 1300 in Middle English, from Old French *host,* guest.]

hos•tel (**hŏs′**təl) *n.* A supervised inexpensive lodging place for travelers, especially young travelers.
❑ *These sound alike:* **hostel, hostile** (showing enmity).

hos•tel•ry (**hŏs′**təl rē) *n., pl.* **hos•tel•ries.** An inn; a hotel.

host•ess (**hō′**stĭs) *n.* **1.** A woman who receives or entertains guests in a social or an official capacity. **2.** A woman who is the keeper of an inn or a hotel. **3.** A woman who is employed to greet and assist patrons, as at a restaurant.

hos•tile (**hŏs′**təl *or* **hŏs′**tīl′) *adj.* **1.** Of, relating to, or characteristic of an enemy: *hostile forces.* **2.** Feeling or showing enmity or ill will: *a hostile crowd.* **3.** Unfavorable to health or well-being: *a hostile climate.* [First written down in 1594 in Modern English, from Latin *hostis,* enemy.] **—hos′tile•ly** *adv.*
❑ *These sound alike:* **hostile, hostel** (lodging).

hos•til•i•ty (hŏ **stĭl′**ĭ tē) *n., pl.* **hos•til•i•ties. 1.** The state of being hostile; antagonism or enmity: *The hostility of the former enemies was felt by everyone.* **2. hostilities.** Acts of war; open warfare: *Hostilities broke out between the two countries.*

hos•tler (**hŏs′**lər *or* **ŏs′**lər) also **os•tler** (**ŏs′**lər) *n.* **1.** A person who is employed to tend horses, especially at an inn. **2.** A person who maintains and repairs a large vehicle or engine, such as a locomotive.

hot (hŏt) *adj.* **hot•ter, hot•test. 1.** Having great heat; being at a high temperature; very warm: *a hot stove; a horse that was hot after working in the sun; a forehead hot with fever.* **2.** Charged with electricity: *a hot wire.* **3.** Radioactive, especially to a dangerous degree: *A reactor's spent fuel remains hot for years.* **4.** Causing a burning sensation, as in the mouth: *hot chile; hot mustard.* **5.** Marked by intense feeling; fiery: *a hot temper; a hot argument.* **6.** Very eager or enthusiastic: *We were hot to go to the beach.* **7.** *Informal.* Most recent; new or fresh: *a hot piece of news.* **8.** *Informal.* Currently very popular: *a hot topic of conversation.* **9.** Close to a successful solution or conclusion: *hot on the trail of the robbers.* **10.** *Slang.* Stolen: *a hot television set.* *—adv.* In a hot manner; with much heat: *The engine runs hot. The sun shone hot on the pavement.* [First written down in 971 in Old English and spelled *hāt.*] **—hot′ly** *adv.* **—hot′ness** *n.*

hot air *n. Slang.* Empty exaggerated talk.

hot•bed (**hŏt′**bĕd′) *n.* **1.** A place that fosters rapid and excessive growth or development, especially of something bad: *a hotbed of intrigue.* **2.** A bed of soil covered with glass and heated by decaying organic matter or electricity, used for growing seeds or protecting young plants.

hot-blood•ed (**hŏt′blŭd′**ĭd) *adj.* Easily excited or aroused.

hot•cake (**hŏt′**kāk′) *n.* A pancake. *—idiom.* **go like hotcakes** or **sell like hotcakes.** *Informal.* To be disposed of quickly and in great amounts: *The raffle tickets are selling like hotcakes.*

hot cross bun *n.* A sweet bun marked on top with a cross of frosting, traditionally eaten during Lent.

hot dog or **hot•dog** (**hŏt′**dôg′ *or* **hŏt′**dŏg′) *n.* A frankfurter, especially one served hot in a long roll.

ho•tel (hō **tĕl′**) *n.* A house or other building that provides lodging and often meals and other services for paying guests.

hot•foot (**hŏt′**fo͝ot′) *intr.v.* **hot•foot•ed, hot•foot•ing, hot•foots.** *Informal.* To go in great haste: *hotfoot it to the market before it closes.*

hot•head•ed (**hŏt′hĕd′**ĭd) *adj.* **1.** Easily angered; quick-tempered: *a crowd of hotheaded protestors.* **2.** Impetuous; rash: *a hotheaded plan.* **—hot′head′ed•ly** *adv.* **—hot′head′ed•ness** *n.*

hot•house (**hŏt′**hous′) *n.* A heated building with a glass roof and sides, used for growing plants; a greenhouse. *—adj.* Grown in a hothouse: *hothouse tomatoes.*

hot line or **hot•line** (**hŏt′**līn′) *n.* **1.** A direct and immediate communications link, usually a telephone line, as between heads of governments for use in a crisis. **2.** A telephone line that provides information or help.

hot•ly (**hŏt′**lē) *adv.* In an intense or fiery manner: *a hotly debated subject.*

hot plate *n.* An electrically heated plate for cooking or warming food.

hot rod *n. Slang.* An automobile rebuilt or modified for greater acceleration and speed.

hot•shot (**hŏt′**shŏt′) *n. Slang.* A person with unusual skill and daring, especially one who is highly successful and self-assured.

hot spot *n.* **1.** A place of dangerous unrest or hostile action. **2.** *Slang.* A lively and popular place, as a nightclub: *a downtown hot spot for food and dancing.* **3.** In geology, a source of great heat in the earth.

hot spring *n.* A spring of warm water, usually having a temperature greater than that of the human body.

hot toddy *n.* A drink made of whiskey or another liquor mixed with hot water, sugar, and spices.

hot water *n. Informal.* A difficult or uncomfortable situation; trouble.

hound (hound) *n.* **1.** Any of various breeds of dog, such as the foxhound and basset, originally bred and used for hunting, usually having short hair and drooping ears. **2.** A dog. **3.** A person who eagerly pursues something: *a mystery hound.* *—tr.v.* **hound•ed, hound•ing, hounds. 1.** To pursue relentlessly: *Reporters hounded the mayor all over town.* **2.** To urge insistently; nag: *The children hounded their parents to let them go to the movies.* [First written down about 725 in Old English and spelled *hund.*]

hour (our) *n.* **1.** A unit of time equal to one of the 24 equal parts of a day; 60 minutes. **2.** One of these units of time as shown on a clock or watch or marked by a bell or other signal: *The hour is 3 p.m. The church clock strikes on the half hour.* **3.** The distance that can be traveled in an hour: *When we cross the bridge we will only be two hours from our destination.* **4.** A particular time of day: *At what hour does the store open?* **5.** A customary or fixed time: *the dinner hour.* **6. hours.** A set period of time for a specified activity: *open hours from eight to three; keeps office hours.* [First written down before 1200 in Middle English and spelled *ure,* from Greek *hōra,* season, time.]
❑ *These sound alike:* **hour, our** (of us).

hour•glass (**our′**glăs′) *n.* An instrument for measuring time, consisting of two glass chambers connected by a narrow neck and containing an amount

hot plate

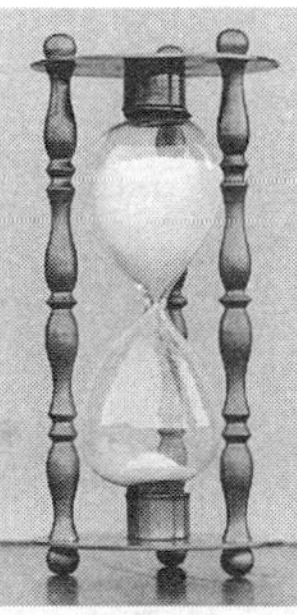

hourglass

ă	pat	oi	boy
ā	pay	ou	out
âr	care	o͝o	took
ä	father	o͞o	boot
ĕ	pet	ŭ	cut
ē	be	ûr	urge
ĭ	pit	th	thin
ī	pie	*th*	this
îr	pier	hw	whoop
ŏ	pot	zh	vision
ō	toe	ə	about
ô	paw	N	*French* bon

houseboat

house sparrow
Male house sparrow

Sam Houston
c. 1845 daguerreotype

of sand or another substance that passes from the top chamber to the bottom one in a fixed amount of time, often an hour.

hour•ly (**our′**lē) *adj.* **1.** Occurring every hour: *hourly temperature readings; hourly news reports during the hurricane.* **2.** By the hour as a unit: *an hourly wage.* **3.** Frequent; continual: *hourly changes to the report.* —*adv.* At or during every hour: *doses of medicine given hourly.*

house (hous) *n., pl.* **hous•es** (**hou′**zĭz *or* **hou′**sĭz). **1.a.** A structure serving as a dwelling for one or more persons; a residence. **b.** A dwelling for a group of people, such as students, who live together as a unit: *a sorority house.* **2.** All of the people living in a house; a household. **3.** A building or another structure used for some special purpose: *an opera house; a movie house.* **4.** The people in an audience: *The actors played to a full house.* **5.** Often **House.** A noble family including its ancestors and descendants. **6.** A business firm: *a banking house; a publishing house.* **7.** Often **House.** An assembly having the duty and power of making laws; a legislature: *The two houses of the U.S. Congress are the Senate and the House of Representatives.* —*tr.v.* (houz). **housed, hous•ing, hous•es. 1.** To provide living quarters for: *The apartment building houses ten families.* **2.** To keep or store in a house or other shelter: *house our car in the garage.* [First written down about 725 in Old English and spelled *hūs.*]

house arrest *n.* Confinement to one's quarters, rather than prison, by court order.

house•boat (**hous′**bōt′) *n.* A barge designed and equipped for use as a dwelling or cruiser.

house•break (**hous′**brāk′) *tr.v.* **house•broke** (**hous′**brōk′), **house•bro•ken** (**hous′**brō′kən), **house•break•ing, house•breaks.** To train (a pet) to have excretory habits that are appropriate for indoor living.

house•break•ing (**hous′**brā′kĭng) *n.* The act of unlawfully breaking into and entering another's house.

house•broke (**hous′**brōk′) *v.* Past tense of **housebreak.**

house•bro•ken (**hous′**brō′kən) *v.* Past participle of **housebreak.** —*adj.* Trained to have excretory habits that are appropriate for indoor living: *a housebroken dog.*

house call *n.* A professional visit made to a home, especially by a physician.

house•clean•ing (**hous′**klē′nĭng) *n.* The cleaning and tidying of a house and its contents.

house•fly (**hous′**flī′) *n.* A common fly that is found in all parts of the world. It feeds on garbage in or around human dwellings and is a carrier of many diseases.

house•hold (**hous′**hōld′) *n.* **1.** The members of a family and others living together as a domestic unit. **2.** The living spaces and possessions belonging to such a unit. —*adj.* Of, relating to, or used in a household: *household appliances; household expenses.*

house•hold•er (**hous′**hōl′dər) *n.* **1.** A person who occupies or owns a house. **2.** The head of a household.

house•hus•band (**hous′**hŭz′bənd) *n.* A married man who manages the household as his main occupation.

house•keep•er (**hous′**kē′pər) *n.* **1.** A person hired to take care of a home. **2.** An employee who manages other employees engaged in domestic tasks in a hospital, hotel, or similar institution.

house•keep•ing (**hous′**kē′pĭng) *n.* **1.** Performance or management of household tasks. **2.** The management of the property and equipment of a hospital, hotel, or similar institution.

house•maid (**hous′**mād′) *n.* A woman or girl employed to do housework.

house•moth•er (**hous′**mŭ*th*′ər) *n.* A woman hired to supervise a residence hall for young people.

House of Commons *n.* The lower house of Parliament in the United Kingdom and Canada.

house of correction *n., pl.* **houses of correction.** An institution for confining persons convicted of minor criminal offenses.

House of Lords *n.* The upper house of Parliament in the United Kingdom, made up of members of the nobility and high-ranking clergy.

House of Representatives *n.* The lower house of the U.S. Congress and of most state legislatures.

house•plant (**hous′**plănt′) *n.* A plant grown indoors, often for decorative purposes.

house sparrow *n.* A small bird having brown and gray feathers and a distinctive black mark on the throat of the male.

house•top (**hous′**tŏp′) *n.* The roof of a house.

house•wares (**hous′**wârz′) *pl.n.* Articles used especially in the kitchen, such as cooking utensils and dishes.

house•warm•ing (**hous′**wôr′mĭng) *n.* A party to celebrate moving into a new home.

house•wife (**hous′**wīf′) *n.* A married woman who manages the household as her main occupation.

house•work (**hous′**wûrk′) *n.* The tasks performed in housekeeping, such as cleaning and cooking.

hous•ing¹ (**hou′**zĭng) *n.* **1.** Buildings or other shelters in which people live. **2.** Provision of lodging or shelter: *The employment agreement included housing.* **3.** Something that covers, contains, or protects a mechanical part. [First written down before 1325 in Middle English and spelled *husing*, from *hus*, house.]

hous•ing² (**hou′**zĭng) *n.* **1.** An ornamental or protective covering for a saddle. **2.** Trappings for a horse. Often used in the plural. [First written down in 1782 in Modern English, from Medieval Latin *hulcia*, protective covering.]

housing project *n.* A group of publicly funded houses or apartment buildings, usually for people with low incomes.

Hous•ton (**hyōō′**stən). The largest city of Texas, in the southeast part of the state east-southeast of Austin. It was founded in 1836. Population, 1,630,553.

Houston, Samuel. 1793–1863. American general and politician who served as president of the Republic of Texas (1836–1838 and 1841–1844).

hove (hōv) *v. & tr.* Past tense and past participle of **heave** (sense 1b). —*intr.* Past tense and past participle of **heave** (sense 5).

hov•el (**hŭv′**əl *or* **hŏv′**əl) *n.* A small miserable dwelling.

hov•er (**hŭv′**ər *or* **hŏv′**ər) *intr.v.* **hov•ered, hov•er•ing, hov•ers. 1.** To stay floating, suspended, or fluttering in the air: *Hummingbirds hover over the flowers they feed on.* **2.** To remain or linger close by. **3.** To be in a state of uncertainty; waver: *The patient hovered between recovery and relapse.* [First written down about 1400 in Middle English and spelled *hoveren.*]

hov•er•craft (**hŭv′**ər krăft′ *or* **hŏv′**ər krăft′) *n.* A vehicle that travels over land or water on a thin cushion of air created by fans blowing downward.

how (hou) *adv.* **1.** In what manner or way; by what means: *The teacher showed us how to use a compass.* **2.** In what state or condition: *How do you feel today?* **3.** To what extent, amount, or degree: *How strong is the rope? How much do these gadgets cost?* **4.** For what reason; why: *How did you manage to miss the train?* **5.** With what meaning: *How* *should I take that remark?* —*conj.* **1.** The manner or way in which: *I forgot how the song goes.* **2.** In whatever way or manner that: *Cook the beans how you like.* —*n.* The way something is done: *I am more interested in the how than the why of a thing.* —***idioms.*** **how about.** What is your thought, feeling, or desire regarding: *How about some ice cream?* **how come.** *Informal.* How is it that; why: *How come you're late?*

how•dah (hou′də) *n.* A seat for riding on the back of an elephant or camel, usually fitted with a canopy and railing.

how•dy (hou′dē) *interj.* An expression used to greet someone.

Howe (hou), **Elias.** 1819–1867. American inventor of early sewing machines (1845 and 1846).

Howe, Julia Ward. 1819–1910. American writer who was active in the women's suffrage movement. She wrote "Battle Hymn of the Republic" (published 1862).

how•ev•er (hou ev′ər) *adv.* **1.** To whatever extent or degree: *However long the process, an education is absolutely necessary.* **2.** In whatever way or manner: *However you manage it, the job must be done.* **3.** Nevertheless; yet: *It was a difficult time; however, there were amusing moments.*

how•it•zer (hou′ĭt sər) *n.* A short cannon that fires shells in a high curving path. [First written down in 1687 in Modern English and spelled *howitz*, from obsolete German *Haufnitz*, catapult.]

howl (houl) *v.* **howled, howl•ing, howls.** —*intr.* **1.** To utter or emit a long, mournful, plaintive sound: *The dogs howled at the loud siren.* **2.** To cry or wail loudly, as in pain, sorrow, or anger: *The patient howled when the dentist pulled the tooth.* See Synonyms at **shout. 3.** *Slang.* To laugh heartily: *The audience howled at the comedian's jokes.* —*tr.* To express or utter with a howl. —*n.* A long wailing cry. [First written down before 1250 in Middle English and spelled *hulen*.]

howl•ing (hou′lĭng) *adj.* **1.** Marked by the sound of howling: *a howling wind.* **2.** *Slang.* Very great: *The party was a howling success.*

how•so•ev•er (hou′sō ev′ər) *adv.* **1.** To whatever extent or degree. **2.** By whatever means.

hoy•den (hoid′n) *n.* A high-spirited boisterous girl.

hp *abbr.* An abbreviation of horsepower.

HQ or **h.q.** or **H.Q.** *abbr.* An abbreviation of headquarters.

hr *abbr.* An abbreviation of hour.

h.r. *abbr.* An abbreviation of home run.

H.R. *abbr.* An abbreviation of House of Representatives.

ht *abbr.* An abbreviation of height.

Huang He (hwäng′ hə′) also **Hwang Ho** (hwäng′ hō′) or **Yel•low River** (yĕl′ō). A river of China rising in the central part of the country and flowing about 3,000 miles (4,827 kilometers) generally eastward to an arm of the Yellow Sea.

hub (hŭb) *n.* **1.** The center part of a wheel, fan, or propeller. **2.** A center of activity or interest; a focal point.

hub•bub (hŭb′ŭb′) *n.* Noisy confusion; uproar: *the hubbub of traffic; the hubbub in a crowded room.*

hub•cap (hŭb′kăp′) *n.* A round covering over an automobile wheel.

huck•le•ber•ry (hŭk′əl bĕr′ē) *n.* **1.** The glossy blackish berry of any of various shrubs related to the blueberries. **2.** A shrub that bears such berries.

huck•ster (hŭk′stər) *n.* **1.** A person who sells goods in the street; a peddler. **2.** A person who used aggressive, sometimes devious methods to promote or sell a product. **3.** *Informal.* A writer of advertising copy, especially for radio or television.

hud•dle (hŭd′l) *n.* **1.** A densely packed group or crowd, as of people or animals. **2.** In football, a brief grouping of a team's players behind the line of scrimmage to plan the next play. **3.** A small private conference or meeting: *The two lawyers went into a huddle.* —*v.* **hud•dled, hud•dling, hud•dles.** —*intr.* **1.** To crowd together, as from cold or fear: *The sheep huddled into a small pen.* **2.** To draw one's limbs close to one's body: *The rabbit huddled under some leaves.* **3.** In football, to gather in a huddle. **4.** *Informal.* To confer; meet: *The two friends huddled and talked over the problem.* —*tr.* To cause to crowd together: *The dog huddled the sheep into a group.* [First written down in 1586 in Modern English, possibly from Low German *hudeln*, to crowd together.]

Hud•son (hŭd′sən), **Henry.** Died 1611. English navigator who explored the Hudson River in 1609.

Hudson Bay. An inland sea of east-central Canada connected to the Atlantic Ocean by **Hudson Strait,** lying between southern Baffin Island and northern Quebec.

Hudson River. A river rising in the Adirondack Mountains of northeast New York and flowing about 315 miles (507 kilometers) generally southward to the Atlantic Ocean at New York City.

hue (hyōō) *n.* **1.** The property of color that distinguishes it from another color, as red from yellow or blue from green; color: *all the hues of the rainbow; the basic hues of red, blue, and yellow.* **2.** A shade or tint of color: *hues of blue from light to dark.* [First written down about 750 in Old English and spelled *hēo*.]

❑ *These sound alike:* **hue, hew** (shape with an ax).

hue and cry *n.* A public clamor, as of protest or demand. [First written down in 1246 in Middle English and spelled *hew and cri*, from Old French *huer*, to shout.]

huff (hŭf) *n.* A fit of anger or annoyance: *left the room in a huff.* —*v.* **huffed, huff•ing, huffs.** —*intr.* To puff; blow: *They huffed all the way up the hill.* —*tr.* To anger; annoy: *Their uncooperative attitude huffed me.*

huff•y (hŭf′ē) *adj.* **huff•i•er, huff•i•est. 1.** Easily offended; touchy: *Why are you so huffy today?* **2.** Irritated or annoyed; indignant: *Their rude remarks made me huffy.* —**huff′i•ly** *adv.* —**huff′i•ness** *n.*

hug (hŭg) *tr.v.* **hugged, hug•ging, hugs. 1.** To clasp or hold closely; embrace: *hug a child.* **2.** To keep or stay close to: *This car hugs the road well on corners.* **3.** To hold steadfastly to; cherish: *hugs his eccentric ideas.* —*n.* An affectionate or tight embrace.

huge (hyōōj) *adj.* **hug•er, hug•est.** Of great size, extent, or quantity; tremendous: *a huge iceberg; a huge difference.* See Synonyms at **large.** —**huge′ly** *adv.* —**huge′ness** *n.*

Hu•go (hyōō′gō), **Victor Marie.** 1802–1885. French writer whose novels include *The Hunchback of Notre Dame* (1831).

Hu•gue•not (hyōō′gə nŏt′) *n.* A French Protestant of the 16th and 17th centuries.

huh (hŭ) *interj.* An expression used to ask a question or show surprise, contempt, or indifference.

hu•la (hōō′lə) *n.* A Polynesian dance characterized by swaying movements of the hips and miming movements of the arms and hands. [First written down in 1835 in Modern English, from Hawaiian.]

hulk (hŭlk) *n.* **1.** The hull of an old, unseaworthy, or wrecked ship. **2.** A heavy unwieldy ship. **3.** A large clumsy person or thing: *a hulk of a football player; a big bus that is a hulk.* **4.** An old or worn-out ship used as a prison or warehouse. Often used in the plural.

Julia Ward Howe

Henry Hudson

Victor Hugo

ă	**pat**	oi	**boy**
ā	**pay**	ou	**out**
âr	**care**	ŏŏ	**took**
ä	**father**	ōō	**boot**
ĕ	**pet**	ŭ	**cut**
ē	**be**	ûr	**urge**
ĭ	**pit**	th	**thin**
ī	**pie**	*th*	**this**
îr	**pier**	hw	**whoop**
ŏ	**pot**	zh	**vision**
ō	**toe**	ə	**about**
ô	**paw**	N	*French* **bon**

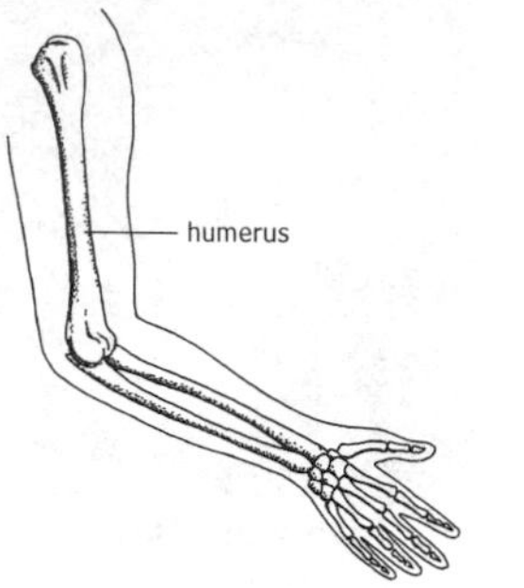

humerus

hummingbird

Word History: **humor**

Everyone likes **humor**, unless someone is in a bad humor. *Humor* goes back to the Latin word *ūmor*, meaning "fluid, especially any of the four fluids of the body." These four *humors* are blood, phlegm, choler (or bile), and melancholy (or black bile). One could explain and interpret a person's current mood or permanent personality according to the four humors in his or her body. Too much choler caused anger. Too much melancholy caused depression: *a melancholic man.* Too much phlegm, sluggishness: *a phlegmatic woman.* To *humor* someone or to be **humorous** originally meant to match another person's *humors.*

hulk•ing (hŭl′kĭng) *adj.* Unwieldy or bulky; massive: *a great hulking St. Bernard.*

hull (hŭl) *n.* **1.** The framework or body of a ship or plane. **2.** The outer covering of certain seeds or fruits; a husk or pod. **3.** The cluster of leaflets at the stem end of certain fruits, such as the strawberry. *—tr.v.* **hulled, hull•ing, hulls.** To remove the hulls of (fruit or seeds): *hull berries.* [First written down about 1000 in Old English and spelled *hulu.*] **—hull′er** *n.*

hul•la•ba•loo (hŭl′ə bə lo͞o′) *n., pl.* **hul•la•ba•loos.** Great noise or excitement; uproar.

hul•lo (hə lō′) *interj. & n.* Variant of **hello.**

hum (hŭm) *v.* **hummed, hum•ming, hums.** *—intr.* **1.** To make the continuous droning sound of a bee in flight; buzz: *Bees hummed around the flower. The television set hums when we turn it on.* **2.** To make a continuous low droning sound like that of the speech sound *m* when prolonged. **3.** To sing without words, with the lips kept closed: *hum while working.* **4.** To be full of or alive with activity: *The street hums with traffic.* *—tr.* To sing (a tune) without opening the lips: *hum a melody.* *—n.* **1.** The act of humming. **2.** The sound produced by humming. *—interj.* An expression used to show surprise, displeasure, or hesitation.

hu•man (hyo͞o′mən) *adj.* **1.** Of, relating to, or characteristic of human beings: *the human body.* **2.** Of or having the qualities of a person or people. **3.** Made up of human beings: *People linked their arms in a human chain.* *—n.* A person; a human being. [First written down about 1450 in Middle English and spelled *humain,* from Latin *hūmānus.*] **—hu′man•ness** *n.*

human being *n.* A person; a woman, man, or child.

hu•mane (hyo͞o mān′) *adj.* Characterized by kindness, compassion, or mercy: *a humane judge.* **—hu•mane′ly** *adv.* **—hu•mane′ness** *n.*

hu•man•ism (hyo͞o′mə nĭz′əm) *n.* **1.** A system of thought that is concerned with human welfare, interests, and values. **2.** The study of the humanities; learning in the liberal arts. **3.** Often **Humanism.** A cultural and intellectual movement of the Renaissance that emphasized secular concerns as a result of the rediscovery and study of the art, literature, and civilization of ancient Greece and Rome.

hu•man•ist (hyo͞o′mə nĭst) *n.* **1.** A believer in the principles of humanism. **2.** A student of the liberal arts. **3.** A person who is concerned with the interest, welfare, and values of human beings.

hu•man•i•tar•i•an (hyo͞o măn′ĭ târ′ē ən) *n.* A person who promotes human welfare and the advancement of social reforms; a philanthropist. *—adj.* Of, relating to, or characteristic of a humanitarian or humanitarianism.

hu•man•i•tar•i•an•ism (hyo͞o măn′ĭ târ′ē ə nĭz′əm) *n.* The belief that human beings have an obligation to work for the improvement of human welfare.

hu•man•i•ty (hyo͞o măn′ĭ tē) *n., pl.* **hu•man•i•ties. 1.** Human beings considered as a group; the human race: *The measles vaccine is of benefit to humanity.* **2.** The quality or fact of being human. **3.** The quality of being humane; kindness: *Taking in the war refugees was an act of great humanity.* **4. humanities.** The branches of knowledge, such as art, philosophy, and literature, that are concerned with human thought and culture.

hu•man•ize (hyo͞o′mə nīz′) *tr.v.* **hu•man•ized, hu•man•iz•ing, hu•man•iz•es. 1.** To make human: *The writer humanizes animal characters by showing how they feel.* **2.** To make humane: *courteous acts that humanize life in the city.* **—hu′man•i•za′tion** (hyo͞o′mə nĭ zā′shən) *n.*

hu•man•kind (hyo͞o′mən kīnd′) *n.* The human race.

hu•man•ly (hyo͞o′mən lē) *adv.* **1.** In a human way. **2.** Within the scope of human means, abilities, or powers: *as soon as is humanly possible.*

human nature *n.* The sum of qualities and characteristics shared by all human beings.

hu•man•oid (hyo͞o′mə noid′) *adj.* Having human characteristics or form: *a humanoid robot.* *—n.* A being that resembles a human.

human rights *pl.n.* The basic rights of all human beings, often held to include the right to life and liberty, freedom of thought and expression, and equality before the law.

hum•ble (hŭm′bəl) *adj.* **hum•bler, hum•blest. 1.** Marked by meekness or modesty in behavior, attitude, or spirit: *a humble manner; humble thanks.* **2.** Low in rank, quality, or station: *My career began as a humble clerk.* *—tr.v.* **hum•bled, hum•bling, hum•bles.** To cause to be meek or modest in spirit; humiliate: *Defeat humbled the proud general.* [First written down about 1275 in Middle English, from Latin *humilis,* low, lowly, from *humus,* ground.] **—hum′ble•ness** *n.* **—hum′bly** *adv.*

hum•bug (hŭm′bŭg′) *n.* **1.** Something meant to deceive; a hoax. **2.** A person who claims to be other than what he or she is; an impostor. **3.** Nonsense; rubbish: *That argument is simply humbug.* *—tr.v.* **hum•bugged, hum•bug•ging, hum•bugs.** To deceive or trick; cheat: *The scheme humbugged many people.*

hum•drum (hŭm′drŭm′) *adj.* Lacking variety or excitement; dull: *the humdrum work of filing papers.*

hu•mer•us (hyo͞o′mər əs) *n., pl.* **hu•mer•i** (hyo͞o′mə rī′). The bone of the upper arm or forelimb, extending from the shoulder to the elbow. [First written down in 1392 in Middle English, from Latin *humerus,* upper arm.]

❑ *These sound alike:* **humerus, humorous** (funny).

hu•mid (hyo͞o′mĭd) *adj.* Having a large amount of water or water vapor; damp; moist: *humid air before a shower of rain.* See Synonyms at **wet.** [First written down before 1400 in Middle English, from Latin *hūmidus,* from *hūmēre,* to be moist.]

hu•mid•i•fy (hyo͞o mĭd′ə fī′) *tr.v.* **hu•mid•i•fied, hu•mid•i•fy•ing, hu•mid•i•fies.** To make moist or damp: *humidify the air in a greenhouse.* **—hu•mid′i•fi′er** *n.*

hu•mid•i•ty (hyo͞o mĭd′ĭ tē) *n.* **1.** The condition of being humid; dampness: *The paintings were damaged by the humidity of the warehouse.* **2.** Relative humidity.

hu•mil•i•ate (hyo͞o mĭl′ē āt′) *tr.v.* **hu•mil•i•at•ed, hu•mil•i•at•ing, hu•mil•i•ates.** To lower the pride, dignity, or self-respect of: *I was humiliated by the rude behavior of my children.*

hu•mil•i•a•tion (hyo͞o mĭl′ē ā′shən) *n.* **1.** The act of humiliating; degradation: *the humiliation of an opponent.* **2.** The condition of being humiliated; disgrace.

hu•mil•i•ty (hyo͞o mĭl′ĭ tē) *n.* The quality or condition of being humble: *accepted the award with humility.*

hum•ming•bird (hŭm′ĭng bûrd′) *n.* Any of numerous very small birds of North and South America, having a long slender bill and usually brightly colored plumage. Hummingbirds move their wings so rapidly they make a humming noise.

hum•mock (hŭm′ək) *n.* **1.** A low mound or ridge, as of earth or snow. **2.** A ridge or hill of ice in an ice field.

hum•mus (ho͝om′əs, hŭm′əs) *n.* A smooth mixture of mashed chickpeas, tahini, garlic, and lemon juice, often eaten as a dip for pita.

hu•mor (hyo͞o′mər) *n.* **1.** The quality of being funny or comical: *We laughed at the humor of the story.*

2. The ability to see or express what is funny or comical: *A sense of humor can help a person in a bad situation.* **3.** An often temporary state of mind; a mood: *The beautiful day put me in good humor.* **4.** That which is intended to induce laughter or amusement: *a writer of humor; an actor known for humor.* —*tr.v.* **hu•mored, hu•mor•ing, hu•mors.** To go along with the wishes or ideas of; indulge: *The babysitter humored the child.* [First written down in 1340 in Middle English and spelled *humor,* fluid, from Latin *ūmor.*] —SEE NOTE.

hu•mor•ist (hyo͞o′mər ĭst) *n.* A person with a sharp sense of humor, especially a writer or performer of humorous material.

hu•mor•less (hyo͞o′mər lĭs) *adj.* **1.** Lacking a sense of humor. **2.** Said or done without humor: *humorless remarks.* —**hu′mor•less•ness** *n.*

hu•mor•ous (hyo͞o′mər əs) *adj.* Characterized by or expressing humor; funny: *a humorous writer; a humorous story.* —**hu′mor•ous•ly** *adv.* —**hu′mor•ous•ness** *n.*

❑ *These sound alike:* **humorous, humerus** (arm bone).

hu•mour (hyo͞o′mər) *n. & v. Chiefly British.* Variant of **humor.**

hump (hŭmp) *n.* **1.** A rounded lump, as on the back of a camel. **2.** A low mound of earth: *a hump in the road.* —*tr.v.* **humped, hump•ing, humps.** To bend or make into a hump; arch. —***idiom.*** **over the hump.** Past the worst or most difficult part or stage: *Once our exams are finished, we'll finally be over the hump.*

hump•back (hŭmp′băk′) *n.* A hunchback. —**hump′backed′** *adj.*

humpback whale *n.* A baleen whale having a rounded back and using complex, distinctive songs to communicate.

humph (hŭmf *or* həmf) *interj.* An expression used to show doubt, contempt, or displeasure.

hu•mus (hyo͞o′məs) *n.* A dark brown or black substance made up of decayed leaves and other organic material that provides nutrients for plants and increases the ability of soil to retain water. [First written down in 1796 in Modern English, from Latin *humus,* soil.]

Hun (hŭn) *n.* **1.** A member of a nomadic pastoral people who invaded Europe in the fourth and fifth centuries A.D. **2.** Often **hun.** A barbarous or destructive person.

hunch (hŭnch) *n.* **1.** A suspicion or an intuition; a premonition: *I had a hunch it would get chilly, so I brought a sweater.* **2.** A hump. —*v.* **hunched, hunch•ing, hunch•es.** —*tr.* To draw up or bend into a hump: *I hunched my shoulders against the cold wind.* —*intr.* To go into a crouched or cramped posture: *The cat hunched in the corner.*

hunch•back (hŭnch′băk′) *n.* **1.** A person having a back with a hump in it caused by a curved spine. **2.** A curved or hunched back. —**hunch′backed′** *adj.*

hun•dred (hŭn′drĭd) *n., pl.* **hundred** or **hun•dreds.** The number, written as 100 or 10^2, that is equal to 10 × 10.

hun•dredth (hŭn′drĭdth) *n.* **1.** The ordinal number matching the number 100 in a series. **2.** One of one hundred equal parts.

hun•dred•weight (hŭn′drĭd wāt′) *n., pl.* **hundredweight** or **hun•dred•weights.** A unit of weight equal to 100 pounds (45.36 kilograms) in the United States.

hung (hŭng) *v.* Past tense and a past participle of **hang.**

Hun•gar•i•an (hŭng gâr′ē ən) *adj.* Of or relating to Hungary or its people, language, or culture. —*n.* **1.** A native or inhabitant of Hungary. **2.** The language that is the official language of Hungary.

Hun•ga•ry (hŭng′gə rē). A country of central Europe east of Austria. Hungary was part of Austria-Hungary from 1867 until 1918, when it gained its independence. Budapest is the capital and the largest city. Population, 10,657,000.

hun•ger (hŭng′gər) *n.* **1.** A strong desire or need for food: *Hunger drove the wolves to hunt closer to the town.* **2.** The discomfort, pain, or weakness caused by a lack of food: *faint with hunger.* **3.** A strong desire or craving: *Scholars have a hunger for learning.* —*intr.v.* **hun•gered, hun•ger•ing, hun•gers.** **1.** To have a need or desire for food: *The hikers hungered for something hot and delicious.* **2.** To have a strong desire or craving: *Our team hungered for victory.* [First written down about 725 in Old English and spelled *hungor.*]

hun•gry (hŭng′grē) *adj.* **hun•gri•er, hun•gri•est.** **1.** Experiencing a need or desire for food. **2.** Having a strong desire or craving: *The students were hungry for knowledge.* **3.** Showing or feeling hunger or need: *shot a hungry glance at my sandwich.* —**hun′gri•ly** *adv.* —**hun′gri•ness** *n.*

hunk (hŭngk) *n. Informal.* A large piece; a chunk: *I broke a hunk of freshly baked bread off the loaf.*

Hunk•pa•pa (hŭngk′pä′pä) *n., pl.* **Hunkpapa** or **Hunk•pa•pas.** A member of a Native American people that is a subdivision of the Sioux, living in North and South Dakota.

Hun•nish (hŭn′ĭsh) *adj.* Of, relating to, or characteristic of the Huns.

hunt (hŭnt) *v.* **hunt•ed, hunt•ing, hunts.** —*tr.* **1.** To chase (game) for food or sport: *Many people hunt animals for food.* **2.** To search for; seek out: *hunting bargains at the local stores.* **3.** To search (a place) thoroughly in pursuit of something: *The detective hunted the streets for the suspect.* —*intr.* **1.** To pursue game. **2.** To search thoroughly; seek: *I hunted for the book at the library.* —*n.* **1.** The act or sport of hunting game. **2.** A group of people hunting together, often with horses and hounds: *a fox hunt.* **3.** A diligent search or pursuit: *I engaged in a prolonged hunt for my missing glasses.*

hunt•er (hŭn′tər) *n.* **1.** A person who hunts. **2.** A dog or horse bred and trained for use in hunting.

hunt•ing (hŭn′tĭng) *n.* The activity or sport of pursuing game.

hunts•man (hŭnts′mən) *n.* **1.** A man who hunts game. **2.** A man who manages the dogs in a hunt.

hur•dle (hûr′dl) *n.* **1.a.** A light portable barrier over which competitors must leap in certain races. **b.** **hurdles.** *(used with a singular verb).* A race in which such barriers must be jumped, without the competitors' breaking their stride. **2.** An obstacle or a problem to be overcome: *Getting the money was the chief hurdle I had in going to college.* —*v.* **hur•dled, hur•dling, hur•dles.** —*tr.* **1.** To jump over (a barrier) in or as if in a race: *The dog hurdled the fence after the rabbit.* **2.** To overcome or deal with successfully. —*intr.* To leap or jump over a hurdle or other barrier. —**hur′dler** *n.*

hur•dy-gur•dy (hûr′dē gûr′dē *or* hûr′dē gûr′dē) *n., pl.* **hur•dy-gur•dies.** A musical instrument played by turning a crank. [First written down in 1749 in Modern English, probably of imitative origin.]

hurl (hûrl) *tr.v.* **hurled, hurl•ing, hurls.** **1.** To throw with great force; fling: *The volcano hurled smoke and ash high into the air.* See Synonyms at **throw.** **2.** To utter vehemently: *The children hurled insults at each other.* —**hurl′er** *n.*

hur•ly-bur•ly (hûr′lē bûr′lē) *n., pl.* **hur•ly-bur•lies.** Noisy confusion; uproar.

Hu•ron (hyo͝or′ən *or* hyo͝or′ŏn′) *n., pl.* **Huron** or **Hu•rons.** **1.** A member of a Native American confederacy formerly living in the region east of Lake Huron, with small groups now living in Quebec

hurdle
Edwin Moses of the United States (#1114) and Allan Ince of Barbados (#77) at the Seoul Summer Olympics, 1988

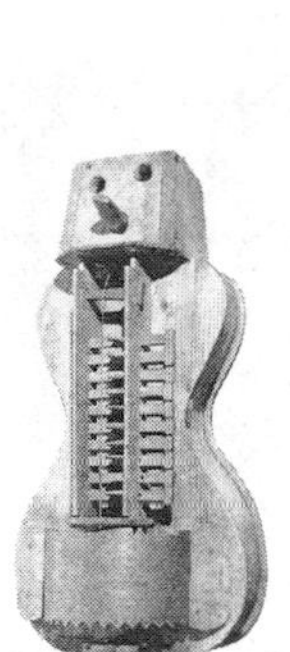

hurdy-gurdy
Early 19th-century American

ă	pat	oi	**boy**
ā	pay	ou	**out**
âr	care	o͝o	**took**
ä	father	o͞o	**boot**
ĕ	pet	ŭ	**cut**
ē	be	ûr	**urge**
ĭ	pit	th	**thin**
ī	pie	*th*	**this**
îr	pier	hw	**whoop**
ŏ	pot	zh	**vision**
ō	toe	ə	**about**
ô	paw	N	*French* **bon**

Zora Neale Hurston

hutch

Anne Hutchinson

hyacinth

and Oklahoma. **2.** The Iroquoian language of the Huron.

Huron, Lake. The second largest of the Great Lakes, between southeast Ontario, Canada, and eastern Michigan. It is part of the Great Lakes–St. Lawrence Seaway system.

hur•rah (ho͞o rä′ *or* hə rä′) also **hoo•ray** (ho͞o rā′ *or* hə rā′) *interj.* An expression used to show approval, pleasure, or victory. —*n.* A shout of "hurrah." —*intr.v.* **hur•rahed, hur•rah•ing, hur•rahs** also **hoo•rayed, hoo•ray•ing, hoo•rays.** To applaud or cheer with shouts of "hurrah."

hur•ri•cane (hûr′ĭ kān′ *or* hŭr′ĭ kān′) *n.* A severe swirling tropical storm with heavy rains and winds exceeding 74 miles (119 kilometers) per hour. Hurricanes originate in the tropical parts of the Atlantic Ocean or the Caribbean Sea and move generally northward. [First written down in 1555 in Modern English and spelled *furacane,* from Spanish *huracán,* from Carib *furacan, huracan.*]

hur•ried (hûr′ēd *or* hŭr′ēd) *adj.* Done very quickly or in haste; rushed: *Because we got up late, we ate a hurried breakfast.* **—hur′ried•ly** *adv.*

hur•ry (hûr′ē *or* hŭr′ē) *v.* **hur•ried, hur•ry•ing, hur•ries.** —*intr.* To move or act very quickly or in haste: *The children hurried along in the rain.* —*tr.* **1.** To cause to move or act with speed or haste: *Parents hurried their children to the bus stop.* **2.** To cause to move or act too quickly; rush: *hurried me into making a choice.* **3.** To speed the progress or completion of: *Using a computer hurried the job along.* —*n., pl.* **hur•ries. 1.** The act or an instance of hurrying: *In my hurry to get to the train, I forgot my wallet.* **2.** The need or wish to hurry; a condition of urgency: *The police were in a hurry to get to the accident.*

Hur•ston (hûr′stən), **Zora Neale.** 1901?–1960. American writer whose novels, such as *Their Eyes Were Watching God* (1937), record the dialect and culture of the American South.

hurt (hûrt) *v.* **hurt, hurt•ing, hurts.** —*tr.* **1.** To cause physical pain to; injure; wound: *The fall hurt my leg.* **2.** To cause mental or emotional suffering to; distress: *The bitter argument hurt both of us.* **3.** To damage or impair: *The dry summer hurt this year's corn crop.* —*intr.* **1.** To have or produce a feeling of physical pain or discomfort: *When I have a cold, my head often hurts.* **2.** To cause distress or damage: *It hurt not to be picked for the team.* —*n.* **1.** Something that hurts; an injury or a wound. **2.** A wrong; harm: *The hurt of smaller paychecks discouraged many people from shopping.*

Synonyms: hurt, injure, damage, spoil. These verbs mean to affect in a bad way. **Hurt** can mean to cause pain, distress, or loss: *Don't try to lift the heavier boxes because you might hurt your back.* **Injure** can mean to harm health, well-being, appearance, or expectations: *Linda didn't want a heavy lunch to injure her chances of winning the race.* **Damage** can mean to injure in a way that decreases value or usefulness: *The movers must have damaged the piano because I never noticed that scratch before now.* **Spoil** means to damage something so that its value, excellence, or strength is ultimately destroyed: *The heavy rains spoiled our picnic.*
Antonyms: heal, help, improve.

hurt•ful (hûrt′fəl) *adj.* Causing injury or suffering; painful: *Air pollution is hurtful to the environment.* **—hurt′ful•ly** *adv.* **—hurt′ful•ness** *n.*

hur•tle (hûr′tl) *intr. & tr.v.* **hur•tled, hur•tling, hur•tles.** To move or cause to move with great speed and a rushing noise: *The speeding train hurtled through the tunnel. The gust of wind hurtled leaves into the air.*

hus•band (hŭz′bənd) *n.* A man married to a woman. —*tr.v.* **hus•band•ed, hus•band•ing, hus•bands.** To use sparingly or economically; conserve: *With so many debts, we had to husband our funds.* [First written down before 1050 in Old English and spelled *hūsbōnda,* from Old Norse *hūsbōndi* : *hūs,* house + *bōndi,* householder.]

hus•band•ry (hŭz′bən drē) *n.* **1.** The work of raising crops and farm animals; farming. **2.** Good or careful management; thrift: *practice husbandry of scarce natural resources.*

hush (hŭsh) *v.* **hushed, hush•ing, hush•es.** —*tr.* **1.** To make silent or quiet: *The parents tried to hush the infant.* **2.** To keep from public knowledge; suppress: *The mayor tried to hush up news of the city scandal.* —*intr.* To be or become silent or still: *The audience hushed as the curtain went up.* —*n.* A silence or stillness; quiet: *When the teacher returned, a hush fell over the classroom.*

husk (hŭsk) *n.* **1.** The dry outer covering of certain seeds or fruits, as of an ear of corn or a nut. **2.** A shell or outer layer, especially one that is considered worthless. —*tr.v.* **husked, husk•ing, husks.** To remove the husk from: *husk ears of corn before cooking them.* **—husk′er** *n.*

husk•y¹ (hŭs′kē) *adj.* **husk•i•er, husk•i•est.** Hoarse or deep in quality: *a husky voice.* [First written down in 1552 in Modern English, from *husk.*] **—husk′i•ly** *adv.* **—husk′i•ness** *n.*

husk•y² (hŭs′kē) *adj.* **husk•i•er, husk•i•est. 1.** Strongly built; burly: *a husky football player.* **2.** Heavily built. —*n., pl.* **husk•ies.** A husky person. [First written down in 1869 in American English, perhaps from *husk.*] **—husk′i•ness** *n.*

hus•ky³ or **Husky** (hŭs′kē) *n., pl.* **hus•kies** or **Hus•kies.** A strong medium-sized dog having a thick coat. The breed originally developed in Siberia and is used in Arctic regions for pulling sleds. [First written down in 1830 in Modern English and spelled *hosky,* probably from shortening and alteration of the word *Eskimo.*]

hus•sar (hə zär′ *or* hə sär′) *n.* A soldier of the light cavalry in some European armies.

hus•sy (hŭz′ē *or* hŭs′ē) *n., pl.* **hus•sies. 1.** A girl considered saucy or impudent. **2.** A woman considered immoral.

hus•tle (hŭs′əl) *v.* **hus•tled, hus•tling, hus•tles.** —*tr.* **1.** To jostle or shove roughly: *The guards hustled the prisoner into a cell.* **2.** To move hurredly; rush: *We hustled the letter to the post office.* —*intr.* **1.** To jostle and push: *We hustled through the busy crowds.* **2.** To work or move energetically and rapidly: *You need to hustle to get the job done.* **3.** *Slang.* To obtain something by deceitful or illicit methods. —*n.* **1.** The act or an instance of hustling: *It was a hustle to get to the airport on time.* **2.** Energetic activity; drive: *The new player shows lots of hustle.* [First written down in 1684 in Modern English, to shake, from Middle Dutch *hustelen.*]

hut (hŭt) *n.* A small crudely made house or shelter; a shack.

hutch (hŭch) *n.* **1.** A pen or coop for small animals, especially rabbits. **2.** A cupboard with drawers for storage and an upper part with usually open shelves. **3.** A chest or bin for storage.

Hutch•in•son (hŭch′ĭn sən), **Anne.** 1591–1643. English-born American religious leader who was banished from Boston (1637) for her religious beliefs.

Hwang Ho (hwäng′ hō′). Huang He.

hwy *abbr.* An abbreviation of highway.

hy•a•cinth (hī′ə sĭnth) *n.* Any of various plants related to the lily that grow from a bulb and have narrow leaves and a long cluster of fragrant, variously colored flowers. [First written down about

1200 in Middle English and spelled *iacinct*, from Greek *huakinthos*, wild hyacinth.]

hy•brid (hī′brĭd) *n.* **1.** A plant or an animal that has parents of different varieties or strains within a species or of different species. **2.** A thing of mixed origin or composition, such as a word whose parts come from different languages. [First written down in 1601 in Modern English, from Latin *hybrida*.]

hy•brid•ize (hī′brĭ dīz′) *intr. & tr.v.* **hy•brid•ized, hy•brid•iz•ing, hy•brid•iz•es.** To produce or cause to produce hybrids; crossbreed. **—hy′brid•i•za′tion** (hī′brĭ dĭ zā′shən) *n.*

Hy•der•a•bad (hī′dər ə băd′ *or* hī′dər ə bäd′). A city of south-central India east-southeast of Bombay. It was founded in the year 1589. Population, 2,187,262.

hy•dra (hī′drə) *n.* Any of several small freshwater animals having a tubular body and a mouth opening surrounded by stinging tentacles. Hydras are related to coral and jellyfish and when cut into pieces can form a new individual from each piece.

Hy•dra (hī′drə) *n.* In Greek mythology, a monster that has many heads and grows back two more if one is cut off.

hy•dran•gea (hī drān′jə *or* hī drăn′jə) *n.* Any of various shrubs having large rounded clusters of white, pink, or blue flowers.

hy•drant (hī′drənt) *n.* A large upright pipe, fitted with a valve and usually placed near a street, from which water can be drawn for fighting fires.

hy•drate (hī′drāt′) *n.* A solid compound produced when certain substances unite chemically with water in definite proportions. *—v.* **hy•drat•ed, hy•drat•ing, hy•drates.** *—tr.* **1.** To combine (a chemical compound) with water, especially to form a hydrate. **2.** To supply water to (a person, for example) in order to restore or maintain a balance of fluids. *—intr.* To combine with water to form a hydrate. **—hy•dra′tion** *n.*

hy•drau•lic (hī drô′lĭk) *adj.* **1.** Operated by the pressure of water or other liquids in motion, especially when forced through an opening: *a hydraulic brake; a hydraulic jack.* **2.** Of or relating to hydraulics. **3.** Capable of hardening under water: *hydraulic cement.* **—hy•drau′li•cal•ly** *adv.*

hy•drau•lics (hī drô′lĭks) *n.* *(used with a singular verb).* The science that deals with water and other liquids at rest or in motion, their uses in engineering, and the laws of their actions.

hy•dra•zine (hī′drə zēn′ *or* hī′drə zĭn) *n.* A colorless liquid compound of nitrogen and hydrogen, used as a jet and rocket fuel.

hy•dride (hī′drīd′) *n.* A compound of hydrogen with another element or radical.

hydro– or **hydr–** *pref.* A prefix that means: **1.** Water: *hydroelectric.* **2.** Hydrogen: *hydrocarbon.* —SEE NOTE.

hy•dro•car•bon (hī′drə kär′bən) *n.* An organic compound that contains only carbon and hydrogen. Hydrocarbons form a large class of chemical compounds and include gasoline, benzene, and butane.

hy•dro•chlo•ric acid (hī′drə klôr′ĭk) *n.* A colorless fuming corrosive solution of hydrogen chloride in water. It is used in food processing, metal cleaning, and dyeing.

hy•dro•cy•an•ic acid (hī′drō sī ăn′ĭk) *n.* A colorless poisonous liquid having an odor of bitter almonds and used in making plastics, pesticides, and dyes.

hy•dro•dy•nam•ic (hī′drō dī năm′ĭk) *adj.* **1.** Of, relating to, or operated by a moving liquid. **2.** Of or relating to hydrodynamics. **—hy′dro•dy•nam′i•cal•ly** *adv.*

hy•dro•dy•nam•ics (hī′drō dī năm′ĭks) *n.* *(used with a singular verb).* The branch of science that deals with the forces exerted by fluids in motion.

hy•dro•e•lec•tric (hī′drō ĭ lĕk′trĭk) *adj.* Generating electricity through the use of water power: *a hydroelectric power station.*

hy•dro•foil (hī′drə foil′) *n.* **1.** One of a set of blades attached to the hull of a boat below the water line so that at high speed the hull is lifted clear of the water, decreasing friction and allowing the boat to travel faster and use less fuel. **2.** A boat equipped with hydrofoils.

hy•dro•gen (hī′drə jən) *n.* *Symbol* **H** A colorless, highly flammable gaseous element present in most organic compounds. Hydrogen is the lightest, most abundant element and combines with oxygen to form water. Atomic number 1. See table at **element.** [First written down in 1791 in Modern English : Greek *hudōr*, water + Greek *-genēs*, born.]

hy•dro•gen•ate (hī′drə jə nāt′ *or* hī drŏj′ə nāt′) *tr. v.* **hy•dro•gen•at•ed, hy•dro•gen•at•ing, hy•dro•gen•ates.** To treat or combine chemically with hydrogen. When a liquid vegetable oil is hydrogenated, it becomes a solid fat. **—hy′dro•gen•a′tion** *n.*

hydrogen bomb *n.* An extremely destructive bomb whose explosive power is derived from the energy released when hydrogen atoms fuse to form helium.

hydrogen chloride *n.* A colorless, fuming, corrosive suffocating gas used in the manufacture of plastics.

hydrogen peroxide *n.* A colorless compound of hydrogen and oxygen having the formula H_2O_2. It is an unstable oxidizing agent, and is often used in water solution as an antiseptic and bleaching agent.

hydrogen sulfide *n.* A poisonous chemical compound containing hydrogen and sulfur and having the formula H_2S. It is a flammable gas having a characteristic odor of rotten eggs.

hy•drog•ra•phy (hī drŏg′rə fē) *n., pl.* **hy•drog•ra•phies.** The scientific study of seas, lakes, rivers, and other surface waters. **—hy•dro•graph•ic** (hī′drə grăf′ĭk) *adj.*

hy•drol•y•sis (hī drŏl′ĭ sĭs) *n.* Decomposition of a chemical compound by reaction with water.

hy•dro•lyze (hī′drə līz′) *tr. & intr.v.* **hy•dro•lyzed, hy•dro•lyz•ing, hy•dro•lyz•es.** To separate or break down by hydrolysis.

hy•drom•e•ter (hī drŏm′ĭ tər) *n.* An instrument used to measure the specific gravity of liquids.

hy•dro•pho•bi•a (hī′drə fō′bē ə) *n.* **1.** Rabies. **2.** An abnormal fear of water.

hy•dro•plane (hī′drə plān′) *n.* **1.** A motorboat with a flattened bottom that skims the surface of the water, allowing it to travel very fast. **2.** A seaplane.

hy•dro•pon•ics (hī′drə pŏn′ĭks) *n.* *(used with a singular verb).* The growing of plants in nutrient solution rather than in soil.

hy•dro•sphere (hī′drə sfîr′) *n.* All the water of the earth, including water vapor in the atmosphere and ice.

hy•dro•stat•ic (hī′drə stăt′ĭk) *adj.* Of or relating to hydrostatics.

hy•dro•stat•ics (hī′drə stăt′ĭks) *n.* *(used with a singular verb).* The branch of physics that deals with fluids at rest and under pressure.

hy•dro•ther•a•py (hī′drə thĕr′ə pē) *n., pl.* **hy•dro•ther•a•pies.** The medical use of water in the treatment of disease.

hy•drot•ro•pism (hī drŏt′rə pĭz′əm) *n.* The tendency of a plant or other organism to grow toward moisture.

hy•drous (hī′drəs) *adj.* Containing water as a constituent: *hydrous salts.*

hy•drox•ide (hī drŏk′sīd′) *n.* A chemical compound consisting of an element or a radical joined to one or more hydroxyl radicals. Metal hydroxides are bases and nonmetal hydroxides are acids.

hy•drox•yl (hī drŏk′sĭl) *n.* The radical or group OH

Word Building: hydro–

The prefix **hydro–** is from the Greek prefix *hudro–* or *hudr–*, which comes from the Greek noun *hudōr*, meaning "water." Thus in the word **hydrophobia**, *hudro–* combines with the suffix *–phobia*, "fear," to mean "an abnormal fear of water." **Hydrophobia** is an example of a Greek word that was later adopted into Latin, then French, and then English. **Hydroelectric**, **hydroplane**, and **hydrosphere** are examples of words more recently formed in English. Before a vowel, **hydro–** sometimes becomes *hydr–*: **hydrate**, **hydrous**.

hydrofoil

hyena
Spotted hyena

ă	**pat**	oi	**boy**
ā	**pay**	ou	**out**
âr	**care**	o͝o	**took**
ä	**father**	o͞o	**boot**
ĕ	**pet**	ŭ	**cut**
ē	**be**	ûr	**urge**
ĭ	**pit**	th	**thin**
ī	**pie**	*th*	**this**
îr	**pier**	hw	**whoop**
ŏ	**pot**	zh	**vision**
ō	**toe**	ə	**about**
ô	**paw**	N	*French* **bon**

Word Building: hyper–

The basic meaning of the prefix **hyper–** is "excessive or excessively." For example, **hyperactive** means "highly or excessively active." **Hyper–** comes from the Greek prefix *huper–*, which comes from the preposition *huper*, meaning "over or beyond." **Hyper–** has been used actively in English since the 17th century and is now frequently used to make up new words, such as **hypercritical** and **hypersensitive**. In fact, most of the words in our language beginning with **hyper–** are relatively recent. Only a few, such as **hyperbole**, are of Greek origin.

Word Building: hypo–

The prefix **hypo–** means "beneath, below, or under." It can be traced back to the Greek prefix *hupo–*, from the word *hupo*, meaning "beneath, under." A few English words, such as **hypocrite**, **hypocrisy**, and **hypochondria**, come from Greek words using *hupo–*. But most English words beginning with **hypo–** have been made up by scientists and physicians. **Hypo–** can mean either "below or under," as in **hypodermic**, or "less than normal," as in **hypoglycemia**.

with a valence of 1 that is present in bases, certain acids, and alcohols.

hy•dro•zo•an (hī′drə zō′ən) *n.* Any of numerous invertebrate water animals, including hydras, corals, and the Portuguese man-of-war. —*adj.* Of or belonging to the hydrozoans.

hy•e•na (hī ē′nə) *n.* Any of several flesh-eating Asian or African mammals having coarse, sometimes spotted or striped hair. Hyenas have powerful jaws for stripping flesh from dead animals and a piercing cry resembling a laugh. [First written down in 1340 in Middle English and spelled *hyane*, from Greek *huaina*.]

hy•giene (hī′jēn′) *n.* **1.** Practices that promote good health and the prevention of disease. **2.** The study of methods that promote and maintain good health and the prevention of disease. [First written down in 1671 in Modern English, from Greek *hugieinē (tekhnē)*, (art) of health, from *hugiēs*, healthy.]

hy•gi•en•ic (hī′jē ĕn′ĭk *or* hī jĕn′ĭk *or* hī jē′nĭk) *adj.* **1.** Of or relating to hygiene: *hygienic studies.* **2.** Tending to promote good health; clean; sanitary: *a hygienic kitchen; food preparation following hygienic practices.* **—hy′gi•en′i•cal•ly** *adv.*

hy•gien•ist (hī jē′nĭst *or* hī jĕn′ĭst) *n.* A specialist in hygiene, especially a person who is trained to clean and examine the teeth.

hy•grom•e•ter (hī grŏm′ĭ tər) *n.* An instrument that measures the humidity of the air.

hy•gro•met•ric (hī′grə mĕt′rĭk) *adj.* Of or relating to the measurement of moisture in the air.

hy•gro•scope (hī′grə skōp′) *n.* An instrument that records changes in the amount of moisture in the air.

hy•gro•scop•ic (hī′grə skŏp′ĭk) *adj.* Tending to absorb moisture from the air: *a hygroscopic salt.*

hy•ing (hī′ĭng) *v.* A present participle of **hie.**

hy•men (hī′mən) *n.* A membrane that partly closes the opening of the vagina.

hymn (hĭm) *n.* **1.** A song of praise to God or to a deity. **2.** A song of praise or joy. [First written down before 1200 in Middle English and spelled *imne*, from Greek *humnos*.]

❑ *These sound alike:* **hymn, him** (pronoun).

hym•nal (hĭm′nəl) *n.* A book or collection of church hymns.

hyper– *pref.* A prefix that means excessively: *hypercritical; hypersensitive.* —See Note.

hy•per•ac•tive (hī′pər ăk′tĭv) *n.* Highly or excessively active: *a hyperactive child; a hyperactive gland.*

hy•per•bo•la (hī pûr′bə lə) *n., pl.* **hy•per•bo•las** or **hy•per•bo•lae** (hī pûr′bə lē). A plane curve having two branches that is formed by the intersection of a plane with two similar cones. The distance of any point on a hyperbola from each of two fixed points differs by a constant.

hy•per•bo•le (hī pûr′bə lē) *n.* A figure of speech in which exaggeration is used for effect; for example, the sentence *It rained last night and our yard is a lake* makes use of hyperbole.

hy•per•bol•ic (hī′pər bŏl′ĭk) *adj.* **1.** Of, relating to, or using hyperbole; exaggerated. **2.** Of, relating to, or shaped like a hyperbola: *a hyperbolic curve.*

hy•per•crit•i•cal (hī′pər krĭt′ĭ kəl) *adj.* Too ready to find fault; overly critical. **—hy′per•crit′i•cal•ly** *adv.*

hy•per•sen•si•tive (hī′pər sĕn′sĭ tĭv) *adj.* Unusually or overly sensitive: *skin that is hypersensitive to the sun.* **—hy′per•sen′si•tive•ness** *n.* **—hy′per•sen′si•tiv′i•ty** (hī′pər sĕn′sĭ tĭv′ĭ tē) *n.*

hy•per•son•ic (hī′pər sŏn′ĭk) *adj.* Moving or able to move at a speed at least five times the speed of sound.

hy•per•ten•sion (hī′pər tĕn′shən) *n.* A condition in which the pressure of the blood, especially in the arteries, is abnormally high; high blood pressure.

hy•per•tro•phy (hī pûr′trə fē) *n., pl.* **hy•per•tro•phies.** An increase in the size of an organ or a tissue, resulting from disease or overuse.

hy•pha (hī′fə) *n., pl.* **hy•phae** (hī′fē). Any of the long slender filaments that form the structural parts of the body of a fungus. Masses of hyphae make up the mycelium.

hy•phen (hī′fən) *n.* A punctuation mark (-) used between the parts of a compound word or between syllables of a word that is divided at the end of a line of text. [First written down about 1620 in Modern English, from Greek *huph' hen*, in one, as one.]

hy•phen•ate (hī′fə nāt′) *tr.v.* **hy•phen•at•ed, hy•phen•at•ing, hy•phen•ates.** To divide or connect (syllables, word elements, or names) with a hyphen. **—hy′phen•a′tion** *n.*

hyp•no•sis (hĭp nō′sĭs) *n., pl.* **hyp•no•ses** (hĭp nō′sēz). **1.** A condition resembling sleep in which a person becomes very responsive to suggestions from another. Hypnosis can be self-induced through concentration and relaxation. **2.** Hypnotism. [First written down in 1876 in Modern English, from Greek *hupnos*, sleep.]

hyp•not•ic (hĭp nŏt′ĭk) *adj.* **1.** Of or relating to hypnosis. **2.** Of or relating to hypnotism. **3.** Causing sleep: *the hypnotic effect of television.* —*n.* A drug or other agent that causes sleep. **—hyp•not′i•cal•ly** *adv.*

hyp•no•tism (hĭp′nə tĭz′əm) *n.* **1.** The theory, method, or process of putting a person into a state of hypnosis. **2.** The act of inducing hypnosis.

hyp•no•tist (hĭp′nə tĭst) *n.* A person who practices hypnotism.

hyp•no•tize (hĭp′nə tīz′) *tr.v.* **hyp•no•tized, hyp•no•tiz•ing, hyp•no•tiz•es. 1.** To put (a person) into a state of hypnosis: *The patient was hypnotized to relieve pain.* **2.** To fascinate by or as if by hypnosis: *The exciting movie hypnotized the audience.* **—hyp′no•tiz′er** *n.*

hy•po (hī′pō) *n., pl.* **hy•pos.** *Informal.* A hypodermic syringe or injection.

hypo– or **hyp–** *pref.* A prefix that means: **1.** Beneath or below: *hypodermic.* **2.** Less than normal: *hypoglycemia.* —See Note.

hy•po•chon•dri•a (hī′pə kŏn′drē ə) *n.* A condition in which a person believes that he or she is ill or worries too much about becoming ill.

hy•po•chon•dri•ac (hī′pə kŏn′drē ăk′) *n.* A person afflicted with hypochondria. —*adj.* Relating to or afflicted with hypochondria.

hy•poc•ri•sy (hĭ pŏk′rĭ sē) *n., pl.* **hy•poc•ri•sies. 1.** The practice of showing or expressing feelings, beliefs, or virtues that one does not actually hold or possess. **2.** The act or an instance of hypocrisy.

hyp•o•crite (hĭp′ə krĭt′) *n.* A person who practices hypocrisy.

hyp•o•crit•i•cal (hĭp′ə krĭt′ĭ kəl) *adj.* **1.** Characterized by hypocrisy: *hypocritical praise.* **2.** Being a hypocrite: *a hypocritical politician.* **—hyp′o•crit′i•cal•ly** *adv.*

hy•po•der•mic (hī′pə dûr′mĭk) *adj.* **1.** Beneath the skin: *a hypodermic injection of penicillin.* **2.** Injected or used to inject beneath the skin: *a hypodermic needle.* —*n.* **1.** An injection given under the skin. **2.** A hypodermic syringe. [First written down in 1863 in Modern English : Greek *hupo*, under + Greek *derma*, skin.]

hypodermic syringe *n.* A syringe that is fitted with a hollow needle and used to inject or remove fluids under the skin.

hy•po•gly•ce•mi•a (hī′pō glī sē′mē ə) *n.* An abnormally low level of sugar in the blood, often resulting from a malfunction of the liver or too much insulin.

hy•po•sul•fite (hī′pō **sŭl′**fīt′) *n.* Sodium thiosulfate.

hy•po•sul•fu•rous acid (hī′pō sŭl **fyo͝or′**əs *or* hī′-pō **sŭl′**fər əs) *n.* An acid related to sulfuric acid, found only in solution, used as a reducing and bleaching agent.

hy•pot•e•nuse (hī **pŏt′**n o͞os′ *or* hī **pŏt′**n yo͞os′) *n.* The side of a right triangle opposite the right angle.

hy•po•thal•a•mus (hī′pō **thăl′**ə məs) *n.* The region of the brain under the thalamus, controlling temperature, hunger, and thirst, and producing hormones that influence the pituitary gland.

hy•poth•e•sis (hī **pŏth′**ĭ sĭs) *n., pl.* **hy•poth•e•ses** (hī **pŏth′**ĭ sēz′). A statement that appears to explain a set of facts; a theory: *If a hypothesis is proved true, it becomes an accepted fact.* [First written down in 1596 in Modern English, from Greek *hupothesis*, basis of an argument, supposition, from *hupotithenai*, to suppose.]

hy•poth•e•size (hī **pŏth′**ĭ sīz′) *intr.v.* **hy•poth•e•sized, hy•poth•e•siz•ing, hy•poth•e•siz•es.** To make a hypothesis.

hy•po•thet•i•cal (hī′pə **thĕt′**ĭ kəl) also **hy•po•thet•ic** (hī′pə **thĕt′**ĭk) *adj.* Of, relating to, or based on a hypothesis; theoretical: *The lawyer made up a hypothetical case to prove a point.* **—hy′po•thet′i•cal•ly** *adv.*

hy•rax (**hī′**răks′) *n., pl.* **hy•rax•es** or **hy•ra•ces** (**hī′**-rə sēz′). Any of several mammals of Africa and Asia that resemble the woodchuck but are more closely related to the hoofed mammals. [First written down in 1832 in Modern English, from Greek *hurax*, shrew mouse.]

hys•sop (**hĭs′**əp) *n.* **1.** A plant having clusters of small blue flowers and a pleasant odor, used for flavoring and in medicine. **2.** In the Bible, a plant whose twigs were used for sprinkling water in certain religious rites.

hys•ter•i•a (hĭ **stĕr′**ē ə *or* hĭ **stîr′**ē ə) *n.* **1.** A mental disorder in which physical symptoms as extreme as blindness or partial paralysis can occur without physical cause. **2.** Uncontrollable excitement or emotion.

hys•ter•ic (hĭ **stĕr′**ĭk) *n.* **1.** A person who suffers from hysteria. **2. hysterics.** *(used with a singular or plural verb).* A fit of uncontrollable laughing or crying. *—adj.* Hysterical.

hys•ter•i•cal (hĭ **stĕr′**ĭ kəl) *adj.* **1.** Of or resulting from hysteria: *hysterical paralysis.* **2.** Having or subject to hysterics: *a screaming and hysterical child.* **3.** *Informal.* Extremely funny: *told a hysterical story.* **—hys•ter′i•cal•ly** *adv.*

Hz *abbr.* An abbreviation of hertz.

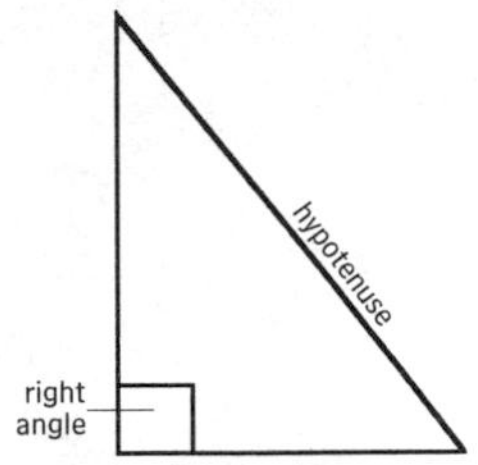

hypotenuse

ă	pat	oi	**boy**
ā	pay	ou	**out**
âr	care	o͝o	**took**
ä	father	o͞o	**boot**
ĕ	pet	ŭ	cut
ē	be	ûr	**ur**ge
ĭ	pit	th	**th**in
ī	pie	*th*	**this**
îr	pier	hw	**wh**oop
ŏ	pot	zh	vision
ō	toe	ə	about
ô	paw	N	*French* bon

Ii

ibis
White ibis

Henrik Ibsen

iceberg

icebreaker

i or **I** (ī) *n., pl.* **i's** or **I's.** **1.** The ninth letter of the English alphabet. **2.** The ninth in a series or group: *row I in a theater.*

I[1] (ī) *pron.* The person who is speaking or writing. [First written down about 725 in Old English and spelled *ic.*] —See Note at **me.**

❑ *These sound alike:* **I**[1], **aye** (yes), **eye** (organ of sight).

I[2] **1.** The symbol for the element **iodine** (sense 1). **2.** The symbol for **current** (sense 1). **3.** Also **i.** The Roman numeral for 1.

i. *abbr.* An abbreviation of: **1.** Island. **2.** Isle.

IA *abbr.* An abbreviation of Iowa.

i•amb (ī′ămb′ *or* ī′ăm′) *n., pl.* **i•ambs.** In poetry, a metrical foot consisting of an unstressed syllable followed by a stressed syllable, as in *delay.* [First written down in 1586 in Modern English and spelled *iambus,* from Greek *iambos.*] —**i•am′bic** *adj. & n.*

–ian *suff.* A suffix that means: **1.** Of, relating to, or resembling: *Bostonian.* **2.** One relating to, belonging to, or resembling: *pediatrician.*

I•be•ri•a (ī bîr′ē ə). **1.** An ancient country in the Caucasus roughly equivalent to the eastern part of present-day Georgia. **2.** Iberian Peninsula.

I•be•ri•an (ī bîr′ē ən) *adj.* **1.** Of or relating to the Iberian Peninsula, its peoples, languages, or cultures. **2.** Of or relating to the ancient peoples that inhabited the Iberian Peninsula or their languages or cultures.

Iberian Peninsula also **I•be•ri•a** (ī bîr′ē ə). A peninsula of southwest Europe occupied by Spain and Portugal. It is separated from the rest of Europe by the Pyrenees and from Africa by the Strait of Gibraltar.

i•bex (ī′bĕks′) *n., pl.* **ibex** or **i•bex•es.** Any of several wild goats of mountainous regions of Europe, Asia, and Africa, having long curving horns in the male.

i•bi•dem (ĭb′ĭ dĕm′ *or* ĭ bī′dəm) *adv.* In the same place. Used in footnotes and bibliographies to refer to something just cited.

i•bis (ī′bĭs) *n., pl.* **ibis** or **i•bis•es.** Any of various large wading birds related to the stork, having a long downward-curving bill. [First written down in 1382 in Middle English and spelled *ibin,* from Greek *ibis.*]

–ible *suff.* Variant of **–able.**

Ib•sen (ĭb′sən *or* ĭp′sən), **Henrik.** 1828–1906. Norwegian playwright whose works include *A Doll's House* (1879).

–ic *suff.* A suffix that means: **1.** Of, relating to, or characterized by: *allergic; atomic.* **2.** Having a higher valence or oxidation state in a compound or ion of an element than indicated by the suffix *-ous*: *ferric; chloric.*

Ic•a•rus (ĭk′ər əs) *n.* In Greek mythology, the son of Daedalus who, in escaping from Crete on wings made by his father, flies close to the sun, so that the wax on his wings melts, causing him to fall into the Aegean Sea.

ice (īs) *n.* **1.** Water frozen solid, normally at or below a temperature of 32 degrees Fahrenheit (0 degrees Celsius). **2.** A surface or mass of frozen water: *Before skating on the pond, test the ice.* **3.** Something resembling frozen water. **4.** A dessert consisting of sweetened and flavored crushed ice. —*v.* **iced, ic•ing, ic•es.** —*tr.* **1.** To coat or cover with ice: *Sleet iced the road.* **2.** To chill with ice: *After catching the fish, we iced them.* **3.** To decorate (a cake or cookies) with icing. —*intr.* To turn into or become covered or blocked with ice; freeze: *The river iced over during the cold spell.* [First written down about 725 in Old English and spelled *īs.*]

ice age *n.* **1.** A cold period during which glaciers covered much of the earth. **2. Ice Age.** The most recent glacial period, which occurred during the Pleistocene epoch.

ice•berg (īs′bûrg′) *n.* A massive body of floating ice that has broken away from a glacier. [First written down in 1774 in Modern English, from Dutch *ijsberg* : *ijs,* ice + *berg,* mountain.]

ice•boat (īs′bōt′) *n.* **1.** A vehicle resembling a boat set on runners and having a sail that can propel it at great speed over ice. **2.** An icebreaker.

ice•bound (īs′bound′) *adj.* **1.** Locked in by surrounding ice: *a ship icebound in the frozen sea.* **2.** Obstructed or covered over by ice: *a harbor icebound during the winter.*

ice•box (īs′bŏks′) *n.* **1.** An insulated box into which ice is put to cool and preserve food. **2.** A refrigerator.

ice•break•er (īs′brā′kər) *n.* A powerful ship with a reinforced hull, built for breaking a passage through icebound water.

ice•cap or **ice cap** (īs′kăp′) *n.* A glacier covering a large area.

ice cream *n.* A smooth sweet frozen food made of a mixture of milk products and flavoring.

ice-cream cone (īs′krēm′) *n.* **1.** A cone-shaped wafer used to hold ice cream. **2.** One of these wafers with ice cream in it.

ice field *n.* A large expanse of ice and snow among the peaks of a mountainous region.

ice hockey *n.* A game played on ice in which two teams of skaters using curved sticks try to drive a puck into the goal of the opposing team.

Ice•land (īs′lənd). An island country in the North Atlantic near the Arctic Circle east of Greenland. Norse settlers arrived here around 850–875. Iceland gained its independence from Denmark in 1944. Reykjavík is the capital and the largest city. Population, 240,443.

Ice•land•ic (īs lăn′dĭk) *adj.* Of or relating to Iceland or its people, language, or culture. —*n.* The Germanic language of Iceland.

ice•man (īs′măn) *n.* A man who delivers or sells ice.

ice pack *n.* **1.** A large mass of floating ice formed from small fragments that have pressed together and frozen solid. **2.** A bag or cloth filled with crushed ice and applied to a sore or swollen part of the body to reduce pain and inflammation.

ice pick *n.* A hand tool with a sharp point, used for chipping or breaking ice.

ice skate *n.* A boot or shoe with a metal runner attached to the sole, used for skating on ice.

ice-skate (īs′skāt′) *intr.v.* **ice-skat•ed, ice-skat•ing, ice-skates.** To skate on ice with ice skates. —**ice skater** *n.*

ich•neu•mon (ĭk nōō′mən *or* ĭk nyōō′mən) *n.* **1.** A large gray mongoose of Africa and southern Europe. **2.** The ichneumon fly.

ichneumon fly *n.* Any of various insects resembling wasps, having larvae that feed on and destroy the larvae of other, often harmful insects.

ich•thy•ol•o•gist (ĭk′thē ŏl′ə jĭst) *n.* A scientist who specializes in ichthyology.

ich•thy•ol•o•gy (ĭk′thē ŏl′ə jē) *n.* The branch of zoology that deals with the study of fishes. [First written down in 1646 in Modern English, from Greek *ikhthus*, fish.]

ich•thy•o•saur (ĭk′thē ə sôr′) *n.* Any of various extinct sea reptiles having a long beak, four flippers, a tapering body, and a tail with a large fin.

i•ci•cle (ī′sĭ kəl) *n.* A hanging spike of ice that is formed by the freezing of dripping or falling water. [First written down before 1325 in Middle English and spelled *isikel* : *is*, ice + Old English *gicel*, icicle.]

i•ci•ly (ī′sə lē) *adv.* In an icy or chilling manner: *an icily cold wind blowing across the lake; eye an opponent icily.*

i•ci•ness (ī′sē nĭs) *n.* The condition or quality of being icy.

ic•ing (ī′sĭng) *n.* A sweet glaze of sugar and egg whites or milk, used to decorate cakes or cookies.

i•con (ī′kŏn′) *n.* A religious image or picture of Jesus, Mary, or a saint, considered sacred in the Eastern Orthodox Church.

i•con•o•clast (ī kŏn′ə klăst′) *n.* **1.** A person who attacks and opposes popular or traditional ideas, beliefs, or practices. **2.** A person who destroys sacred religious images. —**i•con′o•clas′tic** *adj.*

–ics *suff.* A suffix that means: **1.** Art, science, or field of study: *graphics; mathematics.* **2.** Activities, actions, or practices of: *athletics; ceramics.*

ic•y (ī′sē) *adj.* **ic•i•er, ic•i•est. 1.** Containing or covered with ice; frozen: *an icy sidewalk.* **2.** Very cold: *icy waters.* See Synonyms at **cold. 3.** Unfriendly: *an icy stare.*

ID *abbr.* An abbreviation of: **1.** Idaho. **2.** Also **I.D.** Identification.

I'd (īd). Contraction of *I had, I would,* or *I should.*

I•da•ho (ī′də hō′). A state of the northwest United States. It was admitted as the 43rd state in 1890. Boise is the capital and the largest city. Population, 1,011,986. —See Note.

ID card (ī′dē′) *n.* A card, often bearing a photograph, that gives identifying data, such as name, age, and date of birth.

i•de•a (ī dē′ə) *n.* **1.** A product of mental activity, such as a thought, opinion, belief, or fancy: *She developed her idea for the project over several months.* **2.** A plan, scheme, or method: *My idea is to become a doctor.* **3.** The point or purpose of something: *The idea is to get people concerned by publishing the editorial.* [First written down before 1398 in Middle English, from Greek.]

Synonyms: idea, thought, notion, concept. These nouns mean something formed or represented in the mind, a product of mental activity. **Idea** is the most general: *Writers sometimes have many ideas before they begin work.* **Thought** can mean an idea produced by contemplation and reason as opposed, for example, to emotion: *The thoughts of great philosophers are worth our attention.* **Notion** means a vague, general, or even fanciful idea: *Max has a notion to travel around Europe someday.* **Concept** means an idea on a large scale: *He seems to have a very profound concept of time.*

i•de•al (ī dē′əl *or* ī dēl′) *n.* **1.** A standard of perfection: *Equality and justice are some of our society's ideals.* **2.** A person or thing that is regarded as an example of excellence or perfection: *She remains the ideal among mathematics teachers.* **3.** A supreme and worthy end or goal: *Their ideal is to own their own restaurant.* —*adj.* **1.** Perfect or the best possible: *The hot summer sun made this an ideal day for swimming.* **2.** Existing only in the mind; imaginary: *A line without thickness is an ideal geometric object.*

i•de•al•ism (ī dē′ə lĭz′əm) *n.* **1.** The tendency to behave or think mainly in terms of some standard of perfection. **2.** The practice of following one's personal ideals. **3.** A philosophical belief that all things exist only as ideas in the mind, not as objects independent of the mind.

i•de•al•ist (ī dē′ə lĭst) *n.* **1.** A person who creates and follows personal ideals, often with little regard for practical considerations. **2.** A person who believes in philosophical idealism.

i•de•al•is•tic (ī dē′ə lĭs′tĭk) *adj.* Of or relating to idealism or idealists: *an idealistic belief; an idealistic philosopher.* —**i′de•al•is′ti•cal•ly** *adv.*

i•de•al•ize (ī dē′ə līz′) *tr.v.* **i•de•al•ized, i•de•al•iz•ing, i•de•al•iz•es.** To regard as ideal or perfect: *Sometimes we idealize our friends so much that we do not see their faults.* —**i•de′al•i•za′tion** (ī dē′ə lĭ zā′shən) *n.*

i•de•al•ly (ī dē′ə lē) *adv.* **1.** In agreement with an ideal; perfectly: *The two friends were ideally suited to each other.* **2.** In theory or imagination: *Ideally, each classroom should have its own thermostat to adjust the heat.*

i•den•ti•cal (ī dĕn′tĭ kəl) *adj.* **1.** Exactly equal and alike: *We're riding identical bicycles.* **2.** The very same: *The principal used those identical words in his speech.* **3.** Of or relating to twins developed from the same fertilized egg. They are always the same sex and have the same genetic traits. [First written down in 1620 in Modern English, from Late Latin *identitās*, identity, from Latin *idem*, the same.] —**i•den′ti•cal•ly** *adv.*

i•den•ti•fi•ca•tion (ī dĕn′tə fĭ kā′shən) *n.* **1.** The act of identifying or the condition of being identified. **2.** Evidence of a person's identity: *A driver's license is usually accepted as sufficient identification.*

i•den•ti•fy (ī dĕn′tə fī′) *v.* **i•den•ti•fied, i•den•ti•fy•ing, i•den•ti•fies.** —*tr.* **1.** To establish or recognize as a certain person or thing: *We identified the bird as a thrush.* **2.** To consider as identical; equate: *The Greek god Ares is identified with the Roman god Mars.* **3.** To associate or connect closely: *That economist is identified with conservative political groups.* —*intr.* To be or feel closely associated with a person or thing: *He identifies strongly with his grandfather.* —**i•den′ti•fi′a•ble** *adj.*

i•den•ti•ty (ī dĕn′tĭ tē) *n., pl.* **i•den•ti•ties. 1.** The condition of being a certain person or thing; individuality: *The police tried to establish the suspect's identity.* **2.** The condition of being identical: *The identity of the two signatures was established by a handwriting expert.* **3.a.** A mathematical equation that remains true no matter what numbers are substituted for its variables. For example, $x + y = y + x$ is true regardless of the values of x and y. **b.** An identity element.

identity element *n.* An element of a set of numbers that does not change other elements of the set it is combined with in a mathematical operation. For example, 0 is the identity element for addition, since, if a is any real number, $a + 0 = a$. Similarly, 1 is the identity element for multiplication, since $a \times 1 = a$.

ice-skate

Idaho

The origin of the name **Idaho** is not known for certain. It is sometimes claimed to be a Shoshone word that was mistranslated as "gem of the mountains," but no Shoshone source has been confirmed. Congress gave the name first to the territory in 1863 and later to the state.

identical
Identical twins

ă	**pat**	oi	**boy**
ā	**pay**	ou	**out**
âr	**care**	ŏŏ	**took**
ä	**father**	ōō	**boot**
ĕ	**pet**	ŭ	**cut**
ē	**be**	ûr	**urge**
ĭ	**pit**	th	**thin**
ī	**pie**	*th*	**this**
îr	**pier**	hw	**whoop**
ŏ	**pot**	zh	**vision**
ō	**toe**	ə	**about**
ô	**paw**	N	*French* **bon**

ideogram
Top: No parking sign
Bottom: No U-turn sign

igloo

iguana
Common iguana

id•e•o•gram (ĭd′ē ə grăm′ *or* ī′dē ə grăm′) *n.* A written character or symbol that represents an idea or a thing rather than a particular word or phrase.

id•e•o•graph (ĭd′ē ə grăf′) *n.* An ideogram.

i•de•o•log•i•cal (ī′dē ə lŏj′ĭ kəl *or* ĭd′ē ə lŏj′ĭ kəl) *adj.* Of or relating to ideology: *ideological conflicts.* **—i′de•o•log′i•cal•ly** *adv.*

i•de•ol•o•gy (ī′dē ŏl′ə jē *or* ĭd′ē ŏl′ə jē) *n., pl.* **i•de•ol•o•gies.** A set of doctrines or beliefs that are shared by members of a group, such as a political party or social class.

ides (īdz) *pl.n.* *(used with a singular or plural verb).* In the ancient Roman calendar, the 15th day of March, May, July, or October or the 13th day of the other months. [First written down in 1124 in Middle English and spelled *idus*, from Latin *Īdūs*.]

id•i•o•cy (ĭd′ē ə sē) *n., pl.* **id•i•o•cies. 1.** Great foolishness or stupidity. **2.** A foolish or stupid action or remark.

id•i•om (ĭd′ē əm) *n.* **1.** A phrase or expression having a special meaning that cannot be understood from the individual meanings of its words; for example, *fly off the handle* is an idiom in English meaning *lose one's temper.* **2.** The accepted way in which words are used in a language. **3.** The language or dialect of a particular region or group of people: *the idiom of Cajun French.* [First written down in 1588 in Modern English, from Greek *idiōma*, from *idios*, own, personal, private.]

id•i•o•mat•ic (ĭd′ē ə măt′ĭk) *adj.* **1.** Following the pattern of word usage particular to a given language: *It takes many years of study to speak idiomatic Chinese.* **2.** Having the nature of or containing idioms: *writing characterized by many idiomatic sentences.* **—id′i•o•mat′i•cal•ly** *adv.*

id•i•o•syn•cra•sy (ĭd′ē ō sĭng′krə sē) *n., pl.* **id•i•o•syn•cra•sies.** A trait or mannerism peculiar to an individual: *One of my cousin's idiosyncrasies is always taking an umbrella when going out.* **—id′i•o•syn•crat′ic** (ĭd′ē ō sĭn krăt′ĭk) *adj.* **—id′i•o•syn•crat′i•cal•ly** *adv.*

id•i•ot (ĭd′ē ət) *n.* A very foolish or stupid person. [First written down before 1325 in Middle English, from Greek *idiōtēs*, private person, layman, from *idios*, own, private.]

id•i•ot•ic (ĭd′ē ŏt′ĭk) *adj.* Showing stupidity or foolishness: *an idiotic mistake.* **—id′i•ot′i•cal•ly** *adv.*

i•dle (īd′l) *adj.* **i•dler, i•dlest. 1.** Not employed or busy: *idle employees; idle machines; idle time on the holiday.* **2.** Avoiding work; lazy; shiftless. **3.** Not in use or operation: *The presses are idle.* **4.** Lacking substance, value, or basis: *idle talk.* —*v.* **i•dled, i•dling, i•dles.** —*intr.* **1.** To pass time without working or in avoiding work: *The men idled on the park benches.* **2.** To run at a low speed or without transmitting power: *The engine idled smoothly.* —*tr.* **1.** To pass (time) without working or in order to avoid work: *I idled the afternoon away without touching my homework.* **2.** To cause to be unemployed or inactive: *The drivers' strike idled every bus in the city.* [First written down about 725 in Old English and spelled *īdel*.] **—i′dle•ness** *n.* **—i′dly** *adv.*

❑ *These sound alike:* **idle, idol** (image), **idyll** (poem).

i•dler (īd′lər) *n.* A person who idles; a loafer.

i•dol (īd′l) *n.* **1.** An image or object that is worshiped as a god. **2.** A person or thing adored or greatly admired, often to an excessive degree. [First written down about 1250 in Middle English and spelled *idele*, from Greek *eidōlon*, from *eidos*, form.]

❑ *These sound alike:* **idol, idle** (not working), **idyll** (poem).

i•dol•a•ter or **i•dol•a•tor** (ī dŏl′ə tər) *n.* A person who worships idols.

i•dol•a•trous (ī dŏl′ə trəs) *adj.* **1.** Of or relating to idolatry. **2.** Given to idolatry.

i•dol•a•try (ī dŏl′ə trē) *n., pl.* **i•dol•a•tries. 1.** The worship of idols. **2.** Blind admiration or excessive devotion to something: *The fan's idolatry made him blind to the rock star's faults.*

i•dol•ize (īd′l īz′) *tr.v.* **i•dol•ized, i•dol•iz•ing, i•dol•iz•es. 1.** To regard with blind admiration or devotion: *Many fans idolize their favorite performers.* **2.** To worship or treat as an idol: *Early Egyptians idolized cats.* See Synonyms at **revere.**

i•dyll also **i•dyl** (īd′l) *n.* **1.** A short poem or prose work describing a pleasant scene or event of country life. **2.** A scene or event having a simple peaceful nature.

❑ *These sound alike:* **idyll, idle** (not working), **idol** (image).

i•dyl•lic (ī dĭl′ĭk) *adj.* Of or having the nature of an idyll; charming and picturesque: *idyllic countryside.* **—i•dyl′li•cal•ly** *adv.*

i.e. *abbr.* An abbreviation of id est (that is).

–ie *suff.* Variant of **–y³.**

if (ĭf) *conj.* **1.** In the event that; supposing that: *If it rains, then we won't take a walk.* **2.** On condition that: *I'll go only if you do.* **3.** Even though; although possibly: *a handsome if useless gadget.* **4.** Whether: *I asked if they were coming.* **5.** Indicating a strong wish: *If they had only come sooner!*

if•fy (ĭf′ē) *adj.* **if•fi•er, if•fi•est.** *Informal.* Doubtful; uncertain.

–ify *suff.* Variant of **–fy.**

ig•loo (ĭg′lo͞o) *n., pl.* **ig•loos.** An Eskimo dwelling, especially a dome-shaped house built of blocks of packed snow. [First written down in 1824 in Modern English, from Canadian Eskimo *iglu*, house.]

Ig•na•tius of Loy•o•la (ĭg nā′shəs əv loi ō′lə), Saint. 1491–1556. Basque priest who founded the Jesuits.

ig•ne•ous (ĭg′nē əs) *adj.* **1.** Of or relating to fire. **2.** Formed by the cooling and hardening of molten rock: *Basalt is an igneous rock.* [First written down in 1664 in Modern English, from Latin *ignis*, fire.]

ig•nite (ĭg nīt′) *v.* **ig•nit•ed, ig•nit•ing, ig•nites.** —*tr.* To cause to start burning: *A lightning bolt ignited the forest fire.* —*intr.* To begin to burn; catch fire: *Wet logs do not ignite easily.* [First written down in 1666 in Modern English, from Latin *ignis*, fire.]

ig•ni•tion (ĭg nĭsh′ən) *n.* **1.** The act or process of igniting a substance. **2.** An electrical system that provides the spark to ignite the fuel mixture of an internal-combustion engine. **3.** A switch that activates this system: *Pump the gas pedal and turn the ignition.*

ig•no•ble (ĭg nō′bəl) *adj.* **1.** Not noble, as in character or purpose; base; dishonorable: *an ignoble act.* **2.** Not of noble birth or high social standing; common: *Through great good luck, the ignoble scribe became advisor to the king.* **—ig•no′ble•ness** *n.* **—ig•no′bly** *adv.*

ig•no•min•i•ous (ĭg′nə mĭn′ē əs) *adj.* **1.** Characterized by shame or disgrace; humiliating: *The candidate suffered an ignominious defeat at the polls.* **2.** Deserving disgrace or shame; despicable: *an ignominious crime.* **—ig′no•min′i•ous•ly** *adv.* **—ig′no•min′i•ous•ness** *n.*

ig•no•min•y (ĭg′nə mĭn′ē) *n., pl.* **ig•no•min•ies. 1.** Public shame or disgrace; dishonor. **2.** Behavior or action that is shameful.

ig•no•ra•mus (ĭg′nə rā′məs) *n., pl.* **ig•no•ra•mus•es.** An ignorant person.

ig•no•rance (ĭg′nər əns) *n.* The condition of being

ignorant; lack of knowledge: *Ignorance of the law is no excuse for committing a crime.*

ig•no•rant (ĭg′nər ənt) *adj.* **1.** Lacking education or knowledge. **2.** Showing or arising from a lack of knowledge: *an ignorant mistake.* **3.** Unaware or uninformed: *Many pioneers were ignorant of the hardships they were to face.* **—ig′no•rant•ly** *adv.*

ig•nore (ĭg nôr′) *tr.v.* **ig•nored, ig•nor•ing, ig•nores.** To pay no attention to; disregard: *I ignored the sound of the television in the next room.* [First written down in 1611 in Modern English, from Latin *ignōrāre.*]

i•gua•na (ĭ gwä′nə) *n.* Any of various large tropical American lizards having a ridge of spines along the back. [First written down in 1555 in Modern English, from Arawak *iwana.*]

IL *abbr.* An abbreviation of Illinois.

il– *pref.* Variant of **in–**[1].

il•e•um (ĭl′ē əm) *n., pl.* **il•e•a** (ĭl′ē ə). The lowest section of the small intestine.

❑ *These sound alike:* **ileum, ilium** (bone).

il•i•um (ĭl′ē əm) *n., pl.* **il•i•a** (ĭl′ē ə). The uppermost of the three bones that make up each of the hipbones.

❑ *These sound alike:* **ilium, ileum** (intestine).

Il•i•um (ĭl′ē əm). Troy.

ilk (ĭlk) *n.* Type or kind; sort; class: *Flies, mosquitoes, and other insects of that ilk can be annoying.*

ill (ĭl) *adj.* **worse** (wûrs), **worst** (wûrst). **1.** Not healthy; sick: *be ill with a cold.* **2.** Not normal; unsound: *ill health.* **3.** Causing destruction or harm: *the ill effects of the storm.* **4.** Having evil intentions; hostile or unfriendly: *ill feeling between rivals.* **5.** Not favorable or promising: *an ill omen.* *—adv.* **worse, worst. 1.** In a sickly or unsound manner; unwell. **2.** Scarcely or with difficulty: *We can ill afford another mistake.* *—n.* **1.** Evil; wrongdoing: *the choice between doing good or doing ill.* **2.** Harm; disaster: *The drought was a terrible ill for farmers.* **3.** A source of suffering; an affliction: *the ills of living in an overcrowded city.* **4.** Unfavorable or unkind words: *Do not speak ill of him.*

ill. *abbr.* An abbreviation of: **1.** Illustrated. **2.** Illustration.

Ill. *abbr.* An abbreviation of Illinois.

I'll (īl). Contraction of *I will* or *I shall.*

❑ *These sound alike:* **I'll, aisle** (passageway), **isle** (island).

ill-ad•vised (ĭl′əd vīzd′) *adj.* Done with bad advice or with insufficient thinking: *an ill-advised scheme to replace the bridge with a tunnel.*

ill-bred (ĭl′brĕd′) *adj.* Badly brought up; impolite.

il•le•gal (ĭ lē′gəl) *adj.* **1.** Against the law; not legal. **2.** Against the official rules, as of a game: *Fouls are illegal acts in basketball.* **—il•le′gal•ly** *adv.*

il•le•gal•i•ty (ĭl′ē găl′ĭ tē) *n., pl.* **il•le•gal•i•ties. 1.** The condition of being illegal; unlawfulness. **2.** An illegal act.

il•leg•i•ble (ĭ lĕj′ə bəl) *adj.* Impossible or very hard to read: *a note written in an illegible scrawl.* **—il•leg′i•bil′i•ty** *n.* **—il•leg′i•bly** *adv.*

il•le•git•i•mate (ĭl′ĭ jĭt′ə mĭt) *adj.* **1.** Against the law; illegal: *an illegitimate seizure of property.* **2.** Born of parents who are not married to each other. **—il′le•git′i•ma•cy** (ĭl′ĭ jĭt′ə mə sē) *n.* **—il′le•git′i•mate•ly** *adv.*

ill-fat•ed (ĭl′fā′tĭd) *adj.* **1.** Destined for misfortune; doomed: *The ill-fated ship never reached port.* **2.** Marked by or causing misfortune; unlucky: *an ill-fated decision to act too soon.*

ill-fa•vored (ĭl′fā′vərd) *adj.* **1.** Having an ugly or unattractive appearance: *a rundown, ill-favored part of town.* **2.** Objectionable; offensive: *an ill-favored choice of words.*

ill-got•ten (ĭl′gŏt′n) *adj.* Obtained by evil or dishonest means: *ill-gotten wealth.*

ill-hu•mored (ĭl′hyōō′mərd) *adj.* Irritable; disagreeable; cross.

il•lib•er•al (ĭ lĭb′ər əl) *adj.* Narrow-minded; intolerant. **—il•lib′er•al•ly** *adv.*

il•lic•it (ĭ lĭs′ĭt) *adj.* Not permitted by law; unlawful. **—il•lic′it•ly** *adv.* **—il•lic′it•ness** *n.*

❑ *These sound alike:* **illicit, elicit** (evoke).

il•lim•it•a•ble (ĭ lĭm′ĭ tə bəl) *adj.* Impossible to limit; limitless. **—il•lim′it•a•bly** *adv.*

Il•li•nois[1] (ĭl′ə noi′ *or* ĭl′ə noiz′) *n., pl.* **Illinois. 1.** A member of a group of Native American peoples originally living in Illinois, Iowa, Wisconsin, and Missouri, with descendants living in Oklahoma. **2.** The Algonquian language of the Illinois.

Il•li•nois[2] (ĭl′ə noi′ *or* ĭl′ə noiz′). A state of the north-central United States. It was admitted as the 21st state in 1818. Springfield is the capital and Chicago the largest city. Population, 11,466,682. —SEE NOTE.

il•lit•er•a•cy (ĭ lĭt′ər ə sē) *n., pl.* **il•lit•er•a•cies. 1.** The condition of being unable to read and write. **2.** A lack of education or knowledge: *scientific illiteracy.*

il•lit•er•ate (ĭ lĭt′ər ĭt) *adj.* **1.** Unable to read and write. **2.** Showing a lack of knowledge in a certain subject: *illiterate in history.* **—il•lit′er•ate•ly** *adv.*

ill-man•nered (ĭl′măn′ərd) *adj.* Showing a lack of good manners; impolite; rude. **—ill′-man′nered•ly** *adv.*

ill-na•tured (ĭl′nā′chərd) *adj.* Disagreeable, cross, or mean. **—ill′-na′tured•ly** *adv.*

ill•ness (ĭl′nĭs) *n.* **1.** An unhealthy condition; poor health: *often missing school because of illness.* **2.** A disease: *Pneumonia is a serious illness.*

il•log•i•cal (ĭ lŏj′ĭ kəl) *adj.* **1.** Having or showing a lack of sound reasoning; not logical: *Your argument is illogical.* **2.** Unreasonable; senseless: *an illogical fear of dogs.* **—il•log′i•cal•ly** *adv.*

ill-starred (ĭl′stärd′) *adj.* Unlucky; ill-fated.

ill-tem•pered (ĭl′tĕm′pərd) *adj.* Having a bad temper; irritable. **—ill′-tem′pered•ly** *adv.*

ill-timed (ĭl′tīmd′) *adj.* Done or occurring at the wrong time; untimely.

ill-treat (ĭl′trēt′) *tr.v.* **ill-treat•ed, ill-treat•ing, ill-treats.** To treat badly or cruelly; mistreat. **—ill-treat′ment** *n.*

il•lu•mi•nate (ĭ lōō′mə nāt′) *tr.v.* **il•lu•mi•nat•ed, il•lu•mi•nat•ing, il•lu•mi•nates. 1.** To provide with light: *A lamp illuminated the steps.* **2.** To make clear; explain: *The film illuminated the events leading up to the war.* **3.** To decorate with ornamental designs, pictures, or colors: *We do not know how many artists illuminated the manuscript.*

il•lu•mi•na•tion (ĭ lōō′mə nā′shən) *n.* **1.** The act of illuminating or the state of being illuminated: *the illumination of a dark corner.* **2.** An amount of light; brightness: *the soft illumination of a candle.* **3.** Decoration with lights: *festive outdoor illumination.* **4.** Decoration of a book, manuscript, or other writing. **5.** A design, picture, or other adornment in a book or manuscript.

il•lu•mine (ĭ lōō′mĭn) *tr.v.* **il•lu•mined, il•lu•min•ing, il•lu•mines.** To give light to; illuminate.

illus. *abbr.* An abbreviation of: **1.** Illustrated. **2.** Illustrator.

ill-use (ĭl′yōōz′) *tr.v.* **ill-used, ill-us•ing, ill-us•es.** To treat badly or unjustly; mistreat. *—n.* (ĭl′yōōs′). Poor or unjust treatment.

il•lu•sion (ĭ lōō′zhən) *n.* **1.** An unreal or misleading appearance or image: *The painting gives the illusion that we are really looking out to sea.* **2.** An idea or a belief that is mistaken or false: *His illusion that he did not need to study for tests did not last long.*

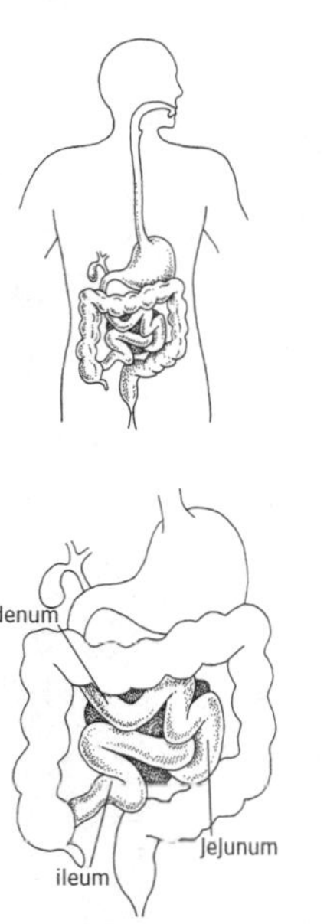

ileum

Illinois[2]

The state of **Illinois** takes its name from the Illinois River. The river's name comes from the name French explorers used for a Native American people of the region. The French learned this name from an Algonquian language, but it is unclear which language. The name was pronounced [ĭl′ə **nō′**wā] and meant "ordinary speaker," that is, "one who speaks a similar language." The final *s* at the end of *Illinois* was added by the French to make the word plural when referring to this group. The pronunciation, with the final *s* silent, comes from the French.

ă	**pat**	oi	**boy**
ā	**pay**	ou	**out**
âr	**care**	ŏŏ	**took**
ä	**father**	ōō	**boot**
ĕ	**pet**	ŭ	**cut**
ē	**be**	ûr	**urge**
ĭ	**pit**	th	**thin**
ī	**pie**	*th*	**this**
îr	**pier**	hw	**whoop**
ŏ	**pot**	zh	**vision**
ō	**toe**	ə	**about**
ô	**paw**	N	*French* **bon**

[First written down about 1350 in Middle English and spelled *illusioun*, from Late Latin *illūsiō*, ridicule, from Latin *illūdere*, to mock.]

il•lu•sive (ĭ lo͞o′sĭv) *adj.* Illusory. —**il•lu′sive•ly** *adv.* —**il•lu′sive•ness** *n.*

❑ *These sound alike:* **illusive, elusive** (tending to elude).

il•lu•so•ry (ĭ lo͞o′sə rē *or* ĭ lo͞o′zə rē) *adj.* Produced by, based on, or having the nature of an illusion; deceptive: *The coach's confidence in the bullpen was illusory.*

il•lus•trate (ĭl′ə strāt′ *or* ĭ lŭs′trāt′) *tr.v.* **il•lus•trat•ed, il•lus•trat•ing, il•lus•trates. 1.** To make clear or explain, as by using examples or comparisons: *The geologist illustrated how the rocks folded by pushing on the ends of a piece of paper.* **2.** To provide with pictures or diagrams that explain or adorn: *The artist illustrated the story.* —**il′lus•tra′tor** *n.*

il•lus•tra•tion (ĭl′ə strā′shən) *n.* **1.** Something, such as a picture, diagram, or chart, that serves to make clear, explain, or decorate something else: *The illustrations improve the book.* **2.** Something serving as an example, a comparison, or a proof: *A ball falling to the ground is an illustration of gravity.* **3.** The act of clarifying or the state of being clarified: *The main idea is interesting but it needs further illustration.* [First written down about 1375 in Middle English and spelled *illustration*, spiritual enlightenment, from Latin *illūstrāre*, to shed light on.]

il•lus•tra•tive (ĭ lŭs′trə tĭv *or* ĭl′ə strā′tĭv) *adj.* Serving as an illustration: *an illustrative example of Baroque art.* —**il•lus′tra•tive•ly** *adv.*

il•lus•tri•ous (ĭ lŭs′trē əs) *adj.* Famous; celebrated: *an illustrious author; illustrious deeds.* See Synonyms at **noted.**

ill will *n.* Unfriendly feeling; hostility.

im– *pref.* Variant of **in–**[1].

I'm (īm). Contraction of *I am.*

im•age (ĭm′ĭj) *n.* **1.** A representation of a person or thing, especially a picture or statue. **2.** A picture or reproduction of an object, especially by reflection in a mirror or refraction through a lens or lens system: *a photographic image.* **3.** A mental picture of something not real or present: *Our image of the new apartment did not conform with reality.* **4.** A vivid description in words, especially a metaphor or simile: *The poem is full of images of country life.* **5.** The concept of a person or thing that is held by the public, especially as a result of advertising or publicity: *The toy company has a friendly image.* **6.** A person or thing that closely resembles another: *a child who is the image of a parent.* [First written down about 1200 in Middle English, from Latin *imāgō*.]

im•age•ry (ĭm′ĭj rē) *n., pl.* **im•age•ries. 1.** The use of figures of speech or vivid descriptions in writing or speaking. **2.** A set of mental pictures or images.

i•mag•i•na•ble (ĭ măj′ə nə bəl) *adj.* Capable of being imagined: *a book that has information on every imaginable topic.* —**i•mag′i•na•bly** *adv.*

i•mag•i•nar•y (ĭ măj′ə nĕr′ē) *adj.* **1.** Existing only in the imagination; not real: *an imaginary illness.* **2.** Of or relating to an imaginary number.

imaginary number *n.* A number whose square is negative.

i•mag•i•na•tion (ĭ măj′ə nā′shən) *n.* **1.** The act or ability of forming mental images of something that is not real or present: *Characters for the story were born in the lively imagination of the writer.* **2.** The ability to use the mind effectively; resourcefulness: *The new mayor solved the city's budget problems with imagination.*

i•mag•i•na•tive (ĭ măj′ə nə tĭv *or* ĭ măj′ə nā′tĭv) *adj.* **1.** Having a strong imagination, especially creative imagination: *an imaginative person.* **2.** Created by or marked by originality and creativity: *an imaginative solution to a problem.* —**i•mag′i•na•tive•ly** *adv.*

i•mag•ine (ĭ măj′ĭn) *v.* **i•mag•ined, i•mag•in•ing, i•mag•ines.** —*tr.* **1.** To form a mental picture of: *Can you imagine what it is like to live in a rain forest?* **2.** To make a guess; suppose: *I imagine this bad weather will make them late.* —*intr.* To use the imagination: *The mind is able to think, remember, and imagine.* [First written down about 1340 in Middle English and spelled *imaginen*, from Latin *imāginārī*, from *imāgō*, image.]

i•ma•go (ĭ mā′gō *or* ĭ mä′gō) *n., pl.* **i•ma•goes** or **i•ma•gi•nes** (ĭ mā′gə nēz′ *or* ĭ mä′gə nēz′). An insect in its fully developed adult stage.

i•mam also **I•mam** (ĭ mäm′) *n.* **1.** A male prayer leader in a mosque. **2.** A male Muslim leader claiming authority on the basis of descent from Muhammad.

im•bal•ance (ĭm băl′əns) *n.* A lack of balance.

im•be•cile (ĭm′bə sĭl) *n.* A stupid or foolish person. —*adj.* Stupid or foolish. [First written down in 1549 in Modern English and spelled *imbecille*, feeble, from Latin *imbēcillus*.] —**im′be•cil′ic** *adj.*

im•bed (ĭm bĕd′) *v.* Variant of **embed.**

im•bibe (ĭm bīb′) *v.* **im•bibed, im•bib•ing, im•bibes.** —*tr.* **1.** To drink. **2.** To absorb or take in as if by drinking: *Thirsty plants imbibe moisture through the roots.* **3.** To take or absorb into the mind: *The painter went to Asia to imbibe new ideas.* —*intr.* To drink alcoholic beverages. [First written down about 1395 in Middle English and spelled *embiben*, to soak up, from Latin *imbibere*, to drink in.] —**im•bib′er** *n.*

im•bro•glio (ĭm brōl′yō) *n., pl.* **im•bro•glios.** A confused or difficult situation; a predicament.

im•bue (ĭm byo͞o′) *tr.v.* **im•bued, im•bu•ing, im•bues. 1.** To inspire or fill: *Reading the novel imbued them with a desire to travel to Africa.* **2.** To stain or dye deeply.

imit. *abbr.* An abbreviation of: **1.** Imitation. **2.** Imitative.

im•i•ta•ble (ĭm′ĭ tə bəl) *adj.* Capable or worthy of being imitated: *imitable behavior.*

im•i•tate (ĭm′ĭ tāt′) *tr.v.* **im•i•tat•ed, im•i•tat•ing, im•i•tates. 1.** To follow as a model or an example: *Your little brother imitates you because he admires you.* **2.** To copy the speech or actions of; mimic: *The actor imitated the President perfectly.* **3.** To copy exactly; reproduce: *Few artists can imitate the paintings of Rembrandt.* **4.** To look like; resemble: *a plastic that imitates the look of leather.* [First written down in 1534 in Modern English, from Latin *imitārī*.] —**im′i•ta′tor** *n.*

Synonyms: imitate, copy, mimic, simulate. These verbs mean to follow something or someone as a model. **Imitate** means to act like another or follow a pattern set by another: *Can you imitate a British accent?* **Copy** means to duplicate an original as closely as possible: *If you were absent, copy the notes from a classmate.* **Mimic** often means to imitate in order to make fun of a person or thing: *The class clown mimicked the teacher in our play about school.* **Simulate** means to falsely take on the appearance or character of something: *They painted the wall to simulate marble.*

im•i•ta•tion (ĭm′ĭ tā′shən) *n.* **1.** The act or an instance of imitating: *I learned the song through imitation.* **2.** Something made to look like something else; a likeness or copy: *This bell is an imitation of the Liberty Bell.* —*adj.* Made to resemble another: *imitation leather.*

im•i•ta•tive (ĭm′ĭ tā′tĭv) *adj.* **1.** Involving imitation: Buzz *and* meow *are imitative words.* **2.** Tending to imitate or copy: *Parrots are imitative birds.* —**im′i·ta′tive·ly** *adv.*

im·mac·u·late (ĭ măk′yə lĭt) *adj.* **1.** Perfectly clean: *the doctor's immaculate white coat.* See Synonyms at **clean. 2.** Free from fault or error; flawless: *an immaculate record as Attorney General.* **3.** Free of sin; pure. —**im·mac′u·late·ness** *n.* —**im·mac′u·late·ly** *adv.*

Immaculate Conception *n.* The doctrine of the Roman Catholic Church that the Virgin Mary was conceived free from original sin.

im·ma·nent (ĭm′ə nənt) *adj.* Existing within; inherent: *They believed that goodness is immanent in all human beings.* [First written down in 1535 in Modern English, from Late Latin *immanēre,* to remain in.]

❑ *These sound alike:* **immanent, imminent** (impending).

im·ma·te·ri·al (ĭm′ə tîr′ē əl) *adj.* **1.** Of no importance or consequence; unimportant: *After losing the tickets, it became immaterial what we decided to do.* **2.** Having no physical body or form; spiritual: *ghosts and other immaterial beings.* —**im′ma·te′ri·al·ly** *adv.*

im·ma·ture (ĭm′ə tyo͝or′ *or* ĭm′ə to͝or′ *or* ĭm′ə cho͝or′) *adj.* Not fully grown or developed; not mature: *immature corn; immature judgment.* —**im′ma·ture′ly** *adv.* —**im′ma·tur′i·ty** *n.*

im·meas·ur·a·ble (ĭ mĕzh′ər ə bəl) *adj.* Impossible to measure: *the immeasurable number of stars in the heavens.* —**im·meas′ur·a·bly** *adv.*

im·me·di·ate (ĭ mē′dē ĭt) *adj.* **1.** Taking place at once or very soon; happening without delay: *needing immediate medical care in an emergency room.* **2.** Of or near the present time: *the immediate future.* **3.** Close at hand; near: *our immediate surroundings.* **4.** Next in line or relation: *the king's immediate successor.* **5.** Occurring with nothing coming between or interfering; direct: *immediate contact with each other.* —**im·me′di·ate·ly** *adv.* —**im·me′di·ate·ness** *n.*

im·me·mo·ri·al (ĭm′ə môr′ē əl) *adj.* Reaching beyond the limits of memory or history: *Insects have lived on the earth since time immemorial.* —**im′me·mo′ri·al·ly** *adv.*

im·mense (ĭ mĕns′) *adj.* Of great size, extent, or degree; huge: *immense rocks; an immense length of time.* —**im·mense′ly** *adv.* —**im·men′si·ty** *n.*

im·merse (ĭ mûrs′) *tr.v.* **im·mersed, im·mers·ing, im·mers·es. 1.** To cover completely with a liquid; submerge: *immerse pots and pans in soapy water.* **2.** To baptize by submerging in water. **3.** To involve deeply; absorb: *I immersed myself in the exciting story.*

im·mer·sion (ĭ mûr′zhən *or* ĭ mûr′shən) *n.* **1.** An act of immersing or the condition of being immersed. **2.** Baptism performed by immersing a person in water.

im·mi·grant (ĭm′ĭ grənt) *n.* A person who leaves one country and settles in another.

im·mi·grate (ĭm′ĭ grāt′) *intr.v.* **im·mi·grat·ed, im·mi·grat·ing, im·mi·grates.** To come into a foreign country to live: *People from many parts of the world immigrate to the United States each year.* —**im′mi·gra′tion** *n.* —SEE NOTE at **emigrate.**

im·mi·nent (ĭm′ə nənt) *adj.* About to happen; looming: *It is cold and windy, and snow seems imminent.* [First written down in 1436 in Middle English and spelled *iminent,* from Latin *imminēre,* to overhang.] —**im′mi·nence** *n.* —**im′mi·nent·ly** *adv.*

❑ *These sound alike:* **imminent, immanent** (inherent).

im·mo·bile (ĭ mō′bəl *or* ĭ mō′bēl′ *or* ĭ mō′bīl′) *adj.* **1.** Not movable; fixed: *A broken axle made the car immobile.* **2.** Not moving; motionless: *The deer stood immobile in the field.* —**im′mo·bil′i·ty** (ĭm′ō bĭl′ĭ tē) *n.*

im·mo·bi·lize (ĭ mō′bə līz′) *tr.v.* **im·mo·bi·lized, im·mo·bi·liz·ing, im·mo·bi·liz·es.** To make immobile; render incapable of moving: *The doctor immobilized the broken finger with a splint.* —**im·mo′bi·li·za′tion** (ĭ mō′bə lĭ zā′shən) *n.*

im·mod·er·ate (ĭ mŏd′ər ĭt) *adj.* Going beyond what is normal or proper; extreme: *loud and immoderate laughter.* —**im·mod′er·ate·ly** *adv.*

im·mod·est (ĭ mŏd′ĭst) *adj.* **1.** Lacking modesty: *She gave an immodest description of her role in the project.* **2.** Not considered proper; indecent or offensive. —**im·mod′est·ly** *adv.* —**im·mod′es·ty** *n.*

im·mo·late (ĭm′ə lāt′) *tr.v.* **im·mo·lat·ed, im·mo·lat·ing, im·mo·lates.** To kill as a sacrifice. —**im′mo·la′tion** *n.*

im·mor·al (ĭ môr′əl *or* ĭ mŏr′əl) *adj.* Contrary to what is considered moral: *immoral behavior.* —**im·mor′al·ly** *adv.*

im·mor·al·i·ty (ĭm′ô răl′ĭ tē) *n., pl.* **im·mor·al·i·ties. 1.** The quality or condition of being immoral: *the immorality of war.* **2.** An immoral act or practice: *The immoralities of a few public officials can weaken the public's confidence in government.*

im·mor·tal (ĭ môr′tl) *adj.* **1.** Never dying; living forever: *The Greek gods were believed to be immortal.* **2.** Having eternal fame: *the immortal words of Shakespeare.* —*n.* **1.** An immortal being: *The ancient Greeks believed their gods were immortals.* **2.** A person with enduring fame: *Mozart and Beethoven are immortals in the field of music.* —**im·mor′tal·ly** *adv.*

im·mor·tal·i·ty (ĭm′ôr tăl′ĭ tē) *n.* **1.** The condition of being immortal. **2.** Enduring fame: *the immortality of Michelangelo.*

im·mor·tal·ize (ĭ môr′tl īz′) *tr.v.* **im·mor·tal·ized, im·mor·tal·iz·ing, im·mor·tal·iz·es.** To make immortal: *Longfellow's poem immortalizes the midnight ride of Paul Revere.*

im·mov·a·ble (ĭ mo͞o′və bəl) *adj.* **1.** Not capable of moving or of being moved: *Mountains are immovable objects.* **2.** Unyielding; steadfast: *an immovable purpose.* —*n.* **immovables.** Property, such as real estate, that cannot be moved. —**im·mov′a·bly** *adv.*

im·mune (ĭ myo͞on′) *adj.* **1.** Protected from disease naturally or by vaccination or inoculation: *I'm immune to chicken pox since I had it when I was young.* **2.** Relating to or producing immunity: *the body's immune response to a vaccine.* **3.** Protected; guarded; safe: *The fort made the harbor immune from attack.* [First written down in 1440 in Middle English, from Latin *immūnis.*]

immune system *n.* The system in humans and other animals that produces white blood cells and antibodies to resist infection by disease.

im·mu·ni·ty (ĭ myo͞o′nĭ tē) *n., pl.* **im·mu·ni·ties. 1.** The ability of an animal or a plant to resist disease, especially through the production of antibodies. **2.** Freedom from certain duties, penalties, or restrictions: *Diplomatic immunity protects ambassadors from being prosecuted for most crimes.*

im·mu·nize (ĭm′yə nīz′) *tr.v.* **im·mu·nized, im·mu·niz·ing, im·mu·niz·es.** To produce immunity in, as by vaccination. —**im′mu·ni·za′tion** (ĭm′yə nĭ zā′shən) *n.*

im·mu·nol·o·gy (ĭm′yə nŏl′ə jē) *n.* The science that deals with the structures and functions of the immune system.

im·mure (ĭ myo͝or′) *tr.v.* **im·mured, im·mur·ing, im·mures.** To confine within walls; imprison.

im·mu·ta·ble (ĭ myo͞o′tə bəl) *adj.* Not subject to change; unchangeable: *nature's immutable laws.*

ă	pat	oi	boy
ā	pay	ou	out
âr	care	o͝o	took
ä	father	o͞o	boot
ĕ	pet	ŭ	cut
ē	be	ûr	urge
ĭ	pit	th	thin
ī	pie	*th*	this
îr	pier	hw	whoop
ŏ	pot	zh	vision
ō	toe	ə	about
ô	paw	N	*French* bon

—im•mu′ta•bil′i•ty, im•mu′ta•ble•ness *n.* —im•mu′ta•bly *adv.*

imp (ĭmp) *n.* **1.** A mischievous child. **2.** A small demon or spirit.

imp. *abbr.* An abbreviation of: **1.** Imperative. **2.** Imperfect. **3.** Imperial. **4.** Imported. **5.** Importer.

im•pact (ĭm′păkt′) *n.* **1.** The action of one body striking against another; collision: *The impact of the meteoroid left a large crater.* **2.** The effect or impression of something: *the emotional impact of a poem; the impact of science on modern society.* [First written down in 1781 in Modern English, from Latin *impāctus*, past participle of *impingere*, to push against.]

impala
Male impala

im•pact•ed (ĭm păk′tĭd) *adj.* **1.** Located inside the gum in such a way as to prevent movement through the gum into a normal position: *an impacted tooth.* **2.** Packed together closely; wedged in place.

im•pair (ĭm pâr′) *tr.v.* **im•paired, im•pair•ing, im•pairs.** To diminish in strength, quantity, or quality; weaken: *An ear infection impaired my hearing for a week.* —**im•pair′ment** *n.*

im•pa•la (ĭm pä′lə) *n.* An African antelope having a yellowish-brown coat and curved spreading horns, noted for its ability to make long high leaps. [First written down in 1875 in Modern English, from Zulu *im-pala*.]

im•pale (ĭm pāl′) *tr.v.* **im•paled, im•pal•ing, im•pales.** **1.** To pierce with a sharp stake or point: *The sales clerk impaled the receipts on a spike.* **2.** To torture or kill by pushing onto a stake.

im•pal•pa•ble (ĭm păl′pə bəl) *adj.* **1.** Not perceptible to the touch: *impalpable shadows.* **2.** Difficult to grasp by the mind: *the impalpable complexity of the atomic theory of matter.* —**im•pal′pa•bil′i•ty** *n.* —**im•pal′pa•bly** *adv.*

im•pan•el (ĭm păn′əl) *tr.v.* **im•pan•eled, im•pan•el•ing, im•pan•els** or **im•pan•elled, im•pan•el•ling, im•pan•els.** **1.** To enroll or place on a panel or list. **2.** To choose (a jury) from a list or lottery. —**im•pan′el•ment** *n.*

im•part (ĭm pärt′) *tr.v.* **im•part•ed, im•part•ing, im•parts.** **1.** To give; bestow: *Bright sunlight imparted a cheerful feeling to the room.* **2.** To make known; disclose; reveal: *impart a secret.*

im•par•tial (ĭm pär′shəl) *adj.* Not favoring either side; fair; unprejudiced: *Sports officials must be impartial in their judgments.* —**im′par•ti•al′i•ty** (ĭm′pär shē ăl′ĭ tē) *n.* —**im•par′tial•ly** *adv.*

im•pass•a•ble (ĭm păs′ə bəl) *adj.* Impossible to travel across or over; not passable: *an impassable gorge.* —**im•pass′a•bil′i•ty** *n.* —**im•pass′a•bly** *adv.*

im•passe (ĭm′păs′) *n.* **1.** A road or passage that has no exit. **2.** A difficult situation that has no practical solution: *When members could not agree, the committee reached an impasse.*

im•pas•sioned (ĭm păsh′ənd) *adj.* Filled with intense feeling; ardent: *an impassioned plea for human rights.*

im•pas•sive (ĭm păs′ĭv) *adj.* Feeling or showing no emotion; calm: *The judge was impassive through all the lawyer's dramatic arguments.* —**im•pas′sive•ly** *adv.* —**im•pas′sive•ness** *n.*

im•pa•tience (ĭm pā′shəns) *n.* The quality or condition of being impatient.

im•pa•tient (ĭm pā′shənt) *adj.* **1.** Unable to wait patiently or endure irritation: *When the line for tickets did not move, she grew impatient and left.* **2.** Expressing or produced by impatience: *an impatient answer.* **3.** Restlessly eager: *impatient to go home.* —**im•pa′tient•ly** *adv.*

im•peach (ĭm pēch′) *tr.v.* **im•peached, im•peach•ing, im•peach•es.** **1.** To charge (a public official) formally with misconduct in office: *The President of the United States can be impeached only before Congress.* **2.** To challenge or discredit; attack: *Scientists impeached the accuracy of the report.* [First written down in 1383 in Middle English and spelled *empechen*, to impede, accuse, from Late Latin *impedicāre*, to entangle, from Latin *pedica*, fetter.] —**im•peach′ment** *n.*

im•pec•ca•ble (ĭm pĕk′ə bəl) *adj.* Having no flaws; faultless: *impeccable table manners.* See Synonyms at **perfect.** [First written down in 1531 in Modern English, from Latin *impeccābilis* : *in-*, not + *peccāre*, to sin.] —**im•pec′ca•bly** *adv.*

im•pe•cu•ni•ous (ĭm′pĭ kyo͞o′nē əs) *adj.* Lacking money; penniless. —**im′pe•cu′ni•ous•ly** *adv.*

im•pede (ĭm pēd′) *tr.v.* **im•ped•ed, im•ped•ing, im•pedes.** To obstruct or slow down; hinder: *Road repairs impeded traffic all summer.* [First written down in 1605 in Modern English, from Latin *impedīre*.]

im•ped•i•ment (ĭm pĕd′ə mənt) *n.* **1.** A physical defect that prevents clear speech. **2.** Something that impedes or incumbers progress; a hindrance or an obstruction: *Youth is no impediment to success in sports and music.*

im•pel (ĭm pĕl′) *tr.v.* **im•pelled, im•pel•ling, im•pels.** **1.** To urge to action; drive; spur: *Their curiosity impelled them to investigate the noise.* **2.** To drive forward; propel: *A strong current impelled the little boat toward the rocks.* [First written down before 1425 in Middle English and spelled *impellen*, from Latin *impellere* : *in-*, against + *pellere*, to drive.]

im•pend (ĭm pĕnd′) *intr.v.* **im•pend•ed, im•pend•ing, im•pends.** To be about to take place: *Her retirement is impending.*

im•pen•e•tra•ble (ĭm pĕn′ĭ trə bəl) *adj.* **1.** Impossible to penetrate or enter: *an impenetrable fortress.* **2.** Impossible to understand; incomprehensible: *an impenetrable mystery.* —**im•pen′e•tra•bly** *adv.*

im•pen•i•tent (ĭm pĕn′ĭ tənt) *adj.* Showing no sorrow for having done something wrong; unrepentant. —**im•pen′i•tent•ly** *adv.*

im•per•a•tive (ĭm pĕr′ə tĭv) *adj.* **1.** In grammar, of or relating to the mood of a verb that expresses a command, an order, or a request. For example, *do* in "Please do it!" and *go* in "Go at once!" are in the imperative mood. **2.** Expressive of a command or an order: *The director's requests were made in an imperative manner.* **3.** Unavoidable; urgent: *It is imperative that we arrive on time.* —*n.* **1.** In grammar: **a.** The imperative mood. **b.** A verb form in the imperative mood. In the sentence *Please do it*, the word *do* is an imperative. **2.** A command; an order: *The boss's suggestions are really imperatives.* [First written down about 1450 in Middle English and spelled *imperatif*, from Late Latin *imperātīvus*, from Latin *imperāre*, to command.] —**im•per′a•tive•ly** *adv.*

im•per•cep•ti•ble (ĭm′pər sĕp′tə bəl) *adj.* Impossible or difficult to perceive or feel: *the ant's imperceptible movement through the grass.* —**im′per•cep′ti•bil′i•ty** *n.* —**im′per•cep′ti•bly** *adv.*

im•per•fect (ĭm pûr′fĭkt) *adj.* **1.** Not perfect; having faults or defects. **2.** Of or relating to the imperfect tense. —*n.* **1.** The imperfect tense. **2.** A verb in the imperfect tense. —**im•per′fect•ly** *adv.*

im•per•fec•tion (ĭm′pər fĕk′shən) *n.* **1.** The condition or quality of being imperfect: *human imperfection.* **2.** A defect; a fault or flaw: *scratches and other imperfections in the surface of the table.*

imperfect tense *n.* A verb tense that expresses incomplete or continuous action, especially in the past.

im•pe•ri•al (ĭm pîr′ē əl) *adj.* Of or relating to an empire, emperor, or empress: *the days of imperial*

Rome; the imperial court. —**im•pe′ri•al•ly** *adv.*

im•pe•ri•al•ism (ĭm pîr′ē ə lĭz′əm) *n.* **1.** The policy of extending and increasing a nation's authority by acquiring territories or by establishing economic and political dominance over other nations. **2.** The system, policies, or practices of an imperial government.

im•pe•ri•al•ist (ĭm pîr′ē ə lĭst) *n.* A person who believes in imperialism. —*adj.* Of, relating to, or supporting imperialism.

im•pe•ri•al•is•tic (ĭm pîr′ē ə lĭs′tĭk) *adj.* Of or relating to imperialism or imperialists. —**im•pe′ri•al•is′ti•cal•ly** *adv.*

im•per•il (ĭm pĕr′əl) *tr.v.* **im•per•iled, im•per•il•ing, im•per•ils** or **im•per•illed, im•per•il•ling, im•per•ils.** To put into peril; endanger: *Pollution imperils the health of the shellfish in the bay.*

im•pe•ri•ous (ĭm pîr′ē əs) *adj.* **1.** Arrogant; overbearing; domineering: *The boss's imperious treatment of the workers caused many to quit.* **2.** Pressing; urgent: *an imperious need.* —**im•pe′ri•ous•ly** *adv.* —**im•pe′ri•ous•ness** *n.*

im•per•ish•a•ble (ĭm pĕr′ĭ shə bəl) *adj.* Not perishable: *imperishable food; imperishable hopes.*

im•per•ma•nent (ĭm pûr′mə nənt) *adj.* Not lasting or durable.

im•per•me•a•ble (ĭm pûr′mē ə bəl) *adj.* Impossible to permeate, as by a liquid or gas: *an impermeable raincoat; an impermeable cell wall.*

im•per•son•al (ĭm pûr′sə nəl) *adj.* **1.** Not referring to or intended for any particular person: *The speaker's remarks were very general and impersonal.* **2.** Showing no emotion; impassive: *an aloof impersonal manner.* **3.** Not existing as a human personality: *A storm is an impersonal force and does not care where it goes.* **4.** Having no subject or having the indefinite *it* as subject. For example, *snow* in the construction *It is snowing* is an impersonal verb. —**im•per′son•al′i•ty** (ĭm pûr′sə năl′ĭ tē) *n.* —**im•per′son•al•ly** *adv.*

im•per•son•ate (ĭm pûr′sə nāt′) *tr.v.* **im•per•son•at•ed, im•per•son•at•ing, im•per•son•ates.** To assume the character or appearance of: *He was arrested for impersonating a police officer.* —**im•per′son•a′tion** *n.* —**im•per′son•a′tor** *n.*

im•per•ti•nence (ĭm pûr′tn əns) *n.* **1.** Rudeness; insolence: *I find your impertinence very annoying.* **2.** An impertinent act or statement. **3.** Irrelevance.

im•per•ti•nent (ĭm pûr′tn ənt) *adj.* **1.** Offensively bold; rude: *The clerk's impertinent manner offended me.* **2.** Not pertinent; irrelevant: *The discussion was interrupted with many impertinent questions and remarks.* —**im•per′ti•nent•ly** *adv.*

im•per•turb•a•ble (ĭm′pər tûr′bə bəl) *adj.* Unshakably calm and collected: *The senator remained imperturbable even in the heat of the debate.* —**im′per•turb′a•bil′i•ty** *n.* —**im′per•turb′a•bly** *adv.*

im•per•vi•ous (ĭm pûr′vē əs) *adj.* **1.** Incapable of being penetrated: *A good raincoat should be impervious to water.* **2.** Incapable of being affected: *The racing driver seemed impervious to fear.* [First written down in 1650 in Modern English, from Latin *impervius* : *in-*, not + *per-*, through + *via*, way.] —**im•per′vi•ous•ly** *adv.* —**im•per′vi•ous•ness** *n.*

im•pe•ti•go (ĭm′pĭ tī′gō) *n., pl.* **im•pe•ti•gos.** A disease often affecting children, characterized by the formation of pimples and thick yellow crusts on the skin.

im•pet•u•os•i•ty (ĭm pĕch′o͞o ŏs′ĭ tē) *n., pl.* **im•pet•u•os•i•ties. 1.** The quality or condition of being impetuous. **2.** An impetuous act.

im•pet•u•ous (ĭm pĕch′o͞o əs) *adj.* **1.** Characterized by rash or hasty actions; impulsive: *This impetuous decision has brought disaster.* **2.** Marked by violent force or motion: *impetuous waves smashing against the pier.* [First written down before 1398 in Middle English, from Latin *impetus*, impetus.] —**im•pet′u•ous•ly** *adv.*

im•pe•tus (ĭm′pĭ təs) *n., pl.* **im•pe•tus•es. 1.** A driving force; a cause of action: *A sense of fairness is often the impetus for reform.* **2.** The force or energy exhibited by a moving body; momentum: *The impetus of the speeding train made it difficult to stop quickly.* [First written down before 1425 in Middle English and spelled *impetous*, rapid movement, from Latin *impetere*, to attack : *in-*, against + *petere*, to go towards, seek.]

im•pi•e•ty (ĭm pī′ĭ tē) *n., pl.* **im•pi•e•ties. 1.** Lack of piety or reverence. **2.** An impious act.

im•pinge (ĭm pĭnj′) *intr.v.* **im•pinged, im•ping•ing, im•ping•es. 1.** To collide; strike: *Light rays impinge on the eye.* **2.** To encroach; infringe; trespass: *Censorship impinges on our right of free speech.* [First written down in 1535 in Modern English, from Latin *impingere*.] —**im•pinge′ment** *n.* —**im•ping′er** *n.*

im•pi•ous (ĭm′pē əs *or* ĭm pī′əs) *adj.* Lacking reverence; not pious. —**im′pi•ous•ly** *adv.* —**im′pi•ous•ness** *n.*

imp•ish (ĭm′pĭsh) *adj.* Of or befitting an imp; mischievous: *an impish grin.* —**imp′ish•ly** *adv.* —**imp′ish•ness** *n.*

im•plac•a•ble (ĭm plăk′ə bəl *or* ĭm plā′kə bəl) *adj.* Impossible to calm or appease: *We are implacable in our demand for better pay.* —**im•plac′a•bil′i•ty** *n.* —**im•plac′a•bly** *adv.*

im•plant (ĭm plănt′) *tr.v.* **im•plant•ed, im•plant•ing, im•plants. 1.** To establish securely; instill; ingrain: *The parents tried to implant a strong sense of values in their children.* **2.** To insert or set in firmly; plant: *We implanted the fence posts around the yard.* **3.** To graft or set (a tissue or a device) within the body. —*n.* (ĭm′plănt′). A tissue or device that has been surgically grafted or inserted within the body. —**im′plan•ta′tion** (ĭm′plăn tā′shən) *n.*

im•plau•si•ble (ĭm plô′zə bəl) *adj.* Difficult to believe; not plausible: *an implausible excuse.* —**im•plau′si•bly** *adv.*

im•ple•ment (ĭm′plə mənt) *n.* A tool or an instrument used in doing a task: *Plows and harrows are farm implements.* —*tr.v.* (ĭm′plə mĕnt′). **im•ple•ment•ed, im•ple•ment•ing, im•ple•ments.** To put into effect; carry out: *We need a plan in order to implement your idea.* [First written down in 1445 in Middle English and spelled *implement*, supplementary payment, from Latin *implēre*, to fill up.] —**im′ple•men•ta′tion** (ĭm′plə mən tā′shən) *n.*

im•pli•cate (ĭm′plĭ kāt′) *tr.v.* **im•pli•cat•ed, im•pli•cat•ing, im•pli•cates.** To show to be involved or connected with an activity, especially a crime: *The witness's testimony implicated several people in the scandal.* [First written down before 1425 in Middle English and spelled *implicaten*, to convey a truth bound up in a fable, from Latin *implicāre*, to entangle, unite.]

im•pli•ca•tion (ĭm′plĭ kā′shən) *n.* **1.** Something implied; an indirect indication: *Although he did not say so directly, his implication was that the operation was a success.* **2.** The act of implying or the condition of being implied: *The writer's thoughts were conveyed more by implication than by direct statement.* **3.** The act of implicating or the condition of being implicated: *The suspect denied any implication in the affair.*

im•plic•it (ĭm plĭs′ĭt) *adj.* **1.** Implied or understood without being directly expressed: *The threat of a lawsuit was implicit in the lawyer's letter.* **2.** Having no doubts; unquestioning: *We have implicit trust in your judgment.* —**im•plic′it•ly** *adv.* —**im•plic′it•ness** *n.*

ă	pat	oi	boy
ā	pay	ou	out
âr	care	o͝o	took
ä	father	o͞o	boot
ĕ	pet	ŭ	cut
ē	be	ûr	urge
ĭ	pit	th	thin
ī	pie	*th*	this
îr	pier	hw	whoop
ŏ	pot	zh	vision
ō	toe	ə	about
ô	paw	N	*French* bon

im•plore (ĭm plôr′) *tr.v.* **im•plored, im•plor•ing, im•plores. 1.** To appeal to (a person) earnestly or anxiously; entreat; beseech: *The students implored the teacher to postpone the test.* **2.** To plead or beg for (something) earnestly: *The defendant implored the judge's mercy.* [First written down about 1500 in Modern English, from Latin *implōrāre*.]

im•ply (ĭm plī′) *tr.v.* **im•plied, im•ply•ing, im•plies. 1.** To say or convey indirectly; suggest without stating outright: *Even though the door was closed, that didn't imply we weren't welcome.* **2.** To involve as a necessary part or consequence: *Life implies growth and eventual death.* [First written down about 1380 in Middle English and spelled *implien*, from Latin *implicāre*.] —SEE NOTE at **infer.**

im•po•lite (ĭm′pə līt′) *adj.* Not polite; discourteous: *an impolite remark.* **—im′po•lite′ly** *adv.* **—im′po•lite′ness** *n.*

im•port (ĭm pôrt′ *or* ĭm′pôrt′) *tr.v.* **im•port•ed, im•port•ing, im•ports. 1.** To bring in (goods) from a foreign country for sale or use. **2.** To convey as a meaning; mean; signify: *The president's speech imported a major change in the country's foreign policy.* —*n.* (ĭm′pôrt′). **1.** Something imported for sale or use. **2.** The act of importing; importation: *The import of fruits and vegetables is strictly regulated.* **3.** Importance; significance: *an event of enormous import.* **4.** Meaning; significance: *Since they found its import unclear, I tried again to explain my letter.*

im•por•tance (ĭm pôr′tns) *n.* The quality or condition of being important; significance.

im•por•tant (ĭm pôr′tnt) *adj.* **1.** Marked by or having great value, significance, or influence: *Coffee is an important crop in South America.* **2.** Having high social rank or influence; prominent: *government leaders and other important people.* **3.** Believing or acting as if one has high social rank or influence: *Some guests strutted about the party in an important manner.* **—im•por′tant•ly** *adv.*

im•por•ta•tion (ĭm′pôr tā′shən) *n.* **1.** The act of importing, especially as a business: *importation of cars and TV's from Japan.* **2.** Something imported; an import: *Many fine shoes are importations from Italy.*

im•port•er (ĭm pôr′tər) *n.* A person, company, or country that imports goods: *Japan is a large importer of North American timber.*

im•por•tu•nate (ĭm pôr′chə nĭt) *adj.* Annoyingly persistent in pressing a request or demand: *We are tired of importunate advertising through the mail.* **—im•por′tu•nate•ly** *adv.* **—im•por′tu•nate•ness** *n.*

im•por•tune (ĭm′pôr to͞on′ *or* ĭm′pôr tyo͞on′ *or* ĭm pôr′chən) *tr.v.* **im•por•tuned, im•por•tun•ing, im•por•tunes.** To beset with frequent requests; ask insistently: *We importuned the management to locate the factory in our town.* **—im′por•tu′ni•ty** *n.*

im•pose (ĭm pōz′) *v.* **im•posed, im•pos•ing, im•pos•es.** —*tr.* **1.** To place (a burden or an obligation) on a person: *impose a tax; impose a punishment.* **2.** To bring about by exercising authority; force to prevail: *The United Nations imposed peace on the warring countries.* **3.** To force (oneself) upon another or others: *Our visitors have imposed themselves on us for too long.* —*intr.* To force oneself upon another or others; take unfair advantage: *We don't mean to impose, but could we stay for dinner?* ***—idiom.*** **impose on** or **impose upon.** To take advantage of: *The guests imposed on the good nature of their host by asking to borrow the car.* [First written down about 1380 in Middle English and spelled *imposen*, from Old French *imposer*, from Latin *impōnere*, to place upon.] **—im•pos′er** *n.*

im•pos•ing (ĭm pō′zĭng) *adj.* Tending to excite awe or admiration; impressive: *The Statue of Liberty is an imposing sight.* See Synonyms at **magnificent. —im•pos′ing•ly** *adv.*

im•po•si•tion (ĭm′pə zĭsh′ən) *n.* **1.** The act of imposing: *the imposition of new taxes.* **2.** Something imposed, such as a tax, burden, or obligation: *The Colonists resented such impositions as the tax on imported tea.* **3.** An unfair demand upon someone's time, friendship, or hospitality: *These daily requests for help have become an imposition.*

im•pos•si•bil•i•ty (ĭm pŏs′ə bĭl′ĭ tē) *n., pl.* **im•pos•si•bil•i•ties. 1.** The quality or condition of being impossible: *the impossibility of being in two places at once.* **2.** Something that is impossible: *I found being a member of the swimming team and singing in the glee club to be an impossibility.*

im•pos•si•ble (ĭm pŏs′ə bəl) *adj.* **1.** Not capable of happening or existing: *A square circle is impossible.* **2.** Not capable of being accomplished: *an impossible task.* **3.** Difficult to tolerate or deal with: *That dog is impossible.* **—im•pos′si•bly** *adv.*

im•post (ĭm′pōst′) *n.* Something, such as a tax or duty, that is imposed or levied.

im•pos•tor (ĭm pŏs′tər) *n.* A person who deceives others by pretending to be someone else.

im•pos•ture (ĭm pŏs′chər) *n.* Deception or fraud by the assumption of a false identity.

im•po•tence (ĭm′pə təns) *n.* The quality or condition of being impotent.

im•po•tent (ĭm′pə tənt) *adj.* **1.** Lacking strength, power, or effectiveness: *The loss of popular support left the government impotent to deal with the crisis.* **2.** Incapable of sexual intercourse. **—im•po′tent•ly** *adv.*

im•pound (ĭm pound′) *tr.v.* **im•pound•ed, im•pound•ing, im•pounds. 1.** To seize and hold in legal custody: *A judge can impound all records in a trial.* **2.** To capture and confine in a pound: *The city impounds stray dogs.* **3.** To collect (water) in a natural or an artificial lake.

im•pov•er•ish (ĭm pŏv′ər ĭsh) *tr.v.* **im•pov•er•ished, im•pov•er•ish•ing, im•pov•er•ish•es. 1.** To make very poor: *Bad harvests impoverished the family.* **2.** To use up the natural richness, strength, or resources of: *Excessive use of pesticides had impoverished the soil.* **—im•pov′er•ish•ment** *n.*

im•prac•ti•ca•ble (ĭm prăk′tĭ kə bəl) *adj.* Impossible to do or carry out: *impracticable ideas for providing health care.* **—im•prac′ti•ca•ble•ness** *n.* **—im•prac′ti•ca•bly** *adv.*

im•prac•ti•cal (ĭm prăk′tĭ kəl) *adj.* **1.** Unwise or foolish to do or carry out: *an impractical plan.* **2.** Incapable of dealing well with practical matters: *an impractical dreamer.* **—im•prac′ti•cal′i•ty** (ĭm-prăk′tĭ kăl′ĭ tē) *n.*

im•pre•ca•tion (ĭm′prĭ kā′shən) *n.* A curse.

im•pre•cise (ĭm′prĭ sīs′) *adj.* Not precise or clear: *an imprecise description.* **—im′pre•cise′ly** *adv.*

im•preg•na•ble (ĭm prĕg′nə bəl) *adj.* **1.** Impossible to capture or enter by force: *an impregnable fort.* **2.** Impossible to refute; firm: *an impregnable argument.* [First written down before 1439 in Middle English and spelled *imprenable*, from Old French : *in-*, not + *prendre*, to seize.] **—im•preg′na•bly** *adv.*

im•preg•nate (ĭm prĕg′nāt) *tr.v.* **im•preg•nat•ed, im•preg•nat•ing, im•preg•nates. 1.** To make pregnant. **2.** To make fertile; fertilize. **3.** To fill completely; saturate: *The smell of roses impregnated the room.* **—im′preg•na′tion** *n.*

im•pre•sa•ri•o (ĭm′prĭ sär′ē ō′ *or* ĭm′prĭ sâr′ē ō′) *n., pl.* **im•pre•sa•ri•os.** A person who organizes, manages, or directs entertainment, such as operas, ballets, or concerts.

im•press¹ (ĭm prĕs′) *tr.v.* **im•pressed, im•press•ing, im•press•es. 1.** To have a strong, often favorable effect on the mind or feelings of: *The worker's performance impressed the manager.* **2.** To fix firmly in the mind, as by force or influence: *The coach impressed upon the team the importance of good defense.* **3.** To mark or stamp with or as if with pressure: *impress a design on soft clay.* —*n.* (ĭm′prĕs′). **1.** The act of impressing. **2.** A mark or an imprint made by pressure. [First written down about 1370 in Middle English and spelled *impressen*, to imprint, from Latin *impressus*, past participle of *imprimere*, to press into.]

im•press² (ĭm prĕs′) *tr.v.* **im•pressed, im•press•ing, im•press•es. 1.** To force (a person) to serve in the military. **2.** To seize (property): *During the war, the government impressed all foreign funds.* [First written down in 1596 in Modern English, from Middle English *prest*, money paid for enlisting.]

im•pres•sion (ĭm prĕsh′ən) *n.* **1.** A marked effect, image, or feeling that stays in the mind: *The new worker made a good impression on everyone.* **2.** A vague notion, memory, or feeling: *I have the impression that we've met before.* **3.** A mark or an imprint made on a surface by pressure: *There was an impression left on the cushion where the dog had slept.* **4.** A humorous imitation of a person's speech and manner: *He gave impressions of movie stars.*

im•pres•sion•a•ble (ĭm prĕsh′ə nə bəl) *adj.* Easily influenced or affected; suggestible. —**im•pres′sion•a•bil′i•ty** *n.*

im•pres•sion•ism (ĭm prĕsh′ə nĭz′əm) *n.* **1.** A style of painting developed in France in the late 19th century, that uses small brush strokes to give the impression of the natural light of a scene or an object. **2.** A musical style of the late 19th century that creates the impression of a mood or a place by the use of colorful and unusual harmonies and other tonal effects.

im•pres•sion•ist (ĭm prĕsh′ə nĭst) *n.* An artist or a musician who uses impressionism. —*adj.* Impressionistic.

im•pres•sion•is•tic (ĭm prĕsh′ə nĭs′tĭk) *adj.* Of or relating to impressionism or the impressionists.

im•pres•sive (ĭm prĕs′ĭv) *adj.* Making a strong or vivid impression; commanding attention: *an impressive monument.* —**im•pres′sive•ly** *adv.* —**im•pres′sive•ness** *n.*

im•print (ĭm prĭnt′) *tr.v.* **im•print•ed, im•print•ing, im•prints. 1.** To make (a mark or pattern) on a surface by pressing: *imprint a name with a rubber stamp.* **2.** To produce a mark on (a surface) by pressure. **3.** To establish firmly, as on the mind or memory: *Memories of childhood are often deeply imprinted on our minds.* —*n.* (ĭm′prĭnt′). **1.** A mark or pattern made by pressing something on a surface: *the imprints in the sand left by the feet of bathers.* **2.** A marked influence or effect; an impression: *Spanish culture has left its imprint on the Southwestern states.* **3.** The publisher's name, often with the date, address, and edition printed on the title page of a book or publication.

im•pris•on (ĭm prĭz′ən) *tr.v.* **im•pris•oned, im•pris•on•ing, im•pris•ons.** To put in or as if in prison; confine. —**im•pris′on•ment** *n.*

im•prob•a•ble (ĭm prŏb′ə bəl) *adj.* Not probable; unlikely: *an improbable tale.* —**im•prob′a•bil′i•ty** *n.* —**im•prob′a•bly** *adv.*

im•promp•tu (ĭm prŏmp′to͞o *or* ĭm prŏmp′tyo͞o) *adj.* Spoken or done with little or no preparation: *The mayor devised an impromptu reply to the unexpected question.* —*adv.* With little or no preparation: *The president commented impromptu on the startling events.* —*n.* Something made or done without rehearsal, as a musical composition or speech.

im•prop•er (ĭm prŏp′ər) *adj.* **1.** Not conforming to accepted standards; incorrect: *an improper diet.* **2.** Not in keeping with circumstances or needs; unsuitable: *A swamp is an improper place to build a house.* **3.** Not conforming to standards of decency; unseemly: *It is improper to interrupt a speaker.* —**im•prop′er•ly** *adv.* —**im•prop′er•ness** *n.*

improper fraction *n.* A fraction in which the numerator is greater than or equal to the denominator: *The fractions 3/2 and 2/2 are improper fractions.*

im•pro•pri•e•ty (ĭm′prə prī′ĭ tē) *n., pl.* **im•pro•pri•e•ties. 1.** The quality or condition of being improper: *the impropriety of playing a radio in the library.* **2.** An improper act or expression.

im•prove (ĭm pro͞ov′) *v.* **im•proved, im•prov•ing, im•proves.** —*tr.* To make better: *The teacher's careful explanation improved my understanding of algebra.* —*intr.* To become or get better: *The patient improved after receiving treatment.* [First written down in 1473 in Middle English and spelled *improwen*, to enclose land for cultivation, from Anglo-Norman *emprouwer*, to turn to profit, from *prou*, profit.]

im•prove•ment (ĭm pro͞ov′mənt) *n.* **1.** A change or an addition that improves something: *A new kitchen was one of our improvements to the house.* **2.** The act or process of improving: *The student's homework shows great improvement.* **3.** A person or thing that is better than another: *This year's science course is an improvement over the one we had last year.*

im•prov•i•dent (ĭm prŏv′ĭ dənt) *adj.* Not planning or providing for the future; careless of one's resources: *Given our meager savings we cannot afford improvident expenditures.* —**im•prov′i•dence** *n.* —**im•prov′i•dent•ly** *adv.*

im•prov•i•sa•tion (ĭm prŏv′ĭ zā′shən *or* ĭm′prə vĭ zā′shən) *n.* **1.** The act of improvising: *Improvisation on the piano is a rare gift.* **2.** Something improvised, such as a dramatic skit.

im•pro•vise (ĭm′prə vīz′) *v.* **im•pro•vised, im•pro•vis•ing, im•pro•vis•es.** —*tr.* **1.** To invent, compose, or perform without preparation: *The comedians improvised several scenes based on suggestions from the audience.* **2.** To make or provide on the spur of the moment from materials found nearby: *The hikers improvised a bridge out of fallen logs.* —*intr.* To invent, compose, or perform something on the spot: *The musicians finished by improvising on the main theme.* [First written down in 1826 in Modern English, from Latin *imprōvīsus*, unforeseen.] —**im′pro•vis′er** *n.*

im•pru•dent (ĭm pro͞od′nt) *adj.* Not prudent; unwise. —**im•pru′dence** *n.* —**im•pru′dent•ly** *adv.*

im•pu•dence (ĭm′pyə dəns) *n.* **1.** The quality of being impudent; insolence. **2.** An impudent act or behavior.

im•pu•dent (ĭm′pyə dənt) *adj.* Offensively bold and disrespectful; insolent: *The impudent student demanded to be assigned another instructor.* [First written down about 1390 in Middle English, from Latin *impudēns* : *in-*, not + *pudēre*, to be ashamed.] —**im′pu•dent•ly** *adv.*

im•pugn (ĭm pyo͞on′) *tr.v.* **im•pugned, im•pugn•ing, im•pugns.** To challenge as false; cast doubt on: *The prosecutor impugned the defendant's testimony.*

im•pulse (ĭm′pŭls′) *n.* **1.** A driving force: *The storm provided the impulse for the huge waves.* **2.** The motion caused by such a force. **3.** A strong motivation; a drive or an instinct: *Most animals have a natural*

impressionism

By the Seashore by Pierre Auguste Renoir

imprint

Rabbit tracks in the snow

ă	pat	oi	boy
ā	pay	ou	out
âr	care	o͝o	took
ä	father	o͞o	boot
ĕ	pet	ŭ	cut
ē	be	ûr	urge
ĭ	pit	th	thin
ī	pie	*th*	this
îr	pier	hw	whoop
ŏ	pot	zh	vision
ō	toe	ə	about
ô	paw	N	*French* bon

Word Building: in–[1]

The basic meaning of the prefix **in–**[1] is "not." Thus **inactive** means "not active." **In–**[1] is related to and sometimes confused with the prefix **un–**[1], which also means "not." In fact, sometimes **in–**[1] is used interchangeably with **un–**[1], as when *incommunicative* is used instead of **uncommunicative**. Before the consonants *l* and *r*, **in–**[1] becomes *il–* and *ir–* respectively: **illogical**, **irregular**. Before the consonants *b*, *m*, and *p*, **in–**[1] becomes *im–*: **imbalanced**, **immeasurable**, **impossible**.

Word Building: in–[2]

Although **in–**[1] and **in–**[2] are both from Latin, they are not related to each other. The basic meaning of **in–**[2] is "in, within, or into." For example, **inlay** means "to set something in something else." **In–**[2] is also a form of the prefix **en–**. And in pairs such as **enclose/inclose** and **enquire/inquire**, the two prefixes can be used somewhat interchangeably. As with the prefix **in–**[1], before the consonants *l* and *r*, **in–**[2] becomes *il–* and *ir–*. And before the consonants *b*, *m*, and *p*, **in–**[2] becomes *im–*.

impulse to care for their young. **4.** A sudden wish or urge: *We had a sudden impulse to go to the movies.* **5.** A surge of electrical power in one direction. **6.** A stimulus or charge transmitted along a nerve cell that excites a muscle, a gland, or another nerve cell. [First written down in 1647 in Modern English, from Latin *impulsus*, from *impellere*, to impel.]

im•pul•sion (ĭm pŭl′shən) *n.* **1.** The act of impelling or the condition of being impelled. **2.** An impelling force; a thrust. **3.** Motion produced by an impelling force; momentum. **4.** A sudden wish or urge; an impulse.

im•pul•sive (ĭm pŭl′sĭv) *adj.* **1.** Tending to act on impulse rather than careful thought: *An impulsive shopper usually doesn't find the best bargains.* **2.** Motivated or caused by impulse: *The wealthy industrialist was given to impulsive acts of generosity.* —**im•pul′sive•ly** *adv.* —**im•pul′sive•ness** *n.*

im•pu•ni•ty (ĭm pyōō′nĭ tē) *n., pl.* **im•pu•ni•ties.** Freedom from punishment, harm, or injury: *Did she really expect to break the law with impunity?* [First written down in 1532 in Modern English, from Latin *impūne*, without punishment.]

im•pure (ĭm pyŏŏr′) *adj.* **im•pur•er, im•pur•est. 1.** Not pure or clean; contaminated: *Polluted water is impure.* **2.** Mixed with other substances often of lower value; adulterated: *an impure diamond.* **3.** Immoral or corrupt; bad: *The Puritans viewed gambling and games of chance as impure.* —**im•pure′ly** *adv.*

im•pu•ri•ty (ĭm pyŏŏr′ĭ tē) *n., pl.* **im•pu•ri•ties. 1.** The quality or condition of being impure. **2.** A substance that makes another substance impure: *The treatment plant filters all the impurities out of our water.*

im•pute (ĭm pyōōt′) *tr.v.* **im•put•ed, im•put•ing, im•putes.** To give the blame or credit for; attribute: *I impute my mistakes to my own carelessness.* [First written down about 1375 in Middle English and spelled *inputen*, from Latin *imputāre*.] —**im′pu•ta′tion** (ĭm′pyōō tā′shən) *n.*

in[1] (ĭn) *prep.* **1.a.** Within the confines or area of; inside: *The students are all in the classroom.* **b.** From outside to a point within; into: *couldn't get in the house.* **2.** Within the time of; after: *I will finish in an hour.* **3.** To or at the condition or situation of: *in good health.* **4.** Wearing; clothed by: *in a bathing suit.* **5.** Having the activity or function of: *a career in politics.* **6.** With the purpose of; for: *follow in pursuit.* **7.** Made with or through the medium of: *a note written in Spanish.* **8.** With reference to; as to: *10 feet in length.* **9.** Among; out of: *One person in five can play a musical instrument.* —*adv.* **1.** To or toward the inside: *coming in out of the rain.* **2.** To or toward a goal: *The researchers are closing in on a cure.* **3.** Within a specified or understood place, situation, or activity: *Is the doctor in? The water is cold and the children won't be in long.* **4.** So as to include: *Did you fold the egg whites in?* —*adj.* **1.** Located inside; inner. **2.** *Informal.* Fashionable; popular; prestigious: *Short haircuts are in.* **3.** Having influence or power: *The in government was made up of a coalition of parties.* **4.** Incoming; inward: *the in bus.* —*n.* **1.** *Informal.* A means of access or influence: *the musician has an in with the conductor.* **2.** A person having power or influence: *The ins are always at an advantage over the outs.* —***idioms.*** **in for.** About to get or have: *We're in for a cold winter.* **in that.** For the reason that; since: *Their arguments are unconvincing in that their reasons are so weak.* **ins and outs.** The details of an activity or a process: *had to learn the ins and outs of local politics.* [First written down before 700 in Old English.]

❑ *These sound alike:* **in**[1] (inside), **inn** (hotel).

in[2] or **in.** *abbr.* An abbreviation of inch.

In The symbol for the element **indium.**

IN *abbr.* An abbreviation of Indiana.

in–[1] or **il–** or **im–** or **ir–** *pref.* A prefix that means not: *inaccurate; illegible; immoral; irresponsible.* —See Note.

in–[2] or **il–** or **im–** or **ir–** *pref.* **1.** A prefix that means *inbound; infield.* **2.** Variant of **en–**. —See Note.

in•a•bil•i•ty (ĭn′ə bĭl′ĭ tē) *n.* Lack of ability or means: *inability to sleep.*

in•ac•ces•si•ble (ĭn′ăk sĕs′ə bəl) *adj.* Not accessible; unapproachable: *an inaccessible cave high on the cliff.* —**in′ac•ces′si•bly** *adv.*

in•ac•cu•ra•cy (ĭn ăk′yər ə sē) *n., pl.* **in•ac•cu•ra•cies. 1.** The quality or condition of being inaccurate: *The report was criticized for its inaccuracy.* **2.** An error; a mistake: *many inaccuracies in their hasty observations.*

in•ac•cu•rate (ĭn ăk′yər ĭt) *adj.* Mistaken or incorrect; not accurate: *an inaccurate description.* —**in•ac′cu•rate•ly** *adv.*

in•ac•tion (ĭn ăk′shən) *n.* Lack or absence of action.

in•ac•tive (ĭn ăk′tĭv) *adj.* Not active; not functioning; idle: *an inactive volcano; an inactive life.* —**in•ac′tive•ly** *adv.*

in•ad•e•qua•cy (ĭn ăd′ĭ kwə sē) *n., pl.* **in•ad•e•qua•cies. 1.** The quality or condition of being inadequate: *a feeling of inadequacy in performing the job.* **2.** A failing or lack.

in•ad•e•quate (ĭn ăd′ĭ kwĭt) *adj.* Not enough; insufficient: *We lost the gymnastics competition because of inadequate practice.* —**in•ad′e•quate•ly** *adv.*

in•ad•mis•si•ble (ĭn′əd mĭs′ə bəl) *adj.* Not admissible: *Inadmissible evidence cannot be used in a trial.* —**in′ad•mis′si•bil′i•ty** *n.*

in•ad•ver•tent (ĭn′əd vûr′tnt) *adj.* **1.** Not meant or intended; unintentional: *an inadvertent error in the bill.* **2.** Not paying attention; not alert; careless. —**in′ad•ver′tence** *n.*

in•ad•vis•a•ble (ĭn′əd vī′zə bəl) *adj.* Not recommended; unwise: *It is inadvisable to swim out past the reef.* —**in′ad•vis′a•bil′i•ty** *n.*

in•al•ien•a•ble (ĭn āl′yə nə bəl *or* ĭn ā′lē ə nə bəl) *adj.* Impossible to give up or take away: *The pursuit of happiness is one of the inalienable rights listed in the Declaration of Independence.* —**in•al′ien•a•bly** *adv.*

in•ane (ĭn ān′) *adj.* **in•an•er, in•an•est.** Lacking sense or substance; empty: *an inane comment.* [First written down in 1662 in Modern English, from Latin *inānis*, empty.] —**in•ane′ly** *adv.*

in•an•i•mate (ĭn ăn′ə mĭt) *adj.* **1.** Not living: *A stone is an inanimate object.* **2.** Not lively; listless; dull. —**in•an′i•mate•ly** *adv.* —**in•an′i•mate•ness** *n.*

in•an•i•ty (ĭ năn′ĭ tē) *n., pl.* **in•an•i•ties. 1.** The quality or condition of being inane. **2.** Something inane, especially a meaningless statement.

in•ap•pli•ca•ble (ĭn ăp′lĭ kə bəl *or* ĭn′ə plĭk′ə bəl) *adj.* Not applicable: *Speed limits are inapplicable to emergency vehicles.* —**in•ap′pli•ca•bil′i•ty** *n.*

in•ap•pre•cia•ble (ĭn′ə prē′shə bəl) *adj.* Too small to be noticed or to make a significant difference; negligible. —**in′ap•pre′cia•bly** *adv.*

in•ap•pro•pri•ate (ĭn′ə prō′prē ĭt) *adj.* Not appropriate; unsuitable. —**in′ap•pro′pri•ate•ly** *adv.* —**in′ap•pro′pri•ate•ness** *n.*

in•apt (ĭn ăpt′) *adj.* **1.** Inappropriate. **2.** Inept. —**in•apt′ly** *adv.* —**in•apt′ness** *n.*

in•ap•ti•tude (ĭn ăp′tĭ tōōd′ *or* ĭn ăp′tĭ tyōōd′) *n.* **1.** Inappropriateness; unfitness. **2.** Lack of talent or skill; ineptitude.

in•ar•tic•u•late (ĭn′är tĭk′yə lĭt) *adj.* **1.** Uttered without the use of normal words or syllables: *an inarticulate cry.* **2.** Unable to speak; speechless: *I was inarticulate with astonishment.* **3.** Unable to speak clearly or effectively. **4.** Unexpressed: *inarticulate sorrow.* **5.** Not having joints or segments: *An amoeba has an inarticulate body.* —**in′ar•tic′u•late•ly** *adv.* —**in′ar•tic′u•late•ness** *n.*

in•ar•tis•tic (ĭn′är tĭs′tĭk) *adj.* Lacking taste or interest in art. —**in′ar•tis′ti•cal•ly** *adv.*

in•as•much as (ĭn′əz mŭch′) *conj.* Because of the fact that; since: *I decided to go swimming inasmuch as it was hot and sunny.*

in•at•ten•tion (ĭn′ə tĕn′shən) *n.* Lack of attention, notice, or regard; heedlessness: *careless mistakes caused by inattention to details.*

in•at•ten•tive (ĭn′ə tĕn′tĭv) *adj.* Showing a lack of attention; negligent: *sleepy and inattentive.* —**in′at•ten′tive•ly** *adv.* —**in′at•ten′tive•ness** *n.*

in•au•di•ble (ĭn ô′də bəl) *adj.* Impossible to hear: *an inaudible conversation.* —**in•au′di•bly** *adv.*

in•au•gu•ral (ĭn ô′gyər əl) *adj.* **1.** Of or relating to an inauguration: *the President's inaugural address.* **2.** First; initial: *an inaugural flight of a new airliner.* —*n.* **1.** An inaugural speech, especially that of the President of the United States. **2.** An inaugural ceremony or activity.

in•au•gu•rate (ĭn ô′gyə rāt′) *tr.v.* **in•au•gu•rat•ed, in•au•gu•rat•ing, in•au•gu•rates. 1.** To install in office by a formal ceremony: *inaugurate a President.* **2.** To open for use with a ceremony; dedicate: *inaugurate a new office building.* **3.** To begin or start officially: *The governor inaugurated a new policy to combat air pollution.* [First written down in 1606 in Modern English, from Latin *inaugurāre* : *in–*, intensive prefix + *augurāre*, to augur (from *augur*, soothsayer.]

in•au•gu•ra•tion (ĭn ô′gyə rā′shən) *n.* **1.** A formal ceremony installing a person in a position or an office. **2.** A formal beginning or introduction.

in•aus•pi•cious (ĭn′ô spĭsh′əs) *adj.* Not auspicious; unfavorable: *Despite an inauspicious weather forecast, we went on the picnic.* —**in′aus•pi′cious•ly** *adv.* —**in′aus•pi′cious•ness** *n.*

in between *prep. & adv.* Between: *mortar in between the bricks; layers with a filling in between.*

in•board (ĭn′bôrd′) *adj.* **1.** In the hull or toward the center of a ship: *an inboard motor.* **2.** Close to the fuselage of an aircraft: *the left inboard engine.*

in•born (ĭn′bôrn′) *adj.* **1.** Present in a person or an animal from birth: *an inborn talent for music.* **2.** Inherited; hereditary: *an inborn disease.*

in•bound (ĭn′bound′) *adj.* Incoming; arriving: *an inbound ship.*

in•bred (ĭn′brĕd′) *adj.* **1.** Produced by inbreeding. **2.** Existing from birth; inborn: *The painter had an inbred sense of color.*

in•breed (ĭn′brēd′) *tr.v.* **in•bred** (ĭn′brĕd′), **in•breed•ing, in•breeds.** To breed by continued mating of closely related individuals.

in•breed•ing (ĭn′brē′dĭng) *n.* The breeding or mating of closely related individuals.

inc. *abbr.* also **Inc.**. An abbreviation of incorporated.

In•ca (ĭng′kə) *n., pl.* **Inca** or **In•cas.** A member of the group of Quechuan peoples who ruled Peru before the Spanish conquest in the 16th century. —**In′can** *adj.*

in•cal•cu•la•ble (ĭn kăl′kyə lə bəl) *adj.* **1.** Too great or too large in number to be calculated or described; enormous: *an incalculable number of ants.* **2.** Impossible to foresee. —**in•cal′cu•la•bil′i•ty** *n.* —**in•cal′cu•la•bly** *adv.*

in•can•des•cent (ĭn′kən dĕs′ənt) *adj.* **1.** Heated to such a high temperature that it gives off light; glowing with heat. **2.** Shining brilliantly; very bright. [First written down in 1794 in Modern English, from Latin *incandēscere*, to begin to glow.] —**in′can•des′cence** *n.* —**in′can•des′cent•ly** *adv.*

incandescent lamp *n.* An electric lamp that produces light by the glow of a wire heated by an electric current.

in•can•ta•tion (ĭn′kăn tā′shən) *n.* **1.** A formula of words or sounds recited or chanted to cast a spell or perform magic. **2.** The act of reciting or chanting such a formula. [First written down before 1393 in Middle English and spelled *incantacioun*, from Latin *incantāre*, to enchant, cast a spell.]

in•ca•pa•ble (ĭn kā′pə bəl) *adj.* Lacking the necessary power or ability; not capable: *Human beings are incapable of breathing on their own under water.* —**in•ca′pa•bil′i•ty** *n.*

in•ca•pac•i•tate (ĭn′kə păs′ĭ tāt′) *tr.v.* **in•ca•pac•i•tat•ed, in•ca•pac•i•tat•ing, in•ca•pac•i•tates.** To deprive of power or ability; disable: *A knee injury incapacitated the wrestler.*

in•ca•pac•i•ty (ĭn′kə păs′ĭ tē) *n., pl.* **in•ca•pac•i•ties. 1.** Inadequate strength or ability: *the mover's incapacity to lift the heavy box.* **2.** A disability or handicap.

in•car•cer•ate (ĭn kär′sə rāt′) *tr.v.* **in•car•cer•at•ed, in•car•cer•at•ing, in•car•cer•ates.** To put in jail; imprison. [First written down in 1560 in Modern English, from Latin *carcer*, prison.] —**in•car′cer•a′tion** *n.*

in•car•nate (ĭn kär′nĭt) *adj.* Embodied in flesh, especially in human form; personified: *a villain who seemed evil incarnate.* —*tr.v.* (ĭn kär′nāt′). **in•car•nat•ed, in•car•nat•ing, in•car•nates.** To be a perfect embodiment of; personify: *a successful leader who incarnated the ideals of her time.*

in•car•na•tion (ĭn′kär nā′shən) *n.* **1.** The taking on of bodily form by a supernatural being: *the incarnation of the devil in the form of a serpent.* **2. Incarnation.** The Christian doctrine that Jesus was conceived in the womb of Mary and that Jesus is both God and man. **3.** A person or thing thought to be the perfect example of a quality or an idea.

in•cau•tious (ĭn kô′shəs) *adj.* Not cautious; rash: *a hasty incautious remark.* —**in•cau′tious•ly** *adv.* —**in•cau′tious•ness** *n.*

in•cen•di•ar•y (ĭn sĕn′dē ĕr′ē) *adj.* **1.** Causing or designed to cause fires: *an incendiary bomb.* **2.** Of or involving arson: *an incendiary fire.* **3.** Tending to arouse anger or conflict; inflammatory: *After the rebel's incendiary speech, the mob rampaged through the streets.* —*n., pl.* **in•cen•di•ar•ies. 1.** An arsonist. **2.** A bomb or an explosive designed to cause fires.

in•cense[1] (ĭn sĕns′) *tr.v.* **in•censed, in•cens•ing, in•cens•es.** To make very angry; enrage: *The factual errors in the article incensed the editor.* [First written down about 1410 in Middle English and spelled *encensen*, from Latin *incēnsus*, set on fire.]

in•cense[2] (ĭn′sĕns′) *n.* **1.** A substance, such as gum or wood, that is burned to produce a pleasant odor. **2.** The smoke or odor produced by the burning of such a substance. **3.** A pleasant smell: *the incense of flowers.* [First written down about 1280 in Middle English and spelled *encens*, from Latin *incēnsum*, from *incendere*, to set on fire.]

in•cen•tive (ĭn sĕn′tĭv) *n.* Something that prompts action or effort; a stimulus: *Seeing his name in print is incentive enough for him to keep writing.* [First written down before 1425 in Middle English, from Late Latin *incentīvus*, inciting.]

in•cep•tion (ĭn sĕp′shən) *n.* The beginning of something; a start: *Fall marks the inception of a new school year.*

in•ces•sant (ĭn sĕs′ənt) *adj.* Continuing without interruption; constant: *The incessant sound of the*

inauguration
Inauguration of Bill Clinton as President, January 20, 1993

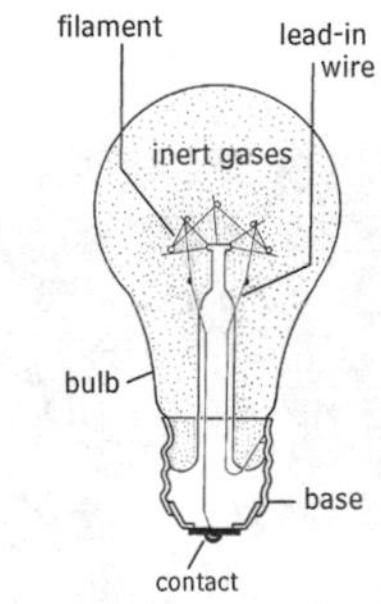

incandescent lamp

ă	pat	oi	boy
ā	pay	ou	out
âr	care	ŏŏ	took
ä	father	ōō	boot
ĕ	pet	ŭ	cut
ē	be	ûr	urge
ĭ	pit	th	thin
ī	pie	*th*	this
îr	pier	hw	whoop
ŏ	pot	zh	vision
ō	toe	ə	about
ô	paw	N	*French* bon

incise

inclined plane

traffic made it difficult to concentrate. **—in•ces′sant•ly** *adv.*

in•cest (ĭn′sĕst′) *n.* Sexual relations between persons who are so closely related that they cannot be legally married.

in•ces•tu•ous (ĭn **sĕs′**cho͞o əs) *adj.* **1.** Of or involving incest. **2.** Having committed incest.

inch (ĭnch) *n.* **1.** A unit of length equal to 1⁄12 of a foot (2.54 centimeters). See table at **measurement**. **2.** A very small degree or amount: *The union would not yield an inch in its demands.* *—intr.v.* **inched, inch•ing, inch•es.** To move or proceed very slowly or by small degrees: *We are inching closer to an understanding of the origin of the universe.* ***—idioms.*** **every inch.** In every detail; entirely: *The actor looked every inch the part.* **inch by inch.** Little by little; very gradually or slowly. **within an inch of.** Almost to the point of; very near: *The team was within an inch of gaining the state championship.* [First written down about 1000 in Old English and spelled *ynce*, from Latin *uncia*, one twelfth.]

inch•worm (**ĭnch′**wûrm′) *n.* A measuring worm.

in•ci•dence (**ĭn′**sĭ dəns) *n.* **1.** The rate or frequency with which something occurs: *The incidence of polio has fallen dramatically since vaccines became available.* **2.** The falling or striking of a ray or beam of light or other radiation upon a surface.

in•ci•dent (**ĭn′**sĭ dənt) *n.* **1.** A particular occurrence; an event, especially one of minor importance: *I cannot remember all the incidents that occurred during our trip.* **2.** A disturbance or mishap: *The damaged plane managed to land without incident.* *—adj.* Tending to happen at the same time; accompanying or related to something else: *His ankle injuries are incident to a career in basketball.* [First written down before 1420 in Middle English, from Old French *incident*, apt to happen, an incident, from Latin *incidere*, to happen, befall.]

in•ci•den•tal (ĭn′sĭ **dĕn′**tl) *adj.* **1.** Occurring or likely to occur as a minor consequence; attendant: *Besides the costs of food and lodging there were many incidental expenses.* **2.** Happening unexpectedly: *The day was marked by several incidental encounters with old friends.* *—n.* A minor item or expense: *We must be careful not to spend our entire budget on mere incidentals.*

in•ci•den•tal•ly (ĭn′sĭ **dĕn′**tl ē) *adv.* **1.** Apart from the main subject; by the way: *Incidentally, what time is it?* **2.** As a minor matter: *She is a stockbroker and incidentally a runner.*

in•cin•er•ate (ĭn **sĭn′**ə rāt′) *tr.v.* **in•cin•er•at•ed, in•cin•er•at•ing, in•cin•er•ates.** To destroy by burning; burn to ashes. [First written down in 1555 in Modern English, from Medieval Latin *incinerāre*, from Latin *cinis*, ashes.] **—in•cin′er•a′tion** *n.*

in•cin•er•a•tor (ĭn **sĭn′**ə rā′tər) *n.* A furnace or other device for burning rubbish.

in•cip•i•ent (ĭn **sĭp′**ē ənt) *adj.* Beginning to exist or appear: *The gathering clouds were the signs of an incipient storm.* **—in•cip′i•en•cy, in•cip′i•ence** *n.*

in•cise (ĭn **sīz′**) *tr.v.* **in•cised, in•cis•ing, in•cis•es.** **1.** To cut into or mark: *incised the wood with the point of a chisel.* **2.** To engrave into a surface; carve: *incise a design into leather.*

in•ci•sion (ĭn **sĭzh′**ən) *n.* **1.** The act of incising: *the incision of a design.* **2.** A cut made into something, especially a surgical cut. [First written down in 1392 in Middle English and spelled *inscicioun*, from Latin *incīdere*, to cut into.]

in•ci•sive (ĭn **sī′**sĭv) *adj.* Sharp and clear; penetrating: *The incisive analysis was clear and to the point.* **—in•ci′sive•ly** *adv.* **—in•ci′sive•ness** *n.*

in•ci•sor (ĭn **sī′**zər) *n.* A tooth having a sharp edge adapted for cutting, located in mammals in the front of the mouth between the canine teeth.

in•cite (ĭn **sīt′**) *tr.v.* **in•cit•ed, in•cit•ing, in•cites.** To provoke; stir up; urge on: *The announcement of a cut in pay incited the workers to strike.* [First written down in 1447 in Middle English and spelled *encyten*, from Latin *incitāre*, to urge forward.] **—in•cite′ment** *n.*

incl. *abbr.* An abbreviation of: **1.** Including. **2.** Inclusive.

in•clem•ent (ĭn **klĕm′**ənt) *adj.* **1.** Stormy; rough: *inclement weather.* **2.** Unmerciful; harsh: *the severe penalties of inclement justice.* **—in•clem′en•cy** *n.*

in•cli•na•tion (ĭn′klə **nā′**shən) *n.* **1.** A natural tendency to be or act in a certain way: *Many people have an inclination to sleep late on weekends.* **2.** The act of inclining or the state of being inclined: *The inclination of the child's head suggested that she was tired.* **3.** A slant or slope: *the steep inclination of the roof.*

in•cline (ĭn **klīn′**) *v.* **in•clined, in•clin•ing, in•clines.** *—intr.* **1.** To slant or slope: *a road that inclines steeply.* **2.** To have a preference; tend: *Diligent students incline to work hard.* **3.** To lower the head or body, as in a nod or bow. *—tr.* **1.** To cause to lean, slant, or slope: *We inclined the boards against the side of the barn.* **2.** To cause to bend or bow: *The conductor inclined his head as a signal for us to get ready to play.* **3.** To influence (a person) to have a certain tendency; dispose: *This book might incline you to change your mind on the issue.* *—n.* (**ĭn′**klīn′). A surface that slants; a slope: *The car skidded down the icy incline of the street.* [First written down before 1325 in Middle English and spelled *enclinen*, from Latin *inclīnāre*.]

in•clined (ĭn **klīnd′**) *adj.* **1.** Sloping, slanting, or leaning. **2.** Having a preference or tendency; disposed: *We are inclined to believe people we respect.*

inclined plane *n.* A plane surface, such as a ramp, set at an acute angle to a horizontal surface. It is a simple machine because it requires less force to slide or roll a body up the plane than to raise the body vertically.

in•close (ĭn **klōz′**) *v.* Variant of **enclose.**

in•clude (ĭn **klo͞od′**) *tr.v.* **in•clud•ed, in•clud•ing, in•cludes.** **1.** To have as a part or member; contain: *The museum's collection includes some masterpieces of modern art.* **2.** To put into a group, class, or total: *I included your whole family in my invitation.* [First written down in 1402 in Middle English and spelled *includen*, from Latin *inclūdere*, to enclose.]

in•clu•sion (ĭn **klo͞o′**zhən) *n.* **1.** The act of including or the condition of being included. **2.** Something that is included.

in•clu•sive (ĭn **klo͞o′**sĭv) *adj.* **1.** Taking everything into account; comprehensive: *The principal had an inclusive list of all the students in the school.* **2.** Including the specified limits as well as what is between them: *The teacher asked us to "read Chapters 1 to 4 inclusive," meaning we are to read from the beginning of Chapter 1 to the end of Chapter 4.* **—in•clu′sive•ly** *adv.* **—in•clu′sive•ness** *n.*

in•cog•ni•to (ĭn′kŏg **nē′**tō *or* ĭn **kŏg′**nĭ tō′) *adv. & adj.* With one's identity hidden or disguised: *The movie star stayed at the hotel incognito.* [First written down in 1649 in Modern English, from Latin *incognitus*, unknown.]

in•co•her•ent (ĭn′kō **hîr′**ənt) *adj.* **1.** Lacking order or logical connection; not coherent: *an incoherent jumble of confused thoughts.* **2.** Unable to think or express one's thoughts in a clear or orderly manner: *The delirious patient was incoherent and confused.* **—in′co•her′ence** *n.* **—in′co•her′ent•ly** *adv.*

in•com•bus•ti•ble (ĭn′kəm **bŭs′**tə bəl) *adj.* Incapable of burning. *—n.* An incombustible material.

in•come (**ĭn′**kŭm′) *n.* The amount of money received for labor or services, from the sale of property or goods, or from financial investments: *One's monthly income is all the money one receives in a month.*

income tax *n.* A tax on the income of a person or business.

in•com•ing (ĭn′kŭm′ĭng) *adj.* **1.** Coming in; entering: *incoming mail.* **2.** About to come in; next in succession: *the incoming president.*

in•com•men•su•rate (ĭn′kə **mĕn′**sər ĭt *or* ĭn′kə **mĕn′**shər ĭt) *adj.* **1.** Not corresponding in size or degree; inadequate: *The salary for the job is incommensurate with the responsibilities.* **2.** Impossible to measure. **—in′com•men′su•rate•ly** *adv.*

in•com•mu•ni•ca•ble (ĭn′kə **myo͞o′**nĭ kə bəl) *adj.* Impossible to communicate: *He found his feelings were so complex as to be incommunicable.*

in•com•mu•ni•ca•do (ĭn′kə myo͞o′nĭ **kä′**dō) *adv.* & *adj.* Without the means or right of communicating with others: *The judge ordered the jurors to remain incommunicado until the trial was over.* [First written down in 1844 in American English, from Spanish *incomunicar*, to deny communication.]

in•com•pa•ra•ble (ĭn **kŏm′**pər ə bəl) *adj.* **1.** Impossible to compare: *The responsibilities of adults are incomparable with those of children.* **2.** Above all comparison; unsurpassed: *the incomparable value of an education.* **—in•com′pa•ra•bly** *adv.*

in•com•pat•i•ble (ĭn′kəm **păt′**ə bəl) *adj.* **1.** Not capable of existing in agreement or harmony with something else: *Speeding is incompatible with safe driving.* **2.** Not capable of living or working together happily or smoothly; antagonistic. **—in′com•pat′i•bil′i•ty** *n.* **—in′com•pat′i•bly** *adv.*

in•com•pe•tent (ĭn **kŏm′**pĭ tənt) *adj.* Not having or showing adequate abilities or qualifications; incapable: *His limited experience means that he is incompetent to do complicated repairs.* —*n.* An incompetent person. **—in•com′pe•tence** *n.* **—in•com′pe•tent•ly** *adv.*

in•com•plete (ĭn′kəm **plēt′**) *adj.* Not complete; unfinished: *The composer's last symphony is incomplete.* **—in′com•plete′ly** *adv.*

in•com•pre•hen•si•ble (ĭn′kŏm prĭ **hĕn′**sə bəl *or* ĭn kŏm′prĭ **hĕn′**sə bəl) *adj.* Difficult or impossible to understand: *an incomprehensible sentence.* **—in′com•pre•hen′si•bil′i•ty** *n.* **—in′com•pre•hen′si•bly** *adv.*

in•com•press•i•ble (ĭn′kəm **prĕs′**ə bəl) *adj.* Impossible to compress. **—in′com•press′i•bil′i•ty** *n.*

in•con•ceiv•a•ble (ĭn′kən **sē′**və bəl) *adj.* Difficult or impossible to understand or imagine: *It would be inconceivable for them to complain about the accommodations.* **—in′con•ceiv′a•bly** *adv.*

in•con•clu•sive (ĭn′kən **klo͞o′**sĭv) *adj.* Not conclusive: *The inclusive election returns left neither candidate sure of victory.* **—in′con•clu′sive•ly** *adv.* **—in′con•clu′sive•ness** *n.*

in•con•gru•i•ty (ĭn′kŏn **gro͞o′**ĭ tē) *n., pl.* **in•con•gru•i•ties. 1.** The quality or condition of being incongruous. **2.** Something that is incongruous.

in•con•gru•ous (ĭn **kŏng′**gro͞o əs) *adj.* **1.** Lacking in harmony; incompatible or inconsistent: *Your proposal is incongruous with our plans.* **2.** Not in keeping with what is correct, proper, or logical; inappropriate: *incongruous behavior.* **—in•con′gru•ous•ly** *adv.* **—in•con′gru•ous•ness** *n.*

in•con•se•quen•tial (ĭn kŏn′sĭ **kwĕn′**shəl *or* ĭn′kŏn sĭ **kwĕn′**shəl) *adj.* Lacking importance; trivial: *an inconsequential and boring debate.* **—in•con′se•quen′tial•ly** *adv.*

in•con•sid•er•a•ble (ĭn′kən **sĭd′**ər ə bəl) *adj.* Too small or unimportant to be worth attention or consideration; trivial. **—in′con•sid′er•a•bly** *adv.*

in•con•sid•er•ate (ĭn′kən **sĭd′**ər ĭt) *adj.* Not considerate; thoughtless: *It is inconsiderate to make noise while we're trying to read.* **—in′con•sid′er•ate•ly** *adv.* **—in′con•sid′er•ate•ness** *n.*

in•con•sis•ten•cy (ĭn′kən **sĭs′**tən sē) *n., pl.* **in•con•sis•ten•cies. 1.** The quality or condition of being inconsistent. **2.** Something that is inconsistent: *inconsistencies in spelling.*

in•con•sis•tent (ĭn′kən **sĭs′**tənt) *adj.* **1.** Not in agreement or harmony: *The witness's version of the story is inconsistent with the facts.* **2.** Not regular or predictable, as in a course of action; erratic: *inconsistent behavior.* **3.** Lacking in logical relation; contradictory. **—in′con•sis′tent•ly** *adv.*

in•con•sol•a•ble (ĭn′kən **sō′**lə bəl) *adj.* Difficult or impossible to console: *The children were inconsolable at the loss of their pet.* **—in′con•sol′a•bly** *adv.*

in•con•spic•u•ous (ĭn′kən **spĭk′**yo͞o əs) *adj.* Not readily noticeable; not obvious: *The flowers of many trees are inconspicuous.* **—in′con•spic′u•ous•ly** *adv.* **—in′con•spic′u•ous•ness** *n.*

in•con•stant (ĭn **kŏn′**stənt) *adj.* Not constant or steady; changeable or fickle. **—in•con′stan•cy** *n.* **—in•con′stant•ly** *adv.*

in•con•tro•vert•i•ble (ĭn kŏn′trə **vûr′**tə bəl *or* ĭn′kŏn trə **vûr′**tə bəl) *adj.* Impossible to dispute; unquestionable: *incontrovertible evidence pointing to the suspect's guilt.* **—in•con′tro•vert′i•bly** *adv.*

in•con•ven•ience (ĭn′kən **vēn′**yəns) *n.* **1.** The quality or condition of being convenient. **2.** Something that causes difficulty, trouble, or discomfort: *Lack of central heating is an inconvenience.* —*tr.v.* **in•con•ven•ienced, in•con•ven•ienc•ing, in•con•ven•ienc•es.** To cause inconvenience to; trouble; bother: *Road construction inconvenienced many drivers.* **—in′con•ven′ient•ly** *adv.*

in•con•ven•ient (ĭn′kən **vēn′**yənt) *adj.* Not convenient; causing difficulty: *It is inconvenient to have no cafeteria in this building.* **—in′con•ven′ient•ly** *adv.*

in•cor•po•rate (ĭn **kôr′**pə rāt′) *tr.v.* **in•cor•po•rat•ed, in•cor•po•rat•ing, in•cor•po•rates. 1.** To include as a part in a whole; combine with something else: *a new car that incorporates features of earlier models.* **2.** To form into a legal corporation: *incorporate a business.* [First written down before 1398 in Middle English and spelled *incorporaten*, from Late Latin *incorporāre*, to form into a body, from Latin *corpus*, body.]

in•cor•po•rat•ed (ĭn **kôr′**pə rā′tĭd) *adj.* Organized and maintained as a legal corporation: *an incorporated business.*

in•cor•po•re•al (ĭn′kôr **pôr′**ē əl) *adj.* Lacking material form or substance; spiritual. **—in′cor•po′re•al•ly** *adv.*

in•cor•rect (ĭn′kə **rĕkt′**) *adj.* **1.** Not correct; faulty; wrong: *The test had many incorrect answers.* **2.** Inappropriate or improper: *incorrect dress for the occasion.* **—in′cor•rect′ly** *adv.* **—in′cor•rect′ness** *n.*

in•cor•ri•gi•ble (ĭn **kôr′**ĭ jə bəl *or* ĭn **kŏr′**ĭ jə bəl) *adj.* Incapable of being corrected or reformed: *an incorrigible habit.* —*n.* A person who cannot be reformed. **—in•cor′ri•gi•bil′i•ty** *n.* **—in•cor′ri•gi•bly** *adv.*

in•cor•rupt•i•ble (ĭn′kə **rŭp′**tə bəl) *adj.* **1.** Incapable of being morally corrupted: *The honest judge is incorruptible.* **2.** Not subject to decay or rot: *Cedar is a nearly incorruptible wood.* **—in′cor•rupt′i•bil′i•ty** *n.* **—in′cor•rupt′i•bly** *adv.*

in•crease (ĭn **krēs′**) *tr.* & *intr.v.* **in•creased, in•creas•ing, in•creas•es.** To make or become greater or larger in size, number, or power: *Machines increase the rate at which goods are manufactured. The world's population increased rapidly over the last decade.* —*n.* (**ĭn′**krēs′). **1.** The act of increasing;

ă	pat	oi	boy
ā	pay	ou	out
âr	care	o͝o	took
ä	father	o͞o	boot
ĕ	pet	ŭ	cut
ē	be	ûr	urge
ĭ	pit	th	thin
ī	pie	*th*	this
îr	pier	hw	whoop
ŏ	pot	zh	vision
ō	toe	ə	about
ô	paw	N	*French* bon

growth: *a steady increase in sales over the last two years.* **2.** The amount or rate by which something is increased: *a ten percent increase in tax rates.* **—*idiom.* on the increase.** Becoming greater or more frequent; increasing. [First written down before 1333 in Middle English and spelled *encresen,* from Latin *incrēscere,* to keep growing.] **—in•creas′ing•ly** *adv.*

Synonyms: increase, expand, enlarge, extend, multiply. These verbs mean to become or make greater or larger. **Increase,** the most general, often means to grow steadily: *The number of students here has increased every year since 1975.* **Expand** means to increase in size, volume, or amount: *The pizza parlor expanded its delivery service to cover a wider area.* **Enlarge** means to make larger: *Sue likes that photograph so much that she wants to enlarge and frame it.* **Extend** means to increase in length: *The transit authority extended the subway line to the suburbs.* **Multiply** means to increase in number: *One of the zoo's roles is to help endangered species multiply.*
Antonym: decrease.

in•cred•i•ble (ĭn krĕd′ə bəl) *adj.* Hard to believe; unbelievable: *The new plane flies at an incredible height.* **—in•cred′i•bly** *adv.*

in•cre•du•li•ty (ĭn′krĭ do͞o′lĭ tē *or* ĭn′krĭ dyo͞o′lĭ tē) *n.* The state or quality of disbelief; doubt.

in•cred•u•lous (ĭn krĕj′ə ləs) *adj.* **1.** Disbelieving or doubtful; skeptical: *incredulous of stories about flying saucers.* **2.** Expressive of disbelief or astonishment: *incredulous gasps at the gymnast's performance.* **—in•cred′u•lous•ly** *adv.*

in•cre•ment (ĭn′krə mənt *or* ĭng′krə mənt) *n.* **1.** An increase in number, size, amount, or extent: *The increment in sales made the company profitable.* **2.** An added amount, especially one of a series of regular additions: *The crowd grew by increments throughout the day.* [First written down about 1425 in Middle English, from Latin *incrēmentum,* from *incrēscere,* to increase.]

in•crim•i•nate (ĭn krĭm′ə nāt′) *tr.v.* **in•crim•i•nat•ed, in•crim•i•nat•ing, in•crim•i•nates. 1.** To accuse of a crime or other wrongful act: *The indictment incriminates six conspirators.* **2.** To cause to appear guilty of a crime or fault; implicate: *The new evidence incriminated other suspects in the robbery.* **—in•crim′i•na′tion** *n.* **—in•crim′i•na′tor** *n.*

in•crust (ĭn krŭst′) *v.* Variant of **encrust.**

in•cu•bate (ĭn′kyə bāt′ *or* ĭng′kyə bāt′) *v.* **in•cu•bat•ed, in•cu•bat•ing, in•cu•bates.** *—tr.* **1.** To warm and hatch (eggs) by bodily heat; brood. **2.** To keep (eggs, organisms, or other living tissue) in conditions favorable to growth and development. **3.** To form or consider slowly: *incubate an outline for a book.* *—intr.* **1.** To sit on eggs; brood. **2.** To go through the process of incubation: *Most colds incubate in about a week.* [First written down in 1641 in Modern English, from Latin *incubāre,* to lie down on.]

in•cu•ba•tion (ĭn′kyə bā′shən *or* ĭng′kyə bā′shən) *n.* **1.** The act of incubating or the condition of being incubated. **2.** The development of a disease from the time of infection until the appearance of symptoms.

in•cu•ba•tor (ĭn′kyə bā′tər *or* ĭng′kyə bā′tər) *n.* **1.** An apparatus in which desired conditions, such as temperature and humidity, can be maintained for hatching eggs artificially and growing cultures of microorganisms. **2.** A similar apparatus supplied with oxygen for the special care of very small or premature babies.

in•cu•des (ĭng kyo͞o′dēz) *n.* Plural of **incus.**

in•cul•cate (ĭn kŭl′kāt′ *or* ĭn′kŭl kāt′) *tr.v.* **in•cul•cat•ed, in•cul•cat•ing, in•cul•cates.** To impress on the mind by persistent teaching; instill: *Our science teacher inculcated the importance of being careful when making measurements.* [First written down in 1550 in Modern English, from Latin *inculcāre,* to force upon.] **—in′cul•ca′tion** *n.*

in•cum•ben•cy (ĭn kŭm′bən sē) *n., pl.* **in•cum•ben•cies. 1.** The quality or condition of being incumbent. **2.** The term of an incumbent.

in•cum•bent (ĭn kŭm′bənt) *adj.* **1.** Currently holding a specified office: *the incumbent mayor.* **2.** Imposed as an obligation or duty; required: *It is incumbent on all citizens to pay their taxes.* **3.** Lying, leaning, or resting on something else: *an incumbent layer of rock.* *—n.* A person currently holding an office. [First written down about 1410 in Middle English, from Latin *incumbere,* to lean upon, apply oneself to.]

in•cur (ĭn kûr′) *tr.v.* **in•curred, in•cur•ring, in•curs. 1.** To acquire or come into (something): *The investor incurred huge profits during the stock market boom.* **2.** To become responsible for or subject to as a result of one's actions; bring upon oneself: *She incurred their resentment because of her incessant wisecracks.* [First written down about 1400 in Middle English and spelled *incurren,* from Latin *incurrere,* to run into.]

in•cur•a•ble (ĭn kyo͝or′ə bəl) *adj.* Incapable of being cured: *an incurable disease.* **—in•cur′a•bly** *adv.*

in•cur•sion (ĭn kûr′zhən *or* ĭn kûr′shən) *n.* A sudden attack on a foreign territory; a raid: *The Vikings made many incursions along the European coast.*

in•cus (ĭng′kəs) *n., pl.* **in•cu•des** (ĭng kyo͞o′dēz). One of the three small bones in the middle ear; the anvil. [First written down in 1669 in Modern English, from Latin *incūs,* anvil.]

Ind. *abbr.* An abbreviation of Indiana.

in•debt•ed (ĭn dĕt′ĭd) *adj.* Owing another money or gratitude for a loan, gift, or useful service; beholden: *We are indebted to you for your hospitality.*

in•debt•ed•ness (ĭn dĕt′ĭd nĭs) *n.* **1.** The state of being indebted. **2.** Something that is owed to another.

in•de•cen•cy (ĭn dē′sən sē) *n., pl.* **in•de•cen•cies. 1.** The quality or condition of being indecent. **2.** Something that is indecent.

in•de•cent (ĭn dē′sənt) *adj.* **1.** Not in good taste; improper; unsuitable: *Our dinner guests left with indecent haste shortly after the meal.* **2.** Morally offensive; obscene; immodest. **—in•de′cent•ly** *adv.*

in•de•ci•sion (ĭn′dĭ sĭzh′ən) *n.* The condition of being unable to make up one's mind.

in•de•ci•sive (ĭn′dĭ sī′sĭv) *adj.* **1.** Unable to make up one's mind; wavering; vacillating: *The indecisive executive constantly put off important purchases.* **2.** Having no clear result; inconclusive: *an indecisive election in which no candidate received a clear majority of the votes.* **—in′de•ci′sive•ly** *adv.* **—in′de•ci′sive•ness** *n.*

in•dec•o•rous (ĭn dĕk′ər əs) *adj.* Not in good taste; lacking propriety: *loud and indecorous behavior.* **—in•dec′o•rous•ly** *adv.*

in•deed (ĭn dēd′) *adv.* **1.** Without a doubt; certainly: *They were indeed happy.* **2.** In fact; in reality: *I said the car would break down and indeed it did.* *—interj.* An expression used to show surprise, irony, or disbelief. [First written down before 1338 in Middle English and spelled *in dede.*]

indef. *abbr.* An abbreviation of indefinite.

in•de•fat•i•ga•ble (ĭn′dĭ făt′ĭ gə bəl) *adj.* Never giving up or becoming tired; tireless: *The indefatigable scientists spent long hours in search of a treatment for the disease.* **—in′de•fat′i•ga•bly** *adv.*

in•de•fen•si•ble (ĭn′dĭ fĕn′sə bəl) *adj.* **1.** Vulnerable to attack: *an indefensible town in the middle of* *a valley.* **2.** Incapable of being justified or excused; inexcusable: *rude and indefensible behavior.* **—in′de•fen′si•bly** *adv.*

in•de•fin•a•ble (ĭn′dĭ fī′nə bəl) *adj.* Impossible to define, describe, or analyze: *a vague and indefinable feeling of suspicion.* **—in′de•fin′a•bly** *adv.*

in•def•i•nite (ĭn **dĕf′**ə nĭt) *adj.* **1.** Not fixed or limited: *an indefinite period of time.* **2.** Not clear or exact; vague: *indefinite outlines of people standing in the shadows.* **3.** Not decided; uncertain: *indefinite plans.* **—in•def′i•nite•ly** *adv.* **—in•def′i•nite•ness** *n.*

indefinite article *n.* An article, in English either *a* or *an,* that does not fix the identity of the noun modified. —SEE NOTE at **a²**.

indefinite pronoun *n.* A pronoun, as English *any* or *some,* that does not specify the identity of its object.

in•del•i•ble (ĭn **dĕl′**ə bəl) *adj.* **1.** Impossible to remove, erase, or wash away; permanent: *an indelible stain.* **2.** Making an indelible mark: *an indelible pen.* [First written down in 1529 in Modern English, from Latin *indēlēbilis* : *in-*, not + *dēlēre*, to wipe out.] **—in•del′i•bil′i•ty, in•del′i•ble•ness** *n.* **—in•del′i•bly** *adv.*

in•del•i•ca•cy (ĭn **dĕl′**ĭ kə sē) *n., pl.* **in•del•i•ca•cies. 1.** The quality or condition of being indelicate. **2.** Something that is indelicate.

in•del•i•cate (ĭn **dĕl′**ĭ kĭt) *adj.* Lacking good taste; crude or improper: *indelicate language.* **—in•del′i•cate•ly** *adv.*

in•dem•ni•fy (ĭn **dĕm′**nə fī′) *tr.v.* **in•dem•ni•fied, in•dem•ni•fy•ing, in•dem•ni•fies. 1.** To protect against possible damage, injury, or loss; insure: *Motorists are indemnified by automobile insurance.* **2.** To make compensation to for damage, injury, or loss suffered: *The shipper indemnified the grower for the lost crate of fruit.* **—in•dem′ni•fi•ca′tion** (ĭn dĕm′nə fĭ **kā′**shən) *n.*

in•dem•ni•ty (ĭn **dĕm′**nĭ tē) *n., pl.* **in•dem•ni•ties. 1.** Insurance or other security against possible damage, loss, or injury. **2.** Payment or compensation for damage, loss, or injury.

in•dent¹ (ĭn **dĕnt′**) *tr.v.* **in•dent•ed, in•dent•ing, in•dents. 1.** To set (the first line of a paragraph) in from the margin. **2.** To make notches in the edge of; make jagged: *He indented the board to make a secure joint.* *—n.* (ĭn **dĕnt′** *or* **ĭn′**dĕnt′). An indentation. [First written down before 1400 in Middle English and spelled *endenten*, to notch, from Medieval Latin *indentāre* : Latin *in-*, in + Latin *dēns*, tooth.]

in•dent² (ĭn **dĕnt′**) *tr.v.* **in•dent•ed, in•dent•ing, in•dents.** To make a dent, recess, or other impression in: *Coves indent the coast.* *—n.* (ĭn **dĕnt′** *or* **ĭn′**dĕnt′). An indentation. [First written down about 1380 and spelled *endenten*, to decorate, as with precious stones, from *denten*, to make a dent in.]

in•den•ta•tion (ĭn′dĕn **tā′**shən) *n.* **1.** The act of indenting or the condition of being indented. **2.** The blank space between a margin and the beginning of an indented line. **3.** A recess or notch, as in a border or coastline.

in•den•ture (ĭn **dĕn′**chər) *n.* A deed or contract between two or more parties, especially one binding a servant or an apprentice to another person for a specified period of time. *—tr.v.* **in•den•tured, in•den•tur•ing, in•den•tures.** To bind by an indenture: *Many 17th-century European immigrants were indentured to American landowners.*

in•de•pend•ence (ĭn′dĭ **pĕn′**dəns) *n.* The quality or condition of being independent: *Many countries of colonial Africa won their independence from European nations during the last fifty years.*

In•de•pend•ence (ĭn′dĭ **pĕn′**dəns). A city of western Missouri east-southeast of Kansas City. It was the home of President Harry S. Truman. Population, 112,301.

Independence Day *n.* A national holiday celebrated on July 4 to commemorate the adoption of the Declaration of Independence in 1776.

in•de•pend•ent (ĭn′dĭ **pĕn′**dənt) *adj.* **1.** Not governed by a foreign country; ruling or governing itself: *The United States became an independent nation after the Revolution.* **2.** Not controlled or guided by others; self-reliant: *an independent mind.* **3.** Not dependent on or connected with a larger or controlling group; separate: *an independent drugstore.* **4.** Not committed to any one political party: *an independent voter.* **5.** Earning one's own living; self-supporting: *With this job I am independent of my parents.* **6.** Providing enough income to allow one to live without working: *a person of independent means.* **—in′de•pend′ent•ly** *adv.*

independent clause *n.* A clause in a sentence that can stand alone as a complete sentence; a main clause. For example, in the sentence *When the sun came out, we went for a walk,* the clause *we went for a walk* is an independent clause.

in-depth (**ĭn′dĕpth′**) *adj.* Detailed; thorough: *an in-depth interview of the candidate.*

in•de•scrib•a•ble (ĭn′dĭ **skrī′**bə bəl) *adj.* Impossible to describe: *indescribable delight.* **—in′de•scrib′a•bly** *adv.*

in•de•struc•ti•ble (ĭn′dĭ **strŭk′**tə bəl) *adj.* Impossible to destroy: *an indestructible stone house.* **—in′de•struc′ti•bly** *adv.*

in•de•ter•mi•nate (ĭn′dĭ **tûr′**mə nĭt) *adj.* Not precisely determined; not defined; vague: *a person of indeterminate age.* **—in′de•ter′mi•nate•ly** *adv.* **—in′de•ter′mi•nate•ness** *n.*

in•dex (**ĭn′**dĕks′) *n., pl.* **in•dex•es** or **in•di•ces** (**ĭn′**dĭ sēz′). **1.** A list of names or subjects arranged in alphabetical order and presented at the end of a printed work, along with the page numbers on which each item is mentioned. **2.** Something that reveals or indicates; a sign: *The baby's face is an index to its feelings.* **3.** An indicator or a pointer, as the arrow on a dial or another device. *—tr.v.* **in•dexed, in•dex•ing, in•dex•es. 1.** To furnish with an index: *index a history textbook.* **2.** To enter (an item) in an index. [First written down before 1398 in Middle English and spelled *index*, forefinger, from Latin.]

index finger *n.* The finger next to the thumb; the forefinger.

index of refraction *n.* The ratio of the speed of light in a vacuum to the speed of light in another medium, such as water or oil.

In•di•a (**ĭn′**dē ə). **1.** A peninsula and subcontinent of southern Asia south of the Himalaya Mountains, occupied by India, Nepal, Bhutan, Pakistan, and Bangladesh. **2.** A country of southern Asia on the Indian Ocean. India was the site of one of the oldest civilizations in the world, centered in the Indus River valley from around 2500 to 1500 B.C. The country gained its independence from Great Britain in 1947. New Delhi is the capital and Calcutta the largest city. Population, 685,184,692.

India ink *n.* Black ink or paint made from lampblack.

In•di•an (**ĭn′**dē ən) *adj.* **1.** Of or relating to India or the East Indies or to their peoples, languages, or cultures. **2.** Of or relating to any of the Native American peoples or their language or culture. *—n.* **1.** A native or inhabitant of India or the East Indies. **2.** A Native American. **3.** Any of the languages of the Native Americans.

In•di•an•a (ĭn′dē **ăn′**ə). A state of the north-central United States east of Illinois. It was admitted as the

Indiana

The name **Indiana** comes from *Indian* plus a Latin ending and means "land of the Indians." It was first used by developers to describe the region and later by Congress when it created the Indiana Territory (1800) and the state of Indiana (1816).

ă	pat	oi	boy
ā	pay	ou	out
âr	care	ŏŏ	took
ä	father	ōō	boot
ĕ	pet	ŭ	cut
ē	be	ûr	urge
ĭ	pit	th	thin
ī	pie	*th*	this
îr	pier	hw	whoop
ŏ	pot	zh	vision
ō	toe	ə	about
ô	paw	N	*French* bon

Indian club

Indian paintbrush

19th state in 1816. Indianapolis is the capital and the largest city. Population, 5,564,228. —SEE NOTE on page 507.

In•di•an•ap•o•lis (ĭn′dē ə **năp′**ə lĭs). The capital and largest city of Indiana, in the central part of the state south-southwest of Fort Wayne. It was settled in 1820. Population, 741,952.

Indian club *n.* A bottle-shaped wooden club held in the hand and swung for exercise.

Indian corn *n.* **1.** The corn plant that is native to North America; maize. **2.** The ears or edible kernels of this plant.

Indian Ocean. A body of water extending from southern Asia to Antarctica and from eastern Africa to southeast Australia.

Indian paintbrush *n.* **1.** Any of various plants having clusters of bright red, yellow, or pink leaves surrounding small greenish flowers. **2.** A North American weed having deep orange flowers.

Indian pipe *n.* A waxy white or pinkish plant having a pipe-shaped flower.

Indian summer *n.* A period of mild weather occurring in late autumn.

Indian Territory. A region and former territory of the south-central United States, mainly in present-day Oklahoma. It was a homeland for forcibly removed Native Americans between 1834 and 1907. —SEE NOTE at **Oklahoma**.

India paper *n.* A thin paper used especially in engraving or in Bibles.

India rubber *n.* Rubber made from the milky sap of the rubber tree.

In•dic (**ĭn′**dĭk) *adj.* **1.** Of or relating to India or its people or cultures. **2.** Of or relating to Indic. —*n.* A branch of the Indo-European language family that includes the languages of the Indian subcontinent and Sri Lanka.

in•di•cate (**ĭn′**dĭ kāt′) *tr.v.* **indi•cat•ed, indi•cat•ing, indi•cates. 1.** To show or point out: *indicate a route on a map.* **2.** To serve as a sign or symptom of: *Dark clouds indicate rain. Fever indicates illness.* **3.** To state or express: *Their faces indicated they did not like spinach at all.*

in•di•ca•tion (ĭn′dĭ **kā′**shən) *n.* **1.** The act of indicating: *His indication of refusal came in the form of a frown.* **2.** Something that indicates; a sign: *flowers, birds, and other indications of spring.* [First written down before 1425 in Middle English and spelled *indicacion*, from Latin *indicāre*, to point to, show, from *index*, forefinger.]

in•dic•a•tive (ĭn **dĭk′**ə tĭv) *adj.* **1.** Serving to indicate: *A cough is often indicative of a cold.* **2.** Of or relating to the mood of a verb used in ordinary statements of fact or in factual questions. For example, in *We went* and *Did they go?*, the words *went* and *go* are in the indicative mood. —*n.* **1.** The indicative mood. **2.** A verb form in this mood.

in•di•ca•tor (**ĭn′**dĭ kā′tər) *n.* **1.** A person or thing that indicates, especially: **a.** A meter or gauge that tells about the operation of an engine or other machine or system. **b.** The needle or dial of such a meter or gauge. **2.** A chemical compound that changes color under certain conditions, used in chemical tests. Litmus is an indicator that shows the amount of acid in a solution by changes in color.

in•di•ces (**ĭn′**dĭ sēz′) *n.* A plural of **index**.

in•dict (ĭn **dīt′**) *tr.v.* **in•dict•ed, in•dict•ing, in•dicts. 1.** To accuse of wrongdoing; charge: *a book that indicts advertisers on charges of corrupting our society.* **2.** To make a formal accusation against and hold (a person) for trial, based on the findings of a grand jury. [First written down about 1303 in Middle English and spelled *enditen*, ultimately from Latin *dīcere*, to say.] —**in•dict′a•ble** *adj.* —**in•dict′er, in•dic′tor** *n.*

in•dict•ment (ĭn **dīt′**mənt) *n.* **1.** The act of indicting or the condition of being indicted: *a bank officer under indictment for embezzlement.* **2.** A written statement issued by a grand jury that charges a person with the commission of a crime.

in•dif•fer•ence (ĭn **dĭf′**ər əns *or* ĭn **dĭf′**rəns) *n.* **1.** Lack of concern or interest: *The regime's indifference to the worsening economic conditions brought about its downfall.* **2.** Lack of importance; insignificance: *Their opinion is a matter of indifference to me.*

in•dif•fer•ent (ĭn **dĭf′**ər ənt *or* ĭn **dĭf′**rənt) *adj.* **1.** Having or showing no interest; not caring one way or the other: *indifferent to the troubles of others; indifferent to weather conditions.* **2.** Showing no preference; impartial: *A jury should be indifferent in viewing the facts of a trial.* **3.** Neither good nor bad; mediocre: *The orchestra gave an indifferent performance.* —**in•dif′fer•ent•ly** *adv.*

in•di•gence (**ĭn′**dĭ jəns) *n.* Poverty; great need.

in•dig•e•nous (ĭn **dĭj′**ə nəs) *adj.* Originally living or growing in a region or environment; native: *The bison and the redwood are indigenous to North America.* [First written down in 1646 in Modern English, from Latin *indigena*, a native.]

in•di•gent (**ĭn′**dĭ jənt) *adj.* Poor; needy. [First written down before 1400 in Middle English, from Latin *indigēre*, to need.]

in•di•gest•i•ble (ĭn′dĭ **jĕs′**tə bəl *or* ĭn′dī **jĕs′**tə bəl) *adj.* Difficult or impossible to digest: *indigestible fatty foods.*

in•di•ges•tion (ĭn′dĭ **jĕs′**chən *or* ĭn′dī **jĕs′**chən) *n.* **1.** Inability to digest or difficulty in digesting food. **2.** Discomfort or illness resulting from this inability or difficulty: *The rich dessert will surely give you indigestion.*

in•dig•nant (ĭn **dĭg′**nənt) *adj.* Feeling or expressing indignation: *I was indignant over their thoughtless remarks.* —**in•dig′nant•ly** *adv.*

in•dig•na•tion (ĭn′dĭg **nā′**shən) *n.* Anger aroused by something unjust, mean, or unworthy: *The voters expressed their indignation over the government's continuing neglect of serious problems.* See Synonyms at **anger.** [First written down before 1200 in Middle English and spelled *indignatio*, from Latin *indignātiō*, from *indignārī*, to regard as unworthy, from *indignus*, unworthy.]

in•dig•ni•ty (ĭn **dĭg′**nĭ tē) *n., pl.* **in•dig•ni•ties.** Something that offends a person's pride and sense of dignity; an insult: *She felt it was an indignity to be asked to do such menial tasks.*

in•di•go (**ĭn′**dĭ gō′) *n., pl.* **in•di•gos** or **in•di•goes. 1.a.** Any of various plants that yield a dark blue dye. **b.** A dark violet-blue dye obtained from these plants or an artificial dye of the same color. **2.** A dark violet blue. [First written down in 1555 in Modern English and spelled *endego*, from Latin *indicum*, from Greek *Indikos*, of India.]

in•di•rect (ĭn′dĭ **rĕkt′** *or* ĭn′dī **rĕkt′**) *adj.* **1.** Not following a direct course; roundabout: *an indirect route.* **2.** Not straight to the point, as in talking: *an indirect answer.* **3.** Not directly connected or planned for; secondary: *The boom in bicycle sales was an indirect effect of the new gasoline tax.* —**in′di•rect′ly** *adv.* —**in′di•rect′ness** *n.*

indirect object *n.* A word or words indirectly affected by the action of a verb. For example, in the sentences *Sing me a song* and *We fed the turtle lettuce,* the words *me* and *turtle* are both indirect objects.

in•dis•creet (ĭn′dĭ **skrēt′**) *adj.* Lacking discretion; unwise or tactless: *an indiscreet remark.* —**in′dis•creet′ly** *adv.* —**in′dis•creet′ness** *n.*

in•dis•cre•tion (ĭn′dĭ **skrĕsh′**ən) *n.* **1.** Lack of discretion. **2.** An indiscreet act or remark.

in•dis•crim•i•nate (ĭn′dĭ **skrĭm′**ə nĭt) *adj.* **1.** Exercising or showing a lack of care in making choices: *an indiscriminate shopper.* **2.** Not sorted out or put in order; random or confused: *an indiscriminate pile of papers on a desk.* **—in′dis•crim′i•nate•ly** *adv.*

in•dis•pen•sa•ble (ĭn′dĭ **spĕn′**sə bəl) *adj.* Not capable of being dispensed with; essential; necessary: *A good education is indispensable to becoming a doctor.* **—in′dis•pen′sa•bly** *adv.*

in•dis•posed (ĭn′dĭ **spōzd′**) *adj.* **1.** Mildly ill: *indisposed with a slight cold.* **2.** Unwilling; reluctant: *indisposed to help at all.*

in•dis•po•si•tion (ĭn dĭs′pə **zĭsh′**ən) *n.* **1.** A minor ailment. **2.** Unwillingness.

in•dis•put•a•ble (ĭn′dĭ **spyo͞o′**tə bəl) *adj.* Beyond doubt; unquestionable: *an indisputable fact.* **—in′dis•put′a•bly** *adv.*

in•dis•sol•u•ble (ĭn′dĭ **sŏl′**yə bəl) *adj.* **1.** Impossible to dissolve. **2.** Not capable of being broken or undone; permanent: *an indissoluble bond between friends.* **—in′dis•sol′u•bly** *adv.*

in•dis•tinct (ĭn′dĭ **stĭngkt′**) *adj.* Not clearly heard, seen, or understood: *an indistinct sound heard from far away; saw an indistinct figure in the distance.* **—in′dis•tinct′ly** *adv.* **—in′dis•tinct′ness** *n.*

in•dis•tin•guish•a•ble (ĭn′dĭ **stĭng′**gwĭ shə bəl) *adj.* Lacking clear differences; impossible to tell apart: *a plain little shop indistinguishable from any other on the street.*

in•di•um (**ĭn′**dē əm) *n. Symbol* **In** A soft, silvery, metallic element that resists abrasion. Atomic number 49. See table at **element.** [First written down in 1864 in Modern English, from *indigo* (so called from the indigo-blue lines in its spectrum).]

in•di•vid•u•al (ĭn′də **vĭj′**o͞o əl) *adj.* **1.** Of or relating to a single human being, animal, or plant: *for each individual child.* **2.** By or for one person: *an individual portion of food.* **3.** Existing as a separate unit; distinct: *individual drops of rain.* **4.** Having a special quality; unique; distinct: *Each variety of apple has its individual flavor.* —*n.* **1.** A single human being: *a pleasant and friendly individual.* **2.** A single animal or plant: *taller individuals in a field of corn; hundreds of individuals in a migrating flock.* [First written down about 1425 in Middle English and spelled *individuall,* single, indivisible, from Latin *indīviduus.*] **—in′di•vid′u•al•ly** *adv.*

in•di•vid•u•al•ism (ĭn′də **vĭj′**o͞o ə lĭz′əm) *n.* **1.** Belief in following one's own interests without concern for the opinions of others or the usual way of doing things. **2.** A way of living based on this belief; personal independence. **3.** The doctrine that an individual should be free from governmental interference or regulation in attempting to acquire wealth.

in•di•vid•u•al•ist (ĭn′də **vĭj′**o͞o ə lĭst) *n.* **1.** A person who is independent in thought and action. **2.** A person who supports or believes in individualism. **—in′di•vid′u•al•is′tic** *adj.* **—in′di•vid′u•al•is′ti•cal•ly** *adv.*

in•di•vid•u•al•i•ty (ĭn′də vĭj′o͞o **ăl′**ĭ tē) *n., pl.* **in•di•vid•u•al•i•ties.** **1.** The condition of being individual; distinctness: *While singing in the chorus, she felt at times she was losing her individuality.* **2.** The qualities that make a person or thing different from others; identity: *He expresses his individuality in the way he dresses.*

in•di•vid•u•al•ize (ĭn′də **vĭj′**o͞o ə līz′) *tr.v.* **in•di•vid•u•al•ized, in•di•vid•u•al•iz•ing, in•di•vid•u•al•iz•es.** **1.** To give individuality to: *The artist individualized his painting when he developed a unique style.* **2.** To change to fit or satisfy an individual: *individualize exercises according to each person's need.*

in•di•vis•i•ble (ĭn′də **vĭz′**ə bəl) *adj.* **1.** Incapable of being divided: *The childhood friends seemed indivisible.* **2.** Incapable of being divided without leaving a remainder; for example, 7 is indivisible by 3. **—in′di•vis′i•bil′i•ty** *n.* **—in′di•vis′i•bly** *adv.*

In•do•chi•na (ĭn′dō **chī′**nə). A peninsula of southeast Asia made up of Vietnam, Laos, Cambodia, Thailand, Burma, and mainland Malaysia.

in•doc•tri•nate (ĭn **dŏk′**trə nāt′) *tr.v.* **in•doc•tri•nat•ed, in•doc•tri•nat•ing, in•doc•tri•nates.** To instruct (a person) in the doctrines or beliefs of a particular group. **—in•doc′tri•na′tion** *n.*

In•do-Eu•ro•pe•an (ĭn′dō yo͝or′ə **pē′**ən) *n.* **1.** A family of languages that includes most of the languages of Europe, along with the languages of Iran, India, and some other parts of Asia. **2.** An unrecorded language that is the ancestor of this family of languages. **3.** One of the peoples who spoke this language. **—In′do-Eu′ro•pe′an** *adj.* —See Note.

In•do-I•ra•ni•an (ĭn′dō ĭ **rā′**nē ən) *n.* **1.** A member of a people who spoke an Indo-European language, lived in Iran, and later conquered India and settled there. **2.** A branch of the Indo-European language family that includes many languages spoken in Iran and India.

in•do•lent (**ĭn′**də lənt) *adj.* Disinclined to work or exertion; lazy. [First written down in 1710 in Modern English, from Late Latin *indolēns,* painless.] **—in′do•lence** *n.*

in•dom•i•ta•ble (ĭn **dŏm′**ĭ tə bəl) *adj.* Incapable of being overcome or subdued; unconquerable: *an indomitable determination to finish.* **—in•dom′i•ta•bly** *adv.*

In•do•ne•sia (ĭn′də **nē′**zhə *or* ĭn′də **nē′**shə). Formerly **Dutch East In•dies** (dŭch ēst **ĭn′**dēz). A country of southeast Asia in the Malay Archipelago made up of Sumatra, Java, Sulawesi, the Moluccas, parts of Borneo, New Guinea, and Timor, and many smaller islands. In 1945 the territory declared its independence from the Netherlands, which was finally achieved in 1949. Jakarta, on the island of Java, is the capital and the largest city. Population, 147,490,298.

In•do•ne•sian (ĭn′də **nē′**zhən *or* ĭn′də **nē′**shən) *n.* **1.** A native or inhabitant of Indonesia. **2.** A dialect of Malay that is the official language of the Republic of Indonesia. —*adj.* Of or relating to Indonesia or its people, languages, or cultures.

in•door (**ĭn′**dôr′) *adj.* Of, situated in, or done within a house or other building: *an indoor pool; an indoor party.*

in•doors (ĭn **dôrz′**) *adv.* In or into a house or building: *staying indoors because of a cold.*

in•dorse (ĭn **dôrs′**) *v.* Variant of **endorse.**

in•du•bi•ta•ble (ĭn **do͞o′**bĭ tə bəl *or* ĭn **dyo͞o′**bĭ tə bəl) *adj.* Too obvious or apparent to be doubted; unquestionable: *the indubitable truth of the evidence.* [First written down about 1461 in Middle English and spelled *indubitabyll,* from Latin *dubitāre,* to hesitate, doubt.] **—in•du′bi•ta•bly** *adv.*

in•duce (ĭn **do͞os′** *or* ĭn **dyo͞os′**) *tr.v.* **in•duced, in•duc•ing, in•duc•es.** **1.** To persuade; influence; lead on: *Nothing could induce me to stay in that awful job.* **2.** To cause to occur; bring about: *induce vomiting in a patient who has swallowed poison.* **3.** To arrive at (a conclusion or general principle) by a reasoned examination of particular facts. **4.** To produce (electricity or magnetism) by induction. [First written down about 1385 in Middle English and spelled *enducen,* from Latin *indūcere,* to lead into.]

in•duce•ment (ĭn **do͞os′**mənt *or* ĭn **dyo͞os′**mənt) *n.* **1.** The act or process of inducing: *the inducement of labor in a pregnant woman.* **2.** Something that helps bring about an action; an incentive: *Free samples are an inducement to try new products.*

in•duct (ĭn **dŭkt′**) *tr.v.* **in•duct•ed, in•duct•ing, in•**

Word History: Indo-European

Most of the languages of Europe and of northern and central India are related to one another like distant cousins of a large family. English, Dutch, Latin, Russian, Armenian, Greek, Sanskrit, Hindi, and Bengali are all "daughter" languages of **Indo-European,** which was originally spoken on the steppes of southern Russia more than 5,000 years ago. English, German, Irish, and Polish are therefore "sister" languages of the *Indo-European* family. Obviously there have been a lot of changes in the family over the centuries, but one can still see the basic family features in a word like *is:* Old English *is,* German *ist,* Old Irish *is,* Latin *est,* ancient Greek *esti,* Lithuanian *esti,* Sanskrit *asti,* all of which came from the original Indo-European *esti.*

ă	pat	oi	boy
ā	pay	ou	out
âr	care	o͝o	took
ä	father	o͞o	boot
ĕ	pet	ŭ	cut
ē	be	ûr	urge
ĭ	pit	th	thin
ī	pie	*th*	this
îr	pier	hw	whoop
ŏ	pot	zh	vision
ō	toe	ə	about
ô	paw	N	*French* bon

ducts. 1. To place formally in office; install: *inducted the officer as treasurer.* **2.** To call into military service; draft. **3.** To admit as a member; initiate: *The honor society inducts new students in the spring.*

in•duc•tance (ĭn **dŭk'**təns) *n.* The property of an electric circuit by which an electromotive force is created in a nearby circuit by a change of current in either circuit.

in•duct•ee (ĭn'dŭk **tē'**) *n.* A person inducted or about to be inducted into the armed forces.

in•duc•tion (ĭn **dŭk'**shən) *n.* **1.** The act of installing formally in office: *the induction of the new president.* **2.** The process of being enrolled in the armed forces. **3.** A method of reasoning in which a conclusion is reached or a general principle is discovered on the basis of particular facts. **4.** The process by which an object having electrical or magnetic properties produces similar properties in a nearby object without direct contact.

induction coil *n.* A type of transformer in which an interrupted direct current of low voltage is changed into a high-voltage alternating current.

in•duc•tive (ĭn **dŭk'**tĭv) *adj.* **1.** Of, relating to, or using logical induction: *inductive reasoning.* **2.** Relating to or caused by electric or magnetic induction. **—in•duc'tive•ly** *adv.*

in•duc•tor (ĭn **dŭk'**tər) *n.* A part of an electric circuit, typically a coil of wire, that works by or produces inductance.

in•dulge (ĭn **dŭlj'**) *v.* **in•dulged, in•dulg•ing, in•dulg•es.** *—tr.* **1.** To yield to the desires of; humor; pamper: *indulge a crying child.* See Synonyms at **pamper. 2.** To give in to or satisfy (a desire): *indulge a craving for rich desserts.* *—intr.* To allow oneself some special pleasure; have or do what one wants: *indulge in a nap; indulge in an afternoon watching old movies.*

in•dul•gence (ĭn **dŭl'**jəns) *n.* **1.** The act of indulging: *surrender to an occasional indulgence in junk food.* **2.** Something indulged in: *A long vacation is a worthwhile indulgence.* **3.** Liberal or lenient treatment; favor: *The child expects to be treated with indulgence.* **4.** In the Roman Catholic Church, the freeing from non-eternal punishment due for a sin that has been pardoned in confession. [First written down before 1376 in Middle English, from Latin *indulgēre*, to indulge.]

in•dul•gent (ĭn **dŭl'**jənt) *adj.* Showing, marked by, or given to indulgence; lenient: *An indulgent owner spoiled the puppy.* **—in•dul'gent•ly** *adv.*

In•dus (**ĭn'**dəs). A river of south-central Asia rising in southwest Tibet and flowing about 1,900 miles (3,057 kilometers) northwest then southwest to the Arabian Sea south of Karachi, Pakistan. Its valley was the site of an advanced civilization lasting from about 2500 to 1500 B.C.

in•dus•tri•al (ĭn **dŭs'**trē əl) *adj.* **1.** Of or relating to industry: *industrial products.* **2.** Having highly developed industries: *an industrial nation.* **3.** Used in industry: *industrial tools and equipment.* **—in•dus'tri•al•ly** *adv.*

in•dus•tri•al•ist (ĭ **dŭs'**trē ə lĭst) *n.* A person who owns or runs an industrial enterprise.

in•dus•tri•al•ize (ĭn **dŭs'**trē ə līz') *v.* **in•dus•tri•al•ized, in•dus•tri•al•iz•ing, in•dus•tri•al•iz•es.** *—tr.* To develop industries in: *Many governments are working to industrialize their economies.* *—intr.* To become industrial. **—in•dus'tri•al•i•za'tion** (ĭn dŭs'trē ə lĭ **zā'**shən) *n.*

industrial revolution also **Industrial Revolution** *n.* A gradual shift from hand tools and home manufacturing to power-driven tools and large-scale factory production that began in England in about 1760 and continued into the 20th century.

in•dus•tri•ous (ĭn **dŭs'**trē əs) *adj.* Working hard as a steady habit; diligent: *An industrious student can get good grades.* **—in•dus'tri•ous•ly** *adv.* **—in•dus'tri•ous•ness** *n.*

in•dus•try (**ĭn'**də strē) *n., pl.* **in•dus•tries. 1.a.** The manufacture or production of goods on a large scale: *Industry has expanded in many Asian nations.* See Synonyms at **business. b.** A specific branch of such activity: *the computer hardware industry.* **2.** Hard work; steady effort: *Most people admire industry and thrift.* [First written down about 1477 in Middle English and spelled *industrie*, skill, from Latin *industrius*, diligent.]

in•e•bri•ate (ĭn **ē'**brē āt') *tr.v.* **in•e•bri•at•ed, in•e•bri•at•ing, in•e•bri•ates.** To intoxicate; make drunk. *—n.* (ĭn **ē'**brē ĭt). An intoxicated person, especially a drunkard.

in•ed•i•ble (ĭn **ĕd'**ə bəl) *adj.* Unfit to be eaten; not edible: *The peel of a banana is inedible.*

in•ef•fa•ble (ĭn **ĕf'**ə bəl) *adj.* Impossible to express; indescribable: *the ineffable majesty of a starlit sky.* **—in•ef'fa•bly** *adv.*

in•ef•fec•tive (ĭn'ĭ **fĕk'**tĭv) *adj.* **1.** Not effective; not producing results: *Their attempt to push the boulder proved ineffective.* **2.** Not performing satisfactorily; incompetent: *The corrupt politician was an ineffective governor.* **—in'ef•fec'tive•ly** *adv.* **—in'ef•fec'tive•ness** *n.*

in•ef•fec•tu•al (ĭn'ĭ **fĕk'**cho͞o əl) *adj.* Not having the desired effect; useless: *Our protests were ineffectual in changing the teacher's mind.* **—in'ef•fec'tu•al•ly** *adv.*

in•ef•fi•cien•cy (ĭn'ĭ **fĭsh'**ən sē) *n., pl.* **in•ef•fi•cien•cies. 1.** The condition, quality, or fact of being inefficient: *The clerk's inefficiency cost the company a great deal of money.* **2.** An inefficient act or procedure: *There are several inefficiencies in the new system for handling business orders.*

in•ef•fi•cient (ĭn'ĭ **fĭsh'**ənt) *adj.* **1.** Wasteful of time, energy, or materials: *an inefficient gasoline engine.* **2.** Lacking in ability; incompetent: *an inefficient manager.* **—in'ef•fi'cient•ly** *adv.*

in•e•las•tic (ĭn'ĭ **lăs'**tĭk) *adj.* Not capable of returning to its original shape or dimensions after being stretched or deformed; stiff or unyielding. **—in'e•las•tic'i•ty** (ĭn'ĭ lă **stĭs'**ĭ tē) *n.*

in•el•e•gant (ĭn **ĕl'**ĭ gənt) *adj.* Not elegant; lacking grace or good taste: *inelegant behavior.* **—in•el'e•gance** *n.* **—in•el'e•gant•ly** *adv.*

in•el•i•gi•ble (ĭn **ĕl'**ĭ jə bəl) *adj.* Not eligible; not qualified: *ineligible to vote; ineligible for citizenship.* **—in•el'i•gi•bil'i•ty** *n.* **—in•el'i•gi•bly** *adv.*

in•ept (ĭn **ĕpt'**) *adj.* **1.** Awkward or clumsy; lacking skill or competence: *an inept actor; an inept performance.* **2.** Not suitable; out of place; inappropriate: *an inept suggestion.* [First written down in 1603 in Modern English, from Latin *ineptus* : *in-*, not + *aptus*, suitable.] **—in•ept'ly** *adv.* **—in•ept'ness** *n.*

in•ep•ti•tude (ĭn **ĕp'**tĭ to͞od' *or* ĭn **ĕp'**tĭ tyo͞od') *n.* **1.** Lack of skill or competence. **2.** An inept act or remark.

in•e•qual•i•ty (ĭn'ĭ **kwŏl'**ĭ tē) *n., pl.* **in•e•qual•i•ties. 1.** The condition of being unequal, as in size, rank, or amount: *the great inequality between the rich and the very poor.* **2.** Lack of regularity; unevenness: *There is a marked inequality in the surface of the old flooring.* **3.** A mathematical statement that one number is greater than or less than another number.

in•eq•ui•ta•ble (ĭn **ĕk'**wĭ tə bəl) *adj.* Not equitable; unfair; unjust: *an inequitable division of work.* **—in•eq'ui•ta•bly** *adv.*

in•eq•ui•ty (ĭn **ĕk'**wĭ tē) *n., pl.* **in•eq•ui•ties.** Lack of equity; injustice; unfairness.

in•ert (ĭn ûrt′) *adj.* **1.** Unable to move or act: *Rock is composed of inert matter.* **2.** Slow to move, act, or respond; sluggish: *the inert forms of lizards sunning on a rock.* **3.** Incapable of reacting with other elements to form chemical compounds: *Helium is an inert gas.* [First written down in 1647 in Modern English, from Latin *iners* : *in-*, not, without + *ars*, skill, ability.] **—in•ert′ly** *adv.*

in•er•tia (ĭ nûr′shə) *n.* **1.** The tendency of a body at rest to remain at rest or of a body in motion to continue moving in a straight line unless a force is applied to it. **2.** Resistance to motion, action, or change: *There is enormous inertia in a big corporation.*

in•es•cap•a•ble (ĭn′ĭ skā′pə bəl) *adj.* Incapable of being escaped or avoided; inevitable: *the inescapable duties of parents.* **—in′es•cap′a•bly** *adv.*

in•es•ti•ma•ble (ĭn ĕs′tə mə bəl) *adj.* Incapable of being estimated: *General Washington performed an inestimable service for the American colonies.* **—in•es′ti•ma•bly** *adv.*

in•ev•i•ta•ble (ĭn ĕv′ĭ tə bəl) *adj.* Impossible to avoid or prevent; certain to happen: *the inevitable delays in trying to drive across town during rush hour.* [First written down about 1443 in Middle English : Latin *in-*, not + Latin *ēvitāre*, to avoid.] **—in•ev′i•ta•bly** *adv.*

in•ex•act (ĭn′ĭg zăkt′) *adj.* Not exact; not quite accurate or precise: *Because of inexact measurements, I cut the boards too short.* **—in′ex•act′ly** *adv.*

in•ex•cus•a•ble (ĭn′ĭk skyo͞o′zə bəl) *adj.* Impossible to excuse, pardon, or justify: *an inexcusable error.* **—in′ex•cus′a•bly** *adv.*

in•ex•haust•i•ble (ĭn′ĭg zô′stə bəl) *adj.* **1.** Not capable of being used up; unlimited: *an inexhaustible supply of food.* **2.** Incapable of being tired out: *a seemingly inexhaustible rescue worker.* **—in′ex•haust′i•bly** *adv.*

in•ex•o•ra•ble (ĭn ĕk′sər ə bəl) *adj.* Not capable of being persuaded or moderated by pleas: *an inexorable judge.* [First written down in 1553 in Modern English, from Latin *inexōrābilis* : *in-*, not + *exōrābilis*, pliant, flexible.] **—in•ex′o•ra•bly** *adv.*

in•ex•pe•di•ent (ĭn′ĭk spē′dē ənt) *adj.* Not expedient; not suitable or wise; inadvisable. **—in′ex•pe′di•ent•ly** *adv.*

in•ex•pen•sive (ĭn′ĭk spĕn′sĭv) *adj.* Not high in price; cheap. **—in′ex•pen′sive•ly** *adv.* **—in′ex•pen′sive•ness** *n.*

in•ex•pe•ri•ence (ĭn′ĭk spîr′ē əns) *n.* Lack of experience or knowledge gained from experience: *The inexperience of the young doctor caused him to hesitate in his decision.*

in•ex•pe•ri•enced (ĭn′ĭk spîr′ē ənst) *adj.* Lacking experience or the knowledge gained from experience: *an inexperienced driver.*

in•ex•pert (ĭn ĕk′spûrt′) *adj.* Not expert; unskilled. **—in•ex′pert′ly** *adv.* **—in•ex′pert′ness** *n.*

in•ex•pli•ca•ble (ĭn ĕk′splĭ kə bəl *or* ĭn′ĭk splĭk′ə bəl) *adj.* Incapable of being explained or understood: *the inexplicable nature of certain violent crimes.* **—in•ex′pli•ca•bly** *adv.*

in•ex•press•i•ble (ĭn′ĭk sprĕs′ə bəl) *adj.* Incapable of being expressed, especially in words; indescribable: *inexpressible joy.* **—in′ex•press′i•bly** *adv.*

in•ex•tin•guish•a•ble (ĭn′ĭk stĭng′gwĭ shə bəl) *adj.* Difficult or impossible to extinguish: *an inextinguishable desire to become a musician.*

in•ex•tri•ca•ble (ĭn ĕk′strĭ kə bəl *or* ĭn′ĭk strĭk′ə bəl) *adj.* **1.** Impossible to escape from: *an inextricable maze.* **2.** Difficult or impossible to disentangle or untie: *an inextricable snarl in my fishing line.* **3.** Too complicated or involved to solve: *an inextricable problem.* **—in•ex′tri•ca•bly** *adv.*

in•fal•li•ble (ĭn făl′ə bəl) *adj.* **1.** Incapable of making a mistake: *We had an infallible guide on our journey.* **2.** Incapable of failing; sure: *an infallible cure.* **—in•fal′li•bil′i•ty** *n.* **—in•fal′li•bly** *adv.*

in•fa•mous (ĭn′fə məs) *adj.* **1.** Having an exceedingly bad reputation; notorious: *an infamous traitor.* **2.** Deserving condemnation; shocking; outrageous: *infamous deeds.* **—in′fa•mous•ly** *adv.*

in•fa•my (ĭn′fə mē) *n., pl.* **in•fa•mies. 1.** The condition of being infamous: *a name that will live in infamy.* **2.** Evil reputation; disgrace: *The infamy of the dishonest politician was known far and wide.* **3.** An evil act that is known publicly; an outrage.

in•fan•cy (ĭn′fən sē) *n., pl.* **in•fan•cies. 1.** The earliest period of childhood, especially before being able to walk. **2.** The earliest stage of something: *Space exploration is still in its infancy.*

in•fant (ĭn′fənt) *n.* **1.** A child in the earliest period of life, especially before being able to walk. **2.** In law, a person who has not yet reached the age of majority; a minor. *—adj.* **1.** Of or relating to an infant: *infant years* **2.** Intended for infants: *infant clothing.* **3.** Newly begun or formed: *The manufacturing of superconductors is an infant industry.* [First written down about 1384 in Middle English and spelled *infaunt*, from Latin *īnfāns*, not able to speak.]

in•fan•tile (ĭn′fən tīl′ *or* ĭn′fən tĭl) *adj.* **1.** Of or relating to infants or infancy: *infantile stages of development.* **2.** Lacking in maturity; childish: *The two leaders showed an infantile reluctance to deal with each other.*

infantile paralysis *n.* Poliomyelitis.

in•fan•try (ĭn′fən trē) *n., pl.* **in•fan•tries.** The branch of an army made up of units trained to fight on foot. [First written down in 1579 in Modern English, from Old Italian *infante*, youth, foot soldier, from Latin *īnfāns*, infant.]

in•fan•try•man (ĭn′fən trē mən) *n.* A soldier in the infantry.

in•fat•u•ate (ĭn făch′o͞o āt′) *tr.v.* **in•fat•u•at•ed, in•fat•u•at•ing, in•fat•u•ates.** To fill with foolish love or attachment: *The stage assistant was infatuated with the famous actress.* **—in•fat′u•a′tion** *n.*

in•fect (ĭn fĕkt′) *tr.v.* **in•fect•ed, in•fect•ing, in•fects. 1.** To cause disease or illness in by introducing bacteria, viruses, fungi, or other organisms. **2.** To transmit a disease to: *The sick child infected the rest of the class.* **3.** To affect as if by a contagious disease: *Their enthusiasm for baseball infected all of us.* [First written down about 1378 in Middle English and spelled *infecten*, from Latin *īnficere*, to stain, infect.]

in•fec•tion (ĭn fĕk′shən) *n.* **1.** The occurrence of disease or illness in people, animals, and plants from the introduction of bacteria, viruses, fungi, or other organisms. **2.** An infectious disease. **3.** The state or condition of being infected.

in•fec•tious (ĭn fĕk′shəs) *adj.* **1.** Caused or spread by infection: *an infectious disease.* **2.** Capable of causing infection: *infectious microorganisms.* **3.** Tending to spread easily or catch on: *infectious laughter.* **—in•fec′tious•ly** *adv.* **—in•fec′tious•ness** *n.*

infectious mononucleosis *n.* A contagious disease caused by a virus and characterized by fever, sore throat, swollen lymph nodes, and white blood cell abnormalities.

in•fer (ĭn fûr′) *tr.v.* **in•ferred, in•fer•ring, in•fers.** To arrive at by reasoning from evidence; conclude: *I inferred from their laughter that the children were having fun.* [First written down in 1526 in Modern English and spelled *enferre*, from Latin *īnferre*, to bring in.] —SEE NOTE.

in•fer•ence (ĭn′fər əns) *n.* **1.** The act or process of inferring: *arrive at a conclusion by inference.* **2.**

Usage: infer

When we say that a speaker or sentence **implies** something, we mean that it is conveyed or suggested without being stated outright: *Even though you say you like sports, your lack of enthusiasm implies that you don't.* To **infer** something, on the other hand, is to draw conclusions that are not explicit in what is said: *I infer from your lack of enthusiasm that even though you say you like sports you really don't.*

ă	pat	oi	boy
ā	pay	ou	out
âr	care	o͝o	took
ä	father	o͞o	boot
ĕ	pet	ŭ	cut
ē	be	ûr	urge
ĭ	pit	th	thin
ī	pie	*th*	this
îr	pier	hw	whoop
ŏ	pot	zh	vision
ō	toe	ə	about
ô	paw	N	*French* bon

Something inferred; a conclusion: *The evidence is too scanty to draw any inferences from it.*

in•fe•ri•or (ĭn fîr′ē ər) *adj.* **1.** Low or lower in order, rank, or importance: *A lieutenant is inferior to a captain.* **2.** Low or lower in quality, value, or estimation: *Boards with many knots are inferior.* —*n.* A person lower in rank, status, or accomplishment than another. [First written down in 1425 in Middle English, from Latin *īnferior*, comparative of *īnferus*, low.]

in•fe•ri•or•i•ty (ĭn fîr′ē ôr′ĭ tē *or* ĭn fîr′ē ŏr′ĭ tē) *n.* The fact or quality of being inferior.

inferiority complex *n.* An enduring feeling of being inferior to others, often accompanied by overly aggressive behavior.

in•fer•nal (ĭn fûr′nəl) *adj.* **1.** Of or relating to hell or a world of the dead: *infernal damnation.* **2.** Outrageous; damnable: *an infernal nuisance.* [First written down about 1385 in Middle English, from Late Latin *īnfernus*, hell, from Latin *infernus*, lower, underground.] —**in•fer′nal•ly** *adv.*

in•fer•no (ĭn fûr′nō) *n., pl.* **in•fer•nos.** A place or condition suggestive of hell, as in being chaotic, noisy, or intensely hot: *The fire flared out of control, becoming a raging inferno.* [First written down in 1834 in Modern English, from Italian *inferno*, hell, from Late Latin *īnfernus.*]

in•fer•tile (ĭn fûr′tl) *adj.* Not fertile; unproductive. —**in′fer•til′i•ty** (ĭn′fər tĭl′ĭ tē) *n.*

in•fest (ĭn fĕst′) *tr.v.* **in•fest•ed, in•fest•ing, in•fests.** To live in or overrun in large numbers so as to be harmful or unpleasant: *Fleas infested the dog's coat.* [First written down before 1425 in Middle English and spelled *infesten*, to distress, from Latin *īnfestus*, hostile.] —**in′fes•ta′tion** *n.*

in•fi•del (ĭn′fĭ dəl *or* ĭn′fĭ dĕl′) *n.* **1.** A person who does not believe in a particular religion, especially Christianity or Islam: *During the Crusades, the invading Christians regarded the Muslims as infidels.* **2.** A person who has no religious beliefs.

in•fi•del•i•ty (ĭn′fĭ dĕl′ĭ tē) *n., pl.* **in•fi•del•i•ties.** **1.** Unfaithfulness to another person, especially by committing adultery. **2.** An unfaithful or adulterous act. **3.** Lack of religious belief.

in•field (ĭn′fēld′) *n.* **1.** The area of a baseball field bounded by all four bases. **2.** The four infielders of a baseball team.

in•field•er (ĭn′fēl′dər) *n.* A baseball player whose defensive position is first base, second base, shortstop, or third base.

in•fight•ing (ĭn′fī′tĭng) *n.* **1.** Fighting or boxing at close range. **2.** Strife or competition among associates in a group or an organization.

in•fil•trate (ĭn fĭl′trāt′ *or* ĭn′fĭl trāt′) *v.* **in•fil•trat•ed, in•fil•trat•ing, in•fil•trates.** —*tr.* **1.a.** To cause (troops) to pass without being noticed into enemy territory. **b.** To penetrate or slip through with hostile intentions: *Enemy troops infiltrated our lines.* **2.** To enter without being noticed for purposes such as spying: *Government agents infiltrated the criminal operation.* **3.** To cause (a liquid or gas) to pass through the small spaces of a substance; filter. **4.** To fill or saturate (a substance) by filtering; permeate. —*intr.* To gain entrance secretly. —**in′fil•tra′tion** *n.*

in•fi•nite (ĭn′fə nĭt) *adj.* **1.** Having no limit or bound; endless: *The universe seems infinite.* **2.a.** Greater in value than any countable number, however large: *an infinite number.* **b.** Having an infinite size or measure; unlimited: *an infinite plane; an infinite set.* **3.** Very great; immense; boundless: *His joy was infinite.* —*n.* Something infinite. —**in′fi•nite•ly** *adv.* —**in′fi•nite•ness** *n.*

in•fin•i•tes•i•mal (ĭn′fĭn ĭ tĕs′ə məl) *adj.* Immeasurably small; minute: *a high-grade steel with only infinitesimal amounts of impurities.* —**in′fin•i•tes′i•mal•ly** *adv.*

inflatable
An inflatable balloon in Macy's Thanksgiving Parade, New York City

in•fin•i•tive (ĭn fĭn′ĭ tĭv) *n.* A verb form that is not inflected to indicate person, number, or tense. In English, it is usually preceded by *to* or by an auxilary verb. For example, in the phrases *wanted to leave* and *will play tomorrow,* the words *leave* and *play* are infinitives.

in•fin•i•ty (ĭn fĭn′ĭ tē) *n., pl.* **in•fin•i•ties.** **1.** A space, period of time, or quantity that is without a limit. **2.** The quality or condition of being infinite. **3.** A quantity that is greater than any other quantity, however large.

in•firm (ĭn fûrm′) *adj.* Weak in body, as from old age or sickness; feeble. —**in•firm′ly** *adv.*

in•fir•ma•ry (ĭn fûr′mə rē) *n., pl.* **in•fir•ma•ries.** A place for the care of sick or injured persons, especially a small hospital or dispensary in a large institution.

in•fir•mi•ty (ĭn fûr′mĭ tē) *n., pl.* **in•fir•mi•ties.** **1.** The condition of being infirm; weakness; frailty: *The doctor hesitated to perform surgery because of the patient's infirmity.* **2.** A sickness; an illness.

in•flame (ĭn flām′) *v.* **in•flamed, in•flam•ing, in•flames.** —*tr.* **1.** To cause redness, swelling, and soreness in. **2.** To stir up anger or other strong emotion; excite: *The speech inflamed the crowd.* —*intr.* To be affected by inflammation.

in•flam•ma•ble (ĭn flăm′ə bəl) *adj.* **1.** Tending to catch fire easily and burn rapidly; flammable: *Gasoline is very inflammable.* **2.** Quickly or easily aroused to strong emotion: *an inflammable boss.*

in•flam•ma•tion (ĭn′flə mā′shən) *n.* **1.** Redness, swelling, heat, and soreness in a part of the body, resulting from injury, infection, or irritation. **2.** The act of inflaming or the condition of being inflamed.

in•flam•ma•to•ry (ĭn flăm′ə tôr′ē) *adj.* **1.** Tending to arouse strong emotion: *a speaker's inflammatory language.* **2.** Characterized by or causing inflammation: *Arthritis is an inflammatory disease.*

in•flat•a•ble (ĭn flā′tə bəl) *adj.* Capable of being inflated: *an inflatable rubber boat.*

in•flate (ĭn flāt′) *v.* **in•flat•ed, in•flat•ing, in•flates.** —*tr.* **1.** To cause to expand with air or gas: *Did you inflate the tires on your bicycle?* **2.** To enlarge or raise abnormally or improperly: *All the attention from the reporters inflated the athlete's notion of his abilities.* —*intr.* To become inflated: *The balloon inflated quickly.* [First written down before 1425 in Middle English and spelled *inflaten*, from Latin *īnflāre*, to blow into.] —**in•flat′er, in•fla′tor** *n.*

in•fla•tion (ĭn flā′shən) *n.* **1.** The act or process of inflating; a swelling: *The inflation of the giant balloon took an hour.* **2.** A continuing rise in prices, caused by an abnormal increase in the amount of money or credit that is available.

in•fla•tion•ar•y (ĭn flā′shə nĕr′ē) *adj.* Of, relating to, or contributing to inflation: *inflationary prices.*

in•flect (ĭn flĕkt′) *tr.v.* **in•flect•ed, in•flect•ing, in•flects.** **1.** To vary the tone or pitch of (the voice), especially in speaking. **2.** To change the form of (a word) to show number, tense, person, comparison, or other grammatical function. For example, *book* is inflected to *books* in the plural. **3.** To bend; curve: *a prism inflects light rays.* [First written down about 1425 in Middle English and spelled *inflecten*, to bend down, from Latin *īnflectere.*]

in•flec•tion (ĭn flĕk′shən) *n.* **1.** A change in the tone or pitch of the voice, especially in speech: *Questions usually end with a rising inflection.* **2.a.** The process that changes the form of a word to indicate number, tense, person, comparison, or other grammatical function. For example, the comparative *quicker* is formed from *quick* by inflection.

b. A word formed by this process; an inflected form. For example, *drives, drove,* and *driven* are all inflections of the word *drive.* **c.** A suffix used in this process. **3.** The act of inflecting or the condition of being inflected. **4.** A bend or curve: *an inflection at an angle of 45°.*

in•flec•tion•al (ĭn **flĕk′**shə nəl) *adj.* Of, relating to, or showing grammatical inflection: *an inflectional language.*

in•flex•i•ble (ĭn **flĕk′**sə bəl) *adj.* **1.** Not flexible; rigid. **2.** Not subject to change or modification: *an inflexible rule.* **3.** Refusing to change; unyielding: *They are inflexible in their demand for better service.* **—in•flex′i•bil′i•ty** *n.* **—in•flex′i•bly** *adv.*

in•flict (ĭn **flĭkt′**) *tr.v.* **in•flict•ed, in•flict•ing, in•flicts. 1.** To give by or as if by attack: *Wasps inflict severe stings. A toothache inflicts pain.* **2.** To cause (something unpleasant) to be suffered or endured; impose: *The law inflicts penalties for criminal behavior.* [First written down in 1566 in Modern English, from Latin *īnflīgere.*]

in•flic•tion (ĭn **flĭk′**shən) *n.* **1.** The act or process of inflicting: *the infliction of punishment.* **2.** Something, such as suffering or a punishment, that is inflicted.

in•flo•res•cence (ĭn′flə **rĕs′**əns) *n.* **1.** The arrangement of flowers in relation to each other on the stem of a plant. **2.** A flower cluster.

in•flow (**ĭn′**flō′) *n.* **1.** The act or process of flowing in or into: *The inflow of requests has increased.* **2.** Something that flows in or into: *a lake fed by an inflow from the mountains.*

in•flu•ence (**ĭn′**flo͞o əns) *n.* **1.** The power to cause changes or have an effect without any apparent use of force: *Public opinion has a great influence on politicians.* **2.** Power that results from wealth or high position in society: *He got the job because of his uncle's influence.* **3.** A person or thing that brings about change without the use of force: *Travel has had a broadening influence on you.* —*tr.v.* **in•flu•enced, in•flu•enc•ing, in•flu•enc•es.** To have an effect on; change: *The automobile has greatly influenced the way people live.* [First written down about 1385 in Middle English, from Medieval Latin *īnfluentia,* influx, from Latin *īnfluēns,* flowing in.]

in•flu•en•tial (ĭn′flo͞o **ĕn′**shəl) *adj.* Having or exercising influence: *an influential newspaper.* **—in′flu•en′tial•ly** *adv.*

in•flu•en•za (ĭn′flo͞o **ĕn′**zə) *n.* A contagious viral disease, characterized by fever, inflammation of the respiratory system, irritation of the intestines, and muscular pain. [First written down in 1743 in Modern English, from Italian, from Medieval Latin *īnfluentia,* influence (so called apparently from the belief that epidemics were due to the influence of the stars).] —SEE NOTE.

in•flux (**ĭn′**flŭks′) *n.* A flowing in: *an influx of tourists to the park.*

in•fo (**ĭn′**fō) *n. Informal.* Information.

in•form (ĭn **fôrm′**) *v.* **in•formed, in•form•ing, in•forms.** —*tr.* To give information to; tell; notify: *The notice informed us of when the meeting would take place.* —*intr.* To give secret or damaging information: *The gang was captured after one of its members informed on the others.*

in•for•mal (ĭn **fôr′**məl) *adj.* **1.** Not following or requiring fixed ceremonies or rules; unofficial: *an informal agreement made with a handshake.* **2.** Suitable for everday use or for casual occasions: *informal dress.* **3.** Not suitable for formal writing but frequently used in conversation and ordinary writing; for example, the use of *kid* to mean "a child" is informal. **—in•for′mal•ly** *adv.*

in•for•mal•i•ty (ĭn′fôr **măl′**ĭ tē) *n., pl.* **in•for•mal•i•ties. 1.** The state or quality of being informal: *the informality of a picnic.* **2.** An informal act; informal behavior.

in•form•ant (ĭn **fôr′**mənt) *n.* A person who provides information to another.

in•for•ma•tion (ĭn′fər **mā′**shən) *n.* **1.** Knowledge or facts learned, especially about a certain event or subject: *The newspaper provides information on the day's events.* **2.** The act of informing or the condition of being informed: *This brochure is for your information.*

in•form•a•tive (ĭn **fôr′**mə tĭv) *adj.* Providing information; instructive: *an informative TV series on dinosaurs.*

in•formed (ĭn **fôrmd′**) *adj.* Provided with information; knowledgable: *That reporter is well informed on the facts of the issue.*

in•form•er (ĭn **fôr′**mər) *n.* A person who notifies authorities of secret and often illegal activities.

infra– *pref.* A prefix that means below or beneath: *infrasonic.*

in•frac•tion (ĭn **frăk′**shən) *n.* A breach or breaking of a law or rule; a violation.

in•fra•red (ĭn′frə **rĕd′**) *adj.* Of or relating to the invisible part of the electromagnetic spectrum with wavelengths longer than those of visible red light but shorter than those of microwaves: *infrared light.* [First written down in 1831 in Modern English and spelled *infra-red* : Latin *īnfrā,* below + *red.*]

in•fra•son•ic (ĭn′frə **sŏn′**ĭk) *adj.* Generating or using sound waves that are too low in frequency to be heard by human ears.

in•fra•struc•ture (**ĭn′**frə strŭk′chər) *n.* An underlying base or foundation for something, especially the basic facilities necessary for a community to function, including roads, bridges, water pipes, and power lines.

in•fre•quent (ĭn **frē′**kwənt) *adj.* Not occurring often; occasional or rare: *an infrequent visitor.* **—in•fre′quen•cy** *n.* **—in•fre′quent•ly** *adv.*

in•fringe (ĭn **frĭnj′**) *tr.v.* **in•fringed, in•fring•ing, in•fring•es.** To fail to obey; break or violate (a law, a right, or an obligation): *Censorship infringes the right to free speech.* ***—idiom.*** **infringe on** or **infringe upon.** To intrude or encroach upon; trespass on: *Reading someone else's mail infringes on that person's privacy.* [First written down about 1467 in Middle English and spelled *enfrangen,* from Latin *īnfringere,* to destroy.] **—in•fring′er** *n.* **—in•fringe′ment** *n.*

in•fu•ri•ate (ĭn **fyo͝or′**ē āt′) *tr.v.* **in•fu•ri•at•ed, in•fu•ri•at•ing, in•fu•ri•ates.** To make furious; enrage: *I was infuriated by their taunting remarks.* **—in•fu′ri•a′tion** *n.*

in•fuse (ĭn **fyo͞oz′**) *tr.v.* **in•fused, in•fus•ing, in•fus•es. 1.** To fill; inspire: *Winning the game infused us with the hope that we might win the championship.* **2.** To put into or introduce; instill: *The executive infused new vigor into the company.* **3.** To steep or soak without boiling in order to extract a substance: *Tea is made by infusing tea leaves in hot water.*

in•fu•sion (ĭn **fyo͞o′**zhən) *n.* **1.** The act or process of infusing. **2.** Something infused or introduced: *With an infusion of money the business recovered.* **3.** A liquid product obtained by infusing: *drank an infusion of medicinal herbs.*

–ing¹ *suff.* A suffix that forms: **1.** The present participle of verbs: *living.* **2.** Adjectives resembling present participles but not formed from verbs: *swashbuckling.*

–ing² *suff.* A suffix that means: **1.** An action or a process: *dancing; thinking.* **2.** An instance of an action or a process: *a meeting.* **3.** The result of an

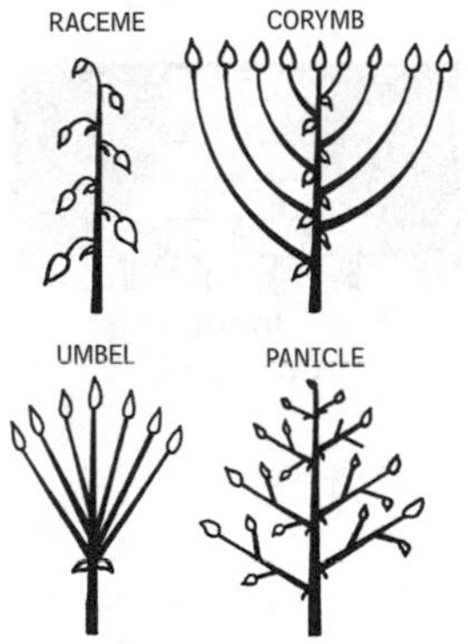

inflorescence

influenza

Since ancient times, **influenza** has periodically swept the world. In just a few years during the early 1900's, 20 million people worldwide died from influenza, which we commonly call the **flu**. Until recently, people could not tell how this illness could spread so widely. Before people knew that organisms cause disease, they thought the stars influenced the spread of influenza. The name for this illness, in fact, reflects that belief. *Influenza* comes from the Latin word *influentia,* meaning "influence." Today, however, the stars are no longer blamed for the flu. Modern medicine has found that inhaling certain viruses, called influenza viruses, causes the spread of this illness.

ă	**pat**	oi	**boy**
ā	**pay**	ou	**out**
âr	**care**	o͝o	**took**
ä	**father**	o͞o	**boot**
ĕ	**pet**	ŭ	**cut**
ē	**be**	ûr	**urge**
ĭ	**pit**	th	**thin**
ī	**pie**	*th*	**this**
îr	**pier**	hw	**whoop**
ŏ	**pot**	zh	**vision**
ō	**toe**	ə	**about**
ô	**paw**	N	*French* **bon**

ingot
Gold ingots

inhalator

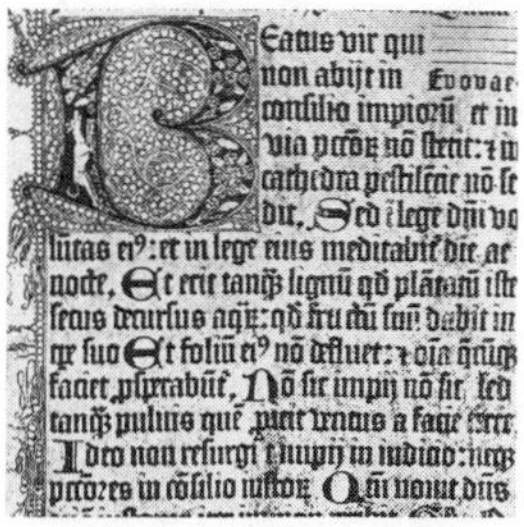

initial

action or a process: *a painting.* **4.** Something used in or connected with an action or a process: *roofing.*

in•gen•ious (ĭn **jēn′**yəs) *adj.* **1.** Clever at devising or making; inventive; creative: *an ingenious storyteller.* **2.** Planned, made, or done with originality and imagination: *The telephone is an ingenious device.* **—in•gen′ious•ly** *adv.* **—in•gen′ious•ness** *n.*

in•gé•nue (**ăɴ′**zhə no͞o′) *n.* **1.** An innocent or naive girl or young woman. **2.** An actress playing an ingénue.

in•ge•nu•i•ty (ĭn′jə **no͞o′**ĭ tē *or* ĭn′jə **nyo͞o′**ĭ tē) *n., pl.* **in•ge•nu•i•ties.** Inventive skill or imagination; cleverness.

in•gen•u•ous (ĭn **jĕn′**yo͞o əs) *adj.* **1.** Frank and open; candid: *They were being quite ingenuous in telling us the whole story.* **2.** Simple and artless; innocent: *The young child had an ingenuous smile.* **—in•gen′u•ous•ly** *adv.* **—in•gen′u•ous•ness** *n.*

in•gest (ĭn **jĕst′**) *tr.v.* **in•gest•ed, in•gest•ing, in•gests.** To take (food) into the body for digestion. **—in•ges′tion** *n.*

in•gle•nook (**ĭng′**gəl no͝ok′) *n.* A nook or corner beside an open fireplace.

in•glo•ri•ous (ĭn **glôr′**ē əs) *adj.* Shameful; dishonorable: *An inglorious incident of cowardice clouded the soldier's career.*

in•got (**ĭng′**gət) *n.* A mass of metal shaped in the form of a bar or block for convenient storage or transportation.

in•grain (ĭn **grān′**) *tr.v.* **in•grained, in•grain•ing, in•grains.** To fix or impress deeply, as in the mind: *ingrain a sense of fairness.*

in•grained (ĭn **grānd′**) *adj.* Firmly established; deep-seated: *an ingrained habit.*

in•grate (**ĭn′**grāt′) *n.* An ungrateful person.

in•gra•ti•ate (ĭn **grā′**shē āt′) *tr.v.* **in•gra•ti•at•ed, in•gra•ti•at•ing, in•gra•ti•ates.** To gain favor for (oneself) from another; make (oneself) agreeable to another: *The class tried to ingratiate itself with the new teacher by being especially attentive.*

in•gra•ti•at•ing (ĭn **grā′**shē ā′tĭng) *adj.* **1.** Agreeable; pleasing: *an ingratiating smile.* **2.** Intended to win favor: *an ingratiating remark.* **—in•gra′ti•at′ing•ly** *adv.*

in•grat•i•tude (ĭn **grăt′**ĭ to͞od′ *or* ĭn **grăt′**ĭ tyo͞od′) *n.* Lack of gratitude; ungratefulness.

in•gre•di•ent (ĭn **grē′**dē ənt) *n.* An element in a mixture or compound: *The main ingredient of bread is flour. Lime is an ingredient of cement.* [First written down before 1425 in Middle English, from Latin *ingredī*, to go into.]

in•gress (**ĭn′**grĕs′) *n.* **1.** A means or place of going in; an entrance. **2.** The right or permission to enter: *Only employees of the company have ingress to its building.* **3.** The act of going in or entering.

in•grown (**ĭn′**grōn′) *adj.* Grown abnormally into the skin or flesh: *an ingrown toenail.*

in•hab•it (ĭn **hăb′**ĭt) *tr.v.* **in•hab•it•ed, in•hab•it•ing, in•hab•its.** To live in; have as a dwelling place: *Dinosaurs inhabited the earth millions of years ago.*

in•hab•it•a•ble (ĭn **hăb′**ĭ tə bəl) *adj.* Suitable for living in: *an inhabitable land.*

in•hab•i•tant (ĭn **hăb′**ĭ tənt) *n.* A permanent resident of a particular place.

in•ha•lant (ĭn **hā′**lənt) *n.* Something, such as a medicine, that is inhaled.

in•ha•la•tion (ĭn′hə **lā′**shən) *n.* The act or an instance of inhaling.

in•ha•la•tor (**ĭn′**hə lā′tər) *n.* A device used to inhale a medicine.

in•hale (ĭn **hāl′**) *v.* **in•haled, in•hal•ing, in•hales.** *—tr.* To draw (air or a fragrance, for example) into the lungs by breathing: *inhaling fresh air.* *—intr.* To breathe in: *inhale deeply.* [First written down in 1725 in Modern English, from Latin *inhālāre*, to breathe upon.]

in•hal•er (ĭn **hā′**lər) *n.* **1.** A person or thing that inhales. **2.** A device used to inhale a medicine.

in•har•mo•ni•ous (ĭn′här **mō′**nē əs) *adj.* **1.** Not in harmony; discordant: *inharmonious music.* **2.** Not in accord or agreement: *inharmonious relations between countries.* **—in′har•mo′ni•ous•ly** *adv.* **—in′har•mo′ni•ous•ness** *n.*

in•her•ent (ĭn **hîr′**ənt *or* ĭn **hĕr′**ənt) *adj.* Being part of the basic nature of a person or thing; essential; intrinsic: *The student's inherent curiosity led to an interest in science.* **—in•her′ent•ly** *adv.*

in•her•it (ĭn **hĕr′**ĭt) *v.* **in•her•it•ed, in•her•it•ing, in•her•its.** *—tr.* **1.** To receive (property or a title) from a person who has died, usually through a will. **2.** To receive or take over from someone else: *Upon taking office, the mayor inherited many serious problems.* **3.** To acquire (characteristics) by genetic transmission from one's parents or ancestors: *I inherited my father's hair color.* *—intr.* To receive an inheritance. [First written down about 1350 in Middle English and spelled *enheriten*, from Late Latin *inhērēditāre*, from Latin *hērēs*, heir.] **—in•her′i•tor** *n.*

in•her•i•tance (ĭn **hĕr′**ĭ təns) *n.* **1.** The act of inheriting: *They gained their wealth by inheritance.* **2.** Something that is inherited or is to be inherited at a person's death. **3.** Something regarded as a heritage: *The concept of democracy is an inheritance from the ancient Greeks.*

in•hib•it (ĭn **hĭb′**ĭt) *tr.v.* **in•hib•it•ed, in•hib•it•ing, in•hib•its.** To restrain or hold back; prevent: *Shyness inhibited the new student from talking freely in class.*

in•hi•bi•tion (ĭn′hə **bĭsh′**ən *or* ĭn′ə **bĭsh′**ən) *n.* **1.** The act of inhibiting or the condition of being inhibited. **2.** A mental or emotional force that restrains an impulse, such as a feeling, an urge, or a biological drive: *My inhibition prevented me from asking a question of the famous writer.*

in•hos•pi•ta•ble (ĭn **hŏs′**pĭ tə bəl *or* ĭn′hŏ **spĭt′**ə bəl) *adj.* **1.** Showing no hospitality to others; unfriendly. **2.** Not providing shelter or food; barren: *the inhospitable Arctic winter.* **—in•hos′pi•ta•bly** *adv.*

in•hu•man (ĭn **hyo͞o′**mən) *adj.* **1.** Lacking kindness or compassion; cruel. **2.** Not suited for human needs: *The moon is an inhuman environment.* **3.** Not of ordinary human form; monstrous. **—in•hu′man•ly** *adv.*

in•hu•mane (ĭn′hyo͞o **mān′**) *adj.* Lacking pity or compassion: *The law punishes inhumane treatment of animals.* **—in′hu•mane′ly** *adv.*

in•hu•man•i•ty (ĭn′hyo͞o **măn′**ĭ tē) *n., pl.* **in•hu•man•i•ties. 1.** Lack of pity or compassion: *the basic inhumanity of war.* **2.** An inhuman or cruel act.

in•im•i•cal (ĭ **nĭm′**ĭ kəl) *adj.* **1.** Harmful or injurious; adverse: *habits inimical to good health.* **2.** Unfriendly; hostile: *The countries have long been inimical neighbors.* [First written down in 1643 in Modern English, from Latin *inimīcus*, enemy.] **—in•im′i•cal•ly** *adv.*

in•im•i•ta•ble (ĭ **nĭm′**ĭ tə bəl) *adj.* Impossible to imitate; unique: *a singer's inimitable style.* **—in•im′i•ta•bil′i•ty** *n.* **—in•im′i•ta•bly** *adv.*

in•iq•ui•tous (ĭ **nĭk′**wĭ təs) *adj.* Unjust; wicked. **—in•iq′ui•tous•ly** *adv.*

in•iq•ui•ty (ĭ **nĭk′**wĭ tē) *n., pl.* **in•iq•ui•ties. 1.** Extreme injustice; wickedness: *The iniquity of the crime aroused great public anger.* **2.** An immoral act; a sin.

in•i•tial (ĭ **nĭsh′**əl) *adj.* Of, relating to, or occurring at the beginning; first: *The initial attempts to correct the problem failed.* *—n.* **1.** The first letter of a word or name. **2.** A large, often decorated letter, as at the beginning of a paragraph or chapter. *—tr.v.* **in•i•tialed, in•i•tial•ing, in•i•tials** also **in•i•tialled, in•i•tial•ling, in•i•tials.** To mark or sign with initials. **—in•i′tial•ly** *adv.*

in•i•ti•ate (ĭ nĭsh′ē āt′) *tr.v.* **in•i•ti•at•ed, in•i•ti•at•ing, in•i•ti•ates. 1.** To begin or start: *The company initiated a new line of clothes.* **2.** To introduce (a person) to a new subject, interest, skill, or activity: *My music teacher initiated me into the world of opera.* **3.** To admit into a group, often with a special ceremony: *Several new members were initiated into the club.* *—n.* (ĭ nĭsh′ē ĭt). A person who is being or has been initiated. **—in•i′ti•a′tor** *n.*

in•i•ti•a•tion (ĭ nĭsh′ē ā′shən) *n.* **1.** The act or process of initiating. **2.** Admission into a club, a society, or an organization. **3.** A ceremony or ritual with which a new member is initiated.

in•i•tia•tive (ĭ nĭsh′ə tĭv) *n.* **1.** The ability to begin a task or put into effect a plan of action; enterprise: *Starting one's own business requires much initiative.* **2.** The first step or action; lead: *Seizing the initiative, I applied for the job before it was advertised.* **3.** The right or procedure by which citizens can propose a new law by petition and have it voted on by the electorate. ***—idiom.* on (one's) own initiative.** Without prompting or direction from others; on one's own.

in•ject (ĭn jĕkt′) *tr.v.* **in•ject•ed, in•ject•ing, in•jects. 1.a.** To force or drive (a liquid or gas) into something: *a mechanism that injects fuel into a cylinder of an engine.* **b.** To introduce (a fluid or medicine) into a body part, especially by a hypodermic syringe. **2.** To introduce; insert: *By mentioning cost, I tried to inject some realism into our planning.* [First written down in 1601 in Modern English, from Latin *iniectus*, past participle of *inicere*, to throw in.] **—in•jec′tor** *n.* —SEE NOTE.

in•jec•tion (ĭn jĕk′shən) *n.* **1.** The act of injecting. **2.** Something that is injected, especially a dose of a liquid medicine injected into the body.

in•ju•di•cious (ĭn′jo͞o dĭsh′əs) *adj.* Showing a lack of judgment; unwise: *an injudicious decision.* **—in′ju•di′cious•ly** *adv.* **—in′ju•di′cious•ness** *n.*

in•junc•tion (ĭn jŭngk′shən) *n.* **1.** An order or a command: *The teacher's injunction to be silent quieted the class.* **2.** A court order prohibiting or requiring a specific course of action: *The judge issued an injunction stopping the strike and requiring further negotiations.* [First written down about 1425 in Middle English and spelled *injunccion*, from Latin *iniungere*, to enjoin.]

in•jure (ĭn′jər) *tr.v.* **in•jured, in•jur•ing, in•jures. 1.** To cause physical harm to; hurt. See Synonyms at **hurt. 2.** To cause damage to; impair: *The faulty computer injured our ability to do business.* **3.** To do an injustice to; wrong: *That remark injured us.*

in•ju•ri•ous (ĭn jo͝or′ē əs) *adj.* Causing injury, damage, or wrong; harmful: *Sunburn is injurious to the skin.* **—in•ju′ri•ous•ly** *adv.* **—in•ju′ri•ous•ness** *n.*

in•ju•ry (ĭn′jə rē) *n., pl.* **in•ju•ries.** Damage or harm done to a person or thing: *The company's reputation escaped injury despite the scandal. I escaped the fall with only a minor leg injury.* [First written down about 1384 in Middle English and spelled *injurie*, from Latin *iniūrius*, unjust.]

in•jus•tice (ĭn jŭs′tĭs) *n.* **1.** Lack of justice; unfairness: *Tyranny always leads to injustice.* **2.** A specific unjust act; a wrong.

ink (ĭngk) *n.* **1.** A colored or black liquid used especially for writing or printing. **2.** A dark liquid ejected for protection by squids and similar marine animals. *—tr.v.* **inked, ink•ing, inks.** To cover with ink; spread ink on: *The rubber stamp must be inked often.* [First written down about 1250 in Middle English and spelled *enke*, from Late Latin *encaustum*, purple ink.]

ink•horn (ĭngk′hôrn′) *n.* A small container made of horn or a similar material, formerly used to hold ink for writing.

in•kling (ĭng′klĭng) *n.* A slight indication or hint; a vague idea: *You haven't an inkling of how much it costs to build a road.*

ink•stand (ĭngk′stănd′) *n.* **1.** A tray or rack for bottles of ink, pens, and other writing implements. **2.** An inkwell.

ink•well (ĭngk′wĕl′) *n.* A small container or reservoir for ink.

ink•y (ĭng′kē) *adj.* **1.** Stained or smeared with ink: *inky fingers.* **2.** Like ink; dark; murky: *inky shadows.* **—ink′i•ness** *n.*

in•laid (ĭn′lād′) *v.* Past tense and past participle of **inlay.** *—adj.* **1.** Set smoothly into a surface to form a pattern or decoration: *inlaid decorative tile in a bathroom wall.* **2.** Decorated with a pattern set into the surface: *a table with an inlaid top of wood.*

in•land (ĭn′lənd) *adj.* Of, relating to, or located in the interior of a country or region: *The Great Lakes are inland waterways.* *—adv.* In, toward, or into the interior of a country or region: *You must travel inland to find the source of a river.* *—n.* (ĭn′lănd′ *or* ĭn′lənd). The interior of a country or region.

in-law (ĭn′lô′) *n.* A relative by marriage.

in•lay (ĭn′lā′ *or* ĭn lā′) *tr.v.* **in•laid** (ĭn′lād′), **in•lay•ing, in•lays. 1.** To set (pieces of wood, for example) into a surface to form a design: *inlay strips of gold on a jewelry box.* **2.** To decorate by setting in such designs: *The floor was inlaid with several different kinds of wood.* *—n.* **1.** Contrasting material set into a surface in pieces to form a design. **2.** An inlaid decoration or design: *There is a rich inlay of ivory and gold on the old book's cover.* **3.** A filling of gold or other solid material, fitted and cemented into a tooth cavity.

in•let (ĭn′lĕt′ *or* ĭn′lĭt) *n.* **1.** A stream or bay leading inland. **2.** A narrow passage of water, as between two islands. **3.** An opening providing a means of entrance.

in•mate (ĭn′māt′) *n.* A person confined to an institution, such as a prison or hospital.

in•most (ĭn′mōst′) *adj.* Farthest within; innermost.

inn (ĭn) *n.* **1.** A hotel or hostel. **2.** A tavern or restaurant. [First written down about 1000 in Old English.]

❑ *These sound alike:* **inn, in**[1] (inside).

in•nards (ĭn′ərdz) *pl.n. Informal.* **1.** The internal organs of the body, especially of the abdomen. **2.** The inner parts, as of a machine.

in•nate (ĭ nāt′ *or* ĭn′āt′) *adj.* **1.** Possessed at birth; inborn: *innate intelligence.* **2.** Existing as a basic or essential characteristic; inherent: *Mountain climbing has certain innate dangers.* [First written down about 1412 in Middle English and spelled *innat*, from Latin *innātus*, past participle of *innāscī*, to be born in.] **—in•nate′ly** *adv.* **—in•nate′ness** *n.*

in•ner (ĭn′ər) *adj.* **1.** Located farther inside: *The inner core of the earth lies under the crust and mantle.* **2.** Of or relating to the spirit or mind: *Sitting beside the brook, he felt an inner peace.* **3.** More exclusive, private, or important: *the inner circles of government.*

inner city *n.* The older central part of a city, especially when run-down and impoverished.

inner ear *n.* The innermost part of the ear of a vertebrate, consisting of the cochlea, vestibule, and semicircular canals. The inner ear contains the essential organs of hearing and of balance.

In•ner Mon•go•li•a (ĭn′ər mŏng gō′lē ə *or* ĭn′ər-mŏng gōl′yə). Nei Monggol.

in•ner•most (ĭn′ər mōst′) *adj.* **1.** Located farthest

Word Building: inject

The word root *-ject-* in English words comes from the past participle *iniectus* of the Latin verb *inicere*, "to throw in, shoot in" (using the prefix *in-*[2], "in, into"). In fact, *iniectus* is the source of our word **inject**, "to shoot in." **Abject** means "thrown away" (*ab-*, "away, away from"); **dejected** is literally "shot down," as we would say informally (*dē-*, "down"); **rejected** means "thrown back" (*re-*, "back, backward"); and **adjective** comes ultimately from *adiectus*, "thrown to or at, placed near" (*ad-*, "at, to, toward"). Thus, an adjective is a word "placed near a noun to modify it."

inlay
Inlaid wood

inlet

ă	pat	oi	boy
ā	pay	ou	out
âr	care	o͝o	took
ä	father	o͞o	boot
ĕ	pet	ŭ	cut
ē	be	ûr	urge
ĭ	pit	th	thin
ī	pie	*th*	this
îr	pier	hw	whoop
ŏ	pot	zh	vision
ō	toe	ə	about
ô	paw	ɴ	*French* bon

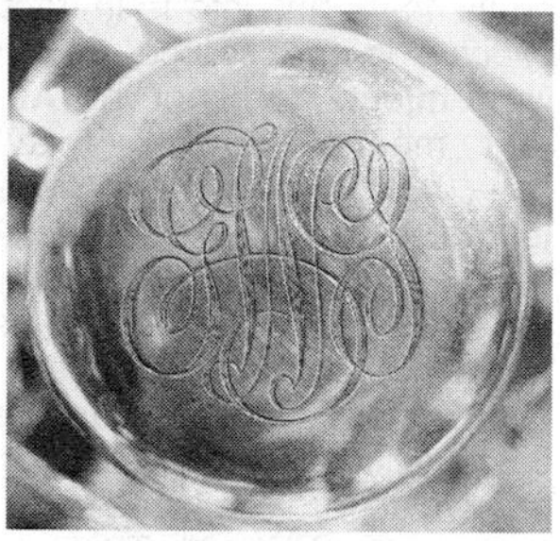

inscription
Monogram on the cover of an inkwell

within: *the innermost room in the palace.* **2.** Most private or intimate: *innermost feelings.*

inner tube *n.* A hollow rubber ring that can be inserted inside the casing of a tire and inflated.

in•ning (ĭn′ĭng) *n.* One of the nine divisions of a baseball game during which each team has a turn at bat.

inn•keep•er (ĭn′kē′pər) *n.* A person who owns or manages an inn.

in•no•cence (ĭn′ə səns) *n.* The condition, quality, or fact of being innocent, especially freedom from guilt.

in•no•cent (ĭn′ə sənt) *adj.* **1.** Free of evil or wrongdoing; not guilty of a crime or sin: *The jury found the the defendant innocent of the crime.* **2.** Unaware of evil or wrongdoing; naive: *We do not remain innocent children for long.* **3.** Not intended to cause harm: *an innocent joke.* —*n.* **1.** A person, especially a child, who is free of evil or sin. **2.** A simple inexperienced person who has no intention of deceiving others. [First written down in 1340 in Middle English, from Latin *innocēns* : *in-*, not + *nocēns*, harming.] —**in′no•cent•ly** *adv.*

in•noc•u•ous (ĭ nŏk′yo͞o əs) *adj.* Harmless; innocent: *an innocuous remark.* —**in•noc′u•ous•ly** *adv.* —**in•noc′u•ous•ness** *n.*

in•no•vate (ĭn′ə vāt′) *v.* **in•no•vat•ed, in•no•vat•ing, in•no•vates.** —*tr.* To begin or introduce for the first time: *The scientist innovated new methods in research.* —*intr.* To begin or introduce something new. [First written down in 1548 in Modern English, from Latin *innovāre*, to renew, from *novus*, new.] —**in′no•va′tor** *n.*

in•no•va•tion (ĭn′ə **vā′**shən) *n.* **1.** The act of innovating: *The Industrial Revolution was a time of great innovation.* **2.** Something newly introduced: *Automatic transmission was a major innovation in automobiles.*

in•no•va•tive (ĭn′ə vā′tĭv) *adj.* Tending to innovate or characterized by innovation: *an innovative architect.*

in•nu•en•do (ĭn′yo͞o **ĕn′**dō) *n., pl.* **in•nu•en•does.** An indirect hint or suggestion, usually intended to hurt the good name or standing of someone; an insinuation.

in•nu•mer•a•ble (ĭ **no͞o′** mər ə bəl *or* ĭ **nyo͞o′**-mər ə bəl) *adj.* Too numerous to be counted: *innumerable difficulties.* —**in•nu′mer•a•ble•ness** *n.* —**in•nu′mer•a•bly** *adv.*

in•oc•u•late (ĭ **nŏk′**yə lāt′) *tr.v.* **in•oc•u•lat•ed, in•oc•u•lat•ing, in•oc•u•lates.** To inject (a person or an animal) with bacteria or a virus that has been weakened or killed in order to make the body resistant to a particular disease. [First written down in 1440 in Middle English and spelled *inoculaten*, to graft a scion onto, from Latin *inoculāre*, from *oculus*, eye, bud.]

in•oc•u•la•tion (ĭ nŏk′yə **lā′**shən) *n.* **1.** The act of inoculating. **2.** An injection, as of a vaccine, given to make the body resistant to a disease.

in•of•fen•sive (ĭn′ə **fĕn′**sĭv) *adj.* Giving no offense; harmless: *an inoffensive joke.* —**in′of•fen′sive•ly** *adv.* —**in′of•fen′sive•ness** *n.*

in•op•er•a•ble (ĭn **ŏp′**ər ə bəl *or* ĭn **ŏp′**rə bəl) *adj.* **1.** Not suitable for surgery. **2.** Not functioning; inoperative.

in•op•er•a•tive (ĭn **ŏp′**ər ə tĭv *or* ĭn **ŏp′**rə tĭv) *adj.* **1.** Not working or functioning: *The computer is inoperative at this time.* **2.** No longer in force: *The governor declared her latest policy inoperative.*

in•op•por•tune (ĭn ŏp′ər **to͞on′** *or* ĭn ŏp′ər **tyo͞on′**) *adj.* Coming at the wrong time; inappropriate: *a telephone call at a most inopportune moment.*

in•or•di•nate (ĭn **ôr′**dn ĭt) *adj.* Exceeding reasonable limits; immoderate; excessive: *a book of inordinate length.* —**in•or′di•nate•ly** *adv.*

in•or•gan•ic (ĭn′ôr **găn′**ĭk) *adj.* **1.** Not involving living organisms or the products of their life processes: *Inorganic matter contains no hydrocarbons.* **2.** Of or relating to mineral matter as opposed to the substance of things that are or were alive: *Sand is considered inorganic matter.* —**in′or•gan′i•cal•ly** *adv.*

in•pa•tient (ĭn′pā′shənt) *n.* A patient who stays overnight in a hospital or clinic for treatment.

in•put (ĭn′po͝ot′) *n.* **1.** Something put into a project or process: *The study requires a large input of money.* **2.** The power supplied to an electronic circuit or device. **3.** The data or programs put into a computer. —*tr.v.* **in•put•ted** or **in•put, in•put•ting, in•puts.** To enter (data or a program) into a computer.

in•quest (ĭn′kwĕst′) *n.* **1.** A legal investigation into the cause of a death, especially one made before a jury or an official. **2.** An investigation.

in•quire (ĭn **kwīr′**) also **en•quire** (ĕn **kwīr′**) *v.* **in•quired, in•quir•ing, in•quires** also **en•quired, en•quir•ing, en•quires.** —*intr.* **1.** To request information; try to find out, as by asking questions: *If you can't find your size, inquire at the sales desk.* See Synonyms at **ask. 2.** To make a search or study; investigate: *inquire into a case.* —*tr.* To ask in order to find out: *inquire the way to the station.* —***idiom.*** **inquire after.** To ask about the health or condition of. [First written down about 1300 in Middle English and spelled *enqueren*, from Latin *inquīrere*.] —**in•quir′er** *n.* —**in•quir′ing•ly** *adv.*

in•quir•y (ĭn **kwīr′**ē *or* ĭn′kwə rē) also **en•quir•y** (ĕn **kwīr′**ē *or* ĕn′kwə rē) *n., pl.* **in•quir•ies** also **en•quir•ies. 1.** The act of inquiring: *engaged in scientific inquiry.* **2.** A request for information; a question: *many inquiries about the new mail rates.* **3.** A detailed examination of a matter; an investigation: *an inquiry into why water bills are so high.*

in•qui•si•tion (ĭn′kwĭ **zĭsh′**ən) *n.* **1.** The act of inquiring; an investigation. **2. Inquisition.** A former tribunal of the Roman Catholic Church established to seek out and punish people considered guilty of heresy. **3.** An investigation that violates the privacy or rights of individuals. **4.** A thorough, harsh questioning.

in•quis•i•tive (ĭn **kwĭz′**ĭ tĭv) *adj.* **1.** Eager to learn; curious: *an inquisitive mind.* See Synonyms at **curious. 2.** Prying into the affairs of others; unduly curious. —**in•quis′i•tive•ly** *adv.* —**in•quis′i•tive•ness** *n.*

in•quis•i•tor (ĭn **kwĭz′**ĭ tər) *n.* A person who conducts an inquisition. —**in•quis′i•to′ri•al** (ĭn kwĭz′ĭ **tôr′**ē əl) *adj.*

in•road (ĭn′rōd′) *n.* **1.** A hostile invasion; a raid. **2.** An advance at another's expense; an encroachment: *Foreign companies have made inroads into American markets.*

in•rush (ĭn′rŭsh′) *n.* A sudden rushing in; an influx: *an inrush of commuter traffic to the city.*

ins. *abbr.* An abbreviation of: **1.** Inches. **2.** Insurance.

in•sane (ĭn **sān′**) *adj.* **1.** Showing or afflicted with insanity; mentally ill. **2.** Characteristic of or intended for insane people: *an insane asylum.* **3.** Very foolish; not sensible: *an insane stunt.* —**in•sane′ly** *adv.*

in•san•i•tar•y (ĭn **săn′**ĭ tĕr′ē) *adj.* Not sanitary; unclean: *insanitary bandages.*

in•san•i•ty (ĭn **săn′**ĭ tē) *n., pl.* **in•san•i•ties. 1.** Mental illness or disorder; madness. **2.** Extreme foolishness; utter folly: *Trying to do three jobs at once is sheer insanity.*

in•sa•tia•ble (ĭn **sā′**shə bəl *or* ĭn **sā′**shē ə bəl) *adj.*

Impossible to satisfy; never satisfied: *an insatiable appetite.* —**in•sa'tia•bly** *adv.*

in•scribe (ĭn **skrīb'**) *tr.v.* **in•scribed, in•scrib•ing, in•scribes. 1.a.** To write, print, carve, or engrave (words, letters, or a design) on a surface: *Inscribe the winners' names on a plaque.* **b.** To mark or engrave (a surface) with words, letters, or design: *inscribe a plaque with the names of the winners.* **2.** To sign one's name or write a brief message in or on (a book or picture given as a gift). **3.** To impress deeply on the mind: *Our last day of school is inscribed on my memory.* **4.** To enter in a list; sign up. **5.** To draw (a geometric figure) within another so that the inner figure touches the outer figure at as many points as possible. [First written down in 1552 in Modern English, from Latin *īnscrībere*, to write on.] —**in•scrib'er** *n.*

in•scrip•tion (ĭn **skrĭp'**shən) *n.* **1.** The act or an example of inscribing: *the inscription of the names of war heroes on a monument.* **2.** Something inscribed: *a wall covered with ancient Egyptian inscriptions.* **3.** A short signed message in a book or on a picture given as a gift.

in•scru•ta•ble (ĭn **skrōō'**tə bəl) *adj.* Difficult or impossible to understand or make out; mysterious: *an inscrutable smile; an inscrutable coded message.* —**in•scru'ta•bil'i•ty, in•scru'ta•ble•ness** *n.* —**in•scru'ta•bly** *adv.*

in•seam (**ĭn'**sēm') *n.* **1.** The inside seam of a pant leg. **2.** The length or measurement of such a seam.

in•sect (**ĭn'**sĕkt') *n.* Any of numerous, usually small animals that in the adult stage have six legs, a body with three main divisions, and usually two pairs of wings. Flies, bees, grasshoppers, butterflies, and moths are insects. [First written down in 1601 in Modern English, from Latin *īnsectum*, from *īnsecāre*, to cut up, divide into segments.]

in•sec•ti•cide (ĭn **sĕk'**tĭ sīd') *n.* A chemical substance used to kill insects.

in•sec•ti•vore (ĭn **sĕk'**tə vôr') *n.* An animal or a plant that feeds mainly on insects.

in•sec•tiv•o•rous (ĭn'sĕk **tĭv'**ər əs) *adj.* Feeding on insects.

in•se•cure (ĭn'sĭ **kyŏŏr'**) *adj.* **1.** Not sure or certain; doubtful: *an insecure future.* **2.** Not secure or safe; not fully protected: *an insecure post on the frontier.* **3.** Not firm or sure; shaky: *an insecure hold on the dog's leash.* **4.** Lacking self-confidence: *an insecure person.* —**in'se•cure'ly** *adv.* —**in'se•cu'ri•ty** (ĭn'sĭ **kyŏŏr'**ĭ tē) *n.*

in•sem•i•nate (ĭn **sĕm'**ə nāt') *tr.v.* **in•sem•i•nat•ed, in•sem•i•nat•ing, in•sem•i•nates.** To introduce semen into (a female); impregnate. —**in•sem'i•na'tion** *n.*

in•sen•sate (ĭn **sĕn'**sāt' *or* ĭn **sĕn'**sĭt) *adj.* **1.** Lacking sensation or awareness; inanimate. **2.** Insensitive; unfeeling: *The insensate official was not interested in my complaints.* **3.** Lacking sense; foolish. —**in•sen'sate'ly** *adv.*

in•sen•si•ble (ĭn **sĕn'**sə bəl) *adj.* **1.** Not noticeable; imperceptible: *an insensible change in the weather.* **2.** Lacking the ability to feel sensation; numb: *insensible to cold.* **3.** Not mindful; unaware: *insensible to good advice.* **4.** Emotionally cold; indifferent: *He is insensible to other people's sorrow.* **5.** Unconscious: *The victim lay insensible on the sidewalk.* —**in•sen'si•bil'i•ty** *n.* —**in•sen'si•bly** *adv.*

in•sen•si•tive (ĭn **sĕn'**sĭ tĭv) *adj.* **1.** Not physically sensitive; numb: *An injection made the tooth insensitive.* **2.** Lacking in sensitivity for others; unfeeling. **3.** Unresponsive: *We must never be insensitive to the needs of our customers.* —**in•sen'si•tive•ly, in•sen'si•tive•ness** *adv.* —**in•sen'si•tiv'i•ty** *n.*

in•sep•a•ra•ble (ĭn **sĕp'**ər ə bəl *or* ĭn **sĕp'**rə bəl) *adj.* Impossible to separate: *inseparable friends.* —**in•sep'a•ra•bil'i•ty, in•sep'a•ra•ble•ness** *n.* —**in•sep'a•ra•bly** *adv.*

in•sert (ĭn **sûrt'**) *tr.v.* **in•sert•ed, in•sert•ing, in•serts.** To put or set into, between, or among: *insert a key in a lock; insert pictures between chapters in the book.* —*n.* (**ĭn'**sûrt'). Something inserted or meant to be inserted, as into a manuscript. *An advertising insert fell out of the magazine.* [First written down in 1529 in Modern English, from Latin *īnserere* : *in-*, in + *serere*, to join.]

in•ser•tion (ĭn **sûr'**shən) *n.* **1.** The act of inserting: *the insertion of proper punctuation.* **2.** Something inserted; an insert: *Please add this insertion to my report.*

in•set (**ĭn'**sĕt' *or* ĭn **sĕt'**) *tr.v.* **in•set, in•set•ting, in•sets.** To set in; insert. —*n.* (**ĭn'**sĕt'). Something set in, as a small map or illustration set within a larger one, or a piece of material set into a dress.

in•shore (**ĭn'shôr'**) *adv. & adj.* **1.** Close to a shore. **2.** Toward or coming toward shore: *an inshore wind.*

in•side (ĭn **sīd'** *or* **ĭn'**sīd') *n.* **1.** An inner part, side, or surface: *the inside of a house; articles on the inside of a magazine.* **2. insides.** *Informal.* **a.** The inner organs, especially those of the abdomen; entrails. **b.** The inner workings: *the insides of a TV set.* —*adj.* **1.** Inner; interior: *the inside pocket of a jacket.* **2.** Of, coming from, or known by those within a group: *inside information; a theft that was definitely an inside job.* **3.** In baseball, passing on the side of home plate nearer the batter: *The first pitch was a fast ball, high and inside.* —*adv.* Into or in the interior; within: *go inside; staying inside.* —*prep.* Into or in the interior of: *inside the package; go inside the house.* —***idioms.*** **inside of.** Within the limits of: *inside of an hour.* **inside out. 1.** With the inner surface turned out; reversed: *wearing his socks inside out.* **2.** *Informal.* Thoroughly: *A taxi driver must know the city inside out.*

in•sid•er (ĭn **sī'**dər) *n.* **1.** An accepted member of a group. **2.** A person who has special knowledge or access to private information.

in•sid•i•ous (ĭn **sĭd'**ē əs) *adj.* **1.** Intended to entrap; treacherous: *an insidious plot.* **2.** Working or spreading harmfully in a subtle or hidden manner: *insidious rumors; an insidious disease.* —**in•sid'i•ous•ly** *adv.* —**in•sid'i•ous•ness** *n.*

in•sight (**ĭn'**sīt') *n.* **1.** The capacity to perceive the true nature of something: *Einstein's insight into the workings of the universe.* **2.** A perception of the true nature of something: *The critic had a brilliant insight about the meaning of the movie.*

in•sight•ful (**ĭn'**sīt'fəl *or* ĭn **sīt'**fəl) *adj.* Showing or having insight; perceptive: *an insightful analysis of the painting.*

in•sig•ni•a (ĭn **sĭg'**nē ə) *n., pl.* **insignia** or **in•sig•ni•as.** A badge of office, rank, membership, or nationality; an emblem. [First written down in 1648 in Modern English, from Latin *īnsigne*, from *īnsignis*, distinguished, marked, from *signum*, sign.]

in•sig•nif•i•cant (ĭn'sĭg **nĭf'**ĭ kənt) *adj.* **1.** Of no importance; trivial: *an insignificant detail.* **2.** Small in size, power, or value: *an insignificant amount of money.* **3.** Having little or no meaning: *insignificant scribbling on the side of the page.* —**in'sig•nif'i•cance** *n.* —**in'sig•nif'i•cant•ly** *adv.*

in•sin•cere (ĭn'sĭn **sîr'**) *adj.* Not sincere; hypocritical: *an insincere apology.* —**in'sin•cere'ly** *adv.* —**in'sin•cer'i•ty** (ĭn'sĭn **sĕr'**ĭ tē) *n.*

in•sin•u•ate (ĭn **sĭn'**yōō āt') *tr.v.* **in•sin•u•at•ed, in•sin•u•at•ing, in•sin•u•ates. 1.** To introduce or suggest in a sly or indirect way: *Are you insinuating that I'm not good enough for the team?* **2.** To introduce or insert (oneself) by artful means: *The*

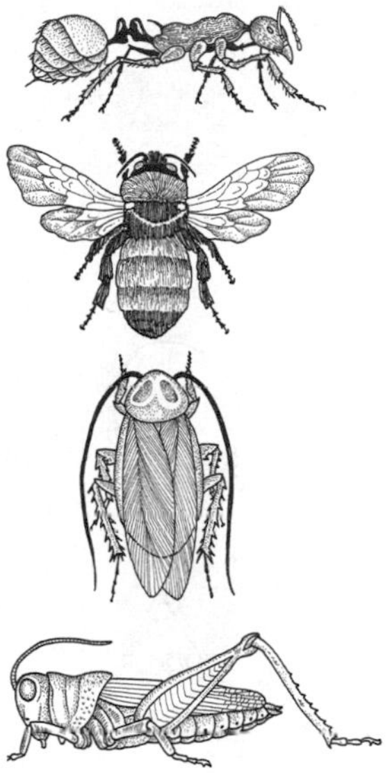

insect

Top to bottom: Ant, bumblebee, cockroach, and grasshopper

insignia

Tufts University insignia

ă	pat	oi	boy
ā	pay	ou	out
âr	care	ŏŏ	took
ä	father	ōō	boot
ĕ	pet	ŭ	cut
ē	be	ûr	urge
ĭ	pit	th	thin
ī	pie	*th*	this
îr	pier	hw	whoop
ŏ	pot	zh	vision
ō	toe	ə	about
ô	paw	N	*French* bon

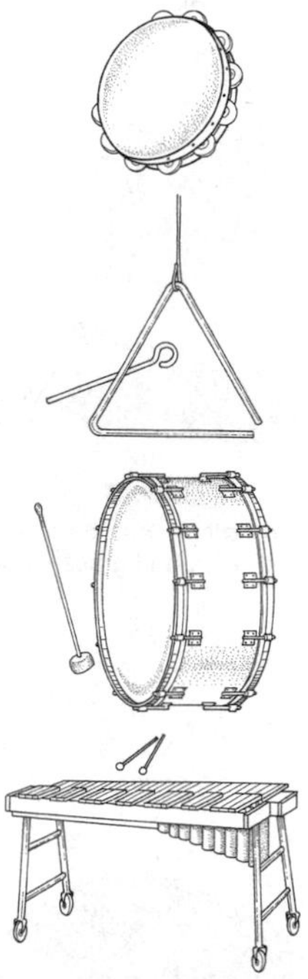

instrument
Top to bottom: Tambourine, triangle, bass drum, and xylophone

stranger insinuated himself into the wedding reception.

in•sin•u•a•tion (ĭn sĭn′yo͞o **ā′**shən) *n.* An indirect hint or suggestion: *an insinuation of wrongdoing.*

in•sip•id (ĭn **sĭp′**ĭd) *adj.* **1.** Lacking flavor; bland: *an insipid watery soup.* **2.** Lacking excitement or interest; dull: *an insipid movie.* [First written down in 1620 in Modern English, from Late Latin *īnsipidus* : Latin *in-*, not, without + Latin *sapere*, to taste.] **—in•sip′id•ly** *adv.* **—in•sip′id•ness** *n.*

in•sist (ĭn **sĭst′**) *v.* **in•sist•ed, in•sist•ing, in•sists.** *—intr.* To be firm in a course or demand; take a strong stand: *I insist on paying my share of the expenses.* *—tr.* To assert or demand vehemently and persistently: *We insist that you stay for dinner.* [First written down in 1586 in Modern English, from Latin *īnsistere*, to persist : *in-*, on + *sistere*, to stand.]

in•sis•tent (ĭn **sĭs′**tənt) *adj.* **1.** Firm or persistent in a course or demand: *The doctor was insistent that the water be boiled before use.* **2.** Demanding notice or attention: *my alarm clock's insistent ring.* **—in•sis′tence** *n.* **—in•sis′tent•ly** *adv.*

in•snare (ĭn **snâr′**) *v.* Variant of **ensnare.**

in•so•far as (ĭn′sō **fär′**) *conj.* To the extent that: *Insofar as I am able, I will carry out your orders.*

in•sole (**ĭn′**sōl′) *n.* **1.** The inner sole of a shoe or boot. **2.** An extra strip of material put inside a shoe for comfort or protection.

in•so•lent (**ĭn′**sə lənt) *adj.* Disrespectfully bold; impudent; rude: *an insolent reply.* **—in′so•lence** *n.* **—in′so•lent•ly** *adv.*

in•sol•u•ble (ĭn **sŏl′**yə bəl) *adj.* **1.** Not capable of being dissolved: *an insoluble salt.* **2.** Difficult or impossible to solve or explain: *an insoluble riddle.* **—in•sol′u•bil′i•ty** *n.* **—in•sol′u•bly** *adv.*

in•sol•vent (ĭn **sŏl′**vənt) *adj.* Unable to pay one's debts; bankrupt: *an insolvent bank.* **—in•sol′ven•cy** *n.*

in•som•ni•a (ĭn **sŏm′**nē ə) *n.* Persistent inability to sleep; sleeplessness. [First written down in 1758 in Modern English, from Latin *īnsomnis*, sleepless : *in-*, not, without + *somnus*, sleep.]

in•so•much as (ĭn′sō **mŭch′**) *conj.* Inasmuch as; because; since.

in•spect (ĭn **spĕkt′**) *tr.v.* **in•spect•ed, in•spect•ing, in•spects. 1.** To examine carefully and critically, especially for flaws: *We inspect all of our products to ensure they are of the highest quality.* **2.** To examine or review formally; evaluate officially: *An officer inspects the troops every Saturday.*

in•spec•tion (ĭn **spĕk′**shən) *n.* **1.** The act of inspecting: *Inspection of the wiring will take two days.* **2.** An official examination or review: *Demerits will be given to anyone who is late for inspection.*

in•spec•tor (ĭn **spĕk′**tər) *n.* **1.** A person who is appointed or employed to inspect something: *Two of our workers serve as inspectors on the job.* **2.** A police officer ranking next below a superintendent.

in•spi•ra•tion (ĭn′spə **rā′**shən) *n.* **1.** The excitement of the mind, emotions, or imagination, as in creating something or solving a problem: *Some writers get inspiration for a story from reading the newspaper.* **2.** A person or thing that excites the mind or the emotions: *The brilliant young scientist was an inspiration to younger colleagues.* **3.** Something, such as an original idea, that is inspired: *Your suggestion to open a store in town was an inspiration.* **4.** The act of breathing in; inhalation. **—in′spi•ra′tion•al** *adj.*

in•spire (ĭn **spīr′**) *v.* **in•spired, in•spir•ing, in•spires.** *—tr.* **1.** To fill with great emotion: *The concerto inspired the entire audience.* **2.** To stimulate to creativity or action: *The story about that great discovery inspired us to look for fossils.* **3.** To cause (a feeling or an attitude) in another or others; influence: *The candidate inspired confidence in the voters.* **4.** To be the cause or source of: *The book inspired a movie.* **5.** To breathe in (air). *—intr.* To inhale. [First written down about 1340 in Middle English and spelled *enspiren*, from Latin *īnspīrāre*, to breathe into.] **—in•spir′er** *n.*

in•spired (ĭn **spīrd′**) *adj.* So superior in brilliance or excellence as to suggest divine inspiration: *an inspired performance.*

in•spir•ing (ĭn **spīr′**ĭng) *adj.* Having an influence; stimulating: *an inspiring story of courage.*

in•sta•bil•i•ty (ĭn′stə **bĭl′**ĭ tē) *n., pl.* **in•sta•bil•i•ties.** Lack of stability; unsteadiness: *The roof collapsed because of the instability of the walls.*

in•stall (ĭn **stôl′**) *tr.v.* **in•stalled, in•stall•ing, in•stalls. 1.** To set in position and connect for use or service: *The company installed the new phones yesterday.* **2.** To place in an office, a rank, or a position, usually with ceremony: *The new mayor was installed soon after election.* **3.** To settle; place: *The mice installed themselves behind the baseboard.* [First written down about 1422 in Middle English and spelled *installen*, to place in office, from Medieval Latin *installāre* : Latin *in-*, in + *stallum*, stall, place.]

in•stal•la•tion (ĭn′stə **lā′**shən) *n.* **1.** The act of installing: *the installation of telephones.* **2.** A system of machinery or other apparatus set up for use: *A computer system is a complicated installation.* **3.** A military base.

in•stall•ment[1] (ĭn **stôl′**mənt) *n.* **1.** One of a series of payments in settlement of a debt: *We paid $400 for our television set in four installments of $100 each.* **2.** A portion of something issued or presented at intervals: *The book came out in installments in a magazine.* [First written down about 1577 in Modern English and spelled *estallment*, from Old French *estaler*, to place, fix.]

in•stall•ment[2] (ĭn **stôl′**mənt) *n.* The act of installing; installation.

in•stance (**ĭn′**stəns) *n.* A case or an example: *This is another instance of her great leadership.* ***—idiom.*** **for instance.** As an example; for example.

in•stant (**ĭn′**stənt) *n.* **1.** A period of time almost too brief to detect; a moment. **2.** A particular point in time: *Please call the instant they arrive.* *—adj.* **1.** Immediate: *an instant success.* **2.** Urgent: *an instant need.* **3.** Prepared by a manufacturer for quick preparation by the consumer: *instant cocoa.*

in•stan•ta•ne•ous (ĭn′stən **tā′**nē əs) *adj.* Happening without delay; immediate: *an instantaneous reaction.* **—in′stan•ta′ne•ous•ly** *adv.*

in•stant•ly (**ĭn′**stənt lē) *adv.* At once: *We recognized our old friends instantly.*

in•stead (ĭn **stĕd′**) *adv.* In place of something previously mentioned; as a substitute or an alternative: *They didn't have cider, so I got apple juice instead.*

instead of *prep.* In place of; rather than: *They walked home instead of taking the bus.*

in•step (**ĭn′**stĕp′) *n.* **1.** The arched middle part of the human foot between the toes and the ankle. **2.** The part of a shoe or stocking covering this part of the foot.

in•sti•gate (**ĭn′**stĭ gāt′) *tr.v.* **in•sti•gat•ed, in•sti•gat•ing, in•sti•gates.** To stir up; urge on; provoke: *instigate a prison riot.* **—in′sti•ga′tion** *n.* **—in′sti•ga′tor** *n.*

in•still (ĭn **stĭl′**) *tr.v.* **in•stilled, in•still•ing, in•stills.** To introduce little by little; fix gradually; implant: *Always playing by the rules instills a sense of fair play.*

in•stinct (**ĭn′**stĭngkt′) *n.* **1.** An inborn pattern of behavior that is characteristic of a given species: *the salmon's instinct to swim upstream to spawn.* **2.** A natural talent or ability: *an instinct for science.* [First written down before 1420 in Middle English, from Latin *īnstinguere*, to incite.]

in•stinc•tive (ĭn **stĭngk′**tĭv) *adj.* Of or arising from instinct: *Building nests is instinctive behavior in most birds.* **—in•stinc′tive•ly** *adv.*

in•sti•tute (**ĭn′**stĭ to͞ot′ *or* ĭn′stĭ tyo͞ot′) *tr.v.* **in•sti•tut•ed, in•sti•tut•ing, in•sti•tutes.** To establish, organize, and set in operation; initiate: *The government instituted a new trade policy.* See Synonyms at **establish.** *—n.* **1.** An organization established to promote a cause: *a research institute.* **2.** An educational institution: *an art institute.* **3.** The building or buildings of such an institution.

in•sti•tu•tion (ĭn′stĭ **to͞o′**shən *or* ĭn′stĭ **tyo͞o′**shən) *n.* **1.** The act or process of instituting: *the institution of new school rules for student conduct.* **2.** A custom, practice, or pattern of behavior that is important in the cultural life of a society: *the institution of marriage.* **3.a.** An organization or foundation, especially one dedicated to public service: *an educational institution.* **b.** The building or buildings housing such an organization. **—in′sti•tu′tion•al** *adj.*

in•sti•tu•tion•al•ize (ĭn′stĭ **to͞o′**shə nə līz′ *or* ĭn′stĭ **tyo͞o′**shə nə līz′) *tr.v.* **in•sti•tu•tion•al•ized, in•sti•tu•tion•al•iz•ing, in•sti•tu•tion•al•iz•es. 1.** To make into, treat as, or give the character of an institution to. **2.** To place (a person) in the care of an institution.

in•struct (ĭn **strŭkt′**) *tr.v.* **in•struct•ed, in•struct•ing, in•structs. 1.** To give knowledge or skill to; teach: *The teacher will instruct the class in how to use these computers.* See Synonyms at **teach. 2.** To give orders to; direct: *The coach instructed us to run around the track.* [First written down about 1425 in Middle English and spelled *instructen*, from Latin *īnstruere*, to prepare, instruct : *in-*, on + *struere*, to build.]

in•struc•tion (ĭn **strŭk′**shən) *n.* **1.** Something that is taught; a lesson: *instructions in modern and classical music.* **2.** The act of teaching or instructing; education. **3. instructions.** Directions; orders: *The model airplane came with clear instructions.* **—in•struc′tion•al** *adj.*

in•struc•tive (ĭn **strŭk′**tĭv) *adj.* Providing knowledge or information: *an instructive example.* **—in•struc′tive•ly** *adv.*

in•struc•tor (ĭn **strŭk′**tər) *n.* **1.** A person who instructs; a teacher. **2.** A college or university teacher ranking below an assistant professor.

in•stru•ment (**ĭn′**strə mənt) *n.* **1.** An implement used to do work, especially one used by a physician, dentist, or scientist. **2.** A device used for making music: *the instruments of an orchestra.* **3.** A device for recording or measuring, as in a control system: *A fuel gauge and a compass are important instruments in an aircraft.* **4.** A means by which something is done: *The law to protect jobs was an important instrument of the governor's policy.* **5.** A legal document. [First written down before 1300 in Middle English, from Latin *īnstrūmentum*, from *īnstruere*, to prepare.]

in•stru•men•tal (ĭn′strə **mĕn′**tl) *adj.* **1.** Serving as the means; useful; helpful: *Our teacher was instrumental in getting the club a place to meet.* **2.** Performed on or written for musical instruments: *instrumental music.* **—in′stru•men′tal•ly** *adv.*

in•stru•men•tal•ist (ĭn′strə **mĕn′**tl ĭst) *n.* A person who plays a musical instrument.

in•stru•men•tal•i•ty (ĭn′strə mĕn **tăl′**ĭ tē) *n., pl.* **in•stru•men•tal•i•ties. 1.** The quality or condition of being instrumental; usefulness. **2.** A means; a help to achieve an end.

in•stru•men•ta•tion (ĭn′strə mĕn **tā′**shən) *n.* **1.** The arrangement or orchestration of music for instruments. **2.** The application or use of instruments.

in•sub•or•di•nate (ĭn′sə **bôr′**dn ĭt) *adj.* Not submissive to authority: *punished for being insubordinate to a superior.* **—in′sub•or′di•nate•ly** *adv.* **—in′sub•or′di•na′tion** (*ĭn′sə{-bôr′dn-ā′shən*) *n.*

in•sub•stan•tial (ĭn′səb **stăn′**shəl) *adj.* **1.** Lacking substance or reality; imaginary: *not facts, but insubstantial visions.* **2.** Not firm; flimsy: *an insubstantial cardboard wall.* **—in′sub•stan′ti•al′i•ty** (ĭn′səb stăn′shē **ăl′**ĭ tē) *n.* **—in′sub•stan′tial•ly** *adv.*

in•suf•fer•a•ble (ĭn **sŭf′**ər ə bəl *or* ĭn **sŭf′**rə bəl) *adj.* Difficult or impossible to endure; intolerable: *insufferable rudeness.* **—in•suf′fer•a•bly** *adv.*

in•suf•fi•cien•cy (ĭn′sə **fĭsh′**ən sē) *n., pl.* **in•suf•fi•cien•cies.** A lack or deficiency: *An insufficiency of funds made it impossible to build a new pool.*

in•suf•fi•cient (ĭn′sə **fĭsh′**ənt) *adj.* Not enough; inadequate: *insufficient rainfall for a good harvest.* **—in′suf•fi′cient•ly** *adv.*

in•su•lar (**ĭn′**sə lər *or* **ĭns′**yə lər) *adj.* **1.** Of, relating to, or forming an island: *England is an insular nation.* **2.** Living or located on an island: *insular people.* **3.** Alone; isolated: *an insular life.* **—in′su•lar′i•ty** (ĭn′sə **lăr′**ĭ tē *or* ĭns′yə **lăr′**ĭ tē) *n.*

in•su•late (**ĭn′**sə lāt′) *tr.v.* **in•su•lat•ed, in•su•lat•ing, in•su•lates. 1.** To cover or surround with a material that prevents the passage of heat, electricity, or sound into or out of: *We insulated our attic to keep out the cold.* **2.** To detach; isolate: *The mountain valley is insulated from outside influences.* [First written down in 1538 in Modern English, from Latin *īnsula*, island.]

in•su•la•tion (ĭn′sə **lā′**shən) *n.* **1.a.** The act of insulating: *Insulation of the windows will keep the cold air out.* **b.** The condition of being insulated: *kept warm by insulation.* **2.** Material that is used for insulating: *There is a layer of fiberglass insulation in the attic.*

in•su•la•tor (**ĭn′**sə lā′tər) *n.* A substance or device that insulates, especially a nonconductor of electricity, heat, or sound.

in•su•lin (**ĭn′**sə lĭn) *n.* **1.** A hormone that is produced in the pancreas and acts to regulate the amount of sugar in the blood. **2.** A drug containing this hormone, obtained from the pancreas of animals or produced synthetically and used in treating diabetes.

in•sult (ĭn **sŭlt′**) *tr.v.* **in•sult•ed, in•sult•ing, in•sults.** To treat with insensitivity or contempt; offend: *She insulted me by saying hello to everyone but me.* *—n.* (**ĭn′**sŭlt′). An offensive action or remark. [First written down about 1570 in Modern English, from Latin *īnsultāre*, to leap at, insult.] **—in•sult′ing•ly** *adv.*

in•su•per•a•ble (ĭn **so͞o′**pər ə bəl) *adj.* Impossible to overcome; insurmountable: *insuperable odds.* **—in•su′per•a•bly** *adv.*

in•sup•port•a•ble (ĭn′sə **pôr′**tə bəl) *adj.* Unbearable; intolerable: *insupportable pain.*

in•sur•ance (ĭn **sho͝or′**əns) *n.* **1.** The act or business of guaranteeing to pay for specified losses in the future, as in case of accident, illness, theft, or death, in return for the continuing payment of regular sums of money. **2.a.** A contract making such guarantees to a person or group in return for regular payments. **b.** The total amount to be paid to the party insured: *bought $100,000 of life insurance.* **c.** A periodic amount paid for such coverage; a premium: *We pay insurance on the first of the month.*

in•sure (ĭn **sho͝or′**) *tr.v.* **in•sured, in•sur•ing, in•sures. 1.** To cover with insurance: *insure a car.* **2.** To make sure or certain; guarantee; ensure: *Proper*

insulation
Installing insulation

ă	pat	oi	boy
ā	pay	ou	out
âr	care	o͝o	took
ä	father	o͞o	boot
ĕ	pet	ŭ	cut
ē	be	ûr	urge
ĭ	pit	th	thin
ī	pie	*th*	this
îr	pier	hw	whoop
ŏ	pot	zh	vision
ō	toe	ə	about
ô	paw	N	*French* bon

Usage: intense

The words **intense** and **intensive** mean two different things in the two phrases *Mark's intense study of German* and *Mark's intensive study of German.* **Intense** suggests that Mark himself is responsible for his concentrated activity, whereas **intensive** suggests that Mark's concentration of activity is set by a program that covers a great deal of material in a brief period.

diet helps to insure good health. —**in•sur′er** *n.* —SEE NOTE at **assure.**

in•sured (ĭn shŏŏrd′) *n., pl.* **insured** or **in•sureds.** A person or thing covered by insurance.

in•sur•gence (ĭn sûr′jəns) *n.* An uprising; a rebellion.

in•sur•gent (ĭn sûr′jənt) *adj.* Rising in revolt: *The insurgent forces overthrew the government.* —*n.* A person who revolts against authority; a rebel.

in•sur•mount•a•ble (ĭn′sər moun′tə bəl) *adj.* Impossible to overcome; insuperable: *an insurmountable obstacle.*

in•sur•rec•tion (ĭn′sə rĕk′shən) *n.* An uprising against an established authority or government; a rebellion. —**in′sur•rec′tion•ist** *n.*

in•tact (ĭn tăkt′) *adj.* Not weakened, injured, damaged, or separated; whole: *The contents were intact in spite of the damage to the box.*

in•take (ĭn′tāk′) *n.* **1.** An opening through which a liquid or gas enters a container or pipe: *an intake clogged with dirt.* **2.a.** The act of taking in: *an efficient air intake.* **b.** Something, or the amount of something, taken in: *an adequate intake of food.*

in•tan•gi•ble (ĭn tăn′jə bəl) *adj.* **1.** Incapable of being touched; lacking physical substance: *Inner satisfaction is one of the intangible rewards of community service.* **2.** Incapable of being defined; vague; elusive: *an intangible change of attitude.* —*n.* Something intangible. —**in•tan′gi•bly** *adv.*

in•te•ger (ĭn′tĭ jər) *n.* A positive or negative whole number or zero. [First written down in 1571 in Modern English, from Latin *integer*, whole, complete.]

in•te•gral (ĭn′tĭ grəl *or* ĭn tĕg′rəl) *adj.* **1.** Necessary to form a whole or make something complete: *Rafters are an integral part of a roof.* **2.** Having everything essential; entire. **3.** Of, involving, or expressed as an integer or integers. —**in′te•gral•ly** *adv.*

in•te•grate (ĭn′tĭ grāt′) *v.* **inte•grat•ed, inte•grat•ing, inte•grates.** —*tr.* **1.** To make into a whole by bringing all parts together; unify: *Our school integrated math and computer courses last fall.* **2.** To open to people of all races or ethnic groups without restriction; desegregate. —*intr.* To become integrated. [First written down in 1638 in Modern English, from Middle English *integrate*, intact, from Latin *integrāre*, to make whole, from *integer*, complete.]

in•te•grat•ed circuit (ĭn′tĭ grā′tĭd) *n.* A tiny wafer of silicon or other semiconducting material on which electronic circuits are etched or imprinted, used in computers and other electronic equipment.

in•te•gra•tion (ĭn′tĭ grā′shən) *n.* **1.** The act or process of integrating. **2.** The bringing of people of different racial or ethnic groups into equal association; desegregation. —**in′te•gra′tion•ist** *n.*

in•teg•ri•ty (ĭn tĕg′rĭ tē) *n.* **1.** Moral uprightness; honesty: *A judge must be a person of integrity.* **2.** Completeness; unity: *The country maintained its integrity by defending its borders.*

in•teg•u•ment (ĭn tĕg′yōō mənt) *n.* A natural outer covering of an animal or a plant, as skin, a seed coat, or a shell.

in•tel•lect (ĭn′tl ĕkt′) *n.* **1.** The power of the mind to think, reason, and learn. **2.** Great intelligence or mental ability: *We admire people of intellect.* **3.** A person of great intellectual ability: *a gathering of scientific intellects.*

in•tel•lec•tu•al (ĭn′tl ĕk′chōō əl) *adj.* **1.** Of or engaging the intellect: *an intellectual discussion.* **2.** Having or showing intelligence: *an intellectual person.* See Synonyms at **smart.** —*n.* A person of intelligence, especially a person who is informed and interested in many things. —**in′tel•lec′tu•al•ly** *adv.*

in•tel•li•gence (ĭn tĕl′ə jəns) *n.* **1.** The capacity to gain and use knowledge; mental ability: *The dolphin is an animal of high intelligence.* **2.** Information or news, especially secret information about an enemy. **3.** An agency or office employed in gathering secret information. [First written down about 1380 in Middle English, from Latin *intellegere*, to perceive.]

intelligence quotient *n.* The ratio of tested mental age to actual age, usually expressed as a quotient multiplied by 100.

intelligence test *n.* A test used to measure intelligence or mental development.

in•tel•li•gent (ĭn tĕl′ə jənt) *adj.* **1.** Having intelligence, especially of a high degree: *an intelligent history student.* See Synonyms at **smart. 2.** Showing intelligence; wise or thoughtful: *an intelligent decision.* —**in•tel′li•gent•ly** *adv.*

in•tel•li•gent•si•a (in tĕl′ə jĕnt′sē ə) *n.* The most educated group of people in a society.

in•tel•li•gi•ble (ĭn tĕl′ĭ jə bəl) *adj.* Capable of being understood; comprehensible: *We need someone to write intelligible instructions on using this computer program.* —**in•tel′li•gi•bly** *adv.*

in•tem•per•ance (ĭn tĕm′pər əns *or* ĭn tĕm′prəns) *n.* Lack of self-control, as in giving in to a craving for food or not controlling one's temper.

in•tem•per•ate (ĭn tĕm′pər ĭt *or* ĭn tĕm′prĭt) *adj.* Not temperate or moderate; excessive. —**in•tem′per•ate•ly** *adv.*

in•tend (ĭn tĕnd′) *tr.v.* **in•tend•ed, in•tend•ing, in•tends. 1.** To have as a purpose; have in mind; plan: *We intend to get an early start.* **2.** To design for a specific purpose or use: *This saw is intended to cut metal.* [First written down about 1300 in Middle English and spelled *entenden*, from Latin *intendere.*]

in•tend•ed (ĭn tĕn′dĭd) *adj.* **1.** Planned; intentional: *an intended result.* **2.** Future; prospective: *their intended trip to Mexico.* —*n. Informal.* A person who is engaged to be married: *My sister and her intended came along.*

in•tense (ĭn tĕns′) *adj.* **in•tens•er, in•tens•est. 1.** Existing in an extreme degree; very strong: *an intense blue; intense heat.* **2.** Having or showing deep feeling: *an intense look; intense words.* [First written down before 1425 in Middle English, from Latin *intēnsus*, stretched, intent, from *intendere*, to stretch, intend.] —**in•tense′ly** *adv.* —SEE NOTE.

in•ten•si•fi•er (ĭn tĕn′sə fī′ər) *n.* **1.** A person or thing that intensifies. **2.** In grammar, an intensive.

in•ten•si•fy (ĭn tĕn′sə fī′) *tr. & intr.v.* **in•ten•si•fied, in•ten•si•fy•ing, in•ten•si•fies.** To make or become intense or more intense: *The police intensified their investigation. Our review sessions intensified as exams drew near.* —**in•ten′si•fi•ca′tion** (ĭn tĕn′sə fĭ kā′shən) *n.*

in•ten•si•ty (ĭn tĕn′sĭ tē) *n., pl.* **in•ten•si•ties. 1.** Extreme force, strength, or concentration: *Our team played with emotional intensity.* **2.** The strength of a color: *The two colors vary in intensity.* **3.** The amount of strength of electricity, heat, light, or sound per unit of area, volume, or mass.

in•ten•sive (ĭn tĕn′sĭv) *adj.* **1.** Of or marked by intensity; deep; concentrated: *intensive study.* **2.** In grammar, giving emphasis: *an intensive adverb.* —*n.* In grammar, a word, phrase, prefix, or suffix that gives force or emphasis. For example, in the sentences *We are very pleased* and *That student is extremely intelligent,* the adverbs *very* and *extremely* are intensives. —**in•ten′sive•ly** *adv.* —SEE NOTE at **intense.**

in•tent (ĭn tĕnt′) *n.* **1.** A purpose or an aim; an intention: *It was never my intent to start an argument.* **2.** Meaning; significance: *The intent of your* *message is unclear.* —*adj.* **1.** Showing concentration; intense: *an intent expression while studying.* **2.** Firmly fixed on some purpose; determined: *We are intent on securing a new trade agreement.* —*idiom.* **for all intents and purposes** or **to all intents and purposes.** In every practical sense; practically. —**in•tent′ly** *adv.* —**in•tent′ness** *n.*

in•ten•tion (ĭn tĕn′shən) *n.* **1.** A plan, purpose, or design. **2. intentions.** Purposes or motives in mind: *with the best of intentions.*

in•ten•tion•al (ĭn tĕn′shə nəl) *adj.* Done deliberately; meant; intended: *an intentional slight.* —**in•ten′tion•al•ly** *adv.*

in•ter (ĭn tûr′) *tr.v.* **in•terred, in•ter•ring, in•ters.** To place in a grave; bury. [First written down in 1303 in Middle English and spelled *enteren*, from Medieval Latin *interrāre* : Latin *in-*, in + Latin *terra*, earth.]

inter– *pref.* A prefix that means: **1.** Between; among: *international.* **2.** Mutually; together: *interact.* —SEE NOTE.

in•ter•act (ĭn′tər ăkt′) *intr.v.* **in•ter•act•ed, in•ter•act•ing, in•ter•acts.** To act on or affect each other: *The mechanic's adjustments made the gears interact more smoothly.* —**in′ter•ac′tion** *n.*

in•ter•ac•tive (ĭn′tər ăk′tĭv) *adj.* **1.** Of or relating to a computer program in which the user and the program interact. For example, computer games are interactive. **2.** Of or relating to a form of television entertainment in which the viewer participates directly.

in•ter•breed (ĭn′tər brēd′) *v.* **in•ter•bred** (ĭn′tər-brĕd′), **in•ter•breed•ing, in•ter•breeds.** —*intr.* **1.** To breed with another kind or species; produce a hybrid. **2.** To breed within a small group or with closely related individuals; inbreed. —*tr.* To cause (a plant or an animal) to breed with one of a different variety or species: *interbreed two varieties of cattle.*

in•ter•cede (ĭn′tər sēd′) *intr.v.* **in•ter•ced•ed, in•ter•ced•ing, in•ter•cedes.** **1.** To plead on another's behalf; seek some favor for another: *The teacher interceded with my parents to let me go on the trip.* **2.** To act as a mediator in a dispute: *The government can appoint people to intercede in certain labor disputes.*

in•ter•cel•lu•lar (ĭn′tər sĕl′yə lər) *adj.* Located between or among cells.

in•ter•cept (ĭn′tər sĕpt′) *tr.v.* **in•ter•cept•ed, in•ter•cept•ing, in•ter•cepts.** **1.** To stop or interrupt the intended course or progress of: *intercept a messenger; intercept a football pass.* **2.** To mark off or bound (a space) between two points or lines. [First written down in 1391 in Middle English and spelled *intercepten*, from Latin *intercipere* : *inter-*, between + *capere*, to seize.] —**in′ter•cep′tion** *n.*

in•ter•cep•tor also **in•ter•cept•er** (ĭn′tər sĕp′tər) *n.* **1.** A person or thing that intercepts. **2.** A fast-climbing, highly maneuverable fighter plane designed to intercept enemy aircraft.

in•ter•ces•sion (ĭn′tər sĕsh′ən) *n.* **1.** The act of interceding. **2.** An earnest request made in favor of another. —**in′ter•ces′sor** *n.*

in•ter•change (ĭn′tər chānj′) *v.* **in•ter•changed, in•ter•chang•ing, in•ter•chang•es.** —*tr.* **1.** To switch each of (two things) into the place of the other: *If you interchange the first and last letters of the word* pal, *it becomes* lap. **2.** To give and receive mutually; exchange: *A vigorous discussion is the best way to interchange ideas.* —*intr.* To change places with each other. —*n.* (ĭn′tər chānj′). **1.** The act of interchanging: *Trade is the interchange of commodities.* **2.** A highway intersection that allows traffic to flow freely from one road to another without crossing another line of traffic.

in•ter•change•a•ble (ĭn′tər chān′jə bəl) *adj.* Capable of being switched or interchanged: *These two cars have interchangeable parts.* —**in′ter•change′a•bly** *adv.*

in•ter•col•le•giate (ĭn′tər kə lē′jĭt *or* ĭn′tər-kə lē′jē ĭt) *adj.* Involving two or more colleges or universities: *an intercollegiate tournament.*

in•ter•com (ĭn′tər kŏm′) *n.* An electronic communication system, as between rooms of a building or areas of a ship.

in•ter•com•mu•ni•cate (ĭn′tər kə myōō′nĭ kāt′) *intr.v.* **in•ter•com•mu•ni•cat•ed, in•ter•com•mu•ni•cat•ing, in•ter•com•mu•ni•cates.** To communicate with each other. —**in′ter•com•mu′ni•ca′tion** *n.*

in•ter•con•nect (ĭn′tər kə nĕkt′) *intr. & tr.v.* **in•ter•con•nect•ed, in•ter•con•nect•ing, in•ter•con•nects.** To connect or be connected with each other. —**in′ter•con•nec′tion** *n.*

in•ter•con•ti•nen•tal (ĭn′tər kŏn′tə nĕn′tl) *adj.* **1.** Involving or extending between two or more continents: *intercontinental weather patterns.* **2.** Having the capability of traveling from one continent to another: *an intercontinental airline.*

in•ter•course (ĭn′tər kôrs′) *n.* **1.** Dealings or communication between persons or groups. **2.** Sexual intercourse.

in•ter•de•nom•i•na•tion•al (ĭn′tər də nŏm′ə nā′shə nəl) *adj.* Involving different religious denominations: *an interdenominational service.*

in•ter•de•pend•ent (ĭn′tər dĭ pĕn′dənt) *adj.* Dependent on one another; mutually dependent. —**in′ter•de•pend′ence** *n.* —**in′ter•de•pend′ent•ly** *adv.*

in•ter•dict (ĭn′tər dĭkt′) *tr.v.* **in•ter•dict•ed, in•ter•dict•ing, in•ter•dicts.** **1.** To prohibit; forbid. **2.** In the Roman Catholic Church, to exclude from participation in most sacraments and from Christian burial. **3.** To halt the activities or entry of; block: *were successful in interdicting the smuggled goods.* —*n.* (ĭn′tər dĭkt′). **1.** A prohibition by court order. **2.** In the Roman Catholic Church, a censure that excludes a person or district from participation in most sacraments and from Christian burial. —**in′ter•dic′tion** *n.*

in•ter•est (ĭn′trĭst *or* ĭn′tər ĭst) *n.* **1.a.** A feeling of curiosity or concern about something: *An exciting story will arouse the reader's interest.* **b.** The quality of arousing such a feeling: *a tedious speech that lacked interest for me.* **c.** A subject that arouses such a feeling: *Music, science fiction, and computer games are among my interests.* **2.** Advantage; benefit. Often used in the plural: *The company's decision to burn coal is not in the public interest.* **3.a.** A right, claim, or legal share in something: *an interest in a business.* **b.** Something in which such a right, claim, or share is held: *American interests in China.* **c.** A group of persons holding such a right, claim, or share. **4.** A charge for borrowing money, usually a percentage of the amount borrowed: *a bank with an interest rate of five percent.* **5.** An excess or a bonus beyond what is expected or due: *Our host paid back the compliment with interest.* —*tr.v.* **in•ter•est•ed, in•ter•est•ing, in•ter•ests.** **1.** To arouse the curiosity or hold the attention of: *Modern sculpture interests me a lot.* **2.** To cause to become involved or concerned: *The salesperson tried to interest us in the options on the car.* —*idiom.* **in the interest of** or **in the interests of.** To the advantage of; for the sake of: *I agreed to switch chores in the interest of peace.* [First written down about 1425 in Middle English, from Latin *interest*, it is of importance.]

in•ter•est•ed (ĭn′trĭ stĭd *or* ĭn′tə rĕs′tĭd) *adj.* **1.** Having or showing interest, fascination, or con-

Word Building: inter–

The prefix **inter–** comes from the Latin prefix *inter–*, from the preposition *inter*, meaning "between, among." Thus the word **intercede**, in which *inter–* combines with the Latin verb *cēdere*, "to go," means "to go between." Similarly, **interject**, which comes from Latin *iacere*, "to throw," means literally "to throw something between or among others." And **intervene**, coming from Latin *venīre*, "to come," means "to come between people or things." In English, **inter–** is still producing new words, such as **interfaith**, **intertwine**, and **intercellular**.

intercom

ă	**pat**	oi	**boy**
ā	**pay**	ou	**out**
âr	**care**	ŏŏ	**took**
ä	**father**	ōō	**boot**
ĕ	**pet**	ŭ	**cut**
ē	**be**	ûr	**urge**
ĭ	**pit**	th	**thin**
ī	**pie**	*th*	**this**
îr	**pier**	hw	**whoop**
ŏ	**pot**	zh	**vision**
ō	**toe**	ə	**about**
ô	**paw**	N	*French* bon

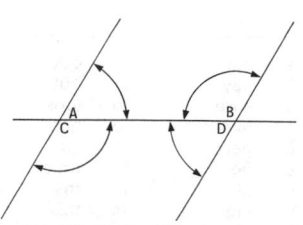

interior angle
A, B, C, and D are interior angles; AD and BC are alternate interior angles

cern: *Good teaching usually produces interested students.* **2.** Having a right, claim, or share: *The interested parties met to settle the dispute.* —**in′ter•est•ed•ly** *adv.*

interest group *n.* A group of persons working to support a particular cause, such as an item of legislation.

in•ter•est•ing (ĭn′trĭ stĭng *or* ĭn′tə rĕs′tĭng) *adj.* Arousing or holding interest or attention; absorbing. —**in′ter•est•ing•ly** *adv.*

Synonyms: interesting, intriguing, fascinating, engaging. These adjectives all mean capable of capturing and holding one's attention. *You may write your report on any subject you find interesting. Sue thought my idea was intriguing and wanted to know more about it. How fascinating that lasers can be used to perform surgery! All the characters in the play are engaging.*

in•ter•face (ĭn′tər fās′) *n.* **1.** A surface forming a common boundary between any two regions, bodies, or phases. **2.** A point at which two systems or groups interact, especially the point at which a computer interacts with another computer or with a human operator. —*tr. & intr.v.* (ĭn′tər **fās′**). **in•ter•faced, in•ter•fac•ing, in•ter•fac•es.** To work together or communicate, especially with a computer or other electronic device.

in•ter•faith (ĭn′tər fāth′) *adj.* Of or involving persons of different religious faiths: *attended an interfaith gathering.*

in•ter•fere (ĭn′tər **fîr′**) *intr.v.* **in•ter•fered, in•ter•fer•ing, in•ter•feres. 1.** To get in the way as an obstacle or a hindrance: *The rain interfered with our plans to go on a picnic.* **2.** To intrude in the affairs of others; meddle. [First written down in 1440 in Middle English and spelled *entiferin,* from Old French *s'entreferer,* to strike one another : *entre-,* between + *ferir,* to strike.]

in•ter•fer•ence (ĭn′tər **fîr′**əns) *n.* **1.** The act or an instance of interfering: *Human interference has upset the balance in the environment.* **2.** In sports, the obstruction of a play or player in a manner prohibited by the rules. **3.** In football, the legal blocking of defensive players to make way for a ball carrier. **4.** The action of two waves of the same frequency in reinforcing or counteracting each other when they meet. **5.** In electronics: **a.** The distortion or interruption of one broadcast signal by others. **b.** The distorted part of a broadcast signal; static.

in•ter•fer•on (ĭn′tər **fîr′**ŏn′) *n.* Any of a group of proteins that are produced by animal cells in response to infection by a virus and that prevent reproduction of the virus.

in•ter•im (ĭn′tər ĭm) *n.* An interval of time between two events, periods, or processes: *During the interim between expeditions, the explorer wrote a book of memoirs.* —*adj.* Of or during an interim; temporary: *After an interim job as a cook, he returned to college.* [First written down in 1548 in Modern English, from Latin, in the meantime.]

in•te•ri•or (ĭn **tîr′**ē ər) *adj.* **1.** Of or located in the inside; inner: *The interior surfaces of the pipe are corroded.* **2.** Located away from a coast or border; inland: *Interior Australia is sparsely populated.* —*n.* **1.** The inner part of something; the inside: *the interior of a house.* **2.** The inland part of a country or geographical area: *The interior of Alaska is very mountainous.* **3.** The affairs within a country; domestic affairs. [First written down in 1490 in Middle English, from Latin, comparative adjective of *inter,* between.]

interior angle *n.* **1.** Any of the four angles formed inside two straight lines intersected by a third straight line. **2.** An angle formed by two adjacent sides of a polygon and included within the polygon.

interior decorator *n.* A person who specializes in the decoration and furnishing of the interiors of homes, offices, or other buildings.

interj. *abbr.* An abbreviation of interjection.

in•ter•ject (ĭn′tər **jĕkt′**) *tr.v.* **in•ter•ject•ed, in•ter•ject•ing, in•ter•jects.** To put in between or among other things; insert: *The speaker paused in the talk to interject a personal remark.* [First written down in 1578 in Modern English, from Latin *interjicere* : *inter-,* between + *iacere,* to throw.]

in•ter•jec•tion (ĭn′tər **jĕk′**shən) *n.* **1.** A sudden phrase or remark that is interjected; an exclamation. **2.** In grammar, a word or phrase that expresses emotion and can stand alone. *Ouch!* and *Hurrah!* are interjections. —**in′ter•jec′tion•al** *adj.*

in•ter•lace (ĭn′tər **lās′**) *tr. & intr.v.* **in•ter•laced, in•ter•lac•ing, in•ter•lac•es.** To weave, lace, or twine together: *A weaver interlaces threads in order to make cloth.*

in•ter•lard (ĭn′tər **lärd′**) *tr.v.* **in•ter•lard•ed, in•ter•lard•ing, in•ter•lards.** To mix something different into; intersperse: *To illustrate the point, the writer interlarded the report with many examples.*

in•ter•lock (ĭn′tər **lŏk′**) *tr. & intr.v.* **in•ter•locked, in•ter•lock•ing, in•ter•locks.** To unite firmly or join tightly, as by hooking: *The dancers form a circle and interlock hands.*

in•ter•lop•er (**ĭn′**tər lō′pər) *n.* A person who intrudes or interferes in the affairs of others; a meddler.

in•ter•lude (**ĭn′**tər lo͞od′) *n.* **1.** An intervening episode or period of time: *There was a brief interlude of sunshine on this mostly cloudy day.* **2.** A short entertainment between the acts of a play. **3.** A short piece of music that occurs between parts of a longer composition. [First written down about 1303 in Middle English and spelled *enterlude,* a dramatic entertainment, from Medieval Latin *interlūdium* : Latin *inter-,* between + Latin *lūdus,* play.]

in•ter•mar•ry (ĭn′tər **măr′**ē) *intr.v.* **in•ter•mar•ried, in•ter•mar•ry•ing, in•ter•mar•ries. 1.** To marry someone of another religion, nationality, or ethnic group. **2.** To be bound together by marriage, as families, religious groups, or ethnic groups, for example. **3.** To marry someone who is a member of one's own family, clan, or tribe. —**in′ter•mar′riage** (ĭn′tər **măr′**ĭj) *n.*

in•ter•me•di•ar•y (ĭn′tər **mē′**dē ĕr′ē) *adj.* **1.** Acting as a mediator: *A labor negotiator plays an intermediary role between management and striking workers.* **2.** Existing or occurring between; intermediate: *A tadpole is an intermediary stage in the development of a frog.* —*n., pl.* **in•ter•me•di•ar•ies.** A person or group acting as a mediator between opposing parties to bring about an agreement.

in•ter•me•di•ate (ĭn′tər **mē′**dē ĭt) *adj.* Being or occurring between; in the middle: *Middle school is intermediate between high school and elementary school.* —*n.* Something intermediate.

in•ter•ment (ĭn **tûr′**mənt) *n.* The act of interring; burial.

in•ter•mez•zo (ĭn′tər **mĕt′**sō *or* ĭn′tər **mĕd′**zō) *n., pl.* **in•ter•mez•zos** or **in•ter•mez•zi** (ĭn′tər **mĕt′**sē or ĭn′tər **mĕd′**zē). **1.** A short piece of music played between sections of a long musical work. **2.** A brief entertainment between two acts of a play.

in•ter•mi•na•ble (ĭn **tûr′**mə nə bəl) *adj.* Having or seeming to have no end; endless: *fell asleep during the second act of the interminable play.* —**in•ter′mi•na•bly** *adv.*

in•ter•min•gle (ĭn′tər **mĭng′**gəl) *tr. & intr.v.* **in•ter•min•gled, in•ter•min•gling, in•ter•min•gles.**

To mix or become mixed together: *A party presents a good chance to intermingle with others.*

in•ter•mis•sion (ĭn′tər **mĭsh′**ən) *n.* An interval between periods of activity; a pause: *The orchestra took a short intermission during the concert.* See Synonyms at **pause.**

in•ter•mit•tent (ĭn′tər **mĭt′**nt) *adj.* Stopping and starting at intervals; not continuous: *The foghorn sounded intermittent blasts at intervals of 15 seconds.* **—in′ter•mit′tent•ly** *adv.*

in•ter•mix (ĭn′tər **mĭks′**) *tr. & intr.v.* **in•ter•mixed, in•ter•mix•ing, in•ter•mix•es.** To mix or become mixed together: *Oil and water do not intermix.*

in•tern (**ĭn′**tûrn′) *n.* An advanced student or recent graduate undergoing practical training, especially a recent medical school graduate who is undergoing supervised training in a hospital or clinic. *—v.* **in•terned, in•tern•ing, in•terns.** *—intr.* To train or serve as an intern. *—tr.* (*also* ĭn **tûrn′**). To detain or confine within a country or place, especially in wartime: *intern an enemy ship.* [First written down in 1879 in American English, from French *interne,* from Latin *internus,* internal.] **—in•tern′ment** *n.*

in•ter•nal (ĭn **tûr′**nəl) *adj.* **1.** Of or located within the limits or surface of something; inner; interior: *the internal workings of a clock.* **2.** Located or acting inside the body: *pills and other internal medicines.* **3.** Of or relating to domestic affairs within a country or an organization: *Environmental issues are no longer internal political matters but require global attention.* **—in•ter′nal•ly** *adv.*

in•ter•nal-com•bus•tion engine (ĭn **tûr′**nəl-kəm **bŭs′**chən) *n.* An engine whose fuel is burned inside the engine itself rather than in an outside furnace or burner. A gasoline or diesel engine is an internal-combution engine; a steam engine is not.

internal medicine *n.* The branch of medicine that deals with the diagnosis and nonsurgical treatment of diseases affecting the internal organs of the body.

in•ter•na•tion•al (ĭn′tər **năsh′**ə nəl) *adj.* Of, relating to, or between two or more nations: *The United Nations is an international organization.* **—in′ter•na′tion•al•ly** *adv.*

International Date Line *n.* An imaginary line through the Pacific Ocean roughly along the 180th meridian, agreed upon as the place where each new calendar day begins. The calendar day to the east of the line is one day earlier than to the west.

in•ter•na•tion•al•ism (ĭn′tər **năsh′**ə nə lĭz′əm) *n.* A policy or principle of cooperation among nations for mutual benefit.

in•ter•na•tion•al•ize (ĭn′tər **năsh′**ə nə līz′) *tr.v.* **in•ter•na•tion•al•ized, in•ter•na•tion•al•iz•ing, in•ter•na•tion•al•iz•es.** To put under international control; make international: *a peace treaty that internationalized the Panama Canal.*

in•ter•nec•ine (ĭn′tər **nĕs′**ēn′ *or* ĭn′tər **nĕs′**ĭn) *adj.* Destructive or fatal to both sides: *an internecine struggle for leadership of the party between the moderates and the liberals.*

in•tern•ee (ĭn′tûr **nē′**) *n.* A person who is interned or confined, especially a prisoner of war.

in•ter•nist (ĭn **tûr′**nĭst) *n.* A physician who specializes in internal medicine.

in•tern•ship (**ĭn′**tûrn shĭp′) *n.* A period of service as an intern.

in•ter•phase (**ĭn′**tər fāz′) *n.* The stage of a cell between two occurrences of mitosis, during which the chromosomes are duplicated.

in•ter•plan•e•tar•y (ĭn′tər **plăn′**ĭ tĕr′ē) *adj.* Located or occurring between planets; in the region of the planets: *interplanetary flight.*

in•ter•play (**ĭn′**tər plā′) *n.* Mutual action or influence; interaction: *The interplay between the two main characters provided most of the humor in the movie.*

in•ter•po•late (ĭn **tûr′**pə lāt′) *tr.v.* **in•ter•po•lat•ed, in•ter•po•lat•ing, in•ter•po•lates. 1.** In mathematics, to estimate (an unknown value, as of a logarithm or trigonometric function) between two known values. **2.** To change (a text) by inserting new material: *This manuscript has been so interpolated it is hard to recognize the original.* **3.** To insert or add (new material) to a text. [First written down in 1612 in Modern English, from Latin *interpolis,* refurbished.] **—in•ter′po•la′tion** *n.*

in•ter•pose (ĭn′tər **pōz′**) *v.* **in•ter•posed, in•ter•pos•ing, in•ter•pos•es.** *—tr.* **1.** To put between parts; insert: *Winter ice interposes a barrier between the harbor and the islands.* **2.** To interject (a remark or question) into a conversation. *—intr.* **1.** To come between. **2.** To come between parties in a dispute; intervene: *The babysitter interposed in the disputes between the children.* **—in′ter•po•si′tion** (ĭn′tər pə **zĭsh′**ən) *n.*

in•ter•pret (ĭn **tûr′**prĭt) *v.* **in•ter•pret•ed, in•ter•pret•ing, in•ter•prets.** *—tr.* **1.** To explain the meaning of: *The critic interprets the poem in an essay.* **2.** To understand in one's own way; construe: *We interpreted his smile to be an agreement.* **3.** To present the meaning of, especially through artistic performance: *an actor interpreting a role.* **4.** To translate (something). *—intr.* **1.** To serve as an interpreter for speakers of a foreign language. **2.** To offer an explanation. [First written down about 1384 in Middle English and spelled *interpreten,* from Latin *interpretārī,* from *interpres,* negotiator, explainer.]

in•ter•pre•ta•tion (ĭn tûr′prĭ **tā′**shən) *n.* **1.** The act or process of interpreting: *Interpretation of statistical data requires both training and care.* **2.** An explanation of the meaning of something, especially of a work of art: *Her interpretation of the movie left us with much to think about.* **3.** A performer's unique version of a work of art, such as a song or dance.

in•ter•pre•ta•tive (ĭn **tûr′**prĭ tā′tĭv) *adj.* Variant of **interpretive.**

in•ter•pret•er (ĭn **tûr′**prĭ tər) *n.* **1.** A person who translates orally from one language to another. **2.** A person who interprets or explains something.

in•ter•pre•tive (ĭn **tûr′**prĭ tĭv) also **in•ter•pre•ta•tive** (ĭn **tûr′**prĭ tā′tĭv) *adj.* Relating to or marked by interpretation; explanatory: *an interpretive comment.*

in•ter•ra•cial (ĭn′tər **rā′**shəl) *adj.* Relating to or involving different races: *an interracial committee.*

in•ter•reg•num (ĭn′tər **rĕg′**nəm) *n., pl.* **in•ter•reg•nums** or **in•ter•reg•na** (ĭn′tər **rĕg′**nə). The period between the end of one ruler's reign and the beginning of the next ruler's reign.

in•ter•re•late (ĭn′tər rĭ **lāt′**) *tr. & intr.v.* **in•ter•re•lat•ed, in•ter•re•lat•ing, in•ter•re•lates.** To place in or come into mutual relationship. **—in′ter•re•la′tion** *n.* **—in′ter•re•la′tion•ship′** *n.*

in•ter•ro•gate (ĭn **tĕr′**ə gāt′) *tr.v.* **in•ter•ro•gat•ed, in•ter•ro•gat•ing, in•ter•ro•gates.** To question formally and closely: *The police interrogated witnesses of the accident.* [First written down in 1483 in Middle English and spelled *enterrogate,* from Latin *interrogāre* : *inter-,* in the presence of + *rogāre,* to ask.] **—in•ter′ro•ga′tion** *n.* **—in•ter′ro•ga′tor** *n.*

interrogation point *n.* A question mark.

in•ter•rog•a•tive (ĭn′tə **rŏg′**ə tĭv) *adj.* **1.** Asking a question or having the nature of a question: *an interrogative sentence.* **2.** Used in asking a question: When, why, *and* where *are interrogative pronouns.*

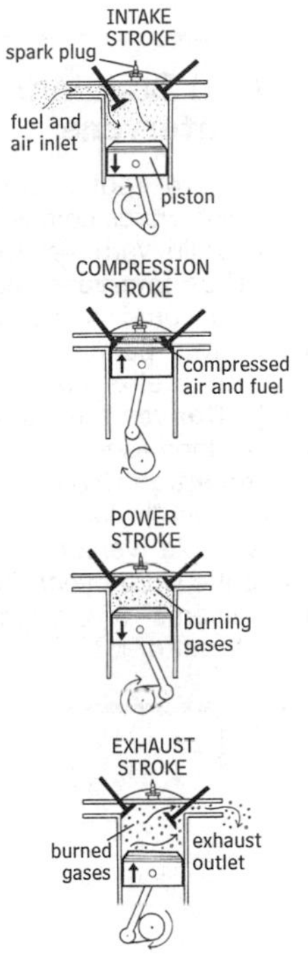

internal-combustion engine

ă	pat	oi	boy
ā	pay	ou	out
âr	care	o͝o	took
ä	father	o͞o	boot
ĕ	pet	ŭ	cut
ē	be	ûr	urge
ĭ	pit	th	thin
ī	pie	*th*	this
îr	pier	hw	whoop
ŏ	pot	zh	vision
ō	toe	ə	about
ô	paw	N	*French* bon

Word Building: intervene

The word root *–ven–* in English words comes from the Latin verb *venīre,* "to come." Thus **intervene** means literally "to come between, as between two people fighting" (using the prefix *inter–,* "between"). **Convene** means "to come together, as for a meeting or a **convention**" (*com–, con–,* "together, with"). *Venīre* has a past participle *ventum,* which provides the word *event,* literally an "outcome" (*ē–,* a form of *ex–,* "out, out of").

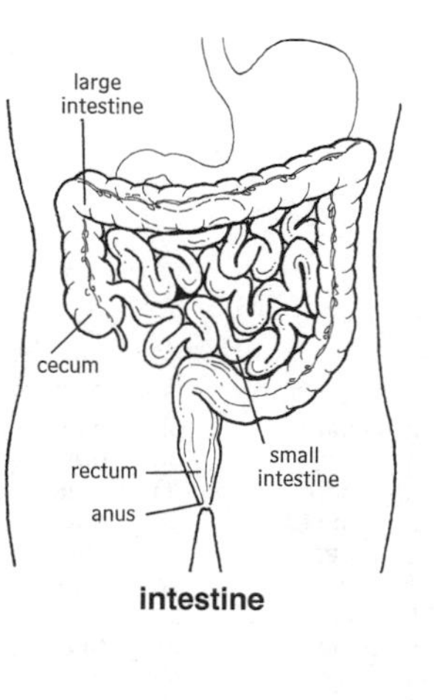

intestine

—*n.* **1.** A word or form used in asking a question. For example, in the questions *Where did you go?* and *Whom did you see?* the words *where* and *whom* are interrogatives. **2.** A question.

in•ter•rog•a•to•ry (ĭn′tə **rŏg′**ə tôr′ē) *adj.* Interrogative.

in•ter•rupt (ĭn′tə **rŭpt′**) *v.* **in•ter•rupt•ed, in•ter•rupt•ing, in•ter•rupts.** —*tr.* **1.** To hinder or stop the action of; break in on: *I was about to finish the joke when my brother interrupted me.* **2.** To break the continuity of: *Rain interrupted our baseball game.* —*intr.* To break in upon or stop something: *It is impolite to interrupt when others are talking.* [First written down before 1400 in Middle English and spelled *interrupten,* from Latin *interrumpere,* to break off.] **—in′ter•rup′tion** *n.*

in•ter•scho•las•tic (ĭn′tər skə **lăs′**tĭk) *adj.* Existing or conducted between or among schools: *an interscholastic tournament.*

in•ter•sect (ĭn′tər **sĕkt′**) *v.* **in•ter•sect•ed, in•ter•sect•ing, in•ter•sects.** —*tr.* To cut across or through; divide: *A fence intersects the pasture.* —*intr.* To cut across each other; overlap: *The road intersects with the highway north of town.* [First written down in 1615 in Modern English, from Latin *intersecāre* : *inter-,* between + *secāre,* to cut.]

in•ter•sec•tion (ĭn′tər **sĕk′**shən) *n.* **1.** The act or result of intersecting. **2.** (*also* **ĭn′**tər sĕk′shən). A place where two or more things intersect, especially a place where two or more roads cross. **3.** In geometry, the point where one line, surface, or solid crosses another: *The intersection of two planes determines a straight line.* **4.** In mathematics, the set that contains only those elements shared by two or more sets.

in•ter•sperse (ĭn′tər **spûrs′**) *tr.v.* **in•ter•spersed, in•ter•spers•ing, in•ter•spers•es. 1.** To scatter or insert here and there among other things: *The florist interspersed greens among the flowers.* **2.** To vary by distributing things here and there: *The magazine is interspersed with advertisements.*

in•ter•state (**ĭn′**tər stāt′) *adj.* Involving, existing between, or connecting two or more states: *An interstate highway runs between cities in different states.*

in•ter•stel•lar (ĭn′tər **stĕl′**ər) *adj.* Between or among the stars: *interstellar gases.*

in•ter•twine (ĭn′tər **twīn′**) *tr. & intr.v.* **in•ter•twined, in•ter•twin•ing, in•ter•twines.** To join or become joined by twining together: *She intertwined the strands into a braid. The dancers' arms intertwined.*

in•ter•val (**ĭn′**tər vəl) *n.* **1.** The amount of time between two events: *We ran laps at 30-second intervals.* **2.** The space between two objects, points, or units: *We set up hurdles at intervals of 15 yards around the track.* **3.** In mathematics and statistics, the set of all numbers between two given numbers. **4.** The difference in pitch between two musical tones. [First written down before 1325 in Middle English and spelled *intervalle,* from Latin *intervallum* : *inter-,* between + *vallum,* rampart.]

in•ter•vene (ĭn′tər **vēn′**) *intr.v.* **in•ter•vened, in•ter•ven•ing, in•ter•venes. 1.** To come or lie between two things: *The road goes nearly to the shore, but a farm intervenes.* **2.** To come between two events: *A period of calm intervened between stormy sessions of the legislature.* **3.a.** To come between so as to hinder or change a course of events: *The teacher intervened to settle the dispute.* **b.** To interfere, usually with force, in the affairs of another nation. [First written down in 1588 in Modern English, from Latin *intervenīre* : *inter-,* between + *venīre,* to come.] —SEE NOTE.

in•ter•ven•tion (ĭn′tər **vĕn′**shən) *n.* **1.** The act or an instance of intervening: *The governor's intervention saved the park from development.* **2.** Interference in the affairs of another nation, usually with force.

in•ter•view (**ĭn′**tər vyo͞o′) *n.* **1.** A face-to-face meeting for a specified purpose: *an interview for a job.* **2.a.** A conversation, such as one between a reporter and another person, for the purpose of obtaining information. **b.** An account or a broadcast of such information. —*tr.v.* **in•ter•viewed, in•ter•view•ing, in•ter•views.** To have an interview with: *The committee interviewed candidates for the job.* **—in′ter•view′er** *n.*

in•ter•weave (ĭn′tər **wēv′**) *v.* **in•ter•wove** (ĭn′tər**wōv′**), **in•ter•wo•ven** (ĭn′tər **wō′**vən), **inter•weav•ing, inter•weaves.** —*tr.* **1.** To weave together: *Cloth is made by interweaving threads.* **2.** To blend; intermix: *The author skillfully interweaves two plots in a single story.* —*intr.* To intertwine.

in•tes•tate (ĭn **tĕs′**tāt′ *or* ĭn **tĕs′**tĭt) *adj.* Having made no legal will: *a person who died intestate.*

in•tes•ti•nal (ĭn **tĕs′**tə nəl) *adj.* Of, relating to, or involving the intestines: *an intestinal parasite.* **—in•tes′ti•nal•ly** *adv.*

in•tes•tine (ĭn **tĕs′**tĭn) *n.* The part of the alimentary canal that extends from the stomach to the anus, consisting of the large intestine and small intestine.

in•ti (**ĭn′**tē) *n.* The basic monetary unit of Peru.

in•ti•ma•cy (**ĭn′**tə mə sē) *n., pl.* **in•ti•ma•cies. 1.** The condition of being intimate, especially personal closeness. **2.** An instance of being intimate.

in•ti•mate¹ (**ĭn′**tə mĭt) *adj.* **1.** Marked by close association or familiarity: *an intimate understanding of children.* **2.** Essential; innermost: *a person's intimate thoughts.* **3.** Very personal; private: *an intimate letter.* —*n.* A close friend or confidant. [First written down in 1632 in Modern English, from Latin *intimātus,* from *intimāre,* to make familiar with.] **—in′ti•mate•ly** *adv.*

in•ti•mate² (**ĭn′**tə māt′) *tr.v.* **in•ti•mat•ed, in•ti•mat•ing, in•ti•mates. 1.** To hint; imply: *He intimated that the award would go to someone in our class.* **2.** To announce; make known. [First written down in 1538 in Modern English, from Latin *intimāre,* to make known, from *intimus,* innermost.] **—in′ti•ma′tion** *n.*

in•tim•i•date (ĭn **tĭm′**ĭ dāt′) *tr.v.* **in•tim•i•dat•ed, in•tim•i•dat•ing, in•tim•i•dates.** To fill with fear; frighten or discourage: *The rough water intimidated us in our light canoe.* **—in•tim′i•da′tion** *n.* **—in•tim′i•da′tor** *n.*

in•to (**ĭn′**to͞o) *prep.* **1.** To the inside of: *going into the house.* **2.** So as to be in or within: *enter into an agreement.* **3.** To the action or occupation of: *go into banking.* **4.** To the condition or form of: *break into pieces.* **5.** To a time or place in the course of: *It's getting well into the week.* **6.** Toward; in the direction of: *looking into the distance.* **7.** Against: *run into a tree.* **8.** *Informal.* Interested in or involved with: *They are into health foods.* **9.** As a divisor of: *5 into 30 is 6.*

in•tol•er•a•ble (ĭn **tŏl′**ər ə bəl) *adj.* Impossible to tolerate; unbearable: *We found the noise in the sawmill intolerable.* **—in•tol′er•a•bly** *adv.*

in•tol•er•ance (ĭn **tŏl′**ər əns) *n.* The quality or condition of being intolerant.

in•tol•er•ant (ĭn **tŏl′**ər ənt) *adj.* **1.** Unwilling to tolerate different opinions or beliefs, or persons of other races, religions, or backgrounds; prejudiced. **2.** Unable or unwilling to endure or tolerate: *Allergies can make a person intolerant of certain foods.*

in•to•na•tion (ĭn′tə **nā′**shən) *n.* **1.** The way in which the speaking voice rises or falls in pitch in order to convey meaning. **2.** An intoned utterance. **3.** The manner in which musical tones are sung or played, especially with regard to accuracy of pitch.

in•tone (ĭn tōn′) *tr. & intr.v.* **in•toned, in•ton•ing, in•tones.** To recite in a singing or chanting voice: *The choir intoned prayers at several points during the church service.*

in•tox•i•cant (ĭn tŏk′sĭ kənt) *n.* Something that intoxicates, especially an alcoholic drink.

in•tox•i•cate (ĭn tŏk′sĭ kāt′) *tr.v.* **in•tox•i•cat•ed, in•tox•i•cat•ing, in•tox•i•cates. 1.** To cause (a person) to lose control of physical or mental powers by means of a chemical substance, such as alcohol. **2.** To fill with great excitement or enthusiasm; exhilarate: *The grandeur of the mountain scenery intoxicated the tourists.* [First written down about 1450 in Middle English, to poison, from Latin *toxicum*, poison.]

in•tox•i•ca•tion (ĭn tŏk′sĭ kā′shən) *n.* **1.** The condition of being intoxicated, especially drunkenness. **2.** Great excitement or enthusiasm.

intra– *pref.* A prefix that means inside of or within: *intravenous.*

in•trac•ta•ble (ĭn trăk′tə bəl) *adj.* **1.** Difficult to manage or control. **2.** Difficult to fix, solve, or cure: *an intractable problem.* **—in•trac′ta•bly** *adv.*

in•tra•mu•ral (ĭn′trə myo͝or′əl) *adj.* Involving members of the same school or institution: *our school's intramural athletic program.*

in•tran•si•gent (ĭn trăn′sə jənt *or* ĭn trăn′zə jənt) *adj.* Refusing to compromise; stubborn. **—in•tran′si•gence** *n.* **—in•tran′si•gent•ly** *adv.*

in•tran•si•tive (ĭn trăn′sĭ tĭv *or* ĭn trăn′zĭ tĭv) *adj.* Of or relating to a verb that does not require a direct object to complete its meaning. For example, in the sentence *The bell rang loudly,* the verb *rang* is intransitive. **—in•tran′si•tive•ly** *adv.* —SEE NOTE at **verb.**

in•tra•ve•nous (ĭn′trə vē′nəs) *adj.* Within or into a vein: *an intravenous injection of serum.* **—in′tra•ve′nous•ly** *adv.*

in•trep•id (ĭn trĕp′ĭd) *adj.* Brave; bold; fearless: *Early explorers of Antarctica were intrepid and resourceful.* **—in′tre•pid′i•ty** (ĭn′trə pĭd′ĭ tē) *n.* **—in•trep′id•ly** *adv.*

in•tri•ca•cy (ĭn′trĭ kə sē) *n., pl.* **in•tri•ca•cies. 1.** The quality or condition of being intricate; complexity: *The intricacy of a maze makes it hard to follow.* **2.** Something intricate; a complication: *The intricacies of human anatomy require years of study.*

in•tri•cate (ĭn′trĭ kĭt) *adj.* **1.** Having a compliment structure or pattern; elaborate: *the intricate arrangement of gears in a clock.* **2.** Difficult to understand: *The document is so intricate that it requires a great deal of study.* [First written down before 1425 in Middle English, from Latin *intrīcāre*, to entangle, perplex, from *trīcae*, perplexities.] **—in′tri•cate•ly** *adv.*

in•trigue (ĭn′trēg′ *or* ĭn trēg′) *n.* **1.a.** Plotting or scheming carried on in secret. **b.** A secret plot or scheme. **2.** A secret love affair. —*v.* (ĭn trēg′). **in•trigued, in•trigu•ing, in•trigues.** —*intr.* To plot or scheme secretly: *The political rivals intrigued against one another.* —*tr.* To excite the interest and curiosity of; fascinate: *The mystery of hibernation has long intrigued biologists.* [First written down in 1612 in Modern English, from Italian *intrigare*, to plot, from Latin *intrīcāre*, to entangle.]

in•trigu•ing (ĭn trē′gĭng) *adj.* Exciting the interest or curiosity; fascinating. See Synonyms at **interesting.**

in•trin•sic (ĭn trĭn′zĭk *or* ĭn trĭn′sĭk) *adj.* Of or relating to the basic nature of a thing; essential; inherent: *He recommended the adventure movie on its intrinsic merits, not on its special effects.* **—in•trin′si•cal•ly** *adv.*

in•tro (ĭn′trō′) *n., pl.* **in•tros.** *Informal.* An introduction.

intro– *pref.* A prefix that means inward: *introvert.*

in•tro•duce (ĭn′trə do͞os′ *or* ĭn′trə dyo͞os′) *tr.v.* **in•tro•duced, in•tro•duc•ing, in•tro•duc•es. 1.** To present (someone) by name to another in order to establish an acquaintance: *Please introduce me to your old friend.* **2.** To bring into use or practice: *That company has introduced several new products.* **3.** To provide (someone) with a first experience of something: *My father introduced me to fishing.* **4.** To present for consideration: *introduce legislation in Congress.* **5.** To talk or write about (something) in advance: *The professor introduced the movie with a short lecture.* **6.** To bring or put (something) in a new place or environment; add: *European starlings were introduced to North America.* **7.** To put in; insert or inject: *introduce a new character into a story.* [First written down before 1425 in Middle English and spelled *introducen*, to bring into, from Latin *intrōdūcere* : *intrō-*, in + *dūcere*, to lead.] **—in′tro•duc′er** *n.*

in•tro•duc•tion (ĭn′trə dŭk′shən) *n.* **1.** The act or process of introducing: *The introduction of printing made books cheaper and more widely available.* **2.** Something introduced or brought into use: *Like many European introductions, the starling has established itself widely in North America.* **3.** The first part of a book, speech, or musical composition. **4.** A first book in a course of study: *This book is an introduction to physics.*

in•tro•duc•to•ry (ĭn′trə dŭk′tə rē) *adj.* Serving to introduce a subject or person: *a few introductory remarks by the speaker.*

in•tro•spec•tion (ĭn′trə spĕk′shən) *n.* The examination of one's own thoughts and feelings.

in•tro•spec•tive (ĭn′trə spĕk′tĭv) *adj.* Given to examining one's own thoughts and feelings: *an introspective philosopher.* **—in′tro•spec′tive•ly** *adv.*

in•tro•vert (ĭn′trə vûrt′) *n.* A person interested mainly in his or her own thoughts and feelings rather than other people or external circumstances.

in•trude (ĭn tro͞od′) *v.* **in•trud•ed, in•trud•ing, in•trudes.** —*tr.* To put or force in without invitation: *They intruded their opinions into our conversation.* —*intr.* To break or come in without being wanted or asked: *The new neighbors were always intruding on her quiet afternoons.* [First written down about 1422 in Middle English and spelled *intruden*, from Latin *intrūdere*, to thrust in : *in-*, in + *trūdere*, to thrust.] **—in•trud′er** *n.*

in•tru•sion (ĭn tro͞o′zhən) *n.* The act of intruding: *Your barging into my room is an intrusion on my privacy.*

in•tru•sive (ĭn tro͞o′sĭv) *adj.* Intruding or tending to intrude: *a rude intrusive question.* **—in•tru′sive•ly** *adv.*

in•tu•i•tion (ĭn′to͞o ĭsh′ən *or* ĭn′tyo͞o ĭsh′ən) *n.* **1.** The power of knowing or understanding something without reasoning or proof: *My intuition tells me that the experiment will work if we try it again.* **2.** Knowledge gained immediately without reasoning or proof; an insight.

in•tu•i•tive (ĭn to͞o′ĭ tĭv *or* ĭn tyo͞o′ĭ tĭv) *adj.* **1.** Of or based on intuition: *an intuitive understanding of musical harmony.* **2.** Having or showing intuition: *an intuitive mind.* **—in•tu′i•tive•ly** *adv.*

In•u•it (ĭn′yo͞o ĭt) *n., pl.* **Inuit** or **In•u•its. 1.** A member of any of the Eskimo peoples of North America and especially of Arctic Canada and Greenland. **2.** Any or all of the languages of the Inuit.

in•un•date (ĭn′ŭn dāt′) *tr.v.* **in•un•dat•ed, in•un•dat•ing, in•un•dates. 1.** To cover with water; flood: *The storm tide inundated the waterfront.* **2.**

ă	pat	oi	boy
ā	pay	ou	out
âr	care	o͝o	took
ä	father	o͞o	boot
ĕ	pet	ŭ	cut
ē	be	ûr	urge
ĭ	pit	th	thin
ī	pie	*th*	this
îr	pier	hw	whoop
ŏ	pot	zh	vision
ō	toe	ə	about
ô	paw	N	*French* bon

To overwhelm as if with a flood: *The store was inundated with shoppers during the holiday sale.* [First written down in 1623 in Modern English, from Latin *inundāre* : *in-*, in + *unda*, wave.] **—in′un•da′tion** *n.*

in•ure (ĭn yo͝or′) *tr.v.* **in•ured, in•ur•ing, in•ures.** To make used to; accustom: *Severe winters inured the pioneers to cold.*

in•vade (ĭn vād′) *v.* **in•vad•ed, in•vad•ing, in•vades.** *—tr.* **1.** To enter by force in order to attack or conquer: *The Romans invaded Britain.* **2.** To enter and spread harm through: *Viruses invade cells of the body.* **3.** To enter as if to take possession of; overrun: *On winter weekends, skiers invade the mountain town.* **4.** To intrude on; violate: *invade someone's privacy.* *—intr.* To make an invasion. **—in•vad′er** *n.*

in•va•lid[1] (ĭn′və lĭd) *n.* A person disabled by disease or injury. *—adj.* **1.** Disabled by disease or injury. **2.** Of, relating to, or intended for invalids. *—tr.v.* **in•va•lid•ed, in•va•lid•ing, in•va•lids.** To disable physically. [First written down in 1707 in Modern English, from *invalid*, not valid.]

in•val•id[2] (ĭn văl′ĭd) *adj.* Not valid or proper; without force, foundation, or authority: *Unless a contract is signed, it is invalid.* [First written down in 1635 in Modern English, from Latin *invalidus*, weak : *in-*, not + *validus*, strong.] **—in•val′id•ly** *adv.*

in•val•i•date (ĭn văl′ĭ dāt′) *tr.v.* **in•val•i•dat•ed, in•val•i•dat•ing, in•val•i•dates.** To make invalid or worthless; nullify: *The lack of a signature invalidated the check.* **—in•val′i•da′tion** *n.*

in•val•u•a•ble (ĭn văl′yo͞o ə bəl) *adj.* Of a value greater than can be measured; priceless: *invaluable art treasures.* **—in•val′u•a•bly** *adv.*

in•var•i•a•ble (ĭn vâr′ē ə bəl) *adj.* Not changing or varying; constant: *the invariable return of spring.* **—in•var′i•a•bil′i•ty** *n.* **—in•var′i•a•bly** *adv.*

in•va•sion (ĭn vā′zhən) *n.* **1.** The act of invading, especially the entry of an armed force in order to conquer another country. **2.** An intrusion or a violation: *The loud music from next door is an invasion of our privacy.*

in•va•sive (ĭn vā′sĭv) *adj.* **1.** Tending to invade, especially tending to invade healthy cells or tissues. **2.** Involving entry into a part of the body, as by surgical incision: *invasive techniques for curing a heart defect.* **3.** Tending to intrude: *was asked to stop his invasive snooping.*

in•vec•tive (ĭn vĕk′tĭv) *n.* Harsh words used to attack; abusive language.

in•veigh (ĭn vā′) *intr.v.* **in•veighed, in•veigh•ing, in•veighs.** To protest by speaking out violently and bitterly: *The tenants inveighed against higher rents.*

in•vei•gle (ĭn vā′gəl *or* ĭn vē′gəl) *tr.v.* **in•vei•gled, in•vei•gling, in•vei•gles.** **1.** To win over by flattery or artful talk: *The saleswoman inveigled me into buying a ring.* **2.** To obtain by flattery or artful talk: *He inveigled free passes from the ticket seller.* **—in•vei′gler** *n.*

in•vent (ĭn vĕnt′) *tr.v.* **in•vent•ed, in•vent•ing, in•vents.** **1.** To produce or create (something new) by using the imagination: *Thomas Edison invented the light bulb.* **2.** To make up; devise in the mind: *They invented an excuse for having to leave earlier than usual.* [First written down about 1475 in Middle English, from Latin *invenīre*, to find : *in-*, on, upon + *venīre*, to come.]

in•ven•tion (ĭn vĕn′shən) *n.* **1.** Something invented, as a new device or process: *The computer is a revolutionary modern invention.* **2.** The act of inventing: *The invention of movable type made books widely available.* **3.** The power or ability to invent: *Only a mystery writer of great invention could create so complicated a plot.* **4.** Something that is made up, especially a falsehood. **—in•ven′tor** *n.*

in•ven•tive (ĭn vĕn′tĭv) *adj.* **1.** Skillful at inventing; creative: *An inventive writer is able to keep the reader's attention.* **2.** Of, relating to, or characterized by invention. **—in•ven′tive•ly** *adv.*

in•ven•to•ry (ĭn′vən tôr′ē) *n., pl.* **in•ven•to•ries.** **1.** A detailed list of goods or possessions, especially a survey of all goods and materials in stock. **2.** The process of making such a survey or list. **3.** The supply of goods on hand; stock: *The store's inventory is getting low.* *—tr.v.* **in•ven•to•ried, in•ven•to•ry•ing, in•ven•to•ries.** To make a detailed list of: *Before reordering, the store inventoried its stock.*

in•verse (ĭn vûrs′ *or* ĭn′vûrs′) *adj.* Opposite or reversed, as in character or order: *CBA is ABC in inverse order.* *—n.* (ĭn′vûrs′ *or* ĭn vûrs′). **1.** Something exactly opposite in order or character. **2.** One of a pair of elements in a set whose result under the operation of the set is the identity element. For example, the inverse of 5 under multiplication is $1/5$, since $5 \times 1/5 = 1$. The inverse of 5 under addition is -5, since $5 + -5 = 0$. **—in•verse′ly** *adv.*

in•ver•sion (ĭn vûr′zhən *or* ĭn vûr′shən) *n.* **1.** The act of inverting or the condition of being inverted. **2.** Something inverted.

in•vert (ĭn vûrt′) *tr.v.* **in•vert•ed, in•vert•ing, in•verts.** **1.** To turn upside down: *invert an hourglass.* **2.** To reverse the order, position, or condition of: *A mirror inverts the placement of things in its reflection.* [First written down in 1533 in Modern English, from Latin *invertere* : *in-*, in + *vertere*, to turn.]

in•ver•te•brate (ĭn vûr′tə brĭt *or* ĭn vûr′tə brāt′) *adj.* Having no backbone or spinal column: *invertebrate animals.* *—n.* An animal, such as an insect or a worm, that has no backbone or vertebrae.

in•vest (ĭn vĕst′) *v.* **in•vest•ed, in•vest•ing, in•vests.** *—tr.* **1.** To put (money) into something, such as property, stocks, or a business, in order to earn interest or make a profit: *Many people invest their savings in mutual funds.* **2.** To devote or spend for future advantage or benefit: *The candidates invested much time and energy in the election campaign.* **3.** To entrust with a right or power: *The Constitution invests Congress with the power to make laws.* **4.** To put in office with a formal ceremony: *The President is invested with an inauguration.* **5.** To provide with a certain quality: *The writer invested the novel with many historical details.* *—intr.* To make an investment: *The bank invested heavily in real estate.* [First written down about 1533 in Modern English, from Latin *investīre*, to clothe, surround.] **—in•ves′tor** *n.*

in•ves•ti•gate (ĭn vĕs′tĭ gāt′) *v.* **in•ves•ti•gat•ed, in•ves•ti•gat•ing, in•ves•ti•gates.** *—tr.* To look into or search carefully for facts, knowledge, or information: *The police investigate crimes to determine who commits them.* *—intr.* To make an investigation. [First written down about 1510 in Modern English, from Latin *investīgāre* : *in-*, in + *vestīgāre*, to track (from *vestīgium*, footprint).]

in•ves•ti•ga•tion (ĭn vĕs′tĭ gā′shən) *n.* A careful examination or search in order to discover facts or gain information.

in•ves•ti•ga•tor (ĭn vĕs′tĭ gā′tər) *n.* A person who investigates, especially a detective.

in•ves•ti•ture (ĭn vĕs′tə cho͝or′ *or* ĭn vĕs′tə chər) *n.* The act or formal ceremony putting a person in a high office or position of authority.

in•vest•ment (ĭn vĕst′mənt) *n.* **1.** The act of investing money for profit or advantage: *The company made an investment in new equipment.* **2.** A sum of money invested: *interest earned on an investment.* **3.** Something in which money is invested: *Land is a* *good investment.* **4.** A commitment, as of time or effort: *I've got a big investment in music lessons.*

in•vet•er•ate (ĭn vĕt′ər ĭt) *adj.* **1.** Fixed in a habit or practice; habitual: *An inveterate reader needs no incentive to pick up a good book.* **2.** Firmly established for a long time; deep-rooted: *Inveterate prejudice is resistant to change or reform.*

in•vid•i•ous (ĭn vĭd′ē əs) *adj.* **1.** Likely to stir up envy or resentment: *Invidious comparisons between the two paintings made it difficult for the artists to remain friends.* **2.** Containing a slight; biased: *Many invidious employment restrictions have been outlawed.* [First written down in 1606 in Modern English, from Latin *invidia*, envy.] **—in•vid′i•ous•ly** *adv.*

in•vig•or•ate (ĭn vĭg′ə rāt′) *tr.v.* **in•vig•or•at•ed, in•vig•or•at•ing, in•vig•or•ates.** To fill with energy, strength, or vigor: *The cool autumn air invigorated us.* **—in•vig′or•a′tion** *n.*

in•vin•ci•ble (ĭn vĭn′sə bəl) *adj.* Incapable of being defeated or overcome: *an invincible army; invincible courage.* **—in•vin′ci•bil′i•ty** *n.* **—in•vin′ci•bly** *adv.*

in•vi•o•la•ble (ĭn vī′ə lə bəl) *adj.* **1.** Regarded as sacred and not to be violated: *an inviolable promise.* **2.** Incapable or being assaulted or trespassed: *an inviolable castle.* **—in•vi′o•la•bly** *adv.*

in•vi•o•late (ĭn vī′ə lĭt) *adj.* Not violated or broken; intact: *Personal integrity requires inviolate honesty in dealing with others.*

in•vis•i•ble (ĭn vĭz′ə bəl) *adj.* Impossible to see; not visible: *Air is colorless and invisible.* **—in•vis′i•bil′i•ty** *n.* **—in•vis′i•bly** *adv.*

in•vi•ta•tion (ĭn′vĭ tā′shən) *n.* **1.** A spoken or written request for a person to come somewhere or do something: *an invitation to a party.* **2.** The act of inviting.

in•vite (ĭn vīt′) *tr.v.* **in•vit•ed, in•vit•ing, in•vites.** **1.** To ask (a person or persons) politely to come somewhere or do something: *invite guests to a party.* **2.** To ask; request: *The author invited questions from the audience.* **3.** To tend to bring on; provoke: *Exercising too much invites injury.* **4.** To tempt, lure, or attract: *After days of rain, the bright sun invited us outside.* [First written down in 1533 in Modern English, from Latin *invītāre*.]

in•vit•ing (ĭn vī′tĭng) *adj.* Attractive; tempting: *A swimming pool looks inviting on a hot day.* **—in•vit′ing•ly** *adv.*

in vi•tro (ĭn vē′trō) *adv. & adj.* In an artificial environment, such as a test tube; not inside a living organism: *grow tissue in vitro.*

in vi•vo (vē′vō) *adv. & adj.* Inside a living organism: *test a new drug in vivo.*

in•vo•ca•tion (ĭn′və kā′shən) *n.* **1.** The act or an instance of invoking, especially an appeal for help from a higher power: *ancient peoples' invocation of their gods for a bountiful harvest.* **2.** A prayer or an appeal used in invoking help or protection, as at the opening of a religious service. **3.** A set of words spoken as a magic charm to bring forth a spirit.

in•voice (ĭn′vois′) *n.* A detailed list of goods shipped to a buyer, with an account of all costs and charges. *—tr.v.* **in•voiced, in•voic•ing, in•voic•es.** To make an invoice of; bill: *The company invoiced the shipment.* [First written down in 1560 in Modern English, from *invoyes*, things sent, from French *envoyer*, to send.]

in•voke (ĭn vōk′) *tr.v.* **in•voked, in•vok•ing, in•vokes.** **1.** To call on for help or protection: *Viking mariners invoked their gods before long voyages at sea.* **2.** To ask or call for earnestly: *The defendant invoked the mercy of the court.* **3.** To use or apply: *In defending their right to protest, the lawyer invoked the Constitution.* **4.** To call up (a spirit) with magic words or spells. [First written down before 1449 in Middle English and spelled *envoken*, from Latin *invocāre* : *in-*, in, on + *vocāre*, to call.]

in•vol•un•tar•y (ĭn vŏl′ən tĕr′ē) *adj.* **1.** Not subject to conscious control; automatic: *Sneezing is involuntary.* **2.** Not done willingly or on purpose; unintentional or accidental: *an involuntary gesture; an involuntary mishap.* **—in•vol′un•tar′i•ly** *adv.*

in•volve (ĭn vŏlv′) *tr.v.* **in•volved, in•volv•ing, in•volves.** **1.** To contain as a part; include: *The recipe involves flour, eggs, and milk.* **2.** To have as a necessary feature or outcome; entail: *His new job involves a lot of travel.* **3.** To draw in; mix up; embroil: *By asking my opinion, he involved me in their argument.* **4.** To hold the interest of; absorb: *The children were completely involved in their game.* [First written down before 1382 in Middle English and spelled *involven*, from Latin *involvere*, to enwrap : *in-*, in + *volvere*, to roll, turn.] **—in•volve′ment** *n.*

in•volved (ĭn vŏlvd′) *adj.* Complicated; complex; intricate: *a long involved sentence.*

in•vul•ner•a•ble (ĭn vŭl′nər ə bəl) *adj.* Impossible to attack, damage, or hurt: *an invulnerable fort; an invulnerable argument.* **—in•vul′ner•a•bil′i•ty** *n.* **—in•vul′ner•a•bly** *adv.*

in•ward (ĭn′wərd) *adj.* **1.** Directed toward the inside: *an inward rush of water into the submarine's holding tanks.* **2.** Located on the inside; inner: *the inward surface of the fuel tank.* **3.** Of, relating to, or existing in the thoughts or mind: *inward feelings.* *—adv.* **1.** Toward the inside or center: *The door swung inward.* **2.** Toward one's own mind or self: *His thoughts turned inward.* **—in′wards** *adv.*

in•ward•ly (ĭn′wərd lē) *adv.* **1.** On or in the inside; internally. **2.** To oneself; privately: *chuckling inwardly.*

i•o•dide (ī′ə dīd′) *n.* A chemical compound of iodine with another element or radical.

i•o•dine (ī′ə dīn′ *or* ī′ə dĭn) *n.* **1.** *Symbol* **I** A nonmetallic grayish-black element of the halogen group. In the body, iodine occurs as part of the thyroid hormones which are secreted by the thyroid gland and control the rate of growth. Atomic number 53. See table at **element.** **2.** An antiseptic solution of iodine and either sodium iodide (NaI) or potassium iodide (KI) dissolved in alcohol.

i•o•dize (ī′ə dīz′) *tr.v.* **i•o•dized, i•o•diz•ing, i•o•diz•es.** To treat or combine with iodine or an iodide: *iodize table salt.*

i•on (ī′ən *or* ī′ŏn′) *n.* An atom or a group of atoms that has an electric charge. Positive ions are formed by the loss of electrons; negative ions are formed by the gain of electrons. [First written down in 1834 in Modern English, from Greek *ion*, something that goes, from *ienai*, to go.]

–ion *suff.* A suffix that means: **1.** Action or process: *completion.* **2.** Result of an action or a process: *indentation.* **3.** State or condition: *elation.*

I•o•ni•a (ī ō′nē ə). An ancient region of western Asia Minor along the coast of the Aegean Sea. Greek settlers lived here before 1000 B.C. **—I•o′ni•an** *adj. & n.*

i•on•ic (ī ŏn′ĭk) *adj.* Of or containing ions.

I•on•ic (ī ŏn′ĭk) *adj.* **1.** Of or belonging to an order of ancient Greek and Roman architecture characterized by columns with two decorative scrolls at the top. **2.** Of or relating to ancient Ionia or the Ionians.

i•on•ize (ī′ə nīz′) *v.* **i•on•ized, i•on•iz•ing, i•on•iz•es.** *—tr.* To produce ions in: *Lightning ionizes the air it moves through.* *—intr.* To break apart or change into ions: *Acids, bases, and salts ionize when they are dissolved in a solution.* **—i′on•i•za′tion** (ī′ə nĭ zā′shən) *n.*

Ionic
Ionic style column

ă	pat	oi	boy
ā	pay	ou	out
âr	care	ŏŏ	took
ä	father	ōō	boot
ĕ	pet	ŭ	cut
ē	be	ûr	urge
ĭ	pit	th	thin
ī	pie	*th*	this
îr	pier	hw	whoop
ŏ	pot	zh	vision
ō	toe	ə	about
ô	paw	N	*French* bon

Iowa[2]

The name of the state of **Iowa** comes from the Iowa River, which had been named by French settlers for an American Indian people who lived on its banks. The French learned the name of the Iowa, earlier pronounced [ī′ə wā′], from the Illinois, who had in turn adapted it from a Sioux designation meaning "sleepy ones."

iris

Irish terrier

i•on•o•sphere (ī ŏn′ə sfîr′) *n.* The region of the atmosphere between the mesosphere and exosphere, extending about 30 miles (50 kilometers) to more than 250 miles (400 kilometers) above the earth. It is composed of layers of ionized gases that assist in the transmission of certain radio waves over long distances.

i•o•ta (ī ō′tə) *n.* **1.** The ninth letter of the Greek alphabet, written Ι, ι. In English it is represented as *I, i.* **2.** A very small amount; a bit: *There is not an iota of truth in that gossip.*

IOU (ī′ō yo͞o′) *n., pl.* **IOU's** or **IOUs.** A written promise to pay a debt, bearing the letters IOU, which stand for "I owe you," followed by the amount owed.

I•o•wa[1] (ī′ə wə) *n., pl.* **Iowa** or **I•o•was.** A member of a Native American people formerly living in Iowa and Minnesota, with descendants living in Nebraska, Kansas, and Oklahoma.

I•o•wa[2] (ī′ə wə). A state of the north-central United States north of Missouri. It was admitted as the 29th state in 1846. The area was inhabited in prehistoric times by a people known as the Mound Builders. Capital, Des Moines. Population, 2,787,424. —See Note.

ip•e•cac (ĭp′ĭ kăk′) *n.* A medicine prepared from the root of a South American shrub, used chiefly to induce vomiting. [First written down in 1710 in Modern English, from Tupi *ipekaaguéne.*]

IQ or **I.Q.** *abbr.* An abbreviation of intelligence quotient.

Ir The symbol for the element **iridium.**

ir– *pref.* Variant of **in–**[1].

I•ran (ĭ răn′ *or* ĭ rän′). Formerly **Per•sia** (pûr′zhə *or* pûr′shə). A country of southwest Asia east of Iraq. The region was first inhabited about 4000 B.C. The name of the country was officially changed to Iran in 1935. Tehran is the capital and the largest city. Population, 40,777,000. **—I•ra′ni•an** (ĭ rā′nē ən *or* ĭ rä′nē ən) *adj. & n.*

I•raq (ĭ răk′ *or* ĭ räk′). A country of southwest Asia north of Saudi Arabia. Iraq is the site of a number of ancient Mesopotamian civilizations. It became an independent kingdom in 1921 and a republic in 1958. Baghdad is the capital and the largest city. Population, 15,584,987. **—I•ra′qi** *adj. & n.*

i•ras•ci•ble (ĭ răs′ə bəl *or* ī răs′ə bəl) *adj.* Easily angered; highly irritable: *The long trip made the children very irascible.* **—i•ras′ci•bly** *adv.*

i•rate (ī rāt′ *or* ī′rāt′) *adj.* Angry; enraged: *A group of irate citizens turned out to protest the tax increase.* **—i•rate′ly** *adv.*

ire (īr) *n.* Anger; wrath. [First written down before 1300 in Middle English, from Latin *īra.*]

ire•ful (īr′fəl) *adj.* Full of ire; wrathful. **—ire′ful•ly** *adv.*

Ire•land (īr′lənd). An island in the northern Atlantic Ocean west of Great Britain. After a civil war (1919–1921) the island was split into the independent Irish Free State (now Ireland) and Northern Ireland, which is joined with Great Britain.

ir•i•des•cence (ĭr′ĭ dĕs′əns) *n.* The quality or state of being iridescent.

ir•i•des•cent (ĭr′ĭ dĕs′ənt) *adj.* Showing a display of lustrous colors: *iridescent soap bubbles.* [First written down in 1796 in Modern English, from Latin *īris,* rainbow.] **—ir′i•des′cent•ly** *adv.*

i•rid•i•um (ĭ rĭd′ē əm) *n. Symbol* **Ir** A yellowish, very hard and brittle metallic element, used as an alloy with platinum in jewelry. Atomic number 77. See table at **element.**

i•ris (ī′rĭs) *n., pl.* **i•ris•es** or **i•ri•des** (ī′rĭ dēz′ *or* ĭr′ĭ dēz′). **1.** The colored part around the pupil of the eye, located between the cornea and lens. The iris regulates the amount of light entering the eye. **2.** Any of numerous plants having long sword-shaped leaves and showy flowers of various colors. [First written down in 1373 in Middle English, from Greek.]

I•rish (ī′rĭsh) *adj.* Of or relating to Ireland or its people, language, or culture. *—n.* **1.** The people of Ireland. **2.** Irish Gaelic.

Irish Gaelic *n.* The Celtic language of Ireland.

I•rish•man (ī′rĭsh mən) *n.* A man of Irish birth or ancestry.

Irish Sea. An arm of the northern Atlantic Ocean between Ireland and Great Britain.

Irish setter *n.* Any of a breed of setters having a silky reddish coat.

Irish terrier *n.* Any of a breed of terriers having a wiry brown coat.

I•rish•wom•an (ī′rĭsh wo͝om′ən) *n.* A woman of Irish birth or ancestry.

irk (ûrk) *tr.v.* **irked, irk•ing, irks.** To annoy, bother, or irritate: *Nothing irks a busy person so much as to be kept waiting.* [First written down about 1330 in Middle English and spelled *irken,* to weary, possibly from Old Norse *yrkja,* to work.]

irk•some (ûrk′səm) *adj.* Tiresome; tedious; annoying: *irksome paperwork.* **—irk′some•ly** *adv.* **—irk′some•ness** *n.*

i•ron (ī′ərn) *n.* **1.** *Symbol* **Fe** A hard, gray, brittle metallic element that can be magnetized and from which steel is made. Iron occurs in red blood cells, helping to carry oxygen to all parts of the body. Atomic number 26. See table at **element. 2.a.** A metal appliance with a handle and flat bottom, used when heated to press wrinkles from cloth. **b.** An implement made of iron or a similar metal: *a branding iron; a curling iron.* **3. irons.** Shackles; fetters: *a prisoner restrained by handcuffs and leg irons.* **4.** A golf club with a metal head. **5.** Great strength, firmness, or hardness: *a grip of iron; a will of iron.* *—adj.* **1.** Very hard, strong, or determined: *an iron fist; an iron will.* **2.** Made of or containing iron: *an iron gate.* *—v.* **i•roned, i•ron•ing, i•rons.** *—tr.* To press or smooth with a heated iron: *iron a shirt.* *—intr.* To press clothes with a heated iron: *I ironed all morning.* ***—idiom.*** **iron out.** To settle through discussion or compromise; work out. [First written down before 830 in Old English and spelled *īren.*]

Iron Age *n.* The period in human history following the Bronze Age, marked by the introduction of iron implements and weapons. The Iron Age in Europe began around the eighth century B.C.

i•ron•clad (ī′ərn klăd′) *adj.* **1.** Covered with iron plates for protection: *an ironclad ship.* **2.** Not easily broken or changed; fixed: *an ironclad rule.* *—n.* A 19th-century warship with protective metal plates.

iron curtain *n.* The military and political barrier separating the Soviet Union and the countries under its influence from the western European nations after World War II.

i•ron•ic (ī rŏn′ĭk) *adj.* Containing or expressing irony: *an ironic comment.* **—i•ron′i•cal•ly** *adv.*

i•ron•ing board (ī′ər nĭng) *n.* A padded board, usually on collapsible legs, for ironing clothing.

iron lung *n.* A metal tank enclosing the entire body except the head and providing artificial respiration through changes in internal air pressure when normal breathing is impaired.

i•ron•wood (ī′ərn wo͝od′) *n.* **1.** Any of numerous trees having very hard wood. **2.** The wood of such a tree.

i•ron•work (ī′ərn wûrk′) *n.* Work in iron, such as gratings and rails.

i•ron•work•er (ī′ərn wûr′kər) *n.* **1.** A person who makes iron or iron articles. **2.** A construction worker who builds steel structures.

i•ron•works (ī′ərn wûrks′) *pl.n. (used with a singular or plural verb).* A place where iron is made or articles made of iron are produced.

i•ro•ny (ī′rə nē *or* ī′ər nē) *n., pl.* **i•ro•nies. 1.** The use of words to express something different to and often opposite from what they mean literally. Referring to a mess as "a pretty sight" is an example of irony. **2.** A conflict between what might be expected and what actually occurs: *We noted the irony that the boy who always complained about the cold weather became a famous skier.* [First written down in 1502 in Modern English, from Greek *eirōneia,* feigned ignorance.]

Ir•o•quoi•an (ĭr′ə **kwoi′**ən) *n.* **1.** A family of Native American languages spoken in Canada and the eastern United States. **2.** A member of a people speaking one of the languages of this family. **—Ir′o•quoi′an** *adj.*

Ir•o•quois (ĭr′ə kwoi′) *n., pl.* **Iroquois** (ĭr′ə kwoi′ *or* ĭr′ə kwoiz′). **1.** A member of a Native American confederacy inhabiting New York State and originally including the Cayuga, Mohawk, Oneida, Onondaga, and Seneca peoples. In 1722, the Tuscaroras joined the Iroquois confederacy. **2.** Any or all of the languages of the Iroquois. **—Ir′o•quois′** *adj.*

ir•ra•di•ate (ĭ **rā′**dē āt′) *tr.v.* **ir•ra•di•at•ed, ir•ra•di•at•ing, ir•ra•di•ates. 1.** To expose to or treat with radiation. **2.** To shed light on; illuminate: *The morning sun irradiated the room.* **3.** To show in a manner suggesting the shining of light: *Her smile irradiated her face.* **—ir•ra′di•a′tion** *n.*

ir•ra•tion•al (ĭ **răsh′**ə nəl) *adj.* **1.** Not capable of reasoning or thinking clearly: *Stunned by the announcement of the award, he was irrational for several minutes.* **2.** Not based on or guided by reason; unreasonable; illogical: *an irrational fear of heights.* **—ir•ra′tion•al•ly** *adv.*

ir•ra•tion•al•i•ty (ĭ răsh′ə **năl′**ĭ tē) *n., pl.* **ir•ra•tion•al•i•ties. 1.** The condition or quality of being irrational. **2.** Something irrational or absurd.

irrational number *n.* A number that cannot be written as an integer or as a fraction whose numerator and denominator are both integers; for example, $\sqrt{2}$ is an irrational number.

ir•re•claim•a•ble (ĭr′ĭ **klā′**mə bəl) *adj.* Impossible to reclaim: *irreclaimable land.* **—ir′re•claim′a•bly** *adv.*

ir•rec•on•cil•a•ble (ĭ rĕk′ən **sī′**lə bəl *or* ĭ **rĕk′**ən sī′lə bəl) *adj.* Impossible to reconcile: *irreconcilable enemies; irreconcilable differences of opinion.*

ir•re•cov•er•a•ble (ĭr′ĭ **kŭv′**ər ə bəl) *adj.* Impossible to recover: *irrecoverable losses.* **—ir′re•cov′er•a•bly** *adv.*

ir•re•deem•a•ble (ĭr′ĭ **dē′**mə bəl) *adj.* **1.** Not capable of being brought back or paid off: *an irredeemable coupon.* **2.** Impossible to remedy or reform: *an irredeemable loss; an irredeemable sinner.* **3.** Not convertible into coin: *irredeemable Confederate dollar bills.* **—ir′re•deem′a•bly** *adv.*

ir•re•duc•i•ble (ĭr′ĭ **do͞o′**sə bəl *or* ĭr′ĭ **dyo͞o′**sə bəl) *adj.* Impossible to reduce to a smaller or simpler amount or form: *¾ is an irreducible fraction.* **—ir′re•duc′i•bly** *adv.*

ir•ref•u•ta•ble (ĭ **rĕf′**yə tə bəl *or* ĭr′ĭ **fyo͞o′**tə bəl) *adj.* Impossible to refute or disprove: *irrefutable facts.* **—ir•ref′u•ta•bly** *adv.*

ir•re•gard•less (ĭr′ĭ **gärd′**lĭs) *adv. Non-Standard.* Regardless. —SEE NOTE.

ir•reg•u•lar (ĭ **rĕg′**yə lər) *adj.* **1.** Not done according to rule, accepted order, or general practice: *a highly irregular proceeding.* **2.** Uneven in occurrence or rate: *an irregular heartbeat.* **3.** Not straight, uniform, or balanced: *an irregular coastline.* **4.** In grammar, not following the usual pattern of inflected forms. For example, *do* is an irregular verb, with the irregular principal parts *did* and *done.* **5.** Not up to standard because of flaws or imperfections: *an irregular piece of cloth.* **—ir•reg′u•lar•ly** *adv.*

ir•reg•u•lar•i•ty (ĭ rĕg′yə **lăr′**ĭ tē) *n., pl.* **ir•reg•u•lar•i•ties. 1.** The quality or condition of being irregular. **2.** Something irregular: *irregularities in the earth's surface.*

ir•rel•e•vant (ĭ **rĕl′**ə vənt) *adj.* Having no relation to the matter at hand; beside the point: *an irrelevant question.* **—ir•rel′e•vance** *n.* **—ir•rel′e•vant•ly** *adv.*

ir•re•lig•ious (ĭr′ĭ **lĭj′**əs) *adj.* **1.** Indifferent to religion. **2.** Contrary or hostile to religion. **—ir′re•lig′ious•ly** *adv.*

ir•re•me•di•a•ble (ĭr′ĭ **mē′**dē ə bəl) *adj.* Impossible to remedy, correct, cure, or repair: *an irremediable blunder.* **—ir′re•me′di•a•bly** *adv.*

ir•rep•a•ra•ble (ĭ **rĕp′**ər ə bəl) *adj.* Impossible to repair, remedy, or set right: *The statue has suffered irreparable damage.* **—ir•rep′a•ra•bly** *adv.*

ir•re•place•a•ble (ĭr′ĭ **plā′**sə bəl) *adj.* Impossible to replace: *irreplaceable natural resources such as coal and oil.*

ir•re•press•i•ble (ĭr′ĭ **prĕs′**ə bəl) *adj.* Impossible to hold back, control, or restrain: *irrepressible laughter.* **—ir′re•press′i•bly** *adv.*

ir•re•proach•a•ble (ĭr′ĭ **prō′**chə bəl) *adj.* Perfect or blameless; faultless: *irreproachable behavior.* **—ir′re•proach′a•bly** *adv.*

ir•re•sis•ti•ble (ĭr′ĭ **zĭs′**tə bəl) *adj.* Too great or overpowering to be resisted; impossible to resist: *an irresistible impulse.* **—ir′re•sist′i•bil′i•ty** *n.* **—ir′re•sist′i•bly** *adv.*

ir•res•o•lute (ĭ **rĕz′**ə lo͞ot′) *adj.* Unsure of how to act; undecided; indecisive: *The irresolute editor was always asking for advice from his colleagues.* **—ir•res′o•lute′ly** *adv.* **—ir•res′o•lute′ness, ir•res′o•lu′tion** *n.*

ir•re•spec•tive of (ĭr′ĭ **spĕk′**tĭv) *prep.* Regardless of: *Anyone can try out for this play, irrespective of past experience.*

ir•re•spon•si•bil•i•ty (ĭr′ĭ spŏn′sə **bĭl′**ĭ tē) *n.* Lack of responsibility or concern for consequences.

ir•re•spon•si•ble (ĭr′ĭ **spŏn′**sə bəl) *adj.* **1.** Showing a lack of responsibility: *Much of our pollution comes from irresponsible manufacturing processes.* **2.** Lacking a sense of responsibility; unreliable or untrustworthy: *an irresponsible driver.* **3.** Not accountable or responsible to a higher authority: *favored representative democracy over irresponsible forms of government such as a dictatorship or monarchy.* **—ir′re•spon′si•bly** *adv.*

ir•re•triev•a•ble (ĭr′ĭ **trē′**və bəl) *adj.* Difficult or impossible to retrieve or recover: *Once the ring fell down the drain, it was irretrievable.* **—ir′re•triev′a•bly** *adv.*

ir•rev•er•ence (ĭ **rĕv′**ər əns) *n.* **1.** Lack of reverence or respect. **2.** A disrespectful act or remark.

ir•rev•er•ent (ĭ **rĕv′**ər ənt) *adj.* Having or showing a lack of reverence or respect; disrespectful: *an irreverent attitude toward the ceremony.* **—ir•rev′er•ent•ly** *adv.*

ir•re•vers•i•ble (ĭr′ĭ **vûr′**sə bəl) *adj.* Impossible to reverse: *rolling on an irreversible downhill path.* **—ir′re•vers′i•bly** *adv.*

ir•rev•o•ca•ble (ĭ **rĕv′**ə kə bəl) *adj.* Not capable of being changed or undone: *an irrevocable judgment.* **—ir•rev′o•ca•bly** *adv.*

ir•ri•gate (ĭr′ĭ gāt′) *tr.v.* **ir•ri•gat•ed, ir•ri•gat•ing, ir•ri•gates. 1.** To supply with water by means of streams, ditches, or pipes: *Ancient Egyptians used water from the Nile to irrigate barren land.* **2.** To wash out (a wound or an opening) with water or

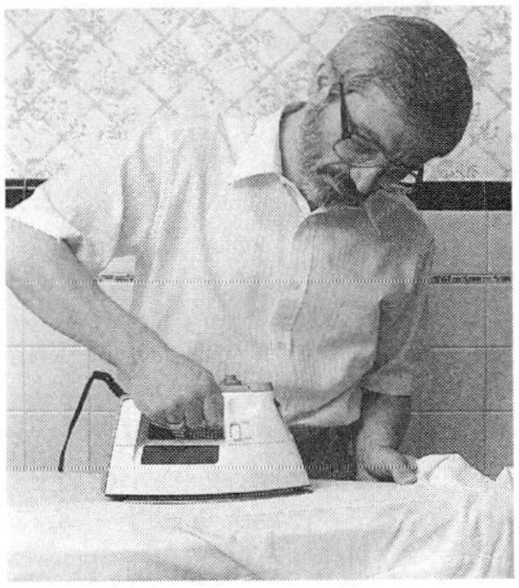

iron

ironwork
Window grille

Usage: irregardless

Many people mistakenly believe that **irregardless** is an acceptable word to use. It is not a correct form, however, and should be carefully avoided. All you need to say is **regardless**, as in *Regardless of what you say, I still like that CD.*

ă	pat	oi	boy
ā	pay	ou	out
âr	care	o͝o	took
ä	father	o͞o	boot
ĕ	pet	ŭ	cut
ē	be	ûr	urge
ĭ	pit	th	thin
ī	pie	*th*	this
îr	pier	hw	whoop
ŏ	pot	zh	vision
ō	toe	ə	about
ô	paw	N	*French* bon

Washington Irving
1832 engraving
by Hatch (1805?–1867)
and Smillie (1807–1885)

Isabella I

Word History: **island**

The two words **island** and **isle** have nothing in common except a misspelling. **Isle** comes from the Old French word *isle*, from an earlier *insla*, which comes from the Latin word *īnsula*, "island." The Latin word also shows up in our **peninsula**, which in both Latin and English means "an almost island" (*paene* in Latin means "almost"). **Island** comes from the Old English word *īegland*, "island" (literally, "waterland" or "land-in-water"). The letter *s* in our modern English *island* dates from the 16th century when people confused the native English word *iland* with the English pronunciation of the French *isle*.

a medicated solution: *The dentist irrigated the infected area around the tooth.* [First written down in 1615 in Modern English, from Latin *irrigāre* : *in-*, in + *rigāre*, to water.] —**ir′ri•ga′tion** *n.*

ir•ri•ta•bil•i•ty (ĭr′ĭ tə **bĭl′**ĭ tē) *n., pl.* **ir•ri•ta•bil•i•ties. 1.** The quality or condition of being irritable. **2.** The capacity to respond to a stimulus: *An amoeba displays irritability by moving away from a stimulus.*

ir•ri•ta•ble (ĭr′ĭ tə bəl) *adj.* **1.** Easily annoyed or angered: *Lack of sleep will make anyone irritable.* **2.** Very sensitive: *irritable skin around a scrape.* **3.** Capable of responding to stimuli. —**ir′ri•ta•ble•ness** *n.* —**ir′ri•ta•bly** *adv.*

ir•ri•tant (ĭr′ĭ tənt) *adj.* Causing irritation. —*n.* Something that irritates: *They found the city air full of irritants such as dust, soot, and smoke.*

ir•ri•tate (ĭr′ĭ tāt′) *tr.v.* **ir•ri•tat•ed, ir•ri•tat•ing, ir•ri•tates. 1.** To make angry or impatient; annoy: *The reporter's repeated questions on the same subject irritated the speaker.* **2.** To make sore or inflamed: *The smoke irritated the firefighter's eyes.* [First written down in 1531 in Modern English, from Latin *irrītāre.*] —**ir′ri•tat′ing•ly** *adv.* —**ir′ri•ta′tor** *n.*

ir•ri•ta•tion (ĭr′ĭ **tā′**shən) *n.* **1.** The act of irritating or the state of being irritated; annoyance. **2.** Soreness or tenderness of a body part: *an irritation of the throat.*

Ir•tysh or **Ir•tish** (ĭr **tĭsh′**). A river rising in northwest China and flowing about 2,650 miles (4,264 kilometers) generally northwest through Kazakhstan and into west-central Russia.

Ir•ving (**ûr′**vĭng), **Washington.** 1783–1859. American writer known for his stories, including "Rip Van Winkle," contained in *The Sketch Book* (1819–1820).

is (ĭz) *v.* Third person singular present tense of **be.** [First written down before 725 in Old English.]

is. or **Is.** *abbr.* An abbreviation of island.

I•saac (ī′zək). In the Bible, the son of Abraham who was offered as a sacrifice to God but was saved by divine intervention.

Is•a•bel•la I (ĭz′ə **bĕl′**ə). 1451–1504. Queen of Castile (1474–1504) who sponsored the voyages of Christopher Columbus.

I•sa•iah (ī **zā′**ə) *n.* **1.** A Hebrew prophet of the eighth century B.C. **2.** A book of the Bible containing the prophecies of Isaiah, which offer an ethical critique of society and a vision of a perfected world.

is•chi•um (ĭs′kē əm) *n., pl.* **is•chi•a** (**ĭs′**kē ə). The lowest of the three large bones forming either side of the pelvis.

–ise *suff.* Variant of **–ize.**

I•seult (ĭ **so͞olt′**) also **I•sol•de** (ĭ **sōl′**də) *n.* In Arthurian legend, an Irish princess who marries the king of Cornwall and falls in love with his knight Tristan.

–ish *suff.* A suffix that means: **1.** Of or relating to: *Finnish.* **2.** Having the character of; like: *sheepish; childish.* **3.** Approximately; somewhat: *greenish.* **4.** Tending toward; interested in: *selfish.*

Ish•tar (**ĭsh′**tär′) *n.* In Assyrian and Babylonian mythology, the goddess of love, fertility, and war.

i•sin•glass (ī′zən glăs′ *or* ī′zĭng glăs′) *n.* **1.** A transparent, almost pure gelatin obtained from the air bladders of sturgeon and certain other fish and used in making glue. **2.** Mica in thin transparent sheets. [First written down in 1545 in Modern English and spelled *Isom glass*, from obsolete Dutch *huizenblas*, from Middle Dutch *huusblase*, sturgeon bladder.]

I•sis (ī′sĭs) *n.* In Egyptian mythology, a goddess of fertility and the sister and wife of Osiris.

Is•lam (ĭs **läm′** *or* ĭz **läm′** *or* **ĭs′**läm′ *or* **ĭz′**läm′) *n.* **1.** A monotheisitc religion marked by submission to God and acceptance of Muhammad as the chief and last prophet of God. Islam is based on God's revelation to Muhammad, contained in the Koran, and on the teachings and example of Muhammad. **2.a.** The people or nations that practice Islam. **b.** The civilization based on Islam. —**Is•lam′ic** *adj.*

Is•lam•a•bad (ĭs **lä′**mə băd′ *or* ĭz **läm′**ə băd′). The capital of Pakistan, in the northeast part of the country east of Kabul, Afghanistan. It replaced Karachi as the capital in 1967. Population, 201,000.

is•land (ī′lənd) *n.* **1.** A body of land, especially one smaller than a continent, entirely surrounded by water: *Iceland is an island in the Atlantic Ocean.* **2.** Something resembling an island that is separated or different in character from what surrounds it: *The library is an island of quiet in the teeming city.* —SEE NOTE.

is•land•er (ī′lən dər) *n.* A person who lives on an island.

is•lands of Lang•er•hans (ī′ləndz əv **läng′**ər-häns′) *pl.n.* Islets of Langerhans.

isle (īl) *n.* An island, especially a small one.

❑ *These sound alike:* **isle, aisle** (passageway), **I'll** (I will).

is•let (ī′lĭt) *n.* A very small island.

❑ *These sound alike:* **islet, eyelet** (small hole).

is•lets of Lang•er•hans (ī′lĭts əv **läng′**ər häns′) *pl.n.* The small scattered endocrine glands in the pancreas that secrete insulin.

–ism *suff.* A suffix that means: **1.** Action, practice, or process: *criticism.* **2.** State or condition: *optimism.* **3.** Characteristic behavior or quality: *heroism.* **4.** A distinctive or characteristic trait, as of a language or people: *Briticism.* **5.** A doctrine, theory, or system: *pacifism.* —SEE NOTE.

is•n't (**ĭz′**ənt). Contraction of *is not.*

i•so•bar (ī′sə bär′) *n.* A line on a weather map connecting places having the same barometric pressure. Isobars show the distribution of atmospheric pressure at a given time, and are used in forecasting the weather.

i•so•late (ī′sə lāt′) *tr.v.* **i•so•lat•ed, i•so•lat•ing, i•so•lates. 1.** To separate from others; set apart: *In the ancient world vast distances isolated peoples from each other.* **2.** To place in quarantine. [First written down in 1807 in Modern English, from *isolated*, from Latin *īnsulātus*, made into an island.]

i•so•la•tion (ī′sə **lā′**shən) *n.* **1.** The condition of being isolated: *living in isolation from the pressures of the industrial world.* **2.** The act of isolating: *the isolation of patients with tuberculosis.*

i•so•la•tion•ism (ī′sə **lā′**shə nĭz′əm) *n.* The policy or principle that a nation should avoid political and economic relationships with other countries. —**i′so•la′tion•ist** *n.*

I•sol•de (ĭ **sōl′**də *or* ĭ **zōl′**də) *n.* Variant of **Iseult.**

i•so•mer (ī′sə mər) *n.* One of two or more compounds composed of the same chemical elements in the same proportions, but differing in at least one physical or chemical property because their atoms are arranged differently.

i•so•met•ric (ī′sə **mĕt′**rĭk) *adj.* Of or involving contraction of a muscle under constant tension without change in length: *isometric exercises.*

i•sos•ce•les triangle (ī **sŏs′**ə lēz′) *n.* A triangle having two sides of equal length.

i•so•therm (ī′sə thûrm′) *n.* A line on a weather map connecting places having the same average temperature.

i•so•tope (ī′sə tōp′) *n.* One of two or more forms of an element that have the same chemical properties and the same atomic number but different atomic weights and slightly different physical properties because of different numbers of neutrons in their atomic nuclei. [First written down in 1913 in Modern English : *iso-*, same, equal + Greek *topos*, place.] **—i'so•top'ic** (ī'sə tŏp'ĭk) *adj.*

Is•ra•el[1] (ĭz'rē əl) *n.* **1.** In the Bible, the name given to Jacob by the angel with whom he wrestled. **2.** The Jewish people past, present, and future, regarded as the chosen people of God.

Is•ra•el[2] (ĭz'rē əl). **1.** An ancient kingdom of Palestine founded in about 1025 B.C. and lasting until it was overthrown by the Assyrians in 721. **2.** A country of southwest Asia on the eastern Mediterranean Sea. It was created in 1948 as a Jewish state on recommendation of the United Nations. Jerusalem is the capital and Tel Aviv–Jaffa the largest city. Population, 4,141,400.

Is•rae•li (ĭz rā'lē) *adj.* Of or relating to modern Israel or its people. *—n., pl.* **Is•rae•lis.** A native or inhabitant of modern Israel.

Is•ra•el•ite (ĭz'rē ə līt') *n.* **1.** A native or inhabitant of the ancient kingdom of Israel. **2.** A descendant of Jacob; a Jew. *—adj.* Of or relating to Israel or the Israelites.

is•su•ance (ĭsh'o͞o əns) *n.* The act of issuing: *the issuance of driver's licenses.*

is•sue (ĭsh'o͞o) *n.* **1.a.** The act of flowing or giving out: *the issue of water from the spring.* **b.** The act of distributing or putting out; release: *The date of issue is indicated on the front of the magazine.* **2.** Something that is distributed or put into circulation: *a new issue of postage stamps.* **3.** A set of newspapers or magazines published at one time: *the June issue of the class newspaper.* **4.** A subject being discussed or disputed; a question under debate: *the issue of reforming campaign laws.* **5.** A place of outflow; an outlet: *The lake has no issue to the sea.* **6.** An outcome or a result. **7.** Offspring; children: *died without issue.* *—v.* **is•sued, is•su•ing, is•sues.** *—intr.* To come out; flow out: *Water issued from the broken pipe.* *—tr.* **1.** To cause to flow out: *The factory issues its waste water into tanks for treatment.* **2.** To put in circulation; publish: *The Postal Service issues stamps.* **3.** To give out; distribute: *issue uniforms to members of the team.* ***—idiom.*** **at issue.** In question; in dispute: *Your conduct is not at issue here.* [First written down before 1300 in Middle English, from Old French, from Latin *exīre*, to go out.] **—is'su•er** *n.*

-ist *suff.* A suffix that means: **1.** A person who performs an action: *lobbyist.* **2.** A person who produces, makes, operates, plays, or is connected with a specified thing: *novelist.* **3.** A person who specializes in a specified art, science, or skill: *biologist.* **4.** A person who believes in a certain doctrine or system: *socialist.* **5.** A person characterized as having a particular trait: *romanticist.* —SEE NOTE.

Is•tan•bul (ĭs'tăn bo͞ol' *or* ĭs'tăn bo͞ol'). Formerly **Con•stan•ti•no•ple** (kŏn'stăn tə nō'pəl). The largest city of Turkey, on the Bosporus at its entrance into the Sea of Marmara. It was founded in about 660 B.C. as Byzantium and renamed Constantinople in A.D. 330 by Constantine the Great. Istanbul was chosen as the official name in 1930. Population, 2,772,708.

isth•mus (ĭs'məs) *n., pl.* **isth•mus•es** or **isth•mi** (ĭs'mī'). A narrow strip of land with water on both sides, connecting two larger masses of land. [First written down in 1555 in Modern English, from Greek *isthmos*.]

it (ĭt) *pron.* **1.** The thing, animal, or person last mentioned or thought to be understood: *I polished the table until it shone. They played with the puppy until it got tired. Whatever you choose, give it your best. I couldn't find out who it was on the telephone.* **2.** Used as the subject of an impersonal verb: *It is snowing.* **3.** Used as the subject of a clause that introduces a phrase or clause that presents the idea of the sentence: *It is important to get enough exercise.* *—n.* In some games, the player who must perform a certain act, such as chasing the other players. [First written down about 725 in Old English and spelled *hit*.]

It. *abbr.* An abbreviation of: **1.** Italian. **2.** Italy.

ital. *abbr.* An abbreviation of italic.

Ital. *abbr.* An abbreviation of: **1.** Italian. **2.** Italy.

I•tal•ian (ĭ tăl'yən) *adj.* Of or relating to Italy, or its people, language, or culture. *—n.* **1.** A native or inhabitant of Italy. **2.** A person of Italian descent. **3.** The Romance language of Italy and a part of Switzerland.

i•tal•ic (ĭ tăl'ĭk *or* ī tăl'ĭk) *adj.* Of or being a style of printing type with the letters slanting to the right, used chiefly to set off a word or passage within a text of roman print: *This is italic print.* *—n.* Italic print or typeface. Often used in the plural. [First written down in 1571 in Modern English, from Latin *Italicus*, Italian.]

i•tal•i•cize (ĭ tăl'ĭ sīz' *or* ī tăl'ĭ sīz') *tr.v.* **i•tal•i•cized, i•tal•i•ciz•ing, i•tal•i•ciz•es.** To print in italic type: *italicize the title of a book.*

It•a•ly (ĭt'l ē). **1.** A peninsula of southern Europe projecting into the Mediterranean Sea between the Tyrrhenian and Adriatic seas. **2.** A country of southern Europe made up of the peninsula of Italy, Sardinia, Sicily, and several smaller islands. It was settled before 800 B.C. The country was unified in 1870. Rome is the capital and the largest city. Population, 56,243,935.

itch (ĭch) *n.* **1.** An irritated feeling in the skin that causes a desire to scratch. **2.** Any of various skin diseases that cause a desire to scratch. **3.** A restless craving or desire: *Every spring I get an itch to go sailing.* *—v.* **itched, itch•ing, itch•es.** *—intr.* **1.** To feel, have, or cause an itch: *I itch all over from mosquito bites.* **2.** To have a restless craving or desire: *They were just itching to show the teacher what they had done.* *—tr.* To cause to have an itch: *This wool shirt itches my back.* [First written down before 800 in Old English and spelled *gicche*.]

itch•y (ĭch'ē) *adj.* **itch•i•er, itch•i•est. 1.** Having or causing an itch: *an itchy bug bite.* **2.** Restless; jumpy: *I get itchy if I have to sit for a long period of time.* **—itch'i•ness** *n.*

-ite *suff.* A suffix that means: **1.** A native or resident of: *Brooklynite.* **2.** Descendant of: *Israelite.* **3.** Rock; mineral: *graphite.*

i•tem (ī'təm) *n.* **1.** A single thing or unit: *I bought a shirt and several other items of clothing. You must show a receipt for each item purchased.* **2.** A piece of news or information: *an interesting item in the newspaper.* [First written down in 1561 in Modern English, from Latin *item*, also.]

i•tem•ize (ī'tə mīz') *tr.v.* **i•tem•ized, i•tem•iz•ing, i•tem•iz•es.** To set down item by item; list: *itemizing all charges on the bill.*

it•er•ate (ĭt'ə rāt') *tr.v.* **it•er•at•ed, it•er•at•ing, it•er•ates.** To say or do again; repeat. [First written down in 1533 in Modern English, from Latin *iterāre*, from *iterum*, again.] **—it'er•a'tion** *n.*

i•tin•er•ant (ī tĭn'ər ənt *or* ĭ tĭn'ər ənt) *adj.* Traveling from place to place: *At harvest time many farmers employ itinerant workers.* *—n.* A person who travels from place to place.

i•tin•er•ar•y (ī tĭn'ə rĕr'ē *or* ĭ tĭn'ə rĕr'ē) *n., pl.* **i•tin•er•ar•ies. 1.** A schedule of places to be visited in the course of a journey: *The tourists' itinerary includes stops in Denver and Salt Lake City.* **2.** An account or record of a journey. **3.** A traveler's guidebook. [First written down before 1425 in Middle English and spelled *itinerarie*, from Latin *iter*, journey.]

Word Building: –ism

The suffix **–ism** is a noun suffix. That is, when added to words or word roots, **–ism** forms nouns. It comes from the Greek noun suffix *-ismos* and means roughly "the act, state, or theory of." Nouns that end in **–ism** often have related verbs that end in **–ize** (**criticism/criticize**), related agent nouns that end in **–ist** (**optimism/optimist**), and related adjectives that end in **–istic** (**optimistic**).

Word Building: –ist

The suffix **–ist**, which comes from the Greek suffix *-istēs*, forms agent nouns, that is, nouns that denote someone who does something. Although **–ist** frequently forms agent nouns from verbs ending in **–ize** or nouns ending in **–ism**, it has also come to be combined with words that do not end in **–ize** or **–ism**. In fact in some cases **–ist** can be used much like the suffix **–er**. In pairs such as **conformer/conformist**, **copier/copyist**, and **cycler/cyclist**, **–ist** and **–er** may be used interchangeably.

ă	pat	oi	boy
ā	pay	ou	out
âr	care	o͝o	took
ä	father	o͞o	boot
ĕ	pet	ŭ	cut
ē	be	ûr	urge
ĭ	pit	th	thin
ī	pie	*th*	this
îr	pier	hw	whoop
ŏ	pot	zh	vision
ō	toe	ə	about
ô	paw	N	*French* bon

Usage: its

The word **its**, the possessive form of the pronoun **it**, is never written with an apostrophe: *I like my house because of its many windows.* The contraction **it's** (for *it is* or *it has*) is always written with an apostrophe: *It's because my house has many windows that I like it.*

ivy

Word Building: –ize

The suffix **–ize**, which comes from the Greek verb suffix *–izein*, has become very important in English as a means of turning nouns and adjectives into verbs. **Formalize**, **jeopardize**, **legalize**, and **modernize** are examples of words that were coined in English hundreds of years ago. Other words that were coined later, in the 19th and 20th centuries, such as **emphasize**, **hospitalize**, **industrialize**, and **computerize**, are now also well established. Words ending in **–ize** often have related nouns ending in *–ization*: **dramatize/dramatization**.

–itis *suff.* A suffix that means an inflammation or inflammatory disease of: *bronchitis.*

it'll (ĭt′l). Contraction of *it will* or *it shall.*

its (ĭts) *adj.* The possessive form of **it.** Of or belonging to the thing just mentioned: *How does the picture look? We just changed its frame.* —See Note.
❑ *These sound alike:* **its, it's** (it is).

it's (ĭts). Contraction of *it is* or *it has.*
❑ *These sound alike:* **it's, its** (of it).

it•self (ĭt sĕlf′) *pron.* **1.** That one that is the same as it: **a.** Used as the direct object or indirect object of a verb or as the object of a preposition to show that the action of the verb refers back to the subject: *The cat scratched itself. Congress voted itself a pay raise. The robot moves by itself.* **b.** Used to give emphasis: *The trouble is in the motor itself.* **2.** Its normal or healthy condition or state: *The dog has not been itself since the hot weather began.*

–ity *suff.* A suffix that means a quality or condition: *authenticity.*

–ive *suff.* A suffix that means tending toward or performing a specified action: *disruptive.*

I've (īv). Contraction of *I have.*

i•vo•ry (ī′və rē *or* īv′rē) *n., pl.* **i•vo•ries. 1.** The hard, smooth, yellowish-white substance forming the tusks of elephants and certain other animals. It was formerly used for making piano keys and decorative objects. **2.** Something made or carved from this substance. **3.** A yellowish white. **4. ivories.** *Slang.* The keys of a piano. —*adj.* **1.** Made of or resembling ivory: *ivory chess pieces.* **2.** Yellowish-white. [First written down in 1263 in Middle English and spelled *ivorie*, from Latin *ebur*.]

I•vo•ry Coast (ī′və rē *or* īv′rē). A country of western Africa on the Atlantic Ocean west of Ghana. It gained its independence from France in 1960. Abidjan is the capital and the largest city. Population, 7,920,000.

i•vy (ī′vē) *n., pl.* **i•vies. 1.** Any of several climbing or trailing plants having evergreen leaves. **2.** Any of several similar plants, such as poison ivy. [First written down about 700 in Old English and spelled *īfig*.]

–ize *suff.* A suffix that means: **1.** To cause to be or become: *dramatize.* **2.** To become; become like: *materialize; crystallize.* **3.** To treat like: *idolize.* **4.** To subject to or with: *satirize; anesthetize.* **5.** To perform, engage in, or produce: *fraternize.* —See Note.

Iz•mir (ĭz mîr′). Formerly **Smyr•na** (smûr′nə). A city of western Turkey on an inlet of the Aegean Sea. It was settled during the Bronze Age. Population, 757,854.

Jj

j or **J** (jā) *n., pl.* **j's** or **J's. 1.** The tenth letter of the English alphabet. **2.** The tenth in a series or group: *row J in a theater.*

jab (jăb) *tr. & intr.v.* **jabbed, jab•bing, jabs. 1.** To poke or thrust, especially with something sharp: *He jabbed the fork into the meat.* **2.** To stab or pierce: *He jabbed the meat with his fork.* **3.** To punch with short quick blows: *jab at a punching bag.* —*n.* **1.** A poke or thrust: *The man sitting next to me gave me a jab in the ribs.* **2.** A short quick blow.

jab•ber (jăb′ər) *intr.v.* **jab•bered, jab•ber•ing, jab•bers.** To talk rapidly and in a senseless manner; chatter: *They jabbered on about their neighbors.* —*n.* Rapid or babbling talk.

ja•bot (zhă bō′ *or* jăb′ō) *n.* A series of frills or ruffles down the front of a shirt, blouse, or dress.

jac•a•ran•da (jăk′ə răn′də) *n.* Any of several tropical American trees or shrubs having feathery leaves and clusters of pale purple flowers.

jack (jăk) *n.* **1.** One who works in a specified manual trade: *a lumberjack; a steeplejack.* **2.** A usually portable device used to raise heavy objects, by means of force applied to a lever, screw, or hydraulic press. **3.** A socket into which a plug is inserted in order to make an electrical connection: *a telephone jack.* **4.** A playing card bearing the figure of a young man and ranking below a queen. **5.a. jacks.** *(used with a singular or plural verb).* A game in which each player in turn bounces and catches a small ball while picking up small six-pointed metal pieces with the same hand. **b.** One of the six-pointed pieces used in this game. **6.** A male donkey. **7.** A small flag flown on a ship, usually to show nationality. —*tr.v.* **jacked, jack•ing, jacks. 1.** To hoist by means of a jack: *The mechanic jacked the rear of the car to fix the tire.* **2.** To raise (something) to a higher level, as in cost: *The landlord jacked rents, causing much concern among tenants.* [First written down in 1391 in Middle English and spelled *jakke,* Jack, possibly from Old French *Jacques.*]

jack•al (jăk′əl *or* jăk′ôl′) *n.* Any of several wild dogs of Africa, Asia, and eastern Europe that hunt and scavenge for food. [First written down in 1603 in Modern English, from Sanskrit *śṛgālaḥ.*]

jack•a•napes (jăk′ə nāps′) *n.* A vain or disrespectful person.

jack•ass (jăk′ăs′) *n.* **1.** A male donkey. **2.** A foolish or stupid person.

jack•boot (jăk′bo͞ot′) *n.* A sturdy military boot extending above the knee.

jack•daw (jăk′dô′) *n.* A small black crow of Europe, North Africa, and Asia.

jack•et (jăk′ĭt) *n.* **1.** A short coat usually extending to the hips. **2.** An outer covering or casing, as of a book. [First written down in 1451 in Middle English and spelled *jaket,* from Old French *jaquet.*]

Jack Frost *n.* Frost or cold weather personified as an old man.

jack•ham•mer (jăk′hăm′ər) *n.* A drill run on compressed air, used especially to drill rock or break up concrete.

jack-in-the-box (jăk′ĭn *thə* bŏks′) *n., pl.* **jack-in-the-box•es** or **jacks-in-the-box** (jăks′ĭn *thə* bŏks′). A toy consisting of a box from which a clownlike puppet springs when the lid is opened.

jack-in-the-pul•pit (jăk′ĭn *thə* po͞ol′pĭt *or* jăk′ĭn *thə* pŭl′pĭt) *n., pl.* **jack-in-the-pulpits.** A North American plant having a hood-shaped sheath arching over an upright flower stalk.

jack•knife (jăk′nīf′) *n.* **1.** A large pocketknife with blades that can be folded back into the handle. **2.** A dive in which the diver bends over in midair, touching the feet while keeping the legs straight, and then straightens out before entering the water hands first. —*intr.v.* **jack•knifed, jack•knif•ing, jack•knifes.** To fold or bend like a jackknife: *The trailer truck jackknifed on the icy road.*

jack-of-all-trades (jăk′əv ôl′trādz′) *n., pl.* **jacks-of-all-trades** (jăks′əv ôl′trādz′). A person who can do many different kinds of work.

jack-o'-lan•tern (jăk′ə lăn′tərn) *n., pl.* **jack-o'-lanterns.** A lantern made from a hollowed out pumpkin with a carved face, used at Halloween.

jack•pot (jăk′pŏt′) *n.* The largest prize or award in various games or contests.

jack•rab•bit or **jack rabbit** (jăk′răb′ĭt) *n.* Any of several hares of western North America having long ears and long very strong hind legs.

Jack•son (jăk′sən). The capital and largest city of Mississippi, in the west-central part of the state west of Montgomery, Alabama. It was chosen as capital in 1821. Population, 196,637.

Jackson, Andrew. 1767–1845. The seventh President of the United States (1829–1837) and a general in the War of 1812.

Jack•son•ville (jăk′sən vĭl′). The largest city of Florida, in the northeast part of the state near the Atlantic Ocean and the Georgia border. It was settled in 1816. Population, 672,971.

jack•stone (jăk′stōn′) *n.* **1. jackstones.** *(used with a singular verb).* The game of jacks. **2.** One of the pieces used in playing jacks; a jack.

jack•straw (jăk′strô′) *n.* **1. jackstraws.** *(used with a singular verb).* A children's game played with straws or thin sticks thrown in a pile from which the players try in turn to remove single sticks without disturbing the others. **2.** One of the straws or sticks used in this game.

Ja•cob (jā′kəb). In the Bible, the son of Isaac whose 12 sons became the ancestors of the 12 tribes of Israel.

jade[1] (jād) *n.* **1.** A hard mineral that is pale green or white and either carved or used as a gemstone. **2.** A light-green color. [First written down in 1598 in Modern English and spelled *iada,* from Spanish *piedra de ijada,* stone of the side (from the belief that it cured kidney disease).] **—jade** *adj.*

jade[2] (jād) *n.* A broken-down or useless horse. [First written down about 1390 in Middle English and spelled *jade.*]

jad•ed (jā′dĭd) *adj.* **1.** Tired or worn out: *a jaded look.* **2.** Dulled by having had too much of something: *a jaded appetite.* **—jad′ed•ly** *adv.* **—jad′ed•ness** *n.*

jag (jăg) *n.* A sharp projecting point. —*tr.v.* **jagged, jag•ging, jags.** To cut or tear unevenly; notch.

jackal

Andrew Jackson

ă	pat	oi	boy
ā	pay	ou	out
âr	care	o͝o	took
ä	father	o͞o	boot
ĕ	pet	ŭ	cut
ē	be	ûr	urge
ĭ	pit	th	thin
ī	pie	*th*	this
îr	pier	hw	whoop
ŏ	pot	zh	vision
ō	toe	ə	about
ô	paw	N	*French* bon

jaguar

jai alai

jasmine
Common white jasmine

javelin

jag•ged (jăg′ĭd) *adj.* Having notches or indentations; irregular: *jagged edges of broken glass; a jagged coastline.* **—jag′ged•ly** *adv.* **—jag′ged•ness** *n.*

jag•uar (jăg′wär′) *n.* A large wild cat of tropical America similar to a leopard, having a coat of tawny fur spotted with black marks. [First written down in 1604 in Modern English, from Guarani *jaguá*, dog.]

jai a•lai (hī′ lī′ *or* hī′ ə lī′ *or* hī′ ə lī′) *n.* A game similar to handball, played on a walled court, in which the participants use a long basket strapped to the wrist to catch and throw the ball.

jail (jāl) *n.* A place in which persons awaiting trial or serving a prison sentence are confined. *—tr.v.* **jailed, jail•ing, jails.** To put into jail; imprison.

jail•er also **jail•or** (jā′lər) *n.* A person in charge of a jail.

Ja•kar•ta or **Dja•kar•ta** (jə kär′tə). The capital and largest city of Indonesia, on the northeast coast of Java. It was founded in about 1619. Population, 6,503,449.

ja•lop•y (jə lŏp′ē) *n., pl.* **ja•lop•ies.** *Informal.* An old automobile that is in bad condition.

jal•ou•sie (jăl′ə sē) *n.* A blind or shutter having horizontal slats that can be tilted to admit or keep out air or light.

jam[1] (jăm) *v.* **jammed, jam•ming, jams.** *—tr.* **1.** To drive or wedge into a tight space: *jam a cork into a bottle.* **2.** To fill (something) to excess: *Holiday shoppers jammed the store.* **3.** To cause to lock in an unworkable position: *Dirt jammed the camera and the film won't advance.* **4.** To crush or bruise: *jam one's finger in the door.* **5.** To apply or activate suddenly: *My bike skidded when I jammed the brakes.* **6.** To make (electronic signals) difficult or impossible to receive by broadcasting an interfering signal. *—intr.* **1.** To become wedged or stuck in a tight space: *The coin jammed in the slot.* **2.** To lock in an unworkable position: *The film jammed in the camera.* **3.** To force one's way into a limited space: *Everyone jammed into the elevator.* *—n.* **1.** A crush or congestion of people or things in a limited space, making it difficult or impossible to move: *a traffic jam; a log jam.* **2.** *Informal.* A difficult situation: *We're really in a jam.* [First written down in 1706 in Modern English.]

❑ *These sound alike:* **jam**[1] (wedge), **jam**[2] (preserve), **jamb** (door post).

jam[2] (jăm) *n.* A preserve made from whole fruit boiled to a pulp with sugar. [First written down about 1730 in Modern English, possibly from *jam*, wedge.]

❑ *These sound alike:* **jam**[2] (preserve), **jam**[1] (squeeze), **jamb** (door post).

Ja•mai•ca (jə mā′kə). An island country in the Caribbean Sea south of Cuba. Explored by Columbus in 1494, the island was settled in 1509. The country gained its independence from Great Britain in 1962. Kingston is the capital and the largest city. Population, 2,190,357.

jamb (jăm) *n.* One of the vertical posts or pieces that form sides of a door or window. [First written down in 1334 in Middle English and spelled *jaumbe*, from Old French *jambe*, leg.]

❑ *These sound alike:* **jamb, jam**[1] (wedge), **jam**[2] (preserve).

jam•bo•ree (jăm′bə rē′) *n.* **1.** A noisy party or celebration. **2.** A large assembly of Boy Scouts or Girl Scouts.

James (jāmz) *n.* A book of the New Testament written in the form of a letter in which Saint James exhorts Christians to act morally.

James[1], Saint. Died A.D. 44. One of the 12 Apostles and brother of John.

James[2], Saint. Died about A.D. 62. The person traditionally regarded as the brother of Jesus and the author of the Epistle of James in the New Testament.

James[3], Saint. Flourished first century A.D. One of the 12 Apostles.

James I. 1566–1625. King of England (1603–1625) and of Scotland as James VI (1567–1625) who was the son of Mary Queen of Scots. He sponsored the King James Bible.

James, Henry. 1843–1916. American writer known for his many novels, such as *The Portrait of a Lady* (1881).

James•town (jāmz′toun′). **1.** The capital of St. Helena in the southern Atlantic Ocean. Population, 1,516. **2.** A former village of southeast Virginia, the first permanent English settlement in America. It was founded in 1607 and named for James I. Jamestown declined after the capital was moved to Williamsburg (1698–1700).

Jam•mu and Kash•mir (jŭm′o͞o ənd kăsh′mîr′- *or* kăsh mîr′). A former state of northern India and Pakistan north of modern Delhi, India.

jam session *n.* A gathering at which a group of musicians improvise together.

Jan. *abbr.* An abbreviation of January.

jan•gle (jăng′gəl) *v.* **jan•gled, jan•gling, jan•gles.** *—intr.* To make a harsh metallic sound: *The coins jangled in my pocket.* *—tr.* **1.** To cause to make a harsh metallic sound: *I jangled my keys.* **2.** To have an irritating effect on: *The racket from the street jangled my nerves.* *—n.* A harsh metallic sound.

jan•i•tor (jăn′ĭ tər) *n.* A person whose job is to clean and take care of a building. [First written down in 1584 in Modern English, from Latin *iānitor*, doorkeeper, from *iānua*, door.]

Jan•u•ar•y (jăn′yo͞o ĕr′ē) *n., pl.* **Jan•u•ar•ies.** The first month of the year in the Gregorian calendar, having 31 days.

Ja•nus (jā′nəs) *n.* In Roman mythology, the god that protects doorways and city gates, shown with two faces looking in opposite directions.

Ja•pan (jə păn′). An island country of Asia in the Pacific Ocean off the northeast coast of the mainland. It is traditionally believed to have been inhabited since about 660 B.C. Tokyo is the capital and the largest city. Population, 121,047,196.

Japan, Sea of. An enclosed arm of the western Pacific Ocean between Japan and the Asian mainland.

Jap•a•nese (jăp′ə nēz′ *or* jăp′ə nēs′) *adj.* Of or relating to Japan or its people, language, or culture. *—n., pl.* **Japanese. 1.** A native or inhabitant of Japan. **2.** The language of Japan.

Japanese beetle *n.* A green and brown beetle native to eastern Asia that is a common plant pest in North America.

jar[1] (jär) *n.* **1.** A cylindrical container of glass or earthenware with a wide mouth and usually no handles. **2.** The amount that a jar can hold: *We ate a jar of peanut butter in two weeks.* [First written down possibly about 1421 in Middle English and spelled *jarre*, a liquid measure, from Arabic *jarrah*, earthen jar.]

jar[2] (jär) *v.* **jarred, jar•ring, jars.** *—intr.* **1.** To make or utter a harsh sound. **2.** To have an irritating effect: *The loud music jars on my nerves.* **3.** To conflict; clash: *The statements of the opposing candidates frequently jarred.* *—tr.* **1.** To bump or cause to shake; rock. **2.** To unsettle or shock: *The defeat jarred everyone on the team.* *—n.* **1.** A jolt or shock. **2.** A harsh or grating sound. [First written down in 1526 in Modern English, perhaps of imitative origin.]

jar•gon (jär′gən) *n.* **1.** Nonsensical or meaningless talk; gibberish. **2.** A mixed language used by people who normally speak different languages; a pidgin.

3. The specialized language of a trade, profession, or class.

jas•mine (jăz′mĭn) also **jes•sa•mine** (jĕs′ə mĭn) *n.* Any of several vines or shrubs having fragrant, usually yellow or white flowers.

Ja•son (jā′sən) *n.* In Greek mythology, the leader of the Argonauts in quest of the Golden Fleece.

jas•per (jăs′pər) *n.* A reddish, brown, or yellow variety of opaque quartz.

jaun•dice (jôn′dĭs *or* jän′dĭs) *n.* An abnormal yellow coloration of the tissues and fluids of the body, resulting from bile pigments that accumulate when the liver does not function properly. *—tr.v.* **jaun•diced, jaun•dic•ing, jaun•dic•es. 1.** To cause jaundice in. **2.** To cause to feel envy, jealousy, prejudice, or hostility.

jaun•diced (jôn′dĭst *or* jän′dĭst) *adj.* **1.** Affected with jaundice. **2.** Showing or feeling envy, jealousy, prejudice, or hostility: *a jaundiced viewpoint.*

jaunt (jônt *or* jänt) *n.* A short trip or excursion; an outing. *—intr.v.* **jaunt•ed, jaunt•ing, jaunts.** To make a short trip or excursion.

jaun•ty (jôn′tē *or* jän′tē) *adj.* **jaun•ti•er, jaun•ti•est. 1.** Having a carefree self-confident air: *a successful jaunty young actor.* **2.** Stylish or smart in appearance: *wearing a jaunty hat.* **—jaun′ti•ly** *adv.* **—jaun′ti•ness** *n.*

Ja•va (jav′ə *or* ja′və) *n. Informal.* Brewed coffee.

Ja•va (jä′və *or* jăv′ə). An island of Indonesia separated from Borneo by the **Java Sea,** an arm of the western Pacific Ocean. It was the center of an early civilization.

Jav•a•nese (jăv′ə nēz′ *or* jăv′ə nēs′) *adj.* Of or relating to Java or its people, language, or culture. *—n., pl.* **Javanese. 1.** A native or inhabitant of Java. **2.** The language spoken by the main ethnic group of Java.

jave•lin (jăv′lĭn *or* jăv′ə lĭn) *n.* **1.** A light spear thrown with the hand and used as a weapon. **2.** A light spear that is thrown for distance in an athletic contest.

jaw (jô) *n.* **1.** Either of two structures of bone or cartilage that in most vertebrates form the framework of the mouth and hold the teeth. **2.** The parts of the body that form the walls of the mouth and serve to open and close it. **3. jaws.** Something resembling a pair of jaws: *the jaws of a large wrench.* *—intr.v.* **jawed, jaw•ing, jaws.** *Slang.* To talk in a gossipy manner; chatter.

jaw•bone (jô′bōn′) *n.* One of the bones in which the teeth are set, especially the lower jaw.

jay (jā) *n.* Any of various birds related to the crow, often having a crest, brightly colored feathers, and a loud harsh call, as the blue jay of North America.

Jay (jā), **John.** 1745–1829. American politician who served in both Continental Congresses and was the first chief justice of the U.S. Supreme Court (1789–1795).

jay•walk (jā′wôk′) *intr.v.* **jay•walked, jay•walk•ing, jay•walks.** To cross a street in violation of the traffic rules, as in the middle of the block or when the light is red. **—jay′walk′er** *n.*

jazz (jăz) *n.* **1.** A style of music native to the United States that has strong and often complex rhythms and melodies that are made up by musicians as variations of a main melody. **2.** *Slang.* Empty talk; nonsense.

jazz•y (jăz′ē) *adj.* **jazz•i•er, jazz•i•est. 1.** Resembling jazz. **2.** *Slang.* Showy; flashy: *a jazzy car.*

jeal•ous (jĕl′əs) *adj.* **1.** Fearful of losing affection or position to another. **2.** Resenting another's success or advantages; envious: *Don't be jealous of his success.* **3.** Careful or watchful in guarding something: *He's jealous of his new stereo.* **4.** Concerning or caused by feelings of envy or the fear of losing position or affection: *jealous thoughts.* [First written down before 1200 in Middle English and spelled *gelus,* from Late Latin *zēlus,* zeal.] **—jeal′ous•ly** *adv.* **—jeal′ous•ness** *n.*

jeal•ous•y (jĕl′ə sē) *n., pl.* **jeal•ous•ies.** A jealous attitude or feeling.

jean (jēn) *n.* **1.** A strong twilled cotton, used in making uniforms and work clothes. **2. jeans.** Pants made of jean or denim.

Jeanne d'Arc (zhän därk′). Joan of Arc.

jeep (jēp) *n.* A small rugged motor vehicle with four-wheel drive, used by the U.S. Army during and after World War II. [First written down in 1941 in American English, probably from *GP,* prefix of the manufacturer's part numbers.]

jeer (jîr) *v.* **jeered, jeer•ing, jeers.** *—intr.* To speak or shout in a mocking or scoffing way. *—tr.* To speak to or shout at in a mocking or scoffing way. *—n.* A mocking or scoffing remark or shout.

Jef•fer•son (jĕf′ər sən), **Thomas.** 1743–1826. The third President of the United States (1801–1809), who was a member of the second Continental Congress and drafted the Declaration of Independence (1776). —See Note.

Jefferson City. The capital of Missouri, in the central part of the state on the Missouri River. It was chosen as the capital in 1821. Population, 35,481.

Je•ho•vah (jĭ hō′və) *n.* God, especially in Christian translations of the Bible.

Je•ho•vah's Witness (jĭ hō′vəz) *n.* A member of a religious group preaching the imminent end of the world and opposed to war and to the authority of the government in matters of conscience.

je•june (jə jo͞on′) *adj.* Not interesting; dull: *another jejune political speech full of empty promises.*

je•ju•num (jə jo͞o′nəm) *n., pl.* **je•ju•na** (jə jo͞o′nə). The part of the small intestine between the duodenum and the ileum.

jell (jĕl) *intr.v.* **jelled, jell•ing, jells. 1.** To thicken or congeal: *The gravy jelled as it cooled.* **2.** To take shape; crystallize: *Plans for the weekend haven't jelled yet.*

❑ *These sound alike:* **jell, gel** (jellylike mixture).

jel•lied (jĕl′ēd) *adj.* **1.** Chilled or otherwise turned into jelly: *a jellied sauce.* **2.** Coated or spread with jelly: *a slice of jellied toast.*

Jell-O (jĕl′ō). A trademark used for a gelatin dessert.

jel•ly (jĕl′ē) *n., pl.* **jel•lies. 1.** A soft clear food with a springy consistency that is made by boiling fruit juice or other liquid with pectin or gelatin. **2.** A substance resembling this: *petroleum jelly.* *—v.* **jel•lied, jel•ly•ing, jel•lies.** *—tr.* To make into jelly. *—intr.* To become thickened; turn into jelly. [First written down in 1381 in Middle English and spelled *gelee,* from Latin *gelāre,* to freeze.] **—jel′ly•like′** *adj.*

jel•ly•bean (jĕl′ē bēn′) *n.* A small chewy candy, shaped somewhat like a bean, with a hard sugar coating.

jel•ly•fish (jĕl′ē fĭsh′) *n.* Any of numerous sea animals having a soft, often umbrella-shaped body. Many jellyfish have tentacles that can cause an uncomfortable sting.

jel•ly•roll (jĕl′ē rōl′) *n.* A thin sheet of sponge cake layered with jelly and then rolled up.

Jen•ner (jĕn′ər), **Edward.** 1749–1823. British physician who developed a vaccine for smallpox.

jen•net (jĕn′ĭt) *n.* A small Spanish horse used for riding.

jen•ny (jĕn′ē) *n., pl.* **jen•nies. 1.** A spinning jenny. **2.** The female of certain animals, especially the donkey.

jeop•ard•ize (jĕp′ər dīz′) *tr.v.* **jeop•ard•ized, jeop•ard•iz•ing, jeop•ard•izes.** To put at risk of loss or

Thomas Jefferson

Thomas Jefferson

Born in Virginia in 1743, Thomas **Jefferson** got involved in politics at an exciting time—just as the American Revolution was brewing. Politics was just one of Jefferson's many lifelong interests, which included the sciences, architecture, and philosophy. Through his extensive studies, Jefferson developed ideas that profoundly influenced the creation of a democratic American government. As the principal author of the Declaration of Independence, he stressed self-government and individual rights, two ideas of long-standing importance in American government. Jefferson went on to serve as the country's third President (1801–1809), during which time he signed the Louisiana Purchase with France (1803), authorized the Lewis and Clark expedition to explore the territory, and prohibited the importation of slaves (1808). In his retirement Jefferson founded the University of Virginia (1819), for which he served as both architect and academic planner.

ă	pat	oi	boy
ā	pay	ou	out
âr	care	o͝o	took
ä	father	o͞o	boot
ĕ	pet	ŭ	cut
ē	be	ûr	urge
ĭ	pit	th	thin
ī	pie	*th*	this
îr	pier	hw	whoop
ŏ	pot	zh	vision
ō	toe	ə	about
ô	paw	N	*French* bon

jerboa

jew's-harp

injury; endanger: *Not getting enough sleep can jeopardize one's health.*

jeop•ard•y (jĕp′ər dē) *n., pl.* **jeop•ard•ies.** Risk of loss or injury; danger or peril: *The active volcano put the nearby city in jeopardy.*

jer•bo•a (jər bō′ə) *n.* Any of various small rodents of Asia and northern Africa having a long tufted tail and long hind legs used for leaping.

Jer•e•mi•ah (jĕr′ə mī′ə) *n.* **1.** A Hebrew prophet of the seventh and sixth centuries B.C. **2.** A book of the Bible in which Jeremiah denounces the sins of the Israelites and prophesies the destruction of Jerusalem.

Jer•i•cho (jĕr′ĭ kō′). An ancient city of Palestine near the northwest shore of the Dead Sea. According to the Bible, it was captured and destroyed by Joshua.

jerk[1] (jûrk) *v.* **jerked, jerk•ing, jerks.** —*tr.* To move (something) with a quick pull, push, or twist: *I jerked my foot out of the cold water.* —*intr.* To move in sudden uneven motions: *The train jerked as we left the station.* —*n.* **1.** A sudden abrupt motion, such as a yank or twist. **2.** A sudden and uncontrolled contraction of a muscle. **3.** *Slang.* A stupid or foolish person. **4.** A lift in weightlifting in which the weight is heaved above the head from shoulder height with a sudden motion. [First written down in 1550 in Modern English.]

jerk[2] (jûrk) *tr.v.* **jerked, jerk•ing, jerks.** To cut (meat) into strips and dry in the sun or cure with smoke. [First written down in 1707 in Modern English, from *jerky*, meat.]

jer•kin (jûr′kĭn) *n.* A short close-fitting jacket having no sleeves, worn by men during the 16th and 17th centuries.

jerk•y[1] (jûr′kē) *adj.* **jerk•i•er, jerk•i•est. 1.** Making sudden starts and stops: *jerky movements.* **2.** *Slang.* Silly; foolish. —**jerk′i•ly** *adv.* —**jerk′i•ness** *n.*

jerk•y[2] (jûr′kē) *n.* Meat, such as beef, that has been cut into strips and dried in the sun or cured with smoke. [First written down in 1850 in Modern English, from Quechua *ch'arki.*]

jer•ry-build (jĕr′ē bĭld′) *tr.v.* **jer•ry-built** (jĕr′ē bĭlt′), **jer•ry-build•ing, jer•ry-builds.** To build hastily, cheaply, and poorly.

jer•sey (jûr′zē) *n., pl.* **jer•seys. 1.** A soft elastic fabric of knitted wool, cotton, or rayon, used for clothing. **2.** A garment made of this or a similar fabric. **3.** Often **Jersey.** Any of a breed of light brown cattle developed on the Island of Jersey and raised for milk.

Jersey. The largest of the Channel Islands in the English Channel. The island has a predominantly French influence.

Je•ru•sa•lem (jə ro͞o′sə ləm *or* jə ro͞o′zə ləm). The capital of Israel, in the east-central part of the country in the West Bank. The city has been occupied as far back as the fourth millennium B.C. and is considered a holy city to Jews, Muslims, and Christians. Population, 446,500.

jes•sa•mine (jĕs′ə mĭn) *n.* Variant of **jasmine.**

jest (jĕst) *n.* **1.** A playful or amusing act. **2.** A playful mood or manner: *Their teasing was only done in jest.* —*intr.v.* **jest•ed, jest•ing, jests. 1.** To act or speak playfully. **2.** To make witty or amusing remarks.

jest•er (jĕs′tər) *n.* A person who jests, especially a person employed to entertain by joking at a medieval court.

Jes•u•it (jĕzh′o͞o ĭt *or* jĕz′o͞o ĭt) *n.* A member of the Society of Jesus, a Roman Catholic religious order for men.

Je•sus (jē′zəs). A teacher and prophet who lived in the early part of the first century of this era. His life and teachings form the basis of Christianity. Christians believe Jesus to be the son of God and the Christ.

jet[1] (jĕt) *n.* **1.** A dense black form of coal that can be polished to a bright shine and used to make beads and other ornaments. **2.** A deep black. [First written down in 1351 in Middle English and spelled *gete*, from Greek *gagatēs*, from *Gagas*, a town of Lycia, an ancient country of southwest Asia Minor.]

jet[2] (jĕt) *n.* **1.** A high velocity stream of liquid or gas forced through a small opening or nozzle under pressure: *A jet of water shot out of the hose.* **2.** An outlet or a nozzle through which a stream is forced: *a gas jet.* **3.a.** An aircraft or other vehicle propelled by a jet engine. **b.** A jet engine. —*v.* **jet•ted, jet•ting, jets.** —*intr.* **1.** To travel by jet plane. **2.** To move very quickly. —*tr.* To propel outward or squirt as under pressure. [First written down in 1696 in Modern English, from Old French *jeter*, to spout forth, from Latin *iactāre*, to throw.]

jet engine *n.* An engine that develops its thrust from a jet of exhaust gases produced by burned fuel.

jet lag *n.* The disruption of body rhythms, such as eating and sleeping times, resulting from high-speed air travel through several time zones.

jet-pro•pelled (jĕt′prə pĕld′) *adj.* Propelled by one or more jet engines: *a jet-propelled airplane.*

jet propulsion *n.* **1.** The driving of an aircraft by the powerful thrust developed when a jet of gas is forced out of a jet engine. **2.** Propulsion by means of any fluid that is forced out in a stream in the opposite direction.

jet•sam (jĕt′səm) *n.* Cargo and other things thrown overboard to lighten a ship in distress.

jet stream *n.* **1.** A strong wind, often reaching very high speeds, that blows from a westerly direction at altitudes of 10 to 15 miles (15 to 25 kilometers). **2.** A rapidly moving stream of liquid or gas as from a jet engine.

jet•ti•son (jĕt′ĭ sən *or* jĕt′ĭ zən) *tr.v.* **jet•ti•soned, jet•ti•son•ing, jet•ti•sons. 1.** To cast (something) overboard, especially as a means of lightening a ship or an aircraft in distress. **2.** *Informal.* To discard (unwanted things).

jet•ty (jĕt′ē) *n., pl.* **jet•ties. 1.** A structure, as of stone, earth, and timbers, projecting into a body of water to affect the current or tide or to protect a harbor or shoreline. **2.** A wharf.

Jew (jo͞o) *n.* **1.** A person whose religion is Judaism. **2.** A member of the widely dispersed people originally descended from the ancient Hebrews and sharing an ethnic heritage based on Judaism.

jew•el (jo͞o′əl) *n.* **1.** A precious stone; a gem. **2.** A costly ornament, such as a ring or necklace, made of precious metal set with gems. **3.** A small gem or crystal used as a bearing in a watch. **4.** A person or thing that is greatly admired or valued: *The only grandchild is the jewel of the family.* —*tr.v.* **jew•eled, jew•el•ing, jew•els** or **jew•elled, jew•el•ling, jew•els.** To adorn with jewels: *a jeweled crown.* [First written down before 1300 in Middle English and spelled *juel*, from Anglo-Norman.]

jew•el•er (jo͞o′ə lər) *n.* A person who makes, repairs, or sells jewelry.

jew•el•ry (jo͞o′əl rē) *n.* Ornaments, such as bracelets or rings, made of precious metals and gems or of inexpensive or imitation materials.

Jew•ish (jo͞o′ĭsh) *adj.* Of or relating to the Jews or their culture or religion. —**Jew′ish•ness** *n.*

Jew•ry (jo͞o′rē) *n.* The Jewish people.

jew's-harp (jo͞oz′härp′) *n.* A small musical instrument consisting of a U-shaped frame that is held in the mouth and an attached blade of flexible metal that is plucked to produce twanging tones.

Jez•e•bel (jĕz′ə bĕl′). Flourished about ninth century B.C. Phoenician princess and queen of Israel.

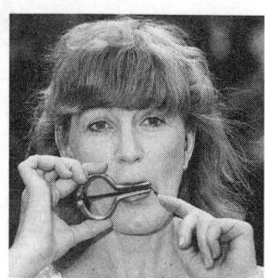

jib (jĭb) *n.* A triangular sail set forward of the mast and stretching to the bow or bowsprit.

jibe[1] (jīb) *v.* **jibed, jib•ing, jibes.** *—intr.* To shift a sail from one side of a boat or ship to the other when sailing before the wind. *—tr.* To cause (a sail) to shift from one side of a boat or ship to the other when sailing before the wind. *—n.* The act of jibing. [First written down in 1693 and spelled *gybe*, from obsolete Dutch *gijben*.]

❑ *These sound alike:* **jibe**[1] (shift a sail), **gibe** (jeer), **jibe**[2] (agree).

jibe[2] (jīb) *intr.v.* **jibed, jib•ing, jibes.** *Informal.* To be in accord; agree: *The account of the other witness doesn't jibe with yours.* [First written down in 1813 in Modern English and spelled *gibe*.]

❑ *These sound alike:* **jibe**[2] (agree), **gibe** (jeer), **jibe**[1] (shift a sail).

jibe[3] (jīb) *v. & n.* Variant of **gibe.**

Jid•da (jĭd′ə). A city of west-central Saudi Arabia on the Red Sea west of Mecca. Population, 1,300,000.

jif•fy (jĭf′ē) *n., pl.* **jif•fies.** *Informal.* A moment; an instant: *I'll have this fixed in a jiffy.*

jig (jĭg) *n.* **1.a.** Any of various lively dances in triple time. **b.** Music written for such a dance. **2.** Any of various devices used to guide a tool or hold work as it is put into a machine, such as a saw or drill. **3.** A metal fishing lure with one or more hooks, designed to bob up and down to attract fish. *—intr.v.* **jigged, jig•ging, jigs. 1.** To dance a jig. **2.** To move up and down or to and fro in a quick, jerky way.

jig•ger (jĭg′ər) *n.* A small cup that holds 1½ ounces (44 milliliters) of liquor.

jig•gle (jĭg′əl) *tr. & intr.v.* **jig•gled, jig•gling, jig•gles.** To shake or cause to shake up and down or back and forth with short quick jerks: *By jiggling the wire we got the light to work. The plane jiggled slightly as it landed on the ground.* *—n.* A jiggling motion.

jig•saw (jĭg′sô′) *n.* A saw with a narrow blade that moves up and down, used for cutting curves.

jigsaw puzzle *n.* A puzzle consisting of a number of irregularly shaped pieces of wood or cardboard that form a picture when fitted together.

ji•had (jĭ häd′) *n.* **1.** A Muslim holy war against unbelievers. **2.** A crusade or struggle.

jilt (jĭlt) *tr.v.* **jilt•ed, jilt•ing, jilts.** To drop or cast aside (a lover or sweetheart).

Jim Crow or **jim crow** (jĭm′ krō′) *Slang. n.* The practice of discriminating against and segregating Black people.

jim•my (jĭm′ē) *n., pl.* **jim•mies.** A short crowbar with curved ends. *—tr.v.* **jim•mied, jim•my•ing, jim•mies.** To pry (something) open with or as with a jimmy: *jimmy a door.*

jim•son•weed (jĭm′sən wēd′) *n.* A tall, coarse, poisonous plant having large, trumpet-shaped white or purplish flowers and prickly seed pods.

jin•gle (jĭng′gəl) *intr. & tr.v.* **jin•gled, jin•gling, jin•gles.** To make or cause to make a tinkling or ringing metallic sound: *Coins jingled in the fare box as the passengers boarded the bus.* *—n.* **1.** A tinkling or ringing sound made by small metal objects striking together: *the jingle of sleigh bells.* **2.** A catchy rhyme or verse often used in radio and television commercials.

jin•go•ism (jĭng′gō ĭz′əm) *n.* Extreme nationalism characterized by hostility to foreign countries.

jin•ni (jĭn′ē *or* jĭ nē′) *n., pl.* **jinn** (jĭn). In Muslim legend, a spirit able to appear in either human or animal form and exercising influence over people. [First written down in 1684 in Modern English and spelled *dgen*, from Arabic *jinnī*.]

jin•rik•sha (jĭn-rĭk′shô′) *n.* A small two-wheeled carriage drawn by one or two people; a ricksha.

jinx (jĭngks) *Informal. n.* **1.** A person or thing that is felt to bring bad luck; a hex. **2.** A condition or period of bad luck that appears to have been caused by a specific person or thing. *—tr.v.* **jinxed, jinx•ing, jinx•es.** To bring bad luck to: *Don't jinx me!* [First written down in 1911 in American English, possibly from *jynx*, a kind of woodpecker, from Greek *iunx*.]

jit•ney (jĭt′nē) *n., pl.* **jit•neys.** A small bus that carries passengers for a low fare: *A jitney runs from the apartment buildings to the shopping center.*

jit•ter•bug (jĭt′ər bŭg′) *n.* **1.** A vigorous energetic dance performed to fast jazz or swing music, popular in the 1940's. **2.** A person who does such a dance. *—intr.v.* **jit•ter•bugged, jit•ter•bug•ging, jit•ter•bugs.** To dance the jitterbug.

jit•ters (jĭt′ərz) *pl.n.* A fit of nervousness: *The exam gave me a case of the jitters.*

jit•ter•y (jĭt′ə rē) *adj.* **jit•ter•i•er, jit•ter•i•est.** Having the jitters; nervous.

jiu•jit•su (jo͞o jĭt′so͞o) *n.* Variant of **jujitsu.**

jive (jīv) *n.* **1.** Jazz or swing music. **2.** The jargon used by jazz musicians and fans. **3.** Nonsensical or deceptive talk.

Joan of Arc (jōn əv ärk), Saint. French name **Jeanne d'Arc** (zhän därk′). 1412?–1431. French military leader and hero who organized the resistance that forced the English to end their siege of Orléans (1429). She was later tried by the English for heresy and sorcery and burned at the stake.

job (jŏb) *n.* **1.** A task that must be done; a duty: *My job is to fix lunch; your job is to wash the dishes.* See Synonyms at **task. 2.** A position at which an activity is regularly done for pay: *I enjoy my job in the bookstore.* **3.** Something resulting from or produced by work: *You did a fine job on the report.* [First written down in 1557 in Modern English and spelled *jobbe*, perhaps from Middle English *gobbe*, lump.]

Job (jōb) *n.* **1.** In the Bible, a man whose faith in God survived the test of repeated troubles. **2.** A book of the Bible in which Job argues with three friends that his sufferings are not a punishment for past sins.

job•ber (jŏb′ər) *n.* A person who buys merchandise from manufacturers and sells it to retailers at a profit.

job•less (jŏb′lĭs) *adj.* **1.** Having no job; unemployed. **2.** Of or relating to those who are without jobs. *—n. (used with a plural verb).* Unemployed people considered as a group. **—job′less•ness** *n.*

Jo•cas•ta (jō kăs′tə) *n.* In Greek mythology, a queen of Thebes who unknowingly marries her son, Oedipus.

jock (jŏk) *n.* **1.** An athlete, especially in college. **2.** An athletic supporter.

jock•ey (jŏk′ē) *n., pl.* **jock•eys.** A person who rides horses in races, especially as a profession. *—v.* **jock•eyed, jock•ey•ing, jock•eys.** *—tr.* **1.** To direct or maneuver by cleverness or skill: *The rowers jockeyed the boat into a good position at the start of the race.* **2.** To ride (a horse) in a race. *—intr.* **1.** To ride a horse as a jockey. **2.** To maneuver for a certain position or advantage: *jockey for a position at the starting line.*

jock•strap (jŏk′străp′) *n.* An athletic supporter.

jo•cose (jō kōs′) *adj.* Given to joking; merry. **—jo•cose′ly** *adv.* **—jo•cose′ness, jo•cos′i•ty** (jō kŏs′ĭ tē) *n.*

joc•u•lar (jŏk′yə lər) *adj.* **1.** Given to joking. **2.** Meant as a joke; humorous: *a jocular remark.* [First written down in 1626 in Modern English, from Latin *ioculus*, joke.] **—joc′u•lar′i•ty** (jŏk′yə lăr′ĭ tē) *n.* **—joc′u•lar•ly** *adv.*

joc•und (jŏk′ənd *or* jō′kənd) *adj.* Having a cheerful

jinriksha
In Hong Kong

Joan of Arc
Detail from a 15th-century illuminated manuscript

ă	pat	oi	boy
ā	pay	ou	out
âr	care	o͝o	took
ä	father	o͞o	boot
ĕ	pet	ŭ	cut
ē	be	ûr	urge
ĭ	pit	th	thin
ī	pie	*th*	this
îr	pier	hw	whoop
ŏ	pot	zh	vision
ō	toe	ə	about
ô	paw	N	*French* bon

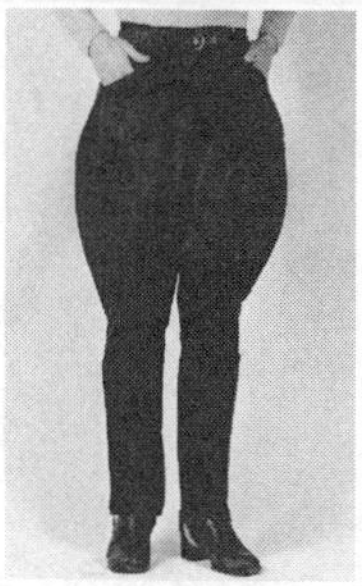

jodhpurs

Andrew Johnson
1865 mezzotint after a photograph by John Sartain (1808–1897)

Lady Bird Johnson

Lyndon B. Johnson
Photographed in 1967

disposition or quality; merry. **—jo•cun′di•ty** (jō **kŭn′**dĭ tē) *n.* **—joc′und•ly** *adv.*

jodh•purs (**jŏd′**pərz) *pl.n.* Pants that fit loosely above the knees and tightly from the knees to the ankles, worn for horseback riding. [First written down in 1899 in Modern English, after *Jodhpur* a city of western India.]

Jo•el (**jō′**əl) *n.* **1.** A Hebrew prophet of the sixth century B.C. **2.** A book of the Bible in which Joel foresees a plague of locusts and a day of judgment by God, and calls for repentance.

jog (jŏg) *v.* **jogged, jog•ging, jogs.** *—tr.* **1.** To move by shoving, bumping, or jerking; jar: *The old horse trotted along jogging me up and down.* **2.** To stir or shake up: *Let's see if I can jog your memory.* *—intr.* **1.** To go or travel at a slow pace: *The old car jogged along until it reached the hill.* **2.** To run at a steady slow trot, especially for exercise. *—n.* **1.** A slight push; a nudge. **2.** A slow steady pace. **3.** A bumping or jolting motion. [First written down in 1548 in Modern English, perhaps from Middle English *shoggen,* to shake.] **—jog′ger** *n.*

jog•gle (**jŏg′**əl) *tr. & intr.v.* **jog•gled, jog•gling, jog•gles.** To shake a little; nudge. *—n.* A shake or nudge.

Jo•han•nes•burg (jō **hăn′**ĭs bûrg′ *or* jō **hä′**nĭs bûrg′). The largest city of South Africa, in the northeast part of the country south of Pretoria. It was founded in 1886 after the discovery of gold nearby. Population, 703,980.

John[1] (jŏn). 1167?–1216. King of England (1199–1216) who was forced to sign the Magna Carta (June 15, 1215), a milestone in English freedom.

John[2] (jŏn) *n.* The fourth Gospel of the New Testament, thought to have been written by Saint John the Evangelist.

John, Saint. Known as "the Evangelist." Flourished about first century A.D. One of the 12 Apostles, traditionally considered the author of the fourth Gospel, three epistles, and the Book of Revelation.

John XXIII. 1881–1963. Pope (1958–1963) who organized the Second Vatican Council (1962), the first general council of the Roman Catholic Church in almost a century.

John Bull *n.* A personification of England or the English people. [First written down in 1714 in Modern English, after *John Bull,* a character in *Law Is a Bottomless Pit* by John Arbuthnot.]

john•ny•cake (**jŏn′**ē kāk′) *n.* Thin flat cornmeal bread, often baked on a griddle.

John Paul II. Born 1920. Pope (since 1978) who is the first Polish-born pope. He supports human rights and conservative doctrine.

John•son (**jŏn′**sən), **Andrew.** 1808–1875. The 17th President of the United States (1865–1869).

Johnson, Claudia Alta Taylor. Known as "Lady Bird." Born 1912. First Lady of the United States (1963–1969) as the wife of Lyndon Johnson. Her work focused on preserving the environment.

Johnson, Lyndon Baines. 1908–1973. The 36th President of the United States (1963–1969), who succeeded to the office after John F. Kennedy was assassinated. He won the 1964 election but faced criticism over U.S. involvement in the Vietnam War (1964–1973).

Johnson, Samuel. 1709–1784. British writer known for his *Dictionary of the English Language* (1755).

John the Bap•tist (**băp′**tĭst), Saint. First century B.C. Jewish prophet who according to the New Testament baptized Jesus.

join (join) *v.* **joined, join•ing, joins.** *—tr.* **1.** To put or bring together; link; connect: *The George Washington Bridge joins New York and New Jersey. The children joined hands.* **2.** To meet and merge with; be united with: *The Missouri River joins the Mississippi near St. Louis.* **3.** To become a member of: *join the photography club.* **4.** To enter into the company of: *Can you join us for lunch?* **5.** To put or bring into close association: *The two families were joined by marriage.* *—intr.* **1.** To come together: *The roads join just before the bridge.* **2.** To act together; join forces: *The two groups joined together to oppose the new law.* **3.** To take part; participate: *Everyone joined in the celebration.* **4.** To become a member of a group. *—n.* A joint; a junction. [First written down before 1300 in Middle English and spelled *joinen,* from Latin *iungere.*]

Synonyms: join, combine, unite, link, connect. These verbs mean to fasten or attach two or more things together. **Join** can mean to bring separate things together physically: *We joined the pipes together and turned on the water.* **Combine** often means to mix or merge different things for a specific purpose: *Jason combined oil, vinegar, and herbs to make a salad dressing.* **Unite** suggests joining of separate parts into a thoroughly blended whole with its own identity: *The prince united the little kingdoms to form a large nation.* **Link** and **connect** can mean to attach firmly without taking away the special characteristics of each part: *The train's engine and wagons are linked together with strong bolts. The new tunnel under the English Channel will connect Great Britain and France.*
Antonyms: separate, divide.

join•er (**joi′**nər) *n.* **1.** A skilled carpenter who makes woodwork, such as doors and stairs, for houses and other buildings. **2.** *Informal.* A person inclined to join many groups or organizations.

joint (joint) *n.* **1.** A place where two or more things are joined together: *a joint in a pipe.* **2.** A point at which movable body parts are connected or come together in an animal: *a knee joint.* **3.** The way in which two parts are joined or the place at which two parts are held together: *A flexible joint allows the table leg to move.* **4.** A part on a plant stem from which a leaf or stem grows. **5.** *Slang.* A cheap or disreputable gathering place. **6.** A large cut of meat for roasting. *—adj.* **1.** Undertaken or shared by two or more people or parties: *a joint effort; a joint bank account.* **2.** Sharing with another or others: *joint owners.* **3.** Involving both houses of a legislature: *a joint session of Congress.* *—tr.v.* **joint•ed, joint•ing, joints.** **1.** To connect with a joint or joints: *Our plumber jointed the new pipes.* **2.** To cut (meat) apart at the joints. ***—idiom.*** **out of joint. 1.** Not in place at the joint; dislocated. **2.** *Informal.* In bad spirits; out of sorts.

Joint Chiefs of Staff (joint) *n.* The principal military advisory group to the President of the United States, composed of the chiefs of the Army, Navy, and Air Force and the commandant of the Marine Corps.

joint•ly (**joint′**lē) *adv.* Together; in common: *The business is owned jointly by three partners.*

joist (joist) *n.* Any of the parallel horizontal beams that support the boards of a floor or ceiling.

joke (jōk) *n.* **1.** Something said or done to cause laughter, especially an amusing story with a punchline. **2.** A mischievous trick; a prank. **3.** A person or thing that is an object of amusement or laughter. *—intr.v.* **joked, jok•ing, jokes.** To tell or play jokes. [First written down in 1670 in Modern English, from Latin *iocus.*]

jok•er (**jō′**kər) *n.* **1.** A person who tells or plays jokes. **2.** A playing card bearing the figure of a jester, used as the highest card or as any card the holder desires.

joke•ster (**jōk′**stər) *n.* A joker.

Jol•li•et also **Jo•li•et** (**jō′**lē ĕt′ *or* jō′lē **ĕt′**), **Louis.** 1645–1700. French-Canadian explorer of the upper

Mississippi Valley who descended the Mississippi River in 1673 to the mouth of the Arkansas River.

jol•li•ty (jŏl′ĭ tē) *n., pl.* **jol•li•ties.** Gaiety; merriment.

jol•ly (jŏl′ē) *adj.* **jol•li•er, jol•li•est. 1.** Full of fun and good spirits. **2.** Showing or causing happiness or mirth; cheerful. *—adv. Chiefly British.* Very: *That's a jolly good idea!*

Jol•ly Rog•er (jŏl′ē rŏj′ər) *n.* A black flag bearing a white skull and crossbones, formerly used on pirate ships.

jolt (jōlt) *v.* **jolt•ed, jolt•ing, jolts.** *—tr.* To shake violently or jar: *The bicycle jolted me off the seat as it bumped over some rocks. —intr.* To move in a bumpy or jerky fashion: *The bus jolted to a stop as the driver jammed on the brakes. —n.* **1.** A sudden jerk or bump. **2.** A sudden shock or surprise: *The news of their arrival came as quite a jolt.*

Jo•nah (jō′nə) *n.* **1.** In the Bible, a Hebrew prophet who, called by God to preach to the Assyrians, tries to escape but is swallowed by a whale and later disgorged unharmed. **2.** A book of the Bible that relates Jonah's eventual success in his mission to the Assyrians.

Jones (jōnz), **John Paul.** 1747–1792. Scottish-born American naval officer in the American Revolution.

Jones, Mary Harris. Known as "Mother Jones." 1830–1930. Irish-born American labor leader and union organizer who in 1905 helped found the Industrial Workers of the World.

jon•quil (jŏng′kwəl *or* jŏn′kwəl) *n.* A garden plant having fragrant yellow flowers resembling those of the daffodil and long narrow leaves.

Jor•dan (jôr′dn). A country of southwest Asia in northwest Arabia east of Israel. It has been inhabited since biblical times. The country gained its independence from Great Britain in 1946. The territory west of the Jordan River is occupied by Israel. Capital, Amman. Population, 2,595,100.

Jordan River. A river of southwest Asia rising in Syria and flowing about 200 miles (322 kilometers) south to the northern end of the Dead Sea.

Jo•seph¹ (jō′zəf *or* jō′səf). In the Bible, a son of Jacob and Rachel and the ancestor of one of the tribes of Israel.

Jo•seph² (jō′zəf *or* jō′səf). Known as "Chief Joseph." 1840?–1904. Nez Percé leader who conducted a retreat of the Nez Percé from U.S. forces (1877) but was forced to surrender before reaching Canada.

Joseph, Saint. Flourished about first century A.D. In the New Testament, the husband of Mary, mother of Jesus.

josh (jŏsh) *v.* **joshed, josh•ing, josh•es.** *—tr.* To tease in a light-hearted playful way. *—intr.* To make or exchange jokes.

Josh•u•a (jŏsh′o͞o ə) *n.* **1.** In the Bible, a Hebrew leader who succeeded Moses as leader of Israel. **2.** A book of the Bible that relates the Israelites' conquest of Canaan.

jos•tle (jŏs′əl) *v.* **jos•tled, jos•tling, jos•tles.** *—tr.* To push and come into rough contact with while moving; bump: *jostled each other on the crowded dance floor. —intr.* **1.** To come into rough contact while moving: *The people jostled on the platform as the train approached.* **2.** To make one's way by pushing or elbowing: *I jostled through the crowd and left the lobby. —n.* A rough shove or push. **—jos′tler** *n.*

jot (jŏt) *n.* A tiny bit; an iota: *They didn't care one jot. —tr.v.* **jot•ted, jot•ting, jots.** To write down briefly and hastily: *I jotted down a few notes.*

joule (jo͞ol *or* joul) *n.* **1.** A unit of energy equal to the work done when a current of 1 ampere is passed through a resistence of 1 ohm for 1 second. **2.** A unit of energy equal to the work done when a force of 1 newton acts through a distance of 1 meter. [First written down in 1882 in Modern English, after James Prescott *Joule* (1818–1889), British physicist.]

jounce (jouns) *intr. & tr.v.* **jounced, jounc•ing, jounc•es.** To move or cause to move with bumps and jolts: *The bus jounced along the bumpy road. —n.* A rough jolting movement.

jour•nal (jûr′nəl) *n.* **1.** A daily record of events, experiences, proceedings, or business transactions; a diary or log. **2.** A periodical containing articles on a particular subject: *a medical journal.* **3.** A newspaper. **4.** The part of an axle or a machine shaft that is supported by a bearing. [First written down in 1355 in Middle English, from Late Latin *diurnālis,* daily.]

jour•nal•ism (jûr′nə lĭz′əm) *n.* The gathering, writing, and presentation of news in newspapers or magazines or in radio or television broadcasts.

jour•nal•ist (jûr′nə lĭst) *n.* A person employed in journalism, especially a reporter or an editor.

jour•nal•is•tic (jûr′nə lĭs′tĭk) *adj.* Of, relating to, or characteristic of journalism or journalists.

jour•ney (jûr′nē) *n., pl.* **jour•neys. 1.** A trip, especially one over a great distance: *a long journey across Europe and Asia.* **2.** The distance traveled on a journey or the time required for such a trip: *a thousand-mile journey; a three-day journey. —intr. v.* **jour•neyed, jour•ney•ing, jour•neys.** To travel; make a trip: *We journeyed throughout India.* [First written down before 1200 in Middle English and spelled *jurnee,* day's travel, from Late Latin *diurnum,* day.]

jour•ney•man (jûr′nē mən) *n.* **1.** A person who has completed an apprenticeship and works for another person. **2.** One who is a competent but undistinguished worker.

joust (joust *or* jŭst) *n.* A combat between two armored knights on horseback armed with lances. *—intr.v.* **joust•ed, joust•ing, jousts.** To take part in a joust.

Jove (jōv) *n.* In Roman mythology, Jupiter.

jo•vi•al (jō′vē əl) *adj.* Full of fun and good cheer; jolly: *a jovial host.* **—jo′vi•al′i•ty** (jō′vē ăl′ĭ tē) *n.* **—jo′vi•al•ly** *adv.*

jowl¹ (joul) *n.* **1.** The jaw, especially the lower jaw. **2.** The cheek. [First written down about 750 in Old English and spelled *ceafl.*]

jowl² (joul) *n.* **1.** The flesh under the lower jaw, especially when plump or hanging loosely. **2.** Loosely hanging flesh on or near the jaw of an animal: *the jowls of a bulldog.* [First written down about 1300 in Middle English and spelled *cholle.*]

joy (joi) *n.* **1.** A feeling of great happiness or delight. **2.** A source or cause of joy: *Some books are a joy to read.*

Joyce (jois), **James.** 1882–1941. Irish writer whose works have greatly influenced modern fiction. His novels include *Finnegans Wake* (1939).

joy•ful (joi′fəl) *adj.* **1.** Full of joy: *a joyful celebration.* See Synonyms at **glad. 2.** Showing or expressing joy: *a joyful shout; a joyful look.* **—joy′ful•ly** *adv.* **—joy′ful•ness** *n.*

joy•less (joi′lĭs) *adj.* Cheerless; dismal.

joy•ous (joi′əs) *adj.* Full of joy; joyful: *a joyous occasion.* **—joy′ous•ly** *adv.* **—joy′ous•ness** *n.*

jr. or **Jr.** *abbr.* An abbreviation of junior.

Juan Car•los (hwän kär′lôs). Born 1938. Spanish king (since 1975) who helped restore democracy.

ju•bi•lant (jo͞o′bə lənt) *adj.* Full of joyful exultation; rejoicing: *A jubilant crowd celebrated their team's victory.* **—ju′bi•lant•ly** *adv.*

ju•bi•la•tion (jo͞o′bə lā′shən) *n.* Great rejoicing: *The good news was greeted with jubilation.*

Mother Jones

jonquil

Chief Joseph

Juan Carlos

ă	pat	oi	boy
ā	pay	ou	out
âr	care	o͝o	took
ä	father	o͞o	boot
ĕ	pet	ŭ	cut
ē	be	ûr	urge
ĭ	pit	th	thin
ī	pie	*th*	this
îr	pier	hw	whoop
ŏ	pot	zh	vision
ō	toe	ə	about
ô	paw	N	*French* bon

judo

Juliana

Word History: jungle

People nearly always think of a **jungle** as a steamy, green, overgrown tropical rain forest, but that wasn't necessarily so originally. Our word comes from the Sanskrit word *jaṅgalam*, "desert, wasteland, uncultivated area." The English word *jungle* therefore comes from the last sense of the Sanskrit word, for a *jungle* is uncultivated. The interior of Iceland is usually described as an "ice desert," as opposed to the more usual sand desert. You could also call Iceland a *jungle*, but perhaps you would have trouble convincing your geography teacher.

ju•bi•lee (jo͞o′bə lē′ *or* jo͞o′bə **lē′**) *n.* **1.** A special anniversary, especially a 50th anniversary, or the celebration of it. **2.** A season or an occasion of joyful celebration.

Ju•dah¹ (jo͞o′də). In the Bible, a son of Jacob and Leah and the ancestor of one of the tribes of Israel.

Ju•dah² (jo͞o′də). An ancient kingdom of southern Palestine between the Mediterranean Sea and the Dead Sea. It lasted from 931 B.C. until 586 B.C.

Ju•da•ic (jo͞o **dā′**ĭk) *adj.* Of, relating to, or characteristic of Jews or Judaism: *Judaic traditions.*

Ju•da•ism (jo͞o′dē ĭz′əm) *n.* The religion of the Jewish people, based on belief in one God and on the teachings set forth in the Bible and the Talmud.

Ju•das (jo͞o′dəs) *n.* A person who betrays others under the appearance of friendship.

Judas Is•car•i•ot (ĭ **skăr′**ē ət). Died about A.D. 30. In the New Testament, one of the 12 Apostles and the betrayer of Jesus.

Jude (jo͞od) *n.* A book of the New Testament written in the form of a letter in which Saint Jude denounces false preachers.

Jude, Saint. Flourished about first century A.D. In the New Testament, one of the 12 Apostles.

Ju•de•a (jo͞o **dē′**ə *or* jo͞o **dā′**ə). An ancient region of southern Palestine made up of present-day southern Israel and southwest Jordan.

judge (jŭj) *v.* **judged, judg•ing, judg•es.** *—tr.* **1.** To form an opinion about or an evaluation of (something): *The critic judged the play to be compelling drama.* **2.** To hear and decide (a case) in a court of law. **3.** To determine the winners of (a contest or an issue): *The teachers judged the school spelling bee.* *—intr.* **1.** To form an opinion or evaluation. **2.** To act or decide as a judge. *—n.* **1.** A person who gives an opinion about the value, quality, or outcome of something: *a good judge of character; a poor judge of painting.* **2.** A public official who hears and decides cases in a court of law. **3.** A person who decides the outcome of a dispute or the winner of a contest or competition. **4. Judges.** *(used with a singular verb).* A book of the Bible containing the history of the Israelites from settlement in Canaan to the establishment of the monarchy. [First written down before 1200 in Middle English and spelled *jugen*, from Latin *iūdicāre*, from *iūdex*, judge.] **—judg′er** *n.*

judge•ship (**jŭj′**shĭp′) *n.* The position of responsibilities of a judge or the period during which a judge is in office.

judg•ment also **judge•ment** (**jŭj′**mənt) *n.* **1.** The ability to make distinctions and form opinions or evaluations: *saving money shows good judgment.* **2.** An opinion or estimate made after careful consideration: *We await the judgment of the referee.* **3.** A decision reached in a court of law: *The high court handed down a judgment holding certain practices illegal.*

Judg•ment Day (**jŭj′**mənt) *n.* In Christian tradition, the last day of the world, when God will pass final judgment on all souls.

ju•di•cial (jo͞o **dĭsh′**əl) *adj.* **1.** Of or relating to courts of law or the administration of justice: *the judicial branch of government.* **2.** Of or appropriate to the office of a judge: *judicial robes.* **3.** Decreed by a court: *a judicial decision.* **—ju•di′cial•ly** *adv.*

ju•di•ci•ar•y (jo͞o **dĭsh′**ē ĕr′ē *or* jo͞o **dĭsh′**ə rē) *n., pl.* **ju•di•ci•ar•ies. 1.** The judicial branch of government. **2.** A system of courts of law and judges. **3.** The judges of these courts.

ju•di•cious (jo͞o **dĭsh′**əs) *adj.* Having or showing wise and sound judgment; prudent: *Conservation involves the judicious use of resources.* **—ju•di′cious•ly** *adv.* **—ju•di′cious•ness** *n.*

ju•do (**jo͞o′**dō) *n.* A sport and method of self-defense developed in Japan and based on jujitsu. [First written down in 1889 in Modern English, from Japanese *jūdō* : *jū*, soft + *dō*, way.]

jug (jŭg) *n.* **1.** A tall, often rounded vessel with a narrow mouth, a handle, and usually a stopper or cap. **2.** The amount that a jug can hold: *We drank a jug of cider.* **3.** A small pitcher.

jug•ger•naut (**jŭg′**ər nôt′) *n.* **1.** Something, such as a belief, to which people blindly devote or sacrifice themselves. **2.** An advancing force or object that crushes or seems to crush everything in its path.

jug•gle (**jŭg′**əl) *v.* **jug•gled, jug•gling, jug•gles.** *—tr.* **1.** To keep (two or more objects) in the air at one time by alternately tossing and catching them. **2.** To have difficulty holding or balancing: *The tourist was juggling luggage and cameras.* **3.** To change or rearrange so as to mislead or cheat: *juggled the figures in the account books.* *—intr.* **1.** To perform as a juggler. **2.** To use trickery to deceive. [First written down about 1378 in Middle English and spelled *jogelen*, to perform tricks, from Latin *ioculārī*, to jest, from *ioculus*, jest.]

jug•gler (**jŭg′**lər) *n.* **1.** An entertainer who juggles balls or other objects. **2.** A person who uses tricks to mislead or cheat.

jug•u•lar (**jŭg′**yə lər) *adj.* Of, relating to, or located in the neck or throat. *—n.* A jugular vein. [First written down in 1597 in Modern English, from Latin *iugulum*, collarbone.]

jugular vein *n.* Either of the two large veins on either side of the neck that drain blood from the head.

juice (jo͞os) *n.* **1.** A liquid naturally contained in plant or animal tissue, especially in plant parts such as fruits, stems, or roots. **2.** A fluid secreted within an organ of the body: *gastric juices.* **3.** *Slang.* Electric current. [First written down about 1300 in Middle English and spelled *jus*, from Latin *iūs*.]

juic•er (**jo͞o′**sər) *n.* An appliance used to extract juice from fruits and vegetables.

juic•y (**jo͞o′**sē) *adj.* **juic•i•er, juic•i•est. 1.** Full of juice: *juicy berries.* **2.** Arousing interest or excitement: *a juicy piece of gossip.* **—juic′i•ly** *adv.* **—juic′i•ness** *n.*

ju•jit•su also **jiu•jit•su** (jo͞o **jĭt′**so͞o) *n.* An art of unarmed self-defense developed in China and Japan that uses techniques that exploit an opponent's weight and strength to one's own advantage.

juke•box (**jo͞ok′**bŏks′) *n.* An automatic phonograph or CD player encased in a large cabinet, operated by inserting money and pressing a button for the desired song.

ju•lep (**jo͞o′**lĭp) *n.* A mint julep.

Ju•li•an•a (jo͞o′lē **ăn′**ə). Born 1909. Queen of the Netherlands (1948–1980) who gave up the throne in favor of her daughter Beatrix.

Jul•ian calendar (**jo͞ol′**yən) *n.* The solar calendar introduced in Rome by Julius Caesar in 46 B.C. having a year of 365 days and a leap year of 366 days every fourth year. It has been replaced by the Gregorian calendar.

ju•li•enne (jo͞o′lē **ĕn′**) *n.* A clear soup or broth containing vegetables cut into long thin strips. *—adj.* Cut into long thin strips: *julienne potatoes.*

Ju•ly (jo͞o **lī′**) *n.* The seventh month of the year in the Gregorian calendar, having 31 days. [First written down before 1121 in Middle English and spelled *Julie*, from Latin *Iūlius*, after *Julius* Caesar.]

jum•ble (**jŭm′**bəl) *tr.v.* **jum•bled, jum•bling, jum•bles.** To mix in a confused way; throw together carelessly: *The shoes were all jumbled together in a heap on the floor.* *—n.* **1.** A confused or disordered mass: *a jumble of socks in a drawer.* **2.** A disordered state; a muddle.

jum•bo (**jŭm′**bō) *n., pl.* **jum•bos.** A very large person, animal, or thing. —*adj.* Very large: *jumbo shrimp; a jumbo jet.* [First written down in 1883 in American English, after *Jumbo*, a large elephant exhibited by P.T. Barnum.]

jump (jŭmp) *v.* **jumped, jump•ing, jumps.** —*intr.* **1.** To rise up off the ground or a surface by pushing with the legs and feet: *The frog jumped into the pond.* **2.** To move suddenly and in one motion: *jump out of bed.* **3.** To move quickly or involuntarily, as in fear or surprise: *I jumped at the sudden noise.* **4.** To enter eagerly into an activity: *She jumped into the race for mayor.* **5.** To form an opinion or a judgment hastily: *Let's not jump to conclusions.* **6.** To rise or increase suddenly: *Prices jumped over the past month.* **7.** To pass from one part to another further on; skip: *We jumped ahead to the middle chapters.* —*tr.* **1.** To leap over or across: *jumped the stream.* **2.** To leap onto: *jump a bus.* **3.** *Slang.* To spring upon in or as if in attack: *The police jumped the thief in the parking lot.* **4.** To cause to leap: *jump a horse over a fence.* **5.** To skip; move ahead: *jump a space in typing.* **6.** To leave (a course or track): *Two subway cars jumped the tracks.* —*n.* **1.** A leap or spring: *The cat made a graceful jump from the floor to the shelf.* **2.** The distance covered by a leap: *a jump of 16 feet.* **3.** Any of several track-and-field events in which contestants jump. **4.** An abrupt rise: *a jump in temperature.* **5.** A sudden involuntary movement; a jerk or start: *gave a jump in surprise.* ***—idiom.*** **jump the gun.** To start doing something too soon.

jump ball *n.* In basketball, a method of starting play or determining which team should have the ball, in which an official tosses the ball up between two opposing players who jump and try to tap it to a teammate.

jump•er[1] (jŭm′pər) *n.* **1.** A person or thing that jumps: *That horse is a good jumper.* **2.** A short length of wire or other electrical conductor used to make a temporary electrical connection.

jump•er[2] (jŭm′pər) *n.* **1.** A sleeveless dress worn over a blouse or sweater. **2.** A loose smock or jacket worn over other clothes to protect them. [First written down in 1653 in Modern English, probably from *jump*, short coat.]

jump•ing bean (jŭm′pĭng) *n.* A seed, as of certain Mexican plants, that contains a moth larva whose movements cause the seed to twist and roll.

jumping jack *n.* **1.** A toy figure with jointed limbs that can be made to dance by pulling an attached string. **2.** An exercise that is performed by jumping to a position with the legs spread wide and the hands touching overhead and then returning to a position with the feet together and the arms at the sides.

jump rope *n.* **1.** A rope held at each end and twirled so that one can jump over it as it touches the ground. **2.** The game or activity played with a jump rope.

jump shot *n.* A basketball shot made by a player at the highest point of a jump.

jump-start (jŭmp′stärt′) *tr.v.* **jump-start•ed, jump-start•ing, jump-starts.** To start (the engine of a motor vehicle) by using a cable connected to the battery of another vehicle or by engaging the clutch when the vehicle is rolling downhill or being pushed. —*n.* The act of jump-starting a motor vehicle.

jump suit *n.* **1.** A parachutist's uniform. **2.** Also **jump•suit** (jŭmp′so͞ot′). A one-piece garment that consists of a shirt and attached pants.

jump•y (jŭm′pē) *adj.* **jump•i•er, jump•i•est. 1.** Moving in jumps; jerky. **2.** Easily upset or excited; nervous. **—jump′i•ness** *n.*

jun•co (jŭng′kō) *n., pl.* **jun•cos** or **jun•coes.** Any of various North American finches having mostly gray or brown feathers.

junc•tion (jŭngk′shən) *n.* **1.** The act of joining or the condition of being joined: *The junction of the Missouri and Mississippi Rivers takes place at St. Louis.* **2.** The place at which two things join or meet: *There is a motel at the junction of the two highways.* [First written down in 1711 in Modern English, from Latin *iūnctiō*, from *iungere*, to join.]

junc•ture (jŭngk′chər) *n.* **1.** The act of joining or the condition of being joined. **2.** The point, line, or seam at which two things join; a joint: *Many small animals live along the juncture between meadow and woodland.* **3.** A point in time, especially a crisis or turning point: *At this juncture, a new government was formed.*

June (jo͞on) *n.* The sixth month of the year in the Gregorian calendar, having 30 days. [First written down about 1050 in Old English and spelled *Junius*, from Latin *Iūno*, Juno.]

Ju•neau (jo͞o′nō′). The capital of Alaska, in the southeast part of the state south-southeast of Whitehorse, Yukon Territory, Canada. It was settled by gold miners in 1880. Population, 26,751.

June bug *n.* Any of various large, brown, North American beetles whose larvae are often destructive to crops.

jun•gle (jŭng′gəl) *n.* **1.** An area of land having a dense growth of tropical trees and plants. **2.** A confused or tangled mass, often the scene of intense competition or violence: *He felt totally out of place in the corporate jungle.* [First written down in 1776 in Modern English, from Sanskrit *jaṅgalam*, desert, wasteland.] —See Note.

jungle gym *n.* A structure of crisscrossing poles and bars on which children can play and climb.

jun•ior (jo͞on′yər) *adj.* **1.** Intended for or including youthful persons: *the junior skating championship.* **2.** Used to distinguish a son from his father when both have the same name. **3.** Lower in rank or shorter in length of service: *a junior partner in a law firm; the junior senator from Texas.* **4.** Of or for the third year of a four-year high school or college: *the junior class.* —*n.* **1.** A person who is younger than another: *I am my aunt's junior by twenty-five years.* **2.** A person of lower rank or shorter service. **3.** A student in the third year at a four-year high school or college. [First written down in 1296 in Middle English, from Latin *iunior*.]

junior college *n.* An educational institution offering a two-year course of undergraduate training.

junior high school *n.* A school attended between elementary and high school that includes the seventh, eighth, and sometimes ninth grades.

ju•ni•per (jo͞o′nə pər) *n.* Any of various evergreen trees or shrubs related to the pine, having small cones used for flavoring gins and liqueurs. [First written down before 1382 in Middle English, from Latin *iūniperus*.]

junk[1] (jŭngk) *n.* **1.** Material of any kind that is old, worn-out, and fit to be discarded, such as scrap metal, rags, or paper; trash. **2.** *Informal.* Something cheap or shoddy: *That cheap toaster is nothing but junk.* —*tr.v.* **junked, junk•ing, junks.** To discard as worn-out or useless. —*adj.* Cheap, flimsy, or worthless: *junk jewelry.* [First written down in 1338 in Middle English and spelled *jonk*, an old cable or rope.]

junk[2] (jŭngk) *n.* A Chinese flat-bottomed ship with a high stern and battened sails. [First written down in 1613 in Modern English, from Javanese *djong*.]

jun•ket (jŭng′kĭt) *n.* **1.** A sweet food made from flavored milk and thickened with rennet. **2.** A trip made by a government official at public expense.

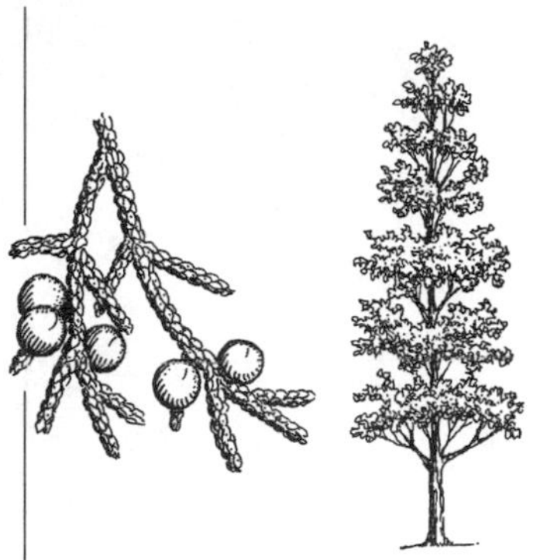

juniper

junk[2]
In Victoria harbor, Hong Kong

ă	**pat**	oi	**boy**
ā	**pay**	ou	**out**
âr	**care**	o͝o	**took**
ä	**father**	o͞o	**boot**
ĕ	**pet**	ŭ	**cut**
ē	**be**	ûr	**urge**
ĭ	**pit**	th	**thin**
ī	**pie**	*th*	**this**
îr	**pier**	hw	**whoop**
ŏ	**pot**	zh	**vision**
ō	**toe**	ə	**about**
ô	**paw**	N	*French* **bon**

junk food *n.* Food that is high in calories but low in nutritional value.

junk•ie (jŭng′kē) *n. Slang.* **1.** A person addicted to narcotics. **2.** A person who has an unflagging interest in something; a devotee: *a video game junkie.*

junk mail *n.* Unrequested mail, such as advertisements and catalogs, sent to large numbers of people.

junk•yard (jŭngk′yärd′) *n.* A yard or other open area used to store junk.

Ju•no (jo͞o′nō) *n.* In Roman mythology, the chief goddess and the wife and sister of Jupiter and patroness primarily of marriage and women. She is identified with the Greek Hera.

jun•ta (ho͝on′tə *or* jŭn′tə) *n.* **1.** A group of military leaders who jointly govern a nation after seizing power. **2.** A council or small legislative body in government, especially in Central and South American countries.

Ju•pi•ter (jo͞o′pĭ tər) *n.* **1.** In Roman mythology, the ruler of the gods and the husband and brother of Juno, identified with the Greek Zeus. **2.** The fifth planet from the sun at a mean distance of about 484 million miles (778 million kilometers) and the largest in the solar system with a mean diameter of about 85,825 miles (138,150 kilometers).

Ju•ras•sic (jo͝o răs′ĭk) *adj.* Of, belonging to, or being the time of the second geologic period of the Mesozoic Era. During the Jurassic, dinosaurs predominated and primitive birds appeared. See table at **geologic time.** —*n.* The Jurassic Period or its series of rocks.

ju•ris•dic•tion (jo͝or′ĭs dĭk′shən) *n.* **1.** The right and power to interpret and apply the law: *A justice of the peace has jurisdiction in a town or village.* **2.** Authority or control; power: *Schools come under the jurisdiction of the state education department.* **3.** The range or extent of authority or control: *Cases of treason are beyond the jurisdiction of local courts.* **4.** A geographic area under a specified authority or control.

ju•ris•pru•dence (jo͝or′ĭs pro͞od′ns) *n.* **1.** The science or philosophy of law. **2.** A division or department of law: *Military jurisprudence is concerned with laws governing the affairs of the army and navy.*

ju•rist (jo͝or′ĭst) *n.* A person who is skilled in the law, especially a judge, lawyer, or legal scholar.

ju•ror (jo͝or′ər *or* jo͝or′ôr′) *n.* A member of a jury.

ju•ry (jo͝or′ē) *n., pl.* **ju•ries. 1.** A body of citizens sworn to hear evidence in a case as presented in a court of law and to hand down a verdict on the basis of the evidence according to the law: *the right to trial by jury.* **2.** A group of people chosen to judge contestants or award prizes, as in a competition. [First written down before 1400 in Middle English and spelled *jure*, from Latin *iūrāre*, to swear.]

just (jŭst) *adj.* **1.** Honorable and fair: *a just ruler of the people.* **2.** Morally right; righteous: *a just cause.* **3.** Properly due or deserved; merited: *just punishment.* **4.** Based on fact or good reason; well-founded: *a just appraisal of his work.* **5.** Valid according to the law; lawful: *a jury's just decision.* —*adv.* (jəst *or* jĭst; jŭst *when stressed*). **1.** Exactly: *Everything went just as we had predicted.* **2.** Only a moment ago: *We've just run out of milk.* **3.** By a small amount; barely: *just made the bus; just after six o'clock.* **4.** Only; merely: *It was just a dream.* **5.** Perhaps; possibly: *I just may go.* ***—idiom.*** **just about.** Almost; very nearly: *We are just about finished.* **—just′ly** *adv.* **—just′ness** *n.*

jus•tice (jŭs′tĭs) *n.* **1.** The quality of being just or fair: *A sense of justice forced the reporter to investigate both sides of the story.* **2.** Moral rightness in action or attitude; righteousness. **3.** Fair treatment in accordance with honor or the law: *We only seek justice for the accused.* **4.** The carrying out of the law or the way in which the law is carried out: *the administration of justice through local and county courts.* **5.** A judge or a justice of the peace: *a local justice; a justice of the Supreme Court.* **6.** Good reason; sound basis: *The customer was angry, and with justice.* ***—idiom.*** **do justice to.** To treat adequately or fairly: *I cannot do justice to her accomplishments in this brief report.*

justice of the peace *n., pl.* **justices of the peace.** A local magistrate having authority to try minor offenses, perform marriages, and administer oaths.

jus•ti•fi•a•ble (jŭs′tə fī′ə bəl *or* jŭs′tə fī′ə bəl) *adj.* Capable of being justified; defensible: *The high price of the piece is justifiable when one considers the fine workmanship.* **—jus′ti•fi′a•bil′i•ty** *n.* **—jus′ti•fi′a•bly** *adv.*

jus•ti•fi•ca•tion (jŭs′tə fĭ kā′shən) *n.* **1.** The act of justifying or the condition of being justified. **2.** Something that justifies; a good reason: *Illness is a justification for not finishing your report on time.*

jus•ti•fy (jŭs′tə fī′) *tr.v.* **jus•ti•fied, jus•ti•fy•ing, jus•ti•fies. 1.** To show or prove to be right, just, or valid: *His fine performance justified the director's decision of casting him in the play.* **2.** To declare innocent; clear of blame: *The jury decided that the evidence justified the defendant's actions.*

jut (jŭt) *intr.v.* **jut•ted, jut•ting, juts.** To extend sharply outward or upward; project: *The branches of that huge tree jut over the street.*

jute (jo͞ot) *n.* **1.** A strong fiber used to make rope, twine, and coarse cloth such as burlap. **2.** Either of two Asian plants that yield such fibers. [First written down in 1746 in Modern English, from Bengali *jhuṭo*, from Sanskrit *jūṭaḥ*, twisted hair.]

Jute (jo͞ot) *n.* A member of a Germanic people who invaded Britain in the fifth and sixth centuries A.D. and settled there with the Angles and Saxons, eventually forming the Anglo-Saxon peoples.

ju•ve•nile (jo͞o′və nīl′ *or* jo͞o′və nəl) *adj.* **1.** Not fully grown or developed; young. **2.** Of or for children or young people: *the juvenile section of the library; a juvenile court.* **3.** Immature; childish: *juvenile behavior.* —*n.* **1.** A young person or animal. **2.** An actor who plays the roles of children. [First written down in 1625 in Modern English, from Latin *iuvenis.*]

juvenile delinquency *n.* Antisocial or criminal behavior by children or adolescents.

juvenile delinquent *n.* A child or an adolescent guilty of juvenile delinquency.

jux•ta•pose (jŭk′stə pōz′) *tr.v.* **jux•ta•posed, jux•ta•pos•ing, jux•ta•pos•es.** To place side by side or close together: *We juxtaposed the two photographs of the house to see how it had changed.* **—jux′ta•po•si′tion** (jŭk′stə pə zĭsh′ən) *n.*

ă	pat	oi	boy
ā	pay	ou	out
âr	care	o͝o	took
ä	father	o͞o	boot
ĕ	pet	ŭ	cut
ē	be	ûr	urge
ĭ	pit	th	thin
ī	pie	*th*	this
îr	pier	hw	whoop
ŏ	pot	zh	vision
ō	toe	ə	about
ô	paw	N	*French* bon

K k

k[1] or **K** (kā) *n., pl.* **k's** or **K's. 1.** The 11th letter of the English alphabet. **2.** The 11th in a series or group: *row k in the bleachers.*
k[2] *abbr.* An abbreviation of karat.
K[1] *n., pl.* **K's.** *Slang.* One thousand dollars.
K[2] The symbol for the element **potassium.**
K[3] *abbr.* An abbreviation of: **1.** Kelvin. **2.** Kilobyte.
k. or **K.** *abbr.* An abbreviation of kopeck.
Kaa•ba (kä′bə) *n.* A Muslim shrine at Mecca that is the goal of pilgrims. Muslims throughout the world turn toward this shrine when praying.
ka•bob (kə bŏb′) *n.* Variant of **kebab.**
ka•bu•ki also **Ka•bu•ki** (kə bo͞o′kē) *n.* A form of traditional Japanese drama with rich costumes and conventional gestures, dances, and songs. It has been performed since the 1600's.
Ka•bul (kä′bo͝ol *or* kə bo͞ol′). The capital and largest city of Afghanistan, in the eastern part of the country on the **Kabul River,** about 300 miles (483 kilometers) long. Population, 913,164.
kaf•tan (kăf′tăn′ *or* kăf tăn′) *n.* Variant of **caftan.**
Kai•ser (kī′zər) *n.* Any of the emperors of the Holy Roman Empire (A.D. 962–1806), of Austria (1804–1918), or of Germany (1871–1918). [First written down in 1858 in Modern English, from German, from Latin *Caesar*, Caesar.]
kale (kāl) *n.* An edible plant having broad wrinkled leaves that do not form a compact head.
ka•lei•do•scope (kə lī′də skōp′) *n.* **1.** A tube in which mirrors reflect light from bits of loose colored glass contained at one end, causing them to appear as changing symmetrical designs when viewed from the other end as the tube is rotated. **2.** A series of changing phases or events: *American politics is a kaleidoscope of ideas.* [First written down in 1817 in Modern English : Greek *kalos*, beautiful + *eidos*, form + *-scope*.] **—ka•lei′do•scop′ic** (kə lī′də skŏp′ĭk) *adj.* **—ka•lei′do•scop′i•cal•ly** *adv.*
Ka•me•ha•me•ha I (kə mā′ə mā′ə). 1758?–1819. King of the Hawaiian Islands (1795–1819) who conquered and united all the islands under his rule.
Kam•pa•la (käm pä′lə). The capital and largest city of Uganda, in the southern part of the country on Lake Victoria. Population, 458,503.
Kam•pu•che•a (kăm′po͞o chē′ə). Cambodia.
kan•ga•roo (kăng′gə ro͞o′) *n., pl.* **kangaroo** or **kan•ga•roos.** Any of various Australian mammals having short forelegs, long hind legs used for leaping, and a long strong tail. The female kangaroo carries the newborn young in a pouch on the outside of her body.
kangaroo rat *n.* Any of various small long-tailed rodents found in the desert regions of southwest North America, having long hind legs for leaping.
Kans. *abbr.* An abbreviation of Kansas.
Kan•sas (kăn′zəs). A state of the central United States north of Oklahoma. It was admitted as the 34th state in 1861. Topeka is the capital and Wichita the largest city. Population, 2,485,600. —SEE NOTE.
Kansas City. 1. A city of northeast Kansas on the Missouri River adjacent to Kansas City, Missouri. Population, 149,767. **2.** A city of western Missouri on the Missouri River west-northwest of St. Louis. It was established as a fur-trading post in the 1820's. Population, 435,146.
ka•o•lin (kā′ə lĭn) *n.* A fine clay used in making ceramics.
ka•pok (kā′pŏk′) *n.* A silky fiber from the seed pods of a tropical tree, used as a stuffing for pillows, mattresses, and life preservers.
kap•pa (kăp′ə) *n.* The tenth letter of the Greek alphabet, written Κ, κ. In English it is represented as *K, k.*
Ka•ra•chi (kə rä′chē). A city of southern Pakistan on the Arabian Sea. It was developed as a trading center in the early 18th century. Population, 4,776,000.
Ka•ra•ko•ram Range (kăr′ə kôr′əm). A mountain range of northern Pakistan and India and southwest China. It rises to 28,250 feet (8,616.3 meters).
kar•a•kul (kăr′ə kəl) *n.* **1.** Any of a breed of Asian sheep bred for the curled glossy fur of the young lambs. **2.** The fur of such a lamb.
kar•at also **car•at** (kăr′ət) *n.* A unit of measure used to indicate the proportion of pure gold contained in an alloy. For example, since 24 karats is pure gold, a bracelet of 12 karat gold contains 12 parts gold and 12 parts alloy.
❑ *These sound alike:* **karat, carat** (weight of gems), **caret** (proofreader's mark), **carrot** (plant).
ka•ra•te (kə rä′tē) *n.* An art of self-defense developed in Japan, in which sharp blows and kicks are delivered to sensitive points on the body of an opponent. [First written down in 1955 in Modern English, from Japanese : *kara*, empty + *te*, hand.]
kar•ma (kär′mə) *n.* **1.** In Hinduism and Buddhism, the effect of a person's conduct, which is believed to determine a person's destiny in this life or when reincarnated in the future. **2.** Fate; destiny. [First written down in 1827 in Modern English and spelled *carme*, from Sanskrit *karman*, doing.]
Kash•mir also **Cash•mere** (kăsh′mîr′ *or* kăsh mîr′). A historical region of northwest India and northeast Pakistan. Conquered by Muslims in the 14th century, it became an independent kingdom in 1751. The region is currently partitioned between India and Pakistan.
Kat•man•du (kăt′măn do͞o′). The capital and largest city of Nepal, in the central part of the country in the eastern Himalaya Mountains. It was founded in about 723. Population, 235,160.
Ka•to•wi•ce (kä′tə vēt′sə). A city of southern Poland southwest of Warsaw. It was chartered in 1865. Population, 363,300.
ka•ty•did (kā′tē dĭd′) *n.* Any of various green insects that have long antennae and are related to the grasshopper. The male rubs its front wings together to make shrill sounds.
Kau•ai (kou′ī′ *or* kou ī′). An island of Hawaii northwest of Oahu. It became part of the kingdom of Hawaii in 1810.
kay•ak (kī′ăk′) *n.* **1.** A watertight Eskimo canoe made of skins stretched over a light wooden or bone frame that leaves only a small opening for the

Kamehameha I

Kansas

The name **Kansas** comes from a Native American people, the Kansa (or Kaw). A possible translation is "people of the south wind." The plural *s* was added to the name when referring to the Native American people, and this form was used for the state.

karate

kayak

John Keats

Helen Keller

Photographed in the 1950's

John F. Kennedy

Kentucky

The name of the state of **Kentucky** probably comes from a Seneca word meaning "field, meadow." The name was applied first to a region and later to the state.

paddler. **2.** A lightweight sports canoe of a similar design. *—intr.v.* **kay•aked, kay•ak•ing, kay•aks.** To travel or race in a kayak. [First written down in 1757 in Modern English and spelled *kajak*, from Eskimo *qajaq*.]

kay•o (kā ō′ *or* kā′ō′) *n., pl.* **kay•os.** A knockout in boxing. *—tr.v.* **kay•oed, kay•o•ing, kay•os.** To knock (someone) out in boxing.

Ka•zakh•stan (kə zäk′stän′). A region south of Russia and northeast of the Caspian Sea. It was part of the Soviet Union from 1936 until 1991. Capital, Alma-Ata. Population, 15,842,000.

ka•zoo (kə zo͞o′) *n., pl.* **ka•zoos.** A musical instrument with a membrane in the mouthpiece that vibrates and produces tones when the player hums into it.

kc *abbr.* An abbreviation of kilocycle.

ke•a (kē′ə) *n.* A brownish-green New Zealand parrot that normally eats insects but sometimes feeds on carrion with its powerful hooked beak.

Keats (kēts), **John.** 1795–1821. British poet whose works include "Ode to a Nightingale" (1819).

ke•bab or **ke•bob** (kə bŏb′) *n.* Shish kebab.

keel (kēl) *n.* **1.** A strong beam, as of wood or metal, that runs along the center line of a vessel from one end to the other. The frame of the entire vessel is built up from the keel. **2.** The part of an aircraft that resembles a ship's keel. ***—idiom.*** **keel over.** To collapse or fall down: *I almost keeled over with surprise.*

keel•haul (kēl′hôl′) *tr.v.* **keel•hauled, keel•haul•ing, keel•hauls. 1.** To drag (a person) under the keel of a ship as punishment. **2.** To scold or criticize harshly.

keen[1] (kēn) *adj.* **keen•er, keen•est. 1.** Having a sharp edge or point: *A keen knife slit the heavy canvas.* **2.** Intense; piercing: *a keen wind.* **3.** Acute; sensitive: *the keen eyes of the owl.* **4.** Intellectually sharp; astute; bright: *a keen observer of politics.* **5.** Eager; enthusiastic: *He's really keen on hunting for fossils.* **6.** *Slang.* Delightful; excellent: *What a keen present!* [First written down before 725 in Old English and spelled *cēne*, brave.] **—keen′ly** *adv.* **—keen′ness** *n.*

keen[2] (kēn) *n.* A crying or wailing in sorrow for the dead. *—intr.v.* **keened, keen•ing, keens.** To cry or wail in sorrow for the dead. [First written down in 1811 in Modern English, from Irish Gaelic *caoineadh*, from Old Irish *coínim*, I lament.]

keep (kēp) *v.* **kept** (kĕpt), **keep•ing, keeps.** *—tr.* **1.** To retain in one's possession; continue to have: *I keep my old photographs.* **2.** To hold for future use; save: *I kept some food for you.* **3.** To put in a customary place; store: *Where do you keep your bike?* **4.** To cause to continue in a certain position or condition: *Keep the boat headed for that island.* **5.** To continue or maintain (an activity, for example): *keep watch.* **6.** To take care of; provide for or manage: *keep house; keep a large family.* **7.** To raise: *We keep ducks and geese.* **8.** To make regular entries in: *keep a record; keep a diary.* **9.** To celebrate or observe: *keeping the Sabbath.* **10.** To carry out; fulfill: *keep a promise.* **11.** To prevent or restrain: *We kept the kite from hitting the tree.* **12.** To refrain from telling: *keep a secret.* **13.** To detain or delay: *I was kept after school.* *—intr.* **1.** To remain in a state or condition: *keep warm; keep in touch.* **2.** To continue or persist: *He kept on talking.* **3.** To restrain oneself: *I could not keep from laughing.* **4.** To stay fresh or unspoiled: *Fruit doesn't keep well.* *—n.* **1.** The things needed to live: *There are many ways to earn one's keep.* **2.** The stronghold of a castle or fort. **3.** Care; charge: *The child was in my keep for the day.* ***—idioms.*** **for keeps.** Permanently: *The kitten was mine for keeps.* **keep (one's) eyes open** or **keep (one's) eyes peeled.** To be on the lookout: *Keep your eyes peeled for fireflies.* **keep to (oneself). 1.** To avoid other people; remain alone. **2.** To refrain from telling others: *We could not keep such good news to ourselves.* **keep up. 1.** To maintain in good condition: *keep up the gardens.* **2.** To continue at the same level or pace: *The wind kept up all night.* **3.** To match others in success or lifestyle: *Our company must keep up with the competition.* [First written down about 1000 in Old English and spelled *cēpan*, to observe, seize.]

Synonyms: keep, retain, withhold, reserve. These verbs mean to maintain something in one's possession or control. **Keep** is the most general: *Sometimes it's easier to earn money than to keep it.* **Retain** means to continue to hold something, especially when in danger of losing it: *No matter what goes wrong, Sarah manages to retain her sense of humor.* **Withhold** means to refuse to give or allow: *The tenants withheld their rent until the landlord repaired the boiler.* **Reserve** means to hold for future use: *Please reserve your questions for the discussion period.*

keep•er (kē′pər) *n.* **1.** A person who watches over or guards something; an attendant or a guard. **2.** A person who takes care of or manages something: *the keeper of a small shop.*

keep•ing (kē′pĭng) *n.* **1.** Care; custody: *documents in the keeping of my lawyer.* See Synonyms at **care. 2.** Agreement; conformity: *wearing formal clothes in keeping with the important occasion.*

keep•sake (kēp′sāk′) *n.* Something kept in memory of the person who gave it or the place from which it came; a memento.

keg (kĕg) *n.* **1.** A small barrel with a capacity of about 30 gallons (114 liters). **2.** A keg and its contents: *a keg of mackerel in brine.*

Kel•ler (kĕl′ər), **Helen Adams.** 1880–1968. American writer who lectured widely on behalf of sightless people. Her books include *Out of the Dark* (1913).

Kel•ley (kĕl′ē), **Florence.** 1859–1932. American social worker whose work prompted legal action against unsafe and unfair labor practices. She was a founder of the NAACP (1909).

kelp (kĕlp) *n.* **1.** Any of various brown, often very large seaweeds. Some kelp have stems over 150 feet (50 meters) long. **2.** The ash of such seaweed, used as a source of potash and iodine.

Kelt (kĕlt) *n.* Variant of **Celt.**

Kelt•ic (kĕl′tĭk) *n. & adj.* Variant of **Celtic.**

kel•vin (kĕl′vĭn) *n.* The temperature scale that has its zero at absolute zero and uses degrees that are the same as those of the Celsius scale. On the Kelvin scale water freezes at 273.15 degrees and boils at 373.15 degrees. [First written down in 1908 in Modern English, after the First Baron *Kelvin* (1824–1907), British physicist.]

ken (kĕn) *n.* **1.** Range of understanding; comprehension: *Many forces of nature are beyond our ken.* **2.** Range of vision: *The powerful telescope brought many unobserved stars within our ken.* *—intr.v.* **kenned** or **kent** (kĕnt), **ken•ning, kens.** *Scots.* To have an understanding of something. [First written down in 1545 in Modern English, from Middle English *kennen*, to recognize, from Old English *cennan*, to declare.]

Ken•ne•dy (kĕn′ĭ dē), **Cape.** Cape Canaveral.

Kennedy, John Fitzgerald. 1917–1963. The 35th President of the United States (1961–1963). Kennedy established the Peace Corps (1961) and advocated civil rights reform. He was assassinated in Dallas, Texas.

ken•nel (kĕn′əl) *n.* **1.** A shelter for a dog or dogs. **2.** An establishment for the breeding, training, or boarding of dogs. *—tr.v.* **ken•neled, ken•nel•ing,**

ken•nels or **ken•nelled, ken•nel•ling, ken•nels.** To place or keep in or as if in a kennel. [First written down in 1301 in Middle English and spelled *kenil*, from Latin *canis*, dog.]

kent (kĕnt) *v. Scots.* A past tense and past participle of **ken.**

Ken•tuck•y (kən tŭk′ē). A state of the east-central United States north of Tennessee. It was admitted as the 15th state in 1792. Frankfort is the capital and Louisville the largest city. Population, 3,698,969. —SEE NOTE.

Ken•ya (kĕn′yə *or* kēn′yə). A country of east-central Africa bordering on the Indian Ocean north of Tanzania. Kenya gained its independence from Great Britain in 1963. Nairobi is the capital and the largest city. Population, 15,327,061.

Ken•yat•ta (kĕn yä′tə), **Jomo.** 1893?–1978. Kenyan politician who was the first president of independent Kenya (1964–1978).

ke•pi (kā′pē *or* kĕp′ē) *n., pl.* **ke•pis.** A French military cap with a flat round top and a visor.

Kep•ler (kĕp′lər), **Johannes.** 1571–1630. German astronomer and mathematician who is considered the founder of modern astronomy.

kept (kĕpt) *v.* Past tense and past participle of **keep.**

ker•a•tin (kĕr′ə tĭn) *n.* A tough fibrous protein that forms the outer layers of hair, nails, horns, feathers, and hoofs.

ker•chief (kûr′chĭf *or* kûr′chēf′) *n., pl.* **ker•chiefs** also **ker•chieves** (kûr′chĭvz *or* kûr′chēvz). **1.** A woman's square scarf worn over the head or around the neck. **2.** A handkerchief.

ker•nel (kûr′nəl) *n.* **1.** A grain or seed, especially of corn, wheat, or a similar cereal plant. **2.** The softer, often edible part inside the shell of a nut or inside the pit of a peach, plum, or other fruit. **3.** The most important or essential part; the core: *the kernel of truth in a witty saying.*

❑ *These sound alike:* **kernel, colonel** (officer).

ker•o•sene (kĕr′ə sēn′ *or* kăr′ə sēn′) *n.* A thin light-colored oil that is obtained from petroleum and used chiefly as a fuel in lamps, home heaters and furnaces, and jet engines.

kes•trel (kĕs′trəl) *n.* Any of various small falcons that have reddish-brown feathers and that can hover for long periods of time while facing into the wind.

ketch (kĕch) *n.* A two-masted fore-and-aft-rigged sailing vessel with a large sail on the mainmast and a shorter mast placed aft.

ketch•up (kĕch′əp *or* kăch′əp) also **cat•sup** (kăt′səp *or* kăch′əp *or* kĕch′əp) *n.* A thick spicy sauce, usually made with tomatoes, used as a seasoning. [First written down in 1711 in Modern English, probably from Malay *kēchap*, fish sauce.]

ket•tle (kĕt′l) *n.* **1.** A metal pot, usually with a lid, for boiling liquids or for cooking. **2.** A teakettle. [First written down before 700 in Old English and spelled *cetil*, from Latin *catīllus*, little bowl.]

ket•tle•drum (kĕt′l drŭm′) *n.* A large drum having a bowl-shaped body of brass or copper and a parchment head that can be tuned by adjusting its tension.

key[1] (kē) *n., pl.* **keys. 1.** A small piece of metal with notches or grooves, that is inserted into a lock to open or close it. **2.** A device that functions like a key: *a key for opening cans; a clock key.* **3.** Something that solves a problem or explains a mystery: *evidence that became the key to solving the crime; the answer key of a test.* **4.** An explanatory table, such as that explaining colors and symbols on a map. **5.** An important or essential person or thing: *The pitcher is the key to our team.* **6.** Any of the buttons or levers moved by the fingers in operating a machine or playing a musical instrument: *a typewriter key; piano keys.* **7.** A scale or group of musical tones related to a primary tone: *a piece written in the key of D.* **8.** The pitch of a voice or other sound. **9.** A general tone or level of intensity: *The candidate spoke in a relaxed and lower key to friends and supporters.* —*adj.* Of crucial importance; significant: *key decisions.* —*tr.v.* **keyed, key•ing, keys. 1.** To tune (a musical instrument) to a particular note: *Key the guitar to E flat.* **2.** To adapt to special conditions; adjust: *Farming methods are keyed to the local weather conditions.* **3.** To lock with or as if with a key. —***idiom.*** **key up.** To make nervous; excite: *I was too keyed up about my trip to eat.* [First written down before 725 in Old English and spelled *cæg.*]

❑ *These sound alike:* **key**[1] (lock opener), **key**[2] (island), **quay** (wharf).

key[2] (kē) *n., pl.* **keys.** A low-lying island or reef along a coast, especially in the Gulf of Mexico. [First written down in 1697 in Modern English, from Spanish *cayo.*]

❑ *These sound alike:* **key**[2] (island), **key**[1] (lock opener), **quay** (wharf).

Key (kē), **Francis Scott.** 1779–1843. American lawyer who wrote a poem in 1814 that was set to music and renamed "The Star-Spangled Banner." In 1931 it was adopted by Congress as the national anthem.

key•board (kē′bôrd′) *n.* A set of keys, as on a piano, an organ, or a typewriter. —*tr.v.* **key•board•ed, key•board•ing, key•boards.** To enter (information) into a computer by using a keyboard. —**key′board′er** *n.*

key•hole (kē′hōl′) *n.* The opening in a lock into which a key fits.

key•note (kē′nōt′) *n.* **1.** The principal tone of a musical scale or key; the tonic. **2.** The basic idea or theme, as of a speech, book, or political campaign.

keynote address *n.* An opening address or speech of a meeting that sets the basic tone or outlines the business to be considered.

key•pad (kē′păd′) *n.* A small panel with a set of buttons for operating a calculator, telephone, or other electronic machine.

key•punch (kē′pŭnch′) *n.* A keyboard machine used to punch holes in cards or tape for data-processing systems.

key signature *n.* The group of sharps or flats placed to the right of the clef on a staff to show the musical key of a piece.

key•stone (kē′stōn′) *n.* **1.** The central wedge-shaped stone of an arch that locks the other stones together. **2.** The essential element that supports a whole: *The keystone of their business was their downtown store.*

key•stroke (kē′strōk′) *n.* A stroke of a key, as on a typewriter or word processor.

Key West. A city of extreme southern Florida on the island of **Key West,** the westernmost of a group of islands off Florida in the Gulf of Mexico. Population, 24,832.

kg *abbr.* An abbreviation of kilogram.

khak•i (kăk′ē *or* kä′kē) *n.* **1.** A yellowish brown. **2.** A strong, heavy, khaki-colored cloth. **3. khakis. a.** Trousers made of this cloth. **b.** A uniform made of this cloth. [First written down in 1857 in Modern English, from Persian *khāk*, dust.] —**khak′i** *adj.*

khan (kän *or* kăn) *n.* **1.** A ruler, an official, or an important person in India and some countries of central Asia. **2.** A medieval ruler of a Mongol, Tartar, or Turkish tribe.

Khar•kov (kär′kôf′). A city of northeast Ukraine east of Kiev. It was founded in 1656. Population, 1,554,000.

Khar•toum (kär to͞om′). The capital and largest city

Jomo Kenyatta

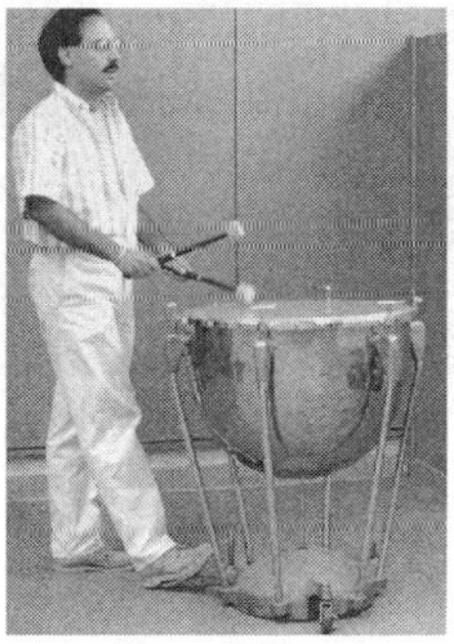

kettledrum

keyboard
Computer keyboard

ă	pat	oi	boy
ā	pay	ou	out
âr	care	o͝o	took
ä	father	o͞o	boot
ĕ	pet	ŭ	cut
ē	be	ûr	urge
ĭ	pit	th	thin
ī	pie	*th*	this
îr	pier	hw	whoop
ŏ	pot	zh	vision
ō	toe	ə	about
ô	paw	N	*French* bon

kickstand
Bicycle kickstand

killer whale

kilt

kimono

of Sudan, in the east-central part of the country on the Nile River. It was founded in about 1821 as an Egyptian army camp. Population, 476,218.

Khmer (kmâr) *n., pl.* **Khmer** or **Khmers. 1.** A member of a people of Cambodia. **2.** The official language of Cambodia.

Kho•mei•ni (kō **mā′**nē), Ayatollah **Ruholla.** 1900–1989. Iranian leader and head of state (1979–1989). His reign was marked by a return to strict observance of the Islamic code.

Khru•shchev (**kro͞osh′**chĕf *or* **kro͞osh′**chôf), **Nikita Sergeyevich.** 1894–1971. Soviet politician who was appointed first secretary of the Communist Party in 1953 and served as Soviet premier (1958–1964).

Khy•ber Pass (**kī′**bər). A narrow pass, about 33 miles (53 kilometers) long, through mountains on the border between western Afghanistan and northern Pakistan. The highest point of the pass is about 3,500 feet (1,068 meters).

kib•ble (**kĭb′**əl) *tr.v.* **kib•bled, kib•bling, kib•bles.** To crush or grind (grain, for example) coarsely. *—n.* A meal ground by this process and used in the form of pellets especially for pet food.

kib•butz (kĭ **bo͞ots′** *or* kĭ **bo͝ots′**) *n., pl.* **kib•but•zim** (kĭb′o͞ot **sēm′** *or* kĭb′o͝ot **sēm′**). A collective farm or settlement in modern Israel.

kib•itz (**kĭb′**ĭts) *intr.v.* **kib•itzed, kib•itz•ing, kib•itz•es.** *Informal.* **1.** To look on and offer unwanted advice. **2.** To chat; converse. **—kib′itz•er** *n.*

kick (kĭk) *v.* **kicked, kick•ing, kicks.** *—intr.* **1.** To strike out with the foot or hoof. **2.** In sports, to score, gain ground, or begin play by kicking a ball. **3.** To recoil when fired: *The rifle kicked after he pulled the trigger.* *—tr.* **1.** To strike with the foot: *The mule kicked the stable door.* **2.** To propel or produce by striking with the foot: *a herd of cattle that kicked up swirls of dust.* **3.** To spring back against suddenly: *The rifle kicked her shoulder when she fired it.* **4.** In sports, to score (a goal or point) by kicking a ball. **5.** *Slang.* To free oneself of; overcome: *kicking a bad habit.* *—n.* **1.** A blow with the foot: *The cow gave the bucket a kick.* **2.a.** The action of kicking a ball, as in a football kickoff or punt. **b.** A kicked ball: *Block that kick!* **c.** The distance covered by a kicked ball. **3.** The recoil of a cannon or firearm. **4.** *Slang.* A feeling of pleasure; a thrill: *They will get a kick out of this greeting card.* ***—idioms.*** **kick around.** *Informal.* **1.** To treat badly; abuse. **2.** To move from place to place. **3.** To think about or discuss: *Several new ideas were kicked around at the meeting.* **kick in.** *Informal.* To contribute (one's share) to a common fund: *kick in a few dollars for the office party.* **kick off.** *Informal.* To begin; start: *kicked off the day with a big breakfast.* **kick out.** *Slang.* To throw out; dismiss: *was kicked out of the library for repeated talking.* **kick up.** *Informal.* To stir up (trouble): *Our cats kick up a fuss until they are fed.* [First written down about 1384 in Middle English and spelled *kiken*, perhaps of Scandinavian origin.] **—kick′er** *n.*

Kick•a•poo (**kĭk′**ə po͞o′) *n., pl.* **Kickapoo** or **Kick•a•poos.** A member of a Native American people formerly living in Wisconsin and Illinois and now living in Kansas, Oklahoma, and Mexico.

kick•back (**kĭk′**băk′) *n.* **1.** A sharp reaction or recoil. **2.** *Slang.* A part of a payment returned by agreement to the payer, especially in the form of a bribe.

kick•ball (**kĭk′**bôl′) *n.* A game similar to baseball but played on a small diamond with an inflated ball that is kicked instead of batted.

kick•off (**kĭk′**ôf′ *or* **kĭk′**ŏf′) *n.* **1.** A kick in football or soccer that begins play. **2.** *Informal.* A beginning: *The concert was the kickoff for the orchestra's new season.*

kick•stand (**kĭk′**stănd′) *n.* A metal bar that can be pushed down to hold a bicycle or motorcycle upright when not being ridden.

kid (kĭd) *n.* **1.a.** A young goat. **b.** Leather made from the skin of a young goat; kidskin. **2.** *Informal.* A child or young person. *—adj.* **1.** Made of kid: *kid gloves.* **2.** Younger than oneself: *my kid brother.* *—v.* **kid•ded, kid•ding, kids.** *Informal.* *—tr.* **1.** To make fun of; tease. **2.** To deceive for fun; fool: *You must be kidding me!* *—intr.* To engage in teasing or good-humored fooling. [First written down before 1200 in Middle English and spelled *kide*, from Old Norse *kidh*.] **—kid′der** *n.*

kid•nap (**kĭd′**năp′) *tr.v.* **kid•napped, kid•nap•ping, kid•naps** or **kid•naped, kid•nap•ing, kid•naps.** To seize and detain (a person or an animal) by force, usually for ransom. **—kid′nap′per, kid′nap′er** *n.*

kid•ney (**kĭd′**nē) *n., pl.* **kid•neys. 1.** Either of a pair of organs that are located in the abdominal cavity of vertebrates close to the back and maintain the proper amount of water in the body and filter out wastes from the bloodstream in the form of urine. **2.** The kidney of certain animals, eaten as food.

kidney bean *n.* A large reddish bean shaped somewhat like a kidney and eaten as a vegetable.

kid•skin (**kĭd′**skĭn′) *n.* Soft leather made from the skin of a young goat.

Kiel (kēl). A city of northern Germany on **Kiel Bay,** an arm of the Baltic Sea. It was chartered in 1242. Population, 245,751.

Ki•ev (**kē′**ĕf *or* **kē′**ĕv). The capital of Ukraine, in the north-central part of the republic west of Kharkov. It is one of the oldest cities in the country and was an early seat of Russian Christianity. Population, 2,448,000.

Ki•ga•li (kĭ **gä′**lē *or* kē **gä′**lē). The capital and largest city of Rwanda, in the central part of the country north-northeast of Bujumbura, Burundi. Population, 156,700.

Kil•i•man•ja•ro (kĭl′ə mən **jär′**ō), **Mount.** The highest mountain in Africa, in northeast Tanzania near the Kenya border, rising 19,340 feet (5,898.7 meters).

kill[1] (kĭl) *v.* **killed, kill•ing, kills.** *—tr.* **1.** To cause the death of; deprive of life. **2.** To put an end to; destroy: *The rainy weekend killed our plans for a picnic.* **3.** To cause severe pain to; hurt intensely: *These narrow boots are killing my feet.* **4.** To pass (time) in idle activity: *kill an hour looking at magazines.* **5.** To thwart passage of; veto: *kill a congressional bill.* **6.** To cause to stop working: *kill a motor.* **7.** To take out; delete: *kill several paragraphs of a news story.* *—intr.* To cause death. *—n.* **1.** An act of killing. **2.** An animal that has just been killed. ***—idiom.*** **kill off.** To destroy totally or on a large scale: *Continued destruction of marshes could kill off several species of fish.* [First written down before 1200 in Middle English and spelled *cullen*.]

kill[2] (kĭl) *n.* A creek. [First written down in 1669 in Modern English, from Dutch *kill*, from Middle Dutch *kille*.] —SEE NOTE at **run.**

kill•deer (**kĭl′**dîr′) *n., pl.* **killdeer** or **kill•deers.** A North American wading bird having a banded breast and a shrill call that sounds like its name. [First written down in 1731 in American English and spelled *kildeer*, imitative of its call.]

kill•er (**kĭl′**ər) *n.* **1.** A person, an animal, or a thing that kills. **2.** *Slang.* Something that is extremely difficult to deal with or withstand: *That test was a killer!*

killer bee *n.* **1.** A black honeybee of Africa, noted for its aggressive behavior. **2.** A hybrid variety of the African bee, prevalent in South and Central America.

killer whale *n.* A black and white whale related to

the dolphins, feeding on fish, seals, porpoises, and penguins.

kill•ing (kĭl′ĭng) *n.* **1.** Murder; homicide. **2.** A sudden large profit: *make a killing in the stock market.* —*adj.* **1.** Apt to kill; fatal. **2.** Exhausting: *walk at a killing pace.*

kill•joy (kĭl′joi′) *n.* A person who spoils the fun of others.

kiln (kĭln *or* kĭl) *n.* Any of various ovens used for hardening, burning, or drying things such as grain or lumber, especially an oven used for firing pottery, porcelain, or brick. [First written down before 800 in Old English and spelled *cyln*, from Latin *culīna*, kitchen, stove.]

ki•lo (kē′lō) *n., pl.* **ki•los. 1.** A kilogram. **2.** A kilometer.

kilo– *pref.* A prefix that means one thousand: *kilowatt.*

kil•o•byte (kĭl′ə bīt′) *n.* A unit of measurement of the memory capacity of a computer, equal to 1024 (2^{10}) bytes.

kil•o•cal•o•rie (kĭl′ə kăl′ə rē) *n.* The quantity of heat needed to raise the temperature of one kilogram of water one degree Celsius.

kil•o•cy•cle (kĭl′ə sī′kəl) *n.* **1.** A unit equal to 1,000 cycles. **2.** A kilohertz.

kil•o•gram (kĭl′ə grăm′) *n.* The basic unit of mass in the metric system equal to 1,000 grams (about 2.2046 pounds). See table at **measurement.**

kil•o•hertz (kĭl′ə hûrts′) *n.* A unit of frequency equal to 1,000 cycles per second, used to express the frequency of radio waves.

kil•o•me•ter (kĭ lŏm′ĭ tər *or* kĭl′ə mē′tər) *n.* A unit of length equal to 1,000 meters (0.62 mile). See table at **measurement.** [First written down in 1810 in Modern English : Greek *khilioi*, thousand + *meter*.]

kil•o•ton (kĭl′ə tŭn′) *n.* **1.** A thousand tons. **2.** A unit of explosive force equal to the force with which 1,000 metric tons of TNT explode, used in expressing the force of nuclear explosions.

kil•o•watt (kĭl′ə wŏt′) *n.* A unit of power, especially electric power, equal to 1,000 watts.

kil•o•watt-hour (kĭl′ə wŏt our′) *n.* A unit of energy, especially electrical energy, equivalent to one kilowatt acting for a period of one hour.

kilt (kĭlt) *n.* **1.** A knee-length pleated skirt, usually of a tartan wool, worn by men in the Scottish Highlands. **2.** A similar skirt worn by women, girls, and boys.

kil•ter (kĭl′tər) *n.* Good condition; proper form: *programs designed to bring the economy back into kilter.*

ki•mo•no (kə mō′nə) *n., pl.* **ki•mo•nos. 1.** A long loose robe with wide sleeves and a broad sash, worn by the Japanese as an outer garment. **2.** A woman's robe resembling this robe. [First written down in 1886 in Modern English, from Japanese : *ki*, to wear + *mono*, object.]

kin (kĭn) *n.* **1.** *(used with a plural verb).* A person's relatives; family: *The kin of many immigrants were left in their native land.* **2.** A kinsman or kinswoman. —*adj.* Related; kindred: *The panda is kin to the raccoon.* [First written down before 725 in Old English and spelled *cyn*.]

kind[1] (kīnd) *adj.* **kind•er, kind•est. 1.** Having a friendly, generous, or warm-hearted nature: *It was kind of you to offer to babysit.* **2.** Showing understanding for others: *kind words.* [First written down about 725 in Old English and spelled *gecynde*, natural.]

kind[2] (kīnd) *n.* **1.** A group sharing common traits or characteristics: *Seals gather with their kind on this island.* **2.** A particular sort or type: *What kind of toothpaste do you use?* **—*idioms.* in kind. 1.** With produce or goods rather than with money: *paying in kind.* **2.** In the same manner or with an equivalent: *return a polite remark in kind.* **kind of.** *Informal.* Rather; somewhat: *I'm kind of hungry.* [First written down before 899 in Old English and spelled *gecynd*.] —See Note.

kin•der•gar•ten (kĭn′dər gär′tn) *n.* A class for children from four to six years of age that prepares them for elementary school.

kind•heart•ed (kīnd′här′tĭd) *adj.* Gentle and generous by nature. **—kind′heart′ed•ly** *adv.* **—kind′heart′ed•ness** *n.*

kin•dle (kĭn′dl) *v.* **kin•dled, kin•dling, kin•dles.** —*tr.* **1.** To build and start (a fire). **2.** To arouse; excite: *The teacher used experiments to kindle our interest in science.* **3.** To cause to glow; light up: *The sunset kindled the skies.* —*intr.* **1.** To catch fire: *The paper kindled on the third match.* **2.** To glow; shine. **3.** To become inflamed or stirred up. **—kin′dler** *n.*

kin•dling (kĭnd′lĭng) *n.* Sticks and other small pieces of material used to start a fire.

kind•ly (kīnd′lē) *adj.* **kind•li•er, kind•li•est. 1.** Considerate and helpful; kind: *a kindly and warm-hearted friend; kindly advice.* **2.** Agreeable; pleasant: *a kindly breeze.* —*adv.* **1.** Out of kindness: *She kindly offered to help.* **2.** In a kind way; cordially, warmly: *greeted them kindly.* **3.** As a matter of courtesy; please: *Kindly read the notice aloud.* **—kind′li•ness** *n.*

kind•ness (kīnd′nĭs) *n.* **1.** The quality or state of being kind; generosity. **2.** A kind act or kind treatment; a favor: *We are grateful for your many kindnesses.*

kin•dred (kĭn′drĭd) *n.* **1.** A group of related persons, such as a clan. **2.** *(used with a plural verb).* A person's family or relatives. —*adj.* Having a similar origin or nature: *kindred feelings.*

kin•e•mat•ics (kĭn′ə măt′ĭks) *n.* *(used with a singular verb).* The branch of physics that deals with the characteristics of motion, without reference to mass or the causes of motion.

ki•net•ic (kĭ nĕt′ĭk *or* kī nĕt′ĭk) *adj.* Of, relating to, or produced by motion.

kinetic energy *n.* The energy possessed by a body because it is in motion.

ki•net•ics (kĭ nĕt′ĭks *or* kī nĕt′ĭks) *n.* *(used with a singular verb).* The branch of physics that deals with forces and motion; dynamics.

kin•folk (kĭn′fōk′) also **kins•folk** (kĭnz′fōk′) or **kin•folks** (kĭn′fōks′) *pl.n.* A person's relatives; kindred.

king (kĭng) *n.* **1.** A man who rules a nation, usually inheriting his position for life. **2.** A person who is the most outstanding or important in a particular group or category: *That reporter is king of sportswriters.* **3.** Something that is regarded as the most powerful or important: *In the South, cotton was once king.* **4.** The most important piece in chess, able to move one square in any direction. **5.** In checkers, a piece that has reached the opponent's side of the board and is able to move both backward and forward. **6.** A playing card bearing the figure of a king and ranking next above a queen. **7. Kings.** Either of the two Biblical books, I Kings or II Kings, that tell the history of the kings of Israel and Judah from Solomon to the fall of Jerusalem. [First written down before 725 in Old English and spelled *cyning*.] —See Note.

King, Coretta Scott. Born 1927. American civil rights leader noted for her work on behalf of the Southern Christian Leadership Conference and the Martin Luther King, Jr., Memorial Foundation.

King, Martin Luther, Jr. 1929–1968. American cleric whose nonviolent tactics helped form the foundation of the civil rights movement of the 1950's

Usage: kind[2]

When the plural **kinds** is used, the demonstrative pronoun and the verb must also be plural: *These* (or *those*) *kinds of films are popular.* When both **kind** and the noun following it are singular, the verb must be singular: *This* (or *that*) *kind of film is popular.*

Word History: king

Our Modern English noun **king** comes from the Old English *cing*, pronounced [kĭng], which is a contraction of the Old English noun *cyning* [kün′ing]. The word root *cyn–* is related to the modern word **kin**, as in "kinfolk, relatives." The suffix *–ing* originally meant "son of, descended from." Thus the family names Browning and Whiting mean "son of Brown, descendant of White," and *cyning* or *cing* means "son of the people, (royal) descendant of the nation."

Martin Luther King, Jr.
Photographed in 1964

ă	**pat**	oi	**boy**
ā	**pay**	ou	**out**
âr	**care**	ŏŏ	**took**
ä	**father**	ōō	**boot**
ĕ	**pet**	ŭ	**cut**
ē	**be**	ûr	**urge**
ĭ	**pit**	th	**thin**
ī	**pie**	*th*	**this**
îr	**pier**	hw	**whoop**
ŏ	**pot**	zh	**vision**
ō	**toe**	ə	**about**
ô	**paw**	N	*French* **bon**

kingdom

Today most scientists agree that there are five major groups, or **kingdoms**, of living organisms on Earth: *Monera* (bacteria), *Protoctista* (seaweed, algae, and similar organisms), *Fungi* (yeasts, molds, and mushrooms), *Plants*, and *Animals*. Scientists long believed that all organisms belonged in one of two groups —animal or vegetable (plant). By this line of thinking, if a creature moved, it was an animal; if it was green, it was a plant. However, centuries of careful observation as well as the development of microscopes and other tools for studying previously unseen organisms helped scientists learn more about life on Earth. Using this knowledge, they were able to devise these five new kingdoms for Earth's organisms.

kingfisher

kinkajou

and 1960's. He won the 1964 Nobel Peace Prize and was assassinated in Memphis, Tennessee.

King, William Lyon Mackenzie. 1874–1950. Canadian politician who three times served as prime minister (1921–1926, 1926–1930, and 1935–1948).

king•bird (kĭng′bûrd′) *n.* Any of various American flycatchers, especially one known for attacking other birds.

king•bolt (kĭng′bōlt′) *n.* A vertical bolt that connects the front axle to the body of a wagon or other vehicle and acts as a pivot when the vehicle turns.

king crab *n.* A large crab found along the coastal waters of Alaska, Japan, and Siberia, valued for its meat.

king•dom (kĭng′dəm) *n.* **1.** A country that is ruled by a king or queen. **2.** An area, province, or realm: *the kingdom of the imagination.* **3.** The highest classification into which living organisms are grouped. One widely accepted system of classification is divided into five kingdoms: monerans, protoctists, fungi, plants, and animals. See table at **taxonomy.** —See Note.

king•fish•er (kĭng′fĭsh′ər) *n.* Any of various colorful birds that feed on fish and have a large bill and a crested head.

King James Bible *n.* An English translation of the Bible from Hebrew and Greek published in 1611 at the direction of James I for the Church of England; the Authorized Version.

king•ly (kĭng′lē) *adj.* **king•li•er, king•li•est.** Of or fit for a king; regal; royal: *a kingly manner.* —*adv.* As a king; royally. —**king′li•ness** *n.*

king•pin (kĭng′pĭn′) *n.* **1.** The front or central pin in a group of bowling pins. **2.** The most important person or part in an organization or system. **3.** A kingbolt.

king•ship (kĭng′shĭp′) *n.* **1.** The position or power of a king. **2.** The area ruled by a king; a kingdom. **3.** The period during which a king rules; a reign.

king-size (kĭng′sīz′) or **king-sized** (kĭng′sīzd′) *adj.* Extra large: *a king-size box of cereal.*

king snake *n.* Any of various nonpoisonous snakes of North America. King snakes are constrictors and eat small animals and other snakes.

King•ston (kĭng′stən). The capital of Jamaica, in the southeast part of the island on the Caribbean Sea. It was founded in about 1692. Population, 586,930.

Kings•town (kĭngz′toun′). The capital of St. Vincent and the Grenadines in the West Indies, on the southwest coast of St. Vincent Island. Population, 18,378.

kink (kĭngk) *n.* **1.** A tight curl or twist, as in a hair, wire, or rope. **2.** A painful cramp or stiffness in a muscle, especially of the neck or back; a crick. **3.** A flaw or difficulty, as in a plan: *Technicians finally got the kinks out of the new computer program.* **4.** A curious idea or turn of mind; a peculiarity. —*intr. & tr.v.* **kinked, kink•ing, kinks.** To form or cause to form a kink; curl or twist sharply: *When the hose kinks, water can't flow through it.*

kink•a•jou (kĭng′kə jo͞o′) *n.* A furry mammal of tropical America that has a long tail, lives in trees, and is related to the raccoon.

kink•y (kĭng′kē) *adj.* **kink•i•er, kink•i•est. 1.** Full of kinks; tightly curled or twisted: *We could not pull the kinky wire through the hole.* **2.** Peculiar or eccentric; odd. —**kink′i•ness** *n.*

kins•folk (kĭnz′fōk′) *pl.n.* Variant of **kinfolk.**

Kin•sha•sa (kĭn shä′sə). The capital and largest city of Zaire, in the western part of the country on the Congo River. It is named for an early village that occupied the site. Population, 2,653,558.

kin•ship (kĭn′shĭp′) *n.* **1.** The condition of being related by blood, marriage, or adoption; family relationship. **2.** A connection or similarity between persons or things.

kins•man (kĭnz′mən) *n.* A male relative.

kins•wom•an (kĭnz′wo͝om′ən) *n.* A female relative.

ki•osk (kē′ŏsk′ *or* kē ŏsk′) *n.* **1.** A small structure often open on one side and used as a newsstand or booth. **2.** A cylindrical structure on which advertisements are posted. [First written down in 1625 in Modern English, from Turkish *köşk.*]

Ki•o•wa (kī′ə wô′ *or* kī′ə wä′ *or* kī′ə wā′) *n., pl.* **Kiowa** or **Ki•o•was. 1.** A member of a Native American people of the southern Great Plains. **2.** The language of the Kiowa.

Kip•ling (kĭp′lĭng), **(Joseph) Rudyard.** 1865–1936. British writer whose works include *The Jungle Book* (1894). He won the 1907 Nobel Prize for literature.

kip•per (kĭp′ər) *n.* A herring or salmon that has been cured by kippering. —*tr.v.* **kip•pered, kip•per•ing, kip•pers.** To cure (fish) by splitting, salting, and smoking.

Kir•ghiz or **Kir•giz** (kîr gēz′). A region in west-central Asia bordering on northwest China. It was part of the Soviet Union from 1936 until 1991. Capital, Bishkek. Population, 3,967,000.

Ki•ri•ba•ti (kēr′ə bä′tē *or* kîr′ə băs′). An island country of the west-central Pacific Ocean near the equator. The country became independent from Great Britain in 1979. Bairiki is the administrative center. Population, 56,213.

kirk (kûrk) *n. Scots.* A church.

Ki•shi•nev (kĭsh′ə nĕf′ *or* kĭsh′ə nôf′). The capital of Moldavia, in the southern part of the republic near the Romanian border. It was founded in the 15th century. Population, 624,000.

kiss (kĭs) *v.* **kissed, kiss•ing, kiss•es.** —*tr.* **1.** To touch with the lips as a sign of affection, greeting, or reverence. **2.** To brush against; touch gently: *Rain kissed the flowers.* —*intr.* To engage in mutual touching or caressing with the lips. —*n.* **1.** A touch with the lips as a token of affection, greeting, or reverence. **2.** A slight or gentle touch. **3.** A small piece of candy, especially of chocolate.

kiss•er (kĭs′ər) *n.* **1.** A person who kisses. **2.** *Slang.* The mouth or face.

kit[1] (kĭt) *n.* **1.a.** A set of articles or tools for a certain purpose: *a first-aid kit; a sewing kit.* **b.** A bag or other container for carrying such a set. **2.** A set of parts or materials to be assembled: *a model airplane kit.* **3.** A collection of clothing and equipment used for traveling. [First written down in 1275 in Middle English and spelled *kitte,* wooden tub, probably from Middle Dutch.]

kit[2] (kĭt) *n.* A young fur-bearing animal; a kitten or cub: *muskrat kits.* [First written down in 1562 in Modern English and spelled *kytte,* from *kitten.*]

kitch•en (kĭch′ən) *n.* A room or an area where food is prepared or cooked. [First written down about 1000 in Old English and spelled *cycene,* from Late Latin *coquīna,* from *coquere,* to cook.]

kitch•en•ette (kĭch′ə nĕt′) *n.* A small kitchen.

kitchen police *n.* **1.** Enlisted military personnel assigned to work in a kitchen. **2.** Military duty helping the cooks in a kitchen.

kite (kīt) *n.* **1.** A light frame, as of wood, covered with paper or similar material and designed to be flown in the wind at the end of a long string. **2.** Any of various hawks having a long, often forked tail and long pointed wings. [First written down before 800 in Old English and spelled *cyta.*]

kith and kin (kĭth′ ən kĭn′) *pl.n.* Friends and relatives.

kit•ten (kĭt′n) *n.* A young cat. [First written down

about 1378 in Middle English and spelled *kitoun*, probably from Late Latin *cattus*, cat.]

kit•ty¹ (kĭt′ē) *n., pl.* **kit•ties.** A sum of money usually consisting of small contributions from a number of people, such as the players in a card game. [First written down in 1887, probably from *kit*, set of articles.]

kit•ty² (kĭt′ē) *n., pl.* **kit•ties.** A kitten or cat. [First written down in 1719 in Modern English, from *kitten*.]

kit•ty-cor•nered (kĭt′ē kôr′nərd) *adj. & adv.* Variant of **cater-cornered.**

Kit•ty Hawk (kĭt′ē hôk′). A village of northeast North Carolina on a sandy peninsula north of Hatteras Island. Nearby is the site of the Wright brothers' first two successful flights (December 17, 1903).

ki•wi (kē′wē) *n., pl.* **ki•wis. 1.** Any of several flightless birds of New Zealand having a long slender bill, a rounded body, and brownish feathers. **2.a.** The oval, brown, fuzzy fruit of a Chinese vine, having sweet green pulp. **b.** The woody vine that bears this fruit.

KKK or **K.K.K.** *abbr.* An abbreviation of Ku Klux Klan.

Klan (klăn) *n.* The Ku Klux Klan.

Klans•man (klănz′mən) *n.* A man who is a member of the Ku Klux Klan.

Kleen•ex (klē′nĕks′). A trademark used for a soft facial tissue.

klep•to•ma•ni•a (klĕp′tə mā′nē ə *or* klĕp′tə mān′yə) *n.* An uncontrollable urge to steal, especially when there is no personal need or desire for the things stolen. **—klep′to•ma′ni•ac′** (klĕp′tə mā′nē ăk′) *n.*

klieg light (klēg) *n.* A powerful lamp used chiefly to light up a scene in filming motion pictures. [First written down in 1923 in American English and spelled *Kleig*, after John H. *Kliegl* (1869–1959) and Anton T. *Kliegl* (1872–1927), German-born American lighting experts.]

Klon•dike (klŏn′dīk′). A region of Yukon Territory, Canada, just east of Alaska and traversed by the **Klondike River,** about 90 miles (145 kilometers) long. Gold was discovered here in August 1896.

klutz (klŭts) *n. Slang.* A clumsy person.

km *abbr.* An abbreviation of kilometer.

knack (năk) *n.* A special talent or skill: *The mechanic has a knack for fixing cars.*

knack•wurst or **knock•wurst** (nŏk′wûrst′ *or* nŏk′wo͝orst′) *n.* A short, thick, highly seasoned sausage.

knap•sack (năp′săk′) *n.* A bag made of sturdy material and having shoulder straps for carrying articles such as camping supplies on the back.

knave (nāv) *n.* **1.** A dishonest crafty man: *The knave got the advantage by trickery.* **2.** A male servant: *a kitchen knave.* **3.** A man of humble birth or position. **4.** A jack in a deck of playing cards. **—knav′ish** *adj.* **—knav′ish•ly** *adv.* **—knav′ish•ness** *n.* —SEE NOTE.

❑ *These sound alike:* **knave, nave** (part of a church).

knav•er•y (nā′və rē) *n., pl.* **knav•er•ies.** Dishonest or crafty dealing.

knead (nēd) *tr.v.* **knead•ed, knead•ing, kneads. 1.** To mix and work (a substance) into a pliable mass, as by folding, stretching, and pressing: *The cook kneaded the pizza dough.* **2.** To squeeze, press, or roll with the hands, as in massaging: *The coach kneaded the runner's sore leg muscles.* **3.** To make or shape by or as if by kneading. **—knead′er** *n.*

❑ *These sound alike:* **knead, need** (necessity).

knee (nē) *n.* **1.a.** The joint at which the human thigh and lower leg come together. **b.** The region around this joint. **2.** A corresponding joint in the leg of another animal. **3.** Something that resembles a knee, as a point where something bends sharply. **4.** The part of a pair of trousers that covers the knee: *The knees of my overalls are patched.* —*tr.v.* **kneed, knee•ing, knees.** To push or strike with the knee: *The waiter kneed the kitchen door open.*

knee•cap (nē′kăp′) *n.* The patella.

knee-deep (nē′dēp′) *adj.* **1.** Reaching as high as the knees: *The prairie grass was knee-deep.* **2.** Submerged to the knees: *The hikers were knee-deep in swampy water.* **3.** Deeply occupied or engaged: *I'm knee-deep in work.*

knee-high (nē′hī′) *adj.* Reaching as high as the knee: *knee-high boots.* —*n.* (nē′hī′). A sock or stocking that extends just below the knee.

kneel (nēl) *intr.v.* **knelt** (nĕlt) or **kneeled, kneel•ing, kneels.** To rest or fall on one or both knees: *The tailor knelt to mark the pants for hemming.* [First written down before 1000 in Old English and spelled *cnēowlian*, from *cnēow*, knee.]

knee•pad (nē′păd′) *n.* A protective covering for the knee, as one used by a player in volleyball.

knell (nĕl) *v.* **knelled, knell•ing, knells.** —*intr.* To ring slowly and solemnly: *The church bells knelled all day.* —*tr.* To announce or summon by or as if by a knell: *The crowd's cheering knelled the coming of the New Year.* —*n.* **1.** The sound of a bell rung slowly and solemnly, as for a funeral. **2.** A signal of disaster, death, or destruction: *Construction of a new highway sounded the knell of the farm.* [First written down about 950 in Old English and spelled *cnyllan*.]

knelt (nĕlt) *v.* A past tense and a past participle of **kneel.**

Knes•set (knĕs′ĕt′) *n.* The parliament of the modern state of Israel.

knew (no͞o *or* nyo͞o) *v.* Past tense of **know.**

❑ *These sound alike:* **knew, gnu** (antelope), **new** (not old).

Knick•er•bock•er (nĭk′ər bŏk′ər) *n.* **1.** A descendant of the Dutch settlers of early New York. **2.** A New Yorker. **3. knick•er•bock•ers.** Loose trousers that are gathered in a band just below the knees. [First written down in 1831 in American English, after Diedrich *Knickerbocker*, fictitious author of *History of New York* by Washington Irving.]

knick•ers (nĭk′ərz) *pl.n.* **1.** Long bloomers formerly worn as underwear by women and girls. **2.** Loose trousers that are gathered in with a band just below the knees.

knick•knack also **nick•nack** (nĭk′năk′) *n.* A small ornamental article; a trinket.

knife (nīf) *n., pl.* **knives** (nīvz). **1.** A tool made of a sharp blade with a handle, used for cutting, carving, or spreading. **2.** A cutting edge or blade of a tool or machine. —*v.* **knifed, knif•ing, knifes.** —*tr.* **1.** To stab with a knife. **2.** *Informal.* To betray by underhand means. —*intr.* To cut or slash a way through something: *The shark's fin knifed through the water.* [First written down before 1100 in Old English and spelled *cnīf*, from Old Norse *knīfr*.]

knight (nīt) *n.* **1.** In the Middle Ages, a man who served a king or lord as a mounted soldier in return for the right to hold and profit from land, especially such a man raised to an order of chivalry after training as a page and squire. **2.** A man given a rank of honor by a sovereign for personal merit or service to the country. **3.** A chess piece shaped like the head of a horse that can be moved two squares horizontally and one vertically or two squares vertically and one horizontally. —*tr.v.* **knight•ed, knight•ing, knights.** To make (a person) a knight. [First written down before 725 in Old English and spelled *cniht*.] **—knight′ly** *adj. & adv.*

❑ *These sound alike:* **knight, night** (darkness).

kiwi

Word History: knave

Our **knave** comes from the Old English noun *cnafa*, which means "boy, male servant." In the thirteenth century, during the Middle English period, the word was also spelled **knave** and acquired its current meaning "rogue, villain." In the sixteenth century, in the Modern English period, **knave** was the name given to the "picture card" that we now usually call the **jack**, as in "the knave of hearts." In modern German the related noun *Knabe* still means "boy."

kneepad

ă	**pat**	oi	**boy**
ā	**pay**	ou	**out**
âr	**care**	o͝o	**took**
ä	**father**	o͞o	**boot**
ĕ	**pet**	ŭ	**cut**
ē	**be**	ûr	**urge**
ĭ	**pit**	th	**thin**
ī	**pie**	*th*	**this**
îr	**pier**	hw	**whoop**
ŏ	**pot**	zh	**vision**
ō	**toe**	ə	**about**
ô	**paw**	N	*French* **bon**

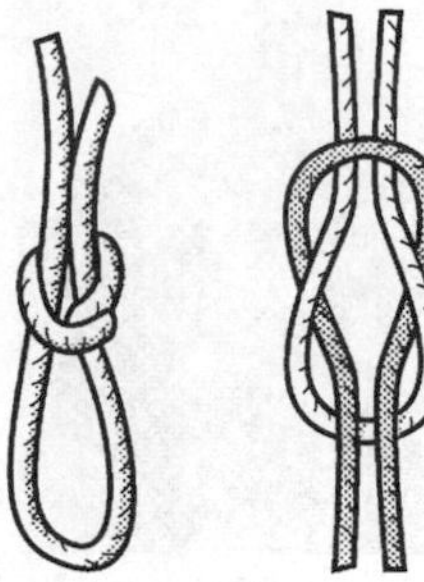

knot
Left: Slipknot
Right: Square knot

koala
Adult female and young koala

Komodo dragon

knight-errant (nīt′ĕr′ənt) *n., pl.* **knights-errant** (nīts′ĕr′ənt). In medieval times, a knight who traveled in search of adventure.

knight•hood (nīt′ho͝od′) *n.* **1.** The rank or dignity of a knight. **2.** The behavior or qualities suitable for a knight; chivalry. **3.** Knights considered as a group.

knish (kə nĭsh′) *n.* A small piece of dough stuffed with a potato, cheese, or other filling, and baked or fried.

knit (nĭt) *v.* **knit** or **knit•ted, knit•ting, knits.** —*tr.* **1.** To make (a fabric or garment) by forming yarn or thread into interlocked loops either by hand with special needles or by machine: *I knit a sweater.* **2.** To join closely; unite securely: *Shared interests knitted the group together.* **3.** To draw together in wrinkles; furrow: *knit one's brows in thought.* —*intr.* **1.** To make a fabric or garment by knitting: *I would like to learn to knit.* **2.** To grow or come together: *A broken bone knits fairly quickly.* —*n.* A fabric or garment made by knitting: *a cotton knit.* [First written down about 1000 in Old English and spelled *cnyttan*, to knot.] —**knit′ter** *n.*

❑ *These sound alike:* **knit, nit** (louse egg).

knit•ting (nĭt′ĭng) *n.* **1.** The act or process of making knitted fabric or garments: *Knitting is a useful skill.* **2.** Fabric or a garment in the process of being knitted: *I brought along my knitting.*

knitting needle *n.* One of two long thin needles, pointed at one or both ends, used in knitting by hand.

knit•wear (nĭt′wâr′) *n.* Knitted garments.

knives (nīvz) *n.* Plural of **knife.**

knob (nŏb) *n.* **1.** A rounded lump or mass: *a brass knob on top of a bedpost.* **2.** A rounded handle or dial: *a control knob on a television set.* [First written down in 1373 in Middle English and spelled *knobe.*] —**knob′by** *adj.*

knock (nŏk) *v.* **knocked, knock•ing, knocks.** —*tr.* **1.** To strike with a hard blow: *knock the ball out of the park.* **2.** To hit and cause to fall: *I accidentally knocked the glass of water over.* **3.** To produce by hitting or striking: *knocked a hole in the wall.* **4.** *Slang.* To criticize; find fault with: *The critic knocked the actor's performance.* —*intr.* **1.** To strike a blow or series of blows causing a noise: *The neighbor knocked on our door.* **2.** To make a pounding or clanking noise: *The old car's engine knocks whenever we drive up a hill.* —*n.* **1.** A sharp blow: *The doctor gave me a knock on the knee.* **2.** The sound of a blow on a hard surface; a rap. **3.** A pounding or clanking noise, as of an engine in need of repairs. —***idioms.*** **knock down.** To break up or take apart: *We knocked down the tent and packed it in the car.* **knock off. 1.** *Informal.* To cease; stop: *knock off work; knock off piano practice.* **2.** *Informal.* To complete, accomplish, or dispose of hastily or easily; finish: *I knocked off several letters this afternoon.* **3.** *Informal.* To eliminate; deduct: *Using the coupon knocked five dollars off our bill.* **knock out. 1.** To make unconscious, as by a blow with the fist. **2.** To make useless or prevent from working: *The storm knocked out power in our neighborhood.* **3.** *Informal.* To exhaust completely: *That long math exam really knocked me out.* [First written down about 1000 in Old English and spelled *cnocian.*]

knock•a•bout (nŏk′ə bout′) *adj.* **1.** Rough and boisterous. **2.** Suitable for rough use. —*n.* A small sailing boat with a mainsail and a jib.

knock•down (nŏk′doun′) *n.* The act of knocking down. —*adj.* **1.** Powerful and overwhelming: *a knockdown punch.* **2.** Designed to be put together and taken apart quickly and easily: *knockdown furniture.*

knock•er (nŏk′ər) *n.* A metal ring, knob, or hammer hinged to a door for use in knocking.

knock-knee (nŏk′nē′) *n.* A deformity of the legs in which the knees are abnormally close together and the ankles are spread apart. —**knock′-kneed′** *adj.*

knock•out (nŏk′out′) *n.* **1.** A victory in boxing in which the loser is unable to rise from the canvas within a specified period of time. **2.** A blow that renders a person unconscious or gains such a victory. **3.** A strikingly attractive person or thing.

knock•wurst (nŏk′wûrst′ *or* nŏk′wo͝orst′) *n.* Variant of **knackwurst.**

knoll (nōl) *n.* A small rounded hill; a hillock. [First written down before 899 in Old English and spelled *cnoll.*]

knot (nŏt) *n.* **1.** A tangle of interlacing thread, cord, hair, or similar material. **2.** A fastening made by tying material such as string, rope, or cord in a certain way: *a square knot.* **3.** A decorative bow of ribbon, fabric, or braid. **4.** A tight cluster of persons or things: *a knot of spectators at the theater's entrance.* **5.** A difficult problem. **6.** A hard lump or swelling, as from an enlarged gland. **7.** The hard dark spot in a board where a branch grew out from a tree trunk. **8.** A unit of speed equal to one nautical mile per hour, about 1.15 statute miles (1.85 kilometers) per hour, used especially by ships and aircraft. —*v.* **knot•ted, knot•ting, knots.** —*tr.* **1.** To tie or fasten in or with a knot: *We knotted the rope around the post.* **2.** To entangle in knots: *The strong current knotted our fishing lines together.* —*intr.* **1.** To become snarled or entangled. **2.** To form a knot or knots. [First written down about 1000 in Old English and spelled *cnotta.*]

❑ *These sound alike:* **knot, not** (in no way).

knot•hole (nŏt′hōl′) *n.* A hole in a piece of lumber where a knot has dropped out or been removed.

knot•ty (nŏt′ē) *adj.* **knot•ti•er, knot•ti•est. 1.** Tied or snarled in knots: *knotty string.* **2.** Having many knots or knobs: *knotty lumber.* **3.** Difficult to solve: *a knotty algebra problem.*

know (nō) *v.* **knew** (no͞o *or* nyo͞o), **known** (nōn), **know•ing, knows.** —*tr.* **1.** To be aware of; realize; sense: *I know what the answer is.* **2.** To regard as true; be sure of: *I know that the play will be a success.* **3.** To have skill in or a practical grasp of: *I know how to make lasagna.* **4.** To be acquainted or familiar with: *I know my neighbors well.* **5.** To recognize: *I know the tune, but I can't remember the words.* **6.** To have fixed in the memory: *The actors must know their lines well.* **7.** To be able to distinguish: *Does that little child know right from left?* —*intr.* **1.** To possess knowledge or understanding: *My sister knows about the history of photography.* **2.** To be aware: *I knew about their plans for the weekend.* —***idiom.*** **in the know.** *Informal.* In possession of special or secret information: *My job at the town hall put me in the know about local politics.* —**know′a•ble** *adj.* —**know′er** *n.*

❑ *These sound alike:* **know, no**[1] (not so), **no**[2] (not any).

know-how (nō′hou′) *n.* Practical knowledge; skill: *Building a house requires lots of know-how.*

know•ing (nō′ĭng) *adj.* **1.** Having knowledge or awareness: *a knowing hiker, wise in the ways of the woods.* **2.** Showing shrewdness or resourcefulness. **3.** Suggestive of inside or secret information: *a knowing glance.* —**know′ing•ly** *adv.*

know-it-all (nō′ĭt ôl′) *n.* *Informal.* A person who claims or pretends to know everything.

knowl•edge (nŏl′ĭj) *n.* **1.** Awareness or understanding gained through experience or study: *He has a thorough knowledge of carpentry.* **2.** The fact or state of knowing: *Knowledge of the company's bad sales record made investors cautious.*

knowl•edge•a•ble (nŏl′ĭ jə bəl) *adj.* Well informed: *The Secretary of State is knowledgeable about foreign policy.*

known (nōn) *v.* Past participle of **know.** *—adj.* Proved or generally recognized: *someone of known talent.*

Knox (nŏks), **Henry.** 1750–1806. American Revolutionary soldier who helped George Washington force the British to evacuate Boston (1776).

Knox, John. 1514?–1572. Scottish religious reformer and founder of Scottish Presbyterianism. He helped Protestantism become the established religion in Scotland.

knuck•le (nŭk′əl) *n.* **1.** A joint of a finger, especially one of the joints connecting a finger to the hand. **2.** The rounded mass formed by the bones in a joint of the finger: *I scraped my knuckles on the sidewalk.* **3.** A cut of meat from a leg joint: *pig's knuckles.* *—tr.v.* **knuck•led, knuck•ling, knuck•les.** To rub, press, or hit with the knuckles. ***—idioms.*** **knuckle down.** To apply oneself earnestly to a task: *We knuckled down and studied for the test.* **knuckle under.** To yield to pressure; give in: *I knuckled under and agreed to go to the store.* [First written down in 1388 in Middle English and spelled *knokel.*]

KO (kā′ō′) *Slang. tr.v.* **KO'd, KO'ing, KO's.** To knock out. *—n.* (kā ō′ *or* kā′ō′). pl. **KO's.** A knockout, as in boxing.

ko•a•la (kō ä′lə) *n.* An Australian mammal that has dense grayish fur, large ears, and sharp claws. Koalas live in eucalyptus trees and feed chiefly on their leaves. The female koala carries her young in a pouch. [First written down in 1808 in Modern English, from Dharuk (Aboriginal language of southeast Australia) *gulawaŋ.*]

Koch (kôk *or* kôKH), **Robert.** 1843–1910. German scientist who discovered the cause of anthrax. He won a 1905 Nobel Prize.

kohl•ra•bi (kōl rä′bē *or* kōl răb′ē) *n., pl.* **kohl•ra•bies.** A plant related to the cabbage, having a thick rounded stem that resembles a turnip and is eaten as a vegetable.

ko•la (kō′lə) *n.* Variant of **cola[3].**

Ko•mo•do dragon (kə mō′dō) *n.* A large lizard of Indonesia measuring up to 10 feet (3 meters) long.

koo•doo (kōō′dōō) *n.* Variant of **kudu.**

kook (ko͝ok) *n. Slang.* An odd or crazy person. [First written down in 1959 in American English, possibly from *cuckoo.*]

kook•a•bur•ra (ko͝ok′ə bûr′ə *or* ko͝ok′ə bŭr′ə) *n.* A large kingfisher native to Australia, having a call that sounds like loud harsh laughter.

kook•y (kōō′kē) *adj.* **kook•i•er, kook•i•est.** *Slang.* Strange or crazy: *a kooky idea.* **—kook′i•ness** *n.*

ko•peck (kō′pĕk) *n.* A Russian coin equal to 1/100 of a ruble.

Ko•ran or **Qur•'an** (kə răn′ *or* kə rän′) *n.* The sacred book of Islam, believed by Muslims to contain the word of Allah as revealed to the prophet Muhammad.

Ko•re•a (kə rē′ə). A peninsula and former country of eastern Asia on the Yellow Sea west of Japan. It is the site of an ancient civilization dating to the 12th century B.C.. The peninsula is now divided between North Korea and South Korea.

Ko•re•an (kə rē′ən) *n.* **1.** A native or inhabitant of Korea. **2.** The language of the Koreans. *—adj.* Of or relating to Korea or its people, language, or culture.

Korean War *n.* A war fought between North Korea, aided by Communist China, and South Korea, aided by United Nations forces consisting mainly of U.S. troops, lasting from 1950 to 1953.

ko•sher (kō′shər) *adj.* **1.** Conforming to or prepared in accordance with Jewish dietary laws. **2.** *Slang.* Proper; correct: *It's not kosher to wear a hat at the dinner table.* *—tr.v.* **ko•shered, ko•sher•ing, ko•shers.** To make proper or ritually pure. [First written down in 1851 in Modern English, from Hebrew *kāšēr*, proper.]

Ko•so•vo (kô′sə vō′). A region of southwest Serbia. It became a region of former Yugoslavia in 1946.

ko•to (kō′tō) *n., pl.* **ko•tos.** A Japanese musical instrument having 7 to 13 strings stretched across an oblong sound box and played by plucking.

kow•tow (kou tou′ *or* kou′tou′) *intr.v.* **kow•towed, kow•tow•ing, kow•tows. 1.** To kneel and touch the forehead to the ground in expression of deep respect, worship, or submission. **2.** To show exaggerated respect or obedience; fawn: *kowtowed to the boss hoping to win favor.* *—n.* The act of kneeling and touching the forehead to the ground. [First written down in 1804 in Modern English and spelled *koo-too*, from Chinese (Mandarin) *kòu tóu*, a kowtow : *kòu*, to knock + *tóu*, head.]

KP (kā′pē′) *n.* Kitchen police.

Kr The symbol for the element **krypton.**

kraal (krôl *or* kräl) *n.* **1.** A village of southern Africa, usually surrounded by a fence or stockade. **2.** A pen for sheep or cattle in southern Africa.

Krem•lin (krĕm′lĭn) *n.* **1.** The citadel of Moscow, housing the major offices of the government. **2.** The government of the former Soviet Union.

krill (krĭl) *n., pl.* **krill.** Very small shellfish that are the chief food of whales and certain other sea animals. [First written down in 1907 in Modern English, from Norwegian *kril*, young fry of fish.]

Krish•na (krĭsh′nə) *n.* A Hindu god worshipped as an incarnation of the god Vishnu.

Kriss Krin•gle (krĭs′ krĭng′gəl) *n.* Santa Claus.

kro•na[1] (krō′nə) *n., pl.* **kro•nur** (krō′nər). The basic monetary unit of Iceland. [First written down in 1886 in Modern English, from Icelandic *krōna.*]

kro•na[2] (krō′nə) *n., pl.* **kro•nor** (krō′nôr′ *or* krō′nər). The basic monetary unit of Sweden. [First written down in 1875 in Modern English, from Swedish.]

kro•ne (krō′nə) *n., pl.* **kro•ner** (krō′nər). The basic monetary unit of Norway and Denmark. [First written down in 1884 in Modern English, from Norwegian and Danish.]

kro•nor (krō′nôr′ *or* krō′nər) *n.* Plural of **krona[2].**

kron•ur (krō′nər) *n.* Plural of **krona[1].**

kryp•ton (krĭp′tŏn′) *n. Symbol* **Kr** A colorless element that is an inert gas, used chiefly in fluorescent lamps and lasers. Atomic number 36. See table at **element.** [First written down in 1898 in Modern English, from Greek *kruptos*, hidden.]

KS *abbr.* An abbreviation of Kansas.

Kua•la Lum•pur (kwä′lə lo͝om po͝or′). The capital and largest city of Malaysia, on the southwest Malay Peninsula northwest of Singapore. It was founded by tin miners in 1857. Population 937,817.

Ku•blai Khan (kōō′blī kän′) also **Ku•bla Khan** (kōō′blə kän′). 1215–1294. Mongol emperor (1260–1294). A grandson of Genghis Khan, he established a great capital, now Beijing.

ku•dos (kōō′dōz′ *or* kōō′dōs′ *or* kyōō′dōz′ *or* kyōō′dōs′) *n.* Praise, fame, or renown for exceptional achievement: *The diplomat received kudos for settling the dispute.* [First written down in 1831 in Modern English, from Greek *kudos*, magical glory.]

ku•du also **koo•doo** (kōō′dōō) *n., pl.* **kudu** or **ku•dus** also **koodoo** or **koo•doos.** An African antelope having a brownish coat marked by white stripes. The male has long horns twisted in a spiral.

kud•zu (ko͝od′zōō) *n.* A fast-growing eastern Asian vine, now common in the southern United States, having clusters of purple flowers.

kookaburra

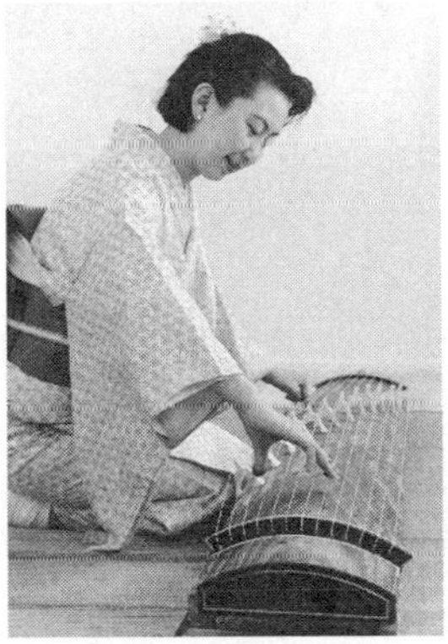

koto

Kublai Khan

ă	pat	oi	boy
ā	pay	ou	out
âr	care	o͝o	took
ä	father	ōō	boot
ĕ	pet	ŭ	cut
ē	be	ûr	urge
ĭ	pit	th	thin
ī	pie	*th*	this
îr	pier	hw	whoop
ŏ	pot	zh	vision
ō	toe	ə	about
ô	paw	N	*French* bon

kumquat

Ku Klux Klan (ko͞o′ klŭks **klăn′** *or* kyo͞o′ klŭks **klăn′**) *n.* **1.** A secret society founded in the southern United States after the Civil War to restore the domination of whites over Blacks through the use of terrorism. **2.** A secret organization of similar purpose founded in Georgia in 1915 and modeled upon the earlier society.

kum•quat (**kŭm′**kwŏt′) *n.* **1.** A small thin-skinned fruit somewhat like an orange but having sweet edible skin and sour pulp. **2.** Any of several trees or shrubs that bear such fruit. [First written down in 1699 in Modern English and spelled *camquit*, from Chinese (Cantonese) *kam kwat* : *kêm*, gold + *kwêt*, orange.]

kung fu (**kŭng′ fo͞o′**) *n.* A Chinese system of unarmed self-defense resembling karate.

kur•cha•tov•i•um (kûr′chə **tō′**vē əm) *n.* Rutherfordium.

Ku•wait (ko͞o **wāt′**). **1.** A country of the Middle East at the northwest end of the Persian Gulf. The city of Kuwait is its capital. Population, 1,355,827. **2.** The capital of Kuwait, in the east-central part of the country on the Persian Gulf. Population, 60,365.

kW *abbr.* An abbreviation of kilowatt.

kWh *abbr.* An abbreviation of kilowatt-hour.

kw-hr *abbr.* An abbreviation of kilowatt-hour.

KY or **Ky.** *abbr.* An abbreviation of Kentucky.

Kyo•to (kē **ō′**tō *or* **kyō′**tō). A city of west-central Honshu, Japan, north-northeast of Osaka. Founded in the eighth century, Kyoto was Japan's capital from 794 until 1869. Population, 1,479,125.

Kyu•shu (kē **o͞o′**sho͞o *or* **kyo͞o′**sho͞o). The southernmost of the major islands of Japan, southwest of Honshu.

Ll

l[1] or **L** (ĕl) *n., pl.* **l's** or **L's. 1.** The 12th letter of the English alphabet. **2.** The 12th in a series or group: *row L in a theater.*
l[2] *abbr.* An abbreviation of liter.
L[1] also **l** The symbol for the Roman numeral 50.
L[2] **L.** *abbr.* An abbreviation of large.
l. *abbr.* An abbreviation of: **1.** Left. **2.** Length.
L. *abbr.* An abbreviation of Latin.
la (lä) *n.* In music, the sixth tone of a major scale.
La The symbol for the element **lanthanum.**
LA or **La.** *abbr.* An abbreviation of Louisiana.
L.A. also **LA** *abbr.* An abbreviation of Los Angeles.
lab (lăb) *n.* A laboratory.
la•bel (lā′bəl) *n.* **1.** A tag, sticker, or piece of paper attached to something such as a container or package to identify it or provide other appropriate information: *the label on a can of peaches; the address label on a package.* **2.** A descriptive word or phrase: *the political labels* liberal *and* conservative. —*tr.v.* **la•beled, la•bel•ing, la•bels** or **la•belled, la•bel•ling, la•bels. 1.** To attach a label to: *label a package for mailing.* **2.** To identify or designate with a label; describe or classify: *The government labeled the writers dissidents.*
la•bi•al (lā′bē əl) *adj.* **1.** Of or relating to the lips. **2.** Articulated by closing or partly closing the lips, as the sounds *b, m,* or *w.* —*n.* A labial consonant. [First written down in 1594 in Modern English, from Latin *labium,* lip.]
la•bor (lā′bər) *n.* **1.** Physical or mental effort; work: *the labor involved in climbing a hill.* **2.** A specific task or piece of work: *the twelve labors of Hercules.* **3.** Work for wages. **4.a.** Workers considered as a group: *negotiations between labor and management.* **b.** Labor unions considered as a group. **5.** The process and effort of childbirth. —*intr.v.* **la•bored, la•bor•ing, la•bors. 1.** To work; toil: *Many workers labored in the fields picking lettuce.* **2.** To move slowly and with difficulty; struggle: *The long freight train labored over the mountain pass.* **3.** To suffer from a burden or disadvantage: *They are laboring under the misconception that others will cooperate.* [First written down before 1325 in Middle English and spelled *labour,* from Latin *labor.*] —**la′bor•er** *n.*
lab•o•ra•to•ry (lăb′rə tôr′ē) *n., pl.* **lab•o•ra•to•ries. 1.** A room or building equipped for scientific research or experiments. **2.** A place where drugs or chemicals are manufactured.
Labor Day *n.* The first Monday in September, celebrated as a holiday in honor of working people.
la•bored (lā′bərd) *adj.* Showing obvious effort; forced; strained: *labored breathing.*
la•bor-in•ten•sive (lā′bər ĭn tĕn′sĭv) *adj.* Requiring more spending for labor than for machines or materials: *An archaeological dig is a labor-intensive undertaking.*
la•bo•ri•ous (lə bôr′ē əs) *adj.* **1.** Demanding great effort; difficult: *a laborious task.* **2.** Hard-working; industrious: *Restoring artworks requires skilled and laborious workers.* —**la•bo′ri•ous•ly** *adv.* —**la•bo′ri•ous•ness** *n.*
la•bor•sav•ing (lā′bər sā′vĭng) *adj.* Designed to save or reduce human labor: *A dishwasher is a laborsaving device.*
labor union *n.* An organization of workers formed to protect and further their mutual interests by bargaining as a group with their employers over wages, working conditions, and benefits.
la•bour (lā′bər) *n. & v. Chiefly British.* Variant of **labor.**
Lab•ra•dor (lăb′rə dôr′). The mainland territory of Newfoundland, Canada, on the northeast portion of the **Labrador Peninsula,** east of Quebec. The area became part of Newfoundland in 1927.
la•bur•num (lə bûr′nəm) *n.* Any of several trees or shrubs planted for their drooping clusters of yellow flowers.
lab•y•rinth (lăb′ə rĭnth′) *n.* **1.** A complex structure of connected passages through which it is difficult to find one's way; a maze. **2. Labyrinth.** In Greek mythology, the maze built by Daedalus in Crete to confine the Minotaur. **3.** Something complicated or confusing in design or construction. [First written down about 1380 in Middle English and spelled *laboryntus,* from Greek *laburinthos.*]
lab•y•rin•thine (lăb′ə rĭn′thĭn *or* lăb′ə rĭn′thēn′) *adj.* Of, relating to, or resembling a labyrinth.
lac (lăk) *n.* A sticky substance resembling resin, secreted by a tropical Asian insect and used in making shellac.
❑ *These sound alike:* **lac, lack** (deficiency).
lace (lās) *n.* **1.** A delicate fabric of fine threads woven in an open weblike pattern with fancy designs. **2.** A cord or string drawn through eyelets or around hooks to pull and tie opposite edges together, as of a shoe. —*v.* **laced, lac•ing, lac•es.** —*tr.* **1.** To thread a lace through the eyelets or around the hooks of: *I laced the boot before trying it on.* **2.** To draw together and tie the laces of: *She laced together the vest.* **3.** To weave, twist, or twine together; interlace: *laced strands of hair into a braid.* **4.** To trim or decorate with lace. —*intr.* To be fastened or tied with a lace or laces: *sneakers that lace easily.* [First written down before 1325 in Middle English, from Latin *laqueus,* noose.]
lac•er•ate (lăs′ə rāt′) *tr.v.* **lac•er•at•ed, lac•er•at•ing, lac•er•ates. 1.** To rip or tear, especially in an injury. **2.** To cause emotional pain to; distress.
lac•er•a•tion (lăs′ə rā′shən) *n.* A jagged wound or cut.
lace•wing (lās′wĭng′) *n.* Any of various insects that have four gauzy wings and feed on and destroy aphids and other insect pests.
lach•ry•mal (lăk′rə məl) *adj.* Of, relating to, or producing tears.
lack (lăk) *n.* **1.** A shortage or an absence: *The lack of electricity during the long power outage made life very hard.* **2.** Something that is needed: *Water is a lack in desert areas.* —*v.* **lacked, lack•ing, lacks.** —*tr.* To have very little of or be without: *Some streets lack trees altogether.* —*intr.* To be needing or deficient: *A diet of nothing but rice is lacking in*

labyrinth

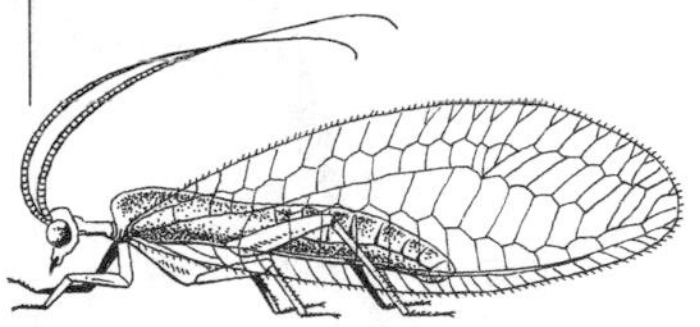

lacewing
Green lacewing

ă	**pat**	oi	**boy**
ā	**pay**	ou	**out**
âr	**care**	o͝o	**took**
ä	**father**	o͞o	**boot**
ĕ	**pet**	ŭ	**cut**
ē	**be**	ûr	**urge**
ĭ	**pit**	th	**thin**
ī	**pie**	*th*	**this**
îr	**pier**	hw	**whoop**
ŏ	**pot**	zh	**vision**
ō	**toe**	ə	**about**
ô	**paw**	N	*French* **bon**

lacrosse

ladder

ladle

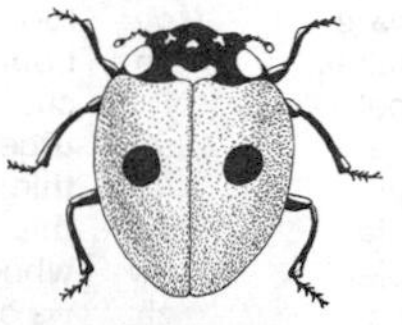
ladybug
Two-spotted ladybug

protein. [First written down before 1300 in Middle English and spelled *lac.*]
❑ *These sound alike:* **lack, lac** (resinous substance).

lack•a•dai•si•cal (lăk′ə dā′zĭ kəl) *adj.* Lacking spirit or interest; listless. **—lack′a•dai′si•cal•ly** *adv.*

lack•ey (lăk′ē) *n., pl.* **lack•eys. 1.** A male servant in uniform; a footman. **2.** A follower who behaves like a servant; a flunky.

lack•lus•ter (lăk′lŭs′tər) *adj.* Lacking luster, brightness, or interest; dull: *Lackluster conversation can be very boring.*

la•con•ic (lə kŏn′ĭk) *adj.* Using few words; terse; concise: *a laconic reply.* **—la•con′i•cal•ly** *adv.*

lac•quer (lăk′ər) *n.* Any of various materials similar to varnish that are applied to a surface and leave a glossy finish when dry. *—tr.v.* **lac•quered, lac•quer•ing, lac•quers.** To coat with lacquer.

la•crosse (lə krôs′ *or* lə krŏs′) *n.* A game played on a field in which two teams of ten players each use sticks with webbed pouches to carry and pass a ball, the object being to send the ball into the opposing team's goal. [First written down in 1718 in American English, from French *(jeu de) la crosse,* (game of) the hooked stick.]

lac•tase (lăk′tās′) *n.* An enzyme, found in some yeasts and in the digestive juices of mammals, that decomposes lactose into simpler sugars.

lac•tate (lăk′tāt′) *intr.v.* **lac•tat•ed, lac•tat•ing, lac•tates.** To secrete milk.

lac•ta•tion (lăk tā′shən) *n.* **1.** The secretion or formation of milk by the mammary glands. **2.** The period during which the mammary glands secrete milk.

lac•tic (lăk′tĭk) *adj.* Of, relating to, or derived from milk.

lactic acid *n.* An organic acid, having the formula $C_3H_6O_3$, produced when milk sours or various fruits ferment, and used as a flavoring and preservative for foods. It is also produced by muscle tissue during exercise.

lac•tose (lăk′tōs′) *n.* A white crystalline sugar that is found in milk and has the formula $C_{12}H_{22}O_{11}$. It is used in infant foods, bakery products, and various sweets.

la•cu•na (lə kyōō′nə) *n., pl.* **la•cu•nae** (lə kyōō′nē) or **la•cu•nas. 1.** An empty space or missing part; a gap. **2.** A space or cavity in bone or tissue.

lac•y (lā′sē) *adj.* **lac•i•er, lac•i•est.** Of, relating to, or resembling lace: *a lacy covering of moss and lichens on the rocks.*

lad (lăd) *n.* A boy or young man.

lad•der (lăd′ər) *n.* **1.** A usually portable device for climbing up or down, consisting of two long side pieces joined by equally spaced rungs or steps. **2.** A means of moving higher or lower: *He used his accomplishments as a ladder to success.* **3.** A series of levels or stages: *She's high on the corporate ladder.* [First written down in 971 in Old English and spelled *hlǣder.*]

lad•die (lăd′ē) *n.* A boy or young man; a lad.

lade (lād) *v.* **lad•ed, lad•en** (lād′n) or **lad•ed, lad•ing, lades.** *—tr.* **1.** To load or burden. **2.** To take up or remove (a liquid) in a ladle. *—intr.* **1.** To take on a load. **2.** To ladle a liquid.

lad•en (lād′n) *adj.* **1.** Weighed down with a load; heavy: *a ship laden with goods from China.* **2.** Oppressed; burdened: *a company laden with debts.*

lad•ing (lā′dĭng) *n.* **1.** The act of loading. **2.** Cargo; freight: *a bill of lading.*

la•dle (lād′l) *n.* A long-handled spoon with a deep bowl used for serving liquids. *—tr.v.* **la•dled, la•dling, la•dles.** To lift out and pour with a ladle. [First written down before 1000 in Old English and spelled *hlædel,* from *hladan,* to draw out, lade.]

la•dy (lā′dē) *n., pl.* **la•dies. 1.** A woman of high social standing or wealth. **2.** A woman with good taste or polite manners. **3.** A woman, especially when spoken of or to in a polite way: *the lady who lives next door.* **4.** A woman who is the head of a household. **5. Lady.** *Chiefly British.* A general feminine title of nobility or other high rank. [First written down before 1121 in Old English and spelled *hlǣfdige.*]

la•dy•bird (lā′dē bûrd′) *n.* The ladybug.

la•dy•bug (lā′dē bŭg′) *n.* Any of numerous small beetles, often reddish with black spots, that feed on and destroy aphids and other insect pests.

lady in waiting *n., pl.* **ladies in waiting.** A woman appointed to attend a queen or princess in a royal court.

la•dy•like (lā′dē līk′) *adj.* Characteristic of or appropriate for a lady.

la•dy•ship also **La•dy•ship** (lā′dē shĭp′) *n.* Used as a title and form of address for a woman holding the rank of lady.

la•dy's slipper (lā′dēz) *n., pl.* **la•dy's slippers.** Any of various wild orchids of North America having flowers that resemble a slipper or shoe.

La•fa•yette (lăf′ē ĕt′ *or* lä′fā ĕt′), Marquis de. 1757–1834. French politician who served on George Washington's staff in the American Revolution and took part in the 1789 and 1830 French revolutions.

La Flesche (lä flĕsh′), **Susette.** Originally Inshta Theumba ("Bright Eyes"). 1854–1903. Omaha lecturer and activist whose work helped bring about more favorable U.S. government policies toward Native Americans.

lag (lăg) *intr.v.* **lagged, lag•ging, lags. 1.** To fail to keep up; straggle: *Several runners began to lag behind the main group in the race.* **2.** To weaken or diminish; slacken: *Our enthusiasm for the hike lagged as the sky clouded over.* *—n.* **1.** The act or condition of lagging: *The cold weather caused a lag in interest in the field trip.* **2.** The extent or degree of lagging; a gap: *A huge lag separated the first and second place finishers in the race.* **—lag′ger** *n.*

la•ger (lä′gər) *n.* A type of beer that is fermented at a low temperature and aged from six weeks to six months before consumption.

lag•gard (lăg′ərd) *n.* A person who lags behind; a straggler. *—adj.* Lagging behind; slow: *a laggard runner.*

la•goon (lə gōōn′) *n.* A shallow body of water separated from the sea by sandbars or reefs. [First written down in 1612 in Modern English and spelled *laguna,* from Latin *lacūna,* pool, hollow, from *lacus,* lake.]

La•gos (lā′gŏs′ *or* lä′gōs). The capital and largest city of Nigeria, in the southwest part of the country east of Porto-Novo, Benin. Population, 1,404,000.

La•hore (lə hôr′). A city of northeast Pakistan near the Indian border northwest of Delhi, India. The city is known for its splendid 16th-century architecture. Population, 2,685,000.

laid (lād) *v.* Past tense and past participle of **lay**[1].

laid-back (lād′băk′) *adj. Informal.* Casual or relaxed in atmosphere or character; easy-going.

lain (lān) *v.* Past participle of **lie**[1].
❑ *These sound alike:* **lain, lane** (path).

lair (lâr) *n.* The den or dwelling place of a wild animal.

laird (lârd) *n. Scots.* The owner of a landed estate; a lord.

lais•sez faire (lĕs′ā fâr′) *n.* An economic doctrine that opposes government regulation of commerce and industry beyond the minimum necessary for free enterprise to operate.

la•i•ty (lā′ĭ tē) *n.* **1.** The laypeople of a religious group as distinguished from the clergy. **2.** Those persons who are not members of a certain profession.

lake (lāk) *n.* A large inland body of fresh or salt water. [First written down in 944 in Old English and spelled *lacu,* from Latin *lacus.*]

lake dwelling *n.* A dwelling, especially a prehistoric dwelling, that rests on piles over a shallow lake. **—lake dweller** *n.*

lake trout *n.* A large North American trout that has dark coloring with pale spots and lives in lakes.

La•ko•ta (lə kō′tə) *n., pl.* **Lakota** or **La•ko•tas.** A Teton.

la•ma (lä′mə) *n.* A Buddhist monk of Tibet or Mongolia.

lamb (lăm) *n.* **1.** A young sheep. **2.** The meat of a young sheep. **3.** Lambskin. **4.** A sweet mild-mannered person. *—intr.v.* **lambed, lamb•ing, lambs.** To give birth to a lamb or lambs. [First written down about 725 in Old English and spelled *lomb.*]

Lamb (lăm), **Charles.** 1775–1834. British critic who with his sister **Mary Ann Lamb** (1764–1847) wrote the children's book *Tales from Shakespeare* (1807).

lam•baste (lăm bāst′) *tr.v.* **lam•bast•ed, lam•bast•ing, lam•bastes.** *Informal.* **1.** To thrash; beat. **2.** To scold; berate: *The two candidates lambasted each other in the debate.*

lamb•da (lăm′də) *n.* The eleventh letter of the Greek alphabet, written Λ, λ. In English it is represented as *L, l.*

lam•bent (lăm′bənt) *adj.* **1.** Flickering gently over a surface: *lambent moonlight.* **2.** Glowing softly; luminous: *lambent eyes.* **3.** Showing effortless brilliance or lightness: *a lambent mind.*

lamb•skin (lăm′skĭn′) *n.* **1.** The hide of a lamb, especially with its wool still on it, as for clothing. **2.** Leather made from the dressed hide of a lamb. **3.** Parchment made from such hide.

lame (lām) *adj.* **lam•er, lam•est. 1.** Unable to walk easily or at all; disabled: *A leg injury made me lame.* **2.** Painful or stiff: *My back is lame after all that heavy lifting.* **3.** Weak and ineffectual; unsatisfactory: *Forgetfulness is a lame excuse for missing our meeting.* *—tr.v.* **lamed, lam•ing, lames.** To make lame; disable. **—lame′ly** *adv.* **—lame′ness** *n.*

la•mé (lă mā′) *n.* A fabric in which flat metal threads, often of gold or silver, are woven with threads of fiber such as silk.

lame duck *n.* **1.** A public officeholder who has not been reelected and is filling out a term of office before the inauguration of a successor. **2.** An ineffective person; a weakling.

la•ment (lə mĕnt′) *v.* **la•ment•ed, la•ment•ing, la•ments.** *—tr.* **1.** To express grief for or about; mourn: *lament the death of a loved one.* **2.** To regret deeply; deplore: *lament the state of the city.* *—intr.* To express or show grief; mourn. *—n.* **1.** An expression of grief: *giving way to tears and laments.* **2.** A sorrowful song or poem. [First written down before 1450 in Middle English and spelled *lementen,* from Latin *lāmentum,* a lament.]

la•men•ta•ble (lə mĕn′tə bəl *or* lăm′ən tə bəl) *adj.* Deserving of lament or regret: *a lamentable mistake.* **—lam′en•ta•bly** *adv.*

lam•en•ta•tion (lăm′ən tā′shən) *n.* **1.** The act of lamenting. **2. Lamentations.** *(used with a singular verb).* A book of the Bible traditionally considered to be written by Jeremiah, in which the fall of Jerusalem is lamented.

lam•i•na (lăm′ə nə) *n., pl.* **lam•i•nae** (lăm′ə nē′) or **lam•i•nas. 1.** A thin plate, scale, or layer. **2.** The flat wide part of a leaf; a blade.

lam•i•nate (lăm′ə nāt′) *tr.v.* **lam•i•nat•ed, lam•i•nat•ing, lam•i•nates. 1.** To beat or press into a thin plate or sheet. **2.** To split into thin layers. **3.** To make (plywood, glass, or plastics) by joining several layers. **4.** To cover with thin layers or sheets. *—n.* Something, such as plywood, made by joining layers together. **—lam′i•na′tor** *n.*

lam•i•na•tion (lăm′ə nā′shən) *n.* **1.** The act or process of laminating or the state of being laminated. **2.** A thin layer.

lamp (lămp) *n.* **1.** A device that gives off light by using oil, gas, or electricity: *When the lights went out we lit a kerosene lamp.* **2.** A device that uses light for heat or radiation: *a sun lamp.* [First written down about 1200 in Middle English and spelled *lampe,* from Greek *lampas,* from *lampein,* to shine.]

lamb

lamp•black (lămp′blăk′) *n.* A gray or black soot that collects when substances containing carbon, such as oil and gas, burn incompletely. Lampblack is used as a pigment.

lamp•light (lămp′līt′) *n.* The light shed by a lamp.

lamp•light•er (lămp′lī′tər) *n.* A person formerly employed to light gas-burning street lights.

lam•poon (lăm po͞on′) *n.* A piece of writing that uses satire to make fun of a person, group, idea, or institution. *—tr.v.* **lam•pooned, lam•poon•ing, lam•poons.** To make fun of with a lampoon: *The comedy lampooned the manners of the upper class.*

lamp•post (lămp′pōst′) *n.* A post supporting a street lamp.

lam•prey (lăm′prē) *n., pl.* **lam•preys.** Any of various fishes having a body like an eel and a jawless sucking mouth. Lampreys attach to other fish in order to feed on their blood.

lamp•shade (lămp′shād′) *n.* A shade placed over a lamp to soften its direct light.

Lan•cas•ter (lăng′kə stər *or* lăn′kə stər). English royal house that from 1399 to 1461 produced three kings of England. During the Wars of the Roses the symbol of the house of Lancaster was a red rose. **—Lan•cas′tri•an** (lăng kăs′trē ən) *adj. & n.*

lance (lăns) *n.* **1.** A long wooden spear with a sharp metal head, used as a weapon, especially by knights or soldiers on horseback. **2.** An implement used for spearing fish. *—tr.v.* **lanced, lanc•ing, lanc•es. 1.** To pierce with a lance. **2.** To make a surgical incision in: *The doctor lanced the swelling.* [First written down before 1300 in Middle English and spelled *launce,* from Latin *lancea.*]

lance corporal *n.* An enlisted person in the U.S. Marine Corps ranking above private first class and below corporal.

Lan•ce•lot (lăn′sə lŏt′) *n.* In Arthurian legend, a knight of the Round Table whose love for Guinevere causes him to go to war with King Arthur.

lanc•er (lăn′sər) *n.* A soldier on horseback equipped with a lance.

lan•cet (lăn′sĭt) *n.* A surgical knife with a short, pointed, double-edged blade.

land (lănd) *n.* **1.** The part of the earth's surface not covered by water: *Only one third of the earth's surface is land.* **2.** Ground or soil: *Farmers plow the land.* **3.** A particular part of the earth, especially a region or country. **4.** The people of a nation, district, or region. **5.** Property; real estate: *buy land in Hawaii.* *—v.* **land•ed, land•ing, lands.** *—tr.* **1.** To bring to and unload on land: *land cargo.* **2.** To set (a vehicle) down on the ground or another surface: *land a plane at New York.* **3.** *Informal.* To cause to arrive in a place or condition: *Their protest landed them in court.* **4.** *Informal.* To catch and pull in (a fish). **5.** To get, secure, or win: *She landed a good job.* **6.** *Informal.* To deliver (a blow). *—intr.* **1.** To

ă	pat	oi	boy
ā	pay	ou	out
âr	care	o͝o	took
ä	father	o͞o	boot
ĕ	pet	ŭ	cut
ē	be	ûr	urge
ĭ	pit	th	thin
ī	pie	*th*	this
îr	pier	hw	whoop
ŏ	pot	zh	vision
ō	toe	ə	about
ô	paw	N	*French* bon

landau
With lowered roof

Dorothea Lange

lantern

come to shore: *The boat landed in heavy surf.* **2.** To go or put ashore; disembark: *We landed on the dock.* **3.** To descend and settle on the ground or another surface: *The plane landed on the lake.* **4.** *Informal.* To arrive in a place or certain condition: *The proposal landed in the file cabinet.* [First written down about 725 in Old English.]

lan•dau (**lăn′**dô′ *or* **lăn′**dou′) *n.* **1.** A four-wheeled carriage with two passenger seats facing each other and a top that can be lowered. **2.** An automobile with a top similar to that of this carriage.

land breeze *n.* A breeze blowing from the land toward open water.

land•ed (**lăn′**dĭd) *adj.* **1.** Owning land: *the landed gentry.* **2.** Consisting of land in the form of property: *a landed estate.*

land•fall (**lănd′**fôl′) *n.* **1.** The act or an instance of sighting or reaching land after a voyage or flight. **2.** The land sighted or reached after a voyage or flight.

land•fill (**lănd′**fĭl′) *n.* **1.** A tract of land in which garbage and trash are buried between layers of dirt. **2.** A method of disposing of garbage and trash using such tracts of land.

land•form (**lănd′**fôrm′) *n.* A feature of the earth's surface, as a plain, plateau, valley, or mountain.

land grant *n.* A grant of public land made by a government for a railroad, state college, or other public use.

land•hold•er (**lănd′**hōl′dər) *n.* A person who owns land. **—land′hold′ing** *n.*

land•ing (**lăn′**dĭng) *n.* **1.** The act or process of coming to land or of coming to rest, as after a voyage or flight: *the landing of a spacecraft on the moon.* **2.** A wharf or pier: *an old boat landing.* **3.** A platform or an area at the top or bottom of a set of stairs.

landing field *n.* An area of level land used by aircraft for landings and takeoffs.

landing gear *n.* The structure attached to the underside of an aircraft that supports it on land or in water.

landing strip *n.* An aircraft runway without airport facilities.

land•la•dy (**lănd′**lā′dē) *n.* **1.** A woman who owns land or buildings rented to tenants. **2.** A woman who runs an inn or a boarding house.

land•less (**lănd′**lĭs) *adj.* Owning or having no land.

land•locked (**lănd′**lŏkt′) *adj.* **1.** Entirely or almost entirely surrounded by land: *Switzerland is a landlocked country.* **2.** Living only in inland waters: *landlocked salmon.*

land•lord (**lănd′**lôrd′) *n.* **1.** A man who owns land or buildings rented to tenants. **2.** A man who runs an inn or a boarding house.

land•lub•ber (**lănd′**lŭb′ər) *n.* A person unfamiliar with sailing or with life aboard a ship or boat.

land•mark (**lănd′**märk′) *n.* **1.** A fixed object that marks a boundary, as a stone or metal post. **2.** A familiar or easily recognized feature of a landscape. **3.** An event that is important in history: *The discovery of penicillin was a landmark in the treatment of certain diseases.* **4.** A building or place preserved for its special historical importance or interest: *Philadelphia has many early American landmarks.*

land•mass (**lănd′**măs′) *n.* A large area of land: *the landmass of Eurasia.*

land mine *n.* A small bomb or similar device buried in the ground and set to explode when stepped on or run over by a vehicle.

land•own•er (**lănd′**ō′nər) *n.* A person who owns land. **—land′own′ing** *adj.*

land•scape (**lănd′**skāp′) *n.* **1.** An expanse of scenery that can be seen from one place. **2.** A painting or picture showing such an expanse of scenery. *—v.* **land•scaped, land•scap•ing, land•scapes.** *—tr.* To change or improve the appearance of (a piece of land) by moving soil and planting trees, shrubs, or flowers. *—intr.* To change or improve grounds as a profession.

land•slide (**lănd′**slīd′) *n.* **1.a.** The loosening and fall of a large mass of soil and rock: *A landslide rumbled down the mountain.* **b.** The mass of soil and rock that moves in this way: *Heavy equipment was needed to clear the landslide.* **2.** A very large majority of votes resulting in victory for a candidate or political party.

land•ward (**lănd′**wərd) *adv. & adj.* To or toward land: *The boat drifted landward.*

lane (lān) *n.* **1.** A narrow path or road, often bordered by hedges, trees, fences, or walls: *a country lane; a lane between old houses.* **2.** A set course or way used by ships or aircraft: *the shipping lanes of the Atlantic.* **3.** A strip marked off on a street or highway to accommodate one line of traffic: *a highway with four lanes.* **4.** A similar strip marked off or divided from others for contestants in a race. **5.** A bowling alley.

❑ *These sound alike:* **lane, lain** (placed oneself flat).

Lange (lăng), **Dorothea.** 1895–1965. American photographer known for her portraits of rural workers during the Depression.

lan•guage (**lăng′**gwĭj) *n.* **1.a.** The use by human beings of voice sounds and often written symbols representing these sounds in organized combinations to express and communicate thoughts and feelings. **b.** A system of such sounds and symbols used by a group of people: *Many languages are spoken in Africa.* **2.** A system of signs, symbols, rules, or gestures used to convey information: *a computer language.* **3.** The study of language; linguistics. **4.** The special words and expressions used by members of a group or profession: *medical language.* **5.** A particular way or style of speaking or writing: *formal language.* **6.** Words or wording, as of a legal document: *the language of a contract.* [First written down about 1280 in Middle English and spelled *langage*, from Latin *lingua*, tongue.]

language arts *pl.n.* Courses that develop the use of language skills with special training in reading, writing, and speaking.

lan•guid (**lăng′**gwĭd) *adj.* **1.** Lacking energy; weak or slow: *a languid wave of the hand.* **2.** Lacking spirit or energy; listless: *a languid mood.* **—lan′guid•ly** *adv.*

lan•guish (**lăng′**gwĭsh) *intr.v.* **lan•guished, lan•guish•ing, lan•guish•es. 1.** To lose strength or vigor; grow weak: *During a long drought crops languish from lack of rain.* **2.** To become listless and depressed; pine: *languish from separation from family and friends.* **3.** To suffer from miserable or depressing conditions.

lan•guor (**lăng′**gər *or* **lăng′**ər) *n.* **1.** Lack of energy; tiredness; listlessness. **2.** A dreamy, lazy mood or quality: *the languor of a summer afternoon.* **3.** Extreme stillness or quiet. **—lan′guor•ous** *adj.*

lank (lăngk) *adj.* **lank•er, lank•est. 1.** Long and lean; slender: *the athlete's lank body.* **2.** Long, straight, and limp: *lank hair.* **—lank′ly** *adv.*

lank•y (**lăng′**kē) *adj.* **lank•i•er, lank•i•est.** Tall, thin, and gawky. **—lank′i•ness** *n.*

lan•o•lin (**lăn′**ə lĭn) *n.* A yellowish-white fatty substance obtained from wool and used in soaps, cosmetics, and ointments.

Lan•sing (**lăn′**sĭng). The capital of Michigan, in the south-central part of the state northwest of Detroit. It became the state capital in 1847. Population, 127,321.

lan•tern (**lăn′**tərn) *n.* **1.** A case or container that protects a light from the weather, usually designed to be carried. **2.** A room at the top of a lighthouse where the light is located. **3.** A structure built on top of a roof as decoration or to let in light and air. [First written down about 1250 in Middle English, from Greek *lamptēr*, from *lampein*, to shine.]

lan•tha•nide (lăn′thə nīd′) *n.* A rare-earth element.

lan•tha•num (lăn′thə nəm) *n. Symbol* **La** A soft silvery element that is one of the rare-earth metals and is used in making glass and in carbon lights for studio lighting. Atomic number 57. See table at **element.**

lan•yard (lăn′yərd) *n.* **1.** A short rope used to secure rigging on a ship. **2.** A cord worn around the neck for carrying a knife, key, or whistle. **3.** A cord with a hook at one end used to fire a cannon.

La•os (lous *or* lä′ōs′). A country of southeast Asia north of Cambodia. It gained its independence from France in 1953. Vientiane is the capital and the largest city. Population, 3,811,000. **—La•o′tian** (lā ō′shən *or* lou′shən) *adj. & n.*

lap[1] (lăp) *n.* **1.** The flat place formed by the front part of the legs above the knees of a person who is sitting: *The puppy curled up in my lap.* **2.** The part of a person's clothing that covers the lap: *the lap of a skirt.* **3.** An area of responsibility, interest, or control: *The opportunity just dropped in my lap.* [First written down before 899 in Old English and spelled *læppa*, flap.]

lap[2] (lăp) *v.* **lapped, lap•ping, laps.** *—tr.* **1.** To fold, wrap, or wind over or around: *Lap the pie dough over the edge of the pan.* **2.** To lie, place, or extend partly over something else; overlap: *The roofer laps the shingles over one another to make the roof watertight.* *—intr.* **1.** To fold or wind around something. **2.** To extend over something else; overlap: *Shingles lap in straight rows.* *—n.* **1.a.** A part folded or extending over something else; an overlapping part: *the front lap of a jacket.* **b.** The amount that a part extends over something else: *The curtains have a lap of three inches.* **2.a.** One complete length or circuit, as of a pool or track: *a race of four laps.* **b.** A part or stage, as of a journey: *The first lap of our trip across the country was from New York to Ohio.* [First written down before 1325 in Middle English and spelled *lappen*, from *lappe*, fold, flap.]

lap[3] (lăp) *v.* **lapped, lap•ping, laps.** *—tr.* **1.** To take up and swallow (a liquid) by using the tongue: *The kitten lapped up the milk.* **2.** To wash or splash with a light slapping sound: *The sea lapped the shore gently.* *—intr.* To wash or splash against something with a light slapping sound: *Waves lapped against the dock.* *—n.* The act or sound of lapping: *each lap of the kitten's tongue; listened to the lap of the waves.* [First written down about 1000 in Old English and spelled *lapian*.]

La Paz (lə päz′ *or* lä päs′). The administrative capital of Bolivia, in the western part of the country southeast of Lima, Peru. It is built on the site of an Inca village and is the highest capital in the world, about 12,000 feet (3,660 meters) above sea level. Population, 992,592.

lap dog *n.* **1.** A small easily held dog kept as a pet. **2.** *Informal.* A person who is eager to do what another asks, especially as a way to maintain a position or privilege.

la•pel (lə pĕl′) *n.* One of the two flaps that extend down from the collar of a coat or jacket and fold back against the chest.

lap•i•dar•y (lăp′ĭ dĕr′ē) *n., pl.* **lap•i•dar•ies.** A person who cuts, polishes, or engraves gems. *—adj.* Of or relating to gemstones or the art of working with them.

lap•is laz•u•li (lăp′ĭs lăz′ə lē *or* lăz′yə lē) *n.* **1.** A typically opaque and deep-blue mineral that is used as a gemstone. **2.** A deep blue.

Lap•land (lăp′lănd′ *or* lăp′lənd). A region of extreme northern Europe including northern Norway, Sweden, and Finland and part of northwest Russia. It is largely within the Arctic Circle.

Lapp (lăp) *n.* **1.** A member of a people of nomadic tradition living in Lapland. **2.** Any of the languages of the Lapps.

lapse (lăps) *intr.v.* **lapsed, laps•ing, laps•es. 1.** To fall to a lower or worse condition: *lapse into bad habits.* **2.** To pass gradually or smoothly; slip: *He lapsed into unconsciousness.* **3.** To be no longer valid or active; end or expire: *I let my membership in the club lapse.* *—n.* **1.** A slip or failure, especially a minor one: *a lapse of memory.* **2.** A fall into a lower or worse condition: *a lapse into bad habits.* **3.** A period of time; an interval: *a lapse of three months between trips.* **4.** The ending of an agreement, right, privilege, or custom through neglect, disuse, or the passage of time: *the lapse of a lease.*

lap•top (lăp′tŏp′) *n.* A portable computer small enough to use on one's lap.

lap•wing (lăp′wĭng′) *n.* Any of several European birds having a narrow wispy crest and a loud piercing call. Their wings have a slow and irregular movement during flight.

lar•board (lär′bərd) *n.* The port side of a ship or boat. *—adj.* On the port side.

lar•ce•nous (lär′sə nəs) *adj.* **1.** Of, relating to, or involving larceny: *Auto theft is a larcenous crime.* **2.** Guilty of larceny.

lar•ce•ny (lär′sə nē) *n., pl.* **lar•ce•nies.** The crime of taking another's property without right or permission; theft.

larch (lärch) *n.* **1.** Any of several tall trees that are related to the pine and shed their needles every year. **2.** The hard strong wood of such a tree.

lard (lärd) *n.* A white waxy substance prepared from the melted fat of a pig and used in cooking. *—tr.v.* **lard•ed, lard•ing, lards. 1.** To cover or coat with lard or a similar fat. **2.** To insert strips of fat or bacon in (meat) before cooking. **3.** To enrich with additions; embellish: *The scholars larded their book with many quotations.*

lar•der (lär′dər) *n.* **1.** A room or cupboard where food is stored. **2.** A supply of food.

large (lärj) *adj.* **larg•er, larg•est.** Greater than average in size, amount, or number; big: *The blue whale is the largest mammal. The Government budget is a large sum of money.* **—*idiom.* at large. 1.** Not in confinement or captivity; at liberty. **2.** As a whole; in general: *The economy at large is doing well.* **3.** Representing a nation, state, or district as a whole. Often used in combination: *a councilor-at-large.* **—large′ness** *n.*

Synonyms: large, big, enormous, great, huge. These adjectives mean notably above the average in size or magnitude. *Los Angeles is a large city. Factory outlet stores usually offer big discounts. A computer can store an enormous amount of information. I'd like to take a cruise on a great ocean liner. Everyone had huge helpings of potato salad at the picnic.* **Antonym: small.**

large calorie *n.* A unit of heat equal to the amount of heat needed to raise the temperature of 1,000 grams of water one degree Celsius.

large-heart•ed (lärj′här′tĭd) *adj.* Having a generous nature; sympathetic.

large intestine *n.* The wide lower section of the intestine that extends from the end of the small intestine to the anus. It absorbs water and eliminates waste matter left after food is digested.

lapel

laptop

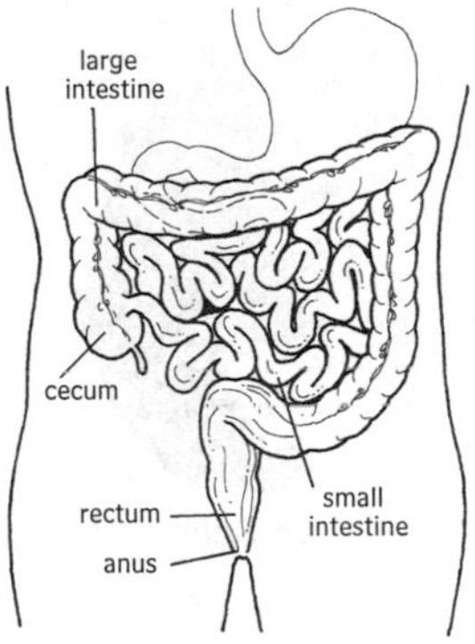

large intestine

ă	pat	oi	boy
ā	pay	ou	out
âr	care	o͝o	took
ä	father	o͞o	boot
ĕ	pet	ŭ	cut
ē	be	ûr	urge
ĭ	pit	th	thin
ī	pie	*th*	this
îr	pier	hw	whoop
ŏ	pot	zh	vision
ō	toe	ə	about
ô	paw	ɴ	*French* bon

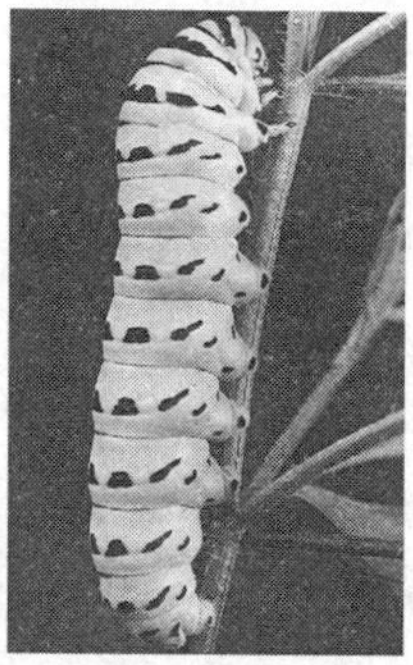

larva
Black swallowtail butterfly larva

La Salle

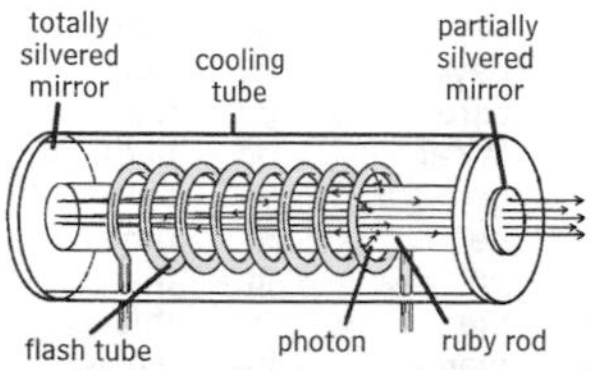

laser
Ruby laser

large•ly (lärj′lē) *adv.* For the most part; mainly: *The hills are largely covered with trees.*

large-scale (lärj′skāl′) *adj.* **1.** Large in scope or effect; extensive: *large-scale farming of crops for export.* **2.** Drawn or made larger in size than average, especially to show detail: *a large-scale map.*

lar•gess also **lar•gesse** (lär zhĕs′ *or* lär jĕs′) *n.* **1.** Generosity in giving gifts. **2.** A generous gift.

lar•go (lär′gō) *adv. & adj.* In music, in a very slow tempo.

lar•i•at (lăr′ē ət) *n.* A lasso.

lark[1] (lärk) *n.* **1.** Any of various songbirds of Europe, Asia, and northern Africa having long hind claws and brown feathers. Larks often sing while flying. **2.** Any of several similar but unrelated birds, such as the meadowlark. [First written down about 700 in Old English and spelled *lāwerce.*]

lark[2] (lärk) *n.* Something done just for fun or adventure: *We went to the zoo on a lark.* —*intr.v.* **larked, lark•ing, larks.** To engage in fun or pranks. [First written down in 1813 in Modern English, perhaps short for *skylark*, to frolic, or possibly from dialectal *lake*, play.]

lark•spur (lärk′spûr′) *n.* The delphinium.

lar•va (lär′və) *n., pl.* **lar•vae** (lär′vē) or **lar•vas. 1.** The immature wormlike form of certain insects, from the time it hatches from the egg until it changes into the adult form. A caterpillar is the larva of a butterfly or moth. **2.** The immature stage of certain animals, differing greatly in form from the parent. A tadpole is the larva of a frog or toad. —**lar′val** *adj.*

la•ryn•ge•al (lə rĭn′jē əl *or* lăr′ən jē′əl) *adj.* Of, relating to, affecting, or near the larynx.

la•ryn•ges (lə rĭn′jēz) *n.* A plural of **larynx.**

lar•yn•gi•tis (lăr′ən jī′tĭs) *n.* Inflammation of the larynx, causing hoarseness and sometimes temporary loss of the voice.

lar•ynx (lăr′ĭngks) *n., pl.* **la•ryn•ges** (lə rĭn′jēz) or **lar•ynx•es.** The upper part of the windpipe, containing the vocal cords.

la•sa•gna (lə zän′yə) *n.* **1.** Flat wide strips of pasta. **2.** A dish made by baking this pasta and layers of tomato sauce, cheese, and other fillings.

La Salle (lə săl), Sieur de. 1643–1687. French explorer in North America who claimed Louisiana for France (1682).

las•civ•i•ous (lə sĭv′ē əs) *adj.* **1.** Feeling or showing lust; lewd. **2.** Tending to excite lust. —**las•civ′i•ous•ly** *adv.* —**las•civ′i•ous•ness** *n.*

la•ser (lā′zər) *n.* A device that emits a very narrow and intense beam of light or other radiation of a single wavelength either continuously or in pulses. Its light is used to cut hard substances, remove diseased tissue, and transmit communications signals.

lash[1] (lăsh) *n.* **1.** A stroke or blow given with or as if with a whip. **2.** The flexible part of a whip. **3.** An eyelash. —*v.* **lashed, lash•ing, lash•es.** —*tr.* **1.** To strike with or as if with a whip. **2.** To strike with force or violence: *The storm lashed the shore with high winds.* **3.** To move or wave rapidly: *The alligator lashed its tail in the water.* **4.** To attack or criticize with harsh language: *Newspaper editorials lashed the government for incompetence.* —*intr.* **1.** To move rapidly or violently; dash: *The waves lashed against the shore.* **2.** To strike with or as if with a whip: *The mule's tail lashed at the flies.* **3.** To make a harsh verbal attack: *The President lashed out against critics of the government.* [First written down before 1300 in Middle English and spelled *las*, probably from *lashen*, to deal a blow.]

lash[2] (lăsh) *tr.v.* **lashed, lash•ing, lash•es.** To fasten or secure, as with a rope or cord: *The crew lashed the cargo firmly in place.* [First written down in 1440 in Middle English and spelled *lasschin*, to lace, from Old French *lachier.*]

lass (lăs) *n.* A girl or young woman.

las•sie (lăs′ē) *n.* A lass.

las•si•tude (lăs′ĭ to͞od′ *or* lăs′ĭ tyo͞od′) *n.* A feeling of weakness or exhaustion; listlessness: *The disease brought on a long period of lassitude and inactivity.*

las•so (lăs′ō *or* lă so͞o′) *n., pl.* **las•sos** or **las•soes.** A long rope with an adjustable loop at one end, used especially to catch horses and cattle. —*tr.v.* **las•soed, las•so•ing, las•sos** or **las•soes.** To catch with a lasso: *lasso a runaway calf.*

last[1] (lăst) *adj.* **1.** Being, coming, or placed after all others; final: *the last day of the school year.* **2.** Being the only one left: *my last dime.* **3.** Most recent; just passed: *last week.* **4.** Most unlikely; least expected: *The last thing you would expect is snow during the summer.* **5.** The latest possible: *We waited until the last second to get on the plane.* —*adv.* **1.** After all others; at the end: *The recipe says to add the flour last.* **2.** Most recently; latest: *I last saw them when I was a child.* —*n.* **1.** A person or thing that is last: *I've read every chapter but the last.* **2.** The end: *They held out until the last.* —***idioms.*** **at last.** After a long time; finally: *At last we fell asleep.* **at long last.** After a lengthy or troublesome wait or delay: *At long last the storm was over.* [First written down before 899 in Old English and spelled *lætest*, latest.] —**last′ly** *adv.*

last[2] (lăst) *v.* **last•ed, last•ing, lasts.** —*intr.* **1.** To continue; go on: *The song lasted three minutes.* **2.** To remain in good condition; endure: *Appliances don't last like they used to.* **3.** To be enough: *The food supply should last for a long time.* —*tr.* To supply adequately; be enough for: *One loaf of bread can't last us a week.* [First written down about 750 in Old English and spelled *læstan.*]

last[3] (lăst) *n.* A block shaped like a human foot and used in making and repairing shoes. [First written down about 1000 in Old English and spelled *læste*, from *læst*, sole of the foot.]

last•ing (lăs′tĭng) *adj.* Continuing or remaining for a long time; enduring: *a lasting peace between nations.* —**last′ing•ly** *adv.*

Last Judgment *n.* The final judgment by God of all human beings, especially as conceived in Christianity, Judaism, and Islam.

last minute *n.* The exact moment before it is too late: *We made our preparations at the last minute before the wedding.* —**last′-min′ute** *adj.*

last straw *n.* The last in a series of annoyances or disappointments that finally leads to loss of patience, trust, or hope.

Last Supper *n.* The last meal of Jesus with the Apostles on the night before his crucifixion.

last word *n.* **1.** The final statement, as in a verbal argument. **2.** The power or authority to make a final decision. **3.** A convincing or authoritative statement or treatment: *This report is the last word on nutrition.* **4.** *Informal.* The newest or most up-to-date style or development; the latest thing: *The model is the last word in racing bikes.*

Las Ve•gas (läs vā′gəs). A city of southeast Nevada near the California and Arizona borders. It is a major tourist center. Population, 258,295.

lat. *abbr.* An abbreviation of latitude.

Lat. *abbr.* An abbreviation of Latin.

latch (lăch) *n.* A fastener for a door, gate, or window, usually consisting of a movable bar that fits into a notch or slot. —*tr. & intr.v.* **latched, latch•ing, latch•es.** To close or be closed with a latch: *Latch the door. Does the door latch securely?* —***idiom.*** **latch on to** or **latch onto.** To get hold of; obtain.

latch•key (lăch′kē′) *n.* A key for unfastening a latch or lock, especially one on a door.

late (lāt) *adj.* **lat•er, lat•est. 1.** Coming or happening after the expected, usual, or proper time; tardy: *I am late for my appointment.* **2.** Coming toward the end or more advanced part of a time period or series of events: *It was late in the meeting when we discussed that issue.* **3.** Of a time just past; recent: *a late model car; the late recession.* **4.** Dead, especially if only recently. **5.** Having recently occupied a position or place: *The late governor is running for office again.* —*adv.* **later, latest. 1.** After the usual, expected, or proper time: *The train arrived late.* **2.** At the end or at an advanced stage: *Our team scored the winning run late in the game.* **3.** Recently: *as late as last week.* —*idiom.* **of late.** Recently; lately: *The trains have been running on a new schedule of late.* [First written down about 725 in Old English and spelled *læt.*] —**late′ness** *n.*

late•com•er (lāt′kŭm′ər) *n.* A person or thing that arrives later than others or has arrived recently: *Latecomers to the show may have difficulty finding seats.*

la•teen (lə tēn′ *or* lă tēn′) *adj.* Being, relating to, or rigged with a triangular sail hung on a long pole attached at an angle to the top of a short mast.

Late Latin *n.* Latin from the third to the seventh century A.D.

late•ly (lāt′lē) *adv.* Not long ago; recently: *The weather has been cold lately.*

la•tent (lāt′nt) *adj.* Present but not evident or active; hidden: *Many of a child's latent talents only emerge in adulthood.* —**la′ten•cy** *n.*

lat•er•al (lăt′ər əl) *adj.* Of, situated on, directed toward, or coming from the side: *Lateral growth on a plant branches out from the stem. A lateral pass in football is to the side of the field.* —*intr.v.* **lat•er•aled, lat•er•al•ing, lat•er•als** also **lat•er•alled, lat•er•al•ling, lat•er•als.** In football, to throw a pass toward the side of the field. [First written down before 1425 in Middle English, from Latin *latus,* side.] —**lat′er•al•ly** *adv.*

la•tex (lā′tĕks′) *n., pl.* **la•ti•ces** (lā′tĭ sēz′ *or* lăt′ĭ-sēz′) or **la•tex•es. 1.** The milky sap of certain trees and plants, such as the milkweed and the rubber tree, that hardens with exposure to air. **2.** A synthetic preparation resembling this, used in paints, adhesives, and other products.

lath (lăth) *n., pl.* **laths** (lă*th*z *or* lăths). **1.** A thin narrow strip of wood or metal used as a supporting structure for plaster, shingles, slates, or tiles. **2.** A quantity of laths or work made using laths. —*tr.v.* **lathed, lath•ing, laths.** To cover or line with laths.

lathe (lā*th*) *n.* A machine on which a piece of wood, metal, or plastic is spun and shaped by a cutting tool.

lath•er (lă*th*′ər) *n.* **1.** Foam formed when soap and water mix. **2.** Froth formed by heavy sweating, especially on a horse. —*v.* **lath•ered, lath•er•ing, lath•ers.** —*tr.* To cover with lather. —*intr.* To produce or form lather: *The race caused the horse to lather heavily.*

la•ti•ces (lā′tĭ sē′ *or* lăt′ĭ sēz′) *n.* A plural of **latex.**

Lat•in (lăt′n) *n.* **1.** The language of the ancient Romans, especially from about 200 B.C. to about A.D. 200. **2.** A native or inhabitant of ancient Rome. **3.** A member of a people who speak a Romance language, especially a native or inhabitant of Latin America. —*adj.* **1.** Of or relating to ancient Rome or its people or culture. **2.** Of or relating to the Latin language. **3.** Of or relating to the peoples or countries of Latin America. **4.** Of or relating to the languages that developed from Latin, such as French, Italian, and Spanish.

Latin A•mer•i•ca (ə mĕr′ĭ kə). The countries of the Western Hemisphere south of the United States, especially those whose peoples speak Spanish, Portuguese, or French.

Latin American *n.* **1.** A native or inhabitant of Latin America. **2.** A person of Latin-American descent. —**Lat′in-A•mer′i•can** *adj.*

La•ti•no (lə tē′nō *or* lă tē′nō) *n., pl.* **La•ti•nos. 1.** A native or inhabitant of Latin America. **2.** A person of Hispanic, especially Latin-American, descent.

lat•i•tude (lăt′ĭ to͞od′ *or* lăt′ĭ tyo͞od′) *n.* **1.** Distance north or south of the equator measured in degrees. A degree of latitude is about 69 statute miles or 60 nautical miles. **2.** A region of the earth indicated by its approximate latitude: *Some of the coldest temperatures on earth occur in the polar latitudes.* **3.** Freedom from confining regulations or restrictions: *The attorney general gave his staff wide latitude in investigating this case.* —**lat′i•tu′di•nal** *adj.*

la•trine (lə trēn′) *n.* A communal toilet of the type often used in camps or military barracks.

lat•ter (lăt′ər) *adj.* **1.** Being the second of two that are mentioned: *Apples and oranges both taste good but I prefer eating the latter.* **2.** Closer to the end: *November comes in the latter part of the year.* —**lat′ter•ly** *adv.*

Lat•ter-day Saint (lăt′ər dā′) *n.* A Mormon.

lat•tice (lăt′ĭs) *n.* **1.** An open framework made of strips of wood, metal, or a similar material overlapping at regular intervals. **2.** A screen, window, or grate made of such a framework. —*tr.v.* **lat•ticed, lat•tic•ing, lat•tic•es. 1.** To form into a lattice: *We latticed strips of cane to make the chair seat.* **2.** To furnish with a lattice. —**lat′ticed** *adj.*

lat•tice•work (lăt′ĭs wûrk′) *n.* **1.** A lattice or structure resembling a lattice. **2.** An open, crisscross pattern or weave.

Lat•vi•a (lăt′vē ə). A country of northern Europe on the Baltic Sea north of Lithuania. Latvia was part of the U.S.S.R. from 1940 to 1991. Capital, Riga. Population, 2,604,000.

Lat•vi•an (lăt′vē ən) *adj.* Of or relating to Latvia or its people, language, or culture. —*n.* **1.** A native or inhabitant of Latvia. **2.** The Baltic language of Latvia.

laud (lôd) *tr.v.* **laud•ed, laud•ing, lauds.** To praise highly: *The principal lauded the school's graduates during commencement.*

laud•a•ble (lô′də bəl) *adj.* Deserving praise; praiseworthy. —**laud′a•bly** *adv.*

lau•da•num (lôd′n əm) *n.* An alcohol solution of opium, formerly used as a painkiller.

laud•a•to•ry (lô′də tôr′ē) *adj.* Expressing or giving praise: *laudatory remarks.*

laugh (lăf) *v.* **laughed, laugh•ing, laughs.** —*intr.* **1.** To make sounds and facial movements to express certain emotions, especially happiness, amusement, scorn, or nervousness. **2.** To express or feel amusement or happiness. —*tr.* To affect or influence by laughter: *We laughed our worries away.* —*n.* The act or sound of laughing: *a good-natured laugh.* —*idiom.* **laugh at.** To treat lightly; mock. [First written down before 725 in Old English and spelled *hlihhan.*]

laugh•a•ble (lăf′ə bəl) *adj.* Causing or deserving of laughter; amusing or ridiculous. —**laugh′a•ble•ness** *n.* —**laugh′a•bly** *adv.*

laugh•ing gas (lăf′ĭng) *n.* Nitrous oxide.

laugh•ing•stock (lăf′ĭng stŏk′) *n.* A person or thing that is made fun of; an object of ridicule.

laugh•ter (lăf′tər) *n.* The act or sound of laughing.

launch¹ (lônch *or* länch) *v.* **launched, launch•ing, launch•es.** —*tr.* **1.** To throw or propel into the air: *launch a spear.* **2.** To put or thrust into motion: *launch a rocket.* **3.** To put (a boat or ship) into the

lateen

lattice
Pattern on a trellis

ă	pat	oi	boy
ā	pay	ou	out
âr	care	o͝o	took
ä	father	o͞o	boot
ĕ	pet	ŭ	cut
ē	be	ûr	urge
ĭ	pit	th	thin
ī	pie	*th*	this
îr	pier	hw	whoop
ŏ	pot	zh	vision
ō	toe	ə	about
ô	paw	N	*French* bon

launch pad
Apollo 15 prior to launching on July 26, 1971

laurel
Abebe Mekonne, winner of the 1989 Boston Marathon

Antoine Lavoisier
Detail from *Antoine Laurent Lavoisier and his Wife* by Jacques Louis David (1748–1825)

water; set afloat. **4.** To set going or start into action: *The institute launched a new research program.* —*intr.* **1.** To set out; make a start: *He launched forth on a new career.* **2.** To enter energetically into something; plunge: *He launched into a review of the new movie.* —*n.* The act of launching something, such as a rocket or spacecraft. [First written down before 1300 in Middle English and spelled *launchen*, from Latin *lanceāre*, to wield a lance.] —**launch′er** *n.*

launch² (lônch *or* länch) *n.* **1.** A large open motorboat. **2.** A large boat carried by a ship. [First written down in 1697 in Modern English, from Malay *lancha*.]

launch•ing pad (**lôn′**chĭng *or* **län′**chĭng) *n.* A launch pad.

launch pad *n.* The platform or base from which a rocket or space vehicle is launched.

laun•der (**lôn′**dər *or* **län′**dər) *v.* **laun•dered, laun•der•ing, laun•ders.** —*tr.* To wash or wash and iron (clothes, for example). —*intr.* To undergo washing in a specific way: *This fabric launders easily in cold water.*

laun•dress (**lôn′**drĭs *or* **län′**drĭs) *n.* A woman employed to wash and iron clothes or linens.

Laun•dro•mat (**lôn′**drə măt′ *or* **län′**drə măt′). A trademark for a self-service laundry where clothes are washed and dried in coin-operated machines.

laun•dry (**lôn′**drē *or* **län′**drē) *n., pl.* **laun•dries. 1.** Clothes and linens that have just been or will be washed: *Sort the laundry by color.* **2.** A place or business establishment where clothes and linens are washed and ironed. [First written down before 1450 in Middle English and spelled *lawndre*, from Latin *lavandāria*, things to be washed, from *lavāre*, to wash.]

lau•re•ate (**lôr′**ē ĭt *or* **lŏr′**ē ĭt) *n.* **1.** A person who has been honored for achievements, especially in the arts or sciences. **2.** A poet laureate.

lau•rel (**lôr′**əl *or* **lŏr′**əl) *n.* **1.a.** A small shrub or tree native to the Mediterranean region, having glossy, spicy-smelling, evergreen leaves. **b.** Any of various related shrubs or trees, such as the mountain laurel. **2.** A wreath of laurel given as a mark of honor. **3.** Honors and glory won for great achievement. Often used in the plural: *She was given laurels for improving so much in math.*

la•va (**lä′**və *or* **lăv′**ə) *n.* **1.** Molten rock that flows from a volcano or from a crack in the earth. **2.** The rock formed when this substance cools and hardens. [First written down in 1750 in Modern English, from Italian.]

lav•a•to•ry (**lăv′**ə tôr′ē) *n., pl.* **lav•a•to•ries. 1.** A room with a sink for washing and often a toilet; a bathroom. **2.** A sink or washbowl, especially one with running water and a drain. **3.** A flush toilet. [First written down before 1382 in Middle English and spelled *lavatory*, basin, from Latin *lavāre*, to wash.]

lave (lāv) *tr. & intr.v.* **laved, lav•ing, laves.** To wash or bathe.

lav•en•der (**lăv′**ən dər) *n.* **1.a.** Any of various plants having small, fragrant purplish flowers that yield an oil used in making perfume. **b.** The dried flowers or leaves of this plant, often placed in a dresser drawer to add fragrance to clothing. **2.** A pale or light purple. [First written down in 1373 in Middle English and spelled *lavandir*, from Medieval Latin *lavendula*.] —**lav′en•der** *adj.*

lav•ish (**lăv′**ĭsh) *adj.* **1.** Given or provided very plentifully: *a party with lavish refreshments.* **2.** Very generous or free in giving: *Be lavish with praise.* —*tr.v.* **lav•ished, lav•ish•ing, lav•ish•es.** To give or bestow in abundance: *The grandparents lavished affection on their grandchildren.* —**lav′ish•ly** *adv.* —**lav′ish•ness** *n.*

La•voi•sier (lä vwä **zyā′**), **Antoine Laurent.** 1743–1794. French scientist who is regarded as the founder of modern chemistry.

law (lô) *n.* **1.** A rule that requires or forbids certain conduct or activities, established by custom or by an authority, such as a legislature. **2.** A set or system of such rules: *Corporate law governs business.* **3.** The condition of social order created by obedience to such rules: *a breakdown of law and order.* **4.** The study of such rules: *a professor of law.* **5.** The profession of a lawyer: *practice the law.* **6.** The system of courts administering the laws of a community: *We are all equal before the law.* **7.** A person or an agency responsible for enforcing the law: *a fugitive pursued by the law.* **8.** A statement or ruling that must be obeyed: *The king's word was law.* **9.** The body of principles held to express the will of God, especially as revealed in the Bible: *Mosaic Law.* **10.** A generally accepted rule, principle, or practice: *the laws of good health.* **11.** A statement or set of statements describing what will always happen when certain conditions exist: *the law of gravity.* [First written down before 1000 in Old English and spelled *lagu*, from Old Norse *lag*, that which is laid down.]

law-a•bid•ing (**lô′**ə bī′dĭng) *adj.* Obeying the law: *law-abiding citizens.*

law•break•er (**lô′**brā′kər) *n.* A person who breaks the law.

law•ful (**lô′**fəl) *adj.* **1.** Allowed by law: *lawful acts.* **2.** Established or recognized by the law: *a lawful heir.* **3.** Law-abiding. —**law′ful•ly** *adv.* —**law′ful•ness** *n.*

law•giv•er (**lô′**gĭv′ər) *n.* A person who establishes a set or system of laws for a people.

law•less (**lô′**lĭs) *adj.* **1.** Not governed by law: *the lawless frontier.* **2.** Disregarding or violating the law: *a lawless mob.* —**law′less•ly** *adv.* —**law′less•ness** *n.*

law•mak•er (**lô′**mā′kər) *n.* A person who participates in writing or passing laws; a legislator. —**law′mak′ing** *n.*

lawn¹ (lôn) *n.* A piece of ground planted with grass that is usually mowed regularly. [First written down in 1548 in Middle English and spelled *laune*, glade, from Old French *launde*, pasture, wooded area.]

lawn² (lôn) *n.* A very fine thin fabric of cotton or linen. [First written down in 1416 in Middle English and spelled *lawnd*, after *Laon*, a city of northern France.]

lawn bowling *n.* A game played on a lawn by rolling an uneven ball as close as possible to a target ball; bowls.

lawn mower also **lawn•mow•er** (**lôn′**mō′ər) *n.* A machine that has rotating blades for cutting grass.

lawn tennis *n.* Tennis played on a grass court.

law•ren•ci•um (lô **rĕn′**sē əm *or* lō **rĕn′**sē əm) *n.* *Symbol* **Lr** A short-lived radioactive element first produced by bombarding californium isotopes with boron isotopes. Atomic number 103. See table at **element.** [First written down in 1961 in Modern English, after Ernest Orlando *Lawrence* (1901–1958), American physicist.]

law•suit (**lô′**so͞ot′) *n.* A suit or case brought before a court of law for settlement.

law•yer (**lô′**yər) *n.* A person who is trained and qualified to give legal advice to clients and represent them in a court of law; an attorney.

lax (lăks) *adj.* **lax•er, lax•est. 1.** Not careful or strict; negligent: *lax about paying bills.* **2.** Not firm; loose; slack: *a lax cable.* [First written down in 1373 in Middle English, from Latin *laxus*, loose.] —**lax′ly** *adv.* —**lax′ness** *n.*

lax•a•tive (lăk′sə tĭv) *n.* A medicine or a food that stimulates bowel movements. *—adj.* Stimulating bowel movements.

lax•i•ty (lăk′sĭ tē) *n.* The quality or condition of being lax.

lay[1] (lā) *v.* **laid** (lād), **lay•ing, lays.** *—tr.* **1.a.** To place or put, especially on a flat surface or in a horizontal position: *I laid the baby in the crib.* **b.** To put or place in a certain position or condition: *They laid themselves open for trouble.* **2.** To put in place; set down: *lay tiles for flooring.* **3.** To produce (an egg or eggs). **4.** To cause to settle, subside, or become calm: *The rain laid the dust.* **5.** To put in order; prepare: *lay the table for dinner.* **6.** To spread over a surface: *lay paint on a canvas.* **7.** To impose as a burden or punishment: *lay a fine on an offender.* **8.** To put forth; present: *lay a case before the court.* **9.** To place or give (importance, for example): *lay emphasis.* **10.** To assign; charge: *They lay the blame on us.* **11.** To place (a bet); wager. *—intr.* To produce an egg or eggs: *The hens stopped laying suddenly.* *—n.* The way or arrangement in which something is situated or organized: *the lay of the land.* ***—idioms.*** **lay aside. 1.** To give up; abandon. **2.** To save for future use. **lay away. 1.** To save for future use. **2.** To reserve (merchandise) until wanted or paid for. **lay by.** To save for future use. **lay down. 1.** To give up and surrender: *laid down their arms.* **2.** To put forth; specify: *lay down rules by which to live.* **lay in.** To store for future use: *lay in supplies for a blizzard.* **lay into.** *Slang.* **1.** To scold harshly. **2.** To beat up physically. **lay off. 1.** To dismiss or suspend from a job. **2.** *Slang.* To stop doing something; quit. **lay out. 1.** To arrange according to plan: *laying out the streets of a new housing development.* **2.** To spend (money). **lay over.** To make a stopover in the course of a journey. **lay up. 1.** To store for future needs. **2.** *Informal.* To keep in bed or out of action with an illness or injury. [First written down before 725 in Old English and spelled *lecgan.*] —SEE NOTE.

❑ *These sound alike:* **lay[1]** (put), **lay[2]** (not of the clergy), **lay[3]** (poem), **lay[4]** (placed oneself flat), **lei** (garland).

lay[2] (lā) *adj.* **1.** Of, relating to, or involving people who are not members of the clergy: *a lay missionary.* **2.** Not of or belonging to a particular profession: *a lay observer accompanying the scientific expedition.* [First written down about 1303 in Middle English, from Late Latin *lāicus*, from Greek *laos*, the people.]

❑ *These sound alike:* **lay[2]** (not of the clergy), **lay[1]** (put), **lay[3]** (poem), **lay[4]** (placed oneself flat), **lei** (garland).

lay[3] (lā) *n.* A poem or song that tells a story; a ballad. [First written down before 1250 in Middle English, from Old French *lai.*]

❑ *These sound alike:* **lay[3]** (poem), **lay[1]** (put), **lay[2]** (not of the clergy), **lay[4]** (placed oneself flat), **lei** (garland).

lay[4] (lā) *v.* Past tense of **lie[1]**.

❑ *These sound alike:* **lay[4]** (placed oneself flat), **lay[1]** (put), **lay[2]** (not of the clergy), **lay[3]** (poem), **lei** (garland).

lay•a•way (lā′ə wā′) *n.* A payment plan in which a seller agrees to hold a piece of merchandise for a customer who has left a deposit until the full price is paid.

lay•er (lā′ər) *n.* **1.** A single thickness of material lying between others or covering a surface: *a cake with three layers.* **2.** A person who lays something: *a carpet layer.* **3.** A hen kept for laying eggs. *—tr. & intr.v.* **lay•ered, lay•er•ing, lay•ers.** To form, arrange, or split into layers. **—lay′er•ing** *n.*

lay•ette (lā ĕt′) *n.* A complete set of clothing, bedding, and other supplies for a newborn child.

lay•man (lā′mən) *n.* **1.** A man who is not a cleric. **2.** A man who does not have the specialized knowledge or training of a member of a profession.

lay•off (lā′ôf′ *or* lā′ŏf′) *n.* **1.** A dismissal or suspension of employees, especially because there is not enough work to be done. **2.** A period of temporary inactivity.

lay•out (lā′out′) *n.* A planned arrangement of parts or areas: *the layout of a factory.*

lay•o•ver (lā′ō′vər) *n.* A short stop or break in a journey.

lay•peo•ple or **lay people** (lā′pē′pəl) *pl.n.* Laymen and laywomen considered as a group.

lay•per•son (lā′pûr′sən) *n.* A layman or laywoman.

lay•wom•an (lā′wo͝om′ən) *n.* **1.** A woman who is not a cleric. **2.** A woman who does not have the specialized knowledge or training of a member of a profession.

Laz•a•rus (lăz′ər əs). In the New Testament, the brother of Mary and Martha.

Lazarus, Emma. 1849–1887. American writer whose poem "The New Colossus" is inscribed on the base of the Statue of Liberty in New York.

laze (lāz) *intr. & tr.v.* **lazed, laz•ing, laz•es.** To relax lazily; loaf.

la•zy (lā′zē) *adj.* **la•zi•er, la•zi•est. 1.** Not willing to work or be energetic: *a lazy person.* **2.** Causing idleness or a lack of energy: *lazy summer afternoons.* **3.** Slow-moving: *lazy clouds floating overhead.* [First written down in 1549 in Modern English and spelled *laysy*, probably of Low German origin.] **—la′zi•ly** *adv.* **—la′zi•ness** *n.*

lb. *abbr.* An abbreviation of pound.

l.c.d. *abbr.* An abbreviation of lowest common denominator.

l.c.m. *abbr.* An abbreviation of least common multiple.

lea (lē *or* lā) *n.* A stretch of grassy ground; a meadow or grassland.

❑ *These sound alike:* **lea, lee** (wind side).

leach (lēch) *tr.v.* **leached, leach•ing, leach•es. 1.** To dissolve out (soluble materials) by passing a liquid through ashes, rock, or other matter: *Heavy rains leached minerals from the soil.* **2.** To pass a liquid through (a substance), dissolving the soluble materials in it: *Heavy rains have leached the soil of minerals and other nutrients.*

❑ *These sound alike:* **leach, leech** (worm).

lead[1] (lēd) *v.* **led** (lĕd), **lead•ing, leads.** *—tr.* **1.** To show the way to, as by going along or ahead; conduct: *The guide will lead us to the top of the mountain.* See Synonyms at **guide. 2.** To guide as by the hand or an attached rope: *I led the pony out of the barn.* **3.** To serve as a channel or passage for: *This pipe leads the water away from the house.* **4.** To be or show the way for: *The trail led us to a cabin.* **5.** To go at the head of; be first in: *She's still leading the race.* **6.** To be the head of; direct: *He led the group in a song.* **7.** To cause to think or act in a certain way: *His remarks led me to conclude that he was a musician.* **8.** To live; experience: *A pilot often leads an exciting life.* *—intr.* **1.** To go first as a guide: *The scouts led as the army followed.* **2.** To be first; be ahead: *Only one runner is now leading in the race.* **3.** To be or form a way, route, or passage: *The trail leads to a little stream.* **4.** To make the first play in a game or contest. *—n.* **1.** The front, foremost, or winning position: *Our team took the lead in the game.* **2.** The amount by which one is ahead: *a five-point lead.* **3.** An example or a preceding event: *They followed the committee's lead and voted against the amendment.* **4.** A guiding indication; a clue or hint: *leads that helped solve the crime.* **5.** The main role, as in a play or movie. **6.** The opening paragraph of a news story. **7.** In

lawn mower

Usage: lay[1]

The words **lay** ("to put, place, or prepare") and **lie** ("to recline or be situated") are frequently confused. **Lay** is basically a transitive verb and takes an object: *I always lay my glasses down carefully. He laid (not lay) the newspaper on the table. The table was laid for four. She was laying carpet.* **Lie** is an intransitive verb and does not take an object: *She often lies down after lunch. When I lay down, I fell asleep. The rubbish had lain there a week. I was lying in bed when he called.*

ă	pat	oi	boy
ā	pay	ou	out
âr	care	o͝o	took
ä	father	o͞o	boot
ĕ	pet	ŭ	cut
ē	be	ûr	urge
ĭ	pit	th	thin
ī	pie	*th*	this
îr	pier	hw	whoop
ŏ	pot	zh	vision
ō	toe	ə	about
ô	paw	N	*French* bon

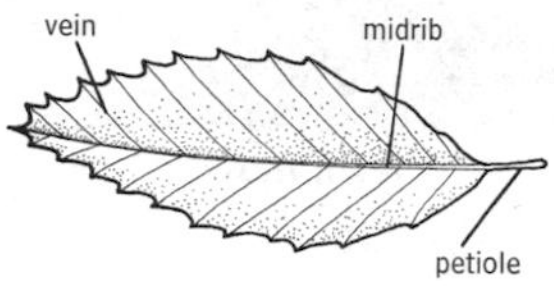

leaf
Simple leaf

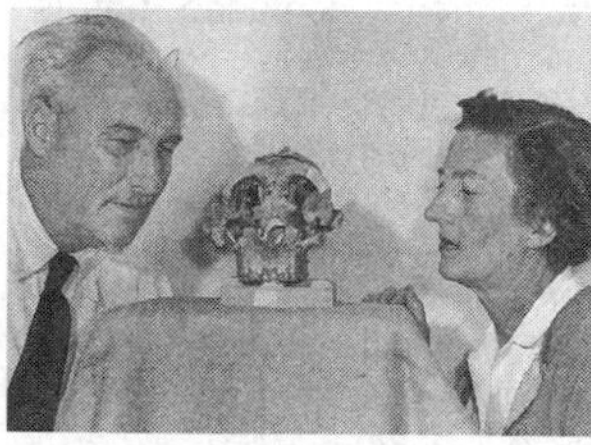

Louis and Mary Leakey
Photographed with the prehistoric skull they discovered

baseball, the position or distance of a base runner away from one base and toward the next. —***idioms.* lead off. 1.** To begin; start. **2.** To be the first batter in an inning of a baseball game. **lead on.** To draw into unwise action or mistaken opinion; deceive: *They led the investors on with false promises of oil discoveries.* **lead up to.** To result in by a series of steps: *These events led up to a change in management of the company.* **led to.** To tend toward or result in: *The discovery of oil led to the development of a city here.* [First written down before 725 in Old English and spelled *lǣdan.*]

lead[2] (lĕd) *n.* **1.** *Symbol* **Pb** A soft, heavy, dull-gray metallic element that is easily worked and shaped. It is used in radiation shields, as a solder, in alloys, and in many other products. Atomic number 82. See table at **element. 2.** A material, often made mostly of graphite, used as the writing substance in pencils. **3.** A piece of lead or other metal attached to a length of line, used in measuring depths. **4.** Bullets from or for firearms; shot. —*tr.v.* **lead•ed, lead•ing, leads.** To cover, join, or weight with lead. [First written down about 750 in Old English and spelled *lēad.*]

❑ *These sound alike:* **lead[2], led** (guided).

lead•en (lĕd′n) *adj.* **1.** Made of lead: *a leaden fishing weight.* **2.** Dull dark gray: *leaden skies.* **3.** Heavy or sluggish: *leaden feet worn out from a long hike.* **4.** Gloomy; depressed: *leaden spirits.*

lead•er (lē′dər) *n.* **1.** A person who leads, guides, or has power over others. **2.** A short length of wire or similar material used to attach a hook or lure to a fishing line.

lead•er•ship (lē′dər shĭp′) *n.* **1.** The position or office of a leader. **2.** The guidance or command of a leader or leaders: *Under the leadership of skillful diplomats, the peace conference was a success.* **3.** Ability to lead: *The mayor showed strong leadership during the crisis.* **4.** A group of leaders: *the leadership of the labor union.*

lead•ing (lē′dĭng) *adj.* **1.** Having the first or front position: *the leading swimmer in the race.* **2.** Most important; main; principal: *the leading industrial countries.*

lead•off (lēd′ôf′ *or* lēd′ŏf′) *n.* **1.** An opening play or move. **2.** A person or thing that leads off. —**lead′off′** *adj.*

leaf (lēf) *n., pl.* **leaves** (lēvz). **1.** A thin, usually flat green plant part that grows on the stem or up from the roots. Leaves take in carbon dioxide and sunlight to carry on the vital process of photosynthesis. **2.** A sheet of paper in a book. **3.a.** A very thin sheet of metal. **b.** Such sheets considered as a group: *gold leaf.* **4.** A movable or removable part of a table top. —*intr.v.* **leafed, leaf•ing, leafs. 1.** To produce or put forth leaves: *Most trees leafed early this spring.* **2.** To turn through pages: *leaf through a book.* [First written down before 725 in Old English and spelled *lēaf.*] —**leaf′less** *adj.*

❑ *These sound alike:* **leaf, lief** (readily).

leaf•let (lē′flĭt) *n.* **1.** A small leaf or leaflike part, especially one of the separate blades or divisions of a compound leaf, as of a clover. **2.** A booklet or small pamphlet.

leaf•stalk (lēf′stôk′) *n.* The stalk by which a leaf is attached to a stem; a petiole.

leaf•y (lē′fē) *adj.* **leaf•i•er, leaf•i•est. 1.** Covered with or having many leaves: *leafy branches.* **2.** Consisting of leaves: *leafy vegetables.* **3.** Similar to or resembling a leaf: *a leafy green.*

league[1] (lēg) *n.* **1.** An association or alliance of nations, organizations, or people working to help one another. **2.** An association of sports teams or clubs that compete chiefly with each other. —*intr.v.* **leagued, leagu•ing, leagues.** To form an association or alliance. —***idiom.* in league.** Joined or working together. [First written down in 1561 in Modern English, from Medieval Latin *liga,* from Latin *ligāre,* to bind.]

league[2] (lēg) *n.* A unit of distance, approximately equal to three miles (4.8 kilometers). [First written down before 1387 in Middle English and spelled *lege,* from Latin *leuga,* a measure of distance, of Celtic origin.]

League of Nations. An organization of nations established after World War I to preserve peace and promote cooperation. It was disbanded in 1946, and the United Nations took over many of its functions.

leagu•er (lē′gər) *n.* A person who belongs to a league.

leak (lēk) *v.* **leaked, leak•ing, leaks.** —*intr.* **1.** To allow something to escape, enter, or pass through an opening or openings: *The roof leaks in a heavy rain.* **2.** To escape or pass through or as if through an opening or a break: *Water leaked from the rusty pail.* **3.** To become known through a break in secrecy: *The news leaked out.* —*tr.* **1.** To let (something) escape or pass through a hole or opening: *The roof leaks water.* **2.** To disclose (secret information) without permission: *Someone leaked the jury's verdict before it was announced in court.* —*n.* **1.** A hole, crack, or similar opening through which something can escape or pass: *I fixed the leak in the roof.* **2.** An escape or passage of something through such an opening or break: *The leak of oil is about a quart every week.* **3.** A disclosure of secret information. [First written down before 1398 in Middle English and spelled *liken,* probably from Middle Dutch *leken.*]

❑ *These sound alike:* **leak, leek** (plant).

leak•age (lē′kĭj) *n.* **1.** The process, act, or an instance of leaking. **2.a.** Something that escapes or enters by leaking. **b.** The amount that leaks in or out.

Lea•key (lē′kē). British family of anthropologists including **Louis Leakey** (1903–1972) and **Mary Leakey** (born 1913), who discovered and analyzed a 1.75-million-year-old skull in Tanzania. Their son **Richard Leakey** (born 1944) has continued their research.

leak•y (lē′kē) *adj.* **leak•i•er, leak•i•est.** Having or allowing a leak or leaks: *a leaky valve.* —**leak′i•ness** *n.*

lean[1] (lēn) *v.* **leaned, lean•ing, leans.** —*intr.* **1.** To slant from an upright position: *The tree leaned in the high wind.* **2.** To rest one's weight on or against for support: *I leaned against the wall to rest.* **3.** To rely for assistance or support; depend: *Friends lean on each other for encouragement.* **4.** To have a tendency or preference: *I lean towards the challenger in this election.* —*tr.* To set or place in a slanting or supported position: *I leaned the ladder against the tree. Lean your head a bit to the right.* —*n.* A slant or an inclination: *The lean of the ladder makes it look as if it will fall.* [First written down about 725 in Old English and spelled *hleonian.*]

❑ *These sound alike:* **lean[1]** (bend), **lean[2]** (thin), **lien** (legal right).

lean[2] (lēn) *adj.* **lean•er, lean•est. 1.** Not fat or fleshy; thin: *a lean cat.* **2.** Containing little or no fat: *lean meat.* **3.** Not productive, plentiful, or satisfying: *The long drought brought a lean harvest.* —*n.* Meat with little or no fat. [First written down about 1000 in Old English and spelled *hlǣne.*] —**lean′ness** *n.*

❑ *These sound alike:* **lean[2]** (thin), **lean[1]** (bend), **lien** (legal right).

Synonyms: lean, thin, slender, spare, skinny, scrawny. These adjectives mean having little or no excess flesh. **Lean** means lacking fat: *Leaner cuts of meat are better for your health.* **Thin** and **slender** mean having a lean body: *It's amazing that Amy can drink a milk shake every day and stay thin. A century ago, heavier builds were considered more beautiful than slender ones.* **Spare** often means trim with good muscle tone: *She has the spare figure of a marathon runner.* **Skinny** and **scrawny** mean unattractively thin, as if undernourished: *The boy had skinny, freckled legs with prominent knees. If you exercise more instead of dieting you won't look so scrawny.*
Antonym: fat.

lean•ing (lē′nĭng) *n.* A tendency; a preference.

leant (lĕnt) *v. Chiefly British.* A past tense and a past participle of **lean[1]**.

lean-to (lēn′to͞o′) *n., pl.* **lean-tos. 1.** A shed with a sloping roof, built against a wall or the side of a building. **2.** A simple shelter, often having a roof that slopes in one direction and an open side.

leap (lēp) *v.* **leaped** or **leapt** (lĕpt *or* lēpt), **leap•ing, leaps.** *—intr.* **1.** To jump or bound upward; spring: *The toad leaped from my hand.* **2.** To move suddenly from one state or subject to another: *A solution leaped into mind.* *—tr.* **1.** To jump or spring over: *The deer leap our garden fence.* **2.** To cause to jump: *leap a horse over a fence.* *—n.* **1.** The act of leaping; a spring or jump. **2.** The distance covered in a jump: *a leap of ten feet.* [First written down about 725 in Old English and spelled *hlēapan.*]

leap•frog (lēp′frôg′ *or* lēp′frŏg′) *n.* A game in which one player bends over while the next in line jumps over him or her. *—tr.v.* **leap•frogged, leap•frog•ging, leap•frogs.** To leap over in a game of leap frog.

leapt (lĕpt *or* lēpt) *v.* A past tense and a past participle of **leap.**

leap year *n.* A year in which there are 366 days, the extra day being February 29. A year is a leap year if its number can be divided exactly by four, except years at the end of a century, which must be exactly divisible by 400.

learn (lûrn) *v.* **learned** also **learnt** (lûrnt), **learn•ing, learns.** *—tr.* **1.** To gain knowledge of or skill in through study or experience: *Is it hard to learn to speak French?* **2.** To find out: *We learned who won the election from the newspaper.* **3.** To memorize: *Learn the tune and then add the words.* *—intr.* To gain knowledge or skill: *I learned of their plans by letter.* [First written down before 725 in Old English and spelled *leornian.*]

learn•ed (lûr′nĭd) *adj.* Having or showing deep knowledge; scholarly: *a learned history professor.* **—learn′ed•ly** *adv.*

learn•ing (lûr′nĭng) *n.* **1.** Instruction; education: *Learning was a lot easier once the noise stopped.* **2.** Thorough knowledge or skill gained by study: *Fortunately I have teachers of great learning.*

learnt (lûrnt) *v.* A past tense and a past participle of **learn.**

lease (lēs) *n.* **1.** A written agreement granting use of property for a certain time in exchange for rent. **2.** The period of time specified in such an agreement. *—tr.v.* **leased, leas•ing, leas•es. 1.** To grant the use of (property) by lease: *The landlord leased the house to new tenants.* **2.** To acquire or hold (property) by lease: *We leased the house from the landlord.* [First written down about 1384 in Middle English and spelled *les,* from Anglo-Norman *lesser,* to let out.]

leash (lēsh) *n.* A cord, chain, or strap attached to a collar or harness and used to hold or lead a dog or other animal. *—tr.v.* **leashed, leash•ing, leash•es.** To restrain with or as if with a leash. [First written down before 1300 in Middle English and spelled *les,* from Old French *laissier,* to let go.]

least (lēst) *adj.* A superlative of **little.** Smallest in degree, size, or importance: *The least money spent on this, the better.* *—adv.* Superlative of **little.** To the smallest degree: *I like vanilla ice cream least.* *—n.* The smallest thing or amount: *The least you could do would be to apologize.* ***—idioms.*** **at least. 1.** According to the lowest estimate; not less than: *I go running at least three days a week.* **2.** In any event; anyway: *You might at least call before you come over.* **in the least.** At all: *I'm not in the least concerned.*

least common denominator *n.* A lowest common denominator.

least common multiple *n.* The smallest number that is a common multiple of two other numbers; for example, 12 is the least common multiple of 3 and 4.

least•wise (lēst′wīz′) *adv. Informal.* In any event; at least.

leath•er (lĕ*th*′ər) *n.* A material made by cleaning and tanning the skin or hide of an animal.

leath•er•ette (lĕ*th*′ə rĕt′) *n.* Imitation leather.

leath•ern (lĕ*th*′ərn) *adj.* Made of or resembling leather.

leath•er•y (lĕ*th*′ə rē) *adj.* Resembling leather: *leathery hands.*

leave[1] (lēv) *v.* **left** (lĕft), **leav•ing, leaves.** *—tr.* **1.** To go out of or go away from: *She just left the room. He left town on Thursday.* **2.** To end one's association with; withdraw from: *He left our band and started another.* **3.** To go without taking; forget: *I left my umbrella on the train.* **4.** To allow to remain unused: *I left some milk in the glass.* **5.** To allow to remain in a certain condition or place: *I left the light on all night.* **6.** To give to another to do or use; entrust: *Leave the job to me.* **7.** To give by will; bequeath: *His uncle left him a piece of land.* **8.** To have as a remainder after subtraction: *12 minus 5 leaves 7.* *—intr.* To go away; depart: *We left after lunch.* ***—idioms.*** **leave alone.** To refrain from disturbing or interfering: *Leave the puzzle alone.* **leave off.** To stop; cease: *Let's start the story where we left off.* **leave out.** To omit: *Don't leave out the pepper from the recipe.* [First written down about 725 in Old English and spelled *lǣfan.*] —See Note.

leave[2] (lēv) *n.* **1.** Permission; consent: *My parents gave me leave to stay up late.* **2.** Official permission to be absent from work or duty; leave of absence. **3.** The length of such an absence. [First written down before 900 in Old English and spelled *lēafe.*]

leave[3] (lēv) *intr.v.* **leaved, leav•ing, leaves.** To put forth leaves; leaf: *The trees leaved early this spring.* [First written down about 1250 in Middle English and spelled *leaven,* from *leaf,* leaf.]

leav•en (lĕv′ən) *n.* **1.** A fermenting substance, such as yeast, used to cause dough or batter to rise. **2.** An influence or element that serves to lighten or enliven the whole: *The leaven of good humor made it a friendly debate.* *—tr.v.* **leav•ened, leav•en•ing, leav•ens. 1.** To add yeast or another fermenting agent to (dough or batter). **2.** To spread through so as to change or enliven. —See Note.

leav•en•ing (lĕv′ə nĭng) *n.* Something that leavens; leaven.

leaves (lēvz) *n.* Plural of **leaf.**

leave-tak•ing (lēv′tā′kĭng) *n.* An exchange of goodbyes; a farewell.

leav•ings (lē′vĭngz) *pl.n.* Scraps left over; remains: *The turkey leavings were fed to the dog.*

Leav•itt (lĕv′ĭt), **Henrietta Swan.** 1868–1921. American astronomer known for her studies of the brightness of stars.

Leb•a•nese (lĕb′ə nēz′ *or* lĕb′ə nēs′) *adj.* Of or re-

Usage: leave[1]

Only **let** should be used in the following examples: *Let me be. Let him go. Let us not quarrel. Let it lie.* Some people use **leave** instead, which is a use that is not acceptable.

Word History: leaven

The word **leaven**, meaning "an agent like yeast added to dough to make the dough rise," comes from the Old French word *levain.* The Old French word comes from the Latin *levāmen,* "something that raises," which is formed from the Latin verb *levāre,* "to raise, lighten, relieve." From the related adjective *levis,* "light," we got **levity**, which is what we have when we lighten up.

ă	pat	oi	**boy**
ā	**pay**	ou	**out**
âr	**care**	o͝o	**took**
ä	**father**	o͞o	**boot**
ĕ	**pet**	ŭ	**cut**
ē	**be**	ûr	**urge**
ĭ	**pit**	th	**thin**
ī	**pie**	*th*	**this**
îr	**pier**	hw	**whoop**
ŏ	**pot**	zh	**vision**
ō	**toe**	ə	**about**
ô	**paw**	N	*French* **bon**

lectern

Robert E. Lee
Photographed in 1865
by Mathew Brady

lating to Lebanon or its people or culture. *—n., pl* **Lebanese.** A native or inhabitant of Lebanon.

Leb•a•non (lĕb′ə nən *or* lĕb′ə nŏn′). A country of southwest Asia on the Mediterranean Sea north of Israel. It has been occupied since ancient times and gained its independence from France in 1945. Beirut is the capital and the largest city. Population, 2,637,000.

lech•er•ous (lĕch′ər əs) *adj.* Given to, characterized by, or inciting lechery. **—lech′er•ous•ly** *adv.* **—lech′er•ous•ness** *n.*

lech•er•y (lĕch′ə rē) *n., pl.* **lech•er•ies.** Excessive indulgence in sexual activity; lewdness.

lec•i•thin (lĕs′ə thĭn) *n.* A fatty substance containing phosphorous, present in all plant and animal tissues but found especially in nerve cells and brain tissue.

lec•tern (lĕk′tərn) *n.* **1.** A desk with a slanted top for holding books from which to read Scriptures during a church service. **2.** A stand that serves as a support for the notes or books of a speaker.

lec•ture (lĕk′chər) *n.* **1.** A prepared talk providing information about a given subject, delivered before an audience or a class. **2.** A serious lengthy warning or scolding: *The judge gave the reckless driver a lecture in court.* *—v.* **lec•tured, lec•tur•ing, lec•tures.** *—intr.* To deliver a lecture or lectures: *lecturing on history at the university.* *—tr.* **1.** To give a lecture to (an audience or a class). **2.** To scold or warn at length. [First written down before 1300 in Middle English and spelled *lecture*, reading, from Medieval Latin *lēctūra*, from Latin *legere*, to read.] **—lec′tur•er** *n.*

led (lĕd) *v.* Past tense and past participle of **lead**[1].
❑ *These sound alike:* **led, lead**[2] (element).

Le•da (lē′də) *n.* In Greek mythology, the mother of Helen of Troy and Pollux by Zeus in the form of a swan, and of Castor and Clytemnestra by her own husband.

ledge (lĕj) *n.* **1.** A narrow shelf projecting from a wall: *a window ledge.* **2.** A cut or projection with a flat horizontal surface on the side of a cliff or rock wall.

ledg•er (lĕj′ər) *n.* An account book in which sums of money received and paid out by a business are recorded.

lee (lē) *n.* **1.** The side away from the wind; the sheltered side: *sailing along the lee of the island.* **2.** A cover or shelter. *—adj.* Sheltered or away from the wind: *the lee side of a ship.* [First written down before 725 in Old English and spelled *hlēo*, shelter, protection.]
❑ *These sound alike:* **lee, lea** (meadow).

Lee (lē), **Ann.** Known as "Mother Ann." 1736–1784. British religious leader and founder (1776) of the Shakers in America.

Lee, Robert Edward. 1807–1870. American Confederate general in the Civil War. His victories included the Second Battle of Bull Run (1862) before he surrendered to Gen. Ulysses S. Grant at Appomattox (1865).

leech (lēch) *n.* **1.** Any of various worms that live in water and suck blood from other animals, including human beings. **2.** A person who constantly attempts to gain from someone else; a parasite. [First written down before 900 in Old English and spelled *lǣce*.]
❑ *These sound alike:* **leech, leach** (dissolve out).

Leeds (lēdz). A borough of north-central England northeast of Manchester. It was incorporated in 1626. Population, 718,100.

leek (lēk) *n.* A vegetable related to the onion, having a narrow white bulb and long dark-green leaves. [First written down about 700 in Old English and spelled *lǣc*.]
❑ *These sound alike:* **leek, leak** (escape).

leer (lîr) *n.* A sly, lustful, or cunning look. *—intr.v.* **leered, leer•ing, leers.** To look with a leer.

leer•y (lîr′ē) *adj.* **leer•i•er, leer•i•est.** Suspicious; wary: *I am very leery of schemes that promise instant riches.* **—leer′i•ly** *adv.*

lees (lēz) *pl.n.* Sediment that settles during fermentation, especially in wine; dregs.

Leeu•wen•hoek or **Leu•wen•hoek** (lā′vən ho͝ok′), **Anton van.** 1632–1723. Dutch naturalist who made early descriptions of bacteria and spermatozoa.

lee•ward (lē′wərd *or* lo͞o′ərd) *adv. & adj.* On or toward the side toward which the wind is blowing: *an island off the leeward side of the boat.* *—n.* The lee side: *a whale to leeward of us.*

Lee•ward Islands (lē′wərd). **1.** The northern group of the Lesser Antilles in the West Indies, extending from the Virgin Islands southeast to Guadeloupe. The islands were visited by Columbus in 1493. **2.** A chain of small islets of Hawaii in the central Pacific Ocean west-northwest of the main islands. The Leewards constitute a government bird sanctuary.

lee•way (lē′wā′) *n.* **1.** Extra space, time, or resources allowing freedom or safety: *We left plenty of leeway to reach the airport during rush hour.* **2.** The drift of a ship or plane to leeward of its course.

left[1] (lĕft) *adj.* **1.a.** Of or belonging to the side of the body to the west when one is facing north: *writes with her left hand.* **b.** Of, relating to, directed toward, or located on the left side: *the left arm of the chair.* **2.** Of or belonging to the political left; leftist. *—n.* **1.a.** The direction or position on the left side: *The sun set on my left as I drove north.* **b.** The left side. **c.** A turn in the direction of the left hand or side **2.** Often **Left.** The people and groups who advocate liberal or radical ways to change society, especially in politics, in an attempt to achieve equality or improve the life of the working classes. *—adv.* On or to the left. [First written down before 1200 in Middle English and spelled *lift*, from Old English *lyft*, weak, useless.]

left[2] (lĕft) *v.* Past tense and past participle of **leave**[1].

left field *n.* **1.** In baseball, the section of the outfield that is to the left, looking from home plate. **2.** The position played by the left fielder.

left fielder *n.* In baseball, the player who defends left field.

left-hand (lĕft′hănd′) *adj.* **1.** Located on the left: *the upper left-hand corner.* **2.** Intended for the left hand or for use by a left-handed person.

left-hand•ed (lĕft′hăn′dĭd) *adj.* **1.** Using the left hand, as for writing or throwing, more skillfully or easily than the right hand. **2.** In sports, swinging from left to right: *a left-handed golfer.* **3.** Designed for use by the left hand: *left-handed scissors.* **4.** Done with the left hand. **5.** Turning or moving from right to left: *a left-handed screw.* **6.** Insincere or doubtful: *a left-handed compliment.* *—adv.* **1.** With the left hand. **2.** From the right to the left: *She bats left-handed.*

left-hand•er (lĕft′hăn′dər) *n.* A person who is left-handed.

left•ist (lĕf′tĭst) *n.* A person who has liberal or radical political views. *—adj.* Of or having liberal or radical political views: *leftist publications.*

left•o•ver (lĕft′ō′vər) *adj.* Remaining unused or uneaten: *leftover fabric; leftover rice.* *—n.* Something remaining unused or uneaten. Often used in the plural: *had leftovers for dinner.*

left wing also **Left Wing** *n.* The liberal or radical faction of a group, especially of a political group. **—left′-wing′** *adj.* **—left′wing′er** *n.*

left•y (lĕf′tē) *n., pl.* **left•ies.** *Informal.* A person who is left-handed.

leg (lĕg) *n.* **1.** A limb of an animal or a human being used for support and for walking. **2.** The part of a garment, especially of a pair of trousers, that covers the leg. **3.** A supporting part resembling a leg in shape or function: *a table leg.* **4.** Either of the sides of a right triangle that is not the hypotenuse. **5.** A stage of a journey or course: *were ahead in the first leg of the relay race.* ***—idioms.*** **leg it.** To walk or run. **on (one's) last legs.** At the end of one's strength or resources; ready to collapse, fail, or die. [First written down before 1300 in Middle English, from Old Norse *leggr.*] **—leg′less** *adj.*

leg•a•cy (lĕg′ə sē) *n., pl.* **leg•a•cies. 1.** Money or property left to a person in a will. **2.** Something passed on to those who come later in time; a heritage: *a legacy of religious freedom.*

le•gal (lē′gəl) *adj.* **1.** Of or relating to the law: *legal knowledge.* **2.** Established or permitted by law: *legal activities.* **3.** Of or characteristic of lawyers or their profession: *legal fees.* [First written down in 1447 in Middle English, from Latin *lēgālis,* from *lēx,* law.] **—le′gal•ly** *adv.*

le•gal•i•ty (lē găl′ĭ tē) *n., pl.* **le•gal•i•ties. 1.** The state of being legal; lawfulness. **2.** Something required by law.

le•gal•ize (lē′gə līz′) *tr.v.* **le•gal•ized, le•gal•iz•ing, le•gal•iz•es.** To make legal. **—le′gal•i•za′tion** (lē′gə lĭ zā′shən) *n.*

legal tender *n.* Money that must by law be accepted in payment of a debt.

leg•ate (lĕg′ĭt) *n.* An official envoy or ambassador, especially one representing the pope.

leg•a•tee (lĕg′ə tē′) *n.* The inheritor of a legacy.

le•ga•tion (lĭ gā′shən) *n.* **1.** A group of diplomatic representatives in a foreign country ranking below an embassy. **2.** The building occupied by such a group.

le•ga•to (lĭ gä′tō) *adv. & adj.* In a musical style in which tones are connected smoothly, without intervening breaks.

leg•end (lĕj′ənd) *n.* **1.a.** A story handed down from earlier times, often believed to be historically true. **b.** A group of such stories. **2.** A person or thing that is famous enough to inspire legends: *He's a legend in his own time.* **3.** An inscription on a coin, a banner, or another object. **4.** An explanatory caption under a map, a chart, or an illustration. [First written down before 1325 in Middle English, from Medieval Latin *(lectiō) legenda,* (lesson) to be read, from Latin *legere,* to read.]

leg•en•dar•y (lĕj′ən dĕr′ē) *adj.* **1.** Of or based on a legend: *legendary heroes.* **2.** Talked about or celebrated in a legend or legends: *The fox's cunning is legendary.* **3.** Very well-known; famous.

leg•er•de•main (lĕj′ər də mān′) *n.* **1.** Skill in performing tricks with the hands, especially by a magician or juggler; sleight of hand. **2.** A display of trickery.

leg•ged (lĕg′id *or* lĕgd) *adj.* Having a certain kind or number of legs: *four-legged animals.*

leg•ging (lĕg′ĭng) *n.* A leg covering of cloth or leather, usually extending from the waist or knee to the ankle.

leg•gy (lĕg′ē) *adj.* **leg•gi•er, leg•gi•est. 1.** Having long awkward legs: *a gangling leggy boy.* **2.** Having attractive long and slender legs.

leg•horn (lĕg′hôrn′ *or* lĕg′ərn) *n.* **1.** A hat made from a plaited straw fabric. **2.** Often **Leghorn.** Any of a breed of white chicken that produces a large number of white eggs.

leg•i•ble (lĕj′ə bəl) *adj.* Capable of being read: *legible handwriting.* **—leg′i•bil′i•ty, leg′i•ble•ness** *n.* **—leg′i•bly** *adv.*

le•gion (lē′jən) *n.* **1.** The major unit of the ancient Roman army, consisting of at least 3,000 foot soldiers and 100 cavalry troops. **2.** A large military unit. **3.** A large group or number of persons or things; a multitude: *legions of insects settled on the fields.* **4.** Often **Legion.** A national organization of people who once served in the armed forces.

le•gion•naire (lē′jə nâr′) *n.* A member of a legion.

le•gion•ar•y (lē′jə nĕr′ē) *adj.* Of or belonging to a legion. *—n., pl.* **le•gion•ar•ies.** A soldier of a legion.

leg•is•late (lĕj′ĭ slāt′) *v.* **leg•is•lat•ed, leg•is•lat•ing, leg•is•lates.** *—intr.* To make or pass laws: *Only Congress is empowered to legislate. —tr.* To create or bring about by making laws: *legislate reforms in the housing code.*

leg•is•la•tion (lĕj′ĭ slā′shən) *n.* **1.** The act or process of making laws: *Our Constitution gives Congress the authority of legislation.* **2.** Proposed or enacted law or group of laws: *legislation being discussed in Congress.*

leg•is•la•tive (lĕj′ĭ slā′tĭv) *adj.* **1.** Of or relating to making laws: *legislative powers.* **2.** Of or relating to a legislature: *legislative decree.* **3.** Having power to make laws: *the legislative branch of government.*

leg•is•la•tor (lĕj′ĭ slā′tər) *n.* A member of a government body that makes laws: *Senators and representatives are legislators.* [First written down in 1605 in Modern English, from Latin *lēgis lātor,* proposer of a law.]

leg•is•la•ture (lĕj′ĭ slā′chər) *n.* A body of persons empowered to make and change the laws of a nation or state.

le•git•i•ma•cy (lə jĭt′ə mə sē) *n.* The quality or fact of being legitimate.

le•git•i•mate (lə jĭt′ə mĭt) *adj.* **1.** In accordance with the law; lawful: *the legitimate owner of the property.* **2.** Supported by logic or common sense; reasonable: *Some problems have more than one legitimate solution.* **3.** Authentic; genuine; real: *We have a legitimate complaint.* **4.** Born of legally married parents: *a legitimate child.* **—le•git′i•mate•ly** *adv.*

le•git•i•mize (lə jĭt′ə mīz′) *tr.v.* **le•git•i•mized, le•git•i•miz•ing, le•git•i•miz•es.** To make legitimate.

leg•ume (lĕg′yo͞om′ *or* lə gyo͞om′) *n.* **1.** Any of a group of related plants having pods that contain a large number of seeds. Beans, peas, clover, and alfalfa are all legumes. **2.** The pod or seed of such a plant, used as food.

le•gu•mi•nous (lə gyo͞o′mə nəs) *adj.* Of or relating to legumes.

leg warmer *n.* A knitted covering for the leg, resembling a sock without a foot.

Le Ha•vre (lə hä′vrə *or* lə häv′). A city of northern France on the English Channel west-northwest of Paris. It is a major port. Population, 199,388.

lei (lā *or* lā′ē) *n., pl.* **leis.** A garland of flowers worn around the neck as an ornament. [First written down in 1843 in Modern English, from Hawaiian.]

❑ *These sound alike:* **lei** (garland), **lay[1]** (put), **lay[2]** (not of the clergy), **lay[3]** (poem), **lay[4]** (placed oneself flat).

Leip•zig (līp′sĭg *or* līp′sĭk). A city of east-central Germany south-southwest of Berlin. At the so-called Battle of the Nations (October 16–19, 1813), Austrian, Russian, and Prussian forces decisively defeated Napoleon I here. Population, 558,994.

lei•sure (lē′zhər *or* lĕzh′ər) *n.* Freedom from work or time-consuming tasks: *Vacation is customarily a time of leisure and relaxation.* ***—idiom.*** **at (one's) leisure.** When one has free time; at one's convenience: *Respond to this letter at your leisure.*

lei•sure•ly (lē′zhər lē *or* lĕzh′ər lē) *adj.* Characterized by leisure; unhurried: *a leisurely lunch. —adv.* In an unhurried manner; slowly: *strolled leisurely toward town.* **—lei′sure•li•ness** *n.*

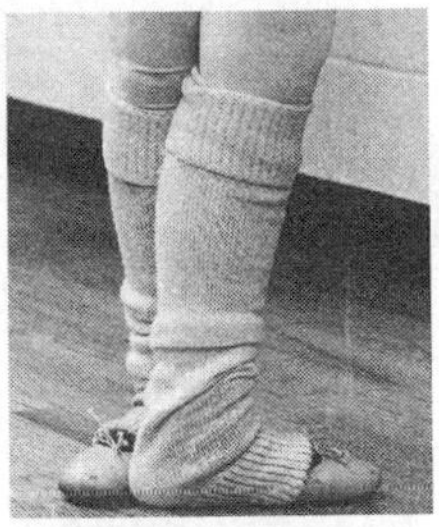

legging
Pair of leggings

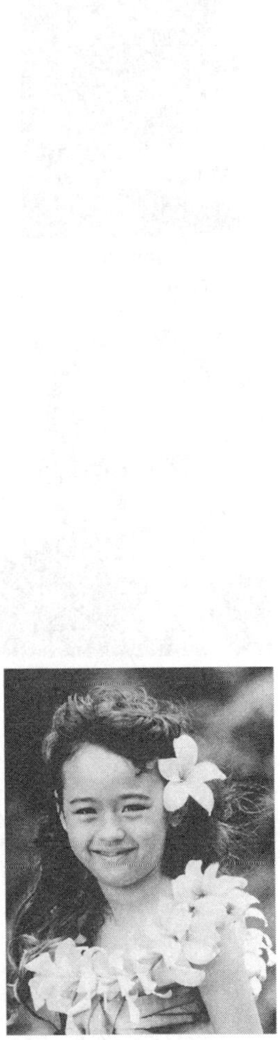

lei

ă	pat	oi	boy
ā	pay	ou	out
âr	care	o͝o	took
ä	father	o͞o	boot
ĕ	pet	ŭ	cut
ē	be	ûr	urge
ĭ	pit	th	thin
ī	pie	*th*	this
îr	pier	hw	whoop
ŏ	pot	zh	vision
ō	toe	ə	about
ô	paw	N	*French* bon

lemming
Collared lemming

lemur
Ring-tailed lemur

Vladimir Lenin

Leonardo da Vinci
c. 1512 self-portrait

leopard

lem•ming (lĕm′ĭng) *n.* Any of various stout rodents somewhat like mice, living in northern regions and noted for their mass migrations that sometimes end in drowning.

lem•on (lĕm′ən) *n.* **1.a.** An egg-shaped yellow citrus fruit having sour juicy pulp. **b.** The spiny evergreen tree that bears such fruit. **2.** A bright clear yellow. **3.** *Informal.* A person or thing that is unsatisfactory or defective: *That car is a lemon and needs to be repaired every two months.* —*adj.* Bright clear yellow. [First written down about 1400 in Middle English and spelled *limon,* from Persian *līmūn.*]

lem•on•ade (lĕm′ə **nād′**) *n.* A drink made of lemon juice, water, and sugar.

le•mur (**lē′**mər) *n.* Any of several small mammals of the island of Madagascar, distantly related to the monkey and having large eyes, soft fur, and a long tail. Lemurs live in trees and are active chiefly at night.

Len•a•pe (**lĕn′**ə pē) *n., pl.* **Lenape** or **Len•a•pes.** A Delaware.

lend (lĕnd) *v.* **lent** (lĕnt), **lend•ing, lends.** —*tr.* **1.** To give or allow the use of (something) with the understanding that it is to be returned: *My parents lent me the car to go to the movies.* **2.** To provide (money) temporarily on condition that the amount borrowed be returned, usually with an interest fee. **3.** To contribute; impart: *The painting lent a feeling of warmth to the room.* **4.** To make available for another's use: *The neighbors lent their help after the storm.* —*intr.* To make a loan. —***idioms.*** **lend a helping hand.** To be of assistance. **lend itself to.** To be suitable for: *This novel lends itself to several interpretations.* [First written down before 725 in Old English and spelled *lǣnan.*] —**lend′er** *n.* —SEE NOTE at **borrow.**

length (lĕngkth *or* lĕngth) *n.* **1.** The measured distance of a thing from end to end along its greatest dimension: *the length of a boat.* **2.** The extent of something: *traveled the length of the Nile River.* **3.** The amount of time something takes; duration: *the length of the meeting.* **4.** The state, quality, or fact of being long: *The length of the journey wore us out.* **5.** The measure of something used as a unit to estimate distances: *two arm's lengths.* **6.** A piece of something, often of a standard size: *a length of wire.* —***idiom.*** **at length. 1.** After some time; eventually: *At length we arrived at the dock.* **2.** In detail; fully: *spoke at length about her travels.*

length•en (**lĕngk′**thən *or* **lĕng′**thən) *tr. & intr.v.* To make or become longer: *lengthen pants legs; shadows that lengthen as sunset approaches.*

length•wise (**lĕngkth′**wīz′ *or* **lĕngth′**wīz′) *adv.* Along the direction of the length: *fold a sheet of paper lengthwise.* —*adj.* In the direction of the length: *lengthwise folds in the paper.*

length•y (**lĕngk′**thē *or* **lĕng′**thē) *adj.* **length•i•er, length•i•est.** Long, especially too long: *a lengthy explanation.* —**length′i•ly** *adv.* —**length′i•ness** *n.*

le•ni•ent (**lē′**nē ənt *or* **lēn′**yənt) *adj.* Inclined to forgive; merciful; generous: *a lenient judge.* [First written down in 1652 in Modern English, from Latin *lēnis,* soft.] —**le′ni•ence, le′ni•en•cy** *n.*

Le•nin (**lĕn′**ĭn), **Vladimir Ilich.** 1870–1924. Russian founder of the Bolsheviks, leader of the Russian Revolution (1917), and first head of the U.S.S.R. (1917–1924).

Len•in•grad (**lĕn′**ĭn grăd′). Saint Petersburg.

Len•ni Len•a•pe (**lĕn′**ē **lĕn′**ə pē) *n.* A Delaware.

lens (lĕnz) *n., pl.* **lens•es. 1.a.** A piece of glass or plastic shaped so as to focus or spread parallel light rays that pass through it to form an image. **b.** A combination of two or more such lenses used to form an image, as in a camera or telescope. **2.** A transparent structure behind the iris of the eye that focuses light entering the eye on the retina. [First written down in 1693 in Modern English, from Latin *lēns,* lentil.]

lent (lĕnt) *v.* Past tense and past participle of **lend.**

Lent (lĕnt) *n.* A time of fasting and penitence observed by Christians during the forty weekdays from Ash Wednesday until Easter. —**Lent′en** *adj.*

len•til (**lĕn′**təl) *n.* **1.** The round flat seed of a pod-bearing plant related to the beans and peas and eaten as a vegetable. **2.** The plant that bears such seeds.

Le•o (**lē′**ō) *n.* **1.** A constellation in the Northern Hemisphere near Cancer. **2.** The fifth sign of the zodiac in astrology.

Le•o•nar•do da Vin•ci (lē′ə **när′**dō də **vĭn′**chē). 1452–1519. Italian artist, scientist, and engineer who is best known for his paintings *The Last Supper* (about 1495) and *Mona Lisa* (about 1503).

le•o•nine (**lē′**ə nīn′) *adj.* Of, relating to, or characteristic of a lion: *a leonine roar.*

leop•ard (**lĕp′**ərd) *n.* A large, meat-eating, wild cat of Africa and Asia, usually having tawny fur with black spots or black fur. [First written down before 1300 in Middle English and spelled *leuparz,* from Greek *leopardos.*]

le•o•tard (**lē′**ə tärd′) *n.* A tight-fitting garment, sometimes with sleeves, originally worn by dancers and acrobats. [First written down in 1920 in Modern English, after Jules *Léotard* (1830–1870), French aerialist.]

lep•er (**lĕp′**ər) *n.* A person who has leprosy.

lep•re•chaun (**lĕp′**rĭ kŏn′ *or* **lĕp′**rĭ kôn′) *n.* In Irish folklore, an elf who can reveal hidden treasure if caught. [First written down in 1604 in Modern English and spelled *lubrican,* from Old Irish *luchorpán,* little figure.]

lep•ro•sy (**lĕp′**rə sē) *n.* An infectious disease caused by bacteria that attack the skin and nerves and form ulcers and sores on the body. If untreated, leprosy causes progressive destruction of affected tissue.

lep•rous (**lĕp′**rəs) *adj.* **1.** Of or resembling leprosy. **2.** Having leprosy.

les•bi•an (**lĕz′**bē ən) *n.* A woman whose sexual feelings are directed toward other women; a homosexual woman. —*adj.* Of, relating to, or being a lesbian.

le•sion (**lē′**zhən) *n.* **1.** A wound or an injury. **2.** An abnormal change in the structure of an organ or a body tissue, caused by disease or injury.

Le•so•tho (lə **sō′**tō *or* lə **sōō′**tōō). A country of southern Africa forming an enclave within east-central South Africa. It gained its independence from Great Britain in 1966. Maseru is the capital. Population, 1,213,960.

less (lĕs) *adj.* A comparative of **little. 1.** Smaller in amount, quantity, or degree; not so much: *less time to spare; less food to eat.* **2.** Lower in importance or rank: *No less a person than the President gave the order.* —*adv.* Comparative of **little.** To a smaller extent, degree, or quantity: *The game was less enjoyable than I had hoped.* —*prep.* Minus; without: *Five less three is two.* —*n.* A smaller amount or quantity: *The house sold for less than we thought.* —***idioms.*** **less than.** Not at all: *a less than satisfactory answer.* **much less** or **still less.** Certainly not: *I'm not blaming anyone, much less you.* —SEE NOTE at **few.**

–less *suff.* **1.** A suffix that means: Without or lacking: *motherless; nameless.* **2.** Not able to act in a certain way: *relentless.* **3.** Not able to be acted on in a certain way: *helpless.* —SEE NOTE.

les•see (lĕ **sē′**) *n.* A tenant holding a lease.

less•en (**lĕs′**ən) *tr. & intr.v.* **less•ened, less•en•ing, less•ens.** To make or become less: *a drug to lessen* *the pain; pain that lessened immediately.* See Synonyms at **decrease.**

❑ *These sound alike:* **lessen, lesson** (instruction).

less•er (lĕs′ər) *adj.* A comparative of **little. 1.** Smaller in amount, value, or importance: *a lesser evil; lesser gods.* **2.** Of a smaller size than other similar forms: *the lesser anteater.*

les•son (lĕs′ən) *n.* **1.** Something to be learned, especially an assignment or exercise in which something is studied or taught: *an algebra textbook divided into 40 lessons.* **2.** A period of time devoted to teaching or learning a certain subject: *three piano lessons a week.* **3.** An experience or example from which one can learn: *The poor grades taught me a lesson in the value of studying.* **4.** A reading from the Bible given as part of a religious service. [First written down before 1200 in Middle English and spelled *lesceun*, from Latin *lēctiō*, a reading.]

❑ *These sound alike:* **lesson, lessen** (make less).

les•sor (lĕs′ôr′ *or* lĕ sôr′) *n.* A person who rents property to another by lease.

lest (lĕst) *conj.* For fear that: *Be careful with the hammer lest you hit your thumb.*

let¹ (lĕt) *v.* **let, let•ting, lets.** *—tr.* **1.a.** To grant permission to; permit: *The crowd let the speaker continue without interruption.* **b.** To permit something to happen; allow: *Let your hot cocoa cool a bit.* **2.** To cause; make: *Let me know what happened.* **3.** Used as an auxiliary verb to express a request, command, or warning: *Let's finish the job!* **4.** Used as an auxiliary verb to express a proposal or an assumption: *Let x equal 3.* **5.** To permit to move in a specified way: *Let the cat out.* **6.** To permit to escape; release: *Who let the air out of the balloon?* **7.** To rent or lease: *They let rooms to students.* *—intr.* To become rented or leased. ***—idioms.*** **let down. 1.** To cause to come down gradually; lower: *The crane let down the piano.* **2.** To fail to meet the expectations of; disappoint: *Don't let me down.* **let off. 1.** To excuse from work or duty: *They let me off so I could go home early.* **2.** To release with little or no punishment: *They were let off with a warning.* **let on. 1.** To allow to be known; admit: *Don't let on that I'm going too.* **2.** To pretend: *They let on that they had been to Europe.* **let out. 1.** To come to a close; end: *School lets out next week.* **2.** To make known; reveal: *Who let that information out?* **3.** To increase the size of (a garment, for example). **let up.** To slow down, diminish, or stop: *The rain finally let up.* [First written down before 725 in Old English and spelled *lǣtan.*] —See Note at **leave¹.**

let² (lĕt) *n.* A stroke in tennis or other net games that must be repeated, especially a serve that has touched the net before falling into the proper part of the court. [First written down before 1200 in Middle English and spelled *lette*, obstacle, from Old English *lettan*, to hinder.]

-let *suff.* A suffix that means: **1.** A small one: *booklet.* **2.** Something worn on: *armlet.*

let•down (lĕt′doun′) *n.* **1.** A decrease or slowing down, as in energy or effort. **2.** A disappointment: *Losing that game was a real letdown.*

le•thal (lē′thəl) *adj.* Causing or capable of causing death: *a lethal disease; a lethal weapon.* [First written down in 1583 in Modern English, from Latin *lētum*, death.] **—le′thal•ly** *adv.*

le•thar•gic (lə thär′jĭk) *adj.* Of, causing, or characterized by lethargy: *spend a lethargic afternoon lying on the beach.* **—le•thar′gi•cal•ly** *adv.*

leth•ar•gy (lĕth′ər jē) *n., pl.* **leth•ar•gies. 1.** Drowsy or sluggish indifference; apathy. **2.** An unconscious state resembling deep sleep.

le•the (lē′thē) *n.* **1. Lethe.** In Greek mythology, the river of forgetfulness that runs through Hades. **2.** A state of forgetfulness.

let's (lĕts). Contraction of *let us.*

Lett (lĕt) *n.* A member of a Baltic people that make up the main population of Latvia.

let•ter (lĕt′ər) *n.* **1.** A written or printed mark that represents a speech sound and is one of the characters of an alphabet. **2.** A written or printed message addressed to a person: *I wrote three letters to friends this week.* **3.** A document giving the person who bears it certain rights or privileges: *carried a letter of safe passage through enemy territory.* **4. letters.** *(used with a singular verb).* Literature: *English letters.* **5.** The exact or literal meaning: *the letter of the law.* **6.** An emblem in the shape of the initial of a school, awarded for achievement in athletics. *—tr.v.* **let•tered, let•ter•ing, let•ters.** To mark or write with letters: *He carefully lettered our name on the mailbox.* ***—idiom.*** **to the letter.** To the last detail; exactly: *We followed the instructions to the letter.* [First written down about 1150 in Middle English and spelled *lettre*, from Latin *littera.*] **—let′ter•er** *n.*

letter carrier *n.* A mail carrier.

let•ter•head (lĕt′ər hĕd′) *n.* **1.** A printed heading at the top of a sheet of letter paper, usually consisting of the name and address of the sender. **2.** Letter paper with such a heading.

let•ter•ing (lĕt′ər ĭng) *n.* **1.** The act of forming letters. **2.** The letters formed, drawn, or painted, as on a sign.

let•ter-per•fect (lĕt′ər pûr′fĭkt) *adj.* Perfect in every detail.

Let•tish (lĕt′ĭsh) *adj.* Of or relating to the Letts or their language or culture. *—n.* The Latvian language.

let•tuce (lĕt′əs) *n.* Any of various plants cultivated for their large edible green or red leaves used in salad. [First written down about 1300 in Middle English and spelled *lettuse*, from Latin *lactūca.*]

let•up (lĕt′ŭp′) *n.* **1.** A reduction in pace, force, or intensity. **2.** A pause or stop: *no letup in the storm.*

leu•co•cyte (lo͞o′kə sīt′) *n.* Variant of **leukocyte.**

leu•ke•mi•a (lo͞o kē′mē ə) *n.* A disease of the blood characterized by the uncontrolled growth in the number of white blood cells.

leu•ko•cyte also **leu•co•cyte** (lo͞o′kə sīt′) *n.* A white blood cell.

Le•vant (lə vănt′). The countries bordering on the eastern Mediterranean Sea from Turkey to Egypt.

lev•ee (lĕv′ē) *n.* **1.** A bank of earth or other material built up along a river to keep it from flooding. **2.** A landing place on a river. [First written down in 1719 in Modern English and spelled *levée*, from Old French *lever*, to raise.]

❑ *These sound alike:* **levee, levy** (collect).

lev•el (lĕv′əl) *n.* **1.** Relative position or rank on a scale: *Science gets more complex at the college level.* **2.a.** A horizontal line or plane, often used to measure heights or depths: *The plane flew at tree level.* **b.** Height or depth: *The divers descended to a level of 60 feet.* **3.** A story or floor of a building. **4.** A flat stretch of land. **5.** An instrument for determining whether a surface is horizontal or vertical, used especially by carpenters and masons. *—adj.* **1.** Having a flat even surface: *level farmland.* **2.** Horizontal: *Is the picture on this wall level?* **3.** Steady; uniform: *a level tone of voice.* **4.** Being at the same height, rank, or position; even: *The two tabletops are level with each other.* **5.** Reasonable and careful; sensible: *a level head.* *—v.* **lev•eled, lev•el•ing, lev•els** or **lev•elled, lev•el•ling, lev•els.** *—tr.* **1.** To make smooth, flat, or horizontal: *level ground for a new building.* **2.** To cut, tear, or knock down to the ground: *A tornado leveled several buildings.* **3.** To

leotard

Word Building: –less

The suffix **–less** comes from the Old English suffix *–lēas*, from the word *lēas*, meaning "without." In Old English and Middle English, **–less** was often used to convey the negative or opposite of words ending in **–ful**, as in **careful/careless** and **fearful/fearless**. But **–less** was also used to coin words that had no counterpart ending in **–ful**: **headless, loveless, motherless.** Although **–less** normally forms adjectives by attaching to nouns, sometimes it attaches to verbs, as in **tireless.**

levee

ă	pat	oi	boy
ā	pay	ou	out
âr	care	o͝o	took
ä	father	o͞o	boot
ĕ	pet	ŭ	cut
ē	be	ûr	urge
ĭ	pit	th	thin
ī	pie	*th*	this
îr	pier	hw	whoop
ŏ	pot	zh	vision
ō	toe	ə	about
ô	paw	N	*French* bon

Meriwether Lewis

place on the same level; equalize: *level differences between schools.* **4.** To aim carefully: *level a rifle at the target.* —*intr. Informal.* To be frank and open: *Let's level with each other.* —***idioms.*** **on the level.** *Informal.* Without deception; honest. **(one's) level best.** The best one can do. [First written down in 1340 in Middle English and spelled *level,* an instrument to check that a surface is horizontal, from Latin *lībella,* balance.] —**lev′el•er, lev′el•ler** *n.* —**lev′el•ly** *adv.* —**lev′el•ness** *n.*

lev•el•head•ed (lĕv′əl hĕd′ĭd) *adj.* Having common sense and good judgment; sensible. —**lev′el•head′ed•ness** *n.*

lev•er (lĕv′ər *or* lē′vər) *n.* **1.** A bar that pivots on a fixed support or fulcrum, used to transmit effort and motion. It is a simple machine that can raise or move a heavy weight at one end as the bar is pushed down at the other end. **2.** A handle or bar used in such a manner, as a crowbar. **3.** A projecting handle used to control, adjust, or operate a device or machine, as a gear shift lever. [First written down about 1300 in Middle English and spelled *levour,* from Old French *lever,* to raise, from Latin *levāre.*]

lev•er•age (lĕv′ər ĭj *or* lē′vər ĭj) *n.* **1.** The action or mechanical advantage of a lever. **2.** An advantage in position or in power to act effectively: *Great wealth gives a person leverage in many business situations.*

Le•vi (lē′vī′). In the Bible, a son of Jacob and Leah and the ancestor of one of the tribes of Israel.

le•vi•a•than (lə vī′ə thən) *n.* **1.** A huge sea creature mentioned in the Bible. **2.** Something of enormous size or bulk.

Le•vi's (lē′vīz′). A trademark for trousers made of denim.

lev•i•tate (lĕv′ĭ tāt′) *intr. & tr.v.* **lev•i•tat•ed, lev•i•tat•ing, lev•i•tates.** To rise or cause to rise into the air and float.

Le•vite (lē′vīt′) *n.* In the Bible, a member of the tribe of Levi, chosen to assist the Temple priests.

Le•vit•i•cus (lə vĭt′ĭ kəs) *n.* A book of the Bible that contains Hebrew ceremonial rituals and laws governing the priests and Levites.

lev•i•ty (lĕv′ĭ tē) *n., pl.* **lev•i•ties.** A light humorous manner or attitude; frivolity.

lev•y (lĕv′ē) *tr.v.* **lev•ied, lev•y•ing, lev•ies. 1.** To impose or collect: *levy a sales tax; levy tariffs.* **2.** To draft into military service. **3.** To declare and carry on (war). —*n., pl.* **lev•ies. 1.** The act of levying. **2.** Money collected as a tax, tariff, or other fee. **3.** A body of troops drafted into military service. [First written down in 1436 in Middle English and spelled *leveien,* from Old French *lever,* to raise.]

❑ *These sound alike:* **levy, levee** (embankment).

lewd (lo͞od) *adj.* **lewd•er, lewd•est. 1.** Lustful. **2.** Obscene; indecent. —**lewd′ly** *adv.* —**lewd′ness** *n.*

Lew•is (lo͞o′ĭs), **Meriwether.** 1774–1809. American explorer who led the Lewis and Clark expedition (1803–1806) from St. Louis to the mouth of the Columbia River.

lex•i•cog•ra•pher (lĕk′sĭ kŏg′rə fər) *n.* A person who writes or compiles a dictionary.

lex•i•cog•ra•phy (lĕk′sĭ kŏg′rə fē) *n.* The process or work of writing or compiling a dictionary.

lex•i•con (lĕk′sĭ kŏn′) *n.* **1.** A dictionary, especially one giving translations of words from an ancient language. **2.** A stock of terms used in a particular subject or profession; a vocabulary.

Lex•ing•ton (lĕk′sĭng tən). **1.** A city of northeast-central Kentucky east of Louisville. It is a noted center for the raising of thoroughbred horses. Population, 204,165. **2.** A town of northeast Massachusetts, northwest of Boston. The Battle of Lexington (April 19, 1775) marked the beginning of the American Revolution. Population, 28,974.

Ley•den jar (līd′n) *n.* An early device for storing electricity that consists of a jar covered inside and out with metal foil and a metal rod that touches the inner foil and passes out of the jar through an insulated stopper.

LF An abbreviation of low frequency.

Lha•sa (lä′sə *or* lăs′ə). The capital of Xizang (Tibet), in southwest China north of Bhutan. Lhasa was long closed to foreign visitors and known as "the Forbidden City." Population, 105,897.

Li The symbol for the element **lithium.**

li•a•bil•i•ty (lī′ə bĭl′ĭ tē) *n., pl.* **li•a•bil•i•ties. 1.** The state of being liable. **2.** Something that one owes; an obligation or a debt. **3.** Something that holds one back; a disadvantage: *Poor spelling is a liability for a secretary.*

li•a•ble (lī′ə bəl) *adj.* **1.** Legally obligated or responsible: *The drivers argued about who was liable to pay for fixing the cars.* **2.** Subject; susceptible; prone: *Delicate glass is especially liable to breakage.* **3.** Likely: *liable to make mistakes.*

li•ai•son (lē′ā zŏn′ *or* lē ā′zŏn′) *n.* **1.** A means of communication between different groups or units of an organization, especially in the military. **2.** A person who maintains communication: *I work as the company's liaison with the people who sell our line of products.* [First written down before 1648 in Modern English, from Latin *ligātiō,* from *ligāre,* to bind.]

li•an•a (lē ä′nə *or* lē ăn′ə) *n.* A climbing tropical vine having woody stems, especially one that grows in a rain forest.

li•ar (lī′ər) *n.* A person who tells lies.

li•bel (lī′bəl) *n.* **1.** A written or printed statement that unjustly damages a person's reputation. **2.** The act or crime of making such a statement. —*tr.v.* **li•beled, li•bel•ing, li•bels** or **li•belled, li•bel•ling, li•bels.** To write or publish a false or damaging statement about (a person). —**li′bel•er** *n.*

li•bel•ous also **li•bel•lous** (lī′bə ləs) *adj.* Involving or being a libel: *a libelous story in the newspaper.*

lib•er•al (lĭb′ər əl *or* lĭb′rəl) *adj.* **1.** Tending to give generously: *a liberal contributor to the charity.* **2.** Generous in amount; ample: *a liberal helping of food.* **3.** Not strict or literal; approximate: *The movie is a liberal adaptation of the story.* **4.** Of or relating to the liberal arts. **5.** Open to new ideas and tolerant of the ideas and behavior of others; broad-minded: *a person with liberal attitudes.* **6. Liberal.** Of or relating to a political party that believes in the natural goodness of human beings and favors civil liberties, democratic reform, and social progress. —*n.* A person with liberal political opinions. [First written down before 1350 in Middle English and spelled *liberal,* noble, generous, from Latin *līber,* free.] —**lib′er•al•ly** *adv.* —**lib′er•al•ness** *n.*

liberal arts *pl.n.* College studies such as languages, history, philosophy, and science that provide general knowledge and the ability to think analytically, rather than practical or professional skills.

lib•er•al•ism (lĭb′ər ə lĭz′əm *or* lĭb′rə lĭz′əm) *n.* Liberal political views and policies.

lib•er•al•i•ty (lĭb′ə răl′ĭ tē) *n., pl.* **lib•er•al•i•ties. 1.** Generosity. **2.** A generous gift. **3.** A broad-minded attitude; tolerance.

lib•er•al•ize (lĭb′ər ə līz′ *or* lĭb′rə līz′) *tr. & intr.v.* **lib•er•al•ized, lib•er•al•iz•ing, lib•er•al•iz•es.** To make or become more liberal: *liberalize government regulations.* —**lib′er•al•i•za′tion** (lĭb′ər ə lĭ zā′shən *or* lĭb′rə lĭ zā′shən) *n.*

lib•er•ate (lĭb′ə rāt′) *tr.v.* **lib•er•at•ed, lib•er•at•ing, lib•er•ates. 1.** To set free, as from confinement or control: *The Emancipation Proclamation liberated the slaves.* **2.** To set free as a result of chemical combination: *liberate a gas.* [First written down in

1623 in Modern English, from Latin *līber*, free.] **—lib′er•a′tion** *n.* **—lib′er•a′tor** *n.*

Li•be•ri•a (lī bîr′ē ə). A country of western Africa on the Atlantic Ocean west of Ivory Coast. It was founded in 1821 and settled mainly by freed slaves from the United States from 1822 to the 1860's. Capital, Monrovia. Population, 1,911,000.

lib•er•tine (lĭb′ər tēn′) *n.* A person who lives an irresponsible immoral life; a rake. *—adj.* Morally unrestrained: *a libertine existence.*

lib•er•ty (lĭb′ər tē) *n., pl.* **lib•er•ties. 1.** Freedom from imprisonment, slavery, or forced labor. **2.** The right and power to act, believe, and express oneself as one chooses. **3.** Political freedom from the control of another government; independence: *In 1776, the United States began the war for its liberty from Britain.* **4.** A legal right to engage in a certain kind of action without control or interference: *liberties of citizens protected by the Bill of Rights.* **5.** An action that is unwarranted or improper. Often used in the plural: *He takes liberties with history to make his argument sound better.* **6.** A period during which a sailor is permitted to go ashore. ***—idiom.* at liberty.** Not in confinement or under constraint; free. [First written down about 1375 in Middle English and spelled *liberte*, from Latin *lībertās*, from *līber*, free.]

Li•bra (lē′brə *or* lī′brə) *n.* **1.** A constellation in the Southern Hemisphere near Scorpius. **2.** The seventh sign of the zodiac in astrology.

li•brar•i•an (lī brâr′ē ən) *n.* A person who is specially trained to work in a library.

li•brar•y (lī′brĕr′ē) *n., pl.* **li•brar•ies. 1.** A building or room where books, magazines, records, and other materials are kept for reading or borrowing. **2.** A collection of such materials. [First written down about 1380 in Middle English and spelled *librarie*, from Latin *liber*, book.]

li•bret•tist (lĭ brĕt′ĭst) *n.* The author of a libretto.

li•bret•to (lĭ brĕt′ō) *n., pl.* **li•bret•tos** or **li•bret•ti** (lĭ brĕt′ē). The text of a dramatic musical work, such as an opera.

Li•bre•ville (lē′brə vĭl′). The capital and largest city of Gabon, in the northwest part of the country on the Atlantic Ocean. It was founded in 1843. Population, 235,700.

Lib•y•a (lĭb′ē ə). A country of northern Africa on the Mediterranean Sea west of Egypt. It became an important oil producer during the 1960's. Tripoli is the capital and the largest city. Population, 3,096,000. **—Lib′yan** *adj. & n.*

lice (līs) *n.* Plural of **louse** (sense 1).

li•cense (lī′səns) *n.* **1.a.** Legal permission to do or own a specified thing: *The group has license to run a daycare center.* **b.** A document, card, plate, or other proof that such permission has been granted: *The doctor's license is hung on the wall.* **2.** Freedom of action: *I took the license to stop by without calling beforehand.* *—tr.v.* **li•censed, li•cens•ing, li•cens•es.** To grant a license to or for. [First written down before 1376 in Middle English and spelled *licence*, from Latin *licentia*, freedom, from *licēre*, to be permitted.]

li•cen•tious (lī sĕn′shəs) *adj.* Lacking moral restraint; immoral. **—li•cen′tious•ly** *adv.* **—li•cen′tious•ness** *n.*

li•chee (lē′chē) *n.* Variant of **litchi.**

li•chen (lī′kən) *n.* An organism that consists of a fungus and an alga growing in close combination. Lichens grow and spread over rocks and tree trunks and look somewhat like moss. [First written down in 1601 in Modern English, from Greek *leikhēn*.]

❑ *These sound alike:* **lichen, liken** (compare).

lick (lĭk) *tr.v.* **licked, lick•ing, licks. 1.a.** To pass the tongue over: *The dog licks her pups.* **b.** To lap up: *The cat licked cream from a dish.* **2.** To move or flicker like a tongue: *Flames lick the burning logs.* **3.** *Slang.* To defeat; beat: *We licked the other team.* **4.** *Slang.* To punish with a beating; thrash. *—n.* **1.** A movement of the tongue over something: *a kitten's wet lick.* **2.** A small quantity; bit: *We couldn't find a lick of evidence.* **3.** A salt lick. **4.** A blow or hard stroke. [First written down in 830 in Old English and spelled *liccian*.]

lic•o•rice (lĭk′ər ĭs *or* lĭk′ər ĭsh) *n.* **1.** A plant having a sweet strong-tasting root used as a flavoring. **2.** The root of this plant. **3.** A chewy, often black candy flavored with an extract from this root. [First written down before 1200 in Middle English and spelled *licoriz*, from Greek *glukurrhiza* : *glukus*, sweet + *rhiza*, root.]

lid (lĭd) *n.* **1.** A removable cover or top for a hollow container: *the lid for a jar; the lid of a box.* **2.** An eyelid. [First written down about 1000 in Old English and spelled *hlid*.]

lie[1] (lī) *intr.v.* **lay** (lā), **lain** (lān), **ly•ing** (lī′ĭng), **lies. 1.** To place oneself in a flat or resting position: *The cow lay down in the pasture.* **2.** To be in a flat or resting position: *I was lying on the floor.* **3.** To be or rest on a surface: *Forks and spoons lay on the table.* **4.** To be located: *Many tiny islands lie off the coast.* **5.** To remain in a certain condition or position: *We let the land lie unused.* **6.** To be a basic quality or characteristic of; exist: *The answer lay in further research.* **7.** To extend: *Our land lies between the river and the trees.* *—n.* The manner or position in which something lies, as the surface or slope of a piece of land. [First written down about 725 in Old English and spelled *licgan*.] —SEE NOTE at **lay**[1].

❑ *These sound alike:* **lie**[1] (be flat), **lie**[2] (falsehood), **lye** (alkaline solution).

lie[2] (lī) *n.* A untrue statement made in order to deceive someone; a falsehood. *—intr.v.* **lied, ly•ing** (lī′ĭng), **lies. 1.** To tell a lie or lies: *The suspect lied to the police.* **2.** To create an illusion or a false impression: *Even photographs can lie.* [First written down about 900 in Old English and spelled *lyge*.]

❑ *These sound alike:* **lie**[2] (falsehood), **lie**[1] (be flat), **lye** (alkaline solution).

Liech•ten•stein (lĭk′tən stīn′ *or* lĭkh′tən shtīn′). A small principality in the Alps of central Europe between Austria and Switzerland. Vaduz is the capital. Population, 27,076.

lie detector *n.* An instrument that records changes in bodily conditions, such as blood pressure and pulse rate, that usually occur when a person is not telling the truth.

lief (lēf) *adv.* **lief•er, lief•est.** Readily; willingly: *I would as lief go now as later.*

❑ *These sound alike:* **lief** (readily), **leaf** (plant part).

liege (lēj) *n.* **1.** A lord to whom subjects owed allegiance and services in feudal times. **2.** A person owing allegiance and services to such a lord; a vassal. *—adj.* Of or relating to the relationship between lord and vassal: *my liege lord.*

liege•man (lēj′mən) *n.* **1.** A feudal vassal or subject. **2.** A loyal supporter, follower, or subject.

lien (lēn *or* lē′ən) *n.* A legal claim on the property of a person as payment for a debt.

❑ *These sound alike:* **lien, lean**[1] (bend), **lean**[2] (thin).

lieu (lo͞o) *n. Archaic.* Place; stead. ***—idiom.* in lieu of.** In place of; instead of: *received a check in lieu of cash.*

lieu•ten•an•cy (lo͞o tĕn′ən sē) *n.* The duty, authority, or rank of a lieutenant.

lieu•ten•ant (lo͞o tĕn′ənt) *n.* **1.a.** A first lieutenant. **b.** A second lieutenant. **2.** An officer in the Navy

library

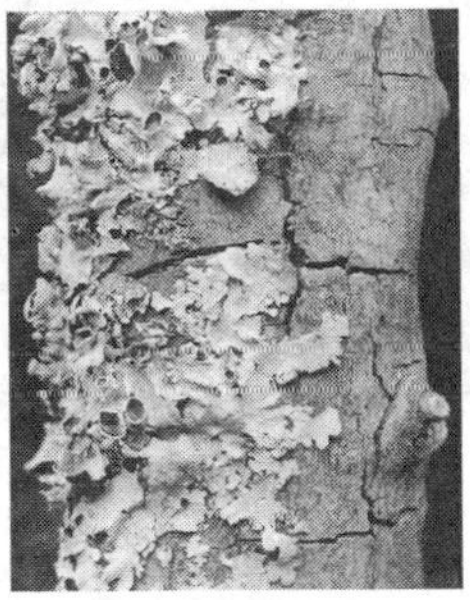

lichen

Growing on a tree limb

ă	pat	oi	boy
ā	pay	ou	out
âr	care	o͝o	took
ä	father	o͞o	boot
ĕ	pet	ŭ	cut
ē	be	ûr	urge
ĭ	pit	th	thin
ī	pie	*th*	this
îr	pier	hw	whoop
ŏ	pot	zh	vision
ō	toe	ə	about
ô	paw	N	*French* bon

life expectancy

The average length of life, or the **life expectancy**, for persons born in the U.S. in 1991 is 75½ years. One hundred or so years ago, life expectancy in the U.S. was about 49 years. And almost 2,000 years ago, in Roman times, a person could expect to live to about age 30. These dramatic increases, especially the more than 25-year increase in just the past century, result from improvements in the way people live. Today's better housing and sanitation, along with widespread availability of food and clean water, help people stay healthy longer. Advances in science and medicine (such as sophisticated surgical techniques, vaccines to prevent disease, and antibiotics to control infection) also help improve a person's life expectancy.

life jacket

life raft

ranking above an ensign and below a lieutenant commander. **3.** An officer in a police or fire department ranking next below a captain. **4.** A chief assistant; a deputy: *a staff member acting as the president's lieutenant.*

lieutenant colonel *n.* An officer in the U.S. Army, Air Force, or Marine Corps, ranking above a major and below a colonel.

lieutenant commander *n.* An officer in the U.S. Navy or Coast Guard ranking above a lieutenant and below a commander.

lieutenant general *n.* An officer in the U.S. Army, Air Force, or Marine Corps, ranking above a major general and below a general.

lieutenant governor *n.* **1.** An elected official ranking just below the governor of a U.S. state. **2.** The nonelected chief of government of a Canadian province.

lieutenant junior grade *n., pl.* **lieutenants junior grade.** An officer in the U.S. Navy or Coast Guard ranking above an ensign and below a lieutenant.

life (līf) *n., pl.* **lives** (līvz). **1.** The property or quality that distinguishes living organisms from dead organisms and nonliving matter. Life is shown in an organism that has the ability to grow, carry on metabolism, respond to stimuli, and reproduce. **2.** The fact of being alive: *risk one's life.* **3.** The period of time between birth and death; a lifetime: *a long and interesting life.* **4.** The time during which something exists and works: *the life of a car.* **5.** Living organisms considered as a group: *plant life; marine life.* **6.** A living being; a person: *That doctor has saved hundreds of lives.* **7.** A way of living: *the outdoor life; city life.* **8.** Liveliness; spirit: *a puppy, curious and full of life.* **9.** An account of a person's life; a biography. **—*idioms.* bring to life. 1.** To cause to regain life or consciousness. **2.** To make lively or lifelike: *A good actor brings a character to life.* **come to life.** To become lively; grow excited: *She always came to life when talking about her favorite writer.* **for life.** Till the end of one's life. **take (someone's) life.** To commit murder. **true to life.** Accurately representing real life: *The movie is true to life.* [First written down about 725 in Old English and spelled *līf.*]

life belt *n.* A life preserver worn like a belt.

life•blood (līf′blŭd′) *n.* **1.** Blood regarded as necessary for life. **2.** An essential or vital part: *The conductor is the lifeblood of the orchestra.*

life•boat (līf′bōt′) *n.* A strong boat carried on a ship or kept along the shore, used if the ship has to be abandoned or for rescue service.

life buoy *n.* A ring made of cork or other buoyant material for keeping a person afloat.

life cycle *n.* The series of changes through which a living organism passes, from its beginning as a fertilized egg to its mature state in which offspring can be produced.

life expectancy *n.* The length of time an organism is expected to live, as determined by statistical studies. —SEE NOTE.

life•guard (līf′gärd′) *n.* A person hired to look out for the safety of bathers at a beach or pool.

life insurance *n.* Insurance on a person's life, paid for by regular premiums and guaranteeing a certain sum of money to a specified person, such as a spouse or child, on the death of the holder.

life jacket *n.* A life preserver in the form of a jacket or vest.

life•less (līf′lĭs) *adj.* **1.** Having no life; dead or inanimate. **2.** Not supporting life; having no living organisms: *a lifeless planet.* **3.** Lacking spirit or vitality; dull: *a lifeless party.* **—life′less•ly** *adv.* **—life′less•ness** *n.*

life•like (līf′līk′) *adj.* Accurately representing real life: *a lifelike statue.*

life•line (līf′līn′) *n.* **1.** An anchored line thrown as a support to someone falling or drowning. **2.** A line used to raise and lower deep-sea divers. **3.** A means or route for transporting vital supplies.

life•long (līf′lông′ *or* līf′lŏng′) *adj.* Lasting over a lifetime: *a lifelong friend; a lifelong ambition.*

life preserver *n.* A device, usually a belt, jacket, or tube filled with a buoyant material, designed to keep a person afloat in the water.

life raft *n.* A raft used by people who have been forced into water as a result of a shipwreck or an airplane crash.

life•sav•er (līf′sā′vər) *n.* **1.** A lifeguard or other person who saves the lives of others. **2.** A person or thing that provides help in a crisis or emergency: *Their call to the fire department was a lifesaver.* **3.** A life preserver shaped like a ring.

life•sav•ing (līf′sā′vĭng) *n.* The skills and methods used in saving lives, especially in keeping people from drowning.

life-size (līf′sīz′) also **life-sized** (līf′sīzd′) *adj.* Being of the same size as the person or object represented: *a life-size statue of a person.*

life span *n.* **1.** The average or longest period of time that an organism can be expected to live. **2.** A lifetime.

life•style (līf′stīl′) *n.* The way of life or style of living of a person or group, including diet, tastes, work, and interests.

life-sup•port system (līf′sə pôrt′) *n.* **1.** Equipment that assists or substitutes for an essential bodily function, such as respiration, enabling a patient who might not otherwise survive to live. **2.** The equipment that supplies oxygen and other essential conditions for human life outside a normal environment.

life•time (līf′tīm′) *n.* The period of time that a person lives or a thing exists or works properly: *the average lifetime of a person; the lifetime of our car.*

life•work (līf′wûrk′) *n.* The chief or entire work of a person's lifetime.

lift (lĭft) *v.* **lift•ed, lift•ing, lifts.** *—tr.* **1.** To raise to a higher position; elevate: *I lifted the suitcase out of the car.* **2.** To raise or improve in condition, status, or estimation: *The news lifted everybody's spirits.* **3.** To end; stop; suspend: *lift a siege.* **4.** *Informal.* To steal; pilfer: *The robber lifted a priceless painting.* **5.** To copy from something already published; plagiarize: *The reporter lifted the paragraph from a magazine article.* *—intr.* **1.** To rise or become raised: *The suitcase is too heavy to lift.* **2.** To rise and disappear: *The heavy fog finally lifted.* *—n.* **1.** The act of lifting or being lifted: *Give me a lift into the saddle.* **2.** A short ride in a vehicle: *Can I have a lift to the store?* **3.** The extent or height something is raised. **4.** An elevation of the spirit: *Good grades give students a big lift.* **5.** An amount or a weight lifted; a load. **6.** One of the layers of leather or rubber in the heel of a shoe. **7.** *Chiefly British.* An elevator. **—*idiom.* lift off.** To begin flight: *The rocket lifted off at dawn.* [First written down about 1200 in Middle English and spelled *liften*, from Old Norse *lypta.*]

lift•off (lĭft′ôf′ *or* lĭft′ŏf′) *n.* The takeoff of a rocket from its launch pad.

lig•a•ment (lĭg′ə mənt) *n.* A sheet or band of tough fibrous tissue that connects two bones or holds an organ of the body in place.

lig•a•ture (lĭg′ə chŏŏr′ *or* lĭg′ə chər) *n.* **1.** Something used for tying or binding. **2.** A thread, wire, or fine cord used in surgery to tie off a bleeding vein or artery. **3.** In printing, two or three letters joined to form a single character, as *œ.*

light¹ (līt) *n.* **1.** A form of radiant energy that can be perceived by the human eye. It is made up of electromagnetic waves that travel at a speed of about 186,282 miles (299,728 kilometers) per second. **2.** Radiant energy that cannot be perceived by the human eye, as infrared light and ultraviolet light. **3.** Illumination; brightness: *The fireworks produced bursts of light.* **4.** A source of light, as the sun or a lamp: *a light in the window.* **5.** A supply of light: *small windows gave little light.* **6.** Daylight: *Flowers need a lot of light to bloom.* **7.** Dawn; daybreak. **8.** A source of fire, as a match. **9.** Understanding through knowledge and information: *Research shed new light on the dinosaurs.* **10.** Public attention; general knowledge: *Reports brought to light the need for improvements in fire protection.* **11.** A famous or outstanding person: *one of the leading lights of the theater.* **12.** A way of looking at or considering a certain matter: *This puts the problem in a different light.* **13.** A light shade or color: *The lights in the photograph are too bright.* —*v.* **light•ed** or **lit** (lĭt), **light•ing, lights.** —*tr.* **1.** To set burning; ignite: *light a fire.* **2.** To cause to give out light; turn on: *light a lamp.* **3.** To provide, cover, or fill with light: *Let's light the room with candles.* **4.** To make lively or bright: *A smile lighted the child's face.* **5.** To guide or direct by means of a light: *A flashlight was enough to light our way along the path.* —*intr.* **1.** To start to burn; become ignited: *The oven won't light for some reason.* **2.** To become light or bright: *The neon sign lighted up after dark.* —*adj.* **light•er, light•est. 1.** Having light: *a nice light room to work in.* **2.** Bright; not dark: *light gray; light hair.* —***idiom.*** **in light of.** In consideration of; in relationship to: *In light of the report, let's try a different approach to the problem.* [First written down about 725 in Old English and spelled *lēoht.*]

light² (līt) *adj.* **light•er, light•est. 1.** Having little weight; not heavy: *a light suitcase; a light jacket.* **2.** Having little force or impact: *a light breeze; a light blow.* **3.** Low in intensity or amount: *a light rain; a light lunch.* **4.** Not serious or profound: *light comedy.* **5.** Not important; slight: *The boat suffered only light damage.* **6.** Carrying little weight or equipment: *light cavalry.* **7.** Free from care or worry: *a light heart.* **8.** Moving easily and quickly; nimble: *light on one's feet.* **9.** Appearing to be graceful and delicate: *light wood carvings; a light structure.* **10.** Requiring little effort or exertion: *light household chores.* **11.** Somewhat unsteady or faint; dizzy: *feel light in the head.* **12.** Having fewer calories; not fatty or rich: *light foods; light soft drinks.* **13.** Spongy or flaky in texture; *light pastries.* **14.** Easily awakened or disturbed: *a light sleeper.* —*adv.* **lighter, lightest.** Lightly, especially with little baggage: *We always travel light.* —*intr.v.* **light•ed** or **lit** (lĭt), **light•ing, lights. 1.** To come to rest; land; perch: *The bird lit on the feeder.* **2.** To get down, as from a mount or vehicle; alight: *Several passengers lighted from the rear of the plane.* —***idioms.*** **light into.** *Informal.* To attack verbally or physically; assail. **light out.** *Informal.* To leave hastily; run off. [First written down before 899 in Old English and spelled *lēoht.*]

light bulb *n.* A glass-covered electric light source in which a wire is heated by an electric current so that it gives off light.

light•en¹ (līt′n) *v.* **light•ened, light•en•ing, light•ens.** —*tr.* To make lighter in color or brighter: *He lightened the blue paint by mixing in some white.* —*intr.* **1.** To become lighter in color or brighter: *The clouds thinned and the sky lightened quickly.* **2.** To give off flashes of lightning.

light•en² (līt′n) *v.* **light•ened, light•en•ing, light•ens.** —*tr.* **1.** To make less heavy; reduce the weight of: *Leaving out those books will lighten the load.* **2.** To make less troublesome or oppressive: *hire an assistant to lighten the load of work.* **3.** To gladden or cheer: *a song to lighten everyone's heart.* —*intr.* **1.** To become less in weight. **2.** To become less troublesome or oppressive. **3.** To become cheerful.

light•er¹ (lī′tər) *n.* A person or device that lights or ignites something: *a lamp lighter; a cigarette lighter.*

light•er² (lī′tər) *n.* A barge used for loading and unloading ships and for carrying cargo short distances. —*tr.v.* **light•ered, light•er•ing, light•ers.** To carry (cargo) in a lighter. [First written down in 1372 in Middle English, perhaps from *lighten,* to make less heavy.]

light•face (līt′fās′) *n.* A typeface that has thin light lines. This definition is in lightface.

light-foot•ed (līt′fo͝ot′ĭd) *adj.* Moving with light and graceful steps; nimble.

light•head•ed (līt′hĕd′ĭd) *adj.* **1.** Giddy, dizzy, or faint, as from fever. **2.** Silly or foolish in one's manner or behavior; flighty. **—light′head′ed•ly** *adv.* **—light′head′ed•ness** *n.*

light•heart•ed (līt′här′tĭd) *adj.* Carefree and cheerful: *a lighthearted attitude.* See Synonyms at **glad.** **—light′heart′ed•ly** *adv.* **—light′heart′ed•ness** *n.*

light•house (līt′hous′) *n.* A tower with a powerful light at the top, used to guide ships and warn ships of dangerous waters.

light•ing (lī′tĭng) *n.* **1.** Light supplied, as for a room or an area; illumination: *right lighting for reading.* **2.** The arrangement or equipment that provides light: *outdoor lighting.*

light•ly (līt′lē) *adv.* **1.** With little pressure or force: *Tread lightly on the floor to avoid waking the baby.* **2.** To a small amount or degree: *The streets were lightly covered with snow.* **3.a.** In a carefree manner; cheerfully: *took the setback lightly.* **b.** Without proper care or consideration: *treated his illness lightly.* **4.** With agility; nimbly: *The deer leaped lightly over the fence.*

light meter *n.* A device that measures the intensity of light, used especially in photography.

light•ness¹ (līt′nĭs) *n.* **1.** The quality or condition of being lighted; brightness. **2.** Paleness of color.

light•ness² (līt′nĭs) *n.* **1.** The property or quality of having little weight or force: *the lightness of straw.* **2.** Ease or quickness of movement; agility: *lightness of step.* **3.** Freedom from worry or trouble: *lightness of heart.* **4.** Lack of appropriate seriousness: *lightness of conduct.*

light•ning (līt′nĭng) *n.* A flash of light in the sky caused by an electrical discharge between clouds or between a cloud and the earth's surface. The flash heats the air and usually causes thunder.

lightning bug *n.* A firefly.

lightning rod *n.* A metal rod that protects a building or another structure from lightning by conducting it along a heavy wire into the ground.

light pen *n.* A small hand-held electronic device shaped like a pen and used to put information into a computer. Light pens read codes on labels by being passed over them or give instructions to the computer by touching particular spaces on the display screen.

light•ship (līt′shĭp′) *n.* A ship with powerful lights and other warning signals, anchored in dangerous waters to alert and guide other vessels.

light•weight (līt′wāt′) *n.* **1.** A person or thing that weighs relatively little. **2.a.** A boxer who weighs more than 126 and not more than 135 pounds (about 57–61 kilograms), heavier than a featherweight and lighter than a welterweight. **b.** A contestant in some other sports in a similar weight class. **3.** A person of little ability, importance, or

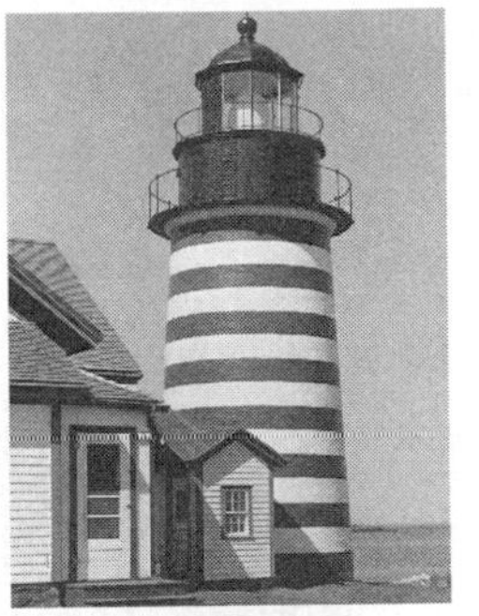

lighthouse
West Quoddy lighthouse, Lubec, Maine

lightning

lightning rod

ă	**pat**	oi	**boy**
ā	**pay**	ou	**out**
âr	**care**	o͝o	**took**
ä	**father**	o͞o	**boot**
ĕ	**pet**	ŭ	**cut**
ē	**be**	ûr	**urge**
ĭ	**pit**	th	**thin**
ī	**pie**	*th*	**this**
îr	**pier**	hw	**whoop**
ŏ	**pot**	zh	**vision**
ō	**toe**	ə	**about**
ô	**paw**	N	*French* **bon**

Liliuokalani

lily of the valley

influence. —*adj.* Not heavy; weighing relatively little: *a lightweight jacket.*

light-year (līt′yîr′) *n.* The distance that light travels in a year, about 5.88 trillion miles (9.46 trillion kilometers).

lig•nite (lĭg′nīt′) *n.* A soft brownish-black form of coal in which the condition of the plant matter is between peat and bituminous coal; brown coal.

lik•a•ble also **like•a•ble** (lī′kə bəl) *adj.* Easy to like; having a pleasing personality: *a pleasant likable classmate.*

like[1] (līk) *v.* **liked, lik•ing, likes.** —*tr.* **1.** To be fond of: *We are old friends and like each other.* See Synonyms at **love. 2.** To find pleasant; enjoy: *They liked the place and decided to stay.* **3.** To feel about; regard: *How do you like your new school?* **4.** To want to have: *Would you like some gravy?* —*intr.* To have a desire or preference: *If you like, we can go home now.* —*n.* Something that is liked; a preference: *my likes and dislikes.* [First written down before 899 in Old English and spelled *līcian*, to please.]

like[2] (līk) *prep.* **1.** Resembling; similar to: *You look a lot like your mother.* **2.** In the same way as: *Don't act like a clown.* **3.** In the typical manner of: *It's not like him to give up easily.* **4.** Such as: *I draw things like buildings and street scenes.* **5.** As if it is likely to be: *It looks like a good year for farmers.* **6.** Inclined to; desirous of: *I felt like going home.* —*adj.* **1.** Having the same or almost the same characteristics; similar: *We made this and like repairs to the car.* **2.** Equivalent: *The company will donate a like amount to the charity.* —*adv.* As if: *We worked like crazy to get the job done on time.* —*n.* Something equal or similar to something else: *Owls eat mice, chipmunks, and the like.* —*conj.* **1.** In the same way that: *To dance like she does takes lots of practice.* **2.** As if: *It looks like we'll finish on time.* [First written down about 725 in Old English and spelled *gelīc.*]

–like *suff.* A suffix that means similar to or characteristic of: *childlike; lifelike.*

like•a•ble (lī′kə bəl) *adj.* Variant of **likable.**

like•li•hood (līk′lē ho͝od′) *n.* The chance of a thing happening; probability: *The likelihood of snow is very remote in July.*

like•ly (līk′lē) *adj.* **like•li•er, like•li•est. 1.** Having or showing a tendency or probability: *It is likely to rain at any moment.* **2.** Seeming to be true; credible: *a likely excuse for being late.* **3.** Appropriate or suitable: *She seems a likely choice for the job.* **4.** Showing promise of success; promising: *a likely way of proceeding.* —*adv.* Probably: *Most likely the barn will need some repairs.*

lik•en (lī′kən) *tr.v.* **lik•ened, lik•en•ing, lik•ens.** To describe as resembling something else; compare: *He likened his youth to a summer day.*

❑ *These sound alike:* **liken, lichen** (organism).

like•ness (līk′nĭs) *n.* **1.** Similarity or resemblance: *an amazing likeness between brothers.* **2.** A copy or picture of a person or thing: *The portrait is a perfect likeness of you.* **3.** Appearance; form: *At once the prince took on the likeness of a frog.*

like•wise (līk′wīz′) *adv.* **1.** Similarly; in like manner: *Once he saw her open her package, he did likewise.* **2.** Moreover; besides: *I enjoyed living in France and likewise learned to speak French.* See Synonyms at **besides.**

lik•ing (lī′kĭng) *n.* A feeling or fondness or affection; a preference: *a special liking for apples.*

li•lac (lī′lək *or* lī′lŏk *or* lī′lăk) *n.* **1.** Any of various shrubs that bear clusters of fragrant purplish or white flowers. **2.** A pale purple.

Li•li•u•o•ka•la•ni (lə lē′ə ō kə lä′nē), **Lydia Kamekeha Paki.** 1838–1917. Queen of the Hawaiian Islands (1891–1893). She was the last Hawaiian ruler to govern the islands.

Li•long•we (lĭ lông′wā). The capital of Malawi, in the south-central part of the country near the border with Mozambique. It was founded in the 1940's. Population, 103,000.

lilt (lĭlt) *n.* **1.** A cheerful lively manner of speaking. **2.** A light happy tune or song. **3.** A light rhythmic manner of moving or walking. —*tr. & intr.v.* **lilt•ed, lilt•ing, lilts.** To sing, play, or speak in a lively rhythmic manner: *the bird lilted its song.*

lil•y (lĭl′ē) *n., pl.* **lil•ies. 1.** Any of various plants having showy flowers shaped like trumpets. Lilies grow from bulbs and produce flowers in many brilliant colors. **2.** Any of various similar or related plants, such as the water lily. **3.** The flower of any of these plants.

lily of the valley *n., pl.* **lilies of the valley.** A plant having a slender one-sided cluster of fragrant, bell-shaped white flowers.

lily pad *n.* One of the broad floating leaves of a water lily.

Li•ma (lē′mə). The capital and largest city of Peru, in the west-central part of the country near the Pacific Ocean. It was largely rebuilt after earthquakes in 1687 and 1746. Population, 371,122.

li•ma bean (lī′mə) *n.* **1.** The light-green kidney-shaped seed of a tropical American plant, eaten as a vegetable. **2.** The plant that bears such seeds.

limb (lĭm) *n.* **1.** A leg, an arm, a wing, or another jointed member of an animal body distinct from the head or trunk. **2.** One of the larger branches of a tree. [First written down about 725 in Old English and spelled *lim.*] **—limb′less** *adj.*

❑ *These sound alike:* **limb, limn** (draw).

lim•ber (lĭm′bər) *adj.* Bending or moving easily; flexible: *limber muscles; a limber athlete.* —*tr. & intr.v.* **lim•bered, lim•ber•ing, lim•bers.** To exercise so as to make or become limber: *She stretched to limber up her muscles. He limbered up before the game.* **—lim′ber•ness** *n.*

lim•bo[1] (lĭm′bō) *n., pl.* **lim•bos. 1.** Often **Limbo.** In Roman Catholic theology, the abode of just or innocent souls kept from heaven but not condemned to Hell or Purgatory. **2.** A place or condition of neglect or oblivion: *Construction for the new pool was kept in limbo until new funds were found.* [First written down about 1378 in Middle English, from Latin *limbus*, border]

lim•bo[2] (lĭm′bō) *n., pl.* **lim•bos.** A West Indian dance in which the dancers bend over backward and pass under a horizontal pole. [First written down in 1956 in Modern English, probably of African origin.]

Lim•burg•er (lĭm′bûr′gər) *n.* A soft white cheese with a strong odor and flavor.

lime[1] (līm) *n.* **1.** An oval fruit related to the lemon and having a green skin and sour juice used as flavoring. **2.** The tree that bears such fruit. [First written down in 1638 in Modern English, from Arabic *līmah.*]

lime[2] (līm) *n.* A European linden. [First written down about 700 in Old English and spelled *lind.*]

lime[3] (līm) *n.* Calcium oxide. —*tr.v.* **limed, lim•ing, limes.** To treat with lime; apply lime to. [First written down about 700 in Old English and spelled *līm*, birdlime.]

lime•light (līm′līt′) *n.* **1.** The center of public attention: *The President is always in the limelight.* **2.** An early type of light used in the theater, in which lime was heated to produce light.

lim•er•ick (lĭm′ər ĭk) *n.* A humorous five-line poem that follows the rhyme scheme *aabba.* [First written down in 1896 in Modern English, after *Limerick*, a borough of southwest Ireland.]

lime•stone (līm′stōn′) *n.* A form of sedimentary rock that consists mainly of calcium carbonate, used as a building material and in making lime and cement.

lime•wa•ter (līm′wô′tər *or* līm′wŏt′ər) *n.* A solution of calcium hydroxide and water, used in calamine lotion and sometimes as an antacid.

lim•it (lĭm′ĭt) *n.* **1.** A point or line beyond which something ends or cannot go: *the 12-mile fishing limit; the limit of my patience.* **2. limits.** The boundary surrounding a certain area: *within the city limits.* **3.** The greatest amount of something allowed: *a speed limit.* —*tr.v.* **lim•it•ed, lim•it•ing, lim•its.** To place a limit on; confine: *Try to limit your talk to ten minutes.* [First written down in 1384 in Middle English, from Latin *līmes*, boundary.]

lim•i•ta•tion (lĭm′ĭ tā′shən) *n.* **1.** Something that limits; a restriction: *Poor ice conditions put limitations on how fast the bobsled could go.* **2.** The act of limiting or the state of being limited.

lim•it•ed (lĭm′ĭ tĭd) *adj.* **1.** Confined within certain limits; restricted: *a small house with limited space.* **2.** Not accomplishing the greatest achievements or possessing the best talent: *a popular but limited actor.* **3.** Traveling fast and making few stops: *a limited train.* —*n.* A limited train or bus.

lim•it•less (lĭm′ĭt lĭs) *adj.* Having no limit or boundary; unrestricted or infinite: *limitless space in the sky.*

limn (lĭm) *tr.v.* **limned, limn•ing** (lĭm′nĭng), **limns.** **1.** To draw or paint. **2.** To describe.
❑ *These sound alike:* **limn, limb** (body part).

lim•ou•sine (lĭm′ə zēn′ *or* lĭm′ə zēn′) *n.* A large luxurious automobile, often with a glass partition between the driver and the passengers. [First written down in 1902 in Modern English, from French, possibly from *Limousin*, a region of France.]

limp (lĭmp) *intr.v.* **limped, limp•ing, limps.** **1.** To walk lamely: *After my knee injury, I limped for several days.* **2.** To move or proceed haltingly or with difficulty: *The damaged ship limped back to port.* —*n.* A lame or irregular way of walking. —*adj.* **limp•er, limp•est.** **1.** Lacking stiffness: *a limp wet towel.* **2.** Not vigorous or strong; weak: *a limp handshake.* [First written down in 1570 in Modern English, probably from Old English *lemphealt*, lame.] —**limp′ly** *adv.* —**limp′ness** *n.*

lim•pet (lĭm′pĭt) *n.* Any of numerous small saltwater shellfish that have a tent-shaped shell and cling to rocks.

lim•pid (lĭm′pĭd) *adj.* Perfectly clear; transparent: *limpid water.*

lim•y (lī′mē) *adj.* **lim•i•er, lim•i•est.** Of, containing, or resembling lime.

linch•pin (lĭnch′pĭn′) *n.* **1.** An iron pin inserted in the end of an axle to prevent a wheel from slipping off. **2.** Something that keeps different parts together and functioning: *The linchpin of the candidate's campaign was his proposal for improving the economy.* [First written down in 1376 in Middle English and spelled *linspin*, from Old English *lynis*.]

Lin•coln (lĭng′kən). The capital of Nebraska, in the southeast part of the state southwest of Omaha. It was chosen as the state capital in 1867. Population, 191,972.

Lincoln, Abraham. 1809–1865. The 16th President of the United States (1861–1865), who led the Union during the Civil War and issued the Emancipation Proclamation (1863), freeing all slaves in the Confederate states.

Lind•bergh (lĭnd′bûrg′ *or* lĭn′bûrg′), **Charles Augustus.** 1902–1974. American aviator who made the first solo flight across the Atlantic Ocean (May 20–21, 1927). His wife, **Anne Morrow Lindbergh** (born 1906), accompanied him on many flights and is known for her books, including *North to the Orient* (1935).

lin•den (lĭn′dən) *n.* Any of various trees having heart-shaped leaves and clusters of fragrant yellowish flowers, often planted for shade. [First written down about 700 in Old English and spelled *lind*.]

line[1] (līn) *n.* **1.** The path traced by a moving point, having length but no thickness: *a curved line.* **2.a.** A thin continuous mark, as one made on paper by a pen or pencil. **b.** Something resembling such a mark: *a brow furrowed with deep lines.* **c.** One of five parallel marks that make a staff in music. **3.** A border or boundary: *the county line; the line between courage and rashness.* **4.** A group of people or things arranged in a row: *a line of customers at the counter.* **5.** Often **lines.** Outline, contour, or styling: *the lines of a new car.* **6.a.** A row of words printed or written across a page or column. **b.** A brief letter: *I'll drop you a line.* **7.a.** A single verse of poetry. **b. lines.** The words recited by an actor in a play. **8.** A cable, rope, cord, or wire: *a fishing line.* **9.** A course or direction; a route: *the line of flight of migrating birds.* **10.** A general method or way of doing something: *Let's continue our present line in teaching safety at school.* **11.** A series of persons or things following one another in time: *the line of French kings.* **12.** Ancestry or lineage: *Her family line goes back to China.* **13.a.** A system of transportation: *a bus line.* **b.** A branch of a transportation system: *all lines go through Detroit.* **c.** A railroad track. **14.a.** A wire or system of wires connecting telephone or telegraph stations. **b.** A telephone connection: *Their line is busy.* **15.** A pipe, channel, or wire used to carry water, gas, or electricity from one point to another. **16.** A range of merchandise having several styles and sizes: *a line of fashionable dresses.* **17.** A person's trade or occupation: *What is your line of work?* **18.** The range of a person's ability or interests: *That sort of work is out of my line.* **19.** In football, the players stationed at the line of scrimmage as a play begins. **20.** The battle area or combat troops closest to the enemy: *The wounded were taken behind the lines.* **21.** *Informal.* False or exaggerated talk intended to impress or deceive a listener: *Disgraced politicians often try to feed voters a line about reforming themselves.* —*v.* **lined, lin•ing, lines.** —*tr.* **1.** To mark or cover with lines: *line paper.* **2.** To form a line along: *Thousands of people lined the sidewalks.* **3.** To place in a line or row: *Line the children up by the door.* **4.** In baseball, to hit (a ball) hard in a straight line. —*intr.* In baseball, to hit a line drive: *The batter lined out to the shortstop.* —***idioms.*** **all along the line.** **1.** In every place. **2.** At every stage or moment: *Building the house has been difficult all along the line.* **in line for.** Next in order for: *She's in line for a promotion.* **line up.** **1.** To arrange in or form a line. **2.** To organize and make ready: *We lined up support for a class in scuba diving.* **out of line.** **1.** Uncalled for; improper: *That remark was out of line.* **2.** Unruly and out of control. [First written down before 900 in Old English and spelled *līne*, from Latin *līnum*, thread, linen.]

line[2] (līn) *tr.v.* **lined, lin•ing, lines.** **1.** To cover the inside surface of with a layer of material: *The tailor lined the coat with satin.* **2.** To serve as a lining for or in: *Tissue paper lined the box.* **3.** To fill plentifully: *The store shelves were lined with toys.* [First written down about 1387 in Middle English and spelled *linen*, from Old English *līn*, linen.]

lin•e•age (lĭn′ē ĭj) *n.* **1.** Direct descent from a particular ancestor; ancestry. **2.** All of the descendants of a particular ancestor.

lin•e•al (lĭn′ē əl) *adj.* **1.** Being in the direct line of

Abraham Lincoln
1863 photograph
by Alexander Gardner
(1821–1882)

Charles Lindbergh and Anne Morrow Lindbergh
Photographed in 1931
on their flight to the Far East

ă	pat	oi	boy
ā	pay	ou	out
âr	care	o͝o	took
ä	father	o͞o	boot
ĕ	pet	ŭ	cut
ē	be	ûr	urge
ĭ	pit	th	thin
ī	pie	*th*	this
îr	pier	hw	whoop
ŏ	pot	zh	vision
ō	toe	ə	about
ô	paw	N	*French* bon

descent: *Without children, the couple had no lineal descendants.* **2.** Linear. **—lin′e•al•ly** *adv.*

lin•e•a•ment (lĭn′ē ə mənt) *n.* A distinctive outline or feature, especially of a face.

lin•e•ar (lĭn′ē ər) *adj.* **1.** Of, relating to, or resembling a line, especially a straight line: *linear distance.* **2.** Consisting of or using lines: *a linear design.* **3.** Of or relating to length: *The meter is a unit of linear measurement.* **—lin′e•ar•ly** *adv.*

linear accelerator *n.* An accelerator for particles, such as electrons, protons, or ions, in which the particles are accelerated in a straight line by means of alternating negative and positive impulses from electric fields.

linear equation *n.* An equation, as $y = 4x + 3$, for example, in which the terms involving variables are of the first degree, so called because the graph of such an equation is a straight line.

linear measure *n.* **1.** Measurement of length. **2.** A system of units, such as a foot and mile, used for measuring length.

line•back•er (līn′băk′ər) *n.* In football, a player stationed just behind a team's defensive line.

line drive *n.* In baseball, a batted ball hit so that it follows a line nearly parallel to the ground.

line•man (līn′mən) *n.* **1.** A person who installs or repairs telephone, telegraph, or electric power lines. **2.** A person who inspects and repairs railroad tracks. **3.** In football, a player positioned on the line of scrimmage.

lin•en (lĭn′ən) *n.* **1.a.** Strong smooth cloth made of flax fibers. **b.** Thread spun from fibers of the flax plant. **2.** Also **linens.** Articles or garments, such as sheets, tablecloths, or shirts, made of linen or a similar material, such as cotton. [First written down before 1325 in Middle English, from Old English *līnen*, made of flax, probably from Latin *līnum*, flax.]

line of force *n., pl.* **lines of force.** An imaginary line in a field of electric or magnetic force that indicates the direction in which the force is acting.

line of scrimmage *n., pl.* **lines of scrimmage.** An imaginary line across a football field on which the ball rests and at which the teams line up for a new play.

lin•er[1] (lī′nər) *n.* **1.** A person or thing that draws lines. **2.** A commercial ship or airplane carrying passengers on a regular route. **3.** In baseball, a line drive.

lin•er[2] (lī′nər) *n.* **1.** A person who makes or puts in linings. **2.** Something used as a lining.

line segment *n.* The part of a line lying between two given points on the line.

lines•man (līnz′mən) *n.* **1.** An official who assists a referee in football, ice hockey, tennis, and other sports. **2.** A person who installs or repairs telephone, telegraph, or electric power lines.

Carolus Linnaeus

line spectrum *n.* A spectrum produced by a luminous gas or vapor and consisting of a series of distinct, fairly narrow lines characteristically produced by the atoms of that gas or vapor.

line•up also **line-up** (līn′ŭp′) *n.* **1.a.** The members of a team chosen to start a game. **b.** A list of such players. **2.** A group of persons lined up, as for purposes of identification: *a police lineup.* **3.** A group of persons, organizations, or things enlisted for a specific purpose.

–ling[1] *suff.* A suffix that means: **1.** A person connected with: *earthling.* **2.** A person or thing having a specified quality: *hireling.* **3.** A person or thing that is small, young, or inferior: *duckling.*

–ling[2] *suff.* A suffix that means in a specified way or condition: *darkling.*

lin•ger (lĭng′gər) *intr.v.* **lin•gered, lin•ger•ing, lin•gers. 1.** To be slow in leaving: *The children lingered in the toy shop until closing.* See Synonyms at **stay**[1]. **2.** To continue or persist: *The taste of cherries lingered in my mouth.* **3.** To be slow in acting: *linger over a decision.* [First written down before 1325 in Middle English and spelled *lengeren*, from Old English *lengan*, to lengthen, prolong.]

lin•ge•rie (län′zhə rā′) *n.* Women's underclothes.

lin•go (lĭng′gō) *n., pl.* **lin•goes.** Language that is difficult to understand, as the jargon of a special group: *Doctors have a lingo all their own.* [First written down in 1660 in Modern English, from Latin *lingua*, language.]

lin•gua fran•ca (lĭng′gwə frăng′kə) *n., pl.* **lingua fran•cas** (frăng′kəz). A language used between people who normally speak different languages.

lin•gual (*lĭng′gwəl*) *adj.* **1.** Of or relating to the tongue. **2.** Produced by the tongue, as the letter *l.*

lin•guist (lĭng′gwĭst) *n.* **1.** A person who speaks several languages fluently. **2.** A specialist in linguistics. [First written down in 1588 in Modern English, from Latin *lingua*, language.]

lin•guis•tic (lĭng gwĭs′tĭk) *adj.* Of or relating to language or linguistics. **—lin•guis′ti•cal•ly** *adv.*

lin•guis•tics (lĭng gwĭs′tĭks) *n. (used with a singular verb).* The study of the nature and structure of human speech.

lin•i•ment (lĭn′ə mənt) *n.* A liquid medicine rubbed on the skin to soothe pain or relieve stiffness, as from bruises or sore muscles.

lin•ing (lī′nĭng) *n.* **1.** An inner covering or coating: *the stomach lining; the lining in a jacket.* **2.** Material used as such a covering or coating.

link (lĭngk) *n.* **1.a.** One of the rings or loops forming a chain. **b.** One of a series of connected units: *a sausage link.* **2.** Something that joins or connects: *a new rail link between the city and the airport.* *—v.* **linked, link•ing, links.** *—tr.v.* To connect or join with or as if with a link: *The telephone links the far corners of the globe.* See Synonyms at **join.** *—intr.v.* To become connected or coupled: *The two expeditions plan to link up by radio.* [First written down before 1415 in Middle English and spelled *linke*, of Scandinavian origin; akin to Old Norse *hlekkr*.]

link•age (lĭng′kĭj) *n.* **1.** The act or process of linking. **2.** The state or condition of being linked. **3.** A system or an arrangement of machine parts, such as rods, springs, or pivots, used to transmit power or motion.

link•ing verb (lĭng′kĭng) *n.* A verb that connects the subject of a sentence with a predicate noun or adjective; a copula. For example, the verbs *are* and *seem* are linking verbs in the sentences *The children are happy* and *You seem sleepy.* —SEE NOTE at **adjective.**

links (lĭngks) *pl.n.* A golf course. [First written down in 1728 in Modern English, from Old English *hlinc*, ridge.]

❑ *These sound alike:* **links, lynx** (wild cat).

Lin•nae•us (lĭ nē′əs *or* lĭ nā′əs), **Carolus.** 1707–1778. Swedish botanist who founded the modern classification system for plants and animals.

lin•net (lĭn′ĭt) *n.* A small brownish finch of Europe, Asia, and Africa.

li•no•le•um (lĭ nō′lē əm) *n.* A sturdy washable material made in sheets by pressing a mixture of hot linseed oil, rosin, powdered cork, and coloring onto a cloth backing, used especially for covering floors.

lin•seed (lĭn′sēd′) *n.* The seed or seeds of the flax plant, pressed to obtain linseed oil.

linseed oil *n.* A yellow oil extracted from flax seeds that thickens and hardens when exposed to air and is used in paints, varnishes, printing inks, and linoleum.

lin•sey-wool•sey (lĭn′zē wo͝ol′zē) *n., pl.* **lin•sey-**

wool•seys. A coarse fabric of cotton or linen woven with wool.

lint (lĭnt) *n.* **1.** Clinging bits of fiber and fluff from a material: *My shirt was covered with lint from the wash.* **2.** Downy material scraped from linen cloth and used to dress wounds. [First written down in 1392 in Middle English and spelled *linet*, from Latin *līnum*, flax.]

lin•tel (lĭn′tl) *n.* The horizontal beam that forms the top of a door or window frame and supports the structure above it.

li•on (lī′ən) *n.* **1.** A very large, meat-eating, wild cat of Africa and India, having a tawny coat and a heavy mane around the neck and shoulders in the male. **2.** A mountain lion. **3.** A very brave person. **4.** A famous person; a celebrity. ***—idiom.*** **lion's share.** The greatest or best part. [First written down about 1175 in Middle English, from Greek *leōn*.]

li•on•ess (lī′ə nĭs) *n.* A female lion.

li•on•heart•ed (lī′ən här′tĭd) *adj.* Extraordinarily courageous.

li•on•ize (lī′ə nīz′) *tr.v.* **li•on•ized, li•on•iz•ing, li•on•iz•es.** To look upon or treat as very important: *The public lionized the popular author.*

lip (lĭp) *n.* **1.** Either of the two fleshy muscular folds of tissue that together surround the mouth. **2.** The edge or rim that surrounds an opening: *the lip of a pitcher.* **3.** Either of the two parts into which the corolla or calyx of certain plants is divided: *the lips of a snapdragon blossom.* **4.** *Slang.* Disrespectful talk. [First written down about 1000 in Old English and spelled *lippa*.]

lip•ase (lĭp′ās′ *or* lī′pās′) *n.* An enzyme that promotes the decomposition of fats to form glycerol and fatty acids.

lip•id (lĭp′ĭd *or* lī′pĭd) also **lip•ide** (lĭp′īd′ *or* lī′pīd′) *n.* Any of a large group of organic compounds, including fats, oils, waxes, and sterols, that have an oily feeling and are insoluble in water. They are a source of stored energy and are a component of cell membranes.

lip-read (lĭp′rēd′) *intr.v.* **lip-read** (lĭp′rĕd′), **lip-read•ing, lip-reads.** To interpret utterances by lip reading.

lip reading *n.* The skill of understanding unheard speech by interpreting movements of the lips and face of the speaker.

lip service *n.* Agreement or respect expressed in words but without sincerity or the intention of doing anything: *He paid lip service to the suggestion that we should volunteer to clean the park.*

lip•stick (lĭp′stĭk′) *n.* A stick of waxy coloring matter applied to the lips and enclosed in a small case.

liq•ue•fac•tion (lĭk′wə făk′shən) *n.* **1.** The act or process of liquefying. **2.** The condition of being liquefied.

liq•ue•fy (lĭk′wə fī′) *tr. & intr.v.* **liq•ue•fied, liq•ue•fy•ing, liq•ue•fies.** To make or become liquid: *Butter liquefies at low heat.* **—liq′ue•fi′er** *n.*

li•queur (lĭ kûr′ *or* lĭ kyŏŏr′) *n.* A sweet syrupy alcoholic beverage usually served after dinner.

liq•uid (lĭk′wĭd) *n.* A substance that is neither a solid nor a gas, with molecules that move freely within the container in which it is put. The volume of a liquid usually remains unchanged or changes only slightly under pressure. *—adj.* **1.** Of or being a liquid: *a liquid rocket fuel.* **2.** Clear and shining like water. **3.** Flowing without abrupt breaks: *a cascade of liquid piano notes.* **4.** Readily converted into cash: *liquid assets such as savings bonds.* [First written down before 1384 in Middle English, from Latin *liquidus*, from *liquēre*, to be liquid.]

liquid air *n.* A very cold liquid formed when air is put under great pressure and cooled. It is used as a source of nitrogen and oxygen and as a refrigerant.

liq•ui•date (lĭk′wĭ dāt′) *tr.v.* **liq•ui•dat•ed, liq•ui•dat•ing, liq•ui•dates.** **1.** To pay off or settle: *liquidate one's debts.* **2.** To close down (a business firm) by settling its accounts and dividing up any remaining assets. **3.** To do away with; put an end to: *Development has liquidated vast tracts of forest.* **4.** To put to death; kill. **—liq′ui•da′tion** *n.*

li•quid•i•ty (lĭ kwĭd′ĭ tē) *n.* **1.** The quality or condition of being liquid. **2.** The quality of being readily convertible to cash.

liquid measure *n.* A system of units for measuring the volume of liquids, as in pints, gallons, or liters.

liquid oxygen *n.* A cold transparent liquid formed when oxygen is put under great pressure and cooled. It is used in rocket fuel and explosives.

liq•uor (lĭk′ər) *n.* **1.** An alcoholic beverage, such as whiskey or gin, made by distillation rather than by fermentation. **2.** A juice or broth produced in cooking or in which food is canned.

li•ra (lîr′ə) *n., pl.* **li•re** (lîr′ā) or **li•ras.** The basic monetary unit of Italy, Malta, San Marino, Turkey, and Vatican City. —SEE NOTE.

Lis•bon (lĭz′bən). The capital and largest city of Portugal, in the western part of the country on an inlet of the Atlantic Ocean. It was almost destroyed by a major earthquake in 1755. Population, 807,167.

lisle (līl) *n.* A fine, smooth, tightly twisted cotton thread or a fabric knitted from it, often used to make underwear, socks, and gloves.

lisp (lĭsp) *n.* A speech defect in which sounds represented by *s* and *z* are pronounced *th* as in *thin* and *then*. *—intr. & tr.v.* **lisped, lisp•ing, lisps.** To speak or say with a lisp.

lis•some also **lis•som** (lĭs′əm) *adj.* Moving or bending easily; lithe. **lis′some•ly** *adv.*

list[1] (lĭst) *n.* A series of names, words, or other items written or printed one after the other: *a guest list; a shopping list.* *—tr.v.* **list•ed, list•ing, lists.** To make a list of; include in a list: *The hotel's guests are listed in the register.* [First written down in 1602 in Modern English, from Old Italian *lista*, of Germanic origin.]

list[2] (lĭst) *n.* A tilt to one side, as of a ship: *a ship's sudden list to starboard.* *—intr. & tr.v.* **list•ed, list•ing, lists.** To lean or cause to lean to one side, as a ship; heel: *The ship listed heavily in the sudden gust of wind.* [First written down in 1626 in Modern English and spelled *lust*.]

list[3] (lĭst) *intr. & tr.v.* **list•ed, list•ing, lists.** *Archaic.* To listen to; hear.

lis•ten (lĭs′ən) *intr.v.* **lis•tened, lis•ten•ing, lis•tens.** **1.** To make an effort to hear something: *I always listen to music in the evening.* **2.** To pay attention; heed: *No one listened to my advice.* ***—idiom.*** **listen in.** **1.** To listen to a conversation between others; eavesdrop. **2.** To tune in and listen to a broadcast. [First written down before 800 in Old English and spelled *hlysnan*.] **—lis′ten•er** *n.*

list•ing (lĭs′tĭng) *n.* **1.** An entry in a list or directory: *a telephone listing.* **2.** A list: *a listing of dentists.*

list•less (lĭst′lĭs) *adj.* Lacking energy or enthusiasm; lethargic: *The long days indoors left us feeling dull and listless.* **—list′less•ly** *adv.* **—list′less•ness** *n.*

list price *n.* A basic price published in a price list, often reduced by a dealer.

Liszt (lĭst), **Franz.** 1811–1886. Hungarian composer and pianist whose compositions include the *Dante Symphony* (1856).

lit[1] (lĭt) *v.* A past tense and a past participle of **light**[1].

lit[2] (lĭt) *v.* A past tense and a past participle of **light**[2].

lit. *abbr.* An abbreviation of: **1.** Liter. **2.** Literature.

lit•a•ny (lĭt′n ē) *n., pl.* **lit•a•nies.** **1.** A liturgical prayer consisting of phrases recited by a leader al-

lion
Female and male lions

Word History: lira

Many of us know that the **lira** is the unit of currency in Italy. As you would expect, the word *lira* is Italian, and it comes from the Latin noun *lībra*, "a pound." The English abbreviation for *pound*, **lb.**, is an abbreviation of *libra*, as is the abbreviation for the British pound sterling, £, which is a cursive form of the letter *L* with a line through it.

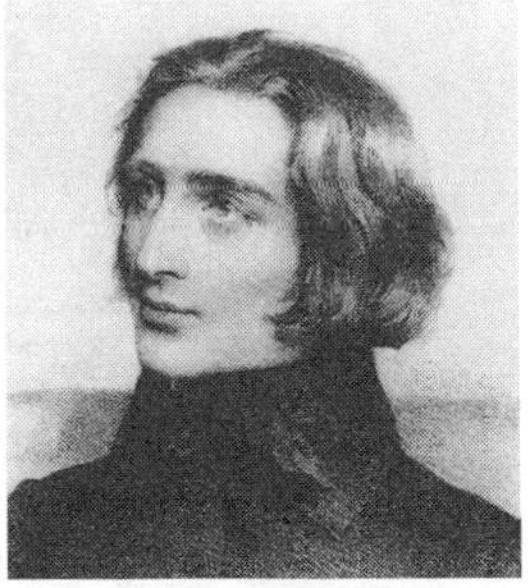

Franz Liszt

ă	**pat**	oi	**boy**
ā	**pay**	ou	**out**
âr	**care**	ŏŏ	**took**
ä	**father**	ōō	**boot**
ĕ	**pet**	ŭ	**cut**
ē	**be**	ûr	**urge**
ĭ	**pit**	th	**thin**
ī	**pie**	*th*	**this**
îr	**pier**	hw	**whoop**
ŏ	**pot**	zh	**vision**
ō	**toe**	ə	**about**
ô	**paw**	N	*French* **bon**

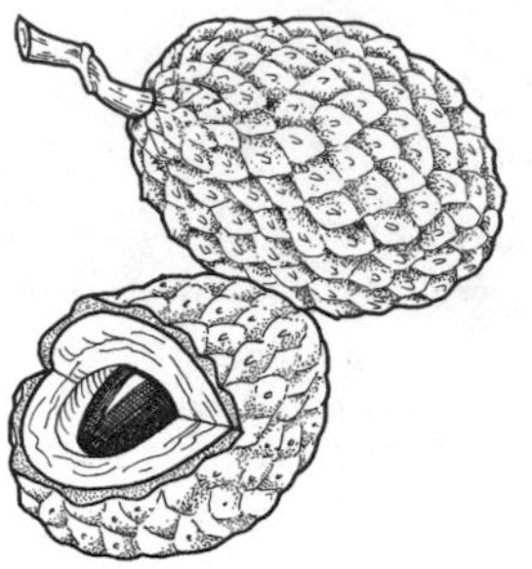

litchi

litter
Boxer puppies

ternating with responses by the congregation. **2.** A similar repetitive series: *Each negotiator recited a familiar litany of grievances and demands.*

li•tchi also **li•chee** (lē′chē) *n.* **1.** A sweet edible fruit of a tree that grows in China, encased in a hard red shell. **2.** The tree that bears such fruit.

li•ter (lē′tər) *n.* A unit of volume that is equal to the volume of one kilogram of pure water at the temperature of its greatest density. A liter is equal to about 1.056 liquid quarts or 0.908 dry quart. See table at **measurement.**

lit•er•a•cy (lĭt′ər ə sē) *n.* **1.** The ability to read or write. **2.** The understanding or knowledge a person has in a particular field: *computer literacy.*

lit•er•al (lĭt′ər əl) *adj.* **1.** Following the usual or exact meaning of a word or group of words: *The literal interpretation of a poem is often too narrow.* **2.** Corresponding word for word with the original: *a literal translation.* **3.** Not exaggerated; factual: *a literal account of events.* [First written down before 1397 in Middle English, from Latin *littera*, letter.]

lit•er•al•ly (lĭt′ər ə lē) *adv.* **1.** In a literal manner: *Translated literally "carte blanche" means "blank card."* **2.** Really; actually: *Literally millions of lives were saved by the vaccine.*

lit•er•ar•y (lĭt′ə rĕr′ē) *adj.* **1.** Of or relating to literature: *a literary critic.* **2.** Of or relating to writers or the profession of writing.

lit•er•ate (lĭt′ər ĭt) *adj.* **1.** Able to read and write. **2.** Familiar with literature; literary. **3.** Having knowledge in a particular field: *literate in architecture.* —*n.* A person who can read and write.

lit•er•a•ture (lĭt′ər ə cho͝or′ *or* lĭt′ər ə chər) *n.* **1.** A body of writing in prose or verse, especially writing having recognized artistic value: *has read much American literature of the 20th century.* **2.** The art or occupation of a literary writer. **3.** The study of literature. **4.** A body of writing on a given subject: *medical literature.* **5.** Printed material: *election campaign literature.*

lithe (lī*th*) *adj.* **lith•er, lith•est.** Easily bent; supple: *a lithe dancer.* **—lithe′ly** *adv.* **—lithe′ness** *n.*

lith•i•um (lĭth′ē əm) *n.* *Symbol* **Li** A soft, silvery metallic element that is highly reactive and occurs in small quantities in some minerals. Lithium is the lightest of all metals and is used in lubricants, ceramics, and welding flux. Atomic number 3. See table at **element.**

lith•o•graph (lĭth′ə grăf′) *n.* A print produced by lithography. —*tr.v.* **lith•o•graphed, lith•o•graph•ing, lith•o•graphs.** To produce by lithography. **—li•thog′ra•pher** (lĭ thŏg′rə fər) *n.* **—lith′o•graph′ic** *adj.*

li•thog•ra•phy (lĭ thŏg′rə fē) *n.* A printing process in which an image is drawn on a flat printing surface such as a metal plate and treated to hold ink. The other areas of the surface are treated to repel ink.

lith•o•sphere (lĭth′ə sfîr′) *n.* **1.** The solid part of the earth, as distinguished from the air and water. **2.** The rocky crust and upper mantle of the earth.

Lith•u•a•ni•a (lĭth′o͞o ā′nē ə). A country of northern Europe on the Baltic Sea south of Latvia. Lithuania was perhaps settled as early as 1500 B.C. and was part of the U.S.S.R. from 1940 to 1991. Capital, Vilnius. Population, 3,570,000.

Lith•u•a•ni•an (lĭth′o͞o ā′nē ən) *n.* **1.** A native or inhabitant of Lithuania. **2.** The Baltic language of the Lithuanians. —*adj.* Of or relating to Lithuania, its people, language, or culture.

lit•i•gant (lĭt′ĭ gənt) *n.* A person who is engaged in a lawsuit.

lit•i•gate (lĭt′ĭ gāt′) *intr.v.* **lit•i•gat•ed, lit•i•gat•ing, lit•i•gates.** To carry on a lawsuit.

lit•i•ga•tion (lĭt′ĭ gā′shən) *n.* **1.** The process of carrying on a lawsuit: *prolonged litigation over a contested will.* **2.** A lawsuit.

lit•mus (lĭt′məs) *n.* A dye, derived from certain lichens, that changes to red in an acid solution and to blue in an alkaline solution. [First written down in 1324 in Middle English and spelled *litmose*, of Scandinavian origin.]

litmus paper *n.* Paper that has been treated with litmus, used to distinguish acid and alkaline solutions.

li•tre (lē′tər) *n. Chiefly British.* Variant of **liter.**

lit•ter (lĭt′ər) *n.* **1.** Carelessly scattered scraps of paper or other waste material. **2.** The young born to a mammal at a single time. **3.a.** Material, such as straw or hay, spread for animals to sleep on. **b.** Loose material, especially clay, spread to absorb the urine and feces of an animal. **4.** A stretcher used to carry a sick or wounded person. **5.** A couch mounted on framework covered with curtains and used to carry a person from place to place. —*v.* **lit•tered, lit•ter•ing, lit•ters.** —*tr.* **1.** To make untidy by scattering things about: *The crowds of revelers littered the street with trash.* **2.** To give birth to (young). —*intr.* **1.** To scatter bits of trash. **2.** To give birth to a litter.

lit•ter•bug (lĭt′ər bŭg′) *n. Informal.* A person who litters public areas with trash.

lit•tle (lĭt′l) *adj.* **lit•tler, lit•tlest** or **less** (lĕs), **least** (lēst). **1.** Small in size, quantity, or degree: *a little book; little money.* **2.** Short in duration: *We have little time left.* **3.** Young or younger: *my little brother.* **4.** Unimportant; trivial: *a little problem.* **5.** Narrow; mean: *a little mind interested only in being pleased.* —*adv.* **less, least. 1.** Not much: *He slept very little that night.* **2.** Not at all: *Little did the class realize the teacher planned a surprise test.* —*n.* **1.** A small amount: *I received only a little of what they owe.* **2.** A short distance or time: *waited a little.* **—*idioms.* a little.** Somewhat; a bit: *She feels a little better now.* **little by little.** By small degrees; gradually. [First written down about 725 in Old English and spelled *lȳtel*.]

Synonyms: little, small, miniature, tiny, wee. These adjectives all mean notably below average in size. *I am knitting a little blanket for the baby. The house would be too small for a large family but it's perfect for newlyweds. Grandmother served delicious miniature cakes at teatime. The recipe calls for a tiny pinch of baking powder. Dan feels a wee bit better now that he has had some rest.*
Antonym: big.

Little Bear *n.* Ursa Minor.

Little Dipper *n.* A group of seven stars in the constellation Ursa Minor that forms the outline of a dipper.

Little League *n.* An organization of baseball teams for children nine to twelve years old.

Little Rock. The capital and largest city of Arkansas, in the central part of the state west of the Mississippi River. It became the state capital in 1836. Population, 175,795.

li•tur•gi•cal (lĭ tûr′jĭ kəl) *adj.* Of, relating to, or used in liturgy.

lit•ur•gy (lĭt′ər jē) *n., pl.* **lit•ur•gies.** The established form for public Christian ceremonies.

liv•a•ble also **live•a•ble** (lĭv′ə bəl) *adj.* **1.** Suitable for living in: *a very livable house.* **2.** Bearable; endurable: *a life of hardship that was barely livable.*

live[1] (lĭv) *v.* **lived, liv•ing, lives.** —*intr.* **1.** To be alive; exist: *Birch trees live only in cold climates.* **2.** To continue to remain alive: *My parents have lived for half a century.* **3.** To support oneself; subsist: *It takes hard work to live off the land.* **4.** To reside or dwell: *They live in an apartment.* **5.** To conduct one's life in a certain manner: *live happily.* **6.** To enjoy life to the utmost: *It is difficult to live in the midst of hardship.* —*tr.* **1.** To spend or pass (one's life): *I have lived my whole life in this town.* **2.** To practice in one's life: *I have always tried to live my ideals.* —***idioms.*** **live down.** To overcome or reduce the shame of (a misdeed, for example) over a period of time. **live up to. 1.** To live or act in accordance with: *I try to live up to my ideals.* **2.** To prove equal to: *The new car did not live up to our expectations.* **3.** To carry out; fulfill: *She lived up to her part of the bargain.* **live with.** To put up with; resign oneself to: *We'll just have to live with the situation.* [First written down about 725 in Old English and spelled *libban, lifian.*]

live[2] (līv) *adj.* **1.** Alive; living: *live animals in the circus.* **2.** Glowing; burning: *live coals.* **3.** Active and energetic: *a live and forceful personality.* **4.** Carrying electric current: *a live circuit.* **5.** Not yet exploded, but capable of being fired: *live ammunition.* **6.** Of current interest or importance: *a live issue.* **7.** Broadcast while actually being performed: *a live television program.* [First written down in 1542 in Modern English, short for *alive.*]

live•li•hood (līv′lē ho͝od′) *n.* The means of supporting life; a way of earning a living: *She earns her livelihood by designing posters.*

live•long (lĭv′lông′ *or* līv′lŏng′) *adj.* Whole; entire: *all the livelong day.*

live•ly (līv′lē) *adj.* **live•li•er, live•li•est. 1.** Full of life, energy, or activity: *a lively baby.* **2.** Full of spirit; exciting: *a lively discussion.* **3.** Tending to bounce or rebound strongly: *a lively soccer ball.* —*adv.* **live•lier, live•liest.** In a lively manner: *The whirling dancers stepped lively about the floor.* —**live′li•ness** *n.*

li•ven (lī′vən) *tr. & intr.v.* **li•vened, li•ven•ing, li•vens.** To make or become lively: *Music livens up a party. The party livened up as more guests arrived.*

live oak (līv) *n.* Any of several evergreen oak trees of the southern United States.

liv•er[1] (lĭv′ər) *n.* **1.** A large, reddish-brown, glandular organ located in the abdomen of vertebrates. The liver secretes bile and acts in the formation of blood and in the absorption and storage of vitamins, minerals, and sugar. **2.** A similar organ of invertebrate animals. **3.** The liver of an animal used as food. [First written down before 899 in Old English and spelled *lifer.*]

liv•er[2] (lĭv′ər) *n.* A person who lives in a specified manner: *city livers.*

liv•er•ied (lĭv′ə rēd *or* lĭv′rēd) *adj.* Wearing livery: *a liveried footman.*

Liv•er•pool (lĭv′ər po͞ol′). A borough of northwest England on the Irish Sea north of Wales. Population, 518,900.

liv•er•wort (lĭv′ər wûrt′ *or* lĭv′ər wôrt′) *n.* Any of numerous small green plants that are related to the mosses and do not bear flowers. Liverworts grow usually in damp areas.

liv•er•wurst (lĭv′ər wûrst′ *or* lĭv′ər wo͝orst′) *n.* A type of sausage containing mostly ground liver.

liv•er•y (lĭv′ə rē *or* lĭv′rē) *n., pl.* **liv•er•ies. 1.** A uniform worn by servants: *a chauffeur dressed in livery.* **2.** The distinctive clothing worn by members of a specific group. **3.** The stabling and care of horses for a fee. **4.** A livery stable.

livery stable *n.* A stable that boards horses and keeps horses and carriages for hire.

lives (līvz) *n.* Plural of **life.**

live•stock (līv′stŏk′) *n.* Domestic animals, such as cattle, horses, sheep, or pigs, raised and kept, as on a farm.

live wire (līv) *n.* **1.** A wire that is charged with an electric current. **2.** *Slang.* An exciting, energetic, or imaginative person.

liv•id (lĭv′ĭd) *adj.* **1.** Discolored, as from a bruise; black-and-blue. **2.** Pale or ashen, as from shock. **3.** Extremely angry; furious. —**liv′id•ly** *adv.*

liv•ing (lĭv′ĭng) *adj.* **1.** Having life; alive: *famous living persons.* **2.** Of or relating to life: *the difficult living conditions of the arctic winter.* **3.** Currently existing or in use: *a living language.* **4.** Enough to live on: *a living wage.* **5.** True to life: *a portrait that is the living image of my parents.* —*n.* **1.** The condition of being alive: *the high cost of living.* **2.** A manner or style of life: *We prefer simple living.* **3.** A means of maintaining life; livelihood: *They make their living by fishing.*

living room *n.* A room in a household for entertaining guests and general use.

Liv•ing•stone (lĭv′ĭng stən), **David.** 1813–1873. Scottish missionary and explorer in Africa. With Henry M. Stanley he tried to find the source of the Nile.

liz•ard (lĭz′ərd) *n.* Any of numerous reptiles having a scaly, often slender body, a tapering tail, and usually four legs. The iguana and chameleon are lizards. [First written down about 1378 in Middle English and spelled *lusarde,* from Latin *lacertus.*]

Lju•blja•na (lo͞o′blē ä′nə). The capital and largest city of Slovenia, in the central part west-northwest of Zagrab, Croatia. Population, 205,600.

lla•ma (lä′mə) *n.* A South American mammal related to the camel, raised for its soft fleecy wool and used for carrying loads. [First written down in 1600 in Modern English, from Spanish, from Quechua.]

lla•no (lä′nō *or* lăn′ō) *n., pl.* **lla•nos.** A broad, grassy, almost treeless plain, as in South America and the southern Great Plains of the United States.

lo (lō) *interj.* An expression used to attract attention.
❑ *These sound alike:* **lo, low[1]** (not high), **low[2]** (bellow).

load (lōd) *n.* **1.** The weight or force supported by a structure or some part of it. **2.a.** Something that is carried, as by a vehicle, a person, or an animal: *a load of firewood.* **b.** The quantity or amount carried: *a wagon with a full load of hay.* **3.** The amount or work required of or done by a person or machine: *The student had a heavy load of homework.* **4.** A single charge of ammunition for a gun. **5.** Something that oppresses or burdens: *That's a load off my mind.* **6.** The mechanical resistance that a machine must overcome. **7.** The power output of a generator or power plant. **8.** *Informal.* A great number or amount. Often used in the plural: *invited to loads of parties.* —*v.* **load•ed, load•ing, loads.** —*tr.* **1.** To put (something) into or onto a structure or vehicle: *load grain onto a train.* **2.** To put something into or onto (a structure or vehicle): *load a ship.* **3.** To provide or fill nearly to overflowing: *Our hosts loaded the table with food.* **4.** To weigh down; burden: *loaded the students with homework.* **5.a.** To put (something necessary) into a device: *load film into a camera.* **b.** To put something necessary into (a device): *load a camera with film.* **c.** To put (a computer program or data) into a computer's memory. **d.** To put ammunition into (a firearm). —*intr.* **1.** To receive a load: *The ship loaded in port.* **2.** To charge a firearm with ammunition. [First written down about 725 in Old English and spelled *lād,* course, way.] —**load′er** *n.*
❑ *These sound alike:* **load, lode** (ore deposit).

load•ed (lō′dĭd) *adj.* **1.** Carrying a load. **2.** Intended to trick or trap by carrying hidden implications: *a loaded question.* **3.** *Slang.* Very wealthy.

load•star (lōd′stär′) *n.* Variant of **lodestar.**

load•stone (lōd′stōn′) *n.* Variant of **lodestone.**

loaf[1] (lōf) *n., pl.* **loaves** (lōvz). **1.** A shaped mass of

David Livingstone

llama

ă pat		oi	boy
ā pay		ou	out
âr care		o͝o	took
ä father		o͞o	boot
ĕ pet		ŭ	cut
ē be		ûr	urge
ĭ pit		th	thin
ī pie		*th*	this
îr pier		hw	whoop
ŏ pot		zh	vision
ō toe		ə	about
ô paw		N	*French* bon

bread baked in one piece. **2.** A shaped mass of food: *a meat loaf.* [First written down before 725 in Old English and spelled *hlāf.*]

loaf[2] (lōf) *intr.v.* **loafed, loaf•ing, loafs.** To spend time lazily or aimlessly; idle: *We loafed all morning accomplishing little.* [First written down in 1835 in American English, probably from *land-loafer,* a vagabond.]

loaf•er (lō′fər) *n.* A person who spends time lazily or idly; an idler.

Loaf•er (lō′fər). A trademark for a shoe that has a broad heel and no laces.

loam (lōm) *n.* Soil composed of sand, clay, silt, and decayed plant matter. **—loam′y** *adj.*

loan (lōn) *n.* **1.** The act of lending: *the loan of a raincoat to a friend.* **2.a.** Something lent for temporary use: *The lamp is a loan from my neighbor.* **b.** A sum of money lent at interest. *—tr.v.* **loaned, loan•ing, loans.** To lend: *Libraries loan books to the public.* —SEE NOTE at **borrow.**

❑ *These sound alike:* **loan, lone** (solitary).

loan word or **loan•word** (lōn′wûrd′) *n.* A word that has been borrowed from a foreign language; for example, *encore, spaghetti,* and *sombrero* are loan words in English.

loath (lōth *or* lō*th*) *adj.* Not willing; reluctant; averse: *They were loath to accept the offer of help from their rivals.*

loathe (lō*th*) *tr.v.* **loathed, loath•ing, loathes.** To dislike greatly; detest: *I loathe cleaning the bathroom.*

loath•ing (lō′*th*ĭng) *n.* Extreme dislike; abhorrence.

loath•some (lō*th*′səm *or* lōth′səm) *adj.* Detestable; abhorrent. **—loath′some•ly** *adv.* **—loath′some•ness** *n.*

loaves (lōvz) *n.* Plural of **loaf[1].**

lob (lŏb) *tr.v.* **lobbed, lob•bing, lobs.** To hit, throw, or propel (a ball) in a high arc. *—n.* A ball hit or thrown in a high arc.

lob•by (lŏb′ē) *n., pl.* **lob•bies. 1.** An entrance hall or a waiting room in a hotel, an apartment house, or a theater. **2.** A group of persons who try to influence lawmakers in favor of a cause. *—v.* **lob•bied, lob•by•ing, lob•bies.** *—intr.* To try to influence lawmakers for or against a cause: *Industry groups often lobby against antipollution laws.* *—tr.* To seek to influence (lawmakers) in their voting: *lobbied Congress to approve the bill.*

lob•by•ist (lŏb′ē ĭst) *n.* A person who tries to influence lawmakers for or against a cause.

lobe (lōb) *n.* A rounded projecting part, as of a leaf or an organ of the body.

lobed (lōbd) *adj.* Having a lobe or lobes: *a lobed leaf.*

lo•be•li•a (lō bē′lē ə *or* lō bēl′yə) *n.* Any of numerous plants having clusters of blue, red, or purplish flowers. [First written down in 1739 in Modern English, after Matthias de *Lobel* (1538–1616), Flemish botanist and physician.]

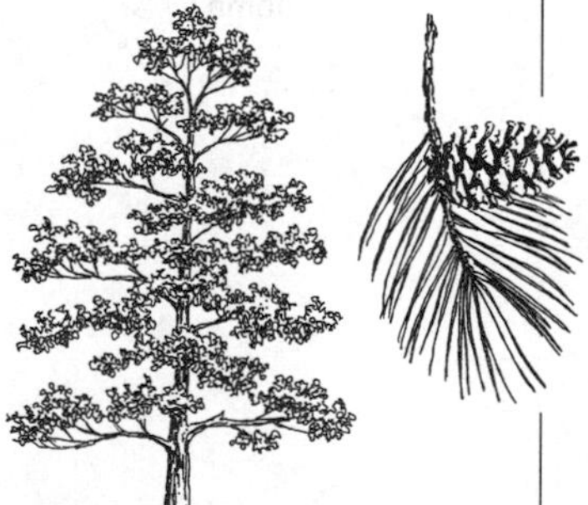

loblolly pine

lob•lol•ly pine (lŏb′lŏl′ē) *n.* **1.** A pine tree of the southeast United States, having coarse bark and strong wood used as lumber and for making paper pulp. **2.** The wood of this tree.

lob•ster (lŏb′stər) *n.* **1.** Any of several sea animals related to the crabs and shrimps, having a long hard-shelled body with five pairs of legs, the first pair of which is often modified into large claws. **2.** The meat of a lobster, used as food.

lobster pot *n.* A cage used for catching lobsters.

lo•cal (lō′kəl) *adj.* **1.** Of, relating to, or characteristic of a particular area or place: *local governments; a local storm.* **2.** Making all stops on a route; not express: *a local train.* **3.** Limited to one part of the body: *a local infection.* *—n.* **1.** A person who lives in a certain region or neighborhood: *The locals are concerned about the town's growth.* **2.** A local branch of an organization, especially of a labor union. **3.** A train or bus that makes all stops along its route. [First written down in 1392 in Middle English, from Latin *locus,* place.] **—lo′cal•ly** *adv.*

lo•cale (lō kăl′) *n.* A place, especially with reference to a particular event or circumstance: *The locale in many of Dickens' stories is London.*

lo•cal•ism (lō′kə lĭz′əm) *n.* A local custom, habit, or expression.

lo•cal•i•ty (lō kăl′ĭ tē) *n., pl.* **lo•cal•i•ties.** A certain neighborhood, place, or region.

lo•cal•ize (lō′kə līz′) *tr. & intr.v.* **lo•cal•ized, lo•cal•iz•ing, lo•cal•iz•es.** To confine or become restricted to a particular area: *The pain localized in my abdomen.*

lo•cate (lō′kāt′ *or* lō kāt′) *v.* **lo•cat•ed, lo•cat•ing, lo•cates.** *—tr.* **1.** To determine or show the position of: *locate Austria on a map.* **2.** To find by searching, inquiring, or examining: *locate information.* **3.** To place or situate: *We located the vegetables in a sunny corner of the garden.* *—intr.* To go and live somewhere; settle: *The family located in Iowa.*

lo•ca•tion (lō kā′shən) *n.* **1.** A place where something is or could be located; a site: *The view makes this a good location for a house.* **2.** The act or process of locating: *the location of water by drilling.* **3.** A site away from a motion-picture studio where filming occurs: *shot on location in Spain.*

loch (lŏKH *or* lŏk) *n. Scots.* **1.** A lake. **2.** An arm of the sea partly surrounded by land.

❑ *These sound alike:* **loch, lock[1]** (security device), **lock[2]** (hair).

lo•ci (lō′sī′) *n.* Plural of **locus.**

lock[1] (lŏk) *n.* **1.** A device used to fasten and secure something, such as a door or lid of a box, operated by a key, combination, or card. **2.** A section of a waterway, closed off with gates, in which a ship can be raised or lowered by pumping water in or out. **3.** A mechanism in a firearm for exploding the charge. **4.** One of several wrestling holds. *—v.* **locked, lock•ing, locks.** *—tr.* **1.** To fasten or secure with a lock or locks: *lock the door.* **2.** To confine by means of a lock: *The keepers locked the animals in their cages.* **3.** To fix in place so that movement is impossible: *The ship was locked in the ice.* **4.** To join or link firmly; intertwine: *The two friends locked arms and walked off.* *—intr.* **1.** To become tightly held, fastened, or secured: *The door locks automatically.* **2.** To become joined or intertwined: *The railroad cars locked as they came together.* [First written down about 750 in Old English and spelled *loc,* bolt, bar.]

❑ *These sound alike:* **lock[1]** (security device), **loch** (lake), **lock[2]** (hair).

lock[2] (lŏk) *n.* **1.** A strand or curl of hair. **2. locks.** The hair of the head: *the baby's red locks.* **3.** A small tuft of wool or cotton. [First written down about 700 in Old English and spelled *locc.*]

❑ *These sound alike:* **lock[2]** (hair), **loch** (lake), **lock[1]** (security device).

lock•er (lŏk′ər) *n.* **1.** A compartment, as in a gymnasium, that can be locked to keep clothes or valuables safe. **2.** A refrigerated cabinet or room for storing frozen foods. **3.** A flat trunk used for storage.

lock•et (lŏk′ĭt) *n.* A small ornamental metal case for a picture, a lock of hair, or another keepsake, usually worn on a chain around the neck.

lock•jaw (lŏk′jô′) *n.* Tetanus.

lock•out (lŏk′out′) *n.* The act of closing a factory or an office during a labor dispute in order to force employees to meet the employer's terms.

lock•smith (lŏk′smĭth′) *n.* A person who makes or repairs locks.

Lock•wood (lŏk′wo͝od′), **Belva Ann Bennett.** 1830–1917. American lawyer and suffragist. She was the first woman to practice law before the U.S. Supreme Court (1879).

lo•co•mo•tion (lō′kə mō′shən) *n.* The act or power of moving from place to place.

lo•co•mo•tive (lō′kə mō′tĭv) *n.* An engine that moves on its own power and is used to pull or push railroad cars. —*adj.* **1.** Able to move independently from place to place. **2.** Of or relating to locomotion.

lo•co•weed (lō′kō wēd′) *n.* Any of several western American plants that cause severe illness when eaten by cattle, sheep, and other grazing animals.

lo•cus (lō′kəs) *n., pl.* **lo•ci** (lō′sī′). **1.** A locality; a place. **2.** A curve, a surface, or another figure that contains all and only the points that satisfy a given mathematical condition.

lo•cust (lō′kəst) *n.* **1.** Any of numerous grasshoppers that travel in large swarms, often doing great damage to crops. **2.** Any of certain cicadas. **3.** Any of several trees having feathery leaves and drooping clusters of fragrant white flowers. [First written down before 1325 in Middle English, from Latin *locusta.*]

lo•cu•tion (lō kyo͞o′shən) *n.* **1.** A particular word, phrase, or expression. **2.** A manner or style of speaking; phraseology.

lode (lōd) *n.* A deposit or vein of a metal-bearing ore: *The miners dug into a rich lode of silver.*
❑ *These sound alike:* **lode, load** (weight).

lode•star also **load•star** (lōd′stär′) *n.* A star, especially Polaris, used as a guide or navigational point.

lode•stone also **load•stone** (lōd′stōn′) *n.* A piece of magnetite that acts like a magnet.

lodge (lŏj) *n.* **1.** A cottage or cabin, especially a temporary house used during a vacation or for recreational activity: *a fishing lodge.* **2.** Any of various Native American dwellings, such as a wigwam or a hogan. **3.** An inn. **4.** The den of certain animals, such as that of beavers. **5.** A branch or meeting place of a fraternal organization or secret society. —*v.* **lodged, lodg•ing, lodg•es.** —*tr.* **1.** To provide with a place to stay temporarily: *We can lodge many guests in our home.* **2.** To rent a room to: *We lodge local students at reasonable rates.* **3.** To fix or implant: *The surveyors lodged stakes in the ground at the corners of the property.* **4.** To present (a charge or complaint) to an appropriate official or office; register: *The angry tenant lodged a complaint with the housing agency.* —*intr.* **1.** To live in a place temporarily: *We lodged in an old hotel.* **2.** To live in a rented room or rooms: *He is lodging above a restaurant this year.* **3.** To be or become fixed or implanted: *The saw blade lodged in the wood.* [First written down in 1231 in Middle English and spelled *lhoge,* from Old French *loge,* of Germanic origin.]

lodg•er (lŏj′ər) *n.* A person who rents a room or rooms in another person's house.

lodg•ing (lŏj′ĭng) *n.* **1.** A temporary place to live or stay: *The vacationers sought lodging for the weekend.* **2. lodgings.** A rented room or rooms.

lodg•ment also **lodge•ment** (lŏj′mənt) *n.* **1.** The act of lodging or the state of being lodged. **2.** Something lodged or deposited.

lo•ess (lō′əs *or* lĕs *or* lŭs) *n.* A yellow to gray fine-grained silt or clay, thought to be deposited as dust blown by the wind.

loft (lôft *or* lŏft) *n.* **1.** A large, open, upper floor in a commercial building or warehouse. **2.** Such a floor used as an apartment or artist's studio. **3.** An open space under a roof; an attic or a garret. **4.** A gallery or balcony, as in a church: *a choir loft.* **5.** A hayloft. —*tr.v.* **loft•ed, loft•ing, lofts.** To send (a ball) in a high arc.

loft•y (lôf′tē *or* lŏf′tē) *adj.* **loft•i•er, loft•i•est. 1.** Of great height; towering: *lofty mountains.* **2.** Elevated in character or spirit; exalted; noble: *lofty thoughts; lofty principles.* **3.** Arrogant; haughty: *Lofty treatment of others does not win friends.* **—loft′i•ly** *adv.* **—loft′i•ness** *n.*

log[1] (lôg *or* lŏg) *n.* **1.** A long thick segment of a tree, used for building, firewood, or lumber. **2.** A device trailed from a ship to determine its speed through the water. **3.a.** An official record of speed, progress, and important events, kept on a ship or an aircraft. **b.** A journal or record. —*v.* **logged, log•ging, logs.** —*tr.* **1.** To cut down the trees on (a section of land). **2.** To cut (trees) into logs. **3.** To enter (something) in a logbook. **4.** To travel (a certain distance or at a certain speed): *We logged several hundred miles in our two-day journey.* —*intr.* To cut down, trim, and haul timber. ***—idioms.*** **log off.** To enter into a computer the command to end a session. **log on.** To enter into a computer the information required to begin a session. [First written down before 1398 in Middle English and spelled *logge.*]

log[2] (lôg *or* lŏg) *n.* A logarithm. [First written down in 1631 in Modern English and spelled *log.*, from *logarithm.*]

lo•gan•ber•ry (lō′gən bĕr′ē) *n.* **1.** The edible dark-red fruit of a prickly plant related to the blackberry and the raspberry. **2.** The plant that bears such fruit. [First written down in 1893 in American English, after James Harvey *Logan* (1841–1928), American horticulturalist.]

log•a•rithm (lô′gə rĭth′əm *or* lŏg′ə rĭth′əm) *n.* The power to which a base, usually 10, must be raised to produce a given number; for example, if the base is 10, then 2 is the logarithm of 100. **—log′a•rith′mic** (lô′gə rĭth′mĭk) *adj.*

log•book (lôg′bo͝ok′ *or* lŏg′bo͝ok′) *n.* The official record book of a ship or an aircraft.

log•ger (lô′gər *or* lŏg′ər) *n.* **1.** A person who logs; a lumberjack. **2.** A tractor, crane, or other machine used for hauling or loading logs.

log•ger•head (lô′gər hĕd′ *or* lŏg′ər hĕd′) *n.* **1.** A large meat-eating sea turtle of warm waters. **2.** *Informal.* A person who acts in a stupid way; a blockhead. ***—idiom.*** **at loggerheads.** In disagreement; at odds.

log•gi•a (lô′jē ə *or* lŏj′ē ə) *n.* A gallery or an arcade along the front or side of a building that is open on at least one side.

log•ging (lô′gĭng *or* lŏg′ĭng) *n.* The work of cutting down trees, sawing them into logs, and moving the logs to a mill.

log•ic (lŏj′ĭk) *n.* **1.** The study of the principles of reasoning; the science of reasoning and of proof. **2.** Sound thinking; clear reasoning: *Their logic is undeniable when it comes to this issue.* **3.** A particular method of reasoning; a way of thinking: *By my logic, the car's starter is faulty, not the battery.* [First written down before 1378 in Middle English and spelled *logik,* from Greek *logos,* reason.]

log•i•cal (lŏj′ĭ kəl) *adj.* **1.** Of, using, or agreeing with the principles of logic: *a logical consequence.* **2.** Reasonably expected: *A small apartment is a logical choice for a single person.* **3.** Reasoning or capable of reasoning clearly and rationally: *a logical mind.* **—log′i•cal•ly** *adv.*

lo•gi•cian (lō jĭsh′ən) *n.* A person who practices or is skilled in logic.

lo•gis•tic (lō jĭs′tĭk) also **lo•gis•ti•cal** (lō jĭs′tĭ kəl) *adj.* Of or relating to logistics.

lo•gis•tics (lō jĭs′tĭks *or* lə jĭs′tĭks) *n.* *(used with a singular or plural verb).* The planning and carrying

locomotive
Diesel locomotive

loganberry

ă	pat	oi	boy
ā	pay	ou	out
âr	care	o͝o	took
ä	father	o͞o	boot
ĕ	pet	ŭ	cut
ē	be	ûr	urge
ĭ	pit	th	thin
ī	pie	*th*	this
îr	pier	hw	whoop
ŏ	pot	zh	vision
ō	toe	ə	about
ô	paw	N	*French* bon

Henry Wadsworth Longfellow
1870 photograph by George K. Warren (1824–1884)

longhorn

long jump

out of a military operation. Logistics includes the transportation, housing, and supplying of troops.

lo•go (lōʹgōʹ) *n.* A name, symbol, or trademark designed for easy recognition.

LO•GO (lōʹgō) *n.* A computer programming language designed for students who use computer terminals in making graphic designs.

log•roll•ing (lôgʹrōʹlĭng *or* lŏgʹrōʹlĭng) *n.* **1.** A sport in which two persons stand on a floating log, spinning it with their feet until one falls. **2.** The exchange of political favors among lawmakers who agree to vote for each other's legislation.

lo•gy (lōʹgē) *adj.* **lo•gi•er, lo•gi•est.** Sluggish; lethargic.

–logy *suff.* A suffix that means: **1.** Oral or written expression: *phraseology.* **2.** Science, theory, or study: *sociology.*

loin (loin) *n.* **1.a.** The part of the sides and back of the body of a person or animal between the ribs and hipbones. **b.** A cut of meat taken from this part of an animal. **2. loins. a.** The region of the hips, groin, and lower abdomen. **b.** The reproductive organs.

loin•cloth (**loinʹ**klôthʹ *or* **loinʹ**klŏthʹ) *n.* A strip of cloth worn around the hips and groin.

Loire (lwär). The longest river of France, rising in south-central France and flowing about 630 miles (1,014 kilometers) north and west to the Bay of Biscay.

loi•ter (**loiʹ**tər) *intr.v.* **loi•tered, loi•ter•ing, loi•ters.** **1.** To stand about idly; linger: *I loitered about the station, waiting for the train to come.* **2.** To go slowly, stopping often: *The shoppers loitered on their way past the store windows.* **—loiʹter•er** *n.*

loll (lŏl) *v.* **lolled, loll•ing, lolls.** *—intr.* **1.** To move, stand, sit, or rest in a lazy way: *The bathers lolled about the side of the pool.* **2.** To hang or let hang loosely or droop: *The limp flag lolled from the pole.* *—tr.* To allow to hang or droop: *The calf lolled its tongue on the hot day.*

lol•li•pop also **lol•ly•pop** (**lŏlʹ**ē pŏpʹ) *n.* A piece of hard candy on the end of a stick.

Lo•mé (lō **mā**ʹ). The capital and largest city of Togo, in the southern part of the country west of Porto-Novo, Benin. Population, 369,926.

Lon•don (**lŭnʹ**dən). The capital and largest city of the United Kingdom, on the Thames River in southeast England. Its growth as an important trade center dates from 886. The old city was devastated by the plague in 1665 and by the Great Fire of 1666; the modern city was damaged severely by bombs during World War II. Population, 6,851,400.

London, John Griffith. Pen name Jack London. 1876–1916. American writer of adventure novels, including *The Call of the Wild* (1903).

lone (lōn) *adj.* **1.** Alone; solitary: *a lone traveler on the deserted road.* **2.** Being the only one of its kind; sole: *the lone hiker to reach the summit.* **3.** Standing by itself; remote: *a lone tree on the hillside.*
❑ *These sound alike:* **lone, loan** (something lent).

lone•ly (**lōnʹ**lē) *adj.* **lone•li•er, lone•li•est.** **1.** Sad at being alone: *feeling lonely with no friends.* **2.** Without companions; alone: *a lonely traveler.* See Synonyms at **alone. 3.** Not used or visited by people; remote: *a lonely road.* **—loneʹli•ness** *n.*

lone•some (**lōnʹ**səm) *adj.* **1.** Sad at being alone. See Synonyms at **alone. 2.** Producing a feeling of loneliness: *a lonesome voyage.* **3.** Not used or visited by people; remote: *a lonesome mountain trail.*

long[1] (lông *or* lŏng) *adj.* **long•er, long•est.** **1.** Measuring a large amount from end to end; having great distance: *The Mississippi is a long river.* **2.** Having great duration: *The candidate gave a long speech.* **3.** Of a certain extent or duration: *The movie was two hours long.* **4.** Made up of many items: *a long shopping list.* **5.** Extending beyond average or standard length: *a long chess game.* **6.** Having an abundance of: *long on kindness.* **7.** Of or relating to the vowel sounds in words such as *mate, meet, mite, mote, moot,* and *mute.* **8.** Stressed or accented: *An iamb has one short and one long syllable.* *—adv.* **longer, longest. 1.** During or for a large amount of time: *Stay as long as you like.* **2.** For or throughout a specific period: *all night long.* **3.** At a very distant time: *That was long before you were born.* *—n.* A long time: *It won't be long before we leave.* ***—idioms.*** **as long as. 1.** Inasmuch as; since: *As long as you're going out, buy me a newspaper.* **2.** On the condition that; if: *You can go as long as you come home early.* **long ago.** At a time or during a period well before the present: *I read that book long ago.* [First written down before 725 in Old English and spelled *lang.*]

long[2] (lông *or* lŏng) *intr.v.* **longed, long•ing, longs.** To have a strong desire; wish very much: *The students longed for summer vacation.* [First written down about 875 in Old English and spelled *langian.*]

long. *abbr.* An abbreviation of longitude.

long•boat (**lôngʹ**bōtʹ *or* **lŏngʹ**bōtʹ) *n.* The longest boat carried by a sailing ship.

long•bow (**lôngʹ**bōʹ *or* **lŏngʹ**bōʹ) *n.* A large bow for shooting arrows, used during the Middle Ages.

long distance *n.* An operator or a system that places long-distance telephone calls.

long-dis•tance (**lôngʹdĭsʹ**təns *or* **lŏngʹdĭsʹ**təns) *adj.* **1.** Covering or carried over a great distance: *a long-distance race.* **2.** Of or involving telephone connections to a distant station. *—adv.* By telephone to a distant station: *They talked long-distance.*

long division *n.* The process of division in arithmetic in which each step of the division is written out.

lon•gev•i•ty (lŏn **jĕvʹ**ĭ tē *or* lôn **jĕvʹ**ĭ tē) *n., pl.* **lon•gev•i•ties.** Long life.

Long•fel•low (**lôngʹ**fĕlʹō *or* **lŏngʹ**fĕlʹō), **Henry Wadsworth.** 1807–1882. American writer whose poems include *The Courtship of Miles Standish* (1858).

long•hand (**lôngʹ**hăndʹ *or* **lŏngʹ**hăndʹ) *n.* Ordinary handwriting in which the words are fully written out.

long•horn (**lôngʹ**hôrnʹ *or* **lŏngʹ**hôrnʹ) *n.* Any of a breed of cattle having long spreading horns, formerly raised in the southwest United States.

long•house or **long house** (**lôngʹ**housʹ) *n.* A long dwelling typically built of poles and bark and housing several families, used especially by the Iroquois.

long•ing (**lôngʹ**ĭng *or* **lŏngʹ**ĭng) *n.* A deep yearning; a strong desire: *a longing for success.* **—longʹing•ly** *adv.*

Long Island (lông *or* lŏng). A long narrow island of southeast New York bordered on the south by the Atlantic Ocean. **Long Island Sound,** an arm of the Atlantic, separates it from Connecticut on the north.

lon•gi•tude (**lŏnʹ**jĭ to͞odʹ *or* **lŏnʹ**jĭ tyo͞odʹ *or* **lônʹ**-jĭ to͞odʹ *or* **lônʹ**jĭ tyo͞odʹ) *n.* Distance east or west on the earth's surface, measured in degrees from a certain meridian, usually the meridian at Greenwich, England.

lon•gi•tu•di•nal (lŏnʹjĭ **to͞odʹ**n əl *or* lŏnʹjĭ **tyo͞odʹ**-n əl *or* lônʹjĭ **to͞odʹ**n əl *or* lônʹjĭ **tyo͞odʹ**n əl) *adj.* **1.** Of or involving length or longitude. **2.** Placed or running lengthwise: *longitudinal stripes running the length of the garter snake.* **—lonʹgi•tuʹdi•nal•ly** *adv.*

long jump *n.* In track and field contests, a jump for distance rather than height, made either from a standing position or a moving start.

long-lived (**lôngʹlīvdʹ** *or* **lôngʹlĭvdʹ** *or* **lŏngʹlīvdʹ**

or lŏng′lĭvd′) *adj.* Having a long life; existing for a long time: *a long-lived partnership.*

long-play•ing (lông′plā′ĭng *or* lŏng′plā′ĭng) *adj.* Of or relating to a phonograph record that turns at 33⅓ revolutions per minute, usually providing about 25 minutes of sound on each side.

long-range (lông′rānj′ *or* lŏng′rānj′) *adj.* **1.** Involving a lengthy period; not immediate: *long-range plans.* **2.** Of or designed for covering great distances: *long-range transport planes.*

long•shore•man (lông′shôr′mən *or* lŏng′shôr′mən) *n.* A dock worker who loads and unloads ships.

long shot *n.* **1.** An entry, as in a horse race, with only a slight chance of winning. **2.** Something that is risky but rewarding if successful.

long-stand•ing (lông′stăn′dĭng *or* lŏng′stăn′dĭng) *adj.* Of long duration: *a longstanding business partnership.*

long-suf•fer•ing (lông′sŭf′ər ĭng *or* lŏng′sŭf′ər ĭng) *adj.* Patiently enduring pain or difficulty.

long-term (lông′tûrm′ *or* lŏng′tûrm′) *adj.* Involving a long period of time: *a long-term investment.*

long ton *n.* A ton weighing 2,240 pounds (1016 kilograms). See table at **measurement.**

long-wind•ed (lông′wĭn′dĭd *or* lŏng′wĭn′dĭd) *adj.* Writing or talking at great length; tiresome. **—long′-wind′ed•ly** *adv.* **—long′-wind′ed•ness** *n.*

look (lo͝ok) *v.* **looked, look•ing, looks.** *—intr.* **1.** To use the eyes to see; perceive by sight: *I looked at the photograph.* **2.** To turn one's gaze or attention: *Everyone looked toward the camera. You must look carefully at all of the facts.* **3.** To appear; seem: *These bananas look ripe.* **4.** To search: *I looked all over for my keys.* **5.** To face in a certain direction: *The house looks on the sea.* *—tr.* **1.** To turn one's eyes upon: *The teacher looked me in the eye.* **2.** To show by one's appearance: *He looks his age.* *—n.* **1.** The action of looking; a gaze or glance: *a quick look at the map.* **2.** An expression or appearance: *The gathering clouds have a threatening look.* **3. looks.** Personal appearance: *The children have their parents' good looks.* ***—idioms.*** **look after.** To take care of: *Someone must look after the baby.* **look alive** or **look sharp.** *Informal.* To act or respond quickly. **look down on.** To regard with contempt or scorn. **look for.** To search for; seek: *a bird looking for food.* **look forward to.** To think of (a future event) with pleasure and excitement. **look on** or **look upon.** To regard; consider: *We look on you as a model student.* **look out.** To be watchful or careful; take care. **look up. 1.** To search for and find, as in a reference book. **2.** To visit: *look up an old friend.* **3.** To become better; improve: *Things are at last looking up.* **look up to.** To admire: *I look up to my grandfather.* [First written down before 899 in Old English and spelled *lōcian.*] **—look′er** *n.*

look•ing glass (lo͝ok′ĭng) *n.* A mirror.

look•out (lo͝ok′out′) *n.* **1.** The act of looking or watching: *keeping a sharp lookout.* **2.** A high place with a wide view for keeping watch. **3.** A person assigned to watch for something: *The captain sent a lookout up the mast.* **4.** A particular worry or concern: *Making sure no one gets hurt is a lifeguard's lookout.*

loom¹ (lo͞om) *intr.v.* **loomed, loom•ing, looms. 1.** To come into view, often with a threatening appearance: *Storm clouds loomed over the mountains.* **2.** To seem close at hand; be about to happen: *The examination loomed before the students.* [First written down in 1591 in Modern English, perhaps of Scandinavian origin.]

loom² (lo͞om) *n.* A machine or frame on which threads or yarns are woven to make cloth. [First written down before 800 in Old English and spelled *gelōma,* tool.]

loon¹ (lo͞on) *n.* Any of several large diving birds having a dark speckled back, a pointed bill, webbed feet, and a cry that resembles a laugh. [First written down in 1634 in Modern English, of Scandinavian origin.]

loon² (lo͞on) *n.* *Informal.* A simple-minded or crazy person. [First written down in 1450 in Middle English and spelled *louen,* rogue.]

loon•y (lo͞o′nē) *Informal. adj.* **loon•i•er, loon•i•est. 1.** Very foolish or silly. **2.** Crazy; insane. *—n., pl.* **loon•ies.** A simple-minded or crazy person.

loop (lo͞op) *n.* **1.** A length of rope, thread, or wire that crosses over itself, making an opening. **2.** A circular path or an oval pattern that closes or nearly closes on itself: *The car followed a loop around the town.* **3.** A fastening or an ornament made from a bent or crossed piece of cloth, cord, or other material: *a belt loop.* **4.** A closed electric circuit. **5.** A series of instructions in a computer program that are repeated until a certain result has been achieved. **6.** A maneuver in which an aircraft flies a circular path in a vertical plane. *—v.* **looped, loop•ing, loops.** *—tr.* **1.** To make into a loop or loops: *loop string and tie the ends.* **2.** To fasten or join with a loop or loops: *looped together the pieces of string.* **3.** To encircle with a loop: *loop the pole with this rope.* **4.** To fly (an aircraft) in a loop or loops. *—intr.* **1.** To form a loop: *yarn that loops easily for knitting.* **2.** To move or fly in a loop.

loop•hole (lo͞op′hōl′) *n.* **1.** A means of escape, especially an omission or an unclear provision in a law or contract that provides a means of evasion: *A loophole in these laws allowed the defendant to escape prosecution.* **2.** A small hole or slit in a wall for looking or shooting through.

loose (lo͞os) *adj.* **loos•er, loos•est. 1.** Not tightly fastened or secured: *a loose shoelace; loose bricks.* **2.** Free from confinement, bonds, or fetters: *The stallion was loose on the prairie.* **3.** Not tight-fitting or tightly fitted: *a loose robe.* **4.** Not tightly stretched; slack: *the loose skin of a turtle's neck.* **5.** Not tightly packed; not compact: *loose gravel.* **6.** Not bound or gathered together: *loose notebook pages.* **7.** Lacking moral restraint: *loose conduct.* **8.** Not strict or exact: *a loose translation.* *—adv.* In a loose manner or condition. *—v.* **loosed, loos•ing, loos•es.** *—tr.* **1.** To set free; release: *We loosed our dog from its leash.* **2.** To make less tight, firm, or compact. **3.** To untie, undo, or unwrap: *We loosed the ribbon from the package.* **4.** To discharge (a missile): *loose an arrow.* *—intr.* **1.** To become loose. **2.** To shoot an arrow or other missile. [First written down before 1200 in Middle English and spelled *louse,* from Old Norse *lauss.*] **—loose′ly** *adv.* **—loose′ness** *n.*

loose-leaf (lo͞os′lēf′) *adj.* Having or being pages that can be easily removed or replaced: *a loose-leaf notebook; loose-leaf paper.*

loos•en (lo͞o′sən) *v.* **loos•ened, loos•en•ing, loos•ens.** *—tr.* **1.** To untie or make looser: *Loosen your tie and relax a while.* **2.** To free of restraint or strictness: *The school loosened its student dress code.* *—intr.* To become loose or looser: *The knot loosened easily.* **—loos′en•er** *n.*

loot (lo͞ot) *n.* **1.** Valuable things pillaged in time of war; spoils. **2.** Stolen goods. **3.** *Slang.* Money *—v.* **loot•ed, loot•ing, loots.** *—tr.* To rob of valuable things by violent means; plunder; pillage: *The burglar looted our house.* *—intr.* To take or steal goods; pillage. **—loot′er** *n.*

❑ *These sound alike:* **loot, lute** (musical instrument).

lop¹ (lŏp) *tr.v.* **lopped, lop•ping, lops. 1.** To cut off (a part); remove: *lopped dead branches from the tree.* **2.** To cut off a part from: *lopped the shrub.*

loom²

loon¹

Common loon

ă	**pat**	oi	**boy**
ā	**pay**	ou	**out**
âr	**care**	o͝o	**took**
ä	**father**	o͞o	**boot**
ĕ	**pet**	ŭ	**cut**
ē	**be**	ûr	**urge**
ĭ	**pit**	th	**thin**
ī	**pie**	*th*	**this**
îr	**pier**	hw	**whoop**
ŏ	**pot**	zh	**vision**
ō	**toe**	ə	**about**
ô	**paw**	N	*French* **bon**

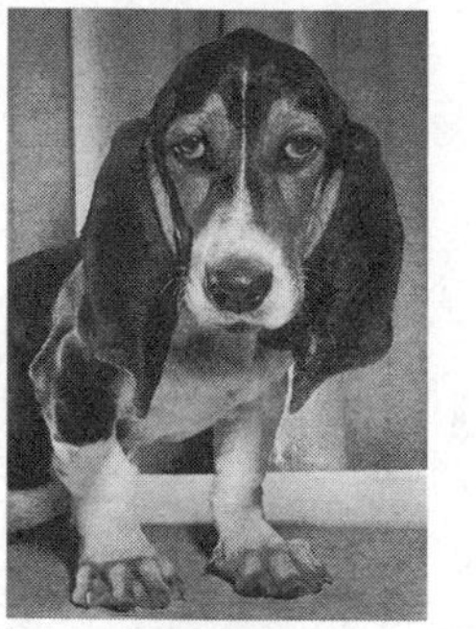

lop-eared
Basset hound

Usage: lot

You will sometimes see the phrase *a lot* as in *a lot of money* spelled as one word, *alot.* This is not an acceptable spelling.

lotus

Louis XIV
1701 portrait
by Hyacinthe Rigaud
(1659–1743)

[First written down in 1519 in Modern English, perhaps from Middle English *loppe*, small branches and twigs.]

lop² (lŏp) *intr.v.* **lopped, lop•ping, lops.** To hang loosely; droop: *The puppy's ears lopped.* [First written down in 1578 in Modern English.

lope (lōp) *intr.v.* **loped, lop•ing, lopes.** To run or ride with a long easy gait: *The horse loped along the trail.* —*n.* An long easy gait [First written down about 1300 in Middle English and spelled *lopen*, to leap, from Old Norse *hlaupa.*]

lop-eared (**lŏp**′îrd′) *adj.* Having bent or drooping ears: *a lop-eared hound.*

lop•sid•ed (**lŏp**′**sī**′dĭd) *adj.* **1.** Heavier or larger on one side than on the other. **2.** Leaning or sagging to one side: *a lopsided stack of books.* —**lop′sid′ed•ly** *adv.* —**lop′sid′ed•ness** *n.*

lo•qua•cious (lō **kwā**′shəs) *adj.* Very talkative; talking a great deal or too much. —**lo•qua′cious•ly** *adv.* —**lo•qua′cious•ness** *n.*

lo•quac•i•ty (lō **kwăs**′ĭ tē) *n.* The tendency to talk a great deal or too much.

lord (lôrd) *n.* **1.** In feudal times, a man of high rank, as a king or the owner of a manor. **2. Lord.** *Chiefly British.* A general masculine title of nobility or other high rank. **3. Lords.** The House of Lords. **4. Lord. a.** God. **b.** Jesus. **5.** A man with great authority or power: *a press lord who owns many newspapers.* —***idiom.*** **lord it over.** To behave in a domineering manner toward: *The older students lorded it over the newcomers.* [First written down about 725 in Old English and spelled *hlāford* : *hlāf*, bread + *weard*, guardian.]

lord•ly (**lôrd**′lē) *adj.* **lord•li•er, lord•li•est. 1.** Of or characteristic of a lord: *a lordly estate; a lordly deed.* **2.** Arrogant; haughty: *a lordly and superior manner.* —**lord′li•ness** *n.*

lord•ship (**lôrd**′shĭp′) *n.* **1.** Often **Lordship.** Used as a title and form of address for a man holding the rank of lord: *your Lordship.* **2.** The rank or domain of a lord.

Lord's Prayer (lôrdz prâr) *n.* The prayer taught by Jesus to his disciples. In English it begins with the words *Our Father.*

Lord's Supper *n.* **1.** The Last Supper. **2.** The sacrament of Holy Communion.

lore (lôr) *n.* **1.** The accumulated facts, traditions, or beliefs about something: *sea lore; animal lore.* **2.** Knowledge acquired by education or experience.

lor•ry (**lôr**′ē *or* **lŏr**′ē) *n., pl.* **lor•ries.** *Chiefly British.* A motor truck.

Los An•ge•les (lôs **ăn**′jə ləs *or* lŏs **ăn**′jə ləs). A city of southern California on the Pacific Ocean north-northwest of San Diego. The so-called City of the Angels was founded by the Spanish in 1781. Population, 3,485,398.

lose (lo͞oz) *v.* **lost** (lôst *or* lŏst), **los•ing, los•es.** —*tr.* **1.** To be unable to find; mislay: *I lost my gloves yesterday.* **2.** To be deprived of (something) by accident, death, or some other circumstance: *We lost our peach trees during the storm.* **3.** To be unable to maintain, sustain, or keep: *Our idea for the play lost the support of our classmates when they saw it had too few parts.* **4.** To fail to win: *They lost the game.* **5.** To fail to use; waste: *lose a chance by hesitating.* **6.** To stray or wander from: *lose one's way.* **7.** To fail to see, hear, understand, or follow: *lose the airplane in the clouds; lose track of what was said.* **8.** To cause the loss of: *Too many mistakes will lose you a good grade on the test.* —*intr.* **1.** To suffer loss or destruction: *Many investors lost heavily in the recession.* **2.** To be defeated: *Their team lost because they were not in good shape.* —***idioms.*** **lose out.** To be unsuccessful. **lose out on.** To fail to win or get; miss: *He lost out on the opportunity because he did not say he was interested.* [First written down before 725 in Old English and spelled *losian*, to perish.] —**los′er** *n.*

los•ing (**lo͞o**′zĭng) *adj.* **1.** Failing to win: *the losing team.* **2.** Of or relating to one that fails to win: *a losing season.* —*n.* **1.** The act of one who loses; loss. **2.** Something lost, such as money. Often used in the plural.

loss (lôs *or* lŏs) *n.* **1.a.** The act or an instance of losing: *a loss of memory; the loss of a game.* **b.** The state of being deprived of a person or thing: *Her loss was made easier by her cheerful outlook.* **2.** A person or thing that is lost: *Because of the accident, our car was a complete loss.* **3.** The suffering or damage caused by losing a person or thing: *The doctor's retirement is a great loss to the community.* **4. losses.** Soldiers killed or wounded; casualties. —***idiom.*** **at a loss. 1.** Below cost: *They sold the cherry crop at a loss.* **2.** Perplexed; puzzled: *I am at a loss to explain his behavior.*

lost (lôst *or* lŏst) *v.* Past tense and past participle of **lose.** —*adj.* **1.** Unable to find the way: *a lost tourist.* **2.a.** No longer possessed or controlled: *a lost fortune; a lost opportunity.* **b.** No longer known or practiced: *a lost art.* **3.** Confused; bewildered: *At first we were lost in the advanced class.* **4.** Ruined or destroyed: *lost honor.* **5.** Completely involved or preoccupied: *lost in thought.*

lot (lŏt) *n.* **1.** *Informal.* A large amount or number: *I have a lot of work to do. We made lots of new friends.* **2.** A number of people or things considered as a group: *We packed this lot of fruit for shipment.* **3.** A piece of land: *the empty lot behind the house.* **4.** A movie studio. **5.** One of a set of objects, such as bits of paper or straw, used to determine something by chance: *They drew lots to see who would go first.* **6.** The use of lots to determine something: *We decided who would go first by lot.* **7.** The decision made in this manner. **8.** What a person gets in determination by lot; a person's portion or share. **9.** Fortune in life; luck: *It is the lot of many to struggle for a living.* [First written down before 800 in Old English and spelled *hlot.*] —SEE NOTE.

lo•tion (**lō**′shən) *n.* A liquid medicine or cosmetic applied to the skin to heal, soften, cleanse, or soothe.

lot•ter•y (**lŏt**′ə rē) *n., pl.* **lot•ter•ies.** A contest in which tickets are sold, the winning ticket or tickets being determined in a random drawing.

lo•tus (**lō**′təs) *n.* **1.** A plant related to the water lily, having large white, pink, or yellow flowers and large, often floating leaves. **2.** In Greek mythology, a fruit that causes a dreamy idle state in those who eat it. [First written down in 1540 in Modern English, from Greek *lōtos.*]

loud (loud) *adj.* **loud•er, loud•est. 1.** Characterized by high volume and intensity of sound: *That band plays loud music.* **2.** Producing loud sounds: *a loud trumpet.* **3.** Clamorous or insistent: *issuing loud denunciations.* **4.** Too bright; gaudy; flashy: *a loud garish suit.* —*adv.* **louder, loudest.** In a loud manner: *Speak louder, please.* [First written down before 725 in Old English and spelled *hlūd.*] —**loud′ly** *adv.* —**loud′ness** *n.*

loud•mouth (**loud**′mouth′) *n.* *Informal.* A person given to loud or unpleasant talk.

loud•speak•er (**loud**′spē′kər) *n.* A device that changes an electric signal into sound.

Lou•is XIV (**lo͞o**′ē). 1638–1715. King of France (1643–1715) whose reign was the longest in French history and was characterized by the expansion of French influence in Europe.

Louis XVI. 1754–1793. King of France (1774–1792) who was executed along with Marie Antoinette during the French Revolution.

Lou•i•si•an•a (lo͞o ē′zē ăn′ə *or* lo͞o′zē ăn′ə). A state of the southern United States on the Gulf of Mexico between Texas and Mississippi. It was admitted as the 18th state in 1812. Baton Rouge is the capital and New Orleans the largest city. Population, 4,238,216. —See Note.

Louisiana French *n.* French as spoken by the descendants of the French settlers of Louisiana.

Louisiana Purchase. A territory of the western United States extending from the Mississippi River to the Rocky Mountains between the Gulf of Mexico and the Canadian border. It was purchased from France on April 30, 1803, for $15 million.

Lou•is•ville (lo͞o′ē vĭl′ *or* lo͞o′ə vəl). The largest city of Kentucky, in the north-central part of the state west of Lexington. Population, 269,063.

lounge (lounj) *intr.v.* **lounged, loung•ing, loung•es. 1.** To move or act in a lazy or relaxed way: *lounge in a comfortable chair.* **2.** To pass time idly: *I lounged around the house on my day off.* —*n.* **1.a.** A waiting room or bar in a hotel or airport terminal. **b.** An informal room for relaxing or gathering: *the new student lounge.* **2.** A long couch or sofa.

lour (lour) *v. & n.* Variant of **lower[1]**.

louse (lous) *n.* **1.** *pl.* **lice** (līs). Any of numerous small, wingless insects that often live as parasites on the bodies of various animals, including human beings. **2.** *pl.* **lous•es.** *Slang.* A mean or contemptible person. [First written down about 700 in Old English and spelled *lūs.*]

lous•y (lou′zē) *adj.* **lous•i•er, lous•i•est. 1.** Covered or overrun with lice. **2.a.** *Slang.* Mean; contemptible. **b.** Of low quality; inferior: *a lousy board full of knots.* —**lous′i•ly** *adv.* —**lous′i•ness** *n.*

lout (lout) *n.* An awkward, often surly and stupid person.

lou•ver (lo͞o′vər) *n.* **1.** An opening, as in a door, fitted with horizontal slats set at a slant so as to keep out rain and admit light and air. **2.** One of the slats used in such an opening. —**lou′vered** *adj.*

lov•a•ble also **love•a•ble** (lŭv′ə bəl) *adj.* Having qualities that attract affection; endearing: *a lovable kitten.* —**lov′a•ble•ness** *n.* —**lov′a•bly** *adv.*

love (lŭv) *n.* **1.** A feeling of affection, concern, or devotion toward a person. **2.a.** A strong liking for something: *a love of reading.* **b.** Something that is very much liked: *Gardening is her great love.* **3.** A beloved person. **4.** A score of zero in tennis. —*v.* **loved, lov•ing, loves.** —*tr.* **1.** To feel love or strong affection for: *We love our parents.* **2.** To like enthusiastically; delight in: *The audience loved the performance.* —*intr.* To be in love; feel affection. —***idiom.* in love.** Feeling love and devotion toward someone. [First written down before 725 in Old English and spelled *lufu.*]

Synonyms: love, like, enjoy, relish, fancy. These verbs mean to be attracted to or to find agreeable. **Love** means to feel a strong emotional attachment or intense affection for: *They love their cat as if it were a member of the family.* **Like** is a less forceful word; it means to be interested in, to approve of, or to favor something: *Erica likes her new school much better than the old one.* **Enjoy** means to feel personal satisfaction or pleasure from: *I would have enjoyed the movie more if the people behind me hadn't been talking so loudly.* **Relish** means to appreciate keenly or zestfully: *We always relish hearing a good joke.* **Fancy** means to find something appealing to one's taste or imagination: *Elvis fancied big flashy cars.*

---

love•a•ble (lŭv′ə bəl) *adj.* Variant of **lovable.**

love•bird (lŭv′bûrd′) *n.* Any of various small parrots that are often kept as pets and seem to show great fondness between mates.

love•less (lŭv′lĭs) *adj.* **1.** Showing or feeling no love: *a loveless tone in his voice.* **2.** Receiving no love; unloved.

love•lorn (lŭv′lôrn′) *adj.* Deprived of love or one's lover.

love•ly (lŭv′lē) *adj.* **love•li•er, love•li•est. 1.** Having attractive qualities of character or appearance; beautiful or endearing: *a lovely person; a lovely house.* **2.** Pleasing or enjoyable; delightful: *We spent a lovely evening with old friends.* —**love′li•ness** *n.*

lov•er (lŭv′ər) *n.* **1.** A person who loves another person. **2.** A person who is fond of or devoted to something: *a lover of jazz.*

love seat or **love•seat** (lŭv′sēt′) *n.* A small sofa that seats two people.

love•sick (lŭv′sĭk′) *adj.* Unable to act normally as a result of feeling love.

lov•ing (lŭv′ĭng) *adj.* Feeling or showing love; affectionate. —**lov′ing•ly** *adv.*

low[1] (lō) *adj.* **low•er, low•est. 1.** Having little height; not high or tall: *a low wall.* **2.** Situated below the surrounding surfaces: *water standing in low spots.* **3.** Near to the ground or horizon: *low branches; low clouds.* **4.** Of less than usual depth; shallow: *The river is low.* **5.a.** Less than usual in degree, intensity, or amount: *a low temperature; a low cost.* **b.** Inferior in rank, position, or status: *a low grade of oil.* **6.** Deep in pitch: *the low tones of a tuba.* **7.** Not loud; soft: *Speak in a low voice.* **8.** Inadequate in amount; almost gone: *Our supplies are low.* **9.** Immoral or contemptible; base: *a low trick.* **10.** Dejected or depressed: *in low spirits.* **11.** Lacking strength or vigor; weak: *a patient in low condition.* **12.** Not favorable; disapproving: *She has a low opinion of his work.* —*adv.* **lower, lowest. 1.** In or to a low position, level, or space: *The plane flew low over the canyon.* **2.** In or to a low condition or rank: *The price of corn fell low after the good harvest.* **3.** Softly; quietly: *speak low.* **4.** With a deep pitch: *sang low.* —*n.* **1.** A low level, position, or degree: *The price of peanuts fell to a new low.* **2.** The gear in a transmission that produces the slowest speed of the vehicle. [First written down about 1175 in Middle English and spelled *lah*, from Old Norse *lāgr.*] —**low′ness** *n.*

❑ *These sound alike:* **low[1]** (not high), **lo** (exclamation), **low[2]** (moo).

low[2] (lō) *n.* The deep sound made by cattle; moo. —*intr.v.* **lowed, low•ing, lows.** To make such a sound; moo. [First written down in 1549 in Modern English, from Old English *hlōwan*, to low.]

❑ *These sound alike:* **low[2]** (moo), **lo** (exclamation), **low[1]** (not high).

low•boy (lō′boi′) *n.* A low chest of drawers with a top that can be used as a table.

low•brow (lō′brou′) *n.* A person who lacks sophisticated interests. —**low′brow′** *adj.*

Low Countries (lō). A region of northwest Europe made up of Belgium, the Netherlands, and Luxembourg.

low•down (lō′doun′) *n.* *Slang.* The whole truth: *the lowdown on the scandal.*

low-down (lō′doun′) *adj.* Despicable; contemptible: *a low-down way of gaining success.*

Low•ell (lō′əl), **Amy.** 1874–1925. American poet whose works include *Sword Blades and Poppy Seed* (1914).

Lowell, James Russell. 1819–1891. American editor, poet, and diplomat who edited the *Atlantic Monthly* (1857–1861) and served as U.S. minister to Spain (1877–1880) and Great Britain (1880–1885).

low•er[1] (lou′ər *or* lour) also **lour** (lour) *intr.v.* **low•ered, low•er•ing, low•ers** also **loured, lour•ing, lours. 1.** To look angry or sullen; scowl. **2.** To appear dark or threatening, as the sky or weather:

Louisiana

The state of **Louisiana** was named by French explorers after Louis XIV, a 17th- and 18th-century French king. The name was first used to refer to a large territory along the Mississippi River that was claimed by France. When this territory was later divided up into several U.S. states, one of the states kept the name **Louisiana**.

Amy Lowell

ă	pat	oi	boy
ā	pay	ou	out
âr	care	o͝o	took
ä	father	o͞o	boot
ĕ	pet	ŭ	cut
ē	be	ûr	urge
ĭ	pit	th	thin
ī	pie	*th*	this
îr	pier	hw	whoop
ŏ	pot	zh	vision
ō	toe	ə	about
ô	paw	N	*French* bon

The sky lowered as the storm approached. —*n.* A sullen or angry look. [First written down about 1225 in Middle English and spelled *luren.*]

low•er[2] (lō′ər) *adj.* Comparative of **low[1]**. **1.** Below another in rank, position, or authority: *the lower court.* **2.** Situated below a similar or comparable thing: *a lower shelf.* **3.** Less advanced in development by evolution: *lower organisms.* **4.** Relating to or being an older division of the geologic period named. —*v.* **low•ered, low•er•ing, low•ers.** —*tr.* **1.** To let, bring, or move something down: *lower the flag; lower one's head.* **2.** To reduce, as in height, amount, degree, or quality: *The company lowered its prices.* **3.** To reduce in strength or intensity: *Lower your voice.* **4.** To reduce in standing or respect: *I wouldn't lower myself to do that.* —*intr.* **1.** To move down: *The helicopter lowered over the clearing.* **2.** To become less: *The temperature lowered after dusk.*

Clare Boothe Luce

Low•er Cal•i•for•nia (lō′ər kăl′ĭ fôr′nyə *or* lō′ər kăl′ĭ fôr′nē ə). Baja California.

low•er•case (lō′ər kās′) *adj.* or **lower-case.** Of or relating to a letter that is smaller than its capital letter. —*n.* Lowercase letters.

lower house or **Lower House** *n.* The larger and more representative branch of a legislature with two branches. The House of Representatives is the lower house of the U.S. Congress.

low•er•most (lō′ər mōst′) *adj.* Lowest.

low•est common denominator (lō′ĭst) *n.* The least common multiple of the denominators of a set of fractions.

lowest common multiple *n.* Least common multiple.

low frequency *n.* A radio-wave frequency in the range between 30 kilohertz and 300 kilohertz.

Low German *n.* **1.** The German dialects spoken in northern Germany. **2.** A group of Germanic languages, including Dutch and Flemish, spoken in the Low Countries.

low•land (lō′lənd) *n.* An area of land that is low in relation to the surrounding country. —*adj.* Relating to or characteristic of a lowland.

low•land•er (lō′lən dər) *n.* A native or inhabitant of a lowland.

low•ly (lō′lē) *adj.* **low•li•er, low•li•est. 1.** Low in rank or position: *a person of lowly birth.* **2.** Meek or humble in manner: *a lowly person.* —*adv.* In a meek and humble manner. —**low′li•ness** *n.*

low-pitched (lō′pĭcht′) *adj.* **1.** Low in tone. **2.** Having little slope: *a low-pitched roof.*

low-pres•sure (lō′prĕsh′ər) *adj.* **1.** Having or using less than the usual pressure: *a low-pressure tire.* **2.** Having a relatively low barometric pressure: *a low-pressure system developing in the atmosphere.*

low profile *n.* Behavior or activity carried out so as not to attract attention.

low-spir•it•ed (lō′spĭr′ĭ tĭd) *adj.* Being in low spirits; depressed; sad. —**low′-spir′it•ed•ly** *adv.* —**low′-spir′it•ed•ness** *n.*

low tide *n.* **1.** The tide as it reaches its lowest point. **2.** The time at which this occurs.

lox (lŏks) *n., pl.* **lox** or **lox•es.** Smoked salmon. [First written down about 1930 in American English, from Yiddish *laks.*]

loy•al (loi′əl) *adj.* **1.** Faithful to a person, an idea, a custom, or a duty: *a loyal worker.* **2.** Faithful to a country or government: *a loyal citizen.* [First written down in 1531 in Modern English, from Latin *lēgālis,* legal.] —**loy′al•ly** *adv.*

loy•al•ist (loi′ə lĭst) *n.* A person who remains loyal to the established government, political party, or ruler, especially during a civil war or revolution.

loy•al•ty (loi′əl tē) *n., pl.* **loy•al•ties.** The condition of being loyal; faithful and loyal conduct.

loz•enge (lŏz′ĭnj) *n.* **1.** A flat diamond-shaped figure. **2.** A small tablet, often having this shape, that contains medicine or is used as a candy.

LP (ĕl′pē′) *n., pl.* **LP's** or **LPs.** A long-playing phonograph record.

Lr The symbol for the element **lawrencium.**

LSD (ĕl′ĕs dē′) *n.* A powerful drug that causes hallucinations and distorted perceptions.

Lt. *abbr.* An abbreviation of lieutenant.

ltd. or **Ltd.** *abbr.* An abbreviation of limited.

Lu The symbol for the element **lutetium.**

Lu•an•da (lo͞o ăn′də) also **Lo•an•da** (lō ăn′də). The capital and largest city of Angola, in the northwest part of the country on the Atlantic Ocean. It was founded in 1575. Population, 1,200,000.

lu•au (lo͞o ou′ *or* lo͞o′ou′) *n.* A Hawaiian feast.

lub•ber (lŭb′ər) *n.* **1.** A clumsy person. **2.** An inexperienced sailor; a landlubber.

lu•bri•cant (lo͞o′brĭ kənt) *n.* A slippery substance, such as oil, grease, or graphite, used to coat the surfaces of objects that move against each other, to reduce friction and wear.

lu•bri•cate (lo͞o′brĭ kāt′) *v.* **lu•bri•cat•ed, lu•bri•cat•ing, lu•bri•cates.** —*tr.* **1.** To apply a lubricant to: *lubricate a car.* **2.** To make slippery or smooth: *lubricate skin with oil.* —*intr.* To act as a lubricant. —**lu′bri•ca′tion** *n.* —**lu′bri•ca′tor** *n.*

Luce (lo͞os), **Clare Boothe.** 1902–1987. American writer and public official whose plays include *The Women* (1936). She served as ambassador to Italy (1953–1956).

Luce, Henry Robinson. 1898–1967. American editor who cofounded *Time* (1923) and founded *Fortune* (1930), *Life* (1936), and *Sports Illustrated* (1954).

lu•cent (lo͞o′sənt) *adj.* **1.** Giving off light; luminous; bright. **2.** Translucent; clear; lucid.

lu•cid (lo͞o′sĭd) *adj.* **1.** Easily understood; clear: *a lucid explanation.* **2.** Mentally sound; sane; rational: *Though unable to speak, the patient was still lucid.* **3.** Transparent: *lucid waters.* —**lu′cid•ness** *n.* —**lu′cid•ly** *adv.*

lu•cid•i•ty (lo͞o cĭd′ĭ tē) *n.* The quality or condition of being lucid, especially in thought or expression.

Lu•ci•fer (lo͞o′sə fər) *n.* In Christian tradition, the archangel cast from heaven for leading a revolt of angels; Satan.

luck (lŭk) *n.* **1.** The chance happening of good or bad events; fate; fortune: *Luck favored our team with a winning season.* **2.** Good fortune; success: *beginner's luck.* —***idioms.*** **in luck.** Enjoying success; fortunate. **out of luck.** Lacking good fortune.

luck•i•ly (lŭk′ə lē) *adv.* With or by favorable chance; fortunately.

luck•less (lŭk′lĭs) *adj.* Having no luck; unlucky.

luck•y (lŭk′ē) *adj.* **luck•i•er, luck•i•est. 1.** Marked by or having good luck; fortunate: *a lucky day; a lucky person.* **2.** Seeming to cause good luck: *a lucky penny.* —**luck′i•ness** *n.*

lu•cra•tive (lo͞o′krə tĭv) *adj.* Producing wealth; profitable: *a lucrative business; a lucrative investment.* —**lu′cra•tive•ly** *adv.*

lu•cre (lo͞o′kər) *n.* Money or profits.

lu•di•crous (lo͞o′dĭ krəs) *adj.* Laughable because of obvious absurdity; ridiculous. —**lu′di•crous•ly** *adv.* —**lu′di•crous•ness** *n.*

luff (lŭf) *n.* **1.** The act of sailing toward the wind. **2.** The forward side of a fore-and-aft sail. —*intr.v.* **luffed, luff•ing, luffs.** To steer a sailing vessel toward the wind.

lug[1] (lŭg) *n.* **1.** A projecting part, as on a machine, used to support something: *take the nuts off the lugs to remove the tire.* **2.** A lugsail. **3.** *Slang.* A clumsy fool; a blockhead. [First written down in 1495 in Middle English and spelled *lugge,* earflap, probably of Scandinavian origin.]

lug[2] (lŭg) *tr.v.* **lugged, lug•ging, lugs.** To drag or haul with great difficulty: *lug boxes up to the attic.* [First written down about 1380 in Middle English and spelled *luggen,* of Scandinavian origin.]

lug•gage (lŭg′ĭj) *n.* The bags, suitcases, boxes, or trunks for carrying belongings on a trip; baggage.

lug•ger (lŭg′ər) *n.* A boat having two or three masts, each with a lugsail.

lug•sail (lŭg′səl) *n.* A four-sided sail that hangs on a yard slanting across the mast.

lu•gu•bri•ous (lo͝o go͞o′brē əs *or* lo͝o gyo͞o′brē əs) *adj.* Sad or mournful; sorrowful: *the lugubrious cry of wolves.* **—lu•gu′bri•ous•ly** *adv.* **—lu•gu′bri•ous•ness** *n.*

lug•worm (lŭg′wûrm′) *n.* Any of various marine worms that burrow in the sand along the seashore, often used as fishing bait.

Luke (lo͝ok) *n.* The third Gospel of the New Testament, thought to have been written by Saint Luke.

Luke, Saint. First century A.D. Companion of Saint Paul traditionally regarded as the author of the third Gospel of the New Testament.

luke•warm (lo͞ok′wôrm′) *adj.* **1.** Neither hot nor cold; mildly warm: *lukewarm water.* **2.** Lacking in enthusiasm; indifferent: *a lukewarm greeting.* **—luke′warm′ly** *adv.* **—luke′warm′ness** *n.*

lull (lŭl) *v.* **lulled, lull•ing, lulls.** *—tr.* To cause to sleep or rest; calm; soothe: *a song to lull a baby to sleep.* *—intr.* To become calm: *The high winds finally lulled.* *—n.* A temporary lessening of activity or noise; a calm interval: *a lull in the storm; a lull in sales.*

lull•a•by (lŭl′ə bī′) *n., pl.* **lull•a•bies.** A soothing song meant to lull a child to sleep.

lum•ba•go (lŭm bā′gō) *n.* A pain that affects the muscles and tendons of the lower back and hips.

lum•bar (lŭm′bər *or* lŭm′bär′) *adj.* Of, near, or situated in the part of the back and sides between the lowest ribs and the hips.

❑ *These sound alike:* **lumbar, lumber[1]** (wood), **lumber[2]** (walk clumsily).

lum•ber[1] (lŭm′bər) *n.* Timber sawed into boards and planks. *—intr.v.* **lum•bered, lum•ber•ing, lum•bers.** To cut down and prepare lumber. [First written down in 1552 in Modern English, perhaps from *lumber,* to walk clumsily.]

❑ *These sound alike:* **lumber[1]** (wood), **lumbar** (lower back), **lumber[2]** (walk clumsily).

lum•ber[2] (lŭm′bər) *intr.v.* **lum•bered, lum•ber•ing, lum•bers.** To walk or move in a clumsy or noisy manner: *The truck lumbered down the bumpy road.* [First written down about 1380 in Middle English and spelled *lomeren,* possibly of Scandinavian origin.]

❑ *These sound alike:* **lumber[2]** (walk clumsily), **lumbar** (lower back), **lumber[1]** (wood).

lum•ber•jack (lŭm′bər jăk′) *n.* A person whose work is to chop down trees and transport timber to a sawmill.

lum•ber•yard (lŭm′bər yärd′) *n.* A business that sells lumber and other building materials from a yard.

lu•men (lo͞o′mən) *n., pl.* **lu•mens** or **lu•mi•na** (lo͞o′mə nə). **1.** The open space within a tubular organ, such as a blood vessel or an intestine. **2.** A unit of measure equal to the flow of light given off by a point source with a brightness of one candela falling on a given curved surface with all points being equally distant from the source.

lu•mi•nar•y (lo͞o′mə nĕr′ē) *n., pl.* **lu•mi•nar•ies. 1.** A celestial body that gives off light, particularly the sun or moon. **2.** A famous person, especially one noted for high achievement: *a luminary of stage and screen.*

lu•mi•nes•cence (lo͞o′mə nĕs′əns) *n.* The production of light accompanied by little heat and at a temperature below that of incandescent bodies. Fluorescence and phosphorescence are examples of luminescence that can be produced by biochemical or chemical processes. **—lu′mi•nes′cent** *adj.*

lu•mi•nos•i•ty (lo͞o′mə nŏs′ĭ tē) *n., pl.* **lu•mi•nos•i•ties. 1.** The condition or property of being luminous. **2.** Something luminous.

lu•mi•nous (lo͞o′mə nəs) *adj.* **1.** Giving off its own light; shining: *the luminous firefly.* **2.** Full of light; bright: *a full luminous moon.* **3.** Easily understood; clear: *simple luminous prose.* [First written down in 1425 in Middle English and spelled *luminose,* from Latin *lūmen,* light.] **—lu′mi•nous•ly** *adv.* **—lu′mi•nous•ness** *n.*

lump[1] (lŭmp) *n.* **1.** An irregularly shaped mass or piece: *a lump of rock.* **2.** A small cube of sugar. **3.** A swelling or bump: *A lump rose on my finger where I was stung.* *—adj.* **1.** Formed into a lump or lumps: *lump sugar.* **2.** Not divided into parts; whole: *We want the entire payment in one lump sum.* *—v.* **lumped, lump•ing, lumps.** *—tr.* To put together; consider as a whole: *The coach lumped the fifth and sixth graders together in one gym class.* *—intr.* To form into a lump or lumps: *The sauce lumped because we didn't stir it.* [First written down before 1325 in Middle English and spelled *lumpe,* of Low German origin.]

lump[2] (lŭmp) *tr.v.* **lumped, lump•ing, lumps.** *Informal.* To endure or put up with something: *You can like my cooking or lump it.* [First written down in 1577 in American English, perhaps from dialectal *lump,* to look sullen.]

lump•y (lŭm′pē) *adj.* **lump•i•er, lump•i•est.** Full of or covered with lumps: *lumpy gravy.* **—lump′i•ness** *n.*

lu•na•cy (lo͞o′nə sē) *n., pl.* **lu•na•cies. 1.** Mental derangement; insanity. **2.** Foolish or reckless conduct.

lu•nar (lo͞o′nər) *adj.* Of or relating to the moon: *a lunar mountain.*

lunar eclipse *n.* The total or partial eclipse of the full moon by the earth's shadow.

lunar month *n.* An interval of about 29 days between one new moon and the next, during which the moon makes one complete revolution around the earth.

lunar year *n.* A period of twelve lunar months, about 354⅓ days.

lu•na•tic (lo͞o′nə tĭk) *n.* An insane person. *—adj.* **1.** Insane; mad. **2.** Of or for the insane: *a lunatic asylum.* **3.** Wildly or recklessly foolish: *a lunatic idea.*

lunch (lŭnch) *n.* **1.** A meal eaten between breakfast and dinner, usually at midday. **2.** The food for this meal. *—intr.v.* **lunched, lunch•ing, lunch•es.** To eat lunch.

lunch•eon (lŭn′chən) *n.* Lunch, often a formal lunch.

lunch•eon•ette (lŭn′chə nĕt′) *n.* A restaurant that serves light meals such as breakfast or lunch.

lunch•room (lŭnch′ro͞om′ *or* lŭnch′ro͝om′) *n.* The cafeteria or room in a building, such as a school, where light meals are served and eaten.

lung (lŭng) *n.* **1.** Either of two spongy organs that occupy the chest cavity of most vertebrates and are the means by which the blood receives oxygen and releases carbon dioxide. **2.** A similar organ found in some invertebrates.

lunge (lŭnj) *n.* **1.** A sudden thrust or pass, as with a sword. **2.** A sudden forward movement: *The fielder made a lunge for the ball.* *—intr.v.* **lunged, lung•ing, lung•es.** To make a sudden forward movement: *The cat lunged at the bird.* **—lung′er** *n.*

lung•fish (lŭng′fĭsh′) *n.* Any of several tropical freshwater fishes of Africa, Australia, and South America, having a long narrow body and gills as

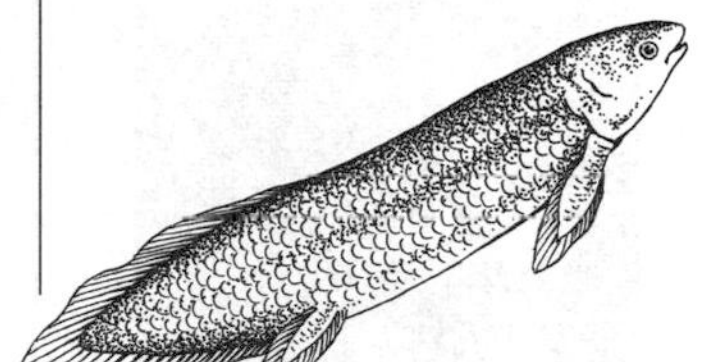

lungfish
Australian lungfish

ă	**pat**	oi	**boy**
ā	**pay**	ou	**out**
âr	**care**	o͝o	**took**
ä	**father**	o͞o	**boot**
ĕ	**pet**	ŭ	**cut**
ē	**be**	ûr	**urge**
ĭ	**pit**	th	**thin**
ī	**pie**	*th*	**this**
îr	**pier**	hw	**whoop**
ŏ	**pot**	zh	**vision**
ō	**toe**	ə	**about**
ô	**paw**	N	*French* **bon**

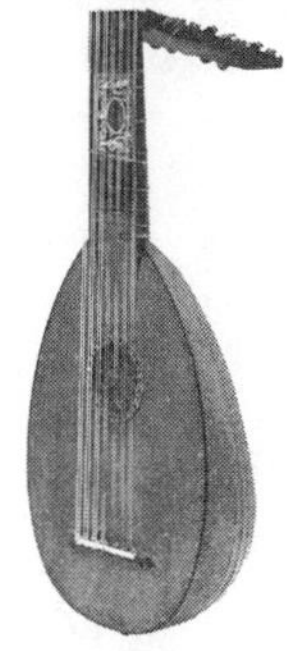

lute
17th-century Italian

Martin Luther
Portrait by Lucas Cranach (1472–1553)

Rosa Luxemburg

lynx

well as organs that enable them to breathe out of water.

lu•pine also **lu•pin** (lo͞o′pən) *n.* Any of numerous plants related to the pea and having leaves with many leaflets and long spikes of variously colored flowers.

lurch[1] (lûrch) *intr.v.* **lurched, lurch•ing, lurch•es. 1.** To move suddenly and unsteadily; stagger: *He lurched forward under the heavy load of his backpack.* **2.** To roll or pitch suddenly: *The ship lurched as the wave hit the bow.* —*n.* **1.** A staggering or tottering movement. **2.** A sudden rolling or pitching: *The train gave a lurch and started out of the station.* [First written down in 1819 in Modern English.]

lurch[2] (lûrch) *n.* A losing position after an overwhelming defeat in the game of cribbage. —***idiom.*** **in the lurch.** In a difficult or embarrassing position. [First written down in 1584 in Modern English, perhaps from Middle English *lurching*, a total victory at *lorche*, a kind of game.]

lure (lo͝or) *n.* **1.** A strong attraction, charm, or enticement: *the lure of fame.* **2.** A decoy used in catching animals, especially an artificial bait used to attract and catch fish. —*tr.v.* **lured, lur•ing, lures.** To attract or tempt, especially with a bait: *We lured the cat inside with a dish of food.*

lu•rid (lo͝or′ĭd) *adj.* **1.** Causing shock or horror: *a lurid description of a train crash.* **2.** Glowing with a fiery glare: *The lurid flames of a distant fire lit up the night sky.* —**lu′rid•ly** *adv.* —**lu′rid•ness** *n.*

lurk (lûrk) *intr.v.* **lurked, lurk•ing, lurks. 1.** To wait out of view; lie in wait: *The cat lurked in the grass, waiting for the mouse to approach.* **2.** To move about secretly; sneak. —**lurk′er** *n.*

Lu•sa•ka (lo͞o sä′kə). The capital and largest city of Zambia, in the south-central part of the country. It was founded in 1905. Population, 535,830.

lus•cious (lŭsh′əs) *adj.* **1.** Having a delicious taste or smell: *a luscious peach.* **2.** Appealing to the senses or the mind: *a luscious singing voice.* —**lus′cious•ly** *adv.* —**lus′cious•ness** *n.*

lush (lŭsh) *adj.* **lush•er, lush•est. 1.** Having or covered in thick plentiful plant growth: *a lush green lawn.* **2.** Juicy and tender: *lush grapes.* **3.** Luxurious; abundant and rich: *lush decorations.* [First written down in 1440 in Middle English and spelled *lusch*, relaxed, soft.] —**lush′ly** *adv.* —**lush′ness** *n.*

lust (lŭst) *n.* **1.** Intense sexual desire. **2.** An overwhelming desire or craving: *a lust for power.* —*intr. v.* **lust•ed, lust•ing, lusts.** To have an intense or overwhelming desire: *The pirates lusted after riches.*

lus•ter (lŭs′tər) *n.* **1.** Soft reflected light; sheen; gloss: *the luster of pearls.* **2.** Radiance of light; brightness: *the luster of the warming sun.* **3.** Glory; splendor: *Her newest discoveries add luster to her name.* **4.** The shiny metallic surface that is found on pottery and china.

lust•ful (lŭst′fəl) *adj.* Full of lust; lewd. —**lust′ful•ly** *adv.* —**lust′ful•ness** *n.*

lus•tre (lŭs′tər) *n. & v. Chiefly British.* Variant of **luster.**

lus•trous (lŭs′trəs) *adj.* Having luster; shining; gleaming: *the tiger's lustrous eyes.* —**lus′trous•ly** *adv.* —**lus′trous•ness** *n.*

lust•y (lŭs′tē) *adj.* **lust•i•er, lust•i•est.** Full of strength and vitality; robust. —**lust′i•ly** *adv.* —**lust′i•ness** *n.*

lute (lo͞ot) *n.* A stringed instrument having a body shaped like a pear sliced lengthwise and a fingerboard that has frets. It is played by plucking.
❑ *These sound alike:* **lute, loot** (stolen goods).

lu•te•ti•um (lo͞o tē′shē əm) *n. Symbol* **Lu** A silvery rare-earth element used in nuclear technology. Atomic number 71. See table at **element.**

Lu•ther (lo͞o′thər), **Martin.** 1483–1546. German theologian, leader of the Reformation, and founder of the Lutheran Church.

Lu•ther•an (lo͞o′thər ən) *adj.* Of or relating to Martin Luther or the branch of the Protestant Church founded on his teachings. —*n.* A member of the Lutheran Church.

Lux•em•bourg also **Lux•em•burg** (lŭk′səm bûrg′). **1.** A country of northwest Europe southwest of Belgium. In 1867 the European powers declared Luxembourg a neutral territory. Luxembourg is the capital. Population, 364,606. **2.** The capital of Luxembourg, in the southern part of the country. Population, 78,924.

Lux•em•burg (lŭk′səm bûrg′), **Rosa.** 1870–1919. German socialist leader who in 1918 cofounded what became the German Communist Party. She was arrested in 1919 and later murdered.

lux•u•ri•ant (lŭg zho͝or′ē ənt *or* lŭk sho͝or′ē ənt) *adj.* **1.** Growing abundantly; lush: *luxuriant vegetation.* **2.** Abundantly productive: *luxuriant fields.* **3.** Highly ornamented: *a luxuriant dining room.* —**lux•u′ri•ance** *n.* —**lux•u′ri•ant•ly** *adv.*

lux•u•ri•ate (lŭg zho͝or′ē āt′ *or* lŭk sho͝or′ē āt′) *intr. v.* **lux•u•ri•at•ed, lux•u•ri•at•ing, lux•u•ri•ates. 1.** To indulge oneself in luxury: *We luxuriated by taking a room in the expensive hotel.* **2.** To take great pleasure or delight: *luxuriate in the warm sunshine.* **3.** To grow in abundance; thrive: *Plants luxuriate in a greenhouse.*

lux•u•ri•ous (lŭg zho͝or′ē əs *or* lŭk sho͝or′ē əs) *adj.* **1.** Fond of luxury: *a luxurious taste for expensive clothes.* **2.** Marked by luxury; sumptuous: *a luxurious apartment.* —**lux•u′ri•ous•ly** *adv.* —**lux•u′ri•ous•ness** *n.*

lux•u•ry (lŭg′zhə rē *or* lŭk′shə rē) *n., pl.* **lux•u•ries. 1.** Something that is not essential but gives pleasure or comfort: *Eating in a good restaurant is a luxury I can't afford these days.* **2.** A way of living that brings comfort; use of the best or most costly things: *live in luxury.*

–ly[1] *suff.* A suffix that means: **1.** Having the characteristics of; like: *sisterly.* **2.** Recurring at a specified interval of time: *hourly.*

–ly[2] *suff.* A suffix that means: **1.** In a specified manner: *gradually.* **2.** At a specified interval: *weekly.*

ly•ce•um (lī sē′əm) *n.* **1.** A hall in which lectures and concerts are presented. **2.** An organization that sponsors educational programs and entertainment.

Lyd•i•a (lĭd′ē ə). An ancient country of west-central Asia Minor on the Aegean Sea in present-day northwest Turkey. It may have been the earliest kingdom to use minted coins (seventh century B.C.).

lye (lī) *n.* **1.** A strong alkaline solution made by allowing water to wash through wood ashes, used in making soap and in cleaning. **2.** Sodium hydroxide.
❑ *These sound alike:* **lye, lie**[1] (be flat), **lie**[2] (falsehood).

ly•ing[1] (lī′ĭng) *v.* Present participle of **lie**[1].

ly•ing[2] (lī′ĭng) *v.* Present participle of **lie**[2]. —*adj.* Given to or marked by falsehood: *a lying witness.*

Lyme disease (līm) *n.* An infectious disease characterized by reddish areas on the skin, chills, fever, fatigue, and sometimes heart and nerve problems as well as arthritis. It is caused by bacteria carried by a species of tick. [First written down about 1980 in Modern English, after *Lyme*, a town of southeast Connecticut.]

lymph (lĭmf) *n.* A nearly colorless liquid that flows through the lymphatic system and serves to bathe and nourish the tissues.

lym•phat•ic (lĭm făt′ĭk) *adj.* **1.** Of, carrying, or relating to lymph. **2.** Lacking vitality; sluggish.

lymphatic system *n.* The network of small vessels, resembling blood vessels, by which lymph circulates throughout the body carrying nutrients from the blood to the cells, picking up fats from the small intestines, and carrying cellular waste to the blood.

lymph node *n.* Any of the numerous round or oval structures, located along the lymphatic vessels, that supply certain white blood cells to the body and remove bacteria and foreign particles from the lymph.

lym•pho•cyte (lĭm′fə sīt′) *n.* A white blood cell of the type that is formed in the lymph nodes.

lym•phoid (lĭm′foid′) *adj.* Of or relating to lymph, lymph cells, or lymph tissue.

lynch (lĭnch) *tr.v.* **lynched, lynch•ing, lynch•es.** To execute, especially by hanging, without due process of law. [First written down in 1811 in American English, after William *Lynch* (died 1820), an organizer of vigilantes who practiced lynching in Virginia.] **—lynch′er** *n.*

lynx (lĭngks) *n., pl.* **lynx** or **lynx•es.** Any of several wild cats having thick soft fur, tufted ears, and a short tail.

❑ *These sound alike:* **lynx, links** (golf course).

ly•on•naise (lī′ə **nāz′** *or* lē′ə **nĕz′**) *adj.* Cooked with onion: *lyonnaise potatoes.*

Ly•ons or **Ly•on** (lē ōɴ′). A city of east-central France on the Rhone River. It was founded in 43 B.C. as a Roman colony. Population, 413,095.

Ly•ra (lī′rə) *n.* A constellation in the Northern Hemisphere thought to resemble a lyre in outline.

lyre (līr) *n.* A stringed instrument related to the harp and used to accompany a singer or reciter of poetry, especially in ancient Greece. [First written down before 1200 in Middle English and spelled *lire*, from Greek *lura.*]

lyre•bird (līr′bûrd′) *n.* An Australian bird, the male of which has a long tail that is shaped like a lyre when spread.

lyr•ic (lĭr′ĭk) *adj.* Of or relating to poetry that expresses personal feelings and thoughts. *—n.* **1.** A lyric poem or poet. **2.** Often **lyrics.** The words of a song.

lyr•i•cal (lĭr′ĭ kəl) *adj.* **1.** Expressing deep personal feelings or thoughts: *a lyrical description of her youth.* **2.** Lyric.

lyr•i•cism (lĭr′ĭ sĭz′əm) *n.* The quality of being lyric; lyric expression.

lyr•i•cist (lĭr′ĭ sĭst) *n.* A writer of lyric poetry or songs.

ly•sin (lī′sĭn) *n.* An antibody capable of destroying or dissolving bacteria, red blood cells, and certain cellular matter.

ly•sis (lī′sĭs) *n., pl.* **ly•ses** (lī sēz). The destruction of a cell by dissolution of the cell wall or membrane, as by a lysin.

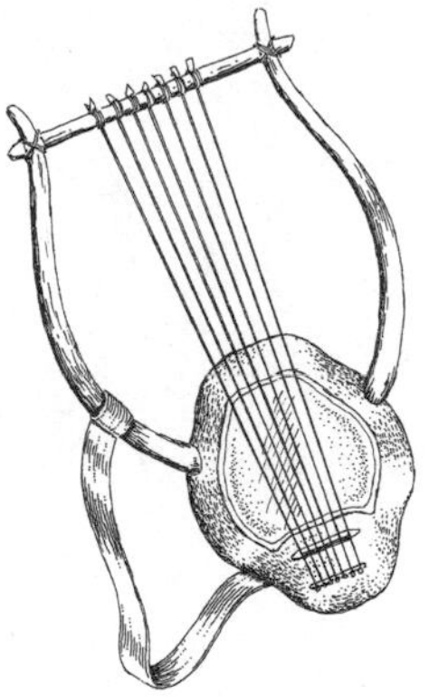

lyre

lyrebird

ă	pat	oi	boy
ā	pay	ou	out
âr	care	ŏŏ	took
ä	father	ōō	boot
ĕ	pet	ŭ	cut
ē	be	ûr	urge
ĭ	pit	th	thin
ī	pie	*th*	this
îr	pier	hw	whoop
ŏ	pot	zh	vision
ō	toe	ə	about
ô	paw	ɴ	*French* bon

Mm

m[1] or **M** (ĕm) *n., pl.* **m's** or **M's. 1.** The 13th letter of the English alphabet. **2.** The 13th in a series or group: *row M in a theater.*

m[2] *abbr.* An abbreviation of: **1.** Mass. **2.** Meter (measurement).

M also **m** The symbol for the Roman numeral 1,000.

m. *abbr.* An abbreviation of: **1.** Male. **2.** Masculine. **3.** Meridian. **4.** Mile. **5.** Month. **6.** Minute.

M. *abbr.* An abbreviation of: **1.** Master. **2.** Monday. **3.** Monsieur.

ma (mä *or* mô) *n. Informal.* Mother.

MA *abbr.* An abbreviation of Massachusetts.

M.A. or **MA** *abbr.* An abbreviation of Master of Arts.

ma'am (măm) *n.* Madam.

ma•ca•bre (mə **kä′**brə *or* mə **käb′**) *adj.* Suggesting the horror of death and decay; gruesome: *a macabre play set during a plague.*

mac•ad•am (mə **kăd′**əm) *n.* Pavement made of layers of small stones packed together, now usually bound with asphalt or tar. [First written down in 1824 in Modern English, after John L. *McAdam* (1756–1836), Scottish civil engineer.]

mac•ad•am•ize (mə **kăd′**ə mīz′) *tr.v.* **mac•ad•am•ized, mac•ad•am•iz•ing, mac•ad•am•iz•es.** To build or pave (a road) with macadam.

ma•caque (mə **kăk′** *or* mə **käk′**) *n.* Any of several monkeys of Asia and northern Africa having short tails.

mac•a•ro•ni (măk′ə **rō′**nē) *n.* A pasta made of wheat flour, usually in the shape of hollow tubes.

mac•a•roon (măk′ə **ro͞on′**) *n.* A chewy cookie made with sugar, egg whites, and ground almonds or coconut.

MacArthur (mək **är′**thər), **Douglas.** 1880–1964. American general who served as U.S. chief of staff (1930–1935) and commanded Allied forces in the South Pacific during World War II.

macaw

ma•caw (mə **kô′**) *n.* Any of various large, often brightly colored Central and South American parrots having long tails and strong beaks.

Mac•beth (mək **bĕth′**). Died 1057. King of Scotland (1040–1057) who gained the throne after killing his cousin King Duncan (died 1040) in battle. Legends about him are the basis of Shakespeare's *Macbeth.*

Mac•ca•bees (**măk′**ə bēz′) *pl. n.* A family of Jewish patriots of the 2nd and 1st century B.C., who led a successful revolt against Syrian rule in Judea.

Mac•don•ald (mĭk **dŏn′**əld), Sir **John Alexander.** 1815–1891. Canadian prime minister (1867–1873 and 1878–1891) who is considered the organizer of the Canadian confederation, established in 1867.

mace[1] (mās) *n.* **1.** A heavy club with a spiked metal head, used as a weapon in medieval times. **2.** A ceremonial staff carried or displayed as a symbol of authority. [First written down before 1300 in Middle English, from Latin *mateola*, mallet.]

mace[2] (mās) *n.* A spice made from the bright red or yellow covering of the seed of the nutmeg. [First written down in 1234 in Middle English and spelled *maces*, from Greek *makir*, a kind of spice.]

Mace (mās). A trademark for an aerosol spray that causes irritation to the eyes, skin, and respiratory tract, used to repel an attacker.

Mac•e•do•ni•a (măs′ĭ **dō′**nē ə *or* măs′ĭ **dōn′**yə). **1.** A region of southeast Europe on the Balkan Peninsula, including modern Macedonia, northern Greece, and southwest Bulgaria. It was a powerful empire in the fourth century B.C. and contributed to the spread of Hellenistic civilization. It was partitioned in 1913 between Yugoslavia and Greece. **2.** A region of the south-central Balkan Peninsula south of Serbia. The region was part of Yugoslavia from 1946 until 1991. Capital, Skopje. Population, 1,623,598.

Mac•e•do•ni•an (măs′ĭ **dō′**nē ən) *adj.* Of or relating to ancient or modern Macedonia or its peoples, languages, or cultures. *—n.* **1.** A native or inhabitant of ancient or modern Macedonia. **2.** The language of ancient Macedonia. **3.** The Slavic language of modern Macedonia.

mac•er•ate (**măs′**ə rāt′) *v.* **mac•er•at•ed, mac•er•at•ing, mac•er•ates.** *—tr.* **1.** To make soft by soaking in a liquid: *Macerate strawberries in sweetened water before serving them.* **2.** To cause (the body) to become thin. *—intr.* To become soft by soaking.

Mach also **mach** (mäk) *n.* Mach number.

ma•chet•e (mə **shĕt′**ē *or* mə **chĕt′**ē) *n.* A large heavy knife with a broad blade, used as a weapon and as a tool for clearing paths and cutting sugar cane. [First written down in 1832 in American English, from Spanish, probably from *maza*, mallet.]

Mach•i•a•vel•li (măk′ē ə **vĕl′**ē), **Niccolò.** 1469–1527. Italian political theorist known for his book *The Prince* (1513) in which he states that a leader should use any means for staying in power, including lying.

Mach•i•a•vel•li•an (măk′ē ə **vĕl′**ē ən) *adj.* **1.** Of or relating to the political theories of Niccolò Machiavelli. **2.** Showing or being deceptive or underhanded; crafty; cunning. *—n.* A person who follows Machiavelli's political principles or is given to deceptive behavior for personal advancement.

mach•i•na•tion (măk′ə **nā′**shən *or* măsh′ə **nā′**shən) *n.* A cunning scheme or plot to do something harmful.

ma•chine (mə **shēn′**) *n.* **1.** A device of fixed and moving parts for performing tasks: *a washing machine.* **2.** A simple device that applies force or changes its direction. The gear, inclined plane, lever, and screw are all simple machines. **3.** A person who acts or performs a task mechanically without thinking. **4.** An organized group of people that controls the policies and activities of a political party in an area: *the key members of the local political machine.* *—tr.v.* **ma•chined, ma•chin•ing, ma•chines.** To cut, shape, or finish by machine: *The workers machine metal at the factory.* [First written down in 1549 in Modern English, from Greek *mēkhanē.*]

machine gun *n.* A gun that fires rapidly and repeatedly when the trigger is pressed.

ma•chine-gun (mə **shēn′**gŭn′) *tr.v.* **ma•chine-**

gunned, ma•chine-gun•ning, ma•chine-guns. To fire at with a machine gun.

ma•chine-read•a•ble (mə shēn′rē′də bəl) *adj.* In a form that can be processed or used directly by a computer: *machine-readable texts.*

ma•chin•er•y (mə shē′nə rē *or* mə shēn′rē) *n., pl.* **ma•chin•er•ies. 1.** Machines or machine parts considered as a group: *The factory is full of machinery.* **2.** The working parts of a particular machine: *The machinery of an automobile engine includes pistons and gears.* **3.** A system of persons or things that operate together to keep something going: *the complex machinery of modern society.*

machine shop *n.* A workshop where machines or machine parts are made, finished, or repaired.

machine tool *n.* A power-driven tool used to cut or shape metal.

ma•chin•ist (mə shē′nĭst) *n.* **1.** A person skilled in the use of machine tools to work metal. **2.** A person who makes, operates, or repairs machines.

ma•chis•mo (mä chēz′mō) *n.* An exaggerated sense of manliness that stresses strength, courage, and aggressiveness.

Mach number also **mach number** (mäk) *n.* The ratio of the speed of a body to the speed of sound in a particular surrounding medium; for example, an aircraft flying through air at twice the speed of sound has a Mach number of 2. [First written down in 1937 in Modern English and spelled *Mach's number*, after Ernst *Mach* (1838–1916), Austrian physicist.]

ma•cho (mä′chō) *adj.* Characterized by or showing machismo: *The cowboy has a macho image.* —*n., pl.* **ma•chos. 1.** Machismo. **2.** A person characterized by machismo.

mac•in•tosh (măk′ĭn tŏsh′) *n.* Variant of **mackintosh.**

Mac•ken•zie (mə kĕn′zē), **Alexander.** 1822–1892. British-born Canadian politician who was the first Liberal prime minister of Canada (1873–1878).

Mackenzie, William Lyon. 1795–1861. British-born Canadian politician who led an armed insurrection in Toronto (1837) to protest colonial rule.

mack•er•el (măk′ər əl *or* măk′rəl) *n., pl.* **mackerel** or **mack•er•els.** Any of several silvery fishes of the north Atlantic ocean, having dark markings on the back and much used as food.

mackerel sky *n.* A sky covered with a series of bands of clouds resembling the markings of a mackerel.

mack•i•naw (măk′ə nô′) *n.* **1.** A short coat of heavy, usually plaid woolen material. **2.** A thick woolen blanket in solid colors or stripes, formerly used in northern and western North America.

mack•in•tosh also **mac•in•tosh** (măk′ĭn tŏsh′) *n. Chiefly British.* A raincoat. [First written down in 1836 in Modern English, after Charles *Macintosh* (1766–1843), Scottish inventor.]

mac•ra•mé (măk′rə mā′) *n.* Coarse lacework made by weaving and knotting threads or cords into a pattern.

macro– *pref.* A prefix that means large: *macronucleus.*

mac•ro•cosm (măk′rə kŏz′əm) *n.* The entire world; the universe.

ma•cron (mā′krŏn′ *or* măk′rŏn′) *n.* A mark (¯) placed over a vowel to show that it has a long sound, as the *ā* in the pronunciation of *make.*

mac•ro•nu•cle•us (măk′rō no͞o′klē əs *or* măk′rō nyo͞o′klē əs) *n., pl.* **mac•ro•nu•cle•i** (măk′rō no͞o′klē ī′ *or* măk′rō nyo͞o′klē ī′). The larger of two types of nuclei in various protozoans, controlling metabolic functions in the cell.

mad (măd) *adj.* **mad•der, mad•dest. 1.** Very irritated; angry: *The unfair accusation made me mad.* **2.** Suffering from a disorder of the mind; crazy; insane. **3.** Very foolish; rash: *a mad idea.* **4.** Liking almost too much; overly enthusiastic: *mad about skiing.* **5.** Wildly excited or confused; frantic: *a mad scramble for the bus.* **6.** Affected by rabies; rabid: *a mad dog.* —***idiom.*** **like mad.** *Informal.* **1.** With great energy; rapidly: *ran like mad.* **2.** To a great extent: *It's snowing like mad.* [First written down before 800 in Old English and spelled *gemǣdde*, from *gemād*, insane.] —**mad′ly** *adv.* —**mad′ness** *n.*

Mad•a•gas•car (măd′ə găs′kər). An island country in the Indian Ocean off the southeast coast of Africa made up of the island of **Madagascar** and several small islands. The country gained its independence from France in 1960. Antananarivo is the capital and the largest city. Population, 9,230,000.

Mad•am (măd′əm) *n., pl.* **Mad•ams** or **Mes•dames** (mā dăm′ *or* mā däm′). Used as a polite form of address for a woman: *Right this way, Madam.*

Ma•dame (mə dăm′ *or* măd′əm) *n., pl.* **Mes•dames** (mā dăm′ *or* mā däm′). Used as a polite form of address for a woman, especially a married woman, in French-speaking areas.

mad•cap (măd′kăp′) *adj.* Not sensible; rash; impulsive: *a madcap idea.*

mad•den (măd′n) *v.* **mad•dened, mad•den•ing, mad•dens.** —*tr.* To make mad: *Heat and the flies maddened the horse.* —*intr.* To become mad.

mad•den•ing (măd′n ĭng) *adj.* Causing great anger; infuriating: *a maddening racket outside my window.* —**mad′den•ing•ly** *adv.*

mad•der (măd′ər) *n.* **1.** A plant of southwest Asia having small yellow flowers and a fleshy red root that is the source of dye. **2.** A red dye made from the root of the madder plant.

made (mād) *v.* Past tense and past participle of **make.** —*adj.* Constructed, shaped, or formed: *a carefully made piece.* —***idiom.*** **made for.** Perfectly suited for: *Those two are made for each other.*

❑ *These sound alike:* **made, maid** (servant).

Ma•dei•ra Islands (mə dîr′ə). A group of islands of Portugal in the northeast Atlantic Ocean west of Morocco. The island of **Madeira** is noted for its wine.

Mad•e•moi•selle (măd′ə mə zĕl′ *or* măd mwä-zĕl′) *n., pl.* **Mad•e•moi•selles** (măd′ə mə zĕlz′ *or* măd mwä zĕlz′) or **Mes•de•moi•selles** (mād′mwä-zĕl′). Used as a polite form of address for a girl or young woman in a French-speaking area.

made-to-or•der (mād′to͞o ôr′dər) *adj.* Made in agreement with particular instructions or requirements; custom-made: *a made-to-order suit.*

made-up (mād′ŭp′) *adj.* **1.** Not real; imaginary; invented: *made-up stories.* **2.** Covered with cosmetics or makeup: *the clown's made-up face.*

mad•house (măd′hous′) *n.* **1.** A hospital or an asylum for the mentally ill. **2.** *Informal.* A place of great confusion or disorder.

Mad•i•son (măd′ĭ sən). The capital of Wisconsin, in the south-central part of the state west of Milwaukee. The city was settled in 1836. Population, 191,262.

Madison, Dolley Payne Todd. 1768–1849. First Lady of the United States (1809–1817) as the wife of President James Madison. She earlier served as White House hostess for the widowed Thomas Jefferson.

Madison, James. 1751–1836. The fourth President of the United States (1809–1817), whose presidency was marked by the War of 1812 with Great Britain (1812–1815).

mad•man (măd′măn′ *or* măd′mən) *n.* A man who is mentally ill.

macramé

Dolley Madison
Detail of an 1804 portrait by Gilbert Stuart (1755–1828)

James Madison

ă	pat	oi	boy
ā	pay	ou	out
âr	care	o͝o	took
ä	father	o͞o	boot
ĕ	pet	ŭ	cut
ē	be	ûr	urge
ĭ	pit	th	thin
ī	pie	*th*	this
îr	pier	hw	whoop
ŏ	pot	zh	vision
ō	toe	ə	about
ô	paw	N	*French* bon

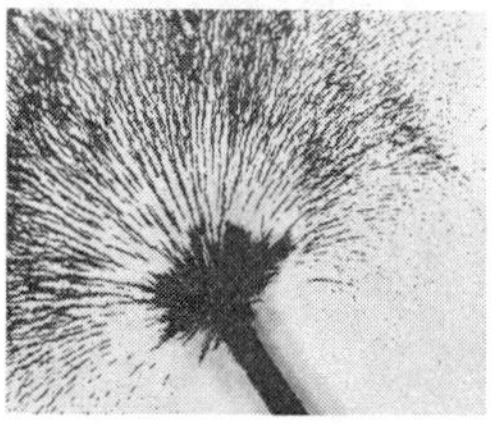

magnetic field
Magnet attracting iron filings

magnetism

The force known as **magnetism** is caused by moving or spinning particles called **electrons**. In an atom, these tiny, negatively charged particles revolve around the nucleus, creating electric currents that produce what is known as a **magnetic field**. This invisible field is made up of closed loops called *lines of force* that surround and run through the atom like tiny raceways. The places where these lines of force come together are strongly magnetic and are called north and south **poles**. In some substances, these tiny magnetic fields naturally align and the entire substance acts like a magnet—with north and south poles and a magnetic field. These naturally magnetic substances are called *permanent magnets*. Other things, such as a coil of wire, can be made magnetic by running electric current through them. These electrically produced magnets, called **electromagnets**, are used in many devices, such as the one that translates electric signals into the voice you hear on the telephone.

Ma•don•na (mə **dŏn′**ə) *n.* The Virgin Mary.

mad•ras (**măd′**rəs *or* mə **drăs′** *or* mə **dräs′**) *n.* A lightweight cotton cloth, usually having a plaid, striped, or checked pattern.

Ma•dras (mə **drăs′** *or* mə **dräs′**). A city of southeast India southeast of Bombay. It was founded in 1639. Population, 3,276,622.

Ma•drid (mə **drĭd′**). The capital and largest city of Spain, in the central part of the country north-northeast of Toledo. It was built on the site of a Moorish fortress captured in the 10th century. Population, 3,200,234.

mad•ri•gal (**măd′**rĭ gəl) *n.* **1.** A musical composition written for two or more unaccompanied voices. **2.** A short poem about love that can be set to music.

mael•strom (**māl′**strəm) *n.* **1.** A large and violent whirlpool. **2.** A violent or turbulent situation: *the maelstrom of war.* [First written down about 1560 in Modern English and spelled *malestrand*, from obsolete Dutch *Maelstrom.*]

maes•tro (**mīs′**trō) *n., pl.* **maes•tros** or **maes•tri** (**mīs′**trē). A master in an art, especially a conductor, composer, or music teacher.

Ma•fi•a (**mä′**fē ə) *n.* **1.** A secret terrorist organization operating in Sicily, Italy since the early 19th century. **2.** A secret organization involved in criminal activities, especially in the United States.

mag•a•zine (**măg′**ə zēn′ *or* măg′ə **zēn′**) *n.* **1.** A publication, often issued weekly or monthly, that contains written matter, such as articles or stories, and usually pictures and advertising. **2.** A building or room in a fort or on a warship where ammunition is stored. **3.** In some firearms, a container in which cartridges are held until they pass into the chamber for firing. [First written down in 1583 in Modern English and spelled *magosine*, from Arabic *maḫāzin*, storehouses.]

Ma•gel•lan (mə **jĕl′**ən), **Ferdinand.** 1480?–1521. Portuguese navigator who led the expedition that included the first ship to sail around the world (1519–1522).

Magellan, Strait of. A channel separating South America from Tierra del Fuego and other islands south of the continent. Ferdinand Magellan sailed through the strait in October and November 1520.

ma•gen•ta (mə **jĕn′**tə) *n.* A bright purplish-red. [First written down in 1860 in Modern English, after *Magenta*, a town of northwest Italy.]

mag•got (**măg′**ət) *n.* The larva of any of various flies, resembling a worm and usually found in decaying matter or as a parasite.

Ma•gi (**mā′**jī′) *pl.n.* In the Bible, the three wise men of the East who traveled to Bethlehem to pay respect to the infant Jesus.

mag•ic (**măj′**ĭk) *n.* **1.** The art that claims to use supernatural powers to control natural events, effects, or forces through charms, spells, or rituals. **2.** The art or skill of using sleight of hand and other tricks to produce entertaining and baffling effects. **3.** A mysterious quality that seems to enchant; a special charm: *the magic of the woods in the fall.* —*adj.* Of or relating to magic and its practice: *a magic trick; a magic wand.* [First written down about 1380 in Middle English and spelled *magik*, from Greek *magikē*, from *magos*, magician.]

mag•i•cal (**măj′**ĭ kəl) *adj.* Of, relating to, or produced by magic: *the magical appearance of a rabbit from a hat.* —**mag′i•cal•ly** *adv.*

ma•gi•cian (mə **jĭsh′**ən) *n.* **1.** A person who uses magic; a sorcerer; a wizard. **2.** An entertainer who performs tricks of magic.

magic lantern *n.* An early kind of slide projector.

mag•is•te•ri•al (măj′ĭ **stîr′**ē əl) *adj.* **1.** Of or relating to a magistrate or a magistrate's official functions: *magisterial duties.* **2.** Having or showing authority; authoritative: *a magisterial account of the American Revolution.* **3.** Domineering; overbearing; dogmatic: *The director's magisterial attitude offended the actors.* —**mag′is•te′ri•al•ly** *adv.*

mag•is•tra•cy (**măj′**ĭs trə sē) *n., pl.* **mag•is•tra•cies. 1.** The position, duties, or term of office of a magistrate. **2.** A body of magistrates.

mag•is•trate (**măj′**ĭ strāt′ *or* **măj′**ĭ strĭt) *n.* **1.** A civil official with the authority to administer the law. **2.** A judge, such as a justice of the peace, who has limited authority.

mag•ma (**măg′**mə) *n., pl.* **mag•ma•ta** (măg **mä′**tə) or **mag•mas.** The molten rock material under the earth's crust that forms igneous rock when it has cooled. [First written down in 1440 in Middle English and spelled *magma*, sediment, dregs, from Greek *magma*, unguent.]

Mag•na Car•ta or **Mag•na Char•ta** (**măg′**nə **kär′**tə) *n.* A document of English political and civil liberties granted by King John in 1215. The Magna Carta guaranteed certain liberties to the people of England and limited the king's power.

mag•na cum lau•de (**mäg′**nə ko͝om **lou′**də) *adv.* With great honor: *graduate magna cum laude*

mag•na•nim•i•ty (măg′nə **nĭm′**ĭ tē) *n., pl.* **mag•na•nim•i•ties.** The quality of being magnanimous; nobility.

mag•nan•i•mous (măg **năn′**ə məs) *adj.* Noble in heart and mind; generous and unselfish: *a magnanimous person.* —**mag•nan′i•mous•ly** *adv.*

mag•nate (**măg′**nāt′ *or* **măg′**nĭt) *n.* A powerful and influential person, especially in business: *a real estate magnate.* [First written down before 1439 in Middle English, from Late Latin *magnātēs*, magnates, from Latin *magnus*, great.]

mag•ne•sia (măg **nē′**zhə *or* măg **nē′**shə) *n.* A white powder used as an antacid or laxative in medicines. [First written down about 1395 in Middle English and spelled *magnasia*, mineral ingredient of the philosophers' stone, from Greek *Magnēsia*, Magnesia, an ancient city of Asia Minor.]

mag•ne•si•um (măg **nē′**zē əm *or* măg **nē′**zhəm) *n.* *Symbol* **Mg** A lightweight, moderately hard, silvery metallic element that burns with an intense flame and is essential for the formation of chlorophyll. Atomic number 12. See table at **element.**

mag•net (**măg′**nĭt) *n.* **1.** A stone, piece of metal, or other solid that has the property, either natural or induced, of attracting iron or steel. **2.** An electromagnet. **3.** A person or place that exerts a powerful attraction: *Our garden is a magnet for rabbits.* [First written down before 1398 in Middle English and spelled *magnes*, from Greek *Magnēs (lithos)*, Magnesian (stone), from *Magnēsia*, Magnesia, an ancient city of Asia Minor.]

mag•net•ic (măg **nĕt′**ĭk) *adj.* **1.** Of or relating to magnetism or magnets. **2.** Having the properties of a magnet; showing magnetism. **3.** Producing, caused by, or operating by magnetism: *a magnetic compass; a magnetic recording.* **4.** Of or relating to the magnetic properties of the earth: *The magnetic north pole is in a different place from the geographic North Pole.* **5.** Having the power to attract or charm: *a popular performer with a magnetic personality.* —**mag•net′i•cal•ly** *adv.*

magnetic field *n.* A condition in the region of space around a magnet or an electric current, in which a magnetic force exists.

magnetic flux *n.* A measure of magnetism, the total number of magnetic lines of force that pass through a specific area.

magnetic needle *n.* A narrow thin piece of magnetized steel for use in a compass. It points toward the earth's magnetic poles.

magnetic north *n.* The direction in which the earth's north magnetic pole lies, to which a magnetic needle of a compass points, differing in most places from the true or geographic north.

magnetic pole *n.* **1.** Either of two regions of a magnet where the magnetic field is strongest. **2.** Either of two variable points on the earth's surface, toward which a compass needle points. The magnetic poles differ from the geographic poles. The North Magnetic Pole is in the Arctic, the South Magnetic Pole is in Antarctica.

magnetic tape *n.* A plastic tape coated with tiny magnetic particles for use in recording sounds or pictures.

mag•net•ism (măg′nĭ tĭz′əm) *n.* **1.** The properties or effects of magnets: *Magnetism causes a compass needle to point north.* **2.** The study of magnets and their effects. **3.** The force produced by a magnetic field. **4.** An unusual power to attract or influence: *The magnetism of the leader's stirring words drew many followers.* —See Note.

mag•net•ite (măg′nĭ tīt′) *n.* A mineral composed of iron oxide that is strongly attracted by a magnet and is an important iron ore.

mag•net•ize (măg′nĭ tīz′) *tr.v.* **mag•net•ized, mag•net•iz•ing, mag•net•iz•es.** To make (an object) magnetic: *magnetize a nail by wrapping it in a wire that will carry an electric current.* —**mag′net•i•za′tion** (măg′nĭ tĭ **zā′**shən) *n.* —**mag′net•iz′er** *n.*

mag•ne•to (măg **nē′**tō) *n., pl.* **mag•ne•tos.** A device that produces alternating current and is used to fire spark plugs in some internal-combustion engines.

magnet school *n.* A school designed to attract students from a wide geographic area by offering special educational programs often with a major focus, as science, the humanities, or art.

mag•ni•fi•ca•tion (măg′nə fĭ **kā′**shən) *n.* The act, process, or degree of magnifying.

mag•nif•i•cence (măg **nĭf′**ĭ səns) *n.* Richness or splendor of surroundings; grand or imposing beauty: *the magnificence of the Grand Canyon.*

mag•nif•i•cent (măg **nĭf′**ĭ sənt) *adj.* **1.** Splendid in appearance; grand; remarkable: *a magnificent cathedral.* **2.** Outstanding of its kind; excellent: *a magnificent athlete.* —**mag•nif′i•cent•ly** *adv.*

Synonyms: magnificent, grand, majestic, imposing, grandiose. These adjectives mean large and impressive. **Magnificent** means full of luxurious splendor and grandeur: *The Taj Mahal is a magnificent example of Indian architecture.* **Grand** and **majestic** suggest lofty dignity or nobility: *The President welcomed the foreign officials with a grand ceremony. The mountain climbers struggled up the majestic slopes of the Alps.* **Imposing** means impressive because of size, bearing, or power: *We stared up at the imposing statue of Abraham Lincoln.* **Grandiose** often means imposing in a pompous, pretentious, or otherwise negative way: *The politician's grandiose speech about world peace turned out to be nothing but empty words.*

mag•ni•fy (măg′nə fī′) *v.* **mag•ni•fied, mag•ni•fy•ing, mag•ni•fies.** —*tr.* **1.** To make (an object) appear larger than it really is: *A microscope magnifies the cell so that you can study it.* **2.** To cause to appear greater or seem more important; exaggerate: *The wind magnifies the effect of the cold.* —*intr.* To make or be capable of making an object appear larger than it really is. [First written down about 1380 in Middle English and spelled *magnifien*, to praise, from Latin *magnificāre*, from *magnificus*, magnificent.] —**mag′ni•fi′er** *n.*

mag•ni•fy•ing glass (**măg′**nə fī′ĭng) *n.* A lens or combination of lenses that makes objects appear larger than they really are.

mag•ni•tude (**măg′**nĭ to͞od′ *or* **măg′**nĭ tyo͞od′) *n.* **1.** Greatness, as of position, size, or significance: *finally understood the magnitude of the problem.* **2.** The relative brightness of a star or another celestial body as measured on a numerical scale. The brightest stars are of the first magnitude.

mag•no•lia (măg **nōl′**yə) *n.* **1.** Any of numerous evergreen trees or shrubs having large showy, usually white, pink, or yellow flowers. **2.** The flower of such a tree or shrub. [First written down in 1748 in Modern English, after Pierre *Magnol* (1638–1715), French botanist.]

mag•pie (**măg′**pī′) *n.* **1.** Any of various noisy black and white birds that are related to the crows and jays and have a long tail. **2.** A person who chatters.

ma•guey (mə **gā′** *or* **măg′**wā) *n., pl.* **ma•gueys. 1.** Any of various plants of the southwest United States and Mexico having large stiff leaves that yield a fiber used for making rope or twine. **2.** The fiber of such a plant.

Mag•yar (**măg′**yär′ *or* **mäg′**yär′) *n.* **1.** A member of the main ethnic group of Hungary. **2.** The language of the Magyars; Hungarian. —**Mag′yar** *adj.*

ma•ha•ra•jah or **ma•ha•ra•ja** (mä′hə **rä′**jə *or* mä′hə **rä′**zhə) *n.* A king or prince in India ranking above a rajah. [First written down in 1698 in Modern English and spelled *mau raja*, from Sanskrit *mahārājā*, great king.]

ma•ha•ra•ni or **ma•ha•ra•nee** (mä′hə **rä′**nē) *n., pl.* **ma•ha•ra•nis** or **ma•ha•ra•nees. 1.** The wife of a maharajah. **2.** A princess in India ranking above a rani.

ma•hat•ma (mə **hät′**mə *or* mə **hăt′**mə) *n.* **1.** In India and Tibet, a wise and compassionate person. **2. Mahatma.** Used as a title of respect for a holy person, especially by Hindus.

Ma•hi•can (mə **hē′**kən) also **Mo•hi•can** (mō **hē′**kən *or* mə **hē′**kən) *n., pl.* **Mahican** or **Ma•hi•cans** also **Mohican** or **Mo•hi•cans. 1.** A member of a Native American people formerly living in the upper Hudson River valley, with descendants now living in Oklahoma and Wisconsin. **2.** The Algonquian language of the Mahican.

mah•jong also **mah•jongg** (**mä′zhŏng′** *or* **mä′zhông′**) *n.* A game of Chinese origin usually played by four persons using tiles bearing various designs. Each player tries to win by forming certain combinations by drawing and discarding tiles.

ma•hog•a•ny (mə **hŏg′**ə nē) *n., pl.* **ma•hog•a•nies. 1.a.** Any of various tropical American trees having hard reddish-brown wood. **b.** The wood of such a tree, much used for making furniture. **2.** A reddish brown. [First written down in 1671 in Modern English and spelled *mohogeney*, from obsolete Spanish *mahogani*, perhaps of Mayan origin.]

maid (mād) *n.* **1.** An unmarried girl or woman. **2.** A female servant. [First written down before 1200 in Middle English and spelled *maide*, from Old English *mægden*, maiden.]

❑ *These sound alike:* **maid, made** (created).

maid•en (**mād′**n) *n.* An unmarried girl or woman. —*adj.* **1.** Of, relating to, or suited to a maiden: *youthful maiden beauty.* **2.** Unmarried: *a maiden aunt.* **3.** First or earliest: *a ship's maiden voyage.*

maid•en•hair fern (**mād′**n hâr′) *n.* Any of various ferns having thin dark stems and feathery fronds with fan-shaped leaflets.

maid•en•hood (**mād′**n ho͝od′) *n.* The quality or condition of being a maiden.

maiden name *n.* A woman's family name before she is married.

maid in waiting *n., pl.* **maids in waiting.** An unmarried woman who attends a queen or princess.

maid of honor *n., pl.* **maids of honor. 1.** An unmarried woman who is the bride's chief attendant

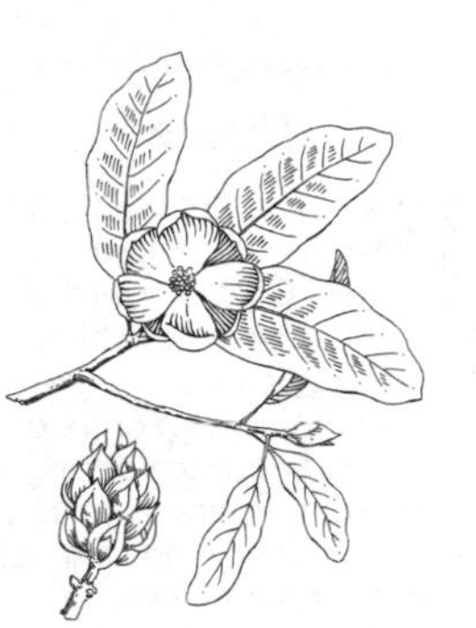

magnolia
Sweet bay magnolia

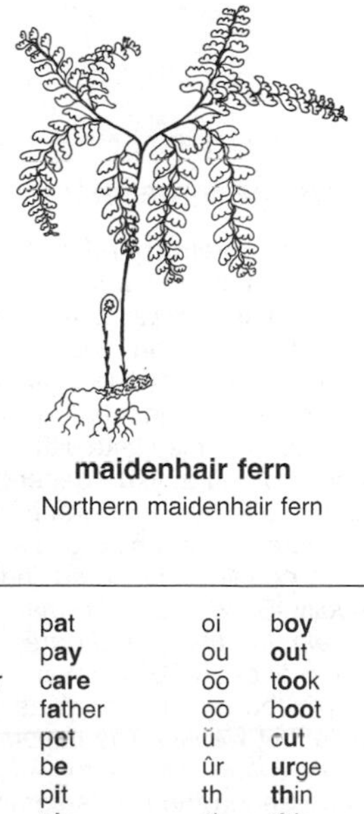

maidenhair fern
Northern maidenhair fern

ă	pat	oi	boy
ā	pay	ou	out
âr	care	o͝o	took
ä	father	o͞o	boot
ĕ	pet	ŭ	cut
ē	be	ûr	urge
ĭ	pit	th	thin
ī	pie	*th*	this
îr	pier	hw	whoop
ŏ	pot	zh	vision
ō	toe	ə	about
ô	paw	N	*French* bon

Maine

The name of the state of **Maine** comes from the archaic English word *main*, also written *maine*, which was used to refer to a continent or mainland. Early explorers of the region needed to distinguish between the many islands and the mainland, and the area soon became known as "the main." **Maine** was made the official name of the state when it was organized in 1820.

maintop

Usage: majority

When **majority** refers to a particular number of votes, it takes a singular verb: *Her majority was five votes.* When it refers to a group of persons or things that are in the majority, it may take either a singular or plural verb, depending on whether the group is considered as a whole or as a set of people considered individually. So we say *The majority elects the candidate it wants,* since the election is accomplished by the group as a whole; but we say *The majority of the voters live in the city,* since living in the city is something that each voter does individually.

at a wedding. **2.** An unmarried noblewoman who attends a queen or princess.

maid•ser•vant (mād′sûr′vənt) *n.* A female servant.

mail[1] (māl) *n.* **1.a.** Letters, postcards, packages, and printed matter sent through the postal system of a country. **b.** Such materials for a specified person or organization: *What came in the mail today?* **2.** A governmental system that handles the postal materials of a country. —*tr.v.* **mailed, mail•ing, mails.** To send by mail. [First written down before 1200 in Middle English and spelled *male*, bag, from Old French, of Germanic origin.]

❑ *These sound alike:* **mail**[1] (postal material), **mail**[2] (armor), **male** (man).

mail[2] (māl) *n.* Flexible armor made of connected metal rings, loops of chain, or overlapping scales, worn to protect the body in battle. —*tr.v.* **mailed, mail•ing, mails.** To cover or protect with such armor. [First written down before 1300 in Middle English, from Old French *maile*, from Latin *macula*, blemish, mesh.]

❑ *These sound alike:* **mail**[2] (armor), **mail**[1] (postal material), **male** (man).

mail•box (māl′bŏks′) *n.* **1.** A public box for depositing outgoing mail. **2.** A private box where incoming mail is delivered.

mail carrier *n.* A person who delivers mail or collects it from mailboxes.

mail•man (māl′măn′ *or* māl′mən) *n.* A man who carries and delivers mail.

mail order *n.* A request for goods to be shipped through the mail.

maim (mām) *tr.v.* **maimed, maim•ing, maims.** To disable, usually by causing the loss of the use of a limb: *Accidents maim many people each year.*

main (mān) *adj.* Most important; principal; chief: *Look for the main idea in each paragraph.* —*n.* **1.** A large pipe, duct, conduit, or conductor used to carry water, oil, gas, or electricity. **2.** The open sea. —***idiom.*** **in the main.** For the most part; on the whole: *Your ideas are, in the main, useful.* [First written down before 1200 in Middle English and spelled *mæin*, from Old English *mægen*, strength.]

❑ *These sound alike:* **main, mane** (neck hair).

Main (mān *or* mīn). A river rising in eastern Germany and flowing about 310 miles (499 kilometers) generally westward to the Rhine River.

main clause *n.* An independent clause.

Maine (mān). A state of the northeast United States northeast of New Hampshire. It was admitted as the 23rd state in 1820. Augusta is the capital and Portland the largest city. Population, 1,125,030. —SEE NOTE.

main•frame (mān′frām′) *n.* A powerful computer that can quickly perform many operations and store great amounts of information, often serving many terminals.

main•land (mān′lănd′ *or* mān′lənd) *n.* The principal land mass of a country, territory, or continent as opposed to its islands or peninsulas: *the mainland of Europe.*

main•ly (mān′lē) *adv.* Most importantly; for the most part: *Homework for history class consists mainly of reading.*

main•mast (mān′məst *or* mān′măst′) *n.* The principal mast of a sailing ship.

main•sail (mān′səl *or* mān′sāl′) *n.* The largest sail set on the mainmast of a sailing ship.

main•spring (mān′sprĭng′) *n.* **1.** The spring that drives a mechanism, especially a clock or watch. **2.** The most important cause or force: *A desire for justice was the mainspring of the reform movement.*

main•stay (mān′stā′) *n.* **1.** A main support: *This player is the mainstay of the team.* **2.** A strong rope or cable that holds in place the mainmast of a sailing vessel.

main•stream (mān′strēm′) *n.* The prevailing current or direction of a movement or an influence: *Her ideas are outside the mainstream.*

main•tain (mān tān′) *tr.v.* **main•tained, main•tain•ing, main•tains. 1.** To keep up; carry on; continue: *The train maintains its speed on hills.* **2.** To keep in a desirable condition: *maintain public roads.* **3.** To provide for the upkeep of; bear the expenses of: *maintain a large family.* **4.** To uphold against attack or danger; defend: *maintain one's independence.* **5.** To declare as true; affirm: *maintain one's innocence.*

main•te•nance (mān′tə nəns) *n.* **1.** The act of maintaining or the condition of being maintained: *maintenance of calm during the emergency; maintenance of the traditions by the family.* **2.** The work involved in maintaining; care; upkeep: *maintenance of an old building.* **3.** Means of support or livelihood: *Wages provide maintenance.*

main•top (mān′tŏp′) *n.* A platform on the mainmast of a ship.

main yard *n.* The yard or pole on which the mainsail of a sailing ship is extended.

maize (māz) *n.* **1.** The corn plant or its edible kernels. **2.** A light to strong yellow. [First written down in 1555 in Modern English, from Spanish *maíz*, from Cariban *mahiz*.]

❑ *These sound alike:* **maize, maze** (labyrinth).

Maj. *abbr.* An abbreviation of major (military rank).

ma•jes•tic (mə jĕs′tĭk) *adj.* Having or showing majesty. See Synonyms at **magnificent.** —**ma•jes′ti•cal** *adj.* —**ma•jes′tic•al•ly** *adv.*

maj•es•ty (măj′ĭ stē) *n., pl.* **maj•es•ties. 1.** The greatness and dignity of a sovereign: *The royal couple arrived at the palace in all their majesty.* **2.** Supreme authority or power: *the majesty of the law.* **3.** A quality of stateliness, splendor, or grandeur: *the majesty of the Rocky Mountains.* **4. Majesty.** Used as a title for a sovereign, such as a king or queen: *Your Majesty.* [First written down about 1300 in Middle English and spelled *maieste*, from Latin *māiestās*.]

Maj. Gen. *abbr.* An abbreviation of major general.

ma•jor (mā′jər) *adj.* **1.** Greater than others in importance or rank: *a major American novelist.* **2.a.** Relating to or based on a major scale: *a major chord.* **b.** Of or relating to a musical tone that is a half step greater than a minor interval. —*n.* **1.** An officer in the Army, Air Force, or Marine Corps ranking above a captain and below a lieutenant colonel. **2.** In schools and colleges, a field of study chosen as a specialty: *My major is French.* **3.** A major scale, key, or interval: *the key of D major.* **4. majors.** The major leagues of a sport, especially baseball. —*intr.v.* **ma•jored, ma•jor•ing, ma•jors.** To study or specialize in a particular subject: *I am majoring in Spanish.* [First written down before 1300 in Middle English and spelled *majour*, from Latin *māior*.]

Ma•jor•ca (mə jôr′kə *or* mə yôr′ə). An island of Spain in the western Mediterranean Sea off the east-central coast of the mainland. It is the largest of the Balearic Islands.

ma•jor-do•mo (mā′jər dō′mō) *n., pl.* **ma•jor-do•mos.** The head steward or butler in the household of a sovereign or great noble.

ma•jor•ette (mā′jə rĕt′) *n.* A drum majorette.

major general *n.* An officer in the Army, Air Force, or Marine Corps ranking above a brigadier general and below a lieutenant general.

ma•jor•i•ty (mə jôr′ĭ tē *or* mə jŏr′ĭ tē) *n., pl.* **ma•jor•i•ties. 1.** The greater number or part of something; a number more than half of a total: *The* *majority of the class did well on the test.* **2.** The amount by which a greater number of votes exceeds the remaining number of votes: *The candidate won by a majority of 5,000 votes.* **3.** A political party or group that has the greater number of members or supporters: *The party is a majority in the city.* **4.** The status of having reached the age of legal responsibility, usually 18 or 21. —SEE NOTE.

major league *n.* **1.** Either of the two principal groups of professional baseball teams in the United States. **2.** A league of principal importance in other professional sports.

ma•jor-league (mā′jər lēg′) *adj.* **1.** Of or relating to a major league: *a major-league player.* **2.** Outstanding of its kind: *a major-league performance.*

ma•jor-lea•guer (mā′jər lē′gər) *n.* A member of a major-league sports team.

major scale *n.* A musical scale in which the third and fourth tones and the seventh and eighth tones are separated by half steps and all other tones are separated by whole steps.

Ma•kas•sar (mə kăs′ər). Ujung Pandang.

make (māk) *v.* **made** (mād), **mak•ing, makes.** —*tr.* **1.** To cause to exist or happen; bring about; create: *The students made noise in the hall.* **2.a.** To bring into existence by shaping, changing, or putting together material: *make a dress; make a wall of stones.* **b.** To draw up; establish; enact: *make rules.* **3.** To cause to be or become: *The invitation made us happy.* **4.a.** To cause to act in a specified way: *The pepper made me sneeze.* **b.** To force; compel: *His allergies made him stay home.* **5.** To prepare; fix: *make breakfast.* **6.** To carry out, perform, or engage in: *make a telephone call; make war.* **7.** To reach in time: *We just made the bus.* **8.** To acquire the rank of or a place on: *made lieutenant; made the baseball team.* **9.** To gain or acquire: *make money; make friends.* **10.** To be suited for: *This area would make a good soccer field.* **11.** To develop into: *She will make a fine doctor.* **12.a.** To formulate or arrive at in one's mind: *make plans; make a decision.* **b.** To determine the meaning of: *What do you make of their proposal?* **13.** To form or amount to; constitute: *Two wrongs don't make a right.* **14.** To assure the success of: *The scenery makes the movie.* —*intr.v.* **1.** To cause something to be in a specified manner: *The actors made ready for the play.* **2.** To go or move, as in a certain direction: *The ship made for harbor.* —*n.* **1.** A style or manner in which something is made: *disliked the make of the coat.* **2.** A specific line of manufactured goods; a brand: *Three makes of small trucks are available.* —***idioms.*** **make away with.** To carry off; steal. **make believe.** To pretend. **make do.** To manage; get along. **make ends meet.** To make enough money to pay one's expenses. **make for.** To be favorable to; help: *The steady breeze made for excellent sailing.* **make fun of.** To mock; ridicule. **make good. 1.** To carry out successfully: *He made good his escape.* **2.** To fulfill: *I will make good my promise.* **3.** To make compensation for; make up for: *He made good the loss.* **4.** To succeed: *She made good as an artist.* **make it.** *Informal.* To be successful. **make light of.** To treat as unimportant: *He made light of his promotion.* **make much of.** To treat as of great importance. **make off with.** To snatch or steal. **make out. 1.** To see or identify, especially with difficulty: *Can you make out that sign?* **2.** To understand: *I can't make out what she means in the letter.* **3.** To write out or fill out: *make out a tax form.* **4.** *Informal.* To represent as being: *You make me out to be a liar.* **5.** To get along in a given way; fare: *How are you making out with the dance lessons?* **make over. 1.** To redo; renovate. **2.** To change or transfer the ownership of, usually by means of a legal document: *They made the house over to their children.* **make the most of.** To use to the greatest advantage. **make up. 1.** To put together; construct or compose: *We made up a model of the new building.* **2.** To constitute; form: *A basketball team is made up of five players.* **3.** To apply cosmetics. **4.** To devise as a fiction or falsehood; invent: *make up a story.* **5.** To compensate for: *We made up the lost time by taking a short cut.* **6.** To resolve a quarrel: *They talked over the their differences and made up.* **7.** To take (an examination or a course) again or at a later time. **make up (one's) mind.** To come to a definite decision or opinion. [First written down before 901 in Old English and spelled *macian.*]

make-be•lieve (māk′bĭ lēv′) *n.* Playful imagining or acting as if one were another person or in an invented place: *Fairies exist in the land of make-believe.* —*adj.* Imaginary; fictional.

mak•er (mā′kər) *n.* **1.** A person or thing that makes. **2. Maker.** God.

make•shift (māk′shĭft′) *n.* Something used or assembled as a temporary substitute: *I didn't have a chair, so I used the crate as a makeshift.* —*adj.* Serving as a temporary substitute: *ate our breakfast at a makeshift table.*

make•up or **make-up** (māk′ŭp′) *n.* **1.** The way in which something is put together or arranged; construction: *What is the makeup of the police department?* **2.** The qualities or temperament that make up a personality; disposition: *It's just not in her makeup to complain.* **3.** Cosmetics applied especially to the face. **4.** A special examination given to a student who has missed or failed a previous one. **5.** The arrangement of type or illustrations on a page or in a book.

mal– *pref.* A prefix that means bad or wrongly: *malpractice; malformed.*

Mal•a•bo (măl′ə bō′ *or* mä lä′bō). The capital and largest city of Equatorial Guinea, on an island off the coast of Cameroon. It was founded in 1827. Population, 30,710.

Mal•a•chi (măl′ə kī′) *n.* **1.** A Hebrew prophet of the sixth century B.C. **2.** A book of the Bible in which Malachi warns the Jews to follow God's laws.

mal•a•chite (măl′ə kīt′) *n.* A green to nearly black copper carbonate mineral used as an ore of copper and in ornamental objects and jewelry and stonework. [First written down before 1398 in Middle English and spelled *melochite,* from Greek *malakhē,* mallow.]

mal•ad•just•ed (măl′ə jŭs′tĭd) *adj.* Poorly adjusted to one's environment or to one's circumstances.

mal•ad•just•ment (măl′ə jŭst′mənt) *n.* Inability to adjust to one's environment or one's circumstances.

mal•a•droit (măl′ə droit′) *adj.* Lacking skill; awkward or inept. —**mal′a•droit′ly** *adv.* —**mal′a•droit′ness** *n.*

mal•a•dy (măl′ə dē) *n., pl.* **mal•a•dies. 1.** A disease, a disorder, or an ailment. **2.** An unwholesome condition.

mal•a•mute or **mal•e•mute** (măl′ə myo͞ot′) *n.* Any of a breed of large strong dog developed in Alaska as a sled dog and having a thick black and white or gray coat and a bushy tail.

ma•lar•i•a (mə lâr′ē ə) *n.* An infectious disease characterized by periods of chills, fever, and sweating. It is caused by parasites in the blood that are transmitted by the bite of a mosquito that has bitten another person infected with malaria. [First written down in 1740 in Modern English, from Italian *mala aria,* bad air.] —**ma•lar′i•al** *adj.*

Ma•la•wi (mə lä′wē). A country of southeast Africa east of Zambia. It was the center of a widespread

major scale

malamute

ă	pat	oi	boy
ā	pay	ou	out
âr	care	o͝o	took
ä	father	o͞o	boot
ĕ	pet	ŭ	cut
ē	be	ûr	urge
ĭ	pit	th	thin
ī	pie	*th*	this
îr	pier	hw	whoop
ŏ	pot	zh	vision
ō	toe	ə	about
ô	paw	ɴ	*French* bon

Malcolm X

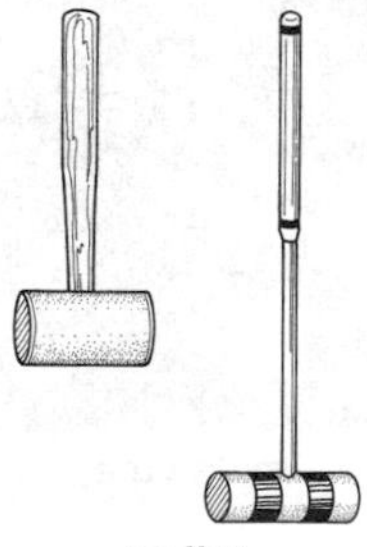

mallet

Left: Carpenter's mallet
Right: Croquet mallet

kingdom from the 15th to the late 18th century and gained its independence from Great Britain in 1964. Lilongwe is the capital and Blantyre the largest city. Population, 6,123,000.

Ma•lay (mə **lā′** *or* **mā′**lā′) *n.* **1.** A member of a people of the Malay Peninsula and some adjacent areas. **2.** The language of this people. —*adj.* **1.** Of or relating to the Malays, their language, or culture. **2.** Of or relating to Malaysia, the Malay Peninsula, or the Malay Archipelago. —**Ma•lay′an** (mə **lā′**ən) *adj. & n.*

Ma•la•ya (mə **lā′**ə *or* mā **lā′**ə). Malay Peninsula.

Mal•a•ya•lam (măl′ə **yä′**ləm) *n.* A language spoken on the southwest coast of India.

Malay Archipelago. An island group of southeast Asia between Australia and mainland Asia. It includes the islands of Indonesia, the Philippines, and Malaysia.

Malay Peninsula. A peninsula of southeast Asia made up of southwest Thailand, western Malaysia, and the island of Singapore.

Ma•lay•sia (mə **lā′**zhə *or* mə **lā′**shə). A country of southeast Asia consisting of the southern Malay Peninsula and the northern part of the island of Borneo. It gained its independence from Great Britain in 1963. Kuala Lumpur is the capital and the largest city. Population, 13,486,433.

Mal•colm X (**măl′**kəm ĕks). Originally Malcolm Little. 1925–1965. American Black activist who advocated separatism and Black Power. In 1964 he founded the Organization of Afro-American Unity.

mal•con•tent (**măl′**kən tĕnt′) *adj.* Dissatisfied with existing conditions. —*n.* A dissatisfied or rebellious person.

Mal•dives (**môl′**dīvz *or* **măl′**dīvz). An island country in the Indian Ocean southwest of Sri Lanka, consisting of 19 groups of coral islands. The Maldives gained independence from Great Britain in 1965. Capital, Male. Population, 181,453.

male (māl) *adj.* **1.** Of, relating to, or characteristic of the sex that can fertilize egg cells and father offspring. **2.** Of or relating to seed plants that have flowers that contain stamens but not pistils. **3.** Composed of men or boys: *a male choir.* **4.** Designed to make a connection by fitting into a corresponding socket or opening: *a male plug.* —*n.* **1.** A male animal or plant. **2.** A man or boy. [First written down in 1373 in Middle English, from Latin *masculus.*] —**male′ness** *n.*

❑ *These sound alike:* **male, mail**[1] (postal material), **mail**[2] (armor).

Ma•le (**mä′**lē). The capital of the Maldives, in the Indian Ocean southwest of Sri Lanka. Population, 46,334.

mal•e•dic•tion (măl′ĭ **dĭk′**shən) *n.* **1.** A curse: *a witch's malediction.* **2.** Evil talk; slander.

mal•e•fac•tor (**măl′**ə făk′tər) *n.* **1.** A person who has committed a crime; a criminal. **2.** An evildoer.

ma•lev•o•lence (mə **lĕv′**ə ləns) *n.* The wish for harm or evil to come to others; ill will; malice.

ma•lev•o•lent (mə **lĕv′**ə lənt) *adj.* Wishing harm to others; malicious. —**ma•lev′o•lent•ly** *adv.*

mal•fea•sance (măl **fē′**zəns) *n.* Wrongdoing or misconduct, especially by a public official: *An official who accepts a bribe is guilty of malfeasance.*

mal•for•ma•tion (măl′fôr **mā′**shən) *n.* An abnormal or imperfect structure or form, as of a part of the body; deformity.

mal•formed (măl **fôrmd′**) *adj.* Having an imperfect or abnormal form: *blight that causes malformed ears of corn.*

mal•func•tion (măl **fŭngk′**shən) *intr.v.* **mal•func•tioned, mal•func•tion•ing, mal•func•tions.** To fail to function properly. —*n.* Failure to function well: *a malfunction in the computer.* [First written down in 1928 in Modern English : *mal-*, wrongly (from Latin *malus*, bad) + *function.*]

Ma•li (**mä′**lē). A country of western Africa west of Niger. It was a powerful empire from the 14th to the 16th century and gained its independence from France in 1960. Capital, Bamako. Population, 6,982,000.

mal•ice (**măl′**ĭs) *n.* The desire to harm others or to see others suffer; ill will; spite. [First written down about 1300 in Middle English, from Latin *malitia*, from *malus*, bad.]

ma•li•cious (mə **lĭsh′**əs) *adj.* Having, showing, or motivated by malice; spiteful: *a malicious lie.* —**ma•li′cious•ly** *adv.* —**ma•li′cious•ness** *n.*

ma•lign (mə **līn′**) *tr.v.* **ma•ligned, ma•lign•ing, ma•ligns.** To speak evil of; slander: *malign a person's reputation.* —*adj.* **1.** Showing or having malice: *a malign look.* **2.** Evil in nature; injurious: *Poverty can be a malign influence.* [First written down before 1420 in Middle English and spelled *malignen*, from Latin *malignus*, evil.]

ma•lig•nan•cy (mə **lĭg′**nən sē) *n., pl.* **ma•lig•nan•cies. 1.** The quality or condition of being malignant. **2.** A malignant tumor or condition.

ma•lig•nant (mə **lĭg′**nənt) *adj.* **1.** Having or showing ill will; malicious: *malignant thoughts.* **2.a.** Threatening to life or health; deadly: *a malignant disease.* **b.** Tending to grow and spread throughout the body; cancerous: *a malignant tumor.* —**ma•lig′nant•ly** *adv.*

ma•lig•ni•ty (mə **lĭg′**nĭ tē) *n., pl.* **ma•lig•ni•ties. 1.** Deep-rooted ill will; malice. **2.** Something evil or of great malice.

ma•lin•ger (mə **lĭng′**gər) *intr.v.* **ma•lin•gered, ma•lin•ger•ing, ma•lin•gers.** To pretend to be ill or injured in order to avoid work or duty. —**ma•lin′ger•er** *n.*

mall (môl *or* măl) *n.* **1.** A large shopping center containing different kinds of stores and businesses. **2.** A street lined with shops and closed to vehicles. **3.** A shady public walk or promenade. [First written down in 1737 in Modern English, after *The Mall* in London, England, originally an alley for playing pall-mall, a kind of croquet.]

❑ *These sound alike:* **mall, maul** (hammer).

mal•lard (**măl′**ərd) *n., pl.* **mallard** or **mal•lards.** A wild duck, the male of which has a glossy green head and a white band on its neck. [First written down before 1300 in Middle English and spelled *maulard*, from Old French *mallart.*]

mal•le•a•ble (**măl′**ē ə bəl) *adj.* **1.** Capable of being shaped or formed, as by pressure or hammering: *copper and other malleable metals.* **2.** Easily controlled or influenced: *a boss who wanted a malleable workforce.* **3.** Able to adjust to a changing circumstances; adaptable. —**mal′le•a•bil′i•ty** *n.*

mal•le•i (**măl′**ē ī′) *n.* Plural of **malleus.**

mal•let (**măl′**ĭt) *n.* **1.** A hammer with a wooden head and a short handle, used to drive a chisel or wedge. **2.** A long-handled hammer used to strike the ball in the games of croquet and polo. [First written down in 1392 in Middle English and spelled *mailet*, from Latin *malleus*, hammer.]

mal•le•us (**măl′**ē əs) *n., pl.* **mal•le•i** (**măl′**ē ī′). The largest and outermost of three small bones in the middle ear; the hammer.

mal•low (**măl′**ō) *n.* Any of various plants having flowers that are usually pink or white and often large and showy.

mal•nour•ished (măl **nûr′**ĭsht *or* măl **nŭr′**ĭsht) *adj.* Suffering from poor food or a lack of food: *emergency food shipments for the malnourished occupants of the refugee camps.*

mal•nu•tri•tion (măl′no͞o **trĭsh′**ən *or* măl′nyo͞o **trĭsh′**ən) *n.* A condition in which the body is not supplied with essential nourishment. Malnutrition usually is caused by a lack of the right foods but can also be caused by a physical condition or a disease.

mal•oc•clu•sion (măl′ə klo͞o′zhən) *n.* A condition in which the upper and lower teeth do not meet properly; a faulty bite.

mal•o•dor•ous (măl ō′dər əs) *adj.* Having a bad odor: *a malodorous swamp.* **—mal•o′dor•ous•ly** *adv.* **—mal•o′dor•ous•ness** *n.*

mal•prac•tice (măl prăk′tĭs) *n.* **1.** Improper or careless treatment of a patient by a doctor. **2.** Improper conduct by a person holding a professional or official position.

malt (môlt) *n.* Barley or other grain that has been soaked in water and allowed to sprout and then dried. It is used chiefly in brewing and distilling. *—tr.v.* **malt•ed, malt•ing, malts. 1.** To make (grain) into malt. **2.** To mix or prepare with malt.

Mal•ta (môl′tə). An island country in the Mediterranean Sea south of Sicily made up of the island of **Malta** and two smaller islands. The country gained its independence from Great Britain in 1964. Valletta is the capital. Population, 331,997.

malt•ed milk (môl′tĭd) *n.* A drink made of milk mixed with a powder of dried milk, malted barley, and wheat flour, often with the addition of ice cream and flavoring.

Mal•tese (môl tēz′ *or* môl tēs′) *adj.* Of or relating to Malta or its people or culture. *—n., pl.* **Maltese. 1.** A native or inhabitant of Malta. **2.** The Semitic language of the Maltese.

Maltese cat *n.* A cat having short bluish-gray fur, kept as a pet.

Maltese cross *n.* A cross having the form of four arrowheads placed with their points toward the center of a circle.

mal•tose (môl′tōs′ *or* môl′tōz′) *n.* A sugar made by the action of various enzymes on starch. It is formed in the body during digestion.

mal•treat (măl trēt′) *tr.v.* **mal•treat•ed, mal•treat•ing, mal•treats.** To treat cruelly or roughly. **—mal•treat′ment** *n.*

ma•ma or **mam•ma** (mä′mə *or* mə mä′) *n. Informal.* Mother.

mam•bo (mäm′bō) *n., pl.* **mam•bos. 1.** A Latin-American dance resembling the rumba. **2.** The music for this dance. *—intr.v.* **mam•boed, mam•bo•ing, mam•bos.** To dance the mambo.

mam•ma (mä′mə *or* mə mä′) *n.* Variant of **mama.**

mam•mal (măm′əl) *n.* Any of various warm-blooded animals that have a backbone, hair or fur, and, in the females, mammary glands that produce milk for feeding their young. Cats, dogs, cows, elephants, whales, and human beings are all mammals. **—mam•ma′li•an** (mă mā′lē ən) *adj. & n.*

mam•ma•ry gland (măm′ə rē) *n.* One of the glands in female mammals that is capable of producing milk.

mam•mo•gram (măm′ə grăm′) *n.* An x-ray image of the human breast.

Mam•mon (măm′ən) *n.* **1.** In the New Testament, riches and avarice personified as a false god. **2.** Often **mammon.** Riches regarded as an evil influence.

mam•moth (măm′əth) *n.* Any of various extinct elephants that had long tusks and thick hair and that lived throughout the Northern Hemisphere during the Ice Age. *—adj.* Huge; gigantic. [First written down in 1706 in Modern English, from obsolete Russian *mamut.*]

man (măn) *n., pl.* **men** (mĕn). **1.** An adult male human being. **2.** A human being without regard to sex or age. **3.** Human beings considered as a group; humanity: *Scientific research has benefited man.* **4.** A human being considered as a member of the species Homo sapiens: *evidence of early man in Africa.* **5.** A male person regarded as having qualities, such as bravery or strength, considered characteristic of manhood. **6.** A husband or lover. **7.** A male servant, employee, or worker: *ten men on the job.* **8.** Any of the pieces used in board games, such as chess or checkers. *—tr.v.* **manned, man•ning, mans. 1.** To take one's place or post at; get ready to work or operate: *Man the oars.* **2.** To supply with men: *The captain manned the ship with a new crew of sailors.* ***—idiom.* to a man.** Without exception: *They supported the new labor contract to a man.* [First written down before 725 in Old English and spelled *mann.*] —See Note.

Man (măn), **Isle of.** An island of Great Britain in the Irish Sea off the northwest coast of England. It is an autonomous possession of the British crown.

Man. *abbr.* Manitoba.

man•a•cle (măn′ə kəl) *n.* **1.** Handcuffs. Often used in the plural. **2.** Something that restricts freedom or restrains. *—tr.v.* **man•a•cled, man•a•cling, man•a•cles. 1.** To put manacles on: *The police officer manacled the thief.* **2.** To restrain; hamper: *manacled by my tiny office.*

man•age (măn′ĭj) *v.* **man•aged, man•ag•ing, man•ag•es.** *—tr.* **1.** To exert control over; be in charge of; direct: *manage a restaurant.* **2.** To direct or control the use of; handle or operate: *manage a bulldozer.* **3.** To succeed in doing or accomplishing; contrive or arrange: *Despite the bitter cold, I managed to stay warm.* *—intr.* **1.** To direct or conduct business affairs: *The book offers advice to executives on how to manage effectively.* **2.** To carry on; get along: *I don't know how we managed without your help.* [First written down in 1561 in Modern English and spelled *manege,* from Italian *maneggiare,* from Latin *manus,* hand.]

man•age•a•ble (măn′ĭ jə bəl) *adj.* Capable of being managed or controlled: *a manageable problem.* **—man′age•a•bil′i•ty** *n.*

man•age•ment (măn′ĭj mənt) *n.* **1.** The act, manner, or practice of managing: *hotel management.* **2.** The persons who manage a business or an organization: *I work for the management.*

man•ag•er (măn′ĭ jər) *n.* **1.** A person who manages a business or another enterprise. **2.** A person who is in charge of the business affairs of an entertainer. **3.** A person who is in charge of the training and performance of an athlete or a team.

man•a•ge•ri•al (măn′ĭ jîr′ē əl) *adj.* Of or characteristic of a manager or management: *learn managerial skills.*

Ma•na•gua (mə näg′wə). The capital and largest city of Nicaragua, in the western part of the country on **Lake Managua.** Population, 644,588.

Ma•na•ma (mə năm′ə) or **Al Ma•na•mah** (ăl mə năm′ə). The capital and largest city of Bahrain, on the Persian Gulf. It became capital in 1971. Population, 108,684.

ma•ña•na (mä nyä′nə) *adv.* **1.** Tomorrow. **2.** In the future. *—n.* Some time in the future.

man-at-arms (măn′ət ärmz′) *n., pl.* **men-at-arms** (mĕn′ət ärmz′). A soldier, especially a heavily armed mounted soldier in the Middle Ages.

man•a•tee (măn′ə tē′) *n.* Any of various plant-eating water mammals of rivers and bays along the tropical Atlantic coast that have flippers shaped like paddles.

Man•ches•ter (măn′chĕs′tər *or* măn′chĭ stər). **1.** A borough of northwest England east-northeast of Liverpool. Founded on the site of Celtic and Roman settlements, it was first chartered in 1301. Population, 464,200. **2.** The largest city of New Hampshire, in the southeast part of the state south-

mammoth

Woolly mammoth

Usage: man

The use of **man** to mean "a human being, regardless of gender," has a long history, but many feel that the sense of "male" is predominant over the sense of "human being." Therefore, many job titles in which **man** occurs are being replaced by neutral terms. For example, *firefighter* is often used instead of *fireman, Member of Congress* instead of *Congressman,* and *chair* or *chairperson* instead of *chairman.* In addition, compounds formed with **woman,** as in *businesswoman, policewoman,* and *chairwoman,* are now used as parallel terms to the compounds formed with **man.**

ă	pat	oi	boy
ā	pay	ou	out
âr	care	o͝o	took
ä	father	o͞o	boot
ĕ	pet	ŭ	cut
ē	be	ûr	urge
ĭ	pit	th	thin
ī	pie	*th*	this
îr	pier	hw	whoop
ŏ	pot	zh	vision
ō	toe	ə	about
ô	paw	N	*French* bon

Nelson Mandela
Photographed in Soweto, South Africa, in 1990

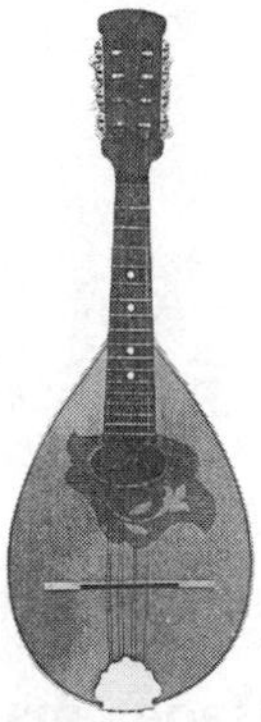

mandolin

mandrill

mane
Lion mane

southeast of Concord. It was an important 19th-century textile center. Population, 99,567.

Man•chu (măn′cho͞o *or* măn **cho͞o′**) *n., pl.* **Manchu** or **Man•chus. 1.** A member of a people native to Manchuria who ruled China from 1644 to 1912. **2.** The language of the Manchu. *—adj.* Of or relating to the Manchu or their language or culture.

Man•chu•ri•a (măn **cho͝or′**ē ə). A historical region of northeast China bordering on modern-day Russia, Nei Monggol (Inner Mongolia), and North Korea. It was the homeland of the Manchu people who conquered China in the 17th century.

man•da•la (**mŭn′**də lə) *n.* Any of various complex geometric designs used in Hinduism and Buddhism as aids to meditation.

Man•da•lay (măn′dl **ā′** *or* **măn′**dl ā′). A city of central Burma north of Rangoon. It was the capital of the kingdom of Burma from 1860 to 1885. Population, 532,895.

Man•dan (**măn′**dăn′) *n., pl.* **Mandan** or **Man•dans. 1.** A member of a Native American people living in North Dakota. **2.** The Siouan language of the Mandan.

man•da•rin (**măn′**də rĭn) *n.* **1.** A member of any of the nine ranks of high public officials in the Chinese Empire. **2.** A high government official or a person having great influence. **3. Mandarin.** The official language of China, which is based on the dialect spoken in and around Beijing. *—adj.* Of or characteristic of a mandarin.

mandarin orange *n.* A small sweet orange having loose skin and parts that separate easily.

man•date (**măn′**dāt′) *n.* **1.** The support or approval of the voters, expressed in the results of an election of their representatives. **2.** An official and authoritative command, order, or instruction, especially one issued by a higher court to a lower court. **3.a.** A commission from the League of Nations giving a member nation control over the government of a territory. **b.** A territory under such control. *—tr.v.* **man•dat•ed, man•dat•ing, man•dates. 1.** To put (a territory) under a mandate. **2.** To make mandatory; require: *The law mandates desegregation in all schools.* [First written down in 1552 in Modern English, from Latin *mandāre*, to order.]

man•da•to•ry (**măn′**də tôr′ē) *adj.* Required; obligatory: *A college degree is mandatory for most teaching jobs.*

Man•de•la (măn **dĕl′**ə), **Nelson Rolihlahla.** Born 1918. South African Black leader imprisoned for nearly 30 years for his political activities.

man•di•ble (**măn′**də bəl) *n.* **1.a.** A jaw of a vertebrate, especially the lower jaw. **b.** The bone of the lower jaw; a jawbone. **2.** An organ in the mouth of many invertebrates for seizing and biting food, especially either of a pair of such organs in an arthropod. **3.** The upper or lower part of a bird's beak. [First written down in 1392 in Middle English, from Late Latin *mandibula*, from Latin *mandere*, to chew.]

man•do•lin (măn′də **lĭn′** *or* **măn′**dl ĭn) *n.* A musical instrument having a body shaped like a pear and a neck that has frets over which four pairs of strings are stretched and played with a pick.

man•drake (**măn′**drāk′) *n.* A low-growing plant having a forked root thought to resemble the human body. The root was once believed to have magical powers and was used in medicines.

man•drill (**măn′**drəl) *n.* A large baboon of western Africa having brightly colored patches of skin on the face and rump in the male.

mane (mān) *n.* The long hair growing from the neck and head of certain animals, such as a horse or a male lion. [First written down before 800 in Old English and spelled *manu*.]

❑ *These sound alike:* **mane, main** (chief).

ma•neu•ver (mə **no͞o′**vər *or* mə **nyo͞o′**vər) *n.* **1.a.** A planned movement of troops or warships: *By a series of brilliant maneuvers, the general outwitted the enemy.* **b.** A large-scale military exercise in which battle movements are practiced. Often used in the plural. **2.** A controlled change in movement or direction of a vehicle or vessel, especially an aircraft. **3.** A movement or procedure that involves skill or cunning. *—v.* **ma•neu•vered, ma•neu•ver•ing, ma•neu•vers.** *—intr.* **1.** To change tactics or approach; plan skillfully: *Our lawyer maneuvered in order to get the trial postponed.* **2.** To carry out a military maneuver. **3.** To make controlled changes in movement or direction: *The ship had to maneuver very carefully to avoid the icebergs.* *—tr.* **1.** To cause (troops or warships) to carry out a military maneuver. **2.** To direct skillfully by changes in course or in position: *They taught me how to maneuver a car on an icy road.* **3.** To manage or direct, especially by trickery: *She maneuvered her opponent into taking a position that lost him the election.* [First written down in 1758 in Modern English and spelled *manœuvre*, from Medieval Latin *manuopera*, hand work.] **—ma•neu′ver•a•bil′i•ty** *n.* **—ma•neu′ver•a•ble** *adj.*

man•ful (**măn′**fəl) *adj.* Brave; resolute; manly: *a manful display of courage.* **—man′ful•ly** *adv.* **—man′ful•ness** *n.*

man•ga•nese (**măng′**gə nēz′ *or* **măng′**gə nēs′) *n.* *Symbol* **Mn** A gray brittle metallic element found in minerals and used in making steel alloys and other industrial products. Atomic number 25. See table at **element.**

mange (mānj) *n.* A skin disease of dogs and other mammals, characterized by itching and loss of hair. [First written down before 1425 in Middle English and spelled *manjeue*, from Old French *mangier*, to eat.]

man•ger (**mān′**jər) *n.* A trough or an open box in which feed for horses or cattle is placed.

man•gle¹ (**măng′**gəl) *tr.v.* **man•gled, man•gling, man•gles. 1.** To disfigure by crushing, hacking, or tearing: *The accident completely mangled our car.* **2.** To ruin; spoil: *The orchestra completely mangled the music.* [First written down before 1400 in Middle English and spelled *manglen*, from Old French *mangoner*, to cut to bits.]

man•gle² (**măng′**gəl) *n.* A machine that presses fabrics by running them between heated rollers. *—tr.v.* **man•gled, man•gling, man•gles.** To smooth or press with a mangle: *mangle sheets.* [First written down in 1774 in Modern English, from Dutch *mangel*.]

man•go (**măng′**gō) *n., pl.* **man•goes** or **man•gos. 1.** A tropical fruit having a smooth rind and sweet, juicy, yellow-orange flesh. **2.** The tree that bears such fruit. [First written down in 1582 in Modern English and spelled *mangas*, from Malay *mangā*, from Tamil *mānkāy*.]

man•grove (**măn′**grōv′ *or* **măng′**grōv′) *n.* Any of several tropical trees or shrubs having many roots growing above the ground that look like extra trunks. The mangrove forms dense thickets in marshes and along shores. [First written down in 1613 in Modern English and spelled *mangrow* : probably Taino *mangue* + *grove*.]

mang•y (**mān′**jē) *adj.* **mang•i•er, mang•i•est. 1.** Having or appearing to have mange: *a mangy stray dog.* **2.** Having many bare spots; shabby: *a mangy old coat.* **—man′gi•ness** *n.*

man•han•dle (**măn′**hăn′dəl) *tr.v.* **man•han•dled, man•han•dling, man•han•dles.** To handle in a rough manner: *The porters manhandled the suitcases.*

Man•hat•tan[1] (măn hăt′n). A borough of New York City in southeast New York, mainly on **Manhattan Island** on the Hudson River between Long Island and northeast New Jersey. Peter Minuit bought the island for the Dutch in 1626 from the Manhattan Indians, supposedly for some $24 worth of merchandise. Population, 1,487,536.

Man•hat•tan[2] (măn hăt′n) *n.* A member of a Native American people formerly inhabiting Manhattan Island.

man•hole (măn′hōl′) *n.* A hole in a street, with a removable cover, that allows a person to reach underground sewers, pipes, or other structures for repair or inspection.

man•hood (măn′ho͝od′) *n.* **1.** The condition of being an adult male person: *He has reached manhood.* **2.** The qualities thought of as appropriate to a man: *Courage is often considered essential to one's manhood.* **3.** Men in general: *the manhood of the country.*

man-hour (măn′our′) *n.* A unit of labor equal to one person working for one hour, used to express industrial production and costs.

ma•ni•a (mā′nē ə *or* mān′yə) *n.* **1.** An intense enthusiasm or desire: *He has a mania for horror movies.* **2.** A form of mental illness in which a patient becomes excessively active and has rapidly changing ideas. [First written down about 1385 in Middle English and spelled *manie*, madness, from Greek *mania*.]

ma•ni•ac (mā′nē ăk′) *n.* **1.** An insane person. **2.** A person who acts in a wildly irresponsible way: *There are too many maniacs driving cars.* —*adj.* Variant of **maniacal**.

ma•ni•a•cal (mə nī′ə kəl) also **ma•ni•ac** (mā′nē ăk′) *adj.* **1.** Mentally ill; insane. **2.** Suggestive of a maniac: *maniacal laughter.*

man•ic (măn′ĭk) *adj.* Relating to or affected by mania.

man•i•cure (măn′ĭ kyo͝or′) *n.* A cosmetic treatment for the fingernails, including shaping and polishing. —*tr.v.* **man•i•cured, man•i•cur•ing, man•i•cures.** To trim, clean, and polish (the fingernails). [First written down in 1880 in Modern English: Latin *manus*, hand + Latin *cūra*, care.]

man•i•cur•ist (măn′ĭ kyo͝or′ĭst) *n.* A person who gives manicures.

man•i•fest (măn′ə fĕst′) *adj.* Clear and apparent; obvious: *It is strange that such a manifest hoax has fooled so many people.* —*tr.v.* **man•i•fest•ed, man•i•fest•ing, man•i•fests.** To reveal; show; display: *Her fidgeting manifested a desire to leave.* —*n.* A list of cargo or passengers: *The ship's manifest was incomplete.* —**man′i•fest•ly** *adv.*

man•i•fes•ta•tion (măn′ə fĕ stā′shən) *n.* **1.** The act of showing, demonstrating, or proving: *a manifestation of bravery.* **2.** Something that reveals a sign or an indication: *Rust on the pipes was a manifestation of tiny leaks.*

man•i•fes•to (măn′ə fĕs′tō) *n., pl.* **man•i•fes•toes** or **man•i•fes•tos.** A public declaration of principles and aims, especially of a political nature.

man•i•fold (măn′ə fōld′) *adj.* **1.** Of many kinds; varied: *This work involves manifold tasks.* **2.** Having many parts, forms, or aspects: *A knowledge of many subjects demonstrates manifold intelligence.* —*n.* A pipe or tube that has several openings for making multiple connections: *The exhaust manifold of an engine connects to each cylinder.*

man•i•kin or **man•ni•kin** (măn′ĭ kĭn) *n.* A mannequin.

ma•nil•a or **ma•nil•la** (mə nĭl′ə) *n.* Manila paper. —*adj.* Made of Manila paper.

Ma•nil•a (mə nĭl′ə). The capital and largest city of the Philippines, on **Manila Bay,** an inlet of the South China Sea. It was founded in 1571. Population, 1,630,485.

Manila hemp *n.* The fiber obtained from the stalks of the abaca plant, used to make rope, fabric, and paper.

Manila paper *n.* A strong paper or thin cardboard with a smooth finish, usually brown or yellow in color, made from manila hemp.

man•i•oc (măn′ē ŏk′) *n.* Cassava.

ma•nip•u•late (mə nĭp′yə lāt′) *tr.v.* **ma•nip•u•lat•ed, ma•nip•u•lat•ing, ma•nip•u•lates. 1.** To operate or control, especially with skill: *manipulate the controls of an airplane.* **2.** To influence or manage in a clever or devious way: *He manipulated public opinion in his favor.* [First written down in 1827 in Modern English, from Latin *manipulus*, handful.] —**ma•nip′u•la′tive** *adj.* —**ma•nip′u•la′tor** *n.*

ma•nip•u•la•tion (mə nĭp′yə lā′shən) *n.* **1.** The act of manipulating. **2.** Clever or devious management: *the manipulation of public opinion by advertising.*

Man•i•to•ba (măn′ĭ tō′bə). A province of south-central Canada west of Ontario. It was admitted to the Canadian confederation in 1870. Winnipeg is the capital and the largest city. Population, 1,026,241. —See Note.

man•i•tou (măn′ĭ to͞o′) *n., pl.* **man•i•tous.** A spirit or force of nature worshiped in Algonquian religious belief.

man•kind (măn′kīnd′) *n.* **1.** The human race; humankind. **2.** Men considered as a group.

man•like (măn′līk′) *adj.* **1.** Resembling a human being. **2.** Belonging to or befitting a man: *manlike courage.*

man•ly (măn′lē) *adj.* **man•li•er, man•li•est. 1.** Having qualities traditionally considered appropriate to a man: *manly courage.* **2.** Of or befitting a man: *a manly voice.* —**man′li•ness** *n.*

man-made (măn′mād′) *adj.* Made by human beings rather than by nature; synthetic: *a man-made hill in the middle of a plain.*

man•na (măn′ə) *n.* **1.** In the Bible, food miraculously provided for the Israelites in the wilderness during their flight from Egypt. **2.** Something of value that a person receives unexpectedly.

manned (mănd) *adj.* Occupied, operated, or performed by a person: *manned spacecraft.*

man•ne•quin (măn′ĭ kĭn) *n.* **1.** A life-size model of the human body, used mainly for displaying clothes. **2.** A person who models clothes; a model. [First written down about 1730 in Modern English and spelled *manequine*, from Middle Dutch *mannekijn*, figurine.]

man•ner (măn′ər) *n.* **1.** The way in which something is done or happens: *We always work in a careful manner.* See Synonyms at **method. 2.** A way of acting; behavior: *The new boss has a gruff manner.* **3. manners.** Socially proper behavior; etiquette: *Did no one ever teach him manners?* **4.** Kind; sort: *We had all manner of incidents on our long trip.* —*idiom.* **in a manner of speaking.** In a way; so to speak. [First written down before 1200 in Middle English and spelled *manere*, from Old French *maniere*, from Latin *manus*, hand.]

❑ *These sound alike:* **manner, manor** (estate).

man•nered (măn′ərd) *adj.* **1.** Having manners of a specific kind: *ill-mannered people.* **2.** Artificial or affected: *quaint and mannered speech.*

man•ner•ism (măn′ə rĭz′əm) *n.* **1.** A distinctive personal trait; a quirk: *People say I have a mannerism of scratching my chin.* **2.** An exaggerated or affected style or habit: *Her scornful laugh was an annoying mannerism.*

manhole

Manitoba

The province of **Manitoba** takes its name from *Lake Manitoba*, which is located there. Where the name *Manitoba* comes from is open to debate. One explanation says that it is from an Ojibwa or Cree word meaning "God's narrows," referring to the narrows at the north end of the lake. Another explanation derives the name from an Assiniboin expression believed to mean "lake of the prairies."

ă	pat	oi	boy
ā	pay	ou	out
âr	care	o͝o	took
ä	father	o͞o	boot
ĕ	pet	ŭ	cut
ē	be	ûr	urge
ĭ	pit	th	thin
ī	pie	*th*	this
îr	pier	hw	whoop
ŏ	pot	zh	vision
ō	toe	ə	about
ô	paw	N	*French* bon

mansard

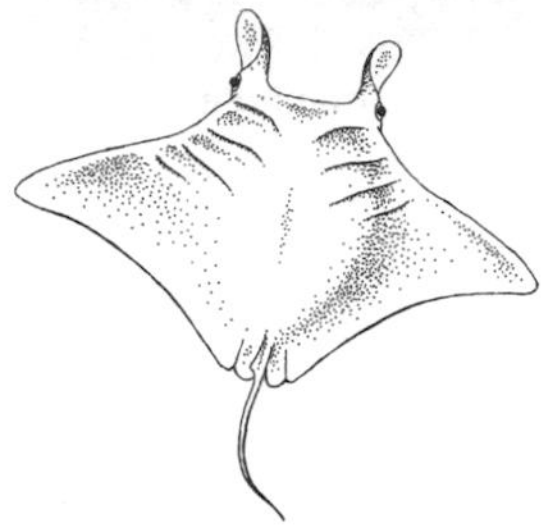

manta

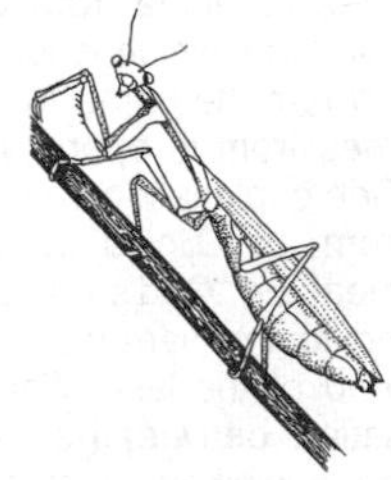

mantis

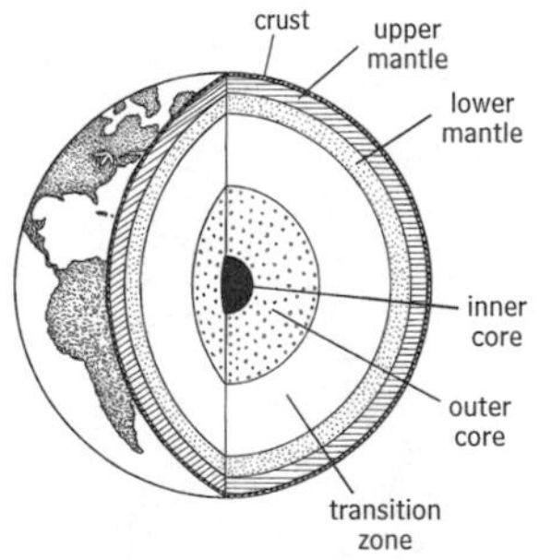

mantle
Cutaway view of Earth

ă	pat	oi	boy
ā	pay	ou	out
âr	care	o͝o	took
ä	father	o͞o	boot
ĕ	pet	ŭ	cut
ē	be	ûr	urge
ĭ	pit	th	thin
ī	pie	*th*	this
îr	pier	hw	whoop
ŏ	pot	zh	vision
ō	toe	ə	about
ô	paw	N	*French* bon

man•ner•ly (măn′ər lē) *adj.* Having good manners; polite. See Synonyms at **polite.** —*adv.* With good manners; politely.

man•ni•kin (măn′ĭ kĭn) *n.* Variant of **manikin.**

man•nish (măn′ĭsh) *adj.* **1.** Characteristic of a man: *a low mannish voice.* **2.** Resembling or suggestive of a man rather than a woman; masculine: *a mannish way of walking.* **—man′nish•ly** *adv.* **—man′nish•ness** *n.*

ma•noeu•vre (mə no͞o′vər *or* mə nyo͞o′vər) *n. & v. Chiefly British.* Variant of **maneuver.**

man-of-war (măn′ə wôr′) *n., pl.* **men-of-war** (mĕn′ə wôr′). A warship, especially a sailing ship.

ma•nom•e•ter (mă nŏm′ĭ tər) *n.* An instrument that measures the pressure of a gas, vapor, or liquid.

man•or (măn′ər) *n.* **1.** An estate including its lands. **2.** The main house on an estate. **3.** The estate of a feudal lord. [First written down about 1300 in Middle English and spelled *maner,* from Latin *manēre,* to remain.]

❑ *These sound alike:* **manor, manner** (way of acting).

ma•no•ri•al (mə nôr′ē əl) *adj.* Of or like a manor: *a manorial estate.*

man•pow•er (măn′pou′ər) *n.* **1.** The power supplied by human physical effort: *Lifting that piano requires a lot of manpower.* **2.** The people working or available for work, especially on a particular task: *Most of their manpower is now devoted to developing new products.*

man•sard (măn′särd′) *n.* A roof having two slopes on all four sides, with the lower slope nearly vertical and the upper nearly horizontal. [First written down in 1734 in Modern English, after François *Mansart* (1598–1666), French architect.]

manse (măns) *n.* A house lived in by a Christian minister.

man•ser•vant (măn′sûr′vənt) *n.* A male servant.

man•sion (măn′shən) *n.* A large stately house. [First written down about 1340 in Middle English, from Latin *mānsiō,* a dwelling, from *manēre,* to dwell, remain.]

man•slaugh•ter (măn′slô′tər) *n.* The unlawful killing of a person without intent to do so, as when a motorist kills a pedestrian through negligence.

man•ta (măn′tə) *n.* Any of several very large ocean fishes having a flattened body with fins resembling wings.

manta ray *n.* The manta.

man•tel also **man•tle** (măn′tl) *n.* **1.** An ornamental facing around a fireplace. **2.** A mantelpiece.

man•tel•piece (măn′tl pēs′) *n.* The shelf over a fireplace.

man•tes (măn′tēz) *n.* A plural of **mantis.**

man•til•la (măn tē′yə *or* măn tĭl′ə) *n.* A scarf, usually of lace, worn over the head and shoulders by women in Spain and Latin America.

man•tis (măn′tĭs) *n., pl.* **man•tis•es** or **man•tes** (măn′tēz). Any of various large insects that look somewhat like a grasshopper. They prey on other insects and hold their front legs up as if praying.

man•tis•sa (măn tĭs′ə) *n.* The fractional part of a logarithm to the base ten. For example, if 2.749 is a logarithm, .749 is the mantissa.

man•tle (măn′tl) *n.* **1.** A loose sleeveless coat worn over outer garments; a cloak. **2.** Something that covers or conceals: *a soft mantle of snow.* **3.** The layer of the earth between the crust and the core. **4.** A sheath of threads that is used in gas lights and lanterns and gives a brilliant light when heated by a flame. **5.** The layer of soft tissue that covers the body of a clam, an oyster, or another mollusk and secretes the material that forms the shell. **6.** The wings, shoulder feathers, and back of a bird when differently colored from the rest of the body. **7.** Variant of **mantel.** —*tr.v.* **man•tled, man•tling, man•tles.** To cover with or as if with a cloak: *Night mantled the earth.* [First written down before 899 in Old English and spelled *mentel,* from Latin *mantellum.*]

man•u•al (măn′yo͞o əl) *adj.* **1.** Of or relating to the hands: *manual dexterity.* **2.** Used by or operated with the hands: *manual controls.* —*n.* A small book of instructions; a handbook. [First written down in 1406 in Middle English and spelled *manuel,* from Latin *manuālis,* from *manus,* hand.] **—man′u•al•ly** *adv.*

manual alphabet *n.* An alphabet of hand signs used for communication by people who are hearing-impaired.

manual training *n.* A course of training in work done with the hands in the practical arts, especially woodworking.

man•u•fac•ture (măn′yə făk′chər) *tr.v.* **man•u•fac•tured, man•u•fac•tur•ing, man•u•fac•tures. 1.** To make or process (a product), especially with the use of machines: *a factory that manufactures cars.* **2.** To make or process (a raw material) into a finished product: *manufacture cotton to make fabric.* —*n.* The act or process of manufacturing products.

man•u•fac•tur•er (măn′yə făk′chər ər) *n.* A person or company that manufactures something, especially the owner or operator of a factory.

ma•nure (mə no͝or′ *or* mə nyo͝or′) *n.* Animal dung, especially the dung of cattle, used as fertilizer. —*tr. v.* **ma•nured, ma•nur•ing, ma•nures.** To apply manure to (soil, for example).

man•u•script (măn′yə skrĭpt′) *n.* **1.** A book or document written by hand, especially one made before the invention of printing. **2.** The form of a book, a paper, or an article as it is submitted for publication in print: *send a manuscript to a publisher.* **3.** Handwriting as opposed to printing.

Manx (măngks) *adj.* Of or relating to the Isle of Man or its people, language, or culture. —*n., pl.* **Manx. 1.** A native or inhabitant of the Isle of Man. **2.** The extinct Celtic language of the Isle of Man.

Manx cat or **manx cat** *n.* Any of a breed of domestic cat that has short hair and a tail that is incompletely developed and invisible outside the body.

man•y (mĕn′ē) *adj.* **more** (môr), **most** (mōst). **1.** Being one of a large number: *Many a brave person has refused to go down these rapids.* **2.** Consisting of or amounting to a large number; numerous: *many friends at the party.* —*n. (used with a plural verb).* **1.** A large number of persons or things: *A good many of us were at the party.* **2.** The majority of the people: *the will of the many.* —*pron. (used with a plural verb).* A large number of persons or things: *Many were invited but few came.*

Mao•ism (mou′ĭz′əm) *n.* The beliefs and practices of Mao Zedong. **—Mao′ist** *adj. & n.*

Mao•ri (mou′rē) *n., pl.* **Maori** or **Mao•ris. 1.** A member of a Polynesian people of New Zealand. **2.** The language of the Maori. —*adj.* Of or relating to the Maori or their language or culture.

Mao Ze•dong (mou′ dzə′dŏng′) also **Mao Tse-tung** (mou′ tsə′to͝ong′). 1893–1976. Chinese Communist leader who helped found the Chinese Communist Party (1921) and served as the first head of state of the People's Republic of China (1949–1959).

map (măp) *n.* **1.** A drawing or chart of a region of the earth, often showing political divisions such as countries and physical features such as mountains and rivers. **2.** A drawing or chart of the moon, a planet, the stars, or other features of the sky. —*tr.v.* **mapped, map•ping, maps. 1.** To make a map of; represent on a map. **2.** To plan in detail: *Let's map* *out our schedule.* [First written down in 1527 in Modern English, from Latin *mappa*, napkin, cloth (on which maps were drawn).]

ma•ple (mā′pəl) *n.* **1.** Any of numerous tall shade trees having broad leaves with deep notches and paired winged seeds. **2.** The hard wood of a maple, often used in making furniture. **3.** The flavor of the concentrated sap of the sugar maple. [First written down about 700 in Old English and spelled *mapul.*]

maple sugar *n.* A sugar made by boiling down maple syrup.

maple syrup *n.* A sweet syrup made from the sap of the sugar maple.

Ma•pu•to (mə **po͞o′**tō). The capital and largest city of Mozambique, in the extreme southern part of the country on the Indian Ocean. It was founded in the late 18th century. Population, 755,300.

mar (mär) *tr.v.* **marred, mar•ring, mars. 1.** To deface or damage: *marred the top of the table with a knife.* **2.** To spoil; ruin: *Rain marred their day at the beach.*

Mar. or **Mar** *abbr.* March.

mar•a•bou (**măr′**ə bo͞o′) *n.* **1.** Any of several large African storks having fluffy down used to trim clothing. **2.** The down of this bird.

ma•ra•ca (mə **rä′**kə) *n.* A percussion instrument consisting of a rattle made from a dried gourd or something shaped like a gourd with pebbles or dried beans inside. Maracas are often played in pairs.

Ma•ra•cai•bo (măr′ə **kī′**bō *or* mä′rä **kī′**bō). A city of northwest Venezuela at the outlet of **Lake Maracaibo,** the largest lake of South America. It was founded in 1571. Population, 929,000.

mar•a•schi•no cherry (măr′ə **skē′**nō *or* măr′ə **shē′**nō) *n.* A cherry preserved in a sweet syrup, used especially in desserts.

Ma•ra•thi (mə **rä′**tē) *n.* The principal language of west-central India.

mar•a•thon (**măr′**ə thŏn′) *n.* **1.** A cross-country footrace of 26 miles, 385 yards (41.3 kilometers). **2.** A long-distance race other than a footrace: *a swimming marathon.* **3.** A contest of endurance: *a dance marathon.*

Mar•a•thon (**măr′**ə thŏn′). A village and plain of ancient Greece northeast of Athens. It was the site of a major victory over the Persians in 490 B.C.

ma•raud (mə **rôd′**) *v.* **ma•raud•ed, ma•raud•ing, ma•rauds.** —*intr.* To roam in search of booty. —*tr.* To raid or pillage for plunder. **—ma•raud′er** *n.*

mar•ble (**mär′**bəl) *n.* **1.** A hard rock made from the action of heat and pressure on limestone or dolomite. Some kinds of marble have irregularly colored marks due to impurities. Marble can be polished to a smooth luster and is used in buildings and statues. **2.a.** A little ball made of a hard substance such as glass. **b. marbles.** *(used with a singular verb).* A children's game played with such balls. —*tr.v.* **mar•bled, mar•bling, mar•bles.** To color and streak (paper, for example) in imitation of marble. —*adj.* Made of or resembling marble: *a marble floor; marble ice cream.* [First written down before 1200 in Middle English and spelled *marbra*, from Greek *marmaros.*]

march¹ (märch) *v.* **marched, march•ing, march•es.** —*intr.* **1.** To walk with measured steps at a steady rate, as in a parade: *The band marched down the street.* **2.** To walk in a purposeful or determined manner; stride: *I marched up to the podium and read my speech.* **3.** To advance with a steady movement: *Time marches on.* —*tr.* To cause to march: *The duck marched its ducklings to the edge of the lake.* —*n.* **1.** The act of marching: *the army's rapid march to the fort.* **2.** A long tiring journey by foot: *a march of ten miles.* **3.** The distance covered by marching: *We were still a march of six hours from camp.* **4.** Forward movement; progress: *the dramatic march of modern science.* **5.** A musical composition written to accompany or as if to accompany marching. [First written down about 1410 in Middle English and spelled *marchen*, from Old French *marchier*, of Germanic origin.]

march² (märch) *n.* A border region; a frontier. [First written down before 1300 in Middle English, from Old French *marche*, of Germanic origin.]

March (märch) *n.* The third month of the year in the Gregorian calendar, having 31 days. [First written down about 1200 in Middle English, from Latin *Mārtius (mēnsis)*, (month) of Mars.]

mar•chio•ness (**mär′**shə nĭs *or* mär′shə **nĕs′**) *n.* **1.** The wife or widow of a marquis. **2.** A noblewoman ranking above a countess and below a duchess.

Mar•co•ni (mär **kō′**nē), **Guglielmo.** 1874–1937. Italian inventor who shared a 1909 Nobel Prize for his work on the long-wave radio.

Mar•di gras or **Mar•di Gras** (**mär′**dē **grä′**) *n.* The day before Ash Wednesday, celebrated as a holiday in many places with carnivals and parades.

mare¹ (mâr) *n.* An adult female horse, zebra, donkey, or other related animal. [First written down before 900 in Old English and spelled *mere.*]

ma•re² (**mä′**rā) *n., pl.* **ma•ri•a** (**mä′**rē ə). Any of the large dark areas on the moon, Mars, or other planets. [First written down in 1860 in Modern English, from Latin *mare*, sea.]

Mar•gar•et of An•jou (**mär′**gə rət əv ăn **jo͞o′** *or* **mär′**grət əv ăn **jo͞o′**). 1430–1482. Queen of England as the wife of Henry VI (1421–1471). She led the Lancastrians in the Wars of the Roses and was captured (1471) and ransomed to France (1476).

mar•ga•rine (**mär′**jər ĭn) *n.* A substitute for butter made from vegetable oils and other ingredients.

mar•gin (**mär′**jĭn) *n.* **1.** An edge or a border: *the margins of the forest.* **2.** The blank space that surrounds the written or printed area on a page. **3.** An extra amount allowed beyond what is needed: *You should allow a 10 minute margin for delays in getting to school.* **4.** A quantity or degree of difference: *We won the election by a large margin.* [First written down before 1350 in Middle English, from Latin *margō.*]

Synonyms: margin, border, edge, brink, rim. These nouns mean the line or narrow area that marks the outside limit of something. **Margin** means an outside area that is different somehow from the inside: *Cornflowers grow along the margin of the meadow.* **Border** can mean a boundary line: *The farmer built a fence along the border of the property.* **Edge** can mean the precise bounding line where two different surfaces meet: *Mark curled his toes over the edge of the diving board.* **Brink** means the upper edge of something steep: *The car teetered on the brink of the canyon.* **Rim** often means the edge of something that is circular or curved: *There is a small nick in the rim of the telescope lens.*

---

mar•gin•al (**mär′**jə nəl) *adj.* **1.** Written or printed in the margin: *There were marginal notes through the whole book.* **2.** Of, in, or on the border or edge: *the northern states marginal to Canada.* **3.** Barely acceptable: *marginal writing ability.* **4.** Making a very small profit: *a marginal business.* **—mar′gin•al•ly** *adv.*

mar•gue•rite (mär′gə **rēt′**) *n.* Any of several plants having white or pale yellow flowers that resemble those of the common American daisy.

ma•ri•a (**mä′**rē ə) *n.* Plural of **mare².**

Mar•i•an•a Islands (măr′ē **ăn′**ə *or* mâr′ē **ăn′**ə). An island group and U.S. commonwealth in the western Pacific Ocean east of the Philippines. Guam, the largest island of the group, is independent of the

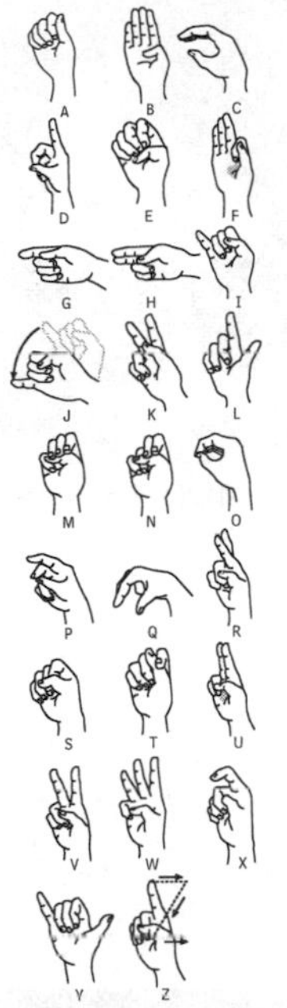

manual alphabet

Mao Zedong

marabou

Maria Theresa

Marie Antoinette
Marie Antoinette with a Rose by Élisabeth Vigée-Lebrun (1755–1842)

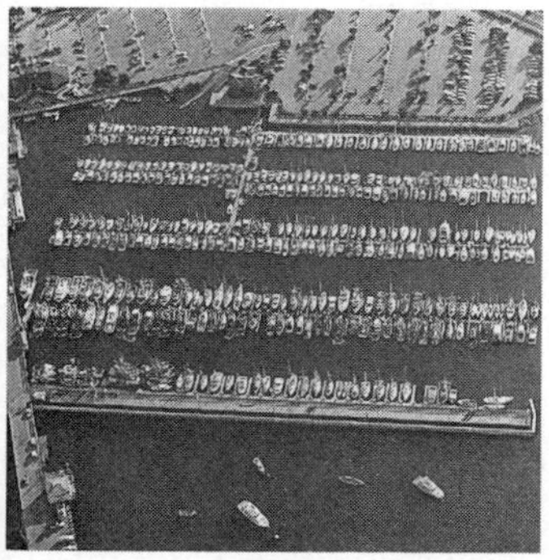

marina

commonwealth, known as the **Northern Mariana Islands.** Population, 16,780.

Ma•ri•a The•re•sa (mə rē′ə tə rā′sə *or* mə rē′ə tə rā′zə). 1717–1780. Queen of Hungary and Bohemia (1740–1780) whose reign was marked by the War of the Austrian Succession (1740–1748) and the Seven Years' War (1756–1763).

Ma•rie An•toi•nette (mə rē′ ăn′twə nĕt′). 1755–1793. Queen of France (1774–1793) as the wife of Louis XVI. She was executed during the French Revolution.

mar•i•gold (măr′ĭ gōld′ *or* mâr′ĭ gōld′) *n.* **1.** Any of various American plants having showy orange, yellow, or reddish flowers. **2.** Any of various related or similar plants, such as the marsh marigold.

mar•i•jua•na or **mar•i•hua•na** (măr′ə wä′nə) *n.* **1.** The dried leaves or flowers of the hemp plant, which contain an intoxicating drug. **2.** The hemp plant.

ma•rim•ba (mə rĭm′bə) *n.* A musical instrument somewhat like a large xylophone, having tuned wooden bars that are struck with wooden mallets.

ma•ri•na (mə rē′nə) *n.* A boat basin that has docks, moorings, supplies, and repair facilities for small boats.

mar•i•nade (măr′ə nād′) *n.* A mixture of oil, vinegar or wine, and spices, used for soaking meat or fish before cooking. *—tr.v.* (măr′ə nād′). **mar•i•nad•ed, mar•i•nad•ing, mar•i•nades.** To marinate.

mar•i•nate (măr′ə nāt′) *tr.v.* **mar•i•nat•ed, mar•i•nat•ing, mar•i•nates.** To soak (meat or fish) in a marinade.

ma•rine (mə rēn′) *adj.* **1.** Of or relating to the sea: *marine zoology.* **2.** Living or found in the sea: *marine life.* **3.** Of or relating to shipping or navigation: *a marine chart.* *—n.* **1.** A soldier serving on a ship or at a naval base. **2. Marine.** A member of the U.S. Marine Corps. [First written down in 1440 in Middle English, from Latin *marīnus*, from *mare*, sea.]

Marine Corps *n.* A branch of the U.S. armed forces whose troops are specially trained for amphibious landings and combat.

mar•i•ner (măr′ə nər) *n.* A person who navigates or helps to navigate a ship.

mar•i•o•nette (măr′ē ə nĕt′) *n.* A puppet controlled from above by strings or wires attached to its limbs.

mar•i•tal (măr′ĭ tl) *adj.* Of or relating to marriage: *marital vows.* **—mar′i•tal•ly** *adv.*

mar•i•time (măr′ĭ tīm′) *adj.* **1.** Located on or near the sea: *a maritime fishing village.* **2.** Of or relating to shipping or navigation: *maritime law.*

Mar•i•time Provinces (măr′ĭ tīm′). The Canadian provinces of Nova Scotia, New Brunswick, and Prince Edward Island, bordering on the Atlantic Ocean.

mar•jo•ram (mär′jər əm) *n.* Any of several plants that are related to the mint and have spicy pleasant-smelling leaves used as flavoring.

mark[1] (märk) *n.* **1.** A visible trace or impression, such as a line or spot, left on a surface. **2.** A written or printed symbol used in punctuation. **3.** An indication of some quality or condition: *Taking responsibility for your own mistakes is a mark of maturity.* **4.** A lasting impression: *The Crusades left their mark on Western civilization.* **5.** Something that is aimed at; a target: *The arrow found its mark.* **6.** A label, a seal, or an inscription placed on an article: *The manufacturer's mark can be found on every product.* **7.** A recognized standard of quality: *Your latest work is not up to the mark.* **8.** A letter or number used to indicate the quality of a person's work: *excellent marks in arithmetic.* **9.** A point that has been or will be reached: *The swimmers just passed the halfway mark.* **10.** A starting line or position, as in a track event. *—v.* **marked, mark•ing, marks.** *—tr.* **1.** To make a mark on: *Someone had marked the important pages of the book.* **2.** To form, make, or write by a mark: *marked a square on the sidewalk.* **3.** To give evidence of; reveal: *The cool winds mark the beginning of fall.* **4.** To be a feature of; distinguish; characterize: *Her painting is marked by an unusual use of color.* **5.** To give attention to; notice: *Mark my words: they are asking for trouble.* **6.** To determine the quality of (something) according to a grade or mark: *The teacher is marking the tests now.* *—intr.* **1.** To make a visible impression: *The pen marks under water.* **2.** To give grades for school work: *I've never had a teacher that marks easily.* ***—idioms.*** **mark down.** To mark for sale at a lower price. **mark time. 1.** To move the feet in a marching step without advancing. **2.** To suspend progress for the time being; wait: *The work crew marked time while the architects changed the plans.* **3.** To perform the actions of a job or task without really accomplishing anything. **mark up. 1.** To cover with marks. **2.** To mark for sale at a higher price. [First written down about 700 in Old English and spelled *mearc.*]

mark[2] (märk) *n.* **1.** A deutsche mark. **2.** An ostmark. [First written down about 960 in Old English and spelled *marc.*]

Mark (märk) *n.* The second Gospel of the New Testament, written by Saint Mark.

Mark, Saint. Author of the second Gospel of the New Testament and disciple of Saint Peter.

mark•down (märk′doun′) *n.* **1.** A reduction in price. **2.** The amount by which a price is reduced.

marked (märkt) *adj.* **1.** Having a mark or marks: *Pedestrians use the marked crosswalk.* **2.** Noticeable; distinct; clear: *a marked difference in price.* **3.** Singled out or distinguished, as for a dire fate: *a marked man.*

mark•ed•ly (mär′kĭd lē) *adv.* In a manner that is noticeable and obvious: *When one works hard, grades should improve markedly.*

mark•er (mär′kər) *n.* **1.** Something used to draw marks on a surface: *We used markers to make posters for the science fair.* **2.** Something that marks a place, as a bookmark or tombstone. **3.** A person who marks, especially a person who gives academic grades.

mar•ket (mär′kĭt) *n.* **1.a.** A public gathering for buying and selling goods: *The farmer took cheese to market.* **b.** A place where goods are offered for sale: *We walked by the market before going home.* **2.** A store that sells a particular type of merchandise: *a fish market.* **3.** The stock market. **4.** The business of buying and selling a particular product: *the international coffee market.* **5.a.** A region or country where goods may be sold: *We produce computers for foreign markets.* **b.** A particular type or group of buyers: *The college market includes people 16 to 22 years old.* **6.** A desire to buy; demand: *There is always a market for our bicycles.* *—v.* **mar•ket•ed, mar•ket•ing, mar•kets.** *—tr.* To sell or offer for sale: *The co-op marketed vegetables from local farmers.* *—intr.* To buy food and household supplies: *We market on Friday.* ***—idioms.*** **in the market.** Interested in buying: *We are in the market for a new car.* **on the market. 1.** Available for buying: *There are several good brands of skis on the market.* **2.** Up for sale: *He put the family business on the market.* [First written down before 1121 in Middle English, from Latin *mercātus*, from *mercārī*, to buy.] **—mar′ket•er** *n.*

mar•ket•a•ble (mär′kĭ tə bəl) *adj.* Fit for sale; salable: *She considered the product a marketable invention.* —**mar′ket•a•bil′i•ty** *n.*

mar•ket•ing (mär′kĭ tĭng) *n.* The business activity involved in moving products from a manufacturer to a consumer, including selling, advertising, and packaging.

mar•ket•place (mär′kĭt plās′) *n.* **1.** A public square or other place in which a market is set up. **2.** The general process of buying and selling; business activities.

mark•ing (mär′kĭng) *n.* **1.** A mark or marks: *markings left along the trail.* **2.** The special way in which an animal or a plant is colored: *a bird with beautiful markings.*

marks•man (märks′mən) *n.* A man skilled at shooting a gun or another weapon.

marks•man•ship (märks′mən shĭp′) *n.* Skill at shooting a gun or another weapon.

marks•wom•an (märks′wo͝om′ən) *n.* A woman skilled at shooting a gun or another weapon.

mark•up (märk′ŭp′) *n.* **1.** An increase in the price of an item for sale. **2.** An amount added to the cost of an item to figure its selling price.

marl (märl) *n.* A kind of rock or a loose soil mixture that contains clay, carbonate of lime, and shells, used as fertilizer.

mar•lin (mär′lĭn) *n.* Any of several large ocean fishes related to the swordfish, often caught for sport.
❑ *These sound alike:* **marlin, marline** (rope).

mar•line (mär′lĭn) *n.* A light rope made of two loosely twisted strands, used to finish off the ends of larger ropes to keep them from unraveling.
❑ *These sound alike:* **marline, marlin** (fish).

mar•line•spike (mär′lĭn spīk′) *n.* A pointed metal tool, used to separate strands of rope in splicing.

mar•ma•lade (mär′mə lād′) *n.* A jam made by boiling the pulp and rind of fruits.

Mar•ma•ra (mär′mər ə), **Sea of.** A sea of northwest Turkey. It is connected to the Black Sea through the Bosporus and to the Aegean Sea through the Dardanelles.

mar•mo•set (mär′mə sĕt′ *or* mär′mə zĕt′) *n.* Any of various small Central and South American monkeys having thick soft fur and a long tail.

mar•mot (mär′mət) *n.* Any of various short-legged burrowing animals having a bushy tail, as the woodchuck.

Marne (märn). A river, about 325 miles (523 kilometers) long, of northeast France flowing in an arc generally northwest to the Seine River near Paris.

ma•roon[1] (mə ro͞on′) *tr.v.* **ma•rooned, ma•roon•ing, ma•roons. 1.** To put (a person) ashore on a deserted island. **2.** To leave alone and helpless: *I was marooned with a cold while everyone else went skating.* [First written down in 1699 in Modern English and spelled *moroon*, from American Spanish *cimarrón*, wild, runaway.]

ma•roon[2] (mə ro͞on′) *n.* A dark purplish red. [First written down in 1594 in Modern English, from Italian *marrone*, a chestnut.]

mar•quee (mär kē′) *n.* A structure that projects over the entrance to a building, such as a theater or hotel, and often bears a signboard.

mar•quess (mär′kwĭs) *n.* Variant of **marquis.**

Marquette (mär kĕt′), Père **Jacques.** 1637–1675. French missionary who in 1673 accompanied Louis Jolliet on an extensive exploration of several American rivers, including the Mississippi River.

mar•quis (mär′kwĭs *or* mär kē′) or **mar•quess** (mär′kwĭs) *n., pl.* **mar•quis•es** (mär′kwĭ sĭz) or **mar•quis** (mär kēz′) or **mar•quess•es** (mär′kwĭ-sĭz). A nobleman ranking below a duke and above an earl or count.

mar•quise (mär kēz′) *n.* A marchioness.

mar•riage (măr′ĭj) *n.* **1.** The state of being married: *Theirs is a happy marriage.* **2.a.** The act of marrying. **b.** The ceremony involved; a wedding. **3.** A close union: *Poetry is a marriage of beautiful sound and intense meaning.*

mar•riage•a•ble (măr′ĭ jə bəl) *adj.* Suitable for marriage.

mar•ried (măr′ēd) *adj.* **1.** Having a husband or wife. **2.** Joined by marriage: *a married couple.* **3.** Of or relating to marriage: *married life.*

mar•row (măr′ō) *n.* **1.** The soft material that fills the cavities inside most bones. It is the source of red blood cells and many white blood cells. **2.** The essential, innermost, or most important part; the pith: *the marrow of an argument.*

mar•ry[1] (măr′ē) *v.* **mar•ried, mar•ry•ing, mar•ries.** —*tr.* **1.** To take (a person) as a husband or wife; wed. **2.** To unite (a couple) as husband and wife: *The judge married them.* **3.** To give in marriage. —*intr.* To take a husband or wife; enter into marriage: *They married in June.* [First written down about 1300 in Middle English and spelled *marien*, from Latin *marītāre*, from *marītus*, married.]

mar•ry[2] (măr′ē) *interj. Archaic.* An expression used as an exclamation of surprise or emphasis. [First written down before 1375 in Middle English and spelled *Marie*, the Virgin Mary, ultimately from Greek *Maria.*]

Mars (märz) *n.* **1.** In Roman mythology, the god of war, identified with the Greek Ares. **2.** The fourth planet from the sun at a mean distance of 142 million miles (228 million kilometers), and the seventh largest in the solar system with a mean diameter of about 4,180 miles (6,726 kilometers).

Mar•seilles (mär sā′). A city of southeast France on an arm of the Mediterranean Sea east of the Rhone River. The oldest city of France, it was founded in about 600 B.C. Population, 874,436.

marsh (märsh) *n.* An area of low-lying wet land; a swamp or bog.

mar•shal (mär′shəl) *n.* **1.a.** In some countries, a military officer of the highest rank. **b.** A field marshal. **2.** In the United States: **a.** A Federal or city officer who carries out court orders and performs duties similar to those of a sheriff. **b.** The head of a police or fire department. **3.** A person in charge of a ceremony or parade. —*tr.v.* **mar•shaled, mar•shal•ing, mar•shals** also **mar•shalled, marshal•ling, mar•shals.** To place in proper or methodical order; organize: *The research team marshaled facts to defend its theory.* [First written down in 1258 in Middle English and spelled *mareschal*, from Old French, of Germanic origin.]
❑ *These sound alike:* **marshal, martial** (of war).

Mar•shall (mär′shəl), **John.** 1755–1835. American politician who served as the chief justice of the U.S. Supreme Court (1801–1835).

Marshall Islands. A self-governing island group in the central Pacific Ocean southwest of Hawaii. In 1986 the islands became a republic. Population, 30,873.

marsh gas *n.* Methane that occurs naturally in swamps.

marsh•land (märsh′lănd′) *n.* A marshy or swampy area.

marsh•mal•low (märsh′mĕl′ō *or* märsh′măl′ō) *n.* **1.** A soft white candy with a spongy texture. **2.** A plant found in marshes of Europe and North America, having pink flowers and a spongy root formerly used in making marshmallow candy.

marsh marigold *n.* Any of several North American plants that grow in wet places and have bright-yellow flowers resembling those of the buttercup.

marsh•y (mär′shē) *adj.* **marsh•i•er, marsh•i•est.**

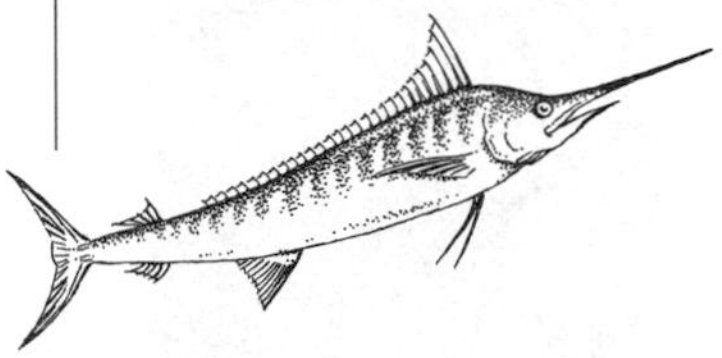

marlin

marmot

marquee

ă	pat	oi	boy
ā	pay	ou	out
âr	care	o͝o	took
ä	father	o͞o	boot
ĕ	pet	ŭ	cut
ē	be	ûr	urge
ĭ	pit	th	thin
ī	pie	*th*	this
îr	pier	hw	whoop
ŏ	pot	zh	vision
ō	toe	ə	about
ô	paw	N	*French* bon

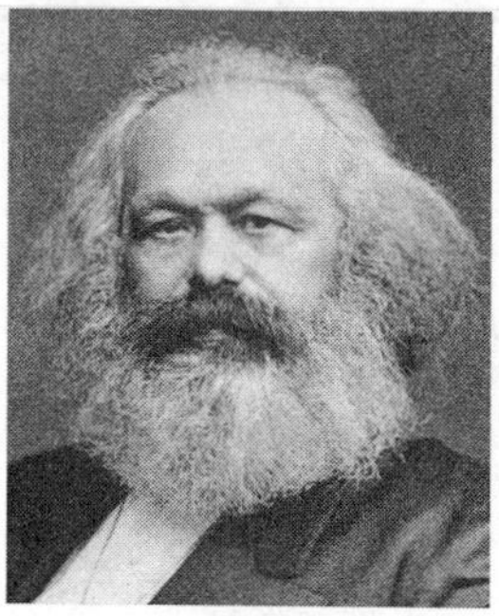

Karl Marx

Maryland

The state of **Maryland** took its name from the colony that was chartered by King Charles I of England in 1632. It was named in honor of Queen Henrietta Maria (1609–1669), Charles's wife.

mask
Top: Surgical mask
Bottom: Catcher's mask

Of or resembling a marsh; wet and swampy. —**marsh′i•ness** *n.*

mar•su•pi•al (mär so͞o′pē əl) *n.* Any of various mammals, such as the kangaroo, opossum, or wombat, whose young continue to develop after birth in a pouch on the outside of the female's body. —*adj.* Of or relating to marsupials. [First written down in 1696 in Modern English, from Greek *marsipion*, pouch.]

mart (märt) *n.* A market or trading center: *a fruit and vegetable mart.*

mar•ten (mär′tn) *n., pl.* **marten** or **mar•tens. 1.** Any of several mammals related to the weasel and the mink, having thick soft brown fur. **2.** The fur of such a mammal.

❑ *These sound alike:* **marten, martin** (bird).

Mar•tha's Vine•yard (mär′thəz vĭn′yərd). An island of southeast Massachusetts off the southwest coast of Cape Cod. Settled in 1642, it was a whaling and fishing center in the 18th and early 19th centuries.

mar•tial (mär′shəl) *adj.* **1.** Of, relating to, or suitable to war: *martial music.* **2.** Of or relating to the armed forces or the military profession: *martial training.* [First written down about 1385 in Middle English and spelled *marcial*, from Latin *Mārtiālis*, from *Mārs*, Mars.]

❑ *These sound alike:* **martial, marshal** (military officer).

martial art *n.* Any of several arts of combat or self-defense that originated in Eastern Asia and include karate and judo.

martial law *n.* Military rule of a civilian population imposed for a time, as in an emergency or during a war.

Mar•tian (mär′shən) *adj.* Of or relating to the planet Mars. —*n.* A being that supposedly lives on the planet Mars.

mar•tin (mär′tn) *n.* Any of various swallows having glossy blue-black feathers and a forked tail.

❑ *These sound alike:* **martin, marten** (weasel).

mar•ti•net (mär′tn ĕt′) *n.* A person who believes in and demands strict obedience to rules. [First written down in 1676 in Modern English, after Jean *Martinet* (died 1672), French army officer.]

mar•tin•gale (mär′tn gāl′) *n.* The strap of a horse's harness that goes from the girth between the front legs to the nose band. It is used to keep a horse from throwing back its head or rearing on its hind legs.

Mar•ti•nique (mär′tn ēk′). An island of France in the Windward Islands of the West Indies. Fort-de-France is the capital. Population, 328,566.

Mar•tin Luther King Day (mär′tn) *n.* The third Monday in January, observed as a holiday by some U.S. states in honor of Martin Luther King, Jr.

mar•tyr (mär′tər) *n.* **1.** A person who chooses to suffer death or torture rather than give up religious principles. **2.** A person who suffers much or makes great sacrifices to further a belief, cause, or principle. **3.** A person who endures great suffering. —*tr.v.* **mar•tyred, mar•tyr•ing, mar•tyrs. 1.** To make a martyr of. **2.** To cause to suffer; torture or torment.

mar•tyr•dom (mär′tər dəm) *n.* **1.** The condition of being a martyr. **2.** The suffering of death by a martyr. **3.** Extreme suffering.

mar•vel (mär′vəl) *n.* A person or thing that causes surprise, astonishment, or wonder: *The digital computer is a marvel of technology.* —*intr.v.* **mar•veled, mar•vel•ing, mar•vels** also **mar•velled, mar•vel•ling, mar•vels.** To be filled with surprise, astonishment, or wonder: *We marveled at the gymnast's strength and grace.* See Synonyms at **wonder.** [First written down before 1300 in Middle English and spelled *merveile*, from Latin *mīrābilis*, wonderful.]

mar•vel•ous also **mar•vel•lous** (mär′və ləs) *adj.* **1.** Causing wonder or astonishment: *a marvelous cure for the disease.* **2.** Excellent; notably superior: *a marvelous performance of the play.* —**mar′vel•ous•ly** *adv.* —**mar′vel•ous•ness** *n.*

Marx (märks), **Karl.** 1818–1883. German philosopher and revolutionary who was the founder of communism.

Marx•ism (märk′sĭz′əm) *n.* The political, economic, and social theories of Karl Marx that predict the eventual change of society from capitalism to communism.

Marx•ist (märk′sĭst) *n.* A person who believes in or follows Marxism. —*adj.* Of or relating to Karl Marx or Marxism.

Mar•y[1] (mâr′ē). The mother of Jesus in the New Testament and the principal saint of many Christian churches.

Mar•y[2] (mâr′ē). In the New Testament, a sister of Lazarus and Martha, and a friend of Jesus.

Mar•y•land (mĕr′ə lənd). A state of the east-central United States south of Pennsylvania. It was admitted as one of the original Thirteen Colonies in 1788. Annapolis is the capital and Baltimore the largest city. Population, 4,798,622. —See Note.

Mary Mag•da•lene (măg′də lən *or* măg′də lēn′). In the New Testament, a repentant woman who washed the feet of Jesus.

Mary Queen of Scots (skŏts) also **Mary Stu•art** (sto͞o′ərt *or* styo͞o′ərt). 1542–1587. Queen of Scotland (1542–1567). The Catholic monarch during the Scottish Reformation, she was imprisoned by Elizabeth I and executed for sedition.

mar•zi•pan (mär′zə păn′) *n.* A very sweet confection flavored with ground almonds. It is molded into decorative shapes and often colored to look like fruit.

masc. *abbr.* An abbreviation of masculine.

mas•car•a (mă skăr′ə) *n.* A cosmetic used to darken the eyelashes.

mas•cot (măs′kŏt′ *or* măs′kət) *n.* An animal, a person, or a thing believed to bring good luck, especially one kept as a symbol of a sports team.

mas•cu•line (măs′kyə lĭn) *adj.* **1.** Of or relating to men or boys: *The group of volunteers was mostly masculine.* **2.** Suggestive of a man; mannish: *a masculine hair style.* **3.** In grammar, relating to or belonging to the gender of nouns that refer to males or to things classified as male: *In French the word for "boat" is masculine.*

mas•cu•lin•i•ty (măs′kyə lĭn′ĭ tē) *n.* The quality or condition of being masculine.

ma•ser (mā′zər) *n.* A device that amplifies or generates microwaves.

Mas•er•u (măz′ə ro͞o′ *or* mä′sə ro͞o′). The capital of Lesotho, in the western part of the country. It was founded in 1869. Population, 14,686.

mash (măsh) *n.* **1.** A mixture of crushed grain and water that ferments and is used in making beer, ale, and whiskey. **2.** A mixture of crushed grain and water fed to livestock and fowl. **3.** A soft pulpy mixture. —*tr.v.* **mashed, mash•ing, mash•es. 1.** To convert (grain) into mash. **2.** To convert into a soft pulpy mixture: *mash potatoes.* **3.** To crush; smash: *I mashed the walnut with a hammer.* —**mash′er** *n.*

mask (măsk) *n.* **1.** A covering, often having openings for the eyes, worn over part or all of the face as a disguise: *a Halloween mask.* **2.** A representation of a face, often made of plaster or clay. **3.** A protective covering for the face: *a welder's mask.* **4.** Something that disguises or conceals: *The faint smile was a mask for the student's disappointment.*

—*tr.v.* **masked, mask•ing, masks.** To cover with a mask: *The robbers masked their faces.*
❑ *These sound alike:* **mask, masque** (masquerade).

masked (măskt) *adj.* **1.** Wearing a mask: *a masked bandit.* **2.** Disguised; hidden: *masked disappointment.*

mask•ing tape (măs′kĭng) *n.* A tape with adhesive on one side used for securing objects and covering areas not to be painted.

mas•och•ism (măs′ə kĭz′əm) *n.* A psychological disorder in which a person derives pleasure from being mistreated or subjected to pain. —**mas′o•chist** *n.*

ma•son (mā′sən) *n.* **1.** A person who builds or works with stone or brick. **2. Mason.** A Freemason.

Ma•son-Dix•on Line (mā′sən dĭk′sən). The boundary between Pennsylvania and Maryland, regarded as the dividing line between free and slave states before the Civil War.

Ma•son•ic (mə sŏn′ĭk) *adj.* Of or relating to Freemasons or Freemasonry.

Mason jar *n.* A glass jar with a wide mouth and an airtight metal lid, used for canning and preserving food. [First written down in 1885 in American English, after John L. *Mason* (1832–1902), American inventor.]

ma•son•ry (mā′sən rē) *n., pl.* **ma•son•ries. 1.** The trade or skill of a mason. **2.** Work done by a mason; stonework or brickwork. **3. Masonry.** Freemasonry.

masque (măsk) *n.* **1.** A dramatic entertainment performed by masked players and popular in European courts in the 16th and 17th centuries. **2.** A masquerade dance or party.
❑ *These sound alike:* **masque, mask** (disguise).

mas•quer•ade (măs′kə rād′) *n.* **1.a.** A dance or party at which masks and fancy costumes are worn. **b.** A costume worn at such a dance or party. **2.** A disguise or false pretense. —*intr.v.* **mas•quer•ad•ed, mas•quer•ad•ing, mas•quer•ades. 1.** To take part in a masquerade. **2.** To have a deceptive appearance; disguise oneself: *The undercover police officer masqueraded as a taxi driver.* —**mas′quer•ad′er** *n.*

mass (măs) *n.* **1.** A unified body of matter with no specific shape: *a mass of clay.* **2.** A large amount or number that is not specified: *A mass of people entered the stadium.* **3.** The major part; the majority: *The mass of voters supported the winning candidate.* **4.** The physical bulk or size of a solid body: *the huge mass of the ocean liner.* **5.** A measure of the amount of matter contained in a physical body. Mass is independent of gravity and therefore is different from weight. **6. masses.** The common people. —*tr. & intr.v.* **massed, mass•ing, mass•es.** To gather into or assemble in a mass: *The army massed its troops at the country's borders. The people massed downtown to watch the parade.* —*adj.* **1.** Of, involving, or attended by large numbers of people: *a mass demonstration.* **2.** Done on a large scale: *mass production.* [First written down before 1382 in Middle English and spelled *masse,* from Greek *maza.*]

Mass also **mass** (măs) *n.* **1.** In the Roman Catholic Church and some Protestant churches, the public celebration of the Eucharist. **2.** A musical composition written for certain parts of the Mass. [First written down before 810 in Old English and spelled *messe,* from Late Latin *missa.*]

Mass. *abbr.* An abbreviation of Massachusetts.

Mas•sa•chu•sett also **Mas•sa•chu•set** (măs′ə chōō′sĭt *or* măs′ə chōō′zĭt) *n., pl.* **Massachusett** or **Mas•sa•chu•setts** also **Massachuset** or **Mas•sa•chu•sets. 1.** A member of a Native American people formerly living along the eastern coast of Massachusetts. **2.** The Algonquian language of the Massachusett.

Mas•sa•chu•setts (măs′ə chōō′sĭts). A state of the northeast United States north of Connecticut. It was admitted as one of the original Thirteen Colonies in 1788. The first settlement was made by the Pilgrims of the *Mayflower* in 1620, and the colony was a leader in the move for independence from Great Britain. Capital, Boston. Population, 6,029,051. —See Note.

mas•sa•cre (măs′ə kər) *n.* A slaughter of a large number of people or animals. —*tr.v.* **mas•sa•cred** (măs′ə kərd), **mas•sa•cring** (măs′ə krĭng *or* măs′ə kər ĭng), **mas•sa•cres.** To kill cruelly; slaughter. [First written down in 1586 in Modern English, from Old French *macecre,* butchery.]

mas•sage (mə säzh′ *or* mə säj′) *n.* The rubbing or kneading of muscles and joints of the body to improve blood circulation and relax muscles. —*tr.v.* **mas•saged, mas•sag•ing, mas•sag•es.** To give a massage to.

Mas•sa•soit (măs′ə soit′). 1580?–1661. Wampanoag leader who aided the Pilgrim colonists and signed a peace treaty with them at Plymouth.

mass-en•er•gy equivalence (măs′ĕn′ər jē) *n.* The principle that a measured quantity of energy is equivalent to a measured quantity of mass.

mas•seur (mă sûr′ *or* mə sûr′) *n.* A man who gives massages professionally.

mas•seuse (mă sœz′) *n.* A woman who gives massages professionally.

mas•sive (măs′ĭv) *adj.* **1.** Bulky, heavy, and solid: *a massive building.* **2.** Unusually large or impressive: *a massive dose of penicillin.* **3.** Large in scope, intensity, degree, or scale: *a massive migration of birds.* —**mas′sive•ly** *adv.* —**mas′sive•ness** *n.*

mass media *pl.n.* The various media of public communication, such as television, radio, films, and newspapers.

mass noun *n.* A noun that refers to something that cannot be counted. *Furniture, honesty,* and *wildlife* are mass nouns.

mass number *n.* The total of the neutrons and protons present in an atomic nucleus.

mass-pro•duce (măs′prə dōōs′ *or* măs′prə dyōōs′) *tr.v.* **mass-pro•duced, mass-pro•duc•ing, mass-pro•duc•es.** To produce in large quantities, especially on an assembly line: *mass-produce cars.*

mass production *n.* The act or process of producing large quantities of a product, as on an assembly line.

mass transit *n.* The public transportation system of a city and the area around it. Buses, subways, and trains are forms of mass transit.

mast (măst) *n.* **1.** An upright pole that supports the sails and rigging of a ship or boat. **2.** An upright pole, as one on a crane. [First written down about 725 in Old English and spelled *mæst.*]

mas•ter (măs′tər) *n.* **1.** A person who directs, rules, or controls others; a ruler: *Caesar was the master of the Roman Empire.* **2.** The owner of a slave or an animal. **3.** A person in control of something: *the master of a banana plantation.* **4.** The captain of a merchant ship. **5.** An artisan who employs others, especially a person who trains apprentices. **6.** A male teacher, schoolmaster, or tutor, especially in a private school. **7.** A person of great learning, skill, or ability; an expert: *a master in metal work.* **8. Master.** A person who has received a Master's degree. **9. Master.** Used as a title before the name of a boy not considered old enough to be addressed as Mister. —*adj.* **1.** Of, relating to, or characteristic of a master. **2.** Principal; chief: *a master bedroom.* **3.** Highly skilled; expert: *a master carpenter.* **4.** Being

Mason jar

Massachusetts

The name **Massachusetts** is of Native American origin. The *Massachusett* Indians took their name, which probably meant "at the big hill," from the Blue Hills south of Boston. The English plural *s* was added to the name when referring to a Native American people of the region, and this form was used for the colony and later for the state.

Massasoit
Detail of bronze statue by Cyrus Dallin (b. 1861), located in Plymouth, Massachusetts

ă	pat	oi	boy
ā	pay	ou	out
âr	care	ŏŏ	took
ä	father	ōō	boot
ĕ	pet	ŭ	cut
ē	be	ûr	urge
ĭ	pit	th	thin
ī	pie	*th*	this
îr	pier	hw	whoop
ŏ	pot	zh	vision
ō	toe	ə	about
ô	paw	N	*French* bon

mastiff

a part of a mechanism that controls all other parts: *a master switch.* **5.** Being the original from which copies are made: *a master recording.* —*tr.v.* **mas•tered, mas•ter•ing, mas•ters. 1.** To become the master of; bring under control: *master one's emotions.* **2.** To become skilled in the use of: *master a foreign language.* [First written down about 1000 in Old English and spelled *mægester*, from Latin *magister.*]

mas•ter•ful (măs′tər fəl) *adj.* **1.** Acting like a master; domineering. **2.** Expert; skillful: *a masterful performance of the concerto.* **—mas′ter•ful•ly** *adv.* **—mas′ter•ful•ness** *n.*

mas•ter•ly (măs′tər lē) *adj.* Knowledgeable and skillful like a master: *a masterly debate.* —*adv.* With the skill of a master. **—mas′ter•li•ness** *n.*

mas•ter•mind (măs′tər mīnd′) *n.* A person who plans or directs something. —*tr.v.* **mas•ter•mind•ed, mas•ter•mind•ing, mas•ter•minds.** To plan or direct (something): *mastermind the team's turnaround.*

Master of Arts *n.* A master's degree in liberal arts.

master of ceremonies *n., pl.* **masters of ceremonies.** A person who acts as the host at a formal gathering and introduces the speakers and entertainers.

Master of Science *n.* A master's degree in science or mathematics.

mas•ter•piece (măs′tər pēs′) *n.* **1.** An outstanding work; something done with skill or brilliance: *The bridge was a masterpiece of engineering.* **2.** The greatest work of an artist or a craftsperson: *This figure is the sculptor's masterpiece.*

mas•ter's degree (măs′tərz) *n.* A degree awarded by a college or university to a student who has completed a prescribed course of study. It ranks above a bachelor's degree and below a doctorate.

master sergeant *n.* **1.** A noncommissioned officer in the U.S. Army and Marine Corps below sergeant major. **2.** A high-ranking noncommissioned officer in the U.S. Air Force.

mas•ter•work (măs′tər wûrk′) *n.* A masterpiece.

mas•ter•y (măs′tə rē) *n., pl.* **mas•ter•ies. 1.** Complete control or domination: *The Iroquois had mastery of the forests.* **2.** Possession of great skill, knowledge, or technique: *the musician's great mastery of the piano.*

mast•head (măst′hĕd′) *n.* **1.** The top of a ship's mast. **2.** The listing in a newspaper, a magazine, or another publication of its owners, staff, and information about its operation.

mas•ti•cate (măs′tĭ kāt′) *tr.v.* **mas•ti•cat•ed, mas•ti•cat•ing, mas•ti•cates.** To chew (food). [First written down in 1649 in Modern English, from Late Latin *masticāre*, from Greek *mastikhan*, to grind the teeth.] **—mas′ti•ca′tion** *n.*

mas•tiff (măs′tĭf) *n.* Any of a breed of large and powerful dog having a short heavy coat and square jaws.

mas•to•don (măs′tə dŏn′) *n.* Any of several extinct mammals resembling an elephant with long curved tusks. It is believed that mastodons lived in North America until the end of the Ice Age. —SEE NOTE.

mastodon

The bones of **mammoths** and **mastodons** indicate that these creatures looked a lot alike. Members of these two groups of extinct mammals were large and elephantlike, and they had extraordinarily long tusks as well as similar coats of thick, shaggy hair. But some researchers who looked carefully at the remains of many of these large mammals found that some remains contained teeth that were flat and ridged while others contained teeth that were knobby, almost cone-shaped. Based on this difference in teeth, scientists decided that two groups of the giant creatures had existed. In fact, they used this difference in teeth to develop a name for the mastodon. *Mastodon* means "breast-shaped tooth."

mas•toid (măs′toid′) *n.* The bone in the lower part of the skull behind the ear.

mas•tur•bate (măs′tər bāt′) *intr.v.* **mas•tur•bat•ed, mas•tur•bat•ing, mas•tur•bates.** To perform an act of masturbation.

mas•tur•ba•tion (măs′tər **bā′**shən) *n.* The act of stimulating the genitals to produce sexual pleasure by means other than sexual intercourse.

mat¹ (măt) *n.* **1.** A flat piece of coarse material, often woven of straw, hemp, or rushes, used as a floor covering or for wiping one's shoes. **2.** A small piece of material put under a dish, vase, or other object to protect or decorate the top of a table. **3.** A thick pad or mattress used on the floor for tumbling, wrestling, or acrobatics. **4.** A dense or tangled mass: *a mat of hair.* —*v.* **mat•ted, mat•ting, mats.** —*tr.* **1.** To tangle into a thick compact mass: *mat fibers together to make felt.* **2.** To cover with a mat or with matting: *They matted the floor of the hut.* —*intr.* To become tangled into a thick compact mass: *The cat's fur matted without brushing.* [First written down before 800 in Old English and spelled *matte*, from Late Latin *matta.*]

mat² (măt) *n.* **1.** A piece of cardboard or other material placed around a picture as a frame or border between the picture and its frame. **2.** also **matte.** A dull finish on something, as of paint or paper. —*tr. v.* **mat•ted, mat•ting, mats.** To put a mat around (a picture). —*adj.* also **matte.** Having a dull finish. [First written down in 1845 in Modern English, from French *mat*, dull.]

mat•a•dor (măt′ə dôr′) *n.* The person who fights and kills the bull in a bullfight.

Ma•ta Ha•ri (mä′tə här′ē *or* măt′ə hăr′ē). 1876–1917. Dutch spy who apparently spied for Germany during World War I and was arrested and executed by the French.

match¹ (măch) *n.* **1.a.** A person or thing exactly like another: *Find the match for this fabric.* **b.** A person or thing that is similar to or goes well with another: *This tie is a good match for your shirt.* **2.** A person or thing with equal or near equal capabilities: *The runners were a good match and ran a very close race.* **3.** A sports contest: *a wrestling match.* **4.a.** A marriage or an arrangement of marriage. **b.** A person viewed as a possible partner in marriage. —*v.* **matched, match•ing, match•es.** —*tr.* **1.** To be alike; correspond exactly to: *This sock doesn't match that one.* **2.** To resemble or harmonize with; be suitable for: *Your shirt matches your slacks.* **3.** To fit together: *Match the edges of the seam and sew them together.* **4.** To find or provide a match for: *We could not match the color of the old paint on the door.* **5.a.** To provide with an opponent or a competitor: *The teacher matched one group against the other in a spelling bee.* **b.** To place in competition: *They matched wits.* **6.** To join or give in marriage. —*intr.* To be alike or equal: *Finally your socks match.* [First written down before 971 in Old English and spelled *gemæcca*, companion, mate.]

match² (măch) *n.* **1.** A strip of wood, cardboard, or wax coated at one end with a substance that catches fire easily when scratched against a surface that has been treated with certain chemicals. **2.** An easily ignited cord or wick, formerly used to fire cannons and muskets or matchlock guns. [First written down about 1378 in Middle English and spelled *macche*, lamp wick, from Greek *muxa.*]

match•book (măch′bo͝ok′) *n.* A small cardboard folder containing safety matches and a surface for striking them.

match•box (măch′bŏks′) *n.* A box for matches that usually has a surface for striking them.

match•less (măch′lĭs) *adj.* Having no rival or equal: *his matchless ability to play the guitar.*

match•lock (măch′lŏk′) *n.* A kind of early musket in which the powder charge is ignited by a wick or match.

match•mak•er (măch′mā′kər) *n.* **1.** A person who arranges or tries to arrange marriages for others. **2.** A person who arranges athletic competitions.

mate¹ (māt) *n.* **1.** One of a matched pair: *Find the mate to this sock.* **2.** A husband or wife. **3.** The male or female of a pair of animals or birds that are breeding. **4.** A close associate; a partner: *We need more help from our mates to finish the job.* **5.a.** An officer on a merchant ship ranking below the master. **b.** An officer of the U.S. Navy ranking below and assisting a warrant officer. *—v.* **mat•ed, mat•ing, mates.** *—tr.* **1.** To join closely; pair. **2.** To unite in marriage. **3.** To bring (a male and a female animal) together for breeding. *—intr.* To pair; breed: *Many animals mate in the spring.* [First written down about 1350 in Middle English, from Middle Low German *māte*, messmate.]

mate[2] (māt) *n.* In chess, a checkmate. *—tr. & intr.v.* **mat•ed, mat•ing, mates.** To checkmate or achieve a checkmate. [First written down before 1300 in Middle English and spelled *mat*, from Arabic *māt*, dead.]

ma•té (**mä**′tā *or* mä **tā**′) *n.* **1.** A drink resembling tea, made from the leaves of an evergreen South American shrub related to holly. **2.** The shrub that bears such leaves.

ma•te•ri•al (mə **tîr**′ē əl) *n.* **1.** The substance or substances from which something is or can be made: *Hemp is often used as material for ropes.* **2.** Cloth or fabric: *a length of silk material.* **3.** Something, such as an idea or information, that is used or developed to make something else: *historical material for a novel.* **4. materials.** Tools or apparatus needed to perform a certain task: *building materials.* *—adj.* **1.** Of, relating to, or composed of matter: *not a ghost, but a material being.* **2.** Of or affecting physical well being: *material comforts.* **3.** Of or concerned with the physical as opposed to the spiritual or intellectual: *I did it not for material gain but for personal satisfaction.* **4.** Important; relevant: *Is your remark material to this discussion?* [First written down about 1340 in Middle English and spelled *materiel*, from Latin *māteria*, matter.] **—ma•te′ri•al•ly** *adv.*

ma•te•ri•al•ism (mə **tîr**′ē ə lĭz′əm) *n.* **1.** The philosophical doctrine that physical matter is the only reality and that everything, including the mind, thoughts, and feelings, can be explained in terms of matter. **2.** The tendency to be concerned with money and possessions rather than with spiritual or intellectual things. **—ma•te′ri•al•is′tic** *adj.* **—ma•te′ri•al•is′ti•cal•ly** *adv.*

ma•te•ri•al•ist (mə **tûr**′ē ə lĭst) *n.* **1.** A person who believes in materialism. **2.** A person who is concerned with money and possessions rather than spiritual or intellectual things.

ma•te•ri•al•ize (mə **tîr**′ē ə līz′) *v.* **ma•te•ri•al•ized, ma•te•ri•al•iz•ing, ma•te•ri•al•iz•es.** *—intr.* **1.** To become real or actual; become a fact: *Support for the project never materialized.* **2.** To appear in material or bodily form: *A mouse materialized in the corner of the room.* *—tr.* To give material form to: *The Wright brothers materialized their ideas by building many models.*

ma•te•ri•el or **ma•té•ri•el** (mə tîr′ē **ĕl**′) *n.* Equipment, apparatus, and supplies, especially those used by a military force.

ma•ter•nal (mə **tûr**′nəl) *adj.* **1.** Relating to or characteristic of a mother or motherhood: *the maternal instinct of a lioness.* **2.** Inherited from one's mother: *a maternal trait.* **3.** Related through one's mother: *maternal aunts and uncles.* [First written down in 1481 in Middle English, from Latin *māter*, mother.] **—ma•ter′nal•ly** *adv.*

ma•ter•ni•ty (mə **tûr**′nĭ tē) *n., pl.* **ma•ter•ni•ties. 1.** The state of being a mother. **2.** The feelings or characteristics that are part of being a mother; motherliness. *—adj.* Relating to or effective during pregnancy, childbirth, or the first months of motherhood: *a maternity dress; maternity care.*

math (măth) *n.* Mathematics.

math•e•mat•i•cal (măth′ə **măt**′ĭ kəl) *adj.* **1.** Of or relating to mathematics. **2.** Precise; exact: *mathematical correctness.* **—math′e•mat′i•cal•ly** *adv.*

math•e•ma•ti•cian (măth′ə mə **tĭsh**′ən) *n.* A person who is skilled in or who specializes in mathematics.

math•e•mat•ics (măth′ə **măt**′ĭks) *n.* *(used with a singular verb).* The study of the relationships and properties of quantities, using numbers and symbols. Arithmetic, algebra, and geometry are branches of mathematics.

mat•i•nee or **mat•i•née** (măt′n **ā**′) *n.* A show or performance given in the afternoon.

mat•ins (**măt**′nz) *n.* *(used with a singular or plural verb).* **1.** The first of the canonical hours in the Roman Catholic Church. **2.** A church service of morning prayer, especially such a service in the Anglican church.

ma•tri•arch (**mā**′trē ärk′) *n.* **1.** A woman who rules a family, clan, or tribe. **2.** A woman who dominates a group or an activity.

ma•tri•ar•chy (**mā**′trē är′kē) *n., pl.* **ma•tri•ar•chies.** A society in which a woman rules a family, clan, or tribe and descent is traced through the mother's side of the family. **—ma′tri•ar′chal** *adj.*

ma•tri•ces (**mā**′trĭ sēz′ *or* **măt**′rĭ sēz′) *n.* A plural of **matrix.**

mat•ri•cide (**măt**′rĭ sīd′) *n.* The act of killing one's mother. **—mat′ri•cid′al** *adj.*

ma•tric•u•late (mə **trĭk**′yə lāt′) *tr. & intr.v.* **ma•tric•u•lat•ed, ma•tric•u•lat•ing, ma•tric•u•lates.** To enroll or allow to enroll in a college or university. **—ma•tric′u•la′tion** *n.*

mat•ri•mo•ny (**măt**′rə mō′nē) *n., pl.* **mat•ri•mo•nies.** The act or condition of being married; marriage. **—mat′ri•mo′ni•al** *adj.*

ma•trix (**mā**′trĭks) *n., pl.* **ma•tri•ces** (**mā**′trĭ sēz′ *or* **măt**′rĭ sēz′) or **ma•trix•es.** A situation or substance within which something is contained, originates, or develops. The mineral grains of a rock in which fossils are embedded are a matrix.

ma•tron (**mā**′trən) *n.* **1.** A married woman or a widow, especially one who is a mother, of mature age or high social position. **2.** A woman who acts as a supervisor or guard in a public institution, such as a school, hospital, or prison. [First written down before 1393 in Middle English and spelled *matrone*, from Latin *mātrōna*, from *māter*, mother.] **—ma′tron•ly** *adv. & adj.*

matron of honor *n., pl.* **matrons of honor.** A married woman who serves as chief attendant of the bride at a wedding.

matte (măt) *n.* Variant of **mat[2]** (sense 2). *—adj.* Variant of **mat[2].**

mat•ted (**măt**′ĭd) *adj.* **1.** Formed into a mass; tangled: *matted underbrush.* **2.** Covered with mats or matting: *a matted floor.*

mat•ter (**măt**′ər) *n.* **1.a.** Something that occupies space, has mass, and can exist ordinarily as a solid, liquid, or gas. **b.** A specific type of substance: *organic matter.* **2.** The substance or content of something: *The matter of the book was very interesting.* See Synonyms at **subject. 3.** A subject of concern, feeling, or action: *For me, this exam is a serious matter.* **4.** Trouble; difficulty: *What's the matter with them?* **5.** A certain quantity, amount, or extent: *The highway construction lasted a matter of years.* **6.** Something written or printed or to be written or printed: *reading matter.* *—intr.v.* **mat•tered, mat•ter•ing, mat•ters.** To be of importance: *Our success mattered a great deal to us.* ***—idioms.*** **as a matter of fact.** In fact; actually. **no matter.** Regardless of: *No matter where you go, I'll be thinking of you.* [First written down before 1200 in Middle English and spelled *materie*, from Latin *māteria.*]

Mat•ter•horn (**măt**′ər hôrn′). A mountain, 14,692

Matterhorn

ă	pat	oi	boy
ā	pay	ou	out
âr	care	ŏŏ	took
ä	father	ōō	boot
ĕ	pet	ŭ	cut
ē	be	ûr	urge
ĭ	pit	th	thin
ī	pie	*th*	this
îr	pier	hw	whoop
ŏ	pot	zh	vision
ō	toe	ə	about
ô	paw	N	*French* bon

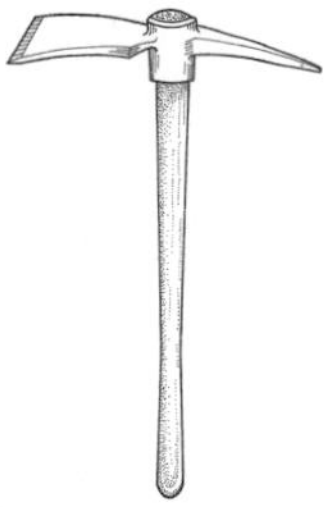

mattock

mausoleum
The Taj Mahal in Agra, India

Barbara McClintock

William McKinley

feet (4,481.1 meters) high, in the Alps on the Italian-Swiss border.

matter of course *n.* Something that is expected; a natural or logical result.

mat•ter-of-fact (măt′ər əv **făkt′**) *adj.* **1.** Adhering strictly to the facts; literal: *a matter-of-fact description of the party.* **2.** Showing no emotion: *a matter-of-fact tone of voice.* **—mat′ter-of-fact′ly** *adv.*

Mat•thew (**măth′**yo͞o) *n.* The first Gospel of the New Testament, thought to have been written by Saint Matthew.

Matthew, Saint. First century A.D. One of the 12 Apostles, traditionally regarded as author of the first Gospel of the New Testament.

mat•ting (măt′ĭng) *n.* **1.** A coarse fabric of woven straw, hemp, or rushes, used especially for making mats or covering floors. **2.** Material formed into a mat: *a matting of leaves on the forest floor.*

mat•tock (măt′ək) *n.* A digging tool with a flat blade, used for cutting roots or breaking up soil.

mat•tress (măt′rĭs) *n.* A pad of heavy cloth filled with soft material or a group of springs, used on or as a bed.

mat•u•ra•tion (măch′ə **rā′**shən) *n.* The process of maturing or ripening.

ma•ture (mə **tyo͝or′** *or* mə **to͝or′** *or* mə **cho͝or′**) *adj.* **ma•tur•er, ma•tur•est. 1.** Having reached full growth or development: *a mature tree.* **2.** Having the mental and emotional qualities associated with an adult: *a mature young person.* **3.** Having characteristics associated with full development: *mature behavior.* **4.** Worked out fully in the mind: *a mature plan of action.* **5.** Having reached the limit of its time; due: *a mature savings bond.* *—v.* **ma•tured, ma•tur•ing, ma•tures.** *—tr.* To bring to full development: *Working in the hospital has matured him.* *—intr.* **1.** To reach full growth or development: *She has matured into a fine actress.* **2.** To become due: *This bond matures in seven years.* [First written down in 1440 in Middle English, from Latin *mātūrus.*] **—ma•ture′ly** *adv.*

ma•tur•i•ty (mə **tyo͝or′**ĭ tē *or* mə **to͝or′**ĭ tē *or* mə-**cho͝or′**ĭ tē) *n., pl.* **ma•tur•i•ties. 1.** The condition of being mature; full growth or development: *Tomatoes reach maturity in late summer.* **2.** The time at which payment of a loan or bond becomes due.

mat•zo or **mat•zah** (**mät′**sə) *n., pl.* **mat•zos** or **mat•zahs** (**mät′**səz) or **mat•zot** or **mat•zoth** (mät-**sôt′**). A brittle flat piece of unleavened bread, eaten especially during Passover. [First written down in 1846 in Modern English, from Yiddish *matse,* from Hebrew *maṣṣâ.*]

maud•lin (**môd′**lĭn) *adj.* Overly or foolishly sentimental. [First written down in 1607 in Modern English, alteration of *(Mary) Magdalene,* who was frequently depicted as a tearful penitent.]

Mau•i (**mou′**ē). An island of Hawaii northwest of Hawaii Island. It is the second-largest island in the state.

maul (môl) *n.* A heavy hammer or mallet, used to drive stakes, piles, or wedges. *—tr.v.* **mauled, maul•ing, mauls. 1.** To injure or damage by beating: *The bear cub mauled the salmon before eating it.* **2.** To handle roughly: *The package was mauled in the mail.*

❑ *These sound alike:* **maul, mall** (shopping center).

Mau•na Lo•a (**mou′**nə **lō′**ə *or* **mô′**nə **lō′**ə). An active volcano, 13,680 feet (4,172.4 meters) high, of south-central Hawaii Island.

maun•der (**môn′**dər *or* **män′**dər) *intr.v.* **maun•dered, maun•der•ing, maun•ders. 1.** To talk in a rambling or confused way. **2.** To wander about in an aimless or confused way.

Mau•ri•ta•ni•a (môr′ĭ **tā′**nē ə). A country of northwest Africa west of Mali and bordering on the Atlantic Ocean. It was settled in about 1000. Mauritania gained its independence from France in 1960. Capital, Nouakchott. Population, 1,727,000.

Mau•ri•tius (mô **rĭsh′**əs *or* mô **rĭsh′**ē əs). An island country in the southwest Indian Ocean made up of the island of **Mauritius** and several smaller islands. Mauritius gained its independence from Great Britain in 1968. Port Louis is the capital and the largest city. Population, 1,023,934.

mau•so•le•um (mô′sə **lē′**əm *or* mô′zə **lē′**əm) *n., pl.* **mau•so•le•ums** or **mau•so•le•a** (mô′sə **lē′**ə *or* mô′zə **lē′**ə). A stately building housing a tomb or tombs. [First written down in 1425 in Middle English, after *Mausolus* (died c. 353 B.C.), a Persian ruler in Asia Minor.]

mauve (mōv) *n.* A light rosy or grayish purple.

mav•er•ick (**măv′**ər ĭk *or* **măv′**rĭk) *n.* **1.** An unbranded calf or colt, traditionally belonging to the first person to brand it. **2.** A person who refuses to go along with the policies or views of a group. [First written down in 1867 in American English, possibly after Samuel Augustus *Maverick* (1803–1870), American cattleman, or perhaps after Samuel *Maverick* (1602?–1676?), American colonist.]

maw (mô) *n.* The mouth, throat, gullet, or stomach of an animal.

mawk•ish (**mô′**kĭsh) *adj.* Excessively and foolishly sentimental: *a mawkish poem about romantic love.* **—mawk′ish•ly** *adv.* **—mawk′ish•ness** *n.*

max. *abbr.* An abbreviation of maximum.

max•il•la (măk **sĭl′**ə) *n., pl.* **max•il•lae** (măk **sĭl′**ē) or **max•il•las. 1.** The jaw or jawbone, especially the upper jawbone in mammals and most vertebrates. **2.** Either of a pair of appendages behind the mandibles in insects, spiders, crabs, and other related animals.

max•il•lar•y (**măk′**sə lĕr′ē) *adj.* Of or relating to the jaw or jawbone, especially the upper jawbone. *—n., pl.* **max•il•lar•ies.** A maxilla or jawbone.

max•im (**măk′**sĭm) *n.* A brief statement of a basic principle or rule of behavior; a proverb.

max•i•ma (**măk′**sə mə) *n.* A plural of **maximum.**

max•i•mize (**măk′**sə mīz′) *tr.v.* **max•i•mized, max•i•miz•ing, max•i•miz•es.** To make as great or large as possible: *Working hard will maximize your opportunities.*

max•i•mum (**măk′**sə məm) *n., pl.* **max•i•mums** or **max•i•ma** (**măk′**sə mə). The greatest known or greatest possible number, measure, quantity, or degree: *The temperature reached a maximum of only 10 degrees today.* *—adj.* Having or being the greatest number, measure, quantity, or degree that is possible: *The train has a maximum speed of 120 miles per hour.* [First written down in 1740 in Modern English, from Latin *maximus,* greatest.]

may (mā) *aux.v.* Past tense **might** (mīt). **1.** To be allowed or permitted to: *May I go outside?* **2.** Used to indicate likelihood or possibility: *It may rain today.* **3.** Used to express a desire or wish: *May your days be filled with laughter.* **4.** Used to express purpose or result in clauses starting with *so that: I tell you this so that you may understand.* [First written down in 650 in Old English and spelled *mæg.*]

May (mā) *n.* The fifth month of the year in the Gregorian calendar, having 31 days. [First written down in 1110 in Middle English, from Latin *Maia,* a goddess of ancient Italy.]

Ma•ya (**mä′**yə) *n., pl.* **Maya** or **Ma•yas. 1.** A member of a Native American people of Central America and southern Mexico whose civilization reached its height around A.D. 1000. **2.** Any of the languages spoken by the Maya.

Ma•yan (**mä′**yən) *adj.* Of or relating to the Maya

or their languages or culture. —*n.* **1.** A Maya. **2.** A family of Indian languages spoken in Central America.

may•be (mā′bē) *adv.* Possibly; perhaps: *Maybe we can go swimming tomorrow.*

may•day (mā′dā′) *n.* An international word used to call for help, especially for planes or ships in trouble. [First written down in 1927 in Modern English, from French *m'aidez*, help me!]

May Day *n.* May 1, celebrated in some countries as a spring holiday, and in others in honor of workers.

may•flow•er (mā′flou′ər) *n.* Any of various plants that bloom in spring, especially the arbutus.

may•fly (mā′flī′) *n.* Any of various insects having transparent wings and long filaments extending from the end of the body. Adult mayflies live for only a day or two.

may•hem (mā′hĕm′ *or* mā′əm) *n.* **1.** In law, the willful maiming or injuring of a person. **2.** A state of confusion or destructive disorder.

may•n't (mā′ənt *or* mānt). Contraction of *may not.*

may•on•naise (mā′ə nāz′ *or* mā′ə nāz′) *n.* A thick dressing made of beaten raw egg yolk, oil, lemon juice or vinegar, and seasonings.

may•or (mā′ər *or* mâr) *n.* The chief government official of a city or town. [First written down about 1300 in Middle English and spelled *mer*, from Latin *māior*, greater, superior.] —**may′or•al** *adj.*

may•or•al•ty (mā′ər əl tē *or* mâr′əl tē) *n., pl.* **may•or•al•ties. 1.** The position of a mayor. **2.** The term of office of a mayor.

May•pole also **may•pole** (mā′pōl′) *n.* A pole decorated with streamers, ribbons, and flowers, around which people dance on May Day.

maze (māz) *n.* **1.** A complicated and often confusing network of pathways. **2.** A muddle or tangle: *a maze of contradictions.*

❑ *These sound alike:* **maze, maize** (corn plant).

ma•zur•ka also **ma•zour•ka** (mə zûr′kə *or* mə-zo͝or′kə) *n.* **1.** A lively Polish dance that resembles a polka. **2.** Music written for this dance.

maz•y (mā′zē) *adj.* **maz•i•er, maz•i•est.** Resembling a maze; complicated.

Mba•bane (əm bä bän′). The capital of Swaziland, in the northwest part of the country near the South African border. Population, 33,000.

MC (em′se′) *n.* A master of ceremonies.

Mc•Clin•tock (mə klĭn′tək *or* mə klĭn′tŏk′), **Barbara.** 1902–1992. American botanist who won a 1983 Nobel Prize for her work on plant cells.

Mc•Cor•mick (mə kôr′mĭk), **Anne Elizabeth O'Hare.** 1882–1954. British-born American journalist who was the first woman to receive a Pulitzer Prize for journalism (1937).

McCormick, Cyrus Hall. 1809–1884. American inventor and manufacturer who developed a mechanical reaper (1831).

Mc•Kin•ley (mə kĭn′lē), **Mount.** Also **De•na•li** (də nä′lē). A peak, 20,320 feet (6,197.6 meters) high, of south-central Alaska. It is the highest point in North America.

McKinley, William. 1843–1901. The 25th President of the United States (1897–1901). His presidency was marked by the Spanish-American War (1898) and the annexation of Cuba and the Philippines.

Md The symbol for the element **mendelevium.**

Md. *abbr.* An abbreviation of Maryland.

MD *abbr.* An abbreviation of **1.** Maryland. **2.** Medicinae Doctor (Doctor of Medicine).

M.D. *abbr.* An abbreviation of Medicinae Doctor (Doctor of Medicine).

me (mē) *pron.* The objective form of **I. 1.** Used as the direct object of a verb: *He helped me.* **2.** Used as the indirect object of a verb: *She sent me a letter.* **3.** Used as the object of a preposition: *They brought the books to me.* —SEE NOTE.

❑ *These sound alike:* **me, mi** (musical tone).

ME *abbr.* An abbreviation of Maine.

Me. *abbr.* An abbreviation of Maine.

mead[1] (mēd) *n.* An alcoholic beverage made of fermented honey and water. [First written down about 725 in Old English and spelled *medu.*]

mead[2] (mēd) *n. Archaic.* A meadow. [First written down before 901 in Old English and spelled *mæd.*]

Mead (mēd), **Margaret.** 1901–1978. American anthropologist noted for her landmark studies of adolescence in primitive cultures.

mead•ow (mĕd′ō) *n.* A stretch of grassy ground, such as one used as a pasture or for growing hay.

mead•ow•lark (mĕd′ō lärk′) *n.* Any of various North American songbirds having a brownish back and a yellow breast with a V-shaped black marking.

mea•ger also **mea•gre** (mē′gər) *adj.* **1.** Lacking in quantity or richness; scanty: *a meager dinner.* **2.** Having little flesh; thin: *a meager face.* —**mea′ger•ly** *adv.* —**mea′ger•ness** *n.*

meal[1] (mēl) *n.* **1.** Grain that has been coarsely ground. **2.** A substance that has been ground. [First written down before 899 in Old English and spelled *melu.*]

meal[2] (mēl) *n.* **1.** The food served and eaten in one sitting. **2.** The customary time for eating food: *Don't eat between meals.* [First written down before 725 in Old English and spelled *mæl.*]

meal•time (mēl′tīm′) *n.* The usual time for eating a meal.

meal•y (mē′lē) *adj.* **meal•i•er, meal•i•est. 1.** Resembling meal in texture and consistency; dry and granular: *a soft and mealy apple.* **2.** Made of or containing meal: *mealy chicken feed.* **3.** Covered with meal: *Sweep the mealy floor.* **4.** Lacking color; pale: *a mealy complexion.* —**meal′i•ness** *n.*

meal•y-mouthed (mē′lē mouthd′ *or* mē′lē-moutht′) *adj.* Unwilling to say directly or simply what one thinks is right or true.

mean[1] (mēn) *v.* **meant** (mĕnt), **mean•ing, means.** —*tr.* **1.** To be used to convey; have the sense of; signify: *The Spanish word* frijol *means "bean."* **2.** To intend to convey or indicate: *What did you mean by that statement?* **3.** To have as a purpose or an intention: *They mean no harm.* **4.** To design or intend for a certain purpose or end: *This building was meant for grain storage.* **5.** To be likely to result in; be attended by: *Dark clouds often mean a storm.* **6.** To bring about or have as a consequence: *Friction means heat.* **7.** To be of a specified importance; matter: *Your friendship means a great deal to me.* —*intr.* To have intentions of a certain kind: *She means well, despite her mistakes.* —***idiom.*** **mean business.** To be in earnest. [First written down about 725 in Old English and spelled *mænan*, to tell of.]

❑ *These sound alike:* **mean[1]** (signify), **mean[2]** (unkind), **mean[3]** (middle point), **mien** (manner).

mean[2] (mēn) *adj.* **mean•er, mean•est. 1.** Lacking kindness and good will: *The teacher was not being mean in asking you to be quiet.* **2.** Cruel; spiteful: *a mean remark made in anger.* **3.** Miserly; stingy. **4.** Low, as in quality, rank, or value; inferior: *rose from mean origins to fame and success.* **5.** *Slang.* Hard to cope with; difficult: *He throws a mean curve ball.* **6.** Excellent: *She plays a mean game of chess.* [First written down about 1000 in Old English and spelled *gemæne*, common.]

❑ *These sound alike:* **mean[2]** (unkind), **mean[1]** (signify), **mean[3]** (middle point), **mien** (manner).

mean[3] (mēn) *n.* **1.** Something that is midway between two extremes. **2.** A number or quantity that has a value that is intermediate between other num-

Usage: me

The correct pronoun to use in sentences like *John and ______ are going home* is the nominative form, such as **I**, **he**, **she**, or **they**, not the objective form, such as **me**, **him**, **her**, or **them**. Therefore you say *John and I are going home*, not *John and me are going home.* You would, after all, say *I am going home* and not *Me am going home.*

Margaret Mead

Usage: mean[3]

When **means** has the meaning of "financial resources," it takes a plural verb: *Her means are more than adequate.* When **means** has the sense of "a way to an end," the word is singular when it refers to a particular method: *The best means of traveling there is by plane.* **Means** is plural when it refers to a group of methods: *What are the most effective means for doing this project?*

ă	pat	oi	boy
ā	pay	ou	out
âr	care	o͝o	took
ä	father	o͞o	boot
ĕ	pet	ŭ	cut
ē	be	ûr	urge
ĭ	pit	th	thin
ī	pie	*th*	this
îr	pier	hw	whoop
ŏ	pot	zh	vision
ō	toe	ə	about
ô	paw	N	*French* bon

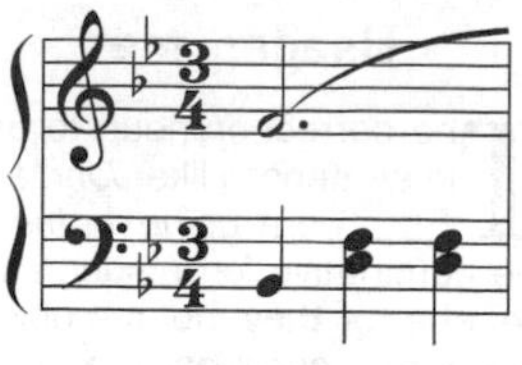

measure
From "Roses of the South," a waltz by Johann Strauss the Younger

measuring worm

bers or quantities, especially an arithmetic mean or average. **3.** Either the second or third term of a proportion of four terms. In the proportion $\frac{2}{3} = \frac{4}{6}$, the means are 3 and 4. **4. means. a.** Something, such as a method or course of action, by which an act or end is achieved: *a practical means of using the sun's energy to generate electricity.* **b.** Money, property, or other wealth: *a person of means.* —*adj.* **1.** Occupying a middle or intermediate position between two extremes: *mean test scores.* **2.** Middling; average. ***—idioms.*** **by all means.** Without fail; certainly. **by any means.** In any way possible; in any case: *We must fix this problem by any means.* **by means of.** With the use of; owing to: *They crossed the river by means of a raft.* **by no means.** In no sense; certainly not: *By no means should you go sailing in rough weather.* [First written down in 1340 in Middle English and spelled *men,* middle, from Latin *mediānus.*] —SEE NOTE on page 607.

❑ *These sound alike:* **mean**[3] (middle point), **mean**[1] (signify), **mean**[2] (unkind), **mien** (manner).

me•an•der (mē ăn′dər) *intr.v.* **me•an•dered, me•an•der•ing, me•an•ders. 1.** To follow a winding and turning course: *The river meanders through the valley.* **2.** To wander aimlessly and idly: *We meandered through the fields and woods.* See Synonyms at **wander.** [First written down in 1576 in Modern English, after the *Maeander* River in Asia Minor.]

mean•ing (mē′nĭng) *n.* **1.** Something that is meant or signified, especially by language: *The word* head *has several meanings.* **2.** Something that one wishes to communicate: *The writer's meaning was easy to understand.* **3.** A goal or purpose: *What is the meaning of all this?* —*adj.* Full of meaning; expressive: *a meaning smile.* **—mean′ing•ly** *adv.*

mean•ing•ful (mē′nĭng fəl) *adj.* Full of meaning; significant: *a meaningful discussion.* **—mean′ing•ful•ly** *adv.* **—mean′ing•ful•ness** *n.*

mean•ing•less (mē′nĭng lĭs) *adj.* Having no meaning or significance: *a meaningless phrase.* **—mean′ing•less•ly** *adv.* **—mean′ing•less•ness** *n.*

mean•ness (mēn′nĭs) *n.* **1.** The condition of being inferior or lacking in quality, character, or value. **2.** Selfishness; stinginess. **3.** A spiteful act.

meant (mĕnt) *v.* Past tense and past participle of **mean**[1].

mean•time (mēn′tīm′) *n.* The time between one occurrence and another: *In the meantime, keep practicing your music.* —*adv.* Meanwhile.

mean•while (mēn′wīl′) *n.* Meantime. —*adv.* **1.** During or in the time between two events: *Meanwhile, she continued to improve her swimming stroke.* **2.** At the same time: *I'll put the food on the plates, and meanwhile, you set the table.*

meas. *abbr.* An abbreviation of measure.

mea•sles (mē′zəlz) *n. (used with a singular or plural verb).* **1.** A highly contagious viral disease with symptoms that include coughing, fever, and a rash. **2.** Any of several milder diseases that have symptoms similar to measles, especially German measles.

mea•sly (mēz′lē) *adj.* **mea•sli•er, mea•sli•est. 1.** *Slang.* Contemptibly small; meager: *A measly dollar is all they gave me.* **2.** Having measles.

meas•ur•a•ble (mĕzh′ər ə bəl) *adj.* Possible to be measured. **—meas′ur•a•ble•ness** *n.* **—meas′ur•a•bly** *adv.*

meas•ure (mĕzh′ər) *n.* **1.** The size or amount of something as determined by comparison with a standard: *What are the measures of that window?* **2.** A unit of measure specified by a scale, as an inch or a pint. **3.** A system of such standards and units, as the metric system. **4.** Something, such as a container or a ruler, used for measuring. **5.** The extent or degree of something: *There is a large measure of planning involved in putting on a play.* **6.** A standard of evaluation or basis for comparison: *A book's sales shouldn't be the only measure of its success.* **7.** Limit; bounds: *His generosity knows no measure.* **8.** An action taken for a specified purpose or end. Often used in the plural: *It took drastic measures to clean up the harbor.* **9.** A legislative bill or act; a law. **10.** Poetic meter. **11.** The music between two bars on a staff. —*v.* **meas•ured, meas•ur•ing, meas•ures.** —*tr.* **1.** To find the size, amount, capacity, or degree of something: *Measure this board for me.* **2.** To serve as a measure of: *The foot measures length.* **3.** To mark off or dole out by measuring: *measure off a yard of fabric.* **4.** To estimate by comparison or evaluation; appraise: *measure the importance of a problem.* **5.** To choose with care; weigh: *I measured my words before answering the question.* —*intr.* **1.** To have a measurement: *The paper measures 8 by 12 inches.* **2.** To take measurements: *Always measure ingredients accurately.* ***—idioms.*** **for good measure.** In addition to the required amount. **measure up.** To have the necessary qualifications: *The baseball player didn't measure up and was sent to the minors.* **measure up to.** To be the equal of; fulfill or meet: *Did the concert measure up to your expectations?*

meas•ured (mĕzh′ərd) *adj.* **1.** Found out by measuring: *the measured distance of almost a mile.* **2.** Regular in rhythm and number: *a measured beat.* **3.** Careful; deliberate: *measured and precise words.* **—meas′ured•ly** *adv.*

meas•ure•less (mĕzh′ər lĭs) *adj.* Having no limits; infinite: *Infinity is measureless.*

meas•ure•ment (mĕzh′ər mənt) *n.* **1.** The act or process of measuring. **2.** A system of measuring: *measurement in inches, feet, and yards.* **3.** The dimension, quantity, or capacity found by measuring and expressed in units: *The tailor took my measurements.* See table on pages 610–611.

meas•ur•ing worm (mĕzh′ə rĭng) *n.* A caterpillar that moves by drawing the rear of its body forward, forming a loop, and then stretching the front forward.

meat (mēt) *n.* **1.** The flesh of an animal eaten as food, especially beef, pork, or lamb, as distinguished from fish or poultry. **2.** The edible part of a nut or fruit: *chop nut meats.* **3.** Food: *meat and drink.* **4.** The essential part of something; the gist: *the meat of the story.* [First written down before 725 in Old English and spelled *mete,* food.]

❑ *These sound alike:* **meat, meet**[1] (come upon), **meet**[2] (fitting), **mete** (allot).

meat•ball (mēt′bôl′) *n.* A small ball of ground meat combined with various ingredients or seasonings and cooked.

meat•y (mē′tē) *adj.* **meat•i•er, meat•i•est. 1.** Full of meat; fleshy: *a large meaty turkey.* **2.** Of or like meat: *a meaty odor.* **3.** Rich in substance; significant: *a meaty book.* **—meat′i•ness** *n.*

mec•ca (mĕk′ə) *n.* A place regarded as a center of activity or interest: *The scientist's lab was a mecca for young chemists.*

Mec•ca (mĕk′ə). A city of western Saudi Arabia near the coast of the Red Sea. The birthplace of Muhammad, it is the holiest city of Islam and a pilgrimage site. Population, 550,000.

me•chan•ic (mĭ kăn′ĭk) *n.* A worker skilled in making, using, or repairing machines and tools. **—me•chan′ic** *adj.*

me•chan•i•cal (mĭ kăn′ĭ kəl) *adj.* **1.** Of, relating to, or involving machines or tools: *mechanical difficulties with the power saw.* **2.** Operated, produced, orperformed by machine. **3.** Performed as if by a machine; showing no variety; dull: *routine mechanical tasks.* **4.** Of or relating to the science of mechanics. [First written down before 1425 in Middle English and spelled *mechanicalle*, from Greek *mēkhanē*, device, machine.] **—me•chan′i•cal•ly** *adv.*

mechanical drawing *n.* **1.** A drawing, as of tools or machines, done with rulers, compasses, and similar instruments. **2.** The technique or art of making such drawings; drafting.

me•chan•ics (mĭ **kăn′**ĭks) *n.* *(used with a singular verb).* **1.** The branch of physics that studies the action of forces on solids, liquids, and gases at rest or in motion. **2.** *(used with a singular or plural verb).* The development, production, and use of machines or mechanical structures. **3.** *(used with a plural verb).* The technical aspects of something, such as an activity or a sport: *the mechanics of swimming.*

mech•a•nism (**mĕk′**ə nĭz′əm) *n.* **1.a.** A machine or mechanical device: *An egg beater is a useful mechanism.* **b.** The working parts of a machine: *an old clock's simple mechanism.* **2.** A system of parts that interact: *the mechanism of the solar system.* **3.** A process or means by which something is done or is brought into being: *A constitution is a mechanism for establishing a democratic government.*

mech•a•nis•tic (mĕk′ə **nĭs′**tĭk) *adj.* **1.** Of or relating to mechanics as a branch of physics. **2.** Of or relating to the philosophy that all natural events can be explained by material causes and mechanical principles.

mech•a•nize (**mĕk′**ə nīz′) *tr.v.* **mech•a•nized, mech•a•niz•ing, mech•a•niz•es.** To equip with machinery: *mechanize a bakery.* **—mech′a•ni•za′tion** (mĕk′ə nĭ **zā′**shən) *n.*

med. *abbr.* An abbreviation of: **1.** Medical. **2.** Medicine. **3.** Medium.

med•al (**mĕd′**l) *n.* A flat piece of metal with a special design, given as an award. [First written down before 1586 in Modern English, from Italian *medaglia*, coin worth half a denarius, from Late Latin *mediālis*, of the middle.]

❑ *These sound alike:* **medal, meddle** (interfere).

med•al•ist (**mĕd′**l ĭst) *n.* **1.** A person who designs, makes, or collects medals. **2.** A person who has received a medal.

me•dal•lion (mĭ **dăl′**yən) *n.* **1.** A large medal. **2.** A round or oval ornament or design resembling a large medal.

med•dle (**mĕd′**l) *intr.v.* **med•dled, med•dling, med•dles. 1.** To interfere in other people's business. **2.** To handle something carelessly or ignorantly; tamper: *Don't meddle with my computer!* [First written down before 1300 in Middle English and spelled *melen*, from Anglo-Norman *medler*, from Latin *miscēre*, to mix.] **—med′dler** *n.*

❑ *These sound alike:* **meddle, medal** (award).

med•dle•some (**mĕd′**l səm) *adj.* Inclined to interfere in other people's business. **—med′dle•some•ness** *n.*

Mede (mēd) *n.* A native or inhabitant of ancient Media.

Me•de•a (mĭ **dē′**ə) *n.* In Greek mythology, a princess and sorceress who helps Jason obtain the Golden Fleece.

me•di•a (**mē′**dē ə) *n.* A plural of **medium.**

Me•di•a (**mē′**dē ə). An ancient country of southwest Asia in present-day northwest Iran. Settled by an Indo-European people, it was conquered by Cyrus the Great, who added it to the Persian Empire.

me•di•ae•val (mē′dē **ē′**vəl *or* mĕd′ē **ē′**vəl) *adj.* Variant of **medieval.**

me•di•al (**mē′**dē əl) *adj.* **1.** Occurring in the middle: *the medial position.* **2.** Average; ordinary. **3.** In mathematics, of or relating to a mean or an average. **—me′di•al•ly** *adv.*

me•di•an (**mē′**dē ən) *adj.* **1.** Located in the middle: *a median barrier.* **2.** Constituting the median of a set of numbers: *median score.* *—n.* **1.** Something that lies halfway between two extremes; a medium. **2.** In mathematics, the middle number of a sequence having an odd number of values or the average of the two middle values if the sequence has an even number of values. For example, in the sequence 3, 4, 5, 6, 7, the median is 5; in the sequence 4, 8, 12, 16, the median is 10. **3.** In geometry: **a.** A line joining a vertex of a triangle to the midpoint of the opposite side. **b.** A line that joins the midpoints of the sides of a trapezoid that are not parallel.

me•di•ate (**mē′**dē āt′) *v.* **me•di•at•ed, me•di•at•ing, me•di•ates.** *—tr.* **1.** To settle (differences) by working with all sides: *mediate a dispute.* **2.** To bring about (an agreement) by working with all sides: *A negotiator mediated the new contract between the company and its workers.* *—intr.* To help the opposing sides in a dispute come to an agreement: *The teacher mediated between the two students.* [First written down in 1542 in Modern English, from Latin *medius*, middle.] **—me′di•a′tion** *n.*

me•di•a•tor (**mē′**dē ā′tər) *n.* A person or an agency that mediates in a dispute.

med•ic (**mĕd′**ĭk) *n.* **1.** A person in a medical corps of the armed services. **2.** A physician or surgeon. **3.** A medical student or intern.

Med•i•caid also **med•i•caid** (**mĕd′**ĭ kād′) *n.* A program in the United States, jointly funded by the federal government and the states, that pays hospitals and physicians for providing medical care to people whose incomes are below a certain level.

med•i•cal (**mĕd′**ĭ kəl) *adj.* Of or relating to the study or practice of medicine: *a medical problem; medical school.* **—med′i•cal•ly** *adv.*

me•dic•a•ment (mĭ **dĭk′**ə mənt *or* **mĕd′**ĭ kə mənt) *n.* A medicine; a medication.

Med•i•care also **med•i•care** (**mĕd′**ĭ kâr′) *n.* A program in the United States, funded by the federal government, that pays hospitals and physicians for medical care provided to people over 65 years old.

med•i•cate (**mĕd′**ĭ kāt′) *tr.v.* **med•i•cat•ed, med•i•cat•ing, med•i•cates. 1.** To treat (a person, an injury, or a part of the body) with medicine. **2.** To put medicine on or in: *medicate a bandage.*

med•i•ca•tion (mĕd′ĭ **kā′**shən) *n.* **1.** A substance that helps to cure a disease, heal an injury, or relieve pain; a medicine. **2.** The act or process of medicating.

Med•i•ci (**mĕd′**ə chē′). Italian noble family that produced three popes and two queens of France. **Lorenzo** "the Magnificent" (1449–1492) was a patron of the arts whose clients included Michelangelo.

me•dic•i•nal (mĭ **dĭs′**ə nəl) *adj.* **1.** Of, relating to, or having the properties of medicine: *medicinal plants.* **2.** Having a bitter taste like many medicines. **—me•dic′i•nal•ly** *adv.*

med•i•cine (**mĕd′**ĭ sĭn) *n.* **1.** The scientific study of diseases and disorders of the body and the methods of diagnosing, treating, and preventing them. **2.** The practice of this science as a profession. **3.** A drug or other substance used to treat a disease or an injury. **4.a.** A group of practices or beliefs, especially among Native Americans, believed to control nature, influence spiritual beings, or prevent or cure disease. **b.** Something, such as a ceremony or a sacred object, believed to have such abilities. [First written down before 1200 in Middle English, from Latin *medicus*, physician.]

medicine ball *n.* A large heavy ball tossed between people for exercise.

medicine man *n.* A Native American who is be-

medal

ă	**pat**	oi	**boy**
ā	**pay**	ou	**out**
âr	**care**	ŏŏ	**took**
ä	**father**	ōō	**boot**
ĕ	**pet**	ŭ	**cut**
ē	**be**	ûr	**urge**
ĭ	**pit**	th	**thin**
ī	**pie**	*th*	**this**
îr	**pier**	hw	**whoop**
ŏ	**pot**	zh	**vision**
ō	**toe**	ə	**about**
ô	**paw**	N	*French* bon

TABLE OF MEASUREMENTS

UNIT	*RELATION TO OTHER U.S. CUSTOMARY UNITS*	*METRIC EQUIVALENT*
LENGTH		
inch	1/12 foot	2.54 centimeters
foot	12 inches or 1/3 yard	0.3048 meter
yard	36 inches or 3 feet	0.9144 meter
mile (statute)	5,280 feet or 1,760 yards	1.6093 kilometers
mile (nautical)	6,076 feet or 2,025 yards	1.852 kilometers
VOLUME OR CAPACITY (LIQUID MEASURE)		
ounce	pint	29.574 milliliters
cup	8 ounces	0.2366 liter
pint	16 ounces	0.4732 liter
quart	2 pints or 1/2 gallon	0.9463 liter
gallon	128 ounces or 8 pints	3.7853 liters
barrel (oil)	42 gallons	159.98 liters
VOLUME OR CAPACITY (DRY MEASURE)		
cup	1/2 pint	0.2753 liter
pint	2 cups or 1/2 quart	0.5506 liter
quart	4 cups or 2 pints	1.1012 liters
peck	8 quarts or 1/4 bushel	8.8098 liters
bushel	4 pecks	35.239 liters
WEIGHT		
grain	1/7000 pound	64.799 milligrams
dram	1/16 ounce	1.7718 grams
ounce	16 drams	28.350 grams
pound	16 ounces	453.6 grams
ton (short)	2,000 pounds	907.18 kilograms
ton (long)	2,240 pounds	1,016.0 kilograms
GEOGRAPHIC AREA		
acre	43,560 square feet or 4,840 square yards	4,047 square meters

COOKING MEASURES

UNIT	*RELATION TO OTHER COOKING MEASURES*	*CONVERSION TO METRIC UNITS*
teaspoon	76 drops or 1/3 tablespoon	4.9288 milliliters
tablespoon	3 teaspoons	14.786 milliliters
cup	16 tablespoons or 1/2 pint	0.2366 liter
pint	2 cups	0.4732 liter
quart	4 cups or 2 pints	0.9463 liter

MEASUREMENT CONVERSIONS

FROM METRIC TO U.S. CUSTOMARY

WHEN YOU KNOW	*MULTIPLY BY*	*TO FIND*
millimeters	0.04	inches
centimeters	0.39	inches
meters	3.28	feet
	1.09	yards
kilometers	0.62	miles
milliliters	0.03	fluid ounces
liters	1.06	quarts
	0.26	gallons
cubic meters	35.32	cubic feet
grams	0.035	ounces
kilograms	2.21	pounds
metric ton (1,000 kg)	1.10	short ton
square centimeters	0.16	square inches
square meters	1.20	square yards
square kilometers	0.39	square miles
hectares	2.47	acres

FROM U.S. CUSTOMARY TO METRIC

WHEN YOU KNOW	*MULTIPLY BY*	*TO FIND*
inches	25.4	millimeters
	2.54	centimeters
feet	30.48	centimeters
yards	0.91	meters
miles	1.61	kilometers
fluid ounces	29.57	milliliters
cups	0.24	liters
pints	0.47	liters
quarts	0.95	liters
gallons	3.79	liters
cubic feet	0.028	cubic meters
ounces	28.35	grams
pounds	0.45	kilograms
short ton (2,000 lbs)	0.91	metric tons
square inches	6.45	square centimeters
square feet	0.09	square meters
square yards	0.84	square meters
square miles	2.60	square kilometers
acres	0.40	hectares

TEMPERATURE CONVERSION BETWEEN CELSIUS AND FAHRENHEIT

$°C = (°F - 32) \div 1.8$ $\qquad$ $°F = (°C \times 1.8) + 32$

METRIC PREFIXES

A multiple of a unit in the metric system is formed by adding a prefix to the name of that unit. The prefixes change the magnitude of the unit by orders of 10 from 10^9 to 10^{-9}.

PREFIX	*SYMBOL*	*MULTIPLYING FACTOR*
giga-	G	$10^9 = 1{,}000{,}000{,}000$
mega-	M	$10^6 = 1{,}000{,}000$
kilo-	K	$10^3 = 1{,}000$
hecto-	h	$10^2 = 100$
deca-	da	$10 = 10$
deci-	d	$10^{-1} = 0.1$
centi-	c	$10^{-2} = 0.01$
milli-	m	$10^{-3} = 0.001$
micro-	μ	$10^{-6} = 0.000{,}001$
nano-	n	$10^{-9} = 0.000{,}000{,}001$

Mediterranean Sea

The word **Mediterranean** is a nice, long, good-for-a-spelling-bee word. It comes from the Latin *mediterrāneus*, "in the middle of the land, inland." The Latin phrase *mare mediterrāneum* therefore means "the sea in the middle of the land." The Latin word root *medi–*, "the middle, in the middle," appears in our words **medium** and **median**. The Latin word *terra*, "land," appears in **territory** and **terrain**.

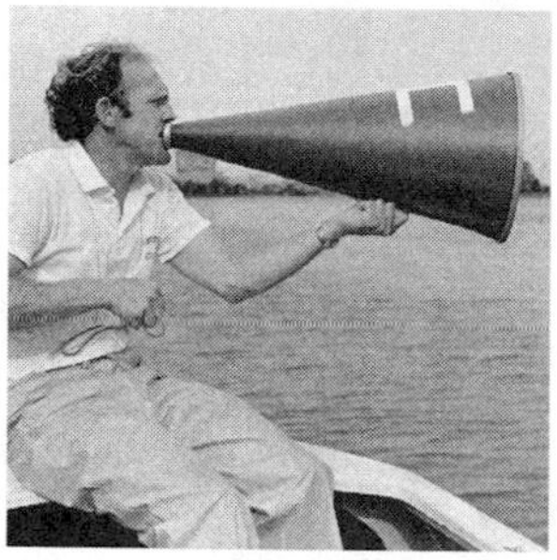

megaphone

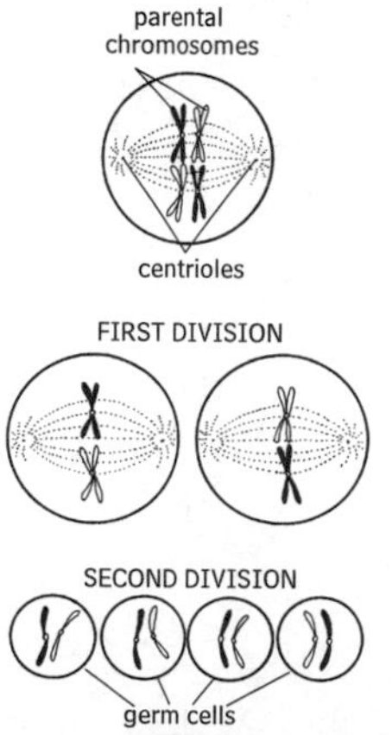

meiosis

lieved to communicate with spirits, control natural events, and cure disease; a shaman.

me•di•e•val also **me•di•ae•val** (mē′dē **ē′**vəl *or* mĕd′ē **ē′**vəl) *adj.* Of or characteristic of the Middle Ages. [First written down in 1827 in Modern English and spelled *mediæval* : Latin *medius*, middle + Latin *aevum*, age.]

Medieval Latin *n.* Latin as used from about 700 to 1500.

Me•di•na (mĭ **dē′**nə). A city of western Saudi Arabia north of Mecca. It is the site of Muhammad's tomb and is a holy site. Population, 290,000.

me•di•o•cre (mē′dē **ō′**kər) *adj.* Neither good nor bad; ordinary; undistinguished: *a mediocre actor.*

me•di•oc•ri•ty (mē′dē **ŏk′**rĭ tē) *n., pl.* **me•di•oc•ri•ties. 1.** The fact or condition of being mediocre. **2.** An ordinary undistinguished quality or performance. **3.** A person of only average ability.

med•i•tate (**mĕd′**ĭ tāt′) *v.* **med•i•tat•ed, med•i•tat•ing, med•i•tates.** *—intr.* **1.** To think deeply and quietly; reflect: *The engineer meditated on the problem and changed the design of the car.* **2.** To reflect deeply on spiritual or religious matters. *—tr.* To consider at length; plan: *meditated a change of jobs.* [First written down in 1560 in Modern English, from Latin *meditārī*.] —**med′i•ta′tor** *n.*

med•i•ta•tion (mĕd′ĭ **tā′**shən) *n.* **1.** The process of meditating; contemplation: *The poet stared out the window, lost in meditation.* **2.** Deep reflection on spiritual or religious matters.

med•i•ta•tive (**mĕd′**ĭ tā′tĭv) *adj.* Devoted to or characterized by meditation. —**med′i•ta′tive•ly** *adv.* —**med′i•ta′tive•ness** *n.*

Med•i•ter•ra•ne•an Sea (mĕd′ĭ tə **rā′**nē ən). An inland sea surrounded by Europe, Asia, Asia Minor, the Near East, and Africa. It connects with the Atlantic Ocean, the Black Sea, and the Red Sea. —SEE NOTE.

me•di•um (**mē′**dē əm) *n., pl.* **me•di•a** (**mē′**dē ə) or **me•di•ums. 1.** A position, choice, or course of action midway between extremes: *a happy medium between hot and cold weather.* **2.a.** The substance or surrounding environment in which an animal, a plant, or another organism normally lives and thrives: *Water is the medium of fish.* **b.** An artificial substance in which bacteria or other microorganisms are grown for scientific purposes. **3.** A substance through which something is transmitted or carried on: *Air is the medium of sound waves.* **4.** An agency by which something is accomplished, transported, or transferred: *Money is a medium of exchange.* **5.** *pl.* **mediums.** A person who claims to be able to communicate with the spirits of the dead. **6.** *pl.* **media.** A means for sending information to large numbers of people: *Television is a good advertising medium.* **7.** *pl.* **media.** *(used with a singular or plural verb).* The group of journalists and others whose work involves communicating information. **8.** One of the techniques, materials, or means of expression available to an artist: *That artist uses the medium of lithography.* *—adj.* Occurring midway between extremes; intermediate: *of medium height.* [First written down in 1584 in Modern English, from Latin.]

medium frequency *n.* A radio-wave frequency lying in the range between 300 and 3,000 kilohertz.

med•ley (**mĕd′**lē) *n., pl.* **med•leys. 1.** A mixture or variety: *a medley of events in the program.* **2.** A musical arrangement that uses a series of melodies from different sources. [First written down before 1400 in Middle English and spelled *mele*, from Anglo-Norman *medlee*, meddling.]

me•dul•la (mĭ **dŭl′**ə) *n., pl.* **me•dul•las** or **me•dul•lae** (mĭ **dŭl′**ē). **1.** The inner core of certain structures of vertebrates, as the marrow of bone. **2.** The medulla oblongata.

medulla ob•lon•ga•ta (ŏb′lông **gä′**tə) *n., pl.* **medulla ob•lon•ga•tas** or **medullae ob•lon•ga•tae** (ŏb′lông **gä′**tē). A mass of nerve tissue located at the top of the spinal cord and at the base of the brain. It controls breathing, circulation, and certain other involuntary functions.

Me•dus•a (mĭ **dōō′**sə *or* mĭ **dyōō′**sə) *n.* In Greek mythology, the Gorgon who is slain by Perseus.

meek (mēk) *adj.* **meek•er, meek•est. 1.** Showing patience and humility; gentle. **2.** Easily imposed upon; submissive: *Meek customers often fail to demand prompt service.* [First written down before 1200 in Middle English and spelled *meok*, of Scandinavian origin; akin to Old Norse *mjūkr*, soft.] —**meek′ly** *adv.* —**meek′ness** *n.*

meer•schaum (**mîr′**shəm *or* **mîr′**shôm′) *n.* **1.** A soft claylike material that is usually white and is used as a building stone and for making tobacco pipes. **2.** A tobacco pipe with a meerschaum bowl. [First written down in 1784 in Modern English, from German : *Meer*, sea + *Schaum*, foam.]

meet¹ (mēt) *v.* **met** (mĕt), **meet•ing, meets.** *—tr.* **1.** To come upon by chance or arrangement: *I met them at the restaurant.* **2.** To be present at the arrival of: *met the train.* **3.** To be introduced to: *Have you met my teacher?* **4.** To come into contact with; join: *The stream meets the river at the rapids.* **5.** To come to the notice of: *There is more here than meets the eye.* **6.** To oppose or fight with: *They met the enemy in the valley.* **7.** To deal or cope with effectively: *We have met every problem and continued our progress.* **8.** To satisfy (a requirement, for example); fulfill: *You meet all the conditions for getting the loan.* **9.** To pay; settle: *Is there enough money to meet our expenses?* *—intr.* **1.** To come together; come face to face: *We'll meet tonight at the ice rink.* **2.** To come into contact; be joined: *The boards meet at the corner.* **3.** To come together as opponents: *The two teams met again last night.* **4.** To become introduced: *My parents met on the ferry.* **5.** To come together in a group; assemble: *The committee meets tonight.* *—n.* A meeting or contest: *a track meet.* ***—idiom.*** **meet with. 1.** To experience or undergo: *The explorers met with great difficulty when crossing the mountains.* **2.** To receive: *Our plan met with their approval.* [First written down about 725 in Old English and spelled *mētan*.]

❑ *These sound alike:* **meet¹** (come upon), **meat** (animal flesh), **meet²** (fitting), **mete** (allot).

meet² (mēt) *adj.* Fitting; proper. [First written down about 961 in Old English and spelled *gemǣte*.] —**meet′ly** *adv.*

❑ *These sound alike:* **meet²** (fitting), **meat** (animal flesh), **meet¹** (come upon), **mete** (allot).

meet•ing (**mē′**tĭng) *n.* **1.** A coming together; an encounter: *a chance meeting of friends.* **2.** A gathering or assembly of people, usually for a business, social, or religious purpose. **3.** A point where two or more things come together; a junction: *the meeting of two railroad lines.* ***—idiom.*** **meeting of the minds.** Agreement; concord.

meet•ing•house (**mē′**tĭng hous′) *n.* A building used for public meetings and especially for Quaker religious services.

mega– *pref.* A prefix that means: **1.** One million: *megahertz.* **2.** Large: *megalith.*

meg•a•cy•cle (**mĕg′**ə sī′kəl) *n.* Megahertz.

meg•a•hertz (**mĕg′**ə hûrts′) *n., pl.* **megahertz.** A unit of frequency equal to one million cycles per second, used to express the frequency of radio waves.

meg•a•lith (mĕg′ə lĭth′) *n.* A very large stone used in the building of prehistoric monuments.

meg•a•lo•ma•ni•a (mĕg′ə lō **mā′**nē ə *or* mĕg′-ə lō **mān′**yə) *n.* A mental disorder in which a person has delusions of being very rich or powerful. **—meg′a•lo•ma′ni•ac′** *n.*

meg•a•lop•o•lis (mĕg′ə **lŏp′**ə lĭs) *n.* A large urban region containing several large cities that border each other.

meg•a•phone (**mĕg′**ə fōn′) *n.* A large funnel-shaped horn, used to direct and amplify the voice.

meg•a•ton (**mĕg′**ə tŭn′) *n.* A unit of power equal to the force with which one million metric tons of TNT explodes, used mainly as a measure of atomic explosive power.

meg•a•watt (**mĕg′**ə wŏt′) *n.* A unit of electrical power equal to one million watts.

Mei•ji (mā′jē′). Mutsuhito.

mei•o•sis (mī **ō′**sĭs) *n., pl.* **mei•o•ses** (mī **ō′**sēz′). The process of cell division that reduces the number of chromosomes in reproductive cells to half the original number, resulting in the production of gametes in animals and spores in plants.

Me•ir (**mī′**ər *or* mā **ĕr′**), **Golda.** 1898–1978. Russian-born Israeli politician who served as minister of labor (1949–1956), foreign minister (1956–1966), and prime minister (1969–1974).

Me•kong (**mā′kông′** *or* **mā′kŏng′**). A river of southeast Asia flowing about 2,600 miles (4,183 kilometers) from southeast China to the South China Sea through southern Vietnam.

mel•an•cho•li•a (mĕl′ən **kō′**lē ə) *n.* A mental disorder in which a person suffers from severe depression.

mel•an•chol•ic (mĕl′ən **kŏl′**ĭk) *adj.* **1.** Sad and gloomy; melancholy. **2.** Of or suffering from melancholia.

mel•an•chol•y (**mĕl′**ən kŏl′ē) *n.* Sadness or depression of the spirits. *—adj.* **1.** Sad; gloomy. See Synonyms at **sad. 2.** Inspiring sadness; depressing: *the melancholy notes of a funeral dirge.* [First written down about 1303 in Middle English and spelled *malincoli*, from Greek *melankholia* : *melas*, black + *kholē*, bile.]

Mel•a•ne•sia (mĕl′ə **nē′**zhə *or* mĕl′ə **nē′**shə). A division of Oceania in the southwest Pacific Ocean made up of the islands northeast of Australia and south of the equator.

Mel•a•ne•sian (mĕl′ə **nē′**zhən *or* mĕl′ə **nē′**shən) *adj.* Of or relating to Melanesia or its peoples, languages, or cultures. *—n.* **1.** A member of any of the peoples of Melanesia. **2.** The group of languages spoken in Melanesia.

mé•lange also **me•lange** (mā **länzh′**) *n.* A mixture.

mel•a•nin (**mĕl′**ə nĭn) *n.* A dark pigment found in the skin, hair, and eyes of human beings and many animals.

mel•a•no•ma (mĕl′ə **nō′**mə) *n.* A dark-colored tumor usually arising in the skin.

Mel•ba toast (**mĕl′**bə) *n.* Crisp thinly sliced toast. [First written down in 1925 in Modern English, after Dame Nellie *Melba* (1861–1931), Australian singer.]

Mel•bourne (**mĕl′**bərn). A city of southeast Australia southwest of Canberra. It was settled in 1835. Population, 2,722,817.

meld (mĕld) *v.* **meld•ed, meld•ing, melds.** *—tr.* In certain card games, to declare or show (a card or combination of cards) as a means of adding points to a score. *—intr.* To meld a card or combination of cards. *—n.* **1.** The act of melding. **2.** A combination of cards to be presented for a score.

me•lee (**mā′**lā′ *or* mā **lā′**) *n.* A confused fight among a number of people.

mel•lif•lu•ous (mə **lĭf′**lo͞o əs) *adj.* Smooth and sweet: *a mellifluous voice.* **—mel•lif′lu•ous•ly** *adv.* **—mel•lif′lu•ous•ness** *n.*

mel•low (**mĕl′**ō) *adj.* **mel•low•er, mel•low•est. 1.a.** Soft, sweet, or juicy; fully ripened: *a mellow peach.* **b.** Rich and full in flavor; properly aged: *mellow wine.* **2.** Rich and soft in quality: *the mellow colors of autumn.* **3.** Having or showing gentleness, wisdom, and tolerance; mature. *—tr. & intr.v.* **mel•lowed, mel•low•ing, mel•lows.** To make or become mellow: *Time often mellows youthful intolerance. Wine mellows over a period of years.* [First written down in 1440 in Middle English and spelled *melwe.*] **—mel′low•ly** *adv.* **—mel′low•ness** *n.*

me•lod•ic (mə **lŏd′**ĭk) *adj.* Of, relating to, or containing melody. **—me•lod′i•cal•ly** *adv.*

me•lo•di•ous (mə **lō′**dē əs) *adj.* Containing pleasant sounds; pleasant to listen to: *a melodious voice.* **—me•lo′di•ous•ly** *adv.* **—me•lo′di•ous•ness** *n.*

mel•o•dra•ma (**mĕl′**ə drä′mə *or* **mĕl′**ə drăm′ə) *n.* **1.** A drama characterized by exaggerated emotions, conflicts between characters, and often a happy ending. **2.** This kind of drama: *Melodrama is common on daytime TV.* **3.** Behavior or occurrences full of exaggerated emotions.

mel•o•dra•mat•ic (mĕl′ə drə **măt′**ĭk) *adj.* **1.** Of, relating to, or characteristic of melodrama: *a melodramatic ending.* **2.** Exaggerated in emotion or sentiment: *a melodramatic speech.* **—mel′o•dra•mat′i•cal•ly** *adv.*

mel•o•dy (**mĕl′**ə dē) *n., pl.* **mel•o•dies. 1.a.** A succession of musical tones making up a particular musical phrase or idea. **b.** The main part in a musical composition that has harmony. **2.** A pleasing arrangement of sounds. [First written down before 1300 in Middle English and spelled *melodie*, from Greek *melōidia*, singing, choral song : *melos*, tune + *aoidē*, song.]

mel•on (**mĕl′**ən) *n.* Any of several large fruits, such as a cantaloupe or watermelon, that grow on a vine and have a hard rind and juicy edible flesh. [First written down about 1395 in Middle English and spelled *meloun*, from Late Latin *mēlō*, from Greek *mēlopepōn.*]

melt (mĕlt) *v.* **melt•ed, melt•ing, melts.** *—intr.* **1.** To be changed from a solid to a liquid state by heat or pressure: *The ice melted in the sun.* **2.** To dissolve: *Sugar melts in water.* **3.** To disappear gradually: *The crowd melted away after the rally.* **4.** To pass or merge into something else: *The blue melted into the green in the painting.* **5.** To become gentle in feeling: *Their hearts melted at the sight of the baby.* *—tr.* **1.** To change (a solid) to a liquid by heat or pressure. **2.** To dissolve: *The tide melted our sand castle.* **3.** To make gentler or milder; soften: *a look to melt the hardest heart.* [First written down about 725 in Old English and spelled *meltan.*] **—melt′er** *n.*

melt•down (**mĕlt′**doun′) *n.* The overheating of the core of a nuclear reactor, resulting in melting of the core and escape of radiation.

melt•ing point (**mĕl′**tĭng) *n.* The temperature at which a given solid becomes a liquid. The melting point of ice is 0°C.

melting pot *n.* **1.** A container in which a substance is melted; a crucible. **2.** A place where people of different cultures or races form a single culture.

Mel•ville (**mĕl′**vĭl), **Herman.** 1819–1891. American writer whose experiences at sea provided the basis of his novel *Moby Dick* (1851).

mem•ber (**mĕm′**bər) *n.* **1.** A part or an organ of a plant, an animal, or a human body, especially a leg, an arm, a wing, or a branch. **2.** A person or thing that belongs to a group: *a member of the cat family; a member of the United Nations.* **3.a.** A quan-

Golda Meir

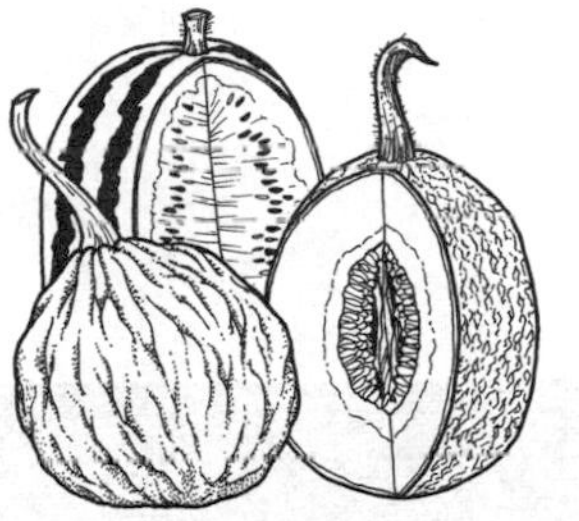

melon

Left to right: Crenshaw melon, watermelon, and cantaloupe

Herman Melville

ă	**pat**	oi	**boy**
ā	**pay**	ou	**out**
âr	**care**	o͝o	**took**
ä	**father**	o͞o	**boot**
ĕ	**pet**	ŭ	**cut**
ē	**be**	ûr	**urge**
ĭ	**pit**	th	**thin**
ī	**pie**	*th*	**this**
îr	**pier**	hw	**whoop**
ŏ	**pot**	zh	**vision**
ō	**toe**	ə	**about**
ô	**paw**	N	*French* **bon**

tity that belongs to a set; an element of a set. **b.** The expression on either side of an equality sign. [First written down about 1280 in Middle English and spelled *membre*, from Latin *membrum*.]

mem•ber•ship (mĕm′bər shĭp′) *n.* **1.** The condition or state of being a member. **2.** The total number of members in a group: *The membership voted in a new club president.*

mem•brane (mĕm′brān′) *n.* A thin flexible layer of plant or animal tissue that covers, lines, separates, or connects parts of an organism.

mem•bra•nous (mĕm′brə nəs) *adj.* **1.** Relating to, made of, or similar to a membrane. **2.** Characterized by the formation of a membrane or a layer like a membrane.

me•men•to (mə mĕn′tō) *n., pl.* **me•men•tos** or **me•men•toes.** A reminder of the past; a keepsake: *These shells are mementos of our trip to the beach.*

mem•o (mĕm′ō) *n., pl.* **mem•os.** *Informal.* A memorandum.

mem•oir (mĕm′wär′ *or* mĕm′wôr′) *n.* **1.** An account of the personal experiences of an author: *a memoir of childhood on a farm.* **2.** An account of a person's own life; an autobiography. Often used in the plural. **3.** A biography. **4. memoirs.** A record of the proceedings of a scholarly organization. [First written down in 1427 in Middle English and spelled *memoire*, from Old French *memoire*, memory.]

mem•o•ra•bil•i•a (mĕm′ər ə bĭl′ē ə *or* mĕm′ər ə bĭl′yə) *pl.n.* Things from the past that are worth remembering or keeping.

mem•o•ra•ble (mĕm′ər ə bəl) *adj.* Worth being remembered or noted: *Memorable events are sometimes pictured on stamps.* **—mem′o•ra•ble•ness** *n.* **—mem′o•ra•bly** *adv.*

mem•o•ran•dum (mĕm′ə răn′dəm) *n., pl.* **me•mo•ran•dums** or **me•mo•ran•da** (mĕm′ə răn′də). **1.** A short note written as a reminder. **2.** An informal letter or note sent between members or offices of an organization. **3.** A short written statement outlining the terms of a legal or business agreement.

memorial
Vietnam Veterans Memorial
by Maya Yang Lin
(b. 1959)

me•mo•ri•al (mə môr′ē əl) *n.* **1.** Something, such as a monument or holiday, established to serve as a remembrance of a person or an event. **2.** A written statement of facts or a petition addressed to a government or legislature. *—adj.* Serving as a remembrance of a person or an event; commemorative: *memorial services; a memorial plaque.*

Memorial Day *n.* May 30, celebrated in the United States in honor of those members of the armed forces killed in war.

me•mo•ri•al•ize (mə môr′ē ə līz′) *tr.v.* **me•mo•ri•al•ized, me•mo•ri•al•iz•ing, me•mo•ri•al•iz•es.** **1.** To honor with a memorial; commemorate. **2.** To address a memorial to; petition.

mem•o•rize (mĕm′ə rīz′) *tr.v.* **mem•o•rized, mem•o•riz•ing, mem•o•riz•es.** To commit to memory; learn by heart. **—mem′o•ri•za′tion** (mĕm′ə rĭ zā′shən) *n.* **—mem′o•riz′er** *n.*

mem•o•ry (mĕm′ə rē) *n., pl.* **mem•o•ries.** **1.** The power or ability of remembering past experiences: *Thanks to a good memory, I could recall the details of what happened.* **2.** The part of the mind where knowledge is stored: *I committed the poem to memory.* **3.** Something remembered: *a pleasant memory of summer vacation.* **4.** The fact of being remembered; remembrance: *a ceremony in memory of our forebears.* **5.** The period of time covered by the ability of a group of people to remember: *the heaviest gale in living memory.* **6.a.** A unit of a computer in which data is stored for later use. **b.** A computer's capacity for storing information: *How much memory does this computer have?* [First written down about 1250 in Middle English and spelled *memorie*, from Latin *memoria*.]

Mem•phis (mĕm′fĭs). **1.** An ancient city of Egypt south of Cairo. It was supposedly founded by the first king of united Egypt. **2.** A city of southwest Tennessee on the Mississippi River near the Mississippi border. It was established in 1819 on the site of a fort built in 1797. Population, 610,337.

men (mĕn) *n.* Plural of **man.**

men•ace (mĕn′ĭs) *n.* **1.** A threat or danger: *a reef that is a menace to passing ships.* **2.** A troublesome or annoying person. *—tr.v.* **men•aced, men•ac•ing, men•ac•es.** To threaten; endanger: *The erupting volcano menaced the nearby town.* [First written down about 1303 in Middle English and spelled *manas*, from Latin *mināx*, threatening.]

me•nag•er•ie (mə năj′ə rē *or* mə năzh′ə rē) *n.* **1.** A collection of wild animals kept in cages or pens on exhibition. **2.** A place where such animals are kept.

men-at-arms (mĕn′ət ärmz′) *n.* Plural of **man-at-arms.**

mend (mĕnd) *v.* **mend•ed, mend•ing, mends.** *—tr.* **1.** To make repairs to; fix: *mend a jacket.* **2.** To reform or correct: *The judge always warns criminals to mend their ways.* *—intr.* **1.** To improve in health: *The patient is mending well.* **2.** To heal: *Her ankle mended slowly.* *—n.* The act of mending. ***—idiom.* on the mend.** Improving, especially in health. [First written down before 1200 in Middle English and spelled *menden*, short for *amenden*, to amend.] **—mend′er** *n.*

men•da•cious (mĕn dā′shəs) *adj.* **1.** False; untrue: *a mendacious explanation.* **2.** Lying; untruthful: *a mendacious person.* [First written down in 1616 in Modern English, from Latin *mendāx*.] **—men•da′cious•ly** *adv.* **—men•da′cious•ness** *n.*

men•dac•i•ty (mĕn dăs′ĭ tē) *n., pl.* **men•dac•i•ties.** **1.** The condition of being mendacious; untruthfulness. **2.** A lie: *The witness's testimony is a complete mendacity.*

Men•del (mĕn′dl), **Gregor Johann.** 1822–1884. Austrian botanist and founder of the science of genetics who discovered the principle of inherited characteristics.

men•de•le•vi•um (mĕn′də lē′vē əm) *n.* *Symbol* **Md** A rare, radioactive, metallic element produced artificially from einsteinium. Mendelevium is chemically similar to thulium. See table at **element.** [First written down in 1955 in Modern English, after D.I. *Mendeleev* (1834–1907), Russian chemist.]

Men•dels•sohn (mĕn′dl sən), **Felix.** 1809–1847. German pianist and composer whose works include the *Reformation* (1830) and *Scotch* (1842) symphonies.

men•di•cant (mĕn′dĭ kənt) *adj.* Depending on alms for a living: *a mendicant order of friars.* *—n.* A beggar. [First written down in 1395 in Middle English and spelled *mendicaunt*, from Latin *mendīcāre*, to beg.] **—men′di•can•cy** *n.*

Men•e•la•us (mĕn′ə lā′əs) *n.* In Greek mythology, a Spartan king who fights in the Trojan War for the return of his wife, Helen.

men•folk (mĕn′fōk′) or **men•folks** (mĕn′fōks′) *pl.n.* **1.** Men considered as a group. **2.** The members of a community or family who are men.

men•ha•den (mĕn hād′n) *n., pl.* **menhaden** or **men•ha•dens.** Any of several fishes of western Atlantic waters, used chiefly as bait and as a source of fish oil and fertilizer.

me•ni•al (mē′nē əl *or* mēn′yəl) *adj.* **1.** Servile; lowly: *They let me run errands and perform other menial tasks for them.* **2.** Of, relating to, or appropriate for a servant. *—n.* A servant who performs the simplest or most unpleasant tasks. **—me′ni•al•ly** *adv.*

me•nin•ges (mə nĭn′jēz) *n.* Plural of **meninx.**

men•in•gi•tis (mĕn′ĭn jī′tĭs) *n.* Inflammation of the

membranes that enclose the brain and spinal cord, usually resulting from a bacterial infection.

me•ninx (mē′nĭngks) *n., pl.* **me•nin•ges** (mə nĭn′jēz). One of the three membranes enclosing the brain and spinal cord.

me•nis•cus (mə nĭs′kəs) *n., pl.* **me•nis•ci** (mə nĭs′ī *or* mə nĭs′kī) or **me•nis•cus•es. 1.** A crescent or crescent-shaped body, as the piece of cartilage at the knee joint. **2.** A lens that is concave on one side and convex on the other. **3.** The curved upper surface of a column of liquid. The surface is concave if the liquid wets the container walls and convex if it does not.

Men•non•ite (mĕn′ə nīt′) *n.* A member of an Anabaptist church noted for its simplicity of living and pacifism. [First written down in 1565 in Modern English, after *Menno* Simons (1492–1559), Frisian religious leader.]

men-of-war (mĕn′ə wôr′) *n.* Plural of **man-of-war.**

Me•nom•i•nee (mə nŏm′ə nē) *n., pl.* **Menominee** or **Menomi•nees. 1.** A member of a Native American people living in northeast Wisconsin. **2.** The Algonquian language of the Menominee.

men•o•pause (mĕn′ə pôz′) *n.* The time at which menstruation ceases, occurring usually between 45 and 55 years of age.

me•no•rah (mə nôr′ə) *n.* A candlestick used in Jewish religious ceremonies, especially one with nine branches used in the celebration of Hanukkah.

men•serv•ants (mĕn′sûr′vənts) *n.* Plural of **manservant.**

men•ses (mĕn′sēz) *pl.n. (used with a singular or plural verb).* The discharge of bloody fluid from the uterus that occurs in women who are not pregnant approximately every four weeks from puberty to menopause. The discharge results from the shedding of the thickened lining of the uterus when fertilization does not take place.

men•stru•al (mĕn′strōō əl) *adj.* Of or involving menstruation.

men•stru•ate (mĕn′strōō āt′) *intr.v.* **men•stru•at•ed, men•stru•at•ing, men•stru•ates.** To undergo menstruation.

men•stru•a•tion (mĕn′strōō ā′shən) *n.* The act or period of discharging the menses.

men•su•ra•tion (mĕn′sə rā′shən *or* mĕn′shə rā′shən) *n.* **1.** The act, process, or technique of measuring. **2.** The branch of mathematics that deals with finding measurements, such as lengths, areas, and volumes.

–ment *suff.* A suffix that means: **1.** Act, action, or process: *statement; government.* **2.** State of being acted upon: *amazement; involvement.* **3.** Result of an action or a process: *advancement.* **4.** Means, instrument, or agent of an action or a process: *inducement.* —SEE NOTE.

men•tal (mĕn′tl) *adj.* **1.** Of or relating to the mind: *mental capacity.* **2.** Occurring in or done by the mind: *a mental image; mental arithmetic.* **3.** Of or having a mental disease or disorder: *a mental patient.* **4.** Intended for the care of the mentally ill: *a mental hospital.* [First written down about 1422 in Middle English, from Latin *mēns*, mind.] **—men′tal•ly** *adv.*

mental age *n.* A measure of mental development, as determined by intelligence tests, and expressed as the age at which that level is average.

men•tal•i•ty (mĕn tăl′ĭ tē) *n., pl.* **men•tal•i•ties. 1.** Mental ability or capacity; intelligence: *a studious group of scholars of high mentality.* **2.** An outlook or characteristic way of thinking: *a cautious mentality.*

mental retardation *n.* A condition of below normal mental ability or intelligence due to disease, injury, or genetic defect.

men•thol (mĕn′thôl′) *n.* A white crystalline compound obtained from peppermint oil and used in perfumes, as a flavoring, and as a mild anesthetic. [First written down in 1876 in Modern English, from German, from Latin *mentha*, mint.]

men•tion (mĕn′shən) *tr.v.* **men•tioned, men•tion•ing, men•tions.** To speak or write about briefly; refer to: *I mentioned your idea during the conversation.* —*n.* The act of referring to something briefly or casually: *He made no mention of the incident in his report.*

men•tor (mĕn′tôr′ *or* mĕn′tər) *n.* **1.** A wise and trusted advisor. **2. Mentor.** In Greek Mythology, Odysseus's trusted counselor.

men•u (mĕn′yōō) *n.* **1.** A list of foods and drinks available or served, as at a restaurant. **2.** The foods served or available at a meal. **3.** A list of available computer commands displayed on a monitor to a user. [First written down in 1837 in Modern English, from Old French *menut*, small, from Latin *minūtus*.]

me•ow (mē ou′) *n.* The high-pitched whining cry of a cat. —*intr.v.* **me•owed, me•ow•ing, me•ows.** To make such a sound.

Meph•i•stoph•e•les (mĕf′ĭ stŏf′ə lēz′) *n.* The devil in the Faust legend to whom Faust sells his soul.

mer•can•tile (mûr′kən tēl′ *or* mûr′kən tīl′) *adj.* **1.** Of or relating to merchants or trade: *mercantile law.* **2.** Of or relating to mercantilism.

mer•can•til•ism (mûr′kən tē lĭz′əm) *n.* The economic system that prevailed in Europe in the 16th and 17th centuries and stressed government regulation of the economy, profit from foreign trade, the founding of colonies and trade monopolies, and the storing of wealth in the form of gold and silver. **—mer′can•til•ist** *n.*

Mer•ca•tor projection (mər kā′tər) *n.* A map projection made with parallel straight lines instead of curved lines for latitude and longitude. In a Mercator projection the areas near the poles appear disproportionately large, because the lines of longitude on the globe decrease in distance from each other as they approach the poles. [First written down in 1669 in Modern English and spelled *Mercator's projection*, after Gerhardus *Mercator* (1512–1594), Flemish cartographer.]

mer•ce•nar•y (mûr′sə nĕr′ē) *adj.* **1.** Working only out of a desire for money. **2.** Hired for service in a foreign army. —*n., pl.* **mer•ce•nar•ies.** A soldier hired to serve in a foreign army.

mer•cer•ize (mûr′sə rīz′) *tr.v.* **mer•cer•ized, mer•cer•iz•ing, mer•cer•iz•es.** To treat (cotton thread) with sodium hydroxide, so as to shrink the fibers, add luster, and make it dye more easily. [First written down in 1859 in Modern English, after John *Mercer* (1791–1866), British calico printer.]

mer•chan•dise (mûr′chən dīz′ *or* mûr′chən dīs′) *n.* Things that may be bought or sold; commercial goods. —*v.* (mûr′chən dīz′). **mer•chan•dised, mer•chan•dis•ing, mer•chan•dis•es.** —*tr.* **1.** To buy and sell (goods). **2.** To promote the sale of, as through advertising. —*intr.* To buy and sell goods; trade commercially. **—mer′chan•dis′er** *n.*

mer•chant (mûr′chənt) *n.* **1.** A person who buys and sells goods for profit. **2.** A person who runs a retail business; a shopkeeper. —*adj.* **1.** Of or relating to trade or commerce; commercial: *a merchant establishment.* **2.** Of or relating to the merchant marine: *a merchant sailor.* [First written down about 1200 in Middle English and spelled *marchaunt*, from Latin *mercārī*, to trade.]

mer•chant•man (mûr′chənt mən) *n.* A ship used in commerce.

merchant marine *n.* **1.** A nation's commercial or

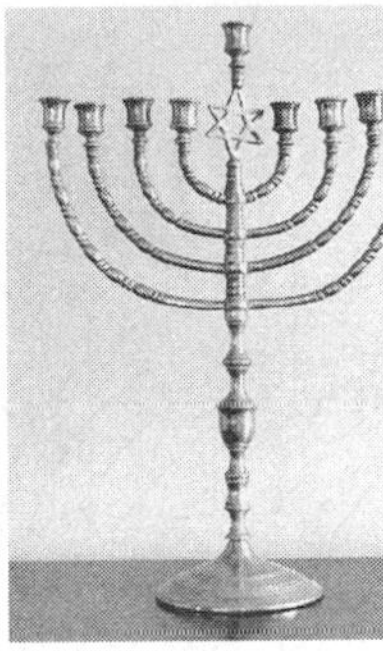

menorah

Word Building: –ment

The suffix **–ment** forms nouns, chiefly by attaching to verbs. It can have several meanings, the most common being "an act or an instance of doing something" or "the state of being acted upon." Thus an **entertainment** can be "an act of entertaining," and **amazement** is "the state of being amazed." The suffix **–ment** can be traced back to the Latin noun suffix *–mentum.* Although its use in English dates back to the 1300's, it wasn't until the 1500's and 1600's that a great number of words were coined with *–ment.*

ă	pat	oi	boy
ā	pay	ou	out
âr	care	ŏŏ	took
ä	father	ōō	boot
ĕ	pet	ŭ	cut
ē	be	ûr	urge
ĭ	pit	th	thin
ī	pie	*th*	this
îr	pier	hw	whoop
ŏ	pot	zh	vision
ō	toe	ə	about
ô	paw	N	*French* bon

meridian
Terrestrial meridian

merino
Merino ram

trading ships considered as a group. **2.** The personnel who serve on such ships.

mer•ci•ful (mûr′sĭ fəl) *adj.* Having, showing, or feeling mercy; compassionate. **—mer′ci•ful•ly** *adv.* **—mer′ci•ful•ness** *n.*

mer•ci•less (mûr′sĭ lĭs) *adj.* Having or showing no mercy; cruel: *a merciless tyrant.* **—mer′ci•less•ly** *adv.* **—mer′ci•less•ness** *n.*

mer•cu•ri•al (mər kyo͝or′ē əl) *adj.* **1.** Clever, shrewd, or quick. **2.** Changeable; fickle: *a mercurial disposition.* **3.** Containing or caused by the action of the element mercury. **—mer•cu′ri•al•ly** *adv.*

mer•cu•ric (mər kyo͝or′ĭk) *adj.* Of or containing mercury with a valence of +2.

mercuric chloride *n.* A poisonous white compound used as an antiseptic, in insecticides and batteries, and in photography.

mercuric sulfide *n.* A poisonous black or red compound formed by the reaction of mercury and sulfur and used as a pigment.

Mer•cu•ro•chrome (mər kyo͝or′ə krōm′). A trademark for an organic compound that contains mercury and is used as an antiseptic.

mer•cu•ry (mûr′kyə rē) *n.* **1.** *Symbol* **Hg** A silvery-white poisonous metallic element that is a liquid at room temperature. Atomic number 80. See table at **element. 2.** The column of mercury in a thermometer or barometer: *The mercury only rose to 25°F today.* [First written down about 1395 in Middle English and spelled *mercurie*, from Latin *Mercurius*, Mercury.]

Mer•cu•ry (mûr′kyə rē) *n.* **1.** In Roman mythology, the god who serves as messenger to the other gods and is himself the god of commerce, travel, and thievery. He is identified with the Greek Hermes. **2.** The planet nearest the sun at a mean distance of about 36 million miles (58 million kilometers) and the smallest with a mean radius of about 1,500 miles (2,414 kilometers).

mer•cy (mûr′sē) *n., pl.* **mer•cies. 1.** Kindness or compassion toward another person: *The victorious army showed great mercy towards the vanquished foe.* **2.** A tendency to be kind and forgiving. **3.** Something for which to be thankful; a blessing: *It's a mercy no one was hurt.* ***—idiom.* at the mercy of.** Without any protection against; helpless before: *Drifting in the boat, they were at the mercy of the weather.* [First written down before 1200 in Middle English and spelled *mearci*, from Old French *merci*, from Latin *mercēs*, reward.]

mercy killing *n.* Euthanasia.

mere (mîr) *adj.* Superlative **mer•est.** Being nothing more than: *The king at that time was a mere child.*

mere•ly (mîr′lē) *adv.* Only; simply.

mer•e•tri•cious (mĕr′ĭ trĭsh′əs) *adj.* **1.** Falsely or offensively attractive. **2.** Of or relating to prostitutes or prostitution. **—mer′e•tri′cious•ly** *adv.* **—mer′e•tri′cious•ness** *n.*

mer•gan•ser (mər găn′sər) *n.* Any of various fish-eating diving ducks having a long narrow hooked bill and usually a crested head.

merge (mûrj) *v.* **merged, merg•ing, merg•es.** *—tr.* To bring together so as to become one; unite: *The new management merged the two companies.* See Synonyms at **mix.** *—intr.* To come together to form one; blend together: *The two streams merge below town.* [First written down in 1636 in Modern English, from Latin *mergere*, to plunge, immerse.]

merg•er (mûr′jər) *n.* The action of merging, especially the union of two or more corporations or organizations.

me•rid•i•an (mə rĭd′ē ən) *n.* **1.a.** An imaginary great circle passing through any place on the earth's surface and through the North and South geographic poles. **b.** Either half of such a circle from pole to pole. All the places on the same meridian have the same longitude. **2.** A similar semicircle that joins the poles of a celestial body or the poles of the celestial sphere. **3.** The highest point; the zenith: *High office is the meridian of a career in politics.*

me•ringue (mə răng′) *n.* **1.** A mixture of stiffly beaten egg whites and sugar, often used as a topping for cakes or pies. **2.** A small pastry shell made of meringue.

me•ri•no (mə rē′nō) *n., pl.* **me•ri•nos. 1.** Any of a breed of sheep originally from Spain, having fine soft wool. **2.** Cloth or yarn made from this wool or any fine wool.

mer•it (mĕr′ĭt) *n.* **1.** Superior worth; excellence: *a painting of great merit.* **2.** Something deserving of praise or reward: *the merits of a good education.* **3. merits.** The actual facts of a matter, whether good or bad: *School grades should reflect the merits of one's work.* *—tr.v.* **mer•it•ed, mer•it•ing, mer•its.** To be worthy of; deserve: *Hard work merits praise.* [First written down before 1200 in Middle English, from Latin *meritum*, something deserved, reward.]

mer•i•to•ri•ous (mĕr′ĭ tôr′ē əs) *adj.* Having merit; deserving praise. **—mer′i•to′ri•ous•ly** *adv.* **—mer′i•to′ri•ous•ness** *n.*

merle also **merl** (mûrl) *n.* A common European blackbird that is a kind of thrush.

Mer•lin (mûr′lĭn) *n.* In Arthurian legend, a magician who serves as the royal counselor to King Arthur.

mer•maid (mûr′mād′) *n.* An imaginary sea creature with the head and upper body of a woman and the tail of a fish.

mer•man (mûr′măn′ *or* mûr′mən) *n.* An imaginary sea creature with the head and upper body of a man and the tail of a fish.

mer•ri•ment (mĕr′ĭ mənt) *n.* Amusement and fun; gaiety.

mer•ry (mĕr′ē) *adj.* **mer•ri•er, mer•ri•est. 1.** Full of fun and gaiety; jolly: *a merry and festive crowd.* **2.** Characterized by fun and gaiety: *a merry celebration.* **—mer′ri•ly** *adv.*

mer•ry-go-round (mĕr′ē gō round′) *n.* **1.** A revolving circular platform having seats, usually in the form of horses, on which people ride for amusement. **2.** A whirl or swift round of activities: *Graduation week was a merry-go-round of parties.*

mer•ry•mak•ing (mĕr′ē mā′kĭng) *n.* **1.** Fun and gaiety; festivity. **2.** A festive party or celebration. *—adj.* Full of fun and gaiety; festive. **—mer′ry•mak′er** *n.*

me•sa (mā′sə) *n.* A high land area with a flat top and steep sides, larger than a butte and smaller than a plateau, common in the southwest United States. [First written down in 1759 in American English, from Spanish, from Latin *mēnsa*, table.]

mes•ca•line (mĕs′kə lēn′ *or* mĕs′kə lĭn) *n.* A hallucinogenic drug derived from certain cactuses.

Mes•dames[1] (mā dăm′ *or* mā dăm′) *n.* A plural of **Madam.**

Mes•dames[2] (mā dăm′ *or* mā dăm′) *n.* Plural of **Madame.**

Mes•de•moi•selles (mād′mwä zĕl′) *n.* A plural of **Mademoiselle.**

mesh (mĕsh) *n.* **1.a.** Any of the open spaces in a net, sieve, or wire screen: *The meshes of this fishnet are one inch square.* **b.** Often **meshes.** The cords, threads, or wires forming a net or screen: *a screen made of wire mesh.* **2.** A net or network: *a fine mesh of interlacing wires.* **3.** A fabric with an open network of interlacing threads. **4. meshes.** An entanglement; a trap: *caught in the meshes of their own bad decisions.* **5.** The engagement of two sets of gear teeth. *—v.* **meshed, mesh•ing, mesh•es.** *—tr.* **1.** To catch in or as if in a net. **2.** To cause (gear teeth) to become engaged. —*intr.* To become engaged or interlocked: *The teeth of the gears failed to mesh.* [First written down in 1343 in Middle English and spelled *mask*, probably from Middle Dutch *maesche*.]

mes•mer•ize (mĕz′mə rīz′ *or* mĕs′mə rīz′) *tr.v.* **mes•mer•ized, mes•mer•iz•ing, mes•mer•iz•es. 1.** To hypnotize. **2.** To fascinate or enthrall: *The performance mesmerized the audience.* [First written down in 1829 in Modern English, after F. *Mesmer* (1734–1815), Austrian physician.]

mes•o•derm (mĕz′ə dûrm′ *or* mĕs′ə dûrm′) *n.* The middle of the three layers of cells found in an early embryo, developing in time into muscles, bones, and cartilage and the circulatory, excretory, and reproductive systems.

Mes•o•po•ta•mi•a (mĕs′ə pə tā′mē ə). An ancient region of southwest Asia between the Tigris and Euphrates rivers in modern-day Iraq. Probably settled before 5000 B.C., the area was the home of many early civilizations. **—Mes′o•po•ta′mi•an** *adj. & n.*

mes•o•sphere (mĕz′ə sfîr′ *or* mĕs′ə sfîr′) *n.* A layer of the atmosphere, between the stratosphere and the ionosphere, that extends from about 20 to about 50 miles (30 to 80 kilometers) above the earth's surface.

Mes•o•zo•ic (mĕz′ə zō′ĭk *or* mĕs′ə zō′ĭk) *adj.* Of, belonging to, or being the third era of geologic time, including the Triassic, Jurassic, and Cretaceous Periods. During the Mesozoic, the dinosaurs appeared and died out, and mammals, birds, and flowering plants developed. See table at **geologic time.** —*n.* The Mesozoic Era.

mes•quite (mĕ skēt′) *n.* Any of several thorny shrubs or trees of southwest North America and Mexico, having pods that are often used as forage for livestock. [First written down in 1759 in American English, from Nahuatl *mizquitl*.]

mess (mĕs) *n.* **1.** A disorderly mass or collection of things: *a mess of toys in the middle of the room.* **2.a.** An untidy or dirty condition: *The kitchen is in a mess.* **b.** A person or thing that is in such a condition: *The house is a mess.* **3.** A confusing or troublesome situation; a muddle: *We're in a mess because we ran out of paper.* **4.** A portion or quantity of food: *caught and cooked a mess of fish.* **5.a.** A meal served to a group of people, especially a military group: *The soldiers lined up for morning mess.* **b.** A group, especially a military group, that takes its meals together. **c.** A room or hall where such a group takes meals. —*v.* **messed, mess•ing, mess•es.** —*tr.* **1.** To make untidy or disorderly: *We took off our muddy boots so as not to mess up the house.* **2.** To manage badly; ruin; spoil: *Losing my notes messed up my chances of doing well on the examination.* —*intr.* **1.** To interfere; meddle: *Who messed with the VCR?* **2.** To take a meal: *The officers messed with their units.* **—*idiom.* mess around.** *Informal.* To pass time aimlessly. [First written down before 1300 in Middle English and spelled *mes*, course of a meal, from Late Latin *missus*, placed, sent, from Latin *mittere*, to place.]

mes•sage (mĕs′ĭj) *n.* **1.** A communication sent from one person or group to another: *I found the message you left at my desk.* **2.** An official statement delivered to a group: *a Presidential message to Congress.* **3.** A basic theme, lesson, or moral: *a movie with a message for all of us.* [First written down about 1300 in Middle English, from Medieval Latin *missaticum*, from Latin *mittere*, to send.]

Mes•sei•gneurs (mā sĕ nyœr′) *n.* Plural of **Monseigneur.**

mes•sen•ger (mĕs′ən jər) *n.* **1.** A person who carries messages or runs errands. **2.** Something that indicates what is about to happen; a forerunner.

messenger RNA *n.* A form of RNA that carries genetic information from the DNA in the nucleus of a cell to the ribosomes in the cytoplasm, specifying the particular protein to be synthesized.

Mes•si•ah (mĭ sī′ə) *n.* **1.** The expected deliverer and king of the Jews, foretold by the prophets of the Bible. **2.** Jesus. **3. messiah.** A leader who is regarded as a savior or liberator of a people.

mes•si•an•ic also **Mes•si•an•ic** (mĕs′ē ăn′ĭk) *adj.* Of or relating to a messiah.

Mes•sieurs (mā syœ′ *or* mĕs′ərz) *n.* Plural of **Monsieur.**

mess kit *n.* A compact kit containing cooking and eating utensils, used by soldiers and campers.

mess•mate (mĕs′māt′) *n.* A member of a group of people who eat together on a regular basis, as in a ship's mess.

Messrs.[1] (mĕs′ərz) *n.* Plural of **Mr.**

Messrs.[2] *abbr.* An abbreviation of Messieurs.

mess•y (mĕs′ē) *adj.* **mess•i•er, mess•i•est. 1.** In a mass; untidy: *a messy house.* **2.** Causing a mess: *the messy work of car repair.* **3.** Difficult or unpleasant; complicated: *a messy situation.* **—mess′i•ly** *adv.* **—mess′i•ness** *n.*

mes•ti•za (mĕs tē′zə) *n.* A woman having European and Native American ancestors.

mes•ti•zo (mĕs tē′zō) *n., pl.* **mes•ti•zos** or **mes•ti•zoes.** A person having European and Native American ancestors. [First written down about 1588 in Modern English, from Spanish, from Late Latin *mixtīcius*, mixed.]

met (mĕt) *v.* Past tense and past participle of **meet**[1].

met•a•bol•ic (mĕt′ə bŏl′ĭk) *adj.* Of, relating to, or resulting from metabolism. **—met′a•bol′i•cal•ly** *adv.*

me•tab•o•lism (mĭ tăb′ə lĭz′əm) *n.* The sum of the physiological processes by which an organism maintains life. In metabolism organic compounds are broken down to yield energy, which is then used by the body to build up new cells and tissues, provide heat, and engage in physical activity. Growth and action depend on metabolism. [First written down in 1878 in Modern English, from Greek *metabolē*, change : *meta-*, aside + *ballein*, to throw.]

met•a•car•pal (mĕt′ə kär′pəl) *adj.* Of or relating to the metacarpus. —*n.* Any of the bones of the metacarpus.

met•a•car•pus (mĕt′ə kär′pəs) *n., pl.* **met•a•car•pi** (mĕt′ə kär′pī). **1.** The part of the human hand that includes the five bones between the wrist and the fingers. **2.** The corresponding part of the forefoot of an animal.

met•al (mĕt′l) *n.* **1.** Any of the elements, such as iron, gold, copper, lead, or magnesium, that usually reflect light and conduct heat and electricity well. Metals form salts by combining with nonmetals, and form alloys by combining with other metals. **2.** An alloy, such as steel or bronze, made of two or more metals. **3.** Strength of character; mettle. [First written down about 1250 in Middle English, from Greek *metallon*.]

❑ *These sound alike:* **metal, mettle** (courage).

me•tal•lic (mə tăl′ĭk) *adj.* **1.** Of, relating to, or having the qualities of a metal: *a metallic gleam.* **2.** Containing metal: *a metallic chemical compound.*

met•al•loid (mĕt′l oid′) *n.* **1.** A nonmetallic element, such as arsenic, having properties of both a metal and a nonmetal. **2.** A nonmetallic element, such as carbon, that can form alloys with metals. —*adj.* Of, relating to, or having the property of a metalloid.

met•al•lur•gist (mĕt′l ûr′jĭst) *n.* A person who specializes in metallurgy.

met•al•lur•gy (mĕt′l ûr′jē) *n.* The science and

mess kit

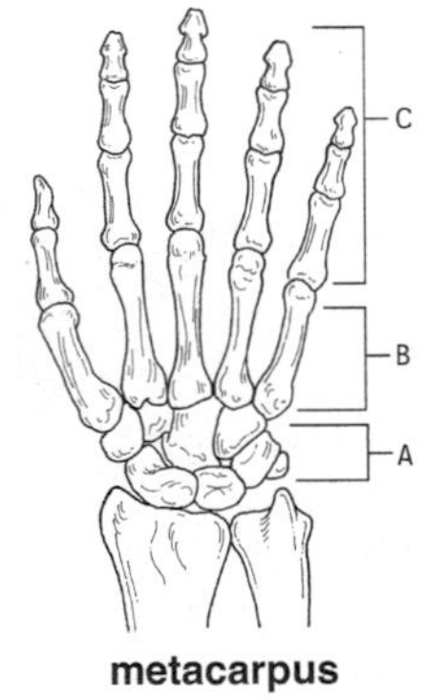

metacarpus
A. Carpus
B. Metacarpus
C. Phalanges

ă	pat	oi	boy
ā	pay	ou	out
âr	care	o͝o	took
ä	father	o͞o	boot
ĕ	pet	ŭ	cut
ē	be	ûr	urge
ĭ	pit	th	thin
ī	pie	*th*	this
îr	pier	hw	whoop
ŏ	pot	zh	vision
ō	toe	ə	about
ô	paw	N	*French* bon

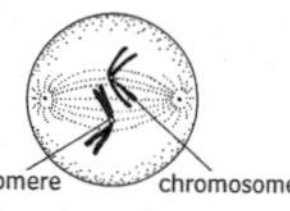

metaphase

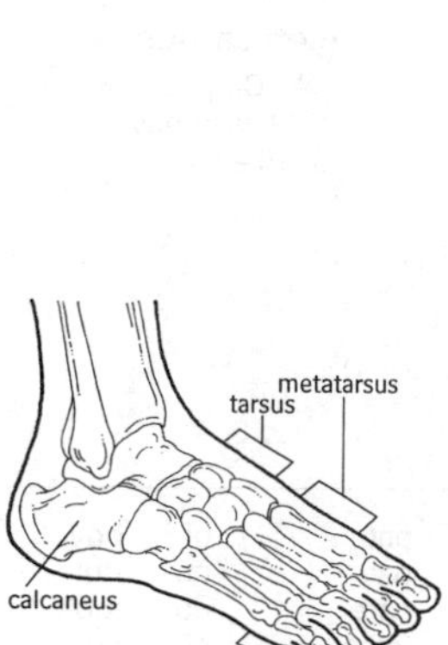

metatarsus

technology of extracting metals from their ores, refining them for use, and creating alloys and useful objects from metals. **—met′al•lur′gi•cal** *adj.*

met•al•work (mĕt′l wûrk′) *n.* **1.** Things made of metal. **2.** The act of making things out of metal.

met•al•work•ing (mĕt′l wûr′kĭng) *n.* The act or process of making or shaping things out of metal.

met•a•mor•phic (mĕt′ə môr′fĭk) *adj.* **1.** Changed by metamorphism: *metamorphic rock.* **2.** Of, relating to, or characterized by metamorphosis: *metamorphic stages of an insect.*

met•a•mor•phism (mĕt′ə môr′fĭz′əm) *n.* The process by which rocks are changed in composition, texture, or internal structure by great heat or pressure.

met•a•mor•phose (mĕt′ə môr′fōz′ *or* mĕt′ə môr′-fōs′) *v.* **met•a•mor•phosed, met•a•mor•phos•ing, met•a•mor•phos•es.** *—intr.* To undergo metamorphism or metamorphosis: *The tadpoles will metamorphose into frogs.* *—tr.* To cause to undergo metamorphism or metamorphosis.

met•a•mor•pho•sis (mĕt′ə môr′fə sĭs) *n., pl.* **met•a•mor•pho•ses** (mĕt′ə môr′fə sēz′). **1.** A marked or complete change in appearance, character, or form. **2.** A change in the form and habits of an animal during natural development after the embryonic stage. Caterpillars become butterflies and tadpoles become frogs by metamorphosis. [First written down in 1533 in Modern English, from Greek *metamorphōsis*, from *metamorphoun*, to transform.]

met•a•phase (mĕt′ə fāz′) *n.* The stage in mitosis and meiosis during which the chromosomes group together toward the center of the cell and line up before separating.

met•a•phor (mĕt′ə fôr′ *or* mĕt′ə fər) *n.* A figure of speech in which a word or phrase that is ordinarily associated with one thing is applied to something else, thus making a comparison between the two. For example, *That boy is a late bloomer* is a metaphor. [First written down about 1477 in Middle English and spelled *methaphor*, from Greek *metaphora* : *meta-*, across + *pherein*, to carry.]

met•a•phor•i•cal (mĕt′ə fôr′ĭ kəl *or* mĕt′ə fŏr′-ĭ kəl) or **met•a•phor•ic** (mĕt′ə fôr′ĭk *or* mĕt′-ə fŏr′ĭk) *adj.* Of, relating to, or using metaphors: *used a metaphorical expression to describe the experience.* **—met′a•phor′i•cal•ly** *adv.*

met•a•phys•i•cal (mĕt′ə fĭz′ĭ kəl) *adj.* **1.** Of or relating to metaphysics. **2.** Hard to understand; highly abstract. **—met′a•phys′i•cal•ly** *adv.*

met•a•phy•si•cian (mĕt′ə fĭ zĭsh′ən) *n.* A person skilled in or familiar with metaphysics.

met•a•phys•ics (mĕt′ə fĭz′ĭks) *n.* *(used with a singular verb).* The branch of philosophy that deals with the ultimate nature of things.

me•tas•ta•sis (mə tăs′tə sĭs) *n., pl.* **me•tas•ta•ses** (mə tăs′tə sēz′). The spread of a disease, cells, or microorganisms from one location in the body to other locations, especially the spread of cancerous cells.

me•tas•ta•size (mə tăs′tə sīz′) *intr.v.* **me•tas•ta•sized, me•tas•ta•siz•ing, me•tas•ta•siz•es.** To spread from one part of the body to another.

met•a•tar•sal (mĕt′ə tär′səl) *adj.* Of or relating to the metatarsus. *—n.* Any of the bones of the metatarsus.

met•a•tar•sus (mĕt′ə tär′səs) *n., pl.* **met•a•tar•si** (mĕt′ə tär′sī). **1.** The part of the human foot that forms the instep and includes the five bones between the ankle and the toes. **2.** The corresponding part of the foot of a bird or the hind foot of a four-legged animal.

met•a•zo•an (mĕt′ə zō′ən) *n.* Any of a large number of animals having a body made up of many cells arranged in tissues and organs. Metazoans include all multi-celled animals except the sponges and certain algae. *—adj.* Of or belonging to the metazoans.

mete (mēt) *tr.v.* **met•ed, met•ing, metes.** To distribute by or as if by measuring portions; allot: *The judge meted out a punishment to fit the crime.* [First written down about 725 in Old English and spelled *metan.*]

❑ *These sound alike:* **mete, meat** (animal flesh), **meet**[1] (come upon), **meet**[2] (fitting).

me•te•or (mē′tē ər *or* mē′tē ôr′) *n.* A bright trail or streak in the night sky, formed when a meteoroid enters the atmosphere and is so heated by friction with air molecules that it glows. [First written down in 1471 in Middle English and spelled *metheour*, atmospheric phenomenon, from Greek *meteōron.*]

me•te•or•ic (mē′tē ôr′ĭk *or* mē′tē ŏr′ĭk) *adj.* **1.** Of, relating to, or produced by meteors: *a meteoric flash.* **2.** Like a meteor in speed, brilliance, or briefness: *the book's meteoric surge in popularity.* **3.** Of or relating to the atmosphere: *Clouds are meteoric phenomena.*

me•te•or•ite (mē′tē ə rīt′) *n.* A meteoroid that has reached the earth without burning up.

me•te•or•oid (mē′tē ə roid′) *n.* A celestial body that travels through interplanetary space and becomes a meteor when it enters the earth's atmosphere.

me•te•or•o•log•i•cal (mē′tē ər ə lŏj′ĭ kəl) *adj.* Of or relating to meteorology. **—me′te•or•o•log′i•cal•ly** *adv.*

me•te•or•ol•o•gist (mē′tē ə rŏl′ə jĭst) *n.* A person who specializes in meteorology.

me•te•or•ol•o•gy (mē′tē ə rŏl′ə jē) *n.* The science that deals with the atmosphere and atmospheric conditions or phenomena, especially as they relate to weather.

me•ter[1] (mē′tər) *n.* **1.** The arrangement of accented and unaccented syllables in a line of poetry; poetic rhythm. **2.** The pattern of beats in a measure of music; musical rhythm. [First written down before 899 in Old English and spelled *meter*, from Greek *metron.*]

me•ter[2] (mē′tər) *n.* The basic unit of length in the metric system, equal to 39.37 inches. See table at **measurement.** [First written down in 1797 in Modern English and spelled *metre*, from French *mètre*, from Greek *metron*, measure.]

me•ter[3] (mē′tər) *n.* A device used to measure and record speed, temperature, or distance, or to indicate the amount of something used, as gas or electricity. *—tr.v.* **me•tered, me•ter•ing, me•ters.** To measure with a meter. [First written down in 1790 in Modern English, from *-meter*, measuring device, from French *-mètre*, from Greek *metron*, measure.]

–meter *suff.* A suffix that means measuring device: *speedometer.*

me•ter-kil•o•gram-sec•ond (mē′tər kĭl′ə grăm-sĕk′ənd) *adj.* Of, relating to, or being a system of measurement based on the meter, the kilogram, the second, and the ampere.

meth•ane (mĕth′ān′) *n.* A colorless, odorless, flammable gas that is the simplest of the hydrocarbons and has the formula CH_4. It is the major constituent of natural gas and forms by the decomposition of plant or other organic compounds, as in marshes and coal mines.

meth•a•nol (mĕth′ə nôl′ *or* mĕth′ə nōl′) *n.* Methyl alcohol.

me•thinks (mĭ thĭngks′) *intr.v.* Past tense **me•thought** (mĭ thôt′). *Archaic.* It seems to me.

meth•od (mĕth′əd) *n.* **1.** A regular or orderly way of doing something: *Boiling is one method of cooking rice.* **2.** Orderliness; regularity: *Lack of method in solving problems wastes time.* [First written down before 1425 in Middle English, from Greek *methodos*.]

Synonyms: method, system, routine, manner. These nouns refer to the plans or procedures followed to accomplish a task or reach a goal. **Method** suggests a detailed, logically ordered plan: *Greg developed a method for finishing his homework in half the time.* **System** means a coordinated group of methods: *Their system of doing experiments was well worked out.* **Routine** means a habitual, often tiresome method: *His routine for cleaning the house never changes.* **Manner** means a personal or distinctive method of action: *I'm probably the only one with my manner of tying knots.*

me•thod•i•cal (mə thŏd′ĭ kəl) also **me•thod•ic** (mə thŏd′ĭk) *adj.* **1.** Arranged or done in regular order; systematic: *a methodical inspection.* **2.** Characterized by orderly habits or behavior: *She's very methodical in her approach to teaching.* **—me•thod′i•cal•ly** *adv.* **—me•thod′i•cal•ness** *n.*

Meth•od•ism (mĕth′ə dĭz′əm) *n.* The beliefs and worship of the Methodists.

Meth•od•ist (mĕth′ə dĭst) *n.* A member of a Protestant church founded in England in the 18th century on the teachings of John and Charles Wesley.

me•thought (mĭ thôt′) *v. Archaic.* Past tense of **methinks.**

Me•thu•se•lah (mə thōō′zə lə). In the Bible, a man said to have lived 969 years.

meth•yl (mĕth′əl) *n.* The organic radical CH_3, derived from methane, having a valence of 1, and occurring in many important chemical compounds.

methyl alcohol *n.* A colorless, flammable, and poisonous liquid compound having the formula CH_3OH. It is used as an antifreeze, a fuel, and a solvent.

me•tic•u•lous (mĭ tĭk′yə ləs) *adj.* Extremely or excessively careful and precise; showing great concern for details. [First written down in 1535 in Modern English, from Latin *metīculōsus*, timid, from *metus*, fear.] **—me•tic′u•lous•ly** *adv.* **—me•tic′u•lous•ness** *n.*

me•tre[1] (mē′tər) *n. Chiefly British.* Variant of **meter[1]**.

me•tre[2] (mē′tər) *n. Chiefly British.* Variant of **meter[2]**.

met•ric (mĕt′rĭk) *adj.* Of or relating to the metric system.

met•ri•cal (mĕt′rĭ kəl) *adj.* **1.** Of, relating to, or composed in poetic meter. **2.** Of or relating to measurement. **—met′ri•cal•ly** *adv.*

met•ri•ca•tion (mĕt′rĭ kā′shən) *n.* Conversion to the metric system of weights and measures.

metric system *n.* A decimal system of weights and measures based on the meter as its unit of length, the kilogram as its unit of mass, and the liter as its unit of volume.

metric ton *n.* A unit of mass or weight equal to 1,000 kilograms (2,205 pounds). See table at **measurement.**

met•ro (mĕt′rō) *n., pl.* **met•ros.** A subway system.

met•ro•nome (mĕt′rə nōm′) *n.* An adjustable device that makes a series of regular clicks at different speeds. It is used to provide a steady beat for practicing music.

me•trop•o•lis (mĭ trŏp′ə lĭs) *n.* **1.** A large important city. **2.** The largest or most important city of a country, state, or region. [First written down about 1386 in Middle English and spelled *metropol*, from Greek *mētropolis*, mother-city : *mētēr*, mother + *polis*, city.]

met•ro•pol•i•tan (mĕt′rə pŏl′ĭ tən) *adj.* Of, relating to, or characteristic of a major city: *metropolitan bus routes.* —*n.* **1.** A person from a major city. **2.** A bishop who presides over a church province.

–metry *suff.* A suffix that means process or science of measurement: *photometry.*

met•tle (mĕt′l) *n.* **1.** Spirit; daring; courage. **2.** Basic character or temperament: *Adversity never fails to test someone's mettle.* [First written down in 1581 in Modern English, variant of *metal.*]

❑ *These sound alike:* **mettle, metal** (element).

met•tle•some (mĕt′l səm) *adj.* High-spirited; full of courage.

mev or **Mev** *abbr.* An abbreviation of million electron volts.

mew[1] (myōō) *intr.v.* **mewed, mew•ing, mews.** To make the high-pitched cry of a cat. —*n.* The crying sound of a cat. [First written down before 1325 in Middle English and spelled *meuen*, of imitative origin.]

mew[2] (myōō) *n.* A gull of northern Europe, northern Asia, and northwest North America. [First written down about 700 in Old English and spelled *mǣw*.]

mewl (myōōl) *intr.v.* **mewled, mewl•ing, mewls.** To cry softly, as a baby does; whimper. —*n.* A weak cry or whimper.

❑ *These sound alike:* **mewl, mule[1]** (animal), **mule[2]** (slipper).

mews (myōōz) *pl.n.* *(used with a singular or plural verb).* **1.** A group of buildings originally containing stables and often converted into apartments. **2.** A street or an alley on which such buildings stand.

❑ *These sound alike:* **mews, muse** (consider), **Muse** (goddess).

Mex. *abbr.* An abbreviation of: **1.** Mexican. **2.** Mexico.

Mex•i•can (mĕk′sĭ kən) *n.* A native or inhabitant of Mexico. —*adj.* Of or relating to Mexico or its people, languages, or cultures.

Mexican Spanish *n.* Spanish as used in Mexico.

Mexican War *n.* A war fought between the United States and Mexico (1846–1848) over possession of Texas and other lands now in the southwest United States.

Mex•i•co (mĕk′sĭ kō′). A country of south-central North America south of the United States. It was originally inhabited by the Aztecs and Maya among others. Mexico was held by the Spanish from 1521 until 1821. Mexico City is the capital. Population, 67,395,826.

Mexico, Gulf of. An arm of the Atlantic Ocean in southeast North America bordering on eastern Mexico, the southeast United States, and Cuba.

Mexico City. The capital and largest city of Mexico, in the central part of the country. It was founded on the site of an ancient Aztec capital. Population, 8,831,079.

me•zu•zah also **me•zu•za** (mə zōōz′ə *or* mə zōō-zä′) *n., pl.* **me•zu•zahs** also **me•zu•zas** (mə zōōz′-əz) or **me•zu•zot** (mə zōō zôt′). A small piece of parchment inscribed with Biblical passages, rolled up in a container and attached by many Jewish families to their door frames as a sign of faith. [First written down in 1650 in Modern English and spelled *Me-zuzah*, from Hebrew *mĕzûzâ*, doorpost.]

mez•za•nine (mĕz′ə nēn′ *or* mĕz′ə nēn′) *n.* **1.** A partial story between two main stories of a building. **2.** The lowest balcony in a theater or the first few rows of the balcony.

mez•zo for•te (mĕt′sō fôr′tā′ *or* mĕd′zō fôr′tā′) *adv. & adj.* In music, moderately loud.

mez•zo-so•pran•o (mĕt′sō sə prăn′ō *or* mĕt′-sō sə prä′nō *or* mĕd′zō sə prăn′ō *or* mĕd′-zō sə prä′nō) *n., pl.* **mez•zo-so•pran•os.** **1.** A woman's singing voice of medium range, lower than a soprano and higher than a contralto. **2.** A woman having such a voice. **3.** A part written in the range of this voice.

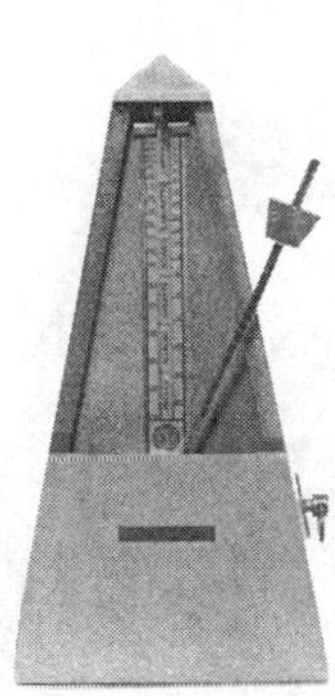

metronome

mezuzah

mezzanine

At the Terra Museum in Chicago

ă	pat	oi	boy
ā	pay	ou	out
âr	care	ŏŏ	took
ä	father	ōō	boot
ĕ	pet	ŭ	cut
ē	be	ûr	urge
ĭ	pit	th	thin
ī	pie	*th*	this
îr	pier	hw	whoop
ŏ	pot	zh	vision
ō	toe	ə	about
ô	paw	N	*French* bon

Michelangelo
Portrait by Daniele de Volterra (1509–1566)

Michigan

The state of **Michigan** gets its name from a Chippewa or Ottawa word meaning "big lake." The name was first applied to **Lake Michigan**, one of the Great Lakes. The state then took its name from the lake.

Word Building: micro–

The basic meaning of the prefix **micro–** is "small." It comes from the Greek prefix *mikro–*, from *mikros*, meaning "small." In English **micro–** has been chiefly used since the 19th century to form science words. It is the counterpart for the prefix **macro–** ("large") in pairs such as **microcosm/macrocosm** and **micronucleus/macronucleus**. And **micro–** is also sometimes the counterpart for the prefix **mega–**, as in *microvolt* ("one millionth of a volt") and *megavolt* ("one million volts").

ă	pat	oi	boy
ā	pay	ou	out
âr	care	o͝o	took
ä	father	o͞o	boot
ĕ	pet	ŭ	cut
ē	be	ûr	urge
ĭ	pit	th	thin
ī	pie	*th*	this
îr	pier	hw	whoop
ŏ	pot	zh	vision
ō	toe	ə	about
ô	paw	N	*French* bon

mg *abbr.* An abbreviation of milligram.
Mg Symbol for the element **magnesium.**
mgr. *abbr.* An abbreviation of manager.
Mgr. *abbr.* An abbreviation of: **1.** Monseigneur. **2.** Monsignor.
MHz *abbr.* An abbreviation of megahertz.
mi (mē) *n.* In music, the third tone of a major scale. ❑ *These sound alike:* **mi, me** (pronoun).
MI *abbr.* An abbreviation of Michigan.
mi. *abbr.* An abbreviation of mile.
Mi•am•i[1] (mī **ăm′**ē *or* mī **ăm′**ə) *n., pl.* **Miami** or **Mi•am•is. 1.** A member of a Native American people originally living in Wisconsin and now living in Indiana and Oklahoma. **2.** The variety of Illinois spoken by the Miami.
Mi•am•i[2] (mī **ăm′**ē *or* mī **ăm′**ə). A city of southeast Florida on the Atlantic Ocean. It was settled in the 1870's. Population, 358,548.
mi•as•ma (mī **ăz′**mə *or* mē **ăz′**mə) *n., pl.* **mi•as•mas** or **mi•as•ma•ta** (mī **ăz′**mə tə *or* mē **ăz′** mə-tə). **1.** A bad-smelling vapor arising from rotting organic matter and formerly thought to cause disease. **2.** A harmful atmosphere or influence. **—mi•as′mal** *adj.*
mi•ca (**mī′**kə) *n.* A member of a group of aluminum silicate minerals that can be split easily into thin, partly transparent sheets. Mica is highly resistant to heat and is used in electric fuses and other electrical equipment. [First written down in 1706 in Modern English, from Latin *mica*, grain.]
Mi•cah (**mī′**kə) *n.* **1.** A Hebrew prophet of the eighth century B.C. **2.** A book of the Bible in which Micah predicts the destruction of Jerusalem as punishment for sinful living and the coming of the Messiah.
mice (mīs) *n.* Plural of **mouse.**
Mich. *abbr.* An abbreviation of Michigan.
Mi•chael (**mī′**kəl) *n.* In the Bible, the guardian archangel of the Jews. In Christian tradition, Michael led the celestial armies against Satan's revolt.
Mich•ael•mas (**mĭk′**əl məs) *n.* September 29, on which a Christian feast in honor of the archangel Michael is observed.
Mi•chel•an•ge•lo Buo•nar•ro•ti (mī′kəl **ăn′**-jə lō′ bwôn′ə **rô′**tē). 1475–1564. Italian Renaissance artist whose works include the marble sculpture *David* (1501).
Mich•i•gan (**mĭsh′**ĭ gən). A state of the north-central United States north of Indiana. It was admitted as the 26th state in 1837. Lansing is the capital and Detroit the largest city. Population, 9,328,784. —SEE NOTE.
Michigan, Lake. The third largest of the Great Lakes, in the north-central United States between Wisconsin and Michigan. The St. Lawrence Seaway links it with the Atlantic Ocean.
Mic•mac (**mĭk′**măk′) *n., pl.* **Micmac** or **Mic•macs. 1.** A member of a Native American people living in Nova Scotia, New Brunswick, and other parts of eastern Canada. **2.** The Algonquian language of the Micmac.
micr– *pref.* Variant of **micro–.**
mi•cra (**mī′**krə) *n.* A plural of **micron.**
micro– or **micr–** *pref.* A prefix that means: **1.** Small or smaller: *microcircuit.* **2.** Requiring or involving magnification or enlargement: *microscope.* **3.** One-millionth: *microsecond.* —SEE NOTE.
mi•crobe (**mī′**krōb′) *n.* A microorganism, especially a bacterium that causes disease.
mi•cro•bi•ol•o•gist (mī′krō bī **ŏl′**ə jĭst) *n.* A scientist who specializes in microbiology.
mi•cro•bi•ol•o•gy (mī′krō bī **ŏl′** ə jē) *n.* The branch of biology that deals with microorganisms. **—mi′cro•bi′o•log′i•cal** (mī′krō bī′ə **lŏj′**ĭ kəl) *adj.*
mi•cro•chip (**mī′**crə chĭp′) *n.* A minute square of semiconducting material on which an electronic component or integrated circuit is etched.
mi•cro•cir•cuit (**mī′**krō sûr′kĭt) *n.* A miniaturized electronic circuit made up of small chips of semiconductor material containing elements of the circuit.
mi•cro•coc•cus (mī′krō **kŏk′**əs) *n., pl.* **mi•cro•coc•ci** (mī′krō **kŏk′**sī′ *or* mī′krō **kŏk′**ī′). Any of a type of spherical bacteria. Certain micrococci cause disease; others produce fermentation.
mi•cro•com•put•er (**mī′**krō kəm pyo͞o′tər) *n.* A small computer, such as a personal computer, containing a microprocessor and designed to be used by one person at a time.
mi•cro•cosm (**mī′**krə kŏz′əm) *n.* Something regarded as a miniature representation of something else: *The problems of the family are the nation's problems in microcosm.* [First written down before 1430 in Middle English and spelled *microcosme*, from Greek *mikros kosmos*, little world.]
mi•cro•film (**mī′**krə fĭlm′) *n.* **1.** A film on which written or printed material can be reproduced in greatly reduced size. **2.** A reproduction made on microfilm. —*tr.v.* **mi•cro•filmed, mi•cro•film•ing, mi•cro•films.** To reproduce on microfilm.
mi•cro•me•te•or•ite (mī′krō **mē′**tē ə rīt′) *n.* A tiny particle of meteorite dust.
mi•crom•e•ter[1] (mī **krŏm′**ĭ tər) *n.* A device for measuring very small distances, angles, or objects. Certain kinds are used with a microscope or telescope.
mi•cro•me•ter[2] (**mī′**krō mē′tər) *n.* A unit of length equal to one millionth (10^{-6}) of a meter.
mi•crom•e•ter caliper (mī **krŏm′**ĭ tər) *n.* A caliper for measuring small distances by the rotation of a finely threaded screw.
mi•cron (**mī′**krŏn′) *n., pl.* **mi•crons** or **mi•cra** (**mī′**-krə). A unit of length equal to one millionth (10^{-6}) of a meter.
Mi•cro•ne•si•a (mī′krō **nē′**zhə *or* mī′krō **nē′**shə). A division of Oceania in the western Pacific Ocean made up of the islands east of the Philippines and north of the equator.
Mi•cro•ne•sian (mī′krə **nē′**zhən *or* mī′krə **nē′**-shən) *adj.* Of or relating to Micronesia or its peoples, languages, or cultures. —*n.* **1.** A member of any of the peoples inhabiting Micronesia. **2.** A group of languages spoken in Micronesia.
mi•cro•nu•cle•us (mī′krō **no͞o′**klē əs *or* mī′-krō **nyo͞o′**klē əs) *n., pl.* **mi•cro•nu•cle•i** (mī′krō-**no͞o′**klē ī′ *or* mī′krō **nyo͞o′**klē ī′) or **mi•cro•nu•cle•us•es.** The smaller of two kinds of nuclei found in protozoans, containing chromatin materials necessary for reproduction.
mi•cro•or•gan•ism (mī′krō **ôr′**gə nĭz′əm) *n.* An organism, such as a bacterium or a protozoan, so small that it can be seen only with the aid of a microscope.
mi•cro•phone (**mī′**krə fōn′) *n.* A device that converts sound waves into electric current, as in recording or radio broadcasting. [First written down in 1683 in Modern English and spelled *microphone*, ear trumpet : Greek *mikros*, small + Greek *phōnē*, sound.]
mi•cro•proc•es•sor (**mī′**krō prŏs′ĕs ər) *n.* An integrated circuit that contains the entire central processing unit of a computer on a single chip.
mi•cro•scope (**mī′**krə skōp′) *n.* An optical instrument consisting of a lens or combination of lenses for magnifying objects that are invisible or indistinct to the unaided eye.
mi•cro•scop•ic (mī′krə **skŏp′**ĭk) *adj.* **1.** Too small to be seen by the eye alone but large enough to be seen through a microscope: *microscopic cells.* **2.** Of,

relating to, or done with a microscope: *microscopic study of a specimen.* **3.** Very small; minute. **4.** Done with great attention to detail: *a microscopic analysis of the city's budget.* **—mi′cro•scop′i•cal•ly** *adv.*

mi•cros•co•py (mī **krŏs′**kə pē) *n., pl.* **mi•cros•co•pies. 1.** The study or use of microscopes. **2.** Investigation using a microscope.

mi•cro•sec•ond (**mī′**krō sĕk′ənd) *n.* A unit of time equal to one millionth (10^{-6}) of a second.

mi•cro•wave (**mī′**krō wāv′) *n.* **1.** A high frequency electromagnetic wave, usually one millimeter to one meter in wavelength. **2.** A microwave oven. *—tr.v.* **mi•cro•waved, mi•cro•wav•ing, mi•cro•waves.** To cook or heat (food) in a microwave oven.

microwave oven *n.* An oven in which microwaves are used to heat and cook food.

mid[1] (mĭd) *adj.* Middle; central. [First written down before 725 in Old English.]

mid[2] (mĭd) *prep.* Amid: *mid smoke and flame.* [First written down before 1400 in Middle English and spelled *midde*, from *amid.*]

mid– *pref.* A prefix that means middle: *midsummer.* —SEE NOTE.

mid•air (**mĭd′âr′**) *n.* A point or region in the air: *a trapeze suspended in midair.*

Mi•das (**mī′**dəs) *n.* In Greek legend, a king who is given the power of turning all that he touches to gold.

mid•brain (**mĭd′**brān′) *n.* The middle section of the brain.

mid•day (**mĭd′**dā′) *n.* The middle of the day; noon.

mid•dle (**mĭd′**l) *adj.* **1.** Equally distant from extremes; central: *the middle seats of the row.* **2.** Being halfway or intermediate in a sequence or series: *the middle child of three in the family.* *—n.* **1.** An area or point equally distant from extremes; a center: *the middle of the room.* **2.** Something between a beginning and an end; an intermediate part: *A story has a beginning, a middle, and an end.* **3.** The middle part of the human body; the waist. [First written down in 785 in Old English and spelled *middel.*]

middle age *n.* The time of human life between youth and old age, usually reckoned as the years between 40 and 60.

mid•dle-aged (**mĭd′**l **ājd′**) *adj.* Of or relating to middle age.

Middle Ages *pl.n.* The period in European history between ancient times and the Renaissance, usually dated from about 500 to about 1450.

middle C *n.* The musical tone represented by a note on the first ledger line above the bass clef.

middle class *n.* The people of a society who occupy a social and economic position between those of the lower working classes and the wealthy. The middle class includes business people, skilled workers, and professionals.

Middle Dutch *n.* The Dutch language from 1150 to 1500.

middle ear *n.* The space between the eardrum and the inner ear. In humans it contains three small bones that carry sound vibrations from the eardrum to the inner ear.

Middle East. An area made up of the countries of southwest Asia and northeast Africa.

Middle English *n.* The English language from about 1100 to 1500, between Old English and Modern English.

Middle Low German *n.* Low German from about 1250 to 1500.

mid•dle•man (**mĭd′**l măn′) *n.* **1.** A trader who buys goods from producers and sells to retailers or consumers. **2.** An intermediary or a go-between.

mid•dle•weight (**mĭd′**l wāt′) *n.* **1.** A boxer weighing between 147 and 160 pounds (66.5–72.5 kilograms). **2.** A contestant in other sports in a similar weight class.

Middle West. Midwest.

mid•dling (**mĭd′**lĭng *or* **mĭd′**lĭn) *adj.* Of medium size, position, or quality; average: *a middling performance on the test.*

mid•dy (**mĭd′**ē) *n., pl.* **mid•dies. 1.** *Informal.* A midshipman. **2.** A middy blouse.

middy blouse *n.* A loose blouse with a wide collar that is designed to resemble a sailor's blouse.

midge (mĭj) *n.* Any of various very small flies; a gnat.

midg•et (**mĭj′**ĭt) *n.* **1.** *Offensive.* A very small person of normal proportions. **2.** A small or miniature version of something. [First written down in 1884 in Modern English, from *midge.*]

mid•land (**mĭd′**lənd) *n.* The middle or interior part of a country or region.

mid•most (**mĭd′**mōst′) *adj.* Situated in the exact middle or nearest the middle.

mid•night (**mĭd′**nīt′) *n.* The middle of the night, specifically twelve o'clock at night.

midnight sun *n.* The sun as seen at midnight during the summer within the Arctic or Antarctic Circle.

mid•point (**mĭd′**point′) *n.* A point halfway between limits or endpoints.

mid•rib (**mĭd′**rĭb′) *n.* The central vein of a leaf.

mid•riff (**mĭd′**rĭf) *n.* The middle part of the human body that extends from just below the chest to the waist.

mid•ship (**mĭd′**shĭp′) *adj.* Of, relating to, or located in the middle of a ship.

mid•ship•man (**mĭd′**shĭp′mən *or* mĭd **shĭp′**mən) *n.* A student training to be an officer at a naval academy.

mid•ships (**mĭd′**shĭps′) *adv.* Amidships.

midst (mĭdst *or* mĭtst) *n.* **1.** The middle position or part; the center: *a tree in the midst of the garden.* **2.** The condition of being surrounded by something: *trouble in the midst of good fortune.* **3.** A position near or among others: *a stranger in our midst.* *—prep.* Among; amid. [First written down before 1325 in Middle English and spelled *middes*, from Old English *midde*, middle.]

mid•stream (**mĭd′**strēm′) *n.* **1.** The middle of a stream. **2.** The middle of a course of action or period of time: *We changed plans in midstream.*

mid•sum•mer (**mĭd′sŭm′**ər) *n.* **1.** The middle of the summer. **2.** The summer solstice, about June 21.

mid•term (**mĭd′**tûrm′) *n.* **1.** The middle of a school term or a political term of office. **2.** An examination given at the middle of a school term.

mid•town (**mĭd′**toun′) *n.* The central part of a town or city.

mid•way (**mĭd′**wā′) *n.* The area of a fair, carnival, or circus where side shows and other amusements are located. *—adv.* In the middle of a distance or period of time.

Mid•way Islands (**mĭd′**wā′). A United States territory made up of two small islands and a surrounding coral reef in the central Pacific Ocean northwest of Honolulu. The Battle of Midway (June 3–6, 1942) was a major victory for Allied forces during World War II.

mid•week (**mĭd′**wēk′) *n.* The middle of the week.

Mid•west (mĭd **wĕst′**) or **Middle West.** A region of the north-central United States around the Great Lakes and the upper Mississippi River valley. The area is known for its rich farmlands and highly industrialized centers.

mid•wife (**mĭd′**wīf′) *n., pl.* **mid•wives** (**mĭd′**wīvz′). A person trained to assist women in childbirth.

mid•win•ter (**mĭd′wĭn′**tər) *n.* **1.** The middle of the

microphone

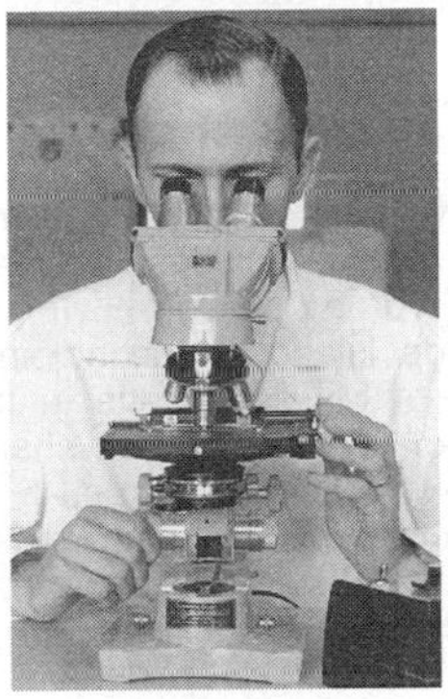

microscope

microwave oven

Interior view of a microwave oven

Word Building: mid–

The prefix **mid–**, which means "middle," combines primarily with nouns to form compounds, most of which represent a time (**midmorning**, **midsummer**, **midyear**) or place (**midbrain**, **midstream**, **midtown**). When **mid–** is affixed to a word beginning with a capital letter, it is always necessary to use a hyphen: *mid-November*, *mid-Atlantic states.* The prefix **mid–** can be traced back to the Old English adjective *midd*, meaning "middle."

Regional Note: milk shake

To most Americans, a **milk shake** includes ice cream. To a person living in Rhode Island or the adjoining part of Massachusetts, a milk shake consists of milk shaken up with flavored syrup. If ice cream is included, the drink is called a *cabinet* or, farther north, a *velvet* or a **frappé**.

milk snake
Eastern milk snake

winter. **2.** The midwinter solstice, occurring about December 22.

mid•wives (mĭd′wīvz′) *n.* Plural of **midwife.**

mid•year (mĭd′yîr′) *n.* **1.** The middle of the year. **2.** An examination given in the middle of a school year.

mien (mēn) *n.* A person's manner of behavior or appearance; bearing: *the mien of a dignified professor.*

❑ *These sound alike:* **mien, mean**[1] (signify), **mean**[2] (unkind), **mean**[3] (middle point).

miff (mĭf) *tr.v.* **miffed, miff•ing, miffs.** To offend or annoy: *I was miffed by their failure to do the job properly.*

might[1] (mīt) *n.* **1.** Great power or force: *the might of a great army.* **2.** Physical strength: *pushed with all my might.* See Synonyms at **strength.** [First written down before 700 in Old English and spelled *mæct.*]

❑ *These sound alike:* **might**[1] (power), **might**[2] (past tense of may[1]), **mite**[1] (small animal), **mite**[2] (small amount of money).

might[2] (mīt) *aux.v.* Past tense of **may. 1.** Used to indicate possibility or probability: *We might go to the beach tomorrow.* **2.** Used to express permission: *She asked if she might stay out late.* [First written down before 830 in Old English and spelled *mæhte.*]

❑ *These sound alike:* **might**[2] (past tense of may[1]), **might**[1] (power), **mite**[1] (small animal), **mite**[2] (small amount of money).

might•y (mī′tē) *adj.* **might•i•er, might•i•est. 1.** Having or showing great power, strength, or skill: *a mighty hunter.* **2.** Great in size, scope, or intensity: *a mighty stone fortress.* —*adv. Informal.* Very; extremely: *They've been gone a mighty long time.* **—might′i•ly** *adv.* **—might′i•ness** *n.*

mi•gnon•ette (mĭn′yə nĕt′) *n.* Any of several garden plants having long clusters of small, fragrant, greenish-white flowers.

mi•graine (mī′grān′) *n.* A very severe headache, often accompanied by nausea, that usually affects only one side of the head and tends to recur. [First written down in 1373 in Middle English and spelled *migrane,* from Greek *hēmikrania* : *hēmi-,* half, one side + *kranion,* head.]

mi•grant (mī′grənt) *n.* **1.** A person or an animal that migrates. **2.** A farm worker who travels from one area to another in search of work. —*adj.* Migratory; migrating.

mi•grate (mī′grāt′) *intr.v.* **mi•grat•ed, mi•grat•ing, mi•grates. 1.** To move from one country or region and settle in another. **2.** To move regularly to a different region, especially at a particular time of the year: *Many birds migrate to southern regions in the fall.* [First written down in 1697 in Modern English, from Latin *migrāre.*]

mi•gra•tion (mī grā′shən) *n.* **1.** The act of migrating. **2.** A group of people or animals migrating together.

mi•gra•to•ry (mī′grə tôr′ē) *adj.* **1.** Traveling from one place to another; migrating regularly: *migratory birds.* **2.** Of or relating to migration: *long migratory flights.*

mi•ka•do (mĭ kä′dō) *n., pl.* **mi•ka•dos.** The emperor of Japan.

mike (mīk) *Informal. n.* A microphone.

mil (mĭl) *n.* A unit of length equal to one thousandth (10^{-3}) of an inch (.0254 millimeter), used chiefly to measure the diameter of wires. [First written down in 1721 in Modern English, from Latin *mīlle,* thousand.]

❑ *These sound alike:* **mil, mill**[1] (grinding machine), **mill**[2] (unit of money).

mi•la•dy (mĭ lā′dē) *n.* Used as a form of address for an English noblewoman.

Mi•lan (mĭ lăn′ *or* mĭ län′). A city of northern Italy northeast of Genoa. It is probably of Celtic origin and was taken by the Romans in 222 B.C. Population, 1,634,638.

milch (mĭlch) *adj.* Giving milk: *a milch cow.*

mild (mīld) *adj.* **mild•er, mild•est. 1.** Gentle or kind in disposition, manner, or behavior: *a mild grandparent.* **2.** Moderate in type, degree, effect, or force: *a mild reprimand; a mild soap.* **3.a.** Not extreme, as in temperature: *a mild climate.* **b.** Warm and full of sunshine: *a mild day.* **—mild′ly** *adv.* **—mild′ness** *n.*

mil•dew (mĭl′do͞o′ *or* mĭl′dyo͞o′) *n.* **1.** Any of various fungi that form a white or grayish coating on surfaces, such as plant leaves, cloth, or leather, especially under damp warm conditions. **2.** The coating formed by such a fungus. —*v.* **mil•dewed, mil•dew•ing, mil•dews.** —*intr.* To become covered or spotted with mildew: *The leather coat mildewed in the damp closet.* —*tr.* To cause to become covered or spotted with mildew. [First written down before 1000 in Old English and spelled *mildēaw,* honeydew, nectar.]

mile (mīl) *n.* **1.** A unit of length equal to 5,280 feet or 1,760 yards (about 1,609 meters). **2.** A nautical mile. See table at **measurement.** [First written down before 800 in Old English and spelled *mīl,* from Latin *mīlia (passuum),* a thousand (double paces).]

mile•age (mī′lĭj) *n.* **1.** Length or distance in miles: *The mileage between the two cities is considerable.* **2.a.** Total miles covered or traveled over a given time: *We haven't put much mileage on the car in the last month.* **b.** The amount of service, use, or wear measured by miles used or traveled: *a tire that gives long mileage.* **3.** The distance a motor vehicle travels on a given amount of fuel: *a mileage of 25 miles per gallon.* **4.** An allowance on a given amount for traveling expenses at a certain rate per mile: *The company pays a mileage of 15¢ per mile when I use my car for business travel.*

mile•post (mīl′pōst′) *n.* A post along a highway that indicates the distance in miles to a certain place.

mile•stone (mīl′stōn′) *n.* **1.** A stone marker set up on a roadside to indicate the distance in miles from a given point. **2.** An important event; a turning point: *The Bill of Rights was a milestone in the history of human rights.*

mi•lieu (mĭl yo͞o′ *or* mē lyœ′) *n., pl.* **mi•lieus** or **mi•lieux** (mē lyœ′). Environment or surroundings: *People often feel most comfortable in their own milieu.*

mil•i•tant (mĭl′ĭ tənt) *adj.* **1.** Fighting or making war: *militant bands of insurgents.* **2.** Aggressive or combative, especially in the service of a cause: *Militant strikers blocked the entrances to the business.* —*n.* A militant person. **—mil′i•tan•cy** *n.* **—mil′i•tant•ly** *adv.*

mil•i•ta•rism (mĭl′ĭ tə rĭz′əm) *n.* **1.** The policy or practice of maintaining strong armed forces. **2.** Glorification of military spirit or ideals. **—mil′i•ta•ris′tic** *adj.*

mil•i•ta•rist (mĭl′ĭ tər ĭst) *n.* A person who supports militarism.

mil•i•ta•rize (mĭl′ĭ tə rīz′) *tr.v.* **mil•i•ta•rized, mil•i•ta•riz•ing, mil•i•ta•riz•es. 1.** To equip or train for war. **2.** To fill with militarism. **—mil′i•ta•ri•za′tion** (mĭl′ĭ tər ĭ zā′shən) *n.*

mil•i•tar•y (mĭl′ĭ tĕr′ē) *adj.* **1.** Of, relating to, or characteristic of the armed forces: *a military base.* **2.** Of or relating to war: *military history.* —*n., pl.* **military** also **mil•i•tar•ies.** The armed forces of a country. [First written down in 1460 in Middle

English, from Latin *mīles*, soldier.] **—mil′i•tar′i•ly** (mĭl′ĭ **târ′**ə lē) *adv.*

mil•i•tate (mĭl′ĭ tāt′) *intr.v.* **mil•i•tat•ed, mil•i•tat•ing, mil•i•tates.** To have force or influence; bring about an effect or a change: *Carelessness militates against doing a good job.*

mi•li•tia (mə **lĭsh′**ə) *n.* An army composed of citizens who are not professional soldiers and who may be called for military service in times of emergency.

mi•li•tia•man (mə **lĭsh′**ə mən) *n.* A member of a militia.

milk (mĭlk) *n.* **1.a.** A white liquid produced by the mammary glands of female mammals for feeding their young. **b.** The milk of cows, used as food by human beings. **2.** A liquid resembling milk: *coconut milk.* —*v.* **milked, milk•ing, milks.** —*tr.* **1.a.** To squeeze milk from the teats or udder of (a cow, goat, or other mammal). **b.** To draw out or extract a liquid from: *milked the snake of its venom.* **2.** To obtain money or benefits from, in order to achieve personal gain: *milk the treasury of its funds.* —*intr.* To draw milk from a cow, goat, or other animal. [First written down before 899 in Old English and spelled *milc.*]

milk•er (**mĭl′**kər) *n.* **1.** A person or machine that milks animals. **2.** An animal kept to give milk, as a cow or goat.

milk•maid (**mĭlk′**mād′) *n.* A girl or woman who milks cows.

milk•man (**mĭlk′**măn′) *n.* A man who sells or delivers milk.

milk of magnesia *n.* A milky white suspension of magnesium hydroxide in water used as an antacid and a laxative.

milk shake *n.* A beverage made of milk, flavoring, and usually ice cream, shaken or whipped until foamy. —SEE NOTE.

milk snake *n.* Any of various nonpoisonous king snakes of North America having brown or gray markings.

milk•sop (**mĭlk′**sŏp′) *n.* A person who lacks courage; a weakling.

milk sugar *n.* Lactose.

milk tooth *n.* Any of the temporary teeth that first grow in the mouth of a young mammal.

milk•weed (**mĭlk′**wēd′) *n.* Any of numerous plants having clusters of purplish flowers, milky juice, and large pods that split open to release downy seeds.

milk•y (**mĭl′**kē) *adj.* **milk•i•er, milk•i•est. 1.** Resembling milk, especially in color. **2.** Consisting of or yielding milk. **—milk′i•ness** *n.*

Milky Way *n.* The galaxy containing the solar system, visible as a broad band of faint light in the night sky.

mill[1] (mĭl) *n.* **1.** A building equipped with machines for grinding grain into flour or meal. **2.** A device or machine that grinds grain. **3.** A device or machine for grinding, crushing, or pressing: *a cider mill.* **4.** A building or group of buildings equipped with machinery for processing a material of some kind: *a steel mill.* —*v.* **milled, mill•ing, mills.** —*tr.* **1.** To grind or crush into powder or fine grains: *mill wheat.* **2.** To process or produce (steel, paper, or another product) in a mill. **3.** To put ridges or grooves on the edge of (a coin). —*intr.* To move around in a confused or disorderly manner: *During the fire drill the students milled about the playground.* [First written down about 961 in Old English and spelled *mylen*, from Late Latin *molīna*, from *molere*, to grind.]

❑ *These sound alike:* **mill**[1] (grinding machine), **mil** (unit of length), **mill**[2] (unit of money).

mill[2] (mĭl) *n.* A unit of money equal to one thousandth of a U.S. dollar, or one tenth of a cent. [First written down in 1791 in American English, from Latin *mīllēsimus*, thousandth.]

❑ *These sound alike:* **mill**[2] (unit of money), **mil** (unit of length), **mill**[1] (grinding machine).

Mill (mĭl), **John Stuart.** 1806–1873. British philosopher and economist whose works include *Principles of Political Economy* (1848).

Mil•lay (mĭ **lā′**), **Edna Saint Vincent.** 1892–1950. American poet whose volumes include *The Harp Weaver and Other Poems* (1923).

mill•dam (**mĭl′**dăm′) *n.* A dam built across a stream to raise the water level and provide water power to turn a mill wheel.

mil•len•ni•um (mə **lĕn′**ē əm) *n., pl.* **mil•len•ni•ums** or **mil•len•ni•a** (mə **lĕn′**ē ə). **1.** A span of one thousand years. **2.** A thousand-year reign of Jesus on earth, mentioned in the Book of Revelation. **3.** A period of joy, prosperity, and peace. [First written down before 1638 in Modern English : Latin *mīlle*, thousand + Latin *annus*, year.] **—mil•len′ni•al** *adj.*

mill•er (**mĭl′**ər) *n.* **1.** A person who owns or operates a mill for grinding grain. **2.** Any of various moths whose wings and body appear as though covered with flour.

mil•let (**mĭl′**ĭt) *n.* **1.** The grain or seeds of a cereal grass, widely used as a food grain in Asia and Europe. **2.** The plant that bears such grain, used as hay. [First written down before 1425 in Middle English and spelled *milet*, from Old French, from Latin *milium.*]

milli– *pref.* A prefix that means one thousandth: *millimeter.*

mil•li•bar (**mĭl′**ə bär′) *n.* A unit of atmospheric pressure.

mil•li•gram (**mĭl′**ĭ grăm′) *n.* A unit of mass or weight equal to one thousandth of a gram.

mil•li•li•ter (**mĭl′**ə lē′tər) *n.* A unit of fluid volume or capacity equal to one thousandth (10^{-3}) of a liter. See table at **measurement.**

mil•li•li•tre (**mĭl′**ə lē′tər) *n. Chiefly British.* Variant of **milliliter.**

mil•li•me•ter (**mĭl′**ə mē′tər) *n.* A unit of length equal to one thousandth (10^{-3}) of a meter. See table at **measurement.**

mil•li•me•tre (**mĭl′**ə mē′tər) *n. Chiefly British.* Variant of **millimeter.**

mil•li•ner (**mĭl′**ə nər) *n.* A person who makes, trims, designs, or sells women's hats.

mil•li•ner•y (**mĭl′**ə nĕr′ē) *n., pl.* **mil•li•ner•ies. 1.** Women's hats, including trimmings for hats. **2.** The business of making, designing, or selling women's hats.

mill•ing (**mĭl′**ĭng) *n.* **1.** The act or process of grinding, especially of grinding grain into flour or meal. **2.** The act or process of cutting ridges on the edges of coins. **3.** The ridges cut on the edges of coins.

mil•lion (**mĭl′**yən) *n., pl.* **million** or **mil•lions. 1.** The number, written as 10^6 or 1 followed by six zeros, that is equal to 1,000 × 1,000. **2.** An indefinitely large number: *There are millions of things to do in a big city.* [First written down before 1376 in Middle English and spelled *milion*, from Old French *milion*, from Latin *mīlle*, thousand.] **—mil′lion** *adj.* **—mil′lionth** *n.*

mil•lion•aire (mĭl′yə **nâr′**) *n.* A person whose wealth amounts to at least a million dollars or a similar amount in another currency.

mil•li•pede or **mil•le•pede** (**mĭl′**ə pēd′) *n.* Any of various small cylindrical animals resembling a centipede, having a body composed of many narrow segments, most of which have two pairs of legs.

mill•pond (**mĭl′**pŏnd′) *n.* A pond formed by a milldam, used to supply water to run a mill.

mill•race (**mĭl′**rās′) *n.* **1.** The fast-moving stream of

milkweed

Edna Saint Vincent Millay
Photographed in 1933

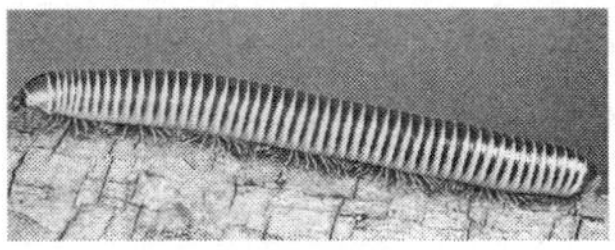

millipede

ă	**pat**	oi	**boy**
ā	**pay**	ou	**out**
âr	**care**	ŏŏ	**took**
ä	**father**	ōō	**boot**
ĕ	**pet**	ŭ	**cut**
ē	**be**	ûr	**urge**
ĭ	**pit**	th	**thin**
ī	**pie**	*th*	**this**
îr	**pier**	hw	**whoop**
ŏ	**pot**	zh	**vision**
ō	**toe**	ə	**about**
ô	**paw**	N	*French* **bon**

mill wheel

mimicry

For many organisms, their chances of survival are improved because they have evolved to imitate the looks, sounds, actions, or other characteristics of different organisms. **Mimicry**, the name for this imitation of one species by another, is common among insects. In one classic example, the viceroy butterfly is protected from being eaten by birds and other predators because its wing markings resemble the striking orange and black markings of the monarch butterfly. The monarch is a dangerous dinner for predators; it contains chemicals that make them so sick that they vomit and their hearts beat dangerously fast. The viceroy, on the other hand, makes a tasty meal, but because it looks like the monarch, predators tend to avoid it.

mine[1]
Coal mine

water that drives a mill wheel. **2.** The channel for the water that drives a mill wheel.

mill•stone (mĭl′stōn′) *n.* One of a pair of large cylindrical stones used to grind grain.

mill wheel *n.* A wheel, usually turned by moving water, that supplies the power for a mill.

mi•lord (mĭ **lôrd′**) *n.* Used to address an English nobleman or gentleman.

milque•toast (**mĭlk′**tōst′) *n.* A person who is meek or timid.

milt (mĭlt) *n.* The sperm cells of male fishes, together with the milky liquid containing them.

Mil•ton (mĭl′tən), **John.** 1608–1674. English poet who is best known for *Paradise Lost* (1667).

Mil•wau•kee (mĭl **wô′**kē). The largest city of Wisconsin, in the southeast part of the state on Lake Michigan. It was a major center of German immigration during the 19th century. Population, 628,088.

mime (mīm) *n.* **1.a.** Acting by means of gestures and movements without speech; pantomime. **b.** An actor in pantomime. **2.** A form of ancient Greek and Roman theatrical entertainment in which actual events and people were made fun of. *—v.* **mimed, mim•ing, mimes.** *—tr.* **1.** To act out (something) with gestures and body movements. **2.** To make fun of by imitation; mimic. *—intr.* To act as a mimic. [First written down in 1616 in Modern English, from Greek *mimos.*] **—mim′er** *n.*

mim•e•o•graph (**mĭm′**ē ə grăf′) *n.* **1.** A machine that makes copies of material that is written, drawn, or typed on a stencil. **2.** A copy made by such a machine. *—tr.v.* **mim•e•o•graphed, mim•e•o•graph•ing, mim•e•o•graphs.** To copy with a mimeograph.

mim•ic (**mĭm′**ĭk) *tr.v.* **mim•icked, mim•ick•ing, mim•ics. 1.** To copy or imitate closely, as in speech, expression, or gesture; ape: *Children often mimic the mannerisms of their parents.* See Synonyms at **imitate. 2.** To resemble closely; simulate: *an insect mimicking a twig.* **3.** To copy or imitate so as to ridicule; mock. *—n.* **1.** A person who imitates, especially a performer or comedian skilled in pantomime. **2.** A copy or imitation. *—adj.* **1.** Of or relating to mimicry; imitative: *the mimic utterances of a parrot.* **2.** Make-believe; mock: *Fire drills are mimic emergencies.* [First written down in 1687 in Modern English, from Greek *mimikos*, of mimes.]

mim•ic•ry (**mĭm′**ĭ krē) *n., pl.* **mim•ic•ries. 1.** The art or practice of mimicking. **2.** The resemblance of one organism to another or to an object in its surroundings for concealment or protection. —SEE NOTE.

mi•mo•sa (mĭ **mō′**sə *or* mĭ **mō′**zə) *n.* Any of various tropical trees or shrubs related to the pea, having leaves that resemble the fronds of a fern and clusters of small yellow, pink, or white flowers.

min. *abbr.* An abbreviation of: **1.** Minimum. **2.** Minute.

min•a•ret (mĭn′ə **rĕt′**) *n.* A tall slender tower on a mosque from which a muezzin summons the people to prayer. [First written down in 1682 in Modern English, from Turkish *minārat*, from Arabic *manārah*, lamp.]

mince (mĭns) *v.* **minced, minc•ing, minc•es.** *—tr.* **1.** To cut or chop into very small pieces. **2.** To change or make (words) less distressing, especially for the sake of politeness: *The doctor minced no words in describing the patient's condition.* *—intr.* To walk in an affected way or with very short steps. *—n.* Mincemeat. [First written down in 1381 in Middle English and spelled *mincen*, from Old French *mincier*, from Latin *minūtia*, smallness.]

mince•meat (**mĭns′**mēt′) *n.* A mixture of finely chopped fruit, spices, suet, and sometimes meat, used especially as a pie filling.

minc•ing (**mĭn′**sĭng) *adj.* Affecting a dainty or refined manner. **—minc′ing•ly** *adv.*

mind (mīnd) *n.* **1.** The human consciousness originating in the brain; the center of thought, perception, emotion, will, memory, and imagination. **2.** The power to think and reason: *Use your mind to solve the problem.* **3.** Focus of thought and attention: *Sometimes it's hard to keep your mind on your work.* **4.** Remembrance; memory: *Keep our invitation in mind.* **5.** Opinion or sentiment; attitude or point of view: *It's not too late to change your mind.* **6.** Desire; purpose: *had half a mind not to go.* **7.** A healthy mental condition; sanity: *lose one's mind.* **8.** A person of great intellect or intelligence: *Newton was one of the great minds of science.* *—v.* **mind•ed, mind•ing, minds.** *—tr.* **1.** To pay attention to; give heed: *Mind what I'm saying.* **2.** To obey: *The children were told to mind the baby sitter.* **3.** To be careful about: *Mind how you swing the hammer.* **4.** To take care of; look after: *stayed home to mind the baby.* **5.** To object to or dislike: *I don't mind mopping the floor.* *—intr.* **1.** To be troubled or concerned: *I don't mind if you borrow the car.* **2.** To behave obediently. **3.** To take notice; pay attention. ***—idiom.* of one mind.** In agreement: *We're of one mind about the proposed tunnel.* [First written down before 725 in Old English and spelled *gemynd.*]

mind-bog•gling (**mīnd′**bŏg′lĭng) *adj. Informal.* Overwhelming; perplexing: *was faced with a mind-boggling problem.*

mind•ed (**mīn′**dĭd) *adj.* **1.** Disposed; inclined: *Come over for a visit if you are so minded.* **2.** Having a specific kind of mind: *a strong-minded person.*

mind•ful (**mīnd′**fəl) *adj.* Attentive; heedful: *always mindful of the importance of reading.* **—mind′ful•ly** *adv.* **—mind′ful•ness** *n.*

mind•less (**mīnd′**lĭs) *adj.* **1.** Lacking intelligence; foolish. **2.** Having no purpose or meaning: *a mindless act.* **—mind′less•ly** *adv.*

mind reading *n.* The ability to know or discern another's thoughts through extrasensory means of communication; telepathy. **—mind reader** *n.*

mind•set or **mind-set** (**mīnd′**sĕt′) *n.* A particular attitude or disposition regarding a situation: *Thanks to his positive mindset, he was able to overcome the setback.*

mind's eye (mīndz) *n.* The ability to imagine or remember.

mine[1] (mīn) *n.* **1.** A hole or passage dug in the earth to extract metals, coal, salt, or other minerals: *a gold mine.* **2.** An abundant supply or source: *The encyclopedia is a mine of information.* **3.** A tunnel dug under enemy positions or fortifications, usually in order to place explosives and destroy them. **4.** An explosive device that can be buried in the ground or concealed in a body of water: *a land mine.* *—v.* **mined, min•ing, mines.** *—tr.* **1.a.** To extract (ores or minerals) from the earth. **b.** To dig or tunnel in (the earth) for this purpose. **2.** To place explosive mines in or under: *mine a harbor.* *—intr.* **1.** To dig in the earth to extract ore or minerals: *The company is mining for diamonds.* **2.** To work in a mine. **3.** To tunnel in the earth, especially under enemy fortifications. [First written down about 1303 in Middle English, from Old French, probably of Celtic origin.]

mine[2] (mīn) *pron. (used with a singular or plural verb).* The one or ones belonging to me: *Your car is different from mine.* *—adj. Archaic.* A possessive form of **I**[1]. Used instead of *my* before a vowel or the letter *h: mine eyes; mine honor.* [First written down about 725 in Old English and spelled *mīn.*]

min•er (mī′nər) *n.* A person who works in a mine, especially to extract ores or minerals from the earth.

❑ *These sound alike:* **miner, minor** (under legal age).

min•er•al (mĭn′ər əl) *n.* **1.** An inorganic solid substance found in nature that has a uniform chemical composition, a regular crystalline form, and a characteristic hardness and color. **2.** A substance, such as gold, iron ore, or stone, that is obtained by mining or quarrying. **3.** A substance that is neither animal nor vegetable. —*adj.* **1.** Of, resembling, or containing a mineral or minerals. **2.** Not animal or vegetable; inorganic. [First written down before 1393 in Middle English, from Medieval Latin *minerālis*, relating to mines.]

min•er•al•o•gy (mĭn′ə rŏl′ə jē *or* mĭn′ə răl′ə jē) *n.* The scientific study of minerals. —**min′er•a•log′i•cal** (mĭn′ər ə lŏj′ĭ kəl) *adj.* —**min′er•a•log′ical•ly** *adv.* —**min′er•al′o•gist** *n.*

mineral oil *n.* A colorless, odorless, tasteless oil distilled from petroleum and used in medicine as a laxative.

Mi•ner•va (mĭ nûr′və) *n.* In Roman mythology, the goddess of wisdom, who is identified with the Greek Athena.

min•e•stro•ne (mĭn′ĭ strō′nē) *n.* A soup containing vegetables, pasta, and herbs in a meat or vegetable broth.

min•gle (mĭng′gəl) *v.* **min•gled, min•gling, min•gles.** —*tr.* To mix or combine; unite: *The poem mingled passion and wit.* See Synonyms at **mix.** —*intr.* **1.** To become mixed or united. **2.** To associate or join with others: *The guests mingled freely at the party.*

min•i (mĭn′ē) *n., pl.* **min•is.** Something smaller or shorter than others of its kind. —**min′i** *adj.*

mini– *pref.* A prefix that means small: *minibike.*

min•i•a•ture (mĭn′ē ə chər *or* mĭn′ə chər) *n.* **1.** A copy or reproduction on a small scale: *The architects made a miniature of the proposed building.* **2.** A very small painting or portrait. —*adj.* Greatly reduced in size or scale. See Synonyms at **little.** [First written down before 1586 in Modern English, from Italian *miniare*, to illuminate manuscripts, from Latin *minium*, red lead.]

min•i•a•tur•ize (mĭn′ē ə chə rīz′ *or* mĭn′ə chə rīz′) *tr.v.* **min•i•a•tur•ized, min•i•a•tur•iz•ing, min•i•a•tur•iz•es.** To plan or make on a very small scale.

min•i•bike (mĭn′ē bīk′) *n.* A small motorcycle.

min•i•com•put•er (mĭn′ē kəm pyo͞o′tər) *n.* A small computer having more memory and speed than a microcomputer.

min•i•ma (mĭn′ə mə) *n.* A plural of **minimum.**

min•i•mal (mĭn′ə məl) *adj.* Smallest in amount or degree; least possible: *a task requiring minimal effort.* —**min′i•mal•ly** *adv.*

min•i•mize (mĭn′ə mīz′) *tr.v.* **min•i•mized, min•i•miz•ing, min•i•miz•es. 1.** To reduce to the smallest possible amount or degree: *In winter, we try to minimize the amount of heat that escapes our house.* **2.** To represent as having little importance, value, or size; depreciate. —**min′i•mi•za′tion** (mĭn′ə mĭ zā′shən) *n.* —**min′i•miz′er** *n.*

min•i•mum (mĭn′ə məm) *n., pl.* **min•i•mums** or **min•i•ma** (mĭn′ə mə). **1.** The smallest amount or degree possible: *We need a minimum of an hour to make dinner.* **2.** The lowest amount or degree reached or recorded: *The temperature's minimum yesterday was 45°.* —*adj.* Representing the least possible or the lowest amount or degree. [First written down in 1663 in Modern English, from Latin, from *minimus*, least.]

minimum wage *n.* The lowest wage, set by law or contract, that an employer may pay an employee for a specified job.

min•ing (mī′nĭng) *n.* **1.** The work, process, or business of extracting coal, minerals, or ore from the earth. **2.** The process of placing explosive mines.

min•ion (mĭn′yən) *n.* **1.** A person who follows or serves another in a slavish or servile manner. **2.** A person who is much loved or admired; a favorite.

min•i•skirt (mĭn′ē skûrt′) *n.* A short skirt with a hemline that falls above the knees.

min•is•ter (mĭn′ĭ stər) *n.* **1.** A person who is authorized to perform religious functions in a Christian church. **2.** A person in charge of a government department: *the minister of finance.* **3.** A diplomat ranking below an ambassador, who represents his or her government in a foreign country. —*intr.v.* **min•is•tered, min•is•ter•ing, min•is•ters.** To attend to another's needs; give aid or comfort: *The nurses ministered to the sick.* [First written down about 1300 in Middle English and spelled *ministre*, from Latin *minister*, servant.] —**min′is•te′ri•al** (mĭn′ĭ stîr′ē əl) *adj.* —**min′is•te′ri•al•ly** *adv.*

min•is•tra•tion (mĭn′ĭ strā′shən) *n.* **1.a.** The act or process of serving or aiding. **b.** The service or aid given. **2.** The act of performing the duties of a minister or cleric.

min•is•try (mĭn′ĭ strē) *n., pl.* **min•is•tries. 1.** The position and duties of a Christian minister or cleric. **2.** The Christian clergy considered as a group. **3.** A department of government under the charge of a minister. **4.** Governmental ministers in general. **5.** The act of serving or aiding.

mink

mink (mĭngk) *n., pl.* **mink** or **minks. 1.** Any of various mammals of North America that resemble the weasel, have thick soft brown fur, and live around water. **2.** The fur of this animal, often used to make or trim clothing. [First written down in 1431 in Middle English, possibly of Scandinavian origin.]

Minn. *abbr.* An abbreviation of Minnesota.

Min•ne•ap•o•lis (mĭn′ē ăp′ə lĭs). The largest city of Minnesota, in the southeast part of the state on the Mississippi River adjacent to St. Paul. It was a leading lumbering center in the 19th century. Population, 368,383.

Min•ne•so•ta (mĭn′ĭ sō′tə). A state of the northern United States north of Iowa and bordering on Lake Superior. It was admitted as the 32nd state in 1858. St. Paul is the capital and Minneapolis the largest city. Population, 4,387,029. —See Note.

Minnesota

The name for the state of **Minnesota** comes from a Dakota name that was first used for the Minnesota River. The name meant "cloudy water." The state was later named after the river.

min•now (mĭn′ō) *n., pl.* **minnow** or **min•nows.** Any of various small freshwater fishes often used as bait. [First written down before 1425 in Middle English and spelled *meneu.*]

Mi•no•an (mĭ nō′ən) *adj.* Of or relating to the Bronze Age culture that flourished in Crete from about 3000 to 1100 B.C. —*n.* A native or inhabitant of ancient Crete.

mi•nor (mī′nər) *adj.* **1.** Lesser or smaller in degree, size, or extent: *a minor change.* **2.** Lesser in importance or rank: *a minor role in the play.* **3.** Lesser in seriousness or danger: *a minor injury.* **4.** Not yet a legal adult: *minor children.* **5.a.** Relating to or based on a minor scale: *a minor key.* **b.** Of or relating to a musical tone that is smaller by a half step than a major interval: *a minor third.* —*n.* **1.** A person who is not yet the legal age of an adult. **2.** A secondary area of academic specialization: *graduated from college with a major in physics and a minor in philosophy.* **3.** A minor key, scale, or interval. **4. minors.** The minor leagues of a sport, especially baseball. —*intr.v.* **mi•nored, mi•nor•ing, mi•nors.** To pursue academic studies in a minor: *This year many students are minoring in history.*

ă	pat	oi	boy
ā	pay	ou	out
âr	care	o͝o	took
ä	father	o͞o	boot
ĕ	pet	ŭ	cut
ē	be	ûr	urge
ĭ	pit	th	thin
ī	pie	*th*	this
îr	pier	hw	whoop
ŏ	pot	zh	vision
ō	toe	ə	about
ô	paw	N	*French* bon

minor scale

minuteman

Statue of Capt. John Parker (1729–1775) in Lexington, Massachusetts, by Henry Kitson (1865–1947)

[First written down about 1410 in Middle English, from Latin.]

❑ *These sound alike:* **minor, miner** (mine worker).

Mi•nor•ca (mĭ nôr′kə). A Spanish island in the Balearics of the western Mediterranean Sea. It was a Loyalist stronghold in the Spanish Civil War.

mi•nor•i•ty (mə nôr′ĭ tē *or* mə nŏr′ĭ tē *or* mī nôr′ĭ tē *or* mī nŏr′ĭ tē) *n., pl.* **mi•nor•i•ties. 1.** The smaller in number of two groups forming a whole. **2.** A racial, religious, political, national, or other group regarded as different from a larger group of which it is a part. **3.** The state or period of being under legal age.

minor league *n.* In sports, a professional league that ranks below a major league.

Mi•nor Prophets (mī′nər) *n.* **1.** The Hebrew prophets Hosea, Joel, Amos, Obadiah, Jonah, Micah, Nahum, Habakkuk, Zephaniah, Haggai, Zechariah, and Malachi. **2.** The books of the Hebrew Scriptures relating the prophecies and experiences of these prophets.

minor scale *n.* A musical scale that has a half step instead of a whole step between the second and third tones as well as flatted sixth and seventh tones when played in descending order.

Mi•nos (mī′nəs *or* mī′nŏs′) *n.* In Greek mythology, a king of Crete who becomes a judge in the underworld after his death.

Min•o•taur (mĭn′ə tôr′ *or* mī′nə tôr′) *n.* In Greek mythology, a monster, half bull and half human, kept in the labyrinth in Crete until Theseus kills him.

Minsk (mĭnsk). The capital of Belorussia, in the central part of the republic. It was occupied (1941–1943) by German forces during World War II. Population, 1,472,000.

min•strel (mĭn′strəl) *n.* **1.** A medieval musician who traveled from place to place, singing and reciting poetry. **2.** A performer in a minstrel show.

minstrel show *n.* A comic variety show in which performers present songs, dances, and comic skits.

min•strel•sy (mĭn′strəl sē) *n.* **1.** The art or profession of a minstrel. **2.** The songs or verses sung or recited by minstrels.

mint[1] (mĭnt) *n.* **1.** A mint where the coins of a country are made by authority of the government. **2.** A large amount, especially of money: *That painting is worth a mint.* —*tr.v.* **mint•ed, mint•ing, mints. 1.** To produce (money) by stamping metal; coin. **2.** To invent; make up: *The scientist minted a name for the newly discovered chemical.* —*adj.* In original condition; undamaged: *an antique car in mint condition.* [First written down about 700 in Old English and spelled *mynet*, coin, from Latin *monēta*.]

mint[2] (mĭnt) *n.* **1.** Any of various plants, such as the spearmint and peppermint, having leaves with a strong pleasant smell and taste that yield an oil used as a flavoring. **2.** A candy flavored with mint. [First written down before 800 in Old English and spelled *minte*, from Latin *menta*.]

mint•age (mĭn′tĭj) *n.* **1.** The act or process of minting coins. **2.** Money manufactured in a mint. **3.** The fee paid to a mint by a government for which coins have been made. **4.** The impression stamped on a coin.

mint julep *n.* A drink made of bourbon or sometimes brandy or rum, sugar, mint leaves, and ice.

min•u•end (mĭn′yo͞o ĕnd′) *n.* A number from which another is to be subtracted; for example, in the expression 100 − 23 = 77, the minuend is 100.

min•u•et (mĭn′yo͞o ĕt′) *n.* **1.** A slow stately dance that originated in 17th-century France. **2.** Music for or in the rhythm of this dance.

Min•u•it (mĭn′yo͞o ĭt), **Peter.** 1580–1638. Dutch colonial administrator who purchased the island of Manhattan from Native Americans, supposedly for the equivalent of $24.

mi•nus (mī′nəs) *prep.* **1.** Reduced by the subtraction of; decreased by: *Seven minus four equals three.* **2.** *Informal.* Without; lacking: *We arrived at the theater minus our tickets.* —*adj.* **1.** Less than zero; negative: *a minus value.* **2.** Slightly lower or less than: *a grade of A minus.* —*n.* **1.** The minus sign. **2.** A negative number or quantity: *My answer was a minus in that problem.* **3.** A disadvantage or drawback: *The lack of good sports facilities at the camp was a minus.* [First written down about 1481 in Middle English, from Latin *minus*, from *minor*, less.]

min•us•cule (mĭn′ə skyo͞ol′ *or* mĭ nŭs′kyo͞ol′) *adj.* Very small; tiny.

minus sign *n.* The symbol −, as in 4 − 2 = 2, that is used to indicate subtraction or a negative quantity.

min•ute[1] (mĭn′ĭt) *n.* **1.** A unit of time equal to 1⁄60 of an hour or 60 seconds. **2.** A unit of angular measurement that is equal to 1⁄60 of a degree or 60 seconds. **3.** A short interval of time; a moment: *Wait a minute.* **4.** A specific point in time: *leaving this very minute.* **5. minutes.** An official record of the events or discussion at a meeting of an organization. [First written down about 1378 in Middle English, from Medieval Latin *(pars) minūta (prīma)*, (primary) small (part).]

mi•nute[2] (mī no͞ot′ *or* mī nyo͞ot′ *or* mĭ no͞ot′ *or* mĭ nyo͞ot′) *adj.* **1.** Exceptionally small; tiny. **2.** Not worth noticing; insignificant: *a minute problem.* **3.** Marked by close examination or careful study of small details: *a minute inspection.* [First written down in 1472 in Middle English, from Latin *minūtus*, diminished, tiny.] —**mi•nute′ly** *adv.* —**mi•nute′ness** *n.*

min•ute•man (mĭn′ĭt măn′) *n.* During the Revolutionary War in the United States, a member of the American militia pledged to be ready to answer a call to fight on a minute's notice.

mi•nu•ti•a (mĭ no͞o′shē ə *or* mĭ nyo͞o′shē ə) *n., pl.* **mi•nu•ti•ae** (mĭ no͞o′shē ē′ *or* mĭ nyo͞o′ shē ē′). A small or trivial detail.

minx (mĭngks) *n.* A girl or young woman who is considered high-spirited, bold, or flirtatious.

Mi•o•cene (mī′ə sēn′) *adj.* Of, belonging to, or being the geologic time of the fourth epoch of the Tertiary Period. During the Miocene, whales, grazing animals, and primitive apes developed. See table at **geologic time.** —*n.* The Miocene Epoch or its series of rocks.

mir•a•cle (mĭr′ə kəl) *n.* **1.** An event believed to be an act of god or of a supernatural power because it appears impossible to explain by the laws of nature. **2.** A person, a thing, or an event that causes great admiration, awe, or wonder: *surgical miracles.* See Synonyms at **wonder.** [First written down in 1137 in Middle English, from Latin *mīrāculum*, from *mīrārī*, to wonder at.]

miracle play *n.* A Christian religious drama of the Middle Ages that portrays miraculous events from the lives of saints and martyrs.

mi•rac•u•lous (mĭ răk′yə ləs) *adj.* **1.** Having the nature of a miracle: *a miraculous event.* **2.** Having the power to work miracles: *a miraculous drug.* —**mi•rac′u•lous•ly** *adv.* —**mi•rac′u•lous•ness** *n.*

mi•rage (mĭ räzh′) *n.* An optical illusion in which nonexistent bodies of water and upside-down reflections of distant objects are seen. It is caused by distortions that occur as light passes between layers of air that are at different temperatures. [First written down in 1812 in Modern English, from French, from *mirer*, to look at.]

mire (mīr) *n.* **1.** An area of wet muddy ground; a bog. **2.** Deep slimy soil or mud. —*v.* **mired, mir•ing, mires.** —*tr.* To cause to sink or become stuck in mire. —*intr.* To sink or become stuck in mire. [First written down in 1219 in Middle English, from Old Norse *mýrr*, bog.]

mir•ror (mĭr′ər) *n.* **1.** A surface that is capable of reflecting light so as to form an image of an object placed in front of it. **2.** Something that reflects or gives a true picture of something else: *The city's progress is a mirror of the nation's progress.* —*tr.v.* **mir•rored, mir•ror•ing, mir•rors.** To reflect in or as if in a mirror: *The lake mirrored the clouds.* [First written down about 1250 in Middle English and spelled *mirour*, from Old French *mireor*, from *mirer*, to look at.]

mirror image *n.* An image that is the exact likeness of another one, but is reversed like an image in a mirror.

mirth (mûrth) *n.* Gaiety or merriment: *shouts of mirth.*

mirth•ful (mûrth′fəl) *adj.* Full of gladness and gaiety; merry. —**mirth′ful•ly** *adv.*

mirth•less (mûrth′lĭs) *adj.* Showing no merriment. —**mirth′less•ly** *adv.*

mir•y (mīr′ē) *adj.* **mir•i•er, mir•i•est. 1.** Full of or resembling mire; swampy. **2.** Smeared with mud; muddy.

mis– *pref.* A prefix that means: **1.** Error or wrongness: *misspell.* **2.** Badness or impropriety: *misbehave.* **3.** Failure or lack of: *misfire; mistrust.* —SEE NOTE.

mis•ad•ven•ture (mĭs′əd vĕn′chər) *n.* An example of misfortune; a mishap.

mis•an•thrope (mĭs′ən thrōp′) *n.* A person who hates or distrusts humankind. [First written down in 1563 in Modern English, from Greek *misanthrōpos*, hating people : *misein*, to hate + *anthrōpos*, person.]

mis•an•throp•ic (mĭs′ən thrŏp′ĭk) *adj.* Of, relating to, or characteristic of a misanthrope. —**mis′an•throp′i•cal•ly** *adv.*

mis•an•thro•py (mĭs ăn′thrə pē) *n.* Hatred or distrust of mankind.

mis•ap•ply (mĭs′ə plī′) *tr.v.* **mis•ap•plied, mis•ap•ply•ing, mis•ap•plies.** To use or apply wrongly: *The word* horns *is often misapplied to include antlers.* —**mis•ap′pli•ca′tion** (mĭs ăp′lĭ kā′shən) *n.*

mis•ap•pre•hend (mĭs ăp′rĭ hĕnd′) *tr.v.* **mis•ap•pre•hend•ed, mis•ap•pre•hend•ing, mis•ap•pre•hends.** To fail to understand correctly; misunderstand: *misapprehend an order.* —**mis•ap′pre•hen′sion** (mĭs ăp′rĭ hĕn′shən) *n.*

mis•ap•pro•pri•ate (mĭs′ə prō′prē āt′) *tr.v.* **mis•ap•pro•pri•at•ed, mis•ap•pro•pri•at•ing, mis•ap•pro•pri•ates.** To take dishonestly for one's own use; embezzle: *misappropriate government funds.* —**mis′ap•pro′pri•a′tion** *n.*

mis•be•got•ten (mĭs′bĭ gŏt′n) *adj.* **1.** Of, relating to, or being a child born to unmarried parents. **2.** Not lawfully obtained: *misbegotten wealth.*

mis•be•have (mĭs′bĭ hāv′) *v.* **mis•be•haved, mis•be•hav•ing, mis•be•haves.** —*intr.* To behave badly. —*tr.* To behave or conduct (oneself) badly. —**mis′be•hav′ior** (mĭs′bĭ hāv′yər) *n.*

misc. *abbr.* An abbreviation of: **1.** Miscellaneous. **2.** Miscellany.

mis•cal•cu•late (mĭs kăl′kyə lāt′) *tr. & intr. v.* **mis•cal•cu•lat•ed, mis•cal•cu•lat•ing, mis•cal•cu•lates.** To calculate or estimate incorrectly. —**mis•cal′cu•la′tion** *n.*

mis•call (mĭs kôl′) *tr.v.* **mis•called, mis•call•ing, mis•calls.** To call by a wrong name.

mis•car•riage (mĭs′kăr′ĭj *or* mĭs kăr′ĭj) *n.* **1.** The birth of a fetus before it is developed enough to survive. **2.** Failure to achieve the proper or desired result: *the miscarriage of a plan.*

mis•car•ry (mĭs′kăr′ē *or* mĭs kăr′ē) *intr.v.* **mis•car•ried, mis•car•ry•ing, mis•car•ries. 1.** To have a miscarriage; abort. **2.** To fail; go wrong: *The plan miscarried.*

mis•cast (mĭs kăst′) *tr.v.* **mis•cast, mis•cast•ing, mis•casts.** To cast (a performer) in an unsuitable role.

mis•ceg•e•na•tion (mĭ sĕj′ə nā′shən *or* mĭs′ĭ jə nā′shən) *n.* Marriage between persons of different races.

mis•cel•la•ne•ous (mĭs′ə lā′nē əs) *adj.* **1.** Made up of a variety of different elements or ingredients: *a miscellaneous assortment of books.* **2.** Concerned with a variety of different subjects or aspects: *Encyclopedias contain miscellaneous information.* [First written down in 1637 in Modern English, from Latin *miscellus*, mixed.]

mis•cel•la•ny (mĭs′ə lā′nē) *n., pl.* **mis•cel•la•nies.** A collection of various items, parts, or ingredients.

mis•chance (mĭs chăns′) *n.* An unfortunate occurrence caused by chance or luck: *If by some mischance I should be late, please wait for me.*

mis•chief (mĭs′chĭf) *n.* **1.a.** Annoying or improper behavior. **b.** Damage, injury, or trouble resulting from such behavior. **2.** A tendency to play pranks or cause trouble. [First written down before 1300 in Middle English and spelled *mischef*, from Old French *meschever*, to end badly.]

mis•chie•vous (mĭs′chə vəs) *adj.* **1.** Causing mischief; naughty: *a mischievous child.* **2.** Showing a tendency to play pranks or tease: *a mischievous look on one's face.* **3.** Causing injury or damage: *a mischievous act.* —**mis′chie•vous•ly** *adv.* —**mis′chie•vous•ness** *n.*

mis•ci•ble (mĭs′ə bəl) *adj.* Capable of being mixed in all proportions: *Water and alcohol are miscible.*

mis•con•ceive (mĭs′kən sēv′) *tr.v.* **mis•con•ceived, mis•con•ceiv•ing, mis•con•ceives.** To interpret incorrectly; misunderstand.

mis•con•cep•tion (mĭs′kən sĕp′shən) *n.* A mistaken idea; a delusion.

mis•con•duct (mĭs kŏn′dŭkt) *n.* Improper conduct or behavior.

mis•con•strue (mĭs′kən stro͞o′) *tr.v.* **mis•con•strued, mis•con•stru•ing, mis•con•strues.** To mistake the meaning of; misinterpret: *misconstrue someone's words.*

mis•count (mĭs kount′) *v.* **mis•count•ed, mis•count•ing, mis•counts.** —*tr.* To count (something) incorrectly. —*intr.* To make an incorrect count. —*n.* (mĭs′kount′). An inaccurate count.

mis•cre•ant (mĭs′krē ənt) *n.* An evil person; a villain.

mis•deal (mĭs dēl′) *tr. & intr.v.* **mis•dealt** (mĭs dĕlt′), **mis•deal•ing, mis•deals.** To deal (playing cards) incorrectly. —**mis′deal′** *n.*

mis•deed (mĭs dēd′) *n.* A wrong or illegal act.

mis•de•mean•or (mĭs′dĭ mē′nər) *n.* In law, an offense less serious than a felony.

mis•did (mĭs dĭd′) *v.* Past tense of **misdo.**

mis•di•rect (mĭs′dĭ rĕkt′ *or* mĭs′dī rĕkt′) *tr.v.* **mis•di•rect•ed, mis•di•rect•ing, mis•di•rects. 1.** To give incorrect or inaccurate instructions to: *misdirect a tourist.* **2.** To put a wrong address on (a piece of mail): *misdirect a letter.* **3.** To aim badly. —**mis′di•rec′tion** *n.*

mis•do (mĭs do͞o′) *tr.v.* **mis•did** (mĭs dĭd′), **mis•done** (mĭs dŭn′), **mis•do•ing, mis•does** (mĭs dŭz′). To do wrongly or poorly. —**mis•do′ing** *n.*

mi•ser (mī′zər) *n.* A stingy person, especially one who lives poorly in order to hoard money. [First written down in 1542 in Modern English, from Latin *miser*, wretched.]

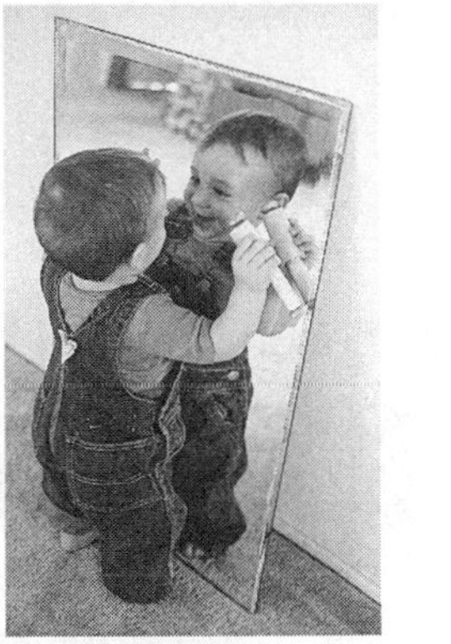

mirror

Word Building: mis–

The basic meaning of the prefix **mis–** is "bad; badly; wrong; wrongly." Thus **misfortune** means "bad fortune" and **misbehave** means "to behave badly." Likewise, a **misdeed** is "a wrong deed" and **misdo** means "to do wrongly." **Mis–** forms compounds primarily by attaching to verbs: *mishear, misremember.* **Mis–** also frequently forms compounds by attaching to nouns that come from verbs: **miscalculation, mismanagement, mispronunciation.** The prefix **mis–** can be traced back to Old English.

ă	pat	oi	boy
ā	pay	ou	out
âr	care	o͝o	took
ä	father	o͞o	boot
ĕ	pet	ŭ	cut
ē	be	ûr	urge
ĭ	pit	th	thin
ī	pie	*th*	this
îr	pier	hw	whoop
ŏ	pot	zh	vision
ō	toe	ə	about
ô	paw	N	*French* bon

mission
San Xavier del Bac Mission, near Tucson, Arizona

Mississippi

The state of **Mississippi** gets its name from the **Mississippi River.** Although the river was known by many different names in different regions, French explorers carried the Illinois name *Missisippi*, meaning "big river," from the northern part of the river south to the Gulf of Mexico. Eventually the entire course of the river came to be called Mississippi.

mis•er•a•ble (mĭz′ər ə bəl *or* mĭz′rə bəl) *adj.* **1.** Very unhappy or uncomfortable; wretched. **2.** Causing discomfort or unhappiness: *miserable weather.* **3.** Mean; shameful; disgraceful. **4.** Wretchedly poor or inadequate: *miserable food.* —**mis′er•a•bly** *adv.*

mi•ser•ly (mī′zər lē) *adj.* Of, relating to, or characteristic of a miser; stingy. —**mi′ser•li•ness** *n.*

mis•er•y (mĭz′ə rē) *n., pl.* **mis•er•ies. 1.** Prolonged suffering or distress. **2.** Miserable conditions of life; dire poverty. [First written down about 1375 in Middle English and spelled *miserie*, from Latin *miseria*, from *miser*, wretched.]

mis•fire (mĭs fīr′) *intr.v.* **mis•fired, mis•fir•ing, mis•fires. 1.** To fail to fire or go off: *The gun misfired.* **2.** To fail to achieve the desired result; go awry: *Their plan misfired.* —**mis′fire′** *n.*

mis•fit (mĭs′fĭt′ *or* mĭs fĭt′) *n.* **1.** Something, especially a garment, that does not fit properly. **2.** A person who has adjusted poorly to his or her situation in life or does not get along well with others.

mis•for•tune (mĭs fôr′chən) *n.* **1.** Bad luck or fortune. **2.** An unfortunate occurrence: *The hurricane was a great misfortune for the fishing industry.*

mis•giv•ing (mĭs gĭv′ĭng) *n.* A feeling of doubt or concern: *We had misgivings about using our savings to buy a new car.*

mis•gov•ern (mĭs gŭv′ərn) *tr.v.* **mis•gov•erned, mis•gov•ern•ing, mis•gov•erns.** To govern or rule badly. —**mis•gov′ern•ment** *n.*

mis•guide (mĭs gīd′) *tr.v.* **mis•guid•ed, mis•guid•ing, mis•guides.** To give wrong or misleading directions to; lead astray. —**mis•guid′ance** *n.*

mis•guid•ed (mĭs gī′dĭd) *adj.* Acting or done out of mistaken or unrealistic opinions or beliefs: *misguided efforts.* —**mis•guid′ed•ly** *adv.*

mis•han•dle (mĭs hăn′dl) *tr.v.* **mis•han•dled, mis•han•dling, mis•han•dles. 1.** To handle roughly: *mishandle a parcel in the mail.* **2.** To manage badly: *mishandle money.*

mis•hap (mĭs′hăp′ *or* mĭs hăp′) *n.* **1.** Bad luck. **2.** An unfortunate accident: *The trip was completed without mishap.*

mish•mash (mĭsh′măsh′) *n.* A random mixture of unrelated things; a hodgepodge.

mis•in•form (mĭs′ĭn fôrm′) *tr.v.* **mis•in•formed, mis•in•form•ing, mis•in•forms.** To give wrong or inaccurate information to. —**mis•in′for•ma′tion** (mĭs ĭn′fər mā′shən) *n.*

mis•in•ter•pret (mĭs′ĭn tûr′prĭt) *tr.v.* **mis•in•ter•pret•ed, mis•in•ter•pret•ing, mis•in•ter•prets.** To interpret or explain incorrectly: *misinterpret someone's remarks.* —**mis′in•ter′pre•ta′tion** *n.*

mis•judge (mĭs jŭj′) *v.* **mis•judged, mis•judg•ing, mis•judg•es.** —*tr.* To judge incorrectly: *misjudge a person.* —*intr.* To be wrong in judging something. —**mis•judg′ment** *n.*

mis•lay (mĭs lā′) *tr.v.* **mis•laid** (mĭs lād′), **mis•lay•ing, mis•lays. 1.** To lay or put down in a place one cannot remember. **2.** To place or put down incorrectly: *They mislaid the carpet.*

mis•lead (mĭs lēd′) *tr.v.* **mis•led** (mĭs lĕd′), **mis•lead•ing, mis•leads. 1.** To lead or guide in the wrong direction: *The sign at the traffic circle completely misled us.* **2.** To lead into error of thought or wrongdoing, especially by intentional deception.

mis•lead•ing (mĭs lē′dĭng) *adj.* Tending to mislead: *misleading information.*

mis•led (mĭs lĕd′) *v.* Past tense of **mislead.**

mis•man•age (mĭs măn′ĭj) *tr.v.* **mis•man•aged, mis•man•ag•ing, mis•man•ag•es.** To manage badly or ineptly. —**mis•man′age•ment** *n.*

mis•match (mĭs măch′) *tr.v.* **mis•matched, mis•match•ing, mis•match•es.** To match in an unsuitable way: *The two teams are mismatched.* —*n.* (mĭs′măch′ *or* mĭs măch′). An unsuitable match.

mis•no•mer (mĭs nō′mər) *n.* **1.** An error in naming a person or place. **2.** A name or designation wrongly or unsuitably applied: *To call a whale "a fish" is to use a misnomer.* [First written down in 1455 in Middle English and spelled *misnoumer*, from Old French *mesnomer*, to misname.]

mi•sog•y•nist (mĭ sŏj′ə nĭst) *n.* A person who hates women.

mis•place (mĭs plās′) *tr.v.* **mis•placed, mis•plac•ing, mis•plac•es. 1.** To put in a wrong place. **2.** To mislay; lose: *misplace one's keys.* **3.** To place (trust, for example) in an improper or unworthy person or idea.

mis•play (mĭs plā′ *or* mĭs′plā′) *n.* A mistaken action in a game or sport. —*tr.v.* (mĭs plā′). **mis•played, mis•play•ing, mis•plays.** To make a misplay of.

mis•print (mĭs prĭnt′) *tr.v.* **mis•print•ed, mis•print•ing, mis•prints.** To print incorrectly. —*n.* (mĭs′prĭnt′ *or* mĭs prĭnt′). An error in printing.

mis•pro•nounce (mĭs′prə nouns′) *tr.v.* **mis•pro•nounced, mis•pro•nounc•ing, mis•pro•nounc•es.** To pronounce incorrectly.

mis•quote (mĭs kwōt′) *tr.v.* **mis•quot•ed, mis•quot•ing, mis•quotes.** To quote incorrectly. —**mis′quo•ta′tion** *n.*

mis•read (mĭs rēd′) *tr.v.* **mis•read** (mĭs rĕd′), **mis•read•ing, mis•reads. 1.** To read incorrectly: *misread a sign.* **2.** To draw the wrong conclusion from; misinterpret: *I misread your nod to mean "yes."*

mis•rep•re•sent (mĭs rĕp′rĭ zĕnt′) *tr.v.* **mis•rep•re•sent•ed, mis•rep•re•sent•ing, mis•rep•re•sents.** To represent in a false or misleading manner: *The newspaper misrepresented the mayor's statements.* —**mis•rep′re•sen•ta′tion** *n.*

mis•rule (mĭs ro͞ol′) *n.* Incompetent or unjust rule. —*tr.v.* **mis•ruled, mis•rul•ing, mis•rules.** To rule incompetely or unjustly.

miss¹ (mĭs) *v.* **missed, miss•ing, miss•es.** —*tr.* **1.** To fail to hit, catch, or make contact with: *The ball missed the basket.* **2.** To fail to see or notice: *We missed the television special last night.* **3.** To fail to attend or be present for: *never missed a day of school.* **4.** To fail to meet: *We missed each other by seconds.* **5.** To fail to understand or grasp: *You're missing my point.* **6.** To fail to accomplish: *just missed winning the race.* **7.** To be late for; not reach on time: *miss a bus.* **8.** To fail to answer correctly; get wrong: *I missed two questions on the test.* **9.** To let slip by; fail to benefit from: *miss one's turn.* **10.** To feel or regret the absence or loss of: *I miss my home town.* **11.** To notice the absence or loss of: *After we left the theater I missed my coat.* **12.** To avoid or escape: *If you go that way, you'll miss most of the traffic.* **13.** To lack: *The book is missing a few pages.* —*intr.* **1.** To fail to hit or make contact with something. **2.** To be unsuccessful; fail. —*n.* A failure to hit, succeed, or find. —***idioms.*** **miss out on.** To lose a chance for: *Don't miss out on this great opportunity.* **miss the boat.** *Informal.* To fail to take advantage of an opportunity. **miss the mark. 1.** To set a goal and fail to fulfill it. **2.** To fail to be correct or exact. [First written down about 725 in Old English and spelled *missan.*]

miss² (mĭs) *n.* **1.** *Informal.* A title of courtesy used before the last name or full name of an unmarried woman or girl. **2. Miss.** Used as a form of polite address for a young woman or girl: *I beg your pardon, miss.* **3.** An unmarried woman or girl. **4. misses.** A range of clothing sizes for girls and women. [First written down in 1645 in Modern English, short for *mistress.*] —SEE NOTE at **Ms.**

Miss. *abbr.* An abbreviation of Mississippi.

mis•sal (mĭs′əl) *n.* A book containing all the prayers and responses necessary for celebrating the Roman

Catholic Mass throughout the year. [First written down before 1300 in Middle English and spelled *messel*, from Medieval Latin *missāle*, from Late Latin *missa*, Mass.]

❑ *These sound alike:* **missal, missile** (weapon).

mis•shape (mĭs shāp′) *tr.v.* **mis•shaped** or **mis•shap•en** (mĭs shā′pən), **mis•shap•ing, mis•shapes.** To shape badly; deform.

mis•sile (mĭs′əl *or* mĭs′īl′) *n.* **1.** An object or a weapon that is thrown, fired, dropped, or otherwise launched at a target. **2.** A guided missile. **3.** A ballistic missile. [First written down in 1656 in Modern English, from Latin *missilis*, throwable, from *mittere*, to let go, throw.]

❑ *These sound alike:* **missile, missal** (prayer book).

miss•ing (mĭs′ĭng) *adj.* **1.** Lost: *missing persons.* **2.** Not present; absent: *Who is missing from class today?* **3.** Lacking; wanting: *Several pages are missing from the book.*

mis•sion (mĭsh′ən) *n.* **1.** An assignment that a person or group of persons is sent to carry out; a task: *a rescue mission.* **2.** A combat operation, especially a flight into a combat zone by military aircraft. **3.** Something that a person assumes to be the main task of his or her life: *My mission in life is to become a teacher.* **4.** A permanent diplomatic office in a foreign country. **5.** A body of persons sent to a foreign land, especially by a Christian organization to spread its religion or provide educational, medical, or other assistance. **6.** An establishment of missionaries in some territory or foreign country: *Los Angeles started as a small Spanish mission.* [First written down in 1598 in Modern English, from Latin *missiō*, a sending, from *mittere*, to send.]

mis•sion•ar•y (mĭsh′ə nĕr′ē) *n., pl.* **mis•sion•ar•ies.** A person sent, especially by a Christian organization, to do religious or charitable work in a territory or foreign country.

Mis•sis•sip•pi (mĭs′ĭ sĭp′ē). A state of the southeast United States west of Alabama. It was admitted as the 20th state in 1817. Jackson is the capital and the largest city. Population, 2,586,443. —See Note.

Mis•sis•sip•pi•an (mĭs′ĭ sĭp′ē ən) *adj.* Of, belonging to, or being the geologic time of the fifth period of the Paleozoic Era. During the Mississippian, much of the Earth was covered by shallow seas. See table at **geologic time.** —*n.* The Mississippian Period or its series of rocks.

Mississippi River. The chief river of the United States, rising in northern Minnesota and flowing about 2,350 miles (3,781 kilometers) generally southward to enter the Gulf of Mexico through a huge delta in southeast Louisiana.

mis•sive (mĭs′ĭv) *n.* A letter or message.

Mis•sou•ri[1] (mĭ zŏŏr′ē) *n., pl.* **Missouri** or **Mis•sou•ris. 1.** A member of a Native American people formerly living in Missouri, with present-day descendants in Oklahoma. **2.** The Siouan language of the Missouri.

Mis•sou•ri[2] (mĭ zŏŏr′ē *or* mĭ zŏŏr′ə). A state of the central United States east of Kansas. It was admitted as the 24th state in 1821. Jefferson City is the capital and St. Louis the largest city. Population, 5,137,804. —See Note.

Missouri River. A river of the United States rising in the Rocky Mountains of southwest Montana. The longest river in the United States, it flows about 2,565 miles (4,127 kilometers) to the Mississippi River north of St. Louis, Missouri.

mis•speak (mĭs spēk′) *tr. & intr.v.* **mis•spoke** (mĭs-spōk′), **mis•spo•ken** (mĭs spō′kən), **mis•speak•ing, mis•speaks.** To pronounce or speak incorrectly: *misspeak one's lines.*

mis•spell (mĭs spĕl′) *tr.v.* **mis•spelled** or **mis•spelt** (mĭs spĕlt′), **mis•spell•ing, mis•spells.** To spell incorrectly.

mis•spend (mĭs spĕnd′) *tr.v.* **mis•spent** (mĭs-spĕnt′), **mis•spend•ing, mis•spends.** To spend improperly, foolishly, or wastefully; squander.

mis•spoke (mĭs spōk′) *v.* Past tense of **misspeak.**

mis•spo•ken (mĭs spō′kən) *v.* Past participle of **misspeak.**

mis•state (mĭs stāt′) *tr.v.* **mis•stat•ed, mis•stat•ing, mis•states.** To state wrongly or falsely. —**mis•state′ment** *n.*

mis•step (mĭs stĕp′) *n.* **1.** A misplaced or awkward step. **2.** A mistake in action or conduct.

miss•y (mĭs′ē) *n., pl.* **miss•ies.** *Informal.* Used as a familiar form of address for a young woman or girl.

mist (mĭst) *n.* **1.** A mass of tiny droplets of water in the air, close to or touching the earth. **2.** Water vapor that condenses on and clouds a surface: *mist on a windowpane.* **3.** A mass of tiny drops of a liquid, such as perfume, sprayed into the air. **4.** Something that dims or obscures; a haze. —*v.* **mist•ed, mist•ing, mists.** —*intr.* **1.** To be or become obscured or blurred by mist. **2.** To rain in a fine shower: *It began to mist at four o'clock.* —*tr.* To conceal or cloud with or as if with mist.

mis•take (mĭ stāk′) *n.* An error or a fault resulting from poor judgment, ignorance, or carelessness. —*tr.v.* **mis•took** (mĭ stŏŏk′), **mis•tak•en** (mĭ stā′kən), **mis•tak•ing, mis•takes. 1.** To understand incorrectly; misinterpret: *mistook politeness as friendliness.* **2.** To recognize or identify incorrectly: *mistook satin for silk.* [First written down in 1638 in Modern English, from Middle English *mistaken*, to do wrong, from Old Norse *mistaka*, to take wrongly.]

mis•tak•en (mĭ stā′kən) *adj.* Wrong; in error: *If I am not mistaken, you were last here a year ago.* —**mis•tak′en•ly** *adv.*

Mis•ter (mĭs′tər) *n.* **1.** Used as a courtesy title before the last name or full name of a man. **2. mister.** *Informal.* Used as a form of polite address for a man: *Do you need directions to town, mister?* [First written down in 1447 in Middle English, alteration of *master*.]

mis•tle•toe (mĭs′əl tō′) *n.* **1.** A plant that grows as a parasite on trees and has leathery evergreen leaves and white berries. **2.** A sprig of this plant, often used as a Christmas decoration. [First written down about 1000 in Old English and spelled *misteltān*, mistletoe twig.]

mis•took (mĭ stŏŏk′) *v.* Past tense of **mistake.**

Mis•tral (mĭ sträl′ *or* mē sträl′), **Gabriela.** 1889–1957. Chilean poet who won the 1945 Nobel Prize for literature.

mis•treat (mĭs trēt′) *tr.v.* **mis•treat•ed, mis•treat•ing, mis•treats.** To treat badly or inconsiderately; abuse. —**mis•treat′ment** *n.*

mis•tress (mĭs′trĭs) *n.* **1.** A woman in a position of authority, control, or ownership, as the head of a household. **2.** A woman owner of an animal or a slave. **3.** A nation or country that has dominance over others. **4.** A man's female lover. **5. Mistress.** Used formerly as a courtesy title and form of address for a woman.

mis•tri•al (mĭs trī′əl *or* mĭs trīl′) *n.* **1.** A trial declared invalid because of a procedural problem or error. **2.** A trial in which the jurors fail to agree on a verdict.

mis•trust (mĭs trŭst′) *n.* Lack of trust; suspicion; doubt. See Synonyms at **uncertainty.** —*tr.v.* **mis•trust•ed, mis•trust•ing, mis•trusts.** To have no trust in; regard with suspicion: *mistrust stangers.* —**mis•trust′ful** *adj.* —**mis•trust′ful•ly** *adv.*

mist•y (mĭs′tē) *adj.* **mist•i•er, mist•i•est. 1.** Consisting of, filled with, or covered by mist: *a misty*

Missouri[2]

The name **Missouri** comes through French from the Illinois name for a Native American people who lived near the **Missouri River**. The name means "those with dug-out canoes."

mistletoe

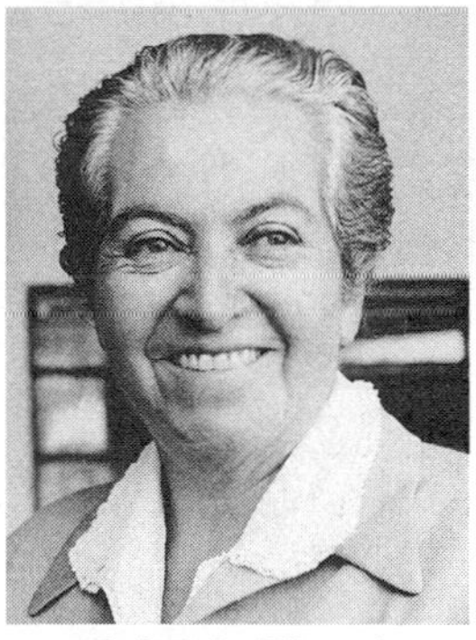

Gabriela Mistral
Photographed in 1948

ă	pat	oi	boy
ā	pay	ou	out
âr	care	ŏŏ	took
ä	father	ōō	boot
ĕ	pet	ŭ	cut
ē	be	ûr	urge
ĭ	pit	th	thin
ī	pie	*th*	this
îr	pier	hw	whoop
ŏ	pot	zh	vision
ō	toe	ə	about
ô	paw	N	*French* bon

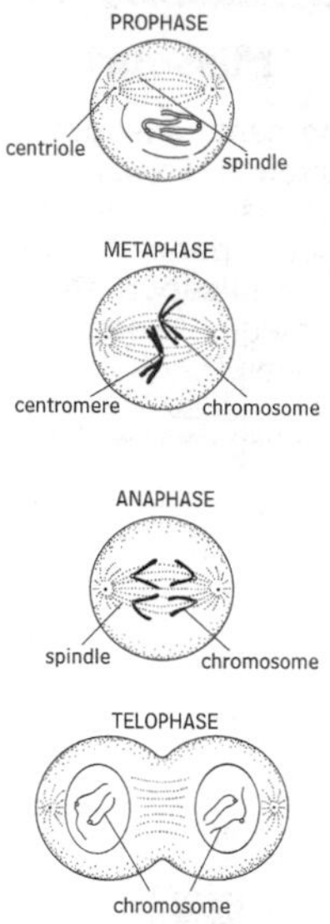

mitosis

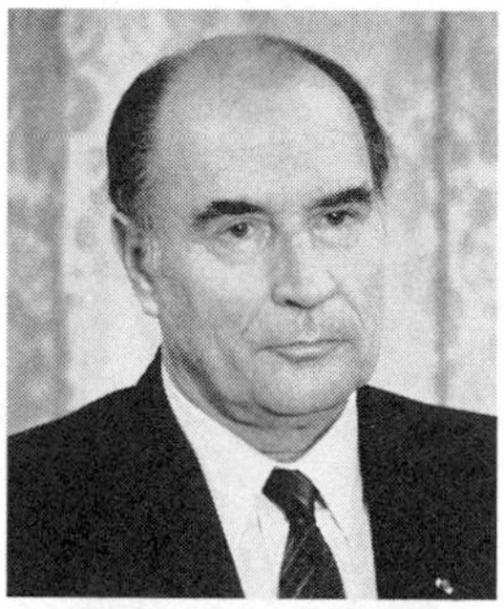
François Mitterrand
Photographed in 1981

morning. **2.** Full of emotion; sentimental. **3.** Obscured by or as by mist; vague: *misty recollections.* **—mist′i•ly** *adv.* **—mist′i•ness** *n.*

mis•un•der•stand (mĭs′ŭn dər **stănd′**) *tr.v.* **mis•un•der•stood** (mĭs′ŭn dər **sto͝od′**), **mis•un•der•stand•ing, mis•un•der•stands.** To understand incorrectly or imperfectly.

mis•un•der•stand•ing (mĭs′ŭn dər **stăn′**dĭng) *n.* **1.** A failure to understand. **2.** A quarrel or disagreement.

mis•un•der•stood (mĭs′ŭn dər **sto͝od′**) *v.* Past tense of **misunderstand.**

mis•use (mĭs **yo͞os′**) *n.* Wrong or improper use: *the misuse of language.* —*tr.v.* (mĭs **yo͞oz′**). **mis•used, mis•us•ing, mis•us•es. 1.** To use wrongly or incorrectly: *misuse a word in a sentence.* **2.** To make improper use of; abuse: *Let's not misuse our natural resources.*

Mitch•ell (**mĭch′**əl), **Maria.** 1818–1889. American astronomer and educator noted for her study of sunspots and for the discovery of a comet (1847).

mite[1] (mīt) *n.* Any of various very small animals related to spiders. Mites often live as parasites on other animals or plants. [First written down about 1000 in Old English and spelled *mīte,* moth, worm, louse.]

❑ *These sound alike:* **mite[1]** (small animal), **mite[2]** (small amount of money), **might[1]** (power), **might[2]** (past tense of may[1]).

mite[2] (mīt) *n.* **1.** A small amount of money, especially one given as a contribution. **2.** A coin of very small value. **3.** A very small creature or object. [First written down before 1375 in Middle English, from Middle Dutch and Middle Low German *mīte,* a small Flemish coin, tiny animal.]

❑ *These sound alike:* **mite[2]** (small amount of money), **mite[1]** (small animal), **might[1]** (power), **might[2]** (past tense of may).

mi•ter (**mī′**tər) *n.* **1.** A tall pointed hat worn by a Christian bishop as a mark of office. **2.a.** A miter joint. **b.** The edge of a piece of material that has been beveled in order to make a miter joint. —*tr.v.* **mi•tered, mi•ter•ing, mi•ters.** To join with a miter joint.

miter box *n.* A device for guiding a handsaw, consisting of two upright sides joined at the bottom and having narrow slots for the saw.

miter joint *n.* A joint made by fitting together two beveled surfaces to form a right angle.

mit•i•gate (**mĭt′**ĭ gāt′) *tr.v.* **mit•i•gat•ed, mit•i•gat•ing, mit•i•gates.** To make less severe or intense; moderate: *The judge mitigated the sentence.* **—mit′i•ga′tion** *n.*

mi•to•chon•dri•on (mī′tə **kŏn′**drē ən) *n., pl.* **mi•to•chon•dri•a** (mī′tə **kŏn′**drē ə). Any of certain microscopic structures found in the cytoplasm of almost all living cells, containing enzymes that act in converting food to usable energy.

mi•to•sis (mī **tō′**sĭs) *n., pl.* **mi•to•ses** (mī **tō′**sēz). **1.** The process in cell division in which the nucleus of a cell divides, producing two new nuclei, each having the same genetic material as the original cell. **2.** A cell division in which this process occurs.

mitt (mĭt) *n.* **1.** A large padded leather glove worn to protect the hand when catching a baseball. **2.** A mitten. **3.** *Slang.* A hand or fist. **4.** A woman's glove that does not fully cover the fingers.

mit•ten (**mĭt′**n) *n.* A covering for the hand, with a separate section for the thumb and one wide section for all four fingers. [First written down about 1390 in Middle English and spelled *mitein,* from Old French *mitaine.*]

Mit•ter•rand (mē′tə **ränd′** *or* mē′tə **räɴ′**), **François Maurice.** Born 1916. President of France (since 1981).

mix (mĭks) *v.* **mixed, mix•ing, mix•es.** —*tr.* **1.** To blend into a single mass, as by pouring, stirring, or shaking: *mix flour, water, and eggs to form dough.* **2.** To make or create by combining different ingredients: *mix cement.* **3.** To combine or join: *mix joy with sorrow.* **4.** To bring into social contact: *The new league mixes boys with girls on the teams.* —*intr.* **1.** To become or be capable of being mixed or blended together: *Oil does not mix with water.* **2.** To associate socially; mingle. **3.** To become involved: *Don't mix in with their argument.* —*n.* **1.** An act of mixing. **2.** A mixture, especially of ingredients packaged and sold commercially: *a brownie mix.* ***—idiom.*** **mix up. 1.** To confuse; confound: *Your directions only mixed us up even more.* **2.** To involve, concern, or implicate: *mixed up in the robbery.* [First written down in 1538 in Modern English, from Middle English *mixt,* mixed, from Latin *mixtus.*]

Synonyms: **mix, blend, merge, fuse, mingle.** These verbs mean to put into or come together in one mass. **Mix** is the most general term: *Julie mixed the blue and yellow paints together on her palette.* **Blend** means to mix thoroughly so that the parts lose their separate characteristics: *They blend coffee and cocoa beans together to make a special mocha drink.* **Merge** means to absorb one thing into another to make a new whole: *Two different rivers merge to form the Nile.* **Fuse** means to make a strong union by merging: *Rust had fused the screw to the metal.* **Mingle** often means to mix without changing the component parts: *They mingled the vinegar and oil in the bowl.*
Antonym: separate.

---

mixed (mĭkst) *adj.* **1.** Blended together into one mass: *mixed baby formula.* **2.** Composed of various elements: *a mixed reaction from the critics.* **3.** Composed of people of different sex, race, or social class.

mixed bag *n.* A collection of dissimilar things; an assortment.

mixed metaphor *n.* A succession of metaphors whose literal meanings form a contradictory or illogical combination, thus producing an absurd effect; for example, *Lying down on the job left me out on a limb* is a mixed metaphor.

mixed number *n.* A number, such as $7\frac{3}{8}$, consisting of a whole number and a fraction.

mix•er (**mĭk′**sər) *n.* **1.** A device that mixes or blends ingredients, especially by mechanical action: *a cement mixer.* **2.** A sociable person who mingles easily with others.

mix•ture (**mĭks′**chər) *n.* **1.** A combination of different ingredients, things, or kinds: *a mixture of roses and carnations in the vase.* **2.** Something made up of substances that are not chemically combined: *Air is a mixture of several gases.* **3.** The act or process of mixing.

mix-up also **mix•up** (**mĭks′**ŭp′) *n.* A state of confusion; a misunderstanding: *a mix-up over the starting time of the game.*

miz•zen (**mĭz′**ən) *n.* **1.** A fore-and-aft sail set on the mizzenmast. **2.** A mizzenmast.

miz•zen•mast or **miz•en•mast** (**mĭz′** ən-məst *or* **mĭz′**ən măst′) *n.* The third mast aft on sailing ships carrying three or more masts.

mks or **MKS** *abbr.* An abbreviation of meter-kilogram second.

ml or **mL** *abbr.* An abbreviation of milliliter.

Mlle. *abbr.* An abbreviation of Mademoiselle.

Mlles. *abbr.* An abbreviation of Mesdemoiselles.

mm *abbr.* An abbreviation of millimeter.

Mme. *abbr.* An abbreviation of Madame.

Mmes. *abbr.* An abbreviation of Mesdames.

Mn The symbol for the element **manganese.**

mne•mon•ic (nĭ **mŏn′**ĭk) *adj.* Relating to or assisting the memory. —*n.* Something, such as a formula or rhyme, that helps one to remember something; for example, *i before e except after c* is a mnemonic.

Mo The symbol for the element **molybdenum.**

MO or **Mo.** *abbr.* An abbreviation of Missouri.

mo. *abbr.* An abbreviation of month.

m.o. or **M.O.** *abbr.* An abbreviation of **1.** Medical Officer. **2.** Also **MO.** Money order.

mo•a (mō′ə) *n.* Any of various large extinct birds of New Zealand that resembled the ostrich.

moan (mōn) *n.* **1.** A low, drawn-out, mournful sound, usually of sorrow or pain. **2.** A similar sound: *the moan of the wind.* —*v.* **moaned, moan•ing, moans.** —*intr.* **1.** To utter a moan or moans. **2.** To make a sound resembling a moan: *The wind moaned in the chimney.* **3.** To complain, lament, or grieve: *They moaned about the lost opportunity.* —*tr.* To utter with a moan or moans: *"We can't seem to win a game," moaned the coach.*

moat (mōt) *n.* A wide deep ditch, usually filled with water, especially one surrounding a medieval town or fortress. [First written down in 1300 in Middle English and spelled *mote,* from Old French *mote,* mound, or Medieval Latin *mota.*]

❑ *These sound alike:* **moat, mote** (dust speck).

mob (mŏb) *n.* **1.** A large disorderly crowd. **2.** The mass of common people. **3.** Often **Mob.** Organized crime. —*tr.v.* **mobbed, mob•bing, mobs. 1.** To crowd around and jostle or annoy, especially in anger or enthusiasm: *Autograph seekers mobbed the stars.* **2.** To crowd into or jam (a place): *Visitors mobbed the museum.*

mo•bile (mō′bəl *or* mō′bēl′ *or* mō′bīl′) *adj.* **1.** Capable of moving or being moved from place to place: *a mobile hospital.* **2.** Capable of moving or changing easily: *mobile features.* **3.** Fluid or flowing freely: *Mercury is a mobile metal.* **4.** Allowing relatively easy movement from one social class to another: *a mobile society.* —*n.* (mō′bēl′). A type of sculpture consisting of parts that move, especially in response to air currents. [First written down in 1490 in Middle English, from Latin *mōbilis,* from *movēre,* to move.] **—mo•bil′i•ty** (mō bĭl′ĭ tē) *n.*

Mo•bile (mō **bēl′** *or* mō′bēl′). A city of southwest Alabama on **Mobile Bay,** an arm of the Gulf of Mexico. The Battle of Mobile Bay (August 1864) was a major Union victory in the Civil War. Population, 196,278.

mobile home *n.* A house trailer that is used as a permanent house and is usually hooked up to utilities.

mo•bi•lize (mō′bə līz′) *v.* **mo•bi•lized, mo•bi•liz•ing, mo•bi•liz•es.** —*tr.* **1.** To assemble or prepare for war or a similar emergency: *mobilize troops.* **2.** To assemble or coordinate for a particular purpose: *mobilize public opinion to support the campaign.* —*intr.* To become prepared for or as if for war. **—mo′bi•li•za′tion** (mō′bə lĭ **zā′**shən) *n.*

Mö•bi•us strip (mœ′bē əs *or* mō′bē əs) *n.* A mathematical surface having a single surface and a single edge. It can be represented as a model by taking a strip of paper, twisting one end through 180°, and attaching it to the other end. [First written down in 1904 in Modern English and spelled *Möbius' strip,* after August Ferdinand *Möbius* (1790–1868), German mathematician.]

mob•ster (mŏb′stər) *n. Informal.* A member of a criminal gang.

moc•ca•sin (mŏk′ə sĭn) *n.* **1.** A soft leather slipper, originally worn by Native Americans. **2.** A shoe resembling a moccasin. **3.** The water moccasin. [First written down in 1612 in American English, of Virginian Algonquian origin.]

moccasin flower *n.* The lady's slipper.

mo•cha (mō′kə) *n.* **1.** A rich Arabian coffee. **2.** A flavoring made of coffee, often mixed with chocolate. [First written down in 1773 in Modern English, after *Mocha,* a town of southwest Yemen.]

mock (mŏk) *v.* **mocked, mock•ing, mocks.** —*tr.* **1.** To make fun of, often by imitating or depicting in an insulting way; ridicule. **2.** To treat with scorn or contempt; deride. —*intr.* To express contempt; scoff. —*adj.* Simulated; false; sham: *a mock battle.* **—mock′er** *n.*

mock•er•y (mŏk′ə rē) *n., pl.* **mock•er•ies. 1.** Ridicule; derision. **2.** An object of ridicule. **3.** A false, offensive, or ridiculous imitation of something: *The trial was a mockery of justice.*

mock•ing•bird (mŏk′ĭng bûrd′) *n.* Any of several birds of the southern and eastern United States that often imitate the songs of other birds.

mock orange *n.* Any of numerous shrubs or trees having flowers or fruit resembling those of an orange.

mock•up also **mock-up** (mŏk′ŭp′) *n.* A full-sized model, as of an airplane or a building, used for demonstration, study, or testing.

mod•al (mōd′l) *adj.* **1.** Of, relating to, or characteristic of a mode. **2.** Of, relating to, or expressing the mood of a verb.

modal auxiliary *n.* One of a set of English verbs, including *can, may, must, ought, shall, should, will,* and *would,* that are used with other verbs to express mood or tense.

mode (mōd) *n.* **1.** A way, manner, or style of doing: *a mode of living; a mode of travel.* **2.** The current fashion or style in dress: *a hat in the latest mode.* **3.** Any of the musical scales produced by starting, in turn, on each of the tones of a major scale and proceeding through an octave. Modes were commonly used in plainsong and ancient church music. **4.** The value that occurs most frequently in a data set or series. For example, in the series 125, 140, 172, 164, 140, and 110, 140 is the mode. [First written down about 1380 in Middle English and spelled *moed,* tune, from Latin *modus,* manner, tune.]

mod•el (mŏd′l) *n.* **1.** A small-scale reproduction or representation of something: *a model of a ship.* **2.** A style or design of something: *This car is last year's model.* **3.** A person or thing serving as an ideal example of something: *The farm is a model of efficient management.* **4.** A person hired to wear clothes in order to show them off, as in fashion shows or advertisements. **5.** A person hired to pose for an artist or a photographer. **6.** In science, a description or concept of a system or set of observable events that accounts for all its known properties in a reasonable way. —*v.* **mod•eled, mod•el•ing, mod•els** also **mod•elled, mod•el•ling, mod•els.** —*tr.* **1.** To make or construct a model of: *The library was modeled after the Library of Congress in Washington.* **2.** To make something by shaping (a plastic substance): *model clay.* **3.** To display (clothing, for example,) to show others how it looks: *She modeled her new dress.* —*intr.* **1.** To serve as a model. **2.** To make a model. —*adj.* **1.** Being, serving, or used as a model: *a model home.* **2.** Serving as a standard of excellence; worthy of imitation: *a model child.* [First written down in 1575 in Modern English, from Italian *modello,* from Latin *modus,* measure, standard.] **—mod′el•er** *n.*

mod•el•ing (mŏd′l ĭng) *n.* **1.** The act or art of constructing a model out of a pliable material. **2.** The act or profession of being a model.

mo•dem (mō′dĕm′) *n.* A device that converts data from one form into another, as from one form usable in data processing to another form usable in transmission by telephone.

mod•er•ate (mŏd′ər ĭt) *adj.* **1.** Kept within reason-

moat

Muiderslot Castle in Holland

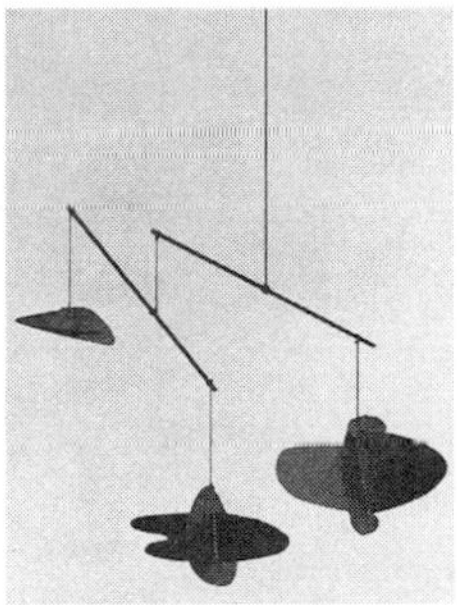

mobile

c. 1934 *Mobile* of sheet metal, metal rods, and cord by Alexander Calder (1898–1976)

moccasin

Huron embroidered black-dyed buckskin moccasins

ă	pat	oi	boy
ā	pay	ou	out
âr	care	o͝o	took
ä	father	o͞o	boot
ĕ	pet	ŭ	cut
ē	be	ûr	urge
ĭ	pit	th	thin
ī	pie	*th*	this
îr	pier	hw	whoop
ŏ	pot	zh	vision
ō	toe	ə	about
ô	paw	N	*French* bon

able limits; not excessive or extreme: *moderate prices.* **2.** Medium or average in amount or quality: *a moderate income.* **3.** Not severe; mild; temperate: *a moderate climate.* **4.** Opposed to radical or extreme views or measures, especially in politics or religion. —*n.* A person who holds moderate views or opinions, especially in politics or religion. —*v.* (mŏd′ə rāt′). **mod•er•at•ed, mod•er•at•ing, mod•er•ates.** —*tr.* **1.** To make less extreme: *moderate one's demands.* **2.** To preside over (a meeting or panel discussion). —*intr.* **1.** To become less extreme. **2.** To act as a moderator. [First written down in 1392 in Middle English and spelled *moderat,* from Latin *moderārī,* to moderate.] **—mod′er•ate•ly** *adv.* **—mod′er•a′tion** *n.*

mod•e•ra•to (mŏd′ə **rä′**tō) *adv. & adj.* In music, in moderate tempo.

mod•er•a•tor (**mŏd′**ə rā′tər) *n.* **1.** The person who presides over a meeting or panel discussion. **2.** A substance, such as graphite or water, placed in a nuclear reactor to slow neutrons down to speeds at which they are likely to cause additional nuclear fission.

mod•ern (**mŏd′**ərn) *adj.* **1.** Of or relating to the present or recent past: *modern history.* **2.** Of or relating to a recently developed style, technique, or technology: *modern methods of farming.* **3.** Experimental; avant-garde. —*n.* **1.** A person who lives in modern times. **2.** A person with modern ideas, tastes, or beliefs. [First written down about 1500 in Modern English, from Late Latin *modernus.*]

Modern English *n.* English since about 1500.

mod•ern•ism (**mŏd′**ər nĭz′əm) *n.* **1.** Modern thought, character, or practice. **2.** Often **Modernism.** The use of innovative forms that characterizes many styles in the art and literature of the 20th century. **—mod′ern•ist** *n.*

mo•der•ni•ty (mŏ **dûr′**nĭ tē *or* mō **dûr′**nĭ tē) *n., pl.* **mo•der•ni•ties.** The quality of being modern.

mod•ern•ize (**mŏd′**ər nīz′) *v.* **mo•dern•ized, mo•dern•iz•ing, mo•dern•iz•es.** —*tr.* To make modern in appearance, style, or character; update: *modernize a kitchen.* —*intr.* To become modern; accept or adopt modern ways. **—mod′ern•i•za′tion** (mŏd′ər nĭ **zā′**shən) *n.*

mod•est (**mŏd′**ĭst) *adj.* **1.** Having or showing a moderate estimation of one's own talents, abilities, or accomplishments. **2.** Retiring or reserved in manner; shy: *a quiet modest demeanor.* **3.** Not elaborate or showy; unpretentious: *a modest house.* **4.** Moderate in size or amount; not large: *a modest salary.* [First written down in 1565 in Modern English, from Latin *modestus.*] **—mod′est•ly** *adv.*

mod•es•ty (**mŏd′**ĭ stē) *n.* **1.** The state or quality of being modest. **2.** Reserve in behavior, dress, or speech. **3.** Lack of pretentiousness; simplicity.

mod•i•cum (**mŏd′**ĭ kəm) *n., pl.* **mod•i•cums** or **mod•i•ca** (**mŏd′**ĭ kə). A small amount: *a subject in which I have only a modicum of interest.*

mod•i•fi•ca•tion (mŏd′ə fĭ **kā′**shən) *n.* **1.** The action or process of modifying: *The theory is still subject to some modification.* **2.** A result of modifying; a change or adaptation: *The design was approved with certain modifications.* **3.** A small alteration, adjustment, or limitation.

mod•i•fi•er (**mŏd′**ə fī′ər) *n.* A word, phrase, or clause that qualifies or limits the sense of another word or phrase.

mod•i•fy (**mŏd′**ə fī′) *v.* **mod•i•fied, mod•i•fy•ing, mod•i•fies.** —*tr.* **1.** To change in form or character; alter: *modify the terms of a deal.* **2.** In grammar, to qualify or limit the meaning of (a word or phrase, for example). —*intr.* To be or become modified; change. [First written down about 1385 in Middle English and spelled *modifien,* from Latin *modificāre,* to measure, limit.]

mod•ish (**mō′**dĭsh) *adj.* Stylish; fashionable. **—mod′ish•ly** *adv.* **—mod′ish•ness** *n.*

mod•u•late (**mŏj′**ə lāt′) *v.* **mod•u•lat•ed, mod•u•lat•ing, mod•u•lates.** —*tr.* **1.** To change or vary the pitch, intensity, or tone of (one's voice or a musical instrument, for example). **2.** To vary the amplitude, frequency, or some other characteristic of (electromagnetic waves) in a way that makes them correspond to a signal or information that is to be transmitted. —*intr.* To pass from one musical key or tonality to another by means of a smooth melodic or chord progression.

mod•u•la•tion (mŏj′ə **lā′**shən) *n.* **1.** The act or process of modulating. **2.** The state of being modulated. **3.** The process by which a characteristic of electromagnetic waves, such as amplitude or frequency, is changed to make the waves correspond to a signal or information that is to be transmitted. **4.** In music, a smooth passage from one key or tonality to another.

mod•u•la•tor (**mŏj′**ə lā′tər) *n.* A device that modulates.

mod•ule (**mŏj′**o͞ol) *n.* **1.** A standard or unit of measurement. **2.** A standard element that is used over and over again in forming a building or structure. **3.** A self-contained unit of electronic components and circuitry that is installed as a unit. **4.** A self-contained unit of a spacecraft that is used for a particular job or set of jobs: *a lunar module.* **—mod′u•lar** (**mŏj′**ə lər) *adj.*

Mog•a•dish•u (mŏg′ə **dĭsh′**o͞o *or* mŏg′ə **dē′**sho͞o). The capital and largest city of Somalia, on the Indian Ocean. It was settled in the ninth or tenth century. Population, 400,000.

Mo•gul (**mō′**gəl *or* mō **gŭl′**) *n.* **1.a.** A member of the force that conquered India in 1526. **b.** A member of the Muslim dynasty that ruled India until 1857. **2.** A Mongol or Mongolian. **3. mogul.** A very rich or powerful person; a magnate.

mo•hair (**mō′**hâr′) *n.* **1.** The soft silky hair of the Angora goat. **2.** Cloth made from this hair. [First written down in 1570 in Modern English and spelled *mocayare,* from Arabic *muḫayyar.*]

Mo•ham•med (mō **hăm′**ĭd *or* mō **hä′**mĭd). Muhammad.

Mo•ham•med•an (mō **hăm′**ĭ dən) *adj. & n.* Variant of **Muhammadan.**

Mo•ha•ve also **Mo•ja•ve** (mō **hä′**vē) *n., pl.* **Mohave** or **Mo•ha•ves** also **Mojave** or **Mo•ja•ves. 1.** A member of a Native American people living along the lower Colorado River in California and Arizona. **2.** The Yuman language of the Mohave.

Mo•hawk (**mō′**hôk′) *n., pl.* **Mohawk** or **Mo•hawks. 1.** A member of a Native American people living in upstate New York and southwest Canada. **2.** The Iroquoian language of the Mohawk.

Mo•he•gan (mō **hē′**gən) *n., pl.* **Mohegan** or **Mo•he•gans. 1.** A member of a Native American people formerly living in Connecticut, with descendants living in Connecticut and Wisconsin. **2.** The Algonquian language of the Mohegan.

Mo•hi•can (mō **hē′**kən *or* mə **hē′**kən) *n.* Variant of **Mahican.**

Mo•ho (**mō′**hō′) *n.* The Mohorovičić discontinuity.

Mo•ho•ro•vi•čić discontinuity (mō′hə **rō′**və chĭch) *n.* The boundary between the earth's crust and mantle, having an average depth of 5 miles (8 kilometers) under oceans and 20 miles (32 kilometers) under continents. [First written down in 1936 in Modern English, after Andrija *Mohorovičić* (1857–1936), Croatian scientist.]

Mohs scale (mōz) *n.* A scale used to measure the relative hardness of a mineral by its resistance to scratching by ten standard minerals ranging from talc, the softest, to diamond, the hardest. [First written down in 1879 in Modern English and spelled *Mohs's scale*, after Friedrich *Mohs* (1773–1839), German mineralogist.]

moi•e•ty (moi′ĭ tē) *n., pl.* **moi•e•ties. 1.** A half. **2.** A part, portion, or share.

moi•ré (mwä rā′ *or* mô rā′) *adj.* Having a wavy or rippled surface pattern. *—n.* **1.** A wavy or rippled pattern pressed on cloth by engraved rollers. **2.** Cloth, especially silk, that has a watery rippled look.

moist (moist) *adj.* **moist•er, moist•est.** Slightly wet; damp. See Synonyms at **wet.** **—moist′ness** *n.*

mois•ten (moi′sən) *tr. & intr.v.* **mois•tened, mois•ten•ing, mois•tens.** To make or become moist.

mois•ture (mois′chər) *n.* **1.** Wetness, especially that caused by water present in the air as vapor or spread thinly over a surface or surfaces. **2.** The state or quality of being damp.

Mo•ja•ve (mō hä′vē) *n.* Variant of **Mohave.**

Mojave Desert also **Mohave Desert.** An arid region of southern California southeast of the Sierra Nevada. The desert was formed by volcanic action and by materials deposited by the Colorado River.

mo•lar (mō′lər) *n.* Any of the teeth located toward the back of the jaws, having broad crowns for grinding food. Humans have 12 molars.

mo•las•ses (mə lăs′ĭz) *n.* A thick syrup produced in refining sugar.

mold[1] (mōld) *n.* **1.** A hollow container of a particular shape, used for shaping a liquid or plastic substance: *pour the batter into a mold.* **2.** Something made or shaped from a mold. **3.** General shape; form: *the round mold of a face.* **4.** Distinctive character, kind, or type: *men and women of serious mold.* *—tr.v.* **mold•ed, mold•ing, molds. 1.** To shape in a mold. **2.** To determine the general character of; shape in a particular way: *mold clay; mold a student's mind.* [First written down before 1200 in Middle English and spelled *molde*, from Latin *modulus*, unit of measure, from *modus*, measure.] **—mold′a•ble** *adj.* **—mold′er** *n.*

mold[2] (mōld) *n.* **1.** Any of various fungi that often form a fuzzy coating on the surface of food and other plant or animal substances. **2.** The coating formed by such a fungus. *—intr.v.* **mold•ed, mold•ing, molds.** To become covered with such a coating. [First written down before 1400 in Middle English and spelled *moulde.*]

mold[3] (mōld) *n.* Loose soil that is rich in humus and fit for planting. [First written down before 725 in Old English and spelled *molde.*]

Mol•da•vi•a (mŏl dā′vē ə *or* mŏl dāv′yə). **1.** A historical region of eastern Romania east of Transylvania. In 1859 Moldavia united with Wallachia to form the core of modern Romania. **2.** A republic of eastern Europe bordering on Romania. Moldavia was a part of the Soviet Union from 1924 to 1991. Capital, Kishinev. Population, 4,111,000.

mold•er (mōl′dər) *v.* **mold•ered, mold•er•ing, mold•ers.** *—intr.* To turn gradually to dust; crumble: *The ancient ruins are beginning to molder away.* *—tr.* To cause to crumble or decay. [First written down in 1531 in Modern English, probably from *mold*, earth.]

mold•ing (mōl′dĭng) *n.* **1.** The act or process of molding. **2.** Something that is molded. **3.** An ornamental strip used to decorate a surface.

mold•y (mōl′dē) *adj.* **mold•i•er, mold•i•est. 1.** Covered with or containing mold: *moldy bread.* **2.** Damp and musty: *a dark moldy cupboard.* **—mold′i•ness** *n.*

mole[1] (mōl) *n.* A small, usually dark growth on the skin. [First written down about 1000 in Old English and spelled *māl.*]

mole[2] (mōl) *n.* Any of various small burrowing mammals having long claws, tiny underdeveloped eyes, a narrow snout, and short silky fur. [First written down in 1362 in Middle English and spelled *mol.*]

mole[3] (mōl) *n.* The amount of a substance that has a mass in grams numerically equal to the molecular weight of the substance. For example, carbon dioxide, CO_2, has a molecular weight of 44; therefore, one mole of it weighs 44 grams. [First written down in 1902 in Modern English, from German *Mol*, from *Molekül*, molecule.]

mo•lec•u•lar (mə lĕk′yə lər) *adj.* Of, caused by, or consisting of molecules. **—mo•lec′u•lar•ly** *adv.*

molecular weight *n.* The sum of the atomic weights of the atoms contained in a molecule.

mol•e•cule (mŏl′ĭ kyo͞ol′) *n.* **1.** A stable, electrically neutral arrangement of atoms. It is the smallest and simplest unit that has the characteristic chemical and physical properties of a compound or an element. **2.** A small particle; a tiny bit. [First written down in 1794 in Modern English, from French *molécule*, from Latin *mōlēs*, mass.]

mole•hill (mōl′hĭl′) *n.* A small mound of earth dug up by a burrowing mole. *—idiom.* **make a mountain out of a molehill.** To give too much weight or importance to a minor problem.

mole•skin (mōl′skĭn′) *n.* **1.** The short, soft, silky fur of the mole. **2.** A sturdy cotton cloth with a thick fine nap on one side.

mo•lest (mə lĕst′) *tr.v.* **mo•lest•ed, mo•lest•ing, mo•lests. 1.** To annoy, bother, or disturb: *Few animals dare molest a badger.* **2.** To subject to unwanted or improper sexual activity. **—mo•lest′er** *n.* **—mo′les•ta′tion** (mō′lĕ stā′shən) *n.*

Mo•lière (mōl yâr′), **Jean Baptiste Poquelin.** 1622–1673. French playwright whose comedies include *Tartuffe* (1664).

mol•li•fy (mŏl′ə fī′) *tr.v.* **mol•li•fied, mol•li•fy•ing, mol•li•fies. 1.** To lessen the anger of; placate: *a new film designed to mollify critics.* **2.** To make less intense; soften or soothe: *The tender words mollified the child's distress.* **—mol′li•fi•ca′tion** (mŏl′ə fĭ kā′shən) *n.*

mol•lusk also **mol•lusc** (mŏl′əsk) *n.* Any of numerous soft-bodied invertebrate animals, such as snails, clams, and oysters, usually living in water and having a hard outer shell. Some mollusks, such as octopuses, squids, and slugs, have no outer shell.

Mo•loch (mō′lŏk′ *or* mŏl′ək) *n.* **1.** In the Bible, a pagan god to whom children were sacrificed. **2.** Something that requires severe sacrifice.

Mo•lo•kai (mŏl′ə kī′ *or* mō′lə kī′). An island of central Hawaii between Oahu and Maui.

molt (mōlt) *v.* **molt•ed, molt•ing, molts.** *—intr.* To shed an outer covering, such as skin or feathers, for replacement by a new growth: *Some snakes molt in spring.* *—tr.* To shed (an outer covering): *molt feathers.* *—n.* The act or process of molting.

mol•ten (mōl′tən) *adj.* Made liquid by heat; melted: *molten metal.*

mol•to (mōl′tō) *adv.* In music, very or very much.

mo•lyb•de•num (mə lĭb′də nəm) *n.* *Symbol* **Mo** A hard gray metallic element that is used to strengthen and harden steel and is a necessary trace element in plant metabolism. Atomic number 42. See table at **element.**

mom (mŏm) *n.* *Informal.* Mother.

mom-and-pop (mŏm′ən pŏp′) *adj.* Of or being a small business that is run by the owners: *a mom-and-pop grocery store.*

mo•ment (mō′mənt) *n.* **1.** A very brief interval of time; an instant. **2.** A certain important point in

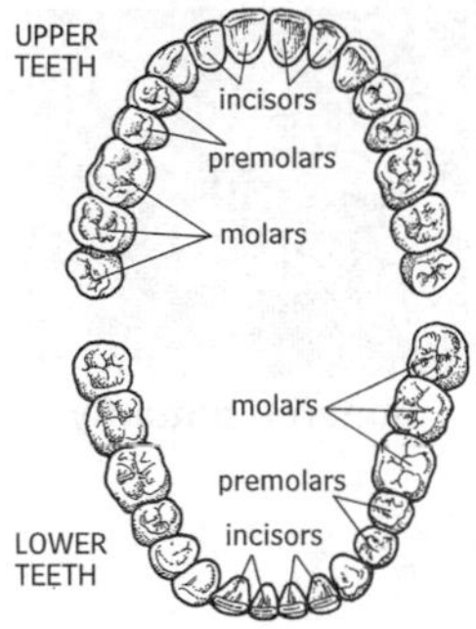

molar

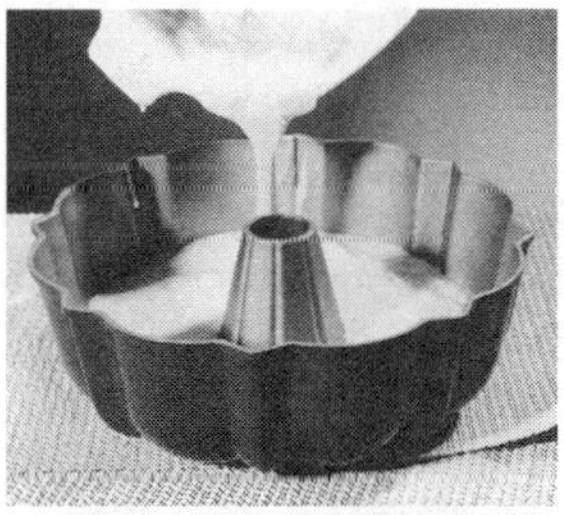
mold[1]
Bundt cake mold

molt
Timber rattlesnake shedding skin

ă	pat	oi	boy
ā	pay	ou	out
âr	care	o͝o	took
ä	father	o͞o	boot
ĕ	pet	ŭ	cut
ē	be	ûr	urge
ĭ	pit	th	thin
ī	pie	*th*	this
îr	pier	hw	whoop
ŏ	pot	zh	vision
ō	toe	ə	about
ô	paw	N	*French* bon

monarch butterfly

Claude Monet
Photographed in 1899
by Paul Nadar (1856–1939)

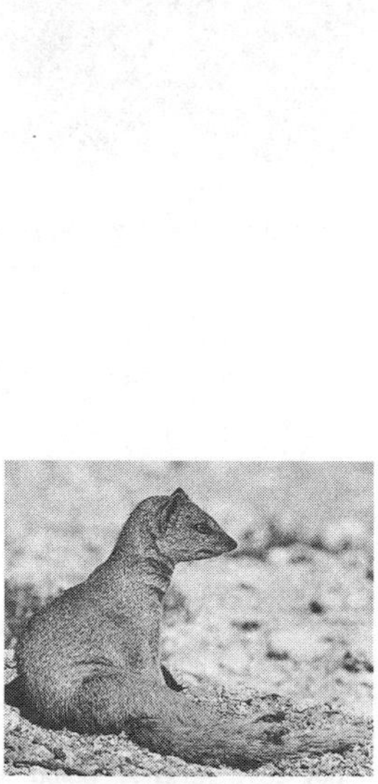

mongoose

time: *the happiest moment of my life.* **3.** The present time: *We are busy at the moment.* **4.** Great significance or importance: *were proud to witness an event of great moment.*

mo•men•ta (mō **mĕn′**tə) *n.* A plural of **momentum.**

mo•men•tar•i•ly (mō′mən **târ′**ə lē) *adv.* **1.** For an instant or a moment: *I was momentarily at a loss for words.* **2.** At any moment; very soon: *The principal will see you momentarily.* **3.** From moment to moment; progressively.

mo•men•tar•y (**mō′**mən tĕr′ē) *adj.* **1.** Lasting only an instant or moment: *a momentary glance.* **2.** Occurring or present at every moment.

mo•men•tous (mō **mĕn′**təs) *adj.* Of the utmost importance or significance: *a momentous occasion.*

mo•men•tum (mō **mĕn′**təm) *n., pl.* **mo•men•ta** (mō **mĕn′**tə) or **mo•men•tums. 1.** The product of the mass and velocity of a moving body. **2.** Force or speed of motion; impetus: *The sled gained momentum as it raced down the hill.*

mom•my (**mŏm′**ē) *n., pl.* **mom•mies.** *Informal.* Mother.

Mon. *abbr.* An abbreviation of Monday.

Mon•a•co (**mŏn′**ə kō′ *or* mə **nä′**kō). A principality on the Mediterranean Sea consisting of an enclave in southeast France. Monaco regained its sovereignty from France in 1861. The village of **Monaco,** or **Monaco-Ville,** is the capital. Population, 27,063.

mon•arch (**mŏn′**ərk *or* **mŏn′**ärk′) *n.* **1.** A ruler or sovereign, such as a king or queen, who reigns over a state, usually for life and by hereditary right. **2.** A monarch butterfly. [First written down before 1439 in Middle English and spelled *monarke,* from Greek *monarkhos.*] **—mo•nar′chic** (mə **när′**kĭk) *adj.* **—mo•nar′chi•cal** *adj.*

monarch butterfly *n.* A large orange and black American butterfly noted for its long-distance migrations.

mon•ar•chism (**mŏn′**ər kĭz′əm *or* **mŏn′**är′kĭz′əm) *n.* **1.** A system of government headed by a single ruler or monarch. **2.** Belief in or support of this system of government.

mon•ar•chist (**mŏn′**ər kĭst *or* **mŏn′**är′kĭst) *n.* A person who believes in or supports monarchy.

mon•ar•chy (**mŏn′**ər kē *or* **mŏn′**är′kē) *n., pl.* **mon•ar•chies. 1.** Government by a monarch. **2.** A country ruled by a monarch.

mon•as•ter•y (**mŏn′**ə stĕr′ē) *n., pl.* **mon•as•ter•ies. 1.** A community of monks. **2.** The building or buildings occupied by monks. **—mon′as•te′ri•al** (mŏn′ə **stîr′**ē əl *or* mŏn′ə **stĕr′**ē əl) *adj.*

mo•nas•tic (mə **năs′**tĭk) *adj.* **1.** Of, relating to, or characteristic of a monastery. **2.** Resembling life in a monastery. *—n.* A monk.

mon•au•ral (mŏn **ôr′**əl) *adj.* Using a single channel to transmit or reproduce sound; monophonic.

Mon•day (**mŭn′**dē *or* **mŭn′**dā′) *n.* The second day of the week. [First written down about 1000 in Old English and spelled *Mōnandæg,* moon's day.]

mo•ne•ran (mə **nîr′**ən) *n.* Any member of the kingdom of one-celled organisms lacking distinct nuclei. Bacteria and blue-green algae are monerans. *—adj.* Of or relating to monerans.

Mo•net (mō **nā′**), **Claude.** 1840–1926. French painter whose works include the *Water Lilies* series (1899–1925).

mon•e•tar•y (**mŏn′**ĭ tĕr′ē) *adj.* **1.** Of or relating to money: *the monetary value of a painting.* **2.** Of or relating to a nation's currency or coinage: *a monetary system.* **—mon′e•tar′i•ly** *adv.*

mon•ey (**mŭn′**ē) *n., pl.* **mon•eys** or **mon•ies. 1.** Something, such as gold or an officially issued coin or paper note, that is legally declared to have a fixed value and to be exchangeable for all goods and services. **2.** The official coins and paper notes issued by a government and used to buy or pay for things; currency. **3.** Wealth; property and assets. **4.** Sums of money collected or stored; funds. Often used in the plural: *state tax moneys.* **5.** An amount of money sufficient for some purpose: *They lacked the money for a vacation.* **6.** Monetary profit or loss: *won big money on the lottery.*

mon•ey•bag (**mŭn′**ē băg′) *n.* **1.** A bag for holding money. **2. moneybags.** *(used with a singular verb). Slang.* A rich and greedy person.

mon•eyed (**mŭn′**ēd) *adj.* **1.** Having much money; wealthy: *the great moneyed corporations.* **2.** Representing or arising from money or wealth.

mon•ey•lend•er (**mŭn′**ē lĕn′dər) *n.* A person whose business is lending money for a fee.

money order *n.* An order for the payment of a specific amount of money that usually can be bought or cashed at a bank or post office.

mon•ger (**mŭng′**gər *or* **mŏng′**gər) *n.* **1.** A dealer in a specific product or commodity: *an ironmonger.* **2.** A person who promotes something undesirable or discreditable: *a scandalmonger.*

Mon•gol (**mŏng′**gəl *or* **mŏng′**gōl′) *n.* **1.** A member of any of the traditionally nomadic peoples of Mongolia. **2.** The language of these peoples; Mongolian. *—adj.* Of or relating to Mongolia, the Mongols, or their language or culture.

Mon•go•li•a (mŏng **gō′**lē ə *or* mŏng **gōl′**yə). **1.** An ancient region of east-central Asia north of China made up of modern-day Nei Monggol (Inner Mongolia) and the country of Mongolia. In the 13th century it was a great empire that eventually stretched from China to the Danube River and into Persia. **2.** Formerly **Out•er Mongolia** (**ou′**tər). A country of north-central Asia between Russia and China. In 1921 Mongolia formed a separate state under the protection of the U.S.S.R. Capital, Ulan Bator. Population, 1,866,300.

Mon•go•li•an (mŏng **gō′**lē ən *or* mŏng **gōl′**yən) *adj.* Of or relating to Mongolia, the Mongols, or their language or culture. *—n.* **1.** A native or inhabitant of Mongolia. **2.** Any of the languages of Mongolia, related to Turkish.

Mon•gol•oid (**mŏng′**gə loid′) *adj.* **1.** Of or relating to a major division of human beings whose members characteristically have yellowish-brown skin, straight black hair, and prominent cheek bones. This division includes peoples of central and eastern Asia. This word is no longer in scientific use. **2.** *Offensive.* Of or relating to Down syndrome.

mon•goose (**mŏng′**go͞os′ *or* **mŏn′**go͞os′) *n., pl.* **mon•goos•es.** Any of various mammals of Asia and Africa that resemble weasels and are noted for their ability to kill poisonous snakes. [First written down in 1698 in Modern English, from Marathi *mangūs.*]

mon•grel (**mŭng′**grəl *or* **mŏng′**grəl) *n.* An animal, especially a dog, of mixed breed. [First written down about 1460 in Middle English, probably from Old English *gemang,* mixture.]

mon•ies (**mŭn′**ēz) *n.* A plural of **money.**

mon•i•tor (**mŏn′**ĭ tər) *n.* **1.** A person who gives warnings, corrective advice, or instruction. **2.** A student who assists a teacher in routine duties such as taking attendance. **3.** A usually electronic device used to record, regulate, or control a process or an activity: *a radiation monitor.* **4.** A receiver that is used to check the quality of an electronic transmission: *a television monitor.* **5.** A device that accepts video signals from a computer and displays information on a screen. *—v.* **mon•i•tored, mon•i•tor•ing, mon•i•tors.** *—tr.* **1.** To keep watch over; supervise. **2.** To keep track of systematically: *monitor a patient's heartbeat.* **3.** To check the quality or content of (an electronic audio or a visual signal) by means of a receiver. *—intr.* To act as a monitor. [First written down in 1546 in Modern English, from Latin, from *monēre*, to warn.]

mon•i•to•ry (**mŏn′**ĭ tôr′ē) *adj.* Giving a warning or reproof: *a monitory glance.*

monk (mŭngk) *n.* A member of a group of men living in a monastery and bound by vows to the rules and practices of a religious order. [First written down before 899 in Old English and spelled *munuc*, from Greek *monakhos*, alone.]

mon•key (**mŭng′**kē) *n., pl.* **mon•keys. 1.** Any of various mammals related to apes and humans and having long tails and hands and feet adapted for grasping. **2.** A playful or mischievous person. **3.** *Slang.* A person made to appear silly or foolish: *We made monkeys out of their team.* *—v.* **mon•keyed, mon•key•ing, mon•keys.** *—intr. Informal.* **1.** To behave in a silly or mischievous way: *Don't monkey around during the ceremony.* **2.** To tamper or meddle with something. *—tr.* To imitate or mimic. [First written down in 1530 in Modern English.]

monkey bars *pl.n.* A jungle gym.

monkey wrench *n.* **1.** A hand tool with adjustable jaws for turning nuts and bolts of various sizes. **2.** Something that disrupts: *Bad weather threw a monkey wrench into our plans.*

monk•ish (**mŭng′**kĭsh) *adj.* Of, relating to, or characteristic of monks or monasticism.

monks•hood (**mŭngks′**ho͝od′) *n.* Any of various usually poisonous plants having hooded flowers of various colors.

mono (**mŏn′**ō) *n. Informal.* Infectious mononucleosis.

mono– or **mon–** *pref.* A prefix that means: **1.** One; only; single: *monogamy.* **2.** Containing a single atom, radical, or group: *monoxide.*

mon•o•chro•mat•ic (mŏn′ə krō **măt′**ĭk) *adj.* **1.** Of or having a single color: *monochromatic light.* **2.** Consisting of a single wavelength of light or other radiation: *monochromatic X rays.*

mon•o•cle (**mŏn′**ə kəl) *n.* An eyeglass, typically having a cord attached, worn in front of one eye.

mon•o•cot (**mŏn′**ə kŏt) *n.* A monocotyledon.

mon•o•cot•y•le•don (mŏn′ə kŏt′l **ēd′**n) *n.* Any of various flowering plants having a single cotyledon. The grasses, palms, lilies, and irises are monocotyledons. **—mon′o•cot′y•le′don•ous** *adj.*

mo•noc•u•lar (mə **nŏk′**yə lər) *adj.* **1.** Of or having a single eye. **2.** Designed for use with only one eye: *a monocular telescope.*

mo•nog•a•my (mə **nŏg′**ə me) *n.* **1.** The custom or condition of being married to only one person at a time. **2.** The condition of having just one mate for life.

mon•o•gram (**mŏn′**ə grăm′) *n.* A design made up of one or more letters, usually the initials of a name. *—tr.v.* **mon•o•grammed, mon•o•gram•ming, mon•o•grams** also **mon•o•gramed, mon•o•gram•ing, mon•o•grams.** To mark with a monogram: *She monogrammed the sheets and towels.* [First written down in 1696 in Modern English : Greek *mono-*, single + Greek *gramma*, letter.]

mon•o•graph (**mŏn′**ə grăf′) *n.* A scholarly book or article on a specific and usually limited subject.

mon•o•lith (**mŏn′**ə lĭth′) *n.* **1.** A large single block of stone. **2.** A memorial, monument, or other structure that is made from a block of stone.

mon•o•lith•ic (mŏn′ə **lĭth′**ĭk) *adj.* **1.** Consisting of a monolith: *a monolithic column.* **2.** Like a monolith in being massive, uniform, or unvarying: *a monolithic business empire.*

mon•o•logue (**mŏn′**ə lôg′ *or* **mŏn′**ə lŏg′) *n.* **1.** A long speech delivered by an actor on the stage or a character in a story or poem. **2.** A series of jokes and stories told by a comedian on the stage alone. **3.** A long speech made by one person in a group: *He kept talking until our conversation turned into a monologue.*

mon•o•ma•ni•a (mŏn′ə **mā′**nē ə *or* mŏn′ə **mān′**yə) *n.* An intense preoccupation with one subject or idea. **—mon′o•ma′ni•ac′** (mŏn′ə **mā′**nē ăk′)

mo•no•mi•al (mŏ **nō′**mē əl) *n.* An algebraic expression consisting of a single term.

mon•o•nu•cle•o•sis (mŏn′ō no͞o′klē **ō′**sĭs *or* mŏn′ō nyo͞o′klē **ō′**sĭs) *n.* Infectious mononucleosis.

mon•o•phon•ic (mŏn′ə **fŏn′**ĭk) *adj.* **1.** Consisting of only one melodic line or part. **2.** Using a single channel to record, store, or reproduce sound: *a monophonic recording.*

mon•o•plane (**mŏn′**ə plān′) *n.* An airplane having a single pair of wings.

mo•nop•o•lis•tic (mə nŏp′ə **lĭs′**tĭk) *adj.* **1.** Maintaining a monopoly. **2.** Of or characteristic of a monopoly or a monopolist.

mo•nop•o•lize (mə **nŏp′**ə līz′) *tr.v.* **mo•nop•o•lized, mo•nop•o•liz•ing, mo•nop•o•liz•es. 1.** To gain and hold a monopoly over. **2.** To get or have control over: *Don't monopolize the conversation.* **—mo•nop′o•li•za′tion** (mə nŏp′ə lĭ **zā′**shən) *n.* **—mo•nop′o•liz′er** *n.*

mo•nop•o•ly (mə **nŏp′**ə lē) *n., pl.* **mo•nop•o•lies. 1.a.** Complete control by one group of the means of producing or selling a product or service: *The early railroads had almost a monopoly on freight and passenger transportation.* **b.** A company having such complete control: *laws to limit the power of monopolies.* **c.** A product, service, or commercial activity completely controlled by one group. **2.** The right given by a government to a person to have exclusive control of the sale and manufacture of commercial goods. **3.** Sole possession or control of something: *The U.S. monopoly on the atomic bomb did not last long.* [First written down in 1534 in Modern English, from Greek *monopōlion* : *mono-*, single + *pōlein*, to sell.]

mon•o•rail (**mŏn′**ə rāl′) *n.* **1.** A single rail serving as a track for cars or trains that travel on it or hang from it. **2.** A railway system using a track with such a rail.

mon•o•so•di•um glu•ta•mate (mŏn′ə **sō′**dē əm **glo͞o′**tə māt′) *n.* A white crystalline compound used to flavor food.

mon•o•syl•lab•ic (mŏn′ə sĭ **lăb′**ĭk) *adj.* **1.** Having only one syllable: *a monosyllabic word.* **2.** Consisting of or characterized by monosyllables.

mon•o•syl•la•ble (**mŏn′**ə sĭl′ə bəl) *n.* A word of one syllable.

mon•o•the•ism (**mŏn′**ə thē ĭz′əm) *n.* The belief that there is only one God. **—mon′o•the′ist** *n.* **—mon′o•the•is′tic** *adj.*

mon•o•tone (**mŏn′**ə tōn′) *n.* **1.** A succession of sounds or words uttered in a single tone of voice. **2.a.** The repeated singing of a single tone with different words and time values, as in chanting. **b.** A chant sung on a single tone. **3.** A tiresome repetition, as in sound, color, or style.

mo•not•o•nous (mə **nŏt′**n əs) *adj.* **1.** Uttered or sounded in one repeated tone; unvarying in pitch: *a monotonous lecture that caused the listener's attention to wander.* **2.** Never varied or enlivened; repetitiously dull: *a monotonous diet.* **—mo•not′o•nous•ly** *adv.*

mo•not•o•ny (mə **nŏt′**n ē) *n., pl.* **mo•not•o•nies.** Tiresome sameness or repetition.

mon•ox•ide (mə **nŏk′**sīd′) *n.* An oxide in which each molecule contains a single atom of oxygen.

Mon•roe (mən **rō′**), **James.** 1758–1831. The fifth President of the United States (1817–1825), whose

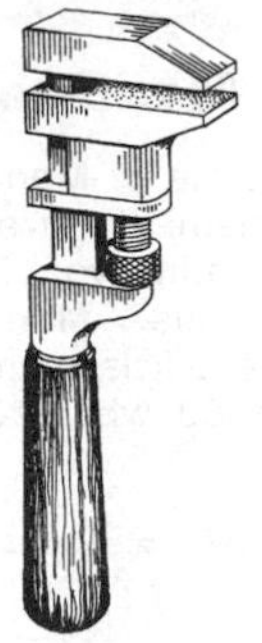

monkey wrench

monocle

James Monroe
Detail of an 1817 portrait by Gilbert Stuart (1755–1828)

ă	pat	oi	boy
ā	pay	ou	out
âr	care	o͝o	took
ä	father	o͞o	boot
ĕ	pet	ŭ	cut
ē	be	ûr	urge
ĭ	pit	th	thin
ī	pie	*th*	this
îr	pier	hw	whoop
ŏ	pot	zh	vision
ō	toe	ə	about
ô	paw	N	*French* bon

Montana

The state of **Montana** gets its name from a Spanish or Latin word meaning "mountainous." **Montana** became the official name of the state in 1889, when it joined the Union.

Maria Montessori

Montezuma II

administration was marked by the acquisition of Florida (1819) and the Missouri Compromise (1820).

Monroe, Marilyn. 1926–1962. American actress noted for her motion pictures, including *Some Like It Hot* (1959).

Mon•ro•vi•a (mən **rō′**vē ə). The capital and largest city of Liberia, in the northwest part of the country on the Atlantic Ocean. It was founded in 1822 as a haven for freed slaves. Population, 243,243.

Mon•sei•gneur (môɴ sĕ **nyœr′**) *n., pl.* **Mes•sei•gneurs** (mā sĕ **nyœr′**). Used as a title of honor or respect in French-speaking areas for princes or highly ranked clergy.

Mon•sieur (mə **syœ′**) *n., pl.* **Mes•sieurs** (mā **syœ′** *or* mĕs′ərz). Used as a courtesy title before the name of a man in a French-speaking area.

mon•soon (mŏn **sōōn′**) *n.* **1.** A system of winds that influences the climate of a large area and that changes direction with the seasons, especially the wind system that produces the wet and dry seasons in southern Asia. **2.** The season during which this wind blows from the southwest, usually accompanied by heavy rains. [First written down in 1584 in Modern English, from Arabic *mawsim*, season.]

mon•ster (**mŏn′**stər) *n.* **1.** An imaginary or legendary creature, such as a centaur or Harpy, that has body parts from various human or animal forms. **2.** A very large animal, plant, or thing: *Fish range from tiny animals to monsters of enormous size.* **3.** An animal or a plant that is abnormal in form or appearance. **4.** A creature having a strange or frightening appearance. [First written down before 1325 in Middle English and spelled *monstre*, from Latin *mōnstrum*, portent.]

mon•stros•i•ty (mŏn **strŏs′**ĭ tē) *n., pl.* **mon•stros•i•ties. 1.** A person or thing that is monstrous. **2.** The quality or condition of being monstrous.

mon•strous (**mŏn′**strəs) *adj.* **1.** Frightful; shocking: *monstrous behavior.* **2.** Huge; enormous: *a monstrous iceberg.* **3.** Abnormal in appearance or structure. **4.** Of or resembling a legendary monster: *monstrous birds called Harpies.* **—mon′strous•ly** *adv.* **—mon′strous•ness** *n.*

Mont. *abbr.* An abbreviation of Montana.

mon•tage (mŏn **täzh′**) *n.* **1.a.** A picture made from many other pictures or designs placed next to or on top of one another. **b.** The art or process of making such a picture. **2.a.** A rapid succession of images or short scenes in a motion picture film. **b.** The use of such images or scenes as a technique of making movies. [First written down in 1929 in Modern English, from French, from *monter*, to mount.]

Mon•tan•a (mŏn **tăn′**ə). A state of the northwest United States north of Wyoming. It was admitted as the 41st state in 1889. Helena is the capital and Billings the largest city. Population, 803,655. —See Note.

mon•tane (mŏn **tān′** *or* **mŏn′**tān′) *adj.* Of or characteristic of mountain areas: *animals adapted to montane forests.*

Mon•te Car•lo (**mŏn′**tē **kär′**lō). A town of Monaco on the Mediterranean Sea and the French Riviera. It is a noted resort. Population, 11,599.

Mon•te•ne•gro (mŏn′tə **nē′**grō *or* mŏn′tə **nĕg′**rō). A region of the western Balkan Peninsula bordering on the Adriatic Sea. With Serbia it formed present-day Yugoslavia in April 1992. Capital, Podgorica. Population, 502,207.

Mon•tes•so•ri (mŏn′tĭ **sôr′**ē), **Maria.** 1870–1952. Italian physician and pioneer educator.

Mon•te•vi•de•o (mŏn′tə vĭ **dā′**ō *or* mŏn′tə **vĭd′**ē ō′). The capital and largest city of Uruguay, in the southern part of the country on the Río de la Plata estuary. It was founded in about 1726. Population, 1,237,227.

Mon•te•zu•ma II (mŏn′tĭ **zōō′**mə). 1466?–1520. Last Aztec emperor in Mexico (1502–1520), who was overthrown by the Spanish.

Mont•gom•er•y (mŏnt **gŭm′**ə rē *or* mŏnt **gŭm′**rē). The capital of Alabama, in the southeast-central part of the state south-southeast of Birmingham. From February to May 1861 it served as the first capital of the Confederate States of America. Population, 187,106.

month (mŭnth) *n.* **1.** One of the twelve calendar divisions of the year, especially according to the Gregorian calendar, lasting about thirty days. **2.** A period extending from a date in one calendar month to the corresponding date in the following month. **3.** A lunar month. [First written down about 750 in Old English and spelled *mōnath*.]

month•ly (**mŭnth′**lē) *adj.* **1.** Occurring, appearing, or payable every month: *a monthly meeting; monthly bills.* **2.** Continuing or lasting for a month: *average monthly rainfall.* *—adv.* Every month: *a magazine published monthly.* *—n., pl.* **month•lies.** A periodical publication appearing once each month.

Mont•pel•ier (mŏnt **pēl′**yər). The capital of Vermont, in the north-central part of the state. It was founded in 1780. Population, 8,247.

Mon•tre•al (mŏn′trē **ôl′**) or **Mont•ré•al** (môɴ′rā **äl′**). A city of southern Quebec, Canada, on **Montreal Island** in the St. Lawrence River. Montreal is Canada's largest city and a major port. Population, 980,354.

mon•u•ment (**mŏn′**yə mənt) *n.* **1.** A structure, such as a tower, statue, or building, erected to honor a person, a group, or an event. **2.** A tombstone. **3.** Something admired for its historical importance. **4.** An outstanding or enduring work: *The book is a monument of scholarship.* **5.** An object, such as a stone or post, placed in the ground to mark a boundary or position. [First written down about 1280 in Middle English, from Latin *monumentum*, from *monēre*, to remind.]

mon•u•men•tal (mŏn′yə **mĕn′**tl) *adj.* **1.** Of, like, or serving as a monument: *a monumental arch.* **2.** Impressively large, sturdy, and enduring: *monumental dams and tunnels.* **3.** Of outstanding significance: *Einstein's monumental discoveries in physics.* **4.** Astounding: *monumental talent.* **—mon′u•men′tal•ly** *adv.*

moo (mōō) *intr.v.* **mooed, moo•ing, moos.** To emit the deep bellowing sound made by a cow; low. *—n., pl.* **moos.** The lowing of a cow or a similar sound.

mooch (mōōch) *v.* **mooched, mooch•ing, mooch•es.** *Slang.* *—tr.* To get or try to get by begging: *always mooching food from me.* *—intr.* To get or try to get something for free: *lived by mooching off friends.* **—mooch′er** *n.*

mood[1] (mōōd) *n.* **1.** A state of mind or feeling: *I was in a good mood after the party.* **2.** An impression on the feelings or spirits of a person: *The painting has a somber mood.* **3.** Inclination; disposition: *I'm in no mood to argue.* [First written down about 725 in Old English and spelled *mōd*.]

mood[2] (mōōd) *n.* A set of verb forms that tells how certain the speaker is of the action expressed. In English, the indicative mood is used to make factual statements, the imperative mood to give commands, and the subjunctive mood to suggest doubt or unlikelihood. [First written down about 1450 in Middle English and spelled *mode*, from Latin *modus*, mode.]

mood•y (**mōō′**dē) *adj.* **mood•i•er, mood•i•est. 1.** Apt to change moods often, especially having spells of anger or gloom. **2.** Gloomy; morose; glum: *his moody silence.* **—mood′i•ly** *adv.* **—mood′i•ness** *n.*

moon (mo͞on) *n.* **1.** The natural satellite of Earth, visible by reflected sunlight and traveling around Earth in a slightly elliptical orbit at an average distance of about 237,000 miles (381,500 kilometers). Its average diameter is 2,160 miles (3,475 kilometers) and its mass about 1⁄80 that of Earth. **2.** A natural satellite of a planet: *the moons of Jupiter.* **3.** The moon as seen at a particular time in its cycle of phases: *a half moon.* **4.** Moonlight. **5.** A month, especially a lunar month. **6.** A disk, ball, or crescent resembling the moon. *—intr.v.* **mooned, moon•ing, moons.** To pass time idly or aimlessly. [First written down before 725 in Old English and spelled *mōna.*]

moon•beam (mo͞on′bēm′) *n.* A ray of moonlight.

moon•calf (mo͞on′kăf′) *n.* A foolish person.

moon•light (mo͞on′līt′) *n.* The light that is reflected from the surface of the moon. *—intr.v.* **moon•light•ed, moon•light•ing, moon•lights.** *Informal.* To work at a second job, often at night, in addition to one's regular job. **—moon′light′er** *n.*

moon•lit (mo͞on′lĭt′) *adj.* Lighted by the moon: *a moonlit pond.*

moon•scape (mo͞on′skāp′) *n.* A view or picture of the surface of the moon.

moon•shine (mo͞on′shīn′) *n.* **1.** Moonlight. **2.** *Informal.* Foolish talk or thinking; nonsense. **3.** Whiskey that is distilled for illegal sale or consumption. *—intr.v.* **moon•shined, moon•shin•ing, moon•shines.** To distill and sell liquor illegally.

moon•stone (mo͞on′stōn′) *n.* Any of several pearly translucent forms of feldspar that are valued as gemstones.

moon•struck (mo͞on′strŭk′) *adj.* **1.** Dazed with romantic love; infatuated. **2.** Affected by insanity; crazed.

moon•y (mo͞o′nē) *adj.* **moon•i•er, moon•i•est. 1.** Of or suggestive of the moon or moonlight: *a moony luster.* **2.** Given to dreamy moods; absent-minded.

moor¹ (mo͝or) *v.* **moored, moor•ing, moors.** *—tr.* **1.** To make fast (a vessel or an aircraft, for example) by means of cables, lines, or anchors. **2.** To fix in place; secure: *moored the boat to the dock.* *—intr.* **1.** To secure a vessel or an aircraft with lines or anchors: *We moored out in the bay.* **2.** To be secured with lines or anchors: *The sloop moored alongside the wharf.* [First written down before 1200 in Middle English and spelled *moren,* to take root.]

moor² (mo͝or) *n.* A broad stretch of open land, often with boggy areas and patches of low shrubs. [First written down about 725 in Old English and spelled *mōr.*]

Moor (mo͝or) *n.* **1.** A member of a Muslim people now living in northwest Africa. **2.** One of the Muslims who invaded Spain in the 8th century and established a civilization that lasted until the late 15th century.

Moore (mo͝or *or* môr), **Marianne Craig.** 1887–1972. American poet whose works are characterized by wit, irony, and unconventional meter.

moor•ing (mo͝or′ĭng) *n.* **1.** A place at which a vessel or an aircraft may be secured. **2.** Equipment, such as anchors, chains, or lines, for making fast a vessel or aircraft. Often used in the plural: *In the storm the boat pulled free from its moorings.*

Moor•ish (mo͝or′ĭsh) *adj.* Of or relating to the Moors or their culture or architecture.

moose (mo͞os) *n., pl.* **moose.** A large mammal of northern regions, related to the deer and having a large head, a dark coat, and broad antlers in the male.

❑ *These sound alike:* **moose, mousse** (dessert).

moot (mo͞ot) *adj.* Open to debate; arguable: *a moot question.* *—tr.v.* **moot•ed, moot•ing, moots. 1.** To bring up as a subject for discussion or debate. **2.** To discuss or debate.

mop (mŏp) *n.* **1.** An implement for washing, dusting, or drying floors, consisting of a sponge or a bundle of yarn or rags attached to a long handle. **2.** A loosely tangled bunch or mass: *a mop of hair.* *—tr.v.* **mopped, mop•ping, mops.** To wash or wipe with or as if with a mop: *mopped the hallway; mopped her forehead with a towel.* ***—idiom.* mop up. 1.** To clear (an area) of remaining enemy troops after a victory. **2.** *Informal.* To finish a nearly completed task. [First written down in 1496 in Middle English and spelled *mappe,* possibly from Latin *mappa,* towel, cloth.]

mope (mōp) *intr.v.* **moped, mop•ing, mopes. 1.** To be gloomy or quietly resentful; sulk. **2.** To move or pass time aimlessly; dawdle. *—n.* **1.** A person who often has gloomy moods. **2. mopes.** Low spirits.

mo•ped (mō′pĕd′) *n.* A lightweight motorized bicycle that can be pedaled.

mop•pet (mŏp′ĭt) *n.* A young child.

mo•raine (mə rān′) *n.* A mass of boulders, stones, and other material that has been carried and deposited by a glacier.

mor•al (môr′əl *or* mŏr′əl) *adj.* **1.** Of or concerned with the judgment of the goodness and badness of human action: *moral principles.* **2.** Teaching or showing good or correct behavior: *a moral lesson.* **3.** Being or acting in accord with standards of what is good and just: *a moral way of living.* **4.** Arising from the inner sense of right and wrong: *She felt she had a moral duty to help.* **5.** Psychological rather than physical or concrete: *a moral victory; gave me some moral support.* **6.** Likely but not proved: *a moral certainty.* *—n.* **1.** The lesson or principle taught by a fable, a story, or an event. **2. morals.** Rules of good or correct conduct. [First written down about 1340 in Middle English, from Latin *mōrālis,* from *mōs,* custom.]

mo•rale (mə răl′) *n.* The state of a person's or group's spirits, as shown in confidence, cheerfulness, and willingness to work toward a goal: *The party boosted morale, and the staff finished the job on schedule.*

mor•al•ist (môr′ə lĭst *or* mŏr′ə lĭst) *n.* **1.** A person who is concerned with moral principles and questions. **2.** A person who follows a system of moral principles. **3.** A person who is unduly concerned with the morals of others.

mor•al•is•tic (môr′ə lĭs′tĭk *or* mŏr′ə lĭs′tĭk) *adj.* **1.** Concerned with morality. **2.** Marked by a narrow-minded morality **—mor′al•is′ti•cal•ly** *adv.*

mo•ral•i•ty (mə răl′ĭ tē *or* mô răl′ĭ tē) *n., pl.* **mo•ral•i•ties. 1.** A set of ideas about what is right and wrong in human conduct and relationships: *religious morality.* **2.** The quality of being moral; goodness or rightness. **3.** Virtuous behavior.

mor•al•ize (môr′ə līz′ *or* mŏr′ə līz′) *v.* **mor•al•ized, mor•al•iz•ing, mor•al•iz•es.** *—intr.* To think about or express moral judgments. *—tr.* **1.** To interpret or explain the moral meaning of; draw a moral from. **2.** To improve the morals of; reform.

mor•al•ly (môr′ə lē *or* mŏr′ə lē) *adv.* **1.** According to moral principles: *Is it morally right to borrow a friend's book without asking?* **2.** According to accepted rules of conduct; virtuously. **3.** According to strong conviction or likelihood: *morally certain.*

mo•rass (mə răs′ *or* mô răs′) *n.* **1.** An area of low soggy ground; a bog or marsh. **2.** A difficult or overwhelming situation: *My paper started out fine, but then I got confused by a morass of details.* [First written down in 1655 in Modern English, from Old French *marais,* probably of Germanic origin.]

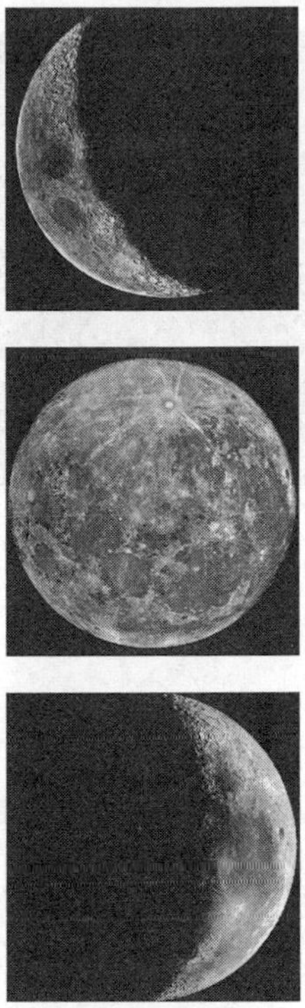

moon
Top: 4th day of new moon
Center: Full moon
Bottom: 24th day of new moon

moose
Bull moose

ă	**pat**	oi	**boy**
ā	**pay**	ou	**out**
âr	**care**	o͝o	**took**
ä	**father**	o͞o	**boot**
ĕ	**pet**	ŭ	**cut**
ē	**be**	ûr	**urge**
ĭ	**pit**	th	**thin**
ī	**pie**	*th*	**this**
îr	**pier**	hw	**whoop**
ŏ	**pot**	zh	**vision**
ō	**toe**	ə	**about**
ô	**paw**	N	*French* **bon**

J.P. Morgan

morning glory

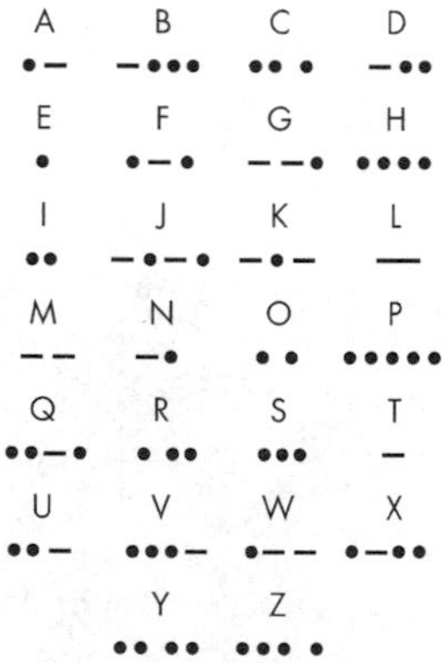

Morse code

mortarboard

mor•a•to•ri•um (môr′ə tôr′ē əm *or* mŏr′ə tôr′ē əm) *n., pl.* **mor•a•to•ri•ums** or **mor•a•to•ri•a** (môr′ə tôr′ē ə *or* mŏr′ə tôr′ē ə). **1.** A stopping of some activity for the time being; a temporary ban or pause. **2.** A period of delay granted before a debt must be paid.

Mo•ra•vi•a (mə rā′vē ə *or* mô rā′vē ə). A region of central and eastern Czech Republic. It was settled by a Slavic people at the end of the sixth century A.D. and became part of Czechoslovakia in 1918.

Mo•ra•vi•an (mə rā′vē ən) *n.* A native or inhabitant of Moravia. **—Mo•ra′vi•an** *adj.*

mo•ray (môr′ā *or* mə rā′) *n.* Any of numerous tropical ocean eels that have sharp teeth and commonly inhabit coral reefs. [First written down in 1624 in American English and spelled *moreraye*, from Greek *muraina*.]

mor•bid (môr′bĭd) *adj.* **1.** Of, caused by, or having to do with disease: *morbid changes in body tissues.* **2.** Preoccupied with death, decay, or other unwholesome matters; gruesome. [First written down in 1656 in Modern English, from Latin *morbidus*, diseased, from *morbus*, disease.] **—mor′bid•ly** *adv.* **—mor′bid•ness** *n.*

mor•bid•i•ty (môr bĭd′ĭ tē) *n., pl.* **mor•bid•i•ties.** **1.** The condition of being morbid. **2.** The rate of occurrence of a disease.

mor•dant (môr′dnt) *adj.* **1.** Bitter; sarcastic: *expressed resentment in mordant remarks.* **2.** Used to fix colors in dyeing. *—n.* **1.** A substance used to fix coloring matter in cloth, leather, or other materials. **2.** A substance, such as an acid, used to etch metal surfaces. **—mor′dan•cy** *n.* **—mor′dant•ly** *adv.*

more (môr) *adj.* Comparative of **many, much. 1.a.** Greater in number: *More people came to the show tonight than ever before.* **b.** Greater in size, amount, extent, or degree: *He does more work than anybody else.* **2.** Additional; extra: *I need more time to finish making dinner.* *—n.* A greater or additional quantity, number, degree, or amount: *More of our textbooks have arrived in the store.* *—pron. (used with a plural verb).* A greater number of persons or things: *I thought I had found all the empty bottles, but there were more in the basement.* *—adv.* Comparative of **much. 1.a.** To or in a greater extent or degree: *After seeing the movie again, we liked it even more.* **b.** Used to form the comparative of many adjectives and adverbs: *more difficult; more intelligently.* **2.** In addition; again: *I telephoned twice more, but got no answer.* ***—idioms.*** **more and more.** To a steadily increasing extent or degree: *got more and more annoyed at the noise.* **more or less. 1.** About; approximately: *The trip takes six hours, more or less.* **2.** To an undetermined degree: *We were more or less in agreement.*

More (*môr*), Sir **Thomas.** 1478–1535. English politician and scholar who was imprisoned and beheaded for treason. His works include the essay *Utopia* (1516).

mo•rel (mə rĕl′ *or* mô rĕl′) *n.* Any of various edible mushrooms having a brown spongy cap.

more•o•ver (môr ō′vər *or* môr′ō′vər) *adv.* Beyond what has been said; besides: *We are, moreover, delighted to report that progress has been made.*

mo•res (môr′āz′ *or* môr′ēz) *pl.n.* **1.** The accepted customs and rules of behavior of a particular social group. **2.** Attitudes about proper behavior; moral conventions: *the manners and mores of suburban life.*

Mor•gan (môr′gən), **John Pierpont.** 1837–1913. American financier and philanthropist noted for his control of major railroads and his consolidation of the U.S. Steel Corporation (1901).

Mor•gan le Fay (môr′gən lə fā′) *n.* In the legend of King Arthur, the sorceress who is Arthur's sister and enemy.

morgue (môrg) *n.* **1.** A place where the bodies of persons found dead are kept until identified or claimed. **2.** A file at a newspaper or magazine office for storing old issues and reference material. [First written down in 1821 in Modern English, from French, from *la Morgue*, building in Paris used as a morgue.]

mor•i•bund (môr′ə bŭnd′ *or* mŏr′ə bŭnd′) *adj.* At the point of death; about to die.

Mo•ri•sot (mô rē zō′), **Berthe.** 1841–1895. French impressionist painter noted for her canvases featuring women and children.

Mor•mon (môr′mən) *n.* **1.** A member of the Mormon Church. **2.** In the Mormon Church, an ancient prophet who appeared to Joseph Smith and imparted to him a sacred history of the Americas, later translated and published by Smith as the Book of Mormon. *—adj.* Of or relating to the Mormons or their church. **—Mor′mon•ism** *n.*

Mormon Church *n.* A Christian church founded by Joseph Smith in 1830, having doctrines based chiefly on the Bible and the Book of Mormon. The church's headquarters have been in Salt Lake City, Utah, since 1847.

morn (môrn) *n.* The morning.
❑ *These sound alike:* **morn, mourn** (grieve).

morn•ing (môr′nĭng) *n.* **1.** The early part of the day, from midnight to noon or from sunrise to noon. **2.** The time of sunrise; dawn. **3.** The first or early part; the beginning: *the morning of a new nation.*
❑ *These sound alike:* **morning, mourning** (grieving).

morning glory *n.* Any of numerous twining vines having showy funnel-shaped flowers that generally close in the afternoon.

morning star *n.* A planet, especially Venus, visible in the eastern sky before sunrise.

Mo•ro (môr′ō) *n., pl.* **Moro** or **Mo•ros.** A member of any of the Muslim Malay peoples of the southern Philippines.

mo•roc•co (mə rŏk′ō) *n., pl.* **mo•roc•cos.** A soft fine leather of goatskin, made originally in Morocco and used chiefly for binding books.

Mo•roc•co (mə rŏk′ō). A country of northwest Africa on the Mediterranean Sea and the Atlantic Ocean. Morocco gained its independence from France in 1956. Rabat is the capital and Casablanca the largest city. Population, 20,419,555.

mo•ron (môr′ŏn′) *n.* A person regarded as very stupid. [First written down in 1910 in American English, from Greek *mōron*, from *mōros*, stupid, foolish.] **—mo•ron′ic** (mə rŏn′ĭk *or* mô rŏn′ĭk) *adj.*

Mo•ro•ni (mə rō′nē). The capital of the Comoros, in the Indian Ocean west of Madagascar. Population, 20,112.

mo•rose (mə rōs′ *or* mô rōs′) *adj.* Ill-humored; gloomy. **—mo•rose′ly** *adv.* **—mo•rose′ness** *n.*

mor•pheme (môr′fēm′) *n.* A unit of language that has meaning and that cannot be divided into smaller meaningful parts. For example, *fire* is a morpheme; the *-s* in *fires* is also a morpheme.

Mor•phe•us (môr′fē əs) *n.* In Greek mythology, the god of dreams.

mor•phine (môr′fēn′) *n.* An addictive narcotic drug extracted from opium and used in medicine as an anesthetic and sedative.

mor•phol•o•gy (môr fŏl′ə jē) *n., pl.* **mor•phol•o•gies.** **1.** The branch of biology that deals with the form and structure of living organisms. **2.** The form and structure of an organism. **3.** In linguistics, the study of the structure and form of words, including inflections and derivations. **—mor′pho•log′i•cal, mor′pho•log′ic** *adj.*

Mor•ris (môr′ĭs *or* mŏr′ĭs), **Gouverneur.** 1752–1816. American political leader who helped produce the final draft of the U.S. Constitution (1787).
Mor•ris•town (môr′ĭs toun′ *or* mŏr′ĭs toun′). A town of northern New Jersey west-northwest of Newark. The Continental Army encamped here during the winters of 1776–1777 and 1779–1780. Population, 16,189.
mor•row (môr′ō *or* mŏr′ō) *n.* **1.** The following day; the next day: *They set out on the morrow.* **2.** *Archaic.* The morning.
Morse (môrs), **Samuel Finley Breese.** 1791–1872. American inventor who patented (1854) the telegraph and developed the Morse code.
Morse code *n.* Either of two codes used for sending messages in which letters of the alphabet and numbers are represented by combinations of short and long sounds or beams of light, known as dots and dashes. [First written down in 1867 in Modern English, after Samuel F.B. *Morse.*]
mor•sel (môr′səl) *n.* **1.** A small piece of food: *ate just a few morsels.* **2.** A small amount; a piece: *a morsel of gossip.*
mor•tal (môr′tl) *adj.* **1.** Subject to death: *All human beings are mortal.* **2.** Of or characteristic of human beings; human: *the mortal limits of endurance.* **3.** Of this world; earthly: *the mortal remains of a hero.* **4.** Causing or accompanying death: *a mortal wound.* **5.** Being so wicked or evil as to bring eternal damnation: *a mortal sin.* **6.** Fought to the death: *mortal battles.* **7.** Unrelenting; deadly: *a mortal enemy.* **8.** Extreme; dire: *in mortal fear.* —*n.* A human being. [First written down about 1370 in Middle English, from Latin *mortālis*, from *mors*, death.] —**mor′tal•ly** *adv.*
mor•tal•i•ty (môr tăl′ĭ tē) *n., pl.* **mor•tal•i•ties. 1.** The condition of being subject to death. **2.** Death, especially of large numbers: *a war accompanied by widespread civilian mortality.* **3.** The proportion of a given group of people that dies in a given period of time; death rate.
mor•tar (môr′tər) *n.* **1.** A bowl used to hold substances while they are crushed or ground with a pestle. **2.** Any of various machines in which substances are ground or crushed. **3.** A building material made of sand, water, lime, and often cement, used to hold together bricks, stones, or building blocks. **4.** A muzzle-loading cannon used to fire shells in a high arc. —*tr.v.* **mor•tared, mor•tar•ing, mor•tars. 1.** To plaster or join with mortar. **2.** To bombard with mortar shells.
mor•tar•board (môr′tər bôrd′) *n.* **1.** A square board with a handle, used for holding and carrying mortar. **2.** An academic cap with a flat square top and a tassel, worn upon graduation, for example.
mort•gage (môr′gĭj) *n.* **1.** A legal pledge of property to a creditor as security for the payment of a loan or debt: *the mortgage of one's house to a bank.* **2.** A written agreement specifying the terms of such a pledge. **3.** The claim that the creditor has on property pledged in this way. —*tr.v.* **mort•gaged, mort•gag•ing, mort•gag•es. 1.** To pledge (property) as security for the payment of a debt. **2.** To put in jeopardy for some immediate benefit; risk: *He mortgaged his future by borrowing lots of money.* [First written down before 1393 in Middle English and spelled *morgage*, from Old French : *mort*, dead + *gage*, pledge.]
mort•ga•gee (môr′gĭ jē′) *n.* The holder of a mortgage.
mort•ga•gor (môr′gĭ jôr′ *or* môr′gĭ jər) also **mort•gag•er** (môr′gĭ jər) *n.* A person who mortgages his or her property.
mor•tice (môr′tĭs) *n. & v.* Variant of **mortise.**
mor•ti•cian (môr tĭsh′ən) *n.* A funeral director; an undertaker.
mor•ti•fi•ca•tion (môr′tə fĭ kā′shən) *n.* **1.** The action or practice of subduing one's body, impulses, and desires by self-denial. **2.** Humiliation; embarrassment. **3.** Death or decay of a part of a living body; gangrene.
mor•ti•fy (môr′tə fī′) *v.* **mor•ti•fied, mor•ti•fy•ing, mor•ti•fies.** —*tr.* **1.** To subdue or discipline (one's body or physical desires) by practicing self-denial. **2.** To cause to feel shame or embarrassment; humiliate: *I was mortified by my cousin's rudeness at the ceremony.* —*intr.* To become gangrenous. [First written down before 1382 in Middle English and spelled *mortifien*, to deaden, subdue, from Latin *mortificāre*, to kill, from *mors*, death.] —**mor′ti•fi′er** *n.*
mor•tise also **mor•tice** (môr′tĭs) *n.* A rectangular hole in a piece of wood or other material, prepared to receive a tenon of another piece, so as to form a joint. —*tr.v.* **mor•tised, mor•tis•ing, mor•tis•es** also **mor•ticed, mor•tic•ing, mor•tic•es. 1.** To cut a mortise in. **2.** To join (two pieces) by means of a mortise and tenon.
mor•tu•ar•y (môr′cho͞o ĕr′ē) *n., pl.* **mor•tu•ar•ies.** A place where dead bodies are prepared or kept before burial or cremation.
mos. *abbr.* An abbreviation of months.
mo•sa•ic (mō zā′ĭk) *n.* **1.** A picture or design made on a surface by fitting and cementing together small colored pieces, as of tile, glass, or stone. **2.** The art or process of making such pictures or designs. **3.** Something that resembles a mosaic: *a mosaic of impressions.* **4.** A virus disease of certain plants, such as tobacco or tomatoes, that causes the leaves to become spotted or wrinkled. **5.** An organism or a part having adjacent cells or tissues of different genetic types.
Mo•sa•ic (mō zā′ĭk) *adj.* Of or relating to Moses or the laws said to have been written by him.
Mos•cow (mŏs′kou *or* mŏs′kō). The capital and largest city of Russia, in the west-central part of the country. It has been inhabited since Neolithic times. Population, 8,408,000.
Mos•es (mō′zĭz *or* mō′zĭs). In the Bible, the Hebrew prophet and lawgiver who led the Israelites out of Egypt.
Moses, Anna Mary Robertson. Known as "Grandma Moses." 1860–1961. American artist known for her colorful paintings of rural scenes.
mo•sey (mō′zē) *intr.v.* **mo•seyed, mo•sey•ing, mo•seys.** *Informal.* **1.** To move slowly or leisurely; stroll. **2.** To get going; leave.
Mos•lem (mŏz′ləm *or* mŏs′ləm) *n. & adj.* Variant of **Muslim.**
mosque (mŏsk) *n.* A Muslim house of worship. [First written down about 1400 in Middle English and spelled *moseak*, from Arabic *masjid.*]
mos•qui•to (mə skē′tō) *n., pl.* **mos•qui•toes** or **mos•qui•tos.** Any of various winged insects of which the females bite and suck blood from animals and human beings. Some kinds transmit diseases such as malaria and yellow fever. [First written down about 1583 in Modern English, from Spanish, gnat, from Latin *musca*, fly.] —SEE NOTE.
moss (môs *or* mŏs) *n.* **1.** Any of various small green or brown plants that do not have flowers and that often form a dense matted growth on damp ground, rocks, or tree trunks. **2.** Any of several similar plants. [First written down in 975 in Old English and spelled *mos*, bog.]
moss•y (mô′sē *or* mŏs′ē) *adj.* **moss•i•er, moss•i•est.** Of, resembling, or covered with moss.
most (mōst) *adj.* Superlative of **many, much. 1.a.** Greatest in number: *Who won the most votes?* **b.**

mosaic
Detail of a portrait of Justinian I (A.D. 483–565) in the Church of San Vitale in Ravenna, Italy

Word History: mosquito

How is a **mosquito** like a **musket**? Both words come from the Latin noun *musca*, "a fly (the insect)." The Latin word becomes *mosca* in Spanish. Spanish adds the diminutive ending *–ito* to *mosca* and changes the meaning to "little fly," and *mosquito* thus becomes the term for the bothersome insect we all love to hate. The Latin *musca* becomes *mosca* in Italian. Italian forms a diminutive noun *moschetta* (literally "little fly") meaning "the bolt or dart fired from a catapult." Later, Italian forms the noun *moschetto,* meaning "a small gun that fires lead balls" (that is, a **musket**), from the noun *moschetta*. French borrows the Italian *moschetto* and changes the spelling to *mousquet.* English borrows *mousquet* from French and changes the spelling to *musket.*

ă	**p**a**t**	oi	**b**oy
ā	**p**a**y**	ou	**out**
âr	**c**are	o͝o	**t**oo**k**
ä	**f**a**th**er	o͞o	**b**oo**t**
ĕ	**p**e**t**	ŭ	**c**u**t**
ē	**b**e	ûr	**u**r**g**e
ĭ	**p**i**t**	th	**th**in
ī	**p**ie	*th*	**th**is
îr	**p**ie**r**	hw	**wh**oop
ŏ	**p**o**t**	zh	vi**s**ion
ō	**t**oe	ə	**a**bout
ô	**p**aw	N	*French* bo**n**

Largest in amount, size, or degree: *the most money.* **2.** In the greatest number of instances: *Most fish have fins.* —*n.* The greatest amount, quantity, or degree; the largest part: *Most of this land is good.* —*pron. (used with a singular or plural verb).* The greatest part or number: *Most of the apples have been picked.* —*adv.* Superlative of **more, much. 1.** In the highest degree, quantity, or extent. Used with many adjectives and adverbs to form the superlative: *most honest; most impatiently.* **2.** Very: *a most impressive piece of work.* **3.** *Informal.* Almost; just about: *Most everybody's here already.* —***idiom.* at most** or **at the most.** At the maximum: *The professor spoke for ten minutes at most. We ran for two miles at the most.*

–most *suff.* A suffix that means most: *innermost.*

most•ly (**mōst′**lē) *adv.* **1.** For the most part; mainly: *The strawberry plants are mostly thriving.* **2.** Generally; usually: *We mostly try to get to bed before midnight.*

Mo•sul (mō **so͞ol′** *or* **mō′**səl). A city of northern Iraq on the Tigris River north-northwest of Baghdad. It was an important center on the historical caravan route across northern Mesopotamia. Population, 570,926.

mote (mōt) *n.* A speck, especially of dust: *Motes drifted in the sunlight near the window.*
❑ *These sound alike:* **mote, moat** (ditch).

mo•tel (mō **tĕl′**) *n.* A hotel for motorists, usually with rooms that open directly on a parking area. [First written down in 1925 in American English, blend of *motor* and *hotel.*]

moth (môth *or* mŏth) *n., pl.* **moths** (mô*thz* *or* mŏ*thz* *or* môths *or* mŏths). Any of numerous insects related to the butterflies but often flying at night and generally having a stouter body and feathery or slender antennae. [First written down about 950 in Old English and spelled *mohthe.*]

moth•ball (**môth′**bôl′ *or* **mŏth′**bôl′) *n.* **1.** A marble-sized ball of naphthalene, stored with clothes to repel moths. **2. mothballs.** A condition of long-term storage with protection against the weather: *After decades of use, the ocean liner was put into mothballs.* —*tr.v.* **moth•balled, moth•ball•ing, moth•balls.** To put into protective storage: *The experimental airplane was mothballed after funds for more research ran out.*

moth-eat•en (**môth′**ēt′n *or* **mŏth′**ēt′n) *adj.* **1.** Eaten away by moths: *a moth-eaten bedspread.* **2.** Old and stale: *a moth-eaten saying.*

moth•er[1] (**mŭ*th*′**ər) *n.* **1.** A woman who gives birth to or raises a child. **2.** A female parent of an animal. **3.** A source or cause: *Poverty is the mother of many ills.* **4.** A mother superior. **5.** A woman who starts or creates something: *Susan B. Anthony was one of the mothers of the women's suffrage movement.* —*adj.* **1.** Being a mother: *a mother hen.* **2.** Of or relating to a mother: *mother love.* **3.** Being the source or origin: *the mother church.* **4.** Native: *one's mother country.* —*tr.v.* **moth•ered, moth•er•ing, moth•ers. 1.** To give birth to. **2.** To watch over or nourish. [First written down before 725 in Old English and spelled *mōdor.*]

moth•er[2] (**mŭ*th*′**ər) *n.* A stringy slime made up of yeast cells and bacteria that forms on the surface of a fermenting liquid. It is often added to wine or cider to start production of vinegar. [First written down in 1538 in Modern English, probably from obsolete Dutch *moeder.*]

Mother Goose *n.* The imaginary author of *Mother Goose's Tales,* a collection of English nursery rhymes published in the 18th century.

moth•er•hood (**mŭ*th*′**ər ho͝od′) *n.* **1.** The condition of being a mother. **2.** Mothers considered as a group.

moth•er-in-law (**mŭ*th*′**ər ĭn lô′) *n., pl.* **moth•ers-in-law** (**mŭ*th*′**ərz ĭn lô′). The mother of one's wife or husband.

moth•er•land (**mŭ*th*′**ər lănd′) *n.* **1.** The country of one's birth. **2.** The land of one's ancestors.

moth•er•less (**mŭ*th*′**ər ləs′) *adj.* Having no living mother.

moth•er•ly (**mŭ*th*′**ər lē) *adj.* **1.** Of, like, or appropriate to a mother: *motherly affection.* **2.** Showing the affection of a mother. —**moth′er•li•ness** *n.*

moth•er-of-pearl (mŭ*th*′ər əv **pûrl′**) *n.* The hard, smooth, pearly layer on the inside of certain oyster shells and other seashells, used to make buttons and jewelry; nacre.

Moth•er's Day (**mŭ*th*′**ərz) *n.* The second Sunday in May, celebrated as a holiday in honor of mothers.

mother superior *n., pl.* **mothers superior** or **mother superiors.** A woman in charge of a religious community of women.

mother tongue *n.* **1.** One's native language. **2.** A language from which another language develops.

mother wit *n.* Natural good judgment that does not come from schooling; common sense.

mo•tif (mō **tēf′**) *n.* **1.** An idea or a symbol that recurs in a literary or artistic work. **2.** A short significant phrase in a piece of music. **3.** A repeated figure or design in architecture or decoration: *a necktie with a floral motif.* [First written down in 1848 in Modern English, from French, from Old French *motif,* motive.]

mo•tile (**mōt′**l *or* **mō′**tīl′) *adj.* Moving or able to move by itself; capable of spontaneous movement.

mo•tion (**mō′**shən) *n.* **1.a.** The process of moving; change of position. **b.** An act of moving; a movement: *the darting motions of dragonflies.* **2.** The ability to move: *The motion in his arm returned after physical therapy.* **3.** Operation; activity: *put the engine in motion.* **4.** A formal application or request: *No state by its own mere motion can get out of the Union.* **5.** A proposal put to a vote in a group following parliamentary procedure: *I moved to adjourn the meeting, and the motion passed by voice vote.* —*v.* **mo•tioned, mo•tion•ing, mo•tions.** —*tr.* To direct by a wave of the hand or another gesture; to signal: *The driver stopped and motioned us to cross.* —*intr.* To make a gesture expressing one's wishes: *motioned for us to enter the room.* —***idiom.* go through the motions.** To do something in a way that shows lack of purpose or interest.

mo•tion•less (**mō′**shən lĭs) *adj.* Not moving. —**mo′tion•less•ly** *adv.*

motion picture *n.* **1.** A movie. **2. motion pictures.** The movie industry.

motion sickness *n.* Nausea and dizziness caused by motion, as from traveling in a car or a ship.

mo•ti•vate (**mō′**tə vāt′) *tr.v.* **mo•ti•vat•ed, mo•ti•vat•ing, mo•ti•vates.** To provide with an incentive; move to action: *The coach motivated us to practice, and we improved dramatically.*

mo•ti•va•tion (mō′tə **vā′**shən) *n.* **1.** The process of providing motives: *studied the motivation of people who run for public office.* **2.** The condition of being motivated, especially to perform well: *These students have a high level of motivation.* **3.** A motive or set of motives; an incentive.

mo•tive (**mō′**tĭv) *n.* **1.** An emotion or need that causes a person to act in a certain way: *Our motive in writing the book was to make people aware of the issue.* **2.** (*also* mō **tēv′**). A motif in art, literature, or music. —*adj.* Causing or able to cause motion: *motive power supplied by a jet engine.* [First written down before 1376 in Middle English and spelled *motif,* from Late Latin *mōtīvus,* of motion, from Latin *movēre,* to move.]

mot•ley (mŏt′lē) *adj.* **1.** Made up of an odd assortment of different types: *a motley group of people from different neighborhoods.* **2.** Made up of many different colors: *the motley suit of a clown.* —*n., pl.* **mot•leys.** A costume of many colors worn by a clown or jester. [First written down about 1380 in Middle English, probably from *mot*, speck.]

mo•tor (mō′tər) *n.* **1.** A device that changes electric energy into mechanical energy. **2.** A device that produces mechanical energy from a fuel; an engine. **3.** Something, such as a machine or an engine, that produces or imparts motion: *the motor of a clock.* —*adj.* **1.** Propelled by an engine or a motor: *a motor ski tow.* **2.** Causing or producing motion: *motor power.* **3.** Of, for, or involving motors or engines: *motor oil.* **4.** Of, involving, or controlling movements of the muscles: *a motor reflex.* —*intr.v.* **mo•tored, mo•tor•ing, mo•tors.** To drive or travel in a motor vehicle. [First written down in 1447 in Middle English and spelled *motour*, Controller (God), from Latin *movēre*, to move.]

mo•tor•bike (mō′tər bīk′) *n.* **1.** A lightweight motorcycle. **2.** A pedal bicycle that has an attached motor.

mo•tor•boat (mō′tər bōt′) *n.* A boat powered by an internal-combustion engine.

mo•tor•cade (mō′tər kād′) *n.* A procession of motor vehicles.

mo•tor•car (mō′tər kär′) *n.* An automobile.

mo•tor•cy•cle (mō′tər sī′kəl) *n.* A vehicle with two wheels, similar to a bicycle but larger and heavier, propelled by an internal-combustion engine. —*intr. v.* **mo•tor•cy•cle, mo•tor•cy•cled, mo•tor•cy•cles.** To ride a motorcycle. —**mo′tor•cy′clist** *n.*

mo•tor•ist (mō′tər ĭst) *n.* A person who drives or rides in an automobile.

mo•tor•ize (mō′tə rīz′) *tr.v.* **mo•tor•ized, mo•tor•iz•ing, mo•tor•iz•es. 1.** To equip with a motor or motors. **2.** To supply with motor-driven vehicles.

motor scooter *n.* A small two-wheeled vehicle that is propelled by a gasoline engine.

motor vehicle *n.* A self-propelled vehicle that travels on wheels but does not run on rails.

Mott (mŏt), **Lucretia Coffin.** 1793–1880. American feminist and abolitionist who with Elizabeth Cady Stanton called the first convention for women's rights, held at Seneca Falls, New York (1848).

mot•tle (mŏt′l) *tr.v.* **mot•tled, mot•tling, mot•tles.** To cover (a surface) with spots or streaks of different colors: *Her arms were lightly mottled with freckles.* —*n.* **1.** One of many little spots or streaks. **2.** A pattern of such markings.

mot•tled (mŏt′ld) *adj.* Spotted or streaked with different colors: *the mottled breast of a bird.*

mot•to (mŏt′ō) *n., pl.* **mot•toes** or **mot•tos. 1.** A phrase or statement expressing a principle, a goal, or an ideal: *"Don't tread on me" was the motto on the flag of the colonies during the American Revolution.* **2.** A brief expression of a guiding principle; a slogan: *His motto has always been "He who hesitates is lost."* [First written down in 1589 in Modern English, from Italian.]

mound (mound) *n.* **1.** A naturally formed area of high ground, as a small hill. **2.** A pile of earth or rocks heaped up, as for protection or concealment: *the mound marking a woodchuck's hole; a burial mound.* **3.** A pile or mass of something: *mounds of mashed potatoes.* **4.** The raised pitcher's area in the middle of a baseball diamond. [First written down in 1515 in Modern English.]

mount[1] (mount) *v.* **mount•ed, mount•ing, mounts.** —*tr.* **1.** To climb; ascend: *mounted the stairs.* **2.a.** To get up on: *mount a bicycle.* **b.** To provide with a riding horse. **3.** To plan and start to carry out: *mounted a campaign for literacy.* **4.** To provide (a theatrical performance) with scenery and costumes; stage. **5.a.** To set in a raised position: *mounted the weathervane on the roof.* **b.** To set (guns) in position for firing. **c.** To place in a secure position for display or study: *mount a specimen on a microscope slide.* **6.** To post (a guard): *mount sentries around the encampment.* —*intr.* **1.** To go upward; rise: *We watched the airplane mount into the sky.* **2.** To get up on something, such as a horse. **3.** To increase; grow higher: *Expenses are mounting quickly.* —*n.* **1.** A horse or another animal for riding. **2.** A frame or structure for holding or supporting something: *the mounts of a telescope.* [First written down before 1300 in Middle English and spelled *mounten*, from Old French *monter*, from Latin *mōns*, mountain.]

mount[2] (mount) *n.* A mountain. [First written down about 750 in Old English and spelled *munt*, from Latin *mōns*.]

moun•tain (moun′tən) *n.* **1.** A raised portion of the earth's surface, generally massive and rising to a great height, having more or less steep sides. **2.** A large heap or quantity: *a mountain of paperwork.* [First written down before 1200 in Middle English and spelled *mountaine*, from Latin *montānus*, of a mountain, from *mōns*, mountain.]

moun•tain•eer (moun′tə nîr′) *n.* **1.** A person who lives in a mountainous area. **2.** A person who climbs mountains for sport. —*intr.v.* **moun•tain•eered, moun•tain•eer•ing, moun•tain•eers.** To climb mountains for sport.

mountain goat *n.* A mammal of the mountains of northwest North America, similar to a goat and having short black horns and thick white hair.

mountain laurel *n.* A shrub of eastern North America having poisonous evergreen leaves and clusters of pink or white flowers.

mountain lion *n.* A large tawny wild cat of mountainous regions of western North America and South America.

moun•tain•ous (moun′tə nəs) *adj.* **1.** Having many mountains: *a mountainous region.* **2.** Huge; massive: *mountainous snowdrifts.*

mountain range *n.* A row or group of connected mountains.

moun•tain•side (moun′tən sīd′) *n.* The side of a mountain.

Mountain Standard Time *n.* Standard time in the seventh time zone west of Greenwich, England, used in the Rocky Mountain states of the United States, for example.

moun•tain•top (moun′tən tŏp′) *n.* The top of a mountain.

moun•te•bank (moun′tə băngk′) *n.* **1.** A seller of quack medicines who attracts customers with stories or tricks. **2.** A swindler; a charlatan.

Mount•ie also **Mount•y** (moun′tē) *n., pl.* **Mount•ies.** *Informal.* A member of the Royal Canadian Mounted Police.

mount•ing (moun′tĭng) *n.* A supporting structure or frame; a mount: *a mounting for a gem.*

Mount Ver•non (mount vûr′nən). An estate of northeast Virginia on the Potomac River near Washington, D.C. It was the home of George Washington from 1752 to 1799.

Mount•y (moun′tē) *n.* Variant of **Mountie.**

mourn (môrn) *v.* **mourned, mourn•ing, mourns.** —*intr.* To feel or express sorrow, especially for a person's death; grieve. —*tr.* **1.** To grieve over (a person who has died). **2.** To feel or express regret about: *mourning his unhappy lot.* [First written down before 725 in Old English and spelled *murnan.*] —**mourn′er** *n.*

❑ *These sound alike:* **mourn, morn** (morning).

mourn•ful (môrn′fəl) *adj.* **1.** Feeling or showing

motorboat

Lucretia Mott

mountain goat

mountain laurel

ă	pat	oi	boy
ā	pay	ou	out
âr	care	ŏŏ	took
ä	father	ōō	boot
ĕ	pet	ŭ	cut
ē	be	ûr	urge
ĭ	pit	th	thin
ī	pie	*th*	this
îr	pier	hw	whoop
ŏ	pot	zh	vision
ō	toe	ə	about
ô	paw	N	*French* bon

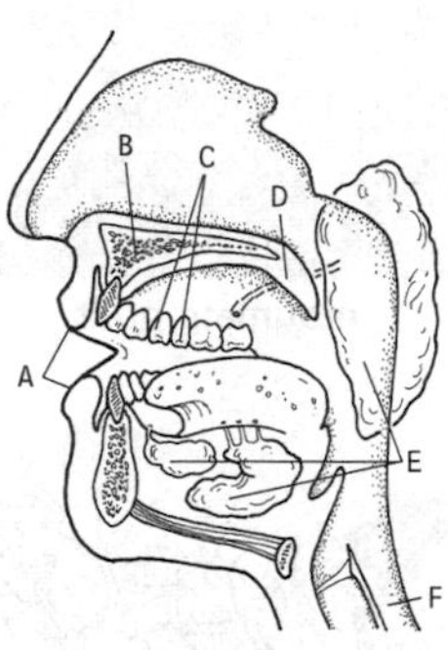

mouth
A. Lips
B. Hard palate
C. Teeth
D. Soft palate
E. Salivary glands
F. Esophagus

grief. **2.** Causing or suggesting grief: *the mournful wail of a foghorn.* **—mourn'ful•ly** *adv.* **—mourn'ful•ness** *n.*

mourn•ing (môr'nĭng) *n.* **1.** The expression of grief and respect for a person who has died: *The flag was flown at half-mast as a sign of mourning.* **2.** The condition of a person showing grief over a death or loss: *in mourning for a friend.* **3.** Traditional signs of grief for the dead, such as black clothes. **4.** The period during which a death is mourned.

❑ *These sound alike:* **mourning, morning** (daybreak).

mourning dove *n.* A North American bird related to the pigeons, having a long tail and a hollow mournful call.

mouse (mous) *n., pl.* **mice** (mīs). **1.** Any of numerous small rodents usually having a pointed snout, rounded ears, and a long narrow tail. Some kinds live in or near human dwellings. **2.** A timid person. **3.** *pl.* **mice** or **mous•es** (mous'ĭz). A device that is moved along a surface to control the movement of a cursor on a computer screen. *—intr.v.* (mouz). **moused, mous•ing, mous•es.** To hunt for mice. [First written down before 700 in Old English and spelled *mūs.*]

mous•er (mou'zər) *n.* An animal, especially a cat, that catches mice.

mouse•trap (mous'trăp') *n.* A trap for catching mice.

mous•ey (mou'sē *or* mou'zē) *adj.* Variant of **mousy.**

mousse (mo͞os) *n.* **1.** A chilled dessert made from whipped cream or beaten egg whites, gelatin, and flavoring. **2.** A molded dish made from meat, fish, or shellfish and whipped cream. **3.** A styling foam for hair. [First written down in 1892 in Modern English, from French, from Old French *mousse,* moss, foam.]

❑ *These sound alike:* **mousse, moose** (deer).

mous•tache (mŭs'tăsh' *or* mə stăsh') *n.* Variant of **mustache.**

mous•y also **mous•ey** (mou'sē *or* mou'zē) *adj.* **mous•i•er, mous•i•est. 1.** Resembling a mouse, especially in color: *mousy brown hair.* **2.** Timid and shy: *a mousy person.*

mouth (mouth) *n., pl.* **mouths** (mou*th*z). **1.a.** The opening of the body through which an animal takes in food. **b.** The group of organs associated with this opening and its function, including the teeth, lips, and tongue. **c.** The opening to a cavity or canal in an organ or organism. **2.** The part of the lips that can be seen on a human face. **3.** A natural opening, such as the opening of a cave or canyon or the part of a river that empties into a larger body of water. **4.** An opening into a container or an enclosure: *the mouth of a bottle.* *—tr.v.* (mou*th*). **mouthed, mouth•ing, mouths. 1.** To utter in a pretentious manner: *mouthed a list of his accomplishments.* **2.** To utter mechanically, without conviction or understanding: *mouthing phrases.* **3.** To hold or move around in the mouth: *The baby was mouthing her spoon.* ***—idiom.*** **mouth off.** *Slang.* To speak impudently; talk back. [First written down before 830 in Old English and spelled *mūth.*]

mouth•ful (mouth'fo͝ol') *n.* **1.** An amount taken into the mouth at one time: *We enjoyed every mouthful of the dessert.* **2.** An important or intelligent remark: *You just said a mouthful.* **3.** A word or phrase that is long and hard to pronounce.

mouth organ *n.* **1.** A harmonica. **2.** A panpipe.

mouth•part (mouth'pärt') *n.* Any of the parts of the mouth of an insect or a similar animal, especially a part adapted to a specific way of feeding.

mouth•piece (mouth'pēs') *n.* **1.** The part of a device that is in or near the mouth when the device is in use: *the mouthpiece of a telephone.* **2.** A protective piece of rubber worn over the teeth, as by a football player. **3.** *Informal.* A person who expresses the viewpoint of another person or of a group.

mouth-to-mouth resuscitation (mouth'tə mouth') *n.* A method of providing air to a person who has stopped breathing, in which the rescuer presses his or her mouth to the mouth of the victim and blows air into the victim's lungs at regular intervals.

mouth•wash (mouth'wŏsh' *or* mouth'wôsh') *n.* A liquid preparation used to cleanse the mouth and freshen the breath.

mov•a•ble also **move•a•ble** (mo͞o'və bəl) *adj.* **1.** Possible to move: *a movable rock.* **2.** Changing its date from year to year: *a movable holiday.* *—n.* Furniture or other personal possessions that can be moved. Often used in the plural.

move (mo͞ov) *v.* **moved, mov•ing, moves.** *—intr.* **1.** To change in position from one place or point to another: *The speaker moved to the middle of the stage.* **2.** To follow a specified course: *Earth moves around the sun.* **3.** To change one's place of residence or business: *Our family moved here last year.* **4.** To advance; progress: *Work on the house was moving slowly.* **5.** To make a formal request or proposal: *move for a court adjournment.* **6.** To be active in a particular social setting: *She moves in the highest diplomatic circles.* **7.** To take action: *If we don't move quickly, there won't be any woods left.* *—tr.* **1.** To change the place or position of: *Let's move the desk against the wall.* **2.** To cause to go from one place to another: *The police moved the crowd away from the stadium gates.* **3.** To change (a piece) to another position on a board, as in chess. **4.** To persuade or motivate: *What moved her to switch schools?* **5.** To arouse the emotions of: *That song moved me the first time I heard it.* **6.** To propose or request in a formal way, as at a meeting: *I move that we adjourn.* **7.** To empty (the bowels). *—n.* **1.** The act of moving: *He made a move to open the door.* **2.** A calculated action to achieve an end: *The opponents, in a surprise move, changed their game plan.* **3.a.** An act of changing the position of a piece in a board game. **b.** A player's turn to move a piece, as in checkers: *It's your move.* ***—idioms.*** **get a move on.** *Informal.* To get started; get going. **move in.** To begin to occupy a residence or place of business. **on the move. 1.** Moving about from one place to another: *The taxi driver was on the move all day.* **2.** Making progress; advancing: *This area of research is really on the move.* [First written down about 1275 in Middle English and spelled *moven,* from Latin *movēre.*]

move•a•ble (mo͞o'və bəl) *adj. & n.* Variant of **movable.**

move•ment (mo͞ov'mənt) *n.* **1.** The act or an instance of moving: *The movement of water in a stream affects what kind of plants can live there. She snatched up the ball in a quick movement.* **2.** A change in the location of military troops, ships, or aircraft. **3.** The activities of a group of people toward a specific goal: *the civil rights movement.* **4.** A tendency or trend: *a movement toward smaller cars.* **5.** A mass migration: *the westward movement of the pioneers.* **6.** An illusion of motion: *The arches and vertical lines emphasized the upward movement of the building.* **7.a.** An emptying of the bowels. **b.** The waste matter removed by this action. **8.** One of the large sections of a musical composition, usually having a distinct beginning and end. **9.** A mechanical device or system that produces or transmits motion: *the movement of a watch.*

mov•er (mo͞o'vər) *n.* **1.** A person or thing that moves: *The railroad became a prime mover of people and products in all directions.* **2.** A person or company that is hired to move furniture and other belongings from one place to another.

mov•ie (mo͞o′vē) *n.* **1.a.** A sequence of photographs projected on a screen in rapid succession, creating the illusion that what is in the pictures moves as in real life. **b.** A story told in such pictures. **2. movies. a.** A showing of a movie: *We went to the movies last night.* **b.** The industry that makes movies.

mov•ing (mo͞o′vĭng) *adj.* **1.** Changing or capable of changing position: *the moving parts of an engine.* **2.** Relating to or involving the transfer of furniture from one location to another: *a moving van.* **3.** Involving a motor vehicle in motion: *got a ticket for a moving violation.* **4.** Affecting the emotions: *a moving love story.* **—mov′ing•ly** *adv.*

moving picture *n.* A movie.

mow[1] (mou) *n.* **1.** A pile of hay or grain, especially one stored in a barn. **2.** The part of a barn where such a pile is stored. [First written down before 800 in Old English and spelled *mūha.*]

mow[2] (mō) *v.* **mowed, mowed** or **mown** (mōn), **mow•ing, mows.** *—tr.* **1.** To cut down (grass or grain) with a scythe or a machine such as a lawn mower: *Mow the grass before it gets too high.* **2.** To cut the grass or grain from: *mow the lawn; mow a field.* *—intr.* To cut down grass or other growth. ***—idiom.* mow down.** To destroy in great numbers as if cutting down, as in battle. [First written down before 899 in Old English and spelled *māwan.*] **—mow′er** *n.*

Mo•zam•bique (mō′zəm **bēk′**). A country of southeast Africa east of Zimbabwe. Mozambique gained its independence from Portugal in 1975. Maputo is the capital and the largest city. Population, 12,130,000.

Mo•zart (mōt′särt), **Wolfgang Amadeus.** 1756–1791. Austrian composer known for his symphonies and operas, including *The Magic Flute* (1791).

moz•za•rel•la (mŏt′sə **rĕl′**ə) *n.* A soft white Italian cheese.

MP or **M.P.** *abbr.* An abbreviation of: **1.** Member of Parliament. **2.** Military police. **3.** Military police officer.

mpg or **m.p.g.** *abbr.* An abbreviation of miles per gallon.

mph or **m.p.h.** *abbr.* An abbreviation of miles per hour.

Mr. (**mĭs′**tər) *n., pl.* **Messrs.** (**mĕs′**ərz). Used as a courtesy title before the last name or full name of a man.

mRNA *abbr.* An abbreviation of messenger RNA.

Mrs. (**mĭs′**ĭz) *n., pl.* **Mmes.** (mā **däm′** *or* mā **dăm′**). Used as a courtesy title before the last name or full name of a married, widowed, or divorced woman. —SEE NOTE at **Ms.**

MS *abbr.* An abbreviation of: **1.** Mississippi. **2.** Multiple sclerosis.

Ms. also **Ms** (mĭz) *n., pl.* **Mses.** also **Mses** also **Mss.** also **Mss** (**mĭz′**ĭz). Used as a courtesy title before the last name or full name of a woman or girl. —SEE NOTE.

MS. or **MS** also **ms.** or **ms** *abbr.* An abbreviation of manuscript.

M.S. *abbr.* An abbreviation of Master of Science.

Mses. also **Mses** (**mĭz′**ĭz) *n.* Plurals of **Ms.**

Msgr. *abbr.* An abbreviation of Monseigneur.

Mss. also **Mss** (**mĭz′**ĭz) *n.* Plurals of **Ms.**

MST or **M.S.T.** *abbr.* An abbreviation of Mountain Standard Time.

mt. or **Mt.** *abbr.* An abbreviation of: **1.** Mount. **2.** Mountain.

mu (myo͞o *or* mo͞o) *n.* The 12th letter of the Greek alphabet, written M, μ. In English it is represented as *M, m.*

much (mŭch) *adj.* **more** (môr), **most** (mōst). Great in quantity, degree, or extent: *much talk and little action.* *—n.* **1.** A large quantity or amount: *Did you get much done?* **2.** Something remarkable or important: *In spite of all our work, the experiment did not amount to much.* *—adv.* **more, most. 1.** To a large extent; greatly: *We are much impressed with the results of your research.* **2.** Just about; almost: *much the same.* [First written down before 725 in Old English and spelled *mycel.*]

much as *conj.* Even though; however much: *Much as I love skating, I'd rather go to the movies.*

mu•ci•lage (**myo͞o′**sə lĭj) *n.* **1.** A clear brown adhesive made from the natural gum of plants. **2.** Any of various sticky gelatinous secretions present in certain plants such as seaweeds.

muck (mŭk) *n.* **1.** Moist animal dung; manure. **2.** Dark soil containing rotting vegetable matter. **3.** A moist sticky mixture, as of mud and filth.

muck•rake (**mŭk′**rāk′) *intr.v.* **muck•raked, muck•rak•ing, muck•rakes.** To search for and expose corruption in public affairs. **—muck′rak′er** *n.*

mu•cous (**myo͞o′**kəs) *adj.* **1.** Of or like mucus. **2.** Producing or secreting mucus.

❑ *These sound alike:* **mucous, mucus** (gland secretion).

mucous membrane *n.* A membrane, covered with glands that secrete mucus, that lines all the passages of the body that connect with the outside. The alimentary canal and the respiratory system are lined with mucous membrane, for example.

mu•cus (**myo͞o′**kəs) *n.* The sticky slippery liquid material secreted by the glands of the mucous membranes as a protective lubricating coating.

❑ *These sound alike:* **mucus, mucous** (like mucus).

mud (mŭd) *n.* **1.** Wet, sticky, soft earth. **2.** Slanderous charges: *sling mud at a political opponent.*

mud•dle (**mŭd′**l) *v.* **mud•dled, mud•dling, mud•dles.** *—tr.* **1.** To make a mess of; bungle: *muddle a task.* **2.** To confuse; befuddle: *I was muddled by the complicated math problem.* *—intr.* To think or act in a confused way: *The band muddled through the rest of the song.* *—n.* A jumble; a mess.

mud•dy (**mŭd′**ē) *adj.* **mud•di•er, mud•di•est. 1.** Covered or soiled with mud: *a muddy field; muddy shoes.* **2.** Cloudy or dull with or as if with mud: *a muddy creek; muddy coffee.* **3.** Confused; vague: *muddy thinking.* *—tr.v.* **mud•died, mud•dy•ing, mud•dies. 1.** To make soiled with mud: *He muddied his boots crossing the yard.* **2.** To make cloudy or dull with or as if with mud: *soil erosion muddies the rivers.* **3.** To confuse: *remarks that only muddied the issue.* **—mud′di•ly** *adv.* **—mud′di•ness** *n.*

mud puppy also **mud•pup•py** (**mŭd′**pŭp′ē) *n., pl.* **mud pup•pies** also **mud•pup•pies.** Any of several North American salamanders of lakes, ponds, and streams, having prominent clusters of dark red external gills.

mud•sling•ing (**mŭd′**slĭng′ĭng) *n.* The practice of making malicious charges against an opponent, especially in a political campaign. **—mud′sling′er** *n.*

mu•ez•zin (myo͞o **ĕz′**ĭn *or* mo͞o **ĕz′**ĭn) *n.* A crier who calls Muslims to prayer.

muff[1] (mŭf) *v.* **muffed, muff•ing, muffs.** *—tr.* **1.** To perform or handle clumsily; bungle: *She played the first song well, but muffed the second. I muffed my chance for the job.* **2.** To fail to make (a catch), as in baseball. *—intr.* To do something clumsily: *The ball was thrown to him, and he muffed.* [First written down in 1841 in Modern English, from *muff,* clumsy person.]

muff[2] (mŭf) *n.* **1.** A tubelike cover of fur or cloth with open ends into which the hands are put for warmth. **2.** A cluster of feathers on the side of the face of certain breeds of fowl. [First written down

Wolfgang Amadeus Mozart

Usage: Ms.

The courtesy title **Ms.** has come to be widely used. It is particularly convenient to use when you are not sure if the woman you are addressing is married. It is parallel to **Mr.**, the courtesy title for men. Many women continue to prefer **Mrs.** or **Miss**, so it is best to use the term preferred by the woman whom you are addressing.

muff[2]

ă	pat	oi	boy
ā	pay	ou	out
âr	care	o͝o	took
ä	father	o͞o	boot
ĕ	pet	ŭ	cut
ē	be	ûr	urge
ĭ	pit	th	thin
ī	pie	*th*	this
îr	pier	hw	whoop
ŏ	pot	zh	vision
ō	toe	ə	about
ô	paw	N	*French* bon

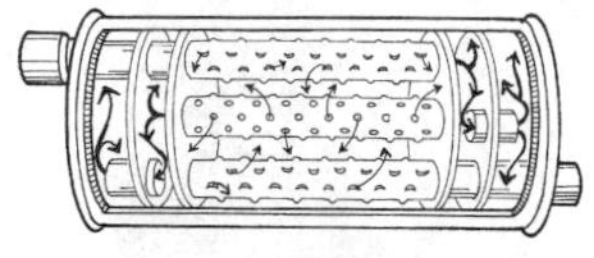

muffler
Reverse-flow muffler

mulberry

mule[1]

in 1599 in Modern English, from Medieval Latin *muffula*, mitten, perhaps of Germanic origin.]

muf•fin (mŭf′ĭn) *n.* A small cup-shaped quick bread, often sweetened.

muf•fle (mŭf′əl) *tr.v.* **muf•fled, muf•fling, muf•fles. 1.** To wrap up in order to keep warm, conceal, or protect: *I muffled the baby in a bunting.* **2.a.** To make less loud or less distinct; deaden: *muffle sound.* **b.** To wrap up or pad in order to deaden the sound of: *muffle a drum.*

muf•fler (mŭf′lər) *n.* **1.** A scarf worn around the neck for warmth. **2.** A device that deadens noise, especially one used on an automobile engine.

muf•ti (mŭf′tē) *n.* Civilian clothes worn by a person who normally wears a uniform.

mug[1] (mŭg) *n.* A large heavy drinking cup, usually having a handle and often used for hot beverages. [First written down in 1570 in Modern English, perhaps of Scandinavian origin.]

mug[2] (mŭg) *n. Informal.* A person's face. *—v.* **mugged, mug•ging, mugs.** *—tr. Informal.* To assault with the intent of robbing. *—intr.* To make faces, especially to be funny. [First written down in 1708 in Modern English, probably from *mug*, drinking cup (possibly in allusion to mugs decorated with grotesque faces).] **—mug′ger** *n.*

mug•gy (mŭg′ē) *adj.* **mug•gi•er, mug•gi•est.** Warm and humid with little or no breeze: *a muggy day in August.* **—mug′gi•ness** *n.*

mug•wump (mŭg′wŭmp′) *n.* A person who acts independently, especially in politics.

Mu•ham•mad (mo͝o hăm′ĭd *or* mo͝o hä′mĭd) also **Mo•ham•med** (mō hăm′ĭd *or* mō hä′mĭd). 570?–632. Arab prophet of Islam who began to convert Arabia to Islam after 622.

Mu•ham•mad•an (mo͝o hăm′ĭ dən) also **Mo•ham•med•an** (mō hăm′ĭ dən) *adj.* Of or relating to Muhammad or Islam; Muslim. *—n. Offensive.* A Muslim.

mu•lat•to (mo͝o lăt′ō *or* myo͝o lăt′ō) *n., pl.* **mu•lat•tos** or **mu•lat•toes. 1.** A person having one white and one Black parent. **2.** A person of mixed white and Black ancestry.

mul•ber•ry (mŭl′bĕr′ē *or* mŭl′bə rē) *n.* **1.a.** Any of several trees having irregularly shaped leaves and sweet purplish or white fruit shaped like blackberries. **b.** The fruit of such a tree. **2.** A grayish to dark purple.

mulch (mŭlch) *n.* A protective covering, as of leaves or hay, placed around growing plants to keep the soil moist, prevent the roots from freezing, and prevent weeds from growing. *—tr.v.* **mulched, mulch•ing, mulch•es.** To cover with mulch. [First written down in 1657 in Modern English, probably from Middle English *molsh*, soft, from Old English *melsc*, mellow, mild.]

mulct (mŭlkt) *tr.v.* **mulct•ed, mulct•ing, mulcts. 1.** To penalize by fining or demanding the surrender of something. **2.** To acquire or take away from by trickery or deception.

mule[1] (myo͞ol) *n.* **1.** A hybrid mammal that is the offspring of a male donkey and a female horse. **2.** *Informal.* A stubborn person. **3.** A spinning machine that draws and twists fibers into yarn and winds the yarn at the same time. [First written down before 830 in Old English and spelled *mūl*, from Latin *mūlus*.]

❑ *These sound alike:* **mule**[1] (animal), **mewl** (whimper), **mule**[2] (slipper).

mule[2] (myo͞ol) *n.* A slipper that leaves the heel bare. [First written down in 1562 in Modern English, ultimately from Latin *mulleus (calceus)*, reddish-purple (ceremonial shoe).]

❑ *These sound alike:* **mule**[2] (slipper), **mewl** (whimper), **mule**[1] (animal).

mul•ish (myo͞o′lĭsh) *adj.* Stubborn; unyielding: *a mulish disposition.* See Synonyms at **obstinate.** **—mul′ish•ly** *adv.* **—mul′ish•ness** *n.*

mull[1] (mŭl) *tr.v.* **mulled, mull•ing, mulls.** To heat and add sugar and spices to (wine, ale, or cider). [First written down in 1607 in Modern English.]

mull[2] (mŭl) *tr. & intr.v.* **mulled, mull•ing, mulls.** To think about; ponder: *He mulled over the idea for days.* [First written down in 1873 in American English, probably from Middle English *mullen*, to moisten, crumble.]

mul•lein (mŭl′ən) *n.* Any of various tall plants having long tight clusters of yellow flowers and leaves covered with woolly down.

mul•let (mŭl′ĭt) *n., pl.* **mullet** or **mul•lets.** Any of various stout gray or red saltwater or freshwater fishes often used as food.

Mul•ro•ney (mŭl rō′nē *or* mŭl ro͞o′nē), **(Martin) Brian.** Born 1939. Canadian prime minister (1984–1993).

multi– *pref.* A prefix that means: **1.** Many; much: *multicolored.* **2.** More than two: *multiracial.* **3.** Many times over: *multimillionaire.*

mul•ti•cel•lu•lar (mŭl′tē sĕl′yə lər) *adj.* Having or consisting of many cells.

mul•ti•col•ored (mŭl′tĭ kŭl′ərd) *adj.* Having many colors.

mul•ti•far•i•ous (mŭl′tə fâr′ē əs) *adj.* Having great variety; diverse: *the multifarious occupations in a modern economy.*

mul•ti•lat•er•al (mŭl′tĭ lăt′ər əl) *adj.* **1.** Having many sides. **2.** Involving more than two sides: *a multilateral trade agreement.*

mul•ti•me•di•a (mŭl′tē mē′dē ə) *adj.* Relating to or using several media, such as videotape, music, lighting, and slides, especially for the purpose of education or entertainment.

mul•ti•mil•lion•aire (mŭl′tē mĭl′yə nâr′) *n.* A person whose financial assets are worth several million dollars.

mul•ti•na•tion•al (mŭl′tē năsh′ə nəl *or* mŭl′tē năsh′nəl) *adj.* **1.** Having operations or smaller divisions in more than two countries: *a multinational corporation.* **2.** Of or involving more than two countries: *a multinational agreement.*

mul•ti•ple (mŭl′tə pəl) *adj.* Having, relating to, or consisting of more than a single element, part, or individual: *a plan with multiple advantages.* *—n.* A number that may be divided by another number with no remainder; for example, 4, 6, 8, and 12 are multiples of 2.

multiple sclerosis *n.* A disease in which there is degeneration of the central nervous system, with hard patches of tissue formed throughout the brain or spinal cord, causing muscular weakness and loss of coordination.

mul•ti•pli•cand (mŭl′tə plĭ kănd′) *n.* A number that is to be multiplied by another number.

mul•ti•pli•ca•tion (mŭl′tə plĭ kā′shən) *n.* **1.** The act or process of multiplying. **2.** A mathematical operation performed on a pair of numbers in order to derive a third number called a product. It is sometimes convenient to consider multiplication as repeated addition in which one number indicates how many times the other is to be added together. For example, $3 \times 4 = 4 + 4 + 4 = 4 \times 3 = 3 + 3 + 3 + 3 = 12$.

multiplication sign *n.* The sign (×) placed between a pair of numbers to show that multiplication is to be performed on them.

mul•ti•plic•i•ty (mŭl′tə plĭs′ĭ tē) *n., pl.* **mul•ti•plic•i•ties.** A great number or variety: *a multiplicity of courses to choose from.*

mul•ti•pli•er (mŭl′tə plī′ər) *n.* **1.** The number by which another number is multiplied. **2.** An instrument or a device that causes an increase of a force or current.

mul•ti•ply (mŭl′tə plī′) *v.* **mul•ti•plied, mul•ti•ply•ing, mul•ti•plies.** —*intr.* **1.** To increase in number or amount. See Synonyms at **increase. 2.** To produce offspring; breed. **3.** To perform multiplication. —*tr.* To perform multiplication on (a pair of numbers).

mul•ti•ra•cial (mŭl′tē rā′shəl) *adj.* Made up of or involving various races: *Hawaii is an example of a multiracial society.*

mul•ti•stage (mŭl′tĭ stāj′) *adj.* Designed to perform a process or operation in more than one stage: *a multistage rocket.*

mul•ti•tude (mŭl′tĭ to͞od′ *or* mŭl′tĭ tyo͞od′) *n.* **1.** A large number: *We face a multitude of challenges.* **2.** The common people: *The multitude rejected both candidates in the election.*

mul•ti•tu•di•nous (mŭl′tĭ to͞od′n əs *or* mŭl′tĭ tyo͞od′n əs) *adj.* Existing in great numbers; very numerous: *the multitudinous stars of our galaxy.*

mum[1] (mŭm) *adj.* Not talking; close-mouthed; silent: *Keep mum.* [First written down before 1376 in Middle English and spelled *mom,* sound made with closed lips.]

mum[2] (mŭm) *n.* A chrysanthemum. [First written down in 1924 in Modern English, short for *chrysanthemum.*]

mum•ble (mŭm′bəl) *tr. & intr.v.* **mum•bled, mum•bling, mum•bles.** To speak or utter in an indistinct manner, as by lowering the voice and partially closing the mouth: *I can't understand you when you mumble. He mumbled a quick apology.* —*n.* A low indistinct sound or utterance: *answered the teacher in a mumble.* [First written down about 1325 in Middle English and spelled *momelen,* from Middle Dutch *mommelen.*] —**mum′bler** *n.*

mum•ble•ty-peg (mŭm′bəl tē pĕg′ *or* mŭm′blē pĕg′) also **mum•ble-the-peg** (mŭm′bəl *th*ə pĕg′) *n.* A game in which the players throw a knife from various positions, with the object being to make the blade stick firmly in the ground.

mum•bo jum•bo or **mum•bo-jum•bo** (mŭm′bō jŭm′bō) *n., pl.* **mum•bo jum•bos** or **mum•bo-jum•bos. 1.** A complicated ceremony or ritual. **2.** Speech or writing that is unclear or impossible to understand.

mum•mer (mŭm′ər) *n.* **1.a.** A person who acts or plays in a pantomime. **b.** An actor. **2.** A masked merrymaker at a festival.

mum•mer•y (mŭm′ə rē) *n., pl.* **mum•mer•ies. 1.** A performance by mummers. **2.** A fake or insincere show or ceremony.

mum•mi•fy (mŭm′ə fī′) *v.* **mum•mi•fied, mum•mi•fy•ing, mum•mi•fies.** —*tr.* To make into a mummy by embalming and drying. —*intr.* To shrivel up like a mummy. —**mum′mi•fi•ca′tion** (mŭm′ə fĭ kā′shən) *n.*

mum•my[1] (mŭm′ē) *n., pl.* **mum•mies. 1.** The body of a human being or an animal embalmed after death, as practiced by the ancient Egyptians. **2.** A dead body shrunken or preserved by a natural process. [First written down in 1392 in Middle English and spelled *mummie,* medicinal material from embalmed corpses, from Arabic *mūmiyā',* from *mūm,* wax.]

mum•my[2] (mŭm′ē) *n., pl.* **mum•mies.** *Informal.* Mother. [First written down in 1784 in Modern English, alteration of *mammy,* mother.]

mumps (mŭmps) *pl.n.* *(used with a singular or plural verb).* A contagious virus disease that causes inflammation of the salivary glands, especially those at the back of the jaw.

munch (mŭnch) *v.* **munched, munch•ing, munch•es.** —*tr.* To chew (food) in a noisy steady manner: *munch popcorn.* —*intr.* To chew food noisily and steadily: *They found the cow munching away in a pasture.*

mun•dane (mŭn dān′ *or* mŭn′dān′) *adj.* Worldly; not spiritual: *mundane interests.*

Mu•nich (myo͞o′nĭk). A city of southeast Germany near the Alps southeast of Bonn. It was founded in 1158 and has long been the center of Bavaria. Population, 1,267,451.

mu•nic•i•pal (myo͞o nĭs′ə pəl) *adj.* Of or relating to a municipality: *municipal politics; the municipal airport.*

mu•nic•i•pal•i•ty (myo͞o nĭs′ə păl′ĭ tē) *n., pl.* **mu•nic•i•pal•i•ties.** A city or town that is self-governing in local matters.

mu•nif•i•cent (myo͞o nĭf′ĭ sənt) *adj.* Very generous: *a munificent reward.* —**mu•nif′i•cence** *n.* —**mu•nif′i•cent•ly** *adv.*

mu•ni•tions (myo͞o nĭsh′ənz) *pl.n.* Supplies for warfare, especially weapons and ammunitions.

Mun•ro (mən rō′), **Alice.** Born 1931. Canadian writer known for her vivid novels and short shories of life in rural Ontario.

mu•ral (myo͝or′əl) *n.* A large picture or decoration applied directly to a wall or ceiling. —*adj.* **1.** Of, relating to, or resembling a wall. **2.** Painted on or applied to a wall. [First written down before 1439 in Middle English, from Latin *mūrus,* wall.]

Mu•ra•sa•ki Shi•ki•bu (mo͞o′rä sä′kē shē′kē boo′), Baroness. 978?–1031?. Japanese writer whose *The Tale of Genji* is considered to be the first full novel.

mur•der (mûr′dər) *n.* The unlawful and deliberate killing of one person by another. —*v.* **mur•dered, mur•der•ing, mur•ders.** —*tr.* **1.** To kill (a person or persons) unlawfully and with deliberate intent. **2.** To ruin; spoil: *a writer who murders the language.* —*intr.* To commit murder. —**mur′der•er** *n.*

mur•der•ous (mûr′dər əs) *adj.* **1.** Guilty of, capable of, or intent on murder: *a murderous mob.* **2.** Of or relating to murder: *murderous acts.* **3.** Angry or savage, as if intent on murder: *a murderous glance.*

mu•rex (myo͝or′ĕks) *n., pl.* **mu•ri•ces** (myo͝or′ĭ sēz′) or **mu•rex•es.** Any of various sea mollusks having a rough or spiny spiral shell. One type of murex was used in ancient times as the source of a highly valued purplish dye.

murk also **mirk** (mûrk) *n.* Darkness; gloom: *groped his way through the murk of the night.*

murk•y (mûr′kē) *adj.* **murk•i•er, murk•i•est. 1.** Dark; gloomy: *a murky dungeon.* See Synonyms at **dark. 2.** Foggy; hazy: *a murky day.* **3.** Cloudy and dark with sediment: *the swamp's murky water.* —**murk′i•ly** *adv.* —**murk′i•ness** *n.*

mur•mur (mûr′mər) *n.* **1.** A low continuous sound: *the murmur of the waves.* **2.** A complaint made in a low voice: *took the scolding without a murmur.* **3.** An abnormal sound made by the heart, lungs, or blood vessels. —*v.* **mur•mured, mur•mur•ing, mur•murs.** —*intr.* **1.** To make a low continuous sound: *The brook murmured through the forest.* **2.** To speak or complain in an undertone: *The students murmured among themselves about the new regulations.* —*tr.* To say in a low voice; utter indistinctly: *murmured his approval.*

Mus•cat (mŭs′kăt′ *or* mŭs′kət). The capital of Oman, in the northern part of the country on an inlet of the Arabian Sea. Population, 30,000.

mus•cle (mŭs′əl) *n.* **1.** A type of body tissue composed of fibers that are capable of contracting and relaxing to cause movement or exert force. **2.** Any of the many structures of the body that are made of such tissue and cause bodily movement. **3.** Muscular strength; brawn: *The swimming team has plenty of muscle.* **4.** *Informal.* Power or authority: *a for-*

mummer

mummy[1]

mural

ă	pat	oi	boy
ā	pay	ou	out
âr	care	o͝o	took
ä	father	o͞o	boot
ĕ	pet	ŭ	cut
ē	be	ûr	urge
ĭ	pit	th	thin
ī	pie	*th*	this
îr	pier	hw	whoop
ŏ	pot	zh	vision
ō	toe	ə	about
ô	paw	N	*French* bon

museum

mushroom

musk ox
Musk ox bull

Benito Mussolini

gotten city ordinance that had no muscle. —*intr.v.* **mus•cled, mus•cling, mus•cles.** *Informal.* To force one's way into a place or situation where one is not wanted: *muscle in on someone else's job.* [First written down in 1392 in Middle English and spelled *mucell,* from Latin *mūsculus,* little mouse.]

❑ *These sound alike:* **muscle, mussel** (mollusk).

mus•cle•bound also **mus•cle-bound** (**mŭs′**-əl bound′) *adj.* Having muscles that are overly developed and stiff, usually as a result of too much exercise.

mus•co•vite (**mŭs′**kə vīt′) *n.* The most common form of mica, a usually colorless to pale gray mineral composed mostly of a silicate of potassium and aluminum.

Muscovite *n.* A native or resident of Moscow.

mus•cu•lar (**mŭs′**kyə lər) *adj.* **1.** Of, relating to, or consisting of muscle: *a muscular organ.* **2.** Having strong well-developed muscles: *a muscular gymnast.* —**mus′cu•lar′i•ty** (mŭs′kyə **lăr′**ĭ tē) —**mus′-cu•lar•ly** *adv.*

Synonyms: muscular, athletic, brawny, burly, sinewy. These adjectives all mean strong and powerfully built. *I lift weights because I want a more muscular body. The athletic young woman won all the races at the company picnic. They need some brawny friends to help move that piano. The wharf was crowded with burly men waiting to unload the ship's cargo. Professional dancers are usually lean and sinewy.* **Antonym: scrawny.**

muscular dys•tro•phy (**dĭs′**trə fē) *n.* A hereditary disease in which a person's muscles gradually and irreversibly deteriorate, causing weakness and finally complete disability.

mus•cu•la•ture (**mŭs′**kyə lə cho͝or′) *n.* The system of muscles of an animal or of a body part.

muse (myo͞oz) *intr.v.* **mused, mus•ing, mus•es.** To consider at length; ponder; meditate: *musing over his chances in tomorrow's game.* [First written down in 1340 in Middle English and spelled *musen,* from Old French *muser,* possibly from *mus,* snout.]

❑ *These sound alike:* **muse, Muse** (goddess), **mews** (alley).

Muse (myo͞oz) *n.* **1.** In Greek mythology, one of the nine sister goddesses who preside over the arts and sciences. **2. muse. a.** A guiding spirit. **b.** A source of inspiration. [First written down about 1380 in Middle English, from Greek *Mousa.*]

❑ *These sound alike:* **Muse, mews** (alley), **muse** (consider).

mu•se•um (myo͞o **zē′**əm) *n.* A building in which objects of artistic, historical, or scientific interest are exhibited. [First written down in 1615 in Modern English, from Greek *Mouseion,* shrine of the Muses.]

mush[1] (mŭsh) *n.* **1.** A porridge made of corn meal boiled in water or milk. **2.** A thick soft mass. **3.** *Informal.* Extreme sentimentality: *That movie was just a lot of mush.* [First written down in 1671 in American English, probably alteration of *mash.*]

mush[2] (mŭsh) *intr.v.* **mushed, mush•ing, mush•es.** To travel over snow with a dogsled. —*interj.* An expression used to command a team of sled dogs to start pulling or go faster. [First written down in 1862 in American English and spelled *mouche,* possibly alteration of French *marchons,* let's go!]

mush•room (**mŭsh′**ro͞om′ *or* **mŭsh′**ro͝om′) *n.* **1.** Any of various types of fungus having a stalk topped by a fleshy umbrella-shaped cap. Some mushrooms are used as food, but many kinds are poisonous. **2.** Something resembling a mushroom in shape. —*intr.* **mush•roomed, mush•room•ing, mush•rooms.** To grow, multiply, or spread quickly: *The population in that suburb mushroomed during the last decade.* —*adj.* **1.** Relating to or containing mushrooms: *mushroom soup.* **2.** Resembling a mushroom in shape: *a mushroom cloud.*

mush•y (**mŭsh′**ē *or* **mo͝osh′**ē) *adj.* **mush•i•er, mush•i•est. 1.** Resembling mush; soft and pulpy: *The apples were mushy and brown inside.* **2.** *Informal.* Very sentimental: *a mushy love story.* —**mush′i•ly** *adv.* —**mush′i•ness** *n.*

mu•sic (**myo͞o′**zĭk) *n.* **1.** The art of arranging sounds in combinations by rhythm, harmony, and melody, to please or interest a listener. **2.** Vocal or instrumental sounds that have rhythm, melody, harmony, or some combination of these. **3.a.** A musical composition. **b.** A group of such compositions that are related in some way: *the music of Bach.* **c.** A written or printed score or part for a musical composition: *Play from the music.* **d.** Such scores or parts considered as a group. **4.** A pleasing sound or combination of sounds: *the music of the wind in the trees.* [First written down about 1250 in Middle English and spelled *musike,* from Greek *(hē) mousikē (tekhnē),* (art) of the Muses.]

mu•si•cal (**myo͞o′**zĭ kəl) *adj.* **1.** Of, involving, or used in producing music: *a musical instrument; musical training.* **2.** Accompanied by or set to music: *a musical play.* **3.** Devoted to or skilled in music. **4.** Pleasing to the ear; melodious: *a musical voice.* —*n.* A play or movie in which songs are included along with the dialogue. —**mu′si•cal•ly** *adv.*

musical comedy *n.* A play or movie that has songs and dialogue; a musical.

mu•si•cale (myo͞o′zĭ **kăl′**) *n.* A musical program performed at a party or social gathering.

mu•si•cal•i•ty (myo͞o′zĭ **kăl′**ĭ tē) *n.* **1.** The quality of being musical. **2.** Musical talent or good taste.

music box *n.* An automatic mechanical device that produces musical sounds, usually by plucking tuned pieces of thin steel.

music drama *n.* A type of opera in which the music and dramatic action go on without interruption rather than being divided into separate pieces such as arias, recitatives, or duets.

music hall *n.* A theater for musical entertainment or vaudeville.

mu•si•cian (myo͞o **zĭsh′**ən) *n.* A person who is skilled in performing or composing music.

mu•si•cian•ship (myo͞o **zĭsh′**ən shĭp′) *n.* Skill, taste, and artistry in performing or composing music.

musk (mŭsk) *n.* **1.** A strong-smelling substance produced by certain glands of the male musk deer of Asia and used in making perfume. **2.** A similar substance produced by other animals, such as the otter, or made artificially. **3.** The odor of musk.

musk deer *n.* A small hornless deer of central and northeast Asia, the male of which secretes musk.

mus•kel•lunge or **mus•ke•lunge** (**mŭs′**kə lŭnj′) *n., pl.* **muskellunge** or **mus•kel•lung•es.** A large North American freshwater fish related to and resembling the pike.

mus•ket (**mŭs′**kĭt) *n.* A long-barreled gun used before the invention of the rifle. [First written down about 1587 in Modern English, ultimately from Italian *moschetto,* a type of crossbow, musket, from *mosca,* fly.]

mus•ket•eer (mŭs′kĭ **tîr′**) *n.* **1.** A soldier armed with a musket. **2.** A member of the French royal household bodyguard in the 17th and 18th centuries.

mus•ket•ry (**mŭs′**kĭ trē) *n.* **1.** Muskets considered as a group. **2.** The technique of firing small arms.

Mus•kho•ge•an (mŭs **kō′**gē ən) *n.* Variant of **Muskogean.**

musk•mel•on (**mŭsk′**mĕl′ən) *n.* Any of several types of melon, such as the cantaloupe, having a rough rind and edible orange or green flesh with a musky odor.

Mus•ko•ge•an also **Mus•kho•ge•an** (mŭs kō′gē ən) *n.* A family of Native American languages of the southeast United States that includes Choctaw, Chickasaw, Creek, and Alabama. **—Mus•ko′ge•an** *adj.*

musk ox *n.* A large animal of northern North America and Greenland, having dark shaggy hair and curved horns and giving off a musky odor.

musk•rat (mŭs′krăt′) *n., pl.* **muskrat** or **musk•rats. 1.** A North American rodent that lives in or near water and has thick brown fur, a flat scaly tail, and a musky odor. **2.** The fur of such an animal.

musk•y (mŭs′kē) *adj.* **musk•i•er, musk•i•est.** Of, relating to, or having the heavy sweet odor of musk. **—musk′i•ness** *n.*

Mus•lim (mŭz′ləm *or* mo͝os′ləm) or **Mos•lem** (mŏz′ləm *or* mŏs′ləm) *n.* A believer in Islam. *—adj.* Of or relating to Islam or its believers.

mus•lin (mŭz′lĭn) *n.* A cotton cloth of plain weave, either coarse or sheer, used especially for sheets.

muss (mŭs) *tr.v.* **mussed, muss•ing, muss•es.** To make untidy or messy: *The wind mussed up my hair.*

mus•sel (mŭs′əl) *n.* Any of several saltwater or freshwater mollusks having a pair of narrow, often dark blue shells.

❑ *These sound alike:* **mussel, muscle** (tissue fiber).

Mus•so•li•ni (mo͞o′sə lē′nē *or* mo͝os′ə lē′nē), **Beni•to.** Known as "Il Duce." 1883–1945. Italian Fascist dictator and prime minister (1922–1943) who brought Italy into World War II (1940). He was assassinated in 1945.

mus•sy (mŭs′ē) *adj.* **muss•i•er, muss•i•est.** In a state of disarray; untidy. **—muss′i•ly** *adv.*

must (mŭst) *aux.v.* **1.** To be required or obliged: *Human beings must have oxygen to live.* **2.** Used to express a command or a warning: *You must be careful when working on a ladder.* **3.** Used to indicate certainty or inevitability: *All good things must come to an end.* **4.** To be determined; be resolved: *If you must talk, do so quietly.* *—n.* Something that is required or necessary: *A good tent is a must when you go camping.*

mus•tache also **mous•tache** (mŭs′tăsh′ *or* mə stăsh′) *n.* The hair growing on a man's upper lip, especially when it is shaped and groomed. [First written down in 1585 in Modern English, from Greek *mustax*, upper lip.]

mus•ta•chio (mə stăsh′ō *or* mə stăsh′ē ō′) *n., pl.* **mus•ta•chios.** A mustache, especially one that is large and full.

mus•tang (mŭs′tăng′) *n.* A small strong horse of the plains of western North America, especially a wild descendant of the horses brought to the New World by Spanish explorers.

mus•tard (mŭs′tərd) *n.* **1.** Any of various plants of Europe and Asia having yellow flowers and small sharp-tasting seeds. **2.a.** The powdered seeds of this plant. **b.** A spicy condiment made from the powdered seeds of this plant. **3.** A dark brownish yellow. ***—idiom.* cut the mustard.** To perform up to expectations or to a required standard. [First written down in 1289 in Middle English and spelled *mostard*, from Old French *mustarde*, from Latin *mustum*, unfermented wine.]

mus•ter (mŭs′tər) *v.* **mus•tered, mus•ter•ing, mus•ters.** *—tr.* **1.** To bring together; assemble: *mustered his troops for inspection.* **2.** To call forth or bring forth: *mustered enough courage to ask the boss for a raise.* *—intr.* To come together; assemble: *The troops mustered for inspection:* *—n.* **1.** A gathering, especially of troops, for inspection, roll call, or some other purpose. **2.** The official roll of persons in a military unit.

must•n't (mŭs′ənt). Contraction of *must not.*

must•y (mŭs′tē) *adj.* **must•i•er, must•i•est. 1.** Stale or moldy: *a musty smell.* **2.** Overused and old-fashioned: *a musty phrase.* **—must′i•ness** *n.*

mu•ta•ble (myo͞o′tə bəl) *adj.* **1.** Capable of or subject to change: *All things in nature are mutable.* **2.** Likely to change: *mutable weather in the mountains.* **—mu′ta•bil′i•ty** *n.*

mu•tant (myo͞ot′nt) *n.* A living thing that, as a result of mutation, has characteristics that are different from those of its parents. *—adj.* Changed as a result of mutation: *a mutant animal.*

mu•tate (myo͞o′tāt *or* myo͞o tāt′) *intr. & tr.v.* **mu•tat•ed, mu•tat•ing, mu•tates.** To undergo or cause to undergo change, especially by mutation. [First written down in 1818 in Modern English, from Latin *mūtāre*, to change.]

mu•ta•tion (myo͞o tā′shən) *n.* **1.a.** A change in the genes or chromosomes of a living thing that can be inherited by its offspring. **b.** A mutant. **2.** A change, as in form: *the mutations in pronunciation since Shakespeare's time.*

mute (myo͞ot) *adj.* **mut•er, mut•est. 1.** Unable to speak. **2.** Refraining from speech; silent: *remained mute under questioning.* **3.** Expressed without speech; unspoken: *the mute approval in his smile.* **4.** Not pronounced; silent: *the mute* e *in* house. *—n.* **1.** *Offensive.* A person incapable of speech. **2.** Any of various attachments used to soften, muffle, or alter the tone of a musical instrument. *—tr.v.* **mut•ed, mut•ing, mutes.** To muffle or soften the sound of: *The additional insulation in the walls muted the noise of the people living next door.* [First written down about 1385 in Middle English and spelled *muwet*, from Old French, from Latin *mūtus*.] **—mute′ly** *adv.* **—mute′ness** *n.*

mu•ti•late (myo͞ot′l āt′) *tr.v.* **mu•ti•lat•ed, mu•ti•lat•ing, mu•ti•lates. 1.** To damage by cutting off or mangling (a necessary part, such as a limb). **2.** To damage badly; ruin: *The photo was mutilated in the mail.* **—mu′ti•la′tion** *n.*

mu•ti•neer (myo͞ot′n îr′) *n.* A person, especially a soldier or sailor, who takes part in a mutiny.

mu•ti•nous (myo͞ot′n əs) *adj.* **1.** Of or being mutiny: *a mutinous act.* **2.** Engaged in or planning to engage in mutiny: *a mutinous officer.* **3.** Unruly; rebellious: *a mutinous child.* **—mu′ti•nous•ly** *adv.*

mu•ti•ny (myo͞ot′n ē) *n., pl.* **mu•ti•nies.** Open rebellion against authority, especially rebellion of sailors against officers in charge. *—intr.v.* **mu•ti•nied, mu•ti•ny•ing, mu•ti•nies.** To engage in mutiny; rebel. [First written down in 1567 in Modern English, from obsolete *mutine*, from Old French *mutin*, rebellious, from Latin *movēre*, to move.]

Mu•tsu•hi•to (mo͞o′tso͞o hē′tō) Called **Mei•ji** (mā′jē′). 1852–1912. Emperor of Japan (1867–1912) who presided over Japan's transformation into a modern state.

mutt (mŭt) *n. Informal.* A dog of mixed breed; a mongrel.

mut•ter (mŭt′ər) *v.* **mut•tered, mut•ter•ing, mut•ters.** *—intr.* **1.** To say or speak in low unclear tones: *She muttered to herself while she worked.* **2.** To complain or grumble: *muttered about the high price of food.* *—tr.* To say in low unclear tones: *He muttered something underneath his breath.* *—n.* Something spoken in low unclear tones.

mut•ton (mŭt′n) *n.* The meat of a fully grown sheep.

mu•tu•al (myo͞o′cho͞o əl) *adj.* **1.** Having the same relationship to each other: *mutual friends.* **2.** Possessed or shared in common: *discussed our mutual problems.* **3.** Given and received in equal amounts:

mustang

mute
On a trumpet

Mutsuhito

ă	**pat**	oi	**boy**
ā	**pay**	ou	**out**
âr	**care**	o͝o	**took**
ä	**father**	o͞o	**boot**
ĕ	**pet**	ŭ	**cut**
ē	**be**	ûr	**urge**
ĭ	**pit**	th	**thin**
ī	**pie**	*th*	**this**
îr	**pier**	hw	**whoop**
ŏ	**pot**	zh	**vision**
ō	**toe**	ə	**about**
ô	**paw**	N	*French* **bon**

mutual respect. [First written down in 1539 in Modern English, from Latin *mūtuus*, borrowed.] **—mu′tu•al•ly** *adv.*

mutual fund *n.* A company that freely buys and sells its own shares and uses the pooled capital of its shareholders to invest in other companies.

muz•zle (mŭz′əl) *n.* **1.** The projecting nose and jaws of certain animals, such as a dog or horse. **2.** A leather or wire device fitted over an animal's snout to prevent biting or eating. **3.** The front end of the barrel of a gun. *—tr.v.* **muz•zled, muz•zling, muz•zles. 1.** To put a muzzle on (an animal). **2.** To prevent (a person) from expressing an opinion. [First written down about 1385 in Middle English and spelled *mosel*, from Medieval Latin *mūsellum*, from Latin *mūsum*, snout.]

muz•zle•load•er (mŭz′əl lō′dər) *n.* A firearm that is loaded at the muzzle. **—muz′zle•load′ing** *adj.*

MW *abbr.* An abbreviation of megawatt.

my (mī) *adj.* The possessive form of **I. 1.** Belonging or relating to me: *my pencil; my good review by the boss.* **2.** Used before various forms of address to indicate politeness or affection: *My friend, you are so right.* **3.** Used in expressions of surprise or dismay: *My word! My goodness! —interj.* An expression used to show surprise or dismay: *My! What a mess!*

Myan•mar (myän mär′). Burma.

my•ce•li•um (mī sē′lē əm) *n., pl.* **my•ce•li•a** (mī-sē′lē ə). A mass of fine branching strands that form the main growing structure of a fungus.

My•ce•nae (mī sē′nē). An ancient Greek city in the northeast Peloponnesus that flourished as the center of an early Bronze Age civilization.

my•col•o•gy (mī kŏl′ə jē) *n., pl.* **my•col•o•gies. 1.** The scientific study of fungi. **2.** The fungi of a particular region or country.

my•e•lin (mī′ə lĭn) *n.* A soft, whitish, fatty substance that forms a sheath about the core of certain nerve fibers.

my•na or **my•nah** also **mi•na** (mī′nə) *n.* Any of various Asian birds related to and resembling the starlings. Some kinds can be taught to imitate human speech. [First written down in 1769 in Modern English, from Hindi *mainā*.]

my•o•pi•a (mī ō′pē ə) *n.* A defect of the eye that makes distant objects appear blurred because their images are focused in front of the retina rather than on it; nearsightedness.

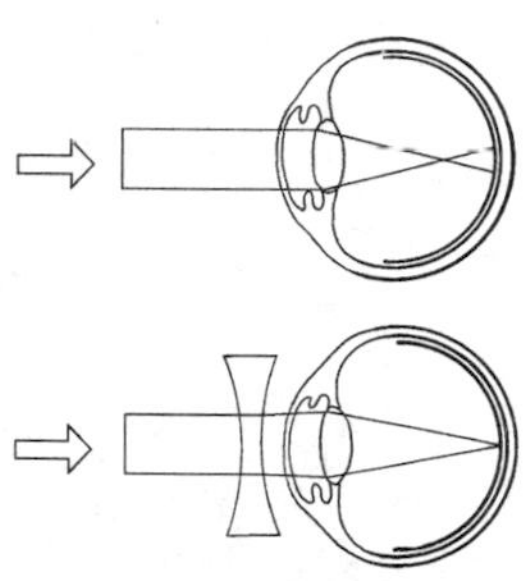

myopia
Top: Before correction
Bottom: After correction

my•op•ic (mī ŏp′ĭk) *adj.* Of or affected with myopia; nearsighted.

myr•i•ad (mĭr′ē əd) *adj.* Amounting to a very large indefinite number: *the myriad fish in the ocean. —n.* A vast number.

myrrh (mûr) *n.* A pleasant-smelling gummy substance obtained from certain African and Asian trees and shrubs and used in perfume and incense. [First written down before 830 in Old English and spelled *myrre*, from Greek *murrha*.]

myr•tle (mûr′tl) *n.* **1.** Any of several shrubs having evergreen leaves, white or pinkish flowers, and blackish berries. **2.** Any of several trailing vines having glossy evergreen leaves and usually blue flowers.

my•self (mī sĕlf′) *pron.* **1.** That one that is the same as me: **a.** Used as the direct object or indirect object of a verb or as the object of a preposition, to show that the action of the verb refers back to the subject: *I injured myself. I gave myself a pep talk. I spent little of the money on myself.* **b.** Used to give emphasis: *I myself had to laugh.* **2.** My normal or healthy self: *I was sick, but I'm feeling myself again.*

mys•te•ri•ous (mĭ stîr′ē əs) *adj.* **1.** Of or implying a mystery: *Antarctica is a strange and mysterious land.* **2.** Difficult or impossible to understand or explain: *the mysterious disappearance of the books.* **—mys•te′ri•ous•ly** *adv.* **—mys•te′ri•ous•ness** *n.*

mys•ter•y (mĭs′tə rē) *n., pl.* **mys•ter•ies. 1.** Something that is difficult to explain or understand: *How he got into the house is a mystery.* **2.** Something that is a secret: *The teacher kept our grades a mystery.* **3.** The quality associated with the unknown or unexplained: *The old house had an air of mystery.* **4.** A piece of fiction dealing with a puzzling crime. **5.** An event such as the Incarnation or Resurrection that serves as a subject for meditation by Roman Catholics. [First written down before 1333 in Middle English and spelled *misterie*, from Greek *mustērion*, secret rite, from *mustēs*, an initiate.]

mystery play *n.* A medieval play based on Biblical events especially in the life of Jesus.

mys•tic (mĭs′tĭk) *adj.* **1.** Of or relating to religious or supernatural rites and practices. **2.** Inspiring a sense of mystery; mysterious: *the mystic effects of a new moon.* **3.** Of or relating to mysticism. *—n.* A person who practices or believes in mysticism.

mys•ti•cal (mĭs′tĭ kəl) *adj.* **1.** Of or relating to the mystics or mysticism and its practices: *the mystical books of the alchemists.* **2.** Based on spiritual insight or intuition rather than experience or reasoning: *mystical spirituality.* **—mys′ti•cal•ly** *adv.*

mys•ti•cism (mĭs′tĭ sĭz′əm) *n.* **1.** The experience of spiritual union or direct communication with God. **2.** The belief that direct communication with God can be attained through deep meditation. **3.** Confused and groundless thinking.

mys•ti•fy (mĭs′tə fī′) *tr.v.* **mys•ti•fied, mys•ti•fy•ing, mys•ti•fies.** To confuse or bewilder: *We were mystified by their response.* **—mys′ti•fi•ca′tion** (mĭs′tə fĭ kā′shən) *n.*

mys•tique (mĭ stēk′) *n.* A feeling of mystery or wonder that surrounds an activity, a person, or a group: *the mystique of the wildlife photographer.*

myth (mĭth) *n.* **1.a.** A traditional story dealing with ancestors, heroes, or supernatural beings, and usually making an attempt to explain a belief, practice, or natural phenomenon: *the myth that gods built the mountains.* **b.** Such stories considered as a group: *Greek myth.* **2.** A fictitious or imaginary story, person, or thing: *the myth of the giant fish in the lake.* **3.** A false belief that is part of an ideology: *the myth that all tax increases are bad.* [First written down in 1830 in Modern English, from Greek *muthos*.]

myth•i•cal (mĭth′ĭ kəl) also **myth•ic** (mĭth′ĭk) *adj.* **1.** Of or existing only in myths: *a mythical beast such as the unicorn.* **2.** Imaginary; fancied: *a mythical account of a voyage to a floating island.*

myth•o•log•i•cal (mĭth′ə lŏj′ĭ kəl) *adj.* **1.** Of or existing in myths: *a mythological animal.* **2.** Fabulous; imaginary.

my•thol•o•gy (mĭ thŏl′ə jē) *n., pl.* **my•thol•o•gies. 1.** A body of myths, especially one dealing with the origin, gods, and heroes of a specific people: *Roman mythology.* **2.** The field of scholarship that deals with the study of myths.

Nn

n[1] or **N** (ĕn) *n., pl.* **n's** or **N's. 1.** The 14th letter of the English alphabet. **2.** The 14th in a series or group: *row n in a theater.*
n[2] *n.* An indefinite number.
N[1] The symbol for the element **nitrogen.**
N[2] *abbr.* An abbreviation of: **1.** North. **2.** Northern.
n. *abbr.* An abbreviation of: **1.** Noun. **2.** Number.
Na The symbol for the element **sodium.**
N.A. *abbr.* An abbreviation of North America.
NAACP or **N.A.A.C.P.** *abbr.* An abbreviation of National Association for the Advancement of Colored People.
nab (năb) *tr.v.* **nabbed, nab•bing, nabs.** *Informal.* **1.** To catch in the act; arrest: *The policeman nabbed the bank robber.* **2.** To grab; snatch: *They nabbed all the tickets before we could get to the box office.*
na•bob (nā′bŏb′) *n.* **1.** A governor in India under the Mogul Empire. **2.** A person of wealth and prominence.
na•celle (nə sĕl′) *n.* A streamlined enclosure mounted on an aircraft to house an engine or shelter cargo or the crew.
na•cho (nä′chō′) *n., pl.* **na•chos.** A small, usually triangular piece of tortilla, often topped with cheese or chili pepper sauce and broiled.
na•cre (nā′kər) *n.* Mother-of-pearl.
na•dir (nā′dər *or* nā′dîr′) *n.* **1.** A point on the celestial sphere directly below the observer, opposite the zenith. **2.** The lowest point: *the nadir of our troubles.*
nag[1] (năg) *v.* **nagged, nag•ging, nags.** —*tr.* **1.** To pester or annoy, as by complaining or scolding. **2.** To cause continuous pain or annoyance to: *My sore shoulder has been nagging me all day.* —*intr.* To scold or complain constantly: *The children have been nagging at me all day.* —*n.* A person who nags. [First written down in 1825 in Modern English, probably of Scandinavian origin; akin to Old Norse *gnaga,* to bite, gnaw.] —**nag′ger** *n.*
nag[2] (năg) *n.* A horse, especially an old or worn-out horse. [First written down before 1400 in Middle English and spelled *nagge,* possibly of Low German origin.]
Na•ga•sa•ki (nä′gə sä′kē *or* năg′ə săk′ē). A city of western Kyushu, Japan, on **Nagasaki Bay,** an inlet of the East China Sea. Nagasaki was destroyed by the second atomic bomb used in World War II (August 9, 1945). Population, 449,382.
Na•hua•tl (nä′wät′l) *n., pl.* **Nahuatl** or **Na•hua•tls. 1.** A member of any of various Native American peoples of Central Mexico, including the Aztecs. **2.** The Uto-Aztecan language of the Nahuatl. —**Na′hua′tl** *adj.*
Na•hum (nā′həm *or* nā′əm) *n.* **1.** A Hebrew prophet of the 7th century B.C. who predicted the fall of Nineveh. **2.** A Book of the Bible that deals with the fall of Nineveh.
nai•ad (nā′ăd′ *or* nī′ăd′) *n., pl.* **nai•a•des** (nā′ə dēz′ *or* nī′ə dēz′) or **nai•ads.** In Greek mythology, one of the nymphs living in and presiding over brooks, fountains, and springs.
nail (nāl) *n.* **1.** A slim pointed piece of metal, often with a head, hammered into wood or other material as a fastener. **2.a.** A fingernail or toenail. **b.** A claw or talon. —*tr.v.* **nailed, nail•ing, nails. 1.** To fasten, join, or attach with or as if with nails: *Nail the boards together.* **2.** *Slang.* To seize; catch: *The police nailed the suspect in his car.* ***—idiom.*** **nail down.** To discover or establish with certainty: *The reporters finally nailed down the facts of the story.*
nail gun *n.* A device, usually powered by compressed air, that drives nails into wood or concrete.
Nai•ro•bi (nī rō′bē). The capital and largest city of Kenya, in the south-central part of the country. It was founded in 1899. Population, 827,775.
na•ive or **na•ïve** (nä ēv′) *adj.* **1.** Simple as a child; unexperienced; artless: *He felt naive as he tried to bargain with the car salesman.* **2.** Showing a lack of experience or judgment; unsophisticated: *naive remarks.* —**na•ive′ly** *adv.*
na•ive•té or **na•ïve•té** (nä′ēv tā′ *or* nä ē′vĭ tā′) *n.* The quality of being naive; natural simplicity.
na•ked (nā′kĭd) *adj.* **1.** Not wearing clothing or other covering; nude. **2.** Having no vegetation or leaves: *trees with naked branches.* **3.** Not concealed, disguised, or added to: *the naked truth.* —**na′ked•ly** *adv.* —**na′ked•ness** *n.*
naked eye *n.* The eye unaided by an optical instrument, such as a telescope.
nam•by-pam•by (năm′bē păm′bē) *adj.* **1.** Insipid and sentimental. **2.** Lacking vigor or decisiveness; weak.
name (nām) *n.* **1.** A word or words by which a person or thing is known or referred to. **2.** A word or group of words used to describe someone, especially as an insult: *Stop calling me names!* **3.a.** General reputation: *That store has a bad name.* **b.** A distinguished reputation: *She has made a name for herself.* **4.** A famous or excellent person: *a big name in the movies.* —*tr.v.* **named, nam•ing, names. 1.a.** To give a name to: *Have you named the baby?* **b.** To call by a name: *They named him "Best in the class."* **2.** To mention or identify by name: *Name the longest river in China.* **3.** To specify, fix, or set: *Name the day for the party.* **4.** To nominate or appoint, as to a specific duty, honor, or office: *He was named coach of the basketball team.* ***—idioms.*** **in the name of.** By the authority of: *Open up in the name of the law!* **to (one's) name.** Belonging to one: *I don't have a dollar to my name.* [First written down about 725 in Old English and spelled *nama.*]
name•less (nām′lĭs) *adj.* **1.** Having or bearing no name: *nameless stars.* **2.** Unknown by name; obscure: *the nameless dead.* **3.** Not designated by name; anonymous: *a nameless benefactor.* **4.** Impossible to describe; inexpressible: *nameless horror.* —**name′less•ly** *adv.* —**name′less•ness** *n.*
name•ly (nām′lē) *adv.* That is to say; specifically: *First-class mail includes written matter, namely letters and postcards.*
name•sake (nām′sāk′) *n.* A person or thing named after another.
Na•mib•i•a (nə mĭb′ē ə). A country of southwest Africa on the Atlantic Ocean south of Angola. Namibia gained its independence from South Africa in

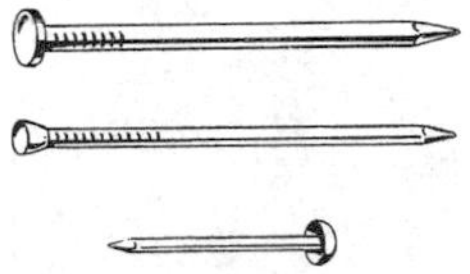

nail
Top: Box nail
Center: Finishing nail
Bottom: Upholstery nail

ă	pat	oi	boy
ā	pay	ou	out
âr	care	ŏŏ	took
ä	father	ōō	boot
ĕ	pet	ŭ	cut
ē	be	ûr	urge
ĭ	pit	th	thin
ī	pie	*th*	this
îr	pier	hw	whoop
ŏ	pot	zh	vision
ō	toe	ə	about
ô	paw	N	*French* bon

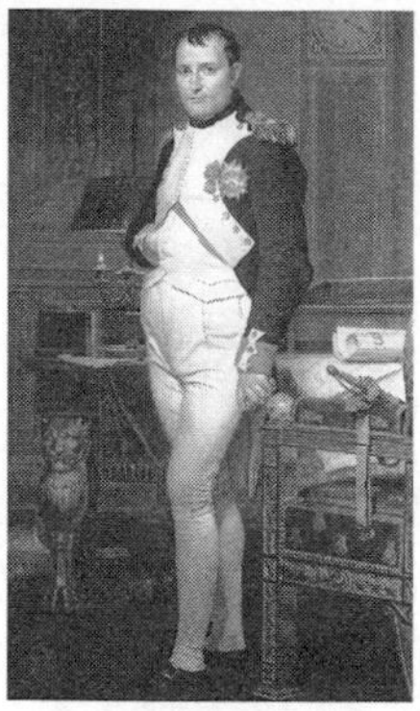

Napoleon I
Detail from *Napoleon in his Study,* 1812, by Jacques Louis David (1748–1825)

narcissus

narwhal
Male and female narwhals

1990. Capital, Windhoek. Population, 1,099,000.

Nan•jing (năn′jĭng′) also **Nan•king** (năn′kĭng′). A city of east-central China on the Yangtze River (Chang Jiang) northwest of Shanghai. Nanjing was captured by the Japanese in 1937 and reclaimed by Chinese forces in 1946. Population, 2,250,000.

nan•ny (năn′ē) *n., pl.* **nan•nies.** A person employed to take care of a child or children.

nanny goat *n.* A female goat.

nano– *pref.* A prefix that means one-billionth (10^{-9}): *nanosecond.*

nan•o•sec•ond (năn′ə sĕk′ənd) *n.* One billionth (10^{-9}) of a second.

Nan•tuck•et (năn tŭk′ĭt). An island of southeast Massachusetts south of Cape Cod. It was settled in 1659 and was a whaling center until the mid-1850's.

nap[1] (năp) *n.* A brief sleep, usually during the day. —*intr.v.* **napped, nap•ping, naps. 1.** To doze or sleep for a brief period. **2.** To be unaware of danger or trouble that is just about to happen. [First written down about 1353 in Middle English and spelled *nappe*, from *nappen*, to doze, from Old English *hnappian*.]

nap[2] (năp) *n.* A soft or fuzzy surface on cloth or leather. —*tr.v.* **napped, nap•ping, naps.** To form or raise a nap on (cloth or leather). [First written down in 1440 in Middle English and spelled *noppe*, from Middle Dutch.]

na•palm (nā′päm′) *n.* A mixture of gasoline and chemicals that makes a flammable jelly for use in flame throwers and bombs.

nape (nāp *or* năp) *n.* The back of the neck.

naph•tha (năf′thə *or* năp′thə) *n.* Any of several flammable liquid hydrocarbons used as solvents, as fuel, and in making various chemicals, especially those derived from petroleum, coal tar, and natural gas.

naph•tha•lene (năf′thə lēn′ *or* năp′thə lēn′) *n.* A white crystalline compound derived from coal tar or petroleum and used to manufacture dyes, moth repellents, explosives, and solvents.

nap•kin (năp′kĭn) *n.* **1.a.** A piece of cloth or soft paper used while eating to protect the clothes or to wipe the mouth and fingers. **b.** A similar cloth or towel. **2.** A sanitary napkin. [First written down in 1384 in Middle English, from Old French *nape*, tablecloth.]

Na•ples (nā′pəlz). A city of south-central Italy on the **Bay of Naples,** an arm of the Tyrrhenian Sea. It was founded in about 600 B.C. Population, 1,210,503.

na•po•le•on (nə pō′lē ən) *n.* A rectangular pastry with flaky layers separated by custard or cream. [First written down in 1892 in Modern English, after *Napoleon I*.]

Na•po•le•on I (nə pō′lē ən) Originally Napoleon Bonaparte. 1769–1821. Emperor of the French (1804–1814) who was a brilliant military strategist and conquered much of Europe but was forced to abdicate (1814). After escaping from exile on the island of Elba, he was ultimately defeated at Waterloo (1815). His Napoleonic Code still forms the basis of French civil law. **—Na•po′le•on′ic** (nə pō′lē ŏn′ik) *adj.*

nar•cis•si (när sĭs′ī′ *or* när sĭs′ē) *n.* A plural of **narcissus.**

nar•cis•sism (när′sĭ sĭz′əm) *n.* Excessive love or admiration of oneself. [First written down in 1905 in Modern English, after *Narcissus*.] **—nar′cis•sist** *n.*

nar•cis•sus (när sĭs′əs) *n., pl.* **nar•cis•sus•es** or **nar•cis•si** (när sĭs′ī′). A garden plant related to the daffodil, having narrow leaves and fragrant yellow or white flowers with a central part that is shaped like a cup or trumpet.

Nar•cis•sus (när sĭs′əs) *n.* In Greek mythology, a young man who pines away in love for his own image in a pool of water and is transformed into the flower that bears his name.

nar•cot•ic (när kŏt′ĭk) *n.* A drug, such as heroin or morphine, that reduces pain, causes sleep, and tends to cause addiction when used regularly. —*adj.* **1.** Tending to cause sleep or stupor. **2.** Of or relating to narcotics. [First written down about 1385 in Middle English and spelled *narcotik*, from Greek *narkōsis*, a numbing, from *narkē*, numbness.]

Nar•ra•gan•sett (năr′ə găn′sĭt) *n., pl.* **Narragansett** or **Nar•ra•gan•setts. 1.** A member of a Native American people living in Rhode Island. **2.** The Algonquian language of the Narragansett.

Narragansett Bay. A deep inlet of the Atlantic Ocean in eastern Rhode Island.

nar•rate (năr′āt′ *or* nă rāt′) *tr.v.* **nar•rat•ed, nar•rat•ing, nar•rates.** To tell (a story, for example) in speech or writing. [First written down in 1656 in Modern English, from Latin *narrāre*, from *gnārus*, knowing.] **—nar′ra′tor** *n.*

nar•ra•tion (nă rā′shən) *n.* **1.** The act of narrating. **2.** Something narrated; an account or a story.

nar•ra•tive (năr′ə tĭv) *n.* A narrated account; a story. —*adj.* **1.** Telling a story: *narrative poems.* **2.** Of or relating to narration: *the narrative skill of an author.*

nar•row (năr′ō) *adj.* **nar•row•er, nar•row•est. 1.** Small or limited in width, especially in comparison with length: *a narrow face.* **2.** Having little room: *narrow quarters.* **3.** Limited in scope or variety: *a narrow selection of products.* **4.** Rigid in views and ideas; narrow-minded: *a man of narrow opinions.* **5.** Just barely successful; close: *a narrow escape.* —*v.* **nar•rowed, nar•row•ing, nar•rows.** —*tr.* **1.** To make narrow or narrower: *He narrowed his eyes.* **2.** To limit or restrict: *Narrow down your topic to something you can handle.* —*intr.* To become narrower: *The stream narrows at the rapids.* —*n.* **1.** A part having little width, such as a mountain pass. **2. narrows.** *(used with a singular or plural verb).* A narrow body of water connecting two larger ones. **—nar′row•ly** *adv.* **—nar′row•ness** *n.*

nar•row-mind•ed (năr′ō mīn′dĭd) *adj.* Lacking in tolerance or sympathy; petty. **—nar′row-mind′ed•ly** *adv.* **—nar′row-mind′ed•ness** *n.*

nar•whal (när′wəl) *n.* A mammal of northern seas, related to the whales and having a single long, spirally twisted tusk.

nar•y (nâr′ē) *adj.* Not one; no: *Nary a leaf was left on the tree.*

NASA (năs′ə) *abbr.* An abbreviation of National Aeronautics and Space Administration.

na•sal (nā′zəl) *adj.* **1.** Of, in, or relating to the nose: *nasal irritation.* **2.a.** Uttered so that most of the air passes through the nose rather than the mouth: *a nasal sound, such as* m *or* n. **b.** Resembling a sound uttered in such a way: *the nasal twang of a guitar.* —*n.* A nasal sound. [First written down before 1425 in Middle English and spelled *nasale*, from Latin *nāsus*, nose.] **—na′sal•ly** *adv.*

na•sal•ize (nā′zə līz′) *tr. & intr.v.* **na•sal•ized, na•sal•iz•ing, na•sal•iz•es.** To make nasal or produce nasal sounds: *nasalize consonants.* **—na′sal•i•za′tion** (nā′zə lĭ zā′shən) *n.*

nas•cent (năs′ənt *or* nā′sənt) *adj.* Coming into existence; emerging: *a nascent movement to reform campaign laws.*

Nash•ville (năsh′vĭl′). The capital of Tennessee, in the north-central part of the state northeast of Memphis. It was founded in 1779 and became the capital in 1843. Population, 488,374.

Nas•sau (năs′ô′). The capital and largest city of the

Bahamas, in the Atlantic Ocean east of Miami, Florida. Population, 135,000.

nas•tur•tium (nə stûr′shəm) *n.* Any of various garden plants having showy orange, yellow, or red flowers and rounded strong-tasting leaves.

nas•ty (năs′tē) *adj.* **nas•ti•er, nas•ti•est. 1.** Disgustingly dirty; filthy. **2.** Morally offensive; indecent: *a nasty word.* **3.** Malicious; spiteful; mean: *a nasty man.* **4.** Unpleasant; annoying: *nasty weather.* **5.** Painful and dangerous: *a nasty cut.* **—nas′ti•ly** *adv.* **—nas′ti•ness** *n.*

na•tal (nāt′l) *adj.* Of, relating to, or accompanying birth: *natal injuries.*

Natch•ez (năch′ĭz) *n., pl.* **Natchez. 1.** A member of a Native American people formerly living on the lower Mississippi River near the city of Natchez, Mississippi. **2.** The language of the Natchez.

Na•than•ael (nə thăn′yəl). Saint Bartholomew.

na•tion (nā′shən) *n.* **1.** A group of people organized under a single government; a country. **2.** The territory occupied by a country: *All across the nation new industries are developing.* **3.** The government of a country. **4.a.** A people who share customs and history and often speak the same language. **b.** A federation or tribe, especially of Native Americans. [First written down before 1300 in Middle English and spelled *nacioun,* from Latin *nātiō,* from *nātus,* born.]

Na•tion (nā′shən), **Carry Amelia Moore.** 1846–1911. American temperance leader in Kansas who organized a branch of the Women's Christian Temperance Union there and conducted a series of raids on saloons.

na•tion•al (năsh′ə nəl *or* năsh′nəl) *adj.* **1.** Relating or belonging to a nation as a whole: *a national anthem; national elections.* **2.** Peculiar to or typical of the people of a nation: *national traits.* **3.** Maintained or supported by the government of a nation: *national parks.* —*n.* A citizen of a particular nation. **—na′tion•al•ly** *adv.*

national bank *n.* **1.** A federally chartered bank in a system of privately owned banks in the United States, each insured by the Federal Deposit Insurance Corporation. **2.** A bank associated with national finances and usually owned or controlled by a government.

national debt *n.* The total amount of money that is owed by a national government.

National Guard *n.* The military reserve units of each state of the United States.

na•tion•al•ism (năsh′ə nə lĭz′əm *or* năsh′nə lĭz′əm) *n.* **1.** Devotion to the interests or culture of a particular nation. **2.** The belief that one's own nation will benefit from acting independently, rather than in coordination with other nations.

na•tion•al•ist (năsh′ə nə lĭst *or* năsh′nə lĭst) *n.* A person who believes in nationalism. —*adj.* Relating to or advocating nationalism: *a nationalist party; a nationalist candidate.* **—na′tion•al•is′tic** *adj.* **—na′tion•al•is′ti•cal•ly** *adv.*

na•tion•al•i•ty (năsh′ə năl′ĭ tē *or* năsh năl′ĭ tē) *n., pl.* **na•tion•al•i•ties. 1.** The status of belonging to a particular nation by origin, birth, or naturalization: *American nationality.* **2.** A people having common origins or traditions: *Many nationalities have settled in America.*

na•tion•al•ize (năsh′ə nə līz′ *or* năsh′nə līz′) *tr.v.* **na•tion•al•ized, na•tion•al•iz•ing, na•tion•al•iz•es. 1.** To remove from private ownership and put under the control of the government: *When did England nationalize its steel industry?* **2.** To make national, as in fame: *TV commercials are nationalizing the candidate's name.* **—na′tion•al•i•za′tion** (năsh′ə nə lĭ zā′shən *or* năsh′nə lĭ zā′shən) *n.*

national monument *n.* A natural landmark or a structure or site of historic interest maintained by a national government for public enjoyment or study.

national park *n.* A tract of land declared public property by a national government in order to preserve and develop it for recreation and study.

National Socialism *n.* Nazism.

na•tion•wide (nā′shən wīd′) *adv. & adj.* Throughout a whole nation: *The speech was broadcast nationwide. There is nationwide interest in recycling.*

na•tive (nā′tĭv) *adj.* **1.** Belonging to one by nature; inborn; natural: *native ability.* **2.** Being such by birth or origin: *a native Englishman.* **3.** Being one's own because of the place of one's birth: *one's native language.* **4.** Originally living, growing, or produced in a particular place: *a plant native to Asia.* **5.** Belonging to or characteristic of the original inhabitants of a region: *a native custom.* **6.** Occurring in nature in pure form or without other substances: *native copper.* —*n.* **1.** A person born in a particular place: *a native of New York now living in California.* **2.** One of the original inhabitants of a region. **3.** An animal or a plant that originated in a particular place. [First written down about 1385 in Middle English and spelled *natif,* from Latin *nātīvus,* from *nāscī,* to be born.] **—na′tive•ly** *adv.*

Native American *n.* A member of any of the peoples living in the Western Hemisphere before the arrival of the Europeans. The ancestors of Native Americans are thought to have come to the Americas from Asia by a land bridge across the Bering Strait during the late Ice Age.

na•tive-born (nā′tĭv bôrn′) *adj.* Belonging to a place by birth.

na•tiv•i•ty (nə tĭv′ĭ tē *or* nā tĭv′ĭ tē) *n., pl.* **na•tiv•i•ties. 1.** Birth, especially the place, condition, or circumstances of being born. **2. Nativity. a.** The birth of Jesus. **b.** A representation, such as a painting, of Jesus's birth.

natl. *abbr.* An abbreviation of national.

NATO *abbr.* An abbreviation of North Atlantic Treaty Organization.

nat•ty (năt′ē) *adj.* **nat•ti•er, nat•ti•est.** Neat and trim; dapper: *a natty suit.* **—nat′ti•ly** *adv.* **—nat′ti•ness** *n.*

nat•u•ral (năch′ər əl *or* năch′rəl) *adj.* **1.** Present in or produced by nature; not artificial or synthetic: *a natural pearl.* **2.** Of or relating to the physical world and the events that occur in it: *natural laws.* **3.** Following the usual course of nature: *a natural death.* **4.a.** Having qualities or abilities that are or seem to be inborn: *a natural leader.* **b.** Present from birth; not acquired: *He has a natural curiosity for how things are put together.* **5.** Not artificial or affected; spontaneous: *a natural way of speaking.* **6.** Expected; accepted: *Their friendship is a natural consequence of their interest in art.* **7.** In music, not having or using any sharps or flats. —*n.* **1.a.** A person having the skills necessary for success: *You are a natural for this job.* **b.** A person suited by nature for something: *She is a natural at mathematics.* **2.a.** In music, a tone that is not altered by a sharp or flat. **b.** A musical sign (♮) indicating that any sharps or flats that would otherwise affect a tone are to be canceled. **—nat′u•ral•ness** *n.*

natural food *n.* Food that contains no additives, such as preservatives or artificial coloring or flavoring.

natural gas *n.* A mixture of hydrocarbon gases, principally methane, that occurs with petroleum deposits. It is used as a fuel and in manufacturing organic compounds.

natural history *n.* The study of living things and natural objects and happenings and of their origins and relationships.

nat•u•ral•ist (năch′ər ə lĭst *or* năch′rə lĭst) *n.* A

nasturtium

Carry Nation

ă	pat	oi	boy
ā	pay	ou	out
âr	care	ŏŏ	took
ä	father	ōō	boot
ĕ	pet	ŭ	cut
ē	be	ûr	urge
ĭ	pit	th	thin
ī	pie	*th*	this
îr	pier	hw	whoop
ŏ	pot	zh	vision
ō	toe	ə	about
ô	paw	N	*French* bon

nautilus
Chambered nautilus

Martina Navratilova
Photographed in 1990
during a U.S. Open tennis match

person who specializes in natural history, especially in the study of plants and animals in their natural surroundings.

nat•u•ral•ize (năch′ər ə līz′ *or* năch′rə līz′) *v.* **nat•u•ral•ized, nat•u•ral•iz•ing, nat•u•ral•iz•es.** —*tr.* **1.** To give full citizenship to (a person of foreign birth). **2.** To adopt (something foreign, such as a word from another language) into general use. **3.** To adapt or accustom (a plant or an animal) to growing or living in new surroundings: *Dandelions are European plants that have been naturalized in North America.* —*intr.* To become adapted or accustomed. **—nat′u•ral•i•za′tion** (năch′ər ə lĭ zā′shən *or* năch′rə lĭ zā′shən) *n.*

nat•u•ral•ly (năch′ər ə lē *or* năch′rə lē) *adv.* **1.** In a natural manner: *behave naturally.* **2.** By nature; inherently: *Children are naturally curious.* **3.** Without a doubt; surely: *Naturally, the faster you grow, the more food you need.*

natural number *n.* A member of the set of positive integers; a whole number greater than zero.

natural resource *n.* Something, such as a forest, a mineral deposit, or fresh water, that is found in nature and is necessary or useful to human beings.

natural science *n.* A science, such as biology, chemistry, or physics, that deals with the objects, occurrences, or laws of nature.

natural selection *n.* The principle that only the organisms best suited to their environment tend to survive and pass on their genetic characteristics to their offspring, so that the proportion of the species having these characteristics increases with each generation.

na•ture (nā′chər) *n.* **1.** The physical world and the events that occur in it. **2.** The forces and processes that produce and control events in the physical world: *the laws of nature.* **3.** The world of living things and the outdoors: *enjoying the beauties of nature.* **4.** A kind or sort: *I like games of that nature.* **5.** The essential characteristics and qualities of a thing: *the mountainous nature of the region.* **6.** The fundamental character or temperament of a person or an animal: *It goes against her nature to complain.* [First written down about 1275 in Middle English, from Latin *nātūra*, from *nāscī*, to be born.]

na•tured (nā′chərd) *adj.* Having a certain kind of nature or temperament: *That child has always had a sweet-natured personality.*

naught also **nought** (nôt) *n.* Zero; the digit 0. —*pron.* Nothing: *All their work was for naught.* [First written down about 830 in Old English and spelled *nāwiht* : *nā*, no + *wiht*, thing.]

naugh•ty (nô′tē) *adj.* **naugh•ti•er, naugh•ti•est. 1.** Disobedient; mischievous: *a naughty boy.* **2.** Bad or improper: *a naughty word.* [First written down about 1378 in Middle English, from Old English *nāwiht*, nothing, naught.] **—naugh′ti•ly** *adv.* **—naugh′ti•ness** *n.*

Na•u•ru (nä o͞o′ro͞o). An island country of the central Pacific Ocean just south of the equator and west of Kiribati. Nauru gained its independence in 1968. Capital, Yaren. Population, 8,000.

nau•se•a (nô′zē ə *or* nô′zhə) *n.* **1.** A feeling of sickness in the stomach, characterized by the need to vomit. **2.** Strong repugnance; disgust. [First written down before 1425 in Middle English, from Greek *nautia*, seasickness, from *nautēs*, sailor.]

nau•se•ate (nô′zē āt′ *or* nô′zhē āt′) *intr. & tr.v.* **nau•se•at•ed, nau•se•at•ing, nau•se•ates.** To feel or cause to feel nausea.

nau•seous (nô′shəs *or* nô′zē əs) *adj.* **1.** Tending to cause nausea; sickening. **2.** Suffering from nausea.

nau•ti•cal (nô′tĭ kəl) *adj.* Of or relating to ships, sailors, or navigation. [First written down in 1552 in Modern English, from Greek *nautikos*, from *nautēs*, sailor, from *naus*, ship.] **—nau′ti•cal•ly** *adv.*

nautical mile *n.* A unit of length used in air and sea navigation, equal to about 6,076 feet (1,852 meters). See table at **measurement.**

nau•ti•lus (nôt′l əs) *n., pl.* **nau•ti•lus•es** or **nau•ti•li** (nôt′l ī′). **1.** A tropical sea mollusk related to the squids and octopuses, having a spiral shell divided into many partitions. **2.** The paper nautilus.

Nav•a•jo also **Nav•a•ho** (năv′ə hō′ *or* nä′və hō′) *n., pl.* **Navajo** or **Nav•a•jos** also **Navaho** or **Nav•a•hos. 1.** A member of a Native American people living in New Mexico, Arizona, and Utah. **2.** The language of the Navajo. **—Nav′a•jo′** *adj.*

na•val (nā′vəl) *adj.* **1.** Of or relating to a navy. **2.** Having a navy: *a great naval power.*

❑ *These sound alike:* **naval, navel** (belly button).

Na•varre (nə vär′). A historical region and former kingdom of southwest Europe in the Pyrenees of northern Spain and southwest France. It was ruled by a Basque dynasty from the 9th to the 13th century.

nave (nāv) *n.* The central part of a church flanked by the side aisles. [First written down in 1673 in Modern English, from Latin *nāvis*, ship.]

❑ *These sound alike:* **nave, knave** (crafty man).

na•vel (nā′vəl) *n.* **1.** The scar left on the abdomen of mammals where the umbilical cord was attached before birth. **2.** A central point; the middle.

❑ *These sound alike:* **navel, naval** (of a navy).

navel orange *n.* A sweet seedless orange having a marking resembling a navel opposite the stem end.

nav•i•ga•ble (năv′ĭ gə bəl) *adj.* **1.** Deep enough or wide enough for navigation. **2.** Capable of being steered: *a navigable aircraft.* **—nav′i•ga•bil′i•ty** *n.*

nav•i•gate (năv′ĭ gāt′) *v.* **nav•i•gat•ed, nav•i•gat•ing, nav•i•gates.** —*tr.* **1.** To plot and control the course of (a ship or an aircraft). **2.** To follow a planned course on, across, or through: *navigate a stream.* —*intr.* To plot and control the course of a ship or an aircraft. [First written down in 1588 in Modern English, from Latin *nāvigāre* : *nāvis*, ship + *agere*, to drive, lead.]

nav•i•ga•tion (năv′ĭ gā′shən) *n.* **1.** The theory and practice of navigating, especially the science of charting a course for a ship or an aircraft. **2.** Travel or traffic by vessels, especially commercial shipping. **—nav′i•ga′tion•al** *adj.*

nav•i•ga•tor (năv′ĭ gā′tər) *n.* **1.** A person who plots the course of a ship or an aircraft. **2.** A device that directs the course of an aircraft or a missile.

Nav•ra•ti•lo•va (năv′rə tĭ lō′və), **Martina.** Born 1956. Czechoslovakian-born American tennis player who won nine Wimbledon women's singles championships between 1978 and 1990.

na•vy (nā′vē) *n., pl.* **na•vies. 1.** All of a nation's warships. **2.** Often **Navy.** A nation's entire organization for sea warfare, including vessels, personnel, and shore establishments. **3.** Navy blue. [First written down before 1338 in Middle English, from Latin *nāvigia*, ships.]

navy bean *n.* A small whitish form of the kidney bean, used for food.

navy blue *n.* A dark grayish blue.

navy yard *n.* A dockyard for the construction, repair, equipping, or docking of naval ships.

nay (nā) *adv.* **1.** No: *All but four Senators voted nay to the treaty.* **2.** And moreover: *That act was disloyal, nay, traitorous to the country.* —*n.* **1.** A vote of "no." **2.** A person who votes "no": *The nays carried it, and the bill was defeated.* [First written down before 1325 in Middle English, from Old Norse *nei*.]

❑ *These sound alike:* **nay, née** (born), **neigh** (whinny).

Naz•a•rene (năz′ə rēn′ *or* năz′ə rēn′) *n.* **1.** A person who was born or lives in Nazareth. **2.** Jesus. **3.** A member of a sect of early Christians who followed many Jewish practices.

Naz•a•reth (năz′ər əth). A town of northern Israel southeast of Haifa. It is mentioned in the New Testament as the boyhood home of Jesus. Population, 46,300.

Na•zi (nät′sē *or* năt′sē) *n., pl.* **Na•zis.** A member of the National Socialist German Workers' Party founded in 1919 and brought to power by Adolf Hitler in 1933. *—adj.* Relating to or typical of Nazis. [First written down in 1930 in Modern English, from German, short for *Nationalsozialist*, National Socialist.]

Na•zism (nät′sĭz′əm *or* năt′sĭz′əm) also **Na•zi•ism** (nät′sē ĭz′əm *or* năt′sē ĭz′əm) *n.* The doctrines and practices of Nazis, especially their policies of racism and aggressive nationalism.

Nb The symbol for the element **niobium.**

NB also **N.B.** *abbr.* An abbreviation of New Brunswick.

n.b. or **N.B.** *abbr.* An abbreviation of nota bene (note well).

NC or **N.C.** *abbr.* An abbreviation of North Carolina.

NCO or **N.C.O.** *abbr.* An abbreviation of noncommissioned officer.

Nd The symbol for the element **neodymium.**

ND *abbr.* An abbreviation of North Dakota.

N.Dak. *abbr.* An abbreviation of North Dakota.

Ndja•me•na or **N'dja•me•na** (ən jä′mə nə). The capital and largest city of Chad, in the southwest part of the country. It was founded in 1900. Population, 303,000.

Ne The symbol for the element **neon.**

NE *abbr.* An abbreviation of: **1.** Northeast. **2.** Nebraska. **3.** New England.

Ne•an•der•thal (nē ăn′dər thôl′) *n.* Neanderthal man. *—adj.* Of or relating to Neanderthal man.

Neanderthal man *n.* An extinct species or race of prehistoric human beings that lived in caves and made and used stone tools.

Ne•a•pol•i•tan (nē′ə pŏl′ĭ tən) *adj.* Of, belonging to, or characteristic of Naples, Italy. *—n.* A native or resident of Naples, Italy.

neap tide (nēp) *n.* A tide in which the difference between high and low tide is the least, occurring twice a month when the sun and moon are about 90° apart.

near (nîr) *adv.* **near•er, near•est. 1.** To, at, or within a short distance or interval in space or time: *a house near the ocean.* **2.** Almost; nearly: *near exhausted by the climb.* *—adj.* **nearer, nearest. 1.** Close in space, time, position, or degree: *near neighbors; near equals.* **2.** Closely related by kinship or association; intimate: *near relatives.* **3.a.** Almost but not actually occurring: *a near victory.* **b.** Just barely avoided: *a near tragedy.* **4.** Bearing a close resemblance: *a near likeness of her.* **5.** Closer of two or more: *the near side of the house.* **6.** Short and direct: *the nearest route to the airport.* *—prep.* Close to, as in time, space, or degree: *We stayed at a little inn near London.* *—v.* **neared, near•ing, nears.** *—tr.* To come close or closer to: *The plane neared the runway.* *—intr.* To draw near or nearer; approach: *The holiday season nears.* [First written down about 725 in Old English and spelled *nēar*, closer.] **—near′ness** *n.*

near•by (nîr′bī′) *adj.* Located a short distance away; close at hand: *a nearby supermarket.* *—adv.* Not far away; close by: *A brook ran nearby.*

Near East (nîr). A region of southwest Asia generally thought to include Turkey, Lebanon, Israel, Iraq, Jordan, Saudi Arabia, the other countries of the Arabian Peninsula, and sometimes Egypt and Sudan.

near•ly (nîr′lē) *adv.* **1.** Almost but not quite: *That coat nearly fits.* **2.** Closely or intimately: *The two girls are nearly related.*

near•sight•ed (nîr′sī′tĭd) *adj.* Unable to see distant objects clearly; myopic. **—near′sight′ed•ly** *adv.* **—near′sight′ed•ness** *n.*

neat (nēt) *adj.* **neat•er, neat•est. 1.** Orderly and clean; tidy: *a neat room; neat handwriting.* **2.** Orderly, as in appearance; not careless or messy: *a neat person.* **3.** Performed with precision and skill: *a neat, graceful takeoff.* **4.** *Slang.* Wonderful; fine: *a neat party.* [First written down in 1542 in Modern English, from Latin *nitidus*, elegant, gleaming.] **—neat′ly** *adv.* **—neat′ness** *n.*

Synonyms: neat, tidy, trim, shipshape. These adjectives mean marked by good order and cleanliness. **Neat** means pleasingly clean and orderly: *Marcia pulled back her hair into a neat ponytail.* **Tidy** suggests precise arrangement and order: *Even their closets and drawers were kept tidy.* **Trim** stresses a smart appearance because of neatness, tidiness, and pleasing proportions: *The trim little boat was all ready to set sail.* **Shipshape** means both neat and tidy: *We'll have the kitchen shipshape in no time.* **Antonyms: messy, sloppy.**

neath or **'neath** (nēth) *prep.* Beneath.

neat's-foot oil (nēts′fo͝ot′) *n.* An oil obtained from the feet and shinbones of cattle, used chiefly to finish leather.

neb•bish (nĕb′ĭsh) *n.* A weak-willed and timid person.

Ne•bras•ka (nə brăs′kə). A state of the central United States in the Great Plains north of Kansas. It was admitted as the 37th state in 1867. Lincoln is the capital and Omaha the largest city. Population, 1,584,617. —See Note.

Neb•u•chad•nez•zar II (nĕb′ə kəd nĕz′ər). 630?–562 B.C. King of Babylonia (605–562) who destroyed Jerusalem in 586 and held the Israelites captive in Babylonia.

neb•u•la (nĕb′yə lə) *n., pl.* **neb•u•lae** (nĕb′yə lē′) or **neb•u•las.** A thinly spread mass of interstellar gas or dust or both, appearing as a bright or dark patch in the night sky depending on the way the light that strikes it is reflected, absorbed, or re-emitted. [First written down before 1449 in Middle English and spelled *nebule*, cloud, mist, from Latin *nebula*.] **—neb′u•lar** *adj.*

neb•u•lous (nĕb′yə ləs) *adj.* **1.** Lacking definite form; vague; unclear. **2.** Of or relating to a nebula. **—neb′u•lous•ly** *adv.* **—neb′u•lous•ness** *n.*

nec•es•sar•i•ly (nĕs′ĭ sâr′ə lē *or* nĕs′ĭ sĕr′ə lē) *adv.* As a necessary result; inevitably: *Playing at home does not necessarily mean that they'll win the game.*

nec•es•sar•y (nĕs′ĭ sĕr′ē) *adj.* **1.** Absolutely essential: *Getting enough sleep is necessary to stay healthy.* **2.** Needed to achieve a certain result or effect; requisite: *Fill out the necessary forms.* **3.** Following as a certain result; inevitable: *Her bad mood was a necessary consequence of not getting enough sleep.* *—n., pl.* **nec•es•sar•ies.** Something essential or needed. [First written down about 1380 in Middle English and spelled *necessarie*, from Latin *necessārius*, from *necesse*.]

ne•ces•si•tate (nə sĕs′ĭ tāt′) *tr.v.* **ne•ces•si•tat•ed, ne•ces•si•tat•ing, ne•ces•si•tates.** To make necessary or unavoidable: *The poor light necessitated the use of a flash to take the picture.* **—ne•ces′si•ta′tion** *n.*

ne•ces•si•ty (nə sĕs′ĭ tē) *n., pl.* **ne•ces•si•ties. 1.** Something needed for the existence, success, or functioning of something; a requirement: *Water is a*

Nebraska

The state of **Nebraska** takes its name from an Omaha word that means "flat water" or "flat river." The Omaha people used this name for the river that was later renamed the **Platte**. The name *Nebraska* was used first for the territory created in 1854 and later for the state.

nebula
Lagoon nebula in Sagittarius

ă	pat	oi	boy
ā	pay	ou	out
âr	care	o͝o	took
ä	father	o͞o	boot
ĕ	pet	ŭ	cut
ē	be	ûr	urge
ĭ	pit	th	thin
ī	pie	*th*	this
îr	pier	hw	whoop
ŏ	pot	zh	vision
ō	toe	ə	about
ô	paw	N	*French* bon

neckerchief

necktie

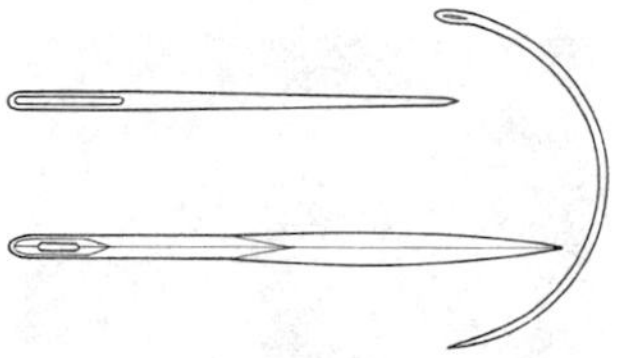

needle

Top: Tapestry needle
Bottom: Sailmaking needle
Right: Curved embroidery needle

Nefertiti

XVIII Dynasty limestone bust

necessity for plant growth. **2.** The quality, condition, or fact of being necessary: *the necessity of sleep.* **3.** Something that must inevitably exist or occur: *the necessity of water freezing when cooled to 32 degrees.* **4.** Pressing or urgent need, especially that arising from poverty.

neck (něk) *n.* **1.** The part of the body that joins the head to the trunk. **2.** The part of a garment that fits around the neck. **3.** A narrow projection or connecting part: *the neck of a bottle.* **4.** The narrow part of a stringed instrument along which the strings extend to the pegs. *—intr.v.* **necked, neck•ing, necks.** *Informal.* To kiss and caress. [First written down before 899 in Old English and spelled *hnecca.*]

neck and neck *adv. & adj.* Even in a close race; nip and tuck.

neck•er•chief (něk′ər chĭf *or* něk′ər chēf′) *n.* A kerchief worn around the neck.

neck•lace (něk′lĭs) *n.* An ornament that goes around the neck, as a string of beads or jewels.

neck•line (něk′līn′) *n.* The line formed by the edge of a garment at or below the neck.

neck•tie (něk′tī′) *n.* A narrow band of cloth worn around the neck beneath the collar and tied in a knot or bow close to the throat.

neck•wear (něk′wâr′) *n.* Articles, such as neckties or scarfs, worn around the neck.

nec•ro•man•cy (něk′rə măn′sē) *n.* **1.** The practice of communicating with the spirits of the dead in order to predict the future. **2.** Black magic; sorcery. **3.** Magical qualities. **—nec′ro•man′cer** *n.* **—nec′ro•man′tic** *adj.*

nec•tar (něk′tər) *n.* **1.** A sweet liquid in certain flowers, used by bees in making honey. **2.** In Greek mythology, the drink of the gods. **3.** A delicious drink. [First written down in 1555 in Modern English, from Greek *nektar.*]

nec•tar•ine (něk′tə rēn′) *n.* **1.** A type of peach having a glossy skin. **2.** The tree that bears such fruit.

née also **nee** (nā) *adj.* Born. Used to indicate the maiden name of a married woman.

❑ *These sound alike:* **née, nay** (no), **neigh** (whinny).

need (nēd) *n.* **1.** A condition or situation in which something is required or wanted: *The school has a need for a new computer.* **2.** Something required or wanted: *Our needs are modest.* **3.** Necessity or obligation: *There wasn't any need for you to pay me back.* **4.** Extreme poverty or misfortune: *living in dire need.* *—v.* **need•ed, need•ing, needs.** *—aux.* To be required or obliged to: *You need not come today.* *—tr.* To require; have need of: *The washing machine needs repairing.* *—intr.* To be in need or want: *You will never need if you inherit a fortune.* ***—idiom.*** **if need be.** If necessary: *I'll go in person, if need be.* [First written down about 750 in Old English and spelled *nēd.*]

❑ *These sound alike:* **need, knead** (press and shape).

need•ful (nēd′fəl) *adj.* Necessary; required. **—need′ful•ly** *adv.* **—need′ful•ness** *n.*

nee•dle (nēd′l) *n.* **1.** A small slender sewing implement, made of polished steel, pointed at one end and having an eye at the other through which a length of thread is passed and held. **2.a.** A slender pointed rod used in knitting. **b.** A similar implement with a hook at one end, used in crocheting. **3.** A slender piece of a jewel or steel that transmits vibrations from the groove of a phonograph record. **4.** The pointer or indicator of a dial, gauge, or compass. **5.** A hypodermic needle. **6.** A sharp pointed instrument used in engraving and etching. **7.** A stiff narrow leaf, as of a pine or related tree. *—tr.v.* **nee•dled, nee•dling, nee•dles.** *Informal.* To goad, provoke, or tease. [First written down about 700 in Old English and spelled *nethle.*]

nee•dle•point (nēd′l point′) *n.* Embroidery on canvas done with even stitches to resemble a woven tapestry.

needless *adj.* Not needed; unnecessary: *Pronouns help a writer avoid needless repetition.* **—need′less•ly** *adv.* **—need′less•ness** *n.*

nee•dle•work (nēd′l wûrk′) *n.* Work, such as sewing or embroidery, that is done with a needle.

need•n't (nēd′nt). Contraction of *need not.*

need•y (nē′dē) *adj.* **need•i•er, need•i•est.** Being in need; impoverished.

ne'er (nâr) *adv.* Never.

ne'er-do-well (nâr′do͞o wěl′) *n.* An irresponsible person who never gets anything done.

ne•far•i•ous (nə fâr′ē əs) *adj.* Evil; wicked: *a nefarious plot.*

Nef•er•ti•ti (něf′ər tē′tē). 14th century B.C. Queen of Egypt (1375?–1358?).

ne•gate (nĭ gāt′) *tr.v.* **ne•gat•ed, ne•gat•ing, ne•gates. 1.** To make ineffective or invalid; nullify: *This new amendment negates the former bill.* **2.** To rule out; deny: *There's no use trying to negate the reality of the problem.* [First written down in 1623 in Modern English, from Latin *negāre.*]

ne•ga•tion (nĭ gā′shən) *n.* **1.** The act or process of negating. **2.** A negative statement; a denial. **3.** The opposite of something regarded as positive or affirmative: *His actions are a negation of everything we believe in.*

neg•a•tive (něg′ə tĭv) *adj.* **1.** Expressing or consisting of a denial or refusal: *a negative answer.* **2.** Not positive or affirmative; not constructive: *a negative outlook.* **3.** Indicating that a suspected disease, disorder, or microorganism is not present: *a negative result of a blood test.* **4.a.** Less than zero. **b.** Relating to or being the sign (−) that indicates a negative number or a number that is to be subtracted. **5.** Relating to or having an electric charge that is like that of an electron and, therefore, tends to repel electrons. **6.** Moving away from a stimulus, such as light: *a negative tropism.* *—n.* **1.** A denial or refusal. **2.** Something that lacks positive or affirmative qualities: *There are many negatives in this proposal.* **3.** In grammar, a word or part of a word that expresses negation; for example, *no, not,* and *un-* are negatives. **4.** The side in a debate that contradicts or opposes the question being debated. **5.a.** An image in which the light areas appear dark and the dark areas appear light. **b.** A film or photographic plate containing such an image. **6.** A negative number. ***—idiom.*** **in the negative.** In a sense or manner indicating a refusal or denial: *answered in the negative.* **—neg′a•tive•ly** *adv.*

ne•glect (nĭ glěkt′) *tr.v.* **ne•glect•ed, ne•glect•ing, ne•glects. 1.** To ignore or pay no attention to; disregard: *He neglected our warnings to stay indoors.* **2.** To fail to care for or give proper attention to: *He neglects his appearance.* **3.** To fail to do, as through carelessness: *We neglected to tell the committee about the extra expenses.* *—n.* **1.** The act or an example of neglecting: *You got into trouble because of your neglect of your homework.* **2.** The condition of being neglected: *The garden has fallen into neglect.* [First written down in 1529 in Modern English, from Latin *neglegere.*]

ne•glect•ful (nĭ glěkt′fəl) *adj.* Marked by neglect; careless; heedless: *neglectful of their responsibility.* **—ne•glect′ful•ly** *adv.*

neg•li•gee also **neg•li•gée** or **neg•li•gé** (něg′lĭ zhā′ *or* něg′lĭ zhā′) *n.* A woman's loose dressing gown, often of soft delicate material.

neg•li•gence (něg′lĭ jəns) *n.* **1.** A failure to act with care or concern. **2.** In law, failure to act with reasonable precaution or care.

neg•li•gent (nĕg′lĭ jənt) *adj.* Guilty of neglect; lacking in proper care or concern: *a negligent worker.* [First written down before 1382 in Middle English and spelled *necgligent,* from Latin *neglegere,* to neglect.] **—neg′li•gent•ly** *adv.*

neg•li•gi•ble (nĕg′lĭ jə bəl) *adj.* Not worth considering; amounting to very little: *a negligible quantity.* **—neg′li•gi•bly** *adv.*

ne•go•tia•ble (nĭ gō′shə bəl *or* nĭ gō′shē ə bəl) *adj.* **1.** Easy or possible to be negotiated: *a negotiable contract.* **2.** Capable of being legally transferred from one person to another: *This certificate is negotiable when signed.* **—ne•go′tia•bil′i•ty** *n.*

ne•go•ti•ate (nĭ gō′shē āt′) *v.* **ne•go•ti•at•ed, ne•go•ti•at•ing, ne•go•ti•ates.** *—tr.* **1.a.** To talk about (something) in hopes of coming to an agreement. **b.** To arrange or settle by discussion: *They agreed to negotiate the new teachers' contract over the summer.* **2.a.** To transfer title to or ownership of (notes, for example) to another person or party in return for value received. **b.** To sell or discount (securities, for example). **3.** To succeed in going over or coping with: *The car negotiated a sharp turn.* *—intr.* To talk with others in order to reach an agreement: *We must be prepared to compromise if we are going to negotiate.* [First written down in 1599 in Modern English, from Latin *negōtium,* business.] **—ne•go′ti•a′tor** *n.*

ne•go•ti•a•tion (nĭ gō′shē ā′shən) *n.* The act or process of negotiating: *secret negotiations between the two nations.*

Ne•gri•to (nĭ grē′tō) *n., pl.* **Ne•gri•tos** or **Ne•gri•toes.** A member of any of various peoples of short stature living in parts of Malaysia, the Philippines, and southeast Asia.

Ne•gro (nē′grō) *n., pl.* **Ne•groes. 1.** A member of a major division of human beings whose members have dark skin, especially a member of various peoples living in central and southern Africa. **2.** A person descended from one of the peoples living in central and southern Africa; a Black person.

Ne•groid (nē′groid′) *adj.* Of or relating to a major division of human beings whose members have dark skin. This division includes peoples living in central and southern Africa. This word is no longer in scientific use.

Ne•he•mi•ah (nē′hə mī′ə *or* nē′ə mī′ə) *n.* **1.** A Jewish leader and governor of Judea in the fifth century B.C. when the Jews were captives in Babylon. **2.** A book of the Bible that relates Nehemiah's plans for rebuilding Jerusalem.

Neh•ru (nā′ro͞o), **Jawaharlal.** 1889–1964. Indian nationalist politician who was the first prime minister of independent India (1947–1964).

neigh (nā) *n.* The long, high-pitched sound made by a horse. *—intr.v.* **neighed, neigh•ing, neighs.** To make the sound of a horse; whinny.

❑ *These sound alike:* **neigh, nay** (no), **née** (born).

neigh•bor (nā′bər) *n.* **1.** A person who lives near or next door to another. **2.** A person or thing adjacent to or near another: *Earth's nearest neighbor is the moon.* **3.** A fellow human being. *—tr.v.* **neigh•bored, neigh•bor•ing, neigh•bors.** To be near or next to: *How many countries neighbor Thailand?* [First written down before 899 in Old English and spelled *nēahgebūr* : *nēah,* near + *gebūr,* dweller.]

neigh•bor•hood (nā′bər ho͝od′) *n.* **1.** A district or area with distinct characteristics. **2.** The people who live in a particular area or district: *The noise upset the entire neighborhood.* **3.** The surrounding area; the vicinity: *I just happened to be in the neighborhood.* ***—idiom.*** **in the neighborhood of.** Approximately: *inflation in the neighborhood of three percent a year.*

neigh•bor•ly (nā′bər lē) *adj.* Having or showing the quality of a friendly neighbor: *a neighborly act of kindness.* **—neigh′bor•li•ness** *n.*

Nei Monggol (nā′ mŏng′gōl′) also **In•ner Mon•go•li•a** (ĭn′ər mŏng gō′lē ə *or* ĭn′ər mŏng gōl′yə). A region of northeast China south of Mongolia. It became part of China in 1911.

nei•ther (nē′*th*ər *or* nī′*th*ər) *adj.* Not either; not one nor the other: *Neither shoe fits comfortably.* *—pron.* Not either one; not the one nor the other: *Neither of the shoes fits.* *—conj.* **1.** Not either; not in either case. Used with *nor*: *They had neither seen nor heard of us.* **2.** Also not; nor: *If you won't go, neither will I.* —SEE NOTE.

nek•ton (nĕk′tən *or* nĕk′tŏn′) *n.* The collection of organisms, such as fish, that possess the power to swim freely in salt and fresh water independent of water movements, in contrast to plankton.

nel•son (nĕl′sən) *n.* One of several holds in wrestling in which a wrestler slips one arm under the opponent's arm and presses the hand against the opponent's neck.

nem•a•to•cyst (nĕm′ə tə sĭst′ *or* nĭ măt′ə sĭst′) *n.* One of the stinging cells in the tentacles of a jellyfish, hydra, or related animal, used to capture prey and ward off attackers.

nem•a•tode (nĕm′ə tōd′) *n.* Any of several slender worms, many of which are parasites that cause disease or damage plants; a roundworm.

nem•e•sis (nĕm′ĭ sĭs) *n., pl.* **nem•e•ses** (nĕm′ĭ-sēz′). **1.a.** A source of harm or ruin: *Carelessness was your nemesis on that math exam.* **b.** Just punishment for wrongdoing. **2.** An unbeatable rival: *He met his nemesis in the tennis finals.* **3. Nemesis.** In Greek mythology, the goddess of retributive justice or vengeance.

neo– *pref.* A prefix that means new or recent: *Neolithic.* —SEE NOTE.

ne•o•dym•i•um (nē′ō dĭm′ē əm) *n.* *Symbol* **Nd** A bright, metallic, rare-earth element, used in lasers, glass, and medicine. Atomic number 60. See table at **element.**

Ne•o•lith•ic (nē′ə lĭth′ĭk) *adj.* Of or relating to the period of human culture that began around 10,000 B.C. in the Middle East and is characterized by the development of farming and the making of polished stone implements.

ne•ol•o•gism (nē ŏl′ə jĭz′əm) *n.* A newly coined word, phrase, or expression or a new meaning for an existing word.

ne•on (nē′ŏn′) *n.* *Symbol* **Ne** A colorless, chemically inert gaseous element, found naturally in minute amounts in the atmosphere. Tubes containing neon are used in electric signs or lamps, giving off a fiery red glow. Atomic number 10. See table at **element.** [First written down in 1898 in Modern English, from Greek *neos,* new.]

ne•o•nate (nē′ə nāt′) *n.* A newborn infant. **—ne′o•na′tal** (nē′ō nāt′l) *adj.*

ne•o•phyte (nē′ə fīt′) *n.* **1.** A recent convert to a belief. **2.** A beginner or novice: *He's a neophyte at politics.*

ne•o•prene (nē′ə prēn′) *n.* A tough synthetic rubber that is resistant to the effects of oils, solvents, heat, and weather.

Ne•pal (nə pôl′ *or* nə päl′). A country of central Asia in the Himalaya Mountains between India and southeast China. It has been inhabited since ancient times. Katmandu is the capital and the largest city. Population, 15,022,839.

neph•ew (nĕf′yo͞o) *n.* The son of one's brother or sister or of the brother or sister of one's spouse.

Jawaharlal Nehru

Usage: neither

When using **neither** as a conjunction, you should follow it with **nor** rather than **or**: *Neither rain nor snow stopped her from going for a walk every day.*

Word Building: neo–

The prefix **neo–**, which comes from Greek, means "new or recent." Thus our word **neophyte**, which means "a recent convert" or "a beginner," comes from Greek *neophutos*, which meant literally "newly planted," from *neo–* + *–phutos*, "planted." Many words beginning with **neo–** do not come from Greek but have been formed in English over the last 150 years. Many of these words refer to a new or a modern form of a movement or doctrine, such as **neoconservatism** or **neofascism**. Many other relatively recent formations are science words, such as **neodymium**.

ă	**pat**	oi	**boy**
ā	**pay**	ou	**out**
âr	**care**	o͝o	**took**
ä	**father**	o͞o	**boot**
ĕ	**pet**	ŭ	**cut**
ē	**be**	ûr	**urge**
ĭ	**pit**	th	**thin**
ī	**pie**	*th*	**this**
îr	**pier**	hw	**whoop**
ŏ	**pot**	zh	**vision**
ō	**toe**	ə	**about**
ô	**paw**	N	*French* bon

Word Building: –ness

The suffix **–ness**, which goes back to Old English, continues to have a productive life. It commonly attaches to adjectives in order to form abstract nouns, such as **artfulness** and **destructiveness**. The suffix **–ness** also forms nouns from adjectives made of participles, such as **contentedness** and **willingness**. It can also form nouns from compound adjectives, such as **kindheartedness** and **straightforwardness**. The suffix **–ness** can even be used with phrases: **matter-of-factness**.

nest
Top: Bird nest
Bottom: c. 1810 English nest of tables once owned by Napoleon Bonaparte

[First written down before 1250 in Middle English and spelled *neweu*, from Latin *nepōs*.]

ne•phri•tis (nə frī′tĭs) *n., pl.* **ne•phrit•i•des** (nə-frĭt′ĭ dēz′) or **ne•phri•tis•es.** Any of various acute or chronic inflammations of the kidneys.

neph•ron (nĕf′rŏn) *n.* Any of the numerous functional units of the kidney, serving to filter waste matter from the blood.

nep•o•tism (nĕp′ə tĭz′əm) *n.* Favoritism shown by persons in high office to relatives. [First written down in 1662 in Modern English, from Latin *nepōs*, nephew.]

Nep•tune (nĕp′to͞on′ *or* nĕp′tyo͞on′) *n.* **1.** In Roman mythology, the god of the sea, identified with the Greek Poseidon. **2.** The eighth planet from the sun at a mean distance of 2.8 billion miles (4.5 billion kilometers), and the fourth largest in the solar system with a mean diameter of about 30,000 miles (48,000 kilometers).

nep•tu•ni•um (nĕp **to͞o′**nē əm *or* nĕp **tyo͞o′**nē əm) *n. Symbol* **Np** A radioactive metallic element, produced by bombarding uranium with neutrons. It has thirteen isotopes with mass numbers ranging from 231 to 241 and half-lives ranging from 7.3 minutes to 2.2 million years. Atomic number 93. See table at **element.**

nerd also **nurd** (nûrd) *n. Slang.* A person regarded as stupid or inept, especially a person who is proficient at science but socially inept.

Ne•ro (nîr′ō *or* nē′rō). A.D. 37–68. Emperor of Rome (54–68) who may have set the Great Fire of Rome (64). He committed suicide because of widespread revolts.

nerve (nûrv) *n.* **1.** Any of the bundles of fibers that extend from the central nervous system to the various organs and parts of the body. They are capable of carrying impulses that represent stimuli to the central nervous system and of carrying impulses that activate muscles and glands. **2.** A sore point; a touchy subject: *She touched a nerve when she criticized my English paper.* **3.a.** Courage and control: *Don't lose your nerve; ask for the job.* **b.** Brazen boldness; effrontery: *He has some nerve, saying that he's better at chess than you.* **4. nerves.** Any of a group of symptoms, such as trembling or restlessness, caused by the reaction of the nervous system to fear, anxiety, or stress: *an attack of nerves.* **—*idioms.* get on (someone's) nerves.** To irritate or exasperate. **strain every nerve.** To make every effort. [First written down about 1385 in Middle English and spelled *nerf*, sinew, nerve, from Latin *nervus*.]

nerve cell *n.* A neuron.

nerve center *n.* **1.** A group of closely connected nerve cells that act together to perform a function. **2.** A source of power or control: *This office is the nerve center of the flood relief effort.*

nerve fiber *n.* Any of the two kinds of threadlike structures that extend from the main body of a nerve cell; an axon or a dendrite.

nerve impulse *n.* The electrical and chemical disturbance that moves along a stimulated nerve fiber.

nerve•less (**nûrv′**lĭs) *adj.* **1.** Lacking strength or energy: *The pipe dropped from his nerveless fingers.* **2.** Not nervous; calm; poised: *nerveless in the face of competition.* **—nerve′less•ly** *adv.*

nerve-rack•ing or **nerve-wrack•ing** (**nûrv′**răk′ĭng) *adj.* Intensely distressing or irritating to the nerves: *As they announced the awards, the suspense was nerve-racking.*

nerv•ous (**nûr′**vəs) *adj.* **1.** Relating to or affecting the nerves or the nervous system: *a nervous disorder.* **2.** Having nerves that are easily affected; high-strung; jittery: *a nervous person.* **3.** Uneasy; anxious: *nervous moments before takeoff.* **—nerv′ous•ly** *adv.* **—nerv′ous•ness** *n.*

nervous breakdown *n.* A severe or disabling emotional disorder marked by depression.

nervous system *n.* The bodily system that regulates internal functions and responses to stimuli. In vertebrates it includes the brain, spinal cord, and nerves.

nerv•y (**nûr′**vē) *adj.* **nerv•i•er, nerv•i•est.** Impudently bold or confident; rude: *a nervy answer.* **—nerv′i•ness** *n.*

–ness *suff.* A suffix that means state, condition, or quality: *brightness.* —SEE NOTE.

nest (nĕst) *n.* **1.a.** A container or shelter made by a bird for holding its eggs and young. **b.** A similar shelter, as of insects, fish, or mammals such as mice or squirrels. **c.** A number of birds, insects, or other animals occupying such a shelter: *a nest of hornets.* **2.** A place of lodging or shelter: *The nest of the newlyweds is a small apartment.* **3.** A place or environment that encourages growth, especially of persons or things: *streets that are a nest of criminal activity.* **4.** A set of objects of different sizes made so that each one fits into or under the one next above it in size: *a nest of tables.* —*v.* **nest•ed, nest•ing, nests.** —*intr.v.* To build or stay in a nest: *Robins nested in the willow tree.* —*tr.v.* **1.** To place in or as if in a nest: *The diamond was nested in cotton fluff.* **2.** To fit snugly together or inside one another: *nest boxes for storage.* [First written down about 750 in Old English.]

nest egg *n.* A sum of money saved for future use; savings.

nes•tle (**nĕs′**əl) *v.* **nes•tled, nes•tling, nes•tles.** —*intr.* **1.** To settle down snugly and comfortably: *The cat nestled among the pillows.* **2.** To press or snuggle close: *The child nestled up to his mother.* **3.** To lie half-sheltered or partly hidden: *Farms nestle in the valley.* —*tr.* **1.** To snuggle or press close: *The baby nestled its head on my shoulder.* **2.** To place or settle as if in a nest: *I nestled the puppy in my arms.*

nest•ling (**nĕst′**lĭng *or* **nĕs′**lĭng) *n.* A bird too young to leave its nest.

Nes•tor (**nĕs′**tər *or* **nĕs′**tôr′) *n.* **1.** In Greek mythology, a hero celebrated for his age and for the wisdom of his counsel among the Greeks at Troy. **2.** Often **nestor.** A venerable and wise old man.

net[1] (nĕt) *n.* **1.** A fabric made of threads, cords, or ropes that are woven or knotted together with holes between them. **2.** A piece of net used for a special purpose, especially: **a.** A device used to catch fish, birds, or insects. **b.** A screen or covering used as protection against insects such as mosquitoes. **c.** A piece of mesh for holding the hair in place. **d.** A fine fabric used for veils or curtains. **3.a.** A barrier of mesh strung between two posts to divide a court in half, as in tennis or volleyball. **b.** The goal in soccer, hockey, or lacrosse. —*tr.v.* **net•ted, net•ting, nets.** **1.** To catch in or as if in a net: *He netted a rare butterfly.* **2.** To cover with or as if with a net. [First written down before 830 in Old English.]

net[2] (nĕt) *adj.* **1.** Remaining after all subtractions have been made: *What was your net income after expenses?* **2.** Final; ultimate: *What was the net result of your efforts?* —*n.* The net amount, as of profit, income, or weight. —*tr.v.* **net•ted, net•ting, nets.** To bring in or yield as profit: *The cargo of spices netted a huge profit.* [First written down before 1300 in Middle English, from Latin *nitidus*, clean, elegant.]

neth•er (**nĕth′**ər) *adj.* Located beneath or below; lower or under: *the nether regions of the earth.* [First written down before 830 in Old English and spelled *niotherra*, from *neother*, down.]

Neth•er•lands (**nĕth′**ər ləndz). Often called **Hol•land** (**hŏl′**ənd). A country of northwest Europe west of Germany on the North Sea. The kingdom of the

Netherlands, proclaimed at the Congress of Vienna (1814–1815), included Belgium until 1830. Amsterdam is the constitutional capital and the largest city; The Hague is the seat of government. Population, 14,394,600.

Netherlands An•til•les (ăn tĭl′ēz). Formerly **Dutch West In•dies** (dŭch wĕst ĭn′dēz). A territory of the Netherlands in the Caribbean Sea, including two islands off the coast of Venezuela and several islands in the northern Windward Islands. Willemstad is the capital. Population, 192,056.

neth•er•most (nĕ*th*′ər mōst′) *adj.* Lowest.

net•ting (nĕt′ĭng) *n.* A fabric made with open spaces between crossing strands; a net.

net•tle (nĕt′l) *n.* Any of numerous plants having stems and leaves covered with hairs that sting when they are touched. —*tr.v.* **net•tled, net•tling, net•tles.** To annoy; irritate: *I was nettled by his constant bragging.* [First written down before 800 in Old English and spelled *netele.*]

net•tle•some (nĕt′l səm) *adj.* Causing annoyance or irritation.

net•work (nĕt′wûrk′) *n.* **1.** An open fabric or structure in which cords, threads, or wires cross at regular intervals: *a network of lace.* **2.** A system or pattern made up of a number of parts, passages, lines, or routes that cross or interconnect: *a network of blood vessels.* **3.a.** A chain of radio or television broadcasting stations, usually sharing a large proportion of their programs. **b.** A company that produces the programs for these stations. **4.a.** A group of electric devices and connecting circuits designed to work in a specific way. **b.** A group of computers connected by cables or telephone lines in order to share information.

neu•ral (no͝or′əl *or* nyo͝or′əl) *adj.* **1.** Of or relating to the nerves or nervous system. **2.** Relating to or situated in the region or side of the body containing the spinal cord; dorsal. —**neu′ral•ly** *adv.*

neu•ral•gia (no͞o răl′jə *or* nyo͞o răl′jə) *n.* A fitful or spasmodic pain that occurs along a nerve.

neu•ri•tis (no͞o rī′tĭs *or* nyo͞o rī′tĭs) *n.* Inflammation of a nerve, with symptoms such as pain, paralysis, and loss of reflexes in the region affected by the nerve.

neu•rol•o•gist (no͞o rŏl′ə jĭst *or* nyo͞o rŏl′ə jĭst) *n.* A person who specializes in neurology.

neu•rol•o•gy (no͞o rŏl′ə jē *or* nyo͞o rŏl′ə jē) *n.* The scientific and medical study of the nervous system and its diseases and disorders. —**neu′ro•log′i•cal** (no͝or′ə lŏj′ĭ kəl *or* nyo͝or′ə lŏj′ĭ kəl) *adj.*

neu•ron (no͝or′ŏn′ *or* nyo͝or′ŏn′) *n.* Any of the cells that make up the tissue of nerves and of the nervous system, consisting typically of a main portion that contains the nucleus and nerve fibers that carry impulses to and away from the cell. [First written down in 1891 in Modern English, from Greek *neuron*, sinew, string, nerve.]

neu•ro•sis (no͞o rō′sĭs *or* nyo͞o rō′sĭs) *n., pl.* **neu•ro•ses** (no͞o rō′sēz *or* nyo͞o rō′sēz). A disorder in which the function of the mind or emotions is disturbed with no apparent physical change in the nervous system, involving symptoms such as anxiety, depression, and fits of anger.

neu•rot•ic (no͞o rŏt′ĭk *or* nyo͞o rŏt′ĭk) *adj.* **1.** Relating to or caused by a neurosis: *neurotic symptoms.* **2.** Suffering from or affected by neurosis: *a neurotic patient.* —*n.* A person suffering from a neurosis. —**neu•rot′i•cal•ly** *adv.*

neu•ro•trans•mit•ter (no͝or′ō trănz′mĭt ər *or* nyo͝or′ō trănz′mĭt ər) *n.* A substance that transmits impulses between nerve cells.

neu•ter (no͞o′tər *or* nyo͞o′tər) *adj.* **1.** In grammar, neither masculine nor feminine in gender; for example, *it* is a neuter pronoun. **2.** Lacking or having undeveloped sex glands or sex organs. —*n.* **1.** In grammar: **a.** The neuter gender. **b.** A neuter word. **2.** A neuter animal or plant. —*tr.v.* **neu•tered, neu•ter•ing, neu•ters.** To castrate or spay (an animal). [First written down before 1398 in Middle English and spelled *neutre*, from Latin *neuter*, neither.]

neu•tral (no͞o′trəl *or* nyo͞o′trəl) *adj.* **1.a.** Not allied with, supporting, or favoring either side in a war, dispute, or contest: *a neutral nation.* **b.** Not belonging to either side in a conflict: *neutral territory.* **2.** Of or indicating a color, such as gray, black, or white, that lacks hue; achromatic. **3.** Without definite or distinctive characteristics: *a neutral personality.* **4.** Neither acid nor alkaline: *a neutral solution.* **5.** Having positive electric charges exactly balanced by negative electric charges: *a neutral atom.* —*n.* **1.** A country or person that does not take part or take sides in a war or other conflict. **2.** A neutral color. **3.** A position in which a set of gears is not engaged and so no power can be transmitted: *Leave the car in neutral while I check the engine.* [First written down in 1471 in Middle English and spelled *neuteral*, from Latin *neuter*, neither.] —**neu′tral•ly** *adv.*

neu•tral•i•ty (no͞o trăl′ĭ tē *or* nyo͞o trăl′ĭ tē) *n.* The condition, quality, or status of being neutral, especially a policy of taking no part in a war.

neu•tral•ize (no͞o′trə līz′ *or* nyo͞o′trə līz′) *tr.v.* **neu•tral•ized, neu•tral•iz•ing, neu•tral•iz•es.** **1.** To cancel or counteract the effect of: *neutralize a poison.* **2.** To counterbalance and reduce to zero: *neutralize an electric charge.* **3.** To declare (a country) neutral and safe from invasion during a war. **4.** To cause to be neither acid nor alkaline: *neutralize a solution.* —**neu′tral•i•za′tion** (no͞o′trə lĭ zā′shən *or* nyo͞o′trə lĭ zā′shən) *n.* —**neu′tral•iz′er** *n.*

neu•tri•no (no͞o trē′nō *or* nyo͞o trē′nō) *n., pl.* **neu•tri•nos.** Any of three electrically neutral subatomic particles that travel at the speed of light and, like photons, are thought to have a mass of zero if at rest.

neu•tron (no͞o′trŏn′ *or* nyo͞o′trŏn′) *n.* An electrically neutral subatomic particle having about the mass of a proton. It is stable when bound in an atomic nucleus, contributing to the mass of the nucleus without affecting atomic number or electric charge. Neutrons are used to bombard the nuclei of various elements to produce fission and other nuclear reactions. [First written down in 1921 in Modern English, from *neutral.*]

Nev. *abbr.* An abbreviation of Nevada.

Ne•vad•a (nə văd′ə *or* nə vä′də). A state of the western United States west of Utah. It was admitted as the 36th state in 1864. Carson City is the capital and Las Vegas is the largest city. Population, 1,206,152. —SEE NOTE.

nev•er (nĕv′ər) *adv.* **1.** At no time; on no occasion; not ever: *I have never been here before.* **2.** Not at all; in no way: *Never fear.* [First written down before 725 in Old English and spelled *nǣfre* : *ne*, not + *ǣfre*, ever.]

nev•er•more (nĕv′ər môr′) *adv.* Never again.

nev•er•the•less (nĕv′ər *thə* lĕs′) *adv.* In spite of that; still; however: *His speech was brief; nevertheless, it drew great applause.*

new (no͞o *or* nyo͞o) *adj.* **new•er, new•est.** **1.a.** Recently made, built, established, created, or formed: *a new law.* **b.** Being or to be made, formed, or created: *cloth for a new dress.* **2.** Just found, discovered, or learned: *new information.* **3.** Recently obtained or acquired: *new political power.* **4.** Never used or worn; not old or secondhand: *a new bicycle.* **5.** Fresh: *a new coat of paint.* **6.** Additional; further: *Industry needed new sources of energy.* **7.** Different from the previous one or ones: *a new edi-*

nettle
Stinging nettle

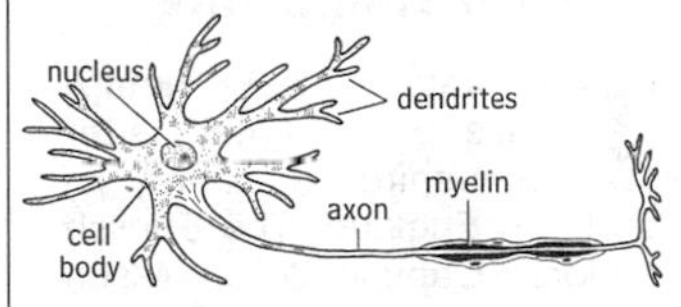

neuron

Nevada

The name **Nevada** was shortened from **Sierra Nevada**, the name of a mountain range in eastern California near what is today the Nevada border. In Spanish the words mean "snow-covered mountains."

ă	pat	oi	boy
ā	pay	ou	out
âr	care	o͝o	took
ä	father	o͞o	boot
ĕ	pet	ŭ	cut
ē	be	ûr	urge
ĭ	pit	th	thin
ī	pie	*th*	this
îr	pier	hw	whoop
ŏ	pot	zh	vision
ō	toe	ə	about
ô	paw	N	*French* bon

New Brunswick

The province of **New Brunswick** was named for King George III of England, who held the title of the German royal house of Brunswick.

Newfoundland[1]

The name **Newfoundland** means exactly that: a "new-found land." It was first explored by John Cabot in 1497, and the name occurs in an English text of 1498.

New Hampshire

The state of **New Hampshire** was named after Hampshire, a county in southern England. The English explorer Captain John Mason (1588–1635) founded and named the colony in 1629.

New Jersey

The state of **New Jersey** gets its name from the island of **Jersey** in the **English Channel**. Jersey was the birthplace of Sir George Carteret (c. 1610–1680), who became a proprietor of the region in 1664.

New Mexico

The name **New Mexico** comes from the Spanish *Nuevo Mexico*, which was used as early as the 1560's by Spanish explorers to describe the territory beyond the northern part of Mexico. In 1848, when the region became part of the United States, the name was translated into its present form.

tion of a book. **8.** Not previously experienced; unfamiliar; novel: *words that are new to you.* **9.** Recently arrived or established in a place, position, or relationship: *the new teacher.* **10.** Inexperienced or untrained: *He is new at this work.* **11.** Fashionable; up-to-date: *a new dance.* —*adv.* Freshly; newly; recently: *new-found friends.* **—new′ness** *n.*

❑ *These sound alike:* **new, gnu** (antelope), **knew** (did know).

New Am•ster•dam (no͞o *or* nyo͞o **ăm′**stər dăm′). A settlement established in 1624 by the Dutch on the southern end of Manhattan Island. It was captured by the British in 1664 and renamed New York.

New•ark (**no͞o′**ərk *or* **nyo͞o′**ərk). A city of northeast New Jersey on **Newark Bay,** an inlet of the Atlantic Ocean, west of New York City. It was settled by Puritans in 1666. Population, 275,221.

new•born (**no͞o′**bôrn′ *or* **nyo͞o′**bôrn′) *adj.* **1.** Just born: *newborn babies.* **2.** Reborn or renewed: *newborn courage.* —*n., pl.* **new•born** or **new•borns.** A newborn child or animal.

New Bruns•wick (**brŭnz′**wĭk). **1.** A province of eastern Canada on the Gulf of St. Lawrence south of Quebec. New Brunswick joined Nova Scotia, Quebec, and Ontario to form the confederated Dominion of Canada in 1867. Fredericton is the capital and St. John the largest city. Population, 696,405. **2.** A city of central New Jersey southwest of Newark. It served as headquarters for both the British and Continental armies during the American Revolution. Population, 41,711. —SEE NOTE.

new•com•er (**no͞o′**kŭm′ər *or* **nyo͞o′**kŭm′ər) *n.* A person, animal, or thing that has only recently arrived in a new place or situation.

New Deal *n.* The programs and policies for economic recovery and social reform introduced during the 1930's by President Franklin D. Roosevelt. **—New Dealer** *n.*

New Del•hi (**dĕl′**ē). The capital of India, in the north-central part of the country south of Delhi. It was constructed between 1912 and 1929 to replace Calcutta as the capital. Population, 273,036.

new•el (**no͞o′**əl *or* **nyo͞o′**əl) *n.* A post that supports a handrail at the bottom of a staircase or at one of the landings. [First written down in 1362 in Middle English and spelled *nowell,* from Latin *nōdulus,* little knot.]

New Eng•land (**ĭng′**glənd). A region of the northeast United States made up of the states of Maine, New Hampshire, Vermont, Massachusetts, Connecticut, and Rhode Island.

new•fan•gled (**no͞o′făng′**gəld *or* **nyo͞o′făng′**gəld) *adj.* New and often unnecessary or undesirable: *newfangled ideas.*

New•found•land[1] (**no͞o′**fən lənd *or* **nyo͞o′**fən lənd). A province of eastern Canada east of Quebec including the island of **Newfoundland** and nearby islands and the mainland area of Labrador with its adjacent islands. Newfoundland joined the Canadian confederation in 1949. St. John's is the capital and the largest city. Population 567,681. —SEE NOTE.

New•found•land[2] (**no͞o′**fən lənd *or* **nyo͞o′**fən lənd) *n.* Any of a breed of large strong dog developed in Newfoundland and having a dark thick coat.

New Guin•ea (**gĭn′**ē). An island in the southwest Pacific Ocean north of Australia, divided between Indonesia to the west and Papua New Guinea to the east.

New Hamp•shire (**hămp′**shər). A state of the northeast United States between Vermont and Maine. It was admitted as one of the original Thirteen Colonies in 1788. New Hampshire was the first colony to declare its independence from Great Britain and the first to establish its own government (January 1776). Capital, Concord. Population, 1,113,915. —SEE NOTE.

New Ha•ven (**hā′**vən). A city of southern Connecticut south-southwest of Hartford on Long Island Sound. It was settled in 1637–1638 by Puritans. Population, 130,474.

New Jer•sey (**jûr′**zē). A state of the east-central United States on the Atlantic Ocean east of Pennsylvania. It was admitted as one of the original Thirteen Colonies in 1787. Trenton is the capital and Newark the largest city. Population, 7,748,634. —SEE NOTE.

New Latin *n.* Latin as used since about 1500.

new•ly (**no͞o′**lē *or* **nyo͞o′**lē) *adv.* **1.** Not long ago; recently: *a newly acquired piece of property.* **2.** In a new or different way; freshly: *an old idea newly stated.*

new•ly•wed (**no͞o′**lē wĕd′ *or* **nyo͞o′**lē wĕd′) *n.* A person recently married.

New Mex•i•co (**mĕk′**sĭ kō′). A state of the southwest United States on the Mexican border east of Arizona. It was admitted as the 47th state in 1912. New Mexico was the site of prehistoric cultures and the Pueblo civilization encountered by the Spanish in the 16th century. Sante Fe is the capital and Albuquerque the largest city. Population, 1,521,779. —SEE NOTE.

new moon *n.* **1.** The phase of the moon that occurs as it passes between the sun and the earth and is invisible or visible only as a thin crescent at sunset. **2.** A crescent moon.

New Neth•er•land (**nĕth′**ər lənd). A Dutch colony in North America along the Hudson River that was annexed by the English and renamed New York in 1664.

New Or•leans (**ôr′**lē ənz *or* **ôr′**lənz *or* ôr **lēnz′**). The largest city in Louisiana, in the southeast part of the state on the Mississippi River. Founded in 1718, it became the capital of a French colony in 1722. French influence continues to dominate the city. Population, 496,938.

news (no͞oz *or* nyo͞oz) *pl.n. (used with a singular verb).* **1.a.** Information about recent events, especially when reported by newspapers, radio, or television. **b.** A presentation of such information, as on a television broadcast: *Did you watch the news last night?* **2.** New information: *The change in the bus schedule was news to me.* **3.** A fact or an event that is interesting enough to be reported: *She is so famous that whatever she does is news.*

news•boy (**no͞oz′**boi′ *or* **nyo͞oz′**boi′) *n.* A boy who sells or delivers newspapers.

news•cast (**no͞oz′**kăst′ *or* **nyo͞oz′**kăst′) *n.* A radio or television program that broadcasts news reports. **—news′cast′er** *n.*

news conference *n.* A press conference.

news•girl (**no͞oz′**gûrl′ *or* **nyo͞oz′**gûrl′) *n.* A girl who sells or delivers newspapers.

news•let•ter (**no͞oz′**lĕt′ər *or* **nyo͞oz′**lĕt′ər) *n.* A printed report giving news or information of interest to a special group.

news•man (**no͞oz′**măn′ *or* **nyo͞oz′**măn′) *n.* A man who gathers, reports, or edits news.

news•pa•per (**no͞oz′**pā′pər *or* **nyo͞oz′**pā′pər) *n.* **1.** A publication, usually issued daily or weekly, containing current news, editorials, articles, and advertisements. **2.** Newsprint.

news•pa•per•man (**no͞oz′**pā′pər măn′ *or* **nyo͞oz′**pā′pər măn′) *n.* **1.** A man who owns or publishes a newspaper. **2.** A man who is a newspaper reporter, writer, or editor.

news•pa•per•wom•an (**no͞oz′**pā′pər wo͝om′ən *or* **nyo͞oz′**pā′pər wo͝om′ən) *n.* **1.** A woman who owns or publishes a newspaper. **2.** A woman who is a newspaper reporter, writer, or editor.

news•print (no͞oz′prĭnt′ *or* **nyo͞oz′**prĭnt′) *n.* Cheap thin paper made from wood pulp and used chiefly to print newspapers.

news•reel (no͞oz′rēl′ *or* **nyo͞oz′**rēl′) *n.* A short motion picture that gives a visual report of recent news events.

news•stand (no͞oz′stănd′ *or* **nyo͞oz′**stănd′) *n.* An open booth or stall where newspapers and magazines are sold.

news•wom•an (no͞oz′wo͝om′ən *or* **nyo͞oz′**wo͝om′ən) *n.* A woman who gathers, reports, or edits news.

news•wor•thy (no͞oz′wûr′*thē* *or* **nyo͞oz′**wûr′*thē*) *adj.* **news•wor•thi•er, news•wor•thi•est.** Interesting or important enough to be worth reporting to the general public: *a newsworthy event.*

news•y (no͞o′zē *or* **nyo͞o′**zē) *adj.* **news•i•er, news•i•est.** *Informal.* Full of news; informative: *a newsy letter.*

newt (no͞ot *or* nyo͞ot) *n.* Any of several small salamanders that live both on land and in the water. [First written down before 1425 in Middle English and spelled *neute*, from the phrase *(an) eute*, from Old English *efete*.]

New Testament *n.* The second of the two main divisions of the Christian Bible, containing the Gospels and other books relating the life and teachings of Jesus and his followers.

new•ton (no͞ot′n *or* **nyo͞ot′**n) *n.* A unit of force equal to the force needed to accelerate a mass of one kilogram one meter per second per second. [First written down in 1904 in Modern English, after Sir Isaac *Newton*.]

New•ton (no͞ot′n *or* **nyo͞ot′**n), Sir **Isaac.** 1642–1727. English mathematician and scientist who developed calculus and formulated a theory of gravitation. **—New•ton′i•an** *adj.*

New World. The Western Hemisphere.

New Year *n.* The first day or days of a calendar year.

New Year's Day (yîrz) *n.* January 1, the first day of the year, celebrated as a holiday in many countries.

New York (yôrk). **1.** A state of the northeast United States north of Pennsylvania. It was admitted as one of the original Thirteen Colonies in 1788. Albany is the capital and New York the largest city. Population, 18,044,505. **2.** Or **New York City.** A city of southern New York on **New York Bay,** an inlet of the Atlantic Ocean at the mouth of the Hudson River. It is the largest city in the country. Population, 7,322,564. —SEE NOTE.

New Zea•land (zē′lənd). An island country in the southern Pacific Ocean southeast of Australia. New Zealand gained its independence from Great Britain in 1931. Wellington is the capital and Auckland the largest city. Population, 3,265,300.

next (nĕkst) *adj.* **1.** Immediately following in time, order, or sequence: *next week; the next item on the list.* **2.** Closest or nearest in space or position: *the next town; the next room.* *—adv.* **1.** In the time, order, or place immediately following: *our next oldest child.* **2.** On the first occasion after the present or previous one: *when you next wash the floor.* ***—idiom.*** **next to. 1.** Adjacent to: *Who is sitting next to you?* **2.** Coming immediately before or after: *She's next to last on the waiting list.* **3.** Almost; practically: *next to impossible.* [First written down about 725 in Old English and spelled *nīehsta*.]

next door *adv.* To or in the adjacent house, building, apartment, or room: *Mike just moved next door to Tom.* *—adj.* **next-door** (**nĕkst′dôr′**). Located or living in the adjacent house, building, apartment, or room: *our next-door neighbors.*

Nez Perce (**nĕz′ pûrs′**) also **Nez Per•cé** (pər **sā′**) *n., pl.* **Nez Perce** or **Nez Per•ces** (**pûr′**sĭz) also **Nez Per•cé** or **Nez Per•cés** (pər **sāz′**). **1.** A member of a Native American people of the northwest United States. **2.** The Sahaptian language of the Nez Perce.

Nfld. *abbr.* An abbreviation of Newfoundland.

NG or **N.G.** *abbr.* An abbreviation of: **1.** National Guard. **2.** No good. **3.** Natural gas.

NH or **N.H.** *abbr.* An abbreviation of New Hampshire.

Ni The symbol for the element **nickel** (sense 1).

ni•a•cin (**nī′**ə sĭn) *n.* A compound containing carbon, hydrogen, oxygen, and nitrogen with the formula $C_6H_5O_2N$. It is a member of the vitamin B complex, is essential to living cells, and is used to treat and prevent pellagra.

Ni•ag•a•ra Falls (nī **ăg′**rə *or* nī **ăg′**ər ə). Falls in the Niagara River between the cities of **Niagara Falls,** New York, and **Niagara Falls,** Ontario, Canada. The falls are divided by an island into the American Falls, 167 feet (50.9 meters) high, and the Canadian Falls, 158 feet (48.2 meters) high.

Niagara River. A river flowing about 34 miles (55 kilometers) from Lake Erie to Lake Ontario.

Nia•mey (nē **ä′**mā). The capital and largest city of Niger, in the southwest part of the country near the borders with Burkina Faso and Benin. Population, 399,100.

nib (nĭb) *n.* **1.** The point of a pen. **2.** A sharp point or tip. **3.** A bird's beak. [First written down about 700 in Old English and spelled *neb*, beak, bill.]

nib•ble (**nĭb′**əl) *v.* **nib•bled, nib•bling, nib•bles.** *—tr.* **1.** To eat with small quick bites: *nibble cheese.* **2.** To bite at gently and repeatedly: *The fish nibbled the bait.* *—intr.* To take small quick bites. *—n.* **1.** A small or hesitant bite. **2.** A small bite or morsel of food. [First written down before 1460 in Middle English and spelled *nebyllen*.]

Nic•a•ra•gua (nĭk′ə **rä′**gwə). A country of Central America north of Costa Rica. Nicaragua gained its independence from Spain in 1821. Managua is the capital and the largest city. Population, 2,823,979.

nice (nīs) *adj.* **nic•er, nic•est. 1.** Good; pleasant; agreeable: *a nice play to stay.* **2.** Having a pleasant appearance; attractive: *a nice dress.* **3.** Courteous and polite; considerate: *It's nice of you to help.* **4.** Morally upright; respectable. **5.** Done with skill and delicacy: *a nice bit of work.* **6.a.** Requiring the ability to notice small differences: *a nice distinction.* **b.** Able to notice small differences: *a nice ear for music.* **7.** Used as an intensive with *and*: *nice and warm.* [First written down before 1300 in Middle English and spelled *nice*, foolish, from Latin *nescius*, ignorant.] **—nice′ly** *adv.* **—nice′ness** *n.* —SEE NOTE.

❑ *These sound alike:* **nice, gneiss** (rock).

Nice (nēs). A city of southeast France on the Mediterranean Sea southwest of Monaco. It is the leading resort city of the French Riviera. Population, 337,085.

Ni•cene Creed (**nī′**sēn′ *or* nī **sēn′**) *n.* A formal statement of doctrine of the Christian faith adopted at the Council of Nicaea in A.D. 325 and expanded in later councils.

ni•ce•ty (**nī′**sĭ tē) *n., pl.* **ni•ce•ties. 1.** Precision or accuracy; exactness: *the nicety of the computer's calculations.* **2.** A fine point, small detail, or subtle distinction. **3.** An elegant or refined feature: *the niceties of civilized life.*

niche (nĭch *or* nēsh) *n.* **1.** A recess or an alcove in a wall, as for holding a statue. **2.** A cranny, hollow, or crevice, as in rock. **3.** A situation or an activity specially suited to a person's abilities or character: *She finally found her niche in life.* **4.** The function or position of an organism within an ecological community. [First written down in 1611 in Modern English, possibly from Old French *nichier*, to nest.]

Nich•o•las (**nĭk′**ə ləs), Saint. Fourth century A.D.

Isaac Newton

c. 1726 painting
by an unknown artist

New York

The state of **New York** was named after the Duke of York, later King James II (1633–1701), who was granted control of the colony after England seized it from the Dutch in 1664. Under the Dutch, the colony had been known as **New Amsterdam**.

Word History: nice

The word **nice** comes from Latin through Old French. In Old French *nice* means "silly." It comes from the Latin word *nescius*, "ignorant." In Middle English *nice* means "foolish" but acquires the sense "foolish about clothes." Then the meaning of *nice* shifts from the clothes to the person who wears them and comes to mean "fussy." A fussy person likes things just so, and *nice* then comes to mean "fine," as in *a nice distinction*; then *nice* finally comes to mean "agreeable."

ă	pat	oi	boy
ā	pay	ou	out
âr	care	o͝o	took
ä	father	o͞o	boot
ĕ	pet	ŭ	cut
ē	be	ûr	urge
ĭ	pit	th	thin
ī	pie	*th*	this
îr	pier	hw	whoop
ŏ	pot	zh	vision
ō	toe	ə	about
ô	paw	N	*French* bon

nighthawk

Florence Nightingale

Nike
Detail from a fifth-century B.C. Greek vase

Bishop in Asia Minor who is often associated with Santa Claus.

nick (nĭk) *n.* A small cut, notch, or chip in a surface or edge: *a plate with a nick in it.* —*tr.v.* **nicked, nick•ing, nicks.** To make a small cut or notch in. —***idiom.*** **in the nick of time.** Just at the critical moment; just in time. [First written down before 1450 in Middle English and spelled *nik*.]

nick•el (nĭk′əl) *n.* **1.** *Symbol* **Ni** A silvery, hard, ductile, metallic element, used in alloys and for electroplating. Atomic number 28. See table at **element. 2.** A U.S. or Canadian coin worth five cents, made of a nickel and copper alloy.

nickel silver *n.* A silvery, hard, malleable alloy of copper, zinc, and nickel that resists corrosion.

nick•nack (nĭk′năk′) *n.* Variant of **knickknack.**

nick•name (nĭk′nām′) *n.* **1.** A descriptive name used instead of or along with the real name of a person, place, or thing. **2.** A familiar or shortened form of a proper name: *Joseph's nickname was Joe.* —*tr.v.* **nick•named, nick•nam•ing, nick•names.** To give a nickname to. [First written down in 1440 in Middle English and spelled *neke name*, from the phrase *an eke name*, an additional name.]

Nic•o•si•a (nĭk′ə sē′ə). The capital and largest city of Cyprus, in the north-central part of the island. It was probably founded before the seventh century B.C. Population, 48,221.

nic•o•tine (nĭk′ə tēn′) *n.* A poisonous addictive alkaloid composed of carbon, hydrogen, and nitrogen in the proportions $C_{10}H_{14}N_2$. It is found in tobacco and is used in medicine and as an insect poison.

nic•o•tin•ic acid (nĭk′ə tĭn′ĭk *or* nĭk′ə tē′nĭk) *n.* Niacin.

niece (nēs) *n.* The daughter of one's brother or sister or of the brother or sister of one's spouse. [First written down about 1300 in Middle English and spelled *nece*, from Latin *neptis*.]

niels•bohr•i•um (nēlz bôr′ē əm) *n.* Element 105. [First written down in 1973 in Modern English, after Niels Henrik David *Bohr* (1885–1962), Danish physicist.]

nif•ty (nĭf′tē) *Slang. adj.* **nif•ti•er, nif•ti•est.** First-rate; great: *a nifty new outfit.*

Ni•ger (nī′jər *or* nē zhâr′). A country of west-central Africa north of Nigeria. It gained its independence from France in 1960. Niamey is the capital and the largest city. Population, 5,772,000.

Ni•ge•ri•a (nī jîr′ē ə). A country of western Africa on the Atlantic Ocean northwest of Cameroon. It gained its independence from Great Britain in 1960. Lagos is the capital and the largest city. Population, 89,117,500.

nig•gard (nĭg′ərd) *n.* A stingy person; a miser. —*adj.* Stingy; miserly.

nig•gard•ly (nĭg′ərd lē) *adj.* **1.** Unwilling to give, spend, or share; stingy: *niggardly in doling out the cookies.* **2.** Small or meager: *a niggardly amount.* —*adv.* Stingily. —**nig′gard•li•ness** *n.*

nig•gling (nĭg′lĭng) *adj.* **1.** Extremely concerned with details; fussy: *a niggling teacher.* **2.** Persistently nagging; petty: *a niggling dispute over trivial details.*

nigh (nī) *adv.* **nigh•er, nigh•est. 1.** Near in time, space, or relationship: *Evening drew nigh.* **2.** Nearly; almost: *talked for nigh onto two hours.* —*adj.* **nigher, nighest.** Being near in time, place, or relationship; close: *sick and nigh to death.* —*prep.* Not far from; near.

night (nīt) *n.* **1.** The period between sunset and sunrise, especially the hours of darkness. **2.** The period between bedtime and morning: *He tossed and turned all night.* **3.** An evening or night devoted to some special purpose or event: *the opening night of a play.* **4.** Nightfall: *They worked from morning to night.* **5.** Darkness: *She ran out into the foggy night.* **6.** A time of gloom, sorrow, or ignorance: *a long night of waiting before our dreams come true.* [First written down about 725 in Old English and spelled *niht*.]

❑ *These sound alike:* **night, knight** (warrior on horseback).

night blindness *n.* Inability to see normally in dim light.

night•cap (nīt′kăp′) *n.* **1.** A cloth cap worn in bed. **2.** A drink taken just before bedtime. **3.** The final game in a baseball double-header.

night•clothes (nīt′klōz′ *or* nīt′klōthz′) *pl.n.* Clothes, such as nightgowns and pajamas, worn in bed.

night•club (nīt′klŭb′) *n.* An establishment that stays open late at night and provides food, drink, and entertainment.

night crawler *n.* Any of various earthworms that come out of the ground at night.

night•fall (nīt′fôl′) *n.* The coming of night; dusk.

night•gown (nīt′goun′) *n.* A loose gown worn in bed by women and girls.

night•hawk (nīt′hôk′) *n.* **1.** Any of several birds related to the whippoorwill that are active at night and have mottled grayish feathers. **2.** *Informal.* A night owl.

night•in•gale (nīt′n gāl′ *or* nī′tĭng gāl′) *n.* A brownish bird of Europe and Asia, noted for the melodious song of the male at night.

Night•in•gale (nīt′n gāl′ *or* nī′tĭng gāl′), **Florence.** 1820–1910. British nurse who is considered the founder of modern nursing.

night-light (nīt′līt′) *n.* A usually small light left on all night.

night•ly (nīt′lē) *adj.* **1.** Of or occurring during the night: *The bears sometimes pay a nightly visit to the dump.* **2.** Happening or done every night: *the nightly news on TV.* —**night′ly** *adv.*

night•mare (nīt′mâr′) *n.* **1.** A dream that is very frightening. **2.** A very frightening experience. [First written down about 1300 in Middle English and spelled *nightmare*, a female demon that afflicts sleeping people : *night*, night + *mare*, goblin.] —**night′mar′ish** *adj.*

night owl *n. Informal.* A person who stays up late at night.

night school *n.* A school that holds classes in the evening.

night•shade (nīt′shād′) *n.* Any of several related plants, such as belladonna, having poisonous black or red berries and small white or purple flowers.

night•shirt (nīt′shûrt′) *n.* A long loose shirt worn in bed, especially by a man.

night•stick (nīt′stĭk′) *n.* A club carried by a police officer.

night•time (nīt′tīm′) *n.* The time between sunset and sunrise. —**night′time′** *adj.*

Ni•ke (nī′kē) *n.* In Greek mythology, the goddess of victory.

nil (nĭl) *n.* Nothing; zero. [First written down in 1833 in Modern English, from Latin *nīl*, contraction of *nihil*.]

Nile (nīl). The longest river in the world, flowing about 4,150 miles (6,677 kilometers) through eastern Africa from Burundi to the Mediterranean Sea in northeast Egypt. The river has been used for irrigation in Egypt since at least 4000 B.C.

nim•bi (nĭm′bī′) *n.* A plural of **nimbus.**

nim•ble (nĭm′bəl) *adj.* **nim•bler, nim•blest. 1.** Quick and light in movement; agile or deft: *nimble fingers.* **2.** Quick and clever in thinking or understanding: *a nimble wit.* [First written down before 1325 in Middle English and spelled *nemel*, from Old English *næmel*, quick to seize, and *numol*, quick at learning.] **—nim′ble•ness** *n.* **—nim′bly** *adv.*

nim•bo•stra•tus (nĭm′bō **strā′** təs *or* nĭm′-bō **străt′**əs) *n., pl.* **nim•bo•stra•ti** (nĭm′bō **strā′**tī *or* nĭm′bō **străt′**ī). A low, gray, often dark cloud usually producing prolonged rain, sleet, or snow.

nim•bus (**nĭm′**bəs) *n., pl.* **nim•bi** (**nĭm′**bī′) or **nim•bus•es. 1.** A halo or cloudy radiance glowing around the head of a god, goddess, saint, or monarch, as in a painting. **2.** A special atmosphere or aura, as of glory or romance, surrounding a person or thing. **3.** A rain cloud. [First written down in 1616 in Modern English, from Latin *nimbus*, cloud.]

nin•com•poop (**nĭn′**kəm po͞op′ *or* **nĭng′**kəm po͞op′) *n.* A stupid or silly person.

nine (nīn) *n.* **1.** The number, written 9, that is equal to 8 + 1. **2.** The ninth in a set or sequence. **3.** The first or second nine holes of an 18-hole golf course. [First written down about 840 in Old English and spelled *nigon.*] **—nine** *adj. & pron.*

nine•teen (nīn **tēn′**) *n.* **1.** The number, written 19, that is equal to 18 + 1. **2.** The 19th in a set or sequence. **—nine•teen′** *adj. & pron.*

nine•teenth (nīn **tēnth′**) *n.* **1.** The ordinal number matching the number 19 in a series. **2.** One of 19 equal parts. **—nine•teenth′** *adj. & adv.*

nine•ti•eth (**nīn′**tē ĭth) *n.* **1.** The ordinal number matching the number 90 in a series. **2.** One of 90 equal parts. **—nine′ti•eth** *adj. & adv.*

nine•ty (**nīn′**tē) *n., pl.* **nine•ties.** The number, written 90, that is equal to 9 × 10. **—nine′ty** *adj. & pron.*

Nin•e•veh (**nĭn′**ə və). An ancient city of Assyria on the Tigris River opposite the site of present-day Mosul, Iraq. It was the capital of the Assyrian Empire and was captured and destroyed by Babylonia in 612 B.C.

nin•ny (**nĭn′**ē) *n., pl.* **nin•nies.** A fool; a simpleton.

ninth (nīnth) *n.* **1.** The ordinal number matching the number nine in a series. **2.** One of nine equal parts. **3.** A musical interval equal to an octave plus a second. **—ninth** *adj. & adv.*

Ni•o•be (**nī′**ə bē) *n.* The daughter of Tantalus who is turned to stone by Zeus while bewailing the death of her children.

ni•o•bi•um (nī **ō′**bē əm) *n. Symbol* **Nb** A soft silvery metallic element used in making stainless steel and in other alloys, in the cores of nuclear reactors, and in making superconducting magnets. Atomic number 41. See table at **element.**

nip¹ (nĭp) *v.* **nipped, nip•ing, nips.** *—tr.* **1.** To seize and pinch or bite: *One pony nipped the other.* **2.** To remove by pinching or snipping: *nipped off the plant leaf.* **3.** To sting or chill with the cold: *The wind nipped our ears.* **4.** To stop the growth or development of: *a plot that was nipped in the bud.* *—intr. Chiefly British.* To move quickly; dart. *—n.* **1.** A small sharp bite, pinch, or snip. **2.** A small bit or portion removed by nipping: *nips of paper on the floor.* **3.** Sharp biting cold: *a nip in the autumn air.* **4.** A sharp biting flavor; tang. [First written down before 1387 in Middle English and spelled *nippen.*]

nip² (nĭp) *Informal. n.* A small amount of liquor. [First written down in 1796 in Modern English, probably short for *nipperkin*, of Dutch or Low German origin.]

nip and tuck *adj.* So close that the advantage or lead shifts from one to another; neck and neck.

nip•per (**nĭp′**ər) *n.* **1.** A tool, such as pliers or pincers, used for grasping or nipping. Often used in the plural. **2.** A part, such as the large claw of a lobster, that resembles such a tool. **3.** *Chiefly British.* A small boy.

nip•ple (**nĭp′**əl) *n.* **1.** A small projection near the center of the mammary gland, as of the human breast, containing in females the outlets of the milk ducts. **2.** A soft rubber cap on a bottle from which a baby nurses. **3.** A device that resembles or functions like a nipple, as a small pipe for releasing a liquid.

nip•py (**nĭp′**ē) *adj.* **nip•pi•er, nip•pi•est. 1.** Sharp or biting in taste: *nippy cheese.* **2.** So cold as to sting: *a nippy fall day.*

nir•va•na (nîr **vä′**nə *or* nər **vä′**nə) *n.* **1.** In Buddhism, the state of wisdom and compassion in which the self is freed from suffering and desire. **2.** An ideal condition of rest, harmony, or joy. [First written down in 1836 in Modern English, from Sanskrit *nirvāṇam*, a blowing out, extinction.]

Ni•sei (nē **sā′** *or* **nē′**sā′) *n., pl.* **Nisei** or **Ni•seis.** A person born in the United States of parents who emigrated from Japan.

nit (nĭt) *n.* The egg or young of a louse or similar insect. [First written down about 700 in Old English and spelled *hnitu.*]

❑ *These sound alike:* **nit, knit** (loop yarn).

ni•ter (**nī′**tər) *n.* A white, gray, or colorless mineral form of potassium nitrate.

ni•trate (**nī′**trāt′ *or* **nī′**trĭt) *n.* **1.** A salt or ester of nitric acid. **2.** A fertilizer containing a salt of nitric acid. *—tr.v.* **ni•trat•ed, ni•trat•ing, ni•trates.** To treat or combine with nitric acid or a nitrate. **—ni•tra′tion** *n.*

ni•tric (**nī′**trĭk) *adj.* Of, derived from, or containing nitrogen, especially in one of its higher valences.

nitric acid *n.* A transparent, colorless to yellowish, corrosive liquid composed of nitrogen, hydrogen, and oxygen and having the formula HNO_3. It is used in making fertilizers, explosives, dyes, and rocket fuels.

ni•tride (**nī′**trīd′) *n.* A compound of nitrogen and another element, such as phosphorus or a metal, in which the nitrogen gains electrons or shares them in a way that makes it the more negative of the two elements.

ni•tri•fy (**nī′**trə fī′) *tr.v.* **ni•tri•fied, ni•tri•fy•ing, ni•tri•fies. 1.** To treat or combine with nitrogen or its compounds. **2.** To oxidize (an ammonium compound) into a nitrite or nitrate, especially in soil by the action of nitrobacteria. **—ni′tri•fi•ca′tion** (nī′-trə fĭ **kā′**shən) *n.*

ni•trite (**nī′**trīt′) *n.* A salt or ester of nitrous acid, important in the nitrogen cycle.

ni•tro•bac•te•ri•um (nī′trō băk **tîr′**ē əm) *n., pl.* **ni•tro•bac•te•ri•a** (nī′trō băk **tîr′**ē ə). Any of various soil bacteria that change ammonium compounds into nitrites or change nitrites into nitrates as part of the nitrogen cycle.

ni•tro•cel•lu•lose (nī′trō **sĕl′**yə lōs′) *n.* An organic compound formed by treating cellulose with sulfuric acid and nitric acid. It is used in making explosives, rocket fuels, and plastics.

ni•tro•gen (**nī′**trə jən) *n. Symbol* **N** A colorless, odorless, gaseous element that makes up nearly four fifths of the atmosphere by volume, is a necessary part of all animal and plant tissues, and is used in the manufacture of explosives and fertilizers. Atomic number 7. See table at **element.**

nitrogen cycle *n.* The continuing process by which nitrogen in the atmosphere forms compounds that are deposited in the soil, taken up by bacteria and living plants that are in turn eaten by animals, and returned to the atmosphere by the decompositon and metabolism of organic substances.

nitrogen fixation *n.* **1.** The conversion of atmospheric nitrogen into nitrogen compounds, either by natural means or by industrial processes. **2.** The conversion by certain algae and soil bacteria of in-

nimbostratus

ă	pat	oi	boy
ā	pay	ou	out
âr	care	o͝o	took
ä	father	o͞o	boot
ĕ	pet	ŭ	cut
ē	be	ûr	urge
ĭ	pit	th	thin
ī	pie	*th*	this
îr	pier	hw	whoop
ŏ	pot	zh	vision
ō	toe	ə	about
ô	paw	N	*French* bon

Richard M. Nixon
Photographed in 1969

organic nitrogen and nitrogen compounds into compounds that plants can use.

ni•trog•e•nous (nī trŏj′ə nəs) *adj.* Of, derived from, or containing nitrogen.

ni•tro•glyc•er•in also **ni•tro•glyc•er•ine** (nī′trō glĭs′ər ĭn) *n.* A thick, pale-yellow, readily explosive liquid formed by treating glycerin with nitric and sulfuric acids. It has the formula $C_3H_5(NO_3)_3$ and is used in making dynamite and in medicine as a drug that dilates the blood vessels.

ni•trous (nī′trəs) *adj.* Of, derived from, or containing nitrogen, especially in one of its lower valences.

nitrous acid *n.* A weak unstable acid composed of nitrogen, hydrogen, and oxygen and having the formula HNO_2.

nitrous oxide *n.* A colorless sweet-smelling gas composed of nitrogen and oxygen and having the formula N_2O. It has an intoxicating effect and is used as a mild anesthetic.

nit•ty-grit•ty (nĭt′ē grĭt′ē) *n. Informal.* The specific or practical details; the heart of the matter.

nit•wit (nĭt′wĭt′) *n.* A stupid or silly person. [First written down in 1922 in American English, probably from obsolete *nit*, nothing.]

nix (nĭks) *Slang. n.* Nothing. *—adv.* Not so; no: *nix on that idea.* *—tr.v.* **nixed, nix•ing, nix•es.** To forbid, refuse, or veto: *My parents nixed my idea of going to the mall.* [First written down in 1789 in Modern English, from Old High German *niwiht*, nothing.]

Nix•on (nĭk′sən), **Richard Milhous.** Born 1913. The 37th President of the United States (1969–1974). When Congress recommended impeachment because of Nixon's involvement in the Watergate scandal, he resigned from office (August 9, 1974).

NJ or **N.J.** *abbr.* An abbreviation of New Jersey.

NM or **N.M.** *abbr.* An abbreviation of New Mexico.

N.Mex. *abbr.* An abbreviation of New Mexico.

no¹ (nō) *adv.* **1.** Not so. Used to express refusal, denial, or disagreement: *No, I'm not going.* **2.** Not at all. Often used with the comparative: *no better; no more.* **3.** Not: *Are you coming or no?* *—n., pl.* **noes** (nōz). **1.** A negative response; a denial or refusal: *The suggestion met with a chorus of noes.* **2.** A negative vote or voter. [First written down before 725 in Old English and spelled *nā*, never.]

❑ *These sound alike:* **no¹** (not so), **know** (have knowledge), **no²** (not any).

no² (nō) *adj.* **1.** Not any; not one: *There are no cookies left.* **2.** Not at all; not close to being: *He's no child; he should know better.* **3.** Hardly any: *We got there in no time at all.* [First written down before 1100 in Old English and spelled *nā*, from *nān*, none.]

❑ *These sound alike:* **no²** (not any), **know** (have knowledge), **no¹** (not so).

No The symbol for the element **nobelium.**

no. *abbr.* An abbreviation of: **1.** North. **2.** Northern. **3.** Number.

No•ah (nō′ə). In the Bible, the man who was chosen by God to build an ark, in which he, his family, and a pair of every animal were saved from the Flood.

No•bel (nō bĕl′), **Alfred Bernhard.** 1833–1896. Swedish scientist who invented dynamite (1866).

no•bel•i•um (nō bĕl′ē əm) *n. Symbol* **No** A radioactive metallic element prepared by bombarding curium with carbon nuclei. It has five isotopes with mass numbers ranging from 252 to 256 and half-lives ranging from 4.5 to 180 seconds. Atomic number 102. See table at **element.** [First written down in 1957 in Modern English, after Alfred *Nobel.*]

Nobel Prize *n.* Any of five international prizes awarded annually for outstanding achievement in physics, chemistry, physiology or medicine, economics, literature, and the promotion of peace. [First written down in 1900 in Modern English, after Alfred *Nobel.*]

no•bil•i•ty (nō bĭl′ĭ tē) *n., pl.* **no•bil•i•ties. 1.** A class of persons distinguished by high birth and hereditary rank, and often having wealth, power, and privilege. **2.** Noble rank or status: *Congress may not grant titles of nobility.* **3.** The state or quality of being noble in character: *There is real nobility in your devoting so much time to volunteer work.*

no•ble (nō′bəl) *adj.* **no•bler, no•blest. 1.** Having high or hereditary rank in society. **2.** Having or showing qualities of high moral character, as courage, generosity, or honor: *a noble spirit.* **3.** Excellent and admirable: *a noble cause.* **4.** Grand; stately; majestic: *noble mountain peaks.* **5.** Chemically inactive or inert. *—n.* A member of the nobility. [First written down before 1200 in Middle English, from Latin *nōbilis.*] **—no′ble•ness** *n.* **—no′bly** *adv.*

no•ble•man (nō′bəl mən) *n.* A man of noble rank.

no•ble•wom•an (nō′bəl wo͝om′ən) *n.* A woman of noble rank.

no•bod•y (nō′bŏd′ē *or* nō′bə dē) *pron.* No person; not anybody: *Nobody stayed after practice was over.* *—n., pl.* **no•bod•ies.** A person of no importance or influence.

noc•tur•nal (nŏk tûr′nəl) *adj.* **1.** Of, relating to, or occurring at night: *a nocturnal breeze.* **2.** Most active at night: *Owls are nocturnal birds.* [First written down in 1485 in Middle English, from Late Latin *nocturnālis*, from Latin *nox*, night.] **—noc•tur′nal•ly** *adv.*

noc•turne (nŏk′tûrn′) *n.* **1.** A painting of a night scene. **2.** A musical composition intended to suggest a dreamy mood.

nod (nŏd) *v.* **nod•ded, nod•ding, nods.** *—intr.* **1.** To lower and raise the head quickly, as in agreement. **2.** To let the head fall forward when getting sleepy: *He began to nod and soon was asleep.* **3.** To be careless for a moment and make a mistake. **4.** To move up and down, sway, or droop: *flowers nodding in the breeze.* *—tr.* **1.** To lower and raise (the head) quickly, as when showing agreement, giving a greeting, or pointing something out. **2.** To express or convey by lowering and raising the head: *He nodded his approval.* *—n.* A nodding movement of the head, as one used to show approval or point something out: *She gave a nod of affirmation.* [First written down about 1390 in Middle English and spelled *nodden.*]

nod•al (nōd′l) *adj.* Of, relating to, or located at or near a node.

node (nōd) *n.* **1.** A knob, knot, or swelling. **2.** The point on a plant stem where a leaf or stem is attached; a joint. **3.** A point or region of a vibrating or oscillating system at which the amplitude of the vibration or oscillation is zero. **4.a.** Either of the two points at which the orbit of a planet intersects the ecliptic. **b.** Either of the two points at which the orbit of a satellite intersects the plane of orbit of a planet. [First written down before 1425 in Middle English, from Latin *nōdus*, knot.]

nod•ule (nŏj′o͞ol) *n.* **1.** A small node, as of body tissue. **2.** A small lump or outgrowth, such as one of those formed on the roots of clover, alfalfa, or soybeans. **3.** A small lump of a mineral or a mixture of minerals.

No•ël also **No•el** (nō ĕl′) *n.* **1.** Christmas. **2. no•ël.** A Christmas carol.

no-fault (nō′fôlt′) *adj.* **1.** Of or relating to a system of automobile insurance in which accident victims are compensated by their insurance companies without assignment of blame. **2.** Of or relating to a type of divorce in which no blame is assigned to either husband or wife.

nog·gin (nŏg′ĭn) *n.* **1.** A small mug or cup. **2.** A small amount of liquid, equal to one-fourth of a pint. **3.** *Slang.* The head.

no-good (**nō′**gŏŏd′) *adj.* **1.** Having no value, use, or excellence. **2.** Gross; hateful: *a no-good criminal.*

noise (noiz) *n.* **1.** Sound or a sound that is loud, unpleasant, unexpected, or undesired: *You're making too much noise. I was awakened by a noise in the alley.* See Synonyms at **uproar. 2.** Sound or a sound of any kind: *The only noise was the wind in the pines.* —*tr.v.* **noised, nois·ing, nois·es.** To spread as a rumor or report: *He noised it about that he won a scholarship.* [First written down before 1200 in Middle English, from Old French, perhaps from Latin *nausea*, seasickness.]

noise·less (**noiz′**lĭs) *adj.* Making little or no noise. —**noise′less·ly** *adv.* —**noise′less·ness** *n.*

noise·mak·er (**noiz′**mā′kər) *n.* **1.** A person or thing that makes noise. **2.** A device, such as a horn or rattle, used to make noise at a party.

noi·some (**noi′**səm) *adj.* **1.** Foul, offensive, or disgusting: *a noisome odor.* **2.** Harmful or dangerous: *noisome fumes from the glue.* —**noi′some·ly** *adv.* —**noi′some·ness** *n.*

nois·y (**oi′**zē) *adj.* **nois·i·er, nois·i·est. 1.** Making a lot of noise: *a noisy engine.* **2.** Full of, characterized by, or accompanied by noise: *noisy streets.* —**nois′i·ly** *adv.* —**nois′i·ness** *n.*

no·mad (**nō′**măd′) *n.* **1.** A member of a group of people who have no fixed home and move about from place to place seeking food, water, and grazing land for their animals. **2.** A person who roams about instead of settling in one place. [First written down in 1555, from Greek *nomas*, wandering in search of pasture.] —**no·mad′ic** *adj.* —**no·mad′i·cal·ly** *adv.*

no man's land (măňz) *n.* **1.** Land under dispute by two opposing parties, especially the field of battle between two opposing entrenched armies. **2.** An area of uncertainty or ambiguity.

nom de plume (nŏm′ də **plo͞om′**) *n., pl.* **noms de plume** (nŏm′). A pen name.

no·men·cla·ture (**nō′**mən klā′chər *or* nō **mĕn′**klə chər) *n.* The system of names used in a particular science or art; terminology: *the nomenclature of anatomy.*

nom·i·nal (**nŏm′**ə nəl) *adj.* **1.** In name only and not in actual fact: *The queen is the nominal ruler, but the prime minister has the real power.* **2.** So small as to be insignificant: *They charged a nominal sum for admission.* **3.** In grammar, of or relating to a noun or a group of words that acts like a noun. [First written down before 1500 in Middle English and spelled *nominalle*, from Latin *nōmen*, name.] —**nom′i·nal·ly** *adv.*

nom·i·nate (**nŏm′**ə nāt′) *tr.v.* **nom·i·nat·ed, nom·i·nat·ing, nom·i·nates. 1.** To propose as a candidate, especially for an elected office. **2.** To appoint to an office or honor: *The President nominated a new chief of staff.* [First written down in 1545 in Modern English, from Latin *nōmen*, name.]

nom·i·na·tion (nŏm′ə **nā′**shən) *n.* **1.** The act or process of nominating. **2.** The state of being nominated: *Her nomination to the court has made her famous.*

nom·i·na·tive (**nŏm′**ə nā′tĭv) *adj.* Of or belonging to a grammatical case of the subject of a verb and of words identified with the subject of a linking verb. For example, in the sentences *These are our children* and *I sang the song* the words *children* and *I* are in the nominative case. —*n.* (**nŏm′**ə nə tĭv). The nominative case.

nom·i·nee (nŏm′ə **nē′**) *n.* **1.** A person proposed or selected as a candidate for an office or award: *the party's Presidential nominee.* **2.** A person appointed to a position, an office, or an honor: *the President's nominee for FBI director.*

non– *pref.* A prefix that means not: *nonconformist.* —See Note.

non·a·gon (**nŏn′**ə gŏn′ *or* **nō′**nə gŏn′) *n.* A polygon with nine sides and containing nine angles.

non·al·co·hol·ic (nŏn′ăl kə **hô′**lĭk *or* nŏn′ăl kə **hŏl′**ĭk) *adj.* Containing no alcohol: *a nonalcoholic beverage.*

non·a·ligned (nŏn′ə **līnd′**) *adj.* Not in alliance with any other nation or group of allies; neutral: *a nonaligned nation.*

nonce (nŏns) *n.* The present time or occasion. Used chiefly in the phrase *for the nonce.*

nonce word *n.* A word made up for use on one particular occasion.

non·cha·lance (nŏn′shə **läns′**) *n.* The state or quality of being nonchalant: *Her nonchalance about the party made us think she didn't want to go.*

non·cha·lant (nŏn′shə **länt′**) *adj.* Seeming to be carefree and unconcerned: *a nonchalant air.* [First written down before 1734 in Modern English and spelled *non chalant*, from Old French *nonchaloir*, to be unconcerned : *non-*, not + Latin *calēre*, to be warm, heat up.] —**non′cha·lance′** *n.* —**non′cha·lant′ly** *adv.*

non·com (**nŏn′**kŏm′) *n. Informal.* A noncommissioned officer.

non·com·bat·ant (nŏn′kəm **băt′**nt *or* nŏn′**kŏm′**bə tnt) *n.* **1.** A person serving in the armed forces, as a chaplain or surgeon, whose duties do not include fighting. **2.** A civilian in wartime.

non·com·mis·sioned officer (nŏn′kə **mĭsh′**ənd) *n.* An enlisted member of the armed forces, as a corporal or sergeant, appointed to a rank conferring leadership over other enlisted people. Noncommissioned officers rank below commissioned officers and warrant officers.

non·com·mit·tal (nŏn′kə **mĭt′**l) *adj.* Not indicating how one feels or thinks: *She gave a noncommittal answer, "We shall see."* —**non′com·mit′tal·ly** *adv.*

non·com·pli·ance (nŏn′kəm **plī′**əns) *n.* Failure or refusal to comply with something, such as a doctor's orders or a law.

non com·pos men·tis (nŏn kŏm′pəs **mĕn′**tĭs) *adj.* Not of sound mind and therefore not legally responsible.

non·con·duc·tor (nŏn′kən **dŭk′**tər) *n.* A substance that conducts little or no electricity, heat, or sound: *Rubber is a nonconductor of electricity.*

non·con·form·ist (nŏn′kən **fôr′**mĭst) *n.* **1.** A person who does not act in accordance with or refuses to follow generally accepted customs, beliefs, or ways of doing things. **2.** Often **Nonconformist.** A member of a Protestant church that does not accept or follow the teachings or practices of a national church, especially the Church of England. —**non′con·form′i·ty** *n.*

non·de·nom·i·na·tion·al (nŏn′dĭ nŏm′ə **nā′**shə nəl) *adj.* Not restricted to or associated with a particular religious denomination: *a nondenominational service.*

non·de·script (nŏn′dĭ **skrĭpt′**) *adj.* Lacking in distinctive qualities and thus difficult to describe: *a nondescript house that looked like any other.*

none (nŭn) *pron.* **1.** Not any: *None of my friends were at the pool.* **2.** Not one; nobody: *None dared to do it.* —*adv.* Not at all: *The coach was none too pleased.* [First written down about 750 in Old English and spelled *nān* : *ne*, no, not + *ān*, one.]

❑ *These sound alike:* **none, nun** (religious woman).

non·en·ti·ty (nŏn **ĕn′**tĭ tē) *n., pl.* **non·en·ti·ties.** A person or thing of no importance or significance.

noisemaker

Word Building: non–

The prefix **non–**, which means "not," comes from Latin *nōn.* The prefix was used primarily in Roman law terms that were adopted into Old French and then into English. By the 16th century, many compounds with **non–**, mostly legal terms, were in use in English. But in the 17th century the prefix began to be used with many different kinds of words. Today **non–** can be added to almost any adjective. Some examples include **nonessential, nonmetallic,** and **nonproductive. Non–** also combines with many nouns, as in **nonentity, nonresident,** and **nonviolence.** Most recently, **non–** is used in combination with some verbs to form adjectives, as in **nonskid** and **nonstop.**

ă	**pat**	oi	**boy**
ā	**pay**	ou	**out**
âr	**care**	o͝o	**took**
ä	**father**	o͞o	**boot**
ĕ	**pet**	ŭ	**cut**
ē	**be**	ûr	**urge**
ĭ	**pit**	th	**thin**
ī	**pie**	*th*	**this**
îr	**pier**	hw	**whoop**
ŏ	**pot**	zh	**vision**
ō	**toe**	ə	**about**
ô	**paw**	N	*French* **bon**

Usage: nonstandard

The term **nonstandard** is used to refer to words such as **ain't** and **irregardless**. The term does not mean that such words are not used by anyone. Rather, the term means that such words are not used in language that is considered standard, as in lectures by teachers or newscasts on television.

non•es•sen•tial (nŏn′ĭ **sĕn′**shəl) *adj.* Having little or no importance; not essential: *nonessential supplies.* —*n.* Something that is not essential: *Do not take any nonessentials on the hike.*

none•the•less (nŭn′*thə* **lĕs′**) *adv.* Nevertheless.

non-Eu•clid•e•an (nŏn′yo͞o **klĭd′**ē ən) *adj.* Of or having to do with any one of several forms of modern geometry that are based on postulates differing from those used by Euclid.

non•ex•ist•ent (nŏn′ĭg **zĭs′**tənt) *adj.* Not existing; entirely lacking: *planets with nonexistent atmospheres.* —**non′ex•ist′ence** *n.*

non•fat (**nŏn′făt′**) *adj.* Lacking fat solids or having the fat content removed: *nonfat milk.*

non•fic•tion (nŏn **fĭk′**shən) *n.* Prose works other than fiction: *I've read his novels but not his nonfiction.* —**non•fic′tion•al** *adj.*

non•flam•ma•ble (nŏn **flăm′**ə bəl) *adj.* Not flammable, especially not easily set fire to and burned. —**non•flam′ma•bil′i•ty** *n.*

non•flow•er•ing (nŏn **flou′**ər ĭng) *adj.* Not producing flowers.

non•in•ter•ven•tion (nŏn′ĭn tər **vĕn′**shən) *n.* Failure or refusal to intervene, especially in the affairs of another nation.

non•judg•men•tal (nŏn′jŭj **mĕn′**tl) *adj.* Refraining from judgment based on one's personal standards.

non•met•al (nŏn **mĕt′**l) *n.* Any of the elements, such as oxygen or sulfur, that usually gain electrons to become more electrically negative in forming a compound and that conduct heat and electricity poorly.

non•me•tal•lic (nŏn′mə **tăl′**ĭk) *adj.* **1.** Not metallic. **2.** Of or relating to a nonmetal: *a nonmetallic element.*

no-no (**nō′**nō′) *n., pl.* **no-noes.** *Informal.* Something that is not acceptable or allowed: *Chewing gum in class is a no-no.*

no-non•sense (nō **nŏn′**sĕns′) *adj.* Practical, serious, and businesslike: *a no-nonsense person.*

non•pa•reil (nŏn′pə **rĕl′**) *adj.* Having no equal; matchless; peerless: *a nonpareil goalie.* —*n.* A person or thing that has no equal.

non•par•ti•san (nŏn **pär′**tĭ zən) *adj.* Not based on, influenced by, or supporting a political party or its interests: *nonpartisan opinions.*

non•plus (nŏn **plŭs′**) *tr.v.* **non•plused, non•plus•ing, non•plus•es** also **non•plussed, non•plus•sing, non•plus•ses.** To put at a loss so that one does not know what to think, say, or do; bewilder.

non•pro•duc•tive (nŏn′prə **dŭk′**tĭv) *adj.* **1.** Not yielding what was expected or wanted: *a nonproductive vineyard.* **2.** Not engaged in the direct production of goods: *productive factory workers and nonproductive clerical personnel.* —**non′pro•duc′tive•ly** *adv.*

non•prof•it (nŏn **prŏf′**ĭt) *adj.* Not set up or managed for the purpose of making a profit: *a nonprofit organization.*

non•res•i•dent (nŏn **rĕz′**ĭ dənt) *adj.* Not making one's home at a particular place, especially not living in the same community where one works, attends school, owns property, or has official duties: *a nonresident taxpayer.* —*n.* A nonresident person.

non•re•stric•tive (nŏn′rĭ **strĭk′**tĭv) *adj.* In grammar, being a clause or phrase that describes a noun but does not restrict the meaning of the sentence and is set off by commas. In the sentence *The Smiths, who live in an apartment, have six cats,* the clause *who live in an apartment* is nonrestrictive.

non•sec•tar•i•an (nŏn′sĕk **târ′**ē ən) *adj.* Not limited to or associated with a particular religious denomination: *a nonsectarian college.*

non•sense (**nŏn′**sĕns′) *n.* **1.** Words or behavior having no sense: *The message was nonsense until we were able to read the handwriting.* **2.** Foolish or senseless talk, writing, or behavior: *Stop the nonsense and pay attention.* **3.** Something that is not important or useful: *You shouldn't waste time on this nonsense.*

non•sen•si•cal (nŏn **sĕn′**sĭ kəl) *adj.* **1.** Making no sense: *a nonsensical message.* **2.** Foolish; absurd: *a nonsensical idea.* —**non•sen′si•cal•ly** *adv.*

non se•qui•tur (nŏn **sĕk′**wĭ tər) *n.* A conclusion or statement that does not follow logically from the statements that preceded it.

non•stan•dard (nŏn **stăn′**dərd) *adj.* **1.** Varying from a standard: *nonstandard lengths of boards.* **2.** Of or relating to a kind of language that is used by uneducated speakers and is not normally considered acceptable by educated speakers. —See Note.

non•stop (**nŏn′stŏp′**) *adj.* Made or done without any stops: *a nonstop flight from New York to Paris.* —*adv.* Without making any stops: *flew nonstop to Los Angeles.*

non•un•ion (nŏn **yo͞on′**yən) *adj.* **1.** Not belonging to a labor union: *nonunion workers.* **2.** Not recognizing or dealing with a labor union or employing union members: *a nonunion shop.*

non•ver•bal (nŏn **vûr′**bəl) *adj.* Not using or relying on words: *Gestures, signs, and symbols are forms of nonverbal communication.*

non•vi•o•lence (nŏn **vī′**ə ləns) *n.* The philosophy, policy, or practice of rejecting violence in favor of peaceful actions as a means of gaining one's ends. —**non•vi′o•lent** *adj.* —**non•vi′o•lent•ly** *adv.*

non•white (nŏn **wīt′**) *n.* A person who is not white. —**non′white′** *adj.*

noo•dle[1] (**no͞od′**l) *n.* A narrow strip of dried dough, usually made of eggs, flour, and water. [First written down in 1779 in Modern English, from German *Nudel.*]

noo•dle[2] (**no͞od′**l) *n. Slang.* **1.** The head. **2.** A silly person; a fool. [First written down in 1753 in Modern English, probably alteration of *noddle,* head.]

nook (no͝ok) *n.* **1.** A corner, alcove, or recess, especially one that is part of a larger room: *a kitchen with a breakfast nook.* **2.** A hidden or secluded spot. [First written down about 1300 in Middle English and spelled *noke,* probably of Scandinavian origin.]

noon (no͞on) *n.* The middle of the day; twelve o'clock in the daytime; midday. [First written down about 725 in Old English and spelled *nōn,* canonical hour of nones (3 P.M. in early Middle Ages), from Latin *nōnus,* ninth.]

noon•day (**no͞on′**dā′) *n.* Noon. —*adj.* Of or occurring at noon: *the noonday heat.*

no one *pron.* No person; nobody: *No one answered, so I thought you were out.*

noon•tide (**no͞on′**tīd′) *n.* Noon.

noon•time (**no͞on′**tīm′) *n.* Noon.

noose (no͞os) *n.* **1.** A loop formed in a rope by means of a slipknot so that it binds tighter as the rope is pulled. **2.** A snare or trap. [First written down about 1450 in Middle English and spelled *nose,* probably from Latin *nōdus,* knot.]

Noot•ka (**no͞ot′**kə *or* **no͝ot′**kə) *n., pl.* **Nootka** or **Noot•kas. 1.** A member of a Native American people of Vancouver Island and adjacent areas of Canada and the United States. **2.** The language of this people.

nor (nôr; nər *when unstressed*) *conj.* And not; or not; not either: *He has neither written nor telephoned me. These life forms are neither plants nor animals.* —See Note at **neither.**

Nor•dic (**nôr′**dĭk) *adj.* **1.** Of, relating to, or characteristic of Scandinavia or its cultures. **2.** Of or relating to a human physical type composed of tall, blond, and light-skinned people, most frequently seen in Scandinavia.

Nor•folk (nôr′fək *or* nôr′fôk). A city of southeast Virginia southeast of Richmond. It was founded in 1682 and is today the largest city of Virginia. Population, 261,229.

norm (nôrm) *n.* **1.** A standard or pattern that is considered to be typical of a group. **2.** An average or a statistical mode. [First written down in 1821 in Modern English, from Latin *norma*, carpenter's square, rule.]

nor•mal (nôr′məl) *adj.* **1.** Conforming with a norm, standard, or type; typical: *normal room temperature.* **2.** Functioning or occurring in a natural healthy way: *normal digestion.* —*n.* Something normal; the standard: *body temperature above normal.* —**nor′mal•ly** *adv.*

nor•mal•cy (nôr′məl sē) *n.* Normality.

nor•mal•i•ty (nôr măl′ĭ tē) *n.* The condition of being normal.

nor•mal•ize (nôr′mə līz′) *tr.v.* **nor•mal•ized, nor•mal•iz•ing, nor•mal•iz•es.** To make normal: *normalized relations with the new foreign government.* —**nor′mal•i•za′tion** (nôr′mə lĭ zā′shən) *n.*

normal school *n.* A school that trains teachers, chiefly for the elementary grades.

Nor•man (nôr′mən) *n.* **1.** A member of a Scandinavian people who settled in Northern France in the tenth century. **2.** One of the descendants of these people who invaded England in 1066. **3.** A native or inhabitant of Normandy. —*adj.* Of or relating to Normandy, the Normans, or their language or culture.

Norman Conquest *n.* The conquest of England by the Normans under William the Conqueror in 1066.

Nor•man•dy (nôr′mən dē). A historical region and former province of northwest France on the English Channel. Its beaches were the site of Allied landings on D-day (June 6, 1944) in World War II.

Norman French *n.* The dialect of Old French used in medieval Normandy.

Norse (nôrs) *adj.* Of or relating to medieval Scandinavia, its peoples, or their languages or cultures. —*n.* **1.** The people of Scandinavia. **2.** The people of Norway; the Norwegians. **3.** North Germanic. **4.** Any of the West Scandinavian languages, especially Norwegian.

Norse•man (nôrs′mən) *n.* A member of one of the peoples of medieval Scandinavia.

north (nôrth) *n.* **1.** The direction to the left of sunrise, directly opposite south. **2.** A region or part of the earth in this direction: *Better farm lands lie in the north of the state.* **3. North.** The northern part of the United States, especially the states that supported the Union during the Civil War. —*adj.* **1.** To, toward, facing, or in the north: *the north shore of Long Island.* **2.** From the north: *a north wind.* —*adv.* In, from, or toward the north. [First written down about 725 in Old English and spelled *north.*]

North A•mer•i•ca (ə mĕr′ĭ kə). The northern continent of the Western Hemisphere, including Central America, Mexico, the islands of the Caribbean Sea, the United States, Canada, the Arctic Archipelago, and Greenland.

north•bound (nôrth′bound′) *adj.* Going toward the north.

North Car•o•li•na (kăr′ə lī′nə). A state of the southeast United States between Virginia and South Carolina on the Atlantic Ocean. It was admitted as one of the original Thirteen Colonies in 1789. Raleigh is the capital and Charlotte the largest city. Population, 6,657,630. —SEE NOTE.

North Da•ko•ta (də kō′tə). A state of the north-central United States east of Montana. It was admitted as the 39th state in 1889. Capital, Bismarck. Population, 641,364. —SEE NOTE.

north•east (nôrth ēst′) *n.* **1.** The direction halfway between north and east. **2.** An area or region lying in this direction. **3. Northeast.** The part of the United States including New England, New York, and sometimes Pennsylvania and New Jersey. —*adj.* **1.** To, toward, facing, or in the northeast. **2.** Coming from the northeast: *northeast winds.* —*adv.* In, from, or toward the northeast.

north•east•er (nôrth ē′stər *or* nôr ē′stər) *n.* A storm or gale blowing from the northeast.

north•east•er•ly (nôrth ē′stər lē) *adj.* **1.** Situated toward or facing the northeast: *a house with a northeasterly view.* **2.** Coming from the northeast: *northeasterly gales.* —**north•east′er•ly** *adv.* —**north•east′ern** *adj.*

north•east•ward (nôrth ēst′wərd) *adv.* To or toward the northeast: *sailed northeastward.* —*adj.* Situated toward or facing the northeast: *a northeastward view.* —*n.* A direction or region to the northeast. —**north•east′wards** *adv.*

north•er (nôr′*th*ər) *n.* A sudden cold gale blowing from the north.

north•er•ly (nôr′*th*ər lē) *adj.* **1.** Situated toward or facing the north: *The compass needle points in a northerly direction.* **2.** Coming from the north: *northerly winds.* —*n., pl.* **north•er•lies.** A storm or wind from the north. —**north′er•ly** *adv.*

north•ern (nôr′*th*ərn) *adj.* **1.** Situated in, toward, or facing the north: *the northern border.* **2.** Coming from the north: *northern winds.* **3.** also **Northern.** Of, relating to, or characteristic of northern regions or the North: *a northern climate.*

north•ern•er also **North•ern•er** (nôr′*th*ər nər) *n.* A person who lives in or comes from the north, especially the northern United States.

Northern Hemisphere *n.* **1.** The half of the earth north of the equator. **2.** The half of the celestial sphere north of the celestial equator.

Northern Ire•land (īr′lənd). A division of the United Kingdom in the northeast part of the island of Ireland. It occupies much of the ancient Irish kingdom of Ulster and is often known by that name. Capital, Belfast. Population, 1,488,077.

northern lights *pl.n.* The aurora borealis.

north•ern•most (nôr′*th*ərn mōst′) *adj.* Farthest north.

Northern Spy *n.* A yellowish-red apple.

North Germanic *n.* A subdivision of the Germanic languages that includes Norwegian, Icelandic, Swedish, and Danish.

north•ing (nôr′thĭng *or* nôr′*th*ĭng) *n.* **1.** The difference in latitude between two positions as a result of northward movement. **2.** Northward movement.

North Island. An island of New Zealand in the Pacific Ocean north of South Island. It is the smaller but more heavily populated of the country's two main islands.

North Ko•re•a (kə rē′ə). A country of northeast Asia west of Japan on the Yellow Sea. It has been inhabited since ancient times. Pyongyang is the capital and the largest city. Population, 18,317,000.

north•land also **North•land** (nôrth′lănd′ *or* nôrth′lənd) *n.* A region in the north of a country or an area.

North•man (nôrth′mən) *n.* A Norseman.

North Pole *n.* **1.** The northern end of the Earth's axis of rotation, a point in the Arctic Ocean. **2. north pole.** The pole of a magnet that tends to point north.

North Sea. An arm of the Atlantic Ocean between Great Britain and northwest Europe.

North Star *n.* Polaris.

North Vi•et•nam (vē ĕt′näm′ *or* vē′ĭt näm′). A for-

North Carolina

The states **North Carolina** and **South Carolina** were one colony, called **Carolina**, until they were formally divided in 1729. The colony was named after King Charles I of England, who granted its first charter. *Carolina* is a form of *Carolus*, the Latin word for Charles.

North Dakota

The states of **North Dakota** and **South Dakota** take their names from the Dakota, a branch of the Sioux people who inhabited the region. The name means "friends." Both sections wished to keep the name *Dakota* when the Dakota Territory was being divided, so *North* and *South* were added to the names when they achieved statehood in 1889.

ă	pat	oi	boy
ā	pay	ou	out
âr	care	o͝o	took
ä	father	o͞o	boot
ĕ	pet	ŭ	cut
ē	be	ûr	urge
ĭ	pit	th	thin
ī	pie	*th*	this
îr	pier	hw	whoop
ŏ	pot	zh	vision
ō	toe	ə	about
ô	paw	N	*French* bon

Northwest Territories

The name **Northwest Territories** describes the location of the territory relative to the rest of Canada. The Northwest Territories were sold by the Hudson's Bay Company to the Canadian confederation in 1870.

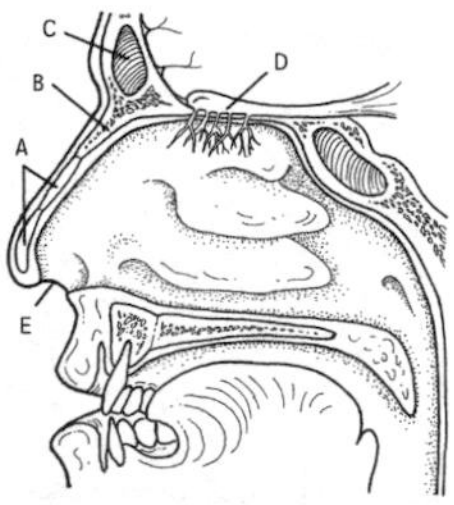

nose
A. Cartilage
B. Bone
C. Frontal sinus
D. Olfactory bulb
E. Nostril

Usage: not

When you use the construction *not only . . . but also,* be sure that each of its parts is parallel to the other. Write *She bought not only a new car but also a new lawnmower* rather than *She not only bought a new car but also a new lawnmower.*

mer country of southeast Asia. It existed from 1954 to 1975, when it became part of the country of Vietnam.

north•ward (nôrth′wərd) *adv. & adj.* Toward, to, or in the north: *turned the ship's prow northward.* —*n.* A direction or region to the north. —**north′wards** *adv.*

north•west (nôrth **wĕst′**) *n.* **1.** The direction halfway between north and west. **2.** An area or region lying in this direction. **3. Northwest.** A northwestern part of a region or country, especially the region of the United States including Washington, Oregon, and Idaho. —*adj.* **1.** Of, in, or toward the northwest. **2.** Coming from the northwest: *northwest winds.* —*adv.* In, from, or toward the northwest. —**north•west′ern** *adj.*

north•west•er (nôrth **wĕs′**tər *or* nôr **wĕs′**tər) *n.* A storm or gale blowing from the northwest.

north•west•er•ly (nôrth **wĕs′**tər lē) *adj.* **1.** Situated toward or facing the northwest: *a northwesterly course.* **2.** Coming from the northwest: *northwesterly breezes.* —**north•west′er•ly** *adv.*

Northwest Pas•sage (**păs′**ĭj). A water route from the Atlantic Ocean to the Pacific Ocean through the Arctic Archipelago of northern Canada and along the northern coast of Alaska. The route's existence was proved in the early 19th century.

Northwest Territories. A territory of northern Canada including the Arctic Archipelago, islands in the northern Hudson Bay, and the mainland north of latitude 60° north. It joined the Canadian confederation in 1870. Yellowknife is the capital and the largest city. Population, 45,741. —SEE NOTE.

Northwest Territory. A historical region of the north-central United States extending from the Ohio and Mississippi rivers to the Great Lakes. The area includes the present-day states of Ohio, Indiana, Illinois, Michigan, Wisconsin, and part of Minnesota.

north•west•ward (nôrth **wĕst′**wərd) *adv. & adj.* Toward, to, or in the northwest: *flying northwestward to Alaska.* —*n.* A northwestward direction or region. —**north•west′wards** *adv.*

Nor•way (**nôr′**wā′). A country of northern Europe on the Scandinavian Peninsula west of Sweden. Norway gained its independence in 1905. Oslo is the capital and the largest city. Population, 4,122,707.

Nor•we•gian (nôr **wē′**jən) *adj.* Of or relating to Norway, or its people, language, or culture. —*n.* **1.** A native or inhabitant of Norway. **2.** The Germanic language of Norway.

nos. or **Nos.** *abbr.* An abbreviation of numbers.

nose (nōz) *n.* **1.** The part of the human face or the forward part of the head of other animals that contains the nostrils and organs of smell and forms the beginning of the respiratory tract. **2.** The sense of smell: *a dog with a good nose.* **3.** The ability to detect things, as if by smell: *a nose for gossip.* **4.** The forward end of an airplane, a rocket, a submarine, or another pointed structure. —*v.* **nosed, nos•ing, nos•es.** —*tr.* **1.** To find out by or as if by smell: *The raccoon nosed the corn stored in the shed.* **2.** To touch with the nose; nuzzle: *cats nosing the stuffed animal.* **3.** To move or push with or as if with the nose: *The cow nosed the calf away from the fence.* **4.** To steer (a vehicle or one's way) ahead cautiously: *He nosed the car into the traffic.* —*intr.* **1.** To smell or sniff. **2.** To search or inquire persistently; snoop or pry: *The police are nosing around for information.* **3.** To move forward cautiously. —***idioms.*** **by a nose.** By a narrow margin. **down (one's) nose.** *Informal.* With disapproval, contempt, or arrogance. **nose out.** To defeat by a narrow margin. **on the nose.** Exactly; precisely. **under (someone's) nose.** In plain view. [First written down before 899 in Old English and spelled *nosu.*]

nose•bleed (**nōz′**blēd′) *n.* An instance of bleeding from the nostrils.

nose cone *n.* The forwardmost, usually separable part of a rocket or missile that is shaped for minimum air resistance and often covered with a heat-resistant material.

nose•dive (**nōz′**dīv′) *n.* **1.** A very steep dive made by an airplane. **2.** A sudden drop or plunge: *The price of tea took a nosedive.*

nose-dive (**nōz′**dīv′) *intr.v.* **nose-dived** or **nose-dove** (**nōz′**dōv′), **nose-div•ing, nose-dives.** To perform a nosedive.

nose•gay (**nōz′**gā′) *n.* A small bunch of flowers.

nos•ey (**nō′**zē) *adj.* Variant of **nosy.**

nos•tal•gi•a (nŏ **stăl′**jə) *n.* **1.** A bittersweet longing for the past: *an old song that filled us with nostalgia.* **2.** Homesickness. [First written down in 1770 in Modern English, from Greek *nostos,* a return home.]

nos•tal•gic (nŏ **stăl′**jĭk) *adj.* Full of nostalgia: *nostalgic memories.* —**nos•tal′gi•cal•ly** *adv.*

nos•tril (**nŏs′**trəl) *n.* Either of the two external openings of the nose. [First written down about 1000 in Old English and spelled *nosthyrl* : *nosu,* nose + *thyrl,* hole.]

nos•trum (**nŏs′**trəm) *n.* **1.** A medicine of doubtful effectiveness and often secret ingredients; a quack remedy. **2.** A favorite but unproved remedy for problems or evils. [First written down in 1602 in Modern English, from Latin *nostrum (remedium),* our (remedy).]

nos•y or **nos•ey** (**nō′**zē) *adj.* **nos•i•er, nos•i•est.** *Informal.* Very curious about other people's affairs; prying. See Synonyms at **curious.** —**nos′i•ly** *adv.* —**nos′i•ness** *n.*

not (nŏt) *adv.* In no way; to no degree. Used to express negation, denial, refusal, or prohibition: *I will not go. You may not have more dessert.* [First written down about 1250 in Middle English, alteration of *naught.*] —SEE NOTE.

❑ *These sound alike:* **not, knot** (tangle).

no•ta•ble (**nō′**tə bəl) *adj.* Worthy of notice; remarkable; striking: *a notable success.* —*n.* A well-known person; a prominent figure. —**no′ta•bly** *adv.*

no•ta•rize (**nō′**tə rīz′) *tr.v.* **no•ta•rized, no•ta•riz•ing, no•ta•riz•es.** To witness and certify (a document) to be authentic by adding one's signature.

no•ta•ry (**nō′**tə rē) *n., pl.* **no•ta•ries.** A notary public. [First written down about 1303 in Middle English and spelled *notarie,* from Latin *notārius,* shorthand writer, from *nota,* mark.]

notary public *n., pl.* **notaries public.** A person legally empowered to witness and certify the validity of documents by signing them.

no•tate (**nō′**tāt) *tr.v.* **no•tat•ed, no•tat•ing, no•tates.** To put into notation, especially musical notation.

no•ta•tion (nō **tā′**shən) *n.* **1.** A system of symbols or figures used in a particular field to represent quantities, tones, or other values: *musical notation.* **2.** Something, especially a piece of music, written in such a system: *played the song without looking at the notation.* **3.** A written comment or explanation: *notations in the margin of a book.* [First written down in 1570 in Modern English, from Latin *notāre,* to note, from *nota,* note.]

notch (nŏch) *n.* **1.** A V-shaped cut. **2.** A narrow pass between mountains. **3.** *Informal.* A level; a degree: *The defeat took him down a notch.* —*tr.v.* **notched, notch•ing, notch•es.** **1.** To cut a notch in: *He notched each tree that he intended to fell.* **2.** To record by making notches: *notched the score on a stick.* [First written down in 1577 in Modern English, probably from Old French *oche*, from *ochier*, to notch.]

note (nōt) *n.* **1.** A brief record of what is heard, seen, or read, written down to aid the memory: *took notes during the lecture.* **2.** A short informal letter or message. **3.** An explanation or comment on a passage in a text, usually printed at the bottom of a page or at the end of a chapter or book. **4.a.** A piece of paper money; a bill. **b.** A certificate representing an amount of money, issued by a government or bank. **c.** A promissory note. **5.a.** A symbol used to represent a musical tone, indicating the pitch by its position on a staff and the relative length by its shape. **b.** A musical tone. **c.** A key, as of a piano or other instrument. **6.** Importance; consequence: *Nothing of note happened.* **7.** Notice; observation: *She peered out the window and took note of the weather.* **8.** The characteristic call or cry of a bird or other animal: *heard the clear note of a cardinal.* **9.** A sign or hint that reveals a certain quality: *ended his plea on a note of hopefulness.* —*tr.v.* **not•ed, not•ing, notes. 1.** To observe; notice: *We noted the shift in the wind.* **2.** To write down; make a brief record of: *She noted the birds she saw in her diary.* **3.** To make mention of; point out. [First written down before 1300 in Middle English, from Latin *nota*, annotation.]

note•book (nōt′bo͝ok′) *n.* A book with blank pages for writing in.

not•ed (nō′tĭd) *adj.* Well-known; famous.

Synonyms: noted, celebrated, famous, illustrious, renowned. These adjectives all mean widely known and esteemed. *Our library has invited a noted author to read from her new book. The concert series features several celebrated musicians. I'd like to be a famous scientist one day. An illustrious judge presided over the case. None of the actors in that movie could be called renowned.* **Antonyms: unknown, obscure.**

note•wor•thy (nōt′wûr′*th*ē) *adj.* **note•wor•thi•er, note•wor•thi•est.** Deserving notice or attention; notable; significant. **—note′wor′thi•ly** *adv.* **—note′wor′thi•ness** *n.*

noth•ing (nŭth′ĭng) *pron.* **1.** Not anything: *I have nothing more to say.* **2.** No part; no portion: *Nothing is left of the old house.* —*n.* **1.** Something that has no quantitative value; zero: *a score of two to nothing.* **2.** A person or thing of no importance: *His concern is nothing to me.* —*adv.* Not at all: *He looks nothing like me.* **—*idiom.* nothing doing.** *Informal.* Certainly not.

noth•ing•ness (nŭth′ĭng nĭs) *n.* **1.** The quality or condition of being nothing; nonexistence. **2.** Empty space.

no•tice (nō′tĭs) *n.* **1.** Perception; observation: *The mistake escaped her notice.* **2.** Respectful attention or consideration: *grateful for the teacher's notice.* **3.** A published or displayed announcement: *post a notice on the bulletin board.* **4.** An announcement of purpose, especially of one's intention to leave a job: *gave a week's notice to the employer.* **5.** A printed review, as of a play. —*tr.v.* **no•ticed, no•tic•ing, no•tic•es. 1.** To perceive with the senses; become aware of: *noticed a cloud of dust in the distance.* See Synonyms at **see**[1]. **2.** To perceive with the mind; take note of: *I could not help noticing a change in her behavior.* [First written down about 1412 in Middle English and spelled *notise*, knowledge, from Latin *nōtitia*, from *nōscere*, to get to know.]

no•tice•a•ble (nō′tĭ sə bəl) *adj.* **1.** Easily observed; evident: *a noticeable change in temperature.* **2.** Worth noting; significant. **—no′tice•a•bly** *adv.*

no•ti•fi•ca•tion (nō′tə fĭ kā′shən) *n.* **1.** The act or an instance of notifying. **2.** Something, such as a letter, that makes something known: *Send me notification when you receive the book.*

no•ti•fy (nō′tə fī′) *tr.v.* **no•ti•fied, no•ti•fy•ing, no•ti•fies.** To give notice to; inform: *notify the police.* **—no′ti•fi′er** *n.*

no•tion (nō′shən) *n.* **1.** A belief or an opinion: *Your notion of how math should be taught is interesting.* **2.** A mental image; an idea: *I haven't the least notion of what you mean.* See Synonyms at **idea. 3.** A fanciful idea or impulse; a whim: *She had a notion to climb the hill.* **4. notions.** Small useful items, such as needles, buttons, and thread. [First written down before 1398 in Middle English and spelled *nocioun*, from Latin *nōtiō*, from *nōtus*, known.]

no•to•chord (nō′tə kôrd′) *n.* A strip of cartilage along the back of certain animals, such as the lancelets, belonging to the same group as the vertebrates. At some stage of embryonic development, all vertebrates have a similar notochord from which the spine develops.

no•to•ri•e•ty (nō′tə rī′ĭ tē) *n.* The quality or condition of being notorious; bad reputation.

no•to•ri•ous (nō tôr′ē əs) *adj.* Known widely and regarded unfavorably; infamous: *a notorious swindler.* [First written down in 1548 in Modern English, from Latin *nōtus*, known.] **—no•to′ri•ous•ly** *adv.* **—no•to′ri•ous•ness** *n.*

Not•ting•ham (nŏt′ĭng əm). A borough of central England northeast of Birmingham. According to tradition, it is the birthplace of Robin Hood. Population, 277,500.

not•with•stand•ing (nŏt′wĭth **stăn′**dĭng *or* nŏt′-wĭ*th* **stăn′**dĭng) *prep.* In spite of: *Notwithstanding the rain, the teams played on.* —*adv.* All the same; nevertheless: *They were exhausted, but proceeded notwithstanding.*

Nouak•chott (nwäk **shŏt′**). The capital and largest city of Mauritania, in the western part of the country on the Atlantic Ocean. Population, 150,000.

nou•gat (no͞o′gət) *n.* A candy made of sugar or honey and nuts.

nought (nôt) *n., pron., & adj.* Variant of **naught.**

noun (noun) *n.* In grammar, a word that is used to name a person, a place, a thing, a quality, or an action and that functions as the subject or object of a verb or as the object of a preposition. [First written down before 1398 in Middle English, from Latin *nōmen*, name.] —SEE NOTE.

nour•ish (nûr′ĭsh *or* nŭr′ĭsh) *tr.v.* **nour•ished, nour•ish•ing, nour•ish•es. 1.** To provide (a living thing) with the food or other substances necessary for life and growth. **2.** To promote the growth or development of; sustain: *She founded the business and nourished it with hard work.* **3.** To keep alive; harbor: *We nourished hope that the party would be a success.* [First written down before 1300 in Middle English and spelled *norisshen*, from Latin *nūtrīre*.]

nour•ish•ment (nûr′ĭsh mənt *or* nŭr′ĭsh mənt) *n.* **1.a.** The act or process of nourishing. **b.** The condition of being nourished. **2.** Something that nourishes; food.

Nov. or **Nov** *abbr.* An abbreviation of November.

no•va (nō′və) *n., pl.* **no•vae** (nō′vē) or **no•vas.** A star that suddenly becomes much brighter, then gradually returns to its original brightness over a period of weeks to years. [First written down in 1877 in Modern English, from New Latin *(stēlla) nova*, new (star), from Latin *novus*, new.]

No•va Sco•tia (nō′və skō′shə). A province of eastern Canada southwest of Newfoundland made up of a mainland peninsula and the adjacent Cape Breton Island. It joined the Canadian confederation in 1867. Halifax is the capital and the largest city. Population, 847,442. —SEE NOTE.

note

Left to right: Whole, half, quarter, eighth, 16th, and 32nd notes

Usage: noun

Every **noun** is either a **common noun** or a **proper noun**. A **common noun** is a noun such as *book* or *student*. Such nouns can stand for one particular item, as in *I want the fifth book on the pile.* Such a noun can also stand for all items referred to by the noun: *The book is the best means of communication ever invented.* A **proper noun** names someone or something that is unique: *Abraham Lincoln, British Columbia.*

Nova Scotia

The words **Nova Scotia** in Latin mean "New Scotland." The province of Nova Scotia received its name in 1621 when King James I of England (who was also King James VI of Scotland) granted territory to the Scot Sir William Alexander (1567–1640), who named it in Latin after his own country.

ă	pat	oi	boy
ā	pay	ou	out
âr	care	o͝o	took
ä	father	o͞o	boot
ĕ	pet	ŭ	cut
ē	be	ûr	urge
ĭ	pit	th	thin
ī	pie	*th*	this
îr	pier	hw	whoop
ŏ	pot	zh	vision
ō	toe	ə	about
ô	paw	N	*French* bon

nozzle

nov•el¹ (nŏv′əl) *n.* A long piece of prose writing that tells an invented story. [First written down in 1566 in Modern English and spelled *novel,* short story, from Latin *novellus,* piece of news, from *novus,* new.]

nov•el² (nŏv′əl) *adj.* Strikingly new or different: *a modern artist using a novel method of painting.* [First written down about 1450 in Middle English, from Latin *novellus,* from *novus.*]

nov•el•ist (nŏv′ə lĭst) *n.* A writer of novels.

no•vel•la (nō vĕl′ə) *n., pl.* **no•vel•las** or **no•vel•le.** A short novel.

nov•el•ty (nŏv′əl tē) *n., pl.* **nov•el•ties. 1.** The quality of being novel; newness: *We liked the new video camera until the novelty wore off.* **2.** Something new and unusual: *Edison's light bulb was at first merely an interesting novelty.* **3.** A small mass-produced article, such as a toy or trinket.

No•vem•ber (nō vĕm′bər) *n.* The 11th month of the year in the Gregorian calendar, having 30 days. [First written down about 1200 in Middle English and spelled *Novembre,* from Latin *November,* ninth month, from *novem,* nine.]

no•ve•na (nō vē′nə) *n., pl.* **no•ve•nas** or **no•ve•nae** (nō vē′nē). In the Roman Catholic Church, a reciting of prayers or devotions for a special purpose during nine consecutive days.

nov•ice (nŏv′ĭs) *n.* **1.** A person new to a field or activity; a beginner. **2.** A person who has entered a religious order but has not yet taken final vows. [First written down in 1340 in Middle English, from Medieval Latin *novīcius,* from Latin *novus,* new.]

no•vi•ti•ate (nō vĭsh′ē ĭt *or* nō vĭsh′ē āt′) *n.* **1.** The period of being a beginner; an apprenticeship. **2.** The period of training served by a novice in a religious order.

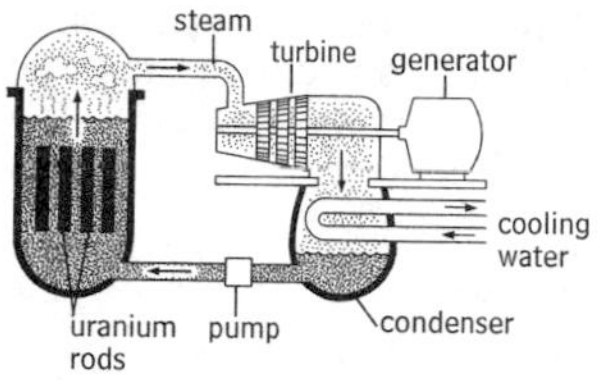

nuclear reactor
Boiling water reactor

No•vo•cain (nō′və kān′). A trademark for a drug used in medicine and dentistry as a local anesthetic.

now (nou) *adv.* **1.** At the present time: *Buildings now stand where there was once a marsh.* **2.** At once; immediately: *We'd better start now.* **3.** Very recently: *He left the room just now.* **4.** At this point in the series of events; then: *The ship now began to sink.* **5.** Nowadays: *You'll rarely see plowing with horses now.* **6.** Used to introduce a command, reproof, or request: *Now, who wants to go to the beach? Now remember to add the flour slowly.* **7.** Used to introduce an idea or a change of subject: *Now bears need more territory than most animals.* —*conj.* Since; seeing that: *Now that spring is here, we can expect milder weather.* —*n.* The present: *Up to now we couldn't hike on that trail.* —***idiom.*** **now and again** or **now and then.** Occasionally: *I like spicy food now and again.* [First written down before 725 in Old English and spelled *nū.*]

now•a•days (nou′ə dāz′) *adv.* In the present times; in these days.

no•way (nō′wā′) also **no•ways** (nō′wāz′) *Informal. adv.* In no way; not at all: *Noway are you going into the woods alone.*

no•where (nō′wâr′) *adv.* **1.** Not anywhere: *The screwdriver was nowhere to be found.* **2.** To no place or result: *Until we found the screwdriver, we were getting nowhere.* —*n.* A remote or unknown place, especially a wilderness: *a cabin in the middle of nowhere.*

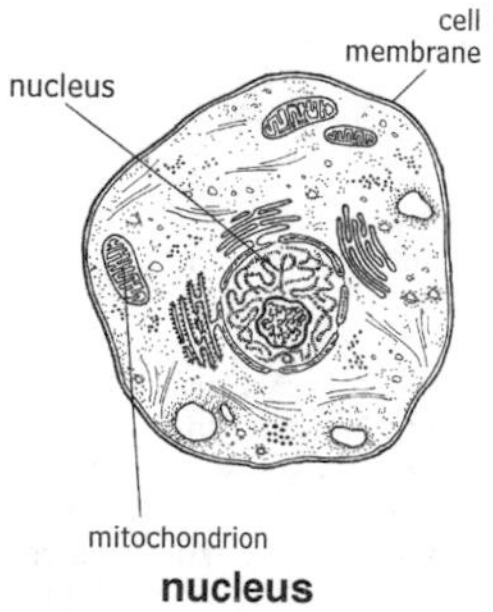

nucleus
Animal cell

no-win (nō′wĭn′) *adj. Informal.* Certain to end in failure or disappointment: *a no-win situation.*

no•wise (nō′wīz′) *adv.* In no way; not at all.

nox•ious (nŏk′shəs) *adj.* **1.** Harmful to the health of living things: *noxious chemicals.* **2.** Harmful to the mind or morals. [First written down before 1500 in Middle English and spelled *noxius,* from Latin, from *noxa,* damage.] —**nox′ious•ly** *adv.*

noz•zle (nŏz′əl) *n.* A projecting part with an opening, as at the end of a hose or the rear of a rocket, through which a liquid or gas is discharged under pressure. [First written down before 1450 in Middle English and spelled *noselle,* socket on a candlestick, from *nose.*]

Np The symbol for the element **neptunium.**

N.S. *abbr.* An abbreviation of Nova Scotia.

NT *abbr.* An abbreviation of New Testament.

nth (ĕnth) *adj.* **1.** Relating to *n,* an indefinitely large whole number: *ten to the nth power.* **2.** Highest; utmost: *delighted to the nth degree.*

nt.wt. *abbr.* An abbreviation of net weight.

nu (no͞o *or* nyo͞o) *n.* The 13th letter of the Greek alphabet, written Ν, ν. It is represented in English as *N, n.*

nu•ance (no͞o′äns′ *or* nyo͞o′äns′) *n.* A subtle variation, as in meaning, color, or tone; a delicate shading. [First written down in 1781 in Modern English, from Old French *nuer,* to shade, cloud, from Latin *nūbēs,* cloud.]

nub (nŭb) *n.* **1.** A lump or knob. **2.** The essence; the core: *the nub of the problem.* —**nub′by** *adj.*

nub•bin (nŭb′ĭn) *n.* **1.** A small imperfectly developed ear of corn. **2.** A fruit that is not fully developed. **3.** A small thing or part that usually projects.

nu•cle•ar (no͞o′klē ər *or* nyo͞o′klē ər) *adj.* **1.** Of, relating to, or forming a nucleus. **2.** Of or relating to atomic nuclei. **3.** Of or using energy derived from the nuclei of atoms: *a nuclear power plant.* **4.** Having or using atomic or hydrogen bombs: *nuclear powers.*

nuclear energy *n.* The energy that is released by alteration of the nuclei of atoms, as in a fission reaction splitting heavy nuclei, or by fusion that combines light nuclei, or by radioactive decay.

nuclear family *n.* A family unit consisting of a mother and father and their children.

nuclear physics *n. (used with a singular verb).* The scientific study of the structure and reactions of atomic nuclei.

nuclear reaction *n.* A reaction, as in fission, fusion, or radioactive decay, that changes the energy, structure, or composition of an atomic nucleus.

nuclear reactor *n.* A device in which a nuclear chain reaction is started and controlled, thus producing heat, which is usually used to generate electricity, and a variety of radioactive isotopes.

nu•cle•i (no͞o′klē ī′ *or* nyo͞o′klē ī′) *n.* A plural of **nucleus.**

nu•cle•ic acid (no͞o klē′ĭk *or* nyo͞o klē′ĭk) *n.* Any of a group of complex organic compounds that are found in living cells and in the form of DNA and RNA are extremely important in cellular functioning and heredity.

nu•cle•o•lus (no͞o klē′ə ləs *or* nyo͞o klē′ə ləs) *n., pl.* **nu•cle•o•li** (no͞o klē′ə lī′ *or* nyo͞o klē′ə lī′). A small, usually round structure found within the nucleus of a cell, containing a high concentration of RNA.

nu•cle•on (no͞o′klē ŏn′ *or* nyo͞o′klē ŏn′) *n.* A proton or a neutron, especially as part of an atomic nucleus. —**nu′cle•on′ic** *adj.*

nu•cle•o•tide (no͞o′klē ə tīd′ *or* nyo͞o′klē ə tīd′) *n.* Any of a group of organic compounds composed of a sugar, a phosphate, and one of several nitrogen bases. Nucleotides are the molecular subunits that make up DNA and RNA.

nu•cle•us (no͞o′klē əs *or* nyo͞o′klē əs) *n., pl.* **nu•cle•i** (no͞o′klē ī′ *or* nyo͞o′klē ī′) or **nu•cle•us•es. 1.** A central or essential part around which other parts are grouped; a core: *the players who formed the nucleus of the team.* **2.** A basis for future growth; a starting point: *a few paintings that formed the nucleus of an art collection.* **3.** A membrane-enclosed structure within a living cell, containing the cell's genetic material and controlling its metabolism, growth, and reproduction. **4.** The positively charged central region of an atom, composed of protons and neutrons and containing most of the mass of the atom. **5.** A specialized mass of gray matter in the brain or spinal cord. [First written down in 1708 in Modern English, from Latin *nucleus*, kernel, from *nucula*, little nut.]

nude (no͞od *or* nyo͞od) *adj.* **nud•er, nud•est.** Being without clothing; naked. *—n.* **1.** An unclothed human figure or a representation of it. **2.** The condition of being unclothed: *in the nude.* **—nude′ly** *adv.* **—nude′ness** *n.*

nudge (nŭj) *tr.v.* **nudged, nudg•ing, nudg•es.** To push or poke gently: *He nudged her with his elbow.* *—n.* A gentle push. [First written down in 1675 in Modern English, probably of Scandinavian origin.]

nu•di•ty (no͞o′dĭ tē *or* nyo͞o′dĭ tē) *n.* The condition of being unclothed.

nug•get (nŭg′ĭt) *n.* **1.** A hard lump of matter, especially of gold. **2.** A small unit or piece: *nuggets of information.* [First written down in 1852 in Modern English, perhaps from English dialectal *nug*, lump.]

nui•sance (no͞o′səns *or* nyo͞o′səns) *n.* A source of inconvenience or annoyance; a bother. [First written down about 1400 in Middle English and spelled *nusaunce*, from Old French *nuire*, to harm, from Latin *nocēre*.]

nuke (no͞ok *or* nyo͞ok) *Slang. n.* **1.** A nuclear weapon. **2.** A plant that generates electricity by nuclear power. *—tr.v.* **nuked, nuk•ing, nukes. 1.** To attack with nuclear weapons. **2.** To heat or cook in a microwave oven.

Nu•ku•a•lo•fa (no͞o′ko͞o ə lô′fə). The capital of Tonga in the southwest Pacific Ocean. Population, 21,745.

null (nŭl) *adj.* **1.** Having no legal force; invalid: *a contract rendered null by a later agreement.* **2.** Having the quantity or value of zero; amounting to nothing. **3.** Of or relating to a set that has no members. *—n.* Zero; nothing. ***—idiom.* null and void.** Having no legal force or effect; not binding. [First written down about 1563 in Modern English, from Latin *nūllus*.]

nul•li•fi•ca•tion (nŭl′ə fĭ kā′shən) *n.* **1.** The act of nullifying: *The nullification of the amendment will take time.* **2.** The state of being nullified.

nul•li•fy (nŭl′ə fī′) *tr.v.* **nul•li•fied, nul•li•fy•ing, nul•li•fies. 1.** To deprive of legal force; invalidate: *The Supreme Court has the right to nullify an act of Congress by finding it unconstitutional.* **2.** To reduce to nothing; make ineffective: *Reading the book nullified his misconceptions.* **—nul′li•fi′er** *n.*

numb (nŭm) *adj.* **numb•er, numb•est. 1.** Deprived of the power to feel or move normally: *toes numb with cold.* **2.** Showing little or no emotion; indifferent: *numb to the same old sales pitch.* *—tr. & intr.v.* **numbed, numb•ing, numbs.** To make or become numb: *The wind numbed our cheeks. My toes numbed with the cold.* [First written down before 1400 in Middle English and spelled *nome*, from Old English *niman*, to seize.] **—numb′ly** *adv.* **—numb′ness** *n.*

num•ber (nŭm′bər) *n.* **1.a.** One of a set of symbols that have unique meaning and that can be derived in a fixed order by counting; a member of the set of positive integers. **b.** A member of any of the further set of mathematical objects, such as the negative integers and real numbers, that can be derived from the positive integers by various mathematical operations. **2. numbers.** Arithmetic: *good at numbers.* **3.** One of a series in numerical order: *What number are you in this line?* **4.** A numeral or series of numerals assigned to a person or thing for reference or identification: *a telephone number.* **5.** A quantity determined by adding up all units or members; a total; a sum: *the number of feet in a mile.* **6.** An indefinite quantity: *The crowd was small in number.* **7. numbers.** A large quantity: *There is strength in numbers.* **8.** A song or other piece of music in a program. **9.** In grammar, the indication by the form of a word of whether it is singular or plural: *The verb must agree in number with the subject.* **10. Numbers.** *(used with a singular verb).* A book of the Bible containing two censuses of the Israelites after the Exodus from Egypt. *—v.* **num•bered, num•ber•ing, num•bers.** *—tr.* **1.** To assign a number to: *Number each item in the list.* **2.** To determine the number of; count: *We numbered the students in each line.* **3.** To amount to; total: *an audience numbering nearly a thousand.* **4.** To include in a certain category: *He was numbered among the better swimmers.* **5.** To mention one by one: *I'll number the advantages of the plan.* **6.** To limit in number: *The days were numbered before cold weather would set in.* *—intr.* **1.** To call off numbers; count. **2.** To amount to a group or number: *The crowd numbered in the thousands.* ***—idiom.* without number** or **beyond number.** Too many to be counted; countless. [First written down before 1300 in Middle English and spelled *noumbre*, from Latin *numerus*.] SEE NOTE.

num•ber•less (nŭm′bər lĭs) *adj.* Too many to be counted; countless.

number line *n.* A line marked with a sequence of numbers at regularly spaced points along its length, especially a line whose points are considered to correspond with the real numbers in a one-to-one way.

number sentence *n.* An equation in arithmetic.

numb•skull (nŭm′skŭl′) *n.* Variant of **numskull.**

nu•mer•a•ble (no͞o′mər ə bəl *or* nyo͞o′mər ə bəl) *adj.* Capable of being counted; countable.

nu•mer•al (no͞o′mər əl *or* nyo͞o′mər əl) *n.* **1.** A symbol or mark used to represent a number. **2. numerals.** The last two digits of a year of graduation, used as a name for the entire class. [First written down in 1530 in Modern English, from Middle English *numeral*, of number, from Latin *numerus*, number.]

nu•mer•ate (no͞o′mə rāt′ *or* nyo͞o′mə rāt′) *tr.v.* **nu•mer•at•ed, nu•mer•at•ing, nu•mer•ates.** To enumerate; count.

nu•mer•a•tion (no͞o′mə rā′shən *or* nyo͞o′mə rā′shən) *n.* **1.** The act or process of counting or numbering. **2.** A system of numbering.

nu•mer•a•tor (no͞o′mə rā′tər *or* nyo͞o′mə rā′tər) *n.* The number written above the line in a common fraction to indicate the number of parts of the whole. For example, in the fraction 2⁄7 the 2 indicates that 2 of 7 equal parts of the whole are compared with the whole itself.

nu•mer•i•cal (no͞o mĕr′ĭ kəl *or* nyo͞o mĕr′ĭ kəl) *adj.* **1.** Of or relating to a number or series of numbers: *numerical order.* **2.** Expressed or measured in numbers: *a numerical grade.* **—nu•mer′i•cal•ly** *adv.*

nu•mer•ous (no͞o′mər əs *or* nyo͞o′mər əs) *adj.* Amounting to a large number; many: *numerous items for sale.* **—nu′mer•ous•ly** *adv.*

nu•mis•mat•ic (no͞o′mĭz măt′ĭk *or* nyo͞o′mĭz-măt′ĭk) *adj.* Of or relating to numismatics. [First written down in 1792 in Modern English, from Greek *nomisma*, custom, coin in circulation.]

nu•mis•mat•ics (no͞o′mĭz măt′ĭks *or* nyo͞o′-mĭz măt′ĭks) *n.* *(used with a singular verb).* The study or collecting of coins, paper money, or medals.

num•skull also **numb•skull** (nŭm′skŭl′) *n.* A stupid person; a blockhead.

nun (nŭn) *n.* A woman who belongs to a religious order, living under vows of poverty, chastity, and

number

Normally when we think of numbers we think of the numbers we count with, called **cardinal numbers**, such as 1, 2, and 3. Or we might think of numbers that we use to describe a sequence, called **ordinal numbers**, such as *first, second,* and *third.* But there are many other ways to think of and classify numbers. The **integers** include all the counting numbers and their negatives, and zero. **Real numbers** include all integers and the infinite set of numbers that can fall between integers, which are usually represented in decimal form. Real numbers are further classified as rational or irrational. **Rational numbers** can be expressed as the ratio of two integers, such as 1⁄3. They include repeating decimals and decimals that expand indefinitely (1⁄3, or 0.33333 . . . , is a rational number). **Irrational numbers**, such as $\sqrt{2}$, cannot be expressed by a ratio of integers. There are still more categories of numbers, including **imaginary numbers**, such as $\sqrt{-1}$ and **transcendental numbers**, such as π (pi). Numbers are much more complicated than 1, 2, 3!

ă	**pat**	oi	**boy**
ā	**pay**	ou	**out**
âr	**care**	o͝o	**took**
ä	**father**	o͞o	**boot**
ĕ	**pet**	ŭ	**cut**
ē	**be**	ûr	**urge**
ĭ	**pit**	th	**thin**
ī	**pie**	*th*	**this**
îr	**pier**	hw	**whoop**
ŏ	**pot**	zh	**vision**
ō	**toe**	ə	**about**
ô	**paw**	N	*French* **bon**

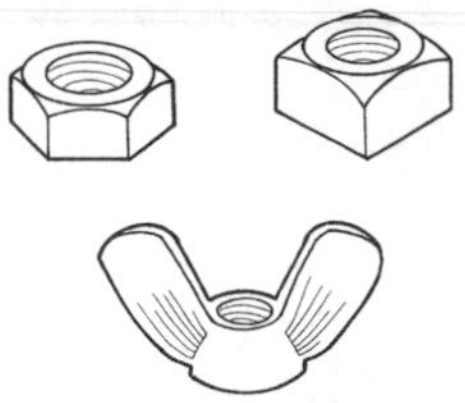

nut
Hexagonal (*top left*), square (*top right*), and wing (*bottom*) nuts

nuthatch
White-breasted nuthatch

nutmeg

ă	pat	oi	boy
ā	pay	ou	out
âr	care	o͝o	took
ä	father	o͞o	boot
ĕ	pet	ŭ	cut
ē	be	ûr	urge
ĭ	pit	th	thin
ī	pie	*th*	this
îr	pier	hw	whoop
ŏ	pot	zh	vision
ō	toe	ə	about
ô	paw	ɴ	*French* bon

obedience. [First written down before 899 in Old English and spelled *nunne*, from Late Latin *nonnus*, tutor, monk.]

❑ *These sound alike:* **nun, none** (not any).

nun•ci•o (nŭn′sē ō′ *or* **no͞on′**sē ō′) *n., pl.* **nun•ci•os.** A papal ambassador or representative.

nun•ner•y (nŭn′ə rē) *n., pl.* **nun•ner•ies.** A place where a group of nuns live; a convent.

nup•tial (nŭp′shəl *or* nŭp′chəl) *adj.* Of or relating to marriage or the wedding ceremony. —*n.* A wedding ceremony. Often used in the plural.

Nu•rem•berg (**no͝or′**əm bûrg′ *or* **nyo͝or′**əm bûrg′). A city of southeast Germany north-northwest of Munich. From 1933 to 1938 it was the site of annual Nazi party congresses and later served as the location for the Allied trials of war criminals (1945–1946). Population, 468,352.

nurse (nûrs) *n.* **1.** A person who is trained to care for sick and disabled persons. **2.** A woman employed to take care of another's children; a nursemaid. —*v.* **nursed, nurs•ing, nurs•es.** —*tr.* **1.** To act as the nurse for; take care of. **2.** To feed (an infant) from the breast; suckle. **3.** To suck (milk) from the breast or mammary gland. **4.** To clasp or hold carefully; fondle: *sat down and nursed the book in his lap.* **5.** To try to cure by special care or treatment: *She's nursed that cough for a week.* **6.** To treat or handle carefully: *He nursed his injured knee by changing his position.* **7.** To drink slowly, as if preserving: *nursed a soda for an hour.* **8.** To keep in the mind; harbor: *Don't nurse a grudge.* —*intr.* **1.** To work or act as a nurse. **2.** To feed at the breast; suckle.

nurse•maid (**nûrs′**mād′) *n.* A woman employed to take care of children.

nurs•er•y (nûr′sə rē *or* **nûrs′**rē) *n., pl.* **nurs•er•ies. 1.** A room set apart for the use of children. **2.** A nursery school. **3.** A place where plants are raised for sale or experimentation.

nursery rhyme *n.* A short rhymed poem for children.

nursery school *n.* A school for children who are not old enough to attend kindergarten.

nurs•ing home (**nûr′**sĭng) *n.* A place that provides living space and care for old people who cannot care for themselves and for people who are chronically ill.

nurs•ling (**nûrs′**lĭng) *n.* An infant that is being nursed.

nur•ture (**nûr′**chər) *n.* **1.** Nourishment; food. **2.** Upbringing; training. —*tr.v.* **nur•tured, nur•tur•ing, nur•tures. 1.** To feed and protect; nourish: *carefully nurtured the plants in a greenhouse.* **2.** To educate or train. **3.** To help grow or develop; cultivate: *nurture a friendship.*

nut (nŭt) *n.* **1.a.** A fruit having a hard shell, one seed, and usually a single kernel, as an acorn. **b.** The seed within such a fruit, as an almond. **c.** The often edible kernel of such a fruit. **2.** *Slang.* **a.** A crazy or eccentric person. **b.** An enthusiast; a buff: *a movie nut.* **3.** A small block of metal or wood having a threaded hole, designed to fit around and hold a bolt or screw. [First written down about 700 in Old English and spelled *hnutu.*]

nut•crack•er (nŭt′krăk′ər) *n.* **1.** An implement for cracking nuts, typically consisting of two hinged metal levers between which the nut is squeezed. **2.** Any of various gray and white birds of the mountains of western North America, related to the crow and having a sharp bill.

nut•hatch (nŭt′hăch′) *n.* Any of several small grayish birds that have a long sharp bill and climb up and down tree trunks.

nut•meat (nŭt′mēt′) *n.* The edible kernel of a nut.

nut•meg (nŭt′mĕg′) *n.* **1.** The hard pleasant-smelling seed of a tropical evergreen tree, used as a spice when ground or grated. **2.** The tree that bears such seeds.

nu•tri•a (**no͞o′**trē ə *or* **nyo͞o′**trē ə) *n.* The coypu. [First written down in 1836 in Modern English, from Spanish, from Latin *lutra.*]

nu•tri•ent (**no͞o′**trē ənt *or* **nyo͞o′**trē ənt) *n.* Something that nourishes, especially an ingredient in a food. —*adj.* Capable of nourishing; having nutritive value.

nu•tri•ment (**no͞o′**trə mənt *or* **nyo͞o′**trə mənt) *n.* Nourishment; food.

nu•tri•tion (no͞o **trĭsh′**ən *or* nyo͞o **trĭsh′**ən) *n.* **1.** The process of nourishing or being nourished, especially the process by which a living thing takes in and uses food. **2.** Nourishment; diet: *Having good nutrition is important for good health.* **3.** The study of food and nourishment. **—nu•tri′tion•al** *adj.* **—nu•tri′tion•al•ly** *adv.*

nu•tri•tious (no͞o **trĭsh′**əs *or* nyo͞o **trĭsh′**əs) *adj.* Providing nourishment; nourishing. **—nu•tri′tious•ly** *adv.* **—nu•tri′tious•ness** *n.*

nu•tri•tive (**no͞o′**trĭ tĭv *or* **nyo͞o′**trĭ tĭv) *adj.* **1.** Nutritious; nourishing. **2.** Of or relating to nutrition.

nuts (nŭts) *Slang. adj.* **1.** Crazy; insane. **2.** Very enthusiastic: *nuts about playing the drums.* —*interj.* Used to express disappointment, contempt, or refusal.

nut•shell (nŭt′shĕl′) *n.* The shell enclosing the meat of a nut. —***idiom.* in a nutshell.** In a few words; concisely.

nut•ty (nŭt′ē) *adj.* **nut•ti•er, nut•ti•est. 1.** Containing or producing nuts: *nutty trees.* **2.** Having the flavor of nuts: *nutty cookies.* **3.** *Slang.* Crazy; silly. **—nut′ti•ly** *adv.* **—nut′ti•ness** *n.*

nuz•zle (nŭz′əl) *v.* **nuz•zled, nuz•zling, nuz•zles.** —*tr.* To rub or push gently with the nose or snout: *The calf nuzzled its mother.* —*intr.* To press close together; nestle. [First written down about 1425 in Middle English and spelled *noselen*, to bend down.]

NV *abbr.* An abbreviation of Nevada.

NW *abbr.* An abbreviation of northwest.

NY or **N.Y.** *abbr.* An abbreviation of New York.

NYC or **N.Y.C.** *abbr.* An abbreviation of New York City.

ny•lon (nī′lŏn′) *n.* **1.** Any of various very strong elastic synthetic resins. **2.** Cloth or yarn made from nylon. **3. nylons.** Stockings made of nylon. [First written down in 1938 in American English, coined by its inventors, E.I. Du Pont de Nemours and Co., Inc.]

nymph (nĭmf) *n.* **1.** In Greek and Roman mythology, one of various goddesses dwelling in woodlands and waters and represented as beautiful young women. **2.** A young incompletely developed form of certain insects, such as the grasshopper or dragonfly, that goes through a series of gradual changes before reaching the adult stage. [First written down about 1385 in Middle English and spelled *nimphe*, from Greek *numphē.*]

N.Z. *abbr.* An abbreviation of New Zealand.

Oo

o or **O** (ō) *n., pl.* **o's** or **O's. 1.** The 15th letter of the English alphabet. **2.** The 15th in a series or group: *row O in a theater.* **3.** A zero. **4.** One of the four types of blood in the ABO system.

O[1] (ō) *interj.* **1.** An expression used before the name of a person or thing being formally addressed. **2.** An expression used to show surprise or strong emotion: *O my goodness!*

❑ *These sound alike:* **O**[1], **oh** (exclamation), **owe** (be indebted).

O[2] The symbol for the element **oxygen.**

oaf (ōf) *n.* A clumsy or stupid person. [First written down in 1610 in Modern English, from Old Norse *alfr*, elf, silly person.] **—oaf′ish** *adj.*

O•a•hu (ō ä′ho͞o). An island of central Hawaii between Molokai and Kauai. It is the chief island of the state.

oak (ōk) *n.* **1.** Any of numerous trees that bear acorns and often have leaves that are irregularly notched or lobed. **2.** The hard strong wood of such a tree. [First written down about 700 in Old English and spelled *āc*.] **—oak′en** *adj.*

Oak•land (ōk′lənd). A city of western California south of Berkeley. It was founded on a site settled by Spanish colonists in 1820. Population, 372,242.

Oak•ley (ōk′lē), **Annie.** 1860–1926. American sharpshooter who was the main attraction of Buffalo Bill's Wild West Show.

oa•kum (ō′kəm) *n.* Loose hemp or jute fiber used for caulking seams in wooden ships and packing pipe joints.

oar (ôr) *n.* **1.** A long thin wooden pole with a blade at one end, used to row or steer a boat. **2.** A person using an oar; a rower. *—v.* **oared, oar•ing, oars.** *—tr.* To propel by using oars: *oaring the boat down the river.* *—intr.* To move forward by rowing.

❑ *These sound alike:* **oar, o'er** (over), **or** (conjunction), **ore** (mineral).

oar•lock (ôr′lŏk′) *n.* A U-shaped metal hoop on a swivel, used to hold an oar in place while rowing.

oars•man (ôrz′mən) *n.* A man who rows a boat; a rower.

oars•wom•an (ôrz′wo͝om′ən) *n.* A woman who rows a boat; a rower.

OAS *abbr.* An abbreviation of Organization of American States.

o•a•sis (ō ā′sĭs) *n., pl.* **o•a•ses** (ō ā′sēz). **1.** A small area in a desert that is fertile because it has a source of water. **2.** A place or situation that provides comfort or refreshment. [First written down in 1616 in Modern English, from Greek, probably of Egyptian origin.]

oat (ōt) *n.* **1.** Any of various cereal grasses having seeds used as food and as fodder for horses. Often used in the plural with a singular or plural verb. **2.** The seed of any of these plants. Often used in the plural with a singular or plural verb. [First written down about 1000 in Old English and spelled *āte*.]

oat•en (ōt′n) *adj.* Of, made of, or containing oats, oatmeal, or oat straw: *oaten fodder.*

Oates (ōts), **Joyce Carol.** Born 1938. American writer whose novels include *A Garden of Earthly Delights* (1967).

oath (ōth) *n., pl.* **oaths** (ō*th*z *or* ōths). **1.** A declaration or promise to act in a certain way, calling on God or some other sacred object as witness: *The President takes an oath to uphold the Constitution.* **2.** A word or phrase that irreverently uses the name of God or something sacred; a profanity. ***—idiom.*** **under oath.** Bound by an oath to tell the truth, as in a court of law. [First written down about 725 in Old English and spelled *āth*.]

oat•meal (ōt′mēl′) *n.* **1.** Meal made from ground oats or from oats that have been pressed flat by rollers. **2.** A porridge made from such meal.

O•ba•di•ah (ō′bə dī′ə) *n.* **1.** A Hebrew prophet of the sixth century B.C. **2.** A book of the Bible in which Obadiah predicts the punishment of the traditional enemies of the Israelites.

ob•bli•ga•to (ŏb′lĭ gä′tō) *adj.* In music, not to be left out; necessary.

ob•du•ra•cy (ŏb′do͝or ə sē *or* ŏb′dyo͝or ə sē) *n.* The quality or condition of being obdurate.

ob•du•rate (ŏb′do͞o rĭt *or* ŏb′dyo͞o rĭt) *adj.* **1.** Hardened against feeling or compassion; hardhearted: *an obdurate miser.* **2.** Unmoved by persuasion; unyielding; stubborn: *obdurate in her refusal to go along.* **—ob′du•rate•ly** *adv.* **—ob′du•rate•ness** *n.*

o•be•di•ence (ō bē′dē əns) *n.* **1.** The act of obeying rules, laws, or requests. **2.** The state of being obedient.

o•be•di•ent (ō bē′dē ənt) *adj.* Willing to obey: *an obedient dog.* **—o•be′di•ent•ly** *adv.*

o•bei•sance (ō bā′səns *or* ō bē′səns) *n.* A bow, curtsy, or other gesture of submission or respect.

ob•e•lisk (ŏb′ə lĭsk) *n.* A tall four-sided shaft of stone, usually tapering to a point.

o•bese (ō bēs′) *adj.* Extremely fat; very overweight. **—o•bese′ness** *n.*

o•be•si•ty (ō bē′sĭ tē) *n.* The condition of being obese.

o•bey (ō bā′) *v.* **o•beyed, o•bey•ing, o•beys.** *—tr.* **1.** To carry out or comply with (a request, an order, or a law): *obeying the traffic regulations.* **2.** To do what is commanded or requested by (a person or other authority): *The girl obeyed her father and picked up her toys.* *—intr.* To be obedient. [First written down before 1300 in Middle English and spelled *obeien*, from Latin *oboedīre*, to listen to.]

o•bi (ō′bē) *n.* A wide sash worn with a kimono by Japanese women.

o•bit•u•ar•y (ō bĭch′o͞o ĕr′ē) *n., pl.* **o•bit•u•ar•ies.** A printed notice of a person's death, often with a short biography.

obj. *abbr.* An abbreviation of: **1.** Object. **2.** Objective.

ob•ject (ŏb′jĕkt′) *n.* **1.** Something that can be seen, touched, or perceived; a material thing. **2.** A thing being viewed, studied, or handled: *Place the object directly beneath the microscope.* **3.** A person or thing toward which emotion, thought, or action is directed: *The new baby was the object of everyone's attention.* **4.** A purpose; a goal: *The object of the project is to learn how people lived in ancient Rome.* **5.a.** A noun, pronoun, or group of words acting like a noun that receives or is affected by the

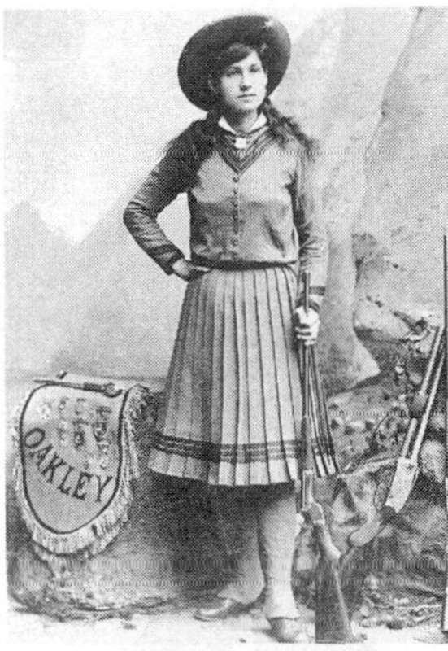

Annie Oakley

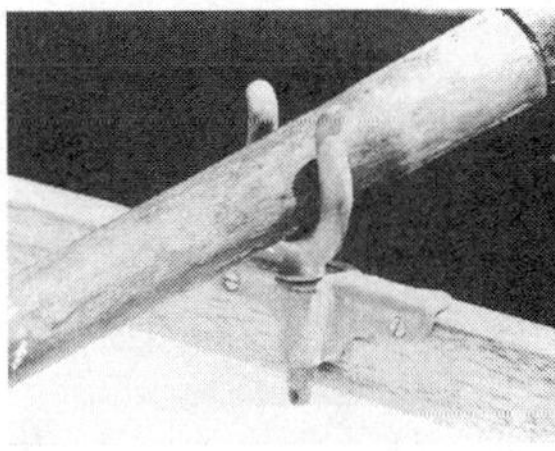

oarlock
With oar

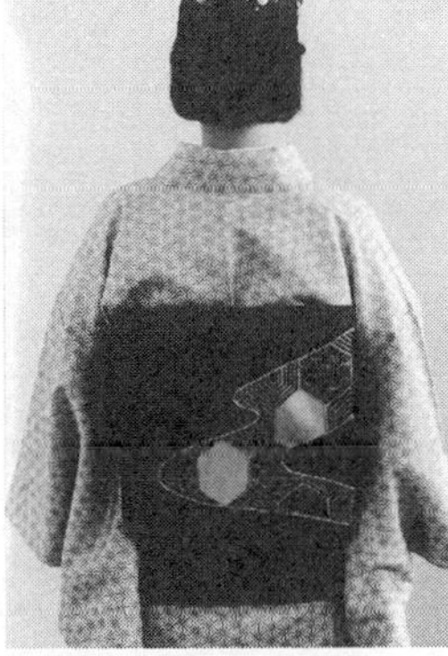

obi

action of a verb. **b.** A noun, pronoun, or group of words acting like a noun that follows and is governed by a preposition. —*v.* (əb **jĕkt′**). **ob•ject•ed, ob•ject•ing, ob•jects.** —*intr.* **1.** To express an opposing opinion or argument; protest. **2.** To be opposed; express disapproval: *We objected to the loud noise downstairs.* —*tr.* To say or offer in opposition or criticism: *We objected that they were being too loud.* [First written down before 1398 in Middle English, from Medieval Latin *obiectum*, something put forward, from Latin *obicere*, to put before.] **—ob•jec′tor** *n.*

ob•jec•tion (əb **jĕk′**shən) *n.* **1.** A statement of an opposing view or argument: *You made no objection when the idea first came up.* **2.** A reason or cause for opposing or disapproving: *His only objection to buying the car was that it was too expensive.*

ob•jec•tion•a•ble (əb **jĕk′**shə nə bəl) *adj.* Causing or apt to cause objection; offensive: *objectionable behavior.* **—ob•jec′tion•a•bly** *adv.*

ob•jec•tive (əb **jĕk′**tĭv) *adj.* **1.** Existing in a material or observable form: *Physics deals with objective phenomena.* **2.** Real; actual: *objective facts.* **3.** Not influenced by emotion or personal prejudice; impartial: *an objective judge of the situation.* **4.** In grammar, of or relating to the case of a noun or pronoun that serves as the object of a verb or preposition. —*n.* **1.** Something worked toward; a goal; a purpose: *Our objective is to plant more trees in town.* **2.** In grammar, the objective case. **3.** The lens or system of lenses in a telescope or microscope that is closest to the object under examination. **—ob•jec′tive•ly** *adj.* **—ob•jec′tive•ness** *n.*

oboe

objective complement *n.* A noun, an adjective, or a pronoun that follows the direct object of certain verbs and is necessary to complete the meaning of the sentence. For example, in the sentence *We elected her governor,* the word *governor* is the objective complement.

ob•jec•tiv•i•ty (ŏb′jĕk **tĭv′**ĭ tē) *n.* The state or quality of being objective.

object lesson *n.* **1.** A lesson taught by using a material object. **2.** A real example of a moral or principle.

ob•jet d'art (ôb′zhĕ **där′**) *n., pl.* **ob•jets d'art** (ôb′-zhĕ **där′**). An object valued for its artistic qualities.

ob•li•gate (**ŏb′**lĭ gāt′) *tr.v.* **ob•li•gat•ed, ob•li•gat•ing, ob•li•gates.** To bind, compel, or constrain by a social, legal, or moral tie: *A doctor is obligated to help every patient.*

ob•li•ga•tion (ŏb′lĭ **gā′**shən) *n.* **1.** A legal, social, or moral requirement, duty, or promise that has the power of binding one to a certain action: *an obligation to vote.* **2.** The binding power of a law, promise, contract, or sense of duty: *the obligation of friendship.* **3.** A debt owed as payment or in return for a special service or favor: *a financial obligation; a social obligation.* **4.** The state or feeling of being obligated to another for a special service or favor: *We felt a sense of obligation toward the teacher.*

o•blig•a•to•ry (ə **blĭg′**ə tôr′ē *or* **ŏb′**lĭ gə tôr′ē) *adj.* Legally or morally binding; required or compulsory: *obligatory attendance.* **—o•blig′a•to′ri•ly** *adv.*

o•blige (ə **blīj′**) *tr.v.* **o•bliged, o•blig•ing, o•blig•es.** **1.** To force by physical, legal, social, or moral means; compel: *The weather obliged him to postpone his trip.* **2.** To make grateful or thankful: *They were obliged to her for her help.* **3.** To do a service or favor for: *The singer obliged the fans with another song.* [First written down about 1280 in Middle English and spelled *oblegen*, from Latin *obligāre*.]

o•blig•ing (ə **blī′**jĭng) *adj.* Ready to do favors for others: *an obliging youth.* **—o•blig′ing•ly** *adv.* **—o•blig′ing•ness** *n.*

o•blique (ō **blēk′**) *adj.* **1.a.** Slanting or sloping, especially in direction. **b.** Neither parallel nor perpendicular. **2.** Indirect or evasive; not straightforward: *an oblique question.* —*n.* Something, such as a line or direction, that is oblique. [First written down before 1425 in Middle English, from Latin *oblīquus*.] **—o•blique′ly** *adv.* **—o•blique′ness** *n.*

oblique angle *n.* An angle that is not a right angle or a multiple of a right angle; an acute angle or obtuse angle.

o•blit•er•ate (ə **blĭt′**ə rāt′) *tr.v.* **o•blit•er•at•ed, o•blit•er•at•ing, o•blit•er•ates.** **1.** To do away with completely; destroy: *The flood obliterated the corn field.* **2.** To cover or hide from view: *The sun obliterated the moon.* [First written down in 1600 in Modern English, from Latin *oblitterāre*, to erase : *ob*, over + *littera*, letter.] **—o•blit′er•a′tion** *n.*

o•bliv•i•on (ə **blĭv′**ē ən) *n.* **1.** The condition of being completely forgotten: *a great writer, in oblivion until the discovery of the manuscript.* **2.** The condition of being oblivious: *the oblivion of a deep sleep.*

o•bliv•i•ous (ə **blĭv′**ē əs) *adj.* Unaware or unmindful: *oblivious to her surroundings.* **—o•bliv′i•ous•ly** *adv.* **—o•bliv′i•ous•ness** *n.*

ob•long (**ŏb′**lông′ *or* **ŏb′**lŏng′) *adj.* Elongated in one direction; shaped like or resembling a rectangle or an ellipse. —*n.* An oblong object or figure. [First written down before 1425 in Middle English, from Latin *oblongus*.]

ob•lo•quy (**ŏb′**lə kwē) *n., pl.* **ob•lo•quies.** **1.** Abusive language that is intended to discredit a person or thing. **2.** The ill repute or discredit suffered because of such abuse.

ob•nox•ious (ŏb **nŏk′**shəs) *adj.* Extremely unpleasant or offensive. **—ob•nox′ious•ly** *adv.*

o•boe (**ō′**bō) *n.* A woodwind instrument with a thin conical shape and a mouthpiece with a double reed. It is played by pressing keys that uncover holes in its body. [First written down in 1724, from French *hautbois* : *haut*, high + *bois*, wood.]

o•bo•ist (**ō′**bō ĭst) *n.* A person who plays the oboe.

ob•scene (ŏb **sēn′**) *adj.* Offensive to accepted standards of decency or modesty: *obscene language.* **—ob•scene′ly** *adv.* **—ob•scene′ness** *n.*

ob•scen•i•ty (ŏb **sĕn′**ĭ tē) *n., pl.* **ob•scen•i•ties.** **1.** Indecency or offensiveness in behavior, appearance, or expression. **2.** Something, such as a word or an act, that is considered obscene.

ob•scure (əb **skyo͝or′**) *adj.* **ob•scur•er, ob•scur•est.** **1.** Dark; gloomy: *the obscure room of the old house.* **2.** Not readily perceived; indistinct: *obscure markings on a stone.* **3.** Difficult to understand; vague: *an obscure reference to a past incident.* See Synonyms at **vague.** **4.** Of humble reputation; known by few people: *an obscure poet.* —*tr.v.* **ob•scured, ob•scur•ing, ob•scures.** **1.** To conceal from view; hide: *Clouds obscured the stars.* **2.** To make difficult to understand: *His vague speech obscured his real intentions.* [First written down before 1400 in Middle English, from Latin *obscūrus*.] **—ob•scure′ly** *adv.* **—ob•scure′ness** *n.*

ob•scu•ri•ty (əb **skyo͝or′**ĭ tē) *n., pl.* **ob•scu•ri•ties.** **1.** The condition of having little or no light; darkness. **2.** The condition of being unknown or inconspicuous: *a great movie star, now in obscurity.* **3.** The condition of being difficult to understand: *the obscurity of the poem.*

ob•se•qui•ous (əb **sē′**kwē əs) *adj.* Overly willing to serve, agree, or obey; fawning: *an obsequious person.* **—ob•se′qui•ous•ly** *adv.* **—ob•se′qui•ous•ness** *n.*

ob•se•quy (**ŏb′**sĭ kwē) *n., pl.* **ob•se•quies.** A funeral rite or ceremony. Often used in the plural.

ob•serv•a•ble (əb zûr′və bəl) *adj.* **1.** Possible to observe: *an observable change in light.* **2.** Deserving note; noteworthy: *an observable anniversary.* **—ob•serv′a•bly** *adv.*

ob•ser•vance (əb zûr′vəns) *n.* **1.** The act of complying with a law, rule, or custom. **2.** The act of keeping or celebrating a holiday or religious festival. **3.** A customary rite or ceremony. **4.** The act of watching; observation.

ob•ser•vant (əb zûr′vənt) *adj.* **1.** Quick to perceive; alert: *an observant student.* **2.** Following or observing a law, custom, or duty: *observant of the speed limit.* **—ob•ser′vant•ly** *adv.*

ob•ser•va•tion (ŏb′zər vā′shən) *n.* **1.** The act of observing: *a tower for the observation of the countryside.* **2.a.** The act of perceiving and recording something, such as a phenomenon, with instruments. **b.** The result or record of such notation: *a meteorological observation.* **3.** A comment or remark: *She made observations about the sculpture.* **—ob′ser•va′tion•al** *adj.*

ob•ser•va•to•ry (əb zûr′və tôr′ē) *n., pl.* **ob•ser•va•to•ries. 1.** A building or room designed and equipped for making observations, as in astronomy or meteorology. **2.** A structure overlooking an extensive view.

ob•serve (əb zûrv′) *tr.v.* **ob•served, ob•serv•ing, ob•serves. 1.** To be aware of; notice: *She observed a skunk crossing the road.* See Synonyms at **see**[1]. **2.** To watch attentively: *I observed how he connected the wires.* **3.** To make a scientific observation of: *observed the migration of the caribou.* **4.** To say; remark: *She observed that math was her best subject.* **5.** To adhere to or abide by: *observe the speed limit.* **6.** To keep or celebrate: *We observed Thanksgiving together.* [First written down about 1390 in Middle English and spelled *observen*, from Latin *observāre*.] **—ob•serv′er** *n.*

ob•sess (əb sĕs′) *tr.v.* **ob•sessed, ob•sess•ing, ob•sess•es.** To preoccupy the mind of abnormally; haunt: *Finding someone to blame for the leak obsessed them for years.*

ob•ses•sion (əb sĕsh′ən) *n.* **1.** Recurring attention to a fixed idea or an unwanted emotion. **2.** An idea, a thought, or an emotion that occupies the mind continually: *Collecting rocks became an obsession.*

ob•ses•sive (əb sĕs′ĭv) *adj.* Of, characteristic of, or causing an obsession: *an obsessive fear of snakes.* **—ob•ses′sive•ly** *adv.* **—ob•ses′sive•ness** *n.*

ob•sid•i•an (ŏb sĭd′ē ən) *n.* A shiny usually black or banded glass of volcanic origin.

ob•so•les•cent (ŏb′sə lĕs′ənt) *adj.* Passing out of use or usefulness; becoming obsolete. [First written down in 1755 in Modern English, from Latin *obsolēscēns*, present participle of *obsolēscere*, to fall into disuse.] **—ob′so•les′cence** *n.*

ob•so•lete (ŏb′sə lēt′ *or* ŏb′sə lēt′) *adj.* No longer useful, in use, or in fashion: *an obsolete word; obsolete technology.* [First written down in 1579 in Modern English, from Latin *obsolētus*, past participle of *obsolēscere*, to fall into disuse.] **—ob′so•lete′ness** *n.*

ob•sta•cle (ŏb′stə kəl) *n.* Something that opposes, holds up, or stands in the way of progress toward a goal. [First written down about 1340 in Middle English and spelled *obstakil*, from Latin *obstāculum*, from *obstāre*, to hinder.]

ob•stet•ric (ŏb stĕt′rĭk) also **ob•stet•ri•cal** (ŏb stĕt′rĭ kəl) *adj.* Of or relating to obstetrics. **—ob•stet′ri•cal•ly** *adv.*

ob•ste•tri•cian (ŏb′stĭ trĭsh′ən) *n.* A physician who specializes in obstetrics.

ob•stet•rics (ŏb stĕt′rĭks) *n.* *(used with a singular verb).* The branch of medicine that deals with the care of women during pregnancy, childbirth, and the period following childbirth.

ob•sti•na•cy (ŏb′stə nə sē) *n., pl.* **ob•sti•na•cies.** The quality or condition of being obstinate; stubbornness.

ob•sti•nate (ŏb′stə nĭt) *adj.* **1.** Stubbornly adhering to an attitude or a course of action. **2.** Difficult to control or cure: *an obstinate headache.* **—ob′sti•nate•ly** *adv.* **—ob′sti•nate•ness** *n.*

Synonyms: **obstinate, stubborn, mulish, headstrong.** These adjectives mean determinedly unwilling to yield. **Obstinate** means unreasonably rigid and difficult to persuade: *Jenny is obstinate about doing things in her own way.* **Stubborn** and **mulish** can mean perversely unyielding by nature: *Robert is too stubborn to admit he was wrong. It's mulish of you to refuse to look at the map until after we're lost.* **Headstrong** means stubbornly, often recklessly willful: *That headstrong child will never follow advice.* Antonyms: **cooperative, flexible.**

ob•strep•er•ous (ŏb strĕp′ər əs) *adj.* Noisily defiant or unruly; boisterous. **—ob•strep′er•ous•ly** *adv.* **—ob•strep′er•ous•ness** *n.*

ob•struct (əb strŭkt′) *tr.v.* **ob•struct•ed, ob•struct•ing, ob•structs. 1.** To make impassable with obstacles; block: *The delivery truck obstructed the alley.* **2.** To interfere with so as to impede or retard; hinder: *obstructing justice.* **3.** To get in the way of so as to hide; cut off from view: *Buildings obstruct our view of the ocean.* [First written down in 1611 in Modern English, from Latin *obstruere*.] **—ob•struc′tive** *adj.*

ob•struc•tion (əb strŭk′shən) *n.* **1.** Something that obstructs or gets in the way: *an obstruction in the road.* **2.** The act or action of obstructing: *the obstruction of justice.* **3.** The condition of being blocked: *an intestinal obstruction.*

ob•struc•tion•ism (*əb-strŭk′shə-nĭz′əm*) *n.* The practice of delaying passage of a bill into law by speechmaking or other types of delay. **—ob•struc′tion•ist** *adj. & n.*

ob•tain (əb tān′) *v.* **ob•tained, ob•tain•ing, ob•tains.** *—tr.* To gain possession of as the result of planning or endeavor; acquire: *obtain an autograph.* *—intr.* To be established or accepted; be in use: *an ancient custom that still obtains.* [First written down about 1412 in Middle English and spelled *opteenen*, from Latin *obtinēre*.] **—ob•tain′a•ble** *adj.* **—ob•tain′er** *n.*

ob•trude (əb tro͞od′) *v.* **ob•trud•ed, ob•trud•ing, ob•trudes.** *—tr.* **1.** To force (ideas or opinions) upon another without invitation: *He tries to obtrude his prejudices on others.* **2.** To push forward; thrust out: *The clam obtruded its siphon.* *—intr.* To force oneself upon another: *She would not obtrude upon their privacy.* **—ob•tru′sion** (əb tro͞o′zhən) *n.*

ob•tru•sive (əb tro͞o′sĭv *or* əb tro͞o′zĭv) *adj.* Tending to obtrude; brash: *obtrusive behavior.* **—ob•tru′sive•ly** *adv.* **—ob•tru′sive•ness** *n.*

ob•tuse (əb to͞os′ *or* əb tyo͞os′) *adj.* **ob•tus•er, ob•tus•est. 1.** Slow in perception or understanding; dull: *an obtuse person.* **2.** Not sharp or pointed in form; blunt. **—ob•tuse′ly** *adv.* **—ob•tuse′ness** *n.*

obtuse angle *n.* An angle that contains more than 90° and less than 180°.

ob•verse (ŏb vûrs′ *or* ŏb′vûrs′) *adj.* Facing or turned toward the observer: *the obverse side of a clock.* *—n.* (ŏb′vûrs′ *or* ŏb vûrs′). The side or face of a coin, medal, or badge that bears the principal stamp or design. **—ob•verse′ly** *adv.*

ob•vi•ate (ŏb′vē āt′) *tr.v.* **ob•vi•at•ed, ob•vi•at•ing, ob•vi•ates.** To anticipate and prevent; make unnecessary: *I obviated the need for a plumber by fixing the leak myself.* **—ob′vi•a′tion** *n.*

ob•vi•ous (ŏb′vē əs) *adj.* Easily perceived or under-

observatory
United States Naval Observatory in Washington, D.C.

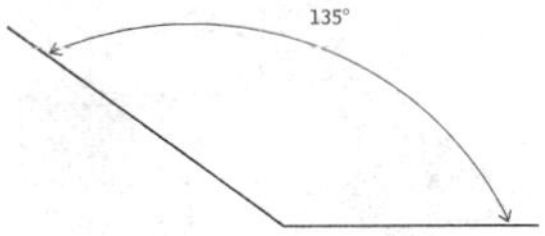

obtuse angle

ă	pat	oi	boy
ā	pay	ou	out
âr	care	o͝o	took
ä	father	o͞o	boot
ĕ	pet	ŭ	cut
ē	be	ûr	urge
ĭ	pit	th	thin
ī	pie	*th*	this
îr	pier	hw	whoop
ŏ	pot	zh	vision
ō	toe	ə	about
ô	paw	N	*French* bon

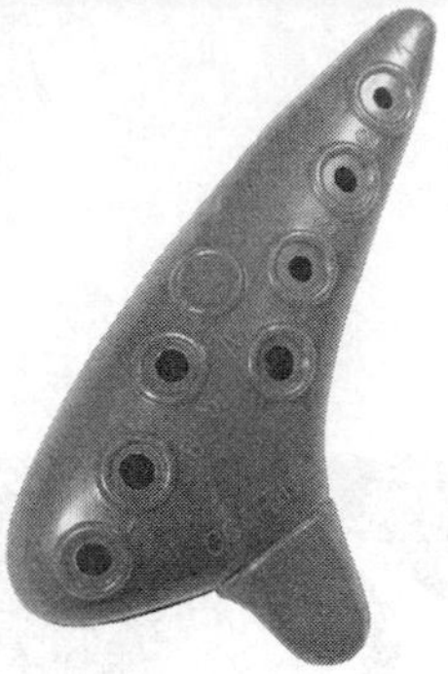
ocarina

ocelot

Sandra Day O'Connor
Photographed in 1985

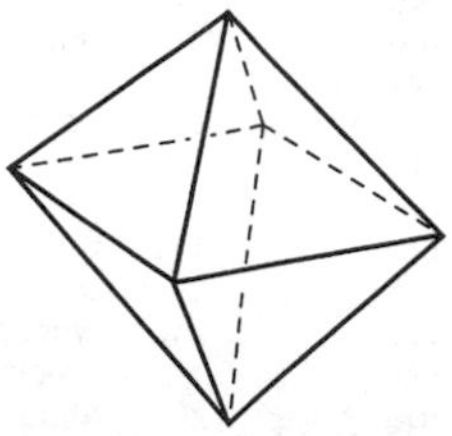
octahedron

stood; evident: *an obvious advantage.* [First written down in 1586 in Modern English, from Latin *obvius*, being in the way.] **—ob′vi•ous•ly** *adv.* **—ob′vi•ous•ness** *n.*

oc•a•ri•na (ŏk′ə **rē′**nə) *n.* A wind instrument with an oval shape, a mouthpiece, and holes that are opened and closed by the fingers.

oc•ca•sion (ə **kā′**zhən) *n.* **1.** An event or a happening: *enjoyable occasions.* **2.** An important event or happening: *Her party was quite an occasion.* **3.** The time of an event or a happening; the moment when something occurs: *shortly before the occasion of their wedding.* **4.** A favorable or suitable time; an opportunity: *There were many occasions when we were able to go sailing.* **5.** A reason or cause: *What was the occasion for all that laughter?* —*tr.v.* **oc•ca•sioned, oc•ca•sion•ing, oc•ca•sions.** To be the reason for; cause: *The need to resolve the dispute occasioned the meeting.* —***idiom.*** **on occasion.** From time to time; now and then. [First written down before 1382 in Middle English, from Latin *occāsiō*, from *occidere*, to fall.]

oc•ca•sion•al (ə **kā′**zhə nəl) *adj.* **1.** Occurring from time to time: *an occasional thunderstorm.* **2.** Intended for use as the need arises: *occasional chairs for a reception.* **3.** Created for a special occasion: *an occasional song.*

oc•ca•sion•al•ly (ə **kā′**zhə nə lē) *adv.* From time to time; now and then.

oc•ci•dent (**ŏk′**sĭ dənt) *n.* **1.** Western lands or regions; the west. **2. Occident.** The countries of Europe and the Western Hemisphere. [First written down about 1375 in Middle English, from Latin *occidēns*, setting (used of the sun).]

oc•ci•den•tal or **Oc•ci•den•tal** (ŏk′sĭ **dĕn′**tl) *adj.* Of or relating to the countries of the Occident or any of their peoples. —*n.* A native or inhabitant of an Occidental country; a westerner.

oc•cip•i•tal (ŏk **sĭp′**ĭ tl) *adj.* Of, belonging to, or situated in the back part of the head or skull. —*n.* The occipital bone.

occipital bone *n.* The compound bone forming the lower back part of the skull.

oc•clude (ə **klo͞od′**) *v.* **oc•clud•ed, oc•clud•ing, oc•cludes.** —*tr.* **1.** To close off or block off: *occlude a passageway.* **2.** To keep from passing: *occlude light.* **3.** To absorb or adsorb large amounts of: *metal that occludes gases.* **4.** To force (air) upward from Earth's surface, as a cold front does when it moves under a warm front. **5.** To bring (the upper and lower teeth) together in proper alignment for chewing. —*intr.* To meet properly for chewing: *The dentist said my jaws do not occlude perfectly.*

oc•clud•ed front (ə **klo͞o′**dĭd) *n.* The front that forms when a cold front occludes a warm front and forces warm air up into the atmosphere.

oc•clu•sion (ə **klo͞o′**zhən) *n.* **1.** The process of occluding. **2.** An obstruction in a bodily passageway, such as a blood vessel. **3.** The manner in which the teeth fit when brought together.

oc•cult (ə **kŭlt′** *or* **ŏk′**ŭlt′) *adj.* **1.** Of, relating to, or dealing with magic, astrology, or supernatural powers. **2.** Beyond human understanding; mysterious. —*n.* Occult practices or teachings.

oc•cul•ta•tion (ŏk′ŭl **tā′**shən) *n.* The passage of a celestial object between an observer and another celestial object, blocking the second object from the observer's view.

oc•cult•ism (ə **kŭl′**tĭz′əm *or* **ŏk′**ŭl tĭz′əm) *n.* A belief in or the study of occult powers and the supernatural. **—oc•cult′ist** *n.*

oc•cu•pan•cy (**ŏk′**yə pən sē) *n., pl.* **oc•cu•pan•cies.** **1.** The act of taking or holding in possession; the act of occupying. **2.** The state of being occupied or rented. **3.** The period during which a person or group stays in, rents, or uses certain premises or land.

oc•cu•pant (**ŏk′**yə pənt) *n.* **1.** A person or thing occupying a place or position: *the occupants of a building.* **2.** A person who has certain legal rights to or control over the premises that are occupied; a tenant or an owner.

oc•cu•pa•tion (ŏk′yə **pā′**shən) *n.* **1.** A means of making a living; a profession or job. **2.** An activity that keeps one busy. **3.** The act or process of holding, possessing, or using a place: *the occupation of the cave by bears.* **4.** The conquest and control of a nation or territory by a foreign military force.

oc•cu•pa•tion•al (ŏk′yə **pā′**shə nəl) *adj.* Of, relating to, or caused by engagement in a particular occupation: *occupational disease.* **—oc′cu•pa′tion•al•ly** *adv.*

oc•cu•py (**ŏk′**yə pī′) *tr.v.* **oc•cu•pied, oc•cu•py•ing, oc•cu•pies.** **1.** To fill; take up: *Reading occupies his free time.* **2.** To dwell in; inhabit: *They occupy a small cabin.* **3.** To hold or control (an office or a position): *She occupies the office of president.* **4.** To seize possession of and maintain control over by force: *The troops occupied the city.* **5.** To employ or busy (oneself). **—oc′cu•pi′er** *n.*

oc•cur (ə **kûr′**) *intr.v.* **oc•curred, oc•cur•ring, oc•curs.** **1.** To take place; come about; happen. **2.** To be found to exist or appear: *Heavy rains occur during the monsoon.* **3.** To come to mind: *That idea never occurred to me.* [First written down in 1527 in Modern English, from Latin *occurrere*, to run into.]

oc•cur•rence (ə **kûr′**əns) *n.* **1.** The fact or condition of occurring: *the occurrence of a rainbow.* **2.** Something that happens; an incident: *a strange occurrence.*

o•cean (**ō′**shən) *n.* **1.** The mass of salt water that covers about 72 percent of the surface of the earth. **2.** Any of the principal divisions of this body of water, including the Atlantic, Pacific, Indian, and Arctic oceans. [First written down about 1300 in Middle English and spelled *occean*, from Greek *Ōkeanos*, the god Oceanus, a great river encircling the earth.]

O•ce•an•i•a (ō′shē **ăn′**ē ə). The islands of the southern, western, and central Pacific Ocean, including Melanesia, Micronesia, and Polynesia. The term sometimes includes Australia, New Zealand, and the Malay Archipelago.

o•ce•an•ic (ō′shē **ăn′**ĭk) *adj.* **1.** Of or relating to the ocean. **2.** Living or found in the ocean, especially in the open sea rather than in coastal waters.

o•cean•og•ra•pher (ō′shə **nŏg′**rə fər) *n.* A scientist who specializes in oceanography.

o•cean•og•ra•phy (ō′shə **nŏg′**rə fē) *n.* The exploration and scientific study of the ocean.

o•cel•lus (ō **sĕl′**əs) *n., pl.* **o•cel•li** (ō **sĕl′**ī′). **1.** A small simple eye, found in many invertebrates. **2.** A marking that resembles an eye; an eyespot. **—o•cel′lar** (ō **sĕl′**ər) *adj.*

oc•e•lot (**ŏs′**ə lŏt′ *or* **ō′**sə lŏt′) *n.* A wild cat of Mexico, Central America, and South America, having a yellowish coat spotted with black.

o•cher or **o•chre** (**ō′**kər) *n.* **1.** Any of several oxides of iron that occur as minerals. Their colors are yellow, brown, and red, and they are used as pigments. **2.** A yellowish or brownish orange.

o'clock (ə **klŏk′**) *adv.* **1.** Of or according to the clock: *three o'clock.* **2.** According to an imaginary clock dial, with the observer at the center and 12 o'clock considered as straight ahead horizontally or straight up vertically: *enemy planes at 10 o'clock.*

O'Con•nor (ō **kŏn′**ər), **Flannery.** 1925–1964. American writer known for her novels, including *The Violent Bear It Away* (1960), and her collections of short stories, including *A Good Man is Hard to Find* (1955).

O'Connor, Sandra Day. Born 1930. American jurist who in 1981 was the first woman appointed associate justice of the U.S. Supreme Court.

Oct. or **Oct** *abbr.* An abbreviation of October.

oct– or **octa–** *pref.* Variants of **octo–**.

oc•ta•gon (ŏk′tə gŏn′) *n.* A plane geometric figure bounded by eight line segments and containing eight angles. [First written down in 1660 in Modern English : Greek *oktō*, eight + Greek *gōnia*, angle.]

oc•tag•o•nal (ŏk tăg′ə nəl) *adj.* Having eight sides and eight angles.

oc•ta•he•dron (ŏk′tə hē′drən) *n., pl.* **oc•ta•he•drons** or **oc•ta•he•dra** (ŏk′tə hē′drə). A solid geometric figure bounded by eight planes.

oc•tal (ŏk′təl) *adj.* Of, relating to, or being a number expressed in a numbering system of base eight.

oc•tane (ŏk′tān′) *n.* Any of several hydrocarbon compounds having the formula C_8H_{18} and occurring in petroleum.

octane number *n.* A number that represents the antiknock rating of gasoline, based on the percentage of a particular form of octane that is contained in the sample of gasoline.

oc•tant (ŏk′tənt) *n.* **1.a.** One eighth of a circle; an arc of 45°. **b.** One eighth of the area of a circle; the area bounded by a pair of radii and an arc of 45° that they intercept. **2.** A navigation instrument similar to a sextant but based on an arc of 45° rather than 60°.

oc•tave (ŏk′tĭv *or* ŏk′tāv′) *n.* **1.** The musical interval between two tones, one of which has twice as many vibrations per second as the other; an interval of eight degrees in a major or minor scale. **2.** A tone that is eight full tones above or below another tone. **3.** A series of tones included in this interval: *the lowest octave of a flute.* [First written down before 1425 in Middle English and spelled *octave*, eighth day after a feast day, from Latin *octāvus*, eighth.]

Oc•ta•vi•an (ŏk tā′ vē ən). Augustus.

oc•ta•vo (ŏk tā′vō *or* ŏk tä′vō) *n., pl.* **oc•ta•vos.** **1.** The page size, from 5 × 8 inches to 6 × 9½ inches, of a book composed of printer's sheets folded into eight leaves. **2.** A book composed of pages of this size.

oc•tet (ŏk tĕt′) *n.* **1.** A musical composition for eight voices or instruments. **2.** Eight singers or instrumentalists. **3.** A group of eight.

octo– or **octa–** or **oct–** *pref.* A prefix that means eight: *octane.*

Oc•to•ber (ŏk tō′bər) *n.* The tenth month of the year in the Gregorian calendar, having 31 days. [First written down about 1050 in Old English, from Latin *Octōber*, eighth month, from *octō*, eight.]

oc•to•ge•nar•i•an (ŏk′tə jə nâr′ē ən) *adj.* Being between 80 and 90 years of age. —*n.* A person between 80 and 90 years of age.

oc•to•pus (ŏk′tə pəs) *n., pl.* **oc•to•pus•es** or **oc•to•pi** (ŏk′tə pī′). Any of numerous sea mollusks having a soft rounded body and eight tentacles bearing suckers used for grasping and holding. [First written down in 1758 in Modern English, from Greek *oktōpous*, eight-footed : *oktō*, eight + *pous*, foot.]

oc•u•lar (ŏk′yə lər) *adj.* **1.** Of or having to do with the eye or the sense of vision. **2.** Seen by the eye; visual: *ocular evidence.* —*n.* The eyepiece of a microscope, telescope, or other optical instrument.

oc•u•list (ŏk′yə lĭst) *n.* **1.** An ophthalmologist. **2.** An optometrist.

odd (ŏd) *adj.* **odd•er, odd•est.** **1.** Differing from what is ordinary or usual; peculiar; strange: *odd behavior; an odd name.* **2.a.** Being one of an incomplete set or pair: *an odd shoe.* **b.** Remaining after others are grouped: *They formed two teams, leaving one odd player.* **3.** Not regular or expected: *telephoned at odd intervals.* **4.** Of or indicating whole numbers that are not divisible by two. **5.** More than the number indicated: *There were 20-odd guests at the party.* [First written down about 1280 in Middle English and spelled *odde*, from Old Norse *oddi*, point of land, triangle.] **—odd′ly** *adv.* **—odd′ness** *n.*

odd•i•ty (ŏd′ĭ tē) *n., pl.* **odd•i•ties.** **1.** A person or thing that is odd or strange. **2.** The condition of being odd; strangeness: *The oddity of his behavior suggested that he wasn't feeling well.*

odd job *n.* Any of various jobs not usually requiring special training.

odd•ment (ŏd′mənt) *n.* Something left over; an item, a fragment, or a remnant. Often used in the plural.

odds (ŏdz) *pl.n.* **1.** The likelihood or probability that one thing rather than another will happen: *The odds are that it will rain tomorrow.* **2.** The ratio of the likelihood of an event's occurring to the likelihood of its not occurring: *The odds are 2 to 1 that the champion will win.* **—*idiom.* at odds.** In disagreement; in conflict: *They were at odds about what to do with the money.*

odds and ends *pl.n.* Miscellaneous items.

ode (ōd) *n.* A lyric poem that expresses in an exalted style the poet's feelings and thoughts. [First written down in 1588 in Modern English, from Greek *aoidē*, song.]

O•des•sa (ō dĕs′ə). A city of southern Ukraine on **Odessa Bay**, an arm of the Black Sea. It is said to occupy the site of an ancient Greek colony that disappeared between the third and fourth centuries A.D. Population, 1,126,000.

O•din (ō′dĭn) *n.* In Norse mythology, the god of wisdom and war, and the creator of the world.

o•di•ous (ō′dē əs) *adj.* Causing repugnance or aversion; abhorrent; hateful. [First written down before 1382 in Middle English, from Latin *odium*, hatred.]

o•di•um (ō′dē əm) *n.* **1.** Intense dislike; hatred. **2.** Disgrace that results from detestable conduct.

o•dom•e•ter (ō dŏm′ĭ tər) *n.* A device that indicates the distance that a vehicle has traveled. [First written down in 1791 in American English, from Greek *hodometron* : *hodos*, journey + *metron*, measure.]

o•dor (ō′dər) *n.* The quality of a thing that affects the sense of smell; scent: *Onions have a pungent odor.* See Synonyms at **scent**.

o•dor•if•er•ous (ō′də rĭf′ər əs) *adj.* Having or giving off an odor, especially a pleasant one.

o•dor•less (ō′dər lĭs) *adj.* Having no odor.

o•dor•ous (ō′dər əs) *adj.* Having a distinct or characteristic odor. **—o′dor•ous•ly** *adv.* **—o′dor•ous•ness** *n.*

o•dour (ō′dər) *n.* *Chiefly British.* Variant of **odor.**

O•dys•se•us (ō dĭs′ē əs) *n.* In Greek mythology, a leader of the Greeks during the Trojan War who reaches home after 10 years of wandering.

od•ys•sey (ŏd′ĭ sē) *n., pl.* **od•ys•seys.** An extended adventurous journey.

Oed•i•pus (ĕd′ə pəs *or* ē′də pəs) *n.* In Greek mythology, the king of Thebes who unknowingly kills his father and marries his mother.

o'er (ôr) *prep. & adv.* Over.

❑ *These sound alike:* **o'er, oar** (wooden pole), **or** (conjunction), **ore** (mineral).

of (ŭv *or* ŏv; əv *when unstressed*) *prep.* **1.** Coming from: *people of the north.* **2.** Caused by; resulting from: *He died of pneumonia.* **3.** At a distance from: *one mile east of here.* **4.** So as to be separated or relieved from: *a prisoner deprived of his freedom; a*

octopus

Odysseus

Oedipus

With the sphinx

ă	pat	oi	boy
ā	pay	ou	out
âr	care	ŏŏ	took
ä	father	ōō	boot
ĕ	pet	ŭ	cut
ē	be	ûr	urge
ĭ	pit	th	thin
ī	pie	*th*	this
îr	pier	hw	whoop
ŏ	pot	zh	vision
ō	toe	ə	about
ô	paw	N	*French* bon

patient cured of an infection. **5.** From the total or group making up: *two of my friends.* **6.** Composed or made from: *shoes of the finest leather.* **7.** Associated with or adhering to: *a person of her religion.* **8.** Belonging or connected to: *the rungs of a ladder.* **9.** Possessing; having: *a man of honor.* **10.** Containing or carrying: *a bag of groceries.* **11.** Named or called: *the busy city of Chicago.* **12.** Centering on or directed toward: *a love of horses.* **13.** Produced by: *the fruits of our orchards.* **14.** Characterized by: *a man of many accomplishments.* **15.** Concerning; about: *We spoke of you last night.* **16.** Set aside for: *a day of rest.* **17.** Before; until: *five minutes of two.* **18.** During: *Of recent years he has devoted himself to gardening.*

off (ôf *or* ŏf) *adv.* **1.** Away from a place: *They drove off.* **2.** At a distance in space or time: *a mile off; a week off.* **3.** So as to be no longer on or connected: *He shaved off his beard.* **4.** So as to be no longer continuing or functioning: *Turn the lights off.* **5.** So as to be smaller, fewer, or less: *Sales are dropping off.* **6.** So as to be away from work or duty: *taking the day off.* —*adj.* **1.** More distant or removed: *the off side of the barn.* **2.** Not on, attached, or connected: *Her shoes were off.* **3.** Not continuing, operating, or functioning: *The oven is off.* **4.** No longer taking place; canceled: *The dance is off.* **5.** Less or smaller: *Production is off this year.* **6.** Below standard: *His performance was somehow off.* **7.** Started on the way; going: *I'm off to the movies.* **8.** In error: *off by several inches.* **9.** Away from work or duty: *I'm off tonight.* —*prep.* **1.** So as to be removed or distant from: *The bird hopped off the branch.* **2.** Away or relieved from: *off duty.* **3.** By consuming or with the means provided by: *living off fruit; living off a pension.* **4.** Extending from: *a little alley off the main street.* **5.** Not up to the usual standard of: *off her game.* **6.** Abstaining from: *staying off tobacco.* **7.** Seaward of: *a mile off the beach.* [First written down before 971 in Old English and spelled *of.*]

of•fal (ô′fəl *or* ŏf′əl) *n.* **1.** Waste parts, especially of a butchered animal. **2.** Refuse; rubbish.
❑ *These sound alike:* **offal, awful** (fearsome).

off•beat (ôf′bēt′ *or* ŏf′bēt′) *n.* A beat in a musical measure that is not normally accented. —*adj.* (ôf′-bēt′ *or* ŏf′bēt′). *Slang.* Not of an ordinary type; unconventional; different: *offbeat humor.*

off-col•or (ôf′kŭl′ər *or* ŏf′kŭl′ər) *adj.* **1.** Improper; in poor taste: *an off-color joke.* **2.** Not of the usual or required color: *an off-color uniform.*

of•fence (ə fĕns′) *n. Chiefly British.* Variant of **offense.**

of•fend (ə fĕnd′) *v.* **of•fend•ed, of•fend•ing, of•fends.** —*tr.* **1.** To cause anger, resentment, or annoyance in; insult or affront: *a remark that offended me.* **2.** To be displeasing to; be disagreeable to: *The smell from the chemicals offended everyone.* —*intr.* **1.** To be the cause of displeasure: *odors that offend.* **2.** To break a moral or spiritual law; sin. **3.** To break a rule or law. [First written down about 1350 in Middle English and spelled *offendien,* from Latin *offendere.*]

of•fend•er (ə fĕn′dər) *n.* A person or thing that offends, especially a violator of a public law.

of•fense (ə fĕns′) *n.* **1.a.** The act of causing anger, resentment, or displeasure. **b.** The state of being offended: *She took offense at the comment.* **2.** A violation of a moral, legal, or social code; a transgression, sin, or crime: *a punishable offense.* **3.** Something that offends: *The building was an offense to the eye.* **4.** (ŏf′ĕns′). The act of attacking or assaulting. **5.** (ŏf′ĕns′). In sports, the team in possession of the ball or puck.

of•fen•sive (ə fĕn′sĭv) *adj.* **1.** Offending the senses; unpleasant: *an offensive smell.* **2.** Causing anger, displeasure, or resentment: *offensive language.* **3.** Of, relating to, or designed for attack: *offensive infantry weapons.* **4.** (ŏf′ĕn sĭv). Of or relating to the offense of a sports team. —*n.* **1.** An attack: *the third offensive of the war.* **2.** An attitude of attack: *She went on the offensive and won the debate.* —**of•fen′sive•ly** *adv.* —**of•fen′sive•ness** *n.*

of•fer (ô′fər *or* ŏf′ər) *tr.v.* **of•fered, of•fer•ing, of•fers.** **1.** To present for acceptance or refusal: *They offered me dessert.* **2.** To put forward for consideration; propose: *offer advice.* **3.** To present for sale or rent: *a store offering suits at a discount.* **4.** To provide; afford: *The new apartment offers many advantages over our old one.* **5.** To present as an act of worship: *offer prayers.* **6.** To show readiness to do; volunteer: *They offered their services.* **7.** To propose as payment: *offer a reward.* **8.** To produce; present to the public: *offered a program of music.* —*n.* **1.** Something, such as a proposal, suggestion, or bid, that is offered: *an offer to teach; an offer for the car.* **2.** The act of offering: *the offer of his services.* [First written down before 830 in Old English and spelled *ofrian,* from Latin *offerre* : *ob-,* to + *ferre,* to bring.]

of•fer•ing (ô′fər ĭng *or* ŏf′ər ĭng) *n.* **1.** The act of making an offer. **2.** Something offered, such as a contribution, gift, or religious sacrifice.

of•fer•to•ry (ô′fər tôr′ē *or* ŏf′ər tôr′ē) *n., pl.* **of•fer•to•ries.** **1.** Often **Offertory.** The part of the Eucharist at which bread and wine are offered to God. **2.** Often **Offertory.** The music accompanying this part of the religious service. **3.** A collection of offerings at a religious service.

off•hand (ôf′hănd′ *or* ŏf′hănd′) *adv.* Without preparation or forethought: *Can you say offhand when they'll call?* —*adj.* Done or said without preparation or forethought: *an offhand reply.* —**off′hand′ed•ly** *adv.*

of•fice (ô′fĭs *or* ŏf′ĭs) *n.* **1.a.** A place in which business, clerical, or professional work is done: *the principal's office.* **b.** The people working in such a place: *The office gave the boss a surprise party.* **2.** A position of authority or trust, as in a government or a corporation: *the office of President.* **3.** A public position: *seek office.* **4.** A branch of a department of a government. **5.** A duty, function, or role: *He did not shirk his office.* **6.** Something performed for another; a service or favor. Often used in the plural: *delighted by the kind offices of their friends.* **7.** A Christian religious ceremony or service, such as a rite for the dead. [First written down about 1250 in Middle English, from Latin *officium.*]

of•fice•hold•er (ô′fĭs hōl′dər *or* ŏf′ĭs hōl′dər) *n.* A person who holds a public office.

of•fi•cer (ô′fĭ sər *or* ŏf′ĭ sər) *n.* **1.** A person who holds an office of authority or trust in a government, corporation, club, or other institution. **2.** A person who holds a commission in the armed forces. **3.** A police officer.

of•fi•cial (ə fĭsh′əl) *adj.* **1.** Of or relating to an office or post of authority: *official duties.* **2.** Authorized by an authority: *an official document.* **3.** Holding office or performing a special duty: *an official mediator.* **4.** Formal or ceremonious: *an official banquet.* —*n.* **1.** A person in a position of authority. **2.** A referee or an umpire in a sports contest. —**of•fi′cial•ly** *adv.*

of•fi•ci•ate (ə fĭsh′ē āt′) *intr.v.* **of•fi•ci•at•ed, of•fi•ci•at•ing, of•fi•ci•ates.** **1.** To perform the duties of a public office: *The mayor officiates at town meetings.* **2.** To perform the duties of a member of the clergy: *The priest officiated at a wedding.* **3.** To serve as a referee or an umpire in a sports contest.

of•fi•cious (ə fĭsh′əs) *adj.* Excessively forward in

offering one's services or advice to others. **—of•fi′cious•ly** *adv.* **—of•fi′cious•ness** *n.*
off•ing (ô′fĭng *or* ŏf′ĭng) *n.* The part of the sea that is distant but visible from the shore. **—*idiom.* in the offing.** In the near or immediate future; soon to come.
off-key (ôf′kē′ *or* ŏf′kē′) *adj.* Higher or lower than the correct notes of a melody. **—off′key′** *adv.*
off-lim•its (ôf lĭm′ĭts *or* ŏf lĭm′ĭts) *adj.* Not to be entered by a certain group: *That district is off-limits to all foreigners.*
off-line (ôf′līn′ *or* ŏf′līn′) *adj.* Not connected to or controlled by a computer.
off•set (ôf′sĕt′ *or* ŏf′sĕt′) *n.* **1.** Something that balances, counteracts, or compensates: *A diver's weighted belt is an offset for the increased buoyancy of the wet suit.* **2.** Offset printing. **3.** A shoot that develops to the side at the base of a plant, often rooting to form a new plant. *—tr.v.* (ôf sĕt′ *or* ŏf sĕt′). **off•set, off•set•ting, off•sets.** To counterbalance or counteract; make up for: *His good passing should offset our weak defense.*
offset printing *n.* A form of printing in which an inked image is transferred from a metal or paper plate to a rotating cylinder, which in turn transfers it onto the paper.
off•shoot (ôf′shoot′ *or* ŏf′shoot′) *n.* **1.** A shoot that branches out from the main stem of a plant. **2.** Something that branches out or originates from a main source.
off•shore (ôf′shôr′ *or* ŏf′shôr′) *adj.* **1.** Moving away from the shore: *an offshore breeze.* **2.** Located at a distance from the shore: *offshore rocks.* *—adv.* **1.** In a direction away from shore: *The breeze was blowing offshore.* **2.** At a distance from shore: *a sea lion swimming a half mile offshore.*
off•side (ôf′sīd′ *or* ŏf′sīd′) also **off•sides** (ôf′sīdz′ *or* ŏf′sīdz′) *adv. & adj.* **1.** In football, ahead of the line of scrimmage before a play begins. **2.** In some other sports, illegally ahead of the ball or puck.
off•spring (ôf′sprĭng′ *or* ŏf′sprĭng′) *n., pl.* **offspring. 1.** The young or descendants of a person, an animal, or a plant. **2.** A result or product: *His design for the garden was the offspring of much research.*
off-stage or **off•stage** (ôf′stāj′ *or* ŏf′stāj′) *adj.* Taking place in an area of a stage that is invisible to the audience: *an off-stage change of costume.* *—adv.* Away from the area of a stage that is visible to the audience: *She walked off-stage.*
off-the-rec•ord (ôf′*thə* rĕk′ərd *or* ŏf′*thə* rĕk′ərd) *adv. & adj.* Not for publication or acknowledgement: *The senator spoke off-the-record to the press. This story should be off-the-record.*
off-white (ôf′wīt′ *or* ŏf′wīt′) *n.* A grayish or yellowish white. **—off′-white′** *adv.*
oft (ôft *or* ŏft) *adv.* Often: *her oft-quoted poem.* [First written down before 725 in Old English.]
of•ten (ô′fən *or* ŏf′ən) *adv.* **of•ten•er, of•ten•est.** Frequently; many times.
of•ten•times (ô′fən tīmz′ *or* ŏf′ən tīmz′) also **oft•times** (ôf′tīmz′ *or* ŏf′tīmz′) *adv.* Often; frequently.
o•gle (ō′gəl *or* ô′gəl) *tr.v.* **o•gled, o•gling, o•gles.** To stare at (someone) in a flirtatious or overly attentive way. **—o′gler** *n.*
O•gle•thorpe (ō′gəl thôrp′), **James Edward.** 1696–1785. English soldier and philanthropist who secured a charter for Georgia (1732) as a refuge for unemployed debtors newly released from prison.
o•gre (ō′gər) *n.* **1.** In legends and fairy tales, a giant or monster that eats human beings. **2.** A person who is especially cruel, brutish, or feared. [First written down in 1786 in Modern English, probably ultimately from Latin *Orcus*, god of the underworld.]
oh (ō) *interj.* **1.** An expression used to show emotion, such as surprise, anger, or pain. **2.** An expression used to address a person directed: *Oh, waiter! Could we have a bill please?*
❑ *These sound alike:* **oh, O**[1] (exclamation), **owe** (be indebted).
OH *abbr.* An abbreviation of Ohio.
O. Hen•ry (ō hĕn′rē). William Sydney Porter.
O•hi•o (ō hī′ō). A state of the north-central United States west of Pennsylvania. It was admitted as the 17th state in 1863. Columbus is the capital and Cleveland the largest city. Population, 10,887,325. —See Note.
Ohio River. A river formed by the confluence of the Allegheny and Monongahela rivers in western Pennsylvania and flowing about 981 miles (1,578 kilometers) to the Mississippi River in southern Illinois.
ohm (ōm) *n.* A unit of electrical resistance, equal to the resistance of a conductor through which a current of one ampere flows when a potential difference of one volt is applied to it. [First written down in 1861 in Modern English and spelled *ohma*, after Georg Simon *Ohm* (1789–1854), German physicist.]
ohm•me•ter (ōm′mē′tər) *n.* An instrument that measures and indicates the resistance of an electrical conductor in ohms.
Ohm's law (ōmz) *n.* A law stating that the current in an electric circuit is equal to the voltage divided by the resistance.
–oid *suff.* A suffix that means like or resembling: *anthropoid.* —See Note.
oil (oil) *n.* **1.** Any of a large class of substances, including animal and vegetable fats as well as substances of mineral or synthetic origin, that are characteristically slippery, capable of being burned, liquid or easily melted, and incapable of mixing with water. **2.a.** Petroleum. **b.** A substance derived from petroleum, as a substance for lubricating machinery. **3.** A liquid that resembles an oil. **4.** Oil paint. **5.** A painting done in oil paint. *—tr.v.* **oiled, oil•ing, oils.** To lubricate, supply, cover, or polish with oil. [First written down before 1200 in Middle English and spelled *eoile*, from Greek *elaion*, from *elaia*, olive.]
oil•cloth (oil′klôth′ *or* oil′klŏth′) *n.* Cloth that has been coated with oil, clay, or paint to make it waterproof.
oil color *n.* Oil paint.
oil of vitriol *n.* Sulfuric acid.
oil paint *n.* A paint that is made with a drying oil.
oil painting *n.* **1.** A painting done in oil paints. **2.** The art or process of painting with oil paints.
oil palm *n.* An African palm tree having fruits resembling nuts that yield a yellowish oil used in making soaps, cosmetics, chocolate, and other products.
oil shale *n.* A dark-brown or black shale containing hydrocarbons yielding petroleum by distillation.
oil•skin (oil′skĭn′) *n.* **1.** Cloth treated with oil so that it is waterproof. **2.** A garment made of oilskin.
oil well *n.* A hole dug or drilled in the earth in order to obtain petroleum.
oil•y (oi′lē) *adj.* **oil•i•er, oil•i•est. 1.** Of or relating to oil: *an oily liquid.* **2.** Covered with, soaked in, or containing oil; greasy: *oily rags.* **3.** Unpleasantly smooth, as in manner or behavior; unctuous: *oily insincere compliments.* **—oil′i•ness** *n.*
oink (oingk) *n.* The characteristic grunting noise of a hog.
oint•ment (oint′mənt) *n.* A thick, often oily substance made to be rubbed on the skin as a medication or cosmetic; a salve. [First written down

Ohio

The state of **Ohio** gets its name from a Seneca name, meaning "beautiful river." The name was first used for the Allegheny and Ohio rivers, and the state was later named after these rivers.

Word Building: –oid

The basic meaning of the suffix **–oid** is "like" or "resembling." Words ending in **–oid** are generally adjectives but can also be nouns. Thus **humanoid** means "having human characteristics or form" (adjective sense) or "a being having human form" (noun sense). Nouns ending in **–oid** form adjectives by adding the suffix **–al: spheroid, spheroidal; trapezoid, trapezoidal.** The suffix **–oid** comes from the Greek suffix *–oeidēs*, from *eidos*, meaning "shape, form."

ă	pat	oi	boy
ā	pay	ou	out
âr	care	ŏŏ	took
ä	father	ōō	boot
ĕ	pet	ŭ	cut
ē	be	ûr	urge
ĭ	pit	th	thin
ī	pie	*th*	this
îr	pier	hw	whoop
ŏ	pot	zh	vision
ō	toe	ə	about
ô	paw	N	*French* bon

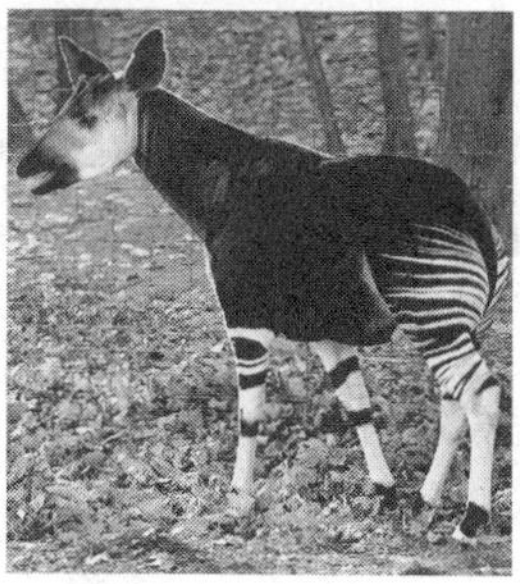

okapi

Georgia O'Keeffe

Oklahoma

The name **Oklahoma** comes from a Choctaw phrase that means "red people." The name "Territory of Oklahoma" was proposed by the Choctaw in 1866 as a substitute for the name **Indian Territory**. When the western section of Indian Territory was organized in 1890, it was called Oklahoma Territory, and this name was later given to the state, organized in 1907.

okra

about 1280 in Middle English and spelled *oinement*, from Latin *unguentum*.]

O•jib•wa (ō jĭb′wā′ *or* ō jĭb′wə) *n., pl.* **Ojibwa** or **O•jib•was. 1.** A member of a Native American people formerly inhabiting the regions around Lake Superior and now living in the northern Great Plains. **2.** The Algonquian language of the Ojibwa.

OK or **o•kay** (ō kā′) *Informal. adj.* All right; acceptable; fine: *The plan is OK with me.* —*adv.* Fairly well; acceptably: *He's doing OK.* —*n., pl.* **OK's** or **o•kays.** Approval; acceptance; agreement: *Get your parents' OK before we start on the trip.* —*tr.v.* **OK'd, OK'ing, OK's** or **o•kayed, o•kay•ing, o•kays.** To approve; agree to: *The governor OK'd the plans for the construction of a new highway.* [First written down in 1839 in American English, abbreviation of *oll korrect*, slang respelling of *all correct*.]

o•ka•pi (ō kä′pē) *n., pl.* **okapi** or **o•ka•pis.** An African mammal related to the giraffe, but having a shorter neck and a dark coat with white stripes on the legs and hindquarters.

o•kay (ō kā′) *adj., adv., n., & v.* Variant of **OK.**

O'Keeffe (ō kēf′), **Georgia.** 1887–1986. American artist known especially for her close-up paintings of flowers.

O•khotsk (ō kŏtsk′), **Sea of.** An arm of the northwest Pacific Ocean north of Japan on the northeast part of Russia.

O•ki•na•wa (ō′kĭ nä′wə *or* ō′kĭ nou′wə). An island group in the western Pacific Ocean southwest of Japan. **Okinawa,** the largest island in the group, was the scene of fierce World War II combat between Japanese and U.S. Army forces (April 1–June 21, 1945).

Okla. *abbr.* An abbreviation of Oklahoma.

O•kla•ho•ma (ō′klə hō′mə). A state of the south-central United States north of Texas. It was admitted as the 46th state in 1907. Oklahoma City is the capital and the largest city. Population, 3,157,604. —SEE NOTE.

Oklahoma City. The capital and largest city of Oklahoma, in the central part of the state. It became the capital in 1910. Population, 444,719.

o•kra (ō′krə) *n.* **1.** The narrow sticky seed pods of a tall tropical plant, used in soups or as a vegetable. **2.** The plant bearing such pods. —SEE NOTE at **goober.**

old (ōld) *adj.* **old•er, old•est. 1.a.** Having lived for a long time; of great age or advanced years: *a gnarled old pine tree.* **b.** Relatively advanced in age: *her older brothers and sisters.* **2.** Of a certain age: *She's 10 years old today.* **3.** In existence for a long time; made long ago: *an old part of the city.* **4.** Showing the effects of time or long use; worn: *an old coat.* **5.** Having the maturity or wisdom of age: *That boy is old for his years.* **6.** Of, belonging to, or associated with an earlier time or period of existence: *visiting his old neighborhood.* **7.** Often **Old.** Being the earlier or earliest of two or more related things, forms, or periods: *the Old Kingdom of ancient Egypt.* **8.** Established by time or tradition: *old customs.* **9.** Known for a long time and well-liked; dear: *an old friend.* **10.** Used as an intensive: *You can't use any old bit with that drill.* —*n.* **1.** A person or thing of a certain age: *That horse is a three-year-old.* **2.** Former times; yore: *in days of old.* [First written down before 725 in Old English and spelled *eald*.]

old country *n.* The native country of an immigrant.

old•en (ōl′dən) *adj.* Of or relating to a time long past; old or ancient: *olden days.*

Old English *n.* The English language from about 450 to 1150; Anglo-Saxon.

old-fash•ioned (ōld′făsh′ənd) *adj.* **1.** Belonging to or typical of an earlier time and no longer in style: *old-fashioned clothes.* **2.** Sticking to, preferring, or in keeping with ways or ideas of an earlier time: *strict old-fashioned grandparents.*

Old French *n.* The French language from about 800 to 1500.

Old Glory *n.* The flag of the United States.

old hand *n.* A person who is experienced; a veteran: *an old hand at politics.*

Old High German *n.* The language of southern Germany from about 850 to 1100.

Old Irish *n.* The Irish language from 725 to about 950.

Old Italian *n.* The Italian language until about 1550.

old maid *n.* **1.** *Offensive.* A woman, especially an older woman, who is not married. **2.** *Informal.* A person who is prim or fussy. **3.** A card game in which the player who holds a specified card at the end loses.

old man *n.* **1.** *Slang.* One's father. **2.** *Slang.* One's husband. **3.** A man who is in charge; a boss.

old master *n.* **1.** An outstanding European artist, especially a painter, chiefly of the period from about 1500 to the early 1700's. **2.** A work by such an artist.

Old Norse *n.* The North Germanic language until about 1350. The Scandinavian languages are descended from Old Norse.

Old North French *n.* The dialects of Old French spoken in northern France.

Old Provençal *n.* The Provençal language before 1550.

Old Testament *n.* The first of the two main divisions of the Christian Bible, corresponding to the Hebrew Scriptures.

old-time (ōld′tīm′) *adj.* Of, relating to, or typical of a time in the past.

old-tim•er (ōld′tī′mər) *n. Informal.* **1.** An elderly person. **2.** A person who has lived in a place or engaged in a certain kind of work or activity for a long time.

old-world also **Old-World** (ōld′wûrld′) *adj.* Of, relating to, or typical of the Old World, especially in earlier times: *an old-world bird; an old-world custom.*

Old World. The Eastern Hemisphere.

o•le•an•der (ō′lē ăn′dər *or* ō′lē ăn′dər) *n.* A poisonous shrub of warm regions, having slender evergreen leaves and showy clusters of fragrant white or reddish flowers. [First written down in 1548 in Modern English, probably from Late Latin *lorandrum*, alteration of Latin *rhododendron*.]

o•le•fin (ō′lə fĭn) *n.* Any of a class of hydrocarbon compounds, such as ethylene, that contain two atoms of hydrogen for each atom of carbon. They are unsaturated and have relatively high chemical activity.

o•le•o (ō′lē ō′) *n., pl.* **o•le•os.** Margarine.

o•le•o•res•in (ō′lē ō rĕz′ĭn) *n.* A naturally occurring mixture of an oil and a resin, as the substance exuded by pine trees.

ol•fac•to•ry (ŏl făk′tə rē *or* ōl făk′tə rē) *adj.* Of, relating to, or contributing to the sense of smell: *olfactory nerves.* [First written down in 1658 in Modern English, from Latin *olfacere*, to smell.]

ol•i•garch (ŏl′ĭ gärk′ *or* ō′lĭ gärk′) *n.* A member of an oligarchy.

ol•i•gar•chy (ŏl′ĭ gär′kē *or* ō′lĭ gär′kē) *n., pl.* **ol•i•gar•chies. 1.** A form of government in which power is exercised by a small group of people. **2.** The people forming such a group. **3.** A state governed by a few persons. [First written down in 1577 in Modern English and spelled *oligarchie*, from Greek *oligarkhia* : *oligos*, few + *arkhein*, to govern.] —**ol′i•gar′chic, ol′i•gar′chi•cal** *adj.*

Ol•i•go•cene (ŏl′ĭ gō sēn′) *adj.* Of, belonging to, or

being the geologic time of the third epoch of the Tertiary Period. During the Oligocene, the first apes appeared and modern mammals became dominant. See table at **geologic time.** *—n.* The Oligocene Epoch or its series of rocks.

ol•ive (ŏl′ĭv) *n.* **1.a.** The small, oval, greenish or blackish fruit of the Mediterranean region, having a single hard seed. Olives are eaten as a relish or pressed to extract olive oil. **b.** The tree bearing such fruit. **2.** A dull yellowish green. [First written down before 1200 in Middle English, from Greek *elaia.*]

olive branch *n.* **1.** A branch of an olive tree, regarded as a symbol of peace. **2.** An offer of peace.

olive drab *n.* **1.** A dull brownish or grayish olive color. **2.** Cloth of this color, often used in military uniforms.

olive oil *n.* Oil pressed from olives, used in salad dressings, for cooking, as an ingredient of soaps, and as an emollient.

Ol•mec (ŏl′mĕk *or* ōl′mĕk) *n., pl.* **Olmec** or **Ol•mecs.** A member of various Native American peoples of southeast Mexico whose civilization flourished before that of the Maya.

O•lym•pi•a[1] (ō lĭm′pē ə *or* ə lĭm′pē ə). A plain of southern Greece in the northwest Peleponnesus. It was the site of the ancient Olympic games. The statue of the Olympian Zeus was one of the Seven Wonders of the World.

O•lym•pi•a[2] (ō lĭm′pē ə *or* ə lĭm′pē ə). The capital of Washington, in the western part of the state on the southern end of Puget Sound southwest of Seattle. It was settled in 1845. Population, 33,840.

O•lym•pi•ad (ō lĭm′pē ad′) *n.* **1.** An interval of four years between celebrations of the Olympic games, by which the ancient Greeks reckoned dates. **2.** A celebration of the modern Olympic games.

O•lym•pi•an (ō lĭm′pē ən) *adj.* **1.** In Greek mythology, of or relating to the greater gods and goddesses who live on Mount Olympus. **2.** Majestic in manner: *Olympian pronouncements from the royal palace.* *—n.* **1.** In Greek mythology, one of the gods or goddesses who live on Mount Olympus. **2.** A contestant in the Olympic games.

O•lym•pic (ō lĭm′pĭk) *adj.* Of or relating to the Olympic games.

Olympic games *pl.n.* **1.** A modern international athletic competition held every four years in a different part of the world. The Olympic games are divided into summer and winter games that now alternate every two years. **2.** An ancient Greek festival of athletic competitions and contests in poetry and dancing, held every four years in Olympia in honor of the god Zeus.

O•lym•pics (ō lĭm′pĭks) *pl.n.* The Olympic games.

O•lym•pus (ə lĭm′pəs *or* ō lĭm′pəs). A mountain range of northern Greece near the Aegean coast. It rises to 9,570 feet (2,918.9 meters) at **Mount Olympus,** the home of the mythical Greek gods.

O•ma•ha[1] (ō′mə hô′ *or* ō′mə hä′) *n., pl.* **Omaha** or **O•ma•has. 1.** A member of a Native American people inhabiting northeast Nebraska. **2.** The Siouan language of the Omaha.

O•ma•ha[2] (ō′mə hô′ *or* ō′mə hä′). A city of eastern Nebraska on the Missouri River and the Iowa border. It was founded in 1854. Population, 335,795.

O•man (ō män′). Formerly **Mus•cat and Oman** (mŭs′kăt′ *or* mŭs′kət). A sultanate of the southeast Arabian Peninsula on the **Gulf of Oman,** an arm of the Arabian Sea. Muscat is the capital. Population, 891,000.

om•buds•man (ŏm′bŭdz′mən *or* ŏm′bo͝odz′mən) *n.* A man who investigates and resolves complaints, especially for a government. [First written down in 1959 in Modern English, from Swedish, from Old Norse *umbodhsmadhr,* deputy.]

o•me•ga (ō mĕg′ə *or* ō mē′gə) *n.* **1.** The 24th and last letter of the Greek alphabet, written Ω, ω. In English it is represented as long O or long *o*. **2.** The last of a series or group. [First written down about 1400 in Middle English, from Greek *ō mega,* large o.]

om•e•let (ŏm′ə lĭt *or* ŏm′lĭt) *n.* A dish of beaten eggs, cooked and often folded around a filling, as of cheese. [First written down in 1611 in Modern English, from Old French *amlette.*]

o•men (ō′mən) *n.* A thing or an event regarded as a sign of future good or bad luck. [First written down in 1582 in Modern English, from Latin *ōmen.*]

om•i•cron (ŏm′ĭ krŏn′ *or* ō′mĭ krŏn′) *n.* The 15th letter of the Greek alphabet, written O, o. In English it is represented as *O, o.* [First written down about 1400 in Middle English, from Greek *o mikron,* small o.]

om•i•nous (ŏm′ə nəs) *adj.* Being a sign of trouble, danger, or disaster; threatening: *ominous clouds.* **—om′i•nous•ly** *adv.* **—om′i•nous•ness** *n.*

o•mis•sion (ō mĭsh′ən) *n.* **1.** The act of omitting something or the state of having been omitted: *the omission of several letters from a word.* **2.** Something that has been omitted: *several omissions from the guest list.*

o•mit (ō mĭt′) *tr.v.* **o•mit•ted, o•mit•ting, o•mits. 1.** To leave out; fail to include or mention: *Omit unnecessary words.* **2.** To fail to do or take advantage of; pass over; neglect: *She omitted no opportunity to tell him how proud she was of him.* [First written down about 1422 in Middle English and spelled *ommitten,* from Latin *omittere.*]

omni– *pref.* A prefix that means all: *omnidirectional.* —SEE NOTE.

om•ni•bus (ŏm′nĭ bŭs′) *n.* **1.** A bus. **2.** A printed collection of the works of one author or of writings on related subjects. *—adj.* Including many different things: *an omnibus bill passed by Congress.* [First written down in 1829 in Modern English, from Latin *omnibus,* for everyone.]

om•ni•di•rec•tion•al (ŏm′nē dĭ rĕk′shə nəl *or* ŏm′nē dī rĕk′shə nəl) *adj.* Capable of transmitting or receiving signals in all directions: *an omnidirectional antenna.*

om•nip•o•tent (ŏm nĭp′ə tənt) *adj.* Having unlimited or universal power, authority, or force; all-powerful. *—n.* **Omnipotent.** God. **—om•nip′o•tence** *n.*

om•ni•pres•ent (ŏm′nĭ prĕz′ənt) *adj.* Present or everywhere at the same time. **—om′ni•pres′ence** *n.*

om•nis•cient (ŏm nĭsh′ənt) *adj.* Having total knowledge; knowing everything. *—n.* **Omniscient.** God. **—om•nis′cience** *n.*

om•ni•vore (ŏm′nə vôr′) *n.* An organism that eats both plant and animal food.

om•niv•o•rous (ŏm nĭv′ər əs) *adj.* **1.** Eating both plant and animal substances or products as food; eating all kinds of food: *Rats are omnivorous.* **2.** Taking in everything one can: *an omnivorous reader.* [First written down in 1656 in Modern English, from Latin *omnivorus* : *omni-,* all + *vorāre,* to devour.] **—om•niv′o•rous•ly** *adv.* **—om•niv′o•rous•ness** *n.*

Omsk (ômsk). A city of south-central Russia on the Irtysh River. It was founded in 1716. Population, 1,108,000.

on (ŏn *or* ôn) *prep.* **1.a.** Used to indicate position upon: *a plate on the table.* **b.** Used to indicate contact with or extent over: *a picture on the wall; a rash on my arm.* **c.** Used to indicate location at or along: *a house on the beach.* **d.** Used to indicate

olive

Word Building: omni–

The prefix **omni–** means "all." It comes from the Latin word *omnis,* also meaning "all." Because the meaning of **omni–** is so clear and easily recognizable, the prefix has long been used in English to make new words. For example, the meanings of words such as *omnipurpose* (all-purpose) and *omnitolerant* (tolerant of all things) are easy to guess, even without a definition. **Omni–** can be compared to the prefix **pan–,** which also means "all." **Pan–,** however, comes from Greek and is most commonly used in English in compounds with names of nationalities: **Pan-American.**

Usage: on

When you use **on** as an adverb attached to a verb, it should not be joined with *to* to form the single word **onto**: *move on to new subjects,* not *move onto new subjects.*

ă	**p**a**t**	oi	**boy**
ā	**pay**	ou	**out**
âr	**care**	o͝o	**took**
ä	**father**	o͞o	**boot**
ĕ	**pet**	ŭ	**cut**
ē	**be**	ûr	**urge**
ĭ	**pit**	th	**thin**
ī	**pie**	*th*	**this**
îr	**pier**	hw	**whoop**
ŏ	**pot**	zh	vi**si**on
ō	**toe**	ə	**a**bout
ô	**paw**	N	*French* bo**n**

Eugene O'Neill

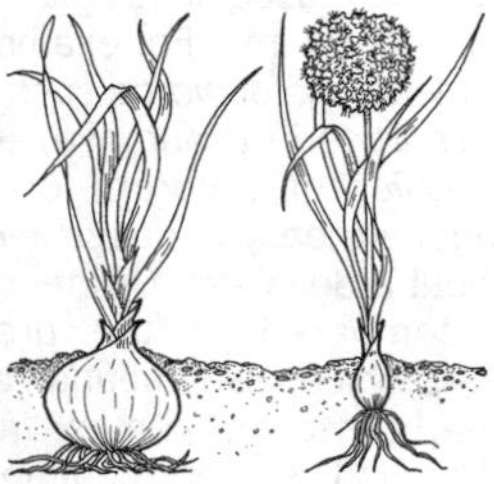

onion

Usage: only

Generally the adverb **only** should be used next to the word or words that it limits. Variation in the placement of **only** can change the meaning of the sentence, as the following examples show: *Dictators respect only force; they are not moved by words. Dictators only respect force; they do not worship it.*

nearness to: *a city on the frontier.* **e.** Used to indicate attachment to or suspension from: *beads on a string.* **2.** Used to indicate motion or direction toward or against: *throwing the books on the floor; the march on Washington.* **3.a.** Used to indicate occurrence during: *on Tuesday.* **b.** Used to indicate the occasion of: *On entering the room, she saw him.* **4.a.** Used to indicate the object affected by an action: *The spotlight fell on the actress.* **b.** Used to indicate the cause or agent of a specified action: *cut his foot on a piece of broken glass; talking on the phone.* **5.** Used to indicate source or basis: *made a decision on the facts.* **6.a.** Used to indicate the state or process of: *on leave; on fire.* **b.** Used to indicate the purpose of: *traveling on business.* **c.** Used to indicate a means of conveyance: *riding on a train.* **d.** Used to indicate availability by means of: *a doctor on call.* **e.** Used to indicate belonging to: *a doctor on the staff.* **f.** Used to indicate addition or repetition: *heaped error on error.* **7.** Concerning; about: *a book on carpentry.* **8.** *Informal.* In one's possession: *I don't have a cent on me.* **9.** At the expense of: *This meal is on me.* —*adv.* **1.** In or into a position of being attached to or covering something: *He pulled his coat on.* **2.** In the direction of something: *She was looking on when the ship came in.* **3.** Forward or ahead: *moving on to the next town.* **4.** In a continuous course: *We worked on quietly.* **5.** In or into action or operation: *Turn the television on.* **6.** In or at the present position or condition: *staying on; hang on.* —*adj.* **1.** Being in operation: *The television is on.* **2.a.** Planned; intended: *We have nothing on for the weekend.* **b.** Taking place or about to take place: *The party is on for tomorrow.* —***idioms.*** **on and off.** Intermittently. **on and on.** Without stopping; continuously. [First written down before 800 in Old English.] —SEE NOTE on page 679.

on•board (ŏn **bôrd′** *or* ôn **bôrd′**) *adj.* Carried aboard a vehicle or vessel. —**on•board′** *adv.*

once (wŭns) *adv.* **1.** One time only: *once a day.* **2.** Formerly: *I was a kid once too.* **3.** At any time; ever: *If he once gets angry, he'll hold a grudge.* —*n.* One single time or occurrence: *Let me go out just this once.* —*conj.* As soon as; if ever; when: *Once we get started, I'll show you what to do.* —*adj.* Having been formerly; former: *the once capital of the nation.* —***idioms.*** **at once. 1.** All at one time; simultaneously. **2.** Immediately; instantly. **once and for all.** Finally; conclusively. **once in a while.** Now and then. **once upon a time.** At some time in the past; long ago.

once-o•ver (**wŭns′**ō′vər) *n. Informal.* A quick but thorough look or going over.

on•com•ing (**ŏn′**kŭm′ĭng *or* **ôn′**kŭm′ĭng) *adj.* Coming nearer or toward a person or thing; approaching: *the oncoming storm.*

one (wŭn) *adj.* **1.** Being a single entity, unit, object, or living being; single; individual: *one dog and three cats.* **2.** Characterized by unity; undivided: *We are of one mind on this question.* **3.** Being a single person or thing that is contrasted with another or others: *He was at one end of the hall and I was at the other.* **4.** Being a particular person or thing: *late one night.* **5.** Occurring or existing indefinitely; some: *One day you will be famous.* **6.** *Informal.* Used as an intensive: *That is one fine mess you've gotten us into!* **7.** Being the same in kind: *three animals of one species.* —*n.* **1.** The number, written 1, that designates the first unit in a series. **2.** A single person or unit: *This is the one I like best.* —*pron.* **1.** A single person or thing: *one of my teammates.* **2.** An unspecified person; anyone: *One should be kind to one's neighbors.* —***idioms.*** **at one.** In accord or unity. **one and all.** Everyone. **one another.** Each other: *They talk to one another every day.* **one by one.** Individually in succession. [First written down about 700 in Old English and spelled *ān.*] —SEE NOTE at **he.**

❑ *These sound alike:* **one, won** (was victorious).

O•nei•da (ō **nī′**də) *n., pl.* **Oneida** or **O•nei•das. 1.** A member of a Native American people of central New York State. **2.** The Iroquoian language of the Oneida.

O'Neill (ō **nēl′**), **Eugene Gladstone.** 1888–1953. American playwright who won the 1936 Nobel Prize for literature.

one•ness (**wŭn′**nĭs) *n.* The condition of being one and the same.

on•er•ous (**ŏn′**ər əs *or* **ō′**nər əs) *adj.* Troublesome or oppressive; burdensome. —**on′er•ous•ly** *adv.* —**on′er•ous•ness** *n.*

one•self (wŭn **sĕlf′**) also **one's self** (wŭn **sĕlf′** *or* wŭnz **sĕlf′**) *pron.* **1.** One's own self: *reading about oneself in the newspaper.* **2.** One's normal or healthy condition: *feeling like oneself again.*

one-sid•ed (**wŭn′sī′**dĭd) *adj.* **1.** Favoring one side or group; partial; biased: *a one-sided version of the disagreement.* **2.** Having one side more prominent, active, or developed than another: *a one-sided game.*

one•time (**wŭn′**tīm′) *adj.* Former: *a onetime TV star.*

one-time (**wŭn′**tīm′) *adj.* Being so on a single occasion: *a one-time winner of the tournament.*

one-to-one (**wŭn′**tə **wŭn′**) *adj.* Matching each member of a class or set with only one member of another class or set.

one-track (**wŭn′**trăk′) *adj.* Narrowly limited to a single idea or way of thinking: *a one-track mind.*

one-way (**wŭn′wā′**) *adj.* Moving or permitting movement in one direction only: *a one-way street.*

on•go•ing (**ŏn′**gō′ĭng *or* **ôn′**gō′ĭng) *adj.* Going onward; continuing or progressing: *the ongoing development of the waterfront.*

on•ion (**ŭn′**yən) *n.* **1.** A plant bulb having a rounded shape and a strong odor and taste, widely grown as a vegetable. **2.** The plant that grows from such a bulb, having long narrow leaves. [First written down in 1130 in Middle English and spelled *ungeon*, from Latin *uniō.*]

on•ion•skin (**ŭn′**yən skĭn′) *n.* A thin, strong, translucent paper.

on•look•er (**ŏn′**lo͝ok′ər *or* **ôn′**lo͝ok′ər) *n.* A person who watches or looks on; a spectator.

on•ly (**ōn′**lē) *adj.* **1.** Alone in kind or class; sole: *our only reason for going; their only child.* **2.** Most suitable of all; excellent or superior: *the only real contenders for the championship.* —*adv.* **1.** Without anyone or anything else; alone: *We have only two sandwiches left.* **2.** Merely; just: *I only followed orders.* **3.** Exclusively; solely: *That train only runs on Sunday.* **4.a.** As recently as: *He called me only last month.* **b.** In the immediate past: *I only just saw her.* —*conj.* With the restriction that; but: *You may climb on the rocks, only be careful.* [First written down about 725 in Old English and spelled *ānlīc.*] —SEE NOTE.

on•o•mat•o•poe•ia (ŏn′ə măt′ə **pē′**ə) *n.* **1.** The forming of a word, such as *buzz*, that imitates the sound of the thing it refers to. **2.** The use of such words. —**on′o•mat′o•poe′ic** *adj.*

On•on•da•ga (ŏn′ən **dô′**gə *or* ŏn′ən **dä′**gə) *n., pl.* **Onondaga** or **On•on•da•gas. 1.** A member of a Native American people of central New York State. **2.** The Iroquoian language of the Onondaga. —**On′on•da′gan** *adj.*

on•rush (**ŏn′**rŭsh′ *or* **ôn′**rŭsh′) *n.* A forward or onward rush or flow.

on•rush•ing (**ŏn′**rŭsh′ĭng *or* **ôn′**rush′ĭng) *adj.*

Rushing or surging onward or forward: *the onrushing tide.*

on•set (ŏn′sĕt′ *or* ôn′sĕt′) *n.* **1.** A beginning; a start: *the onset of a disease.* **2.** An attack or assault.

on•shore (ŏn′shôr′ *or* ôn′shôr′) *adj.* **1.** Moving or directed toward the shore: *an onshore breeze.* **2.** Located on the shore: *an onshore patrol.* —*adv.* Toward the shore: *The wind shifted onshore.*

on•side (ŏn′sīd′ *or* ôn′sīd′) *adv. & adj.* In sports, in a position to receive the ball or puck legally.

on-site (ŏn′sīt′ *or* ôn′sīt′) *adj.* Done or located at the site where something takes place: *an on-site examination of an accident.*

on•slaught (ŏn′slôt′ *or* ôn′slôt′) *n.* A violent attack or charge: *the enemy onslaught.*

Ont. *abbr.* An abbreviation of Ontario.

On•tar•i•o (ŏn târ′ē ō′). A province of east-central Canada west of Quebec. It joined the Canadian confederation in 1867. Toronto is the capital and the largest city. Population, 8,625,107. —SEE NOTE.

Ontario, Lake. The smallest of the Great Lakes, between southeast Ontario, Canada, and northwest New York.

on•to (ŏn′to͞o *or* ôn′to͞o) *prep.* **1.** On top of; to a position on or upon: *The dog jumped onto the chair.* **2.** *Informal.* Aware of; knowing about: *I'm onto his tricks.* —SEE NOTE at **on.**

o•nus (ō′nəs) *n.* A difficult responsibility or necessity.

on•ward (ŏn′wərd *or* ôn′wərd) *adj.* Moving or tending forward: *the onward rush of the train.* —*adv.* Also **on•wards** (ŏn′wərdz. *or* ôn′wərdz). In a direction or toward a position that is ahead in space or time; forward: *The ship sailed onward through the storm.*

–onym *suff.* A suffix that means name; word: *antonym.*

on•yx (ŏn′ĭks) *n.* A type of quartz that occurs in bands of different colors, often black and white.

oo•dles (o͞od′lz) *pl.n. Informal.* A great amount or large number: *oodles of fun.*

ooze[1] (o͞oz) *v.* **oozed, ooz•ing, ooz•es.** —*intr.* **1.** To flow or leak slowly: *Blood oozed from the cut on her finger.* **2.** To disappear as if by slowly leaking or draining: *His courage oozed away.* —*tr.* To give off by flowing slowly: *trees oozing sticky sap.* [First written down before 1387 in Middle English and spelled *wosen*, from Old English *wōs*, juice.]

ooze[2] (o͞oz) *n.* Soft mud or slime, especially that covering the bottoms of oceans and lakes, composed chiefly of the remains of microscopic animals. [First written down before 800 in Old English and spelled *wāse.*]

ooz•y[1] (o͞o′zē) *adj.* **ooz•i•er, ooz•i•est.** Tending to ooze: *an oozy package of ice cream.*

ooz•y[2] (o͞o′zē) *adj.* **ooz•i•er, ooz•i•est.** Of or like ooze; wet and sticky: *oozy ground.*

op. or **Op.** *abbr.* An abbreviation of opus.

o•pac•i•ty (ō păs′ĭ tē) *n., pl.* **o•pac•i•ties.** The quality or condition of being opaque.

o•pal (ō′pəl) *n.* A mineral composed of a form of silica and having an opalescent translucent variety that is often used as a gem. [First written down in 1598 in Middle English and spelled *opale*, from Greek *opallios*, probably from Sanskrit *upalaḥ.*]

o•pal•es•cent (ō′pə lĕs′ənt) *adj.* Having the milky iridescent colors of an opal. —**o′pal•es′cence** *n.*

o•paque (ō pāk′) *adj.* **1.** Not letting light pass through; neither transparent nor translucent: *Metals and some minerals are opaque.* **2.** Not reflecting light; not shiny; dull: *an opaque finish on a surface.* **3.** Hard to understand; obscure. [First written down in 1440 in Middle English and spelled *opake*, shady, from Latin *opācus.*] —**o•paque′ly** *adv.* —**o•paque′ness** *n.*

op. cit. *abbr.* An abbreviation of opere citato (in the book or work already referred to).

ope (ōp) *tr. & intr.v.* **oped, op•ing, opes.** To open. Used chiefly in poetry.

OPEC (ō′pĕk′) *n.* An abbreviation of Organization of Petroleum Exporting Countries.

o•pen (ō′pən) *adj.* **1.** Providing entrance and exit; not shut or closed: *an open door.* **2.** Providing free passage or view; not blocked or enclosed: *open country.* **3.** Having no protecting or concealing cover; exposed: *an open wound.* **4.a.** Not sealed or tied: *an open package.* **b.** Unfolded; spread out: *an open book.* **5.** Having spaces, gaps, or intervals: *a coarse open weave.* **6.a.** Free to be used or participated in; accessible; not restricted: *an open competition.* **b.** Available or obtainable; not closed or decided: *The position is still open.* **7.a.** Liable; susceptible: *The issue is open to question.* **b.** Willing or ready to consider: *I'm open to suggestions.* **8.** Free from pretense or reserve; frank: *I'll be open with you about this.* **9.** Free from prejudice or settled belief: *keeping an open mind.* **10.** Not hidden or secret: *showing open defiance.* **11.** Ready to transact business: *The store is open today.* —*v.* **o•pened, o•pen•ing, o•pens.** —*tr.* **1.** To make no longer shut or fastened: *opened the window.* **2.** To remove the cover or wrapping from: *open the can.* **3.** To spread apart; unfold: *opened the map.* **4.** To begin; commence: *the topic that opens this chapter.* **5.** To begin the operation of: *They opened a new restaurant.* **6.** To make available for use: *The mayor opened the new bridge.* **7.** To make receptive, understanding, or sympathetic: *open one's heart.* —*intr.* **1.** To become open: *The door opened slowly.* **2.** To spread apart; unfold: *The tulips opened yesterday.* **3.a.** To begin; commence: *The meeting opened with her report.* **b.** To begin business or operation. **4.** To have an opening; give access: *Your room opens onto a terrace.* —*n.* **1.** An area of land or water that is not covered or concealed; an opening or a clearing. **2.** The outdoors: *camping in the open.* **3.** A condition free of secrecy or concealment: *bring the facts into the open.* [First written down about 725 in Old English.] —**o′pen•ly** *adv.* —**o′pen•ness** *n.*

o•pen-air (ō′pən âr′) *adj.* Outdoor: *an open-air concert.*

o•pen-and-shut (ō′pən ən shŭt′) *adj.* Presenting no difficulties; easily settled: *an open-and-shut case.*

o•pen-end•ed (ō′pən ĕn′dĭd) *adj.* **1.** Not held back by definite limits, restrictions, or structure: *an open-ended contract.* **2.** Allowing for free response or discussion: *an open-ended question.*

o•pen•er (ō′pə nər) *n.* **1.** A person or thing that opens, especially a device used to cut open cans or pry off bottle caps. **2.** The first act or event in a theatrical show or a series: *Our team won the opener.*

o•pen-eyed (ō′pən īd′) *adj.* **1.** Having the eyes wide open, as in surprise. **2.** Watchful and alert.

o•pen•hand•ed (ō′pən hăn′dĭd) *adj.* Giving freely; generous. —**o′pen•hand′ed•ly** *adv.* —**o′pen•hand′ed•ness** *n.*

o•pen•heart•ed (ō′pən här′tĭd) *adj.* **1.** Frank; candid. **2.** Kindly; generous. —**o′pen•heart′ed•ly** *adv.* —**o′pen•heart′ed•ness** *n.*

o•pen-hearth (ō′pən härth′) *adj.* **1.** Being a furnace that reflects heat onto the material being heated, used in the production of high-quality steel. **2.** Of or relating to steel produced in an open-hearth furnace.

open-heart surgery (ō′pən härt′) *n.* Surgery performed on a heart while it is stopped and its functions are being performed by external devices.

open house *n.* **1.** A party that may be attended by

Ontario

The name **Ontario** comes from a Huron word meaning "beautiful lake." It was first used for **Lake Ontario**, and the province was named after the lake.

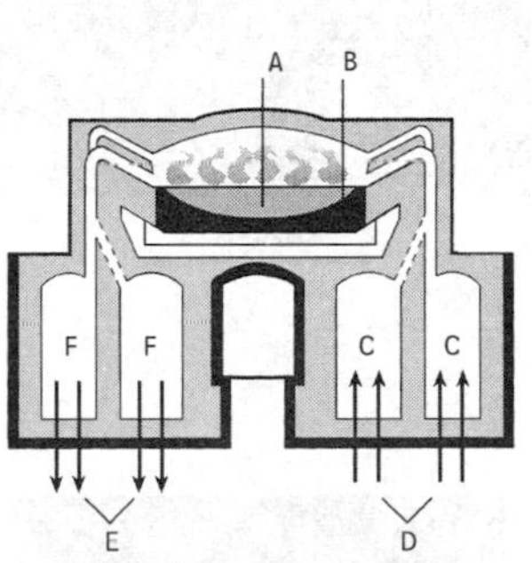

open-hearth

Open-hearth furnace
A. Molten pig iron
B. Hearth
C. Heating chamber (hot)
D. Preheated gas and air entry
E. Gas and air escape
F. Heating chamber (cold)

ă	pat	oi	boy
ā	pay	ou	out
âr	care	o͝o	took
ä	father	o͞o	boot
ĕ	pet	ŭ	cut
ē	be	ûr	urge
ĭ	pit	th	thin
ī	pie	*th*	this
îr	pier	hw	whoop
ŏ	pot	zh	vision
ō	toe	ə	about
ô	paw	N	*French* bon

openwork

opera[1]

opera glasses

opossum

all who wish to do so. **2.** An occasion in which a school or other institution is open for visiting and inspection. **3.** A period during which a house for sale is open to the public.

o•pen•ing (ō′pə nĭng) *n.* **1.** The act or the process of becoming open: *the opening of the wilderness to settlers.* **2.** An open space or clearing: *an opening in the woods.* **3.** The first period or stage of something: *at the opening of the story.* **4.** The first occasion of something, especially of a play or movie. **5.** A favorable opportunity: *He finally found an opening to tell his side of the story.* **6.** An unfilled job or position; a vacancy: *an opening on the teaching staff.*

open letter *n.* A letter on a subject of general interest, addressed to an individual but intended for general readership.

o•pen-mind•ed (ō′pən mīn′dĭd) *adj.* Willing to consider new ideas; unprejudiced. **—o′pen-mind′ed•ly** *adv.* **—o′pen-mind′ed•ness** *n.*

open shop *n.* A business or factory in which membership in a labor union is not a requirement for getting or holding a job.

o•pen•work (ō′pən wûrk′) *n.* Ornamental or structural work, as of embroidery or metal, made with a pattern of holes or open spaces in it.

op•er•a[1] (ŏp′ər ə *or* ŏp′rə) *n.* A theatrical performance in which the words of a play are sung with orchestral accompaniment. [First written down in 1644 in Modern English, from Italian, from Latin *opera,* work.]

o•pe•ra[2] (ō′pər ə *or* ŏp′ər ə) *n.* A plural of **opus.**

op•er•a•ble (ŏp′ər ə bəl *or* ŏp′rə bəl) *adj.* **1.** Being such that use or operation is possible: *a damaged but operable aircraft.* **2.** Possible to put into practice; practicable: *an operable plan.* **3.** Treatable by surgery: *an operable tumor.*

op•er•a glasses (ŏp′ər ə *or* ŏp′rə) *pl.n.* Small low-powered binoculars used especially in a theater.

opera house *n.* A theater designed chiefly for the production of operas.

op•er•ate (ŏp′ə rāt′) *v.* **op•er•at•ed, op•er•at•ing, op•er•ates.** *—intr.* **1.** To perform a function; work: *a machine that operates well.* **2.** To perform surgery. **3.** To produce an effect: *This drug operates quickly.* *—tr.* **1.** To control the functioning of; run: *operate a sewing machine.* **2.** To direct the affairs of; manage: *operate a business.* [First written down in 1606 in Modern English, from Latin *operārī,* from *opera,* work.]

op•er•at•ic (ŏp′ə răt′ĭk) *adj.* Of, related to, or like an opera: *an operatic aria.*

op•er•at•ing system (ŏp′ə rā′tĭng) *n. Computer Science.* A set of programs designed to control the hardware of a computer system.

op•er•a•tion (ŏp′ə rā′shən) *n.* **1.** The act or process of operating or functioning. **2.** The condition of operating or functioning: *a machine no longer in operation.* **3.** A surgical treatment for curing a disease, a disorder, or an injury. **4.** A mathematical process or action performed in a specific way according to specific rules: *Addition is a mathematical operation.* **5.** A military or naval action or series of actions.

op•er•a•tion•al (ŏp′ə rā′shə nəl) *adj.* **1.** Of or relating to an operation or a series of operations. **2.** Fit for proper functioning: *an operational aircraft.*

op•er•a•tive (ŏp′ər ə tĭv *or* ŏp′ə rā′tĭv *or* ŏp′rə tĭv) *adj.* **1.** In effect; in force: *a law of economics that is operative in the stock market.* **2.** Working correctly; efficient: *operative equipment.* **3.** Of, relating to, or resulting from a surgical operation. *—n.* **1.** A skilled worker. **2.** A secret agent; a spy. **3.** A private detective.

op•er•a•tor (ŏp′ə rā′tər) *n.* **1.** A person who operates a machine or device: *a switchboard operator.* **2.** A person who owns or manages a business or an industrial process: *a mine operator.* **3.** A symbol, such as a plus sign, that represents a mathematical operation. **4.** *Informal.* A person who accomplishes goals through shrewd or unfair methods.

o•per•cu•lum (ō pûr′kyə ləm) *n., pl.* **o•per•cu•la** (ō pûr′kyə lə) or **o•per•cu•lums.** A lid or flap covering an aperture, as the gill cover in some fishes or the horny shell cover in snails or other mollusks.

op•e•ret•ta (ŏp′ə rĕt′ə) *n.* A musical play that is similar to an opera but is lighter and more popular in subject and style and contains spoken dialogue.

oph•thal•mol•o•gist (ŏf′thəl mŏl′ə jĭst *or* ŏp′thəl mŏl′ə jĭst) *n.* A physician who specializes in ophthalmology; an eye doctor.

oph•thal•mol•o•gy (ŏf′thəl mŏl′ə jē *or* ŏp′thəl mŏl′ə jē) *n.* The branch of medicine that deals with the structure, functions, diseases, and treatment of the eye.

o•pi•ate (ō′pē ĭt *or* ō′pē āt′) *n.* **1.** A drug containing opium. **2.** A sedative or narcotic drug. *—adj.* **1.** Containing opium. **2.** Causing sleep or sedation.

o•pine (ō pīn′) *tr.v.* **o•pined, o•pin•ing, o•pines.** To hold or state as an opinion; think.

o•pin•ion (ə pĭn′yən) *n.* **1.** A belief or conclusion held with confidence but not supported by positive knowledge or proof. **2.** A judgment based on special knowledge and given by an expert. **3.** A judgment or estimate of the worth or value of a person or thing: *has a high opinion of us.* **4.** The prevailing feeling or view among a group: *public opinion.* [First written down before 1325 in Middle English, from Latin *opīniō.*]

o•pin•ion•at•ed (ə pĭn′yə nā′tĭd) *adj.* Holding stubbornly and often unreasonably to one's own opinions: *an opinionated critic.*

o•pi•um (ō′pē əm) *n.* A bitter addictive yellowish-brown drug prepared from the pods of a certain variety of poppy, and from which codeine, morphine, heroin, and other alkaloid drugs are derived.

o•pos•sum (ə pŏs′əm *or* pŏs′əm) *n., pl.* **opossum** or **o•pos•sums.** Any of various mammals that live mostly in trees, carry their young in a pouch, and have thick fur and a long tail. [First written down in 1610 in American English, of Virginia Algonquian origin.]

op•po•nent (ə pō′nənt) *n.* A person or group that opposes another in a battle, contest, controversy, or debate. *—adj.* Opposing: *opponent armies.* [First written down in 1588 in Modern English, from Latin *oppōnere,* to oppose.]

op•por•tune (ŏp′ər to͞on′ *or* ŏp′ər tyo͞on′) *adj.* **1.** Suited for a particular purpose: *an opportune suggestion.* **2.** Occurring at a time that is advantageous: *an opportune moment.* [First written down about 1408 in Middle English, from Latin *ob portum (veniēns),* (coming) toward port.]

op•por•tun•ist (ŏp′ər to͞o′nĭst *or* ŏp′ər tyo͞o′nĭst) *n.* A person who takes advantage of any opportunity to achieve a goal, usually with no regard for principles of right and wrong. **—op′por•tun′ism** *n.* **—op′por•tun•is′tic** *adj.*

op•por•tu•ni•ty (ŏp′ər to͞o′nĭ tē *or* ŏp′ər tyo͞o′nĭ tē) *n., pl.* **op•por•tu•ni•ties.** **1.** A time or an occasion that is suitable for a certain purpose; a favorable combination of circumstances. **2.** A chance for progress or advancement: *This scholarship presents you with the opportunity of a lifetime.*

op•pose (ə pōz′) *tr.v.* **op•posed, op•pos•ing, op•pos•es.** **1.** To offer resistance to or contend against: *oppose the enemy; oppose a plan of action.* **2.** To place in opposition; contrast: *The sports commentators opposed one football team to another.* [First written down about 1380 in Middle English and spelled *opposen*, to question, interrogate, from Old French *opposer*, from Latin *oppōnere*, to set against.] —**op•pos′er** *n.*

Synonyms: **oppose, fight, combat, contest, resist.** These verbs mean to try to overcome, defeat, or turn back someone or something. **Oppose** is the most general: *They opposed the plan to shut the factory down.* **Fight** and **combat** mean to oppose in an aggressive or active way: *Citizens must work together to fight corruption in government. The development of vaccines was an important step toward combating disease.* **Contest** means to call something into question and take an active stand against it: *The losing candidate contested the election.* **Resist** means to turn aside or counteract the action, effects, or force of someone or something: *The provinces united to resist the invasion.* Antonym: **support.**

---

op•po•site (ŏp′ə zĭt) *adj.* **1.** Placed or located directly across from something else or from each other: *the opposite sides of a house.* **2.** Moving or tending away from each other: *They went off in opposite directions.* **3.** Altogether different, as in nature or significance: *words with opposite meanings.* —*n.* A person or thing that is opposite or contrary to another: *What you're saying today is the exact opposite of what you were saying yesterday.* —*adv.* In an opposite position or positions: *He sat opposite from me.* —*prep.* **1.** Across from or facing: *Park your car opposite the school.* **2.** In a complementary dramatic role to: *She played opposite him.* —**op′po•site•ly** *adv.* —**op′po•site•ness** *n.*

op•po•si•tion (ŏp′ə zĭsh′ən) *n.* **1.a.** The act of opposing: *our vigorous opposition to the law.* **b.** The condition of being in conflict: *The opposition of that country to its neighbor has a long history.* **2.** Something that serves as an opposing force or obstacle: *The old dog was the burglar's only opposition.* **3.** A position or location opposite or opposed to another. **4. Opposition.** A political party or organization opposed to the group, party, or government in power. **5.** An arrangement in which the earth lies along a line segment that extends between the sun and another planet or the moon.

op•press (ə prĕs′) *tr.v.* **op•pressed, op•press•ing, op•press•es. 1.** To keep down by harsh and unjust treatment: *a people who were oppressed by tyranny.* **2.** To weigh heavily on: *Grief oppressed her.* [First written down about 1380 in Middle English and spelled *oppressen*, from Latin *opprimere*, to press against.] —**op•pres′sor** *n.*

op•pres•sion (ə prĕsh′ən) *n.* **1.** The act of oppressing or the condition of being oppressed. **2.** Something that oppresses: *the oppression of too many things to do.* **3.** A feeling of being heavily weighed down, either mentally or physically.

op•pres•sive (ə prĕs′ĭv) *adj.* **1.** Difficult to bear; harsh and unjust: *The government became more oppressive after the demonstration.* **2.** Causing physical or mental distress: *oppressive effects of bad weather; an oppressive silence.* —**op•pres′sive•ly** *adv.* —**op•pres′sive•ness** *n.*

op•pro•bri•ous (ə prō′brē əs) *adj.* **1.** Expressing reproach or scorn: *an opprobrious remark.* **2.** Bringing disgrace; shameful: *opprobrious behavior.* —**op•pro′bri•ous•ly** *adv.*

op•pro•bri•um (ə prō′brē əm) *n.* **1.** Disgrace arising from shameful conduct. **2.** A cause of shame or disgrace.

opt (ŏpt) *intr.v.* **opt•ed, opt•ing, opts.** To make a choice or decision.

op•tic (ŏp′tĭk) *adj.* Of or relating to the eye or vision. [First written down before 1425 in Middle English and spelled *optik*, from Greek *optikos*, from *optos*, visible.]

op•ti•cal (ŏp′tĭ kəl) *adj.* **1.** Of or relating to sight: *an optical defect.* **2.** Designed to assist sight: *optical instruments.* **3.** Of or relating to the science of optics. —**op′ti•cal•ly** *adv.*

optical fiber *n.* A flexible transparent fiber, usually made of glass or plastic, through which light can be transmitted by successive internal reflections.

optical scan•ner (skăn′ər) *n.* A device that converts images and text printed on paper into digital information that can be stored and processed by a computer.

op•ti•cian (ŏp tĭsh′ən) *n.* A person who makes or sells lenses, eyeglasses, or other optical equipment.

optic nerve *n.* The nerve that connects the retina of the eye to the brain.

op•tics (ŏp′tĭks) *n.* *(used with a singular verb).* The scientific study of light and vision.

op•ti•ma (ŏp′tə mə) *n.* A plural of **optimum.**

op•ti•mal (ŏp′tə məl) *adj.* Most favorable or desirable; optimum: *We picked the optimal time to leave for the airport.* —**op′ti•mal•ly** *adv.*

op•ti•mism (ŏp′tə mĭz′əm) *n.* **1.** A tendency to take a hopeful view of a situation or to expect the best possible outcome. **2.** The belief that this world is the best of all possible worlds. **3.** The belief that the universe is improving and that good will ultimately overcome evil. —**op′ti•mist** *n.* —**op′ti•mis′tic** *adj.* —**op′ti•mis′ti•cal•ly** *adv.*

op•ti•mize (ŏp′tə mīz′) *tr.v.* **op•ti•mized, op•ti•miz•ing, op•ti•miz•es. 1.** To make as perfect or effective as possible. **2.** To make the most of: *The general optimized his forces.*

op•ti•mum (ŏp′tə məm) *n., pl.* **op•ti•ma** (ŏp′tə-mə) or **op•ti•mums.** The point at which the condition, degree, or amount of something is the most favorable. —*adj.* Most favorable or advantageous; best: *optimum conditions for long-term investments.* [First written down in 1879 in Modern English, from Latin *optimum*, best.]

op•tion (ŏp′shən) *n.* **1.** The act of choosing; choice. See Synonyms at **choice. 2.** The power or right of choosing; freedom to choose: *had an option to buy the leased equipment.* **3.** Something chosen or available as a choice: *a stereo system that is an option on some new cars.* **4.** The exclusive right to buy or sell something within a specified time at a set price. [First written down in 1604 in Modern English, from Latin *optiō*.]

op•tion•al (ŏp′shə nəl) *adj.* Left to choice; not required or automatic: *an optional ingredient of the recipe.* —**op′tion•al•ly** *adv.*

op•tom•e•trist (ŏp tŏm′ĭ trĭst) *n.* A person who is trained and licensed to practice optometry.

op•tom•e•try (ŏp tŏm′ĭ trē) *n.* The profession of examining, measuring, and treating visual defects by means of corrective lenses or other methods in which the services of a physician are not needed.

op•u•lence (ŏp′yə ləns) *n.* **1.** Great wealth. **2.** A great amount or supply; an abundance.

op•u•lent (ŏp′yə lənt) *adj.* **1.** Having or showing great wealth; rich: *an opulent society.* **2.** Abundant; luxuriant: *opulent vegetation.* —**op′u•lent•ly** *adv.*

o•pus (ō′pəs) *n., pl.* **o•pe•ra** (ō′pər ə *or* ŏp′ər ə) or **o•pus•es.** An artistic work, especially a musical composition numbered to show the order of a composer's works.

or (ôr; ər *when unstressed*) *conj.* **1.a.** Used to indicate an alternative: *hot or cold.* **b.** Used to indicate the second of two alternatives, the first being preceded by *either* or *whether*: *I don't know whether to laugh or cry.* **2.** Used to indicate a synonymous or equivalent expression: *acrophobia, or fear of great heights.* **3.** Used to indicate uncertainty or indefiniteness: *He's called here three or four times already.* —SEE NOTE.

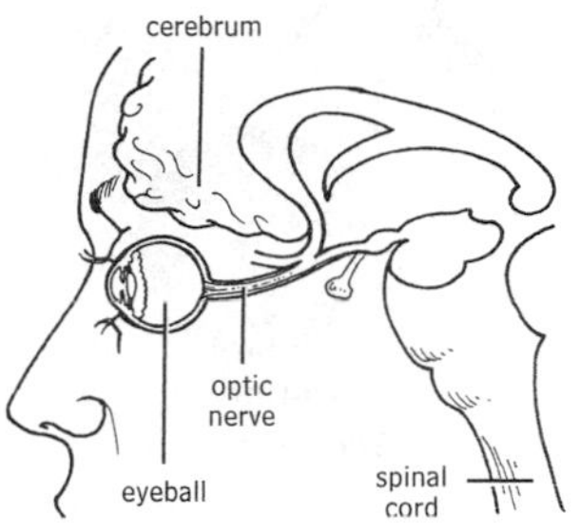

optic nerve

Usage: or

When you connect a series of singular elements by **or**, the verb used with them is singular: *Tom or Jack is coming.* When the elements are plural, the verb is plural: *Either the clowns or the monkeys make you laugh.* When the elements do not agree in number, it is best to find other ways to express what you are trying to say: *Either Tom is coming or his sisters are.*

ă	pat	oi	boy
ā	pay	ou	out
âr	care	ŏŏ	took
ä	father	ōō	boot
ĕ	pet	ŭ	cut
ē	be	ûr	urge
ĭ	pit	th	thin
ī	pie	*th*	this
îr	pier	hw	whoop
ŏ	pot	zh	vision
ō	toe	ə	about
ô	paw	N	*French* bon

orange
Sweet orange

orangutan

orchard
Harvesting an apple orchard

ă	pat	oi	boy
ā	pay	ou	out
âr	care	o͝o	took
ä	father	o͞o	boot
ĕ	pet	ŭ	cut
ē	be	ûr	urge
ĭ	pit	th	thin
ī	pie	*th*	this
îr	pier	hw	whoop
ŏ	pot	zh	vision
ō	toe	ə	about
ô	paw	N	*French* bon

❑ *These sound alike:* **or, oar** (wooden pole), **o'er** (over), **ore** (mineral).

OR *abbr.* An abbreviation of Oregon.

–or[1] *suff.* A suffix that means a person or thing that performs an action: *percolator.*

–or[2] *suff.* A suffix that means state, quality, or activity: *valor.*

or•a•cle (ôr′ə kəl *or* ŏr′ə kəl) *n.* **1.** In ancient Greece, a shrine for the worship and consultation of a god who revealed knowledge or disclosed the future. **2.** The person, such as a priestess, through whom a god is believed to respond to questions of worshipers. **3.** The response to a worshiper's question given by such a person, often in the form of a mysterious statement. **4.** A person considered to be a source of wise counsel or prophetic opinion.

❑ *These sound alike:* **oracle, auricle** (outer ear).

o•rac•u•lar (ô răk′yə lər) *adj.* **1.** Of, relating to, or being an oracle: *oracular sites in ancient Greece.* **2.** Resembling an oracle, especially: **a.** Solemnly prophetic. **b.** Having a difficult or hidden meaning; mysterious. **—o•rac′u•lar•ly** *adv.*

o•ral (ôr′əl) *adj.* **1.** Spoken rather than written: *an oral examination.* **2.** Of or relating to the mouth: *oral hygiene.* **3.** Used in or taken through the mouth: *an oral thermometer; oral medication.* **—o′ral•ly** *adv.*

❑ *These sound alike:* **oral, aural** (of the ear).

or•ange (ôr′ĭnj *or* ŏr′ĭnj) *n.* **1.** Any of several round fruits related to the grapefruit, lemon, and lime, having a reddish-yellow rind and juicy pulp divided into sections. **2.** Any of the trees that bear such fruit, having evergreen leaves and fragrant white flowers. **3.** Any of various colors between yellow and red. [First written down about 1380 in Middle English and spelled *orenge*, ultimately from Sanskrit *nāraṅgaḥ*.]

or•ange•ade (ôr′ĭn **jād′** *or* ŏr′ĭn **jād′**) *n.* A drink consisting of orange juice, sugar, and water.

o•rang•u•tan (ô **răng′**ə tăn′ *or* ə **răng′**ə tăn′) *n.* A large ape of the islands of Borneo and Sumatra, having long arms and a reddish-brown coat. [First written down in 1699 in Modern English and spelled *Orang-Outang*, from Malay *ōrang hūtan* : *ōrang*, man + *hūtan*, jungle.]

o•rate (ô **rāt′** *or* **ôr′**āt′) *intr.v.* **o•rat•ed, o•rat•ing, o•rates.** To speak publicly in a formal, pompous manner.

o•ra•tion (ô **rā′**shən) *n.* A formal address or speech, usually given on a special occasion.

or•a•tor (**ôr′**ə tər *or* **ŏr′**ə tər) *n.* **1.** A person who delivers an oration. **2.** A skilled public speaker.

or•a•to•ri•o (ôr′ə **tôr′**ē ō′ *or* ŏr′ə **tôr′**ē ō′) *n., pl.* **or•a•to•ri•os.** A large musical composition for voices and orchestra, telling a sacred story without costumes, scenery, or dramatic action.

or•a•to•ry[1] (**ôr′**ə tôr′ē *or* **ŏr′**ə tôr′ē) *n.* **1.** The art of public speaking. **2.** Skill or style in public speaking. [First written down before 1586 in Modern English, from Latin *ōrāre*, to speak.]

or•a•to•ry[2] (**ôr′**ə tôr′ē *or* **ŏr′**ə tôr′ē) *n., pl.* **or•a•to•ries.** A place for prayer, as a small private chapel. [First written down before 1325 in Middle English and spelled *oratorie*, from Latin *ōrāre*, to pray.]

orb (ôrb) *n.* **1.** A sphere or spherical object. **2.** Any of a series of transparent spheres that early astronomers thought revolved around the earth carrying the moon, planets, and stars. **3.** A globe surmounted by a cross, used as a ceremonial emblem of an emperor or other ruler.

or•bit (**ôr′**bĭt) *n.* **1.a.** The path of a celestial body or artificial satellite as it travels around another body. **b.** One complete revolution of such a body. **2.** The path of a body in a field of force surrounding another body; for example, the path of an electron in relation to the nucleus of an atom. **3.** Either of two bony depressions in the skull containing the eye and its associated structures. **4.** A range of activity, influence, or control: *a matter that was not within his orbit.* —*v.* **or•bit•ed, or•bit•ing, or•bits.** —*tr.* **1.** To put into orbit: *orbit a satellite.* **2.** To move in an orbit around: *The moon orbits the earth.* —*intr.* To move in an orbit. [First written down in 1392 in Middle English and spelled *orbita*, from Latin.] **—or′bit•al** *adj.*

or•chard (**ôr′**chərd) *n.* **1.** A piece of land on which trees are grown for their fruit. **2.** The trees grown on such land. [First written down before 899 in Old English and spelled *ortgeard*.]

or•ches•tra (**ôr′**kĭ strə) *n.* **1.a.** A large group of musicians who play together on various instruments, including string, woodwind, brass, and percussion instruments. **b.** The instruments played by such a group of musicians. **2.** The area in a theater where the musicians sit, in front of and below the stage. **3.a.** The main floor of a theater. **b.** The seats in the front part of the main floor of a theater. [First written down in 1606 in Modern English, from Greek *orkhēstra*, the space in front of the stage in Greek theaters where the chorus performed.] **—or•ches′tral** (ôr **kĕs′**trəl) *adj.*

or•ches•trate (**ôr′**kĭ strāt′) *tr.v.* **or•ches•trat•ed, or•ches•trat•ing, or•ches•trates.** To compose or arrange (music) for performance by an orchestra. **—or′ches•tra′tion** *n.*

or•chid (**ôr′**kĭd) *n.* **1.a.** Any of many related tropical plants having irregularly shaped flowers. **b.** The flower of such a plant. **2.** A light reddish purple.

or•dain (ôr **dān′**) *tr.v.* **or•dained, or•dain•ing, or•dains.** **1.** To appoint as a minister, priest, or rabbi. **2.** To order by means of superior authority; decree. **3.** To arrange or determine beforehand; predestine: *a destiny that was ordained by fate.* **—or•dain′ment** *n.*

or•deal (ôr **dēl′**) *n.* A difficult or painful experience, especially one that severely tests a person's character or endurance.

or•der (**ôr′**dər) *n.* **1.** A condition or an arrangement of parts or elements that permits proper functioning or appearance: *The soda machine is out of order. Let's put the room in order.* **2.** A sequence or arrangement of things one after the other: *alphabetical order.* **3.** A condition in society marked by peaceful obedience of laws and authority: *The police restored order after the disturbance.* **4.** A command or direction: *a court order.* **5.a.** A commission or an instruction to buy, sell, or supply something: *a government order for 10,000 blankets.* **b.** The thing supplied, bought, or sold: *ships orders postage paid.* **6.** A portion of food in a restaurant: *an order of fried potatoes.* **7.a.** The position and rank of an ordained minister or priest. **b.** The sacrament or ceremony of admission into the priesthood or ministry. Often used in the plural. **8.** A group of persons living according to a religious rule: *the Order of St. Benedict.* **9.** A social organization or club: *the Benevolent and Protective Order of Elks.* **10.** A group of persons upon whom a government has conferred honor for unusual service or merit, or an emblem of such honor. **11.a.** A class or kind: *Photography of that order is very rare.* **b.** Degree of quality or importance; rank; distinctive: *poetry of the highest order.* **12.** Any of several styles of classical architecture distinguished by the type of column employed: *Corinthian order.* **13.** A taxonomic group of plants or animals having certain similar characteristics, ranking between a class and a family. Rodents such as rats, mice, hamsters, and beavers belong to the same order. See table at **tax-**

onomy. —*v.* **or•dered, or•der•ing, or•ders.** —*tr.* **1.** To issue a command or an instruction to: *ordered the platoon to attention.* **2.** To give command or an instruction for: *ordered a review of the budget.* **3.** To give an order for; request to be supplied with: *order supplies for the camping trip.* **4.** To arrange in a sequence; put into an order: *We ordered the books according to subject.* —*intr.* To give an order; request that something be done or supplied. —***idioms.*** **in order that.** So that. **in order to.** With the intention to; so as to: *We built the shed in order to store our tools.* **in short order.** With no delay; quickly. **on order.** Requested but not yet delivered. **on the order of. 1.** Similar to; like: *a building on the order of a pyramid.* **2.** Approximately; about: *a building costing on the order of one million dollars.* **to order.** According to the buyer's wishes: *a coat made to order.* [First written down before 1200 in Middle English and spelled *ordre*, from Latin *ōrdō*.]

or•der•ly (ôr′dər lē) *adj.* **1.** Well arranged; neat: *an orderly kitchen.* **2.** Free from violence or disruption; peaceful: *our right to protest in an orderly manner.* —*n., pl.* **or•der•lies. 1.** An attendant who does nonmedical work in a hospital. **2.** A soldier assigned to a superior officer to carry messages and do other tasks. —**or′der•li•ness** *n.*

or•di•nal (ôr′dn əl) *adj.* Indicating a position in a series: *an ordinal rank of seventh.* —*n.* An ordinal number.

ordinal number *n.* A number indicating position in a series. The ordinal numbers are first, second, third, and so on.

or•di•nance (ôr′dn əns) *n.* A statute or regulation, especially one enacted by a city government.

or•di•nar•i•ly (ôr′dn âr′ə lē *or* ôr′dn ĕr′ə lē) *adv.* **1.** As a general rule; usually: *We ordinarily go shopping for groceries on Tuesday.* **2.** In the regular or usual manner: *ordinarily dressed.*

or•di•nar•y (ôr′dn ĕr′ē) *adj.* **1.** Commonly encountered; usual; normal: *The creek drained back to its ordinary size.* **2.** Average in rank or merit; of no exceptional degree or quality: *lived in an ordinary house.* —*n., pl.* **or•di•nar•ies.** The usual or normal condition or course of events: *Nothing out of the ordinary happened all week.* [First written down before 1402 in Middle English and spelled *ordenarye*, from Latin *ōrdinārius*, from *ōrdō*, order.]

or•di•nate (ôr′dn ĭt *or* ôr′dn āt′) *n.* In a system of plane Cartesian coordinates, the coordinate that represents the distance from a specified point to the *x*-axis, measured parallel to the *y*-axis.

or•di•na•tion (ôr′dn ā′shən) *n.* **1.** The ceremony by which a person is admitted to the ministry of a Christian church. **2.** The act of ordaining or the state of being ordained.

ord•nance (ôrd′nəns) *n.* **1.** Military supplies, including weapons, ammunition, and maintenance equipment. **2.** The branch of a military force that acquires, stores, maintains, and issues weapons, ammunition, and combat vehicles.

Or•do•vi•cian (ôr′də vĭsh′ən) *adj.* Of, belonging to, or being the geologic time of the second period of the Paleozoic Era. See table at **geologic time.** —*n.* The Ordovician Period or its series of rocks.

ore (ôr) *n.* A mineral or rock from which a valuable substance, especially a metal, can be extracted at a reasonable cost.

❑ *These sound alike:* **ore, oar** (wooden pole), **o'er** (over), **or** (alternative).

Ore. *abbr.* An abbreviation of Oregon.

o•reg•a•no (ə rĕg′ə nō′) *n.* An herb similar to marjoram, having spicy strong-tasting leaves used as flavoring for food. [First written down in 1771 in Modern English, from Greek *origanon*.]

Or•e•gon (ôr′ĭ gən *or* ŏr′ĭ gən). A state of the northwest United States north of California. It was admitted as the 33rd state in 1859. The **Oregon Territory** (1848–1859) included all of present-day Washington and Idaho. Salem is the capital and Portland the largest city. Population, 2,853,733. —See Note.

Oregon Trail. A historical trail through the western United States from the Middle West to what is now western Oregon. The trail was opened in 1842 and used by thousands of migrants before it was abandoned with the coming of the railroad.

O•res•tes (ô rĕs′tēz) *n.* In Greek mythology, the son of Agamemnon and Clytemnestra, who, with his sister Electra, avenges his father's murder by killing his mother and Aegisthus.

or•gan (ôr′gən) *n.* **1.** A musical instrument consisting of a number of pipes that sound tones when supplied with air and a keyboard that operates a mechanism controlling the flow of air to the pipes. **2.** Any of various instruments, such as an electric organ, that resemble a pipe organ, either in tone or mechanism. **3.** A distinct part of an organism, adapted for a particular function: *the stomach and other organs of digestion.* **4.** A body or agency that is part of a larger organization: *The FBI is an organ of the Department of Justice.* **5.** A periodical published by a political party, business firm, or other group.

or•gan•dy (ôr′gən dē) *n., pl.* **or•gan•dies.** A stiff transparent cloth of cotton or silk, used for dresses, curtains, and trim.

or•gan•elle (ôr′gə nĕl′) *n.* A structure or part of a cell having a special function, such as the cell wall in plants and algae or the mitochondrion in animal cells.

organ grinder *n.* A street musician who plays a hurdy-gurdy.

or•gan•ic (ôr găn′ĭk) *adj.* **1.** Of or affecting an organ or organs of the body: *an organic disease.* **2.** Of, relating to, or derived from living things: *decaying organic matter.* **3.** Using or produced with fertilizers of animal or vegetable matter and not with artificial fertilizers or pesticides: *organic farming.* **4.** Made up of related parts that work together as a unit: *an organic whole.* **5.** Of or being compounds containing carbon. —**or•gan′i•cal•ly** *adv.*

organic chemistry *n.* The chemistry of carbon compounds.

or•gan•ism (ôr′gə nĭz′əm) *n.* **1.** A living thing, such as a bacterium, a plant, or an animal. **2.** A group of related parts that work together as a whole: *the legislative organism.*

or•gan•ist (ôr′gə nĭst) *n.* A person who plays the organ.

or•gan•i•za•tion (ôr′gə nĭ zā′shən) *n.* **1.** The act of organizing: *planning the organization of a rally.* **2.** The condition of being organized: *a high degree of organization.* **3.** The way in which something is organized: *studying the organization of corporations.* **4.** A group of people united for some purpose or work: *a political organization.*

or•gan•ize (ôr′gə nīz′) *v.* **or•gan•ized, or•gan•iz•ing, or•gan•iz•es.** —*tr.* **1.** To put together or arrange in an orderly systematic way: *organize one's thoughts before speaking.* **2.** To form or establish in order to work together for a particular purpose: *organize a singing group.* **3.a.** To cause (employees) to form or join a labor union: *organize farm workers.* **b.** To cause the employees of (a factory or industry) to form or join a labor union: *organize the shoe industry.* —*intr.* To form or join a group, especially a labor union, devoted to a particular purpose. —**or′gan•iz′er** *n.*

or•gan•ized (ôr′gə nīzd′) *adj.* **1.** Functioning within a formal structure, as in the direction of activities:

orchestra
The Boston Symphony Orchestra

Oregon

The state of **Oregon** takes its name from the Oregon River, the former name of the **Columbia River**. The origin of the river's name, however, is uncertain. It is possible that the name was created when a 17th-century French mapmaker made a mistake in labeling that river, engraving a word onto the map that in English came to be *Oregon*.

organ

oriel

origami

oriole

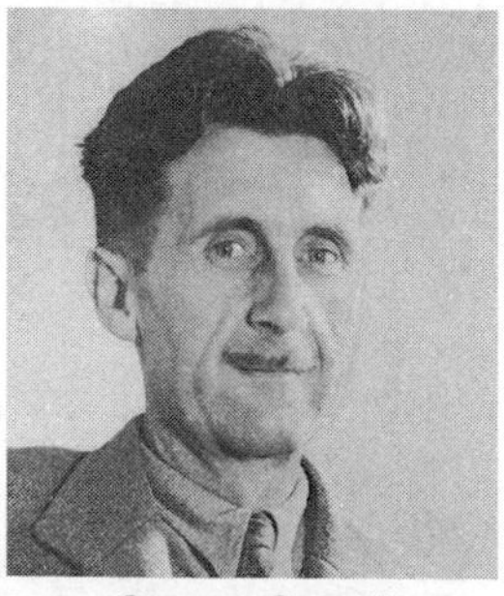
George Orwell

organized soccer games. **2.** Affiliated in an organization, especially a union: *organized labor.* **3.** Efficient and methodical: *an organized employee.*

or•gan•za (ôr găn′zə) *n.* A sheer stiff fabric, as of silk or synthetic material, used for evening dresses or trimmings.

or•gasm (ôr′găz′əm) *n.* The highest point of sexual excitement.

or•gy (ôr′jē) *n., pl.* **or•gies.** A wild, drunken, and often indecent party or celebration.

o•ri•el (ôr′ē əl) *n.* A projecting bay window, supported from below, as by a bracket.

o•ri•ent (ôr′ē ənt *or* ôr′ē ĕnt′) *n.* **Orient.** The countries of Asia, especially of eastern Asia. —*tr.v.* (ôr′ē ĕnt′). **or•i•ent•ed, or•i•ent•ing, or•i•ents. 1.** To set or place in a position relative to the points of the compass: *orient the swimming pool north and south.* **2.** To make (someone) familiar with a new situation: *a book designed to help orient new students.* [First written down about 1375 in Middle English, from Latin *oriēns*, rising.]

o•ri•en•tal (ôr′ē ĕn′tl) *adj.* Often **Oriental.** Of or relating to the countries of the Orient or their peoples or cultures.

or•i•en•tate (ôr′ē ĕn tāt′) *tr.v.* **or•i•en•tat•ed, or•i•en•tat•ing, or•i•en•tates.** To orient.

o•ri•en•ta•tion (ôr′ē ĕn tā′shən) *n.* **1.** Location or position with respect to the points of the compass: *the orientation of a rocket in space.* **2.** Awareness of the outside world in relation to one's self. **3.** Introductory instruction concerning a new situation: *attended an orientation for incoming students.*

or•i•fice (ôr′ə fĭs *or* ŏr′ə fĭs) *n.* An opening, especially into a cavity; a mouth or vent.

o•ri•ga•mi (ôr′ĭ gä′mē) *n., pl.* **o•ri•ga•mis.** The art or process, originating in Japan, of folding paper into shapes representing flowers or birds, for example.

or•i•gin (ôr′ə jĭn *or* ŏr′ə jĭn) *n.* **1.** The source or beginning of something: *the origin of a fire.* **2.** Ancestry: *people of Swedish origin.* **3.** The point at which the axes of a coordinate system intersect. [First written down before 1400 in Middle English and spelled *origine*, ancestry, from Latin *orīgō*.]

o•rig•i•nal (ə rĭj′ə nəl) *adj.* **1.** Existing before all others; first: *the original thirteen states of the Union.* **2.** Fresh and newly created; not copied or based on something else: *an original screenplay.* **3.** Frequently producing new ideas: *an original thinker.* **4.** Being the source from which a copy or translation is made: *an original painting; a book in the original Spanish.* —*n.* The first form of something from which varieties arise or are made: *Later models of the car retained many features of the original.*

o•rig•i•nal•i•ty (ə rĭj′ə năl′ĭ tē) *n., pl.* **o•rig•i•nal•i•ties. 1.** The quality of being original. **2.** The ability to act or think inventively.

o•rig•i•nal•ly (ə rĭj′ə nə lē) *adv.* **1.** At first; in the beginning: *I originally wanted to study French, but decided against it.* **2.** By origin: *I am originally from Oklahoma.* **3.** In a highly distinctive manner: *interpreted the piano piece most originally.*

o•rig•i•nate (ə rĭj′ə nāt′) *v.* **o•rig•i•nat•ed, o•rig•i•nat•ing, o•rig•i•nates.** —*tr.* To bring into being: *Who originated the practice of grading students?* —*intr.* To come into existence; begin: *The idea of mass production originated in the United States.* —**o•rig′i•na′tor** *n.*

O•ri•no•co (ôr′ə nō′kō). A river of Venezuela flowing more than 1,500 miles (2,414 kilometers), partly along the Colombia-Venezuela border, to the Atlantic Ocean.

o•ri•ole (ôr′ē ōl′) *n.* Any of various songbirds that have black and yellow or black and orange feathers in the male and that often build hanging nests. [First written down in 1776 in Modern English, from Latin *aureolus*, golden.]

O•ri•on (ō rī′ən) *n.* A constellation near the celestial equator containing several bright stars.

or•i•son (ôr′ĭ sən *or* ŏr′ĭ sən) *n.* A prayer.

Ork•ney Islands (ôrk′nē). A group of about 70 islands in the Atlantic Ocean and the North Sea off the northeast coast of Scotland. The islands became part of Scotland in 1472.

Or•lé•ans (ôr lā äɴ′). A city of north-central France on the Loire River south-southwest of Paris. The siege of Orléans by the English (1428–1429) was lifted by troops led by Joan of Arc. Population, 102,117.

Or•lon (ôr′lŏn′). A trademark for a synthetic fiber used in a variety of fabrics.

or•na•ment (ôr′nə mənt) *n.* Something that adorns or makes more attractive or beautiful; a decoration. —*tr.v.* (ôr′nə mĕnt′). **or•na•ment•ed, or•na•ment•ing, or•na•ments.** To supply or furnish with ornaments; decorate: *ornament a house for the holidays.* [First written down before 1200 in Middle English and spelled *urnement*, from Latin *ōrnāre*, to adorn.]

or•na•men•tal (ôr′nə mĕn′tl) *adj.* Serving to adorn or ornament: *ornamental jewelry; ornamental plants.*

or•na•men•ta•tion (ôr′nə mĕn tā′shən) *n.* **1.** The act of decorating or the state of being decorated. **2.** Something that ornaments or adorns; a decoration.

or•nate (ôr nāt′) *adj.* Having lavish or elaborate decorations: *an ornate palace.* [First written down before 1400 in Middle English, from Latin *ōrnātus*.] —**or•nate′ly** *adv.* —**or•nate′ness** *n.*

or•ner•y (ôr′nə rē) *adj.* **or•ner•i•er, or•ner•i•est.** Mean and stubborn: *an ornery old dog.*

or•ni•thol•o•gist (ôr′nə thŏl′ə jĭst) *n.* A scientist who specializes in ornithology.

or•ni•thol•o•gy (ôr′nə thŏl′ə jē) *n.* The scientific study of birds.

o•ro•tund (ôr′ə tŭnd′) *adj.* **1.** Full in sound; strong: *an orotund voice.* **2.** Pompous; bombastic: *orotund talk.*

or•phan (ôr′fən) *n.* A child whose parents are dead. —*tr.v.* **or•phaned, or•phan•ing, or•phans.** To make (a child) an orphan.

or•phan•age (ôr′fə nĭj) *n.* A public institution for the care and protection of children without parents.

Or•phe•us (ôr′fē əs) *n.* In Greek mythology, a renowned poet and musician who nearly rescues his wife Eurydice from the underworld, but fails when he looks back at her and breaks the command of Hades.

or•tho•clase (ôr′thə klās′ *or* ôr′thə klāz′) *n.* A type of feldspar found in igneous rock and used in making glass, ceramics, and abrasives.

or•tho•don•tia (ôr′thə dŏn′shə) *n.* Orthodontics. [First written down in 1849 in Modern English : Greek *orthos*, straight + Greek *odous*, tooth.]

or•tho•don•tics (ôr′thə dŏn′tĭks) *n.* *(used with a singular verb).* The dental practice of preventing and correcting abnormal position or alignment of the teeth, often by the use of braces. —**or′tho•don′tic** *adj.*

or•tho•don•tist (ôr′thə dŏn′tĭst) *n.* A dentist who specializes in orthodontics.

or•tho•dox (ôr′thə dŏks′) *adj.* **1.** Adhering to traditional or officially approved doctrines or beliefs: *orthodox theology.* **2. Orthodox. a.** Of or relating to the Eastern Orthodox Church. **b.** Of or relating to Orthodox Judaism. **3.** Adhering to what is commonly accepted, customary, or traditional: *orthodox views on education.* [First written down about 1454 in Middle English and spelled *ortodox* :

Greek *orthos*, straight, right + Greek *doxa*, opinion.]

Orthodox Church *n.* The Eastern Orthodox Church.

Orthodox Judaism *n.* The branch of Judaism that adheres to the Torah as interpreted in the Talmud.

or•tho•dox•y (ôr′thə dŏk′sē) *n., pl.* **or•tho•dox•ies. 1.** The quality or state of being orthodox. **2.** Adherence to traditional practice, custom, or belief.

or•thog•o•nal (ôr **thŏg′**ə nəl) *adj.* Of, containing, or forming right angles: *orthogonal lines.* [First written down in 1571 in Modern English : Greek *orthos*, straight + Greek *gōnia*, angle.]

or•tho•graph•ic (ôr′thə **grăf′**ĭk) *adj.* Of or relating to orthography. **—or′tho•graph′i•cal•ly** *adv.*

or•thog•ra•phy (ôr **thŏg′**rə fē) *n., pl.* **or•thog•ra•phies. 1.** The correct spelling of words. **2.** The study of spelling. **3.** A method of representing the sounds of language by letters or other symbols. [First written down in 1530 in Modern English and spelled *orthographie* : Greek *orthos*, straight, right + Greek *graphein*, to write.]

or•tho•pe•dics (ôr′thə **pē′**dĭks) *n. (used with a singular verb).* The branch of medicine that deals with the correction or treatment, by surgery or manipulation, of disorders or injuries of the bones, joints, and associated muscles. [First written down in 1853 in Modern English : Greek *orthos*, straight, right + Greek *paideia*, child-rearing.] **—or′tho•pe′dist** *n.*

Or•well (**ôr′**wĕl′), **George.** 1903–1950. British writer whose works include *Animal Farm* (1945).

–ory *suff.* A suffix that means: **1.** Of, relating to, or characterized by: *advisory.* **2.** A place or thing used for: *reformatory.*

o•ryx (**ôr′**ĭks *or* **ŏr′**ĭks) *n., pl.* **oryx** or **o•ryx•es.** Any of several antelopes of Africa and south Asia, having a dull coat with dark markings and long, sharp, slightly curved horns.

Os The symbol for the element **osmium.**

O•sage (**ō′**sāj′ *or* ō **sāj′**) *n., pl.* **Osage** or **O•sag•es. 1.** A member of a Native American people formerly living in Missouri and Kansas and now living in Oklahoma. **2.** The Siouan language of this people.

O•sa•ka (ō **sä′**kə). A city of southern Honshu, Japan, on **Osaka Bay,** an inlet of the Pacific Ocean. Population, 2,636,260.

os•cil•late (**ŏs′**ə lāt′) *intr.v.* **os•cil•lat•ed, os•cil•lat•ing, os•cil•lates. 1.** To swing back and forth with a steady rhythm: *a pendulum that oscillates.* **2.** To waver between two or more thoughts or courses of action; vacillate.

os•cil•la•tion (ŏs′ə **lā′**shən) *n.* **1.** The act or process of oscillating. **2.** A single cycle of motion or variation about a central position.

os•cil•la•tor (**ŏs′**ə lā′tər) *n.* Something that oscillates, especially a device that produces electromagnetic waves or an alternating current.

os•cil•lo•scope (ə **sĭl′**ə skōp′) *n.* An electronic instrument that produces a visual display on the screen of a cathode-ray tube representing oscillations of electric current and voltage.

–ose[1] *suff.* A suffix that forms adjectives and means having; full of: *grandiose; verbose.*

–ose[2] *suff.* A suffix that means carbohydrate: *fructose.*

o•sier (**ō′**zhər) *n.* **1.** Any of several willows having long, slender, flexible twigs used in making baskets and wicker furniture. **2.** A twig of such a willow.

O•si•ris (ō **sī′**rĭs) *n.* The ancient Egyptian god of the lower world and judge of the dead. He died and was resurrected annually.

–osis *suff.* A suffix that means: **1.** Condition; process: *osmosis.* **2.** Diseased condition: *tuberculosis.*

Os•lo (**ŏz′**lō *or* **ŏs′**lō). Formerly (1624–1925) **Chris•ti•a•ni•a** (krĭs′chē **ăn′**ē ə). The capital and largest city of Norway, in the southeast part of the country. It was founded in about 1050. Population, 448,747.

os•mi•um (**ŏz′**mē əm) *n. Symbol* **Os** A hard bluish-white metallic element. Osmium is the densest known element and is used for electric light filaments and phonograph needles. Atomic number 76. See table at **element.**

os•mo•sis (ŏz **mō′**sĭs *or* ŏs **mō′**sĭs) *n., pl.* **os•mo•ses** (ŏz **mō′**sēz *or* ŏs **mō′**sēz). **1.** A process in which fluids and substances dissolved in liquids pass through a membrane until all substances involved are present in equal concentrations on both sides of the membrane. **2.** The tendency of fluids to carry on this process. [First written down in 1854 in Modern English and spelled *osmose*, from *endosmose* : Greek *endo-*, within + Greek *ōsmos*, thrust, push.] **—os•mot′ic** (ŏz **mŏt′**ĭk *or* ŏs **mŏt′** ĭk) *adj.*

os•prey (**ŏs′**prē *or* **ŏs′**prā) *n., pl.* **os•preys.** A large hawk having blackish and white feathers and feeding chiefly on fish. [First written down before 1475 in Middle English and spelled *osprai*, from Medieval Latin *avis prede*, bird of prey.]

os•si•fy (**ŏs′**ə fī′) *v.* **os•si•fied, os•si•fy•ing, os•si•fies.** *—intr.* **1.** To change into bone; become bony. **2.** To become rigid or conventional: *His ideas ossified as he grew older. —tr.* **1.** To cause to change into bone. **2.** To cause to become rigid or conventional, as in thinking. **—os′si•fi•ca′tion** (ŏs′ə fĭ **kā′**shən) *n.*

os•ten•si•ble (ŏ **stĕn′**sə bəl) *adj.* Represented or appearing as such, but not actually so: *His ostensible purpose was charity, but his real goal was popularity.* **—os•ten′si•bly** *adv.*

os•ten•ta•tion (ŏs′tĕn **tā′**shən) *n.* Showy display meant to impress others. [First written down in 1436 in Middle English and spelled *ostentacione*, from Latin *ostendere*, to show.]

os•ten•ta•tious (ŏs′tĕn **tā′**shəs) *adj.* Characterized by or given to ostentation; pretentious: *an ostentatious party.* **—os′ten•ta′tious•ly** *adv.*

os•te•o•path (**ŏs′**tē ə păth′) *n.* A physician who practices osteopathy.

os•te•op•a•thy (ŏs′tē **ŏp′**ə thē) *n.* A form of medical practice that stresses the use of manipulation of bones and muscles, along with conventional medical and therapeutic procedures, to treat disease. [First written down in 1891 in American English : Greek *osteon*, bone + *-pathy*, treatment of disease.]

os•te•o•po•ro•sis (ŏs′tē ō pə **rō′**sĭs) *n.* A disease in which the bones become porous and fragile, occurring especially in older women.

os•tler (**ŏs′**lər) *n.* Variant of **hostler.**

ost•mark (**ôst′**märk′ *or* **ŏst′**märk′) *n.* A unit of currency formerly used in East Germany and worth 100 pfennigs.

os•tra•cism (**ŏs′**trə sĭz′əm) *n.* Banishment or exclusion from a group, organization, or society in general.

os•tra•cize (**ŏs′**trə sīz′) *tr.v.* **os•tra•cized, os•tra•ciz•ing, os•tra•ciz•es.** To banish or exclude from a group or from society. [First written down in 1649 in Modern English, from Greek *ostrakon*, shell, potsherd (from the potsherds used as ballots in voting for temporary banishment in ancient Greece).]

os•trich (**ŏs′**trĭch *or* **ôs′**trĭch) *n., pl.* **ostrich** or **os•trich•es.** A very large African bird having a small head, a long neck, and long legs. Ostriches cannot fly but can run very fast.

OT also **O.T.** *abbr.* An abbreviation of: **1.** Old Testament. **2.** Overtime.

oth•er (**ŭth′**ər) *adj.* **1.a.** Being the remaining one of two or more: *Let me look at the other shoe.* **b.** Being the remaining ones of several: *My other friends are away on vacation.* **2.** Different: *Any other kid would have run away.* **3.** Additional; extra:

oryx
Scimitar oryx

osprey

ostrich
Male Masai ostrich

ă	pat	oi	boy
ā	pay	ou	out
âr	care	ŏŏ	took
ä	father	ōō	boot
ĕ	pet	ŭ	cut
ē	be	ûr	urge
ĭ	pit	th	thin
ī	pie	*th*	this
îr	pier	hw	whoop
ŏ	pot	zh	vision
ō	toe	ə	about
ô	paw	N	*French* bon

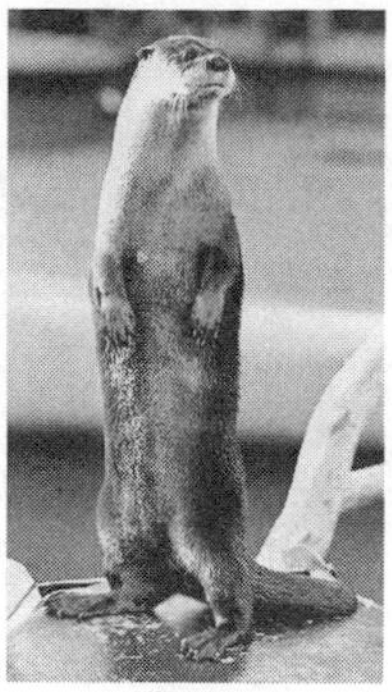

otter
North American river otter

Usage: **ought**

Usually you follow *ought to* with a verb, as in *We ought to go soon.* Sometimes *ought to* is used without a following verb if the meaning is clear: *Should we begin soon? Yes, we ought to.*

Word Building: **–ous**

The suffix **–ous**, which forms adjectives, has the basic meaning "having, full of, or characterized by." *Blusterous*, for example, means "full of or characterized by bluster." The suffix **–ous** can be traced back to the Latin adjective suffix *–ōsus*. Some English words ending in **–ous** that come from Latin adjectives ending in *–ōsus* are: **copious**, **dolorous**, **famous**, **generous**, and **glorious**. Adjectives ending in **–ous** often have related nouns ending in *–ousness* or *–osity*: **copiousness**, **generosity**.

ă	pat	oi	boy
ā	pay	ou	out
âr	care	ŏŏ	took
ä	father	ōō	boot
ĕ	pet	ŭ	cut
ē	be	ûr	urge
ĭ	pit	th	thin
ī	pie	*th*	this
îr	pier	hw	whoop
ŏ	pot	zh	vision
ō	toe	ə	about
ô	paw	N	*French* bon

I have no other shoes. **4.** Opposite or reverse: *Get in on the other side of the boat.* **5.** Alternate; second: *We play tennis every other day.* **6.** Just recent or past: *the other day.* —*n.* **1.a.** The remaining one of two or more: *One took a taxi, and the other walked home.* **b. others.** The remaining ones of several: *How are the others doing now that I'm gone?* **2.a.** A different person or thing: *one hurricane after the other.* **b.** An additional person or thing: *If these are only a few of the guests, how many others are you expecting?* —*pron.* A different or an additional person or thing: *Someone or other will apply for the job.* —*adv.* In another way; otherwise: *He found that he would never succeed other than by work.* [First written down before 899 in Old English and spelled *ōther*.]

oth•er•wise (ŭ*th*′ər wīz′) *adv.* **1.** In another way; differently: *She thought otherwise.* **2.** Under other circumstances: *Experiments make clear some things you might not understand otherwise.* **3.** In other respects: *Hitting the wrong note marred an otherwise perfect performance.* —*adj.* Other than supposed; different: *The truth of the matter was otherwise.*

Ot•ta•wa^1 (ŏt′ə wə) *n., pl.* **Ottawa** or **Ot•ta•was. 1.** A member of a Native American people formerly living along the northern shore of Lake Huron and now living in Ontario, Michigan, and Oklahoma. **2.** The dialect of Ojibwa spoken by the Ottawa.

Ot•ta•wa^2 (ŏt′ə wə). The capital of Canada, in southeast Ontario on the **Ottawa River** west of Montreal, Quebec. It was founded around 1827 and chosen as the capital of the United Provinces of Canada in 1858. Population, 295,163.

ot•ter (ŏt′ər) *n., pl.* **otter** or **ot•ters. 1.** Any of various mammals that resemble the weasel and live in or near water, having webbed feet and thick dark-brown fur. **2.** The fur of such a mammal. [First written down before 700 in Old English and spelled *otor*.]

ot•to•man (ŏt′ə mən) *n., pl.* **ot•to•mans. 1.** A sofa that has no arms or back. **2.** A cushioned footstool. **3.** A heavy fabric with a distinct crosswise rib. [First written down in 1806 in Modern English, from French *ottoman*, Turkish, from Arabic *'Uṯmān*, Osman I, founder of the Ottoman Empire.]

Ot•to•man (ŏt′ə mən) *n., pl.* **Ot•to•mans.** A Turk. —*adj.* **1.** Of or relating to the Ottoman Empire, or its people, language, or culture. **2.** Turkish.

Ottoman Empire. A vast Turkish empire of southwest Asia, northeast Africa, and southeast Europe. It was founded in the 13th century and dissolved after World War I.

Oua•ga•dou•gou (wä′gə **dōō′**gōō). The capital of Burkina Faso, in the central part of the country. It was founded in the late 11th century. Population, 345,150.

ouch (ouch) *interj.* An expression used in response to sudden pain.

ought (ôt) *aux.v.* **1.** To be required by duty or obligation: *We ought to clean up our room.* **2.** To be required by good judgment: *You ought to wear a raincoat.* **3.** To be expected as probable or likely: *Tonight ought to be a good night for looking at stars.* —SEE NOTE.

❑ *These sound alike:* **ought, aught**^{1} (anything), **aught**^{2} (zero).

ounce^1 (ouns) *n.* **1.a.** A unit of avoirdupois weight equal to 1/16 pound and containing 16 drams or 437.5 grains. See table at **measurement. b.** A unit of apothecary weight equal to 480 grains. **2.** A unit of volume or capacity used to measure liquids, equal to 1/16 pint and containing 8 fluid drams or 1.804 cubic inches. See table at **measurement. 3.** A tiny bit: *didn't get an ounce of respect.* [First written down before 1338 in Middle English and spelled *unce*, from Latin *uncia*.]

ounce^2 (ouns) *n.* The snow leopard. [First written down before 1300 in Middle English and spelled *unce*, from Greek *lunx*.]

our (our) *adj.* The possessive form of **we.** Of or belonging to us: *our friends; our house.*

❑ *These sound alike:* **our, hour** (time unit).

Our Father *n.* The Lord's Prayer.

ours (ourz) *pron. (used with a singular or plural verb).* The one or ones belonging to us: *If your car doesn't work, take ours.*

our•selves (our **sĕlvz′** *or* är **sĕlvz′**) *pron.* **1.** Those ones that are the same as us: **a.** Used as a direct object, an indirect object, or an object of a preposition to show that the action of the verb refers back to the subject: *We dressed ourselves. We made ourselves some breakfast. We brought it on ourselves.* **b.** Used to give emphasis: *We ourselves made the same discovery.* **2.** Our normal or healthy condition: *We were soon ourselves again after recovering from the flu.*

–ous *suff.* A suffix that means: **1.** Having; full of: *joyous.* **2.** Having a lower valence than the same element in a compound or ion named with an adjective ending in *-ie: ferrous.* —SEE NOTE.

oust (oust) *tr.v.* **oust•ed, oust•ing, ousts.** To eject; force out: *oust an official from office.* [First written down in 1420 in Middle English and spelled *ousten*, from Latin *obstāre*, to hinder.]

oust•er (**ous′**tər) *n.* An example of ousting or being ousted: *The committee member attributed his ouster to a small group of opponents.*

out (out) *adv.* **1.** Away or forth from inside: *going out of the house.* **2.** Away from the center or middle: *The searchers spread out.* **3.** From a container or source: *Pour the soda out.* **4.** Away from a usual place: *She stepped out for a minute.* **5.** Into or in the open air; outside: *They went out to play. It's raining out.* **6.a.** To depletion or extinction: *Supplies ran out.* **b.** To a finish or conclusion: *Play the game out.* **7.** Into being or view: *The moon came out.* **8.** Without inhibition; boldly: *Speak out.* **9.** Into the possession of someone else: *gave out free tickets.* **10.** Into disuse or an unfashionable status: *Bell-bottom pants went out a long time ago.* **11.** Not in consideration: *Going to the movies is out.* **12.** In or into a non-working condition: *The pump went out.* **13.** So as to be retired in baseball: *He grounded out to the shortstop.* —*adj.* **1.** No longer fashionable. **2.** In baseball, not allowed to continue to bat or be on base; retired. **3.** External; exterior: *the out surface of the wall.* —*prep.* **1.** Through; forth from: *The bird flew out the window.* **2.** Beyond or outside of: *Out this door is the garage.* —*n.* **1.** A person having no power or influence: *the outs versus the ins.* **2.** A means of escape: *Her lawyer discovered an ingenious out for her.* **3.** A play in which a batter or base runner is retired in baseball. [First written down before 725 in Old English and spelled *ūt*.]

out– *pref.* A prefix that means in a way that is better or greater: *outwit.* —SEE NOTE.

out•age (**ou′**tĭj) *n.* An interruption in an operation, such as electric power.

out-and-out (**out′**n **out′**) *adj.* Complete; utter: *an out-and-out liar.*

out•bid (out **bĭd′**) *tr.v.* **out•bid, out•bid•den** (out-**bĭd′**n) or **out•bid, out•bid•ding, out•bids.** To bid higher than: *He outbid his opponents.*

out•board (**out′**bôrd′) *adj.* **1.a.** Situated outside the hull of a vessel. **b.** Being away from the center line of the hull of a ship. **2.** Situated toward or nearer the end of a wing of an aircraft. **—out′board′** *adv.*

outboard motor *n.* A removable engine mounted at

the stern of a boat and linked to a propeller.

out•bound (**out′**bound′) *adj.* Outward bound; headed away: *the outbound train.*

out•break (**out′**brāk′) *n.* A sudden increase or eruption: *an outbreak of disease.*

out•build•ing (**out′**bĭl′dĭng) *n.* A building that is separate from a main building.

out•burst (**out′**bûrst′) *n.* A sudden violent display, as of activity or emotion: *an outburst of laughter.*

out•cast (**out′**kăst′) *n.* A person who has been excluded from a society or system. —*adj.* Cast out; driven out; rejected.

out•class (out **klăs′**) *tr.v.* **out•classed, out•class•ing, out•class•es.** To surpass or excel so as to be of a higher class: *She completely outclassed her opponents.*

out•come (**out′**kŭm′) *n.* A final result: *the outcome of an election.*

out•crop (**out′**krŏp′) *n.* An area of bedrock that is not covered with soil.

out•cry (**out′**krī′) *n., pl.* **out•cries. 1.** A loud cry or clamor. **2.** A strong protest: *The rise in prices provoked a public outcry.*

out•dat•ed (out **dā′**tĭd) *adj.* Out-of-date; old-fashioned: *outdated methods.*

out•did (out **dĭd′**) *v.* Past tense of **outdo.**

out•dis•tance (out **dĭs′**təns) *tr.v.* **out•dis•tanced, out•dis•tanc•ing, out•dis•tanc•es. 1.** To outrun, as in a long-distance race. **2.** To surpass by a wide margin.

out•do (out **do͞o′**) *tr.v.* **out•did** (out **dĭd′**), **out•done** (out **dŭn′**), **out•do•ing, out•does** (out **dŭz′**). To surpass in performance; do better than: *Our team outdid theirs in everything except canoeing.*

out•door (**out′**dôr′) *adj.* Located in, done in, or suitable for the outdoors: *an outdoor game; outdoor clothing.*

out•doors (out **dôrz′**) *adv.* In or into the open; outside: *eat outdoors.* —*n.* An area outside a house or building in the open air.

out•er (**ou′**tər) *adj.* **1.** Located on the outside; external: *outer garments; the outer wall of a fortress.* **2.** Farther from the center: *the outer limits of the universe.*

outer ear *n.* The external ear.

Out•er Mon•go•li•a (**ou′**tər mŏng **gō′**lē ə *or* **ou′**tər mŏng **gōl′**yə). Mongolia (sense 2).

out•er•most (**ou′**tər mōst′) *adj.* Most distant from the center.

outer space *n.* Space between the planets or between the stars.

out•field (**out′**fēld′) *n.* **1.** The playing area extending outward from a baseball diamond, divided into right, center, and left fields. **2.** The members of a baseball team playing in the outfield: *a team with a superb outfield.* **—out′field′er** *n.*

out•fit (**out′**fĭt′) *n.* **1.** A set of equipment for a particular purpose: *a diving outfit.* **2.** A set of clothing and accessories that go together: *She wore a tweed outfit.* **3.** A military unit, business organization, or other association: *an infantry outfit.* —*tr.v.* **out•fit•ted, out•fit•ting, out•fits.** To furnish with the necessary equipment or clothing: *outfit a ship for an expedition.* **—out′fit′ter** *n.*

out•flank (out **flăngk′**) *tr.v.* **out•flanked, out•flank•ing, out•flanks. 1.** To maneuver around and behind the flank of (an opposing force). **2.** To gain an advantage over (a competing business, for example).

out•flow (**out′**flō′) *n.* **1.** The act of flowing out. **2.** Something that flows out: *collect the outflow of the pipe in a barrel.* **3.** The amount flowing out.

out•fox (out **fŏks′**) *tr.v.* **out•foxed, out•fox•ing, out•fox•es.** To outwit; outsmart.

out•go•ing (**out′**gō′ĭng) *adj.* **1.** Leaving; departing: *an outgoing steamship.* **2.** To be taken out: *an outgoing order.* **3.** Friendly; sociable: *an outgoing person.*

out•grow (out **grō′**) *tr.v.* **out•grew** (out **gro͞o′**), **out•grown** (out **grōn′**), **out•grow•ing, out•grows. 1.** To grow too large for: *He outgrew his shoes.* **2.** To discard in the course of growing up or maturing: *She outgrew stuffed animals.* **3.** To grow larger than: *He outgrew his father.*

out•growth (**out′**grōth′) *n.* **1.** Something that grows out of something else: *an outgrowth on a tree branch.* **2.** A result or effect: *The choir's great performance is an outgrowth of many rehearsals.*

out•guess (out **gĕs′**) *tr.v.* **out•guessed, out•guess•ing, out•guess•es.** To guess or anticipate the plans or activities of.

out•house (**out′**hous′) *n.* **1.** A small structure separate from a main building that has a seat with a hole or holes in it built over a pit and is used as a toilet. **2.** An outbuilding.

out•ing (**ou′**tĭng) *n.* An excursion or walk outdoors for pleasure.

out•land•ish (out **lăn′**dĭsh) *adj.* Unconventional; strange: *outlandish clothes.*

out•last (out **lăst′**) *tr.v.* **out•last•ed, out•last•ing, out•lasts.** To last longer than: *Do those batteries really outlast the other brands?*

out•law (**out′**lô′) *n.* **1.** A person who defies the law; a declared criminal. **2.** A person who is excluded from normal legal protection. —*tr.v.* **out•lawed, out•law•ing, out•laws. 1.** To declare illegal: *outlawed the sale of fireworks.* **2.** To deprive (a person) of the protection of the law. [First written down about 1000 in Old English and spelled *ūtlaga,* from Old Norse *ūtlagi.*] —See Note.

out•lay (**out′**lā′) *n.* **1.** The act of spending money. **2.** The total amount spent: *The total outlay was $50.*

out•let (**out′**lĕt′) *n.* **1.** A passage or opening for letting something out; a vent. **2.** A means of releasing energies or desires: *Music was an outlet for her desire to express herself.* **3.** A store that sells the goods of a manufacturer: *a retail outlet.* **4.** An electric receptacle, especially one that is mounted in a wall, connected to a power line, and equipped with a socket for a plug.

out•line (**out′**līn′) *n.* **1.** A line forming the outer edge, limit, or boundary of something. **2.** A drawing that consists of only the outer edge of an object: *Trace an outline of California from the map.* **3.** A short summary, description, or account, usually arranged point by point: *an outline for a composition.* —*tr.v.* **out•lined, out•lin•ing, out•lines. 1.** To draw the outline of: *outline a picture before drawing in the details.* **2.** To give the main points of; summarize: *outline a plan.*

out•live (out **lĭv′**) *tr.v.* **out•lived, out•liv•ing, out•lives.** To live or last longer than: *Women tend to outlive men.*

out•look (**out′**lo͝ok′) *n.* **1.** A point of view; an attitude: *a happy outlook on life.* **2.** The probable situation or result; the expectation: *the weather outlook for tomorrow.* **3.** A place from which something can be viewed: *a photograph taken from an outlook high in the mountains.*

out•ly•ing (**out′**lī′ĭng) *adj.* Lying outside the limits or boundaries of a certain area: *factories being built in the outlying suburbs.*

out•ma•neu•ver (out′mə **no͞o′**vər *or* out′mə **nyo͞o′**vər) *tr.v.* **out•ma•neu•vered, out•ma•neu•ver•ing, out•ma•neu•vers. 1.** To overcome by more artful maneuvering. **2.** To excel in moving easily or skillfully: *The car outmaneuvers all others of its class.*

out•mod•ed (out **mō′**dĭd) *adj.* **1.** No longer in fash-

Word Building: out–

There are many words in English beginning with **out–**. In words such as **outbuilding**, **outcast**, **outpour**, and **outstanding**, **out–** has the same meaning as the adverb **out**. So an **outcast** is "one who is cast out," and one who is **outstanding** "stands out." But in other cases **out–** takes on the sense of doing better, being greater, or going beyond, as in **outdo**, **outnumber**, and **outrun**. Although **out–** can attach to nouns, adjectives, or verbs to form other nouns, adjectives, or verbs, it most frequently attaches to verbs: *outbowl*, *outcook*, *outride*, *outsing*.

outboard motor

Word History: outlaw

Most Americans will say our most famous **outlaw** is *Jesse James*. The word *outlaw* came into English from the Old Norse word *útlagi*, which became the word *ūtlaga* in late Old English and the word *outlawe* in Middle English. In the Viking Age, when Norsemen raided and settled in England, men who caused too much trouble for the community could be publicly declared outside the protection of the law and could even be killed with impunity. In a later age the *outlaw* Jesse James was shot because there was a bounty on him.

ion: *an outmoded style of dress.* **2.** No longer practical: *outmoded methods of production.*

out•num•ber (out nŭm′bər) *tr.v.* **out•num•bered, out•num•ber•ing, out•num•bers.** To be more numerous than; exceed in number.

out of *prep.* **1.a.** From within to the outside of: *got out of the car.* **b.** From a given condition: *came out of a deep sleep.* **c.** From a source, material, or cause: *made out of wood.* **2.a.** Beyond the limits or range of: *The car drove out of view.* **b.** Away from what is expected or usual: *I'm out of practice.* **3.** From among: *five out of six votes.* **4.** In or into a state of being without: *We've run out of paint.*

out-of-bounds (**out′**əv **boundz′**) *adv.* Beyond the designated boundaries or limits.

out-of-date (**out′**əv **dāt′**) *adj.* Outmoded; old-fashioned.

out-of-the-way (**out′**əv *thə* **wā′**) *adj.* Away from areas frequently visited; remote: *an out-of-the-way place.*

out•pa•tient (**out′**pā′shənt) *n.* A person who receives treatment at a hospital or clinic without staying overnight.

out•play (out **plā′**) *tr.v.* **out•played, out•play•ing, out•plays.** To surpass (one's opponent) in playing a game.

out•post (**out′**pōst′) *n.* **1.a.** A detachment of troops stationed at a distance from the main unit to prevent a surprise attack. **b.** The station occupied by such troops. **2.** A remote settlement: *an outpost in the wilderness.*

out•pour•ing (**out′**pôr′ĭng) *n.* **1.** The act of pouring out: *an outpouring of good wishes for the newlywed couple.* **2.** Something that pours out or is poured out; an outflow: *an outpouring of lava from the volcano.*

out•put (**out′**po͝ot′) *n.* **1.** An amount of something produced, especially during a given period of time: *the output of a mine.* **2.a.** The energy, power, or work produced by a system or device: *the output of an engine; the output of a loudspeaker.* **b.** The information that a computer produces by processing a given collection of data.

out•rage (**out′**rāj′) *n.* **1.** An extremely vicious or wicked act. **2.** An offensive or insulting action: *an outrage to common decency.* **3.** Great anger aroused by such an act: *public outrage over the incident.* —*tr.v.* **out•raged, out•rag•ing, out•rag•es.** **1.** To give offense to: *Such an act outrages everyone's sense of justice.* **2.** To make extremely angry or resentful: *We were outraged by his behavior.* [First written down before 1300 in Middle English, from Old French, from *outre*, beyond.]

out•ra•geous (out **rā′**jəs) *adj.* Exceeding all bounds of what is right or proper; immoral or offensive: *an outrageous crime; outrageous prices.* —**out•ra′geous•ly** *adv.*

out•ran (out **răn′**) *v.* Past of tense of **outrun.**

out•rank (out **răngk′**) *tr.v.* **out•ranked, out•rank•ing, out•ranks.** To rank above: *A colonel outranks a major.*

outrigger

out•rig•ger (**out′**rĭg′ər) *n.* **1.** A long thin float attached parallel to a seagoing canoe by projecting spars as a means of preventing it from capsizing. **2.** A canoe fitted with such a float.

out•right (**out′**rīt′ *or* **out′**rīt′) *adv.* **1.** Completely; unconditionally: *accepted her offer outright.* **2.** Openly; straight to one's face: *I decided to tell him the news outright.* **3.** Without delay; on the spot: *denied the accusation outright.* —*adj.* (**out′**rīt′). Complete; unconditional; out-and-out: *an outright gift; an outright lie.*

out•run (out **rŭn′**) *tr.v.* **out•ran** (out **răn′**), **out•run, out•run•ning, out•runs.** **1.** To run faster than: *outran all the opponents.* **2.** To escape from; elude: *They outran three policemen.* **3.** To go beyond; exceed: *Expenses are outrunning those of last year.*

out•sell (out **sĕl′**) *tr.v.* **out•sold** (out **sōld′**), **out•sell•ing, out•sells.** **1.** To sell faster or better than: *a new model car that has outsold all competition.* **2.** To sell more than: *That store consistently outsells the others.*

out•set (**out′**sĕt′) *n.* The beginning; the start.

out•shine (out **shīn′**) *tr.v.* **out•shone** (out **shōn′**), **out•shin•ing, out•shines.** **1.** To shine brighter than. **2.** To be or appear better than: *She outshines her opponents.*

out•side (out **sīd′** *or* **out′**sīd′) *n.* **1.** The outer surface; exterior: *the outside of a house.* **2.** The external or surface aspect: *On the outside, it's very attractive.* —*adj.* **1.** External; outer: *an outside door.* **2.** Not belonging to or originating in a certain group: *a dispute caused by outside influences.* **3.** Being beyond the limits of one's regular occupation: *His outside interests include music and photography.* **4.** Extreme; uttermost: *The outside estimate on that car is $5,000.* **5.** Slight; remote: *an outside possibility.* **6.** In baseball, passing on the side of home plate away from a batter: *an outside pitch.* —*adv.* On or to the external side: *stay outside.* —*prep.* **1.** On or to the outer side of: *going outside the house.* **2.** Beyond the limits of: *going outside the country.* **3.** Except: *no information outside the figures already given.* —***idiom.*** **at the outside.** At the most: *We'll be gone a week at the outside.*

outside of *prep.* Outside: *Outside of my window a bird is building a nest.*

out•sid•er (out **sī′**dər) *n.* A person who is not part of a certain group or activity: *a gate to prevent outsiders from entering.*

out•skirts (**out′**skûrts′) *pl.n.* The regions away from a central district; the surrounding areas: *on the outskirts of town.*

out•smart (out **smärt′**) *tr.v.* **out•smart•ed, out•smart•ing, out•smarts.** To gain the advantage over by cleverness; outwit.

out•sold (out **sōld′**) *v.* Past tense of **outsell.**

out•spo•ken (out **spō′**kən) *adj.* **1.** Spoken without reserve: *outspoken remarks.* **2.** Frank and bold in speech: *an outspoken politician.* —**out•spo′ken•ly** *adv.* —**out•spo′ken•ness** *n.*

out•stand•ing (out **stăn′**dĭng *or* **out′**stăn′dĭng) *adj.* **1.** Standing out among others; prominent; distinguished: *one of the outstanding artists of our age.* **2.** Exceptional; extraordinary: *an outstanding example of modern architecture.* **3.** Not settled or resolved: *outstanding debts.* —**out•stand′ing•ly** *adv.*

out•stretch (out **strĕch′**) *v.* **out•stretched, out•stretch•ing, out•stretch•es.** To spread or stretch out.

out•strip (out **strĭp′**) *tr.v.* **out•stripped, out•strip•ping, out•strips.** **1.** To leave behind; outrun. **2.** To surpass: *Grain came to outstrip cattle in economic importance.*

out•ward (**out′**wərd) *adj.* **1.** Of, located on, or moving toward the outside or exterior: *an outward flow of gold.* **2.** Visible on the surface: *an outward appearance of calm.* —*adv.* Also **outwards.** Away from the center. —**out′ward•ness** *n.*

out•ward•ly (**out′**wərd lē) *adv.* **1.** On the outside. **2.** In appearance: *He seemed outwardly healthy.*

out•wear (out **wâr′**) *tr.v.* **out•wore** (out **wôr′**), **out•worn** (out **wôrn′**), **out•wear•ing, out•wears.** To wear or last longer than: *These shoes will outwear all others.*

out•weigh (out **wā′**) *tr.v.* **out•weighed, out•weigh•ing, out•weighs.** **1.** To weigh more than: *outweighs everyone on the team.* **2.** To be of greater importance or significance than: *an objection that outweighs all others.*

out•wit (out wĭt′) *tr.v.* **out•wit•ted, out•wit•ting, out•wits.** To get the better of with cleverness or cunning; outsmart.

out•wore (out wôr′) *v.* Past tense of **outwear.**

out•work *tr.v.* **out•worked, out•work•ing, out•works.** To work better or faster than: *a mason who outworks everyone else on the job.*

out•worn (out wôrn′) *v.* Past participle of **outwear.**

o•va (ō′və) *n.* Plural of **ovum.**

o•val (ō′vəl) *adj.* Resembling an egg or an ellipse in shape: *an oval face.* —*n.* An oval figure, form, or structure. [First written down in 1577 in Modern English, from Latin *ōvum,* egg.]

o•var•i•an (ō vâr′ē ən) *adj.* Of or relating to an ovary.

o•va•ry (ō′və rē) *n., pl.* **o•va•ries. 1.** Either of the reproductive glands of female animals, producing egg cells and various hormones. **2.** A plant part at the base of the pistil of a flower, in which the seeds are formed.

o•va•tion (ō vā′shən) *n.* A loud and enthusiastic display of approval, usually in the form of applause. [First written down in 1533 in Modern English, from Latin *ovāre,* to rejoice.]

ov•en (ŭv′ən) *n.* An enclosed chamber used for baking, heating, or drying objects. [First written down about 725 in Old English and spelled *ofen.*]

ov•en•bird (ŭv′ən bûrd′) *n.* A small brownish North American bird that has a noisy call and builds a domed nest on the ground.

o•ver (ō′vər) *prep.* **1.** Above; higher than: *a sign over the door.* **2.** Above and across: *hop over the fence.* **3.** To the other side of: *walked over the bridge.* **4.** On the other side of: *a town over the border.* **5.** Upon the surface of: *a coat of varnish over the woodwork.* **6.** Through the extent of: *read over the report.* **7.** Throughout or during: *over the years.* **8.** Through the medium of: *talked over the telephone.* **9.** So as to cover: *put a shawl over her shoulders.* **10.** In excess of; more than: *over ten miles.* **11.** In superiority to: *won a victory over the rivals.* **12.** While engaged in or partaking of: *a chat over coffee.* **13.** On account of or with reference to: *an argument over methods.* —*adv.* **1.** Above the top: *climbed the fence and looked over.* **2.a.** Across to another or opposite side: *flying over to Europe.* **b.** Across the edge or brim: *The coffee spilled over.* **3.** To another place: *move the chair over here.* **4.** To one's home or office: *Let's invite them over.* **5.** Throughout an area: *We went all over.* **6.** To a different opinion or allegiance: *After a long talk, I won her over.* **7.** To a different person, condition, or title: *signing land over to a bank.* **8.** So as to be completely covered: *The river froze over.* **9.** From beginning to end; through: *thinking it over.* **10.a.** From an upright position: *knocked the vase over.* **b.** From an upward to an inverted or reversed position: *Turn the book over.* **11.a.** Again: *He had to do his homework over.* **b.** In repetition: *He sang the same song ten times over.* **12.** In addition or excess: *I have a dollar left over.* —*adj.* In excess: *My guess was $50 over.* [First written down before 725 in Old English and spelled *ofer.*]

o•ver•a•chieve (ō′vər ə chēv′) *intr.v.* **o•ver•a•chieved, o•ver•a•chiev•ing, o•ver•a•chieves.** To perform better than expected, especially in schoolwork. —**o′ver•a•chiev′er** *n.*

o•ver•act (ō′vər ăkt′) *v.* **o•ver•act•ed, o•ver•act•ing, o•ver•acts.** —*tr.* To act (a part, as in a play) with unnecessary exaggeration. —*intr.* To exaggerate a part; overplay.

o•ver•ac•tive (ō′vər ăk′tĭv) *adj.* Active to an excessive or abnormal degree.

o•ver•all (ō′vər ôl′) *adj.* **1.** Including everything; total: *the overall cost of the project.* **2.** Viewed as a whole; general: *The overall effect is very pleasing.*

o•ver•alls (ō′vər ôlz′) *pl.n.* Loose-fitting trousers with a top part that covers the chest, often worn over regular clothes to protect them from dirt.

over and above *prep.* In addition to: *We had to pay a special fee over and above the regular charge.*

over and over *adv.* Again and again; repeatedly.

o•ver•anx•ious (ō′vər ăngk′shəs *or* ō′vər ăng′shəs) *adj.* Too anxious: *He became overanxious about his examination.*

o•ver•arm (ō′vər ärm′) *adj.* Performed or executed with the arm raised above the shoulder; overhand: *an overarm throw.*

o•ver•ate (ō′vər āt′) *v.* Past tense of **overeat.**

o•ver•awe (ō′vər ô′) *tr.v.* **o•ver•awed, o•ver•aw•ing, o•ver•awes.** To overcome with awe.

o•ver•bal•ance (ō′vər băl′əns) *v.* **o•ver•bal•anced, o•ver•bal•anc•ing, o•ver•bal•anc•es.** —*tr.* To have greater weight or importance than. —*intr.* To lose one's balance.

o•ver•bear (ō′vər bâr′) *tr.v.* **o•ver•bore** (ō′vər-bôr′), **o•ver•borne** (ō′vər bôrn′), **o•ver•bear•ing, o•ver•bears. 1.** To crush or press down upon with physical force. **2.** To overcome, as if by superior weight or force.

o•ver•bear•ing (ō′vər bâr′ĭng) *adj.* Arrogant and domineering in manner: *an overbearing person.*

o•ver•board (ō′vər bôrd′) *adv.* Over the side of a boat: *He fell overboard.* —***idiom.*** **go overboard.** To show much enthusiasm.

o•ver•bore (ō′vər bôr′) *v.* Past tense of **overbear.**

o•ver•borne (ō′vər bôrn′) *v.* Past participle of **overbear.**

o•ver•bur•den (ō′vər bûr′dn) *tr.v.* **o•ver•bur•dened, o•ver•bur•den•ing, o•ver•bur•dens. 1.** To burden with excess weight. **2.** To burden with too much work, care, or responsibility.

o•ver•came (ō′vər kām′) *v.* Past tense of **overcome.**

o•ver•cast (ō′vər kăst′ *or* ō′vər kăst′) *adj.* **1.** Covered over, as with clouds or mist; cloudy. **2.** Gloomy; dark. **3.** Sewn with long overlying stitches in order to prevent raveling. —*n.* (ō′vər kăst′). **1.** A covering, as of mist or clouds. **2.** An overcast stitch. —*tr.v.* (ō′vər kăst′ *or* ō′vər kăst′). **o•ver•cast, o•ver•cast•ing, o•ver•casts.** To sew (a cloth edge) with long stitches that go over the edge to prevent raveling.

o•ver•charge (ō′vər chärj′) *tr.v.* **o•ver•charged, o•ver•charg•ing, o•ver•charg•es. 1.** To charge (someone) too high a price for something. **2.** To fill too full; overload. —*n.* (ō′vər chärj′). An excessive price or charge.

o•ver•coat (ō′vər kōt′) *n.* A heavy coat worn over regular clothing in cold weather.

o•ver•come (ō′vər kŭm′) *v.* **o•ver•came** (ō′vər-kām′), **o•ver•come, o•ver•com•ing, o•ver•comes.** —*tr.* **1.** To get the better of; surmount: *overcome a problem.* **2.** To defeat in a conflict or contest: *overcome a powerful team.* **3.** To affect deeply; overpower: *Fear overcame him.* —*intr.* To be victorious.

o•ver•con•fi•dent (ō′vər kŏn′fĭ dənt) *adj.* Excessively confident. —**o′ver•con′fi•dence** *n.* —**o′ver•con′fi•dent•ly** *adv.*

o•ver•crowd (ō′vər kroud′) *tr.v.* **o•ver•crowd•ed, o•ver•crowd•ing, o•ver•crowds.** To cause to be too crowded: *Having two games at once will overcrowd the gym.*

o•ver•de•vel•op (ō′vər dĭ vĕl′əp) *tr.v.* **o•ver•de•vel•oped, o•ver•de•vel•op•ing, o•ver•de•vel•ops. 1.** To develop to excess: *muscles overdeveloped by weightlifting.* **2.** To process (a photographic

ovenbird

overalls

ă	pat	oi	boy
ā	pay	ou	out
âr	care	o͝o	took
ä	father	o͞o	boot
ĕ	pet	ŭ	cut
ē	be	ûr	urge
ĭ	pit	th	thin
ī	pie	*th*	this
îr	pier	hw	whoop
ŏ	pot	zh	vision
ō	toe	ə	about
ô	paw	N	*French* bon

plate or film) too long or in too concentrated a solution. —**o′ver•de•vel′op•ment** *n.*

o•ver•do (ō′vər **dōō′**) *tr.v.* **o•ver•did** (ō′vər **dĭd′**), **o•ver•done** (ō′vər **dŭn′**), **o•ver•do•ing, o•ver•does** (ō′vər **dŭz′**). **1.** To do or use to excess; carry too far: *Don't overdo the workout or you will injure yourself.* **2.** Too cook too long or too much.

❑ *These sound alike:* **overdo, overdue** (unpaid).

o•ver•dose (**ō′**vər dōs′) *n.* An excessively large dose, as of medicine or a drug. —*intr.v.* (ō′vər **dōs′**). **o•ver•dosed, o•ver•dos•ing, o•ver•dos•es.** To take an overdose.

o•ver•draft (**ō′**vər drăft′) *n.* **1.** The act of overdrawing an account. **2.** The amount overdrawn.

o•ver•draw (ō′vər **drô′**) *tr.v.* **o•ver•drew** (ō′vər**drōō′**), **o•ver•drawn** (ō′vər **drôn′**), **o•ver•draw•ing, o•ver•draws. 1.** To withdraw more from (an account) than one has credit for. **2.** To exaggerate; overstate: *I overdrew the seriousness of the problem.*

o•ver•dress (ō′vər **drĕs′**) *tr. & intr.v.* **o•ver•dressed, o•ver•dress•ing, o•ver•dress•es.** To dress in too formal or fancy a way for the occasion.

o•ver•drew (ō′vər **drōō′**) *v.* Past tense of **overdraw.**

o•ver•drive (**ō′**vər drīv′) *n.* **1.** A gear in a motor vehicle transmission that permits cruising at high speed with improved fuel efficiency. **2.** A state of heightened concentration or activity.

o•ver•due (ō′vər **dōō′** *or* ō′vər **dyōō′**) *adj.* **1.** Unpaid after being due: *an overdue bill.* **2.** Later than scheduled or expected: *an overdue train.*

❑ *These sound alike:* **overdue, overdo** (do to excess).

o•ver•eat (ō′vər **ēt′**) *intr.v.* **o•ver•ate** (ō′vər **āt′**), **o•ver•eat•en** (ō′vər **ēt′**n), **o•ver•eat•ing, o•ver•eats.** To eat too much at one time.

o•ver•es•ti•mate (ō′vər **ĕs′**tə māt′) *tr.v.* **o•ver•es•ti•mat•ed, o•ver•es•ti•mat•ing, o•ver•es•ti•mates. 1.** To rate or estimate too highly. **2.** To value or esteem too highly. —*n.* An estimate that is or proves to be too high.

o•ver•ex•pose (ō′vər ĭk **spōz′**) *tr.v.* **o•ver•ex•posed, o•ver•ex•pos•ing, o•ver•ex•pos•es. 1.** To display or expose (someone or something) too much: *overexpose oneself to the sun.* **2.** To expose (a photographic film or plate) too long. —**o′ver•ex•po′sure** (ō′vər ĭk **spō′**zhər) *n.*

o•ver•flow (ō′vər **flō′**) *v.* **o•ver•flowed, o•ver•flow•ing, o•ver•flows.** —*intr.* **1.** To flow or run over the top, brim, or banks. **2.** To be filled beyond capacity: *Your cup is overflowing.* —*tr.* **1.** To flow over (the top, brim, or banks): *The river overflows its banks every year.* **2.** To flow over; flood: *The river overflowed the streets.* **3.** To fill beyond capacity: *The crowd overflowed the stands.* —*n.* (**ō′**vər flō′). **1.** The act of overflowing. **2.** An amount or excess that overflows.

o•ver•grow (ō′vər **grō′**) *v.* **o•ver•grew** (ō′vər**grōō′**), **o•ver•grown** (ō′vər **grōn′**), **o•ver•grow•ing, o•ver•grows.** —*tr.* To cover over with growth: *The bushes overgrew the pathway.* —*intr.* To grow too much or larger than normal.

o•ver•growth (**ō′**vər grōth′) *n.* A growth over or upon something: *an overgrowth of ivy on the house.*

o•ver•hand (**ō′**vər hănd′) also **o•ver•hand•ed** (ō′vər **hăn′**dĭd) *adj.* Performed with the hand brought forward and down from the level of the shoulder: *an overhand stroke.* —*adv.* In an overhand manner: *Throw the ball overhand.*

overhang

o•ver•hang (ō′vər **hăng′**) *v.* **o•ver•hung** (ō′vər**hŭng′**), **o•ver•hang•ing, o•ver•hangs.** —*tr.* To project, extend, or jut out over: *A room overhangs the back porch.* —*intr.* To jut out; extend. —*n.* (**ō′**vər hăng′). Something that overhangs; a projection.

o•ver•haul (ō′vər **hôl′** *or* **ō′**vər hôl′) *tr.v.* **o•ver•hauled, o•ver•haul•ing, o•ver•hauls. 1.** To inspect, examine, or review in order to repair or make changes: *overhaul a car.* **2.** To gain upon in a chase; overtake. —*n.* (**ō′**vər hôl′). The act or an example of overhauling.

o•ver•head (**ō′**vər hĕd′) *adj.* Located above the level of the head: *an overhead light.* —*n.* The operating expenses of a business, as for rent, insurance, taxes, and electricity, that cannot be charged to labor or materials. —*adv.* (ō′vər **hĕd′**). Above one's head: *birds darting overhead.*

o•ver•hear (ō′vər **hîr′**) *tr.v.* **o•ver•heard** (ō′vər**hûrd′**), **o•ver•hear•ing, o•ver•hears.** To hear without being addressed by the speaker; hear accidentally.

o•ver•heat (ō′vər **hēt′**) *tr. & intr.v.* **o•ver•heat•ed, o•ver•heat•ing, o•ver•heats.** To make or become excessively hot: *The furnace overheated the room. The engine overheated.*

o•ver•hung (ō′vər **hŭng′**) *v.* Past tense and past participle of **overhang.**

o•ver•joyed (ō′vər **joid′**) *adj.* Extremely happy or delighted.

o•ver•kill (**ō′**vər kĭl′) *n.* **1.** Destructive nuclear capacity exceeding the amount needed to destroy an enemy. **2.** An excess of what is necessary or appropriate: *Adding two posts to support the beam was overkill.*

o•ver•laid (ō′vər **lād′**) *v.* Past tense and past participle of **overlay.**

o•ver•land (**ō′**vər lănd′ *or* **ō′**vər lənd) *adv. & adj.* Over or across land: *He traveled overland. We made an overland journey.*

o•ver•lap (ō′vər **lăp′**) *v.* **o•ver•lapped, o•ver•lap•ping, o•ver•laps.** —*tr.* **1.** To lie over; cover part of: *The shingles overlap one another.* **2.** To have an area in common with: *The range of the moose overlaps that of the deer.* —*intr.* **1.** To lie or extend over and cover part of another thing: *The scales of a fish overlap, forming a protective covering.* **2.** To have some part in common with something; coincide partly: *Our vacations overlap.* —*n.* (**ō′**vər lăp′). **1.** A part that overlaps. **2.** An example of overlapping.

o•ver•lay (ō′vər **lā′**) *tr.v.* **o•ver•laid** (ō′vər **lād′**), **o•ver•lay•ing, o•ver•lays. 1.** To lay or spread over or on: *We overlay the table with a sheet.* **2.** To cover or decorate with a surface layer: *He overlaid the wood with silver.* —*n.* (**ō′**vər lā′). **1.** Something that is laid over or covers something else. **2.** A layer or decoration, such as gold leaf or wood veneer, applied to a surface.

o•ver•load (ō′vər **lōd′**) *tr.v.* **o•ver•load•ed, o•ver•load•ing, o•ver•loads.** To put too large a load in or on: *overload a bridge; overload an electric circuit.* —*n.* (**ō′**vər lōd′). An excessively large load.

o•ver•look (ō′vər **lo͝ok′**) *tr.v.* **o•ver•looked, o•ver•look•ing, o•ver•looks. 1.a.** To look over from a higher place: *We overlooked the valley from the cliff.* **b.** To provide a view of: *The restaurant overlooks the bay.* **2.** To fail to notice or consider: *overlook an important detail.* **3.** To ignore deliberately; disregard: *I overlooked her rude remark and kept on studying.* —*n.* (**ō′**vər lo͝ok′). An elevated place that provides a view of something.

o•ver•lord (**ō′**vər lôrd′) *n.* **1.** A lord having power or supremacy over other lords. **2.** A person who dominates others.

o•ver•ly (**ō′**vər lē) *adv.* Excessively; unduly; too: *an overly long movie.*

o•ver•much (ō′vər **mŭch′**) *adj.* Too much; excessive.

o•ver•night (**ō′**vər nīt′) *adj.* **1.** Lasting for a night: *an overnight trip.* **2.** For use over a single night: *an overnight bag.* **3.** Happening as if in a single night;

sudden: *an overnight success.* —*adv.* (ō′vər **nīt′**). **1.** During or for the length of a night: *Soak the beans overnight.* **2.** In or as if in the course of a night; suddenly: *became a sensation overnight.*

o•ver•paid (ō′vər **pād′**) *v.* Past tense and past participle of **overpay.**

o•ver•pass (**ō′**vər păs′) *n.* A roadway or bridge that crosses above another roadway or thoroughfare.

o•ver•pay (ō′vər **pā′**) *v.* **o•ver•paid** (ō′vər **pād′**), **o•ver•pay•ing, o•ver•pays.** —*tr.* **1.** To pay (someone) too much. **2.** To pay an amount in excess of (a sum due). —*intr.* To pay too much. —**o′ver•pay′ment** *n.*

o•ver•play (ō′vər **plā′**) *tr.v.* **o•ver•played, o•ver•play•ing, o•ver•plays.** To play (a dramatic role) in an exaggerated manner; overact.

o•ver•pop•u•late (ō′vər **pŏp′**yə lāt′) *tr.v.* **o•ver•pop•u•lat•ed, o•ver•pop•u•lat•ing, o•ver•pop•u•lates.** To fill (an area) with excessive population. —**o′ver•pop′u•la′tion** *n.*

o•ver•pow•er (ō′vər **pou′**ər) *tr.v.* **o•ver•pow•ered, o•ver•pow•er•ing, o•ver•pow•ers. 1.** To get the better of or conquer by superior force: *Our hitters overpowered their pitchers.* **2.** To affect strongly; overwhelm: *The heat overpowered the children and they had to leave the beach.*

o•ver•pow•er•ing (ō′vər **pou′**ər ĭng) *adj.* So strong as not to be withstood.

o•ver•pro•duce (ō′vər prə **dōōs′** *or* ō′vər prə **dyōōs′**) *tr.v.* **o•ver•pro•duced, o•ver•pro•duc•ing, o•ver•pro•duc•es.** To produce too much or too many of: *The factory overproduced that model of truck.* —**o′ver•pro•duc′tion** (ō′vər prə **dŭk′**shən) *n.*

o•ver•ran (ō′vər **răn′**) *v.* Past tense of **overrun.**

o•ver•rate (ō′vər **rāt′**) *tr.v.* **o•ver•rat•ed, o•ver•rat•ing, o•ver•rates.** To rate too highly.

o•ver•reach (ō′vər **rēch′**) *v.* **o•ver•reached, o•ver•reach•ing, o•ver•reach•es.** —*tr.* **1.** To extend or reach over or beyond: *The beam overreaches the post by an inch.* **2.** To miss by reaching too far or attempting too much: *overreach a goal.* **3.** To defeat (oneself) by going too far or doing too much. —*intr.* **1.** To reach or go too far. **2.** To defeat oneself by trying too hard. —**o′ver•reach′er** *n.*

o•ver•ride (ō′vər **rīd′**) *tr.v.* **o•ver•rode** (ō′vər **rōd′**), **o•ver•rid•den** (ō′vər **rĭd′**n), **o•ver•rid•ing, o•ver•rides. 1.** To ride across or beyond: *The cowboys overrode the border and turned back.* **2.** To trample on (something). **3.** To prevail over; surpass: *His concern for you overrides all other considerations.* **4.** To declare null and void; set aside: *The President's veto was overridden by Congress.*

o•ver•rule (ō′vər **rōōl′**) *tr.v.* **o•ver•ruled, o•ver•rul•ing, o•ver•rules. 1.** To decide or rule against: *The judge overruled the objection of the prosecutor.* **2.** To prevail over so as to change an opinion or action; influence: *His argument overruled his opponents, who agreed he was right.*

o•ver•run (ō′vər **rŭn′**) *tr.v.* **o•ver•ran** (ō′vər **răn′**), **o•ver•run, o•ver•run•ning, o•ver•runs. 1.** To invade and occupy: *The army overran the enemy trenches.* **2.** To spread or swarm over destructively: *Weeds overran the garden.* **3.** To overflow: *The river overran its banks.* **4.** To run or extend beyond; exceed: *The plane overran the runway.*

o•ver•saw (ō′vər **sô′**) *v.* Past tense of **oversee.**

o•ver•seas (ō′vər **sēz′** *or* **ō′**vər sēz′) *adv.* Across the sea; abroad: *He was sent overseas.* —*adj.* Of, from, or situated across the sea: *took an overseas flight to Asia.*

o•ver•see (ō′vər **sē′**) *tr.v.* **o•ver•saw** (ō′vər **sô′**), **o•ver•seen** (ō′vər **sēn′**), **o•ver•see•ing, o•ver•sees.** To watch over and direct; supervise.

o•ver•se•er (**ō′**vər sē′ər) *n.* A person who watches over and directs workers.

o•ver•shad•ow (ō′vər **shăd′**ō) *tr.v.* **o•ver•shad•owed, o•ver•shad•ow•ing, o•ver•shad•ows. 1.** To cast a shadow over. **2.** To make insignificant in comparison: *There are some writers who overshadow their contemporaries.*

o•ver•shoe (**ō′**vər shōō′) *n.* A shoe or boot worn over an ordinary shoe for protection from water, snow, or cold.

o•ver•shoot (ō′vər **shōōt′**) *v.* **o•ver•shot** (ō′vər**shŏt′**), **o•ver•shoot•ing, o•ver•shoots.** —*tr.* **1.** To shoot or pass over or beyond: *overshoot a target.* **2.** To fly beyond or past: *The plane overshot the runway.* —*intr.* To shoot or go too far.

o•ver•shot (**ō′**vər shŏt′) *adj.* **1.** Having an upper part that extends out past the lower part: *an overshot jaw.* **2.** Operated or turned by a stream of water that passes over its top: *an overshot water wheel.*

o•ver•sight (**ō′**vər sīt′) *n.* An omission or mistake that is not made on purpose.

o•ver•size (ō′vər **sīz′**) also **o•ver•sized** (ō′vər **sīzd′**) *adj.* Larger than the usual, expected, or required size: *an oversize sofa.*

o•ver•sleep (ō′vər **slēp′**) *intr.v.* **o•ver•slept** (ō′vər**slĕpt′**), **o•ver•sleep•ing, o•ver•sleeps.** To sleep longer than planned.

o•ver•state (ō′vər **stāt′**) *tr.v.* **o•ver•stat•ed, o•ver•stat•ing, o•ver•states.** To state too strongly; exaggerate: *Don't overstate the problem.* —**o′ver•state′ment** *n.*

o•ver•stay (ō′vər **stā′**) *tr.v.* **o•ver•stayed, o•ver•stay•ing, o•ver•stays.** To stay past an expected duration of: *He overstayed his welcome.*

o•ver•step (ō′vər **stĕp′**) *tr.v.* **o•ver•stepped, o•ver•step•ping, o•ver•steps.** To go beyond (a limit or bound): *She overstepped the rules.*

o•ver•stock (ō′vər **stŏk′**) *tr.v.* **o•ver•stocked, o•ver•stock•ing, o•ver•stocks.** To stock with more of (something) than is necessary or desirable. —*n.* (**ō′**vər stŏk′). An excessive supply.

o•ver•sup•ply (**ō′**vər sə plī′) *n., pl.* **o•ver•sup•plies.** A supply in excess of what is required. —*tr.v.* (ō′vər sə **plī′**). **o•ver•sup•plied, o•ver•sup•ply•ing, o•ver•sup•plies.** To supply in excess.

o•vert (ō **vûrt′** *or* **ō′**vûrt′) *adj.* Not concealed or hidden; open: *an overt act of war.* [First written down about 1330 in Middle English, from Old French *overt*, opened, from *ovrir*, to open.] —**o•vert′ly** *adv.*

o•ver•take (ō′vər **tāk′**) *tr.v.* **o•ver•took** (ō′vər**tōōk′**), **o•ver•tak•en** (ō′vər **tā′**kən), **o•ver•tak•ing, o•ver•takes. 1.** To catch up with: *We overtook the other hikers on the mountain road.* **2.** To pass after catching up with: *The car overtook him on the last lap.* **3.** To come upon unexpectedly: *A violent storm overtook him on the road to Cambridge.*

o•ver•tax (ō′vər **tăks′**) *tr.v.* **o•ver•taxed, o•ver•tax•ing, o•ver•tax•es. 1.** To impose an excessive tax or taxes on. **2.** To subject to an excessive burden or strain: *The long drive overtaxed us, and we spent a day recovering.* —**o′ver•tax•a′tion** *n.*

o•ver•throw (ō′vər **thrō′**) *tr.v.* **o•ver•threw** (ō′vər**thrōō′**), **o•ver•thrown** (ō′vər **thrōn′**), **o•ver•throw•ing, o•ver•throws. 1.** To throw over; overturn: *overthrow a table.* **2.** To bring about the downfall or destruction of: *overthrow the government.* **3.** To throw a ball beyond (an intended mark): *She overthrew first base.* —*n.* (**ō′**vər thrō′). **1.** The downfall or destruction, as of a government. **2.** The act of throwing a ball beyond an intended mark.

o•ver•time (**ō′**vər tīm′) *n.* **1.** Time worked in addition to regular working hours. **2.** Payment for this

overpass

ă	pat	oi	boy
ā	pay	ou	out
âr	care	ŏŏ	took
ä	father	ōō	boot
ŏ	pot	ŭ	cut
ē	be	ûr	urge
ĭ	pit	th	thin
ī	pie	*th*	this
îr	pier	hw	whoop
ŏ	pot	zh	vision
ō	toe	ə	about
ô	paw	N	*French* bon

Jesse Owens
Photographed at the 1936 Summer Olympics in Berlin, Germany

owl
Snowy owl

ox

additional time worked. **3.** A period in a sports contest added after the set time limit has passed. *—adv.* Beyond an established time limit, such as working hours: *work overtime.*

o•ver•tone (ō′vər tōn′) *n.* **1.** Any of the pure tones that sound along with a basic tone and give it its characteristic timbre; a harmonic. **2.** An accompanying effect; a suggestion or an implication: *The ambassador's remarks were full of ominous overtones.*

o•ver•took (ō′vər **to͝ok′**) *v.* Past tense of **overtake.**

o•ver•ture (**ō′**vər cho͝or′) *n.* **1.a.** An instrumental composition written as an introduction to an opera, an oratorio, or a suite. **b.** An independent instrumental composition that resembles this. **2.** An offer or a proposal indicating readiness to negotiate or establish something: *making peace overtures.* [First written down in 1249 in Middle English and spelled *overture,* opening, from Old French.]

o•ver•turn (ō′vər **tûrn′**) *v.* **o•ver•turned, o•ver•turn•ing, o•ver•turns.** *—tr.* **1.** To turn over or capsize; upset: *overturn a glass of water.* **2.** To overthrow; defeat. *—intr.* To turn over or capsize: *The raft overturned in the rapids.*

o•ver•use (ō′vər **yo͞oz′**) *tr.v.* **o•ver•used, o•ver•us•ing, o•ver•us•es.** To use to excess. *—n.* (ō′vər **yo͞os′**). Too much or excessive use.

o•ver•view (**ō′**vər vyo͞o′) *n.* A broad comprehensive view; an overall survey.

o•ver•ween•ing (ō′vər **wē′**nĭng) *adj.* Presumptuously arrogant; overbearing. [First written down before 1338 in Middle English and spelled *overwening* : *over* + *wenen,* to think, suppose.]

o•ver•weight (ō′vər **wāt′**) *adj.* Weighing more than is normal or required. *—n.* (**ō′**vər wāt′). Weight that is above normal or usual.

o•ver•whelm (ō′vər **wĕlm′**) *tr.v.* **o•ver•whelmed, o•ver•whelm•ing, o•ver•whelms. 1.** To surge over and submerge; engulf: *Waves overwhelmed the dock.* **2.** To overcome completely; overpower: *The rebels overwhelmed the garrison.* **3.** To affect deeply: *Sadness overwhelmed me.* [First written down before 1338 in Middle English and spelled *overwhelmen* : *over* + *whelmen,* to overturn.]

o•ver•whelm•ing (ō′vər **wĕl′**mĭng) *adj.* Overpowering in effect or strength: *an overwhelming majority.* **—o′ver•whelm′ing•ly** *adv.*

o•ver•work (ō′vər **wûrk′**) *tr.v.* **o•ver•worked, o•ver•work•ing, o•ver•works.** To cause to work too hard: *The manager overworks her.* *—n.* (**ō′**vər wûrk′). Too much work.

o•ver•wrought (ō′vər **rôt′**) *adj.* **1.** Nervous or excited; very agitated. **2.** Extremely elaborate or lavish; overdone: *an overwrought prose style.*

o•vi•duct (**ō′**vĭ dŭkt′) *n.* A tube through which eggs or egg cells travel from an ovary to the uterus in mammals or to the outside of the body in other animals.

o•vip•a•rous (ō **vĭp′**ər əs) *adj.* Producing eggs that hatch outside the body. Birds are oviparous.

o•vi•pos•i•tor (ō′və **pŏz′**ĭ tər) *n.* A tubular part that extends from the end of the abdomen in certain insects, such as grasshoppers or wasps, and is used to lay eggs.

o•void (**ō′**void′) *adj.* Having the shape of an egg: *an ovoid face.* *—n.* Something having this shape.

o•vo•vi•vip•a•rous (ō′vō vī **vĭp′**ər əs) *adj.* Producing eggs that hatch within the female's body. Some fish and reptiles are ovoviviparous.

o•vu•late (**ō′**vyə lāt′ *or* **ŏv′**yə lāt′) *intr.v.* **o•vu•lat•ed, o•vu•lat•ing, o•vu•lates.** To produce or discharge an egg cell. **—o′vu•la′tion** *n.*

o•vule (**ō′**vyo͞ol *or* **ŏv′**yo͞ol) *n.* **1.a.** A small part in a plant ovary that becomes a seed after it has been fertilized by a male cell. **b.** A young seed. **2.** An immature ovum.

o•vum (**ō′**vəm) *n., pl.* **o•va** (**ō′**və). A female reproductive cell; an egg.

owe (ō) *v.* **owed, ow•ing, owes.** *—tr.* **1.a.** To be indebted to the amount of: *He owes five dollars for the meal.* **b.** To be indebted for: *The tenants owe rent for two months.* **c.** To be in debt to: *We owe the plumber for fixing the pipe.* **2.** To be under obligation to give: *owe an apology.* **3.** To have or possess as something derived from or bestowed by; be obliged for: *She owes her good health to exercise.* *—intr.* To be in debt. [First written down before 725 in Old English and spelled *āgan,* to possess.]

❑ *These sound alike:* **owe, O**[1] (exclamation), **oh** (expression of emotion).

Ow•ens (**ō′**ĭnz), **Jesse.** 1913–1980. American athlete who won four gold medals in track and field at the 1936 Olympics.

ow•ing (**ō′**ĭng) *adj.* Still to be paid; owed: *a sum that was owing.*

owing to *prep.* Because of; on account of.

owl (oul) *n.* Any of various birds of prey that usually fly at night and that have a large head, large eyes set forward, a short hooked bill, and a flat round face. [First written down before 800 in Old English and spelled *ūle.*]

owl•et (**ou′**lĭt) *n.* A young or small owl.

own (ōn) *adj.* Of or belonging to oneself or itself: *Jim's own book; my own home.* *—n.* Something that belongs to one: *He built the device but the idea was my own.* *—tr.v.* **owned, own•ing, owns. 1.** To have or possess: *own a car.* **2.** To acknowledge or admit: *I own that I've made a mistake.* ***—idioms.*** **of one's own.** Belonging completely to oneself. **on (one's) own.** By one's own efforts: *I planted the garden on my own.* **own up.** To make a full confession or acknowledgment: *She owned up about the broken window.* [First written down before 725 in Old English and spelled *āgen.*] **—own′er** *n.*

own•er•ship (**ō′**nər shĭp′) *n.* The condition of being an owner; legal right to possess a thing.

ox (ŏks) *n., pl.* **ox•en** (**ŏk′**sən). **1.** A castrated adult male of domestic cattle, used for heavy work or for beef. **2.** Any of several animals, such as the musk ox, related to domestic cattle. [First written down before 830 in Old English and spelled *oxa.*]

ox•al•ic acid (ŏk **săl′**ĭk) *n.* A poisonous acid found in many vegetables and other plants, such as spinach, tomatoes, grapes, and sweet potatoes, composed of carbon, hydrogen, and oxygen and having the formula $C_2H_2O_4 \cdot 2H_2O$. It is used as a general cleanser and bleach.

ox•blood red (**ŏks′**blŭd′) *n.* A deep red or reddish brown.

ox•bow (**ŏks′**bō′) *n.* **1.** A U-shaped piece of wood that fits under the neck of an ox, with its upper ends attached to the bar of the yoke. **2.** A U-shaped bend in a river.

ox•en (**ŏk′**sən) *n.* Plural of **ox.**

ox•eye daisy (**ŏks′**ī′) *n.* The common daisy of North America, having flowers with a yellow center surrounded by white rays resembling petals.

ox•ford (**ŏks′**fərd) *n.* **1.** A low shoe that laces over the instep. **2.** A cotton or rayon cloth used for men's shirts and women's sports clothes.

Ox•ford (**ŏks′**fərd). A borough of south-central England on the Thames River west-northwest of London. It was chartered in 1605. Oxford University was founded here in the 12th century. Population, 114,400.

ox•i•da•tion (ŏk′sĭ **dā′**shən) *n.* **1.** The chemical combination of a substance with oxygen. **2.** A chemical reaction in which the atoms of an element lose electrons, thus undergoing an increase in valence.

ox•ide (ŏk′sīd′) *n.* A compound of oxygen and another element or a radical.

ox•i•dize (ŏk′sĭ dīz′) *v.* **ox•i•dized, ox•i•diz•ing, ox•i•diz•es.** —*tr.* **1.** To combine with oxygen; make into an oxide. **2.** To coat with oxide: *Air oxidizes the surface of aluminum.* **3.** To subject to oxidation. —*intr.* To become oxidized.

ox•i•diz•er (ŏk′sĭ dī′zər) *n.* **1.** An oxidizing agent. **2.** A substance that reacts with a rocket fuel to produce the hot gas used for propulsion.

ox•i•diz•ing agent (ŏk′sĭ dī′zĭng) *n.* A substance that oxidizes another substance or causes it to oxidize.

ox•tail (ŏks′tāl′) *n.* The tail of an ox, especially one used in soup or stew.

ox•y•a•cet•y•lene (ŏk′sē ə sĕt′l ĭn *or* ŏk′sē ə-sĕt′l ēn′) *adj.* Using a mixture of oxygen and acetylene: *an oxyacetylene welding torch.*

ox•y•gen (ŏk′sĭ jən) *n.* *Symbol* **O** A colorless, odorless, gaseous element that occurs in many compounds, such as water. Animals, plants, and most other organisms cannot live without oxygen. Atomic number 8. See table at **element.** [First written down in 1790 in Modern English, from French *oxygène* : Greek *oxus*, sharp, acid + French *-gène*, producer.]

ox•y•gen•ate (ŏk′sĭ jə nāt′) *tr.v.* **ox•y•gen•at•ed, ox•y•gen•at•ing, ox•y•gen•ates.** To combine, treat, or mix with oxygen. —**ox′y•gen•a′tion** *n.*

oxygen mask *n.* A covering that fits closely over the mouth and nose and is connected by a hose to a supply of oxygen.

oxygen tent *n.* An enclosure that is placed over the head and shoulders of a patient who is having difficulty breathing to provide additional oxygen.

ox•y•he•mo•glo•bin (ŏk′sē hē′mə glō′bĭn) *n.* A bright-red chemical complex of hemoglobin and oxygen that transports oxygen from the lungs to the tissues via the blood.

ox•y•mo•ron (ŏk′sē môr′ŏn′) *n., pl.* **ox•y•mo•ra** (ŏk′sē môr′ə) or **ox•y•mo•rons.** An expression combining terms that clash or contradict each other, as *sweet sorrow.* [First written down in 1657 in Modern English, from Greek *oxumōros*, pointedly foolish : *oxus*, sharp + *mōros*, dull.]

o•yez (ō′yĕs′ *or* ō′yĕz′ *or* ō′yā′) *interj.* An expression used three times in a row to introduce the opening of a law court. [First written down about 1425 in Middle English and spelled *oyes*, from Anglo-Norman *oyez*, hear ye.]

oys•ter (oi′stər) *n.* Any of several sea mollusks of shallow waters, having a rough, irregularly shaped, double-hinged shell. Many kinds of oysters are used as food, and some kinds produce pearls inside their shells. [First written down in 1259 in Middle English and spelled *oistre*, from Greek *ostreon.*]

oyster bed *n.* A place where oysters breed or are raised.

oz also **oz.** *abbr.* An abbreviation of ounce.

O•zark Plateau or **O•zark Mountains** (ō′zärk′). An upland region of the south-central United States extending from southwest Missouri into eastern Oklahoma.

o•zone (ō′zōn′) *n.* A poisonous, blue, unstable gaseous form of oxygen that has three atoms per molecule rather than the usual two. It is produced by electricity and is present in the air, especially after a thunderstorm. Commercially, it is produced for use in water purification, air conditioning, and as a bleaching agent. [First written down in 1840 in Modern English, from German *Ozon*, from Greek *ozein*, to smell.]

ozone layer *n.* A region of concentrated ozone in the stratosphere. It shields the earth from excessive ultraviolet radiation.

ă	pat	oi	boy
ā	pay	ou	out
âr	care	o͝o	took
ä	father	o͞o	boot
ĕ	pet	ŭ	cut
ē	be	ûr	urge
ĭ	pit	th	thin
ī	pie	*th*	this
îr	pier	hw	whoop
ŏ	pot	zh	vision
ō	toe	ə	about
ô	paw	N	*French* bon

Pp

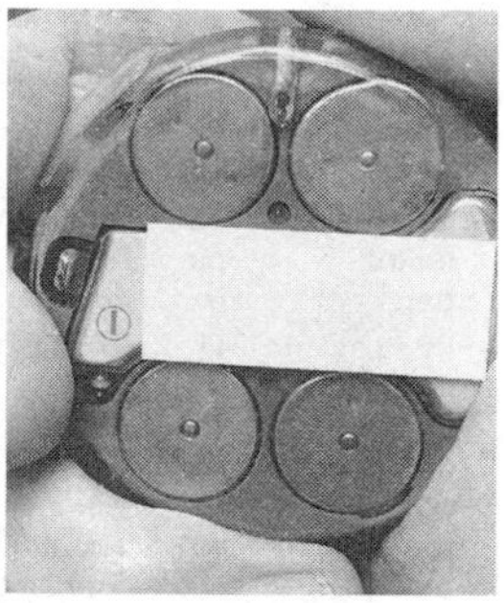

pacemaker

p or **P** (pē) *n., pl.* **p's** or **P's. 1.** The 16th letter of the English alphabet. **2.** The 16th in a series or group: *row P in a theater.*

P The symbol for the element **phosphorus.**

p. *abbr.* An abbreviation of: **1.** Page. **2.** Participle. **3.** Pint.

pa (pä) *n. Informal.* Father.

Pa The symbol for the element **protactinium.**

PA *abbr.* An abbreviation of: **1.** Public-address system. **2.** Or **Pa.** Pennsylvania.

pace (pās) *n.* **1.a.** A step made in walking; a stride. **b.** The distance spanned by such a step, specifically a unit of length equal to 30 inches. **2.a.** The rate of speed at which a person or thing walks or runs. **b.** The speed at which an activity proceeds: *the fast pace of city living.* **3.** A gait of a horse in which the feet on one side leave and return to the ground together. *—v.* **paced, pac•ing, pac•es.** *—tr.* **1.** To walk back and forth across: *He paced the floor impatiently.* **2.** To measure by counting the steps needed to cover a distance: *paced off the distance from the door to the stairs.* **3.** To set or regulate the speed of. *—intr.* To walk with long deliberate steps: *The tiger paced in its cage.* [First written down about 1280 in Middle English and spelled *pas,* from Latin *passus,* stretched out.]

pace•mak•er (**pās′**mā′kər) *n.* **1.** A person or thing that sets the pace in a race; a pacer. **2.** An electronic device used to regulate the heartbeat.

pac•er (**pā′**sər) *n.* A horse trained to move at a pace.

pach•y•derm (**păk′**ĭ dûrm′) *n.* Any of various large thick-skinned mammals, such as the elephant, rhinoceros, or hippopotamus. [First written down in 1838 in Modern English, from Greek *pakhudermos,* thick-skinned : *pakhus,* thick + *derma,* skin.]

pa•cif•ic (pə **sĭf′**ĭk) *adj.* **1.** Loving peace; peaceful: *a pacific people.* **2.** Peaceful in nature; serene: *a pacific scene.* [First written down before 1548 in Modern English and spelled *pacifique,* from Latin *pācificus,* from *pāx,* peace.] **—pa•cif′i•cal•ly** *adv.*

Pa•cif•ic Ocean (pə **sĭf′**ĭk). The largest of the world's oceans, extending from the western Americas to eastern Asia and Australia.

Pacific Standard Time *n.* Standard time as reckoned in the eighth time zone west of Greenwich, England. The west coast of the United States is in this region.

pac•i•fi•er (**păs′**ə fī′ər) *n.* A rubber or plastic nipple or teething ring for a baby to suck on.

pac•i•fism (**păs′**ə fĭz′əm) *n.* Opposition to war or violence as a means of solving disputes.

pac•i•fist (**păs′**ə fĭst) *n.* A person who favors peace and tries to find peaceful means to solving disputes. **—pac′i•fis′tic** *adj.* **—pac′i•fis′ti•cal•ly** *adv.*

pac•i•fy (**păs′**ə fī′) *tr.v.* **pac•i•fied, pac•i•fy•ing, pac•i•fies. 1.** To quiet; calm: *pacify a baby.* **2.** To establish peace in: *pacify the frontier.* **—pac′i•fi•ca′tion** *n.*

pack (păk) *n.* **1.** A collection of items tied up or wrapped together; a bundle. **2.a.** A small package containing a standard number of identical or similar items: *a pack of matches.* **b.** A set of related items: *a pack of cards.* **3.** A group of animals or people: *a pack of wolves.* **4.** A large amount: *a pack of trouble.* **5.** Material, such as gauze, applied to a part of the body or inserted into a body opening or wound as treatment for an injury or a disorder. *—v.* **packed, pack•ing, packs.** *—tr.* **1.a.** To fold, roll, or combine in a bundle; wrap up. **b.** To put into a bag, box, or other container, as for storage, preserving, or selling: *pack groceries; pack clothes.* **2.** To fill with items: *pack a suitcase.* **3.** To press together: *He packed the sugar into the measuring cup.* **4.a.** To bring together; crowd: *The ushers packed the theatergoers into the hall.* **b.** To fill up tight; cram: *The crowd packed the stadium.* **c.** To include in: *A lot of information is packed into a dictionary.* **5.** To wrap tightly for protection or to prevent leakage: *pack a valve stem.* **6.** To treat medically with a pack: *pack a wound.* **7.** *Informal.* To have ready for action: *pack a pistol.* **8.** To arrange (a jury or panel, for example) so as to be favorable to one's purposes. **9.** To cause to go or leave: *pack the kids off to camp.* *—intr.* **1.** To put one's clothes or things into a box or luggage, as for traveling or storage: *I've already packed for my trip.* **2.** To become pressed together: *Brown sugar packs well for measuring.* **3.** To be capable of being stored compactly. [First written down in 1191 in Middle English and spelled *pak,* possibly of Low German origin.]

pack•age (**păk′**ĭj) *n.* **1.** A wrapped or boxed object; a parcel. **2.** A container meant to hold something for storage or transporting. **3.** A proposition or an offer made up of several items, each of which must be accepted. *—tr.v.* **pack•aged, pack•ag•ing, pack•ag•es.** To place in a package or make a package of.

package store *n.* A store that sells sealed bottles of alcoholic beverages for consumption away from its premises; a liquor store.

pack animal *n.* An animal, such as a mule, used to carry loads.

pack•er (**păk′**ər) *n.* A person who packs goods, especially meat products, for transportation and sale.

pack•et (**păk′**ĭt) *n.* **1.** A small package or bundle, as of mail. **2.** A ship that sails on a regular route, carrying freight, passengers, and mail.

pack ice *n.* A large area of sea ice consisting of a mixture of floating ice fragments packed or squeezed together.

pack•ing (**păk′**ĭng) *n.* **1.** The act or process of one that packs, especially the processing and packaging of food products. **2.** A material used to prevent leakage or seepage, as around a pipe joint. **3.** Material inserted into a body opening or wound as part of a medical treatment.

pack•ing•house (**păk′**ĭng hous′) *n.* **1.** A company that slaughters, processes, and packs livestock into meat and meat products. **2.** A company that processes and packs food products other than meat.

pack rat *n.* Any of various North American rats that collect a variety of small objects in their nests.

pack•sack (**păk′**săk′) *n.* A canvas or leather pack carried strapped to the shoulders; a knapsack.

pact (păkt) *n.* **1.** A formal agreement, as between nations; a treaty. **2.** A compact; a bargain.

pad[1] (păd) *n.* **1.** A cushion or mass of soft, firmly packed material used for stuffing, lining, or protection against injury: *chair pads; knee pads.* **2.a.** A small wad of material: *a steel-wool pad for scouring.* **b.** A piece of absorbent material placed in a container and used to hold ink for stamping: *an ink pad.* **3.** A number of sheets of paper of the same size stacked one on top of the other and glued together at one end: *wrote the message on a memo pad.* **4.** The broad floating leaf of a water lily or similar plant. **5.a.** The fleshy underpart of the toes and feet of many animals. **b.** The fleshy tissue at the end of a finger or toe on the side opposite the nail. **6.** A launch pad. **7.** *Slang.* An apartment or a room. *—tr.v.* **pad•ded, pad•ding, pads. 1.** To line, stuff, or cover with soft, firmly packed material: *pad a sleeve.* **2.** To lengthen with unnecessary material: *pad a term paper.* **3.** To add fictitious expenses or costs to: *pad an expense account.* [First written down in 1554 in Modern English.]

pad[2] (păd) *intr.v.* **pad•ded, pad•ding, pads.** To go on foot, especially with a soft, almost inaudible step: *They like to pad about the house barefooted.* *—n.* A muffled sound of or resembling that of soft footsteps: *the soft pad of feet.* [First written down in 1553 in Modern English, probably of Low German origin; akin to *path.*]

pad•ding (păd′ĭng) *n.* **1.** Material used to stuff, fill, protect, or line something. **2.** Unnecessary material added to a speech or written work to lengthen it.

pad•dle[1] (păd′l) *n.* **1.** A short wooden implement with a flat blade at one end, used without an oarlock to propel a small boat, such as a canoe. **2.** Any of various implements with a similar shape and used variously, as for stirring molten ore or playing table tennis. *—v.* **pad•dled, pad•dling, pad•dles.** *—intr.* **1.** To propel a boat with a paddle or paddles. **2.** To swim by repeated short strokes of the limbs. *—tr.* **1.** To propel (a boat) with a paddle or paddles: *Paddle your own canoe.* **2.** To beat or spank with or as if with a paddle. [First written down in 1407 in Middle English and spelled *padell,* implement used for cleaning a plowshare, perhaps from Medieval Latin *padela.*] **—pad′dler** *n.*

pad•dle[2] (păd′l) *intr.v.* **pad•dled, pad•dling, pad•dles.** To splash gently or playfully in shallow water. [First written down in 1530 in Modern English, perhaps of Low German origin.]

pad•dle•fish (păd′l fĭsh′) *n.* A large fish of the Mississippi River and its branches, having a long snout shaped like a paddle.

paddle wheel *n.* A wheel with boards or paddles around its rim, used to propel a ship.

pad•dock (păd′ək) *n.* A fenced field or area, usually near a stable, in which horses are kept, as for grazing or exercising.

pad•dy (păd′ē) *n., pl.* **pad•dies. 1.** A flooded or specially watered field in which rice is grown. **2.** Rice in the husk.

pad•lock (păd′lŏk′) *n.* A detachable lock with a U-shaped bar hinged at one end, designed to be passed through a staple, link, or ring and then snapped into a hole in the body of the lock. *—tr.v.* **pad•locked, pad•lock•ing, pad•locks.** To lock up with or as if with a padlock.

pa•dre (pä′drā) *n.* **1.** A priest in Italy, Spain, Portugal, or Latin America. **2.** A form of address for a priest in any of these countries.

pae•an (pē′ən) *n.* **1.** A fervent expression of joy or praise. **2.** A hymn of thanksgiving to a god.

pa•gan (pā′gən) *n.* **1.** A person who is not a Christian, Muslim, or Jew. **2.** A person who has no religion. *—adj.* Of or relating to pagans or paganism: *pagan gods.*

pa•gan•ism (pā′gə nĭz′əm) *n.* **1.** Pagan beliefs or practices, such as the worship of nature deities. **2.** The condition of being a pagan.

page[1] (pāj) *n.* **1.a.** One side of a printed leaf, as of a book, letter, or newspaper. **b.** The writing or printing on one side of a leaf. **2.** A memorable event: *a new page in the course of human history.* *—v.* **paged, pag•ing, pag•es.** *—tr.* To number the pages of. *—intr.* To turn pages: *paging through a book.* [First written down in 1589 in Modern English, from Latin *pāgina.*]

page[2] (pāj) *n.* **1.** A boy who attended a medieval knight as a first stage of training for knighthood. **2.** A person employed to run errands, carry messages, or act as a guide, as in a hotel or club. *—tr.v.* **paged, pag•ing, pag•es.** To summon or call (a person) by name, as over a loudspeaker. [First written down before 1300 in Middle English, possibly from Italian *paggio,* perhaps ultimately from Greek *paidion,* boy.]

pag•eant (păj′ənt) *n.* **1.** A play or dramatic spectacle usually based on an event in history. **2.** A procession or celebration.

pag•eant•ry (păj′ən trē) *n., pl.* **pag•eant•ries. 1.** Pageants and their presentation. **2.** Grand or showy display.

pag•er (pā′jər) *n.* A beeper.

pa•go•da (pə gō′də) *n.* **1.** A many-storied Buddhist tower, built as a memorial or shrine. **2.** A structure built in imitation of such a tower.

Pa•go Pa•go (päng′ō päng′ō *or* päng′gō päng′gō). The capital of American Samoa, in the Pacific Ocean northeast of New Zealand. Population, 3,075.

paid (pād) *v.* Past tense and past participle of **pay.**

pail (pāl) *n.* **1.** A cylindrical container, open at the top and fitted with a handle; a bucket. **2.a.** A pail with something in it: *carry a pail of water.* **b.** The amount that a pail holds: *pour out a pail of sand.*
❑ *These sound alike:* **pail, pale[1]** (stake), **pale[2]** (whitish).

pail•ful (pāl′fo͝ol′) *n.* The amount that a pail can hold.

pain (pān) *n.* **1.** An unpleasant feeling occurring as a result of injury or disease, usually localized in some part of the body. **2.** Mental or emotional suffering; distress. **3. pains.** Trouble, care, or effort: *take great pains to do something right.* **4.** *Informal.* A source of annoyance; a nuisance: *He's a real pain.* *—tr.v.* **pained, pain•ing, pains. 1.** To cause pain to (a person or an animal); hurt. **2.** To cause to suffer; distress: *It pained her to see him so unhappy.* **—*idiom.* on pain of** or **under pain of.** Subject to the penalty of (a specified punishment, such as death).
❑ *These sound alike:* **pain, pane** (glass).

Paine (pān), **Thomas.** 1737–1809. British-born American writer and Revolutionary leader who wrote and published works arguing in favor of the American Revolution and the French Revolution.

pain•ful (pān′fəl) *adj.* **1.** Causing or full of pain; hurtful: *a painful injury.* **2.** Causing suffering or anxiety; distressing: *a painful decision.* **—pain′ful•ly** *adv.* **—pain′ful•ness** *n.*

pain•kill•er (pān′kĭl′ər) *n.* Something, such as a drug, that relieves pain.

pain•less (pān′lĭs) *adj.* Not painful; causing no unpleasant sensations: *a painless operation.* **—pain′less•ly** *adv.* **—pain′less•ness** *n.*

pains•tak•ing (pānz′tā′kĭng) *adj.* Involving or showing great care or thoroughness; careful: *painstaking research.* **—pains′tak′ing•ly** *adv.*

paint (pānt) *n.* **1.a.** A liquid mixture, usually of a finely ground solid pigment and a liquid, applied to surfaces as a protective or decorative coating. **b.** The thin film formed, as on a surface, when the

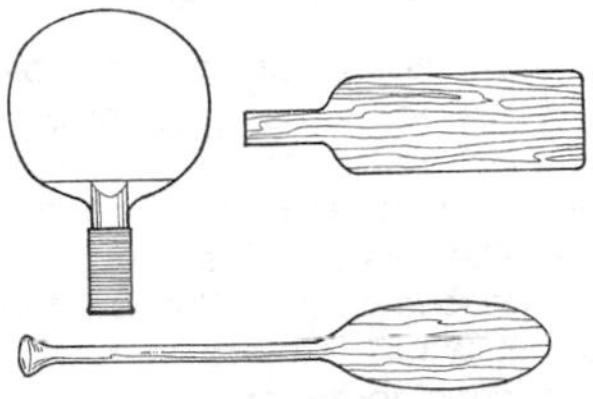

paddle[1]

Table tennis (*top left*), pottery (*top right*), and canoe (*bottom*) paddles

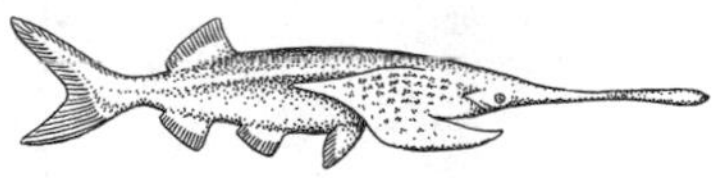

paddlefish

pagoda

ă	pat	oi	boy
ā	pay	ou	out
âr	care	o͝o	took
ä	father	o͞o	boot
ĕ	pet	ŭ	cut
ē	be	ûr	urge
ĭ	pit	th	thin
ī	pie	*th*	this
îr	pier	hw	whoop
ŏ	pot	zh	vision
ō	toe	ə	about
ô	paw	N	*French* bon

Usage: pair

The noun **pair** can be followed by a singular or plural verb. You use the singular when **pair** refers to the set taken as a whole: *This pair of shoes is on sale.* You use the plural when the two members are considered as individuals: *The pair are working together.* After a number other than one, **pair** can be either singular or plural, but the plural is now more common: *She bought six pairs* (or *pair*) *of shoes.*

paisley

palace
Buckingham Palace in London, England

liquid in such a mixture dries and reacts with the air. **c.** The solid pigment before it is mixed with the liquid. **2.** A cosmetic, such as rouge, that colors. **3.** A spotted horse; a pinto. —*v.* **paint•ed, paint•ing, paints.** —*tr.* **1.** To coat or decorate with paint: *paint a house.* **2.** To make (a picture) with paints. **3.a.** To represent in a painting: *She painted a horse.* **b.** To describe vividly in words: *The article painted a lively picture of a typical Mexican fiesta.* **4.** To cover the surface of with a liquid medicine; swab: *paint a sore throat with antiseptic.* —*intr.* **1.** To practice the art of painting pictures. **2.** To cover something with paint.

paint•brush (**pānt′**brŭsh′) *n.* A brush for applying paint.

paint•ed (**pān′**tĭd) *adj.* **1.** Coated or decorated with paint: *a brightly painted cabinet.* **2.** Depicted in paint: *a painted portrait.*

paint•er[1] (**pān′**tər) *n.* A person who paints, either as an artist or a worker.

pain•ter[2] (**pān′**tər) *n.* A rope attached to the bow of a boat, used for tying up. [First written down in 1336 in Middle English and spelled *peintour*, probably from Latin *pendēre*, to hang.]

pain•ter[3] (**pān′**tər) *n.* A mountain lion. [First written down in 1764 in American English, alteration of *panther*.]

paint•ing (**pān′**tĭng) *n.* **1.** The art, process, or occupation of working with paints. **2.** A picture or design in paint.

pair (pâr) *n., pl.* **pair** or **pairs. 1.** A set of two members that are somehow matched or associated in function or form: *a pair of boots.* **2.** An object consisting of two joined or similar parts dependent upon each other: *a pair of binoculars.* **3.a.** Two persons joined together in marriage or engagement. **b.** Two persons, animals, or things having something in common and considered together: *a pair of oxen.* **c.** Two mated animals. **4.** Two playing cards of the same value. —*v.* **paired, pair•ing, pairs.** —*tr.* **1.** To arrange in sets of two; couple: *Pair the questions with the correct answers.* **2.** To provide a partner for: *paired Susan with Alice.* —*intr.* To form pairs or a pair: *paired off at the dance.* —SEE NOTE.

❑ *These sound alike:* **pair, pare** (peel), **pear** (fruit).

pais•ley (**pāz′**lē) *adj.* Having a colorful pattern of curved shapes and swirls: *a paisley dress.*

Pai•ute (**pī′**yo͞ot′) *n., pl.* **Paiute** or **Pai•utes. 1.** A member of a Native American people of the Great Basin region of the western United States. **2.** The Uto-Aztecan language of the Paiute.

pa•ja•mas (pə **jä′**məz *or* pə **jăm′**əz) *pl.n.* A loose-fitting outfit consisting of a jacket and trousers, worn to sleep in or for lounging.

Pak•i•stan (**păk′**ĭ stăn′ *or* pä′kĭ **stän′**). A country of southern Asia west of India. It was the home of the prehistoric Indus Valley civilization, which flourished until about 1500 B.C. Islamabad is the capital and Karachi the largest city. Population, 83,782,000.

pal (păl) *Informal. n.* A friend; a chum. —*intr.v.* **palled, pal•ling, pals.** To associate as friends.

pal•ace (**păl′**ĭs) *n.* **1.** The official residence of a royal person. **2.** A splendid residence.

pal•an•quin (păl′ən **kēn′**) *n.* A covered litter, carried on poles on the shoulders of two or four men, formerly used in eastern Asia.

pal•at•a•ble (**păl′**ə tə bəl) *adj.* **1.** Acceptable to the taste; agreeable enough in flavor to be eaten: *palatable food.* **2.** Acceptable to the mind or sensibilities; agreeable. **—pal′at•a•bil′i•ty** *n.*

pal•ate (**păl′**ĭt) *n.* **1.** The roof of the mouth in vertebrates, forming a complete or partial separation between the mouth cavity and the passages of the nose. **2.** The sense of taste.

❑ *These sound alike:* **palate, palette** (artist's mixing board), **pallet** (hard bed).

pa•la•tial (pə **lā′**shəl) *adj.* Of or like a palace; spacious and magnificent: *a palatial hotel.* **—pa•la′tial•ly** *adv.*

Pa•lau (pə **lou′**). Belau.

pa•lav•er (pə **lăv′**ər) *n.* Idle chatter, especially that meant to flatter or deceive. —*intr.v.* **pa•lav•ered, pa•lav•er•ing, pa•lav•ers.** To chatter idly.

pale[1] (pāl) *n.* **1.** A stake or pointed stick; a picket. **2.** An area enclosed by a fence or boundary. —*tr.v.* **paled, pal•ing, pales.** To enclose with pales; fence in: —***idiom.*** **beyond the pale.** Unacceptable or unreasonable. [First written down before 1200 in Middle English and spelled *pal*, from Latin *pālus*.]

❑ *These sound alike:* **pale[1]** (stake), **pail** (bucket), **pale[2]** (whitish).

pale[2] (pāl) *adj.* **pal•er, pal•est. 1.** Whitish or lighter than normal in complexion. **2.** Containing a large proportion of white; light: *a pale blue.* **3.** Not bright; dim; faint: *a pale moon.* —*v.* **paled, pal•ing, pales.** —*tr.* To make pale. —*intr.* **1.** To lose normal skin coloration; turn pale. **2.** To become pale: *The sky grew red, then paled.* [First written down before 1325 in Middle English, from Latin *pallidus*.]

❑ *These sound alike:* **pale[2]** (whitish), **pail** (bucket), **pale[1]** (stake).

Pa•le•o•cene (**pā′**lē ə sēn′) *adj.* Of, belonging to, or being the geologic time of the first epoch of the Tertiary Period. During the Paleocene, advanced mammals appeared. See table at **geologic time.** —*n.* The Paleocene Epoch or its series of rocks.

Pa•le•o•lith•ic (pā′lē ə **lĭth′**ĭk) *adj.* Of, belonging to, or being the period of human culture that began about 750,000 years ago and ended about 15,000 years ago, marked by the earliest use of tools made of chipped stone. —*n.* The Paleolithic Age.

pa•le•on•tol•o•gist (pā′lē ŏn **tŏl′**ə jĭst) *n.* A scientist who specializes in paleontology.

pa•le•on•tol•o•gy (pā′lē ŏn **tŏl′**ə jē) *n.* The scientific study of fossils and ancient forms of life.

Pa•le•o•zo•ic (pā′lē ə **zō′**ĭk) *adj.* Of, belonging to, or being the geologic time of the era that includes the Cambrian, Ordovician, Silurian, Devonian, Mississippian, Pennsylvanian, and Permian periods. During the Paleozoic, invertebrate sea life, primitive fishes and reptiles, and land plants appeared. See table at **geologic time.** —*n.* The Paleozoic Era.

Pal•es•tine (**păl′**ĭ stīn′). A historical region of southwest Asia on the eastern Mediterranean shore in roughly the same area as modern Israel and the West Bank. It has been occupied since prehistoric times and is often called "the Holy Land." **—Pal′es•tin′i•an** (păl′ĭ **stĭn′**ē ən) *adj. & n.*

pal•ette (**păl′**ĭt) *n.* A thin board, often with a hole for the thumb, upon which an artist mixes colors.

❑ *These sound alike:* **palette, palate** (mouth roof), **pallet** (hard bed).

pal•frey (**pôl′**frē) *n., pl.* **pal•freys.** *Archaic.* A horse used for riding, especially by a woman.

pal•in•drome (**păl′**ĭn drōm′) *n.* A word, phrase, or verse that reads the same backward or forward. For example: *Madam, I'm Adam* is a palindrome.

pal•ing (**pā′**lĭng) *n.* **1.** One or more of the pales or pickets forming a fence. **2.** A fence made of pales or pickets.

pal•i•sade (păl′ĭ **sād′**) *n.* **1.** A fence of stakes forming a fortification. **2. palisades.** A line of high cliffs, usually along a river.

pall[1] (pôl) *n.* **1.** A cloth covering, often of black velvet, for a coffin or tomb. **2.** A coffin, especially one being borne to a grave. **3.** A dark gloomy covering:

a pall of smog over the city. **4.** A gloomy atmosphere: *The bad news cast a pall over the household.* [First written down before 899 in Old English and spelled *pæll,* cloak, covering, from Latin *pallium.*]

❑ *These sound alike:* **pall[1]** (cloth covering), **pall[2]** (grow dull), **pawl** (hinged device).

pall[2] (pôl) *intr.v.* **palled, pall•ing, palls.** To grow dull or tiresome: *a clever idea that begins to pall by the end of the movie.* [First written down before 1325 in Middle English and spelled *pallen,* to grow feeble, probably short for *appallen.*]

❑ *These sound alike:* **pall[2]** (grow dull), **pall[1]** (cloth covering), **pawl** (hinged device).

pal•la•di•um (pə **lā′**dē əm) *n. Symbol* **Pd** A soft white tarnish-resistant metallic element that occurs naturally with platinum. It is used in making scientific instruments, in alloys with precious metals, such as gold and silver, and as a catalyst. Atomic number 46. See table at **element.**

Pal•las Athena (**păl′**əs) *n.* In Greek mythology, the goddess Athena.

pall•bear•er (**pôl′**bâr′ər) *n.* A person who helps carry the coffin at a funeral.

pal•let (**păl′**ĭt) *n.* A narrow hard bed or straw-filled mattress.

❑ *These sound alike:* **pallet, palate** (mouth roof), **palette** (artist's mixing board).

pal•li•ate (**păl′**ē āt′) *tr.v.* **pal•li•at•ed, pal•li•at•ing, pal•li•ates. 1.** To make (an offense or a fault) seem less serious; help to excuse. **2.** To ease the pain or force of; moderate: *took aspirin to palliate his cold symptoms.* **—pal′li•a′tion** *n.*

pal•li•a•tive (**păl′**ē ā′tĭv *or* **păl′**ē ə tĭv) *adj.* Serving to palliate: *a palliative drug.* —*n.* Something that palliates.

pal•lid (**păl′**ĭd) *adj.* Lacking healthy color; pale. **—pal′lid•ly** *adv.* **—pal′lid•ness** *n.*

pal•lor (**păl′**ər) *n.* Unhealthy paleness.

palm[1] (päm) *n.* **1.a.** The inside surface of the hand between the wrist and the base of the fingers. **b.** A similar part of the forefoot of an animal. **2.** A unit of length equal to the width of the hand, or about three inches. —*tr.v.* **palmed, palm•ing, palms. 1.** To conceal (an object) in the palm of the hand. **2.** To pick up secretly. **3.** In basketball, to let (the ball) rest in the palm of the hand when dribbling, in violation of the rules. —***idiom.*** **palm off.** To dispose of or pass off by deception. [First written down before 1300 in Middle English, from Latin *palma,* palm tree, palm of the hand.]

palm[2] (päm) *n.* **1.** Any of various evergreen trees of tropical and subtropical regions, usually having a branchless trunk with a crown of large leaves shaped like feathers or fans. **2.** A leaf or frond of such a tree, used as a symbol of victory, success, or joy. [First written down before 830 in Old English, from Latin *palma,* palm of the hand, palm tree.]

pal•mate (**păl′**māt′ *or* **pä′**māt′) *adj.* **1.** Shaped somewhat like a hand with the fingers spread out: *a palmate leaf.* **2.** Having the front toes joined by a web; web-footed.

pal•met•to (păl **mĕt′**ō) *n., pl.* **pal•met•tos** or **pal•met•toes.** Any of several often small palm trees having leaves shaped like fans.

palm•ist (**pä′**mĭst) *n.* A person who practices palmistry.

palm•is•try (**pä′**mĭ strē) *n.* The practice or art of telling fortunes from the lines, marks, and patterns on the palms of the hands.

palm oil *n.* A yellowish fatty oil that comes from the nut of an African palm and is used in making soaps, chocolates, cosmetics, and candles.

Palm Sunday *n.* The Sunday before Easter, celebrated by Christians in commemoration of Jesus's entry into Jerusalem when palm leaves were strewn before him.

pal•o•mi•no (păl′ə **mē′**nō) *n., pl.* **pal•o•mi•nos.** A horse having a light tan coat and a whitish mane and tail. [First written down in 1914 in American English, from American Spanish, possibly from Italian *palombino,* dove-colored, from Latin *palumbēs,* dove.]

Pa•louse (pə **lo͞os′**) *n., pl.* **Palouse** or **Pa•louses.** A member of a Native American people living in eastern Washington.

palp (pălp) *n.* An organ of touch or taste located near the mouth of invertebrate organisms such as insects and crustaceans.

pal•pa•ble (**păl′**pə bəl) *adj.* **1.** Capable of being touched or felt. **2.** Easily perceived; obvious: *The excitement in the stadium was palpable.* **—pal′pa•bil′i•ty** *n.* **—pal′pa•bly** *adv.*

pal•pate (**păl′**pāt′) *tr.v.* **pal•pat•ed, pal•pat•ing, pal•pates.** To examine or explore (an organ or area of the body) by touching. **—pal•pa′tion** *n.* **—pal′pa′tor** *n.*

pal•pi (**păl′**pī′) *n.* Plural of **palpus.**

pal•pi•tate (**păl′**pĭ tāt′) *intr.v.* **pal•pi•tat•ed, pal•pi•tat•ing, pal•pi•tates. 1.** To shake; quiver. **2.** To beat very rapidly; throb.

pal•pi•ta•tion (păl′pĭ **tā′**shən) *n.* **1.** A trembling or shaking. **2.** Irregular rapid beating of the heart.

pal•pus (**păl′**pəs) *n., pl.* **pal•pi** (**păl′**pī). A palp.

pal•sied (**pôl′**zēd) *adj.* **1.** Afflicted with palsy. **2.** Trembling; shaking.

pal•sy (**pôl′**zē) *n., pl.* **pal•sies.** Complete or partial muscle paralysis, often accompanied by trembling. —*tr.v.* **pal•sied, pal•sy•ing, pal•sies.** To paralyze. [First written down about 1300 in Middle English and spelled *palasie,* from Old French *paralisie,* paralysis.]

pal•try (**pôl′**trē) *adj.* **pal•tri•er, pal•tri•est. 1.** Meager; insignificant: *Jack sold the cow for a few paltry beans.* **2.** Lowly; contemptible: *paltry cowards.* **—pal′tri•ness** *n.*

pam•pa (**păm′**pə) *n., pl.* **pam•pas** (**păm′**pəz *or* **păm′**pəs). The partly grassy, partly arid plain that covers most of central Argentina. Often used in the plural.

pam•per (**păm′**pər) *tr.v.* **pam•pered, pam•per•ing, pam•pers.** To treat with extreme indulgence, especially in an attempt to satisfy luxurious desires.

Synonyms: pamper, indulge, spoil, coddle, baby. These verbs mean to make excessive efforts to please someone. **Pamper** means to satisfy someone's appetites, tastes, or desires for luxurious things: *I pampered myself with a long hot bath.* **Indulge** means to yield to wishes or impulses, especially those that would be better left unfulfilled: *The twins indulged their craving for sweets by sharing a banana split.* **Spoil** means to indulge someone in a way that worsens his or her character: *You are spoiling that child, letting him have every toy he wants.* **Coddle** means to care for in a tender, overprotective way that can weaken character: *Don't coddle her and make her think she can't do the job all by herself.* **Baby** suggests giving someone the kind of attention one might give a baby: *Mike likes to be babied when he has the flu.* **Antonyms: punish, abuse.**

---

pam•phlet (**păm′**flĭt) *n.* A short book or printed essay with a paper cover and no binding; a booklet.

pam•phlet•eer (păm′flĭ **tîr′**) *n.* A writer of pamphlets, especially on political subjects.

pan[1] (păn) *n.* **1.** A wide shallow open container used for holding liquids, cooking, and other household purposes. **2.** A similar flat shallow container, such as one used to separate gold from earth or gravel by washing. —*v.* **panned, pan•ning, pans.** —*tr.* **1.** To wash (earth or gravel) in a pan in search of gold: *panned the debris carefully.* **2.** To cook (food) in a

palette

palm[2]

ă	pat	oi	boy
ā	pay	ou	out
âr	care	o͝o	took
ä	father	o͞o	boot
ĕ	pet	ŭ	cut
ē	be	ûr	urge
ĭ	pit	th	thin
ī	pie	*th*	this
îr	pier	hw	whoop
ŏ	pot	zh	vision
ō	toe	ə	about
ô	paw	N	*French* bon

panda
Giant panda

pangolin

Emmeline Pankhurst

pannier
Bicycle panniers

pan. **3.** *Informal.* To review unfavorably: *The critics panned the musical.* —*intr.* To wash earth or gravel in a pan in search of gold. —***idiom.* pan out.** To turn out well; be successful. [First written down about 700 in Old English and spelled *panne*, probably ultimately from Greek *patanē*, platter.]

pan[2] (păn) *tr. & intr.v.* To turn (a motion-picture or television camera) to follow a moving object or scan a scene. [First written down in 1913 in American English, short for *panoramic.*]

Pan (păn) *n.* In Greek mythology, the god of woodlands, fields, and flocks, having a human head and torso and a goat's legs, horns, and ears.

pan– *pref.* A prefix that means all: *panorama.*

pan•a•ce•a (păn′ə **sē′**ə) *n.* A remedy for all diseases or woes; a cure-all.

pa•nache (pə **năsh′** *or* pə **näsh′**) *n.* Dash; verve: *She trailed the cape behind her with panache.*

Pan•a•ma (**păn′**ə mä′ *or* **păn′**ə mô′). **1.** A country of southeast Central America east of Costa Rica. Panama gained its independence from Colombia in 1903. Capital, Panama. Population, 1,795,012. **2.** Also **Panama City.** The capital and largest city of Panama, in the central part of the country on the **Gulf of Panama,** an inlet of the Pacific Ocean. Population, 389,172.

Panama, Isthmus of. An isthmus of Central America connecting North and South America and separating the Pacific Ocean from the Caribbean Sea.

Panama Canal. A ship canal, about 51 miles (82 kilometers) long, crossing the Isthmus of Panama and connecting the Caribbean Sea with the Pacific Ocean. The canal was opened to traffic in 1914.

Panama City. Panama (sense 2).

Panama hat *n.* A natural-colored hand-plaited hat made from the leaves of a tropical American plant.

Pan-A•mer•i•can (păn′ə **mĕr′**ĭ kən) *adj.* Of, relating to, or including the countries of North, Central, and South America: *Pan-American conferences.*

pan•cake (**păn′**kāk′) *n.* A thin flat cake of batter, cooked on a hot griddle or skillet.

pan•chro•mat•ic (păn′krō **măt′**ĭk) *adj.* Sensitive to light of all colors.

pan•cre•as (**păng′**krē əs *or* **păn′**krē əs) *n.* A long irregularly shaped gland located behind the stomach. It secretes insulin and digestive juices.

pan•cre•at•ic (păng′krē **ăt′**ĭk *or* păn′krē **ăt′**ĭk) *adj.* Of or secreted by the pancreas: *pancreatic juice.*

pan•da (**păn′**də) *n.* **1.** A large mammal of the mountains of China and Tibet, resembling a bear and having woolly fur with black and white markings. **2.** A small mammal of northeast Asia, resembling a raccoon and having reddish fur and a long ringed tail.

pan•dem•ic (păn **dĕm′**ĭk) *adj.* Epidemic through a very wide area: *a pandemic outbreak of influenza.* —*n.* A pandemic disease.

pan•de•mo•ni•um (păn′də **mō′**nē əm) *n.* Wild confusion and noise; uproar.

pan•der (**păn′**dər) *intr.v.* **pan•dered, pan•der•ing, pan•ders.** To profit by exploiting the needs and weaknesses of others: *His movies pander to popular tastes.* —**pan′der•er** *n.*

Pan•do•ra (păn **dôr′**ə) *n.* In Greek mythology, the first woman, who out of curiosity opens a box that releases all the evils into the world.

pane (pān) *n.* **1.** A sheet of glass, especially one in a window or door. **2.** One of the divisions of a window or door, including the glass and its frame. [First written down about 1250 in Middle English, garment, from Latin *pannus*, cloth.]
❑ *These sound alike:* **pane, pain** (hurt).

pan•el (**păn′**əl) *n.* **1.** A flat piece, such as a wooden board, forming part of a surface or overlaying it: *a door with inlaid panels.* **2.** A piece of cloth sewn lengthwise into or onto a skirt or dress. **3.** A board with instruments or controls. **4.** A wooden board used as a surface for oil painting. **5.** A picture painted on such a board. **6.a.** A list or group of persons chosen for jury duty. **b.** A jury. **7.** A group of persons gathered together to discuss or decide something: *a panel of medical and legal experts.* —*tr.v.* **pan•eled** or **pan•elled, pan•el•ing** or **pan•el•ling, pan•els.** To cover or decorate with panels.

pan•el•ing (**păn′**ə lĭng) *n.* A set of wooden panels covering a wall or other surface.

pan•el•ist (**păn′**ə lĭst) *n.* A member of a panel.

panel truck *n.* A small delivery truck with a closed top and back.

pang (păng) *n.* **1.** A brief sharp sensation, as of pain; a spasm: *hunger pangs.* **2.** A brief sharp feeling of strong emotion: *a pang of remorse.*

Pan•gae•a (păn **jē′**ə) *n.* A theoretical continent made up of all the world's present land masses during the Permian and Triassic Periods.

pan•go•lin (**păng′**gə lĭn *or* **păn′**gə lĭn) *n.* Any of several African or Asian mammals having a scaly body, a long tail, and a sticky tongue with which they catch ants. [First written down in 1774 in Modern English, from Malay *pêngguling*, from *guling*, to roll over.]

pan•han•dle[1] (**păn′**hăn′dl) *intr.v.* **pan•han•dled, pan•han•dling, pan•han•dles.** *Informal.* To beg for money on the street or in a public area.

pan•han•dle[2] (**păn′**hăn′dl) *n.* **1.** The handle of a pan. **2.** Often **Panhandle.** A narrow strip of territory extending like the handle of a pan from a broader area: *the Oklahoma Panhandle.*

pan•ic (**păn′**ĭk) *n.* **1.** A sudden overwhelming terror. **2.** A sudden fear of financial loss among investors. —*adj.* Of or relating to panic: *a panic reaction.* —*tr. & intr.v.* **pan•icked, pan•ick•ing, pan•ics.** To cause panic in or be stricken with panic. See Synonyms at **frighten.** [First written down in 1627 in Modern English, from Greek *Panikos*, of Pan (considered a source of terror in flocks of animals).] —**pan′ick•y** *adj.*

pan•ic-strick•en (**păn′**ĭk strĭk′ən) *adj.* Overcome by panic; terrified.

Pank•hurst (**păngk′**hûrst′), **Emmeline Goulden.** 1858–1928. British suffrage leader who with her daughters **Christabel Pankhurst** (1880–1958) and **Sylvia Pankhurst** (1882–1960) founded (1903) the Women's Social and Political Union, a women-only group whose motto was "Deeds, not Words."

pan•nier (**păn′**yər *or* **păn′**ē ər) *n.* A basket, especially one of a pair of baskets carried on either side of a pack animal, bicycle, or motorcycle.

pan•o•ply (**păn′**ə plē) *n., pl.* **pan•o•plies. 1.** A splendid display: *a panoply of flags in the parade.* **2.** Something that covers or protects like armor: *a porcupine's panoply of quills.* **3.** The complete arms and armor of a warrior.

pan•o•ram•a (păn′ə **răm′**ə) *n.* **1.** A view or picture of everything visible over a wide area: *a vast panorama of a mountain range.* **2.** A view or picture of a long series of events, stages, or things: *a book that presents a panorama of world history.* **3.** A wide picture depicting a scene or story that is unrolled or presented a part at a time before spectators.

pan•o•ram•ic (păn′ə **răm′**ĭk) *adj.* Of or like a panorama: *a panoramic photograph.* —**pan′o•ram′i•cal•ly** *adv.*

pan•pipe (**păn′**pīp′) *n.* A musical instrument consisting of a set of tubes or reeds of different lengths bound together, played by blowing air across the tops of the tubes.

pan•sy (**păn′**zē) *n., pl.* **pan•sies.** Any of various garden plants having flowers with rounded velvety petals of various colors. [First written down about 1450 in Middle English and spelled *pancy*, from Old French *pensee*, thought, remembrance.]

pant (pănt) *v.* **pant•ed, pant•ing, pants.** *—intr.* **1.** To breathe in short quick gasps. **2.** To yearn desperately: *panted for the dawn to come.* *—tr.* To utter breathlessly: *Alice managed to pant out a short response.* *—n.* A short quick gasp.

pan•ta•lets also **pan•ta•lettes** (păn′tə **lĕts′**) *pl.n.* Long underpants having frills or ruffles, worn by girls and women in the mid-19th century.

Pan•ta•loon (**păn′**tə lo͞on′) *n.* A comic pantomime character usually portrayed as a foolish old man.

pan•ta•loons (păn′tə **lo͞onz′**) *pl.n.* Trousers, especially loose baggy ones.

pan•the•ism (**păn′**thē ĭz′əm) *n.* **1.** The belief that God is identical with the universe. **2.** The worship of many or all gods. **—pan′the•ist** *n.* **—pan′the•is′tic** *adj.*

pan•the•on (**păn′**thē ŏn′) *n.* **1.** A temple dedicated to all of the gods. **2.** A public building commemorating the great men and women of a nation. **3.** All the gods of a people. [First written down before 1425 in Middle English and spelled *Panteon*, from Greek *Pantheion* : *pan-*, all + *theos*, god.]

pan•ther (**păn′**thər) *n.* **1.** The leopard in its black unspotted form. **2.** The mountain lion. [First written down about 1000 in Old English and spelled *pandher*, from Greek *panthēr*.]

pant•ies (**păn′**tēz) *pl.n.* Short underpants for women or children.

pan•to•mime (**păn′**tə mīm′) *n.* **1.a.** Acting that consists mostly of gestures and other body movement without speech. **b.** A play or an entertainment acted in this way. **2.** Movements of the face and body used in place of words to express a message or meaning. *—tr.v.* **pan•to•mimed, pan•to•mim•ing, pan•to•mimes.** To perform or represent by gestures without speech. **—pan′to•mim′ist** *n.*

pan•try (**păn′**trē) *n., pl.* **pan•tries.** A small room or closet, usually next to a kitchen, where items such as dry goods and silverware are stored.

pants (pănts) *pl.n.* **1.** Trousers. **2.** Underpants.

pant•suit also **pants suit** (**pănt′**so͞ot′) *n.* A woman's suit having trousers and a jacket.

pant•y•hose or **pant•y hose** (**păn′**tē hōz′) *pl.n.* Stockings and underpants woven together and worn as one garment.

pap (păp) *n.* **1.** Soft easily digestible food for infants or invalids. **2.** Matter designed to satisfy or entertain but lacking real value or substance: *the pap on TV every night.*

pa•pa (**pä′**pə *or* pə **pä′**) *n. Informal.* Father.

pa•pa•cy (**pā′**pə sē) *n., pl.* **pa•pa•cies. 1.** The office or authority of the pope. **2.** Often **Papacy.** The system of church government headed by the pope. **3.** All of the popes or a series of popes: *the medieval papacy.* **4.** The period during which a pope is in office.

pa•pal (**pā′**pəl) *adj.* Of or relating to the pope or the office of pope: *papal history.*

pa•paw also **paw•paw** (**pô′**pô′) *n.* **1.** The fleshy fruit of a North American tree, having a taste similar to a banana. **2.** The tree that bears such fruit. [First written down in 1624 in American English, ultimately from Spanish *papaya*, papaya.]

pa•pa•ya (pə **pä′**yə) *n.* **1.** The large yellow fruit of a tropical American tree, having many small seeds and a sweet taste. **2.** The tree that bears such fruit. [First written down in 1598 in Modern English, of Cariban origin.]

pa•per (**pā′**pər) *n.* **1.a.** A material produced, usually in thin sheets, from cellulose pulp derived mainly from wood, rags, and certain grasses. It is used for writing, printing, drawing, wrapping, and covering walls. **b.** A single sheet of this material. **c.** A sheet of this material with writing or printing on it. **2.a.** A document: *legal papers.* **b. papers.** Documents that establish identity or give other information about the bearer. **3. papers.** A collection of letters, diaries, and other personal writings. **4.** A newspaper. **5.** Wallpaper. **6.a.** A report or essay assigned in school. **b.** A scholarly essay: *The professor wrote a paper on the immune system.* *—tr.v.* **pa•pered, pa•per•ing, pa•pers. 1.** To cover or wrap in paper: *Photos of old movie stars papered the mirror.* **2.** To cover with wallpaper. *—adj.* Made of or producing paper: *paper plates; a paper mill.* [First written down in 1364 in Middle English, from Greek *papuros*, papyrus.] **—pa′per•y** *adj.*

pa•per•back (**pā′**pər băk′) *n.* A book with a flexible paper binding.

pa•per•board (**pā′**pər bôrd′) *n.* Cardboard; pasteboard.

pa•per•boy (**pā′**pər boi′) *n.* A boy who sells or delivers newspapers.

paper clip *n.* A piece of wire that is bent and twisted and is used to hold paper together.

pa•per•girl (**pā′**pər gûrl′) *n.* A girl who sells or delivers newspapers.

paper money *n.* Currency in the form of government notes and bank notes.

paper nautilus *n.* A sea mollusk related to the nautilus. The female has a thin papery shell.

pa•per•weight (**pā′**pər wāt′) *n.* A small heavy object for holding down loose papers.

pa•per•work (**pā′**pər wûrk′) *n.* Work involving the handling of reports, letters, and forms.

pa•pier-mâ•ché (**pā′**pər mə **shā′**) *n.* A material made from paper pulp mixed with glue or paste, that can be molded into various shapes when wet. *—adj.* Made of this material: *a papier-mâché piñata.*

pa•pil•la (pə **pĭl′**ə) *n., pl.* **pa•pil•lae** (pə **pĭl′**ē). **1.** A small projection from a body surface, as one of the tiny projections on the top of the tongue. **2.** A pimple or pustule.

pa•pist (**pā′**pĭst) *n. Offensive.* A Roman Catholic.

pa•poose (pă **po͞os′**) *n.* A Native American baby.

pa•pri•ka (pă **prē′**kə *or* **păp′**rĭ kə) *n.* A mild powdered seasoning made from sweet red peppers.

Pap smear (păp) *n.* A test for cancer, especially of a woman's or girl's genital tract, in which a group of cells is spread on a slide, specially stained, and examined under a microscope.

Pap•u•a New Guin•ea (**păp′**yo͞o ə no͞o **gĭn′**ē). An island country of the southwest Pacific Ocean made up of the eastern half of New Guinea, the Bismarck Archipelago, the western Solomons, and adjacent islands. The country gained its independence from Australia in 1975. Capital, Port Moresby. Population, 3,010,727.

pa•py•rus (pə **pī′**rəs) *n., pl.* **pa•py•rus•es** or **pa•py•ri** (pə **pī′**rī′). **1.** A tall water plant similar to a reed, found in northern Africa and nearby regions. **2.** A kind of paper made from the stems and pith of this plant. **3.** A document written on this material.

par (pär) *n.* **1.** An accepted or normal average: *below par in physical condition.* **2.** A level of equality; equal footing: *good food, but not on a par with my grandmother's.* **3.** The number of golf strokes regarded as necessary to complete a given hole or course in expert play. **4.** The value printed on the face of a stock or bond as distinguished from the current market value. *—adj.* Equal to the standard; normal: *a par performance.*

par. *abbr.* An abbreviation of: **1.** Paragraph. **2.** Parallel.

para–[1] or **par–** *pref.* A prefix that means: **1.** Along-

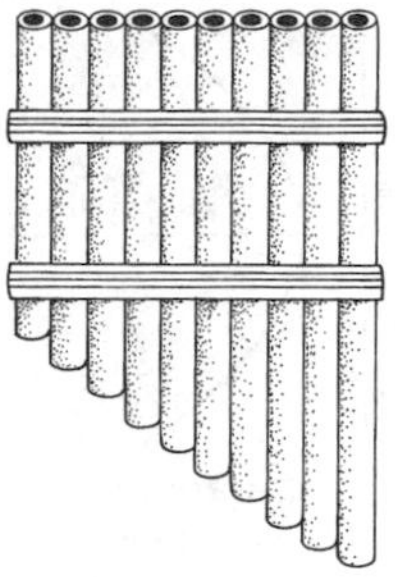

panpipe

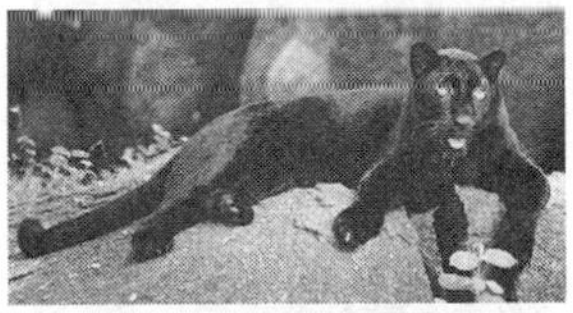

panther

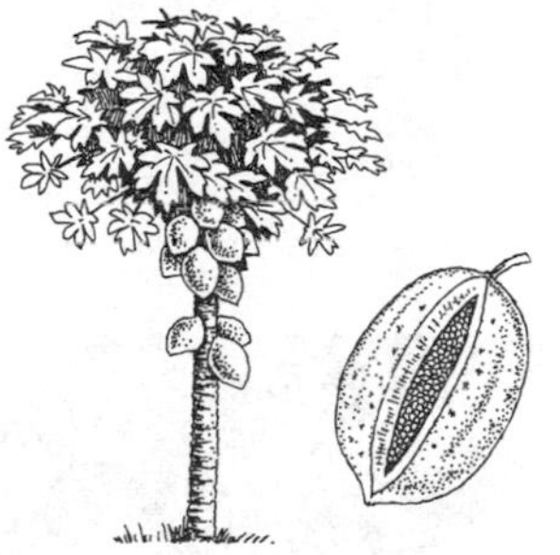

papaya

ă	pat	oi	boy
ā	pay	ou	out
âr	care	o͝o	took
ä	father	o͞o	boot
ĕ	pet	ŭ	cut
ē	be	ûr	urge
ĭ	pit	th	thin
ī	pie	*th*	this
îr	pier	hw	whoop
ŏ	pot	zh	vision
ō	toe	ə	about
ô	paw	N	*French* bon

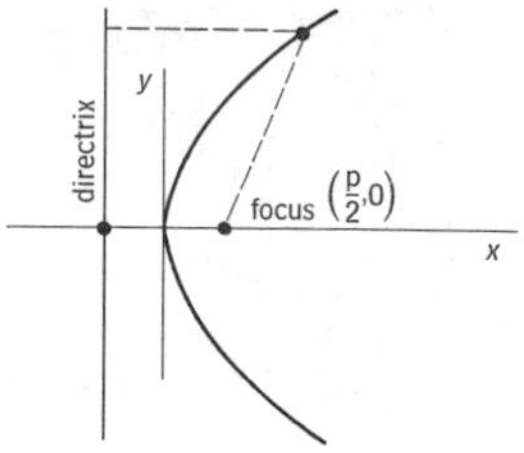

parabola
$y^2 = 2px$

parachute

parallel bars

side; near: *parathyroid gland.* **2.** Assistant: *paramedic.*

para–² *pref.* A prefix that means parachute: *paratrooper.*

par•a•ble (păr′ə bəl) *n.* A simple story illustrating a moral or religious lesson.

pa•rab•o•la (pə răb′ə lə) *n.* The curve formed by the set of points in a plane that are all equally distant from a given line and a given point not on the line.

par•a•bol•ic (păr′ə bŏl′ĭk) *adj.* Of or shaped like a parabola. **—par′a•bol′i•cal•ly** *adv.*

par•a•chute (păr′ə sho͞ot′) *n.* **1.** A foldable device consisting of a large piece of fabric attached by cords to a harness and used to slow the fall of persons or objects from great heights. **2.** A similar device used to slow speeding vehicles. *—v.* **par•a•chut•ed, par•a•chut•ing, par•a•chutes.** *—intr.* To descend by parachute. *—tr.* To drop (supplies, for example) by parachute. [First written down in 1785 in Modern English, from French : *para(sol)*, parasol + *chute*, fall.] **—par′a•chut′ist** *n.*

pa•rade (pə rād′) *n.* **1.a.** A public procession in which assembled people or vehicles pass by spectators, often with music, costumes, and colorful display. **b.** The people participating in such a procession. **2.a.** A formal review of marching military troops. **b.** The grounds on which such reviews are held. **3.** The group participating in such a public event or military review. **4.** A line or group of moving people or things: *a parade of ants.* **5.** An elaborate or vulgar display: *making a parade of his wealth.* *—v.* **pa•rad•ed, pa•rad•ing, pa•rades.** *—intr.* **1.** To take part in a parade: *A company of firefighters paraded in uniform.* **2.** To display oneself proudly or vainly: *a peacock parading before his mate.* *—tr.* **1.** To exhibit proudly or vainly: *paraded his children before the guests.* **2.** To assemble and guide (troops, for example) in a parade. [First written down in 1656 in Modern English, from Old French *parade*, exhibition, from *parer*, to embellish.] **—pa•rad′er** *n.*

par•a•digm (păr′ə dīm′) *n.* **1.** A list of the inflectional forms of a word, considered as a model for determining the forms of other words like it. **2.** An example of how something should be done or treated; a model.

par•a•dise (păr′ə dīs′ *or* păr′ə dīz′) *n.* **1.** Often **Paradise.** The Garden of Eden. **2.** Heaven. **3.** A place or condition of perfect happiness or beauty. **4.** A perfect or ideal place: *a paradise for anglers.* [First written down before 1200 in Middle English, from Greek *paradeisos*, garden, enclosed park.]

par•a•dox (păr′ə dŏks′) *n.* **1.** A statement that contains or implies its own contradiction and therefore has an uncertain meaning or no meaning; for example, "We destroyed the town in order to save it" is a paradox. **2.** A statement that appears to contradict itself or to be untrue but that may be true; for example, "Light consists both of waves and of particles" is a paradox that can be demonstrated in experiments. **3.** A person or thing that is apparently contradictory or inexplicable.

par•a•dox•i•cal (păr′ə dŏk′sĭ kəl) *adj.* Containing a paradox; apparently contradictory. **—par′a•dox′i•cal•ly** *adv.*

par•af•fin (păr′ə fĭn) *n.* A waxy, white or colorless, solid hydrocarbon mixture used in making candles, wax paper, lubricating materials, and sealing materials. *—tr.v.* **par•af•fined, par•af•fin•ing, par•af•fins.** To treat, coat, or seal with paraffin

paraffin series *n.* A family of related hydrocarbon compounds composed so that if *n* is the number of carbon atoms contained, $2n + 2$ is the number of hydrogen atoms contained.

par•a•gon (păr′ə gŏn′) *n.* A model of excellence; a perfect example: *a paragon of honesty.*

par•a•graph (păr′ə grăf′) *n.* **1.** A division of a piece of writing that begins on a new, usually indented line and that consists of one or more sentences on a single idea or aspect of the subject. **2.** A mark (¶) used to indicate where a new paragraph should begin. *—tr.v.* **par•a•graphed, par•a•graph•ing, par•a•graphs.** To divide (a written work) into paragraphs. [First written down before 1500 in Middle English and spelled *paragraf*, from Greek *paragraphein*, to write beside.] **—par′a•graph′ic, par′a•graph′i•cal** *adj.*

Par•a•guay (păr′ə gwī′ *or* păr′ə gwā′). A country of south-central South America between Brazil and Argentina. Paraguay gained its independence from Spain in 1811. Asunción is the capital and the largest city. Population, 3,026,165.

par•a•keet (păr′ə kēt′) *n.* Any of various small parrots usually having a long pointed tail. [First written down in 1621 in Modern English and spelled *parakeete*, from Spanish *periquito*, probably from *Perico*, diminutive of *Pedro*, Peter.]

par•a•le•gal (păr′ə lē′gəl) *adj.* Of, relating to, or being a person with specialized training who assists a lawyer.

par•al•lax (păr′ə lăks′) *n.* An apparent change in the position of an object caused by a change in the observer's position.

par•al•lel (păr′ə lĕl′) *adj.* **1.** Lying in the same plane and not intersecting: *parallel lines.* **2.** Not intersecting: *parallel planes.* **3.** Having corresponding points always separated by the same distance: *a road parallel to the river.* **4.** Matching feature for feature; corresponding: *parallel economic developments in two countries.* **5.** Of, consisting of, or containing electric circuits connected so that a flowing current is divided between them: *The circuit of the lights is parallel, so that if one bulb burns out, the others stay lit.* *—adv.* In a parallel course or direction: *a reef running parallel to the shore.* *—n.* **1.** Any of a set of parallel geometric figures, especially lines. **2.** Something closely resembling something else; a corresponding case or instance. **3.** A comparison showing close resemblance; an analogy. **4.** Any of the lines considered to encircle the earth parallel to the plane of the equator, used to represent degrees of latitude. **5.** An arrangement of an electric circuit that splits the current in two or more paths: *The lights are wired in parallel.* *—tr.v.* **par•al•leled, par•al•lel•ing, par•al•lels** also **par•al•lelled, par•al•lel•ling, par•al•lels.** **1.** To make or place parallel: *paralleled the two edges of the fabric.* **2.** To be or extend parallel to: *The street paralleled a canal.* **3.** To compare; liken: *He paralleled the situation to a gathering storm.* [First written down in 1549 in Modern English, from Greek *parallēlos* : *para*, beside + *allēlōn*, of one another.]

parallel bars *pl.n.* Two horizontal poles set parallel to each other above the floor and used in gymnastic exercises.

par•al•lel•ism (păr′ə lĕl ĭz′əm) *n.* **1.** The condition, position, or relationship of being parallel. **2.** Similarity or correspondence.

par•al•lel•o•gram (păr′ə lĕl′ə grăm′) *n.* A plane four-sided geometric figure in which each pair of opposite sides is parallel.

pa•ral•y•sis (pə răl′ĭ sĭs) *n., pl.* **pa•ral•y•ses** (pə-răl′ĭ sēz′). **1.** Partial or complete loss of the ability to move or feel sensations in a part of the body, resulting from disease or injury that damages the nerves going to and from the part. **2.** An inability to move or function normally. [First written down in 1525 in Modern English, from Greek *paralusis*, from *paraluein*, to cut loose, disable.]

par•a•lyt•ic (păr′ə lĭt′ĭk) *adj.* Of, causing, or affected with paralysis. —*n.* A person affected with paralysis.

par•a•lyze (păr′ə līz′) *tr.v.* **par•a•lyzed, par•a•lyz•ing, par•a•lyz•es. 1.** To affect with paralysis; make unable to move or feel. **2.a.** To make helpless or motionless: *paralyzed by fear.* **b.** To block the normal functioning of; bring to a standstill: *The blizzard paralyzed of the city.*

Par•a•mar•i•bo (păr′ə măr′ə bō′). The capital and largest city of Suriname, in the northern part of the country near the Atlantic Ocean. It was settled in the 1630's. Population, 67,905.

par•a•me•ci•um (păr′ə mē′shē əm *or* păr′ə mē′sē əm) *n., pl.* **par•a•me•ci•a** (păr′ə mē′shē ə *or* păr′ə mē′ sē ə) or **par•a•me•ci•ums.** Any of various freshwater protozoans that are usually oval in shape and that move by means of cilia.

par•a•med•ic (păr′ə mĕd′ĭk) *n.* A person who is trained to give emergency treatment or to assist medical professionals. —**par′a•med′i•cal** *adj.*

pa•ram•e•ter (pə răm′ĭ tər) *n.* **1.** A variable or an arbitrary constant appearing in a mathematical expression, each value of which restricts or determines the specific form of the expression. **2.** A fixed limit or boundary: *We must stay within the parameters of the budget.*

par•a•mil•i•tar•y (păr′ə mĭl′ĭ tĕr′ē) *adj.* Organized or functioning like a military unit but not as part of regular military forces.

par•a•mount (păr′ə mount′) *adj.* **1.** Supreme in rank or position; leading. **2.** Of greatest importance or concern; primary.

par•a•noi•a (păr′ə noi′ə) *n.* **1.** A serious mental disorder marked by delusions of persecution or grandeur. **2.** Irrational fear for one's security.

par•a•noi•ac (păr′ə noi′ăk′) *n.* A person who is affected with paranoia. —*adj.* Of or resembling paranoia.

par•a•noid (păr′ə noid′) *adj.* Relating to, affected with, or characteristic of paranoia. —*n.* A person affected with paranoia.

par•a•pet (păr′ə pĕt′) *n.* **1.** A low wall or railing along the edge of a roof or balcony. **2.** An embankment protecting soldiers from enemy fire.

par•a•pher•na•lia (păr′ə fər nāl′yə) *pl.n. (used with a singular or plural verb).* **1.** A person's personal belongings. **2.** The equipment used in or associated with some activity.

par•a•phrase (păr′ə frāz′) *n.* A restatement in other words. —*tr.v.* **par•a•phrased, par•a•phras•ing, par•a•phras•es.** To restate in other words: *paraphrasing a passage to clarify its meaning.*

par•a•ple•gi•a (păr′ə plē′jē ə *or* păr′ə plē′jə) *n.* Paralysis of the entire lower part of the body, usually caused by injury to the spinal cord.

par•a•ple•gic (păr′ə plē′jĭk) *adj.* Of or affected by paraplegia. —*n.* A person with paraplegia.

par•a•site (păr′ə sīt′) *n.* **1.** An organism that lives in or on a different kind of organism from which it gets nourishment and to which it is sometimes harmful. Lice and tapeworms are parasites. **2.** A person who takes advantage of the generosity of others without making any useful return. [First written down in 1539 in Modern English, from Greek *parasitos*, person who eats at someone else's table : *para-*, beside + *sitos*, grain, food.]

par•a•sit•ic (păr′ə sĭt′ĭk) *adj.* **1.** Of, relating to, or caused by a parasite: *a parasitic disease.* **2.** Living as a parasite: *Mistletoe is a parasitic plant.*

par•a•sol (păr′ə sôl′ *or* păr′ə sŏl′) *n.* A small light umbrella used as a protection against the sun, especially by women. [First written down in 1616 in Modern English, from Italian *parasole* : *parare*, to shield + *sole*, sun.]

par•a•thy•roid gland (păr′ə thī′roid) *n.* Any of four small kidney-shaped glands that lie in pairs at the sides of the thyroid gland, secreting a hormone that controls the metabolism of calcium and phosphorus.

par•a•troop•er (păr′ə tro͞o′pər) *n.* A member of an infantry unit trained and equipped to parachute from airplanes.

par•boil (pär′boil′) *tr.v.* **par•boiled, par•boil•ing, par•boils.** To boil (food) briefly.

par•cel (pär′səl) *n.* **1.** Something wrapped up in a bundle; a package. **2.** A section or piece of land; a plot. **3.** A group; a bunch: *a parcel of assistants.* —*tr.v.* **par•celed, par•cel•ing, par•cels** also **par•celled, par•cel•ling, par•cels.** To divide into parts and distribute; allot: *parcel out work.* [First written down about 1303 in Middle English and spelled *parcelle*, from Latin *particula*, small part.]

parcel post *n.* The branch of the postal service that handles parcels.

parch (pärch) *v.* **parched, parch•ing, parch•es.** —*tr.* **1.** To make very dry, especially by intense heat: *A south wind parched the topsoil.* **2.** To dry or roast (corn or peanuts, for example) by heating. —*intr.* To become very dry, especially from intense heat.

parch•ment (pärch′mənt) *n.* **1.** The skin of a sheep or goat, prepared as a material to write on. **2.** A piece of writing on a sheet or roll of this skin. **3.** A diploma. **4.** Heavy paper that looks like parchment.

par•don (pär′dn) *tr.v.* **par•doned, par•don•ing, par•dons. 1.** To release (a person) from punishment or disfavor. See Synonyms at **forgive. 2.** To let (an offense) pass without punishment. **3.** To make allowance for; excuse: *Pardon me for asking.* —*n.* **1.** The act of pardoning; forgiveness. **2.** Exemption from punishment granted by an official with authority over a legal case. **3.** Polite forgiveness, as for a discourtesy, interruption, or failure to hear: *begged her pardon for being late.* [First written down in 1433 in Middle English and spelled *pardonen*, from Old French *pardoner*, from Latin *dōnāre*, to give, forgive.]

par•don•a•ble (pär′dn ə bəl) *adj.* Easily pardoned; excusable: *displayed her gold medal with pardonable pride.* —**par′don•a•bly** *adv.*

pare (pâr) *tr.v.* **pared, par•ing, pares. 1.** To remove the skin or covering of with a knife: *pare potatoes.* **2.** To remove (a surface part) with a knife; trim off: *held the avocado firmly and pared away the rind.* **3.** To make smaller by or as if by cutting: *pared the budget to a bare minimum.* [First written down before 1300 in Middle English and spelled *paren*, from Latin *parāre*, to prepare.]

❑ *These sound alike:* **pare, pair** (two), **pear** (fruit).

par•e•gor•ic (păr′ə gôr′ĭk *or* păr′ə gŏr′ĭk) *n.* A medicine containing opium and camphor, used to relieve diarrhea and intestinal pain.

pa•ren•chy•ma (pə rĕng′kə mə) *n.* **1.** The essential or characteristic tissue of an organ as distinguished from the connective tissue that holds it in place. **2.** The fundamental tissue of plants, which consists of thin-walled nonspecialized cells, and which, in higher plants, supports the plant body, roots, and leaves, stores water, and contains chloroplasts.

par•ent (pâr′ənt *or* păr′ənt) *n.* **1.** A father or mother. **2.** An ancestor. **3.** A guardian; a protector. **4.** An organism that produces or generates another. **5.** The source or cause of something. [First written down about 1400 in Middle English, from Latin *parēns*.] —**par′ent•hood′** *n.*

par•ent•age (pâr′ən tĭj *or* păr′ən tĭj) *n.* Descent from parents or ancestors; lineage; origin.

pa•ren•tal (pə rĕn′tl) *adj.* Of, relating to, or char-

ă	pat	oi	boy
ā	pay	ou	out
âr	care	o͝o	took
ä	father	o͞o	boot
ĕ	pet	ŭ	cut
ē	be	ûr	urge
ĭ	pit	th	thin
ī	pie	*th*	this
îr	pier	hw	whoop
ŏ	pot	zh	vision
ō	toe	ə	about
ô	paw	N	*French* bon

Rosa Parks

parquetry
Parquet floor

acteristic of a parent: *parental control of a child's money.* —**pa•ren′tal•ly** *adv.*

pa•ren•the•sis (pə rĕn′thĭ sĭs) *n., pl.* **par•en•the•ses** (pə rĕn′thĭ sēz′). **1.** Either or both of the upright curved lines, (or), used to mark off additional or explanatory remarks in printing or writing. **2.** A qualifying or explanatory phrase placed within a sentence in such a way that the sentence is grammatically complete without it. **3.** A comment departing from the main topic.

par•en•thet•i•cal (păr′ən thĕt′ĭ kəl) also **par•en•thet•ic** (păr′ən thĕt′ĭk) *adj.* **1.** Contained or grammatically capable of being contained within parentheses: *a parenthetical construction at the end of a sentence.* **2.** Forming a brief explanation or digression: *a parenthetical aside during a speech.* —**par′en•thet′i•cal•ly** *adv.*

pa•re•sis (pə rē′sĭs *or* păr′ĭ sĭs) *n.* Slight or partial paralysis.

par•fait (pär fā′) *n.* **1.** A sweet frozen dessert made with cream, eggs, and flavoring and served in a tall glass. **2.** A dessert of layers, often of ice cream with various toppings, served in a tall glass. [First written down in 1894 in Modern English, from Old French *parfait*, perfect.]

pa•ri•ah (pə rī′ə) *n.* A person who has been excluded from society; an outcast.

pa•ri•e•tal bone (pə rī′ĭ təl) *n.* Either of the two large bones that form the top and sides of the skull.

par•i-mu•tu•el (păr′ĭ myōō′chōō əl) *n.* **1.** A system of betting on races in which the winners divide the total amount bet in proportion to the amounts they bet individually. **2.** A machine for recording and totaling bets made under this system.

par•ing (pâr′ĭng) *n.* Something, such as a skin or peeling, that has been pared off.

Par•is[1] (păr′ĭs) *n.* In Greek mythology, the Trojan prince whose abduction of Helen causes the Trojan War.

Par•is[2] (păr′ĭs). The capital and largest city of France, in the north-central part of the country on the Seine River. Paris has been the capital of France since 987. Population, 2,149,900.

par•ish (păr′ĭsh) *n.* **1.a.** A division of an Anglican or a Roman Catholic diocese consisting of an area with its own church. **b.** The members of such a division. **2.** An administrative district in Louisiana corresponding to a county in other states.

pa•rish•ion•er (pə rĭsh′ə nər) *n.* A member of a parish.

par•i•ty (păr′ĭ tē) *n., pl.* **par•i•ties. 1.** Equality, as in amount, status, value, or price: *firefighters striking for parity of pay with police officers.* **2.** A fixed relative value between two different kinds of money: *the parity between gold coins and paper currency.* **3.** A level of prices paid to farmers for their products that gives the farmers the same purchasing power they had during a chosen earlier period.

park (pärk) *n.* **1.** A tract of land enclosed for recreational use inside a town or city. **2.** A tract of land kept in its natural state for recreational use. **3.** A fairly large or open area used for recreation or entertainment: *an amusement park.* **4.** A stadium or enclosed playing field: *a baseball park.* **5.** A place for storing or leaving vehicles: *a car park.* —*v.* **parked, park•ing, parks.** —*tr.* **1.** To stop or leave (a vehicle) for a time in a certain place away from traffic. **2.** *Informal.* To place or leave temporarily: *parked his lunch box on the porch while they played.* —*intr.* To park a motor vehicle: *parked in front of the restaurant.* [First written down in 1222 in Middle English, from Old French *parc*, of Germanic origin.]

par•ka (pär′kə) *n.* A warm fur or cloth jacket with a hood.

park•ing lot (pär′kĭng) *n.* An area for parking motor vehicles.

parking meter *n.* A coin-operated device that allows the parking of a motor vehicle for a given period of time.

Par•kin•son's disease (pär′kĭn sənz) *n.* A disease of the nervous system that occurs mainly in people over the age of 50 and tends to become more severe over time. Its symptoms include weakness, muscular tremors, slowing of movement, and partial paralysis of the face. [First written down in 1877 in Modern English, after James *Parkinson* (1755–1824), British physician.]

Parks (pärks), **Rosa.** Born 1913. American civil rights leader who was jailed for her refusal to give up her seat on a bus to a white man in Montgomery, Alabama (1955), which stirred the civil rights movement across the nation.

park•way (pärk′wā′) *n.* **1.** A broad landscaped highway. **2.** A grassy or tree-lined public walk.

par•lance (pär′ləns) *n.* A special kind or style of language: *in the parlance of lawyers.*

par•lay (pär′lā′ *or* pär′lē) *tr.v.* **par•layed, par•lay•ing, par•lays. 1.** To bet (money) on two or more successive events at once, with the winnings of one, plus the original stake, to be automatically risked on the next. **2.** To increase (money) to a much larger amount by repeated investments: *parlayed his small capital into a fortune.* **3.** To use to great advantage or profit: *parlayed a knack for mimicry into a career as an entertainer.* —*n.* A bet made up of the sum of a previous wager plus its winnings.

par•ley (pär′lē) *n., pl.* **par•leys. 1.** A conference, especially between enemies or opponents. **2.** Discussion; conversation: *no time for parley.* —*intr.v.* **par•leyed, par•ley•ing, par•leys.** To hold a parley; confer.

par•lia•ment (pär′lə mənt) *n.* **1.** An assembly of persons that makes the laws of a nation. **2. Parliament.** The national legislature of the United Kingdom, made up of the House of Commons and the House of Lords. [First written down before 1300 in Middle English and spelled *parlement*, from Old French *parler*, to talk.]

par•lia•men•tar•i•an (pär′lə mĕn târ′ē ən) *n.* An expert in parliamentary rules and procedures.

par•lia•men•ta•ry (pär′lə mĕn′tə rē *or* pär′lə mĕn′trē) *adj.* **1.** Of or relating to a parliament. **2.** Following the rules of procedure of a parliament: *parliamentary debate.* **3.** Having a parliament: *parliamentary government.*

par•lor (pär′lər) *n.* **1.** A room, as in a home or dormitory, for entertaining visitors. **2.** A room or a separate section of a building designed for some special use: *a billiard parlor.* [First written down before 1200 in Middle English and spelled *parlur*, from Old French, from *parler*, to talk.]

parlor car *n.* A railroad car for day travel fitted with individual reserved seats.

par•lour (pär′lər) *n. Chiefly British.* Variant of **parlor.**

Par•me•san (pär′mə zän′) *n.* A hard dry Italian cheese, usually served grated.

pa•ro•chi•al (pə rō′kē əl) *adj.* **1.** Of or relating to a parish: *a parochial priest.* **2.** Limited in range or understanding; narrow: *a parochial mind.* —**pa•ro′chi•al•ism** *n.* —**pa•ro′chi•al•ly** *adv.*

parochial school *n.* A school supported by a church parish.

par•o•dy (păr′ə dē) *n.* **par•o•dies. 1.** A comic imitation, as of a person, literary work, or style, that exaggerates the characteristics of the original to make it seem ridiculous. **2.** Something so bad as to appear to be a mockery: *The trial was a parody of justice.* —*tr.v.* **par•o•died, par•o•dy•ing, par•o•**

dies. To present, perform, or be a parody of: *parodied the style of editorial writers.*

pa•role (pə rōl′) *n.* The early release of a prisoner on condition of good behavior. *—tr.v.* **pa•roled, pa•rol•ing, pa•roles.** To release on parole.

par•ox•ysm (păr′ək sĭz′əm) *n.* **1.** A sudden outburst of strong emotion: *a paroxysm of anger.* **2.** A spasm or fit; a convulsion.

par•quet (pär kā′) *n.* **1.** A floor made of parquetry. **2.** The main floor of a theater.

par•quet•ry (pär′kĭ trē) *n., pl.* **par•quet•ries.** Wood, often of contrasting colors, worked into a pattern or mosaic, used especially for floors.

par•ri•cide (păr′ĭ sīd′) *n.* The act of murdering one's own father, mother, or other close relative. **—par′ri•cid′al** (păr′ĭ sīd′l) *adj.*

par•rot (păr′ət) *n.* **1.** Any of numerous tropical birds having a short hooked bill and usually brightly colored feathers. Some kinds are kept as pets and can be taught to imitate spoken words. **2.** A person who repeats or imitates something without understanding it. *—tr.v.* **par•rot•ed, par•rot•ing, par•rots.** To repeat or imitate (another's words or another person), especially without understanding. [First written down about 1525 in Modern English, probably from French dialectal *Perrot,* diminutive of *Pierre,* Peter.]

par•ry (păr′ē) *tr.v.* **par•ried, par•ry•ing, par•ries. 1.** To turn aside; deflect: *parry a thrust in fencing.* **2.** To avoid skillfully; evade: *parried questions of the reporters.* *—n., pl.* **par•ries. 1.** The act or maneuver of deflecting a blow, especially in fencing. **2.** An evasive action or answer: *met the accusation with a deft parry.*

parse (pärs) *v.* **parsed, pars•ing, pars•es.** *—tr.* **1.** To break (a sentence or phrase) down into its parts of speech with an explanation of the form and function of each word. **2.** To indicate the part of speech, form, and function of (a word in a sentence or phrase). *—intr.* To be clearly divisible into parts of speech: *a sentence that parses easily.*

par•sec (pär′sĕk′) *n.* A unit of astronomical distance equal to 3.258 light-years. [First written down in 1913 in Modern English : *par(allax)* + *sec(ond).*]

Par•see (pär′sē *or* pär sē′) *n., pl.* **Par•sees.** A member of a sect of Zoroastrianism in India.

par•si•mo•ni•ous (pär′sə mō′nē əs) *adj.* Marked by parsimony; ungenerous; stingy. **—par′si•mo′ni•ous•ly** *adv.*

par•si•mo•ny (pär′sə mō′nē) *n.* Extreme reluctance to spend money or use resources; stinginess.

pars•ley (pär′slē) *n., pl.* **pars•leys.** A plant having edible, fragrant, feathery leaves used to flavor food and as a garnish. [First written down about 1000 in Old English and spelled *petersilie,* from Greek *petroselinon.*]

pars•nip (pär′snĭp) *n.* **1.** The long whitish root of a plant related to parsley, eaten as a vegetable. **2.** The plant that has such a root.

par•son (pär′sən) *n.* **1.** A cleric in charge of a parish, especially in the Anglican Church. **2.** A member of the Christian clergy, especially a Protestant minister.

par•son•age (pär′sə nĭj) *n.* The official residence of a parson, as provided by the church.

part (pärt) *n.* **1.** A portion, division, or segment of a whole: *arrived late and missed part of the movie; gave her a part of the orange.* **2.a.** One of several equal portions that when combined make up a whole: *For the dressing we mixed two parts olive oil with one part vinegar.* **b.** A fraction: *What part of a quart is a pint?* **3.** An organ, limb, or other division of an animal or a plant. **4.** A piece in a machine or system that can be removed or replaced; a component. **5.** One of the functions or tasks that must be performed in a common effort; a duty or share: *doing one's part.* **6.** A role: *a small part in the play.* **7.a.** One of the melodic lines that go together to make musical harmony: *singing the soprano part.* **b.** A written representation of such a melodic line. **8.** A side in a dispute or controversy: *We took the part of the angry workers.* **9.** A region, an area, or a land. Often used in the plural: *relatives scattered in remote parts.* **10.** Natural ability; talent: *a man of parts.* **11.** The line where the hair on the head is parted. *—v.* **part•ed, part•ing, parts.** *—tr.* **1.** Two divide into two or more parts; split: *parted the log with an ax.* **2.** To break up by separating: *They parted company.* See Synonyms at **separate. 3.** To put or keep apart; come between: *They were good friends until a silly quarrel parted them.* **4.** To comb (hair, for example) away from a dividing line, as on the scalp. *—intr.* **1.** To become divided or separated: *The tree trunk parted into branches higher up.* **2.** To leave one another; separate: *They finally parted when she moved west.* **3.** To go away; depart: *She parted from high school with a sense of accomplishment.* *—adv.* In part; partially: *Her dog is part collie, part German shepherd.* *—adj.* Not full; partial: *owned a part interest in a small business.* ***—idioms.*** **for (one's) part.** So far as one is concerned: *For my part, I have no objections.* **for the most part.** In most cases; chiefly. **in part.** To some extent; partly. **part and parcel.** A basic or essential part: *paying for moving was part and parcel of the job offer.* **part with.** To give up or let go of; yield: *hated to part with her hard-earned salary.* **take part.** To join in; participate: *She took part in the discussion.* [First written down about 1250 in Middle English, from Latin *pars.*]

part. *abbr.* An abbreviation of participle.

par•take (pär tāk′) *intr.v.* **par•took** (pär to͝ok′), **par•tak•en** (pär tā′kən), **par•tak•ing, par•takes. 1.** To take part; participate: *partake in the festivities.* **2.** To take a portion; eat or drink a helping: *invited to partake of their dinner.* **3.** To share some of the properties of something else: *laughter that partook of a chicken's cackle.* [First written down in 1561 in Modern English, from Middle English *part-taker,* one who takes part.] **—par•tak′er** *n.*

par•the•no•gen•e•sis (pär′thə nō jĕn′ĭ sĭs) *n.* Reproduction in which an egg develops without fertilization, as in certain insects. **—par′the•no•ge•net′ic** (pär′thə nō jə nĕt′ĭk) *adj.* **—par′the•no•ge•net′i•cal•ly** *adv.*

Par•the•non (pär′thə nŏn′) *n.* The chief temple of the goddess Athena, built on the Acropolis at Athens, Greece, in the fifth century B.C.

par•tial (pär′shəl) *adj.* **1.** Not total; incomplete: *partial success.* **2.** Favoring one side; biased. **3.** Especially attracted or inclined: *She's partial to detective stories.* [First written down before 1398 in Middle English and spelled *parcial,* from Late Latin *partiālis,* from Latin *pars,* part.]

par•ti•al•i•ty (pär′shē ăl′ĭ tē) *n., pl.* **par•ti•al•i•ties. 1.** An inclination to favor one side over another or others; a bias: *trying to judge without partiality.* **2.** A strong preference; a special fondness: *a partiality for old clothes.*

par•tial•ly (pär′shə lē) *adv.* To a certain degree or extent; incompletely: *partially thawed food.*

partial product *n.* A product formed by multiplying the multiplicand by one digit of the multiplier when the multiplier has more than one digit in its numeral. For example, the product of 67 multiplied by 12 is 134 + 670 = 804. In this example 134 and 670 are partial products.

partial quotient *n.* A quotient that appears after any stage of a division problem requiring two or

parrot

Parthenon

On the Acropolis in Athens, Greece

ă	pat	oi	boy
ā	pay	ou	out
âr	care	o͝o	took
ä	father	o͞o	boot
ĕ	pet	ŭ	cut
ē	be	ûr	urge
ĭ	pit	th	thin
ī	pie	*th*	this
îr	pier	hw	whoop
ŏ	pot	zh	vision
ō	toe	ə	about
ô	paw	N	*French* bon

Usage: participle

You should always avoid the "dangling participle," as in the sentence *Turning the corner, the view was quite different.* This sentence is constructed so that it seems that the present participle *turning* modifies the noun *view.* As you read the sentence, you might at first think that the view is turning the corner. You should rewrite such sentences: *The view was quite different when we turned the corner,* or *Turning the corner, we saw a different view.*

partridge
Male crested wood partridge

more stages and that is added to the other quotients to give the final quotient. For example, in the problem 248 ÷ 4 = 60 + 2 = 62, 60 and 2 are partial quotients.

par•tic•i•pant (pär **tĭs′**ə pənt) *n.* A person who participates: *participants in a card game.*

par•tic•i•pate (pär **tĭs′**ə pāt′) *intr.v.* **par•tic•i•pat•ed, par•tic•i•pat•ing, par•tic•i•pates.** To join with others in doing something; take part: *She participated in a discussion group.* [First written down in 1531 in Modern English, from Latin *participāre*, from *particeps*, partaker.] **—par•tic′i•pa′tion** *n.*

par•tic•i•pa•to•ry (pär **tĭs′**ə pə tôr′ē) *adj.* Involving the active participation of many: *participatory democracy.*

par•ti•cip•i•al (pär′tĭ **sĭp′**ē əl) *adj.* Based on, forming, or formed from a participle: *a participial phrase; a participial adjective.*

par•ti•ci•ple (**pär′**tĭ sĭp′əl) *n.* A verb form, in English ending in *–ing* or *–ed,* that is used with auxiliary verbs to indicate certain tenses and that can also function as an adjective. The past participle is also used to make the passive voice. [First written down before 1397 in Middle English, from Latin *participium*, from *particeps*, partaker.] —See Note.

par•ti•cle (**pär′**tĭ kəl) *n.* **1.** A very small piece of solid matter; a speck: *particles of dust.* **2.** A subatomic particle. **3.a.** The smallest possible unit or portion: *applying every particle of strength she had left.* **b.** The least bit or degree: *hardly a particle of difference between the twins.* **4.** In grammar, any of a class of words, including many prepositions and conjunctions, that have little meaning by themselves but help to specify, connect, or limit the meanings of other words. [First written down before 1398 in Middle English, from Latin *particula*, tiny part.]

particle accelerator *n.* Any of several machines, such as a cyclotron, that greatly increase the speed and energy of protons, electrons, and other atomic particles and direct them at the nuclei of atoms, causing the nuclei to release new particles.

par•ti-col•ored (**pär′**tē kŭl′ərd) *adj.* Having different parts or sections colored differently; pied.

par•tic•u•lar (pər **tĭk′**yə lər) *adj.* **1.** Belonging to or associated with a specific person, group, or thing; not general: *the particular characteristics that distinguish oaks from other trees.* **2.** Distinct from others; specific; certain: *at that particular time of year.* **3.** Exceptional; special: *paying particular attention.* **4.** Providing full details: *a particular account of the incident.* **5.** Giving or demanding close attention to details; fussy: *She's very particular about how her meat is cooked.* —*n.* **1.** A single item, fact, or detail: *correct in every particular.* **2. particulars.** Items of information; detailed news: *reported the particulars of their voyage.* **—*idiom.* in particular.** Particularly; especially. [First written down before 1387 in Middle English and spelled *particuler*, from Latin *particula*, small part.]

par•tic•u•lar•i•ty (pər tĭk′yə **lăr′**ĭ tē) *n., pl.* **par•tic•u•lar•i•ties. 1.** The quality of being particular rather than general or universal: *the particularity of a proper noun, which names only one thing or person.* **2.** The quality of including or providing details: *the particularity of a newspaper story.* **3.** A detail; a particular. **4.** Close attention to details; fussiness.

par•tic•u•lar•ize (pər **tĭk′**yə lə rīz′) *v.* **par•tic•u•lar•ized, par•tic•u•lar•iz•ing, par•tic•u•lar•iz•es.** —*tr.* **1.** To name one by one; itemize: *an indictment that particularized the charges against him.* **2.** To make particular; individualize: *She began with mere stick figures, then particularized them by drawing in faces.* —*intr.* To give details or particulars. **—par•tic′u•lar•i•za′tion** (pər tĭk′yə lər ĭ **zā′**shən) *n.*

par•tic•u•lar•ly (pər **tĭk′**yə lər lē) *adv.* **1.** As one specific case; specifically: *observing the constellations, particularly the Big Dipper.* **2.** To a great degree; especially: *a particularly good play.* **3.** With attention to particulars; in detail: *spread out the chart and studied it particularly.*

par•tic•u•late (pər **tĭk′**yə lĭt *or* pər **tĭk′**yə lāt′) *adj.* Relating to or formed of separate particles.

part•ing (**pär′**tĭng) *n.* **1.** The act of dividing or the state of being divided; separation: *a parting in the trail.* **2.** A departure or leave-taking. —*adj.* Leaving; departing: *a parting friend.*

par•ti•san (**pär′**tĭ zən) *n.* **1.** A strong supporter, as of a party, a cause, a person, or an idea: *the President and his partisans in Congress.* **2.** A member of an organized body of fighters who attack an enemy within occupied territory; a guerilla. —*adj.* **1.** Having or showing a strong preference or bias: *too partisan to give a fair account of the battle.* **2.** Of, relating to, or marked by a partisan or partisans: *partisan politics.* [First written down in 1555 in Modern English, from Old Italian *partigiano*, from *parte*, part.]

par•ti•tion (pär **tĭsh′**ən) *n.* **1.** A usually thin structure, such as a panel or screen, that divides up a room or other enclosure. **2.** A structure that divides a space. **3.a.** The division of something into parts: *the partition of the land into smaller lots.* **b.** The condition of being divided into parts. —*tr.v.* **par•ti•tioned, par•ti•tion•ing, par•ti•tions. 1.** To divide into separate spaces, parts, or sections: *partitioned the room with a curtain.* **2.** To form into a separate space by means of a partition: *partitioned off the dining area from the kitchen.* [First written down about 1400 in Middle English and spelled *partisoun*, from Latin *partīre*, to divide, from *pars*, part.]

part•ly (**pärt′**lē) *adv.* To some extent; in part: *a journey partly by boat and partly on foot.*

part•ner (**pärt′**nər) *n.* **1.** One of two or more persons associated in some common activity, as: **a.** A member of a business partnership. **b.** A friend with whom one lives, travels, or works: *the cowboy and his partner.* **c.** Either of two persons dancing together. **d.** Either of two persons playing a game together. **2.** A spouse. [First written down about 1300 in Middle English and spelled *partiner*, alteration of *parcener*, joint heir, from Latin *partitiō*, partition.]

part•ner•ship (**pärt′**nər shĭp′) *n.* **1.** The condition of being partners: *built the tree house in partnership with two friends.* **2.** A business contract or relationship between two or more persons in which each agrees to work for a common enterprise and to share the profits or losses. **3.** A close relationship in which each member helps or cooperates with the other: *the partnership of science and industry.*

part of speech *n., pl.* **parts of speech.** One of the grammatical classes into which words are placed according to how they function in a given context. Traditionally, the parts of speech in English are *noun, pronoun, verb, adjective, adverb, preposition, conjunction,* and *interjection.* Sometimes *article* is considered a separate part of speech.

par•took (pär **to͝ok′**) *v.* Past tense of **partake.**

par•tridge (**pär′**trĭj) *n., pl.* **partridge** or **par•tridg•es.** Any of several plump birds related to the pheasant, having brownish feathers and often hunted as game.

part-time (**pärt′**tīm′) *adj.* For or during only part of the usual or standard working time: *a part-time job.* **—part′-time′** *adv.*

par•tu•ri•tion (pär′tyo͞o **rĭsh′**ən *or* pär′to͞o **rĭsh′**ən) *n.* The act or process of giving birth; childbirth.

part•way (pärt′wā′) *adv. Informal.* To a part of the way; partly: *pushed a thumbtack partway into the wood.*

par•ty (pär′tē) *n., pl.* **par•ties. 1.** A social gathering for pleasure or entertainment: *a birthday party.* **2.** A group of people participating together in some activity: *a search party.* **3.** A group organized to advance its political views and usually to nominate and support candidates for public office. **4.a.** A person or group involved in a legal proceeding: *the two parties in a lawsuit.* **b.** A person or group taking part in some action or matter; a participant: *She refused to be a party to the dispute.* [First written down before 1300 in Middle English and spelled *partie*, part, side, group, from Old French *partir*, to divide.]

pas•chal (păs′kəl) *adj.* Of or relating to Passover or Easter.

Pa•siph•a•ë (pə sĭf′ə ē′) *n.* In Greek mythology, the wife of Minos and the mother of the Minotaur.

pass (păs) *v.* **passed, pass•ing, pass•es.** —*intr.* **1.** To go or move; proceed: *people passing from shop to shop.* **2.** To extend; run: *The river passes through our town.* **3.** To move by: *The crowd cheered as the band passed.* **4.** To undergo a course of study, an examination, or a difficulty with favorable results: *After studying hard I passed.* **5.** To get through a period of time: *passed through a difficult time.* **6.** To go by in time: *Time seems to pass quickly when you're on vacation.* **7.** To come to an end: *My anger passed.* **8.** To happen; take place: *What passed at the meeting?* **9.** To be allowed to happen without notice or action: *She let his rude remark pass.* **10.** To be transferred: *Ownership of the farm passed to his niece.* **11.** To be approved: *The law passed by a large majority of senators.* **12.** To be changed from one condition to another: *Daylight passed into darkness.* **13.** In sports, to throw or propel a ball or puck to a teammate. —*tr.* **1.** To go by; leave behind: *She passed the lead runner on the home stretch.* **2.** To go beyond; surpass: *The results of the experiment passed all our expectations.* **3.** To go across; go through: *We passed the border into Virginia.* **4.** To undergo (an examination, for example) with favorable results. **5.** To cause to move or go in a certain way: *I passed the bolt through the bracket and secured it.* **6.a.** To transfer; circulate: *passed the news to friends.* **b.** To hand over: *Please pass the beans.* **7.** To allow to go by; spend: *He passed the winter in Vermont.* **8.** In sports, to throw or propel (a ball or puck) to a teammate. **9.** To discharge (bodily waste). **10.a.** To approve or adopt: *The Senate passed the bill.* **b.** To be approved or adopted by: *The bill passed the Senate.* **11.** To pronounce; utter: *pass judgment.* —*n.* **1.** The act of passing; passage. **2.** A way by which one can go through or around an obstacle, especially a gap in a mountain range. **3.a.** A permit or ticket granting the right to come and go at will. **b.** A ticket granting free entrance or transportation. **4.** A motion with the hand or something held in the hand: *made a pass with the sponge over the table.* **5.** An act of passing a ball or puck to a teammate. **6.** A run by a military aircraft over a target area. **7.** A situation, especially a difficult or threatening one: *His own folly brought him to this pass.* —***idioms.*** **bring to pass.** To cause to happen. **come to pass.** To occur. **pass away.** To die. **pass for.** To be accepted as or believed to be: *My mother can pass for my sister.* **pass off.** To describe, offer, or sell as genuine: *passed off the rhinestones as diamonds.* **pass out.** To lose consciousness. **pass over.** To leave out; disregard. **pass up.** *Informal.* To let go by; refuse: *I won't pass up dessert.* —SEE NOTE.

pass•a•ble (păs′ə bəl) *adj.* **1.** Capable of being passed or crossed: *a passable road.* **2.** Satisfactory but not outstanding; adequate: *a passable job of acting.* —**pass′a•bly** *adv.*

pas•sage (păs′ĭj) *n.* **1.** The act or process of passing: *They opened the vents to allow the passage of air.* **2.** A journey, especially by water: *a rough passage across the Atlantic.* **3.** The right to travel on something, especially a ship: *We booked passage to London.* **4.** A narrow path or way between two points: *an underground passage.* **5.** Enactment by a legislature: *the passage of a law.* **6.a.** A channel, duct, or path through or along which something may pass: *the nasal passages.* **b.** A corridor. **7.** Approval of a legislative measure: *Passage of the bill seems assured.* **8.** A section of a written work or speech: *a Biblical passage.* **9.** A section of a musical composition: *a passage for solo violin.*

pas•sage•way (păs′ĭj wā′) *n.* A corridor or hallway.

pass•book (păs′bo͝ok′) *n.* A bankbook.

pas•sé (pă sā′) *adj.* No longer in fashion.

pas•sen•ger (păs′ən jər) *n.* A person riding in a train, an airplane, a ship, a bus, a car, or another vehicle. [First written down in 1337 in Middle English and spelled *passajour*, from Old French *passageor*, from *passage*, passage.]

passenger pigeon *n.* A pigeon that used to be common in North America but has been extinct since the late 19th century.

pas•ser•by (păs′ər bī′) *n., pl.* **pas•sers•by** (păs′ərz-bī′). A person who happens to be passing by, especially by chance.

pas•ser•ine (păs′ə rīn′) *adj.* Of or belonging to the order of perching birds, including more than half of all living birds, such as the songbirds. —*n.* A passerine or perching bird.

pass-fail (păs′fāl′) *adj.* Of or relating to a system of grading in which the student either passes or fails and does not receive a letter grade.

pass•ing (păs′ĭng) *adj.* **1.** Going by: *a passing car.* **2.** Not lasting long; temporary: *a passing fad.* **3.** Superficial; casual: *a passing remark.* **4.** Allowing a person to pass a test, a course of study, or something similar; satisfactory: *a passing grade.* —*n.* **1.** The act of going by or the fact of having passed: *the passing of summer.* **2.** Death: *We mourned his passing.* —***idiom.*** **in passing.** While going by; incidentally.

pas•sion (păsh′ən) *n.* **1.** A powerful feeling such as love, joy, or hatred. See Synonyms at **feeling. 2.a.** Great enthusiasm for a certain activity or subject: *a passion for music.* **b.** The object of such enthusiasm or devotion: *Golf is his passion.* **3. Passion. a.** The sufferings of Jesus on the cross following the Last Supper and including the Crucifixion. **b.** A narrative or musical setting of Jesus's sufferings.

pas•sion•ate (păsh′ə nĭt) *adj.* **1.** Showing or expressing strong feeling: *a passionate speech.* **2.** Arising from or marked by strong feeling: *passionate involvement in a cause.* —**pas′sion•ate•ly** *adv.*

pas•sion•flow•er (păsh′ən flou′ər) *n.* Any of various chiefly tropical American vines having large showy flowers. Some kinds have sweet edible fruit called passion fruit.

passion fruit *n.* The sweet edible fruit of the passionflower.

Passion play *n.* A play representing the Passion of Jesus.

pas•sive (păs′ĭv) *adj.* **1.** Acted upon but not acting in return: *He played a passive role and just went along with what the others wanted.* **2.** Offering no resistance; submissive: *a passive acceptance of one's fate.* **3.** In grammar, of or relating to the passive voice. —*n.* **1.** The passive voice in grammar. **2.** A verb form in the passive voice. [First written down

Usage: pass

The past tense and past participle of the verb **pass** is *passed*: *They passed* (or *have passed*) *our home.* **Past** is the corresponding adjective (*in centuries past*), adverb (*drove past*), preposition (*past midnight; past the crisis*), and noun (*lived in the past*).

passionflower

ă	pat	oi	boy
ā	pay	ou	out
âr	care	o͝o	took
ä	father	o͞o	boot
ĕ	pet	ŭ	cut
ē	be	ûr	urge
ĭ	pit	th	thin
ī	pie	*th*	this
îr	pier	hw	whoop
ŏ	pot	zh	vision
ō	toe	ə	about
ô	paw	N	*French* bon

Louis Pasteur

Word History: pasty[2]

Our humble **pasty** comes from the Middle English word *pastee. Pastee* comes from the Old French word *paste*, which becomes the much more elegant *pâté* in modern French. The Old French word *paste* comes from the Late Latin noun *pasta*, "paste." The Latin *pasta* is also the source of the Italian *pasta*, "dough paste, pasta, a pasta course." Our sweet *pastry* also goes back to Late Latin *pasta*. You could therefore have a dinner of a *pâté* course followed by a *pasta* course followed by a *pasty* course followed by a *pastry* course.

about 1385 in Middle English, from Latin *passīvus*, subject to passion, from *patī*, to experience.] —**pas′sive•ly** *adv.* —**pas′sive•ness** *n.* —SEE NOTE at **verb.**

passive resistance *n.* Resistance to a government or a similar authority by nonviolent methods, such as demonstrating in protest or fasting.

passive smoking *n.* The involuntary inhalation of tobacco smoke in the air, especially by a person who does not smoke.

passive voice *n.* In grammar, a verb form or voice that shows that the subject receives the action expressed by the verb. In the sentence *The trees were planted in a row, were planted* is in the passive voice.

pas•siv•i•ty (pă sĭv′ĭ tē) *n.* The quality or condition of being passive; submissiveness.

pass•key (păs′kē′) *n.* **1.** A master key. **2.** A skeleton key.

Pass•o•ver (păs′ō′vər) *n.* A Jewish holiday lasting eight days in the spring and commemorating the escape of the Jews from Egypt.

pass•port (păs′pôrt′) *n.* **1.** An official document, generally in booklet form, that identifies a person as a citizen of a country and permits that person to travel abroad. **2.** Something that assures the achievement of something else: *Hard work is often a passport to success.*

pass•word (păs′wûrd′) *n.* A secret word or phrase that one uses to get into a place or gain access to information.

past (păst) *adj.* **1.** Gone by; over: *That day is past.* **2.** Having existed or occurred at an earlier time; bygone: *past victories.* **3.** Just ended; just over: *in the past few days.* **4.** Having formerly been or served as: *a past vice president.* **5.** In grammar, of or relating to the past tense. —*n.* **1.** The time before the present: *memories of the past.* **2.** A person's history, background, or former activities: *a woman with a distinguished past.* **3.** The past tense. —*adv.* So as to pass by and go beyond: *He waved as he drove past.* —*prep.* **1.** Beyond in time: *It is well past midnight.* **2.** Beyond in position: *My house is a mile past the river.* **3.** Beyond the power or scope of: *His behavior is past all explanation.* **4.** Beyond the number and amount of: *The child could not count past 20.* —SEE NOTE at **pass.**

pas•ta (päs′tə) *n.* **1.** Dough made from flour and water, formed into shapes and dried for use in recipes after being boiled. **2.** A prepared dish of pasta.

paste (pāst) *n.* **1.** A smooth sticky substance, as that made of flour and water or starch and water, used to fasten light things together. **2.** A dough of flour, water, and shortening, used in making pastry. **3.** A food that has been made soft and creamy by pounding or grinding: *almond paste.* **4.** A hard brilliant glass used in making artificial gems. —*tr.v.* **past•ed, past•ing, pastes. 1.** To fasten or attach with paste: *paste the broken pieces together.* **2.** To cover with something to which paste has been applied: *paste the wall with posters.* [First written down about 1303 in Middle English, from Late Latin *pasta*, from Greek *pasta*, barley-porridge.]

paste•board (pāst′bôrd′) *n.* A thin firm board made of pressed wood pulp or sheets of paper pasted together.

pas•tel (pă stĕl′) *n.* **1.** A crayon resembling a piece of chalk, used in drawing or marking. **2.** A picture drawn or painted with this type of crayon. **3.** A soft delicate color or hue. —*adj.* **1.** Of, relating to, or drawn with pastels. **2.** Pale and soft in color. [First written down in 1662 in Modern English, from Italian *pastello*, material made into a paste, from Late Latin *pasta*, paste.]

pas•tern (păs′tərn) *n.* The part of the leg of a horse or similar hoofed animal that is between the fetlock and the hoof.

Pas•teur (păs tûr′), **Louis.** 1822–1895. French chemist who founded modern microbiology, invented the process of pasteurization, and developed several important vaccines.

pas•teur•i•za•tion (păs′chər ĭ zā′shən) *n.* A process in which milk, beer, and other liquids are heated to a specific temperature for a certain amount of time in order to kill harmful germs or prevent further fermentation.

pas•teur•ize (păs′chə rīz′) *tr.v.* **pas•teur•ized, pas•teur•iz•ing, pas•teur•iz•es.** To treat (a liquid) by pasteurization. [First written down in 1881 in Modern English, after Louis *Pasteur*.]

pas•time (păs′tīm′) *n.* An activity that occupies one's spare time pleasantly.

pas•tor (păs′tər) *n.* A Christian minister or priest who is the leader of a congregation. [First written down before 1376 in Middle English and spelled *pastour*, from Latin *pāstor*, shepherd.]

pas•tor•al (păs′tər əl) *adj.* **1.** Of, relating to, or portraying shepherds or country life: *a pastoral scene.* **2.** Of or relating to a pastor: *pastoral duties.* —**pas′tor•al•ly** *adv.*

pas•tor•ate (păs′tər ĭt) *n.* **1.** The office or term of office of a pastor. **2.** A group of pastors.

past participle *n.* A participle that expresses past or completed action or time. It is used as an adjective, as in the phrase *finished work,* and also to form the passive voice and the perfect tenses of the active voice.

past perfect tense *n.* The pluperfect tense.

pas•tra•mi (pə strä′mē) *n., pl.* **pas•tra•mis.** A seasoned smoked cut of beef, usually taken from the shoulder.

pas•try (pā′strē) *n., pl.* **pas•tries. 1.** Dough of flour, water, and shortening, used for the crusts of pies, tarts, and other baked foods. **2.** Baked food, such as tarts, made with such dough.

past tense *n.* A verb tense used to express an action or a condition that occurred in or during the past. In the sentence *While you were sleeping, I wrote a letter, were sleeping* and *wrote* are in the past tense.

pas•tur•age (păs′chər ĭj) *n.* **1.** The grass and other plants eaten by grazing animals. **2.** Land covered with grass or vegetation suitable for grazing animals.

pas•ture (păs′chər) *n.* **1.** A piece of land covered with grass and other plants eaten by grazing animals such as cattle, horses, or sheep. **2.** Grass and other plants eaten by grazing animals. —*v.* **pas•tured, pas•tur•ing, pas•tures.** —*tr.* To put (animals) in a pasture to graze. —*intr.* To graze in a pasture.

past•y[1] (pā′stē) *adj.* **past•i•er, past•i•est.** Resembling paste in color or texture. [First written down in 1659 in Modern English, from *paste.*] —**past′i•ness** *n.*

pas•ty[2] (păs′tē) *n., pl.* **pas•ties.** *Chiefly British.* A seasoned meat pie. [First written down before 1300 in Middle English and spelled *pastey*, from Old French *paste*, from Late Latin *pasta*, paste.] —SEE NOTE.

pat[1] (păt) *tr.v.* **pat•ted, pat•ting, pats. 1.** To tap or stroke gently with the open hand, often as a sign of affection. **2.** To flatten or shape by tapping gently with the hands or a flat instrument: *pat down the curls.* —*n.* **1.a.** A light stroke or tap. **b.** The sound made by a stroke or tap or by light footsteps. **2.** A small piece or lump: *a pat of butter.* —***idiom.* pat on the back.** A word or gesture of praise or approval. [First written down in 1567 in Modern English, from Middle English *pat*, blow.]

pat[2] (păt) *adj.* **1.** Satisfactory but trite; glib: *He gave* *a pat answer to the reporter's question.* **2.** Suitable; fitting: *We devised a pat way of fixing the problem.* **—*idiom.* have down pat.** To know thoroughly or perfectly: *We have the new computer program down pat.* [First written down in 1578 in Modern English, from *pat*, tap.]

pat. *abbr.* An abbreviation of patent.

Pat•a•go•ni•a (păt′ə **gō′**nē ə *or* păt′ə **gōn′**yə). A plateau region of South America in southern Argentina and Chile extending east from the Andes. The original inhabitants of the area were the Tehuelche ("the Patagonian giants").

patch (păch) *n.* **1.** A small piece of material used to cover a hole, rip, or worn place. **2.a.** A small piece of cloth used for patchwork. **b.** A protective pad, dressing, or bandage worn over a wound or an injured eye. **3.** A small piece of land, usually with plants growing on it: *a berry patch.* **4.** A small part or area that differs from or contrasts with what surrounds it: *a patch of blue sky.* —*tr.v.* **patched, patch•ing, patch•es. 1.** To put a patch or patches on. **2.** To put together or mend: *They patched together the table from broken pieces.* **—*idiom.* patch up.** To settle or smooth over: *They patched up their quarrel.* [First written down before 1382 in Middle English, piece of cloth, perhaps alteration of *pece*, piece.]

patch•work (**păch′**wûrk′) *n.* **1.** Needlework consisting of pieces of cloth of various colors sewn together, as in a quilt. **2.** A mixture of many diverse parts; a jumble: *The wallpaper is a patchwork of many colors.*

patch•y (**păch′**ē) *adj.* **patch•i•er, patch•i•est. 1.** Made up of or marked by patches: *patchy trousers.* **2.** Uneven in quality or performance: *patchy work.* **—patch′i•ly** *adv.* **—patch′i•ness** *n.*

pate (pāt) *n.* The human head, especially the top of the head: *a bald pate.*

pâ•té (pä **tā′**) *n.* A meat paste. [First written down in 1706 in Modern English, from Old French *paste*, paste, pâté.]

pa•tel•la (pə **tĕl′**ə) *n., pl.* **pa•tel•lae** (pə **tĕl′**ē). The small, flat, movable bone at the front of the knee.

pat•ent (**păt′**nt) *n.* A grant made by a government that assures an inventor the exclusive right to manufacture, use, and sell an invention for a stated period of time. —*adj.* (*also* **pāt′**nt). Obvious; plain: *a patent falsehood.* —*tr.v.* **pat•ent•ed, pat•ent•ing, pat•ents. 1.** To obtain a patent on. **2.** To grant a patent to. [First written down before 1376 in Middle English and spelled *patent*, document granting a right, from Old French *(lettre) patente*, open (letter), from Latin *patēns*, open.]

pat•ent•ee (păt′n **tē′**) *n.* A person, group, or business that has been granted a patent.

patent leather *n.* Black leather with a smooth, hard, shiny surface, used for shoes, belts, pocketbooks, and similar items.

pa•ter•nal (pə **tûr′**nəl) *adj.* **1.** Relating to or characteristic of a father; fatherly. **2.** Received from a father: *a paternal trait in his makeup.* **3.** Related through one's father: *my paternal aunt.* **—pa•ter′nal•ly** *adv.*

pa•ter•nal•ism (pə **tûr′**nə lĭz′əm) *n.* The policy or practice of treating or governing people in a fatherly manner by providing for their needs without giving them responsibility. **—pa•ter′nal•is′tic** *adj.*

pa•ter•ni•ty (pə **tûr′**nĭ tē) *n., pl.* **pa•ter•ni•ties. 1.** The fact or condition of being a father. **2.** Ancestry or descent on a father's side.

pa•ter•nos•ter (pā′tər **nŏs′**tər *or* pä′tər **nŏs′**tər) *n.* The Lord's Prayer. [First written down before 900 in Old English, from Latin *pater noster*, our father.]

path (păth) *n., pl.* **paths** (păthz *or* păths). **1.** An track or way made by footsteps: *a path in the woods.* **2.** A road or way made for a particular purpose: *shovel a path through the snow.* **3.** The route or course along which something moves: *the path of a hurricane.* **4.** A course or manner of conduct: *the path of righteousness.*

path. or **pathol.** *abbr.* An abbreviation of: **1.** Pathological. **2.** Pathology.

pa•thet•ic (pə **thĕt′**ĭk) *adj.* **1.** Arousing sympathy or sorrow. **2.** Distressing and inadequate: *a pathetic effort at humor.* [First written down in 1598 in Modern English and spelled *pathetique*, from Greek *pathos*, suffering.] **—pa•thet′i•cal•ly** *adv.*

path•find•er (**păth′**fīn′dər) *n.* A person who discovers a way through or into unexplored regions.

path•o•gen (**păth′**ə jən) *n.* Something that causes disease, especially a virus or microorganism.

path•o•gen•ic (păth′ə **jĕn′**ĭk) *adj.* Capable of causing disease: *pathogenic bacteria.*

path•o•log•i•cal (păth′ə **lŏj′**ĭ kəl) also **path•o•log•ic** (păth′ə **lŏj′**ĭk) *adj.* **1.** Relating to, caused by, or affected with a physical or mental disease: *a pathological liar.* **2.** Of or relating to pathology. **—path′o•log′i•cal•ly** *adv.*

pa•thol•o•gist (pă **thŏl′**ə jĭst) *n.* A physician who specializes in pathology.

pa•thol•o•gy (pă **thŏl′**ə jē) *n., pl.* **pa•thol•o•gies. 1.** The scientific and medical study of disease, its causes, it processes, and its effects. **2.** The physical changes in the body and its functioning as a result of a disease or disorder.

pa•thos (**pā′**thŏs′ *or* **pā′**thôs′) *n.* A quality in a person or thing that arouses feelings of pity, sympathy, tenderness, or sorrow.

path•way (**păth′**wā′) *n.* A path.

pa•tience (**pā′**shəns) *n.* The capacity, quality, or fact of being patient.

pa•tient (**pā′**shənt) *adj.* **1.** Enduring trouble, hardship, annoyance, or delay without complaint or anger. **2.** Persevering; persistent: *the patient piecing together of evidence.* **3.** Showing or expressing patience: *a patient smile.* —*n.* A person who receives medical care or treatment. **—pa′tient•ly** *adv.*

pat•i•o (**păt′**ē ō′) *n., pl.* **pat•i•os. 1.** An outdoor space for dining or recreation, next to a house or an apartment. **2.** An inner courtyard open to the sky.

pat•ois (**păt′**wä′ *or* pă **twä′**) *n., pl.* **pat•ois** (**păt′**wäz′ *or* pă **twä′**). A regional dialect of a language.

pa•tri•arch (**pā′**trē ärk′) *n.* **1.** The father and leader of a family, clan, or tribe. **2.** In certain churches, a high-ranking bishop. **3.** A very old and respected man.

pa•tri•ar•chal (pā′trē **är′**kəl) *adj.* **1.** Relating to or characteristic of a patriarch. **2.** Ruled by a patriarch: *a patriarchal congregation.*

pa•tri•ar•chy (**pā′**trē är′kē) *n.* A society in which a man rules a family, clan, or tribe, and descent is traced through the father's side of the family.

pa•tri•cian (pə **trĭsh′**ən) *n.* **1.** A person of refined upbringing, manners, and tastes. **2.** A member of an aristocracy. **3.** A member of one of the noble families of ancient Rome.

pat•ri•cide (**păt′**rĭ sīd′) *n.* The act of murdering one's father. **—pat′ri•cid′al** (păt′rĭ **sīd′**l) *adj.*

Pat•rick (**păt′**rĭk), Saint. A.D. 389?–461? Christian missionary and patron saint of Ireland.

pat•ri•mo•ny (**păt′**rə mō′nē) *n., pl.* **pat•ri•mo•nies. 1.** Property inherited from a father or other ancestor. **2.** An inheritance or a legacy; a heritage. **3.** Funds or property belonging to a church. **—pat′ri•mo′ni•al** *adj.*

pa•tri•ot (**pā′**trē ət) *n.* One who loves, supports, and defends one's country. [First written down in 1596 in Modern English, from Greek *patriōtēs*, person from the same country, from *patrios*, of one's fathers.]

patchwork
Patchwork quilt

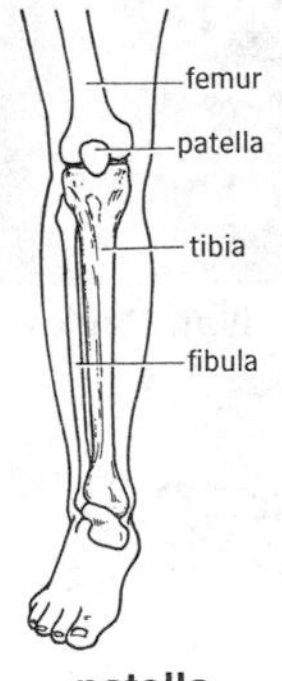

patella

ă	pat	oi	boy
ā	pay	ou	out
âr	care	ŏŏ	took
ä	father	ōō	boot
ĕ	pet	ŭ	cut
ē	be	ûr	urge
ĭ	pit	th	thin
ī	pie	*th*	this
îr	pier	hw	whoop
ŏ	pot	zh	vision
ō	toe	ə	about
ô	paw	N	*French* bon

Alice Paul

pavilion

Ivan Pavlov

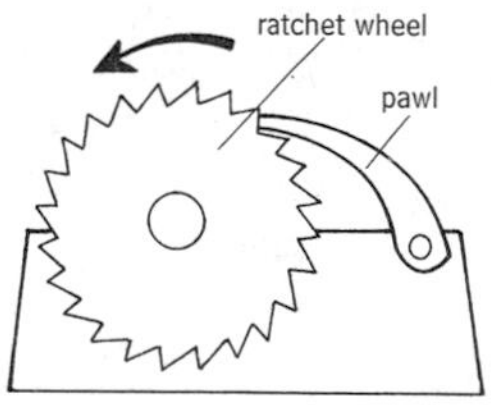

pawl

ă	pat	oi	boy
ā	pay	ou	out
âr	care	o͝o	took
ä	father	o͞o	boot
ĕ	pet	ŭ	cut
ē	be	ûr	urge
ĭ	pit	th	thin
ī	pie	*th*	this
îr	pier	hw	whoop
ŏ	pot	zh	vision
ō	toe	ə	about
ô	paw	N	*French* bon

pa•tri•ot•ic (pā′trē ŏt′ĭk) *adj.* Feeling or expressing love for one's country: *a patriotic song.* —**pa′tri•ot′i•cal•ly** *adv.*

pa•tri•ot•ism (pā′trē ə tĭz′əm) *n.* Love of and devotion to one's country.

pa•trol (pə trōl′) *v.* **pa•trolled, pa•trol•ling, pa•trols.** —*tr.* To walk or travel through (an area) checking for possible trouble or inspecting. —*intr.* To patrol an area: *We're patrolling from midnight until dawn.* —*n.* **1.** The act of patrolling: *The soldiers are out on patrol.* **2.** A group of persons, vehicles, ships, or aircraft that patrols an area. **3.** A division of a Boy Scout troop, consisting of six to eight boys. [First written down in 1691 in Modern English, from Old French *patouiller,* to paddle about in mud.]

patrol car *n.* A squad car.

pa•trol•man (pə trōl′mən) *n.* A policeman who patrols an assigned area.

patrol wagon *n.* A police truck used to convey prisoners.

pa•trol•wom•an (pə trōl′wo͝om′ən) *n.* A policewoman who patrols an assigned area: *a patrolwoman on duty.*

pa•tron (pā′trən) *n.* **1.** A person who supports or champions something, such as an activity or institution, by giving money; a benefactor: *a patron of the arts.* **2.** A regular customer of a store, restaurant, or other business. [First written down about 1300 in Middle English, from Latin *patrōnus,* from *pater,* father.]

pa•tron•age (pā′trə nĭj *or* păt′rə nĭj) *n.* **1.** Support or encouragement from a patron: *dependent upon the patronage of the rich.* **2.** Support or encouragement given with an air of superiority. **3.** The trade given to a store or restaurant by its customers. **4.** Customers; clientele: *The hotel has a very exclusive patronage.* **5.** The power or act of appointing people to governmental or political positions.

pa•tron•ize (pā′trə nīz′ *or* păt′rə nīz′) *tr.v.* **pa•tron•ized, pa•tron•iz•ing, pa•tron•iz•es.** **1.** To act as a patron to; support: *patronize the arts.* **2.** To go to regularly as a customer: *patronize a store.* **3.** To treat (someone) in a condescending way; talk down to.

patron saint *n.* A saint regarded as the special guardian of a country, place, person, trade, or activity.

pa•troon (pə tro͞on′) *n.* Under Dutch colonial rule, a landholder in New York and New Jersey who was granted land and certain rights in exchange for bringing 50 new settlers to the colony.

pat•sy (păt′sē) *n., pl.* **pat•sies.** *Slang.* A person who is cheated, taken unfair advantage of, or made the butt of a joke.

pat•ter¹ (păt′ər) *intr.v.* **pat•tered, pat•ter•ing, pat•ters.** **1.** To make a series of quick light taps: *Rain pattered on the roof.* **2.** To walk or move softly and quickly. —*n.* A series of quick light tapping sounds: *the patter of feet.* [First written down in 1611 in Modern English, from *pat.*]

pat•ter² (păt′ər) *n.* Glib rapid speech, such as that used by a salesperson or comedian. [First written down about 1395 in Middle English and spelled *patren,* to say prayers rapidly, from *paternoster,* the Lord's prayer.]

pat•tern (păt′ərn) *n.* **1.** A person or thing that is used as a guide or considered worth imitating. **2.** An artistic or decorative design: *a floral pattern.* **3.** A diagram, plan, or model used to make things: *a dress pattern.* **4.** A combination of features, actions, or events that are repeated in a recognizable arrangement: *patterns of behavior in monkeys.* —*tr.v.* **pat•terned, pat•tern•ing, pat•terns.** To form or design according to a certain model: *The country's constitution is patterned after our own.*

pat•ty (păt′ē) *n., pl.* **pat•ties.** A small, rounded, flattened mass of ground or minced food.

pau•ci•ty (pô′sĭ tē) *n.* Short supply; scarcity; dearth: *a paucity of natural resources.*

Paul (pôl), Saint. A.D. 5?–67? Apostle to the Gentiles whose life and teachings are set forth in his epistles and the Acts of the Apostles.

Paul, Alice. 1885–1977. American feminist and suffragist who wrote (1923) the first equal rights amendment to be considered by the U.S. Congress.

Paul Bun•yan (pôl′ bŭn′yən) *n.* In American folklore, a giant logger who performs superhuman acts.

paunch (pônch *or* pänch) *n.* The belly, especially a potbelly.

paunch•y (pôn′chē *or* pän′chē) *adj.* **paunch•i•er, paunch•i•est.** Having a protruding abdomen or a potbelly. —**paunch′i•ness** *n.*

pau•per (pô′pər) *n.* A very poor person, often one who lives on charity.

pause (pôz) *intr.v.* **paused, paus•ing, paus•es.** **1.** To stop briefly in the midst of an action or while speaking. **2.** To linger for a time: *We paused under a tree before going on.* —*n.* **1.** A brief stop or break in action or speech. **2.** A sign placed over or below a musical note, chord, or rest, indicating that it is to be held longer than usual.

Synonyms: pause, intermission, recess, suspension. These nouns all mean a temporary stop in activity. *There was a brief pause in the conversation. They planned to serve punch during the play's intermission. Enjoy yourselves during winter recess. The strike caused a suspension of repair work on the highway.*

pa•vane (pə vän′) *n.* **1.** A slow stately court dance of the 16th century. **2.** A piece of music written for this dance.

pave (pāv) *tr.v.* **paved, pav•ing, paves.** To cover with pavement. —***idiom.*** **pave the way.** To make progress or development easier: *His experiments paved the way for new discoveries.* [First written down about 1325 in Middle English and spelled *paven,* from Latin *pavīre,* to beat, tread down.]

pave•ment (pāv′mənt) *n.* **1.** A hard smooth surface of concrete, asphalt, brick, or a similar material, as for a road or sidewalk. **2.** The material used to make such a surface.

pa•vil•ion (pə vĭl′yən) *n.* **1.** An ornate tent. **2.** An open structure with a roof, used at parks or fairs for amusement or shelter. **3.** One of a group of related buildings, as of a hospital.

pav•ing (pā′vĭng) *n.* **1.** A pavement. **2.** Asphalt, cement, and other materials used in making a pavement.

Pav•lov (păv′lôf′ *or* păv′lôv′), **Ivan Petrovich.** 1849–1936. Russian scientist who is best known for discovering psychological conditioning.

paw (pô) *n.* The clawed foot of an animal, especially of an animal that has four legs. —*tr.v.* **pawed, paw•ing, paws.** **1.a.** To touch or strike with a paw. **b.** To scrape or beat with a paw or hoof: *The dog pawed the ground.* **2.** To handle in a clumsy or rude way.

pawl (pôl) *n.* A hinged or pivoted device that fits into a notch of a ratchet wheel, either to drive it forward or to prevent it from moving backward.

❑ *These sound alike:* **pawl, pall¹** (cloth covering), **pall²** (grow dull).

pawn¹ (pôn) *n.* Something given as security for a loan. —*tr.v.* **pawned, pawn•ing, pawns.** To give or leave as security for the payment of money borrowed: *pawn jewels.* [First written down in 1496 in Middle English and spelled *paun,* pledge, security, from Old French *pan,* of Germanic origin.]

pawn[2] (pôn) *n.* **1.** A chess piece of lowest value that can move forward one square at a time or two squares on its first move and capture other pieces by moving one square diagonally forward. **2.** A person used or controlled by others. [First written down about 1369 in Middle English and spelled *poun,* from Medieval Latin *pedō,* foot soldier.]

pawn•bro•ker (pôn′brō′kər) *n.* A person who lends money at interest in exchange for personal property left as security.

Paw•nee (pô nē′) *n., pl.* **Pawnee** or **Paw•nees. 1.** A member of a Native American people formerly living in Nebraska and Kansas, now living in Oklahoma. **2.** The Caddoan language of the Pawnee.

pawn•shop (pôn′shŏp′) *n.* The shop of a pawnbroker.

paw•paw (pô′pô) *n.* Variant of **papaw.**

pay (pā) *v.* **paid** (pād), **pay•ing, pays.** *—tr.* **1.** To give money to in return for goods or services: *I paid her for the newspaper.* **2.** To give (money) in exchange for goods or services: *How much did you pay for the tickets?* **3.** To discharge or settle (a debt or an obligation): *pay the rent.* **4.** To yield as return: *a bond paying eight percent interest.* **5.** To be profitable or worthwhile for: *It paid him to be careful.* **6.** To give, render, or express: *pay attention; pay a compliment.* *—intr.* **1.** To give money in exchange for goods or services. **2.** To discharge a debt or an obligation. **3.** To bear a cost or penalty: *You'll pay for eating so much.* **4.** To be profitable or worthwhile: *It pays to be friendly.* *—adj.* **1.** Of, relating to, giving, or receiving payments: *a pay raise.* **2.** Requiring payment to operate: *a pay telephone.* *—n.* **1.** Money given in return for work done; wages; salary. **2.** Paid employment: *She is in the pay of our company.* ***—idioms.*** **pay off. 1.** To pay the full amount on (a debt). **2.** To be profitable: *an investment that pays off.* **3.** *Informal.* To bribe. **pay (one's) way.** To contribute one's own share; pay for oneself. **pay out. 1.** To give (money) out; spend. **2.** To let out (a line or rope) by slackening. **pay up.** To give all the money owed. [First written down before 1200 in Middle English and spelled *paien,* from Latin *pācāre,* to pacify.]

pay•a•ble (pā′ə bəl) *adj.* **1.** Requiring payment on a certain date; due: *a note payable on demand.* **2.** Specifying payment to a particular person: *Make the check payable to me.*

pay•check (pā′chĕk′) *n.* **1.** A check issued to an employee in payment of salary or wages. **2.** Salary or wages: *The new job means a larger paycheck.*

pay•day (pā′dā′) *n.* The day on which wages are paid.

pay•ee (pā ē′) *n.* A person to whom money is paid.

pay•er (pā′ər) *n.* **1.** A person or an organization that pays. **2.** A person named responsible for paying a bill or note.

pay•load (pā′lōd′) *n.* **1.** The part of a cargo producing revenue as distinguished from the weight of the vehicle. **2.a.** The total weight of passengers and cargo that an aircraft carries or can carry. **b.** The total weight of the instruments, crew, and life-support systems that a spacecraft can carry. **c.** The explosive charge in the warhead of a missile.

pay•mas•ter (pā′măs′tər) *n.* A person in charge of paying wages and salaries.

pay•ment (pā′mənt) *n.* **1.** The act of paying: *Prompt payment of the bill will be appreciated.* **2.** An amount of money paid: *The balance is due in monthly payments.* **3.** Reward, compensation, or punishment: *To see the child healthy again is payment enough for my services.*

pay•off (pā′ôf′ or pā′ŏf′) *n.* **1.** Full payment of a salary or wages. **2.** *Informal.* The most intense part of a narrative or of a sequence of events. **3.** *Informal.* A bribe.

pay•roll (pā′rōl′) *n.* **1.** A list of employees and wages due to each. **2.** The total amount of money paid to employees at a given time.

Pb The symbol for the element **lead[2]** (sense 1).

PC *abbr.* An abbreviation of personal computer.

p.c. *abbr.* An abbreviation of percent.

pct. *abbr.* An abbreviation of percent.

Pd The symbol for the element **palladium.**

pd. *abbr.* An abbreviation of paid.

P.D. *abbr.* An abbreviation of police department.

pea (pē) *n.* **1.** The round green seed of a climbing vine, enclosed in long green pods and eaten as a vegetable. **2.** The plant that bears such seeds. [First written down before 800 in Old English and spelled *piose,* from Greek *pison.*] —See Note.

peace (pēs) *n.* **1.** The absence of war or other hostilities. **2.** A treaty or an agreement ending a war: *Peace was signed in 1918.* **3.** Calm; tranquillity: *a little peace and quiet.* **4.** Inner calm; serenity: *peace of mind.* **5.** Public security; law and order: *He was arrested for disturbing the peace.* ***—idioms.*** **at peace. 1.** In a state of tranquillity; serene: *She is at peace with herself.* **2.** Free from strife: *We all want to live in a world at peace.* **keep one's peace** or **hold one's peace.** To be silent. [First written down before 1140 in Middle English and spelled *pais,* from Latin *pāx.*]

❑ *These sound alike:* **peace, piece** (part).

peace•a•ble (pē′sə bəl) *adj.* **1.** Not quarrelsome, rebellious, or unruly; disposed to peace: *a peaceable disposition.* **2.** Not involving violence or war; peaceful: *a peaceable solution.* **—peace′a•bly** *adv.*

peace•ful (pēs′fəl) *adj.* **1.** Inclined or disposed to peace: *a peaceful nation.* **2.** Calm; tranquil. See Synonyms at **calm.** **—peace′ful•ly** *adv.* **—peace′ful•ness** *n.*

peace•keep•ing (pēs′kē′pĭng) *adj.* Of or relating to the preservation of peace: *a peacekeeping force sent to uphold a ceasefire.*

peace•mak•er (pēs′mā′kər) *n.* A person who makes peace, especially by settling the disputes of others.

peace pipe *n.* A calumet.

peace•time (pēs′tīm′) *n.* A time free from war.

peach (pēch) *n.* **1.a.** A sweet, round, juicy fruit having downy yellowish or reddish skin and a pit with a hard shell. **b.** The tree that bears such fruit. **2.** A light yellowish pink. **3.** An excellent or especially likeable person or thing. —See Note.

peach•y (pē′chē) *adj.* **peach•i•er, peach•i•est. 1.** Resembling a peach, especially in color or texture. **2.** Splendid; fine.

pea•cock (pē′kŏk′) *n.* **1.** The male of the peafowl, having brilliant blue or green feathers and very long tail feathers that are marked with eyespots and can be spread out like a fan. **2.** A vain or showy person.

pea•fowl (pē′foul′) *n., pl.* **peafowl** or **pea•fowls.** Either of two large Asian birds related to the pheasants.

pea•hen (pē′hĕn′) *n.* A female peafowl.

pea jacket *n.* A short, warm, double-breasted coat of heavy wool, worn especially by sailors.

peak (pēk) *n.* **1.a.** The pointed top of a mountain. **b.** The mountain itself. **2.** A tapering point that projects upward: *the peak of a roof.* **3.** The point of greatest development, value, or intensity: *a book written at the peak of her career.* *—intr.v.* **peaked, peak•ing, peaks. 1.** To be formed into a peak or peaks. **2.** To achieve the point of greatest development, value, or intensity: *Sales tend to peak just before the holidays.*

❑ *These sound alike:* **peak, peek** (glance), **pique** (resentment).

Word History: pea

How is a **pea** like a **peafowl**? Both are green? Both are brown? Both have feathers? Actually, there is no connection at all. **Pea** dates only from the 17th century and is made from the word *pease. Pease* was a noun in the singular number and meant "a pea plant, a pea." *Pease* came to be regarded as a plural noun because of expressions such as "alike as two pease in a pod." *Pease* came from the Old English word *pise,* which goes back to the Greek *pison,* "a pea." The **peafowl** is a horse of another color. The Middle English forms for **peacock** are *pecok, pocok,* and *pacok* (similar forms are found for **peahen**) and are all from the Old English word *pāwa,* which came from the Latin *pāvō,* "a peacock, peahen, peafowl."

Word History: peach

When is a **peach** not a peach? Answer: when it's an apple. In Middle English the word is *peche,* and it comes from the Old French word *peche* or *pesche.* The Old French word is from Latin *pessica, persica,* which is from an earlier *Persicum mālum,* "Persian apple." The Latin noun *mālum* originally referred to any soft-skinned fruit that grew on trees, but later it became restricted to the apple. The Romans called the fruit "Persian," meaning "eastern," because the peach originally came from the east, in this case from China.

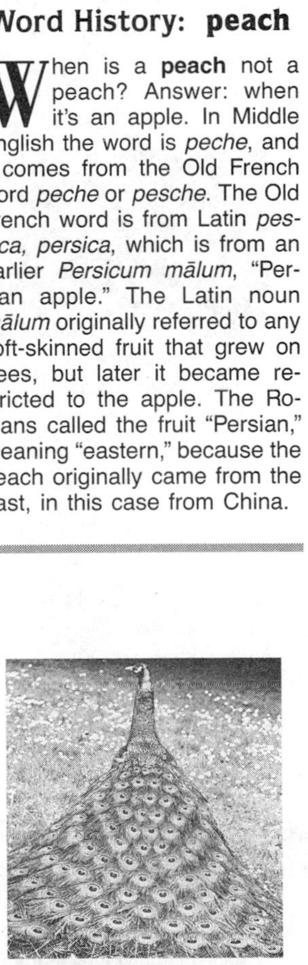

peacock

peaked[1] (pēkt *or* **pē′**kĭd) *adj.* Ending in a peak; pointed: *a peaked cap.* [First written down about 1450 in Middle English and spelled *pekid*, from *pike*, peak.]

peak•ed[2] (**pē′**kĭd) *adj.* Having a sickly appearance: *You look peaked today.* [First written down about 1835 in Modern English, from *peak*, to look sickly.]

peal (pēl) *n.* **1.** A ringing of a set of bells. **2.** A set of bells tuned to each other. **3.** A loud burst of noise: *peals of laughter.* —*tr. & intr.v.* **pealed, peal•ing, peals.** To sound loudly; ring: *The bells pealed joyfully.*

❑ *These sound alike:* **peal, peel** (rind).

pea•nut (**pē′**nŭt′) *n.* **1.** The oily edible seed of a vine that grows in warm regions and bends over so that the light-brown pods containing the seeds ripen underground. **2.** The seed pod of this plant. **3.** The plant that bears such pods.

peanut butter *n.* A paste made from ground roasted peanuts.

peanut oil *n.* The oil pressed from peanuts, used for cooking and in soaps.

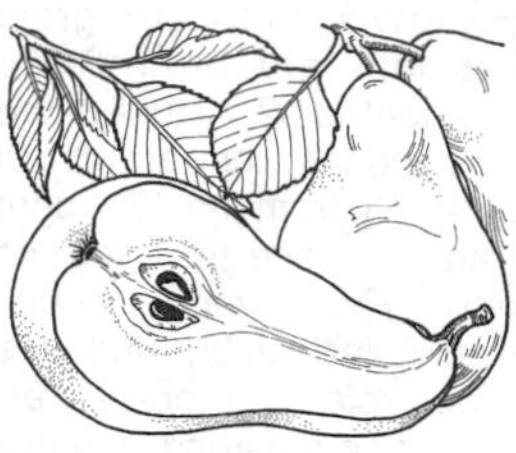

pear

pear (pâr) *n.* **1.** A sweet juicy fruit having a rounded base and a tapering stem end. **2.** The tree that bears such fruit.

❑ *These sound alike:* **pear, pair** (two), **pare** (peel).

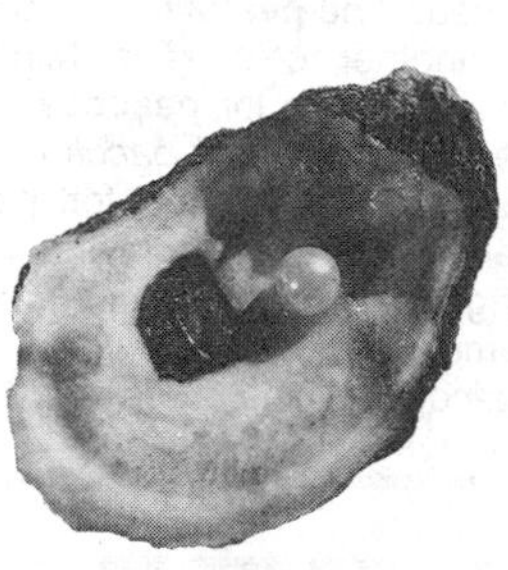

pearl
Pearl in oyster shell

pearl (pûrl) *n.* **1.** A smooth, slightly iridescent white or grayish rounded growth formed inside the shells of some kinds of oysters and valued as a gem. **2.** Mother-of-pearl. **3.** Something resembling a pearl: *pearls of dew.* **4.** A person or thing that is very highly thought of: *pearls of wisdom.*

❑ *These sound alike:* **pearl, purl[1]** (flow), **purl[2]** (knit).

Pearl Harbor (pûrl). An inlet of the Pacific Ocean on the southern coast of Oahu, Hawaii, west of Honolulu. It was the site of a Japanese attack on a U.S. naval base (December 7, 1941), which caused the United States to enter World War II.

pearl•y (**pûr′**lē) *adj.* **pearl•i•er, pearl•i•est. 1.** Resembling pearls, as in whiteness or size. **2.** Covered or decorated with pearls.

Pear•son (**pîr′**sən), **Lester Bowles.** 1897–1972. Canadian politician and prime minister (1963–1968) who won the 1957 Nobel Peace Prize.

peas•ant (**pĕz′**ənt) *n.* A member of the class of small farmers and farm laborers.

peas•ant•ry (**pĕz′**ən trē) *n.* The social class made up of peasants.

peat (pēt) *n.* Rotted vegetable matter, found in bogs, that has been partially converted to carbon. It is used as a fuel and as a fertilizer.

peat moss *n.* **1.** Any of various mosses growing in very wet places. **2.** The dried remains of peat moss, used as a mulch and plant food.

peb•ble (**pĕb′**əl) *n.* A small stone, especially one worn smooth by erosion. —*tr.v.* **peb•bled, peb•bling, peb•bles. 1.** To pave or cover with pebbles. **2.** To give an irregular rough surface to (leather or paper). —**peb′bly** *adj.*

pe•can (pĭ **kän′** *or* pĭ **kăn′** *or* **pē′**kăn) *n.* **1.** An edible nut having a smooth oval shell. **2.** The tree that bears such nuts.

pec•ca•dil•lo (pĕk′ə **dĭl′**ō) *n., pl.* **pec•ca•dil•loes** or **pec•ca•dil•los.** A small sin or fault.

peccary
Collared peccary

pec•ca•ry (**pĕk′**ə rē) *n., pl.* **pec•ca•ries.** Any of several tropical American mammals similar to a pig, having long dark bristles.

peck[1] (pĕk) *v.* **pecked, peck•ing, pecks.** —*tr.* **1.** To strike with a beak or a pointed instrument. **2.** To make (a hole, for example) by striking repeatedly with a beak or a pointed instrument. **3.** To pick up with a beak: *The hungry hens pecked corn off the ground.* —*intr.* To strike something with the beak or a pointed instrument: *The bird pecked at the dead branch.* —*n.* **1.a.** A stroke or light blow with the beak or a pointed instrument. **b.** A hole or mark made by such a blow. **2.** *Informal.* A light quick kiss. [First written down before 1300 in Middle English and spelled *pechen*, probably variant of *piken*.]

peck[2] (pĕk) *n.* **1.** A unit of dry volume or capacity equal to 8 quarts. See table at **measurement. 2.** A container holding or measuring this amount. **3.** *Informal.* A great deal: *a peck of trouble.* [First written down about 1280 in Middle English and spelled *pek*.]

pec•tin (**pĕk′**tĭn) *n.* Any of a group of substances found in ripe fruits, such as apples, that can be made to form gels, used in preparing jellies and in certain medicines and cosmetics.

pec•to•ral (**pĕk′**tər əl) *adj.* Of or located in the chest or breast: *a pectoral muscle.* —*n.* A muscle or an organ of the chest.

pe•cu•liar (pĭ **kyo͞ol′**yər) *adj.* **1.** Unusual or eccentric; strange. **2.** Belonging distinctively to one person, group, or kind; unique: *a fish peculiar to this river.* —**pe•cu′liar•ly** *adv.*

pe•cu•li•ar•i•ty (pĭ kyo͞o′lē **ăr′**ĭ tē *or* pĭ kyo͞ol-**yăr′**ĭ tē) *n., pl.* **pe•cu•li•ar•i•ties. 1.** The quality or condition of being peculiar. **2.** A notable or distinctive feature or characteristic: *the peculiarities of a New York accent.* **3.** Something odd or eccentric; a quirk: *his peculiarities about money.*

pe•cu•ni•ar•y (pĭ **kyo͞o′**nē ĕr′ē) *adj.* Of or relating to money: *a pecuniary loss.*

ped•a•gog•ic (pĕd′ə **gŏj′**ĭk) also **ped•a•gog•i•cal** (pĕd′ə **gŏj′**ĭ kəl) *adj.* Of or relating to teaching: *pedagogic techniques.*

ped•a•gogue (**pĕd′**ə gŏg′ *or* **pĕd′**ə gôg′) *n.* **1.** A schoolteacher; an educator. **2.** A person who teaches in a showy dogmatic manner.

ped•a•go•gy (**pĕd′**ə gō′jē *or* **pĕd′**ə gŏj′ē) *n.* The art or profession of teaching.

ped•al (**pĕd′**l) *n.* A lever operated by the foot, as on a machine such as an automobile or bicycle or on a musical instrument such as a piano or organ. —*v.* **ped•aled, ped•al•ing, ped•als** or **ped•alled, ped•al•ling, ped•als.** —*intr.* **1.** To ride a bicycle. **2.** To operate a pedal or pedals. —*tr.* To operate the pedals of: *pedaled the bike up the hill.* [First written down in 1611 in Modern English, from Latin *pēs*, foot.]

❑ *These sound alike:* **pedal, peddle** (sell).

ped•ant (**pĕd′**nt) *n.* **1.** A person who pays too much attention to book learning and formal rules. **2.** A person who shows off his or her learning.

pe•dan•tic (pə **dăn′**tĭk) *adj.* Characterized by excessive and often showy concern for books and learning: *a pedantic mind.* —**pe•dan′ti•cal•ly** *adv.*

ped•ant•ry (**pĕd′**n trē) *n., pl.* **ped•ant•ries. 1.** Excessive attention to detail or rules. **2.** An instance of pedantic behavior.

ped•dle (**pĕd′**l) *tr.v.* **ped•dled, ped•dling, ped•dles. 1.** To travel about selling (goods): *peddle magazines.* **2.** To spread or deal out: *Don't peddle lies.*

❑ *These sound alike:* **peddle, pedal** (lever).

ped•dler (**pĕd′**lər) *n.* A person who travels about selling goods. [First written down in 1378 in Middle English and spelled *pedlere*, probably from Medieval Latin *pedārius*, crosier bearer.]

ped•es•tal (**pĕd′**ĭ stəl) *n.* **1.** A support or base, as for a column or statue. **2.** A support or foundation. **3.** A position of high regard or admiration: *Putting people on pedestals can lead to disappointment.*

pediment
Above the entrance to the Pantheon in Paris, France

pe•des•tri•an (pə **dĕs′**trē ən) *n.* A person traveling on foot, especially on city streets. —*adj.* **1.** Of or for pedestrians: *a pedestrian crossing.* **2.** Commonplace; ordinary: *pedestrian writing.*

pe•di•a•tri•cian (pē′dē ə trĭsh′ən) *n.* A physician who specializes in pediatrics.

pe•di•at•rics (pē′dē ăt′rĭks) *n.* *(used with a singular verb).* The branch of medicine that deals with the care of infants and children and the treatment of their diseases. **—pe′di•at′ric** *adj.*

ped•i•cel (pĕd′ĭ səl) *n.* A small stalk in a plant, supporting a single flower.

ped•i•cure (pĕd′ĭ kyo͝or′) *n.* A cosmetic treatment of the feet and toenails.

ped•i•gree (pĕd′ĭ grē′) *n.* **1.** A line of ancestors; ancestry. **2.** A list or record of ancestors, especially of a purebred animal.

ped•i•greed (pĕd′ĭ grēd′) *adj.* Having a line of purebred ancestors: *pedigreed cattle.*

ped•i•ment (pĕd′ə mənt) *n.* **1.** A wide triangular gable over the façade of a building in Greek architectural style. **2.** A similar piece used widely in architecture and decoration.

ped•lar (pĕd′lər) *n.* *Chiefly British.* Variant of **peddler.**

pe•dom•e•ter (pĭ dŏm′ĭ tər) *n.* An instrument that measures the approximate distance a person travels on foot by keeping track of the number of steps taken.

pe•dun•cle (pĭ dŭng′kəl *or* pē′dŭng′kəl) *n.* A stalk or stem supporting a flower or an animal organ, as the eyestalk of a lobster.

peek (pēk) *intr.v.* **peeked, peek•ing, peeks. 1.** To look, peer, or glance briefly, as from a place of concealment. **2.** To be partially visible; show: *Crocuses peeked through the snow.* *—n.* A quick sly glance or look.

❑ *These sound alike:* **peek, peak** (mountain top), **pique** (resentment).

peel (pēl) *n.* The skin or rind or certain fruits and vegetables, such as the orange or potato. *—v.* **peeled, peel•ing, peels.** *—tr.* **1.** To remove the skin or rind from: *peel a banana.* **2.** To strip away or pull off (an outer covering): *peel the bark off a tree.* *—intr.* **1.** To come off in thin strips or layers, as skin or paint. **2.** To lose or shed skin or other covering: *The house is peeling and needs to be painted.*

❑ *These sound alike:* **peel, peal** (ringing).

peep[1] (pēp) *n.* A weak high-pitched chirping sound, like that made by a young bird. *—intr.v.* **peeped, peep•ing, peeps.** To make such a sound. [First written down before 1437 in Middle English and spelled *pepe*, probably from Old English *pīpian*, to pipe.]

peep[2] (pēp) *intr.v.* **peeped, peep•ing, peeps. 1.** To look from a concealed place; peek. **2.** To become visible gradually, as though emerging from a hiding place: *At dawn the sun peeped over the horizon.* *—n.* A quick look or glance; a peak. [First written down before 1460 in Middle English and spelled *pepen*, perhaps alteration of *piken*, to peek.]

peep•er[1] (pē′pər) *n.* A creature that makes short high-pitched sounds, especially a frog.

peep•er[2] (pē′pər) *n.* **1.** A person who peeks in a sly manner. **2.** *Slang.* An eye.

peep•hole (pēp′hōl′) *n.* A small hole or crevice through which one may peep.

peer[1] (pîr) *intr.v.* **peered, peer•ing, peers. 1.** To look intently, searchingly, or with difficulty. **2.** To be partially visible; show: *The moon peered from behind a cloud.* [First written down in 1375 in Middle English and spelled *peren*, short for *aperen*, to appear.]

❑ *These sound alike:* **peer[1]** (look), **peer[2]** (equal), **pier** (dock).

peer[2] (pîr) *n.* **1.** A person who has equal standing with others, as in rank, class, or age. **2.** A man who is a member of the nobility, especially in Great Britain. [First written down about 1250 in Middle English and spelled *pere*, from Latin *pār*, equal.]

❑ *These sound alike:* **peer[2]** (equal), **peer[1]** (look), **pier** (dock).

peer•age (pîr′ĭj) *n.* **1.** The rank or title of a peer or peeress. **2.** Peers and peeresses considered as a group. **3.** A book listing the peers.

peer•ess (pîr′ĭs) *n.* **1.** A woman who holds a noble title in her own right; a noblewoman. **2.** The wife or widow of a peer.

peer group *n.* A group of people who are usually of the same age.

peer•less (pîr′lĭs) *adj.* Having no equal; unmatched. **—peer′less•ly** *adv.* **—peer′less•ness** *n.*

peeve (pēv) *tr.v.* **peeved, peev•ing, peeves.** To annoy or make irritable. *—n.* Something that annoys: *Her biggest peeve is the noisy dog next door.*

pee•vish (pē′vĭsh) *adj.* Annoyed; irritable; fretful. **—pee′vish•ly** *adv.* **—pee′vish•ness** *n.*

pee•wee[1] (pē′wē) *n.* *Informal.* A relatively or unusually small person or thing. [First written down in 1848 in American English, probably from *wee.*] **—pee′wee** *adj.*

❑ *These sound alike:* **peewee[1], pewee** (bird).

pee•wee[2] (pē′wē) *n.* Variant of **pewee.**

peg (pĕg) *n.* **1.** A cylindrical or conical pin, often of wood, used to fasten things or to plug a hole. **2.** One of the pins of a stringed musical instrument that are turned to loosen or tighten the strings so as to change their pitch. **3.** A degree, as in estimation: *My opinion of him has gone up a few pegs.* **4.** A throw in baseball. *—tr.v.* **pegged, peg•ging, pegs. 1.** To fasten or plug with a peg. **2.** To set or fix (a price, for example): *peg interest rates to the rate of inflation.* **3.** *Informal.* To classify: *We pegged her as the math expert.* **4.** *Informal.* To throw (a ball).

Peg•a•sus (pĕg′ə səs) *n.* In Greek mythology, a winged horse that with a strike of the hoof causes the fountain Hippocrene to spring forth from Mount Helicon.

peg leg *n.* *Informal.* An artificial leg, especially a wooden one.

peg•ma•tite (pĕg′mə tīt′) *n.* A coarse-grained igneous rock, largely granite. Some pegmatites are sources of tantalum, tungsten, and uranium.

P.E.I. *abbr.* An abbreviation of Prince Edward Island.

Pe•kin•ese (pē′kə nēz′ *or* pē′kə nēs′) *n.* Variant of **Pekingese.**

Pe•king (pē′kĭng′ *or* pā′kĭng′). Beijing.

Pe•king•ese (pē′kĭng ēz′ *or* pē′kĭng ēs′) also **Pe•kin•ese** (pē′kə nēz′ *or* pē′kə nēs′) *n., pl.* **Pekingese** also **Pekinese. 1.** A native or inhabitant of Peking (Beijing). **2.** The dialect of Chinese spoken in and around Peking. **3.** (pē′kə nēz′ *or* pē′kə nēs′). Any of a breed of dog having long hair, large eyes, and a flat face, originally raised in China.

pe•koe (pē′kō) *n.* A type of black tea, consisting of small leaves and sometimes leaf buds.

❑ *These sound alike:* **pekoe, picot** (small loop).

pelf (pĕlf) *n.* Wealth or riches, especially when dishonestly acquired.

pel•i•can (pĕl′ĭ kən) *n.* Any of various large, web-footed water birds of warm regions, having under the lower bill a large pouch used for holding fish.

pel•lag•ra (pə lăg′rə *or* pə lā′grə) *n.* A disease caused by a lack of niacin in the diet, characterized by skin eruptions, nervous digestive disorders, and eventual mental deterioration.

pel•let (pĕl′ĭt) *n.* **1.** A small densely packed ball, as of food, wax, or medicine. **2.** A small bullet or shot.

pell-mell also **pell•mell** (pĕl′mĕl′) *adv.* In a jumbled and confused manner; helter-skelter: *The ducks flew off pell-mell.* **—pell′-mell′** *adj.*

pel•lu•cid (pə lo͞o′sĭd) *adj.* **1.** Admitting the passage

Pegasus
Fourth-century B.C.
Greek coin

Pekingese

pelican
American white pelican

ă	pat	oi	boy
ā	pay	ou	out
âr	care	o͝o	took
ä	father	o͞o	boot
ĕ	pet	ŭ	cut
ē	be	ûr	urge
ĭ	pit	th	thin
ī	pie	*th*	this
îr	pier	hw	whoop
ŏ	pot	zh	vision
ō	toe	ə	about
ô	paw	N	*French* bon

pendant

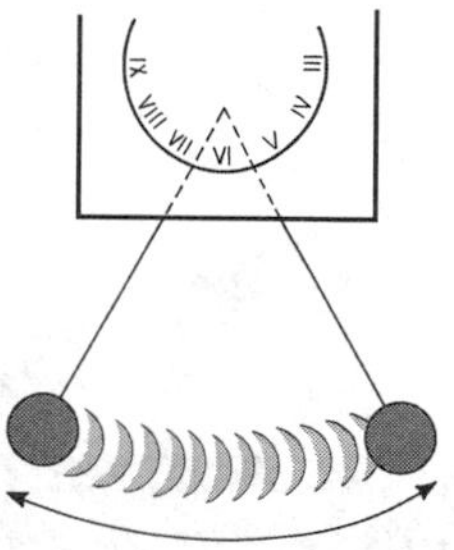

pendulum

penguin
Adélie penguin

William Penn
c. 1700 chalk portrait
by Francis Place
(1647–1728)

of light; transparent. **2.** Easy to understand; clear.

Pel•o•pon•ne•sus or **Pel•o•pon•ne•sos** (pĕl′ə pə **nē′**səs). A peninsula forming the southern part of Greece. It was dominated by Sparta until the fourth century B.C.

pelt[1] (pĕlt) *n.* An animal skin with the fur or hair still on it. [First written down in 1298 in Middle English and spelled *pelet*, probably from Latin *pellis*, skin.]

pelt[2] (pĕlt) *v.* **pelt•ed, pelt•ing, pelts.** *—tr.* **1.** To strike repeatedly with or as if with blows or missiles; bombard: *pelting the sign with snowballs.* **2.** To cast, hurl, or throw (missiles): *pelting stones at tin cans.* *—intr.* To strike or beat heavily: *The rain pelted against the tent.* [First written down before 1200 in Middle English and spelled *pilten*, perhaps ultimately from Latin *pultāre*, to beat.]

pel•ves (**pĕl′**vēz) *n.* A plural of **pelvis.**

pel•vic (**pĕl′**vĭk) *adj.* Of, in, or near the pelvis.

pel•vis (**pĕl′**vĭs) *n., pl.* **pel•vis•es** or **pel•ves** (**pĕl′**vēz). A basin-shaped structure formed of several different bones that rests on the lower limbs and supports the lower end of the spine.

pem•mi•can (**pĕm′**ĭ kən) *n.* **1.** A food made by Native Americans from a paste of lean meat mixed with fat and berries. **2.** A similar food for use in emergencies.

pen[1] (pĕn) *n.* Any of various instruments for writing with ink, including the ballpoint pen and the fountain pen. *—tr.v.* **penned, pen•ning, pens.** To write or compose with a pen. [First written down about 1280 in Middle English and spelled *penne*, from Latin *penna*, feather.]

pen[2] (pĕn) *n.* **1.** A small fenced-in area, especially one in which animals are kept. **2.** The animals kept in such an enclosure. *—tr.v.* **penned** or **pent** (pĕnt), **pen•ning, pens.** To confine in or as if in a pen. [First written down in 957 in Old English.]

pen[3] (pĕn) *n. Informal.* A penitentiary. [First written down in 1884 in American English, from *penitentiary.*]

pe•nal (**pē′**nəl) *adj.* **1.** Of, relating to, or prescribing punishment, as for breaking the law: *a penal colony.* **2.** Subject to punishment: *a penal offense.*

penal code *n.* A body of laws relating to crime and their offenses.

pe•nal•ize (**pē′**nə līz′ *or* **pĕn′**ə līz′) *tr.v.* **pe•nal•ized, pe•nal•iz•ing, pe•nal•iz•es.** To subject to a penalty, as for a legal offense or the breaking of a rule. **—pe′nal•i•za′tion** (pē′nə lĭ **zā′**shən *or* pĕn′ə lĭ **zā′**shən) *n.*

pen•al•ty (**pĕn′**əl tē) *n., pl.* **pen•al•ties.** **1.** A punishment established by law or authority for a crime. **2.** Something, such as a sum of money, that must be given up for an offense. **3.** In sports, a punishment or disadvantage imposed on a team or competitor for breaking a rule. [First written down in 1462 in Middle English and spelled *penalte*, from Latin *poenālis*, penal, from Greek *poinē*, penalty.]

pen•ance (**pĕn′**əns) *n.* **1.** An act of self-denial or devotion performed voluntarily to show sorrow for a sin or other wrongdoing. **2.** In some Christian churches, a sacrament that includes contrition, confession to a priest, acceptance of punishment, and absolution.

pence (pĕns) *n. Chiefly British.* A plural of **penny** (sense 2).

pen•chant (**pĕn′**chənt) *n.* A strong inclination; a definite liking: *a penchant for spicy cooking.*

pen•cil (**pĕn′**səl) *n.* **1.** A thin writing instrument consisting of a stick of graphite or some other material encased in wood or held in a mechanical holder. **2.** Something shaped or used like a pencil: *an eyebrow pencil.* *—tr.v.* **pen•ciled, pen•cil•ing, pen•cils** also **pen•cilled, pen•cil•ling, pen•cils.** To write or mark with a pencil: *penciled her response.*

pen•dant also **pen•dent** (**pĕn′**dənt) *n.* A hanging ornament, such as one worn dangling from a necklace or from the ear.

❑ *These sound alike:* **pendant, pendent** (dangling).

pen•dent also **pen•dant** (**pĕn′**dənt) *adj.* **1.** Hanging down; dangling: *pendent vines.* **2.** Jutting; overhanging: *pendent cliffs.* **3.** Awaiting settlement; pending.

❑ *These sound alike:* **pendent, pendant** (ornament).

pend•ing (**pĕn′**dĭng) *adj.* **1.** Not yet decided or settled; awaiting action: *legislation pending before Congress.* **2.** Impending; about to happen. *—prep.* While awaiting; until: *The bridge is closed pending an investigation of the accident.*

pen•du•lous (**pĕn′**jə ləs *or* **pĕn′**dyə ləs) *adj.* **1.** Hanging loosely; suspended so as to swing or sway. **2.** Wavering; undecided. **—pen′du•lous•ly** *adv.* **—pen′du•lous•ness** *n.*

pen•du•lum (**pĕn′**jə ləm *or* **pĕn′**dyə ləm) *n.* A mass hung from a fixed support so that it is able to swing freely, often used to regulate the action of various devices, especially clocks. [First written down in 1660 in Modern English, from Latin *pendulus*, hanging.]

Pe•nel•o•pe (pə **nĕl′**ə pē) *n.* In Greek mythology, the wife of Odysseus and mother of Telemachus, celebrated for her faithfulness.

pe•ne•plain also **pe•ne•plane** (**pē′**nə plān′) *n.* A large, nearly flat eroded land surface that was formerly a mountainous or hilly area.

pe•nes (**pē′**nēz) *n.* A plural of **penis.**

pen•e•tra•ble (**pĕn′**ĭ trə bəl) *adj.* Capable of being penetrated: *a penetrable fort; a penetrable fabric not for winter use.* **—pen′e•tra•bil′i•ty** *n.*

pen•e•trate (**pĕn′**ĭ trāt′) *v.* **pen•e•trat•ed, pen•e•trat•ing, pen•e•trates.** *—tr.* **1.** To enter or force a way into; pierce: *A shaft of light penetrated the forest canopy.* **2.** To enter into and permeate: *Cold penetrated my bones.* **3.** To grasp the significance of; understand: *penetrating the workings of the immune system.* *—intr.* To pierce or enter something; make a way in or through something.

pen•e•tra•tion (pĕn′ĭ **trā′**shən) *n.* **1.** The act or process of penetrating. **2.** The power or ability to penetrate: *a drill with great penetration.* **3.** The ability to understand; insight.

pen•guin (**pĕng′**gwĭn *or* **pĕn′**gwĭn) *n.* Any of various flightless sea birds that live mostly in or near Antarctica and have webbed feet, narrow wings resembling flippers, and scalelike feathers that are white in front and black on the back.

pen•i•cil•lin (pĕn′ĭ **sĭl′**ĭn) *n.* Any of a group of related antibiotic compounds obtained from penicillium molds and used to treat various diseases and infections.

pen•i•cil•li•um (pĕn′ĭ **sĭl′**ē əm) *n., pl.* **pen•i•cil•li•ums** or **pen•i•cil•li•a** (pĕn′ĭ **sĭl′**ē ə). Any of various green and bluish-green fungi that grow on fruits, cheeses, or bread, including several species used to produce penicillin and other antibiotic drugs.

pen•in•su•la (pə **nĭn′**syə lə *or* pə **nĭn′**sə lə) *n.* A piece of land that projects into a body of water and is connected with a larger land mass. [First written down in 1538 in Modern English : Latin *paene*, almost + Latin *īnsula*, island.] **—pen•in′su•lar** *adj.*

pe•nis (**pē′**nĭs) *n., pl.* **pe•nis•es** or **pe•nes** (**pē′**nēz). **1.** The sex organ of the males of the higher vertebrates, also used by most male mammals for urination. **2.** A similar organ found in the males of lower animals.

pen•i•tent (**pĕn′**ĭ tənt) *adj.* Feeling or showing sorrow for one's sins or misdeeds. —*n.* A person who is penitent. —**pen′i•tence** *n.*

pen•i•ten•tial (pĕn′ĭ **tĕn′**shəl) *adj.* **1.** Of, relating to, or expressing sorrow for one's sins or misdeeds. **2.** Of or relating to penance.

pen•i•ten•tia•ry (pĕn′ĭ **tĕn′**shə rē) *n., pl.* **pen•i•ten•tia•ries.** A prison for those convicted of serious crimes.

pen•knife (**pĕn′**nīf′) *n.* A small pocketknife.

pen•man (**pĕn′**mən) *n.* **1.** An expert in penmanship. **2.** An author; a writer.

pen•man•ship (**pĕn′**mən shĭp′) *n.* The art, skill, style, or manner of handwriting.

Penn (pĕn), **William.** 1644–1718. English Quaker in America who founded the colony of Pennsylvania in 1681.

Penn. *abbr.* An abbreviation of Pennsylvania.

pen name *n.* A fictitious name used by an author.

pen•nant (**pĕn′**ənt) *n.* **1.** A long tapering flag, used on ships for signaling or identification. **2.a.** A flag that serves as the emblem of the championship in professional baseball. **b.** The yearly championship in professional baseball.

pen•ni•less (**pĕn′**ē lĭs) *adj.* Having no money or very little; very poor. —**pen′ni•less•ness** *n.*

pen•non (**pĕn′**ən) *n.* **1.** A long narrow banner borne upon a lance. **2.** A pennant, banner, or flag.

Penn•syl•va•nia (pĕn′səl **vān′**yə *or* pĕn′səl **vā′**nē ə). A state of the eastern United States east of Ohio. It was admitted as one of the original Thirteen Colonies in 1787. Harrisburg is the capital and Philadelphia is the largest city. Population, 11,924,710. —SEE NOTE.

Pennsylvania Dutch *n.* **1.** The descendants of German and Swiss immigrants who settled in Pennsylvania in the 17th and 18th centuries. **2.** The dialect of German spoken by this group. [First written down before 1824 in American English, alteration of German *Deutsch*, German.]

Penn•syl•va•nian (pĕn′səl **vān′**yən *or* pĕn′səl **vā′**nē ən) *adj.* **1.** Of or relating to Pennsylvania. **2.** Of, belonging to, or being the geologic time of the sixth period of the Paleozoic Era. During the Pennsylvanian, rocks bearing coal were formed. See table at **geologic time.** —*n.* **1.** A native or resident of Pennsylvania. **2.** The Pennsylvanian Period or its series of rocks.

pen•ny (**pĕn′**ē) *n., pl.* **pen•nies. 1.** In the United States and Canada, the coin worth one cent. **2.** *pl.* **pence** or **pen•nies. a.** A coin used in Great Britain since 1971, worth 1/100 of a pound. **b.** A coin formerly used in Great Britain, worth 1/12 of a shilling or 1/240 of a pound. **3.** Any of various coins worth a small amount. **4.** A small sum of money: *I haven't a penny to my name.* [First written down before 725 in Old English and spelled *penig.*]

pen•ny•roy•al (pĕn′ē **roi′**əl) *n.* **1.** A plant of Europe and Asia having small blue flowers and round leaves that yield a useful aromatic oil. **2.** A strong-smelling plant of eastern North America having small bluish flowers and hairy leaves that yield an oil used as an insect repellant.

pen•ny•weight (**pĕn′**ē wāt′) *n.* A unit of troy weight equal to 24 grains or 1/20 of a troy ounce.

pen•ny-wise or **pen•ny•wise** (**pĕn′**ē wīz′) *adj.* Careful in dealing with small sums or minor matters.

pen•ny•worth (**pĕn′**ē wûrth′) *n.* **1.** As much as a penny will buy. **2.** A small or trifling amount. **3.** A bargain.

Pe•nob•scot (pə **nŏb′**skət *or* pə **nŏb′**skŏt′) *n., pl.* **Penobscot** or **Pe•nob•scots. 1.** A member of a Native American people living in Maine. **2.** The Algonquian language of the Penobscot. —**Pe•nob′scot** *adj.*

pe•nol•o•gy (pē **nŏl′**ə jē) *n.* The theory and practice of prison management and the rehabilitation of criminals.

pen pal *n.* A friend with whom one is acquainted only by exchanging letters.

pen•sion¹ (**pĕn′**shən) *n.* A sum of money paid regularly as a retirement benefit or by way of patronage. —*tr.v.* **pen•sioned, pen•sion•ing, pen•sions. 1.** To give a pension to. **2.** To retire or dismiss with a pension: *The company reduced its workforce by pensioning off some older workers.* [First written down before 1376 in Middle English and spelled *pencioun*, payment, from Latin *pēnsiō*, from *pendere*, to weigh out, pay.]

pen•sion² (päɴ **syôɴ′**) *n.* A boarding house or small hotel in Europe. [First written down in 1644 in Modern English, from Old French *pension*, payment.]

pen•sion•er (**pĕn′**shə nər) *n.* A person who receives a pension.

pen•sive (**pĕn′**sĭv) *adj.* **1.** Engaged in deep and serious thought. **2.** Showing or suggestive of deep, often sad thoughtfulness: *pensive eyes.* —**pen′sive•ly** *adv.* —**pen′sive•ness** *n.*

pen•stock (**pĕn′**stŏk′) *n.* **1.** A sluice or gate used to control a flow of water. **2.** A pipe used to carry water to a water wheel or turbine.

pent (pĕnt) *v.* A past tense and a past participle of **pen².** —*adj.* Penned or shut up; closely confined.

penta– or **pent–** *pref.* A prefix that means five: *pentatonic.*

pen•ta•cle (**pĕn′**tə kəl) *n.* A five-pointed star formed by five straight lines connecting the vertices of a pentagon and enclosing another pentagon in the completed figure; a pentagram.

pen•ta•gon (**pĕn′**tə gŏn′) *n.* **1.** A plane geometric figure bounded by five line segments and containing five angles. **2. Pentagon. a.** A five-sided building near Washington, D.C., containing the U.S. Department of Defense and the offices of the U.S. Armed Forces. **b.** The U.S. military. [First written down in 1570 in Modern English : Greek *penta-*, five + Greek *gōnia*, angle.] —**pen•tag′o•nal** (pĕn **tăg′**ə nəl) *adj.*

pen•ta•gram (**pĕn′**tə grăm′) *n.* A pentacle.

pen•tam•e•ter (pĕn **tăm′**ĭ tər) *n.* A line of verse composed of five metrical feet.

Pen•ta•teuch (**pĕn′**tə to͞ok′ *or* **pĕn′**tə tyo͞ok′) *n.* The first five books of the Hebrew Scriptures.

pen•tath•lon (pĕn **tăth′**lən *or* pĕn **tăth′**lŏn′) *n.* An athletic contest in which each participant enters five track and field events.

pen•ta•ton•ic (pĕn′tə **tŏn′**ĭk) *adj.* Of or using only five musical tones: *a pentatonic scale.*

Pen•te•cost (**pĕn′**tĭ kôst′ *or* **pĕn′**tĭ kŏst′) *n.* **1.** The seventh Sunday after Easter, observed in Christian churches in commemoration of the descent of the Holy Spirit upon the disciples. **2.** Shavuot. —**Pen′te•cos′tal** *adj.*

pent•house (**pĕnt′**hous′) *n.* An apartment or a dwelling, usually with a terrace, located on the roof of a building.

pent-up (**pĕnt′ŭp′**) *adj.* Not given expression; repressed: *pent-up anger.*

pe•nult (**pē′**nŭlt′ *or* pĭ **nŭlt′**) *n.* The next to the last syllable in a word.

pe•nul•ti•mate (pĭ **nŭl′**tə mĭt) *adj.* Next to last: *the penultimate chapter of the book.*

pe•num•bra (pĭ **nŭm′**brə) *n., pl.* **pe•num•brae** (pĭ**nŭm′**brē) or **pe•num•bras. 1.** A partial shadow between regions of complete shadow and complete illumination, especially in an eclipse. **2.** The partly darkened fringe that surrounds a sunspot. [First written down in 1666 in Modern English : Latin *paene*, almost + Latin *umbra*, shadow.]

pennant

Pennsylvania

The state of **Pennsylvania** was named after its founder, William Penn, and his father, a British admiral. It combines the name *Penn* with a form of the Latin word *silva* (also spelled *sylva*), meaning "woodland."

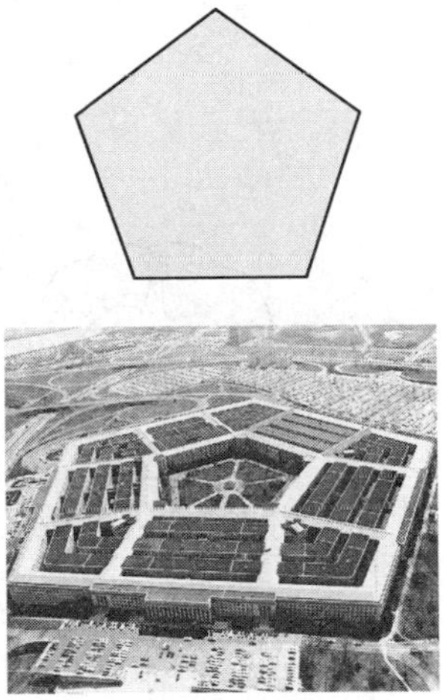

pentagon

Top: Polygonal figure
Bottom: The Pentagon, Arlington, Virginia

ă	**pat**	oi	**boy**
ā	**pay**	ou	**out**
âr	**care**	o͝o	**took**
ä	**father**	o͞o	**boot**
ĕ	**pet**	ŭ	**cut**
ē	**be**	ûr	**urge**
ĭ	**pit**	th	**thin**
ī	**pie**	*th*	**this**
îr	**pier**	hw	**whoop**
ŏ	**pot**	zh	**vision**
ō	**toe**	ə	**about**
ô	**paw**	ɴ	*French* **bon**

pe•nu•ri•ous (pə no͝or′ē əs *or* pə nyo͝or′ē əs) *adj.* **1.** Miserly; stingy. **2.** Extremely needy; poverty-stricken. —**pe•nu′ri•ous•ly** *adv.* —**pe•nu′ri•ous•ness** *n.*

pen•u•ry (pĕn′yə rē) *n.* Extreme poverty.

Pe•nu•ti•an (pə no͞o′tē ən *or* pə no͞o′shən) *n.* A family of Native American languages spoken in Pacific coastal areas from California to British Columbia.

pe•on (pē′ŏn′ *or* pē′ən) *n.* **1.** An unskilled laborer or farm worker in Latin America. **2.** A person once held in a state of servitude to a creditor in Mexico and the southwest United States. **3.** A menial worker; a person who does routine work. [First written down in 1826 in American English, from Medieval Latin *pedō*, foot soldier.]

pe•on•age (pē′ə nĭj) *n.* **1.** The condition of being a peon. **2.** A system by which debtors are bound in servitude to their creditors until their debts are paid.

pe•o•ny (pē′ə nē) *n., pl.* **pe•o•nies. 1.** Any of various garden plants having large pink, red, or white flowers. **2.** The flower of such a plant.

peo•ple (pē′pəl) *n., pl.* **people. 1.** Human beings considered as a group. **2.a.** A group of persons living in the same country under one national government: *the American people.* **b.** The citizens of a political unit: *The people of Alaska will vote tomorrow.* **3.** *pl.* **peoples.** A group of persons sharing a common religion, culture, language, or condition of life: *the peoples of southwest Asia.* **4.** The mass of ordinary persons; the populace: *the rights of the people.* **5.** Family, relatives, or ancestors: *Her people are farmers.* —*tr.v.* **peo•pled, peo•pling, peo•ples.** To furnish with or as if with people; populate: *Many ethnic groups people the city. The bay is peopled with many fish.* —SEE NOTE.

Usage: people

It is all right to use either **people** or **persons** when you refer to a specific number of individuals: *Six people* (or *six persons*) *missed the field trip because of illness.*

pep (pĕp) *Informal. n.* Energy; high spirits. —*tr.v.* **pepped, pep•ping, peps.** To bring energy or liveliness to: *The good news pepped me up.*

pep•per (pĕp′ər) *n.* **1.a.** A black or white pungent spice made from the dried blackish berries of a tropical vine. **b.** The plant that bears such berries. **2.a.** The many-seeded red, yellow, or green fruit of any of several plants, eaten as a vegetable or ground into seasonings. **b.** A plant that bears such fruit. **3.** Any of various seasonings, such as cayenne pepper or chili, made from hot red peppers. —*tr.v.* **pep•pered, pep•per•ing, pep•pers. 1.** To season with pepper. **2.** To sprinkle liberally; dot. **3.** To sprinkle or spray with many small objects: *peppered the newlyweds with rice.* [First written down about 1000 in Old English and spelled *pipor*, from Sanskrit *pippalī*.]

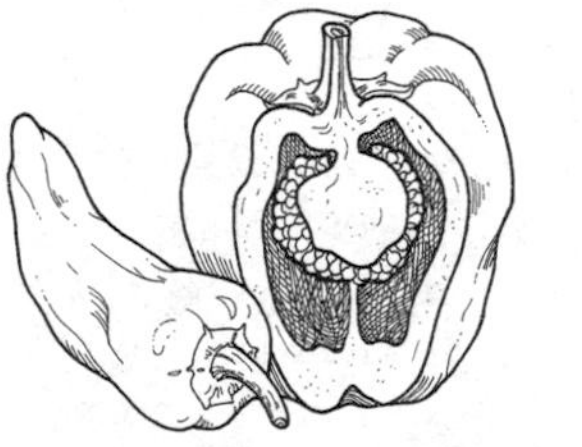

pepper

pep•per•corn (pĕp′ər kôrn′) *n.* A dried blackish berry of the pepper vine.

pep•per•mint (pĕp′ər mĭnt′) *n.* **1.** A plant having small purple or white flowers and leaves that yield an oil having a strong pleasant taste and smell. **2.** The oil or flavoring from this plant. **3.** A candy flavored with this oil.

pep•per•o•ni (pĕp′ə rō′nē) *n., pl.* **pep•per•o•nis.** A highly spiced pork and beef sausage.

pep•per•y (pĕp′ə rē) *adj.* **1.** Of or containing pepper; hot and spicy: *a peppery stew.* **2.** Having a hot temper.

pep•sin also **pep•sine** (pĕp′sĭn) *n.* **1.** An enzyme that is produced in the stomach and acts as a catalyst in one stage of the digestion of protein. **2.** A substance containing this enzyme, obtained from the stomach of hogs and calves and used to aid digestion.

pep talk *n. Informal.* A speech of encouragement, as one given by a coach to a team.

pep•tic (pĕp′tĭk) *adj.* **1.a.** Of, relating to, or assisting digestion: *a peptic secretion.* **b.** Caused by or associated with the action of digestive juices: *a peptic ulcer.* **2.** Of, relating to, or involving pepsin.

Pe•quot (pē′kwŏt′) *n., pl.* **Pequot** or **Pe•quots. 1.** A member of a Native American people living in Connecticut. The Pequot and the Mohegan were the same people until the Mohegan broke away in the 17th century. **2.** The Algonquian language of the Pequot.

per (pûr) *prep.* **1.** To, for, or by each; for every: *eggs at one dollar per dozen.* **2.** According to: *changes made to the play per instructions of the author.*

per•am•bu•late (pə răm′byə lāt′) *v.* **per•am•bu•lat•ed, per•am•bu•lat•ing, per•am•bu•lates.** —*tr.* **1.** To walk through. **2.** To inspect by walking through: *perambulate the plant site.* —*intr.* To walk about; stroll. —**per•am′bu•la′tion** *n.*

per•am•bu•la•tor (pə răm′byə lā′tər) *n. Chiefly British.* A baby carriage.

per•cale (pər kāl′) *n.* A strong closely woven cloth used to make sheets and clothing.

per cap•i•ta (pər kăp′ĭ tə) *adv. & adj.* Per person: *the state's per capita income.*

per•ceive (pər sēv′) *tr.v.* **per•ceived, per•ceiv•ing, per•ceives. 1.** To become aware of through the senses, especially to see or hear. **2.** To achieve understanding of: *We tried to perceive their intentions by analyzing their letter.* —**per•ceiv′er** *n.*

per•cent also **per cent** (pər sĕnt′) *n.* One part in a hundred: *Sixty-two percent of those asked contributed.* —*adj.* Gaining interest at a given rate or percentage: *an eight percent savings account.* [First written down in 1568 in Modern English and spelled *per cent*, from *per centum*, by the hundred.]

per•cent•age (pər sĕn′tĭj) *n.* **1.** A fraction that has 100 understood as its denominator. 0.75 equals a percentage of 75. **2.** A portion or share in relation to the whole: *Teachers made up a sizable percentage of people at the meeting.*

per•cen•tile (pər sĕn′tīl′) *n.* Any of the smaller numerical ranges formed by dividing the total range of a variable into 100 equal parts that do not overlap. The percentile into which a value of this variable falls is determined by the percentage of the other values that it exceeds. For example, an examination score that exceeds 95 percent of the other scores is in the 95th percentile.

per•cep•ti•ble (pər sĕp′tə bəl) *adj.* Capable of being perceived by the senses or by the mind: *a perceptible improvement in the patient's condition.* —**per•cep′ti•bil′i•ty** *n.* —**per•cep′ti•bly** *adv.*

per•cep•tion (pər sĕp′shən) *n.* **1.** The ability, act, or process of perceiving. **2.** Something perceived; an insight: *What an astute perception!*

per•cep•tive (pər sĕp′tĭv) *adj.* **1.** Having the ability to perceive; having keen insight: *a perceptive student of physics.* **2.** Marked by understanding and insight: *a perceptive thought.* —**per•cep′tive•ly** *adv.*

per•cep•tu•al (pər sĕp′cho͞o əl) *adj.* Of, based on, or involving perception.

perch¹ (pûrch) *n.* **1.** A branch or rod that serves as a roost for a bird. **2.** A resting place or vantage point, especially one that is high up: *Lee slid down from a perch in the apple tree.* —*v.* **perched, perch•ing, perch•es.** —*intr.* **1.** To alight or rest on or as if on a perch: *The bird perched on a branch.* **2.** To occupy an elevated positon: *a village perched on the hillside.* —*tr.* To place on or as if on a perch: *She perched the straw hat on her head.* [First written down in 1208 in Middle English and spelled *perche*, from Latin *pertica*, stick, pole.]

perch² (pûrch) *n., pl.* **perch** or **perch•es.** Any of various mostly freshwater food fishes having spiny fins. [First written down before 1300 in Middle

English and spelled *perche*, from Greek *perkē*.]

per•chance (pər chăns′) *adv.* Perhaps; possibly.

per•co•late (pûr′kə lāt′) *v.* **per•co•lat•ed, per•co•lat•ing, per•co•lates.** —*tr.* **1.** To cause (a liquid, for example) to pass through small holes or through a porous substance: *percolate oil through a filter.* **2.** To pass or ooze through: *Water percolated the sand.* —*intr.* **1.** To drain or seep through a porous material or a filter. **2.** *Informal.* To become lively or active: *As she became aware of the new data, her mind began to percolate.* [First written down in 1626 in Modern English, from Latin *percōlāre* : *per-*, through + *cōlum*, sieve, filter.] —**per′co•la′tion** *n.*

per•co•la•tor (pûr′kə lā′tər) *n.* A coffeepot in which boiling water is forced repeatedly to pass up through a center tube and filter through a basket of ground coffee.

per•cus•sion (pər kŭsh′ən) *n.* **1.a.** The striking together of two bodies, especially when noise is produced. **b.** A sound, vibration, or shock produced in this way. **2.** A method of medical examination in which a physician taps areas of the body and draws conclusions on the basis of the sounds produced. **3.a.** The section of a band or an orchestra made up of percussion instruments. **b.** Percussion instruments considered as a group.

percussion cap *n.* A metal cap containing a detonator that explodes on being struck.

percussion instrument *n.* A musical instrument, such as a drum, xylophone, or piano, in which sound is produced by one object striking another.

per di•em (pər dē′əm) *adv.* Per day. —*adj.* On a daily basis; daily.

per•di•tion (pər dĭsh′ən) *n.* **1.a.** The loss of the soul; eternal damnation. **b.** Hell. **2.** *Archaic.* Utter loss or ruin.

per•e•grine falcon (pĕr′ə grĭn) *n.* A swift hawk having gray and white feathers and much used in falconry.

per•emp•to•ry (pə rĕmp′tə rē) *adj.* **1.** Putting an end to all debate or action: *a peremptory decree.* **2.** Not to be denied, refused, or opposed: *a peremptory order.* **3.** Offensively self-assured; dictatorial: *his peremptory manner.* —**per•emp′to•ri•ly** *adv.* —**per•emp′to•ri•ness** *n.*

per•en•ni•al (pə rĕn′ē əl) *adj.* **1.** Living, growing, and flowering and producing seeds for three or more years. **2.** Lasting indefinitely; perpetual: *perennial happiness.* **3.** Repeated regularly; appearing again and again: *perennial fiscal problems.* —*n.* A perennial plant. —**per•en′ni•al•ly** *adv.*

per•fect (pûr′fĭkt) *adj.* **1.a.** Lacking nothing essential to the whole; satisfying all requirements: *Our understanding of the situation is not perfect.* **b.** Completely accurate; exact: *a perfect copy.* **2.** Having no faults, flaws, or defects: *a perfect piece of marble.* **3.a.** Completely suited for a particular purpose or action: *a perfect actor for the part.* **b.** Completely corresponding to a description, standard, or type. **4.** Excellent and delightful in all respects: *perfect weather.* **5.** Pure; undiluted: *the perfect redness of the apple.* **6.** Complete; thorough; utter: *a perfect fool.* **7.** Having a root that is a whole number; formed by raising an integer to an integral power; for example, 25 is a perfect square, and 27 is a perfect cube. **8.** In grammar, of or relating to the perfect tense. —*n.* **1.** The perfect tense. **2.** A verb form in the perfect tense. —*tr.v.* (pər fĕkt′). **per•fect•ed, per•fect•ing, per•fects.** To bring to perfection or completion. [First written down about 1300 in Middle English and spelled *parfijt*, from Latin *perfectus*, past participle of *perficere*, to finish.]

Synonyms: perfect, faultless, flawless, impeccable. These adjectives all mean without any defects or errors. *I think I have found the perfect solution. The lecturer argued her point with faultless logic. That museum owns the largest flawless gem in the world. They spoke impeccable French after spending several years in Paris.*

per•fect•i•ble (pər fĕk′tə bəl) *adj.* Capable of becoming or being made perfect: *a perfectible style of writing.* —**per•fect′i•bil′i•ty** *n.*

per•fec•tion (pər fĕk′shən) *n.* **1.** The quality or condition of being perfect. **2.** The act of process of perfecting. **3.** A person or thing considered to be a perfect example of excellence.

per•fec•tion•ism (pər fĕk′shə nĭz′əm) *n.* **1.** A tendency to set extremely high standards and to be dissatisfied with anything less. **2.** A belief that human beings can achieve moral or spiritual perfection. —**per•fec′tion•ist** *n.*

per•fect•ly (pûr′fĭkt lē) *adv.* **1.a.** In a perfect manner: *She played the piece perfectly.* **b.** To a perfect degree; precisely: *This circle is perfectly round.* **2.** Completely; wholly: *Some mushrooms are perfectly safe to eat.*

perfect number *n.* A positive integer, such as 6 or 28, that equals the sum of all of its divisors other than itself. For example, the divisors of 6, not counting 6 itself, are 1, 2, and 3. Their sum is 6.

perfect pitch *n.* The ability to identify or sing any tone heard; absolute pitch.

perfect tense *n.* In grammar, a verb tense that expresses an action completed prior to a fixed point in time. For example, *she has played* is in the present perfect tense, *she had played* is in the past perfect tense, and *she will have played* is in the future perfect tense.

per•fid•i•ous (pər fĭd′ē əs) *adj.* Disloyal; treacherous. —**per•fid′i•ous•ly** *adv.*

per•fi•dy (pûr′fĭ dē) *n., pl.* **per•fi•dies.** Deliberate breach of faith; treachery.

per•fo•rate (pûr′fə rāt′) *tr.v.* **per•fo•rat•ed, per•fo•rat•ing, per•fo•rates.** **1.** To punch or bore a hole or holes in; pierce: *Perforate the top of the pie to let the steam escape.* **2.** To pierce or stamp with rows of holes to allow easy separation: *a machine that perforates sheets of postage stamps.* [First written down in 1538 in Modern English, from Latin *perforāre* : *per-*, through + *forāre*, to bore.]

per•fo•ra•ted (pûr′fə rā′tĭd) *adj.* Pierced with holes; full of holes: *a perforated spoon.*

per•fo•ra•tion (pûr′fə rā′shən) *n.* **1.** A hole or series of holes, as those between postage stamps. **2.** The act of perforating.

per•force (pər fôrs′) *adv.* By force of circumstance; of necessity: *She must perforce work for wages.*

per•form (pər fôrm′) *v.* **per•formed, per•form•ing, per•forms.** —*tr.* **1.** To begin and carry through to completion; do; execute: *perform an experiment; perform a somersault.* **2.** To carry out or fulfill (a promise, duty, or task, for example). **3.** To present or enact before an audience: *perform a symphony.* —*intr.* **1.** To act or function in a specified manner: *The car performs well on curves.* **2.** To portray a role, present a musical work, or demonstrate a skill before an audience. [First written down about 1300 in Middle English and spelled *parfourmen*, from Anglo-Norman *performer.*] —**per•form′er** *n.*

per•form•ance (pər fôr′məns) *n.* **1.** The act, process, or manner of performing. **2.** The way in which a person or thing functions: *Look for good steady performance when buying a car.* **3.** A public presentation of something, such as a musical or dramatic work. **4.** Something that is performed; an accomplishment.

peregrine falcon
Continental peregrine falcon

ă	pat	oi	boy
ā	pay	ou	out
âr	care	o͝o	took
ä	father	o͞o	boot
ĕ	pet	ŭ	cut
ē	be	ûr	urge
ĭ	pit	th	thin
ī	pie	*th*	this
îr	pier	hw	whoop
ŏ	pot	zh	vision
ō	toe	ə	about
ô	paw	N	*French* bon

Pericles

Copy of a mid fifth-century B.C. bust attributed to Cresilas (fl. 450–430 B.C.)

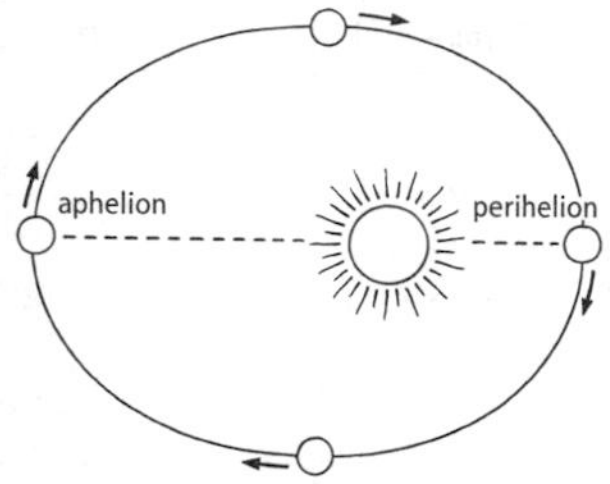

perihelion

Frances Perkins

per•fume (pûr′fyo͞om′ *or* pər **fyo͞om′**) *n.* **1.** A fragrant liquid distilled from flowers or prepared synthetically. **2.** A pleasant scent or odor. —*tr.v.* (pər **fyo͞om′**). **per•fumed, per•fum•ing, per•fumes.** To fill with a fragrance or apply a fragrance to. [First written down in 1533 in Modern English, from Italian *parfumare,* to fill with smoke : Latin *per-,* thoroughly + Latin *fūmus,* smoke.]

per•fum•er•y (pər **fyo͞o′**mə rē) *n., pl.* **per•fum•er•ies. 1.** Perfumes considered as a group. **2.** A business that specializes in making or selling perfume. **3.** The art of making perfume.

per•func•to•ry (pər **fŭngk′**tə rē) *adj.* Done or acting routinely and with little interest or care: *She gave a perfunctory wave and walked away.* —**per•func′to•ri•ly** *adv.*

per•haps (pər **hăps′**) *adv.* Maybe; possibly: *Perhaps he'll come with us.*

peri– *pref.* A prefix that means around, about, or enclosing: *perihelion.*

per•i•car•di•um (pĕr′ĭ **kär′**dē əm) *n., pl.* **per•i•car•di•a** (pĕr′ĭ **kär′**dē ə). The membrane sac that encloses the heart.

Per•i•cles (**pĕr′**ĭ klēz′). Died 429 B.C. Athenian leader known for ordering the construction of the Parthenon.

per•i•gee (**pĕr′**ə jē) *n.* The point in the orbit of a satellite at which it is closest to the body it is orbiting. [First written down in 1594 in Modern English, from Greek *perigeion* : *peri-,* near + *gē,* earth.]

per•i•he•li•on (pĕr′ə **hē′**lē ən) *n., pl.* **per•i•he•li•a** (pĕr′ə **hē′**lē ə). The point in the orbit of a planet or other body that travels around the sun at which it is closest to the sun.

per•il (**pĕr′**əl) *n.* **1.** The condition of being in danger or at risk of harm or loss: *The drought has put the crops in peril.* **2.** Something that is dangerous or risky: *the perils of a journey in a covered wagon.* [First written down before 1200 in Middle English, from Latin *perīculum.*]

per•il•ous (**pĕr′**ə ləs) *adj.* Full of peril; hazardous. —**per′il•ous•ly** *adv.*

pe•rim•e•ter (pə **rĭm′**ĭ tər) *n.* **1.a.** The sum of the lengths of the segments that form the sides of a polygon. **b.** The total length of any closed curve, such as a circle or an ellipse. **2.** The outer limits of an area. **3.** A fortified strip or boundary protecting a military position.

pe•ri•od (**pîr′**ē əd) *n.* **1.** An interval of time having a specified length or characterized by certain conditions or events: *a dormant period in the economy.* **2.** A span of time during which a specified culture, set of beliefs, or technology was predominant; a historical era: *the colonial period.* **3.** Any of various intervals of time, as the divisions of the academic day or of playing time in a game: *I have history in the fifth period.* **4.** A unit of geologic time, longer than an epoch and shorter than an era. **5.** The interval of time between corresponding points in successive occurrences of a repeated action or event; a cycle. **6.** An instance or occurrence of menstruation. **7.** A punctuation mark (.) indicating a full stop, used at the end of declarative sentences and after many abbreviations. [First written down in 1413 in Middle English and spelled *pariode,* from Greek *periodos,* circuit : *peri-,* around + *hodos,* way.]

pe•ri•od•ic (pîr′ē **ŏd′**ĭk) *adj.* **1.** Happening or repeating at regular intervals; cyclic: *the periodic motion of a pendulum.* **2.** Taking place from time to time; intermittent. —**pe′ri•od′i•cal•ly** *adv.*

pe•ri•od•i•cal (pîr′ē **ŏd′**ĭ kəl) *adj.* **1.** Periodic. **2.** Of or relating to a publication that is issued at regular intervals of more than one day. —*n.* A periodical publication, especially a magazine.

periodic table *n.* A table in which the elements are presented in order of increasing atomic number, with the elements that have similar properties usually appearing in columns.

per•i•pa•tet•ic (pĕr′ə pə **tĕt′**ĭk) *adj.* Walking about or traveling on foot from place to place: *peripatetic political candidates.*

pe•riph•er•al (pə **rĭf′**ər əl) *adj.* **1.** Of or located on the periphery: *the peripheral regions of the state.* **2.** Of minor importance or relevance. —**pe•riph′er•al•ly** *adv.*

peripheral nervous system *n.* The part of the vertebrate nervous system that is made up of all the nerves outside the central nervous system.

pe•riph•er•y (pə **rĭf′**ə rē) *n., pl.* **pe•riph•er•ies. 1.** A line that forms a boundary; a perimeter. **2.** The outermost part within a boundary.

per•i•scope (**pĕr′**ĭ skōp′) *n.* Any of several optical instruments in which mirrors or prisms allow observation of objects that are not in a direct line of sight.

per•ish (**pĕr′**ĭsh) *intr.v.* **per•ished, per•ish•ing, per•ish•es. 1.** To die or be destroyed, especially in a violent manner. **2.** To pass from existence; disappear gradually: *The dinosaurs perished from the earth.* [First written down about 1275 in Middle English and spelled *perissen,* from Latin *perīre.*]

per•ish•a•ble (**pĕr′**ĭ shə bəl) *adj.* Liable to decay or spoil easily: *perishable fruits and vegetables.* —*n.* Something, especially food, subject to decay or spoiling. Often used in the plural.

per•i•stal•sis (pĕr′ĭ **stôl′**sĭs *or* pĕr′ĭ **stăl′**sĭs) *n., pl.* **per•i•stal•ses** (pĕr′ĭ **stôl′**sēz *or* pĕr′ĭ **stăl′**sēz). The series of muscle contractions in a tubular organ, such as an intestine, that move the material contained in it along its length.

per•i•to•ne•um (pĕr′ĭ tn **ē′**əm) *n., pl.* **per•i•to•ne•a** (pĕr′ĭ tn **ē′**ə). The membrane that lines the inside of the abdomen and encloses the abdominal organs.

per•i•to•ni•tis (pĕr′ĭ tn **ī′**tĭs) *n.* Inflammation of the peritoneum.

per•i•wig (**pĕr′**ĭ wĭg′) *n.* A wig, especially a peruke.

per•i•win•kle[1] (**pĕr′**ĭ wĭng′kəl) *n.* Any of several small edible sea snails having a broad spiral shell. [First written down probably about 1000 in Old English and spelled *pīnewincle* : Latin *pīna,* mussel (from Greek *pinē*) + Old English *wincel,* snail shell.]

per•i•win•kle[2] (**pĕr′**ĭ wĭng′kəl) *n.* Any of several trailing plants having evergreen leaves and usually blue flowers; myrtle. [First written down before 1475 in Middle English and spelled *pervinkle,* from Old English *pervince,* from Latin *pervincīre,* to wind about.]

per•jure (**pûr′**jər) *tr.v.* **per•jured, per•jur•ing, per•jures.** To make (oneself) guilty of perjury by testifying falsely under oath: *The witness perjured himself.* —**per′jur•er** *n.*

per•ju•ry (**pûr′**jə rē) *n., pl.* **per•ju•ries.** In law, the deliberate giving of false, misleading, or incomplete testimony while under oath.

perk[1] (pûrk) *intr. & tr.v.* **perked, perk•ing, perks.** To raise or stick up: *The dog perked its ears at the noise.* —***idiom.*** **perk up. 1.** To regain or cause to regain one's good spirits or liveliness. **2.** To refresh the appearance of: *New curtains perked up the room.* [First written down perhaps about 1390 in Middle English and spelled *perken,* to perch, from *perk,* perch.]

perk[2] (pûrk) *n.* A perquisite. [First written down in 1824 in Modern English, from *perquisite.*]

Per•kins (**pûr′**kĭnz), **Frances.** 1882–1965. American social reformer and public official who as U.S. secretary of labor (1933–1945) was the first woman to hold a cabinet position.

perk•y (pûr′kē) *adj.* **perk•i•er, perk•i•est.** Cheerful and lively; jaunty. **—perk′i•ly** *adv.*

perm (pûrm) *Informal. n.* A permanent.

per•ma•frost (pûr′mə frôst′ *or* pûr′mə frŏst′) *n.* A layer of permanently frozen subsoil, sometimes reaching a depth of 300 meters or more, found throughout most of the arctic regions.

per•ma•nence (pûr′mə nəns) *n.* The quality or condition of being permanent.

per•ma•nent (pûr′mə nənt) *adj.* Lasting or meant to last indefinitely; enduring: *a permanent settlement on the frontier.* *—n.* A long-lasting hair wave produced by setting the hair with chemicals when wet and drying it with heat. [First written down before 1425 in Middle English, from Latin *permanēre*, to endure.] **—per′ma•nent•ly** *adv.*

permanent press *n.* A chemical process by which fabrics are permanently shaped and treated for resistance to wrinkles. **—per′ma•nent-press′** *adj.*

permanent wave *n.* A permanent.

per•me•a•ble (pûr′mē ə bəl) *adj.* Capable of being passed through or permeated, especially by liquids or gases: *a permeable membrane.* **—per′me•a•bil′i•ty** *n.* **—per′me•a•bly** *adv.*

per•me•ate (pûr′mē āt′) *v.* **per•me•at•ed, per•me•at•ing, per•me•ates.** *—tr.* **1.** To spread or flow throughout: *The smell of baking cookies permeated the house.* **2.** To pass through the tiny openings of: *liquid permeating a membrane.* *—intr.* To spread through or penetrate something.

Per•mi•an (pûr′mē ən) *adj.* Of, belonging to, or being the geologic time of the seventh and last period of the Paleozoic era. During the Permian Period, the reptile ancestors of mammals appeared. See table at **geologic time.** *—n.* The Permian Period or its series of rocks.

per•mis•si•ble (pər mĭs′ə bəl) *adj.* Permitted; allowable: *a permissible error.* **—per•mis′si•bly** *adv.*

per•mis•sion (pər mĭsh′ən) *n.* **1.** The act of permitting. **2.** Consent, especially formal consent; authorization.

per•mis•sive (pər mĭs′ĭv) *adj.* Allowing freedom; tolerant or lenient: *permissive parents.* **—per•mis′sive•ly** *adv.* **—per•mis′sive•ness** *n.*

per•mit (pər mĭt′) *v.* **per•mit•ted, per•mit•ting, per•mits.** *—tr.* **1.** To allow the doing of (something); consent to: *The town permits bicycle riding in the park.* **2.** To give consent or permission to; authorize: *Will the company permit access to its files?* **3.** To afford opportunity to; make possible: *The assembly line permitted mass production.* *—intr.* To afford opportunity; allow: *If weather permits, we will fly.* *—n.* (pûr′mĭt *or* pər mĭt′). A document or certificate giving permission to do something; a license. [First written down in 1429 in Middle English and spelled *permitten*, from Latin *permittere* : *per-*, through + *mittere*, to let go.]

per•mu•ta•tion (pûr′myo͝o tā′shən) *n.* **1.** A complete change; a transformation: *Notice the permutations that certain spices undergo when cooked.* **2.** Any of the ordered subsets that can be formed from the elements of a set. For example, some of the permutations of the set composed of *x, y,* and *z* are *xyz, xzy, yxz, yzx, zxy, zyx.*

per•mute (pər myo͞ot′) *tr.v.* **per•mut•ed, per•mut•ing, per•mutes.** **1.** To change the order of. **2.** To subject (a set) to permutation.

per•ni•cious (pər nĭsh′əs) *adj.* **1.** Tending to cause death or serious injury; deadly: *a pernicious disease.* **2.** Causing great harm; destructive: *a pernicious habit.* **—per•ni′cious•ly** *adv.* **—per•ni′cious•ness** *n.*

per•nick•e•ty (pər nĭk′ĭ tē) *adj.* Persnickety.

per•ox•ide (pə rŏk′sīd′) *n.* **1.** A compound containing the oxygen group O_2, that yields hydrogen peroxide when treated with an acid. **2.** Hydrogen peroxide. *—tr.v.* **per•ox•id•ed, per•ox•id•ing, per•ox•ides.** **1.** To treat with peroxide. **2.** To bleach (hair) with hydrogen peroxide.

per•pen•dic•u•lar (pûr′pən dĭk′yə lər) *adj.* **1.** Intersecting at or forming a right angle or right angles: *perpendicular lines.* **2.** At right angles to the horizontal; vertical. *—n.* **1.** A line or plane perpendicular to a given line or plane. **2.** A vertical or nearly vertical line or plane. [First written down in 1391 in Middle English and spelled *perpendiculer*, from Latin *perpendiculum*, plumb line, from *perpendere*, to weigh carefully.]

per•pe•trate (pûr′pĭ trāt′) *tr.v.* **per•pe•trat•ed, per•pe•trat•ing, per•pe•trates.** To be guilty of; commit: *perpetrate a crime.* **—per′pe•tra′tion** *n.* **—per′pe•tra′tor** *n.*

per•pet•u•al (pər pĕch′o͞o əl) *adj.* **1.** Lasting forever or for an indefinitely long time: *the perpetual ice of the polar regions.* **2.** Ceaselessly repeated or continuing without interruption: *perpetual nagging.* **—per•pet′u•al•ly** *adv.* **—per•pet′u•al•ness** *n.*

per•pet•u•ate (pər pĕch′o͞o āt′) *tr.v.* **per•pet•u•at•ed, per•pet•u•at•ing, per•pet•u•ates.** **1.** To cause to continue indefinitely; make perpetual. **2.** To prolong the existence of; cause to be remembered: *perpetuate a legend.* **—per•pet′u•a′tion** *n.*

per•pe•tu•i•ty (pûr′pĭ to͞o′ĭ tē *or* pûr′pĭ tyo͞o′ĭ tē) *n., pl.* **per•pe•tu•i•ties.** **1.** The quality or condition of being eternal. **2.** Time without end; eternity. ***—idiom.*** **in perpetuity.** For an indefinite period of time; forever.

per•plex (pər plĕks′) *tr.v.* **per•plexed, per•plex•ing, per•plex•es.** **1.** To confuse or puzzle; bewilder. **2.** To make confusingly intricate; complicate. [First written down in 1595 in Modern English, from Latin *perplexus*, confused.]

per•plexed (pər plĕkst′) *adj.* **1.** Confused or puzzled; bewildered: *a perplexed look.* **2.** Full of complexity or complications.

per•plex•i•ty (pər plĕk′sĭ tē) *n., pl.* **per•plex•i•ties.** **1.** The condition of being perplexed; bewilderment. **2.** The state of being intricate or complicated.

per•qui•site (pûr′kwĭ zĭt) *n.* Something received in addition to a regular wage or salary, especially a benefit or something advantageous: *Free use of a car was one of the supervisor's perquisites.*

Per•ry (pĕr′ē), **Oliver Hazard.** 1785–1819. American naval officer in the War of 1812.

per se (pər sā′) *adv.* In or by itself; intrinsically.

per•se•cute (pûr′sĭ kyo͞ot′) *tr.v.* **per•se•cut•ed, per•se•cut•ing, per•se•cutes.** **1.** To oppress or harass, especially because of politics, religion, or race, for example. **2.** To annoy persistently; bother. [First written down in 1450 in Middle English, from Latin *persequī*, to pursue.] **—per′se•cu′tion** (pûr′sĭ kyo͞o′shən) *n.* **—per′se•cu′tor** *n.*

Per•se•id (pûr′sē ĭd) *n.* One of a group of meteors that appear to originate near the constellation Perseus during August.

Per•seph•o•ne (pər sĕf′ə nē) *n.* In Greek mythology, the wife of Hades and queen of the underworld, identified with the Roman Proserpina.

Per•se•us (pûr′sē əs) *n.* **1.** In Greek mythology, a son of Zeus and a mortal and the husband of Andromeda, who kills the Gorgon Medusa. **2.** A constellation in the Northern Hemisphere near Andromeda and Auriga.

per•se•ver•ance (pûr′sə vîr′əns) *n.* The act or quality of holding to a course of action, a belief, or a purpose; steadfastness: *It took great perseverance for the Wright Brothers to build an airplane.*

per•se•vere (pûr′sə vîr′) *intr.v.* **per•se•vered, per•**

ă	pat	oi	boy
ā	pay	ou	out
âr	care	o͝o	took
ä	father	o͞o	boot
ĕ	pet	ŭ	cut
ē	be	ûr	urge
ĭ	pit	th	thin
ī	pie	*th*	this
îr	pier	hw	whoop
ŏ	pot	zh	vision
ō	toe	ə	about
ô	paw	N	*French* bon

Persian cat

persimmon

Word History: person

Our word **person** came from the Old French word *persone,* which came from the Latin noun *persōna.* In Latin *persōna* meant "a mask used by a player in a drama," "a player in a play," "the character acted in a play," and "a person." Indeed, if you look at the very beginning of a play by Shakespeare, you will see the Latin phrase *Dramatis Personae,* which means "Characters of the Drama." The Latin noun perhaps came through the mysterious Etruscans (they lived north of Rome in Italy, and their written language is still undeciphered) from the ancient Greek *prosopon,* which had the same meanings as the Latin word.

se•ver•ing, per•se•veres. To hold to or persist in a course of action, a belief, or a purpose, in spite of opposition or discouragement: *Despite many setbacks, they persevered in their research.* [First written down about 1380 in Middle English and spelled *perseveren,* from Latin *persevērus,* very serious.]

Per•shing (pûr′shĭng *or* pûr′zhĭng), **John Joseph.** 1860–1948. American general who commanded American forces in Europe during World War I.

Per•sia (pûr′zhə *or* pûr′shə). **1.** Also **Per•sian Empire** (pûr′zhən *or* pûr′shən). A vast empire of southwest Asia founded after 546 B.C. and conquered by Alexander the Great in 334 B.C. **2.** Iran.

Per•sian (pûr′zhən *or* pûr′shən) *adj.* Of or relating to Persia or Iran, or their peoples, languages, or cultures. —*n.* **1.** A native or inhabitant of Persia or Iran. **2.** The Indo-European language of Iran. **3.** A Persian cat.

Persian cat *n.* A domestic cat having long silky fur and a broad round head with small ears.

Persian Gulf. An arm of the Arabian Sea between the Arabia Peninsula and southwest Iran. It is an important trade route.

Persian lamb *n.* The glossy tightly curled fur of a lamb of the karakul sheep.

per•sim•mon (pər sĭm′ən) *n.* **1.** The orange-red fruit of any of various chiefly tropical trees, having thin skin, flat seeds, and pulp that is sweet when fully ripe. **2.** A tree that bears such fruit. [First written down in 1612 in American English, of Virginia Algonquian origin.]

per•sist (pər sĭst′) *intr.v.* **per•sist•ed, per•sist•ing, per•sists. 1.** To insist or repeat obstinately; be tenacious: *She persisted in denying her guilt.* **2.** To hold firmly and steadfastly to a purpose, a state, or an undertaking, despite obstacles or setbacks. **3.** To continue in existence; last: *The child's cough persisted for several weeks.* [First written down in 1538 in Modern English, from Latin *persistere* : *per-,* through + *sistere,* to stand.]

per•sist•ence (pər sĭs′təns) *n.* **1.** The act of persisting. **2.** The state or quality of being persistent; perseverance. **3.** The continuance of an effect after the cause is removed: *persistence of vision.*

per•sist•ent (pər sĭs′tənt) *adj.* **1.** Refusing to give up or let go; undaunted: *a persistent salesman.* **2.** Insistently repetitive or continuous: *the persistent ringing of the telephone.* **3.** Existing in the same state for a long period of time; enduring: *The persistent goal of alchemy was to change common metals into gold or silver.* **—per•sist′ent•ly** *adv.*

per•snick•e•ty (pər snĭk′ĭ tē) *adj.* Excessively attentive to detail; fastidious.

per•son (pûr′sən) *n.* **1.** A living human being; an individual. **2.** A human being of a given characteristic: *a person of great resourcefulness.* **3.** The living body of a human being: *He had two wallets on his person.* **4.** Physique and general appearance. **5.** In grammar, any of three groups of pronoun forms with corresponding verb forms that refer to the speaker (first person), the individual addressed (second person), or the individual or thing spoken of (third person). For example, in the sentence *I spoke to you about her, I* is in the first person, *you* is in the second person, and *her* is in the third person. ***—idiom.* in person.** In one's physical presence; personally. [First written down before 1200 in Middle English, from Old French *persone,* from Latin *persōna,* mask, role, person.] —SEE NOTE.

per•son•a•ble (pûr′sə nə bəl) *adj.* Pleasing in appearance or personality; attractive.

per•son•age (pûr′sə nĭj) *n.* **1.** A character in a literary work. **2.a.** A person. **b.** A person of rank or distinction.

per•son•al (pûr′sə nəl) *adj.* **1.** Of or relating to a particular person; private: *the personal correspondence of the college president.* **2.a.** Done, made, or performed in person: *a personal appearance.* **b.** For a particular person: *a personal favor.* **3.** Concerning a particular person and his or her private life; intimate: *a personal conversation.* **4.a.** Aimed at some aspect of a person, especially in a critical or unfriendly manner: *a highly personal remark.* **b.** Tending to make remarks about or pry into another's affairs: *He always becomes personal in an argument.* **5.** Of or relating to the body or physical being: *personal cleanliness.* **6.** In law, relating to a person's movable belongings: *personal property.* —*n.* A personal item or notice in a newspaper.

personal computer *n.* A microcomputer for use by an individual, as in an office or at home or school.

per•son•al•i•ty (pûr′sə năl′ĭ tē) *n., pl.* **per•son•al•i•ties. 1.** The quality or condition of being a person. **2.** The entire group of qualities and traits, as of character or behavior, that are peculiar to each person: *He has a pleasing personality.* **3.** The qualities that make someone socially appealing: *Candidates can win more on personality than on capability.* **4.** A person of importance or renown: *television personalities.* **5.** The characteristics of a place or situation that give it distinctive character: *Colors give a room personality.*

per•son•al•ize (pûr′sə nə līz) *tr.v.* **per•son•al•ized, per•son•al•iz•ing, per•son•al•iz•es. 1.** To perceive (a general remark or characterization) in a personal way. **2.** To make personal, especially by marking as personal property.

per•son•al•ly (pûr′sə nə lē) *adv.* **1.** In person or by oneself; without the help of another: *I thanked her personally.* **2.** As far as oneself is concerned: *Personally, I don't mind.* **3.** As a person: *I don't know him personally.* **4.** In a personal manner: *Try not to take it personally.*

personal pronoun *n.* In grammar, a pronoun that indicates the person speaking *(I, me, we, us),* the person spoken to *(you),* or the person or thing spoken about *(he, she, it, they, him, her, them).*

per•so•na non gra•ta (pər sō′nə nŏn grä′tə) *adj.* Fully unacceptable or unwelcome, especially to a foreign government: *The refugee was persona non grata.*

per•son•i•fi•ca•tion (pər sŏn′ə fĭ kā′shən) *n.* **1.** The act of personifying. **2.** A person or thing that typifies a certain quality or idea; an embodiment: *He is the personification of kindness.* **3.** A figure of speech in which inanimate objects or abstractions are provided with human qualities or are represented as possessing human form, as in *Flowers danced in the garden.*

per•son•i•fy (pər sŏn′ə fī′) *tr.v.* **per•son•i•fied, per•son•i•fy•ing, per•son•i•fies. 1.** To think of or represent (ideas or inanimate objects) as having human qualities or human form: *personifying justice as a blindfolded woman.* **2.** To be the embodiment or perfect example of (a certain quality or idea): *The nurse personified compassion.*

per•son•nel (pûr′sə nĕl′) *n.* **1.** The body of persons employed by or active in an organization, a business, or a service. **2.** The division of an organization concerned with the selection, placement, and training of employees.

per•spec•tive (pər spĕk′tĭv) *n.* **1.** The technique of representing three-dimensional objects and depth relationships on a flat surface. **2.a.** A view or vista: *the perspective of the city as seen from the rooftops.* **b.** A mental view or outlook: *Try to get a new perspective on the issue.* **3.** The appearance of objects from a distance as perceived by normal binocular vision. **4.** A mental view of the relationships of the aspects of a subject to each other and to a whole:

You have a narrow perspective of the situation. **5.** An idea of the relative importance of something; a viewpoint: *I don't want to lose perspective on our disagreement.* —*adj.* Of, seen, or represented in perspective.

per•spi•ca•cious (pûr′spĭ **kā′**shəs) *adj.* Able to perceive, discern, or understand clearly: *a perspicacious student.* **—per′spi•ca′cious•ly** *adv.*

per•spi•cac•i•ty (pûr′spĭ **kăs′**ĭ tē) *n.* The ability to perceive, discern, or understand clearly.

per•spi•ra•tion (pûr′spə **rā′**shən) *n.* **1.** The salty moisture excreted through the skin by the sweat glands; sweat. **2.** The act or process of perspiring.

per•spire (pər **spīr′**) *intr.v.* **per•spired, per•spir•ing, per•spires.** To give off perspiration.

per•suade (pər **swād′**) *tr.v.* **per•suad•ed, per•suad•ing, per•suades.** To cause (someone) to do or believe something by arguing, pleading, or reasoning; convince: *He tried to persuade them to come with us.* [First written down in 1513 in Modern English, from Latin *persuādēre,* from *suādēre,* to urge.] **—per•suad′er** *n.*

per•sua•sion (pər **swā′**zhən) *n.* **1.** The act of persuading or the state of being persuaded. **2.** The ability or power to persuade. **3.a.** A strong belief: *of a certain political persuasion.* **b.** Religious belief; a religion: *people of all persuasions.*

per•sua•sive (pər **swā′**sĭv) *adj.* Tending to or having the power to persuade. **—per•sua′sive•ly** *adv.* **—per•sua′sive•ness** *n.*

pert (pûrt) *adj.* **pert•er, pert•est. 1.** Trim and chic: *a pert dress.* **2.** High-spirited; lively: *a pert little dog.* **3.** Impudently bold or saucy: *a pert answer.* **—pert′ly** *adv.* **—pert′ness** *n.*

per•tain (pər **tān′**) *intr.v.* **per•tained, per•tain•ing, per•tains. 1.** To have reference; relate: *a discussion pertaining to art.* **2.** To belong to as a part or accessory of: *engineering skills that pertain to aeronautics.* **3.** To be fitting or suitable: *conduct that pertains to an officer.* [First written down before 1325 in Middle English and spelled *portenen,* from Latin *pertinēre,* from *tenēre,* to hold.]

Perth (pûrth). A city of southwest Australia near the Indian Ocean. It was founded in 1829. Population, 82,600.

per•ti•na•cious (pûr′tn **ā′**shəs) *adj.* **1.** Holding firmly to some belief, purpose, or opinion. **2.** Stubbornly persistent: *a pertinacious salesman.* **—per′ti•na′cious•ly** *adv.* **—per′ti•na′cious•ness** *n.*

per•ti•nac•i•ty (pûr′tn **ăs′**ĭ tē) *n.* The quality or state of being pertinacious.

per•ti•nent (**pûr′**tn ənt) *adj.* Related to a specific matter at hand; relevant: *discussing pertinent topics.* **—per′ti•nence** *n.*

per•turb (pər **tûrb′**) *tr.v.* **per•turbed, per•turb•ing, per•turbs. 1.** To make uneasy or anxious; disturb; upset: *He was easily perturbed over small matters.* **2.** To throw into great confusion. **—per′tur•ba′tion** (pûr′tər **bā′**shən) *n.*

Pe•ru (pə **ro͞o′**). A country of western South America north of Chile on the Pacific Ocean. It was the center of an Incan empire established after the 12th century A.D. Peru gained its independence from Spain in 1824. Lima is the capital and the largest city. Population, 17,031,221. **—Pe•ru′vi•an** (pə **ro͞o′**vē ən) *adj. & n.*

pe•ruke (pə **ro͝ok′**) *n.* A large powdered wig worn by men in the 17th and 18th centuries. [First written down in 1548 in Modern English, from Old Italian *perrucca,* head of hair.]

pe•rus•al (pə **ro͞o′**zəl) *n.* The act or an instance of perusing; a thorough reading.

pe•ruse (pə **ro͞oz′**) *tr.v.* **pe•rused, pe•rus•ing, pe•rus•es.** To read or examine, especially with great care: *peruse a novel.*

per•vade (pər **vād′**) *tr.v.* **per•vad•ed, per•vad•ing, per•vades.** To spread or be present throughout; permeate: *The sweet scent of gardenias pervaded the house.* [First written down in 1653 in Modern English, from Latin *pervādere* : *per-,* through + *vādere,* to go.]

per•va•sive (pər **vā′**sĭv) *adj.* Tending to pervade or permeate: *a pervasive aroma.* **—per•va′sive•ly** *adv.* **—per•va′sive•ness** *n.*

per•verse (pər **vûrs′** *or* **pûr′**vûrs′) *adj.* **1.** Willfully opposing or resisting what is right, expected, or reasonable: *You're arguing just to be perverse.* **2.** Showing stubbornness or contrariness: *a perverse attitude.* **3.** Morally wrong; wicked. **—per•verse′ly** *adv.* **—per•verse′ness** *n.*

per•ver•sion (pər **vûr′**zhən *or* pər **vûr′**shən) *n.* **1.** The act of perverting or the state of being perverted. **2.** A sexual act or practice that is considered abnormal or deviant.

per•ver•si•ty (pər **vûr′**sĭ tē) *n., pl.* **per•ver•si•ties. 1.** The quality of being perverse. **2.** An instance of being perverse.

per•vert (pər **vûrt′**) *tr.v.* **per•vert•ed, per•vert•ing, per•verts. 1.** To cause to turn from what is considered right, proper, or good; corrupt: *pervert the course of justice.* **2.** To bring to a bad or worse condition; debase. **3.** To put to a wrong or improper use: *The government perverted its responsibility by keeping files on ordinary citizens.* **4.** To interpret wrongly: *He perverted the meaning of the poem.* —*n.* (**pûr′**vûrt′). A person who practices a sexual perversion.

per•vert•ed (pər **vûr′**tĭd) *adj.* **1.** Turned from what is considered right and correct; misguided: *a perverted notion of the truth.* **2.** Misinterpreted; distorted: *a perverted translation of the text.* **3.** Of, relating to, or practicing a sexual perversion.

Pe•sach (**pā′**säκʜ′) *n.* Passover.

pe•se•ta (pə **sā′**tə) *n.* The basic monetary unit of Spain.

pes•ky (**pĕs′**kē) *adj.* **pes•ki•er, pes•ki•est.** *Informal.* Troublesome; annoying: *a pesky gnat.* **—pes′ki•ly** *adv.* **—pes′ki•ness** *n.*

pe•so (**pā′**sō) *n., pl.* **pe•sos.** The basic monetary unit of Chile, Colombia, Cuba, the Dominican Republic, Guinea-Bissau, Mexico, the Philippines, and Uruguay. [First written down in 1555 in Modern English, from Spanish, from Latin *pēnsum,* something weighed.]

pes•si•mism (**pĕs′**ə mĭz′əm) *n.* **1.** A tendency to stress the negative or take the gloomiest possible view. **2.** The belief that the evil in the world outweighs the good. **—pes′si•mist** *n.*

pes•si•mis•tic (pĕs′ə **mĭs′**tĭk) *adj.* Of or marked by pessimism: *a pessimistic person.* **—pes′si•mis′ti•cal•ly** *adv.*

pest (pĕst) *n.* **1.** An annoying person or thing; a nuisance. **2.** A harmful plant or animal, especially one harmful to human beings. **3.** A deadly epidemic disease; a pestilence.

pes•ter (**pĕs′**tər) *tr.v.* **pes•tered, pes•ter•ing, pes•ters.** To harass with petty annoyances; bother.

pes•ti•cide (**pĕs′**tĭ sīd′) *n.* A chemical used to kill harmful animals or plants, especially insects and rodents.

pes•tif•er•ous (pĕ **stĭf′**ər əs) *adj.* Breeding or spreading disease: *pestiferous swamplands.*

pes•ti•lence (**pĕs′**tə ləns) *n.* **1.** A deadly epidemic disease, especially bubonic plague. **2.** An epidemic of such a disease.

pes•ti•lent (**pĕs′**tə lənt) *adj.* **1.** Tending to cause death; deadly; fatal: *a pestilent disease.* **2.** Likely to cause or infect with a contagious disease. **3.** Harmful to law and order, morals, or society: *the pestilent threat of street crime.*

peruke
Portrait of a Man
by Jeremiah Theus (1716–1774)

ă	pat	oi	boy
ā	pay	ou	out
âr	care	o͝o	took
ä	father	o͞o	boot
ĕ	pet	ŭ	cut
ē	be	ûr	urge
ĭ	pit	th	thin
ī	pie	*th*	this
îr	pier	hw	whoop
ŏ	pot	zh	vision
ō	toe	ə	about
ô	paw	N	*French* bon

pestle
In a mortar

Peter the Great

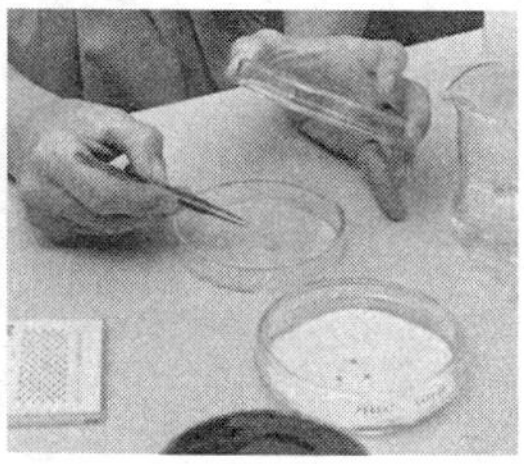

petri dish

ă	pat	oi	boy
ā	pay	ou	out
âr	care	o͝o	took
ä	father	o͞o	boot
ĕ	pet	ŭ	cut
ē	be	ûr	urge
ĭ	pit	th	thin
ī	pie	*th*	this
îr	pier	hw	whoop
ŏ	pot	zh	vision
ō	toe	ə	about
ô	paw	N	*French* bon

pes•ti•len•tial (pĕs′tə **lĕn′**shəl) *adj.* Pestilent.

pes•tle (**pĕs′**əl *or* **pĕs′**təl) *n.* A heavy tool, often with a rounded end, used for mashing substances in a mortar. [First written down in 1326 in Middle English and spelled *pestel*, from Latin *pistillum*.]

pet[1] (pĕt) *n.* **1.** An animal kept for companionship or amusement. **2.** A person or thing of which one is especially fond; a favorite. —*adj.* **1.** Kept as a pet: *a pet cat.* **2.** Being a favorite: *a pet topic.* **3.** Expressing or showing affection: *a pet name.* —*tr.v.* **pet•ted, pet•ting, pets.** To stroke or pat gently; caress. [First written down in 1508 in Modern English, from Old Irish *peata*, tame animal.]

pet[2] (pĕt) *n.* A fit of bad temper or anger. —*intr.v.* **pet•ted, pet•ting, pets.** To be sulky and peevish. [First written down in 1590 in Modern English.]

pet•al (**pĕt′**l) *n.* One of the often brightly colored parts of a flower that are similar to leaves. [First written down in 1704 in Modern English and spelled *petala*, from Greek *petalon*, leaf.]

pe•tard (pĭ **tärd′**) *n.* A small bell-shaped bomb, formerly used to blow apart a gate or wall.

pet•cock (**pĕt′**kŏk′) *n.* A small valve or faucet used to drain or reduce pressure, as from a boiler.

pe•ter (**pē′**tər) *intr.v.* **pe•tered, pe•ter•ing, pe•ters. 1.** To diminish slowly and come to an end; dwindle: *Our supplies petered out.* **2.** To become exhausted: *I petered out on the last lap.*

Pe•ter (**pē′**tər) *n.* Either of two books of the New Testament written in the form of epistles by Saint Peter. The first offers encouragement to persecuted Christians. The second warns against false teachers.

Peter, Saint. Died about 67 A.D. The chief of the 12 Apostles.

Peter I. Known as "Peter the Great." 1672–1725. Russian czar (1682–1725) who extended his territory around the Baltic and Caspian shores.

pet•i•ole (**pĕt′**ē ōl′) *n.* The stalk by which a leaf is attached to a stem; a leafstalk.

pet•it also **pet•ty** (**pĕt′**ē) *adj.* In law, lesser; minor.

pe•tite (pə **tēt′**) *adj.* Small and slender; dainty.

pet•it four (**pĕt′**ē **fôr′**) *n., pl.* **pe•tits fours** or **pe•tits fours** (**pĕt′**ē **fôrz′**). A small square-cut piece of sponge cake or pound cake, frosted and decorated.

pe•ti•tion (pə **tĭsh′**ən) *n.* **1.** An entreaty, especially to a person or group in authority: *a petition for an audience.* **2.** A formal written document requesting a right or benefit from an authority: *collect signatures on a petition for a new school.* —*v.* **pe•ti•tioned, pe•ti•tion•ing, pe•ti•tions.** —*tr.* To address a petition to; entreat: *Hawaii first petitioned Congress for statehood in 1902.* —*intr.* To make a formal request: *The lawyer petitioned for a retrial.* —**pe•ti′tion•er** *n.*

pet•it jury also **pet•ty jury** (**pĕt′**ē) *n.* A jury that sits at civil and criminal trials.

pet•it larceny also **pet•ty larceny** (**pĕt′**ē) *n.* The theft of objects whose value is below a certain set standard.

pet•it point (**pĕt′**ē point′) *n.* Decorative needlework done with a small diagonal stitch.

pet•rel (**pĕt′**rəl) *n.* Any of numerous usually small and darkly colored sea birds that fly close to the surface of the water.

❑ *These sound alike:* **petrel, petrol** (gasoline).

pe•tri dish (**pē′**trē) *n.* A shallow circular glass dish with a loose cover, used in the preparation of bacteriological cultures. [First written down in 1892 in Modern English, after Julius R. *Petri* (1852–1921), German bacteriologist.]

pet•ri•fac•tion (pĕt′rə **făk′**shən) also **pet•ri•fi•ca•tion** (pĕt′rə fĭ **kā′**shən) *n.* The process of turning organic materials into rock by the replacement of the organic matter with minerals.

pet•ri•fy (**pĕt′**rə fī′) *v.* **pet•ri•fied, pet•ri•fy•ing, pet•ri•fies.** —*tr.* **1.** To turn (wood or other organic material) into a stony mass by causing minerals to fill and finally replace its internal structure. **2.** To stun or paralyze with terror. —*intr.* To become stony, especially by petrifaction.

pet•ro•chem•i•cal (pĕt′rō **kĕm′**ĭ kəl) *n.* A chemical derived from petroleum or natural gas. —*adj.* Of or relating to petrochemicals.

Pet•ro•grad (**pĕt′**rə grăd′). Saint Petersburg.

pe•trog•ra•phy (pə **trŏg′**rə fē) *n.* The scientific description and classification of rocks.

pet•rol (**pĕt′**rəl) *n. Chiefly British.* Gasoline.

❑ *These sound alike:* **petrol, petrel** (sea bird).

pet•ro•la•tum (pĕt′rə **lā′**təm) *n.* Petroleum jelly.

pe•tro•le•um (pə **trō′**lē əm) *n.* A thick, yellow-to-black, flammable liquid mixture of hydrocarbons that occurs naturally, mainly below the surface of the earth. [First written down before 1425 in Middle English : Latin *petra*, rock + Latin *ōleum*, oil.]

petroleum jelly *n.* A greasy, usually colorless mixture of hydrocarbons, obtained from petroleum and used in making ointments and lubricants.

pe•trol•o•gy (pə **trŏl′**ə jē) *n.* The science of the origin, composition, and structure of rocks.

pet•ti•coat (**pĕt′**ē kōt′) *n.* A skirt or slip worn by girls and women as an undergarment.

pet•tish (**pĕt′**ĭsh) *adj.* Ill-tempered; peevish. —**pet′tish•ly** *adv.* —**pet′tish•ness** *n.*

pet•ty (**pĕt′**ē) *adj.* **pet•ti•er, pet•ti•est. 1.** Of small importance; trivial: *petty annoyances.* **2.** Narrow-minded; selfish: *petty partisanship.* **3.** Spiteful; mean: *He scolded her in a very petty way.* **4.** Variant of **petit.** [First written down before 1387 in Middle English and spelled *peti*, from Old French *petit.*] —**pet′ti•ly** *adv.* —**pet′ti•ness** *n.*

petty cash *n.* A small fund of money for incidental expenses, as in an office.

petty jury *n.* Variant of **petit jury.**

petty larceny *n.* Variant of **petit larceny.**

petty officer *n.* A noncommissioned officer in the navy.

pet•u•lant (**pĕch′**ə lənt) *adj.* Ill-tempered; peevish. —**pet′u•lance** *n.* —**pet′u•lant•ly** *adv.*

pe•tu•nia (pĭ **to͞on′**yə *or* pĭ **tyo͞on′**yə) *n.* Any of various garden plants having white, reddish, or purple flowers shaped like funnels and sometimes with ruffled petals.

pew (pyo͞o) *n.* One of the long benches with backs arranged in rows for the seating of the congregation in a church.

pe•wee also **pee•wee** (**pē′**wē) *n.* Any of various small brownish North American birds having a call that sounds like its name.

❑ *These sound alike:* **pewee, peewee**[1] (small thing).

pew•ter (**pyo͞o′**tər) *n.* **1.** Any of a number of alloys of tin with varying amounts of antimony, copper, and lead, formerly used for making kitchen utensils and tableware. **2.** Articles made of pewter.

PFC also **Pfc** *abbr.* An abbreviation of private first class.

pfen•nig (**fĕn′**ĭg) *n.* **1.** A monetary unit of Germany equal to 1/100 of a deutsche mark. **2.** A monetary unit formerly used in East Germany, equal to 1/100 of an ostmark.

PG (**pē′jē′**) *n.* A movie rating that allows admission of persons of all ages but suggests parental guidance in the case of children.

pg. *abbr.* An abbreviation of page.

pH (**pē′āch′**) *n.* In chemistry, a numerical measure of the acidity or alkalinity of a solution equal to 7 for neutral solutions, less than 7 for acid solutions, and more than 7 for alkaline solutions.

pha•e•ton (**fā′**ĭ tn) *n.* **1.** A light, four-wheeled open carriage, usually drawn by a pair of horses. **2.** A touring car.

phag•o•cyte (făg′ə sīt′) *n.* A cell, such as a white blood cell, occurring in body fluids or tissues and capable of absorbing and destroying waste or harmful material, such as bacteria that cause disease.

pha•lanx (fā′lăngks′ *or* făl′ăngks′) *n., pl.* **pha•lanx•es** or **pha•lan•ges** (fə lăn′jēz *or* fā lăn′jēz). **1.** A compact gathering of persons: *a solid phalanx of demonstrators on the capitol steps.* **2.** In ancient Greece, a formation of infantry carrying overlapping shields and long spears. **3.** *pl.* **phalanges.** A bone of a finger or toe.

phan•tasm (făn′tăz′əm) *n.* **1.** Something apparently seen but having no physical reality; a phantom or an apparition. **2.** An unreal mental image. **—phan•tas′mal** (făn tăz′məl) *adj.*

phan•tom (făn′təm) *n.* **1.** A ghost; an apparition. **2.** An image that appears only in the mind; an illusion.

Phar•aoh also **phar•aoh** (fâr′ō *or* fā′rō) *n.* A king of ancient Egypt.

phar•i•see (făr′ĭ sē) *n.* **1. Pharisee.** A member of an ancient Jewish sect that believed in strict observance of the Mosaic Law. **2.** A self-righteous hypocrite.

phar•ma•ceu•ti•cal (fär′mə sōō′tĭ kəl) also **phar•ma•ceu•tic** (fär′mə sōō′tĭk) *adj.* Of or relating to pharmacy or pharmacists. *—n.* A pharmaceutical preparation or product; a medicinal drug.

phar•ma•ceu•tics (fär′mə sōō′tĭks) *n. (used with a singular verb).* The science of preparing and dispensing drugs.

phar•ma•cist (fär′mə sĭst) *n.* A person who specializes in pharmacy; a druggist.

phar•ma•col•o•gy (fär′mə kŏl′ə jē) *n.* The scientific study of drugs and their composition, uses, and effects.

phar•ma•cy (fär′mə sē) *n., pl.* **phar•ma•cies. 1.** The art of preparing and dispensing drugs. **2.** A place where drugs are sold; a drugstore. [First written down about 1385 in Middle English and spelled *fermacie,* a drug, from Greek *pharmakon.*]

pha•ryn•ge•al (fə rĭn′jē əl *or* făr′ĭn jē′əl) *adj.* Of, in, or from the pharynx.

phar•ynx (făr′ĭngks) *n., pl.* **pha•ryn•ges** (fə rĭn′jēz) or **phar•ynx•es.** The part of the digestive tract that consists of a short muscular tube extending from the cavities of the nose to the larynx and esophagus. [First written down in 1693 in Modern English, from Greek *pharunx.*]

phase (fāz) *n.* **1.** A distinct stage of development: *the next phase of our space program.* **2.** A temporary manner, attitude, or pattern of behavior: *He's just going through a phase.* **3.** An aspect; a part: *considering every phase of the problem.* **4.** Any of the forms, recurring in cycles, in which the moon or a planet appears. **5.** Any of the forms or states, solid, liquid, or gas, in which matter can exist, depending on temperature and pressure: *Steam and ice are phases of water.* *—tr.v.* **phased, phas•ing, phas•es.** To plan or carry out so as to progress in stages: *The highway construction program was carefully phased.* ***—idioms.*** **phase in.** To introduce, one stage at a time. **phase out.** To bring or come to an end, one stage at a time. [First written down in 1812 in Modern English, from Greek *phasis,* appearance, from *phainein,* to show.]

❑ *These sound alike:* **phase, faze** (upset).

Ph.D. *abbr.* An abbreviation of Doctor of Philosophy.

pheas•ant (fĕz′ənt) *n., pl.* **pheas•ants** or **pheas•ant.** Any of various game birds that have long tails and are often brightly colored in the male. [First written down in 1299 in Middle English and spelled *fesaund,* from Greek *phasianos (ornis),* (bird) of the Phasis River in Asia Minor.]

phe•no•bar•bi•tal (fē′nō bär′bĭ tôl′ *or* fē′nō bär′bĭ tăl′) *n.* A white shiny crystalline compound used in medicine as a sedative and hypnotic drug.

phe•nol (fē′nôl′ *or* fē′nōl′) *n.* A poisonous, irritating, white crystalline compound having the formula C_6H_5OH. It is used as a disinfectant and in making plastics and drugs.

phe•nol•phthal•ein (fē′nōl thăl′ēn′ *or* fē′nōl thā′lēn′) *n.* A white or pale yellow crystalline powder used as an indicator for acid and basic solutions, in making dyes, and as a laxative.

phe•nom•e•na (fĭ nŏm′ə nə) *n.* A plural of **phenomenon.**

phe•nom•e•nal (fĭ nŏm′ə nəl) *adj.* **1.** Of or relating to phenomena or a phenomenon. **2.** Extraordinary; outstanding: *a phenomenal memory.* **—phe•nom′e•nal•ly** *adv.*

phe•nom•e•non (fĭ nŏm′ə nŏn′) *n., pl.* **phe•nom•e•na** (fĭ nŏm′ə nə) also **phe•nom•e•nons. 1.** An occurrence or a fact that can be perceived by the senses or by instruments: *natural phenomena.* **2.** An unusual or unaccountable fact or occurrence; a marvel. **3.** A remarkable or outstanding person; a paragon. [First written down in 1625 in Modern English, from Greek *phainomenon,* from *phainesthai,* to appear.]

phe•no•type (fē′nə tīp′) *n.* The external appearance or discernible characteristics of an organism resulting from the interaction of its genotype and its environment.

phi (fī) *n.* The 21st letter of the Greek alphabet, written Φ, *ϕ*. In English it is represented as *Ph, ph.*

phi•al (fī′əl) *n.* A vial.

Phil•a•del•phi•a (fĭl′ə dĕl′fē ə). **1.** An ancient city of Asia Minor northeast of the Dead Sea in modern-day Jordan. **2.** The largest city of Pennsylvania, in the southeast part of the state southwest of Trenton, New Jersey. The First and Second Continental Congresses (1774 and 1775–1776) and the Constitutional Convention (1787) met here. Population, 1,585,577.

phil•an•throp•ic (fĭl′ən thrŏp′ĭk) *adj.* Of or engaged in philanthropy; charitable. **—phil′an•throp′i•cal•ly** *adv.*

phi•lan•thro•pist (fĭ lăn′thrə pĭst) *n.* A person who is involved in promoting human welfare, as by making charitable donations.

phi•lan•thro•py (fĭ lăn′thrə pē) *n., pl.* **phi•lan•thro•pies. 1.a.** The desire or effort to help humankind, as by making charitable donations. **b.** Love of humankind in general. **2.** Something, such as an institution or a cause, designed to promote human welfare.

phi•lat•e•list (fĭ lăt′l ĭst) *n.* A person who collects and studies postage stamps.

phi•lat•e•ly (fĭ lăt′l ē) *n.* The collection and study of postage stamps. **—phil′a•tel′ic** (fĭl′ə tĕl′ĭk) *adj.*

Phi•le•mon (fĭ lē′mən *or* fī lē′mən) *n.* One of the books of the New Testament, an Epistle of Saint Paul to Philemon, asking Philemon to receive back and forgive a runaway slave.

phil•har•mon•ic also **Phil•har•mon•ic** (fĭl′här mŏn′ĭk) *n.* A symphony orchestra or the group of people that supports it.

Phil•ip (fĭl′ĭp). Died 1676. Wampanoag leader who waged King Philip's War (1675–1676) against New England colonists.

Philip, Saint. Flourished first century A.D. One of the 12 Apostles.

Philip II. 382–336 B.C. King of Macedon (359–336) who achieved a peace settlement in which all the states except Sparta participated.

phi•lip•pic (fĭ lĭp′ĭk) *n.* A passionate speech characterized by harsh, often insulting language; a tirade.

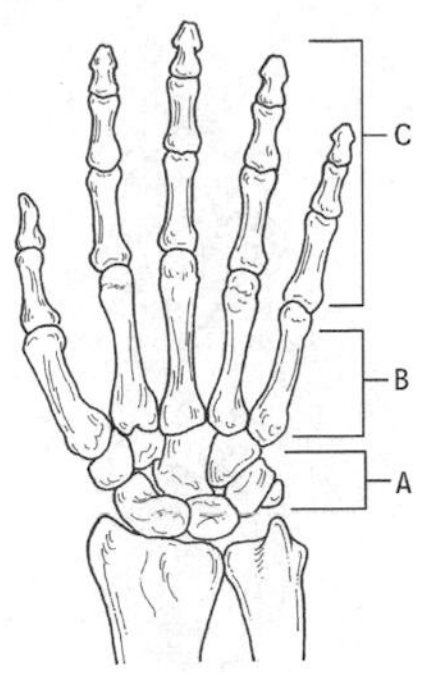

phalanx
A. Carpus
B. Metacarpus
C. Phalanges

Pharaoh
Gold coffin of Tutankhamen

pheasant

King Philip

philodendron

phoenix

phonograph
Early Edison phonograph

Phil•ip•pines (fĭl′ə pēnz′ *or* fĭl′ə **pēnz′**). A country of eastern Asia consisting of the **Philippine Islands** in the western Pacific Ocean southeast of China. The country gained its independence from the United States in 1946. Manila is the capital and the largest city. Population, 48,098,460. —**Phil′ip•pine′** *adj.*

Phil•is•tine (**fĭl′**ĭ stēn′ *or* fĭ **lĭs′**tĭn) *n.* **1.** A member of a people of ancient Palestine who were enemies of the Hebrews. **2.** A smug ignorant person regarded as indifferent or hostile to cultural values. —*adj.* **1.** Of or relating to the ancient Philistines. **2.** Often **philistine.** Boorish; barbarous.

phil•o•den•dron (fĭl′ə **dĕn′**drən) *n., pl.* **phil•o•den•drons** or **phil•o•den•dra** (fĭl′ə **dĕn′**drə). Any of various tropical American climbing plants having evergreen leaves and often grown as house plants. [First written down in 1877 in Modern English, from Greek *philodendros*, fond of trees : *philos*, loving + *dendron*, tree.]

phi•lol•o•gist (fĭ **lŏl′**ə jĭst) *n.* A person who specializes in philology.

phi•lol•o•gy (fĭ **lŏl′**ə jē) *n.* **1.** Literary study or classical scholarship. **2.** Historical linguistics.

phi•los•o•pher (fĭ **lŏs′**ə fər) *n.* **1.** A student of or specialist in philosophy. **2.** A person who lives and thinks according to a particular philosophy. **3.** A person who is calm and rational under any circumstances.

phi•los•o•phers' stone (fĭ **lŏs′**ə fərz) *n.* In medieval alchemy, a substance that was believed to have the power of transmuting base metals into gold.

phil•o•soph•i•cal (fĭl′ə **sŏf′**ĭ kəl) also **phil•o•soph•ic** (fĭl′ə **sŏf′**ĭk) *adj.* **1.** Of or relating to a system of philosophy: *philosophical theories.* **2.** Characteristic of a philosopher, as in calmness and wisdom: *He accepted his fate with philosophical resignation.* —**phil′o•soph′i•cal•ly** *adv.*

phi•los•o•phize (fĭ **lŏs′**ə fīz′) *v.* **phi•los•o•phized, phi•los•o•phiz•ing, phi•los•o•phiz•es.** —*intr.* To speculate in a philosophical manner. —*tr.* To consider (a matter) from a philosophical standpoint.

phi•los•o•phy (fĭ **lŏs′**ə fē) *n., pl.* **phi•los•o•phies.** **1.** Love and pursuit of wisdom by intellectual effort and moral self-discipline. **2.** The study by logical reasoning of the basic truths and laws governing such things as the universe, nature, life, and morals. **3.** A formal system of ideas based upon such study: *the philosophy of Plato.* **4.** The system of values by which one lives: *"Might makes right" was the tyrant's philosophy.* **5.** A basic theory; a viewpoint: *a successful philosophy of coaching.* [First written down about 1300 in Middle English and spelled *philosofie*, from Greek *philosophos*, lover of wisdom : *philos*, loving + *sophia*, knowledge, learning.]

phil•ter also **phil•tre** (**fĭl′**tər) *n.* A magic potion, especially a love potion.

❑ *These sound alike:* **philter, filter** (strainer).

phlegm (flĕm) *n.* Mucus produced by the mucous membranes of the respiratory tract.

phleg•mat•ic (flĕg **măt′**ĭk) *adj.* Having or suggesting a calm sluggish temperament; unemotional. —**phleg•mat′i•cal•ly** *adv.*

phlo•em (**flō′**ĕm′) *n.* Plant tissue consisting mainly of long tubular cells through which food is conducted from the leaves to the rest of the plant.

phlox (flŏks) *n., pl.* **phlox** or **phlox•es.** Any of various plants of North America having clusters of small reddish, purple, or white flowers. [First written down in 1706 in Modern English, from Greek *phlox*, flame, wallflower.]

Phnom Penh (pə **nôm′ pĕn′** *or* **nŏm′ pĕn′**). The capital and largest city of Cambodia, in the southwest part of the country on the Mekong River. It was founded in the 14th century. Population, 400,000.

pho•bi•a (**fō′**bē ə) *n.* An abnormal or unreasonable fear of a thing or a situation: *a phobia about riding in elevators.* [First written down in 1786 in Modern English, from Greek *phobos*, fear.]

phoe•be (**fē′**bē) *n.* Any of several small grayish North American birds having a call that sounds like its name.

Phoe•be (**fē′**bē) *n.* In Greek mythology, Artemis.

Phoe•bus (**fē′**bəs) *n.* **1.** In Greek mythology, Apollo. **2.** The sun.

Phoe•ni•cia (fĭ **nĭsh′**ə *or* fĭ **nē′**shə). An ancient country of southwest Asia along the eastern Mediterranean Sea in present-day Syria and Lebanon. The Phoenicians introduced their alphabet, which was based on symbols for sounds, to the Greeks and other peoples.

Phoe•ni•cian (fĭ **nĭsh′**ən *or* fĭ **nē′**shən) *adj.* Of or relating to ancient Phoenicia or its people, language, or culture. —*n.* **1.** A native or inhabitant of ancient Phoenicia. **2.** The Semitic language of the Phoenicians.

phoe•nix (**fē′**nĭks) *n.* In Egyptian mythology, a bird that consumes itself by fire every 500 years and later rises renewed from its own ashes. [First written down about 750 in Old English and spelled *fēnix*, from Greek *phoinix*.]

Phoe•nix (**fē′**nĭks). The capital and largest city of Arizona, in the south-central part of the state northwest of Tucson. It was settled in about 1868. Population, 983,403.

phone (fōn) *Informal. n.* A telephone. —*v.* **phoned, phon•ing, phones.** —*intr.* To telephone: *He phoned to tell her about the movie.* —*tr.* **1.** To get in touch with by telephone. **2.** To transmit by telephone: *The reporter phoned in her story.*

–phone *suff.* A suffix that means: **1.** Sound: *homophone.* **2.** A device that receives or emits sound: *earphone.*

pho•neme (**fō′**nēm′) *n.* In linguistics, the smallest unit of sound that can distinguish one word from another. For example, the *m* of *mat* and the *b* of *bat* are phonemes.

pho•ne•mic (fə **nē′**mĭk) *adj.* Of or indicating a phoneme or phonemes: *a phonemic sound.*

pho•net•ic (fə **nĕt′**ĭk) *adj.* **1.** Of or relating to phonetics. **2.** Representing the sounds of speech with a set of symbols, each denoting a single sound: *phonetic spelling.* —**pho•net′i•cal•ly** *adv.*

pho•net•ics (fə **nĕt′**ĭks) *n.* *(used with a singular verb).* The study of the sounds of speech and of their representation by symbols. —**pho′ne•ti′cian** (fō′nĭ **tĭsh′**ən) *n.*

pho•ney (**fō′**nē) *adj. & n.* Variant of **phony.**

phon•ic (**fŏn′**ĭk) *adj.* Of or involving sound, especially in speech. —**phon′i•cal•ly** *adv.*

phon•ics (**fŏn′**ĭks) *n.* *(used with a singular verb).* Phonetics.

phono– or **phon–** *pref.* A prefix that means sound, voice, or speech: *phonograph.*

pho•no•graph (**fō′**nə grăf′) *n.* A device that reproduces sound by means of a needle riding in the grooves of a rotating disk. —**pho′no•graph′ic** *adj.*

pho•ny also **pho•ney** (**fō′**nē) *adj.* **pho•ni•er, pho•ni•est.** **1.** Not genuine; fake: *a phony diamond.* **2.** Insincere, hypocritical, or deceitful: *a phony smile.* —*n., pl.* **pho•nies** also **pho•neys.** **1.** Something not genuine; a fake. **2.** A person who is insincere or hypocritical; a fake or an impostor. [First written down in 1900 in American English and spelled *phoney*, from *fawney*, gilt brass ring used by swindlers, from Irish Gaelic *fáinne*, ring.] —**pho′ni•ly** *adv.* —**pho′ni•ness** *n.*

phoo•ey (**fōō′**ē) *interj.* An expression used to show disappointment or contempt.

phos•phate (fŏs′fāt′) *n.* **1.** A salt or an ester of phosphoric acid. **2.** A fertilizer containing compounds of phosphorus.

phos•phor (fŏs′fər) *n.* **1.** A substance that can emit light after absorbing some form of radiation. **2.** Something that shows phosphorescence.

phos•pho•res•cence (fŏs′fə rĕs′əns) *n.* **1.** The process or phenomenon by which a body emits light as a result of and for some time after being exposed to radiation. **2.** The generation of light by a living thing; bioluminescence. **3.** The light that results from either of these. **—phos′pho•res′cent** *adj.*

phos•phor•ic (fŏs fôr′ĭk *or* fŏs fŏr′ĭk) *adj.* Of, relating to, or containing phosphorus, especially with a valence of 5.

phosphoric acid *n.* Any of the three acids that are formed when the oxide of phosphorus that has the formula P_2O_5 reacts with water. The most important of these has the formula H_3PO_4 and is used in fertilizers, detergents, and drugs.

phos•pho•rous (fŏs′fər əs *or* fŏs fôr′əs) *adj.* Of, relating to, or containing phosphorus, especially with a valence of 3.

phos•pho•rus (fŏs′fər əs) *n. Symbol* **P** A highly reactive, poisonous, nonmetallic element occurring in white (or sometimes yellow), red, and black forms. Atomic number 15. See table at **element.** [First written down in 1645 in Modern English, from Greek *phosphorus*, bringing light, morning star : *phōs*, light + *pherein*, to bring.]

pho•to (fō′tō) *Informal. n., pl.* **pho•tos.** A photograph.

photo– or **phot–** *pref.* A prefix that means: **1.** Light: *photosynthesis.* **2.** Photographic: *photocopy.*

pho•to•cell (fō′tō sĕl′) *n.* A photoelectric cell.

pho•to•cop•i•er (fō′tə kŏp′ē ər) *n.* A device for photographically reproducing written, printed, or graphic material.

pho•to•cop•y (fō′tə kŏp′ē) *tr.v.* **pho•to•cop•ied, pho•to•cop•y•ing, pho•to•cop•ies.** To make a photographic reproduction of (printed, written, or graphic material). *—n., pl.* **pho•to•cop•ies.** A photographic reproduction.

pho•to•e•lec•tric (fō′tō ĭ lĕk′trĭk) *adj.* Of or having to do with electrical effects caused by light. **—pho′to•e•lec′tri•cal•ly** *adv.*

photoelectric cell *n.* An electronic device having an electrical output that varies in response to the intensity of the light striking it. It is used to activate mechanisms that set off alarms and measure light intensity.

pho•to•gen•ic (fō′tə jĕn′ĭk) *adj.* Attractive as a subject for photography: *She has a very photogenic smile.* **—pho′to•gen′i•cal•ly** *adv.*

pho•to•graph (fō′tə grăf′) *n.* An image formed on a light-sensitive surface by a camera and developed by chemical means to produce a positive print. *—v.* **pho•to•graphed, pho•to•graph•ing, pho•to•graphs.** *—tr.* To take a photograph of. *—intr.* To be a subject for photographs: *Some subjects photograph better than others.*

pho•tog•ra•pher (fə tŏg′rə fər) *n.* A person who takes photographs, especially professionally.

pho•to•graph•ic (fō′tə grăf′ĭk) *adj.* **1.** Of, relating to, or used in photography or a photograph: *a photographic lens.* **2.** Resembling a photograph, as in accuracy and detail. **3.** Capable of forming accurate and lasting impressions: *a photographic memory.* **—pho′to•graph′i•cal•ly** *adv.*

pho•tog•ra•phy (fə tŏg′rə fē) *n.* **1.** The art or process of creating images on light-sensitive surfaces. **2.** The art, practice, or profession of making photographs. **3.** A collection of photographs or photographic works.

pho•tom•e•ter (fō tŏm′ĭ tər) *n.* An instrument used to measure and indicate some property of light, especially its intensity.

pho•tom•e•try (fō tŏm′ĭ trē) *n.* The measurement of the intensity, brightness, or other properties of light.

pho•ton (fō′tŏn′) *n.* The quantum of light or other electromagnetic energy, considered to be a stable particle that travels at the speed of light and to have a mass of zero. [First written down in 1926 in Modern English, from Greek *phōs*, light.]

photo opportunity *n.* A short period reserved for the press to photograph the participants in a newsworthy event.

pho•to•re•cep•tor (fō′tō rĭ sĕp′tər) *n.* A part of an animal that is specially adapted for sensitivity to light.

pho•to•sen•si•tive (fō′tō sĕn′sĭ tĭv) *adj.* Undergoing or capable of undergoing some chemical or physical change as a result of exposure to light. **—pho′to•sen′si•tiv′i•ty** *n.*

pho•to•sphere (fō′tə sfîr′) *n.* The layer of a star, such as the sun, that emits directly observable light or other radiation.

Pho•to•stat (fō′tə stăt′). A trademark used for a device used to make copies of written or printed material.

pho•to•syn•the•sis (fō′tō sĭn′thĭ sĭs) *n.* The chemical process by which plants that contain chlorophyll, especially green plants, use light to convert carbon dioxide and water to carbohydrates, releasing oxygen as a by-product.

pho•tot•ro•pism (fō tŏt′rə pĭz′əm) *n.* The movement or growth of a living organism in response to light.

phrase (frāz) *n.* **1.** In grammar, a sequence of words that is meaningful but is less than a complete sentence. For example, *on the table* is a phrase. **2.** A brief, apt, and cogent expression. For example, *from the frying pan into the fire* is a phrase. **3.** A short section of a musical composition, typically consisting of four to eight measures. *—v.* **phrased, phras•ing, phras•es.** *—tr.* **1.** To express orally or in writing: *He phrased his answer carefully.* **2.a.** To divide (a musical passage) into phrases. **b.** To combine (notes or measures) into phrases. *—intr.* **1.** To make or render phrases, as in reading aloud. **2.** To perform a passage of music with the correct phrasing. [First written down in 1530 in Modern English, from Greek *phrasis*, speech, diction, phrase, from *phrazein*, to point out, show.] **—phras′al** *adj.*

phra•se•ol•o•gy (frā′zē ŏl′ə jē) *n., pl.* **phra•se•ol•o•gies. 1.** A manner or style of speaking or writing: *difficult phraseology.* **2.** A set of expressions used by a particular person or group: *computer phraseology.*

phre•nol•o•gy (frĭ nŏl′ə jē) *n.* A now disproven method of attempting to determine intelligence and character by studying the shape of a person's skull. [First written down in 1815 in Modern English, from Greek *phrēn*, midriff, heart, mind.]

phy•lum (fī′ləm) *n., pl.* **phy•la** (fī′lə). One of the larger groups into which animals are classified, ranking between a kingdom and a class and including organisms having certain basic similarities. For example, insects, lobsters, spiders, and other invertebrate animals having jointed legs belong to the same phylum. See table at **taxonomy.** [First written down in 1876 in Modern English, from Greek *phulon*, class.]

phys•ic (fĭz′ĭk) *n.* A medicine or drug, especially a laxative.

phys•i•cal (fĭz′ĭ kəl) *adj.* **1.a.** Of or relating to the body rather than the mind or emotions: *physical fitness.* **b.** Involving vigorous bodily activity: *physical exercise.* **2.** Solid; material: *a physical object.* **3.**

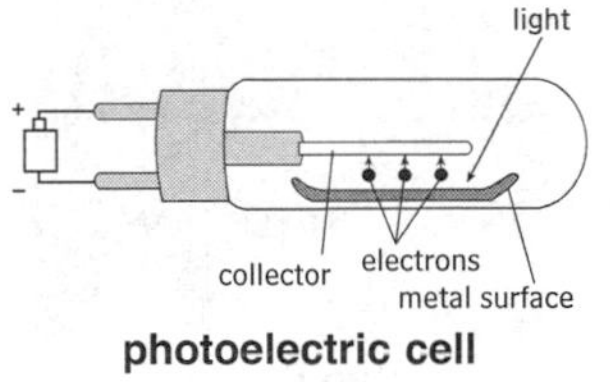

photoelectric cell

ă	pat	oi	boy
ā	pay	ou	out
âr	care	o͝o	took
ä	father	o͞o	boot
ĕ	pet	ŭ	cut
ē	be	ûr	urge
ĭ	pit	th	thin
ī	pie	*th*	this
îr	pier	hw	whoop
ŏ	pot	zh	vision
ō	toe	ə	about
ô	paw	N	*French* bon

piano[1]

piazza
Piazza San Marco in Venice, Italy

Pablo Picasso
Photographed c. 1953

piccolo

Of or relating to non-living matter and energy as distinguished from living phenomena. **4.** Of or relating to the natural phenomena of the earth's surface: *a physical map.* —*n.* A physical examination. [First written down before 1425 in Middle English and spelled *phisical*, medical, from Greek *phusis*, nature.] —**phys′i•cal•ly** *adv.*

physical education *n.* Educaton in the care and development of the human body, including athletics and hygiene.

physical examination *n.* A medical examination to detect illness, impairment, or abnormality and especially to determine physical fitness for a specified activity or service.

physical geography *n.* A branch of geography that deals with the natural features of the earth's surface, such as landforms, climate, winds, and ocean currents.

physical science *n.* Any of the sciences, such as physics, chemistry, astronomy, and geology, that deal mainly with nonliving matter and energy.

physical therapy *n.* The treatment of physical abnormality or injury by such means as exercise, massage, baths, or application of heat or cold.

phy•si•cian (fĭ **zĭsh′**ən) *n.* A person licensed to practice medicine; a medical doctor.

phys•i•cist (**fĭz′**ĭ sĭst) *n.* A specialist in physics.

phys•ics (**fĭz′**ĭks) *n.* (*used with a singular verb*). **1.** The science of matter and energy and the relations between them. **2.** Physical study, analysis, properties, and laws: *the physics of space travel.*

phys•i•og•no•my (fĭz′ē **ŏg′**nə mē) *n., pl.* **phys•i•og•no•mies. 1.** The practice of judging character from facial features. **2.** Facial features, regarded as revealing character. **3.** The aspect and character of an inanimate or abstract thing: *the rugged physiognomy of Colorado.*

phys•i•o•log•i•cal (fĭz′ē ə **lŏj′**ĭ kəl) *adj.* **1.** Of or relating to physiology. **2.** Of, involving, or affecting the processes or functioning of a living thing. —**phys′i•o•log′i•cal•ly** *adv.*

phys•i•ol•o•gy (fĭz′ē **ŏl′**ə jē) *n.* **1.** The scientific study of the processes, activities, and functions essential to and characteristic of living organisms. **2.** The vital processes and functions of a living organism.

phys•i•o•ther•a•py (fĭz′ē ō **thĕr′**ə pē) *n.* Physical therapy.

phy•sique (fĭ **zēk′**) *n.* The body considered in terms of its proportions, muscle development, and appearance: *the physique of a dancer.*

pi (pī) *n., pl.* **pis. 1.** The 16th letter of the Greek alphabet, written Π, π. In English it is represented as *P, p.* **2.** *Symbol* π A transcendental number equal to the quotient of the circumference of a circle divided by its diameter, or approximately 3.14159.
❑ *These sound alike:* **pi, pie** (dessert).

pi•a•nis•si•mo (pē′ə **nĭs′**ə mō′) *adv. & adj.* In music, very softly or quietly.

pi•an•ist (pē **ăn′**ĭst *or* **pē′**ə nĭst) *n.* A person who plays the piano.

pi•an•o[1] (pē **ăn′**ō) *n., pl.* **pi•an•os.** A musical instrument with a manual keyboard that moves hammers that strike wire strings, producing tones. [First written down in 1803 in Modern English, from Italian *pianoforte* : *piano*, soft + *forte*, loud.]

pi•a•no[2] (pē **ä′**nō *or* **pyä′**nō) *adv. & adj.* In music, softly or quietly. [First written down in 1683 in Modern English, from Italian, from Latin *plānus*, flat, smooth.]

pi•an•o•for•te (pē ăn′ō **fôr′**tā *or* pē ăn′ō **fôr′**tē) *n.* A piano.

pi•az•za (pē **ăz′**ə *or* pē **ä′**zə) *n., pl.* **pi•az•zas. 1.** A public square in an Italian town. **2.** A porch.

pi•ca (**pī′**kə) *n.* **1.** A printer's type size equal to 12 points. **2.** The height of this type, about 1/16 inch, used as a unit of measure. **3.** A type size for typewriters.

pic•a•dor (**pĭk′**ə dôr′) *n., pl.* **pic•a•dors** or **pic•a•do•res** (pĭk′ə **dôr′**ās). A horseman in a bullfight who lances the bull's neck muscles so that it will keep its head low for the later stages of the fight.

pic•a•resque (pĭk′ə **rĕsk′** *or* pē′kə **rĕsk′**) *adj.* Of or involving clever rogues or adventurers.

Pi•cas•so (pĭ **kä′**sō *or* pĭ **kăs′**ō), **Pablo.** 1881–1973. Spanish artist known for his many paintings and sculptures, including *Guernica* (1937).

pic•a•yune (pĭk′ə **yo͞on′**) *adj.* **1.** Of little value or importance; paltry: *a picayune amount.* **2.** Spiteful about trivial matters; petty: *Don't be so picayune about everything!*

pic•ca•lil•li (**pĭk′**ə lĭl′ē) *n., pl.* **pic•ca•lil•lis.** A pickled relish of chopped vegetables.

pic•co•lo (**pĭk′**ə lō′) *n., pl.* **pic•co•los.** A small flute with a range an octave above that of an ordinary flute. [First written down in 1856 in Modern English, from Italian *(flauto) piccolo*, small (flute).] —**pic′co•lo′ist** *n.*

pick[1] (pĭk) *v.* **picked, pick•ing, picks.** —*tr.* **1.** To choose or select: *pick the right person for the job.* **2.** To gather in; harvest: *pick peas.* **3.a.** To remove the outer covering of; pluck: *pick a chicken clean of feathers.* **b.** To tear off bit by bit: *pick meat from the bones.* **4.** To poke and pull at with a toothpick or one's finger, for example: *pick one's teeth.* **5.** To separate, detach, or pierce by means of a sharp pointed object. **6.** To take up (food) with the beak; peck. **7.** To open without using a key, as with a piece of wire: *pick a lock.* **8.** To steal the contents of: *pick someone's pocket.* **9.a.** To pluck (the strings) of a musical instrument. **b.** To play (a tune or melody) in this way: *picked a tune on the guitar.* —*intr.* **1.** To decide or choose with care or forethought. **2.** To find fault or make petty criticisms. —*n.* **1.** The act of selecting or choosing; choice: *had first pick of the desserts.* **2.** Something selected as the most desirable; the best or choicest part: *the pick of the crop.* —***idioms.*** **pick and choose.** To select with great care. **pick on.** To tease or bully. **pick out.** To choose or select: *We picked out the juiciest berries.* **pick up. 1.a.** To take up (something) by hand: *pick up a book.* **b.** To collect or gather: *picked up the pieces of broken glass.* **c.** To tidy up: *He picked up the living room.* **2.** To take on (passengers or freight, for example). **3.** To acquire (knowledge) by learning or experience: *picked up Spanish quickly.* **4.** To come down with (a disease): *I picked up the flu last winter.* [First written down about 1225 in Middle English and spelled *picken*, to peck.]

pick[2] (pĭk) *n.* **1.** A tool for loosening or breaking up hard surfaces, consisting of a slightly curved bar sharpened at both ends and fitted to a long handle. **2.** A pointed tool used for piercing, breaking, or picking, as an ice pick or a toothpick. **3.** A small flat piece, as of plastic or bone, used to pluck the strings of an instrument; a plectrum. [First written down before 1200 in Middle English and spelled *pic*, from *pike*, sharp point.]

pick•ax or **pick•axe** (**pĭk′**ăks′) *n.* A pick, especially one having one end of the head pointed and the other with a chisel edge.

pick•er•el (**pĭk′**ər əl *or* **pĭk′**rəl) *n., pl.* **pickerel** or **pick•er•els.** Any of several North American freshwater fishes related to and resembling the pike but generally smaller. [First written down in 1290 in Middle English and spelled *pikerel*, from *pike*, pike (fish).]

pick•et (**pĭk′**ĭt) *n.* **1.** A pointed stake or spike, as one driven into the ground to support a fence, secure a tent, tether an animal, or mark a point in surveying. **2.** A detachment of one or more troops or military vehicles placed in a position to give warning of enemy approach. **3.** A person or group of people stationed outside a building to express a grievance or protest, as during a strike. *—v.* **pick•et•ed, pick•et•ing, pick•ets.** *—tr.* **1.** To support, enclose, secure, tether, or mark with a picket or pickets. **2.** To demonstrate against, as during a strike. **3.** To post as a picket. *—intr.* To act or serve as a picket.

picket fence *n.* A fence of upright pointed pickets.

pick•ing (pĭk′ĭng) *n.* **1.** The act of one that picks: *cotton picking.* **2. pickings. a.** Leftovers or scraps: *We arrived at the picnic only in time for the pickings.* **b.** A share of spoils.

pick•le (pĭk′əl) *n.* **1.** A food, such as a cucumber, that has been preserved and flavored in vinegar and brine. **2.** A preparation of vinegar or brine for preserving and flavoring food. **3.** An acid or other chemical bath used to clean the surface of a metal. **4.** *Informal.* A troublesome or difficult situation. *—tr.v.* **pick•led, pick•ling, pick•les. 1.** To preserve or flavor (food) in vinegar or a brine solution. **2.** To treat (metal) in a chemical bath. [First written down before 1400 in Middle English and spelled *pekill,* highly-seasoned sauce, probably from Middle Dutch *pekel,* pickle, brine.]

pick•led (pĭk′əld) *adj.* Preserved in or treated with pickle: *pickled beets.*

pick•pock•et (pĭk′pŏk′ĭt) *n.* A thief who steals from someone's pockets.

pick•up (pĭk′ŭp′) *n.* **1.** The act or process of picking up, as packages, work, or freight: *The truck made a pickup at 4:00.* **2.** A person or thing that is picked up. **3.** *Informal.* An improvement in condition or activity: *a pickup in attendance.* **4.** The ability to accelerate rapidly: *a car with good pickup.* **5.** The part of a phonograph that changes the variations of the record groove into an electrical signal for conversion into sound. **6.** A pickup truck.

pickup truck *n.* A light truck with an open body and low sides.

pick•y (pĭk′ē) *adj.* **pick•i•er, pick•i•est.** *Informal.* Excessively meticulous; fussy.

pic•nic (pĭk′nĭk) *n.* A meal eaten outdoors, as on an excursion. *—intr.v.* **pic•nicked, pic•nick•ing, pic•nics.** To go on or participate in a picnic. **—pic′nick•er** *n.*

pi•cot (pē′kō *or* pē kō′) *n.* A small embroidered loop forming an ornamental edging, as on ribbon or lace.

❑ *These sound alike:* **picot, pekoe** (tea).

Pict (pĭkt) *n.* One of an ancient people of northern Britain whose descendants joined with the Scots to form Scotland.

pic•to•gram (pĭk′tə grăm′) *n.* A pictograph.

pic•to•graph (pĭk′tə grăf′) *n.* **1.** A picture that represents a word or an idea; a hieroglyph. **2.** A record in hieroglyphic symbols. **3.** A diagram or graph on which numerical data are represented pictorially. **—pic•tog′ra•phy** (pĭk tŏg′rə fē) *n.*

pic•to•ri•al (pĭk tôr′ē əl) *adj.* **1.** Of or characterized by pictures: *pictorial materials.* **2.** Represented as if in pictures; descriptive: *pictorial imagery.* **3.** Composed of or illustrated by pictures: *pictorial representations of planets.* **—pic•to′ri•al•ly** *adv.*

pic•ture (pĭk′chər) *n.* **1.** A visual representation or image that is painted, drawn, photographed, or otherwise represented on a flat surface. **2.a.** A visible image: *a picture reflected in the pond.* **b.** A vivid verbal description; an image in words. **c.** A vivid mental image. **3.** A person or thing that closely resembles another: *He is the picture of his father.* **4.** A person or thing that is a good example of a certain emotion, mood, or state of mind: *The boy was the picture of eagerness.* **5.** A combination of circumstances; the situation: *How does an education figure in the picture?* **6.** An image or a series of images on a television or movie screen. **7.** A movie. *—tr.v.* **pic•tured, pic•tur•ing, pic•tures. 1.** To make a representation or picture of: *A graph is a good way to picture data.* **2.** To form a mental image of; visualize; imagine: *He pictured himself flying over the town.* **3.** To describe vividly; make a verbal image of. [First written down before 1420 in Middle English, from Latin *pictus,* painted, from *pingere,* to paint.]

pic•tur•esque (pĭk′chə rĕsk′) *adj.* **1.** Of or suggesting a picture; striking or interesting: *picturesque Alpine villages.* **2.** Strikingly expressive; vivid: *picturesque language.* **—pic′tur•esque′ly** *adv.* **—pic′tur•esque′ness** *n.*

picture tube *n.* The cathode-ray tube of a television receiver, on which the visual portion of a telecast is shown.

pid•dling (pĭd′lĭng) *adj.* Unimportant; trivial.

pidg•in (pĭj′ən) *n.* A simple form of speech based on a mixture of two or more languages and used for communications between groups speaking different languages.

❑ *These sound alike:* **pidgin, pigeon** (bird).

Pidg•in English *n.* Any of several pidgins based on English and now spoken mostly on the Pacific islands and in West Africa.

pie (pī) *n.* A food consisting of a filling, such as fruit or meat, baked in a pastry shell and often covered with a crust or meringue.

❑ *These sound alike:* **pie, pi** (Greek letter).

pie•bald (pī′bôld′) *adj.* Marked with spots or patches, especially of black and white: *a piebald horse.* *—n.* A piebald animal, especially a horse. [First written down in 1589 in Modern English : *pie,* magpie + *bald.*]

piece (pēs) *n.* **1.** Something considered as a part of a larger quantity or group; a portion: *a piece of land.* **2.** A portion or part that has been separated from a whole: *a piece of pie.* **3.** An object that is one member of a set: *sixty pieces of china.* **4.** An artistic, musical, or literary work: *play a piece on the piano.* **5.** An instance, a specimen, or an example: *What a fine piece of work!* **6.** A coin: *a 50-cent piece.* **7.** A declaration of one's opinions: *She said her piece.* **8.a.** In certain board games, one of the small objects used in playing. **b.** In chess, any of the figures other than a pawn; a king, queen, bishop, knight, or rook. **9.** A firearm. *—tr.v.* **pieced, piec•ing, piec•es. 1.** To join or unite the parts of: *pieced the puzzle together.* **2.** To mend by adding a fragment or part to: *He pieced his ragged trousers.* ***—idioms.*** **a piece of (one's) mind.** Frank and severe criticism; censure: *The principal gave me a piece of her mind for being late again.* **of a piece.** Belonging to the same class or kind.

❑ *These sound alike:* **piece, peace** (tranquillity).

pièce de ré•sis•tance (pyĕs də rā zē stäɴs′) *n., pl.* **pièces de ré•sis•tance** (pyĕs də rā zē stäɴs′). **1.** An outstanding accomplishment. **2.** The principal dish of a meal.

piece goods *pl.n.* Fabrics made and sold in standard lengths.

piece•meal (pēs′mēl′) *adv.* **1.** By a small amount at a time; in stages: *built up the collection piecemeal.* **2.** In pieces; apart: *The puzzle lay piecemeal on the floor.* *—adj.* Done or made in stages: *a piecemeal accumulation.*

piece of eight *n., pl.* **pieces of eight.** An old Spanish silver coin.

piece•work (pēs′wûrk′) *n.* Work paid for by the number of units produced. **—piece′work′er** *n.*

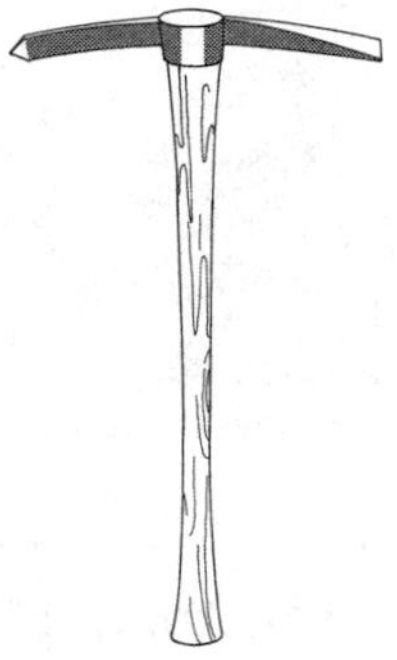

pickax

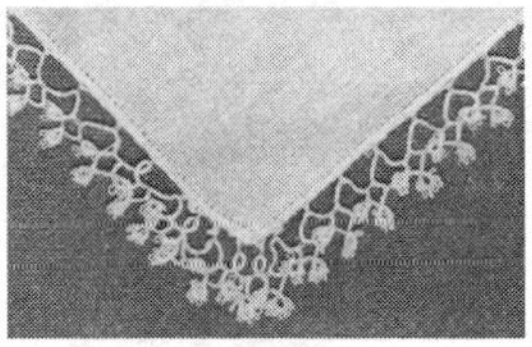

picot

ă	pat	oi	boy
ā	pay	ou	out
âr	care	o͝o	took
ä	father	o͞o	boot
ĕ	pet	ŭ	cut
ē	be	ûr	urge
ĭ	pit	th	thin
ī	pie	*th*	this
îr	pier	hw	whoop
ŏ	pot	zh	vision
ō	toe	ə	about
ô	paw	ɴ	*French* bon

Franklin Pierce

Word History: piety

Both **piety** and **pity** come from the same Latin word through Old French. The Latin source is the adjective *pius*, which means "faithful in one's obligations to one's family as a child, spouse, or parent," "conscientious in doing one's work," "loyal to one's community and country," "devout in one's religion," and "respectful, grateful." The Latin noun formed from *pius* is the word *pietās*, and it acquires the senses "compassion" and "kindness." *Pietās* becomes both *piete* and *pité* in Old French. In English *piety* and *pity* were used interchangeably until the mid 16th century, when they acquired their present meanings.

pika

pillar

pied (pīd) *adj.* Having patches of color; piebald: *a pied flower.*

Pied•mont (pēd′mŏnt′). **1.** A historical region of northwest Italy bordering on France and Switzerland. **2.** A plateau region of the eastern United States extending from New York to Alabama between the Appalachian Mountains and the Atlantic coastal plain.

pier (pîr) *n.* **1.** A platform extending from a shore over water and supported by piles or pillars, used to secure, protect, and provide access to ships or boats. **2.** A supporting structure of a bridge at the points where its spans join. **3.** Any of various other supporting structures, such as a pillar, a buttress, or the part of a wall between two windows.

❑ *These sound alike:* **pier, peer[1]** (look intently), **peer[2]** (member of nobility).

pierce (pîrs) *v.* **pierced, pierc•ing, pierc•es.** —*tr.* **1.** To pass into or through (something) with or as with a sharp instrument: *Arrows pierced the target.* **2.** To make a hole or opening in; perforate: *A nail pierced the tire.* **3.** To make a way through: *explorers piercing the wilderness.* **4.** To sound sharply through: *A cry pierced the air.* —*intr.* To penetrate into or through something: *The rocket pierced through the clouds.*

Pierce (pîrs), **Franklin.** 1804–1869. The 14th President of the United States (1853–1857).

pierc•ing (pîr′sĭng) *adj.* Sharp; penetrating: *piercing cold; piercing eyes.* —**pierc′ing•ly** *adv.*

Pierre (pîr). The capital of South Dakota, in the central part of the state on the Missouri River. It was chosen as state capital in 1889. Population, 12,906.

pi•e•ty (pī′ĭ tē) *n., pl.* **pi•e•ties. 1.** Religious devotion and reverence to God. **2.** Devotion and reverence to parents and family. **3.** A devout act or thought. —See Note.

pi•e•zo•e•lec•tric•i•ty (pī ē′zō ĭ lĕk **trĭs′**ĭ tē *or* pī-ē′zō ē′lĕk **trĭs′**ĭ tē) *n.* A property of certain nonconducting crystals that results in voltages being generated across them when they are subjected to mechanical stress and that causes them to change slightly in shape when voltages are applied across them. [First written down in 1895 in Modern English and spelled *piezo-electricity* : Greek *piezein*, to squeeze + *electricity*.]

pig (pĭg) *n.* **1.** Any of several hoofed mammals having short legs, bristly hair, and blunt snouts used for digging. Pigs are often raised for meat and other food products. **2.** *Informal.* A person regarded as being like a pig, especially a greedy or gross person. **3.a.** A crude block of metal, usually iron or lead, poured from a smelting furnace. **b.** A mold in which such metal is cast.

pi•geon (pĭj′ən) *n.* Any of various birds having short legs, a rounded chest, and a small head, especially one common in cities and often raised for food or trained to carry messages.

❑ *These sound alike:* **pigeon, pidgin** (speech form).

pi•geon•hole (pĭj′ən hōl′) *n.* **1.** A small compartment or recess, as in a desk, for holding papers. **2.** A small hole in which pigeons may nest. **3.** A specific, often oversimplified category. —*tr.v.* **pi•geon•holed, pi•geon•hol•ing, pi•geon•holes. 1.** To place in a small compartment or recess. **2.** To classify into a group; categorize: *a tendency to pigeonhole one's colleagues.*

pi•geon-toed (pĭj′ən tōd′) *adj.* Having the toes or feet turned inward.

pig•gish (pĭg′ĭsh) *adj.* **1.** Greedy. **2.** Stubborn; pigheaded. —**pig′gish•ly** *adv.* —**pig′gish•ness** *n.*

pig•gy•back (pĭg′ē băk′) *adv. & adj.* **1.** On the shoulders or back: *ride piggyback; a piggyback ride.* **2.** In or by means of truck trailers carried on railroad cars: *goods shipped piggyback.*

pig•gy bank (pĭg′ē) *n.* A child's bank for coins, shaped like a pig.

pig•head•ed (pĭg′hĕd′ĭd) *adj.* Stupidly obstinate or stubborn. —**pig′head′ed•ly** *adv.* —**pig′head′ed•ness** *n.*

pig iron *n.* Impure iron as it is drawn from a blast furnace, usually cast in oblong blocks.

pig•let (pĭg′lĭt) *n.* A young small pig.

pig•ment (pĭg′mənt) *n.* **1.** A substance or material used as coloring: *the pigments used in a paint.* **2.** A substance, such as chlorophyll or hemoglobin, that gives a characteristic color to plant or animal tissues. [First written down before 1398 in Middle English, from Latin *pigmentum*, from *pingere*, to paint.]

pig•men•ta•tion (pĭg′mən **tā′**shən) *n.* Coloring of animal or plant tissues by pigments.

Pig•my (pĭg′mē) *n. & adj.* Variant of **Pygmy.**

pig•pen (pĭg′pĕn′) *n.* **1.** A pen for pigs. **2.** A dirty or very untidy place.

pig•skin (pĭg′skĭn′) *n.* **1.** The skin of a pig. **2.** Leather made from the skin of a pig. **3.** A football.

pig•sty (pĭg′stī′) *n., pl.* **pig•sties. 1.** A shelter where pigs are kept. **2.** *Slang.* A dirty or very untidy place.

pig•tail (pĭg′tāl′) *n.* A braid of hair at the back of the head.

pi•ka (pī′kə *or* pē′kə) *n.* Any of several small mammals of the mountains of western North America and Asia, related to the rabbit and having rounded ears and no visible tail.

pike[1] (pīk) *n.* A long spear formerly used by infantry. [First written down about 1511 in Modern English, from Old French *piquer*, to stab.]

pike[2] (pīk) *n., pl.* **pike** or **pikes.** A large freshwater fish having a narrow body and a long snout, often caught for sport. [First written down in 1314 in Middle English, perhaps from Old English *pīc*, sharp point (from its shape).]

pike[3] (pīk) *n.* A turnpike. [First written down in 1837 in American English, short for *turnpike*.]

pike[4] (pīk) *n.* A spike or sharp point, as on the tip of a spear. [First written down about 725 in Old English and spelled *pīc*, pointed tool.]

pik•er (pī′kər) *n. Slang.* **1.** A cautious gambler. **2.** A person regarded as petty or stingy.

Pikes Peak (pīks). A mountain 14,110 feet (4,303.6 meters) high, in the Rocky Mountains of central Colorado.

pike•staff (pīk′stăf′) *n.* **1.** The shaft of a pike. **2.** A walking stick tipped with a metal spike.

pi•laf or **pi•laff** (pĭ **läf′** *or* pē′läf′) *n.* A seasoned dish of steamed rice, often with meat, shellfish, or vegetables.

pi•las•ter (pĭ **lăs′**tər) *n.* A rectangular column set into a wall for decoration.

Pi•late (pī′lət), **Pontius.** Flourished first century A.D. Roman governor of Judea who ordered Jesus's crucifixion.

pile[1] (pīl) *n.* **1.** A mass of objects stacked or thrown together in a heap: *a pile of firewood.* **2.** *Informal.* A large accumulation or quantity: *a pile of complaints.* **3.** *Slang.* A large sum of money; a fortune: *He made his pile and retired.* **4.** A nuclear reactor. —*v.* **piled, pil•ing, piles.** —*tr.* **1.a.** To place or lay in or as if in a pile or heap: *They piled the dishes in the sink.* **b.** To load (something) with a heap or pile: *piled the table with books.* **2.** To place or heap in abundance: *piled honors on him.* —*intr.* **1.** To form a heap or pile. **2.** To move, often in haste, in a disorderly group or mass: *Baseball fans piled out of the stadium.* [First written down about 1410 in Middle English, from Latin *pīla*, pillar.]

pile[2] (pīl) *n.* A heavy beam of timber, concrete, or

steel, driven into the ground as a foundation or support for a structure. [First written down before 1000 in Old English and spelled *pīl*, shaft, stake, from Latin *pīlum*, spear, pestle.]

pile³ (pīl) *n.* **1.** Cut or uncut loops of yarn forming the surface of certain carpets or of fabrics such as velvet and plush. **2.** Soft fine hair, fur, or wool. [First written down about 1350 in Middle English and spelled *pilus*, hair, plumage, from Latin *pilus*, hair.]

pile driver *n.* A machine that drives piles by raising a weight between guideposts and dropping it on the head of the pile.

piles (pīlz) *pl.n.* Hemorrhoids.

pile•up or **pile-up** (pīl′ŭp′) *n.* A serious collision usually involving several motor vehicles.

pil•fer (pĭl′fər) *v.* **pil•fered, pil•fer•ing, pil•fers.** —*tr.* To steal (a small amount or item): *He pilfered some blackberry jam.* —*intr.* To steal or filch. **—pil′fer•er** *n.*

pil•grim (pĭl′grəm) *n.* **1.** A religious devotee who travels to a shrine or sacred place. **2.** A person who embarks on a quest for something conceived of as sacred. **3. Pilgrim.** One of the English separatists who founded the colony of Plymouth in New England in 1620.

pil•grim•age (pĭl′grə mĭj) *n.* **1.** A journey to a sacred place or shrine. **2.** A long journey with a meaningful purpose.

pil•ing (pī′lĭng) *n.* **1.** The act of driving piles. **2.** Building piles considered as a group. **3.** A structure composed of piles.

pill (pĭl) *n.* **1.** A small pellet or tablet of medicine, often coated, taken by swallowing whole or chewing. **2.** Something distasteful or unpleasant that must be accepted. **3.** *Slang.* An ill-natured or disagreeable person.

pil•lage (pĭl′ĭj) *v.* **pil•laged, pil•lag•ing, pil•lag•es.** —*tr.* To rob of goods by force; plunder: *The army pillaged the countryside.* —*intr.* To take booty. —*n.* **1.** The act of pillaging: *the pillage of the city.* **2.** Something pillaged; spoils. **—pil′lag•er** *n.*

pil•lar (pĭl′ər) *n.* **1.a.** A vertical structure used as a support for a building; a column. **b.** Such a structure or one similar to it used for decoration. **2.** A person occupying a central position; a mainstay: *a pillar of the community.* —*tr.v.* **pil•lared, pil•lar•ing, pil•lars.** To support or decorate with a pillar or pillars.

pill•box (pĭl′bŏks′) *n.* **1.** A small box for pills. **2.** A woman's small round hat. **3.** A small concrete structure for a machine gun or other weapon.

pil•lo•ry (pĭl′ə rē) *n., pl.* **pil•lo•ries.** A wooden framework with holes for the head and hands, mounted on a post and formerly used to secure offenders who were subjected to public scorn as punishment. —*tr.v.* **pil•lo•ried, pil•lo•ry•ing, pil•lo•ries. 1.** To expose to ridicule and scorn: *He pilloried his former friends in novels.* **2.** To put in a pillory as punishment.

pil•low (pĭl′ō) *n.* A cloth case stuffed with soft material, such as down, feathers, or foam rubber, used to cushion the head, especially during sleep. —*tr.v.* **pil•lowed, pil•low•ing, pil•lows. 1.** To rest (one's head) on or as if on a pillow: *She pillowed her head on her arms.* **2.** To serve as a pillow for. [First written down before 899 in Old English and spelled *pyle*, from Latin *pulvīnus*.]

pil•low•case (pĭl′ō kās′) *n.* A removable cover for a pillow.

pil•low•slip (pĭl′ō slĭp′) *n.* A pillowcase.

pi•lot (pī′lət) *n.* **1.** A person who operates an aircraft in flight. **2.** A licensed specialist who steers large ships in and out of port or through dangerous waters. **3.** A ship's helmsman. **4.** A person who guides or directs others. **5.** The part of a tool, device, or machine that leads or guides the whole. **6.** A pilot light. **7.** A television program produced as a model of a series being considered for production by a network. —*tr.v.* **pi•lot•ed, pi•lot•ing, pi•lots. 1.** To serve as the pilot of; steer. **2.** To lead, guide, or conduct. —*adj.* Serving as a small-scale model for future work: *a pilot project.* [First written down in 1530 in Modern English, from Greek *pēdon*, steering oar.]

pilot fish *n.* A small ocean fish that often swims along with sharks or other large fish.

pi•lot•house (pī′lət hous′) *n.* An enclosed section on a bridge of a vessel from which the vessel is steered.

pilot light *n.* **1.** A small jet of gas kept burning to ignite a gas burner, as in a stove or water heater. **2.** A small lamp, usually red, used to indicate that an electric circuit, as in an appliance, is turned on.

Pi•ma (pē′mə) *n., pl.* **Pima** or **Pi•mas. 1.** A member of a Native American people of southern Arizona and northern Mexico. **2.** The Uto-Aztecan language of the Pima.

pi•mien•to (pĭ mĕn′tō *or* pĭ myĕn′tō) also **pi•men•to** (pĭ mĕn′tō) *n., pl.* **pi•mien•tos** also **pi•men•tos.** A mild-flavored red pepper, often used as flavoring, as a stuffing for olives, or as a colorful garnish.

pim•per•nel (pĭm′pər nĕl′) *n.* Any of various low-growing plants having small red, pink, or purplish flowers that close in cloudy weather.

pim•ple (pĭm′pəl) *n.* A small swelling on the skin, often red and sore and sometimes containing pus. **—pim′ply** *adj.*

pin (pĭn) *n.* **1.** A short straight stiff piece of wire with a blunt head and a sharp point, used especially for fastening. **2.** Something that resembles a pin in shape or use, as a hairpin, clothespin, or safety pin. **3.** An ornament fastened to clothing by means of a clasp. **4.** A bar or rod of wood or metal that supports or fastens things, especially by passing through or into a series of prepared holes. **5.** On a golf course, a long metal or wooden rod with a small flag at one end, inserted into a cup to indicate its location. **6.** One of the wooden clubs at which the ball is aimed in bowling. —*tr.v.* **pinned, pin•ning, pins. 1.** To fasten or secure with a pin or pins: *pinned the flower to her coat.* **2.** To place in a position of trusting dependence: *We pinned our hopes on him.* **3.** To win a fall from (an opponent) in wrestling: *Joe's teammates wanted him to pin the champ.* **4.** To hold fast; immobilize: *The strong current pinned the canoe against the rock.* ***—idioms.*** **pin down. 1.** To fix or establish clearly: *The researchers finally pinned down the cause of the disease.* **2.** To force (someone) to give firm opinions or precise information: *The school committee pinned down the superintendent on the issue of budget cuts.* **pin on.** To attribute (a wrongdoing or crime): *The theft was pinned on the wrong person.*

pin•a•fore (pĭn′ə fôr′) *n.* A sleeveless garment similar to an apron, especially one worn as a dress or an overdress.

pi•ña•ta (pēn yä′tə) *n.* A decorated container filled with candy and toys and suspended from the ceiling. As part of Christmas and birthday celebrations in certain Latin-American countries, blindfolded children try to break the piñata with a stick.

pince-nez (păns′nā′ *or* pĭns′nā′) *n., pl.* **pince-nez** (păns′nāz′ *or* pĭns′nāz′). Eyeglasses that are clipped to the bridge of the nose.

pin•cers (pĭn′sərz) *pl.n. (used with a singular or plural verb).* **1.** A grasping tool having a pair of jaws and handles pivoted together to work in opposition. **2.** A jointed grasping claw, as of a lobster or crab.

pillory
At Colonial Williamsburg, Virginia

piñata

pince-nez
Worn by Theodore Roosevelt

ă	pat	oi	boy
ā	pay	ou	out
âr	care	o͝o	took
ä	father	o͞o	boot
ĕ	pet	ŭ	cut
ē	be	ûr	urge
ĭ	pit	th	thin
ī	pie	*th*	this
îr	pier	hw	whoop
ŏ	pot	zh	vision
ō	toe	ə	about
ô	paw	N	*French* bon

pineapple

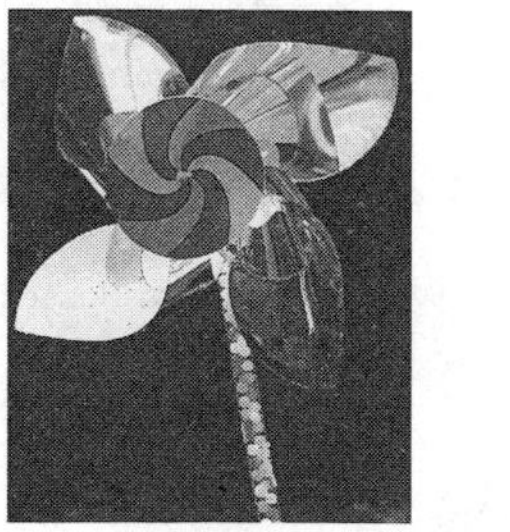

pinwheel

pinch (pĭnch) *v.* **pinched, pinch•ing, pinch•es.** *—tr.* **1.** To squeeze between the thumb and a finger, pincers, or other edges. **2.** To squeeze or compress so as to cause pain or discomfort: *The shoes pinched her feet.* **3.** To nip, wither, or shrivel: *a face pinched by fear and fatigue.* **4.** *Slang.* To steal: *He pinched some doughnuts from the tray.* **5.** *Slang.* To arrest. *—intr.* **1.** To press, squeeze, or bind painfully. **2.** To be miserly or frugal. *—n.* **1.** A squeeze or other pressure caused by pressing between the thumb and a finger, pincers, or other edges: *The crab gave him a pinch on the toe.* **2.** The amount that can be held between the thumb and forefinger: *a pinch of salt.* **3.** A painful, difficult, or straitened circumstance: *the pinch of hard times.* **4.** An emergency situation: *In a pinch she can take over the work.* **5.** *Slang.* A theft. **6.** *Slang.* An arrest. ***—idiom.*** **pinch pennies.** *Informal.* To be thrifty or miserly **—pinch′er** *n.*

pinch-hit (pĭnch′hĭt′) *intr.v.* **pinch-hit, pinch-hit•ting, pinch-hits. 1.** In baseball, to bat as a substitute, especially when a hit is badly needed. **2.** To substitute for another: *I'm pinch-hitting for the mechanic today.* **—pinch hit** *n.* **—pinch hitter** *n.*

pin•cush•ion (pĭn′ko͝osh′ən) *n.* A small firm cushion into which pins and needles are stuck when not in use.

pine[1] (pīn) *n.* **1.** Any of various evergreen trees that bear cones and have clusters of needle-shaped leaves. **2.** The wood of such a tree. [First written down about 1000 in Old English and spelled *pīn*, from Latin *pīnus.*]

pine[2] (pīn) *intr.v.* **pined, pin•ing, pines. 1.** To feel a lingering, often nostalgic desire. **2.** To lose health or waste away from longing or grief. [First written down before 899 in Old English and spelled *pīnian*, to cause to suffer, from Greek *poinē*, penalty.]

pin•e•al gland (pĭn′ē əl *or* pī′nē əl) *n.* A small mass of glandular tissue found in the brain. It is believed its function in humans is to secrete a hormone that helps regulate certain bodily processes.

pine•ap•ple (pīn′ăp′əl) *n.* **1.** A large fleshy tropical fruit having a rough spiny skin and a tuft of narrow prickly leaves at the top. **2.** The plant that bears such fruit.

pine•y (pī′nē) *adj.* Variant of **piny.**

pin•feath•er (pĭn′fĕ*th*′ər) *n.* A feather still enclosed in a narrow horny covering and just beginning to grow out from the skin.

Ping-Pong (pĭng′pông′ *or* pĭng′pŏng′). A trademark used for table tennis and related equipment.

pin•hole (pĭn′hōl′) *n.* A tiny puncture made by or as if by a pin.

pin•ion[1] (pĭn′yən) *n.* A bird's wing. *—tr.v.* **pin•ioned, pin•ion•ing, pin•ions. 1.a.** To clip or tie (the wings) of a bird to prevent it from flying. **b.** To prevent (a bird) from flying by doing this. **2.** To hold or fasten (a person's arms) to prevent movement. [First written down before 1425 in Middle English, from Latin *pinna*, feather.]

pin•ion[2] (pĭn′yən) *n.* A small gearwheel that engages a larger gearwheel or a rack. [First written down in 1659 in Modern English, probably from Old French *peigne*, comb.]

pink[1] (pĭngk) *n.* **1.** A light or pale red. **2.** Any of various plants related to the carnation, grown for their fragrant flowers. **3.** The highest or best degree: *the pink of perfection.* *—adj.* **pink•er, pink•est.** Light or pale red. [First written down in 1573 in Modern English.]

pink[2] (pĭngk) *tr.v.* **pinked, pink•ing, pinks. 1.** To stab lightly or prick with a pointed weapon. **2.** To decorate with a pattern of small holes. **3.** To cut with pinking shears. [First written down about 1325 in Middle English and spelled *pinken*, to punch out, from Latin *pungere*, to prick.]

pink•eye (pĭngk′ī′) *n.* A severe highly contagious inflammation of the mucous membrane of the eyelids and eyeballs that makes the eyes appear pink.

pink•ie also **pink•y** (pĭng′kē) *n., pl.* **pink•ies.** *Informal.* The little finger.

pink•ing shears (pĭng′kĭng) *pl.n.* Sewing scissors with notched blades, used to finish edges of cloth with a zigzag pattern for decoration or to prevent raveling or fraying.

pink•ish (pĭng′kĭsh) *adj.* Somewhat pink in color.

pin money *n.* Money for small expenses.

pin•na•cle (pĭn′ə kəl) *n.* **1.** A small turret or spire on a roof. **2.** A tall pointed formation, as a mountain peak. **3.** The peak or summit of something: *at the pinnacle of his fame.*

pin•nate (pĭn′āt′) *adj.* Having parts or divisions, such as leaflets, in a close arrangement along each side of a stalk. **—pin′nate′ly** *adv.*

pi•noch•le (pē′nŭk′əl *or* pē′nŏk′əl) *n.* A card game for two to four people, played with a deck of 48 cards having no card below a nine.

pi•ñon also **pin•yon** (pĭn′yōn′ *or* pĭn′yən) *n., pl.* **pi•ñons** or **pi•ño•nes** (pĭn yō′nēz) also **pin•yons.** Any of several pine trees of western North and South America, bearing edible seeds.

pin•point (pĭn′point′) *n.* **1.** A very small or sharp point. **2.** Something extremely small or trifling: *bright pinpoints of flame.* *—tr.v.* **pin•point•ed, pin•point•ing, pin•points.** To locate and identify precisely: *We were able to pinpoint the reason for the change.* *—adj.* **1.** Showing care and precision: *pinpoint accuracy.* **2.** Very small; minute: *pinpoint organisms in the sea.*

pin•prick (pĭn′prĭk′) *n.* **1.** A slight puncture made by or as if by a pin. **2.** A small wound. **3.** A minor annoyance.

pin•scher (pĭn′shər) *n.* A Doberman pinscher.

pin•stripe (pĭn′strīp′) *n.* **1.** A very thin stripe on a fabric. **2.** A fabric with very thin stripes.

pint (pīnt) *n.* **1.** A unit of volume or capacity used in liquid measure, equal to 16 fluid ounces or 28.875 cubic inches (about 0.473 liter). **2.** A unit of volume or capacity used in dry measure, equal to ½ quart or 34.6 cubic inches (about 0.551 liter). See table at **measurement. 3.a.** A container that can hold a pint. **b.** The amount of a substance that can be held in such a container.

pin•to (pĭn′tō) *n., pl.* **pin•tos** or **pin•toes.** A horse having irregular spots or markings. *—adj.* Having irregular spots or markings.

pinto bean *n.* A form of string bean that has spotted seeds and is grown chiefly in the southwest United States.

pin•wheel (pĭn′wēl′) *n.* **1.** A toy consisting of blades of colored paper or plastic pinned to the end of a stick so that they revolve in the wind or when blown on. **2.** A firework that forms a rotating wheel of colored flames.

pin•worm (pĭn′wûrm′) *n.* Any of various small parasitic worms that infest the lower part of the intestine and the rectum in human beings and other mammals.

pin•y also **pine•y** (pī′nē) *adj.* **pin•i•er, pin•i•est.** Relating to, suggestive of, or abounding in pines.

pin•yon (pĭn′yōn′ *or* pĭn′yən) *n.* Variant of **piñon.**

pi•o•neer (pī′ə nîr′) *n.* **1.** A person who first enters or settles a region. **2.** A person who opens up new areas of research, thought, or development. **3.** A plant or animal species that is the first kind to grow or live in an environment where there have been no living things. *—adj.* **1.** Of or relating to early settlers. **2.** Leading the way; trailblazing. *—v.* **pi•o•neered, pi•o•neer•ing, pi•o•neers.** *—tr.* **1.a.** To explore or open up (a region): *The expedition pioneered those mountains.* **b.** To settle: *The family* *pioneered North Dakota.* **2.** To take part in the development of: *pioneered a spacecraft to the moon.* —*intr.* To act as a pioneer: *He pioneered in the use of antiseptics in surgery.*

pi•ous (pī′əs) *adj.* **1.** Having or showing religious reverence; devout. **2.a.** Marked by noticeable devoutness: *a pious silence.* **b.** Marked by a false devoutness: *a pious speech.* **3.** Devotional: *pious writings.* —**pi′ous•ly** *adv.*

pip[1] (pĭp) *n.* A small fruit seed, as of an orange or apple. [First written down in 1797 in Modern English, from Middle English *pipin.*]

pip[2] (pĭp) *n.* Any of the dots indicating numerical value on dice or dominoes. [First written down in 1604 in Modern English and spelled *peep.*]

pip[3] (pĭp) *tr.v.* **pipped, pip•ping, pips.** To break through (an eggshell) in hatching. Used of a chick. [First written down in 1879 in Modern English.]

pip[4] (pĭp) *n.* A disease of birds, characterized by a mucous discharge in the mouth and throat. [First written down in 1373 in Middle English and spelled *pipe*, from Latin *pītuīta*, phlegm.]

pipe (pīp) *n.* **1.a.** A tube or hollow cylinder through which a liquid or gas can be made to flow. **b.** A section or piece of such a tube. **2.a.** A device for smoking, consisting of a hollow tube, as of clay or wood, with a mouthpiece at one end and a small bowl at the other. **b.** The amount of smoking material, such as tobacco, needed to fill the bowl of such a pipe. **3.a.** A tubular musical instrument, especially a simple or primitive one, similar to a flute. **b.** Any of the tubes used in an organ to produce musical tones. **c. pipes.** A small wind instrument consisting of a number of tuned tubes bound together. **4. pipes.** A bagpipe. —*v.* **piped, pip•ing, pipes.** —*tr.* **1.** To transport or transmit by means of a pipe or pipes. **2.** To play (music) on a pipe or pipes. **3.** To speak or sing in a shrill tone: *The child piped a question.* **4.** To provide or connect with pipes. —*intr.* **1.** To play on a pipe. **2.** To speak shrilly; make a shrill sound. —***idioms.*** **pipe down.** *Slang.* To stop talking; be quiet. **pipe up.** To speak up. [First written down before 1000 in Old English and spelled *pīpe*, musical pipe, from Latin *pīpāre*, to chirp.]

pipe•line (pīp′līn′) *n.* **1.** A long series of pipes, especially one used to carry water, petroleum, or natural gas over great distances. **2.** A direct line of communication or route of supply. —*tr.v.* **pipe•lined, pipe•lin•ing, pipe•lines.** To transport by or as if by a pipeline.

pipe organ *n.* A musical instrument having a number of pipes that make tones when supplied with air and a keyboard that controls the flow of air.

pip•er (pī′pər) *n.* A person who plays music on a pipe or a bagpipe.

pi•pette (pī pĕt′) *n.* A narrow glass tube, open at both ends and often marked to show volume, used for transferring liquids in a laboratory.

pip•ing (pī′pĭng) *n.* **1.** A system of pipes, such as those used in plumbing. **2.** The act of playing music on a pipe. **3.** A shrill high-pitched sound. **4.** A narrow tube of material, used as a trimming on edges or seams, as on slipcovers. —*adj.* Having a high-pitched sound: *the piping notes of the flute.* —***idiom.*** **piping hot.** Very hot: *piping hot biscuits.*

pip•it (pĭp′ĭt) *n.* Any of various small songbirds having brownish feathers and a streaked breast.

pip•pin (pĭp′ĭn) *n.* Any of several varieties of apple, used mainly in cooking.

pip-squeak (pĭp′skwēk′) *n. Informal.* A person or thing that is small or unimportant.

pi•quant (pē′kənt *or* pē′känt′) *adj.* **1.** Pleasantly pungent or tart in taste; spicy. **2.** Pleasantly disturbing, provocative, or stimulating: *piquant prose.* —**pi′quan•cy, pi′quant•ness** *n.* —**pi′quant•ly** *adv.*

pique (pēk) *n.* A state of vexation caused by a perceived slight or indignity; a feeling of wounded pride. —*tr.v.* **piqued, piqu•ing, piques. 1.** To cause to feel resentment or indignation: *Her arrogant manner piqued her neighbors.* **2.** To arouse; stir: *The unusual objects piqued his curiosity.*

❑ *These sound alike:* **pique, peak** (pointed top), **peek** (glance).

pi•qué (pĭ kā′ *or* pē kā′) *n.* A tightly woven cloth with various raised patterns.

pi•ra•cy (pī′rə sē) *n., pl.* **pi•ra•cies. 1.** Robbery committed at sea. **2.** The unauthorized use of another's invention or creation.

pi•ra•nha (pĭ rän′yə *or* pĭ rä′nə) *n.* Any of several small tropical American freshwater fishes having very sharp teeth. Piranhas school together and sometimes attack human beings and large animals. [First written down in 1869 in Modern English, from Tupi : *pirá*, fish + *ánha*, to cut.]

pi•rate (pī′rĭt) *n.* A person who robs ships at sea or plunders the land from the sea. —*v.* **pi•rat•ed, pi•rat•ing, pi•rates.** —*tr.* **1.** To attack and rob (a ship at sea). **2.** To publish or reproduce (another's invention or creation) without permission. —*intr.* To practice piracy. [First written down before 1300 in Middle English, from Greek *peiratēs*, from *peiran*, to attempt.]

pi•rogue (pĭ rōg′) *n.* A canoe made from a hollowed tree trunk.

pir•ou•ette (pĭr′o͞o ĕt′) *n.* In ballet, a full turn of the body on the tip of the toe or the ball of the foot. —*intr.v.* **pir•ou•et•ted, pir•ou•et•ting, pir•ou•ettes.** To perform a pirouette.

Pi•sa (pē′zə). A city of western Italy near the Tyrrhenian Sea. The famed Leaning Tower of Pisa is here. Population, 104,334.

Pi•sces (pī′sēz) *pl.n. (used with a singular verb).* **1.** A constellation in the equatorial region of the Northern Hemisphere. **2.** The 12th sign of the zodiac in astrology.

pis•ta•chi•o (pĭ stăsh′ē ō′) *n., pl.* **pis•ta•chi•os. 1.** The small hard-shelled nut of a tree of the Mediterranean region and western Asia, having a sweet green kernel. **2.** The tree that bears such nuts. **3.** The flavor of pistachio nuts. [First written down in 1598 in Modern English, from Greek *pistakion.*]

pis•til (pĭs′təl) *n.* The female reproductive organ of a flower, including the ovary, style, and stigma.

❑ *These sound alike:* **pistil, pistol** (gun).

pis•til•late (pĭs′tə lāt′ *or* pĭs′tə lĭt) *adj.* **1.** Having a pistil or pistils. **2.** Having pistils but no stamen: *pistillate flowers.*

pis•tol (pĭs′təl) *n.* A small gun designed to be held and fired with one hand.

❑ *These sound alike:* **pistol, pistil** (flower organ).

pis•ton (pĭs′tən) *n.* **1.** A solid cylinder or disk that fits snugly into a hollow cylinder and moves back and forth under the pressure of a fluid, as in many engines, or moves or compresses a fluid, as in a pump or compressor. **2.** A valve mechanism in brass instruments for changing pitch. [First written down in 1704 in Modern English, from Late Latin *pistāre*, to pound.]

piston ring *n.* An adjustable metal ring that fits around a piston and closes the gap between the piston and cylinder wall.

piston rod *n.* A connecting rod that transmits power to or is powered by a piston.

pit[1] (pĭt) *n.* **1.** A natural or artificial hole or cavity in the ground. **2.a.** A natural depression in the surface of a body, an organ, or a part: *the pit of the stomach.* **b.** A small depression in the skin left by a disease or injury; a pockmark. **3.** A concealed hole

pipeline
Section of the Trans-Alaska Pipeline

piranha

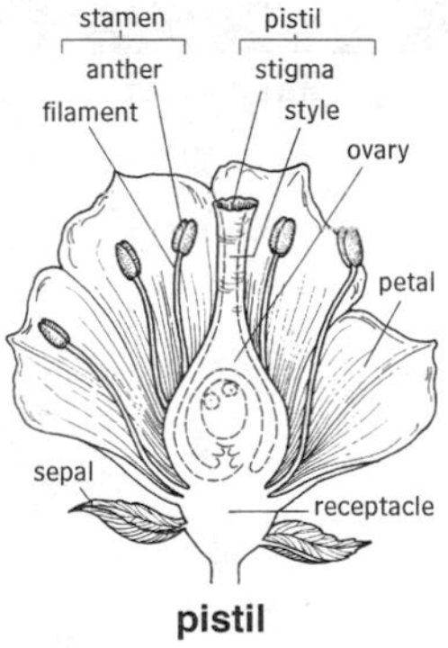

pistil

ă	pat	oi	boy
ā	pay	ou	out
âr	care	o͝o	took
ä	father	o͞o	boot
ĕ	pet	ŭ	cut
ē	be	ûr	urge
ĭ	pit	th	thin
ī	pie	*th*	this
îr	pier	hw	whoop
ŏ	pot	zh	vision
ō	toe	ə	about
ô	paw	N	*French* bon

pitcher plant

pith helmet

in the ground used as a trap; a pitfall. **4.** Hell. **5.** The area directly in front of the stage of a theater in which the musicians sit. **6.a.** A sunken area in a garage where mechanics work underneath automobiles. **b.** The area beside an automobile racecourse where cars may be fueled and serviced during a race. Often used in the plural. **7.** An enclosed space in which animals are kept or are set to fight: *a snake pit.* —*v.* **pit•ted, pit•ting, pits.** —*tr.* **1.** To mark with cavities, depressions, or scars: *The moon appears to have been pitted by meteoroid impacts.* **2.** To set in competition; match: *a tournament that pits one school against another.* **3.** To place, bury, or store in a pit. —*intr.* To become marked with pits. [First written down in 847 in Old English and spelled *pytt*, from Latin *puteus*, well.]

pit[2] (pĭt) *n.* The single hard-shelled seed of certain fruits, such as a peach or cherry; a stone. —*tr.v.* **pit•ted, pit•ting, pits.** To remove the pits from: *We pitted the olives for the salad.* [First written down in 1841 in American English, from Dutch.]

pi•ta (pē′tə) *n.* A round flat bread that can be opened into a pocket for filling. [First written down in 1951 in Modern English and spelled *pitah*, from Modern Greek.]

pit•a•pat (pĭt′ə păt′) *intr.v.* **pit•a•pat•ted, pit•a•pat•ting, pit•a•pats. 1.** To move with a series of quick tapping steps. **2.** To make a repeated tapping sound.

pitch[1] (pĭch) *n.* **1.** Any of various sticky dark thick substances obtained from coal tar, wood tar, or petroleum and used for roofing, waterproofing, and paving. **2.** Any of various natural bitumens, such as asphalt, having similar uses. **3.** A resin derived from the sap of a pine tree or a similar tree that bears cones. —*tr.v.* **pitched, pitch•ing, pitch•es.** To cover with pitch. [First written down about 700 in Old English and spelled *pic*, from Latin *pix*.]

pitch[2] (pĭch) *v.* **pitched, pitch•ing, pitch•es.** —*tr.* **1.** To throw, usually with careful aim: *pitching horseshoes.* See Synonyms at **throw. 2.** To discard by throwing: *pitched the wrapper into the can.* **3.** In baseball: **a.** To throw (the ball) from the mound to the batter. **b.** To play (a game or part of it) as pitcher: *pitched the final game of the Series.* **4.** To set up or establish: *pitch a tent; pitch camp.* **5.** To set at or as if at a given level or degree: *He pitched his hopes too high.* **6.** To set the musical pitch or key of: *Pitch your voice so that it harmonizes with mine.* **7.** To set at a specified downward slant: *pitched the roof at a steep angle.* **8.** To move so that the front end lifts or falls in relation to the stern or tail: *The airplane pitched as it fought the headwind.* —*intr.* **1.** To toss or throw something, such as a baseball or horseshoe. **2.** In baseball, to play in the position of pitcher. **3.** To plunge headlong: *He pitched over the railing.* **4.** To plunge forward and backward alternately, as a ship on the high seas: *Heavy storms made the ship pitch and toss.* **5.** To slope downward: *The hill pitches steeply.* —*n.* **1.** The act or an instance of pitching: *My pitch missed the wastebasket by a mile. The pitch of the boat made the passengers sick.* **2.** In baseball: **a.** A throw of the ball by a pitcher to a batter: *On the next pitch, the batter struck out.* **b.** A ball so thrown. **3.** A degree or level of intensity: *The dispute reached a feverish pitch.* **4.** A steep slope, as of a roof. **5.** The alternating lift and fall of the bow and stern of a ship or the nose and tail of an aircraft or a spacecraft. **6.a.** The quality of a sound by which it can be judged high or low, determined mostly by the frequency of the sound. **b.** The relative position of a tone in a musical scale, as determined by this quality. **c.** Any of several standards that establish the frequency of each musical tone. **7.** The distance between corresponding points on adjoining screw threads or gear teeth. **8.** The forward distance a propeller would travel in one complete revolution through an ideal medium. **9.** *Informal.* A line of talk designed to persuade: *a sales pitch.* —***idiom.*** **pitch in.** *Informal.* **1.** To set to work vigorously. **2.** To join forces with others; help or cooperate. [First written down about 1380 in Middle English and spelled *pichen.*]

pitch-black (pĭch′blăk′) *adj.* Extremely dark; black as pitch.

pitch•blende (pĭch′blĕnd′) *n.* A black, often crusty mineral that is a principal ore of uranium.

pitch-dark (pĭch′därk′) *adj.* Extremely dark.

pitched battle (pĭcht) *n.* A fierce concentrated battle fought by opponents in close contact.

pitch•er[1] (pĭch′ər) *n.* **1.** A person or thing that pitches. **2.** The baseball player who pitches the ball from the mound to the batter.

pitch•er[2] (pĭch′ər) *n.* A container for liquids, usually having a handle and a lip or spout for pouring. [First written down in 1208 in Middle English and spelled *picher*, from Medieval Latin *bicārium*, drinking cup.]

pitcher plant *n.* Any of various plants having pitcher-shaped leaves containing a liquid in which insects are trapped.

pitch•fork (pĭch′fôrk′) *n.* A large fork with sharp, widely spaced prongs, used to lift and pitch hay.

pitch•out (pĭch′out′) *n.* In baseball, a pitch thrown high and away from the batter to make it easier for the catcher to throw out a base runner.

pitch pipe *n.* A small pipe that, when sounded, gives the standard pitch for a piece of music or for tuning an instrument.

pit•e•ous (pĭt′ē əs) *adj.* Demanding or arousing pity. —**pit′e•ous•ly** *adv.*

pit•fall (pĭt′fôl′) *n.* **1.** A hidden danger or unexpected difficulty: *Life is full of pitfalls.* **2.** A concealed hole in the ground for trapping animals.

pith (pĭth) *n.* **1.** The soft spongy substance in the center of the stems of many plants and of some trees. **2.** The central or essential part; the heart or essence: *the pith of her argument.*

pith helmet *n.* A lightweight sun hat made of dried pith.

pith•y (pĭth′ē) *adj.* **pith•i•er, pith•i•est. 1.** Precisely meaningful; forceful and brief: *a pithy sentence.* **2.** Full of or resembling pith: *the pithy stem of a plant.* —**pith′i•ly** *adv.* —**pith′i•ness** *n.*

pit•i•a•ble (pĭt′ē ə bəl) *adj.* Arousing or deserving of pity; lamentable. —**pit′i•a•bly** *adv.*

pit•i•ful (pĭt′ĭ fəl) *adj.* **1.** Inspiring or deserving pity: *The cold and hungry puppy was a pitiful sight.* **2.** Arousing contemptuous pity, as through ineptitude or inadequacy: *a pitiful excuse.* —**pit′i•ful•ly** *adv.* —**pit′i•ful•ness** *n.*

pit•i•less (pĭt′ĭ lĭs) *adj.* Having no pity; merciless. —**pit′i•less•ly** *adv.* —**pit′i•less•ness** *n.*

pit stop *n.* **1.** A stop at a pit in an automobile race for fuel or service. **2.** *Informal.* A brief stop for rest, food, or fuel on a trip.

Pitt (pĭt), **William[1].** Known as "Pitt the Elder." 1708–1778. British politician who directed his country's military effort during the Seven Years' War (1756–1763).

Pitt (pĭt), **William[2].** Known as "Pitt the Younger." 1759–1806. British prime minister (1783–1801 and 1804–1806).

pit•tance (pĭt′ns) *n.* **1.** A meager monetary allowance or wage. **2.** A very small amount: *a pittance of bread.*

pit•ted (pĭt′ĭd) *adj.* **1.** Marked by pits; having pits in the surface: *pitted the surface of the moon.* **2.** Having the pit removed: *pitted olives.*

pit•ter-pat•ter (pĭt′ər păt′ər) *n.* A rapid series of

light tapping sounds: *the pitter-patter of little feet.*

Pitts•burgh (pĭts′bûrg′). A city of southwest Pennsylvania at the head of the Ohio River. The city grew around a fort built by the French in 1750. Population, 369,879.

pi•tu•i•tar•y (pĭ to͞o′ĭ tĕr′ē *or* pĭ tyo͞o′ĭ tĕr′ē) *n., pl.* **pi•tu•i•tar•ies. 1.** The pituitary gland. **2.** Any of various extracts derived from the pituitary glands of domestic animals and used in medicine. *—adj.* Of or relating to the pituitary gland.

pituitary gland *n.* A small oval endocrine gland attached to the base of the brain in vertebrates. Its secretions control the other endocrine glands and influence growth and metabolism.

pit viper *n.* Any of various poisonous snakes, such as the rattlesnake or the copperhead, having a small pit or indentation on each side of the head.

pit•y (pĭt′ē) *n., pl.* **pit•ies. 1.** Sympathy and sorrow aroused by the misfortune or suffering of another. **2.** A matter of regret: *It's a pity you can't go. —v.* **pit•ied, pit•y•ing, pit•ies.** *—tr.* To feel pity for. *—intr.* To feel pity. ***—idiom.*** **have pity on** or **take pity on.** To show compassion for. [First written down before 1250 in Middle English and spelled *pite,* ultimately from Latin *pietās,* piety, compassion.]

Pi•us XII (pī′əs). 1876–1958. Pope (1939–1958) who maintained neutrality during World War II.

piv•ot (pĭv′ət) *n.* **1.** A short rod or shaft on which a related part rotates or swings. **2.** A person or thing on which something depends or turns; the central or crucial factor. **3.** The act or an instance of turning on or as if on a pivot. *—v.* **piv•ot•ed, piv•ot•ing, piv•ots.** *—tr.* **1.** To provide with a pivot or pivots. **2.** To cause to rotate, revolve, or turn. *—intr.* To turn on or as if on a pivot: *The movie pivots on the detective's refusal to believe a witness.* [First written down in 1611 in Modern English, from Old French.]

piv•ot•al (pĭv′ə tl) *adj.* **1.** Of, relating to, or used as a pivot. **2.** Of vital or central importance: *pivotal decisions.* **—piv′ot•al•ly** *adv.*

pix•el (pĭk′səl *or* pĭk′sĕl′) *n.* The smallest unit on a computer or television screen that with many others creates an electronic image.

pix•y or **pix•ie** (pĭk′sē) *n., pl.* **pix•ies.** A creature similar to a fairy or an elf, especially a mischievous playful one.

Pi•zar•ro (pĭ zär′ō), **Francisco.** 1475?–1541. Spanish explorer who conquered the Inca Empire of Peru (1531–1533).

piz•za (pēt′sə) *n.* A baked dish of Italian origin consisting of a shallow crust covered with tomato sauce, cheese, and often other toppings.

piz•zazz or **piz•zaz** (pĭ zăz′) *n. Slang.* Dazzling style; flamboyance; flair.

piz•ze•ri•a (pēt′sə rē′ə) *n.* A place where pizzas are made and sold.

piz•zi•ca•to (pĭt′sĭ kä′tō) *adj.* Played by plucking rather than bowing the strings of an instrument.

pk. *abbr.* An abbreviation of peak.

pkg. *abbr.* An abbreviation of package.

pl. *abbr.* An abbreviation of plural.

plac•ard (plăk′ärd′ *or* plăk′ərd) *n.* A sign or notice for public display. *—tr.v.* **plac•ard•ed, plac•ard•ing, plac•ards.** To post placards on, in, or throughout: *placard a wall.*

pla•cate (plā′kāt′ *or* plăk′āt′) *tr.v.* **pla•cat•ed, pla•cat•ing, pla•cates.** To calm the anger of, especially by making concessions; appease: *placated the child with a cookie.* **—pla′cat′er** *n.* **—pla•ca′tion** *n.*

place (plās) *n.* **1.a.** A particular area or spot with definite or indefinite boundaries. **b.** Room or space, especially adequate space: *There's place for you at the back of the room.* **2.** A city or other locality: *What place were you born in?* **3.** A dwelling; a house: *Come over to my place for supper.* **4.** Often **Place.** A public square or a short city street: *She lives on Butler Place.* **5.** A building or an area set aside for a definite purpose: *a place of worship.* **6.a.** A space occupied by or allocated for a person: *two empty places near the back of the theater.* **b.** A table setting for one person: *Set an extra place for supper.* **7.** Position or rank: *My jam won first place at the fair.* **8.** The position of a person or thing as occupied by a substitute; stead: *I'm going in his place.* **9.** A particular situation or circumstance: *If you were in my place, you'd act differently.* **10.** An appropriate duty, right, or social position: *It's not my place to tell you what to do.* **11.** A job or position: *She found a place with an accounting firm.* **12.** Proper or usual position, order, context, or time: *She felt out of place in the kitchen.* **13.** A particular point that one has reached, as in a book: *mark one's place with a bookmark.* **14.** The position of a digit in relation to the other digits of a numeral. For example, in the number 1.8, the 8 is in the tenths place. *—v.* **placed, plac•ing, plac•es.** *—tr.* **1.a.** To put in a particular spot or position; set: *place cups and saucers on the table.* **b.** To put in a particular order: *place words in alphabetical order.* **2.** To find accommodation or employment for. **3.** To rank in an order or a sequence. **4.** To remember where or how (someone or something) was first encountered: *His face looks familiar, but I can't place him.* **5.** To put; let reside: *place one's trust in the government.* **6.** To apply or arrange for: *placed an order for a dozen new textbooks. —intr.* To arrive among the first three finishers in a race, especially to finish second. ***—idioms.*** **in place. 1.** In the appropriate or usual position or order: *Make sure everything is in place before we start.* **2.** In the same spot; without moving forwards or backwards: *We ran in place for ten minutes.* **in place of.** Instead of. [First written down before 950 in Old English and spelled *plæce,* from Greek *plateia (hodos),* broad street.]

❑ *These sound alike:* **place, plaice** (fish).

pla•ce•bo (plə sē′bō) *n., pl.* **pla•ce•bos** or **pla•ce•boes.** A preparation containing no medicine, given to soothe a patient or used as the control in an experiment to test the effectiveness of a drug.

place•hold•er (plās′hōl′dər) *n.* **1.** A person who acts as a deputy to or in place of someone else. **2.** A person who has been appointed to an office in government. **3.** A digit that has no value in a decimal number. **4.** A symbol that may be replaced by the name of any element in a set in a mathematical expression.

place kick *n.* In football, a kick made while the ball is held or propped up on the ground.

place mat *n.* A protective table mat for a single setting of dishes and flatware at meals.

place•ment (plās′mənt) *n.* **1.a.** The act of placing or arranging. **b.** The state of being placed or arranged. **2.** A particular arrangement or distribution: *a different placement of the pictures on the walls.*

pla•cen•ta (plə sĕn′tə) *n., pl.* **pla•cen•tas** or **pla•cen•tae** (plə sĕn′tē). **1.** A spongy membranous organ that develops in the uterus of a female mammal during pregnancy, lining the uterus and partially surrounding the fetus, to which it is attached by an umbilical cord. It supplies the fetus with nourishment and is expelled after birth. **2.** A similar organ in other animals, such as certain sharks and reptiles.

pla•cen•tal (plə sĕn′tl) *adj.* **1.** Of or relating to the placenta. **2.** Having a placenta.

plac•er (plăs′ər) *n.* A gravel or sand deposit left by a river, containing particles of valuable minerals.

place setting *n.* A table service for one person.

Francisco Pizarro
c. 1760 painting
by an unknown artist

placard

ă	pat	oi	boy
ā	pay	ou	out
âr	care	ŏŏ	took
ä	father	ōō	boot
ŏ	pot	ŭ	cut
ē	be	ûr	urge
ĭ	pit	th	thin
ī	pie	*th*	this
îr	pier	hw	whoop
ŏ	pot	zh	vision
ō	toe	ə	about
ô	paw	N	*French* bon

plac•id (plăs′ĭd) *adj.* **1.** Calm; peaceful. See Synonyms at **calm.** **2.** Satisfied; complacent. —**plac′id•ly** *adv.* —**plac′id•ness** *n.*
pla•cid•i•ty (plə sĭd′ĭ tē) *n.* Calmness; peacefulness.
plack•et (plăk′ĭt) *n.* A slit in a dress, blouse, or skirt.
pla•gia•rism (plā′jə rĭz′əm) *n.* **1.** The act of plagiarizing: *The producers of the show were guilty of plagiarism.* **2.** Something plagiarized: *His poem was a plagiarism from a magazine.* —**pla′gia•rist** *n.*
pla•gia•rize (plā′jə rīz′) *v.* **pla•gia•rized, pla•gia•riz•ing, pla•gia•riz•es.** —*tr.* **1.** To use and pass off as one's own (the ideas or writings of another). **2.** To make use of the passages or ideas from (another) as if they were one's own. —*intr.* To put forth as original to oneself the ideas or words of another.
plague (plāg) *n.* **1.** A widespread calamity or affliction, especially one regarded as a punishment from God. **2.** A very contagious, usually fatal epidemic disease, especially bubonic plague. **3.** A sudden influx or increase, as of something evil. **4.** A cause of annoyance; a nuisance: *The defective printer was a plague to our office.* —*tr.v.* **plagued, plagu•ing, plagues.** **1.** To annoy; pester; harass: *Stop plaguing me with your complaints.* **2.** To cause misery or trouble in or for: *Sleeping sickness has plagued Africa for years.* [First written down before 1382 in Middle English and spelled *plage,* from Latin *plāga,* blow, wound.]
plaice (plās) *n., pl.* **plaice** or **plaic•es.** Any of various large flatfishes of western European waters and of the North Atlantic, related to the flounders and used as food. [First written down in 1267 in Middle English and spelled *plais,* from Late Latin *platessa.*]
❑ *These sound alike:* **plaice, place** (area).
plaid (plăd) *n.* **1.** A woolen scarf of a tartan pattern worn over the left shoulder by Scottish Highlanders. **2.a.** Cloth with a tartan or checked pattern. **b.** A pattern of this kind. [First written down in 1512 in Modern English, from Scottish Gaelic *plaide.*]
plain (plān) *adj.* **plain•er, plain•est.** **1.** Open to view; clear; distinct: *The mountain stood out plain against the sky.* **2.** Obvious to the mind; perfectly clear: *His meaning was quite plain.* **3.** Not elaborate or complicated; simple: *plain food.* **4.** Ordinary; average: *My dog is a plain old mutt.* **5.** Lacking beauty or distinction: *a plain face.* **6.** Marked by little or no ornamentation or decoration: *a plain dress.* **7.** Not pretentious; unaffected. **8.** Frank; candid; down-to-earth: *plain talk.* **9.** Pure; unadulterated; natural: *plain water instead of soda water.* —*n.* A large, flat, mostly treeless area of land. —*adv. Informal.* Clearly; simply: *plain stubborn.* [First written down before 1300 in Middle English, from Latin *plānus.*] —**plain′ly** *adv.* —**plain′ness** *n.*
❑ *These sound alike:* **plain, plane¹** (surface), **plane²** (tool), **plane³** (tree).
plain•chant (plān′chănt′) *n.* A form of early unaccompanied church music; plainsong.
plain•clothes man or **plain•clothes•man** (plān′klōz′mən *or* plān′klōthz′mən) *n.* A member of a police force who wears civilian clothes on duty.
Plains Indian (plānz) *n.* A member of any of the Native American peoples inhabiting the Great Plains of the United States and Canada.
plains•man (plānz′mən) *n.* An inhabitant or a settler of the plains, especially of the prairie regions of the United States.
plain•song (plān′sông′ *or* plān′sŏng′) *n.* **1.** Gregorian chant. **2.** A form of medieval church music traditionally sung without accompaniment.
plain•spo•ken (plān′spō′kən) *adj.* Frank; straightforward: *a plain-spoken critic.*
plaint (plānt) *n.* A complaint.
plain•tiff (plān′tĭf) *n.* The party that institutes a suit in a court of law.
plain•tive (plān′tĭv) *adj.* Expressing sorrow; mournful: *a plaintive song.* —**plain′tive•ly** *adv.* —**plain′tive•ness** *n.*
plait (plāt *or* plăt) *n.* **1.** A braid, especially of hair. **2.** A pleat. —*tr.v.* **plait•ed, plait•ing, plaits.** **1.** To braid: *She plaited her hair.* **2.** To pleat. **3.** To make by braiding: *plait straw hats.*
❑ *These sound alike:* **plait, plate** (dish).
plan (plăn) *n.* **1.** A scheme, program, or method thought out ahead of time for the accomplishment of a goal: *a plan for reorganizing the town government.* **2.** A drawing or diagram showing how to build or assemble something: *plans for a new house.* —*v.* **planned, plan•ning, plans.** —*tr.* **1.** To think out a scheme or program for accomplishing or attaining (something): *plan one's trip.* **2.** To have in mind; intend: *She plans to go to Canada this summer.* **3.** To design (something to be built or made): *plan a new school.* —*intr.* To make a plan or plans. —**plan′ner** *n.*
pla•nar•i•an (plə nâr′ē ən) *n.* Any of various small freshwater flatworms having a broad body.
plane¹ (plān) *n.* **1.** In geometry, a surface that contains all the straight lines required to connect any two points on it. **2.** A flat or level surface. **3.** A level of existence, development, or achievement: *a high moral plane.* **4.** An airplane or a hydroplane. —*adj.* Lying in a plane: *a plane curve.* [First written down in 1696 in Modern English, from Latin *plānus,* flat.]
❑ *These sound alike:* **plane¹** (surface), **plain** (clear), **plane²** (tool), **plane³** (tree).
plane² (plān) *n.* A carpenter's tool with an adjustable blade for smoothing and leveling wood. —*v.* **planed, plan•ing, planes.** —*tr.* To smooth or finish with a plane. —*intr.* To work with a plane. [First written down in 1350 in Middle English, from Late Latin *plāna,* from Latin *plānus,* flat.]
❑ *These sound alike:* **plane²** (tool), **plain** (clear), **plane¹** (surface), **plane³** (tree).
plane³ (plān) *n.* The plane tree. [First written down before 1382 in Middle English, from Greek *platanos.*]
❑ *These sound alike:* **plane³** (tree), **plain** (clear), **plane¹** (surface), **plane²** (tool).
plane geometry *n.* The geometry of plane figures.
plan•er (plā′nər) *n.* A person or thing that planes, especially a machine tool used to smooth or finish the surface of wood or metal.
plan•et (plăn′ĭt) *n.* A celestial body that is larger than an asteroid or a comet and is illuminated by light from a star, about which it moves in an orbit. [First written down before 1300 in Middle English, from Greek *planētēs,* from *planasthai,* to wander.]
plan•e•tar•i•um (plăn′ĭ târ′ē əm) *n., pl.* **plan•e•tar•i•ums** or **plan•e•tar•i•a** (plăn′ĭ târ′ē ə). **1.** A mechanical model of the solar system. **2.** An optical device for projecting images of celestial bodies in their courses onto the ceiling of a dome. **3.** A building or room in which such a device is housed or operated.
plan•e•tar•y (plăn′ĭ tĕr′ē) *adj.* **1.** Of or resembling a planet or the characteristics of a planet. **2.** Of or affecting the entire world; global: *Pollution is a planetary concern.*
plan•e•toid (plăn′ĭ toid′) *n.* An asteroid.
plane tree *n.* Any of several trees, such as the sycamore, having ball-shaped fruit clusters and bark that flakes off in patches.
plank (plăngk) *n.* **1.** A piece of lumber cut thicker than a board. **2.** One of the principles of a political platform. **3.** A foundation; a support. —*tr.v.* **planked, plank•ing, planks.** **1.** To furnish or cover

with planks: *plank a boat.* **2.** To bake or broil and serve (fish or meat) on a board: *plank a steak.*

plank•ton (plăngk′tən) *n.* The collection of plant and animal organisms, usually of very small size, that float or drift in great numbers in bodies of salt or fresh water.

plant (plănt) *n.* **1.** Any of various organisms that can manufacture their own food, cannot move under their own power, and have cells with walls made of cellulose. **2.** One of these organisms that has no permanent woody stem, as distinguished from a tree or shrub. **3.** A factory or similar place where something is produced or processed. **4.** The buildings and equipment of an institution. **5.** A person or thing put into place to mislead or work secretly, especially a person stationed as a spy or a misleading piece of evidence. —*tr.v.* **plant•ed, plant•ing, plants. 1.a.** To place (seeds, for example) in the ground or in soil for growing. **b.** To place seeds or young plants in (land); sow: *plant a field with corn.* **2.** To place (spawn or young fish) in water or an underwater bed for cultivation: *plant salmon.* **3.** To fix or set firmly: *plant one's feet on the ground.* **4.** To start; establish: *plant new colonies.* **5.** To fix firmly in the mind; implant. **6.** To place as a means of trapping or deceiving someone: *plant spies in an organization.* [First written down before 830 in Old English and spelled *plante*, from Latin *planta*, sole of the foot, shoot.]

Plan•tag•e•net (plăn tăj′ə nĭt). Family name of a line of English monarchs from Henry II to Richard III (1154–1485).

plan•tain[1] (plăn′tən) *n.* Any of various weedy plants having large leaves and a dense narrow cluster of small green or whitish flowers. [First written down before 1300 in Middle English and spelled *plauntein*, from Latin *plantāgō*, from *planta*, plant.]

plan•tain[2] (plăn′tən) *n.* **1.** A tropical fruit similar to the banana but not as sweet. **2.** The plant that bears such fruit. [First written down in 1555 in Modern English and spelled *plantan*, from Latin *platanus*, plane tree.]

plan•ta•tion (plăn tā′shən) *n.* **1.** A large farm or estate on which crops are raised, often by resident workers. **2.** A group of cultivated plants or trees or the ground on which they grow.

plant•er (plăn′tər) *n.* **1.** A person or thing that plants, especially a tool or machine for planting seeds. **2.** The owner or manager of a plantation. **3.** A decorative container for a plant or small tree.

plant louse *n.* An aphid.

plaque (plăk) *n.* **1.** An ornamented or engraved plate, slab, or disk, used for decoration or to carry an inscription on a monument. **2.** A film of mucus and bacteria that forms on the surface of the teeth.

plash (plăsh) *n.* A light splash. —*v.* **plashed, plash•ing, plash•es.** —*tr.* To spatter (liquid) about; splash. —*intr.* To cause a light splash.

plas•ma (plăz′mə) *n.* **1.** The clear yellowish liquid part of blood or lymph in which cells are suspended. **2.** Protoplasm or cytoplasm. **3.** An electrically neutral, usually hot gas containing positively charged and negatively charged particles and some neutral particles.

plas•mo•di•um (plăz mō′dē əm) *n., pl.* **plas•mo•di•a** (plăz mō′dē ə). A parasitic protozoan, especially one that causes malaria.

plas•ter (plăs′tər) *n.* **1.** A mixture of sand, lime or gypsum, and water, sometimes with fiber added, that hardens to a smooth solid and is used for covering walls and ceilings. **2.** Plaster of Paris. **3.** A pasty mixture applied to a part of the body, either as a remedy or as a cosmetic. —*v.* **plas•tered, plas•ter•ing, plas•ters.** —*tr.* **1.** To cover with plaster: *plaster cracks in the ceiling.* **2.** To cover as if with plaster: *The students plastered the campus with posters.* **3.** To make adhere to another surface: *plastered posters on the wall.* —*intr.* To apply plaster. [First written down before 1000 in Old English and spelled *plaster*, medical dressing, from Greek *emplastron*, from *emplassein*, to plaster on.] —**plas′ter•er** *n.*

plas•ter•board (plăs′tər bôrd′) *n.* A rigid board or sheet of layers of paper, usually bonded to a plaster core and used to cover walls.

plaster of Paris *n.* Any of a group of cements made by heating gypsum to drive off part of its water of crystallization, forming, when mixed with water, a paste that hardens into a solid.

plas•tic (plăs′tĭk) *adj.* **1.** Capable of being shaped or formed: *Clay is a plastic material.* **2.** Relating to shaping or modeling: *the plastic art of sculpture.* **3.** Giving form or shape to something: *the plastic forces of nature.* **4.** Made of plastic: *a plastic cup.* —*n.* Any of numerous organic chemical compounds formed by repeatedly linking simple units into what is, in effect, a giant molecule. Plastics can be formed into films and objects of practically any shape, or drawn into fibers for use in textiles. [First written down in 1632 in Modern English, from Greek *plastikos*, from *plassein*, to mold.] —**plas•tic′i•ty** (plă stĭs′ĭ tē) *n.*

plastic surgery *n.* Surgery to repair, restore, or remodel injured or malformed body tissue or parts.

plas•tid (plăs′tĭd) *n.* One of several kinds of tiny structures in the protoplasm of plant cells, sometimes containing coloring or starch.

Pla•ta (plä′tə), **Río de la.** A wide estuary of southeast South America between Argentina and Uruguay opening on the Atlantic Ocean.

plate (plāt) *n.* **1.** A thin flat sheet or piece of metal or other material. **2.** A piece of flat metal on which something is engraved, as a license plate or a name plate. **3.** A print of a woodcut or lithograph, especially when reproduced in a book. **4.** A full-page book illustration, often in color and printed on special paper. **5.** A sheet of light-sensitive glass or metal upon which a photographic image can be recorded. **6.** A piece of metal or plastic fitted to the gums to hold false teeth in place. **7.** In baseball, home plate. **8.a.** A shallow usually circular dish from which food is eaten. **b.** The contents of such a dish: *Finish your plate.* **9.** Food and service for one person at a meal: *supper at a dollar a plate.* **10.** Dishes and other household articles made of or plated with gold or silver. **11.** A thin cut of beef from the brisket. **12.a.** An electrode, as in a storage battery or capacitor. **b.** The positive electrode of an electron tube. **13.** In plate tectonics, one of the sections of the earth's crust that is in constant motion along with other sections. —*tr.v.* **plat•ed, plat•ing, plates.** To coat or cover with a thin layer of metal. [First written down about 1250 in Middle English, from Greek *platus*, flat.]

❑ *These sound alike:* **plate, plait** (braid).

pla•teau (plă tō′) *n., pl.* **pla•teaus** or **pla•teaux** (plă tōz′). **1.** An elevated comparatively level expanse of land. **2.** A relatively stable level or stage of growth or development: *The economy has reached a new plateau.* [First written down in 1796 in Modern English, from Old French *platel*, platter, from *plat*, flat.]

plate•ful (plāt′fo͝ol′) *n., pl.* **platefuls.** The amount that a plate will hold.

plate glass *n.* A strong polished glass containing few defects, used for making large windows and mirrors.

plate•let (plāt′lĭt) *n.* Any of the numerous micro-

plaque

ă	pat	oi	boy
ā	pay	ou	out
âr	care	o͝o	took
ä	father	o͞o	boot
ĕ	pet	ŭ	cut
ē	be	ûr	urge
ĭ	pit	th	thin
ī	pie	*th*	this
îr	pier	hw	whoop
ŏ	pot	zh	vision
ō	toe	ə	about
ô	paw	N	*French* bon

Sylvia Plath
Photographed in 1955

Plato
Copy of a mid fourth-century bust attributed to Silanion (fl. 360–330 B.C.)

platypus
Close-up view

scopic bodies, shaped like irregular disks and lacking nuclei, that are found in the blood of mammals and function in the clotting of blood.

plat•en (plăt′n) *n.* The roller of a typewriter or computer printer against which the paper is held.

plate tec•ton•ics (tĕk tŏn′ĭks) *n.* In geology, a theory that the earth's crust is divided into a series of vast platelike sections that move as distinct masses.

plat•form (plăt′fôrm′) *n.* **1.** A floor or horizontal surface higher than an adjoining area: *a speakers' platform.* **2.** A formal declaration of principles, as by a political party or candidate. [First written down in 1550 in Modern English, from Old French *plate-forme*, diagram : *plat*, flat + *forme*, form.]

Plath (plăth), **Sylvia.** 1932–1963. American writer whose poems, collected in *Ariel* (1965), are noted for their technical excellence.

plat•ing (plā′tĭng) *n.* A thin layer or coating of metal, such as gold or silver, deposited on or applied to a surface.

plat•i•num (plăt′n əm) *n. Symbol* **Pt** A silver-white metallic element used as a catalyst, for chemical and industrial equipment, in dentistry, and in jewelry. Atomic number 78. See table at **element.** [First written down in 1812 in Modern English, from Spanish *platina*, from *plata*, silver.]

plat•i•tude (plăt′ĭ to͞od′ *or* plăt′ĭ tyo͞od′) *n.* A trite or banal remark or statement, especially one expressed as if it were original or significant. [First written down in 1812 in Modern English, from French *plat*, flat.]

plat•i•tu•di•nous (plăt′ĭ to͞od′n əs *or* plăt′ĭ tyo͞od′n əs) *adj.* **1.** Commonplace; trite: *a platitudinous remark.* **2.** Full of or inclined to use platitudes: *a platitudinous sermon.*

Pla•to (plā′tō). 427?–347? B.C. Greek philosopher who presented his ideas in the form of dramatic dialogues, as in *Symposium.*

Pla•ton•ic (plə tŏn′ĭk) *adj.* **1.** Of or relating to Plato or his philosophy. **2. platonic.** Not involving physical passion and tending toward the purely spiritual or ideal: *a platonic friendship.*

Pla•to•nism (plāt′n ĭz′əm) *n.* The philosophy of Plato, which asserts that ideal forms are the only eternal reality and everything in the world is but a shadow or reflection of these forms.

pla•toon (plə to͞on′) *n.* **1.** A unit of soldiers smaller than a company but larger than a squad, normally commanded by a lieutenant. **2.** A group of people working, traveling, or assembled together: *a platoon of firefighters.* **3.** In a football team, a group of players specially trained and sent into or withdrawn from a game as a unit.

Platte (plăt). A river, about 310 miles (499 kilometers) long, of central Nebraska formed by the confluence of the **North Platte** and **South Platte** rivers and flowing eastward to the Missouri River.

plat•ter (plăt′ər) *n.* **1.** A large shallow dish or plate for serving food. **2.** A meal or course served on a platter. **3.** *Slang.* A phonograph record.

plat•y•pus (plăt′ĭ pəs) *n., pl.* **plat•y•pus•es.** A furry egg-laying Australian mammal having webbed feet and a snout resembling a duck's bill, living in or near water. [First written down in 1799 in Modern English, from Greek *platupous*, flat-footed : *platus*, flat + *pous*, foot.]

plau•dit (plô′dĭt) *n.* Enthusiastic expression of praise or approval: *the plaudits of the critics.*

plau•si•ble (plô′zə bəl) *adj.* Seemingly true or reasonable: *a plausible excuse.* **—plau′si•bly** *adv.* **—plau′si•bil′i•ty** *n.*

play (plā) *v.* **played, play•ing, plays.** *—intr.* **1.** To have fun; amuse oneself: *The children went outdoors to play.* **2.** To take part in a game. **3.** To act in jest or sport: *She looks angry, but she's just playing.* **4.** To act in a drama: *He played in last season's comedy.* **5.** To be presented for an audience: *What movie is playing tonight?* **6.** To conduct oneself in a particular way: *You're not playing fair.* **7.a.** To perform on a musical instrument: *play on a trumpet.* **b.** To perform music: *The band played.* **8.** To move rapidly, lightly, or irregularly: *A breeze played over the lake.* *—tr.* **1.** To perform or act (a role or part) in a dramatic performance. **2.** To perform (a theatrical work) on or as if on the stage. **3.** To pretend to be; mimic the activities of: *He was playing cowboy.* **4.a.** To engage in (a game or sport): *played tennis.* **b.** To occupy or work at (a position) in a game: *She plays first base.* **c.** To use or move (a card or a piece, for example) in a game or sport: *I'll play the nine of spades next.* **5.** To bet; wager. **6.** To perform or put into effect, especially as a jest or deception: *play a joke on a friend.* **7.a.** To perform on (an instrument): *play the fiddle.* **b.** To perform (a piece of music) on an instrument or instruments. **8.** To cause (a record or phonograph, for example) to emit recorded sounds. **9.** To cause to move rapidly, lightly, or irregularly: *played the flashlight around the dark attic.* *—n.* **1.a.** A literary work written for performance on the stage. **b.** The performance of such a work: *We went to a play last night.* **2.** Activity engaged in for enjoyment or recreation: *Play is important for children and adults.* **3.** The act or manner of playing a game or sport. **4.** A manner of dealing with people: *He believes in fair play.* **5.** A move or an action in a game: *It's your play.* **6.** Movement or freedom of movement: *the play of lights across a stage.* **7.** Action; use: *brought her influence into full play.* **8.** An attempt to obtain something; a bid: *a play for sympathy.* ***—idioms.*** **in play.** In a position to be legally played: *The ball is in play.* **out of play.** Not in a position to be legally played. **play down.** To minimize the importance of; make little of: *The economist played down the fall in stock prices.* **play on** or **play upon.** To take advantage of (another's attitudes or feelings) for one's own interests: *He played on my sympathy when asking for a loan.* **play up to.** To try to win the favor of: *We thought it would help to play up to the new teacher.* **play with fire.** To take part in a dangerous or risky undertaking. [First written down about 830 in Old English and spelled *plegian.*] **—play′a•ble** *adj.*

pla•ya (plī′ə) *n.* An almost level area at the bottom of a desert basin, sometimes temporarily covered with water.

play•bill (plā′bĭl′) *n.* A poster announcing a theatrical performance.

play•boy (plā′boi′) *n.* A man who is devoted to the pursuit of pleasurable activities.

play-by-play (plā′bī plā′) *adj.* Being or giving a detailed running account of the action of an event, especially a sports event, as it occurs.

play•er (plā′ər) *n.* **1.** A person who takes part in a game or sport. **2.** An actor. **3.** A person who plays a musical instrument. **4.** A device that reproduces sound, especially a phonograph.

player piano *n.* A mechanical piano that uses a punched paper roll to control the keys.

play•ful (plā′fəl) *adj.* **1.** Full of fun and high spirits; frolicsome: *a playful cat.* **2.** Humorous; jesting: *a playful discussion.* **—play′ful•ly** *adv.* **—play′ful•ness** *n.*

play•girl (plā′gûrl′) *n.* A woman who is devoted to the pursuit of pleasurable activities.

play•go•er (plā′gō′ər) *n.* A person who attends the theater.

play•ground (plā′ground′) *n.* An outdoor area for recreation and play, especially one having equipment such as seesaws and swings.

play•house (plā′hous′) *n.* **1.** A theater. **2.** A small house for children to play in. **3.** A child's toy house; a doll house.
play•ing card (plā′ĭng) *n.* A card marked with rank and suit and belonging to any of several decks used to play a wide variety of games.
play•mate (plā′māt′) *n.* A companion in play or recreation.
play•off (plā′ôf′ *or* plā′ŏf′) *n.* In sports, a game or series of games played to determine a championship or break a tie.
play•pen (plā′pĕn′) *n.* A portable enclosure in which a baby or a young child can be safely left to play.
play•room (plā′ro͞om′ *or* plā′ro͝om′) *n.* A room designed or set aside for play or recreation.
play•thing (plā′thĭng′) *n.* A thing to play with; a toy.
play•wright (plā′rīt′) *n.* A person who writes plays; a dramatist.
pla•za (plä′zə *or* plăz′ə) *n.* **1.** A public square or similar open area in a town or city. **2.** A shopping center. [First written down in 1836 in American English, from Spanish, from Latin *platea,* broad street.]
plea (plē) *n.* **1.** An appeal or urgent request; an entreaty: *a plea for help.* **2.** An excuse; a pretext. **3.** In law, the answer of the accused to the charges: *a plea of guilty.*
plea-bar•gain (plē′bär′gən) *intr.v.* **plea-bar•gained, plea-bar•gain•ing, plea-bar•gains.** In law, to make an agreement in which a defendant pleads guilty to a lesser charge and the prosecutor in return drops more serious charges.
plead (plēd) *v.* **plead•ed** or **pled** (plĕd), **plead•ing, pleads.** —*intr.* **1.** To appeal earnestly; beg: *They were pleading with him to return.* **2.** To put forward a plea in a court of law: *She pleaded guilty.* —*tr.* **1.** To put forward as a defense or an excuse: *plead illness for being absent.* **2.** To argue (a case) in a court of law. [First written down about 1250 in Middle English and spelled *plaiden,* from Medieval Latin *placitāre,* to appeal to the law.] —**plead′er** *n.*
pleas•ant (plĕz′ənt) *adj.* **pleas•ant•er, pleas•ant•est. 1.** Giving or affording pleasure or enjoyment; agreeable: *a pleasant climate; a pleasant aroma.* **2.** Pleasing in manner, behavior, or appearance: *a pleasant person; a pleasant disposition.* **3.** Fair and comfortable: *pleasant weather.* —**pleas′ant•ly** *adv.* —**pleas′ant•ness** *n.*
pleas•ant•ry (plĕz′ən trē) *n., pl.* **pleas•ant•ries. 1.** A humorous remark or act; a jest. **2.** A polite social remark; a civility.
please (plēz) *v.* **pleased, pleas•ing, pleas•es.** —*tr.* **1.** To give (someone or something) pleasure or satisfaction: *The island pleased the sightseers.* **2.** To be the will or desire of: *May it please the court.* —*intr.* **1.** To give satisfaction or pleasure; be agreeable. **2.** To have the will or desire; wish: *do exactly as they please.* —*adv.* If it is your desire or pleasure; if you please: *Please stand back.* [First written down about 1303 in Middle English and spelled *plesen,* from Latin *placēre.*]
pleas•ing (plē′zĭng) *adj.* Giving pleasure or enjoyment; agreeable: *a pleasing scent.* —**pleas′ing•ly** *adv.* —**pleas′ing•ness** *n.*
pleas•ur•a•ble (plĕzh′ər ə bəl) *adj.* Agreeable; gratifying: *a pleasurable experience.* —**pleas′ur•a•ble•ness** *n.* —**pleas′ur•a•bly** *adv.*
pleas•ure (plĕzh′ər) *n.* **1.** The state or feeling of being pleased or gratified: *She smiled with pleasure.* **2.** A source of enjoyment or delight: *Reading is his chief pleasure.* **3.** Amusement, diversion, or worldly enjoyment: *grew tired of living for pleasure.* **4.** One's preference or wish: *What is your pleasure?*
pleat (plēt) *n.* A flat fold in cloth made by doubling the material on itself and pressing or sewing it in place. —*tr.v.* **pleat•ed, pleat•ing, pleats.** To form pleats in; arrange in pleats: *pleat a ruffle.*
plebe (plēb) also **pleb** (plĕb) *n.* A first year student at the U.S. Military Academy or the U.S. Naval Academy.
ple•be•ian (plĭ bē′ən) *adj.* **1.** Of or relating to the common people of ancient Rome. **2.** Coarse or vulgar: *plebeian tastes.* —*n.* **1.** One of the common people of ancient Rome. **2.** A person considered coarse or vulgar.
pleb•i•scite (plĕb′ĭ sīt′) *n.* A direct vote by an entire people: *She was elected president by plebiscite.*
plec•trum (plĕk′trəm) *n., pl.* **plec•trums** or **plec•tra** (plĕk′trə). A small thin piece of metal, plastic, bone, or similar material, used to pluck the strings of a musical instrument such as a guitar; a pick.
pled (plĕd) *v.* A past tense and a past participle of **plead.**
pledge (plĕj) *n.* **1.** A formal vow; a solemn promise: *made a pledge to do their duty.* **2.a.** Something considered as security to guarantee payment of a debt or an obligation: *a necklace left as a pledge for a loan.* **b.** The condition of something considered as such security: *Her jewels were left in pledge.* **3.** A token or sign: *They exchanged rings as a pledge of devotion.* **4.** A toast to someone. **5.** Someone who has been accepted for membership in a fraternity or similar organization but has not yet been initiated. —*tr.v.* **pledged, pledg•ing, pledg•es. 1.** To guarantee by a solemn promise or vow: *pledged their support.* See Synonyms at **vow. 2.** To bind by a solemn promise or vow: *They pledged themselves to secrecy.* **3.** To deposit as security; pawn: *He pledged his watch for a loan.* **4.a.** To promise to join (a fraternity or similar organization). **b.** To accept as a member of such an organization. **5.** To drink a toast to. [First written down in 1348 in Middle English and spelled *plegge,* from Old French *plege.*]
Pleis•to•cene (plī′stə sēn′) *adj.* Of, belonging to, or being the geologic time of the earlier of the two epochs of the Quaternary Period. During the Pleistocene, glaciers alternately advanced and receded in northern land areas and the first human beings appeared. See table at **geologic time.** —*n.* The Pleistocene Epoch or its series of rocks. [First written down in 1839 in Modern English : Greek *pleistos,* most + Greek *kainos,* recent.]
ple•na (plē′nə *or* plĕn′ə) *n.* A plural of **plenum.**
ple•na•ry (plē′nə rē *or* plĕn′ə rē) *adj.* **1.** Complete in all aspects; full; absolute: *plenary powers.* **2.** Fully attended by all qualified members: *a plenary meeting of the council.*
plen•i•po•ten•ti•ar•y (plĕn′ə pə tĕn′shē ĕr′ē *or* plĕn′ə pə tĕn′shə rē) *adj.* Invested with full powers. —*n., pl.* **plen•i•po•ten•ti•ar•ies.** A diplomatic agent, such as an ambassador, having full powers to represent his or her government.
plen•i•tude (plĕn′ĭ to͞od′ *or* plĕn′ĭ tyo͞od′) *n.* **1.** A large amount; an abundance: *There was a plenitude of vegetables that summer.* **2.** The quality of being abundant or full.
plen•te•ous (plĕn′tē əs) *adj.* Abundant; plentiful. —**plen′te•ous•ly** *adv.* —**plen′te•ous•ness** *n.*
plen•ti•ful (plĕn′tĭ fəl) *adj.* **1.** In abundant supply; ample: *plentiful food.* **2.** Producing or yielding in abundance: *a plentiful land.* —**plen′ti•ful•ly** *adv.* —**plen′ti•ful•ness** *n.*
plen•ty (plĕn′tē) *n.* **1.** An adequate or ample amount or supply: *plenty of time.* **2.** A large amount or number; a lot: *plenty of work to do.* **3.** General abundance or prosperity: *a time of plenty.* —*adj.* Ample; more than enough: *There's plenty room*

player piano

ă	pat	oi	boy
ā	pay	ou	out
âr	care	o͝o	took
ä	father	o͞o	boot
ĕ	pet	ŭ	cut
ē	be	ûr	urge
ĭ	pit	th	thin
ī	pie	*th*	this
îr	pier	hw	whoop
ŏ	pot	zh	vision
ō	toe	ə	about
ô	paw	N	*French* bon

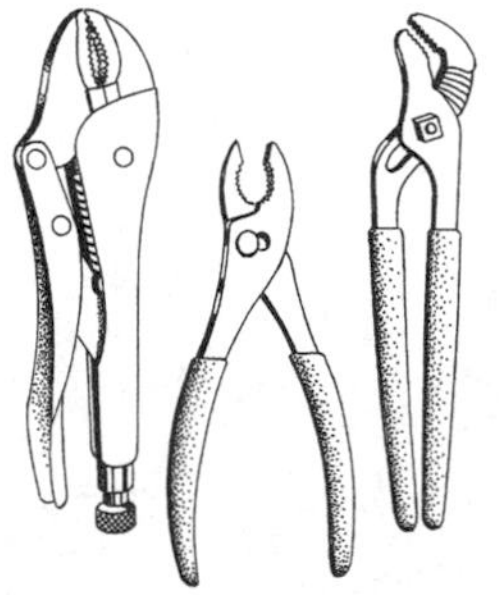

pliers
Left to right: Locking-grip, slip-joint, and multiple-joint pliers

plinth

plow

here. —*adv. Informal.* Excessively; very: *They were plenty hungry.*

ple•num (plē′nəm *or* plĕn′əm) *n., pl.* **ple•nums** or **ple•na** (plē′nə *or* plĕn′ə). **1.** A meeting with all members present. **2.** An enclosure in which air or other gas is kept at a pressure greater than that outside.

ple•si•o•saur (plē′sē ə sôr′) *n.* A large extinct water reptile having a long neck and four flippers. Plesiosaurs lived millions of years ago at about the same time as the dinosaurs. [First written down in 1825 in Modern English and spelled *Plesiosaurus* : Greek *plēsios*, near + New Latin *saurus*, lizard.]

pleu•ra (plo͝or′ə) *n., pl.* **pleu•rae** (plo͝or′ē). A membranous sac that envelops each lung and lines the chest cavity. —**pleu′ral** *adj.*

pleu•ri•sy (plo͝or′ĭ sē) *n.* Inflammation of the pleura, often accompanied by chills, fever, and painful breathing and coughing.

Plex•i•glas (plĕk′sĭ glăs′). A trademark for a light strong transparent plastic.

plex•us (plĕk′səs) *n., pl.* **plexus** or **plex•us•es.** A network, as of nerves or blood vessels in the body.

pli•a•ble (plī′ə bəl) *adj.* **1.** Easily bent or shaped; flexible: *pliable strips of wood.* **2.** Easily influenced or convinced: *a pliable mind.* —**pli′a•bil′i•ty, pli′a•ble•ness** *n.* —**pli′a•bly** *adv.*

pli•ant (plī′ənt) *adj.* **1.** Easily bent or shaped; pliable: *pliant materials.* **2.** Readily changing to fit conditions or to suit others: *He has a pliant personality.* —**pli′an•cy** *n.* —**pli′ant•ly** *adv.*

plied (plīd) *v.* Past tense and past participle of **ply**[2].

pli•ers (plī′ərz) *pl.n. (used with a plural verb).* A tool with two parts attached together in a manner similar to a pair of scissors, used for holding, bending, or cutting.

plies[1] (plīz) *n.* Plural of **ply**[1].

plies[2] (plīz) *v.* Third person singular present tense of **ply**[2].

plight[1] (plīt) *n.* A situation of difficulty or peril. [First written down about 1175 in Middle English and spelled *plihte*, from Anglo-Norman *plit*, fold, wrinkle, situation, from Latin *plicāre*, to fold.]

plight[2] (plīt) *tr.v.* **plight•ed, plight•ing, plights.** To promise or bind by solemn pledge. —***idiom.*** **plight (one's) troth. 1.** To become engaged to marry. **2.** To give one's solemn oath. [First written down before 1016 in Old English and spelled *pligtan*, to endanger, put at risk, from *pliht*, danger, risk.]

plinth (plĭnth) *n.* A block or slab upon which a pedestal, column, or statue is placed.

Pli•o•cene (plī′ə sēn′) *adj.* Of, belonging to, or being the geologic time of the last of the five epochs of the Tertiary Period. During the Pliocene, distinctly modern plants and animals appeared. See table at **geologic time.** —*n.* The Pliocene Epoch or its series of rocks. [First written down in 1833 in Modern English : Greek *pleiōn*, more + Greek *kainos*, recent.]

plod (plŏd) *intr.v.* **plod•ded, plod•ding, plods. 1.** To walk heavily or with great effort: *They plodded wearily home through the twilight.* **2.** To work or act slowly and wearily: *He plodded through his lessons.* —**plod′der** *n.*

plop (plŏp) *v.* **plopped, plop•ping, plops.** —*intr.* **1.** To fall with a sound like that of an object falling into water: *He let the dough plop down into the sink.* **2.** To let one's body drop heavily or wearily: *She plopped into the chair.* —*tr.* To place or drop so as to make a plopping sound: *He plopped the tomatoes onto the plate.* —*n.* A plopping sound: *The pebble fell with a plop into the pool.*

plot (plŏt) *n.* **1.a.** A small piece of ground: *a plot of good land.* **b.** A measured area of land; a lot. **2.** A ground plan, as for a building; a diagram. **3.** The series of actions or events in a novel, movie, or play. **4.** A secret plan to accomplish an often illegal purpose: *a plot against the queen.* —*tr.v.* **plot•ted, plot•ting, plots. 1.** To mark, note, or represent, as on a chart or map: *plotted the ship's course.* **2.** To plan or scheme secretly or deviously: *plot revenge.* —**plot′ter** *n.*

plough (plou) *n. & v.* Variant of **plow.**

plov•er (plŭv′ər *or* plō′vər) *n., pl.* **plover** or **plov•ers.** Any of various small shore birds having short tails and short bills.

plow also **plough** (plou) *n.* **1.** A farm implement consisting of a heavy blade at the end of a beam, drawn either by animals or by a motor vehicle, used for breaking up soil and cutting furrows in preparation for sowing. **2.** A device or vehicle of similar function, as a snowplow. —*v.* **plowed, plow•ing, plows** also **ploughed, plough•ing, ploughs.** —*tr.* **1.** To break and turn over (soil) with a plow. **2.** To make (one's way) steadily and with effort: *plowed her way through the deep snow.* **3.** To remove snow from with a snowplow: *plowed the streets after the blizzard.* —*intr.* To advance or progress steadily and with effort: *The boat plowed through the waves.* —***idiom.*** **plow into.** *Informal.* To strike with force: *The truck plowed into the fence.* [First written down before 1100 in Old English and spelled *plōh.*]

plow•man (plou′mən) *n.* A man who operates a plow.

plow•share (plou′shâr′) *n.* The cutting blade of a plow.

ploy (ploi) *n.* A cunning action designed to obtain advantage over an opponent.

pluck (plŭk) *tr.v.* **plucked, pluck•ing, plucks. 1.** To detach by pulling with the fingers; pick: *pluck a flower.* **2.** To pull out the feathers or hair of: *pluck a chicken.* **3.** To pull abruptly; tug: *pluck a sleeve.* **4.** To sound (a string or strings of an instrument) by stretching and releasing, as with the fingers or a plectrum. —*n.* **1.** A tug; a pull. **2.** Courage and daring; spirit.

pluck•y (plŭk′ē) *adj.* **pluck•i•er, pluck•i•est.** Showing spirit and courage in difficult circumstances.

plug (plŭg) *n.* **1.** A piece of wood, cork, or other material, used to fill a hole. **2.** A device connected to the end of a wire or cable and fitting into a matching socket to make an electrical connection. **3.** A spark plug. **4.** A hydrant. **5.** A flat cake of pressed or twisted tobacco. **6.** *Slang.* Something considered inferior or defective, especially an old horse. **7.** *Informal.* A favorable public mention of something, especially on television or radio. —*v.* **plugged, plug•ging, plugs.** —*tr.* **1.** To fill (a hole) tightly with or as if with a plug or stopper; stop up. **2.** *Informal.* To mention favorably; advertise: *plug a new brand of soap.* —*intr. Informal.* To work doggedly and persistently: *plug away at a job.* —***idioms.*** **plug in. 1.** To connect (an appliance) to an electrical outlet. **2.** To function by being connected to an electrical outlet: *a laptop computer that also plugs in.* **plug into.** To connect or be connected to in the manner of an electrical appliance: *This CD player plugs into the stereo. The computer plugs into a data bank.* —**plug′ger** *n.*

plum (plŭm) *n.* **1.a.** The fruit of any of several small trees, having smooth dark purple skin, juicy flesh, and a hard-shelled pit. **b.** A tree that bears such fruit. **2.** A raisin in a pudding or pie. **3.** A dark purple. **4.** Something very much wanted or envied, such as a job that pays well. [First written down about 700 in Old English and spelled *plūme*, from Latin *prūnum.*]

❑ *These sound alike:* **plum, plumb** (weight).

plum•age (plo͞o′mĭj) *n.* The covering of feathers on a bird.

plumb (plŭm) *n.* A weight hung from the end of a cord, used to measure water depth or test vertical alignment. *—adv.* **1.** Vertically; straight up and down: *a post that stands plumb.* **2.** *Informal.* Completely; utterly: *plumb wrong.* *—adj.* **1.** Exactly vertical: *a plumb wall.* **2.** *Informal.* Utter; sheer: *a plumb fool.* *—tr.v.* **plumbed, plumb•ing, plumbs. 1.** To test the depth or alignment of with or as if with a plumb. **2.** To examine closely; probe into. [First written down before 1325 in Middle English and spelled *plum,* from Latin *plumbum,* lead.]
❑ *These sound alike:* **plumb, plum** (fruit).

plumb bob *n.* A usually conical piece of metal attached to the end of a plumb line.

plumb•er (plŭm′ər) *n.* A person who installs and repairs pipes and plumbing.

plumb•ing (plŭm′ĭng) *n.* **1.** The pipes, fixtures, and other equipment used in a system through which a liquid or gas flows. **2.** The work or occupation of a plumber.

plumb line *n.* A line from which a weight is hung, used to measure depth, as of water, or to determine whether something is vertical.

plume (plo͞om) *n.* **1.** A feather, especially a large or showy one used for decoration. **2.** A large feather or cluster of feathers worn as an ornament or symbol of rank, as on a helmet. **3.** Something resembling a large feather: *A plume of smoke rose from the chimney.* *—tr.v.* **plumed, plum•ing, plumes. 1.** To decorate with or as if with plumes. **2.** To smooth (feathers); preen. [First written down about 1399 in Middle English, from Latin *plūma.*]

plum•met (plŭm′ĭt) *intr.v.* **plum•met•ed, plum•met•ing, plum•mets.** To drop straight down; plunge: *A rock plummeted down from the cliff.*

plump¹ (plŭmp) *adj.* **plump•er, plump•est.** Rounded and full in form: *a plump figure; a plump peach.* *—tr. & intr.v.* **plumped, plump•ing, plumps.** To make or become plump: *He plumped up the pillow. The child plumped out as she grew.* [First written down in 1481 in Middle English and spelled *plump,* blunt, dull, probably from Middle Low German *plomp,* blunt, thick.] **—plump′ly** *adv.* **—plump′ness** *n.*

plump² (plŭmp) *v.* **plumped, plump•ing, plumps.** *—intr.* To drop heavily or abruptly; plop: *She plumped down on the grass.* *—tr.* To place or throw heavily or abruptly: *plumped the books onto the table.* *—n.* **1.** A heavy abrupt fall or impact. **2.** The dull sound of a heavy abrupt fall. *—adv.* With a heavy or abrupt drop: *He fell down plump on the ground.* [First written down before 1300 in Middle English and spelled *plumten,* to immerse quickly, perhaps from Middle Low German.]

plum pudding *n.* A sweet spiced pudding made with flour, suet, raisins, and currants.

plum•y (plo͞o′mē) *adj.* **plum•i•er, plum•i•est. 1.** Consisting of or covered with feathers. **2.** Resembling a feather or plume.

plun•der (plŭn′dər) *tr.v.* **plun•dered, plun•der•ing, plun•ders.** To take booty or valuables from; pillage; rob: *Pirates plundered the coastal city.* *—n.* **1.** The taking of property by force. **2.** Property stolen by force or by fraud; booty: *digging to hide their plunder.* **—plun′der•er** *n.*

plunge (plŭnj) *v.* **plunged, plung•ing, plung•es.** *—tr.* **1.** To thrust, throw, or place forcefully or suddenly into something: *plunged the pitchfork into the hay.* **2.** To cause to enter suddenly or violently into a situation or activity: *events that plunged the world into war.* *—intr.* **1.** To throw oneself suddenly or energetically into a body of water: *He plunged into the lake.* **2.** To throw oneself wholeheartedly into an activity: *She plunged into her work.* **3.** To descend steeply or sharply; fall: *The cliff plunged into the sea.* **4.** To rush or move forward into or toward something quickly and rapidly: *animals plunging through the undergrowth.* *—n.* **1.** The act of plunging: *a plunge into work.* **2.** A swim: *an early morning plunge.* ***—idiom.*** **take the plunge.** *Informal.* To begin an unfamiliar venture, especially after hesitating.

plung•er (plŭn′jər) *n.* **1.** A device consisting of a suction cup attached to the end of a stick, used to clean out clogged drains and pipes. **2.** A machine part, such as a piston, that operates with a repeated thrusting or plunging movement.

plunk (plŭngk) *v.* **plunked, plunk•ing, plunks.** *—tr.* **1.** *Informal.* To throw or place heavily or abruptly: *He plunked the nickel on the table.* **2.** To strum or pluck (the strings of a musical instrument). *—intr.* **1.** To drop or sink heavily or wearily; plop: *They plunked down on the bench.* **2.** To make a short, hollow, twanging sound. *—n.* **1.** A short, hollow, twanging sound. **2.** A heavy blow or hit.

plu•per•fect (plo͞o pûr′fĭkt) *adj.* Of or relating to the pluperfect tense. *—n.* The pluperfect tense.

pluperfect tense *n.* A verb tense that expresses action completed before a specified or implied past time. In English the pluperfect tense is formed with the past participle of a verb and the auxiliary *had,* as *had learned* in the sentence *She had learned to drive before the month was over.*

plu•ral (plo͝or′əl) *adj.* **1.** Relating to or composed of more than one. **2.** In grammar, of or relating to the form of a word that designates more than one. *—n.* The plural form of a word. For example, *birds* is the plural of *bird,* and *children* is the plural of *child.* [First written down about 1378 in Middle English and spelled *plurel,* from Latin *plūrālis,* from *plūs,* more.] **—plu′ral•ly** *adv.*

plu•ral•i•ty (plo͞o răl′ĭ tē) *n., pl.* **plu•ral•i•ties. 1.** The condition of being plural. **2.a.** In a contest of more than two candidates, the number of votes cast for the winner if this number is less than half of the total votes cast. **b.** The number by which the vote of a winning candidate is more than that of the closest opponent.

plus (plŭs) *conj.* **1.** Added to: *Two plus three equals five.* **2.** Increased by; along with: *wages plus bonuses.* *—adj.* **1.** Greater than zero; positive. **2.** Of or indicating an electric charge that is like that of a proton and unlike that of an electron. **3.** Added or extra: *a plus benefit.* **4.** Slightly more than: *a grade of B plus.* *—n., pl.* **plus•es** or **plus•ses. 1.** The plus sign. **2.** A positive number. **3.** A favorable factor or condition.

plush (plŭsh) *n.* A fabric resembling velvet but having a thicker deeper pile. *—adj.* **plush•er, plush•est. 1.** Made of or covered with plush: *a plush sofa.* **2.** Luxurious; elegant: *a plush restaurant.*

plush•y (plŭsh′ē) *adj.* **plush•i•er, plush•i•est. 1.** Resembling plush in texture. **2.** Overly luxurious: *a plushy office.*

plus sign *n.* The symbol (+), as in 2 + 2 = 4, that is used to show addition or a positive quantity.

Plu•to (plo͞o′tō) *n.* **1.** In Roman mythology, the god of the dead and the ruler of the underworld, identified with the Greek Hades. **2.** The ninth planet from the sun at a mean distance of 3.7 billion miles (6.0 billion kilometers), and a mean diameter about one-half that of Earth.

plu•toc•ra•cy (plo͞o tŏk′rə sē) *n., pl.* **plu•toc•ra•cies. 1.** Government by the wealthy. **2.** A wealthy class that controls a government. **3.** A government or state ruled by the wealthy. **—plu′to•crat′ic** *adj.*

Plu•to•ni•an (plo͞o tō′nē ən) also **Plu•ton•ic** (plo͞o tŏn′ĭk) *adj.* **1.** Of or relating to the god Pluto

plum

ă	pat	oi	boy
ā	pay	ou	out
âr	care	o͝o	took
ä	father	o͞o	boot
ĕ	pet	ŭ	cut
ē	be	ûr	urge
ĭ	pit	th	thin
ī	pie	*th*	this
îr	pier	hw	whoop
ŏ	pot	zh	vision
ō	toe	ə	about
ô	paw	N	*French* bon

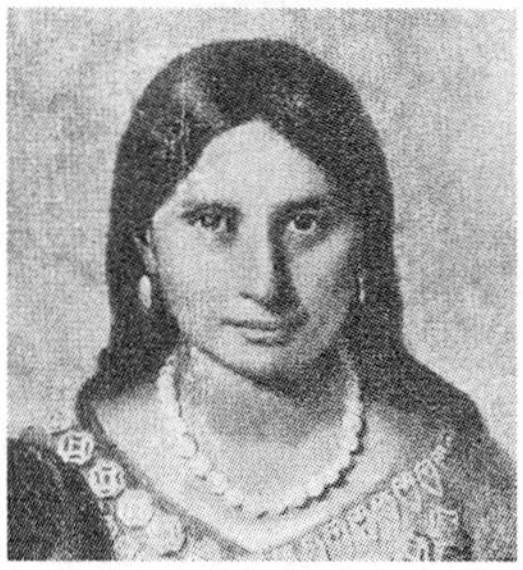
Pocahontas

Edgar Allan Poe

or to the underworld. **2.** Of or relating to the planet Pluto.

plu•to•ni•um (plōō **tō′**nē əm) *n. Symbol* **Pu** A naturally radioactive, silvery metallic element that occurs in trace quantities in uranium ores and is used as a source of energy in nuclear reactors. It is highly poisonous. Atomic number 94. See table at **element.**

plu•vi•al (**plōō′**vē əl) *adj.* **1.** Of or relating to rain; rainy. **2.** Caused by rain.

ply[1] (plī) *n., pl.* **plies** (plīz). **1.** A layer or thickness, as of folded cloth or of wood. **2.** One of the strands twisted together to make yarn, rope, or thread: *three-ply yarn.* [First written down in 1532 in Modern English, from Latin *plicāre*, to fold.]

ply[2] (plī) *tr.v.* **plied** (plīd), **ply•ing, plies** (plīz). **1.** To use or handle (a tool); wield: *ply a broom in sweeping.* **2.** To engage in (a trade or task); perform regularly: *ply the baker's trade.* **3.** To traverse or sail over regularly: *Convoys plied the seas.* **4.** To keep supplying or offering to: *plying her with candy.* [First written down about 1380 in Middle English and spelled *plien*, from *applien*, to apply.]

Plym•outh (**plĭm′**əth). A town of southeast Massachusetts on **Plymouth Bay,** an inlet of the Atlantic Ocean, southeast of Boston. Founded in 1620 by Pilgrims, it was the center of **Plymouth Colony.** Population, 45,608.

ply•wood (**plī′**wŏŏd′) *n.* A building material made of layers of wood glued together, usually with the grains of adjoining layers at right angles.

Pm The symbol for the element **promethium.**

P.M. also **p.m.** *abbr.* An abbreviation of post meridiem.

pneu•mat•ic (nōō **măt′**ĭk *or* nyōō **măt′**ĭk) *adj.* **1.** Of or relating to air or another gas: *pneumatic pressure.* **2.** Filled with or operated by compressed air: *a pneumatic drill.*

pneu•mo•nia (nōō **mōn′**yə *or* nyōō **mōn′**yə) *n.* Any of several diseases, caused by bacteria or viruses, in which the lungs become inflamed. [First written down in 1603 in Modern English, from Greek *pneumonia*, lung disease, from *pleumōn*, lung.]

Po The symbol for the element **polonium.**

PO or **P.O.** *abbr.* An abbreviation of post office.

poach[1] (pōch) *tr.v.* **poached, poach•ing, poach•es.** To cook (eggs or fish, for example) in a liquid that is gently boiling or simmering. [First written down about 1450 in Middle English and spelled *pocchen*, from Old French *poche*, pocket, bag, of Germanic origin.] **—poach′er** *n.*

poach[2] (pōch) *v.* **poached, poach•ing, poach•es.** *—tr.* **1.** To trespass on (a wildlife preserve or private property) in order to hunt or fish. **2.** To take (fish or game) from a wildlife preserve or private property. *—intr.* **1.** To trespass on another's property in order to take fish or game. **2.** To take fish or game illegally. [First written down in 1528 in Modern English, from Old French *pochier*, to poke, gouge, of Germanic origin.] **—poach′er** *n.*

Po•ca•hon•tas (pō′kə **hŏn′**təs). 1595?–1617. The daughter of Powhatan, who aided the English colonists at Jamestown and is said to have saved Captain John Smith from execution.

pock (pŏk) *n.* **1.** A pus-filled swelling of the skin caused by smallpox or a similar disease. **2.** A mark or scar left by such a swelling; a pockmark.

pock•et (**pŏk′**ĭt) *n.* **1.** A small pouch, open at the top, sewn into or onto a garment and used to hold things. **2.** A receptacle, cavity, container, or pouch that resembles a pocket in appearance or function. **3.** A small isolated or protected area or group: *pockets of civilization along the frontier.* **4.** A small cavity in the earth containing ore. *—adj.* Suitable for being carried in one's pocket: *a pocket watch.* *—tr.v.* **pock•et•ed, pock•et•ing, pock•ets. 1.** To place in or as if in a pocket: *pocket a dime.* **2.** To take possession of dishonestly: *pocket the petty cash.* ***—idioms.*** **in (one's) pocket.** In one's power, influence, or possession. **line (one's) pockets.** To make a profit, especially by illegitimate means. [First written down in 1350 in Middle English and spelled *pokete*, pouch, small bag, from Old North French *poke*, bag, sack, of Germanic origin.]

pock•et•book (**pŏk′**ĭt bŏŏk′) *n.* **1.** A container used to hold money, papers, cosmetics, and other small articles; a handbag. **2.** A container for paper money or coins that is small enough to fit into a pocket or handbag. **3.** A supply of money: *too expensive for our pocketbook.* **4.** A small usually paperbound book.

pock•et•ful (**pŏk′**ĭt fŏŏl′) *n., pl.* **pock•et•fuls** or **pock•ets•ful** (**pŏk′**ĭts fŏŏl′). The amount that a pocket will hold.

pock•et•knife (**pŏk′**ĭt nīf′) *n.* A small knife with a blade or blades that fold into the handle.

pock•et-sized (**pŏk′**ĭt sīzd′) or **pock•et•size** (**pŏk′**ĭt sīz′) *adj.* **1.** Of a size suitable to be carried in a pocket: *a pocket-sized radio.* **2.** Small.

pocket veto *n.* The President's veto of a bill that has been presented within ten days of Congress adjourning a session by the President's retaining the bill unsigned until Congress adjourns.

pock•mark (**pŏk′**märk′) *n.* A pit or scar left on the skin as a result of smallpox or a similar disease. **—pock′marked′** *adj.*

po•co (**pō′**kō) *adv.* In music, to a slight degree or amount.

pod (pŏd) *n.* A seed case, as of a pea, bean, or certain other plants, that splits open to release the enclosed seeds.

–pod or **–pode** *suff.* A suffix that means a number or kind of feet: *pseudopod.*

Pod•go•ri•ca (**pŏd′**gə rēt′sə). Formerly (1946–1992) **Ti•to•grad** (**tē′**tō grad′). The capital of Montenegro, in the southeast part near the Albanian border. Population, 73,000.

po•di•a (**pō′**dē ə) *n.* A plural of **podium.**

po•di•a•try (pə **dī′**ə trē) *n.* The branch of medicine that deals with the study and treatment of foot ailments. **—po•di′a•trist** *n.*

po•di•um (**pō′**dē əm) *n., pl.* **po•di•a** (**pō′**dē ə) or **po•di•ums.** An elevated platform, as for an orchestra conductor or a lecturer. [First written down in 1789 in Modern English, from Greek *podion*, base, from *pous*, foot.]

Poe (pō), **Edgar Allan.** 1809–1849. American writer known especially for his short stories and poems, such as "The Raven" (1845).

po•em (**pō′**əm) *n.* A verbal composition that conveys experiences, thoughts, or feelings in a vivid and imaginative way and is characterized by the use of literary techniques such as metaphor, rhyme, and meter. [First written down in 1548 in Modern English, from Greek *poiēma*, from *poiein*, to create.]

po•e•sy (**pō′**ĭ zē *or* **pō′**ĭ sē) *n., pl.* **po•e•sies.** Poetry; verse.

po•et (**pō′**ĭt) *n.* A writer of poems.

po•et•ess (**pō′**ĭ tĭs) *n.* A woman who is a poet.

po•et•ic (pō **ĕt′**ĭk) *adj.* **1.** Of or relating to poetry: *poetic works.* **2.** Having a quality or style characteristic of poetry: *poetic language.* **3.** Of, relating to, or befitting a poet: *poetic thoughts.*

po•et•i•cal (pō **ĕt′**ĭ kəl) *adj.* **1.** Poetic. **2.** Highly fanciful or idealized: *poetical notions about life in the country.* **—po•et′i•cal•ly** *adv.*

poetic justice *n.* The reward of someone who does good, or the punishment of someone who does evil, especially in an appropriate manner: *It was only* *poetic justice that the villain's downfall should come about as a result of his own schemes.*

poet laureate *n., pl.* **poets laureate** or **poet laureates.** **1.** A poet appointed for life by the British sovereign as a member of the royal household and formerly expected to write poems celebrating occasions of national importance. **2.** A poet appointed to a similar position of honor, as in the United States.

po•et•ry (pō′ĭ trē) *n.* **1.** The art or work of a poet. **2.** Poems regarded as a divison of literature: *Our class will be reading poetry for the next two weeks.* **3.** The poems of a given author, country, time period, or kind: *Renaissance poetry.* **4.** A quality that pleases or stirs the imagination; beauty.

po•go stick (pō′gō) *n.* A strong stick with footrests and a heavy spring set into the bottom end, used to propel oneself along the ground by hopping.

po•grom (pə grŏm′ *or* pō′grəm) *n.* An organized and often officially sanctioned massacre or persecution of a minority group, especially one conducted against Jews.

poi (poi) *n.* A Hawaiian food consisting of a starchy fermented paste made from cooked taro root. [First written down in 1823 in Modern English and spelled *poe*, from Hawaiian *poi.*]

poign•ant (poin′yənt) *adj.* **1.** Keenly distressing or painful: *poignant grief.* **2.** Deeply moving; touching: *poignant memories.* **3.** Piercing; incisive; astute: *poignant criticism.* **—poign′an•cy** *n.* **—poign′ant•ly** *adv.*

poin•set•ti•a (poin sĕt′ē ə *or* poin sĕt′ə) *n.* A tropical American plant having small yellowish flowers surrounded by showy, usually bright-red leaves that resemble petals. [First written down in 1836 in Modern English, after Joel Roberts *Poinsett* (1779–1851), American diplomat.]

point (point) *n.* **1.** The sharp or tapered end of something: *the point of a pencil.* **2.** A tapering piece of land that extends into a body of water; a peninsula, cape, or promontory. **3.** A dot or period, as one used to separate the fractional and integral parts of a numeral. **4.** A geometric object having no dimensions and no property other than its location. **5.** Any of the 32 directions indicated on a mariner's compass. **6.** A position or place: *the highest point in the county.* **7.** A specified degree or condition: *the boiling point of water.* **8.** A specific moment in time: *At that point he noticed someone running away.* **9.** The important or essential part or idea: *the point of a story.* **10.** A purpose or goal: *What was the point of her visit?* **11.** A separate item or element: *Let's examine the list point by point.* **12.** A distinctive quality or characteristic: *Making friends quickly is one of his best points.* **13.** A single unit in the score of a game, contest, or test. **14.** In printing, a unit of type size equal to about 1/72 of an inch. **15.** A unit equal to one dollar and used to state the current prices of stocks and commodities. *—v.* **point•ed, point•ing, points.** *—tr.* **1.** To direct or aim: *pointed the flashlight down the road.* **2.** To indicate (a direction or position): *She pointed the way to the river.* **3.** To provide with a point; sharpen: *He pointed the pencil.* *—intr.* **1.** To direct attention toward something with or as if with the finger: *He pointed to the tree.* **2.** To be turned or directed, as in a given direction: *The compass needle pointed north.* **3.** To be an indication of something, especially of a likely event: *All signs point to an improvement in the economy.* **4.** To show the location of animals hunted as game by standing still and facing in that direction. Used of a hunting dog. ***—idioms.*** **beside the point.** Irrelevant to the matter at hand. **make a point of.** To consider or treat (an action of activity) as indispensable: *We made a point of being on time.* **to the point.** Concerning or with relevance to the matter at hand. [First written down before 1200 in Middle English, from Latin *pŭnctum.*]

point-blank (point′blăngk′) *adj.* **1.** Aimed straight at a mark or target: *a point-blank shot.* **2.** Very close to a mark or target: *at point-blank range.* **3.** Straightforward; blunt: *a point-blank answer.* *—adv.* **1.** With a direct aim; straight: *He fired point-blank.* **2.** Without hesitating; bluntly: *answered point-blank.*

point•ed (poin′tĭd) *adj.* **1.** Having a sharp or tapered end or part: *pointed leaves.* **2.** Cutting; piercing: *a pointed manner.* **3.** Clearly directed or aimed, as at a particular person: *a pointed remark.* **—point′ed•ly** *adv.* **—point′ed•ness** *n.*

point•er (poin′tər) *n.* **1.** A person or thing that directs, indicates, or points. **2.** A marker that indicates a number on a scale, as in a clock or meter. **3.** A long stick used for indicating something, as on a map or blackboard. **4.** Any of a breed of dog having a short smooth coat, often trained to point at game. **5.** A piece of advice: *pointers on buying rare stamps.*

point•less (point′lĭs) *adj.* Having no purpose, sense, or meaning: *a pointless regulation.* **—point′less•ly** *adv.* **—point′less•ness** *n.*

point of view *n., pl.* **points of view. 1.** A manner of viewing things; an attitude: *a liberal point of view.* **2.** A position from which something is observed or considered.

point•y (poin′tē) *adj.* **point•i•er, point•i•est.** Having an end tapering to a point.

poise (poiz) *v.* **poised, pois•ing, pois•es.** *—tr.* To balance or hold in equilibrium: *He poised the flashlight on the edge of the table.* *—intr.* **1.** To be balanced: *She poised on the end of the diving board.* **2.** To remain in one spot as if suspended: *A hummingbird poises over a flower.* *—n.* **1.** Balance; stability; equilibrium. **2.** A calm confident manner.

poi•son (poi′zən) *n.* **1.** A substance that causes injury, sickness, or death, especially by chemical means. **2.** Something that causes harm or destruction. *—tr.v.* **poi•soned, poi•son•ing, poi•sons. 1.** To kill or harm with poison. **2.** To put poison on or into: *poisoned arrows; poisoned the drink.* **3.** To have a harmful influence on: *Jealousy poisoned their minds.* *—adj.* Poisonous. **—poi′son•er** *n.*

poison ivy *n.* A shrubby or climbing plant that has small whitish berries and leaflets in groups of three and that can cause a severe itching skin rash if touched.

poison oak *n.* **1.** Either of two shrubs related to and resembling poison ivy and causing a similar skin rash. **2.** Poison ivy.

poi•son•ous (poi′zə nəs) *adj.* **1.** Capable of harming or killing, by or as if by poison. **2.** Containing poison. **3.** Full of ill will; malicious; malevolent: *poisonous remarks.* **—poi′son•ous•ly** *adv.* **—poi′son•ous•ness** *n.*

poison sumac *n.* A swamp shrub of the southeast United States, having compound leaves and greenish-white berries and causing an itching rash on contact with the skin.

poke[1] (pōk) *v.* **poked, pok•ing, pokes.** *—tr.* **1.** To push or jab at (someone), as with a finger or elbow: *poke someone in the ribs.* **2.** To thrust forward; push: *The otter poked its head out of the water.* **3.** To make by thrusting or jabbing: *poke a hole in the canvas.* **4.** To stir (a fire) with a poker or stick. *—intr.* **1.** To make thrusts or jabs, as with a stick. **2.** To pry or meddle; intrude: *poking into someone else's business.* **3.** To look or search in a leisurely manner: *I was just poking around the attic and came across this photograph.* **4.** To proceed in a

poinsettia

pointer
English pointer

ă	pat	oi	boy
ā	pay	ou	out
âr	care	o͝o	took
ä	father	o͞o	boot
ĕ	pet	ŭ	cut
ē	be	ûr	urge
ĭ	pit	th	thin
ī	pie	*th*	this
îr	pier	hw	whoop
ŏ	pot	zh	vision
ō	toe	ə	about
ô	paw	N	*French* bon

polar bear

polecat
European polecat

pole vault

slow or lazy manner: *The old jalopy is still poking along.* —*n.* A push, thrust, or jab. —***idiom.* poke fun at.** To make fun of; ridicule or tease. [First written down before 1300 in Middle English and spelled *puken.*]

poke[2] (pōk) *n.* A large bonnet with a projecting brim in front. [First written down in 1770 in Modern English, from *poke*, to thrust forward.]

poke[3] (pōk) *n.* A sack or bag. [First written down in 1228 in Middle English, probably from Old North French.]

pok•er[1] (pō′kər) *n.* A metal rod used to stir a fire.

pok•er[2] (pō′kər) *n.* Any of various card games played by two or more persons who bet on the value of their hands. [First written down in 1834 in American English.]

po•key (pō′kē) *n., pl.* **po•keys.** *Slang.* A jail.

pok•y also **poke•y** (pō′kē) *adj.* **pok•i•er, pok•i•est.** *Informal.* **1.** Not lively; dull; slow: *a poky little town.* **2.** Small and crowded: *a poky apartment.*

pol (pôl) *n. Informal.* A politician.

Po•land (pō′lənd). A country of central Europe north of Czech Republic and Slovakia on the Baltic Sea. It was unified in the 10th century, and its present boundaries date from the end of World War II. Capital, Warsaw. Population, 37,063,000.

po•lar (pō′lər) *adj.* **1.** Of, indicating, or measured in relation to a pole: *the polar region of a magnet.* **2.** Of, relating to, or near the North Pole or the South Pole: *a polar expedition.*

polar bear *n.* A large white bear of Arctic regions.

polar cap *n.* **1.** The mass of permanent ice that covers either of the earth's polar regions. **2.** The mass of frozen carbon dioxide and water that covers either polar region of Mars.

polar circle *n.* **1.** The Arctic Circle. **2.** The Antarctic Circle.

Po•lar•is (pə lăr′ĭs) *n.* A bright star near the North Pole of the celestial sphere.

po•lar•i•ty (pō lăr′ĭ tē) *n., pl.* **po•lar•i•ties. 1.** The condition of having, being aligned with, or directed toward poles, especially magnetic or electric poles. **2.** The condition of having contrary or opposite tendencies or qualities: *political polarity.*

po•lar•ize (pō′lə rīz′) *v.* **po•lar•ized, po•lar•iz•ing, po•lar•iz•es.** —*tr.* **1.** To cause polarity in; make polar. **2.** To cause the positive and negative electric charges in (a physical body or system) to become separated, either wholly or in part. **3.** To suppress electromagnetic vibrations partially or completely in certain directions so that the directions of electric and magnetic effects can be predicted. **4.** To set at opposite extremes, leaving no middle ground: *polarize public opinion.* —*intr.* To become polarized. **—po′lar•i•za′tion** (pō′lər ĭ zā′shən) *n.*

Po•lar•oid (pō′lə roid′). **1.** A trademark for a specially treated transparent plastic capable of polarizing light passing through it, used in optical devices to reduce glare. **2.** A trademark for a camera and film that produce instant photographs.

pole[1] (pōl) *n.* **1.** Either of the points at which an axis that passes through the center of a sphere intersects the surface of the sphere. **2.** Either of the points at which the earth's axis of rotation intersects the earth's surface; the North Pole or South Pole. **3.** A celestial pole. **4.** A magnetic pole. **5.** Either of a pair of oppositely charged electric terminals. **6.** Either extremity of the main axis of a nucleus, cell, or organism. **7.** The fixed point used as a reference in a system of polar coordinates. [First written down about 1380 in Middle English and spelled *pool*, from Greek *polos*, axis, sky.]

❑ *These sound alike:* **pole[1]** (point on an axis), **pole[2]** (rod), **poll** (voting).

pole[2] (pōl) *n.* **1.** A long slender rod: *a fishing pole.* **2.** An upright post: *a telephone pole.* —*tr.v.* **poled, pol•ing, poles.** To push or move along by using a pole: *pole a boat down the river.* [First written down about 1050 in Old English and spelled *pāl*, from Latin *pālus*, stake.]

❑ *These sound alike:* **pole[2]** (rod), **pole[1]** (point on an axis), **poll** (voting).

Pole (pōl) *n.* **1.** A native or inhabitant of Poland. **2.** A person of Polish descent.

pole•ax or **pole•axe** (pōl′ăks′) *n.* A weapon used in the Middle Ages, consisting of a long pole ending in an ax or a combination of an ax and a hammer.

pole•cat (pōl′kăt′) *n.* **1.** A mammal of Europe, Asia, and northern Africa, related to the weasel and having dark brown fur. **2.** A skunk.

po•lem•ic (pə lĕm′ĭk) *n.* A controversial argument, especially an attack on a specific doctrine or belief. —*adj.* Of or relating to a controversy, argument, or verbal attack. **—po•lem′i•cal•ly** *adv.*

pole•star (pōl′stär′) *n.* Polaris.

pole vault *n.* An athletic contest in which each participant leaps over a high crossbar using a long pole. **—pole′-vault′** *v.*

po•lice (pə lēs′) *n., pl.* **police. 1.** The department of government established to maintain order, enforce the law, and prevent and detect crime. **2.** *(used with a plural verb).* Police officers considered as a group. **3.** A body of persons having a similar function to a police force: *campus police.* —*tr.v.* **po•liced, po•lic•ing, po•lic•es. 1.** To control or keep in order with or as if with a police force. **2.** To clean or tidy up. [First written down in 1530 in Modern English, from Greek *politeia*, the state.]

police dog *n.* **1.** A dog trained to aid the police. **2.** A German shepherd.

police force *n.* A body of persons trained and authorized by a government to enforce laws, detect crimes, and keep order among the public.

po•lice•man (pə lēs′mən) *n.* A man who is a member of a police force.

police officer *n.* A member of a police force.

po•lice•wom•an (pə lēs′wo͝om′ən) *n.* A woman who is a member of a police force.

pol•i•cy[1] (pŏl′ĭ sē) *n., pl.* **pol•i•cies. 1.** A plan or course of action, as of a government or a business. **2.** A guiding principle or course of action considered prudent or helpful: *Honesty is the best policy.* [First written down about 1385 in Middle English and spelled *policie*, from Greek *politeia*, the state.]

pol•i•cy[2] (pŏl′ĭ sē) *n., pl.* **pol•i•cies.** A written contract of insurance, as for medical care. [First written down in 1565 in Modern English and spelled *police*, from Old Italian *polizza*, contract, from Greek *apodeixis*, proof.]

po•li•o (pō′lē ō′) *n.* Poliomyelitis.

po•li•o•my•e•li•tis (pō′lē ō mī′ə lī′tĭs) *n.* A contagious viral disease that occurs mainly in children, causing in its more severe forms damage to the central nervous system that results in paralysis and loss of muscle tissue.

pol•ish (pŏl′ĭsh) *v.* **pol•ished, pol•ish•ing, pol•ish•es.** —*tr.* **1.** To make smooth and shiny, as by rubbing, chemical action, or both: *polish silver.* **2.** To refine or perfect: *polish one's writing.* —*intr.* To become smooth or shiny by or as if by being rubbed. —*n.* **1.** Smoothness and shininess of a surface or finish. **2.** A substance containing chemicals or an abrasive material for smoothing or shining a surface. **3.** A high degree of refinement: *Her performance shows polish.* —***idiom.* polish off.** *Informal.* To finish or dispose of quickly and easily: *polish off a meal.* **—pol′ish•er** *n.*

Po•lish (pō′lĭsh) *adj.* Of or relating to Poland, the

Poles, or their language. —*n.* The Slavic language of the Poles.

pol•ished (pŏl′ĭsht) *adj.* **1.** Made or naturally smooth and shiny: *a polished table; a polished stone.* **2.** Refined; polite; cultured: *polished manners.* **3.** Having no errors or imperfections; flawless: *a polished performance.*

po•lite (pə līt′) *adj.* **po•lit•er, po•lit•est. 1.** Having or showing good manners; courteous: *a polite boy; a polite note.* **2.** Refined; elegant: *polite society.* [First written down before 1398 in Middle English and spelled *polit,* polished, from Latin *polīre,* to polish.] **—po•lite′ly** *adv.* **—po•lite′ness** *n.*

Synonyms: polite, mannerly, civil, courteous. These adjectives mean mindful of, conforming to, or marked by good manners. **Polite** and **mannerly** mean considerate of others, well-bred according to social standards: *You don't have to like all your relatives but you must be polite to them. Are rural people really more mannerly than city dwellers?* **Civil** means having a minimal amount of good manners, neither polite nor rude: *He is barely civil until he has his morning coffee.* **Courteous** means polite in a gracious, courtly way: *She wrote a courteous response accepting their invitation.*

pol•i•tic (pŏl′ĭ tĭk) *adj.* Showing good or pragmatic judgment; prudent; judicious: *a politic decision.*

po•lit•i•cal (pə lĭt′ĭ kəl) *adj.* **1.** Of or relating to the structure or affairs of government: *a political system.* **2.** Relating to or characteristic of politics or politicians: *a political party; a political campaign.* [First written down in 1551 in Modern English, from Greek *politēs,* citizen.] **—po•lit′i•cal•ly** *adv.*

political science *n.* The study of the processes, principles, and structure of government and political institutions.

pol•i•ti•cian (pŏl′ĭ tĭsh′ən) *n.* **1.** A person active in politics, especially one holding a political office. **2.** A person who uses cunning and guile to achieve power or success.

pol•i•tics (pŏl′ĭ tĭks) *n.* **1.** *(used with a singular verb).* The art or science of government or governing, as of a nation. **2.** *(used with a singular or plural verb).* The activities or affairs of a government, politician, or political party: *She never discusses politics at home.* **3.** *(used with a singular or plural verb).* Intrigue or maneuvering within a group: *office politics.* **4.** *(used with a singular or plural verb).* A person's general position or attitude on political subjects: *His politics are conservative.* —See Note.

pol•i•ty (pŏl′ĭ tē) *n., pl.* **pol•i•ties. 1.** The form of government of a nation, a state, or an organization. **2.** A community or society living under a certain form of government. [First written down in 1538 in Modern English, from Late Latin *polītīa,* the Roman government, from Greek *politeia,* the State.]

Polk (pōk), **James Knox.** 1795–1849. The 11th President of the United States (1845–1849).

pol•ka (pōl′kə *or* pō′kə) *n.* **1.** A lively round dance originating in Bohemia and performed by couples. **2.** Music written for this dance. —*intr.v.* **pol•kaed, pol•ka•ing, pol•kas.** To dance the polka.

pol•ka dot (pō′kə) *n.* **1.** One of many round dots that are evenly spaced to form a pattern. **2.** A pattern or fabric with such dots.

poll (pōl) *n.* **1.** The casting and registering of votes in an election. **2.** The place where votes are cast and counted. Often used in the plural. **3.** A survey of the public or of a sample of public opinion to acquire information. **4.** The head, especially the top of the head. —*tr.v.* **polled, poll•ing, polls. 1.** To receive (a given number of votes). **2.** To sample and record the opinions of: *polled the voters.* **3.** To cast (a vote or ballot). **4.** To cut the horns, upper branches, hair, or wool from: *We polled the sheep.*

❑ *These sound alike:* **poll, pole**[1] (point on an axis), **pole**[2] (rod).

pol•len (pŏl′ən) *n.* Powdery grains that contain the male reproductive cells of flowering plants and fertilize female egg cells.

pol•li•nate (pŏl′ə nāt′) *tr.v.* **pol•li•nat•ed, pol•li•nat•ing, pol•li•nates.** To fertilize by transferring pollen to the female part of (a flower or plant). **—pol′li•na′tion** *n.* **—pol′li•na′tor** *n.*

pol•li•wog also **pol•ly•wog** (pŏl′ē wŏg′ *or* pŏl′ē wôg′) *n.* A tadpole.

poll•ster (pōl′stər) *n.* A person who takes surveys of public opinion.

poll tax *n.* A tax imposed on persons rather than on property, often as a requirement for voting.

pol•lut•ant (pə lo͞ot′nt) *n.* Something that pollutes, especially a waste material that makes the environment less suitable for living things.

pol•lute (pə lo͞ot′) *tr.v.* **pol•lut•ed, pol•lut•ing, pol•lutes. 1.** To make unfit for or harmful to living organisms, especially by the addition of waste matter: *Sewage pollutes rivers.* **2.** To render morally impure; corrupt. **—pol•lut′er** *n.*

pol•lu•tion (pə lo͞o′shən) *n.* **1.** The contamination of air, water, or soil by harmful substances. **2.** Something that pollutes.

Pol•lux (pŏl′əks) *n.* In Greek mythology, one of the twin sons of Leda, who along with his brother Castor is transformed by Zeus into the constellation Gemini.

pol•ly•wog (pŏl′ē wŏg′ *or* pŏl′ē wôg′) *n.* Variant of **polliwog.**

po•lo (pō′lō) *n.* A game in which two teams of three or four players on horseback use long-handled mallets to drive a ball into the opposing team's goal.

Po•lo (pō′lō), **Marco.** 1254–1324. Venetian explorer of Asia (1271–1295) who published his account in *Travels of Marco Polo.*

pol•o•naise (pŏl′ə nāz′ *or* pō′lə nāz′) *n.* **1.** A stately dance of Polish origin, consisting mainly of a promenade of couples. **2.** Music written for this dance.

po•lo•ni•um (pə lō′nē əm) *n. Symbol* **Po** A naturally radioactive metallic element produced by the disintegration of radium. Atomic number 84. See table at **element.**

pol•troon (pŏl tro͞on′) *n.* An utter coward.

poly– *pref.* A prefix that means more than one; many: *polygon.*

pol•y•es•ter (pŏl′ē ĕs′tər) *n.* Any of various light, strong, weather-resistant synthetic resins.

pol•y•eth•yl•ene (pŏl′ē ĕth′ə lēn′) *n.* A polymerized ethylene resin, used especially for containers, tubes, and packaging.

po•lyg•a•mist (pə lĭg′ə mĭst) *n.* A person who practices polygamy.

po•lyg•a•my (pə lĭg′ə mē) *n.* The practice or condition of having more than one husband or wife at one time. **—po•lyg′a•mous** *adj.* **—po•lyg′a•mous•ly** *adv.*

pol•y•glot (pŏl′ē glŏt′) *adj.* Knowing or speaking many languages. —*n.* **1.** A person who speaks many languages. **2.** A mixture or confusion of languages.

pol•y•gon (pŏl′ē gŏn′) *n.* A flat closed geometric figure bounded by three or more line segments. **—po•lyg′o•nal** (pə lĭg′ə nəl) *adj.*

pol•y•graph (pŏl′ē grăf′) *n.* An instrument that simultaneously records changes in several body actions, such as blood pressure, pulse rate, and breathing rate, often used to determine if a person is lying.

pol•y•he•dron (pŏl′ē hē′drən) *n., pl.* **pol•y•he•**

Usage: politics

The word **politics** is followed by a singular verb when it refers to the art or science of governing or to political science: *Politics has been a concern of philosophers for centuries.* But in its other senses *politics* can take either a singular or plural verb. Many other nouns that end in *–ics* are similar. Look at specific entries in the dictionary for precise information.

James K. Polk

polo

ă	pat	oi	boy
ā	pay	ou	out
âr	care	o͝o	took
ä	father	o͞o	boot
ĕ	pet	ŭ	cut
ē	be	ûr	urge
ĭ	pit	th	thin
ī	pie	*th*	this
îr	pier	hw	whoop
ŏ	pot	zh	vision
ō	toe	ə	about
ô	paw	N	*French* bon

Pomeranian

pompon
Pompon on a knit cap

Ponce de León

drons or **pol•y•he•dra** (pŏl′ē **hē′**drə). A solid geometric figure bounded by polygons.

pol•y•mer (**pŏl′**ə mər) *n.* Any of a large number of natural or synthetic chemical compounds of extremely high molecular weight, formed of simple molecules linked together into giant molecules.

pol•y•mer•ic (pŏl′ə **mĕr′**ĭk) *adj.* Of, relating to, or consisting of a polymer or polymers.

pol•y•mer•ize (**pŏl′**ə mə rīz′ *or* pə **lĭm′**ə rīz′) *intr. & tr.v.* **pol•y•mer•ized, pol•y•mer•iz•ing, pol•y•mer•iz•es.** To make or combine into a polymer. **—po•lym′er•i•za′tion** (pə lĭm′ər ĭ **zā′**shən) *n.*

Pol•y•ne•sia (pŏl′ə **nē′**zhə *or* pŏl′ə **nē′**shə). A division of Oceania including islands of the central and southern Pacific Ocean roughly between New Zealand, Hawaii, and Easter Island.

Pol•y•ne•sian (pŏl′ə **nē′**zhən *or* pŏl′ə **nē′**shən) *adj.* Of or relating to Polynesia, the Polynesians, or their languages. *—n.* **1.** A native or inhabitant of Polynesia. **2.** A group of related languages spoken in Polynesia.

pol•y•no•mi•al (pŏl′ē **nō′**mē əl) *n.* An algebraic expression that is represented as the sum of two or more terms.

pol•yp (**pŏl′**ĭp) *n.* **1.** A water animal, such as a hydra, having a hollow tube-shaped body and a mouth opening surrounded by tentacles. **2.** An abnormal growth extending from a mucous membrane.

po•lyph•o•ny (pə **lĭf′**ə nē) *n., pl.* **po•lyph•o•nies.** Music with two or more melodic parts sounded together. **—pol′y•phon′ic** (pŏl′ē **fŏn′**ĭk) *adj.*

pol•y•sty•rene (pŏl′ē **stī′**rēn) *n.* A clear, hard, rigid plastic polymer that is easily colored and has a wide variety of uses. It is commonly used in the form of a solid foam as an insulator.

pol•y•syl•lab•ic (pŏl′ē sĭ **lăb′**ĭk) *adj.* Having more than three syllables: *a polysyllabic word.* **—pol′y•syl•lab′i•cal•ly** *adv.*

pol•y•syl•la•ble (pŏl′ē **sĭl′**ə bəl) *n.* A word of more than three syllables.

pol•y•tech•nic (pŏl′ē **tĕk′**nĭk) *adj.* Dealing with or offering instruction in many industrial arts and applied sciences. *—n.* A school specializing in the teaching of industrial arts and applied sciences.

pol•y•the•ism (**pŏl′**ē thē ĭz′əm) *n.* The worship of or belief in more than one god. **—pol′y•the′ist** *n.*

pol•y•un•sat•u•rat•ed (pŏl′ē ŭn **săch′**ə rā′tĭd) *adj.* Of or relating to organic compounds, especially fats, in which more than one pair of carbon atoms are joined by two or more bonds, thus allowing other atoms or radicals to be added.

pol•y•u•re•thane (pŏl′ē **yŏŏr′**ə thān′) *n.* Any of various resins used in making tough resistant coatings, adhesives, and electrical insulation.

po•made (pō **mād′** *or* pŏ **mād′**) *n.* A perfumed ointment, especially for the hair.

pome (pōm) *n.* A fleshy fruit having seeds but no stone, as the apple, pear, or quince.

pome•gran•ate (**pŏm′**grăn′ĭt *or* **pŏm′**ĭ grăn′ĭt) *n.* **1.** A fruit having a tough reddish rind and many small seeds, each enclosed in juicy red flesh. **2.** The tree that bears such fruit. [First written down about 1300 in Middle English and spelled *pommegarnate*, from Old French *pome grenate* : *pome*, apple + *grenate*, having many seeds.]

Pom•er•a•ni•an (pŏm′ə **rā′**nē ən *or* pŏm′ə **rān′**yən) *n.* Any of a breed of small dog having long silky hair, a face like a fox, and a curled bushy tail.

pom•mel (**pŭm′**əl *or* **pŏm′**əl) *tr.v.* **pom•meled, pom•mel•ing, pom•mels** also **pom•melled, pom•mel•ling, pom•mels.** To beat severely. *—n.* **1.** The raised part at the front of a saddle. **2.** A knob on the handle of a sword.

pomp (pŏmp) *n.* Showy or stately display.

pom•pa•dour (**pŏm′**pə dôr′) *n.* A puffed-up hair style in which the hair is brushed or swept up from the forehead. [First written down in 1887 in American English, after the Marquise de *Pompadour* (1721–1764).]

pom•pa•no (**pŏm′**pə nō′) *n., pl.* **pompano** or **pom•pa•nos.** Any of several fishes of warm Atlantic waters, having a flattened silvery body and much valued as food.

Pom•pe•ii (pŏm **pā′** *or* pŏm **pā′**ē). An ancient city of southern Italy southeast of Naples. It was founded in the sixth or early fifth century B.C. and destroyed by an eruption of Mount Vesuvius in A.D. 79.

pom•pon (**pŏm′**pŏn′) or **pom•pom** (**pŏm′**pŏm′) *n.* **1.** A tuft or ball of material such as wool or ribbon, used as a decoration, especially on shoes, caps, or curtains. **2.** A small chrysanthemum or dahlia. **3. pompom.** A ball of material, such as colored paper or feathers, that is waved by cheerleaders and sports fans.

pom•pous (**pŏm′**pəs) *adj.* **1.** Characterized by excessive dignity and self-importance. **2.** Full of high-sounding words and phrases; bombastic: *gave a pompous speech.* **—pom′pous•ly** *adv.* **—pom•pos′i•ty** (pŏm **pŏs′**ĭ tē), **pom′pous•ness** *n.*

Ponce de Le•ón (**pŏns′** də **lē′**ən *or* **pōns′**də lē **ōn′**), **Juan.** 1460–1521. Spanish explorer who discovered Florida (1513) while looking for the legendary Fountain of Youth.

pon•cho (**pŏn′**chō) *n., pl.* **pon•chos. 1.** A cloak with a hole in the center for the head. **2.** A similar garment used as a raincoat and having a hood.

pond (pŏnd) *n.* A still body of water smaller than a lake.

pon•der (**pŏn′**dər) *tr. & intr.v.* **pon•dered, pon•der•ing, pon•ders.** To think or consider carefully and thoroughly: *He pondered the meaning of his dream. She pondered over the decision.*

pon•der•ous (**pŏn′**dər əs) *adj.* **1.** Heavy and massive: *a ponderous dinosaur.* **2.** Dull, graceless, and difficult to read or understand: *a ponderous book.* **—pon′der•ous•ly** *adv.* **—pon′der•ous•ness** *n.*

pon•gee (pŏn **jē′** *or* **pŏn′**jē) *n.* A soft thin cloth woven usually from Chinese or Indian silk.

pon•iard (**pŏn′**yərd) *n.* A dagger typically having a slender square or triangular blade.

pon•tiff (**pŏn′**tĭf) *n.* **1.** The pope. **2.** A bishop.

pon•tif•i•cal (pŏn **tĭf′**ĭ kəl) *adj.* Relating to, characteristic of, or suitable for a pope or bishop.

pon•tif•i•cate (pŏn **tĭf′**ĭ kāt′) *intr.v.* **pon•tif•i•cat•ed, pon•tif•i•cat•ing, pon•tif•i•cates.** To speak in a pompous dogmatic way.

pon•toon (pŏn **tōōn′**) *n.* **1.a.** A flat-bottomed boat or other floating structure used to support a bridge. **b.** A floating structure that serves as a dock. **2.** One of the floats that supports a seaplane on water.

pontoon bridge *n.* A temporary floating bridge using pontoons for support.

po•ny (**pō′**nē) *n., pl.* **po•nies. 1.** Any of several breeds of horses that are small in size when full grown. **2.** A translation of a text in a foreign language, especially one used secretly by students.

pony express *n.* A system of carrying mail by relays of ponies that operated from Missouri to California in 1860–1861.

po•ny•tail (**pō′**nē tāl′) *n.* A hair style in which the hair is held back so as to hang down like a pony's tail.

pooch (pōōch) *n. Slang.* A dog.

poo•dle (**pōōd′**l) *n.* Any of a breed of dog having thick curly hair and varying in size from standard to toy. [First written down in 1825 in Modern English, from German *Pudelhund* : Low German *pudeln*, to splash about + German *Hund*, dog.]

pooh (po͞o) *interj.* An expression used to show disdain or disbelief.

pooh-pooh (po͞o′po͞o′) *tr.v.* **pooh-poohed, pooh-pooh•ing, pooh-poohs.** *Informal.* To express contempt for: *He pooh-poohed the idea.*

pool[1] (po͞ol) *n.* **1.** A small still body of water. **2.** A small collection of a liquid; a puddle: *a pool of molten steel.* **3.** A deep or still place in a stream. **4.** A swimming pool. [First written down before 899 in Old English and spelled *pōl*.]

pool[2] (po͞ol) *n.* **1.** Any of several games played on a table that has pockets on the sides and corners, the object usually being to make a white ball strike one or more variously colored balls so they drop into the pockets. **2.a.** A game of chance, resembling a lottery, in which the contestants put money into a common fund that is later paid to the winner or winners. **b.** The fund containing the money bet in a game of chance or on the outcome of an event, such as a horse race. **3.** A grouping or sharing of resources for the common advantage of the participants: *forming a pool of our talents.* —*tr.v.* **pooled, pool•ing, pools.** To put into a common fund for use by all: *They agreed to pool their resources to finish the project quickly.* [First written down in 1693 in Modern English, from French *poule*, hen, stakes.]

pool•room (po͞ol′ro͞om′ *or* po͞ol′ro͝om′) *n.* A commercial establishment or room for the playing of pool or billiards.

poop[1] (po͞op) *n.* A raised structure at the stern of a ship. [First written down about 1405 in Middle English and spelled *poupe*, from Latin *puppis*.]

poop[2] (po͞op) *tr.v.* **pooped, poop•ing, poops.** *Slang.* To exhaust or tire. [First written down in 1931 in American English.]

poor (po͝or) *adj.* **poor•er, poor•est. 1.** Having little or no money and few or no possessions. **2.** Lacking in a specified quality: *a diet poor in calcium.* **3.** Not adequate in quality; inferior. **4.** Deserving of sympathy or pity; unfortunate. —*n. (used with a plural verb).* People with little or no money or possessions considered as a group. —**poor′ness** *n.*

poor•house (po͝or′hous′) *n.* A place where poor people are housed at public expense.

poor•ly (po͝or′lē) *adv.* In a poor way; badly.

pop[1] (pŏp) *v.* **popped, pop•ping, pops.** —*intr.* **1.** To make a short, sharp, explosive sound. **2.** To burst open with a short, sharp, explosive sound. **3.** To appear suddenly and unexpectedly: *I just popped in to say hello.* **4.** To open wide suddenly: *His eyes popped with astonishment.* **5.** In baseball, to hit a short high fly ball: *She popped out to third base.* —*tr.* **1.** To cause to make a short explosive sound. **2.** To cause to burst open with a short explosive sound. **3.** To put or thrust quickly or suddenly: *He popped dinner into the microwave.* **4.** In baseball, to hit (a ball) high in the air but not far. —*n.* **1.** A sudden sharp, explosive sound. **2.** A soft drink; a soda. [First written down in 1433 in Middle English and spelled *poppen*, from *pop*, a blow, stroke, of imitative origin.]—See Note at **tonic.**

pop[2] (pŏp) *n. Informal.* Father. [First written down in 1838 in American English, from *papa*.]

pop[3] (pŏp) *Informal. adj.* Of or for the general public; popular: *pop culture.* —*n.* Popular music. [First written down in 1926 in American English, short for *popular*.]

pop. *abbr.* An abbreviation of population.

pop•corn (pŏp′kôrn′) *n.* **1.** A type of corn having hard kernels that burst when heated to form white irregularly shaped puffs. **2.** The edible popped kernels of this corn.

pope or **Pope** (pōp) *n.* The bishop of Rome and head of the Roman Catholic Church. [First written down before 899 in Old English and spelled *pāpa*, from Greek *pappas*, father.]

pop fly *n.* In baseball, a short high fly ball.

pop•gun (pŏp′gŭn′) *n.* A toy gun that makes a popping noise.

pop•in•jay (pŏp′ĭn jā′) *n.* A vain talkative person.

pop•lar (pŏp′lər) *n.* **1.** Any of several fast-growing trees having triangular leaves and soft light-colored wood. **2.** The wood of such a tree.

pop•lin (pŏp′lĭn) *n.* A fabric of silk, rayon, wool, or cotton with fine crosswise ridges, used in making clothing and upholstery.

pop•o•ver (pŏp′ō′vər) *n.* A light hollow muffin that expands and pops up over the rim of the pan while baking.

pop•pa (pä′pə) *n.* Variant of **papa.**

pop•py (pŏp′ē) *n., pl.* **pop•pies. 1.** Any of numerous plants having showy, often bright-red flowers and milky juice. The small dark seeds of some kinds are used in cooking and baking. **2.** The flower of any of these plants. **3.** A vivid red to reddish orange.

pop•py•cock (pŏp′ē kŏk′) *n. Informal.* Foolish talk; nonsense.

Pop•si•cle (pŏp′sĭ kəl *or* pŏp′sĭk′əl). A trademark used for a colored flavored ice confection with one or two sticks for a handle.

pop-top (pŏp′tŏp′) *adj.* Having a tab that can be pulled up or off to make an opening: *pop-top soda cans.*

pop•u•lace (pŏp′yə lĭs) *n.* The general public; the masses.

pop•u•lar (pŏp′yə lər) *adj.* **1.** Enjoyed by many people: *a popular pastime.* **2.** Liked by acquaintances; having many friends or admirers: *a popular teacher.* **3.** Of, representing, or carried out by the people at large: *the popular vote.* **4.** Accepted or held by many people; widespread: *a popular notion.* **5.** Suited to or within the means of ordinary people: *popular prices.* [First written down before 1425 in Middle English and spelled *populer*, from Latin *populus*, the people.]

pop•u•lar•i•ty (pŏp′yə lăr′ĭ tē) *n.* The quality of being popular; the state of being liked by many people.

pop•u•lar•ize (pŏp′yə lə rīz′) *tr.v.* **pop•u•lar•ized, pop•u•lar•iz•ing, pop•u•lar•iz•es.** To make popular; make known or understandable to the general public. —**pop′u•lar•i•za′tion** (pŏp′yə lər ĭ zā′shən) *n.*

pop•u•lar•ly (pŏp′yə lər lē) *adv.* Commonly; generally: *Our friend Robert is popularly known as "Bob."*

pop•u•late (pŏp′yə lāt′) *tr.v.* **pop•u•lat•ed, pop•u•lat•ing, pop•u•lates. 1.** To supply with inhabitants: *populate a remote region.* **2.** To live in; inhabit.

pop•u•la•tion (pŏp′yə lā′shən) *n.* **1.a.** All of the people who live in a specified area. **b.** The total number of such people. **2.** The set of individuals, items, or data from which a statistical sample is taken. **3.** All the plants or animals of the same kind living in a particular region.

pop•u•list (pŏp′yə lĭst) *n.* A supporter of the rights and power of ordinary people. —**pop′u•list** *adj.*

pop•u•lous (pŏp′yə ləs) *adj.* Heavily populated; having many inhabitants.

por•ce•lain (pôr′sə lĭn *or* pôrs′lĭn) *n.* **1.** A hard white translucent material made by baking a fine clay at a high temperature and glazing it with one of several variously colored materials. **2.** An object or objects made of this material.

porch (pôrch) *n.* **1.** A roofed platform at the entrance to a house. **2.** A gallery or room attached to the outside of a building.

poncho

poppy

Prickly poppy

ă	pat	oi	boy
ā	pay	ou	out
âr	care	o͝o	took
ä	father	o͞o	boot
ĕ	pet	ŭ	cut
ē	be	ûr	urge
ĭ	pit	th	thin
ī	pie	*th*	this
îr	pier	hw	whoop
ŏ	pot	zh	vision
ō	toe	ə	about
ô	paw	N	*French* bon

porcupine
Old World crested porcupine

porpoise
Common porpoise

portcullis

por•cine (pôr′sīn′) *adj.* Of, resembling, or typical of a pig or pigs: *a porcine snout.*

por•cu•pine (pôr′kyə pīn′) *n.* Any of various rodents covered with long sharp spines that serve as protection.

pore¹ (pôr) *intr.v.* **pored, por•ing, pores.** To read or study with great care and attention: *poring over old documents.* [First written down about 1225 in Middle English and spelled *puren.*]

❑ *These sound alike:* **pore¹** (study), **pore²** (opening), **pour** (make flow).

pore² (pôr) *n.* A tiny opening, as one in an animal's skin or on the surface of a leaf, through which liquids or gases may pass. [First written down before 1387 in Middle English and spelled *poore*, from Greek *poros*, passage.]

❑ *These sound alike:* **pore²** (opening), **pore¹** (study), **pour** (make flow).

por•gy (pôr′gē) *n., pl.* **porgy** or **por•gies.** Any of various saltwater fishes found chiefly in coastal Atlantic waters and used as food.

pork (pôrk) *n.* The meat of a pig or hog used as food.

pork•er (pôr′kər) *n.* A pig raised or fattened for use as food.

por•nog•ra•phy (pôr nŏg′rə fē) *n.* Writing or pictures meant to arouse sexual desire. **—por′no•graph′ic** (pôr′nə grăf′ĭk) *adj.*

po•ros•i•ty (pə rŏs′ĭ tē *or* pô rŏs′ĭ tē) *n., pl.* **po•ros•i•ties. 1.** The condition or property of being porous. **2.** The degree to which something is porous: *a material of high porosity.*

po•rous (pôr′əs) *adj.* **1.** Full of or having pores. **2.** Having pores into or through which a liquid or gas can pass. **—po′rous•ly** *adv.* **—po′rous•ness** *n.*

por•phy•ry (pôr′fə rē) *n., pl.* **por•phy•ries.** A fine-grained igneous rock containing some relatively large crystals, especially of feldspar.

por•poise (pôr′pəs) *n., pl.* **porpoise** or **por•pois•es.** Any of several sea mammals related to the whale but smaller and usually having a short blunt snout.

por•ridge (pôr′ĭj *or* pŏr′ĭj) *n.* Oatmeal or other meal boiled in water or milk until thick.

por•rin•ger (pôr′ĭn jər *or* pŏr′ĭn jər) *n.* A shallow cup or bowl with a handle.

port¹ (pôrt) *n.* **1.** A place on a waterway with facilities for loading or unloading ships. **2.** A city or town with such facilities. **3.** A place that gives shelter for ships; a harbor. [First written down before 899 in Old English, from Latin *portus.*]

port² (pôrt) *n.* The left side of a ship or an aircraft facing forward. *—adj.* Of, relating to, or on the port: *a port cabin.* [First written down about 1625 in Modern English, probably from *port side*, from *port*, harbor.]

port³ (pôrt) *n.* A porthole. [First written down about 1300 in Middle English, from Latin *porta*, gate.]

port⁴ (pôrt) *n.* A sweet fortified wine. [First written down in 1691 in Modern English, from *Oporto*, Portugal.]

port•a•ble (pôr′tə bəl) *adj.* Carried with ease: *a portable radio.* [First written down before 1425 in Middle English, from Latin *portāre*, to carry.]

port•age (pôr′tĭj) *n.* **1.** The carrying of boats and supplies overland between waterways. **2.** A route for such carrying. *—tr. & intr.v.* **port•aged, port•ag•ing, port•ag•es.** To transport or travel by portage.

por•tal (pôr′tl) *n.* A doorway or an entrance, especially a large imposing one.

Port-au-Prince (pôrt′ō prĭns′ *or* pôr′tō prăNs′). The capital and largest city of Haiti, in the southwest part of the country on an arm of the Caribbean Sea. Population, 684,284.

port•cul•lis (pôrt kŭl′ĭs) *n.* A grating of iron or wooden bars or slats, suspended in the gateway of a fortified place so that it can be lowered quickly in case of attack.

por•tend (pôr tĕnd′) *tr.v.* **por•tend•ed, por•tend•ing, por•tends.** To serve as an advance indication of; presage: *an incident that portends further trouble.*

por•tent (pôr′tĕnt′) *n.* **1.** An indication of something important or disastrous that is about to occur. **2.** Great or ominous significance: *a development of great portent.*

por•ten•tous (pôr tĕn′təs) *adj.* **1.** Being a portent; ominous: *a portentous silence.* **2.** Of great significance: *a portentous event.* **—por•ten′tous•ly** *adv.*

por•ter¹ (pôr′tər) *n.* **1.** A person hired to carry baggage, as at a station or hotel. **2.** An attendant who waits on passengers in a railroad car. **3.** A maintenance worker for a building or an institution. [First written down before 1382 in Middle English, from Latin *portāre*, to carry.]

por•ter² (pôr′tər) *n.* A dark beer resembling light stout, made from malt that has been dried at a high temperature. [First written down in 1739 in Modern English, from *porter's ale.*]

Por•ter (pôr′tər), **William Sydney.** Pen name O. Henry. 1862–1910. American writer whose short stories are collected in a number of volumes, including *Cabbages and Kings* (1904).

por•ter•house (pôr′tər hous′) *n.* A cut of beef taken from the loin, having a T-shaped bone and a sizable tenderloin.

port•fo•li•o (pôrt fō′lē ō′) *n., pl.* **port•fo•li•os. 1.** A portable case for holding loose papers or drawings. **2.** The office or post of a cabinet member or minister of state. **3.** A group of investments such as stocks and bonds.

port•hole (pôrt′hōl′) *n.* **1.** A small circular window in a ship's side. **2.** An opening for a gun in a wall or parapet.

por•ti•co (pôr′tĭ kō′) *n., pl.* **por•ti•coes** or **por•ti•cos.** A porch or walkway with a roof supported by columns.

por•tion (pôr′shən) *n.* **1.** A part of a whole; a section or quantity of a larger thing: *A portion of your paycheck is withheld to pay taxes.* **2.** A single helping of food: *a portion of mashed potatoes.* *—tr.v.* **por•tioned, por•tion•ing, por•tions.** To distribute in portions; parcel out. [First written down before 1325 in Middle English and spelled *porcion*, from Latin *portiō.*]

Port•land (pôrt′lənd). **1.** The largest city of Maine, in the southwest part of the state on an arm of the Gulf of Maine southwest of Augusta. It was settled in about 1632 and was state capital from 1820 to 1832. Population, 64,348. **2.** The largest city of Oregon, in the northwest part of the state north-northeast of Salem. It was founded in 1845. Population, 437,319.

Portland cement or **port•land cement** (pôrt′lənd) *n.* A cement made by heating a mixture of limestone and clay in a kiln and pulverizing the resulting material.

Port Lou•is (lo͞o′ĭs *or* lo͞o′ē). The capital and largest city of Mauritius, in the northwest part of the island on the Indian Ocean. It was founded in about 1735. Population, 136,812.

port•ly (pôrt′lē) *adj.* **port•li•er, port•li•est.** Comfortably stout or heavy: *a portly senator.* **—port′li•ness** *n.*

Port Mores•by (môrz′bē). The capital and largest city of Papua New Guinea, on southeast New Guinea. Population, 123,624.

Port of Spain (spān) or **Port-of-Spain** (pôrt′-əv spān′). The capital of Trinidad and Tobago, on the northwest coast of Trinidad on an arm of the Atlantic Ocean. Population, 65,906.

Por•to-No•vo (pôr′tō nō′vō). The capital of Benin, in the southeast part of the country on the Atlantic Ocean west of Lagos, Nigeria. It was probably founded in the 16th century. Population, 123,000.

por•trait (pôr′trĭt *or* pôr′trāt′) *n.* **1.** A painting, photograph, or other likeness of a person, especially one showing the face. **2.** A verbal picture or description, especially of a person.

por•trait•ist (pôr′trə tĭst) *n.* A person who makes portraits, especially a painter or photographer.

por•trai•ture (pôr′trĭ cho͝or′) *n.* **1.** The art of making portraits. **2.** A portrait.

por•tray (pôr trā′) *tr.v.* **por•trayed, por•tray•ing, por•trays. 1.** To show by means of a picture. **2.** To describe or picture through the use of words: *the novel portrays colonial life.* **3.** To play on stage or on the screen: *portray a famous composer.* [First written down about 1250 in Middle English and spelled *purtraien*, from Old French *portraire*.]

por•tray•al (pôr trā′əl) *n.* **1.** The act or process of portraying, representing, or acting: *a brilliant portrayal of the leading role.* **2.** A representation or description.

Por•tu•gal (pôr′chə gəl). A country of southwest Europe on the Iberian Peninsula west of Spain. It includes the Madeira Islands and the Azores in the northern Atlantic Ocean. Lisbon is the capital and the largest city. Population, 9,933,000.

Por•tu•guese (pôr′chə gēz′ *or* pôr′chə gēs′) *adj.* Of or relating to Portugal, or its people, language, or culture. *—n., pl.* **Portuguese. 1.a.** A native or inhabitant of Portugal. **b.** A person of Portuguese descent. **2.** The Romance language of Portugal and Brazil.

Portuguese man-of-war *n.* A colony of tropical sea organisms having a bluish floating bladder and many long stinging tentacles.

pose (pōz) *v.* **posed, pos•ing, pos•es.** *—intr.* **1.** To assume or be in a certain position, as for a portrait or photograph: *The children posed in front of the fireplace.* **2.** To pretend to be someone or something that one is not: *caught posing as a detective.* *—tr.* **1.** To place in a specific position, as for a photograph: *She posed us in front of the fireplace and took several pictures.* **2.** To present, raise, or put forward: *pose a threat; pose a question.* *—n.* **1.** A position assumed or taken, as for a portrait or photograph. **2.** A false appearance or attitude; a pretense: *His scholarliness is only a pose.* [First written down about 1378 in Middle English and spelled *posen*, from Late Latin *pausāre*, to rest.]

Po•sei•don (pō sīd′n *or* pə sīd′n) *n.* In Greek mythology, the god of the sea and the brother of Hera and Zeus, identified with the Roman Neptune.

posh (pŏsh) *adj.* Smart and fashionable.

pos•it (pŏz′ĭt) *tr.v.* **pos•it•ed, pos•it•ing, pos•its.** To put forward as a fact or assumption; postulate.

po•si•tion (pə zĭsh′ən) *n.* **1.** The place where a person or thing is located: *the position of the sun in the sky.* **2.** The right or proper place of a person or thing: *The actors are in position to film the scene.* **3.** The way in which a person or thing is placed or arranged: *Try not to sit in one position too long.* **4.** An advantageous place or location: *jockeys maneuvering for position.* **5.** A situation as it relates to the surrounding circumstances: *You've put me in an awkward position.* **6.** A point of view or an attitude on a certain question: *What is your position on the proposed landfill?* **7.** A post of employment; a job: *a position in the government.* **8.** In sports, the area or station assigned to each member of a team: *defensive positions.* *—tr.v.* **po•si•tioned, po•si•tion•ing, po•si•tions.** To put in place or position: *position the chess pieces on the board.*

pos•i•tive (pŏz′ĭ tĭv) *adj.* **1.** Expressing certainty, acceptance, or affirmation: *a positive answer; a positive statement.* **2.** Making, causing, or focusing on progress; constructive: *positive steps to solve the problem.* **3.** Leaving no room for doubt or question: *positive proof.* **4.** Absolutely certain: *I'm positive about that.* **5.** Indicating that a suspected disease, disorder, or microorganism is present: *a positive test result.* **6.** *Informal.* Utter; absolute: *a positive darling.* **7.a.** Greater than zero: *a positive integer.* **b.** Relating to the sign (+), used to indicate a positive number or one that is to be added. **8.** Relating to or having an electric charge capable of neutralizing a charge like that carried by an electron and therefore tending to attract electrons. **9.** Being a response in which a living thing moves toward a stimulus: *a positive reaction to light.* **10.** In grammar, of or being the simple uncompared degree of an adjective or adverb as opposed to the comparative or superlative degree. *—n.* **1.** An affirmative element or characteristic. **2.a.** In grammar, the positive degree of an adjective or adverb. **b.** A word in this degree. **3.** The side in a debate that agrees with the statement being debated. **4.** A photographic image in which light and dark appear as they do in nature. **5.** A quantity greater than zero. [First written down before 1325 in Middle English and spelled *positive*, laid down, imposed, from Latin *positus*, past participle of *pōnere*, to place.] **—pos′i•tive•ly** *adv.* **—pos′i•tive•ness** *n.*

pos•i•tron (pŏz′ĭ trŏn′) *n.* The antiparticle that corresponds to the electron.

poss. *abbr.* An abbreviation of: **1.** Possession. **2.** Possessive.

pos•se (pŏs′ē) *n.* A body of people summoned by a sheriff to aid in law enforcement.

pos•sess (pə zĕs′) *tr.v.* **pos•sessed, pos•sess•ing, pos•sess•es. 1.** To have as property; own. **2.** To control the mind or thoughts of: *Ambition possessed her.* **3.** To have as a quality, characteristic, or other attribute: *possessed great tact.* [First written down about 1380 in Middle English and spelled *possessen*, from Latin *possidēre*.] **—pos•ses′sor** *n.*

pos•sessed (pə zĕst′) *adj.* **1.** Having or owning something: *possessed of great wealth.* **2.** Controlled by or as if by a spirit or other force; obsessed: *possessed by a desire to become a musician.* **3.** Calm; collected: *possessed even in time of trial.*

pos•ses•sion (pə zĕsh′ən) *n.* **1.** The fact or condition of having or possessing something. **2.** Something that is owned or possessed: *leaving most of their possessions behind.* **3.** A territory subject to foreign control: *The Philippine Islands were once a possession of the United States.* **4.** The state of being dominated by or as if by evil spirits or by an obsession. **5.** In sports, control of the ball or puck by a player or team.

pos•ses•sive (pə zĕs′ĭv) *adj.* **1.** Having a desire to dominate or control. **2.** Of or relating to ownership or possession. **3.** Of or relating to the grammatical case of a noun or pronoun that indicates possession. In the sentences *Bill's car was being repaired* and *Mary lent John her book, Bill's* and *her* are in the possessive case. *—n.* **1.** The possessive case. **2.** A word in the possessive case. **—pos•ses′sive•ly** *adv.* **—pos•ses′sive•ness** *n.*

possessive adjective *n.* An adjective formed from a pronoun indicating possession. In the sentences *This is my duty* and *The boy whose shirt was red left early,* the possessive adjectives are *my* and *whose.*

possessive pronoun *n.* One of several pronouns indicating possession and capable of substituting

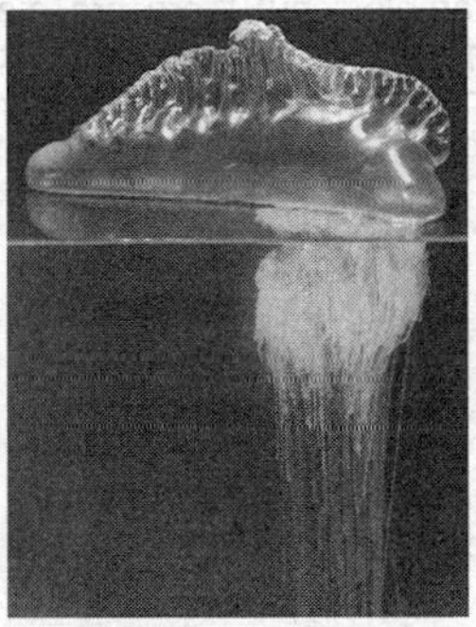

Portuguese man-of-war

ă	pat	oi	boy
ā	pay	ou	out
âr	care	o͝o	took
ä	father	o͞o	boot
ĕ	pet	ŭ	cut
ē	be	ûr	urge
ĭ	pit	th	thin
ī	pie	*th*	this
îr	pier	hw	whoop
ŏ	pot	zh	vision
ō	toe	ə	about
ô	paw	N	*French* bon

Word Building: post–

The basic meaning of the prefix **post–** is "after." It comes from the Latin word *post,* meaning "behind, after." **Post–** is often used in opposition to the prefixes **ante–** and **pre–**: **antedate/postdate** and **prewar/postwar**. And **post–** occurs frequently in medical terminology. **Postnasal** and **postnatal** are just two common examples, but there are many others, such as *postcranial* ("behind the cranium") and *postvertebral* ("behind the vertebrae").

postage stamp
1993 stamp honoring Elvis Presley (1935–1977)

ă	pat	oi	boy
ā	pay	ou	out
âr	care	ŏŏ	took
ä	father	ōō	boot
ĕ	pet	ŭ	cut
ē	be	ûr	urge
ĭ	pit	th	thin
ī	pie	*th*	this
îr	pier	hw	whoop
ŏ	pot	zh	vision
ō	toe	ə	about
ô	paw	N	*French* bon

for noun phrases. The possessive pronouns include *mine, hers, his, ours, yours,* and *theirs.*

pos•si•bil•i•ty (pŏs′ə **bĭl′**ĭ tē) *n., pl.* **pos•si•bil•i•ties. 1.** The fact or condition of being possible: *the possibility of life on Mars.* **2.** Something that is possible: *His promotion now seems a possibility.* **3.** A person or thing that is capable of being chosen or winning a contest: *She seems like a strong possibility in the senatorial race.* **4. possibilities.** Potential for favorable results: *The idea has tremendous possibilities.*

pos•si•ble (**pŏs′**ə bəl) *adj.* **1.** Capable of happening, existing, being true, or being accomplished: *It may be possible to get there by helicopter.* **2.** Capable of being used for a certain purpose: *a possible site for the new capital.* [First written down about 1350 in Middle English and spelled *possibil,* from Latin *possibilis,* from *posse,* to be able.]

pos•si•bly (**pŏs′**ə blē) *adv.* **1.** Perhaps: *He hesitated, possibly remembering his unsuccessful last attempt.* **2.** Conceivably: *Could they possibly be here already?* **3.** Under any circumstances: *I can't possibly do it.*

pos•sum (**pŏs′**əm) *n.* The oppossum. [First written down in 1613 in American English, short for *opossum.*]

post¹ (pōst) *n.* **1.** A piece of wood or other material set upright in the ground to serve as a marker or support. **2.** A support for a beam in the framework of a building. **3.** The starting gate at a racetrack. **4.** A terminal of a battery. **5.** A goal post. **6.** An earring having a short bar that passes through the ear and fits into a cap in the back. *—tr.v.* **post•ed, post•ing, posts. 1.** To put up in a prominent place for public viewing: *The winners' names will be posted on the bulletin board.* **2.** To put up signs on (property) warning against trespassing. [First written down about 1000 in Old English, from Latin *postis.*]

post² (pōst) *n.* **1.** A military base: *an army post.* **2.** A local organization of military veterans. **3.** An assigned position or station, as of a guard or sentry: *a lookout post.* **4.** A position of employment, especially an appointed public office: *a high post in the government.* **5.** A place to which a person is assigned for duty: *an overseas post.* **6.** A trading post. *—tr.v.* **post•ed, post•ing, posts. 1.** To assign to a post or station: *post a sentry.* **2.** To put forward; present: *post bail.* [First written down in 1598 in Modern English, from Latin *positum,* placed, in position, from *pōnere,* to place.]

post³ (pōst) *n.* **1.a.** A delivery of mail. **b.** The mail delivered: *the morning post.* **2.** *Chiefly British.* A governmental system for transporting and delivering the mail. **3.** *Archaic.* One of a series of stations along a mail route, furnishing fresh horses and riders. *—tr.v.* **post•ed, post•ing, posts. 1.** To mail (a letter). **2.** To inform of the latest news: *I try to keep posted on current events.* **3.** In bookkeeping, to transfer (figures) to a ledger. [First written down in 1506 in Modern English, from Old French *post,* relay station for horses.]

post– *pref.* A prefix that means: **1.** After in time; later: *postoperative.* **2.** After in position; behind: *postnasal.* —See Note.

post•age (**pō′**stĭj) *n.* The charge for sending something by mail.

postage stamp *n.* A small, usually adhesive label issued by a government for an amount indicated on the front. It is placed on an item of mail as evidence of the payment of postage.

post•al (**pō′**stəl) *adj.* Of or relating to the post office or mail service: *postal rates.*

postal card *n.* A card printed with the image of a postage stamp, issued by a government and used for sending messages through the mail.

postal service *n.* The post office.

post card also **post•card** (**pōst′**kärd′) *n.* **1.** A commercially printed card with space on one side for a postage stamp and an address, used for sending a short message through the mail. **2.** A postal card.

post chaise *n.* A closed carriage having four wheels and drawn by horses, formerly used to transport mail and passengers.

post•date (pōst **dāt′**) *tr.v.* **post•dat•ed, post•dat•ing, post•dates.** To put a date on (a check, for example) that is later than the actual date.

post•er (**pō′**stər) *n.* A large, usually printed notice or announcement, often illustrated, that is posted to advertise or publicize something.

pos•te•ri•or (pŏ **stîr′**ē ər) *adj.* **1.** Located behind a part or toward the rear of a structure. **2.a.** Of, in, or near the side of the human body in which the spine is located. **b.** Of, in, or near the part of an animal body that is close to the tail. **3.** Coming after in order or time; following. *—n.* The buttocks.

pos•ter•i•ty (pŏ **stĕr′**ĭ tē) *n.* **1.** Future generations: *The author left a rich body of literature to posterity.* **2.** A person's descendants.

pos•tern (**pō′**stərn *or* **pŏs′**tərn) *n.* A small rear gate, especially one in a fort or castle.

Post Exchange A service mark used for a store on a military base that sells merchandise to military personnel and their families.

post•grad•u•ate (pōst **grăj′**ōō ĭt *or* pōst **grăj′**ōō āt′) *adj.* Of, relating to, or pursuing advanced study after graduation from high school or college: *postgraduate courses.* *—n.* A person engaged in postgraduate study.

post•haste (**pōst′hāst′**) *adv.* With great speed; rapidly.

post•hu•mous (**pŏs′**chə məs) *adj.* **1.** Occurring or continuing after one's death: *a posthumous award.* **2.** Published after the author's death: *a posthumous book.* **3.** Born after the death of the father: *a posthumous child.* **—post′hu•mous•ly** *adv.*

pos•til•ion also **pos•til•lion** (pō **stĭl′**yən *or* pŏ**stĭl′**yən) *n.* A person who rides the lead horse on the left to guide the horses drawing a coach.

post•man (**pōst′**mən) *n.* A mailman.

post•mark (**pōst′**märk′) *n.* A mark printed over a postage stamp, especially one that cancels the stamp and records the date and place of mailing. *—tr.v.* **post•marked, post•mark•ing, post•marks.** To stamp with such a mark.

post•mas•ter (**pōst′**măs′tər) *n.* A man in charge of the operations of a local post office.

post me•rid•i•em (mə **rĭd′**ē əm) *adv. & adj.* After noon.

post•mis•tress (**pōst′**mĭs′trĭs) *n.* A woman in charge of the operations of a local post office.

post•mor•tem (pōst **môr′**təm) *adj.* Occurring or done after death. *—n.* **1.** An autopsy. **2.** An analysis or a review of an event that has just taken place.

post•na•sal (pōst **nā′**zəl) *adj.* Located or occurring behind the nose.

post•na•tal (pōst **nāt′**l) *adj.* Occurring or done after birth: *postnatal care.*

post office *n.* **1.** The public department responsible for the transportation and delivery of the mails. **2.** A local office where mail is received, sorted, and delivered, and where stamps and other postal materials are sold.

post•op•er•a•tive (pōst **ŏp′**ər ə tĭv *or* pōst **ŏp′**rə tĭv *or* pōst **ŏp′**ə rā′tĭv) *adj.* Occurring or done after a surgical operation: *postoperative care.*

post•paid (**pōst′pād′**) *adj.* Having the postage paid in advance: *a postpaid reply card.*

post•par•tum (pōst **pär′**təm) *adj.* Of or occurring

in the period shortly after childbirth: *postpartum recovery.*

post•pone (pōst pōn′) *tr.v.* **post•poned, post•pon•ing, post•pones.** To put off until a later time: *You may want to postpone your visit.* **—post•pone′ment** *n.*

post•script (pōst′skrĭpt′) *n.* **1.** A message added at the end of a letter, after the writer's signature. **2.** Additional information added to a manuscript, as of a book or an article.

pos•tu•late (pŏs′chə lāt′) *tr.v.* **pos•tu•lat•ed, pos•tu•lat•ing, pos•tu•lates. 1.** To make claim for; demand. **2.** To assume the truth or existence of (something), especially as a basis of an argument: *Aristotle postulated an "Unmoved Mover" working endlessly to keep the planets in motion.* **3.** To assume as a premise or an axiom; take for granted. *—n.* (pŏs′chə lĭt *or* pŏs′chə lāt′). Something assumed without proof as being self-evident or generally accepted, especially when used as a basis for an argument. [First written down in 1533 in Modern English, from Latin *postulāre*, to request.]

pos•ture (pŏs′chər) *n.* **1.** The way in which one holds or carries one's body; carriage: *a person who has good posture.* **2.** A position or an arrangement of the body or its parts: *a kneeling posture.* **3.** A stance or disposition with regard to something: *a defensive posture.* *—intr.v.* **pos•tured, pos•tur•ing, pos•tures. 1.** To assume an unnatural or exaggerated pose or mental attitude: *We all felt that the speaker was posturing.* **2.** To assume a pose. [First written down in 1605 in Modern English, from Latin *positūra*, position, from *pōnere*, to place.]

post•war (pōst′wôr′) *adj.* Of or belonging to the period after a war: *postwar houses.*

po•sy (pō′zē) *n., pl.* **po•sies.** A flower or bunch of flowers.

pot (pŏt) *n.* **1.** Any of various deep rounded containers made of metal, pottery, or glass, used especially for cooking. **2.** A coffeepot. **3.** A teapot. **4.** A chamberpot. **5.** A flowerpot. **6.a.** A pot with something in it: *a pot of tea.* **b.** The amount that a pot can hold: *drank a pot of coffee.* **7.** A trap for lobsters, fish, or eels, consisting of a wooden, wire, or wicker cage or basket. **8.** The total amount staked by all the players in one hand at cards: *Who won the pot?* **9.** *Informal.* A fund to which the members of a group contribute for their common use. *—tr.v.* **pot•ted, pot•ting, pots. 1.** To plant or put in a pot: *He potted the tulip bulbs.* **2.** To preserve (food) in a pot, jar, or can. **3.** To cook in a pot. **4.** To shoot (game) for food rather than for sport: *She potted a pheasant.* [First written down before 1100 in Old English.]

po•ta•ble (pō′tə bəl) *adj.* Fit to drink: *potable water.* *—n.* A beverage, especially an alcoholic beverage. [First written down before 1425 in Middle English, from Latin *pōtāre*, to drink.]

pot•ash (pŏt′ăsh′) *n.* Any of several chemical compounds that contain potassium, especially a strongly alkaline material obtained from wood ashes.

po•tas•si•um (pə tăs′ē əm) *n. Symbol* **K** A soft, highly reactive, silver-white metallic element. It is essential for the growth of plants, and oxidizes rapidly when exposed to air. Atomic number 19. See table at **element.**

potassium bi•tar•trate (bī tär′trāt′) *n.* A white powder that has the formula $KHC_4H_4O_6$, used in baking powder and in laxatives.

potassium hydroxide *n.* A corrosive solid that is a strong alkali and has the formula KOH. It is used in bleaching and in making soaps and detergents.

potassium nitrate *n.* A transparent white crystalline compound and strong oxidizing agent, KNO_3, used in gunpowder and fireworks, in the manufacture of glass, and in fertilizer.

po•ta•to (pə tā′tō) *n., pl.* **po•ta•toes. 1.** The starchy tuber of a widely grown plant, eaten as a vegetable. **2.** The plant that bears such tubers. **3.** The sweet potato. —See Note.

potato chip *n.* A thin slice of potato fried until crisp and then salted.

Pot•a•wat•o•mi (pŏt′ə wŏt′ə mē) *n., pl.* **Potawatomi** or **Pot•a•wat•o•mis. 1.** A member of a Native American people of the upper Midwest, now living in Michigan, Kansas, Oklahoma, and Ontario. **2.** The Algonquian language of the Potawatomi.

pot•bel•ly (pŏt′bĕl′ē) *n., pl.* **pot•bel•lies.** An abdomen that sags or sticks out.

potbelly stove *n.* A short rounded stove in which wood or coal is burned.

po•ten•cy (pōt′n sē) *n., pl.* **po•ten•cies.** The quality or condition of being potent.

po•tent (pōt′nt) *adj.* **1.** Possessing inner or physical strength; powerful: *a potent ruler.* **2.** Having a powerful influence on the mind or feelings; highly effective: *He made a potent argument for joining the team.* **3.** Having or capable of having strong effects on a living organism: *a potent drug.* [First written down about 1425 in Middle English, from Latin *potēns*, present participle of *posse*, to be able.]

po•ten•tate (pōt′n tāt′) *n.* A person who has the power and position to rule over others; a monarch.

po•ten•tial (pə tĕn′shəl) *adj.* **1.** Capable of being but not yet in existence; latent: *potential buyers; potential problems.* **2.** Having possibility, capability, or power: *the sea as a potential source of minerals.* *—n.* **1.** Capacity for growth, development, or coming into existence: *We see the potential for expanding our business in new markets.* **2.** *Symbol* **V** The potential energy of a unit electric charge at any point in an electric circuit or field, measured with respect to a given reference point in the circuit or field; voltage. [First written down before 1398 in Middle English and spelled *potencial*, from Latin *potentia*, power.] **—po•ten′tial•ly** *adv.*

potential energy *n.* The energy that a particle or system of particles derives from position or condition rather than from motion. A raised weight, coiled spring, or charged battery has potential energy.

po•ten•ti•al•i•ty (pə tĕn′shē ăl′ĭ tē) *n., pl.* **po•ten•ti•al•i•ties. 1.** The state of being potential. **2.** Capacity for growth, development, or existence: *estimating a student's potentiality.* **3.** Something possessing such capacity.

po•ten•ti•om•e•ter (pə tĕn′shē ŏm′ĭ tər) *n.* **1.** An electrical device consisting of a resistor provided with a rotating tap that can be located so that the ratio of the resistance of the two parts into which the resistor is divided has any desired value. Potentiometers are used in radios and television sets as volume controls and brightness controls. **2.** A specially calibrated device used to compare an unknown voltage to a standard voltage.

pot•ful (pŏt′fo͝ol′) *n.* **1.** The amount that a pot can hold. **2.** *Informal.* A large amount: *made a potful of money on the horses.*

pot•herb (pŏt′ûrb′ *or* pŏt′hûrb′) *n.* A plant whose leaves, stems, or flowers are cooked and eaten or used as seasoning.

pot•hold•er (pŏt′hōl′dər) *n.* A small fabric pad used to handle hot cooking utensils.

pot•hole (pŏt′hōl′) *n.* A hole or pit, especially one in a road surface.

pot•hook (pŏt′ho͝ok′) *n.* **1.** A bent or hooked piece of iron for hanging a pot or kettle over a fire. **2.** A

potato

Word History: **potato**

Our English **potato** comes from the Spanish noun *patata.* The Spanish word comes from *batata,* the word for sweet potato in Taino, an extinct language spoken on Haiti. The letter *p* in the Spanish *patata* is probably due to *papa,* the word for "white potato" in Quechua, the language of the Incas in Peru. A **sweet potato** is called a *yam* in the southern United States, but elsewhere the *sweet potato* and the *yam* are different plants. *Yam* comes from the Spanish word *iñame,* which ultimately comes from a West African language such as Fulani, which is spoken from northern Nigeria to Mali and whose word for "eat" is *nyami.*

potbelly stove

curved iron rod with a hooked end used for lifting hot pots, irons, or stove lids.

po•tion (pō′shən) *n.* A liquid dose, especially one of medicinal, magic, or poisonous content. [First written down before 1300 in Middle English and spelled *pocioun*, from Latin *pōtiō*.]

pot•latch (pŏt′lăch′) *n.* A ceremonial feast among certain Native American peoples of the northwest Pacific coast, in which the host gives gifts according to each guest's rank or status. Potlatch may also involve the destruction of valued items as a display of wealth. [First written down in 1845 in American English, from Nootka *p'achitl*, to make a potlatch gift.]

pot•luck (pŏt′lŭk′) *n.* **1.** Whatever food happens to be available for a meal, especially when offered to a guest. **2.** A meal at which each guest brings food to be shared by all.

Po•to•mac River (pə tō′mək). A river of the east-central United States rising in northeast West Virginia and flowing about 285 miles (459 kilometers) along the Virginia-Maryland border to Chesapeake Bay.

pot•pie (pŏt′pī′) *n.* **1.** A mixture of meat or poultry and vegetables covered with a crust of pastry and baked in a deep dish. **2.** A meat or poultry stew with dumplings.

pot•pour•ri (pō′po͝o rē′) *n., pl.* **pot•pour•ris. 1.** A miscellaneous collection or assortment; a medley: *The book was a potpourri of poems, legends, and sayings.* **2.** A fragrant mixture of dried flower petals and spices used to scent the air.

pot roast *n.* A cut of beef that is browned and then cooked until tender, often with vegetables, in a covered pot.

pot•sherd (pŏt′shûrd′) *n.* A fragment of broken pottery, especially one found in an archaeological excavation.

pot•shot also **pot shot** (pŏt′shŏt′) *n.* **1.** A random or easy shot. **2.** A criticism made without careful thought and aimed at a handy target for attack: *reporters taking potshots at the mayor.*

pot•tage (pŏt′ĭj) *n.* A thick soup or stew of vegetables and sometimes meat.

pot•ted (pŏt′ĭd) *adj.* **1.** Placed in a pot: *a potted plant.* **2.** Preserved in a pot, can, or jar: *potted meat.*

pot•ter (pŏt′ər) *n.* A person who makes pottery.

Pot•ter (pŏt′ər), **Beatrix.** 1866–1943. British writer and illustrator whose stories include *The Tale of Peter Rabbit* (1900).

Beatrix Potter

pot•ter's field (pŏt′ərz) *n.* A place for the burial of unknown or impoverished people.

potter's wheel *n.* A revolving disk on which a mass of clay is shaped by hand.

potter's wheel

pot•ter•y (pŏt′ə rē) *n., pl.* **pot•ter•ies. 1.** Objects, such as pots, vases, or dishes, shaped from moist clay and hardened by heat. **2.** The art, craft, or work of a potter. **3.** The place where a potter works.

pouch (pouch) *n.* **1.** A bag often closing with a drawstring and used for holding or carrying various things: *a mail pouch.* **2.** A sealed plastic or foil container used to package frozen or dehydrated food. **3.** A body part similar to a sac or pocket, such as the one in which a kangaroo carries its young. **4.** A puffy part, such as a fold of flesh: *pouches under the eyes.* [First written down in 1299 in Middle English and spelled *puche*, from Old French, of Germanic origin.]

poul•tice (pōl′tĭs) *n.* A soft moist mass of bread, meal, clay, or a similar substance, usually heated, spread on cloth, and applied to an aching or inflamed part of the body. [First written down in 1392 in Middle English and spelled *pultes*, from Medieval Latin *pultēs*, thick paste, from Latin *puls*, pottage.]

poul•try (pōl′trē) *n.* Domestic fowls, such as chickens, turkeys, ducks, or geese, raised for meat or eggs.

pounce (pouns) *intr.v.* **pounced, pounc•ing, pounc•es. 1.** To spring or swoop suddenly so as to seize something: *The kitten pounced on the ball.* **2.** To seize something swiftly and eagerly: *pounce on an opportunity.* —*n.* The act or an instance of pouncing.

pound[1] (pound) *n., pl.* **pound** or **pounds. 1.a.** A unit of avoirdupois weight equal to 16 ounces (about 453.6 grams). See table at **measurement. b.** A unit of apothecary weight equal to 12 ounces (about 373 grams). **2.** A unit of force equal to the downward force exerted by a one-pound weight where the acceleration of gravity is 32.174 feet per second per second. **3.** The basic monetary unit of the United Kingdom, Cyprus, Lebanon, Sudan, Syria, and Egypt. [First written down before 810 in Old English and spelled *pund*, from Latin *(lībra) pondō*, (a pound) by weight.]

pound[2] (pound) *v.* **pound•ed, pound•ing, pounds.** —*tr.* **1.** To strike or beat forcefully and repeatedly: *Pound the nail into the board.* **2.** To crush to a powder or pulp: *pounding corn into meal.* —*intr.* **1.** To strike vigorous repeated blows: *She pounded on the table.* **2.** To move along noisily and heavily: *They pounded up the stairs.* **3.** To pulsate rapidly and heavily; throb: *His heart pounded with excitement.* —*n.* **1.** A heavy blow. **2.** The sound of a heavy blow. [First written down about 1000 in Old English and spelled *pūnian.*]

pound[3] (pound) *n.* **1.** A public enclosure for confining stray animals or livestock. **2.** An enclosure in which animals or fish are trapped. [First written down about 1378 in Middle English, from Old English *pund.*]

pound cake *n.* A rich yellow cake containing a large proportion of eggs, flour, butter, and sugar.

pound-fool•ish (pound′fo͞o′lĭsh) *adj.* Unwise in dealing with large sums of money or important matters.

pound sterling *n.* The basic monetary unit of the United Kingdom.

pour (pôr) *v.* **poured, pour•ing, pours.** —*tr.* **1.** To cause (a fluid or loose particles) to flow or stream, as from a container: *pour the milk.* **2.** To send forth, produce, express, or utter, as if in a stream or flood: *poured money into the project; poured out his story.* —*intr.* **1.a.** To flow or run freely: *Salt pours easily.* **b.** To stream or gush in or as if in a flood: *The water poured down over the rocks.* **c.** To rain hard: *It isn't sprinkling; it's pouring.* **2.** To come or go in large numbers or amounts; swarm or flood: *Fans poured into the arena.* **3.** To serve a beverage, such as tea or coffee, to a gathering: *Will you pour?* [First written down about 1300 in Middle English and spelled *pouren*, from Latin *pūrāre*, to purify.] **—pour′er** *n.*

❑ *These sound alike:* **pour, pore**[1] (tiny opening), **pore**[2] (examine).

pout (pout) *intr.v.* **pout•ed, pout•ing, pouts. 1.** To show disappointment or displeasure; sulk. **2.** To push out the lips, especially as a sign of sullen annoyance. —*n.* A sulky or sullen expression made by pushing out the lips. [First written down before 1325 in Middle English and spelled *pouten*, perhaps of Scandinavian origin.]

pout•er (pou′tər) *n.* Any of a breed of pigeons than can inflate its crop so that its breast puffs out.

pov•er•ty (pŏv′ər tē) *n.* **1.** The state of being poor; lack of the means of providing material needs or comforts. **2.** Deficiency in amount; scantiness: *a poverty of imagination.* **3.** Unproductiveness; infertility: *the poverty of the rocky soil.* [First written down before 1200 in Middle English and spelled *poverte,* from Latin *paupertās,* from *pauper,* poor.]

poverty level *n.* An income level below which a person is officially considered to be living in poverty.

pov•er•ty-strick•en (pŏv′ər tē strĭk′ən) *adj.* Suffering from poverty; very poor.

POW (pē′ō dŭb′əl yo͞o) *n., pl.* **POW's** also **POWs.** A prisoner of war.

pow•der (pou′dər) *n.* **1.a.** A substance in the form of a great number of very fine particles. **b.** Any of various preparations in this form, as certain medicines or cosmetics: *face powder; soap powder.* **2.** An explosive mixture, such as gunpowder. **3.** Light dry snow. *—v.* **pow•dered, pow•der•ing, pow•ders.** *—tr.* **1.** To reduce to powder; pulverize. **2.** To cover, dust, or sprinkle with or as if with powder: *powder cookies with sugar. —intr.* **1.** To become pulverized; turn into powder. **2.** To use powder as a cosmetic. [First written down before 1300 in Middle English and spelled *poudre,* from Latin *pulvis.*]

powder horn *n.* An animal's horn capped at the open end, used to carry gunpowder.

powder keg *n.* **1.** A small cask for holding gunpowder or other explosives. **2.** A potentially explosive thing or situation.

powder puff *n.* A soft pad for applying powder to the skin.

powder room *n.* **1.** A women's bathroom. **2.** A bathroom for guests in a private home.

pow•der•y (pou′də rē) *adj.* **1.** Composed of or similar to powder: *powdery snow.* **2.** Covered or dusted with or as if with powder: *a lily powdery with pollen.* **3.** Easily made into powder; crumbly: *a soft powdery rock.*

pow•er (pou′ər) *n.* **1.** The ability or capacity to act or perform effectively. **2.** A specific ability, capability, or skill. Often used in the plural: *He has great powers of concentration.* **3.** Force or strength: *the pulling power of oxen.* See Synonyms at **strength. 4.** Forcefulness; effectiveness; impact: *a book of unusual power.* **5.** The ability or official capacity to exercise control; authority: *The emperor ruled with absolute power.* **6.** Control or leadership, especially of a government: *the party in power.* **7.** A source of authority or influence, especially a strong influential nation: *a world power.* **8.a.** The rate at which work is done with respect to time, measured in units such as the watt or horsepower. **b.** The rate, with respect to time, at which electricity does work or creates its equivalent in heat. **c.** Relative capability for doing work in a given time: *an engine with lots of power.* **9.a.** Energy that can be used for doing work, derived from such sources as wind, water, fuel, or electricity: *atomic power.* **b.** Electricity: *The power failed during the storm.* **10.** The number of times a number or an expression is multiplied by itself, as shown by an exponent: *ten to the sixth power.* **11.** A number that represents the magnification of an optical instrument, such as a microscope or telescope. *—adj.* **1.** Of or relating to political, social, or economic control: *a power struggle.* **2.** Operating with mechanical or electrical energy in place of bodily exertion: *power tools.* **3.** Of or relating to electricity: *power lines. —tr.v.* **pow•ered, pow•er•ing, pow•ers.** To supply with power, especially mechanical power: *The truck is powered by a gasoline engine.* [First written down before 1300 in Middle English, from Old French *poeir,* to be able, from *potis,* able.]

pow•er•boat (pou′ər bōt′) *n.* A motorboat.

pow•er•ful (pou′ər fəl) *adj.* **1.** Having or capable of exerting power: *powerful machines; a powerful nation.* **2.** Highly effective; potent: *a powerful poison.* **—pow′er•ful•ly** *adv.*

pow•er•house (pou′ər hous′) *n.* **1.** A power plant. **2.** A person or thing that possesses great force or energy.

pow•er•less (pou′ər lĭs) *adj.* Lacking strength, power, or authority to act or resist.

power of attorney *n., pl.* **powers of attorney.** A written document giving someone legal authority to act as another's agent or attorney.

power plant *n.* A building or structure, including all its equipment, that generates electric energy.

Pow•ha•tan[1] (pou′ə tăn′ *or* pou hăt′n). 1550?–1618. Algonquian leader who founded the Powhatan confederacy and maintained peaceful relations with English colonists.

Pow•ha•tan[2] (pou′ə tăn′ *or* pou hăt′n) *n., pl.* **Powhatan** or **Pow•ha•tans. 1.** A member of a confederation of Algonquian-speaking peoples of eastern Virginia. **2.** The Algonquian language of the Powhatan.

pow•wow (pou′wou′) *n.* **1.** A council or meeting of Native Americans. **2.a.** A Native American shaman. **b.** A ceremony conducted by a shaman, as in the performance of healing or hunting rituals. **3.** *Informal.* A conference or gathering.

pox (pŏks) *n.* A disease, such as chicken pox or smallpox, characterized by pus-filled eruptions on the skin.

pp. *abbr.* An abbreviation of: **1.** Pages. **2.** Past participle.

p.p. *abbr.* An abbreviation of: **1.** Past participle. **2.** Parcel post. **3.** Postpaid.

Pr The symbol for the element **praseodymium.**

PR *abbr.* An abbreviation of Puerto Rico.

pr. *abbr.* An abbreviation of: **1.** Pair. **2.** Price.

prac•ti•ca•ble (prăk′tĭ kə bəl) *adj.* **1.** Capable of being done, carried out, or put into effect; possible: *a practicable solution to the problem.* **2.** Usable for a certain purpose: *a practicable ski slope.* **—prac′ti•ca•bil′i•ty** *n.* **—prac′ti•ca•bly** *adv.*

prac•ti•cal (prăk′tĭ kəl) *adj.* **1.** Coming from or involving experience, practice, or use rather than theory, study, or speculation: *practical knowledge as opposed to book learning.* **2.** Manifested in or involving practice: *practical applications of geometry.* **3.** Capable of being used or put into effect; useful: *practical knowledge of Spanish.* **4.** Concerned with the operation or production of something useful: *a practical art.* **5.** Having or showing good judgment; sensible: *If we're practical, we can do the job quickly.* **6.** Being actually so in almost every respect; virtual: *The snowstorm was a practical disaster.* **—prac′ti•cal′i•ty** (prăk′tĭ kăl′ĭ tē) *n.*

practical joke *n.* A mischievous trick or prank played on a person, especially one that causes embarrassment.

prac•ti•cal•ly (prăk′tĭk lē) *adv.* **1.** In a practical way: *They dressed practically for the long hike.* **2.** For all practical purposes; virtually: *The weather was practically perfect.* **3.** Almost but not quite; nearly: *The school year is practically over.*

practical nurse *n.* A professional nurse who has experience but who is not a graduate of a school of nursing.

prac•tice (prăk′tĭs) *v.* **prac•ticed, prac•tic•ing, prac•tic•es.** *—tr.* **1.** To make a habit of; do or perform regularly: *Learn to practice self-control.* **2.** To do or work on over and over in order to gain or polish a skill: *practice the piano.* **3.** To work at, especially as a professional: *practice medicine.* **4.** To carry out in action; observe: *practice what one preaches. —intr.* **1.** To do or perform something regularly. **2.** To do something repeatedly in order to gain or polish a skill: *If you want to improve, you'll*

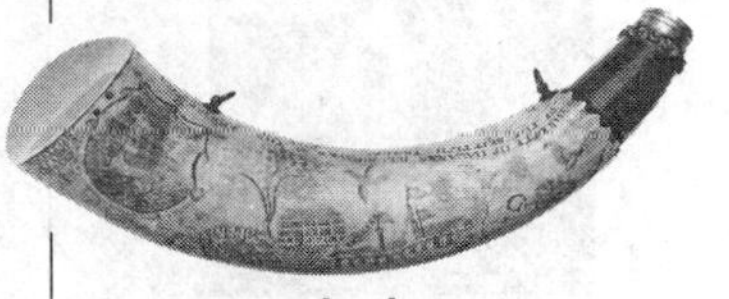

powder horn
1767 American powder horn

ă	pat	oi	boy
ā	pay	ou	out
âr	care	o͝o	took
ä	father	o͞o	boot
ĕ	pet	ŭ	cut
ē	be	ûr	urge
ĭ	pit	th	thin
ī	pie	*th*	this
îr	pier	hw	whoop
ŏ	pot	zh	vision
ō	toe	ə	about
ô	paw	N	*French* bon

prairie dog
Black-tailed prairie dog

prairie schooner

Word Building: pre–

The basic meaning of the prefix **pre–** is "before." It comes from the Latin word *prae*, which means "before, in front." In fact, the word **prefix** comes from *prae* + *fīxus*, a form of the Latin verb *fīgere* ("to fasten"). **Pre–** often appears in combination with verbs of Latin origin. For example, as early as the 16th century we have **preconceive**, **preexist**, and **premeditate**. **Predispose** and **prepossess** came into use in the 17th century, and **prepay** came into use in the 19th century.

have to practice. **3.** To work at a profession. —*n.* **1.** A habitual or customary action or way of doing something: *makes a practice of being on time.* See Synonyms at **habit. 2.a.** Experience or exercise in doing something that develops, maintains, or improves one's skill: *Practice will improve your singing.* **b.** Skill gained or maintained through repeated exercise: *She was out of practice.* **3.** Action, performance, use, or effect: *Put into practice what you have learned.* **4.** Exercise of an occupation or a profession. **5.** The business of a professional person: *She has her own law practice.* [First written down in 1392 in Middle English and spelled *practisen*, from Late Latin *prācticē*, practical.]

prac•ticed (prăk′tĭst) *adj.* Skilled or expert; proficient: *a practiced archer.*

practice teacher *n.* A student teacher.

prac•tise (prăk′tĭs) *v. & n. Chiefly British.* Variant of **practice.**

prac•ti•tion•er (prăk tĭsh′ə nər) *n.* A person who practices something, especially an occupation, a profession, or a technique.

prae•tor (prē′tər) *n.* An elected magistrate of the ancient Roman republic, ranking below a consul but having approximately the same functions.

prae•to•ri•an (prē tôr′ē ən) *adj.* **1.** Of or relating to a praetor. **2. Praetorian.** Of, making up, or belonging to the bodyguard of a Roman emperor. —*n.* **1.** A praetor or a former praetor. **2. Praetorian.** A member of the bodyguard of a Roman emperor.

prag•mat•ic (prăg măt′ĭk) *adj.* **1.** Concerned or dealing with facts and actual occurrences; practical: *a pragmatic approach to solving problems.* **2.** Of or relating to pragmatism. [First written down in 1543 in Modern English and spelled *pragmatical*, from Greek *pragma*, deed.] —**prag•mat′i•cal•ly** *adv.*

prag•ma•tism (prăg′mə tĭz′əm) *n.* **1.** The philosophical theory that the meaning of an idea or a proposition is to be judged by its practical results. **2.** A practical way of approaching or assessing situations or of solving problems.

Prague (präg). The capital and largest city of Czech Republic, in the western part of the country south-southeast of Dresden, Germany. It was the capital of Czechoslovakia from 1918 to 1992. Population, 1,189,828.

Prai•a (prī′ə). The capital of Cape Verde, on the Atlantic Ocean west of Africa. Population, 37,480.

prai•rie (prâr′ē) *n.* A wide area of flat or rolling, mostly treeless grassland, especially the large plain of central North America. [First written down in 1691 in American English, from Latin *prāta*, meadow.]

prairie chicken *n.* Either of two brownish birds of western North America, related to the grouse.

prairie dog *n.* Any of several burrowing rodents of the plains of central North America, living in large colonies and having a call resembling a dog's bark.

prairie schooner *n.* A covered wagon.

prairie wolf *n.* A coyote.

praise (prāz) *n.* **1.** Expression of approval, admiration, or commendation: *Praise from her family meant a lot to her.* **2.** Glory, honor, and adoration as given to a deity, ruler, or hero. —*tr.v.* **praised, prais•ing, prais•es. 1.** To express approval of or admiration for; commend: *Everyone praised her good sense.* **2.** To extol or exalt; worship. [First written down before 1325 in Middle English, from Late Latin *pretiāre*, to prize.] —**prais′er** *n.*

praise•wor•thy (prāz′wûr′thē) *adj.* **praise•wor•thi•er, praise•wor•thi•est.** Deserving praise; highly commendable: *a praiseworthy devotion.*

pram (prăm) *n. Chiefly British.* A baby carriage. [First written down in 1884 in Modern English, short for *perambulator.*]

prance (prăns) *intr.v.* **pranced, pranc•ing, pranc•es. 1.a.** To spring forward on the hind legs. Used of a horse. **b.** To move about by springing on the hind legs. Used of a horse. **2.** To ride a horse moving in such a fashion. **3.** To walk or move in a proud or spirited way; strut: *pranced onstage.* —*n.* The act or an instance of prancing.

prank (prăngk) *n.* A mischievous trick or practical joke. —**prank′ish** *adj.*

prank•ster (prăngk′stər) *n.* A person who plays tricks or pranks.

pra•se•o•dym•i•um (prā′zē ō dĭm′ē əm) *n. Symbol* **Pr** A soft rare-earth element used to tint ceramics green. Atomic number 59. See table at **element.**

prate (prāt) *v.* **prat•ed, prat•ing, prates.** —*intr.* To talk idly and at length; chatter. —*tr.* To utter idly or to little purpose.

prat•tle (prăt′l) *v.* **prat•tled, prat•tling, prat•tles.** —*intr.* To talk or chatter idly or foolishly: *prattling about how much things cost.* —*tr.* To utter or express by chattering foolishly. —*n.* Idle or meaningless chatter; babble.

prawn (prôn) *n.* Any of various shellfishes related to and resembling the shrimp, eaten as food.

pray (prā) *v.* **prayed, pray•ing, prays.** —*intr.* **1.** To say a prayer or prayers to God or a god. **2.** To make a fervent request or an entreaty. —*tr.* **1.** To utter or say a prayer or prayers to; address by prayer. **2.** To ask (someone) imploringly; beseech. **3.** To make a devout or an earnest request for: *I pray your permission to speak.* [First written down before 1225 in Middle English and spelled *preien*, from Latin *precārī.*]

❑ *These sound alike:* **pray, prey** (hunted animal).

prayer (prâr) *n.* **1.** The act of addressing or appealing to God or a god, as in devotion, confession, or pleading. **2.** A special set of words used in addressing or appealing to God. **3. prayers.** A religious service consisting mostly of prayers: *morning prayers.* **4.** An earnest appeal, request, or plea: *a prayer for mercy.* **5.** The slightest chance or hope, as for survival or success: *Without our best player we don't have a prayer.*

prayer book *n.* A book containing religious prayers.

prayer•ful (prâr′fəl) *adj.* Inclined to pray frequently; devout.

pray•ing mantis (prā′ĭng) *n.* A mantis.

pre– *pref.* A prefix that means: **1.** Earlier; before: *prehistoric.* **2.** In advance: *prepay.* —See Note.

preach (prēch) *v.* **preached, preach•ing, preach•es.** —*tr.* **1.** To proclaim or put forth in a sermon: *preaches the gospel.* **2.** To teach or advocate and urge others to accept or follow: *Our leaders preach tolerance of others.* **3.** To deliver (a sermon): *The minister preached the morning sermon.* —*intr.* **1.** To deliver a sermon. **2.** To give religious or moral instruction, especially in a tedious manner: *a writer with an unfortunate tendency to preach.* [First written down before 1200 in Middle English and spelled *preachen*, from Latin *praedicāre*, to proclaim.]

preach•er (prē′chər) *n.* A person who preaches, especially one who proclaims the gospel as an occupation.

preach•y (prē′chē) *adj.* **preach•i•er, preach•i•est.** Inclined to or given to tedious and excessive moralizing.

pre•am•ble (prē′ăm′bəl) *n.* An introductory statement, especially the introduction to a formal document that serves to explain its purpose. [First written down about 1395 in Middle English, from Medieval Latin *preambulum* : *prae-*, in front + *ambulāre*, to walk.]

pre•am•pli•fi•er (prē ăm′plə fī′ər) *n.* An electronic circuit or device designed to amplify and often otherwise process very weak signals before they are further amplified.

pre•ar•range (prē′ə **rānj′**) *tr.v.* **pre•ar•ranged, pre•ar•rang•ing, pre•ar•rang•es.** To arrange in advance.

Pre•cam•bri•an (prē **kăm′**brē ən) *adj.* Of, belonging to, or being the geologic time that preceded the Cambrian Period. During the Precambrian, primitive forms of life appeared. See table at **geologic time.** —*n.* The Precambrian Era or its series of rocks.

pre•car•i•ous (prĭ **kâr′**ē əs) *adj.* **1.** Dangerously lacking in security or stability: *dangling in a precarious position.* **2.** Subject to chance or unknown conditions: *The economic outlook remains precarious.* —**pre•car′i•ous•ly** *adv.*

pre•cau•tion (prĭ **kô′**shən) *n.* **1.** An action taken in advance to guard against possible danger, error, or accident: *take safety precautions.* **2.** Care taken or caution shown in advance; forethought: *a need for precaution.*

pre•cau•tion•ar•y (prĭ **kô′**shə nĕr′ē) *adj.* Of, relating to, or constituting a precaution: *precautionary measures; precautionary advice.*

pre•cede (prĭ **sēd′**) *v.* **pre•ced•ed, pre•ced•ing, pre•cedes.** —*tr.* To come, exist, or occur before in time, order, position, or rank: *A short lecture will precede the movie.* —*intr.* To come or go before in time. [First written down before 1425 in Middle English and spelled *preceden*, from Latin *praecēdere* : *prae-*, before + *cēdere*, to go.]

prec•e•dence (**prĕs′**ĭ dəns *or* prĭ **sēd′**ns) *n.* **1.** The fact, state, or right of preceding; priority: *Business takes precedence over pleasure.* **2.** Priority claimed or received because of preeminence or superiority.

prec•e•dent (**prĕs′**ĭ dənt) *n.* **1.** An act or instance that can serve as an example in dealing with subsequent similar instances. **2.** Convention or custom arising from practice: *The precedent has been to give an exam every six weeks.* —*adj.* (prĭ **sēd′**nt *or* **prĕs′**ĭ dənt). Preceding.

pre•ced•ing (prĭ **sē′**dĭng) *adj.* Existing or coming before another or others in time, place, rank, or sequence: *the preceding winter; the preceding page.*

pre•cept (**prē′**sĕpt′) *n.* A rule or principle of conduct or procedure.

preceptor (prĭ **sĕp′**tər *or* **prē′**sĕp′tər) *n.* **1.** An instructor; a teacher. **2.** An expert or a specialist who gives practical experience and training to a student.

pre•ces•sion (prē **sĕsh′**ən) *n.* **1.** The act or state of preceding; precedence. **2.** The motion of the axis of a spinning body, such as the wobbling of a spinning top, that arises when an external force acts on the axis. **3.** The motion of this kind made by the earth.

pre•cinct (**prē′**sĭngkt′) *n.* **1.** A subdivision or district of a city or town patrolled by a unit of the police force. **2.** An election district of a city or town: *a canvass of the voters in his precinct.* **3.** An area or enclosure with definite boundaries. Often used in the plural: *within the precincts of the university.* **4. precincts.** A neighboring region; environs.

pre•cious (**prĕsh′**əs) *adj.* **1.** Of high cost or worth; valuable: *precious metals.* **2.** Highly esteemed; cherished: *thanked her for her precious advice.* **3.** Dear; beloved. —*n.* A person who is dear or beloved; a darling. —*adv.* Used as an intensive: *We have precious little time.* [First written down about 1250 in Middle English and spelled *preciouse*, from Latin *pretiōsus*, from *pretium*, price.] —**pre′cious•ly** *adv.* —**pre′cious•ness** *n.*

precious stone *n.* Any of several gems, such as the diamond or the ruby, that have high economic value because of their rarity or appearance.

prec•i•pice (**prĕs′**ə pĭs) *n.* A very steep or overhanging mass of rock, such as the face of a cliff. [First written down in 1598 in Modern English, from Latin *praeceps*, headlong.]

pre•cip•i•tate (prĭ **sĭp′**ĭ tāt′) *v.* **pre•cip•i•tat•ed, pre•cip•i•tat•ing, pre•cip•i•tates.** —*tr.* **1.** To throw from or as if from a great height; cast down. **2.** To cause to happen, especially suddenly or prematurely; bring on: *The revelation of the scandal precipitated the director's resignation.* **3.** To cause (water vapor) to condense from the atmosphere and fall as rain or snow. **4.** To separate chemically from a solution in the form of a solid: *We precipitated the minerals from the water by adding borax.* —*intr.* **1.** To condense and fall from the air as rain or snow. **2.** To be separated from a solution as a solid. **3.** To fall or be thrown headlong. —*adj.* (prĭ **sĭp′**ĭ tĭt). **1.** Moving rapidly and heedlessly; speeding headlong: *the precipitate course of a tornado.* **2.** Acting or made hastily or impulsively; rash: *a precipitate decision.* **3.** Occurring suddenly and unexpectedly: *a precipitate drop in prices.* —*n.* (prĭ **sĭp′**ĭ tāt′ *or* prĭ **sĭp′**ĭ tĭt). A solid material separated from a solution by chemical means. [First written down in 1528 in Modern English, from Latin *praeceps*, headlong : *prae-*, before, first + *caput*, head.]

pre•cip•i•ta•tion (prĭ sĭp′ĭ **tā′**shən) *n.* **1.** A headlong fall or rush. **2.** Abrupt or impulsive haste. **3.** A hastening or an acceleration, especially one that is sudden or unexpected. **4.a.** A form of water, such as rain, snow, or sleet, that condenses from the atmosphere and falls to the surface of the earth. **b.** The amount of such water falling in a given area during a given period of time: *Last month's precipitation in our state was 2 inches.* **5.** The production of a precipitate, as in a chemical reaction.

pre•cip•i•tous (prĭ **sĭp′**ĭ təs) *adj.* **1.** Similar to a precipice; extremely steep. **2.** Having several precipices: *a precipitous bluff.* —**pre•cip′i•tous•ly** *adv.* —**pre•cip′i•tous•ness** *n.*

pre•cise (prĭ **sīs′**) *adj.* **1.** Clearly expressed or delineated; definite: *Please be precise in your instructions.* **2.** Distinct from others; particular: *on this precise spot.* **3.** Distinct or correct in sound or meaning: *Can you give me the precise pronunciation of that word?* **4.** Exact, as in performance, execution, or amount; accurate or correct: *a precise measurement.* **5.** Strictly observing established forms and procedures: *a precise gentleman who ate breakfast at 7:15 each morning.* [First written down about 1443 in Middle English, from Latin *praecīsus*, cut short, concise, from *praecīdere*, to cut short.] —**pre•cise′ly** *adv.* —**pre•cise′ness** *n.*

pre•ci•sion (prĭ **sĭzh′**ən) *n.* The state or quality of being precise: *the precision of a chemist's scales.*

pre•clude (prĭ **klo͞od′**) *tr.v.* **pre•clud•ed, pre•clud•ing, pre•cludes.** To make impossible, as by action taken in advance; prevent: *High temperatures on Venus preclude any chance of life as we know it.*

pre•co•cious (prĭ **kō′**shəs) *adj.* Showing skills or abilities, especially mental capabilities, at an earlier age than is normal: *a precocious child.* [First written down in 1650 in Modern English, from Latin *praecox*, premature, from *praecoquere*, to ripen early.] —**pre•co′cious•ly** *adv.* —**pre•co′cious•ness, pre•coc′i•ty** (prĭ **kŏs′**ĭ tē) *n.*

pre-Co•lum•bi•an (prē′kə **lŭm′**bē ən) *adj.* Of or relating to the Americas before the arrival of Columbus: *pre-Columbian empires.*

pre•con•ceive (prē′kən **sēv′**) *tr.v.* **pre•con•ceived, pre•con•ceiv•ing, pre•con•ceives.** To form an opinion or a conception of (something) before adequate knowledge is available; prejudge.

pre•con•cep•tion (prē′kən **sĕp′**shən) *n.* An idea or

precipice
El Capitan in Yosemite National Park in California

pre-Columbian
Gold pendant from west-central Colombia

ă	**pat**	oi	**boy**
ā	**pay**	ou	**out**
âr	**care**	o͝o	**took**
ä	**father**	o͞o	**boot**
ĕ	**pet**	ŭ	**cut**
ē	**be**	ûr	**urge**
ĭ	**pit**	th	**thin**
ī	**pie**	*th*	**this**
îr	**pier**	hw	**whoop**
ŏ	**pot**	zh	**vision**
ō	**toe**	ə	**about**
ô	**paw**	N	*French* **bon**

Word Building: predict

The word root *–dict–* in English words comes from the past participle *dictus* of the Latin verb *dīcere*, "to say." Thus we have **predict**, "to say ahead of time, foretell" (using the prefix *prae–*, "before") and **contradict**, "to speak against" (*contrā–*, "opposite, against").

prefab
Prefabricated building being assembled

opinion formed before adequate knowledge is available; a prejudice.

pre•con•di•tion (prē′kən **dĭsh′**ən) *n.* A condition that must exist or be established before something can occur or be considered; a prerequisite.

pre•cur•sor (prĭ **kûr′**sər *or* **prē′**kûr′sər) *n.* **1.** An indicator of a person or thing to come; a forerunner: *The cool breeze was a precursor of the storm.* **2.** A person or thing that precedes another: *She greeted her precursor, the former principal.* [First written down about 1425 in Middle English and spelled *precursoure*, from Latin *praecursor*, from *praecurrere*, to run before.]

pred. *abbr.* An abbreviation of predicate.

pre•date (prē **dāt′**) *tr.v.* **pre•dat•ed, pre•dat•ing, pre•dates. 1.** To mark with a date earlier than the actual one: *predate a check.* **2.** To precede in time; antedate: *The American Revolution predates the French Revolution.*

pred•a•tor (**prĕd′**ə tər) *n.* An animal that lives by feeding on other animals; a preying animal.

pred•a•to•ry (**prĕd′**ə tôr′ē) *adj.* **1.** Living by preying on other animals: *a predatory animal.* **2.** Living by or given to robbing or destroying others for personal gain. [First written down in 1589 in Modern English, from Latin *praedārī*, to plunder, from *praeda*, booty.]

pred•e•ces•sor (**prĕd′**ĭ sĕs′ər *or* **prē′**dĭ sĕs′) *n.* **1.** A person who precedes another in time, especially in holding an office or a function: *The new mayor's predecessor welcomed her.* **2.** Something that has been succeeded by another: *The new building is more spacious than its predecessor.*

pre•des•ti•na•tion (prē dĕs′tə **nā′**shən) *n.* **1.** The act of predestining or the condition of being predestined. **2.a.** The doctrine that God has planned and ordered all events in advance. **b.** The doctrine that God has assigned every soul to eternal salvation or damnation. **3.** Fate; destiny.

pre•des•tine (prē **dĕs′**tĭn) *tr.v.* **pre•des•tined, pre•des•tin•ing, pre•des•tines.** To fix or decide beforehand, especially by divine decree: *The Greeks believed that the gods predestined the early death of heroes.*

pre•de•ter•mine (prē′dĭ **tûr′**mĭn) *tr.v.* **pre•de•ter•mined, pre•de•ter•min•ing, pre•de•ter•mines. 1.** To determine, decide, or establish in advance: *Climate predetermines the kinds of animals that can live in a region.* **2.** To influence or sway toward an action or opinion; predispose. **—pre′de•ter′mi•na′tion** *n.*

pre•dic•a•ment (prĭ **dĭk′**ə mənt) *n.* A situation, especially an unpleasant or troubling one, from which it is difficult to remove oneself.

pred•i•cate (**prĕd′**ĭ kāt′) *v.* **pred•i•cat•ed, pred•i•cat•ing, pred•i•cates.** *—tr.* **1.** To declare or assert as an attribute or a quality of something: *His article predicated the perfectibility of the new engine.* **2.** To base or establish (a statement or an action, for example): *She predicated her argument on the assumption that inflation would not go up.* **3.** To carry the connotation of; imply. *—intr.* To make a statement or an assertion. *—n.* (**prĕd′**ĭ kĭt). The part of a sentence or clause that expresses the action or condition of the subject and includes the verb and the objects or phrases governed by the verb, as *opened the door* in *Jane opened the door.* *—adj.* (**prĕd′**ĭ kĭt). Of or belonging to the predicate of a sentence or clause. —See Note at **adjective.**

predicate nominative *n.* A noun or pronoun that follows a linking verb and refers to the same person or thing as the subject of the verb, as *President* in *Roosevelt became President.*

pre•dict (prĭ **dĭkt′**) *tr.v.* **pre•dict•ed, pre•dict•ing, pre•dicts.** To tell about or make known in advance, especially on the basis of special knowledge; foretell: *predicted showers for this evening.* [First written down in 1671 in Modern English, from Latin *praedīcere* : *prae-*, before + *dīcere*, to say.] **—pre•dict′a•ble** *adj.* —See Note.

pre•dic•tion (prĭ **dĭk′**shən) *n.* **1.** The act of predicting. **2.** Something that is foretold or predicted: *Her predictions came true.*

pred•i•lec•tion (prĕd′l **ĕk′**shən *or* prēd′l **ĕk′**shən) *n.* A tendency to think favorably of something; a preference.

pre•dis•pose (prē′dĭ **spōz′**) *tr.v.* **pre•dis•posed, pre•dis•pos•ing, pre•dis•pos•es. 1.** To incline or influence beforehand: *Her sense of humor predisposed me in her favor.* **2.** To make susceptible or liable: *conditions that predispose miners to lung disease.*

pre•dis•po•si•tion (prē′dĭs pə **zĭsh′**ən) *n.* The state of being predisposed; tendency, inclination, or susceptibility.

pre•dom•i•nant (prĭ **dŏm′**ə nənt) *adj.* **1.** Greater than all others in strength, authority, or importance; dominant: *the predominant nation.* **2.** Most common or conspicuous: *the predominant color in a design.* **—pre•dom′i•nance** *n.* **—pre•dom′i•nant•ly** *adv.*

pre•dom•i•nate (prĭ **dŏm′**ə nāt′) *intr.v.* **pre•dom•i•nat•ed, pre•dom•i•nat•ing, pre•dom•i•nates. 1.** To have or gain power or controlling influence; prevail. **2.** To be greater than others in number or importance: *People of Italian descent predominate in this neighborhood.*

pre•em•i•nent or **pre-em•i•nent** (prē **ĕm′**ə nənt) *adj.* Superior to or notable above all others; outstanding: *the preeminent artist of the movement.* **—pre•em′i•nence** *n.* **—pre•em′i•nent•ly** *adv.*

pre•empt or **pre-empt** (prē **ĕmpt′**) *tr.v.* **pre•empt•ed, pre•empt•ing, pre•empts** or **pre-empt•ed, pre-empt•ing, pre-empts. 1.** To take for oneself before others: *got to the market early and preempted the bargains.* **2.** To take the place of; displace: *The President's address will preempt the regular shows this evening.* **3.** To gain possession of by prior right, especially to settle on (public land) so as to obtain the right to buy before others. [First written down in 1850 in American English : Latin *prae-*, before + Latin *ēmptiō*, buying.]

preen (prēn) *v.* **preened, preen•ing, preens.** *—tr.* **1.a.** To smooth or clean (feathers) with the beak or bill: *The parrot preened its feathers.* **b.** To trim or clean (fur) with the tongue, as cats do. **2.** To dress or groom (oneself) with elaborate care; primp. **3.** To take self-satisfied pride in (oneself). *—intr.* **1.** To primp. **2.** To swell with pride; gloat.

pre•ex•ist (prē′ĭg **zĭst′**) *intr.v.* **pre•ex•ist•ed, pre•ex•ist•ing, pre•ex•ists.** To exist beforehand.

pre•fab (**prē′**făb′) *Informal. adj.* Prefabricated. *—n.* A prefabricated house or other structure.

pre•fab•ri•cate (prē **făb′**rĭ kāt′) *tr.v.* **pre•fab•ri•cat•ed, pre•fab•ri•cat•ing, pre•fab•ri•cates.** To build or manufacture (a building or section of a building, for example) in advance, especially in sections than can be easily shipped and assembled. **—pre•fab′ri•ca′tion** *n.*

pref•ace (**prĕf′**ĭs) *n.* **1.** An introductory essay, placed at the beginning of a book for explanation. **2.** A statement or series of remarks that introduces or explains what is to come: *a preface to a speech.* *—tr.v.* **pref•aced, pref•ac•ing, pref•ac•es.** To introduce or provide with a preface: *prefaced his lecture with a joke.* [First written down about 1380 in Middle English, from Latin *praefātiō* : *prae-*, before + *fārī*, to speak.] **—pref′ac•er** *n.*

pref•a•to•ry (**prĕf′**ə tôr′ē) *adj.* Of, relating to, or serving as an introduction; preliminary: *prefatory remarks.*

pre•fect (prē′fĕkt′) *n.* **1.** Any of various ancient Roman officials of high rank. **2.** Any of various modern administrative officials, such as a chief of police in Paris, France. **3.** A student monitor or officer, especially in a private school.

pre•fer (prĭ fûr′) *tr.v.* **pre•ferred, pre•fer•ring, pre•fers. 1.** To choose as more desirable; like better: *I prefer tea to coffee.* **2.** To file or present for consideration before a legal authority: *prefer the suit to a higher court.* [First written down before 1393 in Middle English and spelled *preferren*, from Latin *praeferre* : *prae-*, before, in front + *ferre*, to carry.]

pref•er•a•ble (prĕf′ər ə bəl) *adj.* More desirable; preferred. **—pref′er•a•bly** *adv.*

pref•er•ence (prĕf′ər əns) *n.* **1.** A liking for a person or thing over another or others: *had a preference for rice over potatoes.* **2.** The act of preferring; the exercise of choice: *He dressed simply out of preference.* **3.** A person or thing preferred; one's choice: *asked for a window seat, but did not obtain her preference.* See Synonyms at **choice.**

pref•er•en•tial (prĕf′ə rĕn′shəl) *adj.* Showing preference; favoring one over others: *The owner's friends always receive preferential treatment.* **—pref′er•en′tial•ly** *adv.*

pre•fer•ment (prĭ fûr′mənt) *n.* **1.** The act of advancing to a higher position or office; promotion: *the boss's preferment of her to an executive position.* **2.** A position or rank giving advancement, as of profit or prestige. **3.** The act of preferring or the state of being preferred.

pre•fig•ure (prē fĭg′yər) *tr.v.* **pre•fig•ured, pre•fig•ur•ing, pre•fig•ures. 1.** To suggest, indicate, or represent by a preceding form or model; foreshadow. **2.** To imagine or picture to oneself in advance.

pre•fix (prē′fĭks′) *tr.v.* **pre•fixed, pre•fix•ing, pre•fix•es.** To add at the beginning or front: *prefixed the title "Dr." to his name.* —*n.* **1.** An affix placed at the beginning of a word to change its meaning. For example, *un-* in *unable*, *pre-* in *preheat*, and *re-* in *replay* are prefixes. **2.** A title placed before a person's name.

pre•flight (prē′flīt′) *adj.* Occurring before flight.

preg•nan•cy (prĕg′nən sē) *n., pl.* **preg•nan•cies. 1.** The condition of being pregnant. **2.** The time during which one is pregnant.

preg•nant (prĕg′nənt) *adj.* **1.** Carrying developing offspring within the body. **2.** Significant; full of meaning: *a pregnant pause in the campaign speech.* **3.** Full or fraught; replete: *a situation pregnant with danger.*

pre•heat (prē hēt′) *tr.v.* **pre•heat•ed, pre•heat•ing, pre•heats.** To heat (an oven, for example) beforehand: *Preheat the oven to 350° before baking.*

pre•hen•sile (prē hĕn′səl *or* prē hĕn′sīl′) *adj.* Used or adapted for grasping or holding, especially by wrapping around something: *a monkey's prehensile tail.*

pre•his•tor•ic (prē′hĭ stôr′ĭk *or* prē′hĭ stŏr′ĭk) *adj.* Of or belonging to the time before history or events were recorded in writing: *a prehistoric animal.* **—pre′his•tor′i•cal•ly** *adv.*

pre•judge (prē jŭj′) *tr.v.* **pre•judged, pre•judg•ing, pre•judg•es.** To judge beforehand without adequate evidence.

prej•u•dice (prĕj′ə dĭs) *n.* **1.** An adverse judgment or opinion formed unfairly or before one knows the facts; a bias: *a prejudice against unfamiliar foods.* **2.** Irrational suspicion or hatred of a particular race, religion, or group. **3.** Harm or injury caused by the preconceived unfavorable conviction of another or others. —*tr.v.* **prej•u•diced, prej•u•dic•ing, prej•u•dic•es. 1.** To cause (someone) to judge prematurely and irrationally: *an experience that prejudiced her against dogs.* **2.** To affect harmfully by a judgment or an act. [First written down about 1300 in Middle English, from Latin *praeiūdicium* : *prae-*, before + *iūdicium*, judgment.]

prej•u•di•cial (prĕj′ə dĭsh′əl) *adj.* **1.** Harmful; detrimental. **2.** Causing or tending toward preconceived judgment or convictions. **—prej′u•di′cial•ly** *adv.*

prel•ate (prĕl′ĭt) *n.* A high-ranking member of the clergy, especially a bishop.

pre•lim•i•nar•y (prĭ lĭm′ə nĕr′ē) *adj.* Prior to or preparing for the main matter, action, or business; introductory: *preliminary sketches for a building.* —*n., pl.* **pre•lim•i•nar•ies.** Something that leads to or serves as preparation for a main matter, action, or business: *She began her lecture without the usual preliminaries.* [First written down before 1667 in Modern English : Latin *prae-*, before + Latin *līmen*, threshold.]

prel•ude (prĕl′yo͞od′ *or* prā′lo͞od′ *or* prē′lo͞od′) *n.* **1.** An introductory performance, event, or action that precedes a more important one; a preliminary. **2.a.** A piece or movement of music that acts as introduction to a larger work. **b.** A fairly short composition of the 15th and early 16th centuries in a free style, usually for piano or orchestra. —*v.* **prel•ud•ed, prel•ud•ing, prel•udes.** —*tr.* To serve as a prelude to. —*intr.* To serve as a prelude. [First written down in 1561 in Modern English, from Latin *praelūdere*, to play beforehand.]

pre•mar•i•tal (prē măr′ĭ tl) *adj.* Taking place or existing before marriage.

pre•ma•ture (prē′mə tyo͝or′ *or* prē′mə to͝or′- *or* prē′mə cho͝or′) *adj.* **1.** Appearing or occurring before the usual time; unexpectedly early: *a premature death.* **2.** Born after too short a period of development: *a premature baby.* **—pre′ma•ture′ly** *adv.*

pre•med (prē′mĕd′) *Informal. adj.* Premedical. —*n.* **1.** A premedical student. **2.** A premedical program of study.

pre•med•i•cal (prē mĕd′ĭ kəl) *adj.* Of or relating to studies that prepare one for the study of medicine.

pre•med•i•tate (prē mĕd′ĭ tāt′) *tr.v.* **pre•med•i•tat•ed, pre•med•i•tat•ing, pre•med•i•tates.** To plan, arrange, or plot (a crime, for example) in advance. **—pre•med′i•ta′tion** *n.*

pre•mier (prĭ mîr′ *or* prē′mîr) *adj.* **1.** First in status or importance; principal or chief. **2.** Earliest. —*n.* (prĭ mîr′). A prime minister or a chief administrative officer, as of a country or province. [First written down in 1448 in Middle English and spelled *primer*, from Latin *prīmārius*, from *prīmus*, first.]

pre•miere (prĭ mîr′ *or* prĭ myâr′) *n.* The first public performance of a play, motion picture, or other theatrical work.

prem•ise (prĕm′ĭs) *n.* **1.** A proposition upon which an argument is based or from which a conclusion is drawn. **2. premises.** Property and the buildings on it: *The playground is part of the school premises.* —*tr.v.* **prem•ised, prem•is•ing, prem•is•es.** To state in advance as an introduction or explanation. [First written down about 1380 in Middle English and spelled *premisse*, from Latin *praemissus*, set in front, put forward.]

pre•mi•um (prē′mē əm) *n.* **1.** A prize or an award. **2.** Something offered free or at a reduced price as an inducement to buy something else. **3.** An extra or unexpected benefit or sum of money; a bonus: *The store gave out gifts as premiums to the first-day customers.* **4.a.** The amount paid or payable for an insurance policy. **b.** The amount paid to obtain a loan. **5.** An unusual or high value: *Many people*

prehensile
Opossum with prehensile tail

ă	pat	oi	boy
ā	pay	ou	out
âr	care	o͝o	took
ä	father	o͞o	boot
ĕ	pet	ŭ	cut
ē	be	ûr	urge
ĭ	pit	th	thin
ī	pie	*th*	this
îr	pier	hw	whoop
ŏ	pot	zh	vision
ō	toe	ə	about
ô	paw	N	*French* bon

place a premium on a good education. **6.** The amount at which a securities option is bought or sold. *—adj.* Of especially high quality or value: *premium gasoline.* ***—idiom.* at a premium.** More valuable than usual, as from scarcity: *Gasoline was at a premium that summer.* [First written down in 1601 in Modern English, from Latin *praemium.*]

pre•mo•lar (prē **mō′**lər) *n.* Any of eight bicuspid teeth arranged in pairs on both sides of the upper and lower jaws between the canines and molars. **—pre•mo′lar** *adj.*

pre•mo•ni•tion (prē′mə **nĭsh′**ən *or* prĕm′ə **nĭsh′**ən) *n.* **1.** An advance warning: *gave no premonition of her plans.* **2.** A presentiment of the future; a foreboding: *had a premonition of disaster.* [First written down in 1545 in Modern English, from Latin *praemonēre,* to forewarn.]

pre•na•tal (prē **nāt′**l) *adj.* Of or occurring in the time before birth.

pre•oc•cu•pa•tion (prē ŏk′yə **pā′**shən) *n.* **1.** The state of being preoccupied; absorption of the attention or intellect. **2.** Something that preoccupies or engrosses the mind: *Increasing profits was his sole preoccupation.*

pre•oc•cu•pied (prē **ŏk′**yə pīd′) *adj.* **1.** Absorbed in thought; engrossed: *was preoccupied and barely touched her lunch.* **2.** Excessively concerned with something; distracted.

pre•oc•cu•py (prē **ŏk′**yə pī′) *tr.v.* **pre•oc•cu•pied, pre•oc•cu•py•ing, pre•oc•cu•pies.** To hold the attention or interest of; engage deeply or completely: *questions that have preoccupied scientists for decades.*

pre•or•dain (prē′ôr **dān′**) *tr.v.* **pre•or•dained, pre•or•dain•ing, pre•or•dains.** To appoint, decree, or ordain in advance; foreordain.

prep (prĕp) *Informal. adj.* Preparatory. *—n.* A preparatory school.

prep. *abbr.* An abbreviation of preposition.

pre•pack•age (prē **păk′**ĭj) *tr.v.* **pre•pack•aged, pre•pack•ag•ing, pre•pack•ag•es.** To wrap or package (a product) before marketing.

pre•paid (**prē**pād′) *adj.* Paid or paid for in advance: *a prepaid vacation tour.* *—v.* Past tense of **prepay.**

prep•a•ra•tion (prĕp′ə **rā′**shən) *n.* **1.a.** The act or process of preparing: *the preparation of dinner for six persons.* **b.** The condition of having been made ready beforehand; readiness: *a ship in good preparation for a voyage.* **2.** A preliminary measure necessary in getting ready for something: *final preparations for a rocket launch.* **3.** A substance or mixture prepared for a certain use: *a preparation of herbs for seasoning vegetables.*

pre•par•a•to•ry (prĭ **păr′**ə tôr′ē *or* prĭ **pâr′**ə tôr′ē *or* **prĕp′**ər ə tôr′ē) *adj.* Serving to make ready or prepare; introductory: *preparatory exercises before a race.*

preparatory school *n.* A usually private secondary school that prepares students for college.

pre•pare (prĭ **pâr′**) *v.* **pre•pared, pre•par•ing, pre•pares.** *—tr.* **1.** To make ready beforehand for some purpose, task, or event: *prepare the wood surface for painting by cleaning it.* **2.** To put together or make by combining various elements or ingredients: *prepare a book report; prepare the salad dressing.* *—intr.* To put things or oneself in readiness; get ready: *preparing to leave town.* [First written down in 1466 in Middle English and spelled *preparen,* from Latin *praeparāre.*] **—pre•par′er** *n.*

pre•par•ed•ness (prĭ **pâr′**ĭd nĭs) *n.* The state of being prepared, especially military readiness for combat.

pre•pay (prē **pā′**) *tr.v.* **pre•paid, pre•pay•ing, pre•pays.** To pay or pay for beforehand: *She agreed to prepay the rent.* **—pre•pay′ment** *n.*

pre•pon•der•ance (prĭ **pŏn′**dər əns) *n.* Superiority in weight, force, importance, or influence.

pre•pon•der•ant (prĭ **pŏn′**dər ənt) *adj.* Greater in weight, importance, force, or influence. [First written down before 1450 in Middle English, from Latin *praeponderāre,* to outweigh.] **—pre•pon′der•ant•ly** *adv.*

prep•o•si•tion (prĕp′ə **zĭsh′**ən) *n.* **1.** A word placed before a noun or pronoun that indicates the relationship between that noun or pronoun and another word. Some common English prepositions are *at, by, from, in, on, to,* and *with.* **2.** A word or phrase, such as *concerning* or *in regard to,* that functions as a preposition. **—prep′o•si′tion•al** *adj.* **—prep′o•si′tion•al•ly** *adv.*

prep•o•si•tion•al phrase (prĕp′ə **zĭsh′**ə nəl) *n.* A phrase consisting of a preposition and its object, as *by her* in *The book was written by her.*

pre•pos•sess•ing (prē′pə **zĕs′**ĭng) *adj.* Serving to impress favorably; pleasing. **—pre′pos•sess′ing•ly** *adv.*

pre•pos•ter•ous (prĭ **pŏs′**tər əs) *adj.* Contrary to nature, reason, or common sense; absurd. **—pre•pos′ter•ous•ly** *adv.* **—pre•pos′ter•ous•ness** *n.*

prep•py or **prep•pie** (**prĕp′**ē) *n., pl.* **prep•pies.** *Informal.* **1.** A student in a preparatory school. **2.** A person whose manner and dress are considered typical of traditional preparatory schools. **—prep′py, prep′pie** *adj.*

prep school *n. Informal.* A preparatory school.

pre•puce (**prē′**pyo͞os′) *n.* **1.** The foreskin of the penis. **2.** A loose fold of skin at the tip of the clitoris.

pre•req•ui•site (prē **rĕk′**wĭ zĭt) *adj.* Required or necessary as a prior condition: *a course that is prerequisite to more advanced studies.* *—n.* Something that is prerequisite.

pre•rog•a•tive (prĭ **rŏg′**ə tĭv) *n.* A right or privilege, especially one that accompanies the heredity, rank, status, or job of an individual or a group.

pres. *abbr.* An abbreviation of: **1.** Present. **2.** Also **Pres.** President.

pres•age (**prĕs′**ĭj) *n.* **1.** A sign or warning of what is going to happen; an omen. **2.** A feeling about what is going to happen; a presentiment. *—v.* (prĭ **sāj′** *or* **prĕs′**ĭj). **pre•saged, pre•sag•ing, pre•sag•es.** *—tr.* **1.** To indicate or warn of in advance; portend: *A dark sky presaged the coming storm.* **2.** To foretell; prophesy: *a recession presaged by many economists.* *—intr.* To make or utter a prediction. [First written down before 1393 in Middle English, from Latin *praesāgium* : *prae-,* before + *sāgīre,* to perceive.]

pres•by•ter (**prĕz′**bĭ tər *or* **prĕs′**bĭ tər) *n.* **1.** A priest in various hierarchical churches. **2.** An elder in a Presbyterian Church. [First written down in 1597 in Modern English, from Greek *presbuteros,* elder, from *presbus,* old man.]

pres•by•te•ri•an (prĕz′bĭ **tîr′**ē ən *or* prĕs′bĭ **tîr′**ē ən) *n.* **Presbyterian.** A member or an adherent of a Presbyterian Church. *—adj.* **1.** Of or relating to presbyters. **2. Presbyterian.** Of or relating to a Presbyterian Church. **—pres′by•te′ri•an•ism** *n.*

Presbyterian Church *n.* Any of various Protestant churches governed by presbyters and traditionally Calvinist in doctrine.

pre•school (**prē′skōōl′**) *adj.* Of or intended for the years of childhood that precede the beginning of elementary school. *—n.* (**prē′**sko͞ol′). A nursery school.

pre•sci•ence (**prē′**shē əns *or* **prĕsh′**ē əns) *n.* Knowledge of actions or events before they occur; foresight. **—pre′sci•ent** *adj.*

pre•scribe (prĭ **skrīb′**) *v.* **pre•scribed, pre•scrib•ing, pre•scribes.** *—tr.* **1.** To set down as a rule or guide; impose or direct: *The government prescribes* *standards for the purity of food.* **2.** To order or recommend the use of (a drug, for example): *The doctor prescribed bed rest.* —*intr.* **1.** To establish rules, laws, or directions. **2.** To order a medicine or other treatment. [First written down in 1445 in Middle English and spelled *prescriben,* from Latin *praescrībere* : *prae-,* before + *scrībere,* to write.]

pre•scrip•tion (prĭ **skrĭp′**shən) *n.* **1.** The act or process of prescribing. **2.** Something that is prescribed; a recommendation or rule: *prescriptions for correct usage in an English textbook.* **3.a.** A written instruction from a physician indicating what treatment or medication a patient is to receive. **b.** A medicine ordered by prescription. **c.** Specifications for a set of corrective lenses, written by an ophthalmologist or optometrist.

pre•scrip•tive (prĭ **skrĭp′**tĭv) *adj.* **1.** Sanctioned or authorized by long-standing custom or usage. **2.** Making or giving directions, laws, or rules; giving instructions on what to do or how to do it: *a prescriptive grammar.* —**pre•scrip′tive•ly** *adv.*

pres•ence (**prĕz′**əns) *n.* **1.** The fact or condition of being present: *Your presence is required at the meeting.* **2.** The immediate nearness of a person or thing: *Slow oxidation of the metal in the presence of moisture causes rust.* **3.** A person's bearing: *She has great presence on the stage.* **4.** A supernatural influence felt to be nearby: *A mysterious presence frightened them away.* **5.** A person who is present.

presence of mind *n.* The ability to think and act calmly and efficiently, especially in an emergency.

pres•ent[1] (**prĕz′**ənt) *n.* **1.** A moment or period in time that is intermediate between past and future; now. **2.a.** The present tense. **b.** A verb form in the present tense. —*adj.* **1.** Being or occurring now; current: *the present situation.* **2.** Being in attendance or at hand: *The people present broke into loud applause.* **3.** Existing in something specified: *Oxygen is present in blood.* **4.** Of or relating to the present tense. —***idioms.*** **at present.** At the present time; right now. **for the present.** For the time being; temporarily. [First written down about 1303 in Middle English, from Latin *praesēns,* from *praeesse,* to be present.]

pre•sent[2] (prĭ **zĕnt′**) *tr.v.* **pre•sent•ed, pre•sent•ing, pre•sents. 1.a.** To introduce, especially with formal ceremony. **b.** To introduce (a young woman) to society with conventional ceremony. **2.** To bring before the public: *present a drama.* **3.a.** To make a gift or award of: *She presented the pennant to the winners.* **b.** To make a gift or award to: *present the soldier with a medal.* **4.** To offer for observation, examination, or consideration: *Teaching presents many problems.* —*n.* **pres•ent.** (**prĕz′**ənt). Something presented; a gift. [First written down before 1300 in Middle English and spelled *presenten,* from Latin *presentāre,* to show, from *praesēns,* present.]

pre•sent•a•ble (prĭ **zĕn′**tə bəl) *adj.* **1.** Suitable for being given, displayed, or offered: *presentable gifts.* **2.** Fit for introduction to others: *He made himself presentable.* —**pre•sent′a•bil′i•ty** *n.*

pres•en•ta•tion (prĕz′ən **tā′**shən *or* prē′zən **tā′**shən) *n.* **1.** The act of presenting, especially for acceptance or approval. **2.** Something, such as a gift, that is offered or given. **3.** Something presented before an audience, as a play or lecture.

pres•ent-day (**prĕz′**ənt **dā′**) *adj.* Existing or occurring now; current: *present-day attitudes about education.*

pre•sen•ti•ment (prĭ **zĕn′**tə mənt) *n.* A sense that something is about to occur; a premonition.

pres•ent•ly (**prĕz′**ənt lē) *adv.* **1.** In a short time; soon: *We'll be there presently.* **2.** At this time or period; now: *An expedition is presently exploring the area.*

pre•sent•ment (prĭ **zĕnt′**mənt) *n.* **1.** The act of presenting to a view or to the mind; presentation. **2.** Something presented, as a picture or play.

pres•ent participle (**prĕz′**ənt) *n.* A participle that expresses present action or condition. It is formed in English by adding *-ing* to the infinitive, as *playing* in *he is playing,* and is sometimes used as an adjective, as *overwhelming* in *an overwhelming majority.*

pres•ent per•fect (**prĕz′**ənt **pûr′**fĭkt) *n.* A verb tense used to express action or condition completed at the present time. It is formed in English by combining the present tense of *have* with a past participle, as *has spoken* in *He has spoken.*

pres•ent tense (**prĕz′**ənt) *n.* A verb tense used to express action or condition in the present time, as *hits* in *She hits the ball* and *am* in *I am happy.*

pres•er•va•tion (prĕz′ər **vā′**shən) *n.* The act of preserving or the state of being preserved.

pre•ser•va•tive (prĭ **zûr′**və tĭv) *adj.* Tending to preserve or capable of preserving. —*n.* Something used to preserve, especially a chemical added to a food to prevent spoilage.

pre•serve (prĭ **zûrv′**) *tr.v.* **pre•served, pre•serv•ing, pre•serves. 1.** To maintain in safety, as from injury or peril; protect: *laws that help preserve wildlife.* See Synonyms at **defend. 2.** To keep in perfect or unchanged condition or form; maintain intact: *Both countries worked to preserve peaceful relations.* **3.** To protect (food) from spoilage and prepare it for future use, as by pickling or canning. —*n.* **1.** Fruit cooked with sugar to protect against decay or fermentation. Often used in the plural. **2.** An area maintained for the protection of wildlife or natural resources. [First written down in 1392 in Middle English and spelled *preserven,* from Late Latin *praeservāre,* to observe beforehand.] —**pre•serv′er** *n.*

pre•set (prē **sĕt′**) *tr.v.* **pre•set, pre•set•ting, pre•sets.** To set (an automatic control, for example) beforehand: *preset a microwave oven.*

pre•side (prĭ **zīd′**) *intr.v.* **pre•sid•ed, pre•sid•ing, pre•sides. 1.** To hold the position of authority; act as chairperson: *presided over a meeting.* **2.** To possess or exercise authority or control: *Mother presides behind the wheel.* [First written down in 1611 in Modern English, from Latin *praesidēre* : *prae-,* in front + *sedēre,* to sit.] —**pre•sid′er** *n.*

pres•i•den•cy (**prĕz′**ĭ dən sē) *n., pl.* **pres•i•den•cies. 1.** The office, function, or term of a president. **2.** Often **Presidency.** The office of a president of a republic or of the President of the United States.

pres•i•dent (**prĕz′**ĭ dənt) *n.* **1.** The chief officer of an organization or institution, such as a club, corporation, or university. **2.** Often **President.** The chief executive of a republic, such as the United States.

pres•i•dent-e•lect (prĕz′ĭ dənt ĭ **lĕkt′**) *n., pl.* **pres•i•dents-e•lect** (prĕz′ĭ dənts ĭ **lĕkt′**). A person who has been elected president but has not yet begun the term of office.

pres•i•den•tial (prĕz′ĭ **dĕn′**shəl) *adj.* Of or relating to a president or presidency: *a presidential election.*

Pres•i•dents' Day (**prĕz′**ĭ dənts) *n.* The third Monday in February, observed in the United States as a holiday in commemoration of the birthdays of George Washington and Abraham Lincoln.

pre•sid•i•a (prĭ **sĭd′**ē ə) *n.* A plural of **presidium.**

pre•si•di•o (prĭ **sē′**dē ō′ *or* prĭ **sĭd′**ē ō′) *n.* A garrison, especially a fortress in the southwest United States built by the Spanish.

pre•sid•i•um (prĭ **sĭd′**ē əm) *n., pl.* **pre•sid•i•a** (prĭ**sĭd′**ē ə) or **pre•sid•i•ums. 1.** Any of various permanent executive committees in Communist countries having power to act for a larger governing

ă	pat	oi	boy
ā	pay	ou	out
âr	care	o͝o	took
ä	father	o͞o	boot
ĕ	pet	ŭ	cut
ē	be	ûr	urge
ĭ	pit	th	thin
ī	pie	*th*	this
îr	pier	hw	whoop
ŏ	pot	zh	vision
ō	toe	ə	about
ô	paw	N	*French* bon

press conference
President Bill Clinton (*right*) and British Prime Minister John Major (*left*) at a 1993 White House press conference

Word Building: pressure

The word root *–press–* in English words and the English word **press** itself come from the past participle *pressus* of the Latin verb *premere*, "to squeeze, press." Thus we have the noun **pressure** from the Latin noun *pressūra*, "a squeezing, as of the juice from grapes or of the oil from olives." We also have the verbs **compress**, "to squeeze together" (using the prefix *com–*, "together, with"); **depress**, "to squeeze down" (*dē–*, "down"); **express**, "to extract by pressure, expel, force" (*ex–*, "out, out of"); and **impress**, "to press on or against, drive in, imprint" (*in–^{2}*, "into, in").

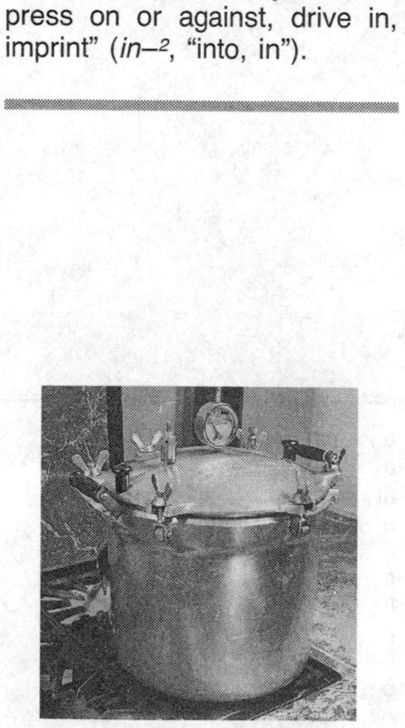

pressure cooker

body. **2. Presidium.** An executive committee of the Supreme Soviet headed by the president.

press^{1} (prĕs) *v.* **pressed, press•ing, press•es.** *—tr.* **1.** To exert force or pressure against; bear down on: *Press the button.* **2.a.** To squeeze the juice or other contents from: *press grapes to make wine.* **b.** To extract (juice or other contents) by squeezing: *press juice from oranges.* **3.a.** To make compact or reshape by applying steady force; compress. **b.** To smooth (clothes or fabric, for example) by applying heat and pressure; iron: *He pressed the trousers.* **4.** To clasp or embrace, as with affection: *Michael pressed her hand with gratitude.* **5.** To try hard to persuade or influence; ask or entreat insistently: *Joy pressed her aunt to stay for the holiday.* **6.** To urge or force to action; impel: *pressing the horses to go faster.* **7.** To carry on or advance vigorously: *Critics charged that the Confederates should have pressed on and taken Washington.* **8.** To place in trying or distressing circumstances; harass or oppress. **9.** To lift (a weight) in a press. *—intr.* **1.** To exert force or pressure. **2.** To weigh heavily, as on the mind. **3.** To advance eagerly; push forward: *The crowd pressed forward to catch a glimpse of the President.* **4.** To require haste; be urgent. **5.** To iron clothes or other material. **6.** To assemble closely and in large numbers; crowd. **7.** To entreat someone or demand something: *He pressed for the new assignment.* **8.** To raise or lift a weight in a press. *—n.* **1.** Any of various machines or devices used to squeeze or exert pressure on something. **2.** A printing press. **3.** A place or an establishment where matter is printed. **4.a.** Journalism in general, especially the collecting and publishing or broadcasting of news. **b.** The people, such as editors and reporters, involved in collecting, publishing, or broadcasting news. **5.** A throng: *a press of people in the square.* **6.** Pressure, haste, or urgency: *The press of business weighs heavily on her time.* **7.** The shape or set of proper creases in a garment or fabric, formed by ironing: *These slacks will keep their press.* **8.** In basketball, an aggressive defense applied over the entire court. **9.** A lift in weightlifting in which the weight is raised to shoulder level and then pushed overhead without movement of the legs. [First written down before 1325 in Middle English and spelled *pressen*, from Latin *pressāre*, from *premere*.]

press^{2} (prĕs) *tr.v.* **pressed, press•ing, press•es.** To force into service in the army or navy. [First written down in 1513 in Modern English, from Middle English *prest*, enlistment money, loan, from Medieval Latin *praestāre*, to lend.]

press agent *n.* A person hired to arrange advertising and publicity, as for a performer or business.

press conference *n.* An interview held for news reporters by a political figure or a famous person.

press•ing (**prĕs′**ĭng) *adj.* Demanding immediate attention; urgent: *the pressing problems of the world.*

press secretary *n.* A person who officially manages the public affairs and press conferences of a public figure.

pres•sure (**prĕsh′**ər) *n.* **1.** The act of pressing or the condition of being pressed. **2.** The application of continuous force on one body by another that it is touching; compression. **3.** The amount of force applied per unit of area of a surface. **4.** A compelling or constraining influence, such as a moral force, on the mind or will: *peer pressure.* **5.** Urgent claim or demand: *I am under great pressure to finish this project.* **6.** A condition of physical, mental, social, or economic distress: *the economic pressures on the farming community.* *—tr.v.* **pres•sured, pres•sur•ing, pres•sures.** To force, as by influencing or persuading: *The studio tried to pressure her into making public appearances.* —SEE NOTE.

pressure cooker *n.* An airtight metal pot that uses steam under pressure to cook food quickly.

pressure suit *n.* A garment that is worn in high-altitude aircraft or in spacecraft to compensate for low-pressure conditions.

pres•sur•ize (**prĕsh′**ə rīz′) *tr.v.* **pres•sur•ized, pres•sur•iz•ing, pres•sur•iz•es.** **1.** To keep (a compartment, as in an aircraft) at normal atmospheric pressure. **2.** To subject (gas or liquid) to a greater pressure than normal. **—pres′sur•i•za′tion** (prĕsh′ər ĭ **zā′**shən) *n.*

pres•ti•dig•i•ta•tion (prĕs′tĭ dĭj′ĭ **tā′**shən) *n.* Skill with one's hands in the execution of tricks; sleight of hand. **—pres′ti•dig′i•ta′tor** *n.*

pres•tige (prĕ **stēzh′** *or* prĕ **stēj′**) *n.* A person's high standing among others; honor or esteem. [First written down in 1656 in Modern English and spelled *prestige*, illusion, from Latin *praestīgiae*, tricks.]

pres•ti•gious (prĕ **stē′**jəs *or* prĕ **stĭj′**əs) *adj.* Having prestige; esteemed: *a prestigious occupation.* **—pres•tig′ious•ly** *adv.* **—pres•tig′ious•ness** *n.*

pres•tis•si•mo (prĕ **stĭs′**ə mō′) *adv. & adj.* In music, as fast a tempo as possible.

pres•to (**prĕs′**tō) *adv.* **1.** In music, in a very fast tempo. **2.** At once; right away.

pre•sum•a•ble (prĭ **zo͞o′**mə bəl) *adj.* Capable of being presumed or taken for granted; reasonably supposed: *a presumable result.* **—pre•sum′a•bly** *adv.*

pre•sume (prĭ **zo͞om′**) *v.* **pre•sumed, pre•sum•ing, pre•sumes.** *—tr.* **1.** To assume to be true in the absence of proof; take for granted: *I presume that she will accept the job.* **2.** To undertake without authority or permission; dare: *He presumed to make arrangements for their vacation without her knowledge.* *—intr.* **1.** To take unfair advantage of something; go beyond the proper limits: *presumed on their hospitality.* **2.** To take for granted that something is true; suppose. [First written down about 1378 in Middle English and spelled *presumen*, from Latin *praesūmere*, to anticipate.] **—pre•sum′ed•ly** (prĭ **zo͞o′**mĭd lē) *adv.* **—pre•sum′er** *n.*

pre•sump•tion (prĭ **zŭmp′**shən) *n.* **1.** Behavior or language that is arrogant or offensive. **2.** The act of presuming or accepting as true without proof: *a presumption of innocence.* **3.** Acceptance or belief based on reasonable evidence.

pre•sump•tive (prĭ **zŭmp′**tĭv) *adj.* **1.** Providing a reason for belief or acceptance. **2.** Based on likelihood or presumption: *an heir presumptive.* **—pre•sump′tive•ly** *adv.*

pre•sump•tu•ous (prĭ **zŭmp′**cho͞o əs) *adj.* Going beyond what is right or proper; excessively forward: *a presumptuous attitude.*

pre•sup•pose (prē′sə **pōz′**) *tr.v.* **pre•sup•posed, pre•sup•pos•ing, pre•sup•pos•es.** **1.** To believe or suppose in advance; take for granted: *The teacher presupposed that we had taken algebra.* **2.** To require as a necessary prior condition: *The charred bits of wood presupposed a fire.* **—pre•sup′po•si′tion** (prē sŭp′ə **zĭsh′**ən) *n.*

pre•teen (**prē′tēn′**) *adj.* **1.** Relating to or designed for children between ages 9 and 12: *preteen clothing.* **2.** Being a child between ages 9 and 12; preadolescent. *—n.* A preadolescent boy or girl.

pre•tend (prĭ **tĕnd′**) *v.* **pre•tend•ed, pre•tend•ing, pre•tends.** *—tr.* **1.** To give a false appearance of: *pretend illness.* **2.** To make believe: *Pretend that you are on another planet.* **3.** To claim or allege insincerely or falsely: *pretended to be an expert.* *—intr.* **1.** To present a false appearance. **2.** To act out an action or a role, as in a play. **3.** To put forward a claim. [First written down in 1382 in Middle English and spelled *pretenden*, from Latin *praetendere* : *prae-*, in front + *tendere*, to extend.]

pre•tend•ed (prĭ **tĕn′**dĭd) *adj.* **1.** Not genuine or sincere; feigned: *had only a pretended interest in the movie.* **2.** Supposed; alleged: *the pretended heir.*

pre•tend•er (prĭ **tĕn′**dər) *n.* **1.** A person who pretends or alleges falsely. **2.** A person who sets forth a claim, especially a person who claims the right to a throne.

pre•tense (**prē′**tĕns′ *or* prĭ **tĕns′**) *n.* **1.** A false appearance or action intended to deceive: *She made a pretense of being worried about us.* **2.** A false reason or excuse: *He came to the meeting under false pretenses.* **3.** Mere show without reality; outward appearance: *There was not even a pretense of justice in the arrest.* **4.** A claim, especially one without support.

pre•ten•sion (prĭ **tĕn′**shən) *n.* **1.** A claim or reason, especially a false one: *made no pretensions to having a classical education.* **2.** Showy or extravagant display.

pre•ten•tious (prĭ **tĕn′**shəs) *adj.* **1.** Making unjustified claims or demands, as to a position of merit. **2.** Extravagantly showy: *a pretentious house.* **—pre•ten′tious•ly** *adv.* **—pre•ten′tious•ness** *n.*

pret•er•it (**prĕt′**ər ĭt) *adj.* Of or relating to the verb tense that describes a past action or state. *—n.* **1.** A preterit tense. **2.** A verb form in the preterit tense.

pre•ter•nat•u•ral (prē′tər **năch′**ər əl *or* prē′-tər **năch′**rəl) *adj.* **1.** Being beyond what is normal or usual. **2.** Supernatural.

pre•text (**prē′**tĕkst′) *n.* A purpose or an excuse given to hide the real reason for something.

Pre•to•ri•a (prĭ **tôr′**ē ə). The administrative capital of South Africa, in the northeast part of the country north of Johannesburg. It was founded in 1855. Population, 435,100.

pre•tri•al (prē **trī′**əl *or* prē **trīl′**) *adj.* Existing or occurring before a trial.

pret•ty (**prĭt′**ē) *adj.* **pret•ti•er, pret•ti•est. 1.** Pleasing or appealing in a graceful or delicate way: *a pretty shell.* **2.** Clever; adroit. **3.** Very bad; terrible: *in a pretty predicament.* **4.** *Informal.* Large in size or extent: *a pretty fortune.* *—adv.* To a fair degree; moderately: *We are in pretty good shape.* *—n., pl.* **pret•ties.** A person or thing that is pretty. *—tr.v.* **pret•tied, pret•ty•ing, pret•ties.** To make pretty: *We can pretty up the spare room for you.* ***—idiom.*** **pretty much.** For the most part; mostly: *We were pretty much exhausted after the hike.* [First written down about 1000 in Old English and spelled *prættig*, cunning, clever.] **—pret′ti•ly** *adv.* **—pret′ti•ness** *n.* —See Note.

pret•zel (**prĕt′**səl) *n.* A glazed brittle biscuit, salted on the outside and baked in the form of a loose knot or stick.

pre•vail (prĭ **vāl′**) *intr.v.* **pre•vailed, pre•vail•ing, pre•vails. 1.** To be greater in strength or influence; triumph: *prevailed against great odds.* **2.** To be most common or frequent; be predominant: *In this region, snow and ice prevail.* **3.** To be in force or use; be current: *an attitude that prevailed in the 1950's.* **4.** To use persuasion or inducement successfully: *The salesperson prevailed upon me to buy a spare tire.* [First written down before 1400 in Middle English and spelled *prevailen*, from Latin *praevalēre*, to be stronger.]

pre•vail•ing (prĭ **vā′**lĭng) *adj.* **1.** Most frequent or common; predominant: *The prevailing winds come from the west.* **2.** Generally current; widespread: *the prevailing attitude.* **—pre•vail′ing•ly** *adv.*

prev•a•lent (**prĕv′**ə lənt) *adj.* Widely existing or commonly occurring: *Certain diseases are more prevalent in hot humid areas.* **—prev′a•lence** *n.* **—prev′a•lent•ly** *adv.*

pre•var•i•cate (prĭ **văr′**ĭ kāt′) *intr.v.* **pre•var•i•cat•ed, pre•var•i•cat•ing, pre•var•i•cates.** To stray from the truth; speak or write evasively. **—pre•var′i•ca′tion** *n.* **—pre•var′i•ca′tor** *n.*

pre•vent (prĭ **vĕnt′**) *tr.v.* **pre•vent•ed, pre•vent•ing, pre•vents. 1.** To keep from happening; avert: *prevent illness.* **2.** To keep (someone) from doing something; impede: *His snoring prevents me from sleeping.* [First written down before 1425 in Middle English and spelled *preventen*, to anticipate, from Latin *praevenīre*, to come before.] **—pre•vent′a•ble, pre•vent′i•ble** *adj.*

pre•ven•ta•tive (prĭ **vĕn′**tə tĭv) *adj.* & *n.* Variant of **preventive.**

pre•ven•tion (prĭ **vĕn′**shən) *n.* The act of preventing or impeding: *the prevention of illness.*

pre•ven•tive (prĭ **vĕn′**tĭv) also **pre•ven•ta•tive** (prĭ **vĕn′**tə tĭv) *adj.* Designed to prevent or hinder: *preventive steps against accidents.* *—n.* **1.** Something that prevents; an obstacle. **2.** Something that prevents or slows the course of an illness or a disease.

pre•view (**prē′**vyōō′) *n.* **1.** An advance showing, as of a motion picture or an art exhibition, to an invited audience prior to presentation to the general public. **2.** An advance viewing, especially of scenes of a forthcoming motion picture. *—tr.v.* **pre•viewed, pre•view•ing, pre•views.** To view or exhibit in advance.

pre•vi•ous (**prē′**vē əs) *adj.* Existing or occurring before something else in time or order: *in the previous chapter.* [First written down in 1625 in Modern English, from Latin *praevius*, going before : *prae-*, before + *via*, way.] **—pre′vi•ous•ly** *adv.*

pre•war (**prē′wôr′**) *adj.* Existing or occurring before a war.

prey (prā) *n.* **1.** An animal hunted or caught for food; quarry. **2.** A person or thing that is defenseless against attack; a victim. **3.** The act or practice of preying. *—intr.v.* **preyed, prey•ing, preys. 1.** To hunt and kill other animals for food: *Owls prey on mice.* **2.** To take unfair advantage of other people, as by swindling. **3.** To have a harmful or troublesome effect: *Worry preyed on his mind.* [First written down about 1225 in Middle English and spelled *preie*, from Latin *praeda*, booty, prey.]

❑ *These sound alike:* **prey, pray** (beseech).

Pri•am (**prī′**əm) *n.* In Greek mythology, the king of Troy and father of Cassandra, Hector, and Paris, who is killed when his city falls to the Greeks.

price (prīs) *n.* **1.** The amount of money or goods asked or given for something: *The price of the book is $5.99.* **2.** The cost, as in suffering, at which something is obtained: *The price of her success was hard work.* **3.** The cost of bribing someone: *Every man has his price.* **4.** A reward offered for the capture or killing of a person. *—tr.v.* **priced, pric•ing, pric•es. 1.** To establish a price for: *priced squash at 89 cents a pound.* **2.** To find out the price of: *Let's go in and price the shirts.* [First written down before 1200 in Middle English and spelled *pris*, from Latin *pretium.*]

price•less (**prīs′**lĭs) *adj.* **1.** Having great worth; invaluable: *priceless treasures.* **2.** Very amusing or odd: *Little children often say priceless things.*

prick (prĭk) *n.* **1.** The act of piercing or puncturing. **2.** The sensation of being pierced. **3.** A hole or mark left by piercing. **4.** A pointed object, such as an ice pick, goad, or thorn. *—tr.v.* **pricked, prick•ing, pricks. 1.** To puncture lightly: *The thorn pricked my finger.* **2.** To sting with emotional pain: *My conscience pricks me at the thought of the deed.* ***—idiom.*** **prick up (one's) ears.** To listen with attentive interest.

prick•er (**prĭk′**ər) *n.* **1.** A person or thing that pricks. **2.** A prickle or thorn.

pressure suit

Regional Note: pretty

The regional word *purty* is probably the most common American example of *metathesis*, the reversal of two adjacent sounds. Metathesis in English often involves the consonant *r* and a vowel. For example, the word *third* used to be *thrid.* By the same process, English *pretty* often is pronounced *purty* in regional speech.

pretzel

ă	pat	oi	boy
ā	pay	ou	out
âr	care	ŏŏ	took
ä	father	ōō	boot
ĕ	pet	ŭ	cut
ē	be	ûr	urge
ĭ	pit	th	thin
ī	pie	*th*	this
îr	pier	hw	whoop
ŏ	pot	zh	vision
ō	toe	ə	about
ô	paw	N	*French* bon

prickly pear

primrose

Prince Edward Island

The province of **Prince Edward Island** was named in honor of the English Prince Edward (1767–1820), who was a son of King George III and the father of Queen Victoria.

Usage: principal

The words **principal** and **principle** are often confused but do not share any meanings. **Principle** is only a noun, and most of its senses refer to that which is basic or to rules and standards: *She really sticks to her principles.* **Principal** is both a noun and an adjective. As a noun it generally refers to a person who has a high position or plays an important role, for example, *a principal of a school.* As an adjective **principal** means "chief" or "leading": *The principal ways to solve these problems are in the third chapter.*

prick•le (prĭk′əl) *n.* **1.** A small sharp point, spine, or thorn. **2.** A tingling sensation. —*v.* **prick•led, prick•ling, prick•les.** —*tr.* **1.** To prick as if with a thorn. **2.** To cause tingling sensations: *This lotion will prickle your face.* —*intr.* To feel a tingling or pricking sensation.

prick•ly (prĭk′lē) *adj.* **prick•li•er, prick•li•est. 1.** Having prickles: *a prickly cactus.* **2.** Tingling or smarting: *a prickly feeling in my foot.* **3.** Easily irritated: *He is quite prickly today.* —**prick′li•ness** *n.*

prickly pear *n.* **1.** The egg-shaped, bristly, but often edible fruit of any of various cacti. **2.** Any of various cacti that bear such fruit.

pride (prīd) *n.* **1.** A sense of one's own proper dignity or worth; self-respect. **2.** Pleasure or satisfaction in one's accomplishments or possessions: *My aunt takes a great deal of pride in her work.* **3.** A source or cause of pleasure or satisfaction; the best of a group: *The painting was the pride of his collection.* **4.** An excessively high opinion of oneself; conceit. **5.** A group of lions. —*tr.v.* **prid•ed, prid•ing, prides.** To indulge (oneself) in a feeling of pleasure or satisfaction: *He prided himself on his ability to fix cars.* [First written down before 1000 in Old English and spelled *prȳde*, from *prūd*, proud.]

pried[1] (prīd) *v.* Past tense and past participle of **pry**[1].

pried[2] (prīd) *v.* Past tense and past participle of **pry**[2].

pries[1] (prīz) *v.* Third person singular present tense of **pry**[1].

pries[2] (prīz) *v.* Third person singular present tense of **pry**[2]. —*n.* Plural of **pry**[2].

priest (prēst) *n.* **1.** In certain Christian churches, a member of the clergy having the authority to administer the sacraments. **2.** In other religions, a person having the authority to administer religious rites. [First written down in 695 in Old English and spelled *prēost*, possibly from Late Latin *presbyter*.]

priest•ess (prē′stĭs) *n.* A woman having the authority to perform and administer various rites, especially of a pagan religion.

priest•hood (prēst′hŏŏd′) *n.* **1.** The office or role of a priest. **2.** The class of priests: *He entered the priesthood two years ago.*

priest•ly (prēst′lē) *adj.* **priest•li•er, priest•li•est.** Of, relating to, or befitting a priest: *priestly garb.*

prig (prĭg) *n.* An arrogant, smug, or narrow-minded person, especially one with an excessive wish to appear proper. —**prig′gish** *adj.*

prim (prĭm) *adj.* **prim•mer, prim•mest.** Stiffly proper or precise in manner or appearance. —**prim′ly** *adv.* —**prim′ness** *n.*

pri•ma•cy (prī′mə sē) *n., pl.* **pri•ma•cies. 1.** The condition of being first or foremost: *the lion's legendary primacy among beasts.* **2.** The office or functions of an ecclesiastical primate.

pri•ma don•na (prē′mə dŏn′ə) *n.* **1.** The leading woman soloist in an opera company. **2.** A conceited person who is easily upset or difficult to please.

pri•mal (prī′məl) *adj.* **1.** Being first in time; original. **2.** Of first importance; primary: *a primal necessity.*

pri•mar•i•ly (prī mâr′ə lē *or* prī mĕr′ə lē) *adv.* In the first place; chiefly: *a forest consisting primarily of hardwoods.*

pri•mar•y (prī′mĕr′ē *or* prī′mə rē) *adj.* **1.** First in importance, rank, or quality; chief: *The primary function of a window is to let in light.* **2.** First in time or sequence; original: *the primary stages of the project.* **3.** Being a fundamental part; basic: *primary needs.* **4.** Of or relating to a primary school. **5.** Of or relating to a primary color. **6.** Of, relating to, or being an inducting current, circuit, or coil. —*n., pl.* **pri•mar•ies. 1.** Something that is first in time, order, quality, or importance. **2.** A primary election. **3.** The circuit, coil, or winding of a transformer into which electricity is fed. [First written down before 1425 in Middle English, from Latin *prīmārius*, from *prīmus*, first.]

primary accent *n.* **1.** The strongest degree of stress placed on a syllable of a word that is pronounced. **2.** The mark (′) used to indicate which syllable of a word receives the strongest degree of stress.

primary color *n.* **1.** Any of the three colors of light, red, green, and blue, from which light of any color can be made by mixing. **2.** Any of the three colors of pigment, purplish red, greenish blue, and yellow, from which pigment of any color can be made by mixing.

primary election *n.* A preliminary election in which registered voters nominate candidates for office.

primary school *n.* A school usually including the first three or four grades of elementary school and sometimes kindergarten.

pri•mate (prī′māt′) *n.* **1.** A member of the group of mammals that includes the lemurs, monkeys, apes, and human beings. Primates have a very highly developed brain and hands that have thumbs and are specially adapted for holding and grasping. **2.** (prī′mĭt *or* prī′māt′). A bishop of the highest rank in a province or country.

prime (prīm) *adj.* **1.** First in excellence, quality, degree, or value: *her prime accomplishments.* **2.** First in degree or rank: *my prime concern.* **3.** Of the highest U.S. Government grade of meat: *prime cuts.* **4.** Of or relating to a prime number. —*n.* **1.** The stage of ideal physical perfection and intellectual vigor in a person's life. **2.a.** A mark (′) placed above and to the right of a letter to distinguish it from the same letter already in use: *compare the angles b and b′.* **b.** The same mark used to represent the units of feet, minutes of arc, or minutes of time: *a 10′ board; an angle of 27°13′.* **3.** A prime number. —*tr. v.* **primed, prim•ing, primes. 1.** To make ready; prepare, as with information: *She primed him for the contest.* **2.** To prepare for operation, as by pouring water into a pump or gasoline into a carburetor. **3.** To prepare (a surface) for painting or finishing by covering with size, primer, or an undercoat. **4.** To prepare (a gun or mine) for firing by inserting a charge of gunpowder or a primer. [First written down about 1385 in Middle English, from Latin *prīmus*, first.]

prime meridian *n.* The zero meridian (0°), used as a reference line from which longitude east and west is measured. It passes through Greenwich, England.

prime minister *n.* **1.** A chief governmental minister appointed by a ruler. **2.** The head of the Cabinet and often also the chief executive of a parliamentary democracy.

prime number *n.* An integer whose only factors that are also integers are itself and 1. For example, 7, 13, and 19 are prime numbers.

prim•er[1] (prĭm′ər) *n.* **1.** An elementary textbook for teaching children to read. **2.** A book that covers the basic elements of a subject. [First written down in 1378 in Middle English and spelled *primer*, prayer book, from Medieval Latin *prīmārius*, first.]

prim•er[2] (prī′mər) *n.* **1.** A coat of paint or similar material applied to prepare a surface, as for painting. **2.** A cap or tube containing a small amount of explosive used to set off the main explosive charge of a firearm or mine.

prime time *n.* The evening hours when the largest television audience is available.

pri•me•val (prī mē′vəl) *adj.* Of or belonging to the earliest ages; ancient or original: *a primeval forest.* —**pri•me′val•ly** *adv.*

prim•ing (prī′mĭng) *n.* **1.** A preliminary coat of

paint applied to a surface. **2.** The explosive used to ignite a charge.

prim•i•tive (prĭm′ĭ tĭv) *adj.* **1.** Not derived from something else; primary or basic. **2.** Of or relating to an early or original stage or state: *a primitive form of life.* **3.** Simple or crude; not sophisticated: *a primitive form of rocket.* [First written down in 1392 in Middle English and spelled *premetif*, from Latin *prīmitīvus*, from *prīmus*, first.] —**prim′i•tive•ly** *adv.* —**prim′i•tive•ness** *n.*

pri•mo•gen•i•ture (prī′mō **jĕn′**ĭ cho͝or′) *n.* **1.** The condition of being the first-born child of one's parents. **2.** In law, the right of the eldest child, especially the eldest son, to inherit the entire estate of one or both parents.

pri•mor•di•al (prī **môr′**dē əl) *adj.* **1.** Being or happening first in sequence of time; original. **2.** Primary or fundamental: *play a primordial role.* —*n.* A basic principle. —**pri•mor′di•al•ly** *adv.*

primp (prĭmp) *v.* **primped, primp•ing, primps.** —*tr.* To dress or groom with considerable attention to detail: *She primped her hair.* —*intr.* To dress or groom oneself with elaborate care: *He primped for hours in front of the mirror.*

prim•rose (**prĭm′**rōz′) *n.* **1.** Any of numerous plants often grown for their clusters of tubular, variously colored flowers. **2.** A plant having four-petaled yellow flowers that open in the evening and close during the day.

prince (prĭns) *n.* **1.** A man or boy who is a member of a royal family other than the monarch, especially a son of the monarch. **2.** The male ruler of a principality. **3.** A king. **4.** A nobleman of varying rank or status. **5.** An outstanding man in a particular group or class. [First written down before 1200 in Middle English, from Latin *prīnceps*.]

prince consort *n.* The husband of a sovereign queen.

prince•dom (**prĭns′**dəm) *n.* **1.** The territory ruled by a prince; a principality. **2.** The rank or status of a prince.

Prince Ed•ward Island (prĭns **ĕd′**wərd). A province of southeast Canada consisting of **Prince Edward Island** in the southern Gulf of St. Lawrence. It joined the Canadian confederacy in 1873. Charlottetown is the capital and the largest city. Population, 122,506. —SEE NOTE.

prince•ly (**prĭns′**lē) *adj.* **prince•li•er, prince•li•est.** Of or befitting a prince: *a princely act.* —**prince′li•ness** *n.*

Prince of Wales (wālz) *n.* The male heir to the British throne.

prin•cess (**prĭn′**sĕs′ *or* prĭn **sĕs′**) *n.* **1.** A woman or girl who is a member of a royal family other than the monarch, especially a daughter of the monarch. **2.** The female ruler of a principality. **3.** A queen. **4.** A noblewoman of varying rank or status. **5.** The wife of a prince.

prin•ci•pal (**prĭn′**sə pəl) *adj.* First or foremost in rank, degree, or importance; chief: *the principal character in the story.* —*n.* **1.** A person who holds a leading position, especially the head of an elementary school or high school. **2.** A main participant, as in a business deal. **3.a.** A financial holding as distinguished from the interest or revenue earned from it. **b.** A sum of money owed as a debt, on which interest is calculated. [First written down about 1300 in Middle English, from Latin *prīnceps*, leader, emperor.] —**prin′ci•pal•ly** *adv.* —SEE NOTE.

❑ *These sound alike:* **principal, principle** (doctrine).

prin•ci•pal•i•ty (prĭn′sə **păl′**ĭ tē) *n., pl.* **prin•ci•pal•i•ties.** The territory ruled by a prince or a princess from which such a title is derived.

principal parts *pl.n.* In inflected languages, the main forms of the verb from which all other forms can be derived. In English the principal parts are the present infinitive (*walk, take*), the past tense (*walked, took*), the past participle (*walked, taken*), and the present participle (*walking, taking*).

prin•ci•ple (**prĭn′**sə pəl) *n.* **1.** A basic or fundamental doctrine: *the principles of Democracy.* **2.a.** A rule or standard, especially of good behavior: *a man of proper principles.* **b.** The general set of moral or ethical standards: *She makes decisions based on principle.* **3.** An underlying quality that determines behavior: *the principles of self-preservation.* **4.** A statement or set of statements describing natural phenomena or mechanical processes: *the principle of conservation of energy.* —***idioms.*** **in principle.** With regard to the basics: *I agree in principle, but we'll see how the details work out.* **on principle.** According to or because of principle: *I objected on principle.* [First written down about 1380 in Middle English, from Latin *prīncipium*, from *prīnceps*, leader, emperor.] —SEE NOTE at **principal.**

❑ *These sound alike:* **principle, principal** (chief).

print (prĭnt) *n.* **1.** A mark or an impression made in or upon a surface by pressure: *The print of footsteps in the sand.* **2.a.** Lettering produced by printing or a similar method. **b.** Matter so produced; printed material. **3.** A design or picture transferred from an engraved plate, wood block, or similar medium. **4.a.** Cloth marked with a dyed pattern or design: *a cotton print.* **b.** The pattern or design on such cloth: *a paisley print.* **5.** A positive photographic image; a photograph. —*v.* **print•ed, print•ing, prints.** —*tr.* **1.** To press (a mark or design, for example) onto or into a surface. **2.** To produce with or as if with a printing press: *The government prints money. The newsletter was just printed.* **3.** To offer in printed form; publish: *The newspaper refused to print the letter.* **4.** To write (something) in block letters similar to those commonly used in printed matter: *Print your name on the dotted line.* **5.** To produce (a photographic print) by passing light through a negative onto a sensitized surface: *Have you printed my pictures yet?* —*intr.* To write block letters similar to those used in print. —***idioms.*** **in print. 1.** In printed or published form: *My letter appeared in print.* **2.** Offered for sale by a publisher: *Her book has been in print now for 20 years.* **out of print.** No longer offered for sale by a publisher: *That book's out of print.* **print out.** To print as a function; produce printed output: *The printer is printing out a document.* [First written down about 1300 in Middle English and spelled *prente*, from Old French *preinte*, from Latin *premere*, to press.]

print•ed circuit (**prĭn′**tĭd) *n.* An electric circuit in which the conducting connections have been deposited in set patterns on an insulating base.

print•er (**prĭn′**tər) *n.* **1.** A person whose job or business is printing. **2.** A device that prints: *a laser printer.*

print•ing (**prĭn′**tĭng) *n.* **1.** The art, process, or business of producing printed matter on a printing press or by similar means. **2.** Printed matter. **3.** All the copies of a publication, such as a book, printed at one time: *the first printing of the dictionary.*

printing press *n.* A machine that transfers letters or images onto sheets of paper or similar material by contact with an inked surface.

print•out (**prĭnt′**out′) *n.* Printed material produced by a printer online with a computer.

pri•or¹ (**prī′**ər) *adj.* **1.** Preceding in time or order: *his prior employment.* **2.** Preceding in importance or value: *a prior consideration.* [First written down in 1714 in Modern English, from Latin.]

printed circuit
On a floppy disk drive

printing press
Offset printing press

ă	pat	oi	boy
ā	pay	ou	out
âr	care	o͝o	took
ä	father	o͞o	boot
ĕ	pet	ŭ	cut
ē	be	ûr	urge
ĭ	pit	th	thin
ī	pie	*th*	this
îr	pier	hw	whoop
ŏ	pot	zh	vision
ō	toe	ə	about
ô	paw	N	*French* bon

prism
Light emanating from a prism

Word Building: pro–¹

The prefix **pro–¹** comes from Latin *pro*, meaning "for." In English, **pro–¹** usually means "favoring" or "supporting," as when it is prefixed to names of nationalities: *pro-American*. In this sense, the opposite of **pro–¹** would be **anti–**: **proslavery/antislavery**. Note that when **pro–¹** precedes a word beginning with a capital letter, a hyphen must be used. The prefix **pro–²** comes from Greek *pro*, meaning "before, in front." The word **prologue** comes from Greek *prologos*, from *pro–* + *logos*, meaning "speech." In English, **pro–²** often means "before" or "earlier" and is used mainly in science terms: **prophase**.

pri•or² (prī′ər) *n.* The monk in charge of a monastery or ranking next below an abbot. [First written down in 1093 in Old English, from Latin *prior*, superior.]

pri•or•ess (prī′ər ĭs) *n.* The nun in charge of a convent or ranking below an abbess.

pri•or•i•ty (prī ôr′ĭ tē *or* prī ŏr′ĭ tē) *n., pl.* **pri•or•i•ties. 1.** Precedence, especially in importance or urgency: *Safety is given high priority in factories.* **2.** Something considered more important than other matters: *Her major priority is finishing college.*

pri•or•y (prī′ə rē) *n., pl.* **pri•or•ies.** A monastery governed by a prior or a convent governed by a prioress.

prism (prĭz′əm) *n.* **1.** A geometric solid or polyhedron having congruent polygons lying in parallel planes as its bases and parallelograms as its sides. **2.** A solid of this type, usually with triangular bases and rectangular sides, made of a transparent material and used to refract light or break it up into a spectrum. [First written down in 1570 in Modern English, from Greek *prisma*, thing sawed off, prism, from *priein*, to saw.]

pris•mat•ic (prĭz măt′ĭk) *adj.* **1.** Of or relating to a prism. **2.** Refracting light as a prism does. **3.** Sparkling with colors, as from refracted light.

pris•on (prĭz′ən) *n.* **1.** A place of confinement for persons convicted or accused of crimes. **2.** A place or condition of confinement: *His job seemed a prison to him.*

pris•on•er (prĭz′ə nər *or* prĭz′nər) *n.* **1.** A person held in custody, especially in a prison. **2.** A person deprived of freedom of action or expression: *He was a prisoner of his fears.*

prisoner of war *n., pl.* **prisoners of war.** A person captured by or surrendering to the enemy in wartime.

pris•sy (prĭs′ē) *adj.* **pris•si•er, pris•si•est.** Excessively prim and proper.

pris•tine (prĭs′tēn′ *or* prĭ stēn′) *adj.* **1.** Of the earliest time or condition; primitive; original: *a pristine form of life.* **2.** Remaining in a pure state; uncorrupted by civilization: *the pristine beauty of snow-covered peaks.*

prith•ee (prĭ*th*′ē *or* prĭth′ē) *interj. Archaic.* An expression used to make a polite request.

pri•va•cy (prī′və sē) *n.* **1.** The condition of being secluded from others: *Her privacy is important to her.* **2.** Freedom from undesired intrusion: *the right of privacy.*

pri•vate (prī′vĭt) *adj.* **1.** Secluded from the sight, presence, or intrusion of others. **2.** Of or confined to one person: *my private opinion.* **3.** Not available for public use, control, or participation: *a private party.* **4.** Owned by a person or group of persons rather than the public or government: *private property.* **5.** Not intended to be known publicly; secret: *private negotiations.* **6.** Not holding public office: *a private citizen.* —*n.* An enlisted person of the lowest rank in the Army or Marine Corps. —***idiom.* in private.** Not in public; secretly or confidentially.

private detective *n.* A privately employed detective as distinguished from one belonging to a public police force.

private enterprise *n.* **1.** Business activities that are not subject to government ownership or control. **2.** A privately owned business, especially one operating in a capitalist economy.

pri•va•teer (prī′və tîr′) *n.* **1.** A ship that is privately owned and operated but authorized by a government to attack and capture enemy vessels during wartime. **2.** The commander or a crew member of such a ship. —*intr.v.* **pri•va•teered, pri•va•teer•ing, pri•va•teers.** To sail as a privateer.

private first class *n., pl.* **privates first class.** An enlisted soldier ranking below corporal and above private in the U.S. Army or Marine Corps.

private school *n.* A secondary or elementary school operated and supported by private individuals or a corporation rather than by a government.

pri•va•tion (prī vā′shən) *n.* **1.** Lack of the basic necessities of life. **2.** An act, a condition, or a result of being deprived.

priv•et (prĭv′ĭt) *n.* Any of several shrubs having small dark-green leaves and clusters of small white flowers, often used for hedges.

priv•i•lege (prĭv′ə lĭj *or* prĭv′lĭj) *n.* A special advantage, right, immunity, benefit, or permission granted to or enjoyed by an individual, a class, or a caste.

priv•i•leged (prĭv′ə lĭjd *or* prĭv′lĭjd) *adj.* Enjoying or having privileges: *the privileged classes.*

priv•i•ly (prĭv′ə lē) *adv.* In a private manner; privately or secretly.

priv•y (prĭv′ē) *adj.* **1.** Provided with knowledge of something private or secret: *I'm not privy to the committee's discussions.* **2.** Belonging to a person, such as the British sovereign, in a private rather than an official capacity. —*n., pl.* **priv•ies.** An outdoor toilet; an outhouse.

Privy Council *n.* A council of the British sovereign that consists of cabinet ministers appointed by reason of their office and others appointed for life.

prize¹ (prīz) *n.* **1.** Something offered or won as an award for superiority or victory, as in a competition or contest. **2.** Something worth having or striving for: *These tomatoes are the prize of the crop.* —*adj.* **1.** Offered or given as a prize: *prize money.* **2.** Given a prize or likely to win a prize: *a prize Siamese cat.* **3.** Worthy of some prize or recognition. —*tr.v.* **prized, priz•ing, priz•es.** To value highly; esteem; treasure: *The Chinese prize jade.* See Synonyms at **appreciate.** [First written down in 1593 in Modern English, from Middle English *pris*, value, price, reward.]

prize² (prīz) *n.* Something seized by force, especially an enemy ship and its cargo captured at sea in wartime. [First written down about 1250 in Middle English and spelled *prise*, from Old French *prise*, something taken, from Latin *prehendere*, to seize.]

prize³ (prīz) *tr.v.* **prized, priz•ing, priz•es.** To move or force with or as if with a lever; pry: *prize a fungus off a tree trunk.* [First written down in 1686 in Modern English, from Middle English *prise*, instrument for prying, probably from *prise*, the taking of something.]

prize•fight (prīz′fīt′) *n.* A match fought between professional boxers for money. **—prize′fight′er** *n.* **—prize′fight′ing** *n.*

prize•win•ning (prīz′wĭn′ĭng) *adj.* Having won a prize or deserving of a prize: *a prize-winning recipe.*

pro¹ (prō) *n., pl.* **pros.** An argument or a consideration in favor of something: *discussed the pros and cons.* —*adv.* In favor; in support: *argue pro and con.* —*adj.* Supporting: *the arguments pro and con.* [First written down before 1430 in Middle English, from Latin *prō*, for.]

pro² (prō) *Informal. n., pl.* **pros.** A professional, especially in sports. —*adj.* Professional: *pro football.* [First written down in 1866 in Modern English, short for *professional.*]

pro–¹ *pref.* A prefix that means: **1.** Favor or support: *pro-choice.* **2.** Acting as; substituting for: *pronoun.* —See Note.

pro–² *pref.* A prefix that means before or earlier: *prophase.*

prob•a•bil•i•ty (prŏb′ə bĭl′ĭ tē) *n., pl.* **prob•a•bil•i•ties. 1.** The condition of being probable; likelihood. **2.** A probable situation, condition, or event. **3.** A number expressing the likelihood of the occurrence of a given event, especially a fraction expressing how many times the event will happen in a given number of trials.

prob•a•ble (prŏb′ə bəl) *adj.* **1.** Likely to happen or be true: *the probable cost of the expedition.* **2.** Likely but not certain; plausible: *a probable explanation.* [First written down before 1387 in Middle English, from Latin *probāre*, to prove.] **—prob′a•bly** *adv.*

pro•bate (prō′bāt′) *n.* Legal establishment of the validity of a will. *—tr.v.* **pro•bat•ed, pro•bat•ing, pro•bates.** To establish the legal validity of (a will).

pro•ba•tion (prō bā′shən) *n.* **1.** A trial period for testing a person's fitness, as for a job or membership in a club. **2.** The release of a convicted criminal on condition of good behavior. **3.** A trial period in which a student may try to redeem failing grades or bad conduct so as not to be suspended.

pro•ba•tion•er (prō bā′shə nər) *n.* A person on probation.

probation officer *n.* An official who supervises persons who have been put on probation after being convicted of a crime.

probe (prōb) *n.* **1.** An exploratory action, expedition, or device, especially one designed to research or investigate a remote or unknown region: *a space probe.* **2.** Any of various long slender tools used to reach into or touch something in order to examine it, especially an instrument used to explore a wound or body cavity. **3.** An examination or study with or as if with a probe. *—v.* **probed, prob•ing, probes.** *—tr.* **1.** To explore or examine (something) with or as if with a probe. **2.** To investigate or explore: *The committee is probing the causes of the strike.* *—intr.* To conduct an investigation or search. [First written down in 1425 in Middle English, from Late Latin *proba*, proof.]

pro•bi•ty (prō′bĭ tē) *n.* Complete integrity; uprightness.

prob•lem (prŏb′ləm) *n.* **1.** A question to be considered, solved, or answered: *math problems; construction problems.* **2.** A situation or person that presents difficulty: *social problems.* *—adj.* Difficult to deal with or control: *a problem child.*

prob•lem•at•ic (prŏb′lə măt′ĭk) also **prob•lem•at•i•cal** (prŏb′lə măt′ĭ kəl) *adj.* Posing a problem or question: *a problematic situation.*

pro•bos•cis (prō bŏs′ĭs) *n., pl.* **pro•bos•cis•es** or **pro•bos•ci•des** (prō bŏs′ĭ dēz′). **1.** A long flexible snout, such as an elephant's trunk. **2.** A slender tubular mouthpart of certain insects, used for sucking food. **3.** An unusually large nose.

pro•caine (prō′kān′) *n.* A drug used as a local anesthetic in medicine and dentistry.

pro•ce•dure (prə sē′jər) *n.* A manner of proceeding; a way of doing something or getting something done: *the procedure for getting a passport.* **—pro•ce′dur•al** *adj.*

pro•ceed (prə sēd′) *intr.v.* **pro•ceed•ed, pro•ceed•ing, pro•ceeds. 1.** To go forward or onward, especially after an interruption; continue: *He ran some errands and then proceeded home.* **2.** To begin to carry on some action or process; continue: *After lunch, she proceeded to talk about the film.* *—n.* **pro•ceeds.** (prō′sēdz′). The amount of money derived from a fund-raising venture. [First written down about 1380 in Middle English and spelled *proceden*, from Latin *prōcēdere* : *prō-*, forward + *cēdere*, to go.]

pro•ceed•ing (prə sē′dĭng) *n.* **1.** A course of action: *a reckless proceeding.* **2. proceedings.** Legal action.

proc•ess (prŏs′ĕs′) *n., pl.* **proc•ess•es** (prŏs′ĕs′ĭz *or* prŏs′ĭ-sēz′). **1.** A series of actions, changes, or functions bringing about a desired result: *a manufacturing process; the process of digestion.* **2.** Course of events or passage of time: *He started playing tennis, and in the process he lost ten pounds.* **3.a.** A summons or writ to appear in court. **b.** The entire course of a judicial proceeding. **4.** A part that extends or projects from the body or one of its organs: *A horn is a bony process that grows from the head of certain animals.* *—tr.v.* **proc•essed, proc•ess•ing, proc•ess•es. 1.** To put through a fixed series of steps: *process an application.* **2.** To prepare, treat, or convert by means of a special process: *process ore to obtain minerals.*

pro•ces•sion (prə sĕsh′ən) *n.* **1.** The act of moving along or forward; progression. **2.** A group of persons, vehicles, or objects moving along in an orderly line: *a royal procession.*

pro•ces•sion•al (prə sĕsh′ə nəl) *adj.* Of, relating to, or suitable for a procession: *She led the processional march.* *—n.* **1.** A book containing the rituals observed during a religious procession. **2.** A musical piece played or sung during a procession.

pro-choice (prō chois′) *adj.* Supporting the legal right of women and girls to choose whether or not to continue a pregnancy.

pro•claim (prə klām′) *tr.v.* **pro•claimed, pro•claim•ing, pro•claims. 1.** To announce officially and publicly; declare: *proclaim a holiday.* **2.** To indicate unmistakably; make plain: *His behavior proclaims him capable of holding the office.*

proc•la•ma•tion (prŏk′lə mā′shən) *n.* **1.** The act of proclaiming. **2.** Something proclaimed, especially an official public announcement.

pro•cliv•i•ty (prō klĭv′ĭ tē) *n., pl.* **pro•cliv•i•ties.** A natural inclination; a predisposition: *her proclivity for the arts.*

pro•con•sul (prō kŏn′səl) *n.* In ancient Rome, a provincial administrator.

pro•cras•ti•nate (prə krăs′tə nāt′) *intr.v.* **pro•cras•ti•nat•ed, pro•cras•ti•nat•ing, pro•cras•ti•nates.** To put off doing something, especially out of habitual carelessness or laziness. [First written down in 1588 in Modern English, from Latin *prōcrāstināre* : *prō-*, forward + *crāstinus*, of tomorrow (from *crās*, tomorrow).] **—pro•cras′ti•na′tion** *n.* **—pro•cras′ti•na′tor** *n.*

pro•cre•ate (prō′krē āt′) *v.* **pro•cre•at•ed, pro•cre•at•ing, pro•cre•ates.** *—tr.* To produce (offspring). *—intr.* To produce offspring. **—pro′cre•a′tion** *n.*

proc•tor (prŏk′tər) *n.* In a school or university, a person appointed to supervise students during examinations. *—tr.v.* **proc•tored, proc•tor•ing, proc•tors.** To supervise (an examination).

pro•cure (prō kyŏŏr′) *tr.v.* **pro•cured, pro•cur•ing, pro•cures. 1.** To get by special effort; obtain or acquire: *procured tickets for the circus.* **2.** To bring about; effect: *striving to procure a solution to the problem.* **—pro•cure′ment** *n.*

prod (prŏd) *tr.v.* **prod•ded, prod•ding, prods. 1.** To jab or poke, as with a pointed object: *She prodded the cattle along.* **2.** To stir to action; urge: *continually prodded him to do his homework.* *—n.* **1.** A pointed object used as a prod: *a cattle prod.* **2.** A stimulus to action. **—prod′der** *n.*

prod•i•gal (prŏd′ĭ gəl) *adj.* **1.** Recklessly or extravagantly wasteful: *our prodigal waste of natural resources.* **2.** Extravagantly generous or abundant: *prodigal praise.* *—n.* An extravagant person; a spendthrift. [First written down about 1500 in Modern English, from Latin *prōdigere*, to drive out, squander.] **—prod′i•gal′i•ty** (prŏd′ĭ găl′ĭ tē) *n.* **—prod′i•gal•ly** *adv.*

pro•di•gious (prə dĭj′əs) *adj.* **1.** Impressively large in size, force, or extent: *a prodigious sea monster.* **2.** Extraordinary: *a prodigious memory.* **—pro•di′gious•ly** *adv.*

proboscis
African elephant eating grass

ă	pat	oi	boy
ā	pay	ou	out
âr	care	ŏŏ	took
ä	father	ōō	boot
ĕ	pet	ŭ	cut
ē	be	ûr	urge
ĭ	pit	th	thin
ī	pie	*th*	this
îr	pier	hw	whoop
ŏ	pot	zh	vision
ō	toe	ə	about
ô	paw	N	*French* bon

Word Building: produce

The word root *–duc–* in English words comes from the Latin verb *dūcere*, "to lead, bring, take." Thus we have **induce**, "to lead on, draw on, as by persuasion" (using the prefix *in–²*, "on, in"); **educe**, "to draw out, bring out, elicit" (*ē–*, "out, out of"); and **produce**, "to bring forth (as a product), lead out" (*prō–*, "forward, in front").

profile
Portrait of Bianca Maria Sforza (1423–1468) by Giovanni de Predis (1450?–1520?)

prod•i•gy (prŏd′ə jē) *n., pl.* **prod•i•gies. 1.** A person with exceptional talents or powers: *a child prodigy.* **2.** An extraordinary act or event; a marvel: *geysers and rock formations that are prodigies of nature.* [First written down before 1470 in Middle English and spelled *prodige*, portent, from Latin *prōdigium.*]

pro•duce (prə **dōōs′** *or* prə **dyōōs′**) *tr.v.* **pro•duced, pro•duc•ing, pro•duc•es. 1.** To bring forth (something); yield: *Seeds grow up to produce plants.* **2.** To create by mental or physical effort: *produce a painting.* **3.** To manufacture: *produce parts for machines.* **4.** To cause to exist; give rise to: *Industrial growth produced a new kind of business organization.* **5.** To bring forward; show; exhibit: *The magician produced a rabbit from the hat.* **6.** To supervise and finance the public presentation of: *produce a movie.* —*n.* (**prŏd′**ōōs *or* **prō′**dōōs). Farm products, especially fruits or vegetables. [First written down before 1425 in Middle English and spelled *producen*, to extend, from Latin *prōdūcere*, to extend, bring forth : *prō-*, forth + *dūcere*, to lead.] —SEE NOTE.

pro•duc•er (prə **dōō′**sər *or* prə **dyōō′**sər) *n.* **1.** A person, an organization, or a thing that produces, especially one that makes something for sale: *a producer of cast iron.* **2.** A person who supervises and manages the making and public presentation of a play, film, television show, or other entertainment.

producer goods *pl.n.* Goods, such as raw materials or tools, used to make consumer goods.

prod•uct (**prŏd′**əkt) *n.* **1.** Something produced, as by human effort or by nature: *farm products.* **2.** A direct result: *His discipline is the product of a strict education.* **3.** The result obtained when multiplication is performed.

pro•duc•tion (prə **dŭk′**shən) *n.* **1.** The act or process of producing: *automobile production.* **2.** An item that has been produced; a product. **3.** A motion picture, play, or television or radio show: *This is the company's finest production to date.* **4.** An amount produced; output or yield: *Production is down this week.*

pro•duc•tive (prə **dŭk′**tĭv) *adj.* **1.** Producing or capable of producing: *productive business.* **2.** Producing abundantly; fertile: *productive farmlands.* **3.** Producing favorable results or conditions; constructive: *a productive life.* —**pro•duc′tive•ly** *adv.* —**pro′duc•tiv′i•ty** (prō′dŭk **tĭv′**ĭ tē *or* **prŏd′**-ək **tĭv′**ĭ tē), **pro•duc′tive•ness** *n.*

prof. *abbr.* An abbreviation of professional.

prof•a•na•tion (prŏf′ə **nā′**shən) *n.* The act of profaning; desecration.

pro•fane (prō **fān′** *or* prə **fān′**) *adj.* **1.** Showing contempt for God or sacred things; irreverent: *profane words.* **2.** Not religious in nature or use; secular: *both sacred and profane music.* **3.** Coarse or vulgar. —*tr.v.* **pro•faned, pro•fan•ing, pro•fanes. 1.** To treat or use (something sacred) in a way that shows contempt or irreverence: *profaning the name of God.* **2.** To put to an unworthy or degrading use; misuse: *profaning lovely Spanish words by mispronunciation.* —**pro•fane′ly** *adv.* —**pro•fane′ness** *n.*

pro•fan•i•ty (prō **făn′**ĭ tē *or* prə **făn′**ĭ tē) *n., pl.* **pro•fan•i•ties. 1.** The quality of being profane; irreverence or vulgarity. **2.a.** Abrasive, vulgar, or irreverent language. **b.** The use of profane language.

pro•fess (prə **fĕs′**) *tr.v.* **pro•fessed, pro•fess•ing, pro•fess•es. 1.** To declare openly; claim: *professed an interest in learning to sail.* **2.** To make a show of; pretend: *professing a sympathy that he did not really feel.* **3.** To claim knowledge of or skill in: *profess medicine.* **4.** To be adherent of (a religion). [First written down before 1333 in Middle English and spelled *professen*, to take vows, from Latin *profitērī*, to affirm openly.]

pro•fes•sion (prə **fĕsh′**ən) *n.* **1.** An occupation that requires training and specialized study: *the profession of engineering.* **2.** The group of qualified persons practicing such an occupation: *the teaching profession.* **3.** The act of professing; an open declaration: *a profession of faith.* [First written down before 1200 in Middle English and spelled *professiun*, vow, from Latin *professiō*, public avowal, from *profitērī*, to affirm openly.]

pro•fes•sion•al (prə **fĕsh′**ə nəl) *adj.* **1.** Of, relating to, or practicing a profession: *lawyers, doctors, and other professional people.* **2.** Having or showing specialized skill: *She did a thoroughly professional repair job on the car.* **3.** Doing specified work for a living or as a career: *a professional writer.* **4.** Performed by or consisting of persons receiving pay; not amateur: *professional golf.* —*n.* **1.** A person who follows a profession, especially a learned profession. **2.** A person who earns a living in a given profession. **3.** A person who is skilled or experienced in a certain field; a qualified expert. —**pro•fes′sion•al•ly** *adv.*

pro•fes•sor (prə **fĕs′**ər) *n.* **1.** A teacher of the highest rank in a college or university. **2.** A teacher or an instructor. [First written down before 1387 in Middle English and spelled *professour*, from Latin *professor*, from *profitērī*, to profess.] —**pro•fes′sor•ship′** *n.*

pro•fes•so•ri•al (prō′fĭ **sôr′**ē əl *or* prŏf′ĭ **sôr′**ē əl) *adj.* Of, relating to, or characteristic of a professor. —**pro′fes•so′ri•al•ly** *adv.*

prof•fer (**prŏf′**ər) *tr.v.* **prof•fered, prof•fer•ing, prof•fers.** To present for acceptance; offer: *proffered her legal services to our school.* —*n.* An offer: *the proffer of help.*

pro•fi•cient (prə **fĭsh′**ənt) *adj.* Performing skillfully; competent; adept: *proficient at playing the harmonica.* —**pro•fi′cien•cy** *n.* —**pro•fi′cient•ly** *adv.*

Synonyms: proficient, adept, skilled, skillful, expert. These adjectives mean having or showing knowledge, ability, or skill, as in a vocation, profession, or branch of learning. **Proficient** suggests advanced ability gained through training: *It takes many years of study and experience to become a proficient surgeon.* **Adept** suggests being naturally good at something that one has improved through practice: *The dressmaker became adept at cutting fabric without a pattern.* **Skilled** suggests sound, thorough ability and often mastery, as in an art, a craft, or a trade: *Only the most skilled gymnasts are accepted for the Olympic team.* **Skillful** means skilled with a natural knack: *She is especially skillful at measuring things by eye.* **Expert** applies to one with absolute skill and command: *A virtuoso is one who is expert in playing a musical instrument.*

pro•file (**prō′**fīl′) *n.* **1.a.** A side view of an object, especially of the human head. **b.** A representation of a human head or other object seen from the side: *the profile of Lincoln on the penny.* **2.** The outline of something: *the jagged profile of the city skyline.* **3.** A biographical sketch. **4.** A summary or an analysis of something: *a profile of the ten best restaurants.* **5.** A vertical section of soil that shows the succession of layers. [First written down in 1656 in Modern English, from Italian *profilare*, to draw in outline.]

prof•it (**prŏf′**ĭt) *n.* **1.** An advantage gained from doing something; a benefit: *There was little profit in complaining.* **2.** The money made in a business venture, sale, or investment after all expenses have been met: *made a profit of five cents on every paper he sold.* —*v.* **prof•it•ed, prof•it•ing, prof•its.** —*intr.* To gain an advantage; benefit: *profiting from the* *experience of others.* —*tr.* To be an advantage to: *It would profit you to pay closer attention to what is being said.* [First written down in 1263 in Middle English, from Latin *prōficere,* to make progress, to profit.] —**prof′it•less** *adj.*

❑ *These sound alike:* **profit, prophet** (person inspired by God).

prof•it•a•ble (prŏf′ĭ tə bəl) *adj.* **1.** Yielding a profit; money-making: *a profitable business.* **2.** Yielding benefits; rewarding; worthwhile: *learned much that proved profitable later.*

prof•it•eer (prŏf′ĭ tîr′) *n.* A person who makes excessive profits on goods in short supply. —*intr.v.* **prof•it•eered, prof•it•eer•ing, prof•it•eers.** To act as a profiteer.

prof•li•gate (prŏf′lĭ gĭt *or* prŏf′lĭ gāt′) *adj.* **1.** Given to extreme self-indulgence; dissolute. **2.** Recklessly wasteful of money or resources. —*n.* A very wasteful or dissolute person. —**prof′li•ga•cy** (prŏf′lĭ gə sē) *n.* —**prof′li•gate•ly** *adv.*

pro•found (prə found′) *adj.* **pro•found•er, pro•found•est. 1.** Extending to or coming from a great depth; deep: *a profound chasm.* **2.** Coming as if from the depths of one's being; deeply felt or held: *profound love of art.* **3.** Far-reaching; thoroughgoing: *a profound change in our society.* **4.** Going well beyond what is apparent or superficial; wise and full of insight: *a profound remark.* **5.** Total; absolute: *a profound silence.* [First written down about 1300 in Middle English, from Latin *profundus* : *prō-,* before + *fundus,* bottom.] —**pro•found′ly** *adv.* —**pro•found′ness** *n.*

pro•fun•di•ty (prə fŭn′dĭ tē) *n., pl.* **pro•fun•di•ties. 1.** Great depth. **2.** Depth of intellect, feeling, or meaning; wisdom. **3.** An idea, a problem, or a subject requiring deep and careful thought.

pro•fuse (prə fyo͞os′) *adj.* **1.** Abundant; plentiful: *a profuse variety of foods.* **2.** Given or giving generously; extravagant; lavish: *profuse praise.* [First written down before 1425 in Middle English, from Latin *profūsus,* from *profundere,* to pour forth.] —**pro•fuse′ly** *adv.* —**pro•fuse′ness** *n.*

pro•fu•sion (prə fyo͞o′zhən) *n.* **1.** The condition of being profuse; abundance. **2.** A great quantity or amount: *a profusion of old books in the attic.* **3.** Lavish or unrestrained expense; extravagance.

pro•gen•i•tor (prō jĕn′ĭ tər) *n.* **1.** A direct ancestor. **2.** A person or thing that originates or sets a pattern for something.

prog•e•ny (prŏj′ə nē) *n., pl.* **progeny** or **prog•e•nies.** Children or descendants considered as a group; offspring.

pro•ges•ter•one (prō jĕs′tə rōn′) *n.* A hormone that readies the lining of the uterus to receive a fertilized ovum.

prog•no•sis (prŏg nō′sĭs) *n., pl.* **prog•no•ses** (prŏg-nō′sēz). **1.a.** A prediction of the likely course or outcome of a disease: *His prognosis was for full recovery.* **b.** The likelihood of recovering from a disease: *a good prognosis.* **2.** A prediction or forecast. [First written down in 1655 in Modern English, from Greek *prognōsis* : *pro-,* before + *gignōskein,* to know.]

prog•nos•tic (prŏg nŏs′tĭk) *adj.* Of, relating to, or useful in prognosis or prediction. —*n.* **1.** A sign or symptom indicating the future course of a disease. **2.** A sign of future events; a portent.

prog•nos•ti•cate (prŏg nŏs′tĭ kāt′) *tr.v.* **prog•nos•ti•cat•ed, prog•nos•ti•cat•ing, prog•nos•ti•cates.** To predict on the basis of present signs or symptoms: *prognosticate a good year for farm crops.* —**prog•nos′ti•ca′tion** *n.* —**prog•nos′ti•ca′tor** *n.*

pro•gram (prō′grăm′ *or* prō′grəm) *n.* **1.** A list of the order of events and other information for a public presentation or entertainment: *a printed program of the concert.* **2.** A public performance, presentation, or entertainment: *We presented a program of folk music.* **3.** A radio or television show. **4.** An ordered list of activities, courses, or procedures; a schedule: *arranged her program so that she could have Mondays off.* **5.** A course of academic study or extracurricular activities: *an excellent African studies program.* **6.** A system of services or projects designed to achieve a goal: *the space program.* **7.a.** The set of steps necessary for a computer to solve a problem, including the collection and processing of data and the presentation of results. **b.** The set of instructions that a computer must execute in carrying out these steps. —*tr.v.* **pro•grammed, pro•gram•ming, pro•grams** or **pro•gramed, pro•gram•ing, pro•grams. 1.** To include in a program; schedule. **2.** To provide (a computer) with a program. **3.** To train or regulate to perform in a certain way: *We have been programmed to expect TV commercials.* [First written down in 1633 in Modern English, from Greek *programma,* public notice : *pro-,* forth, publicly + *graphein,* to write.]

pro•gram•mer or **pro•gram•er** (prō′grăm′ər) *n.* A person who writes programs for computers.

prog•ress (prŏg′rĕs′ *or* prŏg′rəs) *n.* **1.** Onward movement; advance: *made slow progress through the traffic.* **2.** Steady improvement, as of civilization or an individual: *faith in human progress.* —*intr.v.* **pro•gress** (prə grĕs′). **pro•gressed, pro•gress•ing, pro•gress•es. 1.** To move along; advance; proceed: *Work on the new pool has progressed rapidly.* **2.** To make steady or regular improvements: *Medical technology is always progressing.* —***idiom.* in progress.** Going on; under way. [First written down before 1425 in Middle English and spelled *progresse,* from Latin *prōgressus,* from *prōgredī,* to advance : *prō-,* forward + *gradī,* to go, walk.] —SEE NOTE.

pro•gres•sion (prə grĕsh′ən) *n.* **1.** Movement; progress: *limbs adapted for progression on land.* **2.** A series of things or events; a sequence: *a progression of speakers at the rally.* **3.** A sequence of numbers, each derived from the one before by some regular rule.

pro•gres•sive (prə grĕs′ĭv) *adj.* **1.** Moving forward; advancing: *the progressive motion of a wave.* **2.** Continuing steadily by small changes: *progressive erosion in the cliff.* **3.** Tending to spread or grow worse: *progressive paralysis.* **4.** Working for or favoring the changes necessary for progress or steady improvement: *progressive leadership.* **5.** Increasing in rate of tax as the taxable amount increases: *The federal income tax is progressive, but sales taxes are not.* **6.** Indicating a verb form used to express an action or a condition that is in progress. Progressive verb forms in English use a present participle and a form of the verb *be;* for example, *I am sitting. He had been sitting. She will be sitting.* —*n.* A person who works for or favors steady improvements or reforms. —**pro•gres′sive•ly** *adv.* —**pro•gres′sive•ness** *n.*

pro•hib•it (prō hĭb′ĭt) *tr.v.* **pro•hib•it•ed, pro•hib•it•ing, pro•hib•its. 1.** To forbid by law or authority: *The pool rules prohibit diving in the shallow end.* **2.** To prevent: *Laws prohibit employers from discriminating against union members.* [First written down before 1425 in Middle English and spelled *prohibiten,* from Latin *prohibēre* : *pro-,* in front + *habēre,* to hold.]

pro•hi•bi•tion (prō′ə bĭsh′ən) *n.* **1.** The act of prohibiting or the condition of being prohibited. **2.** A law or an order that prohibits something: *a prohibition on smoking.* **3.a.** The forbidding by law of the manufacture, transportation, sale, and possession of alcoholic beverages. **b. Prohibition.** The pe-

Word Building: progress

The word root *–gress–* in English words comes from the past participle *gressus* of the Latin verb *gradī,* "to walk." **Progress** therefore is literally "a walking forward, an advance" (using the prefix *prō–,* "forward"); to **transgress** means "to walk through or over to the other side, pass beyond a limit" (*trans–,* "across"); an **egress** is literally "a way out, an exit" (*ē–,* "out, out of"); and to **digress** means "to go off or astray" (*dī–,* a form of *dis–,* "apart"). The Latin noun derived from *gradī* is *gradus,* "a pace, step, stage in a process," the source of the English **grade.**

ă	**pat**	oi	**boy**
ā	**pay**	ou	**out**
âr	**care**	o͝o	**took**
ä	**father**	o͞o	**boot**
ĕ	**pet**	ŭ	**cut**
ē	**be**	ûr	**urge**
ĭ	**pit**	th	**thin**
ī	**pie**	*th*	**this**
îr	**pier**	hw	**whoop**
ŏ	**pot**	zh	**vision**
ō	**toe**	ə	**about**
ô	**paw**	N	*French* bon

riod from 1920 to 1933 during which a ban on the manufacture and sale of alcoholic beverages was in effect in the United States.

pro•hi•bi•tion•ist (prō′ə **bĭsh′**ə nĭst) *n.* A person in favor of outlawing the manufacture and sale of alcoholic beverages.

pro•hib•i•tive (prō **hĭb′**ĭ tĭv) *adj.* **1.** Prohibiting; forbidding. **2.** Preventing or discouraging purchase or use: *prohibitive prices.* **—pro•hib′i•tive•ly** *adv.* **—pro•hib′i•tive•ness** *n.*

proj•ect (**prŏj′**ĕkt′) *n.* **1.** A plan or proposal. **2.** An undertaking requiring systematic planning and work: *a land-irrigation project.* **3.** A special task undertaken by a student or group of students: *a science project.* **4.** A housing project. *—v.* **pro•ject** (prə **jĕkt′**). **pro•ject•ed, pro•ject•ing, pro•jects.** *—tr.v.* **1.** To thrust forward or outward: *He projected his jaw in defiance.* **2.** To shoot or throw forward; hurl: *project an arrow.* **3.** To cause an image to appear on a surface: *projecting color slides onto a wall.* **4.** To calculate, estimate, or predict (something in the future) based on present data: *project next year's costs.* **5.** To plan; intend: *projecting a new superhighway.* **6.** To direct (one's voice) so as to be heard clearly at a distance. *—intr.* **1.** To extend or jut out: *The second floor projects over the street.* **2.** To project one's voice so as to be heard clearly at a distance. [First written down before 1400 in Middle English and spelled *projecte,* from Latin *prōiectum,* projecting structure, from *prōicere,* to throw out : *prō-,* forth + *iacere,* to throw.]

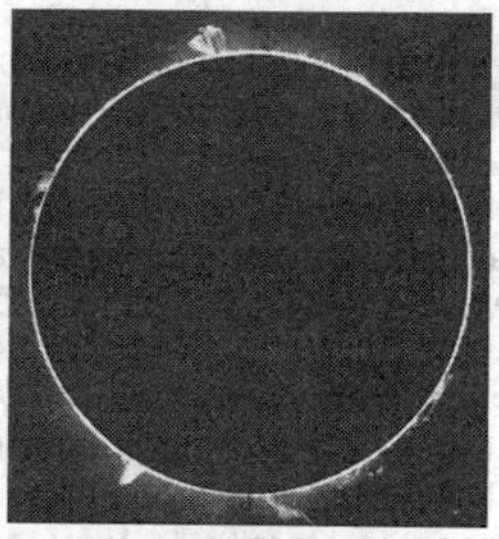

prominence
Solar prominences visible during a total eclipse

pro•jec•tile (prə **jĕk′**təl *or* prə **jĕk′**tīl′) *n.* **1.** An object, such as a bullet or an arrow, that is thrown, fired, or otherwise launched through space. **2.** A missile that can launch itself, such as a rocket.

pro•jec•tion (prə **jĕk′**shən) *n.* **1.** The act of projecting or the condition of being projected. **2.** Something that extends outward beyond a surface: *an insect with spiny projections on its back.* **3.** An image produced by a pattern of light falling on a surface, as when a slide is projected on a screen. **4.** An estimate of what something will be in the future, based on the present trends or data: *Projections indicate that sales will be up.*

pro•jec•tion•ist (prə **jĕk′**shə nĭst) *n.* A person who operates a movie projector

pro•jec•tor (prə **jĕk′**tər) *n.* A machine that uses lenses and a source of light to project images, as of motion pictures, onto a surface.

pro•le•tar•i•an (prō′lĭ **târ′**ē ən) *adj.* Of, connected with, or characteristic of the working class: *a proletarian revolution.* *—n.* A member of the working class. [First written down in 1658 in Modern English, from Latin *prōlētārius,* belonging to the lowest class of Roman citizens.]

pro•le•tar•i•at (prō′lĭ **târ′**ē ĭt) *n.* The class of people who work for wages, especially at industrial jobs, and who do not own property; the working class.

pro-life (prō **līf′**) *adj.* Believing that human embryos or fetuses should have full legal protection and that deliberate abortions should be illegal.

pro•lif•er•ate (prə **lĭf′**ə rāt′) *intr.v.* **pro•lif•er•at•ed, pro•lif•er•at•ing, pro•lif•er•ates. 1.** To produce new growth or offspring rapidly and repeatedly; multiply at a fast rate: *Viruses proliferate in living tissue.* **2.** To increase or spread rapidly: *The branches of physics have proliferated during this century.* **—pro•lif′er•a′tion** *n.*

pro•lif•ic (prə **lĭf′**ĭk) *adj.* **1.** Producing offspring or fruit in great numbers: *Rabbits are prolific animals.* **2.** Producing numerous works: *a prolific author.* [First written down in 1650 in Modern English, from Latin *prōlēs,* offspring.] **—pro•lif′i•cal•ly** *adv.*

pro•lix (prō **lĭks′** *or* **prō′**lĭks′) *adj.* Wordy and tiresome; verbose. **—pro•lix′i•ty** *n.* **—pro•lix′ly** *adv.*

pro•logue (**prō′**lôg′ *or* **prō′**lŏg′) *n.* **1.** A beginning section of a play, an opera, or a literary work that introduces or explains what follows. **2.** An introductory act or event.

pro•long (prə **lông′** *or* prə **lŏng′**) *tr.v.* **pro•longed, pro•long•ing, pro•longs. 1.** To lengthen in duration; protract: *a special diet for prolonging one's life.* **2.** To lengthen in extent or space: *It is unwise to prolong a business letter.* **—pro′lon•ga′tion** (prō′lông **gā′**shən *or* prō′lŏng **gā′**shən) *n.*

prom (prŏm) *n.* A formal dance held for a school class.

prom•e•nade (prŏm′ə **nād′** *or* prŏm′ə **näd′**) *n.* **1.** A leisurely walk, especially in a public place. **2.** A public place for strolling, as a park or mall. **3.** A formal dance. **4.a.** A march performed by the couples in a square dance. **b.** A march by the guests at the opening of a ball. *—tr.v.* **prom•e•nad•ed, prom•e•nad•ing, prom•e•nades. 1.** To go on a leisurely walk; stroll. **2.** To perform a promenade at a square dance or a ball.

Pro•me•the•us (prə **mē′**thē əs) *n.* In Greek mythology, a Titan who steals fire from Olympus and gives it to humankind, for which Zeus chains him to a rock and sets an eagle to eat his liver, which grows back daily.

pro•me•thi•um (prə **mē′**thē əm) *n. Symbol* **Pm** A radioactive rare-earth element produced artificially from uranium and neodymium. Atomic number 61. See table at **element.**

prom•i•nence (**prŏm′**ə nəns) *n.* **1.** The quality or condition of being prominent; eminence or importance: *rose to a position of prominence in government.* **2.** Something that rises sharply upward or outward from its surroundings: *climbed the nearest prominence for a view of the terrain.* **3.** A slender wavy cloud of shining gas that rises from the surface of the sun.

prom•i•nent (**prŏm′**ə nənt) *adj.* **1.** Projecting outward; bulging or jutting: *prominent brows.* **2.** Highly noticeable; conspicuous: *You will find the card catalog in a prominent place in your library.* **3.** Well-known; eminent: *a prominent politician.* [First written down in 1440 in Middle English, from Latin *prōminēre,* to jut out.] **—prom′i•nent•ly** *adv.*

prom•is•cu•i•ty (prŏm′ĭ **skyōō′**ĭ tē *or* prō′mĭ **skyōō′**ĭ tē) *n., pl.* **prom•is•cu•i•ties.** The state or character of being promiscuous.

pro•mis•cu•ous (prə **mĭs′**kyōō əs) *adj.* **1.** Having sexual relations with many persons. **2.** Showing a lack of standards for making choices; indiscriminate: *a gallery with a promiscuous assortment of good and bad paintings.* **—pro•mis′cu•ous•ly** *adv.* **—pro•mis′cu•ous•ness** *n.*

prom•ise (**prŏm′**ĭs) *n.* **1.** A declaration that one will or will not do a certain thing; a vow: *kept her promise to write home once a week.* See Synonyms at **vow. 2.a.** Indication of something favorable to come; grounds for expectation: *a promise of spring in the warm breeze.* **b.** Indication of future success or excellence: *a rookie pitcher who shows promise.* *—v.* **prom•ised, prom•is•ing, prom•is•es.** *—tr.* **1.** To declare with a promise; pledge: *I promised to come home early.* **2.** To give grounds for expecting: *clouds that promised rain.* *—intr.* To make or give a promise. [First written down about 1400 in Middle English and spelled *promis,* from Medieval Latin *prōmissa,* from Latin *prōmittere,* to send forth, promise.]

Prom•ised Land (**prŏm′**ĭst) *n.* **1.** In the Bible, the land of Canaan, promised by God to the descendants of Abraham and Sarah. **2. promised land.** A place of expected or longed-for happiness: *America was once viewed as a promised land by many immigrants.*

prom•is•ing (prŏm′ĭ sĭng) *adj.* Likely to develop as hoped: *a promising career.* **—prom′is•ing•ly** *adv.*

prom•is•so•ry note (prŏm′ĭ sôr′ē) *n.* A written promise to pay a certain sum of money at a stated time or on demand.

pro•mon•to•ry (prŏm′ən tôr′ē) *n., pl.* **prom•on•to•ries.** A high ridge of land or rock jutting out into a body of water. [First written down in 1548 in Modern English, from Latin *prōmunturium*, probably from *prominēre*, to jut out.]

pro•mote (prə mōt′) *tr.v.* **pro•mot•ed, pro•mot•ing, pro•motes. 1.** To raise to a higher rank, position, or class. **2.** To aid the progress or growth of; advance: *promoting the general welfare.* **3.** To urge the adoption or use of; advocate: *promote a measure in Congress.* **4.** To try to sell or make popular, as by advertising; publicize: *promoting a new line of products.* [First written down before 1387 in Middle English and spelled *promoten*, from Latin *prōmovēre*, to move forward.]

pro•mot•er (prə mō′tər) *n.* **1.** An active supporter; an advocate: *promoters of a larger defense budget.* **2.** A person in charge of finance and publicity, as for an artistic performance.

pro•mo•tion (prə mō′shən) *n.* **1.** An advancement to a higher rank, position, or class. **2.** Encouragement; furtherance: *societies for the promotion of knowledge.* **3.** Publicity, as for a product on sale; advertising. **—pro•mo′tion•al** *adj.*

prompt (prŏmpt) *adj.* **prompt•er, prompt•est. 1.** Being on time; punctual: *She was usually prompt in meeting deadlines.* **2.** Done or performed without delay; immediate: *a prompt reply.* *—tr.v.* **prompt•ed, prompt•ing, prompts. 1.** To urge (someone) to some action; incite: *an experience that prompted her to write her family.* **2.** To inspire or lead to: *The poor test scores prompted a review of teaching methods.* **3.** To assist by supplying a forgotten word, a cue, or another reminder: *prompt an actor.* *—n.* **1.** A reminder or cue. **2.** A symbol that appears on a computer monitor to indicate that the computer is ready to receive data. **—prompt′er** *n.* **—prompt′ly** *adv.* **—prompt′ness** *n.*

prom•ul•gate (prŏm′əl gāt′ *or* prō mŭl′gāt′) *tr.v.* **prom•ul•gat•ed, prom•ul•gat•ing, prom•ul•gates.** To announce publicly and officially; proclaim: *promulgate a new constitution.* **—prom′ul•ga′tion** *n.*

pron. *abbr.* An abbreviation of: **1.** Pronoun. **2.** Pronunciation.

prone (prōn) *adj.* **1.** Lying with the front or face downward. **2.** Tending; inclined: *prone to make hasty judgments.* **—prone′ly** *adv.* **—prone′ness** *n.*

prong (prông *or* prŏng) *n.* One of the sharply pointed ends of a fork or other implement.

pronged (prôngd *or* prŏngd) *adj.* Having prongs of a certain number or kind: *a three-pronged electrical plug.*

prong•horn (prông′hôrn′ *or* prŏng′hôrn′) *n., pl.* **pronghorn** or **prong•horns.** A swift-running hoofed mammal of western North America, having short forked horns.

pro•nom•i•nal (prō nŏm′ə nəl) *adj.* Of, relating to, or functioning as a pronoun.

pro•noun (prō′noun′) *n.* In grammar, any of a class of words used as substitutes for nouns or noun phrases. [First written down about 1450 in Middle English : *pro-*, in place of + *noun.*]

pro•nounce (prə nouns′) *v.* **pro•nounced, pro•nounc•ing, pro•nounc•es.** *—tr.* **1.a.** To articulate or produce (a word or speech sound); utter. **b.** To represent (a word) in phonetic symbols. **2.** To deliver formally: *pronounce a speech.* *—intr.* To declare one's opinion: *pronouncing on the issues of the day.* [First written down before 1338 in Middle English and spelled *pronouncen*, to decree, from Latin *prōnūntiāre* : *prō-*, forth + *nūntius*, messenger.] **—pro•nounce′a•ble** *adj.*

pro•nounced (prə nounst′) *adj.* Distinct; marked; unmistakable: *a pronounced limp.*

pro•nounce•ment (prə nouns′mənt) *n.* **1.** A formal expression of opinion. **2.** An authoritative statement.

pron•to (prŏn′tō) *adv. Informal.* Right away; immediately. [First written down in 1850 in American English, from Spanish, from Latin *prōmptus*, prompt.]

pro•nun•ci•a•tion (prə nŭn′sē ā′shən) *n.* **1.** The act or manner of pronouncing words. **2.** A way of speaking a word, especially a way that is generally understood or accepted. **3.** A written representation of the way a word is pronounced, using phonetic symbols.

proof (pro͞of) *n.* **1.** Evidence or demonstration of truth or validity: *Accident figures offer us undeniable proof of the value of using safety belts.* **2.** A demonstration of the truth of a mathematical or logical statement, based on axioms and theorems derived from these axioms. **3.** The act of testing the truth or validity of something by experiment or trial: *The burden of proof is on the prosecution.* **4.a.** A trial sheet of printed material, checked against the original manuscript for errors. **b.** A trial impression or an engraved plate, stone, or block. **c.** A trial print of a photograph. **5.** The alcoholic content of a liquor, expressed in the United States as a given number of parts of alcohol per 200 parts of liquor. Liquor marked 100 proof is 50 percent alcohol. *—adj.* Fully resistant: *a tamperproof lock.*

proof•read (pro͞of′rēd′) *tr.v.* **proof•read** (pro͞of′-rĕd′), **proof•read•ing, proof•reads.** To read and mark corrections in (printed, typed, or written material). **—proof′read′er** *n.*

prop[1] (prŏp) *n.* **1.** An object placed beneath or against a structure to keep it from falling. **2.** A person or an object depended on for support or assistance. *—tr.v.* **propped, prop•ping, props.** To keep from falling by placing something beneath or against: *prop up a shelf with a two-by-four.* [First written down in 1440 in Middle English and spelled *proppe*, probably from Middle Dutch.]

prop[2] (prŏp) *n.* A movable article that is not part of a costume or scenery and is used on stage or in a movie during a dramatic performance. [First written down in 1841 in Modern English, short for *property.*]

prop[3] (prŏp) *n. Informal.* A propeller. [First written down in 1914 in Modern English, short for *propeller.*]

prop•a•gan•da (prŏp′ə găn′də) *n.* **1.** The communication of a doctrine or of information reflecting particular views and interests to large numbers of people, especially by constant repetition and by withholding information that might lead to other conclusions. **2.** Material distributed for the purpose of winning people over to a given doctrine, often without regard to truth or fairness: *wartime propaganda.*

prop•a•gan•dist (prŏp′ə găn′dĭst) *n.* A person engaged in spreading propaganda.

prop•a•gan•dize (prŏp′ə găn′dīz′) *v.* **prop•a•gan•dized, prop•a•gan•diz•ing, prop•a•gan•diz•es.** *—tr.* To influence by or subject to propaganda: *movies that propagandized the population into supporting the war.* *—intr.* To spread propaganda.

prop•a•gate (prŏp′ə gāt′) *v.* **prop•a•gat•ed, prop•**

pronghorn
Male pronghorn

ă	pat	oi	boy
ā	pay	ou	out
âr	care	o͝o	took
ä	father	o͞o	boot
ĕ	pet	ŭ	cut
ē	be	ûr	urge
ĭ	pit	th	thin
ī	pie	*th*	this
îr	pier	hw	whoop
ŏ	pot	zh	vision
ō	toe	ə	about
ô	paw	N	*French* bon

propeller
Airplane propeller

prophase

a•gat•ing, prop•a•gates. —*tr.* **1.** To cause to produce offspring or new individuals; breed: *propagate plants from cuttings.* **2.** To transmit (heat, light, or other energy) through space or a medium. **3.** To make known or accepted among many people; spread: *propagate a rumor.* —*intr.* To produce offspring. —**prop′a•ga′tion** *n.*

pro•pane (prō′pān′) *n.* A colorless gaseous hydrocarbon that has the formula C_3H_8. It is found in petroleum and natural gas and is widely used as a fuel.

pro•pel (prə pĕl′) *tr.v.* **pro•pelled, pro•pel•ling, pro•pels.** To cause to move or continue in motion: *the rearward thrust that propels a jet airplane.* [First written down in 1440 in Middle English and spelled *propellen*, from Latin *prōpellere* : *prō-*, forward + *pellere*, to drive.]

pro•pel•lant also **pro•pel•lent** (prə pĕl′ənt) *n.* **1.** A fuel or an explosive charge used to propel something, especially a rocket or projectile. **2.** The compressed gas used in an aerosol container or a similar device to force out the contents.

pro•pel•ler (prə pĕl′ər) *n.* A rotary device, usually driven by an engine or motor, used to propel an aircraft or boat.

pro•pen•si•ty (prə pĕn′sĭ tē) *n., pl.* **pro•pen•si•ties.** A natural tendency; an inclination: *her propensity to exaggerate.* [First written down in 1570 in Modern English, from Latin *prōpēnsus*, inclined, from *prōpendēre*, to be inclined.]

prop•er (prŏp′ər) *adj.* **1.** Suitable; appropriate: *the proper tools for mending a leaky roof.* **2.** Called for by rules or conventions; correct: *the proper form for a business letter.* **3.** Strictly following the rules or conventions, especially in social behavior; seemly: *a proper gentleman.* **4.** Normally or characteristically belonging to the person or thing in question: *regained his proper frame of mind.* **5.** In the strict sense of the term: *We drove through the suburbs and entered the city proper.* [First written down before 1300 in Middle English and spelled *propre*, from Latin *proprius*.] —**prop′er•ly** *adv.* —**prop′er•ness** *n.*

proper fraction *n.* A common fraction in which the numerator is less than the denominator.

proper noun *n.* A noun that is the name of a unique person, place, or thing. —SEE NOTE at **noun.**

prop•er•ty (prŏp′ər tē) *n., pl.* **prop•er•ties. 1.** A possession or group of possessions: *He could put all his property into two suitcases.* **2.** A piece of land owned by someone: *A stream runs through our property.* **3.** An object or idea that its owner has the legal right to use: *A contribution of one scientist becomes the property of scientists to follow.* **4.** A characteristic quality or attribute, especially one that serves to define or describe something: *the chemical properties of a metal.* See Synonyms at **quality. 5.** A movable object that is not part of a costume or scenery and appears on stage or in a movie during a dramatic performance. [First written down about 1303 in Middle English and spelled *properte*, from Latin *proprietās*, ownership, from *proprius*, one's own.]

pro•phase (prō′fāz′) *n.* The first stage through which a living cell passes in mitosis and meiosis, during which chromatin in the nucleus condenses into chromosomes.

proph•e•cy (prŏf′ĭ sē) *n., pl.* **proph•e•cies** (prŏf′ĭ-sēz). **1.** A statement by a prophet, considered as a revelation of divine will. **2.** A declaration or warning of something to come; a prediction: *prophecies of financial disaster.*

proph•e•sy (prŏf′ĭ sī′) *v.* **proph•e•sied** (prŏf′ĭ sīd′), **proph•e•sy•ing** (prŏf′ĭ sī′ĭng), **proph•e•sies** (prŏf′ĭ-sīz′). —*tr.* **1.** To reveal by divine inspiration: *The soothsayer prophesied that a calf must be sacrificed on the altar.* **2.** To predict (what is to happen) with certainty. —*intr.* **1.** To speak as a prophet. **2.** To predict the future.

proph•et (prŏf′ĭt) *n.* **1.a.** A person who speaks words inspired by God and so expresses God's message. **b. Prophet.** Muhammad. **2.** A person who can foretell the future. **3. Prophets.** *(used with a singular or plural verb).* The second of the three divisions of the Hebrew Scriptures, including the books of Joshua, Judges, Samuel, Kings, Isaiah, Jeremiah, Ezekiel, and the Minor Prophets. [First written down before 1200 in Middle English and spelled *prophete*, from Greek *prophētēs* : *pro-*, before + *phanai*, to speak.]

❑ *These sound alike:* **prophet, profit** (advantage).

pro•phet•ic (prə fĕt′ĭk) *adj.* **1.** Of or characteristic of a prophet. **2.** Predicting the future: *a warning that proved prophetic.* —**pro•phet′i•cal•ly** *adv.*

pro•phy•lac•tic (prō′fə lăk′tĭk) *adj.* Acting to prevent or defend against something, especially a disease. —*n.* A prophylactic medicine, device, or action.

pro•pin•qui•ty (prə pĭng′kwĭ tē) *n.* **1.** Nearness; proximity. **2.** Kinship. **3.** Similarity in nature.

pro•pi•ti•ate (prō pĭsh′ē āt′) *tr.v.* **pro•pi•ti•at•ed, pro•pi•ti•at•ing, pro•pi•ti•ates.** To soothe and win over (an angry or offended person); appease: *propitiate the gods with offerings.* —**pro•pi′ti•a′tion** *n.*

pro•pi•tious (prə pĭsh′əs) *adj.* Favorable; suitable: *a propitious time to ask his mother for a loan.* —**pro•pi′tious•ly** *adv.* —**pro•pi′tious•ness** *n.*

pro•po•nent (prə pō′nənt) *n.* A person who argues in support of something; an advocate: *They are proponents of socialized medicine.* [First written down in 1588 in Modern English, from Latin *prōpōnere*, to set forth, propose.]

pro•por•tion (prə pôr′shən) *n.* **1.** A relationship between quantities such that if one changes the other changes as well. **2.** The size, amount, or extent of one thing compared with that of another thing: *The proportion of flour to milk in the recipe is two to one.* **3.** A pleasing or harmonious relationship between the various parts of a whole; balance or symmetry: *The statue seems out of proportion.* **4.** Size; dimensions. Often used in the plural: *a disease that reached epidemic proportions.* **5.** A relation of equality between two ratios. Four quantities, *a, b, c, d,* are said to be in proportion if $a/b = c/d$. —*tr.v.* **pro•por•tioned, pro•por•tion•ing, pro•por•tions. 1.** To adjust so as to achieve a particular relation between parts: *proportion the oil in the dressing properly.* **2.** To make the parts of harmonious or pleasing: *proportioned the figure nicely.*

pro•por•tion•al (prə pôr′shə nəl) *adj.* **1.** Corresponding in size, amount, or degree; in proportion: *The effects of the drug were proportional to the dose.* **2.** Related by a constant factor. For example, if $y = 6x$, x and y are proportional. —**pro•por′tion•al•ly** *adv.*

pro•por•tion•ate (prə pôr′shə nĭt) *adj.* Being in proportion; corresponding: *a promotion with a proportionate increase in responsibility.* —**pro•por′tion•ate•ly** *adv.*

pro•pos•al (prə pō′zəl) *n.* **1.** The act of proposing; an offer: *a proposal to go fishing.* **2.** A plan or scheme offered for consideration. **3.** An offer of marriage.

pro•pose (prə pōz′) *v.* **pro•posed, pro•pos•ing, pro•pos•es.** —*tr.* **1.** To put forward for consideration or acceptance; suggest: *propose a new law.* **2.** To recommend (a person) for a position, mission, or membership; nominate. **3.** To declare an intention;

intend: *She proposed to beat me at my own game.* —*intr.* To make a proposal, especially an offer of marriage. [First written down in 1340 in Middle English and spelled *proposen*, from Old French *proposer*, from Latin *prōpōnere* : *prō-*, forth + *pōnere*, to put.]

prop•o•si•tion (prŏp′ə **zĭsh′**ən) *n.* **1.** An offer; a proposal: *a business proposition.* **2.** A subject for discussion or analysis. **3.a.** A mathematical statement, as the statement of a theorem. **b.** A statement in logic, especially one that satisfies certain rules or is constructed in a certain form. **4.** A matter to be handled or dealt with; an undertaking: *Finding a cheap apartment is a difficult proposition.* —*tr.v.* **prop•o•si•tioned, prop•o•si•tion•ing, prop•o•si•tions.** *Informal.* To propose a bargain to (someone), especially to propose sexual relations with.

pro•pound (prə **pound′**) *tr.v.* **pro•pound•ed, pro•pound•ing, pro•pounds.** To set forth; propose: *propound a theory.*

pro•pri•e•tar•y (prə **prī′**ĭ tĕr′ē) *adj.* **1.** Of or relating to an owner or ownership: *She has a proprietary interest in the business.* **2.** Owned by an individual or a firm under a trademark or patent: *proprietary medicines.* —**pro•pri′e•tar′i•ly** *adv.*

pro•pri•e•tor (prə **prī′**ĭ tər) *n.* **1.** A person who owns or has legal title to something. **2.** The owner and often manager of a business. —**pro•pri′e•tor•ship′** *n.*

pro•pri•e•ty (prə **prī′**ĭ tē) *n., pl.* **pro•pri•e•ties. 1.** The quality of being proper; suitability; appropriateness. **2.** Conformity to rules and conventions, especially in social conduct: *She insisted on strict propriety at her dinner parties.* **3. proprieties.** The rules and conventions of polite social behavior.

pro•pul•sion (prə **pŭl′**shən) *n.* **1.** The act or process of propelling. **2.** A force that propels. [First written down in 1611 in Modern English, from Latin *prōpulsus*, past participle of *prōpellere*, to drive forward.]

pro•rate (prō **rāt′** *or* **prō′**rāt′) *tr.v.* **pro•rat•ed, pro•rat•ing, pro•rates.** To divide (an expense or a tax, for example) proportionately: *prorating the phone bills among the roommates.*

pro•sa•ic (prō **zā′**ĭk) *adj.* **1.** Characteristic of prose rather than poetry. **2.** Straightforward; matter-of-fact. **3.** Lacking in imagination or powers of fantasy. —**pro•sa′i•cal•ly** *adv.* —**pro•sa′ic•ness** *n.*

pro•scribe (prō **skrīb′**) *tr.v.* **pro•scribed, pro•scrib•ing, pro•scribes. 1.** To forbid; prohibit. **2.** To banish; outlaw: *The queen proscribed the rebels.* [First written down before 1425 in Middle English and spelled *proscriben*, from Latin *prōscribere*, to put up someone's name as outlawed : *prō-*, in front + *scrībere*, to write.] —**pro•scrib′er** *n.*

pro•scrip•tion (prō **skrĭp′**shən) *n.* The act of proscribing or the condition of being proscribed.

prose (prōz) *n.* Ordinary speech or writing as distinguished from verse or poetry.

pros•e•cute (**prŏs′**ĭ kyo͞ot′) *tr.v.* **pros•e•cut•ed, pros•e•cut•ing, pros•e•cutes. 1.** To initiate or conduct a legal action against (someone): *prosecuting people who break federal laws.* **2.** To pursue (an undertaking) to completion; follow to the end: *prosecuting a war.* **3.** To carry on, engage in, or practice: *prosecuting his occupation.* [First written down before 1425 in Middle English and spelled *prosecuten*, from Latin *prōsequī* : *prō-*, forward + *sequī*, to follow.]

pros•e•cu•tion (prŏs′ĭ **kyo͞o′**shən) *n.* **1.a.** The act of prosecuting a person or case in a court of law. **b.** The condition of being thus prosecuted: *risked prosecution by breaking the law.* **2.** A lawyer who initiates and conducts legal cases on behalf of a government and its citizens. **3.** The act of pursuing or performing: *the prosecution of her duties.*

pros•e•cu•tor (**prŏs′**ĭ kyo͞o′tər) *n.* The person who initiates a legal action, especially the public official who represents the state and the people in court.

pros•e•lyte (**prŏs′**ə līt′) *n.* A new convert to a religion, party, or doctrine. —*tr. & intr.v.* **pros•e•lyt•ed, pros•e•lyt•ing, pros•e•lytes.** To proselytize. [First written down about 1384 in Middle English and spelled *proselite*, from Greek *prosēlutos*, stranger, proselyte.]

pros•e•ly•tize (**prŏs′**ə lĭ tīz′) *v.* **pros•e•ly•tized, pros•e•ly•tiz•ing, pros•e•ly•tiz•es.** —*intr.* To try to cause a person to change from one religion, political party, or doctrine to another. —*tr.* To convert (a person) from one religion, political party, or doctrine to another.

Pro•ser•pi•na (prō **sûr′**pə nə) also **Pros•er•pi•ne** (prō **sûr′**pə nē) *n.* In Roman mythology, the daughter of Ceres who is carried away by Pluto to become his wife and the goddess of the underworld. She is identified with the Greek Persephone.

pros•o•dy (**prŏs′**ə dē) *n., pl.* **pros•o•dies. 1.** The study of the form of verse, especially of its meter. **2.** A particular system of form or structure in verse.

pros•pect (**prŏs′**pĕkt′) *n.* **1.** Something expected or foreseen; a possibility: *hurried home with the prospect of a good dinner.* **2. prospects.** Chances for success: *a young woman with prospects.* **3.** A possible customer or client. **4.** A possible candidate, as for a team or position: *a football scout who looked over the college prospects.* **5.** Something presented to the eye; a scene; a view: *a lovely prospect from the tower.* —*v.* **pros•pect•ed, pros•pect•ing, pros•pects.** —*tr.* To explore (a region) in search of mineral deposits or oil: *prospecting the Sierras.* —*intr.* To search for mineral deposits or oil. [First written down before 1425 in Middle English and spelled *prospecte*, from Latin *prōspectus*, distant view, from *prōspicere*, to look out : *prō-*, forward + *specere*, to look at.]

pro•spec•tive (prə **spĕk′**tĭv) *adj.* Likely or expected to be, become, or occur: *prospective budget cuts.* —**pro•spec′tive•ly** *adv.*

pros•pec•tor (**prŏs′**pĕk′tər) *n.* A person who explores an area for valuable mineral deposits or oil.

pro•spec•tus (prə **spĕk′**təs) *n.* A printed description of a business or other venture.

pros•per (**prŏs′**pər) *intr.v.* **pros•pered, pros•per•ing, pros•pers.** To be successful; thrive. [First written down in 1350 in Middle English and spelled *prosperen*, from Latin *prosperāre*, to render fortunate, from *prosperus*, favorable.]

pros•per•i•ty (prŏ **spĕr′**ĭ tē) *n.* The condition of being prosperous; success.

pros•per•ous (**prŏs′**pər əs) *adj.* **1.** Successful; thriving: *a prosperous garden.* **2.** Economically successful; enjoying wealth or profit: *a prosperous business.* —**pros′per•ous•ly** *adv.*

pros•ta•glan•din (prŏs′tə **glăn′**dĭn) *n.* Any of a group of substances similar to hormones, found in various human body tissues and affecting blood pressure and metabolism.

pros•tate (**prŏs′**tāt′) *n.* An organ composed of glandular and muscle tissue, surrounding the urethra of male mammals at the base of the bladder. The prostate controls the release of urine and secretes a fluid that is a major constituent of semen. —*adj.* Of or relating to the prostate.

pros•ti•tute (**prŏs′**tĭ to͞ot′ *or* **prŏs′**tĭ tyo͞ot′) *n.* **1.** A person who performs sexual acts with others for pay. **2.** A person who sells his or her abilities, talent, or name for an unworthy motive. —*tr.v.* **pros•ti•tut•ed, pros•ti•tut•ing, pros•ti•tutes. 1.** To offer (oneself or someone else) for sexual acts in return

prospector
Panning for gold

ă	pat	oi	boy
ā	pay	ou	out
âr	care	o͝o	took
ä	father	o͞o	boot
ĕ	pet	ŭ	cut
ē	be	ûr	urge
ĭ	pit	th	thin
ī	pie	*th*	this
îr	pier	hw	whoop
ŏ	pot	zh	vision
ō	toe	ə	about
ô	paw	N	*French* bon

for pay. **2.** To sell (oneself or one's abilities) for an unworthy purpose.

pros•ti•tu•tion (prŏs′tĭ to͞o′shən *or* prŏs′tĭ **tyo͞o′**-shən) *n.* **1.** The practice or work of performing sexual acts for pay. **2.** The act of prostituting; debasement: *the prostitution of an artist's talents.*

pros•trate (prŏs′trāt′) *tr.v.* **pros•trat•ed, pros•trat•ing, pros•trates. 1.** To throw down flat. **2.** To make (oneself) bow or kneel in humility or adoration. **3.** To exhaust or overcome physically or emotionally; render helpless: *a disease that prostrates its victims.* —*adj.* **1.** Kneeling or lying face down, as in submission: *He fell prostrate before the throne.* **2.** Lying down at full length: *a sleeper prostrate on the floor.* **3.** Exhausted or overcome physically or emotionally; helpless: *prostrate with fear.*

pros•tra•tion (prŏ **strā′**shən) *n.* **1.a.** The act or process or prostrating oneself. **b.** The condition of being prostrate. **2.** Complete mental or physical exhaustion.

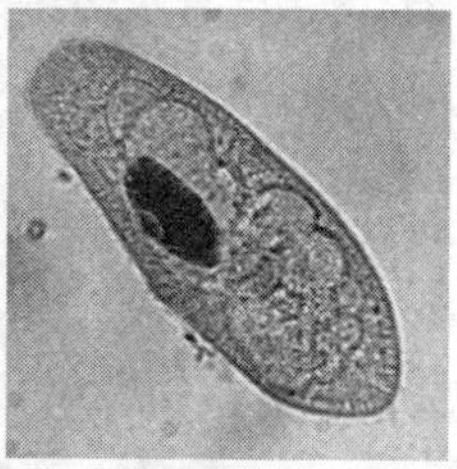

protozoan
Paramecium

Prot. *abbr.* An abbreviation of Protestant.

pro•tac•tin•i•um (prō′tăk **tĭn′**ē əm) *n. Symbol* **Pa** A rare radioactive metallic element chemically similar to uranium. Atomic number 91. See table at **element.**

pro•tag•o•nist (prō **tăg′**ə nĭst) *n.* The main character in a drama or literary work.

pro•te•an (prō′tē ən *or* prō **tē′**ən) *adj.* Taking on many different shapes or forms; highly variable: *a protean talent.* [First written down in 1598 in Modern English, after *Proteus,* Greek sea god who could change his shape at will.]

pro•tect (prə **tĕkt′**) *tr.v.* **pro•tect•ed, pro•tect•ing, pro•tects. 1.** To keep from harm, attack, or injury; guard: *laws that protect certain species of birds.* See Synonyms at **defend. 2.** To help (domestic industry) by placing tariffs or quotas on foreign goods. [First written down about 1456 in Middle English and spelled *protecten,* from Latin *prōtegere* : *prō-,* in front + *tegere,* to cover.]

pro•tec•tion (prə **tĕk′**shən) *n.* **1.a.** The act of protecting. **b.** The condition of being protected: *a hedge for protection against the wind.* **2.** A person or thing that protects: *The thin jacket was his only protection against the wind.* **3.** *Slang.* Money paid to criminals who threaten violence if they are not paid.

pro•tec•tive (prə **tĕk′**tĭv) *adj.* Serving to protect: *a protective coat of shellac.* **—pro•tec′tive•ly** *adv.* **—pro•tec′tive•ness** *n.*

pro•tec•tor (prə **tĕk′**tər) *n.* **1.** A person who protects; a defender or guardian. **2.** Something that protects: *The catcher wears a chest protector.* **3.** A person appointed to rule during the absence or childhood of a monarch.

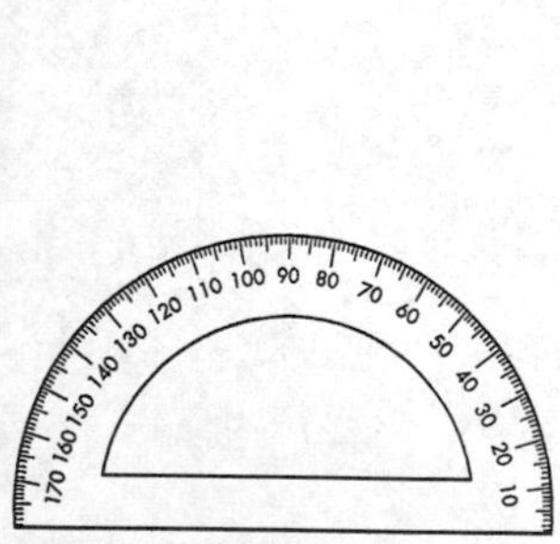

protractor

pro•tec•tor•ate (prə **tĕk′**tər ĭt) *n.* **1.a.** A relationship of protection and partial control assumed by a strong nation over a dependent foreign country. **b.** A dependent country or region in such a relationship. **2.** The office or period of rule of the protector of a country.

pro•té•gé (prō′tə zhā′ *or* prō′tə **zhā′**) *n.* A person whose welfare, training, or career is promoted by another, more influential or experienced person.

pro•tein (**prō′**tēn′) *n.* One of a large class of complex organic chemical compounds that contain nitrogen and have very high molecular weights. Proteins form the basis of living tissues.

pro•test (prə **tĕst′** *or* **prō′**tĕst′) *v.* **pro•test•ed, pro•test•ing, pro•tests.** —*tr.* **1.** To express strong objections to (something), as in a formal statement or public demonstration: *Demonstrators protested the new law.* **2.** To declare earnestly; affirm: *protested his innocence.* —*intr.* To express strong objection. —*n.* (**prō′**tĕst′). **1.** A formal statement of disapproval or objection: *sent a protest to the mayor's office.* **2.** An act expressing disapproval or objection: *refused to buy tea in protest against the new tax.* [First written down in 1430 in Middle English and spelled *protesten,* from Latin *prōtestārī* : *prō-,* forth + *testārī,* to testify.] **—pro•test′er** *n.*

Prot•es•tant (**prŏt′**ĭ stənt) *n.* A member of one of the Western Christian churches descending from those that broke away from the Roman Catholic Church in the 16th century. —*adj.* Of or relating to Protestantism: *the Protestant Bible.* [First written down in 1539 in Modern English, from Latin *prōtestārī,* to protest.]

Prot•es•tant•ism (**prŏt′**ĭ stən tĭz′əm) *n.* **1.** Adherence to the beliefs and practices of Protestants. **2.** Protestants considered as a group.

prot•es•ta•tion (prŏt′ĭ **stā′**shən *or* prō′tĭ **stā′**-shən) *n.* An earnest declaration; an avowal.

pro•tist (**prō′**tĭst) *n.* A protoctist.

pro•ti•um (**prō′**tē əm *or* **prō′**shē əm) *n.* The most abundant isotope of hydrogen, having an atomic mass of 1.

pro•to•col (**prō′**tə kôl′ *or* **prō′**tə kŏl′) *n.* **1.** The form of ceremony and social etiquette observed by diplomats and heads of state. **2.** A record or draft of an agreement, especially one used as the basis for a later, formal document: *the protocol of an international treaty.*

pro•toc•tist (prə **tŏk′**tĭst) *n.* Any of a large group of usually one-celled organisms, considered by many scientists to form a separate kingdom from animals and plants, and including the protozoans, bacteria, certain algae, and the slime molds.

pro•ton (**prō′**tŏn′) *n.* A stable subatomic particle having a positive charge equal in magnitude to that of an electron and a mass equal to 1,836 times that of an electron. [First written down in 1920 in Modern English, from Greek *prōtos,* first.]

pro•to•plasm (**prō′**tə plăz′əm) *n.* A substance resembling jelly that forms the living matter in all plant and animal cells. Protoplasm is made up of proteins, fats, and other substances suspended in water. It includes the nucleus and cytoplasm.

pro•to•type (**prō′**tə tīp′) *n.* **1.** An original example of something, on which later examples are based or judged: *Edison's invention factory was the prototype of modern engineering laboratories.* **2.** An early typical example.

pro•to•zo•an (prō′tə **zō′**ən) *n., pl.* **pro•to•zo•ans** or **pro•to•zo•a** (prō′tə **zō′**ə). Any of a large group of very small one-celled organisms considered to be the simplest forms of animal life. Protozoans are usually too small to be seen without a microscope and include the amoebas and paramecia.

pro•tract (prō **trăkt′**) *tr.v.* **pro•tract•ed, pro•tract•ing, pro•tracts.** To draw out in time; lengthen; prolong. [First written down before 1548 in Modern English, from Latin *prōtrahere* : *prō-,* forth + *trahere,* to drag.] **—pro•trac′tion** *n.*

pro•trac•tor (prō **trăk′**tər) *n.* A semicircular instrument marked off in degrees, used for measuring and drawing angles.

pro•trude (prō **tro͞od′**) *v.* **pro•trud•ed, pro•trud•ing, pro•trudes.** —*tr.* To push or thrust outward: *The cat protruded its nose into the hole in the wall.* —*intr.* To stick out from a surface; project: *Curly hair protruded from the edges of his cap.* [First written down in 1620 in Modern English, from Latin *prōtrūdere* : *prō-,* forward + *trūdere,* to thrust.]

pro•tru•sion (prō **tro͞o′**zhən) *n.* **1.** The act of protruding or the condition of being protruded. **2.** A part or an object that protrudes; a projection.

pro•tu•ber•ance (prō **to͞o′**bər əns *or* prō **tyo͞o′**-bər əns) *n.* **1.** A protuberant part or object; a bulge or knob. **2.** The condition of being protuberant.

pro•tu•ber•ant (prō to͞o′bər ənt *or* prō tyo͞o′bər ənt) *adj.* Bulging or swelling outward from a surface: *slightly protuberant eyes.* **—pro•tu′ber•ant•ly** *adv.*

proud (proud) *adj.* **proud•er, proud•est. 1.a.** Feeling pleasure and satisfaction over something one owns, makes, does, or is a part of: *proud to be a member of the team.* **b.** Calling for or being a reason for pride: *a proud moment when she received her diploma.* **2.a.** Feeling or showing justifiable self-esteem. **b.** Filled with or showing excessive self-esteem. **3.** Highly respected; honored: *a proud name.* **4.** Majestic; magnificent: *the proud mansions of the rich.* [First written down about 1000 in Old English and spelled *prūd*, from Late Latin *prōde*, advantageous.] **—proud′ly** *adv.*

Synonyms: **proud, arrogant, haughty, disdainful.** These adjectives mean filled with or marked by a high opinion of oneself and looking down on what one views as being unworthy. **Proud** often means self-satisfied in a conceited way: *They were too proud to admit that they needed help.* **Arrogant** means overbearingly proud, demanding of more power or consideration than is deserved: *The arrogant man refused to stand in line and wait his turn.* **Haughty** means proud in a condescending way, as because of one's high birth or station: *The duchess turned away with a haughty sniff, ignoring my question.* **Disdainful** means proud in a scornful, mocking way: *My teacher is disdainful of popular music.*

prove (pro͞ov) *v.* **proved** or **prov•en** (pro͞o′vən), **prov•ing, proves.** *—tr.* **1.** To show to be true or valid by giving evidence or arguments: *proved the charge at the trial.* **2.** In law, to establish the authenticity of (a will). **3.** To determine the quality of by testing; try out: *proving a new car on the open road.* **4.** To demonstrate the validity of (a hypothesis or proposition). *—intr.* To be shown to be such; turn out: *The original estimate proved too low.* [First written down before 1200 in Middle English and spelled *pruven*, from Latin *probāre*.] **—prov′a•ble** *adj.*

Pro•ven•çal (prō′vən **säl′** *or* prŏv′ən **säl′**) *adj.* Of or relating to Provence or its people, language, or culture. *—n.* **1.** The Romance language of Provence. **2.** A native or inhabitant of Provence.

Pro•vence (prə **väns′**). A historical region and former province of southeast France on the Mediterranean Sea. It was settled in about 600 B.C. and became part of France in 1486.

prov•en•der (prŏv′ən dər) *n.* **1.** Dry food, such as hay, for livestock; feed. **2.** Food or provisions.

prov•erb (prŏv′ûrb′) *n.* **1.** A short saying that is in frequent use and expresses a basic truth. **2. Proverbs.** A book of the Bible that contains many proverbs and moral sayings. [First written down in 1303 in Middle English and spelled *proverbe*, from Latin *prōverbium*.]

pro•ver•bi•al (prə **vûr′**bē əl) *adj.* **1.** Of the nature of a proverb or proverbs: *proverbial sayings.* **2.** Expressed in a proverb: *slept like the proverbial baby.* **3.** Widely known and spoken of; famous: *Her skill at cards is proverbial.* **—pro•ver′bi•al•ly** *adv.*

pro•vide (prə **vīd′**) *v.* **pro•vid•ed, pro•vid•ing, pro•vides.** *—tr.* **1.** To furnish; supply: *generators that provide electrical energy.* **2.** To make available; afford: *a filling station that provides rest rooms.* **3.** To set down as a stipulation: *The contract provides deadlines for completion of the work.* *—intr.* **1.** To take measures in preparation: *We provided against emergencies by taking extra money and clothing.* **2.** To supply means of subsistence or maintenance: *He worked hard to provide for his large family.* **3.** To set down an instruction, rule, or condition: *He provided for a scholarship fund in his will.* [First written down about 1408 in Middle English and spelled *providen*, from Latin *prōvidēre*, to look ahead : *prō-*, forward + *vidēre*, to see.] **—pro•vid′er** *n.* —SEE NOTE.

pro•vid•ed (prə **vī′**dĭd) *conj.* On the condition; if: *You may go, provided your homework is done.*

prov•i•dence (**prŏv′**ĭ dəns) *n.* **1.** Care or preparation in advance; foresight. **2.** Prudent management; economy. **3.** The control and protection of God; divine direction. **4. Providence.** God.

Providence. The capital and largest city of Rhode Island, in the northeast part of the state on Narragansett Bay. It was founded in 1636 as a refuge for religious dissenters. Population, 160,728.

prov•i•dent (**prŏv′**ĭ dənt) *adj.* **1.** Providing for future needs or events. **2.** Frugal; thrifty. **—prov′i•dent•ly** *adv.*

prov•i•den•tial (prŏv′ĭ **dĕn′**shəl) *adj.* **1.** Of or resulting from divine providence: *the providential mission of a prophet.* **2.** Happening as if through divine intervention; very fortunate: *The providential arrival of reinforcements saved the day.* **—prov′i•den′tial•ly** *adv.*

pro•vid•ing (prə **vī′**dĭng) *conj.* On the condition; provided: *We are going to play volleyball, providing the court is free.*

prov•ince (**prŏv′**ĭns) *n.* **1.** A political subdivision of a country or an empire: *Ontario and Quebec are provinces of Canada.* **2.** A division of territory under the jurisdiction of an archbishop. **3. provinces.** The outlying areas of a country, away from the capital or population center. **4.** The range of one's proper knowledge, functions, or responsibility; scope. **5.** A comprehensive area of knowledge, activity, or interest.

pro•vin•cial (prə **vĭn′**shəl) *adj.* **1.** Of or relating to a province: *a provincial capital.* **2.** Characteristic of people from the provinces; not sophisticated or worldly: *provincial speech and dress.* **3.** Limited in perspective; narrow and self-centered: *provincial attitudes.* *—n.* **1.** A person living in or coming from the provinces. **2.** A person with provincial ideas or habits. **—pro•vin′ci•al′i•ty** (prə vĭn′shē **ăl′**ĭ tē) *n.* **—pro•vin′cial•ly** *adv.*

pro•vi•sion (prə **vĭzh′**ən) *n.* **1.** The act of providing or supplying: *the provision of canteens for the day hike.* **2.** Something that is provided: *A fire escape is an important provision in a building.* **3. provisions.** Stocks of food and other necessary supplies. **4.** A measure taken in preparation: *making provisions for her solo flight.* **5.** A stipulation or qualification, especially a clause in a document or an agreement: *a provision of a peace treaty forbidding rearmament.* *—tr.v.* **pro•vi•sioned, pro•vi•sion•ing, pro•vi•sions.** To supply with provisions.

pro•vi•sion•al (prə **vĭzh′**ə nəl) *adj.* Serving for the time being; temporary: *a provisional government.* **—pro•vi′sion•al•ly** *adv.*

pro•vi•so (prə **vī′**zō) *n., pl.* **pro•vi•sos** or **pro•vi•soes.** A clause in a document making a qualification, condition, or restriction.

prov•o•ca•tion (prŏv′ə **kā′**shən) *n.* **1.** The act of provoking; incitement. **2.** Something that provokes.

pro•voc•a•tive (prə **vŏk′**ə tĭv) *adj.* Tending to provoke: *a provocative new theory.* **—pro•voc′a•tive•ly** *adv.* **—pro•voc′a•tive•ness** *n.*

pro•voke (prə **vōk′**) *tr.v.* **pro•voked, pro•vok•ing, pro•vokes. 1.** To incite to anger or resentment: *His bullying provoked me.* **2.** To stir to action or feeling: *Conscience provoked them to speak out.* **3.** To give rise to; evoke: *The comedy provoked laughter.* **4.** To bring about deliberately; induce: *provoke a fight.* [First written down in 1392 in Middle English and spelled *provoken*, from Latin *prōvocāre*, to

Word History: provide

Our word **provide** comes directly from the Latin verb *prōvidēre*, "to look ahead, see in advance, take care of in advance." The Latin present participle formed from *prōvidēre* has the word root *prōvident–*, from which we get our adjective **provident** and our noun **providence**. Latin also has the word root *prūdent–* (a contracted form of *prōvident–*), from which we get **prudent** and **prudence**.

ă	pat	oi	boy
ā	pay	ou	out
âr	care	o͝o	took
ä	father	o͞o	boot
ĕ	pet	ŭ	cut
ē	be	ûr	urge
ĭ	pit	th	thin
ī	pie	*th*	this
îr	pier	hw	whoop
ŏ	pot	zh	vision
ō	toe	ə	about
ô	paw	N	*French* bon

prow
Of the *Queen Elizabeth 2*

ptarmigan
White-tailed ptarmigan

challenge : *prō-*, forth, out + *vocāre*, to call.] **—pro•vok′ing•ly** *adv.*

pro•vo•lo•ne (prō′və **lō′**nē) *n.* A hard, usually smoked Italian cheese.

pro•vost (**prō′**vōst′ *or* **prŏv′**əst) *n.* **1.** A high-ranking university administrator. **2.** The highest official in certain cathedrals. **3.** The chief magistrate of certain Scottish cities. **4.** The keeper of a prison.

prow (prou) *n.* **1.** The forward part of a ship's hull; the bow. **2.** A projecting front part, such as the nose of an aircraft.

prow•ess (**prou′**ĭs) *n.* **1.** Superior skill or ability: *She showed prowess in mathematics.* **2.** Superior strength, courage, or daring, especially in battle.

prowl (proul) *v.* **prowled, prowl•ing, prowls.** *—tr.* To roam through stealthily, as if in search of prey: *Cats prowl the alleys at night.* *—intr.* To roam furtively or with predatory intent. *—n.* The act or an instance of prowling: *took a prowl through the antique shops.* [First written down about 1395 in Middle English and spelled *prollen*, to move about.] **—prowl′er** *n.*

prowl car *n.* A squad car.

prox•im•i•ty (prŏk **sĭm′**ĭ tē) *n.* The state, quality, or fact of being near; closeness.

prox•y (**prŏk′**sē) *n., pl.* **prox•ies. 1.** A person authorized to act for another; an agent. **2.** The authority to act for another: *vote by proxy.*

prude (pro͞od) *n.* A person who is too concerned with being proper, modest, or righteous.

pru•dence (**pro͞od′**ns) *n.* **1.** The state, quality, or fact of being prudent. **2.** Careful management; economy.

pru•dent (**pro͞od′**nt) *adj.* **1.** Wise in handling practical matters; sensible: *a prudent manager.* **2.** Careful in regard to one's own interests; provident. **3.** Careful about one's conduct; circumspect. [First written down in 1382 in Middle English, from Latin *prūdēns*, from *prōvidēre*, to provide for.] **—pru′dent•ly** *adv.*

pru•den•tial (pro͞o **dĕn′**shəl) *adj.* **1.** Arising from or characterized by prudence. **2.** Showing or using prudence. **—pru•den′tial•ly** *adv.*

prud•er•y (**pro͞o′**də rē) *n., pl.* **prud•er•ies. 1.** The state or quality of being prudish. **2.** An instance of prudish behavior or speech.

prud•ish (**pro͞o′**dĭsh) *adj.* Characteristic of or being a prude; priggish. **—prud′ish•ly** *adv.* **—prud′ish•ness** *n.*

prune[1] (pro͞on) *n.* A dried plum. [First written down in 1345 in Middle English and spelled *prunne*, from Latin *prūnum*, plum.]

prune[2] (pro͞on) *tr.v.* **pruned, prun•ing, prunes. 1.** To cut or trim parts or branches from (a tree or plant) to improve its growth or shape. **2.** To shorten or improve by removing unnecessary parts: *prune a long composition.* [First written down about 1390 in Middle English and spelled *pruinen*, from Old French *proignier*.] **—prun′er** *n.*

Prus•sia (**prŭsh′**ə). A historical region and former kingdom of north-central Europe including present-day northern Germany and Poland. **—Prus′sian** *adj. & n.*

prus•sic acid (**prŭs′**ĭk) *n.* Hydrocyanic acid.

pry[1] (prī) *intr.v.* **pried** (prīd), **pry•ing, pries** (prīz). To look or investigate closely or curiously, often in a secret or furtive manner: *prying into his past.* [First written down in 1307 in Middle English and spelled *prien*.]

pry[2] (prī) *tr.v.* **pried** (prīd), **pry•ing, pries** (prīz). **1.** To raise, move, or force open with a lever: *pry the lid off a box.* **2.** To obtain or extract with difficulty: *pried answers from the child.* *—n., pl.* **pries** (prīz). Something used as a lever. [First written down in 1823 in Modern English, from *prize*, pry.]

P.S. *abbr.* An abbreviation of: **1.** Postscript. **2.** Public school.

psalm (säm) *n.* **1.** A sacred song; a hymn. **2. Psalms.** A book of the Bible containing poems that express devotion to God, sorrow for wrongdoing, and other spiritual concerns.

psalm•ist (**sä′**mĭst) *n.* A writer or composer of psalms.

Psal•ter (**sôl′**tər) *n.* A book containing the Psalms.

psal•ter•y (**sôl′**tə rē) *n., pl.* **psal•ter•ies.** An ancient stringed instrument played by plucking the strings with the fingers or a plectrum.

pseudo– or **pseud–** *pref.* A prefix that means: **1.** False; deceptive: *pseudoscience.* **2.** Apparently similar: *pseudopod.*

pseu•do•nym (**so͞od′**n ĭm′) *n.* A fictitious name assumed by an author; a pen name. [First written down in 1846 in Modern English, from Greek *pseudōnumos*, falsely named : *pseudēs*, false + *onuma*, name.]

pseu•do•pod (**so͞o′**də pŏd′) *n.* A temporary extension of the protoplasm of a one-celled organism such as the amoeba, used for moving about and for surrounding and taking in food.

pseu•do•sci•ence (so͞o′dō **sī′**əns) *n.* A theory or method that is considered to be without scientific foundation.

pshaw (shô) *interj.* An expression used to show impatience, irritation, disapproval, or disbelief.

psi (sī *or* psī) *n.* The 23rd letter of the Greek alphabet, written Ψ, ψ. In English it is represented as *Ps*, *ps*.

psit•ta•co•sis (sĭt′ə **kō′**sĭs) *n.* A viral disease of parrots and related birds, which can be communicated to human beings, producing symptoms similar to pneumonia.

pso•ri•a•sis (sə **rī′**ə sĭs) *n.* A chronic noncontagious skin disease that causes inflammation and white scaly patches on the skin.

PST or **P.S.T.** *abbr.* An abbreviation of Pacific Standard Time.

psych (sīk) *Informal. tr.v.* **psyched, psych•ing, psyches. 1.** To put into the right frame of mind: *The coach psyched the team up before the game.* **2.** To undermine the confidence of; intimidate: *The angry looks of their huge center psyched us out.*

psy•che (**sī′**kē) *n.* **1.** The soul or spirit. **2.** The mind considered as the source and center of thought, feeling, and behavior.

Psy•che (**sī′**kē) *n.* In Greek mythology, a young woman who loves Eros and is united with him after Aphrodite's jealousy is overcome.

psy•che•del•ic (sī′kĭ **dĕl′**ĭk) *adj.* Of or causing hallucinations, distortions of perception, and sometimes mental states that resemble psychosis: *psychedelic drugs.*

psy•chi•a•trist (sĭ **kī′**ə trĭst *or* sī **kī′**ə trĭst) *n.* A physician who specializes in psychiatry.

psy•chi•a•try (sĭ **kī′**ə trē *or* sī **kī′**ə trĭst) *n.* The branch of medicine that deals with the study and treatment of mental illness. [First written down in 1846 in Modern English : Greek *psukhē*, mind + Greek *iatros*, physician.] **—psy′chi•at′ric** (sī′kē **ăt′**rĭk) *adj.*

psy•chic (**sī′**kĭk) *n.* A person who is apparently sensitive to forces that are not physical. *—adj.* **1.** Of or relating to the human mind or psyche. **2.a.** Sensitive to nonphysical forces or capable of extraordinary mental processes, such as extrasensory perception or mental telepathy. **b.** Of or relating to such processes.

psycho– or **psych–** *pref.* A prefix that means the mind or mental processes: *psychoanalysis*

psy•cho•a•nal•y•sis (sī′kō ə **năl′**ĭ sĭs) *n., pl.* **psy•cho•a•nal•y•ses** (sī′kō ə **năl′**ĭ sēz′). A method of psychiatric therapy in which a patient speaks openly to a psychoanalyst about his or her childhood, family relations, behavior, and dreams as a means of investigating mental illness and emotional disorders.

psy•cho•an•a•lyst (sī′kō ăn′ə lĭst) *n.* A person who practices psychoanalysis.

psy•cho•an•a•lyze (sī′kō ăn′ə līz′) *tr.v.* **psy•cho•an•a•lyzed, psy•cho•an•a•lyz•ing, psy•cho•an•a•lyz•es.** To treat (a person) by psychoanalysis.

psy•cho•log•i•cal (sī′kə lŏj′ĭ kəl) *adj.* **1.** Of or relating to psychology. **2.** Of, relating to, or derived from the mind or emotions. **3.** Capable of influencing the mind or emotions: *psychological persuasion.* **—psy′cho•log′i•cal•ly** *adv.*

psy•chol•o•gist (sī kŏl′ə jĭst) *n.* A person trained to perform psychological research, testing, and therapy.

psy•chol•o•gy (sī kŏl′ə jē) *n., pl.* **psy•chol•o•gies.** **1.** The scientific study of mental processes and behavior. **2.** The emotional characteristics and behavior associated with an individual, a group, or an activity: *the psychology of war.* [First written down in 1653 in Modern English : Greek *psukhē*, mind, spirit + Greek *-logia*, study.]

psy•cho•path (sī′kə păth′) *n.* A person who has an antisocial personality disorder, especially one that is shown in aggressive, perverted, or criminal behavior.

psy•cho•sis (sī kō′sĭs) *n., pl.* **psy•cho•ses** (sī kō′sēz). A serious mental disorder in which the mind cannot function normally and the ability to deal with reality is impaired or lost.

psy•cho•so•mat•ic (sī′kō sō măt′ĭk) *adj.* **1.** Of or relating to functions or disorders that originate in the mind but affect the body. **2.** Relating to the influence of the mind on the body.

psy•cho•ther•a•py (sī′kō thĕr′ə pē) *n., pl.* **psy•cho•ther•a•pies.** The treatment of mental and emotional disorders using psychological techniques.

psy•chot•ic (sī kŏt′ĭk) *adj.* Of, relating to, or affected by psychosis. *—n.* A person who is affected by psychosis. **—psy•chot′i•cal•ly** *adv.*

Pt The symbol for the element **platinum.**

pt. *abbr.* An abbreviation of: **1.** Pint. **2.** Point.

PTA or **P.T.A.** *abbr.* An abbreviation of Parent-Teachers Association.

ptar•mi•gan (tär′mĭ gən) *n., pl.* **ptarmigan** or **ptar•mi•gans.** Any of various grouses of northern regions, having feathers that are brownish in summer and white in winter and feathered legs and feet. [First written down in 1599 in Modern English, from Scottish Gaelic *tàrmachan*.]

PT boat (pē tē′) *n.* A fast maneuverable vessel used to torpedo enemy ships.

pte•rid•o•phyte (tə rĭd′ə fīt′ *or* tĕr′ĭ dō fīt′) *n.* Any of various seedless flowerless plants including the ferns and club mosses.

pter•o•dac•tyl (tĕr′ə dăk′təl) *n.* Any of various small pterosaurs. [First written down in 1830 in Modern English and spelled *pterodactyle* : Greek *pteron*, feather, wing + Greek *daktulos*, finger.]

pter•o•saur (tĕr′ə sôr′) *n.* Any of various extinct flying reptiles that had wings formed by a flap of skin extending from a long slender toe on each front leg.

Ptol•e•ma•ic (tŏl′ə mā′ĭk) *adj.* Of or relating to the astronomer Ptolemy.

Ptolemaic system *n.* A description or model of the universe in which the earth is considered to be the center, with all other bodies revolving around it.

Ptol•e•my (tŏl′ə mē). Flourished second century A.D. Alexandrian astronomer who based his astronomy on the belief that all heavenly bodies revolve around the earth.

pto•maine (tō′mān′ *or* tō mān′) *n.* Any of various nitrogen-containing substances, some of which are poisonous, that form when proteins decompose.

pty•a•lin (tī′ə lĭn) *n.* A salivary enzyme that breaks down starches into sugars.

Pu The symbol for the element **plutonium.**

pub (pŭb) *n.* A place of business where alcoholic beverages are sold and drunk.

pu•ber•ty (pyo͞o′bər tē) *n.* The stage in the development of an individual in which the reproductive organs become fully functional, often occurring between ages 13 and 16 in boys and between 12 and 14 in girls.

pu•bes (pyo͞o′bēz) *n.* Plural of **pubis.**

pu•bic (pyo͞o′bĭk) *adj.* Of, relating to, or in the region of the pubis.

pu•bis (pyo͞o′bĭs) *n., pl.* **pu•bes** (pyo͞o′bēz). The forward portion of either of the hipbones, joining to form the front arch of the pelvis.

pub•lic (pŭb′lĭk) *adj.* **1.** Of or affecting the people or community: *public safety.* **2.** Maintained for or used by the people or community; not private: *the public library.* **3.** Serving or acting on behalf of the people or community: *a public official.* **4.** Participated in or attended by the people or community: *a public debate.* **5.** Open to the knowledge or awareness of everybody: *made the testimony public.* *—n.* **1.** The community or people as a whole: *a building open to the public.* **2.** A group of people with a common interest: *the reading public.* **—*idiom.* in public.** In such a way as to be visible to the scrutiny of the people. [First written down in 1394 in Middle English and spelled *pupplik*, from Latin *pūblicus*, from *populus*, people.] —SEE NOTE at **collective noun.**

pub•lic-ad•dress system (pŭb′lĭk ə drĕs′) *n.* An electronic system using amplifiers to project sound throughout a given area.

pub•li•can (pŭb′lĭ kən) *n.* **1.** *Chiefly British.* The keeper of a public house. **2.** A collector of taxes in the ancient Roman empire.

pub•li•ca•tion (pŭb′lĭ kā′shən) *n.* **1.** The act or process of publishing matter in printed or electronic form. **2.** An issue of printed or electronic matter, such as a magazine, offered for sale or distribution. **3.** Communication of information to the public.

public defender *n.* A usually publicly appointed attorney who defends those unable to afford or obtain legal assistance.

public house *n.* *Chiefly British.* A tavern, bar, or similar place licensed to sell alcoholic beverages.

pub•li•cist (pŭb′lĭ sĭst) *n.* A person who publicizes, especially a press or publicity agent.

pub•lic•i•ty (pŭ blĭs′ĭ tē) *n.* **1.** Information given out, as to the press, as a means of attracting public notice to a person, a group, or an event. **2.** Public interest achieved by spreading such information. **3.** The work of a person hired to bring someone or something to public notice.

pub•li•cize (pŭb′lĭ sīz′) *tr.v.* **pub•li•cized, pub•li•ciz•ing, pub•li•ciz•es.** To give publicity to: *publicize a charitable event.*

pub•lic•ly (pŭb′lĭk lē) *adv.* **1.** In a public manner; openly: *They publicly acknowledged the partnership.* **2.** By or with the consent of the public: *a publicly owned water system.*

public opinion *n.* Public consensus, as with respect to an issue or a situation.

public relations *pl.n.* *(used with a singular verb).* The art or science of establishing and promoting a favorable relationship with the public.

public school *n.* **1.** A school supported by public funds and providing free education for the children of a community. **2.** A private boarding school in Great Britain for study before entering a university.

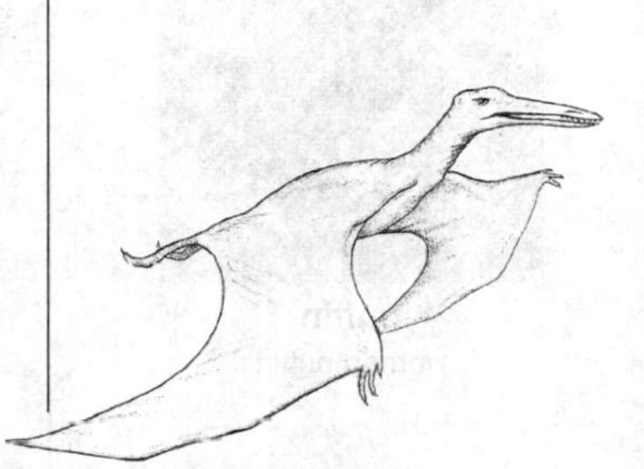

pterodactyl

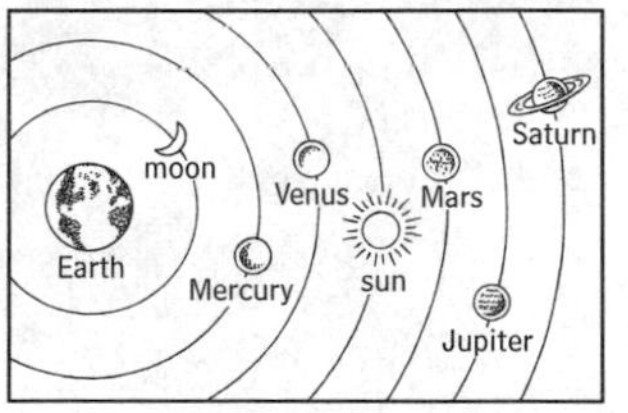

Ptolemaic system

ă	**pat**	oi	**boy**
ā	**pay**	ou	**out**
âr	**care**	o͝o	**took**
ä	**father**	o͞o	**boot**
ĕ	**pet**	ŭ	**cut**
ē	**be**	ûr	**urge**
ĭ	**pit**	th	**thin**
ī	**pie**	*th*	**this**
îr	**pier**	hw	**whoop**
ŏ	**pot**	zh	**vision**
ō	**toe**	ə	**about**
ô	**paw**	N	*French* **bon**

puffin
Horned puffin

pug

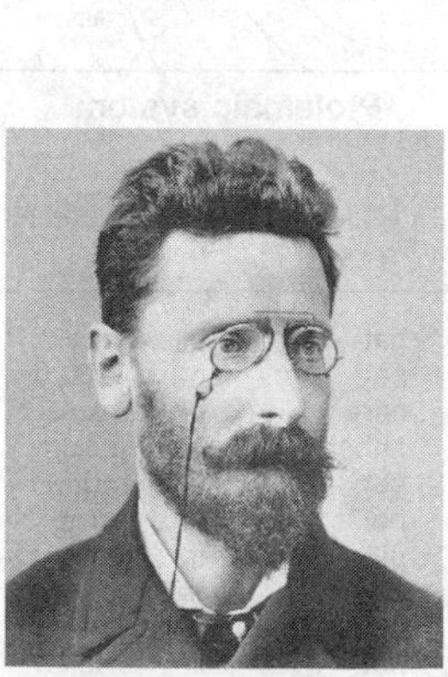
Joseph Pulitzer

public servant *n.* A person who holds a government position.
pub•lic-spir•it•ed (pŭb′lĭk **spĭr′**ĭ tĭd) *adj.* Dedicated to promoting the well-being of the general public: *public-spirited people running for office.*
public television *n.* Television that provides programs, especially of an educational nature, for the public and has few or no commercials.
public utility *n.* A private company subject to governmental regulation that provides an essential service or commodity, such as water, electricity, or communication.
public works *pl.n.* Construction projects, such as highways or dams, financed by public funds and constructed by a government for the benefit or use of the general public.
pub•lish (**pŭb′**lĭsh) *tr.v.* **pub•lished, pub•lish•ing, pub•lish•es. 1.** To prepare and issue (something, such as a book) for public distribution or sale. **2.** To bring to public attention; announce. [First written down before 1338 in Middle English and spelled *publicen*, to make known publicly, from Latin *pūblicāre*.]
pub•lish•er (**pŭb′**lĭ shər) *n.* A person or business that produces and distributes something, such as a book or magazine, in printed or electronic form.
Puc•ci•ni (po͞o **chē′**nē), **Giacomo.** 1858–1924. Italian operatic composer whose works include *Madame Butterfly* (1904).
puce (pyo͞os) *n.* A deep red to dark grayish purple. —*adj.* Deep red or dark grayish purple.
puck (pŭk) *n.* A hard rubber disk used in ice hockey.
Puck (pŭk) *n.* A mischievous sprite in English folklore.
puck•er (**pŭk′**ər) *v.* **puck•ered, puck•er•ing, puck•ers.** —*tr.* To draw up into small wrinkles or folds: *She gathered the cloth to pucker it.* —*intr.* To become gathered, contracted, and wrinkled. —*n.* A small wrinkle or wrinkled part, as in tightly stitched cloth. [First written down in 1598 in Modern English, probably from *pock*, bag, sack, variant of *poke*.]
puck•ish (**pŭk′**ĭsh) *adj.* Mischievous; impish. **—puck′ish•ly** *adv.* **—puck′ish•ness** *n.*
pud•ding (**po͝od′**ĭng) *n.* **1.** A sweet dessert, usually containing flour or a cereal product, that has been boiled, steamed, or baked. **2.** A preparation that is like sausage, made with minced meat stuffed into a bag or skin and boiled. [First written down in 1287 in Middle English and spelled *puding*, a kind of sausage, from Old French *boudin*.]
pud•dle (**pŭd′**l) *n.* **1.** A small pool of water, especially rainwater. **2.** A small pool of a liquid. [First written down before 1338 in Middle English and spelled *podel*, from Old English *pudd*, ditch.]
pudg•y (**pŭj′**ē) *adj.* **pudg•i•er, pudg•i•est.** Short and stocky; chubby. **—pudg′i•ness** *n.*
pueb•lo (**pwĕb′**lō) *n., pl.* **pueb•los. 1. Pueblo,** *pl.* **Pueblo** or **Pueb•los.** A member of any of numerous Native American peoples living in villages in New Mexico and Arizona. **2.** A village or community of any of the Pueblo peoples, typically made up of adobe or stone apartment dwellings of several stories clustered around a central plaza. **—pueb′lo** *adj.*
pu•er•ile (**pyo͞o′**ər əl *or* **pyo͝or′**əl) *adj.* **1.** Belonging to childhood; juvenile. **2.** Immature; childish.
Puer•to Ri•co (pwĕr′tə **rē′**kō *or* pôrt′ə **rē′**kō). A self-governing island commonwealth of the United States in the Caribbean Sea east of Hispaniola. Commonwealth status was proclaimed in 1952. San Juan is the capital and the largest city. Population, 3,522,037.
puff (pŭf) *n.* **1.a.** A short forceful discharge or gust, as of air, smoke, or vapor. **b.** A short abrupt sound produced by such a discharge or gust. **2.** An act of drawing in and expelling the breath, as in smoking tobacco. **3.** Something that looks light and fluffy: *little puffs of white clouds.* **4.** A soft pad for applying powder or lotion. **5.** A light flaky pastry, often filled with custard or cream. **6.** A light padded bed covering. **7.** A section of full gathered fabric that balloons out as though filled with air. —*v.* **puffed, puff•ing, puffs.** —*intr.* **1.** To blow in puffs. **2.** To come forth in puffs: *Smoke puffed from the steamboat.* **3.** To breathe heavily and rapidly, as from fatigue: *He began to puff from the hard climb.* **4.** To take puffs on smoking material. **5.** To swell or seem to swell, as from air or pride. —*tr.* **1.** To smoke (a pipe, for example). **2.** To emit or give forth in puffs: *The train puffed smoke.* **3.** To inflate or distend. **4.** To fill with pride or conceit. [First written down before 1200 in Middle English, from *puffen*, to puff, from Old English *pyffan*.]
puff adder *n.* A poisonous African viper that inflates its body when excited and has crescent-shaped yellowish markings.
puff•ball (**pŭf′**bôl′) *n.* **1.** Any of various ball-shaped fungi that let out a puff of spores when broken open. **2.** *Informal.* The fluffy head of a dandelion that has gone to seed.
puff•er (**pŭf′**ər) *n.* Any of various marine fishes that are capable of swelling up with water or air.
puf•fin (**pŭf′**ĭn) *n.* Any of several small black and white northern sea birds, having a short, flattened, brightly colored bill.
puff•y (**pŭf′**ē) *adj.* **1.** Swollen: *the puffy eyes of a crying child.* **2.** Full and rounded, like a balloon filled with air: *puffy sleeves.* **—puff′i•ness** *n.*
pug (pŭg) *n.* A small short-haired dog having a flattened nose, a wrinkled face, and a curled tail.
Pu•get Sound (**pyo͞o′**jĭt). A deep inlet of the Pacific Ocean in western Washington.
pu•gi•lism (**pyo͞o′**jə lĭz′əm) *n.* Boxing.
pu•gi•list (**pyo͞o′**jə lĭst) *n.* A professional boxer.
pug•na•cious (pŭg **nā′**shəs) *adj.* Combative in nature; belligerent. [First written down in 1642 in Modern English, from Latin *pugnāre*, to fight, from *pugnus*, fist.] **—pug•na′cious•ly** *adv.* **—pug•nac′i•ty** (pŭg **năs′**ĭ tē), **pug•na′cious•ness** *n.*
pug nose *n.* A short nose that is somewhat flattened and turned up at the end.
puis•sance (**pwĭs′**əns *or* **pyo͞o′**ĭ səns) *n.* Power; might. **—puis′sant** *adj.* **—puis′sant•ly** *adv.*
puke (pyo͞ok) *Slang. intr. & tr.v.* **puked, puk•ing, pukes.** To vomit. —*n.* Vomit.
Pu•las•ki (po͞o **lăs′**kē), **Casimir.** 1747–1779. Polish general who aided American forces in the Revolutionary War.
pule (pyo͞ol) *intr.v.* **puled, pul•ing, pules.** To whine; whimper. **—pul′er** *n.*
Pu•lit•zer (**po͝ol′**ĭt sər *or* **pyo͞o′**lĭt sər), **Joseph.** 1847–1911. Hungarian-born American newspaper publisher who established and endowed the Pulitzer Prize for journalism.
pull (po͝ol) *v.* **pulled, pull•ing, pulls.** —*tr.* **1.a.** To apply force to (something), especially so as to cause motion toward the source of the force: *pull the plow.* **b.** To cause (something) to move or tend to move toward a point or center, as by exerting a force; attract: *The force of gravity pulls things toward the center of the earth.* **2.** To take from a fixed position or place; remove: *pull weeds.* **3.** To move: *The driver pulled the car off the road.* **4.** To tug at; jerk: *pulled her hair.* **5.** To draw apart; tear or break: *The puppy pulled the towel into bits.* **6.** To stretch (taffy, for example) repeatedly. **7.** To injure (a muscle) by stretching or straining it too much. **8.** *Informal.* To attract the notice or attendance of; draw: *The play pulls large crowds.* **9.** *Slang.* To draw out (a knife or gun). **10.** To operate (an oar)

in rowing. —*intr.* **1.** To exert force in moving something toward the source of that force. **2.** To drink or inhale deeply. **3.** To row a boat. **4.** *Informal.* To express or feel great empathy or sympathy: *We're pulling for the mayor in the fall election.* —*n.* **1.** The act or process of pulling. **2.** The force used in pulling: *a rope that will stand a 200-pound pull.* **3.** A sustained effort: *a long pull to the summit.* **4.** Something, such as a knob on a drawer, that is used for pulling. **5.** A deep inhalation or draft, as on a cigarette or of a beverage. **6.** *Slang.* Special influence: *He has a lot of pull in his hometown.* —***idioms.*** **pull away.** To move away or backward; withdraw: *I pulled away from the edge of the cliff.* **pull in.** To arrive at a destination. **pull off.** *Informal.* To perform in spite of difficulties or obstacles; bring off: *The team pulled off an upset victory.* **pull (oneself) together.** To regain one's composure. **pull out.** **1.** To leave or depart. **2.** To withdraw, as from a situation or commitment. **pull over.** To bring a vehicle to a stop at a curb or at the side of a road: *I pulled over to look at the view.* **pull through.** To come successfully through trouble or illness. **pull together.** To make a joint effort: *We'll meet the deadline if we all pull together.* [First written down about 1000 in Old English and spelled *pullian.*] —**pull′er** *n.*

Synonyms: pull, drag, draw, tow, tug. These verbs all mean to apply force to something, causing it to move toward that force. *The children pulled their sled up the hill. I had to drag my dog away from the cat in the tree. The weary traveler drew his chair closer to the fire. The car was towing a large trailer. I tugged my desk to the other side of the room.* **Antonym: push.**

pul•let (po͝ol′ĭt) *n.* A young hen, especially one less than a year old. [First written down before 1376 in Middle English and spelled *pulet*, from Latin *pullus*, chicken.]

pul•ley (po͝ol′ē) *n., pl.* **pul•leys. 1.** A simple machine consisting of a freely turning wheel with a groove around its edge through which a rope or chain can run to change the direction of the force exerted on the rope or chain. **2.** A similar wheel that drives or is driven by a belt passing around its edge.

Pullman (po͝ol′mən) *n.* A railroad car having private sleeping compartments or parlors. [First written down in 1867 in American English, after George Mortimer *Pullman* (1831–1897), American industrialist and inventor.]

pull•o•ver (po͝ol′ō′vər) *n.* A garment, such as a sweater, that is put on by being drawn over the head.

pul•mo•nar•y (po͝ol′mə nĕr′ē *or* pŭl′mə nĕr′ē) *adj.* Of, relating to, or affecting the lungs: *a pulmonary infection.* [First written down in 1704 in Modern English, from Latin *pulmō*, lung.]

pulp (pŭlp) *n.* **1.** A soft, moist, shapeless mass of matter. **2.** The soft juicy or fleshy part of fruit or of certain vegetables. **3.** A moist mixture, as of ground wood and rags, used to make paper. **4.** The soft inner part of a tooth, containing blood vessels and nerve tissue. **5.** A magazine containing sensational subject matter. —*tr.v.* **pulped, pulp•ing, pulps.** To reduce to pulp: *pulp logs.* —**pulp′y** *adj.*

pul•pit (po͝ol′pĭt *or* pŭl′pĭt) *n.* **1.** An elevated platform, lectern, or stand used in preaching or conducting a religious service. **2.a.** Clerics considered as a group. **b.** The ministry as a profession. [First written down before 1338 in Middle English, from Latin *pulpitum*, wooden platform.]

pulp•wood (pŭlp′wo͝od′) *n.* Soft wood, such as pine, spruce, or aspen, used in making paper.

pul•sar (pŭl′sär′) *n.* Any of a class of celestial objects that emit radio waves, varying the intensity of radiation at short intervals of precise length.

pul•sate (pŭl′sāt′) *intr.v.* **pul•sat•ed, pul•sat•ing, pul•sates. 1.** To expand and contract rhythmically, as the heart does. **2.** To quiver; vibrate.

pul•sa•tion (pŭl sā′shən) *n.* **1.** The act of pulsating. **2.** A single beat, throb, or vibration.

pulse[1] (pŭls) *n.* **1.** The rhythmical expansion and contraction of the arteries as blood is pumped through them by the beating of the heart. **2.** A regular or rhythmical beating: *the pulse of the drums.* **3.** A single beat or throb; a pulsation. **4.** A short sudden change in a normally constant quantity: *A telegraph message is sent as a series of electrical pulses.* —*intr.v.* **pulsed, puls•ing, puls•es.** To pulsate; beat. [First written down before 1338 in Middle English and spelled *pous*, from Latin *pulsus*, from *pellere*, to beat.]

pulse[2] (pŭls) *n.* **1.** The edible seeds of certain plants, such as peas, beans, or lentils. **2.** A plant that bears such seeds. [First written down in 1297 in Middle English and spelled *pols*, from Latin *puls*, pottage of meal and pulse.]

pul•ver•ize (pŭl′və rīz′) *v.* **pul•ver•ized, pul•ver•iz•ing, pul•ver•iz•es.** —*tr.* To pound, crush, or grind to powder or dust. —*intr.* To be ground or reduced to powder or dust. —**pul′ver•i•za′tion** (pŭl′vər ĭ zā′shən) *n.*

pu•ma (pyo͞o′mə *or* po͞o′mə) *n.* The mountain lion.

pum•ice (pŭm′ĭs) *n.* A porous lightweight rock of volcanic origin, used as an abrasive.

pum•mel (pŭm′əl) *tr.v.* **pum•meled, pum•mel•ing, pum•mels** also **pum•melled, pum•mel•ling, pum•mels.** To beat, as with the fists; pommel.

pump[1] (pŭmp) *n.* A machine for raising, compressing, or transferring fluids. —*v.* **pumped, pump•ing, pumps.** —*tr.* **1.** To raise or cause to flow by means of a pump. **2.** To draw, deliver, or pour forth as if with a pump: *The goal pumped new life into our players.* **3.** To empty of liquid or gas by means of a pump: *pump out a flooded cellar.* **4.** To cause to move up and down in the manner of a pump handle: *a bicyclist pumping the pedals.* **5.** To propel, eject, or insert with or as if with a pump: *pumped bullets into a target.* **6.** To question closely: *pumped him for information.* —*intr.* To raise or move gas or liquid with a pump. —***idiom.*** **pump up.** To inflate with gas by means of a pump: *I pumped up my bicycle tires.* [First written down in 1420 in Middle English and spelled *pomp.*] —**pump′er** *n.*

pump[2] (pŭmp) *n.* A low-cut shoe without laces, straps, or other fasteners. [First written down in 1555 in Modern English.]

pum•per•nick•el (pŭm′pər nĭk′əl) *n.* A dark bread made from whole coarsely ground rye.

pump•kin (pŭmp′kĭn *or* pŭm′kĭn) *n.* **1.** A large round fruit having a thick orange rind and pulp often used for making pies. **2.** The vine that bears such fruit.

pun (pŭn) *n.* A play on words that involves different senses of the same word or the similar sense or sound of different words. —*intr.v.* **punned, pun•ning, puns.** To make a pun. —**pun′ner** *n.*

punch[1] (pŭnch) *n.* **1.** A tool for piercing: *a leather punch.* **2.** A tool for forcing a pin, bolt, or rivet in or out of a hole. **3.** A tool for stamping a design on a surface. —*intr. & tr.v.* **punched, punch•ing, punch•es.** To use a punch or use a punch on. [First written down about 1460 in Middle English and spelled *punche*, from Latin *pungere*, to puncture.]

punch[2] (pŭnch) *tr.v.* **punched, punch•ing, punch•es. 1.** To hit with a sharp blow of the fist. **2.a.** To poke or prod with a stick. **b.** To herd (cattle). **3.** To press in order to operate: *He punched the "exit" key.* —*n.* **1.** A blow with the fist. **2.** Vigor; drive:

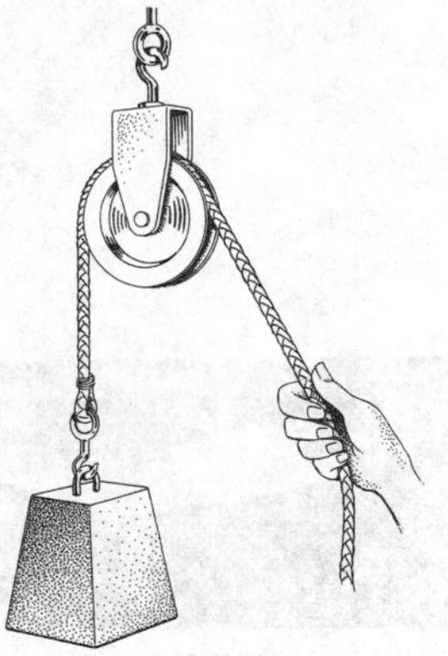

pulley
Simple fixed pulley

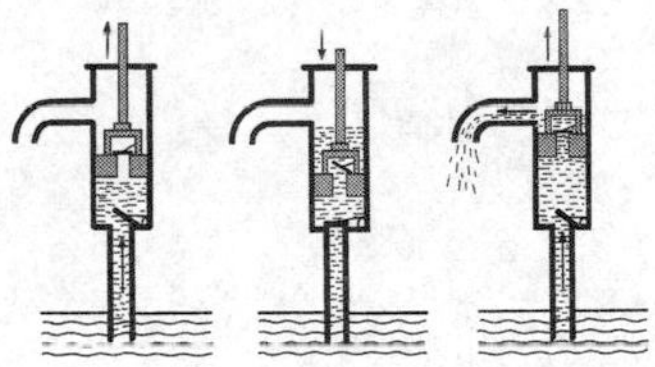

pump[1]

pumpkin

ă	pat	oi	boy
ā	pay	ou	out
âr	care	o͝o	took
ä	father	o͞o	boot
ĕ	pet	ŭ	cut
ē	be	ûr	urge
ĭ	pit	th	thin
ī	pie	*th*	this
îr	pier	hw	whoop
ŏ	pot	zh	vision
ō	toe	ə	about
ô	paw	N	*French* bon

punt[1]
c. 1935 American work punt

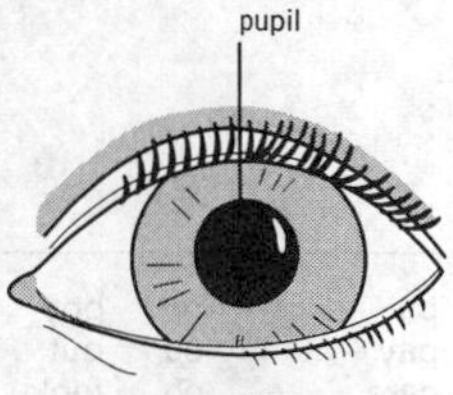

pupil[2]

They were full of punch. [First written down about 1440 in Middle English and spelled *punchen,* to thrust, prod, puncture, from Latin *pungere.*] **—punch′er** *n.*

punch[3] (pŭnch) *n.* A beverage of fruit juices and sometimes soda, sometimes mixed with wine or liquor and spices. [First written down in 1632 in Modern English, perhaps from Hindi *pañc-,* five-(from the hypothesis that it was originally prepared from five ingredients).]

punch card *n.* A card punched with holes or notches to represent letters and numbers or with a pattern of holes to represent related data, formerly used to feed data into a computer.

pun•cheon[1] (pŭn′chən) *n.* **1.** A short upright timber used in structural framing. **2.** A roughly dressed heavy timber, with one face finished flat. **3.** A tool used for punching, perforating, or stamping. [First written down in 1348 in Middle English and spelled *pounchonn,* from Old French *ponchon,* from Latin *pūnctus,* punctured.]

pun•cheon[2] (pŭn′chən) *n.* **1.** A cask that can hold from 70 to 120 U.S. gallons (273 to 454 liters). **2.** The amount that a puncheon can hold. [First written down in 1400 in Middle English and spelled *pinson,* from Old French *poinçon,* punch, cask.]

punch•ing bag (pŭn′chĭng) *n.* A stuffed or inflated bag that is usually suspended so that it can be punched with the fists for exercise.

punch line *n.* The climax of a joke or humorous story.

punch•y (pŭn′chē) *adj.* **punch•i•er, punch•i•est. 1.** Characterized by vigor or drive. **2.** Groggy or dazed from or as if from a punch.

punc•til•i•o (pŭngk tĭl′ē ō′) *n., pl.* **punc•til•i•os.** A fine point of etiquette.

punc•til•i•ous (pŭngk tĭl′ē əs) *adj.* **1.** Attentive to the details of etiquette. **2.** Conscientious and exacting; precise. **—punc•til′i•ous•ly** *adv.*

punc•tu•al (pŭngk′cho͞o əl) *adj.* Acting or arriving exactly on time; prompt. **—punc′tu•al′i•ty** (pŭngk′cho͞o ăl′ĭ tē) *n.* **—punc′tu•al•ly** *adv.*

punc•tu•ate (pŭngk′cho͞o āt′) *v.* **punc•tu•at•ed, punc•tu•at•ing, punc•tu•ates.** *—tr.* **1.** To provide (written or printed material) with punctuation: *punctuate the sentence.* **2.** To interrupt periodically: *The evening silence was punctuated by the hooting of an owl.* *—intr.* To use punctuation.

punc•tu•a•tion (pŭngk′cho͞o ā′shən) *n.* **1.** The use of standard marks in writing and printing to separate sentences and parts of sentences in order to make the meaning clear. **2.** A mark or the marks so used.

punctuation mark *n.* One of the marks or signs, such as the comma (,) or the period (.), used to punctuate written material.

punc•ture (pŭngk′chər) *v.* **punc•tured, punc•tur•ing, punc•tures.** *—tr.* **1.** To pierce with a pointed object: *I punctured the tomato with my fork.* **2.** To cause to collapse or deflate by or as if by piercing with something sharp: *The setback punctured her ego.* *—intr.* To be pierced or punctured. *—n.* **1.** The act or an instance of puncturing. **2.** A hole or depression made by something sharp, especially such a hole in an automotive tire.

pun•dit (pŭn′dĭt) *n.* A learned person, especially an expert or authority: *political pundits.*

pun•gent (pŭn′jənt) *adj.* **1.** Sharp or acrid to the taste or smell: *a pungent sauce; pungent smoke.* **2.** Penetrating, biting, or caustic: *pungent remarks.* **—pun′gen•cy** *n.* **—pun′gent•ly** *adv.*

pun•ish (pŭn′ĭsh) *tr.v.* **pun•ished, pun•ish•ing, pun•ish•es. 1.** To subject to a penalty for an offense, a sin, or a fault: *Society punishes criminals.* **2.** To inflict a penalty for (an offense): *punish cruelty.* **3.** To treat roughly or harshly: *Heavy surf punished the small boat.* **—pun′ish•er** *n.*

pun•ish•a•ble (pŭn′ĭ shə bəl) *adj.* Liable to punishment: *a crime punishable by imprisonment.*

pun•ish•ment (pŭn′ĭsh mənt) *n.* **1.a.** An act of punishing: *the punishment of wrongdoers.* **b.** The condition of being punished. **2.** A penalty for a crime or wrongdoing: *What punishment was given for the crime?* **3.** Rough or harsh handling or treatment: *These shoes have taken a lot of punishment.*

pu•ni•tive (pyo͞o′nĭ tĭv) *adj.* Inflicting or tending to inflict punishment: *a punitive decree.* **—pu′ni•tive•ly** *adv.* **—pu′ni•tive•ness** *n.*

punk (pŭngk) *n.* **1.** *Slang.* A young person, especially a member of a rebellious group. **2.** Dry decayed wood used as tinder. [First written down in 1687 in Modern English and spelled *punk,* rotten wood.]

pun•ster (pŭn′stər) *n.* A person who make puns.

punt[1] (pŭnt) *n.* A flat-bottomed boat with squared ends for use in shallow waters, propelled with a long pole. *—v.* **punt•ed, punt•ing, punts.** *—tr.* **1.** To propel (a boat) with a pole. **2.** To carry in a punt. *—intr.* To go in a punt. [First written down about 1000 in Old English, from Latin *pontō,* pontoon, flat-bottomed boat, from *pōns,* bridge.] **—punt′er** *n.*

punt[2] (pŭnt) *n.* In football, a kick in which the ball is dropped from the hands and kicked before it touches the ground. *—v.* **punt•ed, punt•ing, punts.** *—tr.* To kick (a ball) by means of a punt. *—intr.* To execute a punt. [First written down in 1845 in Modern English, perhaps from alteration of *bunt.*] **—punt′er** *n.*

punt[3] (po͝ont *or* pŭnt) *n.* The basic monetary unit of Ireland. [First written down 1975 in Modern English, from Irish Gaelic, from English *pound,* monetary unit of the United Kingdom.]

pu•ny (pyo͞o′nē) *adj.* **pu•ni•er, pu•ni•est.** Small or inferior in size, strength, or significance; weak. **—pu′ni•ly** *adv.* **—pu′ni•ness** *n.*

pup (pŭp) *n.* **1.** A young dog; a puppy. **2.** The young of certain other animals, such as the seal.

pu•pa (pyo͞o′pə) *n., pl.* **pu•pae** (pyo͞o′pē) or **pu•pas.** The inactive stage in the life cycle of many insects, between the larva and the adult form, during which the larva is often enclosed in a protective covering such as a cocoon.

pu•pal (pyo͞o′pəl) *adj.* **1.** Of or relating to a pupa or pupae: *A cocoon is a pupal case.* **2.** Existing as or having the form of a pupa: *the pupal stage.*

❑ *These sound alike:* **pupal, pupil[1]** (student), **pupil[2]** (iris opening).

pu•pate (pyo͞o′pāt′) *intr.v.* **pu•pat•ed, pu•pat•ing, pu•pates.** To become or exist as a pupa. **—pu•pa′tion** *n.*

pu•pil[1] (pyo͞o′pəl) *n.* A student receiving instruction from a teacher. [First written down in 1384 in Middle English and spelled *pupille,* orphan, from Latin *pūpillus,* from *pūpus,* boy.]

❑ *These sound alike:* **pupil[1]** (student), **pupal** (of a pupa), **pupil[2]** (iris opening).

pu•pil[2] (pyo͞o′pəl) *n.* The opening in the center of the iris through which light enters the eye. [First written down in 1392 in Middle English and spelled *pupilla,* from Latin *pūpilla,* little doll (from the tiny image reflected in the pupil).]

❑ *These sound alike:* **pupil[2]** (iris opening), **pupal** (of a pupa), **pupil[1]** (student).

pup•pet (pŭp′ĭt) *n.* **1.** A small figure of a person or an animal, fitting over the hand or fitted with strings that are moved from above. **2.** A person whose behavior is determined by the will of others.

pup•pet•eer (pŭp′ĭ tîr′) *n.* A person who operates puppets to entertain.

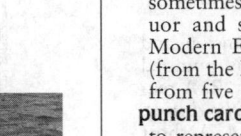

pup•pet•ry (pŭp′ĭ trē) *n., pl.* **pup•pet•ries.** The art of making and operating puppets.
pup•py (pŭp′ē) *n., pl.* **pup•pies.** A young dog.
pup tent *n.* A small tent made of waterproof material.
pur•blind (pûr′blīnd′) *adj.* **1.** Having poor vision; nearly or partly blind. **2.** Slow in understanding or discerning; dull. **—pur′blind′ly** *adv.* **—pur′blind′ness** *n.*
pur•chase (pûr′chĭs) *tr.v.* **pur•chased, pur•chas•ing, pur•chas•es.** To obtain in exchange for money or its equivalent; buy. *—n.* **1.** Something that is bought: *The car was a wise purchase.* **2.** The act or an instance or buying: *the purchase of land.* **3.** A secure position, grasp, or hold: *He got purchase on the ledge and climbed up.* **—pur′chas•a•ble** *adj.* **—pur′chas•er** *n.*
pure (pyŏŏr) *adj.* **pur•er, pur•est. 1.** Having a homogeneous or uniform composition; not mixed: *pure oxygen.* **2.** Free from impurities: *The recipe called for pure chocolate.* **3.** Complete; utter: *pure happiness.* **4.** Without fault or evil; sinless: *a pure heart.* **5.** Chaste; virgin. **6.** Of unmixed blood or ancestry. **7.** Not concerned with or directed toward practical application; theoretical: *pure mathematics.* **—pure′ly** *adv.* **—pure′ness** *n.*
pure•bred (pyŏŏr′brĕd′) *adj.* Having many generations of ancestors of the same breed or kind: *a purebred dog.* *—n.* (pyŏŏr′brĕd′). A purebred animal.
pu•rée (pyŏŏ rā′ *or* pyŏŏr′ā) *tr.v.* **pu•réed, pu•réing, pu•rées.** To put (food) through a strainer or sieve so that it becomes a mushy pulp. *—n.* Food prepared in this way.
pur•ga•tive (pûr′gə tĭv) *adj.* Tending to cleanse or purge, especially tending to cause the bowels to empty. *—n.* A purgative medicine or drug; a laxative.
pur•ga•to•ri•al (pûr′gə tôr′ē əl) *adj.* **1.** Serving to purify of sin. **2.** Of or resembling purgatory.
pur•ga•to•ry (pûr′gə tôr′ē) *n., pl.* **pur•ga•to•ries. 1.** In the Roman Catholic Church, a state in which souls who have died in grace must atone for their sins. **2.** A place or condition of suffering, making amends for sins, or remorse.
purge (pûrj) *v.* **purged, purg•ing, purg•es.** *—tr.* **1.** To cause (the bowels) to empty. **2.** To rid of sin or guilt: *purge one's soul.* **3.** To rid (a nation or a political party, for example) of persons considered undesirable. *—intr.* **1.** To become clean or pure. **2.** To cause or undergo an emptying of the bowels. *—n.* **1.** The act or process of purging. **2.** A medicine or drug used to empty the bowels; a purgative.
pu•ri•fi•ca•tion (pyŏŏr′ə fĭ kā′shən) *n.* The act or an instance of cleansing or purifying.
pu•ri•fy (pyŏŏr′ə fī′) *v.* **pu•ri•fied, pu•ri•fy•ing, pu•ri•fies.** *—tr.* **1.** To rid of impurities; cleanse: *purify water.* **2.** To rid of foreign or objectionable elements. **3.** To free from sin or guilt: *purify the soul.* *—intr.* To become pure: *The air gradually purified.* **—pu′ri•fi′er** *n.*
Pu•rim (pŏŏr′ĭm *or* pŏŏ rēm′) *n.* A Jewish holiday celebrating the rescue of the Jews by Esther from a plot to massacre them.
pu•rine (pyŏŏr′ēn′) *n.* **1.** A colorless crystalline compound, $C_5H_4N_4$, used in organic synthesis and metabolism studies. **2.** Any of a group of naturally occurring organic compounds derived from or having molecular structures related to purine, including uric acid, adenine, guanine, and caffeine.
pur•ist (pyŏŏr′ĭst) *n.* A person who practices or urges strict or traditional correctness, as in the use of words. **—pu•ris′tic** (pyŏŏ rĭs′tĭk) *adj.* **—pu•ris′ti•cal•ly** *adv.*
Pu•ri•tan (pyŏŏr′ĭ tn) *n.* **1.** A member of a group of Protestants in England and the American Colonies in the 16th and 17th centuries who advocated reform of the Church of England and a strict morality. **2. puritan.** A person considered excessively strict in morals.
pu•ri•tan•i•cal (pyŏŏr′ĭ tăn′ĭ kəl) *adj.* **1.** Strict in matters of religious or moral conduct: *a puritanical education.* **2. Puritanical.** Of or relating to the Puritans.
Pu•ri•tan•ism (pyŏŏr′ĭ tn ĭz′əm) *n.* **1.** The practices and doctrines of the Puritans. **2. puritanism.** Moral strictness, especially in regard to social pleasures.
pu•ri•ty (pyŏŏr′ĭ tē) *n.* **1.** The quality or condition of being pure: *the purity of mountain air.* **2.** The degree to which something is homogeneous or uniform. **3.** Freedom from sin or guilt; chastity: *a life of great purity.*
purl[1] (pûrl) *intr.v.* **purled, purl•ing, purls.** To flow or ripple with a murmuring sound, as a brook does. *—n.* The sound made by rippling water. [First written down before 1586 in Modern English, probably of Scandinavian origin.]
❑ *These sound alike:* **purl**[1] (flow), **pearl** (gem), **purl**[2] (knitting stitch).
purl[2] (pûrl) *v.* **purled, purl•ing, purls.** *—tr.* To knit (yarn) with a purl stitch. *—intr.* To do knitting with a purl stitch. *—n.* Inversion of knit stitch; purl stitch. [First written down in 1523 in Modern English and spelled *pirl.*]
❑ *These sound alike:* **purl**[2] (knitting stitch), **pearl** (gem), **purl**[1] (flow).
pur•loin (pər loin′ *or* pûr′loin′) *tr. & intr.v.* **pur•loined, pur•loin•ing, pur•loins.** To steal or commit theft. **—pur•loin′er** *n.*
purl stitch *n.* An inverted knitting stitch, often alternated with the knit stitch to produce a ribbed effect.
pur•ple (pûr′pəl) *n.* **1.** Any of a group of colors with a hue between that of blue and red. **2.** Cloth of this color, formerly worn as a symbol of royalty or high rank. *—adj.* **1.** Of the color purple. **2.** Royal or imperial; regal. **3.** Elaborate and ornate: *purple prose.*
Purple Heart *n.* A U.S. military decoration awarded to members of the armed services who have been wounded in action.
pur•port (pər pôrt′) *tr.v.* **pur•port•ed, pur•port•ing, pur•ports. 1.** To give the often false appearance of being: *He purported to be related to the royal family.* **2.** To have the intention of doing. *—n.* (pûr′pôrt′). **1.** Meaning; significance: *the purport of a letter.* **2.** Intention; purpose: *What was her purport in traveling to Alaska?* **—pur•port′ed•ly** (pər pôr′tĭd lē) *adv.*
pur•pose (pûr′pəs) *n.* **1.** The intended or desired result; a goal; an intent: *The club's purpose is to promote sailing.* **2.** Determination; resolve: *a woman of purpose.* ***—idiom.*** **on purpose.** Intentionally; deliberately: *did it on purpose.* [First written down about 1300 in Middle English and spelled *porpos,* from Anglo-Norman *purposer,* to intend.]
pur•pose•ful (pûr′pəs fəl) *adj.* **1.** Having a purpose; intentional: *a purposeful snub.* **2.** Having or manifesting purpose; determined: *Her stride was sure and purposeful.* **—pur′pose•ful•ly** *adv.* **—pur′pose•ful•ness** *n.*
pur•pose•less (pûr′pəs lĭs) *adj.* Lacking a purpose; aimless or meaningless. **—pur′pose•less•ly** *adv.* **—pur′pose•less•ness** *n.*
pur•pose•ly (pûr′pəs lē) *adv.* With a specific purpose; deliberately.
purr (pûr) *n.* **1.** The soft vibrant sound made by a cat. **2.** A sound similar to that made by a cat: *the purr of the car's engine.* *—v.* **purred, purr•ing, purrs.** *—intr.* To make a purr. *—tr.* To express by a purr.
purse (pûrs) *n.* **1.** A woman's bag for carrying per-

Purple Heart

purse
Change purse

ă	pat	oi	boy
ā	pay	ou	out
âr	care	ŏŏ	took
ä	father	ōō	boot
ĕ	pet	ŭ	cut
ē	be	ûr	urge
ĭ	pit	th	thin
ī	pie	*th*	this
îr	pier	hw	whoop
ŏ	pot	zh	vision
ō	toe	ə	about
ô	paw	N	*French* bon

pushcart
With display of accessories

pushup

pussy willow
American pussy willow

putt

sonal items; a handbag. **2.** A small bag or pouch, used to carry money. **3.** Money; funds; resources: *the family purse.* **4.** A sum of money given as a prize: *a race with a purse of $50,000.* —*tr.v.* **pursed, purs•ing, purs•es.** To gather or contract (the lips or brow) into wrinkles or folds; pucker: *purse one's brow in thought.* [First written down before 1000 in Old English and spelled *purs*, from Greek *bursa*, leather bag, wineskin.]

purs•er (pûr′sər) *n.* The officer in charge of money matters on board a ship or commercial aircraft.

pur•su•ance (pər **sōō′**əns) *n.* The act of putting something into effect.

pur•su•ant (pər **sōō′**ənt) *adj.* Proceeding from and conformable to; in accordance with.

pur•sue (pər **sōō′**) *v.* **pur•sued, pur•su•ing, pur•sues.** —*tr.* **1.** To follow in an effort to overtake or capture; chase: *The hounds pursued the fox.* **2.** To strive to gain or accomplish: *pursue a college degree.* **3.** To proceed along (a course); follow: *The ship pursued a southerly course.* **4.** To carry further; advance: *Do you want to pursue this discussion?* **5.** To engage in; practice: *pursue a hobby.* **6.** To court: *a lady pursued by many suitors.* **7.** To continue to torment or afflict; haunt: *Bad memories pursued him wherever he went.* —*intr.* **1.** To follow in an effort to overtake or capture; chase. **2.** To carry on; continue. [First written down about 1280 in Middle English and spelled *pursuwien*, from Latin *prōsequī*, to follow after.]

pur•suit (pər **sōōt′**) *n.* **1.** The act or an instance of pursuing or chasing: *The police are in pursuit.* **2.** The act of striving to gain or accomplish something: *the pursuit of happiness.* **3.** An activity, such as a vocation or hobby, engaged in regularly.

pur•vey (pər **vā′** *or* pûr′vā′) *tr.v.* **pur•veyed, pur•vey•ing, pur•veys.** To supply or furnish (food, for example): *purvey provisions for an army.* —**pur•vey′ance** *n.* —**pur•vey′or** *n.*

pus (pŭs) *n.* A thick yellowish-white liquid that forms in infected body tissues and consists of mostly white blood cells.

push (po͝osh) *v.* **pushed, push•ing, push•es.** —*tr.* **1.** To apply pressure to (an object) to move it away: *He pushed the rock, but it wouldn't budge.* **2.** To move (an object) by exerting force against it: *push a stalled car out of the intersection.* **3.** To force (one's way): *We pushed our way through the crowd.* **4.** To pressure (someone) for something or to do something: *They pushed him for an answer. They pushed her to try out for the basketball team.* **5.** To extend: *Pioneers pushed their farms westward.* **6.** To press with one's finger: *push a button.* **7.** *Slang.* To promote or try to sell: *push a new brand of toothpaste.* —*intr.* **1.** To exert outward pressure or force against something: *Let's all push to get the door open.* **2.** To advance despite difficulty or opposition; press forward. **3.** To expend great or vigorous effort: *She pushed to finish the report on time.* —*n.* **1.** The act of pushing; a shove: *His car needed a push to get started.* **2.** A vigorous effort: *a real push to finish the project.* **3.** *Informal.* Persevering energy; enterprise. —***idiom.*** **push around.** *Informal.* To treat or threaten to treat roughly; intimidate. [First written down before 1325 in Middle English and spelled *possen*, from Latin *pulsāre*, from *pellere*, to strike, push.]

push•cart (**po͝osh′**kärt′) *n.* A light cart pushed by hand.

push•er (**po͝osh′**ər) *n.* *Slang.* A person who sells drugs illegally.

push•o•ver (**po͝osh′**ō′vər) *n.* **1.** A person or group easily defeated or taken advantage of: *The team we played last week was a pushover.* **2.** Something that is easily done: *an exam that was a pushover.*

push•up (**po͝osh′**ŭp′) *n.* An exercise for strengthening arm muscles, performed by lying facedown and pushing the body up and down with the arms.

push•y (**po͝osh′**ē) *adj.* **push•i•er, push•i•est.** Disagreeably aggressive or forward: *a pushy salesman.*

pu•sil•lan•i•mous (pyo͞o′sə **lăn′**ə məs) *adj.* Lacking courage; cowardly. —**pu′sil•lan′i•mous•ly** *adv.* —**pu′sil•lan′i•mous•ness** *n.*

puss[1] (po͝os) *n.* *Informal.* A cat. [First written down before 1530 in Modern English, probably of Germanic origin.]

puss[2] (po͝os) *Slang.* *n.* **1.** The mouth. **2.** The face. [First written down in 1890 in Modern English, from Irish Gaelic *pus*, mouth.]

puss•y (**po͝os′**ē) *n.*, *pl.* **puss•ies.** **1.** *Informal.* A cat. **2.** A fuzzy catkin, especially of the pussy willow.

puss•y•foot (**po͝os′**ē fo͝ot′) *intr.v.* **puss•y•foot•ed, puss•y•foot•ing, puss•y•foots.** **1.** To move stealthily or cautiously. **2.** *Informal.* To act cautiously or timidly. —**puss′y•foot′er** *n.*

puss•y willow (**po͝os′**ē) *n.* A shrub or small tree that has silky silvery catkins in early spring.

pus•tule (**pŭs′**cho͞ol *or* **pŭs′**tyo͞ol) *n.* **1.** A small inflamed swelling on the skin filled with pus. **2.** A similar swelling, as a blister.

put (po͝ot) *v.* **put, put•ting, puts.** —*tr.* **1.** To place in a specified location; set: *Where did I put my umbrella?* **2.** To cause to be in a given condition: *Her friendly manner put me at ease.* **3.** To cause (someone) to undergo something; subject: *put a prisoner to death.* **4.** To assign; attribute: *He put an unusual interpretation on the tale.* **5.** To impose or levy: *put a tax on gasoline.* **6.** To hurl with an overhand pushing motion: *put the shot.* **7.** To bring up for consideration: *I put a question to the teacher.* **8.** To express; state: *I put my opinions honestly.* **9.** To adapt: *put lyrics to music.* **10.** To apply: *We'll do all right if we put our minds to it.* —*intr.* To proceed. Used of ships: *The ship put into the harbor.* —*n.* An act of putting the shot. —*adj.* *Informal.* Fixed; stationary: *Just stay put for a minute.* —***idioms.*** **put across.** To state so as to be understood clearly or accepted readily: *I put across my ideas to the committee.* **put by.** To save for later use: *We put by four quarts of stewed tomatoes.* **put down.** **1.** To write down. **2.** To bring to an end: *put down a rebellion.* **3.** *Slang.* **a.** To belittle; disparage: *Don't put down your teammates.* **b.** To assign to a category: *We put his bad mood down to a lack of sleep.* **put forth.** To grow: *The tree put forth leaves.* **put forward.** To propose for consideration: *put forward a new theory.* **put in.** **1.** To spend (time) at a location or job: *She put in four years with the armed services.* **2.** To plant: *We put in two rows of rhubarb this year.* **put off.** **1.** To delay; postpone: *I put off taking the test until next week.* **2.** To repel or repulse, as from bad manners: *His harsh tone put me off.* **put on.** **1.** To clothe oneself with: *We put on evening clothes for dinner.* **2.** To assume affectedly: *He put on an accent to amuse his friends.* **3.** *Slang.* To tease or mislead (another): *You're putting me on!* **4.** To add: *put on weight.* **5.** To produce; perform: *put on a play.* **put out.** **1.** To extinguish: *The firefighters arrived in time to put out the flames.* **2.** To inconvenience or offend: *I hope we're not putting you out by arriving on such short notice.* **put (someone) up to.** To cause to commit a funny, mischievous, or malicious act: *I put her up to playing the practical joke.* **put up.** **1.** To erect; build. **2.** To provide (funds) in advance: *They put up money for the new show.* **3.** To provide lodgings for: *They agreed to put me up for the night.* **put up with.** To endure without complaint. [First written down before 1200 in Middle English and spelled *putten*, from Old English *pȳtan*, to put out.]

put•down or **put-down** (po͝ot′doun′) *n. Slang.* A criticism, an insult, or a slight: *She interpreted his remarks as a putdown.*

put-on (po͝ot′ŏn′ *or* po͝ot′ôn′) *adj.* Feigned; pretended: *a put-on air of friendliness.* —*n. Slang.* Something intended to deceive, often as a joke.

pu•tre•fy (pyo͞o′trə fī′) *v.* **put•tre•fied, put•tre•fy•ing, put•tre•fies.** —*tr.* To cause to decay and have a foul odor. —*intr.* To become decayed and have a foul odor. —**pu′tre•fac′tion** (pyo͞o′trə făk′shən) *n.*

pu•trid (pyo͞o′trĭd) *adj.* **1.** Decomposed and having a foul smell; rotten. **2.** Of, showing, or caused by putrefaction: *a putrid smell.*

putt (pŭt) *n.* A light golf stroke made on the green to get the ball into the hole. —*v.* **putt•ed, putt•ing, putts.** —*tr.* To hit (a golf ball) with such a stroke on the green. —*intr.* To putt a golf ball.

put•tee (pŭ tē′ *or* pŭt′ē) *n.* **1.** A strip of cloth wound spirally around the lower leg from the knee to the ankle. Often used in the plural. **2.** A gaiter covering the lower leg. Often used in the plural.

put•ter[1] (pŭt′ər) *n.* **1.** A short golf club used for putting. **2.** A golfer who is putting: *a good putter.*

put•ter[2] *intr.v.* **put•tered, put•ter•ing, put•ters.** To occupy oneself in an aimless or ineffective manner: *puttering around in the garden.* [First written down in 1877 in American English, probably alteration of *potter,* from Old English *potian,* to poke.] —**put′ter•er** *n.*

putt•ing green (pŭt′ĭng) *n.* In golf, the area of short smooth grass that surrounds a hole.

put•ty (pŭt′ē) *n., pl.* **put•ties.** A soft cement made by mixing whiting and linseed oil, used to fill holes in woodwork and secure panes of glass. —*tr.v.* **put•tied, put•ty•ing, put•ties.** To fill, cover, or fasten with putty.

puz•zle (pŭz′əl) *v.* **puz•zled, puz•zling, puz•zles.** —*tr.* **1.** To baffle or confuse by presenting a difficult problem or matter. **2.** To clarify or solve (something confusing) by reasoning or study: *She puzzled out the algebra problem.* —*intr.* **1.** To be perplexed. **2.** To ponder over a problem in order to solve or understand it. —*n.* **1.** Something that confuses or perplexes; a problem or an enigma: *It's a puzzle to me how she can finish her homework so quickly.* **2.** A toy or game that presents one with a perplexing problem or task: *a jigsaw puzzle.* —**puz′zler** *n.*

puz•zle•ment (pŭz′əl mənt) *n.* The state of being confused or baffled: *expressed his puzzlement by a sheepish grin.*

PVT or **Pvt** or **pvt.** *abbr.* An abbreviation of private.

Pyg•my also **Pig•my** (pĭg′mē) *n., pl.* **Pyg•mies** also **Pig•mies. 1. pygmy.** A member of any of various African or Asian peoples having an average height of less than five feet. **2. pygmy.** An individual of unusually small size. —*adj.* **1.** Also **pygmy.** Of or relating to the Pygmies. **2. pygmy.** Much smaller than the usual or typical kind: *a pygmy hippopotamus.*

py•ja•mas (pə jä′məz *or* pə jăm′əz) *pl.n. Chiefly British.* Variant of **pajamas.**

py•lon (pī′lŏn′) *n.* **1.** A steel tower that supports high-tension wires. **2.** A tower marking a turning point in an air race. **3.** A monumental gateway to an Egyptian temple, formed by a pair of flat-topped pyramids. [First written down in 1850 in Modern English and spelled *pylon,* from Greek *pulōn,* gateway, from *pulē,* gate.]

py•lo•rus (pī lôr′əs) *n., pl.* **py•lo•ri** (pī lôr′ī′). The passage that connects the stomach to the small intestine.

Pyong•yang (pyŭng′yăng′ *or* pyŭng′yăng′). The capital and largest city of North Korea, in the southwest-central part of the country. It became the capital of North Korea in 1948. Population, 1,283,000.

py•or•rhe•a (pī′ə rē′ə) *n.* An inflammation of the gums and tooth sockets that causes the teeth to become loose.

pyr•a•mid (pĭr′ə mĭd) *n.* **1.** A solid geometric figure having a polygon as its base and triangular faces that meet at a common vertex. **2.a.** A massive monument found especially in Egypt, having a rectangular base and four triangular faces with a single apex and serving as a tomb or temple. **b.** Any of various similar constructions. [First written down in 1549 in Modern English, from Greek *puramis.*]

py•ram•i•dal (pĭ răm′ĭ dl) *adj.* Having the shape of a pyramid. —**py•ram′i•dal•ly** *adv.*

pyre (pīr) *n.* A pile of wood for burning a corpse as part of a funeral rite.

Pyr•e•nees (pîr′ə nēz′). A mountain range of southwest Europe extending along the French-Spanish border from the Bay of Biscay to the Mediterranean Sea. It rises to 11,168 feet (3,406.2 meters).

Py•rex (pī′rĕks′). A trademark for any of several types of glass that resist heat and chemicals.

pyr•i•dox•ine (pĭr′ĭ dŏk′sēn *or* pĭr′ĭ dŏk′sĭn) *n.* A vitamin of the B complex, found especially in grains, yeast, liver, and fish and acting in various parts of normal metabolism; vitamin B_6.

py•rite (pī′rīt′) *n.* A yellow mineral composed of a sulfide of iron, used as an iron ore and in making sulfur dioxide.

py•ri•tes (pī rī′tēz *or* pī′rīts′) *n., pl.* **pyrites. 1.** Pyrite. **2.** Any of various compounds of sulfur and a metal such as tin.

py•ro•ma•ni•a (pī′rō mā′nē ə *or* pī′rō mān′yə) *n.* An uncontrollable impulse to start fires. [First written down in 1842 in Modern English : Greek *pur,* fire + Greek *mania,* madness.] —**py′ro•ma′ni•ac′** *adj. & n.*

py•ro•tech•nic (pī′rə tĕk′nĭk) *adj.* Of or resembling fireworks: *a pyrotechnic display.* —**py′ro•tech′ni•cal•ly** *adv.*

py•ro•tech•nics (pī′rə tĕk′nĭks) *n. (used with a singular verb).* **1.** The art of manufacturing or setting off fireworks. **2.** A fireworks display. **3.** A brilliant display: *The pyrotechnics of his speech awed the audience.*

Pyr•rhic victory (pĭr′ĭk) *n.* A victory that is offset by staggering losses. [First written down in 1885 in Modern English, after *Pyrrhus* (319–272 B.C.), ancient king who defeated his enemies but had great losses.]

Py•thag•o•ras (pĭ thăg′ər əs). Flourished sixth century B.C. Greek philosopher and mathematician who proved the Pythagorean theorem and is considered the first true mathematician. —**Py•thag′o•re′an** (pĭ thăg′ə rē′ən) *adj. & n.*

Pythagorean theorem *n.* A theorem stating the square of the length of the longest side of a right triangle is equal to the sum of the squares of the lengths of the other sides. [First written down in 1579 in Modern English and spelled *Pythagorian,* after *Pythagoras.*]

Pyth•i•as (pĭth′ē əs) *n.* A legendary Greek man under sentence of death whose friend Damon is willing to die in his place.

py•thon (pī′thŏn′) *n.* Any of various very large nonpoisonous snakes of Africa, Asia, and Australia, that coil around and suffocate their prey. [First written down in 1836 in Modern English, from Latin *Pȳthōn,* mythical serpent killed by Apollo near Delphi.]

pyramid
The Temple of Inscriptions at Palenque, Mexico

python
Ball python

ă	**pat**	oi	**boy**
ā	**pay**	ou	**out**
âr	**care**	o͝o	**took**
ä	**father**	o͞o	**boot**
ĕ	**pet**	ŭ	**cut**
ē	**be**	ûr	**urge**
ĭ	**pit**	th	**thin**
ī	**pie**	*th*	**this**
îr	**pier**	hw	**wh**oop
ŏ	**pot**	zh	vi**s**ion
ō	**toe**	ə	**a**bout
ô	**paw**	N	*French* bo**n**

Qq

q or **Q** (kyo͞o) *n., pl.* **q's** or **Q's. 1.** The 17th letter of the English alphabet. **2.** The 17th in a group or series: *row q in a theater.*

q. *abbr.* An abbreviation of quart.

Qad•da•fi or **Qa•dha•fi** (kə dä′fē), **Muammar al-.** Born 1942. Libyan political leader who seized power in a military coup d'état against the Libyan monarchy (1969).

Qa•tar (kä′tär′ *or* kə tär′). A country of eastern Arabia on a peninsula in the southwest Persian Gulf. It gained its independence from Great Britain in 1971. Capital, Doha. Population, 220,000.

Q.E.D. *abbr.* An abbreviation of quod erat demonstrandum (which was to be demonstrated).

qt or **qt.** *abbr.* An abbreviation of quart.

quack[1] (kwăk) *n.* The sound made by a duck. —*intr. v.* **quacked, quack•ing, quacks.** To make such a sound. [First written down in 1342 in Middle English and spelled *quek*, of imitative origin.]

quack[2] (kwăk) *n.* **1.** An untrained person who pretends to be a physician and gives medical advice and treatment. **2.** A charlatan. —*adj.* Of or characteristic of a quack: *a quack cure.* [First written down in 1638 in Modern English, short for *quacksalver*, from Dutch.]

quail[1]
Male California quail

quack•er•y (kwăk′ə rē) *n., pl.* **quack•er•ies.** The practice of a quack.

quad (kwŏd) *n.* A quadrangle.

quad•ran•gle (kwŏd′răng′gəl) *n.* **1.** A plane geometric figure consisting of four points, no three of which lie on the same straight line, connected by straight lines; a quadrilateral. **2.a.** A rectangular area bordered on all sides by buildings. **b.** The buildings surrounding such an area.

quad•rant (kwŏd′rənt) *n.* **1.a.** An arc equal to one quarter of the circumference of a circle; an arc of 90°. **b.** The region of a plane bounded by such an arc and the pair of radii that extend from its endpoints to the center of the circle of which it is a part. **c.** Any of four regions into which a plane is divided by the axes of a Cartesian coordinate system. **2.** An object, such as a machine part, shaped like a quarter of a circle. **3.** An instrument with an arc of 90°, used to measure angles, as between a celestial object and the horizon.

quad•ra•phon•ic (kwŏd′rə fŏn′ĭk) *adj.* Of or used in a stereophonic sound system that uses four channels and features speakers placed in four corners of a room.

quad•rat•ic (kwŏ drăt′ĭk) *adj.* Of or containing mathematical terms or expressions that are of the second degree and no higher.

quadratic equation *n.* An equation of the general form $ax^2 + bx + c = 0$, where x is the independent variable and a, b, and c are constants.

quad•ren•ni•al (kwŏ drĕn′ē əl) *adj.* **1.** Happening once in four years. **2.** Lasting for four years. **—quad•ren′ni•al•ly** *adv.*

quadri– or **quadru–** or **quadr–** *pref.* A prefix that means: **1.** Four: *quadrilateral.* **2.** Square: *quadrate.*

quad•ri•ceps (kwŏd′rĭ sĕps′) *n.* The large four-part muscle at the front of the thigh that acts to extend the leg.

quad•ri•lat•er•al (kwŏd′rə lăt′ər əl) *n.* A polygon that has four sides. —*adj.* Having four sides.

qua•drille (kwŏ drĭl′) *n.* **1.** A square dance of French origin, performed by four couples. **2.** Music written to accompany this dance.

quad•ril•lion (kwŏ drĭl′yən) *n.* **1.** The number, written as 10^{15} or 1 followed by 15 zeros, that is equal to one thousand times one trillion. **2.** *Chiefly British.* The number, written as 10^{24} or 1 followed by 24 zeros, that is equal to one million times one British trillion. **—quad•ril′lionth** *n.*

quad•ru•ped (kwŏd′rə pĕd′) *n.* A four-footed animal.

quad•ru•ple (kwŏ dro͞o′pəl *or* kwŏ drŭp′əl) *adj.* **1.** Having four parts. **2.** Multiplied by four. —*n.* A number or an amount four times as great as another. —*tr. & intr.v.* **quad•ru•pled, quad•ru•pling, quad•ru•ples.** To make or become four times as great: *Working more hours and getting a raise quadrupled Sue's salary. The population of the town quadrupled.* [First written down before 1398 in Modern English and spelled *quadruply*, from Latin *quadruplus.*]

quad•ru•plet (kwŏ drŭp′lĭt *or* kwŏ dro͞o′plĭt) *n.* **1.** One of four offspring born in a single birth. **2.** A group or combination of four things of one kind.

quaff (kwŏf *or* kwăf *or* kwôf) *tr. & intr.v.* **quaffed, quaff•ing, quaffs.** To drink heartily.

quag•mire (kwăg′mīr′ *or* kwŏg′mīr′) *n.* **1.** Land with a soft muddy surface. **2.** A difficult situation.

qua•hog (kwō′hôg′ *or* kwō′hŏg′) *n.* A clam of the Atlantic coast of North America, having a hard rounded shell and much used as food.

quail[1] (kwāl) *n., pl.* **quail** or **quails.** Any of various small, plump, short-tailed birds having brownish feathers. [First written down about 1380 in Middle English and spelled *quaile*, from Old French.]

quail[2] (kwāl) *intr.v.* **quailed, quail•ing, quails.** To shrink back in fear; cower: *My dog looks ferocious, but he quails at the sight of a stranger.* [First written down before 1425 in Middle English and spelled *wailen*, to break down, from Middle Dutch *quelen*, to suffer, be ill.]

quaint (kwānt) *adj.* **quaint•er, quaint•est. 1.** Odd, especially in an old-fashioned way: *a quaint village.* **2.** Unfamiliar or unusual; curious: *a land full of sloths, kangaroos, and other quaint animals.* [First written down before 1200 in Middle English and spelled *cointe*, clever, cunning, peculiar, from Latin *cognitus*, knowing, from *cognōscere*, to learn.] **—quaint′ly** *adv.* **—quaint′ness** *n.*

quake (kwāk) *intr.v.* **quaked, quak•ing, quakes. 1.** To shake or vibrate, as from shock or lack of balance: *The ground quaked as the stampede passed.* **2.** To shiver or tremble, as from fear or cold: *His legs quaked with fear.* —*n.* **1.** An instance of shaking or quivering: *a quake in one's voice.* **2.** An earthquake. [First written down about 830 in Old English and spelled *cwacian.*]

Quak•er (kwā′kər) *n.* A member of the Society of Friends. **—Quak′er•ism** *n.*

qual•i•fi•ca•tion (kwŏl′ə fĭ kā′shən) *n.* **1.** The act of qualifying or the condition of being qualified:

Her qualification as a surgeon took years of hard work. **2.** A skill or other quality that suits a person for a particular job or task: *What are the qualifications for an airline pilot?* **3.** A restriction or modification: *The group accepted the proposal without qualification.*

qual•i•fied (kwŏl′ə fīd′) *adj.* **1.** Competent or meeting the requirements, as for a job: *a fully qualified doctor.* **2.** Limited; restricted: *an attitude of qualified optimism.* **—qual′i•fied′ly** (kwŏl′ə fīd′-lē *or* kwŏl′ə fī′ĭd lē) *adv.*

qual•i•fi•er (kwŏl′ə fī′ər) *n.* **1.** A person or thing that qualifies. **2.** In grammar, a word or phrase that limits or modifies the meaning of another word or phrase; for example, an adjective is a qualifier of a noun.

qual•i•fy (kwŏl′ə fī′) *v.* **qual•i•fied, qual•i•fy•ing, qual•i•fies.** *—tr.* **1.** To make eligible or qualified, as for a position or task: *Her grades qualify her for the Honor Society.* **2.** To make less harsh or extreme; moderate: *He qualified his remarks to avoid offending anyone.* **3.** To limit the meaning of; modify: *Adjectives qualify other words.* *—intr.* To be or become qualified.

qual•i•ta•tive (kwŏl′ĭ tā′tĭv) *adj.* Of or relating to quality, especially as distinguished from quantity or amount: *qualitative differences between the two bikers.* **—qual′i•ta′tive•ly** *adv.*

qualitative analysis *n.* A testing of a substance or mixture to find out what its chemical constituents are.

qual•i•ty (kwŏl′ĭ tē) *n., pl.* **qual•i•ties. 1.** A characteristic or property that distinguishes something: *the sour quality of vinegar.* **2.** A personal trait, especially a character trait: *He has many good qualities.* **3.** The essential character or nature of something: *capture with watercolors the quality of a sunset.* **4.** Excellence; superiority: *a store that sells only clothes of quality.* **5.** Degree or grade of excellence: *meat of poor quality.* **6.** High social position. [First written down about 1300 in Middle English and spelled *qualite*, from Latin *quālis*, of what kind.]

Synonyms: quality, characteristic, property, attribute, trait. These nouns mean a feature that distinguishes or identifies a person or thing. **Quality** and **characteristic** are the most general: *The voice had a soft, musical quality. Name a common characteristic of mammals.* **Property** means a basic or essential quality possessed by all members of a group: *This experiment will illustrate some of the properties of crystals.* **Attribute** often means a quality that a person or thing is given credit for having: *What are the attributes of a good leader?* **Trait** means a single, clearly defined characteristic: *His jealous streak is a disturbing trait.*

---

qualm (kwäm *or* kwôm) *n.* **1.** A sudden feeling of faintness, nausea, or sickness. **2.** A sudden disturbing feeling: *qualms of homesickness.* **3.** A pang of conscience: *He had no qualms about telling lies.*

quan•da•ry (kwŏn′də rē *or* kwŏn′drē) *n., pl.* **quan•da•ries.** A condition of uncertainty or doubt; a dilemma: *in a quandary over what to do next.*

quan•ta (kwŏn′tə) *n.* Plural of **quantum.**

quan•ti•fy (kwŏn′tə fī′) *tr.v.* **quan•ti•fied, quan•ti•fy•ing, quan•ti•fies.** To determine or express the quantity of.

quan•ti•ta•tive (kwŏn′tĭ tā′tĭv) *adj.* Of or relating to quantity, measurement, or number: *experiments that give quantitative proof of a theory.* **—quan′ti•ta′tive•ly** *adv.*

quantitative analysis *n.* A testing of a substance or mixture to find out the amounts and proportions of its chemical constituents.

quan•ti•ty (kwŏn′tĭ tē) *n., pl.* **quan•ti•ties. 1.** An amount or a number: *The elements are found in nature in various quantities.* **2.** A considerable amount or number: *Pennsylvania was the first state to produce oil in quantity.* **3.** Something, such as a number or symbol that represents a number, on which a mathematical operation is performed. [First written down before 1325 in Middle English and spelled *quantite*, from Latin *quantus*, how great.]

quan•tum (kwŏn′təm) *n., pl.* **quan•ta** (kwŏn′tə). An indivisible unit of energy, such as a photon.

quantum theory *n.* A theory of physics that electromagnetic energy occurs in quanta.

Qua•paw (kwô′pô) *n., pl.* **Quapaw** or **Qua•paws. 1.** A member of a Native American people formerly living in Arkansas along the Arkansas River, now living in Oklahoma. **2.** The Siouan language of the Quapaw.

quar•an•tine (kwôr′ən tēn′ *or* kwŏr′ən tēn′) *n.* **1.a.** A period of time during which a person, vehicle, or material thought to carry a contagious disease can be held at a port of entry and kept in isolation in an effort to prevent the disease from entering the country. **b.** A place where such persons, vehicles, or materials are held. **2.** An enforced confinement or isolation, especially one meant to keep a contagious disease from spreading. *—tr.v.* **quar•an•tined, quar•an•tin•ing, quar•an•tines.** To keep confined or isolated, especially as a way to keep a disease from spreading; place in quarantine. [First written down in 1609 in Modern English, from Italian *quarantina*, from *quaranta (giorni)*, forty (days), from Latin *quadrāgintā*.]

quark (kwôrk *or* kwärk) *n.* Any of a group of hypothetical subatomic particles having electric charges of one-third or two-thirds that of an electron. Quarks have been proposed as fundamental units of matter.

quar•rel (kwôr′əl *or* kwŏr′əl) *n.* **1.** An angry argument or dispute. **2.** A reason for argument or dispute: *I have no quarrel with what you say.* *—intr.v.* **quar•reled, quar•rel•ing, quar•rels** or **quar•relled, quar•rel•ling, quar•rels. 1.** To engage in a quarrel; argue or dispute angrily: *The boys quarreled over the use of the tennis court.* **2.** To disagree or find fault: *quarrel with a court decision.* [First written down in 1340 in Middle English and spelled *querele*, from Latin *querēla*, complaint, from *querī*, to complain.] **—quar′rel•er, quar′rel•ler** *n.*

quar•rel•some (kwôr′əl səm *or* kwŏr′əl səm) *adj.* Tending to quarrel: *a quarrelsome family.* **—quar′-rel•some•ness** *n.*

quar•ry[1] (kwôr′ē *or* kwŏr′ē) *n., pl.* **quar•ries. 1.** An animal hunted or chased. **2.** An object of pursuit. [First written down before 1300 in Middle English and spelled *quirre*, entrails of a deer given to hounds as a reward, from Old French *cuiriee*, from Latin *cor*, heart.]

quar•ry[2] (kwôr′ē *or* kwŏr′ē) *n., pl.* **quar•ries.** An open excavation from which stone is obtained by digging, cutting, or blasting. *—tr.v.* **quar•ried, quar•ry•ing, quar•ries. 1.** To obtain (stone) from a quarry. **2.** To make a quarry in: *quarry a mountain for its marble.* [First written down before 1382 in Middle English and spelled *quarre*, from Old French *quarriere*, from Latin *quadrum*, square.]

quart (kwôrt) *n.* **1.a.** A unit of volume or capacity used for measuring liquids, equal to two pints or 57.75 cubic inches. **b.** A unit of volume or capacity used for measuring dry substances, equal to two pints or 67.2 cubic inches. See table at **measurement. 2.a.** A container having a capacity of one quart. **b.** The amount of a substance that can be held in such a container: *a quart of juice.*

quar•ter (kwôr′tər) *n.* **1.** One of four equal parts. **2.**

quarry[2]

ă	pat	oi	boy
ā	pay	ou	out
âr	care	ŏŏ	took
ä	father	ōō	boot
ĕ	pet	ŭ	cut
ē	be	ûr	urge
ĭ	pit	th	thin
ī	pie	*th*	this
îr	pier	hw	whoop
ŏ	pot	zh	vision
ō	toe	ə	about
ô	paw	N	*French* bon

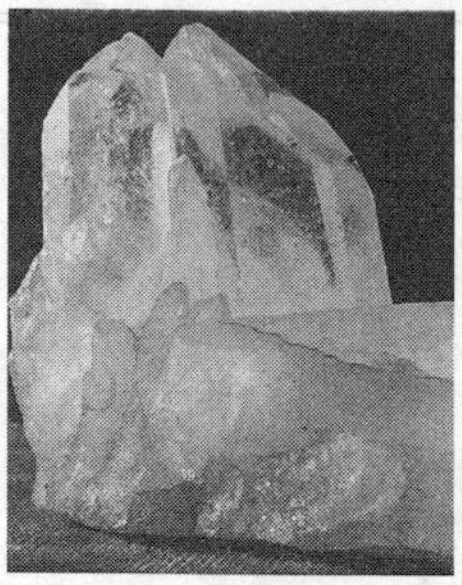
quartz

Quebec

The name **Quebec** comes from a Micmac word that means the "narrows (of a river)." The **Saint Lawrence River** flows through the province, narrowing near Quebec City.

Queen Anne's lace

quetzal
Male resplendent quetzal

A U.S. or Canadian coin worth twenty-five cents. **3.** A period of fifteen minutes; one-fourth of an hour. **4.a.** A period of three months; one-fourth of a year: *Sales picked up in the last quarter.* **b.** A school or college term lasting about three months. **5.** One-fourth of the period of the moon's revolution about Earth. **6.** In football and certain other sports, one of the four equal time periods that make up a game. **7.** One leg of a four-legged animal, including the adjacent parts: *a quarter of beef.* **8.a.** One of the four main divisions of the horizon as outlined by the four major points of the compass. **b.** A region or place: *People came from every quarter.* **9.** Often **Quarter.** A district or section, as of a city: *the Arab Quarter.* **10.** An assigned post or station, as on a ship. Often used in the plural: *a call to quarters.* **11.** **quarters.** A place to which a person is assigned to sleep or reside: *the officers' quarters on a ship.* **12.** An unspecified person or group of persons. Often used in the plural: *Help arrived from an unexpected quarter.* **13.** Mercy, especially when granted to a foe: *They gave no quarter to their enemies.* —*adj.* **1.** Being one of four equal or equivalent parts: *received a quarter share of the inheritance.* **2.** Being equal to one-fourth of a particular unit of measure: *a quarter cup of flour.* —*tr.v.* **quar•tered, quar•ter•ing, quar•ters. 1.** To divide into four equal or equivalent parts: *Mother quartered an orange for us.* **2.** To furnish with housing: *The general quartered the troops in the town.* [First written down before 1300 in Middle English, from Latin *quārtārius*, from *quārtus*, fourth.]

quar•ter•back (kwôr′tər băk′) *n.* In football, the player behind the line of scrimmage who usually calls the signals for the plays.

quar•ter•deck (kwôr′tər dĕk′) *n.* The after part of the upper deck of a ship, usually reserved for officers.

quar•ter•ly (kwôr′tər lē) *adj.* **1.** Made up or being one of four parts. **2.** Occurring or appearing at three-month intervals: *a quarterly magazine; a quarterly payment.* —*n., pl.* **quar•ter•lies.** A magazine published every three months. —*adv.* In or by quarters: *receive dividends quarterly.*

quar•ter•mas•ter (kwôr′tər măs′tər) *n.* **1.** A military officer responsible for the food, clothing, and equipment of troops. **2.** A naval petty officer responsible for the navigation of a ship.

quarter note *n.* A musical note having one-fourth the time value of a whole note.

quar•ter•staff (kwôr′tər stăf′) *n., pl.* **quar•ter•staves** (kwôr′tər stāvz′). A long wooden pole formerly used as a weapon.

quar•tet also **quar•tette** (kwôr tĕt′) *n.* **1.a.** A musical composition for four voices or instruments. **b.** A group of four musicians who perform such a composition. **2.** A group of four people or things. [First written down in 1790 in Modern English, from Italian *quartetto*, from Latin *quārtus*, fourth.]

quar•to (kwôr′tō) *n., pl.* **quar•tos. 1.** The page size obtained by folding a sheet of paper into four leaves. **2.** A book printed on pages of this size.

quartz (kwôrts) *n.* A hard transparent mineral composed of silicon dioxide; the most common of all minerals. It occurs as a component of rocks such as sandstone and granite, and separately in a variety of forms such as rock crystal, flint, and agate. Some crystalline forms, such as amethyst, are considered gemstones. [First written down in 1756 in Modern English, from German *Quarz*, of Slavic origin.]

quartz glass *n.* A type of glass made of pure silica. Quartz glass is highly transparent to ultraviolet light.

quartz•ite (kwôrt′sīt′) *n.* A metamorphic rock essentially of quartz, formed by the heating and compressing of sandstone.

qua•sar (kwā′zär′ *or* kwā′sär′) *n.* An extremely large, radiant, and distant star-like body that gives off radio waves.

quash[1] (kwŏsh) *tr.v.* **quashed, quash•ing, quash•es.** In law, to set aside or annul: *The judge quashed the indictment.* [First written down before 1338 in Middle English and spelled *quassen*, from Medieval Latin *quassāre*, from Latin *cassus*, empty, void.]

quash[2] (kwŏsh) *tr.v.* **quashed, quash•ing, quash•es.** To put down or suppress by force: *quash a rebellion.* [First written down before 1387 in Middle English and spelled *quaschen*, from Latin *quassāre*, to shatter.]

qua•si (kwā′zī′ *or* kwä′zē) *adj.* Resembling but not being: *Phrenology is a quasi science.*

qua•si-stel•lar object (kwā′zī stĕl′ər *or* kwä′zē stĕl′ər) *n.* A quasar.

Qua•ter•nar•y (kwŏt′ər nĕr′ē *or* kwə tûr′nə rē) *adj.* Of, belonging to, or being the geologic time of the later of the two periods of the Cenozoic Era, from the end of the Tertiary Period through the present. During the Quaternary, human beings appeared and developed. See table at **geologic time.** —*n., pl.* **Qua•ter•nar•ies.** The Quaternary Period and its series of rocks.

quat•rain (kwŏt′rān′ *or* kwŏ trān′) *n.* A stanza of four lines in a poem.

qua•ver (kwā′vər) *intr.v.* **qua•vered, qua•ver•ing, qua•vers. 1.** To shake, as from weakness; tremble; quiver. **2.** To speak in a quivering voice or utter a quivering sound. **3.** To produce a trill on a musical instrument or with the voice. —*n.* **1.** A quavering sound. **2.** A trill that is sung or played on a musical instrument. **—qua′ver•y** *adj.*

quay (kē *or* kā) *n.* A wharf or reinforced bank where ships are loaded or unloaded. [First written down in 1306 in Middle English and spelled *caye*, from Old North French *cai*, of Celtic origin.]

❑ *These sound alike:* **quay, key**[1] (lock opener), **key**[2] (island).

Que. *abbr.* An abbreviation of Quebec.

quea•sy (kwē′zē) *adj.* **quea•si•er, quea•si•est. 1.** Sick to one's stomach; nauseated. **2.** Easily nauseated. **3.** Causing nausea; sickening. **4.** Easily troubled or squeamish. **—quea′si•ly** *adv.* **—quea′si•ness** *n.*

Que•bec (kwĭ bĕk′) or **Qué•bec** (kā bĕk′). **1.** A province of eastern Canada east of Ontario. It joined the Canadian confederation in 1867. The region was claimed for France and made a royal colony in 1663. Great Britain was given sovereignty of the territory in 1763, but French influence has remained dominant. Quebec is the capital and Montreal the largest city. Population, 6,438,403. **2.** Also **Quebec City** or **Québec City.** The capital of Quebec, Canada, in the southern part of the province on the St. Lawrence River. A French colony was established here in 1608. Population, 166,474. —SEE NOTE.

que•bra•cho (kā brä′chō) *n., pl.* **que•bra•chos. 1.** Either of two South American trees whose bark yields tannins or other substances used as medicines. **2.** The bark or wood of such a tree.

Quech•ua (kĕch′wə) *n., pl.* **Quechua** or **Quech•uas. 1.** A member of a Native American people that originally made up the ruling class of the Inca Empire. **2.** The language of this people, now widely spoken from Colombia to Chile. **—Quech′uan** *adj.*

queen (kwēn) *n.* **1.a.** A woman who rules a nation, usually inheriting her position for life. **b.** The wife or widow of a king. **2.** Something eminent or considered as the most outstanding in some way: *Paris is regarded as the queen of cities.* **3.a.** A playing card bearing the figure of a queen. It ranks above a jack and below a king. **b.** In chess, a player's most powerful piece, able to move in any direction across any number of unoccupied squares. **4.** In a colony of bees, ants, or termites, a large specially developed female who is able to lay eggs.

Queen Anne's lace (ănz) *n.* A plant having feathery leaves and flat clusters of small white flowers. It is a wild form of the carrot.

queen•ly (**kwēn′**lē) *adj.* **queen•li•er, queen•li•est. 1.** Having the status of a queen. **2.** Of, resembling, or befitting a queen; majestic and regal. **—queen′li•ness** *n.*

queen mother *n.* A widowed queen who is the mother of the ruling monarch.

Queens (kwēnz). A borough of New York City in southeast New York on western Long Island. It was settled in 1635 and became part of New York in 1898. Population, 1,951,598.

queer (kwîr) *adj.* **queer•er, queer•est. 1.** Unusual; odd or unconventional: *a queer expression on his face.* **2.** Feeling slightly ill; queasy. **—queer′ly** *adv.* **—queer′ness** *n.*

quell (kwĕl) *tr.v.* **quelled, quell•ing, quells. 1.** To put down forcibly; suppress: *quell a revolt.* **2.** To allay; calm: *quell one's fears.*

quench (kwĕnch) *tr.v.* **quenched, quench•ing, quench•es. 1.** To put out or extinguish (a fire, for example). **2.** To satisfy (thirst): *quenched his thirst with a can of soda.*

quer•u•lous (**kwĕr′**ə ləs *or* **kwĕr′**yə ləs) *adj.* **1.** Given to complaining or fretting; peevish: *a querulous person.* **2.** Expressing complaints or grievance; grumbling: *the querulous tone of his voice.* **—quer′u•lous•ly** *adv.* **—quer′u•lous•ness** *n.*

que•ry (**kwîr′**ē) *n., pl.* **que•ries.** A question; an inquiry. *—tr.v.* **que•ried, que•ry•ing, que•ries. 1.** To express doubt about; question: *querying the wisdom of his decision.* **2.** To ask questions of: *The police queried the suspect about her recent activities.* [First written down in 1589 in Modern English and spelled *quere*, from Latin *quaerere*, to ask, seek.]

quest (kwĕst) *n.* **1.** A search, especially for something held valuable or precious: *Space exploration represents the latest quest for knowledge of the universe.* **2.** An expedition undertaken in medieval stories by a knight in order to find something or achieve a lofty purpose: *the quest for the Holy Grail.*

ques•tion (**kwĕs′**chən) *n.* **1.** An expression of inquiry that invites or requires a reply. **2.** A subject or point open to debate; an unsettled issue: *Your point raises broad constitutional questions.* **3.** A subject that is being discussed or considered: *The chair called for a vote on the question of building a new library.* **4.** A difficult matter; a problem: *It is only a question of money.* **5.** Uncertainty; doubt: *There is no question about his ability to do the job.* *—tr.v.* **ques•tioned, ques•tion•ing, ques•tions. 1.** To ask a question or questions of: *Dad questioned me about my thoughts on the election.* See Synonyms at **ask. 2.** To express doubt about; dispute: *No one questions her decisions.* ***—idiom.*** **out of the question.** Not to be considered; unthinkable or impossible. [First written down before 1200 in Middle English and spelled *questiun*, from Latin *quaestiō*, act of searching, from *quaerere*, to ask, seek.] **—ques′tion•er** *n.*

ques•tion•a•ble (**kwĕs′**chə nə bəl) *adj.* Open to doubt or suspicion; uncertain: *remedies of questionable value.* **—ques′tion•a•bly** *adv.*

question mark *n.* A punctuation mark (?) written at the end of a sentence or phrase to show that a question is being asked.

ques•tion•naire (kwĕs′chə **nâr′**) *n.* A printed form with a series of questions, often used to obtain statistical information or to sample public opinion on a certain subject.

quet•zal (kĕt **säl′**) *n., pl.* **quet•zals** or **quet•za•les** (kĕt **sä′**lās). **1.** A brilliant green and red Central American bird of which the male has very long tail feathers. **2.** The basic monetary unit of Guatemala.

Quet•zal•co•a•tl (kĕt säl′kō **ät′**l) *n.* The plumed serpent god of the Toltecs and Aztecs.

queue (kyōō) *n.* **1.** A line of people awaiting their turn, as at a ticket window. **2.** A long braid of hair that hangs down the back; a pigtail. **3.** A sequence of stored data or programs waiting to be processed. *—intr.v.* **queued, queu•ing, queues.** To get in line; wait in a queue: *We'll have to queue up for tickets.* [First written down in 1592 in Modern English, from Latin *cauda*, tail.]

❑ *These sound alike:* **queue, cue[1]** (billiards stick), **cue[2]** (signal).

Que•zon City (**kā′**sôn′ *or* **kā′**sōn′). A city of the Philippines adjoining Manila. It was the official capital of the Philippines from 1948 to 1976. Population, 1,165,865.

quib•ble (**kwĭb′**əl) *intr.v.* **quib•bled, quib•bling, quib•bles.** To find fault or criticize for petty reasons: *quibble over details.* *—n.* A minor criticism or an irrelevant objection. **—quib′bler** *n.*

quiche (kēsh) *n.* A rich unsweetened custard baked in a pastry shell often with other ingredients such as vegetables.

quick (kwĭk) *adj.* **quick•er, quick•est. 1.** Moving or acting with speed; fast: *quick on one's feet.* See Synonyms at **fast[1]. 2.** Learning, thinking, or understanding with speed; bright: *a quick mind.* **3.** Perceiving or reacting with speed: *He was quick to sense that something was wrong.* **4.** Occurring or accomplished in a brief space of time: *a quick recovery.* *—n.* **1.** The sensitive tender flesh under the fingernails. **2.** Living persons: *the quick and the dead.* *—adv.* **quicker, quickest.** Quickly; promptly: *Come quick!* [First written down about 725 in Old English and spelled *cwic*, alive.] **—quick′ly** *adv.* **—quick′ness** *n.* —See Note.

quick bread *n.* A bread that is made with a leavening agent, such as baking powder, and may be baked as soon as the ingredients are mixed.

quick•en (**kwĭk′**ən) *v.* **quick•ened, quick•en•ing, quick•ens.** *—tr.* **1.** To make more rapid; accelerate: *quicken one's steps.* **2.** To make keener, livelier, or more intense; stir: *Such stories quicken the imagination.* *—intr.* To become more rapid.

quick-freeze (**kwĭk′**frēz′) *tr.v.* **quick-froze** (**kwĭk′**frōz′), **quick-froz•en** (**kwĭk′**frō′zən), **quick-freez•ing, quick-freez•es.** To freeze (food) quickly enough so that it keeps its natural flavor and nutritional value.

quick•lime (**kwĭk′**līm′) *n.* Calcium oxide; lime.

quick•sand (**kwĭk′**sănd′) *n.* A bed of loose sand mixed with water, forming a soft shifting mass that yields easily to pressure and tends to engulf objects resting on its surface.

quick•sil•ver (**kwĭk′**sĭl′vər) *n.* The element mercury.

quick•step (**kwĭk′**stĕp′) *n.* A fast military march.

quick-tem•pered (**kwĭk′**tĕm′pərd) *adj.* Easily angered.

quick-wit•ted (**kwĭk′**wĭt′ĭd) *adj.* Quick to think and act; mentally alert and sharp.

quid[1] (kwĭd) *n.* A piece of something to be chewed, as tobacco. [First written down before 1000 in Old English and spelled *cwidu*, cud.]

quid[2] (kwĭd) *n., pl.* **quid** or **quids.** *Chiefly British.* A pound sterling. [First written down in 1688 in Modern English, possibly from Latin *quid*, something, what.]

Quetzalcoatl

Word History: quick

When your father yells up the stairs at you to "look alive," you know he means to "be quick." **Quick** comes from the Old English adjective *cwic*, pronounced [kwĭk], which means "alive." This sense is now obsolete except in the phrase *the quick and the dead*, which means "the living and the dead." In Middle English the word *quik* develops the senses "lively, active, swift," which is what your father wants you to be in the first place. A similar development takes place in French. The French adverb *vite* means "quickly," and it comes from the Latin word *vīta*, meaning "with life." The Latin word *vīta* is also the source of **vital** and **vitamin**.

ă	**pat**	oi	**boy**
ā	**pay**	ou	**out**
âr	**care**	ŏŏ	**took**
ä	**father**	ōō	**boot**
ĕ	**pet**	ŭ	**cut**
ē	**be**	ûr	**urge**
ĭ	**pit**	th	**thin**
ī	**pie**	*th*	**this**
îr	**pier**	hw	**whoop**
ŏ	**pot**	zh	**vision**
ō	**toe**	ə	**about**
ô	**paw**	ᴺ	*French* **bon**

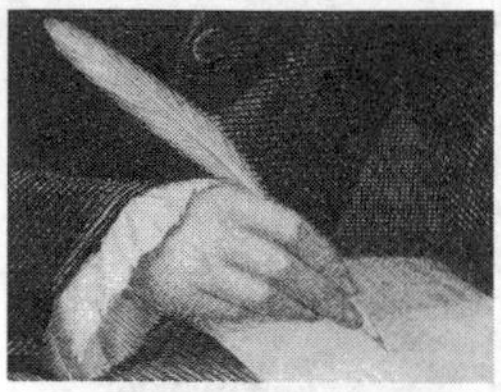

quill
Writing quill

quilt
Patchwork quilt

quirt

Word History: quirt

The word **quirt** looks and sounds strange: it is a riding whip with a short handle and a braided rawhide lash. **Quirt** comes from the Spanish noun *cuerda*, one of whose meanings is "cord," which would be the braided rawhide cord on the whip. *Cuerda* comes from the Latin word *chorda*, "a rope, cord, string on a musical instrument." Latin *chorda* becomes the word *corde* in Old French and acquires the meaning of "vocal cords," and English gets the word **cord** from French. Just about every Latin word spelled with the letters *ch*, *ph*, or *th* comes from Greek, and Latin *chorda* comes from the Greek word *khordē*, which also means a "string of sausage." Our spelling of *chord*, "a straight line connecting two points on a circle," is deliberately modeled on the Latin *chorda*.

qui•es•cent (kwē **ĕs′**ənt *or* kwī **ĕs′**ənt) *adj.* Inactive, quiet, or at rest. —**qui•es′cence** *n.*

qui•et (**kwī′**ĭt) *adj.* **qui•et•er, qui•et•est. 1.** Making little or no noise; silent or almost silent: *quiet neighbors; a quiet engine.* **2.** Free of noise; hushed: *a quiet street.* **3.** Not moving; still; calm: *a quiet lake.* **4.** Tranquil; peaceful; serene: *a quiet place in the country.* **5.** Not showy or bright; subdued: *quiet colors.* —*n.* The quality or condition of being quiet: *the quiet of the forest in winter.* —*tr. & intr.v.* **qui•et•ed, qui•et•ing, qui•ets.** To make or become quiet: *The teacher quieted the class. The audience quieted down.* [First written down before 1382 in Middle English and spelled *quiete*, from Latin *quiētus*.] —**qui′et•er** *n.* —**qui′et•ly** *adv.*

qui•e•tude (**kwī′**ĭ to͞od′ *or* **kwī′**ĭ tyo͞od′) *n.* Calm; tranquillity.

quill (kwĭl) *n.* **1.a.** A long stiff feather, usually from the tail or wing of a bird. **b.** The hollow stem of a feather. **2.** A writing pen made from a feather. **3.** One of the hollow spines of a porcupine. **4.** A plectrum that plucks a string of a harpsichord when a key is pressed.

quilt (kwĭlt) *n.* A bed covering made of two layers of cloth with a layer of batting in between, held together by decorative stitching. —*v.* **quilt•ed, quilt•ing, quilts.** —*tr.* To make into a quilt or construct like a quilt: *quilt a skirt.* —*intr.* To work on or make a quilt or quilts: *They quilt together once a week.* [First written down about 1300 in Middle English and spelled *quilte*, from Latin *culcita*, mattress.]

quilt•ing (**kwĭl′**tĭng) *n.* **1.** The process of doing quilted work. **2.** Material used to make quilts. **3.** Quilted material.

quince (kwĭns) *n.* **1.** A hard pleasant-smelling fruit similar to an apple, used chiefly for making jam or jelly. **2.** The tree that bears such fruit.

qui•nine (**kwī′**nīn′) *n.* A bitter colorless drug derived from certain cinchona barks and used to treat malaria.

quinine water *n.* A carbonated drink flavored with quinine.

quin•sy (**kwĭn′**zē) *n.* Severe inflammation of the tonsils and throat, often leading to the formation of an abscess.

quin•tes•sence (kwĭn **tĕs′**əns) *n.* **1.** The essence or basic element of a thing: *The quintessence of democracy is freedom of choice.* **2.** The purest or most typical example: *Her speech was the quintessence of clear thinking.*

quin•tet (kwĭn **tĕt′**) *n.* **1.a.** A musical composition for five voices or instruments. **b.** A group of five musicians who perform a quintet or quintets. **2.** A group of five people or things. [First written down in 1811 in Modern English, probably from Italian *quintetto*, from Latin *quīntus*, fifth.]

quin•tu•ple (kwĭn **to͞o′**pəl *or* kwĭn **tyo͞o′**pəl *or* kwĭn **tŭp′**əl) *adj.* **1.** Having five parts. **2.** Multiplied by five: *a quintuple increase.* —*n.* A number or amount five times as many or as much as another. —*tr. & intr.v.* **quin•tu•pled, quin•tu•pling, quin•tu•ples.** To make or become five times as great.

quin•tu•plet (kwĭn **tŭp′**lĭt *or* kwĭn **to͞o′**plĭt *or* kwĭn **tyo͞o′**plĭt) *n.* **1.** One of five children born in a single birth. **2.** A group or combination of five related things.

quip (kwĭp) *n.* A clever or witty remark. —*intr.v.* **quipped, quip•ping, quips.** To make a quip or quips.

quire (kwīr) *n.* A unit consisting of 24 or sometimes 25 sheets of paper of the same size and stock; one twentieth of a ream.

❑ *These sound alike:* **quire, choir** (singers).

quirk (kwûrk) *n.* **1.** A peculiarity of behavior: *Everyone has quirks.* **2.** An unpredictable event or act: *a quirk of fate.*

quirt (kwûrt) *n.* A riding whip with a short handle and a braided leather lash. —See Note.

quis•ling (**kwĭz′**lĭng) *n.* A traitor who serves as the puppet of the enemy occupying his or her territory. [First written down in 1940 in Modern English, after Vidkun *Quisling* (1887–1945), head of Norway's government during the Nazi occupation (1940–1945).]

quit (kwĭt) *v.* **quit** or **quit•ted** (**kwĭt′**ĭd), **quit•ting, quits.** —*tr.* **1.** To leave; depart from: *They decided to quit the city for the country.* **2.** To give up; abandon or resign: *quit one's job.* **3.** To discontinue; stop; cease: *Quit bothering me!* See Synonyms at **stop.** —*intr.* **1.** To cease functioning or performing an action: *The motor quit when we were a few miles from home.* **2.** To give up, as in defeat.

quit•claim (**kwĭt′**klām′) *n.* The legal release of a claim or right to another.

quite (kwīt) *adv.* **1.** Completely; altogether: *I am not quite finished with that book.* **2.** Really; actually; truly: *I'm quite positive you're wrong.* **3.** Somewhat; rather: *We plan to leave quite soon.*

Qui•to (**kē′**tō). The capital of Ecuador, in the north-central part of the country. It was settled by the Quito people and captured in 1487 by the Incas who held the city until 1534. Population, 890,355.

quits (kwĭts) *adj.* Even with, as by payment or revenge.

quit•ter (**kwĭt′**ər) *n.* A person who gives up easily.

quiv•er[1] (**kwĭv′**ər) *intr.v.* **quiv•ered, quiv•er•ing, quiv•ers.** To shake with a slight vibrating motion; tremble: *His voice quivered as he spoke.* —*n.* The act or motion of quivering. [First written down in 1490 in Middle English and spelled *quiveren*, perhaps from Old English *cwifer*, nimble.]

quiv•er[2] (**kwĭv′**ər) *n.* A case for holding and carrying arrows. [First written down in 1322 in Middle English, from Anglo-Norman *quiveir*, of Germanic origin.]

quix•ot•ic (kwĭk **sŏt′**ĭk) *adj.* Full of romantic and impractical ideas. —**quix•ot′i•cal•ly** *adv.*

quiz (kwĭz) *tr.v.* **quizzed, quiz•zing, quiz•zes. 1.** To question closely; interrogate. **2.** To test the knowledge of by asking questions. See Synonyms at **ask.** —*n., pl.* **quiz•zes.** A short oral or written examination.

quiz show *n.* A radio or television show in which contestants answer questions, usually for prizes.

quiz•zi•cal (**kwĭz′**ĭ kəl) *adj.* Showing puzzlement; perplexed: *a quizzical look on his face.* —**quiz′zi•cal•ly** *adv.*

quoin (koin *or* kwoin) *n.* **1.a.** An outside corner of a wall. **b.** A stone forming such a corner. **2.** A keystone. **3.** A block shaped like a wedge and used by printers to lock type into a galley.

❑ *These sound alike:* **quoin, coin** (money).

quoit (kwoit *or* koit) *n.* **1. quoits.** *(used with a singular verb).* A game in which players try to toss rings of iron or rope around a peg. **2.** One of the rings used in this game.

quo•rum (**kwôr′**əm) *n.* The minimum number of members of a committee or organization that must be present for the valid transaction of business.

quo•ta (**kwō′**tə) *n.* **1.** An amount of something assigned, as to be done, made, or sold: *a machine shop's production quota.* **2.** The number or proportion of persons or things that may be admitted, as to a country, a group, or an institution: *an immigration quota.*

quot•a•ble (**kwō′**tə bəl) *adj.* Suitable or worthy of quoting. —**quot′a•bil′i•ty** *n.*

quo•ta•tion (kwō **tā′**shən) *n.* **1.** The act of quoting:

These remarks are not for direct quotation. **2.** A passage that is quoted: *read a quotation from Shakespeare.* **3.** A statement of the price of a security or the price itself: *the latest stock market quotations.*

quotation mark *n.* Either of a pair of punctuation marks used to mark the beginning and end of a passage attributed to another person or repeated word for word. They take the form of double quotation marks (" ") and single quotation marks (' '). Single quotation marks usually indicate a quotation within another quotation.

quote (kwōt) *tr.v.* **quot•ed, quot•ing, quotes. 1.a.** To repeat or cite (a sentence, for example): *quote a familiar proverb.* **b.** To repeat a passage in or statement by: *quote the Bible; quote the mayor.* **2.** To cite or refer to for illustration or proof: *quoted statistics to show he was right.* **3.** To state (a price) for securities, goods, or services. —*n.* **1.** *Informal.* A quotation. **2.** A quotation mark. —SEE NOTE.

quoth (kwōth) *tr.v. Archaic.* Said; spoke.

quo•tient (kwō′shənt) *n.* The number that results when one number is divided by another.

Qur•'an (kə rän′ *or* kə răn′) *n.* Variant of **Koran.**

q.v. *abbr.* An abbreviation of quod vide (which see).

quiver[2]
Apache quiver

Usage: quote

The verb **quote** should be used when you are referring to the exact wording of a source: *In her speech she quoted the proverb "A bird in the hand is worth two in the bush."* When you paraphrase or allude to an original source, use **cite**: *He cited three books about architecture in his footnotes.*

ă	pat	oi	boy
ā	pay	ou	out
âr	care	o͝o	took
ä	father	o͞o	boot
ĕ	pet	ŭ	cut
ē	be	ûr	urge
ĭ	pit	th	thin
ī	pie	*th*	this
îr	pier	hw	whoop
ŏ	pot	zh	vision
ō	toe	ə	about
ô	paw	N	*French* bon

Rr

rabbit

rabbit ears

raccoon

r[1] or **R** (är) *n., pl.* **r's** or **R's.** **1.** The 18th letter of the English alphabet. **2.** The eighteenth in a group or series: *the R section of the stadium.*

r[2] or **R** *abbr.* An abbreviation of: **1.** Radius. **2.** Resistance.

R[1] (är) *n.* A movie rating that allows admission only to persons of a certain age, usually 17 and older, unless accompanied by a parent or guardian.

R[2] The symbol for **radical.**

R[3] or **r** *abbr.* An abbreviation of roentgen.

r. or **R.** *abbr.* An abbreviation of: **1.** Right. **2.** River.

R. *abbr.* An abbreviation of: **1.** Rabbi. **2.** Rector. **3.** Republican. **4.** Royal.

Ra[1] (rä) *n.* In ancient Egyptian mythology, the sun god, represented as a man with the head of a hawk crowned with a solar disk and the sacred serpent.

Ra[2] The symbol for the element **radium.**

R.A. *abbr.* An abbreviation of rear admiral.

Ra•bat (rə **bät′**). The capital of Morocco, on the Atlantic Ocean northeast of Casablanca. It was settled in ancient times and became a Muslim fortress in about 700. Population, 518,616.

rab•bi (răb′ī) *n., pl.* **rab•bis.** **1.** A person trained in Jewish law, ritual, and tradition, and ordained for leadership of a Jewish congregation. **2.** A scholar qualified to interpret Jewish law. [First written down before 1325 in Middle English and spelled *rabi*, from Hebrew *rabbî*, my master.]

rab•bin•i•cal (rə **bĭn′**ĭ kəl) *adj.* Made up of, related to, or characteristic of rabbis: *a rabbinical assembly.*

rab•bit (răb′ĭt) *n., pl.* **rab•bits** or **rabbit.** **1.** Any of various burrowing mammals having long ears, soft fur, and a short furry tail. **2.** The fur of such a mammal. [First written down before 1398 in Middle English and spelled *rabbete*, young rabbit, from Middle Dutch *robbe*, rabbit.]

rabbit ears *pl.n. Informal.* An indoor television antenna consisting of two adjustable rods connected to a base and swiveling apart at an angle.

rab•ble (răb′əl) *n.* **1.** A noisy unruly crowd or mob. **2.** The lowest or coarsest class of people.

rab•ble-rous•er (**răb′**əl rou′zər) *n.* A leader or speaker who stirs up the emotions of the public; a demagogue.

rab•id (răb′ĭd) *adj.* **1.** Of or affected by rabies. **2.** Raging; uncontrollable: *rabid thirst.* **3.** Overzealous; fanatical: *a rabid baseball fan.* **—rab′id•ness** *n.* **—rab′id•ly** *adv.*

ra•bies (rā′bēz) *n.* An infectious viral disease that affects mammals, attacks the central nervous system, and usually causes death. It is transmitted by the bite of an infected animal. [First written down in 1598 in Modern English, from Latin *rabiēs*, rage.]

rac•coon (ră **ko͞on′**) *n., pl.* **rac•coons** or **raccoon.** **1.** A North American mammal having grayish-brown fur, black face markings resembling a mask, and a bushy black-ringed tail. **2.** The fur of such a mammal. [First written down in 1608 in American English and spelled *arocoun*, of Virginia Algonquian origin.]

race[1] (rās) *n.* **1.** A group of people considered to be distinct on the basis of physical characteristics that are transmitted genetically. **2.** A group of people classified together on the basis of common history, nationality, or geographic location. **3.** Human beings considered as a group. **4.** A group of plants or animals that have inherited similar characteristics and form a distinct type within a species or breed. [First written down in 1520 in Modern English, from Old Italian *razza.*]

race[2] (rās) *n.* **1.a.** A contest of speed, as in running or riding: *a horse race.* **b. races.** A series of such competitions: *go to the races.* **2.** An extended competition for supremacy: *the presidential race.* *—v.* **raced, rac•ing, rac•es.** *—intr.* **1.** To take part in a race. **2.** To rush at top speed; dash: *raced home.* *—tr.* **1.** To compete against in a race: *I'll race you to the house.* **2.** To enter into a race or races: *She races horses for a living.* **3.** To cause to run at high speed: *race an engine.* [First written down before 1300 in Middle English and spelled *ras*, from Old Norse *rās*, rush, running.]

race•course (rās′kôrs′) *n.* A course laid out for racing; a racetrack.

race•horse (rās′hôrs′) *n.* A horse bred and trained for racing.

ra•ceme (rā **sēm′** *or* rə **sēm′**) *n.* A flower cluster having stalked flowers arranged singly along a stem, as the lily of the valley.

rac•er (rā′sər) *n.* **1.** A person or thing that competes in races or can move at great speed. **2.** Any of various fast-moving North American snakes.

race•track (rās′trăk′) *n.* A usually oval, specially surfaced course on which races are held.

ra•cial (rā′shəl) *adj.* Of, relating to, or based on race or races: *racial discrimination.* **—ra′cial•ly** *adv.*

ra•cism (rā′sĭz′əm) *n.* **1.** The belief that race accounts for differences in human character or ability and that a particular race is superior to others. **2.** Discrimination or prejudice based on race. **—rac′ist** *adj. & n.*

rack (răk) *n.* **1.a.** A frame, stand, or bar in or on which to hang or display certain articles: *a coat rack; a magazine rack.* **b.** A triangular frame for arranging billiard balls at the start of a game. **c.** A frame for holding bombs in an airplane. **2.** A metal bar having teeth that mesh with those of a pinion or gearwheel. **3.** An instrument of torture on which the victim's body was stretched. *—tr.v.* **racked, rack•ing, racks.** **1.** To place (billiard balls, for example) in or on a rack. **2.** To torment or afflict. ***—idiom.*** **rack up.** *Informal.* To accumulate or score: *rack up points.*

❑ *These sound alike:* **rack, wrack**[1] (ruin), **wrack**[2] (wreckage).

rack•et[1] also **rac•quet** (răk′ĭt) *n.* In sports, a device used to strike a ball or shuttlecock, consisting of a frame with tight interlaced strings and a handle. [First written down about 1385 in Middle English and spelled *raket*, a kind of handball, from Old French *rachette*, palm of the hand, racket, from Arabic *rāḥet.*]

rack•et[2] (răk′ĭt) *n.* **1.** A loud unpleasant noise. See Synonyms at **uproar.** **2.** A dishonest business, especially one that obtains money through fraud or extortion. [First written down in 1565 in Modern English.]

rack•et•eer (răk′ĭ tîr′) *n.* A person who runs or works in a criminal racket.

rac•quet (răk′ĭt) *n.* Variant of **racket**[1].

rac•quet•ball (răk′ĭt bôl′) *n.* A game played on a handball court by two to four players with short rackets and a hollow rubber ball.

rac•y (rā′sē) *adj.* **rac•i•er, rac•i•est. 1.** Lively; sprightly. **2.** Slightly improper or indecent; risqué. —**rac′i•ly** *adv.* —**rac′i•ness** *n.*

rad (răd) *n.* A unit of energy absorbed from ionizing radiation, equal to 100 ergs per gram of irradiated material.

ra•dar (rā′där) *n.* **1.** A method of detecting distant objects and determining their position, speed, or other characteristics by causing radio waves to be reflected from them and analyzing the reflected waves. **2.** The equipment used in doing this. [First written down in 1941 in American English, from *ra(dio) d(etecting) a(nd) r(anging).*]

radi– *pref.* Variant of **radio–**.

ra•di•al (rā′dē əl) *adj.* **1.** Of, arranged like, or directed along a radius or radii. **2.** Of or having parts that are arranged like radii: *the radial body of a starfish.* —**ra′di•al•ly** *adv.*

radial symmetry *n.* A pattern in which similar forms or features are arranged around a central point.

radial tire *n.* A tire made up of cords that are placed at approximately right angles to the center of the tread.

ra•di•ance (rā′dē əns) *n.* The quality or state of being radiant.

ra•di•ant (rā′dē ənt) *adj.* **1.** Sending forth light, heat, or other radiation: *a radiant star.* **2.** Consisting of or transmitted as radiation. **3.** Filled with brightness; beaming: *a radiant smile.* —**ra′di•ant•ly** *adv.*

radiant energy *n.* Energy in the form of waves, especially electromagnetic waves. X-rays, radio waves, and visible light are all forms of radiant energy.

ra•di•ate (rā′dē āt′) *v.* **ra•di•at•ed, ra•di•at•ing, ra•di•ates.** —*intr.* **1.** To send out rays or waves. **2.** To be sent forth as radiation: *light that radiates from a star.* **3.** To extend in straight lines from a center. —*tr.* **1.** To send forth (heat, light, or other energy), especially in the form of waves. **2.** To exude; project: *radiate confidence.*

ra•di•a•tion (rā′dē ā′shən) *n.* **1.** The act or process of radiating. **2.a.** The emission and movement of waves or atomic particles through space or other media. **b.** The waves or particles that are emitted and caused to travel.

ra•di•a•tor (rā′dē ā′tər) *n.* **1.** A heating device that circulates steam or hot water so as to radiate heat. **2.** A cooling device, as in an automotive engine, through which water or other fluids circulate as a coolant.

rad•i•cal (răd′ĭ kəl) *adj.* **1.** Going to or coming from a root or source; fundamental; basic: *proposed a radical solution to the problem.* **2.** Advocating extreme or revolutionary changes, as in politics or government. —*n.* **1.** A person who advocates fundamental or revolutionary changes. **2.** A root, such as $\sqrt{2}$, especially as indicated by a radical sign. **3.** A group of atoms that behaves as a unit in chemical reactions and is not stable except as a part of a compound. [First written down before 1398 in Middle English, of a root, from Latin *rādīx,* root.] —**rad′i•cal•ly** *adv.* —**rad′i•cal•ness** *n.*

radical expression *n.* A mathematical expression or form in which radical signs appear.

rad•i•cal•ism (răd′ĭ kə lĭz′əm) *n.* The doctrines or practices of radicals.

radical sign *n.* The sign $\sqrt{\ }$ placed around a number, as in $\sqrt{9}$, to show that a root of the enclosed number is to be taken.

rad•i•cand (răd′ĭ kănd′) *n.* The number or expression written under a radical sign, as the 3 in $\sqrt{3}$ or $x - 5$ in $\sqrt{x-5}$.

rad•i•ces (răd′ĭ sēz′ *or* rā′dĭ sēz′) *n.* A plural of **radix.**

ra•di•i (rā′dē ī′) *n.* A plural of **radius.**

ra•di•o (rā′dē ō) *n., pl.* **ra•di•os. 1.** Electromagnetic waves lying between about 10 kilohertz and 300,000 megahertz and carrying messages or information between points without the use of wires. **2.a.** The equipment used to generate such electromagnetic waves and alter them so that they carry information; a transmitter. **b.** The equipment used to receive such waves; a receiver. **3.** The sending forth of radio signals, as for entertainment or news programs, especially as a business; broadcasting. —*tr.v.* **ra•di•oed, ra•di•o•ing, ra•di•os. 1.** To send (messages) by radio. **2.** To signal or communicate with by radio.

radio– or **radi–** *pref.* A prefix that means radiation: *radiograph.*

ra•di•o•ac•tive (rā′dē ō ăk′tĭv) *adj.* Of, relating to, or showing radioactivity: *a radioactive element.*

ra•di•o•ac•tiv•i•ty (rā′dē ō ăk tĭv′ĭ tē) *n.* **1.** The emission of radiation by atomic nuclei. **2.** The radiation released. —SEE NOTE.

radio astronomy *n.* The scientific study of celestial objects and phenomena by observation of radio waves that reach the earth.

radio beam *n.* A beam of radio signals transmitted by a beacon to guide aircraft or ships.

ra•di•o•car•bon (rā′dē ō kär′bən) *n.* A radioactive isotope of carbon, especially carbon 14.

radiocarbon dating *n.* Carbon dating.

radio compass *n.* A navigational aid consisting of an automatic radio receiver that determines the direction of incoming radio waves.

radio frequency *n.* A frequency in which radio waves can be transmitted, ranging from extremely low frequency (below 300 hertz) to extremely high frequency (between 30 and 300 gigahertz).

ra•di•o•gram (rā′dē ō grăm′) *n.* A message sent by wireless telegraphy.

ra•di•o•graph (rā′dē ō grăf′) *n.* An image produced, as on photographic film, by radiation other than visible light, especially by x-rays. —*tr.v.* **ra•di•o•graphed, ra•di•o•graph•ing, ra•di•o•graphs.** To make a radiograph of.

ra•di•o•i•so•tope (rā′dē ō ī′sə tōp′) *n.* A radioactive isotope of a chemical element.

ra•di•ol•o•gist (rā′dē ŏl′ə jĭst) *n.* A physician who specializes in radiology.

ra•di•ol•o•gy (rā′dē ŏl′ə jē) *n.* **1.** The use of x-rays and other ionizing radiation in medical diagnosis and treatment. **2.** The use of radiation to examine physical objects and structures.

ra•di•om•e•ter (rā′dē ŏm′ĭ tər) *n.* **1.** A device used to detect and measure radiation, consisting of a glass bulb containing a partial vacuum in which a set of vanes, each darkened on one side and shiny on the other, spin about a central axis when radiation strikes them. **2.** An instrument that detects electromagnetic radiation.

ra•di•o•phone (rā′dē ō fōn′) *n.* A radiotelephone.

ra•di•o•sonde (rā′dē ō sŏnd′) *n.* An instrument carried aloft, chiefly by balloon, to gather and transmit information about the weather.

ra•di•o•tel•e•phone (rā′dē ō tĕl′ə fōn′) *n.* A tele-

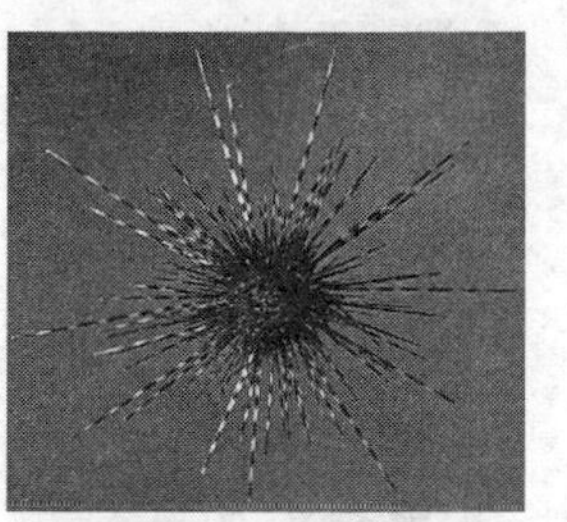

radial symmetry
Long-spined sea urchin

radioactivity

Within the nuclei of some atoms, such as those of lead, the energy holding the protons and neutrons together is great enough to hold the nuclei together, too. In the nuclei of other atoms, such as uranium atoms, this energy is not great enough, and the nuclei are unstable and will not hold together. An unstable nucleus keeps giving off particles and energy in a process known as **radioactivity** or *radioactive decay.* When all the particles and energy have been given off, the radioactivity ceases, and a new element with a stable nucleus is left. For example, uranium 238, a very unstable element, goes through several different stages of radioactive decay. After all the radiation of uranium 238 has been given off, the element lead, which is very stable, is left. All known elements with an atomic number greater than 83 are radioactive. And some elements with an atomic number less than 83 occur in radioactive forms.

ă	pat	oi	**boy**
ā	**pay**	ou	**out**
âr	care	o͝o	took
ä	father	o͞o	boot
ĕ	pet	ŭ	cut
ē	be	ûr	urge
ĭ	pit	th	**thin**
ī	pie	*th*	**this**
îr	pier	hw	**whoop**
ŏ	pot	zh	vision
ō	**toe**	ə	about
ô	**paw**	N	*French* bon

radio telescope

radish

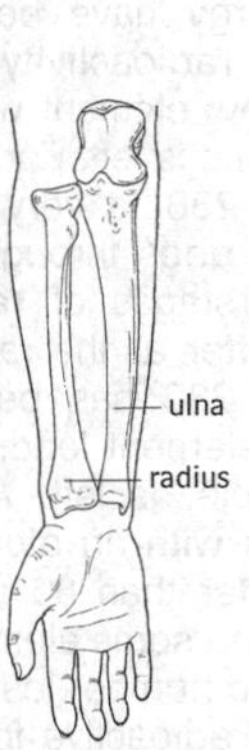

radius

raft[1]

phone in which audible communication is established by radio.

radio telescope *n.* A very sensitive radio receiver, typically equipped with a large reflecting antenna, used to detect radio waves that reach the earth from space.

radio wave *n.* An electromagnetic wave having a frequency in the range used for radio and radar.

rad•ish (răd′ĭsh) *n.* **1.** An edible, strong-tasting, red-skinned or white root, usually eaten raw. **2.** The plant that has such a root. [First written down about 1000 in Old English and spelled *rædic*, from Latin *rādīx*, root.]

ra•di•um (rā′dē əm) *n. Symbol* **Ra** A rare, white, highly radioactive metallic element, used in cancer treatment and nuclear research. Atomic number 88. See table at **element.** [First written down in 1899 in Modern English, from Latin *radius*, ray.]

ra•di•us (rā′dē əs) *n., pl.* **ra•di•i** (rā′dē ī′) or **ra•di•us•es. 1.a.** A line segment that joins the center of a circle with any point on its circumference. **b.** A line segment that joins the center of a sphere with any point on its surface. **2.** The length of such a line segment. **3.** A circular area measured by a given radius: *all houses within a radius of 50 miles.* **4.** The shorter and thicker of the two bones that make up the forearm.

ra•dix (rā′dĭks) *n., pl.* **rad•i•ces** (răd′ĭ sēz′ *or* rā′dĭ sēz′) or **ra•dix•es.** The base of a system of numeration, such as 2 in the binary system or 10 in the decimal system.

ra•don (rā′dŏn) *n. Symbol* **Rn** A colorless, radioactive, inert gaseous element formed by the radioactive decay of radium. Atomic number 86. See table at **element.** [First written down in 1918 in Modern English, from *radium.*]

raf•fi•a (răf′ē ə) *n.* **1.** A fiber obtained from the leaves of an African palm tree, used for baskets and mats. **2.** The tree that yields such fiber.

raf•fle (răf′əl) *n.* A lottery in which a number of persons buy chances to win a prize. **—raf′fle** *v.*

raft[1] (răft) *n.* A floating platform made of planks, logs, or barrels and used for transport or by swimmers. [First written down about 1300 in Middle English, from Old Norse *raptr*, beam, rafter.]

raft[2] (răft) *n. Informal.* A great number or amount. [First written down in 1637 in Modern English, possibly from Middle English *raf*, rubbish, heap.]

raft•er[1] (răf′tər) *n.* A person who travels by raft.

raf•ter[2] (răf′tər) *n.* One of the beams supporting a pitched roof. [First written down about 700 in Old English and spelled *reftras*, rafters, beams.]

rag[1] (răg) *n.* **1.** A scrap of cloth. **2. rags.** Threadbare or tattered clothing. [First written down about 1325 in Middle English and spelled *ragge*, of Scandinavian origin.]

rag[2] (răg) *tr.v.* **ragged, rag•ging, rags.** *Slang.* **1.** To tease; taunt. **2.** To scold. [First written down in 1739 in Modern English.]

rag•a•muf•fin (răg′ə mŭf′ĭn) *n.* A dirty child wearing tattered clothing.

rage (rāj) *n.* **1.** Violent anger or a fit of such anger: *flew into a rage.* See Synonyms at **anger. 2.** A fad or craze: *when torn jeans were the rage. —intr.v.* **raged, rag•ing, rag•es. 1.** To speak or act in violent anger. **2.** To move with great violence: *The storm raged outside.*

rag•ged (răg′ĭd) *adj.* **1.** Torn, frayed, or tattered: *ragged clothes.* **2.** Dressed in threadbare or tattered clothes: *a ragged scarecrow.* **3.** Jagged or uneven: *a ragged edge.* **4.** Imperfect; sloppy: *The actor gave a ragged performance.* **—rag′ged•ly** *adv.* **—rag′ged•ness** *n.*

rag•ged•y (răg′ĭ dē) *adj.* **rag•ged•i•er, rag•ged•i•est.** Worn-out or tattered; ragged.

rag•lan (răg′lən) *adj.* Having or being a sleeve that extends in one piece to the neckline of a garment. *—n.* A loose garment with raglan sleeves. [First written down in 1863 in Modern English, after Fitzroy James Henry Somerset (1788–1855), First Baron *Raglan*, British field marshal.]

ra•gout (ră go͞o′) *n.* A seasoned meat or fish and vegetable stew.

rag•tag (răg′tăg′) *adj.* **1.** Shaggy or unkempt; ragged. **2.** Disorderly and diverse in appearance and composition: *a ragtag gang.*

rag•time (răg′tīm′) *n.* A form of jazz having a steady rhythm and a melody with many notes falling on the unaccented beats.

rag•weed (răg′wēd′) *n.* Any of various weedy plants having narrow clusters of small greenish flowers whose pollen is one of the chief causes of hay fever.

rah (rä) *interj.* An expression used to show approval or encouragement.

raid (rād) *n.* **1.** A sudden attack by a small armed force. **2.** A sudden and forcible entry into a place by police: *a raid on a gambling den. —tr.v.* **raid•ed, raid•ing, raids.** To carry out a raid on. **—raid′er** *n.*

rail[1] (rāl) *n.* **1.** A horizontal bar supported at both ends or at close intervals, as in a fence. **2.** A fence or barrier made of such bars and supports. **3.** A steel bar used, usually as one of a pair, as a track for railroad cars or other wheeled vehicles. **4.** The railroad as a means of transportation: *travel by rail. —tr.v.* **railed, rail•ing, rails.** To enclose or supply with a rail or rails. [First written down in 1294 in Middle English and spelled *reile*, from Latin *rēgula*, straight piece of wood, ruler.]

rail[2] (rāl) *n.* Any of various brownish short-winged marsh birds. [First written down before 1450 in Middle English and spelled *rale*, from Old French *raale.*]

rail[3] (rāl) *intr.v.* **railed, rail•ing, rails.** To object or criticize in bitter, harsh, or abusive language: *railed against the notion of creating another government bureaucracy.* [First written down before 1470 in Middle English and spelled *railen*, from Old Provençal *ralhar*, to chat, joke, from Late Latin *ragere*, to bray.]

rail•ing (rā′lĭng) *n.* **1.** A fence or barrier made of rails. **2.** A banister or handrail.

rail•road (rāl′rōd′) *n.* **1.** A road or path built of parallel steel rails supported by ties and used by trains and other wheeled vehicles. **2.** A system of railroad tracks, together with the stations, land, trains, and other related property under one management. *—v.* **rail•road•ed, rail•road•ing, rail•roads.** *—tr. Informal.* **1.** To rush or push (something) through without adequate consideration: *railroad a bill through the legislature.* **2.** To convict (someone) without a fair trial or on false evidence. *—intr.* To work for a railroad company.

rail•way (rāl′wā′) *n.* **1.** A railroad, especially one operated over a limited area. **2.** A track that acts as a pathway for equipment with wheels.

rai•ment (rā′mənt) *n.* Clothing.

rain (rān) *n.* **1.a.** Water that condenses from vapor in the atmosphere and falls to the earth as drops. **b.** A fall of such water; a rainstorm or shower. **2.** A rainy season. Often used in the plural. *—v.* **rained, rain•ing, rains.** *—intr.* **1.** To fall in drops of water from the clouds: *It may rain tomorrow.* **2.** To release rain: *clouds that rain on the land. —tr.* **1.** To send down like rain: *rained balloons on the delegates to the convention.* **2.** To give or offer in great amounts: *rain gifts on someone.* **—*idioms.* rain cats and dogs.** *Informal.* To rain very heavily. **rain**

out. To force the cancellation or postponement of (an outdoor event) because of rain.

❑ *These sound alike:* **rain, reign** (rule), **rein** (restraint).

rain•bow (rān′bō′) *n.* **1.** An arc-shaped spectrum of color seen in the sky opposite the sun, especially after rain, caused by sunlight refracted by droplets of water. **2.** A similar spectrum, as one seen in the mist of a waterfall.

rain check *n.* **1.** A ticket stub entitling the holder to admission to a future event if the scheduled event is canceled because of rain. **2.** An assurance to a customer that a sold-out sale item may be purchased later at the sale price.

rain•coat (rān′kōt′) *n.* A waterproof or water-resistant coat.

rain•drop (rān′drŏp′) *n.* A drop of rain.

rain•fall (rān′fôl′) *n.* **1.** A fall of rain; a shower. **2.** The amount of water, measured in inches, that falls over a given area during a given time in the form of rain, snow, hail, or sleet.

rain forest *n.* A dense evergreen forest occupying a tropical region with an annual rainfall of at least 100 inches (2.5 meters).

rain•storm (rān′stôrm′) *n.* A storm accompanied by rain.

rain•wear (rān′wâr′) *n.* Waterproof clothing.

rain•y (rā′nē) *adj.* **rain•i•er, rain•i•est.** Characterized by, full of, or bringing rain: *a rainy afternoon; rainy weather.* **—rain′i•ness** *n.*

raise (rāz) *tr.v.* **raised, rais•ing, rais•es. 1.** To move to a higher position; lift: *raise the window slightly.* **2.a.** To set in an upright or erect position: *raise a flagpole.* **b.** To build; erect: *raise a barn.* **3.** To increase in size, quantity, or worth: *raise prices.* **4.** To increase in intensity, degree, strength, or pitch: *Don't raise your voice at me.* **5.** To grow or breed: *raise corn; raise livestock.* **6.** To bring up; rear: *raise children.* **7.** To put forward for consideration: *raise a question.* **8.a.** To stir up; set in motion: *raise a fuss.* **b.** To bring about; provoke: *raise doubts.* **9.** To gather together; collect: *raise money.* —*n.* An increase in wages or salary: *ask for a raise.* **—*idiom.* raise to a power. 1.** To indicate, as by an exponent, that a number or mathematical quantity is to be used a given number of times as a factor. **2.a.** To calculate the value of (a number, such as 9^4, to which an exponent has been applied). **b.** To write (an algebraic expression affected by an exponent, such as $[a + b]^2$) in expanded form, such as $a^2 + 2ab + b^2$. **—rais′er** *n.*

❑ *These sound alike:* **raise, raze** (tear down).

rai•sin (rā′zĭn) *n.* A sweet dried grape.

ra•jah (rä′jə) *n.* A prince, chief, or ruler in India or the East Indies.

rake[1] (rāk) *n.* A long-handled tool with teeth or prongs at one end, used especially to gather leaves or to loosen or smooth earth. —*v.* **raked, rak•ing, rakes.** —*tr.* **1.** To gather or smooth with a rake: *rake leaves; rake the lawn.* **2.** To gain in abundance: *The business suddenly began raking in the money.* **3.** To search or examine thoroughly: *The police raked the apartment for evidence.* **4.** To direct gunfire along the length of (a military position, for example). —*intr.* To use a rake. **—*idiom.* rake up.** To revive or bring to light; uncover: *raking up old gossip.* [First written down before 800 in Old English and spelled *ræce.*]

rake[2] (rāk) *n.* An immoral or dissolute person. [First written down in 1653 in Modern English, short for *rakehell.*]

rake[3] (rāk) *n.* Inclination from the perpendicular, as of a ship's mast. [First written down in 1626 in Modern English.]

rak•ish (rā′kĭsh) *adj.* **1.** Having a trim streamlined appearance, as a boat. **2.** Dashingly or sportingly stylish. **—rak′ish•ly** *adv.*

Ra•leigh (rô′lē *or* rä′lē). The capital of North Carolina, in the east-central part of the state northeast of Charlotte. It was selected as the capital in 1788. Population, 207,951.

ral•ly[1] (răl′ē) *v.* **ral•lied, ral•ly•ing, ral•lies.** —*tr.* **1.** To call together for a common purpose: *trying to rally supporters at a demonstration.* **2.** To reassemble and restore to order: *The general rallied the troops.* **3.** To rouse or revive from inactivity or decline: *rally the team's confidence.* —*intr.* **1.** To come together for a common purpose. **2.** To recover abruptly from a setback or disadvantage: *The stock market rallied in the final hour of trading.* **3.** To show a sudden improvement in health or spirits: *The patient rallied after four days of fever.* —*n., pl.* **ral•lies. 1.** A gathering, especially one intended to inspire enthusiasm for a cause: *a political rally.* **2.** A sudden improvement in health or spirits. [First written down in 1603 in Modern English, from Old French *ralier,* to ally, bring together.]

ral•ly[2] (răl′ē) *v.* **ral•lied, ral•ly•ing, ral•lies.** —*tr.* To tease good-humoredly. —*intr.* To engage in good-humored teasing or jesting. [First written down in 1668 in Modern English, from Old French *railler.*] **—ral′li•er** *n.*

ram (răm) *n.* **1.** A male sheep. **2.** A battering ram. —*tr.v.* **rammed, ram•ming, rams. 1.** To strike or drive against with a heavy impact: *The ship rammed an iceberg.* **2.** To force into a narrow space; jam: *rammed the clothes into a suitcase.*

Ram•a•dan (răm′ə dän′ *or* răm′ə dän′) *n.* The ninth month of the Muslim year, observed with fasting from sunrise to sunset.

ram•ble (răm′bəl) *intr.v.* **ram•bled, ram•bling, ram•bles. 1.** To wander aimlessly; stroll or roam: *The children rambled in the woods.* See Synonyms at **wander. 2.** To follow an irregularly winding course of motion or growth: *The brook rambled through the countryside.* **3.** To speak or write at length, often wandering off the subject: *He rambled on about his recent trip.* —*n.* A leisurely stroll: *an early morning ramble.*

ram•bler (răm′blər) *n.* **1.** A person or thing that rambles. **2.** A climbing rose having many small flowers.

ram•bling (răm′blĭng) *adj.* **1.** Often or habitually roaming: *a rambling herd of buffalo.* **2.** Extending over an irregular area; sprawling: *a rambling estate.* **3.** Lengthy and tending to wander off the subject: *a rambling speech.*

ram•bunc•tious (răm bŭngk′shəs) *adj.* Boisterous and disorderly.

Ram•e•ses II (răm′ĭ sēz′) also **Ram•ses II** (răm′sēz′). 14th–13th century B.C. King of Egypt (1304–1237 B.C.) whose reign was marked by the building of numerous monuments.

ram•i•fi•ca•tion (răm′ə fĭ kā′shən) *n.* **1.** A resulting development; a consequence. **2.** The act or process of branching out. **3.** A branch or an arrangement of branching parts extending from a main body.

ram•i•fy (răm′ə fī′) *intr. & tr.v.* **ram•i•fied, ram•i•fy•ing, ram•i•fies.** To extend or cause to extend in branches or divisions; branch out or cause to branch out. [First written down before 1425 in Middle English and spelled *ramifien,* from Latin *rāmus,* branch.]

ramp (rămp) *n.* **1.** A sloping passage or roadway that leads from one level to another. **2.** A movable stairway used for entering and leaving an airplane.

ram•page (răm′pāj′) *n.* A course of unrestrained, often violent action or behavior. —*intr.v.* (*also* răm pāj′). **ram•paged, ram•pag•ing, ram•**

railroad

rain forest

Rameses II
XIX Dynasty portrait bust

ă	pat	oi	boy
ā	pay	ou	out
âr	care	ŏŏ	took
ä	father	ōō	boot
ĕ	pet	ŭ	cut
ē	be	ûr	urge
ĭ	pit	th	thin
ī	pie	*th*	this
îr	pier	hw	whoop
ŏ	pot	zh	vision
ō	toe	ə	about
ô	paw	N	*French* bon

ranch
Horse ranch

Jeannette Rankin

pag•es. To move about wildly or violently; rage: *a mob rampaging through the streets.*

ram•pant (răm′pənt) *adj.* **1.** Growing or extending unchecked: *a rampant growth of weeds; rampant corruption.* **2.** Rearing up on the hind legs or on a hind leg, especially with the forelegs raised: *a rampant lion on a coat of arms.* **—ram′pant•ly** *adv.*

ram•part (răm′pärt′) *n.* **1.** A wall or bank raised around a fort, city, or other area for protection against attack. **2.** A means of protection or defense; a bulwark.

ram•rod (răm′rŏd′) *n.* **1.** A rod used to force the charge into the muzzle of a gun. **2.** A rod used to clean the barrel of a gun.

ram•shack•le (răm′shăk′əl) *adj.* So poorly made or maintained that disintegration is likely; rickety.

ran (răn) *v.* Past tense of **run.**

ranch (rănch) *n.* **1.** A large farm, especially in the western United States, on which large herds of cattle, sheep, or horses are raised. **2.** A large farm on which a particular crop or kind of animal is raised. *—intr.v.* **ranched, ranch•ing, ranch•es.** To work on or manage a ranch. [First written down in 1808 in American English, ultimately from Old French *renc, reng,* row, line, of Germanic origin.]

ranch•er (răn′chər) *n.* A person who owns or manages a ranch.

ran•che•ro (răn châr′ō) *n., pl.* **ran•che•ros.** A rancher, especially in the southwest United States.

ran•cid (răn′sĭd) *adj.* Having the unpleasant smell or taste of decomposed oils or fats.

ran•cor (răng′kər) *n.* Bitter resentment; deep-seated ill will. **—ran′cor•ous** *adj.*

rand (rănd *or* ränd) *n.* The basic monetary unit of Namibia and South Africa.

Ran•dolph (răn′dŏlf′), **Edmund Jennings.** 1753–1813. American Revolutionary leader and public official who was a member of the Constitutional Convention (1787).

ran•dom (răn′dəm) *adj.* Having no specific pattern, purpose, or objective: *random noise; random movements.* ***—idiom.*** **at random.** Without a method or purpose; unsystematically: *Choose a card at random from the deck.* **—ran′dom•ness** *n.*

rang (răng) *v.* Past tense of **ring[2].**

range (rānj) *n.* **1.** The extent, sphere, or scope of something: *within viewing range; the range of his interests.* **2.** An extent or amount of variation: *a price range.* **3.** The set of values that the dependent variable of a mathematical function can take. **4.** The maximum or effective distance limiting operation, as of a sound, radio signal, or missile: *a radio receiver with a range of 200 miles.* **5.** The maximum distance that a ship, aircraft, or other vehicle can travel before using up its fuel. **6.** The distance between a projectile missile and its target. **7.** A place for practice in shooting at targets. **8.** A testing area in which rockets and missiles are fired and flown. **9.** The geographic area in which a kind of animal or plant normally lives or grows. **10.** A large expanse of open land on which livestock wander and graze. **11.** A stove with spaces for cooking a number of things at the same time: *an electric range.* **12.** An extended group or series, especially a row or chain of mountains. *—v.* **ranged, rang•ing, rang•es.** *—tr.* **1.** To place in a particular order, especially in a row: *ranged the cups on hooks along the wall.* **2.** To assign to a particular category; classify. **3.** To pass over or through (an area): *when buffalo ranged the plains.* *—intr.* **1.** To vary or move between specified limits: *children whose ages ranged from four to ten.* **2.** To extend in a certain direction: *a ridge ranging westward from the peak.* **3.** To live or grow within a certain region. [First written down before 1325 in Middle English and spelled *range,* row, rank, from Old French *rang, reng,* line, of Germanic origin.]

rang•er (rān′jər) *n.* **1.** A wanderer. **2.** A member of an armed troop employed to patrol a specific region. **3.** A person employed to maintain and protect a forest or other natural area.

Ran•goon (răn go͞on′ *or* răng go͞on′). Officially (since 1989) **Yan•gon** (yăng gōn′ *or* yăng gôn′). The capital and largest city of Burma, in the southern part of the country on the **Rangoon River.** It became the capital of Burmese kings after the 1750's. Population, 2,458,712.

rang•y (rān′jē) *adj.* **rang•i•er, rang•i•est.** Having long slender limbs: *a tall rangy young man.*

ra•ni also **ra•nee** (rä′nē) *n., pl.* **ra•nis** also **ra•nees. 1.** A reigning Hindu princess or queen. **2.** The wife of a rajah.

rank[1] (răngk) *n.* **1.** A relative position or degree of value in a graded group: *in the top rank of his class.* **2.** A relative position in a society. **3.** An official position or grade: *an adviser with cabinet rank.* **4.** A row or line, especially of people or things side by side: *The soldiers formed ranks for inspection.* **5. ranks. a.** The armed forces. **b.** Personnel, especially enlisted military personnel. **6.** A body of people classed together; numbers: *joined the ranks of factory workers.* *—v.* **ranked, rank•ing, ranks.** *—tr.* **1.** To place in a row or rows. **2.** To give a particular order or position to; classify: *ranked the children according to age.* *—intr.* To hold a certain rank: *ranked eighth in the class.* ***—idiom.*** **pull rank.** To use one's superior rank to gain an advantage. [First written down before 1325 in Middle English and spelled *rank,* line, row, from Old French *renc,* of Germanic origin.]

rank[2] (răngk) *adj.* **rank•er, rank•est. 1.** Growing thickly or excessively: *rank weeds.* **2.** Strong and unpleasant in odor or taste: *a rank cigar.* **3.** Complete; absolute: *a rank amateur.* [First written down about 1000 in Old English and spelled *ranc,* strong, overbearing.] **—rank′ness** *n.*

rank and file *n.* **1.** The enlisted troops of an army. **2.** The ordinary members of a group or organization, as distinguished from the leaders and officers.

Ran•kin (răng′kĭn), **Jeannette.** 1880–1973. American reformer and politician who was the first woman U.S. representative (1917–1919 and 1941–1943).

rank•ing (răng′kĭng) *adj.* Of the highest rank; preeminent: *the ranking officer.*

ran•kle (răng′kəl) *v.* **ran•kled, ran•kling, ran•kles.** *—intr.* To cause persistent irritation or resentment. *—tr.* To embitter; irritate: *His boasting rankles me.*

ran•sack (răn′săk′) *tr.v.* **ran•sacked, ran•sack•ing, ran•sacks. 1.** To search thoroughly: *ransack a drawer.* **2.** To rob of valuables and leave in disarray; pillage. **—ran′sack′er** *n.*

ran•som (răn′səm) *n.* **1.** The release of property or a person in return for payment of a demanded price. **2.** The price or payment demanded. *—tr.v.* **ran•somed, ran•som•ing, ran•soms. 1.** To obtain the release of by paying a certain price: *The king ransomed his captured knights after the battle.* **2.** To release after receiving such a payment. [First written down before 1200 in Middle English and spelled *rancun,* from Latin *redēmptiō,* a buying back.]

rant (rănt) *intr.v.* **rant•ed, rant•ing, rants.** To speak loudly or violently; rave: *The property owner ranted against high taxes.* *—n.* Loud, violent, or extravagant speech. **—rant′er** *n.*

rap[1] (răp) *tr.v.* **rapped, rap•ping, raps. 1.** To hit sharply and swiftly; strike: *rapped the table with his fist.* **2.** To utter sharply: *rap out a complaint.* **3.** To criticize or blame. *—n.* **1.** A quick light blow or knock. **2.** A knocking or tapping sound. **3.** *Slang.* A reprimand; a rebuke. **4.** *Slang.* A prison sentence. —***idiom.* take the rap.** *Slang.* To accept punishment or take the blame for an offense or error. [First written down before 1350 in Middle English and spelled *rappen*, of imitative origin.]

❑ *These sound alike:* **rap[1]** (knock), **wrap** (envelop), **rap[2]** (talk).

rap[2] (răp) *n.* **1.** *Slang.* A talk, discussion, or conversation. **2.** A form of popular music characterized by a strong rhythm and spoken or chanted rhyming lyrics. —*intr.v.* **rap•ped, rap•ping, raps. 1.** To discuss freely and at length. **2.** To perform rap. [First written down in 1898 in Modern English, possibly from *rap*, to strike.]

❑ *These sound alike:* **rap[2]** (talk), **rap[1]** (knock), **wrap** (envelop).

ra•pa•cious (rə **pā′**shəs) *adj.* **1.** Taking by force; plundering. **2.** Greedy; ravenous. **3.** Living on live prey. —**ra•pa′cious•ly** *adv.* —**ra•pa′cious•ness, ra•pac′i•ty** (rə **păs′**ĭ tē) *n.*

rape[1] (rāp) *n.* **1.** The crime of forcing another person to submit to sexual acts, especially sexual intercourse. **2.** The act of seizing and carrying off by force. —*tr.v.* **raped, rap•ing, rapes. 1.** To force (another person) to submit to sexual acts, especially sexual intercourse. **2.** To seize and carry off (another person) by force. **3.** To plunder. [First written down before 1325 in Middle English, from Latin *rapere*, to seize.]

rape[2] (rāp) *n.* A plant having small seeds used as a source of oil and animal feed. [First written down before 1398 in Middle English, from Latin *rāpa*, turnip.]

Raph•a•el (**răf′**ē əl *or* rä′fē **ĕl′**). 1483–1520. Italian Renaissance painter whose works include religious subjects, portraits, and frescoes.

rap•id (**răp′**ĭd) *adj.* **rap•id•er, rap•id•est.** Fast; swift: *rapid progress; walking with rapid strides.* See Synonyms at **fast[1]**. —*n.* An extremely fast-moving part of a river, caused by a steep descent in the riverbed. Often used in the plural. —**ra•pid′i•ty** (rə **pĭd′**ĭ tē), **rap′id•ness** *n.* —**rap′id•ly** *adv.*

rapid eye movement *n.* REM.

rap•id-fire (**răp′**ĭd **fīr′**) *adj.* **1.** Designed to fire shots in rapid succession. **2.** Marked by continuous rapid occurrence: *rapid-fire questions.*

ra•pi•er (**rā′**pē ər) *n.* A light sword with a sharp point, used for thrusting.

rap•ine (**răp′**ĭn) *n.* The seizure of property by force; plunder.

rap•ist (**rā′**pĭst) *n.* A person who commits the crime of rape.

rap•port (ră **pôr′**) *n.* A relationship of mutual trust and understanding.

rap•scal•lion (răp **skăl′**yən) *n.* A rascal.

rapt (răpt) *adj.* **1.** Deeply moved or delighted; enchanted: *The children were listening with rapt admiration.* **2.** Deeply absorbed; preoccupied: *The painter stood at her easel, rapt in thought.*

❑ *These sound alike:* **rapt, wrapt** (enveloped).

rap•ture (**răp′**chər) *n.* The state of being transported by a lofty emotion; ecstasy. —**rap′tur•ous** *adj.*

rare[1] (râr) *adj.* **rar•er, rar•est. 1.** Occurring infrequently; uncommon: *a rare disease.* **2.** Excellent; extraordinary: *a rare gift for carving.* **3.** Thin in density: *rare gases in the earth's upper atmosphere.* [First written down in 1392 in Middle English and spelled *rere*, from Latin *rārus*.] —**rare′ness** *n.*

rare[2] (râr) *adj.* **rar•er, rar•est.** Cooked a short time: *rare meat.* [First written down about 1000 in Old English and spelled *hrēr*.] —**rare′ness** *n.*

rare•bit (**râr′**bĭt) *n.* Welsh rabbit.

rare earth *n.* **1.** An oxide of a rare-earth element. **2.** A rare-earth element.

rare-earth element (**râr′ûrth′**) *n.* Any of the metallic elements with atomic numbers ranging from 57 to 71.

rar•e•fy (**râr′**ə fī′) *v.* **rar•e•fied, rar•e•fy•ing, rar•e•fies.** —*tr.* **1.** To make thin, less compact, or less dense: *high altitudes that rarefy the air.* **2.** To purify or refine. —*intr.* To become thin or less compact or dense. —**rar′e•fi′a•ble** *adj.*

rare•ly (**râr′**lē) *adv.* Infrequently; seldom. —See Note at **hardly.**

rar•i•ty (**râr′**ĭ tē) *n., pl.* **rar•i•ties. 1.** The quality or condition of being rare; infrequency of occurrence: *the rarity of four-leaf clovers.* **2.** Something that is rare: *Snow is a rarity in Florida.*

ras•cal (**răs′**kəl) *n.* **1.** A person who is playfully mischievous. **2.** A dishonest person; a scoundrel.

ras•cal•i•ty (răs **kăl′**ĭ tē) *n., pl.* **ras•cal•i•ties. 1.** The behavior or character typical of a rascal. **2.** A mean or mischievous act.

rash[1] (răsh) *adj.* **rash•er, rash•est.** Too bold or hasty; reckless. [First written down about 1380 in Middle English and spelled *rasche*.] —**rash′ly** *adv.* —**rash′ness** *n.*

rash[2] (răsh) *n.* **1.** An abnormal eruption of the skin. **2.** An outbreak of many occurrences within a brief period: *a rash of burglaries in the building.* [First written down in 1709 in Modern English, possibly from Old French *raschier*, to scrape, scratch.]

rash•er (**răsh′**ər) *n.* **1.** A thin slice of fried or broiled bacon. **2.** A dish or an order of thin slices of fried or broiled bacon.

rasp (răsp) *v.* **rasped, rasp•ing, rasps.** —*tr.* **1.** To scrape or file using a coarse file with sharp raised points on its surface. **2.** To utter in a grating voice. **3.** To grate on (nerves or feelings). —*intr.* **1.** To make a harsh grating sound. **2.** To scrape harshly; grate. —*n.* **1.** A coarse file with sharp raised points on its surface. **2.** A harsh grating sound.

rasp•ber•ry (**răz′**bĕr′ē) *n.* **1.a.** A sweet, red, many-seeded berry that grows on any of various prickly plants having long woody stems. **b.** A plant that bears such berries. **2.** A dull to dark or deep purplish red. **3.** *Slang.* A jeering sound made by vibrating the tongue between the lips while exhaling.

rasp•y (**răs′**pē) *adj.* **rasp•i•er, rasp•i•est.** Grating; rough: *a raspy voice.*

Ras•ta•far•i•an (răs′tə **fâr′**ē ən) *n.* A person who believes in Rastafarianism. —*adj.* Of or relating to Rastafarianism or Rastafarians.

Ras•ta•fa•ri•an•ism (răs′tə **fâr′**ē ə nĭz′əm) *n.* A religion originating in Jamaica whose members worship Haile Selassie as savior and regard Africa, especially Ethiopia, as the Promised Land.

rat (răt) *n.* **1.** Any of various long-tailed rodents related to and resembling the mouse but larger. **2.** *Informal.* A hateful sneaky person, especially one who informs on associates. —*intr.v.* **rat•ted, rat•ting, rats. 1.** To hunt for or catch rats. **2.** *Slang.* To betray one's comrades by giving information; squeal. [First written down about 1000 in Old English and spelled *ræt*.] —**rat′ter** *n.*

rat cheese *n.* Cheddar.

ratch•et (**răch′**ĭt) *n.* **1.** A mechanism made up of a pawl or hinged catch that fits into the sloping teeth of a wheel or bar, allowing motion in one direction only. **2.** The pawl, wheel, or bar on such a mechanism.

rate (rāt) *n.* **1.** A quantity measured with respect to another measured quantity. For example, the distance that is or could be traveled during a given unit of time is called a rate of speed. **2.** A measure of a part with respect to a whole; proportion: *a national unemployment rate of 4.8 percent.* **3.** The cost or price charged per unit of a commodity or service: *postal rates.* **4.** A level of quality; a grade: *a jewel*

Raphael

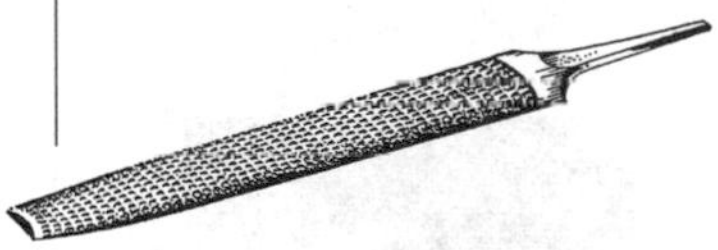

rasp
Half-rounded wood rasp

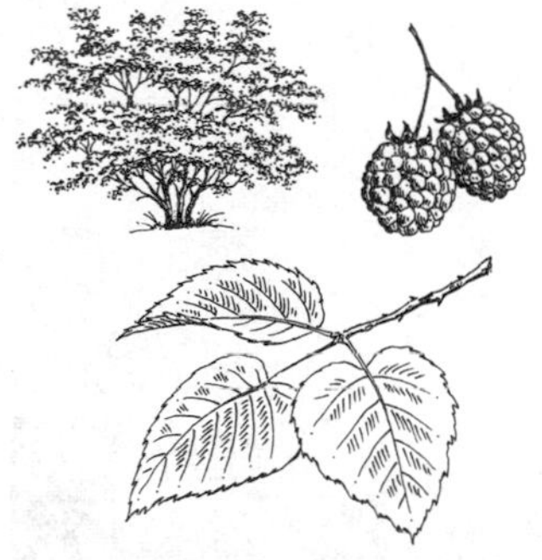

raspberry

ă	pat	oi	boy
ā	pay	ou	out
âr	care	o͝o	took
ä	father	o͞o	boot
ĕ	pet	ŭ	cut
ē	be	ûr	urge
ĭ	pit	th	thin
ī	pie	*th*	this
îr	pier	hw	whoop
ŏ	pot	zh	vision
ō	toe	ə	about
ô	paw	N	*French* bon

rattlesnake

raven

ravine
Jasper National Park
in Alberta, Canada

of no common rate. —*v.* **rat•ed, rat•ing, rates.** —*tr.* **1.** To place in a particular grade or rank: *rated her third in her class.* **2.** To calculate the value of; appraise: *The jeweler rated the quality of the gems.* **3.** To regard or account: *rated the movie excellent.* —*intr.* To hold a certain rank; be valued or placed in a certain class: *This movie rates as the best of the year.* —***idiom.*** **at any rate. 1.** Whatever the case may be. **2.** At least.

rate of exchange *n., pl.* **rates of changes.** The ratio at which the unit of currency of one country may be exchanged for that of another country.

rath•er (răth′ər) *adv.* **1.** Preferably; more willingly: *I'd rather stay home tonight.* **2.** More exactly; more accurately: *She is a businesswoman, or rather a banker.* **3.** To a certain extent; somewhat: *feeling rather sleepy.* **4.** On the contrary: *The photograph did not show the whole family, but rather all the cousins.*

rat•i•fy (răt′ə fī′) *tr.v.* **rat•i•fied, rat•i•fy•ing, rat•i•fies.** To approve and thus make officially valid; confirm: *ratify an amendment to the Constitution.* —**rat′i•fi•ca′tion** (răt′ə fĭ kā′shən) *n.*

rat•ing (rā′tĭng) *n.* **1.** A classification assigned according to quality, performance, skill, or specialty: *beef marked with a "choice" rating.* **2.** An evaluation of the financial status of a person or business: *a high credit rating.* **3.** An estimate of the popularity of a television or radio program, made by polling selected members of the audience.

ra•tio (rā′shō *or* rā′shē ō′) *n., pl.* **ra•tios. 1.** Relation in degree or number between two similar things. **2.** A relationship between the amounts or sizes of two things, expressed as the quotient of one divided by the other; a proportion: *mixed flour and water in the ratio of five to two.* [First written down in 1636 in Modern English, from Latin *ratiō*, calculation, from *rērī*, to reckon, consider.]

ra•tion (răsh′ən *or* rā′shən) *n.* **1.** A fixed amount, especially of food, allotted periodically: *a horse's daily ration of oats.* **2. rations.** Food issued or available to members of a group: *a soldier's rations.* —*tr.v.* **ra•tioned, ra•tion•ing, ra•tions. 1.** To give or make available in fixed limited amounts, as during a period of scarcity: *a drought made it necessary to ration water.* See Synonyms at **distribute. 2.** To supply with allotments of food; give rations to.

ra•tion•al (răsh′ə nəl) *adj.* **1.** Having or using the ability to reason. **2.** Consistent with or based on reason; logical: *rational behavior.* **3.** Of or relating to a rational number. —**ra′tion•al•ly** *adv.*

ra•tion•ale (răsh′ə năl′) *n.* The fundamental reason; the basis.

ra•tion•al•ism (răsh′ə nə lĭz′əm) *n.* The theory that reason provides the only valid basis for action or belief and that reason is the primary source of knowledge and of spiritual truth. —**ra′tion•al•ist** *n.* —**ra′tion•al•is′tic** *adj.* —**ra′tion•al•is′ti•cal•ly** *adv.*

ra•tion•al•i•ty (răsh′ə năl′ĭ tē) *n., pl.* **ra•tion•al•i•ties. 1.** The quality or condition of being rational. **2.** A rational belief or practice.

ra•tion•al•ize (răsh′ə nə līz′) *v.* **ra•tion•al•ized, ra•tion•al•iz•ing, ra•tion•al•iz•es.** —*tr.* **1.** To make rational: *Attempts to rationalize spelling have failed.* **2.** To invent satisfactory but false explanations for (one's behavior). —*intr.* **1.** To think rationally. **2.** To rationalize one's behavior. —**ra′tion•al•i•za′tion** (răsh′ə nə lĭ zā′shən) *n.* —**ra′tion•al•iz′er** *n.*

rational number *n.* A number that can be expressed as an integer or a quotient of integers. For example, 2, 5, and −½ are rational numbers.

rat•line (răt′lĭn) *n.* Any of the small ropes fastened horizontally to the shrouds of a ship and forming a ladder for going aloft.

rat•tan (ră tăn′) *n.* **1.** The stems of a climbing tropical palm tree, used for furniture, canes, and wickerwork. **2.** Any of various trees that have such stems.

rat•ter (răt′ər) *n.* A dog or cat that catches or kills rats.

rat•tle (răt′l) *v.* **rat•tled, rat•tling, rat•tles.** —*intr.* **1.a.** To make a quick succession of short sharp sounds: *so frightened that his teeth rattled.* **b.** To move with such sounds: *The old train rattled along the track.* **2.** To talk rapidly and at length, usually without much thought: *rattled on about his relatives.* —*tr.* **1.** To shake noisily: *rattled the coins in her pocket.* **2.** To utter or perform rapidly or effortlessly: *rattle off a list of names.* **3.** *Informal.* To disturb the composure or confidence of; unnerve. —*n.* **1.** A quick succession of short sharp sounds: *the rattle of the rain on the roof.* **2.** A device that rattles when shaken: *a baby's rattle.* **3.** The series of dry horny rings at the end of a rattlesnake's tail, making a rattling sound when shaken.

rat•tler (răt′lər) *n.* **1.** A person or thing that rattles. **2.** A rattlesnake.

rat•tle•snake (răt′l snāk′) *n.* Any of various poisonous American snakes having at the end of the tail several dry horny rings that can be shaken rapidly to make a rattling sound.

rau•cous (rô′kəs) *adj.* **1.** Rough-sounding and harsh: *the crow's raucous cries.* **2.** Boisterous and disorderly: *a raucous party.* —**rau′cous•ly** *adv.* —**rau′cous•ness** *n.*

raun•chy (rôn′chē *or* rän′chē) *adj.* **raun•chi•er, raun•chi•est.** *Slang.* **1.** Obscene, lewd, or vulgar. **2.** Grimy; unkempt.

rav•age (răv′ĭj) *tr.v.* **rav•aged, rav•ag•ing, rav•ages.** To bring heavy destruction upon; devastate: *A hurricane ravaged the coast.* —*n.* **1.** The act of ravaging; heavy destruction. **2.** Severe damage; havoc: *the ravages of smallpox.* —**rav′ag•er** *n.*

rave (rāv) *intr.v.* **raved, rav•ing, raves. 1.** To speak wildly without making any sense. **2.** To speak with wild enthusiasm or praise: *raving about her new skis.* —*n.* **1.** The act or an instance of raving. **2.** *Informal.* An opinion, a description, or a review full of enthusiastic praise. —*adj. Informal.* Relating to or being an extravagantly enthusiastic review or opinion: *rave reviews.* [First written down before 1325 in Middle English and spelled *reven*, from Old North French *resver*, to dream, wander, rave.]

rav•el (răv′əl) *tr. & intr.v.* **rav•eled, rav•el•ing, rav•els** also **rav•elled, rav•el•ling, rav•els.** To separate or become separated into single loose threads; fray: *Unhappy with her work, she raveled the edge of the sweater. The rug raveled where it was worn.* —*n.* A broken or discarded thread.

ra•ven (rā′vən) *n.* A large black bird having a croaking cry similar to that of a crow. —*adj.* Black and shiny. [First written down before 800 in Old English and spelled *hræfn*.]

rav•en•ing (răv′ə nĭng) *adj.* Greedily seeking and seizing prey; predatory.

rav•en•ous (răv′ə nəs) *adj.* **1.** Greedily eager for food; extremely hungry: *a ravenous appetite.* **2.** Greedy for gratification: *ravenous for power.* —**rav′en•ous•ly** *adv.*

ra•vine (rə vēn′) *n.* A deep narrow valley or gorge in the earth's surface made by running water.

rav•ing (rā′vĭng) *adj.* **1.** Talking or behaving irrationally; wild. **2.** Worthy of admiration: *a raving beauty.* —*n.* Wild irrational speech.

rav•i•o•li (răv′ē ō′lē) *n., pl.* **ravioli** or **ra•vi•o•lis. 1.** A small casing of pasta with various fillings, such as chopped meat or cheese. **2.** A dish made with ravioli.

rav•ish (răv′ĭsh) *tr.v.* **rav•ished, rav•ish•ing, rav•ish•es. 1.** To seize and take by force. **2.** To rape. **3.** To overwhelm with emotion; enrapture. —**rav′ish•ment** *n.* —**rav′ish•er** *n.*

rav•ish•ing (răv′ĭ shĭng) *adj.* Extremely attractive; entrancing: *a ravishing beauty.* —**rav′ish•ing•ly** *adv.*

raw (rô) *adj.* **raw•er, raw•est. 1.** Uncooked: *raw meat.* **2.a.** In a natural condition; not processed or refined: *raw wool.* **b.** Not finished, covered, treated, or coated: *furniture sanded down to raw wood.* **3.** Untrained and inexperienced: *raw recruits.* **4.** Badly irritated; sore: *a raw open wound.* **5.** Powerfully impressive; stark: *raw talent.* **6.** Unpleasantly damp and chilly: *raw weather.* —***idiom.*** **in the raw. 1.** In a crude or unrefined state. **2.** Nude; naked. [First written down about 1000 in Old English and spelled *hrēaw*.]

raw•boned (rô′bōnd′) *adj.* Having a lean gaunt frame with prominent bones.

raw•hide (rô′hīd′) *n.* **1.** The hide of cattle or other animals before it has been tanned. **2.** A whip or rope made of such hide.

raw material *n.* **1.** An unprocessed natural product used in manufacturing. **2.** Unprocessed material of any kind: *These surveys are the raw material for my analysis.*

ray[1] (rā) *n.* **1.** A thin line or narrow beam of light or other radiation. **2.** A small amount; a trace: *a ray of hope.* **3.** A line or part extending from a point. **4.** A narrow flower resembling a petal, as one of those surrounding the dense disk-shaped central flower cluster of a daisy or sunflower. [First written down about 1380 in Middle English, from Latin *radius*.]

❑ *These sound alike:* **ray[1]** (beam), **ray[2]** (fish), **re[1]** (musical tone).

ray[2] (rā) *n.* Any of various ocean fishes having a horizontally flattened body, often with the fins forming extensions resembling wings, and a long narrow tail. [First written down in 1323 in Middle English and spelled *raye*, from Latin *raia*.]

❑ *These sound alike:* **ray[2]** (fish), **ray[1]** (beam), **re[1]** (musical tone).

ray•on (rā′ŏn) *n.* **1.** Any of several types of synthetic fibers made from cellulose. **2.** Fabric made from such fibers.

raze (rāz) *tr.v.* **razed, raz•ing, raz•es.** To destroy or tear down completely; level: *razed old tenements.*

❑ *These sound alike:* **raze, raise** (lift up).

ra•zor (rā′zər) *n.* A sharp cutting instrument, used primarily for shaving the face or removing other body hair.

razz (răz) *Slang. tr.v.* **razzed, razz•ing, razz•es.** To ridicule; heckle.

Rb The symbol for the element **rubidium.**

RBI also **rbi** *abbr.* An abbreviation of run batted in.

RC *abbr.* An abbreviation of: **1.** Red Cross. **2.** Roman Catholic.

rd *abbr.* An abbreviation of rod (unit of measure).

RD *abbr.* An abbreviation of rural delivery.

rd. or **Rd.** *abbr.* An abbreviation of road.

re[1] (rā) *n.* In music, the second tone of a major scale. [First written down about 1325 in Middle English, from Medieval Latin.]

❑ *These sound alike:* **re[1]** (musical tone), **ray[1]** (beam), **ray[2]** (fish).

re[2] (rē) *prep.* Concerning; in reference to. [First written down in 1707 in Modern English, from Latin *rē*, a form of *rēs*, thing.]

Re The symbol for the element **rhenium.**

re– *pref.* A prefix that means: **1.** Again; anew: *reassemble.* **2.** Back; backward: *react.* —SEE NOTE.

reach (rēch) *v.* **reached, reach•ing, reach•es.** —*tr.* **1.** To stretch out or put forth (a body part); extend: *reached out an arm.* **2.** To touch or grasp by stretching out: *couldn't reach the shelf.* **3.** To arrive at; attain: *reached our destination; reaching a conclusion.* **4.** To succeed in communicating with; get in touch with: *reached the fire department in time to save the building.* **5.** To go or extend as far as; get to: *The property reaches the shore.* —*intr.* **1.** To thrust out or extend something. **2.** To try to grasp or touch something: *reached for a book.* **3.** To extend far in space or time: *a coat that reached to the knee; a career that reached over several decades.* —*n.* **1.** The act or an instance of stretching or thrusting out: *The frog seized the butterfly with a sudden reach of its tongue.* **2.** The distance or extent to which something can reach. **3.** The range of a person's understanding; comprehension: *a subject beyond their reach.* [First written down about 725 in Old English and spelled *rǣcan*.]

Synonyms: reach, achieve, attain, gain. These verbs mean to succeed in arriving at a goal or an objective. **Reach** is the most general term: *They reached shelter just before the storm broke.* **Achieve** suggests reaching by applying one's skill or initiative: *Through their pioneering research, the team of chemists achieved international fame.* **Attain** often means to reach because of the force of one's ambitions: *Soon she will attain her dream of becoming a lawyer.* **Gain** suggests making considerable effort to overcome obstacles: *Slowly the new management gained the workers' confidence.*

re•act (rē ăkt′) *intr.v.* **re•act•ed, re•act•ing, re•acts. 1.** To act in response to a stimulus or prompting: *The iris of the eye reacts to bright light.* **2.** To act in opposition to a former condition or act: *musicians who reacted against formal theory.* **3.** To undergo a reaction. —SEE NOTE.

re•ac•tant (rē ăk′tənt) *n.* A substance participating in a chemical reaction, especially a directly reacting substance present at the start of the reaction.

re•ac•tion (rē ăk′shən) *n.* **1.** A response to a stimulus. **2.** A reverse or opposing action: *the body's reaction to a drug.* **3.a.** The process or condition of taking part in a chemical change. **b.** A chemical change. **4.** Political opposition to progress or reform; extreme conservatism.

re•ac•tion•ar•y (rē ăk′shə nĕr′ē) *adj.* Opposing progress or reform; extremely conservative: *a reactionary politician.* —*n., pl.* **re•ac•tion•ar•ies.** An extreme conservative.

re•ac•ti•vate (rē ăk′tə vāt′) *tr.v.* **re•ac•ti•vat•ed, re•ac•ti•vat•ing, re•ac•ti•vates. 1.** To make active again. **2.** To restore (something) to its original effectiveness or ability to function. —**re•ac′ti•va′tion** *n.*

re•ac•tive (rē ăk′tĭv) *adj.* **1.** Tending to be responsive or to react to a stimulus. **2.** Characterized by reaction. **3.** Tending to participate in reactions.

re•ac•tor (rē ăk′tər) *n.* **1.** A person or thing that reacts to a stimulus. **2.** A nuclear reactor.

read (rēd) *v.* **read** (rĕd), **read•ing, reads.** —*tr.* **1.** To look through and take in the meaning of (written or printed characters, words, or sentences): *reading books.* **2.** To speak aloud the words of (something written or printed): *She read the poem while we listened.* **3.** To know (a language or system of notation) well enough to understand written and printed matter: *reads Chinese; reads music.* **4.a.** To examine and take in the meaning of (language in a form other than written or printed words or symbols): *reads American Sign Language; reads Braille.* **b.** To take in the meaning of (a graphic representation): *reading a map.* **5.** To detect by observing closely: *read disappointment in her eyes.* **6.** To indicate or register: *The speedometer read 50 miles*

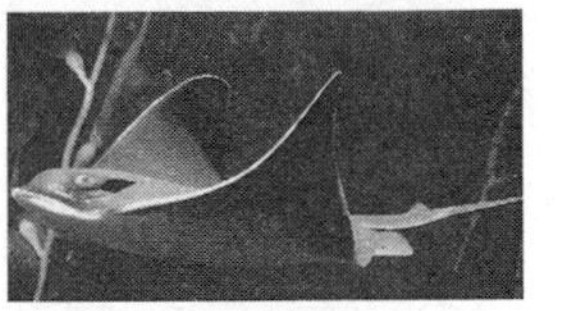

ray[2]

Word Building: re–

The primary meaning of the prefix **re–**, which comes from Latin, is "again." **Re–** combines chiefly with verbs, as in these examples: **rearrange, rebuild, recall, remake, rerun, rewrite**. The prefix has been used with this meaning extensively in English since the 1600's. Sometimes it is necessary to use a hyphen with **re–** to distinguish between pairs such as **recollect** [rĕk′ə **lĕkt′**] and *re-collect* [rē′kə **lĕkt′**] or **recreation** [rĕk′rē **ā′**shən] and *re-creation* [rē′krē **ā′**shən]. A hyphen may also be used when **re–** precedes a word beginning with *e*, as in *re-enact* and *re-enter*.

Word Building: react

The word root *–act–* in English words and the word **act** itself come from the past participle *āctus* of the Latin verb *agere*, "to drive, lead, do, perform, deal with, act." Thus we have **react**, "to respond to a stimulus, act in turn" (using the prefix *re–*, "backward"), and **transact**, "to carry through, manage, do business" (*trans–*, "through, across").

ă	**p**a**t**	oi	**b**oy
ā	**p**a**y**	ou	**ou**t
âr	**c**are	ŏŏ	**t**oo**k**
ä	**f**a**ther**	ōō	**b**oo**t**
ĕ	**p**e**t**	ŭ	**c**u**t**
ē	**b**e	ûr	**u**rge
ĭ	**p**i**t**	th	**th**in
ī	**p**ie	*th*	**th**is
îr	**p**ier	hw	**wh**oop
ŏ	**p**o**t**	zh	vi**s**ion
ō	**t**oe	ə	**a**bout
ô	**p**aw	N	*French* bo**n**

Ronald Reagan

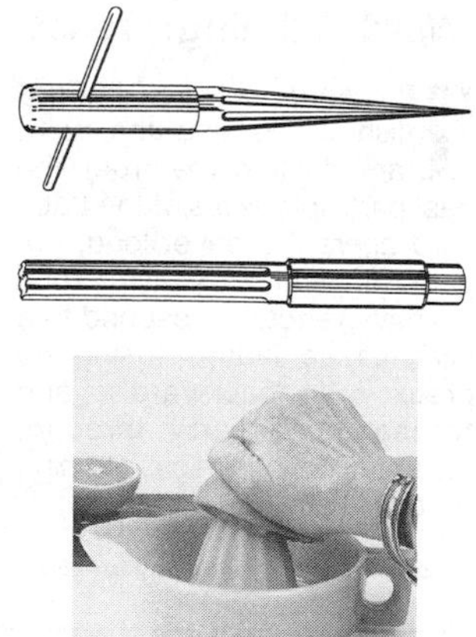

reamer

Top: Pipe (*top*) and fluted (*bottom*) reamers for enlarging holes *Bottom:* Juice reamer

per hour. —*intr.* **1.** To examine and take in the meaning of printed or written characters, as of words or music: *learning to read.* **2.** To speak aloud the words one is reading: *He reads to his children every night.* **3.** To learn by reading: *We read about the elections in the paper.* **4.** To have a certain wording: *Recite the poem exactly as it reads.* **5.** To have a certain character or quality for the reader: *Her prose reads well.* —*idioms.* **read between the lines.** To find a hidden or unexpressed meaning. **read out.** To read aloud. **read up.** To study or learn by reading: *We've been reading up on dinosaurs lately.* [First written down before 899 in Old English and spelled *rǣdan*, to advise.]

❑ *These sound alike:* **read, reed** (grass).

read•a•ble (rē′də bəl) *adj.* **1.** Easily read; legible: *a readable typeface.* **2.** Pleasurable or interesting to read. —**read′a•bil′i•ty, read′a•ble•ness** *n.*

read•er (rē′dər) *n.* **1.** A person who reads. **2.** A textbook with passages for practice in reading. **3.** A teaching assistant who reads and grades examination papers. **4.** An anthology, especially a literary anthology.

read•er•ship (rē′dər shĭp′) *n.* The readers of a publication considered as a group.

read•i•ly (rĕd′ə lē *or* rĕd′l ē) *adv.* **1.** Promptly. **2.** In a cooperative way; willingly: *advice that was readily accepted.* **3.** Without difficulty; easily: *paints that are readily available at a hardware store.*

read•ing (rē′dĭng) *n.* **1.** The act or activity of a person who reads. **2.** An official or public recitation of written material: *a poetry reading.* **3.** A personal interpretation: *We listened to her reading of the political situation.* **4.** Written or printed material. **5.** The data or information shown by a graduated instrument or gauge: *took a reading from the thermometer.*

re•ad•just (rē′ə jŭst′) *tr.v.* **re•ad•just•ed, re•ad•just•ing, re•ad•justs.** To adjust or arrange again: *readjust the settings on a machine.* —**re′ad•just′ment** *n.*

read•y (rĕd′ē) *adj.* **read•i•er, read•i•est. 1.** Prepared or available for action or use: *getting ready for school; ground ready for planting.* **2.** Inclined; willing: *ready to accept any reasonable offer.* **3.** Likely or about to do something: *He seemed ready to go.* **4.** Prompt in apprehending or reacting: *a ready wit; a ready response.* **5.** Available: *ready cash.* —*tr.v.* **read•ied, read•y•ing, read•ies.** To cause to be ready: *readied the boat to go fishing.* —*idiom.* **make ready.** To make preparations. [First written down before 899 in Old English and spelled *rǣde*.] —**read′i•ness** *n.*

read•y-made or **read•y•made** (rĕd′ē mād′) *adj.* **1.** Already made, prepared, or available: *a ready-made dinner.* **2.** Preconceived: *ready-made opinions.*

Rea•gan (rā′gən), **Ronald Wilson.** Born 1911. The 40th President of the United States (1981–1989).

re•a•gent (rē ā′jənt) *n.* A substance used in a chemical reaction to detect, measure, or produce another substance.

re•al¹ (rē′əl *or* rēl) *adj.* **1.** Not imaginary, fictional, or pretended; actual: *a story about real people; concealed his real purpose and identity.* **2.** Authentic and genuine; not artificial: *a real diamond, not a fake one.* See Synonyms at **authentic. 3.** Being no less than what is stated; worthy of the name: *a real friend.* **4.** Serious; not to be taken lightly: *in real trouble.* **5.** Of or indicating an image formed by light rays that converge in space. **6.** Of or relating to a real number. **7.** Of or relating to land, buildings, or other property that cannot be moved by the owner: *a tax on his real property.* —*adv. Informal.* Very: *I'm real sorry about that.* —*idiom.* **for real.** *Slang.* Truly so in fact or actuality: *That description can't be for real.* [First written down before 1325 in Middle English, from Latin *rēs*, thing.]

re•al² (rā äl′) *n., pl.* **re•als** or **re•al•es** (rā ä′lĕs). A silver coin formerly used in Spain and Latin America. [First written down in 1611 in Modern English, from Spanish *real*, royal, from Latin *rēgālis*.]

re•al estate (rē′əl *or* rēl) *n.* Land, including all the permanent buildings and natural resources on it.

re•al•ism (rē′ə lĭz′əm) *n.* **1.** A tendency to accept facts and be practical. **2.** The representation in art and literature of objects, actions, and social conditions as they actually are, without idealizing or presentation in abstract form. —**re′al•ist** *n.*

re•al•is•tic (rē′ə lĭs′tĭk) *adj.* **1.** Accurately represented, as in artistic or literary realism: *realistic characters in a play.* **2.** Tending to or expressing an awareness of facts and things as they actually are; practical: *a realistic admission of defeat.* —**re′al•is′ti•cal•ly** *adv.*

re•al•i•ty (rē ăl′ĭ tē) *n., pl.* **re•al•i•ties. 1.** The quality or condition of being actual or true: *Some scientists questioned the reality of global warming.* **2.** A person or thing that is real: *seeing their dreams become realities.* **3.** The state of things as they actually exist: *The reality of the situation is that we've spent all the money in the budget.* —*idiom.* **in reality.** In fact; actually.

re•al•i•za•tion (rē′ə lĭ zā′shən) *n.* **1.** The act of realizing or the condition of being realized: *shocked by the realization that they had run out of money.* **2.** The result of realizing: *the realization of his hopes.*

re•al•ize (rē′ə līz′) *tr.v.* **re•al•ized, re•al•iz•ing, re•al•iz•es. 1.** To understand completely or correctly; grasp: *He realized that the situation was serious.* **2.** To make real; fulfill: *realized her ambition to succeed.* **3.** To obtain or bring in, as profit or gain: *realized a large sum on the investment.*

re•al•ly (rē′ə lē′ *or* rē′lē) *adv.* **1.** In actual truth or fact: *The horseshoe crab isn't really a crab at all.* **2.** Truly; genuinely: *a really beautiful morning.* **3.** Indeed: *Really, you shouldn't have done it.*

realm (rĕlm) *n.* **1.** A kingdom. **2.** A field, sphere, or province: *the realm of piano music.*

re•al number (rē′əl *or* rēl) *n.* A member of the set of rational numbers or irrational numbers.

re•al•ty (rē′əl tē) *n., pl.* **re•al•ties.** Real estate.

ream¹ (rēm) *n.* **1.** A standard quantity of paper of the same size and stock, now usually 500 sheets. **2.** A very large amount. Often used in the plural. [First written down in 1356 in Middle English and spelled *reme*, from Arabic *rizmah*, bundle.]

ream² (rēm) *tr.v.* **reamed, ream•ing, reams. 1.** To shape, enlarge, or adjust (a hole) with or as if with a reamer: *reamed the hole in the wall after drilling it.* **2.** To squeeze the juice out of (fruit) with a reamer. [First written down in 1815 in Modern English, possibly from Middle English *remen*, to make room, from Old English *rȳman*.]

ream•er (rē′mər) *n.* **1.** A tool for shaping or enlarging holes. **2.** A kitchen utensil consisting of a ridged projection on a bowl, used for extracting juice from citrus fruits.

reap (rēp) *v.* **reaped, reap•ing, reaps.** —*tr.* **1.** To cut (grain or a similar crop) for harvest, as with a scythe: *reap wheat.* **2.a.** To harvest (a crop). **b.** To harvest a crop from: *reaping a field.* **3.** To gain as a result of effort: *Edison reaped fame from his many inventions.* —*intr.* To cut or harvest grain or a similar crop. [First written down before 830 in Old English and spelled *reopan*.]

reap•er (rē′pər) *n.* A person or machine that cuts down and gathers grain or a similar crop.

rear¹ (rîr) *n.* **1.** The part of something that is farthest from or opposite to the front: *the rear of the head.*

2. The part of an army or arrangement of troops or ships that is farthest from the fighting front. **3.** *Informal.* The buttocks. *—adj.* Of, at, or located in the rear: *a rear entrance.* [First written down before 1338 in Middle English and spelled *rere,* rear of an army, short for *rerewarde,* rear guard.]

rear² (rîr) *v.* **reared, rear•ing, rears.** *—tr.* **1.** To care for (children or a child) during the early stages of life; bring up. **2.** To tend (plants or animals): *rearing sheep for their wool.* **3.** To build; erect: *rear a skyscraper.* *—intr.* To rise on the hind legs, as a horse: *The frightened horse reared and neighed.* [First written down before 725 in Old English and spelled *rǣran,* to raise.]

rear admiral *n.* A commissioned officer in the U.S. Navy or Coast Guard, ranking above commodore and below vice admiral.

re•ar•range (rē′ə rānj′) *tr.v.* **re•ar•ranged, re•ar•rang•ing, re•ar•rang•es.** To change the arrangement of. **—re′ar•range′ment** *n.*

rear•ward (rîr′wərd) *adv. & adj.* At, to, or toward the rear. **—rear′wards** *adv.*

rea•son (rē′zən) *n.* **1.** The basis or motive for an action, a decision, or a belief. **2.** A statement or fact that justifies or explains an action, a decision, or a conviction: *I have reason to believe that he is wrong.* **3.** A fact or cause that explains why something exists or occurs: *reasons for being late.* **4.** The ability to think, understand, and make decisions logically and sensibly; intelligence. **5.** A normal mental state; sanity: *lost his reason.* **6.** Sound judgment; good sense: *a woman of reason.* *—v.* **rea•soned, rea•son•ing, rea•sons.** *—intr.* **1.** To use the ability to think logically and sensibly: *reason about the world.* **2.** To argue logically and persuasively: *tried to reason with the angry crowd.* *—tr.* To determine or conclude by logical thinking: *He reasoned out a solution to the problem.* ***—idioms.* by reason of.** Because of. **within reason.** Within the bounds of good sense or practicality. [First written down before 1200 in Middle English and spelled *reison,* from Latin *ratiō,* from *rērī,* to consider, think.]

rea•son•a•ble (rē′zə nə bəl) *adj.* **1.** Capable of reasoning: *a reasonable woman.* **2.** In accordance with reason; logical: *a reasonable solution.* **3.** Not excessive or extreme; fair: *a reasonable price.* **—rea′son•a•ble•ness** *n.* **—rea′son•a•bly** *adv.*

rea•son•ing (rē′zə nĭng) *n.* **1.** The use of reason, especially to form conclusions and judgments. **2.** Evidence or arguments used in thinking or argumentation.

re•as•sem•ble (rē′ə sĕm′bəl) *v.* **re•as•sem•bled, re•as•sem•bling, re•as•sem•bles.** *—tr.* **1.** To fit or join the parts of (something) together again. **2.** To bring or gather together again. *—intr.* To gather together again, especially in a different place.

re•as•sure (rē′ə shŏŏr′) *tr.v.* **re•as•sured, re•as•sur•ing, re•as•sures. 1.** To assure again: *He reassured me he would call back.* **2.** To restore confidence to (someone). **—re′as•sur′ance** *n.* **—re′as•sur′ing•ly** *adv.*

re•bate (rē′bāt′) *n.* A return of part of an amount given in payment or a reduction in an amount to be paid. *—tr.v.* (rē′bāt′ *or* rĭ bāt′). **re•bat•ed, re•bat•ing, re•bates.** To deduct or return (an amount).

re•bel (rĭ bĕl′) *intr.v.* **re•belled, re•bel•ling, re•bels. 1.** To refuse loyalty to and oppose by force an established government or a ruling authority. **2.** To resist or defy an authority or a generally accepted convention: *rebelled against wearing a tie in summer.* *—n.* **reb•el** (rĕb′əl). A person who rebels or is in rebellion. [First written down in 1340 in Middle English and spelled *rebelen,* from Latin *rebellāre,* from *bellum,* war.]

re•bel•lion (rĭ bĕl′yən) *n.* **1.** Open, organized, and armed resistance to an existing government. **2.** An act or a show of defiance toward an authority or established convention.

re•bel•lious (rĭ bĕl′yəs) *adj.* **1.** Prone to or participating in a rebellion. **2.** Of, relating to, or characteristic of a rebellion: *rebellious behavior.* **3.** Resisting treatment: *a rebellious infection.* **—re•bel′lious•ly** *adv.* **—re•bel′lious•ness** *n.*

re•birth (rē bûrth′ *or* rē′bûrth′) *n.* **1.** A second or new birth; reincarnation. **2.** A renaissance; a revival: *the rebirth of classical learning.*

re•born (rē bôrn′) *adj.* Emotionally or spiritually revived.

re•bound (rē′bound′ *or* rĭ bound′) *v.* **re•bound•ed, re•bound•ing, re•bounds.** *—intr.* **1.** To spring or bounce back after hitting or colliding with something. **2.** To recover, as from depression or disappointment. **3.** In basketball, to gain possession of the ball as it bounces off the backboard or rim. *—tr.* To cause to rebound. *—n.* (rē′bound′ *or* rĭ bound′). **1.** A springing or bounding back: *hit the ball on the rebound.* **2.** In basketball, the act or an instance of gaining possession of a ball as it bounces off the backboard or rim.

re•buff (rĭ bŭf′) *n.* An unfriendly reply or response, as to an offer; a blunt refusal, snub, or repulse. *—tr.v.* **re•buffed, re•buff•ing, re•buffs.** To reject bluntly, often disdainfully; snub: *They rebuffed our offer to help.*

re•build (rē bĭld′) *tr.v.* **re•built** (rē bĭlt′), **re•build•ing, re•builds.** To build again; reconstruct: *rebuild a church.*

re•buke (rĭ byōōk′) *tr.v.* **re•buked, re•buk•ing, re•bukes.** To criticize sharply; reprimand. *—n.* An expression of strong disapproval.

re•bus (rē′bəs) *n.* **re•bus•es.** A puzzle composed of words that appear in the form of pictures or symbols.

re•but (rĭ bŭt′) *v.* **re•but•ted, re•but•ting, re•buts.** *—tr.* To prove (something) false, especially by presenting opposing evidence or arguments. *—intr.* To present opposing evidence or arguments.

re•but•tal (rĭ bŭt′l) *n.* **1.** The act of rebutting. **2.** A statement made in rebutting.

re•cal•ci•trant (rĭ kăl′sĭ trənt) *adj.* Marked by stubborn resistance to and defiance of authority and guidance: *a recalcitrant child.* **—re•cal′ci•trance** *n.*

re•call (rĭ kôl′) *tr.v.* **re•called, re•call•ing, re•calls. 1.** To ask or order to return: *The government recalled the ambassador.* **2.** To remember; recollect: *recalling his boyhood love of horses.* **3.** To cancel, take back, or revoke: *recall a promise.* *—n.* (*also* rē′kôl′). **1.** The act of recalling or summoning back, especially an official order to return. **2.** The ability to remember information or experiences. **3.** The procedure by which a public official may be removed from office by popular vote.

re•cant (rĭ kănt′) *v.* **re•cant•ed, re•cant•ing, re•cants.** *—tr.* To take back or deny the validity of (a statement or belief previously held): *recanted his position on the new tax bill.* *—intr.* To make a formal denial or disavowal of a previously held statement or belief. **—re′can•ta′tion** (rē′kăn tā′shən) *n.*

re•ca•pit•u•late (rē′kə pĭch′ə lāt′) *v.* **re•ca•pit•u•lat•ed, re•ca•pit•u•lat•ing, re•ca•pit•u•lates.** *—tr.* To repeat in shorter form; summarize or sum up. *—intr.* To make a summary. **—re′ca•pit′u•la′tion** *n.*

re•cap•ture (rē kăp′chər) *n.* The act of taking again or recovering. *—tr.v.* **re•cap•tured, re•cap•tur•ing, re•cap•tures. 1.** To capture again: *recapture a city.* **2.** To recollect or recall vividly.

re•cast (rē kăst′) *tr.v.* **re•cast, re•cast•ing, re•**

rebus
Detail of a rebus by Benjamin Franklin that reads "embrace these rules and be happy"

ă	pat	oi	boy
ā	pay	ou	out
âr	care	ŏŏ	took
ä	father	ōō	boot
ĕ	pet	ŭ	cut
ē	be	ûr	urge
ĭ	pit	th	thin
ī	pie	*th*	this
îr	pier	hw	whoop
ŏ	pot	zh	vision
ō	toe	ə	about
ô	paw	N	*French* bon

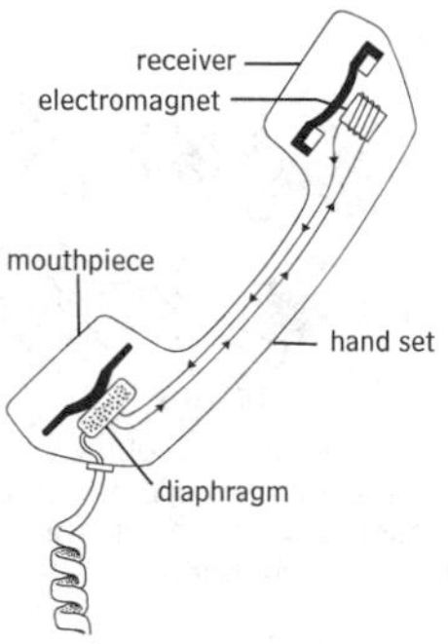

receiver
Telephone hand set

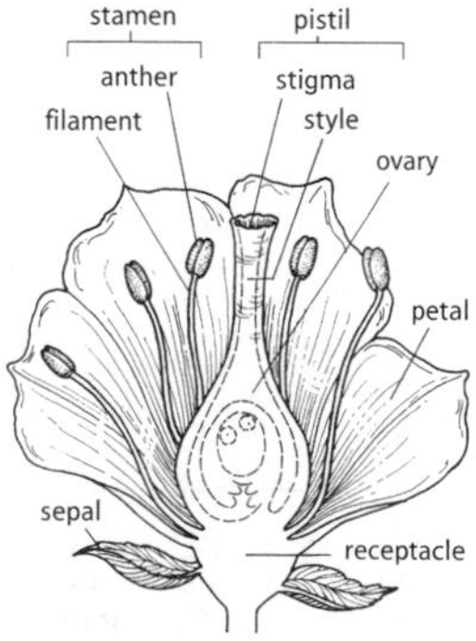

receptacle

casts. 1. To mold again: *She recast the statue.* **2.** To rearrange, as with a new wording or form: *recast a question.*

recd. *abbr.* An abbreviation of received.

re•cede (rĭ sēd′) *intr.v.* **re•ced•ed, re•ced•ing, re•cedes. 1.** To move back or away from a limit, point, or mark: *The flood waters finally receded.* **2.** To slope backward: *a man with a chin that recedes.* **3.** To become fainter or more distant: *Over the years his memory of that summer receded.*

re•ceipt (rĭ sēt′) *n.* **1.** The act of receiving or the fact of being or having been received: *at receipt of word from you.* **2.** The quantity or amount received. Often used in the plural: *box office receipts.* **3.** A written acknowledgment that a specified article, sum of money, or shipment of merchandise has been received. **4.** A recipe. —*tr.v.* **re•ceipt•ed, re•ceipt•ing, re•ceipts. 1.** To mark (a bill) as having been paid. **2.** To give or write a receipt for (money paid or goods or services delivered).

re•ceiv•a•ble (rĭ sē′və bəl) *adj.* Awaiting or requiring payment; due or collectible: *accounts receivable.*

re•ceive (rĭ sēv′) *v.* **re•ceived, re•ceiv•ing, re•ceives.** —*tr.* **1.** To get or acquire (something given, offered, or transmitted): *receive payment.* **2.** To hear or see (information, for example): *received good news.* **3.** To bear the weight of; support: *girders received the weight of the building.* **4.** To experience or be given: *receive a fine.* **5.** To take the force or impact of (a blow, for example): *The island received the full fury of the gale.* **6.** To partake of (Holy Communion). **7.** To greet or welcome: *They received us as if we were royalty.* **8.** To regard with approval or disapproval: *The movie was well received.* —*intr.* **1.** To acquire or get something. **2.** To partake of Holy Communion. **3.** To convert electromagnetic signals into visible or audible signals, as in radio. [First written down before 1300 in Middle English and spelled *resceiven*, from Latin *recipere* : *re-*, back + *capere*, to take.]

re•ceiv•er (rĭ sē′vər) *n.* **1.** A person or thing that receives; a recipient. **2.** A person appointed by a court to hold the funds or property of another while a court case is being decided. **3.** The unit of a communications system, such as radio or television, that receives an incoming signal and converts it, as into a sound or light. **4.** In football, a member of the offensive team who is eligible to catch a forward pass.

re•ceiv•er•ship (rĭ sē′vər shĭp′) *n.* **1.** The office or function of a court-appointed receiver. **2.** The condition of being held by a court-appointed receiver.

re•cent (rē′sənt) *adj.* **1.** Of, belonging to, or occurring at a time immediately before the present. **2. Recent.** Of, belonging to, or indicating the Holocene Epoch. See table at **geologic time.** [First written down before 1425 in Middle English, from Latin *recēns.*] **—re′cent•ly** *adv.* **—re′cent•ness** *n.*

re•cep•ta•cle (rĭ sĕp′tə kəl) *n.* **1.** A container that holds items or matter. **2.** The expanded tip of a stalk or stem that bears a flower or group of flowers.

re•cep•tion (rĭ sĕp′shən) *n.* **1.** The act or process of receiving or of being received. **2.** A welcome, greeting, or acceptance: *a friendly reception.* **3.** A social gathering, especially one honoring or introducing someone: *a wedding reception.* **4.a.** The act or process of receiving electrical or electromagnetic signals. **b.** The quality or condition of the signals received. [First written down before 1393 in Middle English and spelled *recepcion*, from Latin *receptiō*, from *recipere*, to receive.]

re•cep•tion•ist (rĭ sĕp′shə nĭst) *n.* An office worker employed chiefly to receive visitors and answer the telephone.

re•cep•tive (rĭ sĕp′tĭv) *adj.* Ready or willing to receive favorably: *receptive to change.* **—re•cep′tive•ly** *adv.* **—re•cep′tive•ness** *n.*

re•cep•tor (rĭ sĕp′tər) *n.* **1.** A nerve ending specialized to sense or receive stimuli. **2.** A structure or site on a cell that is capable of combining with a hormone, antigen, globulin, or other chemical substance.

re•cess (rē′sĕs′ *or* rĭ sĕs′) *n.* **1.a.** A temporary halt in or stoppage of customary activity: *a court recess ordered by the judge.* See Synonyms at **pause. b.** The period of such a halt: *played games during recess at school.* **2.** A remote, secret, or secluded place. Often used in the plural: *the hidden recesses of her desk.* **3.** A small hollow; an indentation. —*v.* **re•cessed, re•cess•ing, re•cess•es.** —*tr.* **1.** To put in a hollow or an indentation. **2.** To make a hollow place or indentation in: *recessed the wall to provide room for shelves.* —*intr.* To take a recess.

re•ces•sion (rĭ sĕsh′ən) *n.* **1.** The act of withdrawing or going back. **2.** An extended decline in economic activity.

re•ces•sion•al (rĭ sĕsh′ə nəl) *n.* A hymn played as the clergy and choir exit after a church service.

re•ces•sive (rĭ sĕs′ĭv) *adj.* **1.** Tending to recede or go backward. **2.** Of or relating to a gene whose influence on the physical characteristics of an organism is suppressed by the influence of another gene. —*n.* A recessive gene.

rec•i•pe (rĕs′ə pē′) *n.* **1.** A set of directions with a list of ingredients for making or preparing something, especially food. **2.** A formula for accomplishing a certain thing: *a recipe for success.* [First written down in 1584 in Modern English, from Latin, imperative of *recipere*, to take, receive.]

re•cip•i•ent (rĭ sĭp′ē ənt) *adj.* Receiving or able to receive. —*n.* A person or thing that receives something: *the recipient of an award.*

re•cip•ro•cal (rĭ sĭp′rə kəl) *adj.* **1.** Concerning each of two or more persons or things. **2.** Interchanged, given, or owed to each other: *The two countries made reciprocal trade agreements.* **3.** Felt, experienced, or done by both sides; mutual: *reciprocal respect as a basis for true partnership.* **4.** Of or indicating either of a pair of numbers whose product is 1. —*n.* Either of a pair of numbers whose product is 1; for example, the number *a* is the reciprocal of $1/a$. [First written down in 1570 in Modern English, from Latin *reciprocus*, alternating.] **—re•cip′ro•cal•ly** *adv.*

re•cip•ro•cate (rĭ sĭp′rə kāt′) *v.* **re•cip•ro•cat•ed, re•cip•ro•cat•ing, re•cip•ro•cates.** —*tr.* **1.** To give or take mutually: *reciprocating favors.* **2.** To show or feel in return: *reciprocated her love.* —*intr.* **1.** To move back and forth alternately, as a machine part: *a power saw that reciprocates.* **2.** To make a return for something given or done: *You buy lunch today, and I'll reciprocate tomorrow.* **—re•cip′ro•ca′tion** *n.*

rec•i•proc•i•ty (rĕs′ə prŏs′ĭ tē) *n., pl.* **rec•i•proc•i•ties. 1.** A reciprocal condition or relationship. **2.** A mutual exchange or interchange, especially the exchange of rights or privileges of trade between nations.

re•cit•al (rĭ sīt′l) *n.* **1.** The act of reading or reciting in a public performance. **2.** A very detailed account or report of something: *the traveler's recital of his experiences.* **3.** A performance of music or dance, especially one by a solo performer.

rec•i•ta•tion (rĕs′ĭ tā′shən) *n.* **1.** The act of reciting something memorized, as a poem or an oration, in a public performance. **2.** The material presented in a public recitation. **3.** A spoken presentation or report of prepared lessons by a student in school.

rec•i•ta•tive¹ (rĕs′ĭ tā′tĭv *or* rĭ sī′tə tĭv) *adj.* Of, relating to, or being a recital or recitation.

rec•i•ta•tive² (rĕs′ĭ tə tēv′) *n.* **1.** A style of singing in which words are sung with the rhythm of speech, used in opera and oration. **2.** A musical passage sung in this style.

re•cite (rĭ sīt′) *v.* **re•cit•ed, re•cit•ing, re•cites.** —*tr.* **1.** To repeat or say aloud (something prepared or memorized), especially before an audience. **2.** To tell in detail: *recited his difficulties.* —*intr.* **1.** To give a recitation. **2.** To repeat lessons prepared or memorized. [First written down in 1430 in Middle English and spelled *reciten,* from Latin *recitāre,* to read out.]

reck•less (rĕk′lĭs) *adj.* Lacking care or caution; careless: *reckless driving.* [First written down before 899 in Old English and spelled *rēcelēas.*] —**reck′less•ly** *adv.* —**reck′less•ness** *n.*

reck•on (rĕk′ən) *v.* **reck•oned, reck•on•ing, reck•ons.** —*tr.* **1.** To count or calculate; figure: *reckon time.* **2.** To consider as being; regard as: *reckon him an expert in the field.* **3.** *Informal.* To think or assume: *Do you reckon we'll be through in time?* —*intr.* **1.** To make a calculation; figure. **2.** To anticipate; expect: *We didn't reckon on so many guests.* —***idiom.*** **reckon with.** To come to terms or settle accounts with. [First written down before 1000 in Old English and spelled *gerecenian,* to recount, arrange.]

reck•on•ing (rĕk′ə nĭng) *n.* **1.** The act of counting or computing. **2.** A statement of an amount due. **3.** A settlement of accounts: *a day of reckoning.* **4.** The act or process of calculating the position of a ship or an aircraft.

re•claim (rĭ klām′) *tr.v.* **re•claimed, re•claim•ing, re•claims. 1.** To make (land) usable for growing crops or living on, as by draining, irrigating, or fertilizing. **2.** To extract (useful substances) from garbage or waste products. **3.** To turn back, as from error, to a right or proper course; reform. —**re•claim′a•ble** *adj.* —**rec′la•ma′tion** (rĕk′lə mā′shən) *n.*

re•cline (rĭ klīn′) *intr.v.* **re•clined, re•clin•ing, re•clines.** To lie back or down: *reclined on the couch.* [First written down before 1425 in Middle English and spelled *reclinen,* from Latin *reclīnāre* : *re-,* back + *-clīnāre,* to bend, lean.]

re•cluse (rĕk′lo͞os′ *or* rĭ klo͞os′) *n.* A person who withdraws from the world to live in seclusion or solitude. —*adj.* Withdrawn from the world; solitary. [First written down before 1200 in Middle English, from Latin *reclūsus,* shut up : *re-,* back, up + *claudere,* to close.]

rec•og•ni•tion (rĕk′əg nĭsh′ən) *n.* **1.** The act of recognizing or the condition of being recognized. **2.** Acknowledgment or approval: *an award in recognition of excellent service.* **3.** Attention or favorable notice; praise: *world recognition for his work in physics.*

rec•og•nize (rĕk′əg nīz′) *tr.v.* **rec•og•nized, rec•og•niz•ing, rec•og•niz•es. 1.** To know to be something that has been perceived before: *She recognized his face from the photo.* **2.** To know or identify from past experience or knowledge: *I recognized friendliness in her smile.* **3.** To accept as valid or real: *recognize the concerns of taxpayers.* **4.** To acknowledge or approve of: *recognized his right to vote.* **5.** To accept officially the national status of (a new nation). **6.** To permit (someone) to speak at a meeting. —**rec′og•niz′a•ble** *adj.* —**rec′og•niz′a•bly** *adv.*

re•coil (rĭ koil′) *intr.v.* **re•coiled, re•coil•ing, re•coils. 1.** To move or jerk backward, as a gun upon firing. **2.** To shrink back in fear or dislike. **3.** To fall back; return: *Your rudeness will one day recoil upon you.* —*n.* (*also* rē′koil′). **1.** The backward action of a firearm upon firing. **2.** The act of recoiling.

rec•ol•lect (rĕk′ə lĕkt′) *tr. & intr.v.* **rec•ol•lect•ed, rec•ol•lect•ing, rec•ol•lects.** To remember.

rec•ol•lec•tion (rĕk′ə lĕk′shən) *n.* **1.** The act or power of recollecting. **2.** Something recollected: *I have no recollection of meeting him.*

re•com•bi•nant DNA (rē kŏm′bə nənt) *n.* DNA altered through laboratory manipulation in which genes from one organism are transplanted or spliced into the genetic material of an organism of a different species.

rec•om•mend (rĕk′ə mĕnd′) *tr.v.* **rec•om•mend•ed, rec•om•mend•ing, rec•om•mends. 1.** To praise or commend to another as being worthy or desirable: *I highly recommend her for the job.* **2.** To advise or counsel (a course of action). **3.** To make attractive or acceptable: *His honesty recommends him.*

rec•om•men•da•tion (rĕk′ə mĕn dā′shən) *n.* **1.** The act of recommending. **2.** Something that recommends, especially a favorable statement about someone's qualifications or character.

rec•om•pense (rĕk′əm pĕns′) *tr.v.* **rec•om•pensed, rec•om•pens•ing, rec•om•pens•es. 1.** To pay or reward, as for something done: *recompensed her for her services.* **2.** To make up for: *recompense losses.* —*n.* **1.** Amends made for something, such as damage or loss. **2.** Payment in return for something given or done.

rec•on•cile (rĕk′ən sīl′) *tr.v.* **rec•on•ciled, rec•on•cil•ing, rec•on•ciles. 1.** To restore friendship between; make friendly again: *reconcile old enemies.* **2.** To settle or resolve, as a dispute. **3.** To bring (oneself) to accept: *reconciling herself to the loss of a ring.* **4.** To bring into harmony or agreement: *reconcile different points of view.* —**rec′on•cile′ment** *n.* —**rec′on•cil′i•a′tion** (rĕk′ən sĭl′ē ā′shən) *n.*

re•con•di•tion (rē′kən dĭsh′ən) *tr.v.* **re•con•di•tioned, re•con•di•tion•ing, re•con•di•tions.** To restore by repairing, renovating, or rebuilding.

re•con•nais•sance (rĭ kŏn′ə səns) *n.* An inspection or exploration of an area, especially one made to gather information about the presence, arrangement, or activity of military forces.

re•con•noi•ter (rē′kə noi′tər *or* rĕk′ə noi′tər) *v.* **re•con•noi•tered, re•con•noi•ter•ing, re•con•noi•ters.** —*tr.* To make a survey or inspection of, especially to gain information. —*intr.* To make a reconnaisance. —**re′con•noi′ter•er** *n.*

re•con•sid•er (rē′kən sĭd′ər) *tr.v.* **re•con•sid•ered, re•con•sid•er•ing, re•con•sid•ers.** To consider again, especially with the possibility of making a change. —**re′con•sid′er•a′tion** *n.*

re•con•struct (rē′kən strŭkt′) *tr.v.* **re•con•struct•ed, re•con•struct•ing, re•con•structs. 1.** To construct or build again; restore. **2.** To determine or trace from information or clues: *reconstruct the events that preceded the accident.*

re•con•struc•tion (rē′kən strŭk′shən) *n.* **1.** The act or result of reconstructing. **2. Reconstruction.** The period from 1865 to 1877, during which the states of the Confederacy were controlled by the federal government before being readmitted to the Union. —**re′con•struc′tive** *adj.*

re•cord (rĭ kôrd′) *tr.v.* **re•cord•ed, re•cord•ing, re•cords. 1.** To set down for preservation in writing or other permanent form: *She recorded each change of course in the logbook.* **2.** To register or indicate, especially in permanent form: *A thermometer records temperature.* **3.** To store (sound or images) in some permanent form, such as a series of variations in the magnetization of a tape. —*n.* **rec•ord** (rĕk′ərd). **1.** An account usually set down in writing as

ă	pat	oi	boy
ā	pay	ou	out
âr	care	o͝o	took
ä	father	o͞o	boot
ĕ	pet	ŭ	cut
ē	be	ûr	urge
ĭ	pit	th	thin
ī	pie	*th*	this
îr	pier	hw	whoop
ŏ	pot	zh	vision
ō	toe	ə	about
ô	paw	ɴ	*French* bon

recorder

Word Building: rectify

The word roots *–rect–* and *–recti–* in English words come from the past participle *rēctus* of the Latin verb *regere*, "to make or keep straight, guide, direct, rule." Hence we have **rectify**, "to make right, remedy" (using the suffix *–fy*, "to make"); **rectangle**, "a figure with four right angles"; **rectitude**, "uprightness"; and **rectilinear**, "in a straight line." From the same Latin word root *reg–* comes the Latin noun *rēgula*, "a rod for measuring or drawing straight lines; ruler; rule." Its adjective *rēgulāris*, "conforming to the rule, regular," is the source of our word **regular**.

Red Cloud
Photographed in 1880

a means of preserving knowledge: *a record of what happened on the trip.* **2.** Something that records past events: *a fossil record.* **3.** The known history of performance or achievement: *your high-school record.* **4.** The highest or lowest measurement known, as in a sports event or weather readings: *the record for least rainfall in a year.* **5.** A disk designed to be played on a phonograph. **6.** A collection of related data treated as a unit in a computer memory. **—*idioms.* off the record.** Not for publication: *The senator told the reporters that his remarks were off the record.* **on record.** Known to have been stated or to have taken a certain position: *She's on record as opposing the new law.* [First written down before 1200 in Middle English and spelled *recorden*, from Latin *recordārī*, to remember.]

re•cord•er (rĭ **kôr′**dər) *n.* **1.** A person or thing that records. **2.** A flute with a whistlelike mouthpiece and eight holes.

re•cord•ing (rĭ **kôr′**dĭng) *n.* **1.** Something on which sound or visual images have been recorded, as a magnetic tape or a compact disk. **2.** A recorded sound or picture.

re•count (rĭ **kount′**) *tr.v.* **re•count•ed, re•count•ing, re•counts.** To tell in detail; narrate the particulars of: *The book recounts the siege of Troy.*

re•coup (rĭ **ko͞op′**) *tr.v.* **re•couped, re•coup•ing, re•coups. 1.** To receive the equivalent of (something lost); make up for: *recouped his losses when the stock market rebounded.* **2.** To pay back; compensate: *The landlord recouped the tenants for damages.* [First written down about 1450 in Middle English and spelled *recoupen*, to cut short, from Old French *recouper*, to cut back.]

re•course (**rē′**kôrs′ *or* rĭ **kôrs′**) *n.* **1.** The act or an instance of turning or applying to a person or thing for aid or protection: *You have recourse to the courts.* **2.** A person or thing to turn to for help or protection.

re•cov•er (rĭ **kŭv′**ər) *v.* **re•cov•ered, re•cov•er•ing, re•cov•ers.** *—tr.* **1.** To get back; regain: *The police tried to recover the stolen bicycle.* **2.** To regain control over (oneself): *recovered himself sufficiently to speak in public.* **3.** To make up for; compensate for: *She recovered her losses.* *—intr.* To return to a normal or healthy condition: *recover after a long illness.* **—re•cov′er•a•ble** *adj.*

re•cov•er•y (rĭ **kŭv′**ə rē) *n., pl.* **re•cov•er•ies. 1.** A return to a normal condition, as of health. **2.** The act of getting back or regaining.

recovery room *n.* A hospital room equipped for the care and observation of patients immediately following surgery.

rec•re•ant (**rĕk′**rē ənt) *adj.* **1.** Unfaithful or disloyal. **2.** Cowardly. *—n.* **1.** An unfaithful or disloyal person. **2.** A coward.

re-cre•ate (rē′krē **āt′**) *tr.v.* **re-cre•at•ed, re-cre•at•ing, re-cre•ates.** To create again or anew.

rec•re•a•tion (rĕk′rē **ā′**shən) *n.* Refreshment of one's mind or body after work through some activity, such as a sport or game, that amuses or excites. **—rec′re•a′tion•al** *adj.*

re•crim•i•nate (rĭ **krĭm′**ə nāt′) *intr.v.* **re•crim•i•nat•ed, re•crim•i•nat•ing, re•crim•i•nates.** To counter one accusation with another. **—re•crim′i•na′tion** *n.*

re•cruit (rĭ **kro͞ot′**) *tr.v.* **re•cruit•ed, re•cruit•ing, re•cruits. 1.a.** To enlist (persons) in military service. **b.** To raise (an armed force) by enlistment: *recruit a new army.* **2.** To supply with new members or employees: *They recruited new editors for the magazine.* **3.** To enroll or try to enroll: *She's recruiting students for a new course in geology.* *—n.* **1.** A newly enlisted member of the armed forces. **2.** A new member of any organization or body of persons. **—re•cruit′er** *n.* **—re•cruit′ment** *n.*

rec•tal (**rĕk′**təl) *adj.* Of, relating to, or near the rectum.

rec•tan•gle (**rĕk′**tăng′gəl) *n.* A four-sided plane figure with four right angles. [First written down in 1571 in Modern English, from Medieval Latin *rēctangulum*, a right triangle : Latin *rēctus*, right, straight + Latin *angulus*, angle.]

rec•tan•gu•lar (rĕk **tăng′**gyə lər) *adj.* **1.** Having the shape of a rectangle. **2.** Being a system of coordinates using axes that meet at right angles.

rec•ti•fy (**rĕk′**tə fī′) *tr.v.* **rec•ti•fied, rec•ti•fy•ing, rec•ti•fies. 1.** To set right; correct. **2.** To refine or purify, especially by distillation. [First written down in 1392 in Middle English and spelled *rectifien*, from Latin *rēctus*, right.] —SEE NOTE.

rec•ti•lin•e•ar (rĕk′tə **lĭn′**ē ər) *adj.* Moving in, consisting of, bounded by, or characterized by a straight line or lines.

rec•ti•tude (**rĕk′**tĭ to͞od′ *or* **rĕk′**tĭ tyo͞od′) *n.* Moral goodness.

rec•tor (**rĕk′**tər) *n.* **1.** In the Episcopal and Anglican churches, a cleric in charge of a parish. **2.** In the Roman Catholic Church, a priest in a church, seminary, or university who is both its spiritual head and the manager of its affairs. **3.** The principal of certain schools, colleges, or universities.

rec•to•ry (**rĕk′**tə rē) *n., pl.* **rec•to•ries.** The house in which a rector lives.

rec•tum (**rĕk′**təm) *n., pl.* **rec•tums** or **rec•ta** (**rĕk′**tə). The lower end of the alimentary canal, extending from the colon to the anus, where feces are stored until excreted from the body.

re•cum•bent (rĭ **kŭm′**bənt) *adj.* Lying down; reclining. **—re•cum′bent•ly** *adv.*

re•cu•per•ate (rĭ **ko͞o′**pə rāt′ *or* rĭ **kyo͞o′**pə rāt′) *intr.v.* **re•cu•per•at•ed, re•cu•per•at•ing, re•cu•per•ates. 1.** To return to normal health or strength; recover. **2.** To recover from a financial loss. **—re•cu′per•a′tion** *n.* **—re•cu′per•a′tive** *adj.*

re•cur (rĭ **kûr′**) *intr.v.* **re•curred, re•cur•ring, re•curs. 1.** To happen, come up, or show up again or repeatedly; return: *an area where earthquakes recur.* **2.** To return to one's attention or memory: *His name doesn't recur to me.* **3.** To return in thought or in writing or speaking: *The speaker recurred to the main point of his speech.* [First written down in 1529 in Modern English, from Latin *recurrere* : *re-*, back + *currere*, to run.]

re•cur•rent (rĭ **kûr′**ənt *or* rĭ **kŭr′**ənt) *adj.* Occurring or appearing again or repeatedly; returning regularly. **—re•cur′rence** *n.*

re•cy•cle (rē **sī′**kəl) *tr.v.* **re•cy•cled, re•cy•cling, re•cy•cles. 1.** To extract useful materials from (garbage or waste). **2.** To extract and reuse (useful substances found in garbage or waste).

red (rĕd) *n.* **1.** The color of blood or of a ripe strawberry. **2.** Often **Red.** A revolutionary, especially a Communist. *—adj.* **red•der, red•dest. 1.** Having a color resembling that of blood or a ripe strawberry. **2.** Often **Red.** Communist. **—*idiom.* in the red.** Operating at a loss; in debt. [First written down about 700 in Old English and spelled *rēad*.] **—red′ness** *n.*

red•bird (**rĕd′**bûrd′) *n.* Any of various birds having red feathers, such as the cardinal or scarlet tanager.

red blood cell *n.* Any of the cells in the blood that contain hemoglobin and give the blood its red color. Red blood cells carry oxygen from the lungs to various parts of the body.

red-blood•ed (**rĕd′blŭd′**ĭd) *adj.* Strong and full of vigor.

red•breast (**rĕd′**brĕst′) *n.* A bird, such as a robin, that has a red breast.

red•cap (rĕd′kăp′) *n.* A porter, usually in a railroad station.

Red Cloud. 1822–1909. Sioux leader of the resistance against the development of a trail through Wyoming and Montana by the U.S. government (1865–1867).

red•coat (rĕd′kōt′) *n.* A British soldier during the American Revolution and the War of 1812.

Red Cross *n.* An international organization that cares for the victims of war, floods, earthquakes, and other disasters.

red deer *n.* **1.** A European deer having reddish-brown coat and branching antlers. **2.** A North American deer that has a reddish coat in the summer.

red•den (rĕd′n) *tr. & intr.v.* **red•dened, red•den•ing, red•dens.** To make or become red.

red•dish (rĕd′ĭsh) *adj.* Somewhat red.

re•deem (rĭ dēm′) *tr.v.* **re•deemed, re•deem•ing, re•deems. 1.** To recover ownership of by paying a specified sum: *redeemed his ring from the pawnbroker.* **2.** To pay off (a mortgage, for example). **3.** To turn in (coupons, for example) and receive something in exchange. **4.** To exchange (stocks or bonds, for example) for cash. **5.a.** To set free; rescue. **b.** To save from sin and its consequences. **6.** To make up for: *a deed that redeemed her earlier mistake.* [First written down about 1415 in Middle English and spelled *redemen*, from Latin *redimere* : *re-*, *red-*, back + *emere*, to buy.] **—re•deem′a•ble** *adj.*

re•deem•er (rĭ dē′mər) *n.* **1.** A person who redeems. **2. Redeemer.** Jesus.

re•demp•tion (rĭ dĕmp′shən) *n.* **1.** The act of redeeming: *redemption of a promissory note.* **2.** The recovery of something pawned or mortgaged; a repurchase. **3.** The act of rescuing, as by payment of ransom or by complying with demands: *redemption of hostages.* **4.** In Christianity, salvation from sin through Jesus's sacrifice.

red-hand•ed (rĕd′hăn′dĭd) *adv.* In the act of committing something wrong: *The thief was caught red-handed with the loot.*

red•head (rĕd′hĕd′) *n.* A person with red hair.

red•head•ed (rĕd′hĕd′ĭd) *adj.* Having red hair: *a redheaded boy.*

red herring *n.* **1.** A smoked herring having a reddish color. **2.** Something that draws attention away from the subject under notice or discussion.

red-hot (rĕd′hŏt′) *adj.* **1.** Hot enough to glow red: *a red-hot bar of steel.* **2.** Heated, as with excitement or anger. **3.** New; very recent: *red-hot information.*

red-let•ter (rĕd′lĕt′ər) *adj.* Memorably happy; important: *a red-letter day.*

red light *n.* **1.** A red light that signals traffic to stop. **2.** *Informal.* A command to stop.

red•o•lent (rĕd′l ənt) *adj.* **1.** Having or giving off a pleasant odor: *redolent thickets of honeysuckle.* **2.** Suggestive; reminiscent: *a campaign redolent of machine politics.* [First written down about 1400 in Middle English, from Latin *redolēre*, to smell.] **—red′o•lence** *n.* **—red′o•lent•ly** *adj.*

re•dou•ble (rē dŭb′əl) *tr. & intr.v.* **re•dou•bled, re•dou•bling, re•dou•bles.** To make or become twice as great.

re•doubt•a•ble (rĭ dou′tə bəl) *adj.* **1.** Causing awe or fear. **2.** Worthy of respect or honor.

re•dound (rĭ dound′) *intr.v.* **re•dound•ed, re•dound•ing, re•dounds.** To have an effect or a consequence: *Kind acts will redound to your credit.* [First written down in 1382 in Middle English and spelled *redounden*, from Latin *redundāre*, to overflow.]

red pepper *n.* **1.** The ripened fruit of any of several varieties of the pepper plant. **2.** Cayenne pepper.

re•dress (rĭ drĕs′) *tr.v.* **re•dressed, re•dress•ing, re•dress•es.** To set right; remedy or rectify: *The mayor agreed to redress their grievances.* —*n.* (*also* rē′drĕs). **1.** The act of setting right; correction; remedy: *a redress of a wrong.* **2.** Satisfaction for wrong done; reparation.

Red Sea. A long narrow sea between northeast Africa and the Arabian Peninsula. It is linked with the Mediterranean to the north and with the Arabian Sea to the south.

red snapper *n.* Any of several food fishes of tropical and semitropical waters, having red or reddish bodies.

red•start (rĕd′stärt′) *n.* **1.** A small North American bird, the male of which has black feathers and orange patches on the wings and tail. **2.** A European songbird having grayish feathers and a rust-red breast and tail.

red tape *n.* Procedures or practices, especially those connected with the official business of government, that require great attention to detail and often result in delay or inaction.

red tide *n.* Ocean waters colored by the presence of red plankton in sufficient numbers to kill fish.

re•duce (rĭ do͞os′ *or* rĭ dyo͞os′) *v.* **re•duced, re•duc•ing, re•duc•es.** —*tr.* **1.** To make less in amount, degree, or extent; diminish: *reduce the volume of the stereo.* See Synonyms at **decrease. 2.** To gain control of; conquer: *a plan to reduce the rebels.* **3.** To bring into a lower or worse condition or state: *The explosion reduced the building to rubble.* **4.a.** To lower the valence of (an atom or element). **b.** To remove oxygen from chemical combination with or in (an element or compound). **c.** To change to a pure metallic state; smelt. **5.** To change (a mathematical expression) into a simpler form without affecting its value or meaning. —*intr.* To lose body weight, as by dieting. [First written down about 1375 in Middle English and spelled *redusen*, to bring back, bring down, from Latin *redūcere* : *re-*, back + *dūcere*, to lead.] **—re•duc′er** *n.* **—re•duc′i•ble** *adj.*

re•duc•tion (rĭ dŭk′shən) *n.* **1.** The act or process of reducing. **2.** The result of reducing: *a reduction in unemployment.* **3.** The amount by which something is made smaller or less. **4.** The first cell division in meiosis, in which the number of chromosomes in the cell is reduced. **5.** The changing of a fraction into a simpler form, especially by dividing the numerator and denominator by any integral factors that they have in common.

re•dun•dan•cy (rĭ dŭn′dən sē) *n., pl.* **re•dun•dan•cies. 1.** The condition of being redundant. **2.** The use of unnecessary words. —SEE NOTE.

re•dun•dant (rĭ dŭn′dənt) *adj.* **1.** Composed of or containing more words than necessary; verbose: *a redundant paragraph in the speech.* **2.** Exceeding what is necessary; superfluous: *redundant machine parts.* [First written down in 1604 in Modern English, from Latin *redundāre*, to overflow : *re-*, *red-*, back + *unda*, wave.] **—re•dun′dant•ly** *adv.*

red-winged blackbird (rĕd′wĭngd′) *n.* A blackbird, the male of which has bright red patches on the wings.

red•wood (rĕd′wo͝od′) *n.* **1.** A very tall cone-bearing evergreen tree of northwest California, sometimes growing to a height of over 300 feet. **2.** The soft but strong reddish-brown wood of such a tree.

reed (rēd) *n.* **1.** Any of various tall hollow-stemmed grasses or similar plants that grow in wet places. **2.a.** A flexible strip of cane or metal set in the mouthpiece of certain wind instruments to produce tone by vibrating when air passes over it. **b.** A woodwind instrument, such as an oboe or a clari-

red deer

European red deer stag

Usage: redundancy

You should avoid being redundant or needlessly repetitive in your writing. Certain common phrases are redundancies and can be shortened. For example, there is no way to **revert** without *reverting back*, so you can cut out the word *back*. Sometimes, however, people think that a phrase is redundant when it really is not. Thus *a hollow tube* is different from a tube that is blocked up. The best advice in dealing with redundancies is simply to think carefully about what you are trying to say.

redwood

ă	pat	oi	boy
ā	pay	ou	out
âr	care	o͝o	took
ä	father	o͞o	boot
ĕ	pet	ŭ	cut
ē	be	ûr	urge
ĭ	pit	th	thin
ī	pie	*th*	this
îr	pier	hw	whoop
ŏ	pot	zh	vision
ō	toe	ə	about
ô	paw	N	*French* bon

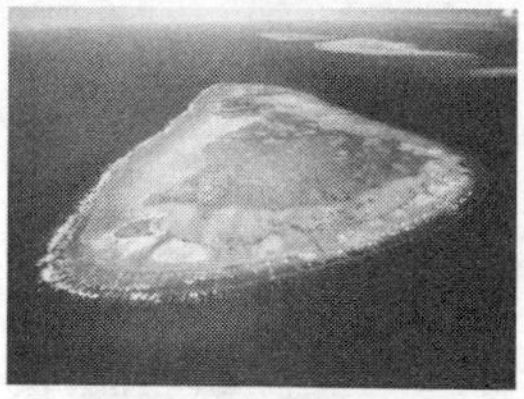

reef[1]
Great Barrier Reef
off the coast of Australia

reel[1]
Top: Reel of film
Bottom: Fishing rod reel

referee

reflector
Bicycle reflector

net, having a reed. [First written down about 700 in Old English and spelled *hrēod.*]

❑ *These sound alike:* **reed, read** (understand writing).

reed•y (rē′dē) *adj.* **reed•i•er, reed•i•est. 1.** Full of reeds: *a reedy marsh.* **2.** Resembling a reed: *a slim reedy girl.* **3.** Having the sound of a reed instrument: *the oboe's reedy tone.* **—reed′i•ness** *n.*

reef[1] (rēf) *n.* An irregular mass, strip, or ridge of rock or coral that rises to or close to the surface of a body of water. [First written down in 1584 in Modern English, from obsolete Dutch *rif,* possibly from Old Norse *rif,* ridge.]

reef[2] (rēf) *n.* A portion of a sail rolled and tied down to decrease the area of the sail that is exposed to the wind. [First written down in 1336 in Middle English and spelled *rif,* from Old Norse *rif,* ridge, reef.]

reek (rēk) *intr.v.* **reeked, reek•ing, reeks.** To give off a strong or unpleasant odor: *a salad reeking of garlic.* —*n.* A strong unpleasant odor. [First written down before 725 in Old English and spelled *rēcan,* to expose to smoke.]

❑ *These sound alike:* **reek, wreak** (inflict).

reel[1] (rēl) *n.* **1.** A device that turns on a central axis and is used for winding and storing rope, film, tape, fishing line, and other flexible materials. **2.** The amount of material wound on a reel. —*tr.v.* **reeled, reel•ing, reels. 1.** To wind onto a reel. **2.** To pull in (a fish) by winding on a reel: *reel in a marlin.* ***—idiom.*** **reel off.** To recite fluently and usually at length: *He reeled off a list of names.* [First written down about 1050 in Old English and spelled *hrēol.*]

reel[2] (rēl) *v.* **reeled, reel•ing, reels.** —*intr.* **1.** To be thrown off balance, as from a blow. **2.** To stagger or sway: *After spinning around, she reeled across the lawn.* **3.** To go round and round in a whirling motion: *The events of the day reeled in his mind.* —*tr.* To cause to reel. —*n.* **1.** A staggering, swaying, or whirling movement. **2.a.** Any of several fast lively folk dances. **b.** Music written to accompany or as if to accompany any of these dances. [First written down in 1375 in Middle English and spelled *relen,* to whirl about, probably from *reel,* spool.]

re•e•lect (rē′ĭ lĕkt′) *tr.v.* **re•e•lect•ed, re•e•lect•ing, re•e•lects.** To elect again. **—re′e•lec′tion** *n.*

re•en•force (rē′ĭn fôrs′) *v.* Variant of **reinforce.**

re•en•ter (rē ĕn′tər) *v.* **re•en•tered, re•en•ter•ing, re•en•ters.** —*intr.* To come in or enter again. —*tr.* To record again on a list or ledger. **—re•en′trance** *n.*

re•en•try (rē ĕn′trē) *n., pl.* **re•en•tries. 1.** The act of reentering; a second or subsequent entry. **2.** The return of a missile or spacecraft to the earth's atmosphere.

re•es•tab•lish (rē′ĭ stăb′lĭsh) *v.* **re•es•tab•lished, re•es•tab•lish•ing, re•es•tab•lish•es.** To establish again; restore. **—re′es•tab′lish•ment** *n.*

re•ex•am•ine (rē′ĭg zăm′ĭn) *tr.v.* **re•ex•am•ined, re•ex•am•in•ing, re•ex•am•ines. 1.** To examine again or anew; review. **2.** In law, to question (a witness) again after cross-examination.

re•fec•to•ry (rĭ fĕk′tə rē) *n., pl.* **re•fec•to•ries.** A room where meals are served.

re•fer (rĭ fûr′) *v.* **re•ferred, re•fer•ring, re•fers.** —*tr.* **1.** To direct to a person or an organization for help or information: *refer a patient to a heart specialist.* **2.** To submit (something) to a person or group for examination or action: *refer a proposed bill to a committee.* —*intr.* **1.** To pertain; concern: *questions that refer to today's lecture.* **2.** To make mention or reference: *referring to Connecticut as the "Nutmeg State."* **3.** To use as a source of information or authority: *refer to a dictionary.* [First written down about 1380 in Middle English and spelled *referren,* from Latin *referre* : *re-,* back + *ferre,* to carry.]

ref•e•ree (rĕf′ə rē′) *n.* **1.** In sports, an official supervising play. **2.** A person to whom something is referred for settlement or decision; an arbitrator or arbiter. —*tr. & intr.v.* **ref•e•reed, ref•e•ree•ing, ref•e•rees.** To judge or act as a referee.

ref•er•ence (rĕf′ər əns *or* rĕf′rəns) *n.* **1.** An act of referring: *Let's file that article away for future reference.* **2.** The state of being related or referred: *I will send a reply in reference to your query.* **3.** A mention of an occurrence or a situation: *He made frequent references to his trip to Europe.* **4.** A note in a book or other publication that directs the reader to another part of the book or to another source of information. **5.a.** A person who is in a position to recommend another or to vouch for his or her fitness, as for a job: *May I use you as a reference?* **b.** A statement about a person's character or qualifications for something. **6.** A person or thing that is referred to.

reference book *n.* A book, such as an encyclopedia, that provides information arranged for easy access.

ref•er•en•dum (rĕf′ə rĕn′dəm) *n.* **1.** The practice of placing a measure directly before the voters rather than deciding it through a legislative body. **2.** Such a vote: *The referendum on the school bond issue passed.*

re•fer•ral (rĭ fûr′əl) *n.* **1.** The act or an instance of referring: *the patient's referral to a specialist.* **2.** A person or thing that has been referred: *The doctor saw many of her own patients plus several referrals.*

re•fill (rē fĭl′) *tr.v.* **re•filled, re•fill•ing, re•fills.** To fill again: *He refilled the glass with water.* —*n.* (rē′fĭl′). **1.** A second or subsequent filling: *held out her glass for a refill.* **2.** A product for replacing the contents of a container when they have been used up.

re•fine (rĭ fīn′) *tr.v.* **re•fined, re•fin•ing, re•fines. 1.** To remove unwanted matter from; make pure: *refine oil; refine sugar.* **2.** To make polished or elegant: *refine one's table manners.* **—re•fin′er** *n.*

re•fined (rĭ fīnd′) *adj.* **1.** Made pure, as through an industrial refining process: *refined uranium.* **2.** Free from coarseness; polite or cultivated: *She is a refined person.*

re•fine•ment (rĭ fīn′mənt) *n.* **1.** The act or process of refining: *Your writing has undergone much refinement.* **2.** A small change or addition intended to improve something: *We made some refinements to the computer program.* **3.** Elegance; cultivation.

re•fin•er•y (rĭ fī′nə rē) *n., pl.* **re•fin•er•ies.** An industrial plant for purifying a crude substance, such as petroleum or sugar.

re•fit (rē fĭt′) *tr.v.* **re•fit•ted, re•fit•ting, re•fits.** To prepare and equip for additional use.

re•flect (rĭ flĕkt′) *v.* **re•flect•ed, re•flect•ing, re•flects.** —*tr.* **1.** To throw or bend back (light, for example) from a surface. **2.** To form an image of; mirror: *The shop window reflected his face.* **3.** To show as a result: *The price of a product reflects the costs of producing it.* —*intr.* **1.** To be thrown or bent back: *light reflecting from the water.* **2.** To think seriously; contemplate. ***—idiom.*** **reflect on. 1.** To form or express thoughts about: *We reflected on the meaning of the poem.* **2.** To give evidence of the qualities of (one): *Keeping your room neat reflects positively on you.* [First written down in 1392 in Middle English and spelled *reflecten,* from Latin *reflectere,* to bend back : *re-,* back + *flectere,* to bend.]

re•flect•ing telescope (rĭ flĕk′tĭng) *n.* A telescope in which light from the object is gathered by a concave mirror.

re•flec•tion (rĭ flĕk′shən) *n.* **1.** The act or process of reflecting: *the reflection of light by a mirror.* **2.a.**

Something, such as sound, light, or heat, that is reflected. **b.** An image formed by reflected light: *the reflection of the trees in the river.* **3.a.** Serious thought; meditation: *After long reflection, he decided to audition for the play.* **b.** An idea, a remark, or a piece of writing resulting from this. **4.** A manifestation or result: *Her achievements are a reflection of her courage.* **5.** An expression of disapproval or blame: *This incident will cast a reflection on your integrity.*

re•flec•tive (rĭ **flĕk′**tĭv) *adj.* **1.a.** Of, relating to, produced by, or resulting from reflection: *the reflective properties of glass.* **b.** Tending to reflect: *a reflective surface.* **2.** Thoughtful; pensive: *a reflective mood.*

re•flec•tor (rĭ **flĕk′**tər) *n.* **1.** Something, such as a surface, that reflects. **2.** A reflecting telescope.

re•flex (**rē′**flĕks′) *n.* **1.** An involuntary response to a stimulus. **2.** An instinctive or unlearned response to a stimulus. **3.** A reflection or an image produced by reflection.

re•flex•ive (rĭ **flĕk′**sĭv) *adj.* **1.** Of or relating to a reflex: *a reflexive twitch.* **2.** Being a verb that has an identical subject and direct object. For example, in the sentence *She dressed herself, dressed* is a reflexive verb. **3.** Being a pronoun used as direct object of a reflexive verb. For example, in the sentence *He blames himself, himself* is a reflexive pronoun. *—n.* A reflexive verb or pronoun. **—re•flex′ive•ly** *adv.*

re•for•est (rē **fôr′**ĭst *or* rē **fŏr′**ĭst) *tr.v.* **re•for•est•ed, re•for•est•ing, re•for•ests.** To replant (an area) with trees. **—re′for•es•ta′tion** *n.*

re•form (rĭ **fôrm′**) *v.* **re•formed, re•form•ing, re•forms.** *—tr.* **1.** To improve, as by correcting errors or removing defects: *a plan to reform the health care system.* **2.** To cause to give up harmful ways: *work designed to reform criminals.* *—intr.* To become changed for the better: *He saw the foolishness of his behavior and reformed.* *—n.* **1.** A change for the better; an improvement: *the reform of city government.* **2.** A movement or policy that aims at this: *prison reform.* **—re•form′er** *n.*

ref•or•ma•tion (rĕf′ər **mā′**shən) *n.* **1.** The act of reforming or the condition of being reformed: *a total reformation of the public school system.* **2. Reformation.** The movement in 16th-century Western Europe that aimed at reforming the Roman Catholic Church and resulted in the establishment of the Protestant churches.

re•for•ma•to•ry (rĭ **fôr′**mə tôr′ē) *n., pl.* **re•for•ma•to•ries.** An institution for disciplining and training young lawbreakers. *—adj.* Reformative.

Reform Judaism *n.* The branch of Judaism founded in the 19th century that does not require strict observance of laws and rituals.

reform school *n.* A reformatory.

re•fract (rĭ **frăkt′**) *tr.v.* **re•fract•ed, re•fract•ing, re•fracts.** To cause the path of (light or other radiation) to bend or deflect by refraction. [First written down in 1612 in Modern English, from Latin *refringere,* to break up.]

re•fract•ing telescope (rĭ **frăk′**tĭng) *n.* A telescope in which the light from an object is gathered by lenses only.

re•frac•tion (rĭ **frăk′**shən) *n.* **1.** The bending or turning of a wave, such as a light or sound wave, when it passes from one medium to another of different density. **2.** The apparent change in position of a celestial body caused by the bending of light as it enters Earth's atmosphere.

re•frac•tor (rĭ **frăk′**tər) *n.* **1.** Something that refracts. **2.** A refracting telescope.

re•frac•to•ry (rĭ **frăk′**tə rē) *adj.* **1.** Stubbornly resistant to authority or control: *a refractory child.* **2.** Difficult to melt or work; resistant to heat: *a refractory ore.* **3.** Not responsive to medical treatment: *a refractory disease.*

re•frain¹ (rĭ **frān′**) *intr.v.* **re•frained, re•frain•ing, re•frains.** To hold oneself back; forbear: *refrain from talking.* [First written down about 1350 in Middle English and spelled *refreinen,* from Latin *refrēnāre,* to restrain : *re-,* back + *frēnum,* bridle.]

re•frain² (rĭ **frān′**) *n.* **1.** A phrase, verse, or group of verses repeated several times throughout the course of a song or poem, especially at the end of each stanza. **2.** The music for the refrain of a song. [First written down about 1385 in Middle English and spelled *refrein,* from Old French *refraindre,* to repeat, from Latin *refringere,* to break back.]

re•fresh (rĭ **frĕsh′**) *tr.v.* **re•freshed, re•fresh•ing, re•fresh•es.** **1.** To revive with or as if with food, drink, or rest: *I refreshed myself with an afternoon nap.* **2.** To make cool, clean, or damp; freshen: *An afternoon shower refreshed the lawn.* **3.** To renew by stimulation: *refresh one's memory.* **—re•fresh′er** *n.*

re•fresh•ing (rĭ **frĕsh′**ĭng) *adj.* **1.** Serving to refresh: *a refreshing breeze.* **2.** New and different in a pleasant way: *a refreshing viewpoint on art.* **—re•fresh′ing•ly** *adv.*

re•fresh•ment (rĭ **frĕsh′**mənt) *n.* **1.** The act of refreshing or the condition of being refreshed. **2.** Something that refreshes. **3. refreshments.** A light meal or snack.

re•fried beans (**rē′**frīd′) *pl.n.* Beans that have been cooked and then mashed and fried.

re•frig•er•ant (rĭ **frĭj′**ər ənt) *n.* A substance used to cool something by absorbing heat from it, either directly or in a refrigerator.

re•frig•er•ate (rĭ **frĭj′**ə rāt′) *tr.v.* **re•frig•er•at•ed, re•frig•er•at•ing, re•frig•er•ates.** **1.** To cool or chill (a substance). **2.** To preserve (food) by storing at a low temperature. [First written down in 1534 in Modern English, from Latin *refrīgerāre,* from *frīgus,* coldness.] **—re•frig′er•a′tion** *n.*

re•frig•er•a•tor (rĭ **frĭj′**ə rā′tər) *n.* An appliance, box, or cabinet for storing food or other substances at a low temperature.

ref•uge (**rĕf′**yo͞oj) *n.* **1.** Protection; shelter: *seeking refuge in the castle.* **2.** A place providing protection or shelter: *a wildlife refuge.* [First written down about 1385 in Middle English, from Latin *refugere,* to run away.]

ref•u•gee (rĕf′yo͞o **jē′**) *n.* A person who flees in search of refuge, as in times of war or religious persecution.

re•ful•gent (rĭ **fo͝ol′**jənt *or* rĭ **fŭl′**jənt) *adj.* Shining radiantly; brilliant: *a diadem refulgent with gems.* **—re•ful′gence** *n.* **—re•ful′gent•ly** *adv.*

re•fund (rĭ **fŭnd′** *or* **rē′**fŭnd′) *tr.v.* **re•fund•ed, re•fund•ing, re•funds.** To pay back (money): *The store refunded the full price of the television set.* *—n.* (**rē′**fŭnd′). **1.** A repayment of funds: *She demanded a refund.* **2.** An amount repaid: *How much was your refund?* **—re•fund′a•ble** *adj.*

re•fur•bish (rē **fûr′**bĭsh) *tr.v.* **re•fur•bished, re•fur•bish•ing, re•fur•bish•es.** To brighten or freshen up; renovate: *refurbish a house.*

re•fus•al (rĭ **fyo͞o′**zəl) *n.* **1.** The act of refusing. **2.** The opportunity or right to accept or reject something before it is offered elsewhere.

re•fuse¹ (rĭ **fyo͞oz′**) *v.* **re•fused, re•fus•ing, re•fus•es.** *—tr.* **1.** To be unwilling (to do something). **2.** To be unwilling to accept; turn down: *refuse an offer.* **3.** To be unwilling to give; deny: *We were refused permission to leave early.* *—intr.* To decline to do, accept, give, or allow something. [First written

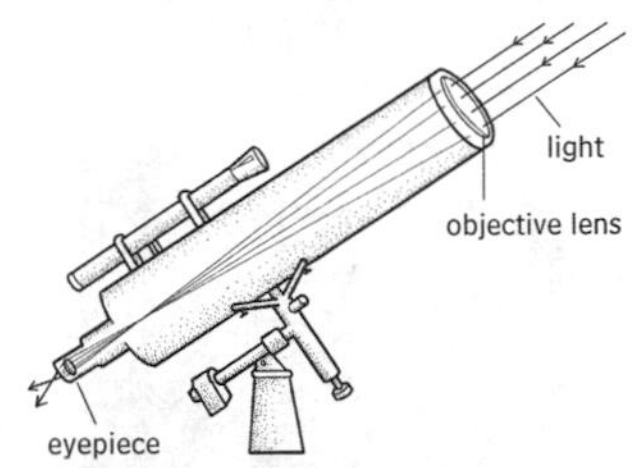

refracting telescope

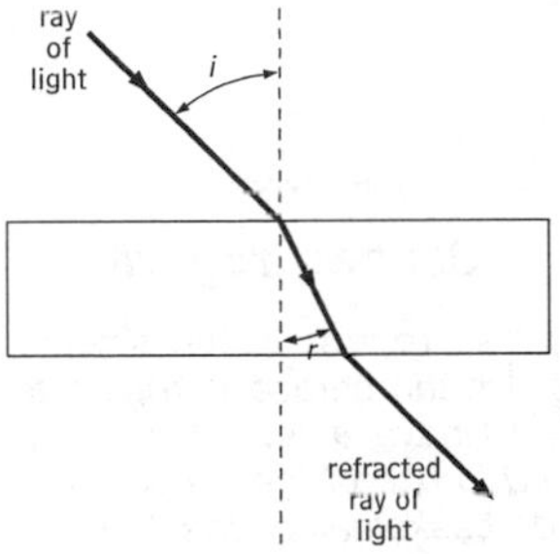

refraction
i, angle of incidence; *r,* angle of refraction

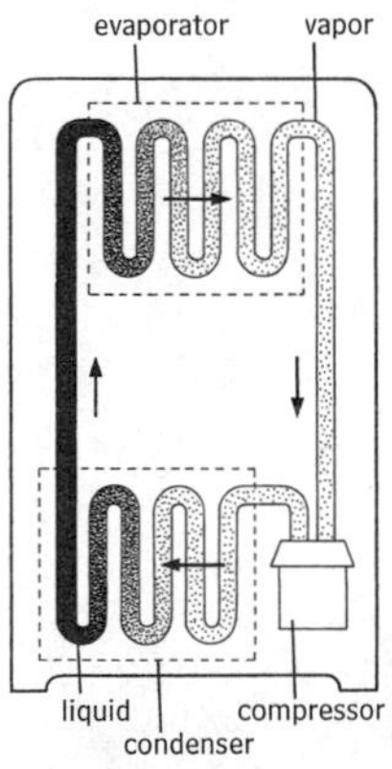

refrigerator
Electric refrigerator

ă	**pat**	oi	**boy**
ā	**pay**	ou	**out**
âr	**care**	o͝o	**took**
ä	**father**	o͞o	**boot**
ĕ	**pet**	ŭ	**cut**
ē	**be**	ûr	**urge**
ĭ	**pit**	th	**thin**
ī	**pie**	*th*	**this**
îr	**pier**	hw	**whoop**
ŏ	**pot**	zh	**vision**
ō	**toe**	ə	**about**
ô	**paw**	N	*French* **bon**

regalia
Queen Elizabeth II

Usage: regard

Use **regard** in the singular in the phrase *in regard to*: *I have a few ideas in regard to use of the school's outside basketball courts.* You can also use *regarding, as regards,* and *with respect to* to mean "with reference to."

regatta
Sailboat race on Lake Huron

down before 1300 in Middle English and spelled *refusen,* from Old French *refuser.*]

Synonyms: refuse, decline, reject. These verbs mean to be unwilling to accept, consider, or receive someone or something. **Refuse** can mean to oppose something in an abrupt, rude way: *The captain refused to hear of any changes to the plan.* **Decline** means to refuse politely: *He declined the job promotion because he wanted to spend more time with his family.* **Reject** suggests casting away someone or something as useless or defective: *The army would reject you because of your flat feet.*

ref•use² (rĕf′yo͞os) *n.* Worthless matter; waste. [First written down before 1338 in Middle English and spelled *refous,* from Old French *refuser,* to refuse.]

ref•u•ta•tion (rĕf′yo͞o tā′shən) *n.* **1.** The act of refuting. **2.** Something, such as an argument, that refutes someone or something.

re•fute (rĭ fyo͞ot′) *tr.v.* **re•fut•ed, re•fut•ing, re•futes.** To prove to be false or wrong: *refuted their statements.* **—re•fut′er** *n.*

re•gain (rē gān′) *tr.v.* **re•gained, re•gain•ing, re•gains. 1.** To recover possession of; get back: *regain one's health.* **2.** To manage to reach again: *regain shore.*

re•gal (rē′gəl) *adj.* **1.** Of or relating to a king; royal: *regal power.* **2.** Befitting a king: *a regal bearing.* [First written down about 1380 in Middle English, from Latin *rēgālis,* from *rēx,* king.]

re•gale (rĭ gāl′) *v.* **re•galed, re•gal•ing, re•gales.** *—tr.* **1.** To entertain or amuse: *regaled us with their stories and jokes.* **2.** To provide a lavish feast for. *—intr.* To feast.

re•ga•lia (rĭ gāl′yə) *pl.n. (used with a singular or plural verb).* **1.** The emblems and symbols of royalty, as the crown and scepter. **2.** The special symbols and costume that distinguish a certain rank, office, or order. **3.** Fine or fancy clothes; finery.

re•gard (rĭ gärd′) *tr.v.* **re•gard•ed, re•gard•ing, re•gards. 1.** To look at closely; observe: *regarded the coyotes with a fixed stare.* **2.** To consider in a particular way: *I regarded her as the brightest of my friends.* **3.** To hold in affection or esteem: *He regards his teachers highly.* **4.** To relate to; concern: *This decision regards the future of our band.* *—n.* **1.** A look or gaze: *a judge's cold regard.* **2.** Careful thought or attention: *She gives little regard to her appearance.* **3.** Esteem or affection: *showing regard for his parents.* **4. regards.** Good wishes; greetings: *Send her my regards, will you?* **5.** A particular point or matter: *I can't help you in that regard.* ***—idiom.*** **in regard to** or **with regard to.** With respect to. —SEE NOTE.

re•gard•ful (rĭ gärd′fəl) *adj.* **1.** Attentive; mindful: *regardful of the feelings of other people.* **2.** Respectful: *addressing her in a regardful voice.*

re•gard•ing (rĭ gär′dĭng) *prep.* In reference to; concerning: *laws regarding sanitation.* —SEE NOTE at **regard.**

re•gard•less (rĭ gärd′lĭs) *adv.* In spite of everything; anyway: *She still loved him, regardless.* *—adj.* Heedless; unmindful. **—re•gard′less•ly** *adv.* —SEE NOTE at **irregardless.**

re•gat•ta (rĭ gä′tə *or* rĭ găt′ə) *n.* A boat race or races, organized as a sporting event.

re•gen•cy (rē′jən sē) *n., pl.* **re•gen•cies. 1.** A group of regents appointed to rule a kingdom jointly. **2.** The government or period of rule of a regent.

re•gen•er•ate (rĭ jĕn′ə rāt′) *v.* **re•gen•er•at•ed, re•gen•er•at•ing, re•gen•er•ates.** *—tr.* **1.** To reform spiritually or morally. **2.** To give new life to; revive: *The reforms were intended to regenerate the nation's economic life.* **3.** To replace (a damaged or lost part or an organ) by growing new tissue: *A starfish that has lost an arm will regenerate a new one.* *—intr.* **1.** To undergo spiritual conversion or renewal; reform. **2.** To become formed or constructed again. *—adj.* (rĭ jĕn′ər ĭt). **1.** Spiritually or morally reformed. **2.** Formed or created anew. **—re•gen′er•a′tion** *n.* **—re•gen′er•a′tive** *adj.*

re•gent (rē′jənt) *n.* **1.** A person appointed to rule when a monarch is absent, too young, or unable to rule. **2.** A member of the governing board of a state university or a state system of schools.

reg•gae (rĕg′ā) *n.* Popular music of Jamaican origin having elements of Calypso, soul, and rock 'n' roll and characterized by rhythm with a strong upbeat.

reg•i•cide (rĕj′ĭ sīd′) *n.* The killing of a king.

re•gime also **ré•gime** (rā zhēm′ *or* rĭ zhēm′) *n.* **1.** A form of government: *a communist regime.* **2.** A government in power; an administration.

reg•i•men (rĕj′ə mən) *n.* A system or method of treatment or cure.

reg•i•ment (rĕj′ə mənt) *n.* A unit of soldiers, composed of two or more battalions. *—tr.v.* (rĕj′ə mĕnt′). **reg•i•ment•ed, reg•i•ment•ing, reg•i•ments. 1.** To put into systematic order. **2.** To force to conform to a single pattern, as by rigid discipline. **—reg′i•men′tal** (rĕj′ə mĕn′tl) *adj.* **—reg′i•men•ta′tion** *n.*

reg•i•men•tals (rĕj′ə mĕnt′lz) *pl.n.* The uniform and insignia of a particular regiment.

Re•gi•na (rĭ jī′nə). The capital and largest city of Saskatchewan, Canada, in the southern part of the province west of Winnepeg, Manitoba. Population, 162,613.

re•gion (rē′jən) *n.* **1.** A large area of a surface or space: *the upper regions of the atmosphere.* **2.** A large portion of the earth's surface. **3.** A section or an area of the body: *the abdominal region.* **4.** A field of interest or activity; a sphere: *The region of music he studies is opera.* [First written down before 1300 in Middle English and spelled *regioun,* from Latin *regiō,* from *regere,* to rule.]

re•gion•al (rē′jə nəl) *adj.* **1.** Of or relating to a large geographic region. **2.** Of or relating to a particular region: *a regional accent.* **—re′gion•al•ly** *adv.*

reg•is•ter (rĕj′ĭ stər) *n.* **1.a.** An official record of items, names, or transactions: *a register of all real-estate properties.* **b.** A book in which such a record is kept. **c.** An entry in such a book. **2.** A person who registers: *a register of deeds.* **3.** A device that automatically records or displays a number or quantity. **4.** A device resembling a grill that can be adjusted to control the flow of heated or cooled air into a room. **5.a.** The range of a voice or musical instrument. **b.** A part of such a range: *the low register of a contralto.* *—v.* **reg•is•tered, reg•is•ter•ing, reg•is•ters.** *—tr.* **1.** To record in a register: *register a birth.* **2.** To set down in writing; record: *register a complaint.* **3.** To indicate, as on a scale or device. **4.** To enroll in order to vote or attend classes. **5.** To show or express: *His face registered no emotion.* **6.** To cause (mail) to be officially recorded by the post office. *—intr.* **1.** To place one's name in a register: *You can register for the conference in the lobby.* **2.** To have one's name placed on a list of eligible voters. **3.** To enroll as a student. **4.** To be shown or expressed: *Recognition did not register on her face.* **5.** To make an impression: *Her name failed to register in my memory.*

reg•is•tered nurse (rĕj′ĭ stərd) *n.* A nurse who has graduated from a nursing school, passed a state registration examination, and been licensed to practice nursing.

reg•is•trar (rĕj′ĭ strär′ *or* rĕj′ĭ strär′) *n.* An official, especially at a university, who is responsible for keeping records.

reg•is•tra•tion (rĕj′ĭ strā′shən) *n.* **1.** The act of registering, as of voters or students. **2.** The number of people registered: *Voter registration in our county is 11,000.* **3.** An entry in a register. **4.** A document showing proof of registration.

reg•is•try (rĕj′ĭ strē) *n., pl.* **reg•is•tries. 1.** The act of registering; registration. **2.** A ship's registered nationality: *The tanker has a Liberian registry.* **3.** A book of official records. **4.** A place where official records are kept.

re•gress (rĭ grĕs′) *intr.v.* **re•gressed, re•gress•ing, re•gress•es.** To go back to a previous condition; revert: *Under hypnosis, the patient regressed to her early childhood.* [First written down in 1552 in Modern English, from Latin *regredī* : *re-*, back + *gradī*, to go.] **—re•gres′sion** (rĭ grĕsh′ən) *n.*

re•gret (rĭ grĕt′) *tr.v.* **re•gret•ted, re•gret•ting, re•grets. 1.** To feel sorry about: *regret an error.* **2.** To remember with a sense of loss; mourn: *regretted leaving her classmates.* *—n.* **1.** A sense of loss and longing for someone or something gone. **2.** A feeling of disappointment or distress. **3. regrets.** A polite reply turning down an invitation: *send one's regrets.* [First written down about 1380 in Middle English and spelled *regretten*, to lament, from Old French *regreter*.] **—re•gret′ta•ble** *adj.*

re•gret•ful (rĭ grĕt′fəl) *adj.* Full of regret; sorrowful or sorry. **—re•gret′ful•ly** *adv.* **—re•gret′ful•ness** *n.*

reg•u•lar (rĕg′yə lər) *adj.* **1.** Customary, usual, or normal: *the train's regular schedule.* **2.** Following an established procedure or discipline: *regular study habits.* **3.** Steady; habitual: *a regular patron.* **4.** Occurring at fixed intervals: *regular meals.* **5.** Orderly, even, or symmetrical: *regular teeth.* **6.** *Informal.* Likable; nice: *He's a regular guy.* **7.** *Informal.* Complete; thorough: *a regular scoundrel.* **8.** Belonging to or constituting the permanent army of a country. **9.** Having all sides equal and all angles equal: *a regular polyhedron.* **10.** In grammar, conforming to the usual pattern of inflection, derivation, or word formation: *a regular verb.* *—n.* **1.** A soldier belonging to a regular army. **2.** A habitual customer: *The waitress recognized him as one of the regulars.* [First written down before 1387 in Middle English and spelled *reguler*, living under religious rule, from Latin *rēgula*, rod, rule.] **—reg′u•lar′i•ty** (rĕg′yə lăr′ĭ tē) *n.* **—reg′u•lar•ly** *adv.*

reg•u•late (rĕg′yə lāt′) *tr.v.* **reg•u•lat•ed, reg•u•lat•ing, reg•u•lates. 1.** To control or direct according to a rule or law: *power to regulate commerce.* **2.** To adjust for proper functioning: *regulate a carburetor.* **3.** To adjust or control according to a requirement: *This valve regulates the flow of water.* **4.** To put or maintain in order: *regulate one's sleeping habits.* **—reg′u•la′tor** *n.*

reg•u•la•tion (rĕg′yə lā′shən) *n.* **1.** The act or process of regulating. **2.** The condition of being regulated: *freedom from government regulation.* **3.** A rule, an order, or a law by which something is regulated: *traffic regulations.*

reg•u•la•to•ry (rĕg′yə lə tôr′ē) *adj.* Having the ability to regulate or oversee.

re•gur•gi•tate (rē gûr′jĭ tāt′) *v.* **re•gur•gi•tat•ed, re•gur•gi•tat•ing, re•gur•gi•tates.** *—intr.* To rush or surge back. *—tr.* To cause to pour back (partially digested food) from the stomach through the mouth; vomit. **—re•gur′gi•ta′tion** *n.*

re•ha•bil•i•tate (rē′hə bĭl′ĭ tāt′) *tr.v.* **re•ha•bil•i•tat•ed, re•ha•bil•i•tat•ing, re•ha•bil•i•tates. 1.** To restore to useful life, as through training or therapy. **2.** To restore the good name of. **3.** To restore the former rank or privileges of. **4.** To restore to good condition or operation: *rehabilitate a house.* **—re′ha•bil′i•ta′tion** *n.*

re•hash (rē hăsh′) *tr.v.* **re•hashed, re•hash•ing, re•hash•es.** To present or go over again, without anything new resulting: *John and Susan rehashed their disagreement.* *—n.* (rē′hăsh′). Something that is rehashed: *His book is a rehash of some earlier ideas.*

re•hears•al (rĭ hûr′səl) *n.* **1.** The act or process of practicing in preparation for a performance or ceremony. **2.** A session devoted to such practice: *a wedding rehearsal.*

re•hearse (rĭ hûrs′) *v.* **re•hearsed, re•hears•ing, re•hears•es.** *—tr.* **1.** To practice (all or part of a program) in preparation for a performance: *The boys rehearsed their skit.* **2.** To train by rehearsal: *rehearse a choir.* *—intr.* To practice something, such as a speech, before presenting it publicly.

Rehn•quist (rĕn′kwĭst′), **William Hubbs.** Born 1924. American jurist who was appointed chief justice of the U.S. Supreme Court in 1986.

reign (rān) *n.* **1.** The exercise of political power by a monarch. **2.** The period during which a monarch rules. *—intr.v.* **reigned, reign•ing, reigns. 1.** To exercise the power of a monarch. **2.** To be predominant or pervasive: *A stillness reigned after the storm.* [First written down about 1225 in Middle English and spelled *rengne*, from Latin *rēgnum*, from *rēx*, king.]

❑ *These sound alike:* **reign, rain** (water drops), **rein** (strap).

re•im•burse (rē′ĭm bûrs′) *tr.v.* **re•im•bursed, re•im•burs•ing, re•im•burs•es.** To pay back; compensate. **—re′im•burs′a•ble** *adj.* **—re′im•burse′ment** *n.*

rein (rān) *n.* **1.** A long narrow leather strap attached to the bit in a horse's mouth and held by the rider or driver to control the horse. Often used in the plural. **2.** A means of restraint or guidance: *the reins of government.* *—v.* **reined, rein•ing, reins.** *—tr.* To check or hold back by or as if by the use of reins: *The police captain reined in the detectives.* *—intr.* To control a horse or other animal with reins. ***—idiom.* give rein to** or **give free rein to.** To release from restraints; allow to go unchecked: *She gave free rein to her feelings.* [First written down before 1300 in Middle English, from Latin *retinēre*, to retain.]

❑ *These sound alike:* **rein, rain** (water drops), **reign** (rule).

re•in•car•nate (rē′ĭn kär′nāt) *tr.v.* **re•in•car•nat•ed, re•in•car•nat•ing, re•in•car•nates.** To cause to be reborn in another body; incarnate again. **—re′in•car•na′tion** *n.* **—re′in•car•na′tion•ist** *n.*

re•in•car•na•tion (rē′ĭn kär nā′shən) *n.* Rebirth of the soul in another body.

rein•deer (rān′dîr′) *n., pl.* **reindeer** or **rein•deers.** A deer of Arctic regions of Europe, Asia, and North America, having large spreading antlers in both the males and females. [First written down before 1400 in Middle English and spelled *raine-dere* : Old Norse *hreinn*, reindeer + Middle English *der*, animal.]

re•in•force or **re•en•force** (rē′ĭn fôrs′) *tr.v.* **re•in•forced, re•in•forc•ing, re•in•forc•es** or **re•en•forced, re•en•forc•ing, re•en•forc•es. 1.** To make stronger by adding extra support to; strengthen: *reinforce a bridge.* **2.** To strengthen (a military force) with additional troops or equipment. **—re′in•force′a•ble** *adj.*

re•in•force•ment (rē′ĭn fôrs′mənt) *n.* **1.** The act or process of reinforcing. **2.** Something that reinforces. **3. reinforcements.** Additional troops or equipment sent to support a military action.

re•in•state (rē′ĭn stāt′) *tr.v.* **re•in•stat•ed, re•in•stat•ing, re•in•states.** To restore to a previous condition or position: *After a leave of absence, she was reinstated in her job.* **—re′in•state′ment** *n.*

register

Top: Hand-cranked
Bottom: Electronic

reindeer

ă	pat	oi	boy
ā	pay	ou	out
âr	care	ŏŏ	took
ä	father	ōō	boot
ĕ	pet	ŭ	cut
ē	be	ûr	urge
ĭ	pit	th	thin
ī	pie	*th*	this
îr	pier	hw	whoop
ŏ	pot	zh	vision
ō	toe	ə	about
ô	paw	N	*French* bon

re•it•er•ate (rē ĭt′ə rāt′) *tr.v.* **re•it•er•at•ed, re•it•er•at•ing, re•it•er•ates.** To say over again; repeat: *The coach reiterated his instructions.* —**re•it′er•a′tion** *n.*

re•ject (rĭ jĕkt′) *tr.v.* **re•ject•ed, re•ject•ing, re•jects. 1.** To refuse to accept, use, or submit to: *We rejected the idea of working overtime.* See Synonyms at **refuse**[1]. **2.** To refuse to consider or grant; deny: *My mother rejected my plans for a big party.* **3.** To fail to give affection or love to (a person). **4.** To throw out; discard. **5.** To resist the introduction of (a transplanted organ or tissue); fail to accept as part of one's own body. —*n.* (rē′jĕkt). A person or thing that has been rejected: *rejects from military service.* [First written down about 1415 in Middle English and spelled *rejecten*, from Latin *rēicere* : *re-*, back + *iacere*, to throw.]

re•jec•tion (rĭ jĕk′shən) *n.* **1.** The act of rejecting or the condition of being rejected: *the rejection of a manuscript by a publisher.* **2.** Something rejected.

re•joice (rĭ jois′) *v.* **re•joiced, re•joic•ing, re•joic•es.** —*intr.* To feel joy; be delighted: *I rejoice in your good fortune.* —*tr.* To fill with joy; gladden.

re•join[1] (rĭ join′) *tr.v.* **re•joined, re•join•ing, re•joins.** To answer; reply: *"I disagree!" Sammy rejoined.* [First written down in 1447 in Middle English and spelled *rejoinen*, from Old French *rejoindre.*]

re•join[2] (rē join′) *tr.v.* **re•joined, re•join•ing, re•joins. 1.** To join together again. **2.** To return to; reunite with: *The explorer rejoined his family.* [First written down in 1541 in Modern English, from *join.*]

re•join•der (rĭ join′dər) *n.* An answer, especially in response to another's answer: *His criticism met with no rejoinder.*

re•ju•ve•nate (rĭ jo͞o′və nāt′) *tr.v.* **re•ju•ve•nat•ed, re•ju•ve•nat•ing, re•ju•ve•nates.** To make young or vigorous again: *Her vacation completely rejuvenated her.* [First written down in 1807 in Modern English, from Latin *iuvenis*, young.] —**re•ju′ve•na′tion** *n.*

re•lapse (rĭ lăps′) *intr.v.* **re•lapsed, re•laps•ing, re•laps•es. 1.** To fall back into a previous condition: *We relapsed into our old sloppy habits.* **2.** To become sick again after a partial recovery. —*n.* (rē′lăps *or* rĭ lăps′). A falling back into a previous condition, especially a return to illness.

relay race
Runner passing baton to a teammate

re•late (rĭ lāt′) *v.* **re•lat•ed, re•lat•ing, re•lates.** —*tr.* **1.** To tell or narrate: *relate a story.* **2.** To bring into association; link or connect: *I related his grumpiness to a lack of sleep.* —*intr.* To interact with other persons in a meaningful way: *She relates well to her classmates.* [First written down in 1530 in Modern English, from Latin *relātus*, carried over.]

re•lat•ed (rĭ lā′tĭd) *adj.* **1.** Connected; associated: *closely related topics.* **2.** Connected by kinship, marriage, or common origin. —**re•lat′ed•ness** *n.*

re•la•tion (rĭ lā′shən) *n.* **1.** A connection or association between two or more things: *the relation of health and a good diet.* **2.** The connection of people by blood or marriage. **3.** A person connected to another by blood or marriage; a relative. **4. relations.** The dealings or associations of persons, groups, or nations: *a country's foreign relations.* **5.** The act of telling; an account: *his relation of his experiences in Alaska.*

re•la•tion•ship (rĭ lā′shən shĭp′) *n.* **1.** The condition or fact of being related; a connection or an association. **2.** A connection or tie between persons: *a business relationship.* **3.** Kinship: *She claimed relationship to the millionaire.*

rel•a•tive (rĕl′ə tĭv) *adj.* **1.** Related or relating: *your comment relative to my work.* **2.** Considered in comparison with something else: *the relative quiet of the suburbs.* **3.** Dependent on something else for meaning; not absolute: *"Expensive" is a relative word.* **4.** In grammar, referring to an antecedent, as the pronoun *who* in *the woman who plays guitar.* —*n.* **1.** A person related by blood or marriage. **2.** In grammar, a relative term, especially a relative pronoun.

relative clause *n.* A dependent clause introduced by a relative pronoun. For example, in the sentence *He who hesitates is lost,* the relative clause is *who hesitates.*

relative humidity *n.* The quotient of the amount of water vapor contained in the air at a given temperature divided by the maximum that the air could contain at that temperature.

rel•a•tive•ly (rĕl′ə tĭv lē) *adv.* In comparison with something else: *a relatively minor problem.*

relative pronoun *n.* A pronoun that introduces a relative clause and refers to an antecedent. For example, in the sentence *The house that I live in has a porch,* the relative pronoun is *that.*

rel•a•tiv•i•ty (rĕl′ə tĭv′ĭ tē) *n.* **1.** The condition of being relative. **2.** The two-part theory of space and time developed by Albert Einstein, the first part stating that the laws of physics apply throughout the universe and that the speed of light is always a constant, and the second part extending the theory to include gravitation and inertia. Among the consequences of the theory are the conclusions that measurements of speed and time depend on the motion of the observer and that mass and energy are equivalent.

re•lax (rĭ lăks′) *v.* **re•laxed, re•lax•ing, re•lax•es.** —*tr.* **1.** To make less tight or tense: *relax one's muscles.* **2.** To make less severe or strict: *relax a dress code.* **3.** To relieve of tension or anxiety: *Listening to jazz relaxes me.* —*intr.* **1.** To take one's ease; rest: *I relaxed on the sofa.* **2.** To become less tight or tense. **3.** To beome less severe or strict. **4.** To become less tense or anxious. [First written down before 1398 in Middle English and spelled *relaxen*, from Latin *relaxāre*, from *laxus*, loose.]

re•lax•a•tion (rē′lăk sā′shən) *n.* **1.** The act or process of relaxing: *a relaxation of the muscles.* **2.** The condition of being relaxed: *She lay in the hammock in perfect relaxation.* **3.** Refreshment of body or mind; fun; diversion.

re•laxed (rĭ lăkst′) *adj.* **1.** Not severe or strict. **2.** Free from tension or anxiety: *a relaxed evening meal.*

re•lay (rē′lā) *n.* **1.** A switch that is operated by an electric current. **2.** A relay race. **3.** A crew of laborers who relieve another crew; a shift. **4.** A fresh team of animals, as for a stagecoach. —*tr.v.* (rē′lā *or* rĭ lā′). **re•layed, re•lay•ing, re•lays.** To pass or send along by or as if by relay: *relay the message to the boss.*

relay race *n.* A race between two or more teams, in which each member of a team goes only a part of the total distance.

re•lease (rĭ lēs′) *tr.v.* **re•leased, re•leas•ing, re•leas•es. 1.** To set free; liberate: *release prisoners.* **2.** To free from something that fastens or holds back; let go: *release balloons.* **3.** To relieve, as from an obligation: *an order that released Private Davis from active duty.* **4.** To make available, as to the public: *release a film.* —*n.* **1.** The act or an instance of releasing, as from confinement or suffering: *release of a prisoner.* **2.** A written discharge, as from a hospital or prison. **3.** A letting go of something caught or held fast: *release of a balloon.* **4.a.** The act or an instance of issuing something to the public. **b.** Something that is issued to the public: *a press release.* **5.** A device for locking or releasing a mechanism. [First written down about 1300 in Middle English and spelled *relesen*, from Latin *relaxāre*, to relax, let go.]

rel•e•gate (rĕl′ĭ gāt′) *tr.v.* **rel•e•gat•ed, rel•e•gat•ing, rel•e•gates. 1.** To send or remove, especially to a place or condition of less importance: *relegated the tools to the shed.* **2.** To refer or assign (a matter or task, for example) to someone else. **—rel′e•ga′tion** *n.*

re•lent (rĭ lĕnt′) *intr.v.* **re•lent•ed, re•lent•ing, re•lents.** To become more lenient, compassionate, or forgiving. **—re•lent′ing•ly** *adv.*

re•lent•less (rĭ lĕnt′lĭs) *adj.* **1.** Mercilessly harsh; unyielding. **2.** Steady and persistent; unremitting: *a relentless wind.* **—re•lent′less•ly** *adv.* **—re•lent′less•ness** *n.*

rel•e•vant (rĕl′ə vənt) *adj.* Related to the matter at hand; pertinent: *relevant questions.* **—rel′e•vance, rel′e•van•cy** *n.* **—rel′e•vant•ly** *adv.*

re•li•a•ble (rĭ lī′ə bəl) *adj.* Capable of being relied upon; dependable. **—re•li′a•bil′i•ty, re•li′a•ble•ness** *n.* **—re•li′a•bly** *adv.*

re•li•ance (rĭ lī′əns) *n.* **1.** The act of relying; dependence: *a reliance on industry.* **2.** Confidence; trust: *complete reliance in their friends.* **3.** A person or thing depended on; a mainstay: *His main reliance was the boat.*

re•li•ant (rĭ lī′ənt) *adj.* Having or showing reliance. **—re•li′ant•ly** *adv.*

rel•ic (rĕl′ĭk) *n.* **1.** An object or a custom surviving from a culture or period that has disappeared: *relics of an ancient civilization.* **2.** Something that is treasured for its age or historic interest. **3.** An object of religious significance, especially something thought to be associated with a saint. **4.** Or **relics.** A corpse. [First written down before 1200 in Middle English and spelled *relik*, object of religious veneration, from Latin *reliquiae*, remains.]

re•lief (rĭ lēf′) *n.* **1.** The easing of distress, such as of pain, anxiety, or oppression: *relief from a cold.* **2.** Something that lessens pain or distress. **3.** Assistance and help, as in the form of food or money, given to the needy, aged, or disaster victims. **4.a.** Release from a job or duty. **b.** A person who takes over the duties of another: *a sentry waiting for his relief.* **5.a.** The projection of a sculptured figure from a flat background. **b.** The apparent projection of a figure in a painting or drawing. **6.** The variations in elevation of an area of the earth's surface: *a map that shows relief.* **7.** Sharpness of outline resulting from contrast: *a white sail in relief against the dark sky.* ***—idiom.*** **on relief.** Receiving assistance from the government because of need or poverty.

relief map *n.* A map that shows the physical features of land, as by using contour lines, colors, or shading.

re•lieve (rĭ lēv′) *tr.v.* **re•lieved, re•liev•ing, re•lieves. 1.** To lessen or reduce (pain or anxiety, for example); ease. **2.** To free from pain, anxiety, or distress: *relieve them of worries.* **3.** To release, as from a duty or position, by providing or acting as a substitute: *The second shift relieves us at 6 o'clock.* **4.** To give assistance or aid to: *relieve the victims of the flood.* **5.** To make less unpleasant, tiresome, or boring: *We sang songs to relieve the monotony of the work.* **6.** *Informal.* To rob or deprive: *Two men relieved me of my wallet.* [First written down about 1370 in Middle English and spelled *releeven*, from Latin *relevare*, from *levāre*, to raise.] **—re•liev′a•ble** *adj.* **—re•liev′er** *n.*

re•lig•ion (rĭ lĭj′ən) *n.* **1.** Belief in and reverence for a supernatural being or beings, usually regarded as creator and governor of the universe. **2.** A particular organized system of such belief: *the Hindu religion.* **3.** A cause, principle, or set of beliefs followed with great feeling: *Ecology is her religion.*

re•lig•ious (rĭ lĭj′əs) *adj.* **1.** Having or showing belief in and reverence for God or a supernatural being. **2.** Of, concerned with, or teaching religion: *a religious book.* **3.** Very faithful; conscientious: *a religious attention to detail.* *—n., pl.* **religious.** A member of a monastic order, as a monk or nun. **—re•lig′ious•ly** *adv.* **—re•lig′ious•ness** *n.*

re•lin•quish (rĭ lĭng′kwĭsh) *tr.v.* **re•lin•quished, re•lin•quish•ing, re•lin•quish•es. 1.** To leave; abandon: *They relinquished camp and traveled inland.* **2.** To give up, put aside, or surrender: *relinquish claim to the land.* **3.** To let go; release: *relinquished her grasp on the fishing pole.* [First written down in 1454 in Middle English and spelled *relinquisshen*, from Latin *relinquere* : *re-*, back + *linquere*, to leave.] **—re•lin′quish•ment** *n.*

rel•ish (rĕl′ĭsh) *n.* **1.** An appetite for something; an appreciation or a liking: *I have a relish for backgammon.* See Synonyms at **love. 2.a.** Great enjoyment; pleasure; zest: *He began the task with relish.* **b.** Something that adds zest or pleasure: *Her wit gave relish to the discussion.* **3.** A spicy condiment, such as chopped pickles, served with food. *—tr.v.* **rel•ished, rel•ish•ing, rel•ish•es.** To take pleasure in; enjoy: *He relished going to the beach at dawn.* [First written down before 1300 in Middle English and spelled *reles*, taste, from Old French *relaissier*, to leave behind.]

re•live (rē lĭv′) *v.* **re•lived, re•liv•ing, re•lives.** *—tr.* To undergo again; live through another time: *We relived our childhood by looking through the photo album.* *—intr.* To live again: *The pioneers relive in her novels.*

re•lo•cate (rē lō′kāt) *tr. & intr.v.* **re•lo•cat•ed, re•lo•cat•ing, re•lo•cates.** To establish or become established in a new place. **—re′lo•ca′tion** *n.*

re•luc•tant (rĭ lŭk′tənt) *adj.* **1.** Unwilling; averse: *reluctant to leave.* **2.** Marked by unwillingness: *a reluctant confession.* [First written down in 1667 in Modern English, from Latin *reluctārī*, to be reluctant.] **—re•luc′tance** *n.* **—re•luc′tant•ly** *adv.*

re•ly (rĭ lī′) *intr.v.* **re•lied, re•ly•ing, re•lies. 1.** To be dependent for support or help: *She's relying on her parents to pay her rent.* **2.** To have trust or confidence: *I'm relying on you to be a good example for the others.*

REM (rĕm) *n.* The rapid jerky movement of the eyes during certain stages of sleep when dreaming takes place.

re•made (rē mād′) *v.* Past tense and past participle of **remake.**

re•main (rĭ mān′) *intr.v.* **re•mained, re•main•ing, re•mains. 1.** To continue to be in the same state or condition: *This issue remains open to debate.* **2.** To continue to be in the same place; stay: *The children remained after their mother left.* See Synonyms at **stay[1]. 3.** To be left over after the loss, removal, or destruction of others: *A few stone columns remained.* **4.** To be left as still to be dealt with: *The solution to the problem remains to be seen.* [First written down before 1425 in Middle English and spelled *remainen*, from Latin *remanēre* : *re-*, back + *manēre*, to remain.]

re•main•der (rĭ mān′dər) *n.* **1.** The remaining part; the rest: *the remainder of the year.* **2.a.** In division, the difference between the dividend and the product of the quotient and divisor. For example, 10 divided by 6 gives 1 with a remainder of 4. **b.** In subtraction, a difference.

re•mains (rĭ mānz′) *pl.n.* **1.** All that remains after the loss, removal, or destruction of other parts: *the remains of last night's supper.* **2.** A corpse. **3.** Ancient ruins or fossils.

relief

Detail of a Roman relief showing woman holding a fan

ă	pat	oi	boy
ā	pay	ou	out
âr	care	o͝o	took
ä	father	o͞o	boot
ĕ	pet	ŭ	cut
ē	be	ûr	urge
ĭ	pit	th	thin
ī	pie	*th*	this
îr	pier	hw	whoop
ŏ	pot	zh	vision
ō	toe	ə	about
ô	paw	N	*French* bon

re•make (rē māk′) *tr.v.* **re•made** (rē mād′), **re•mak•ing, re•makes.** To make again or new. —*n.* (rē′māk′). **1.** The act of making again. **2.** Something made again: *a remake of a motion picture.*

re•mand (rĭ mănd′) *tr.v.* **re•mand•ed, re•mand•ing, re•mands. 1.** To send or order back. **2.** To send back (a prisoner) to another prison, another court, or another agency for further proceedings. **3.** To send back (a legal case) to a lower court for further proceedings. —*n.* **1.** The act of remanding. **2.** The condition of being remanded: *a prisoner on remand.* —**re•mand′ment** *n.*

re•mark (rĭ märk′) *v.* **re•marked, re•mark•ing, re•marks.** —*tr.* **1.** To express as a comment: *He remarked that the book was selling well.* **2.** To notice; observe: *They remarked several changes in the town.* —*intr.* To make a comment or an observation. —*n.* **1.** A casual statement; a comment: *a remark about the weather.* **2.** The act of noticing or observing; mention: *a score worthy of remark.*

Rembrandt
Self-portrait

re•mark•a•ble (rĭ mär′kə bəl) *adj.* **1.** Worthy of notice: *The change in his personality was remarkable.* **2.** Extraordinary; uncommon: *a remarkable achievement.* —**re•mark′a•bly** *adv.*

re•match (rē măch′ *or* rē′măch′) *n.* A second contest between the same opponents.

Rem•brandt van Rijn or **Rem•brandt van Ryn** (rĕm′brănt′ văn rīn′). 1606–1669. Dutch painter whose works include historical and religious scenes, group portraits, and self-portraits.

re•me•di•a•ble (rĭ mē′dē ə bəl) *adj.* Possible to remedy: *remediable problems.* —**re•me′di•a•ble•ness** *n.* —**re•me′di•a•bly** *adv.*

re•me•di•al (rĭ mē′dē əl) *adj.* **1.** Supplying a remedy: *a remedial operation.* **2.** Intended to correct something, especially deficient skills in a subject: *taught remedial reading.* —**re•me′di•al•ly** *adv.*

rem•e•dy (rĕm′ĭ dē) *n., pl.* **rem•e•dies. 1.** Something, such as a medicine or treatment, that relieves pain, cures disease, or corrects a disorder. **2.** Something that corrects a fault, an error, or a wrong: *a remedy for inflation.* —*tr.v.* **rem•e•died, rem•e•dy•ing, rem•e•dies. 1.** To relieve or cure (a disease or disorder). **2.** To set right or correct (an error, for example).

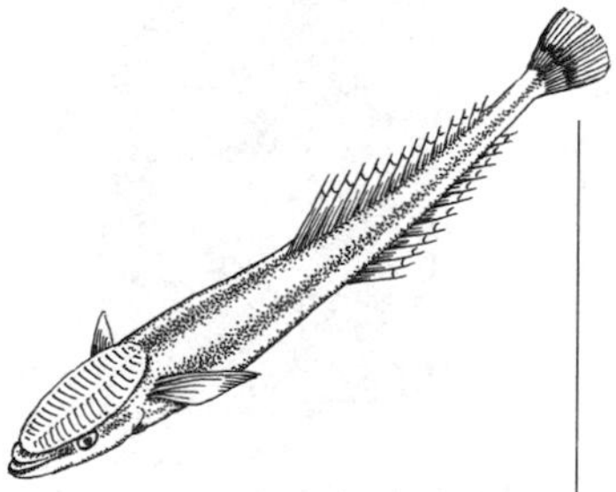

remora

re•mem•ber (rĭ mĕm′bər) *v.* **re•mem•bered, re•mem•ber•ing, re•mem•bers.** —*tr.* **1.** To recall to the mind; think of again: *She remembered how to run the machine.* **2.** To keep carefully in memory: *Remember your doctor's appointment.* **3.** To keep (someone) in mind as worthy of affection or recognition. **4.** To give (someone) a gift or tip: *remembered her nieces at Christmas.* **5.** To give greetings from (someone): *Remember me to your parents.* —*intr.* To have or use the power of memory. [First written down before 1338 in Middle English and spelled *remembren,* from Latin *rememorārī,* to remember again.]

re•mem•brance (rĭ mĕm′brəns) *n.* **1.** The act of remembering: *the remembrance of things past.* **2.** The condition of remembering. **3.** Something remembered; a memory. **4.** Something that serves to remind; a memento or souvenir.

re•mind (rĭ mīnd′) *tr.v.* **re•mind•ed, re•mind•ing, re•minds.** To cause (someone) to remember or think of something: *Remind her to water the plants.* —**re•mind′er** *n.*

rem•i•nisce (rĕm′ə nĭs′) *intr.v.* **rem•i•nisced, rem•i•nisc•ing, rem•i•nisc•es.** To remember and tell of past experiences or events.

rem•i•nis•cence (rĕm′ə nĭs′əns) *n.* **1.** The act or process of recalling the past: *lost in the reminiscence of childhood.* **2.** Something remembered; a memory: *pleasant reminiscences of the summer.* **3.** A narration or an account of past experiences or events. Often used in the plural.

rem•i•nis•cent (rĕm′ə nĭs′ənt) *adj.* **1.** Containing remembered events: *a reminiscent account of her childhood.* **2.** Recalling to the mind; suggestive: *a melody reminiscent of a folk song.*

re•miss (rĭ mĭs′) *adj.* **1.** Careless in attending to duty; negligent: *She's very remiss in answering letters.* **2.** Exhibiting carelessness or slackness: *His performance of his duties was remiss.* —**re•miss′ly** *adv.*

re•mis•sion (rĭ mĭsh′ən) *n.* **1.** Pardon or forgiveness: *the remission of sin.* **2.** Release from a debt, an obligation, or a penalty. **3.** A lessening of the intensity, seriousness, or destructive effect of a pain, disease, or disorder.

re•mit (rĭ mĭt′) *v.* **re•mit•ted, re•mit•ting, re•mits.** —*tr.* **1.** To send or transmit (money) in payment. **2.** To refrain from imposing (a tax or penalty, for example). **3.** To pardon; forgive. **4.** To decrease; reduce: *The storm remitted its fury.* —*intr.* **1.** To transmit money. **2.** To grow less; diminish. [First written down in 1393 in Middle English and spelled *remitten,* to send back, from Latin *remittere* : *re-,* back + *mittere,* to send.] —**re•mit′ter** *n.*

re•mit•tance (rĭ mĭt′ns) *n.* **1.** The act of sending money to someone. **2.** The money sent to someone.

rem•nant (rĕm′nənt) *n.* **1.** A portion or quantity left over; a remainder: *remnants of an old document.* **2.** A surviving trace or vestige: *the last remnants of an ancient empire.* **3.** A leftover piece of cloth remaining after the rest has been sold.

re•mod•el (rē mŏd′l) *tr.v.* **re•mod•eled, re•mod•el•ing, re•mod•els** also **re•mod•elled, re•mod•el•ling, re•mod•els.** To make over in structure or style; reconstruct: *remodel a kitchen.* —**re•mod′el•er** *n.*

re•mon•strance (rĭ mŏn′strəns) *n.* A strong protest or objection.

re•mon•strate (rĭ mŏn′strāt′) *intr.v.* **re•mon•strat•ed, re•mon•strat•ing, re•mon•strates.** To argue or plead in opposition to something.

rem•o•ra (rĕm′ər ə) *n.* Any of several fishes having on the head a sucking disk with which they attach themselves to sharks and other larger fish.

re•morse (rĭ môrs′) *n.* Bitter regret or guilt for having done something wrong. [First written down about 1385 in Middle English and spelled *remors,* from Latin *remordēre,* to torment.]

re•morse•ful (rĭ môrs′fəl) *adj.* Marked by or filled with remorse: *a remorseful sob.* —**re•morse′ful•ly** *adv.*

re•morse•less (rĭ môrs′lĭs) *adj.* Having no pity or compassion; merciless. —**re•morse′less•ly** *adv.* —**re•morse′less•ness** *n.*

re•mote (rĭ mōt′) *adj.* **re•mot•er, re•mot•est. 1.** Located far away: *a remote Arctic island.* **2.** Distant in time: *the remote past.* **3.** Barely perceptible; slight: *There is a remote possibility that it will snow today.* **4.** Far removed in relevance; barely connected: *Her interests are remote from those of most people.* **5.** Distantly related by blood or marriage: *a remote cousin.* [First written down about 1440 in Middle English, from Latin *remōtus,* from *removēre,* to move away.] —**re•mote′ly** *adv.*

remote control *n.* **1.** The control of an activity, a process, or a machine from a distance, especially by radio or coded signals. **2.** A device used to control a device or machine from a distance.

re•mov•al (rĭ mo͞o′vəl) *n.* **1.** The act of removing: *Removal of the piano took four men.* **2.** Relocation: *the removal of the business to New Jersey.* **3.** Dismissal, as from office or duties: *the removal of an adviser.*

re•move (rĭ mo͞ov′) *v.* **re•moved, re•mov•ing, re•**

moves. *—tr.* **1.** To move or convey from a position or place: *remove the pie from the oven.* **2.** To take off or away: *removed his coat.* **3.** To do away with; eliminate: *remove a stain.* **4.** To dismiss from office. *—intr.* To change one's place of residence or business; move. *—n.* Distance or degree of separation or remoteness: *We stood at a safe remove from the demolition site.* **—re•mov′a•ble** *adj.*

re•moved (rĭ mo͞ovd′) *adj.* **1.** Distant; remote. **2.** Separated in relationship by a given degree or descent: *My first cousin's child is my first cousin once removed.* **—re•mov′ed•ly** (rĭ mo͞o′vĭd lē) *adv.* **—re•mov′ed•ness** *n.*

re•mu•ner•ate (rĭ myo͞o′nə rāt′) *tr.v.* **re•mu•ner•at•ed, re•mu•ner•at•ing, re•mu•ner•ates.** To pay (a person) for goods, services, or losses.

re•mu•ner•a•tion (rĭ myo͞o′nə rā′shən) *n.* **1.** An act of remunerating. **2.** A recompense or compensation; a payment or reward.

re•mu•ner•a•tive (rĭ myo͞o′nər ə tĭv *or* rĭ myo͞o′nə rā′tĭv) *adj.* Providing suitable profit; profitable.

Re•mus (rē′məs) *n.* In Roman mythology, the twin brother of Romulus.

ren•ais•sance (rĕn′ĭ säns′ *or* rĕn′ĭ säns′) *n.* **1.** A rebirth or revival: *a renaissance of downtown business.* **2. Renaissance. a.** The humanistic revival of classical art, literature, architecture, and learning in Europe. **b.** The period of this revival, roughly the 14th through the 16th century. *—adj.* **Renaissance.** Of or relating to the Renaissance or its artistic works or styles. [First written down in 1840 in Modern English, from French, from Old French *renaistre,* to be born again.]

re•nal (rē′nəl) *adj.* Of, relating to, or in the region of the kidneys.

re•nas•cence (rĭ năs′əns *or* rĭ nā′səns) *n.* **1.** A renaissance; a rebirth. **2. Renascence.** The Renaissance.

rend (rĕnd) *tr.v.* **rent** (rĕnt) or **rend•ed, rend•ing, rends. 1.** To tear, pull, or wrench apart violently: *The wind rent the flag.* **2.** To remove with force; wrest: *rending the flag from his hand.* **3.** To divide as if by tearing: *This issue rends our student body.*

ren•der (rĕn′dər) *tr.v.* **ren•dered, ren•der•ing, ren•ders. 1.** To cause to become; make: *The hailstorm rendered the crop worthless.* **2.** To give or make available; provide: *render assistance.* **3.** To give in return or as what is owed: *render thanks for her thoughtfulness.* **4.** To give up; surrender; yield: *They rendered their lives in fighting the fire.* **5.** To pronounce; hand down: *render a judgment.* **6.** To represent in words or in art: *render a memory into prose; render a leaf in detail.* **7.** To translate: *render a Latin text into English.* **8.** To perform (a musical composition, for example). **9.** To melt down or process (fat) by heating.

ren•dez•vous (rän′dā vo͞o′) *n., pl.* **ren•dez•vous** (rän′dā vo͞oz′). **1.** A prearranged meeting. **2.** A designated place for a meeting. *—intr. & tr.v.* **ren•dez•voused** (rän′dā vo͞od′), **ren•dez•vous•ing** (rän′dā-vo͞o′ĭng), **ren•dez•vous** (rän′dā vo͞oz′). To meet together or cause to meet together at a certain time and place. [First written down in 1591 in Modern English and spelled *rendevous,* from French *rendez vous,* present yourselves.]

ren•di•tion (rĕn dĭsh′ən) *n.* **1.** The act of rendering. **2.** A translation: *an English rendition of a German phrase.* **3.** An interpretation or a performance of a musical composition or dramatic work.

ren•e•gade (rĕn′ĭ gād′) *n.* **1.** A person who rejects a cause, an allegiance, a religion, or a group for another. **2.** An outlaw. *—adj.* Of, relating to, or resembling a renegade; traitorous.

re•nege (rĭ nĭg′ *or* rĭ nĕg′) *intr.v.* **re•neged, re•neg•ing, re•neges. 1.** To fail to carry out a promise or duty: *renege on a commitment.* **2.** In card games, to fail to follow suit when possible and when required by the rules.

re•new (rĭ no͞o′ *or* rĭ nyo͞o′) *tr.v.* **re•newed, re•new•ing, re•news. 1.** To make new or as if new again; restore: *renew an old building.* **2.** To take up again; resume: *renewed her study of music.* **3.** To arrange for an extension of: *renew a prescription.* **4.** To refill the supply of; replace: *renew supplies.*

re•new•a•ble (rĭ no͞o′ə bəl *or* rĭ nyo͞o′ə bəl) *adj.* **1.** Capable of being renewed: *a renewable membership in the club.* **2.** Capable of being replaced; replaceable: *Wood is a renewable source of energy.*

re•new•al (rĭ no͞o′əl *or* rĭ nyo͞o′əl) *n.* **1.** The act of renewing or the condition of being renewed. **2.** Something renewed.

ren•net (rĕn′ĭt) *n.* **1.** The inner lining of the fourth stomach of calves or the young of related animals. **2.** A dried extract prepared from this lining, used to curdle milk and to make cheese and junket. **3.** Rennin.

ren•nin (rĕn′ĭn) *n.* An enzyme that causes milk to curdle, extracted from rennet and used in making cheeses.

Renoir (rĕn′wär′ *or* rən wär′), **Pierre Auguste.** 1841–1919. French impressionist painter whose works include *Luncheon of the Boating Party* (1881).

Pierre Auguste Renoir

re•nounce (rĭ nouns′) *tr.v.* **re•nounced, re•nounc•ing, re•nounc•es. 1.** To give up (a title, for example), especially by formal announcement: *renounce her title.* **2.** To reject; disown. **—re•nounce′ment** *n.* **—re•nounc′er** *n.*

ren•o•vate (rĕn′ə vāt′) *tr.v.* **ren•o•vat•ed, ren•o•vat•ing, ren•o•vates.** To restore to an earlier condition, as by repairing or remodeling: *renovate a house.* **—ren′o•va′tion** *n.* **—ren′o•va′tor** *n.*

re•nown (rĭ noun′) *n.* The quality of having widespread honor and fame.

re•nowned (rĭ nound′) *adj.* Having renown; famous: *a renowned orator.* See Synonyms at **noted.**

rent¹ (rĕnt) *n.* A contracted payment made at regular intervals for the use of the property of another: *pay the monthly rent.* *—v.* **rent•ed, rent•ing, rents.** *—tr.* **1.** To occupy or use (another's property) in return for regular payments: *rent an apartment; rent a bicycle.* **2.** To grant the use of (one's own property or a service) in return for regular payments. *—intr.* To be for rent: *Rooms rent for 30 dollars a day.* ***—idiom.*** **for rent.** Available for use or service in return for payment. [First written down in 1137 in Middle English and spelled *rente,* from Old French.] **—rent′er** *n.*

rent² (rĕnt) *v.* A past tense and a past participle of **rend.** *—n.* **1.** An opening made by rending: *a rent in the garment.* **2.** A breach of relations between people or groups; a split: *a rent in the family.* [First written down in 1535 in Modern English, from *rend,* to tear, from Old English *rendan.*]

rent•al (rĕn′tl) *n.* **1.** An amount paid or received as rent. **2.** Property for rent: *a summer rental.* **3.** The act of renting: *the rental of a car.*

re•nun•ci•a•tion (rĭ nŭn′sē ā′shən) *n.* The act or an instance of renouncing: *the renunciation of a belief.*

re•o•pen (rē ō′pən) *tr. & intr.v.* **re•o•pened, re•o•pen•ing, re•o•pens. 1.** To open or become open again: *They reopened a trail. The store will reopen after the holiday.* **2.** To take up again or be taken up again; resume.

re•or•gan•ize (rē ôr′gə nīz′) *v.* **re•or•gan•ized, re•or•gan•iz•ing, re•or•gan•iz•es.** *—tr.* To organize again or differently: *She reorganized her ideas and created a new outline for the paper.* *—intr.* To undergo or effect changes in organization: *The group*

ă	pat	oi	boy
ā	pay	ou	out
âr	care	o͝o	took
ä	father	o͞o	boot
ĕ	pet	ŭ	cut
ē	be	ûr	urge
ĭ	pit	th	thin
ī	pie	*th*	this
îr	pier	hw	whoop
ŏ	pot	zh	vision
ō	toe	ə	about
ô	paw	N	*French* bon

is reorganizing. **—re•or′gan•i•za′tion** (rē ôr′gə-nĭ **zā′**shən) *n.* **—re•or′gan•iz′er** *n.*

Rep. *abbr.* An abbreviation of: **1.** Republic. **2.** Representative. **3.** Republican.

re•paid (rĭ**pād′**) *v.* Past tense and past participle of **repay.**

re•pair¹ (rĭ **pâr′**) *tr.v.* **re•paired, re•pair•ing, re•pairs. 1.** To restore to proper or useful condition after damage or injury: *repair an automobile.* **2.** To set right; remedy: *repair an oversight.* —*n.* **1.** The work, act, or process of repairing: *cars in need of repair.* **2.** General condition after use or repairing: *a truck in good repair.* [First written down before 1350 in Middle English and spelled *reparen*, from Latin *reparāre* : *re-*, again + *parāre*, to put in order.] **—re•pair′a•ble** *adj.* **—re•pair′er** *n.*

re•pair² (rĭ **pâr′**) *intr.v.* **re•paired, re•pair•ing, re•pairs.** To go: *The guests repaired to the drawing room.* [First written down before 1300 in Middle English and spelled *repairen*, from Late Latin *repatriāre*, to return to one's country.]

re•pair•man (rĭ **pâr′**măn′) *n.* A man whose job is making repairs.

re•pair•wom•an (rĭ **pâr′**wo͝om′ən) *n.* A woman whose job is making repairs.

rep•a•ra•tion (rĕp′ə **rā′**shən) *n.* **1.** The act or process of repairing or the condition of being repaired. **2.** The act of process of making amends. **3.** Something done or paid to make amends; a compensation. **4. reparations.** Compensation required from a defeated nation for damage or injury during a war.

rep•ar•tee (rĕp′ər **tē′** *or* rĕp′ər **tā′**) *n.* **1.** A swift witty reply. **2.** Conversation marked by the exchange of witty retorts.

re•past (rĭ **păst′**) *n.* A meal or the food provided or eaten at a meal.

re•pa•tri•ate (rē **pā′**trē āt′) *tr.v.* **re•pat•ri•at•ed, re•pat•ri•at•ing, re•pat•ri•ates.** To restore or return to the country of one's birth or citizenship: *repatriated the refugees.*

re•pay (rĭ **pā′**) *tr.v.* **re•paid** (rĭ **pād′**), **re•pay•ing, re•pays. 1.** To pay back: *repaid a debt.* **2.** To give compensation for; make a return for: *repay kindness with kindness.* **3.** To make or do in return: *made a point to repay the visit.* **—re•pay′a•ble** *adj.* **—re•pay′ment** *n.*

re•peal (rĭ **pēl′**) *tr.v.* **re•pealed, re•peal•ing, re•peals.** To withdraw or annul officially; revoke: *repeal a law.* —*n.* The act or process of repealing: *the repeal of an amendment.* [First written down about 1385 in Middle English and spelled *repealen*, from Old French *rapeler* : *re-*, back + *apeler*, to appeal.]

re•peat (rĭ **pēt′**) *v.* **re•peat•ed, re•peat•ing, re•peats.** —*tr.* **1.** To say again: *repeat a question.* **2.** To say in duplication of what another has said: *repeat the phrase after the teacher.* **3.** To recite from memory: *repeat a poem.* **4.** To tell to someone else: *repeat gossip.* **5.** To do, experience, or produce again: *We want to repeat our past successes.* **6.** To express (oneself) in the same way or words: *He's always repeating himself.* —*intr.* To do or say something again. —*n.* **1.** The act of repeating: *the repeat of a performance.* **2.** Something repeated: *This television program is a repeat.* **3.a.** A section of a musical composition that is repeated. **b.** A sign consisting of a pair of vertical dots, used to mark the beginning and end of such a passage. —*adj.* Of or relating to a person or thing that repeats: *a repeat offender; a repeat performance.* [First written down before 1385 in Middle English and spelled *repeten*, from Latin *repetere*, to seek again.] **—re•peat′er** *n.*

re•peat•ed (rĭ **pē′**tĭd) *adj.* Said, done, or occurring again and again: *We heard repeated knocks at the door.* **—re•peat′ed•ly** *adv.*

re•peat•ing decimal (rĭ **pē′**tĭng) *n.* A decimal whose numeral consists of or contains a pattern of digits that is repeated endlessly, as 0.333 . . .

re•pel (rĭ **pĕl′**) *tr.v.* **re•pelled, re•pel•ling, re•pels. 1.** To drive off, force back, or keep away: *repel an enemy attack.* **2.** To be resistant to: *a fabric that repels water.* **3.** To refuse; reject: *repelled her offer of help.* **4.** To cause aversion in: *Her rudeness repels us.* [First written down about 1421 in Middle English and spelled *repellen*, from Latin *repellere* : *re-*, back + *pellere*, to drive.]

re•pel•lent (rĭ **pĕl′**ənt) *adj.* **1.** Acting or tending to repel; capable of repelling: *an odor that is repellent to dogs.* **2.** Causing aversion or disgust: *a repellent manner.* **3.** Resistant or impervious to a specified substance or influence: *a water-repellent cloth.* —*n.* **1.** A substance used to drive off a pest or pests: *an insect repellent.* **2.** A substance used to treat a fabric to make it repellent, as a substance that makes cloth resistant to water.

re•pent (rĭ **pĕnt′**) *v.* **re•pent•ed, re•pent•ing, re•pents.** —*intr.* **1.** To feel remorse or regret for what one has done or failed to do: *We repented later.* **2.** To make a change for the better as a result of remorse or regret for one's sins. —*tr.* To feel regret or remorse for: *repented my bad manners.* [First written down before 1300 in Middle English and spelled *repenten*, from Old French *repentir.*] **—re•pent′er** *n.*

re•pen•tance (rĭ **pĕn′**təns) *n.* **1.** The act or process of repenting. **2.** Remorse or contrition for past conduct or sin.

re•pen•tant (rĭ **pĕn′**tənt) *adj.* Feeling or showing repentance; penitent: *a repentant child.*

re•per•cus•sion (rē′pər **kŭsh′**ən *or* rĕp′ər **kŭsh′**ən) *n.* **1.** An often indirect effect, influence, or result produced by an event or action: *His decision may have alarming repercussions.* **2.** A reflection, especially of sound. **3.** The recoil or rebounding motion of something after impact.

rep•er•toire (**rĕp′**ər twär′) *n.* All of the songs, plays, operas, or other works that a person or company is prepared to perform.

rep•er•to•ry (**rĕp′**ər tôr′ē) *n., pl.* **rep•er•to•ries. 1.** A repertoire. **2.** A theater in which a company presents works from a given repertoire. **3.** A place, such as a storehouse, where a stock of things is kept; a repository. **4.** A stock or collection.

rep•e•ti•tion (rĕp′ĭ **tĭsh′**ən) *n.* **1.** The act or process of repeating or being repeated: *the repetition of a word.* **2.** A recitation or recital, especially of prepared or memorized material.

rep•e•ti•tious (rĕp′ĭ **tĭsh′**əs) *adj.* Filled with repetition, especially needless or tedious repetition: *repetitious arguments.* **—rep′e•ti′tious•ly** *adv.* **—rep′e•ti′tious•ness** *n.*

re•pet•i•tive (rĭ **pĕt′**ĭ tĭv) *adj.* Given to or characterized by repetition. **—re•pet′i•tive•ly** *adv.* **—re•pet′i•tive•ness** *n.*

re•place (rĭ **plās′**) *tr.v.* **re•placed, re•plac•ing, re•plac•es. 1.** To put back into a former position or place: *replaced the dish in the cabinet.* **2.** To take or fill the place of: *automobiles replaced horses.* **3.** To be or provide a substitute for: *replace a broken window.* **4.** To pay back or return; refund. **—re•place′a•ble** *adj.*

re•place•ment (rĭ **plās′**mənt) *n.* **1.** The act or process of replacing or of being replaced: *the replacement of funds.* **2.** A person or thing that replaces: *Stay until your replacement arrives.*

re•play (rē **plā′**) *tr.v.* **re•played, re•play•ing, re•plays.** To play over again: *replay a tape.* —*n.* (**rē′**-plā′). **1.** The act or process of replaying. **2.** Something replayed.

re•plen•ish (rĭ **plĕn′**ĭsh) *tr.v.* **re•plen•ished, re•**

plen•ish•ing, re•plen•ish•es. To fill or complete again; add a new stock or supply to: *replenish the water in the tank.* **—re•plen′ish•er** *n.* **—re•plen′-ish•ment** *n.*

re•plete (rĭ **plēt′**) *adj.* **1.** Plentifully supplied; abounding: *a land replete with streams and forests.* **2.** Filled; gorged: *After two pieces of pie, he felt replete.* **—re•ple′tion** *n.* —SEE NOTE.

rep•li•ca (**rĕp′**lĭ kə) *n.* **1.** A copy or reproduction of a work of art, especially one made by the original artist. **2.** A copy or reproduction, especially one on a smaller scale than the original: *a replica of an early telephone.*

rep•li•cate (**rĕp′**lĭ kāt′) *v.* **rep•li•cat•ed, rep•li•cat•ing, rep•li•cates.** *—tr.* To duplicate, copy, reproduce, or repeat. *—intr.* To become replicated; undergo replication.

rep•li•ca•tion (rĕp′lĭ **kā′**shən) *n.* **1.** A copy or reproduction. **2.** The act or process of duplicating or reproducing.

re•ply (rĭ **plī′**) *v.* **re•plied, re•ply•ing, re•plies.** *—intr.* To say or give an answer: *He replied kindly.* *—tr.* To say or give as an answer: *She replied that she would go.* See Synonyms at **answer.** *—n., pl.* **re•plies.** A response in speech or writing. **—re•pli′er** *n.*

re•port (rĭ **pôrt′**) *n.* **1.** An oral or written account often presented in detail: *a news report.* **2.** Rumor; common talk: *We learned it by report.* **3.** An explosive sound, as of a firearm being discharged. **4.** Reputation: *a person of good report.* *—v.* **re•port•ed, re•port•ing, re•ports.** *—tr.* **1.** To make or present an account of; relate: *report the problem in a memo to the manager.* **2.** To write or provide for publication or broadcast: *report the news.* **3.** To carry back and repeat to another: *reported a message.* **4.** To complain about or denounce: *report them to the police.* *—intr.* **1.** To make a report. **2.** To present oneself: *report for duty.* **3.** To be accountable: *I report directly to the president.* [First written down about 1385 in Middle English, from Latin *reportāre,* to report : *re-,* back + *portāre,* to carry.]

report card *n.* A report of a student's achievement presented at regular intervals to a parent or guardian.

re•port•ed•ly (rĭ **pôr′**tĭd lē) *adv.* By report; supposedly.

re•port•er (rĭ **pôr′**tər) *n.* **1.** A person who investigates, writes, or presents news stories. **2.** A person who writes down the official account of the proceedings in a courtroom.

re•pose[1] (rĭ **pōz′**) *n.* **1.** The act of resting or the state of being at rest. **2.** Peace of mind; freedom from anxiety: *seeking security and repose.* **3.** Calmness; tranquillity: *the repose of the lake.* *—v.* **re•posed, re•pos•ing, re•pos•es.** *—tr.* To lay (oneself) down to rest. *—intr.* **1.** To lie at rest; relax or sleep: *workers reposing at the end of day.* **2.** To lie supported by something: *a dish reposing on the table.* [First written down in 1509 in Modern English, from Late Latin *repausāre,* to cause to rest.]

re•pose[2] (rĭ **pōz′**) *tr.v.* **re•posed, re•pos•ing, re•pos•es.** To place (trust, for example): *They repose their hopes in the new president.* [First written down in 1440 in Middle English and spelled *reposen,* to replace, from Latin *repōnere,* to put away.]

re•pos•i•to•ry (rĭ **pŏz′**ĭ tôr′ē) *n., pl.* **re•pos•i•to•ries.** A place where things may be put for safekeeping.

re•pos•sess (rē′pə **zĕs′**) *tr.v.* **re•pos•sessed, re•pos•sess•ing, re•pos•sess•es.** To retake or regain possession of: *repossess an appliance bought on credit.* **—re′pos•ses′sion** (rē′pə **zĕsh′**ən) *n.*

rep•re•hend (rĕp′rĭ **hĕnd′**) *tr.v.* **rep•re•hend•ed, rep•re•hend•ing, rep•re•hends.** To express disapproval of; reprove: *reprehend their actions.* **—rep′-re•hen′sion** (rĕp′rĭ **hĕn′**shən) *n.*

rep•re•hen•si•ble (rĕp′rĭ **hĕn′**sə bəl) *adj.* Deserving rebuke or censure; worthy of blame: *a reprehensible deed.* **—rep′re•hen′si•bil′i•ty** *n.* **—rep′re•hen′si•bly** *adv.*

rep•re•sent (rĕp′rĭ **zĕnt′**) *tr.v.* **rep•re•sent•ed, rep•re•sent•ing, rep•re•sents.** **1.** To stand for; symbolize: *The rose represents beauty.* **2.** To indicate or communicate by sounds or symbols: *letters represent sounds.* **3.** To portray, as in a picture; depict: *The painting represents a girl with a mischievous smile.* **4.** To describe (something) as having certain characteristics: *represented a product's value falsely.* **5.** To serve as an example of; typify: *Her feelings represent those of the majority.* **6.** To be the equivalent of: *The amount you eat plus the amount you drink represents your total intake.* **7.** To act as the delegate or agent for, especially in a legislative body.

rep•re•sen•ta•tion (rĕp′rĭ zĕn **tā′**shən) *n.* **1.** The act of representing or the condition of being represented. **2.** Something that represents, such as a picture or symbol. **3.** The condition of serving as an official delegate or agent. **4.** The right or privilege of being represented in a governmental body: *no taxation without representation.* **5.** An account or a statement of facts, conditions, or arguments: *improper representations of a product.*

rep•re•sen•ta•tion•al (rĕp′rĭ zĕn **tā′**shə nəl) *adj.* Of or relating to representation, especially realistic graphic representation.

rep•re•sen•ta•tive (rĕp′rĭ **zĕn′**tə tĭv) *n.* **1.** A person or thing that serves as an example or a type for others of the same class. **2.** A person who serves as a delegate or an agent for another. **3.** A member of the U.S. House of Representatives or of the lower house of a state legislature. *—adj.* **1.** Representing, depicting, or portraying or able to do so. **2.** Having power to act as an official delegate or agent. **3.** Of or relating to government by representation. **4.** Serving as a typical example.

re•press (rĭ **prĕs′**) *tr.v.* **re•pressed, re•press•ing, re•press•es.** **1.** To hold back by an act of will: *trying to repress his laughter.* **2.** To put down by force; quell: *repress an uprising.* **3.** To force (painful memories, for example) out of the conscious mind. [First written down about 1385 in Middle English and spelled *repressen,* from Latin *reprimere* : *re-,* back, down + *premere,* to press.]

re•pres•sion (rĭ **prĕsh′**ən) *n.* **1.** The action of repressing or the state of being repressed. **2.** The exclusion of painful desires, impulses, or fears from the conscious mind.

re•pres•sive (rĭ **prĕs′**ĭv) *adj.* Of or tending to cause repression: *repressive measures.* **—re•pres′sive•ly** *adv.*

re•prieve (rĭ **prēv′**) *tr.v.* **re•prieved, re•priev•ing, re•prieves.** **1.** To postpone or cancel the punishment of. **2.** To bring relief to: *The teacher reprieved the proctor from overseeing the examination.* *—n.* **1.** The postponement or cancellation of a punishment. **2.** Temporary relief, as from danger.

rep•ri•mand (**rĕp′**rə mănd′) *tr.v.* **rep•ri•mand•ed, rep•ri•mand•ing, rep•ri•mands.** To rebuke severely or officially. *—n.* A severe or official rebuke. [First written down in 1636 in Modern English, from Latin *reprimenda (culpa),* (fault) to be repressed, from *reprimere,* to restrain.]

re•print (**rē′**prĭnt′) *n.* A new printing, as of a book or a scholarly article, that is identical to an original. *—tr.v.* (rē **prĭnt′**). **re•print•ed, re•print•ing, re•prints.** To print again. **—re•print′er** *n.*

re•pri•sal (rĭ **prī′**zəl) *n.* Retaliation for injury or

Word Building: replete

The word roots *–ple–* and *–plen–* in English words come from the Latin root *plē–,* "full." From the past participle *replētus* of the Latin verb *replēre,* "to fill up again, refill," we have **replete,** "filled, filled up" (using the prefix *re–,* "again"). From the past participle *complētus* of the Latin verb *complēre,* "to fill in, fit," we have **complete,** "entire, finished" (*com–,* "with, together, altogether, completely"). From the Latin adjective *plēnus,* "full, full of," we have **plenitude,** "fullness"; **plenty,** "a full amount"; and **plenipotentiary,** "with full powers."

reporter

ă	pat	oi	boy
ā	pay	ou	out
âr	care	ŏŏ	took
ä	father	ōō	boot
ĕ	pet	ŭ	cut
ē	be	ûr	urge
ĭ	pit	th	thin
ī	pie	*th*	this
îr	pier	hw	whoop
ŏ	pot	zh	vision
ō	toe	ə	about
ô	paw	N	*French* bon

reptile

Top: Common lizard
Center: River turtle
Bottom: Garter snake

damage inflicted, often by one nation against another.

re•prise (rĭ **prēz′**) *n.* **1.** A repetition of a musical phrase or verse. **2.** A musical phrase or verse that is to be repeated.

re•proach (rĭ **prōch′**) *tr.v.* **re•proached, re•proach•ing, re•proach•es. 1.** To express disapproval of, criticism of, or disappointment in (someone). **2.** To bring shame upon; disgrace. *—n.* **1.** Blame; rebuke. **2.** A person or thing that deserves blame or disapproval: *Their behavior was a reproach to the whole school.* **3.** Disgrace; shame.

re•proach•ful (rĭ **prōch′**fəl) *adj.* Expressing blame or reproach: *a reproachful glance.* **—re•proach′ful•ly** *adv.*

rep•ro•bate (**rĕp′**rə bāt′) *n.* A morally unprincipled person. *—adj.* Morally unprincipled; shameless.

re•pro•duce (rē′prə **do͞os′** *or* rē′prə **dyo͞os′**) *v.* **re•pro•duced, re•pro•duc•ing, re•pro•duc•es.** *—tr.* **1.** To make a counterpart, an image, or a copy of: *A phonograph reproduces music.* **2.** To generate or produce (offspring). *—intr.* **1.** To generate or produce offspring. **2.** To undergo copying: *Black-and-white photographs reproduce well.*

re•pro•duc•tion (rē′prə **dŭk′**shən) *n.* **1.** The act of reproducing or the process of being reproduced: *the reproduction of sound.* **2.** Something that is reproduced; a copy: *a reproduction of a painting.* **3.** The process by which organisms produce other organisms of the same kind.

re•pro•duc•tive (rē′prə **dŭk′**tĭv) *adj.* **1.** Of or relating to reproduction, especially by living things. **2.** Tending to reproduce: *a highly reproductive insect.*

re•proof (rĭ **pro͞of′**) *n.* The act or an instance of reproving; a rebuke.

re•prove (rĭ **pro͞ov′**) *tr.v.* **re•proved, re•prov•ing, re•proves. 1.** To express disapproval of (a fault, for example). **2.** To find fault with (someone).

rep•tile (**rĕp′**tīl *or* **rĕp′**tĭl′) *n.* Any of various cold-blooded animals, such as snakes, turtles, and crocodiles, that have a backbone, are covered with scales or horny plates, and breathe by means of lungs. [First written down before 1393 in Middle English and spelled *reptil*, from Latin *rēptilis*, creeping.]

rep•til•i•an (rĕp **tĭl′**ē ən *or* rĕp **tĭl′**yən) *adj.* **1.** Of or relating to reptiles: *reptilian eggs.* **2.** Resembling a reptile, especially in an unpleasant way: *cold reptilian eyes.*

re•pub•lic (rĭ **pŭb′**lĭk) *n.* **1.** A nation whose head of state is not a monarch and in modern times is usually a president. **2.** A nation ruled by officers and representatives elected by the people. **3.** Often **Republic.** A specific republican government of a nation: *the Fourth Republic of France.* [First written down in 1604 in Modern English, from Latin *rēs-pūblica* : *rēs*, thing + *pūblicus*, of the people.]

re•pub•li•can (rĭ **pŭb′**lĭ kən) *adj.* **1.** Of, like, or characteristic of a republic: *a republican form of government.* **2. Republican.** Of, relating to, or belonging to the Republican Party. *—n.* **1.** A person who advocates a republican form of government. **2. Republican.** A member of the Republican Party.

Republican Party *n.* One of the two major political parties of the United States, organized in 1854 to oppose slavery.

re•pu•di•ate (rĭ **pyo͞o′**dē āt′) *tr.v.* **re•pu•di•at•ed, re•pu•di•at•ing, re•pu•di•ates. 1.** To reject the validity or authority of; disavow: *repudiate an agreement.* **2.** To reject as unfounded, untrue, or unjust: *repudiate an accusation.* **3.** To refuse to recognize or pay: *repudiate an old debt.* **—re•pu′di•a′tion** *n.* **—re•pu′di•a′tive** *adj.*

re•pug•nance (rĭ **pŭg′**nəns) *n.* Extreme dislike or aversion.

re•pug•nant (rĭ **pŭg′**nənt) *adj.* Arousing disgust or aversion; offensive or repulsive: *a repugnant odor.*

re•pulse (rĭ **pŭls′**) *tr.v.* **re•pulsed, re•puls•ing, re•puls•es. 1.** To drive back; repel: *repulse the enemy attackers.* **2.** To rebuff or reject with rudeness, coldness, or denial: *She repulsed his offers to help.* *—n.* **1.** The act of repulsing or the state of being repulsed. **2.** A firm rejection. [First written down before 1425 in Middle English and spelled *repulsen*, from Latin *repellere*.]

re•pul•sion (rĭ **pŭl′**shən) *n.* **1.** The act of repulsing or the condition of being repulsed: *the repulsion of a surprise attack.* **2.** Extreme aversion.

re•pul•sive (rĭ **pŭl′**sĭv) *adj.* **1.** Causing repugnance or aversion; disgusting: *a repulsive odor.* **2.** Tending to repel or drive off.

rep•u•ta•ble (**rĕp′**yə tə bəl) *adj.* Having a good reputation; honorable: *a reputable antiques dealer.* **—rep′u•ta•bly** *adv.*

rep•u•ta•tion (rĕp′yə **tā′**shən) *n.* **1.** The general estimation in which a person is held by the public. **2.** A particular characteristic for which a person or thing is noted: *He has a reputation for honesty.*

re•pute (rĭ **pyo͞ot′**) *tr.v.* **re•put•ed, re•put•ing, re•putes.** To consider; suppose: *He is reputed to be honest.* *—n.* Reputation.

re•put•ed (rĭ **pyo͞o′**tĭd) *adj.* Generally supposed to be such: *the reputed leader of the movement.* **—re•put′ed•ly** *adv.*

re•quest (rĭ **kwĕst′**) *tr.v.* **re•quest•ed, re•quest•ing, re•quests. 1.** To express a desire for; ask for: *a letter requesting information.* **2.** To ask (a person) to do something: *I requested him to come along.* *—n.* **1.** The act of asking: *Other sizes are available on request.* **2.** Something asked for: *We received requests for extra copies of the article.*

req•ui•em (**rĕk′**wē əm) *n.* **1.** In the Roman Catholic Church, a mass for a person who has died. **2.** A musical composition for such a mass.

re•quire (rĭ **kwīr′**) *tr.v.* **re•quired, re•quir•ing, re•quires. 1.** To be in need of; need: *Do you require help?* **2.** To call for as necessary; demand: *Skiing requires practice.* **3.** To impose an obligation upon; order: *The school requires all students to study mathematics.*

re•quire•ment (rĭ **kwīr′**mənt) *n.* **1.** Something that is required; a necessity: *a person's daily food requirement.* **2.** Something established as a necessary condition to something else: *What are the requirements for the job?*

req•ui•site (**rĕk′**wĭ zĭt) *adj.* Required; essential. *—n.* Something that is essential; a necessity.

req•ui•si•tion (rĕk′wĭ **zĭsh′**ən) *n.* **1.** A formal written request for something needed. **2.** A necessity; a requirement. *—tr.v.* **req•ui•si•tioned, req•ui•si•tion•ing, req•ui•si•tions. 1.** To demand, as for military needs. **2.** To make demands of: *requisitioned the department for additional supplies.*

re•quite (rĭ **kwīt′**) *tr.v.* **re•quit•ed, re•quit•ing, re•quites. 1.** To make repayment or return for: *requite another's love.* **2.** To avenge. **—re•quit′er** *n.*

re•run (**rē′**rŭn′) *n.* The act or an instance of repeating a recorded movie or a recorded television performance. *—tr.v.* (rē **rŭn′**). **re•ran** (rē **răn′**), **re•run, re•run•ning, re•runs.** To present a rerun of.

re•sale (**rē′**sāl′ *or* rē **sāl′**) *n.* The act of selling again.

re•scind (rĭ **sĭnd′**) *tr.v.* **re•scind•ed, re•scind•ing, re•scinds.** To make void; repeal or annul. **—re•scind′a•ble** *adj.* **—re•scind′er** *n.*

res•cue (**rĕs′**kyo͞o) *tr.v.* **res•cued, res•cu•ing, res•cues.** To set free, as from danger or imprisonment; save. *—n.* An act of rescuing or saving: *A passer-by came to our rescue.* [First written down about 1300 in Middle English and spelled *rescouen*, from Old French *rescourre*.] **—res′cu•er** *n.*

re•search (rĭ **sûrch′** *or* **rē′**sûrch′) *n.* Careful study of a given subject, field, or problem, undertaken to discover facts or principles: *I'm doing research on our town's history.* *—tr.v.* **re•searched, re•search•ing, re•search•es.** To do research on (something); investigate: *He is researching the origins of football.* **—re•search′er** *n.*

re•sem•blance (rĭ **zĕm′**bləns) *n.* The state or quality of resembling, especially similarity in appearance or in external or superficial details.

re•sem•ble (rĭ **zĕm′**bəl) *tr.v.* **re•sem•bled, re•sem•bling, re•sem•bles.** To have a similarity or likeness to; be like. [First written down in 1340 in Middle English and spelled *resemblen*, from Old French *resembler*, from Latin *simulāre*, to imitate.]

re•sent (rĭ **zĕnt′**) *tr.v.* **re•sent•ed, re•sent•ing, re•sents.** To feel angry at (something considered mean, unjust, or offensive): *resent a rude remark.* [First written down in 1605 in Modern English, from Old French *resentir*, to feel strongly, from Latin *sentīre*, to feel.]

re•sent•ful (rĭ **zĕnt′**fəl) *adj.* Full of, characterized by, or inclined to feel resentment. **—re•sent′ful•ly** *adv.* **—re•sent′ful•ness** *n.*

re•sent•ment (rĭ **zĕnt′**mənt) *n.* Anger felt as a result of something considered mean, unjust, or offensive.

res•er•va•tion (rĕz′ər **vā′**shən) *n.* **1.** The act of reserving; a keeping back or withholding. **2.** Something that is kept back or withheld. **3.** A limiting qualification, condition, or exception: *He has certain reservations about the proposal.* **4.** A tract of land set apart by the federal government for a certain purpose, especially one for the use of a Native American people. **5.** An arrangement by which space, as in a hotel or on an airplane, is secured in advance.

re•serve (rĭ **zûrv′**) *tr.v.* **re•served, re•serv•ing, re•serves. 1.** To keep back, as for a particular purpose or later use: *reserve a tablecloth for special occasions.* See Synonyms at **keep. 2.** To order or book in advance for a specified time or date: *reserve a table in a restaurant.* **3.** To keep or retain for oneself: *I reserve the right to reply at a later date.* *—n.* **1.** Something kept back or saved for future use or a special purpose: *a fuel reserve.* **2.** The act of reserving. **3.** A tendency to talk little and keep one's feelings to oneself. **4.** A reservation of public land: *a forest reserve.* **5.** The part of a country's armed forces not on active duty but available in an emergency. Often used in the plural. [First written down in 1357 in Middle English and spelled *reserven*, from Latin *reservāre*, to keep back.]

re•served (rĭ **zûrvd′**) *adj.* **1.** Held in reserve; kept back or set aside: *a reserved seat.* **2.** Marked by self-restraint and reticence: *a shy, reserved person.* **—re•serv′ed•ly** (rĭ **zûr′**vĭd lē) *adv.*

re•serv•ist (rĭ **zûr′**vĭst) *n.* A member of a military reserve.

res•er•voir (**rĕz′**ər vwär′ *or* **rĕz′**ər vwôr′) *n.* **1.** A natural or artificial pond or lake used for the storage of water. **2.** A chamber or receptacle used for storing a fluid: *the reservoir of a fountain pen.* **3.** A large or extra supply; a reserve: *a reservoir of good will.*

re•side (rĭ **zīd′**) *intr.v.* **re•sid•ed, re•sid•ing, re•sides. 1.** To live in a place permanently or for an extended period: *She resides in Miami.* **2.** To lie or be contained: *the spirit of fellowship that resides within us.* [First written down before 1475 in Middle English and spelled *residen*, from Latin *residēre*, to remain behind, reside.] **—re•sid′er** *n.*

res•i•dence (**rĕz′**ĭ dəns) *n.* **1.** The place in which a person lives; a dwelling. **2.** The act or period of residing somewhere: *He learned Spanish during his residence in Mexico.* **3.** A residency.

res•i•den•cy (**rĕz′**ĭ dən sē) *n., pl.* **res•i•den•cies.** The period during which a physician receives specialized clinical training.

res•i•dent (**rĕz′**ĭ dənt) *n.* **1.** A person who resides in a particular place permanently or for an extended period. **2.** A physician serving a period of residency. *—adj.* **1.** Living in a particular place: *a resident alien.* **2.** Living somewhere in connection with one's work: *a resident physician.*

res•i•den•tial (rĕz′ĭ **dĕn′**shəl) *adj.* **1.** Of, relating to, or having residence: *a residential college.* **2.** Of, suitable for, or limited to residences: *a residential neighborhood.*

re•sid•u•al (rĭ **zĭj′**o͞o əl) *adj.* **1.** Of, relating to, or characteristic of a residue. **2.** Remaining as a residue: *the residual solids left when a liquid evaporates.* *—n.* Something left over at the end of a process; a remainder. **—re•sid′u•al•ly** *adv.*

res•i•due (**rĕz′**ĭ do͞o′ *or* **rĕz′**ĭ dyo͞o′) *n.* Something that remains after a part is removed. [First written down before 1350 in Middle English, from Latin *residuus*, remaining, from *residēre*, to remain behind.]

re•sign (rĭ **zīn′**) *v.* **re•signed, re•sign•ing, re•signs.** *—tr.* **1.** To submit (oneself) passively; accept as inevitable: *resigned myself to a long wait.* **2.** To give up (a position, for example), especially by formal notification. *—intr.* To give up one's job or office; quit, especially by formal notification. [First written down about 1370 in Middle English and spelled *resignen*, from Latin *resignāre*, to unseal : *re-*, back, off + *signum*, mark, seal.]

res•ig•na•tion (rĕz′ĭg **nā′**shən) *n.* **1.** The act or an instance of resigning: *The commissioner regretted his resignation.* **2.** Acceptance of something that seems inescapable; submission: *a tone of resignation in her voice.* **3.** An oral or written statement that one is resigning a position or office.

re•signed (rĭ **zīnd′**) *adj.* Feeling or marked by resignation; acquiescent: *a resigned look on his face.* **—re•sign′ed•ly** (rĭ **zī′**nĭd lē) *adv.*

re•sil•ient (rĭ **zĭl′**yənt) *adj.* **1.** Having the ability to recover quickly, as from misfortune. **2.** Capable of returning to an original shape or position, as after having been compressed. [First written down in 1644 in Modern English, from Latin *resilīre*, to leap back.] **—re•sil′ience** *n.*

res•in (**rĕz′**ĭn) *n.* **1.** Any of several clear or translucent yellowish or brownish substances that ooze from certain trees and plants and are used in varnishes, lacquers, and for many other purposes. **2.** Any of various artificial substances that have similar properties and are used in making plastics. [First written down before 1382 in Middle English, from Greek *rhētinē*.]

res•in•ous (**rĕz′**ə nəs) *adj.* Of, containing, or resembling resin: *a resinous substance.*

re•sist (rĭ **zĭst′**) *v.* **re•sist•ed, re•sist•ing, re•sists.** *—tr.* **1.** To strive to fend off or offset the actions, effects, or force of: *resist an attack.* See Synonyms at **oppose. 2.** To undergo little or no change as a result of the action of; withstand: *a material that resists heat.* **3.** To keep from giving in or yielding to: *resist pressure; resist temptation.* *—intr.* To offer resistance. *—n.* A substance used to cover and protect a surface, as against corrosion. [First written down about 1380 in Middle English and spelled *resisten*, from Latin *resistere* : *re-*, back + *sistere*, to place.]

re•sis•tance (rĭ **zĭs′**təns) *n.* **1.** The act, process, or capability of resisting: *The enemy offered little resistance.* **2.** A force that tends to oppose or retard

reservoir

Shasta Dam on the Sacramento River in northern California

ă	pat	oi	boy
ā	pay	ou	out
âr	care	o͝o	took
ä	father	o͞o	boot
ĕ	pet	ŭ	cut
ē	be	ûr	urge
ĭ	pit	th	thin
ī	pie	*th*	this
îr	pier	hw	whoop
ŏ	pot	zh	vision
ō	toe	ə	about
ô	paw	N	*French* bon

motion: *an automobile body shaped to lessen wind resistance.* **3.** Often **Resistance.** An underground organization leading the struggle for national liberation in a country under the control of military forces or an oppressive government. **4.** The capacity of an organism to defend itself against a disease. **5.** The opposition that an object offers to the passage of an electric current, resulting in a change of electric energy into heat.

re•sis•tant (rĭ **zĭs′**tənt) *adj.* Capable of resisting: *a carpet that is resistant to stains.*

re•sist•less (rĭ **zĭst′**lĭs) *adj.* **1.** Impossible to resist; irresistible. **2.** Powerless to resist; unresisting.

re•sis•tor (rĭ **zĭs′**tər) *n.* A device used to control current in an electric circuit by providing resistance.

res•o•lute (**rĕz′**ə lo͞ot′) *adj.* Firm or determined; unwavering: *a resolute voice.* **—res′o•lute′ly** *adv.* **—res′o•lute′ness** *n.*

res•o•lu•tion (rĕz′ə **lo͞o′**shən) *n.* **1.** The state or quality of being resolute; firm determination: *face the future with resolution.* **2.** A resolving to do something: *a resolution to get in shape.* **3.** A formal statement of a decision or an expression of opinion adopted by an assembly, legislature, or other organization. **4.** A solution or explanation; an answer: *the resolution of a problem.* **5.a.** The musical progression of a dissonant tone or chord to a consonant tone or chord. **b.** The tone or chord at which such a progression ends. **6.** The act or process of separating or reducing something into its smaller parts: *the resolution of sunlight into its spectral colors by a prism.*

re•solve (rĭ **zŏlv′**) *v.* **re•solved, re•solv•ing, re•solves.** *—tr.* **1.** To make a firm decision (to do something): *He resolved to work harder.* **2.** To cause (a person) to reach a decision. **3.** To find a solution to; solve: *resolve a conflict.* **4.** To remove or dispel (doubts). **5.** To change or convert: *The issue resolved itself to a single question.* **6.** To cause (a tone or chord) to pass from dissonance to consonance. *—intr.* **1.** To reach a decision or make a determination. **2.** To become separated or reduced to smaller parts. *—n.* **1.** Firmness of purpose; resolution: *work together with resolve.* **2.** A decision or resolution: *a resolve to try harder.*

res•o•nance (**rĕz′**ə nəns) *n.* **1.** The quality or condition of being resonant: *the resonance of a speaker's voice.* **2.a.** The increased response of a physical body or system to an oscillating driving force when the force oscillates at a frequency at which the body or system tends to oscillate naturally. **b.** A frequency at which such a body or system tends to oscillate naturally. **c.** The reinforcement or lengthening of sounds, especially musical tones, as a result of resonances in the room or place in which they are produced.

res•o•nant (**rĕz′**ə nənt) *adj.* **1.** Strong and deep in tone; resounding: *a resonant voice.* **2.** Continuing to sound in the ears or memory; echoing. **3.** Producing or having resonance. **—res′o•nant•ly** *adv.*

re•sort (rĭ **zôrt′**) *intr.v.* **re•sort•ed, re•sort•ing, re•sorts. 1.** To go or turn for help or as a means of achieving something: *The government resorted to censorship.* **2.** To go customarily or frequently. *—n.* **1.** A place where people go for relaxation or recreation: *a ski resort.* **2.** A person or thing turned to for aid or relief: *I would ask him only as a last resort.* **3.** The act of turning to for aid or relief; recourse: *We were able to raise money without resort to borrowing.*

re•sound (rĭ **zound′**) *intr.v.* **re•sound•ed, re•sound•ing, re•sounds. 1.** To be filled with sound; reverberate: *The stadium resounded with cheers.* **2.** To make a loud, long, or reverberating sound: *The music resounded through the hall.*

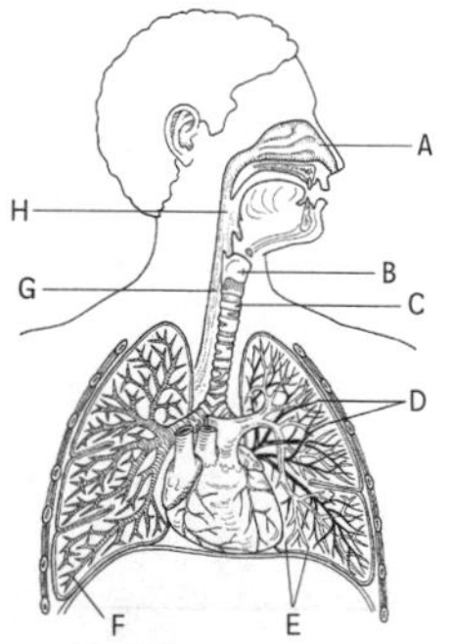

respiratory system

A. Nasal passages
B. Larynx
C. Trachea
D. Veins
E. Arteries
F. Bronchus
G. Esophagus
H. Throat

re•source (**rē′**sôrs′ *or* rĭ **sôrs′**) *n.* **1.** Something that can be used for support or help: *We have exhausted every resource at our disposal.* **2. resources.** An available supply that can be drawn on when needed. **3.** Something that is a source of wealth to a country. **4.** The ability to deal with a situation effectively.

re•source•ful (rĭ **sôrs′**fəl) *adj.* Able to act effectively or imaginatively, especially in a difficult situation: *a resourceful leader.* **—re•source′ful•ly** *adv.* **—re•source′ful•ness** *n.*

re•spect (rĭ **spĕkt′**) *tr.v.* **re•spect•ed, re•spect•ing, re•spects. 1.** To feel or show high regard for; esteem. **2.** To avoid violation of or interference with: *respect the speed limit.* *—n.* **1.** A feeling of high regard; esteem: *respect for one's elders.* **2.** The condition of being regarded with honor or esteem: *She is held in respect by her colleagues.* **3.** Willingness to show consideration or appreciation. **4. respects.** Polite expressions of consideration or regard: *pay one's respects to the family of the deceased.* **5.** A particular aspect or feature: *The two plans differ in one major respect.* **6.** Relation; reference: *I have a comment with respect to your question.* [First written down in 1548 in Modern English, from Latin *respicere*, to look back at, regard : *re-*, back + *specere*, to look at.] —See Note at **regard.**

re•spect•a•ble (rĭ **spĕk′**tə bəl) *adj.* **1.** Worthy of respect or esteem: *respectable people.* **2.** Of or appropriate to proper behavior or conventional conduct. **—re•spect′a•bil′i•ty** *n.* **—re•spect′a•bly** *adv.*

re•spect•ful (rĭ **spĕkt′**fəl) *adj.* Showing or marked by proper respect: *a respectful tone of voice.* **—re•spect′ful•ly** *adv.*

re•spect•ing (rĭ **spĕk′**tĭng) *prep.* With respect to; concerning: *laws respecting personal property.*

re•spec•tive (rĭ **spĕk′**tĭv) *adj.* Relating to each of two or more persons or things; particular: *The delegates to the conference are experts in their respective fields.*

re•spec•tive•ly (rĭ **spĕk′**tĭv lē) *adv.* Each in the order named: *Albany, Augusta, and Atlanta are respectively the capitals of New York, Maine, and Georgia.*

re•spell (rē **spĕl′**) *tr.v.* **re•spelled** or **re•spelt** (rē-**spĕlt′**), **re•spell•ing, re•spells.** To spell again or in a new way, especially by using a phonetic alphabet.

res•pi•ra•tion (rĕs′pə **rā′**shən) *n.* **1.** The act or process of inhaling and exhaling; breathing. **2.** A process of metabolism by which a living organism takes in oxygen and oxidizes nutrients to produce energy, usually releasing carbon dioxide and other products. [First written down in 1392 in Middle English and spelled *respiracioun*, from Latin *respīrāre*, to breathe in and out.]

res•pi•ra•tor (**rĕs′**pə rā′tər) *n.* **1.** A device, usually having a mask that fits over a person's nose and mouth, for giving artificial respiration. **2.** A filter worn over the mouth or nose, or both, to protect the respiratory system.

res•pi•ra•to•ry (**rĕs′**pər ə tôr′ē *or* rĭ **spīr′**ə tôr′ē) *adj.* Of, relating to, or affecting respiration.

respiratory system *n.* The system of organs and passages involved in the intake and exchange of oxygen and carbon dioxide between a living organism and its environment.

re•spire (rĭ **spīr′**) *intr.v.* **re•spired, re•spir•ing, re•spires. 1.** To inhale and exhale; breathe. **2.** To carry on the metabolic process of respiration.

res•pite (**rĕs′**pĭt) *n.* **1.** A usually short interval of rest or relief. **2.** In law, the temporary suspension of a death sentence; a reprieve.

re•splen•dent (rĭ **splĕn′**dənt) *adj.* Splendid or dazzling in appearance; brilliant: *She was resplendent in her jeweled gown.* —**re•splen′dence** *n.*

re•spond (rĭ spŏnd′) *intr.v.* **re•spond•ed, re•spond•ing, re•sponds. 1.** To make a reply; answer. See Synonyms at **answer. 2.** To act in return or in answer: *respond to a challenge.* **3.** To react positively or favorably: *The patient responded well to the treatment.* [First written down about 1300 in Middle English and spelled *responden*, from Latin *respondēre* : *re-*, back + *spondēre*, to promise.]

re•sponse (rĭ spŏns′) *n.* **1.** The act of responding. **2.** An answer or a reply: *Your response to my letter was most heartening.* **3.** A reaction, as that of a living organism or mechanism to a stimulus or an action. **4.** Something that is spoken or sung by a congregation or choir in answer to the minister or priest.

re•spon•si•bil•i•ty (rĭ spŏn′sə bĭl′ĭ tē) *n., pl.* **re•spon•si•bil•i•ties. 1.** The state, quality, or fact of being responsible: *Responsibility usually comes with age.* **2.** Something that one is responsible for; a duty or an obligation: *The two cats are my responsibility.*

re•spon•si•ble (rĭ spŏn′sə bəl) *adj.* **1.** Liable to account for anything that happens or goes wrong: *As the eldest, you'll be responsible while we're away.* **2.** Involving important duties or obligations: *a responsible job.* **3.** Being the cause or source of something: *Viruses are responsible for many diseases.* **4.** Having to account for one's actions; accountable: *a government responsible to the people.* **5.** Dependable; reliable; trustworthy: *a mature and responsible person.* —**re•spon′si•ble•ness** *n.* —**re•spon′si•bly** *adv.*

re•spon•sive (rĭ spŏn′sĭv) *adj.* **1.** Answering or replying; responding. **2.** Reacting readily, as to suggestions or influences: *a responsive student.* **3.** Containing or using responses: *The minister led a responsive reading.* —**re•spon′sive•ly** *adv.* —**re•spon′sive•ness** *n.*

rest[1] (rĕst) *n.* **1.** A period of inactivity, relaxation, or sleep: *The hikers stopped for a brief rest.* **2.** Peace, ease, or relaxation resulting from this: *Be sure to get plenty of rest.* **3.** Mental or emotional tranquillity. **4.** An absence or ending of motion: *The car slowed and came to rest.* **5.** The repose of death: *go to one's eternal rest.* **6.** Relief or freedom from disquiet or disturbance. **7.a.** A musical symbol indicating that a performer or group of performers is to be silent for a time equal to the length of a given note. **b.** The interval of silence corresponding to such a symbol or a series of such symbols. **8.** A device used as a support: *a back rest.* —*v.* **rest•ed, rest•ing, rests.** —*intr.* **1.** To cease motion, work, or activity. **2.** To lie down, especially to sleep. **3.** To be at peace or ease; be tranquil. **4.** To lie or lean on a support: *Her head rested on the pillow.* **5.** To be fixed or directed on something: *His gaze rested on the book.* **6.** To remain; linger. **7.** To depend or rely: *The whole theory rests on one basic assumption.* **8.** To be located or be in a specified place. **9.** To conclude the presentation of evidence in a legal case. —*tr.* **1.** To give rest or repose to: *I rested my eyes.* **2.** To lay or lean for ease, support, or repose: *I rested the rake against the fence.* **3.** To base or ground. **4.** To fix or direct (the gaze, for example). **5.** To conclude the presentation of evidence in (a legal case). [First written down about 725 in Old English and spelled *ræste*.]

❑ *These sound alike:* **rest**[1] (period of inactivity), **rest**[2] (remainder), **wrest** (pull away).

rest[2] (rĕst) *n.* **1.** The part that is left over after something has been taken away; the remainder: *pay the rest on credit.* **2.** That or those remaining: *The beginning was boring, but the rest was interesting.* [First written down about 1440 in Middle English, from Latin *restāre*, to stay behind : *re-*, back, behind + *stāre*, to stand.]

❑ *These sound alike:* **rest**[2] (remainder), **rest**[1] (period of inactivity), **wrest** (pull away).

re•state (rē stāt′) *tr.v.* **re•stat•ed, re•stat•ing, re•states.** To state again or in a new form. —**re•state′ment** *n.*

res•tau•rant (rĕs′tər ənt *or* rĕs′tə ränt′) *n.* A place where meals are served to the public. [First written down in 1827 in Modern English, from French, from *restaurer*, to restore.]

res•tau•ra•teur (rĕs′tər ə tûr′) *n.* The manager or owner of a restaurant.

rest•ful (rĕst′fəl) *adj.* **1.** Affording, marked by, or suggesting rest; tranquil: *a restful vacation.* **2.** Being at rest; quiet. —**rest′ful•ness** *n.*

res•ti•tu•tion (rĕs′tĭ to͞o′shən *or* rĕs′tĭ tyo͞o′shən) *n.* **1.** The act of restoring something to its rightful owner. **2.** The act of making good or compensating for damage, loss, or injury.

res•tive (rĕs′tĭv) *adj.* **1.** Impatient or restless under restriction, opposition, criticism, or delay: *The crowd gradually became restive.* **2.** Resisting control; difficult to control: *a restive horse.* —**res′tive•ly** *adv.* —**res′tive•ness** *n.*

rest•less (rĕst′lĭs) *adj.* **1.** Marked by a lack of quiet, rest, or sleep: *a restless night.* **2.** Unable to rest, relax, or be still: *a restless child.* **3.** Never still or motionless: *the restless sea.* —**rest′less•ly** *adv.* —**rest′less•ness** *n.*

res•to•ra•tion (rĕs′tə rā′shən) *n.* **1.a.** The action of restoring: *The damage was too great for restoration.* **b.** A particular act of restoring: *The restoration of the sculptures was expensive.* **c.** The state of being restored: *The house is now in restoration.* **2.** Something restored: *This building is a restoration of a colonial farmhouse.* **3. Restoration. a.** The return of Charles II to the British throne in 1660. **b.** The period between his return and the Revolution of 1688.

re•stor•a•tive (rĭ stôr′ə tĭv) *adj.* **1.** Of or relating to restoration. **2.** Tending or having the power to restore. —*n.* Something that restores.

re•store (rĭ stôr′) *tr.v.* **re•stored, re•stor•ing, re•stores. 1.** To bring back into existence or use; reestablish: *Such stories restore my faith in humanity.* **2.** To bring back to an original condition: *restore an old building.* **3.** To bring (someone) back to a prior position: *restore an emperor to the throne.* [First written down about 1300 in Middle English and spelled *restoren*, from Latin *restaurāre*.]

re•strain (rĭ strān′) *tr.v.* **re•strained, re•strain•ing, re•strains. 1.** To hold back or keep in check; control. **2.** To hold (a person) back; prevent: *restrained them from going.* **3.** To deprive of freedom or liberty. [First written down before 1349 in Middle English and spelled *restreinen*, from Latin *restringere*, to bind back.]

re•straint (rĭ strānt′) *n.* **1.** The act of restraining. **2.** The condition of being restrained: *He had to be held in restraint.* **3.** Something that holds back or restrains: *a program of wage restraints.* **4.** Control or repression of feelings; constraint.

re•strict (rĭ strĭkt′) *tr.v.* **re•strict•ed, re•strict•ing, re•stricts.** To keep or confine within limits.

re•strict•ed (rĭ strĭk′tĭd) *adj.* **1.** Kept within certain limits: *a restricted number of students.* **2.** Excluding or unavailable to certain groups: *a restricted area.*

re•stric•tion (rĭ strĭk′shən) *n.* **1.a.** The act of limiting or restricting: *restriction of immigration.* **b.** The state of being restricted. **2.** Something that limits or restricts: *The students were subjected to restrictions on their personal liberties.*

re•stric•tive (rĭ strĭk′tĭv) *adj.* **1.** Tending or serving

A B

rest[1]
A. Note
B. Rest

ă	pat	oi	boy
ā	pay	ou	out
âr	care	o͝o	took
ä	father	o͞o	boot
ĕ	pet	ŭ	cut
ē	be	ûr	urge
ĭ	pit	th	thin
ī	pie	*th*	this
îr	pier	hw	whoop
ŏ	pot	zh	vision
ō	toe	ə	about
ô	paw	N	*French* bon

to restrict: *restrictive legislation.* **2.** Of or relating to restriction. **3.** In grammar, being a clause or phrase that describes a noun and restricts the meaning of the sentence. In the sentence *People who read a great deal have large vocabularies,* the clause *who read a great deal* is restrictive. **—re•stric′tive•ly** *adv.* **—re•stric′tive•ness** *n.*

rest•room (rĕst′ro͞om′ *or* rĕst′ro͝om′) *n.* A room with toilets and sinks for public use.

re•sult (rĭ zŭlt′) *intr.v.* **re•sult•ed, re•sult•ing, re•sults. 1.** To come about as a consequence: *Nothing resulted from his efforts.* See Synonyms at **follow. 2.** To end in a certain way: *The negotiations resulted in a new treaty.* —*n.* The consequence of a particular action, operation, or course; an outcome: *The book is the result of years of hard work.*

re•sul•tant (rĭ zŭl′tənt) *adj.* Issuing or following as a result or consequence: *the resultant good feeling after signing the treaty.*

re•sume (rĭ zo͞om′) *v.* **re•sumed, re•sum•ing, re•sumes.** —*tr.* **1.** To begin or take up again after a break: *resumed our dinner.* **2.** To assume, occupy, or take again: *The former prime minister resumed power.* **3.** To take on or take back again. —*intr.* To begin again or continue after interruption: *The meeting will resume after lunch.* [First written down in 1404 in Middle English and spelled *resumen,* from Latin *resūmere* : *re-*, again, back + *sūmere,* to take.]

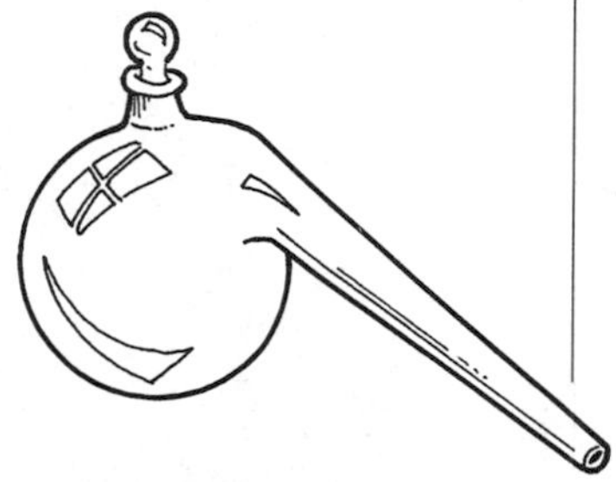
retort²

ré•su•mé (rĕz′o͞o mā′ *or* rĕz′o͞o mā′) *n.* **1.** An outline of one's professional history and experience, submitted when applying for a job. **2.** A summary: *a brief résumé of the week's events.*

re•sump•tion (rĭ zŭmp′shən) *n.* The act or an instance of resuming: *a resumption of diplomatic relations.*

re•sur•gence (rĭ sûr′jəns) *n.* **1.** A continuing after interruption; a renewal. **2.** A restoration to use, acceptance, activity, or vigor; a revival. **—re•sur′gent** *adj.*

res•ur•rect (rĕz′ə rĕkt′) *tr.v.* **res•ur•rect•ed, res•ur•rect•ing, res•ur•rects. 1.** To bring back to life; raise from the dead. **2.** To bring back into practice, notice, or use: *resurrect an old custom.*

res•ur•rec•tion (rĕz′ə rĕk′shən) *n.* **1.** The act of rising from the dead or returning to life. **2.** The act of bringing back into practice, notice, or use: *the resurrection of an ancient practice.* **3. Resurrection.** In Christianity, the rising of Jesus from the dead on the third day after the Crucifixion.

re•sus•ci•tate (rĭ sŭs′ĭ tāt′) *v.* **re•sus•ci•tat•ed, re•sus•ci•tat•ing, re•sus•ci•tates.** —*tr.* To return life or consciousness to; revive. —*intr.* To regain consciousness. **—re•sus′ci•ta′tion** *n.*

re•sus•ci•ta•tor (rĭ sŭs′ĭ tā′tər) *n.* An apparatus that resuscitates by forcing oxygen into a person's lungs.

re•tail (rē′tāl′) *n.* The sale of commodities in small quantities to the general public. —*adj.* Of, relating to, or engaged in the sale of goods at retail. —*adv.* At a retail price: *The radio costs more retail than wholesale.* —*v.* **re•tailed, re•tail•ing, re•tails.** —*tr.* To sell in small quantities directly to consumers. —*intr.* To sell goods at retail. **—re′tail′er** *n.*

re•tain (rĭ tān′) *tr.v.* **re•tained, re•tain•ing, re•tains. 1.** To keep possession of; continue to have: *The new premier retained his post as minister of finance.* See Synonyms at **keep. 2.** To keep or hold in a particular place, condition, or position: *Certain plants retain moisture.* **3.** To keep in mind; remember: *Be sure to take notes since you can't possibly retain everything.* **4.** To hire (an attorney, for example) by the payment of a fee: *retain a lawyer.* [First written down about 1386 in Middle English and spelled *retinen,* from Latin *retinēre* : *re-*, back + *tenēre,* to hold.]

re•tain•er¹ (rĭ tā′nər) *n.* **1.** A person or thing that retains, as a device, frame, or groove that restrains or guides. **2.** An appliance used to hold teeth in position after orthodontic treatment. **3.** A servant or an attendant, especially in a household of a person of high rank.

re•tain•er² (rĭ tā′nər) *n.* **1.** The act of hiring a professional adviser, such as an attorney or a consultant. **2.** The fee paid to hire a professional adviser.

re•tal•i•ate (rĭ tăl′ē āt′) *intr.v.* **re•tal•i•at•ed, re•tal•i•at•ing, re•tal•i•ates.** To return like for like, especially evil for evil: *retaliate against an enemy attack.* [First written down in 1611 in Modern English, from Late Latin *retāliāre* : Latin *re-*, back + Latin *tāliō,* punishment in kind.] **—re•tal′i•a′tion** *n.* **—re•tal′i•a•to′ry** (rĭ tăl′ē ə tôr′ē) *adj.*

re•tard (rĭ tärd′) *v.* **re•tard•ed, re•tard•ing, re•tards.** —*tr.* To slow the progress of; delay; hold back. —*intr.* To be delayed. —*n.* In music, a slackening of tempo. [First written down about 1477 in Middle English and spelled *retarden,* from Latin *retardāre,* from *tardus,* slow.]

re•tar•da•tion (rē′tär dā′shən) *n.* **1.a.** The act or process of retarding: *retardation of growth.* **b.** The condition of being retarded. **2.** In music, a slackening of tempo. **3.** Mental retardation.

re•tard•ed (rĭ tär′dĭd) *adj.* Abnormally slow in mental or emotional development.

retch (rĕch) *intr.v.* **retched, retch•ing, retch•es.** To strain or make an effort to vomit; heave.

re•ten•tion (rĭ tĕn′shən) *n.* **1.** The act of retaining or the condition of being retained: **2.** Capacity or power of retaining. **3.** The ability to retain or remember things: *remarkable powers of retention.*

re•ten•tive (rĭ tĕn′tĭv) *adj.* Having the quality, power, or capacity of retaining: *a retentive memory.* **—re•ten′tive•ness** *n.*

ret•i•cent (rĕt′ĭ sənt) *adj.* **1.** Tending not to speak out; quiet: *a reticent child.* **2.** Restrained or reserved in style. **—ret′i•cence** *n.*

re•tic•u•late (rĭ tĭk′yə lĭt *or* rĭ tĭk′yə lāt′) *adj.* Resembling or forming a net or network: *reticulate veins of a leaf.* **—re•tic′u•late•ly** *adv.* **—re•tic′u•la′tion** *n.*

ret•i•na (rĕt′n ə) *n., pl.* **ret•i•nas** or **ret•i•nae** (rĕt′n ē′). A light-sensitive membrane that lines the back of the inside of the eyeball and is connected to the brain by the optic nerve. [First written down in 1392 in Middle English, from Medieval Latin *rētina,* from Latin *rēte,* net.] **—ret′i•nal** *adj.*

ret•i•nol (rĕt′n ôl′ *or* rĕt′n ŏl′) *n.* Vitamin A.

ret•i•nue (rĕt′n o͞o′ *or* rĕt′n yo͞o′) *n.* A group of servants or attendants accompanying a person of rank.

re•tire (rĭ tīr′) *v.* **re•tired, re•tir•ing, re•tires.** —*intr.* **1.** To withdraw, as for rest or seclusion: *The judge retired to her study.* **2.** To go to bed: *retire for the night.* **3.** To give up one's work, business, or office, usually because of advancing age: *retire from teaching.* **4.** To fall back or retreat, as from battle. —*tr.* **1.** To cause to withdraw from one's usual field of activity. **2.** To lead (troops) away from action; withdraw. **3.** To take out of circulation: *retired the bonds.* **4.** To withdraw from use or active service: *retire an old battleship.* **5.** In baseball, to put out (a batter or a team). [First written down in 1533 in Modern English, from Old French *retirer,* to draw back.]

re•tir•ee (rĭ tīr′ē′) *n.* A person who has retired from active working life.

re•tire•ment (rĭ tīr′mənt) *n.* **1.** The act of retiring or the state of being retired. **2.** Withdrawal from one's job, business, or office. **3.** Withdrawal into privacy or seclusion.

re•tir•ing (rĭ tīr′ĭng) *adj.* Shy and reserved; modest: *He had a retiring manner.*

re•tort[1] (rĭ tôrt′) *v.* **re•tort•ed, re•tort•ing, re•torts.** *—tr.* **1.** To reply, especially to answer in a quick, biting, or witty manner. See Synonyms at **answer. 2.** To return in kind; pay back. *—intr.* **1.** To make a reply, especially a quick, biting, or witty one. **2.** To present a counterargument. *—n.* A quick incisive reply. [First written down about 1557 in Modern English, from Latin *retorquēre*, to bend back.]

re•tort[2] (rĭ tôrt′ *or* rē′tôrt′) *n.* A closed laboratory vessel with an outlet tube, used for distillation or decomposition by heat. [First written down in 1605 in Modern English, from Medieval Latin *retorta*, from Latin *retorquēre*, to bend back.]

re•touch (rē tŭch′) *tr.v.* **re•touched, re•touch•ing, re•touch•es. 1.** To make new details or touches to for correction or improvement; touch up: *retouch a painting.* **2.** To improve or alter (a photographic negative or print), as by removing flaws or adding details.

re•trace (rē trās′) *tr.v.* **re•traced, re•trac•ing, re•trac•es.** To go back over: *retrace one's steps.*

re•tract (rĭ trăkt′) *tr.v.* **re•tract•ed, re•tract•ing, re•tracts. 1.** To take back; disavow: *He refused to retract his statement.* **2.** To pull back or in: *The airplane retracted its landing gear.* **—re•tract′a•ble** *adj.*

re•trac•tion (rĭ trăk′shən) *n.* **1.** The act of retracting or the state of being retracted. **2.** The disavowal of a previously held statement or belief. **3.** The power of drawing back or of being drawn back.

re•tread (rē trĕd′) *tr.v.* **re•tread•ed, re•tread•ing, re•treads.** To fit (a worn automobile tire) with a new tread. *—n.* (rē′trĕd′). A retreaded tire.

re•treat (rĭ trēt′) *n.* **1.** The act or process of withdrawing, especially from something dangerous or unpleasant. **2.** A place affording peace, quiet, privacy, or security. **3.** The withdrawal of a military force when endangered by an enemy attack: *a hasty retreat at dawn.* **4.** The signal for such a withdrawal. **5.** A bugle call or drumbeat sounded during the lowering of the flag at sunset, as on a military base. *—intr.v.* **re•treat•ed, re•treat•ing, re•treats.** To fall or draw back; withdraw or retire. [First written down about 1300 in Middle English and spelled *retret*, from Latin *retrahere*, to draw back, retract.]

re•trench (rĭ trĕnch′) *v.* **re•trenched, re•trench•ing, re•trench•es.** *—tr.* To cut down; reduce; curtail: *retrench expenses.* *—intr.* To curtail expenses; economize.

re•tri•al (rē′trī′əl *or* rē′trīl′) *n.* A second trial, as of a court case.

ret•ri•bu•tion (rĕt′rə byōō′shən) *n.* **1.** Something justly deserved; recompense. **2.** Something given or demanded in repayment, especially punishment.

re•trib•u•tive (rĭ trĭb′yə tĭv) *adj.* Of, involving, or characterized by retribution **—re•trib′u•tive•ly** *adv.*

re•triev•al (rĭ trē′vəl) *n.* **1.** The act or process of retrieving. **2.** The possibility of being retrieved or restored: *lost possessions beyond retrieval.*

re•trieve (rĭ trēv′) *v.* **re•trieved, re•triev•ing, re•trieves.** *—tr.* **1.** To get back; recover: *retrieve a lost glove.* **2.** To bring back again; revive or restore. **3.** To find and carry back; fetch. **4.** To find and read (stored data). Used of a computer. *—intr.* To find and bring back game: *a dog trained to retrieve.*

re•triev•er (rĭ trē′vər) *n.* Any of several breeds of dog trained to find and bring back birds or animals shot by hunters.

retro– *pref.* A prefix that means backward or back: *retrograde.* —See Note.

ret•ro•ac•tive (rĕt′rō ăk′tĭv) *adj.* Applying to a period prior to enactment: *a retroactive pay increase.* **—ret′ro•ac′tive•ly** *adv.*

ret•ro•grade (rĕt′rə grād′) *adj.* **1.** Moving or tending to move backward. **2.** Opposite to the usual order; inverted or reversed.

ret•ro•gress (rĕt′rə grĕs′ *or* rĕt′rə grĕs′) *intr.v.* **ret•ro•gressed, ret•ro•gress•ing, ret•ro•gress•es.** To return to an earlier, inferior, or less complex condition.

ret•ro•rock•et (rĕt′rō rŏk′ĭt) *n.* A rocket engine used to slow, stop, or reverse the motion of an aircraft, a spacecraft, a missile, or another vehicle.

ret•ro•spect (rĕt′rə spĕkt′) *n.* A review, survey, or contemplation of things in the past. ***—idiom.* in retrospect.** Looking backward or reviewing the past: *It's easy to see what went wrong in retrospect.*

ret•ro•spec•tive (rĕt′rə spĕk′tĭv) *adj.* Of, looking back on, or contemplating the past: *a retrospective examination of her career.* *—n.* An extensive exhibition or performance of the work of an artist over a period of years.

ret•ro•vi•rus (rĕt′rō vī′rəs *or* rĕt′rə vī′rəs) *n., pl.* **ret•ro•vi•rus•es.** Any of a group of usually tumor-producing viruses, such as the AIDS virus, containing RNA.

re•turn (rĭ tûrn′) *v.* **re•turned, re•turn•ing, re•turns.** *—intr.* **1.** To go or come back, as to a former condition or place: *return home.* **2.** To revert in speech, thought, or practice: *We finally returned to the discussion.* **3.** To revert to a former owner. **4.** To respond or answer. *—tr.* **1.** To send, put, or carry back. **2.** To give back, as in exchange for or response to something: *return merchandise.* **3.** To give back to the owner: *returned the book to my grandmother.* **4.** To render or deliver (an indictment or a verdict). **5.** To produce or yield (interest or profit) as a payment for labor, investment, or expenditure: *Selling hot dogs returned him about 10 percent.* *—n.* **1.** The act of coming, going, bringing, or sending back: *a return to familiar places.* **2.** Something brought or sent back. **3.** A recurrence, as of an event: *the return of spring.* **4.** The profit or interest earned, as on an investment: *a 5 percent return.* **5.** A formal tax statement on the required official form: *an income tax return.* **6.** A report on the vote in an election. Often used in the plural. **7.** The key or mechanism on a machine, such as a typewriter or computer, that positions the carriage, cursor, or printing element at the beginning of a new line. ***—idiom.* in return.** In repayment or reciprocation. **—re•turn′a•ble** *adj.*

re•turn•ee (rĭ tûr′nē′) *n.* A person who has returned after a long absence, as from a voyage.

re•un•ion (rē yōōn′yən) *n.* **1.** The act of reuniting or the state of being reunited. **2.** A gathering of the members of a group who have been separated: *a yearly family reunion.*

re•u•nite (rē′yōō nīt′) *tr. & intr.v.* **re•u•nit•ed, re•u•nit•ing, re•u•nites.** To bring or come together again.

re•use (rē yōōz′) *tr.v.* **re•used, re•us•ing, re•us•es.** To use again. **—re•us′a•ble** *adj.*

rev (rĕv) *Informal. n.* A revolution, as of a motor. *—tr.v.* **revved, rev•ving, revs.** To increase the speed of (an engine or a motor): *rev the engine.*

Rev. *abbr.* An abbreviation of reverend.

re•vamp (rē vămp′) *tr.v.* **re•vamped, re•vamp•ing, re•vamps.** To patch up, revise, restore, or reconstruct: *revamp a magazine's layout.*

re•veal (rĭ vēl′) *tr.v.* **re•vealed, re•veal•ing, re•veals. 1.** To make known (something concealed or secret); disclose: *reveal a secret.* **2.** To bring to view;

retriever
Golden retriever

Word Building: retro–

The prefix **retro–**, meaning "backward, back," comes from the Latin prefix *retrō–*, meaning "backward, behind." The most common English words beginning with **retro–** are derived from Latin words or elements. **Retroactive** comes from *retrō–* and the verb *agere*, "to drive." **Retrograde** combines *retrō–* with the verb *gradī*, "to walk." **Retrospect** adds *retrō–* to the verb *specere*, "to look at." The 19th and 20th centuries have seen many scientific or technical terms coined with **retro–**, such as **retrorocket**.

ă	pat	oi	boy
ā	pay	ou	out
âr	care	ŏŏ	took
ä	father	ōō	boot
ĕ	pet	ŭ	cut
ē	be	ûr	urge
ĭ	pit	th	thin
ī	pie	*th*	this
îr	pier	hw	whoop
ŏ	pot	zh	vision
ō	toe	ə	about
ô	paw	N	*French* bon

show: *The anecdote revealed much about his character.* [First written down about 1400 in Middle English and spelled *revelen,* from Latin *revēlāre* : *re-,* back, off + *vēlāre,* to cover (from *vēlum,* veil).]

rev•eil•le (rĕv′ə lē) *n.* **1.** The sounding of a bugle early in the morning to awaken people in a camp or garrison. **2.** This bugle call.

rev•el (rĕv′əl) *intr.v.* **rev•eled, rev•el•ing, rev•els** also **rev•elled, rev•el•ling, rev•els. 1.** To take great pleasure or delight: *He revels in our lively discussions.* **2.** To engage in uproarious festivities; make merry. —*n.* A noisy festivity or celebration; merrymaking. Often used in the plural. **—rev′el•er, rev′el•ler** *n.*

rev•e•la•tion (rĕv′ə lā′shən) *n.* **1.** The act of revealing or disclosing. **2.** Something revealed, especially something surprising. **3.** In theology, a manifestation of divine will or truth. **4. Revelation.** The Book of Revelation.

rev•el•ry (rĕv′əl rē) *n., pl.* **rev•el•ries.** Boisterous merrymaking.

re•venge (rĭ vĕnj′) *tr.v.* **re•venged, re•veng•ing, re•veng•es. 1.** To inflict punishment in return for (an injury or insult): *Orestes revenged his father's death.* **2.** To seek or take vengeance for (oneself or another person). —*n.* **1.** The act or an example of revenging. **2.** Something done in vengeance. **—re•venge′ful** *adj.*

rev•e•nue (rĕv′ə no͞o *or* rĕv′ə nyo͞o) *n.* **1.** The income that a government collects for payment of public expenses. **2.** Yield from property or investment; income.

re•ver•ber•ate (rĭ vûr′bə rāt′) *intr.v.* **re•ver•ber•at•ed, re•ver•ber•at•ing, re•ver•ber•ates. 1.** To resound in or as if in a succession of echoes; reecho. **2.** To be repeatedly reflected, as sound waves, heat, or light. **—re•ver′ber•a•tion** *n.*

re•vere (rĭ vîr′) *tr.v.* **re•vered, re•ver•ing, re•veres.** To regard with awe, deference, and devotion. [First written down in 1661 in Modern English, from Latin *reverērī.*]

Synonyms: **revere, worship, adore, idolize.** These verbs mean to regard with the deepest respect and honor. **Revere** means to honor and feel awed by something or someone: *Their ancestor is revered as one of the town's founders.* **Worship** means to feel reverent or devoted love and often religious faith: *The ancient Greeks worshiped many different gods and goddesses.* **Adore** means to worship intensely: *The little girl had such a sweet nature that everyone adored her.* **Idolize** means to worship something as if it were perfect: *Karen still idolizes her older brother.*

Paul Revere

Re•vere (rĭ vîr′), **Paul.** 1735–1818. American silversmith and Revolutionary hero. On April 18, 1775, he made his famous ride to warn of the British advance on Lexington and Concord, Massachusetts.

rev•er•ence (rĕv′ər əns) *n.* **1.** A feeling of profound awe and respect and often love; veneration. **2.** An act showing respect, especially a bow or curtsy. **3. Reverence.** A form of address used for certain members of the Christian clergy: *your Reverence.*

rev•er•end (rĕv′ər ənd) *adj.* **1.** Worthy of or deserving reverence: *a reverend man.* **2.** Relating to or characteristic of the clergy; clerical. **3. Reverend.** A title and form of address used for certain members of the Christian clergy: *the Reverend Martin Chase.* —*n. Informal.* A cleric or minister. [First written down in 1428 in Middle English, from Latin *reverendus,* to be revered, from *reverērī,* to revere.]

rev•er•ent (rĕv′ər ənt) *adj.* Marked by, feeling, or showing reverence: *a reverent hymn.* [First written down about 1380 in Middle English, from Latin *reverēns,* present participle of *reverērī,* to revere.] **—rev′er•ent•ly** *adv.*

rev•er•en•tial (rĕv′ə rĕn′shəl) *adj.* **1.** Expressing reverence; reverent. **2.** Inspiring reverence.

rev•er•ie (rĕv′ə rē) *n.* **1.** A state of abstracted thought; daydreaming: *lost in reverie.* **2.** A daydream.

re•ver•sal (rĭ vûr′səl) *n.* **1.** The act or an example of reversing. **2.** A change for the worse.

re•verse (rĭ vûrs′) *adj.* **1.** Turned backward in position, direction, or order: *the reverse side of the page.* **2.** Causing backward movement: *reverse gear.* —*n.* **1.** The opposite or contrary of something: *His is the exact reverse of my opinion.* **2.** The back or rear of something: *the reverse of a page.* **3.** A mechanism for moving backward, as a gear in an automobile. **4.** A change to an opposite position, condition, or direction. **5.** A change for the worse; a setback: *He has weathered the many reverses in his career.* —*v.* **re•versed, re•vers•ing, re•vers•es.** —*tr.* **1.** To turn around to the opposite direction: *The wind reversed the weather vane.* **2.** To turn inside out or upside down: *reverse a jacket; reverse the painting.* **3.** To exchange the positions of: *reverse the order of the numbers.* **4.** To annul (a decision or decree, for example): *The court reversed the decision.* —*intr.* To move or turn in the opposite direction. [First written down about 1303 in Middle English and spelled *revers,* from Latin *reversus,* past participle of *revertere,* to turn back.] **—re•verse′ly** *adv.* **—re•vers′er** *n.*

re•vers•i•ble (rĭ vûr′sə bəl) *adj.* **1.** Capable of being reversed. **2.** Wearable with either side turned outward: *a reversible vest.*

re•ver•sion (rĭ vûr′zhən) *n.* **1.** A return to a former condition, belief, or interest. **2.** A turning away or in the opposite direction.

re•vert (rĭ vûrt′) *intr.v.* **re•vert•ed, re•vert•ing, re•verts. 1.** To return or go back to a former condition, belief, subject, or practice. **2.** In law, to return (an estate) to the former owner or the former owner's heirs.

re•view (rĭ vyo͞o′) *tr.v.* **re•viewed, re•view•ing, re•views. 1.** To look over, study, or examine again: *Let's review Chapter 5.* **2.** To look back on; think over: *review the day's events.* **3.** To examine so as to correct or criticize: *reviewed the data.* **4.** To write or give a critical report on (a new book or play, for example). **5.** To inspect formally (a group of soldiers or other military personnel). —*n.* **1.** A reexamination or reconsideration. **2.** A studying of something covered earlier in school. **3.** An inspection or examination. **4.** A report or an essay that discusses a work or a performance and attempts to judge its worth: *a book review.* **5.** A formal military inspection. **6.** A revue.

❑ *These sound alike:* **review, revue** (show).

re•view•er (rĭ vyo͞o′ər) *n.* A person who reviews, especially one who writes critical reviews, as for a newspaper or magazine.

re•vile (rĭ vīl′) *v.* **re•viled, re•vil•ing, re•viles.** —*tr.* To denounce with abusive language. —*intr.* To use abusive language.

re•vise (rĭ vīz′) *tr.v.* **re•vised, re•vis•ing, re•vis•es. 1.** To prepare a newly edited version of (a text). **2.** To reconsider and change or modify: *revise an opinion.* [First written down in 1567 in Modern English, from Latin *revīsere,* to look at again : *re-,* again + *vīsere,* to look at (from *vidēre,* to see).]

Re•vised Standard Version (rĭ vīzd′) *n.* A modern American version of the English Bible.

re•vi•sion (rĭ vĭzh′ən) *n.* **1.** The act or process of revising. **2.** A new or revised version, as of a book or other text.

re•viv•al (rĭ vī′vəl) *n.* **1.a.** The act or an instance of reviving. **b.** The condition of being revived. **2.** A restoration to use, acceptance, activity, or vigor after a period of obscurity or inactivity. **3.** A new presentation of an old motion picture or play. **4.** A renewal of interest in religion. **5.** A meeting or meetings promoting such a religious renewal and often characterized by emotional preaching and public testimony.

re•vive (rĭ **vīv′**) *v.* **re•vived, re•viv•ing, re•vives.** —*tr.* **1.** To bring back to life or consciousness: *revive someone who has fainted.* **2.** To give new health, strength, or spirit to: *The music revived me.* **3.** To restore to use: *Congress revived the rank of full general to honor Grant.* —*intr.* **1.** To return to life or consciousness. **2.** To regain health, strength, or good spirits. **3.** To return to use, currency, or notice. —**re•viv′er** *n.*

rev•o•ca•ble (**rĕv′**ə kə bəl) *adj.* Capable of being revoked: *A driver's license is revocable if parking tickets are not paid up.*

rev•o•ca•tion (rĕv′ə **kā′**shən) *n.* The act or an instance of revoking.

re•voke (rĭ **vōk′**) *tr.v.* **re•voked, re•vok•ing, re•vokes.** To make void by reversing, recalling, or withdrawing; cancel: *revoke an edict; revoke a license.* [First written down about 1350 in Middle English and spelled *revoken*, from Latin *revocāre* : *re-*, back + *vocāre*, to call.]

re•volt (rĭ **vōlt′**) *v.* **re•volt•ed, re•volt•ing, re•volts.** —*intr.* **1.** To attempt to overthrow the authority of the state; rebel. **2.** To oppose or refuse to accept something: *We revolted against her notion of what the front page should look like.* **3.** To feel disgust or repugnance. —*tr.* To fill with disgust; repel. —*n.* An act of rebellion against authority; an uprising.

re•volt•ing (rĭ **vōl′**tĭng) *adj.* Causing disgust; offensive: *a revolting display of bad manners.* —**re•volt′ing•ly** *adv.*

rev•o•lu•tion (rĕv′ə **lo͞o′**shən) *n.* **1.a.** Movement around a point in a closed path, especially as distinguished from rotation around an axis. **b.** A spinning or rotation around an axis. **c.** A single complete cycle of motion about a point in a closed path. **2.** The overthrow of one government and its replacement with another. **3.** A sudden or momentous change: *the computer revolution.*

rev•o•lu•tion•ar•y (rĕv′ə **lo͞o′**shə nĕr′ē) *adj.* **1.** Often **Revolutionary.** Of, relating to, or being a revolution: *revolutionary war.* **2.** Of or tending to promote political or social revolution: *revolutionary writings.* **3.** Characterized by or resulting in radical change: *a revolutionary new teaching idea.* —*n., pl.* **rev•o•lu•tion•ar•ies.** A person who is engaged in or favors revolution.

rev•o•lu•tion•ist (rĕv′ə **lo͞o′**shə nĭst) *n.* A revolutionary.

rev•o•lu•tion•ize (rĕv′ə **lo͞o′**shə nīz′) *tr.v.* **rev•o•lu•tion•ized, rev•o•lu•tion•iz•ing, rev•o•lu•tion•iz•es.** **1.** To bring about a radical change in; alter drastically: *The automobile revolutionized travel in the United States.* **2.** To subject to a political or social revolution.

re•volve (rĭ **vŏlv′**) *v.* **re•volved, re•volv•ing, re•volves.** —*intr.* **1.** To orbit a central point: *The earth revolves around the sun.* **2.** To turn on an axis; rotate. —*tr.* To cause to revolve.

re•volv•er (rĭ **vŏl′**vər) *n.* A pistol with a revolving cylinder with chambers for cartridges that may be fired one after another.

re•volv•ing (rĭ **vŏl′**vĭng) *adj.* Tending to revolve or happen repeatedly.

re•vue (rĭ **vyo͞o′**) *n.* A musical show consisting of songs, skits, and dances that often have as a theme current events, trends, and personalities.

❑ *These sound alike:* **revue, review** (examine).

re•vul•sion (rĭ **vŭl′**shən) *n.* **1.** A sudden strong change or reaction in feeling, especially a feeling of violent disgust or loathing. **2.** A turning away or withdrawal from something: *revulsion of public opinion from support of the policy.*

re•ward (rĭ **wôrd′**) *n.* **1.** Something given or received in return for worthy behavior or in retribution for evil acts. **2.** Money offered or given for a special service, such as the return of a lost article or the capture of a criminal. **3.** A satisfying return or result; profit: *an investment with a handsome reward.* —*tr.v.* **re•ward•ed, re•ward•ing, re•wards.** To give a reward to or for: *reward her for bravery.*

re•ward•ing (rĭ **wôr′**dĭng) *adj.* **1.** Offering satisfaction: *a rewarding experience.* **2.** Producing profit: *a rewarding investment.*

re•word (rē **wûrd′**) *tr.v.* **re•word•ed, re•word•ing, re•words.** **1.** To change the wording of: *reword a contract.* **2.** To state or express again in different words: *The speaker reworded the answer to the question.*

re•work (rē **wûrk′**) *tr.v.* **re•worked, re•work•ing, re•works.** To work over again; revise.

re•write (rē **rīt′**) *tr.v.* **re•wrote** (rē **rōt′**), **re•writ•ten** (rē **rĭt′**n), **re•writ•ing, re•writes.** **1.** To write again, especially in a different or improved form. **2.** To put (material submitted to a newspaper or magazine) in a form suitable for publishing. —*n.* (**rē′**-rīt′). Something rewritten. —**re•writ′er** *n.*

Reye's syndrome (rīz *or* rāz) *n.* A rare acute disease of the brain characterized by fever, disorientation, and coma that follows a viral infection such as influenza and occurs mainly in children. [First written down in 1965 in Modern English and spelled *Reye syndrome*, after Ralph Douglas Kenneth Reye (1912–1978), Australian pediatrician.]

Rey•kja•vík (**rā′**kyə vēk′ *or* **rā′**kyə vĭk′). The capital and largest city of Iceland, in the southwest part of the island. Traditionally founded in 874, it became capital of the country in 1918. Population, 88,745.

Rey•nard (**rā′**närd′ *or* **rĕn′**ərd) *n.* A fox.

RFD also **R.F.D.** *abbr.* An abbreviation of rural free delivery.

Rh The symbol for the element **rhodium.**

rhap•so•dy (**răp′**sə dē) *n., pl.* **rhap•so•dies.** **1.** Excessively enthusiastic expression of feeling in speech or writing. **2.** A literary work written in an impassioned or exalted style. **3.** A state of elated bliss; ecstasy. **4.** A musical composition with an irregular form.

rhe•a (**rē′**ə) *n.* Any of several South American birds related to and resembling the ostrich but smaller.

Rhe•a (**rē′**ə) *n.* In Greek mythology, a Titan who is the sister and wife of Cronus and the mother of many of the gods and goddesses.

Rhen•ish (**rĕn′**ĭsh) *adj.* Of or relating to the Rhine River or the lands bordering on it.

rhe•ni•um (**rē′**nē əm) *n. Symbol* **Re** A rare, dense, silvery-white metallic element with a very high melting point that makes it valuable as an ingredient in alloys. Atomic number 75. See table at **element.** [First written down in 1925 in Modern English, from Latin *Rhēnus*, the Rhine.]

rhe•o•stat (**rē′**ə stăt′) *n.* A resistor whose value can be continuously varied between two extremes, used to control the flow of current in an electric circuit.

rhe•sus monkey (**rē′**səs) *n.* A brownish monkey of India, much used in biological experiments.

rhet•o•ric (**rĕt′**ər ĭk) *n.* **1.** The art or study of using language effectively and persuasively. **2.** A style of speaking or writing, especially the language of a particular subject. **3.** Elaborate, pretentious, or insincere writing or speech. —See Note.

rhe•tor•i•cal (rĭ **tôr′**ĭ kəl *or* rĭ **tŏr′**ĭ kəl) *adj.* **1.** Of

rhea
Gray rhea

Usage: rhetoric

The word **rhetoric** was once primarily the name of an important branch of philosophy and an art deserving of serious study. The word now often refers to language that is pretentious, fancy, and insincere, and does not mean much. If your teacher says a speech is full of rhetoric, you know that someone will be doing some rewriting.

ă	**pat**	oi	**boy**
ā	**pay**	ou	**out**
âr	**care**	o͝o	**took**
ä	**father**	o͞o	**boot**
ĕ	**pet**	ŭ	**cut**
ē	**be**	ûr	**urge**
ĭ	**pit**	th	**thin**
ī	**pie**	*th*	**this**
îr	**pier**	hw	**whoop**
ŏ	**pot**	zh	**vision**
ō	**toe**	ə	**about**
ô	**paw**	N	*French* **bon**

rhinoceros
Black rhinoceros

Rhode Island

The state of **Rhode Island** was probably named after Rhodes, a Greek island off the coast of Turkey. It is known that a 16th-century Italian explorer compared the size of an American island that is today part of the state of Rhode Island to that of Rhodes. But the 17th-century Dutch settlers called the same island by a similar-sounding name meaning "red island," which may have also influenced its name. The state later took its name from the island.

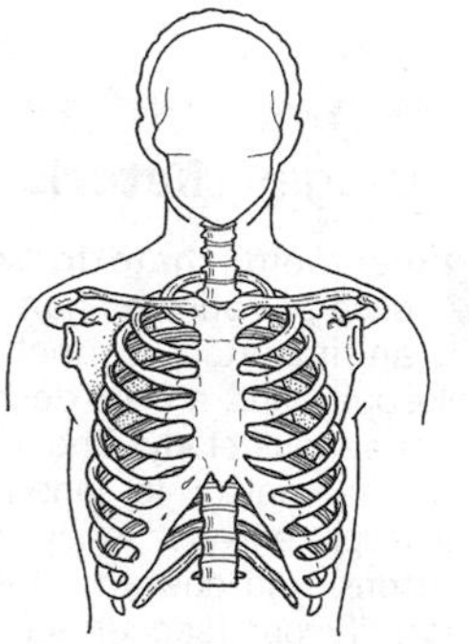

rib

ribbon

or relating to rhetoric. **2.** Concerned primarily with effect; showy. —**rhe•tor′i•cal•ly** *adv.*

rhetorical question *n.* A question to which no answer is expected.

rhet•o•ri•cian (rĕt′ə **rĭsh′**ən) *n.* **1.** An expert in or teacher of rhetoric. **2.** One who speaks or writes eloquently.

rheum (ro͞om) *n.* A thin or watery discharge of mucus from the nose or eyes.

❑ *These sound alike:* **rheum, room** (space).

rheu•mat•ic (ro͞o **măt′**ĭk) *adj.* Of, relating to, or affected with rheumatism. —*n.* A person affected with rheumatism.

rheumatic fever *n.* A severe infectious disease, chiefly of children, with symptoms including fever and painful inflammation of the joints. It often causes permanent damage to the heart.

rheu•ma•tism (**ro͞o′**mə tĭz′əm) *n.* Any of several diseases that affect the muscles, joints, or nerves, causing pain and disability.

Rh factor (**är′āch′**) *n.* Any of several antigens present in the red blood cells of most people. [First written down in 1942 in Modern English, from *rh(esus monkey)*, from its being first detected in the blood of this animal.]

Rhine (rīn). A river of western Europe flowing about 820 miles (1,319 kilometers) from eastern Switzerland north and northwest through Germany and the Netherlands to the North Sea.

Rhine•land (**rīn′**lănd′ *or* **rīn′**lənd). A region along the Rhine River in western Germany. It includes noted vineyards and highly industrial sections.

rhine•stone (**rīn′**stōn′) *n.* A colorless artificial gem of glass or paste, having facets in imitation of a diamond.

rhi•no (**rī′**nō) *n., pl.* **rhi•nos.** *Informal.* A rhinoceros.

rhi•noc•er•os (rī **nŏs′**ər əs) *n., pl.* **rhinoceros** or **rhi•noc•er•os•es.** Any of several large African or Asian mammals having short legs, thick tough skin, and one or two upright horns on the snout. [First written down before 1300 in Middle English and spelled *rinoceros*, from Greek *rhinokerōs* : *rhis*, nose + *keras*, horn.]

rhi•zome (**rī′**zōm′) *n.* A plant stem that grows under or along the ground and that sends out shoots and roots.

rho (rō) *n.* The 17th letter of the Greek alphabet, written Ρ, ρ. In English it is represented as *R, r.*

❑ *These sound alike:* **rho, roe**[1] (fish eggs), **roe**[2] (small deer), **row**[1] (continuous line), **row**[2] (use oars).

Rhode Island (rōd). A state of the northeast United States on the Atlantic Ocean east of Connecticut. It was admitted as one of the original Thirteen Colonies in 1790. Rhode Island was settled by religious exiles from Massachusetts. Providence is the capital and the largest city. Population 1,005,984. —SEE NOTE.

Rho•de•sia (rō **dē′**zhə). **1.** A region of south-central Africa south of Zaire made up of modern-day Zambia and Zimbabwe. **2.** Zimbabwe.

rho•di•um (**rō′**dē əm) *n. Symbol* **Rh** A hard, durable, silvery-white metallic element that is resistant to acid and is used for plating silverware and jewelry. Atomic number 45. See table at **element.**

rho•do•den•dron (rō′də **dĕn′**drən) *n.* Any of numerous evergreen shrubs, having clusters of white, pinkish, or purplish, often bell-shaped flowers. [First written down in 1601 in Modern English, from Greek *rhododendron*, oleander : *rhodon*, rose + *dendron*, tree.]

rhom•bus (**rŏm′**bəs) *n., pl.* **rhom•bus•es** or **rhom•bi** (**rŏm′**bī). A parallelogram that has four equal sides.

Rhone or **Rhône** (rōn). A river rising in south-central Switzerland and flowing about 505 miles (813 kilometers) to Lake Geneva then through eastern and southern France to the Mediterranean Sea.

rhu•barb (**ro͞o′**bärb′) *n.* **1.a.** Any of several plants having large leaves with long fleshy reddish or green stalks. **b.** The stalks of this plant that are edible when sweetened and cooked. **2.** *Informal.* A noisy argument or quarrel. [First written down about 1390 in Middle English and spelled *rubarbe*, from Old French, from Late Latin *rhabarbarum* : Greek *rha*, rhubarb + Latin *barbarus*, foreign.]

rhyme also **rime** (rīm) *n.* **1.** Correspondence or repetition of the final sounds of words or of lines of verse. **2.** A poem having a regular repetition of sounds at the ends of lines. **3.** A word that has the same or similar final sound as another, as *baboon* and *harpoon.* —*v.* **rhymed, rhym•ing, rhymes** also **rimed, rim•ing, rimes.** —*intr.* **1.** To form a rhyme: Hour *rhymes with* power. **2.** To make use of or have rhymes: *Not all poetry rhymes.* —*tr.* To put into a rhyme or compose with rhymes. [First written down about 1200 in Middle English and spelled *rime*, from Old French, of Germanic origin.] —**rhym′er** *n.*

❑ *These sound alike:* **rhyme, rime**[1] (frost).

rhyme scheme *n.* The arrangement of rhymes in a poem or stanza.

rhythm (**rĭth′**əm) *n.* **1.** A movement, an action, or a condition that recurs alternately or in regular sequence: *the rhythm of the tides.* **2.** The pattern of sound in language, especially the regular pattern of stressed and unstressed syllables in poetry. **3.** A musical pattern formed by a series of notes or beats that are of different lengths and stresses. **4.** A particular pattern of rhythm: *a waltz rhythm.* [First written down about 1557 in Modern English, from Greek *rhuthmos.*]

rhythm and blues *pl.n. (used with a singular or plural verb).* A kind of popular music developed by Black Americans that combines blues and jazz, characterized by a strong simple rhythm.

rhyth•mi•c (**rĭth′**mĭk) also **rhyth•mi•cal** (**rĭth′**mĭ kəl) *adj.* Of, relating to, or having rhythm. —**rhyth′mi•cal•ly** *adv.*

RI or **R.I.** *abbr.* An abbreviation of Rhode Island.

ri•al (rē **ôl′** *or* rē **äl′**) *n.* The basic monetary unit of Iran.

rib (rĭb) *n.* **1.** Any of a series of long curved bones, occurring in 12 pairs in human beings, extending from the spine to or toward the breastbone and enclosing the chest cavity. **2.** A part similar to a rib and serving to shape or support: *a rib of an umbrella.* **3.** A cut of meat containing one or more ribs. **4.** One of the main veins of a leaf. **5.** A raised ridge in woven cloth or knitted material. —*tr.v.* **ribbed, rib•bing, ribs. 1.** To support, shape, or provide with a rib or ribs. **2.** *Informal.* To make fun of; tease.

rib•ald (**rĭb′**əld *or* **rī′**bôld′) *adj.* Characterized by or given to using vulgar lewd humor: *a ribald story.* —**rib′ald•ry** *n.*

rib•bon (**rĭb′**ən) *n.* **1.** A narrow strip or band of fine fabric, such as satin or velvet, used for decorating or trimming. **2. ribbons.** Tattered or ragged strips: *torn to ribbons.* **3.** An inked strip of cloth used for making an impression, as in a typewriter. **4.** A strip or band of colored cloth worn or displayed as the symbol of a prize or medal: *won a blue ribbon.*

rib cage *n.* The enclosing structure formed by the ribs and the bones to which they are attached.

ri•bo•fla•vin (**rī′**bō flā′vĭn) *n.* An orange-yellow substance that is the main growth-producing substance of the vitamin B complex; vitamin B_2. Riboflavin is found in milk, leafy vegetables, fresh meat, and egg yolks.

ri•bo•nu•cle•ic acid (rī′bō no͞o **klē′**ĭk *or* rī′bō nyo͞o **klē′**ĭk) *n.* RNA.

ri•bose (**rī′**bōs′) *n.* A simple sugar present in ribonucleic acid, riboflavin, and other nucleotides and nucleic acids, having the formula $C_5H_{10}O_5$.

ri•bo•some (**rī′**bə sōm′) *n.* A small spherical structure in the cytoplasm of living cells where protein is synthesized.

rice (rīs) *n.* **1.** The starchy seeds of a kind of grass much grown in warm regions as a source of food. **2.** The plant that bears such seeds. —SEE NOTE.

rice paper *n.* A thin paper made chiefly from the pith of a small Chinese tree or shrub.

rich (rĭch) *adj.* **rich•er, rich•est. 1.** Having great material wealth: *a rich industrial nation.* **2.** Made of rare or costly materials and often with fine craftsmanship: *a rich brocade.* **3.a.** Having an abundant supply; plentiful: *Milk is rich in protein.* **b.** Abundant in natural resources: *rich land.* **4.** Productive and therefore profitable: *rich soil.* **5.** Containing a large amount of choice ingredients such as butter and sugar, and therefore heavy and sweet: *a rich dessert.* **6.a.** Pleasantly full and mellow: *a rich tenor voice.* **b.** Warm and deep in color: *a rich brown velvet.* **7.** *Informal.* Very funny: *a rich joke.* —*n.* *(used with a plural verb).* Wealthy people considered as a group. **—rich′ly** *adv.* **—rich′ness** *n.*

Rich•ard I (**rĭch′**ərd) Known as "the Lion-Hearted." 1157–1199. King of England (1189–1199) who was a leader of the Third Crusade (1190–1192).

Ri•che•lieu (**rĭsh′**ə lo͞o′), Duc de. 1585–1642. French prelate and politician who led France during the Thirty Years' War (1618–1648).

rich•es (**rĭch′**ĭz) *pl.n.* **1.** Great wealth. **2.** Valuable possessions.

Rich•ler (**rĭch′**lər), **Mordecai.** Born 1931. Canadian writer whose novels include *The Apprenticeship of Duddy Kravitz* (1959).

Rich•mond (**rĭch′**mənd). The capital of Virginia, in the east-central part of the state northwest of Williamsburg. It was settled in the 17th century, became the capital of Virginia in 1779, and was the capital of the Confederacy (1861–1865). Population, 203,056.

Rich•ter scale (**rĭk′**tər) *n.* A scale with no specified upper or lower limits, used to express the magnitude or total energy of an earthquake. On the scale an earthquake with a magnitude of 1 is detectable only by instruments; one with a magnitude of 7 is a major earthquake. [First written down in 1938 in Modern English, after Charles Francis *Richter* (1900–1985), American seismologist.]

rick (rĭk) *n.* A stack of hay, straw, or similar material, especially when covered for protection from the weather.

rick•ets (**rĭk′**ĭts) *n.* *(used with a singular or plural verb).* A disease, found mostly in children, caused by a lack of exposure to sunlight and a lack of vitamin D in the diet. It results in defective or deformed growth of the bones.

rick•et•y (**rĭk′**ĭ tē) *adj.* **rick•et•i•er, rick•et•i•est. 1.** Likely to fall apart or break; shaky: *a rickety old bridge.* **2.** Of, having, or resembling rickets.

rick•rack (**rĭk′**răk′) *n.* A flat narrow braid in zigzag form, used as a trimming for cloth.

rick•sha or **rick•shaw** (**rĭk′**shô) *n.* A jinriksha.

ric•o•chet (rĭk′ə **shā′** *or* **rĭk′**ə shā′) *intr.v.* **ric•o•cheted** (rĭk′ə **shād′**), **ric•o•chet•ing** (rĭk′ə **shā′**ĭng), **ric•o•chets** (rĭk′ə **shāz′**). To rebound at least once from a surface: *A bullet ricocheted off the rock.* —*n.* An example of such a rebound.

rid (rĭd) *tr.v.* **rid** or **rid•ded, rid•ding, rids.** To free from, especially from something objectionable or unwanted: *He rid himself of his financial troubles.*

rid•dance (**rĭd′**ns) *n.* A removal of or deliverance from something.

rid•den (**rĭd′**n) *v.* Past participle of **ride.** —*adj.* Dominated or obsessed by: *disease-ridden; worry-ridden.*

rid•dle¹ (**rĭd′**l) *tr.v.* **rid•dled, rid•dling, rid•dles. 1.** To pierce with numerous holes: *riddle a target with bullets.* **2.** To permeate or spread throughout: *a government riddled with corruption.* —*n.* A coarse sieve. [First written down before 1200 in Middle English and spelled *riddlen,* to sift, probably from Old English *hriddel,* sieve.]

rid•dle² (**rĭd′**l) *n.* **1.** A question or statement requiring thought to answer or understand. **2.** Something that is difficult to understand: *It is a riddle to me why they are so excited.* [First written down about 1000 in Old English and spelled *rǣdels.*]

ride (rīd) *v.* **rode** (rōd), **rid•den** (**rĭd′**n), **rid•ing, rides.** —*intr.* **1.** To be carried or move, as in a vehicle or on horseback: *ride in a car.* **2.** To travel over a surface: *The car rides smoothly.* **3.** To be carried along; move as if on water: *rode to victory on a wave of public support.* **4.** To depend on: *My grade rides on the results of the test.* **5.** To allow to continue: *Let the problem ride.* —*tr.* **1.** To sit on and move or drive: *ride a bicycle; ride a horse.* **2.** To travel over, along, or through: *a delivery van riding the back roads.* **3.** To be supported or carried on: *surfers riding the waves.* **4.** To take part in by riding: *a jockey riding the fourth race.* **5.** *Informal.* To tease or ridicule. —*n.* **1.** The act or an instance of riding, as in a vehicle or on an animal. **2.** A device, such as one at an amusement park, that one rides for pleasure or excitement. **3.** A means of transportation: *waiting for her ride to come.* ***—idiom.* ride out.** To survive or outlast: *rode out the storm.* [First written down about 725 in Old English and spelled *rīdan.*]

Ride (rīd), **Sally.** Born 1951. American astronaut who in 1983 became the first American woman to enter outer space.

rid•er (**rī′**dər) *n.* **1.** A person who rides, especially a person who rides horses. **2.** A clause, usually having little relevance to the main issue, added to a legislative bill.

ridge (rĭj) *n.* **1.** A long narrow upper section or crest: *the ridge of a wave; the ridge of a roof.* **2.** A long narrow chain of hills or mountains, or a long narrow flat-topped strip of high land. **3.** A narrow raised strip, as in cloth or on plowed ground. **4.** A long, narrow, or crested part of the body: *the ridge of the nose.* —*tr.v.* **ridged, ridg•ing, ridg•es.** To mark with, form into, or provide with a ridge or ridges.

ridge•pole (**rĭj′**pōl′) *n.* **1.** A horizontal beam at the ridge of a roof to which sloping beams are attached. **2.** The horizontal pole at the top of a tent.

rid•i•cule (**rĭd′**ĭ kyo͞ol′) *n.* Words or actions intended to cause laughter at or scorn of a person or thing. —*tr.v.* **rid•i•culed, rid•i•cul•ing, rid•i•cules.** To laugh at or make fun of; mock.

ri•dic•u•lous (rĭ **dĭk′**yə ləs) *adj.* Deserving or inspiring ridicule; absurd or silly: *a ridiculous idea.* **—ri•dic′u•lous•ly** *adv.* **—ri•dic′u•lous•ness** *n.*

rid•ing habit (**rī′**dĭng) *n.* The outfit typically worn by a horseback rider.

rife (rīf) *adj.* **rif•er, rif•est. 1.** Widespread; prevalent: *Malaria is rife in these regions.* **2.** Abundant; numerous: *The article is rife with valuable insights.*

riff•raff (**rĭf′**răf′) *n.* **1.** People regarded as disreputable or worthless. **2.** Rubbish; trash.

ri•fle¹ (**rī′**fəl) *n.* A gun designed to be fired from the shoulder, with a barrel containing spiral grooves designed to cause the bullet to spin when fired.

Word History: rice

Our word **rice** is an international word. In Middle English the word is *rys,* and it is a borrowing from the Old French word *ris.* French *ris* and Italian *riso* come from the Latin word *oryza,* which is a borrowing of the Greek word *oruza.* The Greek word comes from some unknown language farther to the east from which Sanskrit also gets its word for rice, *vrīhi.* The Spanish word for rice, *arroz* (as in *arroz con pollo,* "chicken with rice"), does not come from Latin *oryza* but from the Arabic word *ar-rozz,* literally "the rice." The Arabic word *rozz* comes from Greek or from wherever the Greek *oryza* and the Sanskrit *vrīhi* come from. The Japanese now have the word *raisu,* taken from our English word *rice,* and it means "Western rice eaten from a plate with a fork," as opposed to Eastern rice eaten from a bowl with chopsticks.

Sally Ride
Photographed in 1983

ă	pat	oi	boy
ā	pay	ou	out
âr	care	o͝o	took
ä	father	o͞o	boot
ĕ	pet	ŭ	cut
ē	be	ûr	urge
ĭ	pit	th	thin
ī	pie	*th*	this
îr	pier	hw	whoop
ŏ	pot	zh	vision
ō	toe	ə	about
ô	paw	N	*French* bon

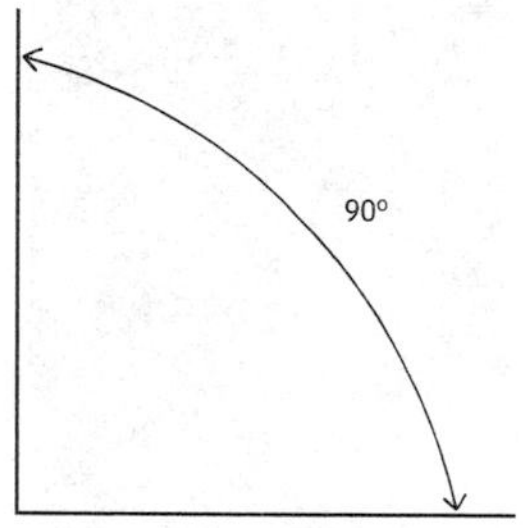

right angle

[First written down before 1751 in Modern English, from *rifle*, to cut spiral grooves in, from Old French *rifler*, to plunder, scratch.]

ri•fle² (rī′fəl) *tr.v.* **ri•fled, ri•fling, ri•fles.** To rob; plunder. [First written down about 1333 in Middle English and spelled *riflen*, to plunder, from Old French *rifler*, probably of Germanic origin.]

ri•fle•man (rī′fəl mən) *n.* **1.** A soldier equipped with a rifle. **2.** A man who shoots a rifle skillfully.

ri•fling (rī′flĭng) *n.* **1.** The process or operation of cutting spiral grooves in a rifle barrel. **2.** Grooves cut in a rifle barrel.

rift (rĭft) *n.* **1.a.** A fault, as in a system of rock. **b.** A narrow break or crack in a rock. **2.** A break in friendly relations. —*v.* **rift•ed, rift•ing, rifts.** —*intr.* To split open; break. —*tr.* To cause to break apart; split. [First written down before 1325 in Middle English, of Scandinavian origin.]

rig (rĭg) *tr.v.* **rigged, rig•ging, rigs. 1.** To provide with equipment; fit out: *rig a garage to store a boat.* **2.a.** To equip (a ship) with sails, shrouds, and yards. **b.** To fit (sails or shrouds, for example) to masts and yards. **3.** To manipulate dishonestly for personal gain: *rig a prize fight.* **4.** To make or construct in haste or in a makeshift manner: *rig up a tent for the night.* —*n.* **1.** The arrangement of masts, spars, and sails on a sailing vessel: *a fore-and-aft rig.* **2.** Special equipment or gear, especially equipment used for drilling oil wells: *a drilling rig.* **3.** A vehicle with one or more horses harnessed to it. **4.** A truck, tractor, or tractor-trailer. **5.** *Informal.* An outfit or a costume.

Ri•ga (rē′gə). The capital of Latvia, in the central part of the republic on the **Gulf of Riga,** an inlet of the Baltic Sea. It was founded as a trading post on a site originally inhabited by Baltic tribes. Population, 883,000.

rig•ger (rĭg′ər) *n.* **1.** A person who rigs something. **2.** A ship with a specific kind of rigging: *a square rigger.*

rig•ging (rĭg′ĭng) *n.* **1.** The system of ropes, chains, and tackle used to support and control the masts, sails, and yards of a sailing vessel. **2.** The supporting material for construction work.

right (rīt) *adj.* **right•er, right•est. 1.** Conforming with justice or morality: *do the right thing.* **2.** In accordance with fact, reason, or truth; correct: *the right answer.* **3.** Fitting, proper, or appropriate: *the right tool for the job.* **4.** Healthy; sound: *not in her right mind.* **5.** Meant to be worn or positioned on the outside, in front, or on top: *wear the jacket with the right side outward.* **6.** Advantageous, desirable, or favorable: *in the right place at the right time.* **7.** Of, relating to, directed toward, or located on the right side. **8.** Often **Right.** Of or belonging to the political Right. —*n.* **1.** That which is just or morally good: *the difference between right and wrong.* **2.** Something that a person has a moral or legal claim to: *the right of free speech.* **3.a.** The direction or position on the right side. **b.** The right side. **c.** A turn in the direction of the right hand or side. **4.** Often **Right.** The people and groups who advocate conservative or reactionary measures, especially in politics. —*adv.* **1.** Toward or on the right: *turning right.* **2.** In a straight line; directly: *came right to the door.* **3.** In a correct manner; properly. **4.** Exactly; just: *right where we were standing.* **5.** Immediately: *called right after breakfast.* **6.** *Informal.* Very: *a right nice place.* **7.** Used as an intensive: *Keep right on going.* —*v.* **right•ed, right•ing, rights.** —*tr.* **1.** To put in or restore to an upright or proper position: *She righted the kayak.* **2.** To make reparation or amends for: *right a wrong.* **3.** To set right; correct: *right unfair hiring practices.* —*intr.* To regain an upright or proper position. ***—idioms.*** **by rights.** In a just manner; properly. **to rights.** In a satisfactory or orderly condition. **—right′ness** *n.*

❑ *These sound alike:* **right, rite** (ceremony), **write** (compose).

right angle *n.* An angle formed by the perpendicular intersection of two straight lines; an angle of 90°.

right-an•gled (rīt′ăng′gəld) *adj.* Containing or forming one or more right angles.

right•eous (rī′chəs) *adj.* Morally right; just: *a righteous cause.* **—right′eous•ly** *adv.* **—right′eous•ness** *n.*

right field *n.* **1.** In baseball, the part of the outfield that is to the right as viewed from home plate. **2.** The position played by the right fielder.

right fielder *n.* In baseball, the player who defends right field.

right•ful (rīt′fəl) *adj.* **1.** Right; just: *a rightful position of honor.* **2.** Having a just, proper, or legal claim: *the car's rightful owner.* **3.** Owned by a just or proper claim: *a rightful share of the money.* **—right′ful•ly** *adv.* **—right′ful•ness** *n.*

right-hand (rīt′hănd′) *adj.* **1.** Of, relating to, or located on the right: *the right-hand margin.* **2.** Relating to, designed for, or done with the right hand: *a right-hand throw.* **3.** Helpful; reliable: *my right-hand assistant.*

right-hand•ed (rīt′hăn′dĭd) *adj.* **1.** Using the right hand more easily than the left: *a right-handed person.* **2.** Done with the right hand: *a right-handed throw.* **3.** Made to be worn on or used by the right hand: *a right-handed glove.* **4.** Turning or spiraling from left to right; clockwise: *a screw with a right-handed thread.* —*adv.* With the right hand: *draws right-handed.* **—right′-hand′ed•ly** *adv.* **—right′-hand′ed•ness** *n.*

right-hand•er (rīt′hănd′ər) *n.* A person who is right-handed.

right•ist (rī′tĭst) *n.* A person who has conservative or reactionary political views. —*adj.* Of or having conservative or reactionary political views.

right•ly (rīt′lē) *adv.* **1.** In a correct or proper manner: *act rightly.* **2.** With honesty; justly. **3.** *Informal.* Really: *I don't rightly know.*

right-mind•ed (rīt′mīn′dĭd) *adj.* Having ideas and views based on what is right or intended to be right.

right of way also **right-of-way** (rīt′əv wā′) *n., pl.* **rights of way** or **right of ways** also **rights-of-way** (rīts′əv wā′) or **right-of-ways** (rīt′əv wāz′). **1.** The right to pass over property owned by someone else. **2.** The strip of land over which structures such as highways, railroads, or power lines are built. **3.** The customary or legal right of a person, vessel, or vehicle to pass in front of another.

right on *interj. Slang.* An expression used to indicate encouragement, support, or enthusiastic agreement.

right-side up (rīt′sīd′) *adv. & adj.* **1.** With the top facing upward. **2.** In or into the correct position: *Turn the painting right-side up.*

right-to-life (rīt′tə līf′) *adj.* Pro-life.

right triangle *n.* A triangle that contains a right angle.

right wing *n.* The conservative or reactionary faction of a group, especially of a political group. **—right′wing′** *adj.* **—right′wing′er** *n.*

right•y (rī′tē) *n., pl.* **right•ies.** *Informal.* A person who is right-handed.

rig•id (rĭj′ĭd) *adj.* **1.** Not changing shape or bending; stiff; inflexible: *a rigid iron frame.* **2.** Harsh and exacting; rigorous: *a rigid examination.* **3.** Strictly maintained or performed: *rigid discipline.* [First written down before 1425 in Middle English and spelled *rigide*, from Latin *rigidus*.] **—rig′id•ly** *adv.* **—rig′id•ness** *n.*

ri•gid•i•ty (rĭ jĭd′ĭ tē) *n., pl.* **ri•gid•i•ties. 1.** The quality or state of being rigid; stiffness; inflexibility. **2.** An instance of being rigid.

rig•ma•role (rĭg′mə rōl′) *n.* **1.** Confused and rambling speech; nonsense. **2.** A complicated and petty set of procedures.

rig•or (rĭg′ər) *n.* **1.** Strictness or severity, as in temperament, action, or judgment. **2.** A harsh or trying circumstance; a hardship. [First written down in 1392 in Middle English and spelled *rigour*, from Latin *rigor*.]

rigor mor•tis (môr′tĭs) *n.* Muscular stiffening following death.

rig•or•ous (rĭg′ər əs) *adj.* **1.** Characterized by or acting with rigor: *The athlete undertook a rigorous training program.* **2.** Severe or harsh: *the rigorous climate of the desert.* **3.** Precisely accurate; strict: *a rigorous examination of policy.* **—rig′or•ous•ly** *adv.* **—rig′or•ous•ness** *n.*

rile (rīl) *tr.v.* **riled, ril•ing, riles.** To anger or irritate; vex.

rill (rĭl) *n.* A small brook.

rim (rĭm) *n.* **1.** The border, edge, or margin of something: *the rim of the cup.* See Synonyms at **margin.** **2.** The outer part of a wheel around which the tire is fitted. *—tr.v.* **rimmed, rim•ming, rims. 1.** To furnish with a rim. **2.** To roll around the rim of (a basket or golf cup, for example) without falling in: *His putt rimmed the cup.*

rime¹ (rīm) *n.* A frost or coating of grains of ice, as on grass or trees; hoarfrost. *—tr.v.* **rimed, rim•ing, rimes.** To cover with or as if with frost or ice. [First written down about 725 in Old English and spelled *hrīm*.]

❑ *These sound alike:* **rime¹** (frost), **rhyme** (poem).

rime² (rīm) *n. & v.* Variant of **rhyme.** —See Note.

rind (rīnd) *n.* A tough outer covering, skin, or coating, as of fruit or cheese.

ring¹ (rĭng) *n.* **1.** A circular object, form, or arrangement with a vacant center: *a ring of flowers.* **2.** A small circular band, often of precious metal, worn on a finger. **3.** A circular band meant to carry, encircle, or hold something: *a napkin ring.* **4.** An enclosed, usually circular area in which exhibitions, sports, or contests take place: *a circus ring.* **5.a.** A rectangular arena, set off by ropes, in which boxing matches are held. **b.** The sport of boxing. **6.** A group of persons acting privately or illegally for their own gain: *a ring of thieves.* **7.** A group of atoms bound together chemically in an arrangement that can be represented as a closed geometric figure: *a benzene ring.* *—v.* **ringed, ring•ing, rings.** *—tr.* **1.** To surround with or as if with a ring; encircle: *Let's ring the statue with rose bushes.* **2.** To ornament or fit with a ring or rings: *ringed the centerpiece with a holly wreath.* **3.** To hem in (cattle or other animals) by riding in a circle around them. **4.** To toss a ring over (a peg), as in horseshoes. *—intr.* To form a ring or rings: *Spectators ringed the wrestlers.* [First written down about 725 in Old English and spelled *hring*.]

❑ *These sound alike:* **ring¹** (circle), **ring²** (sound), **wring** (squeeze).

ring² (rĭng) *v.* **rang** (răng), **rung** (rŭng), **ring•ing, rings.** *—intr.* **1.** To give forth a clear resonant sound, such as that of a bell when struck: *The doorbell rang.* **2.** To sound a bell in order to summon someone. **3.** To hear a persistent buzzing or humming: *ears ringing from the loud music.* **4.** To be filled with talk or rumors: *The town rings with stories of your success.* **5.** To appear to have a certain quality: *That story rings true.* *—tr.* **1.** To cause (a bell, for example) to ring. **2.** To announce or signal by or as if by ringing. **3.** To call (someone) on the telephone: *Ring me this afternoon.* *—n.* **1.** The sound made by a bell or another vibrating object. **2.** A loud sound that is continued or repeated: *the ring of the whistling wind.* **3.** A telephone call: *Give me a ring from the hotel.* **4.** A suggestion of a particular quality: *His offer has a suspicious ring.* **—*idioms.* ring a bell.** *Informal.* To arouse a memory: *That doesn't ring a bell with me.* **ring up.** To record, especially by means of a cash register. [First written down about 725 in Old English and spelled *hringan*.]

❑ *These sound alike:* **ring²** (sound), **ring¹** (circle), **wring** (squeeze).

ringed (rĭngd) *adj.* **1.** Wearing or marked with a ring or rings. **2.** Encircled or surrounded by bands or rings.

ring•er¹ (rĭng′ər) *n.* A horseshoe or quoit thrown so it encircles the peg.

ring•er² (rĭng′ər) *n.* **1.** A person who sounds a bell or chime. **2.** *Slang.* A contestant entered dishonestly into a competition. **3.** *Slang.* A person who bears a striking resemblance to another.

ring•lead•er (rĭng′lē′dər) *n.* A person who leads others, especially in unlawful or improper activities.

ring•let (rĭng′lĭt) *n.* A long curl of hair.

ring•mas•ter (rĭng′măs′tər) *n.* A person who is in charge of and introduces the acts in a circus.

ring•side (rĭng′sīd′) *n.* A place providing a close view of a spectacle, especially the area immediately outside the ring at a prize fight.

ring•worm (rĭng′wûrm′) *n.* Any of a number of contagious skin diseases caused by a fungus and resulting in ring-shaped, scaly, itching patches on the skin.

rink (rĭngk) *n.* **1.** An area surfaced with smooth ice for skating. **2.** A smooth floor suited for roller-skating. [First written down in 1375 in Middle English and spelled *renk*, racecourse, possibly from Old French *renc*, line, of Germanic origin.]

rin•ky-dink (rĭng′kē dĭngk′) *Slang. adj.* **1.** Old-fashioned; worn-out. **2.** Of cheap or poor quality. **3.** Unimportant.

rinse (rĭns) *tr.v.* **rinsed, rins•ing, rins•es. 1.** To wash lightly with water: *rinse the dishes.* **2.** To remove (soap, for example) by washing lightly with water. *—n.* **1.** The act of washing lightly. **2.** The water or other solution used in rinsing. **3.** A solution used in conditioning or coloring the hair.

Ri•o de Ja•nei•ro (rē′ō dā zhə nâr′ō). A city of southeast Brazil on an arm of the Atlantic Ocean. Rio de Janeiro was the capital of the colony of Brazil after 1763, of the Brazilian empire after 1822, and of the independent country from 1889 to 1960. Population, 5,090,700.

Ri•o Grande (rē′ō grănd′ *or* rē′ō grăn′dē). A river, about 1,885 miles (3,033 kilometers) long, rising in southwest Colorado and flowing through central New Mexico to southwest Texas, where it turns southeast and forms the U.S.-Mexican border. It empties into the Gulf of Mexico.

ri•ot (rī′ət) *n.* **1.** A wild disturbance created by a large number of people. **2.** In law, a violent disturbance of the peace by three or more persons assembled for a common purpose. **3.** A profuse display: *The garden was a riot of bright colors.* **4.** *Slang.* An extremely funny person or thing: *That cartoon is a riot.* *—intr.v.* **ri•ot•ed, ri•ot•ing, ri•ots. 1.** To take part in a riot. **2.** To indulge in unrestrained and boisterous merrymaking. **—ri′ot•er** *n.*

Ri•ot Act (rī′ət) *n.* An English law of 1715 providing that groups of 12 or more people that disturb the peace must disperse upon being read part of this act. **—*idiom.* read the riot act.** To warn or reprimand forcefully: *The teacher read the riot act to the rowdy students.*

ri•ot•ous (rī′ət əs) *adj.* **1.** Of, relating to, or resem-

Word History: rime²

The spelling **rhyme** is now the standard usage for similar sounds at the ends of lines of poetry, but it wasn't always the standard. Our English word comes from the Old French word *rime*, which is probably of Germanic origin. The *h* in our present spelling comes from *rhythm*, which goes back to the Latin word *rhythmus*, a word that refers not to the rhyming of words in poetry but to harmony or rhythm in music. Thus, **rhyme** is a compromise between the original Latin *rhythmus* and the French *rime*. It appears in English after 1600 and drives out all the earlier spellings, among them *ryme*, *rithme*, *rythme*, and *rhythme*, except for the now old-fashioned but still acceptable **rime**.

ring¹
Ring set with gemstones

rink
Rockefeller Center ice-skating rink in New York City

ă	pat	oi	boy
ā	pay	ou	out
âr	care	o͝o	took
ä	father	o͞o	boot
ĕ	pet	ŭ	cut
ē	be	ûr	urge
ĭ	pit	th	thin
ī	pie	*th*	this
îr	pier	hw	whoop
ŏ	pot	zh	vision
ō	toe	ə	about
ô	paw	N	*French* bon

bling a riot: *riotous mobs.* **2.** Boisterous or unrestrained: *riotous laughter.* **—ri′ot•ous•ly** *adv.* **—ri′ot•ous•ness** *n.*

rip¹ (rĭp) *v.* **ripped, rip•ping, rips.** *—tr.* **1.** To tear open or split apart: *The cat's claws ripped the curtain.* **2.** To split or saw (wood) along its grain. *—intr.* To become torn or split apart. *—n.* **1.** A torn or split place: *Sew up the rip.* **2.** The act of ripping. ***—idioms.*** **rip into.** To attack vehemently. **rip off.** *Slang.* **1.** To steal from; rob. **2.** To exploit, swindle, or cheat. [First written down before 1400 in Middle English and spelled *rippen*, from Flemish.]

Synonyms: rip, tear, shred, split. These verbs mean to pull apart or separate by physical effort. **Rip** suggests separation by force, often along a dividing line such as a seam or joint: *The nurses ripped sheets into long strips to use as bandages.* **Tear** means to pull something apart or into pieces: *He tore the napkin into bits.* **Shred** means to separate into long, irregular strips: *You should always shred confidential papers before throwing them away.* **Split** means to cut or break something into parts or layers, especially along its entire length: *They split the logs with an ax to make firewood.*

rip² (rĭp) *n.* A stretch of rough water in a river, a channel, or an estuary caused by waves or a tide opposing a current. [First written down in 1775 in American English, probably from *rip*, tear.]

rip•cord (rĭp′kôrd′) *n.* A cord pulled to release a parachute from its pack.

rip current *n.* A strong narrow surface current that flows rapidly away from the shore, returning the water carried shoreward by waves.

ripe (rīp) *adj.* **rip•er, rip•est. 1.** Fully grown and developed: *ripe fruit.* **2.** Aged and ready to be used or eaten: *a ripe cheese.* **3.** Advanced in years: *the ripe age of 85.* **4.** Fully prepared; ready: *a team ripe for its first victory.* **5.** Thoroughly matured; seasoned: *ripe judgment.* [First written down before 899 in Old English and spelled *rīpe.*] **—ripe′ness** *n.* **—ripe′ly** *adv.*

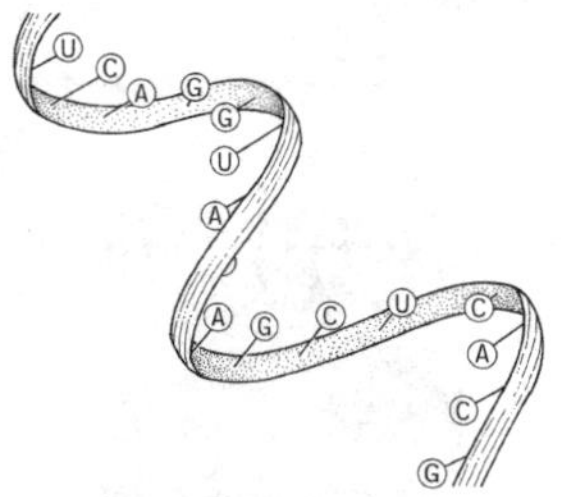

RNA

rip•en (rī′pən) *tr. & intr.v.* **rip•ened, rip•en•ing, rip•ens.** To make or become ripe or riper; mature.

rip-off (rĭp′ôf′ *or* rĭp′ŏf′) *n. Slang.* **1.** A theft. **2.** A thief. **3.** An act of exploitation. **4.** Something, such as a film or story, that is clearly imitative of or based on something else.

rip•ple (rĭp′əl) *v.* **rip•pled, rip•pling, rip•ples.** *—intr.* **1.** To form or show small waves on the surface: *The curtain rippled in the wind.* **2.** To flow with such small waves on the surface: *The stream rippled through the meadow.* *—tr.* To cause to form small waves: *A breeze rippled the prairie grass.* *—n.* **1.** A small wave, such as one formed on the surface of water when it is disturbed. **2.** A motion like that of a wave; an undulation: *the ripple of muscles on the running horse.* **3.** A sound like that made by rippling water: *a ripple of laughter in the audience.*

rip-roar•ing (rĭp′rôr′ĭng) *adj. Informal.* Noisy, lively, and exciting.

rip•saw (rĭp′sô′) *n.* A saw with coarse teeth, used for cutting wood along the grain.

rip tide *n.* A rip current.

rise (rīz) *intr.v.* **rose** (rōz), **ris•en** (rĭz′ən), **ris•ing, ris•es. 1.** To move from a lower to a higher position; ascend: *The kite rose quickly.* **2.** To stand up after sitting or lying. **3.** To exert oneself to deal with a matter: *rise to the challenge of an adventure.* **4.** To get out of bed. **5.** To increase in size, volume, or level: *The creek rose after the heavy rain.* **6.** To increase in number, amount, or value: *Prices of imports rose.* **7.** To increase in intensity, force, or speed: *The wind has risen.* **8.** To increase in pitch or volume: *The sound of their voices rose and fell.* **9.** To advance in status or rank: *He wants to rise in the academic world.* **10.** To slope or extend upward: *Mt. McKinley rises to 20,320 feet.* **11.** To become visible above the horizon: *The sun rises a little later each morning in the fall.* **12.** To appear at the surface of the water or the earth; emerge: *Whales must rise periodically to take in air.* **13.** To become apparent to the mind or senses: *Old doubts rose to challenge me.* **14.** To come back to life: *The phoenix is said to rise from its own ashes.* **15.** To come into existence; spring up: *Many streams rise in the snow-capped Andes.* **16.** To be erected: *New office buildings are rising all around us.* **17.** To puff up; become larger: *Bread dough rises.* **18.** To rebel: *The people rose up against the tyrant.* *—n.* **1.** An act of rising; upward movement. **2.** An increase in height, as of the level of water. **3.** An increase in price, worth, quantity, volume, or degree. **4.** Elevation in status or rank: *her rise to stardom.* **5.** An origin, a beginning, or a source: *the rise of a river.* **6.** A gently sloping hill. [First written down before 830 in Old English and spelled *rīsan.*]

ris•er (rī′zər) *n.* **1.** A person who rises, especially from sleep: *a late riser.* **2.** A vertical part of a stair step.

risk (rĭsk) *n.* **1.** The possibility of suffering harm or loss; danger. **2.** A situation, factor, or course of action involving danger. **3.** A person or thing considered with respect to the possibility of loss: *People who pay their bills are good credit risks.* *—tr.v.* **risked, risk•ing, risks. 1.** To expose to a chance of harm or loss; hazard: *He risked his savings in an investment scheme.* **2.** To incur the possibility of; subject oneself to the chance of: *risking an accident.*

risk•y (rĭs′kē) *adj.* **risk•i•er, risk•i•est.** Involving risk; dangerous. **—risk′i•ness** *n.*

ris•qué (rĭs kā′) *adj.* Close to being improper or indecent.

ri•tar•dan•do (rē′tär dän′dō) *adv. & adj.* In music, gradually slowing in tempo.

rite (rīt) *n.* **1.** A ceremonial act or series of acts: *the rites performed by various peoples before hunting.* **2.** The form required by custom or law for conducting a religious or other solemn ceremony: *the rite of confirmation.* **3. Rite.** The liturgy or forms of worship of a branch of the Christian church. [First written down before 1333 in Middle English, from Latin *rītus.*]

❑ *These sound alike:* **rite, right** (direction), **write** (compose).

rit•u•al (rĭch′o͞o əl) *n.* **1.** The proper form or order of a religious or other ceremony. **2.** The set of ceremonies or rites used in a place of worship. **3.** A method or procedure faithfully followed: *Exercise was part of their daily ritual.* **—rit′u•al•ly** *adv.*

rit•u•al•ism (rĭch′o͞o ə lĭz′əm) *n.* **1.** The practice or observance of religious ritual. **2.** Insistence upon or adherence to ritual.

ritz•y (rĭt′sē) *adj.* **ritz•i•er, ritz•i•est.** *Informal.* Elegant; fancy: *ritzy hotels.*

ri•val (rī′vəl) *n.* **1.** A person who attempts to equal or outdo another; a competitor. **2.** A person or thing that equals or almost equals another: *a performance without rival.* *—tr.v.* **ri•valed, ri•val•ing, ri•vals** or **ri•valled, ri•val•ling, ri•vals. 1.** To compete with; attempt to equal or surpass. **2.** To be the equal of; match in excellence. [First written down in 1577 in Modern English, from Latin *rīvālis*, one using the same stream as another, from *rīvus*, stream.]

ri•val•ry (rī′vəl rē) *n., pl.* **ri•val•ries.** The act of trying to equal or outdo another; competition.

riv•er (rĭv′ər) *n.* **1.** A large natural stream of water that flows into an ocean, a lake, or another body of water, usually fed by smaller streams that flow into it. **2.** A stream or flow resembling a river: *a river of* *tears.* [First written down about 1225 in Middle English and spelled *rivere*, from Latin *rīpārius*, of a bank, from *rīpa*, bank.]

river basin *n.* The land area drained by a river and its tributaries.

riv•et (rĭv′ĭt) *n.* A metal bolt or pin with a head on one end, used to join objects by being set through a hole in each piece and having the headless end hammered to form another head. *—tr.v.* **riv•et•ed, riv•et•ing, riv•ets. 1.** To fasten with a rivet: *rivet leather straps onto the suitcase.* **2.** To fasten or secure firmly; fix: *She stood riveted to the spot.* **3.** To attract or hold unwaveringly: *This book riveted my attention.*

Riv•i•er•a (rĭv′ē ĕr′ə). A narrow coastal region between the Alps and the Mediterranean Sea extending from southeast France to northwest Italy.

riv•u•let (rĭv′yə lĭt) *n.* A small stream or brook.

Ri•yadh (rē yäd′). The capital and largest city of Saudi Arabia, in the east-central part of the country east-northeast of Mecca. It is situated in a desert oasis. Population, 1,250,000.

ri•yal (rē ôl′ *or* rē äl′) *n.* The basic monetary unit of Qatar and Saudi Arabia.

Rn The symbol for the element **radon.**

RNA (är′ĕn ā′) *n.* A nucleic acid found in the nucleus, cytoplasm, and various organelles of all living cells and functioning mainly in the synthesis of proteins; ribonucleic acid.

roach[1] (rōch) *n., pl.* **roach** or **roach•es. 1.** A freshwater fish of northern Europe, related to the carp. **2.** Any of various North American fishes similar or related to the roach. [First written down about 1200 in Middle English and spelled *roche*, from Old French.]

roach[2] (rōch) *n.* A cockroach. [First written down in 1837 in American English, from *cockroach.*]

road (rōd) *n.* **1.** An open way for the passage of vehicles, persons, and animals. **2.** A path or course: *the road to success.* **3.** A railroad. **4.** A roadstead. Often used in the plural. ***—idiom.*** **on the road. 1.** On tour, as a theatrical company. **2.** Traveling, especially as a salesperson. **3.** Wandering, as a vagabond. [First written down in 871 in Old English and spelled *rād*, a riding, road.]

❑ *These sound alike:* **road, rode** (moved in a vehicle), **rowed** (used oars).

road•bed (rōd′bĕd′) *n.* **1.a.** The foundation upon which the ties and rails of a railroad are laid. **b.** A layer of gravel or crushed rock under the ties. **2.** The foundation and surface of a road.

road•block (rōd′blŏk′) *n.* **1.** A barricade or an obstruction across a road set up to prevent the passage of criminals or enemy troops. **2.** Something that prevents progress.

road•run•ner (rōd′rŭn′ər) *n.* A long-tailed swift-running bird of southwest North America, having brownish streaked feathers and a crested head.

road•side (rōd′sīd′) *n.* The area bordering on the side of the road.

road•stead (rōd′stĕd′) *n.* An area offshore where ships can anchor safely.

road•ster (rōd′stər) *n.* An open automobile having a single seat in the front for two or three people and a rumble seat or luggage compartment in the back.

road test *n.* **1.** A test of a motor vehicle under actual road conditions. **2.** A test of driving ability on the road, required of a candidate for a driver's license.

road•way (rōd′wā′) *n.* A road, especially the part over which vehicles travel.

roam (rōm) *v.* **roamed, roam•ing, roams.** *—intr.* To move about without purpose or plan; wander. See Synonyms at **wander.** *—tr.* To travel over or through (an area) without a purpose or plan; wander: *Bears roam the forest.* **—roam′er** *n.*

roan (rōn) *adj.* Brownish or blackish and thickly sprinkled with white or gray hairs: *a roan horse.* *—n.* **1.** The coloring of a roan horse. **2.** A roan horse or other animal.

roar (rôr) *v.* **roared, roar•ing, roars.** *—intr.* **1.** To utter a loud deep sound, especially in distress, rage, or excitement. See Synonyms at **shout. 2.** To make or produce a loud deep sound or noise: *The engines roared.* **3.** To laugh loudly or excitedly. *—tr.* To express with a loud deep noise: *We roared our approval.* *—n.* **1.** The loud deep sound made by a wild animal: *the roar of the lion.* **2.** A loud deep cry of rage or anger. **3.** A loud deep sound or noise: *the roar of a rocket engine.* [First written down before 900 in Old English and spelled *rārian.*]

roar•ing (rôr′ĭng) *adj.* Very lively or successful; thriving: *a roaring business.*

roast (rōst) *v.* **roast•ed, roast•ing, roasts.** *—tr.* **1.** To cook with dry heat, as in an oven or near hot coals. **2.** To dry or brown by heating: *They roasted coffee beans.* **3.** *Informal.* To ridicule or criticize harshly. **4.** To expose to great or excessive heat. **5.** In metallurgy, to heat (ores) in a furnace in order to dehydrate, purify, or oxidize. *—intr.* To cook food in an oven. *—n.* **1.** A cut of meat for roasting. **2.** Something roasted. *—adj.* Roasted: *a roast duck.* [First written down about 1280 in Middle English and spelled *rosten*, from Old French *rostir*, of Germanic origin.]

roast•er (rō′stər) *n.* **1.** A pan or other utensil for roasting. **2.** A chicken or other animal suitable for roasting.

rob (rŏb) *v.* **robbed, rob•bing, robs.** *—tr.* **1.** To take property from (a person or place) unlawfully and with the threat or use of force. **2.** To take valuables unlawfully from: *rob money from a safe.* **3.** To deprive (someone) unjustly or injuriously of something: *The outfielder's great catch robbed him of a home run.* *—intr.* To engage in or commit robbery. **—rob′ber** *n.*

rob•ber•y (rŏb′ə rē) *n., pl.* **rob•ber•ies.** The act or crime of unlawfully taking the property of another with the threat or use of force.

robe (rōb) *n.* **1.** A long, loose, flowing outer garment. **2.** An official garment worn over other clothes on formal occasions to show office or rank: *a judge's robe.* **3.** A bathrobe or dressing gown. **4.** A blanket or covering, especially one for the lap and legs: *a lap robe.* *—v.* **robed, rob•ing, robes.** *—tr.* To cover or dress in or as if in a robe. *—intr.* To put on robes or a robe.

rob•in (rŏb′ĭn) *n.* **1.** A North American songbird having a rust-red breast and a dark gray back. **2.** A small European bird having an orange breast and a brown back.

Rob•in Hood (rŏb′ĭn) *n.* A legendary English outlaw of the 12th century, famous for his courage and practice of robbing the rich to aid the poor.

ro•bot (rō′bət *or* rō′bŏt′) *n.* **1.** A machine having the ability to perform human tasks or to imitate human actions. **2.** A person who works or follows orders mechanically. **3.** A machine that operates automatically or by remote control. [First written down in 1923 in Modern English, from Czech, from *robota*, drudgery.]

ro•bot•ics (rō bŏt′ĭks) *n.* *(used with a singular verb).* The study and use of the technology of robots.

ro•bust (rō bŭst′ *or* rō′bŭst′) *adj.* **1.** Full of health and strength; vigorous: *a robust rosebush with many blooms.* **2.** Characterized by richness; full-bodied: *a robust blend of coffee beans.* [First writ-

roadrunner

roadster

robe

Graduation robes

ă	pat	oi	boy
ā	pay	ou	out
âr	care	o͝o	took
ä	father	o͞o	boot
ĕ	pet	ŭ	cut
ē	be	ûr	urge
ĭ	pit	th	thin
ī	pie	*th*	this
îr	pier	hw	whoop
ŏ	pot	zh	vision
ō	toe	ə	about
ô	paw	N	*French* bon

John D. Rockefeller

rock garden

rocking chair

ten down in 1549 in Modern English, from Latin *rōbustus*, from *rōbus*, oak, strength.]

roc (rŏk) *n.* A legendary bird of prey of enormous size and strength. [First written down in 1579 in Modern English, from Arabic *ruḫḫ*.]

❑ *These sound alike:* **roc, rock[1]** (stone), **rock[2]** (sway).

Ro•cham•beau (rō′shăm **bō′**), **Comte de.** 1725–1807. French army officer who commanded French forces in the defeat of the British at Yorktown (1781) during the American Revolution.

Roch•es•ter (**rŏch′**ĭ stər *or* **rŏch′**ĕs′tər). A city of western New York east-northeast of Buffalo near Lake Ontario. It was first settled about 1812 and grew rapidly after the opening of the Erie Canal (1825). Population, 241,741.

rock[1] (rŏk) *n.* **1.a.** A relatively hard naturally occurring material that is of mineral origin. **b.** A fairly small piece of such material; a stone. **c.** A large mass of such material, as a cliff or peak. **2.** A naturally formed mineral matter that makes up a significant part of the earth's crust. **3.** A person or thing that resembles a rock in firmness or stability. ***—idiom.* on the rocks. 1.** In a state of difficulty, destruction, or ruin. **2.** Without money; bankrupt. **3.** Served over ice cubes, as an alcoholic beverage. [First written down about 1250 in Middle English and spelled *roc*, from Old North French *roque*.]

❑ *These sound alike:* **rock[1]** (stone), **roc** (bird), **rock[2]** (sway).

rock[2] (rŏk) *v.* **rocked, rock•ing, rocks.** *—intr.* **1.** To be moved back and forth or from side to side, especially gently or rhythmically. **2.** To be shaken violently: *The buildings rocked during the earthquake.* *—tr.* **1.** To move back and forth or from side to side, especially in order to soothe: *I rocked the baby to sleep.* **2.** To shake violently, as from a shock or blow: *The earthquake rocked the villages.* **3.** To stun or upset; shock: *a scandal that rocked the town.* *—n.* **1.** An act of rocking. **2.** A rhythmic swaying motion. **3.** Rock 'n' roll. ***—idiom.* rock the boat.** *Slang.* To disturb the balance of a situation or group. [First written down before 1100 in Old English and spelled *roccian*.]

❑ *These sound alike:* **rock[2]** (sway), **roc** (bird), **rock[1]** (stone).

rock-and-roll (**rŏk′**ən **rōl′**) *n.* Variant of **rock 'n' roll.**

rock bottom *n.* The lowest level or absolute bottom: *Prices have reached rock bottom.*

rock candy *n.* A hard candy made by cooling boiled sugar into large clear crystals.

rock crystal *n.* Transparent quartz, especially when colorless, used in optical instruments and as a semiprecious gemstone.

Rock•e•fel•ler (**rŏk′**ə fĕl′ər). American family, including **John Davison** (1839–1937), who gained great wealth through the Standard Oil Company and spent about half of his fortune on charitable works. His grandson **Nelson Aldrich Rockefeller** (1908–1979) was governor of New York (1959–1973) and Vice President of the United States (1974–1977) under Gerald Ford.

rock•er (**rŏk′**ər) *n.* **1.** A person or thing that rocks. **2.** A rocking chair. **3.** A rocking horse. **4.** One of the two curved pieces on which a cradle, rocking chair, or similar device rocks. ***—idiom.* off (one's) rocker.** *Slang.* Out of one's mind; crazy.

rock•et (**rŏk′**ĭt) *n.* **1.a.** A vehicle or device propelled by one or more rocket engines. **b.** A rocket engine. **2.** A projectile weapon carrying a warhead that is propelled by rockets. **3.** A firework that is shot up into the sky. *—v.* **rock•et•ed, rock•et•ing, rock•ets.** *—intr.* **1.** To travel in or by means of a rocket: *rocketing to the moon.* **2.** To move with great speed: *a train that went rocketing by.* *—tr.* To transport or propel by rocket: *rocketing a satellite into orbit.*

rocket engine *n.* An engine that contains all the substances necessary for its operation and is propelled by a jet of hot gases produced by burning fuel. Since they do not rely on air for oxygen, rocket engines can be used in space.

rock•et•ry (**rŏk′**ĭ trē) *n.* The science and technology of designing, building, and flying rockets.

rock garden *n.* A rocky area in which plants are cultivated.

Rock•ies (**rŏk′**ēz). Rocky Mountains.

rock•ing chair (**rŏk′**ĭng) *n.* A chair mounted on rockers or springs.

rocking horse *n.* A toy horse large enough for a child to ride, mounted on rockers or springs.

rock 'n' roll or **rock-and-roll** (**rŏk′**ən **rōl′**) *n.* A form of popular music arising from rhythm and blues, country music, and gospel. It originated in the United States during the 1950's.

rock-ribbed (**rŏk′rĭbd′**) *adj.* **1.** Rocky. **2.** Stern and unyielding.

rock salt *n.* Common salt, mainly sodium chloride, occurring in large solid masses in the earth's crust.

rock wool *n.* A fibrous soundproofing and insulating material that is made from glass.

rock•y[1] (**rŏk′**ē) *adj.* **rock•i•er, rock•i•est. 1.** Consisting of or containing rocks: *rocky soil.* **2.** Resembling or suggesting rock; firm or hard. **3.** Full of obstacles or difficulties: *a rocky career.*

rock•y[2] (**rŏk′**ē) *adj.* **1.** Unsteady or shaky: *a rocky balance.* **2.** Weak, dizzy, or nauseated.

Rock•y Mountains (**rŏk′**ē) also **Rock•ies** (**rŏk′**ēz). A major mountain system of western North America extending more than 3,000 miles (4,827 kilometers) from northwest Alaska to the Mexican border. The system, rising to 14,433 feet (4,402.1 meters) in central Colorado, includes numerous ranges and forms the Continental Divide.

Rocky Mountain sheep *n.* The bighorn.

Rocky Mountain spotted fever *n.* A severe infectious disease having symptoms that include muscle pains, high fever, and skin eruptions. It is caused by microorganisms and transmitted by the bite of infected ticks.

Rocky Mountain States. A region of the western United States including Colorado, Idaho, Montana, Nevada, Utah, and Wyoming.

ro•co•co also **Rococo** (rə **kō′**kō *or* rō′kə **kō′**) *n.* The ornate style of art, especially of architecture, decorative art, and music, that developed in France in the early 18th century. *—adj.* Of or relating to the style of rococo: *a rococo chair.*

rod (rŏd) *n.* **1.** A slender, stiff, straight piece of metal, wood, or other material; a stick or bar: *a curtain rod.* **2.** A fishing rod. **3.** A stick or bunch of sticks used to punish people by whipping. **4.** Punishment; correction. **5.** A measuring stick. **6.** A scepter or staff that symbolizes power or authority. **7.** A unit of length equal to 16.5 feet (5.03 meters). **8.** Any of the elongated cells in the retina of the eye that are sensitive to dim light. **9.** *Slang.* A pistol. [First written down before 1100 in Old English and spelled *rodd*.]

rode (rōd) *v.* Past tense of **ride.**

❑ *These sound alike:* **rode, road** (passage), **rowed** (used oars).

ro•dent (**rōd′**nt) *n.* Any of various related mammals, such as a mouse, rat, squirrel, or beaver, having large front teeth used for gnawing. *—adj.* **1.** Gnawing. **2.** Of or relating to rodents. [First written down in 1835 in Modern English, from Latin *rōdere*, to gnaw.]

ro•de•o (**rō′**dē ō′ *or* rō **dā′**ō) *n., pl.* **ro•de•os.** A public show in which skills such as riding broncos and roping calves are displayed. [First written down in 1834 in Modern English, from Spanish *rodeo*, corral, from Latin *rota*, wheel.]

roe¹ (rō) *n.* The eggs of a fish, often together with the membrane of the ovary in which they are held. [First written down about 1450 in Middle English and spelled *row*.]

❑ *These sound alike:* **roe¹** (fish eggs), **rho** (Greek letter), **roe²** (small deer), **row¹** (continuous line), **row²** (use oars).

roe² (rō) *n., pl.* **roe** or **roes.** The roe deer. [First written down before 700 in Old English and spelled *rāha*.]

❑ *These sound alike:* **roe²** (small deer), **rho** (Greek letter), **roe¹** (fish eggs), **row¹** (continuous line), **row²** (use oars).

roe•buck (rō′bŭk′) *n.* A male roe deer.

roe deer *n.* A small deer of Europe and Asia, having short antlers in the male and a brownish coat.

roent•gen (rĕnt′gən *or* rŭnt′gən) *n.* An obsolete unit used to measure the intensity of exposure to x-rays, gamma rays, and similar ionizing radiation. [First written down in 1896 in Modern English and spelled *Röntgen*, after Wilhelm Konrad *Roentgen* (1845–1923), German physicist.]

rog•er (rŏj′ər) *interj.* An expression used in radio communications to indicate that a message has been received.

rogue (rōg) *n.* **1.** A person who tricks or cheats others; a scoundrel; a rascal. **2.** A mischievous person; a scamp. **3.** An animal, especially an elephant, that lives apart from a herd and that has become vicious and dangerous.

rogu•er•y (rō′gə rē) *n., pl.* **rogu•er•ies. 1.** Behavior characteristic of a rogue. **2.** A mischievous act.

rogues' gallery (rōgz) *n.* A collection of pictures of criminals maintained in police files and used for making identifications.

rogu•ish (rō′gĭsh) *adj.* **1.** Dishonest; unprincipled. **2.** Playfully teasing; mischievous. **—ro′guish•ly** *adv.*

roil (roil) *tr.v.* **roiled, roil•ing, roils. 1.** To make (a liquid) cloudy by stirring up sediment. **2.** To disturb; vex: *We were roiled by their rudeness.*

rois•ter (roi′stər) *intr.v.* **rois•tered, rois•ter•ing, rois•ters. 1.** To engage in boisterous merrymaking; revel noisily. **2.** To behave in a blustering manner; swagger.

Ro•land (rō′lənd) *n.* A legendary defender of Christianity and nephew of Charlemagne, killed in the battle against the Saracens at Roncesvalles (A.D. 778).

role (rōl) *n.* **1.** A character or part played by a performer. **2.** The characteristic or expected social behavior of a person. [First written down in 1606 in Modern English and spelled *rowle*, from Old French *rolle*, roll of parchment, from Latin *rota*, wheel.]

❑ *These sound alike:* **role, roll** (turn over).

role model *n.* A person who serves as a model for another person to imitate.

roll (rōl) *v.* **rolled, roll•ing, rolls.** *—intr.* **1.** To move or travel along a surface by revolving on an axis or repeatedly turning over: *The coin rolled across the sidewalk.* **2.** To move along on wheels or rollers: *The car rolled to a stop.* **3.** To travel or be carried in a vehicle. **4.** To begin to move or operate: *Roll the presses!* **5.** To make progress: *The campaign is rolling.* **6.** To turn over and over: *The puppy rolled in the grass.* **7.** To take the shape of a ball or cylinder: *Yarn rolls easily.* **8.** To become flattened by or as if by applying pressure with a roller: *The dough rolls out smoothly.* **9.** To move steadily or with increasing momentum: *A thick fog was rolling in.* **10.** To move or extend in gentle rises and falls: *The dunes roll to the sea.* **11.** To go by; elapse: *The years rolled by.* **12.** To move or rock from side to side: *The sailboat rolled and pitched in the storm.* **13.** To make a prolonged deep sound: *Thunder rolled in the distance.* **14.** To beat a drum with a continuous series of short blows. **15.** To make a trilling sound, as certain birds do. *—tr.* **1.** To cause to move or travel along a surface by revolving on an axis or repeatedly turning over: *roll a ball.* **2.** To move or push along on wheels or rollers: *rolled the chair under the desk.* **3.** To cause to sway or rock: *Heavy seas rolled the ship.* **4.** To cause to begin moving or operating: *roll the cameras.* **5.** To pronounce or utter with a trill: *You roll your* r*'s in Spanish.* **6.** To beat (a drum) with a continuous series of short blows. **7.** To wrap (something) round and round upon itself: *roll up a poster.* **8.** To flatten or spread by applying pressure with a roller: *roll pastry dough.* **9.a.** To envelop or enfold: *roll dirty laundry in a sheet.* **b.** To make by shaping into a ball or cylinder: *roll a cigarette.* **10.** To throw (dice), as in craps. *—n.* **1.** The act or an instance of rolling: *watched the roll of the golf ball toward the cup.* **2.** Something rolled up: *a roll of tape.* **3.** A tilting, swaying, or rocking motion: *the roll of the ship on the waves.* **4.** A gentle rise and fall in a surface: *the roll of the plains.* **5.** A piece of paper that may be or is rolled up; a scroll. **6.** A list of names of persons belonging to a group: *The roll is called before a council meeting begins.* **7.a.** A small rounded portion of bread. **b.** A portion of food shaped like a tube with a filling: *an egg roll.* **8.** A deep rumble: *a roll of thunder.* **9.** A succession of short sounds, such as those made by beating a drum rapidly. ***—idioms.*** **on a roll.** *Informal.* Undergoing or experiencing sustained, even increasing good fortune or success. **roll back. 1.** To reduce (prices or wages, for example) to a previous lower level. **2.** To cause to turn back or retreat. **roll up. 1.** To arrive in a vehicle. **2.** To acquire; amass: *roll up a fortune.* [First written down about 1300 in Middle English and spelled *rollen*, from Old French *roler*, from Latin *rotula*, little wheel.]

❑ *These sound alike:* **roll, role** (part in a play).

roll call *n.* The reading aloud of a list of names of people to determine who is present.

roll•er (rō′lər) *n.* **1.** A small wheel, as on a roller skate or a caster. **2.** A cylinder around which something is wound: *a window-shade roller.* **3.** A small cylinder of wire mesh or foam rubber around which hair is wound to produce a soft curl or wave. **4.** A cylinder used to flatten, crush, or squeeze things. **5.** A cylinder for applying paint, ink, or a similar substance onto a surface. **6.** A large heavy wave that breaks along a coastline.

roller coaster *n.* An elevated railway with steep inclines and sharp turns that is operated as a ride, especially in an amusement park.

roller skate *n.* A shoe or boot with usually four wheels arranged side by side or in a row, worn for skating on hard surfaces.

roll•er-skate (rō′lər skāt′) *intr.v.* **roll•er-skat•ed, roll•er-skat•ing, roll•er-skates.** To skate on roller skates. **—roller skater** *n.*

rol•lick (rŏl′ĭk) *intr.v.* **rol•licked, rol•lick•ing, rol•licks.** To behave or move in a carefree frolicsome manner; romp. **—rol′lick** *n.* **—rol′lick•some, rol′lick•y** *adj.*

rol•lick•ing (rŏl′ĭ kĭng) *adj.* High-spirited and carefree; boisterous: *a rollicking song.*

roll•ing mill (rō′lĭng) *n.* **1.** A factory in which metal is rolled into sheets, bars, or other forms. **2.** A machine used for rolling metal.

rolling pin *n.* A smooth cylinder, usually of wood, with a handle at each end, used for rolling out dough.

roller coaster

roller skate

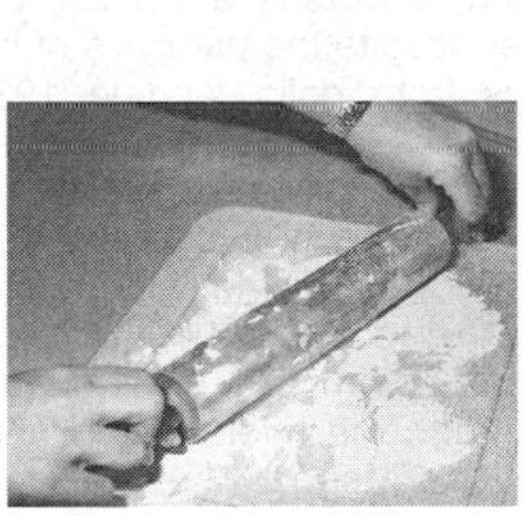

rolling pin

ă	pat	oi	boy
ā	pay	ou	out
âr	care	o͝o	took
ä	father	o͞o	boot
ĕ	pet	ŭ	cut
ē	be	ûr	urge
ĭ	pit	th	thin
ī	pie	*th*	this
îr	pier	hw	whoop
ŏ	pot	zh	vision
ō	toe	ə	about
ô	paw	N	*French* bon

Eleanor Roosevelt

Franklin D. Roosevelt

Eleanor and Franklin Roosevelt

Franklin and Eleanor **Roosevelt** formed a lasting political partnership when they married in 1905. Eleanor Roosevelt encouraged her husband to pursue a political career despite the paralysis of his legs from polio, and in 1932 Franklin Roosevelt was elected President. As President, he initiated a group of programs collectively called the New Deal to get the country out of the Great Depression. As First Lady, Eleanor Roosevelt was an influential adviser to the President and a champion for such groups as civil rights activists, youth leaders, and labor reformers. Franklin Roosevelt led the United States when the nation entered World War II in 1941, but he died suddenly just before the war ended. Eleanor Roosevelt went on to serve as a delegate to the United Nations (1945, 1949–1952, and 1961) and as chairman of the U.N. Commission on Human Rights (1946–1951).

rolling stock *n.* Transportation equipment, such as automobiles, trains, or railroad cars, owned by a company.

ro•ly-po•ly (rō′lē **pō′**lē) *adj.* Short and plump; roundish in shape. *—n., pl.* **ro•ly-po•lies.** A short plump person or thing.

Rom. *abbr.* An abbreviation of: **1.** Roman. **2.** Romance.

ro•maine (rō **mān′**) *n.* A type of lettuce having long crisp leaves forming a narrow head.

Ro•man (**rō′**mən) *adj.* **1.** Of or relating to ancient or modern Rome or its people or culture. **2.** Of or using the Latin alphabet. **3.** Of or relating to the Roman Catholic Church. **4. roman.** Of or being a style of type characterized by upright letters and vertical lines thicker than horizontal lines. *—n.* **1.** A native, inhabitant, or citizen of ancient or modern Rome. **2.** The Italian language as spoken in Rome. **3. roman.** Roman print or style of type. **4. Romans.** A book of the New Testament in the form of a letter of which Saint Paul explains many theological doctrines to the Christian church in Rome.

Roman Catholic *adj.* Of, relating to, or being the Roman Catholic church. *—n.* A member of the Roman Catholic church.

Roman Catholic Church *n.* The Christian church that is organized in a hierarchical structure of bishops and priests with the pope in Rome at its head.

Roman Catholicism *n.* The doctrines, practices, and organization of the Roman Catholic Church.

ro•mance (rō **măns′** *or* **rō′**măns′) *n.* **1.** A love affair. **2.** A strong attachment or enthusiasm for something: *a childhood romance with the sea.* **3.a.** A long narrative in prose or verse that tells of the adventures of heroes and extraordinary events: *a medieval romance.* **b.** The class of literature composed of such stories. **4.** A mysterious quality, as of something adventurous or heroic: *an air of romance about the old castle.* *—v.* (rō **măns′**). **ro•manced, ro•manc•ing, ro•manc•es.** *—intr.* **1.** To invent, write, or tell romances. **2.** To think or behave in a romantic manner. *—tr. Informal.* To carry on a love affair or courtship with (someone).

Romance languages *pl.n.* A group of languages that developed from Latin, including French, Italian, Portuguese, Romanian, and Spanish.

Roman Empire Also called **Rome** (rōm). An empire that succeeded the Roman Republic, lasting from 27 B.C. to A.D. 476. At its greatest extent it included territories stretching from Britain and Germany to North Africa and the Persian Gulf.

Ro•man•esque (rō′mə **nĕsk′**) *adj.* Of, relating to, or being a style of architecture that flourished in Europe in the 11th and 12th centuries, characterized by thick walls and rounded vaults. *—n.* The Romanesque style of architecture.

Ro•ma•ni•a (rō **mā′**nē ə) or **Ru•ma•ni•a** (ro͞o **mā′**nē ə). A country of southeast Europe with a short coastline on the Black Sea. Bucharest is the capital and the largest city. Population, 22,533,074.

Ro•ma•ni•an (rō **mā′**nē ən) *adj.* Of or relating to Romania or its people, language, or culture. *—n.* **1.** A native or inhabitant of Romania. **2.** The Romance language of the Romanians.

Roman nose *n.* A nose with a high prominent bridge.

Roman numeral *n.* Any of the numerals formed with the characters I, V, X, L, C, D, and M in the system of numeration used by the ancient Romans.

ro•man•tic (rō **măn′**tĭk) *adj.* **1.** Of, relating to, or characteristic of romance: *a romantic story.* **2.** Given to thoughts or feelings of romance; sentimental. **3.** Expressive of or conducive to love: *a romantic atmosphere.* **4.** Imaginative but not based on fact: *a romantic interpretation.* **5.** Of or relating to love or a love affair: *a romantic involvement.* **6.** Often **Romantic.** Of or characteristic of Romanticism in art, music, or literature: *a Romantic composer; Romantic dramas.* *—n.* **1.** A romantic person. **2.** Often **Romantic.** A follower of Romanticism. **—ro•man′ti•cal•ly** *adv.*

ro•man•ti•cism (rō **măn′**tĭ sĭz′əm) *n.* **1.** Often **Romanticism.** An artistic and intellectual movement that originated in Europe in the late 18th century and stressed the importance of strong emotion, rich imagination, and rebellion against social and artistic conventions. **2.** The spirit and attitudes characteristic of this movement. **—ro•man′ti•cist** *n.*

ro•man•ti•cize (rō **măn′**tĭ sīz′) *v.* **ro•man•ti•cized, ro•man•ti•ciz•ing, ro•man•ti•ciz•es.** *—tr.* To view or interpret romantically. *—intr.* To think in a romantic way.

Rom•a•ny (**rŏm′**ə nē *or* **rō′**mə nē) *n., pl.* **Rom•a•nies.** **1.** A Gypsy. **2.** The language of the Gypsies, related to Hindi; Gypsy. *—adj.* Of or relating to the Gypsies or their language or culture.

Rome (rōm). **1.** The capital and largest city of Italy, in the west-central part of the country on the Tiber River. It was traditionally founded by Romulus and Remus and was ruled first by Etruscans, who were overthrown in about 500 B.C. As capital of the Roman Empire, Rome was considered the center of the known world, but the city declined after A.D. 323. In the Middle Ages Rome revived as the power of the papacy increased. Population, 2,830,569. **2.** Roman Empire.

Ro•me•o (**rō′**mē ō′) *n.* A man who is devoted to the pursuit of love.

romp (rŏmp) *intr.v.* **romped, romp•ing, romps.** To play or frolic in an excited or lively manner: *dogs romping in a vacant lot.* *—n.* Lively high-spirited play. **—romp′er** *n.*

romp•ers (**rŏm′**pərz) *pl.n.* A child's loose-fitting one-piece play suit with legs like short bloomers.

Rom•u•lus (**rŏm′**yə ləs) *n.* In Roman mythology, the son of Mars and legendary founder of Rome, who with his twin brother Remus was reared by a wolf.

ron•do (**rŏn′**dō *or* rŏn **dō′**) *n., pl.* **ron•dos.** A musical composition in which the principal theme occurs at least three times in its original key between contrasting subordinate themes.

rood (ro͞od) *n.* **1.** A cross or crucifix. **2.** A measure of land area equal to ¼ acre (0.10 hectare).

❑ *These sound alike:* **rood, rude** (crude).

roof (ro͞of *or* ro͝of) *n.* **1.** The exterior covering on the top of a building. **2.** The exterior of something: *the roof of a car.* **3.** The upper part of the mouth. *—tr. v.* **roofed, roof•ing, roofs.** To cover with a roof. [First written down about 725 in Old English and spelled *hrōf*.]

roof•er (**ro͞o′**fər *or* **ro͝of′**ər) *n.* A person who lays or repairs roofs.

roof•ing (**ro͞o′**fĭng *or* **ro͝of′**ĭng) *n.* Materials used in building a roof.

roof•top (**ro͞of′**tŏp′ *or* **ro͝of′**tŏp′) *n.* The outer surface of a roof.

roof•tree (**ro͞of′**trē′ *or* **ro͝of′**trē′) *n.* A long horizontal beam extending along the ridge of a roof; a ridgepole.

rook[1] (ro͝ok) *n.* **1.** A European bird that is related to the crow and nests in large colonies. **2.** A swindler or a cheat, especially at games. *—tr.v.* **rooked, rook•ing, rooks.** To cheat; swindle. [First written down about 725 in Old English and spelled *hrōc*.]

rook[2] (ro͝ok) *n.* A chess piece that may move in a straight line horizontally or vertically across any number of unoccupied squares. [First written down before 1300 in Middle English and spelled *rok*, from Arabic *rukh*, from Persian.]

rook•er•y (ro͝ok′ə rē) *n., pl.* **rook•er•ies. 1.** A place where rooks roost or nest. **2.** A place where certain other birds or animals, such as penguins or seals, gather to breed.

rook•ie (ro͝ok′ē) *n.* **1.** A first-year player, especially in a major-league sport. **2.** *Slang.* A beginner; a novice.

room (ro͞om *or* ro͝om) *n.* **1.** A space that is or may be occupied: *This desk takes up too much room.* **2.a.** An area of a building set off by walls or partitions. **b.** The people present in a room: *The whole room laughed.* **3. rooms.** Living quarters; lodgings. **4.** Occasion; opportunity: *There is room for doubt.* —*intr.v.* **roomed, room•ing, rooms.** To occupy a rented room as a lodger: *rooming with a private family.* [First written down about 725 in Old English and spelled *rūm.*]

❑ *These sound alike:* **room, rheum** (mucus).

room and board *n.* Lodging and meals earned, purchased, or provided.

room•er (ro͞o′mər *or* ro͝om′ər) *n.* A person who rents a room; a lodger.

❑ *These sound alike:* **roomer, rumor** (report).

room•ing house (ro͞o′mĭng *or* ro͝om′ĭng) *n.* A house where lodgers may rent rooms.

room•mate (ro͞om′māt′ *or* ro͝om′māt′) *n.* A person with whom one shares a room or an apartment.

room•y (ro͞o′mē *or* ro͝om′ē) *adj.* **room•i•er, room•i•est.** Having plenty of room; spacious: *a roomy closet.* **—room′i•ness** *n.*

Roo•se•velt (rō′zə vĕlt′ *or* rō′zə vəlt), **(Anna) Eleanor.** 1884–1962. American diplomat and First Lady of the United States (1933–1945) as the wife of Franklin D. Roosevelt. As a delegate to the United Nations (1945, 1949–1952, and 1961), she helped draft the Universal Declaration of Human Rights in 1948. —See Note.

Roosevelt, Franklin Delano. 1882–1945. The 32nd President of the United States (1933–1945). His administration was marked by relief programs, measures to assist recovery from the Depression, and U.S. involvement in World War II. —See Note.

Roosevelt, Theodore. 1858–1919. The 26th President of the United States (1901–1909). He won the 1906 Nobel Peace Prize.

roost (ro͞ost) *n.* **1.** A branch, rod, or similar resting place on which birds perch or settle for the night. **2.** A building or other place where birds perch or settle for the night. **3.** A place for temporary rest or sleep. —*intr.v.* **roost•ed, roost•ing, roosts.** To rest or sleep on or as if on a roost.

roost•er (ro͞o′stər) *n.* A full-grown male chicken.

root[1] (ro͞ot *or* ro͝ot) *n.* **1.** A part of a plant that usually grows down into the ground and that absorbs water and minerals from the soil, stores food, and keeps the plant securely in place. **2.** A usually underground plant part similar to a root, as a tuber or rhizome. **3.** The part of an organ or body structure, as a hair or tooth, that is embedded in other tissue. **4.** The bottom or supporting part of something; a base. **5.** A source; an origin: *the Roman roots of democracy.* **6.** The essential part; core; heart: *the root of the matter.* **7. roots.** The condition of belonging to a particular culture, society, place, or environment: *We've lived here too short a time to have any roots.* **8.** A word or word element from which other words are formed, as by adding affixes. For example, *cheer* is the root of *cheerful* and *cheerless.* **9.a.** A number that when multiplied by itself a given number of times produces a specified number. For example, since $2 \times 2 \times 2 \times 2 = 16$, 2 is a fourth root of 16. **b.** A number that changes an equation to an identity if it is substituted for a variable in that equation; a solution. —*v.* **root•ed, root•ing, roots.** —*intr.* **1.** To send forth or start the growth of a root or roots: *Carrot tops will root in water.* **2.** To become firmly established or settled. —*tr.* **1.** To cause to put out roots and grow. **2.** To implant or fix in place by or as if by roots: *Our love of the mountains has rooted us here.* **3.** To pull up or remove by or as if by the roots: *rooting out tree stumps with a tractor.* [First written down before 1100 in Old English and spelled *rōt,* from Old Norse *rōt.*]

❑ *These sound alike:* **root[1]** (plant part), **root[2]** (dig), **root[3]** (cheer), **route** (road).

root[2] (ro͞ot *or* ro͝ot) *v.* **root•ed, root•ing, roots.** —*tr.* To dig with or as if with the snout or nose: *pigs rooting in the mud.* —*intr.* To rummage for something: *rooting through the drawer looking for an eraser.* [First written down about 725 in Old English and spelled *wrōtan.*] **—root′er** *n.*

❑ *These sound alike:* **root[2]** (dig), **root[1]** (plant part), **root[3]** (cheer), **route** (road).

root[3] (ro͞ot *or* ro͝ot) *intr.v.* **root•ed, root•ing, roots.** To give encouragement by or as if by cheering: *rooting for the home team.* [First written down in 1889 in American English, possibly alteration of *rout,* to bellow.]

❑ *These sound alike:* **root[3]** (cheer), **root[1]** (plant part), **root[2]** (dig), **route** (road).

root beer *n.* A carbonated soft drink made from extracts of certain plant roots and herbs.

root canal *n.* **1.** A passage in the root of a tooth through which nerves and blood vessels reach the interior. **2.** A treatment in which diseased tissue from this part of the tooth is removed and replaced with filling.

root hair *n.* A thin outgrowth of a plant root that absorbs water and minerals from the soil.

root•less (ro͞ot′lĭs *or* ro͝ot′lĭs) *adj.* **1.** Having no roots. **2.** Not belonging to a particular place or society: *rootless refugees in a strange country.*

root•let (ro͞ot′lĭt *or* ro͝ot′lĭt) *n.* A small root or division of a root.

root•stock (ro͞ot′stŏk′ *or* ro͝ot′stŏk′) *n.* **1.** A rhizome. **2.** A root onto which another plant is grafted. **3.** A source or an origin.

rope (rōp) *n.* **1.** A heavy cord made of intertwined strands of fiber or some other material. **2.** A lasso or lariat. **3.** A cord with a noose on one end for hanging a person. **4.** A string of things attached or entwined together: *a rope of onions.* **5.** A sticky formation of stringy matter in a liquid. **6. ropes.** *Informal.* The techniques and procedures involved in a certain task or job: *learning the ropes.* —*tr.v.* **roped, rop•ing, ropes. 1.** To tie or fasten with or as if with a rope. **2.** To catch with a rope or lasso: *rope a calf.* **3.** To enclose or mark with or as if with a rope: *roped off the playing field to keep the crowd away.* **—*idiom.* the end of (one's) rope.** At the end of one's patience, endurance, or resources. [First written down about 725 in Old English and spelled *rāp.*] **—rop′er** *n.*

rop•y (rō′pē) *adj.* **rop•i•er, rop•i•est. 1.** Resembling a rope or ropes. **2.** Forming sticky strings or threads, as some liquids.

Roque•fort (rōk′fərt). A trademark used for a strongly flavored French cheese that has veins of blue mold.

ro•sa•ry (rō′zə rē) *n., pl.* **ro•sa•ries. 1.** A form of devotion to the Virgin Mary consisting of a series of prayers. **2.** A string of beads on which these prayers may be counted.

rose[1] (rōz) *n.* **1.a.** The red, pink, white, or yellow, often very fragrant flower of any of numerous usually prickly shrubs or vines. **b.** A shrub or vine that bears such flowers. **2.** Any of various plants related to or resembling the rose. **3.** A deep pink. —*adj.*

Theodore Roosevelt

rose[1]

ă	pat	oi	boy
ā	pay	ou	out
âr	care	o͝o	took
ä	father	o͞o	boot
ĕ	pet	ŭ	cut
ē	be	ûr	urge
ĭ	pit	th	thin
ī	pie	*th*	this
îr	pier	hw	whoop
ŏ	pot	zh	vision
ō	toe	ə	about
ô	paw	ɴ	*French* bon

rosemary

rotunda
At the New York Botanical Garden

Deep pink. [First written down before 899 in Old English, from Latin *rosa*.]
rose² (rōz) *v.* Past tense of **rise.**
ro•se•ate (rō′zē ĭt *or* rō′zē āt′) *adj.* **1.** Rose-colored. **2.** Cheerful or bright; optimistic: *a roseate outlook.*
Ro•seau (rō **zō′**). The capital of Dominica, in the Windward Islands of the West Indies. Population, 9,348.
rose•bud (**rōz′**bŭd′) *n.* The bud of a rose.
rose•bush (**rōz′**bo͝osh′) *n.* A shrub or vine that bears roses.
rose-col•ored (**rōz′**kŭl′ərd) *adj.* **1.** Having the color rose. **2.** Cheerful or optimistic, especially excessively. ***—idiom.*** **through rose-colored glasses.** With an unduly cheerful, optimistic, or favorable view of things: *Romantics often see the world through rose-colored glasses.*
rose•mar•y (**rōz′**mâr′ē) *n.* **1.** The small, spicy-smelling, grayish-green leaves of an evergreen shrub, used as seasoning in cooking. **2.** The shrub that bears such leaves.
Ro•set•ta stone (rō **zĕt′**ə) *n.* A basalt tablet bearing inscriptions in Greek and Egyptian hieroglyphics and scripts. Discovered in 1799 near Rosetta, Egypt, it provided the key to the decipherment of Egyptian hieroglyphics.
ro•sette (rō **zĕt′**) *n.* **1.** An ornament or badge of ribbon or silk that is gathered or shaped to resemble a rose and is used to decorate clothing. **2.** Something shaped like a rose, as a rounded cluster of leaves or the clusters of spots on a leopard's fur.
rose water *n.* A fragrant preparation made by steeping or distilling rose petals in water, used in cosmetics and cookery.
rose•wood (**rōz′**wo͝od′) *n.* **1.** The hard, reddish, often fragrant wood of any of various tropical trees, used for making furniture. **2.** The tree that yields such wood.
Rosh Ha•sha•nah also **Rosh Ha•sha•na** (rôsh′-hə **shô′**nə *or* rôsh′ hə **shä′**nə) *n.* The Jewish New Year, celebrated in September or October.
ros•in (**rŏz′**ĭn) *n.* A translucent yellowish or brownish substance obtained from the sap of pine trees. It is used to prevent slipping, as on the bows of stringed instruments, and to make varnishes, inks, soldering compounds, and adhesives. *—tr.v.* **ros•ined, ros•in•ing, ros•ins.** To rub or coat with rosin: *rosin a bow.*
Ross (rôs *or* rŏs), **Betsy Griscom.** 1752–1836. American patriot who, according to tradition, made the first American flag (June 1776).
ros•ter (**rŏs′**tər *or* **rô′**stər) *n.* **1.** A list of names or other items. **2.** A list of names of military personnel available for duty.
ros•trum (**rŏs′**trəm *or* **rô′**strəm) *n., pl.* **ros•trums** or **ros•tra** (**rŏs′**trə *or* **rô′**strə). An elevated platform, such as a dais or pulpit, used for public speaking.
ros•y (**rō′**zē) *adj.* **ros•i•er, ros•i•est. 1.** Having a reddish or deep pink color: *rosy cheeks.* **2.** Bright and cheerful; optimistic: *The future looks rosy.* **—ros′i•ly** *adv.* **—ros′i•ness** *n.*
rot (rŏt) *v.* **rot•ted, rot•ting, rots.** *—intr.* **1.** To spoil or decay by the breaking down of plant or animal substances: *The meat may rot if it is not refrigerated.* **2.** To become damaged or useless because of decay: *The roof of the old house had rotted away.* *—tr.* To cause to become rotten; decay. *—n.* **1.** The process of rotting or the result of being rotted; decay. **2.** Any of several destructive plant diseases caused by fungi or bacteria. **3.** Foolish or pointless talk; nonsense. [First written down before 899 in Old English and spelled *rotian*.]
ro•ta•ry (**rō′**tə rē) *adj.* Of, relating to, causing, or characterized by rotation: *rotary motion.* *—n., pl.* **ro•ta•ries. 1.** A device or machine part that rotates. **2.** A traffic circle.
ro•tate (**rō′**tāt) *v.* **ro•tat•ed, ro•tat•ing, ro•tates.** *—intr.* **1.** To turn around on an axis or a center. See Synonyms at **turn. 2.** To proceed in sequence; take turns or alternate: *The order of the classes rotates each day.* *—tr.* **1.** To cause to turn on an axis or a center: *rotate a barrel.* **2.** To plant or grow (crops) in a fixed order of succession. **3.** To cause to alternate: *rotate players on a game.* [First written down in 1808 in Modern English, from Latin *rotāre*, from *rota*, wheel.]
ro•ta•tion (rō **tā′**shən) *n.* **1.a.** The act or process of turning around a center or axis: *the rotation of the earth.* **b.** A complete turn as a result of such motion. **2.** Regular change or variation in a series or sequence: *the rotation of duties in a military unit.*
ro•ta•tor (**rō′**tā′tər) *n.* A person or thing that rotates.
ro•ta•to•ry (**rō′**tə tôr′ē) *adj.* **1.** Of, relating to, causing, or characterized by rotation. **2.** Occurring or proceeding in alternation or succession.
ROTC *abbr.* An abbreviation of Reserve Officers' Training Corps.
rote (rōt) *n.* **1.** A process of memorizing by repetition, often without full understanding: *She learned the French song by rote.* **2.** Mechanical routine.
❑ *These sound alike:* **rote, wrote** (formed letters).
ro•ti•fer (**rō′**tə fər) *n.* Any of various very small water organisms having at the front end a ring of tiny hairs with which they move and take in food.
ro•tis•se•rie (rō **tĭs′**ə rē) *n.* A broiler with a rotating spit for roasting meat.
ro•tor (**rō′**tər) *n.* **1.** A rotating part of an electrical or a mechanical device. **2.** An assembly of airfoils that rotates, as in a helicopter.
ro•to•till•er (**rō′**tə tĭl′ər) *n.* A motorized cultivator having blades that rotate to break up soil.
rot•ten (**rŏt′**n) *adj.* **rot•ten•er, rot•ten•est. 1.** Decayed or decomposed: *rotten meat.* **2.** Having a foul odor that results from or suggests the presence of decay. **3.** Made weak or unsound by rot. **4.** Not honest, honorable, or decent; corrupt. **5.** Very bad; terrible: *rotten luck.* **—rot′ten•ly** *adv.* **—rot′ten•ness** *n.*
Rot•ter•dam (**rôt′**ər **dăm′**). A city of southwest Netherlands south-southeast of The Hague. It was chartered in 1328. Population, 555,341.
ro•tund (rō **tŭnd′**) *adj.* **1.** Rounded in shape or figure; plump. **2.** Full and sonorous: *a rotund voice.* [First written down in 1705 in Modern English, from Latin *rotundus*.] **—ro•tun′di•ty** *n.* **—ro•tund′ly** *adv.* **—ro•tund′ness** *n.*
ro•tun•da (rō **tŭn′**də) *n.* **1.** A circular building, especially one with a dome. **2.** A large area with a high ceiling.
rou•ble (**ro͞o′**bəl) *n.* Variant of **ruble.**
rouge (ro͞ozh) *n.* **1.** A pink or red cosmetic for coloring the cheeks or lips. **2.** A reddish powder, chiefly an oxide of iron, used in polishing metal and glass. *—tr.v.* **rouged, roug•ing, roug•es.** To color with rouge. [First written down in 1753 in Modern English, from Old French *rouge*, red, from Latin *rubeus*.]
rough (rŭf) *adj.* **rough•er, rough•est. 1.** Having an irregular surface; not smooth or even: *a rough bumpy road.* **2.** Coarse to the touch: *rough wool.* **3.** Marked by violent motion: *rough waters.* **4.** Difficult to endure; taxing: *a rough winter.* **5.** Not gentle, polite, or refined: *rough manners.* **6.** Forceful or careless: *a rough push.* **7.** Harsh to the ear: *the rough reedy sound of bagpipes.* **8.** Not finished; in a natural state: *a rough gem.* **9.** Not complete or

fully detailed; tentative: *a rough draft.* —*n.* **1.** Rugged overgrown ground. **2.** The unmowed uncleared part of a golf course that borders the open fairways and greens. —*tr.v.* **roughed, rough•ing, roughs.** To treat (a person) with unnecessary physical violence, especially in certain sports: *penalized for roughing the passer.* —*adv.* In a rough manner; roughly. —***idiom.*** **rough it.** To live without the usual comforts and conveniences: *We roughed it in the mountains for a month.* [First written down about 1000 in Old English and spelled *ruh.*] —**rough'ly** *adv.* —**rough'ness** *n.*

❑ *These sound alike:* **rough, ruff** (collar).

rough•age (rŭf'ĭj) *n.* Dietary fiber.

rough•en (rŭf'ən) *tr. & intr.v.* **rough•ened, rough•en•ing, rough•ens.** To make or become rough.

rough•house (rŭf'hous') *n.* Rowdy uproarious play or behavior. —*intr.v.* (*also* rŭf'houz'). **rough•housed, rough•hous•ing, rough•hous•es.** To engage in roughhouse.

rough•neck (rŭf'nĕk') *n.* A rowdy or unruly person.

rough•shod (rŭf'shŏd') *adj.* Shod with horseshoes having projecting nails or points to prevent slipping. —***idiom.*** **ride roughshod over.** To bully or treat with brutal force.

rou•lette (ro͞o lĕt') *n.* **1.** A gambling game in which players bet on which slot on a rotating disk a ball will come to rest. **2.** A hand tool with a toothed disk for making rows of slits or perforations. [First written down before 1734 in Modern English, from Old French *ruelete*, little wheel, from Latin *rota*, wheel.]

round (round) *adj.* **1.a.** Having a shape that is spherical or nearly spherical; ball-shaped. **b.** Moving in or forming a circle. **c.** Shaped like a cylinder. **d.** Having a curved surface: *a baby's round face.* **2.** Formed with the lips assuming an oval shape: *a round vowel.* **3.** Full in sound or articulation: *round tones.* **4.** Full; complete: *a round dozen.* **5.** Adjusted so as to have less precision; approximate: *round numbers.* **6.** Made with full force: *a round denunciation.* —*n.* **1.** A round object: *a round of bread.* **2.** Movement around or as if in a circle; circuit: *the sun's round.* **3.** A rung of a ladder or chair. **4.** The part of a hind leg of beef between the rump and the shank. **5.** A round dance. **6.** A complete course or series of events: *a round of negotiations.* **7.** A customary course of places visited or duties performed. Often used in the plural: *a doctor on her rounds.* **8.a.** A single shot or volley from a firearm or firearms. **b.** Ammunition for a single shot. **9.** A specified period or unit of play in a game or contest. **10.** A musical composition for two or more voices in which each voice enters at a different time with the same melody. —*v.* **round•ed, round•ing, rounds.** —*tr.* **1.** To make round. **2.** To make a turn about or to the other side of: *The car rounded a bend in the road.* **3.** To make full, complete, or properly balanced: *a description rounded out with details.* **4.** To adjust (a number) to have less precision, as in representing 514 as 510 or 516 as 520. —*intr.* To become round. —*adv.* Around: *a wheel spinning round and round.* —*prep.* Around: *put the rope round the post.* —***idiom.*** **round up. 1.** To seek out and bring together; gather. **2.** To herd (cattle) together from various places. [First written down before 1300 in Middle English, from Latin *rotundus.*] —**round'ness** *n.*

round•a•bout (round'ə bout') *adj.* Not going straight to the goal or conclusion; indirect: *chose a roundabout course to avoid traffic.*

round dance *n.* A folk dance performed with the dancers arranged in a circle.

round•ed (roun'dĭd) *adj.* **1.** Having a curved or spherical shape: *a rounded edge.* **2.** Pronounced with the lips shaped ovally: *a rounded vowel.*

roun•de•lay (roun'də lā') *n.* A poem or song with a regularly recurring refrain.

Round•head (round'hĕd') *n.* A supporter of Parliament during the English Civil War (1642–52) and the Commonwealth.

round•house (round'hous') *n.* **1.** A circular building for housing and switching locomotives. **2.** A cabin on the quarterdeck of a ship. **3.** A meld of four kings and four queens in pinochle. **4.** *Slang.* A punch or swing delivered with a sweeping sidearm movement.

round•ish (roun'dĭsh) *adj.* Somewhat round.

round•ly (round'lē) *adv.* **1.** In the form of a circle or sphere. **2.** With full force or vigor; thoroughly: *roundly applauded.*

round robin *n.* A tournament in which each contestant is matched in turn against every other contestant.

round-shoul•dered (round'shōl'dərd) *adj.* Having the shoulders and upper back bent forward; stooped.

round•ta•ble (round'tā'bəl) *n.* **1.** Often **round table.** A conference or discussion with several participants. **2. Round Table. a.** The circular table of King Arthur and his knights. **b.** King Arthur and his knights considered as a group.

round-the-clock (round'*thə* klŏk') *adj.* Lasting or continuing throughout the entire 24 hours of the day; continuous.

round•trip (round'trĭp') *n.* A trip from one place to another and then back again.

round•up (round'ŭp') *n.* **1.a.** The herding of cattle or other animals together for inspection, branding, or shipping. **b.** The workers and horses that take part in such an act. **2.** A similar gathering up of persons or things: *a roundup of suspects conducted by the police.*

round•worm (round'wûrm') *n.* A nematode.

rouse (rouz) *v.* **roused, rous•ing, rous•es.** —*tr.* **1.** To wake (someone) up; arouse. **2.** To cause to become active, attentive, or excited: *a sight that roused her curiosity.* —*intr.* To wake up; awaken. —**rous'er** *n.*

rous•ing (rou'zĭng) *adj.* **1.** Stirring; inspiring: *a rousing call to action.* **2.** Energetic; vigorous: *a rousing dance tune.*

Rous•seau (ro͞o sō'), **Jean Jacques.** 1712–1778. French philosopher and writer whose works include *The Social Contract* (1762).

roust•a•bout (rous'tə bout') *n.* An unskilled laborer who moves from job to job, especially on docks or ships or in circuses or oil fields.

rout[1] (rout) *n.* **1.** An overwhelming defeat. **2.** A disorderly flight after a defeat: *put all the enemy forces to rout.* —*tr.v.* **rout•ed, rout•ing, routs. 1.** To defeat overwhelmingly; crush: *routed the opposing team.* **2.** To put to disorderly flight; scatter. [First written down before 1225 in Middle English and spelled *route*, gang of soldiers, from Old French *route*, troop, defeat, from Latin *rumpere*, to break.]

rout[2] (rout) *v.* **rout•ed, rout•ing, routs.** —*intr.* To dig with the snout; root. —*tr.* **1.** To dig up or uncover; root: *routing potatoes from the hard earth.* **2.** To drive or force out as if by digging: *routing the cattle from the barn.* [First written down about 1547 in Modern English, variant of *root*, to dig.]

route (ro͞ot *or* rout) *n.* **1.** A road or course for traveling from one place to another. **2.** A highway: *Route 66.* **3.** A fixed course, as of places or customers, visited regularly by a salesperson or delivery person: *a newspaper route.* **4.** A means: *the route to fame and power.* —*tr.v.* **rout•ed, rout•ing, routes.** To send or pass on by a certain route: *route the manuscript to editors.* [First written down be-

ă	pat	oi	boy
ā	pay	ou	out
âr	care	o͝o	took
ä	father	o͞o	boot
ĕ	pet	ŭ	cut
ē	be	ûr	urge
ĭ	pit	th	thin
ī	pie	*th*	this
îr	pier	hw	whoop
ŏ	pot	zh	vision
ō	toe	ə	about
ô	paw	N	*French* bon

rowboat

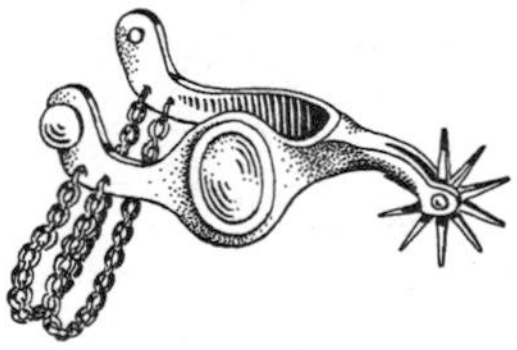

rowel

fore 1200 in Middle English and spelled *rute*, from Latin *rupta (via)*, broken (road), beaten (path).]

❑ *These sound alike:* **route, root**[1] (plant part), **root**[2] (dig), **root**[3] (cheer).

rou•tine (ro͞o **tēn′**) *n.* **1.** A series of activities performed or meant to be performed regularly; a standard or usual procedure. See Synonyms at **method. 2.** A set piece of entertainment, especially in a nightclub or theater. —*adj.* **1.** In accordance with standard procedure: *a routine check of passports.* **2.** Not special; ordinary: *another routine day.* **—rou•tine′ly** *adv.*

rove (rōv) *v.* **roved, rov•ing, roves.** —*intr.* To wander at random, especially over a wide area. —*tr.* To roam or wander around, over, or through: *roving the forest.*

rov•er[1] (rō′vər) *n.* A person or an animal that roves; a wanderer.

ro•ver[2] (rō′vər) *n.* **1.** A pirate. **2.** A pirate vessel. [First written down in Middle English before 1393 and spelled *rovere*, from Middle Dutch *roven*, to rob.]

row[1] (rō) *n.* **1.** A series of persons or things placed next to each other, usually in a straight line: *a row of poplar trees.* **2.** A line of adjacent seats, as in a theater. **3.** A succession without a break or gap in time: *won the title for three years in a row.* **4.** A continuous line of buildings along a street. [First written down in 940 in Old English and spelled *rāw*.]

❑ *These sound alike:* **row**[1] (series), **rho** (Greek letter), **roe**[1] (fish eggs), **roe**[2] (small deer), **row**[2] (use oars).

row[2] (rō) *v.* **rowed, row•ing, rows.** —*intr.* To propel a boat with oars. —*tr.* **1.** To propel (a boat) with oars. **2.** To carry in a boat propelled by oars. —*n.* **1.** A shift at the oars of a rowboat. **2.** A trip in a rowboat. [First written down about 950 in Old English and spelled *rōwan*.] **—row′er** *n.*

❑ *These sound alike:* **row**[2] (use oars), **rho** (Greek letter), **roe**[1] (fish eggs), **roe**[2] (small deer), **row**[1] (series).

row[3] (rou) *n.* **1.** A noisy quarrel or fight; a brawl. **2.** A loud noise; a clamor; a racket. —*intr.v.* **rowed, row•ing, rows.** To participate in a quarrel, a fight, or an uproar. [First written down in 1746 in Modern English.]

row•boat (rō′bōt′) *n.* A small boat propelled by oars.

row•dy (rou′dē) *n., pl.* **row•dies.** A rough disorderly person. —*adj.* **row•di•er, row•di•est.** Rough and disorderly. **—row′di•ness** *n.*

row•el (rou′əl) *n.* A sharp-toothed wheel inserted into the end of the shank of a spur.

row house (rō) *n.* One of a series of identical houses situated side by side and joined by common walls.

row•lock (rō′lŏk′) *n. Chiefly British.* An oarlock.

roy•al (roi′əl) *adj.* **1.** Of or relating to a king or queen. **2.** Fit for a king or queen: *a royal banquet.* **3.** Of, relating to, or serving the government of a king or queen. **4.** Founded or authorized by a king or queen: *a royal society.* [First written down about 1250 in Middle English, from Latin *rēgālis*, from *rēx*, king.] **—roy′al•ly** *adv.*

roy•al•ist (roi′ə lĭst) *n.* **1.** A supporter of government by a king or queen; a monarchist. **2. Royalist. a.** A Cavalier. **b.** An American loyal to British rule during the American Revolution; a Tory.

roy•al•ty (roi′əl tē) *n., pl.* **roy•al•ties. 1.** A person of royal rank or family. **2.** Kings, queens, and their relatives considered as a group. **3.** The rank or power of a sovereign. **4.a.** A share paid to an author or a composer out of the profits resulting from the sale or performance of his or her work. **b.** A share of profits paid to an inventor for the right to use his or her invention.

rpm or **r.p.m.** *abbr.* An abbreviation of revolutions per minute.

R.R. *abbr.* An abbreviation of railroad.

R.S.V.P. or **r.s.v.p.** *abbr.* An abbreviation of répondez s'il vous plaît (please reply).

rt. *abbr.* An abbreviation of right.

rte. *abbr.* An abbreviation of route.

Ru The symbol for the element **ruthenium.**

rub (rŭb) *v.* **rubbed, rub•bing, rubs.** —*tr.* **1.** To press something against (a surface) and move it back and forth: *rub a window with a piece of cloth.* **2.** To cause (something) to move along a surface with pressure: *rub a cloth against a window pane.* **3.** To irritate; annoy. —*intr.* **1.** To move along in contact with a surface; scrape: *He fell, and his knee rubbed on the ground.* **2.** To wear away or chafe with friction: *machine parts with marks showing where they rub together.* **3.** To be removed or transferred by or as if by rubbing: *Her cheerful mood rubbed off on the rest of the group.* —*n.* **1.** The act of rubbing. **2.** An act or a remark that hurts someone's feelings. **3.** A difficulty; a catch. ***—idioms.*** **rub down.** To perform a brisk rubbing of the body, as in massage. **rub in.** To remind someone repeatedly of (an unpleasant matter). **rub (someone) the wrong way.** To annoy; irritate.

rub•ber[1] (rŭb′ər) *n.* **1.** An elastic material prepared from the milky sap of certain tropical plants and used after processing in a great variety of products, including electric insulation and tires. **2.** Any of various synthetic materials having properties that are similar to those of this substance. **3.** A low overshoe made of rubber. **4.** An eraser. **5.** In baseball, the rectangular piece of rubber on which the pitcher stands when making a pitch.

rub•ber[2] (rŭb′ər) *n.* **1.** A series of games, as in bridge, in which two out of three or three out of five must be won to end play. **2.** The deciding game in such a series. [First written down in 1599 in Modern English and spelled *rubbers*.]

rubber band *n.* An elastic loop of natural or synthetic rubber, used to hold objects together.

rub•ber•ize (rŭb′ə rīz′) *tr.v.* **rub•ber•ized, rub•ber•iz•ing, rub•ber•iz•es.** To coat or treat with rubber.

rubber plant *n.* **1.** Any of several tropical plants yielding sap that can be coagulated to form crude rubber. **2.** A small tree that has large, glossy, leathery leaves and is popular as a house plant.

rubber stamp also **rub•ber•stamp** (rŭb′ər **stămp′**) *n.* **1.** A stamp made of rubber, used to print names, dates, and other standard messages. **2.** A person or group that gives quick approval to a program or policy without seriously considering its merits.

rub•ber-stamp (rŭb′ər stămp′) *tr.v.* **rub•ber-stamped, rub•ber-stamp•ing, rub•ber-stamps. 1.** To mark with the imprint of a rubber stamp. **2.** To support, vote for, or approve without question or deliberation.

rub•ber•y (rŭb′ə rē) *adj.* **rub•ber•i•er, rub•ber•i•est.** Of or resembling rubber; elastic or pliable.

rub•bing (rŭb′ĭng) *n.* An image made by placing paper over a surface with raised or indented markings and rubbing the paper with something that marks it, as chalk or charcoal.

rub•bish (rŭb′ĭsh) *n.* **1.** Useless waste material; trash. **2.** Foolish talk or writing; nonsense.

rub•ble (rŭb′əl) *n.* **1.** Fragments of stone or other material left after the destruction or decay of a building. **2.** Irregular broken pieces of rock.

rub•down (rŭb′doun′) *n.* An energetic massage of the body.

ru•bel•la (ro͞o **bĕl′**ə) *n.* An infectious disease that is caused by a virus and resembles measles but has much less severe symptoms; German measles.

ru•bi•cund (ro͞o′bĭ kənd) *adj.* Reddish in complexion; ruddy.

ru•bid•i•um (ro͞o **bĭd′**ē əm) *n. Symbol* **Rb** A soft silvery metallic element with chemical properties that are similar to those of potassium and sodium. Atomic number 37. See table at **element.**

ru•ble also **rou•ble** (**ro͞o′**bəl) *n.* The basic monetary unit of Russia. [First written down in 1554 in Modern English, from Russian *rubl′*.]

ru•bric (**ro͞o′**brĭk) *n.* **1.** A class or category: *In our English book, verb tenses are treated under the rubric of usage.* **2.** A part of a manuscript or book, such as a title, a heading, or an initial letter, that appears in decorative red lettering or is otherwise distinguished from the rest of the text. **3.** A title or heading in a code of law.

ru•by (**ro͞o′**bē) *n., pl.* **ru•bies. 1.** A deep red translucent form of corundum that is greatly valued as a precious stone. **2.** A deep red. [First written down about 1300 in Middle English and spelled *ribe*, from Latin *rubeus*, red.]

ruck•sack (**rŭk′**săk′ *or* **ro͝ok′**săk′) *n.* A knapsack.

ruck•us (**rŭk′**əs) *n. Informal.* A disturbance; a commotion.

rud•der (**rŭd′**ər) *n.* **1.** A flat movable piece of metal or wood hinged at the stern of a vessel for directing its course. **2.** A similar structure in the tail of an aircraft, used for making horizontal changes of course.

rud•dy (**rŭd′**ē) *adj.* **rud•di•er, rud•di•est.** Having a healthy reddish color.

rude (ro͞od) *adj.* **rud•er, rud•est. 1.** Lacking courtesy; ill-mannered: *apologizing for being rude.* **2.** Being in a rough or unfinished state; crude: *a rude tool.* **3.** Relatively undeveloped; primitive: *a rude system of farming.* **4.** Lacking education and refinement. **5.** Sudden and jarring: *a rude shock.* **—rude′ly** *adv.* **—rude′ness** *n.*

❑ *These sound alike:* **rude, rood** (crucifix).

ru•di•ment (**ro͞o′**də mənt) *n.* **1.** A basic principle or skill. Often used in the plural: *learning the rudiments of grammar.* **2.** Something in a beginning or undeveloped form. Often used in the plural: *The children have acquired the rudiments of social behavior.* **3.** An imperfectly or incompletely developed organ or part: *The wings of the kiwi are mere rudiments.*

ru•di•men•ta•ry (ro͞o′də **mĕn′**tə rē *or* ro͞o′də**mĕn′**trē) *adj.* **1.** Of or relating to the basic principles or facts; elementary: *had only a rudimentary knowledge of economics.* **2.** Being in the earliest stages of development. **3.** Imperfectly or incompletely developed: *the rudimentary tail of a Manx cat.*

rue[1] (ro͞o) *tr.v.* **rued, ru•ing, rues.** To feel regret, remorse, or sorrow for. *—n.* Regret. [First written down about 1150 in Middle English and spelled *rewen*, from Old English *hrēowan*, to affect with grief, and *hrēowian*, to repent.]

rue[2] (ro͞o) *n.* Any of various Mediterranean plants having strong-smelling bitter leaves whose juice or oil was formerly used in medicine. [First written down before 1300 in Middle English, from Latin *rūta*.]

rue•ful (**ro͞o′**fəl) *adj.* **1.** Inspiring pity or compassion: *a rueful figure.* **2.** Feeling or expressing sorrow or shame: *a rueful admission of guilt.* **—rue′ful•ly** *adv.* **—rue′ful•ness** *n.*

ruff (rŭf) *n.* **1.** A stiffly starched frilled or pleated collar worn by men and women in the 16th and 17th centuries. **2.** A projecting growth of fur or feathers around the neck of an animal or a bird. **—ruffed** *adj.*

❑ *These sound alike:* **ruff, rough** (not smooth).

ruffed grouse (rŭft) *n.* A North American game bird having mottled brownish feathers, the male of which has a black ruff.

ruf•fi•an (**rŭf′**ē ən) *n.* A tough or rowdy person.

ruf•fle (**rŭf′**əl) *n.* **1.** A strip of gathered or pleated cloth used for a trimming or decoration. **2.** A ruff on a bird. **3.** An irregularity or slight disturbance. *—v.* **ruf•fled, ruf•fling, ruf•fles.** *—tr.* **1.** To disturb the smoothness or evenness of: *The wind ruffled the boy's hair.* **2.** To upset; fluster. **3.** To cause (feathers) to stand up in tufts or projections. **4.** To pleat or gather (fabric) into a ruffle: *ruffle a strip of satin.* *—intr.* **1.** To become irregular or rough. **2.** To become flustered.

rug (rŭg) *n.* **1.** A heavy fabric used to cover a floor. **2.** An animal skin used as a floor covering. **3.** *Chiefly British.* A piece of thick warm fabric or fur used as a blanket or lap robe. [First written down in 1551 in Modern English, of Scandinavian origin.]

Rug•by (**rŭg′**bē) *n.* A form of football in which players may kick, dribble, or run with the ball, and play is continuous. [First written down in 1864 in Modern English, from *Rugby* school in England.]

rug•ged (**rŭg′**ĭd) *adj.* **1.** Having a rough irregular surface: *rugged terrain.* **2.** Having wrinkles and rough features: *a rugged face.* **3.** Sturdy; hardy: *a rugged mountain guide.* **4.** Harsh or difficult: *a rough winter.* [First written down before 1300 in Middle English and spelled *rugged*, shaggy, of Scandinavian origin.] **—rug′ged•ly** *adv.* **—rug′ged•ness** *n.*

Ruhr (ro͝or). A primarily industrial region of northwest Germany along and north of the **Ruhr River,** which flows about 145 miles (233 kilometers) westward to the Rhine River.

ru•in (**ro͞o′**ĭn) *n.* **1.** Total destruction or collapse. **2.** The cause of such destruction: *A refusal to adopt new technology was the ruin of their business.* **3.** The remains of something that has been destroyed or has fallen into pieces from age. Often used in the plural: *Aztec ruins.* *—tr.v.* **ru•ined, ru•in•ing, ru•ins. 1.** To harm greatly; make useless or worthless. **2.** To destroy completely. [First written down about 1375 in Middle English and spelled *ruine*, from Latin *ruīna*.]

Synonyms: ruin, wreck, destroy, demolish. These verbs mean to damage something and deprive it of usefulness, soundness, or value. **Ruin** can mean to harm greatly without necessarily bringing about total destruction: *A flood would ruin all the books in the basement.* **Wreck** can mean to ruin in or as if in a violent collision: *Six cars were wrecked when the crane fell in the parking lot.* **Destroy** can mean to damage something so that it is completely obliterated: *The spy destroyed all evidence of his whereabouts.* **Demolish** means to destroy by pulling down or breaking something to pieces: *The old prison was demolished to build a new hospital.*

ru•in•a•tion (ro͞o′ə **nā′**shən) *n.* Destruction.

ru•in•ous (**ro͞o′**ə nəs) *adj.* **1.** Causing or likely to cause ruin; destructive: *a policy with ruinous consequences.* **2.** Decayed or collapsed. **—ru′in•ous•ly** *adv.*

rule (ro͞ol) *n.* **1.a.** The power of governing; authority. **b.** A period of government: *during the rule of King George III.* **c.** The condition of being governed or controlled; authority: *America under colonial rule.* **2.** A statement that tells how to do something or what may or may not be done: *the rules of tennis.* **3.** A usual or customary course of action. **4.** A statement that tells what is true in most or all cases: *Most mammals are covered with fur, but human beings are an exception to this rule.* **5.** A straightedge; a ruler. **6.** A thin metal strip used by printers to print borders or lines. *—v.* **ruled, rul•**

ruff
Top: Clothing ruff
Bottom: On a rooster

ruffed grouse

ă	pat	oi	boy
ā	pay	ou	out
âr	care	o͝o	took
ä	father	o͞o	boot
ĕ	pet	ŭ	cut
ē	be	ûr	urge
ĭ	pit	th	thin
ī	pie	*th*	this
îr	pier	hw	whoop
ŏ	pot	zh	vision
ō	toe	ə	about
ô	paw	N	*French* bon

rumble seat

Regional Note: run

Words for "a small, fast-flowing stream" vary throughout the United States. Regional terms are **run** (Virginia, West Virginia, Delaware, Maryland, and southern Pennsylvania), *kill* (New York State), **brook** (throughout the Northeast), *branch* (the South), and *crick*, a variant of **creek** (the North).

ing, rules. —*tr.* **1.** To have political control or authority over; govern: *She ruled her country wisely.* **2.** To have great influence over; dominate: *allowed his passions to rule his judgment.* **3.** To declare or decide judicially: *The Supreme Court ruled that the law was unconstitutional.* **4.** To mark (paper or another surface) with straight parallel lines. —*intr.* **1.** To be in control; exercise authority. **2.** To declare a judicial decision. —***idioms.*** **as a rule.** In general; for the most part: *As a rule, I don't like sweets.* **rule out. 1.** To prevent from happening: *The rain ruled out the picnic.* **2.** To remove from consideration; exclude: *We have ruled that option out.* [First written down before 1200 in Middle English and spelled *riwle*, from Latin *rēgula*, rod, measure, principle.]

rul•er (ro͞o′lər) *n.* **1.** A person, such as a king or queen, who governs a country. **2.** A straightedge for drawing straight lines and measuring length.

rul•ing (ro͞o′lĭng) *adj.* **1.** Having control, especially political control; governing: *a ruling body; the ruling classes.* **2.** Prevailing; dominant: *a ruling passion.* —*n.* An official decision.

rum (rŭm) *n.* An alcoholic liquor distilled from sugar cane or molasses. [First written down in 1654 in Modern English, probably short for obsolete *rumbullion*.]

Ru•ma•ni•a (ro͞o mā′nē ə). Romania.

Ru•ma•ni•an (ro͞o mā′nē ən) *adj. & n.* Variant of **Romanian.**

rum•ba also **rhum•ba** (rŭm′bə *or* ro͝om′bə) *n.* **1.** A complex rhythmical dance that originated in Cuba. **2.** A modern ballroom adaptation of the rumba.

rum•ble (rŭm′bəl) *intr.v.* **rum•bled, rum•bling, rum•bles. 1.** To make a deep, long, rolling sound. **2.** To move with such a sound: *A heavy truck rumbled over the wooden bridge.* —*n.* **1.** A deep, long, rolling sound. **2.** *Slang.* A gang fight.

rumble seat *n.* An uncovered passenger seat that opens out from the rear of a car.

ru•men (ro͞o′mən) *n., pl.* **ru•mi•na** (ro͞o′mə nə) or **ru•mens.** The first division of the stomach of a ruminant animal, in which food is partly digested before being regurgitated for further chewing.

ru•mi•nant (ro͞o′mə nənt) *n.* Any of various hoofed mammals, such as cattle, sheep, goats, and deer, that have a stomach divided into four sections and that chew the cud. —**ru′mi•nant** *adj.*

ru•mi•nate (ro͞o′mə nāt′) *intr.v.* **ru•mi•nat•ed, ru•mi•nat•ing, ru•mi•nates. 1.** To chew a cud, as a cow or sheep does. **2.** To spend time thinking about a matter; meditate. [First written down in 1533 in Modern English, from Latin *rūmināre*, from *rūmen*, throat.] —**ru′mi•na′tion** *n.*

rum•mage (rŭm′ĭj) *v.* **rum•maged, rum•mag•ing, rum•mag•es.** —*tr.* **1.** To search thoroughly by turning over or disarranging the contents of: *rummage a trunk for a ball glove.* **2.** To find after a thorough search: *rummaged up an old photograph.* —*intr.* To make an energetic search: *rummaged through the drawers for a bathing suit.* —*n.* A search through a number of things. [First written down in 1544 in Modern English, from Old Provençal *arumar*, to stow.]

rummage sale *n.* **1.** A sale of secondhand objects contributed to raise money for a charity. **2.** A sale, especially of unclaimed or excess goods, as at a warehouse.

rum•my (rŭm′ē) *n.* A card game in which the players try to obtain sets of three or more cards of the same rank or suit.

ru•mor (ro͞o′mər) *n.* **1.** A story or report that is often repeated but has not been established as true. **2.** General talk; gossip; hearsay: *Hints about the scandal had been spreading by rumor for months.* —*tr. v.* **ru•mored, ru•mor•ing, ru•mors.** To spread or tell by rumor. [First written down about 1380 in Middle English and spelled *rumour*, from Latin *rūmor*.]

❑ *These sound alike:* **rumor, roomer** (lodger).

rump (rŭmp) *n.* **1.a.** The fleshy part above the hind legs of a four-footed animal. **b.** A cut of meat from this part. **2.** The human buttocks.

rum•ple (rŭm′pəl) *v.* **rum•pled, rum•pling, rum•ples.** —*tr.* To wrinkle or crease: *Don't rumple the suit.* —*intr.* To become wrinkled or creased. —*n.* A wrinkle or an untidy crease.

rum•pus (rŭm′pəs) *n.* A noisy disturbance or dispute.

run (rŭn) *v.* **ran** (răn), **run, run•ning, runs.** —*intr.* **1.** To move on foot at a pace faster than walking so that both feet leave the ground during each stride. **2.** To move away quickly; flee: *At the first sign of danger we ran.* **3.** To move about or roam freely: *We let the dog run in the yard.* **4.** To go quickly, as when in trouble: *He ran for help.* **5.** To make a quick trip or visit: *I had to run to the store.* **6.a.** To take part in a race: *run in the marathon.* **b.** To compete in a race for elected office: *She's running for governor.* **7.** To move freely on or as if on wheels: *The car ran downhill.* **8.** To be in operation; work: *The engine is running.* **9.** To go along a regular course, especially on a schedule: *The trains are running slow.* **10.a.** To flow: *Turn on the faucet and let the water run.* **b.** To give off pus, mucus, or serous fluid: *My nose is running.* **11.** To extend, spread, or reach: *This road runs all the way through town.* **12.** To tend to persist or recur: *A talent for music runs in that family.* **13.** To take a particular form: *The report runs as follows.* **14.** To be performed for a continuous period of time: *The play ran for six months.* **15.** To pass into a specified condition: *He ran into debt.* —*tr.* **1.** To travel over on foot at a pace faster than a walk: *ran two blocks.* **2.** To do or accomplish by or as if by running: *ran some errands.* **3.** To cause to move quickly: *He ran his fingers over the keyboard.* **4.a.** To cause to compete in a race: *ran a horse in a derby.* **b.** To nominate for elective office: *The party ran her for senate.* **5.** To cause to function; operate: *run a machine.* **6.** To transport: *Run me into town.* **7.** To cause to flow: *run water into a tub.* **8.** To cause to extend or pass: *run a rope between trees.* **9.** To cause (a car, for example) to crash or collide. **10.** To publish in a periodical: *run an advertisement.* **11.** To conduct, manage, or perform: *run an experiment.* **12.** To process or carry out (a computer program or command). **13.** To expose oneself to (a risk). **14.** To have (a fever). —*n.* **1.** A pace faster than a walk. **2.a.** An act of running. **b.** A distance covered by or as if by running. **c.** The time it takes to cover such a distance: *It's a two minutes' run from here.* **3.** A quick trip or visit: *a run into town.* **4.** A regular or scheduled route. **5.** A running race: *a five-mile run.* **6.** In baseball, a point scored by running around all the bases and reaching home plate safely. **7.** In football, a player's attempt to carry the ball past or through the opposing team. **8.** Unrestricted freedom or use: *They gave us the run of the place.* **9.** An athlete's passage down a hill or across country: *The skier had two good runs today.* **10.a.** A continuous period of operation, especially of a machine or factory: *a trial run of a new engine.* **b.** The amount produced during such a period: *a run of 5,000 copies of the book.* **11.** A movement or flow. **12.** A small stream or brook. **13.** A continuous length or extent: *a long run of wire.* **14.** An outdoor enclosure for domestic animals or poultry: *a chicken run.* **15.** A length of torn or unraveled stitches in a knitted fabric: *a run in my stockings.* **16.** An unbroken series: *a run of victories.* **17.** An unbroken sequence of theatrical performances: *a long run on Broadway.* **18.** A rapid sequence of musical notes. **19.** A series of unexpected demands, as by depositors or customers: *a run on a bank.* **20.** A continuing state or condition: *a run of good luck.* **21.** A trend or tendency: *the run of events.* **22.** An execution of a specific computer program or command. **—*idioms.*** **a run for (one's) money.** Strong competition. **in the long run.** Eventually; in the final analysis or outcome. **in the short run.** In the immediate future. **on the run. 1.** In rapid retreat. **2.** In hiding: *fugitives on the run.* **3.** Hurrying busily from place to place: *had lunch on the run.* **run across.** To find by chance; come upon. **run after.** To pursue; chase. **run along.** To go away; leave. **run a temperature.** To have a fever. **run away. 1.** To flee; escape. **2.** To leave home. **run away with.** To make off with hurriedly. **run down. 1.** To stop working because of lack of force or power: *The clock finally ran down.* **2.** To chase and capture. **3.** To say mean or unpleasant things about: *You're always running down my cooking.* **4.** To go over; review: *Run down the list to make sure we didn't forget anything.* **run into. 1.** To meet or find by chance: *ran into an old friend.* **2.** To encounter (something). **3.** To collide with. **run off. 1.** To print, duplicate, or copy: *ran off some more copies of the paper.* **2.** To force or drive off (trespassers, for example). **run on. 1.** To keep going; continue. **2.** To talk without stopping, usually about unimportant matters: *He's always running on about something.* **run out. 1.** To become used up; be exhausted: *Supplies ran out.* **2.** To force to leave: *ran them out of town.* **run out of.** To exhaust the supply of: *We ran out of cookies.* **run out on.** To abandon; forsake: *Don't run out on your friends.* **run over. 1.** To collide with, knock down, and often pass over. **2.** To read or review quickly: *I just need to run over this article.* **3.** To flow over. **4.** To go beyond a limit: *The meeting ran over.* **run short.** To become scanty or insufficient in supply. **run short of.** To use up so that a supply becomes insufficient or scanty. **run through. 1.** To pierce, as with a sword. **2.** To use up quickly: *She ran through all her money.* **3.** To rehearse or examine quickly: *Let's run through the scene again.* **run up.** To make or become greater or larger: *We ran up a huge bill at the restaurant.* [First written down before 1200 in Old English and spelled *rinnan.*] —SEE NOTE.

run•a•bout (rŭn′ə bout′) *n.* **1.** A small motorboat. **2.** A light aircraft. **3.** A small open automobile or carriage.

run•a•round (rŭn′ə round′) *n.* Deception, usually in the form of vague excuses.

run•a•way (rŭn′ə wā′) *n.* **1.** A person who has run away, as from home. **2.** Something that has escaped from control or proper confinement. **3.** *Informal.* An easy victory. *—adj.* **1.** Escaping or having escaped: *runaway horses.* **2.** Out of control: *a runaway car rolling down the hill.* **3.** *Informal.* Easily won: *a runaway victory.*

run•down (rŭn′doun′) *n.* **1.** A point by point summary: *a rundown of the day's news.* **2.** In baseball, a play in which a runner is trapped between bases. *—adj.* also **run-down** (**rŭn′doun′**). **1.** Exhausted or weak: *feeling rundown.* **2.** Old and decayed: *rundown buildings.* **3.** Unwound and not running: *a rundown clock.*

rune (ro͞on) *n.* **1.** Any of the letters of several alphabets used by ancient Germanic peoples. **2.** A similar letter in another alphabet, thought to have magical power. [First written down possibly about 725 in Old English and spelled *rūn.*] **—run′ic** *adj.*

rung[1] (rŭng) *n.* **1.** A rod or bar forming a step of a ladder. **2.** A crosspiece between the legs of a chair. [First written down before 1000 in Old English and spelled *hrung.*]

❑ *These sound alike:* **rung[1]** (rod), **rung[2]** (sounded), **wrung** (twisted).

rung[2] (rŭng) *v.* Past participle of **ring[2]**.

❑ *These sound alike:* **rung[2]** (sounded), **rung[1]** (rod), **wrung** (twisted).

run-in (rŭn′ĭn′) *n.* A quarrel or an argument.

run•ner (rŭn′ər) *n.* **1.** A person who runs, especially in a race. **2.** A messenger. **3.** A person who manages or operates something. **4.** A part on or in which something slides or moves, as the blade of a skate. **5.** A long narrow carpet, as one for a hall or stairway. **6.** A long narrow tablecloth. **7.** A creeping plant stem that puts forth roots at intervals along its length, thus producing new plants.

run•ner-up (rŭn′ər **ŭp′**) *n., pl.* **run•ners-up** (rŭn′ərz-**ŭp′**). A contestant that finishes a competition in second place.

run•ning (rŭn′ĭng) *n.* **1.** The act or an instance of running. **2.** The ability to run. **3.** The sport of someone who runs. *—adj.* Continuous; ongoing: *gave us a running commentary on the game.* *—adv.* Consecutively: *for four years running.* **—*idioms.*** **in the running. 1.** Participating in a competition. **2.** Having the possibility of winning or placing well in a competition. **out of the running. 1.** Not participating in a competition. **2.** Having no possibility of winning or placing well in a competition.

running board

running board *n.* A narrow footboard extending under and beside the doors of some cars and other vehicles.

running light *n.* One of several lights on a vehicle, especially a ship, turned on at night to show position and size.

running mate *n.* The candidate for the lesser of two closely linked political offices.

run•ny (rŭn′ē) *adj.* **run•ni•er, run•ni•est.** Inclined to run or flow: *runny icing.*

Run•ny•mede (rŭn′ē mēd′). A meadow in southeast England on the Thames River west of London. The Magna Carta was accepted by the king here or on a nearby island in 1215.

run•off (rŭn′ôf′ *or* rŭn′ŏf′) *n.* **1.** Rainfall that is not absorbed by the soil, finally reaching streams and rivers. **2.** An extra contest held to break a tie.

run-of-the-mill (rŭn′əv *thə* **mĭl′**) *adj.* Not special or outstanding; average.

run-on sentence (rŭn′ŏn′ *or* rŭn′ôn′) *n.* A sentence in which two or more clauses are joined incorrectly, as by a comma instead of a conjunction. For example, *I was hungry, I missed lunch* is a run-on sentence. It should read *I was hungry because I missed lunch.*

runt (rŭnt) *n.* A very small animal, especially the smallest pig in a litter.

run•way (rŭn′wā′) *n.* **1.** A strip of level, usually paved ground on which aircraft take off and land. **2.** A path, track, or channel over which something runs or passes.

ru•pee (ro͞o **pē′** *or* **ro͞o′**pē) *n.* The basic monetary unit of India, Mauritius, Nepal, Pakistan, Seychelles, and Sri Lanka.

ru•pi•ah (ro͞o **pē′**ə) *n.* The basic monetary unit of Indonesia.

rup•ture (**rŭp′**chər) *n.* **1.** The process of breaking open or bursting. **2.** A break in friendly relations: *a rupture in diplomatic relations.* **3.** A hernia, especially in the groin or intestinal region. *—v.* **rup•tured, rup•tur•ing, rup•tures.** *—tr.* To break open; burst. *—intr.* To undergo or suffer a rupture.

ru•ral (**ro͝or′**əl) *adj.* **1.** Of, relating to, or characteristic of the country: *rural areas.* **2.** Of or relating to people who live in the country: *rural households.*

ă	pat	oi	boy
ā	pay	ou	out
âr	care	o͝o	took
ä	father	o͞o	boot
ĕ	pet	ŭ	cut
ē	be	ûr	urge
ĭ	pit	th	thin
ī	pie	*th*	this
îr	pier	hw	whoop
ŏ	pot	zh	vision
ō	toe	ə	about
ô	paw	N	*French* bon

Mount Rushmore
Left to right: Portraits of Presidents Washington, Jefferson, Theodore Roosevelt, and Lincoln by Gutzon Borglum (1867–1941)

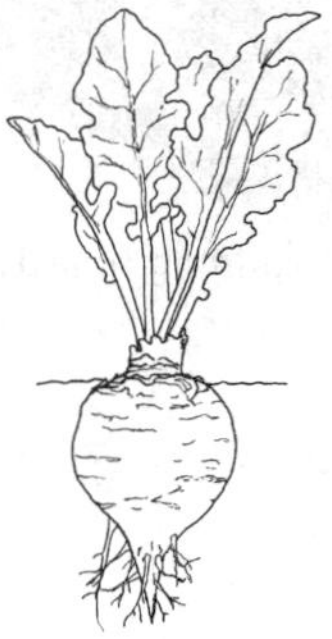

rutabaga

Babe Ruth
Photographed in the 1930's

[First written down before 1425 in Middle English, from Latin *rūs*, country.] —**ru′ral•ly** *adv.*

rural free delivery *n.* Free government delivery of mail in rural areas.

ruse (ro͞os *or* ro͞oz) *n.* A crafty trick or deception.

rush[1] (rŭsh) *v.* **rushed, rush•ing, rush•es.** —*intr.* **1.** To move or act swiftly; hurry: *Fire engines rushed past us.* **2.** To flow or surge rapidly and often with a continuous noise: *Water rushed over the falls.* **3.** In football, to advance the ball by running rather than passing. —*tr.* **1.** To cause to move or act with unusual haste: *Don't rush me.* **2.** To do or perform hastily: *rushed the throw and made an error.* **3.** To attack suddenly; charge: *rushing the barricades.* **4.** To carry or transport hastily: *rushed supplies to the camp.* —*n.* **1.** The act of rushing; a swift forward movement. **2.** An anxious and eager movement to or from a place in large numbers: *a rush for gold in the hills.* **3.** A flurry of hasty activity; a great hurry: *left in such a rush that she forgot her purse.* **4.** A sudden attack; a charge. **5.** A rapid, often noisy flow or passage: *a rush of air; a rush of words.* **6.** The first unedited print of a movie scene. Often used in the plural. [First written down in 1375 in Middle English and spelled *rushen*, from Latin *recūsāre*, to reject.]

rush[2] (rŭsh) *n.* **1.** Any of various tall plants that resemble reeds, grow in wet places, and have hollow or pithy stems. **2.** The stem of any of these plants, used to make chair seats or mats. [First written down about 725 in Old English and spelled *rysc*.]

rush hour *n.* A period of heavy traffic.

Rush•more (**rŭsh′**môr′), **Mount.** A mountain, 5,600 feet (1,708 meters) high, in western South Dakota. A monument here has massive carved likenesses of Washington, Jefferson, Lincoln, and Theodore Roosevelt.

Russ. *abbr.* An abbreviation of: **1.** Russia. **2.** Russian.

rus•set (**rŭs′**ĭt) *n.* **1.** A reddish brown. **2.** A type of apple having reddish-brown skin.

Rus•sia (**rŭsh′**ə). **1.** A former empire of eastern Europe and northern Asia. Originally settled by Slavs from the 3rd to the 8th century, Russia achieved the height of its power and territorial influence in the 17th and 18th centuries. **2.** A region and republic of eastern Europe and northern Asia. It extends from the Gulf of Finland to the Pacific Ocean. Russia was a part of the U.S.S.R. from 1922 to 1991. Capital, Moscow. Population, 143,093,000.

Rus•sian (**rŭsh′**ən) *adj.* Of or relating to Russia or its people, language, or culture: *Russian literature.* —*n.* **1.** A native or inhabitant of Russia. **2.** The Slavic language of Russia.

Russian Orthodox Church *n.* The Eastern Orthodox Church that is under the leadership of the patriarch of Russia or an independent Eastern Orthodox Church that follows Russian religious traditions and rites.

rust (rŭst) *n.* **1.** Any of the various reddish-brown oxides of iron that form on iron and many of its alloys when they are exposed to oxygen in the presence of moisture at ordinary temperatures. **2.a.** Any of various plant diseases caused by parasitic fungi, characterized by reddish or brownish spots on leaves. **b.** Any of the various parasitic fungi that cause such diseases. **3.** A reddish brown. —*tr. & intr.v.* **rust•ed, rust•ing, rusts.** To make or become corroded or oxidized.

rus•tic (**rŭs′**tĭk) *adj.* **1.** Of, relating to, or typical of country life or country people. **2.** Plain and unsophisticated. **3.** Appropriate for use in the country: *rustic boots.* —*n.* **1.** A person from the country. **2.** A crude, coarse, or simple person.

rus•tle (**rŭs′**əl) *v.* **rus•tled, rus•tling, rus•tles.** —*intr.* **1.** To move with soft fluttering or crackling sounds: *leaves rustled in the wind.* **2.** To move or act quickly or energetically. **3.** To steal cattle. —*tr.* **1.** To cause to rustle: *wind rustling the leaves.* **2.** To get quickly or briskly: *rustle up a dinner.* **3.** To steal (cattle). —**rus′tler** *n.*

rust•y (**rŭs′**tē) *adj.* **rust•i•er, rust•i•est. 1.** Covered with rust; corroded. **2.** Consisting of or produced by rust: *a rusty layer on the fender.* **3.** Having a brownish-red color. **4.** Weakened because of lack of use or practice. —**rust′i•ness** *n.*

rut (rŭt) *n.* **1.** A track, as in a dirt road, made by the passage of vehicles. **2.** A fixed, usually boring routine. —*tr.v.* **rut•ted, rut•ting, ruts.** To make ruts in. [First written down in 1580 in Modern English.]

ru•ta•ba•ga (ro͞o′tə **bā′**gə *or* **ro͞o′**tə bā′gə) *n.* A turnip having a yellowish root, used as food and as animal feed. [First written down in 1799 in Modern English, from Swedish dialectal *rotabagge* : *rot*, root + *bagge*, bag.]

Ruth (ro͞oth) *n.* **1.** In the Bible, a widow who left her homeland in order to stay with her mother-in-law, converted to Judaism, and became the great-grandmother of David. **2.** A book of the Bible that tells the story of Ruth.

Ruth, George Herman. Called "Babe." 1895–1948. American baseball player. He hit 714 home runs, played in 10 World Series, and held 54 major-league records.

ru•the•ni•um (ro͞o **thē′**nē əm) *n.* *Symbol* **Ru** A hard white metallic element that resists attack by acids. Atomic number 44. See table at **element.**

Ruth•er•ford (**rŭth′**ər fərd *or* **rŭth′**ər fərd), **Ernest.** 1871–1937. New Zealand-born British physicist who studied radiation and discovered the atomic nucleus. He won the 1908 Nobel Prize in chemistry.

ruth•er•ford•i•um (rŭth′ər **fôr′**dē əm) *n.* Element 104. [First written down in 1969 in Modern English, after Ernest *Rutherford* (1871–1937).]

ruth•less (**ro͞oth′**lĭs) *adj.* Showing no pity; cruel. [First written down about 1330 in Middle English and spelled *rewtheles*, from *reuthe*, pity.] —**ruth′less•ly** *adv.* —**ruth′less•ness** *n.*

RV *abbr.* An abbreviation of recreational vehicle.

Rwan•da (ro͞o **än′**də). A country of east-central Africa north of Burundi. It gained its independence in 1962. Kigali is the capital and the largest city. Population, 5,109,000.

ry. *abbr.* An abbreviation of railway.

rye (rī) *n.* **1.** The seeds of a certain cereal grass, used for making flour and whiskey. **2.** The plant that bears such seeds. **3.** Whiskey made from this grain.
❑ *These sound alike:* **rye, wry** (humorous).

Ss

s[1] or **S** (ĕs) *n., pl.* **s's** or **S's. 1.** The 19th letter of the English alphabet. **2.** The 19th in a series or group: *row S in a stadium.*

s[2] *abbr.* An abbreviation of second[1].

S[1] The symbol for the element **sulfur.**

S[2] *abbr.* An abbreviation of: **1.** South. **2.** Southern.

s. *abbr.* An abbreviation of: **1.** Singular. **2.** Shilling.

–s[1] or **–es** *suff.* A suffix that is used to form plural nouns: *letters.*

–s[2] or **–es** *suff.* A suffix that is used to form the third person singular present tense of most verbs: *talks.*

–s[3] *suff.* A suffix that is used to form certain adverbs, such as *nights,* in *She works nights* or *unawares* in *We were caught unawares.*

–'s *suff.* A suffix that is used to form the possessive case of most nouns: *women's.*

's 1. Contraction of *is: She's happy.* **2.** Contraction of *has: He's been away.* **3.** Contraction of *us: Let's go to lunch.*

S.A. *abbr.* An abbreviation of: **1.** South Africa. **2.** South America.

Saar (sär *or* zär). A river, about 150 miles (241 kilometers) long, rising in northeast France and flowing north and north-northwest to western Germany.

Saar•land (**sär'**lănd' *or* **zär'**lănd') or **Saar** (sär *or* zär). A region of southwest Germany in the Saar River valley on the border with France. Because of its extensive coal deposits, it was long contested between Germany and France.

Sab•bath (**săb'**əth) *n.* **1.** The seventh day of the week, Saturday, observed as a day of rest and worship by Jews and some Christians. **2.** The first day of the week, Sunday, observed as a day of rest and worship by most Christians. [First written down about 950 in Old English and spelled *sabat,* from Hebrew *šabbāt,* from šābat, to rest.]

sab•bat•i•cal (sə **băt'**ĭ kəl) *adj.* **1.** Relating to a sabbatical year. **2. Sabbatical.** Relating to the sabbath as a day of rest. —*n.* A sabbatical year.

sabbatical year *n.* A leave of absence, often with pay, given to some college professors every seven years.

sa•ber (**sā'**bər) *n.* **1.** A heavy cavalry sword with a single-edged, slightly curved blade. **2.** A light flexible sword used in fencing. —*tr.v.* **sa•bered, sa•ber•ing, sa•bers.** To hit, cut, or kill with a saber.

sa•ber-toothed tiger (**sā'**bər to͞otht') *n.* Any of various large extinct mammals of prehistoric times related to the cat, having long upper canine teeth.

Sa•bin (**sā'**bĭn), **Albert Bruce.** Born 1906. American physician who developed a vaccine against polio (1957).

sa•ble (**sā'**bəl) *n.* **1.a.** A mammal of northern Europe and Asia that is related to the mink and weasel and has soft dark fur. **b.** The highly valued fur of this mammal. **2.a.** The color black. **b. sables.** Black garments worn in mourning.

sa•bot (să **bō'** *or* **săb'**ō) *n.* **1.** A shoe carved from a single piece of wood, worn in some European countries. **2.** A shoe with a wooden sole and a leather band across the instep.

sab•o•tage (**săb'**ə täzh') *n.* **1.** The deliberate destruction of property or disruption of work by civilians or enemy agents in wartime. **2.** A deliberate attempt to damage, destroy, or hinder a cause or an activity. —*tr.v.* **sab•o•taged, sab•o•tag•ing, sab•o•tag•es.** To commit sabotage against (something).

sab•o•teur (săb'ə **tûr'**) *n.* A person who commits sabotage.

sa•bre (**sā'**bər) *n. & v. Chiefly British.* Variant of **saber.**

sac (săk) *n.* A part of an animal or a plant that resembles a bag or pouch, often containing a liquid. The human bladder is a sac.

❑ *These sound alike:* **sac, sack**[1] (bag), **sack**[2] (rob), **sack**[3] (wine).

Sac•a•ja•we•a (săk'ə jə **wē'**ə). 1787?–1812. Shoshone guide and interpreter who accompanied (1805–1806) the Lewis and Clark Expedition. —See Note.

sac•cha•rin (**săk'**ər ĭn) *n.* A white crystalline powder composed of carbon, hydrogen, nitrogen, oxygen, and sulfur and having the formula $C_7H_5NO_3S$. It tastes about 500 times sweeter than sugar and is used as a calorie-free sweetener.

❑ *These sound alike:* **saccharin, saccharine** (sweet).

sac•cha•rine (**săk'**ər ĭn *or* **săk'**ə rēn') *adj.* **1.** Of, relating to, or characteristic of sugar; sweet. **2.** Insincerely or cloyingly sweet in tone or character: *a saccharine smile.* [First written down in 1674 in Modern English, from Greek *sakkhar,* sugar, from Sanskrit *śarkarā.*]

❑ *These sound alike:* **saccharine, saccharin** (sweetener).

sac•er•do•tal (săs'ər **dōt'**l *or* săk'ər **dōt'**l) *adj.* Of or relating to priests or the priesthood.

sa•chem (**sā'**chəm) *n.* The chief of a Native American people or confederation.

sa•chet (să **shā'**) *n.* A small bag filled with a perfumed substance and used to scent clothes.

❑ *These sound alike:* **sachet, sashay** (walk casually).

sack[1] (săk) *n.* **1.a.** A large bag of strong coarse material used for holding objects in bulk: *a potato sack.* **b.** A similar bag of paper or plastic: *a brown paper sack.* **c.** The amount that such a container can hold. **2.** A loose-fitting dress or jacket for women and children. **3.** *Informal.* A bed, mattress, or sleeping bag. **4.** *Slang.* Dismissal from a job or position. —*tr.v.* **sacked, sack•ing, sacks. 1.** To put into a sack. **2.** *Slang.* To fire from a job. [First written down about 1000 in Old English and spelled *sacc,* from Greek *sakkos.*]

❑ *These sound alike:* **sack**[1] (bag), **sac** (body part), **sack**[2] (rob), **sack**[3] (wine).

sack[2] (săk) *tr.v.* **sacked, sack•ing, sacks.** To rob (a captured city, for example) of its valuables; loot or plunder. —*n.* The robbing, looting, or plundering of a place captured by the enemy. [First written down in 1549 in Modern English, probably from French *(mettre à) sac,* (to put in) a sack.]

❑ *These sound alike:* **sack**[2] (rob), **sac** (body part), **sack**[1] (bag), **sack**[3] (wine).

sabot
A pair of sabots

Sacajawea

Born around 1787, **Sacajawea** was a Shoshone woman from an area near the current-day Idaho-Montana border. In 1804, while living in what is now North Dakota, Sacajawea encountered Lewis and Clark and joined them the next spring as an interpreter. Meriwether Lewis and William Clark had been commissioned by Thomas Jefferson to explore the Northwest and bring back information about its geography, wildlife, natural resources, and native peoples. In Sacajawea they found a native guide familiar with the region and the language of the Shoshone. Sacajawea secured for the expedition not only safe routes of travel and open communication with Shoshone groups, but also the opportunity to buy horses, which they needed to complete the journey to the coast.

ă	pat	oi	boy
ā	pay	ou	out
âr	care	o͝o	took
ä	father	o͞o	boot
ĕ	pet	ŭ	cut
ē	be	ûr	urge
ĭ	pit	th	thin
ī	pie	*th*	this
îr	pier	hw	whoop
ŏ	pot	zh	vision
ō	toe	ə	about
ô	paw	N	*French* bon

sack[3] (săk) *n.* A strong, light-colored Spanish wine, popular in England in the 16th and 17th centuries. [First written down in 1531 in Modern English, from French *(vin) sec,* dry (wine), from Latin *siccus,* dry.]

❑ *These sound alike:* **sack**[3] (wine), **sac** (body part), **sack**[1] (bag), **sack**[2] (rob).

sack•cloth (săk′klôth′ *or* săk′klŏth′) *n.* **1.** A rough coarse cloth. **2.** Garments made of sackcloth, worn as a symbol of mourning or penitence.

sack•ing (săk′ĭng) *n.* A coarse cloth, such as burlap, used for making sacks.

sa•cra (sā′krə *or* săk′rə) *n.* Plural of **sacrum.**

sac•ra•ment (săk′rə mənt) *n.* **1.** In Christian churches, one of the sacred rites or ceremonies that are considered to have been instituted by Jesus, as Baptism or the Eucharist. **2.** Often **Sacrament. a.** The Eucharist. **b.** The consecrated bread and wine of the Eucharist, or the bread alone. **—sac′ra•men′tal** (săk′rə mĕn′tl) *adj.*

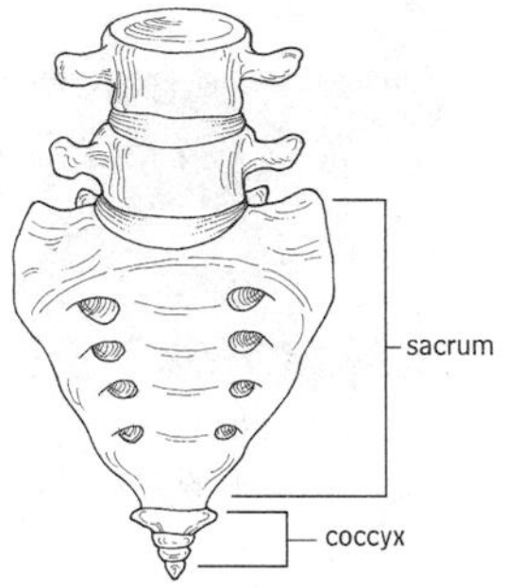

sacrum

Sac•ra•men•to (săk′rə mĕn′tō). The capital of California, in the north-central part of the state northeast of Oakland. It became the state capital in 1854. Population, 369,365.

sa•cred (sā′krĭd) *adj.* **1.** Worthy of religious veneration; holy. **2.** Dedicated to or set apart for the worship of a deity: *a temple sacred to Buddha.* **3.** Dedicated or devoted to a single use, purpose, or person. **4.** Made or declared holy: *sacred bread and wine.* **5.** Of or relating to religious practices or objects. **—sa′cred•ly** *adv.* **—sa′cred•ness** *n.*

sac•ri•fice (săk′rə fīs′) *n.* **1.a.** The act of offering something, such as an animal's life, to a deity in worship or to win favor or forgiveness. **b.** A victim offered this way. **2.a.** The act of giving up something highly valued for the sake of something else considered to be of greater value. **b.** Something given up in this way. **3.** A loss of profit suffered by selling something at less than its value or cost: *forced to sell at a sacrifice.* **4.** A sacrifice fly or sacrifice hit. *—v.* **sac•ri•ficed, sac•ri•fic•ing, sac•ri•fic•es.** *—tr.* **1.** To offer as a sacrifice to a deity. **2.** To give up (one thing) for another thing considered to be of greater value. **3.** To sell or give away at a loss. *—intr.* **1.** To make or offer a sacrifice. **2.** To make a sacrifice hit. [First written down about 1275 in Middle English and spelled *sacrefise,* from Latin *sacrificium* : *sacer,* sacred + *facere,* to make.] **—sac′ri•fi′cial** (săk′rə fĭsh′əl) *adj.*

sacrifice fly *n.* In baseball, a fly ball that allows a runner to score after it is caught by a fielder.

sacrifice hit *n.* In baseball, a bunt that allows a runner to advance a base, but results in the batter being put out.

safety belt

sac•ri•lege (săk′rə lĭj) *n.* An act of disrespect or violence toward something sacred. **—sac′ri•le′gious** (săk′rə lĭj′əs *or* săk′rə lē′jəs) *adj.*

sac•ris•tan (săk′rĭ stən) *n.* **1.** A person in charge of a sacristy. **2.** A sexton.

sac•ris•ty (săk′rĭ stē) *n., pl.* **sac•ris•ties.** A room in a church where vestments and sacred articles are kept; a vestry.

sac•ro•sanct (săk′rō săngkt′) *adj.* Regarded as sacred and not to be violated: *the sacrosanct precincts of the temple.*

sa•crum (sā′krəm *or* săk′rəm) *n., pl.* **sa•cra** (sā′krə *or* săk′rə). A triangular bone, made up of five fused vertebrae, that forms the rear section of the pelvis.

sad (săd) *adj.* **sad•der, sad•dest. 1.** Showing, expressing, or feeling sorrow or unhappiness: *a sad face.* **2.** Causing sorrow, gloom, or regret: *sad memories.* **3.** Sorry; deplorable: *This place is in sad shape.* [First written down before 1000 in Old English and spelled *sæd,* sated, weary.] **—sad′ly** *adv.* **—sad′ness** *n.*

Synonyms: sad, unhappy, melancholy, sorrowful, desolate. These adjectives mean affected with or marked by a lack of joy. **Sad** and **unhappy** are the most general terms: *I was sad when I heard about that beautiful house being destroyed in the fire. He doesn't like movies that make him unhappy.* **Melancholy** means feeling a lingering or habitual sadness: *I kept telling jokes, trying to cheer up our melancholy dinner companion.* **Sorrowful** means experiencing a painful sadness, especially one caused by loss: *One of the mourners let out a sorrowful cry.* **Desolate** means sorrowful beyond consolation: *He has been desolate ever since his friend moved away.* **Antonym: glad.**

sad•den (săd′n) *tr. & intr.v.* **sad•dened, sad•den•ing, sad•dens.** To make or become sad.

sad•dle (săd′l) *n.* **1.a.** A padded leather seat for a rider, strapped onto the back of a horse or other animal. **b.** A similar padded part that fits over an animal's back and supports a pack or forms part of a harness. **2.** The seat of a bicycle, motorcycle, or similar vehicle. **3.** A cut of meat that contains part of the backbone and both loins: *a saddle of veal.* **4.** Something that resembles a saddle in shape. **5.** A saddle-shaped depression in a ridge or between two peaks. *—v.* **sad•dled, sad•dling, sad•dles.** *—tr.* **1.** To put a saddle onto: *saddle a pony.* **2.** To load or burden; encumber: *She was saddled with all the responsibility.* *—intr.* **1.** To saddle a horse. **2.** To get into a saddle: *Saddle up and go.* [First written down about 725 in Old English and spelled *sadol.*]

sad•dle•bag (săd′l băg′) *n.* **1.** A pouch that hangs across the back of a horse, especially one of a pair. **2.** A pouch that hangs over the rear wheel of a bicycle or motorcycle.

saddle horse *n.* A horse bred or trained for riding.

sad•dler (săd′lər) *n.* A person who makes, repairs, or sells equipment for horses.

saddle shoe *n.* A flat casual shoe, usually white, having a band of leather in a contrasting color across the instep.

saddle soap *n.* A mild soap that contains neat's-foot oil and is used for cleaning and softening leather.

sa•dism (sā′dĭz′əm *or* săd′ĭz′əm) *n.* **1.** A psychological disorder in which a person derives pleasure from causing pain to others. **2.** Enjoyment of cruelty or abuse inflicted on others. [First written down in 1888 in Modern English, after Comte Donatien Alphonse François de *Sade* (1740–1814), French writer.] **—sa′dist** *n.* **—sa•dis′tic** (sə dĭs′tĭk) *n.* **—sa•dis′ti•cal•ly** *adv.*

sa•fa•ri (sə fär′ē) *n., pl.* **sa•fa•ris.** A hunting trip or journey of exploration, especially in Africa. [First written down in 1860 in Modern English, from Arabic *safarī,* journey, from *safara,* to travel, set out.]

safe (sāf) *adj.* **saf•er, saf•est. 1.** Secure from danger, risk, or harm. **2.** Providing protection or security: *a safe refuge.* **3.** Free from risk; sure: *a safe bet.* **4.** Free from danger or injury; unhurt: *safe and sound.* **5.** In baseball, having reached a base without being put out: *The runner was safe on third.* *—n.* A strong metal container in which valuables, such as money and jewels, are kept for protection. [First written down about 1280 in Middle English and spelled *sauf,* from Latin *salvus,* healthy.] **—safe′ly** *adv.*

safe-con•duct (sāf′kŏn′dŭkt) *n.* **1.** An official document or an escort that assures safe passage, as through enemy territory. **2.** The protection afforded by such a document.

safe-de•pos•it box (sāf′dĭ pŏz′ĭt) *n.* A fireproof metal box, usually in a bank vault, for the safe storage of valuables.

safe•guard (sāf′gärd′) *n.* Something that provides protection or defense, as a safety precaution or a protective device. —*tr.v.* **safe•guard•ed, safe•guard•ing, safe•guards.** To protect from danger; keep safe and secure: *laws to safeguard individual rights.*

safe•keep•ing (sāf′kē′pĭng) *n.* The act of keeping or the condition of being kept safe; protection.

safe•ty (sāf′tē) *n., pl.* **safe•ties. 1.** The condition of being safe; freedom from danger, risk, or injury. **2.** A device designed to prevent accidents, especially a lock on a gun to keep it from firing accidentally. **3.** In football, a score of two points for the defensive team made by tackling an opponent who is carrying the ball when behind the offensive team's goal line. **4.** One of a football team's two defensive backs.

safety belt *n.* **1.** A seat belt. **2.** A strap or harness used to support someone working at a dangerous height.

safety glass *n.* Glass that resists shattering, especially a composite of two sheets of glass with an intermediate layer of transparent plastic.

safety match *n.* A match that will light only when it is struck on a specially prepared surface.

safety pin *n.* A pin made in the form of a clasp with a guard to cover and hold the pin.

safety valve *n.* **1.** A valve in a pressurized container, such as a steam boiler, that opens if the pressure reaches a dangerous level. **2.** An outlet for the release of bottled-up energy or emotion.

saf•flow•er (săf′lou′ər) *n.* A plant having orange flowers used for making dye and seeds that yield an oil used in cooking.

saf•fron (săf′rən) *n.* **1.** The dried orange-yellow stigmas from the flowers of a kind of crocus, used to flavor food and in making dye. **2.** An orange-yellow color.

sag (săg) *intr.v.* **sagged, sag•ging, sags. 1.** To sink, droop, or settle from pressure or weight: *The large number of fish made the net sag.* **2.** To lose vigor, strength, or firmness: *The old mattress sagged in the middle.* **3.** To decline in amount or value: *Profits sagged.* —*n.* **1.** The act or an instance of sagging or drooping: *the sag of the boards under our feet.* **2.** A sagging or sunken place: *a sag in the ceiling.*

sa•ga (sä′gə) *n.* **1.** A long, usually Icelandic adventure story written during the Middle Ages that deals with historical or legendary heroes, families, deeds, and events. **2.** A modern story that resembles a saga.

sa•ga•cious (sə gā′shəs) *adj.* Prudent; wise. —**sa•gac′i•ty** (sə găs′ĭ tē) *n.* —**sa•ga′cious•ly** *adv.* —**sa•ga′cious•ness** *n.*

sag•a•more (săg′ə môr′) *n.* A subordinate chief among the Algonquian Indians of North America.

sage[1] (sāj) *n.* A person who is highly respected for wisdom, experience, and judgment. —*adj.* **sag•er, sag•est.** Having or showing wisdom and sound judgment. [First written down before 1350 in Middle English, from Old French, from Latin *sapere*, to be wise.] —**sage′ly** *adv.*

sage[2] (sāj) *n.* **1.** Any of various plants related to mint, having grayish-green spicy-smelling leaves used as flavoring in cooking. **2.** Sagebrush. [First written down before 1325 in Middle English, from Latin *salvia*, from *salvus*, healthy.]

sage•brush (sāj′brŭsh′) *n.* Any of several shrubs of dry regions of the Northern Hemisphere, having strong-smelling silver-green leaves and clusters of small white flowers.

Sag•it•tar•i•us (săj′ĭ târ′ē əs) *n.* **1.** A constellation in the Southern Hemisphere near Scorpius and Capricorn. **2.** The ninth sign of the zodiac in astrology.

sa•go (sā′gō) *n., pl.* **sa•gos.** A powdery starch obtained from the pith of various Asian palm trees and used to thicken foods such as puddings.

sa•gua•ro (sə gwär′ō *or* sə wär′ō) *n., pl.* **sa•gua•ros.** A very large cactus of the southwest United States and Mexico, having upward-curving branches, white flowers, and edible red fruit.

Sa•hap•ti•an (sä hăp′tē ən) *n.* A Native American language family spoken in the northwest United States and including the Sahaptin and Nez Perce languages.

Sa•hap•tin (sä hăp′tĭn) *n., pl.* **Sahaptin** or **Sa•hap•tins. 1.** Any of various Native American peoples of Idaho, Oregon, and Washington. **2.** The language of the Sahaptin.

Sa•har•a (sə hâr′ə *or* sə hă′ə *or* sə hä′rə). A vast desert of northern Africa extending east from the Atlantic coast to the Nile Valley and south from the Atlas Mountains to the region of the Sudan.

sa•hib (sä′ĭb *or* sä′ēb *or* sä′hĭb) *n.* Used formerly as a title of respectful address for a European man in colonial India. [First written down in 1673 in Modern English, from Hindi *ṣāḥib*, master.]

said (sĕd) *v.* Past tense and past participle of **say.** —*adj.* In legal use, previously named or mentioned: *The said tenant violated the lease.*

Sai•gon (sī gŏn′). Ho Chi Minh City.

sail (sāl) *n.* **1.a.** A piece of fabric attached to the rigging of a vessel and used to catch the wind and cause the vessel to move over water or ice. **b.** The sails of a boat or ship. **2.** *pl.* **sail** or **sails.** A ship or boat propelled by sails: *a fleet of 50 sail.* **3.** A trip in a sailing craft: *We went for a sail on the lake.* **4.** Something that resembles a sail or catches the wind like a sail, as the blade of a windmill. —*v.* **sailed, sail•ing, sails.** —*intr.* **1.** To travel by ship or boat: *sail around the world.* **2.** To move across the surface of water, especially in a sailing vessel: *The boat sails smoothly.* **3.** To operate a sailing craft: *learn how to sail.* **4.** To start out on a voyage across a body of water: *The ship will sail tomorrow.* **5.** To move swiftly, smoothly, or effortlessly: *She sailed through the test.* —*tr.* **1.** To manage (a sailing vessel). **2.** To voyage upon or across: *sail the Pacific Ocean.* —***idiom.*** **sail into.** To attack or criticize forcefully. [First written down before 899 in Old English and spelled *segl.*]

❑ *These sound alike:* **sail, sale** (act of selling).

sail•board (sāl′bôrd′) *n.* A small light sailboat with a flat hull.

sail•boat (sāl′bōt′) *n.* A boat that has a sail or sails, so that it can be propelled by the wind.

sail•cloth (sāl′klôth′ *or* sāl′klŏth′) *n.* A strong fabric, such as cotton canvas, suitable for making sails or tents.

sail•fish (sāl′fĭsh′) *n.* Any of various large ocean fishes having a large fin resembling a sail along its back and an upper jaw that projects into a bony pointed snout.

sail•ing (sā′lĭng) *n.* **1.** The skill required to operate a vessel; navigation. **2.** The sport of operating or riding in a sailboat. **3.** The departure or time of departure of a sailing vessel.

sail•or (sā′lər) *n.* **1.** A person who is a member of a ship's crew or who serves in a navy. **2.** A straw hat with a low flat crown and a straight brim.

saint (sānt) *n.* **1.a.** A person who has been officially recognized, especially by canonization, as being worthy of special reverence. **b.** A person who has died and gone to heaven. **2.** A person who is very virtuous. —*tr.v.* **saint•ed, saint•ing, saints.** To name, recognize, or venerate as a saint; canonize. [First written down about 1125 in Middle English and spelled *seinte*, from Latin *sānctus*, holy.]

Saint Au•gus•tine (sānt′ ô′gə stēn′). A city of northeast Florida on the Atlantic Ocean south-southeast of Jacksonville. Founded in 1565, it is the

saguaro

sailboat

ă	pat	oi	boy
ā	pay	ou	out
âr	care	o͝o	took
ä	father	o͞o	boot
ĕ	pet	ŭ	cut
ē	be	ûr	urge
ĭ	pit	th	thin
ī	pie	*th*	this
îr	pier	hw	whoop
ŏ	pot	zh	vision
ō	toe	ə	about
ô	paw	N	*French* bon

Saint Bernard

salamander
Spotted salamander

oldest permanent European settlement in the United States. Population, 11,692.

Saint Ber•nard (bər närd′) *n.* Any of a breed of large strong dog developed in Switzerland, having a thick brown and white coat and originally used to rescue people lost in the Alps.

Saint Chris•to•pher-Ne•vis (krĭs′tə fər nē′-vĭs *or* krĭs′tə fər nĕv′ĭs) also **Saint Kitts and Ne•vis** (kĭts ənd nēvĭs *or* kĭts ənd nĕv′ĭs). An island country in the Leeward Islands of the West Indies east-southeast of Puerto Rico. Basseterre is the capital. Population, 44,404.

Saint Croix (kroi). An island of the U.S. Virgin Islands in the West Indies east of Puerto Rico.

saint•ed (sān′tĭd) *adj.* **1.** Considered a saint; canonized. **2.** Of saintly character; holy.

Saint George's (jôr′jəz). The capital of Grenada, on the southwest coast of the island in the Windward Islands of the West Indies. Population, 7,500.

Saint He•le•na (hə lē′nə). A volcanic island in the southern Atlantic Ocean west of Angola. It is best known as Napoleon's place of exile from 1815 until his death in 1821.

Saint Hel•ens (hĕl′ənz), **Mount.** An active volcanic peak of the Cascade Range in southwest Washington. It erupted violently on May 18, 1980, producing an ash plume visible over much of western Washington and Oregon and covering a large area with volcanic ash.

saint•hood (sānt′ho͝od′) *n.* **1.** The status, character, or condition of being a saint. **2.** Saints considered as a group.

Saint John's (jŏnz). **1.** The capital of Antigua and Barbuda, in the Leeward Islands of the West Indies. Population, 24,359. **2.** The capital and largest city of Newfoundland, Canada, on the southeast coast of the island. It is one of the oldest settlements in North America and was first colonized in 1583. Population, 83,770.

Saint Kitts and Ne•vis (kĭts ənd nē′vĭs *or* kĭts ənd nĕv′ĭs). Saint Christopher-Nevis.

Saint Law•rence (lôr′əns *or* lŏr′əns), **Gulf of.** An arm of the northwest Atlantic Ocean off southeast Canada bordered by New Brunswick, Nova Scotia, Newfoundland, and Quebec.

Saint Lawrence River. A river of southeast Canada flowing about 750 miles (1,207 kilometers) northeast from Lake Ontario through southern Quebec to the Gulf of St. Lawrence. It was long used as a water highway by explorers, missionaries, and fur traders.

Saint Lawrence Seaway. An international waterway, about 2,350 miles (3,781 kilometers) long, consisting of canals, dams, and locks in the St. Lawrence River and connecting channels through the Great Lakes. It provides passage for oceangoing ships as far west as Lake Superior.

Saint Lou•is (lo͞o′ĭs). The largest city of Missouri, on the Mississippi River, in the eastern part of the state. It passed to the United States as part of the Louisiana Purchase (1803). Population, 396,685.

Saint Lu•cia (lo͞o′shə *or* lo͞o sē′ə). An island country of the West Indies in the Windward Islands south of Martinique. It gained its independence from Great Britain in 1979. Castries is the capital. Population, 134,006.

saint•ly (sānt′lē) *adj.* **saint•li•er, saint•li•est.** Of, relating to, resembling, or befitting a saint or saints. **—saint′li•ness** *n.*

Saint Pat•rick's Day (păt′rĭks) *n.* March 17, observed in the United States and Ireland in honor of Saint Patrick, the patron saint of Ireland.

Saint Paul (pôl). The capital of Minnesota, in the southeast part of the state on the Mississippi River adjacent to Minneapolis. Population, 272,235.

Saint Pe•ters•burg (pē′tərz bûrg′). Formerly (1924–1991) **Len•in•grad** (lĕn′ĭn grăd′) also **Pet•ro•grad** (pĕt′rə grăd′). A city of northwest Russia northwest of Moscow. It was the capital of Russia from 1712 to 1918. Population, 4,329,000.

Saint Tho•mas (tŏm′əs). An island of the U.S. Virgin Islands in the West Indies east of Puerto Rico.

Saint Val•en•tine's Day (văl′ən tīnz′) *n.* February 14, celebrated in various North American and European countries by the exchange of valentines or love tokens.

Saint Vincent and the Gren•a•dines (vĭn′-sənt ənd *thə* grĕn′ə dēnz′). An island country in the central Windward Islands of the West Indies. Kingstown, on the island of **St. Vincent,** is the capital. Population, 108,704.

saith (sĕth *or* sā′ĭth) *v. Archaic.* A third person singular present tense of **say.**

sake[1] (sāk) *n.* **1.** Purpose; motive: *argue just for the sake of arguing.* **2.** Benefit or interest; welfare: *We bought a humidifier for the sake of the baby.* **3.** Good; advantage: *He moved to a drier climate for the sake of his health.* [First written down about 725 in Old English and spelled *sacu,* lawsuit.]

sa•ke[2] (sä′kē) *n.* A Japanese alcoholic beverage made from fermented rice. [First written down in 1687 in Modern English and spelled *sague,* from Japanese *sake.*]

Sa•kha•lin (săk′ə lēn′ *or* săk′ə lən). An island of southeast Russia in the Sea of Okhotsk north of Hokkaido, Japan. It passed under Russian control in 1875.

sal (săl) *n.* Salt.

sa•laam (sə läm′) *n.* **1.** A ceremonious act of deference or obeisance, especially a low bow performed while placing the right palm on the forehead. **2.** A respectful ceremonial greeting performed especially in Islamic countries. *—tr. & intr.v.* **sa•laamed, sa•laam•ing, sa•laams.** To greet with or perform a salaam.

sal•a•ble also **sale•a•ble** (sā′lə bəl) *adj.* Fit and suitable to sell; capable of attracting buyers. **—sal′-a•bil′i•ty** *n.*

sa•la•cious (sə lā′shəs) *adj.* **1.** Appealing to or stimulating sexual desire. **2.** Lustful; bawdy.

sal•ad (săl′əd) *n.* **1.** A dish consisting of green raw vegetables, such as lettuce, often with cucumbers or tomatoes, served with a dressing. **2.** The course of a meal consisting of this dish. **3.** A cold dish of chopped fruit, potatoes, eggs, or other food, usually prepared with mayonnaise. **4.** A green vegetable used in salad, especially lettuce.

salad bar *n.* A counter in a restaurant from which customers may serve themselves a variety of salad ingredients and dressings.

salad dressing *n.* A sauce, as of mayonnaise or oil and vinegar, that is served on salad.

sal•a•man•der (săl′ə măn′dər) *n.* **1.** Any of various animals that resemble lizards but have smooth moist skin. **2.** In mythology, a creature resembling a lizard, believed to be capable of living in or enduring fire. [First written down in 1340 in Middle English and spelled *salamandre,* from Greek *salamandra.*]

sa•la•mi (sə lä′mē) *n.* A highly spiced and salted sausage of pork or beef or of both these meats.

sal•a•ried (săl′ə rēd) *adj.* Receiving or paying a salary: *a salaried position.*

sal•a•ry (săl′ə rē) *n., pl.* **sal•a•ries.** A set sum of money or other compensation paid to a person on a regular basis in return for work or service. [First written down about 1280 in Middle English and spelled *salerie,* from Latin *salārium,* money given to Roman soldiers to buy salt, from *sāl,* salt.]

sale (sāl) *n.* **1.** The act of selling; an exchange of goods or services for money or other compensation. **2.** An instance of selling. **3.** An occasion when goods or services are offered for purchase at reduced prices: *a half-price sale at the store.* **4. sales. a.** The business of advertising and selling goods or services. **b.** The amount of goods sold or of money brought in by selling goods.

❑ *These sound alike:* **sale, sail** (fabric used to catch wind).

sale•a•ble (sā′lə bəl) *adj.* Variant of **salable.**

Sa•lem (sā′ləm). **1.** A city of northeast Massachusetts northeast of Boston. Founded in 1626, it is noted as the site of witchcraft trials (1692). Population, 38,091. **2.** The capital of Oregon, in the northwest part of the state south-southwest of Portland. It was founded in about 1840 and became state capital in 1859. Population, 107,786.

sales•clerk (sālz′klûrk′) *n.* A person who is employed to sell goods in a store.

sales•man (sālz′mən) *n.* A man who is employed to sell goods or services.

sales•man•ship (sālz′mən shĭp′) *n.* Skill, ability, or persuasiveness in selling.

sales•peo•ple (sālz′pē′pəl) *pl.n.* Persons who are employed to sell goods or services.

sales•per•son (sālz′pûr′sən) *n.* A salesman or saleswoman.

sales tax (sālz) *n.* A tax on the sale of goods or services, representing a fixed percentage of the purchase price and usually collected by the seller.

sales•wom•an (sālz′wo͝om′ən) *n.* A woman who is employed to sell goods or services.

sal•i•cyl•ic acid (săl′ĭ sĭl′ĭk) *n.* A white crystalline acid, $C_7H_6O_3$, used in making aspirin, as a preservative and flavoring agent, and in the external treatment of certain skin conditions such as eczema.

sa•li•ent (sā′lē ənt *or* sāl′yənt) *adj.* **1.** Standing out and attracting attention; striking or conspicuous: *the salient points of a plan.* **2.** Projecting or jutting beyond a line or surface; protruding. —*n.* **1.** A projecting angle or part. **2.** The area of military defense, as a battle line, that projects closest to the enemy. [First written down before 1393 in Middle English and spelled *salience,* leaping, from Latin *salīre,* to leap.]

sa•line (sā′lēn′ *or* sā′līn′) *adj.* Of, relating to, or containing salt; salty. —*n.* A saline solution, especially one used in medicine and surgery. **—sa•lin′i•ty** (sə lĭn′ĭ tē) *n.*

Sa•lish (sā′lĭsh) *n.* A family of Native American languages of the northwest United States and British Columbia. **—Sa′lish•an** *adj.*

sa•li•va (sə lī′və) *n.* The watery tasteless fluid that is secreted into the mouth by various glands, serving to moisten food as it is chewed and to begin the digestion of starches.

sal•i•var•y (săl′ə vĕr′ē) *adj.* Of, relating to, or producing saliva.

salivary gland *n.* A gland that secretes saliva, especially one of three pairs of large glands that secrete saliva into the mouth.

sal•i•vate (săl′ə vāt′) *intr.v.* **sal•i•vat•ed, sal•i•vat•ing, sal•i•vates.** To produce or secrete saliva. **—sal′i•va′tion** *n.*

Salk (sôlk), **Jonas Edward.** Born 1914. American scientist who developed the first effective vaccine against polio (1954). —See Note.

sal•low (săl′ō) *adj.* **sal•low•er, sal•low•est.** Of a sickly yellowish color or complexion.

sal•ly (săl′ē) *intr.v.* **sal•lied, sal•ly•ing, sal•lies. 1.** To rush forth or leap out suddenly. **2.** To set out for a destination in a spirited energetic way: *I sallied forth to seek my fortune.* **3.** To charge at and attack an enemy from a defensive position. —*n., pl.* **sal•lies. 1.** A sudden rush forward; a leap. **2.** A quick, clever, or witty remark; a quip. **3.** A short trip or outing; a jaunt. **4.** An attack from a defensive position. [First written down in 1545 in Modern English, from Latin *salīre,* to leap.]

salm•on (săm′ən) *n., pl.* **salmon** or **salm•ons. 1.** Any of various large food fishes of northern waters, having pinkish flesh and swimming from salt to fresh water to spawn. **2.** A yellowish pink or pinkish orange color. [First written down in 1228 in Middle English, from Latin *salmō.*]

sal•mo•nel•la (săl′mə nĕl′ə) *n., pl.* **sal•mo•nel•lae** (săl′mə nĕl′ē) or **sal•mo•nel•las** or **salmonella.** A type of bacteria that causes food poisoning in humans. [First written down in 1913 in Modern English, after Daniel Elmer *Salmon* (1850–1914), American pathologist.]

Sa•lo•me (sə lō′mē *or* săl′ə mā′). In the New Testament, the niece of Herod Antipas, who granted her the head of John the Baptist in return for her dancing.

sa•lon (sə lŏn′ *or* săl′ŏn′) *n.* **1.** A large room for receiving and entertaining guests. **2.** A regular gathering of prominent persons, such as artists, writers, or politicians. **3.** A hall or gallery in which works of art are exhibited. **4.** A business offering a product or service related to fashion: *a beauty salon.*

sa•loon (sə lo͞on′) *n.* **1.** A place where alcoholic drinks are sold and drunk; a bar or tavern. **2.** A large room or hall for receptions, entertainment, or exhibitions.

sal•sa (säl′sə) *n.* **1.** A spicy sauce made of tomatoes, onions, and peppers, eaten with tortilla chips or other Mexican food. **2.** A popular form of Latin-American dance music, characterized by Cuban melodies and elements of jazz and rock.

sal soda *n.* Sodium carbonate when used as a cleanser.

salt (sôlt) *n.* **1.** A colorless or white crystalline solid, chiefly sodium chloride, widely used as a food seasoning and preservative. **2.** Any of a large class of chemical compounds formed when one or more hydrogen ions of an acid are replaced by metallic ions. **3. salts.** Any of various salts used as laxatives. **4. salts. a.** Smelling salts. **b.** Epsom salts. **5.** Something that is like salt in adding flavor or zest to something. **6.** *Informal.* A sailor. **7.** Sharp humor or wit. —*adj.* **1.** Containing or filled with salt: *a salt mine.* **2.** Having the taste or smell of salt. **3.** Preserved in salt or brine: *salt pork.* —*tr.v.* **salt•ed, salt•ing, salts. 1.** To season or sprinkle with salt: *Salt the stew.* **2.** To preserve (meat or fish, for example) by treating with salt. **3.** To add zest or liveliness to: *salt a lecture with jokes.* **—*idioms.* salt away.** To put aside; save. **worth (one's) salt.** Efficient and capable. [First written down before 830 in Old English.]

salt•cel•lar (sôlt′sĕl′ər) *n.* A small dish or shaker for dispensing salt.

sal•tine (sôl tēn′) *n.* A thin crisp cracker sprinkled with coarse salt.

Salt Lake City (sôlt). The capital and largest city of Utah, in the north-central part of the state near Great Salt Lake. It is the center of the Church of Jesus Christ of Latter-day Saints. Population, 159,936.

salt lick *n.* A natural deposit or block of salt that animals lick.

salt•pe•ter (sôlt′pē′tər) *n.* **1.** Potassium nitrate or sodium nitrate. **2.** Niter.

salt•shak•er (sôlt′shā′kər) *n.* A container with a perforated top for holding and sprinkling salt.

salt•wa•ter or **salt-wa•ter** (sôlt′wô′tər *or* sôlt′wŏt′ər) *adj.* **1.** Relating to or consisting of water that contains a dissolved salt: *a saltwater solution.* **2.** Living in the sea or in salt water.

Jonas Salk

The scientist Jonas **Salk** focused his research studies in the 1940's on creating a vaccine for influenza. At the time, it was thought that the only vaccine that would work on a viral infection was a vaccine using a live virus. A live-virus vaccine generally causes a small risk of infection to the vaccinated person. Salk successfully developed the first killed-virus vaccine, a vaccine for influenza using dead influenza viruses. Salk went on to develop a killed-virus vaccine for polio in the 1950's, when polio was a very real threat, chiefly to children. Salk's polio vaccine was tested in 1955 and found to be safe and effective, and both the polio and the influenza vaccines went into widespread use. It is because of Salk's initial success that researchers today are able to produce vaccines for several new strains of flu each year.

salmon

saltcellar

ă	pat	oi	boy
ā	pay	ou	out
âr	care	o͝o	took
ä	father	o͞o	boot
ĕ	pet	ŭ	cut
ē	be	ûr	urge
ĭ	pit	th	thin
ī	pie	*th*	this
îr	pier	hw	whoop
ŏ	pot	zh	vision
ō	toe	ə	about
ô	paw	N	*French* bon

salute

Deborah Sampson
1797 engraving

salt•y (sôl′tē) *adj.* **salt•i•er, salt•i•est. 1.** Of, containing, or seasoned with salt: *salty food.* **2.** Suggestive of the sea or sailing life. **3.** Witty; pungent: *salty humor.* —**salt′i•ness** *n.*

sa•lu•bri•ous (sə lo͞o′brē əs) *adj.* Good for the health; wholesome. —**sa•lu′bri•ous•ly** *adv.* —**sa•lu′bri•ous•ness** *n.*

sal•u•tar•y (săl′yə tĕr′ē) *adj.* **1.** Helpful; beneficial: *salutary advice.* **2.** Good for the health: *a salutary climate.*

sal•u•ta•tion (săl′yə tā′shən) *n.* **1.** An expression or gesture of greeting or respect. **2.** The word or phrase of greeting used to begin a letter. *Dear Sir or Madam* is a salutation.

sa•lu•ta•to•ri•an (sə lo͞o′tə tôr′ē ən) *n.* In some schools and colleges, the student with the second highest academic rank, who gives the opening address at graduation.

sa•lu•ta•to•ry (sə lo͞o′tə tôr′ē) *n., pl.* **sa•lu•ta•to•ries.** An opening address, especially one delivered at graduation exercises by a salutatorian. —*adj.* Having to do with or expressing a greeting or welcome.

sa•lute (sə lo͞ot′) *v.* **sa•lut•ed, sa•lut•ing, sa•lutes.** —*tr.* **1.** To recognize (a superior officer) with a gesture prescribed by military regulations, especially by raising the hand to the cap. **2.** To greet with a polite, respectful, or friendly gesture. **3.** To pay respect or tribute to; praise. —*intr.* To make a gesture of greeting or respect. —*n.* **1.** An act, gesture, or display of respect. **2.** The act of saluting a military superior. **3.** An act of greeting or recognizing, as a bow, wave, or nod. [First written down before 1383 in Middle English and spelled *saluten*, from Latin *salūtāre*, from *salūs*, health.]

Sal•va•dor (săl′və dôr′). A city of eastern Brazil on the Atlantic Ocean north-northeast of Rio de Janeiro. It was the capital of the Portuguese possessions in the New World from 1549 to 1763. Population, 1,501,981.

Sal•va•do•ran (săl′və dôr′ən) or **Sal•va•do•ri•an** (sălvə dôr′ē ən) *adj.* Of or relating to El Salvador or its people or culture. —*n.* A native or inhabitant of El Salvador.

sal•vage (săl′vĭj) *n.* **1.** The rescue of a ship, crew, or its cargo from fire or shipwreck. **2.** The act of saving endangered property from loss. **3.** Goods or property saved from destruction or disaster. —*tr.v.* **sal•vaged, sal•vag•ing, sal•vag•es. 1.** To save from loss or ruin. **2.** To save (discarded or damaged material) for further use. —**sal′vage•a•ble** *adj.* —**sal′vag•er** *n.*

sal•va•tion (săl vā′shən) *n.* **1.** Preservation or deliverance from destruction, difficulty, or evil. **2.** In Christianity, the saving of the soul from sin and punishment; redemption. **3.** A person or thing that saves, rescues, or preserves: *The emergency supplies were our salvation during the hurricane.*

Salvation Army *n.* An international Christian organization established to spread religious teachings and do charitable work.

salve (săv *or* säv) *n.* **1.** A soothing ointment applied to wounds, burns, or sores to heal them or relieve pain. **2.** Something that soothes or heals; a balm. —*tr.v.* **salved, salv•ing, salves.** To soothe or heal with or as if with salve: *Your praise salved their hurt feelings.*

sal•ver (săl′vər) *n.* A serving tray.

sal•vo (săl′vō) *n., pl.* **sal•vos** or **sal•voes. 1.a.** A simultaneous firing of weapons. **b.** The simultaneous release of a number of bombs from an aircraft. **c.** The projectiles or bombs so released. **2.** A sudden outburst, as of cheers or applause.

Sa•mar•i•tan also **sa•mar•i•tan** (sə măr′ĭ tn) *n.* A Good Samaritan.

sa•mar•i•um (sə mâr′ē əm *or* sə măr′ē əm) *n.* *Symbol* **Sm** A silvery or pale-gray rare-earth element used in control rods in nuclear reactors. Atomic number 62. See table at **element.** [First written down in 1879 in Modern English, after Colonel M. von *Samarski* 19th-century Russian mining official.]

same (sām) *adj.* **1.** Similar in kind, quality, quantity, or degree: *These books are the same size.* **2.** Being the very one; identical: *This is the same seat I had yesterday.* **3.** Being the one previously mentioned: *The same Mr. Johnson also wrote poetry.* —*adv.* In the same way: *The words* sail *and* sale *are pronounced the same.* —*pron.* **1.** A person or thing identical with another. **2.** A person or thing previously mentioned or described: *"Is she the one you mean?" "The same."* [First written down about 1200 in Middle English, from Old Norse *samr.*]

same•ness (sām′nĭs) *n.* **1.** The condition of being the same. **2.** A lack of variety or change; monotony.

Sa•mo•a (sə mō′ə). An island group of the southern Pacific Ocean east-northeast of Fiji, divided between **American Samoa** and **Western Samoa.** The islands were originally populated by Polynesians perhaps as early as 1000 B.C.

Sa•mo•an (sə mō′ən) *adj.* Or or relating to Samoa or its people, language, or culture. —*n.* **1.** A native or inhabitant of Samoa. **2.** The Polynesian language of Samoa.

sam•o•var (săm′ə vär′) *n.* A metal urn with a spigot, used chiefly in Russia to boil water for tea.

sam•pan (săm′păn′) *n.* A small flat-bottomed boat used in Asia and usually propelled by two oars.

sam•ple (săm′pəl) *n.* A part, piece, amount, or selection that is considered representative of the whole: *Could I have a sample of that fabric?* —*tr.v.* **sam•pled, sam•pling, sam•ples.** To take a sample of, especially to test or examine. [First written down about 1300 in Middle English and spelled *saumpel*, from Latin *exemplum*, example.]

sam•pler (săm′plər) *n.* **1.** A person who is employed to take samples. **2.** A piece of cloth embroidered with various designs or mottoes that serves to display fancy stitching or needlework. **3.** A representative selection of something: *a sampler of chocolate candies.*

Samp•son (sămp′sən), **Deborah.** 1760–1827. American Revolutionary soldier who fought disguised as a man (1782–1783) and was granted a full veteran's pension in 1818.

Sam•son (săm′sən). In the Bible, an Israelite judge and warrior who was betrayed to the Philistines by Delilah after she cut off his hair, the source of his great strength.

Sam•u•el (săm′yo͞o əl) *n.* **1.** In the Bible, a Hebrew judge and prophet of the 11th century B.C. who anointed Saul, and later David, as king of Israel. **2.** Either of two books of the Bible that give a history of the prophet Samuel and describe the reigns of Saul and David.

sam•u•rai (săm′ə rī′) *n., pl.* **samurai** or **sam•u•rais. 1.** The military aristocracy of feudal Japan. **2.** A professional warrior belonging to this class.

San (sän) *n., pl.* **San** or **Sans.** A member of a traditionally nomadic hunting people of southwest Africa.

Sa•na or **Sa•n'a** or **Sa•naa** (sä nä′). The capital of Yemen, in the western part of the country. Population, 277,800.

San An•to•ni•o (săn ăn tō′nē ō′). A city of south-central Texas southwest of Austin on the **San Antonio River,** flowing about 200 miles (322 kilometers) southeast to the Gulf of Mexico. The city was founded in 1718. Population, 935,933.

san•a•to•ri•um (săn′ə tôr′ē əm) *n., pl.* **san•a•to•ri•ums** or **san•a•to•ri•a** (săn′ə tôr′ē ə). **1.** An institution for the treatment of chronic diseases. **2.** A health resort, especially for convalescents; a sanitarium.

sanc•ta (**săngk′**tə) *n.* A plural of **sanctum.**

sanc•ti•fy (**săngk′**tə fī′) *tr.v.* **sanc•ti•fied, sanc•ti•fy•ing, sanc•ti•fies. 1.** To make holy or sacred; purify. **2.** To give religious sanction to: *sanctify a marriage.* **3.** To set apart for sacred use.

sanc•ti•mo•ni•ous (săngk′tə **mō′**nē əs) *adj.* Falsely pious or righteous. **—sanc′ti•mo′ni•ous•ly** *adv.* **—sanc′ti•mo′ni•ous•ness** *n.*

sanc•tion (**săngk′**shən) *n.* **1.** Authoritative permission or approval. **2.** An action taken by several nations acting together against a nation that has violated international law. *—tr.v.* **sanc•tioned, sanc•tion•ing, sanc•tions.** To give official approval to; authorize.

sanc•ti•ty (**săngk′**tĭ tē) *n., pl.* **sanc•ti•ties. 1.** Holiness of life; saintliness. **2.** The quality or condition of being considered holy or sacred; sacredness.

sanc•tu•ar•y (**săngk′**cho͞o ĕr′ē) *n., pl.* **sanc•tu•ar•ies. 1.** A sacred place, such as a church, temple, or mosque. **2.** A place of refuge, asylum, or protection. **3.** Immunity to arrest; asylum or protection: *They asked for sanctuary.* **4.** A reserved area in which wildlife is protected by law: *a bird sanctuary.*

sanc•tum (**săngk′**təm) *n., pl.* **sanc•tums** or **sanc•ta** (**săngk′**tə). **1.** A private place where one is free from intrusion. **2.** A sacred or holy place.

sand (sănd) *n.* **1.** Loose grains or particles of disintegrated rock, finer than rice grains and coarser than silt grains. **2.** Land, such as a beach or desert, covered with this material. Often used in the plural. **3.** A light yellowish brown. *—tr.v.* **sand•ed, sand•ing, sands. 1.** To sprinkle or cover with or as if with sand: *sand an icy sidewalk.* **2.** To scrape or rub with sand or sandpaper. [First written down before 830 in Old English.]

san•dal (**săn′**dl) *n.* **1.** A shoe made of a sole and thongs or straps used to fasten it to the foot. **2.** A low-cut shoe fastened to the foot by an ankle strap. [First written down in 1382 in Middle English and spelled *sandalie,* from Greek *sandalon.*]

san•dal•wood (**săn′**dl wo͝od′) *n.* **1.** The pleasant-smelling wood of any of several tropical trees, used for carving decorative objects and for making perfume. **2.** Any of the trees that yield such wood.

sand•bag (**sănd′**băg′) *n.* A bag or sack filled with sand, often used to form protective walls.

sand•bank (**sănd′**băngk′) *n.* A mass of sand that forms a hillside or mound.

sand•bar (**sănd′**bär′) *n.* A long mass or low ridge of sand built up in the water along a shore or beach by the action of waves or currents.

sand•blast (**sănd′**blăst′) *n.* A blast of air or steam carrying sand at high velocity to etch glass or to clean stone or metal surfaces, for example. *—tr.v.* **sand•blast•ed, sand•blast•ing, sand•blasts.** To apply a sandblast to (a building, for example). **—sand′blast′er** *n.*

sand•box (**sănd′**bŏks′) *n.* A low box filled with sand for children to play in.

Sand•burg (**sănd′**bûrg′ *or* **săn′**bûrg′), **Carl.** 1878–1967. American writer known for his poems celebrating American people, geography, and industry.

sand dollar *n.* A thin, flat, circular sea animal related to the starfish, living along sandy shores.

sand•er (**săn′**dər) *n.* **1.** A device, usually attached to a truck, that spreads sand on roads. **2.** A machine with a disk or belt of sandpaper, used for smoothing, polishing, or refinishing: *a floor sander.*

San Di•e•go (dē **ā′**gō). A city of southern California on **San Diego Bay,** an inlet of the Pacific Ocean near the Mexican border. Population, 1,110,549.

sand•lot (**sănd′**lŏt′) *n.* A vacant lot used especially by children for unorganized sports and games.

sand•man (**sănd′**măn′) *n.* A character in fairy tales and folklore who makes children sleep by sprinkling sand in their eyes.

sand•pa•per (**sănd′**pā′pər) *n.* Heavy paper coated on one side with sand or other abrasive material and used for smoothing surfaces. *—tr.v.* **sand•pa•pered, sand•pa•per•ing, sand•pa•pers.** To rub with sandpaper.

sand•pi•per (**sănd′**pī′pər) *n.* Any of various small shore birds having a slender pointed bill.

sand•stone (**sănd′**stōn′) *n.* A type of sedimentary rock that occurs in a variety of colors, formed of sand-size grains of quartz and other minerals held together in most cases by silica and iron oxides.

sand•storm (**sănd′**stôrm′) *n.* A strong wind carrying clouds of sand and dust through the air.

sand•wich (**sănd′**wĭch *or* **săn′**wĭch) *n.* **1.** Two or more slices of bread with a filling, such as meat or cheese, placed between them. **2.** One slice of bread covered with a filling: *an open-faced sandwich.* **3.** Something that resembles a sandwich. *—tr.v.* **sand•wiched, sand•wich•ing, sand•wich•es. 1.** To make into a sandwich. **2.** To insert (one thing) between two other things tightly. **3.** To make room or time for: *sandwiched a meeting into the busy schedule.* [First written down in 1762 in Modern English, after John Montagu, Fourth Earl of *Sandwich* (1718–1792), British politician.]

sand•y (**săn′**dē) *adj.* **sand•i•er, sand•i•est. 1.** Covered with, full of, or consisting of sand. **2.** Of the color of sand; light yellowish brown. **—sand′i•ness** *n.*

sane (sān) *adj.* **san•er, san•est. 1.** Of sound mind; mentally healthy: *a sane person.* **2.** Having or showing good judgment; reasonable: *a sane approach to the problem.* [First written down in 1721 in Modern English, from Latin *sānus,* healthy.] **—sane′ly** *adv.* **—sane′ness** *n.*

❑ *These sound alike:* **sane, seine** (fishing net).

San Fran•cis•co (frən **sĭs′**kō). A city of western California on a peninsula between the Pacific Ocean and **San Francisco Bay,** an inlet of the Pacific. A Spanish fortress and mission were founded here in 1776. Population, 723,959.

sang (săng) *v.* A past tense of **sing.**

san•gui•nar•y (**săng′**gwə nĕr′ē) *adj.* **1.** Accompanied by bloodshed. **2.** Eager for bloodshed; bloodthirsty. **3.** Consisting of blood.

san•guine (**săng′**gwĭn) *adj.* **1.a.** Of the color of blood; red. **b.** Of a healthy reddish color; ruddy: *a sanguine complexion.* **2.** Eagerly optimistic; cheerful. [First written down in 1378 in Middle English and spelled *sanguein,* from Latin *sanguineus,* from *sanguīs,* blood.] **—san′guine•ly** *adv.* **—san•guin′i•ty** *n.*

san•i•tar•i•um (săn′ĭ **târ′**ē əm) *n., pl.* **san•i•tar•i•ums** or **san•i•tar•i•a** (săn′ĭ **târ′**ē ə). A sanatorium.

san•i•tar•y (**săn′**ĭ tĕr′ē) *adj.* **1.** Of or relating to health. **2.** Free of germs; hygienic. [First written down in 1842 in Modern English, from Latin *sānitās,* health.] **—san′i•tar′i•ly** (săn′ĭ **târ′**ə lē) *adv.*

sanitary napkin *n.* A disposable pad of absorbent material worn to absorb menstrual flow.

san•i•ta•tion (săn′ĭ **tā′**shən) *n.* **1.** The study and application of procedures and regulations that are meant to protect public health. **2.** The disposal of sewage and wastes.

san•i•tize (**săn′**ĭ tīz′) *tr.v.* **san•i•tized, san•i•tiz•ing, san•i•tiz•es. 1.** To make sanitary, as by cleaning. **2.** To make more acceptable by removing unpleasant or offensive features from: *a movie that was sanitized for television.*

san•i•ty (**săn′**ĭ tē) *n.* **1.** Soundness of mind; good

Carl Sandburg

sand dollar

Five-holed keyhole urchin

ă	pat	oi	boy
ā	pay	ou	out
âr	care	o͝o	took
ä	father	o͞o	boot
ĕ	pet	ŭ	cut
ē	be	ûr	urge
ĭ	pit	th	thin
ī	pie	*th*	this
îr	pier	hw	whoop
ŏ	pot	zh	vision
ō	toe	ə	about
ô	paw	N	*French* bon

Antonio López de Santa Anna
Detail of a c. 1858 portrait by Paul L'Ouvrier (fl. 1858)

Santa Claus
Illustration from "A Visit from St. Nicholas" by Clement Clarke Moore (1779–1863)

mental health. **2.** The ability to make sound or reasonable judgments.

San Jo•sé (hō zā′). The capital and largest city of Costa Rica, in the central part of the country. It was settled in about 1736 and became the capital in 1823. Population, 277,800.

San Jose scale *n.* A scale insect that does considerable damage to fruit trees and fruit-bearing plants.

San Juan (wän′ *or* hwän′). The capital and largest city of Puerto Rico, in the northeast part of the island on the Atlantic Ocean. It was first settled in 1508–1509. Population, 424,700.

sank (săngk) *v.* A past tense of **sink.**

San Ma•ri•no (mə rē′nō). A country in the Apennines near the Adriatic Sea. It is surrounded by Italy and is the world's smallest republic. The city of **San Marino** is its capital. The country's population is 21,537; the city's, 4,628.

sans (sănz) *prep.* Without.

San Sal•va•dor (săn săl′və dôr′). The capital and largest city of El Salvador, in the west-central part of the country. It was founded in the 16th century. Population, 445,100.

San•skrit (săn′skrĭt′) *n.* An ancient Indo-European language that is the language of Hinduism and the classical literary language of India. **—San′skrit′** *adj.*

San•ta An•na (săn′tə ăn′ə *or* sän′tä ä′nä), **Antonio López de.** 1795?–1876. Mexican military and political leader who was victorious at the Alamo (1836) but was soon after defeated and captured by the Texans.

San•ta Claus (săn′tə klôz′) *n.* The personification of the spirit of Christmas, usually represented as a jolly fat old man with a white beard and red suit, who brings gifts to children on Christmas Eve. [First written down in 1773 in American English, from Middle Dutch *Sinterclaes*, St. Nicholas.]

San•ta Fe (săn′tə fā′). The capital of New Mexico, in the north-central part of the state northeast of Albuquerque. A Spanish settlement was built here in about 1609 on the site of ancient Native American ruins. Population, 55,859.

San•tee (săn tē′) *n., pl.* **Santee** or **San•tees.** A member of the eastern branch of the Sioux peoples.

San•ti•a•go (săn′tē ä′gō *or* sän′tē ä′gō). The capital and largest city of Chile, in the central part of the country. It was founded in 1541. Population, 425,924.

San•to Do•min•go (săn′tō də mĭng′gō). The capital and largest city of the Dominican Republic, in the southeast part of the island of Hispaniola on the Caribbean Sea. It was founded in 1496. Population, 1,313,172.

São Pau•lo (soun pou′lō *or* soun pou′lo͞o). A city of southeast Brazil west-southwest of Rio de Janeiro. Founded in 1554, it is now the largest city in South America. Population, 8,493,226.

São To•mé (tə mā′). An island of São Tomé and Príncipe in the Atlantic Ocean off western Africa. The city of **São Tomé,** the capital of the country, is on the southeast coast. Its population is 17,380.

São Tomé and Prín•ci•pe (prĭn′sə pə). An island country in the Atlantic Ocean off western Africa. It gained its independence from Portugal in 1975. São Tomé is the capital. Population, 73,631.

sap¹ (săp) *n.* **1.** The liquid that circulates through plant tissues, carrying dissolved minerals and other food substances to the various plant parts. **2.** Health and energy; vigor. **3.** *Slang.* A foolish person; a dupe. [First written down about 750 in Old English and spelled *sæp*.]

sap² (săp) *n.* A covered trench or tunnel dug to a point within an enemy position. *—tr.v.* **sapped, sap•ping, saps. 1.** To deplete or weaken gradually: *heat sapping one's strength.* **2.** To undermine the foundations of (a structure). [First written down in 1591 in Modern English and spelled *sappe*, from Late Latin *sappa*, hoe.]

sa•pi•ent (sā′pē ənt) *adj.* Having great wisdom and insight. **—sa′pi•ence** *n.* **—sa′pi•ent•ly** *adv.*

sap•ling (săp′lĭng) *n.* A young tree.

sap•o•dil•la (săp′ə dĭl′ə) *n.* A tropical American tree whose milky juice is the source of chicle, the main ingredient in chewing gum.

sa•pon•i•fi•ca•tion (sə pŏn′ə fĭ kā′shən) *n.* The hydrolysis of an ester by an alkali, producing a free alcohol and an acid salt, especially alkaline hydrolysis of fats to make soap.

sa•pon•i•fy (sə pŏn′ə fī′) *v.* **sa•pon•i•fied, sa•pon•i•fy•ing, sa•pon•i•fies.** *—tr.* **1.** To convert (an ester) by saponification. **2.** To convert (fats) into soap. *—intr.* To undergo saponification. **—sa•pon′i•fi′a•ble** *adj.* **—sa•pon′i•fi′er** *n.*

sap•phire (săf′īr′) *n.* **1.** Any of several fairly pure forms of corundum, especially a blue form valued as a gem. **2.** A gem of this type. **3.** The blue color of the gem sapphire.

Sap•pho (săf′ō). Flourished about 600 B.C. Greek poet considered one of the greatest poets of antiquity. Only fragments of her lyrics survive.

sap•py (săp′ē) *adj.* **sap•pi•er, sap•pi•est. 1.** Full of sap, juice, or vigor. **2.** *Slang.* Foolish; silly.

sap•ro•phyte (săp′rə fīt′) *n.* An organism, such as a mushroom or mold, that lives on and gets its nourishment from dead or decaying organic material. **—sap′ro•phyt′ic** (săp′rə fĭt′ĭk) *adj.*

sap•suck•er (săp′sŭk′ər) *n.* Any of various North American woodpeckers that drill holes into trees to feed on insects and the sap.

sap•wood (săp′wo͝od′) *n.* The outer, newly formed, usually light-colored wood of a tree, through which the sap flows.

Sar•a•cen (săr′ə sən) *n.* **1.** A Muslim, especially of the time of the Crusades. **2.** An Arab.

Sar•ah (sâr′ə). In the Bible, the wife of Abraham and mother of Isaac.

Sa•ra•je•vo (săr′ə yā′vō). The capital and largest city of Bosnia-Herzegovina, in the south-central part southwest of Belgrade, Yugoslavia. Population, 374,500.

sa•ran (sə răn′) *n.* Any of various plastic resins derived from vinyl compounds and used in making transparent films for packaging, bristles, pipes, and fittings, and as a textile fiber.

sa•ra•pe (sə rä′pē) *n.* Variant of **serape.**

sar•casm (sär′kăz′əm) *n.* **1.** A sharply mocking, often ironic remark intended to wound. **2.** The use of sarcasm.

sar•cas•tic (sär kăs′tĭk) *adj.* **1.** Characterized by or expressing sarcasm: *a sarcastic remark.* **2.** Given to using sarcasm: *a sarcastic person.* **—sar•cas′ti•cal•ly** *adv.*

sar•co•din•i•an (sär′kə dĭn′ē ən) *adj.* Of or belonging to a group of protozoans that move and take in food by means of pseudopods. *—n.* A protozoan belonging to this group.

sar•co•ma (sär kō′mə) *n., pl.* **sar•co•mas** also **sar•co•ma•ta** (sär kō′mə tə). A malignant tumor arising from connective tissue.

sar•coph•a•gus (sär kŏf′ə gəs) *n., pl.* **sar•coph•a•gi** (sär kŏf′ə jī′) or **sar•coph•a•gus•es.** A stone coffin, often inscribed or ornamented with sculpture.

sar•dine (sär dēn′) *n.* Any of various small herrings or similar small fishes, often canned for use as food.

Sar•din•i•a (sär dĭn′ē ə). An island of Italy in the Mediterranean Sea south of Corsica. It was settled by Phoenicians, Greeks, and Carthaginians before the sixth century B.C.

sar•don•ic (sär **dŏn′**ĭk) *adj.* Scornfully or cynically mocking; sarcastic. **—sar•don′i•cal•ly** *adv.*

Sar•gas•so Sea (sär **găs′**ō). A part of the northern Atlantic Ocean between the West Indies and the Azores.

sa•ri (**sä′**rē) *n.* An outer garment worn chiefly by women of India and Pakistan, consisting of a length of cloth with one end wrapped about the waist to form a long skirt and the other end draped over the shoulder. [First written down in 1785 in Modern English, from Hindi *sāṛī*, from Sanskrit *śāṭī*.]

sa•rong (sə **rông′** *or* sə **rŏng′**) *n.* A skirt of brightly colored cloth worn wrapped around the waist by men and women in Malaysia, Indonesia, and the Pacific islands.

sar•sa•pa•ril•la (săs′pə **rĭl′**ə *or* särs′pə **rĭl′**ə) *n.* **1.** A soft drink flavored with an extract from the roots of any of several tropical American plants. **2.** A plant that yields this flavoring.

sar•to•ri•al (sär **tôr′**ē əl) *adj.* Of or relating to a tailor, tailoring, or tailored clothing. **—sar•to′ri•al•ly** *adv.*

sash[1] (săsh) *n.* A band or ribbon worn around the waist or over the shoulder as an ornament or symbol of rank. [First written down in 1599 in Modern English and spelled *shash*, from Arabic *šāš*, muslin.]

sash[2] (săsh) *n.* A frame in which the panes of a window or door are set. [First written down in 1681 in Modern English and spelled *shash*, alteration of French *châssis*, frame, chassis.]

sa•shay (să **shā′**) *intr.v.* **sa•shayed, sa•shay•ing, sa•shays.** *Informal.* **1.** To move or walk in an easy or casual manner. **2.** To strut or flounce in a showy manner.

❑ *These sound alike:* **sashay, sachet** (perfumed bag).

sa•shi•mi (sä **shē′**mē) *n.* A Japanese dish consisting of thin slices of fresh raw fish.

Sas•katch•e•wan (să **skăch′**ə wän′). A province of south-central Canada west of Manitoba. It joined the Canadian Confederation in 1905. Regina is the capital and the largest city. Population, 968,313. —SEE NOTE.

sass (săs) *Informal. n.* Impertinent disrespectful speech; back talk. *—tr.v.* **sassed, sass•ing, sass•es.** To talk disrespectfully to.

sas•sa•fras (**săs′**ə frăs′) *n.* **1.** A North American tree having irregularly shaped leaves. Its bark, roots, and leaves have a spicy odor and taste. **2.** The dried root bark of such a tree, used as flavoring and in medicine.

sas•sy (**săs′**ē) *adj.* **sas•si•er, sas•si•est.** Rude and disrespectful; impudent. **—sas′si•ly** *adv.*

sat (săt) *v.* Past tense and past participle of **sit.**

Sat. *abbr.* An abbreviation of Saturday.

Sa•tan (**sāt′**n) *n.* The evil opponent of God; the Devil.

sa•tan•ic (sə **tăn′**ĭk *or* sā **tăn′**ĭk) *adj.* **1.** Relating to the Devil or evil. **2.** Extremely cruel or evil.

satch•el (**săch′**əl) *n.* A small bag, often having a shoulder strap, used for carrying books, clothing, and other small items.

sate (sāt) *tr.v.* **sat•ed, sat•ing, sates. 1.** To satisfy (an appetite) fully. **2.** To satisfy to excess.

sa•teen (să **tēn′**) *n.* A cotton fabric with a satiny finish.

sat•el•lite (**săt′**l īt′) *n.* **1.** A celestial body that travels in an orbit around a planet; a moon. **2.** Any of various objects launched to orbit Earth or another celestial body. **3.** A nation that is dominated politically and economically by another nation. **4.** A subservient follower, especially of a famous person.

sa•ti•ate (**sā′**shē āt′) *tr.v.* **sa•ti•at•ed, sa•ti•at•ing, sa•ti•ates. 1.** To satisfy (an appetite or desire) fully; sate. **2.** To satisfy to excess.

sat•in (**săt′**n) *n.* A smooth fabric, as of silk or rayon, woven with a glossy finish on one side. *—adj.* **1.** Made of or covered with satin. **2.** Glossy and smooth.

sat•in•y (**săt′**n ē) *adj.* Smooth and glossy like satin.

sat•ire (**săt′**īr′) *n.* **1.** A literary work in which human vice and folly are attacked through humor or irony. **2.** The use of humor or irony to attack or expose folly, vice, or stupidity. [First written down in 1509 in Modern English, from Latin *satira*.]

sa•tir•i•cal (sə **tĭr′**ĭ kəl) or **sa•tir•ic** (sə **tĭr′**ĭk) *adj.* Of, relating to, or characterized by satire: *a satirical essay.* **—sa•tir′i•cal•ly** *adv.*

sat•i•rist (**săt′**ər ĭst) *n.* A person who uses satire, especially a writer of satirical works.

sat•i•rize (**săt′**ə rīz′) *tr.v.* **sat•i•rized, sat•i•riz•ing, sat•i•riz•es.** To ridicule or attack by means of satire.

sat•is•fac•tion (săt′ĭs **făk′**shən) *n.* **1.** Fulfillment or gratification of a desire, a need, or an appetite. **2.** Pleasure derived from such fulfillment. **3.** Something that gives fulfillment or gratification: *the satisfactions of life.* **4.** Something given to compensate for a loss or an injury.

sat•is•fac•to•ry (săt′ĭs **făk′**tə rē) *adj.* Sufficient to meet a demand or requirement; adequate: *a satisfactory grade.* **—sat′is•fac′to•ri•ly** *adv.*

sat•is•fy (**săt′**ĭs fī′) *v.* **sat•is•fied, sat•is•fy•ing, sat•is•fies.** *—tr.* **1.** To fulfill or gratify the need, desire, or expectation of: *The actor was satisfied with his performance.* **2.** To fulfill (a need, for example): *satisfy one's hunger.* **3.** To free from doubt or question; convince: *The firefighters were satisfied that the fire was out.* **4.** To fulfill or meet (a standard, for example): *satisfy the requirements to pass the course.* **5.** To compensate for an injury or a loss: *The judgment satisfied the injured parties.* *—intr.* To give satisfaction. [First written down about 1412 in Middle English and spelled *satisfien*, from Latin *satisfacere* : *satis*, sufficient + *facere*, to make.] **—sat′is•fi′er** *n.*

sat•u•rate (**săch′**ə rāt′) *tr.v.* **sat•u•rat•ed, sat•u•rat•ing, sat•u•rates. 1.** To soak, fill, or load to capacity: *Water saturated the cloth.* **2.** To fill thoroughly: *The odor of fish saturated the shop.* **3.** To cause (a solution) to be saturated. **4.** To cause (a compound) to be saturated.

sat•u•rat•ed (**săch′**ə rā′tĭd) *adj.* **1.** Unable to hold or contain more; full. **2.** Having all available valence bonds filled: *a saturated hydrocarbon.* **3.** Soaked with moisture; drenched.

sat•u•ra•tion (săch′ə **rā′**shən) *n.* **1.a.** The act or process of saturating. **b.** The condition of being saturated. **2.** The degree to which a color differs from a gray of the same brightness or lightness. **3.** Containing as much water vapor as is possible at a given temperature; having a relative humidity of 100 percent.

Sat•ur•day (**săt′**ər dē *or* **săt′**ər dā′) *n.* **1.** The seventh day of the week. **2.** The Sabbath for many Jews and some Christians.

Sat•urn (**săt′**ərn) *n.* **1.** In Roman mythology, the god of agriculture. **2.** The sixth planet from the sun at a mean distance of 886 million miles (1.42 billion kilometers) and the second largest in the solar system with a mean diameter of about 74,000 miles (119,000 kilometers). Saturn is encircled by a system of rings that are composed of tiny particles of ice.

sat•ur•na•li•a (săt′ər **nā′**lē ə *or* săt′ər **nāl′**yə) *pl.n.* **Saturnalia. 1.** The ancient Roman seven-day festival of Saturn, which began on December 17. **2.**

sari

Saskatchewan

The name **Saskatchewan** comes from the Cree word *kisiskaaciwan*, meaning "it is a swift current," which referred to the Saskatchewan River. The province was named after the river.

ă	pat	oi	boy
ā	pay	ou	out
âr	care	ŏŏ	took
ä	father	ōō	boot
ĕ	pet	ŭ	cut
ē	be	ûr	urge
ĭ	pit	th	thin
ī	pie	*th*	this
îr	pier	hw	whoop
ŏ	pot	zh	vision
ō	toe	ə	about
ô	paw	N	*French* bon

Word History: **sauce**

Everyone likes **sauce**, especially when it's chocolate over ice cream. Our word came from the Old French word *sauce*, which came from the Latin word *salsa*, which meant "a spicy liquid relish served with food." The Latin word *salsa* in both form and meaning remained unchanged in both Spanish and Italian, and we have adopted the Spanish word. Latin *salsa* came from the word *salsus*, "salty, salted, spiced with salt." There is also a Latin verb *salāre*, "to salt," which has a past participle *salātus*, "salted." This past participle appears in the phrase *herba salāta*, "salted, seasoned herbs," and is the source of our **salad** through the Old French *salade*.

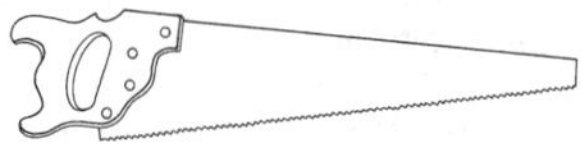

saw[1]

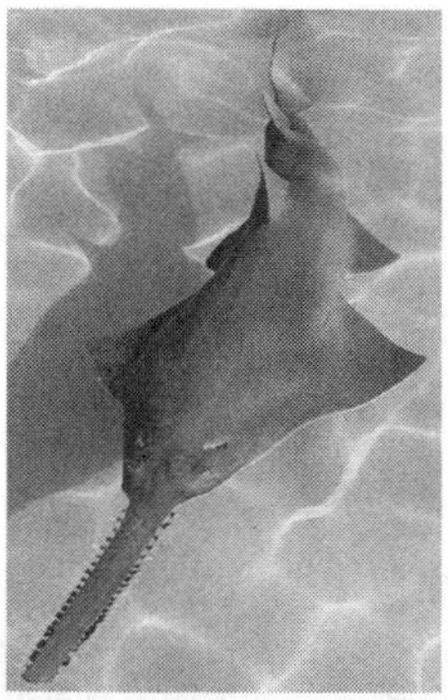

sawfish
Largetooth sawfish

(used with a singular verb). A time of great celebration.

sat•ur•nine (**săt′**ər nīn′) *adj.* **1.** Melancholy or sullen. **2.** Sarcastic or bitter.

sa•tyr (**sā′**tər *or* **săt′**ər) *n.* In Greek mythology, a woodland creature depicted as having the pointed ears, legs, and short horns of a goat. [First written down before 1398 in Middle English and spelled *satire*, from Greek *saturos*.]

sauce (sôs) *n.* **1.** A liquid dressing, seasoning, or topping for food. **2.** Stewed fruit: *cranberry sauce.* **3.** Something that adds zest or flavor. *—tr.v.* **sauced, sauc•ing, sauc•es.** To season or flavor with sauce. —See Note.

sauce•pan (**sôs′**păn′) *n.* A deep cooking pan with a long handle.

sau•cer (**sô′**sər) *n.* A small shallow dish for holding a cup.

sauc•y (**sô′**sē) *adj.* **sauc•i•er, sauc•i•est.** Disrespectful or impertinent, often in an entertaining way. **—sau′ci•ness** *n.*

Sa•u•di A•ra•bi•a (sou**′**dē ə **rā′**bē ə *or* **sô′**dē ə **rā′**bē ə). A country occupying most of the Arabian Peninsula in southwest Asia. Oil was discovered here in 1936. Riyadh is the capital and the largest city. Population, 9,320,000.

sau•er•kraut (**sour′**krout′) *n.* Shredded cabbage, salted and fermented in its own juice.

Sauk (sôk) *n., pl.* **Sauk** or **Sauks. 1.** A member of a Native American people of the upper Midwest, now living mainly in Oklahoma. **2.** The Algonquian language of the Sauk.

Saul (sôl). Flourished 11th century B.C. The first king of Israel, who defended Israel against numerous enemies.

sau•na (**sô′**nə *or* **sou′**nə) *n.* **1.** A steam bath in which the steam is produced by pouring water over heated rocks. **2.** A room for taking a sauna.

saun•ter (**sôn′**tər) *intr.v.* **saun•tered, saun•ter•ing, saun•ters.** To walk at a leisurely pace; stroll: *sauntered across the garden.* *—n.* **1.** A leisurely walk. **2.** A leisurely way of walking.

sau•ri•an (**sôr′**ē ən) *n.* Any of various members of the group of reptiles that includes lizards. *—adj.* Of, belonging to, or typical of the lizards.

sau•sage (**sô′**sĭj) *n.* Chopped and seasoned meat, usually stuffed into a prepared animal intestine or other casing and cooked or cured.

sau•té (sō **tā′** *or* sô **tā′**) *tr.v.* **sau•téed, sau•té•ing, sau•tés.** To fry lightly in fat in a shallow open pan. *—n.* Sautéed food.

sav•age (**săv′**ĭj) *adj.* **1.** Untouched by civilization; not cultivated; wild: *savage lands.* **2.** Not civilized; barbaric: *a savage people.* **3.** Ferocious; vicious or fierce: *a savage attack.* *—n.* **1.** A person regarded as primitive or uncivilized. **2.** A person regarded as fierce or vicious. **3.** A rude person. **—sav′age•ly** *adv.* **—sav′age•ness** *n.*

sav•age•ry (**săv′**ĭj rē) *n., pl.* **sav•age•ries. 1.** The quality or condition of being savage. **2.** Savage action or behavior.

sa•van•na also **sa•van•nah** (sə **văn′**ə) *n.* A flat treeless grassland of warm regions.

Sa•van•nah (sə **văn′**ə). A city of southeast Georgia near the mouth of the **Savannah River.** It was founded in 1733. Population, 137,560.

save[1] (sāv) *v.* **saved, sav•ing, saves.** *—tr.* **1.** To rescue from harm, danger, or loss. **2.** To treat with care to avoid damage or wear; safeguard: *save one's eyesight.* **3.** To prevent the loss or waste of; conserve: *save money at a sale; save energy.* **4.** To make unnecessary; avoid: *saved him a trip to the store.* **5.** To keep for future use; store: *save five dollars a week.* **6.** To set free from sin; redeem. **7.** To copy (a file) from a computer's main memory to a disk or other storage device for later use. *—intr.* **1.** To avoid waste or expense; conserve. **2.** To accumulate money: *saving for a vacation.* *—n.* **1.** In sports, an act of preventing an opponent from scoring a goal. **2.** In baseball, the act of keeping a game from being lost by pitching in relief for the winning pitcher. [First written down before 1200 in Middle English and spelled *sauven*, from Late Latin *salvāre*, from Latin *salvus*, safe.] **—sav′er** *n.*

save[2] (sāv) *prep.* Except; but: *All trains arrived on time save one.* *—conj.* Were it not; except. [First written down about 1300 in Middle English, from Latin *salvō*, from *salvus*, safe.]

sav•ing (**sā′**vĭng) *n.* **1.** Rescue from harm, danger, or loss. **2.** Avoidance of waste or expense: *the saving of energy.* **3. savings.** Money saved: *a bank account for savings.* *—prep.* With the exception of: *All books were ordered, saving this one.* *—conj.* Except; save.

sav•ings account (**sā′**vĭngz) *n.* An account that draws interest at a bank.

savings bank *n.* A bank that receives, invests, and pays interest on the savings of depositors.

savings bond *n.* A registered bond issued by the U.S. Government in denominations of $50 to $10,000.

sav•ior (**săv′**yər) *n.* **1.** A person who saves or delivers another from danger, destruction, or loss. **2. Savior.** Jesus.

sa•vor (**sā′**vər) *n.* **1.** The taste or smell of something. **2.** A specific taste or smell. **3.** A distinctive quality or sensation. *—tr.v.* **sa•vored, sa•vor•ing, sa•vors.** To taste or enjoy heartily; relish.

sa•vor•y[1] (**sā′**və rē) *adj.* **1.** Appetizing to the taste or smell: *a savory plate of lasagna.* **2.** Morally respectable; inoffensive. [First written down about 1200 in Middle English and spelled *savure*, from Latin *sapor*, taste.]

sa•vor•y[2] (**sā′**və rē) *n.* A plant related to mint, having spicy-smelling leaves used as seasoning in cooking. [First written down in 1373 in Middle English, from Latin *saturēia*.]

sav•vy (**săv′**ē) *Informal. adj.* **sav•vi•er, sav•vi•est.** Well informed; shrewd. *—n.* Practical understanding; common sense. *—tr. & intr.v.* **sav•vied** (**săv′**ēd), **sav•vy•ing, sav•vies** (**săv′**ēz). To know or understand.

saw[1] (sô) *n.* Any of various hand-operated or power-driven tools having a thin metal blade or disk with a sharp-toothed edge, used for cutting wood, metal, or other hard materials. *—v.* **sawed, sawed** or **sawn** (sôn), **saw•ing, saws.** *—tr.* **1.** To cut or divide with a saw: *saw off a branch.* **2.** To produce or shape with a saw: *sawing curves in wood.* *—intr.* **1.** To use a saw. **2.** To be capable of being cut with a saw: *Pinewood saws easily.* [First written down about 1000 in Old English and spelled *sagu*.]

saw[2] (sô) *n.* A traditional familiar saying. [First written down before 1000 in Old English and spelled *sagu*.]

saw[3] (sô) *v.* Past tense of **see**[1].

saw•buck (**sô′**bŭk′) *n.* A sawhorse, especially one having a crossed pair of legs at each end.

saw•dust (**sô′**dŭst′) *n.* The small particles of wood or other material that fall from an object being sawed.

sawed-off (**sôd′ôf′** *or* **sôd′ŏf′**) *adj.* Having one end sawed off: *a sawed-off shotgun.*

saw•fish (**sô′**fĭsh′) *n.* Any of various large saltwater fishes related to the rays and skates, having a long snout with teeth along both sides.

saw•horse (**sô′**hôrs′) *n.* A frame with legs, used to support a piece of wood being sawed.

saw•mill (sô′mĭl′) *n.* A place where lumber is sawed into boards.
sawn (sôn) *v.* A past participle of **saw[1]**.
saw•yer (sô′yər) *n.* A person whose work is sawing wood.
sax (săks) *n.* A saxophone.
sax•i•frage (săk′sə frĭj *or* săk′sə frāj′) *n.* Any of numerous plants having small, loosely clustered white, yellow, or reddish flowers.
Sax•on (săk′sən) *n.* **1.** A member of a Germanic people that invaded Britain in the fifth and sixth centuries A.D. and together with the Angles and Jutes formed the Anglo-Saxon peoples. **2.** The West Germanic language of the ancient Saxon peoples.
sax•o•phone (săk′sə fōn′) *n.* A wind instrument having a single-reed mouthpiece, a curved conical body made of metal, and keys operated by the player's fingers. [First written down in 1851 in Modern English, after *Sax*, name of 19th-century Belgian instrument-making family.] **—sax′o•phon′ist** *n.*
say (sā) *v.* **said** (sĕd), **say•ing, says** (sĕz). *—tr.* **1.** To utter aloud; speak: *The children said, 'Good morning.'* **2.** To express in words; state: *The book says that the treaty was signed in 1945.* **3.** To give expression to; show or indicate: *The clock says half past two.* **4.** To repeat or recite: *saying poetry aloud.* **5.** To suppose; assume: *Let's say that you're right.* *—intr.* To make a statement; express oneself: *The story is true, or so they said.* *—n.* **1.** A turn or chance to speak: *Let each one have his or her say.* **2.** The power to influence a decision: *We haven't any say in the matter.* *—adv.* **1.** Approximately: *Let's walk, say, five miles.* **2.** For example: *a tree, say a pine.* *—interj.* An expression used to attract attention or express wonder: *Say, that's some car.* **—*idiom.* that is to say.** In other words. [First written down about 725 in Old English and spelled *secgan.*] **—say′er** *n.*
say•ing (sā′ĭng) *n.* Something that is frequently said; a proverb.
say-so (sā′sō′) *n., pl.* **say-sos.** *Informal.* **1.** An unsupported statement or assurance: *I won't be convicted on your say-so alone.* **2.** An authoritative expression of permission or approval.
Sb The symbol for the element **antimony.**
Sc The symbol for the element **scandium.**
SC or **S.C.** *abbr.* An abbreviation of South Carolina.
scab (skăb) *n.* **1.** The crust discharged from and covering a healing wound. **2.a.** A worker who refuses to join a labor union. **b.** A worker who takes a striker's job. **c.** An employee who works while others are on strike. *—intr.v.* **scabbed, scab•bing, scabs. 1.** To become covered with scabs or a scab. **2.** To work as a scab.
scab•bard (skăb′ərd) *n.* A sheath for the blade of a sword, dagger, or similar weapon.
sca•bies (skā′bēz) *n.* A contagious disease caused by small mites that burrow into the skin and cause severe itching.
scad (skăd) *n. Informal.* A large number or amount. Often used in the plural: *scads of people.*
scaf•fold (skăf′əld *or* skăf′ōld′) *n.* **1.** A temporary platform on which workers sit or stand when performing tasks at heights above the ground. **2.** A platform for the execution of condemned prisoners. **3.** A raised wooden framework or platform.
scaf•fold•ing (skăf′əl dĭng *or* skăf′ōl′dĭng) *n.* **1.** A scaffold or system of scaffolds. **2.** The materials from which a scaffold is made.
scal•a•wag (skăl′ə wăg′) also **scal•ly•wag** (skăl′ē wăg′) *n.* **1.** *Informal.* A shameless person; a rascal. **2.** A white Southerner who supported the federal government during Reconstruction.
scald (skôld) *tr.v.* **scald•ed, scald•ing, scalds. 1.** To burn with or as if with hot liquid or steam. **2.** To treat with or subject to boiling water: *scalded and peeled the peaches.* **3.** To heat (a liquid) almost to the boiling point: *scald milk.* *—n.* Injury or damage caused by scalding. [First written down before 1200 in Middle English and spelled *scalden*, from Late Latin *excaldāre*, to wash in hot water.]
scale[1] (skāl) *n.* **1.a.** One of the small thin plates forming the outer covering of fishes, reptiles, and certain other animals. **b.** A similar part, such as one of the minute structures overlapping to form the covering on the wings of butterflies and moths. **2.** A dry thin flake or crust, as of paint, rust, or dandruff. **3.** A small thin piece. **4.a.** A scale insect. **b.** A plant disease caused by scale insects. *—v.* **scaled, scal•ing, scales.** *—tr.* **1.** To clear or strip of scale or scales: *scale and clean the fish.* **2.** To remove in layers: *scaled off the old paint.* *—intr.* To fall or come off in scales or layers; flake. [First written down about 1300 in Middle English, from Old French *escale*, of Germanic origin.]
scale[2] (skāl) *n.* **1.a.** A system of ordered marks placed at fixed distances, used for measuring. **b.** An instrument having such a system of marks. **2.a.** The proportion used to determine the relationship between the actual dimensions of something and the dimensions to which it is reduced or expanded when represented on a model, map, or drawing: *a scale of 1 inch to 50 miles.* **b.** A line with marks showing the actual dimensions of something represented on a map, plan, or drawing. **3.a.** A progressive classification, as of size, amount, importance, or rank: *a scale of wages.* **b.** The relative size or extent of something: *on a large political scale.* **4.** An ascending or descending series of musical tones that includes all tones that are used in some key, mode, or system of tones and that lie between two limits. *—v.* **scaled, scal•ing, scales.** *—tr.* **1.** To climb up or over: *scale a mountain.* **2.** To draw or arrange in a particular proportion or scale. **3.** To adjust or regulate according to some standard: *scaling back business to curtail spending.* *—intr.* To climb; ascend. [First written down in 1391 in Middle English and spelled *skale*, from Latin *scālae*, ladder.]
scale[3] (skāl) *n.* **1.** An instrument or a machine for weighing. Often used in the plural. **2.** Either of the pans or dishes of a balance. *—v.* **scaled, scal•ing, scales.** *—tr.* To weigh with scales. *—intr.* To have a given weight. [First written down before 1200 in Middle English and spelled *scale*, bowl, balance, from Old Norse *skāl.*]
scale insect *n.* Any of various small insects that feed on plant juices and the females of which secrete and remain under waxy scales on plant tissue.
sca•lene (skā′lēn′ *or* skā lēn′) *adj.* Having three unequal sides: *scalene triangles.*
scal•lion (skăl′yən) *n.* A young onion having a small white bulb and long narrow green leaves.
scal•lop (skŏl′əp *or* skăl′əp) also **scol•lop** (skŏl′əp) *n.* **1.a.** Any of various soft-bodied sea animals having a double, hinged, fan-shaped shell with radiating fluted markings. **b.** The fleshy muscle of such an animal, used as food. **2.** A thin boneless slice of meat. **3.** One of a series of curves shaped like a scallop shell, forming a decorative border. *—tr.v.* **scal•loped, scal•lop•ing, scal•lops. 1.** To bake in a casserole with milk or a sauce and often with bread crumbs: *scallop potatoes.* **2.** To form scallops along the edge of (cloth, for example).
scal•ly•wag (skăl′ē wăg′) *n.* Variant of **scalawag.**
scalp (skălp) *n.* The skin that covers the top of the human head. *—tr.v.* **scalped, scalp•ing, scalps. 1.** To cut or tear the scalp from. **2.** *Slang.* To sell (tickets, for example) at a price higher than their established value. [First written down about 1340 in

sawhorse

saxophone

ă	pat	oi	boy
ā	pay	ou	out
âr	care	ŏŏ	took
ä	father	ōō	boot
ĕ	pet	ŭ	cut
ē	be	ûr	urge
ĭ	pit	th	thin
ī	pie	*th*	this
îr	pier	hw	whoop
ŏ	pot	zh	vision
ō	toe	ə	about
ô	paw	N	*French* bon

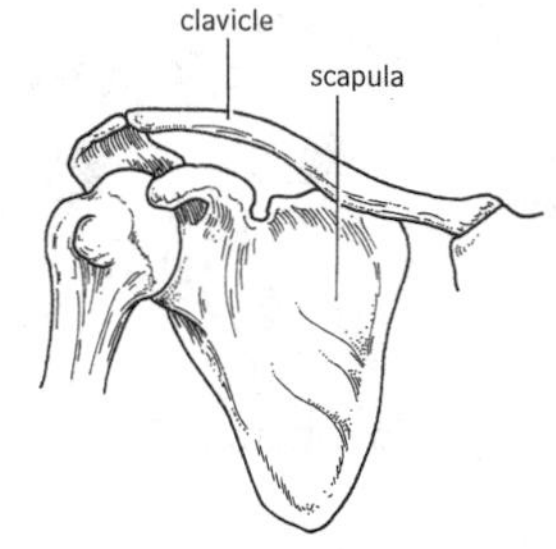

scapula

Usage: scarcely

When you follow the word **scarcely** with a clause, introduce the clause with *when* or *before* but not with *than*: *The meeting had scarcely begun when* (or *before*, but not *than*) *it was interrupted.*

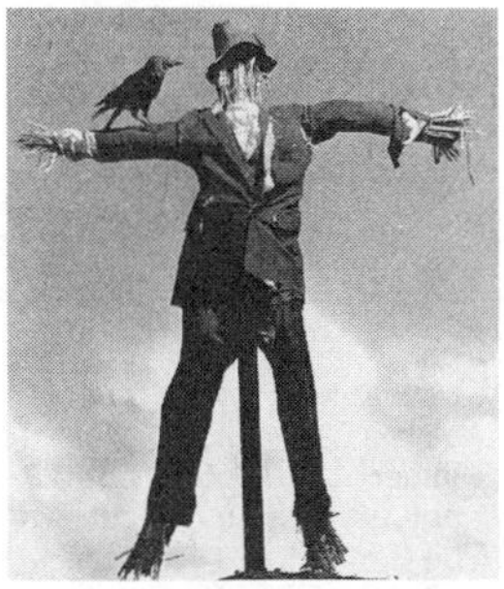
scarecrow

Middle English and spelled *skalp*, top of the head, of Scandinavian origin.]

scal•pel (skăl′pəl) *n.* A small straight knife with a thin pointed blade, used in surgery. [First written down in 1742 in Modern English, from Latin *scalpellum*, from *scalpere*, to scratch, cut.]

scal•y (skā′lē) *adj.* **scal•i•er, scal•i•est. 1.** Covered with scales: *scaly claws.* **2.** Shedding scales: *dry scaly skin.* **—scal′i•ness** *n.*

scaly anteater *n.* The pangolin.

scam (skăm) *n. Slang.* A fraudulent business scheme; a swindle.

scamp (skămp) *n.* **1.** A dishonest or scheming person; a rascal. **2.** A playful mischievous person.

scam•per (skăm′pər) *intr.v.* **scam•pered, scam•per•ing, scam•pers.** To run or go quickly or lightly: *The puppy scampered across the lawn.*

scan (skăn) *v.* **scanned, scan•ning, scans.** *—tr.* **1.** To examine (something) closely: *scan the report card.* **2.** To look (something) over quickly and systematically: *scan the ocean for signs of land.* **3.** To search electronically, as with a radar beam: *scan the skies for incoming aircraft.* **4.** To analyze (verse) to show metrical patterns. **5.** To read (data) for use in a computer. Used especially of an optical scanner. *—intr.* **1.** To undergo electronic scanning. **2.** To analyze verse to show metrical patterns. *—n.* The act or an instance of scanning.

scan•dal (skăn′dl) *n.* **1.** Something that offends the morality of the social community; a public disgrace. **2.** Malicious gossip. [First written down in 1581 in Modern English, from Greek *skandalon*, trap, stumbling block.]

scan•dal•ize (skăn′dl īz′) *tr.v.* **scan•dal•ized, scan•dal•iz•ing, scan•dal•iz•es.** To shock or offend the moral sensibilities of.

scan•dal•ous (skăn′dl əs) *adj.* **1.** Causing scandal; shocking: *scandalous behavior.* **2.** Containing material damaging to reputation; defamatory: *scandalous gossip.* **—scan′dal•ous•ly** *adv.* **—scan′dal•ous•ness** *n.*

Scan•di•na•vi•a (skăn′də nā′vē ə). A region of northern Europe traditionally consisting of Norway, Sweden, and Denmark.

Scan•di•na•vi•an (skăn′də nā′vē ən) *adj.* Of or relating to Scandinavia, its peoples, languages, or cultures. *—n.* **1.** A native or inhabitant of Scandinavia. **2.** North Germanic.

scan•di•um (skăn′dē əm) *n. Symbol* **Sc** A silvery, very lightweight metallic element that is a byproduct in the processing of certain uranium ores. Atomic number 21. See table at **element.**

scan•ner (skăn′ər) *n.* **1.** A person or thing that scans. **2.** An optical scanner. **3.** A radio receiver that continuously searches frequencies and plays aloud any signal it receives.

scan•sion (skăn′shən) *n.* Analysis of verse to show metrical patterns.

scant (skănt) *adj.* **scant•er, scant•est. 1.** Barely sufficient; meager; inadequate: *scant vegetation.* **2.** Falling short of an amount or measure: *a scant six miles away.* *—tr.v.* **scant•ed, scant•ing, scants. 1.** To give an inadequate amount to; skimp on. **2.** To neglect; treat inadequately. **—scant′ly** *adv.* **—scant′ness** *n.*

scant•y (skăn′tē) *adj.* **scant•i•er, scant•i•est. 1.** Barely sufficient; meager: *a scanty water supply.* **2.** Insufficient, as in degree or extent: *a scanty garment.* **—scant′i•ly** *adv.* **—scant′i•ness** *n.*

scape (skāp) *n.* A scene; a view: *cityscape; landscape.*

scape•goat (skāp′gōt′) *n.* A person, group, or thing that unjustly bears the blame of others.

scap•u•la (skăp′yə lə) *n., pl.* **scap•u•las** or **scap•u•lae** (skăp′yə lē′). Either of two flat triangular bones behind the shoulders; a shoulder blade.

scar (skär) *n.* **1.** A mark left on the skin after a wound or an injury has healed. **2.** A mark, as on a plant stem, where a leaf, bud, or other part was once attached. **3.** A mark or sign of damage, either physical or emotional. *—v.* **scarred, scar•ring, scars.** *—tr.* To mark with a scar. *—intr.* To form a scar. [First written down about 1395 in Middle English, from Greek *eskhara*, hearth, scab caused by burning.]

scar•ab (skăr′əb) *n.* **1.** Any of several often large broad-bodied beetles, especially one of a kind regarded as sacred by the ancient Egyptians. **2.** An ornament, sculpture, or cut gem made to look like this beetle, used in ancient Egypt as a symbol of the soul.

scarce (skârs) *adj.* **scarc•er, scarc•est. 1.** Insufficient to meet a demand or requirement: *The pioneers' food and water were beginning to grow scarce.* **2.** Hard to find; rare: *Nickels bearing a buffalo are scarce these days.* *—adv.* Scarcely; hardly. ***—idiom.*** **make (oneself) scarce.** *Informal.* To stay away; be absent. **—scarce′ness** *n.*

scarce•ly (skârs′lē) *adv.* **1.** By a small margin; barely: *We scarcely made it on time.* **2.** Almost not; hardly: *I could scarcely see through the fog.* **3.** Certainly not: *They could scarcely complain after such good service.* —See Note.

scar•ci•ty (skâr′sĭ tē) *n., pl.* **scar•ci•ties.** An insufficient amount or supply; a shortage.

scare (skâr) *v.* **scared, scar•ing, scares.** *—tr.* To frighten or alarm; terrify: *The dog scared the cat.* See Synonyms at **frighten.** *—intr.* To become frightened: *I don't scare easily.* *—n.* A condition, sensation, or state of fear or panic. [First written down about 1200 in Middle English and spelled *skerren*, from Old Norse *skirra*, from *skjarr*, timid.]

scare•crow (skâr′krō′) *n.* **1.** A crude figure of a person set up in a field to scare birds away from crops. **2.** A thin ragged person.

scarf (skärf) *n., pl.* **scarfs** (skärfs) or **scarves** (skärvz). **1.** A rectangular or triangular piece of cloth worn around the neck, head, or shoulders. **2.** A decorative piece of cloth used to cover the top of a piece of furniture, such as a desk or table.

scar•let (skär′lĭt) *n.* A bright red to reddish orange.

scarlet fever *n.* A severe contagious bacterial disease that occurs mainly in children and is characterized by a high fever and a scarlet rash on the skin.

scarlet tanager *n.* A New World songbird, of which the male has bright scarlet plumage with a black tail and wings.

scarves (skärvz) *n.* A plural of **scarf.**

scar•y (skâr′ē) *adj.* **scar•i•er, scar•i•est. 1.** Causing fright or alarm. **2.** Easily frightened; timid. **—scar′i•ly** *adv.*

scat (skăt) *intr.v.* **scat•ted, scat•ting, scats.** *Informal.* To go away hastily; leave at once: *I told the cat to scat.*

scathe (skā*th*) *tr.v.* **scathed, scath•ing, scathes. 1.** To harm or injure severely, especially by fire. **2.** To criticize harshly.

scath•ing (skā′*th*ĭng) *adj.* **1.** Extremely severe; harshly critical: *a scathing verbal attack.* **2.** Harmful or painful. **—scath′ing•ly** *adv.*

scat•ter (skăt′ər) *v.* **scat•tered, scat•ter•ing, scat•ters.** *—tr.* **1.** To cause to separate and go in various directions: *The wind scatters dandelion seeds.* **2.** To distribute loosely by or as if by sprinkling; strew: *scattering confetti during the parade.* **3.** To deflect a stream of (radiation or particles) so that they rebound in different directions. *—intr.* To separate and go in different directions; disperse.

scat•ter•brain (skăt′ər brān′) *n.* A person regarded as flighty, thoughtless, or disorganized. **—scat′ter•brained′** *adj.*

scat•ter•ing (skăt′ər ĭng) *n.* **1.** Something scattered, especially a small or irregular quantity or amount: *a scattering of applause.* **2.** The spreading of a beam of particles or rays over a range of directions as a result of collisions or other physical interactions.

scatter rug *n.* A small rug used to cover part of a floor.

scav•enge (skăv′ənj) *v.* **scav•enged, scav•eng•ing, scav•eng•es.** *—tr.* **1.** To search through for salvageable material: *The cat scavenged the garbage cans for food.* **2.** To collect (something useful or edible) by searching. *—intr.* To search through refuse for useful material.

scav•en•ger (skăv′ən jər) *n.* **1.** An animal, such as a vulture or hyena, that feeds on dead or decaying plant or animal matter. **2.** A person who searches through rubbish or discarded material for food.

sce•nar•i•o (sĭ nâr′ē ō′ *or* sĭ när′ē ō′) *n., pl.* **sce•nar•i•os. 1.** An outline of the plot of a story or play. **2.** The text of a movie; a screenplay. **3.** An outline of an expected or supposed series of events: *In the worst scenario, our plan will still work.*

sce•nar•ist (sĭ nâr′ĭst *or* sĭ när′ĭst) *n.* A writer of screenplays.

scene (sēn) *n.* **1.** A place or an area seen by a viewer; a view from a particular point: *the scene from my window.* **2.** The place where an action or event occurs: *the scene of the crime.* **3.** The place in which the action of a play, movie, novel, or other narrative occurs; a setting. **4.** A part of a movie or play in which the setting is fixed and the action forms a connected unit: *The family reunion scene was the best part of the play.* **5.** A display of temper or behavior that attracts attention in public. ***—idiom.*** **behind the scenes.** In private. [First written down in 1540 in Modern English, from Greek *skēnē*, tent, stage.]

❑ *These sound alike:* **scene, seen** (perceived with the eye).

scen•er•y (sē′nə rē) *n., pl.* **scen•er•ies. 1.** A view or views of natural features, especially in open country: *varied mountain scenery.* **2.** The painted backdrops and other structures used to create the setting for a theatrical production.

sce•nic (sē′nĭk) *adj.* **1.** Having or offering natural scenery, especially attractive landscapes: *a scenic route.* **2.** Of or relating to the stage or theatrical scenery: *scenic design.*

scent (sĕnt) *n.* **1.** A distinctive, often pleasing odor: *the scent of pine.* **2.** A perfume. **3.** The trail of a hunted animal or fugitive: *The dogs lost the deer's scent.* **4.** The sense of smell: *hunting by scent.* **5.** A hint of something; a suggestion: *a scent of excitement with the approach of summer.* *—tr.v.* **scent•ed, scent•ing, scents. 1.** To perceive, identify, or detect by or as if by smelling: *scent danger.* **2.** To provide with an odor; perfume. [First written down in 1375 in Middle English and spelled *sent*, from Latin *sentīre*, to sense.]

❑ *These sound alike:* **scent, cent** (penny), **sent** (transmitted).

Synonyms: scent, aroma, smell, odor. These nouns mean a quality that can be detected by sense organs in the nose. *The scent of pine needles filled the cabin. The aroma of frying onions always makes me hungry. We were alarmed by the smell of gas in the hall. The freshly painted room had a peculiar odor.*

scep•ter (sĕp′tər) *n.* **1.** A staff held by a sovereign as a sign of authority. **2.** Ruling power or authority.

scep•tic (skĕp′tĭk) *n.* Variant of **skeptic.**

scep•ti•cal (skĕp′tĭ kəl) *adj.* Variant of **skeptical.**

scep•ti•cism (skĕp′tĭ sĭz′əm) *n.* Variant of **skepticism.**

sched•ule (skĕj′o͞ol *or* skĕj′o͞o əl *or* skĕj′əl) *n.* **1.** A program of forthcoming events or appointments. **2.** A student's program of classes. **3.** A timetable of departures and arrivals: *a bus schedule.* **4.** A plan for performing work or achieving an objective: *a schedule for success.* **5.** A printed or often written list of items in the form of a table or chart. *—tr.v.* **sched•uled, sched•ul•ing, sched•ules. 1.** To place on a schedule. **2.** To make up a schedule for. **3.** To plan or appoint for a certain time or date: *schedule the trip for next week.*

sche•mat•ic (skē măt′ĭk *or* skĭ măt′ĭk) *adj.* Of, relating to, or in the form of a scheme or diagram. **—sche•mat′i•cal•ly** *adv.*

sche•ma•tize (skē′mə tīz′) *tr.v.* **sche•ma•tized, sche•ma•tiz•ing, sche•ma•tiz•es.** To express or reduce to a scheme.

scheme (skēm) *n.* **1.** A plan of action. **2.** An underhanded or secret plan; a plot. **3.** A chart, a diagram, or an outline of a plan or an object. **4.** An orderly combination or arrangement: *a color scheme.* *—v.* **schemed, schem•ing, schemes.** *—tr.* **1.** To make up a plan or scheme for. **2.** To plot: *scheming their escape.* *—intr.* To make plans, especially secret and devious ones. [First written down in 1553 in Modern English, from Greek *skhēma*, figure, plan.] **—schem′er** *n.*

scher•zo (skĕr′tsō) *n., pl.* **scher•zos** or **scher•zi** (skĕr′tsē). A lively musical movement, commonly in 3/4 time. [First written down in 1852 in Modern English, from Italian *scherzo*, joke.]

schil•ling (shĭl′ĭng) *n.* The basic monetary unit of Austria.

schism (sĭz′əm *or* skĭz′əm) *n.* **1.** A separation or division into opposing groups. **2.** A formal separation of groups within the Christian church.

schis•mat•ic (sĭz măt′ĭk *or* skĭz măt′ĭk) *adj.* Of, relating to, or engaging in a schism. *—n.* A person who encourages or engages in a schism. **—schis•mat′i•cal•ly** *adv.*

schist (shĭst) *n.* A medium-grained metamorphic rock usually composed mostly of mica or similar mineral flakes, that splits easily.

schiz•o•phre•ni•a (skĭt′sə frē′nē ə *or* skĭt′sə frĕn′ē ə) *n.* Any of a group of severe mental disorders in which a person loses touch with reality and withdraws from others, often with disturbances of behavior and the ability to reason. [First written down in 1912 in Modern English : Greek *skhizein*, to split + Greek *phrēn*, mind.]

schiz•o•phren•ic (skĭt′sə frĕn′ĭk) *adj.* Of or affected with schizophrenia. *—n.* A schizophrenic person.

schnau•zer (shnou′zər) *n.* Any of three breeds of dog originally from Germany and having a wiry grayish coat and a blunt muzzle.

schnauzer
Miniature schnauzer

schol•ar (skŏl′ər) *n.* **1.a.** A learned person. **b.** An expert in a particular field: *a scholar of Russian history.* **2.** A pupil or student. **3.** A student who has received a particular scholarship. [First written down about 1000 in Old English and spelled *scolere*, from Latin *schola*, school.]

schol•ar•ly (skŏl′ər lē) *adj.* Of, relating to, or characteristic of scholars or scholarship: *scholarly research.*

schol•ar•ship (skŏl′ər shĭp′) *n.* **1.** The methods, disciplines, and learning of a scholar. **2.** Knowledge resulting from extensive research in a particular field. **3.** A grant of financial aid awarded to a student, as for attending college.

scho•las•tic (skə lăs′tĭk) *adj.* **1.** Of or relating to schools or education; academic: *scholastic standards; scholastic achievement.* **2.** Adhering rigidly

ă	pat	oi	boy
ā	pay	ou	out
âr	care	o͝o	took
ä	father	o͞o	boot
ĕ	pet	ŭ	cut
ē	be	ûr	urge
ĭ	pit	th	thin
ī	pie	*th*	this
îr	pier	hw	whoop
ŏ	pot	zh	vision
ō	toe	ə	about
ô	paw	N	*French* bon

schooner
The *Adventure*

Franz Schubert

Albert Schweitzer

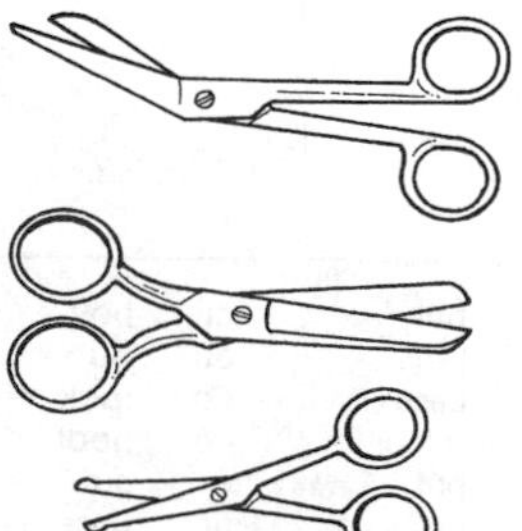

scissors
Top: Bandage scissors
Center: Safety-point scissors
Bottom: Nose and mustache scissors

to scholarly methods; pedantic. **—scho•las′ti•cal•ly** *adv.*

school[1] (sko͞ol) *n.* **1.** An institution for teaching and learning. **2.** A division of an educational institution, especially one for special study within a university: *a law school.* **3.** The student body of an educational institution. **4.** The building or group of buildings housing an educational institution. **5.** The instruction given at a school: *School ends early today.* **6.** The process of being educated formally: *What are your plans when you finish school?* **7.** A group of people, especially artists or writers, whose thought, work, or style shows common influences or underlying beliefs. *—tr.v.* **schooled, school•ing, schools.** To instruct or train in or as if in a school. See Synonyms at **teach.** [First written down before 899 in Old English and spelled *scōl*, from Latin *schola*, from Greek *skholē*.]

school[2] (sko͞ol) *n.* A large group of fish or other water animals that swim together. *—intr.v.* **schooled, school•ing, schools.** To form or swim in such a group. [First written down in 1386 in Middle English and spelled *scoue*, from Middle Dutch *schole*.]

school board *n.* A local board that oversees public schools.

school•book (**sko͞ol′**bo͝ok′) *n.* A textbook or other book for use in school.

school•boy (**sko͞ol′**boi′) *n.* A boy attending school.

school bus *n.* A vehicle that is used for taking schoolchildren to and from school or school-related activities.

school•child also **school child** (**sko͞ol′**chīld′) *n.* A child attending school.

school•girl (**sko͞ol′**gûrl′) *n.* A girl attending school.

school•house (**sko͞ol′**hous′) *n.* A building used as a school.

school•ing (**sko͞o′**lĭng) *n.* **1.** Instruction or training given at school; formal education. **2.** Education obtained through experience or exposure: *Living on a farm has given her valuable schooling.*

school•marm (**sko͞ol′**märm′) *n.* A woman teacher, especially one who is regarded as strict or old-fashioned.

school•mas•ter (**sko͞ol′**măs′tər) *n.* **1.** A man who is a teacher. **2.** A headmaster of a school.

school•mate (**sko͞ol′**māt′) *n.* A companion in one's school.

school•mis•tress (**sko͞ol′**mĭs′trĭs) *n.* **1.** A woman who is a teacher. **2.** A headmistress of a school.

school•room (**sko͞ol′**ro͞om′ *or* **sko͞ol′**ro͝om′) *n.* A classroom.

school•teach•er (**sko͞ol′**tē′chər) *n.* A person who teaches school below the college level.

school•work (**sko͞ol′**wûrk′) *n.* Lessons done at school or to be done at home.

school•yard (**sko͞ol′**yärd′) *n.* An open area next to a school building for play and outdoor activities.

school year *n.* The part of the year during which school is in session, typically from September to June.

schoo•ner (**sko͞o′**nər) *n.* **1.** A fore-and-aft rigged sailing vessel with two or more masts. **2.** A beer glass holding a pint or more.

schot•tische (**shŏt′**ĭsh *or* shŏ **tēsh′**) *n.* **1.** A round dance in 2/4 time. **2.** Music for the schottische.

Schu•bert (**sho͞o′**bərt *or* **sho͞o′**bĕrt′), **Franz Peter.** 1797–1828. Austrian composer of more than 600 vocal and instrumental works.

Schu•mann (**sho͞o′**män′ *or* **sho͞o′**mən), **Robert.** 1810–1856. German composer whose works include symphonies and piano compositions.

schwa (shwä) *n.* A symbol (ə) used to represent certain vowel sounds that in English often occur in unstressed syllables; for example, the sounds of *a* in *alone* and *e* in *linen* are represented by a schwa.

Schweit•zer (**shwīt′**sər *or* **shvīt′**sər), **Albert.** 1875–1965. French philosopher and physician who founded (1913) a missionary hospital in present-day Gabon. He won the 1952 Nobel Peace Prize.

sci. *abbr.* An abbreviation of: **1.** Science. **2.** Scientific.

sci•at•ic (sī **ăt′**ĭk) *adj.* **1.** Of or relating to the ischium. **2.** Of or relating to sciatica.

sci•at•i•ca (sī **ăt′**ĭ kə) *n.* Pain along the sciatic nerve.

sciatic nerve *n.* A sensory and motor nerve that runs through the pelvis and upper leg.

sci•ence (**sī′**əns) *n.* **1.a.** The observation, study, and theoretical explanation of natural phenomena. **b.** Such activities applied to a particular class of phenomena: *the science of living things.* **2.** An activity that requires study and method: *the science of marketing.* **3.** Knowledge, especially knowledge gained through experience. **4.** Systematic activity, discipline, or study: *I've got delivering papers down to a science.* [First written down about 1340 in Middle English and spelled *science*, knowledge, learning, from Latin *scientia*, from *scīre*, to know.]

science fiction *n.* Fiction in which real and imaginary scientific discoveries, such as life on other planets, form part of the plot or background.

sci•en•tif•ic (sī′ən **tĭf′**ĭk) *adj.* Of, relating to, or used in science or a science: *scientific experiments.* **—sci′en•tif′i•cal•ly** *adv.*

scientific method *n.* A method of investigation that typically involves careful observation of phenomena, the formulation of a hypothesis, experimentation to test the hypothesis, and a conclusion that confirms or modifies the hypothesis.

scientific notation *n.* A method of expressing numbers in terms of a decimal number between 1 and 10 multiplied by a power of 10. The scientific notation of 10,492, for example, is 1.0492×10^4.

sci•en•tist (**sī′**ən tĭst) *n.* A person who is an expert in one or more sciences, as a physicist.

scim•i•tar (**sĭm′**ĭ tər *or* **sĭm′**ĭ tär′) *n.* A curved single-edged Asian sword.

scin•til•la (sĭn **tĭl′**ə) *n.* A minute amount; a trace or an iota: *without a scintilla of doubt.*

scin•til•late (**sĭn′**tl āt′) *v.* **scin•til•lat•ed, scin•til•lat•ing, scin•til•lates.** *—intr.* **1.** To throw off sparks; flash or sparkle. **2.** To be animated or brilliant: *The conversation scintillated all evening.* *—tr.* To give off (sparks or flashes). **—scin′til•la′tion** *n.*

sci•on (**sī′**ən) *n.* **1.** A descendant or an heir. **2.** Also **ci•on** (**sī′**ən). A twig or shoot that has been removed from one plant for grafting onto another.

scis•sors (**sĭz′**ərz) *n. (used with a singular or plural verb).* A cutting tool consisting of two blades, each with a ring-shaped handle, joined on a pivot that allows the cutting edges to close against each other. [First written down about 1380 in Middle English and spelled *sisoures*, from Late Latin *cīsōrium*, cutting instrument, from Latin *caedere*, to cut.]

scle•ra (**sklîr′**ə) *n.* The tough, white, fibrous tissue that covers all of the eyeball except the cornea.

scle•ro•sis (sklə **rō′**sĭs) *n., pl.* **scle•ro•ses** (sklə **rō′**sēz). **1.** A thickening or hardening of a body part, such as an artery or the spinal cord. **2.** A disease characterized by sclerosis.

scoff (skŏf *or* skôf) *intr.v.* **scoffed, scoff•ing, scoffs.** To express mocking contempt or derision; jeer: *They scoffed at the idea.* *—n.* An expression of derision or scorn. **—scoff′er** *n.*

scoff•law (**skŏf′**lô′ *or* **skôf′**lô′) *n.* A person who habitually violates the law.

scold (skōld) *tr.v.* **scold•ed, scold•ing, scolds.** To express severe disapproval to; criticize harshly or angrily. —*n.* A person who continually nags or criticizes. [First written down about 1378 in Middle English and spelled *scolden*, to be abusive, from *scolde*, an abusive person, probably of Scandinavian origin.] —**scold′er** *n.*

sco•li•o•sis (skō′lē ō′sĭs) *n.* Abnormal sideways curvature of the spine.

scol•lop (skŏl′əp) *n. & v.* Variant of **scallop.**

sconce (skŏns) *n.* A decorative wall bracket that holds a candle or an electric light.

scone (skōn *or* skŏn) *n.* A small rich pastry that resembles a biscuit.

scoop (sko͞op) *n.* **1.** A small utensil shaped like a shovel with a short handle and a deep curved dish: *a flour scoop.* **2.** The amount that this utensil can hold. **3.a.** A thick-handled utensil with a round bowl, used to dispense balls of ice cream or other semisoft food. **b.** A portion of food served with this utensil. **4.** The bucket of a backhoe, dredge, or similar machine. **5.** A scooping movement or action. **6.** *Informal.* A news story reported by a broadcasting station or newspaper ahead of a competitor. **7.** *Informal.* Current information or details: *What's the scoop on the new neighbors?* —*tr.v.* **scooped, scoop•ing, scoops. 1.** To take up with or as if with a scoop: *scoop out the seeds; scoop up dirt.* **2.** To hollow out or form by digging: *scoop out a hole.* **3.** To grab or gather swiftly: *scoop up a handful of raisins.* **4.** *Informal.* To obtain and report a news story ahead of (rival newspapers, for example). [First written down in 1324 in Middle English and spelled *scope*, from Middle Dutch *schōpe*, bucket for bailing water.]

scoop•ful (sko͞op′fo͝ol′) *n.* The amount that a scoop can hold.

scoot (sko͞ot) *intr.v.* **scoot•ed, scoot•ing, scoots.** To go suddenly or speedily; hurry: *They scooted off into the woods.* —See Note.

scoot•er (sko͞o′tər) *n.* **1.** A child's vehicle consisting of a long footboard between two small end wheels, controlled by an upright steering bar attached to the front wheel. **2.** A motor scooter.

scope (skōp) *n.* **1.** The range of one's perceptions, thoughts, actions, or abilities: *broaden one's scope by reading.* **2.** Room or opportunity to function: *Give full scope to your imagination.* **3.** The area covered by an activity, a situation, or a subject: *The book was very broad in scope.* **4.** A viewing instrument such as a periscope or microscope. [First written down in 1534 in Modern English, from Greek *skopos*, target, aim.]

-scope *suff.* A suffix that means an instrument for viewing or observing: *microscope.*

scorch (skôrch) *v.* **scorched, scorch•ing, scorch•es.** —*tr.* **1.** To burn the surface of. **2.** To wither or parch with intense heat: *The sun scorched the desert.* —*intr.* To become burned. —*n.* **1.** A slight or superficial burn. **2.** A discoloration caused by heat.

scorch•er (skôr′chər) *n. Informal.* An extremely hot day.

score (skôr) *n.* **1.** The number of points made by each competitor or team in a game or contest. **2.** A record of points made in a game or contest: *The score was tied late in the game.* **3.** A result of a test or an examination: *a score of 90 on a math test.* **4.** A debt or wrong that needs to be settled or revenged: *I have an old score to settle with him.* **5.** A reason or ground: *You have nothing to worry about on that score.* **6.** A group of 20 items. **7. scores.** Large numbers: *scores of people.* **8.a.** The written form of a musical composition. **b.** A musical composition written for a film or theater production. **9.** A notch or cut. —*v.* **scored, scor•ing, scores.** —*tr.* **1.a.** To gain (a point or points) in a game or contest. **b.** To count or be worth as points: *That basket scored two points.* **2.** To keep a written record of the score or progress of (a game or contest). **3.** To achieve, gain, or win: *score a touchdown; scored success in the play.* **4.** To evaluate and assign a grade to: *The teacher scored the tests.* **5.** To arrange (a musical composition) for performance. **6.** To mark with lines, notches, or cuts. —*intr.* **1.** To make a point in a game or contest. **2.** To keep the score of a game or contest. [First written down before 1100 in Old English and spelled *scoru*, twenty, from Old Norse *skor.*] —**scor′er** *n.*

score•board (skôr′bôrd′) *n.* A large board that records and indicates the score of a game for spectators.

score•card (skôr′kärd′) *n.* **1.** A printed program or card enabling a spectator to identify players and record the progress of a game. **2.** A small card used, as in golf, to record one's own performance.

score•keep•er (skôr′kē′pər) *n.* An official who records the score throughout a game or competition.

sco•ri•a (skôr′ē ə) *n., pl.* **sco•ri•ae** (skôr′ē ē′). **1.** Rough pieces of crusty lava containing numerous cavities that originated as gas bubbles in the hot lava. **2.** The waste left after a metal or an ore is smelted; slag.

scorn (skôrn) *n.* **1.** A strong feeling that a person or thing is inferior or unworthy; contempt or disdain. **2.** The expression of such a feeling in speech or behavior. **3.** A person or thing considered or treated with contempt. —*v.* **scorned, scorn•ing, scorns.** —*tr.* **1.** To consider or treat as inferior or unworthy: *The artist was scorned by traditional thinkers.* **2.** To reject or refuse because of contempt or disdain: *scorned their offer of help.* —**scorn′er** *n.*

scorn•ful (skôrn′fəl) *adj.* Full of or expressing scorn or contempt: *a scornful laugh.* —**scorn′ful•ly** *adv.* —**scorn′ful•ness** *n.*

Scor•pi•o (skôr′pē ō′) *n.* **1.** Variant of **Scorpius. 2.** The eighth sign of the zodiac in astrology.

scor•pi•on (skôr′pē ən) *n.* Any of various animals related to the spiders and having a narrow jointed body and a tail with a poisonous sting.

Scor•pi•us (skôr′pē əs) also **Scor•pi•o** (skôr′pē ō′) *n.* A constellation in the Southern Hemisphere near Libra and Sagittarius.

Scot (skŏt) *n.* A native or inhabitant of Scotland.

scotch (skŏch) *tr.v.* **scotched, scotch•ing, scotch•es. 1.** To put an end to; crush; stifle: *The governor scotched the rumor in his speech.* **2.** To injure so as to make harmless; wound.

Scotch (skŏch) *n.* **1.** The people of Scotland. **2.** Scots English. **3.** Scotch whisky. —*adj.* Scottish.

Scotch•man (skŏch′mən) *n.* A Scotsman.

Scotch tape *n.* A trademark for a cellulose adhesive tape.

Scotch terrier *n.* A Scottish terrier.

Scotch whisky *n.* A smoky-flavored whiskey distilled in Scotland from malted barley.

Scotch•wom•an (skŏch′wo͝om′ən) *n.* A Scotswoman.

scot-free (skŏt′frē′) *adv.* **1.** Without having to pay. **2.** Without incurring any punishment.

Scot•land (skŏt′lənd). A country of the United Kingdom made up of the northern part of the island of Great Britain and the Hebrides, Shetland Islands, and Orkney Islands. Scotland became a part of the kingdom of Great Britain in 1707. Edinburgh is the capital and Glasgow the largest city. Population, 5,149,500.

Scots (skŏts) *adj.* Scottish. —*n.* The dialect of English used in the lowlands of Scotland.

Scots•man (skŏts′mən) *n.* A man who is a native or inhabitant of Scotland.

Regional Note: scoot

Scoot originally meant "to squirt with water." A more common sense is "to move quickly": *The mouse scooted across the floor.* In areas of the middle portion of the United States, people say *scoot over*, meaning, in its transitive sense, "to push (someone or something) to the side to make room."

scooter

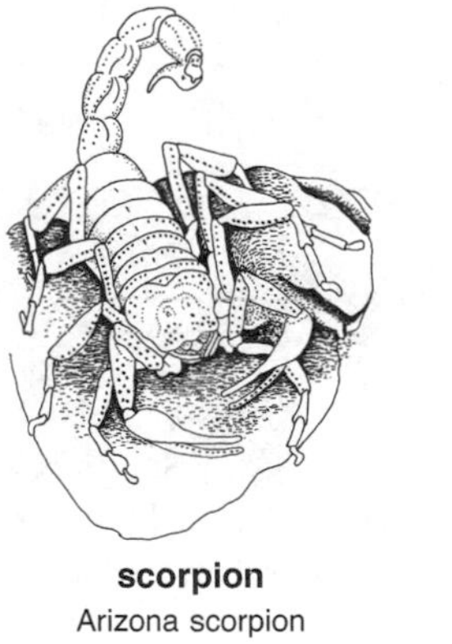

scorpion
Arizona scorpion

ă	pat	oi	boy
ā	pay	ou	out
âr	care	o͝o	took
ä	father	o͞o	boot
ĕ	pet	ŭ	cut
ē	be	ûr	urge
ĭ	pit	th	thin
ī	pie	*th*	this
îr	pier	hw	whoop
ŏ	pot	zh	vision
ō	toe	ə	about
ô	paw	N	*French* bon

Dred Scott
Detail of an 1881 portrait by Louis Schultze after an 1858 photograph

Sir Walter Scott

Scottish terrier

scrapbook

Scots•wom•an (**skŏts′**wo͝om′ən) *n.* A woman who is a native or inhabitant of Scotland.

Scott (skŏt), **Dred.** 1795?–1858. American slave whose lawsuit against his master resulted in the Supreme Court's decision that the Missouri Compromise was unconstitutional (1857).

Scott, Robert Falcon. 1868–1912. British explorer who reached the South Pole (January 1912) one month after Roald Amundsen.

Scott, Sir **Walter.** 1771–1832. British writer whose works include *Ivanhoe* (1819).

Scot•tie (**skŏt′**ē) *n.* A Scottish terrier.

Scot•tish (**skŏt′**ĭsh) *adj.* Of or relating to Scotland or its people, language, or culture. —*n.* **1.** Scots English. **2.** The people of Scotland.

Scottish Gaelic *n.* The Gaelic language of the Scottish Highlanders.

Scottish terrier *n.* A small dog of a breed originally from Scotland, having a dark wiry coat and a blunt muzzle.

scoun•drel (**skoun′**drəl) *n.* A wicked or dishonorable person; a villain. —**scoun′drel•ly** *adv.*

scour[1] (skour) *v.* **scoured, scour•ing, scours.** —*tr.* **1.** To clean or polish by scrubbing vigorously: *scour a dirty pan.* **2.** To remove by scrubbing: *scour grease from a pan.* **3.** To clear (a channel or pipe) by flushing. —*intr.* To scrub something vigorously in order to clean or polish it. —*n.* The act of cleaning or polishing by vigorous scrubbing. [First written down before 1200 in Middle English and spelled *scuren*, from Late Latin *excūrāre*, to clean out.] —**scour′er** *n.*

scour[2] (skour) *v.* **scoured, scour•ing, scours.** —*tr.* To search through or over thoroughly: *scoured the scene of the crime for clues.* —*intr.* To range or travel over or about an area, especially in a search. [First written down before 1425 in Middle English and spelled *scouren*, probably of Scandinavian origin.] —**scour′er** *n.*

scourge (skûrj) *n.* **1.** A cause of widespread suffering, as a disease or war. **2.** A means of inflicting suffering or punishment. **3.** A whip used to inflict punishment. —*tr.v.* **scourged, scourg•ing, scourg•es. 1.** To cause widespread suffering to; devastate. **2.** To punish severely. **3.** To flog. —**scourg′er** *n.*

scout[1] (skout) *v.* **scout•ed, scout•ing, scouts.** —*tr.* **1.** To observe or explore carefully in order to obtain information: *The soldier scouted the woods ahead.* **2.** To observe and evaluate (an athlete or entertainer, for example) for possible hiring. —*intr.* To search: *I scouted around for my baseball glove.* —*n.* **1.** A person who goes out from a main body to gather information. **2.** Often **Scout. a.** A member of the Boy Scouts. **b.** A member of the Girl Scouts. **3.** A person employed to discover and recruit persons with talent. [First written down about 1380 in Middle English and spelled *scouten*, from Latin *auscultāre*, to listen.]

scout[2] (skout) *v.* **scout•ed, scout•ing, scouts.** —*tr.* To reject with scorn. —*intr.* To treat another scornfully; scoff. [First written down in 1605 in Modern English and spelled *scowt*, of Scandinavian origin.]

scout•ing also **Scout•ing** (**skou′**tĭng) *n.* The activities of the Boy Scouts or Girl Scouts.

scout•mas•ter (**skout′**măs′tər) *n.* The adult leader of a troop of Boy Scouts.

scow (skou) *n.* A large flat-bottomed boat or barge that is used to transport sand, gravel, or garbage.

scowl (skoul) *v.* **scowled, scowl•ing, scowls.** —*intr.* To wrinkle or contract the brow as an expression of anger or disapproval. —*tr.* To express with a frowning facial expression. —*n.* An angry frown. —**scowl′er** *n.*

scrab•ble (**skrăb′**əl) *intr.v.* **scrab•bled, scrab•bling, scrab•bles. 1.** To scrape or grope about frantically with the hands: *scrabbled in the dust for the lost tool.* **2.** To struggle: *scrabbled for a living on the farm.*

scrag (skrăg) *n.* **1.** A bony or scrawny person or animal. **2.** A piece of lean or bony meat, especially a neck of mutton.

scrag•gly (**skrăg′**lē) *adj.* **scrag•gli•er, scrag•gli•est.** Ragged; unkempt: *scraggly hair; scraggly undergrowth.*

scrag•gy (**skrăg′**ē) *adj.* **scrag•gi•er, scrag•gi•est. 1.** Jagged; rough: *scraggy cliffs.* **2.** Bony and lean: *a scraggy cat.* —**scrag′gi•ly** *adv.* —**scrag′gi•ness** *n.*

scram (skrăm) *Slang. intr.v.* **scrammed, scram•ming, scrams.** To leave at once; go immediately.

scram•ble (**skrăm′**bəl) *v.* **scram•bled, scram•bling, scram•bles.** —*intr.* **1.** To move or climb hurriedly, especially on the hands and knees: *The children scrambled over the stone wall.* **2.** To struggle or contend in order to get something: *scrambled for the best seats.* **3.** To take off with all possible haste in order to confront enemy aircraft. —*tr.* **1.** To mix or gather together in a confused or disorderly manner: *scrambled the letters of a word.* **2.** To cook (beaten eggs) until firm but moist and soft. **3.** To distort or garble (an electronic signal) so that it cannot be used or understood without a special receiver. **4.** To cause (aircraft) to take off as fast as possible, especially to confront enemy aircraft. —*n.* **1.** The act or an instance of scrambling. **2.** A strenuous climb or hike: *It was quite a scramble to reach the pass.* **3.** A struggle for something: *a scramble for new territory.*

scram•bler (**skrăm′**blər) *n.* An electronic device that scrambles a signal so that it can be received only with special equipment.

scrap[1] (skrăp) *n.* **1.** A small piece or bit; a fragment. **2. scraps.** Leftover bits of food. **3.** Discarded waste material, especially metal suitable for reprocessing: *sold the old car as scrap.* —*tr.v.* **scrapped, scrap•ping, scraps. 1.** To break down into parts for disposal or salvage: *scrap an old stove.* **2.** To discard or abandon as useless; junk: *scrap a plan.* [First written down before 1387 in Middle English, from Old Norse *skrap*, trifles, pieces.]

scrap[2] (skrăp) *intr.v.* **scrapped, scrap•ping, scraps.** To fight, often with the fists. —*n.* A fight or quarrel. [First written down in 1874 in Modern English, perhaps from *scrape*.]

scrap•book (**skrăp′**bo͝ok′) *n.* A book with blank pages for mounting pictures or other mementos.

scrape (skrāp) *v.* **scraped, scrap•ing, scrapes.** —*tr.* **1.** To clean, smooth, or abrade by rubbing: *scrape a carrot.* **2.** To remove (material) from a surface by forceful strokes with a rough or edged instrument: *scraped ice from the windshield.* **3.** To cause to rub or move against something, often with a harsh sound: *scraped her fingernails on the wall.* **4.** To damage or injure the surface of by rubbing against something rough or sharp: *scraped my knee on the sidewalk.* **5.** To amass or produce with difficulty: *scrape together enough money for the rent.* —*intr.* **1.** To rub or move with a harsh grating noise. **2.** To be frugal; scrimp. —*n.* **1.** The act of scraping. **2.** The sound of scraping. **3.** A mark or an injury caused by scraping. **4.a.** An embarrassing or difficult situation. **b.** A fight.

scrap•er (**skrā′**pər) *n.* Something that scrapes, especially a tool for scraping off paint or other material.

scrap•ple (**skrăp′**əl) *n.* A mush of ground pork and cornmeal that is allowed to set and is then sliced and fried.

scrap•py[1] (**skrăp′**ē) *adj.* **scrap•pi•er, scrap•pi•est.** Made up of bits and pieces; fragmentary. [First written down in 1837 in Modern English, from *scrap*, fragment.] —**scrap′pi•ness** *n.*

scrap•py² (skrăp′ē) *adj.* **scrap•pi•er, scrap•pi•est. 1.** Quarrelsome; contentious. **2.** Full of fighting spirit. [First written down in 1895 in American English, from *scrap*, to fight.] **—scrap′pi•ness** *n.*

scratch (skrăch) *v.* **scratched, scratch•ing, scratch•es.** *—tr.* **1.** To make a thin shallow cut or mark on (a surface) with a sharp instrument. **2.** To scrape or injure with the nails or claws: *The cat scratched my arm.* **3.** To rub or scrape (the skin) to relieve itching. **4.a.** To write or draw something by scraping a surface: *scratched a name on a rock.* **b.** To write or mark hastily; scrawl: *scratched notes on a pad.* **5.** To strike out or cancel (a word, for example) by or as if by drawing lines across. **6.** To withdraw from competition: *scratch a horse from a race.* **7.** To make (a living) from hard work and saving money. *—intr.* **1.** To use the nails or claws to scrape or injure: *The dog scratched at the door.* **2.** To rub or scrape the skin to relieve itching. **3.** To make a thin scraping sound: *The pencil scratched on the paper.* *—n.* **1.** A mark or wound made by scratching. **2.** A sound made by scratching. *—adj.* **1.** Done hurriedly or haphazardly: *a scratch outline.* **2.** Assembled at random: *a scratch team.* ***—idioms.*** **from scratch.** From the very beginning: *make a cake from scratch.* **up to scratch.** *Informal.* Meeting the requirements: *The sleepy student's work was not up to scratch.* **—scratch′er** *n.*

scratch•y (skrăch′ē) *adj.* **scratch•i•er, scratch•i•est. 1.** Rough, harsh, or irritating: *was wearing a scratchy sweater.* **2.** Making a harsh scratching sound. **—scratch′i•ly** *adv.* **—scratch′i•ness** *n.*

scrawl (skrôl) *v.* **scrawled, scrawl•ing, scrawls.** *—tr.* To write hastily or carelessly: *scrawl a note on a pad.* *—intr.* To write in a sprawling irregular manner. *—n.* Sprawling or unreadable handwriting. **—scrawl′er** *n.*

scraw•ny (skrô′nē) *adj.* **scraw•ni•er, scraw•ni•est.** Thin and bony; skinny. See Synonyms at **lean²**. **—scraw′ni•ness** *n.*

scream (skrēm) *v.* **screamed, scream•ing, screams.** *—intr.* **1.** To utter a long, loud, piercing cry, as from fear or pain. **2.** To make a loud piercing sound: *The siren screamed.* *—tr.* To utter or say in or as if in a screaming voice: *"Wait!" he screamed.* *—n.* **1.** A loud piercing cry or sound. **2.** *Informal.* A person or thing that is very funny. **—scream′er** *n.*

screech (skrēch) *n.* **1.** A high-pitched harsh cry; a shriek. **2.** A sound resembling this: *the screech of brakes.* *—v.* **screeched, screech•ing, screech•es.** *—tr.* To utter in or as if in a high-pitched harsh voice: *The children screeched an answer.* *—intr.* **1.** To cry out in a high-pitched harsh voice. **2.** To make a shrill grating sound like a screech: *The tires screeched on the wet pavement.*

screech owl *n.* Any of various small owls having tufted ears and a wailing quavering call.

screen (skrēn) *n.* **1.** A light movable device used to divide, conceal, or protect. **2.** Something that serves to conceal: *a screen of shrubs around the yard.* **3.** A frame covered with wire or plastic mesh, used in a window or door to keep out insects and allow air to pass in and out. **4.** A large flat white surface upon which slides or motion pictures are projected. **5.** The phosphorescent surface on which an image appears, as on a television or computer monitor. **6.** The motion-picture industry: *bring a story to the screen.* **7.** A coarse sieve. *—tr.v.* **screened, screen•ing, screens. 1.** To provide with a screen: *screen a porch.* **2.** To shelter, guard, or protect: *The stone wall screened us from the wind.* **3.** To conceal from view with or as if with a screen: *Trees screened the house from the street.* See Synonyms at **hide¹**. **4.** To separate or sift out with a sieve. **5.** To examine systematically in order to determine suitability: *screen job applicants.* **6.** To show (a movie) on a screen. [First written down in 1348 in Middle English and spelled *screne*, from Middle Dutch *scherm*, shield, screen.]

screen•ing (skrē′nĭng) *n.* **1. screenings.** *(used with a singular or plural verb).* Refuse such as waste coal, separated out by a screen. **2.** The mesh material used to make door or window screens. **3.** A presentation of a motion picture.

screen•play (skrēn′plā′) *n.* The script for a motion picture.

screw (skro͞o) *n.* **1.a.** A cylindrical rod having one or more spiral or helical grooves cut into its surface. **b.** The part, cut with a similar groove, into which such a rod fits. **2.** A metal pin having such grooves, fitted with a slotted head so that it can be turned by a screwdriver and used to fasten things together. **3.** A propeller, especially for a ship or motorboat. **4.** A twist or turn of or as if of a screw. *—v.* **screwed, screw•ing, screws.** *—tr.* **1.** To drive or tighten (a screw). **2.a.** To fasten, tighten, or attach by or as if by means of a screw. **b.** To attach (a threaded cap or fitting) by twisting into place: *screw a valve onto the end of a pipe.* **3.** To twist (one's face) out of normal shape. *—intr.* **1.** To turn or twist. **2.** To become attached by means of a screw. ***—idiom.*** **screw up. 1.** To gather or summon up: *I screwed up my courage to face the challenge.* **2.** *Slang.* To make a mess of (an undertaking).

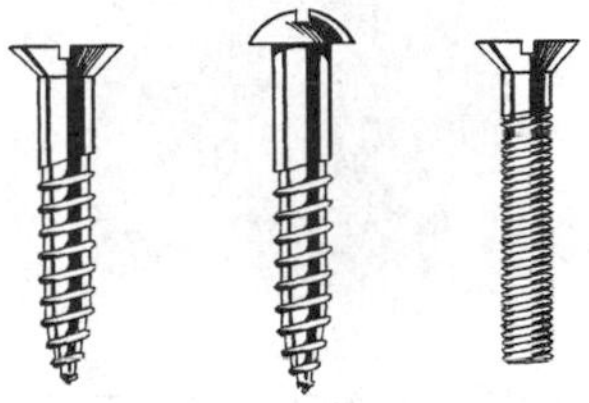

screw
Left to right: Flat head wood screw, round head wood screw, and flat head machine screw

screw•ball (skro͞o′bôl′) *n.* **1.** In baseball, a pitched ball that curves in the direction opposite that of a normal curve ball. **2.** *Slang.* A person regarded as strange or irrational. *—adj. Slang.* Strange or irrational: *That screwball idea will never work.*

screw•driv•er (skro͞o′drī′vər) *n.* A tool used to turn screws.

screw propeller *n.* A propeller.

screw•y (skro͞o′ē) *adj.* **screw•i•er, screw•i•est.** *Slang.* **1.** Crazy or eccentric. **2.** Odd or inappropriate: *There's something screwy with this computer.*

scrib•ble (skrĭb′əl) *v.* **scrib•bled, scrib•bling, scrib•bles.** *—tr.* **1.** To write or draw (something) hastily or carelessly. **2.** To cover with doodles and meaningless marks. *—intr.* To write or draw in a hurried careless way. *—n.* **1.** Careless hurried writing. **2.** Meaningless marks. **—scrib′bler** *n.*

scribe (skrīb) *n.* **1.** A person who copies manuscripts and documents for a living. **2.** A public clerk or secretary, especially in ancient times. **3.** A writer or journalist. **4.** In the New Testament, a Jewish scholar of the Mosaic law. *—tr.v.* **scribed, scrib•ing, scribes.** To draw or mark with a scriber: *scribe a pattern; scribe metal.* [First written down about 1200 in Middle English, from Late Latin *scrība*, from Latin *scrībere*, to write.]

scrib•er (skrī′bər) *n.* A sharply pointed tool for marking lines, as on wood or metal.

scrim•mage (skrĭm′ĭj) *n.* **1.** In football, the action from the time the ball is snapped until it is declared dead. **2.** A practice game between members of the same team. *—intr.v.* **scrim•maged, scrim•mag•ing, scrim•mag•es.** To engage in a scrimmage.

scrimp (skrĭmp) *v.* **scrimped, scrimp•ing, scrimps.** *—intr.* To be very frugal; economize severely: *We scrimped and saved for our trip.* *—tr.* To use sparingly.

scrim•shaw (skrĭm′shô′) *n., pl.* **scrimshaw** or **scrim•shaws. 1.** The art of carving complex and fine designs on whale bone or whale ivory. **2.** An article made by this art.

scrip (skrĭp) *n.* Paper money issued for temporary emergency use.

script (skrĭpt) *n.* **1.a.** Letters or characters written by hand; handwriting. **b.** A particular style of writing: *medieval script.* **2.a.** Printer's type that resembles

ă	pat	oi	**boy**
ā	**pay**	ou	**out**
âr	**care**	o͝o	**took**
ä	**father**	o͞o	**boot**
ĕ	**pet**	ŭ	**cut**
ē	**be**	ûr	**urge**
ĭ	**pit**	th	**thin**
ī	**pie**	*th*	**this**
îr	**pier**	hw	**whoop**
ŏ	**pot**	zh	**vision**
ō	**toe**	ə	**about**
ô	**paw**	N	*French* **bon**

scuba
Scuba diving equipment

sculptor

handwriting. **b.** Something printed with such type. **3.** The text of a play, motion picture, or broadcast. [First written down before 1300 in Middle English and spelled *scrite*, a piece of writing, from Latin *scrīptum*, something written.]

Scrip•ture (skrĭp′chər) *n.* **1.a.** A sacred writing or book. **b.** A passage from such a writing or book. **2.** The sacred writings of the Bible. Often used in the plural. **3.** A statement regarded as authoritative. **—Scrip′tur•al** *adj.*

scriv•en•er (skrĭv′ə nər *or* skrĭv′nər) *n.* **1.** A scribe. **2.** A notary.

scrod (skrŏd) *n.* A young cod or haddock, especially one used for cooking.

scroll (skrōl) *n.* **1.** A roll, as of parchment or papyrus, used especially for writing a document. **2.** An ornamental object or design that resembles a partly rolled scroll of paper. *—v.* **scrolled, scroll•ing, scrolls.** *—tr.* To cause (displayed text or graphics) to move vertically or horizontally across the screen of a computer monitor. *—intr.* To cause displayed text or graphics to move vertically or hoizontally across the screen of a computer monitor: *scrolled down to the end of the document.*

Scrooge also **scrooge** (skro͞oj) *n.* A miserly mean-spirited person. [First written down in 1940 in Modern English, after Ebenezer *Scrooge*, miserly main character in *A Christmas Carol* by Charles Dickens.]

scro•tum (skrō′təm) *n., pl.* **scro•ta** (skrō′tə) or **scro•tums.** The external sac of skin that encloses the testes in most mammals.

scrounge (skrounj) *v.* **scrounged, scroung•ing, scroung•es.** *Slang.* *—tr.* **1.** To obtain by rummaging or foraging: *scrounging old books out of the attic.* **2.** To obtain (something) by begging or borrowing with no intention or returning or repaying: *scrounge a dollar from a friend.* *—intr.* To forage about; search.

scrub[1] (skrŭb) *v.* **scrubbed, scrub•bing, scrubs.** *—tr.* **1.** To rub hard in order to clean. **2.** To remove (dirt or stains) by hard rubbing. **3.** To remove impurities from (a gas). **4.** *Slang.* To cancel or abandon: *scrub a space flight.* *—intr.* To clean or wash something by hard rubbing. [First written down before 1300 in Middle English and spelled *shrubben*, to scratch oneself, from Middle Dutch *schrobben*, to clean by rubbing.] **—scrub′ber** *n.*

scrub[2] (skrŭb) *n.* **1.** A growth of small straggly trees or shrubs. **2.** An undersized poorly developed plant or animal. **3.** In sports, a player not on the varsity or first team. [First written down before 1398 in Middle English, variant of *shrubbe*, shrub.]

scrub•by (skrŭb′ē) *adj.* **scrub•bi•er, scrub•bi•est. 1.** Covered with or consisting of scrub or underbrush. **2.** Straggly or undersized; stunted. **3.** Worthless or contemptible. **—scrub′bi•ness** *n.*

scruff (skrŭf) *n.* The back of the neck or the loose skin covering it; the nape.

scruff•y (skrŭf′ē) *adj.* **scruff•i•er, scruff•i•est.** Shabby; untidy: *a scruffy little house.*

scrump•tious (skrŭmp′shəs) *adj.* Very pleasing to the taste; delicious.

scru•ple (skro͞o′pəl) *n.* **1.** A feeling of uneasiness that is produced by one's conscience and tends to hinder action. **2.** A unit of apothecary weight equal to about 1.3 grams, or 20 grains. *—intr.v.* **scru•pled, scru•pling, scru•ples.** To hesitate as a result of conscience or moral principle.

scru•pu•lous (skro͞o′pyə ləs) *adj.* **1.** Showing extreme care about details; painstaking: *a scrupulous regard for facts.* **2.** Having scruples; ethical: *a scrupulous attorney.* **—scru′pu•lous•ly** *adv.* **—scru′pu•lous•ness** *n.*

scru•ti•nize (skro͞ot′n īz′) *tr.v.* **scru•ti•nized, scru•ti•niz•ing, scru•ti•niz•es.** To observe or examine with great care. **—scru′ti•niz′er** *n.*

scru•ti•ny (skro͞ot′n ē) *n., pl.* **scru•ti•nies. 1.** A close careful examination or study. **2.** Close observation; surveillance.

scu•ba (sko͞o′bə) *n.* A portable device including one or more tanks of compressed air, used by divers to breathe underwater. [First written down in 1952 in American English, from *s(elf-)c(ontained) u(nderwater) b(reathing) a(pparatus).*]

scud (skŭd) *intr.v.* **scud•ded, scud•ding, scuds. 1.** To move along swiftly and easily: *The clouds scudded across the sky.* **2.** To run before a gale with little or no sail set. *—n.* **1.** The act of scudding. **2.** Wind-driven clouds, mist, or rain.

scuff (skŭf) *v.* **scuffed, scuff•ing, scuffs.** *—intr.* To scrape or drag the feet while walking. *—tr.* **1.** To scrape with the feet. **2.** To shuffle (the feet), as in embarrassment. **3.** To scrape or roughen the surface of. *—n.* **1.** The act or sound of scraping. **2.** A worn or rough spot resulting from scraping.

scuf•fle (skŭf′əl) *intr.v.* **scuf•fled, scuf•fling, scuf•fles.** To tussle or fight confusedly at close quarters: *The police scuffled with the thieves.* *—n.* A rough disorderly struggle at close quarters. **—scuf′fler** *n.*

scull (skŭl) *n.* **1.** A long oar moved back and forth from the stern of a boat to propel the boat forward. **2.** One of a pair of short-handled oars used by a single rower. **3.** A small light racing boat. *—tr.v.* **sculled, scull•ing, sculls.** To propel (a boat) with a scull or sculls.

❑ *These sound alike:* **scull, skull** (bones of head).

scul•ler•y (skŭl′ə rē) *n., pl.* **scul•ler•ies.** A room next to the kitchen, where dishwashing and other kitchen chores are done.

scul•lion (skŭl′yən) *n.* A servant employed to do menial tasks in a kitchen.

sculpt (skŭlpt) *v.* **sculpt•ed, sculpt•ing, sculpts.** *—tr.* **1.** To sculpture (an object). **2.** To shape, mold, or fashion, especially artistically. *—intr.* To be a sculptor; produce sculpture. [First written down in 1864 in Modern English, from Latin *sculpere*, to carve.]

sculp•tor (skŭlp′tər) *n.* An artist who makes sculptures.

sculp•ture (skŭlp′chər) *n.* **1.** The art or practice of shaping or making figures or designs, as by carving wood, chiseling stone, or casting metal. **2.a.** A work of art created in this way. **b.** Such works of art considered as a group: *African sculpture.* *—v.* **sculp•tured, sculp•tur•ing, sculp•tures.** *—tr.* **1.** To shape (stone, metal, or wood, for example) into sculpture. **2.** To represent in sculpture: *sculpture a ballerina.* **3.** To ornament with sculpture: *sculptured the portals of the church.* **4.** To change the shape or contour of, as by erosion. *—intr.* To make sculptures or a sculpture. **—sculp′tur•al** *adj.*

scum (skŭm) *n.* **1.** A filmy layer of impure or extraneous matter that forms on or rises to the surface of a liquid or a body of water. **2.** A similar mass of waste material that rises to the surface of a molten metal. **3.** *Slang.* A person or class of people regarded as worthless or contemptible. [First written down in 1340 in Middle English and spelled *scome*, from Middle Dutch *schūm*.]

scup (skŭp) *n., pl.* **scup** or **scups.** A porgy of northern Atlantic waters.

scup•per (skŭp′ər) *n.* An opening in the side of a ship at deck level to allow water to run off.

scurf (skûrf) *n.* **1.** Flaky dry skin, such as dandruff. **2.** A scaly crust on a surface, especially of a plant.

scur•ri•lous (skûr′ə ləs *or* skŭr′ə ləs) *adj.* **1.** Given to the use of coarse, spiteful, and abusive language. **2.** Expressed in coarse, spiteful, and abusive language: *a scurrilous attack.* —**scur′ril•ous•ly** *adv.* —**scur′ril•ous•ness** *n.*

scur•ry (skûr′ē *or* skŭr′ē) *intr.v.* **scur•ried, scur•ry•ing, scur•ries. 1.** To move with light running steps; scamper. **2.** To rush or race about in a hurried or confused manner. —*n., pl.* **scur•ries.** An act or a noise of scurrying.

scur•vy (skûr′vē) *n.* A disease caused by lack of vitamin C and characterized by soft bleeding gums, bleeding under the skin, and extreme weakness. —*adj.* **scur•vi•er, scur•vi•est.** Mean; contemptible.

scutch•eon (skŭch′ən) *n.* An escutcheon.

scut•tle[1] (skŭt′l) *n.* **1.** A small opening or hatch in a ship's deck or hull. **2.** The movable cover for such an opening. —*tr.v.* **scut•tled, scut•tling, scut•tles. 1.** To sink (a ship) by cutting or opening holes in the hull. **2.** *Informal.* To discard or abandon: *We scuttled our vacation plans.* [First written down in 1497 in Middle English and spelled *skottell,* from Old French *escoutille,* possibly from Spanish *escotilla.*]

scut•tle[2] (skŭt′l) *n.* A metal pail for carrying coal. [First written down about 1050 in Old English and spelled *scutel,* dish, from Latin *scutella.*]

scut•tle[3] (skŭt′l) *intr.v.* **scut•tled, scut•tling, scut•tles.** To run or move with quick little steps; scurry: *The crab scuttled over the rocks.* —*n.* A hurried run. [First written down before 1450 in Middle English and spelled *scottlen;* possibly akin to *scud.*]

scut•tle•butt (skŭt′l bŭt′) *n. Slang.* Gossip; rumor.

Scyl•la (sĭl′ə) *n.* In Greek mythology, a female sea monster who devours sailors in the strait separating Italy from Sicily. —***idiom.* between Scylla and Charybdis.** In a position where avoidance of one danger exposes one to another danger.

scythe (sīth) *n.* A tool with a long curved blade and a long bent handle, used for mowing or reaping. —*tr.v.* **scythed, scyth•ing, scythes.** To cut with or as if with a scythe. [First written down about 700 in Old English and spelled *sīthe,* sickle.]

Scyth•i•a (sĭth′ē ə *or* sĭth′ē ə). An ancient region of Eurasia extending from the mouth of the Danube River on the Black Sea to the territory east of the Aral Sea.

SD or **S.D.** *abbr.* An abbreviation of South Dakota.

S.Dak. *abbr.* An abbreviation of South Dakota.

Se The symbol for the element **selenium.**

SE *abbr.* An abbreviation of: **1.** Southeast. **2.** Southeastern.

sea (sē) *n.* **1.a.** The continuous body of salt water that covers most of the surface of the earth. **b.** A region of water within an ocean and partly enclosed by land, as the North Sea. **c.** A large body of either fresh or salt water that is completely enclosed by land, as the Caspian Sea. **2.** The condition of the ocean's surface, especially with respect to its motion or roughness: *a high sea.* **3.** A swell or wave: *choppy seas.* **4.** A vast expanse or extent: *a sea of ice.* **5.** A mare of the moon. —***idiom.* at sea. 1.** On the sea, especially on a sea voyage. **2.** In a state of confusion; at a loss. [First written down about 725 in Old English and spelled *sǣ.*]

❑ *These sound alike:* **sea, see**[1] (perceive with the eyes), **see**[2] (bishop's position), **si** (musical note).

sea anemone *n.* Any of numerous sea animals that remain fastened to a surface underwater and have a mouth opening surrounded by many stinging tentacles.

sea•bed (sē′bĕd′) *n.* The bottom of a sea or an ocean.

sea bird *n.* A bird, such as a petrel or an albatross, that spends much of its time near or on the ocean, especially far from shore.

sea biscuit *n.* Hardtack.

sea•board (sē′bôrd′) *n.* Land along or near the sea.

sea breeze *n.* A cool breeze blowing inland from the sea.

sea•coast (sē′kōst′) *n.* Land along the sea.

sea cow *n.* Any of several large water mammals such as the manatee or dugong.

sea cucumber *n.* Any of various sea animals related to the starfish and sea urchins, having a rough or spiny usually cucumber-shaped body and a mouth surrounded by tentacles.

sea dog *n.* A very experienced sailor.

sea•far•er (sē′fâr′ər) *n.* A sailor or mariner.

sea•far•ing (sē′fâr′ĭng) *n.* The work of a sailor. —*adj.* **1.** Earning one's living at sea: *a seafaring man.* **2.** Fit to travel on the sea.

sea•food (sē′fo͞od′) *n.* Fish or shellfish from the sea eaten as food.

sea•go•ing (sē′gō′ĭng) *adj.* Made or used for ocean voyages: *a seagoing barge.*

sea green *n.* A medium green or bluish green.

sea gull also **sea•gull** (sē′gŭl′) *n.* A gull, especially one that lives along seacoasts.

sea horse *n.* **1.** Any of several small ocean fishes having a head resembling that of a horse, a body covered with bony plates, and a tail that can be curled around a supporting object. **2.** A walrus. **3.** In mythology, an animal, half fish and half horse, ridden by Neptune and other sea gods.

seal[1] (sēl) *n.* **1.a.** An instrument, such as a ring with an engraved design, used to stamp an impression in wax or other soft material. **b.** The impression so made. **c.** A small disk or wafer of wax, lead, or paper bearing such a mark or impression, used to show that a document or statement is genuine or valid or to fasten an envelope. **2.** A design used to identify a person or thing or to show that something is authentic: *The publisher's seal appears on every title page.* **3.** A fitting or closure that prevents a liquid or gas from entering or escaping: *a seal around a window.* **4.** A small paper sticker used to fasten or decorate an envelope. —*tr.v.* **sealed, seal•ing, seals. 1.** To affix a seal to as a mark of genuineness, authority, or legal status: *The duke signed and sealed the letter.* **2.** To close with or as if with a seal: *sealed the envelope; sealed her lips.* **3.** To close so that a liquid or gas cannot enter or escape: *seal a pipe joint.* **4.** To close tightly so that reopening is difficult or impossible: *seal a tunnel with concrete.* **5.** To apply a waterproof coating to: *seal the driveway.* **6.** To establish or determine with no possibility of change: *Their fate was sealed.* —***idiom.* seal off.** To close tightly or surround with a barricade or rope: *They sealed off part of the road for repairs.* [First written down about 1200 in Middle English and spelled *seil,* from Latin *sigillum,* from *signum,* sign, seal.] —**seal′er** *n.*

seal[2] (sēl) *n.* **1.** Any of various sea mammals having a streamlined body, thick fur or hair, and limbs in the form of flippers. **2.** The fur of a seal. **3.** Leather made from the hide of a seal; sealskin. [First written down before 899 in Old English and spelled *seolh.*]

sea-lane (sē′lān′) *n.* An established or frequently used sea route.

seal•ant (sē′lənt) *n.* A substance used to seal, waterproof, or coat something.

sea legs *pl.n.* The ability to walk on board ship with steadiness, especially in rough seas.

sea level *n.* The level of the surface of the ocean, used as a standard in determining land elevation or sea depths.

seal•ing wax (sē′lĭng) *n.* A preparation of shellac and turpentine that is soft and fluid when hot but solid when cold, used to seal letters, jars, or batteries.

sea lion *n.* Any of several large seals, mostly of Pa-

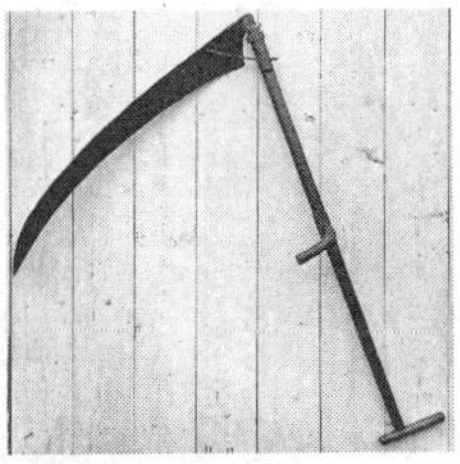

scythe

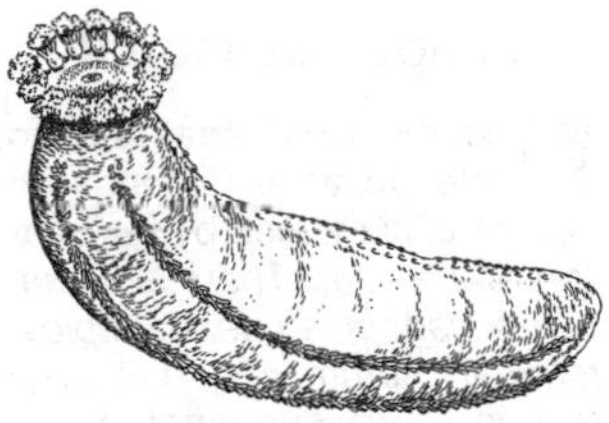

sea cucumber

sea horse

ă	pat	oi	boy
ā	pay	ou	out
âr	care	o͝o	took
ä	father	o͞o	boot
ĕ	pet	ŭ	cut
ē	be	ûr	urge
ĭ	pit	th	thin
ī	pie	*th*	this
îr	pier	hw	whoop
ŏ	pot	zh	vision
ō	toe	ə	about
ô	paw	N	*French* bon

Elizabeth Seaman
"Nellie Bly"

Usage: seasonal

Use the word **seasonal** to refer to what depends on or is controlled by the season of the year: *There is a seasonal rise in student employment in summer.* The closely related word **seasonable** applies to what is appropriate to the season (*seasonable clothing*) or timely (*seasonable intervention in the dispute*).

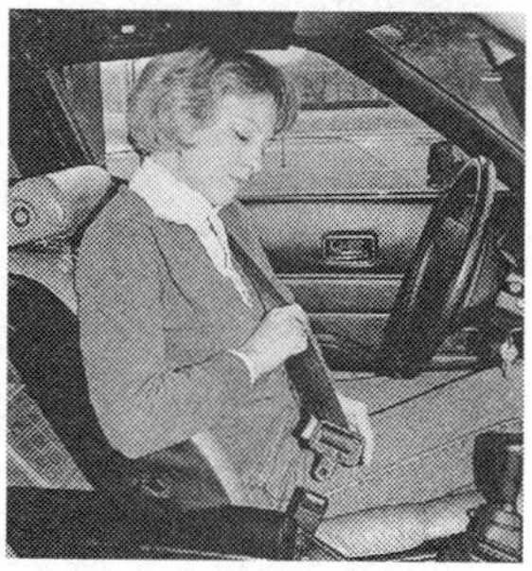

seat belt

cific waters, having a sleek body and brownish fur.

seal•skin (sēl′skĭn′) *n.* **1.** The hide of a seal. **2.** Fur or leather from the pelt or hide of a seal.

seam (sēm) *n.* **1.** A line, ridge, or groove formed by joining two pieces of material together at their edges, as by sewing or welding. **2.** A line across a surface, as a crack or wrinkle. **3.** A thin layer or stratum, as of coal or rock. —*tr.v.* **seamed, seam•ing, seams. 1.** To join with or as if with a seam. **2.** To mark with a groove, wrinkle, scar, or other line. [First written down about 1000 in Old English and spelled *sēam.*] —**seam′er** *n.*

❑ *These sound alike:* **seam, seem** (appear to be).

sea•man (sē′mən) *n.* **1.** A sailor or mariner. **2.** A person in the U.S. Navy or Coast Guard holding any of three noncommissioned ranks below petty officer.

❑ *These sound alike:* **seaman, semen** (sperm).

Sea•man (sē′mən), **Elizabeth Cochrane.** Pen name Nellie Bly. 1867–1922. American journalist whose articles in the *New York World* include an exposé on conditions in mental institutions.

sea•man•ship (sē′mən shĭp′) *n.* Skill in handling or navigating a boat or ship.

seam•stress (sēm′strĭs) *n.* A woman who sews, especially one who makes her living by sewing.

seam•y (sē′mē) *adj.* **seam•i•er, seam•i•est. 1.** Unpleasant; nasty and low: *the seamy side of politics.* **2.** Having or showing a seam.

sé•ance (sā′äns′) *n.* A meeting at which persons attempt to communicate with the dead.

sea otter *n.* A large otter of Pacific waters, having soft dark-brown fur.

sea•plane (sē′plān′) *n.* An airplane equipped with floats for taking off from or landing on water.

sea•port (sē′pôrt′) *n.* A harbor or town having facilities for seagoing ships.

sear (sîr) *tr.v.* **seared, sear•ing, sears. 1.** To scorch or burn the surface of; char. **2.** To cause to dry up or shrivel. —*n.* A scar or mark caused by searing.

❑ *These sound alike:* **sear, seer** (prophet), **sere** (withered).

search (sûrch) *v.* **searched, search•ing, search•es.** —*tr.* **1.** To make a thorough examination of or look over carefully in order to find something: *She searched her room for the missing sock.* **2.** To examine carefully; probe: *searching his soul in order to make the proper decision.* —*intr.* To make a thorough investigation; seek; hunt: *searching for a lost dog.* —*n.* The act of searching: *the search for knowledge.* [First written down before 1300 in Middle English and spelled *serchen*, from Latin *circāre*, to go around.] —**search′er** *n.*

search•ing (sûr′chĭng) *adj.* **1.** Examining closely or thoroughly; scrutinizing: *a searching investigation of stock-market dealings.* **2.** Keenly observant: *some searching insights.* —**search′ing•ly** *adv.*

search•light (sûrch′līt′) *n.* **1.** A light equipped with a reflector to produce a bright beam in which all the rays are approximately parallel. **2.** The beam produced by such a light.

search warrant *n.* A warrant giving authorization to a law officer to search a specified person, building, residence, or area for stolen property or evidence to be used in a case.

sea•shell (sē′shĕl′) *n.* The hard shell of a sea mollusk.

sea•shore (sē′shôr′) *n.* **1.** Land next to the sea. **2.** Ground lying between high-water and low-water marks.

sea•sick•ness (sē′sĭk′nĭs) *n.* Nausea or other discomfort as a result of the pitching and rolling motions of a vessel at sea. —**sea′sick′** *adj.*

sea•side (sē′sīd′) *n.* The seashore.

sea•son (sē′zən) *n.* **1.a.** One of four natural divisions of the year, spring, summer, autumn or fall, and winter, each beginning as the sun passes through a solstice or an equinox. **b.** Either or the two parts, rainy and dry, into which the year is divided in tropical climates. **2.** A period of the year devoted to or marked by a certain activity or by the appearance of something: *the baseball season; the hurricane season.* —*tr.v.* **sea•soned, sea•son•ing, sea•sons. 1.** To give (food) extra flavor by adding salt, pepper, spices, or other flavorings. **2.** To add enjoyment or interest to: *seasoned her writing with wit.* **3.** To dry (lumber) until it is usable; cure. **4.** To accustom or harden (a person or persons) through trial and experience: *hard training to season recruits.* —***idioms.*** **in season. 1.** Available for eating or other use. **2.** Legally permitted to be caught or hunted during a specified period. **3.** At the right moment. **out of season. 1.** Not available, permitted, or ready to be eaten, caught, or hunted. **2.** Not at the right moment. [First written down before 1300 in Middle English and spelled *seisoun*, from Latin *satiō*, act of sowing.]

sea•son•a•ble (sē′zə nə bəl) *adj.* **1.** Suitable for the time or season. **2.** Occurring at the proper time; timely. —**sea′son•a•bly** *adv.* —See Note at **seasonal.**

sea•son•al (sē′zə nəl) *adj.* Of or dependent on a season or seasons: *seasonal variations in temperature.* —**sea′son•al•ly** *adv.* —See Note.

sea•son•ing (sē′zə nĭng) *n.* An ingredient that adds to the flavor of food.

season ticket *n.* A ticket for a specified period of time, as for a series of performances.

seat (sēt) *n.* **1.** Something, such as a chair or bench, that may be sat on. **2.** A place in which a person may sit: *a ticket for a seat on the bus.* **3.** The part of something on which a person sits: *a bicycle seat.* **4.** The buttocks. **5.** The part of a garment covering the buttocks: *the seat of the pants.* **6.** A part that serves as the base or support of something. **7.a.** The place where something is located or based: *the seat of the treasury.* **b.** A capital or center of authority: *the county seat.* **8.** A place of residence, especially a large house on an estate. **9.** Membership in a legislature, stock exchange, or similar organization. **10.** The manner of sitting on a horse. —*tr.v.* **seat•ed, seat•ing, seats. 1.a.** To place in or on a seat. **b.** To assist in sitting down: *The usher sat us in the front row.* **2.** To have seats for: *an auditorium that seats 5,000.* [First written down before 1200 in Middle English and spelled *sete*, probably from Old Norse *sæti.*]

seat belt *n.* A safety strap or harness designed to hold a person securely in a seat, as in a car or airplane.

Se•at•tle (sē ăt′l). The largest city in Washington, in the west-central part of the state on Puget Sound north-northwest of Olympia. It was settled in the 1850's. Population, 516,259.

sea urchin *n.* Any of various sea animals having a soft body enclosed in a spiny shell.

sea•ward (sē′wərd) *adv. & adj.* Toward or at the sea: *a seaward breeze.*

sea•way (sē′wā′) *n.* **1.** A sea route. **2.** An inland waterway for ocean shipping.

sea•weed (sē′wēd′) *n.* Any of various plants or algae that live in ocean waters.

sea•wor•thy (sē′wûr′thē) *adj.* **sea•wor•thi•er, sea•wor•thi•est.** Fit for crossing the sea. —**sea′wor′thi•ness** *n.*

se•ba•ceous (sĭ bā′shəs) *adj.* Relating to or secreting a fatty or oily substance.

sebaceous gland *n.* Any of the tiny glands in the skin that secrete an oily material into the hair follicles.

sec *abbr.* An abbreviation of second (unit of time).

sec. *abbr.* An abbreviation of secant.

se•cant (sē′kănt′) *n.* **1.** A straight line or ray that intersects a curve, especially a circle, at two or more points. **2.** In a right triangle, the ratio of the length of a hypotenuse to the side adjacent to an acute angle.

se•cede (sĭ sēd′) *intr.v.* **se•ced•ed, se•ced•ing, se•cedes.** To withdraw formally from membership in an organization or union: *states that seceded before the Civil War.* [First written down in 1702 in Modern English, from Latin *sēcēdere*, to withdraw : *sē-*, apart + *cēdere*, to go.]

se•ces•sion (sĭ sĕsh′ən) *n.* **1.** The act of seceding. **2.** Often **Secession.** The withdrawal of 11 southern states from the Union in 1860–1861, which brought on the U.S. Civil War. **—se•ces′sion•ism** *n.* **—se•ces′sion•ist** *n.*

se•clude (sĭ klo͞od′) *tr.v.* **se•clud•ed, se•clud•ing, se•cludes.** To set or keep apart, as from social contact with others: *secluded himself from the world.* [First written down in 1451 in Middle English and spelled *secluden*, to shut off, from Latin *sēclūdere* : *sē-*, apart + *claudere*, to shut.]

se•clud•ed (sĭ klo͞o′dĭd) *adj.* **1.** Removed or distant from others; alone: *a secluded life.* **2.** Screened or hidden from view: *a secluded pool.* **—se•clud′ed•ness** *n.*

se•clu•sion (sĭ klo͞o′zhən) *n.* **1.** The act of secluding. **2.** The condition of being secluded; solitude.

sec•ond¹ (sĕk′ənd) *n.* **1.** A unit of time equal to 1/60 of a minute. **2.** A short period of time; a moment. **3.** A unit of angular measure equal to 1/60 of a minute of arc. [First written down in 1391 in Middle English and spelled *seconde*, from Medieval Latin *(pars minūta) secunda*, second (small part).]

sec•ond² (sĕk′ənd) *adj.* **1.** Coming next after the first in order, place, rank, time, or quality: *the second floor.* **2.** Alternate; other: *every second year.* **3.** Inferior to another: *an accomplishment second only to yours.* **4.a.** Having a lower pitch or range: *the second sopranos of a choir.* **b.** Singing or playing a part having a lower range: *the second violins of an orchestra.* **5.** Of or relating to the transmission gear used to produce speeds next highest to those of first in a motor vehicle. *—n.* **1.** The ordinal number matching the number two in a series. **2.** A piece of merchandise of inferior quality. Often used in the plural: *The socks on sale are seconds.* **3.** An attendant of a contestant in a duel or boxing match. **4.a.** The interval between two adjacent tones of a musical scale. **b.** The second tone in a musical scale. **5.** The transmission gear used to produce speeds next highest to those of first in a motor vehicle. *—tr.v.* **sec•ond•ed, sec•ond•ing, sec•onds. 1.** To promote or encourage. **2.** To endorse (a motion or nomination) as a means of bringing it to a vote. *—adv.* **1.** In the second order, place, or rank: *finished second in the race.* **2.** But for one other; save one: *the second-largest seaport.* [First written down about 1300 in Middle English and spelled *secunde*, from Latin *secundus*, following.] **—sec′ond•er** *n.*

sec•ond•ar•y (sĕk′ən dĕr′ē) *adj.* **1.** Of the second rank; not primary: *a secondary cause.* **2.** Derived from what is primary or original: *secondary sources of information.* **3.** Having a current or voltage induced by the magnetic field caused by a current flowing in another coil: *the secondary coil of a transformer.* **4.** Of or relating to a secondary school. *—n., pl.* **sec•ond•ar•ies. 1.** A secondary electric coil or circuit. **2.** In football, the defensive backfield. **—sec′on•dar′i•ly** (sĕk′ən dâr′ə lē) *adv.*

secondary accent *n.* **1.** In a word having more than one accented syllable, the accent or stress that is weaker than the primary one. **2.** A mark, such as (″), used to indicate this accent.

secondary color *n.* A color produced by mixing two primary colors in approximately equal proportions.

secondary school *n.* A school for instruction between elementary school and college.

secondary sex characteristic *n.* Any of various genetically transmitted physical or behavioral characteristics that appear in humans at puberty and distinguish males and females without having a direct relation to reproduction, such as breast development or distribution of body hair.

second base *n.* In baseball, the base that is across the diamond from home plate, touched second by a runner.

second baseman *n.* In baseball, the player defending the area near second base.

second class *n.* **1.** Travel accommodations ranking next below first class, as on a train or an airplane. **2.** Second-class mail.

sec•ond-class (sĕk′ənd klăs′) *adj.* **1.** Of secondary status. **2.** Of or relating to travel accommodations ranking next below first class. **3.** Of or relating to a class of U.S. and Canadian mail consisting of newspapers and periodicals. *—adv.* By means of second-class mail or travel accommodations.

Second Coming *n.* In Christianity, the return of Jesus as judge for the Last Judgment.

sec•ond-de•gree burn (sĕk′ənd dĭ grē′) *n.* A burn that blisters the skin.

sec•ond-guess (sĕk′ənd gĕs′) *tr.v.* **sec•ond•guessed, sec•ond•guess•ing, sec•ond•guess•es.** To criticize or correct (a person or thing) after an outcome is known.

sec•ond•hand (sĕk′ənd hănd′) *adj.* **1.** Previously used by another; not new: *a secondhand coat.* **2.** Dealing in previously used goods: *a secondhand store.* **3.** Obtained or derived from another; not original; borrowed: *secondhand data.* *—adv.* In an indirect manner; indirectly: *news gathered secondhand.*

second hand *n.* The hand of a clock or watch that indicates the seconds.

second lieutenant *n.* An officer holding the lowest commissioned rank in the U.S. Army, Air Force, and Marine Corps.

sec•ond•ly (sĕk′ənd lē) *adv.* In the second place; second.

second nature *n.* A behavior or characteristic that was originally learned, but that comes to seem natural through long practice.

second person *n.* **1.** A set of grammatical forms used in referring to the person addressed. **2.** One of these forms, such as *you* and *are* in *You are my friend.*

sec•ond-rate (sĕk′ənd rāt′) *adj.* Inferior in quality; mediocre.

se•cre•cy (sē′krĭ sē) *n., pl.* **se•cre•cies. 1.** The condition of being secret or hidden; concealment: *work done in secrecy.* **2.** The practice of keeping secrets: *They pledged her to secrecy.*

se•cret (sē′krĭt) *adj.* **1.** Kept hidden from general knowledge or view: *secret plans.* **2.** Working in a hidden or confidential manner: *secret agents.* **3.** Not much visited; secluded: *a secret hiding place.* **4.** Beyond ordinary understanding; mysterious: *God's secret ways.* *—n.* **1.** Something kept hidden or known only to oneself or to a few. **2.** Something beyond understanding or explanation: *the secret of the homing pigeon's instinct.* **3.** A method or formula for accomplishing something: *the secret of making good pie crust.* *—idiom.* **in secret. 1.** Not openly; in a manner unknown to the public. **2.** Privately. [First written down about 1378 in Middle

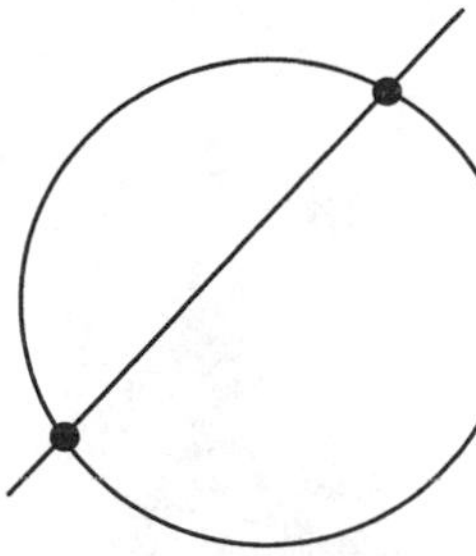

secant
Intersecting a curve

ă	pat	oi	boy
ā	pay	ou	out
âr	care	o͝o	took
ä	father	o͞o	boot
ĕ	pet	ŭ	cut
ē	be	ûr	urge
ĭ	pit	th	thin
ī	pie	*th*	this
îr	pier	hw	whoop
ŏ	pot	zh	vision
ō	toe	ə	about
ô	paw	N	*French* bon

secretary

secretary bird

English, from Latin *sēcrētus*, set apart : *sē-*, apart + *cernere*, to separate.] **—se′cret•ly** *adv.*

sec•re•tar•i•at (sĕk′rĭ târ′ē ĭt) *n.* **1.** The department managed by a governmental secretary, especially for an international organization such as the United Nations. **2.** The headquarters of such a department.

sec•re•tar•y (sĕk′rĭ tĕr′ē) *n., pl.* **sec•re•tar•ies. 1.** A person employed to do clerical work, such as typing, filing, and taking messages. **2.** An officer who takes minutes of meetings, answers correspondence, and keeps records, as for a company. **3.** The head of a governmental department: *the Secretary of State.* **4.** A desk with a small bookcase on top. [First written down before 1387 in Middle English and spelled *secretarie*, someone entrusted with secrets, from Latin *sēcrētus*, secret.] **—sec′re•tar′i•al** (sĕk′rĭ târ′ē əl) *adj.*

secretary bird *n.* A large African bird having long legs and a crest of feathers at the back of the head.

sec•re•tar•y-gen•er•al (sĕk′rĭ tĕr′ē jĕn′ər əl) *n., pl.* **sec•re•tar•ies-gen•er•al** (sĕk′rĭ tĕr′ēz jĕn′ər-əl). A principal executive officer, as of a political party or governmental body such as the United Nations.

se•crete¹ (sĭ krēt′) *tr.v.* **se•cret•ed, se•cret•ing, se•cret•es.** To produce or separate (a substance) from cells or bodily fluids. [First written down in 1707 in Modern English, from Old French *secretion*, separation, from Latin *sēcernere*, to put aside.]

se•crete² (sĭ krēt′) *tr.v.* **se•cret•ed, se•cret•ing, se•cret•es.** To conceal in a hiding place; hide. See Synonyms at **hide¹**. [First written down in 1741 in Modern English, from *secret*.]

se•cre•tion (sĭ krē′shən) *n.* **1.** The act or process of secreting a substance, especially one that is not a waste, from blood or cells. **2.** A substance, such as tears or a hormone, that is secreted.

se•cre•tive (sē′krĭ tĭv *or* sĭ krē′tĭv) *adj.* Practicing or inclined to secrecy. **—se′cre•tive•ly** *adv.* **—se′cre•tive•ness** *n.*

se•cre•to•ry (sĭ krē′tə rē) *adj.* Relating to or performing secretion.

secret police *n.* A police force operating in secret and often using terrorism to crush political opposition to the government.

secret service *n.* **1.** The gathering of secret information by a government; intelligence work. **2. Secret Service.** A branch of the U.S. Treasury Department whose work includes the protection of the President.

sect (sĕkt) *n.* **1.** A group of people forming a distinct unit within a larger group. **2.** A religious group, especially one that has separated from a larger group.

sect. *abbr.* An abbreviation of section.

sec•tar•i•an (sĕk târ′ē ən) *adj.* **1.** Of, relating to, or characteristic of a sect. **2.** Narrow-minded; partisan or parochial. **—sec•tar′i•an•ism** *n.*

sec•tion (sĕk′shən) *n.* **1.** One of several parts that make up something; a piece: *a section of grapefruit.* **2.** A part of a written work: *the sports section of a newspaper.* **3.** A distinct area of a town, country, or city: *the residential section of town.* **4.** The act or process of cutting or separating, especially the separation of tissue in surgery. **5.** A picture or diagram showing the internal structure of a solid object as it would appear if the object were cut by an intersecting plane; a cross section. **6.** A group of musical instruments or voices considered as a unit: *the woodwind section of the orchestra.* *—tr.v.* **sec•tioned, sec•tion•ing, sec•tions. 1.** To separate into parts. **2.** To cut or separate (tissue) surgically. [First written down about 1319 in Middle English and spelled *seccion*, from Latin *sectiō*, a cutting, from *secāre*, to cut.]

sec•tion•al (sĕk′shə nəl) *adj.* **1.** Of, relating to, or characteristic of a particular district. **2.** Composed of or divided into sections: *sectional furniture.* **—sec′tion•al•ly** *adv.*

sec•tion•al•ism (sĕk′shə nə lĭz′əm) *n.* Excessive devotion to local interests and customs. **—sec′tion•al•ist** *adj. & n.*

sec•tor (sĕk′tər *or* sĕk′tôr′) *n.* **1.** The part of a circle bound by two radii and the arc between them. **2.** A particular military area or zone of action. **3.** A division of something: *the manufacturing sector of the economy.* [First written down in 1570 in Modern English, from Latin *sector*, one that cuts, from *secāre*, to cut.]

sec•u•lar (sĕk′yə lər) *adj.* **1.** Worldly rather than spiritual: *secular interests.* **2.** Not related to religion or a religious organization: *a concert of secular music.* **3.** Not bound by monastic rules: *the secular clergy.* [First written down about 1300 in Middle English and spelled *seculer*, from Latin *saeculum*, generation, age.]

sec•u•lar•ize (sĕk′yə lə rīz′) *tr.v.* **sec•u•lar•ized, sec•u•lar•iz•ing, sec•u•lar•iz•es. 1.** To draw (someone) away from religious orientation; make worldly. **2.** To lift the monastic restrictions from (a member of the clergy). **—sec′u•lar•i•za′tion** (sĕk′-yə lər ĭ zā′shən) *n.*

se•cure (sĭ kyŏŏr′) *adj.* **se•cur•er, se•cur•est. 1.** Free from danger or attack: *a secure castle.* **2.** Free from risk of loss; safe: *The jewels are secure in the vault.* **3.** Free from fear, anxiety, or doubt: *feeling secure at home.* **4.** Not likely to fail or give way: *a secure foothold.* **5.** Firmly fastened: *The antenna is secure.* **6.** Assured; certain: *a secure peace.* *—tr.v.* **se•cured, se•cur•ing, se•cures. 1.** To guard from danger or risk of loss: *secured the city against attack.* **2.** To cause to remain firmly in position or place; fasten: *secure the ship's hatches.* **3.** To make certain; ensure: *a constitution designed to secure our freedom.* **4.** To guarantee or make sure with a pledge: *deposited collateral to secure the loan.* **5.** To get possession of; acquire: *secure a job.* **6.** To bring about; effect: *secured their release from prison.* [First written down in 1533 in Modern English, from Latin *sēcūrus* : *sē-*, without + *cūra*, care.] **—se•cure′ly** *adv.*

se•cu•ri•ty (sĭ kyŏŏr′ĭ tē) *n., pl.* **se•cu•ri•ties. 1.** Freedom from risk or danger; safety. **2.** A person, an act, or a thing that gives or assures safety or confidence. **3.** A pledge deposited or given to guarantee fulfillment of an obligation: *an extra month's rent given as security.* **4.** A stock or bond.

secy. *abbr.* An abbreviation of secretary.

se•dan (sĭ dăn′) *n.* **1.** A closed automobile having two or four doors and a front and rear seat. **2.** An enclosed chair for one person, carried on poles by two other people.

se•date¹ (sĭ dāt′) *adj.* Calm and dignified; composed. [First written down in 1663 in Modern English, from Latin *sēdāre*, to settle, calm.] **—se•date′ly** *adv.* **—se•date′ness** *n.*

se•date² (sĭ dāt′) *tr.v.* **se•dat•ed, se•dat•ing, se•dates.** To administer a sedative to. [First written down in 1945 in Modern English, from *sedation*, a calming, from Latin *sēdāre*, to settle, calm.]

se•da•tion (sĭ dā′shən) *n.* **1.** The act or process of calming by administration of a sedative. **2.** The condition brought on by a sedative.

sed•a•tive (sĕd′ə tĭv) *adj.* Having a soothing, calming, or quieting effect. *—n.* A sedative medicine or drug.

sed•en•tar•y (sĕd′n tĕr′ē) *adj.* **1.** Marked by or requiring much sitting: *sedentary work.* **2.** Accustomed to sitting or to taking little exercise. **3.** Living in one place; not migratory: *Pigeons are sedentary birds.* **—sed′en•tar′i•ly** (sĕd′n târ′ə lē) *adv.*

Se•der (sā′dər) *n., pl.* **Se•ders** or **Se•dar•im** (sĭ-där′ĭm *or* sĕ dä rīm′). In Judaism, the feast commemorating the departure of the Jews from Egypt, celebrated on the first two nights of Passover. [First written down in 1865 in Modern English, from Hebrew *sēder*, order, arrangement.]

sedge (sĕj) *n.* Any of numerous grassy plants that grow chiefly in wet places.

sed•i•ment (sĕd′ə mənt) *n.* **1.** Finely divided solid matter that falls to the bottom of a liquid. **2.** Silt, sand, stones, and other matter carried and deposited by water, wind, or ice. [First written down in 1547 in Modern English, from Latin *sedimentum*, act of settling, from *sedēre*, to sit, settle.]

sed•i•men•ta•ry (sĕd′ə mĕn′tə rē *or* sĕd′ə mĕn′-trē) *adj.* **1.** Of, resembling, or derived from sediment. **2.** Of or relating to rocks formed from sediment deposited in water.

sed•i•men•ta•tion (sĕd′ə mən tā′shən) *n.* The act or process of depositing sediment.

se•di•tion (sĭ dĭsh′ən) *n.* **1.** Conduct or language that causes others to rebel against the authority of the government. **2.** Rebellion.

se•di•tious (sĭ dĭsh′əs) *adj.* Of, relating to, or engaged in sedition. **—se•di′tious•ly** *adv.*

se•duce (sĭ dōōs′ *or* sĭ dyōōs′) *tr.v.* **se•duced, se•duc•ing, se•duc•es. 1.** To persuade (someone) to engage in wrongful or immoral behavior. **2.** To persuade (someone) to have sexual intercourse. **—se•duc′er** *n.*

se•duc•tion (sĭ dŭk′shən) *n.* **1.** The act of seducing or the condition of being seduced. **2.** Something that seduces; a temptation.

se•duc•tive (sĭ dŭk′tĭv) *adj.* Tending to seduce; alluring; enticing. **—se•duc′tive•ly** *adv.* **—se•duc′tive•ness** *n.*

sed•u•lous (sĕj′ə ləs) *adj.* Constant in effort or work; diligent; industrious. **—sed′u•lous•ly** *adv.* **—sed′u•lous•ness** *n.*

see¹ (sē) *v.* **saw** (sô), **seen** (sēn), **see•ing, sees.** *—tr.* **1.** To perceive with the eye: *He saw a dog.* **2.** To have a mental picture of; grasp mentally: *They could see their hometown as it once was.* **3.** To understand; comprehend: *I see what you mean.* **4.** To regard; consider to be: *We see her as a world leader.* **5.** To imagine; believe possible: *We can see him as an architect.* **6.** To foresee: *I can see great things in your future.* **7.** To know through actual experience; undergo: *We had seen hard times.* **8.** To be marked by or bring forth: *The 1930's saw the development of antibiotics.* **9.** To find out; ascertain: *See whether that statement is accurate.* **10.** To refer to; read: *See the footnote on the next page.* **11.** To spend time with often or regularly, as in dating: *They've been seeing each other for two years.* **12.a.** To visit socially: *May I see you tonight?* **b.** To visit for consultation: *He saw a lawyer.* **13.** To receive or admit: *The doctor will see you now.* **14.** To attend; view: *We saw a good movie last night.* **15.** To escort; attend: *See her to the bus station.* **16.** To make sure; take care: *Always see that the door is locked.* *—intr.* **1.** To be able to perceive with the eye: *Can you see from there?* **2.** To understand; comprehend. **3.** To consider: *Let's see, what movie should we go to?* ***—idioms.*** **see about. 1.** To attend to. **2.** To investigate. **see after.** To take care of: *Please see after your brother while I go to the store.* **see off.** To take leave of (someone): *saw the guests off at the station.* **see out.** To escort (a guest) to the door: *Will you please see Ms. Smith out?* **see through. 1.** To understand the true character or nature of: *She saw through his sales pitch.* **2.** To support or continue with in good times and bad: *I want to see the project through to the end.* **see to.** To attend to: *See to the chores, please.* [First written down about 725 in Old English and spelled *sēon.*]

❑ *These sound alike:* **see¹** (perceive with the eyes), **see²** (bishop's position), **sea** (body of salt water), **si** (musical note).

Synonyms: see, notice, observe, view. These verbs mean to be visually aware of something. **See** is the most general term: *Did you see the lunar eclipse last night?* **Observe** can mean to look carefully and closely: *We observed a change in the color of the water as it got deeper.* **Notice** can mean to observe closely and form a rather detailed impression: *He didn't notice that frost had formed on the window.* **View** can mean to examine with a particular purpose in mind or in a special way: *The jury wished to view the evidence again.*

---

see² (sē) *n.* The position, authority, or jurisdiction of a bishop. [First written down about 1300 in Middle English and spelled *se*, from Old French, from Latin *sēdēs*, seat.]

❑ *These sound alike:* **see²** (bishop's position), **see¹** (perceive with the eyes), **sea** (body of salt water), **si** (musical note).

seed (sēd) *n., pl.* **seeds** or **seed. 1.** A part of a flowering plant that develops from a fertilized ovule and contains an embryo and the food it will need to grow into a new plant. **2.** Seeds considered as a group. **3.** A source or beginning: *This treaty holds the seeds of a lasting peace.* **4.** Offspring or descendents. *—v.* **seed•ed, seed•ing, seeds.** *—tr.* **1.** To plant seeds in; sow: *seeded four acres of land.* **2.** To remove the seeds from (fruit). **3.** To sprinkle (a cloud or clouds) with particles, as of silver iodide or dry ice, to cause it to disperse or produce rain. *—intr.* **1.** To sow seed. **2.** To go to seed. ***—idiom.*** **go to seed. 1.** To pass the seed-bearing stage. **2.** To become weak or deteriorate. **—seed′less** *adj.*

❑ *These sound alike:* **seed, cede** (give up).

seed coat *n.* The outer protective covering of a seed.

seed•er (sē′dər) *n.* **1.** A machine or tool used for planting seeds. **2.** A machine or tool used to remove seeds from fruit.

seed leaf *n.* An embryonic leaf in the seed of a plant; a cotyledon.

seed•ling (sēd′lĭng) *n.* **1.** A young plant that is grown from a seed. **2.** A young tree less than three feet high.

seed pearl *n.* A very small pearl.

seed•y (sē′dē) *adj.* **seed•i•er, seed•i•est. 1.** Having many seeds: *Raspberries are seedy.* **2.** Shabby and disreputable: *a seedy hotel.* **—seed′i•ness** *n.*

seek (sēk) *v.* **sought** (sôt), **seek•ing, seeks.** *—tr.* **1.** To try to locate or discover; search for: *The elephants moved, seeking a new source of water.* **2.** To try to obtain: *seek a college education.* **3.** To make an attempt; try: *seek to learn a foreign language.* *—intr.* To make a search. **—seek′er** *n.*

seem (sēm) *intr.v.* **seemed, seem•ing, seems. 1.** To give the impression of being; appear to be: *She seems pleased to be in the play.* **2.** To appear to oneself: *I seem unable to finish this book.* **3.** To appear to exist, be true, or be obvious: *There seems to be only one solution.*

❑ *These sound alike:* **seem, seam** (line formed by joining).

seem•ing (sē′mĭng) *adj.* Having an appearance that may or may not be real; apparent: *his seeming friendliness.* **—seem′ing•ly** *adv.*

seem•ly (sēm′lē) *adj.* **seem•li•er, seem•li•est.** Conforming to accepted standards of conduct and good taste; proper: *seemly behavior.*

seen (sēn) *v.* Past participle of **see¹**.

❑ *These sound alike:* **seen, scene** (place).

ă	pat	oi	boy
ā	pay	ou	out
âr	care	ŏŏ	took
ä	father	ōō	boot
ĕ	pet	ŭ	cut
ē	be	ûr	urge
ĭ	pit	th	thin
ī	pie	*th*	this
îr	pier	hw	whoop
ŏ	pot	zh	vision
ō	toe	ə	about
ô	paw	N	*French* bon

seesaw

Word Building: segment

The word root *–seg–*, which is a variant of *–sec–*, in English words comes from the Latin verb *secāre*, "to sever, cut, slice." **Segment** comes from the Latin noun *segmentum*, "a piece removed by cutting off, a section." The past participle of *secāre* is *sectus*, from which we get **bisect**, "cut in half" (using the prefix *bi–*, "twice, in two") and **intersect**, "cut between or among" (*inter–*, "between.") An **insect** is literally "a creature that has been cut into pieces," that is, it has three body segments (*in–²*, "in, into").

Word Building: self–

The prefix **self–** goes back to the Old English word *self*, meaning virtually the same thing it does today. In Old English there were about a dozen compounds with **self–** of which only one has remained common: **self-will**. In Modern English, however, the number of new compounds with **self–** has increased. **Self–** usually forms compounds with adjectives, as in **self-conscious**, **self-employed**, and **self-governing**, and nouns, as in **self-confidence**, **self-improvement**, and **self-satisfaction**, and indicates something about oneself.

seep (sēp) *intr.v.* **seeped, seep•ing, seeps.** To pass slowly through small openings: *Cold air seeped in through the cracks around the window.*

seep•age (sē′pĭj) *n.* **1.** The act or process of seeping; leakage. **2.** The amount of something that has seeped in or out.

seer (sîr) *n.* **1.** A person who sees. *a seer of sights.* **2.** A person who foresees or foretells events.
❑ *These sound alike:* **seer, sear** (scorch), **sere** (withered).

seer•suck•er (sîr′sŭk′ər) *n.* A light thin fabric, generally of cotton or rayon, having a crinkled surface and a usually striped pattern.

see•saw (sē′sô′) *n.* A long plank balanced on a central support so that with a person riding on either end, one goes up as the other goes down. —*intr.v.* **see•sawed, see•saw•ing, see•saws. 1.** To ride on a seesaw. **2.** To move back and forth or up and down.

seethe (sēth) *intr.v.* **seethed, seeth•ing, seethes. 1.** To churn and foam as if boiling. **2.** To be in a state of turmoil or ferment: *The town seethed with excitement.* **3.** To be violently agitated: *She seethed with anger.* [First written down about 725 in Old English and spelled *sēothan*.]

seg•ment (sĕg′mənt) *n.* **1.** A part into which something is or can be divided; a section or division: *the various segments of American society.* **2. a.** The portion of a line between any two of its points. **b.** The region bounded by an arc of a circle and the chord that connects the endpoints of the arc. **c.** The portion of a sphere included between a pair of parallel planes that intersect it or are tangent to it. —*tr. & intr.v.* (sĕg mĕnt′). **seg•ment•ed, seg•ment•ing, seg•ments.** To divide or become divided into segments. [First written down in 1570 in Modern English, from Latin *segmentum*, from *secāre*, to cut.] —SEE NOTE.

seg•men•ta•tion (sĕg′mən tā′shən) *n.* **1.** Division into segments. **2.** The early divisions of a cell into many cells; cleavage.

se•go lily (sē′gō) *n.* A plant of western North America having showy white or purplish flowers and an edible bulb.

seg•re•gate (sĕg′rĭ gāt′) *v.* **seg•re•gat•ed, seg•re•gat•ing, seg•re•gates.** —*tr.* **1.** To separate or isolate from others or from a main body or group: *segregate the sick children from the others.* **2.** To impose the separation of (a race or class) from the rest of society. —*intr.* To practice a policy of racial segregation.

seg•re•ga•tion (sĕg′rĭ gā′shən) *n.* **1.** The act or process of segregating or the condition of being segregated. **2.** The policy and practice of segregating a race, as in schools, housing, and industry, especially so as to discriminate against people of color in a mostly white society. —**seg′re•ga′tion•ist** *adj.*

seg•re•ga•tion•ist (sĕg′rĭ gā′shə nĭst) *n.* A person who advocates racial segregation.

seine (sān) *n.* A large fishing net with weights at the lower edge and floats at the top. —*tr. & intr.v.* **seined, sein•ing, seines.** To fish or catch with a seine. [First written down about 950 in Old English and spelled *segne*, from Greek *sagēnē*.]
❑ *These sound alike:* **seine, sane** (of sound mind).

Seine (sān *or* sĕn). A river of northern France flowing about 480 miles (772 kilometers) generally northwest to an inlet of the English Channel near Le Havre.

seism– *pref.* Variant of **seismo–**.

seis•mic (sīz′mĭk) *adj.* Of, subject to, or caused by an earthquake or earthquakes: *a seismic disturbance.* [First written down in 1858 in Modern English, from Greek *seismos*, earthquake.]

seismo– or **seism–** *pref.* A prefix that means earthquake: *seismology.*

seis•mo•graph (sīz′mə grăf′) *n.* An instrument that detects and records movement in Earth's crust.

seis•mol•o•gy (sīz mŏl′ə jē) *n.* The scientific study of earthquakes and other movements of the earth's crust.

seize (sēz) *tr.v.* **seized, seiz•ing, seiz•es. 1.** To grasp suddenly and forcibly; take or grab: *The police officer seized his arm.* **2.** To comprehend: *seize an idea and develop it.* **3.** To take eagerly: *seize the opportunity to leave.* **4.** To have a sudden effect on; overwhelm: *Stage fright seized the boy.* **5.** To take prisoner; capture. **6.** To take possession of by force: *The agents seized the contraband.*

sei•zure (sē′zhər) *n.* **1.** The act or an instance of seizing or the condition of being seized. **2.** A sudden fit or convulsion, as in epilepsy or a heart attack.

sel•dom (sĕl′dəm) *adv.* Not often; rarely: *A woodchuck seldom strays far from its burrow.*

se•lect (sĭ lĕkt′) *tr.v.* **se•lect•ed, se•lect•ing, se•lects.** To choose from among several; pick out: *select the ripest pears.* —*adj.* **1.** Carefully picked out or chosen: *a select group of students.* **2.** Of special quality; choice: *a select product.* [First written down in 1567 in Modern English, from Latin *sēligere* : *sē-*, apart + *legere*, to choose.]

se•lec•tion (sĭ lĕk′shən) *n.* **1.a.** The act of selecting. See Synonyms at **choice**. **b.** A person or thing selected. **2.** A carefully chosen or representative group of persons or things: *a selection of fine books.* **3.** A literary or musical text chosen for reading or performance. **4.** A natural or artificial process by which certain animals or plants survive and reproduce their kind, while others die or are prevented from breeding.

se•lec•tive (sĭ lĕk′tĭv) *adj.* **1.** Of or characterized by selection: *selective reading.* **2.** Tending to select; fastidious: *He is very selective in his taste in music.* —**se•lec′tive•ly** *adv.*

selective service *n.* A system for calling up people for compulsory military service.

se•lec•tiv•i•ty (sĭ lĕk′tĭv′ĭ tē) *n., pl.* **se•lec•tiv•i•ties.** The state or quality of being selective.

se•lect•man (sĭ lĕkt′măn′) *n.* One of a board of town officers chosen annually in New England communities to manage local affairs.

se•lec•tor (sĭ lĕk′tər) *n.* A person or thing that selects: *a frequency selector.*

se•lect•wom•an (sĭ lĕkt′wo͝om′ən) *n.* A woman who is one of a board of town officers chosen annually in New England communities to manage local affairs.

Se•le•ne (sə lē′nē) *n.* In Greek mythology, the goddess of the moon.

se•le•ni•um (sĭ lē′nē əm) *n. Symbol* **Se** A nonmetallic element that can exist as a red powder, a black glassy material, or a gray crystal, with chemical properties resembling those of sulfur. Because its electrical conductivity increases with the intensity of light striking it, selenium is used in photoelectric cells. Atomic number 34. See table at **element**.

self (sĕlf) *n., pl.* **selves** (sĕlvz). **1.** The total or essential being of a person apart from everyone else; the individual: *one's own self.* **2.** The qualities that distinguish one person from another; individuality: *back to his old cheerful self.* **3.** One's own interests, welfare, or advantage: *thinking of self alone.*

self– *pref.* A prefix that means: **1.** Oneself or itself: *self-evident.* **2.** Automatic or automatically: *self-winding.* —SEE NOTE.

self-ad•dressed (sĕlf′ə drĕst′) *adj.* Addressed to oneself: *a self-addressed stamped envelope.*

self-ap•point•ed (sĕlf′ə point′tĭd) *adj.* Designated

or chosen by oneself rather than by due authority: *a self-appointed judge.*

self-as•sured (sĕlf′ə **shŏŏrd′**) *adj.* Having or showing confidence and sureness. **—self-as•sur′ance** (sĕlf′ə **shŏŏr′**əns) *n.*

self-cen•tered (**sĕlf′sĕn′**tərd) *adj.* Concerned only with one's own needs and interests; selfish. **—self′-cen′tered•ness** *n.*

self-con•fi•dence (**sĕlf′kŏn′**fĭ dəns) *n.* Confidence in oneself or one's abilities. **—self′-con′fi•dent** *adj.*

self-con•scious (**sĕlf′kŏn′**shəs) *adj.* **1.** Excessively conscious of one's appearance or manner; socially ill at ease: *a self-conscious person.* **2.** Not natural; stilted: *a self-conscious laugh.* **—self′-con′scious•ly** *adv.* **—self′-con′scious•ness** *n.*

self-con•tained (sĕlf′kən **tānd′**) *adj.* **1.** Not dependent on others; independent; self-sufficient: *The island was economically self-contained.* **2.** Keeping to oneself; reserved.

self-con•trol (sĕlf′kən **trōl′**) *n.* Control of one's emotions and behavior by one's own will. **—self′-con•trolled′** *adj.*

self-de•fense (sĕlf′dĭ **fĕns′**) *n.* **1.** Defense of oneself against attack. **2.** The legal right to use whatever means are necessary to protect oneself against violence or threatened violence.

self-de•ni•al (sĕlf′dĭ **nī′**əl) *n.* Sacrifice of one's own desires or interests.

self-de•ter•mi•na•tion (sĕlf′dĭ tûr′mə **nā′**shən) *n.* **1.** Determination of one's own fate or course of action without being forced; free will. **2.** Freedom of the people of a given area to determine their own political status; independence.

self-dis•ci•pline (**sĕlf′dĭs′**ə plĭn) *n.* Training and control of oneself and one's conduct, usually for personal improvement.

self-ed•u•cat•ed (**sĕlf′ĕj′**ə kā′tĭd) *adj.* Educated by one's own efforts, without formal instruction.

self-em•ployed (sĕlf′ĕm **ploid′**) *adj.* Earning one's living by working for oneself, rather than for an employer.

self-es•teem (sĕlf′ĭ **stēm′**) *n.* Pride in oneself; self-respect.

self-ev•i•dent (**sĕlf′ĕv′**ĭ dənt) *adj.* Requiring no proof or explanation.

self-ex•plan•a•to•ry (sĕlf′ĭk **splăn′**ə tôr′ē) *adj.* Requiring no explanation; obvious.

self-ex•pres•sion (sĕlf′ĭk **sprĕsh′**ən) *n.* Expression of one's own personality, feelings, or ideas, as through speech or art.

self-ful•fill•ing (sĕlf′fŏŏl **fĭl′**ĭng) *adj.* Achieving fulfillment as a result of having been expected or foretold: *a self-fulfilling prophecy.*

self-gov•ern•ing (**sĕlf′gŭv′**ər nĭng) *adj.* **1.** Exercising control or rule over oneself or itself. **2.** Having the right or power of self-government; independent.

self-gov•ern•ment (**sĕlf′gŭv′**ərn mənt) *n.* **1.** Political independence. **2.** Representative government; democracy.

self-help (**sĕlf′hĕlp′**) *n.* The act or an instance of helping or improving oneself.

self-im•por•tance (sĕlf′ĭm **pôr′**tns) *n.* An excessively high opinion of one's own importance or position; conceit. **—self′-im•por′tant** *adj.*

self-im•prove•ment (sĕlf′ĭm **prōōv′**mənt) *n.* Improvement of one's condition through one's own efforts.

self-in•ter•est (**sĕlf′ĭn′**trĭst *or* **sĕlf′ĭn′**tər ĭst) *n.* **1.** Selfish regard for one's personal advantage or interest. **2.** Personal advantage or interest.

self•ish (**sĕl′**fĭsh) *adj.* **1.** Concerned mainly with oneself with little or no regard for others: *a selfish person.* **2.** Showing lack of regard for others: *a selfish act.* **—self′ish•ly** *adv.* **—self′ish•ness** *n.*

self•less (**sĕlf′**lĭs) *adj.* Having, showing, or based on no concern for oneself; unselfish. **—self′less•ly** *adv.* **—self′less•ness** *n.*

self-made (**sĕlf′mād′**) *adj.* Having achieved success by one's own efforts: *a self-made woman.*

self-pit•y (**sĕlf′pĭt′**ē) *n.* Pity for oneself.

self-pol•li•na•tion (sĕlf′pŏl′ə **nā′**shən) *n.* The transfer of pollen from the anther to the stigma of the same flower or to the stigma of another flower of the same plant.

self-por•trait (**sĕlf′pôr′**trĭt *or* **sĕlf′pôr′**trāt′) *n.* A portrait of oneself made by oneself.

self-pos•ses•sion (sĕlf′pə **zĕsh′**ən) *n.* Full command of one's feelings and behavior; presence of mind; poise. **—self′-pos•sessed′** *adj.*

self-pres•er•va•tion (sĕlf′prĕz′ər **vā′**shən) *n.* **1.** Protection of oneself from harm or destruction. **2.** The instinct for survival.

self-pro•pelled (sĕlf′prə **pĕld′**) *adj.* Containing its own means of propulsion: *a self-propelled golf cart.*

self-re•gard (sĕlf′rĭ **gärd′**) *n.* **1.** Consideration of one's self or one's interests. **2.** Self-respect.

self-re•li•ance (sĕlf′rĭ **lī′**əns) *n.* Reliance on one's own capabilities or resources. **—self′-re•li′ant** *adj.*

self-re•spect (sĕlf′rĭ **spĕkt′**) *n.* Appropriate or due respect for oneself, one's character, and one's behavior. **—self′-re•spect′ing** *adj.*

self-re•straint (sĕlf′rĭ **strānt′**) *n.* Restraint of one's emotions, desires, or inclinations; self-control.

self-right•eous (**sĕlf′rī′**chəs) *adj.* Smugly sure of one's righteousness. **—self′-right′eous•ly** *adv.* **—self′-right′eous•ness** *n.*

self-sac•ri•fice (**sĕlf′săk′**rə fīs′) *n.* Sacrifice of one's own interests or well-being for the sake of others or for a cause. **—self′-sac′ri•fic′ing** *adj.*

self•same (**sĕlf′**sām′) *adj.* Exactly identical; being the very same: *eating the self-same cherries he had picked the day before.*

self-sat•is•fac•tion (sĕlf′săt′ĭs **făk′**shən) *n.* Satisfaction, especially smug satisfaction, with oneself or one's accomplishments. **—self′-sat′is•fied′** (**sĕlf′-săt′**ĭs fīd′) *adj.*

self-seek•ing (**sĕlf′sē′**kĭng) *adj.* Seeking only one's own interests or goals; selfish. *—n.* Determined pursuit of one's own interests or goals.

self-serv•ice (**sĕlf′sûr′**vĭs) *adj.* Being a business or service in which customers help themselves: *a self-service laundry.*

self-serving (**sĕlf′sûr′**vĭng) *adj.* Serving one's own interests or showing concern only for one's own interests: *a speech full of self-serving remarks.*

self-styled (**sĕlf′stīld′**) *adj.* As characterized by oneself, often without justification: *a self-styled artist.*

self-suf•fi•cient (sĕlf′sə **fĭsh′**ənt) *adj.* **1.** Able to provide for oneself without help; independent. **2.** Having excessive confidence in oneself; smug. **—self′-suf•fi′cien•cy** *n.*

self-taught (**sĕlf′tôt′**) *adj.* Having taught oneself without formal training or the help of others.

self-will (**sĕlf′wĭl′**) *n.* Willfulness, especially in satisfying one's own desires or maintaining one's own opinions; stubbornness. **—self′-willed′** *adj.*

self-wind•ing (**sĕlf′wīn′**dĭng) *adj.* Designed so that manual winding is unnecessary: *a self-winding watch.*

sell (sĕl) *v.* **sold** (sōld), **sell•ing, sells.** *—tr.* **1.** To exchange or deliver for money or its equivalent: *sell a bike.* **2.** To offer for sale: *This store sells health foods.* **3.** To surrender in exchange for something: *sell one's integrity for a glamorous career.* **4.** To promote: *Advertising sells many products.* *—intr.* **1.** To engage in selling goods. **2.** To be sold or to be on sale: *Fruit sells in this store.* **3.** To be popular on the market: *This tape is selling well.* *—n.* **1.** The activity or an instance of selling. **2.** *Slang.* An item that

ă	pat	oi	boy
ā	pay	ou	out
âr	care	ŏŏ	took
ä	father	ōō	boot
ĕ	pet	ŭ	cut
ē	be	ûr	urge
ĭ	pit	th	thin
ī	pie	*th*	this
îr	pier	hw	whoop
ŏ	pot	zh	vision
ō	toe	ə	about
ô	paw	N	*French* bon

Word Building: semi–

The prefix **semi–** means "half" or "partially." In general it combines with adjectives: *semiattached, semidry, semisweet.* **Semi–** also combines, less commonly, with nouns: *semidarkness, semidesert, semidome.* **Semi–** can be compared with the prefixes **hemi–** and **demi–**. All three have basically the same meaning, but **semi–** comes from Latin *sēmi–*, meaning "half," and **hemi–** comes from Greek *hēmi–*, meaning "half." **Demi–** comes from Latin *dīmidius*, meaning "divided in half," from *dis–*, "apart, asunder" + *medius*, "half."

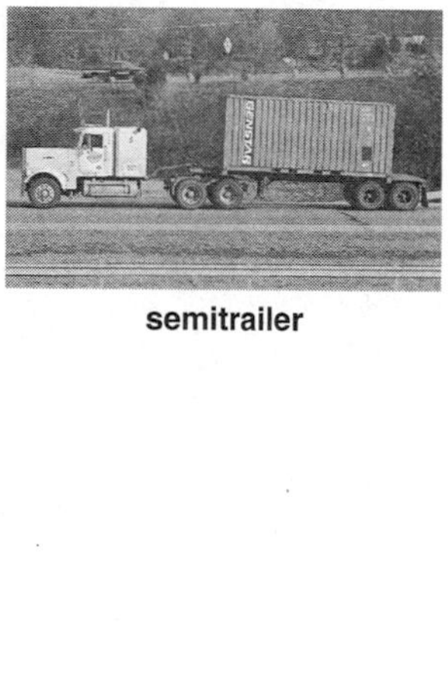

semitrailer

sells in a particular way: *This book was an easy sell.* —*idioms.* **sell off.** To get rid of by selling, often at reduced prices. **sell out. 1.** To put all of one's goods or possessions up for sale. **2.** *Slang.* To betray one's cause or colleagues. [First written down about 725 in Old English and spelled *sellan*, to give, sell.]

❑ *These sound alike:* **sell, cell** (confining room).

sell•er (sĕl′ər) *n.* **1.** A person who sells; a vendor. **2.** An item that sells well or poorly: *This dress has been a very good seller.*

❑ *These sound alike:* **seller, cellar** (basement).

sell•out (sĕl′out′) *n.* **1.** The act of selling out. **2.** An event for which all tickets are sold. **3.** *Slang.* A person who has betrayed a principle or a cause.

selt•zer (sĕlt′sər) *n.* **1.** A naturally bubbly mineral water. **2.** Soda water. [First written down in 1741 in Modern English and spelled *Selters*, from German *Selterser (Wasser)*, (water) of Selters, a village of central Germany.]

sel•vage (sĕl′vĭj) *n.* The edge of a fabric that has been finished so that it will not ravel or fray.

selves (sĕlvz) *n.* Plural of **self.**

se•man•tic (sĭ măn′tĭk) *adj.* **1.** Of or concerned with meaning, especially in language: *a semantic change.* **2.** Of or relating to semantics. [First written down in 1894 in Modern English, from Greek *sēmantos*, marked, significant, from *sēma*, sign.]

se•man•ti•cist (sĭ măn′tĭ sĭst) *n.* A person who specializes in semantics.

se•man•tics (sĭ măn′tĭks) *n.* *(used with a singular or plural verb).* In linguistics, the study of meaning in language forms.

sem•a•phore (sĕm′ə fôr′) *n.* **1.** A visual signaling device with flags, lights, or movable indicators, as on a railroad. **2.** A system for signaling that uses an alphabetic code based on positions of the arms. [First written down in 1816 in Modern English : Greek *sēma*, sign + Greek *-phoros*, carrying.]

sem•blance (sĕm′bləns) *n.* **1.** The appearance of something, whether it is really present or not; show: *keeping up a semblance of dignity.* **2.** A representation; a likeness: *cupped his hands together in the semblance of a heart.*

se•men (sē′mən) *n.* A whitish fluid that carries sperm cells, produced by the male reproductive organs.

❑ *These sound alike:* **semen, seaman** (sailor).

se•mes•ter (sə mĕs′tər) *n.* One of two divisions of 15 to 18 weeks each of a school year. [First written down in 1827 in Modern English, from Latin *(cursus) sēmēstris*, (course) of six months : *sex*, six + *mēnsis*, month.]

semi– *pref.* A prefix that means: **1.** Half: *semicircle.* **2.** Partial or partially: *semiconscious.* **3.** Occurring twice during: *semimonthly.* —See Note.

sem•i•an•nu•al (sĕm′ē ăn′yo͞o əl) *adj.* Occurring or issued twice a year: *semiannual payments; a semiannual magazine.* —**sem′i•an′nu•al•ly** *adv.*

sem•i•ar•id (sĕm′ē ăr′ĭd) *adj.* Characterized by light annual rainfall and sustaining only short grasses and shrubs: *a semiarid region.* —**sem′i•a•rid′i•ty** (sĕm′ē ə rĭd′ĭ tē *or* sĕm′ē ă rĭd′ĭ tē) *n.*

sem•i•au•to•mat•ic (sĕm′ē ô′tə măt′ĭk) *adj.* **1.** Partially automatic. **2.** Being a firearm that ejects the shell and loads the next round of ammunition automatically after each shot has been fired. —*n.* A semiautomatic firearm.

sem•i•cir•cle (sĕm′ĭ sûr′kəl) *n.* An arc of 180 degrees; a half circle. —**sem′i•cir′cu•lar** (sĕm′ĭ sûr′kyə lər) *adj.*

semicircular canal *n.* Any of three tubular looped structures in the labyrinth of the inner ear that act together in maintaining the sense of balance.

sem•i•co•lon (sĕm′ĭ kō′lən) *n.* A punctuation mark (;) used to connect independent clauses and indicating a closer relationship between them than a period does.

sem•i•con•duc•tor (sĕm′ē kən dŭk′tər) *n.* Any of various solid crystalline substances, such as silicon or germanium, that conduct electricity more easily than insulators but less easily than conductors.

sem•i•con•scious (sĕm′ē kŏn′shəs) *adj.* Partially conscious. —**sem′i•con′scious•ly** *adv.* —**sem′i•con′scious•ness** *n.*

sem•i•fi•nal (sĕm′ē fī′nəl) *n.* A match, a competition, or an examination that precedes the final one. —**sem′i•fi′nal** *adj.* —**sem′i•fi′nal•ist** *n.*

sem•i•month•ly (sĕm′ē mŭnth′lē) *adj.* Occurring or issued twice a month: *semimonthly visits.* —*n., pl.* **sem•i•month•lies.** A semimonthly publication. —*adv.* Twice a month: *We meet semimonthly.* —See Note at **biweekly.**

sem•i•nal (sĕm′ə nəl) *adj.* **1.** Of, relating to, or containing semen or sperm cells: *seminal fluid.* **2.** Giving rise to something new: *seminal ideas.*

sem•i•nar (sĕm′ə när′) *n.* **1.** A small group of advanced students who do independent research on a specialized subject and meet regularly with professors to discuss their reports. **2.** A course of study pursued by such a group. **3.** A meeting of such a group. [First written down in 1887 in American English, from Latin *sēminārium*, seed plot.]

sem•i•nar•i•an (sĕm′ə nâr′ē ən) *n.* A student at a seminary.

sem•i•nar•y (sĕm′ə nĕr′ē) *n., pl.* **sem•i•nar•ies. 1.** A school for the training of priests, ministers, or rabbis. **2.** A school of higher education, especially a private school for girls.

Sem•i•nole (sĕm′ə nōl′) *n., pl.* **Seminole** or **Sem•i•noles. 1.** A member of a Native American people made up of mostly Creek groups who moved to Florida in the 18th and 19th centuries, many of whom were forcibly moved to Oklahoma. **2.** Either of the Muskogean languages of the Seminole.

sem•i•of•fi•cial (sĕm′ē ə fĭsh′əl) *adj.* Having some official authority or authorization.

sem•i•pre•cious stone (sĕm′ē prĕsh′əs) *n.* A gem, such as topaz, amethyst, or jade, that has commercial value but is less rare and expensive than a precious stone.

sem•i•pro•fes•sion•al (sĕm′ē prə fĕsh′ə nəl) *adj.* **1.** Taking part in a sport for pay, but not as a full-time occupation: *a semiprofessional baseball player.* **2.** Composed of such players: *a semiprofessional team.*

sem•i•skilled (sĕm′ē skĭld′) *adj.* **1.** Having some skills but not enough to do specialized work. **2.** Requiring limited skills: *a semiskilled job.*

sem•i•sol•id (sĕm′ē sŏl′ĭd) *adj.* Intermediate in properties, especially in rigidity, between solids and liquids. —*n.* (sĕm′ē sŏl′ĭd). A semisolid substance, such as a stiff dough or firm gelatin.

Sem•ite (sĕm′īt′) *n.* A member of a group of Semitic-speaking peoples of the Near East and northern Africa, including Arabs, Babylonians, Ethiopians, and Jews.

Se•mit•ic (sə mĭt′ĭk) *adj.* **1.** Of or relating to the Semites or their languages or cultures. **2.** Of or relating to a division of the Afro-Asiatic languages that includes Hebrew and Arabic. —*n.* The Semitic languages.

sem•i•tone (sĕm′ē tōn′) *n.* A half step in a musical scale.

sem•i•trail•er (sĕm′ē trā′lər) *n.* A trailer with a set or sets of wheels at the rear only, the forward portion being supported by the truck tractor or towing vehicle.

sem•i•trop•i•cal (sĕm′ē trŏp′ĭ kəl) *adj.* Partly tropical; subtropical.

sem•i•week•ly (sĕm′ē wēk′lē) *adj.* Occurring or issued twice a week. —*adv.* Twice a week. —SEE NOTE at **biweekly.**

sen. or **Sen.** *abbr.* An abbreviation of: **1.** Senate. **2.** Senator. **3.** Senior.

sen•ate (sĕn′ĭt) *n.* **1. Senate.** The upper house of the U.S. Congress, to which two members are elected by the people of each state for a six-year term. **2.** Often **Senate.** The upper house of the legislature in many states of the United States. **3. Senate.** The upper house of the national legislature of Canada, France, and some other countries. **4.** The governing council of the ancient Roman republic and later of the Roman Empire. **5.** A governing or advisory council of some colleges and universities. [First written down before 1200 in Middle English and spelled *senaht*, from Latin *senātus*, from *senex*, old, an elder.]

sen•a•tor (sĕn′ə tər) *n.* A member of a senate.

sen•a•to•ri•al (sĕn′ə tôr′ē əl) *adj.* **1.** Of, concerning, or appropriate to a senator. **2.** Made up of senators: *a senatorial advisory group.*

send (sĕnd) *v.* **sent** (sĕnt), **send•ing, sends.** —*tr.* **1.** To cause to be conveyed to a place: *We sent supplies to the disaster area by airlift.* **2.** To dispatch, as by mail or telegraph; transmit: *Send me a letter. Send my regards.* **3.** To direct to go to a place: *sent me to the store to buy milk.* **4.** To enable to go to a place, as by providing money: *She worked hard to send herself to college.* **5.** To direct (a person) to a source of information: *The teacher sent us to the library.* **6.** To give off (heat, for example); emit: *The beacon sends a bright light.* **7.** To hit so as to direct with force: *The batter sent the ball to the left field.* **8.** To put into a given condition or kind of behavior: *The long delay sent the train passengers into a rage.* —*intr.* **1.** To cause someone to do an errand or to convey a message: *He sent out for pizza.* **2.** To convey a request or an order, especially by mail: *send away for a catalogue.* —***idiom.*** **send for.** To request to come by means of a message or messenger; summon. [First written down about 725 in Old English and spelled *sendan.*] —**send′er** *n.*

send•off (sĕnd′ôf′ *or* sĕnd′ŏf′) *n.* A demonstration of affection and good wishes for the beginning of a new undertaking.

Sen•e•ca (sĕn′ĭ kə) *n., pl.* **Seneca** or **Sen•e•cas. 1.** A member of a Native American people living in western New York State and southeast Ontario. **2.** The Iroquoian language of the Seneca.

Seneca Falls. A village of west-central New York east-southeast of Rochester. The first women's rights convention was held here in 1848. Population, 7370.

Sen•e•gal (sĕn′ĭ gôl′ *or* sĕn′ĭ gäl′). A country of western Africa on the Atlantic Ocean south of Mauritania. It was first settled in prehistoric times. Senegal gained its independence from France in 1960. Capital, Dakar. Population, 6,038,000.

sen•e•schal (sĕn′ə shəl) *n.* An official appointed to manage a medieval noble household and its servants; a steward.

se•nile (sē′nīl′ *or* sĕn′īl′) *adj.* Of, showing, or characteristic of senility. [First written down in 1661 in Modern English, from Latin *senīlis*, from *senex*, old.]

se•nil•i•ty (sĭ nĭl′ĭ tē) *n.* The weakening of a person's mental or physical abilities due to old age.

sen•ior (sēn′yər) *adj.* **1.** Of, relating to, or being the older of two, especially the older of two persons having the same name, as father and son. **2.** Of or being in a higher position, rank, or grade than one's peers: *a senior editor.* **3.** Of or relating to the fourth and last year of a high school or college: *the senior class.* —*n.* **1.** A person who is older than another: *My brother is my senior by four years.* **2.** A senior citizen. **3.** A person in a higher position, rank, or grade than another. **4.** A student in the fourth and last year of a high school or college. [First written down in 1287 in Middle English and spelled *seniore*, from Latin *senior*, older, from *senex*, old.]

senior high school *n.* A high school usually made up of the 10th, 11th, and 12th grades.

sen•ior•i•ty (sēn yôr′ĭ tē *or* sēn yŏr′ĭ tē) *n.* **1.** The condition of being older or of higher rank. **2.** Priority over others, especially because of greater length of service.

sen•na (sĕn′ə) *n.* **1.** Any of various plants having yellow flowers and leaves with many leaflets. **2.** The dried leaves of such a plant or a preparation made from them, used in medicine as a laxative. [First written down in 1543 in Modern English, from Arabic *sanā′*.]

se•ñor (sān yôr′ *or* sĕ nyôr′) *n., pl.* **se•ño•res** (sān-yôr′ās *or* sĕ nyô′rĕs). **1.** Used as a courtesy title for a man in a Spanish-speaking region. **2.** A Spanish or Spanish-speaking man. [First written down in 1622 in Modern English and spelled *sennor*, from Spanish *señor*, from Latin *senior*, senior.]

se•ño•ra (sān yôr′ə *or* sĕ nyô′rä) *n.* **1.** Used as a courtesy title for a woman in a Spanish-speaking region. **2.** A Spanish or Spanish-speaking woman.

se•ño•ri•ta (sān′yə rē′tə *or* sĕ′nyô rē′tä) *n.* **1.** Used as a courtesy title for a girl or young woman in a Spanish-speaking region. **2.** A Spanish or Spanish-speaking unmarried woman or girl.

sen•sa•tion (sĕn sā′shən) *n.* **1.a.** A feeling or an awareness that results from the stimulation of a sense organ or from some condition of the body: *the sensation of heat.* **b.** The ability to perceive or feel: *a loss of sensation in the fingers due to frostbite.* **2.** A state of unusually strong interest or emotion: *a sensation of great joy.* **3.a.** A condition of lively public interest and excitement: *News of the first artificial satellite caused a sensation.* **b.** A person, an event, or an object that arouses lively interest, excitement, or admiration. See Synonyms at **wonder.**

sen•sa•tion•al (sĕn sā′shə nəl) *adj.* **1.** Of or relating to sensation or the senses. **2.** Arousing great interest or excitement, especially by shocking: *a sensational television report.* **3.** Extraordinary; outstanding: *a sensational dinner.* —**sen•sa′tion•al•ly** *adv.*

sen•sa•tion•al•ism (sĕn sā′shə nə lĭz′əm) *n.* The deliberate use of sensational subject matter or highly dramatic style, especially in writing, journalism, or politics.

sense (sĕns) *n.* **1.a.** Any of the functions or abilities by which a living thing can perceive or feel its environment or certain of its own internal conditions: *the sense of smell.* **b.** A perception or feeling due to stimulation of one or more of these functions or abilities: *have a sense of being tired.* **2.** An ability to understand or appreciate something: *a sense of humor.* **3.** A vague feeling about something; an impression: *I have a sense that our team's going to win.* **4.** Good judgment; practical intelligence. Often used in the plural: *I had the sense to go to bed early. Come to your senses!* **5.a.** Speech, thought, or reasoning that is sound and practical: *Talk sense!* **b.** Something reasonable: *saw no sense in hurrying.* **6.a.** A meaning conveyed by speech or writing: *tried to understand the sense of the poem's last line.* **b.** One of the meanings of a word or phrase: *Words sometimes have many different senses.* **7.** Consensus: *The sense of the group was that we should go ahead.* —*tr.v.* **sensed, sens•ing, sens•es. 1.** To become aware of through the senses. **2.** To understand; grasp: *The teacher sensed that we were confused.* **3.** To detect automatically: *A geiger*

ă	pat	oi	boy
ā	pay	ou	out
âr	care	o͝o	took
ä	father	o͞o	boot
ĕ	pet	ŭ	cut
ē	be	ûr	urge
ĭ	pit	th	thin
ī	pie	*th*	this
îr	pier	hw	whoop
ŏ	pot	zh	vision
ō	toe	ə	about
ô	paw	N	French bon

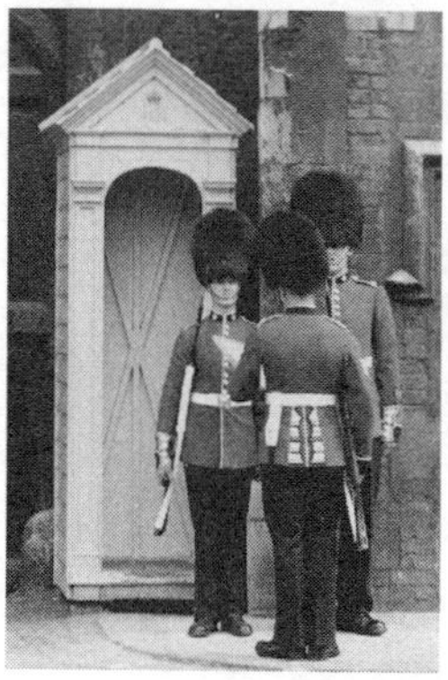

sentry box
At Saint James's Palace in London, England

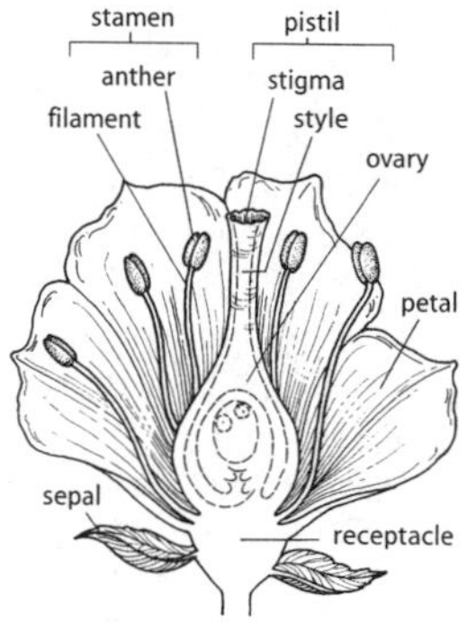

sepal

ă	**pat**	oi	**boy**
ā	**pay**	ou	**out**
âr	**care**	ŏŏ	**took**
ä	**father**	ōō	**boot**
ĕ	**pet**	ŭ	**cut**
ē	**be**	ûr	**urge**
ĭ	**pit**	th	**thin**
ī	**pie**	*th*	**this**
îr	**pier**	hw	**whoop**
ŏ	**pot**	zh	**vision**
ō	**toe**	ə	**about**
ô	**paw**	N	*French* **bon**

counter senses radioactivity. [First written down before 1382 in Middle English and spelled *sense,* meaning, from Latin *sēnsus,* the faculty of perceiving, from *sentīre,* to feel.]

sense•less (sĕns′lĭs) *adj.* **1.** Lacking meaning or sense: *senseless drivel.* **2.** Lacking good judgment; foolish. **3.** Deprived of sensation; unconscious: *knocked senseless.* **—sense′less•ly** *adv.* **—sense′less•ness** *n.*

sense organ *n.* An organ or a structure of the body, as the eye or ear, that is specially developed to receive stimuli.

sen•si•bil•i•ty (sĕn′sə bĭl′ĭ tē) *n., pl.* **sen•si•bil•i•ties. 1.** The ability to feel or perceive. **2.** The ability to receive and appreciate sensations and feelings in the mind: *her acute sensibility to the feelings of others.* **3.** The capacity to respond intelligently to refined emotions, especially in art.

sen•si•ble (sĕn′sə bəl) *adj.* **1.** Perceptible through or as if through one or more of the senses: *a sensible difference of temperature.* **2.** Capable of feeling or perceiving; sensitive: *sensible to pain.* **3.** Showing or in accordance with good judgment; reasonable: *a sensible decision.* **4.** Aware; conscious: *We are sensible of your objections.* **—sen′si•ble•ness** *n.* **—sen′si•bly** *adv.*

sen•si•tive (sĕn′sĭ tĭv) *adj.* **1.** Capable of perceiving with a sense or senses: *Bats are sensitive to sounds that we cannot hear.* **2.** Responsive to or affected by an external condition or stimulus: *Photographic film is sensitive to light.* **3.** Responsive to the feelings, attitudes, or circumstances of others: *a sensitive and sympathetic listener.* **4.** Quick to take offense; touchy: *He was sensitive about his poor performance in the race.* **5.** Easily irritated: *sensitive skin.* **6.** Designed to indicate or measure small changes of condition: *a sensitive thermometer.* **7.** Requiring careful or discreet handling; delicate: *a matter too sensitive to be discussed.* **—sen′si•tive•ly** *adv.* **—sen′si•tiv′i•ty, sen′si•tive•ness** *n.*

sensitive plant *n.* Any of various plants having leaflets that fold together or droop when touched.

sen•si•tize (sĕn′sĭ tīz′) *tr. & intr.v.* **sen•si•tized, sen•si•tiz•ing, sen•si•tiz•es.** To make or become sensitive or more sensitive.

sen•sor (sĕn′sər *or* sĕn′sôr′) *n.* A device, such as a photocell or thermocouple, that responds to a particular type of change in its condition or environment.

sen•so•ry (sĕn′sə rē) *adj.* **1.** Of or relating to the senses or sensation. **2.** Transmitting data or impulses from sense organs to the central nervous system: *sensory nerves.*

sen•su•al (sĕn′shōō əl) *adj.* **1.** Relating to or affecting the senses; sensory. **2.** Of, relating to, or giving pleasure to the body; physically gratifying: *the sensual experience of a warm bath.* **3.** Suggesting sexuality; voluptuous. **4.** Physical rather than spiritual or intellectual. **—sen′su•al′i•ty** (sĕn′shōō ăl′ĭ tē) *n.* **—sen′su•al•ly** *adv.*

sen•su•ous (sĕn′shōō əs) *adj.* **1.** Of, relating to, or derived from the senses: *both a sensuous and an intellectual response to the music.* **2.** Appealing to the senses: *sensuous curves and floral patterns.* **3.** Easily affected through the senses. **—sen′su•ous•ly** *adv.* **—sen′su•ous•ness** *n.*

sent (sĕnt) *v.* Past tense and past participle of **send.**
❑ *These sound alike:* **sent, cent** (penny), **scent** (smell).

sen•tence (sĕn′təns) *n.* **1.** An independent grammatical unit that has a subject that is either expressed or implied and a predicate containing at least one finite verb. For example, *It's almost midnight* and *Stop!* are sentences. **2.a.** The judgment of a court of law; a verdict. **b.** The penalty given by a court to a convicted person: *a sentence of four years in prison.* —*tr.v.* **sen•tenced, sen•tenc•ing, sen•tenc•es.** To pass sentence upon (a defendant). [First written down before 1200 in Middle English and spelled *sentence,* opinion, from Latin *sententia,* from *sentīre,* to feel.]

sen•ten•tious (sĕn tĕn′shəs) *adj.* **1.** Brief and pointed in meaning or expression; pithy. **2.** Full of proverbs. **3.** Giving moral advice, especially in a pompous way. **—sen•ten′tious•ly** *adv.* **—sen•ten′tious•ness** *n.*

sen•ti•ment (sĕn′tə mənt) *n.* **1.** A general attitude or inclination: *His sentiment is to root for the underdog.* **2.** An opinion; a view: *I expressed my sentiments in favor of the idea.* **3.a.** Emotion; feeling: *Different music arouses different kinds of sentiment.* See Synonyms at **feeling. b.** Tender or romantic emotion. **4.** Sentimentality. [First written down about 1385 in Middle English and spelled *sentement,* from Latin *sentīre,* to feel.]

sen•ti•men•tal (sĕn′tə mĕn′tl) *adj.* **1.** Of or relating to the feelings; emotional: *We have sentimental ties to this town.* **2.** Marked by emotion that is excessive or foolish: *read us a sentimental story.* **3.** Ruled or influenced by one's emotions rather than reason or practicality: *a sentimental man.* **—sen′ti•men′tal•ly** *adv.*

sen•ti•men•tal•ism (sĕn′tə mĕn′tl ĭz′əm) *n.* A tendency to be ruled or influenced by excessive or foolish emotion. **—sen′ti•men′tal•ist** *n.*

sen•ti•men•tal•i•ty (sĕn′tə mĕn tăl′ĭ tē) *n., pl.* **sen•ti•men•tal•i•ties. 1.** The quality or condition of being excessively sentimental. **2.** An expression of excessive sentiment.

sen•ti•nel (sĕn′tə nəl) *n.* A guard; a sentry. [First written down in 1579 in Modern English, probably from Old Italian *sentina,* vigilance, from *sentire,* to watch.]

sen•try (sĕn′trē) *n., pl.* **sen•tries.** A guard, especially a soldier posted at a given spot to prevent the passage of unauthorized persons. [First written down in 1632 in Modern English, perhaps alteration of obsolete *sentrinel,* variant of *sentinel.*]

sentry box *n.* A small shelter for a posted sentry.

Seoul (sōl). The capital and largest city of South Korea, in the northwest part of the country. It was founded in the 14th century and became the capital in 1948. Population, 9,646,000.

se•pal (sē′pəl) *n.* One of the divisions forming the calyx of a flower. Sepals are usually green and resemble leaves but are sometimes brightly colored and resemble petals. [First written down in 1829 in Modern English, from New Latin *sepalum.*]

sep•a•ra•ble (sĕp′ər ə bəl *or* sĕp′rə bəl) *adj.* Capable of being separated.

sep•a•rate (sĕp′ə rāt′) *v.* **sep•a•rat•ed, sep•a•rat•ing, sep•a•rates.** —*tr.* **1.** To put or keep apart: *separated the rolls in the pan.* **2.** To keep apart by occupying a position between: *the channel that separates Great Britain from France.* **3.** To place in different categories; sort: *separating the list of words into nouns and verbs.* **4.** To make a distinction between; distinguish: *It was hard to separate facts from opinion in the editorial.* **5.** To divide into parts: *Draw a line that separates a square into two triangles.* **6.** To end a relationship with; part: *He was separated from his wife.* **7.** To remove from a mixture; extract: *We separated the coarse sand in a sieve.* —*intr.* **1.** To come apart. **2.** To withdraw; leave: *The state separated from the Union.* **3.** To part company: *We set out together, then separated at Nashville.* **4.** To stop living together as a couple. **5.** To become removed from a mixture: *The oil separated from the peanut butter.* —*adj.* (sĕp′ər ĭt *or* sĕp′rĭt). **1.** Set apart from the rest: *Libraries* *have a separate section for reference books.* **2.** Distinct from others; individual or independent: *a separate treaty between two of the members of the alliance.* **3.** Not identical or alike; different: *The ships took separate courses.* —*n.* (**sĕp′**ər ĭt *or* **sĕp′**-rĭt). A garment, such as a skirt, shirt, or pair of slacks, that may be bought separately and worn with other clothes in various combinations. [First written down before 1425 in Middle English and spelled *separaten*, from Latin *sēparāre* : *sē-*, apart + *parāre*, to prepare.] —**sep′a•rate•ly** *adv.*

Synonyms: **separate, divide, part, sever.** These verbs mean to cause to become disconnected or disunited. **Separate** means to put apart or to keep apart: *A mountain range separates France and Spain.* **Divide** means to separate by cutting, splitting, or branching into parts: *The orange was divided into segments.* **Part** often means to separate closely associated persons or things: *A difference of opinion parted the old friends.* **Sever** often means to divide or cut off something abruptly and violently: *The United States severed diplomatic relations with Cuba in 1961.*

sep•a•ra•tion (sĕp′ə **rā′**shən) *n.* **1.a.** The act or process of separating: *the separation of cream from milk.* **b.** The condition of being separated: *her separation from the rest of the runners.* **2.** An intervening space; a gap: *a separation between electrical circuits.* **3.** A legal agreement by which a husband and wife live apart.

sep•a•ra•tist (**sĕp′**ər ə tĭst *or* **sĕp′**rə tĭst) *n.* **1.** A person who advocates the withdrawal of a group from a larger group, as from a political union or an established church. **2.** A person who advocates cultural, ethnic, or racial separation.

sep•a•ra•tor (**sĕp′**ə rā′tər) *n.* A person or thing that separates, such as a device for separating cream from milk.

se•pi•a (**sē′**pē ə) *n.* **1.** A dark-brown ink or coloring material originally prepared from the liquid secreted by cuttlefish. **2.** A dark brown. [First written down before 1398 in Middle English and spelled *sepia*, cuttlefish, from Greek.]

Sept. or **Sept** *abbr.* An abbreviation of September.

sep•ta (**sĕp′**tə) *n.* Plural of **septum.**

Sep•tem•ber (sĕp **tĕm′**bər) *n.* The ninth month of the year in the Gregorian calendar, having 30 days. [First written down about 1050 in Middle English, from Latin *September*, the seventh month, from *septem*, seven.]

sep•tet (sĕp **tĕt′**) *n.* **1.a.** A musical composition for seven voices or instruments. **b.** A group of seven musicians who perform such a composition. **2.** A group of seven people or things.

sep•tic (**sĕp′**tĭk) *adj.* Of, relating to, or caused by the presence of disease-causing microorganisms or their toxins in the blood: *septic shock.* [First written down in 1605 in Modern English, from Greek *sēptikos*, putrefying, from *sēpein*, to make rotten.]

sep•ti•ce•mi•a (sĕp′tĭ **sē′**mē ə) *n.* A disease caused by microorganisms or their toxins in the blood; blood poisoning.

septic tank *n.* A tank in which sewage is decomposed by bacteria.

sep•tum (**sĕp′**təm) *n., pl.* **sep•ta** (**sĕp′**tə). A thin partition or membrane between two cavities or soft masses of tissue in a plant or animal part.

sep•ul•cher (**sĕp′**əl kər) *n.* A burial vault.

se•pul•chral (sə **pŭl′**krəl *or* sə **pool′**krəl) *adj.* **1.** Of or relating to a sepulcher: *sepulchral inscriptions.* **2.** Suggestive of the grave; funereal.

sep•ul•chre (**sĕp′**əl kər) *n. Chiefly British.* Variant of **sepulcher.**

se•quel (**sē′**kwəl) *n.* **1.** A thing or an event that follows; a continuation. **2.** A book complete in itself but continuing the story of an earlier work. **3.** A result; an outcome. [First written down in 1439 in Middle English and spelled *sequele*, from Latin *sequēla*, from *sequī*, to follow.]

se•quence (**sē′**kwəns) *n.* **1.** A following of one thing after another; succession: *the sequence of cause and effect.* **2.** The order in which things or events occur or are arranged: *following the sequence of steps outlined in the manual.* **3.** A related or continuous series: *a sequence of incidents that led to civil war.* **4.** The order of subunits in a polymer, especially the order of nucleotides in a nucleic acid or of the amino acids in a protein.

se•ques•ter (sĭ **kwĕs′**tər) *tr.v.* **se•ques•tered, se•ques•ter•ing, se•ques•ters. 1.** To cause to withdraw to a private or out-of-the-way place; seclude: *sequestered himself in his room to think over what had happened.* **2.** To take possession of (property) until a legal claim is settled.

se•ques•tra•tion (sē′kwĭ **strā′**shən) *n.* **1.** The act of sequestering; segregation. **2.a.** Seizure of property. **b.** A writ authorizing seizure of property.

se•quin (**sē′**kwĭn) *n.* A small shiny disk or spangle, often sewn on cloth or clothes for decoration. —**se′quined** *adj.*

se•quoi•a (sĭ **kwoi′**ə) *n.* **1.** A very large cone-bearing evergreen tree of the mountains of southern California. **2.** The redwood. [First written down in 1869 in American English, after *Sequoya.*]

Se•quoy•a or **Se•quoy•ah** (sĭ **kwoi′**ə). 1770?–1843. Cherokee scholar who developed a system of transcribing the Cherokee language. —See Note.

se•ra (**sîr′**ə) *n.* A plural of **serum.**

se•ra•glio (sə **răl′**yō) *n., pl.* **se•ra•glios. 1.** A large harem. **2.** A sultan's palace.

se•ra•pe (sə **rä′**pē) *n.* A long, often brightly colored shawl resembling a blanket, worn especially by Mexican men.

ser•aph (**sĕr′**əf) *n., pl.* **ser•a•phim** (**sĕr′**ə fĭm) or **ser•aphs.** An angel of high rank. —**se•raph′ic** (sə **răf′**ĭk) *adj.*

Serb (sûrb) *n.* A member of a southern Slavic people that is the principal ethnic group of Serbia.

Ser•bi•a (**sûr′**bē ə). A region and former kingdom of the central Balkan Peninsula. Serbia was a constituent republic of Yugoslavia from 1946 to 1991, and with Montenegro it established a new Yugoslavian nation in 1992. Capital, Belgrade. Population, 11,596,572.

Serbian (**sûr′**bē ən) *n.* **1.** A Serb. **2.** Serbo-Croatian as used in Serbia, almost identical with Croatian but written in a Cyrillic alphabet. —*adj.* Of or relating to Serbia, Serbian, the Serbs, or their culture.

Ser•bo-Cro•a•tian (sûr′bō krō **ā′**shən) *n.* The Slavic language of the Serbs and Croats. —*adj.* Of or relating to Serbo-Croatian or its speakers.

sere (sîr) *adj.* Withered. [First written down in 824 in Old English and spelled *sēar.*]

❑ *These sound alike:* **sere, sear** (scorch), **seer** (prophet).

ser•e•nade (sĕr′ə **nād′** *or* **sĕr′**ə nād′) *n.* A musical performance given to honor or express love for someone. —*v.* **ser•e•nad•ed, ser•e•nad•ing, ser•e•nades.** —*tr.* To perform a serenade for. —*intr.* To perform a serenade. [First written down in 1649 in Modern English, from Latin *serēnus*, serene.]

ser•en•dip•i•ty (sĕr′ən **dĭp′**ĭ tē) *n.* The knack for making fortunate discoveries by accident.

se•rene (sə **rēn′**) *adj.* **1.** Peaceful and untroubled; perfectly tranquil or composed: *the serene face of a Greek statue.* See Synonyms at **calm. 2.** Unclouded; clear and bright: *serene skies.* **3.** Often **Serene.** Used as part of a title and form of address for certain royal persons: *Her Serene Majesty.* [First writ-

Sequoya

Sequoya

While growing up in what is now Tennessee, **Sequoya** was fascinated by the writing systems of English and other languages. In 1809 he began his work on an alphabet for the Cherokee language and finally settled on an 86-character alphabet using characters adapted from the English, Greek, and Hebrew alphabets. By 1821 this alphabet was completed and approved by the Cherokee chieftains, and thousands of people were being taught to read and write. As a result of Sequoya's alphabet, the *Cherokee Phoenix,* a weekly newspaper printed in Cherokee and English, was begun in 1828, and books began appearing in Cherokee. In 1828 Sequoya moved west to Indian Territory (later Oklahoma) and became a teacher in Indian schools.

serape

ten down in 1440 in Middle English, from Latin *serēnus.*] —**se•rene′ly** *adv.*

se•ren•i•ty (sə rĕn′ĭ tē) *n.* The quality of being serene; tranquillity.

serf (sûrf) *n.* A member of a class of laborers in Europe who were owned by lords and bound to the land where they lived and worked. If the land was sold, the serfs were sold with it. [First written down in 1483 in Middle English, from Latin *servus*, slave.] —**serf′dom** *n.*

❑ *These sound alike:* **serf, surf** (waves).

serge (sûrj) *n.* A strong wool cloth often used for suits.

❑ *These sound alike:* **serge, surge** (rush).

ser•geant (sär′jənt) *n.* **1.** A noncommissioned officer in the U.S. Army, Air Force, or Marine Corps holding any of several ranks just below lieutenant. **2.** A police officer ranking just below a captain, lieutenant, or inspector. [First written down before 1200 in Middle English and spelled *sergante*, servant, soldier, from Late Latin *serviēns*, public official, from Latin *servīre*, to serve.]

sergeant at arms *n., pl.* **sergeants at arms.** An officer whose job is to keep order at the meetings of a legislature, club, or other group.

sergeant major *n., pl.* **sergeants major** or **sergeant majors.** A noncommissioned officer of the highest rank in the U.S. Army, Air Force, or Marine Corps.

se•ri•al (sîr′ē əl) *adj.* **1.** Of, arranged in, or forming a series. **2.** Presented in installments: *a serial television drama.* —*n.* A story or play presented in installments. —**se′ri•al•ly** *adv.*

❑ *These sound alike:* **serial, cereal** (grain).

se•ri•al•ize (sîr′ē ə līz′) *tr.v.* **se•ri•al•ized, se•ri•al•iz•ing, se•ri•al•iz•es.** To write or publish in installments: *serialize a novel in a magazine.*

serial number *n.* A number that is one of a series and is used for identification, as of a machine: *the serial number of a car.*

se•ries (sîr′ēz) *n., pl.* **series. 1.** A number of similar things or events that occur in a row or follow one another in time; a succession: *a series of tracks in the snow.* **2.** An arrangement in an electric circuit in which the current passes through a number of devices in a single path. **3.** A group of rock formations that were deposited in the same geologic period or epoch. [First written down in 1611 in Modern English, from Latin *seriēs*, from *serere*, to join.]

se•ri•ous (sîr′ē əs) *adj.* **1.** Thoughtful and earnest; grave: *gave me a serious look.* **2.a.** Carried out in earnest: *She did a serious study of the matter.* **b.** Deeply interested or involved: *a serious musician.* **3.** Intended to arouse deep thought or emotion: *a serious play.* **4.** Not joking: *I'm serious. Get moving.* **5.** Worthy of concern or anxiety: *a serious situation.* —**se′ri•ous•ly** *adv.* —**se′ri•ous•ness** *n.*

ser•mon (sûr′mən) *n.* **1.** A talk on a religious subject or text delivered as part of a church service. **2.** A solemn, lengthy, and boring talk.

ser•mon•ize (sûr′mə nīz′) *v.* **ser•mon•ized, ser•mon•iz•ing, ser•mon•iz•es.** —*tr.* To deliver a sermon to (someone). —*intr.* To deliver or speak as though delivering a sermon. —**ser′mon•iz′er** *n.*

Sermon on the Mount *n.* In the New Testament, a sermon delivered by Jesus including the Beatitudes.

se•rous (sîr′əs) *adj.* Of, resembling, containing, or producing serum.

ser•pent (sûr′pənt) *n.* **1.** A snake. **2.** A sly or treacherous person. [First written down before 1300 in Middle English, from Latin *serpēns*, from *serpere*, to creep.]

ser•pen•tine (sûr′pən tēn′ *or* sûr′pən tīn′) *adj.* **1.** Of, resembling, or typical of a serpent: *serpentine movements.* **2.** Having many bends or curves: *a serpentine river.*

ser•rate (sĕr′āt′) *adj.* Having an edge with notched projections resembling teeth: *a serrate leaf.*

ser•rat•ed (sĕr′ā′tĭd) *adj.* Serrate.

se•rum (sîr′əm) *n., pl.* **se•rums** or **se•ra** (sîr′ə). **1.** The clear yellowish liquid obtained when all solid particles are removed from whole blood. **2.** A liquid extracted from the tissues of an immunized animal, containing antibodies and used to transfer immunity to another individual. **3.** A watery fluid derived from animal tissue, such as lymph.

ser•vant (sûr′vənt) *n.* **1.** A person, such as a butler, cook, or housekeeper, who works for wages in the household of someone else. **2.** A person publicly employed to perform services for others: *Presidents often declare that they are servants of the people.* **3.** A person who expresses submission, debt, or deep respect to another: *your humble servant.*

serve (sûrv) *v.* **served, serv•ing, serves.** —*tr.* **1.a.** To work for. **b.** To be a servant to: *The steward serves the king.* **2.a.** To prepare and offer (food): *serve dinner.* **b.** To provide food for (someone): *serving the children first.* **3.** To provide goods and services for (customers), as in a store or restaurant; wait on. **4.** To assist; promote: *serving the national interest.* **5.** To spend (a period of time) in fulfillment of an obligation: *served 12 years in the Senate.* **6.** To fight or undergo military service for: *served her country in the army.* **7.** To give homage and obedience to: *served God.* **8.** To be used profitably by: *a port that serves a wide region.* **9.** To fulfill (a task or function): *The old car served its purpose.* **10.** To deliver (a legal writ or summons) to the person named. **11.** To put (a ball or shuttlecock) in play by hitting it, as in tennis or badminton. **12.** To assist a priest during (Mass). —*intr.* **1.** To work as a servant. **2.** To do a term of duty: *He served in the Air Force during the war.* **3.** To act in a given capacity: *serve as a clerk.* **4.** To be of use; function: *Let this serve as a reminder.* —*n.* The right to serve or the manner or act of serving a ball or shuttlecock. —***idiom.*** **serve (someone) right.** To be deserved under the circumstances. [First written down about 1175 in Middle English and spelled *serven*, from Latin *servīre*, from *servus*, slave.]

serv•er (sûr′vər) *n.* **1.** A person who serves food and drink. **2.** Something, such as a tray or a bowl, used in serving food. **3.** A person who assists a priest at Mass.

serv•ice (sûr′vĭs) *n.* **1.** Work or employment for another or others: *years of hard service.* **2.** A branch of the government and its employees: *the diplomatic service.* **3.** The armed forces or a branch of the armed forces: *joined the service.* **4.** Work or duties done for another, as for a superior or a client: *provides full catering service; the services of a doctor.* **5.** Installation, maintenance, or repairs provided by a dealer or manufacturer. **6.** A facility providing the public with use of something: *Is there telephone service in this building?* **7.** An act of assistance to another or others: *performing a valuable service for the family.* **8.a.** The act or manner of serving food or fulfilling the demands of customers: *a hotel with poor service.* **b.** A set of dishes and table utensils for serving and eating food: *a service for eight persons.* **9.** A religious ceremony; a rite: *a church service.* **10.** The presentaton of a legal writ or summons to the person named. **11.** The act, manner, or right of serving, as in tennis or badminton. —*tr.v.* **serv•iced, serv•ic•ing, serv•ic•es. 1.** To maintain or repair: *The mechanic serviced my car.* **2.** To provide services to: *Our business services the entire city.* —*adj.* **1.** Of or relating to the armed forces: *a service medal.* **2.** Reserved for the use of employees and messengers rather than the general public: *a service entrance.* **3.** Of or for the maintenance and repair of products sold: *a service guarantee.* **4.** Of or concerned with the serving of customers: *a service manager of a department store.*

serv•ice•a•ble (sûr′vĭ sə bəl) *adj.* **1.** Ready or fit for service; usable. **2.** Wearing well; sturdy; durable: *serviceable work boots.* **—serv′ice•a•bil′i•ty** *n.* **—serv′ice•a•bly** *adv.*

serv•ice•man (sûr′vĭs măn′) *n.* **1.** A man who is a member of the armed forces. **2.** Also **service man.** A man whose job is to maintain and repair equipment.

service station *n.* A business that refuels, services, and often repairs motor vehicles.

serv•ice•wom•an (sûr′vĭs wo͝om′ən) *n.* **1.** A woman who is a member of the armed forces. **2.** Also **service woman.** A woman whose job is to maintain and repair equipment.

ser•vile (sûr′vəl *or* sûr′vīl′) *adj.* **1.** Submissive; slavish. **2.** Of or appropriate to slaves or servants: *servile tasks.* **—ser′vile•ly** *adv.* **—ser•vil′i•ty** (sər vĭl′ĭ tē) *n.*

serv•ing (sûr′vĭng) *n.* A single portion of food or drink; a helping.

ser•vi•tude (sûr′vĭ to͞od′ *or* sûr′vĭ tyo͞od′) *n.* **1.** The condition of being a slave or serf. **2.** Forced labor imposed as a punishment.

ses•a•me (sĕs′ə mē) *n.* **1.** The small flat seeds of a tropical Asian plant, used as food and as a source of oil. **2.** The plant that bears such seeds. [First written down about 1425 in Middle English and spelled *sisamie,* from Greek *sēsamē.*]

ses•sile (sĕs′īl′ *or* sĕs′əl) *adj.* **1.** Sedentary; fixed to one spot: *Some barnacles are sessile.* **2.** Attached by the base instead of by a stem: *sessile leaves.*

ses•sion (sĕsh′ən) *n.* **1.** A meeting or series of meetings of a judicial or legislative body. **2.** A period of time during the day or year when a school holds classes: *a summer session.* **3.** A meeting of a school class, a club, or another group assembled to do or discuss something of common interest: *a recording session; a gossip session.* [First written down about 1387 in Middle English, from Latin *sessiō,* act of sitting, from *sedēre,* to sit.]

set[1] (sĕt) *v.* **set, set•ting, sets.** *—tr.* **1.** To put in a specified position; place: *set the book on the table.* **2.** To put in a specified condition: *setting him at liberty; set the wagon in motion.* **3.** To place in a firm or unmoving position: *set the post in a bed of concrete.* **4.** To restore (a broken or dislocated bone) to a proper or normal state. **5.** To adjust for proper functioning: *setting a mouse trap.* **6.** To adjust (an instrument, tool, or other device) so that some desired condition of operation is established: *set the television to channel eight.* **7.** To arrange tableware on (a table) or at (a place) in preparation for a meal. **8.** To arrange (hair) in a certain style, as by rolling it up with clips and curlers. **9.a.** To arrange (type) into words, lines, and columns in preparation for printing. **b.** To arrange (matter to be printed) into type. **10.a.** To compose (music) to fit a text. **b.** To write (words) to fit a melody. **11.** To represent as happening in a certain place or at a certain time: *setting her story in Detroit.* **12.** To establish: *setting an example; set a record.* **13.** To decide on; appoint or designate: *They set June 9 as the day of the wedding.* **14.** To assign (someone) to a given task or station: *set us to work.* **15.a.** To place or fix (a jewel or an ornament, for example) in a setting: *set a diamond in a crown.* **b.** To decorate or stud, as jewels mounted in a setting: *set a bracelet with rubies.* **16.** To cause to sit. **17.** To point toward (game) by holding a fixed position, as hunting dogs do. *—intr.* **1.** To disappear behind the horizon: *The sun sets in the west.* **2.** To sit on eggs in order to hatch them: *The hens were sitting.* *—adj.* **1.** Fixed and established: *a set purpose.* **2.** Unwilling to change: *set in her ways.* **3.** Determined; intent: *He's dead set against it.* *—n.* **1.** The act or process of setting. **2.** The manner in which something is set: *the set of his cap.* ***—idioms.*** **set about.** To begin or start: *She quickly set about solving the problem.* **set apart. 1.** To reserve for a specific use. **2.** To make noticeable: *characteristics that set them apart.* **set aside. 1.** To separate and reserve for a special purpose. **2.** To discard or reject. **set back.** To slow down the progress of; hinder. **set down. 1.** To cause to sit; seat: *He set his child down beside him.* **2.** To put in writing; record. **3.a.** To regard; consider. **b.** To assign to a cause; attribute: *Just set the mistake down to inexperience.* **set fire to.** To cause to ignite and burn. **set forth. 1.** To present for consideration; propose: *set forth a plan.* **2.** To express in words: *She set forth her idea very convincingly.* **set in.** To begin to happen or be apparent: *A storm was just setting in.* **set off. 1.a.** To give rise to; cause to occur: *set off a chemical reaction.* **b.** To cause to explode: *set off fireworks.* **2.** To direct attention to by contrast; accentuate: *set off a passage by highlighting it.* **3.** To start on a journey. **set on fire.** To cause to ignite and burn. **set out. 1.** To begin an earnest attempt; undertake: *set out to solve the problem.* **2.** To display for exhibition or sale. **3.** To start a journey. **set sail.** To begin a voyage on water. **set the pace. 1.** To go at a speed that other competitors attempt to match or surpass. **2.** To behave or perform in a way that others try to match. **set the stage for.** To provide the underlying basis for. **set to.** To begin working energetically; start in. **set up. 1.** To place in an upright position. **2.** To assemble or erect: *set up a stereo system.* **3.** To establish; found: *set up a business.* **4.** To establish in business by providing money, equipment, or other backing: *set them up in a small store.* **5.** *Informal.* To put (someone else) into a difficult situation by deceit or trickery: *Don't set me up when you're the one responsible.* **set upon.** To attack violently. [First written down about 725 in Old English and spelled *settan.*] —SEE NOTE.

set[2] (sĕt) *n.* **1.** A group of matching or related things that have the same use or purpose or that form a unit: *a set of china.* **2.** A group of persons having a common interest: *the younger set.* **3.a.** The scenery constructed for a theatrical performance. **b.** The enclosure in which a movie is filmed. **4.** The collection of parts or apparatus that makes up a radio or television receiver. **5.** In mathematics, a collection of distinct elements that have something in common: *the set of all positive integers.* **6.** In tennis and other sports, a group of games that forms one unit or part of a match. [First written down in 1443 in Middle English and spelled *sette,* from Medieval Latin *secta,* retinue, from Latin *sequī,* to follow.]

set•back (sĕt′băk′) *n.* A sudden check or reverse in progress; a change from better to worse.

Se•ton (sēt′n), Saint **Elizabeth Ann Bayley.** Known as "Mother Seton." 1774–1821. American religious leader who converted to Catholicism and founded a religious order, the Sisters of Charity (1809).

set•tee (sĕ tē′) *n.* A small or medium-sized sofa.

set•ter (sĕt′ər) *n.* **1.** A person or thing that sets: *a setter of printing type.* **2.** Any of several breeds of dog having smooth silky hair, often trained and used in hunting. Setters indicate the presence of game animals by crouching in a set position.

set theory *n.* The mathematical study of the properties of sets.

set•ting (sĕt′ĭng) *n.* **1.** The way in which something, such as an automatic control, is set. **2.a.** A

Usage: set[1]

The verb **set** is usually transitive and has an object: *He sets the table.* **Sit** is generally intransitive and has no object: *She sits at the table.* There are some exceptions: *The sun sets* (not *sits*). *A hen sets* (or *sits*) *on her eggs.*

Elizabeth Seton

setter

English setter

ă	**pat**	oi	**boy**
ā	**pay**	ou	**out**
âr	**care**	o͝o	**took**
ä	**father**	o͞o	**boot**
ĕ	**pet**	ŭ	**cut**
ē	**be**	ûr	**urge**
ĭ	**pit**	th	**thin**
ī	**pie**	*th*	**this**
îr	**pier**	hw	**whoop**
ŏ	**pot**	zh	**vision**
ō	**toe**	ə	**about**
ô	**paw**	N	*French* **bon**

surrounding area; environment: *animals in a natural setting.* **b.** The place where a narrative, drama, or film takes place: *the setting for a novel.* **3.** The scenery constructed for a play or movie. **4.** A framework or border, as of precious metal, in which a jewel is firmly fixed: *a turquoise stone in a silver setting.* **5.** Music composed or arranged so that a particular poem or other text can be sung to it: *a musical setting for a psalm.* **6.** A set of eggs in a hen's nest.

set•tle (sĕt′l) *v.* **set•tled, set•tling, set•tles.** *—tr.* **1.** To put into order; arrange or fix as desired: *settle the matter with the bank.* **2.** To put securely into a desired position or place: *She settled herself by the fire.* **3.** To establish as a resident or residents: *settled her family in Utah.* **4.** To establish residence in (a region): *pioneers who settled Nebraska.* **5.** To restore calmness or comfort to: *The music settled her nerves.* **6.** To cause to sink, condense, or come to rest. **7.a.** To make compensation for (a claim). **b.** To pay (a debt). **8.** To end or resolve: *settle a dispute.* **9.** To decide (a lawsuit) by mutual agreement. *—intr.* **1.** To stop moving and come to rest in one place. **2.** To descend or sink gradually: *Dust settled on the road.* **3.** To establish one's home in: *settled in Canada.* **4.** To reach a decision: *We finally settled on a solution to the problem.* *—n.* A long wooden bench with a low back. ***—idioms.*** **settle down. 1.** To begin living a stable and orderly life. **2.** To become less nervous or restless. **settle for.** To accept in spite of incomplete satisfaction: *It's not what I wanted, but I guess I'll settle for it.* [First written down about 1000 in Old English and spelled *setlan,* to seat, from *setl,* seat.]

set•tle•ment (sĕt′l mənt) *n.* **1.** The act or process of settling: *the settlement of differences; land open to settlement.* **2.a.** Establishment, as of a person in a business or people in a new region. **b.** A newly colonized region. **3.** A small community. **4.** An adjustment or understanding reached, as in financial matters or business proceedings. **5.a.** The transfer of property to provide for a person's future needs. **b.** Property thus transferred. **6.** A center providing community services in a poor area.

set•tler (sĕt′lər) *n.* A person who settles in a new region.

set-to (sĕt′to͞o′) *n., pl.* **set-tos.** A brief but usually heated contest or conflict.

set•up (sĕt′ŭp′) *n.* The way in which something is organized or planned.

sev•en (sĕv′ən) *n.* **1.** The number, written 7, that is equal to 6 + 1. **2.** The seventh in a set or series. [First written down about 725 in Old English and spelled *seofon.*] **—sev′en** *adj. & pron.*

seven seas also **Seven Seas** *pl.n.* All the oceans of the world.

sev•en•teen (sĕv′ən tēn′) *n.* **1.** The number, written 17, that is equal to 16 + 1. **2.** The 17th in a set or sequence. [First written down about 900 in Old English and spelled *seofontīne.*] **—sev′en•teen′** *adj. & pron.*

sev•en•teenth (sĕv′ən tēnth′) *n.* **1.** The ordinal number matching the number 17 in a series. **2.** One of 17 equal parts. **—sev′en•teenth′** *adj. & adv.*

sev•enth (sĕv′ənth) *n.* **1.** The ordinal number matching the number seven in a series. **2.** One of seven equal parts. **3.a.** Any of three intervals formed by tones that are seven steps apart in a musical scale. **b.** The seventh tone of a musical scale. **—sev′enth** *adj. & adv.*

Sev•enth-day Adventist (sĕv′ənth dā′) *n.* A member of a sect of Adventists who observe the Sabbath on Saturday.

sev•en•ti•eth (sĕv′ən tē ĭth) *n.* **1.** The ordinal number matching the number 70 in a series. **2.** One of 70 equal parts. **—sev′en•ti•eth** *adj. & adv.*

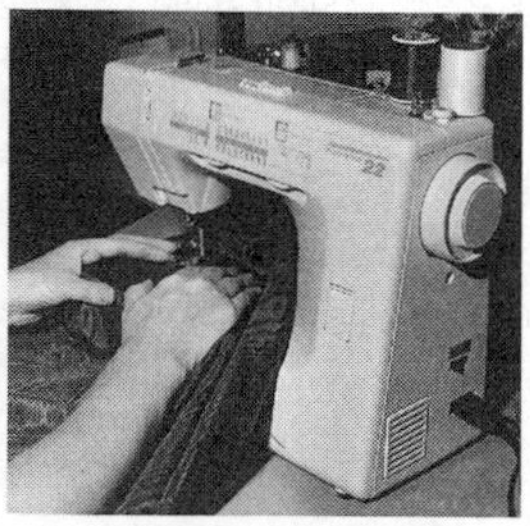

sewing machine

sev•en•ty (sĕv′ən tē) *n.* The number, written 70, that is equal to 7 × 10. [First written down about 1200 in Middle English and spelled *seofenntig,* from Old English *hundseofontig.*] **—sev′en•ty** *adj. & pron.*

sev•er (sĕv′ər) *v.* **sev•ered, sev•er•ing, sev•ers.** *—tr.* **1.** To divide, separate, or keep apart: *a clash that severed the Union.* See Synonyms at **separate. 2.** To cut or break off from a whole: *sever a limb from a tree.* *—intr.* To become cut or broken apart. [First written down about 1300 in Middle English and spelled *severen,* from Latin *sēparāre,* to separate.]

sev•er•al (sĕv′ər əl *or* sĕv′rəl) *adj.* **1.** Being of a number more than two or three but not many: *several miles away.* **2.** Distinct; various: *They parted and went their several ways.* *—pron. (used with a plural verb).* An indefinite but small number; some or a few: *He saw several of his classmates.* [First written down about 1421 in Middle English and spelled *saverale,* separate, from Medieval Latin *sēparālis,* from Latin *sēparāre,* to separate.] **—sev′er•al•ly** *adv.*

sev•er•ance (sĕv′ər əns *or* sĕv′rəns) *n.* **1.a.** The act or process of severing: *the severance of political ties.* **b.** The condition of being severed. **2.** Separation; partition.

severance pay *n.* Extra pay given an employee upon leaving a job.

se•vere (sə vîr′) *adj.* **se•ver•er, se•ver•est. 1.** Unsparing or harsh; strict: *a severe law.* **2.** Grim or stern in manner or appearance: *a severe voice.* **3.** Extremely plain: *severe clothes.* **4.** Causing great distress; sharp: *a severe pain.* **5.** Very serious; extreme: *severe damage.* **6.** Very difficult; trying: *a severe test of our friendship.* [First written down in 1548 in Modern English, from Latin *sevērus.*] **—se•vere′ly** *adv.* **—se•vere′ness** *n.*

se•ver•i•ty (sə vĕr′ĭ tē) *n., pl.* **se•ver•i•ties. 1.** The state or quality of being severe. **2.** The act or an instance of severe behavior, especially punishment.

Se•ville (sə vĭl′). A city of southwest Spain southwest of Córdoba. It was settled in ancient times. Population, 672,435.

sew (sō) *v.* **sewed, sewn** (sōn) or **sewed, sew•ing, sews.** *—tr.* To make, repair, or fashion by stitching, as with a needle and thread or a sewing machine: *sew a new dress; sew up a seam.* *—intr.* To work with a needle and thread or a sewing machine: *Tailors and seamstresses sew for a living.* ***—idiom.*** **sew up.** *Informal.* To complete successfully: *Our volleyball team sewed up the championship.* [First written down before 800 in Old English and spelled *siowian.*] **—sew′er** *n.*

❑ *These sound alike:* **sew, so**[1] (thus), **so**[2] (musical note), **sow**[1] (plant seeds).

sew•age (so͞o′ĭj) *n.* Liquid and solid waste carried off in sewers or drains.

Sew•ard (so͞o′ərd), **William Henry.** 1801–1872. American politician who arranged the purchase of Alaska from Russia (1867).

sew•er[1] (so͞o′ər) *n.* An underground pipe or channel built to carry off sewage or rainwater. [First written down in 1279 in Middle English and spelled *suere,* from Anglo-Norman *sewere.*]

sew•er[2] (sō′ər) *n.* A person or thing that sews: *a sewer of fine clothing.*

sew•er•age (so͞o′ər ĭj) *n.* **1.** A system of sewers. **2.** The removal of waste materials by a system of sewers. **3.** Sewage.

sew•ing (sō′ĭng) *n.* **1.** The act, occupation, or hobby of one who sews. **2.** The article on which a person is working with needle and thread.

sewing machine *n.* A machine for sewing.

sewn (sōn) *v.* A past participle of **sew.**

sex (sĕks) *n.* **1.** Either of two divisions, male and female, into which most organisms are grouped according to their functions in the process of reproduction. **2.** The combination of characteristics that are typical of each of these groups: *Sex is often recognized by marked physical differences.* **3.** The condition or character of being male or female. **4.** Sexual intercourse.

sex chromosome *n.* Either of a pair of chromosomes, usually called X and Y, that in combination determine the sex of an individual in human beings, most animals, and some plants, with XX resulting in a female and XY in a male.

sex gland *n.* A gonad.

sex•ism (**sĕk′**sĭz′əm) *n.* Discrimination based on gender, especially discrimination against women. **—sex′ist** *adj. & n.*

sex-linked (**sĕks′**lĭngkt′) *adj.* **1.** Carried by a sex chromosome, especially an X chromosome. Used of genes. **2.** Sexually determined. Used especially of inherited traits.

sex•tant (**sĕk′**stənt) *n.* A navigation instrument used to measure the altitude between the plane of the horizon and a celestial body.

sex•tet (sĕk **stĕt′**) *n.* **1.a.** A musical composition for six voices or instruments. **b.** A group of six musicians who perform such a composition. **2.** A group of six persons or things. [First written down in 1801 in Modern English and spelled *sestet*, from Latin *sextus*, sixth.]

sex•ton (**sĕk′**stən) *n.* A person employed to take care of a church and its property and sometimes to ring bells and dig graves.

Sex•ton (**sĕk′**stən), **Anne.** 1928–1974. American poet whose works include the collection *Live or Die* (1966).

sex•u•al (**sĕk′**shōō əl) *adj.* **1.** Of, affecting, or typical of sex, sexuality, the sexes, or the sex organs and their functions: *sexual development.* **2.** Of or involving the union of male and female sex cells: *sexual reproduction.* **—sex′u•al•ly** *adv.*

sexual harassment *n.* Unwanted and offensive sexual behavior or remarks.

sexual intercourse *n.* Intimate physical contact between human beings, usually involving insertion of the penis into the vagina.

sex•u•al•i•ty (sĕk′shōō **ăl′**ĭ tē) *n.* **1.** The condition of being characterized and distinguished by sex. **2.** Concern with or interest in sexual activity.

Sey•chelles (sā **shĕl′** *or* sā **shĕlz′**). An island country in the western Indian Ocean north of Madagascar. It gained its independence from Great Britain in 1976. Capital, Victoria. Population, 64,718.

Sgt. *abbr.* An abbreviation of sergeant.

sh (sh) *interj.* An expression used to urge silence.

shab•by (**shăb′**ē) *adj.* **shab•bi•er, shab•bi•est. 1.** Dressed in threadbare clothes. **2.** Worn-out, frayed, and faded; threadbare: *shabby clothes.* **3.** Dilapidated; deteriorated: *shabby houses.* **4.** Despicable or unfair; mean: *shabby treatment.* [First written down in 1669 in Modern English, from obsolete *shab*, scab, from Old English *sceabb.*] **—shab′bi•ly** *adv.* **—shab′bi•ness** *n.*

shack (shăk) *n.* A small crudely built cabin. [First written down in 1878 in American English, possibly from American Spanish *jacal*, from Nahuatl *xacalli*, adobe hut.]

shack•le (**shăk′**əl) *n.* **1.** A metal ring fastened or locked around the wrist or ankle of a prisoner or captive. **2.** A restraint or check to action or progress. Often used in the plural: *the shackles of ignorance.* —*tr.v.* **shack•led, shack•ling, shack•les. 1.** To put a shackle or shackles on: *shackle a prisoner.* **2.** To confine, restrain, or hamper.

shad (shăd) *n., pl.* **shad** or **shads.** Any of several food fishes that are related to the herrings and that swim from salt to fresh water to spawn.

shade (shād) *n.* **1.** Light that has been diminished in strength by partial blocking or deflection of its rays; partial darkness. **2.** An area or a space of such partial darkness. **3.** Cover or shelter from the sun or its rays. **4.** Any of various devices used to reduce light or heat, as that from the sun: *a window shade.* **5.** The degree to which a color is mixed with black or less than fully lighted. **6.** A slight difference; a nuance: *a shade of meaning.* **7.** A small amount; a trace: *a shade under forty miles.* **8.** A spirit; a ghost. **9. shades.** Reminders; echoes: *shades of 1776.* —*tr. v.* **shad•ed, shad•ing, shades. 1.** To screen from light or heat: *Trees shaded the street.* **2.** To represent or produce degrees of shade or shadow in: *shade a drawing.* [First written down before 900 in Old English and spelled *sceadu.*]

shad•ing (**shā′**dĭng) *n.* **1.** A screening against light or heat. **2.** The lines or other marks used in a drawing, an engraving, or a painting to represent gradations of color or darkness. **3.** A small change or difference.

shad•ow (**shăd′**ō) *n.* **1.** An area from which light or other radiation is wholly or partly blocked due to the presence of an opaque object between it and the source of radiation. **2.** The rough image cast by an object blocking rays of light: *shadows of leaves on the wall.* **3.** An imperfect imitation or copy. **4. shadows.** The darkness following sunset: *evening shadows.* **5.** Gloom or unhappiness. **6.** A shaded area in a picture or photograph. **7.** A phantom; a ghost. **8.** A person, such as a detective or spy, who follows another in secret. **9.** A faint indication; a premonition: *shadows of future events.* **10.** A slight trace: *beyond a shadow of a doubt.* —*tr.v.* **shad•owed, shad•ow•ing, shad•ows. 1.** To cast a shadow on; shade. **2.** To follow after, especially in secret; trail. [First written down before 1200 in Middle English and spelled *schadewe*, from Old English *sceaduwe*, form of *sceadu*, shade.]

shad•ow•y (**shăd′**ō ē) *adj.* **shad•ow•i•er, shad•ow•i•est. 1.** Relating to or resembling a shadow: *shadowy forms moving underwater.* **2.** Full of or dark with shadows: *shadowy woods.* See Synonyms at **dark. 3.** Vague; indistinct: *shadowy ideas.*

shad•y (**shā′**dē) *adj.* **shad•i•er, shad•i•est. 1.** Full of shade; shaded: *a shady street.* See Synonyms at **dark. 2.** Casting shade: *shady trees.* **3.** Of doubtful character or honesty; questionable: *a shady deal.* **—shad′i•ly** *adv.* **—shad′i•ness** *n.*

shaft (shăft) *n.* **1.a.** The long narrow body of a spear or an arrow. **b.** A spear or an arrow. **2.** A ray or beam of light. **3.** The handle of any of various tools or implements: *the shaft of a hammer.* **4.** The rib of a feather. **5.** The section of a column between the capital and the base. **6.** One of the two parallel poles between which an animal drawing a vehicle is hitched. **7.** A long, generally cylindrical bar, especially one that turns and transmits power, as the drive shaft of an engine. **8.** A long narrow passage or conduit: *a mine shaft.* [First written down about 1000 in Old English and spelled *sceaft.*]

shag (shăg) *n.* **1.** A tangle or mass, especially of rough matted hair. **2.a.** A coarse long nap, as on a woolen cloth. **b.** Cloth having such a nap.

shag•bark (**shăg′**bärk′) *n.* A North American hickory tree having shaggy bark and edible hard-shelled nuts.

shag•gy (**shăg′**ē) *adj.* **shag•gi•er, shag•gi•est. 1.** Having, covered with, or resembling long rough hair or wool: *a shaggy dog.* **2.** Rough and bushy: *shaggy hair.*

shah (shä) *n.* Used formerly as a title for the king of

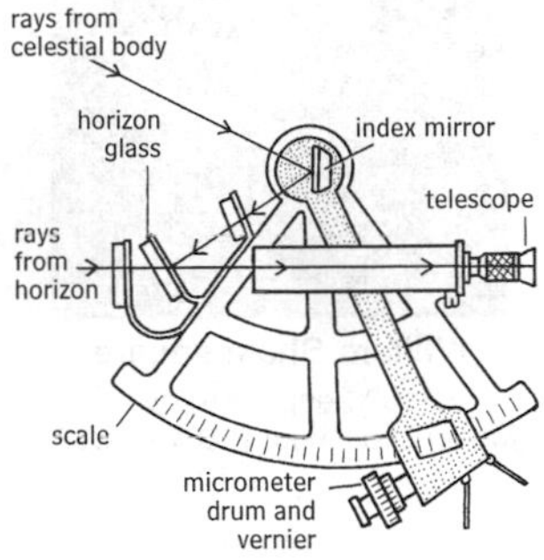

sextant

Anne Sexton

ă	pat	oi	boy
ā	pay	ou	out
âr	care	ŏŏ	took
ä	father	ōō	boot
ĕ	pet	ŭ	cut
ē	be	ûr	urge
ĭ	pit	th	thin
ī	pie	*th*	this
îr	pier	hw	whoop
ŏ	pot	zh	vision
ō	toe	ə	about
ô	paw	N	*French* bon

William Shakespeare
1623 engraving by
Martin Droeshout (1601–1650?)

Usage: shall

It is now all right to use the word **will** instead of **shall** to refer to the future whether you are speaking in the first, second, or third persons: *I, we* (or *you* or *he, she, it, they*) *will be leaving soon.*

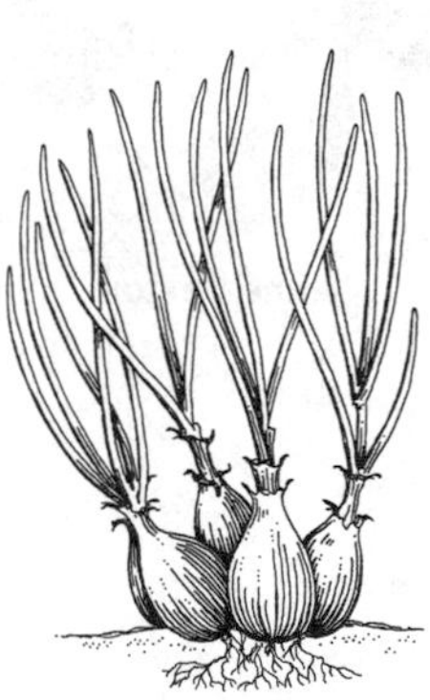

shallot

Iran. [First written down in 1566 in Modern English and spelled *shaugh*, from Persian *shāh*.]

shake (shāk) *v.* **shook** (shŏŏk), **shak•en** (shā′kən), **shak•ing, shakes.** —*tr.* **1.** To move or cause to move to and fro with jerky movements: *shake a tambourine.* **2.** To cause to tremble, vibrate, or rock: *The earthquake shook the ground.* **3.** To cause to waver; unsettle: *Nothing could shake him from his belief.* **4.** To remove or dislodge by jerky movements: *shake snow from the boots.* **5.** To make uneasy; disturb; agitate: *The bad news shook her.* **6.** To brandish or wave, especially in anger: *shake one's fist.* **7.** To clasp (hands) in greeting or leave-taking or as a sign of agreement. —*intr.* **1.** To move to and fro in short, irregular, often jerky movements. **2.** To tremble, as from cold or in anger. **3.** To be unsteady; totter or waver. **4.** To move something vigorously up and down, as in mixing. **5.** To shake hands: *Let's shake on it.* —*n.* **1.** The act of shaking: *a shake of the head.* **2.** A trembling or vibrating movement. **3.** *Informal.* A moment: *We'll be there in a shake.* **4.** A beverage mixed by shaking, especially a milkshake. **5. shakes.** *Informal.* Uncontrollable trembling. ***—idioms.*** **shake off.** To free oneself of; get rid of: *We shook off our fears.* **shake up. 1.** To upset by or as if by a physical jolt or shock. **2.** To subject to a drastic rearrangement or reorganization: *The new director decided to shake up the entire organization.* [First written down about 725 in Old English and spelled *sceacan*.]

shak•er (shā′kər) *n.* **1.** A person or thing that shakes. **2.** A container used for shaking: *a pepper shaker.* **3. Shaker.** A member of a Christian group originating in England in 1747 and practicing communal living and celibacy.

Shake•speare (shāk′spîr), **William.** 1564–1616. English writer whose plays include historical works, comedies, and tragedies, such as *Hamlet.* **—Shake•spear′e•an, Shake•spear′i•an** *adj.*

shake•up (shāk′ŭp′) *n.* A drastic reorganization: *a shakeup of government personnel.*

shak•o (shăk′ō *or* shā′kō) *n., pl.* **shak•os** or **shak•oes.** A military cap with a visor in front and an upright plume on top.

shak•y (shā′kē) *adj.* **shak•i•er, shak•i•est. 1.** Trembling or quivering: *a shaky voice.* **2.** Unsteady or unsound: *a shaky old dock.* **3.** Not to be depended on; wavering or doubtful: *a shaky alliance.* **—shak′i•ly** *adv.*

shale (shāl) *n.* Any of various easily split sedimentary rocks consisting of layers of clay and particles smaller than fine sand grains pressed together.

shall (shăl) *aux.v.* past tense **should** (shŏŏd). **1.** Used to express future action or condition: *I shall return tomorrow.* **2.** Used to express an order, a promise, a requirement, or an obligation: *You shall pay for your misdeeds.* **3.** Used to express determination: *I shall go if I want to.* —See Note.

shal•lop (shăl′əp) *n.* An open boat fitted with oars or sails or both.

shal•lot (shə lŏt′ *or* shăl′ət) *n.* **1.** A plant closely related to the onion, cultivated for its edible bulb. **2.** The mild-flavored bulb of the shallot.

shal•low (shăl′ō) *adj.* **shal•low•er, shal•low•est. 1.** Measuring little from the bottom to the top or surface; not deep: *a shallow lake; a shallow pan.* **2.** Lacking depth of thought, feeling, or knowledge; superficial: *shallow ideas.* —*n.* A shallow part of a body of water. Often used in the plural: *went swimming in the shallows.* [First written down before 1387 in Middle English and spelled *schalowe*.] **—shal′low•ly** *adv.* **—shal′low•ness** *n.*

shalt (shălt) *aux.v. Archaic.* A second person singular present tense of **shall.**

sham (shăm) *n.* Something false that is deceitfully passed off as genuine; a fraudulent imitation: *The antique turned out to be a sham.* —*adj.* Fake; not genuine: *sham diamonds.* —*tr.v.* **shammed, sham•ming, shams.** To pretend to have or feel; feign: *shamming ignorance.* [First written down in 1677 in Modern English, possibly from *shame*.]

sha•man (shä′mən *or* shā′mən) *n.* A member of certain societies who acts as an intermediary between the visible world and an invisible spirit world and who heals people and foretells or controls events. [First written down in 1698 in Modern English, ultimately from Sanskrit *śramaṇaḥ*, a Buddhist monk.]

sham•ble (shăm′bəl) *intr.v.* **sham•bled, sham•bling, sham•bles.** To walk in an awkward or lazy way, dragging the feet; shuffle. —*n.* An awkward shuffling walk.

sham•bles (shăm′bəlz) *pl.n. (used with a singular verb).* A scene or condition of great disorder or destruction.

shame (shām) *n.* **1.** A painful emotion caused by a strong sense of guilt, embarrassment, unworthiness, or disgrace. **2.** Capacity for such an emotion: *Have you no shame?* **3.** A source of disgrace or embarrassment: *It's a shame that none of you offered to help the strangers.* **4.** A condition of disgrace or dishonor. **5.** A great disappointment: *It would be a shame to miss the circus.* —*tr.v.* **shamed, sham•ing, shames. 1.** To cause to feel shame: *He lies because the truth shames him.* **2.** To bring disgrace upon: *shamed their good name.* **3.** To force (someone) by arousing a feeling of shame or guilt: *He was shamed into making an apology.* ***—idiom.*** **put to shame. 1.** To fill with shame; disgrace. **2.** To outdo thoroughly; surpass: *Her batting record put the rest of us to shame.* [First written down before 800 in Old English and spelled *sceamu*.]

shame•faced (shām′fāst′) *adj.* **1.** Ashamed. **2.** Very shy; bashful. **—shame′fac′ed•ly** (shām′fā′sĭd lē) *adv.*

shame•ful (shām′fəl) *adj.* Causing shame; disgraceful: *shameful behavior.* **—shame′ful•ly** *adv.* **—shame′ful•ness** *n.*

shame•less (shām′lĭs) *adj.* **1.** Feeling no shame: *a shameless liar.* **2.** Marked by a lack of shame: *a shameless lie.* **—shame′less•ly** *adv.*

sham•poo (shăm po͞o′) *n., pl.* **sham•poos. 1.** Any of various preparations of soap or detergent used to wash the hair and scalp. **2.** Any of various cleaning agents for rugs, upholstery, or cars. **3.** The act or process of washing the hair or cleaning something with shampoo. —*tr. & intr.v.* **sham•pooed, sham•poo•ing, sham•poos.** To wash or be washed with shampoo. [First written down in 1838 in Modern English, from Hindi *cāpō*, imperative of *cāpnā*, to press, massage.]

sham•rock (shăm′rŏk′) *n.* A clover or similar plant having leaves with three small leaflets, regarded as the national emblem of Ireland. [First written down in 1577 in Modern English, from Irish Gaelic *seamróg*, diminutive of *seamar*, clover.]

shang•hai (shăng hī′ *or* shăng′hī′) *tr.v.* **shang•haied, shang•hai•ing, shang•hais. 1.** To kidnap (a person), especially by making the person unconscious with a drug or liquor, for forced service aboard a ship. **2.** To force (a person) to do something by deceitful or dishonest means.

Shang•hai (shăng hī′). The largest city in China, in the eastern part of the country at the mouth of the Yangtze River (Chang Jiang) on the East China Sea. Population, 6,980,000.

shank (shăngk) *n.* **1.a.** The part of the human leg between the knee and ankle. **b.** The corresponding part of the leg of a vertebrate animal. **2.** A long narrow part of an object: *the shank of an anchor.* **3.** A cut of meat from the leg of a steer, calf, sheep, or lamb.

shan't (shănt). Contraction of *shall not.*

shan•tung (shăn tŭng′) *n.* A heavy fabric with a rough nubby surface, made of rayon, cotton, or wild silk.

shan•ty (shăn′tē) *n., pl.* **shan•ties.** A roughly built or ramshackle cabin; a shack.
❑ *These sound alike:* **shanty, chantey** (song).

shape (shāp) *n.* **1.** The outward appearance of a thing; form. **2.** Something distinguished from its surroundings by its outline: *dark shapes on the horizon that might have been houses.* **3.** The outline of a person's body; the figure. **4.a.** A definite distinctive form: *Our discussion took the shape of an argument.* **b.** A desirable form: *a fabric that holds its shape.* **5.** A form or condition in which something may exist or appear: *a god in the shape of a swan.* **6.** A device for giving or determining form; a mold or pattern. **7.** Proper condition for action, effectiveness, or use: *an athlete out of shape.* —*tr.v.* **shaped, shap•ing, shapes. 1.** To give a certain shape or form to: *shape clay into bowls.* **2.** To change to a particular shape or form; mold: *shape a sculpture out of ice.* **3.** To modify; adapt: *shaped their plans to fit ours.* **4.** To direct the course of: *shaping a child's education.* —**idiom. shape up.** *Informal.* **1.** To turn out; develop: *I wondered how the game was shaping up.* **2.** To improve so as to meet a standard. [First written down before 1000 in Old English and spelled *gesceap,* a creation.]

shape•less (shāp′lĭs) *adj.* **1.** Having no definite shape; formless: *a shapeless cloud.* **2.** Lacking a pleasing shape; not shapely: *a shapeless figure.* —**shape′less•ly** *adv.* —**shape′less•ness** *n.*

shape•ly (shāp′lē) *adj.* **shape•li•er, shape•li•est.** Having a shape that is pleasing to look at; well-proportioned. —**shape′li•ness** *n.*

shard (shärd) *n.* **1.** A piece of broken pottery, especially one found in an archaeological dig. **2.** A fragment, as of glass or metal.

share[1] (shâr) *n.* **1.** A part belonging to, distributed, contributed by, or owned by a person or group; a portion. **2.** A fair or full portion: *did her share to make the play a success.* **3.** Any of the equal parts into which the capital stock of a business is divided. —*v.* **shared, shar•ing, shares.** —*tr.* **1.** To divide and distribute. **2.** To use or experience in common with another or others: *sharing the responsibility; share a room.* **3.** To disclose or present to others: *He shared his adventure with the class.* —*intr.* To participate: *We shared in applauding the suggestion.* [First written down about 1000 in Old English and spelled *scearu,* division.] —**shar′er** *n.*

share[2] (shâr) *n.* A plowshare. [First written down before 800 in Old English and spelled *scēar.*]

share•crop•per (shâr′krŏp′ər) *n.* A tenant farmer who pays a share of the crops as rent to the landowner.

share•hold•er (shâr′hōl′dər) *n.* A person who owns a share or shares in the stock of a company; a stockholder.

shark (shärk) *n.* **1.** Any of numerous often large and voracious ocean fishes having sharp teeth and tough skin. **2.** A person regarded as ruthless, greedy, or dishonest. [First written down in 1569 in Modern English.]

sharp (shärp) *adj.* **sharp•er, sharp•est. 1.** Having a thin edge or fine point for cutting or piercing: *a sharp razor.* **2.** Having an edge or a point: *sharp rocks.* **3.** Clear and distinct: *a sharp image.* **4.** Abrupt; not gradual: *a sharp drop to the sea.* **5.** Intelligent; smart: *a sharp mind.* **6.** Acute: *the sharp eyes of a falcon.* **7.** Watchful; alert: *keep a sharp lookout.* **8.** Crafty or deceitful: *a sharp politician.* **9.** Cold and cutting: *a sharp wind.* **10.** Harsh; caustic: *a sharp tongue.* **11.** Fierce or impetuous; violent: *a sharp blow.* **12.** Felt suddenly and intensely: *a sharp pain.* **13.** Sudden and shrill: *a sharp whistle.* **14.** Having a strong odor and flavor: *a sharp cheese.* **15.a.** Higher in musical pitch than is correct: *a sharp note.* **b.** Higher in pitch by a half step than a corresponding natural tone or key: *a C sharp.* **16.** *Informal.* Stylish or attractive: *a sharp dresser.* —*adv.* **sharper, sharpest. 1.** In a sharp manner. **2.** Promptly; exactly: *at 3 o'clock sharp.* **3.** Above the correct pitch: *Nervousness caused him to sing sharp.* —*n.* **1.** A musical note or tone that is a half step higher than a corresponding natural note or tone. **2.** The symbol (♯) attached to a note to indicate that it is a sharp. —*intr.v.* **sharped, sharp•ing, sharps.** To sing or play sharp. [First written down before 830 in Old English and spelled *scearp.*] —**sharp′ly** *adv.* —**sharp′ness** *n.*

sharp•en (shär′pən) *tr. & intr.v.* **sharp•ened, sharp•en•ing, sharp•ens.** To make or become sharp or sharper. —**sharp′en•er** *n.*

sharp•shoot•er (shärp′shōō′tər) *n.* A person expert at shooting a gun.

Shatt al Ar•ab or **Shatt-al-Ar•ab** (shăt′ ăl ăr′əb). A river channel, about 120 miles (193 kilometers) long, of southeast Iraq formed by the junction of the Tigris and Euphrates rivers and flowing southeast to the Persian Gulf.

shat•ter (shăt′ər) *v.* **shat•tered, shat•ter•ing, shat•ters.** —*tr.* **1.** To cause to break suddenly into pieces, as with a violent blow; smash. **2.** To damage seriously. **3.** To destroy beyond hope of repair; ruin: *shattered his hopes.* —*intr.* To break into pieces; smash or burst. See Synonyms at **break.**

shave (shāv) *v.* **shaved, shaved** or **shav•en** (shā′vən), **shav•ing, shaves.** —*tr.* **1.a.** To remove hair from, especially with a razor: *shave a man's face.* **b.** To cut (the beard or hair) at the surface of the skin with a razor. **2.** To cut thin slices from: *shaving a board.* **3.** To cut or scrape into small pieces; shred: *shave chocolate.* **4.** To touch gently in passing; graze. —*intr.* To cut hair, especially the hair on a man's face, at the surface of the skin with a razor: *Tom shaves every morning.* —*n.* The act, process, or result of shaving: *a smooth shave.*

shav•er (shā′vər) *n.* **1.** A person who shaves. **2.** A device for shaving, especially an electric razor. **3.** *Informal.* A young boy; a lad.

shav•ing (shā′vĭng) *n.* **1.** A thin slice or sliver, as of wood or metal that is shaved off. **2.** The action of a person that shaves.

Sha•vu•ot (shə vōō′ōt′ *or* shə vōō′əs) *n.* A Jewish festival that commemorates God's revelation of the Torah on Mount Sinai.

shawl (shôl) *n.* A large piece of cloth worn as a covering for the shoulders, neck, or head.

Shaw•nee (shô nē′) *n., pl.* **Shawnee** or **Shaw•nees. 1.** A member of a Native American people formerly living in the Cumberland and Ohio valleys and now living in Oklahoma. **2.** The Algonquian language of the Shawnee.

shay (shā) *n. Informal.* A chaise.

she (shē) *pron.* **1.** The woman or girl previously mentioned: *Nancy left, but she will be back.* **2.** The female animal previously mentioned: *Our cat likes fish, but she won't eat chicken.* **3.** Something previously mentioned that is traditionally personified as female: *Britain was bombed heavily, but she would not surrender.* —*n.* A female person or animal: *Is the baby a he or a she?* —SEE NOTE.

sheaf (shēf) *n., pl.* **sheaves** (shēvz). **1.** A bundle of cut stalks of grain or similar plants bound with

shark

shay

Usage: she

Many people feel it is fairest to use phrases such as *he or she* when referring to someone who could be either male or female: *Every student must hand in his or her assignment today.* You can also rewrite such sentences using plural nouns and pronouns: *All students must hand in their assignments today.* This issue comes up with words such as **any**, **anyone**, **each**, **every**, **neither**, and **one**.

ă	pat	oi	**boy**
ā	**pay**	ou	**out**
âr	**care**	ŏŏ	**took**
ä	**father**	ōō	**boot**
ĕ	**pet**	ŭ	**cut**
ē	**be**	ûr	**urge**
ĭ	**pit**	th	**thin**
ī	**pie**	*th*	**this**
îr	**pier**	hw	**whoop**
ŏ	**pot**	zh	**vision**
ō	**toe**	ə	**about**
ô	**paw**	N	*French* **bon**

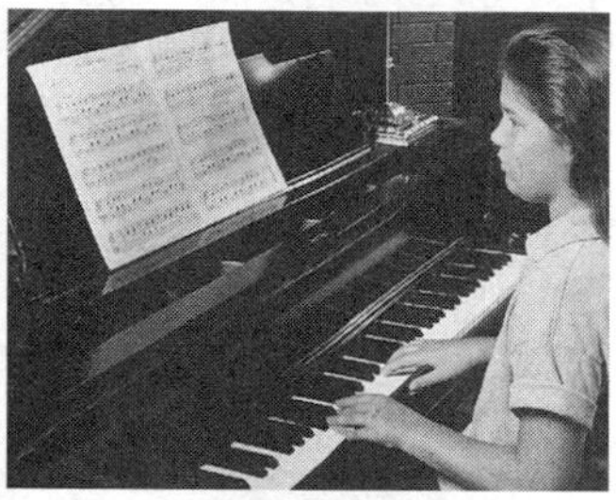

sheet music

Mary Wollstonecraft Shelley
Detail of a c. 1840 portrait
by Richard Rothwell (1800–1868)

Percy Bysshe Shelley
1819 portrait
by Amelia Curran (1775–1847)

straw or twine. **2.** A collection of things held or bound together.

shear (shîr) *tr.v.* **sheared, sheared** or **shorn** (shôrn), **shear•ing, shears. 1.** To remove (fleece or hair) by clipping with a sharp instrument. **2.** To remove the fleece or hair from: *shearing a ram.* **3.** To cut with or as if with shears: *shearing a hedge.* **4.** To deprive; divest: *sheared of all privileges.* —*n.* A pair of scissors or a similar cutting tool. Often used in the plural. [First written down about 725 in Old English and spelled *sceran.*] —**shear'er** *n.*

❑ *These sound alike:* **shear, sheer**[1] (swerve), **sheer**[2] (thin).

sheath (shēth) *n., pl.* **sheaths** (shēthz *or* shēths). **1.** A case into which the blade of a knife or sword fits. **2.** Any of various similar coverings. **3.** A close-fitting dress. —*tr.v.* **sheathed, sheath•ing, sheaths** (shēthz *or* shēths). To sheathe.

sheathe (shēth) *tr.v.* **sheathed, sheath•ing, sheathes. 1.** To insert into or provide with a sheath: *sheath a sword.* **2.** To provide with a protective covering: *sheathe electric wires with rubber.*

sheath•ing (**shē'**thĭng) *n.* **1.** A layer of boards or other materials applied to the frame of a building to strengthen and protect it from weather. **2.** A protective covering on the underwater part of a ship's hull.

sheave (shēv) *tr.v.* **sheaved, sheav•ing, sheaves.** To gather and bind (grain) into a sheaf.

sheaves (shēvz) *n.* Plural of **sheaf.**

She•ba (**shē'**bə). An ancient country of southern Arabia in present-day Yemen. Its people colonized Ethiopia in the tenth century B.C.

shed[1] (shĕd) *tr.v.* **shed, shed•ding, sheds. 1.** To rid oneself of: *shed his clothes and jumped into the pool.* **2.** To send forth; give off: *The moon shed a pale light on the pond.* **3.** To repel: *This coat sheds water.* **4.** To lose by a natural process: *trees that shed their leaves in autumn.* **5.** To cause to pour forth: *shed tears.* —***idiom.*** **shed blood.** To take life; kill. [First written down about 1000 in Old English and spelled *scēadan,* to divide, separate.] —**shed'der** *n.*

shed[2] (shĕd) *n.* A small structure for storage or shelter: *a tool shed.* [First written down in 1481 in Middle English and spelled *shadde,* perhaps variant of *shade,* shade.]

she'd (shēd). Contraction of *she had* or *she would.*

sheen (shēn) *n.* Glistening brightness; luster.

sheep (shēp) *n., pl.* **sheep. 1.** Any of various hoofed mammals having a thick fleecy coat, widely raised for their wool, meat, and skin. **2.** A weak person who is easily led or influenced.

sheep•cote (**shēp'**kōt' *or* **shēp'**kŏt') *n. Chiefly British.* A sheepfold.

sheep•dog also **sheep dog** (**shēp'**dôg' *or* **shēp'**dŏg') *n.* A dog trained to guard and herd sheep.

sheep•fold (**shēp'**fōld') *n.* A pen for sheep.

sheep•herd•er (**shēp'**hûr'dər) *n.* A person who herds sheep; a shepherd.

sheep•ish (**shē'**pĭsh) *adj.* **1.** Embarrassed, as by being aware of a fault: *a sheepish grin.* **2.** Meek or stupid. —**sheep'ish•ly** *adv.* —**sheep'ish•ness** *n.*

sheep•skin (**shēp'**skĭn') *n.* **1.** The skin of a sheep, either with the fleece left on or in the form of leather or parchment. **2.** *Informal.* A diploma.

sheer[1] (shîr) *intr. & tr.v.* **sheered, sheer•ing, sheers.** To swerve or cause to swerve from a course. [First written down in 1626 in Modern English, probably partly from Low German *scheren,* to move to and from (said of boats), and partly from Dutch *scheren,* to withdraw.]

❑ *These sound alike:* **sheer**[1] (swerve), **shear** (cut), **sheer**[2] (thin).

sheer[2] (shîr) *adj.* **sheer•er, sheer•est. 1.** Thin, fine, and transparent: *sheer stockings.* **2.** Complete; utter: *dropped from sheer exhaustion.* **3.** Almost perpendicular; steep: *sheer cliffs.* [First written down in 1565 in Modern English and spelled *shere,* thin, clear, partly from Middle English *shir,* bright, clear (from Old English *scīr*) and partly from Middle English *skir,* bright, clean (from Old Norse *skærr*).]

❑ *These sound alike:* **sheer**[2] (thin), **shear** (cut), **sheer**[1] (swerve).

sheet[1] (shēt) *n.* **1.** A large piece of cloth, used as a bed covering, especially in pairs, one under and one over the sleeper. **2.** A broad, thin, usually rectangular piece of material, such as paper, metal, or glass. **3.** A broad continuous expanse of material covering a surface: *a sheet of ice.* —*tr.v.* **sheet•ed, sheet•ing, sheets.** To cover or provide with sheets, especially bed sheets. [First written down before 800 in Old English and spelled *scēte.*]

sheet[2] (shēt) *n.* A rope attached to one or both of the lower corners of a sail to move or extend it. [First written down in 1294 in Middle English and spelled *shete,* from Old English *scēat(line),* sheet (line), from *scēata,* corner of a sail.]

sheet•ing (**shē'**tĭng) *n.* Material, such as metal or cloth, used to make a sheet.

sheet lightning *n.* Lightning that appears as a broad sheet of light across a part of the sky, caused by reflection of a distant flash of lightning by clouds.

sheet metal *n.* Metal that has been rolled into a sheet.

sheet music *n.* Music printed on unbound sheets of paper.

sheik also **sheikh** (shēk *or* shāk) *n.* **1.** A Muslim religious official. **2.** The leader of an Arab family or village.

❑ *These sound alike:* **sheik, chic** (fashionable).

shek•el (**shĕk'**əl) *n.* **1.** The basic monetary unit of Israel. **2.** An ancient Hebrew unit of weight equal to about half an ounce. **3.** An ancient Hebrew coin weighing this amount in silver or gold.

shel•duck (**shĕl'**dŭk') *n.* **1.** Any of various large ducks of Europe, North America, and Asia, having mostly black and white feathers. **2.** The merganser.

shelf (shĕlf) *n., pl.* **shelves** (shĕlvz). **1.** A flat, usually rectangular piece of wood, metal, or glass, fastened at right angles to a wall or other vertical surface and used to hold or store objects. **2.** An object resembling a shelf, as a flat ledge of rock jutting out from a cliff. **3.** A reef, sandbar, or shoal.

shelf life *n.* The length of time a product may be stored, as on a supermarket shelf, without deteriorating.

shell (shĕl) *n.* **1.a.** The usually hard outer covering of certain animals, such as mollusks, insects, and turtles. **b.** The material of which such a covering is made. **c.** A similar hard or brittle outer covering on an egg, nut, or fruit. **2.** An outer covering or framework resembling or having the form of a shell: *a pastry shell for a pie.* **3.** A long narrow boat used in rowing races. **4.a.** A projectile or piece of ammunition, especially the hollow tube containing explosives used to propel a projectile. **b.** A cartridge for a shotgun. **5.** A pattern of electrons surrounding the nucleus of an atom. All of the electrons in a given shell have approximately the same energy. —*v.* **shelled, shell•ing, shells.** —*tr.* **1.** To remove the shells of; shuck: *shell peas for dinner.* **2.** To fire shells at; bombard: *shell a fortress.* —*intr.* To search for or gather shells, as along a beach. —***idiom.*** **shell out.** *Informal.* To hand over; pay: *had to shell out fifty dollars for the food.* —**shelled** *adj.*

she'll (shēl). Contraction of *she will* or *she shall.*

shel•lac (shə **lăk'**) *n.* **1.** A purified lac in the form of yellow or orange flakes, often bleached white and used in varnishes, paints, and sealing wax and formerly in making phonograph records. **2.** A solution of flakes of this material in alcohol, making a thin varnish used for finishing wood surfaces and as a sealer. —*tr.v.* **shel•lacked, shel•lack•ing, shel•lacs. 1.** To apply shellac to (a wooden surface, for example). **2.** *Slang.* To defeat decisively.

Shel•ley (shĕl′ē), **Mary Godwin Wollstonecraft.** 1797–1851. British writer best known for the Gothic novel *Frankenstein* (1818).

Shelley, Percy Bysshe. 1792–1822. British poet whose works include "To a Skylark" (1820).

shell•fish (shĕl′fĭsh′) *n.* A water animal, such as a clam or lobster, that has a shell or a similar outer covering.

shell shock *n.* Any of various severe nervous or emotional disorders caused by the experience of combat. **—shell′-shocked′** *adj.*

shel•ter (shĕl′tər) *n.* **1.** Something that provides cover or protection: *used an abandoned shack as a shelter for the night.* **2.** A refuge; a haven: *seeking shelter from the storm.* **3.** An institution providing temporary housing for the homeless. —*v.* **shel•tered, shel•ter•ing, shel•ters.** —*tr.* To provide cover or protection for. —*intr.* To take cover or refuge: *sheltering by day and traveling by night.*

shelve (shĕlv) *tr.v.* **shelved, shelv•ing, shelves. 1.** To place or arrange on a shelf or shelves. **2.** To put aside as though on a shelf; postpone: *shelved the trip because we couldn't afford it.*

shelves (shĕlvz) *n.* Plural of **shelf.**

shelv•ing (shĕl′vĭng) *n.* **1.** Shelves considered as a group. **2.** Material for shelves.

Shen•an•do•ah Valley (shĕn′ən dō′ə). A valley of northern Virginia between the Allegheny Mountains and the Blue Ridge. The valley was an important gateway to the frontier.

she•nan•i•gan (shə năn′ĭ gən) *n. Informal.* **1.a.** A playful trick or prank. **b.** Mischief. **2.** A deceitful trick or remark. Often used in the plural.

shep•herd (shĕp′ərd) *n.* **1.** A person who herds, guards, and tends sheep. **2.** A person who cares for and guides a group of people, as a minister or teacher. —*tr.v.* **shep•herd•ed, shep•herd•ing, shep•herds.** To herd, guard, tend, or guide in the manner of a shepherd. See Synonyms at **guide.**

shep•herd•ess (shĕp′ər dĭs) *n.* A woman or girl who herds, guards, and tends sheep.

sher•bet (shûr′bĭt) *n.* A frozen dessert made of fruit juice, sugar, water, milk, and egg whites or gelatin.

Sher•i•dan (shĕr′ĭ dn), **Philip Henry.** 1831–1888. American Union general in the Civil War.

sher•iff (shĕr′ĭf) *n.* The chief law enforcement officer for the courts in a U.S. county. [First written down about 1024 in Old English and spelled *scīr-gerēfa* : *scīr*, shire + *gerēfa*, officer.]

Sher•man (shûr′mən), **William Tecumseh.** 1820–1891. American Union general who as commander of Union troops in the West led a destructive March to the Sea (1864) in the Civil War.

sher•ry (shĕr′ē) *n., pl.* **sher•ries.** An amber-colored dry or sweet Spanish wine.

Sher•wood Forest (shûr′wo͝od′). A former royal forest of central England known in legend as the home of Robin Hood and his followers.

she's (shēz). Contraction of *she is* or *she has.*

Shet•land Islands (shĕt′lənd). A group of islands of northern Scotland in the Atlantic Ocean northeast of the Orkney Islands. The islands became part of Scotland in 1472.

Shetland pony *n.* A small, sturdy, long-maned pony of a breed originally from the Shetland Islands north of Scotland.

Shetland sheepdog *n.* A dog of a breed developed in the Shetland Islands, having a rough coat and resembling a small collie.

shf or **SHF** *abbr.* An abbreviation of super high frequency.

shib•bo•leth (shĭb′ə lĭth) *n.* **1.** A custom, use of language, or other characteristic that serves to identify the members of a certain group. **2.** A slogan, saying, or theme repeated by the supporters of a certain party or cause.

shied[1] (shīd) *v.* Past tense and past participle of **shy**[1].

shied[2] (shīd) *v.* Past tense and past participle of **shy**[2].

shield (shēld) *n.* **1.** A piece of armor carried on the arm for protection against arrows, swords, and similar weapons. **2.** A person or thing that provides protection: *raised her arm as a shield against the glare.* **3.** A concrete or lead structure built around a nuclear reactor to prevent radiation from escaping. **4.** An emblem or a badge: *a police shield.* —*tr.v.* **shield•ed, shield•ing, shields.** To protect with or as if with a shield. See Synonyms at **defend.**

shi•er (shī′ər) *adj.* A comparative of **shy**[1].

shies[1] (shīz) *v.* Third person singular present tense of **shy**[1]. —*n.* Plural of **shy**[1].

shies[2] (shīz) *v.* Third person singular present tense of **shy**[2]. —*n.* Plural of **shy**[2].

shi•est (shī′ĭst) *adj.* A superlative of **shy**[1].

shift (shĭft) *v.* **shift•ed, shift•ing, shifts.** —*tr.* **1.** To exchange (one thing) for another of the same class: *shifted game plans.* **2.** To move from one place or position to another; transfer. **3.** To change (gears), as in driving a car. —*intr.* **1.** To change position, direction, place, or form. **2.** To provide for one's needs; get along: *I can shift for myself.* **3.** To shift gears, as when driving a car. —*n.* **1.** A change from one person or setup to another; a substitution. **2.a.** A group of workers on duty at the same time, as at a factory. **b.** The period during which such a group works: *the 9-to-5 shift.* **3.** A change in direction, attitude, judgment, or emphasis: *a shift in the wind; a shift toward greater tolerance.* **4.** A change in position. **5.** A change in the position of the spectral lines from a celestial body, either toward red or toward blue. **6.a.** A loosely fitting dress that hangs straight from the shoulders. **b.** A woman's slip or chemise. **7.** A means to an end; a strategy.

shift•less (shĭft′lĭs) *adj.* Lacking ambition or purpose; lazy. **—shift′less•ly** *adv.*

shift•y (shĭf′tē) *adj.* **shift•i•er, shift•i•est. 1.** Evasive or untrustworthy; deceitful. **2.** Changing direction frequently: *shifty winds.* **—shift′i•ly** *adv.*

Shi•ite (shē′īt′) *n.* A member of a branch of Islam that regards Ali and his descendants as the true successors of Muhammad.

shil•le•lagh (shə lā′lē) *n.* A wooden club or cudgel, traditionally used in Ireland.

shil•ling (shĭl′ĭng) *n.* **1.** A coin used in the United Kingdom worth one twentieth of a pound, 5 new pence, or 12 old pence prior to 1971. **2.** The basic monetary unit of Kenya, Somalia, Tanzania, and Uganda.

shil•ly-shal•ly (shĭl′ē shăl′ē) *intr.v.* **shil•ly-shal•lied** (shĭl′ē shăl′ēd), **shil•ly-shal•ly•ing, shil•ly-shal•lies** (shĭl′ē shăl′ēz). **1.** To waste time or delay. **2.** To be unable to reach a decision. **—shil′ly-shal′li•er** *n.*

shim•mer (shĭm′ər) *intr.v.* **shim•mered, shim•mer•ing, shim•mers. 1.** To shine with a flickering light; glimmer. **2.** To appear as a wavering or flickering image: *Heat waves shimmered above the road ahead.* —*n.* A flickering light; a glimmer.

shim•my (shĭm′ē) *n., pl.* **shim•mies. 1.** Abnormal vibration or wobbling, as of the wheels of an automobile. **2.** A dance popular in the 1920's, characterized by rapid shaking of the body. —*intr.v.*

William Tecumseh Sherman

Shetland pony

ă	pat	oi	boy
ā	pay	ou	out
âr	care	o͝o	took
ä	father	o͞o	boot
ĕ	pet	ŭ	cut
ē	be	ûr	urge
ĭ	pit	th	thin
ī	pie	*th*	this
îr	pier	hw	whoop
ŏ	pot	zh	vision
ō	toe	ə	about
ô	paw	N	*French* bon

Word Building: –ship

The suffix **–ship** has a long history in English. It goes back to the Old English suffix *–scipe,* which was attached frequently to adjectives and nouns to indicate a particular state or condition: **hardship**, **friendship**. In Modern English the suffix has been added only to nouns and usually indicates a state or condition (**authorship**, **kinship**, **partnership**, **relationship**), the qualities belonging to a class of human beings (**craftsmanship**, **horsemanship**, **sportsmanship**), or rank or office (**ambassadorship**).

shipyard

Word History: shirt

The nouns **shirt** and **skirt** are related to the adjective **short**. *Shirt* came from the Old English word *scyrte,* which in Middle English referred to an undergarment worn on the upper part of the body. In Old Norse, which was closely related to Old English, the word *skyrta* meant "a short shirt, knee-length shirt or tunic, nightshirt." The Old Norse word kept getting longer and lower, so to speak, and wound up being used for a short garment below the waist, while the English word stayed put for a short garment above the waist.

shim•mied, shim•my•ing, shim•mies. 1. To vibrate or wobble abnormally. **2.** To shake the body, as in dancing the shimmy.

shin (shĭn) *n.* **1.** The front part of the human leg below the knee and above the ankle. **2.** A corresponding part of the leg of an animal. **3.** The shinbone. *—v.* **shinned, shin•ning, shins.** *—tr.* To climb (a rope or pole, for example) by gripping and pulling with hands and legs: *shinning a tree.* *—intr.* To climb something by shinning it.

shin•bone (**shĭn′**bōn′) *n.* The tibia.

shin•dig (**shĭn′**dĭg′) *n.* A large party, often with dancing.

shine (shīn) *v.* **shone** (shōn) or **shined, shin•ing, shines.** *—intr.* **1.** To emit light: *The sun shone on the mountains.* **2.** To reflect light; gleam: *We polished the table until it shone.* **3.** To distinguish oneself in an activity; excel: *Our band shines when we play the songs we know best.* **4.** To be apparent: *Delight shone in his eyes.* *—tr.* **1.** To aim the beam or glow of (a light). **2.** *past tense and past participle* **shined.** To make glossy or bright by polishing. *—n.* **1.** Brightness from a source of light; radiance. **2.** Brightness from reflected light. **3.** A shoeshine. **4.** Excellence in quality or appearance; splendor. **5.** Fair weather: *We'll have a picnic, rain or shine.* **—*idiom.* take a shine to.** *Informal.* To like spontaneously.

shin•er (**shī′**nər) *n.* **1.** A person or thing that shines. **2.** *Slang.* A black eye.

shin•gle[1] (**shĭng′**gəl) *n.* **1.** A thin oblong piece of wood or other material laid in overlapping rows to cover the roof or sides of a building. **2.** A small signboard, as one hung outside the office of a professional: *The dentist hung out her shingle.* *—tr.v.* **shin•gled, shin•gling, shin•gles.** To cover (a roof or wall) with shingles. [First written down about 1200 in Middle English and spelled *scincle,* from Old English *scindel,* from Late Latin *scindula.*]

shin•gle[2] (**shĭng′**gəl) *n.* **1.** Beach gravel consisting of smooth pebbles with no finer material mixed in. **2.** A stretch of shore or beach covered with such gravel. [First written down in 1421 in Middle English and spelled *chingell.*]

shin•gles (**shĭng′**gəlz) *pl.n. (used with a singular or plural verb).* A painful viral infection marked by skin eruptions along a nerve path, usually only on one side of the body. [First written down before 1398 in Middle English and spelled *schingles,* from Medieval Latin *cingulus,* belt, girdle.]

shin•ny[1] (**shĭn′**ē) *n., pl.* **shin•nies. 1.** Field hockey that is played informally with curved sticks and a ball, can, or similar object. **2.** A curved stick used in this game. [First written down in 1672 in Modern English and spelled *shinnie,* probably from the phrase *shin ye,* a call used in the game.]

shin•ny[2] (**shĭn′**ē) *intr.v.* **shin•nied** (**shĭn′**ēd), **shin•ny•ing, shin•nies** (**shĭn′**ēz). To climb by shinning: *shinny up a pole.* [First written down in 1888 in American English, from *shin.*]

shin splints also **shin•splints** (**shĭn′**splĭnts′) *pl.n. (used with a singular or plural verb).* Pain or soreness in the shin caused by excessive running or jumping.

Shin•to (**shĭn′**tō) *n.* The traditional religion of the Japanese, marked by worship of nature spirits and ancestors and by a lack of formal dogma. **—Shin′to•ism** *n.* **—Shin′to•ist** *adj. & n.*

shin•y (**shī′**nē) *adj.* **shin•i•er, shin•i•est. 1.** Sending forth light; bright: *shiny stars.* **2.** Bright from reflecting light; glistening: *a shiny brass knocker.* **3.** Glossy from being rubbed or worn smooth: *shiny red apples.* **—shin′i•ness** *n.*

ship (shĭp) *n.* **1.a.** A large vessel for traveling over deep water. **b.** A sailing vessel with three or more masts. **2.** An aircraft or a spacecraft. **3.** A ship's crew: *Most of the ship was on deck.* *—tr.v.* **shipped, ship•ping, ships. 1.** To send or transport: *shipping goods by truck.* **2.** To take (water) in over the side of a boat: *We're shipping a lot of water.* **—*idiom.* ship out. 1.** To leave, as for a distant place. **2.** To send, as to a distant place.

–ship *suff.* A suffix that means: **1.** Condition or quality: *friendship.* **2.** Rank or office: *professorship.* **3.** Art, skill, or craft: *penmanship.* **4.** A collective body: *readership.* —See Note.

ship biscuit *n.* Hardtack.

ship•board (**shĭp′**bôrd′) *n.* The condition of being aboard a ship: *The supplies are on shipboard.* *—adj.* Existing or occurring on board a ship: *a shipboard friendship.*

ship•build•ing (**shĭp′**bĭl′dĭng) *n.* The art or business of building or designing ships. **—ship′build′er** *n.*

ship•load (**shĭp′**lōd′) *n.* The amount that a ship can carry.

ship•mas•ter (**shĭp′**măs′tər) *n.* The officer in command of a merchant ship.

ship•mate (**shĭp′**māt′) *n.* A sailor serving on the same ship as another; a fellow sailor.

ship•ment (**shĭp′**mənt) *n.* **1.** The act or an instance of shipping goods: *iron ore for shipment abroad.* **2.** A quantity of goods shipped together: *a new shipment of automobiles.*

ship•per (**shĭp′**ər) *n.* A person or company engaged in the business of transporting or receiving goods.

ship•ping (**shĭp′**ĭng) *n.* **1.** The act or business of transporting goods. **2.** The body of ships belonging to one port, industry, or country.

ship•shape (**shĭp′shāp′**) *adj.* Neatly arranged; in good order. See Synonyms at **neat.**

ship•worm (**shĭp′**wûrm′) *n.* Any of various marine mollusks that resemble worms and bore into wood, often doing extensive damage.

ship•wreck (**shĭp′**rĕk′) *n.* **1.** The destruction of a ship, as by storm or collision. **2.** A wrecked ship. *—tr.v.* **ship•wrecked, ship•wreck•ing, ship•wrecks. 1.** To cause (a ship) to be destroyed. **2.** To cause (a person) to suffer shipwreck.

ship•yard (**shĭp′**yärd′) *n.* A yard in which ships are built or repaired.

shire (shīr) *n.* A former division of Great Britain equivalent to a county.

shirk (shûrk) *tr.v.* **shirked, shirk•ing, shirks.** To avoid or neglect (a task or duty). **—shirk′er** *n.*

shirr (shûr) *tr.v.* **shirred, shirr•ing, shirrs. 1.** To gather (cloth) into decorative rows by parallel stitching. **2.** To bake (unshelled eggs) until set.

shirt (shûrt) *n.* **1.** A garment for the upper part of the body, generally having a collar, sleeves, and a front opening. **2.** An undershirt. **3.** A nightshirt. —See Note.

shirt•ing (**shûr′**tĭng) *n.* Cloth for making shirts.

shirt•waist (**shûrt′**wāst′) *n.* A tailored blouse.

shish ke•bab (**shĭsh′** kə bŏb′) *n.* A dish consisting of pieces of seasoned meat and sometimes vegetables roasted on skewers.

Shi•va (**shē′**və) *n.* One of the principal Hindu gods, worshiped as the destroyer and restorer of worlds and in numerous other forms.

shiv•er[1] (**shĭv′**ər) *intr.v.* **shiv•ered, shiv•er•ing, shiv•ers.** To shake with or as if with cold; tremble. *—n.* An instance of shivering. [First written down about 1200 in Middle English and spelled *chiveren.*]

shiv•er[2] (**shĭv′**ər) *intr. & tr.v.* **shiv•ered, shiv•er•ing, shiv•ers.** To break or cause to break into fragments or splinters; shatter. *—n.* A fragment or sliver. [First written down before 1200 in Middle English and spelled *shivren,* from *shivere,* splinter.]

shiv•er•y (**shĭv′**ə rē) *adj.* **1.** Trembling, as from cold or fear. **2.** Causing shivers; chilling.

shoal[1] (shōl) *n.* **1.** A shallow place in a body of water. **2.** A sandbank or sandbar at the bottom of a body of water. *—adj.* Shallow: *places where the water is shoal.* [First written down about 1375 in Middle English and spelled *schald*, from Old English *sceald*, shallow.]

shoal[2] (shōl) *n.* A large school of fish or other water animals. *—intr.v.* **shoaled, shoal•ing, shoals.** To come together in large numbers. [First written down in 1579 in Modern English and spelled *shole*, probably from Middle Low German or Middle Dutch *schōle*.]

shoat also **shote** (shōt) *n.* A young pig.

shock[1] (shŏk) *n.* **1.** A violent collision or impact; a heavy blow. **2.** Something that upsets the mind or emotions as if with a violent unexpected blow. **3.** The sudden disturbance of the mind or emotions caused by such an occurrence. **4.** A generally temporary reaction to severe bodily injury, usually consisting of a loss of blood pressure and a slowing down of vital functions. **5.** The sensation and muscular spasm caused by the passage of an electric current through the body or a body part. *—tr.v.* **shocked, shock•ing, shocks. 1.** To surprise and disturb greatly. **2.** To offend. **3.** To cause a state of shock in (a living organism). **4.** To subject (a person or an animal) to an electric shock. [First written down in 1565 in Modern English, from French *choquer*, to collide with.] **—shock′er** *n.*

shock[2] (shŏk) *n.* **1.** A pile of sheaves of grain stacked upright in a field to dry. **2.** A thick heavy mass: *a shock of fair hair.* *—tr.v.* **shocked, shock•ing, shocks.** To gather (grain) into shocks. [First written down before 1325 in Middle English and spelled *scholke*.]

shock absorber *n.* A device used to absorb mechanical shocks, as in a moving car.

shock•ing (**shŏk′**ĭng) *adj.* **1.** Highly disturbing emotionally. **2.** Highly offensive; distasteful or indecent. **—shock′ing•ly** *adv.*

shock troops *pl.n.* Soldiers trained to lead attacks.

shock wave *n.* A wave formed by the sudden compression of the medium through which the wave moves. Shock waves can be caused by explosions or objects moving at supersonic speeds.

shod (shŏd) *v.* Past tense and a past participle of **shoe.**

shod•den (**shŏd′**n) *v.* A past participle of **shoe.**

shod•dy (**shŏd′**ē) *adj.* **shod•di•er, shod•di•est. 1.** Made of or containing inferior material. **2.** Of poor quality or craft: *shoddy toys; a shoddy job.* **3.** Dishonest: *shoddy politicians.* *—n., pl.* **shod•dies. 1.** Woolen yarn made from scraps or used clothing, with some new wool added. **2.** Cloth made from or containing such yarn.

shoe (sho͞o) *n.* **1.** An outer covering for the human foot, especially one of a pair having a rigid sole and heel and a flexible upper part. **2.** A horseshoe. **3.** The part of a brake that presses against a wheel or drum to slow its motion. **4. shoes.** *Informal.* Position or situation: *I wouldn't want to be in your shoes.* *—tr.v.* **shod** (shŏd), **shod** or **shod•den** (**shŏd′**n), **shoe•ing, shoes.** To furnish or fit with shoes. [First written down about 950 in Old English and spelled *scōh*.]

❑ *These sound alike:* **shoe, shoo** (scare away).

shoe•horn (**sho͞o′**hôrn′) *n.* A curved implement, often of plastic or metal, used at the heel to help put on a shoe.

shoe•lace (**sho͞o′**lās′) *n.* A string or cord used for lacing and fastening shoes.

shoe•mak•er (**sho͞o′**mā′kər) *n.* A person who makes or repairs shoes.

shoe•string (**sho͞o′**strĭng′) *n.* A shoelace. *—adj.* Consisting of a small amount of money: *a shoestring budget.* ***—idiom.*** **on a shoestring.** With a small amount of money: *The company started out on a shoestring.*

shoe•tree (**sho͞o′**trē′) *n.* A form inserted into a shoe to preserve its shape.

sho•far (**shō′**fär′ *or* **shō′**fər) *n.* A trumpet made of a ram's horn, sounded in synagogues during Rosh Hashanah and at the end of Yom Kippur. [First written down in 1864 in Modern English and spelled *shophar*, from Hebrew *šôpār*.]

sho•gun (**shō′**gən) *n.* Any of the military commanders who ruled Japan until 1867.

shone (shōn) *v.* A past tense and a past participle of **shine.**

❑ *These sound alike:* **shone, shown** (displayed).

shoo (sho͞o) *interj.* An expression used to scare away animals or birds. *—tr.v.* **shooed, shoo•ing, shoos.** To drive or scare away by or as if by crying "shoo."

❑ *These sound alike:* **shoo, shoe** (foot covering).

shook (sho͝ok) *v.* Past tense of **shake.**

shoon (sho͞on) *n.* *Archaic.* A plural of **shoe.**

shoot (sho͞ot) *v.* **shot** (shŏt), **shoot•ing, shoots.** *—tr.* **1.a.** To hit, wound, or kill with a missile fired from a weapon. **b.** To fire (a gun, bow, or similar weapon). **c.** To fire (a bullet, arrow, or other missile) from a weapon. **2.** To discharge or explode; set off: *shooting off firecrackers.* **3.** To propel or launch with great force: *shoot a rocket toward the moon.* **4.** To propel in a rapid stream or flow: *a volcano shooting lava.* **5.** To pass swiftly through: *shooting the narrows in a sailboat.* **6.** To record on film: *shot the scene in one take.* **7.a.** To throw or propel (a ball or puck, for example) in a specific direction or toward the goal. **b.** To score (a basket, point, or goal) in this way. **8.** To play (a round of golf or craps, for example). **9.** To slide (a door bolt) into or out of place. **10.** To streak or spot with a different color or substance: *brown hair shot with gray.* *—intr.* **1.** To fire a missile from a weapon. **2.** To fire; go off. **3.** To appear or spurt suddenly: *Water shot out of the fountain. The sun shot through a break in the clouds.* **4.** To move quickly; dart. **5.** To be felt moving or as if moving through the body: *A shiver shot through my body.* **6.** To engage in hunting or the firing of weapons, especially for sport. **7.** To put forth new growth, as a plant. **8.** To take pictures or begin filming a scene in a movie. **9.** To propel a ball or other object in a specific direction or toward the goal. **10.** To play a game involving a ball or other projectile. *—n.* **1.** A plant or plant part, such as a stem, leaf, or bud, that has just begun to grow, sprout, or develop. **2.** An organized hunt: *a turkey shoot.* *—interj.* An expression used to show surprise, annoyance, or disappointment. ***—idioms.*** **shoot down. 1.** To bring down (an aircraft, for example) by hitting and damaging with gunfire or a missile. **2.** *Informal.* To ruin the hopes of; disappoint. **3.** *Informal.* To put an end to; defeat: *shot down the proposal.* **shoot for** or **shoot at.** *Informal.* To strive or aim for; have as a goal. **shoot up. 1.** *Informal.* To grow or get taller rapidly. **2.** To increase dramatically in amount. [First written down before 899 in Old English and spelled *scēotan*.] **—shoot′er** *n.*

❑ *These sound alike:* **shoot, chute** (inclined trough).

shoot•ing star (**sho͞o′**tĭng) *n.* A meteor.

shop (shŏp) *n.* **1.** A small retail store or a specialty department in a large store. **2.** A workshop or studio, as of an artist. **3.** A place where certain goods are made or repaired. **4.a.** A schoolroom equipped with machinery and tools for instruction in industrial arts. **b.** A course of study in an industrial art.

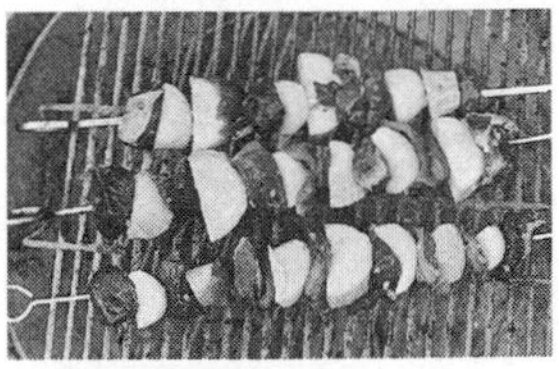

shish kebab

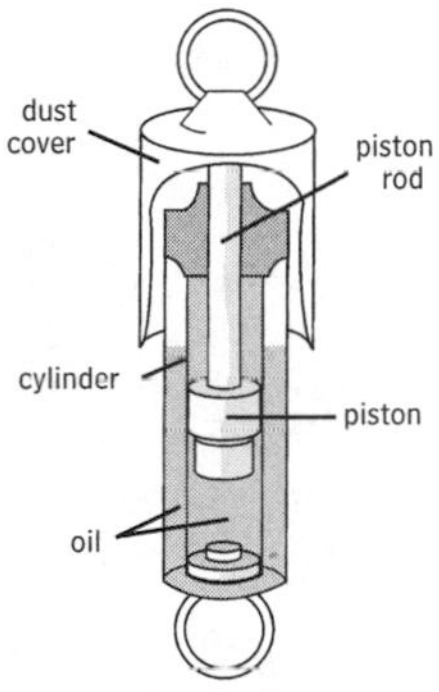

shock absorber

Hydraulic shock absorber

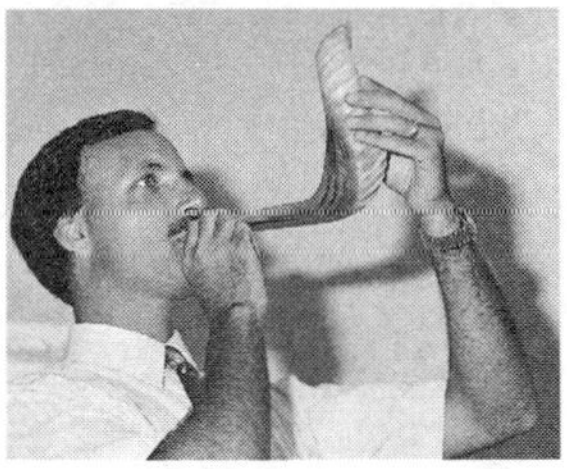

shofar

ă	pat	oi	boy
ā	pay	ou	out
âr	care	o͝o	took
ä	father	o͞o	boot
ĕ	pet	ŭ	cut
ē	be	ûr	urge
ĭ	pit	th	thin
ī	pie	*th*	this
îr	pier	hw	whoop
ŏ	pot	zh	vision
ō	toe	ə	about
ô	paw	N	*French* bon

—*intr.v.* **shopped, shop•ping, shops.** To visit stores to look at or buy things. —***idioms.*** **shop around. 1.** To go from store to store in search of merchandise or bargains. **2.** To look for something, such as a better job. **talk shop.** To talk about one's work. [First written down before 1050 in Old English and spelled *scoppa*, work shed.] —**shop'per** *n.*

shop•keep•er (shŏp'kē'pər) *n.* A person who owns or manages a shop.

shop•lift (shŏp'lĭft') *v.* **shop•lift•ed, shop•lift•ing, shop•lifts.** —*intr.* To steal merchandise from a store. —*tr.* To steal from a store.

shop•ping center (shŏp'ĭng) *n.* A group of stores and often restaurants and other businesses having a common parking lot.

shop•talk (shŏp'tôk') *n.* **1.** Talk or conversation concerning one's business. **2.** The jargon used in a specific business or field.

shop•worn (shŏp'wôrn') *adj.* Soiled, faded, frayed, or otherwise damaged from being displayed in a store.

shore[1] (shôr) *n.* **1.** The land along the edge of a body of water. **2.** Land within national or other boundaries. Often used in the plural: *immigrants who came to these shores.* [First written down before 1100 in Old English and spelled *scora.*]

shore[2] (shôr) *tr.v.* **shored, shor•ing, shores.** To support by or as if by a prop: *shore up a sagging floor.* —*n.* A beam or timber propped against a structure to provide support. [First written down in 1340 in Middle English and spelled *ssoren*, from *shore*, a prop.]

shore bird *n.* Any of various birds, such as a sandpiper, plover, and snipe, that live on the shores of coastal or inland waters.

shore•line (shôr'līn') *n.* The edge of a body of water.

shorn (shôrn) *v.* A past participle of **shear.**

short (shôrt) *adj.* **short•er, short•est. 1.a.** Having little length; not long: *a short fuse.* **b.** Having little height; not tall: *a short building.* **2.** Covering a relatively small distance: *a short walk; a short toss.* **3.** Lasting a brief time: *a short vacation; a short speech.* **4.** Insufficient in length or amount: *The ladder is 2 feet short.* **5.** Having an inadequate or insufficient supply: *I'm short of money.* **6.** Of or relating to the vowel sounds in words such as *pat, pet, pit, pot, putt, and put.* **7.** Unstressed or unaccented: *a poetic meter in which a long syllable is followed by two short syllables.* **8.** Curt; abrupt: *He was very short with the salesclerk.* **9.** Easily provoked: *a short temper.* **10.** Containing a large amount of shortening; flaky: *a short pie crust.* —*adv.* **shorter, shortest. 1.** Abruptly; quickly: *stopped short.* **2.** Before a given point or goal: *The arrow fell short of the target.* —*n.* **1.** A short movie. **2.** A short circuit. **3. shorts.** Short trousers with legs that extend to the knee or above. —*v.* **short•ed, short•ing, shorts.** —*tr.* To cause a short circuit in. —*intr.* To short-circuit. —***idioms.*** **for short.** As an abbreviation: *His name is Joseph, but he's called "Joe" for short.* **in short.** In summary; briefly. **short for.** An abbreviation of: *"Jo" is short for "Joanna."* **short of. 1.** Less than: *Nothing short of winning satisfies her.* **2.** Other than; without resorting to: *Nothing short of a siren would have caught their attention.* [First written down before 899 in Old English and spelled *sceort.*] —**short'ness** *n.*

short•age (shôr'tĭj) *n.* A lack in the amount needed; deficiency: *a food shortage.*

short•bread (shôrt'brĕd') *n.* A cookie made of flour, sugar, and much butter or other shortening.

short•cake (shôrt'kāk') *n.* A dessert consisting of a crisp light cake served with fruit and topped with cream.

short•change (shôrt'chānj') *tr.v.* **short•changed, short•chang•ing, short•chang•es. 1.** To give (someone) less change than is due. **2.** *Informal.* To swindle, cheat, or trick. —**short'chang'er** *n.*

short circuit *n.* A path that allows most of the current in an electric circuit to flow around or away from the principal elements or devices in the circuit.

short-cir•cuit (shôrt'sûr'kĭt) *v.* **short-cir•cuit•ed, short-cir•cuit•ing, short-cir•cuits.** —*tr.* To cause to have a short circuit. —*intr.* To become affected with a short circuit.

short•com•ing (shôrt'kŭm'ĭng) *n.* An inadequacy; a flaw.

short•cut (shôrt'kŭt') *n.* **1.** A route that is quicker or more direct than the one usually taken. **2.** A means of saving effort or time.

short division *n.* A division of one number by another, usually of no more than two digits, without writing out the remainders.

short•en (shôr'tn) *v.* **short•ened, short•en•ing, short•ens.** —*tr.* **1.** To make short or shorter. **2.** To add shortening to (dough). —*intr.* To become short or shorter.

short•en•ing (shôr'tn ĭng *or* shôrt'nĭng) *n.* A fat, such as butter, lard, or vegetable oil, used to make cake or pastry rich and flaky.

short•fall (shôrt'fôl') *n.* **1.** A failure to attain a specified amount or level; a shortage. **2.** The amount by which a supply falls short of expectation, need, or demand.

short•hand (shôrt'hănd') *n.* A system of rapid handwriting using symbols to represent words, phrases, and letters.

short-hand•ed (shôrt'hăn'dĭd) *adj.* Lacking the usual or necessary number of employees, players, workers, or assistants.

short•horn (shôrt'hôrn') *n.* Any of a breed of cattle having short curved horns.

short-lived (shôrt'līvd' *or* shôrt'lĭvd') *adj.* Living or lasting only a short time: *short-lived joy.*

short•ly (shôrt'lē) *adv.* **1.** In a short time; soon: *We will leave shortly.* **2.** In a few words; briefly: *To put it shortly, we've got to finish now or not at all.* **3.** In a curt or abrupt manner: *"Why shouldn't I?" Charles demanded rather shortly.*

short-range (shôrt'rānj') *adj.* **1.** Made for use over short distances: *short-range airlines.* **2.** Of or relating to the near future: *short-range goals.*

short shrift *n.* **1.** Brief or hasty consideration: *I gave short shrift to the invitation.* **2.** Quick work; rapid settlement: *The debater made short shrift of her opponent's arguments.* **3.** A short delay before punishment, death, or some other harsh fate.

short•sight•ed (shôrt'sī'tĭd) *adj.* **1.** Nearsighted; lacking clear vision of distant objects. **2.** Lacking foresight: *The land policy was shortsighted in its neglect of the peasant.* —**short'sight'ed•ly** *adv.* —**short'sight'ed•ness** *n.*

short•stop (shôrt'stŏp') *n.* The baseball player defending the area between second base and the third baseman.

short story *n.* A short piece of prose fiction.

short-tem•pered (shôrt'tĕm'pərd) *adj.* Easily losing one's temper; quickly angered.

short ton *n.* A unit of weight equal to 2,000 pounds (0.907 metric ton). See table at **measurement.**

short wave *n.* A radio wave having a wavelength between about 10 and 200 meters.

short-wind•ed (shôrt'wĭn'dĭd) *adj.* **1.** Breathing with quick labored breaths. **2.** Likely to have difficulty in breathing, especially after physical stress.

Sho•sho•ne (shō shō'nē) *n., pl.* **Shoshone** or **Sho•sho•nes. 1.** A member of a Native American people living mostly in Idaho, Nevada, and Wyoming. **2.**

Any of the languages of the Shoshone. —**Sho•sho′ne•an** *adj.*

shot¹ (shŏt) *n.* **1.** The discharge of a gun or similar weapon: *a rifle shot.* **2.** The distance over which something is shot. **3.** An attempt to hit something with a projectile: *took a shot at the bear.* **4.** An attempt to score in a game such as soccer. **5.** A throw, drive, or stroke, as of a ball or puck, toward a goal or target: *a nice shot onto the green.* **6.** *Informal.* A chance; a try: *had a shot at a good job.* **7.a.** A solid projectile, such as a ball or bullet, designed to be fired from a firearm or cannon: *A blast of shot ripped through the door.* **b.** *pl.* **shot.** Such projectiles considered as a group. **8.** A person who shoots, considered with regard to his or her accuracy: *He is the best shot on the hockey team.* **9.a.** A photograph. **b.** A single, continuously photographed scene or view in a motion picture. **10.** A hypodermic injection: *a shot of penicillin.* **11.** A drink of liquor, especially a measure of about 1½ ounces. **12.** The heavy metal ball used in the shot put. —***idioms.*** **like a shot.** Very quickly. **shot in the dark.** *Informal.* A wild guess. [First written down before 899 in Old English and spelled *sceot.*]

shot² (shŏt) *v.* Past tense and past participle of **shoot.**

shote (shōt) *n.* Variant of **shoat.**

shot•gun (**shŏt′**gŭn′) *n.* A gun with a smooth bore that fires shot at close range.

shot put *n.* **1.** An athletic event in which participants put a heavy metal ball as far as possible. **2.** The ball used in this competition. —**shot′-put′er** (**shŏt′**po͝ot′ər) *n.*

should (sho͝od) *aux.v.* Past tense of **shall. 1.** Used to express obligation or duty: *You should send her a note.* **2.** Used to express probability or expectation: *They should arrive at noon.* **3.** Used to express condition as opposed to present fact: *If they should call while I'm out, tell them I'll be right back.* —SEE NOTE.

shoul•der (**shōl′**dər) *n.* **1.a.** The part of the human body between the neck and upper arm. **b.** The joint that connects the arm with the trunk. **c.** The corresponding part of the body of an animal. **2.** The area of the back from one shoulder to the other. Often used in the plural: *a boy with broad shoulders.* **3.** The part of a garment that covers the shoulder. **4.** A sloping or jutting side of something: *the shoulder of a mountain; the shoulder of a vase.* **5.** The edge or border running on either side of a roadway. —*v.* **shoul•dered, shoul•der•ing, shoul•ders.** —*tr.* **1.** To place on the shoulder or shoulders for carrying: *The porters shouldered their loads.* **2.** To take on; bear; assume: *shouldering the blame for the others.* **3.** To push or apply force to with or as if with the shoulders. —*intr.* To push with the shoulders. —***idiom.*** **shoulder to shoulder. 1.** Side by side. **2.** In close cooperation. [First written down before 800 in Old English and spelled *sculdor.*]

shoulder blade *n.* Either of the two large flat bones that form the rear of the shoulder; the scapula.

shoulder strap *n.* A strap worn over the shoulder to support a garment or another item, such as a bag.

should•n't (**sho͝od′**nt). Contraction of *should not.*

shouldst (sho͝odst) *aux.v. Archaic.* Second person singular past tense of **should.**

shout (shout) *n.* A loud cry. —*tr. & intr.v.* **shout•ed, shout•ing, shouts.** To say with or utter a shout: *shouted orders; shouted at the umpire.* —***idiom.*** **shout down.** To silence by shouting loudly. [First written down in 1375 in Middle English and spelled *schout,* perhaps from Old Norse *skūta,* a taunt.] —**shout′er** *n.*

Synonyms: **shout, holler, howl, roar, yell.** These verbs all mean to say with or make a loud, strong cry. *The children shouted and ran around the playground. She hollered a warning at the trespassers. Kevin dropped the bowling ball on his foot and started howling with pain. The audience roared with laughter at the clowns. Several people were yelling at the umpire.*

shove (shŭv) *v.* **shoved, shov•ing, shoves.** —*tr.* **1.** To push forward or along: *shoved the table against the wall.* **2.** To push roughly or rudely. —*intr.* To push a person or thing along. —*n.* The act of shoving; a push. [First written down about 725 in Old English and spelled *scūfan.*] —**shov′er** *n.*

shov•el (**shŭv′**əl) *n.* **1.** A tool with a handle and a wide scoop or blade for digging and moving material, such as dirt or snow. **2.** A large mechanical machine used for heavy digging. **3.** The amount that a shovel can hold: *put a shovel of coal into the furnace.* —*v.* **shov•eled, shov•el•ing, shov•els** also **shov•elled, shov•el•ling, shov•els.** —*tr.* **1.** To move or remove with a shovel: *shovel snow.* **2.** To clear or make with a shovel: *shovel the walk; shovel a path.* **3.** To place, throw, or move as if with a shovel: *shovel food into his mouth.* —*intr.* To dig or work with a shovel. [First written down before 800 in Old English and spelled *scofl.*]

shov•el•er also **shov•el•ler** (**shŭv′**ə lər *or* **shŭv′**lər) *n.* **1.** A person or thing that shovels. **2.** A duck having a long broad bill, which it uses to strain food from mud and water.

shov•el•ful (**shŭv′**əl fo͝ol′) *n.* The amount that a shovel can hold.

show (shō) *v.* **showed, shown** (shōn) or **showed, show•ing, shows.** —*tr.* **1.a.** To cause or allow to be seen; display: *She showed them her new computer programs. The dog showed his teeth.* **b.** To present in public exhibition, for sale, or in competition: *show goods in a store.* **2.** To point out: *Show him the way.* **3.** To indicate or reveal: *His expression showed interest.* **4.** To conduct; guide: *She showed us around the village.* **5.** To demonstrate by reasoning or example: *showed that her hypothesis was correct; He showed us how to cook squash.* **6.** To grant or allow: *They showed no mercy in their treatment of the prisoners.* —*intr.* **1.** To be or become visible. **2.** To become revealed: *Your intelligence shows in your selection of books.* **3.** *Slang.* To appear at an event or appointment: *We gave a party, but our friends didn't show.* —*n.* **1.** A display: *a show of power.* **2.** A trace or indication: *no show of his former might.* **3.** An insincere display; a pretense: *put on quite a show of prestige.* **4.a.** A striking appearance or display; a spectacle: *the fiery show of a volcanic eruption.* **b.** A pompous or ostentatious display: *They rented the limousine just to make a show.* **5.a.** A public exhibition or entertainment: *a puppet show.* **b.** A radio or television program. **6.** *Informal.* An undertaking: *She ran the whole show.* **7.** Third place in a sports contest. —***idioms.*** **get the show on the road.** *Slang.* To get started. **show off.** To display or behave in a proud or showy manner: *He keeps trying to show off in his new sports car.* **show up. 1.** To be clearly visible. **2.** To put in an appearance; arrive: *I waited half an hour, but they never showed up.* **3.** *Informal.* To surpass, as in ability or intelligence: *Their team really showed us up.* [First written down about 725 in Old English and spelled *scēawian,* to look at, display.] —**show′er** *n.*

show bill *n.* An advertising poster.

show•boat (**shō′**bōt′) *n.* A river steamboat with a troupe of performers and a theater aboard for the performance of plays.

shot put
Preparing to put the shot

Usage: should

Be sure to say or write *should have* instead of *should of: They should have been here long before now.* Sometimes people use *should of* because they incorrectly think that is what the contraction *should've* stands for.

shovel
Left: Rounded mouth
Right: Tapered mouth

ă	pat	oi	boy
ā	pay	ou	out
âr	care	o͝o	took
ä	father	o͞o	boot
ĕ	pet	ŭ	cut
ē	be	ûr	urge
ĭ	pit	th	thin
ī	pie	*th*	this
îr	pier	hw	whoop
ŏ	pot	zh	vision
ō	toe	ə	about
ô	paw	N	*French* bon

show business *n.* The entertainment industry.
show•case (shō′kās′) *n.* **1.** A display case, as in a store or museum. **2.** A setting in which something may be displayed to advantage.
show•down (shō′doun′) *n.* An event, especially a confrontation, that forces an issue to a conclusion.
show•er (shou′ər) *n.* **1.a.** A brief fall of rain, snow, hail, or sleet. **b.** A fall of a group of objects, especially from the sky: *a meteor shower.* **2.** An abundant flow or outpouring: *a shower of praise.* **3.a.** A bath in which the water is sprayed on the bather, especially from overhead. **b.** The stall or tub in which such a bath is taken. **4.** A party held to honor and present gifts to someone: *a bridal shower.* —*v.* **show•ered, show•er•ing, show•ers.** —*tr.* **1.** To pour down in a shower: *showered confetti on the parade.* **2.** To bestow or pour forth abundantly: *showered presents on the child.* —*intr.* **1.** To fall or pour down in or as if in a shower. **2.** To wash oneself in a shower. [First written down about 950 in Old English and spelled *scūr.*]
shower bath *n.* A bath in which the water is sprayed on the bather.
show•ing (shō′ĭng) *n.* **1.** The act of presenting or displaying. **2.** Performance, as in a competition or test of skill: *a good showing.* **3.** A presentation of evidence, facts, or figures.
show•man (shō′mən) *n.* **1.** A person who produces shows. **2.** A man having a flair for dramatic effectiveness. —**show′man•ship′** *n.*
shown (shōn) *v.* A past participle of **show.**
❑ *These sound alike:* **shown, shone** (put forth light).
show•off (shō′ôf′ *or* shō′ŏf′) *n.* A person who seeks attention by showing off.
show•piece (shō′pēs′) *n.* Something shown, especially as an outstanding example of its kind.
show room *n.* A room in which merchandise is displayed.
show•y (shō′ē) *adj.* **show•i•er, show•i•est. 1.** Attracting attention; striking: *a plant with showy flowers.* **2.** Marked by or given to striking display; flashy: *made a showy catch in the outfield.* —**show′i•ly** *adv.* —**show′i•ness** *n.*
shrank (shrăngk) *v.* A past tense of **shrink.**
shrap•nel (shrăp′nəl) *n., pl.* **shrapnel. 1.** An artillery shell filled with metal balls and designed to explode in the air over enemy troops. **2.** Shell fragments from an exploded shell. [First written down in 1806 in Modern English, after Henry *Shrapnel* (1761–1842), British army officer.]
shred (shrĕd) *n.* **1.** A long irregular strip cut or torn from something: *shreds of cloth.* **2.** A small amount; a bit: *not a shred of evidence.* —*tr.v.* **shred•ded** or **shred, shred•ding, shreds.** To cut or tear into small strips: *shred cabbage.* See Synonyms at **rip**[1]. [First written down about 1000 in Old English and spelled *scrēade.*]
shrew (shro͞o) *n.* **1.** Any of various small mammals that resemble a mouse and have a narrow pointed snout. **2.** A scolding woman. [First written down before 800 in Old English and spelled *scrēawa.*]

shrew

shrewd (shro͞od) *adj.* **shrewd•er, shrewd•est. 1.** Clever, sharp, and practical: *a shrewd person.* **2.** Tricky and artful. [First written down about 1280 in Middle English and spelled *schrewede,* wicked.] —**shrewd′ly** *adv.* —**shrewd′ness** *n.*
shrew•ish (shro͞o′ĭsh) *adj.* Ill-tempered; nagging. —**shrew′ish•ly** *adv.* —**shrew′ish•ness** *n.*
shriek (shrēk) *n.* A shrill, often frantic cry: *shrieks of laughter; the shriek of a fire engine.* —*v.* **shrieked, shriek•ing, shrieks.** —*intr.* To utter a shriek: *The children shrieked in play.* —*tr.* To say with a shriek: *shriek a warning.* [First written down in 1590 in Modern English, from Middle English *skriken, shriken,* to shriek, of Scandinavian origin.] —**shriek′er** *n.*
shrike (shrīk) *n.* Any of various usually gray, black, and white birds of prey having a short hooked bill.
shrill (shrĭl) *adj.* **shrill•er, shrill•est.** High-pitched and piercing: *a shrill whistle.* —*tr. & intr.v.* **shrilled, shrill•ing, shrills.** To utter with or make a shrill sound or cry: *He shrilled his complaint. The wind shrilled outside.* [First written down about 1380 in Middle English and spelled *schrille.*] —**shril′ly** *adv.* —**shrill′ness** *n.*
shrimp (shrĭmp) *n., pl.* **shrimp** or **shrimps. 1.** Any of various small, usually salt-water animals related to the lobsters and crayfish, often used as food. **2.** *Slang.* A small or unimportant person. [First written down in 1327 in Middle English and spelled *shrimpe,* possibly of Low German origin.]
shrine (shrīn) *n.* **1.** A receptacle for sacred relics. **2.** The tomb of a saint or other venerated person. **3.** A site or object that is hallowed or revered for its history or associations. [First written down about 1000 in Old English and spelled *scrīn,* box, from Latin *scrīnium,* case for books or papers.]
shrink (shrĭngk) *v.* **shrank** (shrăngk) or **shrunk** (shrŭngk), **shrunk** or **shrunk•en** (shrŭng′kən), **shrink•ing, shrinks.** —*intr.* **1.** To become reduced in size, amount, or value; become smaller. **2.** To draw back; recoil: *They shrank from giving up their favorite dessert.* —*tr.* To cause to shrink. —*n.* **1.a.** The act of shrinking. **b.** Shrinkage. **2.** *Slang.* A psychiatrist. [First written down before 899 in Old English and spelled *scrincan,* to shrivel up.] —**shrink′a•ble** *adj.* —**shrink′er** *n.*
shrink•age (shrĭng′kĭj) *n.* **1.** The process of shrinking; constriction in size. **2.** The amount by which something shrinks. **3.** A reduction in value; depreciation.
shrive (shrīv) *tr.v.* **shrove** (shrōv) or **shrived, shriv•en** (shrĭv′ən) or **shrived, shriv•ing, shrives.** To hear the confession of and give absolution to (a penitent person). —**shriv′er** *n.*
shriv•el (shrĭv′əl) *intr. & tr.v.* **shriv•eled, shriv•el•ing, shriv•els** or **shriv•elled, shriv•el•ling, shriv•els.** To become or make shrunken or wrinkled: *Leaves fall and shrivel. Heat shriveled the grapes into raisins.*
shriv•en (shrĭv′ən) *v.* A past participle of **shrive.**
shroud (shroud) *n.* **1.** A cloth used to wrap a body for burial. **2.** Something that conceals, protects, or hides: *a shroud of silence.* **3.** One of the set of ropes or cables stretched to support the mast of a vessel. —*tr.v.* **shroud•ed, shroud•ing, shrouds. 1.** To wrap (a corpse) in a shroud. **2.** To conceal; screen; hide.
shrove (shrōv) *v.* A past tense of **shrive.**
Shrove Tuesday *n.* The day before Ash Wednesday.
shrub (shrŭb) *n.* A woody plant that is smaller than a tree and generally has several separate stems rather than a single trunk; a bush.
shrub•ber•y (shrŭb′ə rē) *n., pl.* **shrub•ber•ies.** A group of shrubs.
shrub•by (shrŭb′ē) *adj.* **shrub•bi•er, shrub•bi•est. 1.** Consisting of, planted with, or covered with shrubs. **2.** Of or resembling a shrub. —**shrub′bi•ness** *n.*
shrug (shrŭg) *v.* **shrugged, shrug•ging, shrugs.** —*tr.* To raise (the shoulders), especially to show doubt, disdain, or indifference. —*intr.* To shrug the shoulders. —*n.* The gesture of raising the shoulders to show doubt, disdain, or indifference. —***idiom.*** **shrug off. 1.** To consider as being of little importance: *She shrugged off the home run and continued pitching.* **2.** To get rid of: *I can't seem to shrug off this cold.*

shrunk (shrŭngk) *v.* A past tense and a past participle of **shrink.**

shrunk•en (shrŭng′kən) *v.* A past participle of **shrink.**

shuck (shŭk) *n.* An outer covering, such as a corn husk, a pea pod, or an oyster shell. *—tr.v.* **shucked, shuck•ing, shucks. 1.** To remove the husk or shell from: *shuck corn; shuck oysters.* **2.** *Informal.* To remove or strip (clothing or a similar outer covering): *shucked his jacket in the heat of the afternoon.* *—interj.* **shucks** (shŭks). An expression used to show disappointment or annoyance. **—shuck′er** *n.*

shud•der (shŭd′ər) *intr.v.* **shud•dered, shud•der•ing, shud•ders.** To tremble or shiver, as from fear or horror. *—n.* A shiver, as from fear or horror.

shuf•fle (shŭf′əl) *v.* **shuf•fled, shuf•fling, shuf•fles.** *—tr.* **1.** To slide (the feet) along the floor or ground. **2.** To mix together (playing cards, tiles, or dominoes) so as to make a random order of arrangement. **3.** To shift about from one place to another: *shuffled the papers around.* *—intr.* To move with a shambling idle gait: *shuffled across the road.* *—n.* **1.** A short sliding step or movement. **2.** The mixing of cards, dominoes, or tiles.

shuf•fle•board (shŭf′əl bôrd′) *n.* A game in which the players use pronged sticks to slide disks along a flat surface that has marked scoring areas.

shul (shōōl *or* shŏŏl) *n.* A synagogue.

shun (shŭn) *tr.v.* **shunned, shun•ning, shuns.** To avoid deliberately and consistently; keep away from: *shunned a person; shun a task.* **—shun′ner** *n.*

shunt (shŭnt) *n.* **1.** The act or process of turning aside or moving to an alternate course. **2.** A railroad switch. **3.** A low-resistance connection between two points in an electric circuit that forms an alternative path for a portion of the current. *—tr.v.* **shunt•ed, shunt•ing, shunts. 1.** To move aside or onto an alternate course: *shunt traffic around a bottleneck.* **2.** To avoid by putting aside or ignoring: *problems we should not shunt aside.* **3.** To switch (a railroad car or train) from one track to another. **4.a.** To provide (current) by means of a shunt. **b.** To divert (current) by means of a shunt. **—shunt′er** *n.*

shush (shŭsh) *interj.* An expression used to demand silence. *—tr.v.* **shushed, shush•ing, shush•es.** To demand silence from by saying "shush": *She shushed the children.*

shut (shŭt) *v.* **shut, shut•ting, shuts.** *—tr.* **1.** To move (a door or lid, for example) so as to block passage through an opening; close. **2.** To block entrance to or exit from; close: *shut the garage.* **3.** To fasten with a lock or latch. **4.** To lock up or confine: *She shut herself up in her room to prepare the surprise.* **5.** To exclude from a closed space: *shut the cat out of the house.* **6.** To cause to stop operating: *School was shut for vacation.* *—intr.* **1.** To move or be moved so as to block passage; close: *a door that shuts by itself.* **2.** To stop operating, especially automatically: *The light shuts off at dawn.* ***—idioms.*** **shut off. 1.** To stop the flow or passage of; cut off: *Be sure to shut off the water when you finish washing.* **2.** To close off; isolate: *During their camping trip they were completely shut off from everybody.* **shut up. 1.** To cause (someone) to stop speaking; silence. **2.** To stop speaking.

shut•down (shŭt′doun′) *n.* A stoppage of operation, as of a factory.

shut-in (shŭt′ĭn′) *n.* A person confined indoors because of illness or disability. *—adj.* (shŭt ĭn′). Confined to a house or hospital, as by illness.

shut•out (shŭt′out′) *n.* A game in which one side does not score.

shut•ter (shŭt′ər) *n.* **1.** A hinged cover or screen for a window, usually fitted with slanted slats. **2.** A device that opens and shuts the lens opening of a camera to expose a plate or film.

shut•tle (shŭt′l) *n.* **1.** A device used in weaving to carry the woof threads back and forth between the warp threads. **2.** A device for holding the thread on a sewing machine. **3.** A vehicle that takes short frequent trips over an established route: *We took the shuttle to the airport.* *—tr. & intr.v.* **shut•tled, shut•tling, shut•tles.** To move or cause to move back and forth by or as if by a shuttle.

shut•tle•cock (shŭt′l kŏk′) *n.* A small rounded piece of cork or rubber with a crown of feathers or plastic, hit back and forth in badminton.

shy[1] (shī) *adj.* **shi•er** (shī′ər), **shi•est** (shī′ĭst) or **shy•er, shy•est. 1.** Easily startled; timid: *a shy deer.* **2.** Avoiding contact or familiarity with others; reserved: *a shy person.* **3.** Distrustful; wary: *shy of strangers.* **4.** Short; lacking: *He is three inches shy of six feet.* *—intr.v.* **shied** (shīd), **shy•ing, shies** (shīz). To move suddenly, as if startled: *The horse shied at the sound.* [First written down about 1000 in Old English and spelled *scēoh.*] **—shy′ly** *adv.* **—shy′ness** *n.*

shy[2] (shī) *v.* **shied** (shīd), **shy•ing, shies** (shīz). *—tr.* To throw (something) with a swift motion; fling. *—intr.* To throw something with a swift motion. *—n., pl.* **shies** (shīz). A quick throw; a fling. [First written down in 1787 in Modern English.]

shy•ster (shī′stər) *n.* *Slang.* An unethical or unscrupulous lawyer or politician.

si (sē) *n.* The seventh tone of a major scale; ti.

❑ *These sound alike:* **si, sea** (ocean), **see[1]** (perceive with the eyes), **see[2]** (bishop's position).

Si The symbol for the element **silicon.**

Si•am (sī ăm′). Thailand. **—Si′a•mese′** *n. & adj.*

Si•a•mese cat (sī′ə mēz′ *or* sī′ə mēs′) *n.* A cat of an Asian breed having blue eyes and short tan or gray fur with darker ears, face, tail, and feet.

Siamese twin *n.* One of a pair of twins born with their bodies joined together at some point. [First written down in 1829 in Modern English, after Chang and Eng (1811–1874), joined Chinese twins born in *Siam* (Thailand).]

Si•be•ri•a (sī bîr′ē ə). A region of central and eastern Russia stretching from the Ural Mountains to the Pacific Ocean. The area was annexed by Russia during the 16th and 17th centuries and settled by Russians after the construction of the Trans-Siberian Railroad (completed in 1905).

Si•be•ri•an husky (sī bîr′ē ən) *n.* A breed of dog developed in Siberia and having a large build and thick fur.

sib•i•lant (sĭb′ə lənt) *adj.* Producing a hissing sound. *—n.* A speech sound that suggests hissing. For example, (s), (sh), (z), and (zh) are sibilants. **—sib′i•lance** *n.* **—sib′i•lant•ly** *adv.*

sib•ling (sĭb′lĭng) *n.* One of two or more people having one or both parents in common; a brother or a sister.

sib•yl (sĭb′əl) *n.* **1.** One of a number of women who were regarded as prophets by the ancient Greeks and Romans. **2.** A woman who is a prophet.

sic[1] (sĭk) *adv.* Thus; so. Used in written texts to show that a word or phrase that is misspelled in a quotation appears with this spelling in the document quoted. [First written down in 1887 in Modern English, from Latin *sīc.*]

❑ *These sound alike:* **sic[1]** (thus), **sic[2]** (attack), **sick[1]** (ill).

sic[2] also **sick** (sĭk) *tr.v.* **sicced, sic•cing, sics** also **sicked, sick•ing, sicks. 1.** To set upon; attack. **2.** To urge to attack: *He sicced his dog on the burglar.*

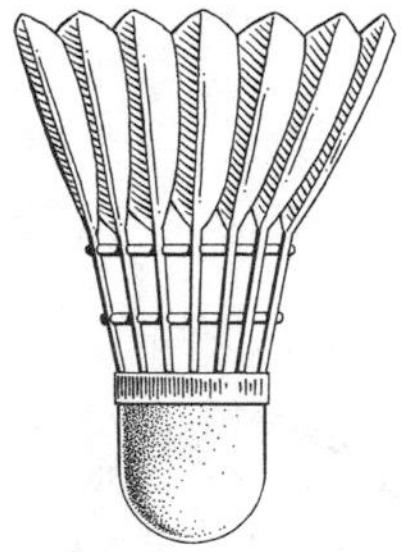

shuttlecock

Siamese cat

ă	**pat**	oi	**boy**
ā	**pay**	ou	**out**
âr	**care**	ŏŏ	**took**
ä	**father**	ōō	**boot**
ĕ	**pet**	ŭ	**cut**
ē	**be**	ûr	**urge**
ĭ	**pit**	th	**thin**
ī	**pie**	*th*	**this**
îr	**pier**	hw	**whoop**
ŏ	**pot**	zh	**vision**
ō	**toe**	ə	**about**
ô	**paw**	N	*French* **bon**

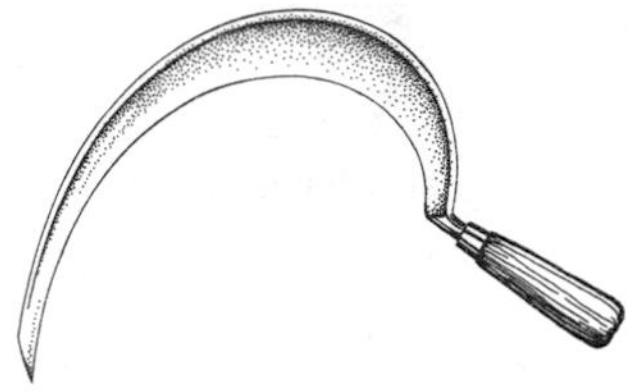

sickle

[First written down in 1845 in American English and spelled *sick*, dialectal variant of *seek*.]

❑ *These sound alike:* **sic²** (attack), **sic¹** (thus), **sick¹** (ill).

Si•ci•ly (sĭs′ə lē). An island of southern Italy in the Mediterranean Sea west of the southern end of the Italian peninsula. It became part of Italy in 1860.

sick¹ (sĭk) *adj.* **sick•er, sick•est. 1.a.** Suffering from or affected with a physical or mental illness; ill. **b.** Nauseated; queasy: *Riding over the rough road made her sick.* **c.** Of or for sick persons: *sick wards.* **2.** Morbid or unwholesome: *a sick sense of humor.* **3.** Not dependable; unsound: *a sick economy.* **4.a.** Deeply distressed; upset: *sick at heart.* **b.** Disgusted; revolted. **c.** Weary; tired: *sick of work.* **—*idiom.* sick and tired.** Thoroughly weary, discouraged, or bored. [First written down before 899 in Old English and spelled *sēoc*.]

❑ *These sound alike:* **sick¹** (ill), **sic¹** (thus), **sic²** (attack).

sick² (sĭk) *v.* Variant of **sic²**.

sick•bay (sĭk′bā′) *n.* **1.** The hospital of a ship. **2.** A place where the sick or injured are treated.

sick•bed (sĭk′bĕd′) *n.* A sick person's bed.

sick•en (sĭk′ən) *tr. & intr.v.* **sick•ened, sick•en•ing.** To make or become sick.

sick•en•ing (sĭk′ə nĭng) *adj.* **1.** Revolting or disgusting: *a sickening smell.* **2.** Causing sickness.

sick•ish (sĭk′ĭsh) *adj.* **1.** Somewhat sick. **2.** Somewhat nauseated: *The boat's rocking made me feel sickish.* **3.** Somewhat revolting or nauseating.

sick•le (sĭk′əl) *n.* A tool for cutting grain or tall grass, consisting of a semicircular blade attached to a short handle. [First written down about 1000 in Old English and spelled *sicol*, from Latin *sēcula*.]

sick leave *n.* A leave of absence given to a worker because of illness.

sickle cell anemia *n.* A hereditary disease characterized by red blood cells that are sickle-shaped instead of round because of an abnormality in the hemoglobin.

sick•ly (sĭk′lē) *adj.* **sick•li•er, sick•li•est. 1.** Tending to become sick easily; having delicate health. **2.** Of, caused by, or associated with sickness: *a sickly appearance.* **—sick′li•ness** *n.*

sick•ness (sĭk′nĭs) *n.* **1.** The condition of being sick; illness. **2.** A particular disease, disorder, or illness. **3.** Nausea.

sid•dur (sĭd′ər *or* sĭd′o͝or′) *n., pl.* **sid•du•rim** (sĭ do͝or′ĭm *or* sĭ′do͝o-rĭm′). A Jewish prayer book.

side (sīd) *n.* **1.a.** A line segment that forms a part of the boundary of a plane geometric figure. **b.** A segment of a plane that forms a part of the boundary of a three-dimensional geometric figure. **2.** A surface of an object, especially one joining a top and a bottom: *the side of the box.* **3.** Either of two surfaces of a flat object, such as a piece of paper. **4.a.** Either of two halves into which an object is divided by an axis. **b.** Either the right or left half of a human or animal body. **5.** The space immediately next to a person or thing: *walking at her side; drove onto the side of the road.* **6.** An area contrasted against another, especially when separated by an intervening object: *this side of the river.* **7.** One of two or more opposing individuals, groups, teams, or sets of opinions: *Our side won the debate.* **8.** A distinct aspect or quality of something: *the spiritual side of love.* **9.** Line of descent: *On her side, there are five brothers.* —*adj.* **1.** Located on or to the side: *a side door.* **2.** From or to one side; oblique: *a side view.* **3.** Incidental; minor: *a little side trip.* **4.** In addition to the main part: *a side order of French fries.* —*intr.v.* **sid•ed, sid•ing, sides.** To be on a particular side in a dispute: *She's always siding with her brother and against her sister.* **—*idioms.* on the side. 1.** In addition to the main portion: *We'll have some broccoli on the side.* **2.** In addition to the main occupation or activity: *He works as a doctor and plays violin on the side.* **side by side.** Next to each other; close together. [First written down before 800 in Old English and spelled *sīde*.]

side•arm (sīd′ärm′) *adj.* In sports, thrown with or characterized by a sweep of the arm between shoulder and hip height: *a sidearm curve ball.* **—side′-arm** *adv.*

side arm *n.* A small weapon, such as a pistol, carried at the side or waist.

side•board (sīd′bôrd′) *n.* A piece of dining room furniture containing drawers and shelves for linens and tableware.

side•burns (sīd′bûrnz′) *pl.n.* Growths of hair down the sides of a man's face in front of the ears, especially when worn with the rest of the beard shaved off. [First written down in 1887 in American English, alteration of *burnsides*, after General Ambrose *Burnside* (1824–1881), American army officer.]

sid•ed (sī′dĭd) *adj.* Having a specified number or kind of sides: *a three-sided figure.*

side effect *n.* A usually undesirable reaction that results in addition to the intended effect of a drug.

side•kick (sīd′kĭk′) *n. Slang.* A close friend or associate.

side•light (sīd′līt′) *n.* **1.** A light coming from the side. **2.** Either of two lights, red to port, green to starboard, shown by ships at night. **3.** Incidental or extra information.

side•line (sīd′līn′) *n.* **1.** A boundary line along either of the two sides of a playing area, such as a soccer field. **2. sidelines.** The space immediately outside these lines. **3.** A secondary or subsidiary line of merchandise. **4.** An activity pursued in addition to one's regular occupation.

side•long (sīd′lông′ *or* sīd′lŏng′) *adj.* Directed to one side: *a sidelong glance.* —*adv.* Toward the side: *glancing sidelong.*

si•de•re•al (sī dîr′ē əl) *adj.* Of, concerned with, or measured by the stars: *sidereal time.*

side•sad•dle (sīd′săd′l) *n.* A saddle designed so that a rider may sit with both legs on the same side of the horse. —*adv.* On a sidesaddle: *riding sidesaddle.*

side•show (sīd′shō′) *n.* A small show offered as part of a larger one, as at a circus.

side•step (sīd′stĕp′) *v.* **side•stepped, side•step•ping, side•steps.** —*intr.* **1.** To step aside: *sidestepped to make room for the runner.* **2.** To dodge an issue or a responsibility. —*tr.* **1.** To step out of the way of or aside: *The quarterback sidestepped the tackler.* **2.** To evade (an issue or a responsibility). **—side′step′per** *n.*

side•stroke (sīd′strōk′) *n.* A swimming stroke in which a person swims on one side and thrusts one arm forward while pushing the other backward and performing a scissors kick.

side•swipe (sīd′swīp′) *tr.v.* **side•swiped, side•swip•ing, side•swipes.** To strike (a vehicle, for example) along the side in passing: *The car sideswiped the truck as it started to turn.* —*n.* A glancing blow on or along the side.

side•track (sīd′trăk′) *tr.v.* **side•tracked, side•track•ing, side•tracks. 1.** To divert from a main issue or course. **2.** To switch (a train or railroad car) from a main track onto a siding. —*n.* A railroad siding.

side•walk (sīd′wôk′) *n.* A paved walkway along the side of a road.

side•wall (sīd′wôl′) *n.* **1.** A wall that forms the side of something. **2.** A side surface of an automobile tire.

side•ways (sīd′wāz′) also **side•way** (sīd′wā′) *adv. & adj.* **1.** Toward one side: *turn sideways; a sideways glance.* **2.** From one side: *sideways pressure.* **3.** With one side forward: *crabs moving sideways; a sideways view.*

side•wind•er (sīd′wīn′dər) *n.* A rattlesnake of the southwest United States and Mexico that moves by looping its body with a sideways motion.

sid•ing (sī′dĭng) *n.* **1.** Material, such as boards or shingles, used for covering the outside walls of a frame building. **2.** A short section of railroad track connected by switches with a main track.

si•dle (sīd′l) *intr.v.* **si•dled, si•dling, si•dles. 1.** To move sideways. **2.** To move forward in a quiet or sly manner.

siege (sēj) *n.* **1.** The surrounding and blockading of a town or fortress by an army attempting to capture it. **2.** A prolonged period, as of illness.

si•en•na (sē ĕn′ə) *n.* **1.** A special clay, containing oxides of iron and manganese, used as a pigment in making paints. **2.** A yellowish or reddish brown.

si•er•ra (sē ĕr′ə) *n.* A rugged range of mountains having an irregular outline somewhat like the teeth of a saw. [First written down in 1613 in Modern English, from Spanish *sierra*, saw, sierra, from Latin *serra*, saw.]

Si•er•ra Le•one (sē ĕr′ə lē ōn′). A country of western Africa on the Atlantic Ocean south of Guinea. It gained its independence from Great Britain in 1961. Freetown is the capital and the largest city. Population, 3,381,000.

Sierra Ne•va•da (nə văd′ə *or* nə vä′də). A mountain range of eastern California extending southeast about 400 miles (644 kilometers) from northeast California just west of the Nevada border. It rises to 14,494 feet (4,420.7 meters) at Mount Whitney.

si•es•ta (sē ĕs′tə) *n.* A rest or nap after the midday meal.

sieve (sĭv) *n.* A utensil made of mesh or having small holes, used to strain solids from liquids or to separate fine particles of loose matter from coarse ones. —*tr.v.* **sieved, siev•ing, sieves.** To pass (something) through a sieve.

sift (sĭft) *v.* **sift•ed, sift•ing, sifts.** —*tr.* **1.** To put through a sieve or other straining device to separate fine from coarse particles: *Sift a cup of flour.* **2.** To examine carefully: *sift the evidence.* —*intr.* To make a careful examination: *sifted through the data.* **—sift′er** *n.*

sigh (sī) *v.* **sighed, sigh•ing, sighs.** —*intr.* **1.** To exhale a long deep breath while making a sound, as of weariness, sorrow, or relief. **2.** To make a similar sound: *trees sighing in the wind.* **3.** To feel longing or grief; mourn. —*tr.* To express with or as if with a sigh: *"Oh well," he sighed.* —*n.* The act or sound of sighing. **—sigh′er** *n.*

sight (sīt) *n.* **1.** The ability to see. **2.** The act or fact of seeing: *The sight of land thrilled the sailors.* **3.** The range that can be seen; the field of vision: *out of our sight.* **4.** A view; a glimpse: *catch sight of her.* **5.** Something seen or worth seeing: *the sights of Rome.* **6.** *Informal.* An unpleasant sight; an unsightly scene, person, or object: *We were a sight after crossing the swamp.* **7.a.** A device used to help in aiming, as on a firearm or telescope. **b.** An aim or observation made with the aid of such a device. —*tr.v.* **sight•ed, sight•ing, sights. 1.** To see or observe: *sight land.* **2.** To observe with the help of a sight: *sight a target.* **3.** To adjust the sights of (a firearm). [First written down about 950 in Old English and spelled *gesiht*, something seen.]

❑ *These sound alike:* **sight, cite** (quote), **site** (place).

sight•ed (sī′tĭd) *adj.* **1.** Having the ability to see. **2.** Having eyesight of a specified kind: *keen-sighted.*

sight•less (sīt′lĭs) *adj.* Unable to see with the eyes; blind.

sight•ly (sīt′lē) *adj.* **sight•li•er, sight•li•est. 1.** Pleasing to see; handsome. **2.** Affording a fine view. **—sight′li•ness** *n.*

sight-read (sīt′rēd′) *v.* **sight-read** (sīt′rĕd′), **sight-read•ing, sight-reads.** —*tr.* To read or perform (music, for example) without having seen or studied it. —*intr.* To read or perform something without having seen or studied it.

sight•see•ing (sīt′sē′ĭng) *n.* The act or pastime of touring places of interest. **—sight′see′ing** *adj.* **—sight′se′er** *n.*

sig•ma (sĭg′mə) *n.* The 18th letter of the Greek alphabet, written Σ, σ. In English it is represented as *S, s.*

sign (sīn) *n.* **1.** Something that suggests a fact, quality, or condition not immediately evident; an indication: *A high temperature is a sign of an infection.* **2.** An act or a gesture that conveys an idea, a desire, information, or a command: *gave the go-ahead sign.* **3.** A board, poster, or placard bearing lettering or symbols and conveying information: *a street sign.* **4.** A mark, figure, or character that represents a word, a phrase, or an operation, as in mathematics or musical notation. **5.** Remaining evidence; a trace or vestige: *looked for signs of life.* **6.** An event or incident regarded as foretelling something: *People once thought that eclipses were signs of coming disaster.* **7.** One of the 12 divisions of the zodiac, each named for a constellation and represented by a symbol. —*v.* **signed, sign•ing, signs.** —*tr.* **1.** To affix one's signature to: *sign a document.* **2.** To write (one's signature): *Sign your name.* **3.** To approve or guarantee (a document) by affixing one's signature. **4.** To hire by getting a signature on a contract: *signed three new players.* **5.** To communicate with a sign or by sign language: *signed the lecture to a hearing-impaired audience.* —*intr.* **1.** To make a sign; signal. **2.** To use sign language. ***—idioms.*** **sign in.** To record the arrival of (another or oneself) by signing a register. **sign off.** To announce the end of a communication or broadcast. **sign out.** To record the departure of (another or oneself) by signing a register. **sign up.** To agree to be a participant or recipient by signing one's name; enlist: *I signed up for art classes.* [First written down before 1200 in Middle English and spelled *sine*, from Latin *signum*.] **—sign′er** *n.* —SEE NOTE.

❑ *These sound alike:* **sign, sine** (function of an acute angle).

sig•nal (sĭg′nəl) *n.* **1.a.** A sign, gesture, or device that conveys information: *a traffic signal; finger signals to the pitcher.* **b.** A message conveyed by such means. **2.** Something that is the cause of action: *The news of the peace treaty was the signal for rejoicing.* **3.** An electric current or radio wave that represents sound or images. **4.** The sound, image, or message transmitted or received, as in radio or television. —*adj.* Out of the ordinary; remarkable: *a signal victory.* —*v.* **sig•naled, sig•nal•ing, sig•nals** or **sig•nalled, sig•nal•ling, sig•nals.** —*tr.* **1.** To make a signal to: *They signaled the engineer to start.* **2.** To make known or relate by signals: *A period signals the end of a sentence.* —*intr.* To make a signal or signals. **—sig′nal•er** *n.*

sig•nal•ize (sĭg′nə līz′) *tr.v.* **sig•nal•ized, sig•nal•iz•ing, sig•nal•iz•es. 1.** To make well-known or conspicuous. **2.** To point out in detail. **—sig′nal•i•za′tion** (sĭg′nə lĭ zā′shən) *n.*

sig•nal•ly (sĭg′nə lē) *adv.* To a remarkable degree; notably: *We defeated them signally.*

sig•na•ture (sĭg′nə chər) *n.* **1.** One's name as written by oneself. **2.** The act of signing. **3.** A distinctive characteristic indicating identity: *humor is her sig-*

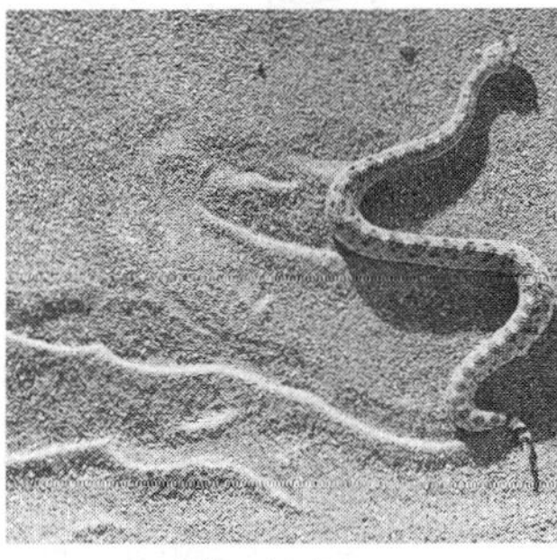

sidewinder

Word Building: sign

The word root *–sign–* in English words comes from the Latin verb *signāre*, "to mark, put one's mark, seal, or name to." This Latin verb is the source of our verb **sign**, "to sign one's name on (a document)." **Signature** comes from the Latin *signatūra*, which means "a person's name as proof of the authenticity of a document." **Signal** comes from the Latin *signāle*, "a sign or token of recognition." **Assign** comes from the Latin verb *assignāre*, "to mark something or someone for a purpose" (using the prefix *as–*, a form of *ad–*, "to, toward"). **Resign** comes from the Latin verb *resignāre*, "to unseal, cancel, give up" (*re–*, "back again, back over to").

ă	pat	oi	boy
ā	pay	ou	out
âr	care	ŏŏ	took
ä	father	ōō	boot
ĕ	pet	ŭ	cut
ē	be	ûr	urge
ĭ	pit	th	thin
ī	pie	*th*	this
îr	pier	hw	whoop
ŏ	pot	zh	vision
ō	toe	ə	about
ô	paw	N	*French* bon

silhouette
By an unidentified 18th-century artist

Word History: sill

On a window, which is the **sill** and which is the **lintel**, the top or the bottom? *Sill* came from the Old English noun *syll* or *sylle*, "sill." The Old English word is related to the Latin noun *solea*, which means "sole of the foot," and that should help you remember that the *sill* is on the bottom; therefore the *lintel* is on the top.

silo

nature. **4.** A section of a book that is made up of a large sheet printed with four or a multiple of four pages and folded to page size.

sign•board (sīn′bôrd′) *n.* A board bearing a sign.

sig•net (sĭg′nĭt) *n.* A seal, especially one used to stamp documents officially. [First written down about 1380 in Middle English and spelled *singnette*, from Old French *signet*, small sign.]
❑ *These sound alike:* **signet, cygnet** (swan).

sig•nif•i•cance (sĭg nĭf′ĭ kəns) *n.* **1.** The state and quality of being significant; importance: *a development of great significance.* **2.** The sense of something; meaning.

sig•nif•i•cant (sĭg nĭf′ĭ kənt) *adj.* **1.** Having a meaning; meaningful: *a significant detail.* **2.** Full of hidden meaning: *a significant glance.* **3.** Having or likely to have a major effect; important: *a significant historical event.* **—sig•nif′i•cant•ly** *adv.*

sig•ni•fy (sĭg′nə fī′) *v.* **sig•ni•fied, sig•ni•fy•ing, sig•ni•fies.** *—tr.* **1.** To be a sign or an indication of; represent or mean: *What does this monument signify?* **2.** To make known: *Peter signified that he wanted to leave early.* *—intr.* To have meaning or importance. [First written down about 1275 in Middle English and spelled *signefien*, from Latin *significāre*.]

sign language *n.* A language that uses hand movements to express words, grammar, and meaning.

si•gnor (sēn yôr′) *n., pl.* **si•gno•ri** (sēn yôr′ē) also **si•gnors.** Used as a title of courtesy for a man in an Italian-speaking area.

si•gno•ra (sēn yôr′ə) *n., pl.* **si•gno•re** (sēn yôr′ā) or **si•gno•ras.** Used as a title of courtesy for a married woman in an Italian-speaking area.

si•gno•re (sēn yôr′ā) *n., pl.* **si•gno•ri** (sēn yô′rē). Used as a title of courtesy for a man in an Italian-speaking area.

si•gno•ri•na (sēn′yə rē′nə) *n., pl.* **si•gno•ri•ne** (sēn′yə rē′nā) or **si•gno•ri•nas.** Used as a title of courtesy for an unmarried woman in an Italian-speaking area.

sign•post (sīn′pōst′) *n.* **1.** A post supporting a sign that has information or directions. **2.** An indication, a sign, or a guide.

Sikh (sēk) *n.* A member of a religion that was founded in India in the 16th century, believing in one God and combining elements of Hinduism and Islam.

si•lage (sī′lĭj) *n.* Fodder consisting of green plants that have fermented in a silo.

si•lence (sī′ləns) *n.* **1.** The quality or condition of being still and silent. **2.** The absence of sound; stillness. **3.** A period of time without speech or noise. **4.** Refusal or failure to speak out. *—tr.v.* **si•lenced, si•lenc•ing, si•lenc•es. 1.** To make silent or bring to silence; quiet: *The teacher's stern look silenced the children.* **2.** To stop, prevent, or cut short the expression of; suppress: *The government tried to silence all criticism.*

si•lenc•er (sī′lən sər) *n.* A device attached to the muzzle of a firearm to muffle the sound it makes when fired.

si•lent (sī′lənt) *adj.* **1.** Having no sound or noise; quiet: *the silent night.* **2.** Refraining from speech; saying nothing: *remained respectfully silent.* **3.** Not disposed to speak; not talkative. **4.** Not voiced or expressed; unspoken: *a silent admission of guilt.* **5.** Inactive: *a silent volcano.* **6.** Not pronounced or sounded, as a letter in a word: *The* k *in* knight *is silent.* **7.** Having no spoken dialogue and usually no soundtrack: *a silent movie.* [First written down before 1500 in Middle English, from Latin *silēre*, to be silent.] **—si′lent•ly** *adv.*

Si•le•sia (sī lē′zhə *or* sī lē′shə). A region of central Europe primarily in southwest Poland and northern Czech Republic. It was settled by Slavic peoples in about A.D. 500.

sil•hou•ette (sĭl′o͞o ĕt′) *n.* **1.** A drawing consisting of the outline of something, especially a human profile, filled in with a solid color. **2.** An outline of something that appears dark against a light background. *—tr.v.* **sil•hou•et•ted, sil•hou•et•ting, sil•hou•ettes.** To cause to be seen as a silhouette. [First written down in 1798 in Modern English, after Étienne de *Silhouette* (1709–1767), French finance minister.]

sil•i•ca (sĭl′ĭ kə) *n.* Silicon dioxide, SiO_2, a compound that occurs widely in rocks and mineral forms, such as quartz, sand, and flint, and is used in making glass, concrete, and other materials.

sil•i•cate (sĭl′ĭ kāt′ *or* sĭl′ĭ kĭt) *n.* Any of a large class of chemical compounds composed of silicon, oxygen, and at least one metal, found widely in rocks and forming the principal substance of bricks.

sil•i•con (sĭl′ĭ kən *or* sĭl′ĭ kŏn′) *n. Symbol* **Si** A metalloid element that occurs in both gray crystalline and brown amorphous forms and is used in glass, semiconductors, concrete, bricks, and ceramics. Atomic number 14. See table at **element.**

silicon carbide *n.* A bluish-black crystalline compound of silicon and carbon, SiC, used as an abrasive.

sil•i•cone (sĭl′ĭ kōn′) *n.* Any of a class of chemical compounds that are polymers based on the unit $RSiO_2$, in which R is an organic radical. They are used in making adhesives, lubricants, protective coatings, and synthetic rubber.

silk (sĭlk) *n.* **1.** A fine glossy fiber produced by a silkworm to form its cocoon. **2.** Thread or fabric made from this fiber. **3.** A garment made from this fabric. **4. silks.** The brightly colored garments that identify a jockey or harness driver in a horse race. **5.** A fine silky material, such as the tuft at the end of an ear of corn. *—adj.* Made of or similar to silk. [First written down before 899 in Old English and spelled *sioloc*, ultimately from Chinese.]

silk•en (sĭl′kən) *adj.* **1.** Made of silk: *a silken scarf.* **2.** Having the look or feel of silk; smooth and glossy: *silken hair.*

silk•worm (sĭlk′wûrm′) *n.* Any of various caterpillars that produce silk cocoons, especially the caterpillar of a moth native to Asia that spins a cocoon of fine glossy fiber used to make silk fabric and thread.

silk•y (sĭl′kē) *adj.* **silk•i•er, silk•i•est.** Soft, smooth, and glossy like silk: *silky fur.* **—silk′i•ly** *adv.* **—silk′i•ness** *n.*

sill (sĭl) *n.* A horizontal piece that holds up the vertical part of a frame, especially the piece that forms the base of a window. [First written down about 725 in Old English and spelled *syll.*] —SEE NOTE.

sil•ly (sĭl′ē) *adj.* **sil•li•er, sil•li•est. 1.** Showing lack of good sense or reason; stupid: *silly mistakes.* **2.** Lacking seriousness; playful: *a silly game.* **3.** Partly conscious or dazed, as from a blow. **—sil′li•ness** *n.*

si•lo (sī′lō) *n., pl.* **si•los. 1.** A tall cylindrical building in which fodder is stored. **2.** An underground shelter for a missile, usually equipped to launch the missile or to raise it to a launching position.

silt (sĭlt) *n.* A material consisting of mineral particles smaller than those of sand and larger than those of clay, often found at the bottom of bodies of water. *—tr. & intr.v.* **silt•ed, silt•ing, silts.** To fill or become filled with silt: *The flow of water had silted up the channel. A pond will silt up after a time.* [First written down in 1440 in Middle English and spelled *cylte*, probably of Scandinavian origin.]

Si•lu•ri•an (sĭ lo͝or′ē ən *or* sī lo͝or′ē ən) *adj.* Of, belonging to, or being the geologic time of the third period of the Paleozoic Era. During the Silurian, land plants first appeared. See table at **geologic time.** —*n.* The Silurian period or its series of rocks.

sil•van (sĭl′vən) *adj. & n.* Variant of **sylvan.**

sil•ver (sĭl′vər) *n.* **1.** *Symbol* **Ag** A soft, shiny, white metallic element that is superior to any other metal in its ability to conduct heat and electricity. Atomic number 47. See table at **element. 2.** This metal used as money or a commodity. **3.** Coins made of this metal. **4.** Tableware or other household articles made of or plated with this metal. **5.** A light, shiny, or metallic gray. —*adj.* **1.** Made of or containing silver. **2.** Having a light gray color like that of the metal silver: *silver hair.* —*tr.v.* **sil•vered, sil•ver•ing, sil•vers.** To cover or plate with silver or something that resembles silver. [First written down before 830 in Old English and spelled *seolfor.*]

sil•ver•fish (sĭl′vər fĭsh′) *n.* **1.** Any of various silvery fishes, such as the tarpon. **2.** A silvery wingless insect that feeds on and can damage materials containing starch, such as bookbindings, wallpaper, and clothing.

silver lining *n.* A hopeful aspect of a bad situation.

silver nitrate *n.* A poisonous, clear, crystalline compound of silver, nitrogen, and oxygen, $AgNO_3$, that darkens when exposed to light, used in photography and silver plating and as an external antiseptic.

silver plate *n.* **1.** A coating or plating of silver. **2.** Tableware made of or plated with silver.

sil•ver•smith (sĭl′vər smĭth′) *n.* A person who makes, repairs, or replates articles of silver.

sil•ver-tongued (sĭl′vər tŭngd′) *adj.* Having the power to speak smoothly and persuasively; eloquent.

sil•ver•ware (sĭl′vər wâr′) *n.* Metal eating and serving utensils, especially ones made of or plated with silver.

sil•ver•y (sĭl′və rē) *adj.* **1.** Containing or coated with silver. **2.** Resembling silver in color or appearance: *silvery fish.* **3.** Having a clear ringing sound: *a silvery voice.*

sim•i•an (sĭm′ē ən) *adj.* Relating to, characteristic of, or resembling an ape or a monkey. —*n.* An ape or a monkey.

sim•i•lar (sĭm′ə lər) *adj.* **1.** Related in appearance or nature; alike though not exactly the same: *a wild cat similar to but smaller than a lion.* **2.** Having corresponding angles equal and corresponding line segments proportional in length: *similar triangles.* [First written down in 1611 in Modern English, from Latin *similis,* like.] —**sim′i•lar•ly** *adv.*

sim•i•lar•i•ty (sĭm′ə lăr′ĭ tē) *n., pl.* **sim•i•lar•i•ties. 1.** The quality or condition of being similar. **2.** A corresponding feature or property: *a similarity of style.*

sim•i•le (sĭm′ə lē) *n.* A figure of speech in which unlike things are compared, often in a phrase introduced by *like* or *as.* For example, *She runs like a gazelle* and *That house is as big as a ship* are similes.

si•mil•i•tude (sĭ mĭl′ĭ to͞od′ *or* sĭ mĭl′ĭ tyo͞od′) *n.* Similarity; resemblance; likeness.

sim•mer (sĭm′ər) *v.* **sim•mered, sim•mer•ing, sim•mers.** —*intr.* To be cooked gently or just at the boiling point. —*tr.* To cook gently or just at the boiling point: *simmered the sauce.* —*n.* The condition or process of simmering. —***idiom.* simmer down.** To become calm after excitement or anger. [First written down in 1477 in Middle English and spelled *simperen.*]

si•mo•ny (sī′mə nē *or* sĭm′ə nē) *n.* The buying or selling of church pardons, offices, or salaries.

Si•mon Ze•lo•tes (sī′mən zē lō′tēz) or **Simon the Ca•naan•ite** (kā′nə nīt′). First century A.D. One of the 12 Apostles.

sim•per (sĭm′pər) *intr.v.* **sim•pered, sim•per•ing, sim•pers.** To smile in a silly or self-conscious manner. —*n.* A silly or self-conscious smile.

sim•ple (sĭm′pəl) *adj.* **sim•pler, sim•plest. 1.** Having or composed of a single part or unit; not compound. **2.** Not involved or complicated; easy: *a simple explanation.* See Synonyms at **easy. 3.** Having no additions or qualifications; bare; mere: *a simple "yes" or "no."* **4.** Not showy, elaborate, or luxurious; plain: *a simple wedding dress; simple everyday words.* **5.** Not vain, showy, or deceitful. **6.** Having or showing little intelligence, education, or experience: *a simple man who is easily cheated.* **7.** Humble or lowly in condition or rank: *simple farm folk.* **8.** Ordinary; common: *a simple head cold.* [First written down before 1200 in Middle English, from Latin *simplus.*]

simple fraction *n.* A fraction in which both the numerator and denominator are whole numbers.

simple fracture *n.* A bone fracture that causes little or no damage to the surrounding tissues.

simple machine *n.* A simple device for doing work, such as a lever or pulley.

sim•ple-mind•ed or **sim•ple•mind•ed** (sĭm′pəl mīn′dĭd) *adj.* **1.** Not sophisticated; artless or naive. **2.** Stupid or silly. **3.** Mentally impaired. —**sim′ple-mind′ed•ly** *adv.* —**sim′ple-mind′ed•ness** *n.*

simple sentence *n.* A sentence consisting of one independent clause with no dependent clauses, as *The two boys played chess.*

sim•ple•ton (sĭm′pəl tən) *n.* A person who lacks common sense or intelligence.

sim•plic•i•ty (sĭm plĭs′ĭ tē) *n., pl.* **sim•plic•i•ties. 1.** The property, condition, or quality of being simple; absence of complexity or difficulty. **2.** Absence of luxury or showiness; plainness. **3.** Absence of vanity or deceitfulness; sincerity: *childlike simplicity.* **4.** Lack of good sense or intelligence; foolishness.

sim•pli•fy (sĭm′plə fī′) *tr.v.* **sim•pli•fied, sim•pli•fy•ing, sim•pli•fies.** To make simple or simpler. —**sim′pli•fi•ca′tion** (sĭm′plə fĭ kā′shən) *n.* —**sim′pli•fi′er** *n.*

sim•ply (sĭm′plē) *adv.* **1.** In a simple manner; plainly: *They live very simply.* **2.** Clearly: *She explained it quite simply.* **3.** Merely; only; just: *We knew him simply as Joe.* **4.** Absolutely; altogether: *The meal was simply delicious.*

sim•u•late (sĭm′yə lāt′) *tr.v.* **sim•u•lat•ed, sim•u•lat•ing, sim•u•lates. 1.** To have or take on the appearance, form, or sound of; imitate: *a device that simulates space flight.* See Synonyms at **imitate. 2.** To make a pretense of; pretend; feign: *simulated interest.* [First written down in 1652 in Modern English, from Latin *similis,* like.] —**sim′u•la′tor** *n.*

sim•u•la•tion (sĭm′yə lā′shən) *n.* **1.** The act or process of simulating. **2.** An imitation or a false appearance: *a simulation of conditions on the moon.*

si•mul•cast (sī′məl kăst′) *tr.v.* **si•mul•cast•ed, si•mul•cast•ing, si•mul•casts.** To broadcast (a program) simultaneously by FM and AM radio or by radio and television. —*n.* A simulcasted broadcast.

si•mul•ta•ne•ous (sī′məl tā′nē əs) *adj.* Happening, existing, or done at the same time. —**si′mul•ta′ne•ous•ly** *adv.*

sin¹ (sĭn) *n.* **1.** The act of breaking a religious or moral law, especially when done deliberately. **2.** An act considered shameful or wrong. —*intr.v.* **sinned, sin•ning, sins. 1.** To violate a religious or moral law. **2.** To commit an offense; do wrong. [First written down before 830 in Old English and spelled *synn.*] —**sin′ner** *n.*

sin² *abbr.* An abbreviation of sine.

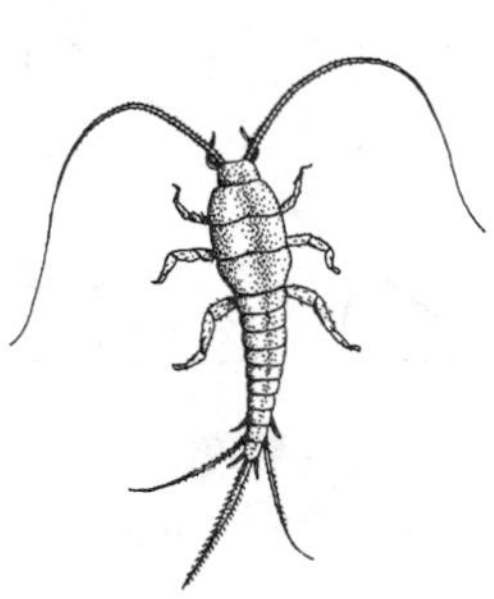

silverfish

ă	pat	oi	boy
ā	pay	ou	out
âr	care	o͝o	took
ä	father	o͞o	boot
ĕ	pet	ŭ	cut
ē	be	ûr	urge
ĭ	pit	th	thin
ī	pie	*th*	this
îr	pier	hw	whoop
ŏ	pot	zh	vision
ō	toe	ə	about
ô	paw	N	*French* bon

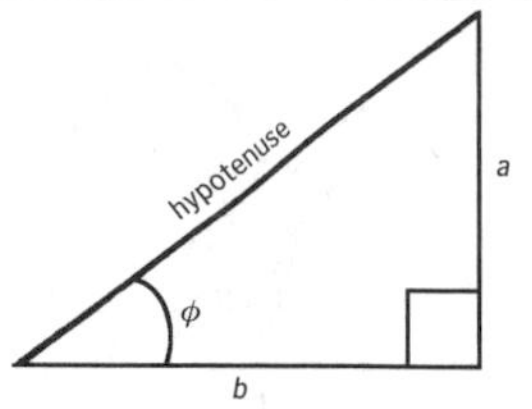

sine

$\text{sine } \phi = \frac{a}{Hyp}$

single file

Word History: sirloin

Some of you may know the story of how King Henry VIII dubbed the upper, choice loin of beef *Sir Loin* because it was so good. The story is old (it goes back to 1655, at least) but not factual. The original spelling in 15th-century English is *surloyn*; it was probably pronounced about the same as it is now and came from the Old French word *surloigne*, "(the meat) above the loin." The Old French word *sur* came from the Latin word *super*, "above, beyond, in addition," and we see *sur* in **surcharge**, "an additional charge," and **surname**, "an additional name, a name added on to one's given name." The modern spelling of **sirloin** therefore would have been *surloin*, except probably for that story about King Henry; the variant spelling *sirloin* was supported by the story.

Si•nai (sī′nī′), **Mount.** A mountain, about 7,500 feet (2,288 meters) high, of the south-central Sinai Peninsula. It is thought to be the biblical peak on which Moses received the Ten Commandments.

Sinai Peninsula. A peninsula linking southwest Asia with northeast Africa at the northern end of the Red Sea.

since (sĭns) *adv.* **1.** From then until now, or between then and now: *He left town and hasn't been here since.* **2.** Before now; ago: *long since forgotten.* —*prep.* From (a given time): *They've been friends since childhood.* —*conj.* **1.** During the time after which: *She hasn't been home since she graduated.* **2.** Continuously from the time when: *He hasn't spoken since he sat down.* **3.** Because; inasmuch as: *Since you're not interested, I won't tell you about it.*

sin•cere (sĭn sîr′) *adj.* **sin•cer•er, sin•cer•est.** Not false or affected; genuine or true: *sincere friends; a sincere apology.* —**sin•cere′ly** *adv.*

sin•cer•i•ty (sĭn **sĕr′**ĭ tē) *n.* The quality or condition of being sincere; genuineness or honesty.

sine (sīn) *n.* In a right triangle, a function of an acute angle equal to the length of the side opposite the angle divided by the length of the hypotenuse.
❑ *These sound alike:* **sine, sign** (indication).

si•ne•cure (**sī′**nĭ kyo͝or′ *or* **sĭn′**ĭ kyo͝or′) *n.* A position that requires little or no work yet provides a salary. [First written down in 1662 in Modern English, from Medieval Latin *(beneficium) sine cūrā*, (church appointment) without care (of souls).]

sin•ew (**sĭn′**yo͞o) *n.* **1.** A tendon. **2.** Vigorous strength; muscular power. [First written down about 725 in Old English and spelled *seonowe*.]

sin•ew•y (**sĭn′**yo͞o ē) *adj.* **1.** Consisting of or resembling sinew. **2.** Lean and muscular. See Synonyms at **muscular. 3.** Strong; vigorous.

sin•ful (**sĭn′**fəl) *adj.* Characterized by or full of sin; wicked. —**sin′ful•ly** *adv.* —**sin′ful•ness** *n.*

sing (sĭng) *v.* **sang** (săng) or **sung** (sŭng), **sung, sing•ing, sings.** —*intr.* **1.** To utter a series of words or sounds in musical tones. **2.** To perform songs or other vocal selections. **3.** To produce musical sounds: *birds that sing in tropical forests.* **4.** To make a high-pitched whining, humming, or whistling sound: *The teakettle sang.* **5.** To tell or proclaim something in song or verse: *poets singing of Greece's glory.* —*tr.* **1.** To produce the musical sound of: *sang a love song.* **2.** To bring to a specified condition by singing: *sang the baby to sleep.* **3.** To tell or proclaim (something), especially in song or verse: *sang her praises.* —***idiom.*** **sing out.** To call out loudly. [First written down about 725 in Old English and spelled *singan*.]

sing. *abbr.* An abbreviation of singular.

Sin•ga•pore (**sĭng′**gə pôr′ *or* **sĭng′**ə pôr′). A country of southeast Asia made up of **Singapore Island** and adjacent smaller islands. It gained its independence in 1965. The city of **Singapore** is the capital. Population, 2,529,100.

singe (sĭnj) *tr.v.* **singed, singe•ing, sing•es. 1.** To burn slightly; scorch. **2.** To burn the ends of: *singed his hair.* **3.** To burn off the feathers or bristles of by holding briefly to a flame. —*n.* A slight burn. [First written down about 1000 in Old English and spelled *sengan*.]

sing•er (**sĭng′**ər) *n.* **1.** A person who sings, especially one who has had special training or sings professionally. **2.** A songbird.

Sin•gha•lese (sĭng′gə **lēz′** *or* sĭng′gə **lēs′**) or **Sin•ha•lese** (sĭn′hə **lēz′** *or* sĭn′hə **lēs′**) *n., pl.* **Singhalese** or **Sinhalese. 1.** A member of a people constituting the major portion of the population of Sri Lanka. **2.** The language of the Singhalese that is the chief language of Sri Lanka. —*adj.* Of or relating to Sri Lanka, the Singhalese, or their language or culture.

sin•gle (**sĭng′**gəl) *adj.* **1.** Not accompanied by another or others; alone. **2.** Consisting of one thing, part, or section: *a single layer.* **3.** Separate from others; individual: *Every single person will receive a free gift.* **4.** Intended or designed for use by one person: *a single bed.* **5.** Unmarried. **6.** Having only one row of petals: *the single flowers of a tulip.* —*n.* **1.** An accommodation for one person, as a room in a hotel. **2.** In baseball, a hit that allows the batter to reach first base. **3.** A tennis or badminton match between two players. Often used in the plural. **4. singles.** Unmarried persons considered as a group. —*v.* **sin•gled, sin•gling, sin•gles.** —*tr.* To choose or distinguish from others: *He singled out two students for praise.* —*intr.* In baseball, to hit a single. [First written down before 1300 in Middle English and spelled *sengle*, from Latin *singulus*.]

sin•gle-breast•ed (sĭng′gəl **brĕs′**tĭd) *adj.* Closing with a narrow overlap and fastened down the front with a single row of buttons: *He wore a single-breasted jacket.*

single file *n.* A line of people, animals, or things standing or moving one behind the other.

sin•gle-hand•ed (**sĭng′**gəl **hăn′**dĭd) *adj.* **1.** Working or done without help; unassisted. **2.** Having or using only one hand. —**sin′gle-hand′ed•ly** *adv.*

sin•gle-mind•ed (**sĭng′**gəl **mīn′**dĭd) *adj.* **1.** Having one purpose or opinion: *a single-minded approach to tax reform.* **2.** Steadfast; not wavering: *the single-minded pursuit of a dream.* —**sin′gle-mind′ed•ly** *adv.* —**sin′gle-mind′ed•ness** *n.*

sin•gle•tree (**sĭng′**gəl trē′) *n.* A whiffletree.

sin•gly (**sĭng′**glē) *adv.* **1.** Without the company or help of others; alone. **2.** One by one; individually: *materials used singly or in combinations.*

sing•song (**sĭng′**sông′ *or* **sĭng′**sŏng′) *n.* **1.** Verse or song having a mechanical regularity of rhythm and rhyme. **2.** A manner of speaking marked by a monotonous rising and falling of sound. —*adj.* Having a monotonous rhythm or manner of speaking.

sin•gu•lar (**sĭng′**gyə lər) *adj.* **1.** Being only one; individual. **2.** Being the only one of a kind; unique. **3.a.** Of or relating to a noun, pronoun, or adjective that refers to a single person or thing or a group considered as a unit. For example, *I* and *he* are singular pronouns and *house* is a singular noun. **b.** Of or relating to a verb expressing the action or state of a single subject. **4.** Deviating from the usual or expected; remarkable. **5.** Very strange; peculiar: *singular arrivals and departures at midnight.* —*n.* The form taken by a word indicating one person or thing. —**sin′gu•lar•ly** *adv.*

sin•gu•lar•i•ty (sĭng′gyə **lăr′**ĭ tē) *n., pl.* **sin•gu•lar•i•ties. 1.** The quality or condition of being singular. **2.** A distinguishing trait; a peculiarity. **3.** Something uncommon or unusual.

Sin•ha•lese (sĭn′hə **lēz′** *or* sĭn′hə **lēs′**) *n. & adj.* Variant of **Singhalese.**

sin•is•ter (**sĭn′**ĭ stər) *adj.* **1.** Suggesting or threatening evil: *a sinister smile.* **2.** Promising trouble; ominous: *sinister storm clouds.* [First written down in 1411 in Middle English and spelled *sinistre*, false, from Latin *sinister*, on the left, unlucky.] —**sin′is•ter•ly** *adv.*

sink (sĭngk) *v.* **sank** (săngk) or **sunk** (sŭngk), **sunk, sink•ing, sinks.** —*intr.* **1.** To descend to the bottom; submerge: *The anchor sank to the bottom.* **2.** To move to a lower level, especially slowly or in stages: *He sank into the chair.* **3.** To appear to move downward, as the sun or moon in setting. **4.** To pass into a specified condition: *She sank into a deep sleep.* **5.** To worsen in condition or quality: *The business sank into bankruptcy.* **6.** To diminish or become weaker, as in strength, vitality, or value: *His voice sank to a faint whisper. Farm prices sank steadily.* **7.** To seep or soak; penetrate: *Rainfall could barely sink into the sodden earth.* **8.** To become felt or understood: *Let the meaning sink in.* —*tr.* **1.** To cause to descend beneath the surface: *Heavy storms can sink ships.* **2.** To cause to drop or lower: *sank the ladle into the soup.* **3.** To force or drive (a piling or post, for example) into the ground. **4.** To dig or drill (a mine or well) in the earth. **5.** To bring to a worse condition or quality: *Poor management sank the project in confusion.* **6.** To make weaker, quieter, or less forceful. **7.** To invest: *He sank a small fortune into real estate.* **8.** In basketball and golf, to place (a ball) into a hole or basket. —*n.* **1.** A water basin having a drainpipe and usually a piped supply of water. **2.** A low land area in a rock formation where water collects. **3.** A sinkhole. —***idiom.*** **sink or swim.** *Informal.* To succeed or fail without alternative. [First written down about 950 in Old English and spelled *sincan.*] —**sink′a•ble** *adj.*

sink•er (sĭng′kər) *n.* A person or thing that sinks, as a weight used for sinking fishing lines or nets.

sink•hole (sĭngk′hōl′) *n.* A natural depression in a land surface joining with an underground passage or cavern.

sin•ner (sĭn′ər) *n.* A person who sins or does wrong.

sin•u•os•i•ty (sĭn′yo͞o ŏs′ĭ tē) *n., pl.* **sin•u•os•i•ties. 1.** The quality or condition of being sinuous. **2.** A bending or curving shape or movement.

sin•u•ous (sĭn′yo͞o əs) *adj.* Having many curves or turns; winding. —**sin′u•ous•ly** *adv.* —**sin′u•ous•ness** *n.*

si•nus (sī′nəs) *n.* Any of several air-filled cavities in the bones of the skull, especially one that connects with the nose.

si•nus•i•tis (sī′nə sī′tĭs) *n.* Inflammation of the sinuses or a sinus, especially in the region near the nose.

Si•on (sī′ən) *n.* Variant of **Zion.**

Siou•an (so͞o′ən) *n.* **1.** A large family of North American Indian languages spoken over an extensive area of the Midwest. **2.** A member of a Siouan-speaking people. —**Siou′an** *adj.*

Sioux (so͞o) *n., pl.* **Sioux** (so͞o *or* so͞oz). **1.** A member of any of a group of Native American peoples living in the west and north-central United States and parts of Canada. **2.** Any of the Siouan languages of these peoples.

sip (sĭp) *v.* **sipped, sip•ping, sips.** —*tr.* To drink in small quantities. —*intr.* To drink something in sips. —*n.* **1.** The act of sipping: *smiled after his first sip.* **2.** A small quantity of liquid sipped: *took a sip of coffee.*

si•phon also **sy•phon** (sī′fən) *n.* **1.** A pipe or tube in the form of an inverted U, filled with liquid and arranged so that the pressure of the atmosphere forces liquid from a container to flow through the tube, over a barrier, and into a lower container. **2.** A tubular animal part as of a clam, through which water is taken in or expelled. —*v.* **si•phoned, si•phon•ing, si•phons.** —*tr.* To draw off or transfer (a liquid) through or as if through a siphon. —*intr.* To pass through a siphon. [First written down before 1398 in Middle English, from Greek *siphōn.*]

sir (sûr) *n.* **1.** Used as a polite form of address for a man. **2. Sir.** A title of honor used before the given name or the full name of a knight or baronet.

sire (sīr) *n.* **1.** A father or forefather. **2.** The father of an animal, especially a domesticated animal such as a horse. **3.** *Archaic.* A form of address for a superior, especially for a king. —*tr.v.* **sired, sir•ing, sires.** To be the father or male ancestor of. [First written down before 1200 in Middle English, from Latin *senior*, older.]

si•ren (sī′rən) *n.* **1.** A device in which compressed gas is driven against a rotating disk that is full of holes, making a loud whistling or wailing sound as a signal or warning. **2.** An electronic device that makes a similar sound as a signal or warning.

Si•ren (sī′rən) *n.* **1.** In Greek mythology, one of a group of sea nymphs whose sweet singing lures sailors to destruction on the rocks surrounding their island. **2. siren.** A woman regarded as beautiful and captivating.

Sir•i•us (sĭr′ē əs) *n.* The brightest star seen in the night sky.

sir•loin (sûr′loin′) *n.* A cut of meat, especially beef, from the upper part of the loin. —SEE NOTE.

si•roc•co (sə rŏk′ō) *n., pl.* **si•roc•cos.** A hot, humid south or southeast wind of southern Italy, Sicily, and the Mediterranean islands, originating in the Sahara as a dry dusty wind but becoming moist as it passes over the Mediterranean.

sir•up (sĭr′əp *or* sûr′əp) *n.* Variant of **syrup.**

sis (sĭs) *n. Informal.* Sister.

si•sal (sī′səl) *n.* **1.** A stiff fiber obtained from the leaves of a tropical plant and used for making rope and twine. **2.** The plant that yields such a fiber.

sisal

sis•sy (sĭs′ē) *n., pl.* **sis•sies. 1.** A boy or man regarded as effeminate. **2.** A person regarded as timid or cowardly. **3.** *Informal.* Sister.

sis•ter (sĭs′tər) *n.* **1.** A girl or woman having the same mother and father as someone else. **2.** A girl or woman having one parent in common with someone else; a half sister. **3.** A stepsister. **4.** A fellow woman or girl. **5.** A woman fellow member, as of a sorority. **6. Sister.** A member of a Christian religious order of women; a nun. [First written down in 835 in Old English and spelled *sweostor.*]

sis•ter•hood (sĭs′tər ho͝od′) *n.* **1.** The relationship of being a sister or sisters. **2.** The quality of being sisterly. **3.** A group of women united by a common purpose or by vows, especially a religious order of women.

sis•ter-in-law (sĭs′tər ĭn lô′) *n., pl.* **sis•ters-in-law** (sĭs′tərz ĭn lô′). **1.** The sister of one's husband or wife. **2.** The wife of one's brother. **3.** The wife of the brother of one's husband or wife.

sis•ter•ly (sĭs′tər lē) *adj.* **1.** Suitable for a sister or sisters: *took a sisterly interest in her education.* **2.** Showing affection. —**sis′ter•li•ness** *n.*

sit (sĭt) *v.* **sat** (săt), **sit•ting, sits.** —*intr.* **1.** To rest with the body supported on the buttocks and the torso upright: *He sat on the bench.* **2.** To perch: *The robin sat on the branch.* **3.** To cover eggs so that they will hatch; brood. **4.** To be situated or located; lie: *The farmhouse sits on a hill.* **5.** To remain inactive or unused: *The school building sits until the next term begins.* **6.** To lie or rest: *dishes sitting on the shelf.* **7.** To pose for an artist or a photographer. **8.** To occupy a seat as a member of a body of officials: *She was the first woman to sit in the Senate.* **9.** To be in session: *Normally the Supreme Court does not sit in the summer.* **10.** To affect one with or as if with a burden; weigh: *Responsibility sat heavy on the President.* **11.** To be agreeable to one; please: *The idea did not sit well with us.* **12.** To fit, fall, or drape in a specified manner: *The jacket sits perfectly on you.* **13.** To keep watch or take care of a child; babysit. —*tr.* **1.** To cause to sit; seat. **2.** To provide seating for: *This restaurant sits forty people.* —***idioms.*** **sit down.** To take a seat. **sit in.** To attend or participate in as a visitor. **sit out.** To refrain from taking part in: *sit out a dance.* **sit pretty.** *Informal.* To be in a very favorable position. **sit tight.** *Informal.* To be patient and wait. **sit up. 1.** To rise from lying down to

ă	pat	oi	**boy**
ā	pay	ou	**out**
âr	care	o͝o	**took**
ä	father	o͞o	**boot**
ĕ	pet	ŭ	**cut**
ē	be	ûr	**urge**
ĭ	pit	th	**thin**
ī	pie	*th*	**this**
îr	pier	hw	**whoop**
ŏ	pot	zh	**vision**
ō	toe	ə	**about**
ô	paw	N	*French* bon

sitar

Sitting Bull
Photographed in the 1880's

skateboard

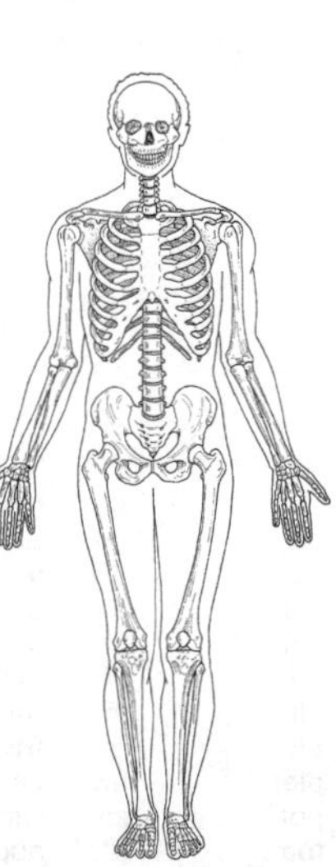
skeleton

a sitting position. **2.** To sit with the spine erect. **3.** To stay up later than the customary bedtime. [First written down about 725 in Old English and spelled *sittan.*] **—sit′ter** *n.* —See Note at **set¹**.

si•tar (sĭ tär′) *n.* A stringed instrument of India, made of seasoned gourds and teak and having 20 metal frets with 6 or 7 main playing strings above and 13 resonating strings below. [First written down in 1845 in Modern English, from Hindi *sitār*, from Persian : *si*, three + *tār*, string.]

sit•com also **sit-com** (sĭt′kŏm′) *n. Informal.* A situation comedy.

sit-down strike (sĭt′doun′) *n.* A protest in which workers stop working and refuse to leave their place of employment until their demands are considered or met.

site (sīt) *n.* **1.** The place where something was, is, or will be located: *a good site for a park.* **2.** The place or setting of an event: *the site of a historic battle.*
❑ *These sound alike:* **site, cite** (quote), **sight** (perception).

sit-in (sĭt′ĭn′) *n.* A demonstration in which persons protesting against certain conditions sit down in an appropriate place and refuse to move until their demands are considered or met.

sit•ter (sĭt′ər) *n.* **1.** A person who cares for children when the parents are not home; a babysitter. **2.** A person who poses or models for an artist.

sit•ting (sĭt′ĭng) *n.* **1.** The act or position of one that sits. **2.** A period during which one is seated and occupied with a single activity, such as posing for an artist or reading a book. **3.** A session, as of a legislature or court.

Sit•ting Bull (sĭt′ĭng bo͝ol′). 1834?–1890. Hunkpapa Sioux leader who guided his people to victory at the Battle of the Little Bighorn (1876).

sitting duck *n. Informal.* An easy target or victim.

sitting room *n.* A living room.

sit•u•ate (sĭch′o͞o āt′) *tr.v.* **sit•u•at•ed, sit•u•at•ing, sit•u•ates.** To place in a certain spot or position; locate.

sit•u•a•tion (sĭch′o͞o ā′shən) *n.* **1.** The place in which something is situated; location. **2.** A person's position or status with respect to specified conditions: *a favorable economic situation.* **3.** A combination of circumstances at a given moment; state of affairs. **4.** A position of employment.

situation comedy *n.* A humorous television or radio series in which the comedy arises from the interactions between a regular cast of characters.

sit-up (sĭt′ŭp′) *n.* An exercise in which a person lying on his or her back rises to a sitting position using the abdominal muscles and then lies down again without moving the legs.

Si•va (shē′və *or* sē′və) *n.* Variant of **Shiva.**

six (sĭks) *n.* **1.** The number, written 6, that is equal to 5 + 1. **2.** The sixth in a set or sequence.

Six Nations *pl.n.* The Iroquois confederacy after it was joined by the Tuscarora in 1722.

six•pence (sĭks′pəns) *n. Chiefly British.* A coin formerly used in Britain and worth six pennies.

six-shoot•er (sĭks′sho͞o′tər) *n. Informal.* A revolver that can be fired six times before it has to be reloaded.

six•teen (sĭk stēn′) *n.* **1.** The number, written 16, that is equal to 15 + 1. **2.** The 16th in a set or sequence. **—six′teen′** *adj. & pron.*

six•teenth (sĭk stēnth′) *n.* **1.** The ordinal number matching the number 16 in a series. **2.** One of 16 equal parts. **—six•teenth′** *adj. & adv.*

sixteenth note *n.* A musical note having one sixteenth the time value of a whole note.

sixth (sĭksth) *n.* **1.** The ordinal number matching the number six in a series. **2.** One of six equal parts. **3.a.** The interval covering six tones in a musical scale. **b.** The sixth tone in a musical scale. **—sixth** *adj. & adv.*

sixth sense *n.* A power of perception seemingly independent of the five senses; keen intuition.

six•ti•eth (sĭk′stē ĭth) *n.* **1.** The ordinal number matching the number 60 in a series. **2.** One of 60 equal parts. **—six′ti•eth** *adj. & adv.*

six•ty (sĭks′tē) *n., pl.* **six•ties. 1.** The number, written 60, that is equal to 6 × 10. **2.** A decade or the numbers from 60 to 69. **—six′ty** *adj. & pron.*

six•ty-fourth note (sĭks′tē fôrth′) *n.* A musical note having one sixty-fourth the time value of a whole note.

siz•a•ble also **size•a•ble** (sī′zə bəl) *adj.* Of considerable size; fairly large. **—siz′a•ble•ness** *n.* **—siz′a•bly** *adv.*

size¹ (sīz) *n.* **1.** The physical dimensions, proportions, or extent of an object. **2.** Any of a series of standard dimensions with which certain objects, such as clothing, are manufactured. **3.** Considerable extent, amount, or dimensions: *We had no difficulties of any size.* **4.** The actual state of affairs; the true situation: *We had succeeded—that was the size of it.* —*tr.v.* **sized, siz•ing, siz•es. 1.** To arrange, classify, or distribute according to size. **2.** To make, cut, or shape to a required size: *sized material for tents.* **—*idiom.* size up.** To make an estimate, an opinion, or a judgment of: *She sized up her opponent.* [First written down before 1300 in Middle English and spelled *sise*, from Old French *assise*, court session, law.]

size² (sīz) *n.* Any of several gelatinous or sticky substances made from glue, wax, or clay and used as a filler or glaze for porous materials such as paper, cloth, or wall surfaces. —*tr.v.* **sized, siz•ing, siz•es.** To treat or coat with size or a similar substance. [First written down about 1325 in Middle English and spelled *sise*, probably from Old French *sise*, a setting.]

size•a•ble (sī′zə bəl) *adj.* Variant of **sizable.**

sized (sīzd) *adj.* Having a particular or specified size: *a medium-sized car.*

siz•ing (sī′zĭng) *n.* **1.** A substance used as a filler or glaze; size. **2.** The treatment of fabric or another surface with size.

siz•zle (sĭz′əl) *intr.v.* **siz•zled, siz•zling, siz•zles. 1.** To make the hissing sound characteristic of frying fat. **2.** To be very hot: *a summer day that sizzled.* —*n.* A hissing sound.

S.J. *abbr.* An abbreviation of Society of Jesus.

skate¹ (skāt) *n.* **1.** An ice skate. **2.** A roller skate. —*intr.v.* **skat•ed, skat•ing, skates.** To glide or move along on or as if on skates. [First written down in 1662 in Modern English and spelled *skeat*, from Dutch *schaats*, from Old North French *escache*, stilt.] **—skat′er** *n.*

skate² (skāt) *n.* Any of various ocean fishes related to the rays, having a broad flat body with fins resembling wings. [First written down about 1340 in Middle English and spelled *schat*, from Old Norse *skata.*]

skate•board (skāt′bôrd′) *n.* A short narrow board having a set of four wheels mounted under it and usually ridden in a standing or crouched position. —*intr.v.* **skate•board•ed, skate•board•ing, skate•boards.** To ride on a skateboard. **—skate′board′er** *n.* **—skate′board′ing** *n.*

skeet (skēt) *n.* A form of trapshooting in which clay targets are used to simulate birds in flight. [First written down in 1926 in American English, alteration of *shoot.*]

skein (skān) *n.* **1.** A length of thread or yarn wound in a long loose coil. **2.** Something resembling this: *Skeins of mist floated above the lake.*

skel•e•tal (**skĕl′ĭ** tl) *adj.* Of, relating to, forming, or like a skeleton.

skel•e•ton (**skĕl′ĭ** tn) *n.* **1.a.** The internal structure composed of bone and cartilage that supports and protects the soft organs of a vertebrate. **b.** The hard protective covering or supporting structure of many invertebrates, such as crustaceans and insects. **2.** A supporting structure or framework, as of a building. **3.** An outline or a sketch: *the skeleton of a research paper.* **4.** A very thin person or animal. [First written down in 1578 in Modern English and spelled *sceleton,* from Greek *skeletos,* dried up.]

skeleton key *n.* A key with a large part of the bit filed off so that it can open many different locks.

skep•tic also **scep•tic** (**skĕp′**tĭk) *n.* **1.** A person who habitually questions or doubts the truth of generally accepted beliefs or conclusions. **2.** A person inclined to skepticism in religious matters.

skep•ti•cal also **scep•ti•cal** (**skĕp′**tĭ kəl) *adj.* Of, relating to, or characterized by skepticism; doubting or disbelieving: *a skeptical attitude.* **—skep′ti•cal•ly** *adv.*

skep•ti•cism also **scep•ti•cism** (**skĕp′**tĭ sĭz′əm) *n.* **1.** A doubting or questioning attitude or state of mind. **2.** Doubt or disbelief of religious doctrines.

sketch (skĕch) *n.* **1.** A rough preliminary drawing or painting: *a sketch of the park.* **2.** A brief composition or outline: *a biographical sketch.* **3.** A brief, light, or informal story or play. *—v.* **sketched, sketch•ing, sketch•es.** *—tr.* To make a sketch of: *sketch his face.* *—intr.* To make a sketch: *She loves to sketch in the park.* **—sketch′er** *n.*

sketch•book (**skĕch′**bo͝ok′) *n.* **1.** A pad of paper used for sketching. **2.** A book of literary sketches.

sketch•y (**skĕch′**ē) *adj.* **sketch•i•er, sketch•i•est.** Lacking in substance or completeness: *sketchy information.* **—sketch′i•ly** *adv.* **—sketch′i•ness** *n.*

skew (skyo͞o) *tr.v.* **skewed, skew•ing, skews. 1.** To turn or place at an angle; slant. **2.** To distort in meaning or effect; give a bias to: *The article was skewed in favor of the proposal.* *—adj.* Turned or placed to one side.

skew•er (**skyo͞o′**ər) *n.* A long pin of wood or metal, used to hold or suspend meat during cooking. *—tr. v.* **skew•ered, skew•er•ing, skew•ers.** To hold together or pierce with or as if with a skewer.

ski (skē) *n., pl.* **skis.** One of a pair of long, narrow, flat runners of wood, metal, or plastic that are fastened to a boot or shoe for gliding or traveling over snow. *—v.* **skied, ski•ing, skis.** *—intr.* To glide or travel on skis. *—tr.* To travel over on skis: *She skied a new trail.* [First written down in 1755 in Modern English, from Old Norse *skīdh,* stick, snowshoe.] **—ski′er** *n.*

skid (skĭd) *n.* **1.** The act of slipping or sliding over a surface: *The car went into a skid on the slippery pavement.* **2.** A plank or log, usually one of a pair, used as a support or track for sliding or rolling heavy objects. **3.** A runner forming part of the landing gear of an aircraft, such as a helicopter. **4.** A shoe or wedge that applies pressure to a wheel to keep it from turning. *—v.* **skid•ded, skid•ding, skids.** *—intr.* **1.** To slip or slide out of control over a slippery surface. See Synonyms at **slide. 2.** To slide over a surface without turning, as a wheel. *—tr.* **1.** To move (something) on a skid or skids. **2.** To brake (a wheel) with a skid.

skies (skīz) *n.* Plural of **sky.**

skiff (skĭf) *n.* A flat-bottomed boat with a pointed bow and a square stern, propelled by oars, sail, or motor.

ski jump *n.* **1.** A jump made by a person on skis. **2.** A course or run prepared for making jumps while on skis.

ski lift *n.* An apparatus that transports skiers to the top of a ski trail or mountain, usually consisting of a moving cable with attached bars, chairs, or gondolas.

skill (skĭl) *n.* **1.** Ability resulting from training or experience. **2.** An art, a trade, or a technique, especially one requiring use of the hands or body: *a carpenter's skills.* **3.** A developed ability: *He has excellent writing skills.* [First written down about 1175 in Middle English, from Old Norse *skil,* discernment.]

skilled (skĭld) *adj.* **1.** Having or showing skill; expert: *a skilled hunter.* See Synonyms at **proficient. 2.** Requiring specialized ability or training: *a skilled occupation.*

skil•let (**skĭl′**ĭt) *n.* A frying pan. [First written down in 1404 in Middle English and spelled *skelett,* from Latin *scutella,* plate.] —See Note at **frying pan.**

skill•ful (**skĭl′**fəl) *adj.* **1.** Having or using skill; expert: *a skillful cook.* See Synonyms at **proficient. 2.** Characterized by or requiring skill: *skillful violin playing.* **—skill′ful•ly** *adv.* **—skill′ful•ness** *n.*

skim (skĭm) *v.* **skimmed, skim•ming, skims.** *—tr.* **1.a.** To remove (floating matter) from a liquid: *skim cream off the top of the milk.* **b.** To remove floating matter from (a liquid): *skim milk.* **2.** To throw so as to bounce or slide: *skim stones over the pond.* **3.** To move or glide lightly and quickly over. **4.** To read, glance at, or consider superficially: *skim a book.* *—intr.* **1.** To move or glide lightly and quickly over a surface: *The sailboat skimmed across the lake.* **2.** To give a quick and superficial reading or consideration.

skim•mer (**skĭm′**ər) *n.* **1.** A person or thing that skims. **2.** A flat utensil used for skimming liquids. **3.** Any of several sea birds having long narrow wings and a long bill with a longer lower jaw used to skim the surface of the water for fish and other food.

skim milk *n.* Milk from which the cream has been removed.

skimp (skĭmp) *v.* **skimped, skimp•ing, skimps.** *—tr.* **1.** To deal with hastily, carelessly, or with poor material: *I had to concentrate on my science project, skimping other things.* **2.** To give inadequate funds to; be stingy with. *—intr.* To be stingy or very thrifty.

skimp•y (**skĭm′**pē) *adj.* **skimp•i•er, skimp•i•est.** Inadequate, as in size or amount; scanty: *a skimpy meal.* **—skimp′i•ly** *adv.* **—skimp′i•ness** *n.*

skin (skĭn) *n.* **1.** The membranous tissue that forms the outer covering of the body of an animal. **2.** A hide or pelt removed from the body of an animal: *a tent made of buffalo skins.* **3.** An outer layer, covering, or coating: *the skin of an apple.* **4.** A container for liquids that is made from an animal's skin. *—tr.v.* **skinned, skin•ning, skins. 1.** To remove the skin from: *skin a sheep.* **2.** To injure by scraping: *fell and skinned her knee.* **3.** To remove (an outer covering): *skinned off the thin bark.* **4.** *Slang.* To cheat; swindle. ***—idiom.*** **by the skin of (one's) teeth.** By the smallest margin; just barely.

skin-deep (**skĭn′dēp′**) *adj.* Superficial; shallow.

skin-dive (**skĭn′**dīv′) *intr.v.* **skin-dived, skin-div•ing, skin-dives.** To engage in skin diving.

skin diving *n.* The sport of underwater swimming in which the swimmer is equipped with flippers and a face mask and usually a snorkel rather than a portable air supply. **—skin diver** *n.*

skin•flint (**skĭn′**flĭnt′) *n.* A miser.

skink (skĭngk) *n.* Any of numerous lizards having a smooth shiny body and short legs.

skin•ner (**skĭn′**ər) *n.* **1.** A person who strips, dresses, or sells animal skins. **2.** A mule driver.

skin•ny (**skĭn′**ē) *adj.* **skin•ni•er, skin•ni•est.** Very thin: *skinny legs.* See Synonyms at **lean**[2]. **—skin′ni•ness** *n.*

ski

skin diving

ă	**pat**	oi	**boy**
ā	**pay**	ou	**out**
âr	**care**	o͝o	**took**
ä	**father**	o͞o	**boot**
ĕ	**pet**	ŭ	**cut**
ē	**be**	ûr	**urge**
ĭ	**pit**	th	**thin**
ī	**pie**	*th*	**this**
îr	**pier**	hw	**whoop**
ŏ	**pot**	zh	**vision**
ō	**toe**	ə	**about**
ô	**paw**	N	*French* **bon**

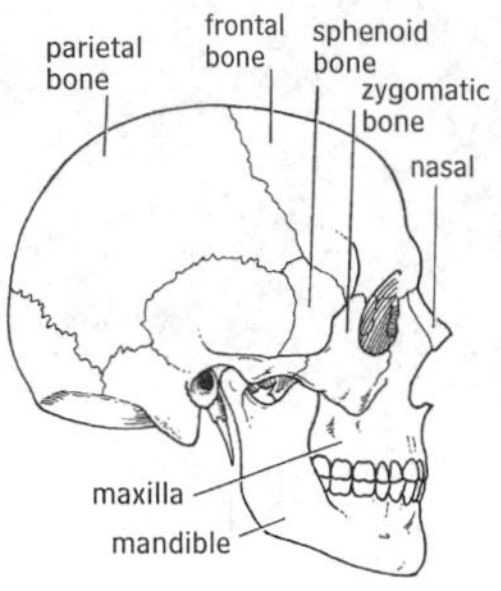

skull

skunk

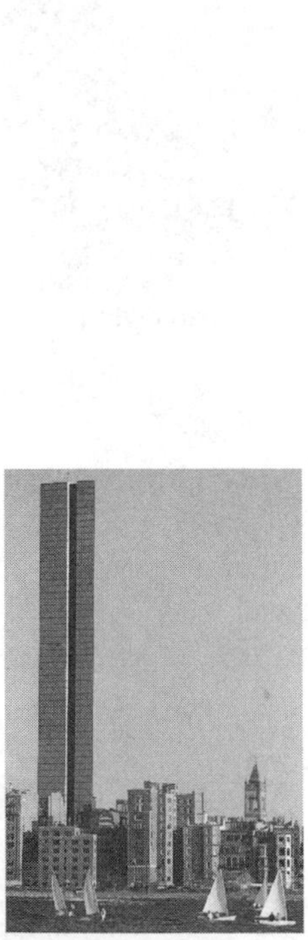
skyscraper

skin•tight (skĭn′tīt′) *adj.* Fitting or clinging closely to the skin.

skip (skĭp) *v.* **skipped, skip•ping, skips.** *—intr.* **1.a.** To move by hopping on one foot and then the other. **b.** To leap lightly about. **2.** To bounce over or be deflected from a surface: *The stone I threw skipped over the water six times.* **3.** To pass quickly from point to point: *skipping through the list hurriedly.* **4.** To be promoted in school beyond the next class or grade. **5.** *Informal.* To leave hastily. *—tr.* **1.** To leap or jump lightly over: *skip rope.* **2.** To pass over without mentioning; omit: *skipped the unimportant details.* **3.** To cause to bounce over a surface; skim. **4.** To be promoted beyond (the next class or grade). **5.** To leave hastily: *skip town.* *—n.* **1.** A gait in which hops and steps alternate. **2.** The act of passing over something; an omission. [First written down before 1300 in Middle English and spelled *skippen.*]

skip•per[1] (skĭp′ər) *n.* The captain of a ship. [First written down in 1391 in Middle English, from Middle Dutch, from *scip,* ship.]

skip•per[2] (skĭp′ər) *n.* **1.** A person or thing that skips. **2.** Any of numerous stout hairy butterflies that dart as they fly.

skir•mish (skûr′mĭsh) *n.* **1.** A minor battle between small bodies of troops. **2.** A minor conflict. *—intr.v.* **skir•mished, skir•mish•ing, skir•mish•es.** To engage in a minor battle or dispute.

skirt (skûrt) *n.* **1.** A garment that hangs from the waist and is worn by women and girls. **2.** The part of a garment, such as a dress or coat, that hangs from the waist down. **3.** Something that hangs like a skirt, as a cloth covering the legs of a piece of furniture. **4.** A border, a margin, or an outer edge: *The sheep grazed at the skirt of the hill.* *—v.* **skirt•ed, skirt•ing, skirts.** *—tr.* **1.** To form the border of, lie along, or surround: *The road skirted the park.* **2.** To pass around rather than across or through: *We skirted the marshes.* **3.** To evade (a topic or an issue, for example) in a roundabout way. *—intr.* To lie along, move along, or be an edge or a border.

skit (skĭt) *n.* A short, usually humorous theatrical sketch.

skit•ter (skĭt′ər) *v.* **skit•tered, skit•ter•ing, skit•ters.** *—intr.* To glide or move rapidly along a surface. *—tr.* To cause to skitter.

skit•tish (skĭt′ĭsh) *adj.* **1.** Excitable or nervous: *a skittish colt.* **2.** Frivolous in action or character; capricious or fickle. **—skit′tish•ly** *adv.* **—skit′tish•ness** *n.*

skit•tles (skĭt′lz) *n. (used with a singular verb).* A British form of the game ninepins.

skoal (skōl) *interj.* An expression used as a toast.

Skop•je (skôp′yā′ *or* skŏp′yə). The capital of Macedonia, in the north-central part south-southeast of Belgrade, Yugoslavia. Population, 406,400.

skul•dug•ger•y (skŭl dŭg′ə rē) *n.* Variant of **skullduggery.**

skulk (skŭlk) *intr.v.* **skulked, skulk•ing, skulks.** To move about stealthily.

skull (skŭl) *n.* The part of the skeleton that forms the framework of the head, consisting of the bones that protect the brain and the bones of the face. [First written down before 1200 in Middle English and spelled *sculle,* probably of Scandinavian origin.]

❑ *These sound alike:* **skull, scull** (oar).

skull and crossbones *n.* A representation of a human skull above two crossed bones, a symbol of death once used by pirates and now used as a warning label on poisons.

skull•cap (skŭl′kăp′) *n.* A small, close-fitting, brimless cap sometimes worn indoors.

skull•dug•ger•y or **skul•dug•ger•y** (skŭl dŭg′ə rē) *n., pl.* **skull•dug•ger•ies** or **skul•dug•ger•ies.** Crafty deception or trickery.

skunk (skŭngk) *n.* **1.** Any of several small mammals that have black and white fur and a bushy tail and can spray a foul-smelling liquid from glands near the base of the tail. **2.** *Slang.* An annoying or despicable person. *—tr.v.* **skunked, skunk•ing, skunks.** *Slang.* To defeat overwhelmingly, especially by keeping from scoring.

sky (skī) *n., pl.* **skies** (skīz). **1.** The atmosphere, as seen from a given point on Earth's surface. **2.** The appearance of the upper atmosphere, especially with respect to weather. Often used in the plural: *threatening skies.* [First written down before 1200 in Middle English, from Old Norse *ský,* cloud.]

sky blue *n.* A light to pale blue.

sky•dive (skī′dīv′) *intr.v.* **sky•dived, sky•div•ing, sky•dives.** To jump and fall freely from an airplane, performing various maneuvers before opening a parachute. **—sky′div′er** *n.* **—sky′div′ing** *n.*

sky-high (skī′hī′) *adv.* **1.** To a very high level: *garbage piled sky-high.* **2.** In a lavish or enthusiastic manner: *The critics praised the movie sky-high.* **3.** To pieces or in pieces; apart: *The explosives blew the old bridge sky-high.* *—adj.* Exorbitantly high: *sky-high prices.*

sky•jack (skī′jăk′) *tr.v.* **sky•jacked, sky•jack•ing, sky•jacks.** To hijack (an airplane) through the use or threat of force. **—sky′jack′er** *n.*

sky•lark (skī′lärk′) *n.* A brownish European songbird that sings while in flight. *—intr.v.* **sky•larked, sky•lark•ing, sky•larks.** To romp playfully; frolic.

sky•light (skī′līt′) *n.* An overhead window that admits daylight.

sky•line (skī′līn′) *n.* **1.** The line along which the earth and sky appear to meet; the horizon. **2.** The outline of a mountain range or group of buildings seen against the sky.

sky•rock•et (skī′rŏk′ĭt) *n.* A firework that ascends high into the air, where it explodes in a cascade of flares and sparks. *—intr. & tr.v.* **sky•rock•et•ed, sky•rock•et•ing, sky•rock•ets.** To rise or cause to rise rapidly or suddenly: *Prices skyrocketed.*

sky•scrap•er (skī′skrā′pər) *n.* A very tall building.

sky•ward (skī′wərd) *adv. & adj.* Toward the sky: *turn skyward.* **—sky′wards** *adv.*

sky•writ•ing (skī′rī′tĭng) *n.* **1.** The process of writing in the sky by releasing a visible vapor from an airplane. **2.** The letters or words so formed. **—sky′writ′er** *n.*

slab (slăb) *n.* A broad, flat, thick piece of something, as of cake, stone, or cheese.

slack[1] (slăk) *adj.* **slack•er, slack•est. 1.** Slow; dull; sluggish: *a slack pace.* **2.** Not busy: *the slack moments of the day.* **3.** Not tense or taut; loose: *a slack rope.* **4.** Careless; negligent: *a slack performance.* *—v.* **slacked, slack•ing, slacks.** *—tr.* To make slower or looser; slacken. *—intr.* **1.** To be or become slack. **2.** To avoid work. *—n.* **1.** A loose part of something: *take up some of the slack in the rope.* **2.** A period of little activity. **3. slacks.** Casual trousers that are not part of a suit. ***—idiom.*** **slack off.** To decrease in activity or diligence. [First written down about 725 in Old English and spelled *slæc.*] **—slack′ness** *n.*

slack[2] (slăk) *n.* A mixture of chunks of coal, coal dust, and dirt that remains after coal has been screened. [First written down about 1440 in Middle English and spelled *sleck.*]

slack•en (slăk′ən) *tr. & intr.v.* **slack•ened, slack•en•ing, slack•ens. 1.** To make or become slower; slow down: *The dogs slackened their pace. The plane's air speed slackened.* **2.** To make or become less vigorous or intense: *High rates slackened the demand for loans. Business slackened.* **3.** To make or become less taut or firm: *I slackened the leash to let the dog run. The tension in the room slackened.*

slack•er (**slăk′**ər) *n.* A person who tries to avoid work or responsibility.

slag (slăg) *n.* **1.** The glassy refuse that remains after a metal has been removed from an ore by smelting. **2.** Angular porous fragments of solidified lava from a volcano; scoria.

slain (slān) *v.* Past participle of **slay.**

slake (slāk) *tr.v.* **slaked, slak•ing, slakes. 1.** To satisfy (a craving): *slaked her thirst.* **2.** To lessen the force of; moderate: *slaking his anger.* **3.** To combine (lime) chemically with water, either directly or by exposure to moist air.

sla•lom (**slä′**ləm) *n.* **1.** The act or sport of skiing in a zigag manner. **2.** A skiing race down a zigzag course marked with flags. [First written down in 1921 in Modern English, from Norwegian *slalåm* : *slad*, sloping + *låm*, path.]

slam¹ (slăm) *v.* **slammed, slam•ming, slams.** *—tr.* **1.** To shut forcefully and with a loud noise: *slam a door.* **2.** To throw, move, or strike forcefully and loudly: *slammed down the telephone receiver.* *—intr.* **1.** To close or swing into place forcefully and with a loud noise: *The door slammed in the wind.* **2.** To hit something with force; crash: *The meteorite slammed into the side of a hill.* *—n.* **1.** An act of slamming. **2.** The noise of a forceful impact; a bang. [First written down in 1691 in Modern English, perhaps of Scandinavian origin.]

slam² (slăm) *n.* In certain card games, such as bridge, the winning of all the tricks or all but one during the play of one hand. [First written down in 1621 in Modern English.]

slan•der (**slăn′**dər) *n.* **1.** A false statement reported or uttered maliciously to damage someone's reputation. **2.** The act or crime of uttering or reporting such false statements. *—tr.v.* **slan•dered, slan•der•ing, slan•ders.** To utter or report against (someone); defame. **—slan′der•er** *n.*

slan•der•ous (**slăn′**dər əs) *adj.* Making or containing false and damaging charges about someone: *a slanderous speech.* **—slan′der•ous•ly** *adv.*

slang (slăng) *n.* **1.** A kind of language occurring most often in casual speech, consisting of made-up words and figures of speech that are deliberately used in place of standard terms to add vividness, humor, irreverence, or other effect. For example, slang terms include *cool* meaning "excellent" and *split* meaning "to leave." **2.** Language peculiar to a certain group of people; jargon: *surfers' slang.* **—slang′y** *adj.*

slant (slănt) *v.* **slant•ed, slant•ing, slants.** *—tr.* **1.** To give a direction other than horizontal or vertical to; cause to slope. **2.** To present (news or information, for example) in a way that conforms with a particular opinion; bias. *—intr.* To have or go in a direction other than horizontal or vertical; slope: *My handwriting slants to the right.* *—n.* **1.** A sloping line, plane, direction, or course. **2.** A personal point of view or opinion. **3.** A bias.

slant•wise (**slănt′**wīz′) *adv.* At a slant or slope; obliquely. *—adj.* Slanting; oblique.

slap (slăp) *n.* **1.a.** A sharp blow with the open hand or some other flat object. **b.** The sound made by such a blow. **2.** An injury or sharp insult: *a slap to one's pride.* *—v.* **slapped, slap•ping, slaps.** *—tr.* **1.** To strike with a flat object, such as the palm of the hand: *Grandpa slapped his knee and chuckled.* **2.** To put or place with a loud sharp sound: *slapping a price tag on the package.* *—intr.* To strike or beat with the force or sound of a slap: *waves slapping against the canoe.* [First written down about 1450 in Middle English and spelled *slappe.*]

slap•dash (**slăp′**dăsh′) *adj.* Characterized by haste or carelessness: *slapdash work.* *—adv.* In a reckless haphazard manner.

slap•stick (**slăp′**stĭk′) *n.* A form of comedy marked by chases, collisions, and crude practical jokes.

slash (slăsh) *v.* **slashed, slash•ing, slash•es.** *—tr.* **1.** To cut or form with forceful sweeping strokes: *We slashed a path through the jungle.* **2.** To lash with sweeping strokes. **3.** To make a gash or gashes in: *slashed the screen with a knife.* **4.** To cut a decorative slit or slits in (a garment or fabric). **5.** To criticize severely. **6.** To reduce greatly: *slash prices for a sale.* *—intr.* **1.** To make forceful sweeping strokes with or as if with a sharp instrument. **2.** To cut one's way with such strokes. *—n.* **1.** A forceful sweeping stroke made with a sharp instrument. **2.** A long cut or opening made by such a stroke. **3.** A sharp reduction: *making slashes in the national budget.* **4.** A diagonal mark (/) used in writing and printing to separate alternatives, as in *and/or,* or to mean "per" as in *miles/hour.* **5.** A decorative slit in a fabric or garment.

slat (slăt) *n.* A narrow strip of metal or wood, as in a Venetian blind.

slate (slāt) *n.* **1.** A fine-grained metamorphic rock that splits into thin layers with smooth surfaces. **2.a.** A piece of such rock cut for use as a roofing material or as a writing surface. **b.** A writing tablet made of this or a similar material. **3.** A dark bluish gray. **4.** A record of past performance or activity: *starting with a clean slate.* **5.** A list of the candidates of a political party running for office. *—tr.v.* **slat•ed, slat•ing, slates. 1.** To cover (a roof, for example) with slates. **2.** To put on a list of candidates. **3.** To schedule or designate: *slated the appointment for Tuesday.*

slath•er (**slăth′**ər) *tr.v.* **slath•ered, slath•er•ing, slath•ers.** *Informal.* **1.** To use or give in great amounts; lavish: *slathered attention on the child.* **2.** To spread thickly: *slather cream cheese on a bagel.*

slat•tern (**slăt′**ərn) *n.* A woman who is careless or sloppy in her appearance or personal habits. **—slat′tern•ly** *adj.*

slat•y (**slā′**tē) *adj.* **slat•i•er, slat•i•est. 1.** Composed of or resembling slate. **2.** Having the color of slate.

slaugh•ter (**slô′**tər) *n.* **1.** The killing of animals for food. **2.** The killing of a large number of people; a massacre. *—tr.v.* **slaugh•tered, slaugh•ter•ing, slaugh•ters. 1.** To kill (an animal) for food. **2.** To kill (people) brutally or in large numbers. **—slaugh′ter•er** *n.*

slaugh•ter•house (**slô′**tər hous′) *n.* **1.** A place where animals are butchered. **2.** A scene of massacre or carnage.

Slav (släv) *n.* A member of one of the Slavic-speaking peoples of eastern Europe.

slave (slāv) *n.* **1.** A person who is owned by and forced to work for someone else. **2.** A person completely controlled by a specified person or influence: *a slave to his appetites.* **3.** A person who works very hard. *—intr.v.* **slaved, slav•ing, slaves.** To work very hard; toil. [First written down about 1300 in Middle English and spelled *sclave,* from Old French *esclave,* from Medieval Latin *Sclāvus,* a Slav.]

slave driver *n.* **1.** An overseer of slaves at work. **2.** An extremely demanding employer or supervisor.

slave•hold•er (**slāv′**hōl′dər) *n.* A person who owns slaves.

slav•er¹ (**slăv′**ər) *intr.v.* **slav•ered, slav•er•ing, slav•ers.** To let saliva dribble from the mouth; drool. *—n.* Saliva drooling from the mouth. [First written down before 1325 in Middle English and spelled *slaveren,* probably from Old Norse *slafra.*]

slav•er² (**slā′**vər) *n.* **1.** A ship engaged in slave traffic. **2.** A person who sells and trades slaves.

ă	pat	oi	boy
ā	pay	ou	out
âr	care	o͝o	took
ä	father	o͞o	boot
ĕ	pet	ŭ	cut
ē	be	ûr	urge
ĭ	pit	th	thin
ī	pie	*th*	this
îr	pier	hw	whoop
ŏ	pot	zh	vision
ō	toe	ə	about
ô	paw	N	*French* bon

sledge

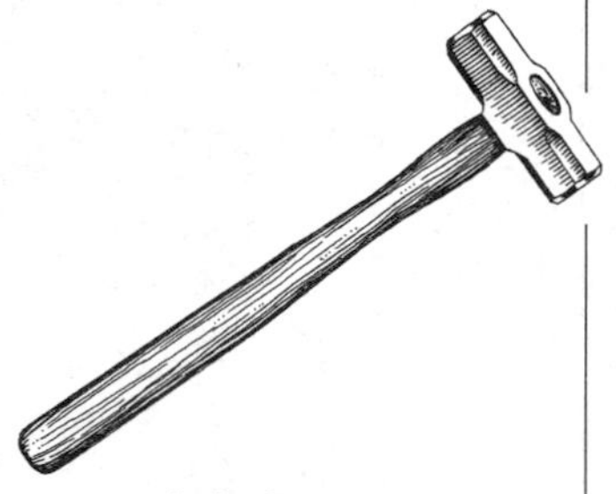
sledgehammer

sleigh

slav•er•y (slā′və rē *or* slāv′rē) *n., pl.* **slav•er•ies. 1.** The condition of being a slave. **2.** The practice of owning slaves. **3.** Hard work or subjection like that of a slave. **4.** The condition of being subject or addicted to a specified influence.

slave state *n.* Any of the 15 states of the Union in which slavery was legal before the Civil War.

Slav•ic (slä′vĭk) *adj.* Of or relating to the Slavs or their languages. —*n.* A branch of the Indo-European language family that includes Russian, Czech, Bulgarian, Polish, and Serbo-Croatian.

slav•ish (slā′vĭsh) *adj.* **1.** Of or characteristic of a slave; servile or submissive: *slavish devotion.* **2.** Showing no originality; blindly imitative: *a slavish copy of another artist's work.* **—slav′ish•ly** *adv.* **—slav′ish•ness** *n.*

Sla•vo•ni•a (slə vō′nē ə *or* slə vō′nyə). A historical region of northern Croatia. It became a Slavic state in the seventh century and has long been allied with Croatia.

slaw (slô) *n.* Coleslaw.

slay (slā) *tr.v.* **slew** (slo͞o), **slain** (slān), **slay•ing, slays. 1.** To kill violently. **2.** *Slang.* To overwhelm, as with laughter or love: *Those old jokes still slay me.* **—slay′er** *n.*

❑ *These sound alike:* **slay, sleigh** (sledge).

slea•zy (slē′zē) *adj.* **slea•zi•er, slea•zi•est. 1.** Shabby, dirty, and tawdry: *a sleazy tavern.* **2.** Disreputable or dishonest; corrupt: *a sleazy character.* **3.** Made of low-quality materials; cheap. **4.** Thin and loosely woven. **—slea′zi•ly** *adv.* **—slea′zi•ness** *n.*

sled (slĕd) *n.* **1.** A vehicle mounted on runners, used for carrying people or loads over snow and ice. **2.** A light frame mounted on runners, used by children for coasting over snow and ice. —*v.* **sled•ded, sled•ding, sleds.** —*tr.* To carry on a sled. —*intr.* To ride on a sled. [First written down before 1325 in Middle English and spelled *sledde,* from Middle Dutch.]

sledge (slĕj) *n.* A vehicle on runners, drawn by horses, dogs, or reindeer and used for transporting loads across snow and ice. [First written down in 1617 in Modern English, from Dutch dialectal *sleedse.*]

sledge•ham•mer (slĕj′hăm′ər) *n.* A long heavy hammer, often wielded with both hands, used for driving posts and other heavy work. —*tr.v.* **sledge•ham•mered, sledge•ham•mer•ing, sledge•ham•mers.** To strike with or as if with a sledgehammer.

sleek (slēk) *adj.* **sleek•er, sleek•est. 1.** Smooth and glossy: *the sleek coat of a horse.* **2.** Neat, trim, and graceful in appearance: *a sleek racing car.* **3.** Healthy or well-fed; thriving: *a sleek pig ready for the market.* [First written down in 1589 in Modern English, variant of *slick.*] **—sleek′ly** *adv.* **—sleek′ness** *n.*

sleep (slēp) *n.* **1.** A natural condition of rest, occurring periodically in many animals, that is characterized by unconsciousness and a decrease in bodily movement. **2.** A period of this form of rest. **3.** A similar condition of inactivity, such as hibernation or unconsciousness. —*v.* **slept** (slĕpt), **sleep•ing, sleeps.** —*intr.* **1.** To be in or pass into a state of sleep. **2.** To be inactive or inattentive: *The sudden question caught me sleeping.* —*tr.* **1.** To pass or get rid of by sleeping: *slept away the afternoon.* **2.** To provide with beds: *This cabin sleeps four.* **—*idioms.*** **sleep on it.** *Informal.* To consider something overnight before deciding. **sleep over.** To spend the night as a guest in another's home. **sleep with.** To have sexual relations with. [First written down about 725 in Old English and spelled *slæp.*]

sleep•er (slē′pər) *n.* **1.** A person or an animal that sleeps: *a sound sleeper.* **2.** A sleeping car on a train. **3.** Something, such as a movie, play, or contestant, that gets little attention at first but then becomes unexpectedly popular or successful. **4.** A horizontal beam on or near the ground that supports weight.

sleep•ing bag (slē′pĭng) *n.* A large warmly lined bag in which a person may sleep, especially outdoors.

sleeping car *n.* A railroad car with small bedrooms for overnight passengers.

sleeping sickness *n.* An often fatal infectious disease of human beings and animals in tropical Africa. It is caused by parasitic protozoans, spread by the bite of the tsetse fly, and is marked by fever and extreme sluggishness.

sleep•less (slēp′lĭs) *adj.* **1.** Unable to sleep; restless or insomniac. **2.** Marked by a lack of sleep; wakeful: *sleepless nights.* **3.** Never resting; always alert or active. **—sleep′less•ly** *adv.* **—sleep′less•ness** *n.*

sleep•walk•ing (slēp′wô′kĭng) *n.* The act or an instance of walking about while asleep or in a condition resembling sleep; somnambulism. **—sleep′walk′er** *n.*

sleep•y (slē′pē) *adj.* **sleep•i•er, sleep•i•est. 1.** Ready for or needing sleep. **2.** Dulled or sluggish from sleep: *sleepy eyes.* **3.** Quiet; inactive: *a sleepy town.* **—sleep′i•ly** *adv.* **—sleep′i•ness** *n.*

sleep•y•head (slē′pē hĕd′) *n. Informal.* A sleepy person.

sleet (slēt) *n.* **1.** Water that falls to the earth in the form of frozen or partially frozen raindrops. **2.** A thin coating of ice that forms on trees or road surfaces as a result of sleet or freezing rain. —*intr.v.* **sleet•ed, sleet•ing, sleets.** To fall as sleet.

sleeve (slēv) *n.* **1.** The part of a garment that covers all or part of the arm. **2.** A case or covering into which an object or a device fits: *a record sleeve.* —*tr.v.* **sleeved, sleev•ing, sleeves.** To furnish or fit with a sleeve or sleeves. **—*idiom.*** **up (one's) sleeve.** Hidden but ready to be used: *I still have a few tricks up my sleeve.* **—sleeve′less** *adj.*

sleigh (slā) *n.* A light vehicle on low runners for use on snow or ice, having one or more seats and usually drawn by a horse. —*intr.v.* **sleighed, sleigh•ing, sleighs.** To ride in or drive a sleigh. [First written down in 1400 in Middle English and spelled *sceye,* from Middle Dutch *slēde.*]

❑ *These sound alike:* **sleigh, slay** (kill).

sleight (slīt) *n.* **1.** Quickness or skillfulness; dexterity. **2.** A clever or skillful trick or deception.

sleight of hand *n., pl.* **sleights of hand.** A trick or set of tricks performed by a juggler or magician so quickly that one cannot see how it is done.

slen•der (slĕn′dər) *adj.* **slen•der•er, slen•der•est. 1.** Having little width as compared to length or height; long and thin: *a slender church spire.* See Synonyms at **lean**[2]. **2.** Small in amount or extent: *a slender chance of winning.* **—slen′der•ly** *adv.* **—slen′der•ness** *n.*

slept (slĕpt) *v.* Past tense and past participle of **sleep.**

sleuth (slo͞oth) *n.* A detective. —*v.* **sleuthed, sleuth•ing, sleuths.** —*tr.* To track or follow. —*intr.* To act as a detective.

slew[1] (slo͞o) *n. Informal.* A large amount or number: *caught a whole slew of fish.* [First written down in 1840 in American English, from Irish Gaelic *sluagh,* multitude.]

❑ *These sound alike:* **slew**[1] (large amount), **slew**[2] (killed), **slough**[1] (a hollow), **slue** (turn).

slew[2] (slo͞o) *v.* Past tense of **slay.**

❑ *These sound alike:* **slew**[2] (killed), **slew**[1] (large amount), **slough**[1] (hollow), **slue** (turn).

slew[3] (slo͞o) *n.* Variant of **slough**[1].

slew[4] (slo͞o) *v.* Variant of **slue.**

slice (slīs) *n.* **1.** A thin broad piece cut from a larger amount: *a slice of bread.* **2.** A share or portion: *a slice of the profits.* **3.a.** The path of a ball that curves to the right when hit by a righthander or to the left when hit by a lefthander. **b.** A ball that follows such a path. *—v.* **sliced, slic•ing, slic•es.** *—tr.* **1.** To cut into slices: *slice a loaf of bread.* **2.** To cut from a larger piece: *slicing off a piece of salami.* **3.** To divide into portions. **4.** To hit (a ball) with a slice. *—intr.* **1.** To move like a knife: *The airplane sliced through the clouds.* **2.** To hit a ball with a slice. [First written down before 1300 in Middle English, from Old French *esclicier*, to splinter, of Germanic origin.] **—slic′er** *n.*

slick (slĭk) *adj.* **slick•er, slick•est. 1.** Smooth, glossy, and slippery: *slick ice.* **2.** Acting or done with skill and ease; deft; adroit: *a slick tennis shot.* **3.** Shrewd; crafty: *a slick business deal.* **4.** Attractive at first, but really shallow or insincere; glib: *a slick writing style.* *—n.* A smooth or slippery surface or area. *—tr.v.* **slicked, slick•ing, slicks.** To make smooth, glossy, or oily: *slicked back his hair with water.* [First written down before 1325 in Middle English and spelled *slike*.]

slick•er (slĭk′ər) *n.* **1.** A long waterproof coat, usually made of oilskin. **2.** A raincoat made of a glossy or shiny material. **3.** *Informal.* A person with stylish clothing and fancy manners: *a city slicker.*

slide (slīd) *v.* **slid** (slĭd), **slid•ing, slides.** *—intr.* **1.** To move smoothly over a surface while maintaining continuous contact. **2.** To move or pass quietly: *I slid past the door to his office.* **3.** To lose a secure footing; slip. **4.** In baseball, to drop down and skid into a base to avoid being tagged out. **5.** To move downward or into a less favorable position: *Prices began to slide.* **6.** To go unacted upon: *Let the matter slide.* *—tr.* To cause to slip or slide: *Slide that box over here.* *—n.* **1.** A sliding action or movement. **2.** A smooth surface or track for sliding that usually is inclined, especially a playground apparatus that includes a smooth chute for sliding down. **3.** An image formed on a transparent piece of material for projection on a screen. **4.** A small glass plate on which things are placed or mounted for examination by microscope. **5.** A fall of a mass of rock, earth, or snow down a slope; an avalanche or a landslide. [First written down before 950 in Old English and spelled *slīdan*.]

Synonyms: slide, glide, skid, coast. These verbs mean to move smoothly and continuously over or as if over a slippery surface. **Slide** suggests rapid, easy movement without loss of contact with the surface: *A tear slid down my cheek.* **Glide** means to move in a smooth, free-flowing, seemingly effortless way: *A submarine glided silently through the water.* **Skid** means to slide uncontrollably, often in a sideways direction: *The car skidded on a patch of ice.* **Coast** often means to slide downward, especially as a result of gravity: *We coasted down the hill on our sleds.*

slide projector *n.* A machine that projects an image from a slide on a screen.

slide rule *n.* A device that consists of two scaled rules arranged to slide along each other, having scales that correspond to the logarithms of numbers, allowing its use in performing multiplication, division, and more complex mathematical operations. Slide rules have now been largely replaced by pocket calculators.

sli•er (slī′ər) *adj.* A comparative of **sly.**

sli•est (slī′ĭst) *adj.* A superlative of **sly.**

slight (slīt) *adj.* **slight•er, slight•est. 1.** Small in size, amount, or degree: *a slight change in temperature.* **2.** Small and slender in build or construction; delicate. **3.** Of little importance; trifling: *a slight misunderstanding.* **4.** Lacking in strength or substance: *There was slight evidence he was right.* *—tr.v.* **slight•ed, slight•ing, slights. 1.** To treat as of small importance; underestimate. **2.** To snub or insult. **3.** To neglect: *Don't slight your schoolwork.* *—n.* An act of slighting, especially an insult to one's pride or self-esteem. **—slight′ness** *n.*

slight•ing (slī′tĭng) *adj.* Constituting or conveying a slight; disrespectful; discourteous. **—slight′ing•ly** *adv.*

slight•ly (slīt′lē) *adv.* **1.** To a small degree or extent; somewhat. **2.** Slenderly; delicately: *slightly built.*

slim (slĭm) *adj.* **slim•mer, slim•mest. 1.** Small in thickness as compared to height; slender; thin: *a slim person.* **2.** Small in quantity or amount; scant: *a slim chance of success.* *—intr. & tr.v.* **slimmed, slim•ming, slims. 1.** To become or make slim. **2.** To lose or cause to lose weight, as by diet or exercise. [First written down in 1657 in Modern English, from Middle Dutch *slimp*, bad, crooked.]

slime (slīm) *n.* **1.** Thick, sticky, slippery mud or a similar substance. **2.** A slippery mucous substance secreted by certain animals, such as slugs or snails.

slime mold *n.* An organism that in one stage of its development forms a slimy moving mass of protoplasm and in another stage forms a growth that resembles a fungus and produces spores.

slim•y (slī′mē) *adj.* **slim•i•er, slim•i•est. 1.** Consisting of or resembling slime. **2.** Vile or disgusting. **3.** Covered with or secreting slime. **—slim′i•ness** *n.*

sling (slĭng) *n.* **1.a.** A looped rope, strap, or chain for hoisting or supporting something. **b.** An adjustable strap for carrying a rifle over the shoulder. **c.** A band of cloth suspended from the neck to support an injured arm or hand. **2.a.** A weapon made from a looped strap in which a stone is whirled and then let fly. **b.** A slingshot. *—tr.v.* **slung** (slŭng), **sling•ing, slings. 1.** To raise, lower, or move (a load) in a sling. **2.** To place or carry in a sling. **3.** To hurl with or as if with a sling. **4.** To place so as to hang loosely: *We slung the hammock between two trees.*

sling•shot (slĭng′shŏt′) *n.* A Y-shaped stick with an elastic strap attached to the prongs, used for shooting small stones.

slink (slĭngk) *intr.v.* **slunk** (slŭngk) also **slinked, slink•ing, slinks.** To move in a quiet sneaky way.

slip¹ (slĭp) *v.* **slipped, slip•ping, slips.** *—intr.* **1.** To move smoothly, easily, and quietly: *slipped past the guards.* **2.** To pass gradually, easily, or unnoticed: *weeks slipping away.* **3.** To lose one's balance or foothold. **4.** To slide out of place; shift position: *The beams supporting the mine's roof were beginning to slip.* **5.** To escape from a hold, grip, or restraint: *The dog slipped out of its collar.* **6.** To fall into fault or error. **7.** To decline from a former standard or level; fall: *The senator's popularity has slipped.* *—tr.* **1.** To cause to move in a smooth, easy, or sliding motion: *slipped the rope over the branch.* **2.** To place or insert smoothly and quietly: *slip a note under the door.* **3.** To put on or remove (clothing) easily or quickly: *slipped off her shoes.* **4.** To get loose or free from: *The cat slipped my grasp.* *—n.* **1.** The act or an instance of slipping or sliding. **2.** An accident, especially a loss of one's balance or footing. **3.** An error or oversight; a mistake. **4.** A docking place for a ship between two piers. **5.a.** A woman's undergarment that hangs from shoulder straps. **b.** A half-slip. **6.** A pillowcase. ***—idioms.*** **give (someone) the slip.** *Slang.* To escape from. **let slip.** To say unintentionally or thoughtlessly. [First written down before 1325 in Middle English and spelled *slippen*, probably of Middle Low German or Middle Dutch origin.]

slip² (slĭp) *n.* **1.** A part of a plant cut or broken off for planting or grafting; a cutting. **2.** A small piece or strip, especially of paper: *a sales slip.* **3.** A slender youthful person: *a slip of a girl.* [First written down in 1555 in Modern English and spelled

slide

slide projector

ă	**pat**	oi	**boy**
ā	**pay**	ou	**out**
âr	**care**	ŏŏ	**took**
ä	**father**	ōō	**boot**
ĕ	**pet**	ŭ	**cut**
ē	**be**	ûr	**urge**
ĭ	**pit**	th	**thin**
ī	**pie**	*th*	**this**
îr	**pier**	hw	**whoop**
ŏ	**pot**	zh	**vision**
ō	**toe**	ə	**about**
ô	**paw**	N	*French* **bon**

sloth
Brown-throated three-toed sloth

slippe, probably from Middle Low German or Middle Dutch *slippe*.]

slip•cov•er (slĭp′kŭv′ər) *n.* A removable cover of cloth or plastic that fits over a piece of upholstered furniture, such as a sofa.

slip•knot (slĭp′nŏt′) *n.* **1.** A knot made with a loop so that it can slip easily along the rope around which it is tied. **2.** A knot made so that it can be untied by pulling one free end of the rope.

slip-on (slĭp′ŏn′ *or* slĭp′ôn′) *n.* A piece of clothing, such as a glove or shoe, that is easily slipped on and off.

slip•o•ver (slĭp′ō′vər) *n.* A garment, such as a sweater, designed to be put on or taken off over the head.

slip•page (slĭp′ĭj) *n.* **1.** The act or an instance of slipping. **2.** The amount that something has slipped: *a slippage of 20 points in the stock market.*

slip•per (slĭp′ər) *n.* A low shoe that can be slipped on and off easily and is usually worn indoors.

slip•per•y (slĭp′ə rē) *adj.* **slip•per•i•er, slip•per•i•est. 1.** Causing or tending to cause slipping, as a surface that is oily or wet. **2.** Not trustworthy; elusive or tricky: *a slippery character.* **—slip′per•i•ness** *n.*

slip•shod (slĭp′shŏd′) *adj.* **1.** Done carelessly. **2.** Untidy or slovenly in appearance.

slip-up (slĭp′ŭp′) *n.* A mistake or an oversight.

slit (slĭt) *n.* A long, straight, narrow cut or opening: *slits between the boards of a fence.* *—tr.v.* **slit, slit•ting, slits. 1.** To cut a slit or slits in. **2.** To cut lengthwise into strips; split. **—slit′ter** *n.*

slith•er (slĭth′ər) *intr.v.* **slith•ered, slith•er•ing, slith•ers. 1.** To move along by sliding or gliding like a snake. **2.** To slip and slide, as on a loose or uneven surface.

sliv•er (slĭv′ər) *n.* A slender piece cut, split, or broken off, as of wood or glass; a splinter. *—tr. & intr.v.* **sliv•ered, sliv•er•ing, sliv•ers.** To split or become split into slender pieces.

slob (slŏb) *n. Informal.* A person regarded as dirty, crude, and slovenly.

slob•ber (slŏb′ər) *intr.v.* **slob•bered, slob•ber•ing, slob•bers. 1.** To let saliva or liquid dribble from the mouth; drool. **2.** To express emotion in an overexcited or exaggerated way; gush. *—n.* **1.** Saliva or liquid spilled from the mouth. **2.** Sentimental or confused speech or writing. **—slob′ber•y** *adj.*

sloe (slō) *n.* **1.** A tart dark purple, red, or yellow fruit similar to a plum. **2.** Either of two eastern North American shrubs that bear such fruit. [First written down before 800 in Old English and spelled *slā*, blackthorn fruit.]

❑ *These sound alike:* **sloe, slow** (not quick).

slog (slŏg) *v.* **slogged, slog•ging, slogs.** *—intr.* **1.** To walk with a slow heavy gait; plod. **2.** To work very hard for long hours. *—tr.* To make (one's way) slowly, heavily, and with great effort. *—n.* **1.** Long hard work. **2.** A long exhausting march or hike. **—slog′ger** *n.*

slo•gan (slō′gən) *n.* **1.** A phrase expressing the aims or nature of an enterprise, an organization, or a political candidate; a motto. **2.** A phrase used repeatedly to advertise a commercial product or service. [First written down in 1513 in Modern English and spelled *slogorne*, from Scottish Gaelic *sluagh-ghairm*, battle cry.]

sloop (slo͞op) *n.* A single-masted, fore-and-aft-rigged sailing vessel.

slop (slŏp) *n.* **1.** Watery mud or a similar substance. **2.** Spilled or splashed liquid. **3.** Unappetizing watery food. **4.** Waste food fed to animals. Often used in the plural. **5.** Overly gushy writing or speech. *—v.* **slopped, slop•ping, slops.** *—intr.* **1.** To be spilled or splashed: *Soup slopped over the edge of the bowl.* **2.** To walk heavily or messily, as through mud or puddles. *—tr.* **1.** To spill (liquid). **2.** To feed slops to (animals).

slope (slōp) *v.* **sloped, slop•ing, slopes.** *—intr.* To incline upward or downward; be slanted. *—tr.* To cause to slope. *—n.* **1.** An inclined line, plane, surface, direction, or position. **2.** A part of Earth's surface forming a natural or artificial incline: *ski slopes.* **3.a.** A deviation from the horizontal plane or direction. **b.** The amount or measure of such a deviation: *a slope of 20 degrees.*

slop•py (slŏp′ē) *adj.* **slop•pi•er, slop•pi•est. 1.** Messy; untidy: *a sloppy room.* **2.** Carelessly done; full of oversights or mistakes: *a sloppy research paper.* **3.** *Informal.* Overly sentimental; gushy: *a sloppy greeting card.* **4.** Covered or spattered with watery mud or slush; muddy. **5.** Watery and disagreeable: *a sloppy stew.* **—slop′pi•ly** *adv.* **—slop′pi•ness** *n.*

slosh (slŏsh) *v.* **sloshed, slosh•ing, slosh•es.** *—tr.* To spill or splash (a liquid). *—intr.* To flounder or splash in water or another liquid.

slot (slŏt) *n.* **1.** A narrow groove or opening: *a mail slot.* **2.** An assigned place or position; a niche: *a new time slot for the TV program.* *—tr.v.* **slot•ted, slot•ting, slots.** To cut or make a slot or slots in.

sloth (slôth *or* slōth *or* slŏth) *n.* **1.** Dislike and avoidance of work; laziness. **2.** Any of various slow-moving tropical American mammals that live in trees and hang upside-down from branches by their claws.

sloth•ful (slôth′fəl *or* slōth′fəl *or* slŏth′fəl) *adj.* Sluggishly idle; lazy. **—sloth′ful•ly** *adv.* **—sloth′ful•ness** *n.*

slot machine *n.* A vending or gambling machine operated by inserting coins into a slot.

slouch (slouch) *intr.v.* **slouched, slouch•ing, slouch•es.** To sit, stand, or walk with an awkward, drooping, bent posture. *—n.* **1.** An awkward, drooping, overly relaxed posture or gait. **2.** *Slang.* A lazy or incompetent person. **—slouch′y** *adj.*

slouch hat *n.* A soft hat with a broad flexible brim.

slough[1] (slo͞o *or* slou) also **slew** (slo͞o) *n.* **1.** A hollow or depression in the ground, usually filled with mud or mire. **2.** A stagnant swamp, bog, or marsh. [First written down before 899 in Old English and spelled *slōh*.]

❑ *These sound alike:* **slough[1], slew[1]** (large amount), **slew[2]** (killed), **slue** (turn).

slough[2] (slŭf) *n.* **1.** The dead outer skin shed by a reptile or an amphibian. **2.** An outer layer or covering that is shed. *—tr. & intr.v.* **sloughed, slough•ing, sloughs.** To cast off or come off; shed: *The snake sloughed its old skin. The scab on his knee sloughed off.* [First written down before 1325 in Middle English and spelled *slughe*.]

Slo•vak (slō′väk′ *or* slō′văk′) *n.* **1.** A member of a Slavic people living in Slovakia. **2.** The Slavic language of the Slovaks. *—adj.* Of or relating to Slovakia, or its people, language, or culture.

Slo•va•ki•a (slō vä′kē ə *or* slō văk′ē ə). A country of central Europe. It was settled in about the sixth century A.D. and became part of Czechoslovakia in 1918. Slovakia and Czech Republic split into two countries on January 1, 1993. Capital, Bratislava. Population, 4,991,168. **—Slo•va′ki•an** *n. & adj.*

slov•en (slŭv′ən) *n.* A person who is careless in personal appearance or work.

Slo•vene (slō′vēn′) *n.* **1.** A native or inhabitant of Slovenia. **2.** The Slavic language of Slovenia.

Slo•ve•ni•a (slō vē′nē ə *or* slō vēn′yə). A region of the northwest Balkan Peninsula. Slovenia became part of Yugoslavia in 1918 and declared its independence in 1991. Capital, Ljubljana. Population, 1,697,068.

slov•en•ly (slŭv′ən lē) *adj.* **1.** Untidy, as in dress or appearance: *slovenly garments.* **2.** Careless: *slovenly work.* —**slov′en•li•ness** *n.*

slow (slō) *adj.* **slow•er, slow•est. 1.** Not moving, acting, or capable of moving or acting quickly: *a slow train.* **2.** Taking or requiring a long time or more time than usual: *a slow dinner.* **3.** Not suitable or made for rapid movement: *a slow track.* **4.** Behind the correct time: *My watch is slow.* **5.** Not quick or willing: *We were slow to volunteer for such a boring job.* **6.** Sluggish; inactive: *Business is slow.* **7.** Not having or showing mental quickness: *a slow learner.* **8.** Lacking excitement or interest; boring: *a slow party.* —*adv.* **slower, slowest. 1.** In a slow manner; not quickly or rapidly. **2.** So as to fall behind the correct time or rate: *This watch runs slow.* —*tr. & intr.v.* **slowed, slow•ing, slows.** To make or become slow or slower: *The wind slowed the car. The pace of the runners slowed.* [First written down before 899 in Old English and spelled *slāw*.] —**slow′ly** *adv.* —**slow′ness** *n.*

❑ *These sound alike:* **slow, sloe** (fruit).

slow•down (slō′doun′) *n.* The act or process of slowing down, especially an intentional slowing down of production by labor or management.

slow motion *n.* A filmmaking technique in which the action as projected is slower than the original action.

slow•poke (slō′pōk′) *n. Informal.* A person who works, acts, or moves slowly.

sludge (slŭj) *n.* **1.** Semisolid material, as that formed from the treatment of sewage. **2.** Mire, mud, or ooze covering the ground or forming a deposit, as on a river bed. **3.** Finely broken or half-formed ice on a body of water. —**sludg′y** *adj.*

slue also **slew** (slo͞o) *v.* **slued, slu•ing, slues** also **slewed, slew•ing, slews.** —*tr.* **1.** To turn (something) on an axis; rotate. **2.** To turn sharply. —*intr.* **1.** To turn about an axis; pivot. **2.** To turn or slide sideways; skid.

❑ *These sound alike:* **slue, slew**[1] (large amount), **slew**[2] (killed), **slough**[1] (hollow).

slug[1] (slŭg) *n.* **1.** A bullet. **2.** A small metal disk for use in a vending or gambling machine, especially one used illegally. [First written down in 1622 in Modern English, perhaps from *slug*, animal (from its shape).]

slug[2] (slŭg) *n.* **1.** Any of various land mollusks related to the snails but having no shell. **2.** *Informal.* A lazy idle person; a sluggard. [First written down in 1408 in Middle English and spelled *slogge*, sluggard, probably of Scandinavian origin.]

slug[3] (slŭg) *tr.v.* **slugged, slug•ging, slugs.** To strike hard, especially with the fist or a bat. —*n.* A hard blow, as with the fist or a baseball bat. [First written down in 1862 in Modern English, possibly from *slug*, bullet.] —**slug′ger** *n.*

slug•gard (slŭg′ərd) *n.* A lazy idle person.

slug•gish (slŭg′ĭsh) *adj.* **1.** Showing little activity or movement; slow: *a sluggish stream.* **2.** Lacking alertness, vigor, or energy: *a sluggish response.* **3.** Slow to perform or respond. —**slug′gish•ly** *adv.* —**slug′gish•ness** *n.*

sluice (slo͞os) *n.* **1.a.** An artificial channel for conducting water, with a gate to regulate the flow. **b.** The gate used in such a channel; a floodgate. **2.** A body of water confined and controlled by such a gate. **3.** A long inclined trough, as for moving logs or separating gold ore. —*tr.v.* **sluiced, sluic•ing, sluic•es. 1.** To flood or drench with a sudden flow of water. **2.** To draw off or let out by a sluice. **3.** To wash with water flowing from a sluice: *sluice sand for gold.*

slum (slŭm) *n.* An overcrowded urban area marked by squalor and poor housing conditions.

slum•ber (slŭm′bər) *intr.v.* **slum•bered, slum•ber•ing, slum•bers. 1.** To sleep or doze. **2.** To be calm or inactive: *The city slumbers.* —*n.* **1.** Sleep. **2.** A state of inactivity or dormancy. —**slum′ber•er** *n.*

slum•ber•ous (slŭm′bər əs) or **slum•brous** (slŭm′brəs) *adj.* **1.** Sleepy; drowsy. **2.a.** Suggesting or resembling sleep. **b.** Quiet; tranquil. **3.** Causing or inducing sleep; soporific. —**slum′ber•ous•ly** *adv.* —**slum′ber•ous•ness** *n.*

slump (slŭmp) *intr.v.* **slumped, slump•ing, slumps. 1.** To fall or sink heavily; collapse: *She slumped onto the sofa.* **2.** To droop or slouch: *The new recruits slumped outside their barracks.* **3.** To decline or sink suddenly: *Business slumped badly during the spring.* —*n.* **1.** A sudden decline: *a stock market slump.* **2.** A drooping or slouching posture. **3.** An extended period of poor performance, especially in a sport: *a slump in his batting average.*

slung (slŭng) *v.* Past tense and past participle of **sling.**

slunk (slŭngk) *v.* A past tense and a past participle of **slink.**

slur (slûr) *tr.v.* **slurred, slur•ring, slurs. 1.** To pronounce carelessly or indistinctly: *slur words.* **2.** To speak badly of; disparage. **3.** To pass over or treat carelessly. **4.** To sing or play (a series of musical tones) smoothly and without a break. —*n.* **1.** A discourteous or disparaging remark. **2.** A slurred sound. **3.a.** A curved line connecting a series of notes on a musical score to indicate that they are to be played or sung smoothly. **b.** A passage played or sung in this manner.

slurp (slûrp) *tr. & intr.v.* **slurped, slurp•ing, slurps.** To eat or drink noisily. —*n.* A sucking noise made when eating or drinking.

slush (slŭsh) *n.* **1.** Partially melted snow or ice. **2.** Soft mud; mire. **3.** Sentimental speech or writing. —**slush′i•ness** *n.* —**slush′y** *adj.*

slut (slŭt) *n.* **1.** A woman considered immoral and sexually promiscuous. **2.** A dirty untidy woman.

sly (slī) *adj.* **sli•er** (slī′ər), **sli•est** (slī′ĕst) also **sly•er, sly•est. 1.** Clever or cunning. **2.** Secretive or dishonest: *a sly trick.* **3.** Playfully mischievous; roguish: *a sly wink.* —***idiom.*** **on the sly.** In a way intended to escape notice; secretly: *had another job on the sly.* —**sly′ness** *n.*

Sm The symbol for the element **samarium.**

smack[1] (smăk) *v.* **smacked, smack•ing, smacks.** —*tr.* **1.** To press together and open (the lips) quickly and noisily, as in eating. **2.** To kiss noisily. **3.** To slap or strike with a loud sound. —*intr.* **1.** To make or give a smack. **2.** To collide loudly and sharply: *The notebook smacked against the floor.* —*n.* **1.** The sound made by smacking the lips. **2.** A noisy kiss. **3.** A sharp blow or loud slap. —*adv.* **1.** With a smack: *She flopped smack on her back.* **2.** Directly: *We're smack in the middle of a slump.* [First written down in 1557 in Modern English.]

smack[2] (smăk) *n.* **1.** A distinctive flavor or taste. **2.** A suggestion or trace. —*intr.v.* **smacked, smack•ing, smacks. 1.** To have a distinctive flavor or taste. **2.** To give an indication or suggestion: *This plan does not smack of success.* [First written down before 1000 in Old English and spelled *smæc*.]

smack[3] (smăk) *n.* A fore-and-aft-rigged fishing vessel, especially one used to transport fish to market. [First written down in 1611 in Modern English, from Dutch or Low German *smak*, from *smakken*, to fling, dash.]

small (smôl) *adj.* **small•er, small•est. 1.** Being below the average in size, number, quantity, or extent; little: *a small car; a small business.* See Synonyms at **little. 2.** Limited in importance; trivial: *a small matter.* **3.** Carrying on an activity in a limited way: *a small farmer.* **4.** Not fully grown; very young: *a*

sluice

ă	pat	oi	boy
ā	pay	ou	out
âr	care	o͝o	took
ä	father	o͞o	boot
ĕ	pet	ŭ	cut
ē	be	ûr	urge
ĭ	pit	th	thin
ī	pie	*th*	this
îr	pier	hw	whoop
ŏ	pot	zh	vision
ō	toe	ə	about
ô	paw	N	*French* bon

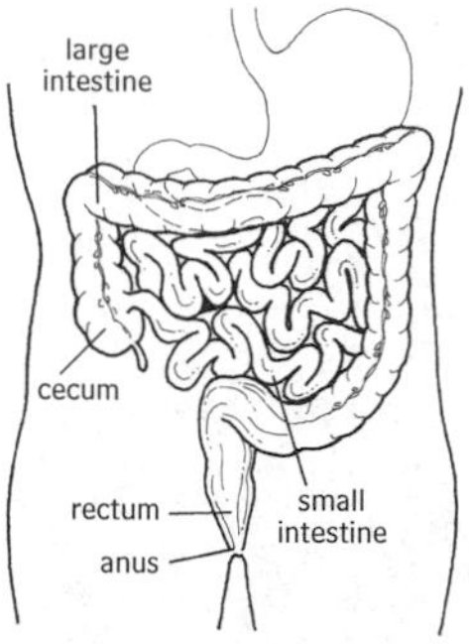

small intestine

Bessie Smith

Joseph Smith
Portrait executed in 1971
by Adrian Lamb (1901–1988)

small child. **5.** Narrow in outlook; petty: *a small mind.* **6.** Soft; low: *a small voice.* —*n.* Something that is smaller and especially narrower than the rest: *the small of the back.* **—small′ish** *adj.* **—small′ness** *n.*

small arms *pl.n.* Firearms that can be carried in the hand.

small calorie *n.* A unit of heat equal to the amount of heat needed to raise the temperature of one gram of water one degree Celsius.

small change *n.* **1.** Coins of low denomination. **2.** Something of little value or significance.

small fry *n. Informal.* Young or small children.

small intestine *n.* The part of the alimentary canal in which digestion is completed and nutrients are absorbed by the blood, extending from the outlet of the stomach to the beginning of the large intestine. The human small intestine consists of the duodenum, the jejunum, and the ileum.

small-mind•ed (smôl′mīn′dĭd) *adj.* **1.** Having a narrow or selfish attitude. **2.** Characterized by pettiness or selfishness. **—small′-mind′ed•ly** *adv.* **—small′-mind′ed•ness** *n.*

small•pox (smôl′pŏks′) *n.* A serious, often fatal, highly infectious viral disease having symptoms that include chills, fever, and headache, followed by the eruption of pimples that form pus and develop into pockmarks.

small talk *n.* Casual or ordinary conversation.

smart (smärt) *adj.* **smart•er, smart•est. 1.** Intelligent, clever, or bright: *a smart student.* **2.** Shrewd in dealing with others: *a smart business person.* **3.** Rudely flippant; impertinent: *That's enough of your smart talk!* **4.** Quick or energetic in movement: *a smart pace.* **5.** Fashionable; elegant: *a smart new coat.* —*intr.v.* **smart•ed, smart•ing, smarts.** To cause or feel a sharp stinging pain: *My leg began to smart from the hornet's sting.* —*n.* A stinging mental or physical pain. [First written down before 1023 in Old English and spelled *smeart*, stinging.] **—smart′ly** *adv.* **—smart′ness** *n.*

Synonyms: **smart, intelligent, bright, brilliant, intellectual.** These adjectives all mean talented in using one's mind. **Smart** means able to learn quickly and often also able to look out for oneself: *Judy was smart to tune up her bicycle before the long ride.* **Intelligent** means able to handle new situations and problems and good at figuring things out: *Only the most intelligent students can keep up with the teacher's rapid pace.* **Bright** means able to learn quickly and easily: *He is so bright, he learned to play chess in one hour.* **Brilliant** means unusually and impressively intelligent: *The most brilliant minds in the country have gathered for this meeting.* **Intellectual** means able to understand difficult or abstract concepts: *Her intellectual abilities help her to appreciate difficult poetry.*

smart al•eck (ăl′ĭk) *n. Informal.* A person regarded as obnoxiously assertive or conceited. [First written down in 1865 in American English and spelled *smart Aleck*, perhaps after *Aleck* Hoag, 19th-century American confidence man and thief.]

smart bomb *n.* A bomb that can be guided by radio waves or a laser beam to its target.

smart•en (smär′tn) *v.* **smart•ened, smart•en•ing, smart•ens.** —*tr.* **1.** To improve in appearance; spruce up. **2.** To make quicker: *smarten the pace.* —*intr.* To make oneself smart or smarter.

smash (smăsh) *v.* **smashed, smash•ing, smash•es.** —*tr.* **1.** To break (something) into pieces noisily and violently; shatter: *smash an egg.* **2.** To throw, dash, or strike (something) violently and suddenly: *The wind smashed the tree into the house.* **3.** To destroy or crush completely: *The troops smashed the rebellion.* —*intr.* **1.** To strike or collide noisily and violently: *The car smashed into the guard rail.* **2.** To break into pieces: *The vase smashed on the floor.* **3.** To be destroyed or ruined: *a bank that smashed up during the Depression.* —*n.* **1.** The act or sound of smashing. **2.** A collision; a crash. **3.** *Informal.* A total success: *The new musical proved to be a smash.* **—smash′er** *n.*

smash•ing (smăsh′ĭng) *adj. Informal.* Unusually impressive or fine; wonderful: *a smashing time at the party.*

smash•up (smăsh′ŭp′) *n.* **1.** A total collapse; a failure. **2.** A serious collision between vehicles.

smat•ter•ing (smăt′ər ĭng) *n.* Superficial or piecemeal knowledge: *He has a smattering of Latin.*

smear (smîr) *v.* **smeared, smear•ing, smears.** —*tr.* **1.** To spread, cover, or stain with a sticky, greasy, or dirty substance: *smeared the wall with plaster.* **2.** To put (a sticky, greasy, or dirty substance) on a surface; apply: *I smeared suntan lotion on my arms.* **3.** To blacken or destroy the reputation of: *The ad campaign smeared the candidate.* —*intr.* To be or become stained or dirtied. —*n.* **1.** A stain or mark made by smearing. **2.** An attempt to destroy someone's reputation; slander. **3.** A substance or preparation placed on a slide for microscopic study.

smell (smĕl) *v.* **smelled** or **smelt** (smĕlt), **smell•ing, smells.** —*tr.* To detect or notice the odor of (something) by means of the nerves located in the nose: *smell smoke.* —*intr.* **1.a.** To have or give off an odor. **b.** To have or give off an unpleasant odor; stink. **2.** To use the sense of smell; detect the scent of something. —*n.* **1.** The sense by which odors are perceived; the ability to smell. **2.** The quality that permits something to be perceived by the sense of smell; odor. See Synonyms at **scent. 3.** The act or an instance of smelling. **4.** A distinctive quality; an aura or a feeling: *This plan has a smell of success.*

smell•ing salts (smĕl′ĭng) *pl.n. (used with a singular or plural verb).* Any of several preparations based on ammonia, sniffed to relieve faintness and dizziness.

smell•y (smĕl′ē) *adj.* **smell•i•er, smell•i•est.** *Informal.* Having an unpleasant or offensive odor.

smelt[1] (smĕlt) *v.* **smelt•ed, smelt•ing, smelts.** —*tr.* To melt or fuse (ores) in order to extract the metals they contain. —*intr.* To undergo such melting or fusing, as an ore does. [First written down in 1543 in Modern English, from Middle Dutch or Middle Low German *smelten.*]

smelt[2] (smĕlt) *n., pl.* **smelts** or **smelt.** Any of various small, silvery, saltwater or freshwater fishes used as food. [First written down before 800 in Old English.]

smelt[3] (smĕlt) *v.* A past tense and a past participle of **smell.**

smelt•er (smĕl′tər) *n.* **1.a.** An apparatus or device for smelting ore. **b.** An establishment for smelting. **2.** A person whose work is smelting.

smid•gen also **smid•geon** (smĭj′ən) *n.* A very small quantity; a bit: *Add a smidgen of nutmeg.*

smile (smīl) *n.* A facial expression formed by an upward curving of the corners of the mouth and indicating pleasure, affection, amusement, or contempt. —*v.* **smiled, smil•ing, smiles.** —*intr.* **1.** To have or form a smile. **2.** To express favor or approval: *The committee smiled on our proposal.* —*tr.* To express with a smile: *He smiled his agreement.* **—smil′er** *n.* **—smil′ing•ly** *adv.*

smirch (smûrch) *tr.v.* **smirched, smirch•ing, smirch•es. 1.** To soil, stain, or dirty. **2.** To dishonor or disgrace: *smirch the family's reputation.* —*n.* Something that smirches; a blot or stain.

smirk (smûrk) *intr.v.* **smirked, smirk•ing, smirks.** To smile in an annoying manner that expresses too much satisfaction in oneself. —*n.* A smile made in such a way. **—smirk′er** *n.*

smite (smīt) *tr.v.* **smote** (smōt), **smit•ten** (**smĭt′**n) or **smote, smit•ing, smites. 1.** To hit with a heavy blow: *The sword smote the shield.* **2.** To attack, damage, or destroy by or as if by blows. **3.** To affect or afflict suddenly: *He was smitten with remorse.* **—smit′er** *n.*

smith (smĭth) *n.* A person who forges and shapes metal: *a blacksmith.*

Smith (smĭth), **Bessie.** 1894?–1937. American singer who became a leading jazz and blues singer in the 1920's.

Smith, John. 1580?–1631. English colonist whose accounts of his explorations in Virginia and New England aided later explorers and colonists.

Smith, Joseph. 1805–1844. American religious leader who founded (1830) the Church of Jesus Christ of Latter-day Saints.

smith•er•eens (smĭ*th*′ə **rēnz′**) *pl.n. Informal.* Splintered pieces; bits: *The vase smashed to smithereens.*

smith•y (**smĭth′**ē *or* smĭ*th*′ē) *n., pl.* **smith•ies.** The shop of a blacksmith; a forge.

smit•ten (**smĭt′**n) *v.* A past participle of **smite.**

smock (smŏk) *n.* A long loose garment resembling a coat, worn over other clothes to protect them. *—tr. v.* **smocked, smock•ing, smocks. 1.** To clothe in a smock. **2.** To decorate with smocking.

smock•ing (**smŏk′**ĭng) *n.* Needlework decoration of small regularly spaced gathers stitched into a honeycomb pattern.

smog (smŏg *or* smôg) *n.* Fog that has become polluted with smoke and chemical pollutants, usually present in large urban or industrial areas. [First written down in 1905 in Modern English : *sm(oke)* + *(f)og*.] **—smog′gy** *adj.*

smoke (smōk) *n.* **1.** A mixture of carbon dioxide, water vapor, and various other gases, usually containing small suspended particles of soot or other solids and resulting from incomplete burning of materials such as wood or coal. **2.** A mixture consisting of fine particles suspended in a gas. **3.** The act of smoking tobacco. **4.** *Informal.* A cigarette or other form of tobacco that is smoked. *—v.* **smoked, smok•ing, smokes.** *—intr.* **1.** To draw in and exhale smoke from a cigarette, cigar, or pipe. **2.** To emit smoke, especially excessively. *—tr.* **1.** To draw in and exhale smoke from (a cigarette, cigar, or pipe). **2.** To preserve (meat or fish) by exposing to wood smoke. **3.** To expose to smoke or fumigate: *smoked the wasps' nest.* ***—idiom.*** **smoke out.** To force (someone or something) out of a place of hiding by or as if by the use of smoke.

smoke•house (**smōk′**hous′) *n.* An enclosure in which meat or fish is cured by exposing it to smoke.

smoke•less (**smōk′**lĭs) *adj.* Producing or giving off little or no smoke.

smok•er (**smō′**kər) *n.* **1.** A person who smokes tobacco. **2.** A railroad car in which smoking is permitted. **3.** An informal social gathering for men.

smoke screen or **smoke•screen** (**smōk′**skrēn′) *n.* **1.** A mass of artificial smoke used to conceal military operations from an enemy. **2.** An action or a statement used to conceal actual plans or intentions.

smoke•stack (**smōk′**stăk′) *n.* A large chimney or vertical pipe through which smoke and waste gases and vapors are discharged.

smok•y (**smō′**kē) *adj.* **smok•i•er, smok•i•est. 1.** Producing or giving off a large amount of smoke: *a smoky furnace.* **2.** Mixed or filled with smoke: *smoky air.* **3.** Resembling smoke in smell, taste, or appearance. **—smok′i•ness** *n.*

smol•der also **smoul•der** (**smōl′**dər) *intr.v.* **smol•dered, smol•der•ing, smol•ders** also **smoul•dered, smoul•der•ing, smoul•ders. 1.** To burn with little smoke and no flame. **2.** To show signs of repressed anger or hatred: *He sat, still smoldering from the insult.* **3.** To exist in a restrained state: *Revolution smoldered among the common people.*

smooth (smo͞o*th*) *adj.* **smooth•er, smooth•est. 1.** Having a surface free from irregularities; not rough; even: *smooth skin.* **2.** Having a fine consistency or texture: *the smooth side of the fabric.* **3.** Having an even or gentle motion or movement: *a smooth ride.* **4.** Serene; mild: *a smooth manner.* **5.** Flattering; ingratiating: *a smooth talker.* **6.** Having no obstructions or difficulties: *a smooth operation.* See Synonyms at **easy.** *—v.* **smoothed, smooth•ing, smoothes.** *—tr.* **1.** To make (something) smooth: *smooth out the wrinkles in a dress.* **2.** To make calm; soothe: *He smoothed over our disagreement.* **3.** To make less crude; refine. *—intr.* To become smooth. **—smooth′ly** *adv.* **—smooth′ness** *n.*

smooth•bore also **smooth bore** (**smo͞o*th*′bôr′**) *adj.* Having no rifling within the barrel of a firearm. *—n.* A firearm having no rifling.

smor•gas•bord (**smôr′**gəs bôrd′) *n.* A buffet meal with a variety of dishes.

smote (smōt) *v.* Past tense and a past participle of **smite.**

smoth•er (**smŭ*th*′**ər) *v.* **smoth•ered, smoth•er•ing, smoth•ers.** *—tr.* **1.** To cause (someone) to die from lack of oxygen; suffocate. **2.** To cause (a fire) to go out because of lack of oxygen. **3.** To cover (food) with another food: *smother the hotdog with onions.* **4.** To conceal or hide: *smothered the facts.* **5.** To lavish attention on (someone). *—intr.* **1.** To suffocate. **2.** To be concealed or hidden.

smoul•der (**smōl′**dər) *v.* Variant of **smolder.**

smudge (smŭj) *v.* **smudged, smudg•ing, smudg•es.** *—tr.* **1.** To smear or blur: *The rain smudged the paint.* **2.** To fill (an orchard or other planted area) with smoke from a smudge pot in order to prevent damage from insects or frost. *—intr.* To become smudged. *—n.* **1.** A blotch or smear. **2.** A smoky fire used against insects or frost. **—smudg′y** *adj.*

smudge pot *n.* A container in which oil or some other smoky fuel is burned to protect an orchard from insects or frost.

smug (smŭg) *adj.* **smug•ger, smug•gest.** Satisfied or contented while having little concern for others: *had a smug sense of well-being.* **—smug′ly** *adv.* **—smug′ness** *n.*

smug•gle (**smŭg′**əl) *v.* **smug•gled, smug•gling, smug•gles.** *—tr.* **1.** To bring or take by stealth. **2.** To import or export without paying custom charges. *—intr.* To engage in smuggling. **—smug′gler** *n.*

smut (smŭt) *n.* **1.** A smudge made by dirt, smoke, or soot. **2.** Obscene material, such as pictures or writing. **3.a.** Any of various plant diseases caused by parasitic fungi and resulting in the formation of black powdery masses on the affected plant parts. **b.** A fungus that causes such a disease. **—smut′ty** *adj.*

Smyr•na (**smûr′**nə). Izmir.

Sn The symbol for the element **tin** (sense 1).

snack (snăk) *n.* **1.** A quick light meal. **2.** Food eaten between meals. *—intr.v.* **snacked, snack•ing, snacks.** To eat a snack.

snaf•fle (**snăf′**əl) *n.* A bit for a horse, consisting of two bars joined at the center. *—tr.v.* **snaf•fled, snaf•fling, snaf•fles.** To put on or control with a snaffle.

snag (snăg) *n.* **1.** A sharp, rough, or jagged projection. **2.** A tree or part of a tree that sticks out above the surface in a body of water. **3.** A break, pull, or tear in fabric. **4.** An unforeseen or hidden obstacle. *—v.* **snagged, snag•ging, snags.** *—tr.* To catch, damage, or destroy by or as if by a snag: *snagged my coat on a branch.* *—intr.* To be damaged by a snag.

snail (snāl) *n.* **1.** Any of numerous slow-moving,

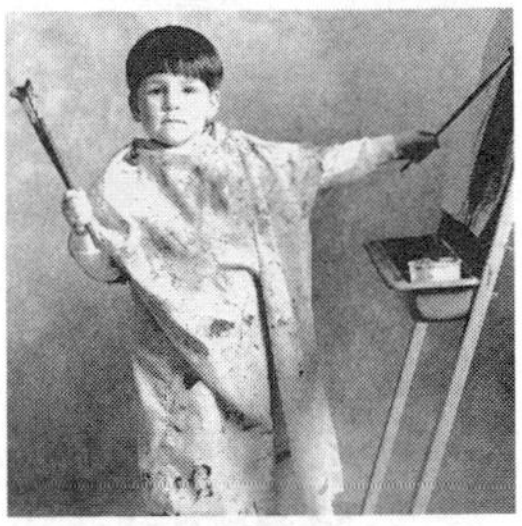

smock

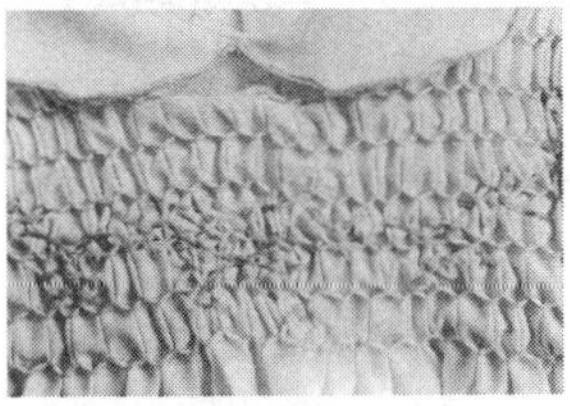

smocking

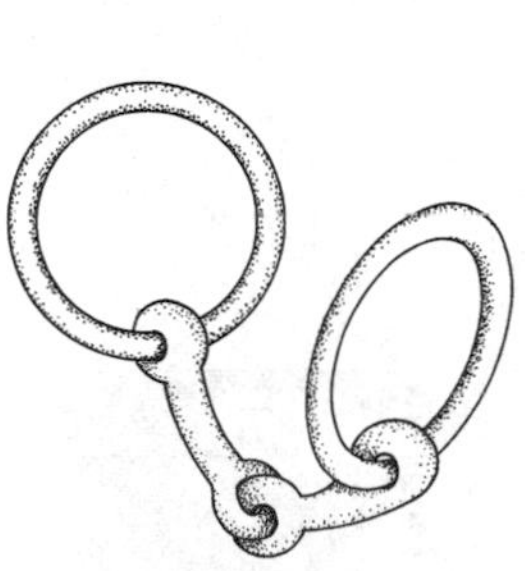

snaffle

snail

ă	**pat**	oi	**boy**
ā	**pay**	ou	**out**
âr	**care**	o͝o	**took**
ä	**father**	o͞o	**boot**
ĕ	**pet**	ŭ	**cut**
ē	**be**	ûr	**urge**
ĭ	**pit**	th	**thin**
ī	**pie**	*th*	**this**
îr	**pier**	hw	**whoop**
ŏ	**pot**	zh	**vision**
ō	**toe**	ə	**about**
ô	**paw**	N	*French* **bon**

snapdragon

snare drum

Usage: sneak

The word **sneak** has two past tense and past participle forms: **sneaked** and **snuck**. When you write or speak in a more formal style, as in your school essays and tests, it is best to use the original past tense form **sneaked**.

soft-bodied land or water animals having a coiled spiral shell. **2.** A slow-moving, lazy, or sluggish person. [First written down before 800 in Old English and spelled *snægl.*]

snake (snāk) *n.* **1.** Any of numerous reptiles having a long narrow body and no legs. Some snakes have venom glands and sharp fangs that can give a poisonous bite. **2.** A sneaky or untrustworthy person. **3.** A long flexible wire used for cleaning drains. [First written down about 1000 in Old English and spelled *snaca.*]

snake in the grass *n., pl.* **snakes in the grass.** A person who is sneaky or untrustworthy.

snake•root (**snāk′**ro͞ot′ *or* **snāk′**ro͝ot′) *n.* Any of various plants having roots believed to cure the bite of a snake.

snake•skin (**snāk′**skĭn′) *n.* The skin of a snake, especially when prepared as leather.

snak•y (**snā′**kē) *adj.* **snak•i•er, snak•i•est. 1.** Relating to or characteristic of snakes. **2.** Having the form or movement of a snake; serpentine. **3.** Overrun with snakes. **4.** Treacherous; sly. **—snak′i•ly** *adv.* **—snak′i•ness** *n.*

snap (snăp) *v.* **snapped, snap•ping, snaps.** *—intr.* **1.** To make a sharp cracking sound: *The burning log snapped in the fireplace.* **2.** To break suddenly with a sharp sound: *The twigs snapped underfoot.* **3.** To break under pressure or tension: *The rope snapped.* **4.** To bite, seize, or grasp at suddenly and eagerly: *The dog snapped at the bone.* **5.** To speak abruptly or sharply: *She snapped at him.* **6.** To move swiftly and smartly: *The soldiers snapped to attention.* **7.** To open or close with a sharp sound: *The lid snapped shut.* *—tr.* **1.** To bite or snatch at with the teeth. **2.** To break with a sharp sound. **3.** To cause to make a cracking sound: *snap one's fingers.* **4.** To close or shut with a sharp sound: *snap the lid on the jar.* **5.** To utter sharply or abruptly. **6.** To take (a photograph). **7.** In football, to put (the ball) in play by passing it from the line of scrimmage to a player in the backfield. *—n.* **1.** A sharp cracking sound. **2.** A sudden breaking of something under strain. **3.** A fastener that closes and opens with a snapping sound. **4.** A thin crisp cookie. **5.** A brief spell of cold weather. **6.** *Informal.* An easy task. **7.** A snapshot. *—adj.* **1.** Made or done on the spur of the moment: *a snap decision.* **2.** *Informal.* Simple; easy. ***—idiom.*** **snap up.** To acquire quickly: *snapped up the tickets.*

snap•drag•on (**snăp′**drăg′ən) *n.* Any of several garden plants having clusters of variously colored flowers with a narrow two-lipped opening.

snap•per (**snăp′**ər) *n.* **1.** A person or thing that snaps. **2.** Any of numerous tropical and semitropical ocean fishes used as food, as the red snapper of southern Atlantic waters. **3.** A snapping turtle.

snap•ping turtle (**snăp′**ĭng) *n.* Any of several large American freshwater turtles having a rough shell and powerful hooked jaws.

snap•pish (**snăp′**ĭsh) *adj.* **1.** Likely to snap or bite, as a dog. **2.** Sharp in speech; irritable; curt. **—snap′pish•ly** *adv.* **—snap′pish•ness** *n.*

snap•py (**snăp′**ē) *adj.* **snap•pi•er, snap•pi•est. 1.** *Informal.* Lively; brisk: *a snappy rhythm.* **2.** *Informal.* Smart or chic in appearance: *a snappy dresser.* **3.** Irritable; snappish: *snappy because of lack of sleep.* **—snap′pi•ly** *adv.* **—snap′pi•ness** *n.*

snap•shot (**snăp′**shŏt′) *n.* A photograph taken with a small hand-held camera.

snare[1] (snâr) *n.* **1.** A trapping device, usually consisting of a noose, used for capturing birds and small animals. **2.** Something that entangles unsuspecting people: *The agents bought stolen goods as part of a snare to catch thieves.* *—tr.v.* **snared, snar•ing, snares.** To trap with or as if with a snare: *snare a rabbit; snare a thief.* [First written down before 1100 in Old English and spelled *snearu.*]

snare[2] (snâr) *n.* **1.** Any of the wires or cords stretched across the lower head of a snare drum to give it a sharp rattling tone. **2.** A snare drum. [First written down in 1688 in Modern English, probably from Middle Dutch *snāre,* string.]

snare drum *n.* A small double-headed drum having a snare or snares stretched across the lower head to make the tone rattling and sharp.

snarl[1] (snärl) *v.* **snarled, snarl•ing, snarls.** *—intr.* **1.** To growl angrily or threateningly while baring the teeth. **2.** To speak angrily or threateningly. *—tr.* To utter with anger or hostility: *snarled an answer.* *—n.* **1.** An angry or threatening growl, often made with bared teeth. **2.** A sound or tone of voice resembling this: *He made his demands in a grumpy snarl.* [First written down in 1589 in Modern English and spelled *snarle,* from *snar.*]

snarl[2] (snärl) *n.* **1.** A tangled mass, as of hair or yarn. **2.** A confused, complicated, or tangled situation: *a traffic snarl.* *—v.* **snarled, snarl•ing, snarls.** *—intr.* To become tangled: *My fishing line snarled as I made a cast.* *—tr.* **1.** To tangle: *The kitten snarled the wool.* **2.** To confuse: *Snow snarled the morning commute.* [First written down before 1387 in Middle English and spelled *snarle,* trap, probably from *snare.*]

snatch (snăch) *v.* **snatched, snatch•ing, snatch•es.** *—tr.* **1.** To grasp or grab hastily or eagerly: *snatch an apple off the tree.* **2.** To take unlawfully: *snatch a purse.* *—intr.* To make grasping motions: *snatched at the rope.* *—n.* **1.** The act of snatching. **2.** A small amount; a fragment: *a snatch of an old song.* **—snatch′er** *n.*

sneak (snēk) *v.* **sneaked** also **snuck** (snŭk), **sneak•ing, sneaks.** *—intr.* **1.** To go or move in a quiet stealthy way: *She sneaked onto one of the boats.* **2.** To behave in a cowardly underhand manner: *Don't sneak around.* *—tr.* To move, give, or take in a quiet stealthy manner: *sneaked the photo into his pocket; sneak a peek at the present.* *—n.* **1.** A person regarded as cowardly or underhanded. **2.** A quiet stealthy movement or action. —See Note.

sneak•er (**snē′**kər) *n.* A canvas sport shoe with a soft, flat rubber sole.

sneak•ing (**snē′**kĭng) *adj.* **1.** Acting in a stealthy furtive way. **2.** Not known or expressed: *a sneaking ambition to take over.* **3.** Gradually growing or persistent: *a sneaking suspicion.* **—sneak′ing•ly** *adv.*

sneak•y (**snē′**kē) *adj.* **sneak•i•er, sneak•i•est.** Like a sneak; sly; furtive: *A sneaky cat ate my goldfish.* **—sneak′i•ly** *adv.* **—sneak′i•ness** *n.*

sneer (snîr) *n.* **1.** A scornful facial expression made by raising one corner of the upper lip slightly. **2.** A scornful expression, sound, or statement. *—v.* **sneered, sneer•ing, sneers.** *—tr.* To utter with a sneer. *—intr.* To show contempt or scorn with a sneer: *fairly sneered at my suggestion.* [First written down in 1707 in Modern English, from Middle English *sneren,* to mock, from Old English *fnǣran,* to breathe heavily.] **—sneer′er** *n.*

sneeze (snēz) *intr.v.* **sneezed, sneez•ing, sneez•es.** To force air from the nose and mouth in an involuntary convulsive action that results from irritation of the mucous membranes of the nose. *—n.* The act or the sound of sneezing. [First written down about 1000 in Old English and spelled *fnēosan.*] **—sneez′er** *n.*

snick•er (**snĭk′**ər) *intr.v.* **snick•ered, snick•er•ing, snick•ers.** To utter a snide, partly stifled laugh. *—n.* A snide, partly stifled laugh.

snide (snīd) *adj.* **snid•er, snid•est.** Sarcastic, disparaging, or cruel: *a snide remark.* **—snide′ly** *adv.*

sniff (snĭf) *v.* **sniffed, sniff•ing, sniffs.** *—intr.* **1.** To inhale a short audible breath through the nose, as in smelling something: *He sniffed at the jar.* **2.** To regard something with contempt or scorn: *She sniffed at those who knew less than she.* *—tr.* **1.** To inhale (something) through the nose: *sniffed the cold air.* **2.** To smell, as in enjoyment or investigation: *sniffed the roses.* **3.** To perceive or detect by or as if by sniffing: *The dog sniffed the bear's trail.* *—n.* **1.** The act or the sound of sniffing. **2.** Something noticed or detected by or as if by sniffing: *a sniff of perfume; a sniff of scandal.*

snif•fle (snĭf′əl) *intr.v.* **snif•fled, snif•fling, snif•fles.** To breathe noisily through an inflamed or partially blocked nose, as when suffering from a head cold. *—n.* **1.** The act or sound of sniffling. **2. sniffles.** A condition, such as a head cold, that makes a person sniffle.

snig•ger (snĭg′ər) *n.* A snicker.

snip (snĭp) *tr.v.* **snipped, snip•ping, snips.** To cut or clip (something) with short quick strokes. *—n.* **1.** A small piece cut or clipped off. **2.** An instance of snipping or the sound so produced. **3. snips.** *(used with a singular or plural verb).* Hand shears used to cut sheet metal.

snipe (snīp) *n., pl.* **snipe** or **snipes.** Any of various brownish wading birds having a long bill. *—intr.v.* **sniped, snip•ing, snipes. 1.** To shoot at others from a hiding place. **2.** To hunt for snipe.

snip•er (snī′pər) *n.* A person who shoots at others from a hiding place.

snip•pet (snĭp′ĭt) *n.* A tidbit or morsel.

snip•py (snĭp′ē) *adj.* **snip•pi•er, snip•pi•est.** *Informal.* **1.** Impertinent or insolent. **2.** Fragmentary.

snitch (snĭch) *Slang. v.* **snitched, snitch•ing, snitch•es.** *—tr.* To steal (something of little value): *snitch candy.* *—intr.* To tell on someone; turn informer: *snitched on his brother.* *—n.* **1.** A thief. **2.** An informer. **—snitch′er** *n.*

sniv•el (snĭv′əl) *intr.v.* **sniv•eled, sniv•el•ing, sniv•els** or **sniv•elled, sniv•el•ling, sniv•els. 1.** To complain or whine tearfully. **2.** To sniffle. **—sniv′el•er, sniv′el•ler** *n.*

snob (snŏb) *n.* **1.** A person who despises or ignores those he or she considers inferior. **2.** A person who is convinced of his or her superiority in matters of taste or intellect.

snob•ber•y (snŏb′ə rē) *n., pl.* **snob•ber•ies.** Snobbish behavior.

snob•bish (snŏb′ĭsh) *adj.* Of, befitting, or characteristic of a snob; pretentious: *a snobbish attitude.* **—snob′bish•ly** *adv.* **—snob′bish•ness** *n.*

snood (sno͞od) *n.* A small net cap worn on the head to keep the hair in place.

snoop (sno͞op) *intr.v.* **snooped, snoop•ing, snoops.** To look, pry, or search in a sneaky manner. *—n.* A person who snoops. **—snoop′er** *n.*

snoop•y (sno͞o′pē) *adj.* **snoop•i•er, snoop•i•est.** Likely to snoopy; nosy. See Synonyms at **curious.**

snoot•y (sno͞o′tē) *adj.* **snoot•i•er, snoot•i•est.** *Informal.* **1.** Snobbishly aloof; haughty. **2.** High-class; exclusive. **—snoot′i•ly** *adv.* **—snoot′i•ness** *n.*

snooze (sno͞oz) *intr.v.* **snoozed, snooz•ing, snooz•es.** To take a light nap; doze. *—n.* A light nap.

snore (snôr) *intr.v.* **snored, snor•ing, snores.** To breathe through the nose and mouth while sleeping, making snorting noises caused by vibrations of the soft palate. *—n.* The act or the sound of snoring. [First written down about 1400 in Middle English and spelled *snoren,* to snort, from Old English *fnora,* sneezing.] **—snor′er** *n.*

snor•kel (snôr′kəl) *n.* **1.** A breathing apparatus used by skin divers, consisting of a long tube curved at one end and fitted with a mouthpiece. **2.** A retractable tube that can be extended from a submarine, allowing it to draw in fresh air and expel waste gases while submerged. *—intr.v.* **snor•keled, snor•kel•ing, snor•kels.** To swim using a snorkel. [First written down in 1944 in Modern English and spelled *Schnorkel,* from German *Schnorchel.*]

snort (snôrt) *n.* **1.** A rough noisy sound made by breathing forcefully through the nostrils, as that made by a horse or pig. **2.** A sound resembling this: *the snort of a steam engine.* *—v.* **snort•ed, snort•ing, snorts.** *—intr.* **1.** To breathe noisily and forcefully through the nostrils: *The frightened horses reared and snorted.* **2.** To make a sound resembling a snort. **3.** To make a noise expressive of ridicule, disbelief, or contempt. *—tr.* To express with a snort: *She snorted her disapproval.* **—snort′er** *n.*

snout (snout) *n.* **1.** The projecting nose, jaws, or front part of the head of an animal. **2.** A spout or nozzle shaped like such a projection. [First written down about 1225 in Middle English and spelled *snute.*] **—snout′ed** *adj.*

snow (snō) *n.* **1.** Crystals of ice that form from water vapor in the atmosphere and fall to earth. **2.** A falling of snow; a snowstorm. **3.** Specks of white that appear on a television screen as a result of weak reception of the video signal. *—v.* **snowed, snow•ing, snows.** *—intr.* To fall to the earth as snow. *—tr.* To isolate, block, or cover with or as if with snow: *We were snowed in.* ***—idiom.* snow under.** To overwhelm: *I was snowed under with work.* [First written down before 830 in Old English and spelled *snāw.*]

snow•ball (snō′bôl′) *n.* **1.** A mass of soft wet snow packed into a ball that can be thrown. **2.** Any of several shrubs having large rounded clusters of white flowers. *—intr.v.* **snow•balled, snow•ball•ing, snow•balls.** To grow rapidly, as in importance or size: *The minor problems snowballed into a huge mess.*

snow•bird (snō′bûrd′) *n.* Any of several birds, such as the junco, common in snowy regions.

snow blindness *n.* A usually temporary loss of vision and irritation of the eyes caused by exposure of the eyes to bright sunlight reflected from snow or ice.

snow•bound (snō′bound′) *adj.* Confined to one place because of heavy snow: *snowbound travelers.*

snow bunting *n.* A bird of northern regions, having predominantly white winter feathers.

snow•cap (snō′kăp′) *n.* A cap of snow, as on a mountaintop. **—snow′capped′** *adj.*

snow•drift (snō′drĭft′) *n.* A large mass of snow that has been piled up by the wind.

snow•drop (snō′drŏp′) *n.* Any of several plants having drooping white flowers that bloom early in spring.

snow•fall (snō′fôl′) *n.* **1.** A falling of snow. **2.** The amount of snow in a given area over a given period of time.

snow•flake (snō′flāk′) *n.* A single crystal or flake of snow.

snow leopard *n.* A large wild cat of the mountains of central Asia, having long, thick, whitish fur with dark spots.

snow line *n.* **1.** The boundary marking the lowest altitude at which a given area is always covered with snow, as the top of a mountain. **2.** The varying boundary marking the lowest latitude around the polar regions at which there is snow cover.

snow•man (sno′măn′) *n.* A figure of a person made from packed and shaped snow, usually formed by piling large snowballs on top of each other.

snow•mo•bile (snō′mō bēl′) *n.* A vehicle with runners resembling skis that is used for traveling over ice and snow.

snow•plow (snō′plou′) *n.* **1.** A vehicle or machine

snorkel

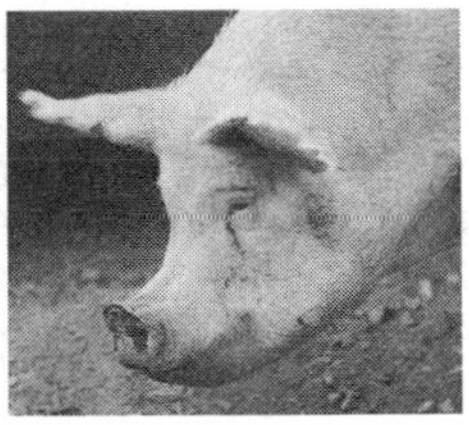
snout
Of a pig

ă	pat	oi	boy
ā	pay	ou	out
âr	care	o͝o	took
ä	father	o͞o	boot
ĕ	pet	ŭ	cut
ē	be	ûr	urge
ĭ	pit	th	thin
ī	pie	*th*	this
îr	pier	hw	whoop
ŏ	pot	zh	vision
ō	toe	ə	about
ô	paw	N	*French* bon

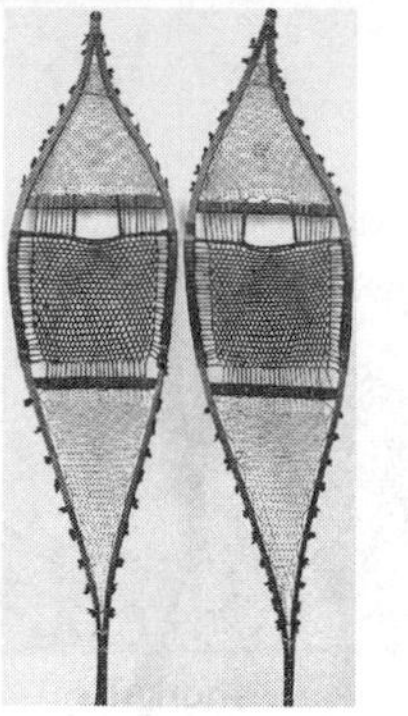

snowshoe
19th-century Eastern Plains Indians snowshoes

Usage: so[1]

You can use either the word **so** or the phrase *so that* when you introduce a clause giving the reason for or purpose of an action: *He stayed so* (or *so that*) *he could see the second feature.* You can also use *so* or *so that* to introduce clauses that state a result or consequence: *The bridge was still closed, so* (or *so that*) *the drive took an hour.*

equipped with a flat or slightly curved surface used to remove snow, as from roads and railroad tracks. **2.** A skiing maneuver for stopping or slowing in which the tips of the skis are angled together.

snow•shoe (snō′sho͞o′) *n.* A frame strung with strips of leather and worn under the shoe to keep the foot from sinking in deep snow. —*intr.v.* **snow•shoed, snow•shoe•ing, snow•shoes.** To walk or travel on snowshoes.

snowshoe rabbit *n.* A hare of northern North America, having large furry feet and fur that is white in winter and brown in summer.

snow•storm (snō′stôrm′) *n.* A storm with heavy snowfall and high winds.

snow•y (snō′ē) *adj.* **snow•i•er, snow•i•est. 1.a.** Full of or covered with snow. **b.** Subject to snowfall. **2.** Resembling snow; white: *snowy petals.*

snub (snŭb) *tr.v.* **snubbed, snub•bing, snubs. 1.** To treat with scorn or contempt. **2.a.** To check the movement of (a rope or cable) by securing it to a post. **b.** To secure (a boat) in this manner. —*n.* **1.** A deliberate slight; scornful treatment. **2.** A sudden securing or checking of a rope.

snub-nosed (snŭb′nōzd′) *adj.* **1.** Having a short turned-up nose. **2.** Having an extremely short barrel: *a snub-nosed pistol.*

snuck (snŭk) *v.* A past tense and a past participle of **sneak.**

snuff[1] (snŭf) *v.* **snuffed, snuff•ing, snuffs.** —*tr.* **1.** To inhale (something) through the nose; sniff. **2.** To examine (something) by smelling; sniff at. —*intr.* To sniff; inhale. [First written down before 1477 in Middle English and spelled *snoffen*, to sniffle, probably from *snoffe*, burned part of a candle.]

snuff[2] (snŭf) *tr.v.* **snuffed, snuff•ing, snuffs. 1.** To put out; extinguish: *snuff out a candle.* **2.** To put an end to; destroy. **3.** To cut off the charred portion of (a candlewick). [First written down before 1450 in Middle English and spelled *snuffen*, possibly of Low German origin.]

snuff[3] (snŭf) *n.* A preparation of finely pulverized tobacco that can be drawn up into the nostrils by inhaling. —***idiom.* up to snuff.** Up to standard; adequate. [First written down in 1683 in Modern English, from Dutch *snuffen*, to sniff.]

snuff•box (snŭf′bŏks′) *n.* A small box used for carrying snuff.

snuf•fle (snŭf′əl) *v.* **snuf•fled, snuf•fling, snuf•fles.** —*intr.* To breathe noisily through the nose; sniffle. —*tr.* To utter in a sniffling tone. —*n.* The act or sound of snuffling.

snug (snŭg) *adj.* **snug•ger, snug•gest. 1.** Pleasant and comfortable; cozy: *a snug apartment.* **2.** Close-fitting: *a snug sweater.* **3.** Secure; safe: *a snug hideout; a snug living.* —**snug′ly** *adv.*

snug•gle (snŭg′əl) *intr. & tr.v.* **snug•gled, snug•gling, snug•gles.** To lie or press close together; nestle or cuddle: *snuggle up under the covers.*

so[1] (sō) *adv.* **1.** In a condition or manner expressed or indicated; thus: *He got sick last week and has been so ever since.* **2.** To such an extent: *I'm so happy that I could cry.* **3.** To a great extent: *The idea is so obvious.* **4.** Consequently; as a result: *He refused to study for the exam and so nearly failed.* **5.** Approximately that amount or number; thereabouts: *The student fare is only $10 or so.* **6.** In the same way; also; likewise: *She likes the book and so do I.* **7.** Then; apparently: *So you think you've got troubles?* **8.** In truth; indeed: *"You aren't telling the truth." " I am so."* —*adj.* True; factual: *I wouldn't have told you this if it weren't so.* —*conj.* **1.** With the result or consequence that: *He failed to show up, so we went without him.* **2.** In order that: *I stayed so I could see you.* —*interj.* An expression used to show surprise or comprehension: *So, you finished on time after all.* —***idioms.* and so on** or **and so forth.** And similarly; and continuing in a like manner. **so as to.** In order to: *Go early so as to be sure to get a good seat.* **so that. 1.** In order that: *I stopped so that you could catch up.* **2.** With the result or consequence that: *The draw bridge got stuck, so that the boats could not pass.* [First written down about 700 in Old English and spelled *swā.*] —See Note.

❑ *These sound alike:* **so[1]** (thus), **sew** (stitch), **so[2]** (musical note), **sow[1]** (plant seed).

so[2] (sō) *n.* Variant of **sol.**

❑ *These sound alike:* **so[2]** (musical note), **sew** (stitch), **so[1]** (thus), **sow[1]** (plant seed).

so. or **So.** *abbr.* An abbreviation of: **1.** South. **2.** Southern.

soak (sōk) *v.* **soaked, soak•ing, soaks.** —*tr.* **1.** To make thoroughly wet by or as if by immersing in a liquid: *Soak the beans in water until soft.* **2.** To absorb (liquid, for example): *Sponges soak up moisture.* **3.** *Slang.* To overcharge. —*intr.* **1.** To become completely saturated. **2.** To penetrate; permeate: *She paused to let her words soak in.* —*n.* The act or process of soaking. [First written down about 1000 in Old English and spelled *socian.*]

so-and-so (sō′ən sō′) *n., pl.* **so-and-sos.** An unnamed or unspecified person or thing.

soap (sōp) *n.* A cleansing agent, manufactured in the form of bars, granules, flakes, or liquid, consisting of a mixture of the sodium or potassium salts of fatty acids that occur in natural fats and oils. —*tr.v.* **soaped, soap•ing, soaps.** To treat or cover with or as if with soap. [First written down about 1000 in Old English and spelled *sāpe.*]

soap•box (sōp′bŏks′) *n.* **1.** A carton in which soap is packed. **2.** A temporary platform used while making an unprepared public speech.

soap opera *n.* A drama, typically performed as a serial on daytime radio or television and characterized by conventional situations, sentimentality, and melodrama.

soap•stone (sōp′stōn′) *n.* A soft metamorphic rock composed mostly of the mineral talc.

soap•suds (sōp′sŭdz′) *pl.n.* Suds from soapy water.

soap•y (sō′pē) *adj.* **soap•i•er, soap•i•est. 1.** Covered or filled with soap: *soapy water.* **2.** Resembling soap: *a soapy texture.* —**soap′i•ness** *n.*

soar (sôr) *intr.v.* **soared, soar•ing, soars. 1.** To rise, fly, or glide high, especially by using rising air currents and moving with little apparent effort, as eagles and hawks do. **2.** To rise suddenly, especially above what is normal: *The cost of living soared.*

❑ *These sound alike:* **soar, sore** (painful).

sob (sŏb) *v.* **sobbed, sob•bing, sobs.** —*intr.* **1.** To weep aloud with gasps and sniffles; cry uncontrollably. See Synonyms at **cry. 2.** To utter with gasps and sniffles. —*tr.* **1.** To utter with sobs. **2.** To put or bring (oneself) to a specific state or condition by sobbing: *sob oneself to sleep.* —*n.* The act or sound of sobbing. [First written down before 1200 in Middle English and spelled *sobben*, perhaps of Low German origin.]

so•ber (sō′bər) *adj.* **so•ber•er, so•ber•est. 1.** Not intoxicated or affected by the use of alcoholic beverages or drugs. **2.** Serious or grave: *a sober temperament.* **3.** Plain or subdued: *sober clothing.* **4.** Lacking frivolity or exaggeration: *a sober assessment of the situation.* **5.** Showing self-control or restraint; reasonable. —*tr. & intr.v.* **so•bered, so•ber•ing, so•bers.** To make or become sober: *The news sobered us to the difficulties we could face.* [First written down in 1340 in Middle English, from Latin *sōbrius.*] —**so′ber•ly** *adv.* —**so′ber•ness** *n.*

so•bri•e•ty (sə brī′ĭ tē) *n.* **1.** Seriousness in bearing, manner, or treatment; solemnity. **2.** Moderation in or abstinence from the use of alcoholic beverages or drugs.

so•bri•quet (sō′brĭ kā′ *or* sō′brĭ kĕt′) *n.* **1.** A humorous nickname. **2.** An assumed name.

so-called (sō′kôld′) *adj.* **1.** Commonly called. **2.** Incorrectly termed: *a so-called musician.*

soc•cer (sŏk′ər) *n.* A game played on a rectangular field with net goals at either end, in which two teams maneuver a ball mainly by kicking, the object being to propel the ball into the opposing team's goal. [First written down in 1889 in Modern English, alteration of *association*, abbreviation of *association football.*]

so•cia•ble (sō′shə bəl) *adj.* **1.** Liking company; friendly: *a sociable person.* **2.** Pleasant: *Dinner is often the most sociable meal of the day.* **—so′cia•bil′i•ty, so′cia•ble•ness** *n.* **—so′cia•bly** *adv.*

so•cial (sō′shəl) *adj.* **1.a.** Living together in communities or similar organized groups: *Bees and ants are social insects.* **b.** Of or relating to this way of life: *the social behavior of bees.* **2.** Of or relating to the upper classes: *wealth and social position.* **3.** Sociable or companionable: *a social person.* **4.** Of, relating to, or occupied with matters affecting human welfare: *the state's social policy.* —*n.* An informal social gathering: *a church social.* [First written down before 1387 in Middle English and spelled *sociale*, domestic, from Latin *socius*, companion.]

so•cial•ism (sō′shə lĭz′əm) *n.* **1.** A social system in which the government or the whole community owns the means of production, such as land and factories, and controls the distribution of goods and services. **2.** The theory or practice of people who support such a system.

so•cial•ist (sō′shə lĭst) *n.* **1.** A person who believes in or advocates socialism. **2.** Often **Socialist.** A member of a party or group that advocates socialism. —*adj.* Of or relating to socialism.

so•cial•is•tic (sō′shə lĭs′tĭk) *adj.* Of, advocating, or tending toward socialism. **—so′cial•is′ti•cal•ly** *adv.*

so•cial•ite (sō′shə līt′) *n.* A person who is prominent in fashionable society.

so•cial•ize (sō′shə līz′) *v.* **so•cial•ized, so•cial•iz•ing, so•cial•iz•es.** —*tr.* **1.** To place under government or group ownership or control: *a proposal to socialize the medical system.* **2.** To make fit for companionship with others. —*intr.* To take part in social activities. **—so′cial•i•za′tion** (sō′shə lĭ zā′shən) *n.*

so•cial•ly (sō′shə lē) *adv.* **1.** In a social manner: *He is socially successful.* **2.** With regard to society: *socially important government policies.* **3.** By society: *socially acceptable behavior.*

social science *n.* The study of human society and of individual relationships in and to society, including sociology, psychology, anthropology, economics, political science, and history. **—social scientist** *n.*

social security *n.* A government program that provides financial assistance to the elderly, unemployed, or disabled, financed by a tax on employers and employees.

social studies *pl.n. (used with a singular or plural verb).* A course of study that includes geography, history, government, and sociology, taught in elementary and secondary schools.

social work *n.* Organized work and social services intended to improve the social condition of a community, especially of the poor, elderly, or disabled. **—social worker** *n.*

so•ci•e•tal (sə sī′ĭ tl) *adj.* Of or relating to the structure, organization, or functioning of society.

so•ci•e•ty (sə sī′ĭ tē) *n., pl.* **so•ci•e•ties. 1.** A group of people distinct from other groups and sharing a common culture. **2.** An organization or association of people sharing common interests or activities: *an archaeological society.* **3.** The rich, privileged, and fashionable social class. **4.** Companionship or company: *enjoying the society of friends.* **5.** A group of living things, usually of the same kind, living and functioning together: *a society of bees forming a single hive.*

So•ci•e•ty Islands (sə sī′ĭ tē). An island group in the southern Pacific Ocean east of Samoa. The islands became a French protectorate in 1843.

Society of Friends *n.* A Christian group, founded in the mid-17th century in England, that is opposed to war, oathtaking, and rituals; the Quakers.

Society of Jesus *n.* A Roman Catholic religious order for men; the Jesuits.

so•ci•ol•o•gy (sō′sē ŏl′ə jē *or* sō′shē ŏl′ə jē) *n.* The scientific study of human social behavior and its origins, development, organizations, and institutions. **—so′ci•o•log′i•cal** (sō′sē ə lŏj′ĭ kəl *or* sō′shē ə lŏj′ĭ kəl) *adj.* **—so′ci•ol′o•gist** *n.*

sock¹ (sŏk) *n.* **1.** *pl.* **socks** or **sox.** A short stocking reaching a point between the ankle and the knee. **2.a.** A light shoe worn by comic actors in ancient Greek and Roman plays. **b.** Comedy. [First written down before 800 in Old English and spelled *socc*, a light shoe, from Latin *soccus*.]

sock² (sŏk) *tr.v.* **socked, sock•ing, socks.** To hit forcefully: *socked the ball out of the park.* —*n.* A punch. [First written down before 1700 in Modern English.]

sock•et (sŏk′ĭt) *n.* **1.** An opening or a cavity into which an inserted part is designed to fit: *a light bulb socket.* **2.a.** A hollow part in a bone into which a projection from another bone fits, as at a joint. **b.** A hollow part or hole into which a body part, such as an eye, fits.

Soc•ra•tes (sŏk′rə tēz′). 470?–399 B.C. Greek philosopher whose method of teaching has survived through the writings of Plato.

sod (sŏd) *n.* **1.** A piece of grass and soil held together by matted roots; turf. **2.** The ground, especially when covered by grass. —*tr.v.* **sod•ded, sod•ding, sods.** To cover with sod.

so•da (sō′də) *n.* **1.a.** Carbonated water; soda water. **b.** A soft drink containing soda water. **2.** A drink made from carbonated water and ice cream. **3.** Any of various salts of sodium. —See Note at **tonic.**

soda fountain *n.* A counter equipped for preparing and serving soft drinks, sandwiches, and ice-cream.

so•dal•i•ty (sō dăl′ĭ tē) *n., pl.* **so•dal•i•ties. 1.** An association, especially a devotional or charitable society in the Roman Catholic Church. **2.** Fellowship.

soda pop *n.* A soft drink.

soda water *n.* Water that has been charged with carbon dioxide under pressure, used in various drinks and refreshments.

sod•den (sŏd′n) *adj.* **1.** Thoroughly soaked; saturated: *sodden land.* **2.** Stupid or dull, especially from drink. **3.** Soggy and heavy from improper cooking. **—sod′den•ly** *adv.* **—sod′den•ness** *n.*

so•di•um (sō′dē əm) *n. Symbol* **Na** A soft, light, silver-white metallic element that reacts explosively with water and is naturally abundant in combined forms, especially in common salt. Atomic number 11. See table at **element.**

sodium benzoate *n.* The sodium salt of benzoic acid, C_6H_5COONa, used as a food preservative and antiseptic.

sodium bicarbonate *n.* Baking soda.

sodium carbonate *n.* A white powdery salt of sodium, Na_2CO_3, with a strongly alkaline reaction, used in preparing other compounds of sodium and

soccer
1982 World Cup soccer competition in Madrid, Spain

Socrates
Copy of an early fourth-century B.C. bust

ă	pat	oi	boy
ā	pay	ou	out
âr	care	o͝o	took
ä	father	o͞o	boot
ĕ	pet	ŭ	cut
ē	be	ûr	urge
ĭ	pit	th	thin
ī	pie	*th*	this
îr	pier	hw	whoop
ŏ	pot	zh	vision
ō	toe	ə	about
ô	paw	N	*French* bon

softball

solarium

solar system

Usually we think of the **solar system** as including the sun and the nine planets with their moons. Actually, the solar system contains millions of other objects as well. There are thousands of asteroids, millions of meteoroids, and many comets. These objects all travel around the sun at high speeds in paths called **orbits**. Some of the orbits, like those of the near planets, are almost circular. Other orbits, like those of the comets, are highly elongated ellipses. Of the many objects in the solar system, few can be seen with the unaided eye. You can see the sun and our own moon. You can see five planets—Mercury, Venus, Mars, Jupiter, and Saturn—if you know where to look. Meteoroids are visible only when they enter the earth's atmosphere and burn, forming meteors. But a telescope is needed to see Uranus, Neptune, Pluto, the satellites of all the other planets besides Earth, the asteroids, and most comets.

in making glass, detergents, soaps, and other industrial products.

sodium chloride *n.* A colorless crystalline salt of sodium, NaCl, used in making chemicals and as a preservative and seasoning for foods; common salt.

sodium fluoride *n.* A colorless crystalline salt, NaF, used in the fluoridation of water, in the treatment of tooth decay, and as an insecticide and a disinfectant.

sodium glu•ta•mate (**glo͞o′**tə māt′) *n.* Monosodium glutamate.

sodium hydroxide *n.* A strongly alkaline compound of sodium, NaOH, used in making chemicals and soaps, in refining petroleum, and as a cleansing agent; lye.

sodium nitrate *n.* A white crystalline compound, $NaNO_3$, used in solid rocket propellants, in the manufacture of explosives, and as a fertilizer.

sodium thi•o•sul•fate (thī′ō **sŭl′**fāt′) *n.* A white crystalline compound, $Na_2S_2O_3{\cdot}5H_2O$, used as a photographic fixing agent and as a bleach.

so•di•um-va•por lamp (**sō′**dē əm **vā′**pər) *n.* An electric lamp containing neon and a small amount of sodium. It generates a powerful yellow light and is often used for lighting streets.

Sod•om (**sŏd′**əm). A city of ancient Palestine that in the Bible was destroyed along with Gomorrah because of its wickedness.

so•fa (**sō′**fə) *n.* A long upholstered seat with a back and arms.

so far as *conj.* In so far as: *So far as I'm concerned, the project is finished.*

So•fi•a (**sō′**fē ə *or* sō **fē′**ə). The capital and largest city of Bulgaria, in the west-central part of the country. It became the capital in 1879. Population, 1,102,100.

soft (sôft *or* sŏft) *adj.* **soft•er, soft•est. 1.** Not hard or firm; easily molded or cut: *a soft squishy melon; soft snow.* **2.** Smooth or fine to the touch: *the soft fur of a kitten.* **3.** Not loud or harsh; quiet: *a soft voice.* **4.** Not brilliant or glaring; subdued: *a soft pink.* **5.** Containing relatively little dissolved mineral matter: *soft water.* **6.** Mild; balmy: *a soft breeze.* **7.** Out of condition; flabby. **8.** *Informal.* Easy: *a soft job.* **9.** Tender or affectionate. **10.** Not stern; lenient: *The coach is never soft on his players.* **11.** Weak in character. **12.** Of or relating to the hissing sound of the letters *c* and *g* as they are pronounced in *receive*and *general.* —*adv.* In a soft manner; gently. **—soft′ly** *adv.* **—soft′ness** *n.*

soft•ball (**sôft′**bôl′ *or* **sŏft′**bôl′) *n.* **1.** A game similar to baseball but played with a larger softer ball that is pitched underhand. **2.** The ball used in this game.

soft-boiled (**sôft′boild′** *or* **sŏft′boild′**) *adj.* Boiled in the shell to a soft consistency. Used of an egg.

soft coal *n.* Bituminous coal.

soft drink *n.* A carbonated nonalcoholic beverage, usually commercially prepared and sold in cans or bottles.

soft•en (**sô′**fən *or* **sŏf′**ən) *tr. & intr.v.* **soft•ened, soft•en•ing, soft•ens.** To make or become soft or softer. **—soft′en•er** *n.*

soft•heart•ed (**sôft′här′**tĭd *or* **sŏft′här′**tĭd) *adj.* Easily moved; tender. **—soft′heart′ed•ly** *adv.* **—soft′heart′ed•ness** *n.*

soft landing *n.* The landing of a space vehicle on a celestial body or Earth in such a way as to prevent damage or destruction.

soft palate *n.* The movable fold, consisting of muscle fibers enclosed in mucous membrane, that hangs from the back of the hard palate and closes off the nasal cavity from the mouth cavity during swallowing and sucking.

soft-shoe (**sôft′sho͞o′** *or* **sŏft′sho͞o′**) *n.* Tap dancing performed in shoes with soft soles and no metal taps.

soft-spo•ken (**sôft′spō′**kən *or* **sŏft′spō′**kən) *adj.* Speaking with a soft or gentle voice.

soft spot *n.* **1.** A tender or sentimental feeling. **2.** A weak or vulnerable point.

soft•ware (**sôft′**wâr′ *or* **sŏft′**wâr′) *n.* The programs, routines, and symbolic languages that control the operation of a computer.

soft•wood (**sôft′**wo͝od′ *or* **sŏft′**wo͝od′) *n.* **1.** The wood of a cone-bearing tree, such as a pine, fir, or cedar. **2.** A tree bearing such wood.

soft•y or **soft•ie** (**sôf′**tē *or* **sŏf′**tē) *n., pl.* **soft•ies.** *Informal.* A weak or sentimental person.

sog•gy (**sŏg′**ē *or* **sô′**gē) *adj.* **sog•gi•er, sog•gi•est. 1.** Saturated with moisture; soaked: *soggy bread.* **2.** Hot and humid. **—sog′gi•ly** *adv.* **—sog′gi•ness** *n.*

soil[1] (soil) *n.* **1.** The loose top layer of the earth's surface, a mixture of rock and mineral particles with organic matter, suitable for the growth of plant life. **2.** A particular kind of earth or ground: *sandy soil.* **3.** Country; region: *native soil.* [First written down before 1300 in Middle English and spelled *sol*, from Latin *solium*, seat.]

soil[2] (soil) *v.* **soiled, soil•ing, soils.** —*tr.* **1.** To make dirty. **2.** To disgrace; tarnish: *soil one's reputation.* —*intr.* To become dirty or tarnished: *a fabric that soils easily.* [First written down before 1250 in Middle English and spelled *soillen*, from Old French *souiller.*]

so•journ (**sō′**jûrn′ *or* sō **jûrn′**) *intr.v.* **so•journed, so•journ•ing, so•journs.** To stay for a time; reside temporarily: *Thoreau sojourned at Walden pond.* —*n.* A temporary stay. **—so′journ′er** *n.*

sol (sōl) also **so** (sō) *n.* In music, the fifth tone of a major scale. [First written down before 1380 in Middle English, from Medieval Latin.]

❑ *These sound alike:* **sol** (musical syllable), **sole**[1] (foot part), **sole**[2] (only), **sole**[3] (fish), **soul** (spirit).

sol•ace (**sŏl′**ĭs) *n.* **1.** Comfort in distress, sorrow, or misery. **2.** Something that gives such comfort or consolation. —*tr.v.* **sol•aced, sol•ac•ing, sol•ac•es.** To provide solace; comfort.

so•lar (**sō′**lər) *adj.* **1.** Of or relating to the sun: *solar radiation.* **2.** Using or operating by energy from the sun: *a solar heating system.* **3.** Measured with respect to the sun: *solar time.* [First written down about 1450 in Middle English, from Latin *sōlāris*, from *sōl*, sun.]

solar battery *n.* An electrical battery consisting of a number of solar cells connected together.

solar cell *n.* A semiconductor device that converts solar radiation into electrical energy, often used in space vehicles.

solar flare *n.* A temporary outburst of gases from a small area of the sun's surface.

solar furnace *n.* A device equipped with a large reflector that focuses the sun's rays, producing temperatures as high as 7,200°F (4,000°C).

so•lar•i•um (sō **lâr′**ē əm) *n., pl.* **so•lar•i•a** (sō **lâr′**ē-ə) or **so•lar•i•ums.** A room or glassed-in porch that is exposed to the sun.

solar plexus *n.* **1.** The large network of nerves and nerve tissue located in the abdomen behind the stomach, having branches that supply nerves to the abdominal organs. **2.** The pit of the stomach.

solar system *n.* The sun together with the nine planets and other bodies, such as asteroids and comets, that orbit the sun. —SEE NOTE.

solar wind (wĭnd) *n.* The flow of charged atomic particles that radiates from the sun.

solar year *n.* The period of time required for the earth to make one complete revolution around the sun, from one vernal equinox to the next. The solar year is 365 days, 5 hours, 48 minutes, 45.51 seconds.

sold (sōld) *v.* Past tense and past participle of **sell.**

sol•der (sŏd′ər) *n.* Any of various alloys, mainly of tin and lead, that melt at low temperatures and are applied in the molten state to metal parts in order to join them. *—tr. & intr.v.* **sol•dered, sol•der•ing, sol•ders.** To join, mend, or unite with solder: *soldering the wires together.* [First written down about 1320 in Middle English and spelled *soudour,* from Latin *solidāre,* to make solid.]

sol•dier (sōl′jər) *n.* **1.** A person who serves in an army. **2.** An enlisted person or noncommissioned officer. **3.** A dedicated and militant follower. *—intr. v.* **sol•diered, sol•dier•ing, sol•diers.** To be or serve as a soldier. [First written down before 1300 in Middle English and spelled *souder,* mercenary, from Late Latin *solidus,* gold coin.]

sol•dier•ly (sōl′jər lē) *adj.* Of, relating to, or befitting a soldier: *soldierly courage.*

soldier of fortune *n., pl.* **soldiers of fortune.** A person willing to serve in any army for personal gain or love of adventure.

sole[1] (sōl) *n.* **1.** The bottom surface of the foot. **2.** The bottom surface of a shoe or boot, often excluding the heel. *—tr.v.* **soled, sol•ing, soles.** To put a sole on (a shoe or boot): *The cobbler soled the shoes.* [First written down about 1325 in Middle English, from Latin *solum,* bottom, sole of the foot.]

❑ *These sound alike:* **sole**[1] (foot part), **sol** (musical note), **sole**[2] (only), **sole**[3] (fish), **soul** (spirit).

sole[2] (sōl) *adj.* **1.** Being the only one; single; only: *Her sole purpose in coming is to see you.* **2.** Belonging or relating exclusively to one person or group: *She took sole command of the ship.* [First written down about 1395 in Middle English, from Latin *sōlus.*]

❑ *These sound alike:* **sole**[2] (only), **sol** (musical note), **sole**[1] (foot part), **sole**[3] (fish), **soul** (spirit).

sole[3] (sōl) *n., pl.* **sole** or **soles.** Any of various flatfishes related to the flounders and used as food. [First written down in 1252 in Middle English, from Latin *solea,* sandal, flatfish.]

❑ *These sound alike:* **sole**[3] (fish), **sol** (musical note), **sole**[1] (foot part), **sole**[2] (only), **soul** (spirit).

sol•e•cism (sŏl′ĭ sĭz′əm *or* sō′lĭ sĭz′əm) *n.* **1.** A nonstandard use of language or grammar. **2.** A violation of etiquette.

sole•ly (sōl′lē *or* sō′lē) *adv.* **1.** Alone; singly: *solely responsible.* **2.** Entirely; exclusively: *judging solely from these passages.*

sol•emn (sŏl′əm) *adj.* **1.** Deeply serious or earnest: *a solemn scholar.* **2.** Seriously impressive; grave: *a solemn occasion* **3.** Having the force of a religious ceremony; sacred: *took a solemn oath.* **4.** Performed with full ceremony: *held a solemn mass at the funeral service.* **5.** Gloomy: *He looks solemn.* **—sol′emn•ly** *adv.* **—sol′emn•ness** *n.*

so•lem•ni•ty (sə lĕm′nĭ tē) *n., pl.* **so•lem•ni•ties.** **1.** The quality or condition of being solemn; seriousness. **2.** A solemn event or occasion.

sol•em•nize (sŏl′əm nīz′) *tr.v.* **sol•em•nized, sol•em•niz•ing, sol•em•niz•es.** **1.** To celebrate or observe with dignity and gravity: *solemnize the occasion.* **2.** To perform with formal ceremony: *solemnize a marriage.* **3.** To make serious or grave. **—sol′em•ni•za′tion** (sŏl′əm nĭ zā′shən) *n.*

so•le•noid (sō′lə noid′) *n.* A coil of wire that acts as a magnet when an electric current passes through it. A solenoid often has a movable iron rod that is pulled into the coil when current flows through the wire, thus allowing the entire device to act as a switch.

so•lic•it (sə lĭs′ĭt) *v.* **so•lic•it•ed, so•lic•it•ing, so•lic•its.** *—tr.* **1.** To seek to obtain: *solicit votes.* **2.** To ask or petition (someone) persistently; entreat: *solicited all his neighbors for donations.* *—intr.* To ask or petition for something desired. **—so•lic′i•ta′tion** *n.*

so•lic•i•tor (sə lĭs′ĭ tər) *n.* **1.** A person who solicits, especially one who seeks contributions or business. **2.** The chief law officer for a city, town, or government department. **3.** *Chiefly British.* A lawyer who is not a member of the bar and who may be heard only in the lower courts.

so•lic•i•tous (sə lĭs′ĭ təs) *adj.* **1.** Anxious and concerned; attentive: *a solicitous parent.* **2.** Full of desire; eager: *solicitous to move ahead.* **—so•lic′i•tous•ly** *adv.* **—so•lic′i•tous•ness** *n.*

so•lic•i•tude (sə lĭs′ĭ to͞od′ *or* sə lĭs′ĭ tyo͞od′) *n.* The state of being solicitous; care or concern, as for another person.

sol•id (sŏl′ĭd) *adj.* **sol•id•er, sol•id•est.** **1.** Having a definite shape and volume; not liquid or gaseous. **2.** Firm or compact in substance: *a solid wall.* **3.** Not hollowed out: *a solid block of ice.* **4.** Being the same substance or color throughout: *solid gold.* **5.** Of or relating to three-dimensional geometric figures. **6.** Having no breaks; continuous: *a solid line of people.* **7.** Of good quality or substance; well-made: *a solid foundation.* **8.** Substantial; hearty: *a solid breakfast.* **9.** Upstanding and dependable: *a solid citizen.* **10.** Acting together; unanimous: *a solid voting bloc.* **11.** Financially sound. *—n.* **1.** A substance made up of atoms, molecules, or ions that have little or no ability to exchange places; a substance that has a definite shape and volume. **2.** A geometric figure that has three dimensions. [First written down in 1391 in Middle English and spelled *solide,* from Latin *solidus.*] **—sol′id•ly** *adv.* **—sol′id•ness** *n.*

sol•i•dar•i•ty (sŏl′ĭ dăr′ĭ tē) *n.* Unity of purpose, interest, or sympathy.

solid geometry *n.* The geometry of three-dimensional figures and surfaces.

so•lid•i•fy (sə lĭd′ə fī′) *tr. & intr.v.* **so•lid•i•fied, so•lid•i•fy•ing, so•lid•i•fies.** To make or become solid.

so•lid•i•ty (sə lĭd′ĭ tē) *n.* **1.** The condition or property of being solid. **2.** Soundness of mind, character, or finances.

sol•id-state (sŏl′ĭd stāt′) *adj.* **1.** Of or concerned with the physical properties of crystalline solids: *solid-state physics.* **2.** Based on or using transistors or related semiconductor devices: *a solid-state radio receiver.*

so•lil•o•quy (sə lĭl′ə kwē) *n., pl.* **so•lil•o•quies.** **1.** A literary or dramatic discourse in which a character reveals his or her thoughts when alone or unaware of the presence of other characters. **2.** The act of speaking to oneself.

sol•i•taire (sŏl′ĭ târ′) *n.* **1.** Any of a number of card games played by one person. **2.** A diamond or other gemstone set alone, as in a ring.

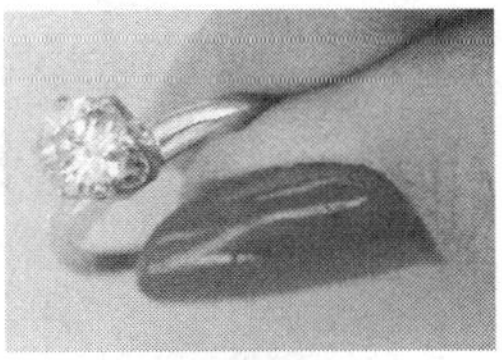

solitaire
Diamond solitaire

sol•i•tar•y (sŏl′ĭ tĕr′ē) *adj.* **1.** Existing or living alone: *a solitary traveler.* See Synonyms at **alone.** **2.** Happening, done, or made alone: *a solitary evening.* **3.** Remote; secluded: *solitary places.* **4.** Having no or few companions; lonely.

sol•i•tude (sŏl′ĭ to͞od′ *or* sŏl′ĭ tyo͞od′) *n.* **1.** The state or quality of being alone or remote from others; isolation. **2.** A lonely or secluded place.

so•lo (sō′lō) *n., pl.* **so•los.** **1.** A musical composition or passage for a single voice or instrument, with or without accompaniment. **2.** A performance by or intended for a single individual. *—adj.* **1.** Composed, arranged for, or performed by a single voice or instrument. **2.** Made or done by a single individual. *—adv.* Alone or without accompani-

ă	pat	oi	boy
ā	pay	ou	out
âr	care	o͝o	took
ä	father	o͞o	boot
ĕ	pet	ŭ	cut
ē	be	ûr	urge
ĭ	pit	th	thin
ī	pie	*th*	this
îr	pier	hw	whoop
ŏ	pot	zh	vision
ō	toe	ə	about
ô	paw	N	*French* bon

sombrero

ment: *Lacking a pianist, he had to perform solo.* —*intr.v.* **so•loed, so•lo•ing, so•los. 1.** To perform a solo. **2.** To fly an airplane without an instructor or companion. [First written down in 1695 in Modern English, from Italian, from Latin *sōlus*, alone.] —**so'lo•ist** *n.*

Sol•o•mon (sŏl'ə mən). Flourished about tenth century B.C. King of Israel famous for his wisdom.

Solomon Islands. An island country in the western Pacific Ocean east of New Guinea. It gained its independence from Great Britain in 1978. Capital, Honiara. Population, 212,868.

sol•stice (sŏl'stĭs *or* sōl'stĭs) *n.* Either of the two times of year, approximately June 21, the summer solstice, and December 21, the winter solstice, at which the sun reaches an extreme of its northward or southward motion and appears not to move in either of these directions.

sol•u•bil•i•ty (sŏl'yə bĭl'ĭ tē) *n., pl.* **sol•u•bil•i•ties. 1.** The quality or condition of being soluble. **2.** The amount of a substance that is soluble in a particular liquid, especially water.

sol•u•ble (sŏl'yə bəl) *adj.* **1.** Capable of being dissolved. **2.** Capable of being solved or explained.

sol•ute (sŏl'yo͞ot *or* sō'lo͞ot) *n.* A substance that is dissolved in another substance.

so•lu•tion (sə lo͞o'shən) *n.* **1.** A mixture of two or more substances that appears to be uniform throughout except at the molecular level, and that is capable of forming by itself when the substances are in contact: *a solution of salt in water.* **2.** The act or process of forming such a mixture. **3.** The condition or property of being dissolved. **4.** An answer to a problem. **5.** The method or procedure used in solving an equation or problem.

solv•a•ble (sŏl'və bəl *or* sôl'və bəl) *adj.* Capable of being solved: *a solvable riddle.*

solve (sŏlv *or* sôlv) *tr.v.* **solved, solv•ing, solves.** To find an answer or solution to (a problem or an equation, for example).

sol•vent (sŏl'vənt *or* sôl'vənt) *adj.* **1.** Capable of meeting financial obligations: *a solvent business.* **2.** Capable of dissolving another substance. —*n.* **1.** A substance in which another substance is dissolved. **2.** A liquid that is capable of dissolving another substance. —**sol'ven•cy** *n.*

So•ma•li•a (sō mä'lē ə *or* sō mäl'yə). A country of extreme eastern Africa on the Gulf of Aden and the Indian Ocean. Mogadishu is the capital and the largest city. Population, 3,645,000.

so•mat•ic (sō măt'ĭk) *adj.* Of, relating to, or affecting the body, especially as distinguished from a body part, the mind, or the germ cells.

somatic cell *n.* Any of the cells of an organism that are not germ cells.

som•ber (sŏm'bər) *adj.* **1.** Dark; gloomy: *a somber color.* **2.** Melancholy; dismal: *a somber mood.* **3.** Serious; grave. [First written down in 1760 in Modern English and spelled *sombre*, from Late Latin *subumbrāre*, to cast a shadow.] —**som'ber•ly** *adv.* —**som'ber•ness** *n.*

som•bre•ro (sŏm brâr'ō) *n., pl.* **som•bre•ros.** A large straw or felt hat with a broad brim and tall crown, worn especially in Mexico and the southwest United States. [First written down in 1598 in Modern English, from Spanish, perhaps from *sombra*, shade, probably from Late Latin *subumbrāre*, to cast a shadow.]

some (sŭm) *adj.* **1.** Being an unspecified number or quantity; a few or a little: *some people; some sugar.* **2.** Unknown or unspecified by name: *Some student was just here and left you this note.* **3.** *Informal.* Considerable; remarkable: *Mary's some skier.* —*pron.* **1.** An indefinite or unspecified number or quantity: *We took some of the books to the library.* **2.** An indefinite additional quantity: *From here to the lake is 100 miles and then some.* —*adv.* **1.** Approximately; about: *Some 40 people were at the party.* **2.** *Informal.* Somewhat: *He's improved some but not much.* [First written down about 725 in Old English and spelled *sum.*]

❑ *These sound alike:* **some, sum** (amount).

–some¹ *suff.* A suffix that means characterized by a specified quality, condition, or action: *bothersome.*

–some² *suff.* A suffix that means a group of a specified number of members: *threesome.*

some•bod•y (sŭm'bŏd'ē *or* sŭm'bŭd'ē *or* sŭm'bə dē) *pron.* An unspecified or unknown person; someone: *Somebody's been here, but who?* —*n., pl.* **some•bod•ies.** *Informal.* A person of importance: *He really thinks he's somebody.*

some•day (sŭm'dā') *adv.* At some time in the future.

some•how (sŭm'hou') *adv.* In a way that is not specified or understood: *I couldn't remember the formula, but somehow I got the right answer.*

some•one (sŭm'wŭn') *pron.* Somebody: *Someone called, but she didn't leave her name.*

some•place (sŭm'plās') *adv.* Somewhere: *I don't like it here, so let's go someplace else.*

som•er•sault also **sum•mer•sault** (sŭm'ər sôlt') *n.* An acrobatic stunt in which the body rolls in a complete circle, heels over head. —*intr.v.* **som•er•sault•ed, som•er•sault•ing, som•er•saults.** To perform a somersault: *Children were somersaulting on the grass.*

some•thing (sŭm'thĭng) *pron.* An unspecified or unknown thing: *Something's wrong, but I'm not sure what it is.* —*n. Informal.* A remarkable or important thing or person: *That concert was really something.* —*adv.* Somewhat: *She looks something like her mother.* —***idiom.*** **something of.** To some extent: *He's something of a computer expert.*

some•time (sŭm'tīm') *adv.* At an indefinite or unstated time in the future: *I'll see you sometime around six.* —*adj.* Former: *our sometime king.*

some•times (sŭm'tīmz') *adv.* Now and then: *I see them sometimes but not often.*

some•way (sŭm'wā') also **some•ways** (sŭm'wāz') *adv.* In some way or other; somehow: *Don't worry—I'll fix up something someway.*

some•what (sŭm'wŏt' *or* sŭm'wŭt' *or* sŭm'wət) *adv.* To some extent or degree; rather: *He resembles his brother somewhat.*

some•where (sŭm'wâr') *adv.* **1.** At, in, or to a place not specified or known: *I found this turtle somewhere near the edge of the swamp.* **2.** To a place or state of further development or progress: *Good writers make sure that their essays lead somewhere and end with a definite point.* **3.** Approximately; roughly: *somewhere about halfway through.* —*n.* An unknown or unspecified place: *I wish I had somewhere to park my bike.*

som•nam•bu•lism (sŏm năm'byə lĭz'əm) *n.* The act or an instance of walking while asleep or in a condition resembling sleep. —**som•nam'bu•list** *n.* —**som•nam'bu•lis'tic** *adj.*

som•no•lence (sŏm'nə ləns) *n.* A state of drowsiness; sleepiness.

som•no•lent (sŏm'nə lənt) *adj.* **1.** Drowsy; sleepy. **2.** Causing or tending to cause sleepiness: *the somnolent sound of rain.* —**som'no•lent•ly** *adv.*

son (sŭn) *n.* **1.** A person's male child. **2.** A male descendant: *sons of Abraham.* **3.** A man or boy regarded as if in a relationship of child to parent: *sons of freedom.* **4. Son.** Jesus. **5.** Used as a familiar form of address for a young man. [First written down about 725 in Old English and spelled *sunu.*]

❑ *These sound alike:* **son, sun** (planet).

so•nar (sō′när′) *n.* **1.** A system that uses reflected sound waves to detect and locate underwater objects. **2.** An apparatus using such a system, as for detecting submarines. [First written down in 1946 in American English, from *so(und) n(avigation) a(nd) r(anging).*]

so•na•ta (sə nä′tə) *n.* A musical composition for one to four instruments, one of which is usually a keyboard instrument, consisting of several movements that vary in key, mood, and tempo.

sonata form *n.* A musical form consisting of an opening section in which two or more themes are introduced, a middle section in which the themes are developed and elaborated, and a third section in which the opening themes are restated, often followed by a coda.

song (sông *or* sŏng) *n.* **1.** A brief musical composition that is meant to be sung. **2.** The act or art of singing. **3.** A distinctive or characteristic sound made by an animal, such as a bird. **4.a.** Poetry; verse. **b.** A lyric poem or ballad. ***—idiom.* for a song.** *Informal.* At a low price: *bought the old books for a song.*

song•bird (sông′bûrd′ *or* sŏng′bûrd′) *n.* A bird having a melodious song or call.

Song of Solomon *n.* The Song of Songs.

Song of Songs *n.* A book of the Bible consisting of a dramatic and emotional love poem, traditionally attributed to Solomon.

song•writ•er (sông′rī′tər *or* sŏng′rī′tər) *n.* A person who writes lyrics or composes tunes for songs.

son•ic (sŏn′ĭk) *adj.* **1.** Of sound, especially audible sound. **2.** Having a speed equal to that of sound in air, about 760 miles per hour (1229 kilometers per hour) at sea level at normal temperatures.

sonic barrier *n.* The sudden sharp increase in drag exerted by the atmosphere on an aircraft approaching the speed of sound.

sonic boom *n.* The shock wave caused by an aircraft traveling at a supersonic speed, sometimes causing damage to structures on the ground and often audible as a loud explosive sound.

son-in-law (sŭn′ĭn lô′) *n., pl.* **sons-in-law** (sŭnz′ĭn-lô′). The husband of one's daughter.

son•net (sŏn′ĭt) *n.* A 14-line poem usually having one of several conventional rhyme schemes.

son•net•eer (sŏn′ĭ tîr′) *n.* **1.** A composer of sonnets. **2.** An inferior poet.

son•ny (sŭn′ē) *n., pl.* **son•nies.** Used as a familiar form of address for a boy or young man.
❑ *These sound alike:* **sonny, sunny** (cheerful).

so•nor•i•ty (sə nôr′ĭ tē *or* sə nŏr′ĭ tē) *n., pl.* **so•nor•i•ties. 1.** The quality or property of being sonorous; resonance. **2.** A sound, especially one used in music or speech: *The work is a masterful study in orchestral sonorities.*

so•no•rous (sə nôr′əs *or* sŏn′ər əs) *adj.* **1.** Having or producing sound, especially full, deep, or rich sound. **2.** Impressive in style of speech: *sonorous prose.* **—so•no′rous•ly** *adv.* **—so•no′rous•ness** *n.*

soon (so͞on) *adv.* **soon•er, soon•est. 1.** In the near future: *Soon you'll have to leave.* **2.** Before the usual or appointed time; early: *He got there not an instant too soon.* **3.** Immediately; promptly: *Phone your mother as soon as we get into the house.* **4.** Gladly; willingly: *I'd as soon leave right now.* ***—idiom.* sooner or later.** At some time; eventually. [First written down before 830 in Old English and spelled *sōna,* immediately.] —See Note.

soot (so͝ot *or* so͞ot) *n.* A fine black powdery substance consisting chiefly of carbon and produced when wood, coal, or hydrocarbon fuels burn incompletely. [First written down before 800 in Old English and spelled *sōt.*]

sooth (so͞oth) *Archaic. adj.* **1.** Real; true. **2.** Soft; smooth. *—n.* Truth; reality. —See Note.

soothe (so͞o*th*) *v.* **soothed, sooth•ing, soothes.** *—tr.* **1.** To calm or quiet: *sang a lullabye to soothe the baby.* **2.** To ease or relieve (pain, discomfort, or distress): *The massage soothed the ache in his back. —intr.* To bring comfort, composure, or relief. **—sooth′er** *n.*

sooth•ing (so͞o′*th*ĭng) *adj.* Tending to soothe; bringing relief or comfort: *soothing words.* **—sooth′ing•ly** *adv.*

sooth•say•er (so͞oth′sā′ər) *n.* A person who claims to be able to foretell events or predict the future; a seer.

sooth•say•ing (so͞oth′sā′ĭng) *n.* **1.** The art or practice of foretelling events. **2.** A prediction; a prophecy.

soot•y (so͝ot′ē *or* so͞o′tē) *adj.* **soot•i•er, soot•i•est. 1.** Covered with or as if with soot. **2.** Of, relating to, or producing soot: *a sooty fire.*

sop (sŏp) *v.* **sopped, sop•ping, sops.** *—tr.* **1.** To dip, soak, or drench in a liquid: *sop the bread in the beaten eggs.* **2.** To take up by absorption; soak up: *sop up water with a towel. —intr.* To be or become thoroughly soaked. *—n.* **1.** A piece of food soaked or dipped in a liquid. **2.** Something yielded to placate or soothe a person.

soph•ist (sŏf′ĭst) *n.* **1.** A person skilled in elaborate and often deceptive methods of argumentation. **2. Sophist.** One of a group of ancient Greek philosophers known for their elaborate and often misleading methods of argumentation.

so•phis•ti•cate (sə fĭs′tĭ kāt′) *tr.v.* **so•phis•ti•cat•ed, so•phis•ti•cat•ing, so•phis•ti•cates. 1.** To make less natural; cause to become less naive and more worldly: *Travel tends to sophisticate a person.* **2.** To make more complex or complicated; refine: *sophisticate the communications system. —n.* (sə fĭs′tĭ kĭt). A sophisticated person. **—so•phis′ti•ca′tion** *n.*

so•phis•ti•cat•ed (sə fĭs′tĭ kā′tĭd) *adj.* **1.** Having acquired worldly knowledge or refinement; lacking natural simplicity. **2.** Elaborate, complex, or complicated: *sophisticated technology.* **3.** Suitable for or appealing to the tastes of sophisticates: *a sophisticated play.*

soph•is•try (sŏf′ĭ strē) *n., pl.* **soph•is•tries. 1.** Argumentation that is seemingly valid but actually false or misleading. **2.** An attractive but misleading or false argument.

Soph•o•cles (sŏf′ə klēz′). 496?–406 B.C. Greek dramatist whose plays include *Oedipus Rex.*

soph•o•more (sŏf′ə môr′ *or* sŏf′môr′) *n.* **1.** A second-year student in a U.S. college. **2.** A tenth-grade student in a U.S. high school.

soph•o•mor•ic (sŏf′ə môr′ĭk *or* sŏf′ə mŏr′ĭk) *adj.* **1.** Of or characteristic of a sophomore. **2.** Immature and foolish.

sop•o•rif•ic (sŏp′ə rĭf′ĭk *or* sō′pə rĭf′ĭk) *adj.* **1.** Inducing or tending to induce sleep. **2.** Drowsy. *—n.* A drug or other substance that induces sleep.

sop•ping (sŏp′ĭng) *adj.* Thoroughly soaked; drenched. *—adv.* Extremely; very: *sopping wet.*

sop•py (sŏp′ē) *adj.* **sop•pi•er, sop•pi•est. 1.** Soaked; sopping. **2.** Rainy. **3.** *Slang.* Sentimental.

so•pran•o (sə prăn′ō *or* sə prä′nō) *n., pl.* **so•pran•os. 1.** A highest singing voice of a woman or young boy. **2.** A singer having such a voice. **3.** A part written in the range of such a voice. **4.** An instrument with the range of such a voice.

sor•cer•er (sôr′sər ər) *n.* A man who practices sorcery; a wizard.

sor•cer•ess (sôr′sər ĭs) *n.* A woman who practices sorcery.

sor•cer•y (sôr′sə rē) *n.* The use of supernatural

Usage: **soon**

When you use *no sooner* as a comparative adverb, follow it with *than,* not *when,* as in *No sooner had she left than he called.*

Word History: **sooth**

The words **sooth** and **soothe**—are they related, or is the resemblance accidental? Yes and no: that is, yes, they are related; no, it is not accidental. *Sooth* comes from the Old English word *sōth,* "true," "the truth," and a *soothsayer* is "one who tells the truth." *Soothe* comes from the Old English verb *sōthian,* "to prove to be true." The verb later developed the senses "to tell the truth," "confirm as true," "encourage," "please by agreeing," and "calm down."

Sophocles

ă	pat	oi	boy
ā	pay	ou	out
âr	care	o͝o	took
ä	father	o͞o	boot
ĕ	pet	ŭ	cut
ē	be	ûr	urge
ĭ	pit	th	thin
ī	pie	*th*	this
îr	pier	hw	whoop
ŏ	pot	zh	vision
ō	toe	ə	about
ô	paw	N	*French* bon

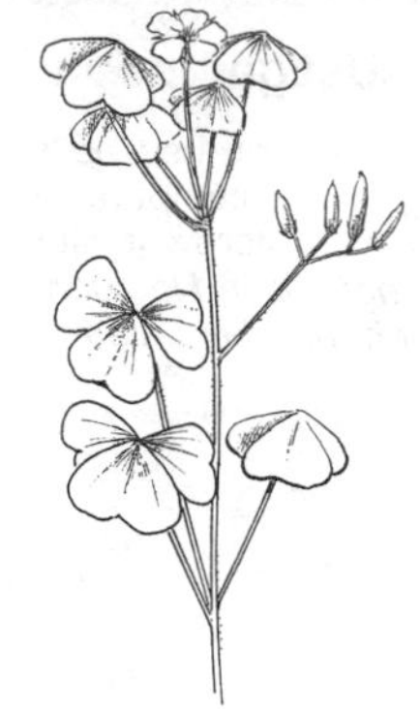

sorrel[1]

sound[1]

The form of energy called **sound** is produced when matter moves or vibrates. The vibrations are transferred to another medium, usually the air, and travel through the medium as sound waves. You hear a sound when its vibrations reach your eardrum, causing it to vibrate. People with excellent hearing can hear sounds with vibrations from 20 to 20,000 times a second. Other animals can hear sounds at higher vibrations. Bats, for instance, can hear sounds with vibrations as high as 100,000 times a second. The loudness, or intensity, of sound is measured in decibels. For each increase of 10 decibels, the sound wave has 10 times as much energy. For example, a sound of 20 decibels is twice as loud as one of 10 decibels, but has 10 times the energy. The softest sound humans can hear, at the very threshold of hearing, has a loudness of 0 decibels. A moderate conversation has a loudness of about 60 decibels, and thunder has a loudness of about 140 decibels. Sound with intensity greater than 85 decibels can cause ear damage; sound with intensity above 120 decibels causes pain.

power over others through the aid of spirits; witchcraft.

sor•did (sôr′dĭd) *adj.* **1.** Filthy or squalid: *a sordid neighborhood.* **2.** Morally degraded; base: *a sordid motive.* **—sor′did•ly** *adv.* **—sor′did•ness** *n.*

sore (sôr) *adj.* **sor•er, sor•est. 1.** Painful to the touch; tender: *His sore leg made him walk with a limp.* **2.** Feeling physical pain; hurting: *sore all over.* **3.** Causing misery, sorrow, or distress; grievous: *in sore need.* **4.** Causing embarrassment or irritation: *a sore subject.* **5.** *Informal.* Angry; offended. *—n.* An open skin wound or ulcer. [First written down before 899 in Old English and spelled *sār.*] **—sore′ness** *n.*

❑ *These sound alike:* **sore, soar** (rise).

sore•ly (sôr′lē) *adv.* **1.** Painfully; grievously: *She was sorely distressed.* **2.** Extremely; greatly: *sorely needed expertise.*

sor•ghum (sôr′gəm) *n.* **1.** A grain-bearing grass grown as feed for animals and as a source of syrup. **2.** Syrup made from the juice of this plant.

so•ri (sôr′ī) *n.* Plural of **sorus.**

so•ror•i•ty (sə rôr′ĭ tē *or* sə rŏr′ĭ tē) *n., pl.* **so•ror•i•ties. 1.** A chiefly social organization of women students at a college or university. **2.** An association of women.

sor•rel[1] (sôr′əl *or* sŏr′əl) *n.* Any of several plants having sour-tasting leaves sometimes used in salads. [First written down in 1373 in Middle English and spelled *sorell,* from Old French *surele,* from *sur,* sour, of Germanic origin.]

sor•rel[2] (sôr′əl *or* sŏr′əl) *n.* **1.** A brownish orange to light brown. **2.** A sorrel-colored horse or other animal. [First written down in 1340 in Middle English and spelled *sorel,* from Old French *sor,* red-brown, of Germanic origin.]

sor•row (sŏr′ō) *n.* **1.** Mental pain or suffering caused by loss, injury, or despair. **2.** Something that causes sadness or grief; a misfortune. **3.** The expression of sadness or grief: *He looked at them with sorrow.* *—intr.v.* **sor•rowed, sor•row•ing, sor•rows.** To feel or display sorrow; grieve. [First written down about 725 in Old English and spelled *sorg.*] **—sor′row•er** *n.*

sor•row•ful (sŏr′ō fəl) *adj.* Causing, feeling, or expressing sorrow: *a sorrowful event; a sorrowful voice.* See Synonyms at **sad. —sor′row•ful•ly** *adv.* **—sor′row•ful•ness** *n.*

sor•ry (sŏr′ē) *adj.* **sor•ri•er, sor•ri•est. 1.** Feeling or expressing sympathy, pity, or regret. **2.** Worthless or inferior; poor; paltry: *a sorry excuse.* **3.** Causing sorrow or grief; grievous; sad: *a sorry development.* [First written down about 725 in Old English and spelled *sārig,* sad, from *sār,* sore.] **—sor′ri•ly** *adv.*

sort (sôrt) *n.* **1.** A group or collection of similar persons or things; a class; a kind: *What sort of machine is it?* **2.** The character or nature of something; type; quality: *a person of an interesting sort.* *—tr.v.* **sort•ed, sort•ing, sorts. 1.** To arrange according to class, kind, or size; classify: *sorted the mail.* **2.** To separate (one kind) from the rest: *She sorted out the nails of the largest size.* ***—idioms.*** **of sorts** or **of a sort. 1.** Of a mediocre or inferior kind: *a democracy of a sort.* **2.** Of one kind or another: *knew many stories of sorts.* **out of sorts. 1.** Slightly ill. **2.** Irritable; cross. **sort of.** *Informal.* Somewhat; rather: *They were sort of interested in the question.* **—sort′er** *n.*

sor•tie (sôr′tē *or* sôr tē′) *n.* **1.** An armed attack made from a place surrounded by enemy forces. **2.** A flight of an aircraft on a combat mission. [First written down in 1778 in Modern English, from French, from *sortir,* to go out.]

so•rus (sôr′əs) *n., pl.* **so•ri** (sôr′ī). One of the clusters of spore cases formed on the undersides of fern fronds.

S O S (ĕs′ō ĕs′) *n.* **1.** The letters represented by the signal • • • — — — • • •, used as an international distress signal by ships and aircraft. **2.** A signal for help.

so-so (sō′sō′) *adj.* Neither very good nor very bad; just passable: *a so-so party.* *—adv.* Indifferently; tolerably; passably: *performed so-so.*

sot (sŏt) *n.* A drunkard.

sou (so͞o) *n.* A coin formerly used in France and worth a small amount.

sou•bri•quet (so͞o′brĭ kā′ *or* so͞o′brĭ kĕt′) *n.* Variant of **sobriquet.**

souf•flé (so͞o flā′) *n.* A light, fluffy baked dish made of eggs combined with other ingredients. [First written down in 1813 in Modern English, from French, from *souffler,* to puff up.]

sough (sŭf *or* sou) *intr.v.* **soughed, sough•ing, soughs.** To make a soft murmuring or rustling sound. *—n.* A soft murmuring or rustling sound, as of the wind or a gentle surf.

sought (sôt) *v.* Past tense and past participle of **seek.**

soul (sōl) *n.* **1.** The spiritual nature of a person, regarded as the source of thought and emotion, and often believed to separate from the body after death and live forever. **2.** A spirit; a ghost. **3.** A human being: *not a soul in sight.* **4.** The central or vital part of something: *The soul of that business is its sales force.* **5.** A sense of ethnic pride among Black people and especially African-Americans. **6.** A strong, deeply felt emotion conveyed by a speaker or an artist. **7.** Soul music. [First written down about 725 in Old English and spelled *sāwol.*]

❑ *These sound alike:* **soul, sol** (musical note), **sole[1]** (foot part), **sole[2]** (only), **sole[3]** (fish).

soul•ful (sōl′fəl) *adj.* Full of or expressing a deep feeling. **—soul′ful•ly** *adv.* **—soul′ful•ness** *n.*

soul•less (sōl′lĭs) *adj.* Lacking sensitivity or the capacity for deep feeling. **—soul′less•ly** *adv.*

soul music *n.* Popular music developed by Black Americans and combining elements of gospel music and rhythm and blues.

sound[1] (sound) *n.* **1.** A type of wave motion that travels through air and other elastic materials as variations of internal pressure and density, detectable by human ears in air when the variation of pressure is between about 20 and 20,000 hertz. **2.a.** The sensation produced in the organs of hearing by waves of this type. **b.** Sensations of this type considered as a group. **3.** A distinctive noise: *the sound of laughter.* **4.** The distance over which something can be heard; earshot: *within the sound of my voice.* **5.** A noise made as part of human speech: *the sound of* y *in* try. **6.** A mental impression; import; implication: *He did not like the sound of the invitation.* **7.** Recorded material, as for a motion picture: *a good film but the sound was bad.* *—v.* **sound•ed, sound•ing, sounds.** *—intr.* **1.** To make a sound: *The whistle sounded.* **2.** To produce a certain audible effect: *The words* break *and* brake *sound alike.* **3.** To seem to be: *The news sounds good.* *—tr.* To summon, announce, or signal by a sound: *sound a warning.* ***—idiom.*** **sound off.** To express one's views vigorously: *sounding off about the unexpected test.* [First written down about 1280 in Middle English and spelled *soun,* from Latin *sonus.*] —SEE NOTE.

sound[2] (sound) *adj.* **sound•er, sound•est. 1.** Free from defect, decay, or damage; in good condition: *The bridge is sound.* **2.** Free from disease or injury. **3.** Solid and firm: *a sound foundation.* **4.** Financially secure: *a sound economy.* **5.** Logical and correct: *sound reasoning.* **6.** Complete or thorough. **7.**

Deep and unbroken: *a sound sleep.* **8.** Legally valid; good: *sound title.* —*adv.* Thoroughly; deeply: *sound asleep.* [First written down about 725 in Old English and spelled *gesund.*] **—sound′ly** *adv.* **—sound′ness** *n.*

sound[3] (sound) *n.* **1.** A long body of water, wider than a strait or channel, connecting larger bodies of water. **2.** A long wide inlet of the ocean. [First written down about 725 in Old English and spelled *sund,* swimming, sea.]

sound[4] (sound) *v.* **sound•ed, sound•ing, sounds.** —*tr.* **1.** To measure the depth of (water), especially by means of a weighted line. **2.** To try to learn (someone's) attitudes or opinions: *I want to sound her out on this before we begin.* —*intr.* **1.** To measure depth: *sounding with a long pole.* **2.** To dive swiftly downward: *The whale sounded and did not reappear.* [First written down about 1385 in Middle English and spelled *sounden,* from Old French *sonder,* from *sonde,* sounding line.]

sound barrier *n.* The sonic barrier.

sound box *n.* A hollow chamber in the body of a musical instrument, such as a violin, that intensifies the resonance of the tone.

sound•er (**soun′**dər) *n.* A person or device that measures the depth of water.

sound•ing[1] (**soun′**dĭng) *n.* **1.** The act or process of making measurements of depth, especially of a body of water. **2.** A measured depth of water. **3.** An investigation, as of the atmosphere, to obtain information.

sound•ing[2] (**soun′**dĭng) *adj.* **1.** Emitting a full sound; resonant. **2.** Noisy but with little significance.

sounding board *n.* **1.** A thin board forming the upper portion of the resonant chamber of a musical instrument, such as a violin or piano, and serving to increase resonance. **2.** A structure placed over or behind a podium to reflect music or a speaker's voice to the audience. **3.** A person or group whose reactions to an idea or opinion will serve as a measure of its effectiveness or acceptability. **4.** A device or means serving to spread or popularize an idea or point of view: *using the press as a sounding board.*

sound•less (**sound′**lĭs) *adj.* Having or making no sound. **—sound′less•ly** *adv.*

sound•proof (**sound′**pro͞of′) *adj.* Designed or treated to allow no audible sound to pass through or enter: *a soundproof room.* **—sound′proof′** *v.*

sound•track (**sound′**trăk′) *n.* **1.** The narrow strip at the edge of a motion-picture film that carries a recording of the sound. **2.** The music that accompanies a movie. **3.** A recording of such music available for purchase.

sound wave *n.* A series of vibrations carried through a material, such as air or water, by which sounds are transmitted.

soup (so͞op) *n.* A liquid food prepared from meat, fish, or vegetable stock, often with other ingredients added. [First written down before 1325 in Middle English and spelled *soupe,* from Old French, of Germanic origin.]

soup kitchen *n.* A place where food is offered free or at a very low cost to the needy.

soup•y (**so͞o′**pē) *adj.* **soup•i•er, soup•i•est. 1.** Having the consistency or appearance of soup. **2.** *Slang.* Foggy. **3.** *Informal.* Sentimental

sour (sour) *adj.* **sour•er, sour•est. 1.** Having an acid taste; sharp, tart, or tangy: *sour lemonade.* **2.** Spoiled; rancid: *The milk became sour.* **3.** Bad-tempered; cross; peevish: *a sour temper.* **4.** Worse than expected or than usual; bad: *His career went sour.* **5.** Of or relating to soil that is so acidic as to harm crops. —*n.* **1.** The sensation of a sharp acid taste. **2.** A thing that is sour. —*tr. & intr.v.* **soured, sour•ing, sours.** To make or become sour. [First written down about 1000 in Old English and spelled *sūr.*] **—sour′ly** *adv.* **—sour′ness** *n.*

source (sôrs) *n.* **1.** A place or thing from which something comes; a point of origin: *used the sea as a source of food.* **2.** The beginning of a stream or river. **3.** A person or thing that supplies information: *Who is your source for that story?* [First written down in 1346 in Middle English, from Old French *sourse,* from Latin *surgere,* to rise.]

sour cream *n.* Cream that has soured naturally, used in soups, salads, and various meat dishes.

sour•dough (**sour′**dō′) *n.* Sour fermented dough used as a leaven for bread.

sour grapes *pl.n.* The denying that something is desirable after one has learned it cannot be had.

Sou•sa (**so͞o′**zə *or* **so͞o′**sə), **John Philip.** 1854–1932. American composer who wrote marches such as *Stars and Stripes Forever* (1897).

John Philip Sousa

sou•sa•phone (**so͞o′**zə fōn′) *n.* A large brass wind instrument similar to a tuba, designed for use in marching bands. [First written down in 1925 in Modern English, after John Philip *Sousa.*]

souse (sous) *tr.v.* **soused, sous•ing, sous•es. 1.** To plunge into a liquid. **2.** To make soaking wet; drench. **3.** To steep in a brine or other liquid, as in pickling. **4.** *Slang.* To make drunk. —*n.* **1.** Something pickled in brine, especially the feet or ears of a pig. **2.** The brine used in pickling. **3.** *Slang.* A drunkard.

south (south) *n.* **1.** The direction to the right of sunrise, directly opposite north. **2.** Often **South.** A region or part of a country in this direction. **3. South.** The southern part of the United States, especially the states that fought for the Confederacy in the Civil War. —*adj.* **1.** Of, in, or toward the south: *the south side of the mountain.* **2.** From the south: *a dry south wind.* —*adv.* In, from, or toward the south: *He pointed south. We hiked south.* [First written down about 725 in Old English and spelled *sūth.*]

South Af•ri•ca (**ăf′**rĭ kə). A country of southern Africa on the Atlantic and Indian oceans. Pretoria is the administrative capital; Cape Town, the legislative capital; Bloemfontein, the judicial capital. Population, 24,208,140. **—South Af′ri•can** *adj. & n.*

sousaphone

South A•mer•i•ca (ə **mĕr′**ĭ kə). A continent of the southern Western Hemisphere southeast of North America between the Atlantic and Pacific oceans.

South•amp•ton (south **hămp′**tən *or* sou **thămp′**tən). A borough of south-central England on an inlet of the English Channel. Population, 208,800.

south•bound (**south′**bound′) *adj.* Going toward the south.

South Car•o•li•na (kăr′ə **lī′**nə). A state of the southeast United States on the Atlantic Ocean northeast of Georgia. It was admitted as one of the original Thirteen Colonies in 1788. South Carolina was a leader in the movement for independence from Great Britain and was the first state to secede from the Union (1860) before the Civil War. Capital, Columbia. Population, 3,505,707. —SEE NOTE at **North Carolina.**

South Chi•na Sea (**chī′**nə). An arm of the western Pacific Ocean bounded by southeast China, Taiwan, the Philippines, Borneo, and Vietnam.

South Da•ko•ta (də **kō′**tə). A state of the north-central United States north of Nebraska. It was admitted as the 40th state in 1889. Pierre is the capital and Sioux Falls the largest city. Population, 699,999. —SEE NOTE at **North Dakota.**

south•east (south **ēst′**) *n.* **1.** The direction halfway between east and south. **2.** An area or a region that lies in this direction. **3. Southeast.** A part of the southeast United States generally including Ala-

ă	pat	oi	boy
ā	pay	ou	out
âr	care	o͝o	took
ä	father	o͞o	boot
ĕ	pet	ŭ	cut
ē	be	ûr	urge
ĭ	pit	th	thin
ī	pie	*th*	this
îr	pier	hw	whoop
ŏ	pot	zh	vision
ō	toe	ə	about
ô	paw	N	*French* bon

sow[2]

Word History: soy

Most people know that **soy** or **soya sauce** goes with rice and comes from the Far East, but from where in the Far East? The Chinese expression for **soy sauce** is *jiàng yóu* ("soy" + "sauce"), but *jiàng* would have become *jang*, or something like that, in English, not *soy*. The Japanese, however, got much of their civilization from China, and *siayau-yu* or *shō-yu* is the Japanese pronunciation of the Chinese phrase *jiàng yóu*, and there is a variant Japanese pronunciation *sōyu*. Thus Japanese is the source of our *soy*, but not directly, because *soy* first appears in English in 1679, 55 years after the English were expelled from Japan. In 1679 the only Westerners allowed to trade in Japan were the Dutch, and it is from the Dutch word *soya* that English gets the words *soya* and *soy*.

bama, Georgia, South Carolina, and Florida. —*adj.* **1.** To, toward, or in the southeast: *the southeast corner.* **2.** Coming from the southeast: *a southeast wind.* —*adv.* In, from, or toward the southeast: *walking southeast.* —**south•east′ern** *adj.*

Southeast A•sia (ā′zhə *or* ā′shə). A region of Asia bounded roughly by the Indian subcontinent on the west, China on the north, and the Pacific Ocean on the east. It includes Indochina, the Malay Peninsula, and the Malay Archipelago.

south•east•er (south ē′stər) *n.* A storm or gale that blows from the southeast.

south•east•er•ly (south ē′stər lē) *adj.* **1.** Situated toward or facing the southeast: *a southeasterly direction.* **2.** Coming from the southeast: *a southeasterly breeze.* —**south•east′er•ly** *adv.*

south•east•ward (south ēst′wərd) *adv. & adj.* To or toward the southeast: *journeyed southeastward.* —*n.* A direction or region to the southeast. —**south•east′wards** *adv.*

south•er (sou′*th*ər) *n.* A strong wind from the south.

south•er•ly (sŭ*th*′ər lē) *adj.* **1.** Situated toward or facing the south: *a southerly direction.* **2.** Coming from the south: *a southerly wind.* —*n., pl.* **south•er•lies.** A storm or wind from the south. —**south′er•ly** *adv.*

south•ern (sŭ*th*′ərn) *adj.* **1.** Situated in, toward, or facing the south: *the southern side of the mountain.* **2.** Coming from the south: *a southern breeze.* **3.** Often **Southern.** Of, relating to, or characteristic of southern regions or the South: *a southern climate.*

Southern Cross *n.* A constellation in the Southern Hemisphere.

south•ern•er also **South•ern•er** (sŭ*th*′ər nər) *n.* A person who lives in or comes from the south, especially the southern United States.

Southern Hemisphere *n.* **1.** The half of the earth south of the equator. **2.** The half of the celestial sphere south of the celestial equator.

southern lights *pl.n.* The aurora australis.

south•ern•most (sŭ*th*′ərn mōst′) *adj.* Farthest south.

Southern Yem•en (yĕm′ən *or* yā′mən). A former country of southwest Asia on the Arabian Peninsula. It gained its independence from Great Britain in 1967 and united with North Yemen in 1990 to form the new country of Yemen.

south•ing (sou′*th*ĭng) *n.* **1.** The difference in the latitudes between two positions as a result of southward movement. **2.** Southward movement.

South Island. An island of New Zealand southwest of North Island. It is the larger but less populous of the country's two principal islands.

South Ko•re•a (kə rē′ə). A country of eastern Asia west of Japan on the Yellow Sea. It was part of the ancient country of Korea. Seoul is the capital and the largest city. Population, 39,951,000.

south•land or **South•land** (south′lănd′) *n.* A region in the south of a country or an area.

south•paw (south′pô′) *n. Slang.* A left-handed person, especially a left-handed baseball pitcher.

South Pole *n.* **1.** The southern end of Earth's axis of rotation, a point in Antarctica. **2. south pole.** The pole of a magnet that tends to point south.

South Sea Islands. The islands of the southern Pacific Ocean, roughly including the same islands as Oceania.

South Seas. The oceans south of the equator, especially the southern Pacific Ocean.

South Vi•et•nam (vē ĕt′näm′ *or* vē′ĭt näm′). A former country of southeast Asia on the South China Sea. It existed from 1954 to 1975 and is now part of the country of Vietnam.

south•ward (south′wərd) *adv. & adj.* Toward, to, or in the south: *He gazed southward. She went on a southward hike.* —*n.* A direction or region to the south: *traveled to the southward.* —**south′ward•ly** *adj. & adv.* —**south′wards** *adv.*

south•west (south wĕst′) *n.* **1.** The direction halfway between south and west. **2.** An area or a region lying in this direction. **3. Southwest.** A region of the southwest United States generally considered to include New Mexico, Arizona, Texas, California, and Nevada and sometimes Utah and Colorado. —*adj.* **1.** Of, in, or toward the southwest: *a southwest window.* **2.** Coming from the southwest. —*adv.* In, from, or toward the southwest: *facing southwest.* —**south•west′ern** *adj.*

south•west•er (south wĕs′tər) also **sou′•west•er** (sou wĕs′tər) *n.* **1.** A storm or gale from the southwest. **2.** A waterproof hat with a broad brim in back to protect the neck.

south•west•er•ly (south wĕs′tər lē) *adj.* **1.** Situated toward or facing the southwest: *a southwesterly march.* **2.** Coming from the southwest: *a southwesterly wind.*

south•west•ward (south wĕst′wərd) *adv. & adj.* Toward, to, or in the southwest: *sailing southwestward; a southwestward journey.* —*n.* A southwestward direction or region.

sou•ve•nir (so͞o′və nîr′ *or* so͞o′və nîr′) *n.* A token kept as a remembrance, as of a place or an occasion; a memento.

sou′•west•er (sou wĕs′tər) *n.* Variant of **southwester.**

sov•er•eign (sŏv′ər ĭn *or* sŏv′rĭn) *n.* **1.** A person or group of persons with supreme authority over a state, especially a king or queen. **2.** A gold coin formerly used in Great Britain. —*adj.* **1.** Independent; self-governing: *sovereign states.* **2.** Having supreme rank or power: *a sovereign leader.* **3.** Highest; supreme: *sovereign wisdom.* [First written down about 1280 in Middle English and spelled *soverain*, from Old French, from Latin *super*, above.]

sov•er•eign•ty (sŏv′ər ĭn tē *or* sŏv′rĭn tē) *n., pl.* **sov•er•eign•ties. 1.** Supremacy of authority or rule: *sovereignty over a territory.* **2.** Royal rank, authority, or power: *They did not dispute his sovereignty.* **3.** Freedom from foreign control; independence: *Each state values its sovereignty.*

so•vi•et (sō′vē ĕt′ *or* sō′vē ĭt) *n.* **1.** One of the elected legislative assemblies that existed at the local, regional, and national levels in the Soviet Union. **2. Soviet.** A native or inhabitant of the Soviet Union. **3. Soviets.** The government of the Soviet Union. —*adj.* **1.** Often **Soviet.** Of or relating to the Union of Soviet Socialist Republics. **2.** Of or relating to a soviet.

Soviet Union. Union of Soviet Socialist Republics. —SEE NOTE at **Union of Soviet Socialist Republics.**

sow[1] (sō) *tr.v.* **sowed, sown** (sōn) or **sowed, sow•ing, sows. 1.** To plant (seeds) to produce a crop: *The farmer sowed wheat and corn.* **2.** To plant or scatter seed in or on: *She sowed her fields in the spring.* **3.** To propagate; spread: *sow rumors.* [First written down before 830 in Old English and spelled *sāwan*.]

❑ *These sound alike:* **sow**[1], **sew** (stitch), **so**[1] (thus), **so**[2] (musical note).

sow[2] (sou) *n.* **1.** An adult female pig. **2.** The adult female of certain other animals, such as the bear. [First written down before 800 in Old English and spelled *sugu*.]

sow bug (sou) *n.* Any of various small land crustaceans, commonly found under logs or stones and having an oval segmented body.

So•we•to (sə wĕ′tō *or* sə wā′tō). A city of northeast South Africa southwest of Johannesburg. Population, 868,580.

sown (sōn) *v.* A past participle of **sow**[1].

sox (sŏks) *n.* A plural of **sock**[1] (sense 1).

soy (soi) *n.* **1.** The soybean. **2.** Soy sauce. —SEE NOTE.

soy•a (soi′ə) *n.* The soybean.

soy•bean (soi′bēn′) *n.* **1.** The edible, highly nutritious seed of a plant native to Asia, used to make vegetable oil, flour, and many other products. **2.** The plant that bears such seeds.

soy sauce *n.* A brown salty liquid made by fermenting soybeans in brine and used to flavor food.

spa (spä) *n.* **1.** A resort providing therapeutic baths. **2.** A resort area having mineral springs. **3.** A business offering facilities and equipment for physical exercise.

space (spās) *n.* **1.a.** A set of points that satisfies some set of geometric rules: *a space of five dimensions.* **b.** The familiar three-dimensional region or field of everyday experience. **2.a.** The expanse in which the solar system, stars, and galaxies exist; the universe. **b.** The part of the universe beyond the solar system or beyond Earth's atmosphere. **3.** A blank or empty area: *Fill in the blank space.* **4.** An area provided for a particular purpose: *a parking space.* **5.a.** A period or interval of time. **b.** A little while: *Let's rest for a space.* **6.** Sufficient freedom to develop or explore one's needs, interests, and individuality. **7.** Any of the blank areas between the lines of a musical staff. **8.** In a telegraph system, an interval when the key is open or not in contact. —*tr.v.* **spaced, spac•ing, spac•es. 1.** To arrange or organize with spaces between: *Carefully space the words on the poster.* **2.** To separate or keep apart. [First written down before 1300 in Middle English, from Latin *spatium.*]

space•craft (spās′krăft′) *n., pl.* **spacecraft.** A vehicle designed for space travel.

space flight *n.* Flight beyond the atmosphere of Earth.

space probe *n.* A spacecraft carrying instruments designed for use in exploring the physical properties of outer space or of celestial bodies other than Earth.

space•ship (spās′shĭp′) *n.* A spacecraft.

space shuttle *n.* A reusable space vehicle designed to transport astronauts between Earth and space.

space sickness *n.* Motion sickness that results from space travel.

space station *n.* A large satellite equipped to support a human crew and designed to remain in orbit around Earth for a long period.

space suit *n.* A protective pressurized suit designed to allow the wearer to move about freely in space.

space-time (spās′tīm′) *n.* The four-dimensional continuum in which events or objects are located, consisting of the three dimensions of ordinary space plus the dimension of time.

space walk *n.* An excursion by an astronaut outside a spacecraft in space. —**space walker** *n.*

spac•ing (spā′sĭng) *n.* **1.** The act or result of arranging things so that they are separated by spaces. **2.** The spaces or a space between things.

spa•cious (spā′shəs) *adj.* **1.** Having much space; roomy; extensive: *a spacious room.* **2.** Vast in range or scope: *a spacious landscape.* —**spa′cious•ly** *adv.* —**spa′cious•ness** *n.*

spade[1] (spād) *n.* A digging tool with a thick handle and a flat heavy blade that can be pressed into the ground with the foot. —*tr.v.* **spad•ed, spad•ing, spades.** To dig with a spade: *spade the garden.* [First written down before 800 in Old English and spelled *spadu.*]

spade[2] (spād) *n.* **1.** A black leaf-shaped figure on a playing card. **2.** A playing card with this figure. **3.** also **spades.** *(used with a singular or plural verb).* The suit of cards having this figure as its symbol. [First written down in 1598 in Modern English, from Italian *spada,* from Greek *spathē,* broad blade.]

spa•dix (spā′dĭks) *n., pl.* **spa•di•ces** (spā′dĭ sēz′). A fleshy spike bearing tiny flowers, often surrounded by a part resembling a leaf or petal, as in the jack-in-the-pulpit.

spa•ghet•ti (spə gĕt′ē) *n.* A pasta made into long solid strings and cooked by boiling.

Spain (spān). A country of southwest Europe made up of most of the Iberian Peninsula and the Balearic and Canary Islands. It has been inhabited since the Stone Age and was united in 1492 under Ferdinand of Aragon and Isabella of Castile. Madrid is the capital and the largest city. Population, 38,872,389.

spake (spāk) *v. Archaic.* A past tense of **speak.**

span[1] (spăn) *n.* **1.** The distance between two points or ends, as of a bridge. **2.** A section of a bridge between two vertical supports. **3.** The distance from the tip of the thumb to the tip of the little finger when the hand is fully extended, formerly used as a unit of measure equal to about nine inches (23 centimeters). **4.** A period of time: *a span of four hours.* —*tr.v.* **spanned, span•ning, spans. 1.** To measure with or as if with the extended hand. **2.** To encircle with the hand or hands in or as if in measuring. **3.** To extend across in space or time: *a career that spans 30 years.* [First written down before 899 in Old English and spelled *spann,* hand's breadth.]

span[2] (spăn) *n.* A pair of animals matched in size, strength, or color and driven as a team: *a span of oxen.* [First written down in 1769 in American English, from Dutch *spannen,* to harness.]

span•dex (spăn′dĕks) *n.* A fiber or fabric made of a polymer containing polyurethane and used in elastic clothing.

span•gle (spăng′gəl) *n.* **1.** A small piece of sparkling metal or plastic sewn especially on clothes for decoration. **2.** A small sparkling object, drop, or spot: *spangles of sunlight.* —*v.* **span•gled, span•gling, span•gles.** —*tr.* To decorate with or as if with spangles. —*intr.* To sparkle in the manner of spangles.

Span•iard (spăn′yərd) *n.* A native or inhabitant of Spain.

span•iel (spăn′yəl) *n.* Any of several breeds of small to medium-sized dogs having drooping ears, short legs, and a silky wavy coat.

Span•ish (spăn′ĭsh) *adj.* Of or relating to Spain or its people, language, or culture. —*n.* **1.** The Romance language of the largest part of Spain and most of Central and South America. **2.** The people of Spain.

Spanish A•mer•i•ca (ə mĕr′ĭ kə). The former Spanish possessions in the New World, including most of South and Central America, Mexico, Cuba, Puerto Rico, and the Dominican Republic.

Spanish American *n.* **1.** A native or inhabitant of Spanish America. **2.** A U.S. citizen or resident of Hispanic descent. —*adj.* **Span•ish-A•mer•i•can.** (spăn′ĭsh ə mĕr′ĭ kən). **1.** Of or relating to Spanish America or its peoples or cultures. **2.** Of or relating to Spain and America, especially the United States.

Spanish Main (mān). **1.** The coastal region of mainland Spanish America in the 16th and 17th centuries. **2.** The section of the Caribbean Sea crossed by Spanish ships in colonial times.

Spanish moss *n.* A plant of the southeast United States and tropical America that grows on trees and hangs down in long grayish masses.

spank (spăngk) *tr.v.* **spanked, spank•ing, spanks.**

soybean

space shuttle
Atlantis landing
at Edwards Air Force Base
in California, March 1990

space suit
Edwin E. Aldrin, Jr., on the moon,
July 1969

ă	pat	oi	boy
ā	pay	ou	out
âr	care	ŏŏ	took
ä	father	ōō	boot
ĕ	pet	ŭ	cut
ē	be	ûr	urge
ĭ	pit	th	thin
ī	pie	*th*	this
îr	pier	hw	whoop
ŏ	pot	zh	vision
ō	toe	ə	about
ô	paw	N	*French* bon

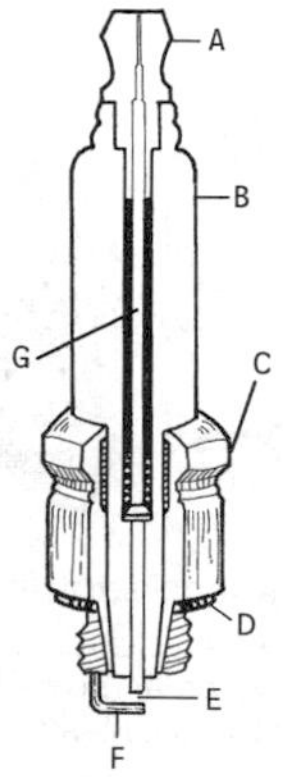

spark plug
Cross section of a spark plug
A. Terminal
B. Insulator
C. Body
D. Gasket
E. Gap
F. Ground electrode
G. Center electrode

sparrow
Song sparrow

To slap on the buttocks with a flat object or the open hand. —*n.* A slap on the buttocks.

spank•ing (spăng′kĭng) *adj.* **1.** *Informal.* Exceptional; remarkable. **2.** Bright; fast: *a spanking pace.* **3.** Brisk and fresh: *a spanking breeze.* —*adv.* Used as an intensive: *a spanking new kitchen.* —*n.* A series of slaps on the buttocks, given as punishment.

span•ner (spăn′ər) *n. Chiefly British.* A wrench.

spar[1] (spär) *n.* A pole, such as a mast, boom, yard, or bowsprit, used on a sailing vessel. [First written down before 1325 in Middle English and spelled *sparre,* rafter.]

spar[2] (spär) *intr.v.* **sparred, spar•ring, spars. 1.** To participate in a practice boxing match. **2.** To exchange words in a quarrel or an argument. [First written down about 1380 in Middle English and spelled *sparren,* to go quickly.]

spare (spâr) *tr.v.* **spared, spar•ing, spares. 1.** To treat mercifully; deal with leniently. **2.** To refrain from destroying or harming: *spared the trees.* **3.** To save or relieve from experiencing or doing: *I spared you the trouble of returning the books.* **4.** To hold back or avoid: *We spared no expense for the party.* **5.** To use in small amounts: *Don't spare the pepper.* **6.** To give or grant out of one's resources: *Can you spare ten minutes?* —*adj.* **spar•er, spar•est. 1.a.** Kept in reserve: *a spare tire.* **b.** Being in excess of what is needed; extra: *spare cash.* **c.** Free for other use: *spare time.* **2.a.** Not abundant; meager: *a spare breakfast.* **b.** Thin or lean. See Synonyms at **lean[2]**. —*n.* **1.** A replacement, such as a tire, reserved for future need. **2.a.** The act of knocking down all ten pins with two rolls of a bowling ball. **b.** The score so made. —***idiom.* to spare.** In addition to what is needed: *We have ice cream to spare.* —**spare′ly** *adv.* —**spare′ness** *n.*

spare•ribs (spâr′rĭbz′) *pl.n.* Pork ribs with most of the meat trimmed off.

spar•ing (spâr′ĭng) *adj.* Thrifty; frugal. —**spar′ing•ly** *adv.* —**spar′ing•ness** *n.*

spark (spärk) *n.* **1.** A glowing particle, such as one thrown off or left over from a fire or one caused by friction. **2.a.** A flash of light, especially one produced by electric discharge. **b.** A short pulse of electric current. **3.** Something small that starts or remains of something; a seed or trace: *the spark of rebellion; no spark of interest in continuing the club.* —*v.* **sparked, spark•ing, sparks.** —*intr.* To give off sparks. —*tr.* To set in motion or rouse to action: *His speech sparked a controversy.*

spar•kle (spär′kəl) *intr.v.* **spar•kled, spar•kling, spar•kles. 1.** To give off sparks. **2.** To give off or reflect flashes of light; glitter. **3.** To be brilliant in performance: *She sparkled on the piano.* **4.** To be lively: *The conversation sparkled at the dinner table.* **5.** To release bubbles of gas; effervesce. —*n.* **1.** A small spark or glowing particle. **2.** Liveliness; vivacity. **3.** The releasing of bubbles of gas; effervescence.

spar•kler (spär′klər) *n.* **1.** A person or thing that sparkles. **2.** A firework that burns slowly and produces a shower of sparks.

spark plug *n.* A device that fits into the combustion chamber of an internal-combustion engine and produces an electric spark to ignite the fuel mixture.

spar•row (spăr′ō) *n.* **1.** Any of various small brownish or grayish finches. **2.** Any of several similar or related birds, such as the house sparrow. [First written down before 800 in Old English and spelled *spearwa.*]

sparrow hawk *n.* **1.** A small North American falcon that preys on small birds and animals. **2.** A European hawk similar to this hawk.

sparse (spärs) *adj.* **spars•er, spars•est.** Not dense or crowded: *sparse vegetation; a sparse population.* —**sparse′ly** *adv.* —**sparse′ness** *n.* —**spar′si•ty** (spär′sĭ tē) *n.*

Spar•ta (spär′tə). A city-state of ancient Greece in the southeast Peloponnesus. It was noted for its militaristic policies and reached the height of its power in the sixth century B.C.

Spar•tan (spär′tn) *adj.* **1.** Of or relating to Sparta or its people. **2.** Simple, frugal, or self-disciplined: *Spartan furnishings; a Spartan lifestyle.* —*n.* **1.** A citizen of Sparta. **2.** A person of Spartan character.

spasm (spăz′əm) *n.* **1.** A sudden involuntary contraction of a muscle or group of muscles. **2.** A sudden burst of energy, activity, or emotion. [First written down in 1373 in Middle English and spelled *spasom,* from Greek *spasmos,* from *span,* to pull.]

spas•mod•ic (spăz mŏd′ĭk) *adj.* **1.** Relating to, affected by, or resembling a spasm. **2.** Happening intermittently; fitful: *spasmodic attempts to change jobs.* **3.** Given to sudden outbursts of energy or feeling; excitable.

spas•tic (spăs′tĭk) *adj.* **1.** Of, relating to, or marked by spasms. **2.** Affected with spastic paralysis. —*n.* A person affected with spastic paralysis.

spastic paralysis *n.* A chronic condition that involves exaggerated reflexes of the tendons and muscular spasms because of damage to motor nerves of the central nervous system.

spat[1] (spăt) *v.* A past tense and a past participle of **spit[1]**.

spat[2] (spăt) *n., pl.* **spat** or **spats.** The spawn of an oyster or a similar shellfish. —*intr.v.* **spat•ted, spat•ting, spats.** To spawn. Used of oysters and similar shellfish. [First written down in 1376 in Middle English.]

spat[3] (spăt) *n.* A cloth or leather covering for the ankle and the top part of the shoe, fastening under the shoe with a strap. Often used in the plural. [First written down in 1779 in Modern English and spelled *spatt,* short for *spatterdash.*]

spat[4] (spăt) *n.* A brief quarrel. —*intr.v.* **spat•ted, spat•ting, spats.** To engage in a brief quarrel. [First written down in 1804 in American English.]

spate (spāt) *n.* **1.** A sudden flood, rush, or outpouring: *a spate of words.* **2.** *Chiefly British.* A flash flood.

spathe (spāth) *n.* A plant part that resembles a leaf or petal and surrounds a fleshy flower spike, as in the jack-in-the-pulpit.

spa•tial (spā′shəl) *adj.* Of, relating to, or involving space. —**spa′tial•ly** *adv.*

spat•ter (spăt′ər) *v.* **spat•tered, spat•ter•ing, spat•ters.** —*tr.* **1.** To scatter in drops or small splashes: *She spattered paint on her dress.* **2.** To spot or soil with a liquid: *spattered his tie with gravy.* —*intr.* **1.** To come forth in drops or small splashes: *Mud from the passing car spattered on my shoes.* **2.** To fall in drops or splashes: *Rain spattered into the pool.* —*n.* **1.** The act of spattering. **2.** A spattering sound: *the spatter of raindrops.* **3.** A drop, splash, or small amount: *spatters of grease on the stove.*

spat•u•la (spăch′ə lə) *n.* A tool with a broad, flat, flexible blade, used to mix, spread, or lift material, such as paint or food. [First written down in 1525 in Modern English, from Latin *spatula,* flat piece of wood, splint, from *spatha,* broadsword.]

spav•in (spăv′ĭn) *n.* A disease of the hock joint of horses, causing stiffness and lameness.

spawn (spôn) *n.* **1.** The eggs of water animals such as fishes, amphibians, and mollusks. **2.** Offspring produced in large numbers. —*v.* **spawned, spawn•ing, spawns.** —*intr.* To lay eggs; produce spawn: *Salmon swim up streams to spawn.* —*tr.* **1.** To produce from such eggs: *Thousands of frogs were* *spawned in that pond.* **2.** To give rise to; bring about: *an act that spawned a revolution.*

spay (spā) *tr.v.* **spayed, spay•ing, spays.** To remove the ovaries of (a female animal).

SPCA *abbr.* An abbreviation of Society for the Prevention of Cruelty to Animals.

SPCC *abbr.* An abbreviation of Society for the Prevention of Cruelty to Children.

speak (spēk) *v.* **spoke** (spōk), **spo•ken** (**spō′**kən), **speak•ing, speaks.** *—intr.* **1.** To utter words; talk: *They spoke about the weather.* **2.** To express thoughts or feelings: *He spoke of his desire to travel.* **3.** To be on speaking terms: *They haven't spoken for years.* **4.** To deliver an address or a lecture: *She's speaking tonight at the rally.* *—tr.* **1.** To pronounce; utter: *He spoke kind words.* **2.** To converse in or be able to converse in (a language): *She speaks Chinese.* **3.** To express in words; tell: *speak the truth.* **4.** To communicate without words: *His eyes spoke volumes.* ***—idioms.*** **so to speak.** In a manner of speaking; as it were. **speak out.** To talk freely and fearlessly, as about a public issue. **speak up. 1.** To speak loud enough to be heard. **2.** To speak without fear or hesitation. [First written down about 725 in Old English and spelled *sprecan.*]

Synonyms: speak, talk, converse. These verbs mean to express one's thoughts by uttering words. **Speak** and **talk** are both very general: *The movie star refuses to speak to reporters about her private life. I want to talk to you about your book report.* **Converse** means to interchange thoughts and ideas by talking: *They spent the evening laughing and conversing about old times.*

speak•eas•y (**spēk′**ē′zē) *n., pl.* **speak•eas•ies.** A place for the illegal sale of alcoholic drinks, especially during Prohibition in the United States.

speak•er (**spē′**kər) *n.* **1.** A person who speaks: *speakers of Swahili.* **2.** A spokesperson. **3.** A person who delivers a speech in public. **4.** Often **Speaker.** The presiding officer of a legislative body. **5.** A loudspeaker.

speak•ing (**spē′**kĭng) *adj.* **1.** Capable of or involving speech: *a speaking voice.* **2.** Highly expressive: *speaking eyes.* **3.** True to life; striking: *a speaking likeness.* ***—idiom.*** **on speaking terms.** Friendly enough to exchange superficial remarks: *We're on speaking terms with our neighbors.*

spear¹ (spîr) *n.* **1.** A weapon consisting of a long shaft with a sharply pointed head. **2.** A device with a sharp point and barbs for spearing fish. *—tr.v.* **speared, spear•ing, spears.** To pierce with or as if with a spear. [First written down before 800 in Old English and spelled *spere.*]

spear² (spîr) *n.* A slender stalk, as of asparagus. *—intr.v.* **speared, spear•ing, spears.** To sprout like a spear. [First written down in 1509 in Modern English, variant of *spire*, tapering point.]

spear•fish (**spîr′**fĭsh′) *intr.v.* **spear•fished, spear•fish•ing, spear•fish•es.** To fish with a spear or spear gun.

spear gun *n.* A device that shoots a short spear under water, used to spear fish.

spear•head (**spîr′**hĕd′) *n.* **1.** The head of a spear. **2.** The front forces in a military campaign. **3.** The driving force in an endeavor. *—tr.v.* **spear•head•ed, spear•head•ing, spear•heads.** To lead: *spearheaded the effort to develop solar energy.*

spear•mint (**spîr′**mĭnt′) *n.* A common mint plant that yields an oil used as flavoring.

spe•cial (**spĕsh′**əl) *adj.* **1.** Surpassing what is common or usual; exceptional: *a special occasion.* **2.** Distinct among others of a kind: *a special camera.* **3.** Peculiar to a specific person or thing: *special interests.* **4.** Having a specific function or application: *special training.* **5.** Particularly dear and esteemed: *special friends.* **6.** Additional; extra: *a special flight.* *—n.* **1.** Something arranged or designed for a particular service or occasion. **2.** A featured attraction, such as a reduced price: *a special on peaches.* **3.** A single television production that features a specific work, topic, or performer. **—spe′cial•ly** *adv.*

special delivery *n.* The delivery of a piece of mail, for an additional charge, by special messenger rather than by scheduled delivery.

special education *n.* Instruction designed for students whose needs cannot be met by standard classroom education.

special interest *n.* A group or an organization attempting to influence legislators in favor of a particular interest or issue.

spe•cial•ist (**spĕsh′**ə lĭst) *n.* A person whose work is restricted to a particular activity or to a particular branch of study or research, as a doctor who practices a particular branch of medicine.

spe•cial•ize (**spĕsh′**ə līz′) *intr.v.* **spe•cial•ized, spe•cial•iz•ing, spe•cial•iz•es. 1.** To focus on a special study, activity, or product: *specialized in underwater photography; a shop that specializes in sports clothes.* **2.** To develop so as to become adapted to a particular environment, function, or way of life: *Some worms have specialized so that they are parasites of only one kind of animal.* **—spe′cial•i•za′tion** (spĕsh′ə lĭ **zā′**shən) *n.*

spe•cial•ty (**spĕsh′**əl tē) *n., pl.* **spe•cial•ties. 1.** A special pursuit, occupation, talent, or skill: *His specialty is portrait painting.* **2.** A special item or feature: *The restaurant's specialty is pastry.*

spe•cie (**spē′**shē *or* **spē′**sē) *n.* Coined money.

spe•cies (**spē′**shēz *or* **spē′**sēz) *n., pl.* **species. 1.a.** A group of similar animals or plants that are regarded as of the same kind and that are able to produce fertile offspring. See table at **taxonomy. b.** An animal or a plant belonging to such a group, identified by a scientific name consisting of two Latin terms. **2.** A type, kind, or sort.

spe•cif•ic (spĭ **sĭf′**ĭk) *adj.* **1.** Stating or stated clearly and in detail: *Be specific about what you want.* **2.** Of or relating to a biological species: *The specific name of human beings is* Homo sapiens. **3.** Special, distinctive, or unique: *a specific trait.* **4.** Intended for or acting on one particular thing: *a specific remedy for the infection.* *—n.* **1.** Something designed for a particular use or purpose, especially a remedy intended for a particular disorder. **2. specifics.** Details; particulars: *Tell me what happened and give me the specifics.* **—spe•cif′i•cal•ly** *adv.*

spec•i•fi•ca•tion (spĕs′ə fĭ **kā′**shən) *n.* **1.** The act of specifying. **2.a. specifications.** A statement giving an exact description, as of a product or a structure to be constructed. **b.** A single item that has been specified.

specific gravity *n.* **1.** The quotient of the measure of the mass of a solid or liquid divided by the measure of the mass of an equal volume of water at 4°C (39°F). **2.** The quotient of the measure of the mass of a gas divided by the measure of the mass of an equal volume of air or hydrogen under prescribed conditions of temperature and pressure.

specific heat *n.* **1.** The ratio of the amount of heat needed to raise the temperature of a unit mass of a substance by one unit to the amount of heat needed to raise the temperature of a unit mass of a reference substance, usually water, by the same amount. **2.** The amount of heat, measured in calories, needed to raise the temperature of one gram of a substance by one degree Centigrade.

spec•i•fy (**spĕs′**ə fī′) *tr.v.* **spec•i•fied, spec•i•fy•ing, spec•i•fies. 1.** To state clearly or in detail. **2.** To include in a specification.

ă	pat	oi	boy
ā	pay	ou	out
âr	care	o͝o	took
ä	father	o͞o	boot
ĕ	pet	ŭ	cut
ē	be	ûr	urge
ĭ	pit	th	thin
ī	pie	*th*	this
îr	pier	hw	whoop
ŏ	pot	zh	vision
ō	toe	ə	about
ô	paw	N	*French* bon

Word Building: spectator

The word root *–spec–* in English words comes from the Latin verb *specere,* "to look at, observe." A **spectator,** therefore, is literally "a watcher." To **inspect** means "to look into, inquire into" (using the prefix *in–²,* "in, into"); **introspection** is literally "a mental look within oneself" (*intrō–,* "inside"); **retrospection** means "a review, a backward look at the past" (*retrō–,* "backward"); and a **prospect** is literally "something seen ahead of one or presented to one, view" (*pro–,* "in front of, before").

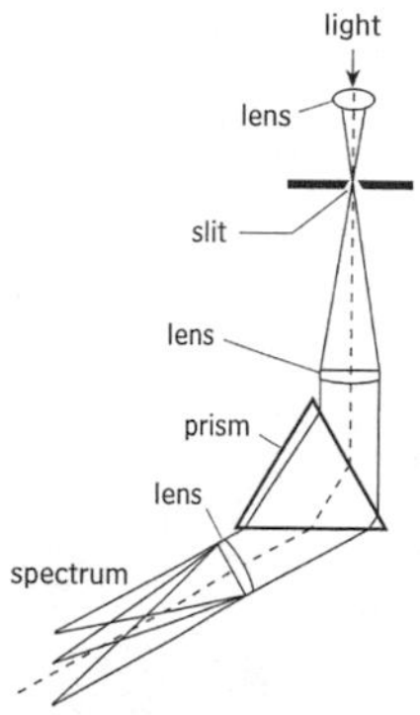

spectroscope

Edmund Spenser

spec•i•men (spĕs′ə mən) *n.* **1.** An element of a set or a part of a whole, taken as representative of the entire set or the whole. **2.** A sample, as of blood, tissue, or urine, used for analysis.

spe•cious (spē′shəs) *adj.* Seemingly fair, sound, or true, but actually false: *specious reasoning.*

speck (spĕk) *n.* **1.** A small spot, mark, or discoloration: *brown specks on the paper.* **2.** A small amount; a bit: *a speck of dust.* —*tr.v.* **specked, speck•ing, specks.** To mark with specks: *Her jeans were specked with mud.*

speck•le (spĕk′əl) *n.* A speck or small spot, especially a natural marking on skin, feathers, or leaves.

speck•led (spĕk′əld) *adj.* Covered with speckles or small spots.

spec•ta•cle (spĕk′tə kəl) *n.* **1.** Something that can be seen, especially a remarkable or impressive sight: *The meteor shower was quite a spectacle.* **2.** A public performance or display, especially on a grand scale. **3.** A regrettable display: *He got angry and made a spectacle of himself.* **4. spectacles.** A pair of eyeglasses.

spec•tac•u•lar (spĕk tăk′yə lər) *adj.* Of the nature of a spectacle; impressive or sensational: *a spectacular view.* —**spec•tac′u•lar•ly** *adv.*

spec•ta•tor (spĕk′tā′tər) *n.* An observer of an event. [First written down before 1586 in Modern English, from Latin *spectāre,* to watch.] —SEE NOTE.

spec•ter (spĕk′tər) *n.* **1.** A ghost; a phantom. **2.** A haunting or disturbing image or prospect.

spec•tra (spĕk′trə) *n.* A plural of **spectrum.**

spec•tral (spĕk′trəl) *adj.* **1.** Of or resembling a specter; ghostly. **2.** Of or produced by a spectrum. —**spec′tral•ly** *adv.*

spec•trom•e•ter (spĕk trŏm′ĭ tər) *n.* **1.** A spectroscope equipped with devices for measuring the wavelengths of the radiation observed by it. **2.** An instrument used to measure the index of refraction of a substance. —**spec•trom′e•try** *n.*

spec•tro•scope (spĕk′trə skōp′) *n.* Any of various instruments used to resolve radiation into spectra and to make observations or recordings.

spec•trum (spĕk′trəm) *n., pl.* **spec•tra** (spĕk′trə) or **spec•trums. 1.** A band of colors seen when white light is broken up according to wavelengths, as when passing through a prism or striking water drops. **2.** A broad range of related qualities, ideas, or activities: *a wide spectrum of ideas.* [First written down in 1611 in Modern English, from Latin *spectrum,* appearance, from *specere,* to look at.]

spec•u•late (spĕk′yə lāt′) *v.* **spec•u•lat•ed, spec•u•lat•ing, spec•u•lates.** —*intr.* **1.** To think deeply on a subject; ponder. **2.** To buy or sell something that involves a risk on the chance of making a profit: *speculating on the stock exchange.* —*tr.* To assume to be true without conclusive evidence: *speculated that there were mineral deposits in the rocks.* [First written down in 1599 in Modern English, from Latin *speculārī,* to observe, from *specula,* watchtower.]

spec•u•la•tion (spĕk′yə lā′shən) *n.* **1.a.** The act of thinking deeply about a subject; consideration; contemplation. **b.** A conclusion, an idea, or an opinion reached by guessing. **2.a.** A business deal involving speculation. **b.** Involvement in such business deals.

spec•u•la•tive (spĕk′yə lə tĭv *or* spĕk′yə lā′tĭv) *adj.* **1.** Of or based on mental speculation. **2.** Given to making guesses. **3.** Engaging in or involving financial speculation. —**spec′u•la•tive•ly** *adv.* —**spec′u•la•tive•ness** *n.*

spec•u•la•tor (spĕk′yə lā′tər) *n.* A person who speculates.

sped (spĕd) *v.* A past tense and a past participle of **speed.**

speech (spēch) *n.* **1.** The act of speaking. **2.** The ability to speak. **3.** Something spoken; an utterance. **4.** Communication by speaking; conversation. **5.** A talk or address. **6.** The manner in which a person speaks. **7.** The language or dialect of a nation or region: *American speech.* **8.** The study of oral communication. [First written down before 800 in Old English and spelled *sprǣc.*]

speech•less (spēch′lĭs) *adj.* **1.** Unable to speak. **2.** Temporarily unable to speak, as through astonishment. **3.** Not speaking; silent. **4.** Not expressed or not expressible in words: *speechless admiration.* —**speech′less•ly** *adv.* —**speech′less•ness** *n.*

speed (spēd) *n.* **1.** The rate at which an object changes position, especially the distance an object travels divided by the time of travel. **2.** Swiftness of action. **3.** The condition or act of moving rapidly; swiftness: *He finished the race with a show of speed.* **4.** A transmission gear or set of gears in a motor vehicle. **5.a.** A number that expresses the sensitivity to light of a photographic film, plate, or paper. **b.** The capacity of a lens to admit light at a particular aperture. **c.** The length of time the shutter of a camera is open to admit light. **6.** *Archaic.* Prosperity; luck. —*v.* **sped** (spĕd) or **speed•ed, speed•ing, speeds.** —*tr.* **1.** To cause to go or move rapidly. **2.** To increase the speed or rate of; accelerate: *speed up a mechanism.* **3.** To wish Godspeed to. —*intr.* **1.** To go or move quickly. **2.** To drive at a speed that exceeds a legal limit. **3.** To pass quickly: *The days sped by.* **4.** To move, work, or happen at a faster rate: *The phonograph speeded up.* —***idiom.*** **up to speed. 1.a.** Operating at maximum speed. **b.** Producing something or performing at an acceptable rate or level. **2.** *Informal.* Fully informed: *Bring me up to speed on the issue.* [First written down before 800 in Old English and spelled *spēd,* success, swiftness.]

speed•boat (spēd′bōt′) *n.* A fast motorboat.

speed•er (spē′dər) *n.* A person or thing that speeds, especially a driver who exceeds a legal or safe speed.

speed•om•e•ter (spĭ dŏm′ĭ tər) *n.* **1.** An instrument that indicates speed. **2.** An odometer.

speed-read•ing (spēd′rē′dĭng) *n.* A method of reading rapidly by skipping unimportant words in a text and by understanding groups of words at a time.

speed•up (spēd′ŭp′) *n.* **1.** An increase in speed; acceleration. **2.** Acceleration of production without increase in pay.

speed•way (spēd′wā′) *n.* **1.** A course for automobile or motorcycle racing. **2.** A road designed for high-speed traffic; an expressway.

speed•well (spēd′wĕl′) *n.* Any of various plants having clusters of small, usually blue flowers.

speed•y (spē′dē) *adj.* **speed•i•er, speed•i•est. 1.** Swift; quick: *a speedy runner.* **2.** Done without delay; prompt: *a speedy reply.* —**speed′i•ly** *adv.* —**speed′i•ness** *n.*

spe•le•ol•o•gy (spē′lē ŏl′ə jē) *n.* The study and exploration of caves. —**spe′le•ol′o•gist** *n.*

spell¹ (spĕl) *v.* **spelled** or **spelt** (spĕlt), **spell•ing, spells.** —*tr.* **1.** To name or write in order the letters forming (a word or part of a word). **2.** To be the letters of; form (a word or part of a word): *These letters spell* animal. **3.** To add up to; signify: *Her efforts spelled success.* —*intr.* To form a word or words by letters: *learned to spell.* —***idiom.*** **spell out.** To make perfectly clear and understandable: *spelled out the instructions for us.* [First written down before 1325 in Middle English and spelled *spellen,* from Old French *espeller* (of Germanic origin).]

spell² (spĕl) *n.* **1.** A word or group of words believed to have magic power. **2.** The condition of being bewitched or enchanted; a trance. **3.** Fascination;

charm: *the spell of a tropical island.* [First written down about 725 in Old English and spelled *spell*, discourse.]

spell³ (spĕl) *n.* **1.** A short indefinite period of time: *Let's visit for a spell.* **2.** *Informal.* A period of weather of a particular kind: *a cold spell.* **3.** A period of work; a shift: *a spell at the plane's controls.* **4.** *Informal.* A period or fit of illness: *a coughing spell.* —*tr.v.* **spelled, spell•ing, spells.** To relieve (someone) from work temporarily by taking a turn. [First written down in 1593, from Middle English *spellen*, to spare, from Old English *spelian*, to represent, substitute for.]

spell•bind (**spĕl′**bīnd′) *tr.v.* **spell•bound** (**spĕl′**-bound′), **spell•bind•ing, spell•binds.** To hold under or as if under a spell; enchant or fascinate.

spell•bound (**spĕl′**bound′) *adj.* Held as if under a spell; entranced; fascinated.

spell•er (**spĕl′**ər) *n.* **1.** A person who spells words: *good spellers.* **2.** A textbook with exercises that teach spelling.

spell•ing (**spĕl′**ĭng) *n.* **1.** The forming of words with letters in an accepted order. **2.** The way in which a word is spelled.

spelling bee *n.* A spelling contest in which participants drop out when they fail to spell a given word correctly.

spelt (spĕlt) *v.* A past tense and a past participle of **spell¹**.

spe•lunk•er (spĭ **lŭng′**kər *or* **spē′**lŭng′kər) *n.* One who explores and studies caves. —**spe′lunk′ing** *n.*

spend (spĕnd) *v.* **spent** (spĕnt), **spend•ing, spends.** —*tr.* **1.** To use or put out; expend: *spent an hour practicing.* **2.** To pass (time) in a specified place or manner: *spent my vacation hiking.* **3.** To pay out or squander (money): *spending my last five dollars.* **4.** To wear out; exhaust. —*intr.* To pay out money. —**spend′er** *n.*

spend•thrift (**spĕnd′**thrĭft′) *n.* A person who spends money wastefully or foolishly. —*adj.* Wasteful; extravagant.

Spen•ser (**spĕn′**sər), **Edmund.** 1552?–1599. English poet known chiefly for his epic romance *The Faerie Queene* (1590–1596).

spent (spĕnt) *v.* Past tense and past participle of **spend.** —*adj.* **1.** Used up; consumed: *spent mineral resources.* **2.** Having no more energy, force, or strength: *a spent horse.*

sperm (spûrm) *n., pl.* **sperm** or **sperms. 1.** A male reproductive cell; a spermatozoon. **2.** Semen.

sper•ma•ce•ti (spûr′mə **sē′**tē *or* spûr′mə **sĕt′**ē) *n., pl.* **sper•ma•ce•tis.** A white waxy substance obtained from the head of the sperm whale and used in making candles, ointments, and cosmetics.

sper•mat•o•phyte (spər **măt′**ə fīt′ *or* **spûr′**-mə tə fīt′) *n.* A plant that produces seeds, as a conifer or a flowering plant.

sper•mat•o•zo•on (spər măt′ə **zō′**ŏn′ *or* spûr′-mə tə **zō′**ŏn′) *n., pl.* **sper•mat•o•zo•a** (spər măt′ə-**zō′**ə *or* spûr′mə tə **zō′**ə). A male reproductive cell, usually having a long tail and uniting with an egg in the process of sexual reproduction.

sperm oil *n.* A yellow waxy oil obtained from the sperm whale, used as an industrial lubricant.

sperm whale *n.* Any of several whales having a long, narrow, toothed lower jaw and a large head in which there are cavities containing spermaceti and sperm oil.

spew (spyo͞o) *v.* **spewed, spew•ing, spews.** —*tr.* **1.** To send or force out in or as if in a stream: *volcanoes spewing out lava.* **2.** To vomit or cast out through the mouth. —*intr.* **1.** To flow or gush forth: *water spewed out.* **2.** To vomit.

sp gr *abbr.* An abbreviation of specific gravity.

sphag•num (**sfăg′**nəm) *n.* Any of various grayish mosses that grow in swamps and bogs and decompose to form peat.

sphe•noid bone (**sfē′**noid′) *n.* A bone with projections resembling wings, situated at the base of the skull.

sphere (sfîr) *n.* **1.** A three-dimensional geometric surface having all of its points the same distance from a given point. **2.** An object or a figure having this shape. **3.** A planet, star, or other celestial body. **4.** In ancient astronomy, any of a series of transparent revolving globes thought to have Earth as a center and to contain the sun, moon, planets, and stars. **5.** The extent of a person's knowledge, interests, or social position. **6.** An area of power, control, or influence: *Poland was once in the sphere of the Soviet Union.* [First written down before 1300 in Middle English and spelled *spere*, from Greek *sphaira*.]

spher•i•cal (**sfîr′**ĭ kəl *or* **sfĕr′**ĭ kəl) *adj.* **1.** Having the shape of a sphere. **2.** Of or relating to a sphere. **3.** Of or relating to celestial bodies. —**spher′i•cal•ly** *adv.*

sphe•roid (**sfîr′**oid′ *or* **sfĕr′**oid′) *n.* **1.** A three-dimensional geometric surface generated by rotating an ellipse on or about one of its axes. **2.** A figure or an object having such a shape.

sphinc•ter (**sfĭngk′**tər) *n.* A circular muscle that usually remains contracted and keeps the opening of a bodily passage closed, relaxing as required by normal functioning.

sphinx (sfĭngks) *n., pl.* **sphinx•es** or **sphin•ges** (**sfĭn′**jēz′). **1.** In Egyptian mythology, a figure having the body of a lion and the head of a man, ram, or hawk. **2.** In Greek mythology, a winged creature having the body of a lion and the head of a woman, noted for killing those who could not answer its riddle. **3.** A puzzling or mysterious person.

sphyg•mo•ma•nom•e•ter (sfĭg′mō mə **nŏm′**ĭ tər) *n.* An instrument used to measure the pressure of the blood in the arteries.

spice (spīs) *n.* **1.a.** Any of various plant substances having a pleasant or strong smell and taste, as cinnamon, nutmeg, pepper, or cloves, used to flavor food. **b.** Such substances considered as a group. **2.** A pungent odor or fragrance: *the spice of ripening fruit.* **3.** Something that adds zest or flavor: *Variety is the spice of life.* —*tr.v.* **spiced, spic•ing, spic•es. 1.** To flavor with spices. **2.** To add zest or flavor to: *She spiced her conversation with Spanish words.* [First written down before 1200 in Middle English, from Late Latin *speciēs*, wares, spices.]

spick-and-span (spĭk′ən **spăn′**) *adj.* Neat and clean; spotless.

spic•ule (**spĭk′**yo͞ol) *n., pl.* **spic•ules.** A small structure or part resembling a needle, as one of the mineral structures supporting the soft tissue of certain invertebrates, especially sponges.

spic•y (**spī′**sē) *adj.* **spic•i•er, spic•i•est. 1.** Having the flavor, smell, or quality of spice: *spicy pumpkin pie.* **2.** Lively; high-spirited. **3.** Slightly scandalous: *spicy stories.* —**spic′i•ly** *adv.* —**spic′i•ness** *n.*

spi•der (**spī′**dər) *n.* Any of numerous small animals that have eight legs and a body divided into two parts and that usually spin webs to trap insects. Spiders are sometimes confused with insects but belong to a different group, the arachnids, which also includes the scorpions, mites, and ticks. [First written down about 950 in Old English and spelled *spīthra*.]

spider monkey *n.* Any of several tropical American monkeys having long legs and a long tail.

spi•der•y (**spī′**də rē) *adj.* **1.** Resembling a spider in form, characteristics, or behavior: *the robot's spidery legs.* **2.** Resembling a spider's web in delicacy; very fine: *spidery handwriting.*

sphinx

c. 530 B.C. Greek grave monument

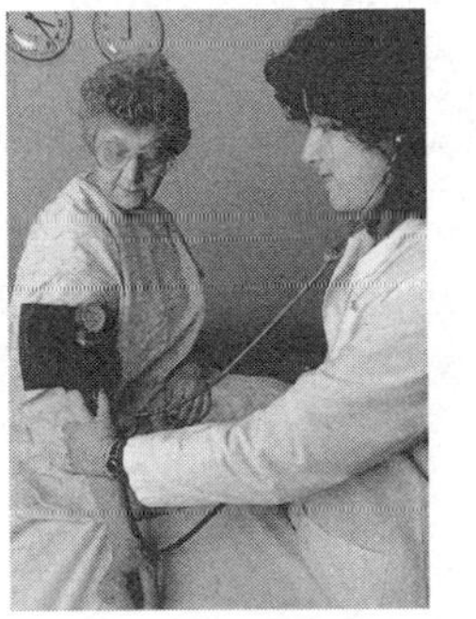

sphygmomanometer

spider monkey

ă	pat	oi	**boy**
ā	pay	ou	**out**
âr	care	o͝o	**took**
ä	father	o͞o	**boot**
ĕ	pet	ŭ	**cut**
ē	be	ûr	**urge**
ĭ	pit	th	**thin**
ī	pie	*th*	**this**
îr	pier	hw	**whoop**
ŏ	pot	zh	**vision**
ō	toe	ə	**about**
ô	paw	N	*French* **bon**

spied (spīd) *v.* Past tense and past participle of **spy.**

spies (spīz) *n.* Plural of **spy.** —*v.* Third person singular present tense of **spy.**

spiff•y (spĭf′ē) *adj.* **spiff•i•er, spiff•i•est.** *Informal.* Smart in appearance or dress; stylish.

spig•ot (spĭg′ət) *n.* **1.** A faucet. **2.** A plug or peg used to stop up the opening of a barrel.

spike[1] (spīk) *n.* **1.a.** A long, thick, sharp-pointed piece of wood or metal. **b.** A long heavy nail. **2.** A sharp-pointed projection along the top of a fence or wall. **3.** One of a number of sharp metal projections set in the soles of athletic shoes for grip. —*tr.v.* **spiked, spik•ing, spikes. 1.** To fasten or provide with a spike or spikes: *spiked the rails to the railroad ties.* **2.** To pierce or injure with a spike. **3.** To put an end to; thwart; block: *spiked the rumor.* **4.** *Informal.* To add alcoholic liquor to: *spiked the punch.* [First written down in 1345 in Middle English, from Old Norse *spīk.*]

spike[2] (spīk) *n.* **1.** An ear of grain. **2.** A long cluster of flowers lacking or nearly lacking stalks. [First written down before 1300 in Middle English and spelled *spic,* from Latin *spīca.*]

spike•nard (spīk′närd′) *n.* **1.** A fragrant plant from which a pleasant-smelling ointment was made in ancient times. **2.** The ointment made from this plant. **3.** A North American plant having small greenish flowers and an aromatic root.

spik•y (spī′kē) *adj.* **spik•i•er, spik•i•est.** Having projecting sharp points: *The bird had a spiky tail.* **—spik′i•ness** *n.*

spill[1] (spĭl) *v.* **spilled** or **spilt** (spĭlt), **spill•ing, spills.** —*tr.* **1.** To cause or allow to run or fall out of a container: *spilled water from the bucket.* **2.** To scatter (objects): *spilled the nails on the desk.* **3.** To shed (blood). **4.** To cause to fall; throw: *the bronco that spilled every rider.* **5.** *Informal.* To divulge; make known: *spill the news.* —*intr.* **1.** To run or fall out of a container: *milk spilling over the top of the glass.* **2.** To spread beyond limits: *Fans spilled onto the playing field.* —*n.* **1.** An act of spilling: *pollution caused by oil spills.* **2.** The amount spilled. **3.** A fall, as from a horse. [First written down about 950 in Old English and spelled *spillan,* to kill.]

spill[2] (spĭl) *n.* **1.** A piece of wood or rolled paper used to light a fire. **2.** A small peg, especially one used as a plug. [First written down about 1300 in Middle English and spelled *spille.*]

spill•age (spĭl′ĭj) *n.* **1.** The act of spilling. **2.** An amount spilled: *The spillage from the tanker has spread two miles.*

spill•way (spĭl′wā′) *n.* A channel for an overflow of water, as from a reservoir.

spilt (spĭlt) *v.* A past tense and a past participle of **spill**[1].

spin (spĭn) *v.* **spun** (spŭn), **spin•ning, spins.** —*tr.* **1.a.** To draw out and twist (fibers, as of cotton or wool) into thread. **b.** To make (thread or yarn) by drawing out and twisting fibers: *spinning yarn on a spindle.* **2.** To form (a web or cocoon, for example) from a fluid emitted from the body, as spiders and certain insects do. **3.** To relate; tell: *spin tales of the sea.* **4.** To cause to turn or rotate rapidly: *He spun the top.* —*intr.* **1.** To spin thread or yarn. **2.** To spin a web or cocoon. **3.** To rotate or turn rapidly: *wheels spinning.* See Synonyms at **turn. 4.** To seem to be whirling, as from dizziness; reel: *his head was spinning.* —*n.* **1.** The act of spinning. **2.** A rapid rotating motion. **3.** *Informal.* A short drive in a vehicle. [First written down before 800 in Old English and spelled *spinnan.*]

spin•ach (spĭn′ĭch) *n.* **1.** The edible dark green leaves of a garden plant, eaten as a vegetable. **2.** The plant that bears such leaves.

spinning wheel
Foot-operated spinning wheel

spi•nal (spī′nəl) *adj.* **1.** Of, relating to, or near the spine or spinal cord. **2.** Resembling a spine or similar part. —*n.* An injection of an anesthetic into the spinal canal.

spinal canal *n.* The passage formed by successive openings in the bones of the spinal column, containing the spinal cord and the membranes that enclose it.

spinal column *n.* In vertebrate animals, the series of jointed bones enclosing the spinal cord and forming the main support of the part of the body between the pelvis and head; the spine.

spinal cord *n.* The part of the central nervous system that extends from the brain and through the spinal canal, branching to form smaller nerves that serve the various parts or regions of the body.

spin•dle (spĭn′dl) *n.* **1.a.** A slender rounded rod on which fibers are spun by hand into thread and then wound. **b.** A similar rod on a spinning wheel or machine. **2.** A spike on which papers are stuck to keep them in place. **3.** A machine part that rotates or serves as an axis on which other parts rotate. **4.** The cellular structure along which the chromosomes are distributed during cell division. —*v.* **spin•dled, spin•dling, spin•dles.** —*tr.* To punch a hole or holes in: *Do not spindle, fold, or mutilate this card.* —*intr.* To grow into a thin, elongated, or weakly form. [First written down before 800 in Old English and spelled *spinel.*]

spin•dling (spĭnd′lĭng) *adj.* Spindly.

spin•dly (spĭnd′lē) *adj.* **spin•dli•er, spin•dli•est.** Slender and elongated, especially in a way that suggests weakness.

spin•drift (spĭn′drĭft′) *n.* Windblown sea spray.

spine (spīn) *n.* **1.** The spinal column of a vertebrate animal; the backbone. **2.** A sharp-pointed projecting plant or animal part, such as a thorn or quill. **3.** The supporting part at the back of a book, to which the covers are hinged. [First written down about 1400 in Middle English, from Latin *spīna.*]

spine•less (spīn′lĭs) *adj.* **1.** Lacking courage or will power. **2.** Having no spiny plant or animal parts. **3.** Lacking a spinal column. **—spine′less•ness** *n.*

spin•et (spĭn′ĭt) *n.* **1.** A small, compact, upright piano. **2.** A small harpsichord having a single keyboard.

spin•na•ker (spĭn′ə kər) *n.* A large triangular sail set on a spar swinging out opposite the mainsail on a racing yacht, used when running before the wind.

spin•ner (spĭn′ər) *n.* **1.** A person or thing that spins: *a spinner of yarn.* **2.** A fishing lure that spins rapidly.

spin•ner•et (spĭn′ə rĕt′) *n.* **1.** In spiders or insect larvae that spin silk, one of the small openings in the back part of the body through which a sticky fluid flows to form a fine thread. **2.** A device for making rayon, nylon, and other synthetic fibers, consisting of a plate pierced with holes through which plastic material is forced out in the form of fine threads.

spin•ning jenny (spĭn′ĭng) *n.* An early form of power-operated spinning machine having several spindles.

spinning wheel *n.* A device for spinning fibers into thread or yarn, consisting of a hand-operated or foot-operated wheel and one spindle.

spin•off or **spin-off** (spĭn′ôf′ *or* spĭn′ŏf′) *n.* An object, a product, or a process derived from a larger or more complex item or enterprise.

spin•ster (spĭn′stər) *n.* A woman who has remained single beyond the traditional age for marrying.

spin•y (spī′nē) *adj.* **spin•i•er, spin•i•est. 1.** Full of or covered with spines, thorns, or similar growth: *spiny undergrowth; a spiny hedgehog.* **2.** Shaped like a spine or spines: *spiny prickles.*

spir•a•cle (spĭr′ə kəl *or* spī′rə kəl) *n.* An opening through which certain animals breathe, as one of the openings in the exoskeleton of an insect or the blowhole of a whale.

spi•ral (spī′rəl) *n.* **1.** A curve that winds around a fixed center at a distance that constantly increases or decreases. **2.** A helix. **3.** An object or a figure having the shape of a spiral: *A spiral of smoke came from the chimney.* **4.** A course or path that takes the form of a spiral. —*intr.v.* **spi•raled, spi•ral•ing, spi•rals** also **spi•ralled, spi•ral•ling, spi•rals. 1.** To take a spiral form or course: *Smoke spiraled from the chimney.* **2.** To rise or fall with steady acceleration: *Costs are spiraling.* [First written down in 1656 in Modern English, from Latin *spīra*, coil.]

spire[1] (spīr) *n.* **1.** A top part or point that tapers upward. **2.** The pointed top of a tower. [First written down before 1000 in Old English and spelled *spīr*.]

spire[2] (spīr) *n.* **1.** A spiral. **2.** A single turn of a spiral. [First written down in 1572 in Modern English and spelled *spyre*, from Greek *speira*, coil.]

spi•ril•lum (spī rĭl′əm) *n., pl.* **spi•ril•la** (spī rĭl′ə). Any of various bacteria having a long, spirally twisted form.

spir•it (spĭr′ĭt) *n.* **1.** The force thought to give the body life. **2.** The soul, believed to depart from the body at death. **3.** The part of a human being associated with the mind, will, and feelings: *Though they can't be here, they're with us in spirit.* **4.** One's essential nature: *her sweet and gentle spirit.* **5.** A quality that distinguishes a person, a movement, or an epoch: *the daring spirit of the early aviators.* **6. spirits.** A mood or an emotional state: *in high spirits.* **7.** A particular mood marked by vigor, courage, or liveliness: *Their team showed a lot of spirit.* **8.** Strong loyalty or dedication: *school spirit.* **9.** A prevailing mood or attitude: *a spirit of rebellion in the land.* **10. Spirit. a.** Spiritual power in the universe, often identified as God. **b.** The Holy Spirit. **11.** A supernatural being such as a ghost, a fairy, an angel, or a demon. **12.** The real meaning, sense, or intent of something: *the spirit of the law.* **13.** An alcohol solution of an essential substance. Often used in the plural with a singular verb. **14. spirits.** An alcoholic beverage. —*tr.v.* **spir•it•ed, spir•it•ing, spir•its.** To carry off mysteriously or secretly: *Someone spirited the papers away.* [First written down about 1250 in Middle English, from Latin *spīritus*, breath, from *spīrāre*, to breathe.]

spir•it•ed (spĭr′ĭ tĭd) *adj.* **1.** Full of or marked by life, vigor, or courage: *a spirited defense of her rights.* **2.** Having a specified mood or nature. *high-spirited.*

spir•it•less (spĭr′ĭt lĭs) *adj.* Lacking energy or enthusiasm; listless. **—spir′it•less•ly** *adv.* **—spir′it•less•ness** *n.*

spir•i•tu•al (spĭr′ĭ cho͞o əl) *adj.* **1.** Of, relating to, or having the nature of spirit; not physical or material. **2.** Of, concerned with, or affecting the soul: *spiritual welfare.* **3.** Of, from, or relating to God. **4.** Of or relating to religion; sacred. **5.** Supernatural. —*n.* A religious folk song of Black American origin or a song composed in imitation of such a song. **—spir′i•tu•al•ly** *adv.*

spir•i•tu•al•ism (spĭr′ĭ cho͞o ə lĭz′əm) *n.* **1.** The belief that the dead communicate with the living, as through a medium. **2.** A philosophy, doctrine, or religion emphasizing the spiritual aspect of being. **—spir′i•tu•al•ist** *n.*

spir•i•tu•al•i•ty (spĭr′ĭ cho͞o ăl′ĭ tē) *n., pl.* **spir•i•tu•al•i•ties.** The state, quality, or fact of being spiritual.

spi•ro•chete (spī′rə kēt′) *n.* Any of various microorganisms having a slender, flexible, twisted form, including those that cause syphilis and other diseases.

spi•ro•gy•ra (spī′rə jī′rə) *n.* Any of various freshwater green algae having chloroplasts in spirally twisted bands.

spit[1] (spĭt) *n.* **1.** Saliva, especially when ejected from the mouth. **2.** The act of ejecting something from the mouth. —*v.* **spat** (spăt) or **spit, spit•ting, spits.** —*tr.* **1.** To eject (something) from the mouth: *Rinse your mouth with water and spit it out.* **2.** To utter in a violent manner: *spat out an oath.* —*intr.* **1.** To eject something from the mouth. **2.** To make a hissing or sputtering noise, as a cat does. **3.** To rain or snow in light, scattered drops or flakes. ***—idiom.*** **spit up.** To vomit. [First written down before 1325 in Middle English, from Old English *spittan*, to spit.]

spit[2] (spĭt) *n.* **1.** A slender pointed rod on which meat is speared and broiled. **2.** A narrow point of land extending into a body of water. —*tr.v.* **spit•ted, spit•ting, spits.** To place on or as if on a spit. [First written down about 1000 in Old English and spelled *spitu*.]

spit•ball (spĭt′bôl′) *n.* **1.** A piece of paper chewed and shaped into a lump for use as a projectile. **2.** In baseball, an illegal pitch in which a substance, such as saliva or grease, is put on the ball before it is thrown.

spite (spīt) *n.* Ill will that causes a person to wish to hurt or humiliate another. —*tr.v.* **spit•ed, spit•ing, spites.** To show spite toward. ***—idiom.*** **in spite of.** Not stopped by; regardless of: *They went on in spite of their fears.*

spite•ful (spīt′fəl) *adj.* Filled with, caused by, or showing spite; malicious. **—spite′ful•ly** *adv.* **—spite′ful•ness** *n.*

spit•fire (spĭt′fīr′) *n.* A quick-tempered or very excitable person.

spit•ting image (spĭt′ĭng) *n.* A perfect likeness or counterpart.

spit•tle (spĭt′l) *n.* Spit; saliva.

spit•toon (spĭ to͞on′) *n.* A bowl-shaped receptacle into which tobacco chewers spit.

spitz (spĭts) *n.* A dog of any of several breeds originating in Germany, having a long, thick, usually white coat and a tail curled over the back.

splash (splăsh) *v.* **splashed, splash•ing, splash•es.** —*tr.* **1.** To dash or scatter (a liquid) about in flying masses. **2.** To dash liquid upon; wet or soil with flying masses of liquid. —*intr.* **1.** To cause a liquid to fly in scattered masses. **2.** To fall into or move through liquid so as to make it fly: *splashing in the ocean.* **3.** To spill or fly about in scattered masses. —*n.* **1.** The act or sound of splashing. **2.** A flying mass of liquid. **3.** A marking produced by or as if by scattered liquid: *splashes of color.* **4.** A strong but often short-lived impression; a stir: *made a splash with her new novel.* ***—idiom.*** **splash down.** To land in water. Used of a spacecraft or missile. **—splash′er** *n.*

splash•down (splăsh′doun′) *n.* The landing of a missile or spacecraft in water.

splash•y (splăsh′ē) *adj.* **splash•i•er, splash•i•est. 1.** Making or liable to make splashes. **2.** Covered with splashes of color. **3.** Showy; ostentatious: *a splashy wedding reception.*

splat•ter (splăt′ər) *v.* **splat•tered, splat•ter•ing, splat•ters.** —*tr.* To spatter (something), especially so as to soil with splashes of liquid. —*intr.* To move or fall so as to cause heavy splashes. —*n.* A splash of liquid.

splay (splā) *adj.* **1.** Spread or turned out. **2.** Clumsy or clumsily formed; awkward. —*tr.v.* **splayed, splay•ing, splays. 1.** To spread out or apart: *The*

spire[1]

ă	pat	oi	boy
ā	pay	ou	out
âr	care	o͝o	took
ä	father	o͞o	boot
ĕ	pet	ŭ	cut
ē	be	ûr	urge
ĭ	pit	th	thin
ī	pie	*th*	this
îr	pier	hw	whoop
ŏ	pot	zh	vision
ō	toe	ə	about
ô	paw	N	*French* bon

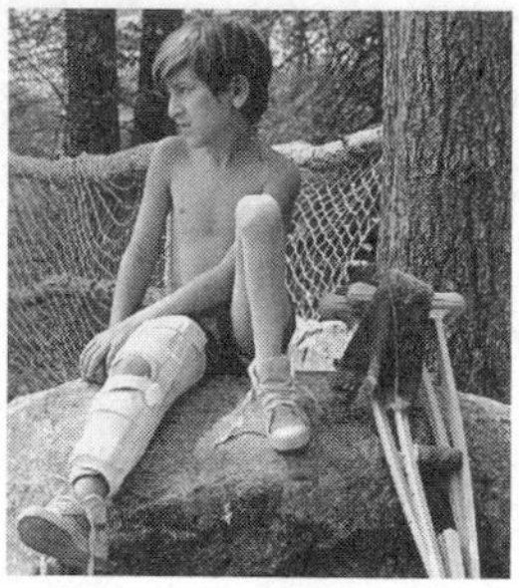
splint

Usage: split infinitive

When one or more words are placed between *to* and the verb in a sentence, this causes a **split infinitive**: *She wanted to quickly go.* Sometimes you will find that it improves your style if you avoid the split infinitive. The sentence *We want a plan to gradually and economically improve our drama program* becomes clearer if you say *We want a plan to improve our drama program gradually and economically.* Sometimes using a split infinitive is better stylistically. In *We expect attendance to more than double in a year,* the phrase *more than* is necessary to the sense of the infinitive phrase *to double in a year,* though the split infinitive could be avoided by use of another phrase, such as *to increase by more than 100 percent.*

sponge

eagle splayed its feathers. **2.** To make slanting or sloping; bevel.

spleen (splēn) *n.* **1.** An organ that is located in the left side of the human body near the stomach and is composed of a mass of lymph nodes and blood vessels. It stores and filters blood, destroys old blood cells, and produces white blood cells. **2.** A similar organ found in other vertebrates. **3.** Ill temper; anger: *an outburst that was caused by spleen.*

splen•did (splĕn′dĭd) *adj.* **1.** Brilliant with light or color: *a splendid lighting display.* **2.** Grand; magnificent: *splendid costumes.* **3.** Excellent; praiseworthy: *a splendid record.* **—splen′did•ly** *adv.* **—splen′did•ness** *n.*

splen•dor (splĕn′dər) *n.* **1.** Great light or luster; brilliance. **2.** Magnificent appearance or display; grandeur. **3.** Distinction; fame; glory.

splice (splīs) *tr.v.* **spliced, splic•ing, splic•es. 1.a.** To join (film, for example) at the ends. **b.** To join (ropes, for example) by weaving together strands. **2.** To join (pieces of wood) by overlapping them and binding the ends together. **3.** To join together or insert (segments of DNA or RNA) so as to form new genetic combinations or alter a genetic structure. *—n.* A joining made by splicing. [First written down in 1524 in Modern English and spelled *splise,* from Middle Dutch *splissen.*] **—splic′er** *n.*

splint (splĭnt) *n.* **1.** A strip of rigid material bound to an injured joint or to the ends of a fractured bone to prevent movement. **2.** A thin flexible strip of wood, as one used in making baskets. [First written down in 1267 in Middle English and spelled *splente.*]

splin•ter (splĭn′tər) *n.* A sharp slender piece, as of wood, bone, or glass, split or broken off from a main body. *—v.* **splin•tered, splin•ter•ing, splin•ters.** *—intr.* To split or break into sharp slender pieces. See Synonyms at **break.** *—tr.* To cause to splinter. [First written down before 1325 in Middle English and spelled *splentre,* from Middle Dutch.]

split (splĭt) *v.* **split, split•ting, splits.** *—tr.* **1.** To divide from end to end or along the grain: *split the log.* **2.** To break, burst, or rip apart with force: *split the nut.* See Synonyms at **rip**[1]. **3.** To separate (persons or groups); disunite: *issues that split the party.* **4.** To divide and share: *agreed to split the reward.* **5.** To mark (a vote or ballot) in favor of candidates from different parties: *split the ticket.* *—intr.* **1.** To become separated into parts, especially lengthwise. **2.** To become open or ripped apart. *—n.* **1.** The act or result of splitting. **2.** A division within a group; a breach; a rupture: *a split in the party.* **3.** Something divided and portioned out; a share. **4.** An acrobatic feat in which the legs are stretched out in opposite directions at right angles to the trunk. Often used in the plural. **5.** In bowling, an arrangement of two or more pins left standing after some pins between them have been knocked down. *—adj.* **1.** Divided or separated. **2.** Cracked lengthwise; cleft. ***—idiom.*** **split hairs.** To see or make trivial distinctions; quibble. [First written down in 1590 in Modern English, from Middle Dutch *splitten.*] **—split′ter** *n.*

split infinitive *n.* An infinitive verb form with a word or words placed between *to* and the verb; for example, *to suddenly remember* is a split infinitive. —See Note.

split-lev•el (splĭt′lĕv′əl) *adj.* Having the floor levels of adjoining rooms separated by about half a story: *a split-level ranch house.*

split second *n.* An instant; a flash: *I'll be there in a split second.*

split•ting (splĭt′ĭng) *adj.* Very severe and painful, as a headache.

splotch (splŏch) *n.* An irregularly shaped stain, spot, or discolored area. *—tr.v.* **splotched, splotch•ing, splotch•es.** To mark with a splotch or splotches. **—splotch′y** *adj.*

splurge (splûrj) *intr.v.* **splurged, splurg•ing, splurg•es.** To spend money extravagantly or wastefully, as on luxuries. *—n.* An act of spending extravagantly.

splut•ter (splŭt′ər) *v.* **splut•tered, splut•ter•ing, splut•ters.** *—intr.* **1.** To make a spitting sound. **2.** To speak in a hurried or confused way, as when angry. *—tr.* To utter or express in a hurried or confused way: *spluttered out the wrong answer in his haste.* *—n.* A spluttering noise. **—splut′ter•er** *n.*

spoil (spoil) *v.* **spoiled** or **spoilt** (spoilt), **spoil•ing, spoils.** *—tr.* **1.** To damage, as in value or quality; flaw or ruin: *Rain spoiled our picnic.* See Synonyms at **hurt. 2.** To do harm to the character of by praising too much or being too lenient: *spoiled their children.* See Synonyms at **pamper.** *—intr.* To become unfit for use or consumption, as from decay: *Milk spoils quickly if it is not kept cold.* *—n.* **1. spoils.** Goods or property seized or robbed, especially after a military victory. **2. spoils.** Benefits gained by a victor, especially political appointments or jobs that a winning candidate or party has control over after an election. ***—idiom.*** **spoil for.** To be eager for: *spoiling for a fight.* **—spoil′er** *n.*

spoil•age (spoi′lĭj) *n.* **1.a.** The process of becoming spoiled. **b.** The condition of being spoiled. **2.a.** Something that has been spoiled. **b.** The degree to which something has been spoiled.

spoils system (spoilz) *n.* The post-election practice of rewarding loyal supporters of the winning candidates or party with political jobs or appointments.

spoilt (spoilt) *v.* A past tense and a past participle of **spoil.**

spoke[1] (spōk) *n.* **1.** One of the rods or braces that connect the rim of a wheel to its hub. **2.** One of the handles that project from the rim of a ship's wheel. **3.** A rod or stick that can be inserted into a wheel to keep it from turning. **4.** A rung of a ladder. *—tr. v.* **spoked, spok•ing, spokes. 1.** To equip with spokes. **2.** To keep (a wheel) from turning by inserting a rod. [First written down before 899 in Old English and spelled *spāca.*]

spoke[2] (spōk) *v.* **1.** Past tense of **speak. 2.** *Archaic.* A past participle of **speak.**

spo•ken (spō′kən) *v.* Past participle of **speak.** *—adj.* **1.** Utttered; expressed orally: *spoken dialogue in an opera.* **2.** Speaking or using speech in a specified manner or voice: *a soft-spoken man.*

spoke•shave (spōk′shāv′) *n.* A tool having a blade set between two handles, used for trimming and smoothing rounded surfaces.

spokes•man (spōks′mən) *n.* A man who speaks on behalf of another or others.

spokes•per•son (spōks′pûr′sən) *n.* A spokesman or spokeswoman.

spokes•wom•an (spōks′wo͝om′ən) *n.* A woman who speaks on behalf of another or others.

spon•dee (spŏn′dē′) *n.* In poetry, a metrical foot consisting of two stressed syllables.

sponge (spŭnj) *n.* **1.** Any of numerous simple water animals that have a soft or bony skeleton and that often form large irregularly shaped colonies attached to an underwater surface. **2.a.** The soft, porous, absorbent skeleton of certain of these animals, used for bathing, cleaning, and other purposes. **b.** A piece of porous absorbent rubber or other material, used for similar purposes. **3.** A gauze pad used to absorb blood and other fluids, as in surgery or in dressing a wound. **4.** A person who lives by relying on the generosity of others. *—v.* **sponged, spong•ing, spong•es.** *—tr.* **1.** To wash, wipe, or moisten with or as if with a sponge: *She sponged her face* *with a wet hankerchief. Sponge the water off the table.* **2.** *Informal.* To get (something) without paying for it: *She sponged a free meal from the cook at the cafeteria.* —*intr.* To live by relying of the generosity of others: *sponged off his friends until he found a job.* [First written down about 1000 in Old English, from Greek *spongos.*]

sponge cake *n.* A light porous cake made with flour, sugar, and eggs and containing no shortening.

spong•er (spŭn′jər) *n.* **1.** A person or boat engaged in gathering sponges. **2.** *Informal.* A person who lives off the generosity of others; a parasite.

spong•y (spŭn′jē) *adj.* **spong•i•er, spong•i•est.** Resembling a sponge; soft, porous, and elastic: *a spongy bed of moss.* **—spong′i•ness** *n.*

spon•sor (spŏn′sər) *n.* **1.** A person who assumes responsibility for another person or group during a period of instruction or training. **2.** A person who supports a candidate for admission to an organization, for example. **3.** A member of a lawmaking body who proposes and works for passage of a bill. **4.** A person who presents a candidate for baptism or confirmation; a godparent. **5.** A person, group, or business that financially supports a project, an event, or a program: *Most television shows have several corporate sponsors.* —*tr.v.* **spon•sored, spon•sor•ing, spon•sors.** To act as a sponsor for. [First written down in 1651 in Modern English, from Late Latin *spōnsor*, godparent, from Latin *spondēre*, to pledge.] **—spon′sor•ship′** *n.*

spon•ta•ne•i•ty (spŏn′tə nē′ĭ tē *or* spŏn′tə nā′ĭ tē) *n., pl.* **spon•ta•ne•i•ties.** The quality or condition of being spontaneous.

spon•ta•ne•ous (spŏn tā′nē əs) *adj.* **1.** Happening or arising without apparent outside cause. **2.** Arising from a natural inclination or impulse: *spontaneous cheers.* [First written down about 1200 in Middle English and spelled *sponntaneuss*, from Late Latin *spontāneus*, of one's own accord, from Latin *sponte.*] **—spon•ta′ne•ous•ly** *adv.*

spontaneous combustion *n.* The bursting into flame of a mass of material, such as oily rags or damp hay, as a result of heat generated by slow oxidation.

spoof (spo͞of) *n.* **1.** A joke or hoax. **2.** An imitation of something that pokes fun at it; a light satire: *a spoof of grand opera.* —*tr.v.* **spoofed, spoof•ing, spoofs. 1.** To deceive or trick. **2.** To do a spoof of; satirize.

spook (spo͝ok) *Informal. n.* A ghost. —*v.* **spooked, spook•ing, spooks.** —*tr.* **1.** To haunt. **2.** To frighten. —*intr.* To become frightened or nervous: *The horse spooked at the sound of thunder.*

spook•y (spo͞o′kē) *adj.* **spook•i•er, spook•i•est.** *Informal.* Ghostly; eerie. **—spook′i•ness** *n.*

spool (spo͞ol) *n.* **1.** A cylinder upon which thread, wire, tape, or a similar material is wound. **2.** The amount of something wound on such a cylinder: *Sewing the coat used up a whole spool of thread.* —*tr.v.* **spooled, spool•ing, spools.** To wind on or unwind from a spool: *spool thread.*

spoon (spo͞on) *n.* **1.** A utensil consisting of a small shallow bowl at the end of a handle, used in preparing, serving, or eating food. **2.** Something similar to this utensil in shape or function, as a curved metal fishing lure. —*v.* **spooned, spoon•ing, spoons.** —*tr.* To lift or scoop up with or as if with a spoon. —*intr. Informal.* To show affection, as by kissing or caressing. [First written down before 800 in Old English and spelled *spōn*, chip of wood.]

spoon•bill (spo͞on′bĭl′) *n.* Any of several wading birds having long legs and a long flat bill with a broad rounded tip.

spoon-feed (spo͞on′fēd′) *tr.v.* **spoon-fed** (spo͞on′fĕd′), **spoon-feed•ing, spoon-feeds. 1.** To feed with a spoon. **2.** To discourage from independent thought or action, as by overindulgence: *The professor spoonfed her students, who never questioned what she said.* **3.** To provide (knowledge or information) in an oversimplified way.

spoon•ful (spo͞on′fo͝ol′) *n., pl.* **spoon•fuls.** The amount that a spoon holds.

spoor (spo͝or) *n.* The track or trail of an animal, especially a wild animal.

spo•rad•ic (spə răd′ĭk) *adj.* Occurring at irregular intervals; having no pattern or order: *sporadic applause.* **—spo•rad′i•cal•ly** *adv.*

spo•ran•gi•um (spə răn′jē əm) *n., pl.* **spo•ran•gi•a** (spə răn′jē ə). A plant part in which spores are formed, as in ferns, fungi, mosses, and algae; a spore case.

spore (spôr) *n.* **1.** A tiny, usually one-celled reproductive body that can become a new organism, produced by certain bacteria, fungi, algae, and nonflowering plants. **2.** An inactive form of certain bacteria. [First written down in 1836 in Modern English, from Greek *spora*, seed.]

spore case *n.* A sporangium.

spo•ro•phyte (spôr′ə fīt′) *n.* The spore-producing phase in the life cycle of certain plants.

spo•ro•zo•an (spôr′ə zō′ən) *n.* Any of numerous parasitic protozoans that reproduce by means of spores. **—spo′ro•zo′an** *adj.*

spor•ran (spôr′ən *or* spŏr′ən) *n.* A leather or fur pouch worn at the front of the kilt in the traditional dress of men of the Scottish Highlands.

sport (spôrt) *n.* **1.** An activity involving physical exercise and skill that is governed by rules and often done in competition. **2.** An active pastime; recreation. **3.** Light mockery; jest; fun: *They made sport of my new hat.* **4.** A person judged by the manner of accepting the rules of a game or a difficult situation: *a good sport.* **5.** *Informal.* A person who lives a jolly extravagant life. —*v.* **sport•ed, sport•ing, sports.** —*intr.* **1.** To play or frolic. **2.** To joke or trifle. —*tr.* To wear, display, or show off: *He sported a bright red necktie.* —*adj.* or **sports. 1.** Of, relating to, or appropriate for sports. **2.** Suitable for outdoor or informal wear: *sport clothes; a sport shirt.* [First written down about 1400 in Middle English and spelled *sporte*, short for *disporte*, from Old French *desporter*, to divert.]

sport•ing (spôr′tĭng) *adj.* **1.** Used in or appropriate for sports: *sporting goods.* **2.** Marked by sportsmanship. **3.** Of or associated with gambling. **—sport′ing•ly** *adv.*

sporting chance *n. Informal.* A fair chance for success.

spor•tive (spôr′tĭv) *adj.* Playful; frolicsome. **—spor′tive•ly** *adv.* **—spor′tive•ness** *n.*

sports car (spôrts) *n.* An automobile equipped for racing and designed to be driven at high speeds with precise control.

sports•man (spôrts′mən) *n.* **1.** A man who is active in sports. **2.** A man whose conduct and attitude exhibit sportsmanship. **—sports′man•like′** *adj.*

sports•man•ship (spôrts′mən shĭp′) *n.* The attitude and conduct suitable to one who participates in sports, especially fair play, courtesy, and grace in losing.

sports•wear (spôrts′wâr′) *n.* Clothes designed for comfort and casual wear.

sports•wom•an (spôrts′wo͝om′ən) *n.* **1.** A woman who is active in sports. **2.** A woman whose conduct and attitude exhibit sportsmanship.

sport•y (spôr′tē) *adj.* **sport•i•er, sport•i•est. 1.** Appropriate to sports or participation in sports. **2.** Flashy, especially in dress.

spot (spŏt) *n.* **1.** A mark on a surface differing sharply in color from the surroundings, especially a

spoonbill
Roseate spoonbill

ă	**pat**	oi	**boy**
ā	**pay**	ou	**out**
âr	**care**	o͝o	**took**
ä	**father**	o͞o	**boot**
ĕ	**pet**	ŭ	**cut**
ē	**be**	ûr	**urge**
ĭ	**pit**	th	**thin**
ī	**pie**	*th*	**this**
îr	**pier**	hw	**whoop**
ŏ	**pot**	zh	**vision**
ō	**toe**	ə	**about**
ô	**paw**	N	*French* **bon**

stain or blot: *spots on the tablecloth.* **2.** A position; a location: *a good spot for watching birds.* **3.** *Informal.* A situation, especially a difficult one. **4.** A flaw or defect in one's reputation. —*v.* **spot•ted, spot•ting, spots.** —*tr.* **1.** To cause to become marked or soiled with spots: *Soot spotted the curtains.* **2.** To place in a particular location; situate. **3.** To detect or recognize: *spotted him on the subway.* **4.** To give a handicap or favorable scoring margin to: *spotted her opponent six points.* —*intr.* To become marked or soiled with spots. —*adj.* **1.** Made, paid, or delivered immediately: *spot cash; a spot sale.* **2.** Presented between major television or radio programs: *a spot announcement.* ***—idiom.*** **on the spot. 1.** Without delay; at once. **2.** At the scene of action. **3.** In a difficult position. [First written down before 1200 in Middle English.]

spot check *n.* A random or limited inspection or investigation.

spot-check (spŏt′chĕk′) *tr. & intr.v.* **spot-checked, spot-check•ing, spot-checks.** To subject to or make a spot check.

spot•less (spŏt′lĭs) *adj.* Perfectly clean; free from stain or blemish: *spotless linen; a spotless reputation.* See Synonyms at **clean.** **—spot′less•ly** *adv.* **—spot′less•ness** *n.*

spot•light (spŏt′līt′) *n.* **1.** A strong beam of light that illuminates only a small area, often used to draw attention to an actor on a stage. **2.** A lamp that produces such a light. **3.** Public attention or prominence: *She was in the spotlight after winning the race.* —*tr.v.* **spot•light•ed** or **spot•lit** (spŏt′lĭt), **spot•light•ing, spot•lights. 1.** To shine a spotlight on. **2.** To focus attention on.

spot•ted (spŏt′ĭd) *adj.* Marked or stained with spots.

spot•ty (spŏt′ē) *adj.* **spot•ti•er, spot•ti•est. 1.** Having or marked with spots; spotted. **2.** Lacking consistency; uneven in quality or occurrence. **—spot′ti•ly** *adv.* **—spot′ti•ness** *n.*

spouse (spous *or* spouz) *n.* A marriage partner; one's husband or wife.

spout (spout) *v.* **spout•ed, spout•ing, spouts.** —*intr.* **1.** To gush forth in a rapid stream or in spurts: *lava spouting up from a volcano.* **2.** To give off a liquid or other substance continuously or in spurts: *whales spouting offshore.* **3.** *Informal.* To speak in a wordy, dull, and pompous manner. —*tr.* **1.** To cause to flow or spurt out. **2.** To utter pompously and tediously. —*n.* **1.** A tube, mouth, or pipe through which liquid is released or discharged: *the spout of a coffeepot.* **2.** A continuous stream of liquid. [First written down before 1325 in Middle English and spelled *sputen.*] **—spout′er** *n.*

sprain (sprān) *n.* An injury caused by a painful twisting or tearing of the ligaments of a joint. —*tr. v.* **sprained, sprain•ing, sprains.** To cause a sprain to (a joint or muscle).

sprang (sprăng) *v.* A past tense of **spring.**

sprat (sprăt) *n.* **1.** A small edible ocean fish of northeast Atlantic waters that is eaten fresh or smoked and is often canned in oil as a sardine. **2.** Any of various other similar fishes, such as a small herring.

sprawl (sprôl) *intr.v.* **sprawled, sprawl•ing, sprawls. 1.** To sit or lie with the body and limbs spread out awkwardly. **2.** To spread out in a straggling or disordered fashion. —*n.* A sprawling posture or condition. [First written down about 1300 in Middle English and spelled *sprawlen,* from Old English *sprēawlian,* to writhe.]

spray[1] (sprā) *n.* **1.** Water or other liquid moving in a mass of finely dispersed droplets or mist. **2.** A fine jet of liquid shot from a pressurized container. **3.** A pressurized container that shoots such a jet; an atomizer. **4.** Any of a large number of commercial products, including paints, insecticides, and cosmetics, that are dispensed from containers in this manner. —*v.* **sprayed, spray•ing, sprays.** —*tr.* **1.** To scatter (a liquid) in the form of a spray. **2.** To apply a spray to (a surface). —*intr.* To shoot sprays of liquid. [First written down in 1621 in Modern English, from obsolete *spray,* to sprinkle, from Middle Dutch *sprayen.*] **—spray′er** *n.*

spray[2] (sprā) *n.* **1.** A small branch bearing flowers, leaves, or berries. **2.** An ornament that resembles such a branch. [First written down about 1250 in Middle English.]

spread (sprĕd) *v.* **spread, spread•ing, spreads.** —*tr.* **1.** To open to a full or fuller extent or width; unfold: *spread out a tablecloth; a bird spreading its wings.* **2.** To widen the gap between; move farther apart: *spread her fingers wide.* **3.a.** To distribute over a surface in a layer; apply: *spread varnish on the table.* **b.** To cover with a layer: *spread bread with jelly.* **4.** To distribute widely: *storms that spread destruction.* **5.** To arrange over a wide area or over a period of time: *We spread the payments over six months.* **6.** To cause to become widely known or seen: *spread the news.* **7.** To lay out; display: *spread his merchandise in the window.* **8.a.** To prepare (a table) for a meal; set. **b.** To arrange (food) on a table. —*intr.* **1.** To become extended or enlarged: *The table spread out to accommodate more people.* **2.** To become distributed or widely dispersed: *The news spread quickly.* **3.** To cover a surface in a layer: *The paint spreads nicely.* **4.** To become separated. —*n.* **1.a.** The act of spreading. **b.** Dissemination or flow, as of news: *the spread of information.* **2.** An open area of land; an expanse. **3.a.** The extent or limit to which something can be spread or unfolded: *wings with a six-foot spread.* **b.** Range or scope: *a wide spread of development.* **4.** A cloth covering for a bed, table, or other piece of furniture. **5.** *Informal.* An abundant meal laid out on a table. **6.** A soft food that can be spread on bread or crackers. **7.** The difference, as between two figures or totals. **8.a.** Two facing pages, as of a magazine or newspaper, often with related matter extending across the fold. **b.** A story or advertisement running across two or more columns of a magazine or newspaper. **—spread′a•bil′i•ty** *n.* **—spread′a•ble** *adj.*

spread-eagle (sprĕd′ē′gəl) *adj.* Placed with the arms and legs stretched out. —*tr.v.* **spread-ea•gled, spread-ea•gling, spread-ea•gling.** To place with the arms and legs stretched out, especially as a form of punishment.

spread•er (sprĕd′ər) *n.* **1.** Something that spreads, such as a butter knife. **2.** A farm or garden tool for scattering fertilizer or seed.

spree (sprē) *n.* **1.** A carefree lively outing. **2.** Overindulgence in an activity, especially drinking or spending: *a shopping spree.*

spri•er (sprī′ər) *adj.* A comparative of **spry.**

spri•est (sprī′ĭst) *adj.* A superlative of **spry.**

sprig (sprĭg) *n.* **1.** A small twig or shoot of a plant. **2.** A design or decoration in this shape. —*tr.v.* **sprigged, sprig•ging, sprigs.** To decorate with a design of sprigs.

spright•ly (sprīt′lē) *adj.* **spright•li•er, spright•li•est.** Full of vitality and spirit; brisk. **—spright′li•ness** *n.*

spring (sprĭng) *v.* **sprang** (sprăng) or **sprung** (sprŭng), **sprung, spring•ing, springs.** —*intr.* **1.** To move upward or forward in a single quick motion or a series of such motions; leap: *springing up from her chair.* **2.** To issue or emerge suddenly: *A thought springs to mind.* **3.** To appear or come into being suddenly: *The mushroom sprang up overnight.* **4.** To move suddenly on or as if on a spring:

The door sprang shut. **5.** To become warped, bent, or cracked: *This board has sprung.* **6.** To move out of place; come loose, as a machine part. *—tr.* **1.** To cause to move, leap, or come forth suddenly. **2.** To have as a sudden condition: *The pipe sprang a leak.* **3.** To cause to operate or close suddenly: *spring a trap.* **4.** To cause to warp, bend, or crack, as a piece of wood. **5.** To present or produce unexpectedly: *spring a surprise party.* *—n.* **1.** An elastic device, such as a coil of wire, that returns to its original shape after being compressed or extended. **2.** The quality or condition of being elastic. **3.** The act of springing, especially a leap or jump. **4.** A small stream of water flowing naturally from the earth. **5.** The season of the year occurring between winter and summer. In the Northern Hemisphere it lasts from the vernal equinox to the summer solstice, or in ordinary usage, from March until June. **6.** A source, an origin, or a beginning. *—adj.* Of, occurring in, or appropriate to the season of spring: *spring showers.* [First written down about 725 in Old English and spelled *springan.*]

spring•board (**sprĭng′**bôrd′) *n.* **1.** A flexible board, secured at one end and mounted on a fulcrum, used by gymnasts to gain momentum in leaping or tumbling. **2.** A diving board. **3.** Something that helps to launch a career or an activity: *athletic fame as a springboard for a career in politics.*

spring•bok (**sprĭng′**bŏk′) *n., pl.* **springbok** or **spring•boks.** A small brown and white African gazelle that can leap high into the air.

spring fever *n.* A feeling of laziness or a yearning for change brought on by the arrival of spring.

Spring•field (**sprĭng′**fēld′). The capital of Illinois, in the central part of the state. It is the site of Abraham Lincoln's grave. Population, 105,227.

spring tide *n.* The tide in which the difference between high and low tides is greatest, occurring at or near a new moon or full moon when the sun, moon, and earth are aligned.

spring•time (**sprĭng′**tīm′) *n.* The season of spring.

spring•y (**sprĭng′**ē) *adj.* **spring•i•er, spring•i•est.** Capable of springing back; elastic: *a springy footstep.* **—spring′i•ly** *adv.* **—spring′i•ness** *n.*

sprin•kle (**sprĭng′**kəl) *v.* **sprin•kled, sprin•kling, sprin•kles.** *—tr.* **1.** To scatter or release in drops or small particles: *sprinkle sand on the icy steps.* **2.** To scatter drops or particles upon: *sprinkle the garden with water.* *—intr.* To rain or fall in small or infrequent drops. *—n.* **1.** A small amount. **2.** A light rainfall; a drizzle. **3.** The act of sprinkling. [First written down before 1382 in Middle English and spelled *sprinkklen,* perhaps of Middle Dutch or Middle Low German origin.]

sprin•kler (**sprĭng′**klər) *n.* **1.** One of the outlets in a sprinkler system. **2.** A device, attached to the end of a hose, for sprinkling water on a lawn.

sprinkler system *n.* A system for extinguishing fires, consisting of pipes that release water automatically when the temperature reaches a certain level.

sprin•kling (**sprĭng′**klĭng) *n.* A small amount of something, especially when sparsely distributed.

sprint (sprĭnt) *n.* A short race at top speed. *—intr.v.* **sprint•ed, sprint•ing, sprints.** To run or move at top speed for a brief period. **—sprint′er** *n.*

sprit (sprĭt) *n.* A pole extending diagonally across a fore-and-aft sail from the lower part of the mast to the peak of the sail.

sprite (sprīt) *n.* A small or elusive supernatural being; an elf or a pixy. [First written down about 1303 in Middle English and spelled *sprit,* from Latin *spīritus,* spirit.]

sprit•sail (**sprĭt′**səl *or* **sprĭt′**sāl′) *n.* A sail extended by a sprit.

sprock•et (**sprŏk′**ĭt) *n.* Any of various parts that project from the rim of a wheel to fit into the links of a chain.

sprocket wheel *n.* A wheel having sprockets around its rim.

sprout (sprout) *v.* **sprout•ed, sprout•ing, sprouts.** *—intr.* **1.** To begin to grow; produce or appear as a bud, shoot, or new growth: *The newly planted corn sprouted after the rain.* **2.** To emerge or develop rapidly: *New businesses sprouted up across the state.* *—tr.* To cause to come forth and grow: *The abandoned farmland again sprouted buckwheat and clover.* *—n.* **1.** A young plant growth, such as a bud or shoot. **2. sprouts.** Brussels sprouts. [First written down before 1200 in Middle English and spelled *spruten.*]

spruce[1] (spro͞os) *n.* **1.** Any of various evergreen trees having short needles, drooping cones, and soft wood often used for paper pulp. **2.** The wood of such a tree. [First written down in 1670 in Modern English, from Middle English *spruce,* Prussia, from Medieval Latin *Prussia.*]

spruce[2] (spro͞os) *adj.* **spruc•er, spruc•est.** Neat, trim, and smart in appearance. *—tr. & intr.v.* **spruced, spruc•ing, spruc•es.** To make or become neat and trim: *We spruced up the house with a new coat of paint. He really spruced up for the date.* [First written down in 1589 in Modern English, perhaps from obsolete *spruce leather,* Prussian leather, from Middle English *spruce,* Prussia.] **—spruce′ly** *adv.* **—spruce′ness** *n.*

sprung (sprŭng) *v.* A past tense and the past participle of **spring.**

spry (sprī) *adj.* **spri•er** (**sprī′**ər), **spri•est** (**sprī′**ĭst) or **spry•er, spry•est.** Active; nimble; lively. **—spry′ly** *adv.* **—spry′ness** *n.*

spud (spŭd) *n.* **1.** *Slang.* A potato. **2.** A sharp tool resembling a spade, used for rooting or digging out weeds.

spume (spyo͞om) *n.* Foam or froth on a liquid, as on the sea. *—intr.v.* **spumed, spum•ing, spumes.** To froth or foam.

spu•mo•ni or **spu•mo•ne** (spo͞o **mō′**nē) *n.* An Italian ice cream having layers of different colors and flavors and often containing fruit and nuts.

spun (spŭn) *v.* Past tense and past participle of **spin.**

spunk (spŭngk) *n.* *Informal.* Spirit; courage.

spunk•y (**spŭng′**kē) *adj.* **spunk•i•er, spunk•i•est.** *Informal.* Spirited; plucky. **—spunk′i•ly** *adv.* **—spunk′i•ness** *n.*

spun sugar *n.* Cotton candy.

spur (spûr) *n.* **1.** A short spike or sharp-toothed wheel that attaches to the heel of a rider's boot and is used to urge the horse forward. **2.** Something that urges one to action, an incentive; a stimulus: *Ambition was the spur for her great achievements.* **3.** A pointed projecting part, as on the back of a rooster's leg or on some flowers. **4.** A relatively short ridge that projects from the side of a mountain or mountain range. **5.** A short side track that connects with the main track of a railroad system. *—tr.v.* **spurred, spur•ring, spurs.** **1.** To urge (a horse) on by the use of spurs: *The rider spurred the horse to a gallop.* **2.** To move to action; incite; stimulate: *The reward spurred us on.* ***—idiom.*** **on the spur of the moment.** Without planning; suddenly; impulsively. [First written down before 800 in Old English and spelled *spura.*]

spu•ri•ous (**spyo͝or′**ē əs) *adj.* Lacking authenticity; false; counterfeit. **—spu′ri•ous•ly** *adv.* **—spu′ri•ous•ness** *n.*

spurn (spûrn) *v.* **spurned, spurn•ing, spurns.** *—tr.* To reject or refuse with disdain; scorn. *—intr.* To reject something contemptuously. *—n.* A contemptuous rejection.

ă	pat	oi	boy
ā	pay	ou	out
âr	care	o͝o	took
ä	father	o͞o	boot
ĕ	pet	ŭ	cut
ē	be	ûr	urge
ĭ	pit	th	thin
ī	pie	*th*	this
îr	pier	hw	whoop
ŏ	pot	zh	vision
ō	toe	ə	about
ô	paw	N	*French* bon

spurred (spûrd) *adj.* **1.** Wearing spurs. **2.** Having a spur or spurs: *spurred flowers.*

spurt (spûrt) *n.* **1.** A sudden and forcible gush or jet. **2.** A sudden short burst, as of energy or activity. —*v.* **spurt•ed, spurt•ing, spurts.** —*intr.* **1.** To gush forth suddenly in a stream or jet. **2.** To show a brief intense effort: *The team spurted late in the season.* —*tr.* To force in a sudden jet or squirt.

spu•ta (spyo͞o′tə) *n.* Plural of **sputum.**

sput•nik (spo͝ot′nĭk *or* spŭt′nĭk) *n.* Any of the artificial satellites put into orbit around the earth by the Soviet Union.

sput•ter (spŭt′ər) *v.* **sput•tered, sput•ter•ing, sput•ters.** —*intr.* **1.** To spit out or spray small particles of saliva or food from the mouth in noisy bursts. **2.** To make sporadic spitting or coughing noises: *The engine sputtered and died.* **3.** To spit out words or sounds in an excited or confused manner. —*tr.* **1.** To eject in short bursts with spitting or coughing sounds. **2.** To utter in an excited or confused manner. —*n.* **1.** The act or sound of sputtering. **2.** The particles spit out during sputtering. **3.** Excited or confused speech. **—sput′ter•er** *n.*

spu•tum (spyo͞o′təm) *n., pl.* **spu•ta** (spyo͞o′tə). Matter that is spit out; spit; spittle.

spy (spī) *n., pl.* **spies** (spīz). **1.** An agent employed by a state or company to obtain secret information about another state or a competitor. **2.** A person who secretly keeps watch on another or others. —*v.* **spied** (spīd), **spy•ing, spies** (spīz). —*tr.* **1.** To watch or observe secretly. **2.** To catch sight of; see: *spied a turtle on a log.* —*intr.* **1.** To act as a spy. **2.** To investigate or observe something secretly and closely. [First written down about 1250 in Middle English and spelled *spie*, from Old French *espier*, to watch, of Germanic origin.]

spy•glass (spī′glăs′) *n.* **1.** A small telescope. **2. spyglasses.** Binoculars.

sq. *abbr.* An abbreviation of: **1.** Squadron. **2.** Square.

squab (skwŏb) *n.* A young pigeon. —*adj.* Young or newly hatched: *a squab chick.*

squab•ble (skwŏb′əl) *intr.v.* **squab•bled, squab•bling, squab•bles.** To engage in an argument, usually over a trivial matter; bicker: *squabbling over the morning paper.* —*n.* A noisy quarrel. [First written down in 1602 in Modern English, probably of Scandinavian origin.] **—squab′bler** *n.*

squad (skwŏd) *n.* **1.** A small organized group of people who work for a common goal or cause. **2.** A small unit of police officers or military personnel. **3.** An athletic team.

squad car *n.* A police patrol car connected by radio with headquarters.

squad•ron (skwŏd′rən) *n.* **1.** Any of various military units, as of soldiers, planes, or ships. **2.** An organized group or gathering: *squadrons of flies.*

squal•id (skwŏl′ĭd) *adj.* **1.** Having a dirty or wretched appearance: *squalid buildings.* **2.** Sordid; morally repulsive: *leading a squalid existence.* **—squal′id•ly** *adv.* **—squal′id•ness** *n.*

squall[1] (skwôl) *n.* A loud harsh cry. —*intr.v.* **squalled, squall•ing, squalls.** To scream or cry harshly and loudly. [First written down before 1631 in Modern English, probably of Scandinavian origin.]

squall[2] (skwôl) *n.* A brief, sudden, and violent windstorm, often accompanied by rain or snow. —*intr.v.* **squalled, squall•ing, squalls.** To blow strongly for a short time. [First written down in 1719 in Modern English, probably of Scandinavian origin.]

squall•y (skwô′lē) *adj.* **squall•i•er, squall•i•est. 1.** Characterized by squalls; gusty. **2.** *Informal.* Marked by disturbance or trouble.

squal•or (skwŏl′ər) *n.* The quality or condition of being squalid; wretched.

squa•mous (skwā′məs) also **squa•mose** (skwā′mōs′) *adj.* **1.** Covered with or formed of scales; scaly. **2.** Resembling a scale or scales.

squan•der (skwŏn′dər) *tr.v.* **squan•dered, squan•der•ing, squan•ders.** To use or spend wastefully or extravagantly: *squander money.*

Squanto

Squan•to (skwŏn′tō). Died 1622. Native American who taught the Massachusetts colonists agricultural methods and acted as interpreter between the colonists and the Wampanoag.

square (skwâr) *n.* **1.** A rectangle having four equal sides. **2.** A figure or an object having this shape. **3.** An L-shaped or T-shaped instrument or tool, used for drawing or testing right angles. **4.** The product that results when a number or quantity is multiplied by itself. **5.a.** An open area at the intersection of two or more streets. **b.** A rectangular space enclosed by streets; a block. **6.** *Slang.* A person considered dull, conventional, and out of touch with current trends. —*adj.* **squar•er, squar•est. 1.** Having four equal sides and four right angles. **2.** Forming a right angle: *a board with square corners.* **3.** Similar to a square in form: *a square field.* **4.** Of, being, or using units that express the measure of area: *square miles.* **5.** Honest; direct: *a square answer.* **6.** Just; equitable: *a square deal.* **7.** *Slang.* Dull and conventional. —*v.* **squared, squar•ing, squares.** —*tr.* **1.** To cut or form into a square or rectangular shape: *square a board.* **2.** To test (a joint, for example) to ensure that its parts meet at right angles. **3.** To multiply (a number, a quantity, or an expression) by itself. **4.** To find a square whose area is equal to (the area of a given figure). **5.** To bring into agreement or conformity: *We must square his story with ours.* **6.** To settle; bring into balance: *square an account.* —*intr.* **1.** To be at right angles. **2.** To agree or conform: *That story doesn't square with the facts.* —*adv.* **1.** In a square shape or form. **2.** Directly; straight: *ran square into the wall.* **3.** In a solid, honest, or firm manner. **—*idioms.* square away.** To put away or in order. **square off.** To assume a fighting stance; prepare to fight. [First written down about 1250 in Middle English and spelled *squire*, from Old French *esquarre.*] **—square′ly** *adv.* **—square′ness** *n.*

square dance

square dance *n.* **1.** A dance in which sets of four couples form squares. **2.** Any of various similar group dances.

square-dance (skwâr′dăns′) *intr.v.* To perform a square dance.

square knot *n.* A common double knot with the loose ends parallel to the standing parts.

square measure *n.* A system for expressing the measure of surfaces using units, such as square feet and square meters, that are the squares of linear units.

square-rigged (skwâr′rĭgd′) *adj.* Fitted with square sails as the principal sails: *a square-rigged ship.*

square-rig•ger (skwâr′rĭg′ər) *n.* A square-rigged vessel.

square root *n.* A divisor of a number that when squared gives the number; if *a* is a square root of *b* (written $a = \sqrt{b}$), then $a \times a = b$, for example.

squash[1]

squash[1] (skwŏsh *or* skwôsh) *n.* **1.** Any of various types of fleshy fruit related to the pumpkins and the gourds, eaten as a vegetable. **2.** A vine that bears such fruit. [First written down in 1643 in American English, from alteration of Narragansett *askútasquash.*]

squash[2] (skwŏsh *or* skwôsh) *v.* **squashed, squash•ing, squash•es.** —*tr.* **1.** To beat or flatten into a pulp; crush: *squashed the peach on the pavement.* **2.** To suppress; quash: *squash a revolt.* —*intr.* **1.** To become crushed or flattened: *The tomato squashed when it hit the floor.* **2.** To move with a sloshing or splashing sound: *squashed through the slush.* —*n.* **1.** The act or sound of squashing. **2.** A crowd. **3.** In sports, a game played in a walled court in which the players hit a hard rubber ball with a racket. [First written down before 1325 in Middle English and spelled *squachen*, from Old French *esquasser*.]

squash•y (**skwŏsh′**ē *or* **skwô′**shē) *adj.* **squash•i•er, squash•i•est.** **1.** Easily squashed. **2.** Overripe and soft; pulpy. **3.** Boggy; marshy. —**squash′i•ly** *adv.*

squat (skwŏt) *v.* **squat•ted, squat•ting, squats.** —*intr.* **1.** To sit in a low crouching position with the knees bent: *squat down to watch an ant.* **2.** To settle on unoccupied land without legal claim. **3.** To occupy a given piece of public land in order to acquire title to it. —*tr.* **1.** To put (oneself) into a crouching position. **2.** To occupy as a squatter. —*adj.* **squat•ter, squat•test.** Short and thick; low and broad: *a squat shape.* —*n.* **1.** The act of squatting. **2.** A squatting position.

squat•ter (**skwŏt′**ər) *n.* **1.** A person who settles on land without legal claim. **2.** A person who occupies public land in order to acquire title to it.

squaw (skwô) *n. Offensive.* **1.** A Native American woman. **2.** A woman or wife. [First written down in 1634 in American English, from Massachusett *squa*, younger woman.]

squawk (skwôk) *intr.v.* **squawked, squawk•ing, squawks.** **1.** To utter a harsh scream; screech. **2.** *Informal.* To complain or protest loudly and angrily. —*n.* **1.** A loud harsh screech: *the squawk of an automobile horn.* **2.** *Informal.* A loud angry complaint or protest. —**squawk′er** *n.*

squeak (skwēk) *v.* **squeaked, squeak•ing, squeaks.** —*intr.* **1.** To make a short, high-pitched cry or sound. **2.** *Slang.* To turn informer; squeal. —*tr.* To utter in a thin, high-pitched voice. —*n.* **1.** A thin, high-pitched cry or sound. **2.** An escape: *a tight squeak.* —***idiom.*** **squeak by** or **squeak through.** To manage barely to pass, win, or survive: *He just squeaked by in his final exams.* [First written down before 1387 in Middle English and spelled *squeken*, perhaps of Scandinavian origin.]

squeak•y (**skwē′**kē) *adj.* **squeak•i•er, squeak•i•est.** Having or making squeaking tones: *a squeaky door; squeaky shoes.*

squeal (skwēl) *v.* **squealed, squeal•ing, squeals.** —*intr.* **1.** To make a loud shrill cry or sound: *The bus squealed as it stopped.* **2.** *Slang.* To turn informer; betray another by giving away information. —*tr.* To utter or produce with a squeal. —*n.* A loud shrill cry or sound. —**squeal′er** *n.*

squea•mish (**skwē′**mĭsh) *adj.* **1.** Easily nauseated or sickened. **2.** Easily shocked or disgusted. —**squea′mish•ly** *adv.* —**squea′mish•ness** *n.*

squee•gee (**skwē′**jē) *n.* A tool having a rubber blade that is drawn across a surface to remove water from it, as in washing windows.

squeeze (skwēz) *v.* **squeezed, squeez•ing, squeez•es.** —*tr.* **1.** To press hard on or together; compress: *The baby squeezed the rubber toy.* **2.** To exert pressure on, as by way of extracting liquid: *squeeze an orange.* **3.** To extract by or as if by applying pressure: *squeeze juice from a lemon; squeezed a confession out of a suspect.* **4.** To press gently, as in affection or sympathy: *squeezed her mother's hand.* **5.** To crowd; cram: *She squeezed her books onto the crowded shelf.* —*intr.* **1.** To exert pressure. **2.** To give way under pressure. **3.** To force one's way: *squeeze through a crowd.* —*n.* **1.** An act or instance of squeezing: *gave his hand a squeeze.* **2.** *Informal.* Pressure exterted to obtain something: *They put the squeeze on him and he confessed.* —**squeez′a•ble** *adj.* —**squeez′er** *n.*

squelch (skwĕlch) *v.* **squelched, squelch•ing, squelch•es.** —*tr.* **1.** To crush by or as if by trampling; squash: *squelched a revolt.* **2.** To silence, as with a crushing remark: *squelch a rumor.* —*intr.* To make a splashing squishing sound, as when walking in mud. —*n.* **1.** A crushing reply. **2.** A squishing sound. —**squelch′er** *n.*

squib (skwĭb) *n.* **1.a.** A small firecracker. **b.** A broken firecracker that burns but does not explode. **2.** A brief witty literary effort, such as a lampoon.

squid (skwĭd) *n., pl.* **squids** or **squid.** Any of various soft-bodied sea animals related to the octopuses and cuttlefish and having a long body, ten arms surrounding the mouth, and a pair of triangular or rounded fins.

squig•gle (**skwĭg′**əl) *n.* A small wiggly mark or scrawl.

squint (skwĭnt) *intr.v.* **squint•ed, squint•ing, squints.** **1.** To look with the eyes partly closed, as in bright sunlight. **2.** To look or glace to the side. **3.** To be cross-eyed. —*n.* **1.** The act or an instance of squinting. **2.** The condition of being cross-eyed.

squire (skwīr) *n.* **1.** A man who attends or escorts a woman. **2.** An English country gentleman. **3.** A judge or another local dignitary. **4.** A young man of noble birth serving as a knight's attendant. —*tr.v.* **squired, squir•ing, squires.** To attend as a squire; escort. [First written down about 1225 in Middle English and spelled *squier*, esquire, from Old French *esquier*.]

squirm (skwûrm) *intr.v.* **squirmed, squirm•ing, squirms.** **1.** To twist about in a wriggling motion; writhe. **2.** To feel or exhibit signs of humiliation or embarrassment. —*n.* The act of squirming or a squirming movement.

squir•rel (**skwûr′**əl *or* **skwŭr′**əl) *n.* **1.** Any of various rodents that live in trees and have gray or reddish-brown fur and a bushy tail. **2.** The fur of such a rodent. —*tr.v.* **squir•reled, squir•rel•ing, squir•rels** or **squir•relled, squir•rel•ling, squir•rels.** To hide or store: *squirreled away her money.* [First written down in 1327 in Middle English and spelled *scurelle*, from Greek *skiouros* : *skia*, shadow + *oura*, tail.]

squirt (skwûrt) *v.* **squirt•ed, squirt•ing, squirts.** —*intr.* **1.** To come out in a thin forceful stream or jet; spurt. **2.** To eject liquid in a jet. —*tr.* **1.** To eject (liquid) in a thin stream through a narrow opening. **2.** To wet with a spurt of liquid. —*n.* **1.** The act of squirting. **2.a.** A device used to squirt. **b.** The stream squirted. **3.** *Informal.* An insignificant but arrogant person. —**squirt′er** *n.*

squish (skwĭsh) *v.* **squished, squish•ing, squish•es.** —*tr.* To squash or squeeze together: *squish a ripe tomato.* —*intr.* To make a noise like that of soft mud being walked on. —*n.* A squishing sound.

Sr The symbol for the element **strontium.**

Sr. *abbr.* An abbreviation of: **1.** Or **sr.** Senior. **2.** Señor. **3.** Sister (religious).

Sri Lan•ka (srē **lăng′**kə). Formerly **Cey•lon** (sĭ **lŏn′** *or* sā **lŏn′**). An island country in the Indian Ocean off southeast India. It gained its independence from Great Britain in 1948. Colombo is the capital and the largest city. Population, 14,848,364.

SS (**ĕs′ĕs′**) *n.* An elite military unit of the Nazi party that served as Hitler's personal guard and as a special security force.

S.S. *abbr.* An abbreviation of: **1.** Social Security. **2.** **SS.** Steamship.

SST *abbr.* An abbreviation of supersonic transport.

ST *abbr.* An abbreviation of standard time.

St. *abbr.* An abbreviation of saint.

stab (stăb) *v.* **stabbed, stab•bing, stabs.** —*tr.* **1.** To pierce or wound with or as if with a pointed weapon: *stabbed the fish with a spear.* **2.** To plunge (a

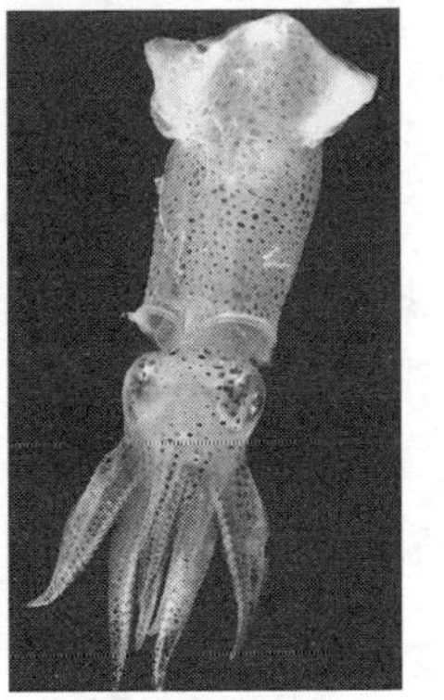

squid

squirrel
Eastern gray squirrel

ă	pat	oi	boy
ā	pay	ou	out
âr	care	o͝o	took
ä	father	o͞o	boot
ĕ	pet	ŭ	cut
ē	be	ûr	urge
ĭ	pit	th	thin
ī	pie	*th*	this
îr	pier	hw	whoop
ŏ	pot	zh	vision
ō	toe	ə	about
ô	paw	N	*French* bon

stagecoach
c. 1890 Concord stagecoach

pointed weapon or instrument) into something: *stabbed a fork into the meat.* —*intr.* **1.** To thrust with or as if with a pointed weapon. **2.** To inflict a wound with or as if with a pointed weapon. —*n.* **1.** A thrust made with a pointed weapon or instrument. **2.** A wound inflicted with a pointed weapon. **3.** An attempt; a try: *He thought he would take a stab at painting for a living.* [First written down in 1375 in Middle English and spelled *stabben.*] —**stab′ber** *n.*

sta•bil•i•ty (stə **bĭl′**ĭ tē) *n., pl.* **sta•bil•i•ties. 1.** The condition or property of being stable. **2.** The degree to which something is stable.

sta•bi•lize (**stā′**bə līz′) *v.* **sta•bi•lized, sta•bi•liz•ing, sta•bi•liz•es.** —*tr.* **1.** To make stable. **2.** To maintain the stability of (a plane or ship, for example) by means of a stabilizer. **3.** To fix the level of; keep from fluctuating: *stabilize interest rates.* —*intr.* To become stable. —**sta′bi•li•za′tion** (stā′-bə lĭ **zā′**shən) *n.*

sta•bi•liz•er (**stā′**bə lī′zər) *n.* **1.** Something that stabilizes. **2.** A device, such as a fin controlled by a gyroscope, used to keep a ship steady in heavy seas. **3.** A fixed airfoil used to keep an aircraft steady in flight.

sta•ble[1] (**stā′**bəl) *adj.* **sta•bler, sta•blest. 1.a.** Not likely to change position; firm: *a stable foundation of a house.* **b.** Not likely to change, as in condition: *a stable economy.* **2.** Not likely to be affected or overthrown: *a stable government.* **3.** Firm or steady, as in purpose or character. **4.** Mentally or emotionally sound; sane or rational. **5.** Not known to decay; existing for an indefinitely long time, as an atomic particle. **6.** Not easily decomposed, as a chemical compound. [First written down about 1150 in Middle English, from Latin *stabilis.*] —**sta′bly** *adv.*

sta•ble[2] (**stā′**bəl) *n.* **1.a.** A building for the shelter of horses or other domestic animals. **b.** The animals inhabiting such a building. **2.** All of the racehorses belonging to a single owner. —*tr.v.* **sta•bled, sta•bling, sta•bles.** To put or keep (an animal) in or as if in a stable: *stable a horse at the end of the day.* [First written down about 1225 in Middle English, from Latin *stabulum*, standing place.]

stac•ca•to (stə **kä′**tō) *adv. & adj.* In a musical style in which tones are short and unconnected.

stack (stăk) *n.* **1.** A large, usually conical pile of straw or food. **2.** An orderly pile, especially one arranged in layers: *a stack of firewood.* **3.** *Informal.* A large quantity: *a stack of work to do.* **4.** A group of three or more rifles supporting each other butt downward and forming a cone. **5.** A chimney or vertical exhaust pipe. **6.a.** An extensive arrangement of shelves. **b.** The part of a library where books are stored on such shelves. Often used in the plural: *You'll find that novel in the stacks.* —*v.* **stacked, stack•ing, stacks.** —*tr.* **1.** To arrange in a stack: *stacking hay; stack the books neatly.* **2.a.** To prearrange the order of (a deck of cards) so as to increase one's chance of winning. **b.** To prearrange or fix unfairly; cheat. —*intr.* To form a stack. —***idiom.*** **stack up.** *Informal.* To measure up or equal: *Our team stacks up well against the competition.* [First written down about 1300 in Middle English and spelled *stac*, from Old Norse *stakkr.*]

sta•di•um (**stā′**dē əm) *n., pl.* **sta•di•ums** or **sta•di•a** (**stā′**dē ə). **1.** A large, usually open structure for sports events with tiered seating for spectators. **2.** A course for foot races in ancient Greece, usually semicircular and surrounded with tiers of seats. **3.** An ancient Greek measure of distance equal to about 607 feet (185 meters). [First written down about 1380 in Middle English and spelled *stadie*, unit of length, from Greek *stadion.*]

staff (stăf) *n., pl.* **staffs** or **staves** (stāvz). **1.a.** A long stick or cane used as an aid in walking or as a weapon. **b.** A rod carried as a symbol of authority. **c.** A pole on which a flag is displayed. **2.** *pl.* **staffs.** A long measuring stick, as used in surveying. **3.** *pl.* **staffs. a.** A group of assistants who serve a person of authority: *the senator's campaign staff.* **b.** A group of military officers who assist and advise a commander. **c.** An organized group of employees working together on a project or enterprise: *the hospital's nursing staff.* **4.** The set of five horizontal lines and the spaces between them on which musical notes are written. —*tr.v.* **staffed, staff•ing, staffs.** To provide with assistants or employees. [First written down before 800 in Old English and spelled *stæf.*]

staff•er (**stăf′**ər) *n. Informal.* A member of a staff: *White House staffers.*

stag (stăg) *n.* **1.** The adult male of various deer. **2.a.** A man who attends a social gathering unaccompanied by a woman. **b.** A woman who attends a social gathering unaccompanied by a man. —*adj.* Of or for men only: *a stag party.*

stage (stāj) *n.* **1.** A raised and level platform, especially one in a theater on which actors and other entertainers perform. **2.** The acting profession or the world of theater: *The stage is her life.* **3.** The scene or setting of an event or series of events: *The stage was set for a summit conference.* **4.** Part of a journey. **5.** A stagecoach. **6.** A level, degree, or period of time in the course of a process; a step in development: *a disease in its early stages.* **7.** Any of a series of rocket propulsion units, each of which fires after the preceding one has finished burning and been cast away. —*tr.v.* **staged, stag•ing, stag•es. 1.** To produce or direct (a theatrical performance). **2.** To arrange and carry out: *students staging a protest march.* **3.** To exhibit or present on or as if on a stage: *stage a boxing match.*

stage•coach (**stāj′**kōch′) *n.* A closed horsedrawn vehicle with four wheels, used to transport mail and passengers over a regular route.

stage•hand (**stāj′**hănd′) *n.* A person who works backstage during a theater production.

stag•ger (**stăg′**ər) *v.* **stag•gered, stag•ger•ing, stag•gers.** —*intr.* **1.** To move or stand unsteadily, as if carrying a great weight; totter. **2.** To begin to lose confidence or sense of purpose; waver. —*tr.* **1.** To cause to totter or sway. **2.** To overwhelm with emotion or astonishment. **3.** To cause to waver or lose confidence. **4.** To arrange in parallel horizontal rows that form zigzags when viewed vertically: *stagger theater seats.* **5.** To arrange or schedule in overlapping time periods: *The terms of U.S. senators are staggered, so that only one-third are elected every two years.* —*n.* **1.** An act of staggering; a tottering motion or walk. **2.** A staggered pattern, arrangement, or order. **3. staggers.** *(used with a singular verb).* Any of various diseases of horses, cattle, or other domestic animals, marked by a staggering gait and frequent falling.

stag•ger•ing (**stăg′**ər ĭng) *adj.* Causing great astonishment, amazement, or dismay: *a staggering achievement.* —**stag′ger•ing•ly** *adv.*

stag•nant (**stăg′**nənt) *adj.* **1.** Not moving or flowing; motionless. **2.** Foul or polluted as a result of not moving: *stagnant water.* **3.** Not changing or growing; inactive: *a stagnant industry.* —**stag′nan•cy** *n.* —**stag′nant•ly** *adv.*

stag•nate (**stăg′**nāt′) *intr.v.* **stag•nat•ed, stag•nat•ing, stag•nates.** To be or become stagnant. —**stag•na′tion** *n.*

staid (stād) *adj.* **1.** Serious and drab in style, manner, or behavior; grave; sedate. **2.** Fixed; unchanging. —**staid′ly** *adv.* —**staid′ness** *n.*

stain (stān) *v.* **stained, stain•ing, stains.** —*tr.* **1.** To discolor, soil, or spot. **2.** To taint or tarnish (someone's reputation, for example). **3.** To color (wood, for example) with a dye or tint mixed with a penetrating liquid. **4.** To treat (microscopic specimens) with chemicals or dyes that make certain features visible through a microscope. —*intr.* **1.** To produce a discoloration. **2.** To become discolored. —*n.* **1.** A discolored or soiled spot or smudge. **2.** A blemish on one's character or reputation. **3.** A liquid preparation applied especially to wood in order to color it. **4.** A solution used for staining microscopic specimens. **—stain′er** *n.*

stained glass (stānd) *n.* Glass colored by mixing pigments into the glass, by fusing colored metallic oxides onto the glass, or by painting and baking transparent colors on the glass surface.

stain•less (stān′lĭs) *adj.* **1.** Free of stains or blemishes: *a stainless reputation.* **2.** Resisting stain or corrosion: *stainless alloys.*

stainless steel *n.* Any of various steel alloys that contain enough chromium to be resistant to rusting and corrosion.

stair (stâr) *n.* **1.** A series or flight of steps; a staircase. Often used in the plural. **2.** One of a flight of steps. [First written down about 1000 in Old English and spelled *stæger.*]
❑ *These sound alike:* **stair, stare** (gaze).

stair•case (stâr′kās′) *n.* A flight of steps and its supporting structure.

stair•way (stâr′wā′) *n.* A staircase.

stair•well (stâr′wĕl′) *n.* A vertical shaft containing a staircase.

stake (stāk) *n.* **1.** A piece of wood or metal pointed on one end and driven into the ground as a marker, fence pole, or tent support. **2.a.** A post to which a condemned person is bound for execution by burning. **b.** Execution by burning. **3.a.** The amount of money or the property risked in a bet or gambling game. Often used in the plural. **b.** The prize awarded to a contest winner. **c.** A race, especially a horse race, offering a prize to the winner. Often used in the plural. **4.** A share or an interest: *We all have a stake in completing this project on time.* —*tr.v.* **staked, stak•ing, stakes. 1.** To mark the location or boundaries of with or as if with stakes: *stake out a piece of land.* **2.** To fasten, secure, or support with a stake or stakes: *stake a plant.* **3.** To gamble or risk: *stake two dollars on the game.* **4.** To provide with the capital for or finance: *The bank will stake the new company.* **—*idioms.* at stake.** At risk; in jeopardy. **stake out.** To keep close watch over a person or thing: *The police staked out the jewelry store.* [First written down before 899 in Old English and spelled *staca.*]
❑ *These sound alike:* **stake, steak** (meat).

stake•out (stāk′out′) *n.* The watching of an area, a building, or a person, especially by the police.

sta•lac•tite (stə lăk′tīt′) *n.* A cylindrical or conical mineral deposit projecting downward from the roof of a cave or cavern, formed by dripping mineral water. [First written down in 1677 in Modern English, from Greek *stalaktos*, dripping, from *stalassein*, to drip.]

sta•lag•mite (stə lăg′mīt′) *n.* A cylindrical or conical mineral deposit built up from the floor of a cave or cavern and formed by dripping mineral water. [First written down in 1681 in Modern English, from Greek *stalagma*, a drop, from *stalassein*, to drip.]

stale (stāl) *adj.* **stal•er, stal•est. 1.** Having lost freshness or flavor: *stale bread.* **2.** Lacking originality; overused: *stale jokes.* **3.** Weakened by inactivity or boredom: *Some athletes work out on holidays, for fear of getting stale.*

stale•mate (stāl′māt′) *n.* **1.** A situation in which further action is blocked; a deadlock: *The peace talks have reached a stalemate.* **2.** A position in chess that results in a draw because the only piece that can be moved is the king and every move the king can make puts the king in check. —*tr.v.* **stale•mat•ed, stale•mat•ing, stale•mates.** To bring into a stalemate; deadlock.

Sta•lin (stä′lĭn), **Joseph.** 1879–1953. Soviet politician who served as premier (1941–1953) of the Soviet Union and oversaw the growth of industry and Soviet involvement in World War II. His rule was marked by extreme political repression.

Sta•lin•grad (stä′lĭn grăd′). Volgograd.

Sta•lin•ism (stä′lə nĭz′əm) *n.* The authoritarian exercise of state power associated with Stalin and characterized by repression of political opponents. **—Sta′lin•ist** *adj.* & *n.*

stalk[1] (stôk) *n.* **1.** The main stem of a plant or a stem or similar slender part supporting a leaf, flower, or other plant structure. **2.** A similar supporting or connecting part. [First written down before 1325 in Middle English, probably from *stale*, upright of a ladder, post, handle, from Old English *stalu.*]

stalk[2] (stôk) *v.* **stalked, stalk•ing, stalks.** —*intr.* **1.** To walk in a stiff, haughty, or angry manner: *He stalked past me in stony silence.* **2.** To move in a threatening manner, as if tracking prey or a victim: *The hungry tiger stalked through the jungle.* —*tr.* To pursue or track in a threatening manner. [First written down before 1000 in Old English and spelled *stealcian*, to move stealthily.] **—stalk′er** *n.*

stall[1] (stôl) *n.* **1.** A compartment for a domestic animal in a barn or stable. **2.** A small booth or stand used for selling or displaying goods, as at a fair. **3.** A small compartment or booth: *a shower stall.* **4.** A pew in a church. **5.** A designated parking space provided for an automobile. **6.** A protective covering for a finger or toe. **7.** A sudden unintended loss of power or effectiveness in an engine. —*v.* **stalled, stall•ing, stalls.** —*tr.* **1.** To put or lodge (an animal) in a stall. **2.** To slow down or halt the progress of; bring to a standstill: *Opponents of the bill have stalled it in Congress.* **3.** To cause (an engine or a motor) to stop running. **4.** To cause (an aircraft) to go into a stall. —*intr.* **1.** To live or be lodged in a stall. **2.** To come to a standstill: *The project stalled because of a lack of money.* **3.** To stop running because of mechanical failure. [First written down before 800 in Old English and spelled *steall*, standing place.]

stall[2] (stôl) *n.* A tactic used to mislead or delay. —*v.* **stalled, stall•ing, stalls.** —*tr.* To use delaying tactics against: *stall off creditors.* —*intr.* To use delaying tactics: *stalling for time.* [First written down before 1425 in Middle English and spelled *stal*, decoy, from Anglo-Norman *estale*, of Germanic origin.]

stal•lion (stăl′yən) *n.* An adult male horse that has not been castrated, especially one kept for breeding.

stal•wart (stôl′wərt) *adj.* **1.** Physically strong; sturdy; robust. **2.** Not easily deterred or defeated; brave and resolute: *stalwart defenders of their country.* —*n.* **1.** A person who is physically and morally strong. **2.** A loyal supporter; a dependable ally. **—stal′wart•ly** *adv.* **—stal′wart•ness** *n.*

sta•men (stā′mən) *n.*, *pl.* **sta•mens** or **sta•mi•na** (stā′mə nə *or* stăm′ə nə). The male reproductive organ of a flower, usually consisting of a slender stalk with a pollen-bearing part at its tip.

stam•i•na[1] (stăm′ə nə) *n.* The power to resist fatigue or illness while working hard; endurance. [First written down before 1676 in Modern English, from Latin *stāmina*, plural of *stamen*, thread.

stalactite and stalagmite

Joseph Stalin

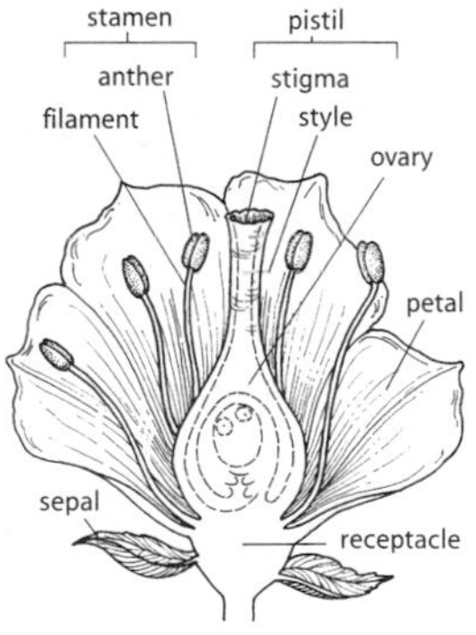

stamen

ă	pat	oi	boy
ā	pay	ou	out
âr	care	ŏŏ	took
ä	father	ōō	boot
ĕ	pet	ŭ	cut
ē	be	ûr	urge
ĭ	pit	th	thin
ī	pie	*th*	this
îr	pier	hw	whoop
ŏ	pot	zh	vision
ō	toe	ə	about
ô	paw	N	*French* bon

sta•mi•na² (stā′mə nə *or* stăm′ə nə) *n.* A plural of **stamen.**

sta•mi•nate (stā′mə nĭt *or* stā′mə nāt′ *or* stăm′ə nĭt *or* stăm′ə nāt′) *adj.* Having stamens but lacking pistils: *staminate flowers.*

stam•mer (stăm′ər) *v.* **stam•mered, stam•mer•ing, stam•mers.** *—intr.* To speak with involuntary pauses or repetitions, as from nervousness or confusion. *—tr.* To say or utter with involuntary pauses or repetitions. *—n.* A manner of speaking marked by stammering. **—stam′mer•er** *n.*

stamp (stămp) *v.* **stamped, stamp•ing, stamps.** *—tr.* **1.a.** To bring down (the foot) forcefully: *We stamped our feet to shake off the snow.* **b.** To bring the foot down onto (an object or surface) forcefully. **2.** To extinguish or destroy by or as if by trampling underfoot: *stamp out a fire.* **3.** To imprint or impress with a seal: *The border guard stamped our passports.* **4.** To put a postage stamp on: *Don't forget to stamp the letter before mailing it.* **5.** To shape or cut out by forcing into or against a mold, form, or die: *a factory that stamps metal parts.* **6.** To impress deeply or permanently: *an image stamped in her memory.* **7.** To make, characterize, or reveal: *His accent stamped him as a foreigner.* *—intr.* **1.** To thrust the foot forcefully downward. **2.** To walk with heavy forceful steps. *—n.* **1.** The act of stamping. **2.** A device used to impress, shape, or cut out something to which it is applied. **3.** The impression or shape formed by such a device. **4.a.** A postage stamp. **b.** A similar piece of gummed paper issued for a specific purpose: *a trading stamp.* **5.** A characteristic mark; a clear indication: *the stamp of truth on a witness's face.* **6.** Characteristic nature or quality: *a person of her stamp.* [First written down about 1200 in Middle English and spelled *stampen*, possibly from Old English *stempan*, to pound in a mortar.] —See Note at **stomp.**

stam•pede (stăm pēd′) *n.* **1.** A sudden violent rush of frightened animals, as of a herd of cattle. **2.** A sudden headlong rush or flight of a crowd of people. *—v.* **stam•ped•ed, stam•ped•ing, stam•pedes.** *—tr.* To cause (animals or people) to stampede. *—intr.* To flee in a sudden rush. [First written down in 1826 in American English and spelled *stompado*, from Spanish *estampida*, from Provençal *estampir*, to stamp, of Germanic origin.]

stance (stăns) *n.* **1.** The position or manner in which a person or an animal stands, especially the position taken by an athlete about to go into action: *the erect stance of a diver.* **2.** An attitude or a point of view regarding some issue: *a judge with a tough stance toward repeating offenders.*

stanch¹ (stônch *or* stänch *or* stănch) also **staunch** (stônch *or* stänch) *tr.v.* **stanched, stanch•ing, stanch•es** also **staunched, staunch•ing, staunch•es. 1.** To stop or check the flow of (blood or tears, for example). **2.** To stop or check the flow of blood from (a wound). [First written down before 1325 in Middle English and spelled *staunchen*, from Old French *estanchier*.]

stanch² (stônch *or* stänch *or* stănch) *adj.* Variant of **staunch¹.**

stan•chion (stăn′chən *or* stăn′shən) *n.* An upright pole, post, or support.

stand (stănd) *v.* **stood** (stŏŏd), **stand•ing, stands.** *—intr.* **1.** To rise to an upright position on the feet: *I stood up from my chair to answer the telephone.* **2.** To maintain an upright position on the feet or on a base or support: *Stand straight. The rocket stood on a launching pad.* **3.** To measure a certain height when in an upright position: *stood six feet tall.* **4.** To be located or situated: *The building stands at the corner.* **5.** To be at a specified level, position, or rank: *stand 12th in line.* **6.** To come to a stop; remain motionless or undisturbed: *Let the mixture stand overnight. Cars may not stand on this street.* **7.** To remain in effect or existence: *Exceptions are made, but the rule still stands.* **8.** To take up or maintain a specified position or attitude: *How do you stand on the issue?* **9.** To be in a specified state or condition: *My client stands accused of a serious crime.* **10.** To be in a position of possible gain or loss: *She stands to make a fortune.* *—tr.* **1.** To cause to stand; place upright. **2.** To engage in or encounter: *stand battle.* **3.** To resist successfully; withstand: *a metal that can stand high temperatures.* **4.** To tolerate; endure: *I can't stand all of this noise.* **5.** To submit to or undergo: *stand trial.* **6.** *Informal.* To bear the expense of; pay for: *I'll stand you a dinner to celebrate.* *—n.* **1.** An act of standing: *endured a long stand in a line.* **2.** A place or station where a person, such as a guard, stands. **3.** A place reserved for the stopping or parking of certain vehicles: *a taxi stand.* **4.** A booth, stall, or counter for the display of goods for sale: *a flower stand.* **5.** A small rack, prop, or receptacle for holding something: *an umbrella stand.* **6.** A raised structure on which someone can sit or stand and be clearly seen: *a witness stand.* **7. stands.** The seating area at a playing field or stadium. **8.** A halt in progress, advance, or work. **9.** A stop on a performance tour: *a one-show stand.* **10.** A desperate or final effort at defense or resistance, as in battle: *made their stand at the river.* **11.** A position or an opinion that one is prepared to defend against the arguments of others. **12.** A group or growth of tall plants or trees: *a stand of pine trees.* ***—idioms.*** **stand a chance.** To have a chance or hope for gaining or accomplishing something. **stand bail for.** To provide bail for (a person under arrest). **stand by. 1.** To be ready or available to act. **2.** To remain uninvolved; refrain from acting: *stood by and let her get away.* **3.** To remain loyal to; aid or support. **4.** To keep or maintain: *I stand by my promise to you.* **stand down.** To leave a witness stand at a trial. **stand for. 1.** To represent; symbolize: *The rose in the poem stands for beauty.* **2.** To advocate or support: *We stand for freedom of the press.* **3.** To put up with; tolerate: *He won't stand for another delay.* **stand in.** To act as a stand-in. **stand off. 1.** To stay at a distance; remain apart or aloof. **2.** To withstand; repel: *stood off the attack.* **stand on. 1.** To be based on; depend on: *Our success stands on her approval.* **2.** To demand observance of: *standing on his constitutional rights.* **stand out. 1.** To protrude; project. **2.** To be distinctive or prominent; attract attention: *Brightly colored clothing stands out in a crowd.* **stand up. 1.** To remain valid, sound, or durable: *His claim will not stand up in court.* **2.** *Informal.* To fail to keep a date with. **stand up for.** To side with; defend; be loyal to. **stand up to.** To confront fearlessly; face up to. [First written down about 725 in Old English and spelled *standan*.]

stan•dard (stăn′dərd) *n.* **1.** A flag or banner, especially one used as the emblem of a nation, military unit, or city. **2.a.** A widely known and accepted measure used as a basis for a system of measures. **b.** A physical object from which such a measure can be determined under a given set of conditions. **3.** A rule or model used to judge the quality, value, or rightness of something. **4.** A level of quality, value, or achievement that is required or aimed for: *an artist who sets high standards for herself.* **5.** The commodity or commodities used to back a monetary system: *the gold standard.* **6.** A stand on which something is mounted or supported; a pedestal. *—adj.* **1.** Serving as a standard of measurement, value, or quality: *a standard unit of volume.* **2.** Conforming to a standard, as in size, weight, or quality:

bolts of standard length and thickness. **3.** Normal; familiar; usual: *a standard excuse.* **4.** Widely accepted as reliable or excellent: *a standard reference work.* **5.** Of or relating to a kind of language that is most widely accepted by educated speakers. [First written down in 1138 in Middle English, from Old French *estandard,* rallying place, of Germanic origin.]

standard candle *n.* A candela.

Standard English *n.* The variety of the English language that is most widely accepted and used by educated speakers.

standard gauge *n.* **1.** A railroad track having a width of 56½ inches (143.5 centimeters). **2.** A railroad or railroad car built to this specification.

stan•dard•ize (stăn′dər dīz′) *tr.v.* **stan•dard•ized, stan•dard•iz•ing, stan•dard•iz•es.** To cause to conform to a standard: *standardized the old electrical fixtures.* **—stan′dard•i•za′tion** (stăn′-dər dĭ **zā′**shən) *n.*

standard time *n.* The time in any of the 24 time zones into which the earth is divided, computed from the position of the sun at the central meridian of each zone.

stand•by (stănd′bī′) *n., pl.* **stand•bys. 1.** A person or thing that can always by depended on, as in an emergency. **2.** A person or thing kept ready and available for service as a substitute. **3.** A favorite or frequent choice.

stand•ee (stăn **dē′**) *n.* A person who stands because no seats are available, as on a bus or in a theater.

stand-in (**stănd′**ĭn′) *n.* **1.** A substitute. **2.** A person who takes the place of another performer while the lights and camera are adjusted or during dangerous action.

stand•ing (stăn′dĭng) *n.* **1.** Status with respect to rank, reputation, or position, as in society, a profession, or a sport. **2.** High reputation; esteem: *a person of standing in the community.* **3.** Persistence in time; duration: *a friend of long standing.* —*adj.* **1.** Remaining upright; erect: *standing timber.* **2.** Performed or done from an upright position: *a standing jump.* **3.** Remaining in effect or existence; permanent: *a standing invitation; a standing army.* **4.** Not flowing or circulating; stagnant: *several feet of standing water.*

Stan•dish (stăn′dĭsh′), **Miles** or **Myles.** 1584?–1656. English colonist in America who was a military and political leader in the difficult early years of the colony at Plymouth.

stand•off (**stănd′**ôf′ *or* **stănd′**ŏf′) *n.* **1.** A tie or draw, as in a contest. **2.** A situation in which one force neutralizes or counterbalances another.

stand•off•ish (stănd **ô′**fĭsh *or* stănd **ŏf′**ĭsh) *adj.* Unfriendly; aloof.

stand•pipe (stănd′pīp′) *n.* A large vertical pipe into which water is pumped in order to produce a desired pressure.

stand•point (stănd′point′) *n.* A position from which things are considered or judged; a point of view.

stand•still (stănd′stĭl′) *n.* A halt; a stop: *Work came to a standstill.*

stank (stăngk) *v.* A past tense of **stink.**

Stan•ley (stăn′lē), Sir **Henry Morton.** 1841–1904. British journalist and explorer known for his expedition into Africa in search of David Livingstone.

stan•nic (stăn′ĭk) *adj.* Of, relating to, or containing tin, especially with a valence of +4. [First written down in 1790 in Modern English, from Late Latin *stannum,* tin.]

stan•nous (stăn′əs) *adj.* Of, relating to, or containing tin, especially with a valence of +2.

Stan•ton (stăn′tən), **Elizabeth Cady.** 1815–1902. American feminist and reformer who helped organize the first women's rights convention, held in Seneca Falls, New York (1848).

stan•za (stăn′zə) *n.* One of the divisions of a poem, composed of two or more lines usually with a common pattern of meter and rhyme. [First written down in 1588 in Modern English and spelled *stanze,* from Italian *stanza,* stopping place.]

sta•pes (stā′pēz) *n., pl.* **stapes** or **sta•pe•des** (**stā′**-pĭ dēz′). The innermost of the three small bones of the middle ear; the stirrup.

staph•y•lo•coc•cus (stăf′ə lō **kŏk′**əs) *n., pl.* **staph•y•lo•coc•ci** (stăf′ə lō **kŏk′**sī *or* stăf′ə lō **kŏk′**ī). Any of several round bacteria that usually occur in clusters like grapes and that often cause boils and other infections.

sta•ple[1] (stā′pəl) *n.* **1.** A major product grown or produced in a region: *Rice and rubber are the staples of this Asian country.* **2.** A basic food item, such as flour or rice. **3.** A raw material. **4.** A basic or principal element or feature: *the classics that are the staples of every good library.* **5.** The fiber of cotton, wool, or flax, graded as to length or fineness. —*adj.* **1.** Produced or stacked in large quantities to meet a steady demand: *Wheat is a staple crop.* **2.** Principal; main. [First written down before 1350 in Middle English and spelled *stapel,* official market for purchase of export goods, from Anglo-Norman *estaple.*]

Miles Standish

sta•ple[2] (stā′pəl) *n.* **1.** A U-shaped metal loop with pointed ends, driven into a surface to hold a hook or bolt or to hold wiring in place. **2.** A similar thin piece of wire, used for fastening papers together. —*tr.v.* **sta•pled, sta•pling, sta•ples.** To secure or fasten by means of a staple or staples. [First written down about 725 in Old English and spelled *stapol,* post, pillar.]

stapler (stā′plər) *n.* A device used to fasten papers or other materials together by means of staples.

star (stär) *n.* **1.** A celestial body consisting of extremely hot gases that emit radiation, including visible light. **2.** Any of the luminous, relatively stationary celestial bodies visible from Earth at night. **3. stars. a.** The celestial bodies, regarded as determining and influencing human events. **b.** Fate; fortune. **4.** Something resembling a star, especially a design with several points radiating from a center. **5.** An asterisk. **6.a.** An actor who plays a leading role in a movie, drama, or other performance. **b.** An outstanding and widely admired performer, as in movies or sports. —*adj.* Of, relating to, or being an outstanding and famous performer: *a star tennis player.* —*v.* **starred, star•ring, stars.** —*tr.* **1.** To ornament with stars. **2.** To award or mark with a star for excellence. **3.** To present or feature (a performer) in a leading role: *a television series starring a famous actor.* —*intr.* **1.** To play the leading role in a theatrical or film production: *She's now starring in a Broadway show.* **2.** To perform excellently.

Elizabeth Cady Stanton
Photographed in the 1890's

star•board (stär′bərd) *n.* The right-hand side of a ship or an aircraft as one faces forward. —*adj.* On the right-hand side as one faces forward: *the starboard bow.* —*adv.* To or toward the right-hand side as one faces forward. [First written down before 899 in Old English and spelled *stēorbord* : *stēor-,* steering + *bord,* side.]

starch (stärch) *n.* **1.** A nutrient carbohydrate that occurs widely in nature, chiefly in parts of plants, especially wheat, corn, rice, and potatoes, and that appears as a white tasteless powder when purified. **2. starches.** Foods having a high content of starch, as rice, beans, and potatoes. **3.** Any of various substances, such as natural starch, used to stiffen fabrics. **4.** Stiff behavior. —*tr.v.* **starched, starch•ing, starch•es.** To stiffen with starch. [First written down in 1440 in Middle English and spelled

ă	pat	oi	boy
ā	pay	ou	out
âr	care	ŏŏ	took
ä	father	ōō	boot
ĕ	pet	ŭ	cut
ē	be	ûr	urge
ĭ	pit	th	thin
ī	pie	*th*	this
îr	pier	hw	whoop
ŏ	pot	zh	vision
ō	toe	ə	about
ô	paw	N	*French* bon

starfish

statehouse
The state capitol in Sacramento, California

starche, substance used to stiffen cloth, from *sterchen*, to stiffen.]

starch•y (stär′chē) *adj.* **starch•i•er, starch•i•est. 1.a.** Containing starch. **b.** Stiffened with starch, as a fabric. **2.** Of or resembling starch. **3.** Stiff; formal.

star-crossed (stär′krôst′ *or* stär′krŏst′) *adj.* Opposed by fate; ill-fated.

star•dom (stär′dəm) *n.* The status of a performer or an entertainer acknowledged as a star.

stare (stâr) *v.* **stared, star•ing, stares.** —*intr.* To look steadily and directly, often with a wide-eyed gaze. —*tr.* To look at steadily and directly: *stared him in the eyes.* —*n.* An intent gaze. [First written down about 725 in Old English and spelled *starian.*]

❑ *These sound alike:* **stare, stair** (step).

star•fish (stär′fĭsh′) *n.* Any of various sea animals having a star-shaped body and usually five arms.

star•gaze (stär′gāz′) *intr.v.* **star•gazed, star•gaz•ing, star•gaz•es. 1.** To gaze at the stars. **2.** To daydream.

stark (stärk) *adj.* **stark•er, stark•est. 1.** Bare and blunt; unadorned: *the stark landscape of the moon.* **2.** Utter; complete; total: *in stark contrast.* **3.** Harsh; grim: *a stark future.* —*adv.* Utterly; completely: *stark raving mad.* [First written down about 750 in Old English and spelled *stearc*, stiff, strong.] —**stark′ly** *adv.* —**stark′ness** *n.*

star•let (stär′lĭt) *n.* A young film actress publicized as a future star.

star•light (stär′līt′) *n.* The light that reaches Earth from the stars.

star•ling (stär′lĭng) *n.* Any of various common birds having a short dark tail, pointed wings, and dark glossy feathers.

star•lit (stär′lĭt′) *adj.* Illuminated by starlight.

star•ry (stär′ē) *adj.* **star•ri•er, star•ri•est. 1.** Shining like stars: *starry eyes.* **2.** Full of stars; starlit: *a starry night.* —**star′ri•ness** *n.*

star•ry-eyed (stär′ē īd′) *adj.* Full of youthful hope and confidence; naively optimistic.

Stars and Stripes *n.* *(used with a singular or plural verb).* The flag of the United States.

Star-Span•gled Banner (stär′spăng′gəld) *n.* The flag of the United States.

start (stärt) *v.* **start•ed, start•ing, starts.** —*intr.* **1.** To begin an action or a movement; set out: *Having started at dawn, we reached the summit by nightfall.* See Synonyms at **begin. 2.** To come into operation or being; have a beginning: *School starts in September.* **3.** To move suddenly and involuntarily; startle: *The horse started at the loud noise.* **4.** In sports, to be in the first lineup of a game or race. —*tr.* **1.** To begin or commence (something): *start a new job; start reading a book.* **2.** To set into motion, operation, or activity: *start a car.* **3.** To found; establish: *start a business.* **4.** To help or tend in an early stage of development: *start seedlings.* **5.** To rouse (game) from a resting or hiding place; flush. **6.a.** To enter (a participant) into a race or game: *start a horse.* **b.** To play in the initial lineup of (a game): *The coach decided not to start the injured goalie.* —*n.* **1.** A beginning. **2.** A place or time at which a person or thing begins: *At the start of our trip we were cheerful.* **3.** A sudden or involuntary movement of the body; a startled reaction: *awoke with a start.* **4.** A position of advantage over rivals, as in a race; a lead. **5.** An opportunity to pursue a career or course of action: *She got her start by acting in commercials.* [First written down about 975 in Old English and spelled *sturtan*, to jump up.]

start•er (stär′tər) *n.* **1.** A person or thing that starts. **2.** A device, usually an electric motor, that turns an internal-combustion engine through several revolutions to make it start. **3.** A person who signals the start of a race. **4.a.** A contestant at the beginning of a race. **b.** A player who is a member of the starting lineup of a sports team.

star•tle (stär′tl) *v.* **star•tled, star•tling, star•tles.** —*tr.* **1.** To cause to make a sudden involuntary movement or start: *A thud on the roof startled us.* **2.** To alarm, frighten, or surprise suddenly: *The ambassador's angry reaction startled our allies.* —*intr.* To become alarmed, frightened, or surprised. —*n.* A sudden mild shock; a start. [First written down about 1025 in Old English and spelled *steartlian*, to kick.]

star•va•tion (stär vā′shən) *n.* **1.** The act or process of starving. **2.** The condition of being starved.

starve (stärv) *v.* **starved, starv•ing, starves.** —*intr.* **1.** To suffer or die from prolonged lack of food. **2.** To suffer because of a lack of something necessary: *a puppy starving for attention.* **3.** *Informal.* To be hungry. —*tr.* **1.** To cause to starve. **2.** To force to a specified state by starving: *The invading troops starved the town into submission.* [First written down about 1000 in Old English and spelled *steorfan*, to die.]

starve•ling (stärv′lĭng) *n.* A person or an animal that is starving or being starved. —*adj.* **1.** Starving. **2.** Poor in quality; inadequate.

stash (stăsh) *Slang. tr.v.* **stashed, stash•ing, stash•es.** To hide or store in a secret place: *stashing her comic books under her mattress.* —*n.* **1.** A hiding place for money or valuables. **2.** Something hidden away.

state (stāt) *n.* **1.** A condition or mode of being: *a state of confusion.* **2.** One of the three principal conditions, solid, liquid, or gaseous, in which material substances occur: *Ice is water in the solid state.* **3.** A stage or form in development: *the fetal state.* **4.** Social position or rank. **5.** A mental or emotional disposition; a mood: *in a calm rational state.* **6.** *Informal.* A condition of excitement, confusion, or disorder: *got into a state over the preparations for the party.* **7.a.** A body of people living under a single independent government; a nation: *the state of Israel.* **b.** The political organization or government of such a body of people. **c.** The territory of such a government. **8.** The power or scope of authority of a government: *the separation of church and state.* **9.** One of the political and geographic subdivisions of a country such as the United States of America. **10.** A grand and formal style; pomp: *a queen riding in state.* —*adj.* **1.** Owned and operated by a state: *state universities.* **2.** Of or relating to a nation or a political and geographic subdivision of a nation: *state security.* —*tr.v.* **stat•ed, stat•ing, states.** To express in words; declare: *stating a problem.* [First written down before 1200 in Middle English, from Latin *status.*]

state•hood (stāt′ho͝od′) *n.* The condition of being a state, especially a state of the United States.

state•house also **state house** (stāt′hous′) *n.* A building in which a state legislature meets; a state capitol.

state•less (stāt′lĭs) *adj.* Not being a citizen of any state or nation.

state•ly (stāt′lē) *adj.* **state•li•er, state•li•est. 1.** Marked by a graceful dignity or formality: *a dance with a slow stately rhythm.* **2.** Impressive in size or proportions; majestic: *stately columns; a stately oak.* —**state′li•ness** *n.*

state•ment (stāt′mənt) *n.* **1.** The act of stating or declaring. **2.** Something stated or declared: *a statement of purpose.* **3.** A written summary of a financial account: *a monthly bank statement.*

Stat•en Island (stăt′n). A borough of New York City made up of **Staten Island** in southeast New York southwest of Manhattan Island. It was permanently settled in the 1600's and became part of New York City in 1898. Population, 378,977.

state of the art *n.* The highest level of development, as of a device, technique, or scientific field, achieved at a particular time: *the state of the art in computers.* **—state′-of-the-art′** *adj.*

state•room (**stāt′**ro͞om′ *or* **stāt′**ro͝om′) *n.* A private room with sleeping accommodations on a ship or train.

state•side (**stāt′**sīd′) *adj.* Of or in the continental United States: *Soldiers undergo stateside training before being shipped abroad.* —*adv. Informal.* To or toward the continental United States.

states•man (**stāts′**mən) *n.* A man who is a leader in national or international affairs. **—states′man•ship′** *n.*

states' rights also **States' rights** (stāts) *pl.n.* **1.** The rights and powers of the state governments, especially those not granted to the federal government by the Constitution of the United States. **2.** A political belief in limiting the powers of the federal government and defending or extending those of the individual states.

states•wom•an (**stāts′**wo͝om′ən) *n.* A woman who is a leader in national or international affairs.

stat•ic (**stăt′**ĭk) *adj.* **1.a.** Having no motion; being at rest. **b.** Fixed; stationary. **2.** Of or relating to bodies at rest or forces that balance each other. **3.** Of, relating to, or producing stationary electric charges; electrostatic. **4.** Of, related to, or produced by random radio noise. —*n.* Random noise, such as crackling in a radio receiver or specks on a television screen, produced by atmospheric disturbance of the signal.

static electricity *n.* **1.** An electric charge accumulated on an insulated body. **2.** An electric discharge resulting from the accumulation of such a charge.

stat•ics (**stăt′**ĭks) *n.* *(used with a singular or plural verb).* The branch of physics that deals with balanced forces on and within stationary physical systems.

sta•tion (**stā′**shən) *n.* **1.** A place or location where a person or thing stands or is assigned to stand; a post: *a guard station.* **2.** A place, a building, or an establishment from which a service is provided or certain activities are directed: *a fire station.* **3.** A stopping place along a route, especially a stop for taking on passengers or refueling: *a bus station.* **4.** An establishment equipped to transmit radio or television signals. **5.** An establishment set up for the purpose of study or observation: *a radar station.* **6.** Social position; rank: *content with his station in life.* —*tr.v.* **sta•tioned, sta•tion•ing, sta•tions.** To assign to a position; post. [First written down about 1280 in Middle English and spelled *stacioun*, from Latin *statiō*.]

sta•tion•ar•y (**stā′**shə nĕr′ē) *adj.* **1.** Not moving. **2.** Not capable of being moved; fixed: *a stationary bridge.* **3.** Unchanging: *a stationary sound.* [First written down before 1430 in Middle English and spelled *stacionarie*, from Medieval Latin *statiōnārius*, from Latin *statiō*, station.]

❑ *These sound alike:* **stationary, stationery** (paper).

sta•tion•er (**stā′**shə nər) *n.* A person who sells stationery.

sta•tion•er•y (**stā′**shə nĕr′ē) *n.* **1.** Writing paper and envelopes. **2.** Writing materials and office supplies, including pens and paper. [First written down in 1727 in Modern English and spelled *stationary*, from Middle English *staciouner*, bookseller, from Medieval Latin *statiōnārius*, shopkeeper.]

❑ *These sound alike:* **stationery, stationary** (not moving).

station house *n.* A police or fire station.

sta•tion•mas•ter (**stā′**shən măs′tər) *n.* A person in charge of a railroad or bus station.

station wagon *n.* An automobile having a large interior with a third row of seats or a luggage platform and a tailgate.

sta•tis•tic (stə **tĭs′**tĭk) *n.* An item of numerical data.

sta•tis•ti•cal (stə **tĭs′**tĭ kəl) *adj.* Of, relating to, or employing statistics. **—sta•tis′ti•cal•ly** *adv.*

stat•is•ti•cian (stăt′ĭ **stĭsh′**ən) *n.* A person who specializes in statistics.

sta•tis•tics (stə **tĭs′**tĭks) *n.* **1.** *(used with a singular verb).* The branch of mathematics that deals with the collection, organization, analysis, and interpretation of numerical data. **2.** *(used with a plural verb).* A collection or set of numerical data.

sta•tor (**stā′**tər) *n.* The stationary part around which a piece of machinery, such as a motor, generator, or turbine, rotates.

stat•u•ar•y (**stăch′**o͞o ĕr′ē) *n., pl.* **stat•u•ar•ies. 1.** Statues considered as a group: *American war memorial statuary.* **2.** The art of making statues. —*adj.* Of, relating to, or suitable for a statue.

stat•ue (**stăch′**o͞o) *n.* A form or likeness sculpted, cast, modeled, or carved in a material such as stone, clay, metal, or wood. [First written down about 1375 in Middle English, from Latin *statua*, from *statuere*, to set up.]

stat•u•esque (stăch′o͞o **ĕsk′**) *adj.* Suggestive of a statue, as in size, proportions, or dignity; stately.

stat•u•ette (stăch′o͞o **ĕt′**) *n.* A small statue.

stat•ure (**stăch′**ər) *n.* **1.** The natural height of a person or an animal in an upright position. **2.** A level of development or achievement: *chess players of equal stature.*

sta•tus (**stā′**təs *or* **stăt′**əs) *n.* **1.** Social position relative to that of others; rank or standing: *Her status is that of an observer.* **2.** High standing; prestige: *seeking status by buying an expensive car.* **3.** The legal condition of a person or thing: *marital status.* **4.** A state of affairs; a situation: *the status of a bill in Congress.*

status quo (kwō) *n.* The existing state of affairs.

stat•ute (**stăch′**o͞ot) *n.* A law enacted by a legislative body.

statute mile *n.* A unit of length equal to 5,280 feet or 1,760 yards (1,609 meters); a mile. See table at **measurement.**

stat•u•to•ry (**stăch′**ə tôr′ē) *adj.* Of, defined by, or regulated by statute.

staunch[1] (stônch *or* stänch) also **stanch** (stônch *or* stänch *or* stănch) *adj.* **staunch•er, staunch•est** also **stanch•er,** also **stanch•est. 1.** Firm and steadfast; loyal: *a staunch ally.* **2.** Strongly made or built: *staunch roots; staunch boards.* [First written down before 1393 in Middle English and spelled *staunche*, from Old French *estanchier*, to stanch.] **—staunch′ly** *adv.* **—staunch′ness** *n.*

staunch[2] (stônch *or* stänch) *v.* Variant of **stanch[1].**

stave (stāv) *n.* **1.** A strip of wood forming a part of the side of a barrel, tub, or similar structure. **2.** A rung of a ladder or chair. **3.** A heavy stick or pole; a staff. **4.** A musical staff. **5.** A set of verses; a stanza. —*tr.v.* **staved** or **stove** (stōv), **stav•ing, staves. 1.** To break or puncture the staves or side of: *We almost stove the boat on a reef.* **2.** To break or smash a hole in. **3.** To furnish with staves. —***idiom.*** **stave off.** To keep or hold off; repel: *stave off the threat of disaster.*

staves (stāvz) *n.* A plural of **staff.**

stay[1] (stā) *v.* **stayed, stay•ing, stays.** —*intr.* **1.** To continue to be in a place or condition: *stay home; stay awake.* **2.** To remain or reside as a guest: *stay at a hotel.* **3.** To endure; persist: *We voted to stay with the original plan.* **4.** To stop moving; cease or halt. **5.** To wait; pause. —*tr.* **1.** To stop; halt: *stay*

station wagon

ă	pat	oi	boy
ā	pay	ou	out
âr	care	o͝o	took
ä	father	o͞o	boot
ĕ	pet	ŭ	cut
ē	be	ûr	urge
ĭ	pit	th	thin
ī	pie	*th*	this
îr	pier	hw	whoop
ŏ	pot	zh	vision
ō	toe	ə	about
ô	paw	N	*French* bon

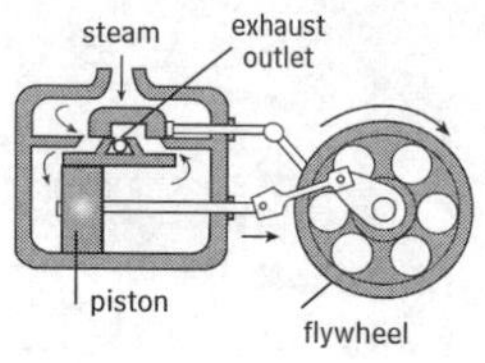

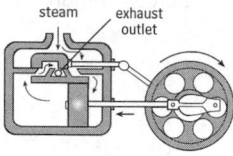

steam engine
Rightward (*top*) and leftward (*bottom*) movements of a slide valve steam engine

steamroller

steel band

one's tongue. **2.** To postpone; delay: *stay a prisoner's execution.* **3.** To satisfy or moderate temporarily: *stayed her appetite with an orange.* **4.** To remain during: *stayed the week with my grandparents.* —*n.* **1.** A brief period of residence or visiting. **2.** A halt or pause. **3.** A postponement, as of an execution or a legal action. [First written down in 1440 in Middle English and spelled *steien*, from Latin *stāre*.]

Synonyms: stay, remain, wait, linger. These verbs mean to continue to be in a given place. **Stay** is the most general: *We stayed at home all evening.* **Remain** often means to continue to be left after others have gone: *One person should remain on watch at night.* **Wait** means to stay in readiness, anticipation, or expectation: *I was waiting for you in the car.* **Linger** means to be slow in leaving: *I lingered, enjoying the starry night after the fireworks had ended.*

stay² (stā) *tr.v.* **stayed, stay•ing. 1.** To support, brace, or prop up. **2.** To strengthen or sustain mentally. —*n.* **1.** A support or brace. **2.** A strip of bone, plastic, or metal used to stiffen a garment or part, such as a corset or a shirt collar. **3. stays.** A corset. [First written down in 1423 in Middle English and spelled *staien*, from Old French *estaie*, a support, of Germanic origin.]

stay³ (stā) *n.* **1.** A heavy rope or cable, usually of wire, used to brace or support a mast or spar. **2.** A rope used to steady, guide, or brace. —*tr. & intr.v.* **stayed, stay•ing, stays.** To put (a ship) on the opposite tack or to come about. [First written down before 1100 in Old English and spelled *stæg*.]

stay•ing power (**stā′ĭng**) *n.* The ability to endure or last.

stay•sail (**stā′**səl *or* **stā′**sāl′) *n.* A triangular sail hoisted on a stay.

stead (stĕd) *n.* **1.** The place, position, or function that belongs to or is usually occupied by another: *Zeus overthrew his father and ruled the world in his stead.* **2.** Advantage; service; purpose: *Knowing how to use a computer stood me in good stead.*

stead•fast (**stĕd′**făst′) *adj.* **1.** Not moving; fixed; steady: *standing steadfast.* **2.** Firmly loyal or constant; faithful: *a steadfast friend.* **—stead′fast′ly** *adv.* **—stead′fast′ness** *n.*

stead•y (**stĕd′**ē) *adj.* **stead•i•er, stead•i•est. 1.** Firm in position or place; fixed: *a steady grip on the wheel.* **2.** Free or almost free from change or variation; constant; uniform: *a steady wind; a steady income.* **3.** Direct and unfaltering; sure: *sewing with a steady hand.* **4.** Not easily excited or disturbed; composed: *steady nerves.* **5.** Reliable; dependable: *steady workers.* **6.** Unwavering, as in purpose; steadfast. —*v.* **stead•ied, stead•y•ing, stead•ies.** —*tr. & intr.v.* To make or become steady; stabilize. —*n., pl.* **stead•ies.** The person whom one dates regularly and usually exclusively. **—stead′i•ly** *adv.* **—stead′i•ness** *n.*

stead•y-state theory (**stĕd′**ē **stāt′**) *n.* A theory that assumes that the average density of matter in the universe is constant and that as the universe expands, new matter is continuously being created.

steak (stāk) *n.* A slice of meat, typically beef, usually broiled or fried. [First written down in 1440 in Middle English and spelled *steike*, from Old Norse *steik*.]

❑ *These sound alike:* **steak, stake** (post).

steal (stēl) *v.* **stole** (stōl), **sto•len** (**stō′**lən), **steal•ing, steals.** —*tr.* **1.** To take (someone else's property) without right or permission. **2.** To get or enjoy secretly or furtively: *steal an hour to play video games; steal a look in the teacher's grade book.* **3.** To move, carry, or place secretly. **4.** In baseball, to advance safely to (another base) by running to the base during the delivery of a pitch. —*intr.* **1.** To commit theft. **2.** To move or happen secretly or stealthily: *The hours stole by.* **3.** In baseball, to steal a base. —*n.* **1.** The act of stealing; theft. **2.** *Slang.* Something acquired at a very low price; a bargain. **—steal′er** *n.*

❑ *These sound alike:* **steal, steel** (metal).

stealth (stĕlth) *n.* **1.** The act of moving or proceeding in a quiet secretive way so as to avoid notice: *The leopard uses stealth to catch its prey.* **2.** The quality or characteristic of being furtive or secretive.

stealth•y (**stĕl′**thē) *adj.* **stealth•i•er, stealth•i•est.** Quiet, secretive, and cautious, so as to avoid notice; furtive: *stealthy steps.* **—stealth′i•ly** *adv.* **—stealth′i•ness** *n.*

steam (stēm) *n.* **1.a.** Water in the gaseous state; vapor. **b.** The mist that forms when hot water vapor cools and condenses into tiny droplets. **2.** Power generated by water vapor under pressure. **3.** Power; energy: *running out of steam.* —*v.* **steamed, steam•ing, steams.** —*intr.* **1.** To produce or emit steam. **2.** To become or rise up as steam. **3.** To become misted or covered with steam: *The bathroom mirror steams up when the shower is used.* **4.** To move by means of steam power: *The ship steamed into the harbor.* **5.** *Informal.* To become very angry; fume. —*tr.* To expose to steam, as in cooking. [First written down before 1000 in Old English and spelled *stēam*.]

steam•boat (**stēm′**bōt′) *n.* A steamship, especially one used on rivers and inland waterways.

steam engine *n.* An engine in which the energy of hot steam is converted into mechanical power, especially one in which the steam expands in a closed cylinder and drives a piston.

steam•er (**stē′**mər) *n.* **1.** A steamship. **2.** A vehicle, a machine, or an engine driven by steam. **3.** A container in which something is steamed: *a rice steamer.* **4.** A soft-shell clam cooked by steaming.

steam•fit•ter (**stēm′**fĭt′ər) *n.* A person who installs and repairs heating, ventilating, refrigerating, and air-conditioning systems.

steam•rol•ler (**stēm′**rō′lər) *n.* **1.** A vehicle, formerly powered by a steam engine but now powered by an internal-combustion engine, equipped with a heavy roller for smoothing road surfaces. **2.** A crushing or overpowering force. —*v.* **steam•rol•lered, steam•rol•ler•ing, steam•rol•lers.** —*tr.* **1.** To smooth or level (a road) with a steamroller. **2.** To defeat or overwhelm ruthlessly; crush. —*intr.* To move or proceed with an overwhelming force: *The team steamrollered over every opponent.*

steam•ship (**stēm′**shĭp′) *n.* A large vessel propelled by one or more steam-driven engines.

steam shovel *n.* A large steam-driven machine for digging.

steam•y (**stē′**mē) *adj.* **steam•i•er, steam•i•est. 1.** Filled with or emitting steam: *a steamy kitchen.* **2.** Hot and humid: *another steamy August afternoon.* **—steam′i•ness** *n.*

ste•a•tite (**stē′**ə tīt′) *n.* Soapstone.

steed (stēd) *n.* A horse, especially a spirited one used for riding.

steel (stēl) *n.* **1.** Any of various hard strong alloys of iron and carbon, often with other metals added to give certain desired properties, widely used as a structural material. **2.** Something, such as a sword, that is made of steel. **3.** A quality suggestive of this alloy; hardness or strength: *nerves of steel.* **4.** Steel gray. —*adj.* **1.** Made with, relating to, or consisting of steel: *steel beams; the steel industry.* **2.** Very firm or strong. **3.** Of the color steel gray. —*tr.v.* **steeled, steel•ing, steels. 1.** To cover, plate, edge, or point with steel. **2.** To strengthen; brace: *steel oneself* *against disappointment.* [First written down about 725 in Old English and spelled *stȳle.*]

❑ *These sound alike:* **steel, steal** (take without right).

steel band *n.* A musical band that originated in Trinidad and is composed chiefly of tuned percussion instruments fashioned from oil drums.

steel gray *n.* A dark to purplish gray.

steel wool *n.* A matted or woven mass of fine steel fibers, used for cleaning, smoothing, or polishing.

steel•work (stēl′wûrk′) *n.* **1.** Something made of steel. **2. steelworks.** *(used with a singular verb).* A plant where steel is made; a foundry. **—steel′work′er** *n.*

steel•y (stē′lē) *adj.* **steel•i•er, steel•i•est. 1.** Made of steel. **2.** Resembling steel, as in color or hardness: *fixed me with a steely gaze.* **—steel′i•ness** *n.*

steel•yard (stēl′yärd′) *n.* A weighing device made of a horizontal bar marked off in units of weight, with a hook at the shorter end for holding the object to be weighed and a sliding counterweight at the other end that indicates the correct weight when the bar is balanced.

steep[1] (stēp) *adj.* **steep•er, steep•est. 1.** Rising or falling abruptly; sharply sloped: *a steep hill.* **2.** Very high; excessive: *a steep price to pay.* [First written down about 725 in Old English and spelled *stēap.*] **—steep′ly** *adv.* **—steep′ness** *n.*

steep[2] (stēp) *v.* **steeped, steep•ing, steeps.** *—tr.* **1.** To soak in a liquid: *steep a tea bag in boiling water; steeped the cloth in red dye.* **2.** To involve or preoccupy thoroughly; immerse: *As a child, she steeped herself in adventure stories.* *—intr.* To undergo soaking in a liquid: *Let the tea steep five minutes.* *—n.* The act or process of steeping. [First written down before 1325 in Middle English and spelled *stepen*, perhaps of Old English origin.]

steep•en (stē′pən) *tr. & intr.v.* **steep•ened, steep•en•ing, steep•ens.** To make or become steep or steeper.

stee•ple (stē′pəl) *n.* A tall tower rising from the roof of a building, especially from a church or courthouse.

stee•ple•chase (stē′pəl chās′) *n.* A horse race across open country or over an obstacle course.

stee•ple•jack (stē′pəl jăk′) *n.* A person who builds or maintains steeples or other high structures.

steer[1] (stîr) *v.* **steered, steer•ing, steers.** *—tr.* **1.** To direct the course of (an automobile, for example). **2.** To set and follow (a course): *We steered a course around the rocks.* **3.** To guide or maneuver (a person) into a place or course of action: *I steered the tourists toward downtown.* See Synonyms at **guide.** *—intr.* **1.** To guide a vehicle or vessel. **2.** To follow a set course. **3.** To be guided: *This car steers easily.* *—n.* A piece of advice; a tip: *gave me a bum steer about the movie.* [First written down before 899 in Old English and spelled *stēran.*]

steer[2] (stîr) *n.* A young male of domestic cattle, castrated before reaching maturity and raised for beef. [First written down before 800 in Old English and spelled *stēor.*]

steer•age (stîr′ĭj) *n.* **1.** The act or practice of steering a boat or a ship. **2.** The section of a passenger ship, originally near the rudder, providing the cheapest accommodations.

steer•ing wheel (stîr′ĭng) *n.* A wheel that controls steering, as on a boat or in an automobile.

steers•man (stîrz′mən) *n.* A person who steers a ship.

steg•o•saur (stĕg′ə sôr′) also **steg•o•sau•rus** (stĕg′ə sôr′əs) *n.* Any of several plant-eating dinosaurs having a double row of upright bony plates along the back.

stein (stīn) *n.* A beer mug usually holding about a pint.

Stein (stīn), **Gertrude.** 1874–1946. American writer known for her experimental novels, essays, and plays. Her works include *The Autobiography of Alice B. Toklas* (1933).

Stein•beck (stīn′bĕk′), **John Ernst.** 1902–1968. American writer known for his short stories and novels, including *The Grapes of Wrath* (1939). He won the 1962 Nobel Prize for literature.

Stein•em (stī′nəm), **Gloria.** Born 1934. American feminist who was a founding editor of *Ms.* magazine (1972).

stel•lar (stĕl′ər) *adj.* **1.** Of, relating to, or consisting of stars. **2.** Of or relating to a star performer: *a stellar cast for the play.* **3.** Outstanding; prominent: *stellar achievements.* [First written down in 1656 in Modern English, from Latin *stēlla*, star.]

stem[1] (stĕm) *n.* **1.a.** The main, often long or slender supporting part of a plant, usually growing above the ground. **b.** A slender plant part attached to or supporting a leaf, fruit, or flower; a stalk. **2.** A connecting or supporting part resembling such a plant part: *the stem of a pipe; the stem of a goblet.* **3.** The small shaft by which a watch is wound. **4.** The curving upright beam at the fore of a ship or boat. **5.** The main part of a word, to which affixes may be added to form various inflections or derivative words. *—v.* **stemmed, stem•ming, stems.** *—intr.* **1.** To derive; originate; spring: *His financial problems stem from an income that varies too much.* **2.** To make progress against: *We're stemming the tide of orders from our customers.* *—tr.* To remove the stem of: *stem and pit cherries for a pie.* ***—idiom.*** **from stem to stern.** From one end to another. [First written down before 899 in Old English and spelled *stefn, stemn.*]

stem[2] (stĕm) *tr.v.* **stemmed, stem•ming, stems. 1.** To stop or hold back by or as if by damming; stanch. **2.** To plug or fill (a hole, for example). [First written down before 1325 in Middle English and spelled *stemmen*, from Old Norse *stemma.*]

stemmed (stĕmd) *adj.* **1.** Having a stem or a specific type of stem: *a stemmed goblet; a prickly-stemmed plant.* **2.** Having the stems removed.

stench (stĕnch) *n.* A strong unpleasant smell; a stink.

sten•cil (stĕn′səl) *n.* **1.** A sheet, as of plastic or cardboard, in which letters or figures have been cut so that when ink or paint is applied to the sheet the patterns will appear on the surface beneath. **2.** The lettering or pattern produced with such a sheet. *—tr.v.* **sten•ciled, sten•cil•ing, sten•cils** or **sten•cilled, sten•cil•ling, sten•cils. 1.** To mark with a stencil. **2.** To produce by means of a stencil.

ste•nog•ra•pher (stə nŏg′rə fər) *n.* A person who is skilled in shorthand, especially one employed to transcribe dictation or testimony.

ste•nog•ra•phy (stə nŏg′rə fē) *n.* The art or process of writing in shorthand.

sten•to•ri•an (stĕn tôr′ē ən) *adj.* Very loud and powerful: *a stentorian voice.* [First written down in 1605 in Modern English, after *Stentor*, a loud-voiced Greek herald in the *Iliad.*]

step (stĕp) *n.* **1.** The single complete movement of raising one foot and putting it down in another spot, as in walking. **2.** The sound of someone walking: *heard his step in the corridor.* **3.** A footprint: *steps in the sand.* **4.a.** A manner of walking; a gait: *moving with a light step.* **b.** A fixed rhythm or pace, as in dancing or marching: *keep step to the music.* **5.a.** The distance covered by moving one foot ahead of the other. **b.** A short walking distance: *The bus stop is just a step from my front door.* **c. steps.** A course; a path: *turned her steps toward home.* **6.a.**

steeple

Gertrude Stein
Photographed in the 1930's

John Steinbeck

ă	pat	oi	boy
ā	pay	ou	out
âr	care	ŏŏ	took
ä	father	ōō	boot
ĕ	pet	ŭ	cut
ē	be	ûr	urge
ĭ	pit	th	thin
ī	pie	*th*	this
îr	pier	hw	whoop
ŏ	pot	zh	vision
ō	toe	ə	about
ô	paw	N	*French* bon

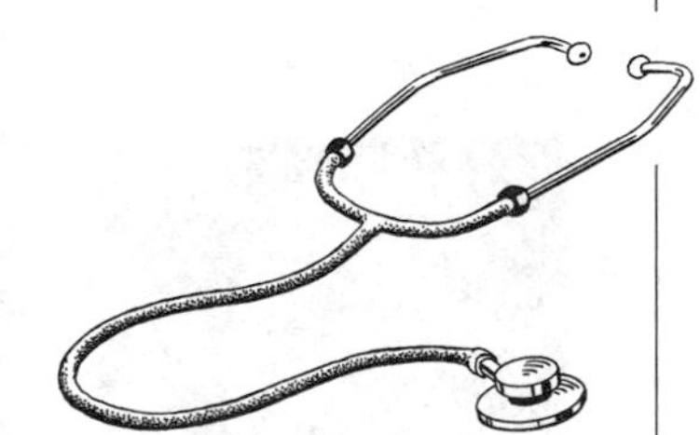
stethoscope

Baron von Steuben

A rest for the foot in ascending or descending, as a stair or a rung of a ladder. **b. steps.** Stairs. **7.a.** One of a series of actions or measures taken to achieve a goal: *taking steps to preserve the wildlife of a region.* **b.** A stage in a process or action. **8.** A grade or rank in a scale: *a step up in the corporation.* **9.** The interval that separates two successive tones of a musical scale. **10.** The block in which the base of a ship's mast is held. *—v.* **stepped, step•ping, steps.** *—intr.* **1.** To put or press the foot: *Don't step on the grass.* **2.** To move with the feet in a certain manner: *step lively.* **3.** To shift or move slightly by taking a step: *Please step back.* *—tr.* **1.** To put or set (the foot) down: *step foot on land.* **2.** To measure (a distance) by pacing: *step off ten yards on the field.* **3.** To place (a ship's mast) in its step. ***—idioms.*** **step by step.** By degrees. **step down. 1.** To resign from a high post. **2.** To reduce, especially in stages: *stepping down our use of water.* **step in. 1.** To enter into an activity or a situation. **2.** To intervene. **step on it.** *Informal.* To go faster; hurry. **step out. 1.** To walk briskly. **2.** To go outside for a short time. **step up. 1.** To increase, especially in stages: *step up production.* **2.** To come forward: *step up and be counted.* [First written down before 830 in Old English and spelled *stæpe.*]

❑ *These sound alike:* **step, steppe** (plain).

step– *pref.* A prefix that means related through the remarriage of a parent rather than by blood: *stepbrother.*

step•broth•er (**stĕp′**brŭ*th*′ər) *n.* A son of one's stepparent.

step•child (**stĕp′**chīld′) *n.* A child of one's wife or husband by an earlier marriage.

step•daugh•ter (**stĕp′**dô′tər) *n.* A daughter of one's husband or wife by an earlier marriage.

step•fa•ther (**stĕp′**fä′*th*ər) *n.* The husband of one's mother and not one's natural father.

step•lad•der (**stĕp′**lăd′ər) *n.* A portable ladder with a hinged supporting frame and usually topped with a small platform.

step•moth•er (**stĕp′**mŭ*th*′ər) *n.* The wife of one's father and not one's natural mother.

step•par•ent (**stĕp′**pâr′ənt *or* **stĕp′**păr′ənt) *n.* A stepfather or stepmother.

steppe (stĕp) *n.* A vast semiarid, grass-covered plain as found in southeast Europe, Siberia, and central North America. [First written down in 1671 in Modern English and spelled *step,* from Russian *step'.*]

❑ *These sound alike:* **steppe, step** (foot movement).

step•ping•stone (**stĕp′**ĭng stōn′) *n.* **1.** A stone that provides a place to step, as in crossing a stream. **2.** A step or means toward the achievement of a goal.

step•sis•ter (**stĕp′**sĭs′tər) *n.* A daughter of one's stepparent.

step•son (**stĕp′**sŭn′) *n.* A son of one's spouse by an earlier marriage.

–ster *suff.* A suffix that means someone who does, performs, or takes part in something: *gangster.*

ster•e•o (**stĕr′**ē ō′ *or* **stîr′**ē ō′) *n., pl.* **ster•e•os. 1.** A stereophonic system of sound reproduction. **2.** Stereophonic sound: *a performance reproduced in stereo.* *—adj.* **1.** Stereophonic. **2.** Stereoscopic.

ster•e•o•phon•ic (stĕr′ē ə **fŏn′**ĭk *or* stîr′ē ə **fŏn′**ĭk) *adj.* Of or used in a system of sound reproduction that uses two or more separate channels to give a more natural distribution of sound. **—ster′e•o•phon′i•cal•ly** *adv.*

ster•e•o•scope (**stĕr′**ē ə skōp′ *or* **stîr′**ē ə skōp′) *n.* An optical instrument through which two slightly different views of the same scene are presented, one to each eye, giving a three-dimensional illusion.

ster•e•o•scop•ic (stĕr′ē ə **skŏp′**ĭk *or* stîr′ē ə **skŏp′**ĭk) *adj.* **1.** Of or relating to vision that sees objects in three dimensions. **2.** Of or relating to a stereoscope.

ster•e•o•type (**stĕr′**ē ə tīp′ *or* **stîr′**ē ə tīp′) *n.* **1.** A conventional or oversimplified idea or image: *the stereotype of the meek librarian.* **2.** A metal printing plate cast from a matrix that is molded from a raised surface, such as type. *—tr.v.* **ster•e•o•typed, ster•e•o•typ•ing, ster•e•o•types. 1.** To make a stereotype of: *a movie that stereotypes farmers as unsophisticated yokels.* **2.** To print or reproduce from stereotypes. **—ster′e•o•typ′er** *n.*

ster•e•o•typed (**stĕr′**ē ə tīpt′ *or* **stîr′**ē ə tīpt′) *adj.* **1.** Lacking originality or creative force. **2.** Printed or reproduced from stereotype plates.

ster•ile (**stĕr′**əl *or* **stĕr′**īl′) *adj.* **1.** Not able to produce offspring, seeds, or fruit. **2.** Producing little or no plant life; barren: *a desolate sterile region.* **3.** Free from living microorganisms, especially those that cause disease: *a sterile bandage.* **4.** Not productive or effective; fruitless: *a sterile discussion.* **5.** Lacking imagination, creativity, or vitality: *a sterile recreation of the colonial period.* **—ster′ile•ly** *adv.* **—ste•ril′i•ty** (stə **rĭl′**ĭ tē) *n.*

ster•il•i•za•tion (stĕr′ə lĭ **zā′**shən) *n.* **1.** The act or procedure of sterilizing. **2.** The condition or being sterile or sterilized.

ster•il•ize (**stĕr′**ə līz′) *tr.v.* **ster•il•ized, ster•il•iz•ing, ster•il•iz•es.** To make sterile, especially to rid of live microorganisms or deprive of the ability to produce offspring. **—ster′il•iz′er** *n.*

ster•ling (**stûr′**lĭng) *n.* **1.** British money. **2.a.** Sterling silver. **b.** Articles, such as tableware, made from sterling silver. *—adj.* **1.** Consisting of or relating to British money: *sterling prices.* **2.** Made of sterling silver: *sterling knives.* **3.** Of the highest quality; very fine: *She has sterling qualifications.*

sterling silver *n.* **1.** An alloy containing 92.5 percent silver with copper or another metal. **2.** Objects made of this alloy.

stern[1] (stûrn) *adj.* **stern•er, stern•est. 1.** Hard, harsh, or severe in manner or character: *a stern look of reproach.* **2.** Firm or unyielding; uncompromising: *stern resistance.* **3.** Grim or gloomy in appearance or outlook: *a stern fate.* [First written down before 1000 in Old English and spelled *styrne.*] **—stern′ly** *adv.* **—stern′ness** *n.*

stern[2] (stûrn) *n.* The rear part of a ship or boat. [First written down about 1225 in Middle English and spelled *sterne,* perhaps of Scandinavian origin.]

ster•num (**stûr′**nəm) *n., pl.* **ster•nums** or **ster•na** (**stûr′**nə). A long flat bone located in the center of the chest, serving as a support for the collarbone and ribs; the breastbone.

stern-wheel•er (**stûrn′**wē′lər) *n.* A steamboat propelled by a paddle wheel at the stern.

ster•oid (**stîr′**oid′ *or* **stĕr′**oid′) *n.* **1.** Any of a large class of naturally occurring fat-soluble organic compounds based on a structure having 17 carbon atoms arranged in 4 rings and including many hormones, sterols, natural drugs, and substances related to vitamins. **2.** An anabolic steroid. **—ster′oid′, ste•roi′dal** (stĭ **roid′**l *or* stĕ **roid′**l) *adj.*

ster•ol (**stîr′**ôl′ *or* **stĕr′**ôl′) *n.* Any of various steroid alcohols, such as cholesterol, found in fatty tissues of plants and animals.

steth•o•scope (**stĕth′**ə skōp′) *n.* Any of various instruments used to listen to sounds, such as the heartbeat, made within the body.

Steu•ben (**stōō′**bən *or* **styōō′**bən), Baron **Friedrich Wilhelm Ludolf Gerhard Augustin von.** 1730–1794. Prussian-born American Revolutionary military leader who trained General George Washington's troops.

ste•ve•dore (stē′vĭ dôr′) *n.* A person whose job is the loading and unloading of ships.

Ste•ven•son (stē′vən sən), **Robert Louis Balfour.** 1850–1894. British writer whose novels include *The Strange Case of Dr. Jekyll and Mr. Hyde* (1886).

stew (sto͞o *or* styo͞o) *v.* **stewed, stew•ing, stews.** —*tr.* To cook (food) by simmering or boiling slowly: *stewing a chicken.* —*intr.* **1.** To undergo cooking by simmering or boiling slowly. **2.** *Informal.* To suffer from intense heat; swelter. **3.** *Informal.* To worry or be angry. —*n.* **1.** A dish cooked by stewing, especially a mixture of meat or fish and vegetables in stock. **2.** *Informal.* Mental agitation: *in a stew over her lost keys.*

stew•ard (sto͞o′ərd *or* **styo͞o′**ərd) *n.* **1.** A person who manages another's property, finances, or other affairs. **2.** A person in charge of the household affairs of a large estate, club, hotel, or resort. **3.** An attendant on a ship or an airplane. [First written down about 900 in Old English and spelled *stīward* : *stig,* hall + *weard,* keeper.] **—stew′ard•ship′** *n.*

stew•ard•ess (sto͞o′ər dĭs *or* **styo͞o′**ər dĭs) *n.* A woman who is a flight attendant.

stewed (sto͞od *or* styo͞od) *adj.* Cooked by stewing: *stewed tomatoes.*

stick (stĭk) *n.* **1.** A long slender piece of wood, such as a branch cut or fallen from a tree. **2.** A piece of wood that is used for fuel, cut for lumber, or shaped for a specific purpose: *a walking stick; a hockey stick.* **3.** Something slender and often cylindrical in form: *a stick of dynamite.* **4.** The control lever that operates the elevators and ailerons of an airplane. **5.a. sticks.** *Informal.* A remote area; the backwoods. **b.** A city or town regarded as dull or unsophisticated. **6.** *Informal.* A person regarded as stiff, listless, or boring. **7.** A poke or thrust with a pointed object. —*v.* **stuck** (stŭk), **stick•ing, sticks.** —*tr.* **1.** To pierce or prick with a pointed instrument or object: *sticking her finger on a thorn.* **2.** To push or thrust (something pointed) into or through a surface: *stuck the knife in the board.* **3.** To kill by piercing. **4.** To fasten or attach, as with a pin or nail: *stick a note on the door with a thumb tack.* **5.** To fasten or attach with an adhesive material, such as glue or tape: *stick a ticket on a car window.* **6.** To put, thrust, or push: *stuck a flower in his buttonhole; sticking her head out the window.* **7.** To detain or delay: *We were stuck in traffic for an hour.* **8.** *Informal.* To put blame or responsibility on; burden: *stuck me with the bill.* —*intr.* **1.** To be or become fixed or embedded in place by having the point thrust in: *The arrow stuck in the tree.* **2.** To become attached or fastened: *Mud stuck to my shoes.* **3.** To be in close association; cling: *Let's stick together or we'll get lost in this crowd.* **4.a.** To remain faithful or loyal: *stick by a friend in trouble.* **b.** To continue; persist: *I stuck with the lessons until the end.* **5.** To be at or come to a standstill; become fixed or obstructed: *The wheels stuck in the mud.* **6.** To extend; project: *hair sticking up on his head.* **—*idioms.* stick around.** *Informal.* To remain; linger. **stick out.** To be prominent or obvious: *That hat sticks out in a crowd.* **stick up.** To rob, especially at gunpoint. **stick up for.** To defend or support. [First written down about 1000 in Old English and spelled *sticca.*]

stick•ball (stĭk′bôl′) *n.* A form of baseball played with a rubber ball and a stick, such as one made from a broom handle.

stick•er (stĭk′ər) *n.* **1.** A gummed or adhesive label, seal, or sign. **2.** A thorn, prickle, or barb.

stick•le (stĭk′əl) *intr.v.* **stick•led, stick•ling, stick•les. 1.** To argue or raise objections stubbornly, especially about trivial or petty points. **2.** To have objections; scruple.

stick•le•back (stĭk′əl băk′) *n.* Any of various small freshwater and marine fishes having erectile spines along the back.

stick•ler (stĭk′lər) *n.* **1.** A person who stubbornly insists on something: *Be on time, because the interviewer is a stickler for promptness.* **2.** Something, such as a problem, that is puzzling or difficult.

stick•pin (stĭk′pĭn′) *n.* A decorative pin used to hold a necktie in place.

stick•up (stĭk′ŭp′) *n. Slang.* A robbery, especially at gunpoint.

stick•y (stĭk′ē) *adj.* **stick•i•er, stick•i•est. 1.** Having the property of sticking to a surface; adhesive: *sticky paste; sticky candy.* **2.** Hot and humid; muggy. **3.** *Informal.* Difficult or unpleasant: *a sticky situation.* **—stick′i•ly** *adv.* **—stick′i•ness** *n.*

sties[1] (stīz) *n.* Plural of **sty**[1].

sties[2] (stīz) *n.* Plural of **sty**[2].

stiff (stĭf) *adj.* **stiff•er, stiff•est. 1.** Difficult to bend; not flexible or pliant: *a stiff new pair of shoes.* **2.** Not moving or operating easily or freely: *a stiff joint; a stiff doorknob.* **3.** Not liquid, loose, or fluid; thick: *a stiff mixture.* **4.** Rigidly formal; not easy or graceful: *a stiff writing style.* **5.** Moving with or having a strong steady force: *a stiff current.* **6.** Firm, as in purpose; resolute. **7.** Difficult or laborious: *a stiff entrance requirement.* **8.** Harsh; severe: *stiff penalties.* **9.** Strong or potent: *a stiff dose of medicine.* **10.** Excessively high: *stiff prices.* —*adv.* **1.** In a stiff manner: *frozen stiff.* **2.** To a complete extent; totally: *bored stiff.* —*n. Slang.* **1.** A corpse. **2.** A person regarded as inhibited, dull, and overly formal. **3.** A person: *those lucky stiffs.* [First written down in 1000 in Old English and spelled *stīf.*] **—stiff′ly** *adv.* **—stiff′ness** *n.*

stiff•en (stĭf′ən) *tr. & intr.v.* **stiff•ened, stiff•en•ing, stiff•ens.** To make or become stiff or stiffer. **—stiff′en•er** *n.*

stiff-necked (stĭf′**nĕkt′**) *adj.* Stubborn and arrogant; unyielding.

sti•fle (stī′fəl) *v.* **sti•fled, sti•fling, sti•fles.** —*tr.* **1.** To keep in or hold back; suppress or stop: *stifled a laugh.* **2.** To kill by depriving of air or oxygen; smother. —*intr.* **1.** To feel smothered or suffocated by or as if by a lack of air, as in a stuffy room. **2.** To die from lack of oxygen; suffocate.

sti•fling (stī′flĭng) *adj.* Very hot or stuffy, almost to the point of being suffocating: *a stifling room.*

stig•ma (stĭg′mə) *n., pl.* **stig•ma•ta** (stĭg **mä′**tə) or **stig•mas. 1.** A mark of shame, disgrace, or reproach: *There should be no stigma attached to doing strenuous physical work.* **2.a.** A small mark; a scar or birthmark. **b.** A mark on the skin that bleeds as a symptom of hysteria. **3. stigmata.** Marks or sores that resemble the crucifixion wounds of Jesus, sometimes appearing on the bodies of persons in a state of religious ecstasy. **4.** The sticky tip of a flower pistil, on which pollen is deposited in the process of pollination. [First written down about 1400 in Middle English and spelled *stigme,* from Greek *stigma,* tattoo mark.]

stig•ma•tize (stĭg′mə tīz′) *tr.v.* **stig•ma•tized, stig•ma•tiz•ing, stig•ma•tiz•es.** To brand or characterize as shameful or dishonorable. **—stig′ma•ti•za′tion** (stĭg′mə tĭ **zā′**shən) *n.*

stile (stīl) *n.* **1.** A set of steps for crossing a fence or wall. **2.** A turnstile.

❑ *These sound alike:* **stile, style** (manner).

sti•let•to (stĭ **lĕt′**ō) *n., pl.* **sti•let•tos** or **sti•let•toes. 1.** A small dagger with a slender tapering blade. **2.** A small sharp-pointed instrument used for making eyelet holes in needlework. [First written down in 1611 in Modern English, from Italian, di-

Robert Louis Stevenson

ă	pat	oi	boy
ā	pay	ou	out
âr	care	o͝o	took
ä	father	o͞o	boot
ĕ	pet	ŭ	cut
ē	be	ûr	urge
ĭ	pit	th	thin
ī	pie	*th*	this
îr	pier	hw	whoop
ŏ	pot	zh	vision
ō	toe	ə	about
ô	paw	N	*French* bon

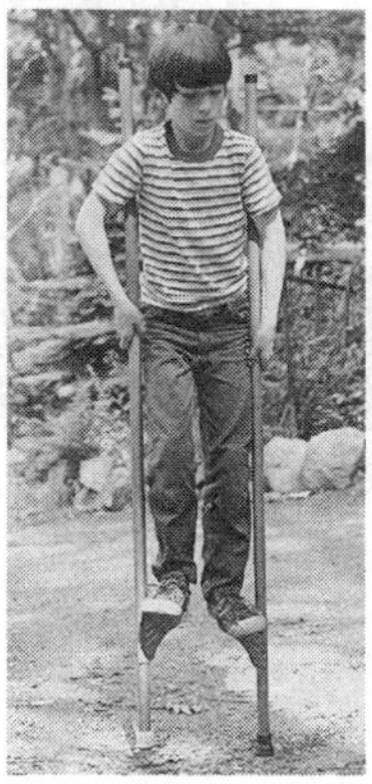

stilt
Walking on stilts

stingray

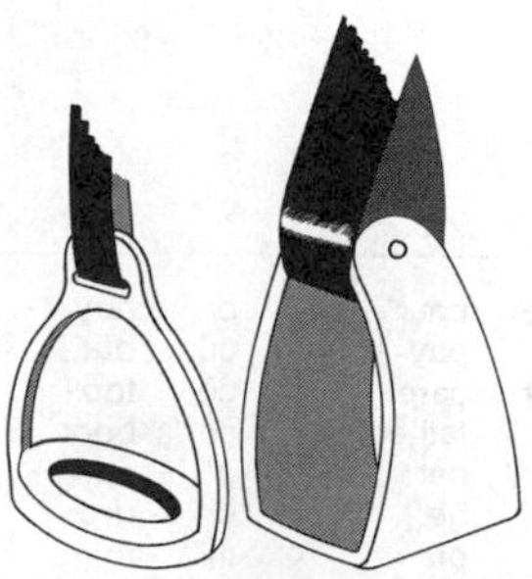

stirrup
Left: English
Right: Western

minutive of *stilo*, dagger, from Latin *stilus*, stylus, spike.]

still[1] (stĭl) *adj.* **still•er, still•est. 1.** Silent; quiet: *He was still for a moment and then started talking again.* **2.** Not moving; motionless: *still water.* **3.** Free from commotion or disturbance; peaceful: *the still countryside.* **4.** Not carbonated: *still wine.* **5.** Of or relating to a single or static photograph, as distinguished from a movie. —*n.* **1.** Silence; quiet; calm: *the still of the night.* **2.** A still photograph. —*adv.* **1.** Without movement: *Please stand still.* **2.** Up to or at the time indicated; yet: *The book will still be here tomorrow.* **3.** In increasing amount or degree: *I've got still more good news for you.* **4.** Nevertheless; all the same: *a painful but still necessary decision.* —*v.* **stilled, still•ing, stills.** —*tr.* **1.** To make still or tranquil. **2.** To make calm; allay: *stilled their fears.* —*intr.* To become still. [First written down about 725 in Old English and spelled *stille*.]

still[2] (stĭl) *n.* **1.** An apparatus for distilling liquids, especially alcohols. **2.** A distillery. [First written down in 1562 in Modern English, from Middle English *stillen*, to distill.]

still•born (stĭl′bôrn′) *adj.* Dead at birth.

still life *n., pl.* **still lifes. 1.** Representation of inanimate objects, such as flowers or fruit, in painting or photography. **2.** A painting, picture, or photograph of inanimate objects. **—still′-life′** *adj.*

still•ness (stĭl′nĭs) *n.* The state or an instance of being quiet or calm.

stilt (stĭlt) *n.* **1.** Either of a pair of long slender poles, each with a raised footrest, that enables the user to walk elevated above the ground. **2.** Any of various tall posts or pillars used as supports, as for a building or dock. **3.** A long-legged American wading bird having black and white feathers and a long bill. [First written down before 1300 in Middle English and spelled *stilte*.]

stilt•ed (stĭl′tĭd) *adj.* Stiffly or artificially formal; pompous: *stilted conversation.*

stim•u•lant (stĭm′yə lənt) *n.* **1.** Something, especially a medicine or drug, that temporarily speeds up or excites the function of the body or one of its systems or parts. **2.** A stimulus or an incentive.

stim•u•late (stĭm′yə lāt′) *v.* **stim•u•lat•ed, stim•u•lat•ing, stim•u•lates.** —*tr.* **1.** To rouse to activity or increased action; stir or excite: *music that stimulates the imagination.* **2.** To increase temporarily the activity of (a body organ or part). **3.** To excite or invigorate (a person, for example) with a stimulant. —*intr.* To act or serve as a stimulant or stimulus. **—stim′u•la′tion** *n.*

stim•u•lus (stĭm′yə ləs) *n., pl.* **stim•u•li** (stĭm′yə-lī′). **1.** Something causing or regarded as causing a response: *Many hope the road repairs will be a stimulus to the state's economy.* **2.** Something that causes an organism or a body part to change or respond. [First written down in 1684 in Modern English, from Latin *stimulus*, goad.]

sting (stĭng) *v.* **stung** (stŭng), **sting•ing, stings.** —*tr.* **1.** To pierce or wound with or as if with a sharp-pointed part or organ, as that of certain insects, such as bees. **2.** To cause to feel a sharp smarting pain by or as if by pricking with a sharp point: *Smoke began to sting her eyes.* **3.** To cause to suffer emotionally or feel keen unhappiness: *The angry words stung him bitterly.* —*intr.* **1.** To have, use, or wound with or as if with a sharp-pointed part or organ. **2.** To cause or feel a sharp smarting pain. —*n.* **1.** The act of stinging. **2.** A wound or pain caused by or as if by stinging. **3.** A sharp stinging part or organ, such as that of a bee, wasp, or scorpion, used for stinging and often injecting a poisonous or irritating substance. **4.** A keen stimulus; a goad or spur. [First written down before 899 in Old English and spelled *stingan*.] **—sting′ing•ly** *adv.*

sting•er (stĭng′ər) *n.* Something that stings, such as the sharp stinging organ of a bee, wasp, or scorpion.

sting•ray (stĭng′rā′) *n.* Any of various rays having a broad flattened body and a long tail with a sharp poisonous spine that can cause severe injury.

stin•gy (stĭn′jē) *adj.* **stin•gi•er, stin•gi•est. 1.** Giving or spending reluctantly. **2.** Scanty; meager: *a stingy meal.* **—stin′gi•ly** *adv.* **—stin′gi•ness** *n.*

stink (stĭngk) *v.* **stank** (stăngk) or **stunk** (stŭngk), **stunk, stink•ing, stinks.** —*intr.* **1.** To give off a strong foul odor. **2.** To be highly offensive. **3.** *Slang.* To be of extremely poor quality: *This movie stinks.* —*tr.* To cause to stink: *The wet dog stunk up the room.* —*n.* A strong offensive odor.

stint (stĭnt) *v.* **stint•ed, stint•ing, stints.** —*tr.* To restrict or limit, as in amount or number; be sparing with. —*intr.* To be frugal: *Don't stint on food.* —*n.* **1.** A fixed amount of work: *a stint as a clerk in her family's business.* **2.** A limitation or restriction: *working without stint.*

sti•pend (stī′pĕnd′) *n.* A fixed or regular payment, such as a salary or an allowance.

stip•ple (stĭp′əl) *tr.v.* **stip•pled, stip•pling, stip•ples.** To draw, engrave, or paint in dots or short strokes. —*n.* **1.** A method of drawing, engraving, or painting using dots or short strokes. **2.** The effect produced by stippling.

stip•u•late (stĭp′yə lāt′) *tr.v.* **stip•u•lat•ed, stip•u•lat•ing, stip•u•lates.** To specify or demand as a condition of an agreement; require by contract.

stip•u•la•tion (stĭp′yə lā′shən) *n.* **1.** The act of stipulating. **2.** Something stipulated, especially a term or condition in an agreement.

stip•ule (stĭp′yo͞ol) *n.* One of the usually small paired parts resembling leaves at the base of a leafstalk in certain plants.

stir (stûr) *v.* **stirred, stir•ring, stirs.** —*tr.* **1.** To pass an implement through (a liquid, for example) in circular motions so as to mix or cool the contents: *Stir the soup.* **2.** To mix or add by using an implement in this way: *Stir flour into the sauce.* **3.** To cause to move or change position: *The wind stirred the bird's feathers.* **4.** To rouse, as from sleep or indifference. **5.** To incite or provoke deliberately: *stir up trouble.* **6.** To excite strong feelings in: *The music stirred her heart.* —*intr.* **1.** To change position slightly: *The dog stirred in its sleep.* **2.** To move about actively: *Who's that stirring in the hall?* **3.** To be roused or affected by strong feelings. —*n.* **1.** A stirring or mixing movement. **2.** A disturbance or commotion. **3.** An excited reaction. **4.** A slight movement. [First written down about 725 in Old English and spelled *styrian*, to agitate.] **—stir′rer** *n.*

stir•ring (stûr′ĭng) *adj.* **1.** Exciting strong feelings: *a stirring song of peace.* **2.** Active; lively: *a stirring march.* **—stir′ring•ly** *adv.*

stir•rup (stûr′əp *or* stĭr′əp) *n.* A loop or ring with a flat base, hung by a strap from either side of a saddle on a horse to support the rider's foot. [First written down about 1000 in Old English and spelled *stīgrāp* : *stīgan*, to mount + *rāp*, rope.]

stirrup bone *n.* The stapes.

stitch (stĭch) *n.* **1.a.** A single complete movement of a threaded needle, as in sewing fabric or closing a wound during surgery. **b.** A single loop of yarn or thread around a knitting needle or crochet hook. **c.** A link, loop, or knot made in this way. **2.** A method or style or arranging thread or yarn in sewing, knitting, crocheting: *a purl stitch.* **3.** *Informal.* An article of clothing: *a baby without a stitch on.* **4.** A sudden sharp pain, especially in the side. **5.** The least part; a bit: *didn't do a stitch of work.* —*v.* **stitched, stitch•ing, stitch•es.** —*tr.* To fasten, join, or ornament with stitches: *stitch on a pocket; stitch a sampler.* —*intr.* To make stitches; sew.

stoat (stōt) *n., pl.* **stoat** or **stoats.** *Chiefly British.* The ermine, especially when its fur is brown. [First written down before 1475 in Middle English and spelled *stote.*]

stock (stŏk) *n.* **1.** A supply accumulated for future use; a store: *grain stocks.* **2.** The total merchandise kept on hand by a merchant or commercial establishment. **3.** All the animals kept or raised on a farm; livestock. **4.** The main stem or trunk of a tree or plant, especially one used for grafting. **5.** A line or group of ancestors from which persons, animals, or plants are descended. **6.** The raw material out of which something is made. **7.** Broth from boiled meat, fish, or vegetables, used in making soup, gravy, or sauces. **8.** A supporting structure, block, or frame, such as one around a ship during construction. **9.** The rear metal, wooden, or plastic handle or part of a firearm. **10.a.** The money invested in a corporation by the buying of shares of ownership, each share entitling the owner to voting rights at meetings and often dividends. **b.** A number of shares owned by a stockholder: *I have stock in that company.* **11. stocks.** A device consisting of a heavy wooden frame with holes for the ankles and often the wrists, formerly used to punish offenders. **12.** A theatrical activity, especially one outside a main theatrical center: *playing in summer stock.* **13.** Any of several garden plants having long showy clusters of fragrant flowers. —*v.* **stocked, stock•ing, stocks.** —*tr.* **1.** To provide with a stock of something: *stock a pond with trout.* **2.** To keep for future sale or use: *We stock canned goods.* —*intr.* To gather or lay in a supply of something: *stock up on canned foods.* —*adj.* **1.** Kept regularly available for sale or use: *Bread is a stock item.* **2.** Commonplace; not original: *a stock answer.* —***idioms.* in stock.** Available for sale or use; on hand. **out of stock.** Not available for sale or use. [First written down in 862 in Old English and spelled *stocc,* tree trunk.]

stock•ade (stŏ **kād′**) *n.* **1.** A defensive barrier made of strong upright posts driven into the ground. **2.** A similar fenced or enclosed area, such as a jail on a military base.

stock•bro•ker (**stŏk′**brō′kər) *n.* A person who buys or sells stocks, bonds, and other securities for a client and receives a commission in return; a broker.

stock car *n.* **1.** An automobile of standard make modified for racing. **2.** A railroad car for carrying livestock.

stock company *n.* **1.** A company or corporation whose capital is divided into shares. **2.** A permanent theatrical company that performs a fixed group of plays, usually at a single theater.

stock exchange *n.* A place where stocks, bonds, or other securities are bought and sold.

stock•hold•er (**stŏk′**hōl′dər) *n.* A person who owns a share or shares of stock in a company.

Stock•holm (**stŏk′**hōlm′ *or* **stŏk′**hōm′). The capital and largest city of Sweden, in the eastern part of the country on the Baltic Sea. It was founded in the mid-13th century. The Nobel Institute is here. Population, 653,455.

stock•ing (**stŏk′**ĭng) *n.* A close-fitting, usually knitted covering for the foot and leg made from nylon, cotton, wool, and similar yarns.

stocking cap *n.* A close-fitting knitted cap, often having a long tapering tail with a tassel attached.

stock•man (**stŏk′**mən) *n.* **1.** A man who owns or raises livestock. **2.** A man who is employed in a stockroom or warehouse.

stock market *n.* **1.** A stock exchange. **2.** The business transacted at a stock exchange.

stock•pile (**stŏk′**pīl′) *n.* A supply of material stored for future use. —*tr.v.* **stock•piled, stock•pil•ing, stock•piles.** To accumulate a stockpile of for future use: *stockpile supplies.*

stock•room also **stock room** (**stŏk′**ro͞om′ *or* **stŏk′**ro͝om′) *n.* A room in which a store of goods or materials is kept.

stock-still (**stŏk′stĭl′**) *adj.* Completely still; motionless.

stock•y (**stŏk′**ē) *adj.* **stock•i•er, stock•i•est.** Solidly built; squat and thick: *a stocky boy.* **—stock′i•ness** *n.*

stock•yard (**stŏk′**yärd′) *n.* A large enclosed yard in which livestock, such as cattle or pigs, are kept until slaughtered, sold, or shipped elsewhere.

stodg•y (**stŏj′**ē) *adj.* **stodg•i•er, stodg•i•est. 1.** Dull, unimaginative, and commonplace: *a stodgy person.* **2.** Heavy and indigestible: *stodgy food.* **3.** Solidly built; stocky. **—stodg′i•ly** *adv.* **—stodg′i•ness** *n.*

sto•gy or **sto•gie** (**stō′**gē) *n., pl.* **sto•gies. 1.** A cheap cigar. **2.** A roughly made heavy shoe or boot.

sto•ic (**stō′**ĭk) *n.* **1.** A person who is seemingly indifferent to joy, grief, pleasure, or pain. **2. Stoic.** A member of an ancient Greek school of philosophy believing that human beings should be free from all passion and accept all occurrences as resulting from a divine will or natural forces. —*adj.* also **sto•i•cal** (**stō′**ĭ kəl). Seemingly indifferent to or unaffected by pleasure or pain. **—sto′i•cal•ly** *adv.*

sto•i•cism (**stō′**ĭ sĭz′əm) *n.* **1.** Indifference to pain or pleasure; impassiveness. **2. Stoicism.** The doctrines or philosophy of the Stoics.

stoke (stōk) *tr.v.* **stoked, stok•ing, stokes.** To feed fuel to and tend (a fire or furnace).

stoke•hold (**stōk′**hōld′) *n.* The area or compartment into which a ship's furnaces or boilers open.

stoke•hole (**stōk′**hōl′) *n.* **1.** The space about the opening in a furnace or boiler. **2.** A stokehold.

stok•er (**stō′**kər) *n.* **1.** A person employed to feed fuel to and tend a furnace, as on a steam locomotive. **2.** A mechanical device for feeding coal to a furnace.

stole¹ (stōl) *n.* **1.** A long narrow scarf, usually of embroidered silk or linen, worn by deacons, priests, and bishops while officiating. **2.** A long scarf of cloth or fur worn by women about the shoulders. [First written down about 950 in Old English, from Greek *stolē,* robe.]

stole² (stōl) *v.* Past tense of **steal.**

sto•len (**stō′**lən) *v.* Past participle of **steal.**

stol•id (**stŏl′**ĭd) *adj.* **stol•id•er, stol•id•est.** Having or showing little movement or emotion; impassive: *a stolid soldier.* **—sto•lid′i•ty** (stŏ **lĭd′**ĭ tē) *n.* **—stol′id•ly** *adv.*

sto•lon (**stō′**lŏn′ *or* **stō′**lən) *n.* A shoot that grows along the ground and produces roots and shoots at the nodes; a runner.

sto•ma (**stō′**mə) *n., pl.* **sto•ma•ta** (**stō′**mə tə) or **sto•mas.** One of the tiny openings in the outer surface of a plant leaf or stem, through which gases and water vapor pass.

stom•ach (**stŭm′**ək) *n.* **1.a.** The enlarged portion of the alimentary canal, located in vertebrates between the esophagus and the small intestine and serving as one of the main organs of digestion. **b.** A similar part of the digestive system of many invertebrates. **2.** The part of the body that contains the stomach; the abdomen or belly. **3.** An appetite for food. **4.** A desire or an inclination: *I don't have the stomach for such adventures.* —*tr.v.* **stom•ached, stom•ach•ing, stom•achs.** To bear, tolerate, or endure: *She had to stomach his rudeness.* [First written

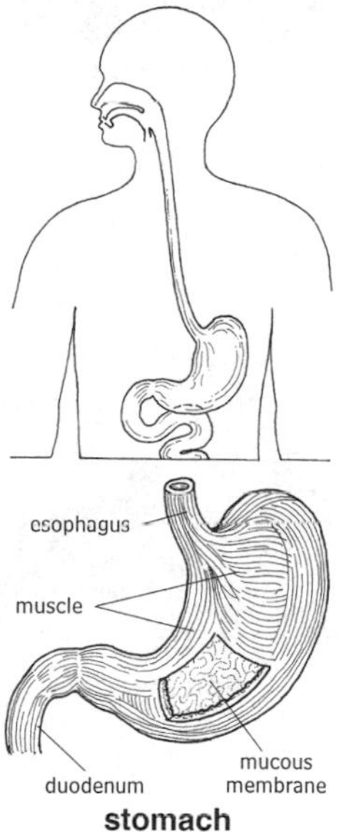

stomach

ă	pat	oi	boy
ā	pay	ou	out
âr	care	o͝o	took
ä	father	o͞o	boot
ĕ	pet	ŭ	cut
ē	be	ûr	urge
ĭ	pit	th	thin
ī	pie	*th*	this
îr	pier	hw	whoop
ŏ	pot	zh	vision
ō	toe	ə	about
ô	paw	N	*French* bon

Usage: stomp

You can use **stomp** or **stamp** to mean "to trample" or "to tread on violently": *stomping* (or *stamping*) *horses.* Only **stamp** is used in the sense "to eliminate": *stamp out a fire.* Also use *stamp* when referring to the action of striking the ground with the foot, as in anger or frustration: *He stamped his foot and began to cry.*

Lucy Stone

Stonehenge

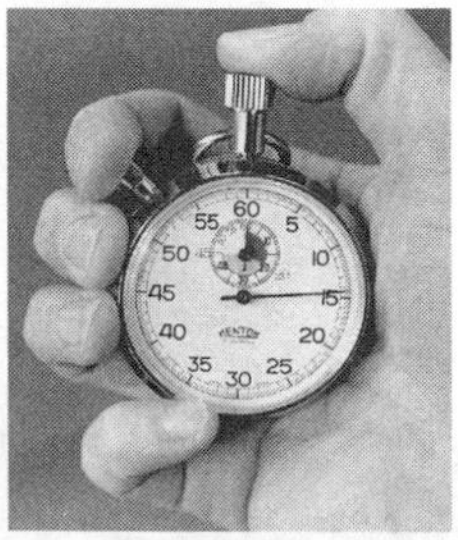

stopwatch

down before 1325 in Middle English and spelled *stomak*, from Greek *stomakhos*, from *stoma*, mouth.]

stom•ach•ache (**stŭm′**ək āk′) *n.* Pain in the stomach or abdomen.

sto•ma•ta (**stō′**mə tə) *n.* A plural of **stoma.**

stomp (stŏmp *or* stômp) *v.* **stomped, stomp•ing, stomps.** *—tr.* To tread or trample heavily or violently on. *—intr.* To tread or trample heavily or violently: *He stomped in frustration.* —See Note.

stone (stōn) *n.* **1.** Hard or compacted mineral or earthy matter; rock. **2.** A small piece of rock. **3.** A piece of rock cut or shaped for a particular purpose, as a tombstone or milestone. **4.** A gem or precious stone. **5.** A seed with a hard covering, as of a cherry or plum; a pit. **6.** A hard mass of mineral matter that collects in a hollow organ of the body, such as a kidney; a calculus. **7.** A unit of weight in Great Britain, equal to 14 pounds (6.4 kilograms). *—adj.* Relating to or made from stone: *a stone wall.* *—tr. v.* **stoned, ston•ing, stones. 1.** To throw stones at. **2.** To remove the stones or pits from. [First written down before 830 in Old English and spelled *stān*.]

Stone (stōn), **Lucy.** 1818–1893. American feminist and reformer who was a founder of the American Woman Suffrage Association (1869).

Stone Age *n.* The earliest known period of human culture, characterized by the use of stone tools.

stone-blind (**stōn′blind′**) *adj.* Completely blind.

stone•cut•ter (**stōn′**kŭt′ər) *n.* **1.** A person who cuts or carves stone. **2.** A machine used to finish the surface of stone.

stoned (stōnd) *adj. Slang.* Drunk or drugged.

stone-deaf (**stōn′dĕf′**) *adj.* Completely deaf.

Stone•henge (**stōn′**hĕnj′). A group of standing stones on Salisbury Plain in southern England. The stones date to about 2000–1800 B.C., and their arrangement suggests that Stonehenge was used as a religious center and also as an astronomical observatory.

stone•ma•son (**stōn′**mā′sən) *n.* A person who prepares and lays stones in building.

stone's throw (stōnz) *n.* A short distance.

stone•wall (**stōn′**wôl′) *v.* **stone•walled, stone•wall•ing, stone•walls.** *—intr. Informal.* **1.** To delay or stall. **2.** To refuse to answer or cooperate: *The witness tried to stonewall as long as possible.* *—tr. Informal.* To refuse to answer or cooperate with; resist or rebuff: *The government official stonewalled the investigating committee.*

stone•ware (**stōn′**wâr′) *n.* A heavy nonporous pottery, fired at a high temperature.

stone•work (**stōn′**wûrk′) *n.* **1.** The technique or process of building or making things from stone: *a mason skilled in stonework.* **2.** Something built or made of stone. **—stone′work′er** *n.*

ston•y (**stō′**nē) *adj.* **ston•i•er, ston•i•est. 1.** Covered with or full of stones: *stony soil.* **2.** Resembling stone, as in hardness. **3.** Hardhearted and unfeeling: *a stony gaze.* **—ston′i•ly** *adv.* **—ston′i•ness** *n.*

stood (sto͝od) *v.* Past tense and past participle of **stand.**

stooge (sto͞oj) *n.* **1.** A person who allows himself or herself to be used for another's profit or advantage; a puppet. **2.** The straight man of a comedy team.

stool (sto͞ol) *n.* **1.** A single seat having no back or arms and supported on legs or a pedestal. **2.** A low bench or support for the feet or knees in sitting or kneeling. **3.a.** A bowel movement. **b.** Waste matter expelled in a bowel movement.

stool pigeon *n.* **1.** *Slang.* A person who acts as a decoy or an informer, especially for the police. **2.** A pigeon used as a decoy.

stoop¹ (sto͞op) *v.* **stooped, stoop•ing, stoops.** *—intr.* **1.** To bend forward and down from the waist or middle of the back: *stooping to pick up the newspaper.* **2.** To walk or stand with the head and upper back bent forward. **3.** To lower or debase oneself: *He wouldn't stoop to such behavior.* *—tr.* **1.** To bend (the head and body) forward and down. **2.** To debase; humble. *—n.* **1.** The act of stooping. **2.** A forward bending of the head and body, especially when habitual: *walk with a stoop.* [First written down before 899 in Old English and spelled *stūpian*.]

❑ *These sound alike:* **stoop¹** (bend forward), **stoop²** (small porch), **stoup** (church basin).

stoop² (sto͞op) *n.* A small porch, staircase, or platform leading to the entrance of a house or building. [First written down in 1755 in American English, from Dutch *stoep*, front verandah.]

❑ *These sound alike:* **stoop²** (small porch), **stoop¹** (bend forward), **stoup** (church basin).

stop (stŏp) *v.* **stopped, stop•ping, stops.** *—tr.* **1.** To cause to halt or cease moving, progressing, acting, or operating: *The officer stopped the car.* **2.** To bring to an end; cease: *stop running.* **3.** To close or block (an opening) by covering, plugging up, or filling in: *stop up the drain.* **4.** To prevent the flow or passage of: *stop traffic; stop the bottle from leaking.* **5.a.** To press down (a string on a stringed instrument) to produce a tone of a desired pitch. **b.** To close (a hole on a woodwind instrument) to produce a tone of a desired pitch. **6.** To order a bank to withhold payment of: *stopped the check.* *—intr.* **1.** To cease moving, progressing, acting, or operating; come to a halt: *The clock stopped during the night.* **2.** To interrupt one's course or journey for a brief visit or stay: *stop at the store on the way home.* *—n.* **1.** The act of stopping or the condition of being stopped; a halt. **2.** A stay or visit: *We made a stop at Austin.* **3.** A place at which a person or thing stops: *a bus stop.* **4.** A device or means that stops, blocks, or regulates movement. **5.a.** A tuned set of pipes, as in an organ. **b.** A knob, lever, or key that controls such a series of pipes. **6.** The aperture of a lens, as on a camera. [First written down about 950 in Old English and spelled *stoppian*.]

Synonyms: stop, cease, halt, quit. These verbs mean to bring or come to an end. *Stop making so much noise; I'm trying to sleep! The siren ceased abruptly. We were halted at the checkpoint on the border. They quit riding at sundown.*

stop•gap (**stŏp′**găp′) *n.* A temporary substitute or expedient.

stop•light (**stŏp′**līt′) *n.* **1.** A traffic light. **2.** A light on the rear of a vehicle that goes on when the brakes are applied.

stop•o•ver (**stŏp′**ō′vər) *n.* **1.** A brief stay or visit, as in the course of a journey. **2.** A place visited briefly.

stop•page (**stŏp′**ĭj) *n.* The act of stopping or the condition of being stopped; a halt.

stop•per (**stŏp′**ər) *n.* A device, such as a cork or plug, that is inserted into an opening to close it. *—tr.v.* **stop•pered, stop•per•ing, stop•pers.** To close with or as if with a stopper.

stop•watch (**stŏp′**wŏch′) *n.* A watch that can be instantly started and stopped by pushing a button, used for measuring exact intervals of time.

stor•age (**stôr′**ĭj) *n.* **1.** The act of storing or the state of being stored: *goods in storage.* **2.** A space for storing: *We have storage in the attic.* **3.** The price charged for storing goods: *How much is storage per month?*

storage battery *n.* A group of rechargeable electric cells acting as a unit.

store (stôr) *n.* **1.** A place where merchandise is offered for sale; a shop. **2.** A stock or supply reserved for future use. **3.** **stores.** Supplies, especially of food, clothing, or arms. **4.** A great quantity or number; an abundance: *a store of knowledge.* *—tr.v.* **stored, stor•ing, stores. 1.** To put away for future use: *Squirrels store acorns for winter.* **2.** To fill, supply, or stock. ***—idiom.*** **in store.** Forthcoming: *A great opportunity was in store for her.* [First written down before 1300 in Middle English and spelled *stor*, supply, from Latin *īnstaurāre*, to restore.]

store•house (stôr′hous′) *n.* **1.** A place or building in which goods are stored; a warehouse. **2.** An abundant source or supply: *a storehouse of knowledge.*

store•keep•er (stôr′kē′pər) *n.* A person who runs a retail shop or store.

store•room (stôr′ro͞om′ *or* stôr′ro͝om′) *n.* A room in which things are stored.

sto•rey (stôr′ē) *n.* *Chiefly British.* Variant of **story[2]**.

sto•ried[1] (stôr′ēd) *adj.* Famous in story or history: *the storied ruins of Pompeii.* [First written down in 1481 in Middle English, from *storie*, a tale.]

sto•ried[2] (stôr′ēd) *adj.* Having or consisting of a certain number of stories: *a five-storied house.* [First written down in 1624 in Modern English, from *story*, a story in a building.]

stork (stôrk) *n.* Any of various large wading birds having long legs and a long straight bill.

storm (stôrm) *n.* **1.** A disturbance of the atmosphere in which strong winds appear, usually accompanied by rain, snow, or other precipitation, often with thunder and lightning. **2.** A violent disturbance or upheaval, as in political, social, or domestic affairs. **3.** A strong or violent outburst, as of emotion or excitement. **4.** A heavy shower of objects, such as bullets or missiles. **5.** A violent sudden attack on a fortified place. *—v.* **stormed, storm•ing, storms.** *—intr.* **1.** To be stormy; blow forcefully and often rain, snow, hail, or sleet: *It stormed for an hour yesterday.* **2.** To be very angry; rant and rage. **3.** To move or rush about angrily: *He stormed into the room.* *—tr.* To assault or capture by a violent sudden attack: *storm the gates.* [First written down about 725 in Old English.]

storm cellar *n.* A cyclone cellar.

storm center *n.* **1.** The central area of a storm, especially the point of lowest barometric pressure within a storm. **2.** A center of trouble, disturbance, or argument.

storm door *n.* An outer or additional door added for protection against stormy weather.

storm petrel *n.* Any of various small sea birds of the North Atlantic and the Mediterranean, usually having dark feathers with white markings.

storm window *n.* A secondary window set outside of the usual window to protect against the wind and cold.

storm•y (stôr′mē) *adj.* **storm•i•er, storm•i•est. 1.** Subject to, affected by, or characterized by storms: *stormy weather.* **2.** Characterized by violent emotions, passions, speech, or actions: *a stormy meeting.* **—storm′i•ly** *adv.* **—storm′i•ness** *n.*

sto•ry[1] (stôr′ē) *n., pl.* **sto•ries. 1.** An account of an event or a series of events, either true or fictitious. **2.** A fictional prose or verse narrative; a tale. **3.** A short story. **4.** A news article or broadcast: *The reporter covered three stories today.* **5.** A lie: *Don't tell stories.* **6.** A statement, a report, or an allegation of facts: *That's his story.* [First written down before 1200 in Middle English and spelled *storie*, from Latin *historia*.]

sto•ry[2] (stôr′ē) *n., pl.* **sto•ries.** A complete horizontal division of a building, consisting of an area between two levels or floors. [First written down before 1384 in Middle English and spelled *storie*, *story*, from Medieval Latin *historia*, picture, story.]

sto•ry•book (stôr′ē bo͝ok′) *n.* A book containing a collection of stories, usually for children. *—adj.* Occurring in or resembling the style or content of a storybook: *a storybook romance.*

sto•ry•tell•er (stôr′ē tĕl′ər) *n.* A person who tells or writes stories.

stoup (sto͞op) *n.* A basin for holy water in a church. ❑ *These sound alike:* **stoup, stoop[1]** (bend forward), **stoop[2]** (small porch).

stout (stout) *adj.* **stout•er, stout•est. 1.** Determined, bold, or brave: *a stout heart.* **2.** Strong in body or structure; sturdy: *the stout back of a donkey.* **3.** Bulky in figure; fat: *a stout man.* *—n.* A strong dark beer or ale. **—stout′ly** *adv.* **—stout′ness** *n.*

stout•heart•ed (stout′här′tĭd) *adj.* Brave; courageous. **—stout′heart′ed•ly** *adv.* **—stout′heart′ed•ness** *n.*

stove[1] (stōv) *n.* An apparatus that furnishes heat for warmth or cooking, using fuel or electricity as a source of power. [First written down in 1456 in Middle English and spelled *stove*, heated room, probably from Middle Low German or Middle Dutch.]

stove[2] (stōv) *v.* A past tense and a past participle of **stave.**

stove•pipe (stōv′pīp′) *n.* **1.** A metal pipe used to carry smoke or fumes from a stove to a chimney. **2.** A man's tall silk hat.

stow (stō) *tr.v.* **stowed, stow•ing, stows. 1.** To place or arrange, especially neatly: *stowed her equipment in the locker.* **2.** To store for future use: *stow the wood in the cellar.* ***—idiom.*** **stow away.** To hide oneself aboard a train or ship, for example, in order to obtain free transportation.

stow•a•way (stō′ə wā′) *n.* A person who hides aboard a ship or other vehicle in order to obtain free passage.

Stowe (stō), **Harriet (Elizabeth) Beecher.** 1811–1896. American writer known for her antislavery novel *Uncle Tom's Cabin* (1852).

strad•dle (străd′l) *v.* **strad•dled, strad•dling, strad•dles.** *—tr.* **1.** To sit or stand with a leg on each side of: *She straddled the horse.* **2.** To appear to favor both sides of: *straddle a political issue.* *—intr.* To sit astride. **—strad′dler** *n.*

strafe (strāf) *tr.v.* **strafed, straf•ing, strafes.** To attack (troops, for example) with machine-gun fire from low-flying aircraft.

strag•gle (străg′əl) *intr.v.* **strag•gled, strag•gling, strag•gles. 1.** To stray or fall behind: *The cows straggled in the pastures.* **2.** To proceed or spread out in a scattered or irregular group: *caribou straggling north to the tundra.* **—strag′gler** *n.*

straight (strāt) *adj.* **straight•er, straight•est. 1.** Extending continuously in the same direction without curving: *a straight line.* **2.** Having no waves or bends: *straight hair.* **3.** Erect; upright: *a straight back.* **4.** Perfectly horizontal or vertical; level. **5.** Direct and candid: *do some straight talking.* **6.** Neatly or properly arranged; orderly: *He can't keep his desk straight.* **7.** Not interrupted; consecutive: *ended the season with six straight wins.* **8.** Not deviating politically: *a straight party line.* **9.** Not mixed with anything else; undiluted. **10.** Not deviating from what is considered socially acceptable; conventional. *—adv.* **1.** In a straight line; directly: *The arrow flew straight at the target.* **2.** In an erect posture; upright: *stand straight.* **3.** Without detour or delay: *went straight home.* **4.** Candidly: *Tell me straight.* **5.** Without stopping; continuously: *It snowed for five days straight.* *—n.* In poker, a series of five cards of different suits in numerical order. [First written down before 1325 in Middle English and spelled *streit*, from past participle of *strecchen*,

stork
Yellow-billed stork

Harriet Beecher Stowe

ă	pat	oi	boy
ā	pay	ou	out
âr	care	o͝o	took
ä	father	o͞o	boot
ĕ	pet	ŭ	cut
ē	be	ûr	urge
ĭ	pit	th	thin
ī	pie	*th*	this
îr	pier	hw	whoop
ŏ	pot	zh	vision
ō	toe	ə	about
ô	paw	N	*French* bon

to stretch.] —**straight′ly** *adv.* —**straight′ness** *n.*

❑ *These sound alike:* **straight, strait** (channel).

straight angle *n.* An angle of 180 degrees.

straight•a•way (strāt′ə wā′) *adj.* Extending in a straight line or course without a curve or turn. —*n.* A straight road, course, or track. —*adv.* (strāt′ə wā′). At once; immediately.

straight•edge (strāt′ĕj′) *n.* A stiff, flat, rectangular bar, as of wood or metal, with a straight edge for drawing or testing straight lines.

straight•en (strāt′n) *tr. & intr.v.* **straight•ened, straight•en•ing, straight•ens.** To make or become straight or straighter: *straighten hair; straighten up a room.*

❑ *These sound alike:* **straighten, straiten** (confine).

straight•for•ward (strāt fôr′wərd) *adj.* **1.** Proceeding in a straight course; direct: *a straightforward approach to a problem.* **2.** Not evasive; honest and frank: *a straightforward reply.* —**straight•for′ward•ly** *adv.* —**straight•for′ward•ness** *n.*

straight•jack•et (strāt′jăk′ĭt) *n.* Variant of **straitjacket.**

straight man *n.* The partner in a comedy team who feeds lines to the other comedian, who then makes witty replies.

straight•way (strāt′wā′ *or* strāt′wā′) *adv.* **1.** In a direct course. **2.** Without delay; at once.

strain¹ (strān) *v.* **strained, strain•ing, strains.** —*tr.* **1.** To pull, draw, or stretch tight: *The weight of the pulley strains the rope.* **2.** To exert or tax to the utmost; strive hard: *strained my eyes to read the sign.* **3.** To injure or impair by overuse or overexertion: *strain a muscle.* **4.** To force or stretch beyond a proper or legitimate limit: *strain a point.* **5.** To pass through a strainer; filter. —*intr.* **1.** To make violent or steady efforts: *strained to reach the finish line.* **2.** To be or become wrenched or twisted. **3.** To pull forcibly or violently: *The dog strained at its leash.* **4.** To stretch or exert one's muscles or nerves to the utmost. —*n.* **1.** The act of straining or the state of being strained. **2.** A pressure, stress, or force: *felt a strain on the line.* **3.** An injury resulting from excessive effort or twisting: *a muscle strain.* **4.** Great pressure or demands on one's mind, body, or resources: *felt the strain of the extra homework.* [First written down about 1300 in Middle English and spelled *streinen*, from Latin *stringere*, to bind.]

strain² (strān) *n.* **1.** The collective descendants of a common ancestor; a race, stock, line, or breed. **2.** A group of organisms of the same species, not usually considered a separate breed or variety. **3.** A kind or sort. **4.** An inborn or inherited tendency or characteristic. **5.** The tone, tenor, or substance of something: *spoke in an academic strain.* **6.** A piece, passage, or sound of music. Often used in the plural: *the strains of the waltz.* [First written down about 950 in Old English and spelled *strēon*, gain.]

strained (strānd) *adj.* **1.** Passed through a strainer: *strained peaches.* **2.** Done with or marked by excessive effort; forced: *strained humor.* **3.** Under severe stress; on the point of collapse: *strained relations between the two countries.*

strain•er (strā′nər) *n.* Something that strains, especially a device used for separating liquids from solids.

strait (strāt) *n.* **1.** A narrow channel that connects two larger bodies of water. Often used in the plural. **2.** A position of difficulty, perplexity, distress, or need. Often used in the plural: *He was in desperate straits for money.* —*adj.* **1.** Difficult; stressful. **2.** Having or marked by limited funds or resources. [First written down about 1390 in Middle English and spelled *straite*, from Latin *strictus*, narrow.]

❑ *These sound alike:* **strait, straight** (erect).

strait•en (strāt′n) *tr.v.* **strait•ened, strait•en•ing, strait•ens. 1.** To make narrow; restrict. **2.** To enclose in a limited area; confine. **3.** To put or bring into financial difficulties.

❑ *These sound alike:* **straiten, straighten** (make straight).

strait•jack•et also **straight•jack•et** (strāt′jăk′ĭt) *n.* **1.** A long-sleeved garment of strong material used to bind the arms tightly against the body as a means of restraining a violent patient or prisoner. **2.** Something that restricts, hinders, or confines.

strait-laced (strāt′lāst′) *adj.* Excessively strict in behavior, morality, or opinions.

strand¹ (strănd) *n.* The land bordering a body of water; a beach. —*tr. & intr.v.* **strand•ed, strand•ing, strands. 1.** To drive or be driven ashore or aground. **2.** To leave or be left in a difficult or helpless position. [First written down about 1000 in Old English.]

strand² (strănd) *n.* **1.** A complex of fibers or filaments that have been twisted together to form a rope, cord, yarn, or cable. **2.** A single filament, such as a fiber or thread, of a woven or braided material. **3.** Something, such as a string of pearls, that is plaited or twisted together into a length. [First written down in 1497 in Middle English and spelled *strond.*]

strange (strānj) *adj.* **strang•er, strang•est. 1.** Previously unknown; unfamiliar: *a strange fish of tropical waters.* **2.** Out of the ordinary; unusual or striking: *a strange feeling.* **3.** Not of one's own particular locality, environment, or kind: *a strange language.* **4.** Reserved in manner; distant. **5.** Not accustomed: *strange to her new duties.* [First written down about 1280 in Middle English and spelled *strounge*, from Latin *extrāneus*, foreign.] —**strange′ly** *adv.* —**strange′ness** *n.*

strang•er (strān′jər) *n.* **1.** A person who is neither a friend nor an acquaintance. **2.** A foreigner, a newcomer, or an outsider.

stran•gle (străng′gəl) *tr.v.* **stran•gled, stran•gling, stran•gles. 1.a.** To kill by choking or suffocating. **b.** To deprive of oxygen; smother. **2.** To suppress or stifle: *strangle a cry.* **3.** To restrict or limit the growth or action of: *strangle the enemy's supply lines.* —**stran′gler** *n.*

stran•gu•la•tion (străng′gyə lā′shən) *n.* The act of strangling or the state of being strangled.

strap (străp) *n.* **1.** A long narrow strip of leather or other pliant material, used to hold things down, bind things together, or keep things in place: *the straps of an evening gown.* **2.** A narrow band formed into a loop for grasping with the hand: *pulled the suitcase along by its strap.* **3.** A strip of leather used in flogging. —*tr.v.* **strapped, strap•ping, straps. 1.** To fasten or secure with a strap: *strapped an air tank to the diver's back.* **2.** To beat with a strap.

strap•ping (străp′ĭng) *adj.* Having a sturdy muscular physique; robust.

stra•ta (strā′tə *or* străt′ə) *n.* A plural of **stratum.**

strat•a•gem (străt′ə jəm) *n.* **1.** A military maneuver designed to deceive or surprise an enemy. **2.** A clever, often underhanded scheme for achieving an objective.

stra•te•gic (strə tē′jĭk) *adj.* **1.** Of or relating to strategy: *the strategic importance of the Panama Canal.* **2.** Essential in relation to a plan of action: *strategic locations.* —**stra•te′gi•cal•ly** *adv.*

strat•e•gist (străt′ə jĭst) *n.* A person who is skilled in strategy.

strat•e•gy (străt′ə jē) *n., pl.* **strat•e•gies. 1.** The science of using all the forces of a nation as effectively as possible during peace or war. **2.** A plan of action arrived at by means of this science or intended to accomplish a specific goal.

Strat•ford-up•on-Av•on (străt′fərd ə pŏn ā′vən *or* străt′fərd ə pôn ā′vən). A borough of central England south-southeast of Birmingham. William Shakespeare was born and died here. Population, 20,800.

stra•ti (strā′tī *or* străt′ī) *n.* Plural of **stratus.**

strat•i•fi•ca•tion (străt′ə fĭ kā′shən) *n.* **1.** Formation or deposition of layers, as of rock or sediments. **2.** The condition of being stratified. **3.** A layered arrangement.

strat•i•fy (străt′ə fī′) *v.* **strat•i•fied, strat•i•fy•ing, strat•i•fies.** —*tr.* To form, arrange, or deposit in layers. —*intr.* To become layered; form strata.

stra•to•cu•mu•lus (strā′tō kyo͞om′yə ləs *or* străt′ō kyo͞om′yə ləs) *n., pl.* **stra•to•cu•mu•li** (strā′tō-kyo͞om′yə lī′ *or* străt′ō kyo͞om′yə lī′). A low-lying cloud formation occurring in extensive horizontal layers with massive rounded tops.

strat•o•sphere (străt′ə sfîr′) *n.* The layer of the earth's atmosphere that lies above the troposphere and below the mesosphere, having a relatively even temperature throughout.

strat•o•spher•ic (străt′ə sfîr′ĭk *or* străt′ə sfĕr′ĭk) *adj.* Of or relating to the stratosphere.

stra•tum (strā′təm *or* străt′əm) *n., pl.* **stra•ta** (strā′tə *or* străt′ə) or **stra•tums. 1.** A horizontal layer of material, especially one made up of several parallel layers arranged one on top of another. **2.** A bed or layer of rock whose composition is more or less the same throughout. **3.** A level of society composed of people with similar social, cultural, or economic status.

stra•tus (strā′təs *or* străt′əs) *n., pl.* **stra•ti** (strā′tī *or* străt′ī). A low-lying grayish cloud that resembles a layer of fog.

Strauss (strous *or* shtrous), **Johann.** Known as "the Elder." 1804–1849. Austrian violinist and composer. His son **Johann** (1825–1899), known as "the Younger," is best known for his waltzes, such as "The Blue Danube" (1867).

Strauss, Richard. 1864–1949. German composer whose works include the opera *Salome* (1905).

Stra•vin•sky (strə vĭn′skē), **Igor Fyodorovich.** 1882–1971. Russian-born composer whose works include the ballet *The Rite of Spring* (1913).

straw (strô) *n.* **1.a.** Stalks of wheat, oats, or other grain from which the seeds have been removed by threshing, used as bedding and food for animals, as stuffing or padding, and for making such items as hats and baskets. **b.** A single stalk of such grain. **2.** A slender tube used to suck up liquids. **3.** Something of minimal value or importance: *not worth a straw.* —*adj.* Of, relating to, or made of straw: *a straw hat.* [First written down about 950 in Old English and spelled *strēaw.*]

straw•ber•ry (strô′bĕr′ē) *n.* **1.** A sweet, red, fleshy fruit of any of various plants, having many small seeds on the surface. **2.** A low-growing plant that bears such fruit.

straw man *n.* **1.** A person who is set up as a cover or front for a questionable enterprise. **2.** An argument or opponent set up so as to be easily refuted or defeated. **3.** A bundle of straw made into the likeness of a man and often used as a scarecrow.

straw vote *n.* An unofficial vote or poll indicating the trend of opinion.

stray (strā) *intr.v.* **strayed, stray•ing, strays. 1.** To wander about or roam, especially beyond established limits: *The woodchuck seldom strays far from its burrow.* **2.** To follow a winding course; meander. **3.** To become diverted from a subject: *Don't stray from the topic.* —*n.* A person or an animal that has strayed and is lost. —*adj.* **1.** Strayed or having strayed; lost: *a stray cat.* **2.** Scattered or separate: *stray shafts of sunlight.*

streak (strēk) *n.* **1.** A line, mark, smear, or band different in color or texture from its surroundings. **2.** A slight contrasting element; a trace: *a mean streak.* **3.** *Informal.* A brief run or stretch, as of luck: *a winning streak.* —*v.* **streaked, streak•ing, streaks.** —*tr.* To mark with a streak: *Dog tracks streaked the floor.* —*intr.* **1.** To form a streak or streaks. **2.** To move at high speed; rush: *Lightning streaked across the sky.*

streak•y (strē′kē) *adj.* **streak•i•er, streak•i•est. 1.** Marked with, characterized by, or occurring in streaks. **2.** Variable or uneven in character or quality. **—streak′i•ly** *adv.* **—streak′i•ness** *n.*

stream (strēm) *n.* **1.a.** A body of running water that flows in a more or less regular course, as a brook or small river. **b.** A steady current in such a body of water. **2.** A steady flow or succession of something: *a stream of electrons; a stream of questions.* —*v.* **streamed, stream•ing, streams.** —*intr.* **1.** To flow in or as if in a stream: *Water streamed into the reservoir.* **2.** To pour forth or give off a stream; flow: *His eyes streamed with tears.* **3.** To move or travel in large numbers. —*tr.* To give off or discharge (a body fluid, for example). [First written down before 850 in Old English and spelled *strēam.*]

stream•er (strē′mər) *n.* **1.** A long narrow flag or banner. **2.** A long narrow strip of material used for ornament or decoration: *a hall decked with streamers of crepe paper.*

stream•let (strēm′lĭt) *n.* A small stream.

stream•line (strēm′līn′) *tr.v.* **stream•lined, stream•lin•ing, stream•lines. 1.** To construct or design so as to offer the least resistance to the flow of a fluid. **2.** To improve the appearance or efficiency of; modernize: *streamline a computer design; streamline a factory process.*

stream•lined (strēm′līnd′) *adj.* **1.** Designed or constructed to offer the least resistance to the flow of a fluid. **2.** Reduced to essentials; lacking anything extra: *a streamlined procedure.* **3.** Improved in appearance or efficiency; modernized: *a streamlined factory.*

street (strēt) *n.* **1.** A public way or road in a city or town. **2.** A public way or road along with its houses and buildings and the people living and working in them. —*adj.* **1.** Taking place in the street: *a street performance.* **2.** Living or making a living on the streets: *a street vendor.* **3.** Crude; vulgar: *street language.* **4.** Appropriate for wear or use in public: *street clothes.*

street•car (strēt′kär′) *n.* A public vehicle operated on rails and providing transportation along a regular route.

street-smart (strēt′smärt′) *adj. Informal.* Having or showing a shrewd awareness of how to survive in a city.

strength (strĕngkth *or* strĕngth *or* strĕnth) *n.* **1.** The state, quality, or property of being strong: *strength in battle.* **2.** The power to resist force, stress, or attack: *the strength of steel.* **3.** Concentration or potency, as of a solution or a drug. **4.** Effective or binding force: *the strength of an argument.* **5.** The ability to maintain a moral or an intellectual position firmly. **6.** A source of power or force: *Religion is his strength.* **7.** The number of people making up a normal or ideal organization: *at full strength.* **—*idiom.*** **on the strength of.** On the basis of: *gave her an "A" on the strength of her*

Johann Strauss the Younger
Photographed in the 1890's

strawberry

ă	**pat**	oi	**boy**
ā	**pay**	ou	**out**
âr	**care**	o͝o	**took**
ä	**father**	o͞o	**boot**
ĕ	**pet**	ŭ	**cut**
ē	**be**	ûr	**urge**
ĭ	**pit**	th	**thin**
ī	**pie**	*th*	**this**
îr	**pier**	hw	**whoop**
ŏ	**pot**	zh	**vision**
ō	**toe**	ə	**about**
ô	**paw**	N	*French* **bon**

essay. [First written down before 899 in Old English and spelled *strengthu.*]

Synonyms: strength, power, might, force. These nouns mean the capacity to act or work effectively. **Strength** means great physical, mental, or moral energy: *Jennifer gathered her strength and moved the boulder out of the way.* **Power** means the ability to do something and especially to produce an effect: *Only the king had the power to call the legislature together.* **Might** often means great power: *We would devote all our might to a just cause.* **Force** often means the application of strength or power: *He used great force in moving the furniture.*

strength•en (strĕngk′thən *or* strĕng′thən *or* strĕn′-thən) *tr. & intr.v.* **strength•ened, strength•en•ing, strength•ens.** To make or become strong or stronger.

stren•u•ous (strĕn′yo͞o əs) *adj.* **1.** Requiring great effort or energy: *strenuous exercise.* **2.** Vigorously active; energetic: *a strenuous child.* [First written down before 1460 in Middle English, from Latin *strēnuus.*] **—stren′u•ous•ly** *adv.* **—stren′u•ous•ness** *n.*

strep (strĕp) *adj.* Streptococcal.

strep throat *n.* An infection of the throat caused by certain streptococci and characterized by fever and inflamed tonsils.

strep•to•coc•cal (strĕp′tə kŏk′əl) *adj.* Of, relating to, or caused by a streptococcus.

strep•to•coc•cus (strĕp′tə kŏk′əs) *n., pl.* **strep•to•coc•ci** (strĕp′tə kŏk′sī *or* strĕp′tə kŏk′ī). Any of several rounded or oval bacteria that form pairs or chains and cause various diseases in human beings.

strep•to•my•cin (strĕp′tə mī′sĭn) *n.* An antibiotic drug produced by certain bacteria and used to treat tuberculosis and other bacterial infections.

stress (strĕs) *n.* **1.** Importance, significance, or emphasis placed on something: *puts too much stress on money.* **2.** The relative force given to a sound or syllable in a spoken word or phrase. **3.** The relative force of sound given to a syllable or word according to a metrical pattern. **4.** A musical accent, such as one beat of a measure. **5.** A force that tends to strain or deform something: *The stress of the books caused the wood to warp.* **6.** An influence that disrupts mentally or emotionally. **7.** A state of extreme difficulty, pressure, or strain. *—tr.v.* **stressed, stress•ing, stress•es. 1.** To place stress on; emphasize; accent: *stress quality; stresses the first syllable.* **2.** To subject to physical or mental pressure, tension, or strain.

stretch (strĕch) *v.* **stretched, stretch•ing, stretch•es.** *—tr.* **1.** To lengthen, widen, or distend: *stretch a rubber band.* **2.** To cause to extend from one place to another or across a given space: *Stretch the canvas over the frame.* **3.** To make taut; tighten: *stretched the plastic wrap.* **4.** To reach or put forth; extend: *stretch out her hand.* **5.** To extend (oneself) when lying down: *stretched herself out on the couch.* **6.** To expand in order to fulfill a larger function: *stretch one's paycheck.* **7.** To extend or enlarge beyond the usual or proper limits: *stretch the meaning of the law.* **8.** To wrench or strain (a muscle, for example). *—intr.* **1.** To become lengthened, widened, or distended. **2.** To extend or reach over a distance or an area or in a given direction: *The wheat field stretched to the north.* **3.** To lie down at full length: *stretched out on the bed.* **4.** To extend one's muscles or limbs, as after sleep. *—n.* **1.** The act of stretching or the state of being stretched. **2.** The extent to which something can be stretched; elasticity. **3.a.** A continuous or unbroken length, area, or expanse. **b.** A straight section of a course or track leading to the finish line. **4.** A continuous period of time. *—adj.* Made of an elastic material that stretches easily: *stretch pants.* ***—idiom.*** **stretch (one's) legs.** To go for a walk, especially after a lengthy period of sitting. [First written down before 899 in Old English and spelled *streccan.*]

stretch•er (strĕch′ər) *n.* **1.** A movable bed or cot on which a person can be carried in a lying position. **2.** Any of various devices for stretching or shaping, as a wooden frame for canvas.

strew (stro͞o) *tr.v.* **strewed, strewn** (stro͞on) or **strewed, strew•ing, strews. 1.** To spread here and there; scatter: *strewed the papers on the floor.* **2.** To cover (an area or a surface) with scattered or sprinkled things: *The beach was strewn with debris.*

stri•ate (strī′āt′) also **stri•at•ed** (strī′ā′tĭd) *adj.* Marked with striations; striped, grooved, or ridged.

stri•a•tion (strī ā′shən) *n.* One of a number of parallel lines or grooves on the surface of a rock, formed when pieces of rock frozen into the base of a glacier moved across the rock and scratched it.

strick•en (strĭk′ən) *v.* A past participle of **strike.** *—adj.* **1.** Struck or wounded, as by a projectile. **2.** Affected by something overwhelming, such as disease, trouble, or painful emotion.

strict (strĭkt) *adj.* **strict•er, strict•est. 1.** Precise; exact: *in strict accordance with the law.* **2.** Complete; absolute: *strict control.* **3.** Demanding or imposing an exacting discipline: *a strict teacher.* **4.** Exacting in enforcement, observance, or requirement: *a strict school.* **5.** Rigidly conforming to established rule, principle, or condition: *a strict Catholic.* [First written down about 1400 in Middle English and spelled *strecte,* narrow, small, from Latin *strictus,* tight, strict, past participle of *stringere,* to draw tight.] **—strict′ly** *adv.* **—strict′ness** *n.*

stric•ture (strĭk′chər) *n.* **1.** A restraint, limit, or restriction. **2.** An adverse remark or criticism; a censure. **3.** An abnormal narrowing of a duct or passage of the body.

stride (strīd) *v.* **strode** (strōd), **strid•den** (strĭd′n), **strid•ing, strides.** *—intr.* **1.** To walk vigorously with long steps. **2.** To take a single long step, as in passing over an obstruction. *—tr.* **1.** To walk with long steps on, along, or over. **2.** To step over or across. *—n.* **1.** The act of striding. **2.** A single long step. **3.** The distance traveled in such a step. **4.** A step forward: *new strides in the field of medicine.* ***—idiom.*** **take in (one's) stride.** To cope with calmly, without interrupting one's normal routine: *took the postponement of the recital in stride.* [First written down before 800 in Old English and spelled *strīdan.*]

stri•dent (strīd′nt) *adj.* Loud, harsh, grating, or shrill: *a strident voice.* **—stri′den•cy** *n.*

strife (strīf) *n.* A bitter conflict or struggle.

strike (strīk) *v.* **struck** (strŭk), **struck** or **strick•en** (strĭk′ən), **strik•ing, strikes.** *—tr.* **1.** To hit with or as if with the hand, the fist, or a weapon. **2.** To inflict (a blow): *strike a blow at injustice.* **3.** To collide with or crash into: *She struck the desk with her knee.* **4.** To make a military attack on; assault. **5.** To afflict suddenly, as with a disease or an impairment. **6.** To produce or play by hitting some device, as a key on a piano: *struck the opening chords of the sonata.* **7.** To indicate with a sound: *The clock struck five.* **8.** To form by stamping, printing, or punching: *strike a medal.* **9.** To ignite by friction: *strike a match.* **10.** To impress strongly or anew: *struck her as a good idea.* **11.** To come upon; reach; discover: *strike gold.* **12.** To make or conclude: *strike a bargain.* **13.** To take on or assume: *strike a pose.* *—intr.* **1.** To deal a blow or blows with or as if with the fist or a weapon; hit. **2.** To aim a stroke or blow. **3.** To make contact suddenly and violently; collide. **4.** To begin a military attack: *The army struck at dawn.* **5.** To set out or proceed, especially in a new direction. **6.** To indicate the time with a sound: *The clock struck at noon.* **7.** To catch fire. **8.** To discover something suddenly or unexpectedly: *struck on an idea.* **9.** To have an effect; make an impression. **10.** To engage in a strike against an employer. *—n.* **1.** An act or a gesture of striking. **2.** An attack, especially a military air attack. **3.** The stopping of work by employees in an attempt to force an employer to meet certain demands. **4.** In baseball, a pitched ball that is counted against the batter, typically one swung at and missed or one taken and judged to have passed through the strike zone. **5.** In bowling, the knocking down of all ten pins with one roll of the ball. ***—idioms.*** **on strike.** Refusing to work in an attempt to force an employer to meet a demand: *on strike for better wages.* **strike down. 1.** To cause to fall by a blow. **2.** To render ineffective; cancel: *The court struck down the judgment.* **strike out. 1.** To set out energetically: *decided to strike out for the mountains on foot.* **2.a.** In baseball, to pitch three strikes to (a batter), putting the batter out. **b.** In baseball, to be struck out. **3.** To fail in an endeavor: *I auditioned for a part in the play, but I struck out.* **strike up.** To initiate or begin: *struck up a friendship with the new student.* [First written down before 1000 in Old English and spelled *strīcan*, to stroke, rub.]

strike•break•er (strīk′brā′kər) *n.* A person who works or provides an employer with workers during a strike.

strike•out (strīk′out′) *n.* In baseball, an example of striking out a batter or of a batter being struck out.

strik•er (strī′kər) *n.* **1.** An employee on strike against an employer. **2.** A person or thing that strikes.

strike zone *n.* In baseball, the area over home plate through which a pitch must pass to be called a strike, roughly between the batter's armpits and knees.

strik•ing (strī′kĭng) *adj.* Capturing the attention and making a vivid impression on the sight or mind. **—strik′ing•ly** *adv.*

string (strĭng) *n.* **1.** A cord usually made of fiber, used for fastening, lacing, or tying. **2.** Something shaped into a long thin line: *a string of lights.* **3.** A set of things threaded together: *a string of beads.* **4.a.** A cord stretched across a musical instrument and struck, plucked, or bowed to produce tones. **b.** Also **strings.** Stringed instruments or their players considered as a group. **5.** *Informal.* A limiting or hidden condition. Also used in the plural: *a gift with no strings attached.* **6.** In sports, a group of players constituting a ranked team within a team: *plays first string.* *—tr.v.* **strung** (strŭng), **string•ing, strings. 1.** To fit or furnish with a string or strings: *string a piano.* **2.** To thread on a string: *string beads.* **3.** To arrange in a string or series. **4.** To fasten, tie, or hang with a string or strings. **5.** To stretch out or extend. ***—idiom.*** **string along.** *Informal.* **1.** To go along with something; agree. **2.** To fool, cheat, or deceive. [First written down about 725 in Old English and spelled *streng*.]

string bean *n.* **1.** A long, narrow green bean pod eaten as a vegetable. **2.** The bushy or climbing plant that bears such pods.

stringed instrument (strĭngd) *n.* A musical instrument, such as a guitar or violin, played by plucking, bowing, or striking tightly stretched strings.

strin•gent (strĭn′jənt) *adj.* Rigorous; severe: *stringent restrictions.* **—strin′gent•ly** *adv.*

string•er (strĭng′ər) *n.* **1.** A person or thing that strings. **2.** A long heavy bar or timber that connects or supports parts of a structure. **3.** A part-time reporter for the news media.

string•y (strĭng′ē) *adj.* **string•i•er, string•i•est. 1.** Resembling, made of, or having strings: *stringy hair.* **2.** Slender and sinewy: *a stringy piece of meat.* **—string′i•ness** *n.*

strip[1] (strĭp) *v.* **stripped, strip•ping, strips.** *—tr.* **1.** To remove clothing or covering from. **2.** To deprive of (clothing or covering). **3.** To remove all excess detail from; reduce to essentials. **4.** To clear of a natural covering or growth; make bare: *strip a tree trunk of its bark.* **5.** To rob of wealth or property; plunder: *The invaders stripped the countryside.* *—intr.* **1.** To undress completely. **2.** To fall away or be removed; peel. [First written down before 1200 in Middle English and spelled *strupen*, from Old English *bestrȳpan*, to plunder.]

strip[2] (strĭp) *n.* **1.** A long narrow piece or area of approximately even width: *a strip of paper; a strip of desert.* **2.** A comic strip. **3.** An airstrip. [First written down in 1459 in Middle English, perhaps from Middle Low German *strippe*, strap, thong.]

stripe (strīp) *n.* **1.** A long narrow band that differs, as in color or texture, from the area on either side: *a zebra's stripes.* **2.** A strip of cloth or braid worn on a uniform to show rank, awards received, or length of service: *a sergeant's stripes.* **3.** Sort; kind: *film directors of a bold new stripe.* *—tr.v.* **striped, strip•ing, stripes.** To mark with a stripe or stripes.

strip•ling (strĭp′lĭng) *n.* An adolescent boy.

strip mine *n.* An open mine, especially a coal mine, whose seams or outcrops run close to ground level and are exposed by the removal of overlying soil and rocks. **—strip′-mine′** *v.*

strive (strīv) *intr.v.* **strove** (strōv), **striv•en** (strĭv′ən) or **strived, striv•ing, strives. 1.** To exert much effort or energy: *strive to improve working conditions.* **2.** To struggle or fight forcefully; contend: *The pioneers had to strive against great odds.*

strobe (strōb) *n.* A strobe light.

strobe light *n.* A lamp that produces very short, intense flashes of light by means of an electric discharge in a gas. [First written down in 1942 in Modern English, from Greek *strobos*, spinning.]

strode (strōd) *v.* Past tense of **stride.**

stroke[1] (strōk) *n.* **1.** The act or an instance of striking, as with the hand or a weapon; a blow: *a stroke of the sword.* **2.a.** The striking of a bell or gong. **b.** The sound so produced. **c.** The time so indicated: *at the stroke of midnight.* **3.** A sudden action, event, or process having a strong impact or effect: *a stroke of lightning.* **4.a.** A sudden severe attack, as of paralysis or sunstroke. **b.** A sudden loss of brain function caused by a blockage or rupture of a blood vessel to the brain, marked by loss of muscular control, loss of sensation or consciousness, dizziness, or slurred speech. **5.** An inspired or effective idea or act: *a stroke of genius.* **6.** A single uninterrupted movement, especially when repeated or in a back-and-forth motion. **7.** Any of a series of movements of a piston from one end of the limit of its motion to another. **8.** A single completed movement of the limbs and body, as in swimming or rowing. **9.** A movement of the upper body and arms for the purpose of striking a ball, as in golf or tennis. **10.** A single mark made by a writing or marking implement, such as a pen. *—v.* **stroked, strok•ing, strokes.** *—tr.* **1.** To hit or propel (a ball, for example) with a smooth swinging motion. **2.** To set the pace for (a rowing crew). *—intr.* **1.** To make or perform a stroke. **2.** To row at a particular rate per minute. [First written down before 1300 in Middle English.]

stroke[2] (strōk) *tr.v.* **stroked, strok•ing, strokes.** To rub lightly, with or as if with the hand or something held in the hand; caress: *stroked the cat's head.* *—n.* A light caressing movement, as of the

stringed instrument
Top: Violin
Center: Cello
Bottom: Guitar

ă	**p**a**t**	oi	**boy**
ā	**pay**	ou	**out**
âr	**care**	o͝o	**took**
ä	**f**a**ther**	o͞o	**boot**
ĕ	**pet**	ŭ	**cut**
ē	**be**	ûr	**urge**
ĭ	**pit**	th	**thin**
ī	**pie**	*th*	**this**
îr	**pier**	hw	**whoop**
ŏ	**pot**	zh	**vision**
ō	**toe**	ə	**about**
ô	**paw**	N	*French* **bon**

stroller

hand. [First written down before 899 in Old English and spelled *strācian*.]

stroll (strōl) *v.* **strolled, stroll•ing, strolls.** —*intr.* To walk or wander at a leisurely pace: *People strolled about the park.* —*tr.* To walk along or through at a leisurely pace: *stroll the beach.* —*n.* A leisurely walk.

stroll•er (strō′lər) *n.* **1.** A person who strolls. **2.** A light four-wheeled chair for transporting small children.

strong (strông) *adj.* **strong•er, strong•est. 1.** Physically powerful; capable of exerting great physical force: *The ox is a strong animal.* **2.** In good or sound health; robust: *a strong constitution.* **3.** Having force of character, will, morality, or intelligence: *a strong personality.* **4.** Capable of enduring force or wear; not easily broken: *strong furniture.* **5.** Intense in degree or quality: *strong feelings; a strong wind.* **6.** Having great mental or spiritual force: *a strong belief.* **7.** Extreme; drastic: *strong measures.* **8.** Persuasive, effective, and cogent: *a strong argument.* **9.** Concentrated: *a strong vinegar.* **10.** Highly active chemically: *a strong acid.* **11.** Having a specified number of units or members: *Five hundred strong, they marched forward.* **12.** Of high saturation; vivid: *a strong color.* [First written down about 725 in Old English and spelled *strang*.] **—strong′ly** *adv.*

strong•box (strông′bŏks′) *n.* A stoutly made box or safe for storing valuables.

strong•hold (strông′hōld′) *n.* **1.** A fortress or fortified place. **2.** A place of survival or refuge. **3.** An area dominated or occupied by a special group.

stron•ti•um (strŏn′chē əm *or* strŏn′tē əm) *n. Symbol* **Sr** A soft, silvery, metallic element that is chemically active and is used in making alloys, fireworks, and signal flares. Atomic number 38. See table at **element.**

strontium 90 *n.* A radioactive isotope of strontium with a mass number of 90 and a half-life of 28 years that occurs in the fallout from nuclear explosions. It poses a health hazard to humans because it can be absorbed by the body.

strop (strŏp) *n.* **1.** A strap, especially a short rope whose ends are spliced together to make a ring. **2.** A flexible strip of leather or canvas used for sharpening a razor. —*tr.v.* **stropped, strop•ping, strops.** To sharpen (a razor) on a strop.

stro•phe (strō′fē) *n.* A stanza of a poem.

strove (strōv) *v.* Past tense of **strive.**

struck (strŭk) *v.* Past tense and a past participle of **strike.**

struc•tur•al (strŭk′chər əl) *adj.* **1.** Of, relating to, characterized by, or having structure. **2.** Used in or necessary to construction: *structural steel.* **—struc′tur•al•ly** *adv.*

structural formula *n.* A chemical formula that shows how the atoms making up a compound are arranged within the molecule.

struc•ture (strŭk′chər) *n.* **1.** Something made up of a number of parts that are held together or put together in a particular way. **2.** The way in which parts are arranged or put together to form a whole. **3.** Something constructed, such as a building or bridge: *They completed work on the structure last May.* **4.** A plant or animal part or organ: *A paramecium moves by means of tiny hairlike structures called cilia.* —*tr.v.* **struc•tured, struc•tur•ing, struc•tures.** To give form or arrangement to: *I structured my day around my dance lessons.* [First written down in 1440 in Middle English and spelled *structure*, building materials, from Latin *strūctūra*, structure, from *struere*, to construct.]

strug•gle (strŭg′əl) *intr.v.* **strug•gled, strug•gling, strug•gles. 1.** To exert muscular energy, as against a physical force or mass: *We struggled to control the fire.* **2.** To make a strenuous effort: *struggled to stay awake.* **3.** To compete or contend: *Passengers struggled for room on the subway.* —*n.* **1.** The act of struggling. **2.** Strenuous effort or striving: *the struggle for survival.* **3.** Combat; battle or strife: *hand-to-hand struggles; a legal struggle.* [First written down about 1395 in Middle English and spelled *struglen*.] **—strug′gler** *n.*

strum (strŭm) *v.* **strummed, strum•ming, strums.** —*tr.* To play (a stringed instrument or a tune on a stringed instrument) by stroking or brushing the strings. —*intr.* To strum a stringed instrument or a tune on such an instrument. —*n.* The act or sound of strumming.

strung (strŭng) *v.* Past tense and past participle of **string.**

strut (strŭt) *v.* **strut•ted, strut•ting, struts.** —*intr.* To walk with pompous bearing; swagger. —*tr.* **1.** To display in order to impress others. **2.** To brace or support with a strut or struts. —*n.* **1.** A vain or pompous way of walking. **2.** A bar or rod used to brace a mechanical structure against forces applied from the side.

strych•nine (strĭk′nīn′ *or* strĭk′nĭn) *n.* An extremely poisonous white crystalline compound composed of carbon, hydrogen, nitrogen, and oxygen in the proportions $C_{21}H_{22}O_2N_2$.

Stu•art (sto͞o′ərt *or* styo͞o′ərt). Ruling house of Scotland (1371–1603) and of England and Scotland (1603–1649 and 1660–1714).

stub (stŭb) *n.* **1.** The usually short end remaining after something bigger has been used up: *the stub of a pencil.* **2.a.** The part of a check or receipt retained as a record. **b.** The part of a ticket returned as a voucher of payment. —*tr.v.* **stubbed, stub•bing, stubs.** To strike (one's toe or foot) against something.

stub•ble (stŭb′əl) *n.* **1.** The short stiff stalks of grain or hay left after a crop has been harvested. **2.** Something resembling this, especially a short stiff growth of beard or hair.

stub•born (stŭb′ərn) *adj.* **stub•born•er, stub•born•est. 1.** Unreasonably, often perversely unyielding: *a stubborn child.* See Synonyms at **obstinate. 2.** Continuously enduring; persistent: *a stubborn idea.* **3.** Difficult to treat or deal with: *a stubborn stain.* **—stub′born•ly** *adv.* **—stub′born•ness** *n.*

stub•by (stŭb′ē) *adj.* **stub•bi•er, stub•bi•est. 1.** Short, broad, and stocky: *stubby legs.* **2.** Full of stubs: *stubby grass.* **—stub′bi•ness** *n.*

stuc•co (stŭk′ō) *n., pl.* **stuc•coes** or **stuc•cos.** A durable finish for walls, usually of plaster or cement.

stuck (stŭk) *v.* Past tense and past participle of **stick.**

stuck-up (stŭk′ŭp′) *adj. Informal.* Snobbish; conceited.

stud[1] (stŭd) *n.* **1.** An upright post in the framework of a wall for supporting lath, plasterboard, or similar material. **2.** Any of various projecting pins or pegs, as in machinery. **3.** A removable button used to fasten and ornament, as on a dress shirt. —*tr.v.* **stud•ded, stud•ding, studs. 1.** To provide with or construct with studs or a stud. **2.** To set with objects that project or stand out from the surface: *stud a bracelet with turquoise.* **3.** To be dotted about on; strew: *Daisies studded the meadow.* [First written down about 850 in Old English and spelled *studu*.]

stud[2] (stŭd) *n.* **1.** A male animal, especially a stallion, kept for breeding. **2.** A group of horses or other animals kept for breeding. [First written down about 1000 in Old English and spelled *stōd*, a place for breeding horses.]

stu•dent (sto͞od′nt *or* styo͞od′nt) *n.* **1.** A person who attends a school, college, or university. **2.** A person who studies something: *a student of languages.*

student teacher *n.* A college student who teaches in a classroom under a teacher's supervision as part of a degree in education.

stud•ied (stŭd′ēd) *adj.* **1.** Carefully contrived; deliberate: *a studied pose.* **2.** Learned; knowledgeable.

stu•di•o (sto͞o′dē ō *or* styo͞o′dē ō) *n., pl.* **stu•di•os. 1.** An artist's workroom. **2.** A photographer's place of business. **3.** A place where an art is taught or studied: *a ceramics studio.* **4.** A room or building for motion-picture, television, or radio productions. **5.** A room or building where tapes and records are produced.

studio couch *n.* A couch that can be made to serve as a double bed by sliding the frame of a cot from beneath it.

stu•di•ous (sto͞o′dē əs *or* styo͞o′dē əs) *adj.* **1.** Devoted to study: *a studious life.* **2.** Marked by steady attention and effort; assiduous: *a studious avoidance of anything silly.* **—stu′di•ous•ly** *adv.* **—stu′di•ous•ness** *n.*

stud•y (stŭd′ē) *n., pl.* **stud•ies. 1.** The act or process of studying; pursuit of knowledge: *years of devoted study.* **2.** Attentive observation or examination. **3.** A branch of knowledge; a subject: *technical studies.* **4.** A work on a particular subject: *presented a study of dreams.* **5.** A musical composition written or played as an exercise; an étude. **6.** An artist's preliminary sketch. **7.** A room intended for or equipped for studying. *—v.* **stud•ied, stud•y•ing, stud•ies.** *—tr.* **1.** To apply one's mind to gaining knowledge and understanding of (a subject): *study French.* **2.** To read carefully. **3.** To memorize. **4.** To take (a course) at a school: *He studies law at night.* **5.** To investigate: *She studied the behavior of bees.* **6.** To examine closely; scrutinize: *She studied his face.* *—intr.* **1.** To apply oneself to learning, especially by reading. **2.** To pursue a course of study.

stuff (stŭf) *n.* **1.** The material out of which something is made or formed; substance. **2.** The basic elements of something; essence: *the stuff of which fear is made.* **3.** *Informal.* Unspecified material or articles: *venders selling stuff on the street.* **4.** *Slang.* Specific talk or actions: *Don't give me that stuff about being tired.* **5.** Special capability: *They showed their stuff on the debate team.* *—tr.v.* **stuffed, stuff•ing, stuffs. 1.a.** To pack tightly: *stuffed the Christmas stockings.* **b.** To block a passage; obstruct: *stuffed the hole in the window with cardboard.* **2.** To fill with an appropriate stuffing: *stuff a pillow.* **3.** To cram with food: *He stuffed himself at dinner.*

stuffed shirt *n. Informal.* A person regarded as stiff or pompous.

stuff•ing (stŭf′ĭng) *n.* **1.** Padding put in things made of or covered with cloth, as upholstered furniture or cushions: *a doll with the stuffing coming out.* **2.** Food put into the cavity of a piece of meat or a hollowed-out vegetable.

stuff•y (stŭf′ē) *adj.* **stuff•i•er, stuff•i•est. 1.** Lacking sufficient ventilation; close: *an overheated stuffy room.* **2.** Having blocked breathing passages: *a stuffy nose.* **3.** Dull and boring: *a stuffy party.* **—stuff′i•ly** *adv.* **—stuff′i•ness** *n.*

stul•ti•fy (stŭl′tə fī′) *tr.v.* **stul•ti•fied, stul•ti•fy•ing, stul•ti•fies. 1.** To make useless or ineffectual: *customs that stultify free thought.* **2.** To cause to appear stupid or foolish. **—stul′ti•fi•ca′tion** (stŭl′tə fĭ kā′shən) *n.*

stum•ble (stŭm′bəl) *v.* **stum•bled, stum•bling, stum•bles.** *—intr.* **1.a.** To trip and almost fall: *The horse stumbled.* **b.** To move unsteadily or falteringly: *He stumbled out of bed.* **2.** To make a mistake; blunder: *Do you stumble over words?* **3.** To come upon accidentally or unexpectedly: *They stumbled upon the clue.* *—tr.* To cause to stumble. *—n.* **1.** The act of stumbling; a fall. **2.** A mistake or blunder. **—stum′bler** *n.*

stum•bling block (stŭm′blĭng) *n.* An obstacle or impediment.

stump (stŭmp) *n.* **1.** The part of a tree trunk left protruding from the ground after the tree has fallen or been cut down. **2.** A short or broken part left after the main part has been cut away, broken off, or worn down: *a stump of a tail.* **3.** A place or an occasion used for making political speeches. *—tr.v.* **stumped, stump•ing, stumps. 1.** To reduce to a stump. **2.** To clear stumps from: *stump a field.* **3.** To stub (a toe or foot). **4.** To go about (an area) making political speeches. **5.** *Informal.* To puzzle or baffle completely. [First written down about 1350 in Middle English and spelled *stompe*, possibly from Middle Low German *stump*.] **—stump′y** *adj.*

stun (stŭn) *tr.v.* **stunned, stun•ning, stuns. 1.** To daze or render senseless, by or as if by a blow. **2.** To overwhelm or daze by a loud noise. **3.** To shock or stupefy, as with the emotional impact of an experience: *The scandal stunned the neighborhood.* [First written down before 1325 in Middle English and spelled *stunen*, from Old French *estoner* : Latin *ex-*, out + Latin *tomāre*, to thunder.]

stung (stŭng) *v.* Past tense and past participle of **sting.**

stunk (stŭngk) *v.* A past tense and the past participle of **stink.**

stun•ning (stŭn′ĭng) *adj.* **1.** Causing or capable of causing emotional shock or loss of consciousness. **2.** Of a strikingly attractive appearance: *a stunning suit.* **3.** Impressive or suprising: *a stunning performance.* **—stun′ning•ly** *adv.*

stunt¹ (stŭnt) *tr.v.* **stunt•ed, stunt•ing, stunts.** To stop or interfere with the growth or development of: *Air pollution may stunt many kinds of plants.* [First written down in 1583 in Modern English, from Middle English *stunnt*, foolish, short-witted, from Old English *stunt*.]

stunt² (stŭnt) *n.* **1.** A feat displaying unusual strength, skill, or daring. **2.** Something of an unusual nature done for publicity. [First written down in 1878 in American English.]

stu•pe•fy (sto͞o′pə fī′ *or* styo͞o′pə fī′) *tr.v.* **stu•pe•fied, stu•pe•fy•ing, stu•pe•fies. 1.** To dull the senses or consciousness of: *The dull routine stupefied them.* **2.** To amaze; astonish: *a record-breaking time that stupefied the sports world.* **—stu′pe•fac′tion** (sto͞o′pə făk′shən *or* styo͞o′pə făk′shən) *n.*

stu•pen•dous (sto͞o pĕn′dəs *or* styo͞o pĕn′dəs) *adj.* **1.** Of astonishing force, volume, degree, or excellence; marvelous: *stupendous risks.* **2.** Amazingly large; huge: *stupendous temple ruins.* **—stu•pen′dous•ly** *adv.*

stu•pid (sto͞o′pĭd *or* styo͞o′pĭd) *adj.* **stu•pid•er, stu•pid•est. 1.** Slow to learn or understand. **2.** Not sensible; unintelligent: *a stupid answer.* **3.** In a stupor; stupefied. **4.** In a dazed or stunned state. **5.** Pointless; worthless: *a stupid task.* [First written down in 1541 in Modern English, from Latin *stupidus*, from *stupēre*, to be stunned.] **—stu′pid•ly** *adv.*

stu•pid•i•ty (sto͞o pĭd′ĭ tē *or* styo͞o pĭd′ĭ tē) *n., pl.* **stu•pid•i•ties. 1.** The quality or condition of being stupid. **2.** A stupid act, remark, or idea.

stu•por (sto͞o′pər *or* styo͞o′pər) *n.* A state of reduced sensibility or consciousness; a daze.

stur•dy (stûr′dē) *adj.* **stur•di•er, stur•di•est. 1.** Having or showing rugged physical strength. **2.** Substantially made or built; stout: *a sail made of*

ă	pat	oi	boy
ā	pay	ou	out
âr	care	o͝o	took
ä	father	o͞o	boot
ĕ	pet	ŭ	cut
ē	be	ûr	urge
ĭ	pit	th	thin
ī	pie	*th*	this
îr	pier	hw	whoop
ŏ	pot	zh	vision
ō	toe	ə	about
ô	paw	N	*French* bon

sturgeon

Peter Stuyvesant
c. 1660 portrait
attributed to Henri Couturrier

Word Building: sub–

The prefix **sub–** can be traced back to the Latin preposition *sub*, meaning "under." Some words beginning with **sub–** that came into English from Latin include **submerge**, **suburb**, and **subvert**. When **sub–** is used to form words in English, it can mean "under" (**submarine**, **subsoil**, **subway**), "subordinate" (**subcommittee**, **subplot**, **subset**), or "less than completely" (**subhuman**, **substandard**). **Sub–** can form compounds by combining with verbs as well as with adjectives and nouns, as in **subdivide**, **sublease**, and **sublet**.

sturdy canvas. **3.** Marked by determination; firm. **—stur′di•ly** *adv.* **—stur′di•ness** *n.*

stur•geon (stûr′jən) *n.* Any of various large edible freshwater or saltwater fishes having bony plates rather than true scales on its body. Its roe is a source of caviar. [First written down about 1300 in Middle English and spelled *sturgiun*, from Old French *estourgeon*, of Germanic origin.]

stut•ter (stŭt′ər) *v.* **stut•tered, stut•ter•ing, stut•ters.** *—intr.* To speak with constant hesitations or repetitions of sounds. *—tr.* To utter with constant hesitations or repetitions of sounds: *stuttered a response.* *—n.* The act or habit of stuttering. **—stut′ter•er** *n.*

Stuy•ve•sant (stī′vĭ sənt), **Peter.** 1592?–1672. Dutch colonial administrator who was forced in 1664 to surrender the colony of New York (then New Netherland) to England.

sty¹ (stī) *n., pl.* **sties** (stīz). **1.** An enclosure for pigs. **2.** A very dirty or untidy place. [First written down before 1100 in Old English and spelled *stig*.]

sty² (stī) *n., pl.* **sties** (stīz). Inflammation of one or more of the oil-producing glands of an eyelid. [First written down in 1601 in Modern English and spelled *styan*, alteration of Middle English *styanye* : *styan*, sty + *eye*, eye.]

style (stīl) *n.* **1.** The way or manner in which something is said, done, expressed, or performed: *a style of speech; a writing style.* **2.** Sort; kind; type: *a style of furniture.* **3.** A comfortable and elegant mode of existence: *living in style.* **4.a.** A particular fashion, especially of dressing: *the styles of the 1920's.* **b.** The fashion of the moment: *Dresses of various lengths are in style.* **5.** A quality of imagination and individuality expressed in one's actions and tastes: *She does things with style.* **6.** The slender stalk of a flower pistil, rising from the ovary and tipped by the stigma. *—tr.v.* **styled, styl•ing, styles.** To arrange, design, or fashion in a special way. [First written down before 1325 in Middle English, from Latin *stilus*, stylus.]

❑ *These sound alike:* **style, stile** (turnstile).

sty•li (stī′lī) *n.* A plural of **stylus.**

styl•ish (stī′lĭsh) *adj.* Conforming to the current style; fashionable: *a stylish outfit.* **—styl′ish•ly** *adv.* **—styl′ish•ness** *n.*

styl•ist (stī′lĭst) *n.* **1.** A writer or speaker who cultivates an artful literary style. **2.** A designer of or an expert on styles in decorating, dress, or beauty: *a hair stylist.*

sty•lis•tic (stī lĭs′tĭk) *adj.* Of or relating to style, especially literary style.

styl•ize (stī′līz′) *tr.v.* **styl•ized, styl•iz•ing, styl•iz•es.** To restrict or make conform to a particular style.

sty•lus (stī′ləs) *n., pl.* **sty•lus•es** or **sty•li** (stī′lī). **1.** A sharp pointed instrument used for writing, marking, or engraving. **2.** A phonograph needle.

sty•mie (stī′mē) *tr.v.* **sty•mied** (stī′mēd), **sty•mie•ing** (stī′mē ĭng), **sty•mies** (stī′mēz). To block or thwart: *The setback stymied their hopes.*

styp•tic (stĭp′tĭk) *adj.* Contracting the blood vessels so as to stop bleeding; astringent. *—n.* A styptic drug or substance.

sty•rene (stī′rēn′) *n.* A colorless oily liquid hydrocarbon, $C_6H_5CH{:}CH_2$, from which polystyrene is made.

Sty•ro•foam (stī′rə fōm′). A trademark used for a light resilient polystyrene plastic.

Styx (stĭks) *n.* In Greek mythology, the river across which the souls of the dead are ferried, one of the five rivers in Hades.

sua•sion (swā′zhən) *n.* Persuasion: *moral suasion.*

suave (swäv) *adj.* **suav•er, suav•est.** Smoothly agreeable and courteous: *a suave gentleman.* [First written down about 1501 in Modern English, from Latin *suāvis*, delightful, sweet.] **—suave′ly** *adv.* **—suav′i•ty, suave′ness** *n.*

sub¹ (sŭb) *n. Informal.* **1.** A submarine. **2.** A submarine sandwich.

sub² (sŭb) *Informal. n.* A substitute. *—intr.v.* **subbed, sub•bing, subs.** To act as a substitute.

sub– *pref.* A prefix that means: **1.** Under; beneath: *submarine.* **2.** A subordinate or secondary part: *subplot; subdivision.* **3.** Less than completely or normally; almost: *subtropical.* —See Note.

sub•a•tom•ic (sŭb′ə tŏm′ĭk) *adj.* **1.** Of or relating to the parts of the atom. **2.** Having dimensions or participating in reactions characteristic of the parts of the atom.

subatomic particle *n.* One of the fundamental units of which atoms and all matter are made; an elementary particle: *Protons and quarks are subatomic particles.*

sub•com•mit•tee (sŭb′kə mĭt′ē) *n.* A subordinate committee composed of members appointed from a main committee.

sub•com•pact (sŭb kŏm′păkt′) *n.* An automobile smaller than a compact.

sub•con•scious (sŭb kŏn′shəs) *adj.* Not wholly conscious; partially or imperfectly conscious. *—n.* The unconscious. **—sub•con′scious•ly** *adv.*

sub•con•ti•nent (sŭb′kŏn′tə nənt *or* sŭb kŏn′tə nənt) *n.* A large landmass, such as India, that is part of a continent but is considered as an independent entity.

sub•cu•ta•ne•ous (sŭb′kyōō tā′nē əs) *adj.* Located or found just beneath the skin. **—sub′cu•ta′ne•ous•ly** *adv.*

sub•di•vide (sŭb′dĭ vīd′ *or* sŭb′dĭ vīd′) *v.* **sub•di•vid•ed, sub•di•vid•ing, sub•di•vides.** *—tr.* To divide into smaller parts, especially to divide (land) into lots. *—intr.* To form into subdivisions.

sub•di•vi•sion (sŭb′dĭ vĭzh′ən *or* sŭb′dĭ vĭzh′ən) *n.* **1.** The act of process of subdividing. **2.** A subdivided part. **3.** An area composed of subdivided lots.

sub•dom•i•nant (sŭb dŏm′ə nənt) *n.* The fourth tone of a musical scale, next below the dominant. *—adj.* Less than dominant; ranking below one that is dominant: *the subdominant male in a pride of lions.*

sub•due (səb dōō′ *or* səb dyōō′) *tr.v.* **sub•dued, sub•du•ing, sub•dues.** **1.** To conquer; vanquish. **2.** To quiet or bring under control by physical force or persuasion: *subdue the wild horse.* **3.** To make less intense; tone down: *Hearing that you weren't going subdued my excitement about the party.*

sub•fam•i•ly (sŭb′făm′ə lē) *n.* **1.** A taxonomic category ranking between a family and a genus. **2.** A division of languages ranking below a family and above a branch.

sub•head (sŭb′hĕd′) *n.* **1.** The heading or title of a subdivision of a printed subject. **2.** A subordinate heading or title.

sub•hu•man (sŭb hyōō′mən) *adj.* **1.** Below the human race in evolutionary development. **2.** Regarded as not being fully human.

sub•ject (sŭb′jĭkt) *adj.* **1.** Under the power or authority of another: *subject to the jurisdiction of a government.* **2.** Prone; disposed: *Are you subject to colds?* **3.** Likely to incur or receive; exposed: *a statement subject to misinterpretation.* **4.** Contingent or dependent: *The project was subject to approval by the board.* *—n.* **1.** A person who owes allegiance to a government or ruler: *a subject of the throne.* **2.a.** A person or thing about which something is said or done: *a subject of discussion.* **b.** Something that is treated in a work of art. **3.** A theme of a musical composition. **4.** A course or an area of study: *Her favorite subject is math.* **5.** An individual used as the object of clinical study: *the subjects of an experiment.* **6.** The part of a sentence or clause that identifies who or what does the action or what is described by the predicate. The subject is often a noun, noun phrase, or pronoun. —*tr. v.* (səb **jĕkt′**). **sub•ject•ed, sub•ject•ing, sub•jects. 1.** To bring under control or authority: *The ancient Romans subjected many peoples.* **2.** To cause to undergo or experience: *subjected me to many tests.* **—sub•jec′tion** *n.*

Synonyms: subject, matter, topic, theme. These nouns mean the principal idea or point of a speech, a piece of writing, or a work of art. **Subject** is the most general: *Many 18th-century paintings have historical subjects.* **Matter** often means the material that is the object of thought: *This will be an interesting matter for you to discuss.* **Topic** means a subject of discussion, argument, or conversation: *The hospital is giving a series of lectures on the topic of nutrition.* **Theme** often means a subject, idea, point of view, or perception that is developed in a work of art: *The theme of this poem is the healing power of love.*

sub•jec•tive (səb **jĕk′**tĭv) *adj.* **1.** Coming from or taking place within the mind; unaffected by the external world. **2.** Particular to a given person; personal: *a subjective experience.*

subject matter *n.* Matter considered in a written work or speech; a theme.

sub•ju•gate (**sŭb′**jə gāt′) *tr.v.* **sub•ju•gat•ed, sub•ju•gat•ing, sub•ju•gates.** To bring under control; conquer. [First written down before 1425 in Middle English and spelled *subjugaten*, from Latin *subiugāre* : *sub-*, under + *iugum*, yoke.] **—sub′ju•ga′tion** *n.*

sub•junc•tive (səb **jŭngk′**tĭv) *adj.* Of, relating to, or being a mood of a verb used to express an uncertainty, a wish, or an unlikely condition. For example, in the sentence *If I were you, I would go,* the word *were* is a subjunctive form. —*n.* **1.** The subjunctive mood. **2.** A subjunctive construction.

sub•king•dom (**sŭb′**kĭng′dəm) *n.* A taxonomic category constituting a major division of a kingdom.

sub•lease (**sŭb′lēs′**) *tr.v.* **sub•leased, sub•leas•ing, sub•leas•es. 1.** To sublet (property). **2.** To rent (property) under a sublease.

sub•let (**sŭb′lĕt′**) *tr.v.* **sub•let, sub•let•ting, sub•lets.** To rent (property one holds by lease) to another. —*n.* (**sŭb′**lĕt′). Property, especially an apartment, rented by a tenant to another party.

sub•li•mate (**sŭb′**lə māt′) *v.* **sub•li•mat•ed, sub•li•mat•ing, sub•li•mates.** —*tr.* To cause (a solid or gas) to change state without becoming liquid. —*intr.* To be sublimated: *The block of dry ice sublimated, producing wisps of white gas.*

sub•li•ma•tion (sŭb′lə **mā′**shən) *n.* **1.** The act or process of sublimating. **2.** Something that has been sublimated.

sub•lime (sə **blīm′**) *adj.* **1.** Characterized by nobility; majestic. **2.** Not to be excelled; supreme. **3.** Inspiring awe; impressive: *a sublime performance.* —*v.* **sub•limed, sub•lim•ing, sub•limes.** —*tr.* To sublimate (a solid or gas). —*intr.* To sublimate. **—sub•lime′ly** *adv.*

sub•ma•chine gun (sŭb′mə **shēn′**) *n.* A lightweight automatic or semiautomatic gun fired from the shoulder or the hip.

sub•ma•rine (**sŭb′**mə rēn′ *or* sŭb′mə **rēn′**) *n.* **1.** A ship that can operate underwater. **2.** A large meat and cheese sandwich on a long roll. —*adj.* Beneath the surface of the sea; undersea: *a submarine volcano.* —SEE NOTE.

sub•merge (səb **mûrj′**) *v.* **sub•merged, sub•merg•ing, sub•merg•es.** —*tr.* **1.** To place under water: *submerged the dish.* **2.** To cover with water: *The flood submerged the island.* —*intr.* To go under or as if under water. [First written down in 1606 in Modern English, from Latin *submergere* : *sub-*, under + *mergere*, to plunge.]

sub•merse (səb **mûrs′**) *tr.v.* **sub•mersed, sub•mers•ing, sub•mers•es.** To submerge. **—sub•mer′sion** (səb **mûr′**zhən *or* səb **mûr′**shən) *n.*

sub•mis•sion (səb **mĭsh′**ən) *n.* **1.** The act of submitting to the power of another. **2.** The condition of being submissive or compliant: *forced into submission.* **3.a.** The act of submitting something for consideration: *the submission of a manuscript to a publisher.* **b.** Something submitted for consideration: *received a number of submissions in the mail.*

sub•mis•sive (səb **mĭs′**ĭv) *adj.* Inclined or willing to submit: *a submissive personality.*

sub•mit (səb **mĭt′**) *v.* **sub•mit•ted, sub•mit•ting, sub•mits.** —*tr.* **1.** To yield or surrender (oneself) to the will or authority of another: *They submitted themselves to his judgment.* **2.** To subject to a condition or process. **3.** To commit (something) to the consideration of another: *We submitted our ideas to her.* **4.** To offer as a proposition or contention: *I submit that the terms of the contract are unreasonable.* —*intr.* To yield; surrender; acquiesce: *He submitted to their demands.* [First written down about 1380 in Middle English and spelled *submitten*, from Latin *submittere*, to set under : *sub-*, under + *mittere*, to cause to go.] **—sub•mit′tal** *n.*

sub•or•di•nate (sə **bôr′**dn ĭt) *adj.* **1.** Belonging to a lower or inferior rank; secondary: *a subordinate position.* **2.** Subject to the authority or control of another. —*n.* A person or thing that is subordinate: *He is courteous to his subordinates.* —*tr.v.* (sə **bôr′**dn āt′). **sub•or•di•nat•ed, sub•or•di•nat•ing, sub•or•di•nates.** To put in a lower or inferior rank or class: *subordinate a court to a higher one.* **—sub•or′di•nate•ly** *adv.* **—sub•or′di•na′tion** *n.*

subordinate clause *n.* A dependent clause.

subordinate conjunction *n.* A conjunction such as *that, who, which,* or *where,* that introduces a dependent clause.

sub•orn (sə **bôrn′**) *tr.v.* **sub•orned, sub•orn•ing, sub•orns. 1.a.** To cause (a person) to commit an unlawful or evil act. **b.** To cause (a person) to commit perjury. **2.** To pay someone to give (perjured testimony). **—sub′or•na′tion** (sŭb′ôr **nā′**shən) *n.* **—sub•orn′er** *n.*

sub•poe•na (sə **pē′**nə) *n.* A writ requiring a person to appear in court and give testimony. —*tr.v.* **sub•poe•naed, sub•poe•na•ing, sub•poe•nas.** To serve or summon with such a writ. [First written down before 1461 in Middle English and spelled *sub pena*, from Medieval Latin *sub poenā*, under a penalty : Latin *sub*, under + Latin *poena*, penalty.]

sub•scribe (səb **skrīb′**) *v.* **sub•scribed, sub•scrib•ing, sub•scribes.** —*tr.* **1.** To pledge or contribute (a sum of money). **2.** To sign (one's name) at the end of a document. **3.** To sign one's name to in testimony or consent: *subscribe a will.* —*intr.* **1.** To contract to receive and pay for a certain number of things, as issues of a periodical or tickets to a series of performances: *subscribe to a magazine.* **2.** To promise to pay or contribute money: *subscribe to a charity.* **3.** To feel or express hearty approval: *I subscribe to your opinion.* **4.** To sign one's name. [First written down in 1425 in Middle English and spelled *subscriben*, from Latin *subscrībere* : *sub-*, under + *scrībere*, to write.] **—sub•scrib′er** *n.*

sub•script (**sŭb′**skrĭpt′) *n.* A symbol or character written directly beneath or next to and slightly below another symbol or character, as in a mathematical expression or chemical formula. **—sub′script′** *adj.*

sub•scrip•tion (səb **skrĭp′**shən) *n.* **1.** A purchase made by a signed order, as for issues of a periodical

submarine

Regional Note: submarine

The long sandwich featuring layers of meat and cheese on a crusty Italian roll goes by a variety of names. **Submarine**, **sub**, and **hero** are widespread. Localized terms are *bomber* (upstate New York), *wedge* (downstate New York), *hoagie* (Delaware Valley, including Philadelphia and southern New Jersey), *grinder* (New England), *Cuban sandwich* (Miami), *Italian sandwich* (Maine), *Italian* (southern Midwest), and *poor boy* (New Orleans).

ă	pat	oi	boy
ā	pay	ou	out
âr	care	o͝o	took
ä	father	o͞o	boot
ĕ	pet	ŭ	cut
ē	be	ûr	urge
ĭ	pit	th	thin
ī	pie	*th*	this
îr	pier	hw	whoop
ŏ	pot	zh	vision
ō	toe	ə	about
ô	paw	N	*French* bon

or a series of theatrical performances: *a subscription to the ballet.* **2.** Acceptance, as of articles of faith, demonstrated by the signing of one's name. **3.** The signing of one's name, as to a legal document.

sub•se•quent (sŭb′sĭ kwĕnt′) *adj.* Following in time or order; succeeding: *heavy rains and subsequent floods.* **—sub′se•quence** *n.* **—sub′se•quent•ly** *adv.*

sub•serve (səb sûrv′) *tr.v.* **sub•served, sub•serv•ing, sub•serves.** To be useful to (a purpose or an end).

sub•ser•vi•ent (səb sûr′vē ənt) *adj.* **1.** Subordinate in capacity or function. **2.** Inclined or willing to submit to others; obsequious. **—sub•ser′vi•ence** *n.*

sub•set (sŭb′sĕt′) *n.* A set that has all of its members contained in another set. For example, if *A* is a set and *B* is a set and every member of *A* is a member of *B*, then *A* is a subset of *B*.

sub•side (səb sīd′) *intr.v.* **sub•sid•ed, sub•sid•ing, sub•sides. 1.** To sink to a lower or normal level: *The flood waters subsided.* **2.** To become less agitated or active; abate: *The wind finally subsided.* [First written down in 1681 in Modern English, from Latin *subsīdere* : *sub-*, under, down + *sīdere*, to settle.]

sub•sid•i•ar•y (səb sĭd′ē ĕr′ē) *adj.* **1.** Serving to assist or supplement; auxiliary: *subsidiary roads.* **2.** Secondary in importance; subordinate: *a subsidiary aim of the project.* *—n., pl.* **sub•sid•i•ar•ies. 1.** Something that is subsidiary to another. **2.** A company having more than half of its stock owned by another company.

sub•si•dize (sŭb′sĭ dīz′) *tr.v.* **sub•si•dized, sub•si•diz•ing, sub•si•diz•es.** To assist or support with a subsidy: *The committee appropriated funds to subsidize the investigation.* **—sub′si•diz′er** *n.*

sub•si•dy (sŭb′sĭ dē) *n., pl.* **sub•si•dies.** Financial assistance, as that granted by a government to a private commercial enterprise.

sub•sist (səb sĭst′) *intr.v.* **sub•sist•ed, sub•sist•ing, sub•sists. 1.** To exist; be. **2.** To continue or remain in existence. **3.** To maintain life; live: *Horses can subsist on grass.*

sub•sis•tence (səb sĭs′təns) *n.* **1.** The act or state or subsisting. **2.** A means of subsisting.

sub•soil (sŭb′soil′) *n.* The layer of earth below the surface soil.

sub•son•ic (sŭb sŏn′ĭk) *adj.* Having a speed less than that of sound.

sub•spe•cies (sŭb′spē′shēz *or* sŭb′spē′sēz) *n., pl.* **subspecies.** A subdivision of a taxonomic species, usually based on geographic distribution.

sub•stance (sŭb′stəns) *n.* **1.a.** That which has mass and occupies space; matter. **b.** A material of a particular kind or composition. **2.** The essence of what is said or written; the gist: *the substance of the report.* **3.** That which is solid or real; reality as opposed to appearance: *a dream without substance.* **4.** Density; body: *Air has little substance.* **5.** Material possessions; wealth: *a person of substance.* [First written down before 1300 in Middle English and spelled *substaunce*, from Latin *substāre*, to be present : *sub-*, under + *stāre*, to stand.]

substance abuse *n.* Excessive use of addictive substances, especially alcohol and narcotic drugs.

sub•stan•dard (sŭb stăn′dərd) *adj.* **1.** Failing to meet a standard; below standard. **2.** Of or relating to linguistic usage that does not conform to that of the standard language.

sub•stan•tial (səb stăn′shəl) *adj.* **1.** Of or having substance; material. **2.** Not imaginary; true; real. **3.** Solidly built; strong: *substantial houses.* **4.** Ample; sustaining: *a substantial meal.* **5.** Considerable in importance, value, degree, amount, or extent: *making substantial progress.* **6.** Possessing wealth or property; well-to-do. **—sub•stan′tial•ly** *adv.*

sub•stan•ti•ate (səb stăn′shē āt′) *tr.v.* **sub•stan•ti•at•ed, sub•stan•ti•at•ing, sub•stan•ti•ates.** To support with proof or evidence; verify: *substantiate a claim.*

sub•stan•tive (sŭb′stən tĭv) *adj.* **1.** Substantial; considerable. **2.** Independent in existence or function; not subordinate. **3.** Not imaginary; real. *—n.* In grammar, a word or a group of words functioning as a noun.

sub•sti•tute (sŭb′stĭ to͞ot′ *or* sŭb′stĭ tyo͞ot′) *n.* A person or thing that takes the place of another; a replacement. *—v.* **sub•sti•tut•ed, sub•sti•tut•ing, sub•sti•tutes.** *—tr.* To put or use (a person or thing) in place of another: *substitute walnuts for pecans in the recipe.* *—intr.* To take the place of another: *I substituted for him in the game.* [First written down in 1413 in Middle English, from Latin *substituere*, to substitute : *sub-*, in place of + *statuere*, to cause to stand.] **—sub′sti•tu′tion** *n.*

sub•stra•tum (sŭb′strā′təm *or* sŭb′străt′əm) *n., pl.* **sub•stra•ta** (sŭb′strā′tə *or* sŭb′străt′ə) or **sub•stra•tums. 1.a.** An underlying layer. **b.** A layer of earth beneath the surface soil; subsoil. **2.** The foundation or groundwork for something. **3.** The material upon which another material is coated or fabricated.

sub•ter•fuge (sŭb′tər fyo͞oj′) *n.* A deceptive trick or device.

sub•ter•ra•ne•an (sŭb′tə rā′nē ən) *adj.* **1.** Located or operating beneath the earth's surface; underground. **2.** Hidden; secret. **—sub′ter•ra′ne•an•ly** *adv.*

sub•ti•tle (sŭb′tīt′l) *n.* **1.** A secondary and usually explanatory title, as of a literary work. **2.a.** A printed translation of the dialogue of a foreign-language film shown at the bottom of the screen. **b.** A printed narration or portion of dialogue flashed on the screen between the scenes of a silent film.

sub•tle (sŭt′l) *adj.* **sub•tler, sub•tlest. 1.** So slight as to be difficult to detect or analyze; elusive: *subtle changes.* **2.** Not immediately obvious; abstruse: *a subtle problem.* **3.** Able to make fine distinctions; keen: *a subtle mind.* **4.** Characterized by skill or ingenuity; clever. [First written down before 1325 in Middle English and spelled *sutile*, from Latin *subtīlis*.] **—sub′tle•ness** *n.* **—sub′tly** *adv.*

sub•tle•ty (sŭt′l tē) *n., pl.* **sub•tle•ties. 1.** The state or quality of being subtle: *the subtlety of his plan.* **2.** Something subtle, especially a nicety of thought or a fine distinction.

sub•to•tal (sŭb′tōt′l) *n.* The total of part of a set of numbers. *—tr.v.* **sub•to•taled, sub•to•tal•ing, sub•to•tals** also **sub•to•talled, sub•to•tal•ling, sub•to•tals.** To total (a subset of a set of numbers).

sub•tract (səb trăkt′) *v.* **sub•tract•ed, sub•tract•ing, sub•tracts.** *—tr.* To take away; deduct: *subtract five from seven.* *—intr.* To perform the arithmetic operation of subtraction.

sub•trac•tion (səb trăk′shən) *n.* **1.** The act or process of subtracting; deduction. **2.** The mathematical operation of finding the difference between two numbers.

sub•trac•tive (səb trăk′tĭv) *adj.* Producing or involving subtraction.

sub•tra•hend (sŭb′trə hĕnd′) *n.* A number that is to be subtracted from another number; for example, in the expression 8 − 5, 5 is the subtrahend.

sub•trop•i•cal (sŭb trŏp′ĭ kəl) *adj.* Of, relating to, or being the regions bordering on the Tropics.

sub•trop•ics (sŭb trŏp′ĭks) *pl.n.* Subtropical regions.

sub•urb (sŭb′ûrb′) *n.* **1.** A usually residential area or community outside or near a city. **2. suburbs.** The usually residential region around a major city.

[First written down before 1325 in Middle English and spelled *suburbe*, from Latin *suburbium* : *sub-*, under + *urbs*, city.]

sub•ur•ban (sə **bûr′**bən) *adj.* **1.** Of, relating to, or characteristic of a suburb: *a suburban area.* **2.** Located or residing in a suburb: *a suburban school.* **3.** Of, relating to, or characteristic of the culture typical of life in the suburbs.

sub•ur•ban•ite (sə **bûr′**bə nīt′) *n.* A person who lives in a suburb.

sub•ur•bi•a (sə **bûr′**bē ə) *n.* Suburbs or suburbanites considered as a group.

sub•ver•sion (səb **vûr′**zhən *or* səb **vûr′**shən) *n.* **1.** The act or an instance of subverting. **2.** The condition of being subverted.

sub•ver•sive (səb **vûr′**sĭv *or* səb **vûr′**zĭv) *adj.* Intended or serving to overthrow: *subversive plots.*

sub•vert (səb **vûrt′**) *tr.v.* **sub•vert•ed, sub•vert•ing, sub•verts. 1.** To overthrow or destroy: *subvert a government.* **2.** To undermine the character, morals, or allegiance of; corrupt: *Socrates denied he had subverted the youth of Athens.* [First written down about 1375 in Middle English and spelled *subverten*, from Latin *subvertere* : *sub-*, under + *vertere*, to turn.]

sub•way (**sŭb′**wā′) *n.* **1.a.** An underground urban railroad, usually operated by electricity. **b.** A passage for such a railroad. **2.** An underground tunnel or passage, as for pedestrians.

suc•ceed (sək **sēd′**) *v.* **suc•ceed•ed, suc•ceed•ing, suc•ceeds.** —*intr.* **1.** To follow or come next in time or order; replace another in an office or position: *She succeeded to the throne.* **2.** To accomplish something desired or attempted: *He succeeded in repairing the watch.* —*tr.* **1.** To come after in time or order; follow. See Synonyms at **follow. 2.** To come after and take the place of: *Who succeeded Taft as President?* [First written down in 1375 in Middle English and spelled *succeden*, from Latin *succēdere* : *sub-*, near + *cēdere*, to go.] —**suc•ceed′er** *n.*

suc•cess (sək **sĕs′**) *n.* **1.** The achievement of something desired, planned, or attempted: *the success of the experiment.* **2.** The gaining of fame or prosperity: *an athlete spoiled by success.* **3.** A person or thing that is successful: *The project was a big success.*

suc•cess•ful (sək **sĕs′**fəl) *adj.* **1.** Having a favorable outcome: *a successful attempt.* **2.** Having gained something desired or intended. **3.** Having achieved fame or prosperity: *She is a successful actor.* —**suc•cess′ful•ly** *adv.*

suc•ces•sion (sək **sĕsh′**ən) *n.* **1.** The act or process of following in order or sequence: *the succession of events.* **2.** A group of persons or things arranged or following in order; a sequence: *We heard a succession of sharp sounds.* **3.** The sequence or right of one person after another to succeed to a title, a throne, a dignity, or an estate: *a war over the succession to the Spanish throne.*

suc•ces•sive (sək **sĕs′**ĭv) *adj.* Following in uninterrupted order; consecutive: *three successive years.* —**suc•ces′sive•ly** *adv.*

suc•ces•sor (sək **sĕs′**ər) *n.* A person or thing that succeeds another.

suc•cinct (sək **sĭngkt′**) *adj.* **suc•cinct•er, suc•cinct•est.** Characterized by clear precise expression in few words; concise and terse: *gave a succinct explanation.* —**suc•cinct′ly** *adv.* —**suc•cinct′ness** *n.*

suc•cor (**sŭk′**ər) *n.* Assistance in time of distress; relief. —*tr.v.* **suc•cored, suc•cor•ing, suc•cors.** To give assistance to in time of distress, difficulty, or want.

❑ *These sound alike:* **succor, sucker** (dupe).

suc•co•tash (**sŭk′**ə tăsh′) *n.* A dish made with kernels of corn and beans, often lima beans. [First written down in 1751 in American English and spelled *suckatash*, from Narragansett *msíckquatash*, boiled whole-kernel corn.]

Suc•coth (**sŏŏk′**əs *or* sōō **kōs′** *or* sōō **kôt′**) *n.* A Jewish harvest festival celebrated in the autumn and commemorating the booths in which the Israelites lived during their 40 years in the wilderness.

suc•cu•lent (**sŭk′**yə lənt) *adj.* **1.** Full of juice or sap; juicy: *succulent berries.* **2.** Having thick, fleshy, water-storing leaves or stems: *a succulent plant.* —*n.* A succulent plant, such as a cactus. —**suc′cu•lence** *n.* —**suc′cu•lent•ly** *adv.*

suc•cumb (sə **kŭm′**) *intr.v.* **suc•cumbed, suc•cumb•ing, suc•cumbs. 1.** To submit to something overpowering or overwhelming; give up or give in: *succumb to the pressures of one's friends.* **2.** To die.

such (sŭch) *adj.* **1.** Of this kind or a similar kind: *an eye specialist, one of many such doctors in the hospital.* **2.** Of a degree or quality indicated: *Their happiness was such that they were in tears.* **3.** Of so extreme a degree or quality: *We never dreamed of such wealth.* —*adv.* **1.** To so extreme a degree; so: *She is such a good friend.* **2.** Very; especially: *He has done such good work lately.* —*pron.* **1.** Such a person or persons or thing or things: *We expected problems, and such occurred.* **2.** A person or thing implied or indicated: *Such are the fortunes of love.* **3.** Similar things or people; the like: *pins, needles, and such.* —***idiom.* such as.** For example. [First written down about 725 in Old English and spelled *swylc.*]

suck (sŭk) *v.* **sucked, suck•ing, sucks.** —*tr.* **1.** To draw (liquid) into the mouth by moving the tongue and lips. **2.** To draw in (something) by lowering the pressure inside: *a vacuum cleaner sucking up dirt.* **3.** To hold or move inside the mouth: *suck a cough drop.* —*intr.* To suckle. —*n.* The act or sound of sucking.

suck•er (**sŭk′**ər) *n.* **1.** A person or thing that sucks, especially a young farm animal. **2.** A part by which an animal or plant clings to something by suction. **3.** Any of numerous chiefly North American freshwater fishes having thick lips adapted for feeding by suction. **4.** A shoot growing from the base of a tree or shrub. **5.** A lollipop. **6.** *Informal.* A person who is easily fooled.

❑ *These sound alike:* **sucker, succor** (help).

suck•le (**sŭk′**əl) *v.* **suck•led, suck•ling, suck•les.** —*tr.* **1.** To allow to take milk from the breast or udder; nurse: *Mammals suckle their young.* **2.** To nourish or nurture. —*intr.* To suck at the breast or udder.

suck•ling (**sŭk′**lĭng) *n.* A baby or young animal that is still being nursed by its mother. —*adj.* Not yet weaned: *a suckling pig.*

su•cre (**sōō′**krā) *n.* The basic unit of money of Ecuador. [First written down in 1886 in Modern English, after Antonio José de *Sucre* (1795–1830), Venezuelan military leader.]

Su•cre (**sōō′**krā). The constitutional capital of Bolivia, in the south-central part of the country southeast of La Paz. Population, 86,609.

su•crose (**sōō′**krōs′) *n.* A crystalline sugar having the formula $C_{12}H_{22}O_{11}$, found in many plants, especially sugar cane, sugar beets, and sugar maple, and widely used as a sweetener.

suc•tion (**sŭk′**shən) *n.* A force that causes a fluid or solid to be drawn into a space because of a difference in pressures. —*adj.* Creating, using, or done by suction: *a suction pump.*

Su•dan (sōō **dăn′**). **1.** A region of northern Africa south of the Sahara and north of the equator. It extends across the continent from the Atlantic coast to Ethiopia. **2.** A country of northeast Africa south

subway
Subway system
in Prague, Czech Republic

ă	pat	oi	boy
ā	pay	ou	out
âr	care	ŏŏ	took
ä	father	ōō	boot
ĕ	pet	ŭ	cut
ē	be	ûr	urge
ĭ	pit	th	thin
ī	pie	*th*	this
îr	pier	hw	whoop
ŏ	pot	zh	vision
ō	toe	ə	about
ô	paw	N	*French* bon

suffragist
Demonstrating outside the White House in 1917

sugar cane
Harvesting sugar cane

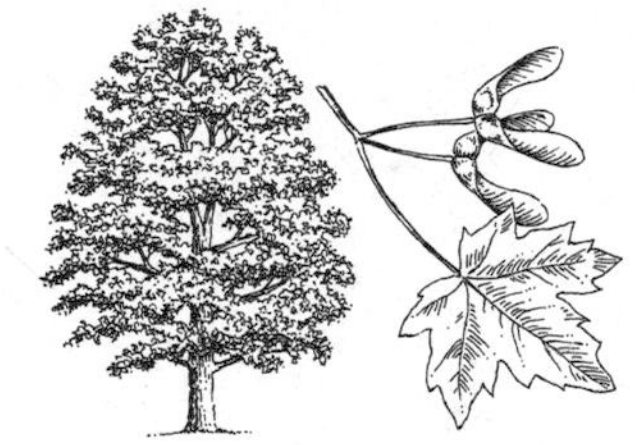

sugar maple

of Egypt. It has been inhabited since prehistoric times. Sudan gained its independence from Great Britain and Egypt in 1956. Capital, Khartoum. Population, 20,564,364.

sud•den (sŭd'n) *adj.* **1.** Happening without warning; unforeseen: *a sudden storm.* **2.** Hasty; abrupt: *a sudden change of mind.* **—*idiom.* all of a sudden.** Very quickly and unexpectedly; suddenly. [First written down about 1300 in Middle English and spelled *soden,* from Latin *subitāneus.*] **—sud'den•ly** *adv.* **—sud'den•ness** *n.*

sudden death *n.* Extra play added to a tied game, the winner being the first team to score.

suds (sŭdz) *pl.n.* **1.** Soapy water. **2.** Foam; lather. **—suds'y** *adj.*

sue (so͞o) *v.* **sued, su•ing, sues.** *—tr.* To bring legal action against (a person) in order to satisfy a claim or grievance. *—intr.* **1.** To institute legal proceedings: *He sued for his right to the property.* **2.** To make an appeal or entreaty: *sue for peace.* [First written down before 1200 in Middle English and spelled *sewen,* from Latin *sequī,* to follow.]

suede also **suède** (swād) *n.* **1.** Leather with a soft velvety nap. **2.** Cloth made to resemble suede. [First written down in 1884 in Modern English and spelled *Suède,* from French *Suède,* Sweden.]

su•et (so͞o'ĭt) *n.* The hard fatty tissue around the kidneys of cattle and sheep, used in cooking and in making tallow.

Su•ez Canal (so͞o ĕz' *or* so͞o'ĕz'). A ship canal, about 103 miles (166 kilometers) long, linking the Red Sea with the Mediterranean Sea. It was opened in November 1869.

suf•fer (sŭf'ər) *v.* **suf•fered, suf•fer•ing, suf•fers.** *—intr.* **1.** To feel or endure pain or distress: *suffer from disease.* **2.** To be or appear at a disadvantage: *The film suffered from a poor sound track.* *—tr.* **1.** To undergo or be subject to (something painful, injurious, or unpleasant): *suffer a defeat.* **2.** To endure or bear; stand: *She does not suffer fools easily.* **3.** To permit; allow: *The children were not suffered to go outside of the hospital grounds.* **—suf'fer•er** *n.*

suf•fer•ance (sŭf'ər əns *or* sŭf'rəns) *n.* Consent or permission implied or given by failure to prohibit.

suf•fer•ing (sŭf'ər ĭng *or* sŭf'rĭng) *n.* **1.** The condition of a person or thing that suffers. **2.** Pain or distress.

suf•fice (sə fīs') *v.* **suf•ficed, suf•fic•ing, suf•fic•es.** *—intr.* **1.** To meet present needs; be sufficient: *The food will suffice until next week.* **2.** To be capable or competent: *No words can suffice to convey my gratitude.* *—tr.* To be sufficient or adequate for: *enough water to suffice them for three days.*

suf•fi•cien•cy (sə fĭsh'ən sē) *n., pl.* **suf•fi•cien•cies. 1.** The quality or condition of being sufficient. **2.** An adequate amount or quantity.

suf•fi•cient (sə fĭsh'ənt) *adj.* As much as is needed; enough; adequate: *Are these really sufficient reasons for going?* **—suf•fi'cient•ly** *adv.*

suf•fix (sŭf'ĭks) *n.* In grammar, an affix added to the end of a word serving to form a new word or indicate a grammatical function by adding an inflectional ending; for example, *-ness* in *gentleness* and *-es* in *boxes* are suffixes. *—tr.v.* **suf•fixed, suf•fix•ing, suf•fix•es.** To add as a suffix.

suf•fo•cate (sŭf'ə kāt') *v.* **suf•fo•cat•ed, suf•fo•cat•ing, suf•fo•cates.** *—tr.* **1.** To stop the breathing of; kill by depriving of oxygen. **2.** To cause to suffer discomfort by or as by cutting off a supply of air. *—intr.* **1.** To die from a lack of oxygen. **2.** To feel discomfort from a lack of fresh air. **—suf'fo•ca'tion** *n.*

suf•frage (sŭf'rĭj) *n.* **1.** The right to vote. **2.** The act of voting.

suf•fra•gette (sŭf'rə jĕt') *n.* A woman who advocates suffrage for women, especially during the woman suffrage movement in the United Kingdom.

suf•fra•gist (sŭf'rə jĭst) *n.* A person who advocates extending voting rights, especially to women.

suf•fuse (sə fyo͞oz') *tr.v.* **suf•fused, suf•fus•ing, suf•fus•es.** To spread through or over, as with liquid, color, or light: *A greenish haze suffused the woods.*

sug•ar (sho͝og'ər) *n.* **1.** Any of a class of crystalline carbohydrates, such as sucrose, glucose, or lactose, that dissolve in water and have a characteristic sweet taste. **2.** Sucrose. *—tr.v.* **sug•ared, sug•ar•ing, sug•ars.** To coat or sweeten with sugar. [First written down about 1325 in Middle English and spelled *sucre,* from Sanskrit *śarkarā,* grit, ground sugar.]

sugar beet *n.* A type of beet having whitish roots from which sugar is obtained.

sugar cane *n.* A tall grass grown in warm regions, having thick juicy stems that are one of the chief sources of sugar.

sug•ar•coat (sho͝og'ər kōt') *tr.v.* **sug•ar•coat•ed, sug•ar•coat•ing, sug•ar•coats. 1.** To cause to seem more appealing: *The governor sugarcoated the budget cuts by promising to cut taxes.* **2.** To coat with sugar: *The manufacturer sugarcoats the pills to make them easier to take.*

sug•ar•less (sho͝og'ər lĭs) *adj.* **1.** Containing no sugar. **2.** Sweetened with a substance other than sucrose: *sugarless gum.*

sugar loaf *n.* **1.** A large loaf of sugar shaped into a cone. **2.** A mountain or hill shaped like a sugar loaf.

sugar maple *n.* An eastern North American maple tree having sap that is the source of maple syrup.

sug•ar•plum (sho͝og'ər plŭm') *n.* A small round piece of sugary candy.

sug•ar•y (sho͝og'ə rē) *adj.* **sug•ar•i•er, sug•ar•i•est. 1.** Containing, resembling, or tasting like sugar. **2.** Excessively kind or sentimental: *sugary compliments.*

sug•gest (səg jĕst' *or* sə jĕst') *tr.v.* **sug•gest•ed, sug•gest•ing, sug•gests. 1.** To offer for consideration or action: *I suggest that we take a walk.* **2.** To bring or call to mind by association; evoke: *a cloud that suggests a dragon.* **3.** To make evident indirectly; imply: *a silence that suggests disapproval.*

sug•gest•i•ble (səg jĕs'tə bəl *or* sə jĕs'tə bəl) *adj.* Easily influenced by suggestions.

sug•ges•tion (səg jĕs'chən *or* sə jĕs'chən) *n.* **1.** The act of suggesting. **2.** Something suggested: *Let's follow her suggestion.* **3.** A trace; a touch.

sug•ges•tive (səg jĕs'tĭv *or* sə jĕs'tĭv) *adj.* **1.** Tending to bring something to mind: *These ruins are suggestive of a highly developed civilization.* **2.** Giving a suggestion: *a suggestive message in an advertisement.* **3.** Tending to imply something improper or indecent: *suggestive song lyrics.* **—sug•ges'tive•ly** *adv.*

su•i•cid•al (so͞o'ĭ sīd'l) *adj.* **1.** Of, relating to, or causing suicide. **2.** Dangerous to oneself; self-destructive; ruinous: *a suicidal plan to climb the mountain alone.*

su•i•cide (so͞o'ĭ sīd') *n.* **1.** The act or an instance of intentionally killing oneself. **2.** A person who commits suicide. **3.** The destruction or ruin of one's own interests: *Refusing to follow company policy would be professional suicide.* [First written down in 1651 in Modern English : Latin *suī,* of oneself + Latin *caedere,* to kill.]

suit (so͞ot) *n.* **1.** A set of matching outer garments designed to be worn together, especially a jacket with trousers or a skirt. **2.** An outfit worn for a special activity or purpose: *a gym suit.* **3.** One of the four sets, spades, clubs, hearts, or diamonds, in a deck of playing cards. **4.** A court action to recover a right or claim; a lawsuit. *—v.* **suit•ed, suit•ing, suits.** *—tr.* **1.** To meet the requirements of: *The house suited them.* **2.a.** To be appropriate or acceptable for: *The song suited the occasion.* **b.** To make appropriate; adapt: *They suited the play to their audience.* **3.** To please; satisfy: *This choice suits me just fine.* *—intr.* To be suitable or acceptable.

suit•a•ble (sōō′tə bəl) *adj.* Appropriate to a given purpose or occasion: *suitable shelter; suitable clothes.* **—suit′a•bil′i•ty** *n.* **—suit′a•bly** *adv.*

suit•case (sōōt′kās′) *n.* A usually rectangular piece of luggage for carrying clothing.

suite (swēt) *n.* **1.** A series of connected rooms used as a living unit. **2.** A staff of attendants; a retinue. **3.** (*also* sōōt). A set of matching furniture. **4.** An instrumental musical composition consisting of a set of pieces in the same or closely related keys.

❑ *These sound alike:* **suite, sweet** (sugary).

suit•or (sōō′tər) *n.* **1.** A man who is courting a woman. **2.** A person who sues in court.

su•ki•ya•ki (sōō′kē **yä′**kē *or* skē **yä′**kē) *n.* A Japanese dish of sliced meat, bean curd, and vegetables fried together.

Suk•koth (sŏŏk′əs *or* sōō **kōs′** *or* sōō **kôt′**) *n.* Variant of **Succoth.**

sul•fate (sŭl′fāt′) *n.* A compound, especially a salt, formed when sulfuric acid reacts with another substance. Epsom salt is a sulfate of magnesium. Gypsum is a sulfate of calcium.

sul•fide (sŭl′fīd′) *n.* A compound of sulfur having a valence of −2 with another element.

sul•fite (sŭl′fīt′) *n.* A salt or an ester of sulfurous acid.

sul•fur also **sul•phur** (sŭl′fər) *n. Symbol* **S** A pale yellow nonmetallic element that is used in making matches and gunpowder, in vulcanizing rubber, and in medicine. Atomic number 16. See table at **element.** [First written down about 1380 in Middle English and spelled *soulfre*, from Latin *sulfur.*]

sulfur dioxide *n.* A colorless, extremely irritating gas or liquid having the formula SO_2, used in many industrial processes, especially the manufacture of sulfuric acid.

sul•fu•ric (sŭl **fyŏŏr′**ĭk) *adj.* Of or containing sulfur, especially with a valence of 6.

sulfuric acid *n.* A strong acid composed of sulfur, hydrogen, and oxygen and having the formula H_2SO_4.

sul•fur•ous (sŭl′fər əs *or* sŭl′fyər əs) *adj.* **1.** Of or containing sulfur, especially with a valence of 4. **2.** Characteristic of or given off by burning sulfur: *sulfurous vapors.* **3.** also **sul•phur•ous.** Of or relating to the fires of hell; infernal.

sulk (sŭlk) *intr.v.* **sulked, sulk•ing, sulks.** To be sullenly silent or withdrawn. *—n.* A mood or display of sullen silence or withdrawal.

sulk•y[1] (sŭl′kē) *adj.* **sulk•i•er, sulk•i•est.** Sullenly silent or withdrawn. [First written down in 1744 in Modern English, perhaps from *sulke*, sluggish, perhaps from Old English *āseolcan*, to become sluggish.]

sulk•y[2] (sŭl′kē) *n., pl.* **sulk•ies.** A light two-wheeled vehicle with room only for a driver and pulled by a single horse, especially in harness racing. [First written down in 1756 in Modern English, from *sulky*, aloof (because it only has one seat).]

sul•len (sŭl′ən) *adj.* **sul•len•er, sul•len•est.** Showing a brooding ill humor or resentment; morose; sulky: *a sullen disposition.* **—sul′len•ly** *adv.* **—sul′len•ness** *n.*

sul•ly (sŭl′ē) *tr.v.* **sul•lied, sul•ly•ing, sul•lies.** To tarnish; stain: *sullied his reputation.*

sul•phur (sŭl′fər) *n.* Variant of **sulfur.**

sul•phur•ous (sŭl′fər əs *or* sŭl′fyər əs) *adj.* Variant of **sulfurous** (sense 3).

sul•tan (sŭl′tən) *n.* The ruler of a Muslim country. [First written down in 1555 in Modern English, from Arabic *sulṭān.*]

sul•tan•a (sŭl **tăn′**ə) *n.* **1.** The wife, mother, sister, or daughter of a sultan. **2.** A small yellow seedless raisin of a kind originally produced in Asia Minor.

sul•tan•ate (sŭl′tə nāt′) *n.* **1.** The office, power, or reign of a sultan. **2.** A country ruled by a sultan.

sul•try (sŭl′trē) *adj.* **sul•tri•er, sul•tri•est.** Very hot and humid: *a sultry summer day.*

sum (sŭm) *n.* **1.** A number obtained as a result of adding numbers. **2.** The whole amount, quantity, or number: *the sum of our knowledge.* **3.** An amount of money: *the sum of $10,000.* **4.** An arithmetic problem: *He's good at sums.* **5.** A summary: *That is my view, in sum.* *—tr.v.* **summed, sum•ming, sums.** To add (numbers). **—*idiom.* sum up.** To present (material) in a condensed form; summarize. [First written down about 1300 in Middle English and spelled *summe*, from Latin *summa*, from *summus*, highest.]

❑ *These sound alike:* **sum, some** (a few).

su•mac also **su•mach** (sōō′măk *or* shōō′măk) *n.* Any of various shrubs or small trees having feathery leaves and small, usually red berries. Some kinds, such as the poison sumac, can cause an itching rash when touched.

Su•ma•tra (sōō **mä′**trə). An island of western Indonesia in the Indian Ocean south of the Malay Peninsula. It joined Indonesia in 1949.

Su•mer (sōō′mər). An ancient country of southern Mesopotamia in present-day southern Iraq. The Sumerians are believed to have invented the cuneiform system of writing.

Su•me•ri•an (sōō **mîr′**ē ən *or* sōō **mĕr′**ē ən) *adj.* Of or relating to ancient Sumer or its people, language, or culture. *—n.* **1.** A member of an ancient people whose civilization in Mesopotamia flourished around 3000 B.C. **2.** The language of the Sumerians, having no relation to any known language.

sum•ma cum lau•de (sŏŏm′ə kŏŏm **lou′**də) *adv. & adj.* With the greatest academic honor: *She graduated summa cum laude from college.*

sum•mar•i•ly (sə **mĕr′**ə lē) *adv.* In a summary manner; speedily and without ceremony: *The dishonest broker was summarily dismissed.*

sum•ma•rize (sŭm′ə rīz′) *tr.v.* **sum•ma•rized, sum•ma•riz•ing, sum•ma•riz•es.** To make a summary of; restate briefly: *summarized his views.* **—sum′ma•ri•za′tion** (sŭm′ər ĭ **zā′**shən) *n.*

sum•ma•ry (sŭm′ə rē) *n., pl.* **sum•ma•ries.** A brief statement mentioning the main points of something: *a summary of our findings.* *—adj.* **1.** Presented in condensed form; brief. **2.** Done speedily and without ceremony: *a summary rejection of a proposal.*

❑ *These sound alike:* **summary, summery** (like summer).

sum•ma•tion (sə **mā′**shən) *n.* **1.a.** The act or process of adding; addition. **b.** A number obtained by adding; a sum. **2.** A concluding part of an argument containing a summary of the main points, especially in a court of law.

sum•mer (sŭm′ər) *n.* The season of the year occurring between spring and autumn. In the Northern Hemisphere it lasts from the summer solstice to the autumnal equinox or, in ordinary usage, from June until September. *—v.* **sum•mered, sum•mer•ing, sum•mers.** *—tr.* To keep or place during the summer: *summered my house plants outside.* *—intr.* To pass the summer: *They summered at a beach resort.* *—adj.* Of, occurring in, or appropriate to the summer: *a summer wedding; summer clothing.* [First

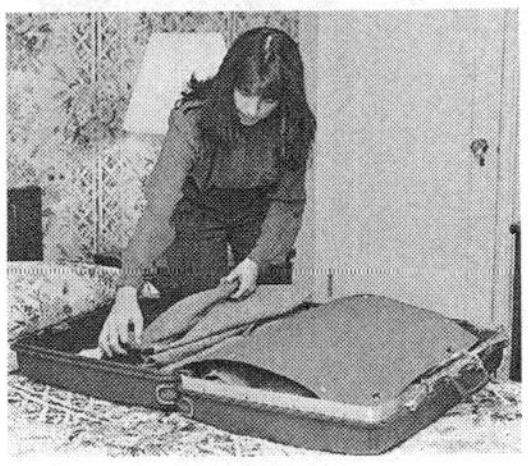

suitcase
Packing a suitcase

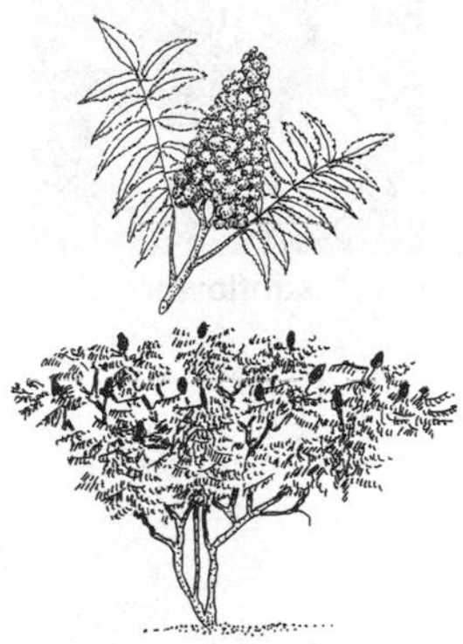

sumac

ă	**pat**	oi	**boy**
ā	**pay**	ou	**out**
âr	**care**	ŏŏ	**took**
ä	**father**	ōō	**boot**
ĕ	**pet**	ŭ	**cut**
ē	**be**	ûr	**urge**
ĭ	**pit**	th	**thin**
ī	**pie**	*th*	**this**
îr	**pier**	hw	**whoop**
ŏ	**pot**	zh	**vision**
ō	**toe**	ə	**about**
ô	**paw**	N	*French* **bon**

sundial

sunflower

written down before 830 in Old English and spelled *sumor.*]

sum•mer•house (sŭm′ər hous′) *n.* A small roofed structure in a park or garden, used for a shady place to rest.

summer school *n.* A session of school held during the summer vacation.

summer solstice *n.* In the Northern Hemisphere, the solstice that occurs around June 21.

summer squash *n.* Any of several kinds of squash that are eaten shortly after being picked rather than kept in storage.

sum•mer•time (sŭm′ər tīm′) *n.* The summer season.

sum•mer•y (sŭm′ə rē) *adj.* Of, intended for, or suggesting summer: *summery weather.*
❑ *These sound alike:* **summery, summary** (brief).

sum•mit (sŭm′ĭt) *n.* **1.** The highest point or part; the top, especially of a mountain. **2.** The highest level, as of government officials. [First written down before 1400 in Middle English and spelled *somet*, from Old French *sommette*, from Latin *summus*, highest.]

summit conference *n.* A conference of government leaders of two or more countries.

sum•mon (sŭm′ən) *tr.v.* **sum•moned, sum•mon•ing, sum•mons. 1.** To call together; convene: *summon a meeting of the delegates.* **2.** To send for; request to appear: *summoned her to the principal's office.* **3.** To order (someone) to appear in court by issuing a summons. **4.** To call forth; muster: *I summoned up my will power not to laugh.* [First written down before 1200 in Middle English and spelled *sumunen*, from Latin *summonēre*, to remind privately, hint to : *sub-*, secretly + *monēre*, to warn.]

sum•mons (sŭm′ənz) *n., pl.* **sum•mons•es. 1.** A document ordering a defendant, witness, or juror to appear in court. **2.** A call or an order to appear or do something.

sump (sŭmp) *n.* A pit or low-lying place that collects liquids.

sump•tu•ous (sŭmp′cho͞o əs) *adj.* Of a size or splendor suggesting great expense; lavish: *a sumptuous feast.* [First written down about 1410 in Middle English and spelled *sumptous*, from Latin *sūmptus*, expense.] **—sump′tu•ous•ly** *adv.* **—sump′tu•ous•ness** *n.*

sun (sŭn) *n.* **1.** The star that is orbited by all of the planets and other bodies of the solar system and that supplies the energy that sustains life on Earth. It has a diameter of about 864,000 miles (1,390,000 kilometers), a mass about 330,000 times that of the earth, and is at an average distance of about 93 million miles (150 million kilometers) from Earth. **2.** A star that is the center of a system of planets. **3.** The radiation given off by the sun, especially infrared light, visible light, and ultraviolet light. *—v.* **sunned, sun•ning, suns.** *—tr.* To expose to the sun, as for warming, drying, or tanning. *—intr.* To bask in the sun; sunbathe. [First written down about 725 in Old English and spelled *sunne.*]
❑ *These sound alike:* **sun, son** (male offspring).

Sun. *abbr.* An abbreviation of Sunday.

sun•bathe (sŭn′bā*th*′) *intr.v.* **sun•bathed, sun•bath•ing, sun•bathes.** To expose the body to the sun.

sun•beam (sŭn′bēm′) *n.* A ray of sunlight.

sun•bon•net (sŭn′bŏn′ĭt) *n.* A woman's bonnet having a wide brim and a flap at the back to protect the neck from the sun.

sun•burn (sŭn′bûrn′) *n.* Inflammation or blistering of the skin caused by overexposure to direct sunlight. *—tr. & intr.v.* **sun•burned** or **sun•burnt** (sŭn′bûrnt′), **sun•burn•ing, sun•burns.** To affect or be affected with sunburn.

sun•dae (sŭn′dē *or* sŭn′dā′) *n.* Ice cream with toppings such as syrup, fruit, and nuts.

Sun•day (sŭn′dē *or* sŭn′dā′) *n.* **1.** The first day of the week. **2.** The Sabbath for many Christians. [First written down before 700 in Old English and spelled *sunnandæg.*]

Sunday school *n.* A school, usually associated with a church or synagogue, that provides religious education on Sundays.

sun•der (sŭn′dər) *v.* **sun•dered, sun•der•ing, sun•ders.** *—tr.* To force or break apart: *A misunderstanding sundered their friendship.* *—intr.* To break into parts; come apart. [First written down about 950 in Old English and spelled *sundrian.*]

sun•di•al (sŭn′dī′əl) *n.* An instrument that indicates the time of day by the shadow cast by a central pointer on a dial.

sun•down (sŭn′doun′) *n.* The time of sunset.

sun•dries (sŭn′drēz) *pl.n.* Miscellaneous articles; various things.

sun•dry (sŭn′drē) *adj.* Various; miscellaneous: *a drawer full of pens, paper clips, and sundry items.* [First written down before 899 in Old English and spelled *syndrig*, separate.]

sun•fish (sŭn′fĭsh′) *n.* **1.** Any of various small North American freshwater fishes having a flat, often brightly colored body. **2.** Any of several large ocean fishes having a rounded short-tailed body.

sun•flow•er (sŭn′flou′ər) *n.* Any of several tall plants having large flower heads with yellow rays and dark centers and bearing edible seeds that are rich in oil.

sung (sŭng) *v.* A past tense and the past participle of **sing.**

sun•glass•es (sŭn′glăs′ĭz) *pl.n.* Eyeglasses having tinted lenses to protect the eyes from the sun's glare.

sunk (sŭngk) *v.* A past tense and the past participle of **sink.**

sunk•en (sŭng′kən) *adj.* **1.** Fallen in or depressed: *sunken eyes.* **2.** Situated beneath the surface of the water or ground; submerged: *a sunken reef.* **3.** Below the surrounding level: *a sunken bathtub.*

sun lamp *n.* **1.** A lamp that gives off radiation similar to that of sunlight, used in therapeutic and cosmetic treatments. **2.** A very bright lamp equipped with a reflector, used in photography.

sun•light (sŭn′līt′) *n.* The light of the sun.

sun•lit (sŭn′lĭt′) *adj.* Illuminated by the sun: *a sunlit prairie.*

Sun•na (so͝on′ə) *n.* The proper way of life in Islam, based on the teachings and practices of Muhammad and on the guidance of the Koran.

Sun•ni (so͝on′ē) *n.* The branch of Islam that accepts the first four caliphs as the rightful successors of Muhammad.

Sun•nite (so͝on′īt′) *n.* A Muslim belonging to the Sunni branch.

sun•ny (sŭn′ē) *adj.* **sun•ni•er, sun•ni•est. 1.** Full of sunshine: *a sunny day.* **2.** Cheerful: *a sunny mood.*
❑ *These sound alike:* **sunny, sonny** (little boy).

sun•rise (sŭn′rīz′) *n.* **1.** The daily first appearance of the sun above the eastern horizon. **2.** The time at which this occurs.

sun•screen (sŭn′skrēn′) *n.* A cream or lotion used to protect the skin from the damaging ultraviolet rays of the sun.

sun•set (sŭn′sĕt′) *n.* **1.** The daily disappearance of the sun below the western horizon. **2.** The time at which this occurs.

sun•shade (sŭn′shād′) *n.* Something, such as an awning, used as protection from the sun.

sun•shine (sŭn′shīn′) *n.* **1.** The light of the sun; sunlight. **2.** Happiness or cheerfulness.

sun•spot (sŭn′spŏt′) *n.* Any of the dark spots that appear on the surface of the sun and that are associated with strong magnetic fields.

sun•stroke (sŭn′strōk′) *n.* A severe form of heat stroke caused by exposure to the sun.

sun•tan (sŭn′tăn′) *n.* A tan color of the skin resulting from exposure to the sun. **—sun′tanned′** *adj.*

sun•up (sŭn′ŭp′) *n.* The time of sunrise.

sun•ward (sŭn′wərd) *adv. & adj.* Toward or at the sun: *bathers facing sunward.*

Sun Yat-sen (so͞on′ yät′sĕn′). 1866–1925. Chinese politician who served as president of the republic (1911–1912).

sup[1] (sŭp) *tr. & intr.v.* **supped, sup•ping, sups.** To eat or drink by taking small amounts. *—n.* A small swallow or mouthful of liquid; a sip. [First written down before 899 in Old English and spelled *sūpan.*]

sup[2] (sŭp) *intr.v.* **supped, sup•ping, sups.** To eat supper. [First written down about 1300 in Middle English and spelled *supen*, from Old French *soupe*, soup.]

su•per (so͞o′pər) *n. Informal.* A superintendent in a building. *—adj. Informal.* **1.** Very large, great, or extreme: *a super skyscraper.* **2.** Excellent: *a super party.*

super– *pref.* A prefix that means: **1.** Above; over; upon: *superimpose.* **2.** Superior in size, quality, number, or degree: *superhuman.* **3.** Exceeding a standard or norm: *supersonic.* **4.** Excessive in degree or intensity: *supersensitive.*

su•per•a•bun•dant (so͞o′pər ə bŭn′dənt) *adj.* More than sufficient; excessive: *superabundant zeal.* **—su′per•a•bun′dance** *n.*

su•per•an•nu•at•ed (so͞o′pər ăn′yo͞o ā′tĭd) *adj.* **1.** Retired or ineffective because of advanced age. **2.** Outdated; obsolete: *superannuated laws.*

su•perb (so͞o pûrb′) *adj.* **1.** Of unusual quality; excellent: *a superb meal.* **2.** Majestic; imposing: *a superb view.* [First written down in 1549 in Modern English, from Latin *superbus*, arrogant, superior.] **—su•perb′ly** *adv.*

su•per•charge (so͞o′pər chärj′) *tr.v.* **su•per•charged, su•per•charg•ing, su•per•charg•es.** To increase the power of (an internal-combustion engine) with a supercharger.

su•per•charg•er (so͞o′pər chär′jər) *n.* A blower or fan that forces air under high pressure into the cylinders of an internal-combustion engine, thereby increasing power.

su•per•cil•i•ous (so͞o′pər sĭl′ē əs) *adj.* Feeling or showing arrogant disdain; haughty: *a supercilious smile.* [First written down before 1529 in Modern English, from Latin *supercilium*, eyebrow, pride : *super-*, above + *cilium*, lower eyelid.] **—su′per•cil′i•ous•ly** *adv.*

su•per•com•put•er (so͞o′pər kəm pyo͞o′tər) *n.* A mainframe computer that can process information extremely rapidly.

su•per•con•duc•tiv•i•ty (so͞o′pər kŏn′dŭk tĭv′ĭ tē) *n.* The flow of electric current almost without resistance in certain metals, alloys, and ceramics at temperatures near absolute zero and in some cases several hundred degrees higher.

su•per•con•duc•tor (so͞o′pər kən dŭk′tər) *n.* A metal or an alloy that at a very low temperature conducts electric current almost without resistance.

su•per•con•ti•nent (so͞o′pər kŏn′tə nənt) *n.* A large continent that is thought to have split into smaller continents in the geologic past.

su•per•cool (so͞o′pər ko͞ol′) *tr.v.* **su•per•cooled, su•per•cool•ing, su•per•cools.** To cool (a liquid) below the freezing point without causing solidification.

su•per•e•rog•a•to•ry (so͞o′pər ĭ rŏg′ə tôr′ē) *adj.* **1.** Performed or observed beyond the required or expected degree. **2.** Unnecessary; superfluous.

su•per•fi•cial (so͞o′pər fĭsh′əl) *adj.* **1.** Of, affecting, or being on or near the surface: *a superficial wound.* **2.** Concerned only with what is apparent or obvious; shallow: *a superficial person.* [First written down in 1392 in Middle English, from Latin *superficiēs*, surface.] **—su′per•fi′ci•al′i•ty** (so͞o′pər fĭsh′ē ăl′ĭ tē) *n.* **—su′per•fi′cial•ly** *adv.*

su•per•fine (so͞o′pər fīn′) *adj.* **1.** Of exceptional quality; excellent. **2.** Excessively delicate or refined: *a superfine distinction.* **3.** Having extremely fine texture: *superfine sandpaper.*

su•per•flu•i•ty (so͞o′pər flo͞o′ĭ tē) *n., pl.* **su•per•flu•i•ties. 1.** The quality or condition of being superfluous. **2.** Something superfluous.

su•per•flu•ous (so͞o pûr′flo͞o əs) *adj.* Being beyond what is required or sufficient: *Many items on the budget are superfluous.* **—su•per′flu•ous•ly** *adv.* **—su•per′flu•ous•ness** *n.*

su•per•heat (so͞o′pər hēt′) *tr.v.* **su•per•heat•ed, su•per•heat•ing, su•per•heats. 1.** To heat excessively; overheat. **2.** To heat (steam or other vapor) to increase its pressure. **3.** To heat (a liquid) above its boiling point at a given pressure without allowing it to vaporize. *—n.* (so͞o′pər hēt′). The heat that something absorbs when superheated.

su•per•high frequency (so͞o′pər hī′) *n.* A radio-wave frequency between 3,000 and 30,000 megahertz.

su•per•high•way (so͞o′pər hī′wā′) *n.* A broad highway having six or more lanes for high-speed traffic.

su•per•hu•man (so͞o′pər hyo͞o′mən) *adj.* **1.** Beyond what is human; divine or supernatural: *superhuman beings.* **2.** Beyond ordinary or normal human ability or power.

su•per•im•pose (so͞o′pər ĭm pōz′) *tr.v.* **su•per•im•posed, su•per•im•pos•ing, su•per•im•pos•es.** To lay or place (something) over or upon something else.

su•per•in•tend (so͞o′pər ĭn tĕnd′ *or* so͞o′prĭn tĕnd′) *tr.v.* **su•per•in•tend•ed, su•per•in•tend•ing, su•per•in•tends.** To have charge of; oversee; supervise. **—su′per•in•ten′dence** *n.*

su•per•in•ten•dent (so͞o′pər ĭn tĕn′dənt *or* so͞o′prĭn tĕn′dənt) *n.* **1.** A person who supervises or is in charge of something. **2.** A janitor or custodian in a building.

su•pe•ri•or (so͞o pîr′ē ər) *adj.* **1.** High or higher in order, degree, or rank: *a superior court; a superior officer.* **2.** Higher in quality or nature: *a superior product.* **3.** Excellent; extraordinary. **4.** Greater in number or amount than another: *There are superior numbers of warblers in the park in your town.* **5.** Disdainful or conceited; snobbish: *What makes him feel so superior?* **6.** Situated over or above another; higher. *—n.* **1.** A person who surpasses another in rank or quality. **2.** The head of religious community, such as a monastery or convent. [First written down before 1393 in Middle English and spelled *superiour*, from Latin *superior*, from *super*, over.]

Su•pe•ri•or (so͞o pîr′ē ər), **Lake.** The largest and westernmost of the Great Lakes, between the north-central United States and southern Ontario.

su•pe•ri•or•i•ty (so͞o pîr′ē ôr′ĭ tē *or* so͞o pîr′ē ŏr′ĭ tē) *n.* The fact or quality of being superior.

su•per•la•tive (so͞o pûr′lə tĭv) *adj.* **1.** Of the highest order, quality, or degree: *a superlative specimen.* **2.** In grammar, of or relating to the extreme degree of comparison of an adjective or adverb, as in *best, brightest,* or *most comfortable.* *—n.* **1.** In grammar, the superlative degree of an adjective or adverb. **2.** An adjective or adverb expressing the superlative degree. *Brightest* is the superlative of the adjective

Sun Yat-sen
Photographed in the 1920's

superhighway
Route 128 in Massachusetts

ă	pat	oi	**boy**
ā	pay	ou	**out**
âr	care	o͝o	**took**
ä	father	o͞o	**boot**
ĕ	pet	ŭ	**cut**
ē	be	ûr	**urge**
ĭ	pit	th	**thin**
ī	pie	*th*	**this**
îr	pier	hw	**whoop**
ŏ	pot	zh	vision
ō	toe	ə	about
ô	paw	N	*French* bon

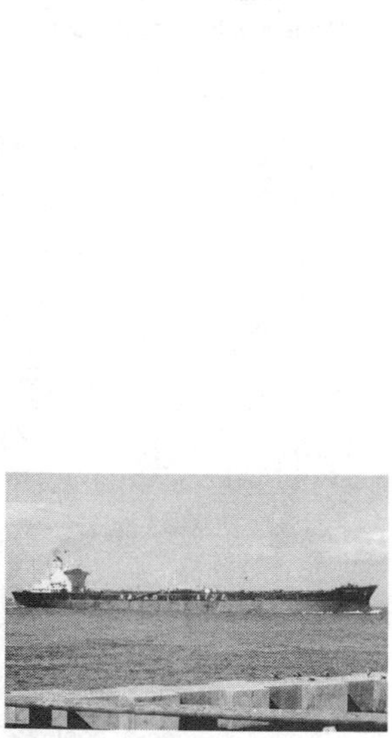
supertanker

bright, and *most brightly* is the superlative of the adverb *brightly*. **—su·per′la·tive·ly** *adv.* **—su·per′la·tive·ness** *n.*

su·per·man (so͞o′pər măn′) *n.* A man with superhuman powers.

su·per·mar·ket (so͞o′pər mär′kĭt) *n.* A large self-service retail store that sells food and household goods.

su·per·nal (so͞o pûr′nəl) *adj.* **1.** Of or relating to heaven; heavenly. **2.** Of, coming from, or being in the sky.

su·per·nat·u·ral (so͞o′pər năch′ər əl) *adj.* Of or relating to existence outside the natural world; spiritual or divine. *—n.* Something supernatural.

su·per·no·va (so͞o′pər nō′və) *n., pl.* **su·per·no·vae** (so͞o′pər nō′vē) or **su·per·no·vas.** An extremely large explosion of a star that for a short time gives off vast amounts of radiation.

su·per·nu·mer·ar·y (so͞o′pər no͞o′mə rĕr′ē *or* so͞o′pər nyo͞o′mə rĕr′ē) *adj.* Exceeding a fixed or required number; extra. *—n., pl.* **su·per·nu·mer·ar·ies. 1.** A person or thing that is in excess of the regular or required amount. **2.** An actor who has no speaking part in a play or movie: *She was a supernumerary in the crowd scene.*

su·per·pow·er (so͞o′pər pou′ər) *n.* A powerful and influential nation, especially a nuclear power that dominates its allies.

su·per·sat·u·rate (so͞o′pər săch′ə rāt′) *tr.v.* **su·per·sat·u·rat·ed, su·per·sat·u·rat·ing, su·per·sat·u·rates.** To cause (a chemical solution) to be more concentrated than is normally possible under given conditions of temperature or pressure.

su·per·script (so͞o′pər skrĭpt′) *n.* A character written or printed just above and to one side of another character. For example, in *light*[1], the superscript is 1. **—sup′er·script′** *adj.*

su·per·scrip·tion (so͞o′pər skrĭp′shən) *n.* Something written above or outside something else, as on a package.

su·per·sede (so͞o′pər sēd′) *tr.v.* **su·per·sed·ed, su·per·sed·ing, su·per·sedes. 1.** To take the place of; replace or succeed: *Electric light bulbs superseded candles and kerosene lamps as the major source of indoor light.* **2.** To cause to be set aside or displaced: *Supreme Court decisions supersede those of lower courts.*

su·per·sen·si·tive (so͞o′pər sĕn′sĭ tĭv) *adj.* Hypersensitive.

su·per·son·ic (so͞o′pər sŏn′ĭk) *adj.* Relating to, traveling at, or caused by a speed greater than the speed of sound in a given medium, especially air.

supersonic transport *n.* An aircraft designed to carry passengers or cargo at supersonic speeds.

su·per·star (so͞o′pər stär′) *n.* A widely acclaimed performer, as in films, music, or sports.

su·per·sti·tion (so͞o′pər stĭsh′ən) *n.* **1.** A belief that some object, action, or circumstance not logically related to a course of events influences its outcome. For example, the belief that walking under a ladder brings bad luck is a superstition. **2.** An action or a practice that is based on faith in magic or chance: *the superstition that carrying a crystal will protect the bearer from bad luck.*

su·per·sti·tious (so͞o′pər stĭsh′əs) *adj.* **1.** Inclined to believe in superstition: *a superstitious person.* **2.** Of or proceeding from superstition: *a superstitious fear of Fridays.* **—su′per·sti′tious·ly** *adv.* **—su′per·sti′tious·ness** *n.*

su·per·struc·ture (so͞o′pər strŭk′chər) *n.* **1.** The part of a building that is above the foundation. **2.** The parts of a ship that are above the main deck.

su·per·tank·er (so͞o′pər tăng′kər) *n.* A very large ship used for transporting oil and other liquids in large quantities.

su·per·vene (so͞o′pər vēn′) *intr.v.* **su·per·vened, su·per·ven·ing, su·per·venes. 1.** To come or occur as something additional or unexpected. **2.** To follow immediately; ensue.

su·per·vise (so͞o′pər vīz′) *tr.v.* **su·per·vised, su·per·vis·ing, su·per·vis·es.** To direct, oversee, and manage: *She supervises a staff of chemists. Who supervises your work?* [First written down in 1475 in Middle English and spelled *supervisen*, from Medieval Latin *supervidēre* : Latin *super-*, over + Latin *vidēre*, to see.]

su·per·vi·sion (so͞o′pər vĭzh′ən) *n.* The act or process of supervising; control; direction.

su·per·vi·sor (so͞o′pər vī′zər) *n.* A person who supervises.

su·per·vi·so·ry (so͞o′pər vī′zə rē) *adj.* Of or relating to supervision or a supervisor: *She works in a supervisory capacity.*

su·pine (so͞o pīn′ *or* so͞o′pīn′) *adj.* **1.** Lying on the back or having the face upward. **2.** Not inclined to act; lethargic; passive.

sup·per (sŭp′ər) *n.* **1.** An evening meal, especially dinner when eaten in the evening. **2.** A social gathering at which supper is served. [First written down about 1250 in Middle English and spelled *sopere*, from Old French *souper*, to sup.]

sup·plant (sə plănt′) *tr.v.* **sup·plant·ed, sup·plant·ing, sup·plants.** To take the place of; supersede: *The word processor has supplanted the typewriter.*

sup·ple (sŭp′əl) *adj.* **sup·pler, sup·plest. 1.** Easily bent or folded: *supple leather.* **2.** Moving easily; agile; limber: *a supple body.* **3.** Yielding or changing easily; adaptable: *a supple mind.* [First written down about 1300 in Middle English and spelled *souple*, from Latin *supplex*, suppliant.] **—sup′ple·ly** *adv.* **—sup′ple·ness** *n.*

sup·ple·ment (sŭp′lə mənt) *n.* **1.** Something added to complete a thing, make up for a deficiency, or extend or strengthen the whole: *This book is a supplement to the regular required reading.* **2.** A section added to a newspaper, book, or document to give further information or correct errors. **3.** A supplementary angle. *—tr.v.* (sŭp′lə mĕnt′). **sup·ple·ment·ed, sup·ple·ment·ing, sup·ple·ments.** To provide a supplement to: *The teacher supplemented our reading with films.*

sup·ple·men·ta·ry (sŭp′lə mĕn′tə rē *or* sŭp′lə mĕn′trē) *adj.* Added or serving as a supplement; additional: *supplementary information.*

supplementary angle *n.* One of a pair of angles whose sum is 180 degrees.

sup·pli·ant (sŭp′lē ənt) *adj.* Asking humbly and earnestly; beseeching: *a suppliant beggar.* *—n.* A supplicant.

sup·pli·cant (sŭp′lĭ kənt) *n.* A person who supplicates. *—adj.* Supplicating.

sup·pli·cate (sŭp′lĭ kāt′) *v.* **sup·pli·cat·ed, sup·pli·cat·ing, sup·pli·cates.** *—tr.* **1.** To ask for humbly or earnestly, as by praying. **2.** To make an earnest appeal to; beseech: *supplicated his captors for mercy.* *—intr.* To make a humble earnest petition or request; beg. **—sup′pli·ca′tion** *n.*

sup·ply (sə plī′) *tr.v.* **sup·plied, sup·ply·ing, sup·plies. 1.** To make available for use; provide: *Most hotels supply their guests with towels.* **2.** To furnish or equip with: *Supply sheets for every bed.* **3.** To fill sufficiently; satisfy: *supply a need.* **4.** To compensate or make up for (a loss, for example). *—n., pl.* **sup·plies. 1.** The act of supplying. **2.** An amount available or adequate for a given use; stock: *Our supply of milk is low.* **3.** Materials or provisions stored and dispensed when needed. Often used in the plural. [First written down in 1375 in Middle English and spelled *supplien*, from Latin *supplēre*, to fill up : *sub-*, from below + *plēre*, to fill.] —**sup•pli′er** *n.*

sup•port (sə pôrt′) *tr.v.* **sup•port•ed, sup•port•ing, sup•ports. 1.** To bear or carry the weight of (a structure or an object): *Beams support the floor joists.* **2.** To hold up or in position: *supported the baby's head with his hand.* **3.** To be capable or bearing; withstand: *This elevator won't support more than 300 pounds.* **4.** To provide for or maintain by supplying with money or other necessities: *She supports two children.* **5.** To provide evidence for; show to be true: *The experiment supports his theory.* **6.** To aid the cause, policy, or interest of: *support a political candidate.* **7.** To act a part or role that is secondary or subordinate to (a leading performer). —*n.* **1.a.** The act or process of supporting. **b.** The condition of being supported. **2.** A person or thing that supports. [First written down about 1384 in Middle English and spelled *supporten*, from Latin *supportāre*, to carry : *sub-*, from below + *portāre*, to carry.]

sup•port•a•ble (sə pôr′tə bəl) *adj.* Bearable; endurable. —**sup•port′a•bly** *adv.*

sup•port•er (sə pôr′tər) *n.* **1.** A person or thing that supports. **2.** A person who promotes or favors someone or something; an advocate: *the candidate's loyal supporters.* **3.** An athletic supporter.

sup•por•tive (sə pôr′tĭv) *adj.* Providing support or assistance.

sup•pose (sə pōz′) *v.* **sup•posed, sup•pos•ing, sup•pos•es.** —*tr.* **1.** To assume to be true or real for the sake of an argument or illustration: *Suppose we were rich.* **2.** To believe, especially on uncertain grounds: *Scientists suppose that dinosaurs lived in swamps.* **3.** To consider as a suggestion: *Suppose we stop and rest a minute.* —*intr.* To guess or imagine: *We'll just have to go inside, I suppose.* [First written down about 1303 in Middle English and spelled *supposen*, from Old French *supposer*, from Latin *suppōnere*, to put under.]

sup•posed (sə pōzd′ *or* sə pō′zĭd) *adj.* **1.** Presumed to be true or real; reputed: *the supposed model for a fictional character.* **2.** Intended or imagined: *a medicine that is supposed to relieve pain.* **3.a.** Required: *He's supposed to be at school.* **b.** Permitted: *We are not supposed to be here at night.* **c.** Believed; expected: *You're supposed to be my friend.* —**sup•pos′ed•ly** (sə pō′zĭd lē) *adv.*

sup•po•si•tion (sŭp′ə zĭsh′ən) *n.* **1.** The act of supposing: *an argument based on supposition, not fact.* **2.** Something supposed; an assumption: *made plans based on the supposition of good weather.*

sup•pos•i•to•ry (sə pŏz′ĭ tôr′ē) *n., pl.* **sup•pos•i•to•ries.** A medication prepared in a solid form, designed to be inserted into a body cavity other than the mouth, especially in the rectum.

sup•press (sə prĕs′) *tr.v.* **sup•pressed, sup•press•ing, sup•press•es. 1.** To put an end to forcibly; subdue; crush: *suppress a rebellion.* **2.** To restrict or forbid the activities of: *The government was accused of suppressing the opposition party.* **3.** To keep from being revealed or published: *suppress news of the leader's illness.* **4.** To keep back, restrain; check: *suppress a laugh.* [First written down about 1400 in Middle English and spelled *suppressen*, from Latin *supprimere* : *sub-*, down + *premere*, to press.]

sup•pres•sion (sə prĕsh′ən) *n.* **1.** The act of suppressing. **2.** The condition of being suppressed.

sup•pu•rate (sŭp′yə rāt′) *intr.v.* **sup•pu•rat•ed, sup•pu•rat•ing, sup•pu•rates.** To form or fill with pus: *The infected wound suppurated.* —**sup′pu•ra′tion** *n.*

su•pra•re•nal gland (so͞o′prə rē′nəl) *n.* An adrenal gland.

su•prem•a•cy (so͞o prĕm′ə sē) *n., pl.* **su•prem•a•cies. 1.** The quality or condition of being supreme: *a struggle for supremacy between two colonial powers.* **2.** Supreme power or authority.

su•preme (so͞o prēm′) *adj.* **su•prem•er, su•prem•est. 1.** Greatest in power, authority, or rank; dominant over others: *a supreme commander.* **2.** Greatest in importance, degree, or achievement: *supreme intelligence.* **3.** Ultimate; final: *the supreme sacrifice.* —**su•preme′ly** *adv.*

Supreme Being *n.* God.

Supreme Court *n.* **1.** The highest Federal court in the United States, consisting of nine justices and having legal authority over all other courts in the nation. **2. supreme court.** The highest court in most states within the United States.

Supreme Soviet *n.* The legislature of the Soviet Union, consisting of two houses, one whose members were elected on the basis of population and another whose members were elected by the national republics of the Soviet Union.

supt. or **Supt.** *abbr.* An abbreviation of superintendent.

sur•cease (sûr′sēs′ *or* sər sēs′) *tr. & intr.v.* **sur•ceased, sur•ceas•ing, sur•ceas•es.** To bring or come to an end; stop. —*n.* Cessation.

sur•charge (sûr′chärj′) *n.* **1.** An additional sum added to the usual amount or cost. **2.** An overcharge, especially an illegal one. **3.** An additional or excessive burden; an overload: *words carrying a surcharge of emotion.* **4.** A new value printed over the face value of a stamp. —*tr.v.* **sur•charged, sur•charg•ing, sur•charg•es. 1.** To charge (a person) an additional sum. **2.** To overcharge (a person). **3.** To overload or overburden. **4.** To print a surcharge on (a stamp).

sur•coat (sûr′kōt′) *n.* **1.** A loose outer coat or gown. **2.** A tunic worn in the Middle Ages by a knight over his armor.

surd (sûrd) *n.* A mathematical expression that contains at least one irrational root of a number, as $1 + \sqrt{3}$. [First written down in 1551 in Modern English, from Latin *surdus*, speechless.]

sure (sho͝or) *adj.* **sur•er, sur•est. 1.** Impossible to doubt or dispute; certain: *sure proof of her innocence.* **2.** Bound or destined to happen: *a sure victory for the team.* **3.** Steady; unwavering; firm: *a sure hold on the suitcase.* **4.** Confident, as of something awaited or expected: *I'm sure the package will come today.* **5.** Dependable; reliable: *The surest way of seeing that something gets done right is to do it yourself.* **6.** Careful to do something: *Be sure to brush your teeth.* —*adv. Informal.* Surely; certainly. —***idioms.*** **for sure.** *Informal.* Certainly; unquestionably: *We'll win today for sure.* **make sure.** To make certain; establish something without doubt: *I think the play starts at 5:00, but I'll call to make sure.* **to be sure.** Indeed; certainly. [First written down about 1250 in Middle English, from Latin *sēcūrus*.] —**sure′ness** *n.*

sure-fire (sho͝or′fīr′) *adj. Informal.* Bound to be successful or perform as expected: *a sure-fire solution to the problem.*

sure-foot•ed or **sure•foot•ed** (sho͝or′fo͝ot′ĭd) *adj.* **1.** Not likely to stumble or fall: *a sure-footed mule.* **2.** Confident and capable. —**sure′foot′ed•ness** *n.*

sure•ly (sho͝or′lē) *adv.* **1.** Certainly; without doubt: *Surely you can't be serious.* **2.** Without fail: *Slowly but surely spring returns.*

sur•e•ty (sho͝or′ĭ tē) *n., pl.* **sur•e•ties. 1.** The condition of being sure, especially of oneself; self-assurance. **2.** Something beyond a doubt; a certainty. **3.** A formal promise or pledge to take responsibility in case of loss or damage; a guaran-

ă	**pat**	oi	**boy**
ā	**pay**	ou	**out**
âr	**care**	o͝o	**took**
ä	**father**	o͞o	**boot**
ĕ	**pet**	ŭ	**cut**
ē	**be**	ûr	**urge**
ĭ	**pit**	th	**thin**
ī	**pie**	*th*	**this**
îr	**pier**	hw	**whoop**
ŏ	**pot**	zh	**vision**
ō	**toe**	ə	**about**
ô	**paw**	N	*French* **bon**

surfboard

tee. **4.** A person who agrees to be responsible if another does not pay a debt or fulfill a promise.

surf (sûrf) *n.* The waves of the sea as they break upon a shore or reef. *—intr.v.* **surfed, surf•ing, surfs.** To ride on a surfboard.

❑ *These sound alike:* **surf, serf** (slave).

sur•face (sûr′fəs) *n.* **1.a.** The outermost layer or boundary of an object. **b.** A material layer that makes up such a boundary. **2.** The outward or superficial appearance: *On the surface, the house looked new.* **3.a.** A portion of space that has length and breadth but no thickness; a geometric figure that has only two dimensions. **b.** The boundary of a three-dimensional geometric figure. *—v.* **sur•faced, sur•fac•ing, sur•fac•es.** *—tr.* To form or shape the surface of: *surfaced the driveway with asphalt.* *—intr.* **1.** To rise to the surface, as of a body of water. **2.** To emerge after being hidden: *She knew the lost book would surface when she cleaned her room.* [First written down in 1611 in Modern English, from French : *sur-*, above + *face*, face.]

surf•board (sûrf′bôrd′) *n.* A long narrow board used for surfing.

sur•feit (sûr′fĭt) *tr.v.* **sur•feit•ed, sur•feit•ing, sur•feits.** To feed or supply to excess; satiate. *—n.* **1.** An excessive amount. **2.a.** Indulgence in something, such as food, to excess. **b.** A result of such overindulgence; a feeling of fullness or disgust.

surf•er (sûr′fər) *n.* A person who surfs.

surf•ing (sûr′fĭng) *n.* The sport of riding waves, especially while standing or lying on a surfboard.

surge (sûrj) *intr.v.* **surged, surg•ing, surg•es. 1.** To move with a gathering force and fullness, in or as if in waves. **2.** To move like advancing waves: *The crowd surged forward.* **3.** To increase suddenly: *Excitement surged through his veins.* **4.** To roll or be tossed about on waves, as a boat. *—n.* **1.** A powerful wave or swell of water. **2.** A heavy swelling motion like that of great waves. **3.a.** A sudden onrush or increase: *a surge of excitement.* **b.** A sudden increase or change in electric current or voltage. [First written down in 1511 in Modern English, from Latin *surgere*, to rise.]

❑ *These sound alike:* **surge, serge** (cloth).

sur•geon (sûr′jən) *n.* A doctor specializing in surgery.

Surgeon General *n., pl.* **Surgeons General. 1.** The chief medical officer of the U.S. Army, Navy, or Air Force. **2.** The chief medical officer in the U.S. Public Health Service.

sur•ger•y (sûr′jə rē) *n., pl.* **sur•ger•ies. 1.** The branch of medicine that deals with the diagnosis and treatment of injury, deformity, and disease by physical manipulation or adjustment of the affected part or parts, often involving the cutting and reattachment of body tissues. **2.** A surgical operation or procedure, especially one involving the removal or replacement of a diseased organ or tissue. **3.** An operating room or a laboratory of a surgeon or surgical staff: *He's in surgery right now.* **4.** The skill or work of a surgeon. [First written down about 1300 in Middle English and spelled *sirgirie*, from Greek *kheirourgia* : *kheir*, hand + *ourgos*, working.]

sur•gi•cal (sûr′jĭ kəl) *adj.* Of, relating to, or characteristic of surgeons or surgery: *surgical instruments.* **—sur′gi•cal•ly** *adv.*

Su•ri•na•me (so͞o′rē nä′mə). Formerly **Dutch Gui•a•na** (dŭch gē ăn′ə *or* dŭch gē ä′nə). A country of northeast South America on the Atlantic Ocean west of French Guiana. It gained its independence from the Netherlands in 1975. Paramaribo is the capital and the largest city. Population, 354,860.

sur•ly (sûr′lē) *adj.* **sur•li•er, sur•li•est.** Ill-humored; gruff; sullen. **—sur′li•ness** *n.*

sur•mise (sər mīz′) *v.* **sur•mised, sur•mis•ing, sur•mis•es.** *—tr.* To conclude or infer (something) on slight evidence; suppose: *Astronomers surmise that there is life elsewhere in the universe.* *—intr.* To guess. *—n.* An idea or opinion based on slight evidence; a guess.

sur•mount (sər mount′) *tr.v.* **sur•mount•ed, sur•mount•ing, sur•mounts. 1.** To climb up and over: *surmount a hill.* **2.** To overcome; triumph over: *surmount a weakness.* **3.** To be placed or located above; top: *A weathervane surmounted the steeple.*

sur•name (sûr′nām′) *n.* One's family name as distinguished from one's given name.

sur•pass (sər păs′) *tr.v.* **sur•passed, sur•pass•ing, sur•pass•es. 1.** To go beyond the limit, powers, or capacity of: *a palace that surpasses description.* **2.** To be or go beyond, as in degree or quality; exceed: *The success of the program surpassed their expectations.*

sur•pass•ing (sər păs′ĭng) *adj.* Excellent; exceeding: *surpassing skill as a painter.*

sur•plice (sûr′plĭs) *n.* A loose-fitting white garment with full flowing sleeves, worn over a cleric's cassock in certain churches.

sur•plus (sûr′pləs *or* sûr′plŭs′) *adj.* Being more than or in excess of what is needed or required: *Surplus grain is usually sold abroad or stored.* *—n.* An amount or a quantity in excess of what is needed. [First written down about 1385 in Middle English, from Medieval Latin *superplūs* : Latin *super-*, over + Latin *plūs*, more.]

sur•prise (sər prīz′) *tr.v.* **sur•prised, sur•pris•ing, sur•pris•es. 1.** To come upon suddenly or unexpectedly; catch unawares. **2.** To attack or capture suddenly and without warning. **3.** To cause to feel wonder, astonishment, or amazement, as at something unexpected: *The low price of the antique surprised me.* *—n.* **1.** The act of surprising or the condition of being surprised. **2.** Something, such as an attack, a gift, or an event, that surprises. [First written down about 1390 in Middle English and spelled *surprisen*, to overcome, from Old French *surprendre*, to surprise : *sur-*, over + *prendre*, to take.] **—sur•pris′ing•ly** *adv.*

Synonyms: **surprise, astonish, amaze, astound.** These verbs mean to affect a person strongly as being unexpected or unusual. **Surprise** means to fill with often sudden wonder or disbelief: *It surprises me that you would want a job like that.* **Astonish** means to overwhelm with surprise: *The sight of such an enormous crowd outside the house astonished them.* **Amaze** means to affect with great wonder: *The daredevil's feats have amazed audiences around the world.* **Astound** means to shock with surprise: *They were astounded by the waiter's rudeness.*

sur•re•al (sə rē′əl) *adj.* **1.** Having qualities attributed to or associated with surrealism. **2.** Having strange qualities like those of a dream. **—sur•re′al•ly** *adv.*

sur•re•al•ism (sə rē′ə lĭz′əm) *n.* **1.** A 20th-century literary and artistic movement attempting to depict dreams and other products of the unconscious mind. **2.** Literature or art produced in this style. **—sur•re′al•ist** *adj. & n.*

sur•re•al•is•tic (sə rē′ə lĭs′tĭk) *adj.* **1.** Of or relating to surrealism. **2.** Having a dreamlike or unreal quality. **—sur•re′al•is′ti•cal•ly** *adv.*

sur•ren•der (sə rĕn′dər) *v.* **sur•ren•dered, sur•ren•der•ing, sur•ren•ders.** *—tr.* **1.** To give up (something) to another on demand or under pressure: *surrendered the coast to the invading army.* See Synonyms at **yield. 2.** To give over (oneself) entirely to something such as an emotion, influence, or effort. **3.** To give up or abandon: *surrender a right.* *—intr.* To give oneself up, as to the enemy. *—n.* The act or an instance of surrendering: *pre-*

ferred death to surrender. [First written down in 1441 in Middle English and spelled *surrendouren,* from Old French *surrendre* : *sur-,* over + *rendre,* to deliver.]

sur•rep•ti•tious (sûr′əp **tĭsh′**əs) *adj.* Obtained, done, or made in secret; stealthy: *a surreptitious glance at his watch.* **—sur′rep•ti′tious•ly** *adv.* **—sur′rep•ti′tious•ness** *n.*

sur•rey (**sûr′**ē *or* **sŭr′**ē) *n., pl.* **sur•reys.** A four-wheeled horse-drawn carriage having two or four seats.

sur•ro•gate (**sûr′**ə gĭt *or* **sûr′**ə gāt′) *n.* **1.** A person or thing that takes the place of another; a substitute. **2.** A judge in some states having jurisdiction over the probate of wills and settlement of estates. *—adj.* Substitute: *a surrogate parent.*

sur•round (sə **round′**) *tr.v.* **sur•round•ed, sur•round•ing, sur•rounds. 1.** To extend on all sides of; encircle: *the field of gravitation surrounding the earth; the hills that surround the town.* **2.** To shut in or enclose on all sides so as to prevent escape or outside communication. [First written down in 1423 in Middle English and spelled *surrounden,* to inundate, from Late Latin *superundāre* : Latin *super-,* over + Latin *unda,* wave.]

sur•round•ings (sə **roun′**dĭngz) *pl.n.* The things and circumstances that affect and surround one; environment.

sur•tax (**sûr′**tăks′) *n.* An additional tax.

sur•veil•lance (sər **vā′**ləns) *n.* **1.** Close observation of a person or group, especially one under suspicion. **2.** The act of observing or the condition of being observed.

sur•vey (sər **vā′** *or* **sûr′**vā′) *v.* **sur•veyed, sur•vey•ing, sur•veys.** *—tr.* **1.** To look over the parts or features of; view broadly: *surveyed the neighborhood from a rooftop.* **2.** To inspect or examine carefully: *surveyed the damage done by the storm.* **3.** To determine the area, boundaries, or elevation of (land or features of the earth's surface) by measuring angles and distances and using geometry and trigonometry. *—intr.* To make a survey. *—n.* (**sûr′**vā′). pl. **sur•veys. 1.** A general or comprehensive view of something. **2.** A detailed inspection or investigation: *a survey of public opinion.* **3.a.** The act or process of surveying. **b.** A map or report of what has been surveyed. [First written down about 1400 in Middle English and spelled *servaien,* from Medieval Latin *supervidēre* : Latin *super-,* over + Latin *vidēre,* to look.]

sur•vey•ing (sər **vā′**ĭng) *n.* The measurement and description of a region, part, or feature on the earth's surface, especially for use in locating property boundaries and mapmaking. **—sur•vey′or** *n.*

sur•viv•al (sər **vī′**vəl) *n.* **1.a.** The act or process of surviving. **b.** The fact of having survived. **2.** A person or thing that has survived: *a custom that is a survival of an ancient tradition.*

sur•vive (sər **vīv′**) *v.* **sur•vived, sur•viv•ing, sur•vives.** *—intr.* To stay alive or in existence: *trying to survive in the woods; a folktale that has survived for centuries. tr.* **1.** To live longer than; outlive. **2.** To live or persist through: *The plants survived the frost.* [First written down in 1473 in Middle English and spelled *surviven,* from Latin *supervīvere* : *super-,* over + *vīvere,* to live.]

sur•vi•vor (sər **vī′**vər) *n.* **1.** A person who has survived an accident or disaster that caused the death of others. **2.** A living descendant, relative, or heir of a person who has died.

sus•cep•ti•bil•i•ty (sə sĕp′tə **bĭl′**ĭ tē) *n., pl.* **sus•cep•ti•bil•i•ties. 1.** The quality or condition of being susceptible. **2.** The capacity to be affected by deep emotions or strong feelings; sensitivity. **3. susceptiblilities.** Feelings; sensibilities.

sus•cep•ti•ble (sə **sĕp′**tə bəl) *adj.* **1.** Easily influenced or affected: *She is simply not susceptible to persuasion.* **2.** Especially sensitive; highly impressionable: *a susceptible child.* **3.** Having little resistance: *susceptible to colds.* **4.** Capable of accepting or permitting a treatment or process: *a poem susceptible to several interpretations.*

su•shi (**sōō′**shē) *n.* Small cakes of cold cooked rice wrapped in seaweed and topped or wrapped with slices of raw or cooked fish, egg, or vegetables.

sus•pect (sə **spĕkt′**) *v.* **sus•pect•ed, sus•pect•ing, sus•pects.** *—tr.* **1.** To consider to be true or probable without being sure; imagine: *The early Greeks were the first to suspect that the earth is round.* **2.** To have doubts about; distrust: *We suspected his intentions.* **3.** To consider (someone) guilty without proof: *The police suspect her of fraud.* *—intr.* To have suspicion. *—n.* (**sŭs′**pĕkt′). A person who is suspected, especially of having committed a crime. *—adj.* (**sŭs′**pĕkt′ *or* sə **spĕkt′**). Open to or viewed with suspicion: *suspect motives; a suspect policy.* [First written down before 1325 in Middle English and spelled *suspecten,* from Latin *suspectāre* : *sub-,* from below + *specere,* to look at.]

sus•pend (sə **spĕnd′**) *tr.v.* **sus•pend•ed, sus•pend•ing, sus•pends. 1.** To bar temporarily from a position, membership, or privilege, usually as a punishment: *suspend a student from school.* **2.** To cause to stop for a period; interrupt: *suspended her work to have lunch.* **3.** To put off for the time being; postpone: *suspend judgment until all the facts are known.* **4.** To render temporarily ineffective: *suspended his driver's license.* **5.** To hang so as to allow free movement: *suspended a swing from the tree.* **6.** To support or keep from falling without apparent attachment; cause to float: *For an instant the acrobat seemed to suspend himself in midair.* [First written down about 1300 in Middle English and spelled *suspenden,* from Latin *suspendere* : *sub-,* from below + *pendere,* to hang.]

sus•pend•ers (sə **spĕn′**dərz) *pl.n. (used with a plural verb).* A pair of straps worn over the shoulders to hold up one's pants.

sus•pense (sə **spĕns′**) *n.* **1.** The condition of being suspended, as in the air. **2.** The state or quality of being undecided or uncertain. **3.** Excitement, worry, or fear resulting from an uncertain or mysterious situation.

sus•pen•sion (sə **spĕn′**shən) *n.* **1.** The act of suspending or the condition of being suspended: *a suspension of the rules; his suspension from school.* See Synonyms at **pause. 2.** A dispersion of solid particles in a liquid or gas. **3.** The system of springs, shock absorbers, and associated parts by which the wheels of a vehicle are connected to its chassis.

suspension bridge *n.* A bridge in which the roadway is hung from cables anchored at both ends and supported at intervals by towers.

sus•pi•cion (sə **spĭsh′**ən) *n.* **1.** The act of suspecting something on little evidence or without proof: *She had a strong suspicion that she was being double-crossed.* **2.** The condition of being suspected, especially of wrongdoing: *held under suspicion of theft.* **3.** A state of uncertainty; doubt: *eyeing the stranger with suspicion.* See Synonyms at **uncertainty. 4.** A minute amount; a trace; a hint.

sus•pi•cious (sə **spĭsh′**əs) *adj.* **1.** Arousing suspicion; inviting distrust: *suspicious behavior.* **2.** Tending to suspect; distrustful: *She was suspicious of anything out of the ordinary.* **3.** Expressing suspicion: *a suspicious glance.* **—sus•pi′cious•ly** *adv.* **—sus•pi′cious•ness** *n.*

Sus•que•han•na River (sŭs′kwə **hăn′**ə). A river of the northeast United States rising in central New

surveying

suspension bridge
San Francisco–Oakland Bay Bridge

ă	pat	oi	boy
ā	pay	ou	out
âr	care	ŏŏ	took
ä	father	ōō	boot
ĕ	pet	ŭ	cut
ē	be	ûr	urge
ĭ	pit	th	thin
ī	pie	*th*	this
îr	pier	hw	whoop
ŏ	pot	zh	vision
ō	toe	ə	about
ô	paw	N	*French* bon

Bertha von Suttner

swallowtail
Tiger swallowtail

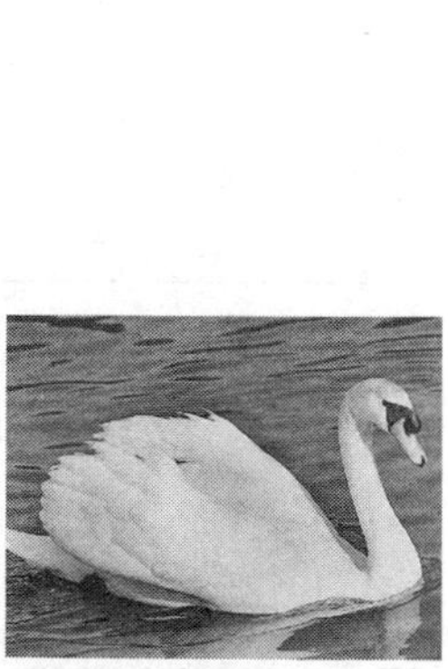

swan

York and flowing about 444 miles (714 kilometers) south to Chesapeake Bay.

sus•tain (sə stān′) *tr.v.* **sus•tained, sus•tain•ing, sus•tains. 1.** To keep in existence; maintain: *sustain an effort; sustain a note for four beats.* **2.** To keep alive; supply with needed nourishment: *the grasses that sustain antelope.* **3.** To support from below; keep from falling or sinking: *strong beams that sustain the weight of the roof.* **4.** To support the spirits of; encourage. **5.** To experience or suffer: *sustained minor injuries in the accident.* **6.** To affirm the validity of; uphold: *The judge sustained the objection of the prosecutor.* [First written down before 1300 in Middle English and spelled *sustenen*, from Latin *sustinēre* : *sub-*, from below + *tenēre*, to hold.] **—sus•tain′able** *adj.* **—sus•tain′er** *n.*

sus•te•nance (sŭs′tə nəns) *n.* **1.** The act of sustaining or the condition of being sustained. **2.** The support of life, as with food and other necessities. **3.** Something that supports life, especially food.

Sutt•ner (zo͝ot′nər *or* so͝ot′nər), **Bertha von.** 1843–1914. Austrian pacifist who was the first woman to receive the Nobel Peace Prize (1905).

su•ture (so͞o′chər) *n.* **1.** The process of joining two surfaces or edges together along a line by or as if by sewing. **2.a.** The fine thread or other material used in surgery to close a wound or join tissues. **b.** A stitch used in such surgery. **3.** The line where bones connect in an immovable joint: *the sutures of the skull.* *—tr.v.* **su•tured, su•tur•ing, su•tures.** To join by means of sutures, as in surgery. [First written down before 1425 in Middle English, from Latin *sūtūra*, from *suere*, to sew.]

Su•va (so͞o′və). The capital of Fiji, in the South Pacific Ocean. Population, 74,000.

su•ze•rain (so͞o′zər ən *or* so͞o′zə rān′) *n.* **1.** A nation that controls the foreign affairs of another nation but allows it to govern its domestic affairs. **2.** In feudal times, a lord to whom vassals gave service in return for use of land.

su•ze•rain•ty (so͞o′zər ən tē *or* so͞o′zə rān′tē) *n., pl.* **su•ze•rain•ties.** The power of or the area controlled by a suzerain.

svelte (svĕlt) *adj.* **svelt•er, svelt•est.** Slender or graceful in figure or outline; slim. [First written down about 1817 in Modern English and spelled *svelt*, from French, from Italian *svelto*.]

SW *abbr.* An abbreviation of southwest.

swab also **swob** (swŏb) *n.* **1.** A small piece of cotton, sponge, or other absorbent material attached to the end of a stick or wire and used for cleansing or for applying medicine. **2.** A mop used for cleaning floors or decks. *—tr.v.* **swabbed, swab•bing, swabs** also **swobbed, swob•bing, swobs. 1.** To use a swab on: *swab the skin with antiseptic.* **2.** To clean with a swab: *swab the decks.* **—swab′ber** *n.*

swad•dle (swŏd′l) *tr.v.* **swad•dled, swad•dling, swad•dles. 1.** To wrap, envelop, or bind in bandages. **2.** To wrap (an infant) in swaddling clothes. *—n.* A band or cloth used for swaddling.

swad•dling clothes (swŏd′lĭng) *pl.n.* Long narrow strips of cloth wrapped around a newborn infant to hold its legs and arms still.

swag (swăg) *n.* **1.a.** An ornamental drapery that hangs in a curve between two points. **b.** A decorative carved, painted, or molded representation of such a drapery. **2.** *Slang.* Stolen property; loot.

swag•ger (swăg′ər) *intr.v.* **swag•gered, swag•ger•ing, swag•gers. 1.** To walk with an insolent air; strut. **2.** To brag; boast. *—n.* **1.** A swaggering movement or gait. **2.** Boastful or conceited expression.

Swa•hi•li (swä hē′lē) *n., pl.* **Swahili** or **Swa•hi•lis. 1.** A member of a predominantly Muslim people inhabiting eastern Africa. **2.** The Bantu language of the Swahili, widely used in trade and as a general means of communication in eastern and east-central Africa. [First written down in 1814 in Modern English and spelled *Sowauli*, from Arabic *sawāḥilīy*, belonging to the coasts.]

swain (swān) *n.* **1.** A country lad, especially a shepherd. **2.** A beau.

swal•low¹ (swŏl′ō) *v.* **swal•lowed, swal•low•ing, swal•lows.** *—tr.* **1.** To cause (food or drink) to pass from the mouth through the throat and esophagus into the stomach by muscular action. **2.** To put up with (something unpleasant); tolerate: *swallow an insult.* **3.** To refrain from expressing; suppress: *swallow one's feelings.* **4.** To consume or destroy as if by ingestion; devour: *a building that was swallowed by fire.* **5.** *Slang.* To believe without question: *She swallowed their story about why they were late.* **6.** To take back; retract: *swallow one's words.* *—intr.* To perform the act of swallowing. *—n.* **1.** The act of swallowing. **2.** An amount swallowed. [First written down about 1000 in Old English and spelled *swelgan*.]

swal•low² (swŏl′ō) *n.* Any of various small swift-flying birds having narrow pointed wings, a forked or notched tail, and a large mouth for catching flying insects. [First written down before 800 in Old English and spelled *swealwe*.]

swal•low•tail (swŏl′ō tāl′) *n.* **1.** A deeply forked tail of or like that of a swallow. **2.** Any of various large, often colorful butterflies having a projection on the end of each hind wing, so that together they resemble the tail of certain swallows. **3.** *Informal.* A swallow-tailed coat.

swal•low-tailed (swŏl′ō tāld′) *adj.* **1.** Having a deeply forked tail. Used of various birds. **2.** Resembling the forked tail of a swallow.

swallow-tailed coat *n.* A man's coat worn for formal daytime occasions, divided in back into two long tapered ends.

swam (swăm) *v.* Past tense of **swim.**

swa•mi (swä′mē) *n., pl.* **swa•mis.** A Hindu religious teacher.

swamp (swŏmp *or* swômp) *n.* A low-lying region that is sometimes covered with water. *—v.* **swamped, swamp•ing, swamps.** *—tr.* **1.** To drench in or cover with or as if with water: *The road is swamped with rain water.* **2.** To inundate or burden; overwhelm: *swamped with work.* **3.** To fill (a boat) with water to the point of sinking. *—intr.* To become full of water or sink. [First written down before 1500 in Middle English and spelled *swam*, perhaps of Low German origin.] **—swamp′y** *adj.*

swamp•land (swŏmp′lănd′ *or* swômp′lănd′) *n.* Land of swampy consistency or having many swamps on it.

swan (swŏn) *n.* Any of various large, usually white water birds having webbed feet and a long slender neck. [First written down about 750 in Old English.]

swan dive *n.* A dive performed with the legs straight together, the back arched, and the arms stretched out from the sides.

swank (swăngk) *adj.* **swank•er, swank•est.** Very fashionable or elegant; grand: *a swank hotel.* *—n.* **1.** Elegance. **2.** An excessive display of style or arrogance in behavior; swagger.

swank•y (swăng′kē) *adj.* **swank•i•er, swank•i•est.** Very fashionable or elegant; swank. **—swank′i•ly** *adv.* **—swank′i•ness** *n.*

swan's-down also **swans•down** (swŏnz′doun′) *n.* **1.** The soft fluffy down of a swan. **2.** A soft thick fabric used especially for baby clothes.

swan song *n.* A farewell or last appearance, work, or action, as by an actor, a writer, or an athlete before death or retirement.

swap also **swop** (swŏp) *Informal.* *tr. & intr.v.*

swapped, swap•ping, swaps also **swopped, swop•ping, swops.** To trade (one thing) for another; exchange. *—n.* An exchange of one thing for another. **—swap′per** *n.*

sward (swôrd) *n.* Ground covered with short, thickly growing grass.

swarm[1] (swôrm) *n.* **1.** A large number of insects or other small creatures, especially when in motion: *a swarm of mosquitoes; swarms of microbes.* **2.** A group of bees, together with a queen bee, moving together to find a new hive. **3.** A group of people or animals, especially when agitated or moving in mass: *His friends came in a swarm to congratulate him.* *—v.* **swarmed, swarm•ing, swarms.** *—intr.* **1.** To move in or form a swarm, as bees or other insects. **2.** To move or gather in large numbers: *Fans swarmed onto the playing field after the game.* **3.** To be filled or overrun: *The streams swarmed with fish.* *—tr.* To fill with a crowd: *Thousands of fans swarmed the stadium.* [First written down before 800 in Old English and spelled *swearm.*]

swarm[2] (swôrm) *tr. & intr.v.* **swarmed, swarm•ing, swarms.** To climb by gripping with the arms and legs. [First written down about 1500 in Modern English.]

swarth•y (swôr′*thē*) *adj.* **swarth•i•er, swarth•i•est.** Having a dark complexion. **—swarth′i•ly** *adv.* **—swarth′i•ness** *n.*

swash (swŏsh *or* swôsh) *n.* **1.** A splash of liquid. **2.** The sound of such a splash. *—v.* **swashed, swash•ing, swash•es.** *—intr.* To strike, move, or wash with a splashing sound: *water swashing around his feet.* *—tr.* **1.** To splash (a liquid). **2.** To splash a liquid against.

swash•buck•ler (swŏsh′bŭk′lər *or* swôsh′bŭk′lər) *n.* **1.** A sword-wielding adventurer. **2.** A dramatic or literary work full of swordplay and romantic adventure. **—swash′buck′ling** *adj. & n.*

swas•ti•ka (swŏs′tĭ kə) *n.* **1.** The emblem of Nazi Germany. **2.** An ancient religious symbol formed by a Greek cross with the ends of the arms bent at right angles. [First written down in 1871 in Modern English, from Sanskrit *svastikaḥ*, sign of good luck, from *svasti*, well-being.]

swat (swŏt) *tr.v.* **swat•ted, swat•ting, swats.** To deal a sharp blow to; slap. *—n.* A quick blow; a slap. **—swat′ter** *n.*

swatch (swŏch) *n.* A small sample strip of cloth or other material.

swath (swŏth *or* swôth) *n.* **1.** The width of a scythe stroke or a mowing-machine blade. **2.** A path of this width made in mowing. **3.** The mown grass or grain lying on such a path. ***—idiom.*** **cut a swath.** To create a great stir, impression, or display. [First written down about 725 in Old English and spelled *swæth*, track.]

swathe (swŏ*th* *or* swô*th* *or* swā*th*) *tr.v.* **swathed, swath•ing, swathes. 1.** To wrap or bind with or as if with strips of cloth: *His right ankle was swathed in bandages.* **2.** To cover or wrap with something that envelops or encloses: *The actress was swathed in a long black cape.* *—n.* A bandage, binding, or other wrapping.

sway (swā) *v.* **swayed, sway•ing, sways.** *—intr.* **1.** To move back and forth or from side to side: *trees swaying in the wind.* **2.** To lean or bend to one side; veer: *She swayed and put out a hand to steady herself.* *—tr.* **1.** To cause to move back and forth or from side to side: *The wind swayed the trees.* **2.** To cause to lean or bend to one side: *The heavy load made the ship sway to the right.* **3.** To have influence on or control over: *issues most likely to sway voters.* *—n.* **1.** The act of moving from side to side with a swinging motion. **2.** Power; influence: *when the liberals held sway.* [First written down before 1325 in Middle English and spelled *swie*, probably of Scandinavian origin.]

sway•back (swā′băk′) *n.* An abnormal inward or downward curve of the spine. **—sway′backed′** *adj.*

Swa•zi•land (swä′zē lănd′). A country of southeast Africa between South Africa and Mozambique. It gained its independence from Great Britain in 1968. Mbabane is the capital and the largest city. Population, 585,000.

swear (swâr) *v.* **swore** (swôr), **sworn** (swôrn), **swear•ing, swears.** *—intr.* **1.** To make a solemn statement while calling on a sacred person or thing to confirm the honesty or truth of what is spoken. **2.** To make a solemn promise; vow: *swore to the authenticity of her claim.* See Synonyms at **vow. 3.** To use profane oaths; curse; blaspheme. *—tr.* **1.** To declare or affirm by calling on a sacred person or thing. **2.** To pledge or promise with a solemn oath; vow: *swore to do his duty.* **3.** To bind by means of an oath: *swore them to secrecy.* **4.** To administer a legal oath to: *swearing each juror in turn.* ***—idioms.*** **swear by. 1.** To have great reliance on or confidence in: *He swears by his personal physician.* **2.** To take an oath by. **swear in.** To administer a legal or official oath to: *swear in the new mayor.* **swear off.** *Informal.* To pledge to renounce or give up: *swore off sweets.* **swear out.** To obtain (a warrant for arrest) by making a charge under oath. [First written down about 725 in Old English and spelled *swerian.*] **—swear′er** *n.*

sweat (swĕt) *v.* **sweat•ed** or **sweat, sweat•ing, sweats.** *—intr.* **1.** To give off a salty liquid through pores in the skin; perspire. **2.** To give off a liquid in droplets, as moisture from certain cheeses or sap from a tree. **3.** To collect moisture in small drops from the air, as a cold water pipe. **4.** *Informal.* To work long and hard. **5.** *Informal.* To suffer, as for a misdeed. *—tr.* **1.** To give off (moisture) through a porous surface, such as skin. **2.** To cause to sweat, as by drugs, heat, or strenuous exercise. **3.** To make wet by perspiration: *His shirt was sweated through.* **4.** To overwork and underpay (employees). *—n.* **1.** The salty liquid given off by the sweat glands of the skin. **2.** Water that condenses on a surface and forms small drops. **3.** The act or process of sweating. **4.** Strenuous exhaustive labor; drudgery. **5.** *Informal.* An anxious fretful condition; impatience: *The painters were in a sweat to get started.* ***—idioms.*** **sweat blood.** *Informal.* To work extremely hard. **sweat out.** *Slang.* **1.** To endure anxiously: *sweat out an examination.* **2.** To await (something) anxiously: *sweat out one's final grades.*

sweat•er (swĕt′ər) *n.* A knitted or crocheted jacket or pullover made especially of wool, cotton, or acrylic yarn.

sweat gland *n.* Any of the tiny tubular glands that are found nearly everywhere in the skin of human beings and that give off sweat through pores.

sweat•pants (swĕt′pănts′) *pl.n.* Cotton jersey pants usually having a drawstring or elasticized waistband, worn especially for exercising.

sweat•shirt (swĕt′shûrt′) *n.* A long-sleeved pullover usually made of cotton jersey and having a fleeced backing.

sweat•shop (swĕt′shŏp′) *n.* A shop or factory where employees work long hours for low wages under poor conditions.

sweat•y (swĕt′ē) *adj.* **sweat•i•er, sweat•i•est. 1.** Covered with, wet with, or smelling of sweat. **2.** Causing sweat. **—sweat′i•ly** *adv.*

swede (swēd) *n.* The rutabaga.
❑ *These sound alike:* **swede, Swede** (Swedish person).

Swede (swēd) *n.* A native or inhabitant of Sweden.
❑ *These sound alike:* **Swede, swede** (rutabaga).

sweatpants

ă	pat	oi	boy
ā	pay	ou	out
âr	care	ŏŏ	took
ä	father	ōō	boot
ĕ	pet	ŭ	cut
ē	be	ûr	urge
ĭ	pit	th	thin
ī	pie	*th*	this
îr	pier	hw	whoop
ŏ	pot	zh	vision
ō	toe	ə	about
ô	paw	N	*French* bon

sweet William

Swe•den (swēd′n). A country of northern Europe east of Norway. Stockholm is the capital and the largest city. Population, 8,342,621.

Swed•ish (swē′dĭsh) *adj.* Of or relating to Sweden or the Swedes, their culture, or their language. —*n.* The North Germanic language of Sweden.

sweep (swēp) *v.* **swept** (swĕpt), **sweep•ing, sweeps.** —*tr.* **1.** To clean or clear with or as if with a broom or brush: *swept the hallway.* **2.** To clear away with or as if with a broom or brush: *sweep snow from the steps.* **3.** To clear (a space or path) with or as if with a broom. **4.** To move, remove, or convey by force: *flood waters sweeping away everything in their path.* **5.** To remove or carry off with a swift brushing motion: *swept the cards off the table.* **6.a.** To search thoroughly: *The counselor swept the dormitory during the fire drill.* **b.** To search for and remove (eavesdropping devices) from a place. **7.** To touch or brush lightly: *branches sweeping the river's surface.* **8.** To pass over or through a surface or medium with a continuous movement: *The conductor swept her baton through the air.* **9.** To drag the bottom of (a body of water). **10.** To win all the stages or parts of (a game or contest): *swept the playoffs.* —*intr.* **1.** To clean or clear a surface with or as if with a broom or brush. **2.** To search for and remove eavesdropping devices. **3.** To move swiftly with a strong steady force: *The wind swept over the plain.* **4.** To move swiftly and majestically: *The dancer swept through the crowd.* **5.** To trail, as a long garment. **6.** To extend gracefully, especially in a curve: *wildflowers sweeping down the slopes.* **7.** To extend in a wide range: *Searchlights swept the sky.* —*n.* **1.** A clearing out or removal with or as if with a broom or brush. **2.** The act or an instance of searching for and removing eavesdropping devices. **3.** A wide curving motion: *the sweep of the oars.* **4.** The range or scope covered by sweeping: *the sweep of a flashlight beam.* **5.** A broad reach or extent: *a sweep of glistening snow.* **6.** A curve or contour: *the sweep of her hair.* **7.** A person who sweeps, especially a chimney sweep. **8.** Victory in all stages of a game or contest. **9.** A long oar used to propel a boat. **10.** A long pole attached to a pivot and used to raise and lower a bucket in a well. [First written down before 1325 in Middle English and spelled *swepen*, perhaps from Old English *swēop*, past tense of *swāpan*.] —**sweep′er** *n.*

sweep•ing (swē′pĭng) *adj.* **1.** Having wide-ranging influence or effect: *sweeping changes.* **2.** Moving in or as if in a long curve: *sweeping gestures.* **3.** Overwhelming; complete: *a sweeping victory.* —*n.* **1.** The action or work of a person who sweeps. **2. sweepings.** Things swept up. —**sweep′ing•ly** *adv.*

sweep•stakes (swēp′stāks′) *pl.n. (used with a singular or plural verb).* **1.** A lottery in which the participants' contributions form a fund that is awarded as a prize to one or several winners. **2.** An event or a contest, especially a horse race, whose result determines the winner of such a lottery. **3.** The prize won in such a lottery.

sweet (swēt) *adj.* **sweet•er, sweet•est. 1.** Having the taste of sugar or a substance containing or resembling sugar, such as honey. **2.** Containing or made with sugar: *a sweet wine.* **3.** Pleasing to the senses, feelings, or mind; agreeable: *a sweet melody.* **4.** Having a pleasing disposition; lovable: *a sweet child.* **5.** Not salted: *sweet butter.* **6.** Not spoiled; fresh: *milk that is still sweet.* **7.** Free of acid: *sweet soil.* —*n.* **1.** Sweet taste or quality; sweetness. **2. sweets.** Foods, such as candy or pastries, that are high in sugar content. **3.** *Chiefly British.* A sweet dish, such as pudding, served as a dessert. **4.** A dear or beloved person. [First written down before 830 in Old English and spelled *swēte.*] —**sweet′ly** *adv.* —**sweet′ness** *n.*

❑ *These sound alike:* **sweet, suite** (series of rooms).

sweet•bread (swēt′brĕd′) *n.* The thymus gland or pancreas of an animal, especially a calf or lamb, used for food.

sweet•bri•er also **sweet•bri•ar** (swēt′brī′ər) *n.* A wild rose having prickly stems, fragrant leaves, and fragrant pink flowers.

sweet corn *n.* A type of corn having kernels that are sweet and juicy when young, commonly cooked and eaten as food.

sweet•en (swēt′n) *v.* **sweet•ened, sweet•en•ing, sweet•ens.** —*tr.* **1.** To make sweet or sweeter by adding sugar or another sweet substance: *sweetened his coffee.* **2.** To make more pleasant or agreeable: *sweeten a job offer with added benefits.* —*intr.* To become sweet.

sweet•en•er (swēt′n ər) *n.* A substance, such as sugar or saccharin, that sweetens.

sweet•en•ing (swēt′n ĭng) *n.* **1.** The act or process of making sweet. **2.** A sweetener.

sweet•heart (swēt′härt′) *n.* **1.** A person whom one loves. **2.** *Informal.* A person regarded as lovable.

sweet•ie (swē′tē) *n. Informal.* Sweetheart; dear.

sweet•meat (swēt′mēt′) *n.* A piece of candy or other sweet delicacy.

sweet pea *n.* A climbing plant related to the pea, having fragrant variously colored flowers.

sweet potato *n.* **1.** The thick, sweet yellowish or reddish root of a tropical vine, cooked and eaten as a vegetable. **2.** The vine that has such a root.

sweet tooth *n. Informal.* A fondness or desire for sweets.

sweet William *n.* A garden plant having dense clusters of flowers in various combinations of red, pink, and white.

swell (swĕl) *v.* **swelled, swelled** or **swol•len** (swō′lən), **swell•ing, swells.** —*intr.* **1.** To increase in size or volume as a result of internal pressure; expand: *The balloon swelled as I filled it with helium.* **2.a.** To increase in force, size, number, or degree: *Membership in the club swelled.* **b.** To increase in loudness or intensity, as a sound. **3.** To bulge out, as a sail. **4.a.** To rise in billows, as clouds. **b.** To rise in swells, as the sea. **5.a.** To be or become filled or puffed up, as with pride, arrogance, or anger. **b.** To rise from within: *Pride swelled within me.* —*tr.* **1.** To cause to increase in volume, size, number, degree, or intensity: *The new students swelled our class.* **2.** To fill with emotion: *Joy swelled her heart.* —*n.* **1.a.** The act or process of swelling. **b.** The condition of being swollen. **2.** A long wave that moves continuously through the water without breaking. **3.** A gentle rise in the surface of the earth; a rounded hill. **4.** In music: **a.** A crescendo followed by a diminuendo. **b.** The sign that indicates such a crescendo. **c.** A device on an instrument, such as an organ, for regulating volume. **5.** *Informal.* A person who is fashionably dressed or of high social position. —*adj.* **swell•er, swell•est.** *Informal.* **1.** Fine; excellent: *had a swell time.* **2.** Stylish; elegant. [First written down about 725 in Old English and spelled *swellan.*]

swell•ing (swĕl′ĭng) *n.* **1.** The condition of being swollen or expanded. **2.** Something swollen, especially a part of the body that has become abnormally swollen, as through disease or injury.

swel•ter (swĕl′tər) *v.* **swel•tered, swel•ter•ing, swel•ters.** —*intr.* To suffer from oppressive heat: *We sweltered in the stuffy room.* —*tr.* To affect with oppressive heat. —*n.* A condition of oppressive heat. [First written down about 1350 in Middle English and spelled *swelteren*, from *swelten*, to faint from heat, from Old English *sweltan*, to perish.]

swel•ter•ing (swĕl′tər ĭng) *adj.* **1.** Oppressively hot and humid. **2.** Suffering from heat.

swept (swĕpt) *v.* Past tense and past participle of **sweep.**

swept•back (swĕpt′băk′) *adj.* Extending sharply rearward from the points of attachment: *sweptback airplane wings.*

swerve (swûrv) *tr. & intr.v.* **swerved, swerv•ing, swerves.** To turn aside or be turned aside from a straight course: *I swerved my bike to avoid the tree. The bus swerved into the passing lane.* —*n.* The act of swerving.

swift (swĭft) *adj.* **swift•er, swift•est. 1.** Moving or capable of moving with great speed; fast. See Synonyms at **fast**[1]. **2.** Coming, occurring, or accomplished quickly: *a swift response.* —*adv.* Quickly: *swift-flowing streams.* —*n.* **1.** Any of various small, fast-flying, gray or blackish birds having long narrow wings, as the chimney swift. **2.** Any of various small, fast-moving, long-tailed lizards. [First written down about 725 in Old English.] **—swift′ly** *adv.* **—swift′ness** *n.*

Swift (swĭft), **Jonathan.** 1667–1745. Irish-born English writer whose works include *Gulliver's Travels* (1726).

swig (swĭg) *Informal. n.* A large swallow, especially of liquor; a gulp. —*tr. & intr.v.* **swigged, swig•ging, swigs.** To drink (liquid) or engage in drinking liquid in large gulps.

swill (swĭl) *v.* **swilled, swill•ing, swills.** —*tr.* **1.** To drink eagerly or greedily. **2.** To feed (animals) with swill. —*intr.* To eat or drink eagerly or greedily. —*n.* **1.** A mixture of liquid and solid food given to animals, especially pigs. **2.** Garbage; refuse. **3.** A large swallow of liquor. [First written down before 800 in Old English and spelled *swilian.*]

swim (swĭm) *v.* **swam** (swăm), **swum** (swŭm), **swim•ming, swims.** —*intr.* **1.** To move through water by means of the limbs, fins, or tail. **2.** To float on water or another liquid: *leaves swimming on the lake.* **3.** To be covered or flooded with or as if with a liquid: *The french fries swam in ketchup.* **4.** To experience a floating or giddy sensation; be dizzy: *a thought that made his head swim.* **5.** To appear to spin or reel: *The room swam before my eyes.* —*tr.* **1.** To move through or across (a body of water) by swimming. **2.** To perform (a swimming stroke). —*n.* **1.a.** The act of swimming. **b.** The period of time spent swimming. **2.** A state of dizziness. —*adj.* Of, relating to, or used for swimming: *a swim mask.* [First written down about 725 in Old English and spelled *swimman.*] **—swim′mer** *n.* **—swim′ming** *adj. & n.*

swim•mer•et (swĭm′ə rĕt′ *or* swĭm′ə rĕt′) *n.* One of the paired appendages along the abdomen of a shrimp, lobster, or related animal, used primarily for carrying the eggs in females and usually adapted for swimming.

swim•ming•ly (swĭm′ĭng lē) *adv.* With great ease and success: *School is going swimmingly.*

swimming pool *n.* A structure that is filled with water and used for swimming.

swim•suit (swĭm′so͞ot′) *n.* A garment worn while swimming; a bathing suit.

swin•dle (swĭn′dl) *tr.v.* **swin•dled, swin•dling, swin•dles. 1.** To cheat or defraud of money or property. **2.** To obtain by cheating or fraud: *swindled money from gullible people.* —*n.* The act or an instance of swindling; a fraud. **—swin′dler** *n.*

swine (swīn) *n., pl.* **swine. 1.** Any of various mammals, including pigs, hogs, and boars, that have a stout body with thick skin, a short neck, and a movable snout. **2.** A person regarded as brutish or contemptible.

swine•herd (swīn′hûrd′) *n.* A person who tends swine.

swing (swĭng) *v.* **swung** (swŭng), **swing•ing, swings.** —*intr.* **1.** To move back and forth, suspended or as if suspended from above: *a pendulum swinging from the ceiling.* **2.** To hit at something with a sweeping motion of the arm: *swing at the ball.* **3.** To ride on a swing. **4.** To turn in place on or as if on a hinge: *shutters swinging.* **5.** To move along with an easy swinging gait. **6.** To move laterally or in a curve; turn: *The car swung over to the curb.* **7.** *Slang.* To be put to death by hanging. —*tr.* **1.** To cause to move back and forth, as on a swing: *She swung her arms as she walked.* **2.** To lift or hoist with a sweeping motion: *swung the pouch over his shoulder.* **3.** To cause to move in a broad arc or curve: *swing a bat.* **4.** *Informal.* To manage or arrange successfully: *swing a deal.* —*n.* **1.** The act of swinging, especially a back-and-forth movement, as of a pendulum. **2.** A sweep or stroke of something that swings. **3.** The manner in which a person or thing swings something, such as a baseball bat. **4.** A shift from one attitude or condition to another: *a swing toward conservatism.* **5.** Freedom of movement or action: *He was given full swing in operating the business.* **6.** A seat suspended from above, on which one may ride back and forth for recreation. **7.a.** A type of popular dance music that developed about 1935 from jazz and using a large band and simpler harmony and rhythm patterns. **b.** The rhythmic quality or character of this music. —*idiom.* **in full swing.** At the highest level of activity or operation. [First written down before 800 in Old English and spelled *swingan*, to flog, swing.] **—swing′er** *n.*

swin•ish (swī′nĭsh) *adj.* **1.** Resembling or befitting swine. **2.** Bestial or brutish.

swipe (swīp) *n.* A sweeping blow or stroke. —*v.* **swiped, swip•ing, swipes.** —*tr.* **1.** To hit with a sweeping blow. **2.** *Informal.* To steal. —*intr.* To make a sweeping stroke.

swirl (swûrl) *v.* **swirled, swirl•ing, swirls.** —*intr.* To move with a twisting whirling motion: *The dancers swirled around the room.* See Synonyms at **turn.** —*tr.* To cause to move with a twisting or whirling motion. —*n.* **1.** The motion of whirling or twisting. **2.** Something that swirls, coils, or whirls. [First written down before 1398 in Middle English and spelled *swirlen*, probably of Low German or Scandinavian origin.]

swish (swĭsh) *v.* **swished, swish•ing, swish•es.** —*intr.* **1.** To move with a whistling or hissing sound, as a whip. **2.** To rustle, as certain fabrics such as silk. —*tr.* To cause to make a swishing sound or movement. —*n.* **1.** A sharp hissing or rustling sound. **2.** A movement making such a sound.

Swiss (swĭs) *adj.* Of or relating to Switzerland or its people or culture. —*n., pl.* **Swiss.** A native or inhabitant of Switzerland.

Swiss chard *n.* A variety of beet having large succulent leaves used as a vegetable.

Swiss cheese *n.* A firm whitish cheese with many large holes and a nutty flavor.

switch (swĭch) *n.* **1.** A slender flexible rod, stick, or twig, especially one used for whipping. **2.** A flailing or lashing, as with a slender rod. **3.** A device used to open or close an electric circuit or to make a connection to another circuit. **4.** A device consisting of two sections of railroad track and various movable parts, used to transfer rolling stock from one track to another. **5.** A shift, as of attention or opinion. **6.** A thick strand of real or artificial hair worn as part of a hairdo. —*v.* **switched, switch•ing, switch•es.** —*tr.* **1.** To whip with or as if with a switch. **2.** To jerk or swish abruptly or sharply: *The*

Jonathan Swift
Detail of a c. 1718 portrait
by Charles Jervas (1675–1739)

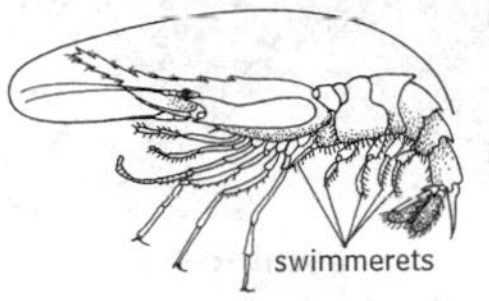

swimmeret
Of a shrimp

ă	**pat**	oi	**boy**
ā	**pay**	ou	**out**
âr	**care**	o͝o	**took**
ä	**father**	o͞o	**boot**
ĕ	**pet**	ŭ	**cut**
ē	**be**	ûr	**urge**
ĭ	**pit**	th	**thin**
ī	**pie**	*th*	**this**
îr	**pier**	hw	**whoop**
ŏ	**pot**	zh	**vision**
ō	**toe**	ə	**about**
ô	**paw**	N	*French* **bon**

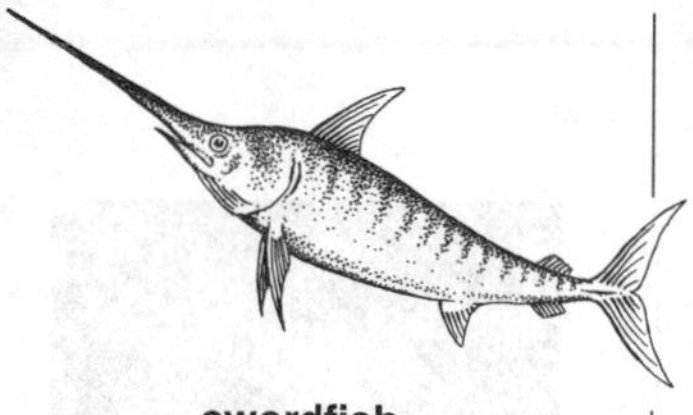

swordfish

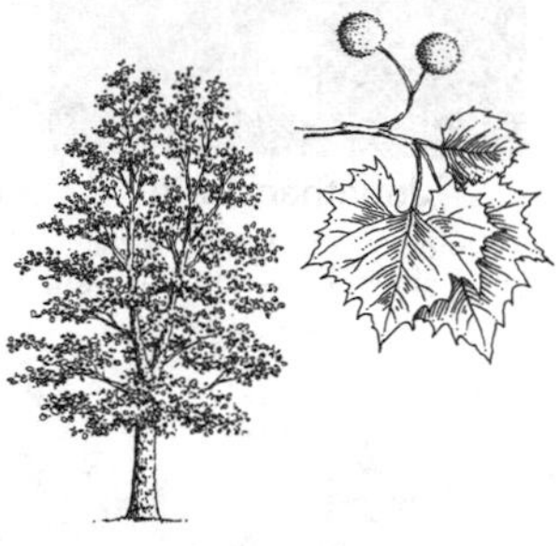

sycamore
American sycamore

symbiosis
Egret and hippopotamus

symbiosis

Two organisms that live together in **symbiosis** may have one of three kinds of relationships: **mutualism**, **commensalism**, or **parasitism**. The **mutualism** shown by the rhinoceros and birds such as the tickbird benefits both. Riding on the rhino's back, the bird eats its fill of the ticks that bother the rhino, while the rhino gets warning calls from the bird when it senses danger. In **commensalism**, one member benefits and the other is unaffected. The ocean fish known as the remora attaches to a shark by a suction disk on its head and gets to eat the scraps left after the shark feeds. But the shark is unaffected by the remora's presence. In **parasitism**, though, one species always gets hurt, as when fleas infest a dog's coat and feed on its blood.

cat switched its tail. **3.** To shift, transfer, or change: *switch the conversation to a more interesting topic.* **4.** To exchange: *We switched seats.* **5.** To control (an electric current) by operating a switch. **6.** To cause (an electrical device) to begin or cease operation by controlling the current to it with a switch: *Switch on the lights.* **7.** To move (rolling stock) from one railroad track to another. —*intr.* **1.** To make or undergo a shift or an exchange. **2.** To swish sharply from side to side. [First written down in 1592 in Modern English, probably of Low German or Flemish origin.] —**switch′er** *n.*

switch•blade (swĭch′blād′) *n.* A pocketknife with a blade that is quickly pushed open by a spring when a button on the handle is pressed.

switch•board (swĭch′bôrd′) *n.* One or more panels containing switches and other equipment for controlling electric circuits.

switch hitter *n.* In baseball, a player who can bat either right-handed or left-handed.

switch•man (swĭch′mən) *n.* A man who operates railroad switches.

Swit•zer•land (swĭt′sər lənd). A country of west-central Europe north of Italy. Switzerland maintained a policy of neutrality through both World Wars. Capital, Bern. Population, 6,455,900.

swiv•el (swĭv′əl) *n.* **1.** A link, pivot, or other fastening designed so that attached parts can turn freely. **2.** A pivoted support that allows an attached object, such as a chair, to turn around. —*tr. & intr. v.* **swiv•eled, swiv•el•ing, swiv•els** or **swiv•elled, swiv•el•ling, swiv•els.** To turn or rotate on or as if on a swivel. [First written down in 1307 in Middle English and spelled *swyvel.*]

swivel chair *n.* A chair that swivels on its base.

swob (swŏb) *n. & v.* Variant of **swab.**

swol•len (swō′lən) *v.* A past participle of **swell.** —*adj.* **1.** Expanded by or as if by internal pressure. **2.** Overblown; exaggerated: *swollen praise.*

swoon (swo͞on) *intr.v.* **swooned, swoon•ing, swoons.** To faint. —*n.* A fainting spell; a faint.

swoop (swo͞op) *v.* **swooped, swoop•ing, swoops.** —*intr.* To move with a sudden sweeping motion: *The hungry owl swooped down and caught the mouse.* —*tr.* To snatch or take with a sudden sweeping motion: *She swooped the cat up in her arms.* —*n.* The act or an instance of swooping. [First written down before 1000 in Old English and spelled *swāpan,* to sweep, swing.]

swoosh (swo͝osh *or* swo͞osh) *v.* **swooshed, swoosh•ing, swoosh•es.** —*intr.* To move with or make a rushing sound: *The jet swooshed over the airfield.* —*tr.* To cause to move with or make a rushing or swirling sound.

swop (swŏp) *v. & n.* Variant of **swap.**

sword (sôrd) *n.* **1.** A hand weapon consisting of a long pointed blade set in a handle or hilt. **2.** Military power or the use of force, as in war. [First written down about 725 in Old English and spelled *sweord.*]

sword•fish (sôrd′fĭsh′) *n.* A large ocean fish having a long pointed upper jaw that projects forward like a sword.

sword•play (sôrd′plā′) *n.* The act or art of using a sword, as in fencing.

swords•man (sôrdz′mən) *n.* A man who is skilled in the use of swords. —**swords′man•ship′** *n.*

sword•tail (sôrd′tāl′) *n.* A small tropical freshwater fish that has a long narrow point extending from the tail fin of the male and is often kept in home aquariums.

swore (swôr) *v.* Past tense of **swear.**

sworn (swôrn) *v.* Past participle of **swear.**

swum (swŭm) *v.* Past participle of **swim.**

swung (swŭng) *v.* Past tense and past participle of **swing.**

syc•a•more (sĭk′ə môr′) *n.* **1.** Any of various trees having leaves resembling those of the maple, ball-shaped seed clusters, and bark that flakes off in large patches. **2.** A kind of maple tree native to Europe and Asia. **3.** A kind of fig tree native to Africa and southwest Asia, having clusters of figs on short leafless twigs. [First written down about 1350 in Middle English and spelled *sicamour,* a kind of fig tree, from Greek *sukomoros.*]

syc•o•phant (sĭk′ə fənt *or* sī′kə fənt) *n.* A person who attempts to win favor or advancement by flattering influential people.

Syd•ney (sĭd′nē). The largest city of Australia, in the southeast part of the country northeast of Canberra. Population, 3,358,550.

syl•la•bi (sĭl′ə bī′) *n.* A plural of **syllabus.**

syl•lab•ic (sĭ lăb′ĭk) *adj.* **1.** Of, relating to, or consisting of a syllable or syllables. **2.** Relating to a consonant that forms a syllable without a vowel, as the *l* in *riddle.* **3.** Pronounced with every syllable distinct. —*n.* A syllabic sound.

syl•lab•i•fy (sĭ lăb′ĭ fī′) or **syl•lab•i•cate** (sĭ lăb′ĭ kāt′) *tr.v.* **syl•lab•i•fied** (sĭ lăb′ĭ fīd′), **syl•lab•i•fy•ing, syl•lab•i•fies** (sĭ lăb′ĭ fīz′) or **syl•lab•i•cat•ed, syl•lab•i•cat•ing, syl•lab•i•cates.** To form or divide into syllables. —**syl•lab′i•fi•ca′tion** (sĭ lăb′ĭ fĭ kā′shən), **syl•lab′i•ca′tion** *n.*

syl•la•ble (sĭl′ə bəl) *n.* A single uninterrupted sound forming part of a word or in some cases an entire word. [First written down about 1380 in Middle English and spelled *sillable,* from Greek *sullabē.*]

syl•la•bus (sĭl′ə bəs) *n., pl.* **syl•la•bus•es** or **syl•la•bi** (sĭl′ə bī′). An outline or a summary of the main points of a text, lecture, or course of study.

syl•lo•gism (sĭl′ə jĭz′əm) *n.* **1.** A form of reasoning in which two propositions, the first called the major premise and the second called the minor premise, are stated, followed by a conclusion that is logically derived from them. An example of a syllogism is *All horses have tails* (major premise); *Big Red is a horse* (minor premise); *therefore Big Red has a tail* (conclusion). **2.** Reasoning from the general to the specific; deduction.

sylph (sĭlf) *n.* A slim graceful woman or girl.

syl•van also **sil•van** (sĭl′vən) *adj.* **1.** Relating to or characteristic of woodlands or forests: *sylvan life.* **2.** Located in or inhabiting a wood or forest. **3.** Having many trees; wooded: *sylvan slopes.*

sym•bi•o•sis (sĭm′bē ō′sĭs *or* sĭm′bī ō′sĭs) *n., pl.* **sym•bi•o•ses** (sĭm′bē ō′sēz *or* sĭm′bī ō′sēz). The close association between two or more different organisms of different species, often but not necessarily benefiting each member. —SEE NOTE.

sym•bi•ot•ic (sĭm′bē ŏt′ĭk *or* sĭm′bī ŏt′ĭk) *adj.* Of, relating to, or characterized by symbiosis. —**sym′bi•ot′i•cal•ly** *adv.*

sym•bol (sĭm′bəl) *n.* **1.** Something that stands for something else, as by association, resemblance, or convention: *The lamb is a symbol of innocence.* **2.** A printed or written sign used to represent an operation, element, quantity, quality, or relation, as in mathematics or music. [First written down about 1434 in Middle English and spelled *simbal,* creed, from Greek *sumbolon,* token for identification (by comparison with a counterpart) : *sun-,* together + *ballein,* to throw.]

❑ *These sound alike:* **symbol, cymbal** (musical instrument).

sym•bol•ic (sĭm bŏl′ĭk) also **sym•bol•i•cal** (sĭm bŏl′ĭ kəl) *adj.* **1.** Of, relating to, or expressed by means of a symbol or symbols. **2.** Serving as a symbol. **3.** Using symbolism, as a work of art. —**sym•bol′i•cal•ly** *adv.*

sym•bol•ism (sĭm′bə lĭz′əm) *n.* **1.a.** The practice of representing things by means of symbols. **b.** The attachment of symbolic meaning or significance to objects, events, or relationships. **2.** A system of symbols or representation. **3.** A symbolic meaning or representation.

sym•bol•ize (sĭm′bə līz′) *v.* **sym•bol•ized, sym•bol•iz•ing, sym•bol•iz•es.** *—tr.* **1.** To serve as a symbol of: *The poet uses rain to symbolize grief.* **2.** To represent or identify by a symbol. *—intr.* To use symbols.

sym•met•ri•cal (sĭ mĕt′rĭ kəl) also **sym•met•ric** (sĭ mĕt′rĭk) *adj.* Of or showing symmetry.

sym•me•try (sĭm′ĭ trē) *n., pl.* **sym•me•tries. 1.** An exact matching of form and arrangement of parts on opposite sides of a boundary, such as a plane or line, or around a point or axis. **2.** A relationship in which there is a characteristic correspondence, equivalence, or identity between parts. [First written down in 1563 in Modern English, from Greek *summetros*, of like measure : *sun-*, together + *metron*, measure.]

sym•pa•thet•ic (sĭm′pə thĕt′ĭk) *adj.* **1.** Of, feeling, expressing, or resulting from sympathy: *a sympathetic person; a sympathetic glance.* **2.** In agreement; favorable; inclined: *They were sympathetic to the plan.* **—sym′pa•thet′i•cal•ly** *adv.*

sym•pa•thize (sĭm′pə thīz′) *intr.v.* **sym•pa•thized, sym•pa•thiz•ing, sym•pa•thiz•es. 1.** To feel or express sympathy or compassion for another. **2.** To share or understand the feelings or ideas of another. **—sym′pa•thiz′er** *n.*

sym•pa•thy (sĭm′pə thē) *n., pl.* **sym•pa•thies. 1.** Mutual understanding or affection between persons. **2.a.** The act or capacity of sharing or understanding the feelings of another. **b.** A feeling or expression of pity or sorrow for the distress of another; compassion. **3.** Favor; agreement; accord: *in sympathy with their beliefs.* [First written down in 1579 in Modern English, from Greek *sumpathēs*, affected by like feelings : *sun-*, together + *pathos*, emotion.]

sym•phon•ic (sĭm fŏn′ĭk) *adj.* **1.** Relating to or having the character or form of a symphony. **2.** Harmonious in sound.

symphonic poem *n.* A piece of music based on a story or an ideal and consisting of a single movement for a symphony orchestra.

sym•pho•ny (sĭm′fə nē) *n., pl.* **sym•pho•nies. 1.a.** A long and elaborate musical composition for orchestra, usually consisting of four movements. **b.** An instrumental passage in a vocal piece, such as an opera or oratorio. **2.** A symphony orchestra.

symphony orchestra *n.* A large orchestra composed of string, wind, and percussion sections.

sym•po•si•um (sĭm pō′zē əm) *n., pl.* **sym•po•si•ums** or **sym•po•si•a** (sĭm pō′zē ə). **1.** A meeting or conference for discussion of a topic. **2.** A collection of writings on a particular topic. [First written down before 1586 in Modern English, from Greek *sumposion*, drinking party : *sun-*, together + *posis*, drinking.]

symp•tom (sĭm′təm *or* sĭmp′təm) *n.* **1.** An indication or a characteristic sign of the existence of something else: *The scarcity of birds was a symptom of broader problems in the environment.* **2.** A sign or an indication of disorder or disease, especially a change from normal bodily function, feeling, or appearance. [First written down in 1541 in Modern English, from Greek *sumptōma*, from *sumpiptein*, to coincide.]

syn. *abbr.* An abbreviation of: **1.** Synonym. **2.** Synonymous. **3.** Synonymy.

syn•a•gogue also **syn•a•gog** (sĭn′ə gŏg′ *or* sĭn′ə gôg′) *n.* **1.** A building or place of meeting for worship and religious instruction in the Jewish faith. **2.** A congregation of Jews for the purpose of worship or religious study. [First written down before 1225 in Middle English and spelled *sinagoga*, from Greek *sunagōgē*, from *sunagein*, to bring together.]

syn•apse (sĭn′ăps′ *or* sĭ năps′) *n.* The point at which a nerve impulse passes from one nerve cell to another nerve cell, a muscle cell, or a gland cell.

sync or **synch** (sĭngk) *Informal. n.* **1.** Synchronization. **2.** Harmony; accord.

syn•chro•ni•za•tion (sĭng′krə nĭ zā′shən *or* sĭn′krə nĭ zā′shən) *n.* The state of being synchronous.

syn•chro•nize (sĭng′krə nīz′ *or* sĭn′krə nīz′) *v.* **syn•chro•nized, syn•chro•niz•ing, syn•chro•niz•es.** *—intr.* **1.** To occur at the same time; be simultaneous. **2.** To operate at the same rate and time. *—tr.* To cause to occur or operate at the same rate and time: *Let's synchronize our watches.*

syn•chro•nous (sĭng′krə nəs *or* sĭn′krə nəs) *adj.* **1.** Occurring or existing at the same time. **2.** Moving or operating at the same rate and together in time. **3.** Having identical periods or identical periods and phases, as two waves, satellites, or pendulums.

syn•chro•tron (sĭng′krə trŏn′ *or* sĭn′krə trŏn′) *n.* A machine in which charged subatomic particles are accelerated to high energies by electric fields. The particles are held in a circular path by an increasing magnetic field.

syn•cline (sĭn′klīn′) *n.* A fold of rock layers that slope downward on both sides to a common low point.

syn•co•pate (sĭng′kə pāt′ *or* sĭn′kə pāt′) *tr.v.* **syn•co•pat•ed, syn•co•pat•ing, syn•co•pates. 1.** To shorten (a word) by syncope. **2.** To change (a musical rhythm) by syncopation.

syn•co•pa•tion (sĭng′kə pā′shən *or* sĭn′kə pā′shən) *n.* **1.** In music, a shift of accent in a passage or a composition that occurs when a normally weak beat is stressed. **2.** Something, such as a rhythm, that is syncopated. **3.** Syncope.

syn•co•pe (sĭng′kə pē *or* sĭn′kə pē) *n.* **1.** The shortening of a word by omission of a sound, letter, or syllable from the middle of a word; for example, *bos'n* for *boatswain.* **2.** A brief loss of consciousness caused by a temporary deficiency of oxygen in the brain; a blackout.

syn•di•cate (sĭn′dĭ kĭt) *n.* **1.** An association of people or firms authorized to carry out a specific business enterprise. **2.** An association of people or firms formed to promote a common interest. **3.** An agency that sells articles or photographs for simultaneous publication in a number of newspapers or periodicals. *—v.* (sĭn′dĭ kāt′). **syn•di•cat•ed, syn•di•cat•ing, syn•di•cates.** *—tr.* **1.** To organize into or manage as a syndicate. **2.** To sell (an article, for example) through a syndicate for publication. *—intr.* To join together in a syndicate.

syn•drome (sĭn′drōm′) *n.* A set of symptoms and signs that together indicate the presence of a disease, mental disorder, or other abnormal condition. [First written down in 1541 in Modern English, from Greek *sundromos*, running together.]

syn•fu•el (sĭn′fyōō′əl) *n.* A liquid or gaseous fuel derived from coal, shale, or tar sand, or obtained by fermentation of certain substances, such as grain.

syn•od (sĭn′əd) *n.* A council or assembly of churches or church officials.

syn•o•nym (sĭn′ə nĭm′) *n.* A word having the same or almost the same meaning as that of another word. For example, the words *wide* and *broad* are synonyms.

syn•on•y•mous (sĭ nŏn′ə məs) *adj.* Having the same or a similar meaning: *synonymous words.*

syn•on•y•my (sĭ nŏn′ə mē) *n., pl.* **syn•on•y•mies. 1.** The quality of being synonymous. **2.** Study or

synagogue
Temple Ohabei Shalom in Brookline, Massachusetts

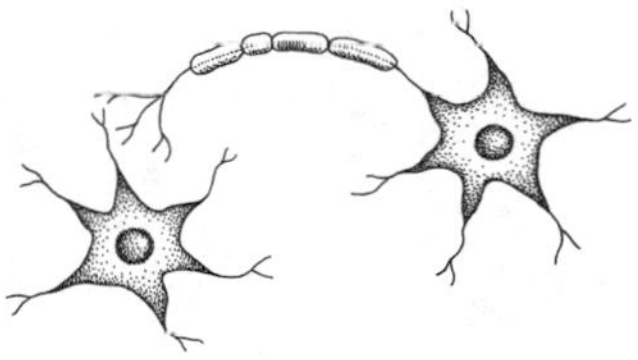

synapse

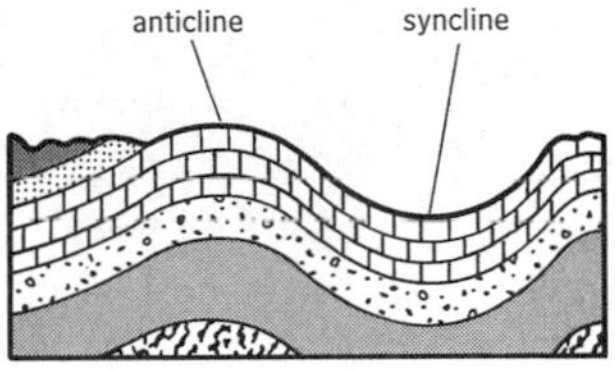

syncline

ă	pat	oi	boy
ā	pay	ou	out
âr	care	ŏŏ	took
ä	father	ōō	boot
ĕ	pet	ŭ	cut
ē	be	ûr	urge
ĭ	pit	th	thin
ī	pie	*th*	this
îr	pier	hw	whoop
ŏ	pot	zh	vision
ō	toe	ə	about
ô	paw	N	*French* bon

synthesizer

classification of synonyms. **3.** A list, book, or system of synonyms.

syn•op•sis (sĭ nŏp′sĭs) *n., pl.* **syn•op•ses** (sĭ nŏp′sēz). A brief summary or outline of a subject or written work: *a synopsis of a play.*

syn•op•size (sĭ nŏp′sīz′) *tr.v.* **syn•op•sized, syn•op•siz•ing, syn•op•siz•es.** To make a synopsis of; summarize.

syn•tac•tic (sĭn tăk′tĭk) or **syn•tac•ti•cal** (sĭn tăk′tĭ kəl) *adj.* Of, relating, or conforming to the rules or patterns of syntax. **—syn•tac′ti•cal•ly** *adv.*

syn•tax (sĭn′tăks′) *n.* The way in which words are put together to form phrases and sentences.

syn•the•sis (sĭn′thĭ sĭs) *n., pl.* **syn•the•ses** (sĭn′thĭ-sēz′). **1.** The combination of separate elements or substances into a single unit or whole. **2.** The single unit or whole formed in this way. **3.** The formation of a chemical compound by combining simpler compounds or elements. [First written down in 1611 in Modern English, from Greek *sunthesis*, from *suntithenai*, to put together.]

syn•the•size (sĭn′thĭ sīz′) *v.* **syn•the•sized, syn•the•siz•ing, syn•the•siz•es.** *—tr.* To make or produce by a process of synthesis: *synthesize an antibiotic.* *—intr.* To form a synthesis.

syn•the•siz•er (sĭn′thĭ sī′zər) *n.* **1.** A person or thing that synthesizes. **2.** An electronic musical instrument that can be made to produce a wide range of musical sounds, including sounds that imitate those of conventional instruments.

syn•thet•ic (sĭn thĕt′ĭk) *adj.* **1.** Relating to or involving synthesis. **2.** Produced by synthesis; not of natural origin: *synthetic rubber; synthetic fabrics.* *—n.* A synthetic chemical compound or material. **—syn•thet′i•cal•ly** *adv.*

syph•i•lis (sĭf′ə lĭs) *n.* An infectious venereal disease caused by a spirochete, progressing through three stages marked first by hard sores on or near the genitalia, second by ulcerous skin eruptions, and third by infection, often fatal, of the entire body.

syph•i•lit•ic (sĭf′ə lĭt′ĭk) *adj.* Of, relating to, or affected wtih syphilis. *—n.* A person who has syphilis.

sy•phon (sī′fən) *n. & v.* Variant of **siphon.**

Sy•ri•a (sîr′ē ə). A country of southwest Asia on the eastern Mediterranean coast west of Iraq. It gained its independence in 1944. Damascus is the capital and the largest city. Population, 9,052,628.

sy•rin•ga (sə rĭng′gə) *n.* The mock orange.

sy•ringe (sə rĭnj′ *or* sîr′ĭnj) *n.* **1.** A medical instrument used to inject fluids into the body or draw fluids from the body. **2.** A hypodermic syringe. [First written down before 1398 in Middle English and spelled *suringa*, from Greek *surinx*, shepherd's pipe.]

syr•inx (sîr′ĭngks) *n., pl.* **sy•rin•ges** (sə rĭn′jēz *or* sə-rĭng′gēz) or **syr•inx•es.** **1.** The panpipe. **2.** The vocal organ of a bird, situated at or near the division of the trachea into the right and left bronchi.

syr•up also **sir•up** (sĭr′əp *or* sûr′əp) *n.* **1.** A thick, sweet, sticky liquid, consisting of sugar, water, and flavoring or medicine. **2.** The juice of a fruit or plant boiled with sugar until thick and sticky. [First written down in 1392 in Middle English and spelled *sirip*, from Arabic *šarāb*.] **—syr′up•y** *adj.*

sys•tem (sĭs′təm) *n.* **1.** A group of elements or parts that interact to form a complex whole. **2.** Something formed of a group of elements or parts that function together, especially: **a.** The human body considered as a working unit. **b.** A group of related organs or parts: *the skeletal system.* **c.** A set of mechanical or electrical parts that work together: *the transmission system of an automobile.* **d.** A network of pathways or channels, as for travel or communications: *a transport system; a telephone system.* **3.** An organized set of related principles or rules. See Synonyms at **method.** **4.** A social, economic, or political organizational form: *a system of government.* [First written down in 1619 in Modern English, from Greek *sustēma* : *sun-*, together + *histanai*, set up, establish.]

sys•tem•at•ic (sĭs′tə măt′ĭk) also **sys•tem•at•i•cal** (sĭs′tə măt′ĭ kəl) *adj.* **1.** Of, characterized by, based on, or forming a system. **2.** Carried on or done in a step-by-step manner: *a systematic review.* **3.** Orderly or methodical: *a systematic worker.*

sys•tem•a•tize (sĭs′tə mə tīz′) *tr.v.* **sys•tem•a•tized, sys•tem•a•tiz•ing, sys•tem•a•tiz•es.** To form or organize into a system.

sys•tem•ic (sĭ stĕm′ĭk) *adj.* **1.** Of or relating to an entire system: *The recession is not limited to one area of the economy, but is systemic.* **2.** Of, relating to, or affecting the entire body: *systemic poisoning.*

sys•to•le (sĭs′tə lē) *n.* The rhythmic contraction of the heart, especially of the ventricles, by which blood is driven through the aorta and pulmonary artery. **—sys•tol′ic** (sĭ stŏl′ĭk) *adj.*

Tt

t or **T** (tē) *n., pl.* **t's** or **T's. 1.** The 20th letter of the English alphabet. **2.** The 20th in a series or group. ***—idiom.*** **to a T.** Perfectly; precisely: *The jacket fit me to a T.*

T *abbr.* An abbreviation of temperature.

Ta The symbol for the element **tantalum.**

tab[1] (tăb) *n.* **1.** A projection, flap, or short strip attached to an object to aid in opening, handling, or identifying it. **2.** A small, usually decorative flap or tongue on a garment. **3.** A small auxiliary control surface attached to a larger one, as on an aircraft. [First written down in 1607 in Modern English.]

tab[2] (tăb) *n.* **1.** *Informal.* A bill or check, as for a meal in a restaurant: *I'll pay the tab.* **2.** A tabulator on a typewriter. ***—idiom.*** **keep tabs on.** To watch or observe carefully: *kept tabs on the children during the trip to the museum.* [First written down in 1889 in Modern English, partly from *tab,* flap.]

tab•ard (**tăb′**ərd) *n.* **1.** A sleeveless or short-sleeved tunic worn by a knight over his armor and embroidered with his coat of arms. **2.** A similar garment worn by a herald and bearing his lord's coat of arms.

Ta•bas•co (tə **băs′**kō). A trademark used for a spicy sauce made from a strong-flavored red pepper.

tab•by (**tăb′**ē) *n., pl.* **tab•bies.** A cat having striped gray or tawny fur.

tab•er•na•cle (**tăb′**ər năk′əl) *n.* **1.** Often **Tabernacle. a.** The portable sanctuary in which the Jews carried the Ark of the Covenant during their wanderings through the desert. **b.** The Jewish temple. **2.** Often **Tabernacle.** A case or box on a church altar containing the consecrated host and wine of the Eucharist. **3.a.** A place of worship. **b.** The Mormon temple.

ta•ble (**tā′**bəl) *n.* **1.** A piece of furniture supported by one or more vertical legs and having a flat horizontal surface. **2.** The objects laid out on a table for a meal. **3.** The food and drink served at a meal: *sets a fine table.* **4.** The people assembled at a table, especially for a meal: *The entire table burst into laughter.* **5.** A plateau or tableland. **6.** An orderly presentation of data, especially one in which the data are arranged in columns and rows in an essentially rectangular form. *—tr.v.* **ta•bled, ta•bling, ta•bles.** To postpone consideration of; shelve: *table a piece of legislation.* ***—idiom.*** **under the table.** In secret: *The business deal was under the table.* [First written down before 899 in Old English and spelled *tabule,* from Latin *tabula,* board.]

tab•leau (**tăb′**lō′ *or* tă **blō′**) *n., pl.* **tab•leaux** or **tab•leaus** (**tăb′**lōz′ *or* tă **blōz′**). **1.** A vivid graphic description. **2.** A silent part of a scene when all the performers onstage freeze in position and then resume action as before.

ta•ble•cloth (**tā′**bəl klôth′ *or* **tā′**bəl klŏth′) *n.* A cloth to cover a table, especially during a meal.

ta•ble•land (**tā′**bəl lănd′) *n.* A flat elevated region; a plateau or mesa.

table linen *n.* Tablecloths and napkins.

table salt *n.* **1.** A refined mixture of salts, chiefly sodium chloride, used in cooking and as a seasoning. **2.** Sodium chloride.

ta•ble•spoon (**tā′**bəl spo͞on′) *n.* **1.** A large spoon used for serving food. **2.** A household cooking measure equal to three teaspoons or ½ fluid ounce (about 15 milliliters). See table at **measurement.**

ta•ble•spoon•ful (**tā′**bəl spo͞on fo͝ol′) *n.* The amount that a tablespoon can hold.

tab•let (**tăb′**lĭt) *n.* **1.** A slab or plaque, as of stone, with a surface bearing an inscription. **2.** A thin sheet or leaf used as a writing surface. **3.** A pad of writing paper glued together along one edge. **4.** A small flat pellet of medicine to be taken orally.

table tennis *n.* A game similar to tennis, played an a table with wooden paddles and a small hollow plastic ball.

ta•ble•ware (**tā′**bəl wâr′) *n.* The dishes, glassware, and silverware used in setting a table for a meal.

tab•loid (**tăb′**loid′) *n.* A newspaper of small size presenting the news in condensed form and often having much sensational material.

ta•boo (tə **bo͞o′** *or* tă **bo͞o′**) *n., pl.* **ta•boos. 1.** A ban or an inhibition resulting from social custom or tradition. **2.** A prohibition preventing certain things considered sacred from being used, approached, or mentioned. **3.** A word or an act prohibited for cultural reasons. *—adj.* Excluded or forbidden from use, approach, or mention: *a taboo subject. —tr.v.* **ta•booed, ta•boo•ing, ta•boos.** To place under taboo. [First written down in 1777, from Tongan *tabu,* under prohibition.]

ta•bor (**tā′**bər) *n.* A small drum used by a fife player to accompany the fife.

tab•u•lar (**tăb′**yə lər) *adj.* **1.** Having a plane surface; flat: *a tabular crystal.* **2.** Organized or presented in the form of a table or list: *tabular data.* **3.** Calculated from information given in a mathematical table, as of square roots and sines and cosines.

tab•u•late (**tăb′**yə lāt′) *tr.v.* **tab•u•lat•ed, tab•u•lat•ing, tab•u•lates. 1.** To arrange in tabular form; condense and list. **2.** To cut or form with a plane surface. **—tab′u•la′tion** *n.*

tab•u•la•tor (**tăb′**yə lā′tər) *n.* **1.** A person or thing that tabulates, especially a machine that reads, sorts, and prints out data from punched cards. **2.** A mechanism on a typewriter for setting automatic stops or margins for columns.

ta•chom•e•ter (tə **kŏm′**ĭ tər) *n.* An instrument used to measure the rotations per minute of a rotating shaft. [First written down in 1810 in Modern English, from Greek *takhos,* speed.]

tac•it (**tăs′**ĭt) *adj.* Implied from actions; not spoken or written: *a tacit agreement.*

tac•i•turn (**tăs′**ĭ tûrn′) *adj.* Not inclined to talk much; untalkative.

tack (tăk) *n.* **1.** A short light nail with a sharp point and a flat head. **2.a.** A rope for holding down the lower forward corner of a fore-and-aft sail. **b.** The lower forward corner of a fore-and-aft sail. **3.a.** The direction of a ship in relation to the position of its sails: *the starboard tack.* **b.** In sailing, the act of changing from one position or direction to another. **4.** A course of action or an approach, especially

tabard
Worn by armored knight

ă	**pat**	oi	**boy**
ā	**pay**	ou	**out**
âr	**care**	o͝o	**took**
ä	**father**	o͞o	**boot**
ĕ	**pet**	ŭ	**cut**
ē	**be**	ûr	**urge**
ĭ	**pit**	th	**thin**
ī	**pie**	*th*	**this**
îr	**pier**	hw	**whoop**
ŏ	**pot**	zh	**vision**
ō	**toe**	ə	**about**
ô	**paw**	N	*French* **bon**

taco

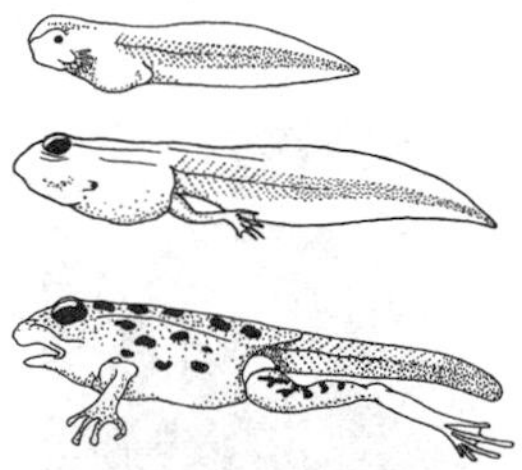

tadpole
Development of a northern leopard frog

Word History: taffeta

The word for the smooth, glossy silk we call **taffeta** first appears in English in 1355 and is spelled *taffata.* Our word comes through French *taffetas* or Italian *taffetà* or Latin *taffata* from Persian *tāftah,* "silk or linen cloth." The Persian noun comes from the Persian verb *tāftan,* "to shine, twist, spin."

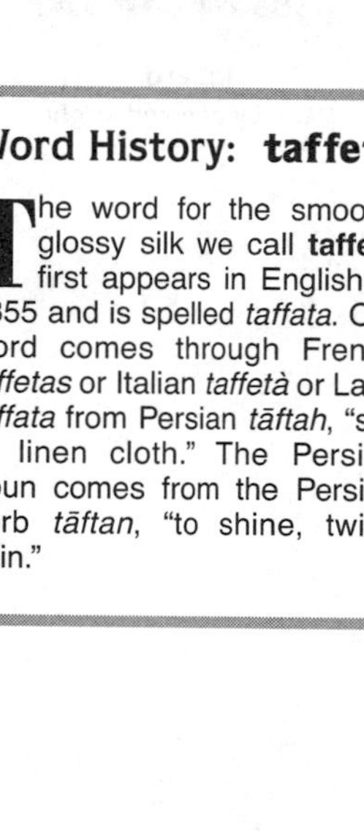

William Howard Taft

when differing from a previous one: *try a new tack.* **5.** A large loose stitch used to hold edges together temporarily or to mark places on a fabric. *—v.* **tacked, tack•ing, tacks.** *—tr.* **1.** To fasten or attach with or as if with a tack. **2.** To sew with a loose temporary stitch: *Tack the facing to the seams.* **3.** To add as an extra item: *tack two dollars onto the bill.* **4.** To change the course of (a boat or ship) by turning into the wind. *—intr.* **1.** To change the direction or course of a boat or ship. **2.** To change one's course of action. [First written down in 1283 in Middle English and spelled *tak*, probably of Germanic origin.]

tack•le (tăk′əl) *n.* **1.** The equipment used in a sport or an occupation, especially in fishing; gear. **2.** (*also* **tā′**kəl). **a.** A system of ropes and pulleys for raising and lowering heavy objects, such as the spars on a ship. **b.** A rope and its pulley. **3.** In football: **a.** Either of the two line players on a team positioned between the guard and the end. **b.** The act of stopping an opposing player carrying the ball by seizing and throwing the player down. *—tr.v.* **tack•led, tack•ling, tack•les. 1.** To take on and wrestle with (an opponent or a problem, for example). **2.** In football, to seize and throw down (an opposing player carrying the ball). **—tack′ler** *n.*

tack•y[1] (tăk′ē) *adj.* **tack•i•er, tack•i•est.** Slightly adhesive or gummy to the touch; sticky: *a tacky surface.* [First written down in 1788 in Modern English, from *tack*, small nail.]

tack•y[2] (tăk′ē) *adj.* **tack•i•er, tack•i•est.** *Informal.* Lacking style or good taste: *tacky clothes.* [First written down in 1862 in American English, from *tackey*, an inferior horse.]

ta•co (tä′kō) *n., pl.* **ta•cos.** A corn tortilla folded around a filling such as ground meat or cheese. [First written down before 1940 in Modern English, from American Spanish *taco*, plug, wad of bank notes.]

Ta•co•ma (tə kō′mə). A city of west-central Washington on an arm of Puget Sound south of Seattle. Population, 176,664.

tac•o•nite (tăk′ə nīt′) *n.* A low-grade iron ore consisting mainly of magnetite, hematite, and quartz.

tact (tăkt) *n.* The ability to speak or act without offending others.

tact•ful (tăkt′fəl) *adj.* Having or showing tact; considerate and discreet: *a tactful person.* **—tact′ful•ly** *adv.* **—tact′ful•ness** *n.*

tac•tic (tăk′tĭk) *n.* A plan or measure for achieving a goal; a maneuver.

tac•ti•cal (tăk′tĭ kəl) *adj.* **1.** Of, relating to, or using tactics: *a tactical maneuver.* **2.** Characterized by ingenuity or skill: *a tactical decision.*

tac•tics (tăk′tĭks) *n.* **1.** *(used with a singular verb).* The military science of deploying and directing troops, ships, and aircraft against an enemy. **2.** *(used with a plural verb).* Maneuvers used against an enemy: *Guerrilla tactics were used during the war.* **3.** *(used with a singular or plural verb).* A set of procedures or methods used to achieve a goal: *The candidate used scare tactics during the campaign.* [First written down in 1626 in Modern English, from Greek *taktikē (tekhnē)*, (science) of arranging.]

tac•tile (tăk′təl *or* tăk′tīl′) *adj.* **1.** Capable of being felt by the sense of touch; tangible. **2.** Used for feeling: *tactile organs such as antennae.*

tact•less (tăkt′lĭs) *adj.* Lacking or showing a lack of tact; inconsiderate or indiscreet. **—tact′less•ly** *adv.* **—tact′less•ness** *n.*

tad (tăd) *n. Informal.* A small amount or degree.

tad•pole (tăd′pōl′) *n.* A frog or toad in its early, newly hatched stage, when it lives in the water and has a tail and gills that disappear as the legs develop and the adult stage is reached. [First written down about 1450 in Middle English and spelled *taddepol* : *tadde, tode,* toad + *pol,* head.]

Ta•dzhik•i•stan (tä jĭk′ĭ stăn′ *or* tä jĭk′ĭ stän′). A region of west-central Asia bordering on Afghanistan and China. It was settled by the tenth century. The region was part of the Soviet Union from 1929 until 1991. Capital, Dushanbe. Population, 4,499,000.

taf•fe•ta (tăf′ĭ tə) *n.* A crisp smooth fabric with a slight sheen, made of a fiber such as silk or rayon and used especially for women's garments. [First written down in 1355 in Middle English and spelled *taffata*, from Persian *tāftah*, silk or linen cloth, from *tāftan*, to twist, spin.] —SEE NOTE.

taf•fy (tăf′ē) *n., pl.* **taf•fies.** A sweet chewy candy of molasses or brown sugar boiled until very thick and then pulled until the candy is glossy and holds it shape.

Taft (tăft), **William Howard.** 1857–1930. The 27th President of the United States (1909–1913). He later served as the chief justice of the U.S. Supreme Court (1921–1930).

tag[1] (tăg) *n.* **1.** A strip, as of paper, metal, or leather, attached to something or worn by someone for the purpose of identifying, classifying, or labeling: *a name tag; a price tag.* **2.** The plastic or metal tip at the end of a shoelace. **3.** A saying or quotation used as ornamentation in speech or writing. *—v.* **tagged, tag•ging, tags.** *—tr.* **1.** To label, recognize, or identify with or as if with a tag: *She tagged the teacher a stickler.* **2.** To put a ticket on (a vehicle) for a traffic or parking violation. *—intr.* To follow after; accompany: *My little sister always wants to tag along.* [First written down before 1400 in Middle English and spelled *tagges*, dangling pieces of cloth on a garment, possibly of Scandinavian origin.]

tag[2] (tăg) *n.* **1.** A children's game in which one player pursues the others until he or she is able to touch one of them, who then in turn becomes the pursuer. **2.** In baseball, the act of putting a base runner out by touching the base runner with the ball. *—tr.v.* **tagged, tag•ging, tags. 1.** To touch (another player) in a game of tag. **2.** In baseball, to touch (a runner or a base) with the ball in order to put the runner out. ***—idiom.*** **tag up.** In baseball, to return to a base before running to the next base after a fielder has caught a fly ball. [First written down in 1738 in Modern English, perhaps variant of Scots *tig*, touch, tap.]

Ta•ga•log (tə gä′lôg) *n., pl.* **Tagalog** or **Ta•ga•logs. 1.** A member of a people native to the Philippines. **2.** The language of this people.

tag sale *n.* A garage sale.

Ta•hi•ti (tə hē′tē). An island of the southern Pacific Ocean in the Society Islands. It was first settled by Polynesians in the 14th century.

Ta•hi•tian (tə hē′shən) *adj.* Of or relating to Tahiti or its people, language, or culture. *—n.* **1.** A native or inhabitant of Tahiti. **2.** The Polynesian language of Tahiti.

tai•ga (tī′gə) *n.* The northernmost forest region of the earth, having a growth of cone-bearing evergreens.

tail (tāl) *n.* **1.** The hindmost part of an animal, especially when extending beyond the main part of the body. **2.** The hindmost, rear, or bottom part: *the tail of a kite.* **3.** The rear end of a vehicle, especially an automobile. **4.** The rear portion of the fuselage of an aircraft. **5.** A braid of hair; a pigtail. **6. tails.** The side of a coin not having the principal design and the date. Often used in the plural: *heads or tails.* **7.** *Informal.* The trail of a person or an animal in flight: *on the criminal's tail.* **8.** *Informal.* A person assigned to follow and report on someone else: *The police put a tail on the suspect.* **9. tails. a.** A formal evening costume typically worn by men. **b.** A swallow-tailed coat. *—tr.v.* **tailed, tail•ing, tails.** *Informal.* To follow and observe: *The detective tailed the suspect.* **—tail′less** *adj.*

❑ *These sound alike:* **tail, tale** (story).

tail•board (tāl′bôrd′) *n.* A tailgate.

tail•coat (tāl′kōt′) *n.* A swallow-tailed coat.

tail end *n.* **1.** The rear or hindmost part. **2.** The very end: *the tail end of the day.*

tail•gate (tāl′gāt′) *n.* A hinged board or panel at the rear of a vehicle, such as a station wagon, that can be lowered for loading and unloading. *—v.* **tail•gat•ed, tail•gat•ing, tail•gates.** *—tr.* To drive too closely behind (another vehicle). *—intr.* To follow another vehicle too closely.

tail•light (tāl′līt′) *n.* A red light or one of a pair mounted on the rear of a vehicle to make it visible in the dark.

tai•lor (tā′lər) *n.* A person who makes, mends, and alters garments such as suits, coats, and dresses. *—v.* **tai•lored, tai•lor•ing, tai•lors.** *—tr.* To make (clothing), especially to specific requirements or measurements. *—intr.* To pursue the trade of a tailor. [First written down in 1287 in Middle English, from Anglo-Norman *taillour*, from Old French *taillier*, to cut.] **—tai′lored** *adj.*

tail•pipe (tāl′pīp′) *n.* The pipe through which exhaust gases from an engine are discharged.

tail•spin (tāl′spĭn′) *n.* The rapid descent of an aircraft in a steep spiral spin.

tail•stock (tāl′stŏk′) *n.* The movable part of a lathe, containing a center that does not rotate.

tail wind *n.* A wind blowing in the same direction as that of the course of a vehicle.

Tai•no (tī′nō) *n., pl.* **Taino** or **Tai•nos. 1.** A member of an Arawak people of the West Indies who became extinct during the 16th century. **2.** The Arawakan language of this people.

taint (tānt) *v.* **taint•ed, taint•ing, taints.** *—tr.* **1.** To affect slightly with something bad or undesirable: *a reputation that was tainted by rumors of unlawful activity.* **2.** To affect with decay or rot; spoil: *The fish was tainted.* **3.** To corrupt morally. *—intr.* To become affected with decay or rot; spoil. *—n.* **1.** A moral defect considered as a stain or spot. **2.** An infecting influence or trace. [First written down in 1591 in Modern English, partly from obsolete *taynt*, to color, dye (from Anglo-Norman *teindre*, from Latin *tingere*) and partly from Middle English *tainten*, to convict (from Old French *attaindre*, to attain, touch upon).]

Tai•pei also **Tai•peh** (tī′pā′ *or* tī′bā′). The capital and largest city of Taiwan, in the northern part of the country. It was founded in the 18th century. Population, 2,327,641.

Tai•wan (tī′wän′). Officially Republic of **Chi•na** (chī′nə). Formerly **For•mo•sa** (fôr mō′sə). A country off the southeast coast of China made up of the island of **Taiwan** and other smaller islands. Taiwan separated from mainland China in 1949. Capital, Taipei. Population, 18,457,923.

take (tāk) *v.* **took** (to͝ok), **tak•en** (tā′kən), **tak•ing, takes.** *—tr.* **1.** To capture physically; seize: *take an enemy fortress.* **2.** To kill, snare, or trap (fish or game, for example). **3.** To acquire in a game or competition; win: *took the crown in horseracing.* **4.** To grasp with the hands; grip: *Take your partner's hand.* **5.** To affect or attack, as an infection: *The child has been taken with the flu.* **6.** To encounter or catch in a particular situation; come upon: *Your actions took me by surprise.* **7.** To charm or captivate: *She was taken by the puppy.* **8.a.** To put (food or drink, for example) into the body; eat or drink: *took a little soup for dinner.* **b.** To draw in; inhale: *took a deep breath.* **9.** To accept and place under one's care or keeping: *I wanted to take the stray kitten.* **10.** To claim for oneself: *take all the credit.* **11.** To pledge one's obedience to; impose upon oneself: *take an oath.* **12.** To subject oneself to: *We took extra time to do the job properly.* **13.** To require or have as a fitting or proper accompaniment: *Intransitive verbs take no direct object. She takes cream in her coffee.* **14.** To pick out; select: *Take any card.* **15.** To use (something) as when in operation: *This camera takes 35mm film.* **16.** To use (something) as a means of transportation: *take a train to Philadelphia.* **17.** To choose and then adopt (a particular route or direction): *Take a right at the next corner.* **18.** To assume occupancy of: *take a seat.* **19.** To require (something) as a basic necessity: *It takes money to live in that town.* **20.** To obtain, as through measurement or a specified procedure: *took the patient's temperature.* **21.** To make an image or representation of, as by photography: *took a picture of us.* **22.** To accept, withstand, or endure (something) reluctantly or willingly: *He does not take criticism well.* **23.** To accept or believe (something) as true: *I'll take your word.* **24.** To follow (advice or a suggestion, for example): *I took your advice and studied for the exam.* **25.** To allow to come in; give access or admission to: *The boat took a lot of water but remained afloat. We can't take more than 100 guests.* **26.** In baseball, to refrain from swinging at (a pitch). **27.** To perceive or feel; experience: *She takes pride in her work.* **28.** To carry, convey, lead, or cause to go along to another place: *Don't forget to take your umbrella.* **29.** To remove from a place: *take the dishes from the sink.* **30.** To subtract: *take 15 from 30.* **31.** To apply oneself to the study of: *take art lessons; take Spanish.* *—intr.* **1.** To acquire possession of something. **2.** To start growing; root or germinate: *Have the seeds taken?* **3.** To have the intended effect; operate or work: *The transfusion apparently took.* **4.** To become: *He took sick.* *—n.* **1.a.** The act or process of taking. **b.** Something that is taken. **2.** A quantity collected at one time, especially the amount of profit or receipts taken by a business: *counted today's take.* **3.a.** A scene filmed or televised without stopping the camera. **b.** A recording made in a single session. ***—idioms.*** **take advantage of. 1.** To put to good use; avail oneself of: *take advantage of the sale.* **2.** To use unfairly and selfishly; exploit: *They took advantage of our friendship just to get a ride to the movies.* **take after.** To resemble in appearance, temperament, or character: *He takes after his grandfather.* **take apart.** To divide into parts; disassemble: *We had to take the chair apart to refinish it.* **take back.** To retract something stated or written: *I took back my promise when I saw I had been cheated.* **take care.** To be careful: *Take care when you cross the street.* **take care of.** To assume responsibility for the maintenance, support, or treatment of: *I'm taking care of the puppy now.* **take charge.** To assume control or command. **take effect.** To become operative, as under law or regulation: *The new rules are to take effect today.* **take for. 1.** To regard as: *Many take him for a genius.* **2.** To consider mistakenly: *The teacher took me for my sister.* **take for granted. 1.** To consider as true, real, or forthcoming; anticipate correctly: *took it for granted that he would pass the test.* **2.** To underestimate the value of. **take hold. 1.** To seize, as by grasping. **2.** To become established: *The new shrubs took hold on the hill.* **take in. 1.** To grant admittance to; receive as a guest or an employee. **2.** To reduce in size; make smaller or shorter: *He had to take in the slacks before he could wear them.* **3.** To understand: *We took in the lecture despite its*

ă	**pat**	oi	**boy**
ā	**pay**	ou	**out**
âr	**care**	o͝o	**took**
ä	**father**	o͞o	**boot**
ĕ	**pet**	ŭ	**cut**
ē	**be**	ûr	**urge**
ĭ	**pit**	th	**thin**
ī	**pie**	*th*	**this**
îr	**pier**	hw	**whoop**
ŏ	**pot**	zh	**vision**
ō	**toe**	ə	**about**
ô	**paw**	N	*French* **bon**

takeoff

Word History: talc

The word **talc** has a long and complicated history. The word first appears in English about 1582 in the spelling *talke*; the spelling *talc* appears in 1601. The English word comes from the French word *talc*, which comes from both the Spanish word *talco* and the Latin word *talcum*. The Spanish and Latin words in turn are derived from the Arabic word *ṭalq*. The Arabic word goes back to the Persian word *talk*, "talc."

talon
Of a bald eagle

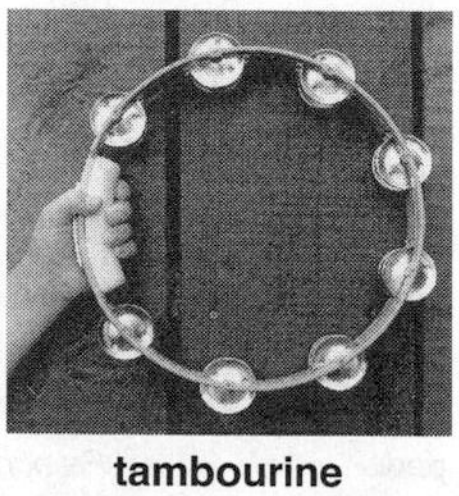

tambourine

complexity. **4.** To look at thoroughly; view: *We took in the scenery.* **take into account.** To take into consideration. **take off. 1.** To remove, as clothing: *took off our coats in the hallway.* **2.** *Slang.* To go off; leave: *She took off early from practice.* **3.** To rise in flight: *A flock of geese took off from the pond.* **take offense.** To become angered, resentful, or displeased: *I took offense at his comment.* **take on. 1.** To undertake or begin to handle: *took on some extra duties while a coworker was out.* **2.** To hire; engage. **3.** To oppose in competition: *offered to take on any opponent.* **take (one's) time.** To act slowly or at one's leisure. **take out. 1.** To extract; remove: *had to have two teeth taken out.* **2.** *Informal.* To escort, as a date. **take over.** To assume the control or management of. **take place.** To happen; occur: *When did the event take place?* **take sides.** To associate with and support a particular faction, group, cause, or person. **take to. 1.** To go to, as for safety: *took to the hills.* **2.** To become fond of or attached to: *The new kitten really took to me.* **take up. 1.** To accept (an option, a bet, or a challenge) as offered. **2.** To develop an interest in or devotion to: *decided to take up stamp collecting.* **take up with.** *Informal.* To begin to associate with; consort with. [First written down about 1100 in Old English and spelled *tacan*, from Old Norse *taka*.] **—tak′er** *n.*

take•off (tāk′ôf′ *or* tāk′ŏf′) *n.* **1.** The act or process of rising in flight. Used of an airplane or a rocket. **2.** *Informal.* An amusing imitation or caricature.

take•out (tāk′out′) *adj.* Intended to be eaten off the premises: *takeout pizza.*

take•o•ver (tāk′ō′vər) *n.* The act or an instance of assuming control or management of something, especially the seizure of power.

talc (tălk) *n.* A fine-grained white, greenish, or gray mineral that is a silicate of magnesium and has a soft soapy texture. It is used in face powder and talcum powder, for coating paper, and as a filler in paints and plastics. [First written down in 1582 in Modern English and spelled *talke*, ultimately from Arabic *ṭalq*, from Persian *talk*.] —SEE NOTE.

tal•cum powder (tăl′kəm) *n.* A fine, often perfumed powder made from purified talc for use on the skin.

tale (tāl) *n.* **1.** Something told or related; a recital of events or happenings: *told us a tale of suspense.* **2.** A narrative of real or imaginary events; a story. **3.** A falsehood; a lie: *Don't tell tales.* [First written down about 950 in Old English and spelled *talu*.]
❑ *These sound alike:* **tale, tail** (hindmost part).

tal•ent (tăl′ənt) *n.* **1.a.** A marked natural ability, as for artistic accomplishment. **b.** A person or group of people with such ability: *a great literary talent.* **2.** An ancient coin or weight in the Middle East, Greece, and Rome. [First written down before 1300 in Middle English and spelled *talent*, inclination, disposition, from Greek *talanton*, sum of money.] **—tal′ent•ed** *adj.*

ta•li (tā′lī′) *n.* Plural of **talus**[1].

tal•is•man (tăl′ĭs mən) *n., pl.* **tal•is•mans.** An object marked with magic signs and believed to give supernatural powers or protection to its bearer.

talk (tôk) *v.* **talked, talk•ing, talks.** *—tr.* **1.** To utter or pronounce (words): *The two-year-old is talking sentences now.* **2.** To speak of or discuss (something) or give expression to in words: *talk music; talk treason.* **3.** To speak or know how to speak in (an idiom or a language): *talked French with the flight crew.* **4.** To gain, influence, or bring into a specified state by talking: *talked me into coming.* **5.** To spend (a period of time) by or as if by talking: *talked the evening away.* *—intr.* **1.** To converse by means of spoken language: *We talked for hours.* **2.** To utter or pronounce words: *The baby can talk.* **3.** To imitate the sounds of human speech: *The parrot talks.* **4.** To express one's thoughts or emotions by means of a spoken language: *talked about the issue.* See Synonyms at **speak. 5.** To convey one's thoughts in a way other than by spoken words: *talk with one's hands.* **6.** To express one's thoughts in writing: *The author of this book talks about geology.* **7.** To spread rumors; gossip: *If you do that, people will talk.* **8.** To consult or confer with someone: *I talked with the doctor.* **9.** To reveal information concerning oneself or others, especially under pressure: *Has the prisoner talked?* *—n.* **1.** An exchange of ideas or opinions; a conversation. **2.** A speech or lecture. **3.** Hearsay, rumor, or speculation. **4.** A subject of conversation: *a musical that is the talk of the town.* **5.** Empty speech or unnecessary discussion: *all talk and no action.* **6.** A particular manner of speech: *baby talk.* ***—idioms.*** **talk back.** To make a rude reply: *You'll be sorry if you talk back.* **talk down.** To address someone in a condescending manner: *The speaker talked down to the young audience.* **talk over.** To consider thoroughly in conversation; discuss: *We talked over the problem and decided what to do.* **talk sense.** To speak rationally and coherently. [First written down before 1200 in Middle English and spelled *talken*.]

talk•a•tive (tô′kə tĭv) *adj.* Tending to talk a great deal. **—talk′a•tive•ly** *adv.* **—talk′a•tive•ness** *n.*

talk•er (tô′kər) *n.* A person who talks, especially a talkative person.

talk•ing-to (tô′kĭng to͞o′) *n., pl.* **talk•ing-tos.** *Informal.* A scolding.

tall (tôl) *adj.* **tall•er, tall•est. 1.** Having greater than ordinary height: *a tall tree.* **2.** Having a specified height: *a plant three feet tall.* **3.** *Informal.* Imaginary; fanciful or boastful: *a tall tale.* **4.** Impressively great or difficult: *a tall order to fill.* *—adv.* **taller, tallest.** With proud bearing; straight: *stand tall.* [First written down before 1325 in Middle English, brave, large, from Old English *getæl*, swift.] **—tall′ness** *n.*

Tal•la•has•see (tăl′ə hăs′ē). The capital of Florida, in the northwest part of the state west of Jacksonville. It was originally a Native American village. Population, 124,773.

Tal•linn (tăl′ĭn *or* tä′lĭn). The capital of Estonia, in the northwest part of the country on an arm of the Baltic Sea opposite Helsinki, Finland. Population, 464,000.

tal•lith (tä′lĭs *or* tä lēt′) *n., pl.* **tal•lith•im** (tä lē′sĭm *or* tä′lē tēm′) or **tal•liths.** A ritually fringed shawl worn by Jews, especially at morning prayer.

tal•low (tăl′ō) *n.* A mixture of fats obtained from animals, such as cattle, sheep, or horses, and used to make candles, soaps, and lubricants. [First written down before 1307 in Middle English and spelled *talough*.]

tal•ly (tăl′ē) *n., pl.* **tal•lies. 1.** A reckoning or score. **2.** A stick on which notches are made to keep a count or score. *—v.* **tal•lied, tal•ly•ing, tal•lies.** *—tr.* **1.** To reckon or record: *tallied up our bill.* **2.** To cause to correspond or agree. *—intr.* To be alike; correspond or agree: *The two accounts tallied in every detail.*

tal•ly•ho (tăl′ē hō′) *interj.* An expression used to urge hounds on during fox hunting.

Tal•mud (täl′mo͝od *or* tăl′məd) *n.* The collection of ancient Rabbinic writings that constitutes the basis of religious authority in Orthodox Judaism.

tal•on (tăl′ən) *n.* **1.** The claw of a bird or an animal that seizes other animals as prey. **2.** Something similar to or suggesting an animal's claw.

ta•lus[1] (tā′ləs) *n., pl.* **ta•li** (tā′lī′). **1.** The bone that forms a joint with the tibia and fibula, making up the main bone of the ankle. **2.** The ankle. [First written down in 1693 in Modern English, from Latin *tālus*, ankle.]

ta•lus² (tā′ləs) *n., pl.* **ta•lus•es.** A sloping mass of rock debris at the base of a cliff. [First written down in 1645 in Modern English, from Latin *talūtium*, gold-bearing outcrop.]

tam (tăm) *n.* A tam-o'-shanter.

ta•ma•le (tə mä′lē) *n.* A highly seasoned Mexican dish made of fried chopped meat and crushed peppers or other foods rolled in cornmeal dough, wrapped in corn husks, and steamed.

tam•a•rack (tăm′ə răk′) *n.* A North American larch tree.

tam•a•rind (tăm′ə rĭnd′) *n.* **1.** The pulpy seed pod of a tropical tree, having a pleasant sharp taste and used as food and flavoring. **2.** The tree that bears such pods. [First written down about 1425 in Middle English, from Arabic *tamr hindī* : *tamr*, date + *hindī*, of India.]

tam•a•risk (tăm′ə rĭsk′) *n.* Any of numerous shrubs or trees of warm regions, having small leaves and clusters of pink flowers.

tam•bour (tăm′bo͝or′ *or* tăm **bo͝or′**) *n.* **1.** A drum or drummer. **2.** A small wooden embroidery frame consisting of two hoops that fit one inside the other and between which fabric is stretched.

tam•bou•rine (tăm′bə **rēn′**) *n.* A percussion instrument consisting of a small drumhead with small metal disks fitted into the rim that jingle when the instrument is struck or shaken.

tame (tām) *adj.* **tam•er, tam•est. 1.** Brought from wildness into a domesticated state. **2.** Naturally unafraid; not timid: *The dodo was very tame and soon became extinct.* **3.** Submissive; docile. **4.** Unexciting or uninteresting; dull: *The ride home seemed very tame after watching the car race.* —*tr. v.* **tamed, tam•ing, tames. 1.** To make tame; domesticate: *tame a wild horse.* **2.** To subdue or curb: *The pioneers tamed the wilderness.* —**tame′ly** *adv.* —**tame′ness** *n.* —**tam′er** *n.*

Tam•il (tăm′əl *or* tŭm′əl *or* tä′məl) *n., pl.* **Tamil** or **Tam•ils. 1.** A member of a people of southern India and northern Sri Lanka. **2.** The language of the Tamil.

tam-o'-shan•ter (tăm′ə shăn′tər) *n.* A tight-fitting Scottish cap, sometimes having a pompon, feather, or tassle in the center. [First written down about 1840 in Modern English, after the hero of *"Tam o' Shanter,"* a poem by Robert Burns.]

tamp (tămp) *tr.v.* **tamped, tamp•ing, tamps. 1.** To pack down tightly: *tamp the gravel.* **2.** To pack clay, sand, or dirt into (a hole) above an explosive.

Tam•pa (tăm′pə). A city of west-central Florida on **Tampa Bay,** an inlet of the Gulf of Mexico. It was first visited by the Spanish in 1528. Population, 280,015.

tam•per (tăm′pər) *intr.v.* **tam•pered, tam•per•ing, tam•pers. 1.** To interfere in a harmful manner: *caught tampering with the switches.* **2.** To engage in secret or improper dealings, as in an effort to influence: *tamper with the jury.* —**tam′per•er** *n.*

tam•pon (tăm′pŏn′) *n.* A plug of absorbent material inserted into a wound or body cavity to stop a flow of blood or absorb secretions

tam-tam (tŭm′tŭm′ *or* tăm′tăm′) *n.* Variant of **tom-tom.**

tan¹ (tăn) *v.* **tanned, tan•ning, tans.** —*tr.* **1.** To convert (animal hides) into leather, as by treating with tannin. **2.** To make brown by exposure to the sun. —*intr.* To become brown or tawny from exposure to the sun. —*n.* **1.** A light or moderate yellowish brown to brownish orange. **2.** The brown color that sun rays impart to the skin. **3.** Tannin or a solution made from it. —*adj.* **tan•ner, tan•nest. 1.** Light or moderate yellowish brown to brownish orange. **2.** Having a suntan. [First written down about 1000 in Old English and spelled *getannede*, tanned, from Medieval Latin *tannum*, tanbark.]

tan² *abbr.* An abbreviation of tangent.

tan•a•ger (tăn′ĭ jər) *n.* Any of various small American birds that are often brightly colored in the male.

Ta•nakh (tä **näKH′**) *n.* The Hebrew Scriptures.

tan•bark (tăn′bärk′) *n.* The bark of certain oaks and other trees, used as a source of tannin for tanning leather, and then shredded and used as a ground covering for circus rings and racetracks.

tan•dem (tăn′dəm) *n.* **1.** A two-wheeled carriage drawn by horses harnessed one before the other. **2.** A team of carriage horses harnessed in single file. **3.** A tandem bicycle. **4.** An arrangement of two or more people or things placed on behind the other. —*adv.* One behind the other: *riding tandem.* [First written down in 1785 in Modern English, from Latin *tandem*, at last, at length.]

tandem bicycle *n.* A bicycle built for two or more people sitting one behind the other.

tang (tăng) *n.* **1.** A sharp distinctive flavor, taste, or odor, as that of orange juice. **2.** A trace or hint of something. **3.** A sharp point, tongue, or prong. **4.** A projection by which a tool such as a file, chisel, or knife is attached to its handle.

tan•ge•lo (tăn′jə lō′) *n., pl.* **tan•ge•los. 1.** A citrus fruit that is a cross between a grapefruit and a tangerine. **2.** The tree that bears such fruit.

tan•gent (tăn′jənt) *adj.* Making contact at a point or along a line; touching but not intersecting. —*n.* **1.** A line, curve, or surface touching but not intersecting another. **2.** A function of an acute angle in a right triangle, equal to the length of the side opposite the angle divided by the length of the side adjacent to the angle. **3.** A sudden digression or change of course: *go off on a different tangent.* [First written down in 1594 in Modern English, from Latin *(līnea) tangēns*, touching (line), from *tangere*, to touch.]

tan•gen•tial (tăn **jĕn′**shəl) *adj.* **1.** Of, relating to, or moving along in the direction of a tangent. **2.** Only superficially relevant to the matter at hand. —**tan•gen′tial•ly** *adv.*

tan•ger•ine (tăn′jə **rēn′** *or* tăn′jə rēn′) *n.* **1.** A fruit related to the orange but somewhat smaller, having deep orange skin that peels easily. **2.** The tree that bears such fruit. **3.** A strong reddish orange to strong or vivid orange.

tan•gi•ble (tăn′jə bəl) *adj.* **1.** Capable of being touched: *a tangible product like steel.* **2.** Capable of being treated as fact; real or concrete: *tangible evidence.* **3.** Capable of being understood or realized: *a tangible benefit.* —*n.* **1.** Something palpable or concrete. **2. tangibles.** Material assets. —**tan′gi•bly** *adv.*

Tan•gier (tăn **jîr′**) also **Tan•giers** (tăn **jîrz′**). A city of northern Morocco at the west end of the Strait of Gibraltar. It was founded in Roman times. Population, 266,346.

tan•gle (tăng′gəl) *v.* **tan•gled, tan•gling, tan•gles.** —*tr.* **1.** To mix together or intertwine in a confused mass; snarl: *A bad cast tangled my fishing line.* **2.** To catch or hold in or as if in a net; entrap. —*intr.* **1.** To be or become entangled. **2.** *Informal.* To enter into an argument, dispute, or conflict: *We tangled over the wording of our editorial.* —*n.* **1.** A confused snarled mass: *a tangle of vines.* **2.** A confused state or condition. **3.** *Informal.* An argument: *They got into a tangle over who should go first.*

tan•go (tăng′gō) *n., pl.* **tan•gos. 1.** A Latin American ballroom dance in 2/4 or 4/4 time. **2.** The music for this dance. —*intr.v.* **tan•goed, tan•go•ing, tan•gos.** To perform this dance.

tandem bicycle

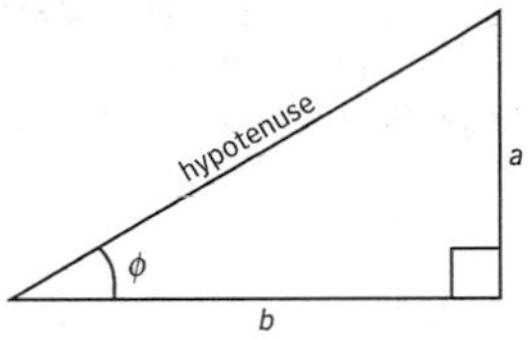

tangent

tangent $\phi = \frac{a}{b}$

tangerine

ă	pat	oi	boy
ā	pay	ou	out
âr	care	o͝o	took
ä	father	o͞o	boot
ĕ	pet	ŭ	cut
ē	be	ûr	urge
ĭ	pit	th	thin
ī	pie	*th*	this
îr	pier	hw	whoop
ŏ	pot	zh	vision
ō	toe	ə	about
ô	paw	N	*French* bon

tap dance
Ginger Rogers and Fred Astaire in the 1930's

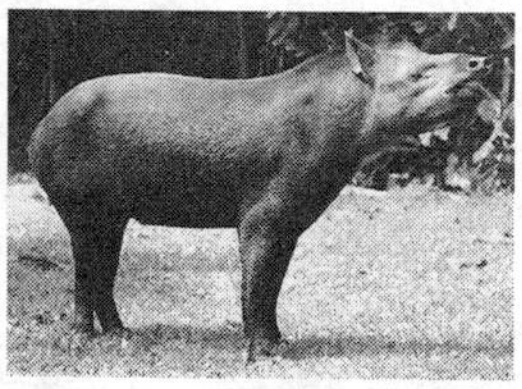

tapir
South American tapir

tang•y (tăng′ē) *adj.* Having a sharp distinctive flavor, taste, or odor: *a tangy cheese.*

tank (tăngk) *n.* **1.a.** A large, often metallic container for holding or storing fluids or gases: *a gasoline tank.* **b.** The amount that such a container can hold: *Buy a tank of gas.* **2.** A usually artificial pool, pond, or reservoir, especially one used to hold water for drinking or irrigation. **3.** An enclosed, heavily armored combat vehicle mounted with a cannon and guns and moving on treads.

tank•ard (tăng′kərd) *n.* A large drinking cup having a single handle and often a hinged cover.

tank•er (tăng′kər) *n.* A ship, truck, or plane equipped to transport liquids, such as oil, in bulk.

tank top *n.* A sleeveless, tight-fitting, usually knit shirt with wide shoulder straps.

tan•ner (tăn′ər) *n.* A person who tans hides.

tan•ner•y (tăn′ə rē) *n., pl.* **tan•ner•ies.** A place where hides are tanned.

tan•nic (tăn′ĭk) *adj.* Of, relating to, or derived from tannin.

tannic acid *n.* A yellowish to light-brown substance obtained from the fruit and bark of certain plants and used in tanning hides, in dyeing and winemaking, and as a medicine.

tan•nin (tăn′ĭn) *n.* **1.** Tannic acid. **2.** Any of various other chemicals or mixtures used in tanning hides, making ink, and in medicine.

tan•ning (tăn′ĭng) *n.* **1.** The art or process of making leather from animal hides. **2.** Browning of the skin from exposure to sun and weather.

Ta•no•an (tä′nō ən) *n.* A family of Native American languages of New Mexico and northeast Arizona.

tan•sy (tăn′zē) *n., pl.* **tan•sies.** Any of several strong-smelling plants having feathery leaves and broad clusters of yellow flowers.

tan•ta•lite (tăn′tə līt′) *n.* A black to red-brown mineral that contains tantalum and some niobium and is used as an ore for both.

tan•ta•lize (tăn′tə līz′) *tr.v.* **tan•ta•lized, tan•ta•liz•ing, tan•ta•liz•es.** To excite (another) by presenting something desirable while keeping it out of reach. **—tan′ta•liz′er** *n.*

tan•ta•lum (tăn′tə ləm) *n. Symbol* **Ta** A hard, heavy gray metallic element that is very resistant to corrosion at temperatures below 150°C. It is used as an alloy in nuclear reactors and in surgical and dental equipment. Atomic number 73. See table at **element.**

tan•ta•mount (tăn′tə mount′) *adj.* Equivalent in effect or value: *a rule tantamount to a dictatorship.*

tan•trum (tăn′trəm) *n.* A fit of bad temper.

Tan•za•ni•a (tăn′zə nē′ə). A country of east-central Africa on the Indian Ocean south of Kenya. It has been inhabited since prehistoric times. Dar es Salaam is the de facto capital and the largest city, and Dodoma is the official capital. Population, 17,557,000.

Tao•ism (tou′ĭz′əm *or* dou′ĭz′əm) *n.* A principal philosophy and system of religion of China that emphasizes living simply and in harmony with nature and is based on the teachings of Lao-tzu, a sixth century B.C. philosopher.

tap[1] (tăp) *v.* **tapped, tap•ping, taps.** *—tr.* **1.** To strike gently with a light blow or blows: *tap him on the shoulder.* **2.** To give a light rap with: *tap a pencil on the desk.* **3.** To produce with a succession of light blows: *tap out a rhythm.* **4.** To repair or reinforce (shoe heels or toes) by putting on a tap or taps. *—intr.* **1.** To deliver a gentle light blow or blows. **2.** To walk making light clicks. *—n.* **1.a.** A gentle blow. **b.** The sound made by such a blow. **2.a.** A layer of leather or other material used to repair and reinforce the worn heel or toe of a shoe. **b.** A metal plate attached to the toe or heel of a shoe, as for tap-dancing. [First written down before 1200 in Middle English and spelled *tepen*, possibly from Old French *taper*.]

tap[2] (tăp) *n.* **1.a.** A valve and spout used to regulate the flow of a fluid at the end of a pipe. **b.** A plug for a hole in a cask from which a liquid is drained or poured out. **2.** A tool for cutting a screw thread into the inner wall of a drilled hole. **3.** A point at which a connection is made in an electric circuit to add another element in parallel with an existing load. *—tr.v.* **tapped, tap•ping, taps. 1.** To furnish with a spigot or tap. **2.** To pierce in order to draw off liquid: *tap a maple tree.* **3.** To draw (liquid) from a vessel or container: *tap a barrel.* **4.** To make a connection with, as to divert part of a flow: *tap an electric circuit.* **5.** To wiretap (a telephone). ***—idiom.*** **on tap.** Ready to be drawn; in a tapped cask. [First written down about 1050 in Old English and spelled *tæpa.*]

ta•pa (tä′pə *or* tăp′ə) *n.* **1.** The fibrous inner bark of a kind of mulberry tree. **2.** A cloth made in the islands of the Pacific Ocean by pounding this bark.

tap dance *n.* A dance in which the rhythm is sounded out by the clicking taps on the heels and toes of a dancer's shoes. **—tap dancer** *n.*

tap-dance (tăp′dăns′) *intr.v.* **tap-danced, tap-danc•ing, tap-danc•es.** To perform a tap dance.

tape (tāp) *n.* **1.** A narrow strip of strong woven fabric, as that used in sewing. **2.** A continuous narrow, flexible strip of cloth, metal, paper, or plastic, as adhesive tape, magnetic tape, or ticker tape. **3.** A string or strip stretched across the finish line of a race to be broken by the winner. **4.** A tape recording. *—tr.v.* **taped, tap•ing, tapes. 1.** To fasten, wrap, or bind with tape: *tape a bow on a package; tape a sprained wrist.* **2.** To measure with a tape measure. **3.** To record (sounds or pictures) on magnetic tape. [First written down about 1000 in Old English and spelled *tæppe.*]

tape deck *n.* A tape recorder and player having no built-in amplifiers or speakers, used as a component in an audio system.

tape measure *n.* A tape of cloth, paper, or metal marked off in a scale, as of inches or centimeters, used for taking measurements.

tape player *n.* A machine for playing back recorded magnetic tapes, having a built-in amplifier and speakers.

ta•per (tā′pər) *n.* **1.** A small or slender candle. **2.** A gradual decrease in thickness or width of an elongated object: *the taper of a cone. —v.* **ta•pered, ta•per•ing, ta•pers.** *—intr.* **1.** To become gradually thinner toward one end: *a candle tapering to a point.* **2.** To diminish or lessen gradually: *The storm tapered off. —tr.* **1.** To make thinner or narrower at one end: *tapered the board to fit the slot.* **2.** To make smaller gradually.
❑ *These sound alike:* **taper, tapir** (animal).

tape-re•cord (tāp′rĭ kôrd′) *tr.v.* **tape-re•cord•ed, tape-re•cord•ing, tape-re•cords.** To record on magnetic tape.

tape recorder *n.* A mechanical device for recording on magnetic tape and usually for playing back the recorded material.

tape recording *n.* **1.** A magnetic tape on which sound or visual images have been recorded. **2.** The act of recording on magnetic tape.

tap•es•try (tăp′ĭ strē) *n., pl.* **tap•es•tries.** A heavy cloth woven with rich, often many-colored designs and scenes, usually hung on walls for decoration and sometimes used to cover furniture.

tape•worm (tāp′wûrm′) *n.* Any of various long flatworms that live as parasites in the intestines of human beings and other animals.

tap•i•o•ca (tăp′ē ō′kə) *n.* A starch obtained from the root of the cassava, used in puddings and sometimes to thicken foods such as soups.

ta•pir (tā′pər *or* tə pîr′) *n.* Any of several tropical American or Asian mammals having a heavy body, short legs, and a long fleshy snout.
❑ *These sound alike:* **tapir, taper** (candle).

tap•root (tăp′ro͞ot′ *or* tăp′ro͝ot′) *n.* The main, often thick root of a plant, growing straight downward from the stem.

taps (tăps) *pl.n.* *(used with a singular or plural verb).* A bugle call or drum signal sounded at night, as at a military camp, as an order to put out lights, or at funerals and memorial services.

tar¹ (tär) *n.* **1.** A thick oily dark mixture consisting mainly of hydrocarbons, made by destructive distillation of wood, coal, peat, or other organic materials. **2.** Coal tar. —*tr.v.* **tarred, tar•ring, tars.** To coat with or as if with tar. [First written down before 700 in Old English and spelled *teru.*]

tar² (tär) *n.* *Informal.* A sailor. [First written down in 1676 in Modern English, possibly short for *tarpaulin.*]

tar•an•tel•la (tăr′ən tĕl′ə) *n.* **1.** A lively whirling dance of southern Italy. **2.** The music for this dance. [First written down in 1782 in Modern English, from Italian, after *Taranto*, Italy.]

ta•ran•tu•la (tə răn′chə lə) *n., pl.* **ta•ran•tu•las** or **tarantu•lae** (tə răn′chə lē′). Any of various large, hairy, mostly tropical spiders that have a painful but not seriously poisonous bite. [First written down in 1561 in Modern English, from Medieval Latin, from Old Italian *tarantola*, after *Taranto*, Italy.]

tar•dy (tär′dē) *adj.* **tar•di•er, tar•di•est. 1.** Occurring, arriving, acting, or done later than expected; delayed: *a tardy guest.* **2.** Moving slowly; sluggish: *tardy acceptance of new ideas.* **—tar′di•ly** *adv.* **—tar′di•ness** *n.*

tare¹ (târ) *n.* Any of several troublesome weeds that grow in grain fields. [First written down before 1300 in Middle English.]
❑ *These sound alike:* **tare¹** (weed), **tare²** (weight), **tear¹** (rend).

tare² (târ) *n.* The weight of a container or wrapper that is subtracted from the gross weight to obtain the net weight. [First written down in 1429 in Middle English, from Old French, ultimately from Arabic *ṭarḥah*, that which is thrown away.]
❑ *These sound alike:* **tare²** (weight), **tare¹** (weed), **tear¹** (rend).

tar•get (tär′gĭt) *n.* **1.** An object that is shot at to test accuracy in rifle or archery practice. **2.** Something aimed or fired at: *The target of the snowball was a trash can.* **3.** An object of criticism or attack: *the target of her satire.* **4.** A desired goal or aim: *the target of the research program.*

tar•iff (tăr′ĭf) *n.* **1.** A list or system of duties imposed by a government on imported or exported goods. **2.** A duty or duties imposed by a government on imported or exported goods: *a tariff on wool.* **3.** A schedule of prices or fees.

tar•nish (tär′nĭsh) *v.* **tar•nished, tar•nish•ing, tar•nish•es.** —*tr.* **1.** To dull the luster of; discolor: *Being in the ground for so long had tarnished the old coins.* **2.** To detract from or stain; disgrace: *The scandal tarnished his reputation.* —*intr.* **1.** To lose luster; become discolored: *The silver cup tarnished as it sat on the shelf.* **2.** To diminish or become tainted. —*n.* **1.** The condition of being tarnished. **2.** Discoloration of a metal surface, as from oxidation.

ta•ro (tär′ō *or* tăr′ō) *n., pl.* **ta•ros. 1.** A tropical plant having broad leaves and a large starchy root used as food. **2.** The root of this plant, similar to a potato.

tarp (tärp) *n.* *Informal.* A tarpaulin.

tar•pa•per (tär′pā′pər) *n.* Heavy paper coated or saturated with tar, used as a waterproof protective material in building.

tar•pau•lin (tär pô′lĭn *or* tär′pə lĭn) *n.* **1.** Material, such as waterproof canvas, used to cover and protect things from moisture. **2.** A sheet of this material: *put a tarpaulin over the boat.*

tar•pon (tär′pən) *n., pl.* **tarpon** or **tar•pons.** Any of several large silvery fishes of the Caribbean Sea and Atlantic coastal waters, often caught for sport.

tar•ra•gon (tăr′ə gŏn′) *n.* The mildly spicy pleasant-smelling leaves of a plant native to Europe and Asia, used to flavor salads and cooked foods.

tar•ry¹ (tăr′ē) *intr.v.* **tar•ried, tar•ry•ing, tar•ries. 1.** To delay or be late in coming, going, or doing: *tarry on the way to school.* **2.** To remain or stay temporarily, as in a place. [First written down before 1325 in Middle English and spelled *tarien.*]

tar•ry² (tär′ē) *adj.* **tar•ri•er, tar•ri•est.** Of, resembling, or covered with tar: *a tarry substance.* [First written down in 1552 in Modern English, from *tar.*]

tar•sal (tär′səl) *adj.* Of, relating to, or near the ankle.

tar•si (tär′sī) *n.* Plural of **tarsus.**

tar•si•er (tär′sē ər *or* tär′sē ā′) *n.* Any of several small mammals of the East Indies that are similar to monkeys, having large eyes, long fingers and toes, and a long tail.

tar•sus (tär′səs) *n., pl.* **tar•si** (tär′sī). **1.** The section of the vertebrate foot located between the leg and the metatarsus; the ankle. **2.** The seven bones making up this section.

tart¹ (tärt) *adj.* **tart•er, tart•est. 1.** Having a sharp pungent taste; sour: *tart cranberries.* **2.** Sharp or bitter in tone or meaning; biting: *a tart answer.* [First written down about 1000 in Old English and spelled *teart*, sharp, severe.] **—tart′ly** *adv.* **—tart′ness** *n.*

tart² (tärt) *n.* A small pie having a sweet filling and no crust on top. [First written down before 1370 in Middle English, perhaps from Late Latin *torta*, a kind of bread.]

tar•tan (tär′tn) *n.* **1.** Any of a number of fabric patterns consisting of stripes in different colors and widths crossed at right angles against a solid background, each forming a distinctive design worn by the members of a Scottish clan. **2.** A twilled wool fabric or garment having such a pattern. **3.** A plaid fabric.

tar•tar (tär′tər) *n.* **1.** A hard yellowish deposit that collects on the teeth, consisting of food particles and secretions held together by insoluble salts such as calcium carbonate. **2.** A reddish acid substance, chiefly a potassium salt of tartaric acid, found in the juice of grapes and deposited on the sides of casks during winemaking.

Tar•tar (tär′tər) *n.* A member of any of the Turkic and Mongolian peoples of central Asia who invaded western Asia and eastern Europe in the Middle Ages. **—Tar′tar** *adj.*

tar•tar•ic acid (tär tăr′ĭk) *n.* Any of four organic acids having the composition $C_4H_6O_6$ and used in tanning, to make cream of tartar, and in various foods, beverages, and chemicals.

tartar sauce *n.* Mayonnaise mixed with chopped onion, olives, pickles, and capers and served as a sauce with fish.

Tar•ta•rus (tär′tər əs) *n.* In Greek mythology, the regions below Hades where the gods confine the Titans.

Tash•kent (tăsh kĕnt′ *or* täsh kĕnt′). The capital of Uzbekistan, in the eastern part of the republic north of Dushanbe, Tadzhikistan. It is one of the oldest

target
Archery target

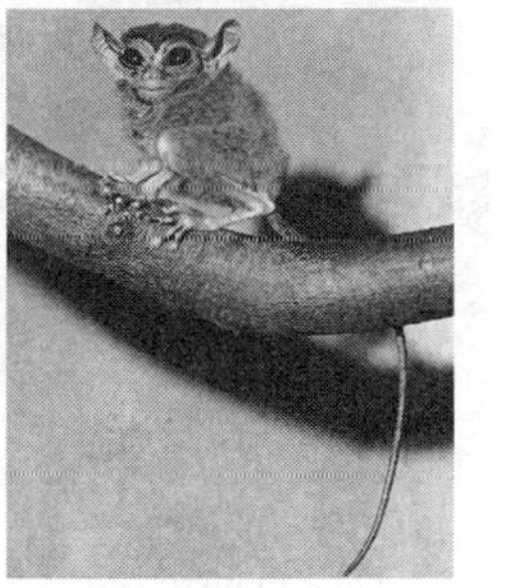

tarsier

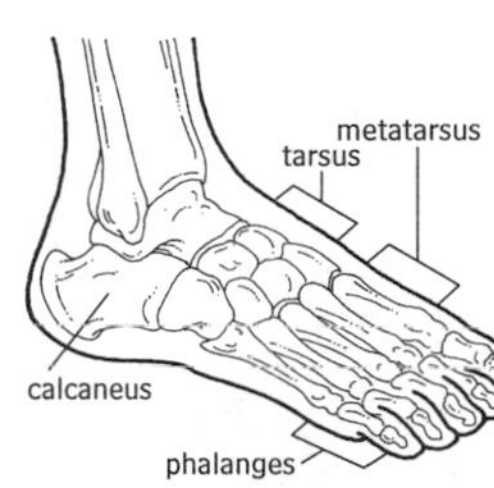

tarsus

ă	pat	oi	boy
ā	pay	ou	out
âr	care	o͝o	took
ä	father	o͞o	boot
ĕ	pet	ŭ	cut
ē	be	ûr	urge
ĭ	pit	th	thin
ī	pie	*th*	this
îr	pier	hw	whoop
ŏ	pot	zh	vision
ō	toe	ə	about
ô	paw	N	*French* bon

cities of central Asia. Population, 2,030,000.

task (tăsk) *n.* **1.** A piece of work assigned or done as part of one's duties. **2.** A difficult or tedious undertaking: *the task of building a nation.* —*tr.v.* **tasked, task•ing, tasks. 1.** To assign a task to or impose a task on: *She tasked us with cleaning out the attic.* **2.** To burden with too many tasks.

Synonyms: task, job, chore, assignment. These nouns mean a piece of work that one must do. **Task** means a well-defined responsibility that is sometimes burdensome and is usually required by someone else: *The receptionist's main task is to answer the telephones.* **Job** often means a specific short-term piece of work: *We spent the day doing odd jobs around the house.* **Chore** often means a minor, routine, or odd job: *I have to finish my chores before I'm allowed to go out.* **Assignment** usually means a task given to one by a person in authority: *For tonight's assignment, read the first chapter.*

task force *n.* A temporary grouping of forces and resources for a specific goal: *a military task force.*

task•mas•ter (**tăsk′**măs′tər) *n.* A person who assigns tasks, especially difficult or burdensome ones.

Tas•ma•ni•a (tăz **mā′**nē ə *or* tăz **mān′**yə). An island of Australia in the Indian Ocean south of Melbourne. It joined Australia in 1901.

tassel
On a mortarboard

tas•sel (**tăs′**əl) *n.* **1.** A bunch of loose threads or cords bound at one end and hanging free at the other, used as an ornament on curtains and clothing, for example. **2.** Something resembling such an ornament, especially the pollen-bearing flower cluster of a corn plant. —*tr.v.* **tas•seled, tas•sel•ing, tas•sels** or **tas•selled, tas•sel•ling, tas•sels.** To decorate or fringe with tassels.

taste (tāst) *v.* **tast•ed, tast•ing, tastes.** —*tr.* **1.** To distinguish the flavor of (something) by taking it into the mouth. **2.** To eat or drink a small quantity of: *I've already eaten, so I'll just taste the salmon.* **3.** To partake of, especially for the first time; experience: *tasted freedom and loved it.* —*intr.* **1.** To distinguish flavors in the mouth. **2.** To have a distinct flavor: *The stew tastes salty.* **3.** To eat or drink a small amount. —*n.* **1.** The sense that distinguishes the sweet, sour, salty, and bitter qualities of substances in contact with the taste buds. **2.** A sensation produced by this sense; a flavor. **3.** A distinctive perception as if by the sense of taste: *an experience that left a bad taste in my mouth.* **4.** A small quantity eaten or tasted: *Have a taste of this.* **5.** A limited or first experience; a sample. **6.** A personal preference or liking: *a taste for mysteries.* **7.** The ability to recognize and appreciate what is beautiful, excellent, or appropriate: *good taste in clothes.* **8.** The sense of what is proper, seemly, or least likely to offend in a given social situation: *a remark made in bad taste.* [First written down before 1300 in Middle English and spelled *tasten,* to touch, taste, from Old French *taster.*]

taste bud *n.* Any of numerous rounded structures on the surface of the tongue that contain cells producing nerve impulses corresponding to sweet, sour, salty, or bitter stimuli.

taste•ful (**tāst′**fəl) *adj.* Having, showing, or being in keeping with good taste: *a tasteful reply.* **—taste′ful•ly** *adv.* **—taste′ful•ness** *n.*

taste•less (**tāst′**lĭs) *adj.* **1.** Lacking in flavor: *a tasteless dish.* **2.** Having or showing poor taste: *a tasteless remark.* **—taste′less•ly** *adv.* **—taste′less•ness** *n.*

tast•y (**tā′**stē) *adj.* **tast•i•er, tast•i•est.** Having a pleasing flavor: *a tasty meal.* **—tast′i•ly** *adv.* **—tast′i•ness** *n.*

tat (tăt) *intr. & tr.v.* **tat•ted, tat•ting, tats.** To do tatting or to produce (something) by tatting.

Ta•tar (**tä′**tər) *n.* **1.** A member of a group of Turkic peoples living in southeast Europe and west-central Asia. **2.** Any of the Turkic languages of the Tatars.

tat•ter (**tăt′**ər) *n.* **1.** A torn and hanging piece of cloth; a shred. **2. tatters.** Torn and ragged clothing; rags. —*tr. & intr.v.* **tat•tered, tat•ter•ing, tat•ters.** To make or become ragged.

tat•tered (**tăt′**ərd) *adj.* **1.** Torn into shreds; ragged: *tattered clothes.* **2.** Dressed in ragged clothes: *a tattered ragamuffin.* **3.** Shabby or dilapidated.

tat•ting (**tăt′**ĭng) *n.* **1.** Handmade lace made by looping and knotting a single strand of heavy thread on a small hand shuttle. **2.** The act or art of making such lace.

tat•tle (**tăt′**l) *v.* **tat•tled, tat•tling, tat•tles.** —*intr.* **1.** To reveal the plans or activities of another; gossip: *The boy tattled on his sister.* **2.** To talk idly; prate: *He tattled endlessly over the book.* —*tr.* To reveal (something) through gossiping. **—tat′tler** *n.*

tat•tle•tale (**tăt′**l tāl′) *n.* A person who tattles on others.

tat•too[1] (tă **to͞o′**) *n., pl.* **tat•toos. 1.** A signal sounded on a drum or bugle to summon soldiers or sailors to their quarters at night. **2.** A display of military exercises. **3.** A continuous even drumming or rapping. [First written down in 1644 in Modern English and spelled *tap-too,* from Dutch *taptoe,* tap-shut (closing time for taverns), tattoo : *tap,* spigot, tap + *toe,* shut.]

tat•too[2] (tă **to͞o′**) *n., pl.* **tat•toos.** A permanent mark or design made on the skin by a process of pricking and ingraining an indelible dye or by raising scars. —*tr.v.* **tat•tooed, tat•too•ing, tat•toos.** To mark (the skin) with a tattoo. [First written down in 1769 in Modern English, of Polynesian origin.]

tau (tou *or* tô) *n.* The 19th letter of the Greek alphabet, written Τ, τ. In English it is represented as *T, t.*

taught (tôt) *v.* Past tense and past participle of **teach.**

❑ *These sound alike:* **taught, taut** (tense).

taunt (tônt) *tr.v.* **taunt•ed, taunt•ing, taunts.** To mock or reproach in an insulting or scornful manner. —*n.* A scornful remark; a jeer.

taupe (tōp) *n.* A brownish gray.

Tau•rus (**tôr′**əs) *n.* **1.** A constellation in the Northern Hemisphere. **2.** The second sign of the zodiac in astrology.

taut (tôt) *adj.* **taut•er, taut•est. 1.** Pulled or drawn tight: *sails taut with wind.* **2.** Strained; tense: *taut nerves.* **3.** Kept in trim shape; neat. **—taut′ly** *adv.* **—taut′ness** *n.*

❑ *These sound alike:* **taut, taught** (instructed).

tau•tol•o•gy (tô **tŏl′**ə jē) *n., pl.* **tau•tol•o•gies. 1.** Needless repetition of the same information in different words; redundancy. **2.** A statement made up of simpler statements that is logically true whether the simpler statements are true or false; for example, the statement *Either it will rain tomorrow or it will not rain tomorrow* is a tautology.

tav•ern (**tăv′**ərn) *n.* **1.** A place licensed to sell alcoholic beverages to be drunk on the premises. **2.** An inn for travelers. [First written down about 1300 in Middle English and spelled *taverne,* from Latin *taberna,* hut, tavern.]

taw (tô) *n.* **1.** A large fancy marble used for shooting. **2.** The line from which a player shoots in marbles.

taw•dry (**tô′**drē) *adj.* **taw•dri•er, taw•dri•est.** Cheap and gaudy in nature or appearance. [First written down in 1676 in Modern English, from *tawdry lace,* lace necktie, alteration of *Saint Audrey's lace* (sold at the annual Saint Audrey's fair, Ely, England) after *Saint Audrey* (Saint Etheldreda), queen of Northumbria, who died in 679 of a throat tumor, supposedly because she delighted in fancy necklaces as a young woman.] **—taw′dri•ness** *n.*

taw•ny (tô′nē) *n.* A light brown to brownish orange. **—taw′ny** *adj.*

tax (tăks) *n.* **1.** A contribution for the support of the government required of persons, groups, or businesses within the domain of that government. **2.** A burdensome or excessive demand; a strain: *The extra orders are a tax on our system of production.* *—tr.v.* **taxed, tax•ing, tax•es. 1.** To place a tax on (income, property, or goods). **2.** To require a tax from: *tax the people.* **3.** To make difficult or excessive demands upon: *Don't tax my patience.* [First written down about 1325 in Middle English, from *taxen*, to tax, from Latin *taxāre*, to touch, reproach, reckon.]

tax•a•ble (tăk′sə bəl) *adj.* Subject to taxation: *taxable income.*

tax•a•tion (tăk sā′shən) *n.* The act or practice of imposing taxes: *no taxation without representation.*

tax•i (tăk′sē) *n., pl.* **tax•is** or **tax•ies.** A taxicab. *—intr.v.* **tax•ied** (tăk′sēd), **tax•i•ing** or **tax•y•ing, tax•ies** or **tax•is** (tăk′sēz). **1.** To be transported by taxi. **2.** To move slowly over the surface of the ground or water before takeoff or after landing: *The airplane taxied to the runway.*

tax•i•cab (tăk′sē kăb′) *n.* An automobile that carries passengers for a fare, usually calculated on a meter.

tax•i•der•my (tăk′sĭ dûr′mē) *n.* The art or process of preparing, stuffing, and mounting the skins of animals for exhibition in a lifelike state. **—tax′i•der′mist** *n.*

tax•o•nom•ic (tăk′sə nŏm′ĭk) *adj.* Of or relating to taxonomy: *a taxonomic name.*

tax•on•o•my (tăk sŏn′ə mē) *n., pl.* **tax•on•o•mies.** The science of classifying organisms into specially named groups based on shared characteristics and natural relationships. [First written down in 1828 in Modern English : Greek *taxis*, arrangement + Greek *-nomia*, system of rules.]

tax•pay•er (tăks′pā′ər) *n.* A person who pays or is required to pay taxes.

Tay•lor (tā′lər), **Zachary.** 1784–1850. The 12th President of the United States (1849–1850).

Tb The symbol for the element **terbium.**

TB also **T.B.** *abbr.* An abbreviation of tuberculosis.

Tbi•li•si (tə bə lē′sē). The capital of Georgia, in the southeast part of the region west-northwest of Baku, Azerbaijan. Population, 1,158,000.

tbs. *abbr.* An abbreviation of: **1.** Tablespoon. **2.** Tablespoonful.

tbsp. *abbr.* An abbreviation of: **1.** Tablespoon. **2.** Tablespoonful.

Tc The symbol for the element **technetium.**

T cell *n.* A major type of white blood cell that recognizes specific foreign antigens in the body and activates and deactivates other immune cells.

Tchai•kov•sky (chī kôf′skē), **Peter Ilich.** 1840–1893. Russian composer whose works include symphonies and ballets.

Te The symbol for the element **tellurium.**

tea (tē) *n.* **1.a.** The young dried leaves of an eastern Asian evergreen shrub or small tree having fragrant white flowers and glossy leaves. **b.** The shrub or small tree that bears such leaves. **2.** An aromatic beverage made by steeping tea leaves in hot water. **3.** *Chiefly British.* **a.** A light afternoon meal consisting usually of sandwiches and cakes served with tea. **b.** An afternoon reception or social gathering at which tea is served.

❑ *These sound alike:* **tea, tee** (peg for a golf ball), **ti** (musical tone).

teach (tēch) *v.* **taught** (tôt), **teach•ing, teach•es.** *—tr.* **1.** To give knowledge or skill to: *He teaches children.* **2.** To provide knowledge of; give instruction in: *She teaches math.* **3.** To advocate or preach: *teach religious tolerance.* **4.** To carry on instruction on a regular basis in: *taught third grade for years.* *—intr.* To give instruction or be employed as a teacher. [First written down before 899 in Old English and spelled *tǣcan.*]

Synonyms: teach, train, instruct, educate, school. These verbs mean to pass on knowledge or skill. **Teach** is the most general: *Your sister can teach you how to ride a bicycle.* **Train** means to teach particular skills intended to fit a person for a certain role, such as a job: *It is the manager's responsibility to train all new employees.* **Instruct** usually means to teach in an organized way: *The manual instructs you how to assemble the stereo.* **Educate** often means to instruct in a formal way: *They wanted their children to be educated in the very best schools.* **School** often means to teach with a hard, demanding process: *The violinist has been schooled to practice slowly.*

teach•a•ble (tē′chə bəl) *adj.* **1.** Capable of being taught: *Geometry is a teachable subject.* **2.** Able and willing to be taught: *teachable students.*

teach•er (tē′chər) *n.* A person who teaches, especially one hired to teach.

teach•ing (tē′chĭng) *n.* **1.** The act, practice, occupation, or profession of a teacher. **2.** Something taught, especially a precept or doctrine: *the teachings of Confucius.*

tea•cup (tē′kŭp′) *n.* A small cup for drinking tea.

tea•house (tē′hous′) *n.* A public establishment serving tea and light refreshments.

teak (tēk) *n.* **1.** A tall Asian tree having large evergreen leaves and hard, strong, heavy wood. **2.** The dark or yellowish-brown wood of such a tree, used for furniture and shipbuilding.

tea•ket•tle (tē′kĕt′l) *n.* A covered kettle with a spout and handle, used for boiling water, as for tea.

teal (tēl) *n., pl.* **teal** or **teals.** Any of several small freshwater ducks, often having brightly marked feathers. [First written down before 1300 in Middle English and spelled *tele.*]

team (tēm) *n.* **1.** A group on the same side, as in a game. **2.** Two or more people organized to work together: *a team of scientists.* **3.** Two or more animals used to pull a vehicle or farm implement: *a team of horses.* *—v.* **teamed, team•ing, teams.** *—tr.* **1.** To harness or join together so as to form a team. **2.** To transport or haul with a draft team. *—intr.* To form a team or an association: *We teamed up to clean the beach.* [First written down about 825 in Old English and spelled *tēam*, team of draft animals.] —SEE NOTE at **collective noun.**

❑ *These sound alike:* **team, teem** (abound).

team•mate (tēm′māt′) *n.* A member of one's own team.

team•ster (tēm′stər) *n.* **1.** A truck driver. **2.** A person who drives a team.

team•work (tēm′wûrk′) *n.* Cooperative effort by members of a group or team to achieve a common goal.

tea•pot (tē′pŏt′) *n.* A covered pot with a handle and spout, used for making and pouring tea.

tear[1] (târ) *v.* **tore** (tôr), **torn** (tôrn), **tear•ing, tears.** *—tr.* **1.** To pull apart or into pieces by force; rend: *Tear the paper in half.* See Synonyms at **rip[1]. 2.** To make (an opening) by ripping: *tore a hole in my sock.* **3.** To injure by cutting or ripping. **4.** To separate forcefully: *tore the wrapping off the present.* **5.** To divide or disrupt emotionally: *He is torn between duty and loyalty to his friends.* *—intr.* **1.** To become torn. **2.** To move with great speed; rush

Zachary Taylor

Peter Ilich Tchaikovsky
Photographed in 1888

teapot

ă	**pat**	oi	**boy**
ā	**pay**	ou	**out**
âr	**care**	o͝o	**took**
ä	**father**	o͞o	**boot**
ĕ	**pet**	ŭ	**cut**
ē	**be**	ûr	**urge**
ĭ	**pit**	th	**thin**
ī	**pie**	*th*	**this**
îr	**pier**	hw	**whoop**
ŏ	**pot**	zh	vi**si**on
ō	**toe**	ə	**a**bout
ô	**paw**	N	*French* bo**n**

TAXONOMY

The taxonomy of all life on earth is organized so that each species belongs to a genus, each genus to a family, and so on through order, class, phylum, and kingdom. These categories indicate how closely or distantly organisms are related to each other, based on structural and genetic similarities.

The table below compares the taxonomy of two common living things, a dog and a goldfish. As the table shows, although dogs and goldfish are different in many ways, they also share certain important taxonomic characteristics.

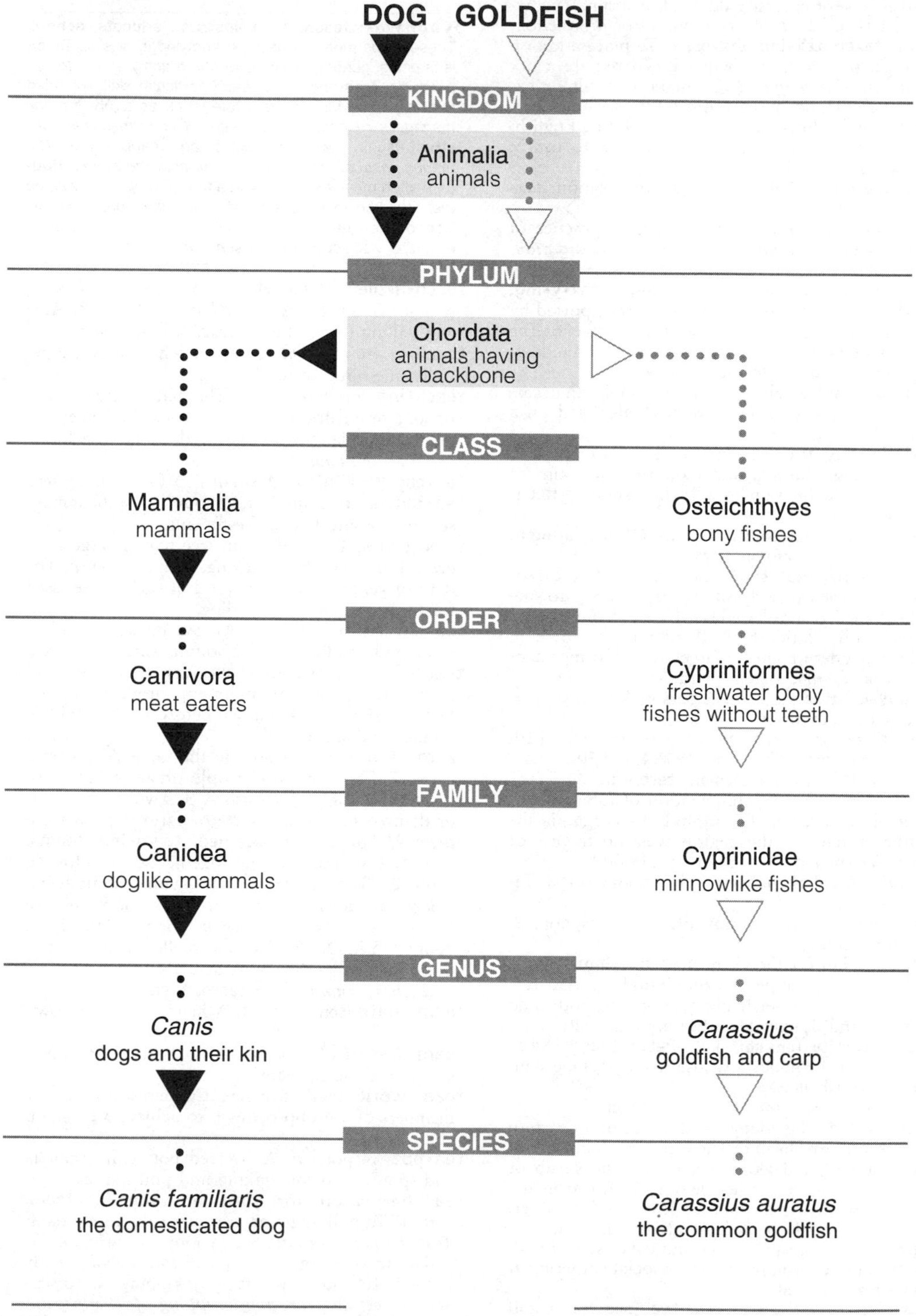

headlong: *He went tearing into town.* —*n.* **1.** The act of tearing. **2.** The result of tearing; a rip or rent. —***idioms.*** **tear down.** To demolish: *They had to tear down what was left of the building after the fire.* **tear up.** To tear to pieces: *Tear up the letter when you've read it.* [First written down before 850 in Old English and spelled *teoran.*]

❑ *These sound alike:* **tear[1], tare[1]** (weed), **tare[2]** (weight).

tear[2] (tîr) *n.* A drop of the clear salty liquid secreted by glands of the eyes. —*intr.v.* **teared, tear•ing, tears.** To fill with tears: *The vapor of an onion will make your eyes tear.* [First written down about 725 in Old English and spelled *tæhher.*]

❑ *These sound alike:* **tear[2], tier** (row).

tear•drop (tîr′drŏp′) *n.* **1.** A tear. **2.** An object shaped like a tear.

tear•ful (tîr′fəl) *adj.* **1.** Filled with or accompanied by tears: *a tearful farewell.* **2.** So piteous as to bring forth tears: *a tearful movie.* —**tear′ful•ly** *adv.* —**tear′ful•ness** *n.*

tear gas (tîr) *n.* Any of various chemicals that when dispersed as a gas or mist irritate the eyes and breathing passages severely, causing choking and heavy tears.

tease (tēz) *v.* **teased, teas•ing, teas•es.** —*tr.* **1.** To annoy or pester; vex: *teasing the cat by pulling its tail.* **2.** To make fun of; mock playfully. **3.** To urge persistently; coax: *teased our mother to let us stay up late.* **4.** To disentangle and dress the fibers of: *tease wool.* **5.** To raise a nap (on cloth), as with a teasel. **6.** To brush or comb (the hair) toward the scalp for a full airy effect. —*intr.* To annoy or make fun of persistently: *Quit teasing!* —*n.* **1.** The act of teasing. **2.** A person or a remark that teases.

tea•sel (tē′zəl) *n.* **1.** Any of several plants having flowers surrounded by stiff bristles. **2.** The flower head of such a plant, used to brush the surface of fabrics so as to form a nap.

tea•spoon (tē′spo͞on′) *n.* **1.** The common small spoon used especially in serving and consuming coffee and desserts. **2.** A household cooking measure equal to ⅓ tablespoon (about 5 milliliters). See table at **measurement.**

tea•spoon•ful (tē′spo͞on fo͝ol′) *n.* The amount that a teaspoon can hold.

teat (tēt *or* tĭt) *n.* The part of an udder or a breast through which milk is taken; a nipple.

tech. *abbr.* An abbreviation of: **1.** Technical. **2.** Technician.

tech•ne•ti•um (tĕk nē′shē əm) *n. Symbol* **Tc** A silvery-gray, radioactive, metallic element used to remove corrosion from steel. Atomic number 43. See table at **element.**

tech•ni•cal (tĕk′nĭ kəl) *adj.* **1.** Of, relating to, or derived from technique: *technical ability.* **2.** Used in or peculiar to a particular subject; specialized: *technical language.* **3.** Of, relating to, or involving the practical, mechanical, or industrial arts or the applied sciences: *a technical school.* **4.** Industrial and mechanical; technological: *technical assistance overseas.* **5.** According to a principal or rule: *a technical foul.* [First written down in 1617 in Modern English, from Greek *tekhnikos,* of art, from *tekhnē,* art.] —**tech′ni•cal•ly** *adv.*

tech•ni•cal•i•ty (tĕk′nĭ kăl′ĭ tē) *n., pl.* **tech•ni•cal•i•ties. 1.** The quality or condition of being technical. **2.** Something meaningful or relevant only to a specialist: *caught on a legal technicality.*

tech•ni•cian (tĕk nĭsh′ən) *n.* A person who is skilled in a certain technical field or process: *a dental technician.*

Tech•ni•col•or (tĕk′nĭ kŭl′ər). A trademark used for a method of making motion pictures in color.

tech•nique (tĕk nēk′) *n.* **1.** A procedure or method for accomplishing a complicated task, as in a science or an art. **2.** Skill in handling such procedures or methods: *As a pianist, she has nearly perfect technique.* [First written down in 1817 in Modern English, from Greek *tekhnikos,* technical.]

tech•no•log•i•cal (tĕk′nə lŏj′ĭ kəl) *adj.* Of, relating to, or resulting from technology: *technological developments.* —**tech′no•log′i•cal•ly** *adv.*

tech•nol•o•gist (tĕk nŏl′ə jĭst) *n.* A specialist in technology.

tech•nol•o•gy (tĕk nŏl′ə jē) *n., pl.* **tech•nol•o•gies. 1.** The use of scientific knowledge to solve practical problems, especially in industry and commerce. **2.** The methods and materials used to solve practical problems: *aerospace technology.*

Te•cum•seh (tĭ kŭm′sə). 1768–1813. Shawnee leader who attempted to establish a confederacy of Native Americans against white settlement in the Northwest Territory.

Tecumseh

ted•dy bear (tĕd′ē) *n.* A child's toy bear, usually stuffed with soft material. [First written down in 1906 in American English, after *Teddy,* nickname of Theodore Roosevelt, who was depicted in a cartoon sparing the life of a bear cub.]

Te De•um (tā′ dā′əm) *n.* A hymn of praise to God sung as part of a liturgy.

te•di•ous (tē′dē əs) *adj.* Tiresome because of slowness, dullness, or length; boring: *a tedious lecture.* See Synonyms at **boring.** —**te′di•ous•ly** *adv.* —**te′di•ous•ness** *n.*

te•di•um (tē′dē əm) *n.* The quality or condition of being tedious; boredom. [First written down in 1662 in Modern English, from Latin *taedium,* from *taedēre,* to weary.]

tee (tē) *n.* **1.** A small peg stuck in the ground to support a golf ball for a shot. **2.** A raised area from which a golfer hits the first shot toward a hole. —*tr.v.* **teed, tee•ing, tees.** To place (a golf ball) on a tee. —***idiom.*** **tee off. 1.** To drive a golf ball from a tee. **2.** *Slang.* To make (someone) angry or irritated.

❑ *These sound alike:* **tee, tea** (drink), **ti** (musical tone).

tee
Golf tee

teem (tēm) *intr.v.* **teemed, teem•ing, teems.** To be full of things; swarm or abound: *The pond water teemed with microbes.* [First written down about 1000 in Old English and spelled *tīeman, tēman.*]

❑ *These sound alike:* **teem, team** (group).

teen (tēn) *n.* **1. teens. a.** The numbers 13 through 19. **b.** The 13th through 19th items in a series or scale, as years of a century or degrees of temperature. **2.** A teenager.

teen•age or **teen-age** (tēn′āj′) *adj.* Of, relating to, or applicable to those aged 13 through 19.

teen•ag•er (tēn′ā′jər) *n.* A person between the ages of 13 and 19.

tee•ny (tē′nē) also **teen•sy** (tēn′sē) *adj.* **tee•ni•er, tee•ni•est** also **teen•si•er, teen•si•est.** *Informal.* Tiny.

tee•pee (tē′pē) *n.* Variant of **tepee.**

tee shirt *n.* Variant of **T-shirt.**

tee•ter (tē′tər) *intr.v.* **tee•tered, tee•ter•ing, tee•ters. 1.** To walk or move unsteadily; totter. **2.** To seesaw. —*n.* A seesaw.

tee•ter-tot•ter (tē′tər tŏt′ər) *n.* A seesaw.

teeth (tēth) *n.* Plural of **tooth.**

teethe (tē*th*) *intr.v.* **teethed, teeth•ing, teethes.** To have teeth coming through the gums.

tee•to•tal•er or **tee•to•tal•ler** (tē′tōt′l ər) *n.* A person who abstains completely from drinking alcoholic beverages.

Tef•lon (tĕf′lŏn′). A trademark for a durable plastic based on compounds of carbon and fluorine, used to coat certain cooking utensils and to prevent sticking of machine parts.

ă	**pat**	oi	**boy**
ā	**pay**	ou	**out**
âr	**care**	o͝o	**took**
ä	**father**	o͞o	**boot**
ĕ	**pet**	ŭ	**cut**
ē	**be**	ûr	**urge**
ĭ	**pit**	th	**thin**
ī	**pie**	*th*	**this**
îr	**pier**	hw	**whoop**
ŏ	**pot**	zh	**vision**
ō	**toe**	ə	**about**
ô	**paw**	N	*French* **bon**

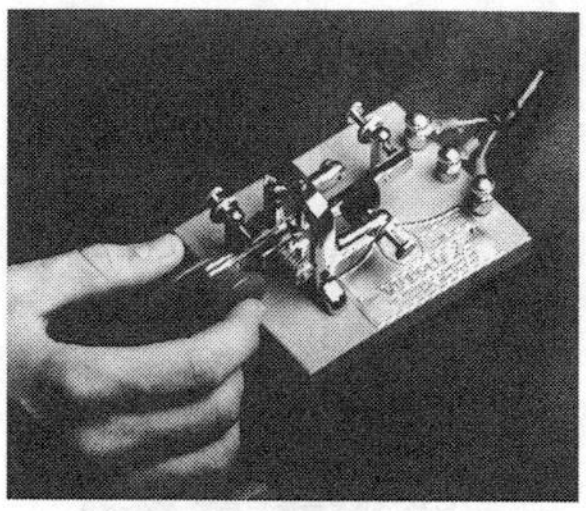

telegraph
Telegraph keypad

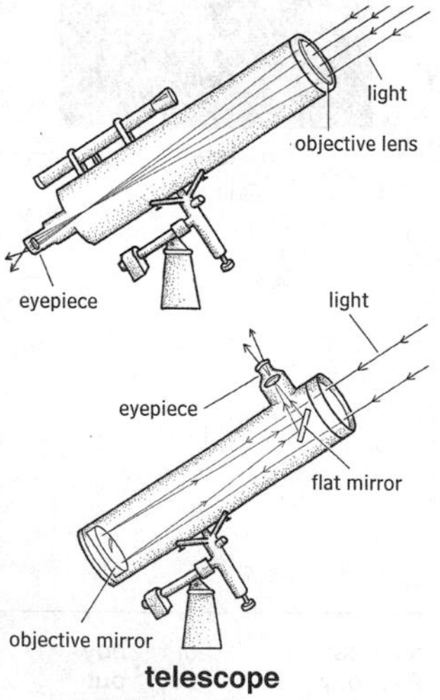

telescope
Top: Refracting telescope
Bottom: Reflecting telescope

Te•gu•ci•gal•pa (tə go͞o′sə **găl′**pə *or* tĕ go͞o′-sē **gäl′**pä). The capital and largest city of Honduras, in the south-central part of the country. It was founded in the late 16th century. Population, 532,500.

Teh•ran or **Te•he•ran** (tĕ **răn′** *or* tĕ **rän′**). The capital and largest city of Iran, in the north-central part of the country south of the Caspian Sea. It became capital in the late 1700's. Population, 5,734,199.

Te•huel•che (tə **wĕl′**chē *or* tā **wĕl′**chā) *n., pl.* **Te-huelche** or **Te•huel•ches. 1.** A member of a Native American people of Patagonia, who were killed off by the European settlers. **2.** The language of the Tehuelche.

tek•tite (**tĕk′**tīt′) *n.* Any of numerous dark-brown to green glassy objects, usually small and round, composed of silica and various oxides and found in several parts of the world. They are thought to have come from the moon or to have resulted from impacts of large meteorites with Earth's surface.

tel. *abbr.* An abbreviation of: **1.** Telegram. **2.** Telegraph. **3.** Telephone.

Tel A•viv–Jaf•fa (tĕl′ ə **vēv′jăf′**ə). The largest city in Israel, on the Mediterranean Sea west-northwest of Jerusalem. Tel Aviv, founded in 1909, and the ancient city of Jaffa merged in 1950. Population, 323,400.

tele– *pref.* A prefix that means: **1.** Distance; distant: *telemetry.* **2.** Telegraph or telephone: *telegram.* **3.** Television: *telecast.*

tel•e•cast (**tĕl′**ĭ kăst′) *tr.v.* **tel•e•cast** or **tel•e•cast•ed, tel•e•cast•ing, tel•e•casts.** To broadcast (a program or programs) by television. —*n.* A television broadcast.

tel•e•com•mu•ni•ca•tion (**tĕl′**ĭ kə myo͞o′nĭ **kā′**-shən) *n.* The science and technology of sending messages over long distances, especially by electrical or electronic means. Often used in the plural with a singular verb.

teleg. *abbr.* An abbreviation of: **1.** Telegram. **2.** Telegraph. **3.** Telegraphy.

tel•e•gram (**tĕl′**ĭ grăm′) *n.* A message transmitted by telegraph.

tel•e•graph (**tĕl′**ĭ grăf′) *n.* **1.** A communications system in which a message in the form of electric impulses is sent, either by wire or radio, to a receiving station. **2.** A message sent by such a system; a telegram. —*tr.v.* **tel•e•graphed, tel•e•graph•ing, tel•e•graphs. 1.** To transmit (a message) by telegraph: *telegraph our congratulations.* **2.** To send or convey a message to (someone) by telegraph.

tel•e•graph•ic (tĕl′ĭ **grăf′**ĭk) *adj.* Of, relating to, or sent by telegraph.

te•leg•ra•phy (tə **lĕg′**rə fē) *n.* Communication by means of telegraph.

Te•lem•a•chus (tə **lĕm′**ə kəs) *n.* In Greek mythology, the son of Odysseus and Penelope, who helps his father kill Penelope's suitors.

tel•e•mar•ket•ing (**tĕl′**ə mär′kĭ tĭng) *n.* Use of the telephone in marketing goods or services.

tel•e•me•ter (**tĕl′**ə mē′tər *or* tə **lĕm′**ĭ tər) *n.* A measuring, transmitting, and receiving device used in telemetry. —*tr.v.* (**tĕl′**ə mē′tər). **tel•e•me•tered, tel•e•me•ter•ing, tel•e•me•ters.** To measure, transmit, and receive (data) automatically from a distant source, such as a spacecraft.

te•lem•e•try (tə **lĕm′**ĭ trē) *n.* The automatic measurement and transmission of data from a distant source to a receiving station.

tel•e•path•ic (tĕl′ə **păth′**ĭk) *adj.* Of, transmitted by, or possessing telepathy.

te•lep•a•thy (tə **lĕp′**ə thē) *n.* Communication from one mind to another through means other than the senses.

tel•e•phone (**tĕl′**ə fōn′) *n.* An instrument for transmitting speech or other sounds over a distance by changing the sounds into electric impulses and by receiving electric impulses and converting them into sounds. —*tr.v.* **tel•e•phoned, tel•e•phon•ing, tel•e•phones. 1.** To call or communicate with (a person) by telephone. **2.** To transmit (a message or information) by telephone. [First written down in 1844 in Modern English : Greek *tēle*, far off + Greek *phonos*, sound.]

telephone book *n.* A listing of the names of telephone subscribers with their numbers and often their addresses.

telephone exchange *n.* A central system of switches and other equipment that establish connections between individual telephones.

tel•e•phon•ic (tĕl′ə **fŏn′**ĭk) *adj.* **1.** Of or relating to telephones. **2.** Transmitted by or conveyed by telephone.

te•leph•o•ny (tə **lĕf′**ə nē) *n.* **1.** The transmission of sound between distant points, especially by radio or telephone. **2.** The technology and manufacture of telephone equipment.

tel•e•pho•to•graph (tĕl′ə **fō′**tə grăf′) *n.* **1.** A photograph made with a telephoto lens. **2.** A photograph that is transmitted and reproduced by telephotography.

tel•e•pho•tog•ra•phy (tĕl′ə fə **tŏg′**rə fē) *n.* **1.** The photographing of distant objects using a telephoto lens on a camera. **2.** The transmission of photographs, pictures, and charts over a distance.

tel•e•pho•to lens (**tĕl′**ə fō′tō) *n.* A lens that produces a large image of a distant object.

Tel•e•Promp•Ter (**tĕl′**ə prŏmp′tər) *n.* A trademark used for a device that shows an actor or a speaker a script that is unseen by a television audience.

tel•e•scope (**tĕl′**ĭ skōp′) *n.* **1.** A device that uses an arrangement of lenses, mirrors, or both to collect visible light, allowing observation or photographic recording of distant objects. **2.** Any of various devices, such as a radio telescope, used to collect and analyze electromagnetic radiation other than light coming from distant sources. —*tr.v.* **tel•e•scoped, tel•e•scop•ing, tel•e•scopes. 1.** To slide or cause to slide inward or outward in overlapping sections, as the tube sections of a small hand telescope. **2.** To make more compact or concise; condense: *telescoping several instructions for a recipe into one sentence.* [First written down in 1648 in Modern English and spelled *telescopio*, from Greek *tēleskopos*, far-seeing : *tēle-*, far off + *skopos*, watcher.]

tel•e•scop•ic (tĕl′ĭ **skŏp′**ĭk) *adj.* **1.** Of or relating to a telescope. **2.** Seen or obtained by means of a telescope: *telescopic data.* **3.** Visible only by means of a telescope: *a telescopic binary star.* **4.** Capable of discerning distant objects: *telescopic vision.* **5.** Capable of sliding inward or outward in overlapping sections: *a telescopic antenna.*

tel•e•thon (**tĕl′**ə thŏn′) *n.* A lengthy television program to raise funds for a charity.

Tel•e•type (**tĕl′**ĭ **tīp′**). A trademark used for a teletypewriter.

tel•e•type•writ•er (tĕl′ĭ **tīp′**rī′tər) *n.* A device similar to a typewriter that either transmits or receives telegraph or telephone messages.

tel•e•vise (**tĕl′**ə vīz′) *tr.v.* **tel•e•vised, tel•e•vis•ing, tel•e•vis•es.** To broadcast by television: *Four channels televised the presidential debate.*

tel•e•vi•sion (**tĕl′**ə vĭzh′ən) *n.* **1.** The transmission and reception of visual images of moving and stationary objects, usually with accompanying sound, as electrical waves through the air or through wires. **2.** A device that receives such electrical waves and reproduces the transmitted images on a screen. **3.** The industry of producing and broadcasting television programs.

tell (tĕl) *v.* **told** (tōld), **tell•ing, tells.** —*tr.* **1.** To give an account of; describe or relate: *tell a story.* **2.** To express in words; say: *tell the truth.* **3.** To make known; indicate or inform: *The temperature of something tells how hot or cold it is.* **4.** To discover by observation; perceive or identify: *It is hard to tell how far a teacher's influence extends.* **5.** To command; order: *told us to stand in line.* —*intr.* **1.** To give an account or a description of something. **2.** To reveal secrets; inform: *You shouldn't tell on your friends.* [First written down before 899 in Old English and spelled *tellan.*]

tell•er (**tĕl′**ər) *n.* **1.** A person who tells: *a teller of tall tales.* **2.** A bank employee who receives and pays out money. **3.** A person appointed to count votes in a legislative assembly.

tell•ing (**tĕl′**ĭng) *adj.* Having force and producing a striking effect: *a telling remark.* **—tell′ing•ly** *adv.*

tell•tale (**tĕl′**tāl′) *n.* A person or thing that reveals information. —*adj.* Serving to indicate or reveal: *a telltale sign.*

tel•lu•ride (**tĕl′**yə rīd′) *n.* A chemical compound of tellurium and another element.

tel•lu•ri•um (tĕ **lo͝or′**ē əm) *n. Symbol* **Te** A brittle, silvery-white, metalloid element that is used in stainless steel and lead alloys. Atomic number 52. See table at **element.**

tel•o•phase (**tĕl′**ə fāz′ *or* **tē′**lə fāz′) *n.* The final phase of mitosis and meiosis, in which the chromosomes of the daughter cells are grouped in new nuclei.

te•mer•i•ty (tə **mĕr′**ĭ tē) *n.* Foolish disregard of danger; recklessness.

temp. *abbr.* An abbreviation of: **1.** Temperature. **2.** Temporary.

tem•per (**tĕm′**pər) *tr.v.* **tem•pered, tem•per•ing, tem•pers. 1.** To lessen the harshness or severity of; moderate: *tempering justice with mercy.* **2.** To bring (a substance) to a desired physical condition by mixing with something else or treating in some special way: *tempered the paint with oil.* **3.** To harden or strengthen (metal or glass) by applying heat or by heating and cooling. —*n.* **1.** A state of mind or emotions; a disposition: *an even temper.* **2.** Calmness of mind or emotions; composure: *Don't lose your temper.* **3.** A tendency to become angry or irritable: *has a quick temper.* **4.a.** The condition of being tempered. **b.** The degree of hardness and elasticity of a metal, especially steel, achieved by tempering.

tem•per•a (**tĕm′**pər ə) *n.* **1.** A type of paint made by mixing pigment with a substance such as egg yolk that is soluble in water. **2.** Painting done with this type of paint.

tem•per•a•ment (**tĕm′** prə mənt *or* **tĕm′**pər ə mənt) *n.* The manner of thinking, behaving, or reacting characteristic of a specific person: *a nervous temperament.*

tem•per•a•men•tal (tĕm′ prə **mĕn′**tl *or* tĕm′pər ə **mĕn′**tl) *adj.* **1.** Relating to or caused by temperament. **2.** Excessively sensitive, irritable, or moody: *a temperamental person.*

tem•per•ance (**tĕm′**pər əns *or* **tĕm′**prəns) *n.* **1.** Moderation and self-restraint, as in behavior or expression. **2.** Restraint in the use of or abstinence from alcoholic beverages.

tem•per•ate (**tĕm′**pər ĭt *or* **tĕm′**prĭt) *adj.* **1.** Exercising moderation and self-restraint. **2.** Moderate in degree or quality; restrained. **3.** Characterized by moderate temperatures, weather, or climate; neither hot nor cold.

Tem•per•ate Zone (**tĕm′**pər ĭt *or* **tĕm′**prĭt). Either of two intermediate latitude zones of the earth, the **North Temperate Zone,** between the Arctic Circle and the Tropic of Cancer, or the **South Temperate Zone,** between the Antarctic Circle and the Tropic of Capricorn.

tem•per•a•ture (**tĕm′**pər ə cho͝or′ *or* **tĕm′**prə cho͝or′) *n.* **1.a.** The relative hotness or coldness of a body or an environment. **b.** A numerical measure of hotness or coldness on a standard scale. **2.** An abnormally high body temperature that is caused by a disease or disorder; a fever. —SEE NOTE.

tem•pered (**tĕm′**pərd) *adj.* **1.** Having a specified temper or disposition: *sweet-tempered.* **2.** Strengthened, hardened, or toughened by tempering: *a tempered steel blade.*

tem•pest (**tĕm′**pĭst) *n.* **1.** A violent windstorm, often accompanied by rain, snow, or hail. **2.** A violent commotion or tumult; an uproar.

tem•pes•tu•ous (tĕm **pĕs′**cho͞o əs) *adj.* **1.** Of, relating to, or resembling a tempest: *tempestuous winds.* **2.** Tumultuous; noisy: *a tempestuous meeting.* **—tem•pes′tu•ous•ly** *adv.* **—tem•pes′tu•ous•ness** *n.*

tem•pi (**tĕm′**pē) *n.* A plural of **tempo.**

tem•plate (**tĕm′**plĭt) *n.* A pattern or gauge, such as a thin metal plate cut to a definite pattern, used in making something accurately, as in carpentry.

tem•ple[1] (**tĕm′**pəl) *n.* **1.** A building dedicated to religious ceremonies or worship: *the temple of Athena.* **2.** A synagogue, especially of a Reform or Conservative congregation. [First written down before 830 in Old English and spelled *tempel,* from Latin *templum.*]

tem•ple[2] (**tĕm′**pəl) *n.* Either of the flat regions at the sides of the head next to the forehead. [First written down about 1330 in Middle English, from Latin *tempus.*]

tem•po (**tĕm′**pō) *n., pl.* **tem•pos** or **tem•pi** (**tĕm′**pē). **1.** The relative speed at which music is or ought to be played. **2.** A characteristic rate or rhythm of something; a pace: *the tempo of life in a city.*

tem•po•ral[1] (**tĕm′**pər əl *or* **tĕm′**prəl) *adj.* **1.** Of, relating to, or limited by time: *temporal boundaries.* **2.** Of or relating to worldly affairs, especially as distinguished from religious concerns: *the temporal powers of the church.* **3.** Lasting only for a time; not eternal. [First written down about 1350 in Middle English and spelled *temperel,* from Latin *temporālis,* from *tempus,* time.] **—tem′po•ral•ly** *adv.*

tem•po•ral[2] (**tĕm′**pər əl *or* **tĕm′**prəl) *adj.* Of, relating to, or near the temples of the skull. [First written down before 1425 in Middle English and spelled *temperal,* from Latin *tempora,* temples.]

tem•po•rar•y (**tĕm′**pə rĕr′ē) *adj.* Lasting, used, serving, or enjoyed for a limited time only; not permanent: *a temporary job.* —*n., pl.* **tem•po•rar•ies.** *Informal.* An employee who works for a limited time only: *Her position is being filled for now by a temporary.*

tem•po•rize (**tĕm′**pə rīz′) *intr.v.* **tem•po•rized, tem•po•riz•ing, tem•po•riz•es.** To compromise or act evasively in order to gain time, avoid an argument, or postpone a decision. **—tem′po•ri•za′tion** (tĕm′pər ĭ **zā′**shən) *n.* **—tem′po•riz′er** *n.*

tempt (tĕmpt) *tr.v.* **tempt•ed, tempt•ing, tempts. 1.** To try to get (someone) to do wrong, especially by a promise of reward. **2.** To be inviting or attractive to: *Your offer tempts me.* **3.** To provoke or risk provoking: *Do not tempt fate.* [First written down before 1200 in Middle English and spelled *tempti,* from Latin *temptāre,* to feel, try.]

temp•ta•tion (tĕmp **tā′**shən) *n.* **1.** The act of tempting or the condition of being tempted. **2.** Something tempting or enticing: *Desserts were a real temptation for her.*

tempt•ing (**tĕmp′**tĭng) *adj.* Having strong appeal; enticing: *a tempting offer.*

tem•pu•ra (**tĕm′**po͝o rə *or* tĕm **po͝or′**ə) *n.* A Japa-

temperature

What is the difference between **temperature** and heat? Think of a teacup and a spaghetti pot, both filled with water. If both start at the same temperature, it takes more energy to boil the water in the pot than the water in the cup. Heat is the sum of two kinds of energy—**kinetic** energy and **potential** energy—in the particles of a given amount of matter. The heat contained in an object depends on the mass of the object—that is, on the amount of matter or stuff in the object. Since there is more water in the pot than in the cup, there is more total heat energy in the pot of water than in the cup of water. Temperature, however, does not depend on the mass of the water but on the speed of the particles in that mass. When a material receives more heat energy, the atoms in the material vibrate or move faster and faster. For this reason a pot of boiling water and a cup of boiling water can have the same **temperature** (100° C) but still contain a different amount of **heat.**

ă	**pat**	oi	**boy**
ā	**pay**	ou	**out**
âr	**care**	o͝o	**took**
ä	**father**	o͞o	**boot**
ĕ	**pet**	ŭ	**cut**
ē	**be**	ûr	**urge**
ĭ	**pit**	th	**thin**
ī	**pie**	*th*	**this**
îr	**pier**	hw	**whoop**
ŏ	**pot**	zh	**vision**
ō	**toe**	ə	**about**
ô	**paw**	N	*French* **bon**

Word Building: tenacious

The word root *–ten–* in English words comes from the Latin verb *tenēre*, "to hold." The root appears in **tenacious**, which comes from the Latin adjective *tenāc–*, "holding fast, persistent." The Latin word root *–ten–* often has the form *–tain–* in French, and English has words from both forms. A **tenant** is one "holding land from a lord or holding something on lease." **Contain** means "to have with it or in it, keep within limits" (using the prefix *com–*, "with, together"). **Retain** is "to keep back, keep possession of" (*re–*, "back").

Tennessee

The name of **Tennessee** comes from the Cherokee name for the Tennessee River, which was also used for a Cherokee town in the area. The name of the river was later used for the state.

Alfred, Lord Tennyson

tentacle
Octopus tentacles

nese dish of vegetables and shrimp or other seafood dipped in batter and fried.

ten (tĕn) *n.* **1.** The number, written 10, that is equal to 9 + 1. **2.** The tenth in a set or sequence. **—ten** *adj. & pron.*

ten•a•ble (tĕn′ə bəl) *adj.* Defensible or logical: *His theory is tenable.* **—ten′a•bil′i•ty, ten′a•ble•ness** *n.* **—ten′a•bly** *adv.*

te•na•cious (tə nā′shəs) *adj.* **1.** Holding or tending to hold firmly to something, such as a point of view: *a man tenacious in his convictions.* **2.** Holding together firmly; cohesive. **3.** Clinging to another object or surface. **4.** Tending to retain; retentive: *a tenacious memory.* **—te•nac′i•ty** (tə năs′ĭ tē) *n.* —See Note.

ten•an•cy (tĕn′ən sē) *n., pl.* **ten•an•cies. 1.** Possession or occupancy of lands, buildings, or other property, as by lease or rent. **2.** The period of a tenant's occupancy or possession.

ten•ant (tĕn′ənt) *n.* **1.** A person who pays rent to use or occupy land, a building, or other property owned by another. **2.** A dweller in a place; an occupant.

tenant farmer *n.* A person who lives on and farms land owned by another and pays rent in cash or with a share of the produce.

Ten Commandments *pl.n.* In the Bible, the ten laws given to Moses by God.

tend[1] (tĕnd) *intr.v.* **tend•ed, tend•ing, tends. 1.** To have a tendency: *Pressure at the office tends to make her grouchy.* **2.** To be disposed or inclined: *She tends toward conservatism in economic matters.* **3.** To move or extend in a certain direction: *Our course tended toward the north.* [First written down about 1380 in Middle English and spelled *tenden*, from Latin *tendere*.]

tend[2] (tĕnd) *v.* **tend•ed, tend•ing, tends.** *—tr.* **1.** To have the care of; look after: *tend a sick child.* **2.** To manage the activities and transactions of: *tend a sales counter.* *—intr.* **1.** To be an attendant or a servant. **2.** To apply one's attention; attend: *tend to one's own business.* [First written down about 1330 in Middle English and spelled *tenden*, short for *attenden*, to wait on.]

ten•den•cy (tĕn′dən sē) *n., pl.* **ten•den•cies. 1.** Movement or prevailing movement in a given direction. **2.** A characteristic likelihood: *Linen has a tendency to wrinkle.* **3.** A leaning or an inclination to think, act, or behave in a certain way: *He has a tendency to write long sentences.*

ten•der[1] (tĕn′dər) *adj.* **ten•der•er, ten•der•est. 1.** Easily crushed or bruised; fragile: *tender flowers.* **2.** Easily chewed or cut: *a tender steak.* **3.** Young and vulnerable: *of tender age.* **4.a.** Easily hurt; sensitive: *tender skin.* **b.** Painful; sore: *a tender tooth.* **5.** Gentle and loving: *a tender heart; a tender glance.* [First written down before 1200 in Middle English and spelled *tendre*, from Latin *tener*.]

ten•der[2] (tĕn′dər) *n.* **1.** A formal offer or bid. **2.** Something, especially money, offered in payment. *—tr.v.* **ten•dered, ten•der•ing, ten•ders.** To offer formally: *tender a letter of resignation.* [First written down in 1542 in Modern English, from Latin *tendere*, to hold forth, extend.]

tend•er[3] (tĕn′dər) *n.* **1.** A person who tends something: *a furnace tender.* **2.** A boat that ferries supplies between a larger ship and shore. **3.** A railroad car attached to the rear of a locomotive, carrying fuel and water.

ten•der•foot (tĕn′dər fo͝ot′) *n., pl.* **ten•der•foots** or **ten•der•feet** (tĕn′dər fēt′). **1.** A newcomer not yet hardened to rough outdoor life. **2.** An inexperienced person; a beginner.

ten•der•heart•ed (tĕn′dər här′tĭd) *adj.* Easily moved by another's distress; compassionate.

ten•der•ize (tĕn′də rīz′) *tr.v.* **ten•der•ized, ten•der•iz•ing, ten•der•iz•es.** To make (meat) tender, as by marinating or pounding.

ten•der•iz•er (tĕn′də rī′zər) *n.* A substance applied to meat to make it tender.

ten•der•loin (tĕn′dər loin′) *n.* The tenderest part, as of a loin of beef.

ten•don (tĕn′dən) *n.* A band of tough fibrous tissue that connects a muscle to a bone. [First written down in 1543 in Modern English, from Greek *tenōn*.]

ten•dril (tĕn′drəl) *n.* **1.** One of the slender coiling parts resembling stems by means of which a climbing plant clings to something to help support it. **2.** Something, such as a ringlet of hair, that is long, slender, and curling.

ten•e•ment (tĕn′ə mənt) *n.* **1.** A building for human habitation, especially one that is rented to tenants. **2.** An apartment house that is poorly maintained and often overcrowded.

ten•et (tĕn′ĭt) *n.* An opinion, a doctrine, or a principle held as being true by a person or an organization.

ten-gal•lon hat (tĕn′găl′ən) *n.* A cowboy hat.

Tenn. *abbr.* An abbreviation of Tennessee.

Ten•nes•see (tĕn′ĭ sē′ *or* tĕn′ĭ sē′). A state of the southeast United States west of North Carolina. It was admitted as the 16th state in 1796. Nashville is the capital and Memphis the largest city. Population, 4,896,641. —See Note.

ten•nis (tĕn′ĭs) *n.* A game played with rackets and a light ball by two players or two pairs of players on a rectangular court, as of grass or clay, divided by a net.

tennis shoe *n.* A sneaker.

Ten•ny•son (tĕn′ĭ sən), **Alfred.** Known as Alfred, Lord Tennyson. 1809–1892. British poet who was appointed poet laureate in 1850.

ten•on (tĕn′ən) *n.* A projection on the end of a piece of wood designed to fit into a mortise to make a joint.

ten•or (tĕn′ər) *n.* **1.** A continuous unwavering course: *The tenor of his career has been steadily upwards.* **2.** The general meaning; gist; drift: *He knew enough German to get the tenor of what was being said.* **3.a.** The highest natural adult male voice. **b.** A person having such a voice. **c.** A part for this voice.

ten•pin (tĕn′pĭn′) *n.* **1.** One of the bottle-shaped pins used in bowling. **2.** **tenpins.** *(used with a singular verb).* Bowling.

tense[1] (tĕns) *adj.* **tens•er, tens•est. 1.** Taut; tightly stretched: *tense muscles.* **2.** Characterized by nervous tension or suspense: *a tense situation.* *—tr. & intr.v.* **tensed, tens•ing, tens•es.** To make or become tense: *I could feel my neck muscles tense up.* [First written down in 1670 in Modern English, from Latin *tēnsus*, past participle of *tendere*, to stretch.]

tense[2] (tĕns) *n.* **1.** Any of the inflected forms of a verb that indicate the time, such as past or present, and continuance or completion of the action or state. **2.** A set of tense forms indicating a particular time: *the future tense.* [First written down before 1333 in Middle English, from Latin *tempus*.]

ten•sile (tĕn′səl *or* tĕn′sīl′) *adj.* **1.** Of or relating to tension. **2.** Capable of being stretched or extended.

tensile strength *n.* The resistance of a material to a force that tends to pull it apart, usually expressed as the measure of the largest force that can be applied in this way before the material breaks apart.

ten•sion (tĕn′shən) *n.* **1.a.** The act or process of stretching something tight. **b.** The condition of being so stretched; tautness. **2.a.** A force that tends to stretch or elongate something. **b.** A measure of such a force: *a tension of 50 pounds.* **3.** Mental, emotional, or nervous strain: *working under great tension.* **4.** Unfriendliness or hostility between persons or groups: *tension among the teammates.* **5.** A difference of electrical potential; voltage.

ten•sor (tĕn′sər *or* **tĕn′**sôr′) *n.* A muscle that stretches or tightens a body part.

tent (tĕnt) *n.* A portable shelter, as of canvas, stretched over a supporting framework of poles with ropes and pegs. [First written down before 1300 in Middle English, from Old French *tente*, from Latin *tendere*, to stretch out.]

ten•ta•cle (tĕn′tə kəl) *n.* **1.** One of the narrow, flexible, unjointed parts extending from the body of certain animals, such as an octopus, jellyfish, or sea anemone, that are used for feeling, grasping, or moving. **2.** One of the sensitive hairs on the leaves of certain plants. **3.** Something resembling a tentacle, especially in the ability to grasp or hold.

ten•ta•tive (tĕn′tə tĭv) *adj.* **1.** Not fully worked out, concluded, or agreed on: *a tentative production schedule.* **2.** Uncertain; hesitant.

tent caterpillar *n.* Any of several destructive caterpillars whose colonies construct silken webs in the branches of trees.

ten•ter (tĕn′tər) *n.* A frame on which cloth is stretched while it dries to keep it from shrinking.

ten•ter•hook (tĕn′tər ho͝ok′) *n.* A hooked nail used to fasten cloth on a tenter. —***idiom.* on tenterhooks.** In a state of uneasiness, suspense, or anxiety: *I was on tenterhooks before the party.*

tenth (tĕnth) *n.* **1.** The ordinal number matching the number ten in a series. **2.** One of ten equal parts. —**tenth** *adv. & adj.*

ten•u•ous (tĕn′yo͞o əs) *adj.* **1.** Long and thin; slender: *a tenuous nylon rope.* **2.** Having little substance; flimsy: *the tenuous character of his political ideas.* [First written down in 1597 in Modern English, from Latin *tenuis*, thin.] —**ten′u•ous•ly** *adv.* —**ten′u•ous•ness** *n.*

ten•ure (tĕn′yər *or* tĕn′yo͝or′) *n.* **1.** The holding of something in one's possession, as an office; an occupation. **2.** The terms under which something is held. **3.a.** The period of holding something. **b.** The status of holding one's position on a permanent basis without renewing one's contract of appointment: *academic tenure.*

te•pee also **tee•pee** (tē′pē) *n.* A portable dwelling of certain Native American peoples, consisting of a conical framework of poles covered with skins or bark. [First written down in 1743 in American English and spelled *ti pee*, from Sioux *tʰipi*, dwelling.]

tep•id (tĕp′ĭd) *adj.* Moderately warm; lukewarm: *tepid water.*

te•qui•la (tə kē′lə) *n.* An alcoholic liquor made from the juice of a Central American century plant.

ter•bi•um (tûr′bē əm) *n. Symbol* **Tb** A rare-earth element used in x-ray and color television tubes. Atomic number 65. See table at **element.**

Te•re•sa (tə rē′sə *or* tə rē′zə), Mother. b. 1910. Albanian-born Indian nun who won the 1979 Nobel Peace Prize.

term (tûrm) *n.* **1.a.** A limited period of time: *worked in a mine for a term.* **b.** An assigned period for a person to serve: *served a six-year term as senator.* **c.** A period when a school or court is in session. **2.** A point in time at which something ends; a termination: *Our lease is approaching its term.* **3.a.** A word or group of words having a particular meaning: *used a series of medical terms.* **b. terms.** Language of a certain kind; chosen words: *He spoke to us in no uncertain terms.* **4.** An element of an agreement; a condition. Often used in the plural: *peace terms.* **5. terms.** The relation between two persons or groups: *We're on good terms with the neighbors.* **6.a.** Each of the quantities or expressions that form the parts of a ratio or the numerator and denominator of a fraction. **b.** Any of the quantities in an equation that are connected to other quantities by a plus sign or minus sign. —*tr.v.* **termed, term•ing, terms.** To call by a particular term or name; designate. [First written down before 1200 in Middle English and spelled *terme*, from Latin *terminus*, boundary.]

ter•mi•nal (tûr′mə nəl) *adj.* **1.** Of, relating to, situated at, or forming a limit, an end, or a boundary. **2.** Causing, ending in, or approaching death; fatal: *a terminal disease.* —*n.* **1.** A point or part that forms the end. **2.** A point at which another conductor can be connected to an electric device or component. **3.** The station at the end of a railway, a bus line, or an airline. **4.** A device, often having a keyboard and a video display, through which data or information can enter or leave a computer system.

ter•mi•nate (tûr′mə nāt′) *v.* **ter•mi•nat•ed, ter•mi•nat•ing, ter•mi•nates.** —*tr.* **1.** To bring to an end or a halt: *terminate an employee's contract.* **2.** To occur at or form the end of; conclude: *A sonata terminated the concert.* —*intr.* **1.** To come to an end: *The lecture terminated in a question and answer period.* **2.** To have as an end or a result: *The negotiations terminated in a new treaty.* —**ter′mi•na′tion** *n.*

ter•mi•ni (tûr′mə nī′) *n.* A plural of **terminus.**

ter•mi•nol•o•gy (tûr′mə nŏl′ə jē) *n., pl.* **ter•mi•nol•o•gies.** The group of technical terms used in a particular trade, science, or art.

ter•mi•nus (tûr′mə nəs) *n., pl.* **ter•mi•nus•es** or **ter•mi•ni** (tûr′mə nī′). **1.** The final point; the end. **2.** An end point on a transportation line or the town in which it is located.

ter•mite (tûr′mīt′) *n.* Any of numerous pale-colored insects that live in large colonies and that feed on and destroy wood. Termites resemble ants in appearance and manner of living but are not related to them. [First written down in 1781 in Modern English, from Late Latin *termes*, wood-eating worm.]

tern (tûrn) *n.* Any of various sea birds related to and resembling the gulls, but generally smaller and having a forked tail. [First written down in 1678 in Modern English, of Scandinavian origin.]

❑ *These sound alike:* **tern, turn** (rotate).

terr. *abbr.* An abbreviation of: **1.** Territorial. **2.** Territory.

ter•race (tĕr′ĭs) *n.* **1.** A porch or walkway bordered by colonnades. **2.** A platform extending outdoors from a floor of a house or an apartment building. **3.** An open area adjacent to a house; a patio. **4.** A raised bank of earth having vertical or sloping sides and a flat top. **5.** A row of buildings erected on raised ground or on a sloping site. —*tr.v.* **ter•raced, ter•rac•ing, ter•rac•es.** To form into a terrace or terraces: *terraced the hillside.*

ter•ra cot•ta (tĕr′ə kŏt′ə) *n.* **1.** A hard, waterproof ceramic clay used in pottery and building construction. **2.** Ceramic wares made of this material.

terra fir•ma (fûr′mə) *n.* Solid ground; dry land: *back on terra firma after our long ocean voyage.*

ter•rain (tə rān′) *n.* **1.** An area of land; a region. **2.** The surface features of an area of land: *The trail led us over some rough terrain.*

Ter•ra•my•cin (tĕr′ə mī′sĭn). A trademark used for an antibiotic drug extracted from a soil mold and used against bacterial infections.

ter•ra•pin (tĕr′ə pĭn) *n.* Any of various North American turtles of ponds or coastal waters, often valued as food.

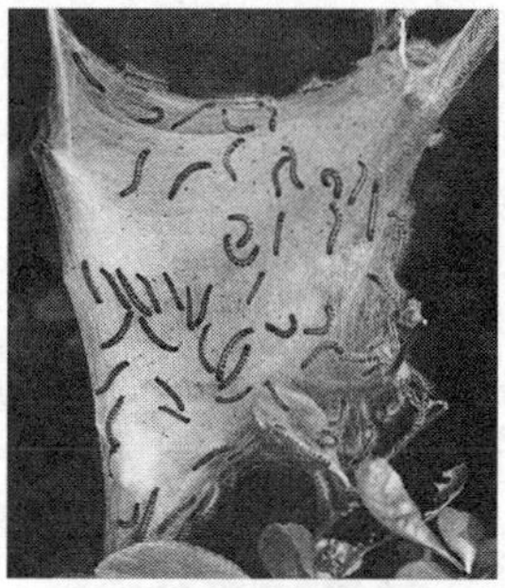

tent caterpillar
Tent caterpillars in nest

tepee
Modern Cheyenne tepee

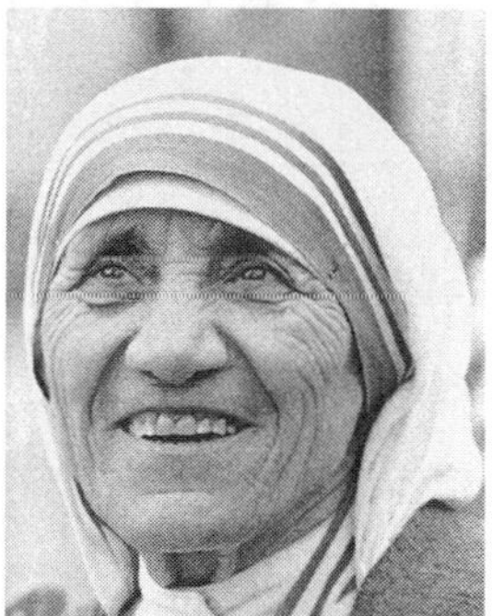

Mother Teresa

ă	pat	oi	boy
ā	pay	ou	out
âr	care	o͝o	took
ä	father	o͞o	boot
ĕ	pet	ŭ	cut
ē	be	ûr	urge
ĭ	pit	th	thin
ī	pie	*th*	this
îr	pier	hw	whoop
ŏ	pot	zh	vision
ō	toe	ə	about
ô	paw	N	*French* bon

terrarium

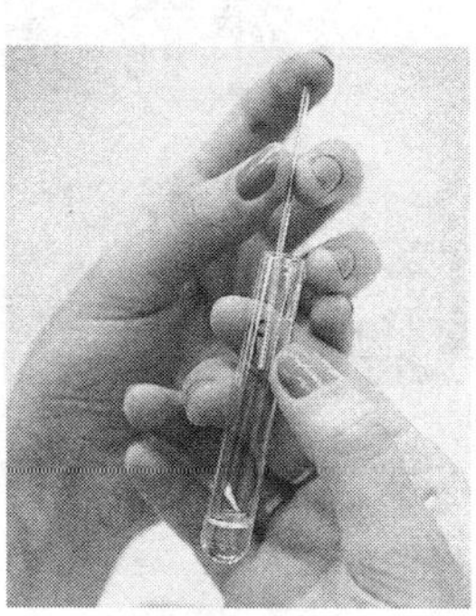
test tube

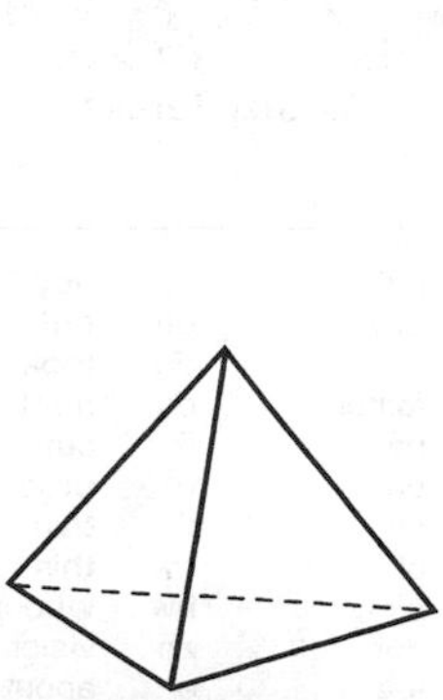
tetrahedron

ter•rar•i•um (tə râr′ē əm) *n., pl.* **ter•rar•i•ums** or **ter•rar•i•a** (tə râr′ē ə). A small enclosure or closed container in which selected plants and sometimes small animals, such as turtles, are kept and observed. [First written down in 1890 in Modern English, from Latin *terra*, earth.]

ter•res•tri•al (tə rĕs′trē əl) *adj.* **1.** Of or relating to Earth or its inhabitants: *The craters of the moon look like some terrestrial craters.* **2.** Of, relating to, or consisting of land. **3.** Living or growing on land.

ter•ri•ble (tĕr′ə bəl) *adj.* **1.** Causing great alarm or fear; dreadful: *a terrible storm.* **2.** Extreme in extent or degree: *the terrible heat in the tropics.* **3.** Unpleasant; disagreeable: *We had a terrible time at the party.* **4.** Very bad in quality: *a terrible movie.* [First written down about 1400 in Middle English, from Latin *terribilis*, from *terrēre*, to frighten.] **—ter′ri•bly** *adv.*

ter•ri•er (tĕr′ē ər) *n.* Any of several usually small active dogs originally used for hunting small burrowing animals.

ter•ri•fic (tə rĭf′ĭk) *adj.* **1.** Causing terror or great fear; terrifying: *a terrific storm.* **2.** Very bad or unpleasant: *a terrific headache.* **3.** Very good: *a terrific party.* **4.** Awesome; astounding: *a train moving at a terrific speed.* **—ter•rif′i•cal•ly** *adv.*

ter•ri•fy (tĕr′ə fī′) *tr.v.* **ter•ri•fied, ter•ri•fy•ing, ter•ri•fies.** To fill with terror; alarm: *Heights terrified her.* See Synonyms at **frighten.**

ter•ri•to•ri•al (tĕr′ĭ tôr′ē əl) *adj.* **1.** Of or relating to the geographic area under a given jurisdiction. **2.** Relating or restricted to a particular territory; regional.

territorial waters *pl.n.* Inland and coastal waters under the jurisdiction of a nation or state.

ter•ri•to•ry (tĕr′ĭ tôr′ē) *n., pl.* **ter•ri•to•ries. 1.** An area of land; a region. **2.** The land and waters under the jurisdiction of a government. **3.** Also **Territory. a.** A political subdivision of a country, especially one that is not a state but has its own legislature. **b.** A geographic region that is dependent on an external government. **4.** An area for which a person is responsible as a representative or an agent: *Oregon is his territory for sales.* **5.** An area, such as a nesting ground, in which an animal lives and from which it keeps out intruders, especially others of the same species. **6.** In sports, the area of a field defended by a team. [First written down before 1398 in Middle English and spelled *territorie*, from Latin *territōrium*, from *terra*, earth.]

ter•ror (tĕr′ər) *n.* **1.** Intense overpowering fear. **2.** A cause of intense fear: *Outlaws were the terror of the ranchers.* **3.** Violence committed by a group in order to frighten people or accomplish a goal, especially as part of a political policy. [First written down about 1375 in Middle English and spelled *terroure*, from Latin *terror*, from *terrēre*, to frighten.]

ter•ror•ism (tĕr′ə rĭz′əm) *n.* The unlawful use of violence to frighten people or accomplish a goal, often for political reasons. **—ter′ror•ist** *adj. & n.*

ter•ror•ize (tĕr′ə rīz′) *tr.v.* **ter•ror•ized, ter•ror•iz•ing, ter•ror•iz•es. 1.** To fill or overpower with terror. **2.** To force (someone to do something) by fear and intimidation.

ter•ry (tĕr′ē) *n.* A pile fabric, usually of cotton, with uncut loops on one or both sides, used for towels and bathrobes.

terse (tûrs) *adj.* **ters•er, ters•est.** Brief and to the point; concise: *Give that letter a terse reply.* **—terse′ly** *adv.* **—terse′ness** *n.*

ter•ti•ar•y (tûr′shē ĕr′ē) *adj.* **1.** Third in place, order, degree, or rank. **2. Tertiary.** Of, belonging to, or being the geologic time of the first period of the Cenozoic Era. During the Tertiary Period, modern plant life and apes and other large mammals appeared. See table at **geologic time.** *—n.* The Tertiary Period.

test (tĕst) *n.* **1.** A means of determining the presence, quality, or truth of something; a trial: *a vision test.* **2.** A series of questions, problems, or physical responses designed to determine knowledge, intelligence, or ability. **3.** A basis for evaluation or judgment: *This slope will provide a good test of our skiing skills.* **4.a.** A physical or chemical reaction for determining the properties or presence of a particular substance or class of substances, such as disease germs of a particular type. **b.** The procedure, reagents, and stains used in producing this reaction. *—v.* **test•ed, test•ing, tests.** *—tr.* To subject to a test; try: *test one's strength; test a food for purity.* *—intr.* To undergo a test, especially with an indicated result: *The ore tested high in uranium content.* **—test′er** *n.*

Test. *abbr.* An abbreviation of Testament.

tes•ta•ment (tĕs′tə mənt) *n.* **1.** Something that serves as tangible proof or evidence. **2.** A statement of belief; a credo. **3.** A document providing for the disposing of a person's property after death; a will. **4. Testament.** Either of the two main divisions of the Christian Bible.

tes•tate (tĕs′tāt′) *adj.* Having made a legally valid will before death.

tes•ta•tor (tĕs′tā′tər *or* tĕ stā′tər) *n.* A person who has made a legally valid will before death.

test-drive (tĕst′drīv′) *tr.v.* **test-drove** (tĕst′drōv′), **test-driv•en** (tĕst′drĭv′ən), **test-driv•ing, test-drives.** To drive (a motor vehicle) to test its performance and condition.

tes•tes (tĕs′tēz) *n.* Plural of **testis.**

tes•ti•cle (tĕs′tĭ kəl) *n.* A testis, especially one contained within a scrotum.

tes•ti•fy (tĕs′tə fī′) *v.* **test•i•fied, test•i•fy•ing, test•i•fies.** *—intr.* **1.** To make a declaration of truth or fact under oath: *Two witnesses testified against him in court.* **2.** To express or declare a strong belief. *—tr.* **1.** To declare publicly; make known. **2.** To state or affirm under oath: *testified in court that she saw the defendant.* [First written down about 1387 in Middle English and spelled *testifien*, from Latin *testificārī*, from *testis*, witness.]

tes•ti•mo•ni•al (tĕs′tə mō′nē əl) *n.* **1.** A statement in support of a particular fact, truth, or claim. **2.** A statement or letter affirming the quality of another's character or worth; a recommendation. **3.** Something given as a tribute for a person's achievement.

tes•ti•mo•ny (tĕs′tə mō′nē) *n., pl.* **tes•ti•mo•nies. 1.** A declaration by a witness under oath. **2.** Evidence in support of a fact or an assertion; proof.

tes•tis (tĕs′tĭs) *n., pl.* **tes•tes** (tĕs′tēz). A reproductive gland in male animals, usually one of a pair in which sperm is produced.

tes•tos•ter•one (tĕs tŏs′tə rōn′) *n.* A hormone produced primarily in the testes and responsible for male secondary sex characteristics.

test pilot *n.* A pilot who flies new or experimental aircraft in order to test them.

test tube *n.* A cylindrical tube of clear glass, usually open at one end and rounded at the other, used in laboratory tests and experiments.

test-tube baby (tĕst′to͞ob′ *or* tĕst′tyo͞ob′) *n.* A baby developed from an egg fertilized outside the body and then placed in the uterus of the mother.

tes•ty (tĕs′tē) *adj.* **tes•ti•er, tes•ti•est.** Irritable, impatient, or exasperated: *I was testy after being stuck in traffic.* **—tes′ti•ly** *adv.* **—tes′ti•ness** *n.*

tet•a•nus (tĕt′n əs) *n.* A serious, often fatal disease caused by bacteria that generally enter the body through a deep wound. The main symptoms are muscular rigidity and muscular spasms.

tête-à-tête (tāt′ə **tāt′** *or* tĕt′ə **tĕt′**) *n.* A private conversation between two people.

teth•er (**tĕth′**ər) *n.* **1.** A rope or chain that is secured to keep an animal within a small area. **2.** The range or scope of one's resources or abilities: *an overworked intern at the end of his tether.* —*tr.v.* **teth•ered, teth•er•ing, teth•ers.** To fasten or restrict with or as if with a tether. [First written down in 1376 in Middle English and spelled *tethir,* from Old Norse *tjōdhr.*]

Te•ton (**tē′**tŏn′) *n., pl.* **Teton** or **Te•tons.** A member of the largest group of the Sioux peoples, living in the western Great Plains.

tet•ra (**tĕt′**rə) *n.* Any of numerous small, brightly colored tropical freshwater fishes, often kept in home aquariums.

tet•ra•he•dron (tĕt′rə **hē′**drən) *n., pl.* **tet•ra•he•drons** or **tet•ra•he•dra** (tĕt′rə **hē′**drə). A solid geometric figure with four triangular faces.

te•tram•e•ter (tĕ **trăm′**ĭ tər) *n.* In poetry, a line of verse made up of four metrical feet.

tet•rarch (**tĕt′**rärk′ *or* **tē′**trärk′) *n.* **1.** A governor of one of the four divisions of a country or province, especially in the Roman Empire. **2.** A subordinate ruler.

Teu•ton (**to͞ot′**n *or* **tyo͞ot′**n) *n.* **1.** A member of an ancient people who lived in Denmark and northern Germany until about 100 B.C. **2.** A German.

Teu•ton•ic (to͞o **tŏn′**ĭk *or* tyo͞o **tŏn′**ĭk) *adj.* **1.** Of or relating to the ancient Teutons. **2.** Germanic. —*n.* Of or relating to the Germanic languages.

Tex. *abbr.* An abbreviation of Texas.

Tex•as (**tĕk′**səs). A state of the south-central United States south of Oklahoma. It was admitted as the 28th state in 1845. Texas won its independence from Mexico in 1836 and formed an independent republic that lasted until 1845. Austin is the capital and Houston is the largest city. Population, 17,059,805. —SEE NOTE.

text (tĕkst) *n.* **1.** The original wording or words of something written or printed. **2.** The main body of a printed work as distinguished from a preface, footnote, or illustration. **3.** A passage of a written work, especially the Bible, used as the starting point of a sermon or discussion. **4.** A subject; a topic: *the text of a discussion.* **5.** A textbook. [First written down in 1369 in Middle English, from Latin *textus,* structure, context, body of a passage, from *texere,* to weave, fabricate.]

text•book (**tĕkst′**bo͝ok′) *n.* A book used in schools or colleges for the formal study of a subject.

tex•tile (**tĕks′**tīl′ *or* **tĕks′**təl) *n.* **1.** A cloth or fabric, especially when woven or knitted. **2.** Fiber or yarn for weaving or knitting into cloth. [First written down in 1626 in Modern English, from Latin *textilis,* woven, from *texere,* to weave.]

tex•tu•al (**tĕks′**cho͞o əl) *adj.* Of, relating to, or conforming to a text. **—tex′tu•al•ly** *adv.*

tex•ture (**tĕks′**chər) *n.* **1.** The structure of the interwoven threads or strands of a fabric: *Burlap has a coarse texture.* **2.** The appearance and feel of a surface: *The plaster gives the wall a rough texture.* **3.** The characteristic composition or structure of a substance or object: *soil with a sandy texture.*

Th The symbol for the element **thorium.**

-th *suff.* A suffix used to form ordinal numbers: *hundredth.*

Thai (tī) *n., pl.* **Thai** or **Thais. 1.** A native or inhabitant of Thailand. **2.** The official language of Thailand. —*adj.* Of or relating to Thailand or its peoples, languages, or cultures.

Thai•land (**tī′**lănd′ *or* **tī′**lənd). Formerly **Si•am** (sī **ăm′**). A country of southeast Asia on the **Gulf of Thailand,** an arm of the South China Sea. Bangkok is the capital and the largest city. Population, 49,515,074.

thal•a•mus (**thăl′**ə məs) *n., pl.* **thal•a•mi** (**thăl′**ə mī′). A large rounded mass of gray nerve tissue located under the cerebrum, to which it relays sensory stimuli.

thal•li (**thăl′**ī) *n.* A plural of **thallus.**

thal•li•um (**thăl′**ē əm) *n. Symbol* **Tl** A soft, highly poisonous metallic element used in making glass of high refractive power. Atomic number 81. See table at **element.**

thal•lo•phyte (**thăl′**ə fīt′) *n.* Any of a group of organisms similar to plants but having no true roots, leaves, or stems, as the algae and fungi. Thallophytes were formerly considered plants.

thal•lus (**thăl′**əs) *n., pl.* **thal•li** (**thăl′**ī) or **thal•lus•es.** A plant body that is not divided into stem, root, or leaf.

Thames (tĕmz). A river of southern England flowing about 210 miles (338 kilometers) eastward to the North Sea.

than (*th*ăn *or th*ən) *conj.* Used to introduce the second element or clause of an unequal comparison: *She's a better skier than I am.* —*prep.* In comparison with: *We admire no one more than him.*

thane (thān) *n.* **1.** In Anglo-Saxon England, a freeman granted land by the king in return for military service. **2.** A feudal lord or baron in Scotland.

thank (thăngk) *tr.v.* **thanked, thank•ing, thanks.** To express gratitude to: *We thanked her for the kind offer.* [First written down about 725 in Old English and spelled *thancian.*]

thank•ful (**thăngk′**fəl) *adj.* Showing or feeling gratitude; grateful. **—thank′ful•ly** *adv.* **—thank′ful•ness** *n.*

thank•less (**thăngk′**lĭs) *adj.* **1.** Not feeling or showing gratitude; ungrateful. **2.** Not likely to be appreciated: *a thankless task.*

thanks (thăngks) *pl.n.* An acknowledgment of a favor or gift. —*interj.* An expression used to show gratitude. **—*idiom.* thanks to.** On account of; because of.

thanks•giv•ing (thăngks **gĭv′**ĭng) *n.* **1.** An act of giving thanks; an expression of gratitude, especially to God. **2. Thanksgiving.** A holiday for giving thanks, celebrated in the United States on the fourth Thursday of November and in Canada on the second Monday of October.

that (*th*ăt *or th*ət) *pron.* pl. **those** (*th*ōz). **1.** Used to refer to the one mentioned or understood: *What kind of soup is that?* **2.** Used to indicate the farther or less immediate one: *That is for sale; this is not.* **3. those.** Used to indicate an unspecified number of people: *those who refused to join.* **4.** Used as a relative pronoun to introduce a clause, especially a restrictive clause: *the car that has the flat tire.* **5.** In, on, by, or with which: *each summer that the concerts are performed.* —*adj.* pl. **those. 1.** Being the one singled out, implied, or understood: *that place; those mountains.* **2.** Being the one further removed or less obvious: *That route is shorter than this one.* —*adv.* To such an extent or degree: *Is your problem that complicated?* —*conj.* **1.** Used to introduce a subordinate clause stating a result, wish, purpose, reason, or cause: *We hope that you will enjoy the book.* **2.a.** Used to introduce a subordinate clause modifying an adverb or adverbial expression: *The dogs will go anywhere that they are welcome.* **b.** Used to introduce a subordinate clause that is joined to an adjective or a noun as a complement: *I was sure that she was right. He has a feeling that interest rates will rise soon.* **—*idiom.* that is.** To explain more clearly; in other words: *on the first floor, that is, the floor at street level.* [First written

Texas

The name **Texas** comes from a Caddo word meaning "friend" or "ally" that the Spaniards applied to the area in eastern Texas where the Caddo lived. The state later took its name from this area.

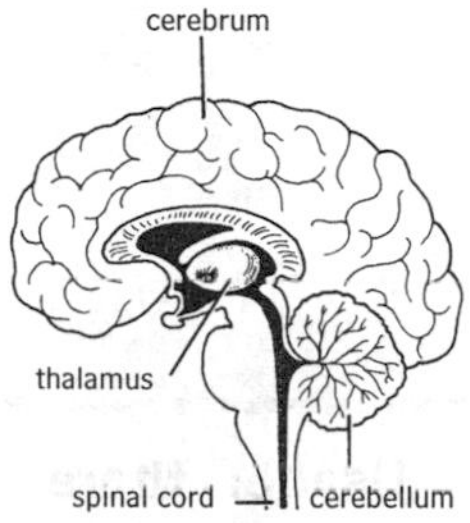

thalamus

Usage: that

Use **that** to introduce a restrictive relative clause, which serves to identify what is being talked about: *The house that Jack built has been torn down.* In this sentence the clause *that Jack built* tells which house was torn down. Use **which** with a nonrestrictive clause, which gives additional information about something that has already been identified: *The students in Chemistry 10 have been complaining about the textbook, which is hard to follow.* We know that the textbook under discussion is the one used in Chemistry 10. The fact that the textbook is hard to follow is additional information.

ă	pat	oi	boy
ā	pay	ou	out
âr	care	o͝o	took
ä	father	o͞o	boot
ĕ	pet	ŭ	cut
ē	be	ûr	urge
ĭ	pit	th	thin
ī	pie	*th*	this
îr	pier	hw	whoop
ŏ	pot	zh	vision
ō	toe	ə	about
ô	paw	N	*French* bon

Margaret Thatcher

Usage: there

When you use **there** before a verb such as *be*, *seem*, or *appear*, make sure that the verb agrees in number with the following subject: *There is a great pizza place across the street. There are beautiful wildflowers in the meadow.*

Word Building: thermo–

The prefix **thermo–** comes from the Greek word *thermos*, meaning "warm, hot." When used to form words in English, **thermo–** generally refers to heat, as in **thermodynamic**, or sometimes to thermoelectricity, as in **thermocouple**. Most of the words that begin with **thermo–**, such as **thermodynamics**, **thermoelectricity**, **thermostat**, and **thermosphere**, have only come into being in the 19th and 20th centuries. Sometimes before a vowel **thermo–** becomes **therm–**, as in *thermanesthesia*, "inability to feel hot or cold."

down about 725 in Old English and spelled *thæt*.] —See Note on page 973.

thatch (thăch) *n*. **1**. Plant stalks or leaves, such as straw, reeds, or palm fronds, used for roofing. **2**. Something resembling this, such as a thick growth of hair on the head. —*tr.v*. **thatched, thatch•ing, thatch•es.** To cover with or as if with thatch: *thatch a cottage*. [First written down about 725 in Old English and spelled *thæc*.]

Thatch•er (thăch′ər), **Margaret Hilda.** Born 1925. British Conservative politician who served as prime minister (1979–1990).

thaw (thô) *v*. **thawed, thaw•ing, thaws.** —*intr*. **1**. To change from a frozen solid to a liquid by gradual warming; melt. **2**. To lose stiffness or numbness by being warmed: *I thawed my feet by the fire*. **3**. To become warm enough for snow and ice to melt: *It often thaws in January*. **4**. To become less formal or reserved: *Relations between the countries began to thaw*. —*tr*. To cause to thaw: *thaw out the chicken*. —*n*. **1**. The process of thawing. **2**. A period of warm weather during which snow and ice melt.

the[1] (*thē before a vowel; thə before a consonant*) *def. art*. **1**. Used before nouns or noun phrases that refer to specified persons or things: *The pen that I was looking for was under the newspaper*. **2**. Used before a noun to stress its uniqueness or importance: *Last night's party was the event of the year*. **3**. Used before a singular noun to make it general: *The buffalo is an endangered species*. **4**. Used before a proper name, as of a monument or ship: *the Alamo*. **5**. Used before an adjective to make it function as a noun and signify a class: *the rich and the powerful*. **6**. Used before a noun, meaning "per" or "each": *She can have my entire stock at one dollar the box*. [First written down about 950 in Old English and spelled *the*, alteration of *se*, masculine demonstrative pronoun.] —See Note at **article.**

the[2] (*thē before a vowel; thə before a consonant*) *adv*. **1**. Because of that: *thinks the better of you*. **2**. To that extent; by that much: *the sooner the better*. **3**. Beyond any other: *Of all my cousins, I like you the best*. [First written down before 899 in Old English and spelled *thȳ, thē*.]

the•a•ter or **the•a•tre** (thē′ə tər) *n*. **1**. A building, a room, or an outdoor structure where plays or motion pictures are presented. **2**. Dramatic literature or its performance; drama. **3**. A place that is the setting for dramatic events.

the•at•ri•cal (thē ăt′rĭ kəl) *adj*. **1**. Of, relating to, or suitable for the theater. **2**. Marked by self-display or exaggerated behavior; affectedly dramatic: *had a theatrical way of saying good-bye*. —*n*. Stage performances, or a stage performance, especially by amateurs. Often used in the plural: *He likes directing theatricals*. —**the•at′ri•cal•ly** *adv*.

Thebes (thēbz). **1**. An ancient city on the Nile River in present-day central Egypt. It flourished from the mid 22nd to the 18th century B.C. The tomb of Tutankhamen is nearby. **2**. An ancient city of east-central Greece northwest of Athens. It reached the height of its power in the fourth century B.C.

thee (*thē*) *pron*. The objective case of **thou.**

theft (thĕft) *n*. The act or an instance of stealing; larceny.

their (*thâr*) *adj*. The possessive form of **they.** Belonging to or relating to them: *Pittsburgh is their home town*. [First written down about 1200 in Middle English and spelled *theggre*, from Old Norse *theira*, theirs.]

❑ *These sound alike:* **their, there** (at that place), **they're** (they are).

theirs (*thârz*) *pron*. *(used with a singular or plural verb)*. The one or ones belonging to them: *If your car is not working, use theirs*.

them (*thĕm or thəm*) *pron*. The objective case of **they. 1**. Used as the direct object of a verb: *I helped them fix a flat tire*. **2**. Used as the indirect object of a verb: *I paid them a visit*. **3**. Used as the object of a preposition: *I saved the best seats for them*. [First written down about 1200 in Middle English and spelled *theggm*, from Old Norse *theim* and Old English *thǣm*.] —See Note at **me.**

the•mat•ic (thĭ măt′ĭk) *adj*. Of, relating to, or being a theme or themes. —**the•mat′i•cal•ly** *adv*.

theme (thēm) *n*. **1**. A topic of discussion or discourse. See Synonyms at **subject. 2**. A short written composition, especially a school composition. **3**. The principal melody in a musical composition. [First written down before 1325 in Middle English and spelled *teme*, from Greek *thema*.]

them•selves (*thĕm* sĕlvz′ *or thəm* sĕlvz′) *pron*. **1**. The ones that are the same as them. **a**. Used as the direct or indirect object of a verb or as the object of a preposition, to show that the action of the verb refers back to the subject: *They prepared themselves for the trip. The travelers gave themselves plenty of time. They saved the best for themselves*. **b**. Used to give emphasis: *The cooks themselves will eat in the kitchen*. **2**. Their normal or healthy selves: *After getting over their jet lag, they're themselves again*.

then (*thĕn*) *adv*. **1**. At that time: *We were younger then*. **2**. Next in time, space, or order; immediately afterward: *We'll get ice cream, and then we'll go home*. **3**. Moreover; besides: *He wasn't feeling well and then he was in a bad mood anyway*. **4.a**. In that case: *If you want to go, then go*. **b**. Therefore; consequently: *If x equals 11 and y equals 3, then xy equals 33*. —*n*. That time or moment: *From then on, we were close friends*. —*adj*. Being so at the time: *the then President*. —***idiom*. and then some.** *Informal*. With considerably more in addition: *I made enough to serve all the guests and then some*. [First written down about 725 in Old English and spelled *thenne*.]

thence (*thĕns or* thĕns) *adv*. From there on: *We flew to Chicago and thence to St. Louis*.

thence•forth (*thĕns* fôrth′ *or* thĕns fôrth′) *adv*. From that time forward; thereafter: *Thenceforth she became steadily more conservative*.

thence•for•ward (*thĕns* fôr′wərd *or* thĕns fôr′-wərd) *adv*. **1**. Thenceforth. **2**. From that time or place on.

the•oc•ra•cy (thē ŏk′rə sē) *n*., *pl*. **the•oc•ra•cies. 1**. A government ruled by or subject to religious authority. **2**. A state so governed.

the•o•crat•ic (thē′ə krăt′ĭk) *adj*. Of, relating to, or based on theocracy.

theol. *abbr*. An abbreviation of: **1**. Theological. **2**. Theology.

the•o•lo•gi•an (thē′ə lō′jən) *n*. A person who is learned in theology.

the•o•log•i•cal (thē′ə lŏj′ĭ kəl) *adj*. Of or relating to theology.

the•ol•o•gy (thē ŏl′ə jē) *n*., *pl*. **the•ol•o•gies.** The study of the nature of God and religious truth; rational inquiry into religious questions. [First written down before 1376 in Middle English and spelled *teologie*, from Greek *theologia* : *theos*, god + *-logia*, study.]

the•o•rem (thē′ər əm *or* thîr′əm) *n*. **1**. An idea that is demonstrably true or is assumed to be so. **2**. A mathematical statement whose truth can be proved on the basis of a given set of axioms or assumptions.

the•o•ret•i•cal (thē′ə rĕt′ĭ kəl) also **the•o•ret•ic** (thē′ə rĕt′ĭk) *adj*. **1**. Of, based on, or relating to theory. **2**. Restricted to theory; not practical: *theoretical physics*. —**the′o•ret′i•cal•ly** *adv*.

the•o•re•ti•cian (thē′ər ĭ **tĭsh′**ən *or* thîr′ĭ **tĭsh′**ən) *n.* A person who formulates, studies, or is expert in the theory of a science or an art.

the•o•rist (**thē′**ər ĭst *or* **thîr′**ĭst) *n.* A person who formulates a theory; a theoretician.

the•o•rize (**thē′**ə rīz′ *or* **thîr′**īz) *intr.v.* **the•o•rized, the•o•riz•ing, the•o•riz•es.** To formulate a theory or theories; speculate.

the•o•ry (**thē′**ə rē *or* **thîr′**ē) *n., pl.* **the•o•ries. 1.a.** A statement or set of statements designed to explain an event or a group of events. **b.** Knowledge of such statements as distinguished from experiment or practice. **2.** A belief that guides action or assists comprehension or judgment: *We went fishing on the theory that the rain would cause the fish to bite.* **3.** An assumption based on limited information or knowledge; a guess. [First written down in 1597 in Modern English, from Greek *theōria.*]

ther•a•peu•tic (thĕr′ə **pyōō′**tĭk) *adj.* Having the capability of healing or curing: *a therapeutic bath.* **—ther′a•peu′ti•cal•ly** *adv.*

ther•a•peu•tics (thĕr′ə **pyōō′**tĭks) *n. (used with a singular verb).* The medical treatment of disease.

ther•a•pist (**thĕr′**ə pĭst) *n.* A person who specializes in a particular kind of therapy.

ther•a•py (**thĕr′**ə pē) *n., pl.* **ther•a•pies. 1.** A procedure designed to heal or cure an illness or a disability. **2.** Psychotherapy. **3.** Healing power or quality: *the therapy of fresh air and exercise.* [First written down in 1846 in Modern English, from Greek *therapeia.*]

there (*th*âr) *adv.* **1.** At or in that place: *Set the package over there.* **2.** To, into, or toward that place: *How long did it take to get there?* **3.** At that stage, moment, or point: *The violins come in there.* **4.** In that matter: *I can't agree with you there.* *—pron.* **1.** Used to introduce a clause or sentence: *There are different kinds of pepper.* **2.** Used to indicate a person in direct address: *Hello there.* *—n.* That place or point: *I'll never know how we got out of there.* *—interj.* An expression used to show feelings such as satisfaction, sympathy, relief, or anger: *There, there, you'll be fine.* [First written down before 800 in Old English and spelled *thǣr.*] —SEE NOTE.

❑ *These sound alike:* **there, their** (belonging to them), **they're** (they are).

there•a•bouts (*th*âr′ə **bouts′**) *adv.* **1.** Near that place; about there: *somewhere in the Rockies or thereabouts.* **2.** About that number, amount, or time: *at 8 o'clock or thereabouts.*

there•af•ter (*th*âr **ăf′**tər) *adv.* From a specified time onward; from then on: *Thereafter, people were glad to come to our concerts.*

there•at (*th*âr **ăt′**) *adv.* **1.** At that place; there. **2.** At the event; on account of that: *I replied sharply, and thereat the man kept quiet.*

there•by (*th*âr **bī′**) *adv.* By that means; because of that: *We put down the storm windows to keep out drafts and thereby conserve heat.*

there•fore (***th*âr′**fôr′) *adv.* For that reason or cause; consequently: *The fungi lack chlorophyll and are therefore dependent upon other plants and animals for their food.*

there•from (*th*âr **frŭm′** *or* *th*âr **frŏm′**) *adv.* From that place, time, or thing.

there•in (*th*âr **ĭn′**) *adv.* **1.** In that place, time, or thing: *the house and everything therein.* **2.** In that respect: *He was never elected President; therein lay his great frustration.*

there•of (*th*âr **ŭv′** *or* *th*âr **ŏv′**) *adv.* Of or concerning this, that, or it: *born in the United States and subject to the jurisdiction thereof.*

there•on (*th*âr **ŏn′** *or* *th*âr **ôn′**) *adv.* On or upon this, that, or it.

there•to (*th*âr **tōō′**) *adv.* To that, this, or it: *She got a house with furnishings in addition thereto.*

there•to•fore (***th*âr′**tə fôr′) *adv.* Until that time; before that: *a house where none had been theretofore.*

there•un•der (*th*âr **ŭn′**dər) *adv.* Under this, that, or it: *the floor planks and all stowed thereunder.*

there•un•to (*th*âr′ŭn **tōō′**) *adv. Archaic.* To that, this, or it; thereto.

there•up•on (*th*âr′ə **pŏn′** *or* *th*âr′ə **pôn′**) *adv.* After that; directly following that: *He criticized the judge and was thereupon summoned to court.*

there•with (*th*âr **wĭth′** *or* *th*âr **wĭ*th*′**) *adv.* With this, that, or it: *He got a microscope, and therewith his fate was sealed—he had to become a scientist.*

ther•mal (**thûr′**məl) *adj.* **1.** Of, relating to, using, producing, or caused by heat. **2.** Intended or designed to help retain body heat: *thermal underwear.* *—n.* A current of warm air that rises because it is less dense than the air around it. [First written down in 1756 in Modern English, from Greek *thermē,* heat.] **—ther′mal•ly** *adv.*

therm•i•on (**thûr′**mī′ən) *n.* An electrically charged particle or ion that is emitted by a conducting material as a result of heat.

thermo– or **therm–** *pref.* A prefix that means heat: *thermometer.* —SEE NOTE.

ther•mo•cou•ple (**thûr′**mə kŭp′əl) *n.* A thermoelectric device used to measure temperatures, especially high temperatures, accurately. It usually consists of a junction of dissimilar metals across which a voltage that varies with temperature is produced. Thermocouples are used as thermometers, to generate electricity, and to make refrigeration devices.

ther•mo•dy•nam•ic (thûr′mō dī **năm′**ĭk) *adj.* **1.** Of or having to do with thermodynamics. **2.** Of or operating by mechanical power derived from heat.

ther•mo•dy•nam•ics (thûr′mō dī **năm′**ĭks) *n. (used with a singular verb).* The part of physics that deals with the relationships between heat and other forms of energy.

ther•mo•e•lec•tric (thûr′mō ĭ **lĕk′**trĭk) *adj.* Of or having to do with electricity that is generated by the action of heat.

ther•mo•e•lec•tric•i•ty (thûr′mō ĭ lĕk **trĭs′**ĭ tē *or* thûr′mō ē′lĕk **trĭs′**ĭ tē) *n.* Electricity generated by a flow of heat, as in a thermocouple.

ther•mo•graph (**thûr′**mə grăf′) *n.* A thermometer that records the temperatures it measures, usually indicating the time at which each measurement was made.

ther•mom•e•ter (thər **mŏm′**ĭ tər) *n.* An instrument that measures and indicates temperature, especially one that consists of a glass tube in which a liquid expands or contracts as the temperature increases or decreases.

ther•mo•nu•cle•ar (thûr′mō **nōō′**klē ər *or* thûr′mō **nyōō′**klē ər) *adj.* **1.** Of or derived from the fusion of atomic nuclei at high temperatures or the energy produced in this way. **2.** Of or relating to weapons based on nuclear fusion, especially as distinguished from those based on nuclear fission.

ther•mo•plas•tic (thûr′mə **plăs′**tĭk) *adj.* Soft and pliable when heated but hard when cooled. *—n.* A thermoplastic material.

Ther•mop•y•lae (thər **mŏp′**ə lē). A narrow pass of east-central Greece that was the site of a battle between the Spartans and the Persians in 480 B.C.

Ther•mos (**thûr′**məs). A trademark used for a brand of vacuum bottles and other insulated containers.

ther•mo•sphere (**thûr′**mə sfîr′) *n.* The outermost layer of the atmosphere, extending from the mesosphere to outer space, having temperatures that increase steadily with altitude.

ther•mo•stat (**thûr′**mə stăt′) *n.* A device that automatically controls a piece of heating or cooling

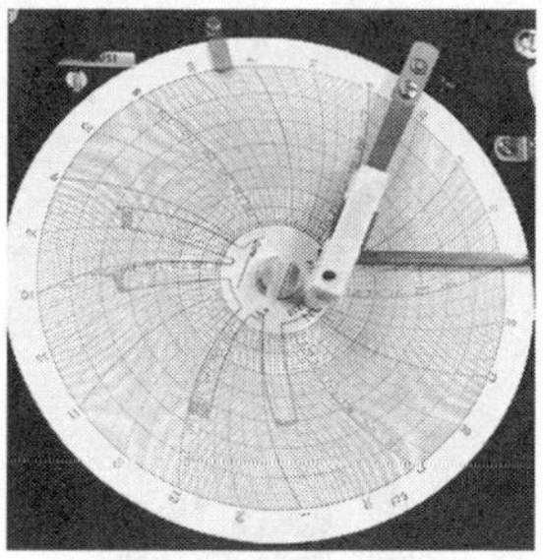

thermograph

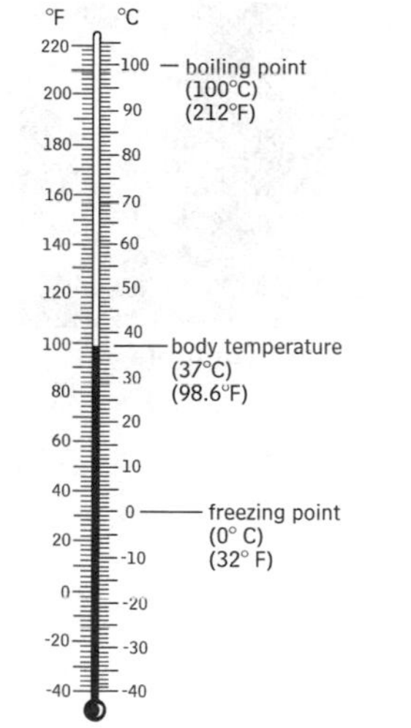

thermometer

ă	pat	oi	boy
ā	pay	ou	out
âr	care	ŏŏ	took
ä	father	ōō	boot
ĕ	pet	ŭ	cut
ē	be	ûr	urge
ĭ	pit	th	thin
ī	pie	*th*	this
îr	pier	hw	whoop
ŏ	pot	zh	vision
ō	toe	ə	about
ô	paw	N	*French* bon

Theseus
Theseus and the Minotaur
by Antoine Louis Barye
(1796–1875)

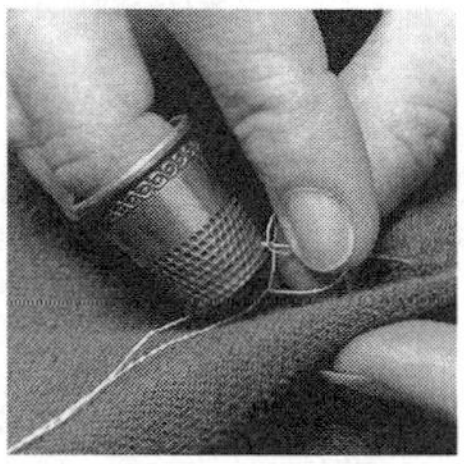

thimble

Usage: this

You can use either **this** or **that** to refer to a thought expressed earlier: *The letter was unopened; that* (or *this*) *in itself casts doubt on the detective's theory.* Only use **this** when you are referring to something that is yet to be mentioned: *This is what bothers me: we don't have enough time to get there.*

equipment in such a way as to keep the temperature nearly constant.

the•sau•rus (thĭ sôr′əs) *n., pl.* **the•sau•ri** (thĭ sôr′-ī′) or **the•sau•rus•es. 1.** A book of synonyms, often including antonyms. **2.** A book that lists all the words relating to a general idea or to a specific subject, such as medicine or music. [First written down in 1823 in Modern English, from Greek *thēsauros*, treasury.]

these (*th*ēz) *pron. & adj.* Plural of **this.**

the•ses (thē′sēz) *n.* Plural of **thesis.**

The•se•us (thē′sē əs) *n.* In Greek mythology, the king of Athens who slays the Minotaur.

the•sis (thē′sĭs) *n., pl.* **the•ses** (thē′sēz). **1.** A statement put forth for consideration, especially when supported by an argument. **2.** A long essay resulting from original research written especially by a candidate for an academic degree. [First written down in 1579 in Modern English, from Greek, from *tithenai*, to put.]

thes•pi•an (thĕs′pē ən) *adj.* Of or relating to drama; dramatic. —*n.* An actor or actress.

the•ta (thā′tə *or* thē′tə) *n.* The eighth letter of the Greek alphabet, written Θ, ϑ. In English it is represented as *Th, th.*

thew (thyo͞o) *n.* **1.** A well-developed sinew or muscle. **2.** Muscular power or strength. Often used in the plural.

they (*th*ā) *pron.* **1.** The persons, animals, or things previously mentioned: *Paula and Dick worked here last summer, but now they are back in school.* **2.** People considered as a group: *He's as smart as they come.* [First written down before 1200 in Middle English, from Old Norse *their.*] —SEE NOTE at **me.**

they'd (*th*ād). Contraction of *they had* or *they would.*

they'll (*th*āl). Contraction of *they will* or *they shall.*

they're (*th*âr). Contraction of *they are.*
❑ *These sound alike:* **they're, their** (belonging to them), **there** (at that place).

they've (*th*āv). Contraction of *they have.*

thi•a•mine (thī′ə mĭn *or* thī′ə mēn′) *n.* A vitamin of the B complex, found in bran, yeast, and meat, and necessary for carbohydrate metabolism and normal activity of the nervous system; vitamin B_1.

thick (thĭk) *adj.* **thick•er, thick•est. 1.** Relatively great in depth or in extent from one surface to the opposite; not thin: *a thick board.* **2.** Measuring in this dimension: *a board two inches thick.* **3.** Heavy in form or build; thickset: *a thick neck.* **4.** Flowing slowly; heavy or viscous: *thick oil.* **5.** Dense or concentrated: *thick fog; a thick forest.* **6.** Very noticeable; pronounced; heavy: *speaking with a thick accent.* **7.** *Informal.* Mentally slow; stupid. **8.** *Informal.* Very friendly: *The two are thick friends.* —*adv.* So as to be thick; thickly: *Slice it thick.* —*n.* **1.** The thickest part. **2.** The most active or intense part: *in the thick of the battle.* ***—idiom.* thick and thin.** Good and bad times: *promised to be there to help through thick and thin.* [First written down before 899 in Old English and spelled *thicce.*] **—thick′ly** *adv.*

thick•en (thĭk′ən) *tr. & intr.v.* **thick•ened, thick•en•ing, thick•ens. 1.** To make or become thick or thicker: *We thickened the gravy. The fog thickened.* **2.** To make or become more intricate or complex. **—thick′en•er** *n.*

thick•en•ing (thĭk′ə nĭng) *n.* **1.** The act or process of making or becoming thick. **2.** A substance, such as corn starch, used to thicken a liquid.

thick•et (thĭk′ĭt) *n.* A dense growth of shrubs or underbrush. [First written down before 1000 in Old English and spelled *thiccet*, from *thicce*, thick.]

thick•set (thĭk′sĕt′) *adj.* **1.** Having a solid stocky form or body; stout: *a thickset man.* **2.** Placed or positioned closely together: *thickset rose bushes.*

thick-skinned (thĭk′skĭnd′) *adj.* **1.** Having a thick skin or rind. **2.** Not easily offended, as by criticism or insult.

thief (thēf) *n., pl.* **thieves** (thēvz). A person who steals, especially one who steals by stealth rather than force. [First written down about 688 in Old English and spelled *thēof.*]

thieve (thēv) *tr. & intr.v.* **thieved, thiev•ing, thieves.** To take (something) by theft or commit theft.

thieves (thēvz) *n.* Plural of **thief.**

thigh (thī) *n.* **1.** The part of the human leg between the hip and the knee. **2.** A similar part of the body of an animal.

thigh•bone (thī′bōn′) *n.* The femur.

thim•ble (thĭm′bəl) *n.* A small cup, usually of metal or plastic, worn for protection on the finger that pushes the needle in sewing. [First written down about 1000 in Old English and spelled *thȳmel*, leather finger covering, from *thūma*, thumb.]

Thim•bu (thĭm′bo͞o′ *or* tĭm′bo͞o′). The capital of Bhutan, in the western part of the country in the eastern Himalaya Mountains. Population, 8,982.

thin (thĭn) *adj.* **thin•ner, thin•nest. 1.a.** Relatively small in extent from one surface to the opposite; not thick: *a thin board.* **b.** Not great in diameter or cross section; fine: *thin wire.* **2.** Lean or slender in form or build: *a thin man.* See Synonyms at **lean**^{2}. **3.** Not dense or concentrated; sparse: *hair that was thin on top.* **4.a.** Flowing with relative ease; not viscous: *a thin oil.* **b.** Watery: *thin soup.* **5.** Lacking substance or force; flimsy: *a thin excuse.* **6.** Lacking in strength or resonance, as a sound or tone. —*adv.* So as to be thin; thinly: *Slice the bread thin.* —*tr. & intr.v.* **thinned, thin•ning, thins.** To make or become thin or thinner: *I thinned the gravy. Wait until the crowd thins out.* [First written down in 849 in Old English and spelled *thynne.*] **—thin′ly** *adv.* **—thin′ness** *n.*

thine (*th*īn) *pron. (used with a singular or plural verb).* The one or ones belonging to thee. —*adj. Archaic.* A possessive form of **thou.** Used instead of *thy* before an initial vowel or *h*: *Know thine enemy.*

thing (thĭng) *n.* **1.** Something that can be perceived, known, or thought to have existence; an entity, an idea, or a quality. **2.** An individual object, especially an inanimate object: *not a thing in sight.* **3.** A creature: *That baby is the sweetest thing!* **4.** An article of clothing: *I can't wear that thing to the dance!* **5.** An act, a deed, or a work: *That was a nice thing to do for your sister.* **6.** The result of work or activity: *He's always drawing things.* **7.** A thought or an utterance: *What a rotten thing to say!* **8.** A goal or an objective: *In golf, the thing is to make the fewest strokes possible.* **9. things.** Personal possessions; belongings: *Have you packed your things for the weekend?* **10.** A matter of concern: *many things on my mind.* **11.** A turn of events; a circumstance: *The flood was a terrible thing.* **12. things.** The general state of affairs; conditions: *Things are really looking up.* **13.** *Informal.* The latest fashion or fad: *Long sweaters are the thing this fall.* **14.** *Slang.* An activity uniquely suitable or satisfying to one: *doing his own thing.* ***—idioms.* first thing.** *Informal.* Right away; before anything else: *We'll get the kitten vaccinated first thing.* **sure thing.** *Informal.* Of course; certainly: *Are you coming? Sure thing!* [First written down in 685 in Old English and spelled *thing*, assembly.]

think (thĭngk) *v.* **thought** (thôt), **think•ing, thinks.** —*tr.* **1.** To have or form in the mind: *Think what we could do with a computer.* **2.a.** To reason about or reflect on; ponder: *Think the matter through.* **b.** To decide by reasoning: *thinking what to do.* **3.** To judge or regard; look upon: *I think it only fair.* **4.** To believe; suppose: *He always thought he was right.* **5.** To devise; invent: *thought up a plan to improve the library.* —*intr.* **1.** To use the power of reason, as by conceiving ideas or making judgments. **2.** To weigh or consider an idea: *They are thinking about moving.* **3.a.** To bring a thought to mind by imagination or invention: *No one before had thought of bifocal glasses.* **b.** To recall a thought or an image to mind: *She thought of her childhood when she saw the movie.* **4.** To believe; suppose: *It's later than you think.* **5.** To have care or consideration: *Think first of the ones you love.* [First written down about 725 in Old English and spelled *thencan.*]

think tank *n.* A group or an institution organized for intensive research and solving of problems in such areas as technology and political strategy.

thin•ner (thĭn′ər) *n.* A liquid, such as turpentine, that is mixed with a paint or varnish to make it flow more easily as it is applied.

thin-skinned (thĭn′skĭnd′) *adj.* **1.** Having a thin rind or skin. **2.** Easily offended, as by criticism or insult.

third (thûrd) *n.* **1.** The ordinal number matching the number three in a series. **2.** One of three equal parts. **3.a.** The interval covering three tones in a musical scale. **b.** The third tone in a musical scale. **4.** The transmission gear used to produce speeds next highest to those of second in a motor vehicle. [First written down about 750 in Old English and spelled *thridda.*] **—third** *adv. & adj.*

third base *n.* **1.** In baseball, the base that must be touched last by a runner before reaching home plate, located to the left as one looks toward the pitcher from home plate. **2.** The position played by a third baseman.

third baseman *n.* The baseball player defending the area near third base.

third class *n.* **1.** A class of U.S. mail including all printed matter, except newspapers and magazines, that weighs less than 16 ounces and is unsealed. **2.** Accommodations, as on a ship or an airplane, of the third and usually lowest order of luxury and price. **—third′-class′** *adj.*

third-de•gree burn (thûrd′dĭ grē′) *n.* A severe burn in which the outer layer of skin is destroyed and sensitive nerve endings are exposed.

third person *n.* **1.** A set of grammatical forms used in referring to a person or thing other than the speaker or the one spoken to. **2.** A grammatical form belonging to such a set, as *he, she,* and *they.*

Third World *n.* The developing nations of Africa, Asia, and Latin America.

thirst (thûrst) *n.* **1.a.** A sensation of dryness in the mouth and throat related to a need or desire to drink. **b.** The desire to drink. **2.** An insistent desire; a craving: *a thirst for adventure.* —*intr.v.* **thirst•ed, thirst•ing, thirsts. 1.** To feel a need to drink. **2.** To have a strong craving; yearn: *thirsting for knowledge.* [First written down about 1000 in Old English and spelled *thurst.*]

thirst•y (thûr′stē) *adj.* **thirst•i•er, thirst•i•est. 1.** Desiring to drink: *Salty foods make one thirsty.* **2.** Arid; parched: *fields thirsty for rain.* **3.** Having a strong desire: *thirsty for knowledge.*

thir•teen (thûr tēn′) *n.* **1.** The number, written 13, that is equal to 12 + 1. **2.** The 13th in a set or sequence. **—thir•teen′** *adj. & pron.*

thir•teenth (thûr tēnth′) *n.* **1.** The ordinal number matching the number 13 in a series. **2.** One of 13 equal parts. **—thir′teenth′** *adv. & adj.*

thir•ti•eth (thûr′tē ĭth) *n.* **1.** The ordinal number matching the number 30 in a series. **2.** One of 30 equal parts. **—thir′ti•eth** *adv. & adj.*

thir•ty (thûr′tē) *n., pl.* **thir•ties.** The number, written 30, that is equal to 3 × 10.

thir•ty-sec•ond note (thûr′tē sĕk′ənd) *n.* A musical note having the time value of 1/32 of a whole note.

this (*th*ĭs) *pron.* pl. **these** (*th*ēz). **1.** Used to refer to the person or thing present, nearby, or just mentioned: *This is my friend Judy. This is my house.* **2.** Used to refer to what is about to be said: *This will really make you laugh.* **3.** Used to refer to the present occasion or time: *Jim's been out later than this.* **4.** Used to indicate the nearer or the more immediate one: *That little scene was nothing compared to this.* —*adj.* pl. **these. 1.** Being just mentioned or present in space, time, or thought: *We left early this morning.* **2.** Being nearer or more immediate: *Walk on this side of the street, not that side.* **3.** Being about to be stated or described: *Just wait until you hear this story.* —*adv.* To this extent; so: *I never stayed up this late before.* [First written down in 670 in Old English.] —SEE NOTE.

this•tle (thĭs′əl) *n.* Any of numerous prickly plants having usually purplish flowers and seeds tufted with silky fluff. [First written down about 700 in Old English and spelled *thistel.*]

this•tle•down (thĭs′əl doun′) *n.* The silky fluffy material attached to the seeds of a thistle, by means of which they float through the air.

thith•er (thĭ*th*′ər *or* *th*ĭ*th*′ər) *adv.* To or toward that place; in that direction; there: *running hither and thither.*

thole pin (thōl) *n.* A peg set in pairs in the gunwales of a boat to serve as an oarlock. [First written down about 725 in Old English and spelled *thol.*]

Thom•as (tŏm′əs), Saint. One of the 12 Apostles, who doubted that Jesus had risen from the dead until he saw the wounds.

Thomas, Dylan Marlais. 1914–1953. Welsh writer known especially for his poetry. He also wrote essays, short fiction, and works for radio.

thong (thông *or* thŏng) *n.* **1.** A narrow strip, as of leather, used for binding or lashing. **2.** A whip of plaited leather or cord. **3.** A sandal held on the foot by a strip that passes between the toes.

Thor (thôr) *n.* In Norse mythology, the god of thunder.

tho•ra•ces (thôr′ə sēz′) *n.* A plural of **thorax.**

tho•rac•ic (thə răs′ĭk) *adj.* Of, relating to, in, or near the thorax.

thoracic duct *n.* The main lymph duct of the body, rising along the spinal column and joining a vein near the heart.

tho•rax (thôr′ăks′) *n., pl.* **tho•rax•es** or **tho•ra•ces** (thôr′ə sēz′). **1.** The part of the human body between the neck and the diaphragm, enclosed partly by the ribs; the chest. **2.** A similar part in other animals. **3.** The middle division of the three-part body of an insect, bearing the true legs and wings.

Tho•reau (thə rō′ *or* thôr′ō), **Henry David.** 1817–1862. American writer whose works include *Walden* (1854).

tho•ri•um (thôr′ē əm) *n. Symbol* **Th** A silvery-white metallic element used in magnesium alloys and as a source of nuclear energy. Atomic number 90. See table at **element.**

thorn (thôrn) *n.* **1.** A sharp woody spine growing from the stem of a plant. **2.** Any of various shrubs, trees, or plants bearing such spines. **3.** Any of various sharp spiny projections; a prickle. **4.** A person or thing that causes sharp pain, irritation, or discomfort. [First written down about 750 in Old English.] **—thorn′less** *adj.*

thorn•y (thôr′nē) *adj.* **thorn•i•er, thorn•i•est. 1.** Full of or covered with thorns: *thorny branches.* **2.**

thistle
Scotch thistle

Dylan Thomas

Henry David Thoreau

ă	pat	oi	boy
ā	pay	ou	out
âr	care	o͝o	took
ä	father	o͞o	boot
ĕ	pet	ŭ	cut
ē	be	ûr	urge
ĭ	pit	th	thin
ī	pie	*th*	this
îr	pier	hw	whoop
ŏ	pot	zh	vision
ō	toe	ə	about
ô	paw	N	*French* bon

thrasher
Brown thrasher

Spiny: *a porcupine's thorny quills.* **3.** Painfully controversial; difficult: *a thorny situation.*

thor•ough (thûr′ō *or* thŭr′ō) *adj.* **1.** Complete in all respects: *a thorough search.* **2.** Painstakingly accurate or careful: *a thorough worker.* **3.** Absolute; utter: *a thorough success.* [First written down about 1000 in Old English and spelled *thuruh*, from end to end, through.] **—thor′ough•ly** *adv.* **—thor′ough•ness** *n.*

thor•ough•bred (thûr′ō brĕd′ *or* thŭr′ō brĕd′) *n.* **1.** An animal bred of pure or pedigreed stock. **2. Thoroughbred.** Any of a breed of horses resulting from the mating of English mares and certain Arabian stallions in the 18th century. **3.** A well-bred person. *—adj.* Bred of pure stock: *thoroughbred cattle.*

thor•ough•fare (thûr′ō fâr′ *or* thŭr′ō fâr′) *n.* **1.** A main road or public highway. **2.** A heavily traveled passage, such as a channel.

thor•ough•go•ing (thûr′ō gō′ĭng *or* thŭr′ō gō′ĭng) *adj.* Very thorough; complete: *a thoroughgoing overhaul of the company's management.*

those (*th*ōz) *pron.* *&* *adj.* Plural of **that.**

thou (*th*ou) *pron.* Used to address one person, especially a familiar person in literary or religious writing. [First written down about 725 in Old English and spelled *thū*.] —SEE NOTE at **you-all.**

though (*th*ō) *conj.* **1.** Despite the fact that; although: *He walked to work even though it was raining.* **2.** Even if: *Though our chances of winning are slim, I think we should play.* *—adv.* However; nevertheless: *It's not going to snow; it may rain, though.*

thought (thôt) *v.* Past tense and past participle of **think.** *—n.* **1.** The act or process of thinking: *spending hours in thought.* **2.** A product of thinking; an idea: *Let me have your thoughts on this subject.* See Synonyms at **idea. 3.** The intellectual activity or the ideas of a particular time or group: *ancient Greek thought.* **4.** Consideration; attention: *giving serious thought to the matter.* **5.** Intention; purpose: *She had no thought of hurting his feelings.*

thought•ful (thôt′fəl) *adj.* **1.** Occupied with thought; contemplative: *was thoughtful for a minute.* **2.** Showing or marked by careful thought: *a thoughtful paper.* **3.** Having or showing concern for others; considerate: *a thoughtful gesture.* **—thought′ful•ly** *adv.* **—thought′ful•ness** *n.*

thought•less (thôt′lĭs) *adj.* **1.** Characterized by or showing lack of thought or care; careless: *It was thoughtless of her to forget your birthday.* **2.** Inconsiderate; inattentive: *thoughtless of the feelings of others.* **—thought′less•ly** *adv.* **—thought′less•ness** *n.*

thou•sand (thou′zənd) *n.* The number, written as 1000 or 10^3, that is equal to 10×100. [First written down about 725 in Old English and spelled *thūsend*.] **—thou′sand** *adj.* *&* *pron.*

Thou•sand Islands (thou′zənd). A group of more than 1,800 islands of New York and Ontario, Canada, in the St. Lawrence River at the outlet of Lake Ontario.

thou•sandth (thou′zəndth *or* thou′zənth) *n.* **1.** The ordinal number matching the number 1000 in a series. **2.** One of 1000 equal parts. **—thou′sandth** *adv.* *&* *adj.*

thrash (thrăsh) *v.* **thrashed, thrash•ing, thrash•es.** *—tr.* **1.** To beat or flog with or as if with a flail, especially as a punishment. **2.** To defeat utterly. **3.** To thresh. *—intr.* To move wildly or violently: *a crocodile thrashing around in the water.*

thrash•er (thrăsh′ər) *n.* Any of various songbirds of North America having a long tail, a long curved beak, and often a spotted breast.

thrash•ing (thrăsh′ĭng) *n.* A severe beating; a whipping.

thread (thrĕd) *n.* **1.a.** Fine thin cord made of two or more strands of fiber twisted together and used in sewing and weaving cloth. **b.** A piece of such cord. **2.** Something that resembles a thread in thinness or fineness: *a thread of smoke coming out the chimney.* **3.** Something that suggests the continuousness of such a strand: *He lost the thread of his argument.* **4.** A helical or spiral ridge on a screw, nut, or bolt. *—v.* **thread•ed, thread•ing, threads.** *—tr.* **1.a.** To pass one end of a thread through the eye of (a needle, for example). **b.** To pass (something) through in the manner of thread: *thread the film through the projector.* **2.** To pass a thread, tape, or film into or through (a device): *thread the sewing machine; thread a film projector.* **3.** To connect by running a thread through; string: *thread beads.* **4.** To cut a thread onto (a screw, nut, or bolt). **5.** To make (one's way) cautiously through something: *pedestrians threading their way through a crowd.* *—intr.* **1.** To make one's way cautiously. **2.** To proceed in a winding course. [First written down before 800 in Old English and spelled *thrǣd*.] **—thread′er** *n.* **—thread′like′** *adj.*

thread•bare (thrĕd′bâr′) *adj.* **1.** Having the nap worn down so that the threads show through; shabby or frayed: *a threadbare rug.* **2.** Wearing old shabby clothing. **3.** Overused; hackneyed; trite: *threadbare excuses.*

thread•y (thrĕd′ē) *adj.* **thread•i•er, thread•i•est. 1.** Consisting of or resembling thread. **2.** Lacking fullness of tone; thin: *a thready voice.*

threat (thrĕt) *n.* **1.** An expression of an intention to inflict pain, injury, evil, or punishment. **2.** An indication of impending danger or harm: *The night air held a threat of frost.* **3.** Something, such as a person, a thing, or an idea, regarded as a possible danger. [First written down about 725 in Old English and spelled *thrēat*, oppression.]

threat•en (thrĕt′n) *v.* **threat•ened, threat•en•ing, threat•ens.** *—tr.* **1.** To utter a threat against (someone). **2.** To be a source of danger to; menace: *Landslides threatened the mountain village.* **3.** To give signs or warning of; portend: *Dark skies threaten rain.* **4.** To announce the possibility of, in or as in a threat: *They are always threatening to move to the suburbs.* *—intr.* **1.** To utter or use threats. **2.** To indicate danger or harm.

three (thrē) *n.* **1.** The number, written 3, that is equal to 2 + 1. **2.** The third in a set or sequence. [First written down before 830 in Old English and spelled *thrī*.] **—three** *adj.* *&* *pron.*

three-di•men•sion•al (thrē′dĭ mĕn′shə nəl) *adj.* **1.** Of or having three dimensions. **2.** Of or producing visual images in which there is an illusion of depth and perspective: *a three-dimensional image projected with light from a laser.*

three•score (thrē′skôr′) *adj.* Being three times twenty; sixty.

three•some (thrē′səm) *n.* **1.** A group of three persons or things. **2.** An activity, especially a golf match, that involves three people.

thren•o•dy (thrĕn′ə dē) *n., pl.* **thren•o•dies.** A poem or song of mourning or lamentation.

thresh (thrĕsh) *v.* **threshed, thresh•ing, thresh•es.** *—tr.* **1.a.** To separate the seeds from (grain-bearing plants) by striking or beating: *The workers threshed the wheat with a machine.* **b.** To separate (grains or seeds) in this manner. **2.** To beat severely; thrash. *—intr.* **1.** To use a machine to separate grain or seeds from straw. **2.** To thrash about; toss.

thresh•er (thrĕsh′ər) *n.* **1.** A person or thing that threshes. **2.** A threshing machine. **3.** Any of various large sharks having a tail with a long upper lobe with which it strikes the surface of the water.

thresh•ing machine (**thrĕsh′**ĭng) *n.* A farm machine used in threshing grain or seed plants; a thresher.

thresh•old (**thrĕsh′**ōld′ *or* **thrĕsh′**hōld′) *n.* **1.** The piece of wood or stone placed beneath a door; a doorsill. **2.** An entrance or a doorway. **3.** The place or point of beginning; the outset: *Science is on the threshold of a better understanding of the atmosphere.* **4.** The lowest level or intensity at which a stimulus can be perceived or can produce a given effect: *a sound at the threshold of hearing.*

threw (thro͞o) *v.* Past tense of **throw.**

❑ *These sound alike:* **threw, through** (in and out of).

thrice (thrīs) *adv.* Three times: *She was thrice named class president.*

thrift (thrĭft) *n.* Wisdom in the management of money and other resources; frugality. [First written down before 1300 in Middle English and spelled *thrift*, prosperity, perhaps from Old Norse, from *thrīfask*, to thrive.] **—thrift′less** *adj.*

thrift•y (**thrĭf′**tē) *adj.* **trift•i•er, trift•i•est.** Practicing thrift; economical and frugal. **—thrift′i•ly** *adv.* **—thrift′i•ness** *n.*

thrill (thrĭl) *v.* **thrilled, thrill•ing, thrills.** *—tr.* To cause to feel a sudden intense sensation, as of joy, fear, or excitement: *The news of his promotion thrilled him.* *—intr.* To feel a sudden quiver of excitement or emotion. *—n.* **1.** A quivering or trembling caused by sudden excitement or emotion. **2.** A source or cause of excitement or emotion.

thrill•er (**thrĭl′**ər) *n.* Something that thrills, especially an exciting or suspenseful book, story, play, or movie.

thrive (thrīv) *intr.v.* **thrived** or **throve** (thrōv), **thrived** or **thriv•en** (**thrĭv′**ən), **thriv•ing, thrives. 1.** To grow vigorously; flourish: *Some plants thrive in sandy soil.* **2.** To make steady progress; prosper: *The town thrived and grew larger.* [First written down about 1200 in Middle English and spelled *thrifenn*, from Old Norse *thrīfask*.]

throat (thrōt) *n.* **1.a.** The front portion of the neck. **b.** The part of the digestive tract that forms a passage between the rear of the mouth and the esophagus and includes the pharynx and the larynx. **2.** A narrow passage or part suggesting the human throat: *the throat of a bottle.* [First written down before 700 in Old English and spelled *throte*.]

throat•y (**thrō′**tē) *adj.* **throat•i•er, throat•i•est.** Uttered or sounding as if uttered deep in the throat; guttural, hoarse, or husky: *a throaty growl.* **—throat′i•ly** *adv.* **—throat′i•ness** *n.*

throb (thrŏb) *intr.v.* **throbbed, throb•bing, throbs. 1.** To beat rapidly or violently; pound: *His heart was throbbing with excitement.* **2.** To vibrate or sound with a slow steady rhythm: *hearing the boat's engines throbbing all night.* *—n.* The act of throbbing; a beating or vibration.

throe (thrō) *n.* **1.** A severe pang or spasm of pain, as in childbirth. **2. throes.** A condition of great struggle or trouble: *a country in the throes of an economic depression.*

throm•bi (**thrŏm′**bī) *n.* Plural of **thrombus.**

throm•bin (**thrŏm′**bĭn) *n.* An enzyme in the blood that aids blood clotting by reacting with fibrinogen to form fibrin.

throm•bo•sis (thrŏm **bō′**sĭs) *n., pl.* **throm•bo•ses** (thrŏm **bō′**sēz). The formation or presence of a thrombus.

throm•bus (**thrŏm′**bəs) *n., pl.* **throm•bi** (**thrŏm′**bī). A blood clot that forms in a blood vessel or a chamber of the heart and obstructs the circulation.

throne (thrōn) *n.* **1.** The chair occupied by a monarch or an honored person on ceremonial occasions. **2.** The power, rank, or authority of a monarch; sovereignty: *succeed to the throne.* [First written down before 1200 in Middle English and spelled *trone*, from Greek *thronos*.]

❑ *These sound alike:* **throne, thrown** (propelled through the air).

throng (thrông *or* thrŏng) *n.* A large group of people or things gathered or crowded closely together. *—v.* **thronged, throng•ing, throngs.** *—tr.* To crowd into; fill: *People thronged the platforms of the subway station.* *—intr.* To gather, press, or move in a throng: *People thronged to the new restaurant.* [First written down in 993 in Old English and spelled *gethrang*.]

throt•tle (**thrŏt′**l) *n.* **1.** A valve that regulates the flow of a fluid, such as the valve in an internal-combustion engine that controls the flow of fuel to the combustion chamber. **2.** A pedal or lever that controls such a valve. *—tr.v.* **throt•tled, throt•tling, throt•tles. 1.** To control (an engine, its fuel, or working fluid) with or as if with a throttle. **2.** To strangle; choke. **3.** To suppress: *The dictator tried to throttle the press.*

through (thro͞o) *prep.* **1.** In one side and out the opposite or another side of: *going through the door.* **2.** Among or between; in the midst of: *a walk through the flowers.* **3.** By way of: *He entered through a side door.* **4.** By means of: *getting an apartment through an agency.* **5.** Here and there in; around: *a tour through France.* **6.** From the beginning to the end of: *staying up through the night.* **7.** At or near the end of: *We are through our testing period.* **8.** Without stopping for: *driving through a red light.* **9.** Because of; on account of: *We succeeded through hard work.* *—adv.* **1.** From one end or side to another or an opposite end or side: *I opened the window and climbed through.* **2.** From beginning to end; completely: *I glanced at the article but haven't read it through.* **3.** Thoroughly: *We got soaked through in the rain.* **4.** Over the total distance; all the way: *We drove straight through to Toledo.* **5.** To the end or conclusion: *I mean to see this matter through.* *—adj.* **1.** Allowing continuous passage without obstruction: *a through street.* **2.** Going all the way to the end without stopping: *This is a through flight.* **3.** Passing from one end or side to another: *a through beam.* **4.** Finished; done: *Are you through with your homework?* **5.** Finished; no longer effective or capable: *If he injures that knee again, he's through as a basketball player.* **6.** Having no further dealings or connection: *Jane and I are through.* [First written down about 750 in Old English and spelled *thurh*.]

❑ *These sound alike:* **through, threw** (propelled through the air).

through•out (thro͞o **out′**) *prep.* In, to, through, or during every part of: *throughout the country; throughout the night.* *—adv.* **1.** In or through all parts; everywhere: *The house is beautiful throughout.* **2.** During the entire time or extent: *She was questioned for two hours and remained calm throughout.*

through•way (**thro͞o′**wā′) *n.* Variant of **thruway.**

throve (thrōv) *v.* A past tense of **thrive.**

throw (thrō) *v.* **threw** (thro͞o), **thrown** (thrōn), **throw•ing, throws.** *—tr.* **1.** To propel through the air with or as if with a motion of the hand or arm: *throw a ball.* **2.** To hurl or fling with great force and speed: *threw themselves at the food.* **3.** To cast: *throw a glance at the window displays; throw a shadow.* **4.** To put on or off quickly or carelessly: *throwing a cape over her shoulders.* **5.** To hurl to the ground or floor: *The horse threw its rider.* **6.** To arrange or give: *throw a party.* **7.** *Informal.* To lose (a fight, for example) purposely. **8.** To put (suddenly or forcefully) into a specified condition: *new reg-*

threshing machine

ă	**pat**	oi	**boy**
ā	**pay**	ou	**out**
âr	**care**	o͝o	**took**
ä	**father**	o͞o	**boot**
ĕ	**pet**	ŭ	**cut**
ē	**be**	ûr	**urge**
ĭ	**pit**	th	**thin**
ī	**pie**	*th*	**this**
îr	**pier**	hw	**whoop**
ŏ	**pot**	zh	**vision**
ō	**toe**	ə	**about**
ô	**paw**	N	*French* **bon**

ulations that threw the players into confusion. **9.** To move (a switch or control lever) in order to activate or deactivate a device. **10.** To form on a potter's wheel: *throw a vase.* **11.a.** To roll (dice). **b.** To roll (a particular combination) with dice. **12.** To discard or play (a card). **13.** To send forth; project: *She threw me an encouraging look.* **14.** *Informal.* To disconcert or perplex: *Don't let his friendly manner throw you.* —*intr.* To cast, fling, or hurl something. —*n.* **1.** The act or an instance of throwing. **2.** The distance to which something can be thrown. **3.** A scarf, shawl, or light coverlet. **4.** The distance or region through which a mechanical part moves. **5.a.** A roll or cast of dice. **b.** The combination of numbers so obtained. —***idioms.*** **throw away. 1.** To discard as useless: *threw away the empty box.* **2.** To fail to take advantage of: *threw away a chance to make a fortune.* **throw in. 1.** To add (an extra thing or amount) with no additional charge. **2.** To engage (a clutch, for example). **throw off. 1.** To cast out; rid oneself of. **2.** To give off; emit: *The blanket threw off an unusual odor.* **throw out. 1.** To reject or discard: *Threw out yesterday's paper.* **2.** To disengage (a clutch, for example). **3.** In baseball, to put out (a base runner) by throwing the ball to the player guarding the base to which the base runner is moving. **throw up.** To vomit. [First written down about 1000 in Old English and spelled *thrāwan.*] **—throw′er** *n.*

Synonyms: **throw, hurl, fling, pitch, toss.** These verbs mean to shoot something through the air with a motion of the hand or arm. **Throw** is the most general: *Toby threw a life preserver to the struggling swimmer.* **Hurl** and **fling** mean to throw with great force: *In Greek mythology Zeus hurls lightning bolts from Olympus as if they were spears. The paper carrier had flung the newspaper onto the porch.* **Pitch** often means to throw with careful aim: *She pitched the wad of paper into the wastebasket.* **Toss** usually means to throw lightly or casually: *He tossed the day's mail onto the desk.*

throw•back (thrō′băk′) *n.* A return to a former type or an ancestral characteristic.

thrown (thrōn) *v.* Past participle of **throw.** ❑ *These sound alike:* **thrown, throne** (monarch's chair).

throw rug *n.* A scatter rug.

thru (thro͞o) *prep., adv., & adj. Informal.* Through.

thrum (thrŭm) *v.* **thrummed, thrum•ming, thrums.** —*tr.* To play (a stringed instrument) in an idle or monotonous way. —*intr.* To strum idly on a stringed instrument. —*n.* The sound made by thrumming.

thrush[1] (thrŭsh) *n.* Any of numerous songbirds usually having a brownish back and a spotted breast. [First written down about 1000 in Old English and spelled *thrysce.*]

thrush[2] (thrŭsh) *n.* An infection caused by a fungus that produces white spots on the mouth, throat, and tongue. [First written down in 1665 in Modern English, probably of Scandinavian origin.]

thrust (thrŭst) *v.* **thrust, thrust•ing, thrusts.** —*tr.* **1.** To push or drive quickly and forcibly. **2.** To issue or extend: *thrust out his fingers.* **3.** To force into a specified condition or situation: *She thrust herself into our conversation.* **4.** *Archaic.* To stab; pierce. —*intr.* **1.** To shove something into or at something else; push. **2.** To pierce or stab with or as if with a pointed weapon. **3.** To force one's way. —*n.* **1.** A forceful shove or push. **2.** A force that tends to move an object, especially an airplane or a rocket. **3.** A piercing movement; a stab. **4.** The essence or main point: *the thrust of the governor's proposal.*

thru•way also **through•way** (thro͞o′wā′) *n.* An expressway.

thud (thŭd) *n.* **1.** A dull sound. **2.** A blow or fall causing such a sound. —*intr.v.* **thud•ded, thud•ding, thuds.** To make a heavy dull sound.

thug (thŭg) *n.* A hoodlum.

thu•li•um (tho͞o′lē əm *or* thyo͞o′lē əm) *n.* *Symbol* **Tm** A rare-earth element used in portable medical x-ray units. Atomic number 69. See table at **element.**

thumb (thŭm) *n.* **1.** The short thick first digit of the human hand, which can be moved so that it is opposite each of the other fingers. **2.** A similar digit of an animal, especially a monkey, ape, or other primate. **3.** The part of a glove or mitten that covers the thumb. —*v.* **thumbed, thumb•ing, thumbs.** —*tr.* **1.** To scan (written matter) by turning pages with or as if with the thumb. **2.** To soil or wear by careless or frequent handling, as the pages of a book. **3.** *Informal.* To ask for (a ride) from a passing automobile by signaling with the thumb. —*intr.* *Informal.* To hitchhike. —***idioms.*** **all thumbs.** Clumsy; awkward. **thumbs down.** An expression of rejection, refusal, or disapproval. **thumbs up.** An expression of approval, success, or hope. **under (one's) thumb.** Under the control of influence of someone. [First written down before 800 in Old English and spelled *thūma.*]

thumb•nail (thŭm′nāl′) *n.* The nail of the thumb. —*adj.* **1.** Of, relating to, or the size of a thumbnail. **2.** Brief; cursory: *a thumbnail biography.*

thumb•screw (thŭm′skro͞o′) *n.* **1.** A screw made so that it can be turned with the thumb and fingers. **2.** An instrument of torture formerly used to compress the thumb.

thumb•tack (thŭm′tăk′) *n.* A tack with a smooth rounded head that can be pressed into place with the thumb.

thump (thŭmp) *n.* **1.** A blow with a blunt instrument. **2.** The muffled sound produced by or as if by such a blow; a thud. —*v.* **thumped, thump•ing, thumps.** —*tr.* To strike with a blunt instrument, so as to produce a muffled sound or thud: *thumping the desk with her fist.* —*intr.* **1.** To beat, hit, or fall in such a way as to produce a thump: *The book thumped on the floor.* **2.** To beat or palpitate violently: *His heart thumped with fear.*

thun•der (thŭn′dər) *n.* **1.** The explosive noise that accompanies a stroke of lightning. **2.** A noise that resembles or suggests thunder: *the thunder of applause.* —*v.* **thun•dered, thun•der•ing, thun•ders.** —*intr.* **1.** To produce thunder: *It stormed and thundered.* **2.** To produce sounds like thunder: *guns thundering in the distance.* —*tr.* To utter loudly or threatenly: *The captain thundered orders to the sailors.* [First written down before 800 in Old English and spelled *thuner.*]

thun•der•bolt (thŭn′dər bōlt′) *n.* A stroke of lightning accompanied by thunder.

thun•der•clap (thŭn′dər klăp′) *n.* A single sharp crash of thunder.

thun•der•cloud (thŭn′dər kloud′) *n.* A large dark cloud carrying an electric charge and producing lightning and thunder; a cumulonimbus cloud.

thun•der•head (thŭn′dər hĕd′) *n.* The billowy upper part of a thundercloud.

thun•der•ous (thŭn′dər əs) *adj.* Producing thunder or a similar sound: *thunderous applause.* **—thun′der•ous•ly** *adv.*

thun•der•show•er (thŭn′dər shou′ər) *n.* A short, often heavy rainstorm accompanied by thunder and lightning.

thun•der•storm (thŭn′dər stôrm′) *n.* A storm of heavy rain accompanied by lightning and thunder and sometimes hail.

thun•der•struck (thŭn′dər strŭk′) *adj.* Amazed; astonished: *He stood thunderstruck at the sidelines watching the team's defeat.*

Thur. *abbr.* An abbreviation of Thursday.

Thurs•day (**thûrz′**dē *or* **thûrz′**dā′) *n.* The fifth day of the week. [First written down about 1000 in Old English and spelled *thurresdæg,* alteration of *thunres dæg,* Thor's day.]

thus (*th*ŭs) *adv.* **1.** In this manner: *Lay the pieces out thus.* **2.** To a stated degree or extent; so: *She has evaluated my work thus far.* **3.** Consequently; therefore.

thwack (thwăk) *tr.v.* **thwacked, thwack•ing, thwacks.** To strike or hit with a flat object; whack. —*n.* A sharp blow with a flat object.

thwart (thwôrt) *tr.v.* **thwart•ed, thwart•ing, thwarts.** To prevent from taking place; frustrate; block: *They thwarted his plans.* —*n.* A seat across a boat on which a rower may sit.

thy (*th*ī) *adj.* The possessive form of **thou.**

thyme (tīm) *n.* **1.** The spicy-smelling leaves of any of several low-growing plants, used as a seasoning. **2.** A plant that bears such leaves. [First written down before 1398 in Middle English, from Greek *thumon.*]

❑ *These sound alike:* **thyme, time** (moment).

thy•mine (**thī′**mēn′) *n.* A base that is a component of DNA.

thy•mus (**thī′**məs) *n., pl.* **thy•mus•es. 1.** A ductless glandular organ located behind the top of the breastbone, having a role in building resistance to disease. It reaches maximum development in early childhood and is absent or very small in adults. **2.** A similar structure in other vertebrate animals.

thy•roid (**thī′**roid′) *n.* **1.** The thyroid gland. **2.** The thyroid cartilage.

thyroid cartilage *n.* The largest cartilage of the larynx, having two broad projections that join in front to form the Adam's apple.

thyroid gland *n.* An endocrine gland having two lobes, located in front of and to either side of the windpipe in human beings. It is found in all vertebrates and produces the hormone thyroxine.

thy•rox•ine (thī **rŏk′**sēn′ *or* thī **rŏk′**sĭn) also **thy•rox•in** (thī **rŏk′**sĭn) *n.* A hormone that contains iodine, produced by the thyroid gland and acting to regulate body metabolism. It is also produced synthetically for the treatment of thyroid disorders.

thy•self (*th*ī **sĕlf′**) *pron. Archaic.* Yourself.

ti (tē) *n.* In music, the seventh tone of a major scale.

❑ *These sound alike:* **ti, tea** (drink), **tee** (peg for a golf ball).

Ti The symbol for the element **titanium.**

Tian•jin (**tyän′jĭn′**). A city of northeast China southeast of Beijing. It developed rapidly after 1860. Population, 5,380,000.

ti•ar•a (tē **ăr′**ə *or* tē **är′**ə) *n.* **1.** An ornament that looks like a small crown, often is set with jewels, and is worn on the head by women on formal occasions. **2.** The tall three-tiered crown worn by the pope.

Ti•ber (**tī′**bər). A river of central Italy flowing about 252 miles (406 kilometers) south and southwest through Rome to the Tyrrhenian Sea.

Ti•bet (tə **bĕt′**). A historical region of central Asia north of the Himalayas. Tibet came under Chinese control in 1720.

Ti•bet•an (tĭ **bĕt′**n) *adj.* Of or relating to Tibet, the Tibetans, or their language or culture. —*n.* **1.** A native or inhabitant of Tibet. **2.** A member of a Buddhist people who make up the largest ethnic group in Tibet.

tib•i•a (**tĭb′**ē ə) *n., pl.* **tib•i•ae** (**tĭb′**ē ē′) or **tib•i•as. 1.** The inner and larger of the two bones of the human leg between the knee to the ankle; the shinbone. **2.** A similar bone in an animal.

tic (tĭk) *n.* A recurring spasmodic contraction or twitching of a set of muscles, usually in the face or limbs.

❑ *These sound alike:* **tic, tick[1]** (clicking sound), **tick[2]** (insect), **tick[3]** (cloth case).

tick[1] (tĭk) *n.* **1.** A light sharp clicking sound made repeatedly by a machine, such as a clock. **2.** A light mark used to check off or call attention to an item. —*v.* **ticked, tick•ing, ticks.** —*intr.* **1.** To produce recurring clicking sounds. **2.** To function characteristically: *What makes him tick?* —*tr.* To count, record, or check off with a tick: *a clock ticking the hours; tick off each name.* [First written down in 1440 in Middle English and spelled *tek,* light tap.]

❑ *These sound alike:* **tick[1]** (clicking sound), **tic** (muscle contraction), **tick[2]** (insect), **tick[3]** (cloth case).

tick[2] (tĭk) *n.* **1.** Any of numerous small animals related to spiders. Ticks attach themselves to and suck blood from the skin of human beings and animals and often carry microorganisms that cause disease. **2.** Any of various small bloodsucking insects resembling lice that are parasites on sheep, goats, and other animals. [First written down about 1310 in Middle English and spelled *tik.*]

❑ *These sound alike:* **tick[2]** (insect), **tic** (muscle contraction), **tick[1]** (clicking sound), **tick[3]** (cloth case).

tick[3] (tĭk) *n.* The sturdy cloth case of a mattress or pillow that encloses the stuffing. [First written down in 1342 in Middle English and spelled *tike,* probably from Middle Dutch *tīke,* ultimately from Latin *thēca,* receptacle.]

❑ *These sound alike:* **tick[3]** (cloth case), **tic** (muscle contraction), **tick[1]** (clicking sound), **tick[2]** (insect).

tick•bird (**tĭk′**bûrd′) *n.* Either of two kinds of African starlings that feed on ticks found on the hides of large animals.

tick•er (**tĭk′**ər) *n.* **1.** A type of telegraphic instrument that receives news reports and prints them on paper tape. **2.** Any of various devices that receive and record similar information, such as stock-market quotations, by electronic means.

ticker tape *n.* The strip of paper on which a telegraphic ticker prints.

tick•et (**tĭk′**ĭt) *n.* **1.** A paper slip or card that entitles the holder to a specified service or right: *a bus ticket; a theater ticket.* **2.** A tag attached to and giving information about merchandise; a label. **3.** A list of candidates in an election, entered or backed by a particular party or group. **4.** A legal summons, especially one for a traffic violation: *I got a ticket for speeding.* —*tr.v.* **tick•et•ed, tick•et•ing, tick•ets. 1.** To provide with a ticket for admission or passage. **2.** To attach a tag to; label. **3.** To mark or intend for a specified use: *cars ticketed for shipment.* **4.** To give a legal summons to.

tick•ing (**tĭk′**ĭng) *n.* Strong tightly woven cloth of cotton or linen used to make pillow and mattress coverings.

tick•le (**tĭk′**əl) *v.* **tick•led, tick•ling, tick•les.** —*tr.* **1.** To touch (the body) lightly, causing laughter or twitching movements. **2.** To delight or amuse; please. —*intr.* To feel or cause a tingling sensation. —*n.* The act or sensation of tickling. —***idiom.* tickle (one) pink.** *Informal.* To please; delight: *I was tickled pink by the compliment.* —**tick′ler** *n.*

tick•lish (**tĭk′**lĭsh) *adj.* **1.** Sensitive to tickling: *a ticklish child.* **2.** Easily offended or upset; touchy. **3.** Requiring skillful handling: *a ticklish problem.* —**tick′lish•ness** *n.*

tick•tack•toe also **tick-tack-toe** (tĭk′tăk′**tō′**) *n.* A game played by two persons, each trying to make a line of three X's or three O's in a square figure with

tiara
Jeweled tiara

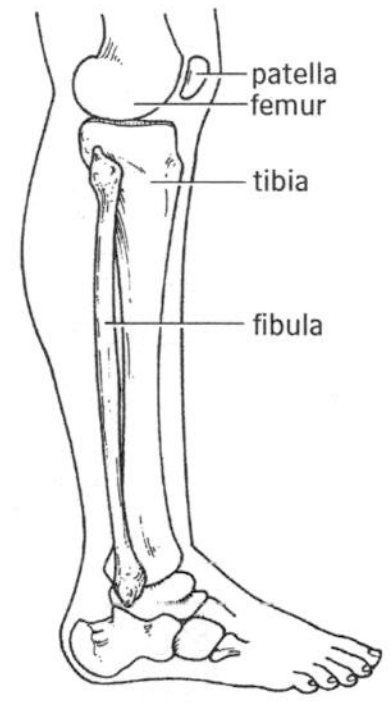

tibia

ă	**p**a**t**	oi	**boy**
ā	**pay**	ou	**out**
âr	**care**	o͝o	**took**
ä	**father**	o͞o	**boot**
ĕ	**pet**	ŭ	**cut**
ē	**be**	ûr	**urge**
ĭ	**pit**	th	**thin**
ī	**pie**	*th*	**this**
îr	**pier**	hw	**whoop**
ŏ	**pot**	zh	**vision**
ō	**toe**	ə	**about**
ô	**paw**	N	*French* **bon**

tide
Top: High tide in the Bay of Fundy in southeast Canada
Bottom: Low tide from the same perspective

tiger lily

nine spaces. [First written down in 1884 in Modern English, probably imitative of the sounds of the original children's game, in which players brought pencils down on a numbered slate with their eyes shut.]

Ti•con•der•o•ga (tī′kŏn də **rō′**gə). A resort village of northeast New York at the southern end of Lake Champlain. Fort Carillon, renamed Fort Ticonderoga in 1759 by the British, is here.

tid•al (**tīd′**l) *adj.* Relating to or affected by tides: *tidal marshes.*

tidal wave *n.* **1.** An unusual rise in the level of water along a seacoast, as from a storm or a combination of wind and tide. **2.** A tsunami.

tid•bit (**tĭd′**bĭt′) *n.* A choice morsel, as of food or gossip.

tid•dly•winks (**tĭd′**lē wĭngks′) *pl.n.* *(used with a singular verb).* A game in which the players try to pop small disks into a cup by pressing them on the edge with a larger disk.

tide (tīd) *n.* **1.a.** The periodic variation in the surface level of the oceans, seas, and bays of the earth caused by the gravitational attraction of the moon and to a lesser extent the sun. **b.** A particular occurrence of such a variation. **c.** The water that moves when such a variation occurs. **2.** A stress or change in shape that a body undergoes as a result of the gravitational attraction of another body. **3.** Something that fluctuates like the waters of the tide: *the rising tide of immigration.* **4.** A favorable occasion; an opportunity. **5.** A time or season: *eveningtide; Christmastide.* —*intr.v.* **tid•ed, tid•ing, tides.** To drift or ride with the tide: *Our boat tided up the river.* ***—idiom.*** **tide over.** To support through a difficult period: *lent me $100 to tide me over until payday.* [First written down about 725 in Old English and spelled *tīd*, division of time.]

tide•land (**tīd′**lănd′) *n.* Land along a coast that is under water at high tide.

tide•wa•ter (**tīd′**wô′tər *or* **tīd′**wŏt′ər) *n.* **1.** Water that flows onto the land when the tide is very high. **2.** Water, especially water in streams or rivers, that is affected by tides. **3.** Low coastal land drained by streams that are affected by tides.

tid•ings (**tī′**dĭngz) *pl.n.* News; information: *tidings of great joy.* [First written down in 1069 in Old English and spelled *tīdung*.]

ti•dy (**tī′**dē) *adj.* **ti•di•er, ti•di•est. 1.** Orderly and neat: *a tidy room.* See Synonyms at **neat. 2.** *Informal.* Considerable: *a tidy sum of money.* —*tr. & intr.v.* **ti•died, ti•dy•ing, ti•dies.** To put in order; make neat: *Tidy up your room. We tidied up after dinner.* —*n., pl.* **ti•dies.** A decorative protective covering for the arms or headrest of a chair. [First written down about 1250 in Middle English and spelled *tidi*, in season, healthy, from *tide*, time.] **—ti′di•ly** *adv.* **—ti′di•ness** *n.*

tie (tī) *v.* **tied, ty•ing** (**tī′**ĭng), **ties.** —*tr.* **1.** To fasten or secure with or as if with a cord, rope, or strap: *tie up a parcel; tie a dog to a fence.* **2.** To fasten by drawing together the parts of (something) and knotting with strings or laces: *bending to tie her shoes.* **3.** To make by fastening ends or parts: *tie a knot.* **4.** To put a knot or bow in: *tie a necktie; tie a scarf.* **5.a.** To equal (an opponent or a score, for example) in a contest: *He tied the pole-vaulting record last year.* **b.** To equal a score in (a contest): *tied the game with minutes remaining.* **6.** To bring together in a relationship; connect or unite: *people who are tied by marriage or family.* **7.** To join (successive musical tones of the same pitch) so that there is no break between them. —*intr.* **1.** To be fastened or attached: *an apron that ties in back.* **2.** To achieve equal scores in a contest. —*n.* **1.** A cord, string, rope, or other means by which something is tied. **2.** A necktie. **3.** Something that connects or unites; a bond: *the ties of friendship; family ties.* **4.** An equality of scores, votes, or performances in a contest: *The game ended in a tie.* **5.** A beam or rod that joins parts of a structure and gives support. **6.** One of the timbers laid across a railroad bed to support the rails. **7.** A curved line above or below two musical notes of the same pitch, indicating that they are to be played or sung with no break. ***—idioms.*** **tie in.** To bring into or have a close relation with; connect or coordinate: *Your story ties in with what she told me.* **tie up. 1.** To secure or be secured to a shore or pier; dock. **2.** To block or stop: *an accident that tied up traffic.* **3.** To keep busy; engage: *I will be tied up in meetings all day.* **4.** To place or invest (money) so that it cannot be used freely: *tied up her money in a new house.* [First written down about 1000 in Old English and spelled *tīgan*.]

tie clasp *n.* An ornamental pin or clip that holds the ends of a necktie to the front of a shirt.

tie-dye (**tī′**dī′) *tr.v.* **tie-dyed, tie-dye•ing, tie-dyes.** To dye (a fabric) after tying parts of the fabric so that they will not absorb the dye, giving the fabric a streaked or mottled look.

tier (tîr) *n.* One of a series of rows placed one above another: *a stadium with four tiers of seats.* —*tr. & intr.v.* **tiered, tier•ing, tiers.** To arrange in or form tiers: *tier a wedding cake; seats that tier upward.*
❑ *These sound alike:* **tier, tear²** (eye drop).

Ti•er•ra del Fue•go (tē ĕr′ə dĕl **fwā′**gō). A group of islands of Chile and Argentina off southern South America separated from the mainland by the Strait of Magellan. The main island, also called **Tierra del Fuego,** is divided between Chile and Argentina.

tie tack *n.* A short decorative pin used to fasten a necktie to a shirt.

tie-up (**tī′**ŭp′) *n.* A temporary stoppage, as of work or traffic: *The strike caused a work tie-up at the factory.*

tiff (tĭf) *n.* **1.** A fit of irritation. **2.** A petty quarrel.

ti•ger (**tī′**gər) *n.* **1.** A very large wild cat of Asia, having tawny fur with crosswise black stripes. **2.** A person regarded as enthusiastic, fierce, or aggressive. [First written down before 1000 in Old English and spelled *tigras*, tigers, from Greek *tigris*, tiger.]

ti•ger-eye (**tī′**gər ī′) also **ti•ger's-eye** (**tī′**gərz ī′) *n.* A yellow-brown gemstone.

tiger lily *n.* A tall lily having black-spotted orange flowers.

tiger moth *n.* Any of numerous often brightly colored moths having wings marked with spots or stripes.

tight (tīt) *adj.* **tight•er, tight•est. 1.** Fastened, held, or closed securely: *a tight knot; a tight lid.* **2.** Stretched or drawn out to the fullest extent: *a tight rope.* **3.** Of such close construction as to be impermeable, especially by water or air: *a tight roof.* **4.** Leaving little empty space between; compact: *planes flying in tight formation.* **5.** Leaving little time to spare; full: *a tight schedule.* **6.** Fitting close or too close to some part of the body; snug: *The tight shoes hurt his feet.* **7.** Constricted: *a tight feeling in the chest.* **8.** Reluctant to give or spend money; stingy. **9.a.** Difficult to obtain: *Money was tight.* **b.** Affected by scarcity: *a tight money market.* **10.** Difficult to deal with or get out of: *in a tight spot.* **11.** Closely contested; close: *a tight race; a tight game.* —*adv.* **tighter, tightest. 1.** Firmly; securely: *Screw the lid on tight.* **2.** Soundly: *sleep tight.* [First written down about 1325 in Middle English and spelled *tigt*, dense, of Scandinavian origin.] **—tight′ly** *adv.* **—tight′ness** *n.*

tight•en (**tīt′**n) *tr. & intr.v.* **tight•ened, tight•en•**

ing, tight•ens. To make or become tight or tighter.
tight•fist•ed (tīt′fĭs′tĭd) *adj.* Stingy.
tight•lipped also **tight-lipped** (tīt′lĭpt′) *adj.* **1.** Having the lips pressed together. **2.** Secretive; reticent; silent: *He was tight-lipped about the meeting.*
tight•rope (tīt′rōp′) *n.* A tightly stretched rope, usually of wire, on which acrobats perform high above the ground.
tights (tīts) *pl.n.* **1.** A snug stretchable garment covering the body from the waist or neck down, designed for general wear by women and girls. **2.** A similar garment designed for athletics, worn especially by dancers and acrobats.
tight•wad (tīt′wŏd′) *n. Slang.* A stingy person.
ti•gress (tī′grĭs) *n.* A female tiger.
Ti•gris (tī′grĭs). A river rising in eastern Turkey and flowing about 1,150 miles (1,850 kilometers) southeast through Iraq to the Euphrates River.
tike (tīk) *n.* Variant of **tyke.**
til•de (tĭl′də) *n.* A diacritical mark (˜) used in Spanish and Portuguese to indicate certain nasal sounds, as in the word *cañon.*
tile (tīl) *n.* **1.** A thin flat slab of baked clay, plastic, concrete, or other hard material, laid in rows as a covering for floors, walls, and roofs. **2.** A short length of clay or concrete pipe, used in sewers and drains. **3.** A block of concrete or fired clay used for building walls. **4.** Tiles considered as a group. **5.** A marked playing piece used in certain games. *—tr.v.* **tiled, til•ing, tiles.** To cover or provide with tiles.
til•ing (tī′lĭng) *n.* **1.** The laying of tiles. **2.** Tiles considered as a group. **3.** A tiled surface.
till[1] (tĭl) *tr.v.* **tilled, till•ing, tills.** To prepare (land) for the raising of crops, as by plowing and harrowing; cultivate. [First written down before 850 in Old English and spelled *tilian.*] **—till′a•ble** *adj.*
till[2] (tĭl) *prep.* Until: *I won't see you till tomorrow.* *—conj.* Until: *I can't help you till you tell me what's wrong.* [First written down before 800 in Old English and spelled *til,* from Old Norse.] —SEE NOTE.
till[3] (tĭl) *n.* A drawer or compartment for money, especially in a store. [First written down before 1450 in Middle English and spelled *tille.*]
till[4] (tĭl) *n.* A mass of material deposited by a glacier; a mixture containing clay, sand, gravel, and boulders. [First written down in 1765 in Modern English.]
till•age (tĭl′ĭj) *n.* **1.** The cultivation of land. **2.** Tilled land.
till•er[1] (tĭl′ər) *n.* A person who tills land.
til•ler[2] (tĭl′ər) *n.* A lever used to turn a boat's rudder. [First written down before 1325 in Middle English and spelled *tiler,* stock of a crossbow, from Latin *tēla,* loom.]
tilt (tĭlt) *v.* **tilt•ed, tilt•ing, tilts.** *—tr.* **1.** To cause to slope, as by raising one end; incline; tip: *The children tilted the barrel to empty it.* **2.** To aim or thrust (a lance) in a joust. *—intr.* **1.** To slope; incline. **2.** To favor one side over another in a dispute: *Her political views tilt to the right.* **3.a.** To joust. **b.** To engage in combat; fight: *tilting at injustices.* *—n.* **1.** A slant; a slope. **2.** A joust. **3.** A combat, especially a verbal duel. ***—idiom.* at full tilt.** *Informal.* At full speed. [First written down about 1350 in Middle English and spelled *tulten,* to cause to fall, perhaps of Scandinavian origin.]
tilth (tĭlth) *n.* **1.** Cultivation of land; tillage. **2.** Tilled earth.
tim•ber (tĭm′bər) *n.* **1.** Trees or wooded land considered as a source of wood. **2.** Wood for building; lumber. **3.** A beam or shaped piece of wood, as one used in forming a ship's frame. **4.** Personal quality; character: *a man of heroic timber.* *—tr.v.* **tim•bered, tim•ber•ing, tim•bers.** To support or frame with timbers. [First written down before 750 in Old English and spelled *timber,* building, trees for building.]
❑ *These sound alike:* **timber, timbre** (sound quality).
tim•bered (tĭm′bərd) *adj.* **1.** Covered with trees; wooded: *a timbered slope.* **2.** Made of or framed by timbers, especially exposed timbers: *a timbered barn.*
timber hitch *n.* A knot used to fasten a rope around a log, pole, or spar that is to be towed or hoisted.
tim•ber•land (tĭm′bər lănd′) *n.* Wooded land, especially land used for the commercial production of timber.
tim•ber•line (tĭm′bər līn′) *n.* In mountainous or arctic regions, the height or limit beyond which trees do not grow.
timber wolf *n.* The gray wolf.
tim•bre (tăm′bər *or* tĭm′bər) *n.* **1.** The quality or characteristic of a sound that distinguishes it from other sounds of the same pitch and volume. **2.** The tone or quality that is characteristic of an instrument or voice: *the timbre of a clarinet.*
❑ *These sound alike:* **timbre, timber** (trees).
tim•brel (tĭm′brəl) *n.* An ancient musical instrument similar to the tambourine.
Tim•buk•tu (tĭm′bŭk to͞o′ *or* tĭm bŭk′to͞o). A city of central Mali northeast of Bamako. It was founded in the 11th century. Population, 19,166.
time (tīm) *n.* **1.** A continuous measurable quantity, ordinarily distinct from space, in which events occur in an order that does not seem to be reversible, proceeding from the past through the present to the future. **2.a.** An interval bounded by two points of this quantity, as by the beginning and end of an event: *the time it takes to go from one place to another.* **b.** A number, as of years, days, or minutes, representing such an interval. **c.** A similar number representing a given point, such as the present, reckoned in hours and minutes: *The time was 5:15.* **d.** A system by which such intervals are measured or such numbers are reckoned: *standard time; solar time.* **3.** The characteristic beat of a musical rhythm: *three-quarter time.* **4.a.** A moment or period designated for a given activity: *harvest time; time for bed.* **b.** A period at one's disposal: *Do you have time for dinner?* **5.a.** A period, especially a span of years marked by similar events and conditions, or associated with certain historical figures. Often used in the plural: *Victorian times; a time of famine.* **b. times.** The present: *a sign of the times.* **6.a.** An appointed or fated moment, especially of death or giving birth: *She died before her time.* **b.** A person's experience during a specific period or occasion: *had a good time at the party.* **7.a.** The customary period of work of an employee: *working full time.* **b.** The hourly pay rate: *She gets double time on weekends.* **8.a.** One of several instances: *I let the phone ring three times.* **b. times.** Used to indicate the number of instances by which something is multiplied or divided: *This building is three times taller than that one.* *—adj.* Of, relating to, or measuring time. *—tr.v.* **timed, tim•ing, times. 1.** To set the time at which (something) happens or is to happen. **2.** To adjust (a clock or watch, for example) so that it keeps time accurately. **3.** To regulate or adjust so that an action occurs or force is applied at the correct time: *time a leap carefully; time an automobile engine.* **4.** To record or register the speed or duration of: *We timed the game at two hours even.* ***—idioms.* against time.** With a quickly approaching time limit: *working against time.* **at one time. 1.** Simultaneously. **2.** At a period or moment in the past: *At one time they were classmates.* **at the same time.** However; nonetheless. **at times.** On occasion; sometimes. **behind the times.** Out-

Usage: till[2]

You can usually use either **till** or **until.** Use **until** as the first word in a sentence, however: *Until you get that paper written, don't plan to go out.*

ă	pat	oi	boy
ā	pay	ou	out
âr	care	o͝o	took
ä	father	o͞o	boot
ĕ	pet	ŭ	cut
e	be	ûr	urge
ĭ	pit	th	thin
ī	pie	*th*	this
îr	pier	hw	whoop
ŏ	pot	zh	vision
ō	toe	ə	about
ô	paw	N	*French* bon

timpani

of-date; old-fashioned. **for the time being.** Temporarily. **from time to time.** Once in a while; at intervals. **high time.** Long overdue: *It's high time that you went to bed.* **in good time. 1.** In a reasonable length of time. **2.** Quickly. **in no time.** Almost instantly; immediately. **in time. 1.** Before a time limit expires: *They had to hurry to arrive in time for the movie.* **2.** In the end; eventually: *In time you will see that she is right.* **3.** In the proper musical tempo. **on time. 1.** According to schedule; punctually. **2.** By paying in installments: *buy a car on time.* **time after time.** Again and again; repeatedly. **time and again.** Again and again; repeatedly. [First written down before 899 in Old English and spelled *tīma.*]

❑ *These sound alike:* **time, thyme** (plant).

time bomb *n.* A bomb that can be set to explode at a certain time.

time clock *n.* A device that records the starting and quitting times of employees.

time exposure *n.* **1.** A photographic exposure in which light stikes the film or plate for a relatively long time. **2.** A photograph made by such an exposure.

time frame *n.* A period during which something takes place or is expected to take place.

time-hon•ored (tīm′ŏn′ərd) *adj.* Honored or adhered to because of age or age-old observance: *time-honored customs.*

time•keep•er (tīm′kē′pər) *n.* A person who keeps track of time, as in a sports event.

time•less (tīm′lĭs) *adj.* **1.** Independent of time; eternal: *the timeless universe.* **2.** Unaffected by time; ageless: *the timeless mountains of the Alps.* **—time′less•ness** *n.*

time•ly (tīm′lē) *adj.* **time•li•er, time•li•est.** Occurring at a suitable or opportune time; well-timed: *a timely remark.*

time-out also **time out** (tīm′out′) *n.* In sports, a brief period in a game for rest, consultation, or substitution, during which play is stopped.

time•piece (tīm′pēs′) *n.* An instrument, such as a watch or clock, that measures, records, or indicates time.

tim•er (tī′mər) *n.* **1.** A person or thing that measures time; a timekeeper. **2.** A timepiece, especially one used to measure intervals of time. **3.** A switch that controls another mechanism at set times.

times (tīmz) *prep.* Multiplied by: *Eight times three equals twenty-four.*

time-shar•ing (tīm′shâr′ĭng) *n.* A system whereby many users at different locations share a single computer.

time signature *n.* A musical sign placed on a staff to indicate the meter.

time•ta•ble (tīm′tā′bəl) *n.* A schedule listing the times at which certain events are expected to occur, as the arrival and departure of trains at a station.

time•worn (tīm′wôrn′) *adj.* **1.** Showing the effects of long use or wear. **2.** Used too often; trite: *a time-worn joke.*

time zone *n.* Any of 24 areas into which the earth is divided for purposes of keeping standard time. Time is reckoned one hour earlier in each successive zone to the east and one hour later in each successive zone to the west.

tim•id (tĭm′ĭd) *adj.* **tim•id•er, tim•id•est.** Easily frightened; hesitant and fearful; shy. **—ti•mid′i•ty** *n.* **—tim′id•ly** *adv.*

tim•ing (tī′mĭng) *n.* The art or process of regulating occurrence, pace, or coordination to achieve the most desirable effects, as in music, theater, sports, or mechanics.

Ti•mor (tē′môr *or* tē môr′). An island of southeast Indonesia, east of Java in the Indian Ocean.

tim•or•ous (tĭm′ər əs) *adj.* Easily frightened; timid. **—tim′or•ous•ly** *adv.* **—tim′or•ous•ness** *n.*

tim•o•thy (tĭm′ə thē) *n., pl.* **tim•o•thies.** Any of several grasses having long, narrow, dense flower clusters, widely grown for hay. [First written down before 1736 in American English, probably after *Timothy* Hanson, an 18th-century American farmer.]

Tim•o•thy (tĭm′ə thē) *n.* Either of two books of the New Testament, traditionally attributed to Saint Paul. The books are letters to Timothy, one of Paul's followers, and discuss the organization of the Church and Paul's imprisonment in Rome.

tim•pa•ni also **tym•pa•ni** (tĭm′pə nē) *pl.n.* A set of kettledrums.

tim•pa•num (tĭm′pə nəm) *n.* Variant of **tympanum.**

tin (tĭn) *n.* **1.** *Symbol* **Sn** A soft, silvery metallic element that is used to coat other metals to prevent corrosion and is a part of numerous alloys, such as pewter and bronze. Atomic number 50. See table at **element. 2.** Tin plate. **3.** A tin container or box. *—tr.v.* **tinned, tin•ning, tins. 1.** To plate or coat with tin. **2.** To preserve or pack in tins; can. *—adj.* Of, relating to, or made of tin. [First written down before 899 in Old English.]

tin can *n.* A container made of thin steel coated on the inside with tin or some other corrosion-resistant material, used for preserving food.

tinc•ture (tĭngk′chər) *n.* An alcohol solution of a medicine: *tincture of iodine.*

tin•der (tĭn′dər) *n.* A material that catches fire easily, used to kindle fires: *We use dry twigs as tinder.*

tin•der•box (tĭn′dər bŏks′) *n.* **1.** A metal box for holding tinder. **2.** A potentially dangerous or explosive situation.

tine (tīn) *n.* A prong or similar narrow or pointed part, as of a fork or of a deer's antlers.

tin•foil also **tin foil** (tĭn′foil′) *n.* A thin pliable sheet of aluminum or a tin-lead alloy, used as a protective wrapping, as for foods.

ting (tĭng) *n.* A light metallic sound, as of a small bell. *—intr.v.* **tinged** (tĭngd), **ting•ing, tings.** To give forth a light metallic sound.

tinge (tĭnj) *tr.v.* **tinged** (tĭnjd), **tinge•ing** or **ting•ing** (tĭn′jĭng), **ting•es. 1.** To color slightly; tint: *The sunset tinged the sky with red.* **2.** To affect slightly, as with a contrasting quality. *—n.* A small amount of color or some other property or quality: *a tinge of sadness in her remarks.* [First written down in 1471 in Middle English and spelled *tingen,* from Latin *tingere.*]

tin•gle (tĭng′gəl) *v.* **tin•gled, tin•gling, tin•gles.** *—intr.* To have a prickling stinging sensation, as from cold or excitement. *—tr.* To cause to tingle. *—n.* A prickling or stinging sensation.

tin•ker (tĭng′kər) *n.* **1.** A person who travels about fixing metal household utensils. **2.** A person who enjoys experimenting with and repairing machine parts. **3.** A poor worker. *—intr.v.* **tin•kered, tin•ker•ing, tin•kers. 1.** To work as a tinker. **2.** To make unskilled and experimental efforts at repair.

tin•kle (tĭng′kəl) *intr. & tr.v.* **tin•kled, tin•kling, tin•kles.** To make or cause to make light metallic sounds, as of a small bell. *—n.* A light clear metallic sound.

tin•ny (tĭn′ē) *adj.* **tin•ni•er, tin•ni•est. 1.** Of or containing tin. **2.** Tasting or smelling of tin: *tinny canned food.* **3.** Having a thin metallic sound: *a tinny voice.*

tin plate *n.* Thin sheet iron or steel coated with tin to prevent rusting.

tin-plate (tĭn′plāt′) *tr.v.* **tin-plat•ed, tin-plat•ing, tin-plates.** To coat with tin, as by dipping or electroplating.

tin•sel (tĭn′səl) *n.* **1.** Very thin sheets, strips, or threads of a glittering material used as a decoration. **2.** Something that is superficially showy but basically valueless. —*tr.v.* **tin•seled, tin•sel•ing, tin•sels** or **tin•selled, tin•sel•ling, tin•sels.** To decorate with or as if with tinsel.

tin•smith (tĭn′smĭth′) *n.* A person who works with light metal, such as tin.

tint (tĭnt) *n.* **1.** A shade of a color, especially a pale or delicate variation. **2.** A slight coloration; a tinge: *a tint of red in the sky.* **3.** A gradation of color made by adding white. —*tr.v.* **tint•ed, tint•ing, tints.** To give a tint to; color: *tint hair.* [First written down in 1717 in Modern English, from Latin *tīnctus*, dyeing.] **—tint′er** *n.*

tin•tin•nab•u•la•tion (tĭn′tĭ năb′yə lā′shən) *n.* The ringing or sounding of bells.

ti•ny (tī′nē) *adj.* **ti•ni•er, ti•ni•est.** Extremely small. See Synonyms at **little.**

tip[1] (tĭp) *n.* **1.** The end or extremity of something: *a house on the tip of the island; asparagus tips.* **2.** A piece meant to be fitted to the end of something: *the barbed tip of a harpoon.* —*tr.v.* **tipped, tip•ping, tips. 1.** To furnish with a tip. **2.** To decorate or cover the tip of. **3.** To remove the tip of: *tip artichokes.* [First written down before 1200 in Middle English and spelled *tippe.*]

tip[2] (tĭp) *v.* **tipped, tip•ping, tips.** —*tr.* **1.** To push or knock over; overturn or topple: *The wind tipped over the vase on the table.* **2.** To slant; tilt: *a weight that tipped the balance.* **3.** To touch or raise (one's hat) in greeting. —*intr.* **1.** To topple over; overturn. **2.** To become tilted; slant. [First written down about 1380 in Middle English and spelled *tipen.*]

tip[3] (tĭp) *v.* **tipped, tip•ping, tips.** —*tr.* **1.** To strike gently; tap. **2.a.** In baseball, to hit (a pitched ball) with the side of the bat so that it glances off. **b.** To tap or deflect (a ball or puck, for example), especially in scoring. —*intr.* To deflect or glance off. Used of a ball or puck. [First written down in 1567 in Modern English, from Middle English *tippe*, a tap, perhaps of Low German origin.]

tip[4] (tĭp) *n.* **1.** A small sum of money given to someone for performing a service; a gratuity. **2.** Useful information; a helpful hint: *a book with tips on car repair.* —*v.* **tipped, tip•ping, tips.** —*tr.* **1.a.** To give a tip to: *tipped the waiter generously.* **b.** To give as a tip: *tipped a dollar.* **2.** To provide with useful information: *tipped the police about the robbery.* —*intr.* To give tips or a tip: *tips generously.* [First written down in 1755 in Modern English.] **—tip′per** *n.*

tip-off[1] (tĭp′ôf′ *or* tĭp′ŏf′) *n. Informal.* **1.** A piece of secret, advance, or exclusive information. **2.** Something that signals a previously unknown fact or probability: *Her smile was a tip-off that the test had gone well.* [First written down in 1901 in American English, from *tip*, light blow, tap.]

tip-off[2] (tĭp′ôf′ *or* tĭp′ŏf′) *n.* In basketball, an act of starting play at the beginning of a period with a jump ball. [First written down in 1924 in Modern English : *tip*, light blow, tap + *(kick)off.*]

tip•pet (tĭp′ĭt) *n.* **1.** A scarf, cape, or other covering for the shoulders with long ends that hang down in front. **2.** A long hanging part, as of a sleeve, hood, or cape. **3.** A long stole worn by members of the Anglican clergy.

tip•ple (tĭp′əl) *tr. & intr.v.* **tip•pled, tip•pling, tip•ples.** To drink (alcoholic liquor) or engage in such drinking, especially habitually or to excess. **—tip′pler** *n.*

tip•sy (tĭp′sē) *adj.* **tip•si•er, tip•si•est. 1.** Slightly drunk. **2.** Unsteady or crooked. **—tip′si•ly** *adv.* **—tip′si•ness** *n.*

tip•toe (tĭp′tō′) *intr.v.* **tip•toed, tip•toe•ing, tip•toes.** To walk or move quietly on one's toes. —*n.* The tip of a toe. —*adj.* **1.** Standing or walking on one's toes. **2.** Stealthy; wary. —*adv.* **1.** On tiptoe. **2.** Stealthily; warily.

tip•top (tĭp′tŏp′) *n.* The highest point; the summit. —*adj.* Excellent; first-rate: *feeling in tiptop shape.*

ti•rade (tī′rād′ *or* tī **rād′**) *n.* A long angry or violent speech, usually denouncing or criticizing something or someone; a diatribe.

Ti•ra•në (tə rä′nə). The capital and largest city of Albania, in the west-central part of the country. It became capital in 1920. Population, 206,100.

tire[1] (tīr) *v.* **tired, tir•ing, tires.** —*intr.* **1.** To become weary or fatigued: *She does not tire easily.* **2.** To become bored; lose interest: *The audience tired after the first act of the play.* —*tr.* **1.** To make tired; fatigue: *The long walk tired me.* **2.** To exhaust the interest or patience of; bore: *His long speech tired the listeners.* [First written down before 800 in Old English and spelled *tīorian.*]

tire[2] (tīr) *n.* **1.** A covering for a wheel, usually made of rubber reinforced with cords of nylon, fiberglass, or other material and filled with compressed air. Tires are fitted around the wheels of automobiles, for example, to absorb shocks and provide traction. **2.** A hoop of metal or rubber fitted around a wheel. [First written down in 1485 in Middle English and spelled *tire*, iron rim of a wheel, probably from *tir*, attire.]

tired (tīrd) *adj.* **1.a.** Exhausted; fatigued: *a tired athlete.* **b.** Impatient; bored: *a tired audience.* **2.** Overused; hackneyed; trite: *a tired joke.*

tire•less (tīr′lĭs) *adj.* Not tiring easily; indefatigable: *a tireless worker.* **—tire′less•ly** *adv.*

tire•some (tīr′səm) *adj.* Causing fatigue or boredom; wearisome: *a tiresome job; a long tiresome speech.* See Synonyms at **boring. —tire′some•ly** *adv.* **—tire′some•ness** *n.*

'tis (tĭz). Contraction of *it is.*

tis•sue (tĭsh′o͞o) *n.* **1.** A group of animal or plant cells that are similar in form and function and often make up a particular organ or part: *connective tissue.* **2.** Tissue paper. **3.** A piece of soft absorbent paper used as toilet paper, a handkerchief, or a towel. **4.** A fine, very thin fabric such as gauze.

tissue paper *n.* Light thin paper used for wrapping, packing, or protecting breakable objects.

tit[1] (tĭt) *n.* **1.** The titmouse. **2.** Any of various similar or related birds. [First written down in 1706 in Modern English, short for *titmouse.*]

tit[2] (tĭt) *n.* A teat. [First written down about 950 in Old English and spelled *titt.*]

Ti•tan (tīt′n) *n.* **1.** In Greek mythology, one of a family of giants who are overthrown and supplanted by the family of Zeus. **2. titan.** A person of great size, strength, or importance.

ti•tan•ic[1] (tī tăn′ĭk) *adj.* Having great size, strength, or importance. [First written down in 1656 in Modern English, from *Titan.*]

ti•tan•ic[2] (tī tăn′ĭk *or* tĭ tăn′ĭk) *adj.* Relating to or containing titanium, especially with a valence of 4. [First written down in 1826 in Modern English, from *titanium.*]

ti•ta•ni•um (tī tā′nē əm *or* tĭ tā′nē əm) *n. Symbol* **Ti** A shiny, white metallic element that is strong, light, and highly resistant to corrosion. Atomic number 22. See table at **element.**

tit for tat *n.* Repayment in kind, as for an injury; retaliation.

tithe (tī*th*) *n.* **1.** A tenth part of one's annual income, especially for the financial support of a church or clergy. **2.** A tenth part. —*tr.v.* **tithed, tith•ing, tithes. 1.** To pay or give one tenth of (one's annual income). **2.** To levy a tithe on.

tit•il•late (tĭt′l āt′) *tr.v.* **tit•il•lat•ed, tit•il•lat•**

tippet

ă	pat	oi	boy
ā	pay	ou	out
âr	care	o͝o	took
ä	father	o͞o	boot
ĕ	pet	ŭ	cut
ē	be	ûr	urge
ĭ	pit	th	thin
ī	pie	*th*	this
îr	pier	hw	whoop
ŏ	pot	zh	vision
ō	toe	ə	about
ô	paw	N	*French* bon

titmouse
Tufted titmouse

toadstool
Jack-o'-lantern (*left*), death cap (*top right*), and fly agaric (*bottom right*) toadstools

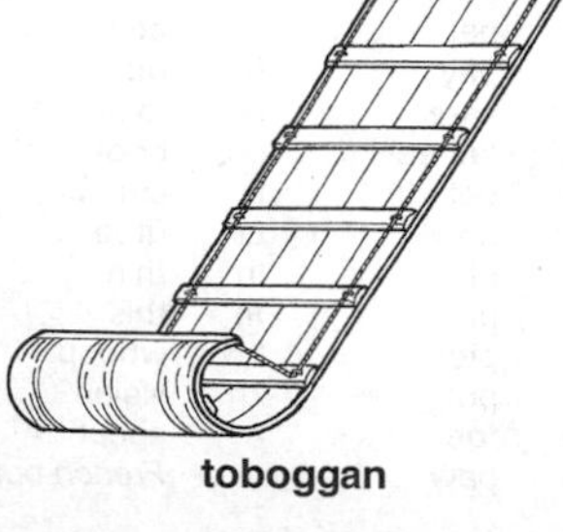

toboggan

ing, tit•il•lates. To excite or stimulate (another) in a pleasurable way: *an author expert in titillating the reader's interest.* **—tit′il•la′tion** *n.*

ti•tle (tīt′l) *n.* **1.a.** An identifying name given to a book, painting, musical composition, or other work. **b.** A general or descriptive heading, as of a book chapter. **2.** A word attached to a person's name as a mark of distinction showing rank, office, or noble birth, or used as a sign of respect. **3.a.** The legal right or claim to ownership or possession. **b.** The document, such as a deed, that serves as evidence of such a legal right: *receiving title to their house.* **4.** A championship in sports. *—tr.v.* **ti•tled, ti•tling, ti•tles.** To give a title to.

ti•tled (tīt′ld) *adj.* Having a title, especially a noble title.

tit•mouse (tĭt′mous′) *n.* Any of numerous small grayish birds, such as the chickadee, related to and resembling the sparrows.

Ti•to•grad (tētō grăd′). Podgorica.

tit•ter (tĭt′ər) *intr.v.* **tit•tered, tit•ter•ing, tit•ters.** To laugh in a restrained nervous way; giggle. *—n.* A nervous giggle. **—tit′ter•er** *n.*

tit•tle (tĭt′l) *n.* **1.** A small diacritic mark, such as an accent, a vowel mark, or a dot over an *i.* **2.** The tiniest bit.

tit•tle-tat•tle (tĭt′l tăt′l) *n.* Petty gossip; foolish talk. *—intr.v.* **tit•tle-tat•tled, tit•tle-tat•tling, tit•tle-tat•tles.** To talk idly or foolishly; gossip.

tit•u•lar (tĭch′ə lər) *adj.* **1.** Relating to, constituting, or bearing a title: *the titular role in a play.* **2.** Existing in name only; nominal: *the titular ruler of a country.*

tiz•zy (tĭz′ē) *n., pl.* **tiz•zies.** *Slang.* A state of nervous excitement or confusion; a dither.

Tl The symbol for the element **thallium.**

Tlin•git (tlĭng′gĭt *or* tlĭng′ĭt) *n., pl.* **Tlingit** or **Tlin•gits. 1.** A member of a Native American people living in southeast Alaska. **2.** The language of the Tlingit.

Tm The symbol for the element **thulium.**

TNT (tē′ĕn **tē′**) *n.* A yellow crystalline compound used mainly as an explosive.

to (to͞o; tə *when unstressed*) *prep.* **1.** In the direction of; so as to reach: *a trip to Paris.* **2.** Toward: *He turned to me.* **3.** Reaching as far as: *The water was clear to the bottom.* **4.** Toward or reaching a certain state: *the Governor's rise to power.* **5.** In contact with: *cheek to cheek.* **6.** In front of: *We stood face to face.* **7.** For the attention, benefit, or possession of: *Tell it to me.* **8.** For the purpose of; for: *We went out to lunch.* **9.** Used to indicate belonging or appropriateness: *Do you have the belt to this dress?* **10.** Concerning or regarding: *Did you get an answer to your letter?* **11.** In a relationship with: *The brook runs parallel to the road.* **12.** With the resulting condition of: *torn to shreds.* **13.** As an accompaniment of: *singing to an old tune.* **14.** Composing or constituting; in: *two pints to a quart.* **15.** In accord with: *That's not really to my liking.* **16.** As compared with: *This book is superior to her others.* **17.** Before: *The time is ten to five.* **18.** In honor of: *a toast to our visitors.* **19.a.** Used before a verb to indicate the infinitive: *I'd like to go.* **b.** Used alone when the infinitive is understood: *Go if you want to.* *—adv.* **1.** In a shut position: *slammed the door to.* **2.** Into consciousness: *The patient came to.* **3.** Into a state of action or attentiveness: *They sat down for lunch and everybody fell to.*
❑ *These sound alike:* **to, too** (also), **two** (number).

toad (tōd) *n.* Any of numerous animals related to and resembling the frogs, but having rougher drier skin and living mostly on land when full grown.
❑ *These sound alike:* **toad, toed** (having toes), **towed** (pulled).

toad•stool (tōd′sto͞ol′) *n.* A mushroom considered unfit for eating, especially a poisonous one.

toad•y (tō′dē) *n., pl.* **toad•ies.** A person who flatters others for the sake of gain; a sycophant. *—tr. & intr.v.* **toad•ied** (tō′dēd), **toad•y•ing, toad•ies** (tō′dēz). To be a toady or behave like a toady: *shamelessly toadying to his boss.*

to and fro *adv.* Back and forth: *She's always running to and fro.*

toast[1] (tōst) *v.* **toast•ed, toast•ing, toasts.** *—tr.* **1.** To heat and brown (bread or marshmallows, for example) by placing in an oven, a toaster, or close to a fire. **2.** To warm thoroughly, as before a fire: *toast one's feet by the fireplace.* *—intr.* To become toasted. *—n.* Sliced bread heated and browned. [First written down before 1398 in Middle English and spelled *tosten,* from Old French *toster.*]

toast[2] (tōst) *n.* **1.a.** The act of raising the glass and drinking in honor of or to the health of a person or thing. **b.** A person or thing honored in this way. **2.** A person who receives much attention or acclaim: *The star of the play became the toast of London.* *—v.* **toast•ed, toast•ing, toasts.** *—tr.* To drink in honor of or to the health of: *The guests toasted the bride.* *—intr.* To propose or drink a toast. [First written down in 1700 in Modern English, perhaps from *toast,* from the use of spiced toast to flavor drinks.]

toast•er (tō′stər) *n.* An electrical appliance used to toast bread.

toast•mas•ter (tōst′măs′tər) *n.* A man who proposes the toasts and introduces the speakers at a banquet.

toast•mis•tress (tōst′mĭs′trĭs) *n.* A woman who proposes the toasts and introduces the speakers at a banquet.

to•bac•co (tə băk′ō) *n., pl.* **to•bac•cos** or **to•bac•coes. 1.** The leaves of any of various tropical American plants, processed for use in cigarettes, cigars, or snuff or for smoking in pipes. **2.** A plant that bears such leaves. **3.** Products, such as cigarettes, cigars, or snuff, made from tobacco. **4.** The habit of smoking tobacco: *He gave up tobacco years ago.*

to•bac•co•nist (tə băk′ə nĭst) *n.* A person who sells tobacco and smoking supplies.

To•ba•go (tə bā′gō). An island of Trinidad and Tobago in the southeast West Indies northeast of Trinidad. It gained independence with Trinidad in 1962.

to•bog•gan (tə bŏg′ən) *n.* A long narrow sled without runners, made of thin boards curved upward at the front end. *—intr.v.* **to•bog•ganed, to•bog•gan•ing, to•bog•gans.** To ride on a toboggan.

toc•ca•ta (tə kä′tə) *n.* A musical composition, usually for the organ or another keyboard instrument, in a free style with full chords and elaborate passages.

toc•sin (tŏk′sĭn) *n.* **1.a.** An alarm sounded on a bell. **b.** A bell used to sound an alarm. **2.** A warning; an omen.

to•day (tə dā′) *n.* The present day, time, or age: *the schedule for today; the composers of today.* *—adv.* **1.** During or on the present day: *He will arrive today.* **2.** During or at the present time: *Today more vitamins are sold than ever before.*

tod•dle (tŏd′l) *intr.v.* **tod•dled, tod•dling, tod•dles.** To walk with short unsteady steps, as a small child does. *—n.* An unsteady gait.

tod•dler (tŏd′lər) *n.* A young child who is just learning how to walk.

tod•dy (tŏd′ē) *n., pl.* **tod•dies. 1.** A hot toddy. **2.a.** The sweet sap of certain tropical Asian palm trees. **b.** A fermented beverage made from this sap.

to-do (tə do͞o′) *n., pl.* **to-dos** (tə do͞oz′). *Informal.* A commotion or stir.

toe (tō) *n.* **1.** One of the extensions from the foot of a human being or other vertebrate. **2.** The part of a sock, stocking, shoe, or boot that fits over the toes. —*v.* **toed, toe•ing, toes.** —*tr.* **1.** To touch, kick, or reach with the toes. **2.a.** To drive (a nail or spike) at an oblique angle. **b.** To fasten or secure with nails or spikes driven in this way. —*intr.* To walk, stand, or move with the toes pointed in a specified direction: *She toes out.* —***idioms.*** **on (one's) toes.** Ready to act; alert. **step** or **tread on (someone's) toes.** To hurt or offend the feelings of.

❑ *These sound alike:* **toe, tow**[1] (pull), **tow**[2] (flax).

toed (tōd) *adj.* Having toes, especially a certain kind or number of toes: *a long-toed bird; a two-toed sloth.*

❑ *These sound alike:* **toed, toad** (animal), **towed** (pulled).

toe•nail (tō′nāl′) *n.* **1.** A nail on a toe. **2.** A nail driven at an oblique angle, as in joining a vertical beam to a horizontal beam. —*tr.v.* **toe•nailed, toe•nail•ing, toe•nails.** To join or secure (beams) with nails driven at an oblique angle.

tof•fee (tô′fē *or* tŏf′ē) *n.* A hard chewy candy made of brown sugar or molasses and butter.

to•fu (tō′fo͝o) *n.* A soft white food that is made from soybeans, has a high protein content, and is used in salads and cooked foods.

tog (tŏg *or* tôg) *Informal. n.* **togs.** Clothing: *gardening togs.* —*tr.v.* **togged, tog•ging, togs.** To dress or clothe.

to•ga (tō′gə) *n.* **1.** A loose one-piece outer garment worn in public by citizens of ancient Rome. **2.** A robe of office; a professional or ceremonial gown.

to•geth•er (tə gĕth′ər) *adv.* **1.** In or into a single group, mass, or place: *Many people were crowded together.* **2.** In or into contact: *rubbing one's hands together.* **3.** In association with or in relationship to another: *My cats get along together.* **4.** By cooperative effort: *We built the deck together.* **5.** Simultaneously: *The bells rang out together.* **6.** *Informal.* Into an effective condition to do something: *Get yourself together.* **—to•geth′er•ness** *n.* —SEE NOTE.

tog•gle (tŏg′əl) *n.* A pin, rod, or bolt fitted or inserted into a loop in a rope, chain, or strap to prevent slipping, to tighten, or to hold something. —*tr. v.* **tog•gled, tog•gling, tog•gles.** To furnish or fasten with a toggle.

toggle bolt *n.* A fastener consisting of a threaded bolt and toggle, used to attach objects to thin walls.

toggle joint *n.* A joint consisting of two arms attached by a pivot shaped like an elbow that allows force to be applied to the ends of the levers as the joint is expanded.

toggle switch *n.* An electrical switch that is opened and closed by a toggle joint that is loaded with a spring, with one of the levers projecting outward so that it can be moved by a finger.

To•go (tō′gō′). A country of western Africa on the Atlantic Ocean west of Benin. It gained its independence from France in 1960. Capital, Lomé. Population, 2,742,945.

toil[1] (toil) *intr.v.* **toiled, toil•ing, toils. 1.** To labor continuously; work strenuously: *We toiled all day at cleaning up the yard.* **2.** To proceed with difficulty: *toiling up a steep hill.* —*n.* Exhausting labor or effort. [First written down before 1300 in Middle English and spelled *toilen,* from Latin *tudiculāre,* to stir up, from *tudicula,* a machine for bruising olives.] **—toil′er** *n.*

toil[2] (toil) *n.* Something that binds, snares, or entangles; an entrapment. Often used in the plural: *caught in the toils of despair.* [First written down before 1529 in Modern English, from French *toile,* cloth, from Latin *tēla,* web.]

toi•let (toi′lĭt) *n.* **1.** A fixture for urination and defecation, consisting of a bowl fitted with a hinged seat and having a flushing device. **2.** A room or booth containing such a fixture. **3.** The act or process of grooming or dressing oneself; toilette.

toilet paper *n.* Thin absorbent paper, usually in rolls, used to clean oneself after defecation or urination.

toi•let•ry (toi′lĭ trē) *n., pl.* **toi•let•ries.** An article, such as toothpaste or a hairbrush, used in dressing or grooming oneself.

toi•lette (twä lĕt′) *n.* **1.** The act or process of dressing or grooming oneself. **2.** A person's dress or style of dress.

toilet water *n.* A scented liquid used for bathing or applied as a skin freshener.

toil•some (toil′səm) *adj.* Characterized by or requiring toil.

to•ken (tō′kən) *n.* **1.** Something that serves as an indication or a representation of something else; a sign: *A white flag is a token of surrender.* **2.** Something that signifies or gives proof of authority, validity, or identity: *The crown is a token of royal status.* **3.** A keepsake; a souvenir: *This ring was a token of our wedding anniversary.* **4.** A piece of stamped metal used as a substitute for currency: *subway tokens.* —*tr.v.* **to•kened, to•ken•ing, to•kens.** To symbolize or serve as a warning of. —*adj.* **1.** Done as an indication or pledge: *a token payment.* **2.** Minimal or merely symbolic: *token resistance to the new leader.* —***idioms.*** **by the same token.** In like manner; similarly. **in token of.** As an indication of: *a ring given in token of love.*

to•ken•ism (tō′kə nĭz′əm) *n.* The policy of making only a superficial effort or symbolic gesture toward the accomplishment of a goal, such as racial integration.

To•ky•o (tō′kē ō′ *or* tō′kyō). The capital and largest city of Japan, in east-central Honshu on **Tokyo Bay,** an inlet of the Pacific Ocean. It is the world's most populous city. Population, 8,353,674.

told (tōld) *v.* Past tense and past participle of **tell.**

To•le•do (tə lē′dō). **1.** A city of central Spain south-southwest of Madrid. As a Moorish capital (712–1031) it was a center of Arab and Hebrew learning. Population, 57,778. **2.** A city of northwest Ohio on Lake Erie. It was incorporated in 1837. Population, 332,943.

tol•er•a•ble (tŏl′ər ə bəl) *adj.* **1.** Able to be tolerated; endurable: *tolerable food.* **2.** Fairly good; passable: *in tolerable health.* **—tol′er•a•bly** *adv.*

tol•er•ance (tŏl′ər əns) *n.* **1.** The capacity for or the practice of recognizing and respecting the beliefs or practices of others. **2.** The capacity to endure hardship or pain. **3.** The amount that something is allowed to vary from the value intended: *The bolt was made to a tolerance of .001 inch.* **4.** The ability of an organism to resist the effects of a poison or drug.

tol•er•ant (tŏl′ər ənt) *adj.* **1.** Inclined to tolerate the beliefs or practices of others. **2.** Able to withstand or endure an adverse environmental condition: *plants tolerant of extreme heat.*

tol•er•ate (tŏl′ə rāt′) *tr.v.* **tol•er•at•ed, tol•er•at•ing, tol•er•ates. 1.** To allow without prohibiting or opposing; permit. **2.** To recognize and respect (the beliefs, rights, or practices of others). **3.** To put up with; endure: *I won't tolerate your bad manners.* **4.** To have a tolerance for (a drug or poison). [First written down in 1531 in Modern English, from Latin *tolerāre.*]

tol•er•a•tion (tŏl′ə rā′shən) *n.* **1.** Tolerance of the

Usage: together

You can use *together with* following the subject of a sentence or clause to introduce an addition: *The king, together with two aides, is expected in an hour.* Notice that the addition does not change the number of the verb that follows the original subject: *The king . . . is.* The same is true of the words or phrases *along with, besides,* and *in addition to.*

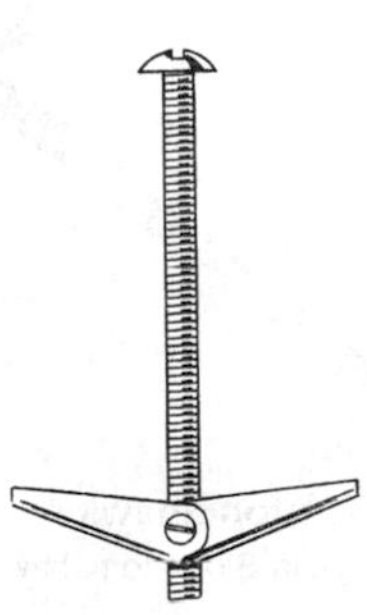

toggle bolt

ă	pat	oi	boy
ā	pay	ou	out
âr	care	o͝o	took
ä	father	o͞o	boot
ĕ	pet	ŭ	cut
ē	be	ûr	urge
ĭ	pit	th	thin
ī	pie	*th*	this
îr	pier	hw	whoop
ŏ	pot	zh	vision
ō	toe	ə	about
ô	paw	N	*French* bon

Leo Tolstoy

actions or beliefs of others. **2.** Official recognition of the rights of individuals or groups who hold different views than the majority of the population, especially in matters of religion.

toll¹ (tōl) *n.* **1.** A fixed charge or tax for a privilege, especially for passage across a bridge or along a road. **2.** A charge for a service, as a long-distance telephone call. **3.** An amount of people or things destroyed or adversely affected, as in a disaster: *The hurricane took a heavy toll along the coast.* [First written down about 1000 in Old English, from Latin *telōnēum*, tollbooth, from Greek *telos*, tax.]

toll² (tōl) *v.* **tolled, toll•ing, tolls.** —*tr.* **1.** To sound (a bell) slowly at regular intervals: *tolling the church bells.* **2.** To announce or summon by tolling: *The bell tolled the hour. The church bells tolled the monks to Vespers.* —*intr.* To sound in slowly repeated single tones. —*n.* **1.** The act of tolling. **2.** The sound of a bell being struck. [First written down in 1452 in Middle English and spelled *tollen*, to ring an alarm, perhaps from *tollen*, to entice, pull, variant of *tillen*.]

toll•booth (**tōl′**bo͞oth′) *n.* A booth where a toll is collected.

toll•gate (**tōl′**gāt′) *n.* A gate barring passage of vehicles to a road, tunnel, or bridge until a toll is paid.

Tol•stoy (**tōl′**stoi *or* **tŏl′**stoi), Count **Leo.** 1828–1910. Russian writer and philosopher whose novels include *War and Peace* (1864–1869).

Tol•tec (**tōl′**tĕk′ *or* **tŏl′**tĕk′) *n., pl.* **Toltec** or **Tol•tecs.** A member of an ancient Nahuatl-speaking people of central and southern Mexico. —*adj.* also **Tol•tec•an** (tōl **tĕk′**ən *or* tŏl **tĕk′**ən). Of or relating to the Toltec or their culture.

tol•u•ene (**tŏl′**yo͞o ēn′) *n.* A colorless liquid related to benzene that burns easily, is composed of carbon and hydrogen, and has the formula $CH_3C_6H_5$. It is used in making fuels, dyes, explosives, and other industrial chemicals.

tom (tŏm) *n.* The male of various animals, especially a male cat or turkey.

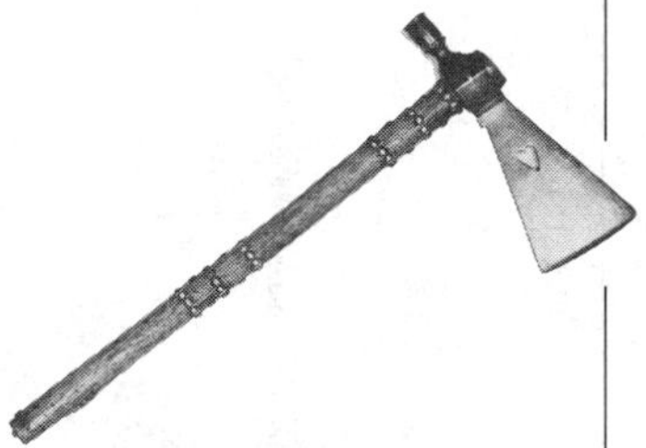

tomahawk

Oglala Sioux tomahawk

tom•a•hawk (**tŏm′**ə hôk′) *n.* A light ax formerly used as a weapon and tool by certain Native American peoples. [First written down in 1612 in American English and spelled *tamahaac*, from Virginia Algonquian.]

to•mal•ley (tə **măl′**ē *or* **tŏm′**ăl′ē) *n., pl.* **to•mal•leys.** The greenish liver of cooked lobster, considered a delicacy.

to•ma•to (tə **mā′**tō *or* tə **mä′**tō) *n., pl.* **to•ma•toes. 1.** The fleshy, usually reddish fruit of a widely cultivated South American plant, eaten raw or cooked as a vegetable. **2.** The plant that bears such fruit. [First written down in 1604 in Modern English and spelled *tomate*, from Spanish, from Nahuatl *tomatl*.]

tomb (to͞om) *n.* **1.** A place of burial; a grave. **2.** A vault or chamber for the burial of the dead.

tom•boy (**tŏm′**boi′) *n.* A girl who is considered boyish in manner or behavior.

tomb•stone (**to͞om′**stōn′) *n.* A gravestone.

tom•cat (**tŏm′**kăt′) *n.* A male cat.

tome (tōm) *n.* **1.** One of the books in a work of several volumes. **2.** A book, especially a large or scholarly one.

tom•fool•er•y (tŏm **fo͞o′**lə rē) *n., pl.* **tom•fool•er•ies.** Foolish behavior; silliness; nonsense.

to•mor•row (tə **môr′**ō *or* tə **mŏr′**ō) *n.* **1.** The day following today. **2.** The near future: *space flights of tomorrow.* —*adv.* On or for the day following today: *I will return your book tomorrow.*

Tom Thumb (tŏm) *n.* A hero of English folklore who was no larger than his father's thumb.

tom-tom

tom•tit (**tŏm′**tĭt′) *n.* A small bird, such as a titmouse.

tom-tom (**tŏm′**tŏm′) also **tam-tam** (**tŭm′**tŭm′ *or* **tăm′**tăm′) *n.* Any of various small-headed drums, usually tall and narrow, that are beaten with the hands. [First written down in 1693 in Modern English, from Hindi *ṭamṭam*, probably of imitative origin.]

ton (tŭn) *n.* **1.a.** A unit of weight equal to 2,000 pounds; a short ton. **b.** A unit of weight equal to 2,240 pounds; a long ton. **c.** A metric ton. See table at **measurement. 2.** *Informal.* A very large quantity of something: *buying tons of books.*

❑ *These sound alike:* **ton, tun** (cask).

ton•al (**tō′**nəl) *adj.* Of or relating to tones, a tone, or tonality. —**ton′al•ly** *adv.*

to•nal•i•ty (tō **năl′**ĭ tē) *n., pl.* **to•nal•i•ties. 1.a.** A system or an arrangement of seven tones built on a tonic key. **b.** The arrangement of all of the tones and chords of a musical composition with respect to a tonic. **2.** The arrangement or scheme of the tones in a painting.

tone (tōn) *n.* **1.a.** A sound that has a distinct pitch, quality, and duration; a note. **b.** The interval of a major second in a musical scale; a whole step. **2.a.** The quality or character of sound. **b.** The characteristic quality or timbre of a particular instrument or voice. **3.a.** A color or shade of color. **b.** Quality of color. **4.a.** The tension that normally remains in a muscle when it is at rest. **b.** Normal firmness of body tissue or an organ. **5.** A manner of expression in speech or writing: *an angry tone of voice.* **6.** A general quality or atmosphere: *the tone of the debate; a quiet tone of elegance in the room.* —*v.* **toned, ton•ing, tones.** —*tr.* **1.** To give a particular tone or inflection to. **2.** To soften or change the color of (a painting or photograph, for example). —*intr.* To harmonize in color. —***idioms.*** **tone down.** To make less vivid, harsh, or violent; moderate. **tone up.** To make or become brighter or more vigorous. [First written down before 1300 in Middle English and spelled *ton*, from Greek *tonos*, a stretching.]

tone arm *n.* The pivoted arm of a phonograph turntable that holds the cartridge.

tone poem *n.* A symphonic poem.

Ton•ga (**tŏng′**gə). A country in the southwest Pacific Ocean east of Fiji made up of about 150 islands, of which about 36 are inhabited. It gained its independence from Great Britain in 1970. Capital, Nukualofa. Population, 96,592.

Ton•gan (**tŏng′**gən *or* **tŏng′**ən) *adj.* Of or relating to Tonga or its people, language, or culture. —*n.* **1.** A native or inhabitant of Tonga. **2.** The Polynesian language of Tonga.

tongs (tôngz *or* tŏngz) *pl.n.* *(used with a singular or plural verb).* A device consisting of two arms joined at one end by a pivot or hinge, used for holding, lifting, or grasping objects.

tongue (tŭng) *n.* **1.** The fleshy muscular organ, attached in most vertebrates to the bottom of the mouth, that is the main organ of taste, moves to aid in chewing and swallowing, and, in human beings, acts in speech. **2.** A similar part, as in an insect. **3.** The tongue of an animal, such as a cow, used as food. **4.** A strip that projects from the edge of a board and fits into a matching groove on another board. **5.** Something that resembles a tongue in shape or function, as the flap of material under the laces or buckles of a shoe. **6.** A spoken language: *Her native tongue is Swedish.* **7.a.** Speech; talk. **b.** The act or power of speaking. **8.** A manner of speech: *He has a sharp tongue.* **9.** The part of a bell that hangs inside and strikes the walls to create the ringing noise. —*tr.v.* **tongued, tongu•ing, tongues.** To separate (notes played on a brass or wind instrument) by shutting off the stream of air with the tongue. ***—idioms.*** **hold (one's) tongue.** To be or keep silent. **on the tip of one's tongue.** On the verge of being recalled or spoken. [First written down before 899 in Old English and spelled *tunge.*]

tongue-tied (tŭng**'**tīd') *adj.* Speechless or confused in expression, as from shyness or embarassment.

tongue twister *n.* **1.** A word or group of words that is difficult to speak rapidly. **2.** Something that is difficult to pronounce.

ton•ic (tŏn**'**ĭk) *n.* **1.** A medicine or other agent that restores, refreshes, or invigorates the body. **2.** The first note of a musical scale; the keynote. **3.** Quinine water. *—adj.* In music, of or based on the keynote. —SEE NOTE.

to•night (tə nīt**'**) *adv.* On or during the present or coming night: *I'll see you tonight at ten. —n.* This night or the night of this day: *Tonight is a very special occasion.*

Ton•kin (tŏn**'**kĭn**'** *or* tŏng**'**kĭn**'**). A historical region of southeast Asia on the **Gulf of Tonkin,** an arm of the South China Sea, now forming most of northern Vietnam.

ton•nage (tŭn**'**ĭj) *n.* **1.** The number of tons of water a ship displaces when afloat. **2.** The capacity of a merchant ship in units of 100 cubic feet. **3.** A charge per ton on cargo. **4.** The total shipping of a country or port, figured in tons. **5.** Weight measured in tons.

ton•sil (tŏn**'**səl) *n.* Either of a pair of oval masses of tissue located on either side of the inner wall of the throat, believed to help protect the body from respiratory infections. [First written down in 1601 in Modern English, from Latin *tōnsillae,* tonsils.]

ton•sil•lec•to•my (tŏn'sə lĕk**'**tə mē) *n., pl.* **ton•sil•lec•to•mies.** The removal of a tonsil or tonsils by means of surgery.

ton•sil•li•tis (tŏn'sə lī**'**tĭs) *n.* Inflammation of a tonsil or tonsils.

ton•so•ri•al (tŏn sôr**'**ē əl) *adj.* Of or relating to a barber or barbering.

ton•sure (tŏn**'**shər) *n.* **1.** The act of shaving the head or part of the head, especially as a preliminary to becoming a priest or a member of a monastic order. **2.** The part of a monk's or priest's head so shaven. *—tr.v.* **ton•sured, ton•sur•ing, ton•sures.** To shave the head of.

too (to͞o) *adv.* **1.** In addition; also: *I can play the piano too.* See Synonyms at **besides. 2.** More than enough; excessively: *You worry too much.* **3.** Very; extremely: *I'm only too happy to be of service.* **4.** *Informal.* Indeed; so: *You will too do it!*

❑ *These sound alike:* **too, to** (toward), **two** (number).

took (to͝ok) *v.* Past tense of **take.**

tool (to͞ol) *n.* **1.** A device, especially a mechanical one held in the hand, used to do work or perform a task. **2.a.** A machine, such as a lathe, used to make machine parts and other objects. **b.** The part of such a machine that cuts or shapes. **3.** Something used in the performance of an operation; an instrument: *the necessary fiscal and monetary tools to stop inflation.* **4.** Something regarded as necessary to the carrying out of one's occupation: *Words are the tools of her trade.* **5.** A person used to carry out the designs of another; a dupe. *—v.* **tooled, tool•ing, tools.** *—tr.* To form, work, or decorate with a tool. *—intr.* To work with a tool. ***—idiom.*** **tool up.** To provide an industry or a factory with machinery and tools for a particular job.

❑ *These sound alike:* **tool, tulle** (fabric).

tool•box (to͞ol**'**bŏks') *n.* A case for carrying or storing tools.

toot (to͞ot) *v.* **toot•ed, toot•ing, toots.** *—intr.* **1.** To sound a horn or whistle in short blasts. **2.** To make a sound resembling that of a horn or whistle blown in short blasts. *—tr.* To blow or sound (a horn or whistle). *—n.* A blast, as of a horn.

tooth (to͞oth) *n., pl.* **teeth** (tēth). **1.** Any of a set of hard bony structures set in sockets around the jaws of most vertebrates, used to grasp, hold, and chew and as weapons of attack and defense. **2.** A similar structure in an invertebrate. **3.** A projecting part resembling a tooth in shape or function, as on a gearwheel, saw, or comb. *—tr.v.* (to͞oth *or* to͞oth). **toothed, tooth•ing, tooths.** To provide (a tool or machine part, for example) with teeth. ***—idiom.*** **to the teeth.** Lacking nothing; completely: *armed to the teeth.* [First written down before 800 in Old English and spelled *tōth.*]

tooth•ache (to͞oth**'**āk') *n.* An aching pain in or near a tooth.

tooth•brush (to͞oth**'**brŭsh') *n.* A brush used for cleaning the teeth.

toothed (to͞otht *or* to͞othd) *adj.* Having teeth, especially a certain number or type: *sharp-toothed jaws.*

tooth•paste (to͞oth**'**pāst') *n.* A paste used to clean the teeth.

tooth•pick (to͞oth**'**pĭk') *n.* A small piece of wood or other material for removing food particles from between the teeth.

tooth•pow•der (to͞oth**'**pou'dər) *n.* A powder used to clean the teeth.

tooth•some (to͞oth**'**səm) *adj.* **1.** Delicious; savory: *a toothsome pie.* **2.** Pleasant; attractive.

top[1] (tŏp) *n.* **1.** The uppermost part, point, surface, or end: *read the words at the top of the page; luggage on the top of the car.* **2.** Something, such as a lid or cap, that covers or forms an uppermost part: *the top of a trash can.* **3.** The upper half of a two-piece garment. **4.a.** The highest rank or position: *He is at the top of the company.* **b.** The highest degree, point, or pitch; the acme: *singing at the top of her powers.* **5.** The earliest part or beginning: *take it from the top.* **6.** The first half of an inning in baseball. *—adj.* **1.** Situated at the top: *the top drawer.* **2.** Of the highest degree, amount, or quality: *She's in top form today. —v.* **topped, top•ping, tops.** *—tr.* **1.** To furnish with, form, or serve as a top: *top a cake with frosting.* **2.** To reach the top of: *We topped the hill and started to climb down.* **3.** To exceed or surpass: *He just topped the old record.* **4.** To be at the head of: *She tops her class. —intr.* To make a finish, an end, or a conclusion. ***—idioms.*** **off the top of (one's) head.** *Informal.* Without preparation or previous thought: *I don't have any figures, but I can give you an estimate off the top of my head.* **on top of.** *Informal.* **1.** In control of: *It's a touchy situation, but she's on top of it.* **2.** In addition to; besides: *two papers due next week and an exam on top of that.* [First written down about 1000 in Old English.]

top[2] (tŏp) *n.* A toy having one end tapered to a point, allowing it to be spun, as by suddenly pulling a string wound around it. [First written down about 1060 in Old English.]

to•paz (tō**'**păz') *n.* **1.** A colorless, blue, yellow, brown, or pink mineral consisting largely of aluminum silicate and valued as a gem. **2.** Any of various yellow gemstones, especially a yellow variety of sapphire or corundum. **3.** A light yellow variety of quartz.

top•coat (tŏp**'**kōt') *n.* A lightweight overcoat.

To•pe•ka (tə pē**'**kə). The capital of Kansas, in the northeast part of the state west of Kansas City. It became capital in 1861. Population, 119,883.

top•flight (tŏp**'**flīt**'**) *adj. Informal.* First-rate; excellent.

top•gal•lant (tə găl**'**ənt *or* tŏp găl**'**ənt) *adj.* Of or relating to the mast above the topmast or its sails or rigging.

Regional Note: tonic

Probably the two most common generic terms for carbonated soft drinks in the United States are **soda**, used in the northeast United States, and **pop**, used from the Midwest westward. Speakers in Western Maryland and Boston and its environs call a carbonated soft drink a *tonic.*

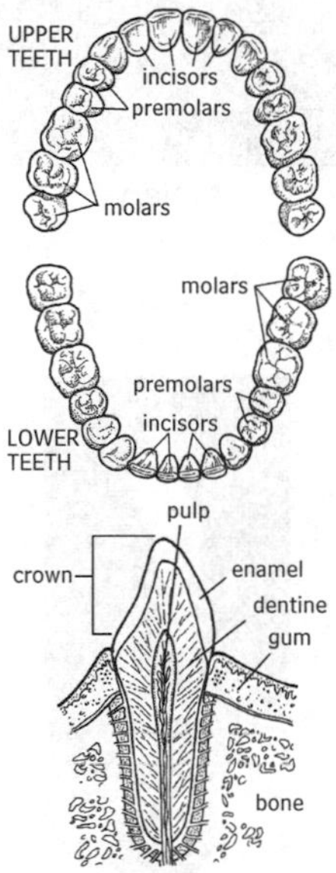

tooth

Top: Permanent teeth of an adult human
Bottom: Cross section of an incisor

ă	pat	oi	boy
ā	pay	ou	out
âr	care	o͝o	took
ä	father	o͞o	boot
ĕ	pet	ŭ	cut
ē	be	ûr	urge
ĭ	pit	th	thin
ī	pie	*th*	this
îr	pier	hw	whoop
ŏ	pot	zh	vision
ō	toe	ə	about
ô	paw	N	*French* bon

top hat

topiary

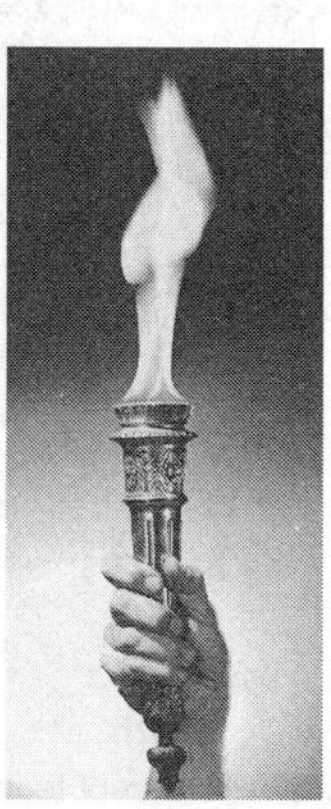
torch

tornado

top hat *n.* A man's hat having a narrow brim and a tall crown shaped like a cylinder.

top-heav•y (tŏp′hĕv′ē) *adj.* **top-heav•i•er, top-heav•i•est.** Having too much weight at the top and therefore likely to topple.

to•pi•ar•y (tō′pē ĕr′ē) *adj.* Of or characterized by the clipping of live shrubs or trees into decorative shapes, as of animals.

top•ic (tŏp′ĭk) *n.* **1.** The subject of a speech or a piece of writing. See Synonyms at **subject. 2.** A subject of discussion or conversation. [First written down in 1634 in Modern English, from Greek *topikos*, of a place.]

top•i•cal (tŏp′ĭ kəl) *adj.* **1.** Of or belonging to a particular location or place; local: *topical news items.* **2.** Currently of interest; contemporary: *ecology and other topical issues.* **3.** Of or on a particular part of the body: *topical application of an ointment.* **—top′i•cal•ly** *adv.*

top•knot (tŏp′nŏt′) *n.* A crest or knot of hair or feathers on the crown of the head.

top•most (tŏp′mōst′) *adj.* Highest; uppermost.

top•notch (tŏp′nŏch′) *adj. Informal.* First-rate; excellent.

topog. *abbr.* An abbreviation of topography.

to•pog•ra•pher (tə pŏg′rə fər) *n.* A person who is skilled in or whose work is topography.

top•o•graph•ic (tŏp′ə grăf′ĭk) or **top•o•graph•i•cal** (tŏp′ə grăf′ĭ kəl) *adj.* Of or relating to topography.

to•pog•ra•phy (tə pŏg′rə fē) *n., pl.* **to•pog•ra•phies. 1.** The detailed description or drawing of the physical features of a place or region. **2.** The physical features of a place or region.

top•o•log•i•cal (tŏp′ə lŏj′ĭ kəl) *adj.* Of or relating to topology. **—top′o•log′i•cal•ly** *adv.*

to•pol•o•gy (tə pŏl′ə jē) *n., pl.* **to•pol•o•gies.** The mathematical study of the properties of geometric figures that are not normally affected by changes in size or shape.

top•ping (tŏp′ĭng) *n.* A sauce, frosting, or garnish for food.

top•ple (tŏp′əl) *v.* **top•pled, top•pling, top•ples.** *—tr.* To push or throw over; overturn or overthrow. *—intr.* To totter and fall: *The pile of books toppled over.*

tops (tŏps) *adj. Slang.* First-rate; excellent.

top•sail (tŏp′səl *or* tŏp′sāl′) *n.* A square sail set above the lowest sail on the mast of a square-rigged ship.

top-se•cret (tŏp′sē′krĭt) *adj.* Containing information of the highest level of national security classification.

top•soil (tŏp′soil′) *n.* The layer of soil at the surface of the ground.

top•sy-tur•vy (tŏp′sē tûr′vē) *adv.* **1.** Upside-down. **2.** In a state of utter disorder or confusion: *turned the room topsy-turvy looking for the keys. —adj.* **top•sy-tur•vi•er, top•sy-tur•vi•est.** Confused; disordered: *a topsy-turvy political situation.*

toque (tōk) *n.* A small close-fitting hat with no brim, worn by women.

To•rah also **to•rah** (tôr′ə *or* tô rä′) *n.* **1.** The body of Jewish religious law and learning including both sacred literature and oral tradition. **2.a.** The first five books of the Hebrew Scriptures. **b.** A scroll on which these books are written, used in a synagogue during services.

torch (tôrch) *n.* **1.a.** A portable light produced by the flame of a stick of wood or of a flammable material wound about the end of a stick of wood. **b.** *Chiefly British.* A flashlight. **2.** Something that serves to enlighten, guide, or illuminate: *passing the torch of learning to the new generation.* **3.** A portable device that burns a fuel, usually a gas, to produce a flame hot enough for welding, soldering, brazing, or cutting metals. [First written down about 1250 in Middle English and spelled *torche*, from Latin *torqua*, from *torquēre*, to twist.]

tore (tôr) *v.* Past tense of **tear**[1].

tor•e•a•dor (tôr′ē ə dôr′) *n.* A person who performs the central action in a bullfight; a bullfighter.

tor•ment (tôr′mĕnt′) *n.* **1.** Great physical pain or mental anguish: *the torment of a toothache; the torments of jealousy.* **2.** A source of harrassment, annoyance, or pain: *That dog is the torment of its owners. —tr.v.* (tôr mĕnt′ *or* tôr′mĕnt′). **tor•ment•ed, tor•ment•ing, tor•ments. 1.** To cause to undergo great pain or anguish. **2.** To annoy, pester, or harass: *Stop tormenting me with silly questions.* [First written down before 1300 in Middle English and spelled *tourment*, from Latin *tormentum*, from *torquēre*, to twist.] **—tor•men′tor** *n.*

torn (tôrn) *v.* Past participle of **tear**[1].

tor•na•do (tôr nā′dō) *n., pl.* **tor•na•does** or **tor•na•dos. 1.** A violent atmospheric disturbance in the form of a column of air several hundred yards wide spinning at speeds of up to 500 miles (800 kilometers) per hour, usually accompanied by a funnel-shaped extension of a thundercloud. **2.** A whirlwind or hurricane. [First written down in 1556 in Modern English and spelled *ternado*, from Spanish *tronada*, thunderstorm.]

To•ron•to (tə rŏn′tō). The capital and largest city of Ontario, Canada, in the southern part of the province on Lake Ontario. It was founded as York in 1793 and renamed Toronto in 1834. Population, 599,217.

tor•pe•do (tôr pē′dō) *n., pl.* **tor•pe•does.** A cylindrical, self-propelled underwater projectile launched from an airplane, a ship, or a submarine and designed to explode against or near a target. *—tr.v.* **tor•pe•doed, tor•pe•do•ing, tor•pe•does.** To attack, strike, or sink with a torpedo. [First written down about 1520 in Modern English and spelled *torpedo*, ray that gives off an electric shock, from Latin *torpēdō*, numbness.]

tor•pid (tôr′pĭd) *adj.* **1.** Unable to move or feel; numb. **2.** Dormant; hibernating. **3.** Sluggish or dull. [First written down in 1613 in Modern English, from Latin *torpidus*.]

tor•por (tôr′pər) *n.* A state of mental or physical inactivity or insensibility.

torque (tôrk) *n.* **1.** The tendency or capability of a force for producing rotation about an axis. **2.** A force that tends to cause twisting or rotation.

tor•rent (tôr′ənt *or* tŏr′ənt) *n.* **1.** A swift-flowing stream. **2.** A heavy downpour; a deluge: *rain falling in torrents.* **3.** A heavy uncontrolled outpouring: *a torrent of insults.*

tor•ren•tial (tô rĕn′shəl *or* tə rĕn′shəl) *adj.* Caused by or resembling a torrent: *torrential rain.*

tor•rid (tôr′ĭd *or* tŏr′ĭd) *adj.* **tor•rid•er, tor•rid•est. 1.** Very dry and hot; scorching: *torrid weather.* **2.** Passionate; ardent: *a torrid romance.* [First written down in 1586 in Modern English, from Latin *torridus*, from *torrēre*, to punch.] **—tor′rid•ly** *adv.*

Tor•rid Zone (tôr′ĭd *or* tŏr′ĭd). The central latitude zone of the earth, between the Tropic of Cancer and the Tropic of Capricorn.

tor•si (tôr′sē) *n.* A plural of **torso.**

tor•sion (tôr′shən) *n.* **1.a.** The act or process of twisting or turning. **b.** The condition of being twisted or turned. **2.** The stress that an object undergoes when one of its ends is twisted out of line with the other end.

tor•so (tôr′sō) *n., pl.* **tor•sos** or **tor•si** (tôr′sē). The human body except for the head and limbs; the trunk.

tort (tôrt) *n.* In law, a damage, an injury, or a

wrongful act that does not involve a breach of contract and that can be made the cause of a civil suit.
❑ *These sound alike:* **tort, torte** (cake).

torte (tôrt *or* tôr′tə) *n.* A rich cake made with many eggs and nuts.
❑ *These sound alike:* **torte, tort** (wrongful act).

tor•til•la (tôr tē′yə) *n.* A round, flat Mexican bread made from cornmeal or wheat flour and water and baked on a grill.

tor•toise (tôr′tĭs) *n.* Any of various turtles that live on land.

tor•toise•shell (tôr′tĭs shĕl′) *n.* The mottled, horny, brownish outer covering of certain sea turtles, used to make combs and jewelry.

tor•tu•ous (tôr′cho͞o əs) *adj.* **1.** Winding; twisting: *a tortuous road.* **2.** Not straightforward; devious: *a tortuous argument.* [First written down about 1390 in Middle English, from Latin *tortus*, a twisting, from *torquēre*, to twist.] **—tor′tu•ous•ly** *adv.* **—tor′tu•ous•ness** *n.*

tor•ture (tôr′chər) *n.* **1.** Infliction of severe physical pain in order to punish someone or force someone to do something or provide information. **2.** Excruciating physical or mental pain. *—tr.v.* **tor•tured, tor•tur•ing, tor•tures. 1.** To subject to torture. **2.** To bring great pain or anguish upon (another): *He is tortured by anxiety.* [First written down before 1425 in Middle English, from Late Latin *tortūra*, from Latin *torquēre*, to twist.] **—tor′tur•er** *n.*

tor•tur•ous (tôr′chər əs) *adj.* **1.** Of, relating to, or causing torture. **2.** Twisted; strained.

To•ry (tôr′ē) *n., pl.* **To•ries. 1.** A member of a British political party founded in 1689 that was the rival of the Whigs and has been known as the Conservative Party since 1832. **2.** An American siding with the British during the American Revolution. **3.** A political conservative.

toss (tôs *or* tŏs) *v.* **tossed, toss•ing, toss•es.** *—tr.* **1.a.** To throw lightly or casually: *toss a ball to a teammate.* See Synonyms at **throw. b.** To heave, fling, or throw continuously about; pitch to and fro: *Heavy seas tossed the ship.* **2.** To move or lift (the head) with a sudden movement. **3.** To flip (a coin) to decide something. **4.** To mix (a salad) lightly with a dressing. *—intr.* **1.** To be thrown here and there; be flung to and fro. **2.** To move about restlessly; twist and turn: *I tossed in my sleep all night.* *—n.* **1.** The act of tossing or the condition of being tossed. **2.** A rapid upward movement, as of the head.

toss•up (tôs′ŭp′ *or* tŏs′ŭp′) *n. Informal.* An even chance or choice: *It's a tossup as to who will win.*

tot (tŏt) *n.* **1.** A small child. **2.** A small amount, as of liquor.

to•tal (tōt′l) *n.* **1.** An amount obtained by addition; a sum. **2.** A whole quantity; an entirety. *—adj.* **1.** Of, relating to, or constituting the whole: *the total population of the state.* **2.** Complete; absolute; utter: *a total eclipse.* *—v.* **to•taled, to•tal•ing, to•tals** or **to•talled, to•tal•ling, to•tals.** *—tr.* **1.** To find the sum of; add up: *totaling expenses.* **2.** To equal a total of; amount to: *Your bill totals $25.* *—intr.* To add up; amount: *It totals to three dollars.* [First written down about 1390 in Middle English, from Latin *tōtus*.] **—to′tal•ly** *adv.*

to•tal•i•tar•i•an (tō tăl′ĭ târ′ē ən) *adj.* Of or relating to a form of government in which one political party exercises absolute control over society and uses falsehood and violence to silence opposition. *—n.* A person who supports or practices such a form of government. **—to•tal′i•tar′i•an•ism** *n.*

to•tal•i•ty (tō tăl′ĭ tē) *n., pl.* **to•tal•i•ties. 1.** The quality or state of being total. **2.** A total amount; a sum.

tote (tōt) *tr.v.* **tot•ed, tot•ing, totes.** *Informal.* To haul; carry.

tote bag *n.* A large handbag or shopping bag.

to•tem (tō′təm) *n.* **1.** An animal, a plant, or a natural object that serves among certain peoples as the emblem of a clan or family and is sometimes claimed by the members as an ancestor, a founder, or a guardian. **2.** A representation of such an object. [First written down about 1760 in American English, from Ojibwa *nindoodem*, my totem.] **—to•tem′ic** *adj.*

totem pole *n.* A post carved and painted with a series of totemic symbols and put up before a dwelling, as among certain Native American peoples of the northwest Pacific coast.

tot•ter (tŏt′ər) *intr.v.* **tot•tered, tot•ter•ing, tot•ters. 1.** To sway as if about to fall: *A pile of books tottered at the edge of the table.* **2.** To walk unsteadily; stagger: *The baby tottered and fell down.*

tou•can (to͞o′kăn′ *or* to͞o kăn′) *n.* Any of various tropical American birds having brightly colored plumage and a very large bill. [First written down in 1568 in Modern English, from Tupi *tucano*, bird.]

touch (tŭch) *v.* **touched, touch•ing, touch•es.** *—tr.* **1.** To cause a part of the body, especially the hand or fingers, to feel: *I touched the statue.* **2.** To bring something into contact with: *touched the sore spot with a probe; touching fire to a fuse.* **3.** To press or push lightly; tap: *touched a control to improve the TV picture.* **4.** To lay hands on in violence. **5.** To eat or drink; taste: *She didn't touch her food.* **6.** To disturb or move by handling: *Just don't touch anything in my room!* **7.** To meet without going beyond; adjoin: *the line where his property touches mine.* **8.** To affect the emotions of; move to tender response: *an appeal that touched us deeply.* **9.** To color slightly; tinge: *a white petal touched with pink.* *—intr.* **1.** To touch a person or thing. **2.** To be or come into contact: *Don't let the live wires touch.* *—n.* **1.** The act or an instance of touching. **2.** The sense by which external objects or forces are perceived through contact with the body. **3.** A sensation experienced in touching something with a characteristic texture: *felt the touch of snowflakes on her face.* **4.** A light push; a tap: *a switch that requires just a touch.* **5.** A small change or addition, or the effect achieved by it: *Candlelight provided just the right touch.* **6.a.** A suggestion, hint, or tinge: *a touch of jealousy.* **b.** A mild attack: *a touch of the flu.* **c.** A small amount; a dash: *a touch of paprika.* **7.** A facility; a knack: *She has a fine touch.* **8.** The state of being in contact or communication: *kept in touch with several classmates.* ***—idioms.*** **touch down.** To make contact with the ground; land: *The plane touched down smoothly.* **touch up.** To improve by making minor corrections, changes, or additions: *I touched up the painting before submitting it.* [First written down before 1300 in Middle English and spelled *touchen*, from Old French *touchier*.]

touch-and-go (tŭch′ən gō′) *adj.* Dangerous and uncertain in nature or outcome; precarious.

touch•back (tŭch′băk′) *n.* In football, an instance of touching the ball to the ground behind one's goal line after the ball has been kicked or passed over the line by an opponent. The team with the ball resumes play on its own 20-yard line.

touch•down (tŭch′doun′) *n.* **1.** In football, the act of having possession of the ball on or across the opponent's goal line for a score of six points. **2.** The contact or moment of contact of an aircraft or a spacecraft with the surface on which it lands.

touched (tŭcht) *adj.* **1.** Emotionally affected; moved. **2.** Somewhat demented or mentally unbalanced.

totem pole

toucan

ă	pat	oi	boy
ā	pay	ou	out
âr	care	o͝o	took
ä	father	o͞o	boot
ĕ	pet	ŭ	cut
ē	be	ûr	urge
ĭ	pit	th	thin
ī	pie	*th*	this
îr	pier	hw	whoop
ŏ	pot	zh	vision
ō	toe	ə	about
ô	paw	N	*French* bon

Usage: toward

The words **toward** and **towards** mean the same thing. **Toward** is more commonly used by American speakers of English. **Towards** is the main form used by British speakers of English.

tower
Eiffel Tower in Paris, France

towhee

touch football *n.* A variety of football played without protective clothing in which players tag rather than tackle each other.

touch•ing (tŭch′ĭng) *adj.* Causing a sympathetic reaction; moving: *a touching speech.* —*prep.* Concerning; about: *I have heard nothing touching his departure.* —**touch′ing•ly** *adv.*

touch-me-not (tŭch′mē nŏt′) *n.* **1.** The jewelweed. **2.** The sensitive plant.

touch•stone (tŭch′stōn′) *n.* **1.** A hard black stone, such as jasper or basalt, formerly used to test a sample of silver or gold. The streak left by rubbing the sample on the touchstone was compared with the streak left by a standard alloy. **2.** An excellent quality or example used for testing the value or genuineness of something; a standard.

touch-tone (tŭch′tōn′) *adj.* Of or relating to a telephone with which the user places calls by pressing buttons that produce tones corresponding to the digits of the number being called.

touch•y (tŭch′ē) *adj.* **touch•i•er, touch•i•est. 1.** Tending to take offense easily; oversensitive. **2.** Requiring special tact or skill; delicate: *a touchy operation.*

tough (tŭf) *adj.* **tough•er, tough•est. 1.** Able to withstand heavy strain or load without tearing or breaking; strong and resilient. **2.** Difficult to cut or chew: *a tough steak.* **3.** Physically hardy; rugged. **4.** Demanding or troubling; difficult: *a tough lesson.* **5.** Strong-minded; resolute: *a tough man to convince.* **6.** Aggressive; pugnacious: *tough criminals.* **7.** *Slang.* Too bad; unfortunate: *a tough break.* —*n.* A thug or hoodlum. [First written down about 700 in Old English and spelled *tōh.*] —**tough′ly** *adv.* —**tough′ness** *n.*

❑ *These sound alike:* **tough, tuff** (rock).

tough•en (tŭf′ən) *tr. & intr.v.* **tough•ened, tough•en•ing, tough•ens.** To make or become tough. —**tough′en•er** *n.*

tou•pee (to͞o pā′) *n.* A small wig or hairpiece worn to cover a bald spot.

tour (to͝or) *n.* **1.** A trip with visits to many places of interest for business, pleasure, or instruction: *a tour of Europe.* **2.** A brief trip to or through a place for the purpose of seeing it: *a tour of the printing plant.* **3.** A journey to fulfill a round of engagements in several places: *a concert tour.* **4.** A period of duty at a single place or job. —*intr. & tr.v.* **toured, tour•ing, tours.** To go on a tour or make a tour of: *touring through Spain; touring Canada.* [First written down about 1300 in Middle English and spelled *tour,* a turn, from Latin *tornus,* lathe.]

tour de force (to͝or′ də fôrs′) *n., pl.* **tours de force** (to͝or′ də fôrs′). A feat requiring great skill or strength, often deliberately undertaken for its difficulty.

tour•ism (to͝or′ĭz′əm) *n.* **1.** The practice of traveling for pleasure. **2.** The business of providing tours and services for travelers.

tour•ist (to͝or′ĭst) *n.* A person who travels for pleasure.

tourist class *n.* The lowest class of accommodations on some passenger ships and airplanes.

tour•ma•line (to͝or′mə lĭn *or* to͝or′mə lēn′) *n.* A complex crystalline silicate mineral containing aluminum, boron, and other elements. It is used in electronic instruments and in certain varieties as a gemstone.

tour•na•ment (to͝or′nə mənt *or* tûr′nə mənt) *n.* **1.** A contest made up of a series of games or trials: *a tennis tournament.* **2.** A medieval jousting match.

tour•ne•dos (to͝or′nə dō′) *n., pl.* **tour•ne•dos** (to͝or′nə dō′ *or* to͝or′nə dōz′). A cut of beef from the tenderloin, often bound in bacon or suet for cooking.

tour•ney (to͝or′nē *or* tûr′nē) *n., pl.* **tour•neys.** A tournament.

tour•ni•quet (to͝or′nĭ kĭt *or* tûr′nĭ kĭt) *n.* A device, such as a tightly encircling bandage, used to stop temporarily the flow of blood in a large artery in one of the limbs.

Tours (to͝or). A city of west-central France on the Loire River. It dates to pre-Roman times. Population, 132,209.

tou•sle (tou′zəl) *tr.v.* **tou•sled, tou•sling, tou•sles.** To disarrange or rumple; dishevel.

tout (tout) *v.* **tout•ed, tout•ing, touts.** —*intr.* To try to obtain customers, votes, or patronage, especially aggressively. —*tr.* To promote or praise energetically; publicize: *touting the proposal at the town meeting.*

tow[1] (tō) *tr.v.* **towed, tow•ing, tows.** To draw or pull along behind by a chain or line: *tow a car.* See Synonyms at **pull.** —*n.* **1.** The act or an instance of towing: *trying to get a tow from a police truck.* **2.** The condition of being towed: *The tugboat had a rowboat in tow.* [First written down about 1000 in Old English and spelled *togian.*]

❑ *These sound alike:* **tow**[1] (pull), **toe** (foot part), **tow**[2] (flax).

tow[2] (tō) *n.* Coarse broken flax or hemp fibers that are ready for spinning. [First written down before 1387 in Middle English, possibly from Old English *tōw-,* spinning.]

❑ *These sound alike:* **tow**[2] (flax), **toe** (foot part), **tow**[1] (pull).

to•ward (tôrd *or* tə wôrd′) also **to•wards** (tôrdz *or* tə wôrdz′) *prep.* **1.** In the direction of: *driving toward the river.* **2.** In a position facing: *She had her back toward me.* **3.** Somewhat before in time: *It started raining toward dawn.* **4.** In relation to; regarding: *a positive attitude toward the future.* **5.** In furtherance or partial fulfillment of: *a payment toward the house.* **6.** With a view to: *efforts toward peace.* —See Note.

tow•el (tou′əl) *n.* A piece of absorbent cloth or paper used for wiping or drying. —*tr.v.* **tow•eled, tow•el•ing, tow•els** or **tow•elled, tow•el•ling, tow•els.** To wipe or rub dry with a towel. [First written down about 1250 in Middle English and spelled *towaille,* from Old French *toaille,* of Germanic origin.]

tow•el•ing (tou′ə lĭng) *n.* Any of various fabrics of cotton or linen used for making towels.

tow•er (tou′ər) *n.* **1.** A building or part of a building that is high in proportion to its width and length. **2.** A tall slender structure used for observation, signaling, or pumping: *a control tower.* **3.** A person who embodies a virtue such as strength or firmness: *His father is a tower of strength.* —*intr.v.* **tow•ered, tow•er•ing, tow•ers.** To rise to a conspicuous height: *skyscrapers towering over New York.* [First written down about 899 in Old English and spelled *torr,* from Latin *turris.*]

tow•er•ing (tou′ər ĭng) *adj.* **1.** Of imposing height; very tall: *towering peaks.* **2.** Outstanding; preeminent. **3.** Intense; extreme: *in a towering rage.*

tow•head (tō′hĕd′) *n.* A person having white-blond hair resembling tow. —**tow′head′ed** *adj.*

tow•hee (tō′hē *or* tō hē′) *n.* **1.** A North American bird having black, white, and rust-colored feathers. **2.** Any of several finches having brownish feathers.

town (toun) *n.* **1.** An area in which people live and that is larger than a village and smaller than a city. **2.** The residents of such a population center. **3.** *Informal.* A city. **4.** The commerical center or district of an area: *She goes into town every Tuesday.* [First written down about 601 in Old English and spelled *tūn,* enclosed place, village.]

town crier *n.* A person formerly employed to walk

about the streets of a town shouting public announcements.

town hall *n.* The building that contains the offices of the public officials of a town and that houses the town council and courts.

town•ship (toun′shĭp′) *n.* **1.** A subdivision of a county in most northeast and Midwest U.S. states. **2.** A unit of land area used in surveying, equal to 36 square miles.

towns•peo•ple (tounz′pē′pəl) *pl.n.* The inhabitants or citizens of a town or city.

tow•path (tō′păth′) *n.* A path along a canal or river used by animals towing boats.

tox•e•mi•a (tŏk sē′mē ə) *n.* A condition in which the blood contains toxins, either produced by body cells at a local source of infection or by the growth of microorganisms.

tox•ic (tŏk′sĭk) *adj.* **1.** Of, relating to, or caused by a toxin or other poison: *a toxic condition.* **2.** Capable of causing injury or death, especially by chemical means; poisonous: *toxic industrial wastes.* [First written down in 1664 in Modern English, from Greek *toxikon*, poison for arrows, from *toxon*, bow.]

tox•ic•i•ty (tŏk sĭs′ĭ tē) *n., pl.* **tox•ic•i•ties.** **1.** The condition or property of being toxic. **2.** The degree to which a substance is toxic.

tox•i•col•o•gist (tŏk′sĭ kŏl′ə jĭst) *n.* A physician or scientist who specializes in toxicology.

tox•i•col•o•gy (tŏk′sĭ kŏl′ə jē) *n.* The scientific and medical study of poisons, their effects and detection, and the treatment of poisoning.

tox•in (tŏk′sĭn) *n.* A poison produced by a plant, an animal, or a microorganism, having a protein structure and capable of causing poisoning when introduced into the body but also often capable of stimulating production of an antitoxin.

toy (toi) *n.* **1.** An object for children to play with. **2.** Something of little importance; a trifle. **3.** A dog of a very small breed or of a variety smaller than the standard variety of its breed. *—intr.v.* **toyed, toy•ing, toys.** To amuse oneself idly; trifle: *talking on the phone and toying with a pencil.*

tpk. *abbr.* An abbreviation of turnpike.

tr. *abbr.* An abbreviation of: **1.** Transitive. **2.** Translation. **3.** Treasurer.

trace[1] (trās) *n.* **1.** A visible mark made or left by the passage of a person, a thing, or an animal. **2.** A barely perceivable indication; a touch. **3.a.** An extremely small amount. **b.** Something, such as an element or a chemical compound, that is present in a substance or mixture in very small amounts. **4.** A line drawn on a graph to represent a continuous set of values of a variable: *the trace made by a seismograph.* *—v.* **traced, trac•ing, trac•es.** *—tr.* **1.** To follow the course or trail of: *trace a lost letter.* **2.** To follow the history or development of: *trace the beginnings of the Industrial Revolution.* **3.** To locate or discover by searching or researching evidence. **4.** To draw or sketch (a figure). **5.** To form (letters) with special care. **6.** To copy by following lines seen through a sheet of transparent paper. *—intr.* **1.** To make one's way along a trail or course. **2.** To have origins; be traceable. [First written down before 1300 in Middle English, from Old French *tracier*, to make one's way.] **—trace′a•ble** *adj.*

trace[2] (trās) *n.* One of two side straps or chains connecting a harnessed draft animal to a vehicle. [First written down about 1330 in Middle English and spelled *trais*, from Old French, from Latin *tractus*, a hauling.]

trac•er (trā′sər) *n.* **1.a.** A person employed to locate missing persons or goods. **b.** A search instituted to locate missing persons or goods. **2.** A bullet that leaves a luminous or smoky trail. **3.** An identifiable substance, such as a dye or radioactive isotope, that can be followed through the course of a mechanical, chemical, or biological process, providing information about details of the process or the distribution of the substances involved in it.

trac•er•y (trā′sə rē) *n., pl.* **trac•er•ies.** Ornamental work of interlaced and branching lines.

tra•che•a (trā′kē ə) *n., pl.* **tra•che•ae** (trā′kē ē′) or **tra•che•as.** A thin-walled tube of cartilage and membrane leading from the larynx to the bronchi and carrying air to the lungs; the windpipe.

tra•che•ot•o•my (trā′kē ŏt′ə mē) *n., pl.* **tra•che•ot•o•mies.** The act or procedure of cutting into the trachea through the neck, as to make an artificial opening for breathing.

tra•cho•ma (trə kō′mə) *n.* A contagious disease caused by bacteria that results in severe inflammation of the membranes that line the eyelid and cover the eyeball.

track (trăk) *n.* **1.** A mark or trail of marks left by something that has passed: *tire tracks.* **2.** A pathway or course over which something moves: *a bicycle track in the park.* **3.** A course of action or way of proceeding: *on the right track.* **4.** Awareness of something occurring or passing: *Keep track of the score.* **5.** A rail or set of parallel rails on which a train or trolley runs: *railroad tracks.* **6.** A groove or ridge that holds or guides a moving part or device: *The curtain had come off its track.* **7.** A tread, as on a bulldozer or tank. **8.** A racetrack. **9.** Track and field. **10.** A path or band on a film or magnetic tape on which sound or other information is recorded. **11.** A selection from a sound recording: *the title track of the album.* **12.** One of the separate sound recordings that are combined to produce a stereophonic sound reproduction: *the vocal track of a song.* *—tr.v.* **tracked, track•ing, tracks.** **1.** To follow the footprints or trail of: *They tracked the animal through the woods.* **2.** To carry on the feet and deposit as tracks: *Don't track mud on the floor.* **3.** To follow and find: *We tracked him down in the library.* **4.** To observe or monitor the course of: *Radar is used to track weather balloons.* **5.** To watch the progress of; follow: *She tracked the performance of their best pitcher.* [First written down before 1470 in Middle English, from Old French *trac*, perhaps of Germanic origin.] **—track′er** *n.*

track and field *n.* Athletic events performed on a running track and the field associated with it. **—track′-and-field′** *adj.*

track•ing station (trăk′ĭng) *n.* A facility containing instruments for observing and maintaining contact with an artificial satellite or spacecraft.

track meet *n.* A track-and-field competition between two or more teams.

track record *n.* *Informal.* A record of actual performance or accomplishment.

tract[1] (trăkt) *n.* **1.** An expanse of land or water. **2.a.** A system of body organs and tissues that together perform a specialized function: *the digestive tract.* **b.** A bundle of nerve fibers that begin and end at the same places and have the same function. [First written down in 1441 in Middle English and spelled *tract*, period of time, from Latin *tractus*, course, space, period of time, from *trahere*, to draw.]

tract[2] (trăkt) *n.* A leaflet or pamphlet containing a declaration, especially one put out by a religious or political group. [First written down before 1398 in Middle English and spelled *tracte*, treatise, probably short for Latin *tractātus*, from *tractāre*, to discuss.]

trac•ta•ble (trăk′tə bəl) *adj.* **1.** Easily managed or controlled; governable: *a tractable child.* **2.** Easily worked; malleable: *tractable metals.* **—trac′ta•bly** *adv.*

track and field
Top: Foot race
Bottom: Long jump by Carl Lewis in 1987

ă	pat	oi	boy
ā	pay	ou	out
âr	care	o͝o	took
ä	father	o͞o	boot
ĕ	pet	ŭ	cut
ē	be	ûr	urge
ĭ	pit	th	thin
ī	pie	*th*	this
îr	pier	hw	whoop
ŏ	pot	zh	vision
ō	toe	ə	about
ô	paw	N	*French* bon

tractor

traffic light

trac•tion (trăk′shən) *n.* **1.** The act of drawing or pulling, especially the drawing of a vehicle or load over a surface. **2.** The condition of being drawn or pulled. **3.** Pulling power, as of a draft animal or an engine. **4.** The friction that prevents a wheel from slipping or skidding over the surface on which it runs. **5.a.** A pulling force applied to a part of the body, as to correct a broken or dislocated bone. **b.** The condition of having such force applied: *a leg in traction.* [First written down in 1615 in Modern English, from Latin *tractus,* past participle of *trahere,* to pull, draw.]

trac•tor (trăk′tər) *n.* **1.** A vehicle powered by a gasoline or diesel engine, equipped with large tires that have deep treads, and used in moving, farming, and other applications. **2.** A truck having a cab and no body, used for pulling large vehicles such as trailers and vans. [First written down in 1798 in Modern English and spelled *tractor,* something that pulls, from Latin *tractus,* past participle of *trahere,* to draw.]

trade (trād) *n.* **1.** The business of buying and selling goods; commerce. See Synonyms at **business. 2.** The people who work in a particular business or industry: *the building and construction trades.* **3.** Customers or patrons; clientele. **4.** An exchange of one thing for another, as by bartering: *Everyone brings something to market for sale or trade.* **5.** An occupation, especially one requiring special skill with the hands; a craft: *the tailor's trade.* **6.** The trade winds. Often used in the plural. —*v.* **trad•ed, trad•ing, trades.** —*intr.* **1.** To engage in buying, selling, or bartering: *He traded for furs along the Oregon coast.* **2.** To exchange one thing for another. **3.** To shop regularly: *He trades at the local grocery store.* —*tr.* **1.** To exchange or swap: *trade books with a friend.* **2.** To buy and sell (stocks, for example). —***idiom.*** **trade in.** To surrender or sell (an old or used item), using the proceeds as partial payment on a new purchase. [First written down about 1375 in Middle English and spelled *trade,* course, from Middle Low German.]

trade-in (trād′ĭn′) *n.* Something accepted as partial payment for a new purchase.

trade•mark (trād′märk′) *n.* A name, symbol, or other device identifying a product, which is registered with the government and legally restricted to the use of the owner or manufacturer. —*tr.v.* **trade•marked, trade•mark•ing, trade•marks. 1.** To label (a product) with a trademark. **2.** To register as a trademark.

trade name *n.* **1.** A name used to identify a commercial product or service. **2.** The name by which a commodity, service, or process is known to the trade.

trade•off (trād′ôf′ *or* trād′ŏf′) *n.* An exchange of one thing in return for another, especially a giving up of something desirable for something else regarded as more desirable.

trad•er (trā′dər) *n.* **1.** A person who trades; a dealer. **2.** A ship employed in foreign trade.

trade school *n.* A school that offers training in skilled trades; a vocational school.

trades•man (trādz′mən) *n.* **1.** A man engaged in retail trade. **2.** A craftsman.

trades•peo•ple (trādz′pē′pəl) *pl.n.* **1.** People engaged in retail trade. **2.** Skilled workers.

trade union *n.* A labor union.

trade wind *n.* Any of a consistent system of winds blowing over most of the Torrid Zone, blowing northeasterly in the Northern Hemisphere and southeasterly in the Southern Hemisphere. Often used in the plural.

trad•ing post (trā′dĭng) *n.* A station or store in a sparsely settled area established by traders for bartering.

tra•di•tion (trə dĭsh′ən) *n.* **1.** The passing down of elements of a culture from generation to generation, especially orally. **2.** A custom or usage handed down from generation to generation. **3.** A set of such customs or usages: *We follow our family tradition and have a reunion each fall.* [First written down about 1382 in Middle English and spelled *tradicion,* from Latin *trāditiō,* from *trādere,* to hand over : *trāns-,* over + *dare,* to give.]

tra•di•tion•al (trə dĭsh′ə nəl) *adj.* Of, relating to, or in accord with tradition. —**tra•di′tion•al•ly** *adv.*

Tra•fal•gar (trə făl′gər), **Cape.** A cape on the southwest coast of Spain northwest of the Strait of Gibraltar. The British navy defeated the French and Spanish here in 1805.

traf•fic (trăf′ĭk) *n.* **1.a.** The commercial exchange of goods; trade. See Synonyms at **business. b.** Illegal or improper commercial activity: *traffic in drugs.* **2.** The movement of vehicles, people, or messages along routes of transportation or communication. **3.** The amount, as of vehicles, people, or aircraft, in movement: *Traffic is heavy during rush hour.* —*intr.v.* **traf•ficked, traf•fick•ing, traf•fics.** To carry on trade or other dealings. —**traf′fick•er** *n.*

traffic circle *n.* A circular intersection of roads around which traffic moves in one direction.

traffic light *n.* A road signal for directing traffic by means of colored lights.

tra•ge•di•an (trə jē′dē ən) *n.* **1.** A writer of tragedies. **2.** An actor who performs tragic roles in the theater.

tra•ge•di•enne (trə jē′dē ĕn′) *n.* A woman who performs tragic roles in the theater.

trag•e•dy (trăj′ĭ dē) *n., pl.* **trag•e•dies. 1.** A serious play or literary work that ends with great misfortune or ruin for the main character or characters, especially as a result of some personal flaw or weakness. **2.** The branch of literature including such works. **3.** A disastrous event; a calamity. [First written down about 1375 in Middle English and spelled *tragedie,* from Greek *tragōidia.*]

trag•ic (trăj′ĭk) *adj.* **1.** Of or relating to dramatic tragedy. **2.** Writing or performing tragedy. **3.** Bringing or involving death, grief, or destruction. —**trag′i•cal•ly** *adv.*

trag•i•com•e•dy (trăj′ĭ kŏm′ĭ dē) *n.* A play that has qualities of both tragedy and comedy.

trail (trāl) *v.* **trailed, trail•ing, trails.** —*tr.* **1.** To allow to drag or stream behind, as along the ground: *a child trailing a toy dog.* **2.** To drag (the body, for example) wearily. **3.** To follow the traces or scent of, as in hunting; track: *hounds trailing a bear.* **4.** To follow behind: *The great ship was trailed by a dozen small boats.* **5.** To lag behind: *The home team trailed by 10 points.* —*intr.* **1.** To drag or be dragged along, brushing the ground: *Her long skirt was trailing on the floor.* **2.** To extend, grow, or droop loosely over a surface. **3.** To drift in a thin stream, as smoke. **4.** To become gradually fainter: *Her voice tailed off.* **5.** To walk or proceed with dragging steps. —*n.* **1.** A path or beaten track. **2.** A mark or trace left by a moving body: *The car left a trail of dust.* **3.** The scent of a person or an animal: *hounds following the trail of a bear.* **4.** Something that hangs loose and long. **5.** Something that is drawn along or follows behind; a train: *The mayor came down the street followed by a trail of reporters.* [First written down about 1303 in Middle English and spelled *trailen,* probably from Old French *trailler,* to hunt without a foreknown course.]

trail•blaz•er (trāl′blā′zər) *n.* **1.** A person who blazes a trail. **2.** An innovative leader in a field; a pioneer.

trail•er (trā′lər) *n.* **1.** A large transport vehicle hauled by a tractor or truck. **2.** A furnished van that can be hauled by an automobile or a truck and used when parked as a home or an office. **3.** A person or thing that trails. **—trail′er•a•ble** *adj.*

train (trān) *n.* **1.a.** A series of connected railroad cars pulled or pushed by one or more locomotives. **b.** An underground railroad in a city; a subway. **2.** A long line of moving people, animals, or vehicles: *a wagon train.* **3.** A part of a gown that trails behind the wearer. **4.** A staff of followers; a retinue: *persons in the king's train.* **5.** An orderly succession of related events or thoughts; a sequence: *The ring of the telephone interrupted my train of thought.* **6.** A set of linked mechanical parts: *a train of gears.* —*v.* **trained, train•ing, trains.** —*tr.* **1.** To instruct or show a certain way of acting or behaving: *training a child to be polite.* **2.** To make proficient with specialized instruction and practice. See Synonyms at **teach. 3.** To prepare physically, as with regular exercise: *coaches training the players for the championship game.* **4.** To cause (a plant or one's hair) to take a desired course or shape. —*intr.* To give or undergo a course of training: *trained daily for the marathon.* [First written down before 1338 in Middle English and spelled *train*, a drawing out, from Old French, from *trainer*, to drag.]

train•ee (trā nē′) *n.* A person who is being trained.

train•er (trā′nər) *n.* A person who trains, especially one who coaches athletes, racehorses, or show animals.

train•ing (trā′nĭng) *n.* **1.** The process or routine of one who trains. **2.** The state of being trained.

train•load (trān′lōd′) *n.* The number of occupants or the amount of material that a passenger or freight train can hold.

train•man (trān′mən) *n.* A member of the operating crew on a railroad train, especially the brakeman.

traipse (trāps) *intr.v.* **traipsed, traips•ing, traips•es.** To walk or wander about. [First written down in 1593 in Modern English, possibly from Old French *trespasser*, to trespass.]

trait (trāt) *n.* **1.** A distinctive feature, as of a person's character. See Synonyms at **quality. 2.** A genetically determined characteristic or condition.

trai•tor (trā′tər) *n.* **1.** A person who commits treason. **2.** A person who betrays a cause or trust. [First written down before 1300 in Middle English and spelled *traitur*, from Latin *trāditor*, from *trādere*, to betray.]

trai•tor•ous (trā′tər əs) *adj.* **1.** Having the character of a traitor; disloyal: *traitorous behavior.* **2.** Constituting treason: *a traitorous act.*

tra•jec•to•ry (trə jĕk′tə rē) *n., pl.* **tra•jec•to•ries.** The path of a moving body or particle. [First written down in 1696 in Modern English, from Latin *trāiectus*, past participle of *trāicere*, to throw across.]

tram (trăm) *n.* **1.** *Chiefly British.* A streetcar. **2.** An open wagon or car run on tracks in a coal mine.

tram•mel (trăm′əl) *n.* **1.** A shackle used to teach a horse to amble. **2.** Something that restricts activity or free movement; a restraint. —*tr.v.* **tram•meled, tram•mel•ing, tram•mels** or **tram•melled, tram•mel•ling, tram•mels.** To hinder the activity or free movement of.

tramp (trămp) *v.* **tramped, tramp•ing, tramps.** —*intr.* To walk with a firm heavy step: *tramp up the stairs.* —*tr.* **1.** To traverse on foot: *tramp the fields in search of wild berries.* **2.** To tread down; trample: *tramp down snow.* —*n.* **1.** A heavy footfall. **2.** A walking trip; a hike: *We took a long tramp through the woods.* **3.** A person who travels aimlessly about as a vagrant. **4.** A cargo vessel that has no regular schedule but takes on freight whenever hired to do so.

tram•ple (trăm′pəl) *v.* **tram•pled, tram•pling, tram•ples.** —*tr.* To tread heavily so as to crush, bruise, or destroy: *The dog trampled the flowers.* —*intr.* To treat harshly, as if tramping upon: *He is always trampling on her feelings.* —*n.* The action or sound of trampling. **—tram′pler** *n.*

tram•po•line (trăm′pə lēn′ *or* trăm′pə lĭn) *n.* A sheet of taut canvas attached with springs to a metal frame and used for gymnastic springing and tumbling. [First written down in 1798 in Modern English and spelled *trampolin*, from Italian *tràmpoli*, stilts, of Germanic origin.]

trance (trăns) *n.* **1.** A condition of altered consciousness during which voluntary movement is lost, produced by hypnotism, drugs, or catalepsy. **2.** A dazed condition, as between sleeping and waking. **3.** A condition in which little or no attention is paid to one's surroundings, as in daydreaming or deep thought. [First written down about 1385 in Middle English and spelled *traunce*, from Latin *trānsīre*, to go over or across.]

tran•quil (trăng′kwəl *or* trăn′kwəl) *adj.* **1.** Free from commotion or disturbance: *a tranquil lake.* See Synonyms at **calm. 2.** Free from anxiety, tension, or restlessness: *leading a tranquil life.* [First written down before 1450 in Middle English and spelled *tranquill*, from Latin *tranquillus.*] **—tran′quil•ly** *adv.*

tran•quil•ize (trăng′kwə līz′ *or* trăn′kwə līz′) *tr. & intr.v.* **tran•quil•ized, tran•quil•iz•ing, tran•quil•iz•es.** To make or become tranquil or calm.

tran•quil•iz•er (trăng′kwə līz′ər *or* trăn′kwə līz′ər) *n.* Any of various drugs used to relieve tension, anxiety, or mental upset.

tran•quil•li•ty or **tran•quil•i•ty** (trăng kwĭl′ĭ tē *or* trăn kwĭl′ĭ tē) *n.* The quality or condition of being tranquil; serenity.

trans. *abbr.* An abbreviation that means: **1.** Transitive. **2.** Translation. **3.** Transportation.

trans– *pref.* A prefix that means: **1.** Across; beyond: *transpolar.* **2.** Through: *transcontinental.* **3.** Change; transfer: *transliterate.* —SEE NOTE.

trans•act (trăn săkt′ *or* trăn zăkt′) *v.* **trans•act•ed, trans•act•ing, trans•acts.** —*tr.* To do, carry out, or conduct (business or affairs). —*intr.* To conduct business.

trans•ac•tion (trăn săk′shən *or* trăn zăk′shən) *n.* **1.** The act of transacting or the fact of being transacted: *the transaction of business.* **2.** Something transacted, especially a business agreement or exchange: *cash transactions only.*

trans•at•lan•tic (trăns′ət lăn′tĭk *or* trănz′ət lăn′tĭk) *adj.* **1.** Situated on or coming from the other side of the Atlantic Ocean: *transatlantic military bases.* **2.** Spanning or crossing the Atlantic Ocean: *a transatlantic flight.*

tran•scend (trăn sĕnd′) *tr.v.* **tran•scend•ed, tran•scend•ing, tran•scends. 1.** To pass beyond the limits of: *an experience that transcends human understanding.* **2.** To be greater than, as in intensity or power; surpass: *a composition that transcends all his previous ones.* [First written down about 1340 in Middle English and spelled *transcenden*, from Latin *trānscendere* : *trāns-*, over + *scandere*, to climb.]

tran•scen•dent (trăn sĕn′dənt) *adj.* Surpassing others; pre-eminent or supreme: *a scientist of transcendent genius.*

tran•scen•den•tal (trăn′sĕn dĕn′tl) *adj.* **1.** Beyond common thought or experience; mystical or supernatural. **—tran′scen•den′tal•ly** *adv.*

transcendental number *n.* An irrational number

trampoline

Word Building: trans–

The prefix **trans–** goes back to the Latin prefix *trāns–*, from the Latin preposition *trāns*, meaning "across, beyond, through." Many of the most common English words beginning with **trans–** are derived from Latin words or elements, as in **transfer**, **transfuse**, **translate**, **transmit**, **transpire**, and **transport**. Another large group of words has **trans–** in combination with English adjectives, as in **transatlantic**, **transcontinental**, **transoceanic**, **transpacific**, and **transpolar**, with the meaning "across" or "through" a particular geographic element.

ă	pat	oi	boy
ā	pay	ou	out
âr	care	ŏŏ	took
ä	father	ōō	boot
ĕ	pet	ŭ	cut
ē	be	ûr	urge
ĭ	pit	th	thin
ī	pie	*th*	this
îr	pier	hw	whoop
ŏ	pot	zh	vision
ō	toe	ə	about
ô	paw	N	*French* bon

Word Building: transfer

The word root *–fer–* in English words comes from the Latin verb *ferre,* "to carry, bear." **Transfer**, then, is literally "to carry from place to place or from person to person" (using the prefix *trans–,* "across, through, change in"); **refer** means "to carry back (to an earlier condition)" (*re–,* "back"); and to **offer** is literally "to bring to or present in worship, propose" (*of–,* a form of *ob–,* "toward").

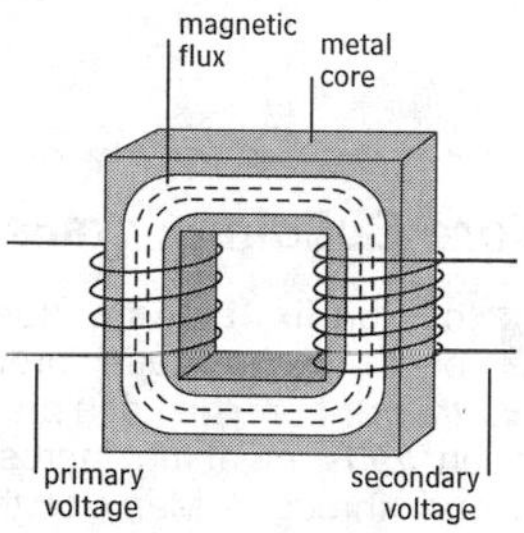

transformer

Iron core transformer

Word Building: transfusion

The word root *–fus–* in English words comes from the Latin word *fūsus,* the past participle of the verb *fundere,* "to pour." A **transfusion**, then, is literally "a pouring out of one thing into another" (using the prefix *trans–,* "across, through, change in"). **Diffuse** means "widespread, scattered," literally "poured out all over the place" (*dif–,* a form of *dis–,* "apart, in different directions"). **Profuse** means "generous, abundant," literally "poured forth freely" (*pro–,* "forth").

that is not a solution of a polynomial equation with rational coefficients. For example, the irrational number pi is a transcendental number.

trans•con•ti•nen•tal (trăns′kŏn tə **nĕn′**tl) *adj.* Spanning or crossing a continent: *a transcontinental flight.*

tran•scribe (trăn **skrīb′**) *tr.v.* **tran•scribed, tran•scrib•ing, tran•scribes. 1.** To write or type a copy of: *transcribe a dictated letter.* **2.** To adapt or arrange (a musical composition). **3.** To record, usually on tape, for broadcast at a later date. **4.** To transfer (information) from one computer recording and storing system to another. [First written down in 1552 in Modern English, from Latin *trānscrībere* : *trāns-,* over + *scrībere,* to write.]

tran•script (**trăn′**skrĭpt′) *n.* Something transcribed, especially a written, typed, or printed copy.

tran•scrip•tion (trăn **skrĭp′**shən) *n.* **1.** The act or process of transcribing. **2.** An adaptation of a musical composition. **3.** A recorded radio or television program. **4.** A representation of speech sounds in phonetic symbols. **5.** The process of messenger RNA synthesis, in which genetic information is transferred from a DNA molecule to the messenger RNA.

tran•sept (**trăn′**sĕpt′) *n.* Either of the two lateral arms of a church built in the shape of a cross.

trans•fer (trăns **fûr′** *or* **trăns′**fər) *v.* **trans•ferred, trans•fer•ring, trans•fers.** —*tr.* **1.** To move or cause to pass from one place, person, or thing to another: *Bees transfer pollen from one flower to another.* **2.** To shift the ownership of (property) to another. **3.** To move (a design, for example) from one surface to another, as by impression: *Trace the design, then transfer it to the leather.* —*intr.* **1.** To move oneself from one location or job to another. **2.** To change from one public conveyance to another: *transferred to another bus.* —*n.* (**trăns′**fər). **1.** Also **transferal.** The conveyance or removal of something from one place, person, or thing to another: *the transfer of land by purchase.* **2.** A person or thing that transfers or is transferred, as a student who changes schools. **3.** A design conveyed by contact from one surface to another. **4.a.** A ticket entitling a passenger to change from one public conveyance to another as part of one trip. **b.** A place where such a change is made. [First written down about 1380 in Middle English and spelled *transferren,* from Latin *trānsferre* : *trāns-,* across + *ferre,* to carry.] —See Note.

trans•fer•a•ble (trăns **fûr′**ə bəl) *adj.* Capable of being transferred: *a check that is not transferable.*

trans•fer•al (trăns **fûr′**əl) *n.* Variant of **transfer** (sense 1).

trans•fer•ence (trăns **fûr′**əns *or* **trăns′**fər əns) *n.* **1.** The act or process of transferring. **2.** The fact of being transferred.

transfer RNA *n.* A form of RNA that delivers amino acids to the ribosomes during protein synthesis.

trans•fig•u•ra•tion (trăns fĭg′yə **rā′**shən) *n.* **1.** A marked change in form or appearance, especially one that exalts or glorifies. **2. Transfiguration.** In the New Testament, the sudden radiant change in Jesus's appearance that took place on a mountain in the presence of the Apostles James, John, and Peter.

trans•fig•ure (trăns **fĭg′**yər) *tr.v.* **trans•fig•ured, trans•fig•ur•ing, trans•fig•ures. 1.** To change the outward appearance of; transform. **2.** To glorify or exalt.

trans•fi•nite number (trăns **fī′**nīt′) *n.* A number that is greater than any finite number.

trans•fix (trăns **fĭks′**) *tr.v.* **trans•fixed, trans•fix•ing, trans•fix•es. 1.** To pierce with or as if with a pointed weapon. **2.** To fix fast; impale. **3.** To render motionless, as with terror.

trans•form (trăns **fôrm′**) *tr.v.* **trans•formed, trans•form•ing, trans•forms. 1.** To change markedly the form or appearance of. **2.** To change the nature, function, or condition of; convert: *A steam engine transforms heat into energy.* **3.** To perform a mathematical transformation on. **4.** To subject (electricity) to the action of a transformer. —*n.* (**trăns′**fôrm′). The result of a transformation, especially in mathematics.

trans•for•ma•tion (trăns′fər **mā′**shən) *n.* **1.** The act or an instance of transforming. **2.** The state of being transformed. **3.** A marked change, as in appearance, usually for the better. **4.a.** The conversion of an algebraic expression to another expression of a different form. **b.** The replacement of the variables in an algebraic expression or equation by their values in terms of another set of variables. —**trans′for•ma′tion•al** *adj.*

trans•form•er (trăns **fôr′**mər) *n.* A device used to transfer electrical energy from one circuit to another, often with a change of voltage or current.

trans•fuse (trăns **fyo͞oz′**) *tr.v.* **trans•fused, trans•fus•ing, trans•fus•es. 1.** To pour (something) out of one vessel into another. **2.** To cause to be instilled or imparted. **3.** To diffuse through; permeate: *The glade was transfused with sunlight.* **4.** To give a transfusion of or to: *transfuse blood; transfuse a patient.* [First written down before 1425 in Middle English and spelled *transfusen,* to transmit, from Latin *trānsfundere,* to transfuse : *trāns-,* across + *fundere,* to pour.]

trans•fu•sion (trăns **fyo͞o′**zhən) *n.* **1.** The act or process of transfusing. **2.** The transfer of blood from one person to another. —See Note.

trans•gress (trăns **grĕs′** *or* trănz **grĕs′**) *v.* **trans•gressed, trans•gress•ing, trans•gress•es.** —*tr.* **1.** To go beyond or over (a limit or boundary): *His conduct transgressed the boundaries of politeness.* **2.** To act in violation of (a law, for example). —*intr.* To commit an offense by violating a law or command. [First written down about 1475 in Middle English and spelled *transgressen,* from Latin *trānsgredī,* to step across.] —**trans•gres′sor** *n.*

trans•gres•sion (trăns **grĕsh′**ən *or* trănz **grĕsh′**ən) *n.* A violation of a law, command, or duty.

tran•sient (**trăn′**shənt *or* **trăn′**zhənt *or* **trăn′**zē ənt) *adj.* **1.** Passing away with time; transitory: *transient happiness.* **2.** Remaining in a place only a brief time: *a transient guest at a hotel.* —*n.* A person or thing that is transient, especially a person making a brief stay at a hotel or boarding house. [First written down in 1612 in Modern English, from Latin *trānsiēns,* present participle of *trānsīre,* to go over.] —**tran′sience, tran′sien•cy** *n.*

tran•sis•tor (trăn **zĭs′**tər *or* trăn **sĭs′**tər) *n.* **1.** A semiconductor device having at least three electrical contacts and used for amplification and switching. **2.** A radio equipped with transistors.

tran•sis•tor•ize (trăn **zĭs′**tə rīz′ *or* trăn **sĭs′**tə rīz′) *tr.v.* **tran•sis•tor•ized, tran•sis•tor•iz•ing, tran•sis•tor•iz•es.** To equip (an electronic circuit or device) with transistors.

tran•sit (**trăn′**sĭt *or* **trăn′**zĭt) *n.* **1.** The act of passing over, across, or through; passage. **2.** The moving of people or goods from one place to another, especially on a local public transportation system. **3.a.** The passage of a celestial body across the meridian of an observer. **b.** The passage of a celestial body or its shadow across the disk of a larger celestial body. **4.** A surveying instrument consisting of a telescope provided with scales for measuring horizontal and vertical angles. —*tr.v.* **tran•sit•ed, tran•sit•ing, tran•sits.** To pass over, across, or through.

tran•si•tion (trăn **zĭsh′**ən *or* trăn **sĭsh′**ən) *n.* **1.** Passage from one form, state, style, or place to another. **2.** Passage from one subject to another in discourse. **—tran•si′tion•al** *adj.*

tran•si•tive (trăn′sĭ tĭv *or* trăn′zĭ tĭv) *adj.* In grammar, of or relating to a verb that requires a direct object to complete its meaning. In the sentence *I bought a book on Monday,* the verb *bought* is transitive. **—tran′si•tive•ly** *adv.* —SEE NOTE at **verb.**

transitive property *n.* The property of a mathematical relation that, if it holds true for *a* and *b,* and for *b* and *c,* then it must hold true for *a* and *c* as well. For example, if 12 is greater than 6, and 6 is greater than 3, then 12 must be greater than 3.

tran•si•to•ry (trăn′sĭ tôr′ē *or* trăn′zĭ tôr′ē) *adj.* Existing or lasting only briefly; shortlived: *transitory happiness.*

trans•late (trăns lāt′ *or* trănz lāt′) *v.* **trans•lat•ed, trans•lat•ing, trans•lates.** *—tr.* **1.** To express in another language: *translate a book.* **2.** To put into simpler terms; explain or interpret: *It is difficult to see how you could translate his silence.* *—intr.* **1.a.** To make a translation. **b.** To work as a translator. **2.** To be capable of being expressed in another language: *Her poetry translates well.* [First written down before 1325 in Middle English and spelled *translaten,* from Latin *trānslātus,* past participle of *trānsferre,* to transfer.]

trans•la•tion (trăns lā′shən *or* trănz lā′shən) *n.* **1.** The act or process of translating. **2.** A translated version of a text: *translations from the French.* **3.** The process by which messenger RNA directs the amino acid sequence of a growing protein during protein synthesis.

trans•la•tor (trăns lā′tər *or* trănz lā′tər) *n.* A person who translates, especially a person employed to render written works into another language.

trans•lit•er•ate (trăns lĭt′ə rāt′ *or* trănz lĭt′ə rāt′) *tr.v.* **trans•lit•er•at•ed, trans•lit•er•at•ing, trans•lit•er•ates.** To represent (letters or words) in the corresponding characters of another alphabet. **—trans•lit′er•a′tion** *n.*

trans•lu•cent (trăns lo͞o′sənt *or* trănz lo͞o′sənt) *adj.* Transmitting light, but scattering it enough so that images become blurred or are indistinct. **—trans•lu′cence, trans•lu′cen•cy** *n.*

trans•mi•gra•tion (trăns′mī grā′shən *or* trănz′mī grā′shən) *n.* In theology, the passing of a soul at death into another body; reincarnation.

trans•mis•sion (trăns mĭsh′ən *or* trănz mĭsh′ən) *n.* **1.a.** The act or process of transmitting: *the transmission of news; the transmission of a disease.* **b.** The fact of being transmitted. **2.** Something, such as a message, that is transmitted. **3.** An automotive assembly of gears and associated parts by which power is carried from an engine to a driving axle. **4.** The sending of a signal wave, as in radio, television, or telegraphy.

trans•mit (trăns mĭt′ *or* trănz mĭt′) *tr.v.* **trans•mit•ted, trans•mit•ting, trans•mits.** **1.** To send or pass on from one person, place, or thing to another: *transmit a message; transmit an infection.* **2.** To pass on (a trait or traits) by biological inheritance. **3.** To send out (an electric or electronic signal), as by wire or radio. **4.** To cause or allow (energy or a disturbance) to travel or spread, as through a medium: *Glass transmits light.* **5.** To carry (power, force, or energy) from one part of a machine to another. [First written down before 1400 in Middle English and spelled *transmitten,* from Latin *trānsmittere* : *trāns-,* across + *mittere,* to send.]

trans•mit•tal (trăns mĭt′l *or* trănz mĭt′l) *n.* The act or process of transmitting; a transmission.

trans•mit•ter (trăns mĭt′ər *or* trănz mĭt′ər) *n.* **1.** A person or thing that transmits. **2.** A device used in a communications system to send forth information, especially: **a.** A switching device that opens and closes a telegraph circuit. **b.** The part of a telephone that changes sounds into electrical impulses that are sent over wires. **c.** A device that generates a radio signal, modulates it with information, often a voice or music signal, and radiates it by means of an antenna.

trans•mu•ta•tion (trăns′myo͞o tā′shən *or* trănz′myo͞o tā′shən) *n.* In physics, the changing of one element into another by one or more nuclear reactions.

trans•mute (trăns myo͞ot′ *or* trănz myo͞ot′) *tr.v.* **trans•mut•ed, trans•mut•ing, trans•mutes.** To change from one form, nature, state, or substance into another; transform: *Socialism transmuted the political life of the country.* [First written down in 1392 in Middle English and spelled *transmuten,* from Latin *trānsmūtāre* : *trāns-,* over + *mūtāre,* to change.]

trans•o•ce•an•ic (trăns′ō shē ăn′ĭk *or* trănz′ō shē ăn′ĭk) *adj.* **1.** Situated beyond or on the other side of the ocean. **2.** Spanning or crossing the ocean: *transoceanic flight.*

tran•som (trăn′səm) *n.* **1.a.** A horizontal crosspiece over a door. **b.** A small hinged window above a door or another window. **2.** A horizontal dividing piece in a window.

transom

tran•son•ic (trăn sŏn′ĭk) *adj.* Of or relating to conditions of flight or airflow at speeds close to the speed of sound.

trans•pa•cif•ic (trăns′pə sĭf′ĭk *or* trănz′pə sĭf′ĭk) *adj.* **1.** Situated on or coming from the other side of the Pacific Ocean. **2.** Spanning or crossing the Pacific Ocean: *a transpacific flight.*

trans•par•en•cy (trăns pâr′ən sē *or* trăns păr′ən sē) *n., pl.* **trans•par•en•cies.** **1.** A transparent object, especially a photographic slide. **2.** The condition or state of being transparent.

trans•par•ent (trăns pâr′ənt *or* trăns păr′ənt) *adj.* **1.** Capable of transmitting light so that objects and images are clearly visible, as if there were nothing between the observer and the light source. **2.** Allowing electromagnetic radiation of a specified frequency, such as x-rays, light, or radio waves, to pass with little or no interference. **3.** So fine in texture that it can be seen through; sheer: *a transparent fabric.* **4.** Easily seen through or detected: *transparent lies.* [First written down before 1425 in Middle English, from Medieval Latin *trānspārēre,* to show through.] **—trans•par′ent•ly** *adv.*

tran•spire (trăn spīr′) *v.* **tran•spired, tran•spir•ing, tran•spires.** *—tr.* To give off (vapor containing waste products) through pores or similar small openings, as of plant leaves or the skin. *—intr.* **1.** To become known; come to light. **2.** To happen; take place. [First written down in 1597 in Modern English, from Medieval Latin *trānspīrāre* : Latin *trāns-,* across + Latin *spīrāre,* to breathe.]

trans•plant (trăns plănt′) *v.* **trans•plant•ed, trans•plant•ing, trans•plants.** *—tr.* **1.** To uproot and replant (a growing plant). **2.** To transfer to and establish in a new place: *The early colonists transplanted their customs to the New World.* **3.** To transfer (tissue or an organ) from one body or body part to another. *—intr.* To be capable of being transplanted. *—n.* (**trăns′**plănt′). **1.** The act or process of transplanting. **2.** Something transplanted. **3.** An operation in which tissue or an organ is transplanted: *The doctor performed a heart transplant.* **—trans•plant′a•ble** *adj.* **—trans′plan•ta′tion** *n.*

trans•po•lar (trăns pō′lər) *adj.* Extending across or crossing either of the polar regions: *a transpolar flight.*

trans•port (trăns pôrt′) *tr.v.* **trans•port•ed, trans•**

ă	pat	oi	boy
ā	pay	ou	out
âr	care	o͝o	took
ä	father	o͞o	boot
ĕ	pet	ŭ	cut
ē	be	ûr	urge
ĭ	pit	th	thin
ī	pie	*th*	this
îr	pier	hw	whoop
ŏ	pot	zh	vision
ō	toe	ə	about
ô	paw	N	*French* bon

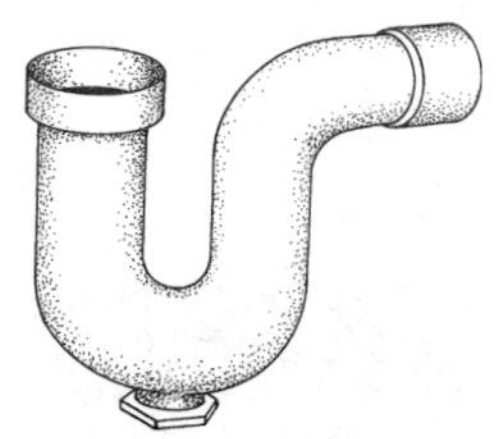

trap
Drainpipe trap

trapeze

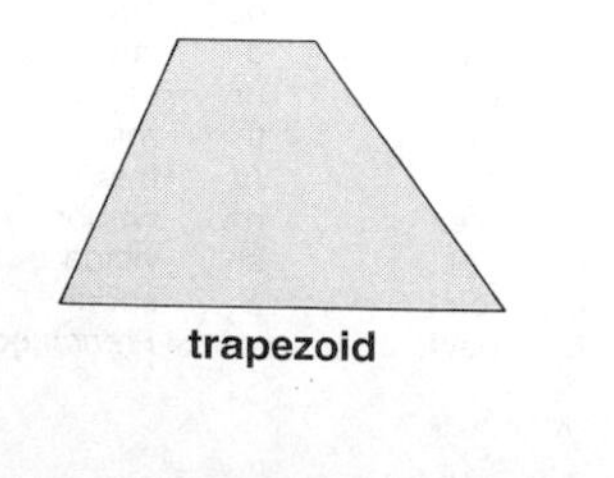

trapezoid

port•ing, trans•ports. 1. To carry from one place to another; convey: *transport cargo; transport passengers.* **2.** To move to strong emotion; enrapture: *She was transported with joy.* —*n.* (**trăns′**pôrt′). **1.** An act of transporting: *goods lost in transport.* **2.** A ship or an aircraft used to transport troops or military equipment. **3.** A vehicle, such as an aircraft, used to transport passengers, mail, or freight. **4.** A system for transporting passengers: *public transport.* [First written down about 1380 in Middle English and spelled *transporten,* from Latin *trānsportāre* : *trāns-*, across + *portāre*, to carry.]

trans•por•ta•tion (trăns′pər **tā′**shən) *n.* **1.** The act or an instance of transporting: *the transportation of mail.* **2.** A means of transport; a conveyance: *Planes are fast transportation.* **3.** The business of conveying passengers or goods: *a company engaged in transportation.* **4.** A charge for transporting; a fare: *paying his own transportation.*

trans•pose (trăns **pōz′**) *tr.v.* **trans•posed, trans•pos•ing, trans•pos•es. 1.** To reverse or transfer the order or place of; interchange: *transpose the letters of a word.* **2.** To move (an algebraic term) from one side of an equation to the other by adding or subtracting that term to or from both sides. **3.** To write or perform (a musical composition) in a key other than the original or given key. **—trans′po•si′tion** (trăns′pə **zĭsh′**ən) *n.*

trans•ship (trăns **shĭp′**) *tr. & intr.v.* **trans•shipped, trans•ship•ping, trans•ships.** To transfer or be transferred from one conveyance to another for reshipment. **—trans•ship′ment** *n.*

tran•sub•stan•ti•a•tion (trăn′səb stăn′shē **ā′**shən) *n.* **1.** Conversion of one substance into another. **2.** In theology, the doctrine holding that the bread and wine of the Eucharist are transformed into the body and blood of Jesus, although their appearances remain the same.

trans•u•ran•ic (trăns′yo͞o **răn′**ĭk *or* trănz′yo͞o **răn′**ĭk) *adj.* Having an atomic number greater than 92, the atomic number of uranium.

trans•ver•sal (trăns **vûr′**səl *or* trănz **vûr′**səl) *n.* A line that intersects a system of lines.

trans•verse (trăns **vûrs′** *or* trănz **vûrs′** *or* **trăns′**vûrs′ *or* **trănz′**vûrs′) *adj.* Situated or lying across; crosswise: *a transverse beam.* —*n.* Something, such as a part or beam, that is transverse. **—trans•verse′ly** *adv.*

Tran•syl•va•nia (trăn′sĭl **vān′**yə *or* trăn′sĭl **vā′**nē ə). A historical region of western Romania. Transylvania became part of modern-day Romania after World War II.

trap (trăp) *n.* **1.** A device for catching and holding animals, as a concealed pit or a clamp that springs shut suddenly. **2.** A stratagem for catching or tricking an unsuspecting person. **3.a.** A device for separating and collecting solids or other materials from the liquid that flows through a drain. **b.** A device for keeping a drain sealed against a backward flow of foul gases, especially a U-shaped or S-shaped bend in a pipe that remains full of liquid. **4.** A device that hurls clay pigeons into the air to be shot at in trapshooting. **5.** A sandy depression in a golf course that stops a ball from going any farther and is hard to hit out of. **6. traps.** Percussion instruments, such as snare drums and cymbals, especially in a jazz band. —*v.* **trapped, trap•ping, traps.** —*tr.* **1.** To catch in or as if in a trap; ensnare. **2.** To provide with traps or a trap. **3.** To seal off (gases) with a trap, as in a pipe. —*intr.* To trap animals, especially for their fur. [First written down before 1000 in Old English and spelled *træppe.*]

trap door *n.* A hinged or sliding door in a floor, roof, or ceiling.

tra•peze (tră **pēz′**) *n.* A short horizontal bar hung from two parallel ropes, used for exercises or for acrobatic stunts. [First written down in 1861 in Modern English, from Greek *trapezion,* small table.]

tra•pe•zi•um (trə **pē′**zē əm) *n., pl.* **tra•pe•zi•ums** or **tra•pe•zi•a** (trə **pē′**zē ə). A quadrilateral having no parallel sides.

trap•e•zoid (**trăp′**ĭ zoid′) *n.* A quadrilateral having two parallel sides. **—trap′e•zoi′dal** *adj.*

trap•per (**trăp′**ər) *n.* A person who traps animals for their fur.

trap•ping (**trăp′**ĭng) *n.* **1.** An ornamental covering or harness for a horse. Often used in the plural. **2. trappings.** Articles of dress or adornment, especially accessories: *They enjoyed their fancy car and all the trappings of success.*

trap•shoot•ing (**trăp′**sho͞o′tĭng) *n.* The sport of shooting at clay pigeons hurled into the air by a spring trap.

trash (trăsh) *n.* **1.** Worthless or discarded material or objects; refuse or rubbish. **2.** Empty expressions or ideas. **3.** A person or group of people regarded as worthless or contemptible.

trash•y (**trăsh′**ē) *adj.* **trash•i•er, trash•i•est. 1.** Resembling or containing trash. **2.** In very poor taste or of very poor quality: *a trashy motion picture.* **—trash′i•ness** *n.*

trau•ma (**trou′**mə *or* **trô′**mə) *n., pl.* **trau•mas** or **trau•ma•ta** (**trou′**mə tə *or* **trô′**mə tə). **1.** A serious wound or injury, as from violence or an accident. **2.** An emotional shock that causes serious and lasting damage to one's personality. [First written down in 1693 in Modern English, from Greek.]

trau•mat•ic (trou **măt′**ĭk *or* trô **măt′**ĭk) *adj.* Of, relating to, or caused by a trauma: *a traumatic experience.* **—trau•mat′i•cal•ly** *adv.*

trau•ma•tize (**trou′**mə tīz′ *or* **trô′**mə tīz′) *tr.v.* **trau•ma•tized, trau•ma•tiz•ing, trau•ma•tiz•es.** To subject to a trauma.

tra•vail (trə **vāl′** *or* **trăv′**āl′) *n.* **1.** Work, especially when arduous or involving painful exertion; toil. **2.** Tribulation or agony; anguish. **3.** The labor of childbirth. —*intr.v.* **tra•vailed, tra•vail•ing, tra•vails. 1.** To work strenuously; toil. **2.** To be in the labor of childbirth. [First written down about 1275 in Middle English, from Late Latin *tripālium,* instrument of torture.]

trav•el (**trăv′**əl) *v.* **trav•eled, trav•el•ing, trav•els** or **trav•elled, trav•el•ling, trav•els.** —*intr.* **1.** To go from one place to another, as on a trip; journey: *travel through Mexico.* **2.** To journey from place to place as a salesperson or an agent: *He travels for a publishing house.* **3.** To be transmitted, as light or sound; move or pass. **4.** To keep or be in company: *travel in wealthy circles.* **5.** In basketball, to walk or run illegally while holding the ball. —*tr.* To pass or journey over or through; traverse: *travel the countries of Africa.* —*n.* **1.** The act or process of traveling: *Travel is slow in the mountains.* **2. travels.** A series of journeys. [First written down in 1375 in Middle English and spelled *travelen,* alteration of *travailen,* to toil, from Old French *travailler,* to toil, travail.]

trav•eled (**trăv′**əld) *adj.* **1.** Having made journeys; experienced in travel. **2.** Frequented by travelers: *a heavily traveled road.*

trav•el•er or **trav•el•ler** (**trăv′**əl ər *or* **trăv′**lər) *n.* A person who travels or has traveled, as to distant places.

trav•el•er's check (**trăv′**əl ərz *or* **trăv′**lərz) *n.* A check or draft purchased in various denominations from a bank or travel agency and signed by a traveler upon purchase and again later in the presence of the person cashing it.

trav•el•ing salesman (**trăv′**ə lĭng *or* **trăv′**lĭng) *n.* A man who travels from place to place soliciting business orders.

trav•el•ler (trăv′əl ər *or* trăv′lər) *n.* Variant of **traveler.**

trav•e•logue also **trav•e•log** (trăv′ə lôg′ *or* trăv′ə lŏg′) *n.* **1.** A lecture illustrated by travel slides or films. **2.** A narrated film about travels.

tra•verse (trə vûrs′ *or* trăv′ərs) *v.* **tra•versed, tra•vers•ing, tra•vers•es.** *—tr.* **1.** To travel or pass across, over, or through: *traversed the desert safely.* **2.** To move to and fro over: *Searchlights traversed the sky.* **3.** To extend across; cross: *A bridge traversed the mountain stream.* *—intr.* To move to the side or back and forth. *—n.* **trav•erse** (trăv′ərs *or* trə vûrs′). **1.** A passing over, across, or through. **2.** Something lying across something else, such as a beam or a rung of a ladder. *—adj.* **trav•erse** (trăv′ərs *or* trə vûrs′). Lying or extending across: *a traverse curtain rod.* [First written down before 1325 in Middle English and spelled *traversen*, from Late Latin *trānsversāre.*]

trav•es•ty (trăv′ĭ stē) *n., pl.* **trav•es•ties. 1.** A grotesque imitation, such as a parody of a literary work. **2.** A grotesque likeness. *—tr.v.* **trav•es•tied** (trăv′ĭ stēd), **trav•es•ty•ing, trav•es•ties** (trăv′ĭ stēz). To make a travesty of; parody or ridicule.

tra•vois (trə voi′) *n., pl.* **tra•vois** (trə voiz′) also **tra•vois•es** (trə voi′zĭz). A frame slung between trailing poles and pulled by a dog or horse, formerly used by Plains Indians to transport goods and belongings.

trawl (trôl) *n.* **1.** A large tapered fishing net that is towed along the sea bottom. **2.** A long fishing line towed by a boat and supporting many smaller lines bearing baited hooks. *—v.* **trawled, trawl•ing, trawls.** *—tr.* To catch (fish) with a trawl. *—intr.* To fish with a trawl.

trawl•er (trô′lər) *n.* **1.** A boat used for trawling. **2.** A person who trawls.

tray (trā) *n.* A flat shallow receptacle with a raised edge or rim, used for carrying, holding, or displaying articles.

treach•er•ous (trĕch′ər əs) *adj.* **1.** Marked by betrayal of fidelity, confidence, or trust; disloyal: *a treacherous friend.* **2.** Not to be relied on; not dependable: *He has a treacherous memory.* **3.** Marked by unforeseen hazards; dangerous: *a beach with a treacherous surf.*

treach•er•y (trĕch′ə rē) *n., pl.* **treach•er•ies. 1.** Willful betrayal of confidence, fidelity, or trust; perfidy. **2.** An act of such willful betrayal.

trea•cle (trē′kəl) *n. Chiefly British.* Molasses.

tread (trĕd) *v.* **trod** (trŏd), **trod•den** (trŏd′n) or **trod, tread•ing, treads.** *—tr.* **1.** To walk on, over, or along: *people treading the sidewalks on their way to work.* **2.** To stamp or trample: *They threshed the rice by treading it on a hard earthen floor.* **3.** To make (a path or trail) by walking or trampling. **4.** To perform or execute by walking or dancing: *tread a measure of the minuet.* *—intr.* **1.** To go on foot; walk. **2.** To set down the foot; step. **3.** To press, crush, or injure something by or as if by trampling: *Their careless remarks trod upon her feelings.* *—n.* **1.a.** The act, manner, or sound of treading: *the swift tread of a horse.* **b.** An instance of treading; a step. **2.** The upper horizontal part of a step in a staircase. **3.** The part of a wheel or tire that makes contact with the road or rails. **4.** The pattern of grooves or raised ridges on a tire. **5.** The part of a shoe sole that touches the ground. **6.** Either of the continuous metal belts with which bulldozers, tanks, and some tractors move over the ground. *—idiom.* **tread water. 1.** To keep the head above water while in an upright position by pumping the legs. **2.** To expend effort but make little or no progress toward achieving a goal. [First written down about 725 in Old English and spelled *tredan.*]

tread•le (trĕd′l) *n.* A pedal or lever operated by the foot to drive a wheel, as in a sewing machine or potter's wheel. *—intr.v.* **tread•led, tread•ling, tread•les.** To operate a treadle.

tread•mill (trĕd′mĭl′) *n.* **1.a.** A device rotated by people treading on the moving steps of a wheel. **b.** A similar device operated by an animal treading on an endless sloping belt. **2.** An exercise device consisting of an endless moving belt on which a person can walk or run while remaining in the same place. **3.** A monotonous task or routine.

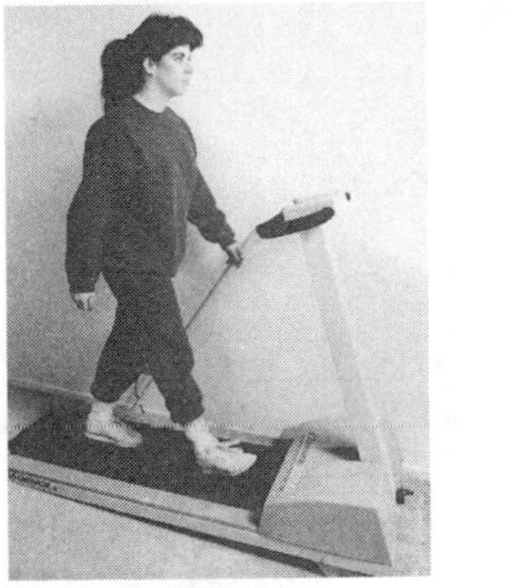

treadmill

treas. *abbr.* An abbreviation of: **1.** Treasurer. **2.** Treasury.

trea•son (trē′zən) *n.* Betrayal of one's country, especially by giving aid to an enemy or by waging war against it. [First written down before 1200 in Middle English and spelled *treison*, from Latin *trāditiō*, a handing over.]

trea•son•a•ble (trē′zə nə bəl) *adj.* Treasonous: *his treasonable actions.*

trea•son•ous (trē′zə nəs) *adj.* Relating to, constituting, or involving treason; treasonable.

treas•ure (trĕzh′ər) *n.* **1.** Accumulated or stored wealth in the form of money or valuables such as jewels. **2.** A person or thing considered especially precious or valuable. *—tr.v.* **treas•ured, treas•ur•ing, treas•ures.** To value highly; cherish: *He treasures the gold watch his colleagues gave him.* See Synonyms at **appreciate.** [First written down in 1137 in Middle English and spelled *tresor*, from Greek *thēsauros.*]

treas•ur•er (trĕzh′ər ər) *n.* A person having charge of funds or revenues, especially the chief financial officer of a government, a corporation, or an association.

treas•ure-trove (trĕzh′ər trōv′) *n.* **1.** Treasure found hidden. **2.** A discovery of great value.

treas•ur•y (trĕzh′ə rē) *n., pl.* **treas•ur•ies. 1.** A place in which treasure is kept. **2.** A place in which private or public funds are received, kept, managed, and given or paid out. **3.** Public funds or revenues. **4.** A collection of literary or artistic treasures: *a treasury of good music.* **5. Treasury.** The department of a government in charge of collecting, managing, and paying out public funds.

Treasury bill *n.* A U.S. Treasury bond that is sold at a discount from its face value and reaches face value in one year or less.

treat (trēt) *v.* **treat•ed, treat•ing, treats.** *—tr.* **1.** To act or behave in a specified manner toward: *We will treat you fairly.* **2.** To regard or handle in a certain way: *treated the matter seriously.* **3.** To deal with in speech, writing, or art: *The essay treats the subject with humor.* **4.** To provide food, entertainment, or gifts at one's own expense: *Did you say you'd treat us today?* **5.** To subject to a physical or chemical process or action in order to change in some way: *treating cloth with bleach.* **6.** To give medical care to (a person) or for (a disease). *—intr.* **1.** To deal with a subject or topic in writing or speech: *The book treats of the early experimenters in science.* **2.** To pay for another's entertainment, food, or drink. *—n.* **1.** A meal, an entertainment, or something similar that is paid for by someone else: *Let this lunch be my treat.* **2.** A source of special delight or pleasure: *What a treat it was to visit the museum!* [First written down about 1300 in Middle English and spelled *tretien*, from Latin *tractare*, from *trahere*, to draw.]

treat•a•ble (trē′tə bəl) *adj.* Possible to treat; responsive to treatment: *a treatable disorder.*

trea•tise (trē′tĭs) *n.* A systematic, usually extensive written discourse on a subject.

ă	pat	oi	boy
ā	pay	ou	out
âr	care	o͝o	took
ä	father	o͞o	boot
ĕ	pet	ŭ	cut
ē	be	ûr	urge
ĭ	pit	th	thin
ī	pie	*th*	this
îr	pier	hw	whoop
ŏ	pot	zh	vision
ō	toe	ə	about
ô	paw	N	*French* bon

treble clef

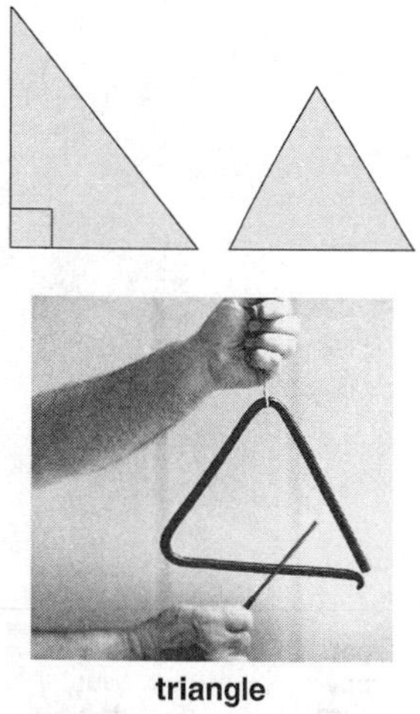
triangle
Top: Right triangle (*left*) and equilateral triangle (*right*)
Bottom: Musical instrument

treat•ment (trēt′mənt) *n.* **1.** The act, manner, or method of handling or dealing with a person or thing: *equal treatment under the law.* **2.a.** The use or application of a remedy to relieve or cure a disease or disorder; therapy. **b.** The substance or remedy so applied.

trea•ty (trē′tē) *n., pl.* **trea•ties. 1.** A formal agreement between two or more states, as in reference to terms of peace or trade. **2.** A document containing this agreement. **3.** A contract or an agreement.

treb•le (trĕb′əl) *adj.* **1.** Triple. **2.** Relating to or having the highest musical part, voice, or range. —*n.* The highest musical voice, part, instrument, or range. —*tr. & intr.v.* **treb•led, treb•ling, treb•les.** To make or become triple.

treble clef *n.* A symbol on a musical staff indicating that the G above middle C is on the second line of the staff.

tree (trē) *n.* **1.** A usually tall woody plant having a single main stem or trunk. **2.** Something resembling a tree, as a pole with pegs or hooks for hanging clothes. **3.** A diagram with a branching form, as one used to show family lineage. —*tr.v.* **treed, tree•ing, trees.** To force up a tree: *The dogs treed a raccoon.* —***idiom.*** **up a tree.** *Informal.* In a situation of great difficulty or perplexity; helpless. [First written down before 830 in Old English and spelled *trēow.*] —**tree′less** *adj.* —**tree′like′** *adj.*

tree fern *n.* Any of various treelike ferns having a woody stem and large feathery fronds.

tree frog *n.* Any of various small frogs that live in trees and that have toes with sticky pads used for clinging to tree trunks and branches.

tree house *n.* A structure built in the limbs of a tree and usually used for recreation.

tree line *n.* The timberline.

tree-of-heaven (trē′əv hĕv′ən) *n.* A rapidly growing tree native to China and widely planted in the United States because of its ability to resist pollution, disease, and insects.

tree•top (trē′tŏp′) *n.* The uppermost part of a tree.

tre•foil (trē′foil′ *or* trĕf′oil′) *n.* **1.** Any of various plants, such as a clover, having compound leaves with three leaflets. **2.** An ornament, a symbol, or an architectural form having three divisions like those of a clover leaf. [First written down in 1384 in Middle English and spelled *treifoile,* from Latin *trifolium* : *tri-*, three + *folium,* leaf.]

trek (trĕk) *intr.v.* **trekked, trek•king, treks. 1.** To make a slow or arduous journey. **2.** To journey on foot, especially to hike. —*n.* A journey, especially a long and difficult one.

trel•lis (trĕl′ĭs) *n.* A lattice used for training creeping plants.

trem•a•tode (trĕm′ə tōd′) *n.* Any of numerous flatworms that are parasites in animals and use suckers or hooks to attach to their hosts.

trem•ble (trĕm′bəl) *intr.v.* **trem•bled, trem•bling, trem•bles. 1.** To shake involuntarily, as from excitement, weakness, or anger. **2.** To feel fear or anxiety: *I tremble to think what has happened.* **3.** To vibrate or quiver: *leaves trembling in the breeze.* —*n.* The act of trembling; a shudder. [First written down about 1303 in Middle English and spelled *tremlen,* from Old French *trembler,* from Latin *tremulus,* trembling.]

tre•men•dous (trĭ mĕn′dəs) *adj.* **1.a.** Extremely large in amount, extent, or degree; enormous: *traveling at a tremendous speed.* **b.** *Informal.* Marvelous; wonderful: *a tremendous party.* **2.** Capable of making one tremble; terrible: *witnessed a tremendous accident.* [First written down in 1632 in Modern English and spelled *tremenduous,* from Latin *tremendus,* causing dread, from *tremere,* to tremble.] —**tre•men′dous•ly** *adv.* —**tre•men′dous•ness** *n.*

trem•o•lo (trĕm′ə lō′) *n., pl.* **trem•o•los. 1.a.** A rapid repetition of a single musical tone. **b.** A rapid alternation of two musical tones. **2.** A vibrato in a singing voice, especially one that is excessive or poorly controlled.

trem•or (trĕm′ər) *n.* **1.** A shaking or vibrating movement, as of the earth. **2.** A rapid involuntary shaking or twitching of muscles.

trem•u•lous (trĕm′yə ləs) *adj.* **1.** Marked by quivering, trembling, or shaking: *speaking with a tremulous voice.* **2.** Timid; fearful: *He was tremulous in the presence of the queen.*

trench (trĕnch) *n.* **1.** A deep furrow or ditch. **2.** A long ditch used as protection for soldiers in warfare. **3.** A long deep valley on the ocean floor. —*tr. v.* **trenched, trench•ing, trench•es.** To cut a trench in: *trench a field.* [First written down about 1395 in Middle English, from Old French, from *trenchier,* to cut.]

trench•ant (trĕn′chənt) *adj.* **1.** Keen; incisive: *a trenchant remark.* **2.** Forceful, effective, and vigorous: *a trenchant argument.* —**trench′an•cy** *n.* —**trench′ant•ly** *adv.*

trench coat *n.* A belted raincoat in a military style, having straps on the shoulders and deep pockets.

trench•er (trĕn′chər) *n.* A wooden board or platter on which food is served or carved.

trench foot *n.* Frostbite of the feet, often affecting soldiers who must stand in cold water for long periods of time.

trench mouth *n.* A painful infection of the mouth and throat caused by certain bacteria and marked by ulcers, bleeding, and bad breath.

trend (trĕnd) *n.* **1.** The general direction in which something tends to move. **2.** A general tendency or inclination. **3.** Current style; vogue: *the latest trend in fashion.* —*intr.v.* **trend•ed, trend•ing, trends. 1.** To extend, incline, or veer in a specified direction: *The mountain road trends westward.* **2.** To show a general tendency; tend: *In the 1950's jazz trended away from big bands to small groups of musicians.* [First written down about 1630 in Modern English, from Middle English *trenden,* to revolve, from Old English *trendan.*]

trend•y (trĕn′dē) *adj.* **trend•i•er, trend•i•est.** *Informal.* Of or in accord with the latest fad or fashion: *trendy clothes.*

Tren•ton (trĕn′tən). The capital of New Jersey, in the west-central part of the state northeast of Philadelphia. It was settled about 1679 by Quakers. Population, 88,675.

tre•pan (trĭ păn′) *n.* A tool used in mining for boring shafts in rock. —*tr.v.* **tre•panned, tre•pan•ning, tre•pans.** To bore (a shaft) through rock with a trepan. —**trep′a•na′tion** (trĕp′ə nā′shən) *n.*

trep•i•da•tion (trĕp′ĭ dā′shən) *n.* A state of alarm or dread; apprehension: *We approached the rapids with trepidation.*

tres•pass (trĕs′pəs *or* trĕs′păs′) *intr.v.* **tres•passed, tres•pass•ing, tres•pass•es. 1.** To commit an offense or a sin; err or transgress. **2.** To invade the property or rights of another without consent, especially to enter another's land wrongfully. **3.** To commit an unlawful act against the person, rights, or property of another: *trespass on someone's privacy.* —*n.* (trĕs′păs′ *or* trĕs′pəs). **1.** A transgression of a moral law or duty; a sin. **2.** An illegal act committed against the person, rights, or property of another, especially the illegal entry onto another's land. [First written down about 1303 in Middle English and spelled *trespassen,* from Old French *trespasser* : *tres-*, over + *passer,* to pass.] —**tres′pass•er** *n.*

tress (trĕs) *n.* A long lock or ringlet of hair.

tres•tle (trĕs′əl) *n.* **1.** A horizontal beam or bar extending between two pairs of legs that spread outward at an angle, used as a support. **2.** A framework made up of vertical, horizontal, and slanting supports, used to hold up a bridge. [First written down about 1330 in Middle English, from Latin *trānstrum*, beam.]

tri– *pref.* A prefix that means three: *tripartite.*

tri•ad (trī′ăd′) *n.* **1.** A group of three. **2.** In music, a chord of three tones, especially a chord that consists of a tone and the third and fifth tones above it.

tri•al (trī′əl *or* trīl) *n.* **1.** The examination of evidence, charges, and claims made in a case in court. **2.** The act or process of testing and trying by use and experience: *the trial of a new aircraft.* **3.** An effort or attempt: *He succeeded on his second trial.* **4.** Something, such as an annoying person or a state of anguish, that tries one's patience, endurance, or belief: *The lack of water was a trial to the hikers.* —*idiom.* **on trial.** In the process of being tried, as in a court of law.

tri•an•gle (trī′ăng′gəl) *n.* **1.** A closed plane geometric figure formed by three points not in a straight line connected by three line segments; a polygon with three sides. **2.** Something shaped like such a figure. **3.** Any of various flat objects having the outline of a triangle and used as guides in drawing or drafting. **4.** A percussion instrument consisting of a bar of metal in the shape of a triangle that is left open at one angle.

tri•an•gu•lar (trī ăng′gyə lər) *adj.* **1.** Of, relating to, or shaped like a triangle. **2.** Having a base that is a triangle: *a triangular prism.*

tri•an•gu•late (trī ăng′gyə lāt′) *tr.v.* **tri•an•gu•lat•ed, tri•an•gu•lat•ing, tri•an•gu•lates. 1.** To divide into triangles. **2.** To survey by means of triangulation. **3.** To make triangular. **4.** To measure by using trigonometry.

tri•an•gu•la•tion (trī ăng′gyə lā′shən) *n.* **1.** A method used in surveying in which a region is divided into a set of triangular elements based on a line of known length, so that an accurate determination of distances and directions can be made by using trigonometry. **2.** The set of triangles laid out for this purpose. **3.** The location of an unknown point, as in navigation, by means of trigonometry.

Tri•as•sic (trī ăs′ĭk) *adj.* Of, belonging to, or being the geologic time of the first period of the Mesozoic Era. During the Triassic, dinosaurs and other reptiles became the dominant form of animal life on Earth and mammals appeared. See table at **geologic time.** —*n.* The Triassic Period or its series of rocks.

tri•ath•lon (trī ăth′lən *or* trī ăth′lŏn′) *n.* An athletic competition consisting of three successive events, usually swimming, bicycling, and running.

trib•al (trī′bəl) *adj.* Of, relating to, or characteristic of a tribe: *tribal customs.*

tribe (trīb) *n.* **1.** A unit of social organization consisting of a number of families, clans, or other groups who share a common ancestry, culture, and leadership. **2.** A group of related organisms usually containing several genera. [First written down about 1250 in Middle English and spelled *tribu*, from Latin *tribus*, division of the Roman people.]

trib•u•la•tion (trĭb′yə lā′shən) *n.* **1.** Great affliction or distress; suffering: *a time of great tribulation.* **2.** An experience that tests one's endurance, patience, or faith; a trial. [First written down before 1200 in Middle English and spelled *tribulaciun*, from Latin *trībulāre*, to oppress.]

tri•bu•nal (trī byo͞o′nəl *or* trĭ byo͞o′nəl) *n.* **1.** A seat or court of justice. **2.** A committee or board appointed to judge or settle a particular matter or dispute. **3.** Something that has the power to judge or determine: *the tribunal of public opinion.*

trib•une (trĭb′yo͞on′ *or* trĭ byo͞on′) *n.* **1.** An official of ancient Rome chosen by the common people to protect their rights. **2.** A protector or champion of the people. [First written down about 1375 in Middle English, from Latin *tribūnus*, from *tribus*, tribe.]

trib•u•tar•y (trĭb′yə tĕr′ē) *adj.* **1.** Making additions or yielding supplies; contributory. **2.** Paying tribute: *a tributary colony.* —*n., pl.* **trib•u•tar•ies. 1.** A stream that flows into a larger river or stream. **2.** A ruler or nation that pays tribute.

trib•ute (trĭb′yo͞ot) *n.* **1.** A gift, payment, or other acknowledgment of gratitude, respect, or admiration. **2.a.** A sum of money paid by one ruler or nation to another as acknowledgment of submission or as the price for protection by that nation. **b.** A forced payment or contribution. [First written down about 1350 in Middle English and spelled *tribit*, from Latin *tribūtum*, from *tribuere*, to pay, distribute.]

trice (trīs) *n.* A very short period of time; an instant: *I'll do it for you in a trice.*

tri•ceps (trī′sĕps′) *n., pl.* **tri•ceps•es** (trī′sĕp′sĭz) also **triceps.** A large muscle that runs along the back of the upper arm, having three points of attachment at one end and serving to extend the forearm.

tri•cer•a•tops (trī sĕr′ə tŏps′) *n.* A large plant-eating dinosaur having three sharp horns on its head and a bony plate covering the back of the neck. —SEE NOTE.

tri•chi•na (trĭ kī′nə) *n., pl.* **tri•chi•nae** (trĭ kī′nē) or **tri•chi•nas.** A very small parasitic worm that lives in the intestines and muscles of pigs and other mammals and that causes trichinosis. [First written down in 1835 in Modern English, from Greek *trikhinos*, hairy.]

trich•i•no•sis (trĭk′ə nō′sĭs) *n.* A disease that results from eating incompletely cooked pork that contains trichinae, marked by intestinal disorders, fever, and pain.

trick (trĭk) *n.* **1.** An act or a procedure intended to achieve an end by deceptive means. **2.** A mischievous action; a prank: *Did you play a trick on your brother?* **3.a.** A special skill; a knack: *There's a trick to making a good soufflé.* **b.** A convention or specialized method peculiar to a certain field or activity: *the tricks of the trade.* **4.** A deception or an optical illusion: *This landscape can play tricks on the eyes.* **5.** A feat of magic or sleight of hand: *showed us a card trick.* **6.** A mean, stupid, or childish act: *That was a dirty trick.* **7.** All of the cards played in a single round of a card game. —*v.* **tricked, trick•ing, tricks.** —*tr.* To cheat or deceive. —*intr.* To practice trickery or deception. —*adj.* **1.** Of, relating to, or involving tricks: *trick photography.* **2.** Capable of doing tricks: *a trick dog.* **3.** Used to play tricks: *a trick deck of cards.* **4.** Weak and liable to give way: *a trick knee.* —*idioms.* **do the trick.** To bring about the desired result: *On a hot day an iced lemonade will just do the trick.* **not miss a trick.** To be extremely alert: *an accompanist who doesn't miss a trick.* [First written down about 1412 in Middle English and spelled *trik*, from Old North French *trikier*, to deceive, probably from Latin *trīcae*, tricks.]

trick•er•y (trĭk′ə rē) *n., pl.* **trick•er•ies.** The practice or use of tricks; deception: *He got the money by trickery.*

trick•le (trĭk′əl) *v.* **trick•led, trick•ling, trick•les.** —*intr.* **1.** To flow or fall in drops or in a thin stream: *Sand trickled through his fingers.* **2.** To move or proceed slowly or bit by bit: *The audience trickled in before curtain time.* —*tr.* To cause to

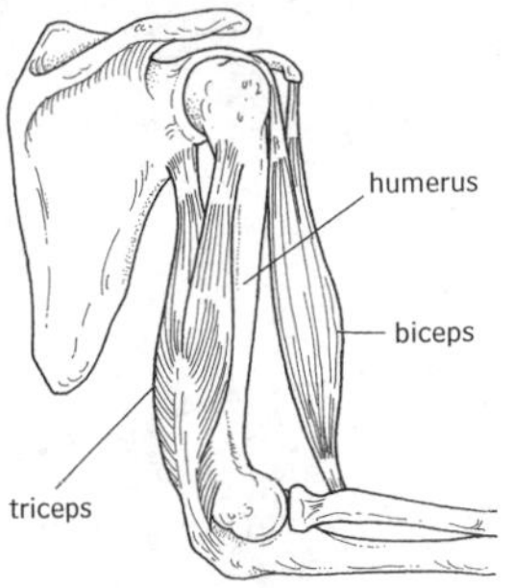

triceps

triceratops

Word History: triceratops

The animal **triceratops** first appeared in the American West during the late Cretaceous Period and was perhaps the very last species of dinosaur to exist; the word *triceratops* first appeared considerably later and farther away, in 1892 in England. The word is composed of three easy Greek roots: *tri–*, "three," as in **tripod** (literally, "a three-foot"); *kerat–*, "horn, head"; and *ōps*, "face." *Kerat–* is the source of our word *keratin*, the substance that hair is made of. *Ōps* is related to other Greek words meaning "eye" and "see" and appears in our word **autopsy**, which originally meant a "personal inspection." Thus, a *triceratops* is a "three-horned face."

ă	pat	oi	boy
ā	pay	ou	out
âr	care	o͝o	took
ä	father	o͞o	boot
ĕ	pet	ŭ	cut
ē	be	ûr	urge
ĭ	pit	th	thin
ī	pie	*th*	this
îr	pier	hw	whoop
ŏ	pot	zh	vision
ō	toe	ə	about
ô	paw	N	*French* bon

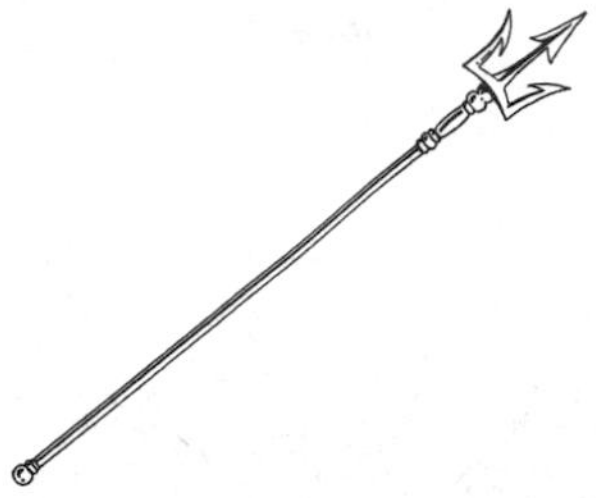

trident

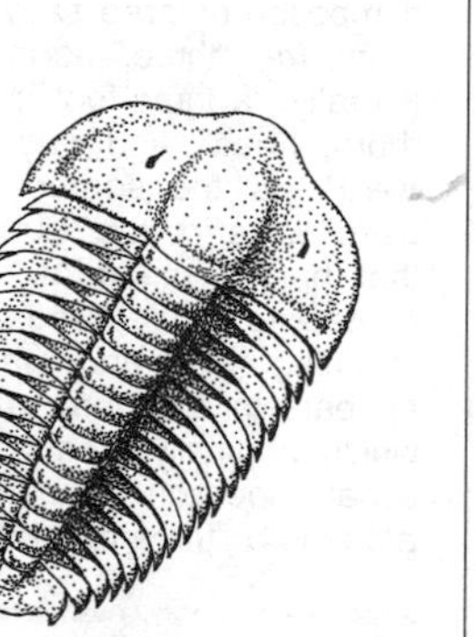

trilobite

trickle: *trickled the syrup on the waffle.* —*n.* **1.** The act or condition of trickling. **2.** A slow, small, or irregular quantity that moves, proceeds, or occurs intermittently: *a trickle of water from the roof; a trickle of orders in the mail.*

trick•ster (trĭk′stər) *n.* A person who swindles or plays tricks.

trick•y (trĭk′ē) *adj.* **trick•i•er, trick•i•est. 1.** Given to or characterized by trickery. **2.** Requiring caution or skill: *a tricky situation.*

tri•col•or (trī′kŭl′ər) *n.* **1.** A flag with three colors. **2.** Also **Tricolor.** The French flag. —*adj.* Having three colors.

tri•cot (trē′kō) *n.* A plain knitted fabric.

tri•cus•pid (trī kŭs′pĭd) *n.* A tooth having three points. —*adj.* Having three points, as one of the molar teeth.

tri•cy•cle (trī′sĭk′əl *or* trī′sĭ kəl) *n.* A vehicle used especially by small children, having three wheels and moved by pedals.

tri•dent (trīd′nt) *n.* **1.** A long three-pronged fork or weapon, especially a spear. **2.** In Greek and Roman mythology, the three-pronged spear carried by Poseidon or Neptune. [First written down about 1450 in Middle English, from Latin *tridēns* : *tri-*, three + *dēns*, tooth.]

tried (trīd) *v.* Past tense and past participle of **try.** —*adj.* Thoroughly tested and proved to be good or trustworthy: *a tried recipe.*

tri•en•ni•al (trī ĕn′ē əl) *adj.* **1.** Occurring every third year. **2.** Lasting three years. —*n.* **1.** A third anniversary. **2.** A ceremony or celebration occurring every three years.

tries (trīz) *v.* Third person singular present tense of **try.** —*n.* Plural of **try.**

tri•fle (trī′fəl) *n.* **1.** Something of little importance or value. **2.** A small amount; a little. **3.** A dessert of cake soaked in brandy or another sweet liquid and topped with jam, custard, and whipped cream. —*intr.v.* **tri•fled, tri•fling, tri•fles. 1.** To deal with something as if it were of little significance or importance: *Don't trifle with me!* **2.** To play or toy with something: *trifle with a pencil.* —*idiom.* **a trifle.** Very little; somewhat: *I had just a trifle too much to eat.*

tri•fling (trī′flĭng) *adj.* **1.** Of slight worth or importance: *a trifling sum.* **2.** Frivolous or idle. —**tri′fling•ly** *adv.*

trig•ger (trĭg′ər) *n.* The lever pressed by the finger to discharge a gun. —*tr.v.* **trig•gered, trig•ger•ing, trig•gers.** To start; set off: *His thoughtless remark triggered an argument.* [First written down in 1621 in Modern English and spelled *tricker*, from Dutch *trekker*, from Middle Dutch *trecken*, to pull.]

trig•o•no•met•ric function (trĭg′ə nə mĕt′rĭk) *n.* A function of an angle, as the sine, cosine, or tangent, whose value is expressed as a ratio of two of the sides of a right triangle in which the angle is included.

trig•o•nom•e•try (trĭg′ə nŏm′ĭ trē) *n.* The study of the properties and uses of trigonometric functions. [First written down in 1614 in Modern English : Greek *trigōnon*, triangle + Greek *-metria*, measuring.]

trill (trĭl) *n.* **1.** A fluttering or tremulous sound, as that made by certain birds; a warble. **2.** The rapid alternation of two musical tones that are either a half or a whole tone apart. **3.** A rapid vibration of one organ of speech against another, as of the tip of the tongue against the ridge behind the upper front teeth. —*v.* **trilled, tril•ling, trills.** —*tr.* **1.** To sound, sing, or play with a trill. **2.** To make (a sound) with a trill: *In Spanish you trill the* r*'s.* —*intr.* To produce or give forth a trill.

tril•lion (trĭl′yən) *n.* **1.** The number, written as 10^{12} or 1 followed by 12 zeros, that is equal to one thousand times one billion. **2.** *Chiefly British.* The number, written as 10^{18} or 1 followed by 18 zeros, that is equal to one million times one British billion. [First written down in 1690 in Modern English, from French : *tri-*, third power + *million*, million.] —**tril′lionth** *n.*

tril•li•um (trĭl′ē əm) *n.* Any of various plants having three leaves grouped together and a single flower with three petals.

tri•lo•bate (trī lō′bāt′) *adj.* Having three lobes: *trilobate leaves.*

tri•lo•bite (trī′lə bīt′) *n.* Any of numerous extinct sea animals that lived during the Paleozoic Era and that had a body with a hard outer covering divided by grooves into three lengthwise sections.

tril•o•gy (trĭl′ə jē) *n., pl.* **tril•o•gies.** A group of three related dramatic or literary works.

trim (trĭm) *tr.v.* **trimmed, trim•ming, trims. 1.** To make neat, even, or tidy by clipping, smoothing, or pruning: *Trim the hedges.* **2.** To remove or reduce by cutting: *trim the crust off the bread; trim a budget.* **3.** To decorate, ornament, or embellish: *trim a Christmas tree.* **4.** In sailing, to adjust (the sails and yards) so that they receive the wind properly: *trimmed sail and steered the ship past the sandbar.* —*n.* **1.** Proper shape, order, or condition: *in good trim for the game.* **2.** Ornamentation on the surface of something, as braid on clothing or moldings on windows. **3.** A cutting or clipping to make neat: *Your beard needs a trim.* **4.a.** The readiness of a ship for sailing. **b.** The balance of a ship. **5.** The position of an aircraft when compared to how it flies parallel to the ground. —*adj.* **trim•mer, trim•mest. 1.** In good or neat order: *He looked very trim in his new suit.* See Synonyms at **neat. 2.** Well designed or proportioned, with simple or slim lines: *a trim schooner; a trim figure.* [First written down before 1460 in Middle English and spelled *trimmen*, to make firm, from Old English *trum*, strong.] —**trim′ly** *adv.* —**trim′mer** *n.* —**trim′ness** *n.*

tri•mes•ter (trī mĕs′tər *or* trī′mĕs′tər) *n.* **1.** A period or term of three months. **2.** One of three terms making up an academic year at some schools and colleges.

trim•ming (trĭm′ĭng) *n.* **1.** The act of trimming. **2.** Something added as decoration; an ornament: *fur trimming on a coat.* **3. trimmings.** Accessories; extras: *roast turkey with all the trimmings.* **4. trimmings.** Scraps or material removed when something is trimmed.

Trin•i•dad (trĭn′ĭ dăd′). An island of Trinidad and Tobago in the Atlantic Ocean off northeast Venezuela. It was settled in the 1570's. —**Trin′i•dad′i•an** *adj. & n.*

Trinidad and To•ba•go (tə bā′gō). A country of the southeast West Indies in the Atlantic Ocean off northeast Venezuela. It is made up of the islands of Trinidad and Tobago, which gained independence from Great Britain in 1962. Port of Spain, on Trinidad, is the capital. Population, 1,059,825.

tri•ni•tro•tol•u•ene (trī nī′trō tŏl′yo͞o ēn′) *n.* TNT.

trin•i•ty (trĭn′ĭ tē) *n., pl.* **trin•i•ties. 1.** A group made up of three closely related members. **2. Trinity.** In Christianity, the union of the Father, Son, and Holy Spirit as three divine persons in one God. [First written down before 1200 in Middle English and spelled *trinite*, from Latin *trīnitās*, from *trīnus*, triple.]

trin•ket (trĭng′kĭt) *n.* A small ornament, such as a piece of jewelry.

tri•no•mi•al (trī nō′mē əl) *adj.* Consisting of three algebraic terms connected by plus signs or minus signs or some combination of the two. —*n.* A trinomial algebraic expression.

tri•o (trē′ō) *n., pl.* **tri•os. 1.** A group of three people or things joined or associated. **2.a.** A musical composition for three performers. **b.** The group performing such a composition. **c.** The middle section of a minuet or scherzo, a march, or one of various dances.

tri•ode (trī′ōd′) *n.* An electron tube having three electrodes, usually an anode, a cathode, and a grid that controls the flow of current between the anode and cathode.

tri•ox•ide (trī ŏk′sīd′) *n.* An oxide that contains three atoms of oxygen per molecule.

trip (trĭp) *n.* **1.** A going from one place to another; a journey: *a trip from Cleveland to Pittsburgh.* **2.** A stumble or fall. **3.** A maneuver causing someone to stumble or fall. **4.** A mistake or blunder. **5.** A device, such as a catch for triggering a mechanism. —*v.* **tripped, trip•ping, trips.** —*intr.* **1.** To stumble: *He tripped over a root and fell.* **2.** To move nimbly with light rapid steps; skip: *The children tripped happily over the bridge.* **3.** To be released, as a tooth on an escapement wheel in a watch. **4.** To make a trip. —*tr.* **1.** To cause to stumble or fall. **2.** To catch or trap in an error or an inconsistency: *The police tripped up the suspect during questioning.* **3.** To release (a catch, trigger, or switch), thereby setting something in operation.

tri•par•tite (trī pär′tīt) *adj.* **1.** Composed of or divided into three parts. **2.** Relating to or executed by three parties: *a tripartite agreement.*

tripe (trīp) *n.* **1.** The rubbery lining of the stomach of cattle or similar animals, used as food. **2.** *Informal.* Something with no value; rubbish.

tri•ple (trĭp′əl) *adj.* **1.** Consisting of three parts. **2.** Three times as much or as many. **3.** Repeated three times. —*n.* **1.** A number or amount three times as great as another. **2.** A group or set of three; a triad. **3.** In baseball, a hit that enables the batter to reach third base safely. —*v.* **tri•pled, tri•pling, tri•ples.** —*tr.* To make three times as great in number or amount. —*intr.* **1.** To become three times as great in number or amount: *Prices tripled in 20 years.* **2.** In baseball, to hit a triple.

triple play *n.* In baseball, a defensive play in which three outs are made during a single turn at bat.

trip•let (trĭp′lĭt) *n.* **1.** A group or set of three of one kind. **2.** One of three children born at one birth. **3.** A group of three musical notes having the time value of two notes of the same kind.

triple time *n.* A musical time or rhythm having three beats to the measure, with the accent on the first beat.

trip•li•cate (trĭp′lĭ kĭt) *n.* One of a set of three identical objects or copies. —*tr.v.* (trĭp′lĭ kāt′). **trip•li•cat•ed, trip•li•cat•ing, trip•li•cates. 1.** To make threefold; triple. **2.** To make three identical copies of.

tri•pod (trī′pŏd′) *n.* An adjustable stand with three legs, as one used to support a camera.

Trip•o•li (trĭp′ə lē). The capital and largest city of Libya, in the northwest part of the country on the Mediterranean Sea. Population, 858,500.

trip•tych (trĭp′tĭk) *n.* A painting or carving consisting of three panels hinged together.

tri•sect (trī′sĕkt′ *or* trī sĕkt′) *tr.v.* **tri•sect•ed, tri•sect•ing, tri•sects.** To divide into three equal parts. **—tri•sec′tion** *n.*

Tris•tan (trĭs′tən *or* trĭs′tăn′) or **Tris•tram** (trĭs′trəm) *n.* In Arthurian legend, a knight who falls in love with the Irish princess Iseult.

trite (trīt) *adj.* **trit•er, trit•est.** Lacking the power to evoke interest because of overuse or repetition: *a trite expression.* **—trite′ly** *adv.* **—trite′ness** *n.*

trit•i•um (trĭt′ē əm *or* trĭsh′ē əm) *n.* A rare radioactive isotope of hydrogen having a nucleus that consists of a proton and two neutrons and an atomic mass of 3. It is made artificially and is used as a tracer and in nuclear weapons.

tri•ton (trīt′n) *n.* Any of various tropical sea animals having a large, pointed, spiral shell.

Tri•ton (trīt′n) *n.* In Greek Mythology, a god of the sea portrayed as having the head and trunk of a man and the tail of a fish.

tri•umph (trī′əmf) *intr.v.* **tri•umphed, tri•umph•ing, tri•umphs. 1.** To be victorious or successful; win: *triumph over adversity.* **2.** To rejoice over a success or victory; exult. —*n.* **1.** The fact of being victorious; success: *Her political campaign ended in triumph.* **2.** A noteworthy or spectacular success: *The bridge is a triumph of engineering.* **3.** Exultation or rejoicing over success or victory: *a cry of triumph.* [First written down before 1450 in Middle English and spelled *triomfen,* from Latin *triumphus,* triumph.]

tri•um•phal (trī ŭm′fəl) *adj.* Relating to, of the nature of, or celebrating a triumph: *a triumphal march.*

tri•um•phant (trī ŭm′fənt) *adj.* **1.** Rejoicing over success or victory: *the team's triumphant return home.* **2.** Victorious; successful: *a triumphant political campaign.*

tri•um•vir (trī ŭm′vər) *n., pl.* **tri•um•virs** or **tri•um•vi•ri** (trī ŭm′və rī′). One of three men sharing civil authority in ancient Rome.

tri•um•vi•rate (trī ŭm′vər ĭt) *n.* **1.** Government by triumvirs. **2.** The office or term of a triumvir. **3.** An association or group of three: *a triumvirate of business leaders.*

tri•va•lent (trī vā′lənt) *adj.* In chemistry, having valence +3 or −3.

triv•et (trĭv′ĭt) *n.* **1.** A metal stand with short feet, placed under a hot dish on a table. **2.** A three-legged metal stand for holding a kettle or pot in a hearth.

triv•i•a (trĭv′ē ə) *pl.n. (used with a singular or plural verb).* Insignificant or inessential matters; trifles.

triv•i•al (trĭv′ē əl) *adj.* **1.** Of little significance or value; trifling: *trivial matters.* **2.** Ordinary; commonplace: *a trivial occurrence.* **3.** Concerned with or involving trivia. **—triv′i•al′i•ty** (trĭv′ē ăl′ĭ tē) *n.* **—triv′i•al•ly** *adv.*

tRNA (tē′är ĕn ā′) *n.* Transfer RNA.

tro•che (trō′kē) *n.* A small, circular medicinal lozenge.

❑ *These sound alike:* **troche, trochee** (metrical foot in poetry).

tro•chee (trō′kē) *n.* In poetry, a metrical foot consisting of a stressed syllable followed by an unstressed syllable.

❑ *These sound alike* : **trochee, troche** (lozenge).

trod (trŏd) *v.* Past tense and a past participle of **tread.**

trod•den (trŏd′n) *v.* A past participle of **tread.**

trog•lo•dyte (trŏg′lə dīt′) *n.* A member of a fabulous or prehistoric people that lived in caves, dens, or holes.

Tro•jan (trō′jən) *n.* A native or inhabitant of ancient Troy. —*adj.* Of or relating to ancient Troy or its inhabitants.

Trojan horse *n.* **1.** In Greek mythology, the hollow wooden horse in which Greeks hid and gained entrance to Troy during the Trojan War. **2.** A subversive group or device placed within enemy ranks.

Trojan War *n.* In Greek mythology, the ten-year war waged against Troy by the Greeks, caused by the carrying off of Helen by Paris.

troll[1] (trōl) *v.* **trolled, troll•ing, trolls.** —*tr.* **1.** To fish for or in by trailing a line from behind a slowly

tripod

Triton

Trojan horse
Engraving after a painting by Henri Paul Motte (1846–1922)

ă	pat	oi	boy
ā	pay	ou	out
âr	care	ŏŏ	took
ä	father	ōō	boot
ĕ	pet	ŭ	cut
ē	be	ûr	urge
ĭ	pit	th	thin
ī	pie	*th*	this
îr	pier	hw	whoop
ŏ	pot	zh	vision
ō	toe	ə	about
ô	paw	N	*French* bon

moving boat: *troll bass; troll a bay.* **2.** To sing in succession the parts of (a round, for example). —*intr.* **1.** To fish by trailing a line, as from a moving boat. **2.** To sing heartily or gaily. [First written down before 1387 in Middle English and spelled *trollen*, to wander about, from Old French *troller*, of Germanic origin.]

troll² (trōl) *n.* A creature of Scandinavian folklore, variously described as a friendly or mischievous dwarf or as a giant, that lives in caves, in the hills, or under bridges. [First written down in 1616 in Modern English, ultimately from Old Norse.]

trol•ley (trŏl′ē) *n., pl.* **trol•leys. 1.** A streetcar. **2.** A device that makes contact with an overhead wire, a third rail, or an underground conductor and supplies current to an electrically powered vehicle. **3.** A carriage or basket that hangs from wheels that run on an overhead track.

trolley bus *n.* An electric bus that runs without tracks and is powered by electricity from an overhead wire.

trolley car *n.* A streetcar.

trom•bone (trŏm bōn′ *or* trəm bōn′) *n.* A brass instrument consisting of a long, looped cylindrical tube, a movable U-shaped slide for producing different pitches, and a flaring bell. [First written down in 1724 in Modern English, from Italian, from *tromba*, trumpet, of Germanic origin.]

trombone

troop (tro͞op) *n.* **1.** A group or company of people, animals, or things: *a troop of students on a field trip.* **2.** A group of soldiers. **3. troops.** Military units; soldiers. **4.** A unit of Boy Scouts or Girl Scouts under the guidance of an adult leader. —*intr.v.* **trooped, troop•ing, troops.** To move or go as a group: *children trooping home from school.* [First written down in 1545 in Modern English, from Old French *trope.*]

❑ *These sound alike:* **troop, troupe** (group of actors).

troop•er (tro͞o′pər) *n.* **1.a.** A member of a unit of cavalry. **b.** A cavalry horse. **2.** A mounted police officer. **3.** A state police officer.

troop•ship (tro͞op′shĭp′) *n.* A ship designed for transporting troops.

trop. *abbr.* An abbreviation of: **1.** Tropic. **2.** Tropical.

tro•phy (trō′fē) *n., pl.* **tro•phies. 1.** A prize or memento received as a symbol of victory, especially in sports. **2.** A specimen or part, such as the antlers of a deer, preserved as a token of a successful hunt. **3.** A memento, as of one's personal achievements. [First written down in 1513 in Modern English, from Latin *trophaeum*, monument to victory.]

trophy
Hollis Stacy, winner of the U.S. Women's Open golf tournament in 1984

trop•ic (trŏp′ĭk) *n.* **1.** Either of two parallels of latitude on Earth at 23° 27′ north and south of the equator that form the boundaries of the Torrid Zone. **2. Tropics** or **tropics** The region of the earth bounded by these parallels. **3.** The corresponding lines on the celestial sphere that mark the limits of the apparent north-to-south motion of the sun. —*adj.* Of or relating to the Tropics; tropical. [First written down in 1391 in Middle English and spelled *tropik*, from Greek *tropikos*, of turning, from *tropē*, a turning.]

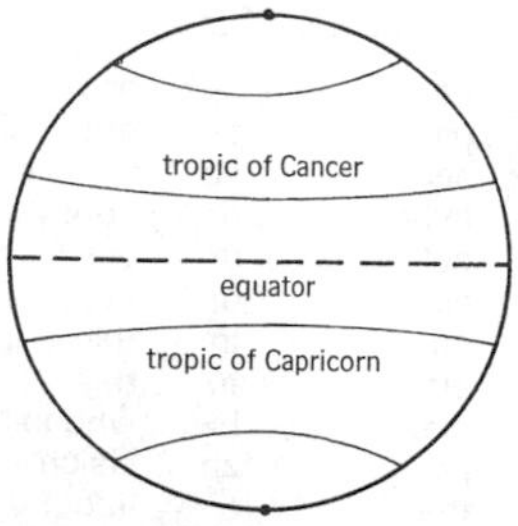

tropic

trop•i•cal (trŏp′ĭ kəl) *adj.* **1.** Of, occurring in, or characteristic of the Tropics. **2.** Hot and humid; torrid. **—trop′i•cal•ly** *adv.*

tropical fish *n.* Any of various small, usually brightly colored fishes native to tropical waters and often kept in home aquariums.

tropic of Cancer *n.* The parallel of latitude 23° 27′ north of the equator, forming the northern boundary of the Torrid Zone.

tropic of Capricorn *n.* The parallel of latitude 23° 27′ south of the equator, forming the southern boundary of the Torrid Zone.

tro•pism (trō′pĭz′əm) *n.* Growth or movement of a plant or animal toward or away from an external stimulus, such as light, heat, or gravity. **—tro•pis′tic** *adj.*

tro•po•pause (trō′pə pôz′ *or* trŏp′ə pôz′) *n.* The boundary between the upper troposphere and the lower stratosphere, varying in altitude from approximately 5 miles (8 kilometers) at the poles to 11 miles (18 kilometers) at the equator.

tro•po•sphere (trō′pə sfîr′ *or* trŏp′ə sfîr′) *n.* The lowest region of the atmosphere, bounded by the surface of the earth and the tropopause and characterized by temperatures that decrease with increasing altitude. Weather and most cloud formations occur in the troposphere.

trot (trŏt) *n.* **1.** A running gait of a horse or other four-footed animal in which diagonal pairs of legs move forward together. **2.** A gait of a person, faster than a walk; a jog: *a trot around the playing field.* **3.** A word-for-word translation of a work in a foreign language, sometimes used secretly in preparing a class assignment; a pony. —*v.* **trot•ted, trot•ting, trots.** —*intr.* **1.** To go or move at a trot: *The horses trotted down the road.* **2.** To proceed rapidly; hurry: *trotted up and down the stairs doing chores.* —*tr.* To cause to trot: *She trotted her pony around the ring.* ***—idiom.*** **trot out.** *Informal.* To bring out and show for inspection or admiration: *The trainer trotted out the show dogs one by one.* [First written down before 1325 in Middle English and spelled *trott*, from Old French *troter*, to trot, of Germanic origin.]

troth (trôth *or* trŏth *or* trōth) *n.* **1.** Betrothal. **2.** A person's pledged faithfulness.

Trot•sky (trŏt′skē), **Leon.** 1879–1940. Russian revolutionary who was a leader of the Bolshevik Revolution (1917). He was later expelled from the Communist Party (1927) and banished (1929) for his opposition to Stalin.

trot•ter (trŏt′ər) *n.* **1.** A horse that trots, especially one trained for harness racing. **2.** *Informal.* A foot, especially the foot of a pig or sheep prepared as food.

trou•ba•dour (tro͞o′bə dôr′ *or* tro͞o′bə do͝or′) *n.* A poet of the 12th and 13th centuries in Provence, northern Italy, and northern Spain, who composed and sang songs and poems, often about love.

trou•ble (trŭb′əl) *n.* **1.** A state of distress, affliction, danger, or need: *The ship was in trouble and signaled for help.* **2.** A cause or source of distress, disturbance, or difficulty: *Minding the baby won't be any trouble.* **3.** An effort, especially one that causes inconvenience or bother: *They went to a lot of trouble on our account.* **4.** A condition of pain, disease, or malfunction: *stomach trouble.* —*v.* **troub•led, troub•ling, troub•les.** —*tr.* **1.** To agitate; stir up: *A stiff wind troubled the lake.* **2.** To afflict with pain or discomfort: *My stomach is troubling me.* **3.** To cause mental agitation or distress to; worry: *I am troubled by your lack of interest.* **4.** To inconvenience; bother: *May I trouble you for the time?* —*intr.* To take pains: *Don't trouble to see me off.* [First written down about 1200 in Middle English and spelled *trubuil*, from Old French *troubler*, to trouble, from Late Latin *turbidāre.*]

trou•ble•mak•er (trŭb′əl mā′kər) *n.* A person or thing that stirs up trouble or strife.

trou•ble•shoot•er (trŭb′əl sho͞o′tər) *n.* A person whose job is to locate and eliminate sources of trouble.

trou•ble•some (trŭb′əl səm) *adj.* **1.** Causing trouble or anxiety; worrisome: *a troublesome car.* **2.** Difficult; trying: *a troublesome situation.*

trough (trôf *or* trŏf) *n.* **1.** A long, narrow, generally shallow receptacle, especially one for holding water or feed for animals. **2.** A gutter under the eaves of a roof. **3.** A long narrow depression, as between waves or ridges. **4.** An extended region of low atmospheric pressure, often associated with a front. [First written down about 700 in Old English and spelled *trog*.]

trounce (trouns) *tr.v.* **trounced, trounc•ing, trounc•es. 1.** To thrash; beat. **2.** To defeat decisively: *trounced the opposing field hockey team.*

troupe (tro͞op) *n.* A company or group, especially of touring actors, singers, or dancers. [First written down in 1825 in American English, from French *troupe*, troop.]

❑ *These sound alike:* **troupe, troop** (group).

trou•sers (trou′zərz) *pl.n.* An outer garment for covering the body from the waist to the ankles, divided into sections to fit each leg separately.

trous•seau (tro͞o′sō *or* tro͞o **sō′**) *n., pl.* **trous•seaux** (tro͞o′sōz *or* tro͞o **sōz′**) or **trous•seaus.** The possessions, such as clothing and linens, that a woman assembles for her marriage.

trout (trout) *n., pl.* **trout** or **trouts.** Any of various chiefly freshwater fishes usually having a speckled body and valued as food. [First written down about 1050 in Old English and spelled *trūht*, from Late Latin *tructa*.]

trow•el (trou′əl) *n.* **1.** A hand tool with a flat blade for spreading or smoothing such substances as mortar and cement. **2.** A tool with a scoop-shaped blade used for digging, as in setting plants.

troy (troi) *adj.* Of, measured in, or expressed in troy weight.

Troy (troi) Also **Il•i•um** (ĭl′ē əm). An ancient city of northwest Asia Minor. It is the legendary site of the Trojan War.

troy weight *n.* A system of weights in which the grain is the same as in the avoirdupois system, one ounce equals 480 grains, and one pound equals 12 ounces.

tru•an•cy (tro͞o′ən sē) *n., pl.* **tru•an•cies.** The act or condition of being absent without permission.

tru•ant (tro͞o′ənt) *n.* **1.** A person who is absent without permission. **2.** A person who shirks work or duty. —*adj.* **1.** Absent without permission, especially from school: *a truant pupil.* **2.** Idle, lazy, or neglectful: *a truant worker.*

truant officer *n.* An official who investigates unauthorized absences from school.

truce (tro͞os) *n.* A temporary stopping of fighting by mutual agreement.

truck[1] (trŭk) *n.* **1.** Any of various heavy motor vehicles designed for carrying or pulling loads. **2.** A two-wheeled barrow used for moving heavy objects by hand. **3.** A wheeled, sometimes motorized platform for conveying loads in a warehouse or freight yard. **4.** One of the swiveling frames of wheels under each end of a railroad car or trolley car. —*v.* **trucked, truck•ing, trucks.** —*tr.* To transport (goods) by truck. —*intr.* **1.** To carry goods by truck. **2.** To drive a truck. [First written down in 1611 in Modern English and spelled *truck*, small wheel, perhaps short for *truckle*.]

truck[2] (trŭk) *n.* **1.** Articles of commerce; trade goods. **2.** Vegetables and fruit raised for marketing. **3.** *Informal.* Worthless stuff; rubbish. **4.** *Informal.* Dealings: *He is too high and mighty to have any truck with us.* [First written down in 1533 in Modern English, from Old North French *troquer*, to barter.]

truck•er (trŭk′ər) *n.* A person who drives a truck.

truck farm *n.* A farm producing vegetables for the market.

truck•le (trŭk′əl) *n.* A small wheel or roller.

truck•load (trŭk′lōd′) *n.* The amount that a truck can hold.

truc•u•lent (trŭk′yə lənt) *adj.* **1.** Ready or willing to fight. **2.** Scathingly harsh; caustic: *a truculent article.* **3.** Savage and cruel; fierce: *truculent warriors.* [First written down about 1540 in Modern English, from Latin *truculentus*, from *trux*, fierce.] **—truc′u•lent•ly** *adv.*

Tru•deau (tro͞o **dō′** *or* tro͞o′dō′), **Pierre Elliot.** Born 1919. Canadian prime minister (1968–1979 and 1980–1984) whose administration was marked by the Constitution Act of 1982, which granted Canada full independence.

trudge (trŭj) *intr.v.* **trudged, trudg•ing, trudg•es.** To walk in a laborious heavy-footed way; plod.

true (tro͞o) *adj.* **tru•er, tru•est. 1.** Consistent with fact or reality; not false or erroneous: *Is this statement true or false?* **2.** Not imitation or counterfeit; real or genuine: *true gold.* See Synonyms at **authentic. 3.** Reliable; accurate: *a true prophecy.* **4.** Sincerely felt or expressed; unfeigned: *true sorrow.* **5.** Faithful; loyal: *Be true to your friends.* **6.** Rightful; legitimate: *the true heir to the land.* **7.** Having the characteristics of a certain group or type; typical: *The horseshoe crab is not a true crab.* **8.** Exactly conforming to a rule, standard, or pattern. **9.** Determined with reference to the earth's axis, not the magnetic poles: *true north.* —*adv.* **1.** In accord with reality, fact, or truthfulness: *She speaks true.* **2.** Without swerving from a course; exactly: *I'll sail the ship straight and true.* —*tr.v.* **trued, tru•ing** or **true•ing, trues.** To adjust or fit (something) so as to make it balanced, level, or square: *true the edges of a seam.* [First written down about 725 in Old English and spelled *trēowe*, firm, trustworthy.]

true-blue (**tro͞o′ blo͞o′**) *adj.* Loyal or faithful; staunch: *my true-blue friend.*

truf•fle (trŭf′əl) *n.* Any of various fleshy blackish or light-brown fungi that grow underground and are regarded as a food delicacy.

tru•ism (tro͞o′ĭz′əm) *n.* A statement of obvious truth.

tru•ly (tro͞o′lē) *adv.* **1.** Sincerely; genuinely: *I am truly sorry.* **2.** Truthfully; accurately: *The newspaper reported the story truly.* **3.** Indeed: *The view from the hilltop is truly magnificent.*

Tru•man (tro͞o′mən), **Harry S.** 1884–1972. The 33rd President of the United States (1945–1953). He authorized the use of the atomic bomb against Japan (1945) and ordered U.S. involvement in the Korean War (1950–1953).

trump (trŭmp) *n.* In card games, a suit declared to outrank all other suits during the play of a hand. Often used in the plural. —*v.* **trumped, trump•ing, trumps.** —*tr.* To take (a card or trick) with a trump. —*intr.* To play a trump. **—*idiom.* trump up.** To devise fraudulently: *The dictator trumped up charges against his opponents.*

trump•er•y (trŭm′pə rē) *n., pl.* **trump•er•ies. 1.** Showy but worthless finery. **2.** Nonsense; rubbish.

trum•pet (trŭm′pĭt) *n.* **1.** A high-pitched brass instrument consisting of a long metal tube, looped once and having a mouthpiece at one end and a flaring bell at the other. Modern trumpets are equipped with three valves for producing variations in pitch. **2.** Something shaped like a trumpet: *the yellow trumpets of the daffodils.* **3.** A resounding call, as that of the elephant. —*v.* **trum•pet•ed, trum•pet•ing, trum•pets.** —*intr.* **1.** To play a trumpet. **2.** To make a loud resounding sound like that of a trumpet: *Elephants trumpeted in the distance.* —*tr.* To shout or announce loudly. [First written down before 1393 in Middle English and spelled *trompette*, from Old French *trompette*, from

Harry S. Truman
Photographed c. 1945

trumpet

ă	pat	oi	boy
ā	pay	ou	out
âr	care	o͝o	took
ä	father	o͞o	boot
ĕ	pet	ŭ	cut
ē	be	ûr	urge
ĭ	pit	th	thin
ī	pie	*th*	this
îr	pier	hw	whoop
ŏ	pot	zh	vision
ō	toe	ə	about
ô	paw	N	*French* bon

Sojourner Truth
Photographed c. 1870

Usage: try

When you write on a formal level, as in your school work, avoid using the phrase *try and* instead of *try to*: *Could you try to* (not *and*) *make less noise?*

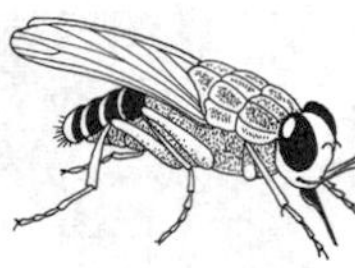

tsetse fly

tuatara

trompe, horn, from Old High German *trumpa*.] **—trum′pet•er** *n.*

trumpet creeper *n.* A woody vine of the United States having reddish-orange flowers shaped like trumpets.

trun•cate (trŭng′kāt′) *tr.v.* **trun•cat•ed, trun•cat•ing, trun•cates.** To shorten by or as if by cutting off. *—adj.* Appearing to end abruptly, as a leaf of a tulip tree.

trun•cheon (trŭn′chən) *n.* A short stick carried by police officers; a billy club.

trun•dle (trŭn′dl) *v.* **trun•dled, trun•dling, trun•dles.** *—tr.* To push or propel on wheels or rollers: *trundling a wheelbarrow.* *—intr.* To move along by or as if by rolling. **—trun′dler** *n.*

trundle bed *n.* A low bed on casters that can be rolled under another bed when not in use.

trunk (trŭngk) *n.* **1.** The woody main stem of a tree. **2.** The main part of the body, not including the arms, legs, and head. **3.** A long flexible snout, especially of an elephant, used for grasping and holding. **4.** A main body, not including parts that branch off: *the trunk of a nerve.* **5.** A trunk line. **6.** A covered compartment of an automobile, used for luggage or storage. **7.** A large box or case with a lid that clasps shut, used as luggage or for storage. **8.** **trunks.** Men's shorts worn for swimming or athletics. [First written down in 1440 in Middle English and spelled *trunke*, from Latin *truncus*.]

trunk line *n.* **1.** A line that makes a direct connection between two telephone switchboards. **2.** The main line of a communications system or transportation system.

truss (trŭs) *n.* **1.** A device worn to support a hernia so that it will not enlarge or spread. **2.** A framework, as of beams or bars, used to support a roof, bridge, or other structure. *—tr.v.* **trussed, truss•ing, truss•es. 1.** To tie up securely; bind. **2.** To bind the wings and legs of (a fowl) before cooking. **3.** To support or brace with a truss.

trust (trŭst) *n.* **1.** Firm reliance on the integrity, ability, or character of a person or thing. **2.** Custody; care: *The children are in my trust.* See Synonyms at **care. 3.** The condition and resulting obligation of having confidence placed in one: *violated a public trust.* **4.** Reliance on something in the future; hope. **5.** Reliance on the intention and ability of a purchaser to pay in the future; credit: *goods bought on trust.* **6.** The confidence placed in a person who has been given legal control of property for the benefit of someone else. **7.** The property under such control. **8.** A combination of business firms and corporations, joined for the purpose of reducing competition and controlling prices. *—v.* **trust•ed, trust•ing, trusts.** *—intr.* **1.** To have or place confidence; depend: *Trust in me.* **2.** To be confident; hope. *—tr.* **1.** To have or place confidence in; depend on: *Trust me.* **2.** To expect with assurance; assume: *I trust that you will be on time.* **3.** To believe: *I trust what you say.* **4.** To grant discretion to confidently: *Can I trust them with the boat?* ***—idiom.*** **in trust.** In the possession or care of a trustee. [First written down before 1200 in Middle English and spelled *truste*, perhaps from Old Norse *traust*, confidence.]

trus•tee (trŭ stē′) *n.* **1.** A person or firm that has legal control of property for another person's benefit. **2.** A member of a group or board that manages the affairs of an institution.

trus•tee•ship (trŭ stē′shĭp′) *n.* **1.** The position or function of a trustee. **2.a.** Administration of a territory by a country or countries so commissioned by the United Nations. **b.** A trust territory.

trust•ful (trŭst′fəl) *adj.* Inclined to believe or confide readily; full of trust: *a child's trustful eyes; a trustful person.* **—trust′ful•ly** *adv.* **—trust′ful•ness** *n.*

trust fund *n.* Property placed under the legal control of a trustee for the benefit of someone else.

trust territory *n.* A colony or territory placed under the administration of a country or countries by the United Nations.

trust•wor•thy (trŭst′wûr′thē) *adj.* **trust•wor•thi•er, trust•wor•thi•est.** Warranting trust; reliable: *a trustworthy assistant.*

trust•y (trŭs′tē) *adj.* **trust•i•er, trust•i•est.** Reliable; trustworthy. *—n., pl.* **trust•ies.** A trusted person, especially a convict regarded as trustworthy and therefore granted special privileges.

truth (trōōth) *n., pl.* **truths** (trōōthz *or* trōōths). **1.** Accordance with fact or actuality: *a story with an appearance of truth.* **2.** A statement proven to be or accepted as true: *scientific truths.* **3.** Sincerity; integrity: *There was no truth in his speech.* **4.** Reality; actuality: *At Appomattox, the Civil War was in truth over.* [First written down before 899 in Old English and spelled *trēowth*, loyalty.]

Truth (trōōth), **Sojourner.** 1797?–1883. American abolitionist and feminist. After she escaped from slavery in 1827, she lectured widely against slavery and for the rights of women.

truth•ful (trōōth′fəl) *adj.* **1.** Consistently telling the truth; honest: *a truthful person.* **2.** Corresponding to reality; true: *a truthful account of the events.* **—truth′ful•ly** *adv.* **—truth′ful•ness** *n.*

try (trī) *v.* **tried** (trīd), **try•ing, tries** (trīz). *—tr.* **1.** To make an effort (to do or accomplish something); attempt: *Try to understand.* **2.** To taste, sample, or otherwise test in order to determine something, such as quality: *Let's try the pasta dish.* **3.a.** To examine or hear (a case) in a court of law. **b.** To put (an accused person) on trial in a court. **4.** To subject to great strain or hardship; tax: *a task that tried his strength.* **5.** To melt (fat, for example) to separate out impurities; render. *—intr.* To make an effort; strive. *—n., pl.* **tries** (trīz). An attempt; an effort. ***—idioms.*** **try on.** To put on (a garment) to test its fit: *tried on the pants in the dressing room.* **try (one's) hand.** To attempt to do something for the first time: *thought he would try his hand at making an omelette.* **try out. 1.** To undergo a competitive qualifying test, as for a job or athletic team: *I wanted to try out for the basketball team.* **2.** To test or use experimentally: *tried out her new showshoes.* [First written down before 1325 in Middle English and spelled *trien*, from Old French *trier*, to pick out.] —See Note.

try•ing (trī′ĭng) *adj.* Causing strain, hardship, or distress: *trying circumstances.*

try•out (trī′out′) *n.* A test to evaluate or find out qualifications of applicants, as for a theatrical role.

try•pan•o•some (trĭ păn′ə sōm′) *n.* Any of various parasitic protozoans that are carried into the bloodstream of human beings and other animals by the bite of certain insects and that can cause serious diseases such as sleeping sickness.

tryp•sin (trĭp′sĭn) *n.* An enzyme of pancreatic juice that breaks down proteins.

try square *n.* A carpenter's tool consisting of a straightedge set at right angles to a straight bar, used for measuring and marking square work.

tryst (trĭst) *n.* **1.** An agreement, as between lovers, to meet at a certain time and place. **2.** The meeting or meeting place so arranged.

tsar (zär *or* tsär) *n.* Variant of **czar** (sense 1).

tsetse fly (tsĕt′sē *or* tsē′tsē) *n.* Any of several bloodsucking African flies that carry and transmit by their bite the protozoans that cause sleeping sickness.

T-shirt also **tee shirt** (tē′shûrt′) *n.* A short-sleeved collarless shirt or undershirt.

tsp. or **tsp** *abbr.* An abbreviation of: **1.** Teaspoon. **2.** Teaspoonful.

T-square (tē′skwâr′) *n.* A ruler with a short crosspiece at one end, used for drawing parallel lines.

tsu•na•mi (tso͝o nä′mē) *n., pl.* **tsu•na•mis.** A very large ocean wave that is caused by an underwater earthquake or volcanic eruption and often causes extreme destruction when it strikes land. [First written down in 1904 in Modern English, from Japanese.]

Tu. *abbr.* An abbreviation of Tuesday.

tu•a•ta•ra (to͞o′ə tär′ə) *n.* A reptile of New Zealand that resembles a lizard and is the only living member of a group that flourished during the time of the dinosaurs. [First written down in 1820 in Modern English, from Maori *tuatàra.*]

tub (tŭb) *n.* **1.** An open, flat-bottomed, usually round container used for washing, packing, or storing. **2.** The amount that such a container can hold. **3.** A bathtub. [First written down in 1384 in Middle English and spelled *tobbe*, from Middle Dutch or Middle Low German *tubbe.*]

tu•ba (to͞o′bə *or* tyo͞o′bə) *n.* A large brass instrument having a bass range and several valves to change its pitch. [First written down in 1852 in Modern English, from Latin *tuba*, trumpet.]

tub•by (tŭb′ē) *adj.* **tub•bi•er, tub•bi•est.** Short and fat.

tube (to͞ob *or* tyo͞ob) *n.* **1.** A hollow cylinder, especially one that conveys a fluid or functions as a passage. **2.** An organ of the body having the shape or function of a tube: *the bronchial tubes.* **3.** A small flexible container with a screw cap at one end, used for holding toothpaste and similar substances that can be squeezed out. **4.** The part of a wind instrument that extends from the mouthpiece to the end that is open to the air. **5.** *Chiefly British.* A subway. **6.** An inner tube. **7.** *Slang.* Television. [First written down in 1611 in Modern English, from Latin *tubus.*] **—tube′less** *adj.*

tube•less tire (to͞ob′lĭs *or* tyo͞ob′lĭs) *n.* A tire, as for an automobile, in which the air is contained between the body of the tire itself and the rim on which it is mounted, with no inner tube.

tu•ber (to͞o′bər *or* tyo͞o′bər) *n.* A swollen, usually underground stem, such as a potato, bearing buds from which new plants grow. [First written down in 1668 in Modern English, from Latin *tūber*, lump.]

tu•ber•cle (to͞o′bər kəl *or* tyo͞o′bər kəl) *n.* **1.** A small swelling, as on the roots of certain plants or on skin or a bone. **2.** A swelling of this kind caused by tuberculosis.

tu•ber•cu•lar (to͝o bûr′kyə lər *or* tyo͝o bûr′kyə lər) *adj.* **1.** Of, relating to, or covered with tubercles. **2.** Of, relating to, or affected with tuberculosis. *—n.* A person having tuberculosis.

tu•ber•cu•late (to͝o bûr′kyə lĭt′ *or* tyo͝o bûr′kyə lĭt) *adj.* Tubercular.

tu•ber•cu•lin (to͝o bûr′kyə lĭn *or* tyo͝o bûr′kyə lĭn) *n.* A liquid derived from cultures of the bacteria that cause tuberculosis, used in testing for the disease.

tu•ber•cu•lo•sis (to͝o bûr′kyə lō′sĭs *or* tyo͝o bûr′kyə lō′sĭs) *n.* **1.** An infectious disease of human beings and animals, caused by bacteria and producing lesions of the lungs, bones, and other body tissues. **2.** Tuberculosis of the lungs.

tu•ber•cu•lous (to͝o bûr′kyə ləs *or* tyo͝o bûr′kyə ləs) *adj.* Of, having, or caused by tuberculosis or tubercles.

tube•rose (to͞ob′rōz′ *or* tyo͞ob′rō′) *n.* A Mexican plant having a tuberous root and highly fragrant white flowers.

tu•ber•ous (to͞o′bər əs *or* tyo͞o′bər əs) *adj.* Producing, consisting of, or resembling a tuber: *tuberous roots.*

tub•ing (to͞o′bĭng *or* tyo͞o′bĭng) *n.* **1.** Tubes considered as a group. **2.** A system of tubes. **3.** A piece or length of tube.

Tub•man (tŭb′mən), **Harriet.** 1820?–1913. American abolitionist who escaped from slavery in 1849 and became the most famous conductor on the Underground Railroad, leading more than 300 slaves to freedom. —SEE NOTE.

tu•bu•lar (to͞o′byə lər *or* tyo͞o′byə lər) *adj.* **1.** Of or relating to a tube. **2.** Made of or being tubes or a tube. **3.** Shaped like a tube.

tu•bule (to͞o′byo͞ol *or* tyo͞o′byo͞ol) *n.* A very small tube or tubular structure.

tuck (tŭk) *v.* **tucked, tuck•ing, tucks.** *—tr.* **1.** To make a fold or folds in. **2.** To gather up and fold or turn under in order to secure or confine: *He tucked the shirt into his trousers.* **3.** To cover or wrap snugly: *tucked in the baby and turned off the light.* **4.a.** To put in an out-of-the-way and snug place: *a cabin tucked among the pines.* **b.** To store in a safe spot; save: *tuck away a bit of lace.* *—intr.* To make tucks. *—n.* **1.** The act of tucking. **2.** A flattened pleat or fold, especially a narrow one stitched in place. [First written down in 1440 in Middle English and spelled *tukken*, possibly from Middle Low German or Middle Dutch *tocken, tucken.*]

tuck•er[1] (tŭk′ər) *n.* **1.** A person or thing that tucks, especially an attachment on a sewing machine for making tucks. **2.** A piece of lace, linen, or other material formerly worn by women around the neck and shoulders.

tuck•er[2] (tŭk′ər) *tr.v.* **tuck•ered, tuck•er•ing, tuck•ers.** *Informal.* To make weary; exhaust: *The long climb up the hill tuckered him out.* [First written down in 1833 in American English.]

Tuc•son (to͞o′sŏn′). A city of southeast Arizona south-southeast of Phoenix. A Spanish mission was founded nearby in 1700, and the present city was first settled in 1775. Population, 405,390.

Tudor[1] (to͞o′dər *or* tyo͞o′dər). English ruling dynasty (1485–1603).

Tu•dor[2] (to͞o′dər *or* tyo͞o′dər) *adj.* **1.** Of or relating to the royal house of Tudor. **2.** Of, relating to, or characteristic of the period of the Tudors, especially in architectural style.

Tues•day (to͞oz′dē *or* to͞oz′dā′ *or* tyo͞oz′dē *or* tyo͞oz′dā′) *n.* The third day of the week.

tu•fa (to͞o′fə *or* tyo͞o′fə) *n.* **1.** The rock material, rich in calcium and silicon, deposited by lakes, springs, or ground water. **2.** Tuff.

tuff (tŭf) *n.* A rock made up of particles of volcanic ash, varying in size from fine sand to coarse gravel.
❑ *These sound alike:* **tuff, tough** (rugged).

tuft (tŭft) *n.* A short cluster of strands, as of hair, grass, or yarn, attached at the base or growing close together. *—tr.v.* **tuft•ed, tuft•ing, tufts. 1.** To decorate or supply with a tuft or tufts. **2.** To pass threads through the layers of (a quilt, a mattress, or upholstery), securing the thread ends with a knot or button.

tug (tŭg) *v.* **tugged, tug•ging, tugs.** *—tr.* **1.** To pull at vigorously; strain at: *The puppy was tugging the leash.* **2.** To move by pulling with great effort or exertion; drag: *I tugged a chair across the room.* See Synonyms at **pull. 3.** To tow by a tugboat. *—intr.* To pull hard: *kept tugging until the boot came off.* *—n.* **1.** A strong pull or pulling force. **2.** A tugboat. [First written down before 1200 in Middle English and spelled *toggen*, from Old English *tēon.*]

tug•boat (tŭg′bōt′) *n.* A small powerful boat designed for towing or pushing larger vessels.

Harriet Tubman

Harriet Tubman

Born and raised a slave on a Maryland plantation, Harriet **Tubman** was the most famous and successful of conductors on the Underground Railroad, leading over 300 slaves to freedom in the North and Canada. Harriet Tubman left her family in 1849 to escape to freedom in the North. Over the next 12 years she returned at least 19 times to lead other slaves along similar routes, successfully evading bounty hunters seeking the often huge rewards for her capture. Among the many slaves Tubman conducted to the North were her own parents, in 1857. At the outbreak of the Civil War, Tubman was commissioned by the Union to work among the wounded soldiers in the South as a nurse, scout, and spy. In this position, Tubman was able to gain information about rebel supplies and sources of ammunition, which proved valuable in several Union raids on coastal areas in the Carolinas.

ă	pat	oi	boy
ā	pay	ou	out
âr	care	o͝o	took
ä	father	o͞o	boot
ĕ	pet	ŭ	cut
ē	be	ûr	urge
ĭ	pit	th	thin
ī	pie	*th*	this
îr	pier	hw	whoop
ŏ	pot	zh	vision
ō	toe	ə	about
ô	paw	N	*French* bon

tulip

tumbleweed

tumbrel

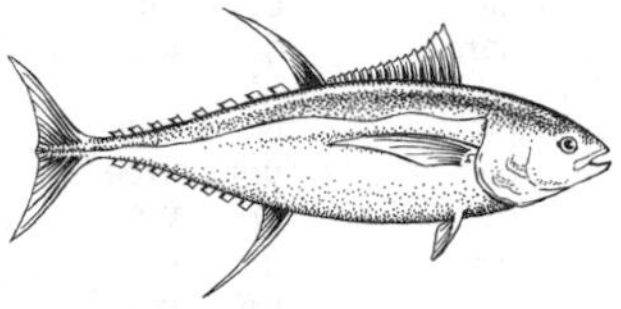

tuna¹
Yellowfin tuna

tug of war *n., pl.* **tugs of war.** A contest of strength in which two teams tug on opposite ends of a rope, each trying to pull the other across a dividing line.

tu•i•tion (to͞o **ĭsh′**ən *or* tyo͞o **ĭsh′**ən) *n.* **1.** A fee for instruction, especially at a college or private school. **2.** Instruction; teaching.

tu•la•re•mi•a (to͞o′lə **rē′**mē ə *or* tyo͞o′lə **rē′**mē ə) *n.* An infectious disease of rodents and other small mammals, caused by bacteria and transmitted to human beings through the bite of various insects or contact with infected animals.

tu•lip (**to͞o′**lĭp *or* **tyo͞o′**lĭp) *n.* **1.** The colorful cup-shaped flower of any of several plants that grow from a bulb. **2.** A plant that bears such a flower. [First written down in 1578 in Modern English, from Turkish *tülbend*, muslin, gauze.]

tulle (to͞ol) *n.* A fine, often starched net used especially for veils, gowns, and tutus.
❑ *These sound alike:* **tulle, tool** (device).

Tul•sa (**tŭl′**sə). A city of northeast Oklahoma northeast of Oklahoma City. Population, 367,302.

tum•ble (**tŭm′**bəl) *v.* **tum•bled, tum•bling, tum•bles.** —*intr.* **1.** To perform acrobatic feats, such as somersaults, rolls, or twists. **2.** To fall or roll end over end: *The kittens tumbled over each other.* **3.** To spill or roll out in confusion or disorder: *Schoolchildren tumbled out of the bus.* **4.** To pitch headlong; fall: *He tumbled on the ice.* **5.** To drop: *Prices tumbled.* **6.** To collapse: *The tower of blocks tumbled down.* —*tr.* **1.** To cause to fall; bring down. **2.** To put, spill, or toss haphazardly: *tumbling logs out of a truck.* —*n.* **1.** An act of tumbling; a fall. **2.** Confusion; disorder. [First written down before 1300 in Middle English and spelled *tumblen*, from Old English *tumbian*, to dance about.]

tum•ble•down (**tŭm′**bəl doun′) *adj.* Being in such bad repair as to seem in danger of collapsing; very rickety: *a tumbledown shack.*

tum•bler (**tŭm′**blər) *n.* **1.** An acrobat or a gymnast who tumbles. **2.** A drinking glass having no handle or stem. **3.** The part in a lock that releases the bolt when turned by a key. **4.** The drum of a clothes dryer.

tum•ble•weed (**tŭm′**bəl wēd′) *n.* Any of various densely branched plants that break off from the roots at the end of the growing season and are rolled about by the wind.

tum•bling (**tŭm′**blĭng) *n.* Gymnastics, such as somersaults and handsprings, performed without specialized equipment.

tum•brel or **tum•bril** (**tŭm′**brəl) *n.* **1.** A two-wheeled cart, especially a farmer's cart that can be tilted to dump a load. **2.** A cart used to carry condemned prisoners to their execution, as during the French Revolution.

tu•mes•cence (to͞o **mĕs′**əns *or* tyo͞o **mĕs′**əns) *n.* **1.** A swelling or an enlarging. **2.** A swollen condition.

tu•mes•cent (to͞o **mĕs′**ənt *or* tyo͞o **mĕs′**ənt) *adj.* Swollen or becoming swollen.

tu•mid (**to͞o′**mĭd *or* **tyo͞o′**mĭd) *adj.* Swollen or distended.

tum•my (**tŭm′**ē) *n., pl.* **tum•mies.** *Informal.* The human stomach or belly.

tu•mor (**to͞o′**mər *or* **tyo͞o′**mər) *n.* A growth of tissue having an abnormal structure and rate of growth and serving no function within the body. [First written down before 1425 in Middle English and spelled *tumour*, from Latin *tumor*, a swelling, from *tumēre*, to swell.]

tu•mult (**to͞o′**mŭlt′ *or* **tyo͞o′**mŭlt′) *n.* **1.** The din and commotion of a great crowd. **2.** A disorderly commotion or disturbance. **3.** Agitation of the mind or emotions.

tu•mul•tu•ous (to͞o **mŭl′**cho͞o əs *or* tyo͞o **mŭl′**cho͞o əs) *adj.* Characterized by tumult; noisy and disorderly: *a tumultuous crowd.*

tun (tŭn) *n.* **1.** A large cask for liquids, especially wine. **2.** A measure of liquid capacity, especially one equal to approximately 252 gallons (954 liters).
❑ *These sound alike:* **tun, ton** (weight unit).

tu•na¹ (**to͞o′**nə) *n., pl.* **tuna** or **tu•nas. 1.a.** Any of various often large ocean fishes, such as the albacore, that have greatly reduced or absent scales. Many kinds of tuna are important sources of canned fish. **b.** Any of several related food fishes, such as the bonito. **2.** The edible flesh of tuna, often canned or processed. [First written down in 1881 in American English, from Arabic *at-tūn*, from Latin *thunnus*.]

tu•na² (**to͞o′**nə) *n.* Any of several spiny tropical American cacti related to the prickly pear. [First written down in 1555 in Modern English, from Taino.]

tun•a•ble also **tune•a•ble** (**to͞o′**nə bəl *or* **tyo͞o′**nə bəl) *adj.* Capable of being tuned: *a tunable wind instrument.*

tun•dra (**tŭn′**drə) *n.* A cold treeless area of arctic regions, having permanently frozen subsoil and only low-growing mosses, lichens, and stunted shrubs as plant life.

tune (to͞on *or* tyo͞on) *n.* **1.** A melody, especially a simple and easily remembered one. **2.a.** Correct musical pitch. **b.** Agreement in musical pitch or key: *a piano soloist and orchestra not in tune.* **3.** Agreement or harmony: *ideas in tune with the times.* —*tr. v.* **tuned, tun•ing, tunes. 1.** To put in proper musical pitch: *tune a guitar.* **2.** To adjust (an engine, for example) for top performance. **3.** To adjust (a radio, for example) to a desired frequency. ***—idioms.*** **to the tune of.** To the sum or extent of: *paid extra for the tickets to the tune of 20 dollars each.* **tune in.** To adjust an electronic receiver to receive signals at a particular frequency or to receive a desired program. **tune out.** To adjust an electronic receiver so as not to receive a particular signal. [First written down before 1325 in Middle English, variant of *tone*, tone.]

tune•a•ble (**to͞o′**nə bəl *or* **tyo͞o′**nə bəl) *adj.* Variant of **tunable.**

tune•ful (**to͞on′**fəl *or* **tyo͞on′**fəl) *adj.* Full of tune; melodious. —**tune′ful•ly** *adv.*

tun•er (**to͞o′**nər *or* **tyo͞o′**nər) *n.* **1.** A person or thing that tunes: *a piano tuner.* **2.** A device for tuning, especially an electronic circuit or device used to select signals at a specific radio frequency for amplification and conversion to sound.

tune-up (**to͞on′**ŭp′ *or* **tyo͞on′**ŭp′) *n.* An adjustment, as of a motor or an engine, made to improve working order or efficiency.

tung oil (tŭng) *n.* A yellowish or brownish oil extracted from the seeds of an Asian tree and used as a drying agent in paints and varnishes and for waterproofing.

tung•sten (**tŭng′**stən) *n. Symbol* **W** A hard gray to white metallic element that is very resistant to corrosion and high temperatures. It is used in making electric light-bulb filaments, surgical instruments, and solar energy devices. Atomic number 74. See table at **element.**

tu•nic (**to͞o′**nĭk *or* **tyo͞o′**nĭk) *n.* **1.** A loose-fitting, knee-length garment worn in ancient Greece and Rome. **2.** A long, plain military jacket, usually having a high stiff collar. **3.** A short pleated and belted dress worn by women for some sports.

tun•ing fork (**to͞o′**nĭng *or* **tyo͞o′**nĭng) *n.* A small two-pronged metal device that when struck produces a tone of fixed pitch that is used as a reference, as in tuning musical instruments.

Tu•nis (**to͞o′**nĭs *or* **tyo͞o′**nĭs). The capital and largest city of Tunisia, in the northern part of the country on the **Gulf of Tunis**, an inlet of the Mediterranean Sea. Population, 550,404.

Tu•ni•sia (tōō **nē′**zhə *or* tyōō **nē′**zhə). A country of northern Africa on the Mediterranean Sea between Algeria and Libya. It gained its independence from France in 1956. Tunis is the capital and the largest city. Population, 5,588,209.

tun•nel (tŭn′əl) *n.* **1.** An underground or underwater passage. **2.** A passage through or under a barrier. *—v.* **tun•neled, tun•nel•ing, tun•nels** or **tun•nelled, tun•nel•ling, tun•nels.** *—tr.* **1.** To make a tunnel under or through: *tunneling the granite.* **2.** To produce, shape, or dig in the form of a tunnel: *tunnel a passage under a wall.* *—intr.* To make a tunnel: *tunneled under the harbor.*

tun•ny (tŭn′ē) *n., pl.* **tunny** or **tun•nies.** Any of various large ocean fishes, such as the albacore, that have greatly reduced or absent scales; tuna.

tu•pe•lo (tōō′pə lō′ *or* tyōō′pə lō′) *n., pl.* **tu•pe•los. 1.** Any of several trees having bluish-black berries and soft light wood. **2.** The wood of such a tree.

Tu•pi (tōō′pē *or* tōō **pē′**) *n., pl.* **Tupi** or **Tu•pis. 1.** A member of any of a group of Native American peoples living along the coast of Brazil, in the Amazon River valley, and in Paraguay. **2.** The language of the Tupi. **—Tu′pi•an** *adj.*

tur•ban (tûr′bən) *n.* **1.** A traditionally Muslim headdress consisting of a long scarf of cotton, linen, or silk, that is wound around a small cap or directly around the head. **2.** A similar headdress or hat. [First written down in 1561 in Modern English and spelled *tolipane*, from Turkish *tülbend*, muslin, gauze.]

tur•bid (tûr′bĭd) *adj.* **1.** Having sediment or foreign particles stirred up or suspended: *turbid water.* **2.** Heavy, dark, or dense: *turbid smoke.* **3.** In a state of turmoil; muddled: *turbid feelings.* **—tur′bid•ness, tur•bid′i•ty** *n.*

tur•bine (tûr′bĭn *or* tûr′bīn′) *n.* Any of various machines in which the kinetic energy of a moving fluid is converted to rotary motion as the fluid pushes against a series of vanes or paddles arranged about the circumference of one or more wheels.

tur•bo•charg•er (tûr′bō chär′jər) *n.* A device that uses the exhaust gas of an internal-combustion engine to drive a turbine that in turn drives a supercharger attached to the engine.

tur•bo•jet (tûr′bō jĕt′) *n.* **1.** A jet engine in which the exhaust gas operates a turbine that in turn drives a compressor that forces air into the intake of the engine. **2.** An aircraft powered by an engine or engines of this type.

tur•bo•prop (tûr′bō prŏp′) *n.* **1.** A turbojet engine that drives an external propeller as well as producing jet propulsion. **2.** An aircraft powered by an engine or engines of this type.

tur•bot (tûr′bət) *n., pl.* **turbot** or **tur•bots.** A European flatfish that has a brown knobby upper surface and is highly regarded as food.

tur•bu•lence (tûr′byə ləns) *n.* **1.** The state or quality of being turbulent. **2.** Turbulent flow. **3.** An eddying motion of the atmosphere that interrupts the flow of wind.

tur•bu•lent (tûr′byə lənt) *adj.* **1.** Violently agitated or disturbed: *turbulent waters.* **2.** Causing unrest or disturbance. [First written down before 1425 in Middle English, from Latin *turbulentus*, from *turba*, turmoil.]

turbulent flow *n.* Movement of a fluid in which the pressure and velocity in any small region of the fluid fluctuate at random.

tu•reen (tōō **rēn′** *or* tyōō **rēn′**) *n.* A broad deep dish with a cover, used for serving soups or stews at the table.

turf (tûrf) *n., pl.* **turfs** also **turves** (tûrvz). **1.a.** A surface layer of earth containing a dense growth of grass and its matted roots; sod. **b.** An artificial substitute for such a grassy layer, as on a playing field. **2.** A piece cut from a layer of earth or sod. **3.** A piece of peat that is burned for use as fuel. **4.** *Slang.* The area claimed by a neighborhood gang as its territory. **5.a.** A racetrack. **b.** The sport or business of horse racing. [First written down before 800 in Old English.]

tur•gid (tûr′jĭd) *adj.* **1.** Excessively ornate or complex in style or language: *The description runs on for 20 turgid pages.* **2.** Swollen or distended, as by a fluid or inner pressure. **—tur•gid′i•ty, tur′gid•ness** *n.* **—tur′gid•ly** *adv.*

Turk (tûrk) *n.* A native or inhabitant of Turkey.

tur•key (tûr′kē) *n., pl.* **tur•keys. 1.** A large, brownish North American bird having a bare head and neck with fleshy wattles. It is widely domesticated as a source of food. **2.** The meat of a turkey.

Tur•key (tûr′kē). A country of southwest Asia and southeast Europe between the Mediterranean Sea and the Black Sea. It is one of the oldest inhabited regions in the world. Ankara is the capital and Istanbul the largest city. Population, 44,736,957.

turkey vulture *n.* An American vulture having dark feathers and a bare red head and neck.

Turk•ic (tûr′kĭk) *n.* A group of languages related to Turkish. *—adj.* Of or relating to Turkic or the peoples who speak these languages.

Turk•ish (tûr′kĭsh) *adj.* Of or relating to Turkey or its peoples, languages, or cultures. *—n.* The language of the Turks, used mainly in Turkey, Cyprus, and the Balkan States.

Turk•men•i•stan (tûrk′mĕn ĭ **stăn′** *or* tûrk′-mĕn ĭ **stän′**). A region of west-central Asia east of the Caspian Sea. It has been inhabited since the tenth century. Turkmenistan was part of the Soviet Union from 1925 to 1991. Capital, Ashkabad. Population, 3,189,000.

tur•mer•ic (tûr′mər ĭk) *n.* **1.** A yellowish spicy powder obtained from the root of an Asian plant, used as a seasoning, especially in curries. **2.** The plant that yields such powder. [First written down before 1425 in Middle English and spelled *termeryte*, from Old French *terre-merite*, saffron : Latin *terra*, earth + Latin *merita*, deserving.]

tur•moil (tûr′moil′) *n.* A state of extreme confusion or agitation; commotion or tumult: *a country in turmoil over labor strikes.*

turn (tûrn) *v.* **turned, turn•ing, turns.** *—tr.* **1.** To cause to move around an axis or a center; cause to rotate or revolve. **2.** To cause to move around in order to achieve a result, such as opening or loosening: *turn the key; turn a screw.* **3.** To perform or accomplish by rotating or revolving: *turn a somersault.* **4.** To change the position of so that the underside becomes the upper side: *turn a page.* **5.** To give a rounded form to (wood, for example) by rotating against a cutting tool. **6.** To change the position of by moving in an arc of a circle; pivot: *turned his chair toward the speaker.* **7.a.** To fold, bend, or twist (something). **b.** To injure by twisting: *turn an ankle.* **c.** To upset or make nauseated: *That story turns my stomach.* **8.** To change the direction or course of: *turn the car to the left.* **9.** To make a course around or about: *turn a corner.* **10.** To present in a specified direction: *turn one's face to the wall.* **11.** To aim or focus; train: *turn one's gaze to the sky.* **12.** To cause to act or go against; make opposed: *News of the scandal turned public opinion against the candidate.* **13.** To cause to change; transform: *Autumn turns the green leaves golden.* **14.** To get by buying and selling: *turn a fair profit.* *—intr.* **1.** To move around an axis or a center; ro-

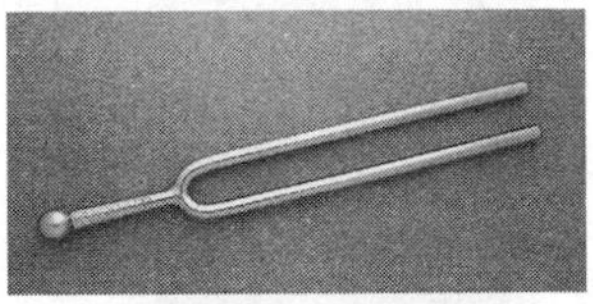

tuning fork

turban

turkey vulture

ă	pat	oi	boy
ā	pay	ou	out
âr	care	ŏŏ	took
ä	father	ōō	boot
ĕ	pet	ŭ	cut
ē	be	ûr	urge
ĭ	pit	th	thin
ī	pie	*th*	this
îr	pier	hw	whoop
ŏ	pot	zh	vision
ō	toe	ə	about
ô	paw	N	*French* bon

turnstile

turtle
Florida box turtle

turtleneck

tusk
Bull walrus

tate or revolve: *How fast is the wheel turning?* **2.** To have a sensation of revolving or whirling, especially as a result of dizziness or giddiness. **3.** To change position from side to side or back and forth: *I tossed and turned all night.* **4.** To progress through pages so as to arrive at a given place: *Please turn to page 361.* **5.** To direct one's way or course: *The truck turned into the service station.* **6.** To change or reverse one's way, course, or direction: *Too tired to go farther, we turned and went home.* **7.** To have a specific reaction or effect, especially when adverse: *The milk turned sour.* **8.** To become hostile or opposed: *The peasants turned against the cruel king.* **9.** To direct one's attention, interest, or thought toward or away from something: *Let's turn to another subject.* **10.** To have recourse to a person or thing for help, support, or information: *You can always turn to your parents.* **11.a.** To change so as to be; become: *His hair turned gray. The night turned into day.* **b.** To reach and pass (a certain age, for example): *My niece has turned three.* **12.** To change color: *The leaves have turned.* —*n.* **1.** The act of turning or the condition of being turned; rotation or revolution. **2.** A change of direction, motion, or position: *Make a left turn at the corner.* **3.** A curve, as in a road or path: *a sharp turn in the road.* **4.** A departure or change, as in a trend: *a strange turn of events.* **5.** One of a series of opportunities that occur in succession or in scheduled order: *waiting for her turn at bat.* **6.** A movement or development in a particular direction: *a turn for the worse.* **7.** A deed or an action having a good or bad effect on another: *She did me a good turn.* **8.** A winding of one thing about another. ***—idioms.*** **at every turn.** In every place; at every moment. **in turn.** In the proper order or sequence. **out of turn.** Not in the proper order or sequence. **turn away.** To send away; dismiss: *turned away the canvassers who came to the door.* **turn back. 1.** To reverse one's direction of motion: *stopped on the road and had to turn back.* **2.** To fold down: *turned back the covers before getting into bed.* **turn down. 1.** To lessen the speed, volume, intensity, or flow of: *I turned down the radio.* **2.** To reject or refuse, as a person, advice, or a suggestion: *was turned down for the job.* **3.** To fold or be capable of folding down: *turn down the bed.* **turn in. 1.** To hand in; give over: *She turned in her keys at the end of the lease.* **2.** To inform on or deliver: *One of his classmates found out he was cheating and turned him in.* **3.** *Informal.* To go to bed: *She was tired and so decided to turn in.* **turn off. 1.** To stop the operation, activity, or flow of; shut off: *Turn off the TV.* **2.** *Slang.* To affect with dislike, displeasure, or revulsion: *Brussels sprouts really turn me off.* **turn on. 1.** To cause to begin the operation, activity, or flow of: *Turn on the porch light.* **2.** To begin to display or use: *a politician who knows how to turn on the charm.* **turn out. 1.** To arrive or assemble, as for a public event or entertainment: *A good crowd turned out for the picnic.* **2.** To end up; result: *The cake turned out beautifully.* **3.** To evict; expel: *They were turned out of the apartment when the lease was up.* **turn over. 1.** To change the position of so that the bottom is on top or the top is on bottom. **2.** To shift one's position by rolling from one side to the other. **3.** To think about; consider: *turning over the lecture in my mind.* **4.** To transfer to another; surrender: *turned over the keys to a more experienced driver.* **turn up. 1.** To increase the speed, volume, intensity, or flow of: *Turn up the radio so we can hear the news.* **2.** To find: *Our investigation turned up several clues.* **3.** To be found: *A stray kitten turned up on our doorstep one morning.* **4.** To make an appearance; arrive: *He turned up just in time for supper.* [First written down about 1000 in Old English and spelled *turnian, tyrnan*, from Latin *tornāre*, to turn in a lathe.]

❑ *These sound alike:* **turn, tern** (sea bird).

Synonyms: turn, rotate, spin, whirl, swirl. These verbs all mean to move or cause to move in a circle. **Turn** is the most general: *The boy in front of me turned and stared at my desk.* **Rotate** means to move around an axis or a center: *The top rotated with decreasing speed and finally fell over.* **Spin** means to rotate rapidly, often within a narrow space: *The sheets were spinning in the clothes dryer.* **Whirl** means to rotate or turn rapidly or forcefully: *They saw the whirling snowflakes and knew the blizzard had started.* **Swirl** often means to move rapidly in a circle: *Flood waters swirled wildly under the bridge.*

turn•a•round (tûrn′ə round′) *n.* **1.** A space, as in a driveway, permitting the turning around of a vehicle. **2.** A reversal: *a turnaround in stock prices.*

turn•buck•le (tûrn′bŭk′əl) *n.* A device for adjusting the tension of a rope or cable, consisting of an oblong center section with threaded holes at the ends that receive threaded rods to which the ends of the rope or cable are fastened.

turn•coat (tûrn′kōt′) *n.* A person who goes over to the opposite party; a traitor.

Tur•ner (tûr′nər), **Nat.** 1800–1831. American slave leader who led a rebellion in Virginia, killing about 50 whites (1831). He was captured and executed.

tur•nip (tûr′nĭp) *n.* **1.** A plant having a large edible yellowish or white root. **2.** The root of this plant, eaten as a vegetable.

turn•key (tûrn′kē′) *n., pl.* **turn•keys.** The keeper of the keys in a prison; a jailer.

turn•off (tûrn′ôf′ *or* tûrn′ŏf′) *n.* A branch of a road or path leading away from a main thoroughfare, especially an exit on a highway.

turn•out (tûrn′out′) *n.* **1.** The number of people at a gathering; attendance: *a great turnout for the picnic.* **2.** A number of things produced; output: *The factory increased its turnout.* **3.** The act or an instance of turning out.

turn•o•ver (tûrn′ō′vər) *n.* **1.** The act of turning over; an upset. **2.** An abrupt change; a reversal: *a turnover in public opinion.* **3.** A small pastry made by spreading a filling on half of a piece of dough, turning the other half over the filling, and sealing the edges. **4.** The number of times a particular stock of goods is sold and restocked during a given period. **5.** The amount of business transacted during a given period. **6.** The number of workers hired by an establishment to replace those who have left in a given period of time. **7.** In sports, a loss of possession of the ball to the opposing team, as by a misplay or a violation of the rules.

turn•pike (tûrn′pīk′) *n.* A toll road, especially an expressway with tollgates.

turn•stile (tûrn′stīl′) *n.* A device for controlling or counting the number of persons entering a public area by admitting them one at a time between horizontal bars revolving on a post.

turn•ta•ble (tûrn′tā′bəl) *n.* **1.a.** The rotating circular platform of a phonograph on which the record is placed. **b.** A phonograph without amplifiers or loudspeakers. **2.** A circular platform equipped with a railway track and capable of rotating, used for turning locomotives. **3.** A rotating platform or disk, such as a lazy Susan.

tur•pen•tine (tûr′pən tīn′) *n.* **1.** A thin, easily vaporized oil composed of carbon and hydrogen and having the formula $C_{10}H_{16}$. It is distilled from the wood or resin of certain pine trees and used as a paint thinner, solvent, and liniment. **2.** The sticky mixture of resin and oil from which this oil is distilled.

tur•pi•tude (tûr′pĭ to͞od′ *or* tûr′pĭ tyo͞od′) *n.* Baseness; depravity.

tur•quoise (tûr′kwoiz′ *or* tûr′koiz′) *n.* **1.** A bluish-green mineral containing aluminum and copper, valued in certain of its forms as a gem. **2.** A light to brilliant bluish green. [First written down before 1398 in Middle English and spelled *turkeis*, from Old French *(pierre) turqueise*, Turkish (stone), turquoise.] **—tur′quoise′** *adj.*

tur•ret (tûr′ĭt *or* tŭr′ĭt) *n.* **1.** A small tower or tower-shaped projection on a building. **2.** A low, usually rotating structure containing guns, as on a tank or warship. **3.** An attachment for a lathe consisting of a rotating cylinder holding various cutting tools. [First written down about 1300 in Middle English and spelled *turet*, from Old French *torete*, from *tor*, tower.]

tur•tle (tûr′tl) *n.* Any of various reptiles living either in water or on land and having a bony or leathery shell into which the head, legs, and tail can be pulled for protection. [First written down in 1657 in Modern English, perhaps from French *tortue*, from Old French.]

tur•tle•dove (tûr′tl dŭv′) *n.* A European dove having a white-edged tail and a soft purring voice.

tur•tle•neck (tûr′tl nĕk′) *n.* **1.** A high, tubular, turned-down collar that fits closely around the neck. **2.** A garment, such as a sweater, having such a collar.

turves (tûrvz) *n.* A plural of **turf**.

Tus•ca•ro•ra (tŭs′kə rôr′ə) *n., pl.* **Tuscarora** or **Tus•ca•ro•ras. 1.** A member of a Native American people formerly living in North Carolina and now living in western New York and southeast Ontario. The Tuscarora joined the Iroquois confederacy in 1722. **2.** The Iroquoian language of the Tuscarora.

tusk (tŭsk) *n.* **1.** A long pointed tooth, usually one of a pair, projecting outside of the mouth of certain animals, such as the elephant or walrus. **2.** A long projecting tooth or part similar to a tooth. [First written down before 899 in Old English and spelled *tūx, tūsc*, canine tooth.]

tus•sle (tŭs′əl) *intr.v.* **tus•sled, tus•sling, tus•sles.** To fight roughly; scuffle. *—n.* A rough or vigorous fight; a scuffle.

tus•sock (tŭs′ək) *n.* A clump or tuft, as of growing grass. [First written down in 1530 in Modern English.]

Tut•ankh•a•men (to͞ot′äng kä′mən). Flourished about 1358 B.C. King of Egypt during the XVIII Dynasty. His tomb was found almost intact in 1922.

tu•te•lage (to͞ot′l ĭj *or* tyo͞ot′l ĭj) *n.* **1.** The activity or capacity of a guardian; guardianship. **2.** The act or capacity of a tutor; instruction. **3.** The state of being under the direction of a guardian or tutor.

tu•tor (to͞o′tər *or* tyo͞o′tər) *n.* **1.** A private instructor. **2.** In law, the guardian of a minor and the minor's property. *—tr.v.* **tu•tored, tu•tor•ing, tu•tors.** To act as tutor to; instruct or teach privately: *tutored the boy in math.* [First written down before 1376 in Middle English and spelled *tutour*, from Latin *tūtor*, from *tuērī*, to guard.]

tu•to•ri•al (to͞o tôr′ē əl *or* tyo͞o tôr′ē əl) *adj.* Of or relating to a tutor or private instructor.

tut•ti-frut•ti (to͞o′tē fro͞o′tē) *n., pl.* **tut•ti-frut•tis.** A confection, especially ice cream, containing a variety of chopped and usually candied fruits. [First written down in 1834 in American English, from Italian : *tutti*, all + *frutti*, fruits.]

Tu•tu (to͞o′to͞o), **Desmond.** Born 1931. South African archbishop. An antiapartheid leader, he won the 1984 Nobel Peace Prize.

Tu•va•lu (to͞o vä′lo͞o *or* to͞o′və lo͞o′). An island country of the western Pacific Ocean north of Fiji. It gained its independence from Great Britain in 1978. Capital, Fongafale. Population, 7,349.

tux (tŭks) *n. Informal.* A tuxedo.

tux•e•do (tŭk sē′dō) *n., pl.* **tux•e•dos** or **tux•e•does.** A man's formal suit, including a usually black jacket with satin lapels, trousers, a bow tie, and often a cummerbund.

TV (tē′vē′) *n., pl.* **TVs** or **TV's.** Television.

TVA *abbr.* An abbreviation of Tennessee Valley Authority.

TV dinner *n.* A frozen prepared meal that only needs to be heated before serving.

twad•dle (twŏd′l) *intr.v.* **twad•dled, twad•dling, twad•dles.** To talk foolishly. *—n.* Foolish, trivial, or idle talk.

twain (twān) *n., adj., & pron.* Two.

Twain (twān), **Mark.** Samuel Langhorne Clemens.

twang (twăng) *v.* **twanged, twang•ing, twangs.** *—intr.* To emit a sharp vibrating sound, as the string of a musical instrument does when plucked. *—tr.* **1.** To cause to make a sharp vibrating sound. **2.** To utter with a strongly nasal tone of voice. *—n.* **1.** A sharp vibrating sound, as that of a plucked string. **2.** A stongly nasal tone of voice.

'twas (twŭz *or* twŏz; twəz *when unstressed*) Contraction of *it was.*

tweak (twēk) *tr.v.* **tweaked, tweak•ing, tweaks.** To pinch, pluck, or twist sharply: *He tweaked her nose playfully.* *—n.* A sharp twisting pinch.

tweed (twēd) *n.* **1.** A coarse woolen fabric made in a twill weave and used chiefly for casual suits and coats. **2. tweeds.** Clothes made of this fabric.

tweet (twēt) *n.* A weak chirping sound, as of a small bird. *—intr.v.* **tweet•ed, tweet•ing, tweets.** To utter a weak chirping sound.

tweet•er (twē′tər) *n.* A small loudspeaker designed to reproduce high-pitched sounds in a high-fidelity sound system.

tweez•ers (twē′zərz) *pl.n. (used with a singular or plural verb).* Small pincers used for plucking or handling small objects.

twelfth (twĕlfth) *n.* **1.** The ordinal number matching the number 12 in a series. **2.** One of 12 equal parts. **—twelfth** *adv. & adj.*

twelve (twĕlv) *n.* **1.** The number, written 12, that is equal to 11 + 1. **2.** The 12th in a set or sequence. [First written down before 899 in Old English and spelled *twelf.*] **—twelve** *adj. & pron.*

twelve•month (twĕlv′mŭnth′) *n.* A year.

twen•ti•eth (twĕn′tē ĭth *or* twŭn′tē ĭth) *n.* **1.** The ordinal number matching the number 20 in a series. **2.** One of 20 equal parts. **—twen′ti•eth** *adv. & adj.*

twen•ty (twĕn′tē *or* twŭn′tē) *n.* **1.** The number, written 20, that is equal to 2 × 10. **2.** The 20th in a set or sequence. [First written down before 899 in Old English and spelled *twēntig.*] **—twen′ty** *adj. & pron.*

twen•ty-one (twĕn′tē wŭn′ *or* twŭn′tē wŭn′) *n.* The game of blackjack.

twerp (twûrp) *n. Slang.* A person regarded as silly and contemptible.

twice (twīs) *adv.* **1.** In two cases or on two occasions; two times: *He saw the movie twice.* **2.** In doubled degree or amount: *She works twice as hard as her colleagues.*

twice-told (twīs′tōld′) *adj.* Very familiar because of repeated telling.

twid•dle (twĭd′l) *v.* **twid•dled, twid•dling, twid•dles.** *—tr.* To turn over or around idly or lightly; fiddle with. *—intr.* To trifle with something. *—n.* The act or an instance of twiddling. ***—idiom.*** **twiddle (one's) thumbs.** To do little or nothing; be idle.

twig (twĭg) *n.* A small branch or slender shoot of a

Tutankhamen
Gold portrait mask

Desmond Tutu

tuxedo

ă	pat	oi	boy
ā	pay	ou	out
âr	care	o͝o	took
ä	father	o͞o	boot
ĕ	pet	ŭ	cut
ē	be	ûr	urge
ĭ	pit	th	thin
ī	pie	*th*	this
îr	pier	hw	whoop
ŏ	pot	zh	vision
ō	toe	ə	about
ô	paw	N	*French* bon

Word Building: –ty

The suffix **–ty** forms nouns from adjectives. The word **subtlety**, for example, means "the quality or state of being subtle." **Subtlety** comes from the Latin noun *subtīlitās*, from the adjective *subtīlis* ("subtle") + *–tās*, the ancestor of our suffixes **–ty** and **–ity**. Some other words that end in **–ty** are: **certainty**, **cruelty**, **frailty**, **loyalty**, and **royalty**. In English the suffix **–ity** is now more common, as in **eccentricity**, **electricity**, **peculiarity**, **similarity**, and **technicality**. The suffixes **–ty** and **–ity** can be compared in meaning to the suffix **–ness**. Whereas **–ty** and **–ity** come from Latin, however, **–ness** comes from Old English.

John Tyler
Detail of an 1842 portrait by George Peter Alexander Healy (1813?–1894)

tree or shrub. [First written down about 950 in Old English and spelled *twigge*.]

twi•light (twīʹlīt′) *n.* **1.** The diffused light from the sky during the early evening or early morning when the sun is below the horizon. **2.** The interval of time during which the sun is just below the horizon; the period between sunset and night. **3.** A period or condition of decline following growth, glory, or success: *a man in the twilight of his life.*

twill (twĭl) *n.* **1.** A fabric having diagonal parallel ribs. **2.** A weave that produces diagonal ribs on the surface of a fabric. —*tr.v.* **twilled, twill•ing, twills.** To weave (cloth) so as to produce diagonal ribs.

twin (twĭn) *n.* **1.** One of two offspring born at the same birth. **2.** One of two identical or similar persons, animals, or things; a counterpart: *looking for a twin to a sock.* —*adj.* **1.** Being two or one of two offspring born at the same birth: *her twin sister; twin brothers.* **2.** Being two or one of two identical or similar persons, animals, or things: *a twin bed; twin cities.* [First written down about 1000 in Old English and spelled *twinn*, twofold.]

twine (twīn) *v.* **twined, twin•ing, twines.** —*tr.* **1.** To twist together (threads, for example); intertwine. **2.** To form by twisting or interlacing: *twine a garland.* **3.** To encircle or coil about: *A vine twined the fence.* —*intr.* **1.** To become twisted, interlaced, or interwoven. **2.** To go in a winding course: *a stream twining through the valley.* —*n.* A strong cord or string made of threads twisted together. [First written down before 1200 in Middle English and spelled *twinen*, from Old English *twīn*, double thread.]

twinge (twĭnj) *n.* **1.** A sudden and sharp physical pain. **2.** A mental or emotional pain. —*intr.v.* **twinged, twing•ing, twing•es.** To feel a twinge.

twin•kle (twĭngʹkəl) *intr.v.* **twin•kled, twin•kling, twin•kles.** **1.** To shine with slight intermittent gleams; sparkle: *stars twinkling in the sky.* **2.** To be bright or sparkling, as with merriment or delight: *Her eyes twinkle.* —*n.* **1.** A slight intermittent gleam of light; a glimmer. **2.** A sparkle of merriment or delight in the eye. **3.** A brief interval; a twinkling. [First written down before 899 in Old English and spelled *twinclian*.]

twin•kling (twĭngʹklĭng) *n.* **1.** The act of blinking. **2.** A blink or twinkle. **3.** The time that it takes to blink; an instant.

twirl (twûrl) *tr. & intr.v.* **twirled, twirl•ing, twirls.** To rotate or revolve briskly: *twirl a baton; pinwheels twirling in the wind.* —*n.* The act of twirling or the condition of being twirled; a sharp quick spin or whirl. —**twirlʹer** *n.*

twist (twĭst) *v.* **twist•ed, twist•ing, twists.** —*tr.* **1.a.** To wind together (threads, for example) so as to produce a single strand. **b.** To form in this manner: *twist a length of rope.* **2.** To wind or coil (rope, for example) about something. **3.** To turn so as to face another direction: *They twisted their heads around at the sound.* **4.** To form into a spiral, as by turning the ends in opposite directions: *twisting wire into a loop.* **5.a.** To turn or open by turning: *twisted off the bottle cap.* **b.** To pull, break, or snap by turning: *twist off a dead branch.* **6.** To injure by wrenching; sprain: *twist one's ankle.* **7.** To alter or distort the intended meaning of: *The prosecutor twisted the words of the witness.* —*intr.* **1.** To be or become twisted. **2.** To move or progress in a winding course; meander: *The river twisted toward the sea.* **3.** To squirm; writhe: *twist with pain.* —*n.* **1.** Something twisted or formed by twisting, as a length of yarn or cord. **2.** A sliver of citrus peel twisted over or dropped into a beverage for flavoring. **3.** The act of twisting or the condition of being twisted; a spin, twirl, or rotation. **4.** A change in direction; a turn: *a sharp twist in the path.* **5.** An unexpected change in a process or a departure from a pattern: *a story with a twist.* [First written down before 1200 in Middle English and spelled *tweasten*, from *twist*, a divided object, fork, rope, from Old English *twist*, rope.] —**twistʹa•ble** *adj.*

twist•er (twĭsʹtər) *n. Informal.* A tornado.

twit (twĭt) *tr.v.* **twit•ted, twit•ting, twits.** To taunt or tease, especially for mistakes or faults. —*n. Slang.* A person regarded as foolishly annoying.

twitch (twĭch) *v.* **twitched, twitch•ing, twitch•es.** —*intr.* To move with a jerk or spasm. —*tr.* To pull, jerk, or move sharply: *The bird twitched its tail.* —*n.* **1.** A sudden involuntary or spasmodic movement, as of a muscle. **2.** A sudden pull; a tug.

twit•ter (twĭtʹər) *v.* **twit•tered, twit•ter•ing, twit•ters.** —*intr.* **1.** To utter a series of light chirping sounds made by certain birds. **2.** To speak rapidly and softly. —*tr.* To utter or say with a twitter. —*n.* **1.** The light chirping sound made by certain birds. **2.** A similar sound, especially light speech or laughter. **3.** A state of agitation or excitement. [First written down about 1380 in Middle English and spelled *twiteren*, of imitative origin.]

two (to͞o) *n.* **1.** The number, written 2, that is equal to 1 + 1. **2.** The second in a set or sequence. [First written down about 725 in Old English and spelled *twā*.] —**two** *adj. & pron.*

❑ *These sound alike:* **two, to** (toward), **too** (also).

two-bit (to͞oʹbĭt′) *adj.* **1.** *Informal.* Costing or worth 25 cents. **2.** *Slang.* Worth very little; petty or insignificant.

two-by-four (to͞oʹbī fôr′) *adj.* Measuring two units by four units, especially inches. —*n.* A length of lumber that is 2 inches thick and 4 inches wide.

two-faced (to͞oʹfāst′) *adj.* **1.** Having two faces or surfaces. **2.** Hypocritical or double-dealing; deceitful.

two-ply (to͞oʹplī′) *adj.* **1.** Made of two interwoven layers. **2.** Consisting of two thicknesses or strands: *two-play yarn.*

two•some (to͞oʹsəm) *n.* **1.** Two people or things together; a pair or couple. **2.** A round of golf played by two people.

two-step (to͞oʹstĕp′) *n.* A ballroom dance in 2/4 time, characterized by long sliding steps.

two-time (to͞oʹtīm′) *tr.v.* **two-timed, two-tim•ing, two-times.** *Slang.* **1.** To be unfaithful to (a spouse or lover). **2.** To deceive; double-cross.

two-way (to͞oʹwā′) *adj.* **1.a.** Affording passage in two directions: *a two-way street.* **b.** Moving in two directions: *two-way traffic.* **2.** Permitting communication in two directions: *a two-way radio.*

–ty *suff.* A suffix that means condition or quality: *loyalty.* —SEE NOTE.

ty•coon (tī ko͞onʹ) *n.* A wealthy and powerful person in business or industry. [First written down in 1857 in Modern English, from Japanese *taikun*, title of a military leader.]

ty•ing (tīʹĭng) *v.* Present participle of **tie.**

tyke also **tike** (tīk) *n.* **1.** A small child. **2.** A mongrel dog.

Ty•ler (tīʹlər), **John.** 1790–1862. The 10th President of the United States (1841–1845).

tym•pa•na (tĭmʹpə nə) *n.* A plural of **tympanum.**

tym•pa•ni (tĭmʹpə nē) *pl.n.* Variant of **timpani.**

tym•pan•ic membrane (tĭm pănʹĭk) *n.* The eardrum.

tym•pa•num also **tim•pa•num** (tĭmʹpə nəm) *n., pl.* **tym•pa•na** (tĭmʹpə nə) or **tym•pa•nums** also **tim•pa•na** (tĭmʹpə nə) or **tim•pa•nums.** **1.** The middle ear. **2.** The eardrum.

type (tīp) *n.* **1.** A number of people or things having in common traits or characteristics that set them apart as a distinct class. **2.** A person or thing having the characteristics of a group or class: *the type of hero popular in Victorian novels.* **3.** An example or a model having the ideal features of a group or class: *He was the perfect type of coach.* **4.a.** In printing, a small block of metal or wood with a raised letter or character on the upper end that leaves a printed impression when inked and pressed on paper. **b.** Such pieces considered as a group. **c.** Printed or typewritten characters; print. —*v.* **typed, typ•ing, types.** —*tr.* **1.** To write (something) with a typewriter. **2.** To classify according to a particular type or class: *type the rock samples by studying each; type an actor as a villain.* —*intr.* To write with a typewriter; typewrite. [First written down about 1470 in Middle English and spelled *type*, symbol, from Latin *typus*, image, from Greek *tupos*, impression.]

type•face (tīp′fās′) *n.* **1.** In printing, the surface of a block of type that makes the impression. **2.** The impression made by this surface. **3.** The size or style of the letters on blocks of type.

type•script (tīp′skrĭpt′) *n.* A typewritten copy, as of a manuscript.

type•set (tīp′sĕt′) *tr.v.* **type•set, type•set•ting, type•sets.** In printing, to set (written material) into type.

type•set•ter (tīp′sĕt′ər) *n.* A person who sets type; a compositor.

type•write (tīp′rīt′) *intr. & tr.v.* **type•wrote** (tīp′rōt′), **type•writ•ten** (tīp′rĭt′n), **type•writ•ing, type•writes.** To engage in writing or to write (something) with a typewriter; type.

type•writ•er (tīp′rī′tər) *n.* A writing machine that produces characters similar to print by means of a hand-operated keyboard that moves a set of raised blocks, which strike the paper through an inked ribbon.

type•writ•ten (tīp′rĭt′n) *v.* Past participle of **typewrite.**

type•wrote (tīp′rōt′) *v.* Past tense of **typewrite.**

ty•phoid (tī′foid′) *n.* Typhoid fever.

typhoid fever *n.* An infectious, often fatal disease caused by bacteria transmitted in contaminated food or water. Its symptoms include high fever, intestinal bleeding, and rose-colored spots on the skin.

ty•phoon (tī fo͞on′) *n.* A hurricane occurring in the western Pacific.

ty•phus (tī′fəs) *n.* Any of several forms of an infectious disease caused by bacteria, especially those transmitted by fleas, lice, or mites, and characterized generally by sustained high fever, delirium, and red rashes.

typ•i•cal (tĭp′ĭ kəl) *adj.* Showing the traits or characteristics that identify a kind, group, or category: *a typical college campus.* **—typ′i•cal•ly** *adv.*

typ•i•fy (tĭp′ə fī′) *tr.v.* **typ•i•fied** (tĭp′ə fīd′), **typ•i•fy•ing, typ•i•fies** (tĭp′ə fīz′). To serve as a typical example of.

typ•ist (tī′pĭst) *n.* A person who operates a typewriter.

typo. *abbr.* An abbreviation of: **1.** Typographer. **2.** Typography.

ty•pog•ra•pher (tī pŏg′rə fər) *n.* A person who sets written material into type; a printer or compositor.

ty•po•graph•i•cal (tī′pə grăf′ĭ kəl) *adj.* Of or relating to typography.

ty•pog•ra•phy (tī pŏg′rə fē) *n., pl.* **ty•pog•ra•phies. 1.** The art and technique of printing with movable type. **2.** The arrangement and appearance of printed matter.

ty•ran•ni•cal (tĭ răn′ĭ kəl *or* tī răn′ĭ kəl) *adj.* Of, relating to, or characteristic of a tyrant or tyranny. **—ty•ran′ni•cal•ly** *adv.*

tyr•an•nize (tĭr′ə nīz′) *v.* **tyr•an•nized, tyr•an•niz•ing, tyr•an•niz•es.** —*tr.* To treat or govern tyrannically. —*intr.* **1.** To exercise absolute power. **2.** To rule as a tyrant.

ty•ran•no•saur (tĭ răn′ə sôr′ *or* tī răn′ə sôr′) also **ty•ran•no•saur•us** (tĭ răn′ə sôr′əs *or* tī răn′ə sôr′əs) *n.* A large meat-eating dinosaur having small front legs, a large head, and sharp teeth.

tyr•an•ny (tĭr′ə nē) *n., pl.* **tyr•an•nies. 1.** A government in which a single ruler has absolute power. **2.** The office, authority, or jurisdiction of an absolute ruler. **3.** Absolute power, especially when exercised unjustly or cruelly.

ty•rant (tī′rənt) *n.* **1.** An absolute ruler who governs without legal restrictions. **2.** A ruler who exercises power in a harsh cruel manner; an oppressor. **3.** A person who uses authority in a harsh or cruel manner. [First written down before 1300 in Middle English and spelled *tiraunt*, from Greek *turannos*.]

Tyre (tīr). An ancient Phoenician city on the eastern Mediterranean Sea in present-day southern Lebanon. It was the capital of Phoenicia after the 11th century B.C.

ty•ro (tī′rō) *n., pl.* **ty•ros.** A beginner in learning something.

Tyr•rhe•ni•an Sea (tə rē′nē ən). An arm of the Mediterranean Sea between the Italian peninsula and the islands of Corsica, Sardinia, and Sicily.

tzar (zär *or* tsär) *n.* Variant of **czar** (sense 1).

typewriter

tyrannosaur
Tyrannosaurus rex

ă	pat	oi	boy
ā	pay	ou	out
âr	care	o͝o	took
ä	father	o͞o	boot
ĕ	pet	ŭ	cut
ē	be	ûr	urge
ĭ	pit	th	thin
ī	pie	*th*	this
îr	pier	hw	whoop
ŏ	pot	zh	vision
ō	toe	ə	about
ô	paw	N	*French* bon

Uu

ukulele

umbrella

umiak

umpire
Baseball umpire

u or **U** (yo͞o) *n., pl.* **u's** or **U's. 1.** The 21st letter of the English alphabet. **2.** The 21st in a series or group.

U The symbol for the element **uranium.**

U. or **U** *abbr.* An abbreviation of university.

u•biq•ui•tous (yo͞o **bĭk′**wĭ təs) *adj.* Being or seeming to be everywhere at the same time: *a ubiquitous bird throughout South Dakota.* [First written down in 1837 in Modern English, from Latin *ubīque*, everywhere.] **—u•biq′ui•tous•ly** *adv.*

u•biq•ui•ty (yo͞o **bĭk′**wĭ tē) *n.* Existence or apparent existence everywhere at the same time: *the ubiquity of television in modern society.*

ud•der (**ŭd′**ər) *n.* A bag-shaped part of a cow or certain other female mammals, in which milk is formed and stored and from which it is taken in suckling or milking.

UFO (yo͞o′ĕf **ō′**) *n., pl.* **UFOs** or **UFO's.** An unidentified flying object.

U•gan•da (yo͞o **găn′**də). A country of east-central Africa west of Kenya. It gained its independence from Great Britain in 1962. Kampala is the capital and the largest city. Population, 12,636,179.

ugh (ŭg *or* ŭk) *interj.* An expression used to show disgust or horror.

ug•ly (**ŭg′**lē) *adj.* **ug•li•er, ug•li•est. 1.** Displeasing to the eye: *an ugly building.* **2.** Repulsive or offensive: *an ugly remark.* **3.** Disagreeable; unpleasant: *an ugly temper.* [First written down about 1250 in Middle English and spelled *uglike*, frightful, repulsive, from Old Norse *uggligr*, from *uggr*, fear.] **—ug′li•ness** *n.*

uh (ŭ) *interj.* An expression used to show hesitation or uncertainty.

uhf or **UHF** *abbr.* An abbreviation of ultrahigh frequency.

uh-huh (ə **hŭ′**) *interj. Informal.* An expression used to show agreement.

U•jung Pan•dang (o͞o jo͝ong′ pän **däng′**). Formerly **Ma•kas•sar** (mə **kăs′**ər). A city of central Indonesia on southwest Celebes Island. Population, 709,038.

U.K. or **UK** *abbr.* An abbreviation of United Kingdom.

U•kraine (yo͞o **krān′**). A region of eastern Europe bordering on the Black Sea. It was part of the U.S.S.R. from 1922 to 1991. Capital, Kiev. Population, 50,840,000.

U•krain•i•an (yo͞o **krā′**nē ən) *n.* **1.** A native or inhabitant of the Ukraine. **2.** The Slavic language of the Ukrainians.

u•ku•le•le (yo͞o′kə **lā′**lē) *n.* A small four-stringed guitar, first popular in Hawaii. [First written down in 1896 in American English, from Hawaiian *'ukulele.*]

U•lan Ba•tor (o͞o′län **bä′**tôr′). The capital and largest city of Mongolia, in the north-central part of the country. It was founded in 1649. Population, 488,200.

ul•cer (**ŭl′**sər) *n.* An inflamed, often pus-filled sore or lesion on the skin or a mucous membrane of the body. [First written down before 1400 in Middle English, from Latin *ulcus.*]

ul•cer•ate (**ŭl′**sə rāt′) *tr. & intr.v.* **ul•cer•at•ed, ul•cer•at•ing, ul•cer•ates.** To affect or become affected with an ulcer.

ul•cer•a•tion (ŭl′sə **rā′**shən) *n.* **1.** Development of an ulcer. **2.** An ulcer or an ulcerous condition.

ul•cer•ous (**ŭl′**sər əs) *adj.* Of or affected with an ulcer or ulcers.

ul•na (**ŭl′**nə) *n., pl.* **ul•nas** or **ul•nae** (**ŭl′**nē). **1.** The bone that in humans extends from the elbow to the wrist on the side of the arm opposite to the thumb. **2.** The corresponding bone in the foreleg of other vertebrates. [First written down in 1541 in Modern English, from Latin *ulna*, elbow, forearm.]

Ul•ster (**ŭl′**stər). A historical region and ancient kingdom of northern Ireland. It is now divided between Ireland and Northern Ireland, which is often called Ulster.

ul•te•ri•or (ŭl **tîr′**ē ər) *adj.* **1.** Lying beyond what is evident or admitted, especially when intentionally concealed: *ulterior motives.* **2.** Lying beyond or outside the area of immediate interest: *the ulterior parts of the island.*

ul•ti•mate (**ŭl′**tə mĭt) *adj.* **1.** Final; last: *the ultimate stop on the rail line.* **2.** Greatest possible in size or significance: *the ultimate act of courage.* **3.** Basic; fundamental: *ultimate truths.* —*n.* The greatest extreme; the maximum: *the ultimate in stereo systems.* [First written down in 1654 in Modern English, from Latin *ultimus.*] **—ul′ti•mate•ly** *adv.*

ul•ti•ma•tum (ŭl′tə **mā′**təm) *n., pl.* **ul•ti•ma•tums** or **ul•ti•ma•ta** (ŭl′tə **mā′**tə). A final statement of terms that expresses or implies the threat of serious penalties if the terms are not accepted.

ul•tra (**ŭl′**trə) *adj.* Extreme, as in following a belief, fashion, or course of action: *an ultra conservative.* —*n.* A person with extreme views or opinions.

ultra– *pref.* A prefix that means beyond the range, limit, or normal degree of: *ultrasonic; ultraviolet.*

ul•tra•high frequency (ŭl′trə **hī′**) *n.* A band of radio frequencies from 300 to 3,000 megahertz.

ul•tra•ma•rine (ŭl′trə mə **rēn′**) *n.* **1.** A blue pigment made from a powder of the mineral lapis lazuli. **2.** A bright or strong blue to purplish blue. —*adj.* Having the color ultramarine. [First written down in 1686 in Modern English and spelled *ultra marine*, from Medieval Latin *ultrāmarīnus*, from beyond the sea.]

ul•tra•son•ic (ŭl′trə **sŏn′**ĭk) *adj.* Consisting of or using sound that is too high in frequency to be heard by human beings: *ultrasonic waves.*

ul•tra•son•ics (ŭl′trə **sŏn′**ĭks) *n. (used with a singular verb).* The scientific study and practical application of ultrasonic sounds.

ul•tra•sound (**ŭl′**trə sound′) *n.* **1.** Ultrasonic sound. **2.** The medical use of ultrasonic waves, especially to produce images of internal structures of the body or to observe a developing fetus.

ul•tra•vi•o•let (ŭl′trə **vī′**ə lĭt) *adj.* Of or relating to electromagnetic radiation having wavelengths shorter than those of visible light but longer than those of x-rays. —*n.* Ultraviolet light or the ultraviolet part of the spectrum.

U•lys•ses (yo͞o **lĭs′**ēz′) *n.* Odysseus.

um•bel (**ŭm′**bəl) *n.* A flat or rounded flower cluster in which the individual flower stalks arise from about the same point on the stem. [First written down in 1597 in Modern English and spelled *umbell*, from Latin *umbella*, parasol.]

um•ber (ŭm′bər) *n.* **1.** A natural brown earth composed of oxides of iron, silicon, aluminum, calcium, and manganese, used as a pigment. **2.** A dark reddish brown. —*adj.* Dark reddish-brown.

um•bil•i•cal (ŭm bĭl′ĭ kəl) *adj.* Of or relating to a navel or an umbilical cord: *an umbilical hernia.*

umbilical cord *n.* **1.** The flexible cord-shaped structure connecting a fetus at the abdomen to the placenta, containing blood vessels that supply nourishment to the fetus and remove its wastes. **2.** One of the tubes, wires, or cables that are connected to a rocket and removed shortly before launching.

um•bil•i•cus (ŭm bĭl′ĭ kəs) *n., pl.* **um•bil•i•ci** (ŭm-bĭl′ĭ sī′). The navel.

um•bra (ŭm′brə) *n., pl.* **um•bras** or **um•brae** (ŭm′-brē). **1.** A dark area, especially the darkest part of a shadow. **2.a.** The completely dark portion of the shadow cast by the earth, moon, or other body during an eclipse. **b.** The darkest region of a sunspot. [First written down in 1599 in Modern English, from Latin *umbra*, shadow.]

um•brage (ŭm′brĭj) *n.* Offense; resentment: *Don't take umbrage at my question.*

um•brel•la (ŭm brĕl′ə) *n.* A device for protection from the rain or sun, consisting of a collapsible, usually circular piece of cloth or other material mounted on a rod. [First written down in 1610 in Modern English and spelled *umbrello*, from Latin *umbella*, parasol.]

u•mi•ak (o͞o′mē ăk′) *n.* A large open Eskimo boat made of skins stretched on a wooden frame.

um•pire (ŭm′pīr′) *n.* **1.** A person appointed to rule on plays, especially in baseball. **2.** A person empowered to settle a dispute. —*v.* **um•pired, um•pir•ing, um•pires.** —*tr.* To act as an umpire for: *umpire a game.* —*intr.* To be or act as an umpire. [First written down about 1350 in Middle English and spelled *noumpere*, mediator, altered to *(an) oumpere*, from the phrase *(a) noumpere*, from Old French *nonper* : *non-*, not + *per*, equal, even, paired.]

ump•teen (ŭmp′tēn′) *adj. Informal.* Large but unspecified in number: *I have umpteen reasons for not wanting to go.* —**ump′teenth′** *adj.*

UN or **U.N.** *abbr.* An abbreviation of United Nations.

un–[1] *pref.* A prefix that means: **1.** Not: *unattached.* **2.** Contrary to: *unrest.* —See Note.

un–[2] *pref.* A prefix that means: **1.** To reverse or undo an action: *unbar.* **2.** To deprive of or remove a thing: *unburden.* **3.** To release, free, or remove from: *untie.* **4.** Used as an intensive: *unloose.*

un•a•bashed (ŭn′ə băsht′) *adj.* Not embarrassed or ashamed: *unabashed sentimentality.* —**un′a•bash′-ed•ly** (ŭn′ə băsh′ĭd lē) *adv.*

un•a•ble (ŭn ā′bəl) *adj.* **1.** Lacking the necessary power, authority, or means to do something: *unable to go to the party.* **2.** Lacking mental or physical capability or efficiency: *With a sprained ankle, she was unable to walk to school.*

un•a•bridged (ŭn′ə brĭjd′) *adj.* Not condensed: *an unabridged book.*

un•ac•cent•ed (ŭn ăk′sĕn tĭd) *adj.* Having weak stress or no stress: *an unaccented syllable.*

un•ac•com•pa•nied (ŭn′ə kŭm′pə nēd) *adj.* **1.** Being without a companion: *traveling unaccompanied.* **2.** Performed or designed to be performed without accompaniment; solo: *a composition for unaccompanied flute.*

un•ac•count•a•ble (ŭn′ə koun′tə bəl) *adj.* **1.** Impossible to explain: *an unaccountable absence from class.* **2.** Not accountable to a higher authority; not responsible: *unaccountable for his actions.* —**un′-ac•count′a•bly** *adv.*

un•ac•cus•tomed (ŭn′ə kŭs′təmd) *adj.* **1.** Not customary; unusual: *treated me with unaccustomed politeness.* **2.** Not habituated or accustomed: *unaccustomed to the cold.*

un•ac•quaint•ed (ŭn′ə kwān′tĭd) *adj.* **1.** Not familiar or acquainted with another person. **2.** Not informed or knowledgeable: *unacquainted with the necessary procedures.*

un•a•dorned (ŭn′ə dôrnd′) *adj.* Lacking adornment or embellishment; simple or plain.

un•a•dul•ter•at•ed (ŭn′ə dŭl′tə rā′tĭd) *adj.* **1.** Not mixed or diluted; pure. **2.** Thorough; utter: *unadulterated joy.*

un•af•fect•ed (ŭn′ə fĕk′tĭd) *adj.* **1.** Not changed, modified, or affected: *Our plans were unaffected by the rain.* **2.** Marked by a lack of affectation; sincere.

un•al•ter•a•ble (ŭn ôl′tər ə bəl) *adj.* Impossible to alter; unchangeable. —**un•al′ter•a•bly** *adv.*

u•na•nim•i•ty (yo͞o′nə nĭm′ĭ tē) *n.* The condition of being unanimous; complete agreement.

u•nan•i•mous (yo͞o năn′ə məs) *adj.* **1.** Sharing the same opinion: *Critics were unanimous about the play.* **2.** Based on or characterized by complete agreement: *a unanimous vote.* [First written down before 1619 in Modern English, from Latin *ūnanimus* : *ūnus*, one + *animus*, mind.] —**u•nan′i•mous•ly** *adv.*

un•ap•proach•a•ble (ŭn′ə prō′chə bəl) *adj.* **1.** Not friendly; aloof: *an unapproachable boss.* **2.** Not easily reached; not accessible: *an unapproachable cabin in the woods.*

un•armed (ŭn ärmd′) *adj.* Having no weapons.

un•as•sum•ing (ŭn′ə so͞o′mĭng) *adj.* Not boastful or pretentious; modest.

un•at•tached (ŭn′ə tăcht′) *adj.* **1.** Not attached or joined, especially to surrounding tissue. **2.** Not engaged, married, or involved in a serious romantic relationship.

un•at•test•ed (ŭn′ə tĕs′tĭd) *adj.* Not found in a written document: *Scholars sometimes construct unattested words as possible sources of familiar ones.* —See Note.

un•a•vail•ing (ŭn′ə vā′lĭng) *adj.* Not effective; unsuccessful: *her unavailing efforts to apologize.*

un•a•void•a•ble (ŭn′ə voi′də bəl) *adj.* Impossible to avoid; inevitable: *an unavoidable discussion.* —**un′a•void′a•bly** *adv.*

un•a•ware (ŭn′ə wâr′) *adj.* Not aware: *She was unaware of his presence.*

un•a•wares (ŭn′ə wârz′) *adv.* By surprise; unexpectedly: *I caught them unawares.*

un•bal•anced (ŭn băl′ənst) *adj.* **1.** Not in balance or in proper balance: *an unbalanced scale.* **2.** Not mentally sound; irrational: *an unbalanced mind.* **3.** Not balanced financially; having debits and credits that do not correspond to each other.

un•bar (ŭn bär′) *tr.v.* **un•barred, un•bar•ring, un•bars.** To remove the bars from; open: *unbar a window.*

un•bear•a•ble (ŭn bâr′ə bəl) *adj.* So unpleasant or painful as to be intolerable: *unbearable heat.* —**un•bear′a•bly** *adv.*

un•beat•a•ble (ŭn bē′tə bəl) *adj.* Impossible to surpass or defeat: *a team that was unbeatable.*

un•beat•en (ŭn bēt′n) *adj.* **1.** Never defeated: *an unbeaten swim team.* **2.** Never having been traveled or walked on: *an unbeaten path through the woods.* **3.** Not beaten or pounded, as in cooking: *unbeaten eggs.*

un•be•com•ing (ŭn′bĭ kŭm′ĭng) *adj.* **1.** Not attractive or flattering: *unbecoming clothes.* **2.** Not suitable or proper: *unbecoming behavior.*

Word Building: un–[1]

The prefix **un–**[1], which goes back to Old English, has the basic meaning "not." Thus **unhappy** means "not happy." **Un–**[1] chiefly attaches to adjectives, as in **unable**, **unclean**, **unequal**, **uneven**, **unripe**, and **unsafe**, and adjectives made of participles, as in **unfeeling**, **unfinished**, **unflinching**, and **unsaid**. Less frequently **un–**[1] attaches to nouns: **unbelief**, **unconcern**, **unrest**. Although **un–**[2] is also from Old English, it is not related to **un–**[1]. Whereas **un–**[1] forms adjectives and nouns, **un–**[2] forms verbs and expresses removal, reversal, or deprivation: **undress**, **unnerve**, **unravel**.

Word History: unattested

Etymologists use the word **unattested** to refer to words that have not been found written down but have been put together or reconstructed by etymologists from clues left behind by other words. For example, the ancestor of our word *is*, the Indo-European word *esti*, is *unattested* because it was only spoken and never written down. But the languages descended from Indo-European preserved different parts of the word *esti*, like pieces to a puzzle. English has *is*, Gothic *ist*, Latin *est*, Greek *esti*, and Sanskrit *asti–*. Scholars have constructed the unattested Indo-European word *esti* from these clues.

ă	pat	oi	**boy**
ā	**pay**	ou	**out**
âr	**care**	o͝o	**took**
ä	**father**	o͞o	**boot**
ĕ	pet	ŭ	cut
ē	be	ûr	**urge**
ĭ	pit	th	**thin**
ī	**pie**	*th*	**this**
îr	**pier**	hw	**whoop**
ŏ	pot	zh	vision
ō	**toe**	ə	about
ô	**paw**	N	*French* bon

I WANT YOU
for the U.S. ARMY
Uncle Sam
World War I poster
by James Montgomery Flagg
(1877–1960)

un•be•known (ŭn′bĭ nōn′) *adj.* Unknown: *a problem unbeknown to us.*
un•be•knownst (ŭn′bĭ nōnst′) *adj.* Unknown. *—adv.* Without the knowledge of someone: *Our cousin had come to town, unbeknownst to us.*
un•be•lief (ŭn′bĭ lēf′) *n.* Lack of belief or faith, especially in religious matters.
un•be•liev•a•ble (ŭn′bĭ lē′və bəl) *adj.* Not to be believed; incredible: *an unbelievable tale.* **—un′be•liev′a•bly** *adv.*
un•be•liev•er (ŭn′bĭ lē′vər) *n.* A person who lacks belief or faith, especially in a particular religion.
un•be•liev•ing (ŭn′bĭ lē′vĭng) *adj.* Not believing; doubting: *an unbelieving facial expression.*
un•bend (ŭn bĕnd′) *v.* **un•bent** (ŭn bĕnt′), **un•bend•ing, un•bends.** *—tr.* **1.** To straighten (something crooked or bent): *unbend a paper clip.* **2.** To free from tension or strain: *unbend one's mind.* *—intr.* **1.** To become less tense; relax: *unbend at the beach.* **2.** To become straight: *muscles bending and unbending.*
un•bend•ing (ŭn bĕn′dĭng) *adj.* Not flexible; uncompromising: *an unbending will.*
un•bent (ŭn bĕnt′) *v.* Past tense and past participle of **unbend.**
un•bi•ased (ŭn bī′əst) *adj.* Without bias or prejudice; impartial: *A judge must be unbiased.*
un•bid•den (ŭn bĭd′n) *adj.* Not asked or invited: *unbidden guests.*
un•bind (ŭn bīnd′) *tr.v.* **un•bound** (ŭn bound′), **un•bind•ing, un•binds. 1.** To untie or unfasten: *unbinding the bunch of candy canes.* **2.** To set free; release: *unbind a prisoner.*
un•bolt (ŭn bōlt′) *tr.v.* **un•bolt•ed, un•bolt•ing, un•bolts.** To remove the bolts of; unlock: *unbolt a door.*
un•born (ŭn bôrn′) *adj.* **1.** Not yet born: *an unborn child.* **2.** Not yet in existence: *unborn scientific theories.*
un•bound (ŭn bound′) *v.* Past tense and past participle of **unbind.** *—adj.* **1.** Not having a binding: *an unbound book.* **2.** Freed from bonds or restraints.
un•bound•ed (ŭn boun′dĭd) *adj.* **1.** Having no boundaries or limits: *unbounded space.* **2.** Not kept within bounds; unrestrained: *unbounded joy.*
un•bri•dled (ŭn brīd′ld) *adj.* **1.** Unrestrained; uncontrolled: *moments of unbridled joy.* **2.** Not fitted with a bridle.
un•bro•ken (ŭn brō′kən) *adj.* **1.** Not broken; whole; intact. **2.** Not violated: *an unbroken promise.* **3.** Uninterrupted: *unbroken silence.* **4.** Not tamed or broken: *an unbroken pony.*
un•buck•le (ŭn bŭk′əl) *tr.v.* **un•buck•led, un•buck•ling, un•buck•les.** To loosen or undo the buckle or buckles of.
un•bur•den (ŭn bûr′dn) *tr.v.* **un•bur•dened, un•bur•den•ing, un•bur•dens.** To free from or relieve of a burden: *unburden one's mind.*
un•but•ton (ŭn bŭt′n) *tr.v.* **un•but•toned, un•but•ton•ing, un•but•tons.** To unfasten the buttons of: *Unbutton your coat.*
un•called-for (ŭn kôld′fôr′) *adj.* Unwanted, undeserved, or inappropriate: *an uncalled-for remark.*
un•can•ny (ŭn kăn′ē) *adj.* **un•can•ni•er, un•can•ni•est. 1.** Arousing wonder and fear, as if supernatural; eerie: *an uncanny light coming out of the ruins.* **2.** So keen and perceptive as to seem supernatural: *uncanny wisdom.* **—un•can′ni•ly** *adv.*
un•ceas•ing (ŭn sē′sĭng) *adj.* Not stopping; continuous: *unceasing activity.* **—un•ceas′ing•ly** *adv.*
un•cer•e•mo•ni•ous (ŭn sĕr′ə mō′nē əs) *adj.* Without appropriate courtesy or formality: *an unceremonious departure.*
un•cer•tain (ŭn sûr′tn) *adj.* **1.** Not known or established; questionable: *The results of the experiment are uncertain.* **2.** Not definite; undecided: *uncertain plans.* **3.** Not having sure knowledge: *uncertain of the answers.* **4.** Subject to change: *uncertain weather.* **—un•cer′tain•ly** *adv.*
un•cer•tain•ty (ŭn sûr′tn tē) *n., pl.* **un•cer•tain•ties. 1.** The condition of being uncertain. **2.** Something that is uncertain: *the uncertainties of life.*

Synonyms: uncertainty, doubt, suspicion, mistrust. These nouns mean a condition of being unsure about a person or thing. **Uncertainty** is the least forceful: *I looked back on my decision with growing uncertainty.* **Doubt** refers to a questioning state of mind that leads to hesitation in accepting something or making a decision: *If there is any doubt about his story, you can call his office to confirm it.* **Suspicion** often suggests an uneasy feeling that a person or thing is evil: *The leaders from the warring countries regarded each other with suspicion at the start of the conference.* **Mistrust** means a lack of trust or confidence arising from suspicion: *After the strike, the company was filled with an atmosphere of general mistrust.*

un•char•i•ta•ble (ŭn chăr′ĭ tə bəl) *adj.* **1.** Not generous. **2.** Unfair or unkind: *uncharitable remarks.*
un•chart•ed (ŭn chär′tĭd) *adj.* **1.** Not recorded on a map. **2.** Unknown.
un•chris•tian (ŭn krĭs′chən) *adj.* **1.** Not Christian in religion. **2.** Not in accordance with the spirit or principles of Christianity.
un•cial (ŭn′shəl *or* ŭn′sē əl) *adj.* Of or relating to a script with rounded capital letters found especially in Greek and Latin manuscripts of the fourth to the eighth century A.D. *—n.* **1.** A style of writing characterized by rounded capital letters. **2.** A capital letter written in this style. [First written down in 1650 in Modern English and spelled *unciall,* from Latin *uncia,* a twelfth part, ounce, inch.]
un•civ•il (ŭn sĭv′əl) *adj.* Impolite; discourteous.
un•civ•i•lized (ŭn sĭv′ə līzd′) *adj.* Not civilized; barbaric.
un•clad (ŭn klăd′) *adj.* Not wearing clothes; naked.
un•cle (ŭng′kəl) *n.* **1.** The brother of one's mother or father. **2.** The husband of one's aunt. [First written down about 1300 in Middle English, from Latin *avunculus,* maternal uncle.]
un•clean (ŭn klēn′) *adj.* **un•clean•er, un•clean•est. 1.** Not clean; dirty. **2.** Morally impure. **—un•clean′ness** *n.*
un•clean•ly (ŭn klĕn′lē) *adj.* **un•clean•li•er, un•clean•li•est.** Unclean. *—adv.* (ŭn klēn′lē). In an unclean manner. **—un•clean′li•ness** *n.*
un•clear (ŭn klîr′) *adj.* **un•clear•er, un•clear•est.** Not clear or explicit.
Uncle Sam (săm) *n.* The United States Government, often personified as a tall thin man dressed in the national colors and sporting a white beard and a top hat.
un•clothe (ŭn klōth′) *tr.v.* **un•clothed, un•cloth•ing, un•clothes.** To remove the clothing or cover from.
un•coil (ŭn koil′) *tr. & intr.v.* **un•coiled, un•coil•ing, un•coils.** To unwind or become unwound: *Uncoil the hose. The snake uncoiled.*
un•com•fort•a•ble (ŭn kŭm′fər tə bəl *or* ŭn kŭmf′tə bəl) *adj.* **1.** Experiencing physical discomfort. **2.** Ill at ease; uneasy: *I'm uncomfortable with the committee's decision.* **3.** Causing discomfort: *an uncomfortable chair.* **—un•com′fort•a•bly** *adv.*
un•com•mit•ted (ŭn′kə mĭt′ĭd) *adj.* Not pledged to a specific cause or course of action: *uncommitted delegates at the convention.*
un•com•mon (ŭn kŏm′ən) *adj.* **un•com•mon•er, un•com•mon•est. 1.** Not common; rare; unusual: *words used in uncommon ways.* **2.** Wonderful; remarkable. **—un•com′mon•ly** *adv.*
un•com•pro•mis•ing (ŭn kŏm′prə mī′zĭng) *adj.*

Not willing to make compromises; inflexible: *took an uncompromising stance during negotiations.* —**un•com′pro•mis′ing•ly** *adv.*

un•con•cern (ŭn′kən **sûrn′**) *n.* **1.** Lack of interest; indifference: *From the beginning he viewed the assignment with unconcern.* **2.** Lack of worry or anxiety.

un•con•cerned (ŭn′kən **sûrnd′**) *adj.* **1.** Not interested; indifferent. **2.** Not worried or anxious. —**un′con•cern′ed•ly** (ŭn′kən **sûr′**nĭd lē) *adv.*

un•con•di•tion•al (ŭn′kən **dĭsh′**ə nəl) *adj.* Without conditions or limitations; absolute: *unconditional surrender.* —**un′con•di′tion•al•ly** *adv.*

un•con•quer•a•ble (ŭn **kŏng′**kər ə bəl) *adj.* Impossible to overcome or defeat: *With her unconquerable spirit, she will recover quickly from this setback.*

un•con•scion•a•ble (ŭn **kŏn′**shə nə bəl) *adj.* **1.** Not restrained by conscience; unscrupulous: *an unconscionable act.* **2.** Beyond reason; excessive: *an unconscionable price.* —**un•con′scion•a•bly** *adv.*

un•con•scious (ŭn **kŏn′**shəs) *adj.* **1.** Temporarily lacking consciousness: *The patient was still unconscious from the anesthesia.* **2.** Lacking awareness: *He was unconscious of their wishes.* **3.** Occurring without one's awareness or conscious thought: *unconscious fears.* **4.** Not done on purpose; accidental: *an unconscious mistake.* —*n.* The part of the mind that contains desires, fears, or memories that are not subject to conscious awareness or control. —**un•con′scious•ly** *adv.* —**un•con′scious•ness** *n.*

un•con•sid•ered (ŭn′kən **sĭd′**ərd) *adj.* Not done with reason or consideration; rash: *an unconsidered remark.*

un•con•sti•tu•tion•al (ŭn′kŏn stĭ **to͞o′**shə nəl *or* ŭn′kŏn stĭ **tyo͞o′**shə nəl) *adj.* Not in agreement with the principles set forth in the constitution of a nation or state. —**un′con•sti•tu′tion•al•ly** *adv.* —**un′con•sti•tu′tion•al′i•ty** (ŭn′kŏn stĭ to͞o′shə **năl′**ĭ tē *or* ŭn′kŏn stĭ tyo͞o′shə **năl′**ĭ tē) *n.*

un•con•trol•la•ble (ŭn′kən **trō′**lə bəl) *adj.* Impossible to control or govern: *an uncontrollable urge to laugh.* —**un′con•trol′la•bly** *adv.*

un•con•trolled (ŭn′kən **trōld′**) *adj.* Not under control or restraint: *an uncontrolled drug; uncontrolled anger.*

un•con•ven•tion•al (ŭn′kən **vĕn′**shə nəl) *adj.* Not conforming to convention or accepted social norms; out of the ordinary: *unconventional forms of art.* —**un′con•ven′tion•al′i•ty** (ŭn′kən vĕn′shə **năl′**ĭ tē) *n.* —**un′con•ven′tion•al•ly** *adv.*

un•cork (ŭn **kôrk′**) *tr.v.* **un•corked, un•cork•ing, un•corks.** To remove the cork from (a bottle, for example).

un•count•ed (ŭn **koun′**tĭd) *adj.* **1.** Not counted: *The uncounted money is in the safe.* **2.** Not capable of being counted; innumerable: *uncounted millions calling for change.*

un•coup•le (ŭn **kŭp′**əl) *v.* **un•cou•pled, un•cou•pling, un•cou•ples.** —*tr.* To disconnect: *uncouple railroad cars.* —*intr.* To come or break loose.

un•couth (ŭn **ko͞oth′**) *adj.* **1.** Not refined; crude: *uncouth behavior.* **2.** Awkward; clumsy. [First written down about 725 in Old English and spelled *uncūth*, unknown : *un-*, not + *cūth*, known, knowing.]

un•cov•er (ŭn **kŭv′**ər) *tr.v.* **un•cov•ered, un•cov•er•ing, un•cov•ers. 1.** To remove a cover from: *uncovered a jar.* **2.** To reveal or disclose: *uncover a plot.* **3.** To remove the hat from, as in respect: *He uncovered his head as he marched past his friends.*

un•cross (ŭn **krôs′** *or* ŭn **krŏs′**) *tr.v.* **un•crossed, un•cross•ing, un•cross•es.** To move (one's legs, for example) from an uncrossed position.

unc•tion (**ŭngk′**shən) *n.* **1.** The act of anointing as part of a religious, ceremonial, or healing ritual. **2.** An ointment or oil; a salve. **3.** Something that serves to soothe. [First written down before 1387 in Middle English and spelled *unccioun*, from Latin *ūnctiō*, from *unguere*, to anoint.]

unc•tu•ous (**ŭngk′**cho͞o əs) *adj.* **1.** Exaggerated or insincere: *an unctuous sales pitch.* **2.** Oily; greasy. —**unc′tu•ous•ly** *adv.* —**unc′tu•ous•ness** *n.*

un•cul•ti•vat•ed (ŭn **kŭl′**tə vā′tĭd) *adj.* **1.** Not prepared for growing crops: *uncultivated land.* **2.** Not refined or cultured: *an uncultivated person.*

un•cut (ŭn **kŭt′**) *adj.* **1.** Not cut, trimmed, or sliced: *uncut hair; uncut bread.* **2.** Not ground or polished: *an uncut gem.* **3.** Not abridged or shortened: *an uncut novel.*

un•daunt•ed (ŭn **dôn′**tĭd *or* ŭn **dän′**tĭd) *adj.* Not discouraged; resolutely courageous. —**un•daunt′ed•ly** *adv.*

un•de•cid•ed (ŭn′dĭ **sī′**dĭd) *adj.* **1.** Not yet settled; open: *plans still undecided.* **2.** Having reached no decision: *undecided whether to hire new workers.*

un•de•clared (ŭn′dĭ **klârd′**) *adj.* **1.** Not formally declared: *an undeclared war.* **2.** Not having formally revealed something about oneself: *an undeclared candidate for governor.*

un•de•ni•a•ble (ŭn′dĭ **nī′**ə bəl) *adj.* Difficult or impossible to deny: *undeniable facts.* —**un′de•ni′a•bly** *adv.*

un•der (**ŭn′**dər) *prep.* **1.** In a lower position or place than: *a cat under the table.* **2.** Beneath the surface of: *under the ground.* **3.** Beneath the guise of: *under a false name.* **4.** Less than; smaller than: *under 20 years of age.* **5.** Less than the required amount or degree of: *under voting age.* **6.** Inferior to in rank or status: *a general with thousands of troops under him.* **7.** Subject to the authority, rule, or control of: *under a dictatorship.* **8.** Undergoing or receiving the effects of: *under the care of a physician.* **9.** Subject to the obligation of: *under contract.* **10.** Within the group or classification of: *books listed under biology in the card catalog.* **11.** In the process of: *The proposal is under discussion.* **12.** In view of; because of: *Under these conditions, it would be wiser to postpone your trip.* —*adv.* In or into a place below or beneath: *The frog put its head under and swam off.* —*adj.* Located lower than or beneath something else: *the under parts of a machine.* [First written down about 725 in Old English.]

under– *pref.* A prefix that means: **1.** Beneath or below in position: *underground.* **2.** Inferiority in rank or importance: *undersecretary.* **3.** Less in degree, rate, or quantity than normal or proper: *underestimate.* —SEE NOTE.

un•der•a•chieve (ŭn′dər ə **chēv′**) *intr.v.* **un•der•a•chieved, un•der•a•chiev•ing, un•der•a•chieves.** To perform worse or achieve less than expected. —**un′der•a•chiev′er** *n.*

un•der•age (ŭn′dər **āj′**) *adj.* Below the customary or required age, as for voting.

un•der•arm (**ŭn′**dər ärm′) *adj.* **1.** Located, placed, or used under the arm. **2.** Performed with the hand brought forward and up from below the level of the shoulder; underhand. —*n.* The armpit. —**un′der•arm′** *adv.*

un•der•bel•ly (**ŭn′**dər bĕl′ē) *n.* **1.** The underside of an animal's body. **2.** A weak or vulnerable part: *The underbelly of his argument is that it runs counter to the facts.*

un•der•bid (ŭn′dər **bĭd′**) *tr.v.* **un•der•bid, un•der•bid•ding, un•der•bids. 1.** To bid lower than (a competitor). **2.** To bid less than the value of (one's hand) in bridge.

un•der•brush (**ŭn′**dər brŭsh′) *n.* Small trees, shrubs, or similar plants growing thickly beneath taller trees.

un•der•car•riage (**ŭn′**dər kăr′ĭj) *n.* **1.** A supporting

Word Building: under–

The prefix **under–**, which can be traced back to Old English, has essentially the same meaning as the preposition **under**. For example, in words such as **underbelly**, **undercurrent**, **underlie**, and **undershirt**, **under–** denotes a position beneath or below. **Under–** also frequently conveys incompleteness or falling below a certain standard. Some examples are **undercharge**, **underdeveloped**, **underestimate**, and **underfeed**. Note that in this sense words beginning with **under–** often have counterparts beginning with **over–**: **overcharge**, **overestimate**.

ă	pat	oi	boy
ā	pay	ou	out
âr	care	o͝o	took
ä	father	o͞o	boot
ĕ	pet	ŭ	cut
ē	be	ûr	urge
ĭ	pit	th	thin
ī	pie	*th*	this
îr	pier	hw	whoop
ŏ	pot	zh	vision
ō	toe	ə	about
ô	paw	N	*French* bon

underhand
Underhand softball pitch

framework or structure, as for the body of a car. **2.** The landing gear of an aircraft.

un•der•charge (ŭn′dər **chärj′**) *tr.v.* **un•der•charged, un•der•charg•ing, un•der•charg•es.** To charge (a customer, for example) too little.

un•der•clothes (**ŭn′**dər klōz′ *or* **ŭn′**dər klō*th*z′) *pl.n.* Clothes worn next to the skin, beneath one's outer clothing; underwear.

un•der•cloth•ing (**ŭn′**der klō′*th*ĭng) *n.* Underclothes.

un•der•coat (**ŭn′**dər kōt′) *n.* **1.** A coat worn beneath another coat. **2.** A covering of short hair lying underneath the longer outer hair of an animal's coat. **3.** A coat of material applied to a surface to seal it or otherwise prepare it for a final coat, as of paint.

un•der•cov•er (ŭn′dər **kŭv′**ər) *adj.* **1.** Performed or occurring in secret: *an undercover investigation.* **2.** Engaged in spying or secret investigations: *undercover FBI agents.*

un•der•cur•rent (**ŭn′**dər kûr′ənt *or* **ŭn′**dər kŭr′-ənt) *n.* **1.** A current, as of air or water, flowing beneath a surface or another current. **2.** A partly hidden tendency, force, or influence that is often contrary to what is obvious.

un•der•cut (ŭn′dər **kŭt′**) *tr.v.* **un•der•cut, un•der•cut•ting, un•der•cuts. 1.** To diminish or destroy the effectiveness of; undermine: *The scandal undercut the senator's influence.* **2.** To sell or work for less money than (a competitor). **3.** To make a cut under or below (something) so as to leave an overhanging projection. *—n.* (**ŭn′**dər kŭt′). **1.** A cut made in the lower part of something. **2.** A notch cut in a tree to direct its fall.

un•der•de•vel•oped (ŭn′dər dĭ **vĕl′**əpt) *adj.* **1.** Not developed in a full or normal way, as a living thing or one of its parts. **2.** Having a low level of economic development and technology in comparison to other societies: *an underdeveloped nation.*

un•der•dog (**ŭn′**dər dôg′ *or* **ŭn′**dər dŏg′) *n.* A person or thing that is expected to lose a contest or struggle, as in sports or politics.

un•der•done (ŭn′dər **dŭn′**) *v.* Past participle of **underdo.** *—adj.* Not sufficiently cooked.

un•der•em•ployed (ŭn′dər ĕm **ploid′**) *adj.* **1.** Employed in a part-time job when one needs or desires a full-time job. **2.** Employed at a job that requires less skill or training than one possesses.

un•der•es•ti•mate (ŭn′dər **ĕs′**tə māt′) *tr.v.* **un•der•es•ti•mat•ed, un•der•es•ti•mat•ing, un•der•es•ti•mates.** To make too low an estimate of the value, amount, or quality of: *We underestimated how long it would take to build the shed. Don't underestimate their defense.* *—n.* (ŭn′dər **ĕs′**tə mĭt). An estimate that is or proves to be too low.

un•der•ex•pose (ŭn′dər ĭk **spōz′**) *tr.v.* **un•der•ex•posed, un•der•ex•pos•ing, un•der•ex•pos•es.** To expose (film) to light for too short a time to produce an image with good contrast. **—un′der•ex•po′sure** (ŭn′dər ĭk **spō′**zhər) *n.*

un•der•feed (ŭn′dər **fēd′**) *tr.v.* **un•der•fed** (ŭn′dər-**fĕd′**), **un•der•feed•ing, un•der•feeds.** To feed insufficiently.

un•der•foot (ŭn′dər **fo͝ot′**) *adv.* **1.** Below or under the foot or feet. **2.** In the way: *too many toys underfoot.*

un•der•gar•ment (**ŭn′**dər gär′mənt) *n.* A garment worn under outer garments, especially one worn next to the skin.

un•der•go (ŭn′dər **gō′**) *tr.v.* **un•der•went** (ŭn′dər-**wĕnt′**), **un•der•gone** (ŭn′dər **gôn′** *or* ŭn′dər **gŏn′**), **un•der•go•ing, un•der•goes** (ŭn′dər **gōz′**). **1.** To experience: *Many insects undergo several changes in body form during their development.* **2.** To endure; suffer through: *undergo hardship.*

un•der•grad•u•ate (ŭn′dər **grăj′**o͞o ĭt) *n.* **1.** A student who has entered a college or university but has not yet received a bachelor's or similar degree. **2.** A high-school student who has not yet received a diploma. *—adj.* **1.** Of, for, or characteristic of an undergraduate: *undergraduate courses.* **2.** Being an undergraduate: *undergraduate students.*

un•der•ground (**ŭn′**dər ground′) *adj.* **1.** Located or occurring below the surface of the earth: *an underground passage.* **2.** Acting or done in secret; hidden: *underground resistance to the tyrant.* **3.** Of or relating to an avant-garde or experimental movement or its films, publications, or art: *the underground press.* *—n.* **1.** A secret organization working against a government in power. **2.** *Chiefly British.* A subway system. *—adv.* (ŭn′dər **ground′**). **1.** Below the surface of the earth: *miners digging underground.* **2.** In secret: *spies working underground.*

Underground Railroad *n.* A secret system that helped fugitive slaves reach freedom in the free states and in Canada before slavery was abolished in the United States.

un•der•growth (**ŭn′**dər grōth′) *n.* Low-growing plants, shrubs, or young trees beneath trees in a forest.

un•der•hand (**ŭn′**dər hănd′) also **un•der•hand•ed** (ŭn′dər **hăn′**dĭd) *adj.* **1.** Done deceptively, slyly, or secretly. **2.** In sports, performed with the hand brought forward and up from below the level of the shoulder. **—un′der•hand′, un′der•hand′ed** *adv.*

un•der•lie (ŭn′dər **lī′**) *tr.v.* **un•der•lay** (ŭn′dər **lā′**), **un•der•lain** (ŭn′dər **lān′**), **un•der•ly•ing, un•der•lies. 1.** To be located under or below: *Roman roads underlie many modern European highways.* **2.** To be the basis for; account for: *These things underlie her decision.*

un•der•line (**ŭn′**dər līn′ *or* ŭn′dər **līn′**) *tr.v.* **un•der•lined, un•der•lin•ing, un•der•lines. 1.** To draw a line under; underscore. **2.** To stress or emphasize: *He underlined their desire to cooperate.*

un•der•ling (**ŭn′**dər lĭng) *n.* A person of lesser rank or authority than another; a subordinate.

un•der•ly•ing (**ŭn′**dər lī′ĭng) *adj.* **1.** Located under or beneath something: *the underlying bedrock of the Sierras.* **2.** Basic; fundamental: *underlying values.* **3.** Present but not obvious; implied: *an underlying meaning.*

un•der•mine (ŭn′dər **mīn′**) *tr.v.* **un•der•mined, un•der•min•ing, un•der•mines. 1.** To weaken or impair by or as if by wearing away a base or foundation: *waters undermining the foundation of a house; bad habits undermining his health.* **2.** To dig a mine or tunnel beneath: *undermine a wall.*

un•der•most (**ŭn′**dər mōst′) *adj.* Lowest in position, rank, or place. *—adv.* In or to the lowest place.

un•der•neath (ŭn′dər **nēth′**) *adv.* In or to a place beneath; below. *—prep.* Beneath; below; under: *put a coaster underneath a glass.* *—n.* The part or side below or under; the underside. [First written down before 899 in Old English and spelled *underneothan* : *under*, under + *neothan*, below.]

un•der•nour•ished (ŭn′dər **nûr′**ĭsht *or* ŭn′-dər **nŭr′**ĭsht) *adj.* Lacking sufficient nourishment for proper health and growth.

un•der•pants (**ŭn′**dər pănts′) *pl.n.* Briefs or shorts worn as underwear.

un•der•pass (**ŭn′**dər păs′) *n.* A passage underneath something, especially a part of a road that passes under another road or a railroad.

un•der•pin•ning (**ŭn′**dər pĭn′ĭng) *n.* **1.** Material used to support a structure, such as a wall. **2.** A support or foundation. Often used in the plural.

un•der•priv•i•leged (ŭn′dər **prĭv′**ə lĭjd) *adj.* Lacking advantages or opportunities enjoyed by other members of one's society.

un•der•rate (ŭn′dər rāt′) *tr.v.* **un•der•rat•ed, un•der•rat•ing, un•der•rates.** To judge or rate too low; underestimate.

un•der•score (ŭn′dər skôr′) *tr.v.* **un•der•scored, un•der•scor•ing, un•der•scores. 1.** To underline. **2.** To emphasize; stress.

un•der•sea (ŭn′dər sē′) *adj.* Existing, done, used, or operating beneath the surface of the sea: *undersea life; undersea exploration.* —*adv.* (ŭn′dər sē′) also **un•der•seas** (ŭn′dər sēz′). Beneath the surface of the sea.

un•der•sec•re•tar•y (ŭn′dər sĕk′rə tĕr′ē) *n.* An official directly subordinate to a cabinet member.

un•der•sell (ŭn′dər sĕl′) *tr.v.* **un•der•sold** (ŭn′dər-sōld′), **un•der•sell•ing, un•der•sells. 1.** To sell for a lower price than (another seller). **2.** To sell (a product) at a price less than the actual value.

un•der•shirt (ŭn′dər shûrt′) *n.* An undergarment worn next to the skin under a shirt.

un•der•shoot (ŭn′dər sho͞ot′) *tr.v.* **un•der•shot** (ŭn′dər shŏt′), **un•der•shoot•ing, un•der•shoots. 1.** To shoot a missile so that it falls short of (a target). **2.** To land or begin to land an aircraft short of (a landing area).

un•der•shot (ŭn′dər shŏt′) *adj.* **1.** Driven by water passing from below: *an undershot water wheel.* **2.** Having the lower jaw or teeth projecting beyond the upper.

un•der•side (ŭn′dər sīd′) *n.* The side or surface that is underneath; the bottom side.

un•der•signed (ŭn′dər sīnd′) *adj.* **1.** Having a signature at the end: *an undersigned document.* **2.** Having signed at the end of a document: *the undersigned persons.* —*n., pl.* **undersigned.** A person whose name appears at the end of a document.

un•der•sized (ŭn′dər sīzd′) also **un•der•size** (ŭn′-dər sīz′) *adj.* Smaller than the usual, expected, or required size: *an undersized garment.*

un•der•sold (ŭn′dər sōld′) *v.* Past tense and past participle of **undersell.**

un•der•stand (ŭn′dər stănd′) *v.* **un•der•stood** (ŭn′dər sto͝od′), **un•der•stand•ing, un•der•stands.** —*tr.* **1.** To grasp the nature and significance of: *Do you understand how soap works?* **2.** To know well by long experience or close contact with: *That teacher understands kids.* **3.** To grasp the meaning intended or expressed by: *She speaks Russian and can understand your new neighbors.* **4.** To be tolerant or sympathetic toward: *I don't agree, but I can still understand your point.* **5.** To learn indirectly, as by hearsay: *We understand she had a baby on Thanksgiving.* **6.** To draw as a conclusion; infer: *Am I to understand that you are staying for the weekend?* **7.** To accept as an agreed fact: *Are the terms of our agreement understood?* **8.** To supply or add (words, for example) mentally: *The subject of an imperative verb is understood.* —*intr.* **1.a.** To have knowledge or understanding. **b.** To have sympathy or tolerance. **2.** To learn something indirectly; gather. [First written down before 899 in Old English and spelled *understandan.*] **—un′der•stand′a•ble** *adj.* **—un′der•stand′a•bly** *adv.*

un•der•stand•ing (ŭn′dər stăn′dĭng) *n.* **1.** The quality or condition of one who understands; comprehension. **2.** The ability to understand; intelligence: *a person of great understanding.* **3.** Individual judgment; opinion: *In my understanding, this plan makes sense.* **4.** An agreement between two or more people or groups. **5.** A reconciliation of differences; a state of agreement: *After long negotiations they finally reached an understanding.* **6.** A disposition to appreciate or share the thoughts or feelings of others: *Show some understanding!* —*adj.* **1.** Characterized by or having comprehension or good sense. **2.** Compassionate; sympathetic: *a kind and understanding friend.*

un•der•state (ŭn′dər stāt′) *tr.v.* **un•der•stat•ed, un•der•stat•ing, un•der•states. 1.** To state incompletely or without full information: *They have understated the problem in order to avoid punishment.* **2.** To express with little emphasis, especially for an ironic effect.

un•der•state•ment (ŭn′dər stāt′mənt *or* ŭn′-dər stāt′mənt) *n.* **1.** A statement that is less than complete. **2.** Lack of emphasis in expression, especially for rhetorical effect: *He often uses understatement, as in saying "not bad" to mean "very good."*

un•der•stood (ŭn′dər sto͝od′) *v.* Past tense and past participle of **understand.** —*adj.* **1.** Agreed upon: *We recalled that the understood fee is 50 dollars.* **2.** Not expressed but implied: *the understood subject in the sentence* Get going.

un•der•stud•y (ŭn′dər stŭd′ē) *tr.v.* **un•der•stud•ied** (ŭn′dər stŭd′ēd), **un•der•stud•y•ing, un•der•stud•ies** (ŭn′dər stŭd′ēz). **1.** To study or know (a role) so as to be able to substitute for the regular actor. **2.** To act as an understudy to (an actor). —*n., pl.* **un•der•stud•ies.** An actor trained to substitute for the regular actor.

un•der•take (ŭn′dər tāk′) *tr.v.* **un•der•took** (ŭn′-dər to͝ok′), **un•der•tak•en, un•der•tak•ing, un•der•takes. 1.** To take upon oneself; decide or agree to do: *undertake a difficult job.* **2.** To agree or promise: *She undertook to inspect the building.*

un•der•tak•er (ŭn′dər tā′kər) *n.* A funeral director.

un•der•tak•ing (ŭn′dər tā′kĭng) *n.* **1.** A task or an assignment undertaken; a venture. **2.** The occupation of a funeral director.

un•der•tone (ŭn′dər tōn′) *n.* **1.** An underlying or implied sense or meaning. **2.** A speech tone of low pitch or volume.

un•der•took (ŭn′dər to͝ok′) *v.* Past tense of **undertake.**

un•der•tow (ŭn′dər tō′) *n.* A current beneath the surface of a body of water running in a direction opposite to that of the current at the surface.

un•der•val•ue (ŭn′dər văl′yo͞o) *tr.v.* **un•der•val•ued, un•der•val•u•ing, un•der•val•ues. 1.** To value at less than real worth: *Houses are undervalued in this neighborhood.* **2.** To have too little regard for: *Don't undervalue his abilities.*

un•der•wa•ter (ŭn′dər wô′tər *or* ŭn′dər wŏt′ər) *adj.* Used, done, or existing under the surface of water. **—un′der•wa′ter** *adv.*

un•der way or **un•der•way** (ŭn′dər wā′) *adv. & adj.* **1.** In motion or operation: *The boat got under way.* **2.** In progress: *Plans for a new stadium are under way.*

un•der•wear (ŭn′dər wâr′) *n.* Underclothes.

un•der•weight (ŭn′dər wāt′) *adj.* Weighing less than is normal or required. —*n.* Weight that is below normal or usual.

un•der•went (ŭn′dər wĕnt′) *v.* Past tense of **undergo.**

un•der•world (ŭn′dər wûrld′) *n.* **1.** The part of society engaged in crime and vice. **2.** In Greek and Roman mythology, the world of the dead, located beneath the world of the living.

un•der•write (ŭn′dər rīt′) *tr.v.* **un•der•wrote** (ŭn′dər rōt′), **un•der•writ•ten** (ŭn′dər rĭt′n), **un•der•writ•ing, un•der•writes. 1.** To assume financial responsibility for; guarantee against failure: *The corporation underwrote the movie.* **2.** To sign (an insurance policy), thus guaranteeing payment in the event of losses or damage. **3.** To agree to buy (the stock in a new enterprise not yet sold publicly) at a fixed time and price. **4.** To write underneath or

ă	pat	oi	boy
ā	pay	ou	out
âr	care	o͝o	took
ä	father	o͞o	boot
ĕ	pet	ŭ	cut
ē	be	ûr	urge
ĭ	pit	th	thin
ī	pie	*th*	this
îr	pier	hw	whoop
ŏ	pot	zh	vision
ō	toe	ə	about
ô	paw	N	*French* bon

Word Building: uni–

The basic meaning of the prefix **uni–** is "one." It comes from the Latin prefix *ūni–*, from the word *ūnus*, meaning "one." Many English words beginning with **uni–** were formed in Latin. The word **unicorn**, for example, comes from *ūni–* + *cornū*, meaning "horn," and refers to a one-horned animal. **Uniform** comes from *ūni–* + *fōrma*, "shape," and means "always the same" or literally "one shape." And **unison**, which comes from *ūni–* + *sonus*, "sound," means literally "one sound." The majority of new words with **uni–**, such as **unicellular**, **unicycle**, **unilateral**, and **univalent**, are from the 19th century. **Uni–** can be compared to the prefix **mono–**, which is from Greek.

unicorn
Detail of late 18th- to early 19th-century American watercolor and ink drawing

below, especially to endorse (a document). —**un′der•writ′er** *n.*

un•de•sir•a•ble (ŭn′dĭ **zīr′**ə bəl) *adj.* Not desirable; not wanted. —*n.* A person who is not wanted or whose behavior is objectionable. —**un′de•sir′a•bil′i•ty** *n.* —**un′de•sir′a•bly** *adv.*

un•did (ŭn **dĭd′**) *v.* Past tense of **undo.**

un•dies (**ŭn′**dēz) *pl.n. Informal.* Underwear.

un•dig•ni•fied (ŭn **dĭg′**nə fīd′) *adj.* Lacking in or harmful to dignity: *undignified behavior.*

un•do (ŭn **do͞o′**) *tr.v.* **un•did** (ŭn **dĭd′**), **un•done** (ŭn-**dŭn′**), **un•do•ing** (ŭn **do͞o′**ĭng), **un•does** (ŭn **dŭz′**). **1.** To do away with or reverse the result or effect of (a previous action): *trying to undo mistakes.* **2.** To untie, unfasten, or loosen: *undo a knot.* **3.** To open; unwrap: *undo a package.* **4.** To cause the ruin or downfall of.

❑ *These sound alike:* **undo, undue** (excessive).

un•do•ing (ŭn **do͞o′**ĭng) *n.* **1.** The act of fastening or loosening. **2.** Ruin; destruction. **3.** A cause of ruin; a downfall: *Greed was his undoing.* **4.** The act of reversing or canceling something.

un•done (ŭn **dŭn′**) *v.* Past participle of **undo.**

un•doubt•ed (ŭn **dou′**tĭd) *adj.* Not doubted or questioned; accepted: *undoubted talent.* —**un•doubt′ed•ly** *adv.*

un•dreamed (ŭn **drēmd′**) also **un•dreamt** (ŭn **drĕmt′**) *adj.* Not believed possible; unimaginable: *undreamed wealth; discoveries undreamed of by scientists.*

un•dress (ŭn **drĕs′**) *v.* **un•dressed, un•dress•ing, un•dress•es.** —*tr.* To remove the clothing of; disrobe. —*intr.* To take off one's clothing. —*n.* Nakedness: *in a state of undress.*

un•due (ŭn **do͞o′** *or* ŭn **dyo͞o′**) *adj.* **1.** Beyond what is normal or appropriate; excessive: *an undue amount of noise.* **2.** Not proper or legal: *undue powers.* **3.** Not yet payable or due: *an undue loan.*

❑ *These sound alike:* **undue, undo** (reverse).

un•du•late (**ŭn′**jə lāt′ *or* **ŭn′**dyə lāt′) *v.* **un•du•lat•ed, un•du•lat•ing, un•du•lates.** —*tr.* **1.** To cause to move in waves: *The wind undulated the wheat.* **2.** To give a wavy appearance or form to: *The hills undulate the land for miles.* —*intr.* **1.** To move in waves or with a smooth wavy motion: *wheat undulating in the breeze.* **2.** To have a wavy appearance or form. [First written down in 1664 in Modern English, from Late Latin *undula*, small wave.]

un•du•la•tion (ŭn′jə **lā′**shən *or* ŭn′dyə **lā′**shən) *n.* **1.** A regular rising and falling or movement from side to side; movement in waves. **2.** A wavy form, outline, or appearance. **3.** One of a series of waves or parts of waves.

un•du•ly (ŭn **do͞o′**lē *or* ŭn **dyo͞o′**lē) *adv.* Excessively; immoderately: *unduly fearful.*

un•dy•ing (ŭn **dī′**ĭng) *adj.* Endless; everlasting: *undying gratitude.*

un•earned (ŭn **ûrnd′**) *adj.* **1.** Not gained by work: *unearned income.* **2.** Not deserved: *unearned praise.* **3.** Not yet earned: *unearned interest.*

un•earth (ŭn **ûrth′**) *tr.v.* **un•earthed, un•earth•ing, un•earths. 1.** To bring up out of the earth; dig up: *unearthing pottery.* **2.** To bring to public notice; uncover: *unearthing evidence about the crime.*

un•earth•ly (ŭn **ûrth′**lē) *adj.* **un•earth•li•er, un•earth•li•est. 1.** Not of the earth or this world; supernatural: *unearthly creatures.* **2.** Unnaturally strange and frightening. *an unearthly scream.* **3.** Not customary or reasonable; absurd: *gets up at an unearthly hour.* —**un•earth′li•ness** *n.*

un•eas•y (ŭn **ē′**zē) *adj.* **un•eas•i•er, un•eas•i•est. 1.** Lacking a sense of security: *The farmers were uneasy until the crop was in.* **2.** Awkward or unsure in manner: *The dog is uneasy with strangers.* —**un•eas′i•ly** *adv.* —**un•eas′i•ness** *n.*

un•ed•u•cat•ed (ŭn **ĕj′**ə kā′tĭd) *adj.* Lacking education, especially in formal schooling; not educated.

un•em•ploy•a•ble (ŭn′ĕm **ploi′**ə bəl) *adj.* Not able to find or hold a job.

un•em•ployed (ŭn′ĕm **ploid′**) *adj.* **1.** Out of work; jobless. **2.** Not being used; idle: *an unemployed lathe.* —*pl.n.* People who are out of work.

un•em•ploy•ment (ŭn′ĕm **ploi′**mənt) *n.* The condition of being unemployed.

un•e•qual (ŭn **ē′**kwəl) *adj.* **1.** Not the same in any measurable way; not equal: *unequal numbers.* **2.** Not the same in rank or social position. **3.** Having opponents that are unevenly matched: *an unequal race.* **4.** Not having the required ability; not adequate: *unequal to the task.* **5.** Not fair: *unequal distribution of income.*

un•e•qualed also **un•e•qualled** (ŭn **ē′**kwəld) *adj.* Not matched by others of its kind; exceptional.

un•e•quiv•o•cal (ŭn′ĭ **kwĭv′**ə kəl) *adj.* Admitting of no doubt; clear: *an unequivocal success.* —**un′e•quiv′o•cal•ly** *adv.*

un•err•ing (ŭn **ûr′**ĭng *or* ŭn **ĕr′**ĭng) *adj.* Making no mistakes; consistently accurate. —**un•err′ing•ly** *adv.*

UNESCO *abbr.* An abbreviation of United Nations Educational, Scientific, and Cultural Organization.

un•e•ven (ŭn **ē′**vən) *adj.* **un•e•ven•er, un•e•ven•est. 1.** Not equal, as in size, length, or quality. **2.** Having opponents that are poorly matched: *an uneven contest.* **3.** Not uniform or consistent; varying, as in quality or form: *an uneven performance; a lamp giving very uneven light.* **4.** Not level or smooth: *the uneven surface of a cobblestone road.* **5.** Not straight or parallel: *a book with uneven margins.* —**un•e′ven•ly** *adv.* —**un•e′ven•ness** *n.*

un•e•vent•ful (ŭn′ĭ **vĕnt′**fəl) *adj.* Having no significant events. —**un′e•vent′ful•ly** *adv.*

un•ex•cep•tion•a•ble (ŭn′ĭk **sĕp′**shə nə bəl) *adj.* Beyond any reasonable objection; irreproachable.

un•ex•cep•tion•al (ŭn′ĭk **sĕp′**shə nəl) *adj.* Not varying from what is usual or expected. —**un′ex•cep′tion•al•ly** *adv.*

un•ex•pect•ed (ŭn′ĭk **spĕk′**tĭd) *adj.* Not expected; coming without warning. —**un′ex•pect′ed•ly** *adv.* —**un′ex•pect′ed•ness** *n.*

un•fail•ing (ŭn **fā′**lĭng) *adj.* **1.** Not running out; inexhaustible: *a source of unfailing amusement.* **2.** Constant; reliable: *an unfailing friend.* —**un•fail′ing•ly** *adv.*

un•fair (ŭn **fâr′**) *adj.* **un•fair•er, un•fair•est.** Not fair, right, or just: *unfair laws.* —**un•fair′ly** *adv.* —**un•fair′ness** *n.*

un•faith•ful (ŭn **fāth′**fəl) *adj.* **1.** Not faithful; disloyal. **2.** Not true to one's spouse or lover. **3.** Not reflecting the original contents; inaccurate: *an unfaithful copy.* —**un•faith′ful•ness** *n.*

un•fa•mil•iar (ŭn′fə **mĭl′**yər) *adj.* **1.** Not acquainted: *unfamiliar with that subject.* **2.** Not within one's knowledge; strange: *an unfamiliar face.* —**un′fa•mil•iar′i•ty** (ŭn′fə mĭl **yăr′**ĭ tē) *n.* —**un′fa•mil′iar•ly** *adv.*

un•fas•ten (ŭn **făs′**ən) *v.* **un•fas•tened, un•fas•ten•ing, un•fas•tens.** —*tr.* To separate the connected parts of; open: *unfastened the belt.* —*intr.* To become opened or untied: *The buckle unfastens easily.*

un•fa•vor•a•ble (ŭn **fā′**vər ə bəl *or* ŭn **fāv′**rə bəl) *adj.* **1.** Likely to be a hindrance; disadvantageous: *unfavorable winds.* **2.** Opposed; adverse: *unfavorable criticism.* —**un•fa′vor•a•bly** *adv.*

un•feel•ing (ŭn **fē′**lĭng) *adj.* **1.** Having no sensation; numb. **2.** Not sympathetic; callous.

un•feigned (ŭn**fānd′**) *adj.* Not feigned; genuine or sincere.

un•fet•ter (ŭn **fĕt′**ər) *tr.v.* **un•fet•tered, un•fet•ter•ing, un•fet•ters.** To set free or keep free from restrictions or bonds.

un•fin•ished (ŭn **fĭn′**ĭsht) *adj.* **1.** Not finished; incomplete: *unfinished business.* **2.** Not processed in a specific way; natural: *unfinished furniture.*

un•fit (ŭn **fĭt′**) *adj.* **1.** Not suitable or adapted for a given purpose; inappropriate: *a paint that is unfit for use on metal.* **2.** Performing below a standard; incompetent or unqualified: *an unfit teacher.* **3.** Not in good health.

un•flap•pa•ble (ŭn **flăp′**ə bəl) *adj.* Not easily upset or excited; calm. **—un•flap′pa•bil′i•ty** *n.*

un•fledged (ŭn **flĕjd′**) *adj.* **1.** Having incompletely developed feathers and still unable to fly: *an unfledged bird.* **2.** Inexperienced; immature.

un•flinch•ing (ŭn **flĭn′**chĭng) *adj.* Not showing fear or indecision; steadfast: *an unflinching determination to find out all the facts.* **—un•flinch′ing•ly** *adv.*

un•fold (ŭn **fōld′**) *v.* **un•fold•ed, un•fold•ing, un•folds.** *—tr.* **1.** To open or spread out: *unfolded the map.* **2.** To reveal gradually; make known: *unfolding the details of her plans.* *—intr.* **1.** To become spread out or open: *The flower unfolded during the day.* **2.** To develop: *Their rivalry unfolded over the summer.* **3.** To be revealed gradually: *The truth unfolded as the investigation proceeded.*

un•fore•seen (ŭn′fər **sēn′** *or* ŭn′fôr **sēn′**) *adj.* Not foreseen; unexpected.

un•for•get•ta•ble (ŭn′fər **gĕt′**ə bəl) *adj.* Permanently impressed on one's memory; memorable. **—un′for•get′ta•bly** *adv.*

un•formed (ŭn **fôrmd′**) *adj.* **1.** Having no definite shape or form. **2.** Not yet developed: *unformed ideas.*

un•for•tu•nate (ŭn **fôr′**chə nĭt) *adj.* **1.** Having undeserved bad luck; unlucky. **2.** Causing misfortune; disastrous. **3.** Regrettable or inappropriate: *an unfortunate remark.* *—n.* A person who has undeserved bad luck. **—un•for′tu•nate•ly** *adv.*

un•found•ed (ŭn **foun′**dĭd) *adj.* Having no basis in fact; groundless: *unfounded accusations.*

un•friend•ly (ŭn **frĕnd′**lē) *adj.* **un•friend•li•er, un•friend•li•est. 1.** Not friendly. **2.** Unpleasant or unfavorable: *unfriendly clouds on the horizon.* **—un•friend′li•ness** *n.*

un•furl (ŭn **fûrl′**) *tr. & intr.v.* **un•furled, un•furl•ing, un•furls.** To open or spread out or become open or spread out; unroll: *Let's unfurl the flag. The banner unfurled for everyone to see.*

un•gain•ly (ŭn **gān′**lē) *adj.* **un•gain•li•er, un•gain•li•est.** Lacking grace or ease of movement; awkward; clumsy. [First written down in 1611 in Modern English and spelled *ungainely* : *un-*, not + *gainli*, proper (from Old Norse *gegn*, direct).] **—un•gain′li•ness** *n.*

un•god•ly (ŭn **gŏd′**lē) *adj.* **un•god•li•er, un•god•li•est. 1.** Not revering God; impious. **2.** Sinful; wicked. **3.** Outrageous: *waking him up at that ungodly hour.*

un•gov•ern•a•ble (ŭn **gŭv′**ər nə bəl) *adj.* Incapable of being governed or controlled: *an ungovernable mob.*

un•gra•cious (ŭn **grā′**shəs) *adj.* Impolite; discourteous; rude.

un•gram•mat•i•cal (ŭn′grə **măt′**ĭ kəl) *adj.* Not in accord with the rules or standards of grammar.

un•grate•ful (ŭn **grāt′**fəl) *adj.* **1.** Not feeling or expressing thanks. **2.** Disagreeable; unpleasant: *an ungrateful task.* **—un•grate′ful•ly** *adv.* **—un•grate′ful•ness** *n.*

un•guard•ed (ŭn **gär′**dĭd) *adj.* **1.** Lacking a guard or defense: *an unguarded gate.* **2.** Having or showing no caution or thought; careless: *The question caught her during an unguarded moment.*

un•guent (**ŭng′**gwənt) *n.* A salve for soothing or healing; an ointment. [First written down before 1425 in Middle English, from Latin *unguentum.*]

un•gu•late (**ŭng′**gyə lĭt *or* **ŭng′**gyə lāt′) *adj.* Having hoofs. *—n.* A hoofed animal, such as a horse, cow, or deer. [First written down in 1802 in Modern English, from Latin *ungula*, hoof.]

un•hand (ŭn **hănd′**) *tr.v.* **un•hand•ed, un•hand•ing, un•hands.** To remove one's hands from; let go of: *Unhand me!*

un•hap•py (ŭn **hăp′**ē) *adj.* **un•hap•pi•er, un•hap•pi•est. 1.** Not happy; sad: *feeling unhappy.* See Synonyms at **sad. 2.** Not satisfied; displeased: *She's unhappy with her performance.* **3.** Not bringing good fortune; unlucky: *In an unhappy moment he made a wrong decision.* **4.** Not suitable; inappropriate: *an unhappy choice of words.* **—un•hap′pi•ly** *adv.* **—un•hap′pi•ness** *n.*

un•health•y (ŭn **hĕl′**thē) *adj.* **un•health•i•er, un•health•i•est. 1.** Being in a state of poor health; ill; sick. **2.** Being a sign or symptom of poor health: *a pale unhealthy appearance.* **3.** Causing or tending to cause poor health; not wholesome: *an unhealthy diet.* **4.** Harmful to character or moral health; corruptive: *an unhealthy influence on her younger sister.* **5.** Risky; dangerous: *an unhealthy situation.*

un•heard-of (ŭn **hûrd′**ŭv′) *adj.* Not previously known or done; without an earlier example: *living in unheard-of luxury.*

un•hinge (ŭn **hĭnj′**) *tr.v.* **un•hinged, un•hing•ing, un•hing•es. 1.** To remove from hinges: *unhinged the door.* **2.** To remove the hinges from. **3.** To confuse, upset, or derange: *The conductor was unhinged by the poor performance of the choir.*

un•ho•ly (ŭn **hō′**lē) *adj.* **un•ho•li•er, un•ho•li•est. 1.** Wicked; immoral. **2.** Not holy or sacred. **3.** *Informal.* Dreadful; outrageous: *an unholy mess.*

un•hook (ŭn **ho͝ok′**) *tr.v.* **un•hooked, un•hook•ing, un•hooks. 1.** To release or remove from a hook: *unhooked the porch screen.* **2.** To unfasten the hooks of: *unhook a dress.*

un•horse (ŭn **hôrs′**) *tr.v.* **un•horsed, un•hors•ing, un•hors•es.** To cause (a rider) to fall from a horse.

uni– *pref.* A prefix that means one or single: *unilateral.* —SEE NOTE.

u•ni•cam•er•al (yo͞o′nĭ **kăm′**ər əl) *adj.* Having or consisting of a single legislative chamber: *a unicameral parliament.*

UNICEF *abbr.* An abbreviation of United Nations Children's Fund.

u•ni•cel•lu•lar (yo͞o′nĭ **sĕl′**yə lər) *adj.* Having or consisting of a single cell; one-celled: *unicellular microorganisms.*

u•ni•corn (**yo͞o′**nĭ kôrn′) *n.* A legendary animal resembling a horse and having a single long horn projecting from its forehead. [First written down before 1200 in Middle English and spelled *unicorne*, from Latin *ūnicornis*, having one horn : *ūnus*, one + *cornū*, horn.]

u•ni•cy•cle (**yo͞o′**nĭ sī′kəl) *n.* A vehicle consisting of a frame mounted over a single wheel and usually propelled by pedals.

un•i•den•ti•fied flying object (ŭn′ī **dĕn′**tə fīd′) *n.* A flying object of an unknown nature, especially one suspected to have been sent by extraterrestrial beings.

u•ni•form (**yo͞o′**nə fôrm′) *adj.* **1.** Always the same; not changing or varying: *planks of uniform length.* **2.** Being the same as or consistent with another or others: *rows of uniform brick houses.* *—n.* A suit of clothing intended to identify the persons who wear it as members of a specific group. [First written

unicycle

uniform
Park ranger

ă	pat	oi	boy
ā	pay	ou	out
âr	care	o͝o	took
ä	father	o͞o	boot
ĕ	pet	ŭ	cut
ē	be	ûr	urge
ĭ	pit	th	thin
ī	pie	*th*	this
îr	pier	hw	whoop
ŏ	pot	zh	vision
ō	toe	ə	about
ô	paw	N	*French* bon

Union Jack

Union of Soviet Socialist Republics

The **Union of Soviet Socialist Republics** (or **Soviet Union**) was created in December 1922 by the Communists who overthrew the czars. It included Russia (or "Great Russia," which included Siberia), the Ukraine (or "Little Russia"), Belorussia (or "White Russia"), the Baltic States (Latvia, Lithuania, and Estonia), and the lands of the Caucasus and central Asia. During the crisis in the Soviet Union in 1990–1991, the Baltic states declared complete independence. Russia, the Ukraine, Belorussia, and many of the other members of the Soviet Union declared independence as well and formed the Commonwealth of Independent States in 1991. The Soviet Union was formally dissolved on December 31, 1991.

down in 1540 in Modern English, from Latin *ūniformis* : *ūni-*, one + *forma*, shape.] **—u′ni•formed′** *adj.* **—u′ni•for′mi•ty** *n.* **—u′ni•form′ly** *adv.*

u•ni•fy (yo͞o′nə fī′) *tr. & intr.v.* **u•ni•fied** (yo͞o′nə fīd), **u•ni•fy•ing, u•ni•fies** (yo͞o′nə fīz). To make into or become a unit; unite. **—u′ni•fi•ca′tion** (yo͞o′nə fĭ **kā′**shən) *n.*

u•ni•lat•er•al (yo͞o′nə **lăt′**ər əl) *adj.* **1.** Of, on, or affecting only one side. **2.** Done or undertaken by only one side: *unilateral disarmament.* **—u′ni•lat′er•al•ly** *adv.*

un•im•peach•a•ble (ŭn′ĭm **pē′**chə bəl) *adj.* **1.** Difficult or impossible to impeach. **2.** Beyond reproach; blameless: *unimpeachable behavior.* **3.** Beyond doubt or question; unquestionable: *unimpeachable honesty.*

un•im•por•tant (ŭn′ĭm **pôr′**tnt) *adj.* Not important; petty. **—un′im•por′tance** *n.*

un•in•hab•it•ed (ŭn′ĭn **hăb′**ĭ tĭd) *adj.* Not inhabited; having no residents.

un•in•hib•it•ed (ŭn′ĭn **hĭb′**ĭ tĭd) *adj.* **1.** Open and unrestrained: *uninhibited laughter.* **2.** Free from social or moral restraints.

un•in•tel•li•gent (ŭn′ĭn **tĕl′**ə jənt) *adj.* Lacking in intelligence. **—un′in•tel′li•gent•ly** *adv.*

un•in•tel•li•gi•ble (ŭn′ĭn **tĕl′**ĭ jə bəl) *adj.* Difficult or impossible to understand. **—un′in•tel′li•gi•bil′i•ty** *n.* **—un′in•tel′li•gi•bly** *adv.*

un•in•ten•tion•al (ŭn′ĭn **tĕn′**shə nəl) *adj.* Not done or said on purpose. **—un′in•ten′tion•al•ly** *adv.*

un•in•ter•est•ed (ŭn **ĭn′**trĭ stĭd *or* ŭn **ĭn′**tə rĕs′tĭd) *adj.* **1.** Having no stake or interest; impartial. **2.** Not interested; indifferent.

un•in•vit•ed (ŭn′ĭn **vī′**tĭd) *adj.* Not invited or welcome.

un•ion (**yo͞on′**yən) *n.* **1.a.** The act of uniting or the state of being united: *union of the two colleges into one.* **b.** A combination formed by uniting, especially a number of persons or groups joined together for a purpose: *plans for the union of all colonies under one government.* **2.** A mathematical set having the property that each of its elements is also an element of two or more given sets. **3.** A partnership in marriage: *a happy union.* **4.** A labor union. **5.** A device used for joining parts, such as pipes or rods. **6.** A design on or part of a flag that symbolizes the union of two or more independent states or regions. For example, the blue part with stars is the union of the U.S. flag. **7. Union.** The United States of America, especially during the Civil War. *—adj.* **1. Union.** Of, relating to, or loyal to the United States of America during the Civil War. **2.** Of or relating to a labor union. [First written down in 1410 in Middle English and spelled *unioun*, from Late Latin *ūniō*, from Latin *ūnus*, one.]

un•ion•ize (**yo͞on′**yə nīz′) *tr.v.* **un•ion•ized, un•ion•iz•ing, un•ion•iz•es.** To organize into or cause to join a labor union: *unionize factory workers.* **—un′ion•i•za′tion** (yo͞on′yə nĭ **zā′**shən) *n.*

Union Jack *n.* The flag of the United Kingdom.

Union of So•vi•et Socialist Republics (**sō′**vē ĕt′ *or* **sō′**vē ĭt). Commonly called **Soviet Union.** A former country of eastern Europe and northern Asia with coastlines on the Baltic and Black seas and the Arctic and Pacific oceans. It was established in December 1922 and was officially dissolved on December 31, 1991. —See Note.

union shop *n.* A business or industrial establishment whose employees are required to be or become members of a labor union.

u•nique (yo͞o **nēk′**) *adj.* **1.** Being the only one of its kind: *the unique manuscript of a medieval poem.* **2.** Having no equal or equivalent: *a unique opportunity to buy a house.* [First written down in 1602 in Modern English, from Latin *ūnicus.*] **—u•nique′ly** *adv.* **—u•nique′ness** *n.* —See Note.

u•ni•sex (**yo͞o′**nĭ sĕks′) *adj.* Suitable to both males and females: *unisex clothes.*

u•ni•son (**yo͞o′**nĭ sən *or* **yo͞o′**nĭ zən) *n.* **1.** In music, the combination of two or more tones of the same pitch at the same time. **2.** Agreement; harmony. ***—idiom.* in unison. 1.** In complete agreement; harmonizing exactly. **2.** At the same time; at once.

u•nit (**yo͞o′**nĭt) *n.* **1.** A thing, person, group, or structure regarded as a part of a whole: *adding an extra unit to a bookcase.* **2.** A single group regarded as a distinct part within a larger group: *an army unit.* **3.** A mechanical part or piece of equipment: *an air-conditioning unit.* **4.** A precisely defined quantity used as a standard for measuring quantities of the same kind: *The meter is a unit of distance.* **5.a.** The number located just to the left of the decimal point in the Arabic numeral system. **b.** The lowest whole number; 1: *to count in units, tens, and hundreds.* **6.** A section of a course of study focusing on one subject: *a unit on Native Americans.* [First written down in 1570 in Modern English, from *unity*.]

U•ni•tar•i•an (yo͞o′nĭ **târ′**ē ən) *n.* **1.** A person who believes in Unitarian Universalism. **2.** A Christian who does not believe in the Trinity or the divinity of Jesus, but who believes that God is a single being. **—U′ni•tar′i•an** *adj.* **—U′ni•tar′i•an•ism** *n.*

Unitarian U•ni•ver•sal•ism (yo͞o′nə **vûr′**sə lĭz′əm) *n.* A member of a religious association of Christian origin that has no official creed and that considers God to be a single being and salvation to be granted to everyone.

u•nite (yo͞o **nīt′**) *v.* **u•nit•ed, u•nit•ing, u•nites.** *—tr.* **1.** To bring together or join so as to form a whole: *The chemist united the substances to form a new compound.* See Synonyms at **join. 2.** To join together or to bring into close association for a common purpose: *a treaty to unite all nations in the fight against disease.* **3.** To join (a couple) in matrimony. *—intr.* **1.** To become joined or combined into a unit: *The two firms united to form a large business.* **2.** To join and act together for a common purpose: *Let's unite and stop pollution.* [First written down before 1425 in Middle English and spelled *uniten*, from Latin *ūnus*, one.]

u•nit•ed (yo͞o **nī′**tĭd) *adj.* **1.** Combined into one. **2.** Concerned with or resulting from joint action: *a united effort to preserve the meadow.* **3.** Being in harmony; agreed: *On that point we are united.*

Unit•ed Arab E•mir•ates (ĭ **mîr′**ĭts *or* **ĕm′**ər ĭts). A country of eastern Arabia on the Persian Gulf. It was formed in 1971. Capital, Abu Dhabi. Population, 980,000.

United Arab Republic. 1. A former union of Egypt and Syria that lasted from 1958 until 1961. **2.** Egypt.

United Kingdom or **United Kingdom of Great Britain and Northern Ireland.** Commonly called **Great Britain** or **Britain.** A country of western Europe made up of England, Scotland, Wales, and Northern Ireland. It reached the height of its power in the 19th century. London is the capital and the largest city. Population, 55,648,994.

United Nations. An international organization composed of most of the countries of the world. It was founded in 1945.

United States or **United States of America.** A country of central and northwest North America with coastlines on the Atlantic and Pacific oceans. It includes the states of Alaska and Hawaii and various island territories in the Caribbean Sea and Pacific Ocean. The original Thirteen Colonies declared their independence from Great Britain in

1776. Washington, D.C., is the capital and New York is the largest city. Population, 249,632,692.

unit pricing *n.* The pricing of goods on the basis of cost per unit of measure.

u•ni•ty (yo͞o′nĭ tē) *n., pl.* **u•ni•ties. 1.** The condition of being one. **2.** Accord; harmony: *a period of great national unity and purpose.* **3.** The combination or arrangement of parts, as in a work of art or literature, into a complete whole. **4.** The number 1. [First written down about 1300 in Middle English and spelled *unite,* from Latin *ūnus,* one.]

univ. *abbr.* An abbreviation of: **1.** Universal. **2.** University.

u•ni•va•lent (yo͞o′nĭ **vā′**lənt) *adj.* In chemistry, having valence 1.

u•ni•valve (**yo͞o′**nĭ vălv′) *adj.* **1.** Having a single shell: *a univalve mollusk.* **2.** Consisting of a single part: *a univalve shell.* —*n.* A mollusk, such as a snail, having a single shell.

u•ni•ver•sal (yo͞o′nə **vûr′**səl) *adj.* **1.** Relating to, extending to, or affecting the whole world; worldwide: *universal peace.* **2.** Including, relating to, or affecting all members of a class or group: *the universal delight of critics regarding her new movie.* **3.** Of or relating to the universe: *universal laws.* —**u′ni•ver•sal′i•ty** (yo͞o′nə vər **săl′**ĭ tē) *n.* —**u′ni•ver′sal•ly** *adv.*

U•ni•ver•sal•ist (yo͞o′nə **vûr′**sə lĭst) *n.* A person who believes in Unitarian Universalism.

universal joint *n.* A joint or coupling that transmits rotary motion from one point to another that is not in line with it.

Universal Product Code *n.* A series of vertical bars of varying widths printed on a consumer product and designed to be read by a computer scanner to identify the price and keep track of the inventory.

universal time *n.* The time at the meridian at Greenwich, England (0° longitude), used as a basis for reckoning time throughout the world.

u•ni•verse (**yo͞o′**nə vûrs′) *n.* **1.** All matter and energy considered as a whole; the cosmos. **2.** In mathematics, a set that contains all the objects and sets under discussion as elements or subsets. [First written down about 1374 in Middle English, from Latin *ūniversus,* whole : *ūnus,* one + *versus,* turned.]

u•ni•ver•si•ty (yo͞o′nə **vûr′**sĭ tē) *n., pl.* **u•ni•ver•si•ties.** An institution of higher learning that includes one or more colleges and a graduate school and professional schools.

un•just (ŭn **jŭst′**) *adj.* Not just or fair; unfair. —**un•just′ly** *adv.*

un•kempt (ŭn **kĕmpt′**) *adj.* **1.** Not combed: *unkempt hair.* **2.** Not neat or tidy; messy: *an unkempt lawn; unkempt clothes.* [First written down before 1393 in Middle English and spelled *unkemd* : *un-,* not + *kembed,* combed (from Old English *cemban,* to comb).]

un•kind (ŭn **kīnd′**) *adj.* **un•kind•er, un•kind•est.** Not kind or sympathetic. —**un•kind′ly** *adv.* —**un•kind′ness** *n.*

un•know•a•ble (ŭn **nō′**ə bəl) *adj.* Impossible to know; beyond human understanding.

un•known (ŭn **nōn′**) *adj.* **1.** Not known or familiar; strange: *a town unknown to us.* **2.** Not identified or ascertained: *an unknown quantity.* **3.** Not widely known: *an unknown painter.* —*n.* A person or thing that is unknown.

un•lace (ŭn **lās′**) *tr.v.* **un•laced, un•lac•ing, un•lac•es.** To loose or undo the laces of.

un•latch (ŭn **lăch′**) *tr.v.* **un•latched, un•latch•ing, un•latch•es.** To unfasten or open by releasing a latch.

un•law•ful (ŭn **lô′**fəl) *adj.* Being in violation of the law; illegal. —**un•law′ful•ly** *adv.*

un•lead•ed (ŭn **lĕd′**ĭd) *adj.* Not containing lead or lead compounds: *unleaded gasoline.*

un•learn (ŭn **lûrn′**) *tr.v.* **un•learned** also **un•learnt** (ŭn **lûrnt′**), **un•learn•ing, un•learns. 1.** To put (something learned) out of the mind; forget. **2.** To stop practicing (a habit).

un•learn•ed (ŭn **lûr′**nĭd) *adj.* **1.** Not educated; ignorant or illiterate. **2.** Not known or acquired by training or studying: *an unlearned sense of balance.*

un•learnt (ŭn **lûrnt′**) *v.* A past tense and past participle of **unlearn.**

un•leash (ŭn **lēsh′**) *tr.v.* **un•leashed, un•leash•ing, un•leash•es.** To release from or as if from a leash: *unleashed the dog; unleashed his anger.*

un•leav•ened (ŭn **lĕv′**ənd) *adj.* Made without yeast or other leaven: *unleavened bread.*

un•less (ŭn **lĕs′**) *conj.* Except on the condition that: *You can't write the report unless you do the research first.* [First written down in 1438 in Middle English and spelled *onlesse* : *on,* on + *lesse,* less.]

un•let•tered (ŭn **lĕt′**ərd) *adj.* Not skilled at reading and writing.

un•like (ŭn **līk′**) *adj.* **1.** Not alike; different. **2.** Not equal, as in amount: *unlike sums.* —*prep.* **1.** Different from; not like: *That band has a sound unlike any other.* **2.** Not typical of: *It is unlike him not to call if he cannot come.*

un•like•ly (ŭn **līk′**lē) *adj.* **un•like•li•er, un•like•li•est. 1.** Not likely; improbable: *an unlikely story.* **2.** Likely to fail; unpromising: *an unlikely business venture.*

un•lim•it•ed (ŭn **lĭm′**ĭ tĭd) *adj.* Having no limits or bounds: *unlimited possibilities.*

un•list•ed (ŭn **lĭs′**tĭd) *adj.* Not appearing on a list: *an unlisted telephone number.*

un•load (ŭn **lōd′**) *tr.v.* **un•load•ed, un•load•ing, un•loads. 1.a.** To remove the load or cargo from: *unload a truck.* **b.** To remove (cargo): *unload furniture from the van.* **2.** To give expression to (one's troubles or feelings). **3.** To remove the charge from (a firearm). **4.** To dispose of, especially by selling in large quantities; dump: *unloading textiles at low prices.*

un•lock (ŭn **lŏk′**) *tr.v.* **un•locked, un•lock•ing, un•locks. 1.** To undo (a lock), as by turning a key or executing a combination. **2.** To undo the lock of: *unlock the trunk.* **3.** To set free; release: *The news unlocked a torrent of emotion.* **4.** To solve, disclose, or reveal: *unlock a mystery.*

un•looked-for (ŭn **lo͝okt′**fôr′) *adj.* Not expected; unforeseen.

un•loose (ŭn **lo͞os′**) *tr.v.* **un•loosed, un•loos•ing, un•loos•es. 1.** To unfasten. **2.** To set free; release.

un•loos•en (ŭn **lo͞o′**sən) *tr.v.* **un•loos•ened, un•loos•en•ing, un•loos•ens.** To unloose.

un•luck•y (ŭn **lŭk′**ē) *adj.* **un•luck•i•er, un•luck•i•est. 1.** Marked by or having bad luck: *an unlucky occurrence; an unlucky person.* **2.** Seeming to cause bad luck: *an unlucky number.* —**un•luck′i•ly** *adv.*

un•made (ŭn **mād′**) *adj.* Not made: *an unmade bed.*

un•man•age•a•ble (ŭn **măn′**ĭ jə bəl) *adj.* Difficult or impossible to manage: *an unmanageable pony; an unmanageable amount of work.*

un•manned (ŭn **mănd′**) *adj.* Lacking a crew or designed to operate without a crew: *an unmanned spacecraft.*

un•man•ner•ly (ŭn **măn′**ər lē) *adj.* Having bad manners; impolite: *unmannerly behavior.*

un•mar•ried (ŭn **măr′**ēd) *adj.* Not married.

un•mask (ŭn **măsk′**) *v.* **un•masked, un•mask•ing, un•masks.** —*tr.* **1.** To remove a mask from. **2.** To disclose the true nature of; reveal: *finally unmasked his resentment.* —*intr.* To remove one's mask.

un•men•tion•a•ble (ŭn **mĕn′**shə nə bəl) *adj.* Not fit to be mentioned or discussed. —*n.* **1.** A person

Usage: unique

The word **unique** is used in its most meaningful way when you are referring to something that really is one of a kind or in a class by itself. Although advertisements often tell you that a product is unique when it only differs slightly in color or taste from another, there is no reason for you to use **unique** in the same way in your writing.

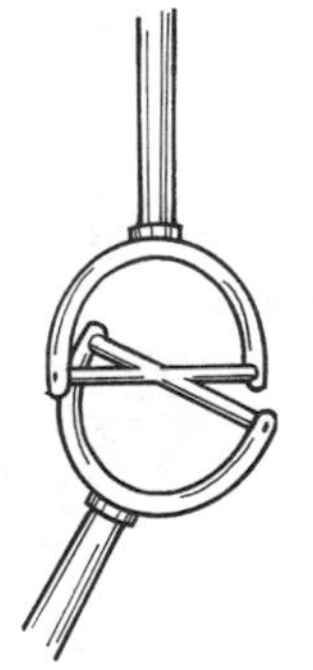

universal joint
Yoke and spider model

ă	**pat**	oi	**boy**
ā	**pay**	ou	**out**
âr	**care**	o͝o	**took**
ä	**father**	o͞o	**boot**
ĕ	**pet**	ŭ	**cut**
ē	**be**	ûr	**urge**
ĭ	**pit**	th	**thin**
ī	**pie**	*th*	**this**
îr	**pier**	hw	**whoop**
ŏ	**pot**	zh	**vision**
ō	**toe**	ə	**about**
ô	**paw**	N	*French* **bon**

or thing that is not to be mentioned. **2. unmentionables.** Underwear.

un•mer•ci•ful (ŭn mûr′sĭ fəl) *adj.* **1.** Having or showing no mercy; merciless. **2.** Excessive; extreme: *unmerciful heat.* **—un•mer′ci•ful•ly** *adv.*

un•mind•ful (ŭn mīnd′fəl) *adj.* Not giving enough care or attention; careless: *unmindful of the time.* **—un•mind′ful•ly** *adv.*

un•mis•tak•a•ble (ŭn′mĭ stā′kə bəl) *adj.* Impossible to mistake: *the unmistakable sound of a hyena.* **—un′mis•tak′a•bly** *adv.*

un•mit•i•gat•ed (ŭn mĭt′ĭ gā′tĭd) *adj.* **1.** Not diminished in intensity; without relief: *unmitigated heat.* **2.** Absolute; unqualified: *an unmitigated lie.*

un•moved (ŭn mo͞ovd′) *adj.* Emotionally unaffected.

un•nat•u•ral (ŭn năch′ər əl) *adj.* **1.** Not in accordance with what usually occurs in nature; abnormal or unusual. **2.** Strained, stiff, or affected; artificial: *an unnatural manner.* **3.** Against natural feelings; inhuman. **—un•nat′u•ral•ly** *adv.*

un•nec•es•sar•y (ŭn nĕs′ĭ sĕr′ē) *adj.* Not necessary; needless. **—un•nec′es•sar′i•ly** (ŭn nĕs′ĭ sâr′ə lē) *adv.*

un•nerve (ŭn nûrv′) *tr.v.* **un•nerved, un•nerv•ing, un•nerves.** To cause to lose strength or firmness of purpose: *The heated argument unnerved him.*

un•ob•served (ŭn′əb zûrvd′) *adj.* **1.** Not seen or noticed: *We crept up the walkway unobserved.* **2.** Not kept or complied with: *unobserved regulations; an unobserved holiday.*

un•ob•tru•sive (ŭn′əb tro͞o′sĭv) *adj.* Not undesirably blatant or noticeable; inconspicuous. **—un′ob•tru′sive•ly** *adv.* **—un′ob•tru′sive•ness** *n.*

un•oc•cu•pied (ŭn ŏk′yə pīd′) *adj.* **1.** Not occupied or being used; vacant: *unoccupied seats.* **2.** Not busy; idle: *unoccupied workers.*

un•of•fi•cial (ŭn′ə fĭsh′əl) *adj.* Not official: *unofficial reports.* **—un′of•fi′cial•ly** *adv.*

un•op•posed (ŭn′ə pōzd′) *adj.* Not challenged by another: *The candidate was unopposed.*

un•or•gan•ized (ŭn ôr′gə nīzd′) *adj.* **1.** Lacking order, system, or unity; disorganized. **2.** Not represented by a labor union.

un•or•tho•dox (ŭn ôr′thə dŏks′) *adj.* Breaking with tradition or convention; not orthodox: *her unorthodox approach to a problem.*

un•pack (ŭn păk′) *v.* **un•packed, un•pack•ing, un•packs.** *—tr.* **1.** To remove the contents of (a suitcase, for example). **2.** To remove from a container or from packaging: *unpack groceries.* *—intr.* To remove objects from a container.

un•paid (ŭn pād′) *adj.* **1.** Not yet paid: *an unpaid bill.* **2.** Receiving no pay; not salaried: *an unpaid volunteer.*

un•par•al•leled (ŭn păr′ə lĕld′) *adj.* Without parallel or match; unequaled: *unparalleled beauty.*

un•pleas•ant (ŭn plĕz′ənt) *adj.* Not pleasing; disagreeable. **—un•pleas′ant•ly** *adv.*

un•plug (ŭn plŭg′) *tr.v.* **un•plugged, un•plug•ging, un•plugs.** **1.** To remove a plug from. **2.** To disconnect (an electric appliance) by removing a plug from an outlet.

un•pop•u•lar (ŭn pŏp′yə lər) *adj.* Lacking general approval or acceptance.

un•prac•ticed (ŭn prăk′tĭst) *adj.* **1.** Not yet tested or tried: *unpracticed methods.* **2.** Lacking experience; unskilled: *unpracticed volunteers.*

un•prec•e•dent•ed (ŭn prĕs′ĭ dĕn′tĭd) *adj.* Having no previous example: *an unprecedented demand for housing.*

un•pre•dict•a•ble (ŭn′prĭ dĭk′tə bəl) *adj.* Difficult to foretell or foresee. **—un′pre•dict′a•bly** *adv.*

un•pre•pared (ŭn′prĭ pârd′) *adj.* **1.** Having made no preparations: *unprepared for school.* **2.** Done without preparation; impromptu: *an unprepared speech.*

un•pre•pos•sess•ing (ŭn′prē pə zĕs′ĭng) *adj.* Failing to impress favorably; nondescript: *an unprepossessing motel like any other.*

un•pre•ten•tious (ŭn′prĭ tĕn′shəs) *adj.* Lacking pretention or affectation; modest.

un•prin•ci•pled (ŭn prĭn′sə pəld) *adj.* Lacking principles or moral scruples; immoral.

un•print•a•ble (ŭn prĭn′tə bəl) *adj.* Not proper for publication for legal or social reasons: *an unprintable story.*

un•pro•fes•sion•al (ŭn′prə fĕsh′ə nəl) *adj.* **1.** Not a member of a professional group. **2.** Not meeting the standards of a profession: *unprofessional behavior.*

un•prof•it•a•ble (ŭn prŏf′ĭ tə bəl) *adj.* **1.** Bringing in no profit: *an unprofitable business.* **2.** Serving no useful purpose: *got into an unprofitable argument.* **—un•prof′it•a•bly** *adv.*

un•qual•i•fied (ŭn kwŏl′ə fīd′) *adj.* **1.** Without the necessary or required qualifications. **2.** Without reservation; complete: *an unqualified success.*

un•ques•tion•a•ble (ŭn kwĕs′chə nə bəl) *adj.* Beyond question or doubt; certain. **—un•ques′tion•a•bly** *adv.*

un•rav•el (ŭn răv′əl) *v.* **un•rav•eled, un•rav•el•ing, un•rav•els** or **un•rav•elled, un•rav•el•ling, un•rav•els.** *—tr.* **1.a.** To undo (a knitted fabric); reduce to yarn. **b.** To separate (entangled threads). **2.** To separate the elements of (a mystery or problem). *—intr.* To become unraveled.

un•read (ŭn rĕd′) *adj.* **1.** Not read, studied, or examined: *an unread book.* **2.** Having read little; lacking in knowledge acquired by reading.

un•read•y (ŭn rĕd′ē) *adj.* **un•read•i•er, un•read•i•est.** **1.** Not ready or prepared. **2.** Slow to see or respond.

un•re•al (ŭn rē′əl *or* ŭn rēl′) *adj.* **1.** Not real; imaginary. **2.** *Slang.* So remarkable as to be hard to believe. **3.** Surreal.

un•re•al•is•tic (ŭn′rē ə lĭs′tĭk) *adj.* Unreasonably idealistic. **—un′re•al•is′ti•cal•ly** *adv.*

un•rea•son•a•ble (ŭn rē′zə nə bəl) *adj.* **1.** Not subject to reason: *an unreasonable attitude.* **2.** Exceeding reasonable limits; immoderate: *an unreasonable amount.* **—un•rea′son•a•bly** *adv.*

un•re•gen•er•ate (ŭn′rĭ jĕn′ər ĭt) *adj.* **1.** Not spiritually renewed or reformed; not repentant: *an unregenerate sinner.* **2.** Not reconciled to change; stubborn: *an unregenerate conservative.*

un•re•lent•ing (ŭn′rĭ lĕn′tĭng) *adj.* **1.** Not yielding, as in resolution; inflexible: *an unrelenting opponent.* **2.** Not diminishing in intensity: *She works at an unrelenting pace.*

un•re•li•a•ble (ŭn′rĭ lī′ə bəl) *adj.* Characterized by or showing a lack of reliability. **—un′re•li′a•bil′i•ty** *n.* **—un′re•li′a•bly** *adv.*

un•re•mit•ting (ŭn′rĭ mĭt′ĭng) *adj.* Not letting up; persistent: *an unremitting struggle for survival.* **—un′re•mit′ting•ly** *adv.*

un•re•pent•ant (ŭn′rĭ pĕn′tənt) *adj.* Having or showing no remorse.

un•re•quit•ed (ŭn′rĭ kwī′tĭd) *adj.* Not reciprocated or returned in kind: *unrequited love.*

un•re•served (ŭn′rĭ zûrvd′) *adj.* **1.** Not held for a particular person: *an unreserved seat.* **2.** Given without reservation: *unreserved praise.* **3.** Showing no reserve: *unreserved laughter.*

un•rest (ŭn rĕst′ *or* ŭn′rĕst′) *n.* An uneasy or troubled condition: *social unrest.*

un•re•strained (ŭn′rĭ strānd′) *adj.* **1.** Not controlled or held in check; immoderate: *unrestrained spread of weeds.* **2.** Not constrained; spontaneous and natural: *unrestrained laughter.*

un•ripe (ŭn rīp′) *adj.* **un•rip•er, un•rip•est. 1.** Not ripe; immature. **2.** Not fully prepared or ready: *The time is yet unripe for such a plan.*

un•ri•valed or **un•ri•valled** (ŭn rī′vəld) *adj.* Having no rival or equal; incomparable: *the unrivaled champion.*

un•ruf•fled (ŭn rŭf′əld) *adj.* **1.** Not agitated; calm: *He was unruffled after the coach's reprimand.* **2.** Regular and smooth, as the surface of water.

un•ru•ly (ŭn ro͞o′lē) *adj.* **un•ru•li•er, un•ru•li•est.** Difficult or impossible to discipline or control.

un•sad•dle (ŭn săd′l) *tr.v.* **un•sad•dled, un•sad•dling, un•sad•dles. 1.** To remove the saddle from. **2.** To throw (a rider) from a saddle. Used of a horse.

un•safe (ŭn sāf′) *adj.* **un•saf•er, un•saf•est.** Not safe; dangerous.

un•said (ŭn sĕd′) *adj.* Not said, especially not uttered out loud: *angry thoughts left unsaid.*

un•san•i•tar•y (ŭn săn′ĭ tĕr′ē) *adj.* Not sanitary; unclean.

un•sat•is•fac•to•ry (ŭn săt′ĭs făk′tə rē) *adj.* Not satisfactory; inadequate: *unsatisfactory living conditions.*

un•sat•u•rat•ed (ŭn săch′ə rā′tĭd) *adj.* **1.** Of or indicating a chemical compound, especially of carbon, in which two atoms are joined by more than a single bond: *unsaturated fats.* **2.** Capable of dissolving more of a solute: *an unsaturated solution.*

un•sa•vor•y (ŭn sā′və rē) *adj.* **1.** Unpleasant to the taste or smell; not savory. **2.** Distasteful or disagreeable: *an unsavory situation.* **3.** Morally offensive: *an unsavory character.*

un•scathed (ŭn skā*th*d′) *adj.* Not harmed or injured.

un•sci•en•tif•ic (ŭn′sī ən tĭf′ĭk) *adj.* **1.** Not according to the principles of science. **2.** Not knowledgeable about science.

un•scram•ble (ŭn skrăm′bəl) *tr.v.* **un•scram•bled, un•scram•bling, un•scram•bles. 1.** To straighten out or disentangle (a jumble or tangle); resolve. **2.** To restore (a scrambled message) to intelligible form: *She unscrambled the coded message.*

un•screw (ŭn skro͞o′) *v.* **un•screwed, un•screw•ing, un•screws.** —*tr.* **1.** To remove the screws from: *unscrewed the hinges.* **2.** To loosen, adjust, or remove by turning: *unscrewed the lid off the jar.* —*intr.* To become or allow to become unscrewed: *This lid unscrews easily.*

un•scru•pu•lous (ŭn skro͞o′pyə ləs) *adj.* Without scruples or principles; not honorable. —**un•scru′pu•lous•ly** *adv.* —**un•scru′pu•lous•ness** *n.*

un•seal (ŭn sēl′) *tr.v.* **un•sealed, un•seal•ing, un•seals.** To break open or remove the seal of; open.

un•sea•son•a•ble (ŭn sē′zə nə bəl) *adj.* Occurring or done out of season; not suitable for or characteristic of the season: *unseasonable weather.*

un•sea•soned (ŭn sē′zənd) *adj.* **1.** Inexperienced: *unseasoned campers.* **2.** Not ripe or mature: *unseasoned wood.* **3.** Having no added seasoning: *unseasoned meat.*

un•seat (ŭn sēt′) *tr.v.* **un•seat•ed, un•seat•ing, un•seats. 1.** To remove from a seat, especially from a saddle. **2.** To remove or force out of a position or office: *unseated the Senator in the election.*

un•seem•ly (ŭn sēm′lē) *adj.* **un•seem•li•er, un•seem•li•est.** Not in good taste; improper. —**un•seem′ly** *adv.*

un•seen (ŭn sēn′) *adj.* Not seen or noticed; invisible.

un•self•ish (ŭn sĕl′fĭsh) *adj.* Not selfish; generous. —**un•self′ish•ly** *adv.* —**un•self′ish•ness** *n.*

un•set•tle (ŭn sĕt′l) *tr.v.* **un•set•tled, un•set•tling, un•set•tles. 1.** To move from a settled condition; disrupt: *strikes unsettling the economy.* **2.** To make uneasy; disturb: *The news unsettled him.*

un•set•tled (ŭn sĕt′ld) *adj.* **1.** Not in a state of order or calmness; disturbed: *unsettled times.* **2.** Uncertain; variable: *unsettled weather.* **3.** Not determined or resolved: *an unsettled legal case.* **4.** Not paid: *unsettled accounts.* **5.** Not populated; uninhabited: *a vast unsettled region.*

un•shack•le (ŭn shăk′əl) *tr.v.* **un•shack•led, un•shack•ling, un•shack•les.** To release from or as if from shackles; set free.

un•shak•a•ble (ŭn shā′kə bəl) *adj.* Not capable of being shaken; firm: *a woman of unshakable convictions.* —**un•shak′a•bly** *adv.*

un•sheathe (ŭn shē*th*′) *tr.v.* **un•sheathed, un•sheath•ing, un•sheathes.** To remove from or as if from a sheath.

un•shod (ŭn shŏd′) *adj.* Not having or wearing shoes or a shoe: *an unshod horse.*

un•sight•ly (ŭn sīt′lē) *adj.* **un•sight•li•er, un•sight•li•est.** Not pleasant to look at; unattractive. —**un•sight′li•ness** *n.*

un•skilled (ŭn skĭld′) *adj.* **1.** Lacking skill or technical training: *unskilled workers.* **2.** Requiring no special training or skills: *unskilled work.*

un•so•phis•ti•cat•ed (ŭn′sə fĭs′tĭ kā′tĭd) *adj.* Not sophisticated; naive.

un•sound (ŭn sound′) *adj.* **un•sound•er, un•sound•est. 1.** Not dependably strong or solid: *a house with unsound foundations.* **2.** Not physically or mentally healthy. **3.** Not logical; fallacious: *an unsound argument.*

un•speak•a•ble (ŭn spē′kə bəl) *adj.* **1.** Beyond description; indescribable: *unspeakable anxiety.* **2.** Bad beyond description; totally objectionable: *unspeakable wickedness.* **3.** Not to be spoken: *an unspeakable word.* —**un•speak′a•bly** *adv.*

un•spoiled (ŭn spoild′) *adj.* Not spoiled: *an unspoiled landscape.*

un•spo•ken (ŭn spō′kən) *adj.* Not expressed in words; unsaid: *an unspoken wish.*

un•sta•ble (ŭn stā′bəl) *adj.* **un•sta•bler, un•sta•blest. 1.** Having a strong tendency to change: *unstable prices.* **2.** Not firm; unsteady: *an unstable ladder.* **3.** Lacking control of one's emotions; characterized by unpredictable behavior. **4.** Tending to decompose easily, as a chemical compound. **5.a.** Decaying after a relatively short time, as an atomic particle. **b.** Radioactive, as an element, isotope, or atomic nucleus.

un•stead•y (ŭn stĕd′ē) *adj.* **un•stead•i•er, un•stead•i•est. 1.** Not steady; unstable: *an unsteady chair.* **2.** Wavering; uneven: *an unsteady voice.* —**un•stead′i•ly** *adv.* —**un•stead′i•ness** *n.*

un•stop (ŭn stŏp′) *tr.v.* **un•stopped, un•stop•ping, un•stops. 1.** To remove the stopper from: *unstop a bottle.* **2.** To remove an obstruction from; open: *unstop a drain.*

un•stressed (ŭn strĕst′) *adj.* **1.** Not accented or stressed: *an unstressed syllable.* **2.** Not exposed or subjected to stress.

un•strung (ŭn strŭng′) *adj.* **1.** Having a string or strings loosened or removed. **2.** Emotionally upset.

un•stud•ied (ŭn stŭd′ēd) *adj.* Not contrived for effect; natural: *unstudied grace.*

un•sub•stan•tial (ŭn′səb stăn′shəl) *adj.* **1.** Lacking material substance; insubstantial. **2.** Lacking a factual basis: *unsubstantial hopes.*

un•suc•cess•ful (ŭn′sək sĕs′fəl) *adj.* Not succeeding; without success: *an unsuccessful plan; an unsuccessful person.* —**un′suc•cess′ful•ly** *adv.*

un•suit•a•ble (ŭn so͞o′tə bəl) *adj.* Not appropriate: *an unsuitable outfit for a wedding.* —**un•suit′a•bil′i•ty** *n.* —**un•suit′a•bly** *adv.*

un•sung (ŭn sŭng′) *adj.* **1.** Not honored or praised; uncelebrated: *unsung heroes.* **2.** Not sung.

un•sus•pect•ed (ŭn′sə spĕk′tĭd) *adj.* **1.** Not under

ă	pat	oi	boy
ā	pay	ou	out
âr	care	o͝o	took
ä	father	o͞o	boot
ĕ	pet	ŭ	cut
ē	be	ûr	urge
ĭ	pit	th	thin
ī	pie	*th*	this
îr	pier	hw	whoop
ŏ	pot	zh	vision
ō	toe	ə	about
ô	paw	N	*French* bon

suspicion. **2.** Not known; unexpected: *Unsuspected wealth lay hidden there.*

un•sus•pect•ing (ŭn′sə **spĕk′**tĭng) *adj.* Not suspicious; trusting: *an unsuspecting child.* —**un′sus•pect′ing•ly** *adv.*

un•tan•gle (ŭn **tăng′**gəl) *tr.v.* **un•tan•gled, un•tan•gling, un•tan•gles. 1.** To free from a tangle; disentangle: *untangle a fishing line.* **2.** To settle; clarify; resolve: *untangle a problem.*

un•tapped (ŭn **tăpt′**) *adj.* **1.** Not tapped: *an untapped keg.* **2.** Not utilized: *untapped resources.*

un•taught (ŭn **tôt′**) *adj.* **1.** Not instructed; ignorant. **2.** Not acquired by instruction; natural: *untaught musical skill.*

un•ten•a•ble (ŭn **tĕn′**ə bəl) *adj.* Not capable of being defended or maintained: *an untenable position.* —**un•ten′a•bly** *adv.*

un•think•a•ble (ŭn **thĭng′**kə bəl) *adj.* Impossible to imagine; inconceivable. —**un•think′a•bly** *adv.*

un•think•ing (ŭn′**thĭng′**kĭng) *adj.* **1.** Heedless or thoughtless: *an unthinking remark.* **2.** Showing lack of thought: *an unthinking conviction.*

un•ti•dy (ŭn **tī′**dē) *adj.* **un•ti•di•er, un•ti•di•est.** Not tidy and neat; sloppy. —**un•ti′di•ly** *adv.* —**un•ti′di•ness** *n.*

un•tie (ŭn **tī′**) *v.* **un•tied, un•ty•ing** (ŭn **tī′**ĭng), **un•ties.** —*tr.* **1.** To undo or loosen (a knot). **2.** To free from something that binds or restrains. —*intr.* To become untied.

un•til (ŭn **tĭl′**) *prep.* **1.** Up to the time of: *They danced until dawn.* **2.** Before (a specified time): *You can't have the bike until tomorrow.* —*conj.* **1.** Up to the time that: *We worked until it got dark.* **2.** Before: *Don't leave until we talk.* **3.** To the point or extent that: *He talked until he was worn out.* [First written down about 1200 in Middle English and spelled *untill.*] —See Note at **till**[2].

un•time•ly (ŭn **tīm′**lē) *adj.* **un•time•li•er, un•time•li•est. 1.** Occurring at an inappropriate or unsuitable time: *an untimely visit.* **2.** Occurring too soon; premature: *an untimely death.*

un•tir•ing (ŭn **tīr′**ĭng) *adj.* **1.** Not tiring: *The swimmer seemed untiring during practice.* **2.** Not ceasing; persistent: *untiring efforts.* —**un•tir′ing•ly** *adv.*

un•to (**ŭn′**to͞o) *prep.* **1.** To. **2.** Until.

un•told (ŭn **tōld′**) *adj.* **1.** Not told or revealed: *untold secrets.* **2.** Without limit; beyond description: *untold millions.*

un•touch•a•ble (ŭn **tŭch′**ə bəl) *adj.* **1.** Not to be touched. **2.** Out of reach; unobtainable. **3.** Beyond the reach of criticism or attack: *His work has been untouchable.* **4.** Unpleasant to the touch. —*n.* Also **Untouchable.** A member of the Hindu class considered ritually unclean by the other Hindu classes.

un•to•ward (ŭn **tôrd′**) *adj.* **1.** Not favorable; troublesome: *untoward circumstances.* **2.** Improper; unseemly: *untoward behavior.*

un•tried (ŭn **trīd′**) *adj.* **1.** Not tried, tested, or proved. **2.** Not tried in court; without a trial.

un•trod•den (ŭn **trŏd′**n) *v.* A past participle of **untread.**

un•true (ŭn **tro͞o′**) *adj.* **un•tru•er, un•tru•est. 1.** Not true; false. **2.** Not faithful; disloyal.

un•truth (ŭn **tro͞oth′**) *n.* **1.** Something untrue; a lie. **2.** The condition of being false.

un•ty•ing (*ŭn-tī′ĭng*) *v.* Present participle of **untie.**

un•used (ŭn **yo͞ozd′**) *adj.* **1.** Not used or never having been used. **2.** (*also* ŭn **yo͞ost′**). Not accustomed: *He is unused to working so late.*

un•u•su•al (ŭn **yo͞o′**zho͞o əl) *adj.* Not usual, common, or ordinary. —**un•u′su•al•ness** *n.*

un•ut•ter•a•ble (ŭn **ŭt′**ər ə bəl) *adj.* Being such as cannot or must not be uttered or expressed: *an unutterable word; unutterable beauty.* —**un•ut′ter•a•bly** *adv.*

un•veil (ŭn **vāl′**) *tr.v.* **un•veiled, un•veil•ing, un•veils. 1.** To remove a veil or covering from: *unveil a statue.* **2.** To reveal: *unveil secrets.*

un•voiced (ŭn **voist′**) *adj.* **1.** Not uttered or expressed. **2.** Uttered without vibrating the vocal cords; voiceless: *an unvoiced consonant.*

un•war•rant•ed (ŭn **wôr′**ən tĭd *or* ŭn **wŏr′**ən tĭd) *adj.* Having no justification; groundless: *an unwarranted judgment lacking basis in fact.*

un•war•y (ŭn **wâr′**ē) *adj.* **un•war•i•er, un•war•i•est.** Not alert to danger; careless.

un•well (ŭn **wĕl′**) *adj.* Being in poor health; ill.

un•whole•some (ŭn **hōl′**səm) *adj.* **1.** Not healthful or healthy: *unwholesome foods.* **2.** Offensive or loathsome: *unwholesome behavior.*

un•wield•y (ŭn **wēl′**dē) *adj.* **un•wield•i•er, un•wield•i•est.** Difficult to carry or handle because of shape or size: *an unwieldy bundle.*

un•will•ing (ŭn **wĭl′**ĭng) *adj.* **1.** Not willing; hesitant or loath: *unwilling to face facts.* **2.** Done reluctantly: *unwilling help.* —**un•will′ing•ly** *adv.* —**un•will′ing•ness** *n.*

un•wind (ŭn **wīnd′**) *v.* **un•wound** (ŭn **wound′**), **un•wind•ing, un•winds.** —*tr.* To unroll: *unwind cable.* —*intr.* **1.** To become unrolled. **2.** To become free of anxiety, worry, or tension: *went to the park to unwind.*

un•wise (ŭn **wīz′**) *adj.* **un•wis•er, un•wis•est.** Showing lack of wisdom; foolish: *an unwise decision.* —**un•wise′ly** *adv.*

un•wit•ting (ŭn **wĭt′**ĭng) *adj.* **1.** Not knowing; unaware: *an unwitting victim of fraud.* **2.** Not intended; unintentional: *an unwitting remark.*

un•wont•ed (ŭn **wôn′**tĭd *or* ŭn **wōn′**tĭd) *adj.* Not ordinary; unusual.

un•world•ly (ŭn **wûrld′**lē) *adj.* **un•world•li•er, un•world•li•est. 1.** Concerned with matters of the spirit or soul rather than of this world. **2.** Not wise to the ways of the world; naive.

un•wor•thy (ŭn **wûr′**thē) *adj.* **un•wor•thi•er, un•wor•thi•est. 1.** Not deserving: *a play unworthy of the award.* **2.** Not suiting or befitting: *a remark unworthy of her.* —**un•wor′thi•ness** *n.*

un•wound (ŭn **wound′**) *v.* Past tense and past participle of **unwind.**

un•wrap (ŭn **răp′**) *v.* **un•wrapped, un•wrap•ping, un•wraps.** —*tr.* To remove the wrapping from: *unwrap a gift.* —*intr.* To have the wrapping removed.

un•writ•ten (ŭn **rĭt′**n) *adj.* **1.** Not written or recorded. **2.** Having authority based on custom or tradition rather than documentation: *an unwritten law.*

un•yield•ing (ŭn **yēl′**dĭng) *adj.* **1.** Not bending or flexible. **2.** Not yielding or giving in to pressure or persuasion; firm.

up (ŭp) *adv.* **1.** In or to a higher position: *looking up.* **2.** In or to an upright position: *She helped me up.* **3.a.** Above a surface: *come up for air.* **b.** So as to detach or unearth: *pulling up weeds.* **c.** Above the horizon: *The sun came up.* **4.** Into view or existence: *write up a report.* **5.** Into consideration: *You never brought this up before.* **6.** In or toward a position conventionally regarded as higher, as on a map: *going up to Canada.* **7.** To or at a higher price: *Fares are going up again.* **8.** So as to advance, increase, or improve: *His hopes keep going up.* **9.** With or to a greater intensity, pitch, or volume: *Turn the radio up.* **10.** Into a state of excitement or turbulence: *A great wind came up.* **11.** Completely; entirely: *ate it all up.* **12.** Used as an intensive with certain verbs: *cleaning up the room.* **13.** Apart; into pieces: *tore the paper up.* —*adj.* **1.** Being above an earlier position or level: *My grades are up.* **2.** Being out of bed: *Are you up yet?* **3.** Raised; lifted: *a switch in the up position.* **4.** Moving or directed upward: *an up elevator.* **5.** Excited or cheerful: *Our spirits were up.* **6.** Actively functioning: *The computer's are up.* **7.** *Informal.* Going on; happening: *What's up?* **8.** Being considered: *a contract up for renewal.* **9.** Finished; over: *Time's up!* **10.** *Informal.* Well-informed or prepared: *I'm not up on sports.* **11.** Being ahead of an opponent: *up two holes in a golf match.* **12.** At bat in baseball: *You're up!* —*prep.* **1.** To or toward a higher point on: *up the mountain.* **2.** Toward or at a point farther along: *up the road.* **3.** In a direction toward the source of: *up the Hudson.* —*n.* **1.** An upward slope; a rise. **2.** *Slang.* A feeling of excitement. —*v.* **upped, up•ping, ups.** —*tr.* To increase: *upping prices.* —*intr. Informal.* To act suddenly or unexpectedly: *We voted his proposal down, so he upped and left the meeting.* —***idioms.*** **up against.** Confronted with; facing: *up against a strong opponent.* **up to. 1.** Occupied with, especially devising or scheming: *up to more tricks.* **2.** Able to do or deal with: *It was hard, but she proved up to it.* **3.** Dependent on: *Winning the game is up to us.* [First written down about 725 in Old English and spelled *ūp, uppe.*]

up-and-com•ing (ŭp′ən **kŭm′**ĭng) *adj.* Showing signs of future success: *an up-and-coming neighborhood.*

up•beat (**ŭp′**bēt′) *n.* An unaccented musical beat, especially the last beat of a measure. —*adj. Informal.* Optimistic or cheerful.

up•braid (ŭp **brād′**) *tr.v.* **up•braid•ed, up•braid•ing, up•braids.** To scold; reproach. [First written down about 1000 in Old English and spelled *ūpbrēdan,* to bring forward as a ground for censure : *ūp-,* up + *bregdan,* to turn, lay hold of.]

up•bring•ing (**ŭp′brĭng′**ĭng) *n.* The care and training received during childhood.

up•coun•try (**ŭp′**kŭn′trē) *n.* The interior of a country. —*adj.* Of, located in, or coming from the upcountry: *their home in upcountry Maine.* —*adv.* (*also* ŭp **kŭn′**trē). In, to, or toward the upcountry: *traveling upcountry.*

up•date (ŭp **dāt′**) *tr.v.* **up•dat•ed, up•dat•ing, up•dates.** To bring up to date: *update a map.*

up•draft (**ŭp′**drăft′) *n.* A current of air that flows upward.

up•end (ŭp **ĕnd′**) *v.* **up•end•ed, up•end•ing, up•ends.** —*tr.* To set or turn on one end: *upend a boat.* —*intr.* To become upended.

up-front or **up•front** (**ŭp′frŭnt′**) *adj. Informal.* Straightforward and direct; frank.

up•grade (**ŭp′**grād′) *tr.v.* **up•grad•ed, up•grad•ing, up•grades.** To raise to a higher grade or standard: *upgrading all their products.* —*n.* **1.** The act or an instance of upgrading. **2.** Something that upgrades: *an upgrade for computer software.* **3.** An upward incline.

up•heav•al (ŭp **hē′**vəl) *n.* **1.** A sudden and violent disturbance. **2.** A lifting or upward movement of the earth's crust.

up•held (ŭp **hĕld′**) *v.* Past tense and past participle of **uphold.**

up•hill (**ŭp′**hĭl′) *adj.* **1.** Going up a hill or slope: *an uphill street.* **2.** Marked by difficulty or strong resistance: *an uphill struggle to finish on time.* —*adv.* (**ŭp′hĭl′**). To or toward higher ground: *going uphill.* —*n.* An upward slope or incline.

up•hold (ŭp **hōld′**) *tr.v.* **up•held** (ŭp **hĕld′**), **up•hold•ing, up•holds. 1.** To raise: *uphold a banner.* **2.** To prevent from falling; support: *The pillars uphold the roof.* **3.** To maintain in the face of a challenge: *upholding her political opinions.*

up•hol•ster (ŭp **hōl′**stər *or* ə **pōl′**stər) *tr.v.* **up•hol•stered, up•hol•ster•ing, up•hol•sters.** To supply (furniture) with stuffing, springs, cushions, and a fabric covering. [First written down in 1853 in American English, from *upholsterer,* from Middle English *upholdester,* from *upholden,* to repair.] —**up•hol′ster•er** *n.*

up•hol•ster•y (ŭp **hōl′**stə rē *or* ə **pōl′**stə rē) *n.* **1.** The materials used in upholstering. **2.** The craft, trade, or business of upholstering.

up•keep (**ŭp′**kēp′) *n.* **1.** Maintenance in proper operation, condition, and repair. **2.** The cost of such maintenance.

up•land (**ŭp′**lənd) *n.* **1.** Land of high elevation, especially when level. **2.** Land in the interior of a country.

up•lift (ŭp **lĭft′**) *tr.v.* **up•lift•ed, up•lift•ing, up•lifts. 1.** To raise; elevate. **2.** To raise to a higher social, moral, or intellectual level. —*n.* (**ŭp′**lĭft′). **1.** The act, process, or result of lifting up. **2.** An effort or a movement to raise social, moral, or intellectual standards. **3.** A geologic upheaval.

up•on (ə **pŏn′** *or* ə **pôn′**) *prep.* On: *We stopped and sat down upon a flat rock.* [First written down in 1121 in Middle English and spelled *uppon.*]

up•per (**ŭp′**ər) *adj.* **1.** Higher in place, position, or rank: *the upper floors of a building; the upper classes of society.* **2.** Situated on higher ground: *upper regions.* **3.** Northern. —*n.* The part of a shoe or boot above the sole.

up•per•case (ŭp′ər **kās′**) *adj.* Belonging to, set, or printed in capital letters: *an uppercase A.*

upper class *n.* The highest social and economic class in a society. —**up′per-class′** *adj.*

up•per•cut (**ŭp′**ər kŭt′) *n.* In boxing, a swinging blow directed upward, as to an opponent's chin.

upper hand *n.* A position of control or advantage.

upper house *n.* The branch of a bicameral legislature, such as the U.S. Senate, that is smaller and less representative of the population.

up•per•most (**ŭp′**ər mōst′) *adv. & adj.* In the highest place, position, or rank: *the uppermost rung of a ladder; finished uppermost in the standings.*

Upper Vol•ta (**vŏl′**tə *or* **vōl′**tə). Burkina Faso.

up•pi•ty (**ŭp′**ĭ tē) *adj. Informal.* Taking liberties or assuming airs beyond one's station; presumptuous.

up•raise (ŭp **rāz′**) *tr.v.* **up•raised, up•rais•ing, up•rais•es.** To raise or lift up; elevate.

up•right (**ŭp′**rīt′) *adj.* **1.** In a vertical position; erect: *an upright post.* **2.** Morally respectable; honorable: *an upright person.* —*adv.* Vertically. —*n.* **1.** A part of an object or structure that stands upright, as a beam. **2.** An upright piano. —**up′right′ness** *n.*

upright piano *n.* A piano in which the strings are mounted vertically in a rectangular case with the keyboard at a right angle to the case.

up•ris•ing (**ŭp′**rī′zĭng) *n.* A popular revolt against a government or its policies.

up•roar (**ŭp′**rôr′) *n.* A condition of noisy excitement and confusion; a tumult.

Synonyms: uproar, din, racket, noise. These nouns mean loud, confused, or disagreeable sound or sounds. **Uproar** means disorder with loud, bewildering sound: *Even indoors we could hear the uproar of the crowd, cheering during the parade.* **Din** means a jumble of loud sounds that usually clash: *The din in the factory ends abruptly when the noon whistle sounds.* **Racket** means loud, distressing noise: *The toddlers were making a racket clanging pots and pans together.* **Noise** is the most general term: *Ear plugs cannot completely protect your hearing from damage due to noise.*

up•roar•i•ous (ŭp **rôr′**ē əs) *adj.* **1.** Caused or accompanied by an uproar. **2.** Loud and full; boisterous: *uproarious laughter.* **3.** Extremely funny: *an uproarious comedy.* —**up•roar′i•ous•ly** *adv.*

up•root (ŭp **ro͞ot′** *or* ŭp **ro͝ot′**) *tr.v.* **up•root•ed, up•**

upholster
Upholstering a chair

upright piano

ă	pat	oi	boy
ā	pay	ou	out
âr	care	o͝o	took
ä	father	o͞o	boot
ĕ	pet	ŭ	cut
ē	be	ûr	urge
ĭ	pit	th	thin
ī	pie	*th*	this
îr	pier	hw	whoop
ŏ	pot	zh	vision
ō	toe	ə	about
ô	paw	N	*French* bon

root•ing, up•roots. 1. To tear or remove (a plant and its roots) from the ground. **2.** To destroy or get rid of completely; do away with: *It is not easy to uproot old customs.* **3.** To force to leave a familiar or native place: *The government uprooted many people in order to build the highway.*

up•set (ŭp **sĕt′**) *tr.v.* **up•set, up•set•ting, up•sets. 1.** To cause to overturn; tip over: *upset a vase of flowers.* **2.** To disturb the functioning, order, or course of: *The move to the new building upset our schedule of deliveries.* **3.** To distress mentally or emotionally: *The news upset him.* **4.** (**ŭp′**sĕt′). To defeat unexpectedly (an opponent favored to win). —*n.* (**ŭp′**sĕt′). **1.** The act of upsetting or the condition of being upset: *Who is responsible for the upset of our plans?* **2.** A game or contest in which the favorite is defeated. —*adj.* **1.** Overturned: *an upset boat.* **2.** Showing symptoms of indigestion: *an upset stomach.* **3.** Mentally or emotionally disturbed: *feeling upset by the news.* [First written down about 1440 in Middle English and spelled *upsetten*, to set up.]

up•shot (**ŭp′**shŏt′) *n.* The final result; outcome.

up•side down (**ŭp′**sīd′) *adv.* **1.** So that the upper or proper side is down: *Turn your cards upside down.* **2.** In great disorder: *The room had been turned upside down.*

up•si•lon (**ŭp′**sə lŏn′ *or* **yo͞op′**sə lŏn′) *n.* The 20th letter of the Greek alphabet, written Υ, υ. In English it is represented as *U, u,* or often also as *Y, y.*

up•stage (**ŭp′stāj′**) *adv.* On, at, to, or toward the rear of a stage. —*adj.* Of or relating to the rear of a stage. —*tr.v.* (ŭp **stāj′**). **up•staged, up•stag•ing, up•stag•es. 1.** To distract audience attention from (another actor) by moving upstage. **2.** To steal attention or praise from: *He upstaged his rivals by announcing his discovery first.*

up•stairs (**ŭp′stârz′**) *adv.* **1.** Up the stairs: *plodded upstairs.* **2.** To or on a higher floor: *slept upstairs.* —*adj.* (**ŭp′**stârz′). Of or located on a higher floor: *an upstairs bedroom.* —*n.* (**ŭp′**stârz′). *(used with a singular verb).* The part of a building above the ground floor.

up•stand•ing (ŭp **stăn′**dĭng *or* **ŭp′**stăn′dĭng) *adj.* **1.** Standing erect or upright. **2.** Morally upright; honest: *a fine upstanding woman.*

up•start (**ŭp′**stärt′) *n.* A person of humble origin who has suddenly risen to wealth or high position, especially one who becomes arrogant because of success. —*adj.* **1.** Suddenly raised to an important position. **2.** Self-important; arrogant.

up•state (**ŭp′**stāt′) *n.* The northerly part of a state in the United States. —*adv. & adj.* To, from, or in the northerly part of a state: *traveling upstate; upstate New York.*

up•stream (**ŭp′strēm′**) *adv. & adj.* In a direction opposite to the current of a stream: *fish swimming upstream; upstream waters.*

up•surge (**ŭp′**sûrj′) *n.* A rapid or abrupt rise.

up•swing (**ŭp′**swĭng′) *n.* **1.** An upward swing or trend. **2.** An increase, as in movement or business.

up•take (**ŭp′**tāk′) *n.* **1.** A passage for drawing up smoke or air. **2.** Understanding; comprehension: *quick on the uptake.*

up•tight (**ŭp′tīt′**) *adj. Slang.* Tense or nervous: *an uptight person.*

up-to-date (ŭp′tə **dāt′**) *adj.* Reflecting or informed of the latest information, changes, improvements, or style: *an up-to-date encyclopedia.*

up•town (**ŭp′**toun′) *n.* The upper part of a town or city. —*adv.* (**ŭp′toun′**). To, toward, or in the upper part of a town or city: *move uptown.* —*adj.* Of, relating to, or located uptown: *an uptown store.*

up•turn (**ŭp′**tûrn′) *v.* **up•turned, up•turn•ing, up•turns.** —*tr.* To turn up or over: *upturn the sail.* —*intr.* To turn over or up. —*n.* An upward movement, curve, or trend, as in business.

up•ward (**ŭp′**wərd) *adv.* In, to, or toward a higher place, level, or position: *The hawk flew upward and out of sight.* —*adj.* Directed toward a higher place or position: *upward movement.* —***idiom.*** **upward of** or **upwards of.** More than; in excess of: *a reading attended by upward of 100 people.*

Ur (ûr *or* o͝or). A city of ancient Sumer in southern Mesopotamia on a site in present-day southeast Iraq. It was one of the oldest cities in Mesopotamia.

u•ra•cil (**yo͝or′**ə sĭl) *n.* A base that is a component of RNA.

U•ral Mountains (**yo͝or′**əl). A range of western Russia forming the traditional boundary between Europe and Asia and extending about 1,500 miles (2,414 kilometers) from the Arctic Ocean southward to Kazakhstan.

Ural River. A river of western Russia and western Kazakhstan rising in the southern Ural Mountains and flowing about 1,574 miles (2,533 kilometers) to the Caspian Sea.

U•ralsk (yo͞o **rälsk′**). A city of northwest Kazakhstan on the Ural River southeast of Moscow, Russia. It was founded about 1622. Population, 192,000.

u•ra•ni•um (yo͞o **rā′**nē əm) *n. Symbol* **U** A heavy, toxic, silvery-white metallic element that is radioactive and easily oxidized. Uranium is the main source of nuclear energy. Atomic number 92. See table at **element.** [First written down in 1797 in Modern English, after *Uranus.*]

uranium 235 *n.* The isotope of uranium that has a mass number of 235 and a half-life of 713 million years. Uranium 235 undergoes nuclear fission when it collides with a slow neutron, and it is capable of sustaining a chain reaction that can become explosive.

uranium 238 *n.* The most common isotope of uranium, having a mass number of 238 and a half-life of 4.51 billion years. It is only capable of fission under very special conditions but can capture neutrons to form plutonium 239, which is capable of fission.

U•ra•nus (**yo͝or′**ə nəs *or* yo͞o **rā′**nəs) *n.* **1.** In Greek mythology, the earliest supreme god, the son of Gaea and the father of the Titans. **2.** The seventh planet from the sun at a mean distance of 1,790 million miles (2,869 million kilometers), and the third largest in the solar system with a mean diameter of 32,480 miles (52,290 kilometers). It has fifteen moons or satellites and a system of thin rings around it.

ur•ban (**ûr′**bən) *adj.* **1.** Of, relating to, or located in a city: *urban traffic; urban dwellers; urban housing.* **2.** Characteristic of the city or city life: *urban pollution.* [First written down in 1619 in Modern English, from Latin *urbs*, city.]

ur•bane (ûr **bān′**) *adj.* **ur•ban•er, ur•ban•est.** Polite, refined, and often elegant in manner.

urban renewal *n.* The rebuilding of impoverished urban neighborhoods by major renovation or reconstruction of housing and public works.

ur•chin (**ûr′**chĭn) *n.* **1.** A playful or mischievous child. **2.** A sea urchin. [First written down about 1300 in Middle English and spelled *irichen*, hedgehog, from Latin *ēricius.*]

Ur•du (**o͝or′**do͞o *or* **ûr′**do͞o) *n.* An Indic language that is the official literary language of Pakistan. It is written in an Arabic alphabet and is also widely used in India, especially by Muslims.

-ure *suff.* A suffix that means: **1.** Act or process: *erasure.* **2.** Function or office: *legislature.*

u•re•a (yo͞o **rē′**ə) *n.* A chemical compound of carbon, hydrogen, nitrogen, and oxygen having the formula $CO(NH_2)_2$. It occurs in the urine of mammals and is also produced synthetically for use in fertilizers and medicine.

u•re•ter (yo͞o rē′tər *or* **yo͝or′**ĭ tər) *n.* The long narrow duct that carries urine from the kidney to the urinary bladder.

u•re•thra (yo͞o rē′thrə) *n., pl.* **u•re•thras** or **u•re•thrae** (yo͞o rē′thrē). The duct from which urine is discharged in most mammals and through which semen is discharged in males.

urge (ûrj) *tr.v.* **urged, urg•ing, urg•es. 1.** To push, force, or drive onward; impel. **2.** To entreat earnestly and repeatedly; exhort: *The coach urged us to stay in shape over summer vacation.* **3.** To advocate earnestly the doing, consideration, or approval of: *urge the passage of new crime laws.* —*n.* An impulse that prompts action or effort. [First written down in 1560 in Modern English, from Latin *urgēre.*]

ur•gen•cy (ûr′jən sē) *n., pl.* **ur•gen•cies.** The quality or condition of being urgent: *the urgency of the political situation.*

ur•gent (ûr′jənt) *adj.* **1.** Calling for immediate action or attention; pressing: *an urgent situation.* **2.** Conveying a sense of pressing importance or necessity: *an urgent tone of voice.* **—ur′gent•ly** *adv.*

u•ri•nal (yo͝or′ə nəl) *n.* **1.** An upright wall fixture used by men and boys for urinating. **2.** A portable receptacle for urine.

u•ri•nal•y•sis (yo͝or′ə năl′ĭ sĭs) *n., pl.* **u•ri•nal•y•ses** (yo͝or′ə năl′ĭ sēz′). The chemical analysis of urine, used to diagnose disease or to detect the presence of a specific substance, such as a drug.

u•ri•nar•y (yo͝or′ə nĕr′ē) *adj.* **1.** Of or relating to urine or its production, function, or excretion. **2.** Of or relating to the organs that produce and discharge urine.

urinary bladder *n.* An elastic muscular sac located in the forward part of the lower abdomen, in which urine is stored until excreted.

u•ri•nate (yo͝or′ə nāt′) *intr.v.* **u•ri•nat•ed, u•ri•nat•ing, u•ri•nates.** To discharge urine. **—u′ri•na′tion** *n.*

u•rine (yo͝or′ĭn) *n.* A fluid containing body wastes extracted from the blood by the kidneys, stored in the urinary bladder, and discharged from the body through the urethra.

urn (ûrn) *n.* **1.** A vase, usually having a footed base or pedestal. **2.** A metal container with a spigot, used for warming or serving tea or coffee. [First written down about 1385 in Middle English and spelled *urne*, from Latin *urna.*]
❑ *These sound alike:* **urn, earn** (gain by work).

Ur•sa Major (ûr′sə) *n.* A constellation near the north celestial pole. Seven of its stars form the Big Dipper.

Ursa Minor *n.* A constellation that includes the star Polaris. Seven of its stars form the Little Dipper.

U•ru•guay (yo͝or′ə gwī′ *or* **yo͝or′**ə gwā′). A country of southeast South America on the Atlantic Ocean and the Río de la Plata. It gained its independence from Spain in 1814 and severed its union with Brazil in 1828. Capital, Montevideo. Population, 2,788,429.

us (ŭs) *pron.* The objective case of **we. 1.** Used as the direct object of a verb: *The movie impressed us greatly.* **2.** Used as the indirect object of a verb: *She gave us free tickets to the show.* **3.** Used as the object of a preposition: *Tom sent his regards to us.* [First written down before 830 in Old English and spelled *ūs.*]

U.S. or **US** *abbr.* An abbreviation of United States.

USA *abbr.* An abbreviation of: **1.** United States Army. **2.** United States of America.

us•a•ble also **use•a•ble** (yo͞o′zə bəl) *adj.* **1.** Capable of being used: *separating usable ore from waste.* **2.** In a fit condition for use: *The little room seemed usable as an office.*

USAF also **U.S.A.F.** *abbr.* An abbreviation of United States Air Force.

us•age (yo͞o′sĭj *or* yo͞o′zĭj) *n.* **1.** The act or manner of using something: *a gauge that measures water usage.* **2.** A usual or accepted practice. **3.** The way in which words or phrases are used, spoken, or written: *contemporary English usage.*

USCG also **U.S.C.G.** *abbr.* An abbreviation of United States Coast Guard.

U.S. Customary System *n.* The standard system of measurement in the United States, including linear measure, liquid measure, and dry measure, for example. A yard, an acre, a pint, and a bushel are all units of measure in the U.S. Customary System.

use (yo͞oz) *v.* **used, us•ing, us•es.** —*tr.* **1.** To bring or put into service; employ for some purpose: *I used a whisk to beat the eggs.* **2.** To avail oneself of; practice: *Use caution when driving at night.* **3.** To achieve a goal by means of; exploit: *He used his connections to get a job in the mayor's office.* —*intr.* (yo͞os). Used in the past tense followed by *to* to indicate a former state, practice, or custom: *I used to go there often.* —*n.* (yo͞os). **1.** The act of using: *the use of a pencil for writing.* **2.** The condition or fact of being used: *The telephone is in use right now.* **3.** The manner of using; usage: *the proper use of power tools.* **4.a.** The permission or privilege of using something: *I have the use of the car on Sundays.* **b.** The power or ability of using something: *lost the use of one arm.* **5.** The need or occasion to use: *Do you have any use for this book?* **6.** The quality of being suitable or adaptable to an end; usefulness: *old pieces of equipment of no practical use.* **—*idiom.* use up.** To consume completely: *We used up the peanut butter yesterday.* [First written down before 1200 in Middle English and spelled *usen*, from Latin *ūtī.*] —See Note at **utilize.**

use•a•ble (yo͞o′zə bəl) *adj.* Variant of **usable.**

used (yo͞ozd) *adj.* **1.** Not new; secondhand. **2.** (*also* yo͞ost). Accustomed; habituated: *getting used to the cold weather; was used to taking a swim in the morning.*

use•ful (yo͞os′fəl) *adj.* Capable of being used for some purpose; being of use or service: *a useful map.* **—use′ful•ly** *adv.* **—use′ful•ness** *n.*

use•less (yo͞os′lĭs) *adj.* **1.** Being or having no use: *a useless new gadget.* **2.** Unable to function or assist: *When it comes to protecting the house, the dog is useless.* **—use′less•ly** *adv.* **—use′less•ness** *n.*

us•er (yo͞o′zər) *n.* A person or thing that uses: *a personal computer user.*

us•er-friend•ly (yo͞o′zər frĕnd′lē) *adj.* Easy to use or learn to use: *a user-friendly software program; a user-friendly income tax form.*

ush•er (ŭsh′ər) *n.* **1.** A person employed to escort people to their seats, as in a theater. **2.** A man who attends a bridal party at a wedding. —*v.* **ush•ered, ush•er•ing, ush•ers.** —*tr.* **1.** To serve as an usher to; escort. See Synonyms at **guide. 2.** To precede and introduce: *usher in a new era.* —*intr.* To work as an usher: *ushered at the concert.* [First written down about 1280 in Middle English and spelled *usschere*, doorkeeper, from Latin *ōstiārius*, from *ōstium*, door.]

USMC also **U.S.M.C.** *abbr.* An abbreviation of United States Marine Corps.

USN also **U.S.N.** *abbr.* An abbreviation of United States Navy.

U.S.S. *abbr.* An abbreviation of: **1.** United States Senate. **2.** United States Ship.

U.S.S.R. *abbr.* An abbreviation of Union of Soviet Socialist Republics.

urn
c. 1450 Flemish urn

ă	pat	oi	boy
ā	pay	ou	out
âr	care	o͝o	took
ä	father	o͞o	boot
ĕ	pet	ŭ	cut
ē	be	ûr	urge
ĭ	pit	th	thin
ī	pie	*th*	this
îr	pier	hw	whoop
ŏ	pot	zh	vision
ō	toe	ə	about
ô	paw	N	*French* bon

Utah

The name for the state of **Utah** comes from *Ute*, the name of a Native American people who lived in the region. The name was also used for Utah Lake and the river flowing out of it. The name of the river and the lake was adopted for the state in 1850.

Usage: utilize

You can often simply say **use** instead of the longer word **utilize**. *Utilize*, however, can mean "to find a profitable or practical use for." Thus the sentence *They were unable to use the new computers* might mean only that people were unable to turn the computers on. The sentence *The teachers were unable to utilize the new computers* suggests that the teachers could not find ways to employ the computers in instruction.

u•su•al (yōō′zhōō əl) *adj.* **1.** Commonly encountered, experienced, or observed; ordinary: *the usual traffic jams during rush hour.* **2.** Regularly or customarily used: *the usual expressions of thanks.* **3.** In conformity with regular practice or procedure: *Come at the usual time.* **—*idiom.* as usual.** As commonly or habitually happens: *She jogged that morning as usual.* [First written down before 1387 in Middle English and spelled *usualle*, from Latin *ūsus*, use.] **—u′su•al•ly** *adv.*

u•su•rer (yōō′zhər ər) *n.* A person who lends money at interest, especially at an excessively high or unlawfully high rate.

u•surp (yōō sûrp′ *or* yōō zûrp′) *tr.v.* **u•surped, u•surp•ing, u•surps.** To seize and hold (the power or rights of another, for example) by force and without legal authority: *usurp a throne.* **—u′sur•pa′tion** *n.* **—u•surp′er** *n.*

u•su•ry (yōō′zhə rē) *n., pl.* **u•su•ries. 1.** The practice of lending money at interest, especially at an excessively high or unlawfully high rate. **2.** An excessively or unlawfully high rate of interest.

U•tah (yōō′tô′ *or* yōō′tä′). A state of the western United States north of Arizona. It was admitted as the 45th state in 1896. Salt Lake City is the capital and the largest city. Population, 1,727,784. —See Note.

Ute (yōōt) *n., pl.* **Ute** or **Utes. 1.** A member of a Native American people living in Utah and along the Colorado–New Mexico border. **2.** The Uto-Aztecan language of the Ute.

u•ten•sil (yōō tĕn′səl) *n.* An instrument, an implement, or a container, such as one used in a kitchen. [First written down about 1375 in Middle English, from Latin *ūtēnsilis*, fit for use, from *ūtī*, to use.]

u•ter•us (yōō′tər əs) *n., pl.* **u•ter•i** (yōō′tə rī′) or **u•ter•us•es.** A hollow muscular organ of female mammals, in which a fertilized egg implants and develops; the womb.

U•ther Pen•dra•gon (yōō′thər pĕn drăg′ən) *n.* In Arthurian legend, a king of Britain and the father of King Arthur.

u•til•i•ty (yōō tĭl′ĭ tē) *n., pl.* **u•til•i•ties. 1.** The quality of being useful; usefulness. **2.** A public service, such as electricity, water, or transportation.

u•til•ize (yōōt′l īz′) *tr.v.* **u•til•ized, u•til•iz•ing, u•til•iz•es.** To put to use, especially for a practical purpose: *utilizing the stream's water to run the mill.* **—u′ti•li•za′tion** (yōōt′l ĭ zā′shən) *n.* **—u′til•iz′er** *n.* —See Note.

ut•most (ŭt′mōst′) *adj.* Of the highest or greatest degree, amount, or intensity: *matters of the utmost importance.* **—*n.*** The greatest possible degree, amount, or extent; the maximum.

U•to-Az•tec•an (yōō′tō ăz′tĕk′ən) *n.* **1.** A large family of North and Central American languages that includes Ute and Hopi. **2.** A member of a tribe speaking a Uto-Aztecan language. **—*adj.*** Of or relating to the Uto-Aztecans or their languages.

u•to•pi•a (yōō tō′pē ə) *n.* Often **Utopia. 1.** A place that is ideal, especially in morals and social and political life. **2.** A work of fiction describing such a place. **—u•to′pi•an** *adj. & n.*

ut•ter[1] (ŭt′ər) *tr.v.* **ut•tered, ut•ter•ing, ut•ters. 1.** To give forth with the voice: *utter a sigh.* **2.** To pronounce or speak; say: *utter a word.* [First written down before 1400 in Middle English and spelled *utteren*, partly from Middle Low German *uteren*, and partly alteration of Middle English *outen*, to disclose.]

ut•ter[2] (ŭt′ər) *adj.* Complete; absolute: *utter darkness.* [First written down before 901 in Old English and spelled *ūtera*, outer.] **—ut′ter•ly** *adv.*

ut•ter•ance (ŭt′ər əns) *n.* **1.** The act of uttering: *She found his continued utterance of old jokes quite irritating.* **2.** Something uttered or expressed; a statement.

ut•ter•ly (ŭt′ər lē) *adv.* Completely; absolutely.

U-turn (yōō′tûrn′) *n.* A turn, as by a vehicle, completely reversing the direction of travel.

u•vu•la (yōō′vyə lə) *n.* The small cone-shaped mass of fleshy tissue that hangs from the end of the soft palate above the tongue. [First written down in 1392 in Middle English, from Late Latin *ūvula*, diminutive of Latin *ūva*, grape (from its shape).] **—u′vu•lar** *adj.*

Uz•bek•i•stan (ōōz bĕk′ĭ stăn′ *or* ōōz bĕk′ĭ stän′). A region of west-central Asia. It was settled in ancient times. Uzbekistan was part of the Soviet Union from 1924 to 1991. Capital, Tashkent. Population, 17,974,000.

V v

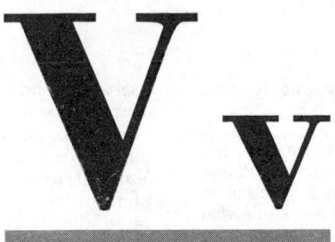

v or **V** (vē) *n., pl.* **v's** or **V's. 1.** The 22nd letter of the English alphabet. **2.** The 22nd in a series or group.

V[1] **1.** The symbol for the element **vanadium. 2.** The symbol for **potential** (sense 2). **3.** The symbol for the Roman numeral 5.

V[2] *abbr.* An abbreviation of: **1.** Velocity. **2.** Victory. **3.** Volt. **4.** Volume.

V-1 (**vē′wŭn′**) *n.* A robot bomb used by the Germans in World War II.

V-2 (**vē′to͞o′**) *n.* A long-range rocket that burned liquid fuel, used by the Germans as a ballistic missile in World War II.

v. *abbr.* An abbreviation of: **1.** Verb. **2.** Verse. **3.** Version. **4.** Versus. **5.** Violin. **6.** Volume (book). **7.** Vowel.

V. *abbr.* An abbreviation of: **1.** Venerable (in titles). **2.** Viscount. **3.** Viscountess.

VA or **Va.** *abbr.* An abbreviation of Virginia.

va•can•cy (vā′kən sē) *n., pl.* **va•can•cies. 1.** The condition of being vacant or unoccupied. **2.** A position, office, or space that is unfilled or unoccupied. **3.** Emptiness of mind.

va•cant (vā′kənt) *adj.* **1.** Containing nothing; empty. See Synonyms at **empty. 2.** Not occupied or taken: *vacant seats.* **3.** Not put to use: *vacant lands.* **4.a.** Lacking intelligence or knowledge. **b.** Expressionless; blank: *a vacant stare.* [First written down about 1300 in Middle English and spelled *vacaunt*, from Latin *vacāre*, to be empty.] **—va′cant•ly** *adv.*

va•cate (vā′kāt′ *or* vā **kāt′**) *tr. & intr.v.* **va•cat•ed, va•cat•ing, va•cates.** To cease to occupy or hold; give up: *vacate an apartment.*

va•ca•tion (vā **kā′**shən) *n.* **1.** An interval of time devoted to rest or relaxation, especially one with pay granted to an employee. **2.** A holiday. *—intr.v.* **va•ca•tioned, va•ca•tion•ing, va•ca•tions.** To take or spend a vacation: *He vacationed on the island.* **—va•ca′tion•er** *n.*

vac•ci•nate (**văk′**sə nāt′) *tr.v.* **vac•ci•nat•ed, vac•ci•nat•ing, vac•ci•nates.** To inoculate (a person or an animal) with a vaccine in order to give immunity against an infectious disease.

vac•ci•na•tion (văk′sə **nā′**shən) *n.* **1.** Inoculation with a vaccine in order to give immunity against an infectious disease. **2.** A scar left on the skin where such an inoculation was made.

vac•cine (văk **sēn′** *or* **văk′**sēn′) *n.* A preparation containing weakened or killed disease germs, injected into a person or animal to stimulate the production of antibodies against the disease. [First written down in 1799 in Modern English, from Latin *vaccīnus*, of cows, from *vacca*, cow.] —See Note.

vac•il•late (**văs′**ə lāt′) *intr.v.* **vac•il•lat•ed, vac•il•lat•ing, vac•il•lates. 1.** To sway from one side to the other; oscillate. **2.** To swing indecisively from one course of action or opinion to another; waver: *vacillate between hope and despair.* [First written down in 1597 in Modern English, from Latin *vacillāre*, to waver.] **—vac′il•la′tion** *n.*

vac•u•a (**văk′**yo͞o ə) *n.* A plural of **vacuum.**

va•cu•i•ty (vă **kyo͞o′**ĭ tē) *n., pl.* **vac•u•i•ties. 1.** Total absence of matter; emptiness. **2.** An empty space; a vacuum. **3.** Absence of meaningful occupation; idleness. **4.** The quality or fact of lacking something specified: *a vacuity of emotions.*

vac•u•ole (**văk′**yo͞o ōl′) *n.* A small cavity in the cytoplasm of a cell, surrounded by a membrane and containing water, food, or metabolic waste. **—vac′u•o′lar** (văk′yo͞o **ō′**lər) *adj.*

vac•u•ous (**văk′**yo͞o əs) *adj.* **1.** Devoid of matter; empty: *a vacuous space.* **2.** Lacking intelligence; stupid: *a vacuous remark.* **—vac′u•ous•ly** *adv.*

vac•u•um (**văk′**yo͞o əm *or* **văk′**yo͞om) *n., pl.* **vac•u•ums** or **vac•u•a** (**văk′**yo͞o ə). **1.a.** The absence of matter. **b.** A space that is empty of matter. **c.** A space containing a gas at a very low pressure. **2.** *pl.* **vac•u•ums.** A vacuum cleaner. *—tr. & intr.v.* **vac•u•umed, vac•u•um•ing, vac•u•ums.** To clean with or use a vacuum cleaner. [First written down in 1550 in Modern English, from Latin, from *vacuus*, empty.]

vacuum bottle *n.* A small container with a double wall and a partial vacuum in the space between the two walls, used to minimize the transfer of heat between the inside and the outside and thus keep the contents at a desired temperature.

vacuum cleaner *n.* An electrical appliance that draws up dirt by suction.

vac•u•um-packed (**văk′**yo͞o əm păkt′ *or* **văk′**yo͞om păkt′) *adj.* **1.** Packed in an airtight container. **2.** Sealed under low pressure or in a partial vacuum.

vacuum tube *n.* An electron tube in which there is a vacuum to such a high degree that the likelihood of an electron striking a gas atom is small enough to be ignored. Cathode-ray tubes, which include television picture tubes and other video display tubes, are the most widely employed vacuum tubes.

Va•duz (vä **do͞ots′** *or* fä **do͞ots′**). The capital of Liechtenstein, in the western part of the country on the Rhine River. Population, 4,927.

vag•a•bond (**văg′**ə bŏnd′) *n.* **1.** A person who moves from place to place and has no permanent home. **2.** A vagrant; a tramp. *—adj.* **1.** Of, relating to, or characteristic of a wanderer; nomadic: *leading a vagabond life.* **2.** Aimless; drifting.

va•ga•ry (**vā′**gə rē *or* və **gâr′**ē) *n., pl.* **va•ga•ries.** An extravagant or erratic notion or action.

va•gi•na (və **jī′**nə) *n., pl.* **va•gi•nas** or **va•gi•nae** (və **jī′**nē). The passage leading from the uterus to the outside of the body in female mammals.

vag•i•nal (**văj′**ə nəl) *adj.* Of or relating to the vagina. **—vag′i•nal•ly** *adv.*

va•grant (**vā′**grənt) *n.* **1.** A person who wanders from place to place and has no permanent home or means of livelihood. **2.** A wanderer; a rover. *—adj.* Wandering from place to place and lacking any means of support. **—va′gran•cy** *n.*

vague (vāg) *adj.* **vagu•er, vagu•est. 1.** Not clearly expressed; lacking clarity: *a vague statement; a vague promise.* **2.** Not thinking or expressing oneself clearly or precisely: *The Senator was vague to avoid being asked questions.* **3.** Lacking definite shape, form, or character: *the vague outline of a ship on the horizon.* **4.** Indistinctly felt, perceived, understood, or recalled; hazy: *a vague sense of fear.* [First written down in 1548 in Modern English,

vaccine

For centuries, smallpox was a leading cause of death all over the world. If victims survived, they often had terrible scars. Nowadays, however, smallpox has been virtually eradicated, thanks to the work of Edward Jenner, an English surgeon. In the late 18th century, Jenner observed that people who had cowpox, a mild disease contracted from milking infected cows, did not get smallpox. Jenner took liquid from the cowpox sores of a milkmaid and injected a boy with it. Later, Jenner exposed him to smallpox, but the boy remained healthy. Jenner had thus discovered a safe way to prevent smallpox. His use of cowpox, or *variolae vaccinae* ("smallpox of a cow"), the Latin name he gave it, became known as **vaccination** and the liquid he injected as a **vaccine.**

ă	pat	oi	boy
ā	pay	ou	out
âr	care	o͝o	took
ä	father	o͞o	boot
ĕ	pet	ŭ	cut
ē	be	ûr	urge
ĭ	pit	th	thin
ī	pie	*th*	this
îr	pier	hw	whoop
ŏ	pot	zh	vision
ō	toe	ə	about
ô	paw	N	*French* bon

Saint Valentine

valley
Along Fedafjord
in southern Norway

from Latin *vagus*, wandering.] **—vague′ly** *adv.* **—vague′ness** *n.*

Synonyms: vague, ambiguous, obscure, cryptic. These adjectives mean lacking a clear meaning. **Vague** means unclear because of a lack of clarity or precision in expression or thought: *I have only a vague idea of what the book is about.* **Ambiguous** means having two or more possible meanings: *Frustrated by ambiguous instructions, the parents had difficulty assembling the swing set.* **Obscure** suggests a hidden meaning: *The document makes several obscure references to a hidden treasure.* **Cryptic** suggests something that is overly brief and is meant to be puzzling: *The club used cryptic abbreviations for everything in order to seem mysterious.*

vain (vān) *adj.* **vain•er, vain•est. 1.** Not yielding the desired outcome; fruitless: *a vain effort to regain her balance.* **2.** Lacking substance or worth; hollow: *vain promises.* **3.** Showing undue preoccupation with one's appearance or accomplishments; conceited: *He was a vain and disagreeable fellow.* **—*idiom.* in vain. 1.** To no avail; without success: *We tried in vain to open the window.* **2.** In an irreverent or disrespectful manner: *One of the Ten Commandments forbids taking God's name in vain.* [First written down before 1200 in Middle English and spelled *veine*, from Latin *vānus*, empty.] **—vain′ly** *adv.*

❑ *These sound alike:* **vain, vane** (weathervane), **vein** (blood vessel).

vain•glo•ri•ous (vān **glôr′**ē əs) *adj.* Characterized by or showing excessive pride or vanity; boastful: *being vainglorious about his athletic record.*

vain•glo•ry (**vān′**glôr′ē) *n.* Boastful unwarranted pride or excessive vanity.

val. *abbr.* An abbreviation of value.

val•ance (**văl′**əns *or* **vā′**ləns) *n.* **1.** An ornamental drapery hung across a top edge, as of a bed, table, or canopy. **2.** A short drapery, decorative board, or metal strip extending across the top of a window to conceal structural fixtures.

vale (vāl) *n.* A valley; a dale.

❑ *These sound alike:* **vale, veil** (mesh fabric).

val•e•dic•to•ri•an (văl′ĭ dĭk **tôr′**ē ən) *n.* The student with the highest academic rank in a class, who delivers the valedictory at graduation.

val•e•dic•to•ry (văl′ĭ **dĭk′**tə rē) *n., pl.* **val•e•dic•to•ries.** A closing or farewell statement or address, especially one delivered at graduation exercises. *—adj.* Of, relating to, or expressing a farewell: *a valedictory oration.*

va•lence (**vā′**ləns) *n.* **1.** The capability of an atom or a group of atoms to combine with other atoms or groups of atoms, determined by the number of electrons that an atom will lose, add, or share. **2.** A whole number, often one of several for a given element, that represents this capability.

Va•len•ci•a (və **lĕn′**shē ə *or* və **lĕn′**chə *or* və **lĕn′**sē ə). A region and former kingdom of eastern Spain on the Mediterranean coast. It was inhabited by Iberian peoples in early times.

Va•len•ci•ennes (və lĕn′sē **ĕnz′**). A city of northern France near the Belgian border. It has been noted for its lace industry since the 15th century. Population, 40,275.

val•en•tine (**văl′**ən tīn′) *n.* **1.** A sentimental card sent to a sweetheart, friend, or family member on Saint Valentine's Day. **2.** A person singled out as one's sweetheart on Saint Valentine's Day.

Val•en•tine (**văl′**ən tīn′), Saint. Flourished third century A.D. Roman Christian who according to tradition was martyred.

Val•en•tine's Day (**văl′**ən tīnz′) *n.* Saint Valentine's Day.

val•et (**văl′**ĭt *or* **văl′**ā *or* vă **lā′**) *n.* **1.** A man's male servant, who takes care of his clothes and performs other personal services. **2.** An employee, as in a hotel, who performs various personal services for guests or passengers.

Val•hal•la (văl **hăl′**ə) *n.* In Norse mythology, the hall in which the souls of slain heroes are received by Odin. [First written down before 1768 in Modern English, from Old Norse *Valhöll* : *valr*, the slain in battle + *höll*, hall.]

val•iant (**văl′**yənt) *adj.* **1.** Possessing valor; brave. See Synonyms at **brave. 2.** Marked by or done with valor. **—val′iant•ly** *adv.* **—val′iant•ness** *n.*

val•id (**văl′**ĭd) *adj.* **1.** Well-grounded; just: *a valid objection.* **2.** Having legal force: *a valid passport.* [First written down in 1571 in Modern English, from Latin *validus*, strong.] **—va•lid′i•ty** (və **lĭd′**ĭ tē) *n.*

val•i•date (**văl′**ĭ dāt′) *tr.v.* **val•i•dat•ed, val•i•dat•ing, val•i•dates. 1.** To make or declare legally valid: *validate a contract.* **2.** To establish the soundness of; corroborate: *validate a theory.*

va•lise (və **lēs′**) *n.* A small piece of hand luggage.

Val•kyr•ie (văl **kîr′**ē *or* **văl′**kə rē) *n.* In Norse mythology, one of Odin's women attendants who conduct the souls of the slain warriors to Valhalla. [First written down before 1768 in Modern English and spelled *Valkyria*, from Old Norse *Valkyrja*.]

Val•let•ta (və **lĕt′**ə). The capital of Malta, on the Mediterranean Sea south of Sicily. Population, 14,013.

val•ley (**văl′**ē) *n., pl.* **val•leys. 1.** A long narrow region of low land between ranges of mountains, hills, or other uplands, often having a river or stream running along the bottom. **2.** A large region of land drained or irrigated by a river system: *the Connecticut River valley.* [First written down before 1300 in Middle English and spelled *valey*, from Latin *vallēs*.]

Val•ley Forge (**văl′**ē). A village of southeast Pennsylvania northwest of Philadelphia. The Continental Army headquarters encampment here was subjected to severe winter weather (1777–1778).

val•or (**văl′**ər) *n.* Courage and boldness, as in combat; bravery.

val•or•ous (**văl′**ər əs) *adj.* Showing or having great personal bravery; valiant: *valorous deeds.*

val•our (**văl′**ər) *n. Chiefly British.* Variant of **valor.**

val•u•a•ble (**văl′**yo͞o ə bəl *or* **văl′**yə bəl) *adj.* **1.** Having high monetary or material value for use or exchange: *a valuable piece of jewelry.* **2.** Of great importance, use, or service: *acquire valuable information.* **3.** Having admirable or esteemed qualities: *a valuable friend.* *—n.* A valuable personal possession, as a piece of jewelry. Often used in the plural.

val•u•a•tion (văl′yo͞o **ā′**shən) *n.* **1.** The act or process of assessing value or price; an appraisal: *valuation of imported merchandise.* **2.** Assessed value or price.

val•ue (**văl′**yo͞o) *n.* **1.** The amount, as of goods, services, or money, that is considered a fair equivalent for something else: *walking shoes that will give you good value for your money.* **2.** Monetary or material worth: *the value of a rare stamp.* **3.** Worth in usefulness or importance to the possessor; utility or merit: *the value of a good education.* **4.** A principle, standard, or quality considered worthwhile or desirable: *traditional values such as honesty and integrity.* **5.** Precise meaning or import, as of a word. **6.** An assigned or calculated numerical quantity. **7.** The relative duration of a musical note or rest. **8.** The relative lightness or darkness of a color. *—tr.v.* **val•ued, val•u•ing, val•ues. 1.** To determine or estimate the worth or value of; appraise: *value a piece of jewelry.* **2.** To consider of great worth or importance; prize: *valued the team of horses highly.* See

Synonyms at **appreciate. 3.** To rate according to worth or desirability: *Don't we all value health above money?* [First written down about 1303 in Middle English and spelled *valeu*, from Old French, from *valoir*, to be worth.]

valve (vălv) *n.* **1.** A structure located in a hollow organ or passage, such as an artery or a vein, that prevents the backward flow of a body fluid. **2.a.** Any of various mechanical devices that control the flow of liquids, gases, or loose material through pipes or channels by blocking and uncovering openings. **b.** The movable part or element of such a device. **c.** A device in a brass wind instrument that changes the pitch by changing the length of the air column in a tube. **3.** One of the paired hinged shells of certain mollusks, such as clams and oysters. [First written down before 1387 in Middle English and spelled *valve*, half of a folding door, from Latin *valva*.]

va•moose (vă **mōōs′**) *intr.v.* **va•moosed, va•moos•ing, va•moos•es.** *Slang.* To leave hastily.

vamp (vămp) *n.* The upper part of a shoe or boot covering the instep and sometimes extending over the toes. —*tr.v.* **vamped, vamp•ing, vamps.** To provide (a shoe) with a new vamp.

vam•pire (**văm′**pīr′) *n.* **1.** A corpse believed to rise from its grave at night to suck the blood of sleeping people. **2.** A person who preys on or victimizes others. **3.** Any of various tropical American bats that feed on the blood of mammals and birds through a bite in the skin. [First written down in 1734 in Modern English, from German *Vampir*, of Slavic origin.]

van¹ (văn) *n.* **1.** An enclosed motor vehicle having rear or side doors and side panels, used especially for transporting people. **2.** A covered or enclosed truck or wagon used for transporting goods or livestock. [First written down in 1829 in Modern English, short for *caravan*.]

van² (văn) *n.* The vanguard; the forefront. [First written down in 1610 in Modern English, short for *vanguard*.]

va•na•di•um (və **nā′**dē əm) *n.* *Symbol* **V** A soft, bright white, metallic element, used especially in making various strong alloys of steel. Atomic number 23. See table at **element.**

Van Al•len belt (văn **ăl′**ən) *n.* Either of two zones of high-intensity radiation surrounding the earth. In these zones a large number of atomic particles with high energies are trapped by the earth's magnetic field. [First written down in 1959 in Modern English, after J.A. *Van Allen* (born 1914), American physicist.]

Van Bu•ren (văn **byŏŏr′**ən), **Martin.** 1782–1862. The eighth President of the United States (1837–1841).

Van•cou•ver (văn **kōō′**vər). The largest city in British Columbia, Canada, in the southwest part of the province on an inlet of the Pacific Ocean opposite **Vancouver Island.** Population, 414,281.

van•dal (**văn′**dl) *n.* A person who willfully or maliciously defaces or destroys public or private property.

Van•dal (**văn′**dl) *n.* A member of a Germanic people that overran Gaul, Spain, northern Africa, and Rome in the fourth and fifth centuries A.D.

van•dal•ism (**văn′**dl ĭz′əm) *n.* Willful or malicious damage to or destruction of public or private property.

van•dal•ize (**văn′**dl īz′) *tr.v.* **van•dal•ized, van•dal•iz•ing, van•dal•iz•es.** To destroy or damage (public or private property) willfully or maliciously.

Vandyke or **Van Dyck** (văn **dīk′**), Sir **Anthony.** 1599–1641. Flemish painter whose numerous portraits include many of the English court.

Vandyke beard *n.* A short pointed beard. [First written down in 1909 in Modern English, after Sir Anthony *Vandyke*.]

vane (vān) *n.* **1.** A weathervane. **2.** Any of several usually rigid blades mounted around an axis and turned by or used to direct the motion of a fluid. **3.** The thin flat part of a feather, extending from each side of a main shaft or quill. **4.** One of the stabilizing fins attached to the tail of a bomb or other missile.

❑ *These sound alike:* **vane, vain** (proud), **vein** (blood vessel).

van Gogh (văn **gō′**), **Vincent.** 1853–1890. Dutch painter whose works include numerous self-portraits, a series of sunflower paintings (1888), and *Starry Night* (1889).

van•guard (**văn′**gärd) *n.* **1.** The front or leading position in an army or a fleet. **2.** The foremost or leading position in a trend or movement.

va•nil•la (və **nĭl′**ə) *n.* **1.** Any of various tropical American orchids having seedpods from which a flavoring extract is obtained. **2.** The long seedpods of this plant. **3.** A flavoring extract made from the cured seedpods of this plant or produced synthetically.

va•nil•lin (və **nĭl′**ĭn *or* **văn′**ə lĭn) *n.* A white or yellow crystalline compound of carbon, hydrogen, and oxygen, having the formula $C_8H_8O_3$. It is found in vanilla beans and certain balsams and resins and used in perfumes, flavorings, and drugs.

van•ish (**văn′**ĭsh) *intr.v.* **van•ished, van•ish•ing, van•ish•es. 1.** To pass out of sight, especially quickly; disappear: *The sun vanished behind a cloud.* See Synonyms at **disappear. 2.** To pass out of existence: *The dinosaurs vanished from Earth.*

van•ish•ing point (**văn′**ĭ shĭng) *n.* A point in a drawing or a work of art at which parallel lines drawn in perspective converge or seem to converge.

van•i•ty (**văn′**ĭ tē) *n., pl.* **van•i•ties. 1.** Excessive pride; conceit. **2.** Futility; worthlessness: *the vanity of trying to hold back the forces of change.* **3.** A vanity case. **4.** A dressing table.

vanity case *n.* A small handbag or case used by women for carrying cosmetics or toiletries.

van•quish (**văng′**kwĭsh *or* **văn′**kwĭsh) *tr.v.* **van•quished, van•quish•ing, van•quish•es. 1.** To defeat or conquer in battle; subjugate. **2.** To defeat in a conflict, contest, or competition. **3.** To overcome or subdue (an emotion, for example); suppress. **—van′quish•er** *n.*

van•tage (**văn′**tĭj) *n.* **1.** An advantage in a competition. **2.** A position, a condition, or an opportunity that provides superiority or an advantage. **3.** A position that affords a broad view or perspective.

Va•nu•a•tu (vä′nōō **ä′**tōō). An island country of the southern Pacific Ocean east of northern Australia. The islands gained independence from Great Britain and France as Vanuatu in 1980. Capital, Vila. Population, 138,000.

vap•id (**văp′**ĭd *or* **vā′**pĭd) *adj.* **1.** Lacking liveliness, animation, or interest; dull: *vapid conversation.* **2.** Lacking taste, zest, or flavor; flat: *a restaurant with cheap but vapid food.* **—vap′id•ly** *adv.*

va•por (**vā′**pər) *n.* **1.** Faintly visible suspension of fine particles of matter in the air, as mist, fumes, or smoke. **2.a.** The state of a substance that is in gaseous form but at a low enough temperature to be liquefied by the application of pressure. **b.** The gaseous state of a substance that is solid or liquid at normal temperatures. **c.** A mixture of a vapor and air, as the fuel mixture of an internal-combustion engine **3. vapors.** *Archaic.* A nervous condition such as depression or hysteria.

va•por•ize (**vā′**pə rīz′) *tr. & intr.v.* **va•por•ized, va•por•iz•ing, va•por•iz•es.** To convert or be con-

Martin Van Buren

Vincent van Gogh
1889 self-portrait

vanilla

ă	**pat**	oi	**boy**
ā	**pay**	ou	**out**
âr	**care**	ŏŏ	**took**
ä	**father**	ōō	**boot**
ĕ	**pet**	ŭ	**cut**
ē	**be**	ûr	**urge**
ĭ	**pit**	th	**thin**
ī	**pie**	*th*	**this**
îr	**pier**	hw	**whoop**
ŏ	**pot**	zh	**vision**
ō	**toe**	ə	**about**
ô	**paw**	N	*French* **bon**

verted into vapor. —**va′por•i•za′tion** (vā′pər ĭ **zā′**-shən) *n.*

va•por•iz•er (**vā′**pə rī′zər) *n.* A device that converts a substance into vapor, especially a device used to vaporize medicine for inhalation.

va•por•ous (**vā′**pər əs) *adj.* **1.** Relating to or like vapor. **2.** Producing vapors; volatile. **3.** Insubstantial or vague. —**va′por•ous•ly** *adv.*

va•pour (**vā′**pər) *n. Chiefly British.* Vapor.

va•que•ro (vä **kâr′**ō) *n., pl.* **va•que•ros.** A cowboy.

var. *abbr.* An abbreviation of: **1.** Variable. **2.** Variant. **3.** Variation. **4.** Variety. **5.** Various.

var•i•a•ble (**vâr′**ē ə bəl *or* **văr′**ē ə bəl) *adj.* **1.** Subject to variation; changeable: *a variable climate.* **2.** Capable of assuming any of a set of two or more values, as a mathematical function or symbol; not fixed in value. —*n.* **1.** Something that varies or is prone to variation. **2.** A variable mathematical quantity or a symbol that represents it. —**var′i•a•bil′i•ty, var′i•a•ble•ness** *n.* —**var′i•a•bly** *adv.*

var•i•ance (**vâr′**ē əns *or* **văr′**ē əns) *n.* **1.a.** The act of varying. **b.** The state or quality of being variable. **c.** A difference between what is expected and what actually occurs. **2.** The state or fact of differing or of being in conflict. **3.** Legal permission to do something contrary to established rules: *had to get a variance to add a room to the historic house.* —***idiom.*** **at variance.** In a state of discrepancy; differing: *Your view of the issue is at variance with mine.*

var•i•ant (**vâr′**ē ənt *or* **văr′**ē ənt) *adj.* **1.** Having or exhibiting variation; differing: *words with variant spellings.* **2.** Tending or liable to vary; variable. —*n.* Something that differs in form only slightly from something else, as a different spelling or pronunciation of the same word.

var•i•a•tion (vâr′ē **ā′**shən *or* văr′ē **ā′**shən) *n.* **1.** The act, process, or result of varying. **2.** The state or fact of being varied. **3.** The extent or degree to which something varies: *temperature variations of more than 50 degrees Fahrenheit.* **4.** Something that is slightly different from another of the same type. **5.** A mathematical function that relates values of a variable to values of other variables. **6.** A musical form that is an altered version of a given theme, diverging from it by melodic ornamentation and by changes in harmony, rhythm, or key.

var•i•cel•la (văr′ĭ **sĕl′**ə) *n.* Chicken pox.

var•i•col•ored (**vâr′**ĭ kŭl′ərd *or* **văr′**ĭ kŭl′ərd) *adj.* Having a variety of colors; variegated.

var•i•cose (**văr′**ĭ kōs′) *adj.* Abnormally swollen or knotted: *varicose veins.*

var•ied (**vâr′**ēd *or* **văr′**ēd) *adj.* Having or consisting of various forms or types; diverse: *a varied assortment of candy.* —**var′ied•ly** *adv.*

var•i•e•gat•ed (**vâr′**ē ĭ gā′tĭd *or* **văr′**ē ĭ gā′tĭd) *adj.* Having streaks, marks, or patches of a different color or colors: *butterflies with variegated wings.*

va•ri•e•ty (və **rī′**ĭ tē) *n., pl.* **va•ri•e•ties. 1.** The quality or condition of being various or varied; diversity. **2.** A number or collection of varied things, usually within the same general grouping; an assortment: *a variety of outdoor activities.* **3.** A group that is distinguished from other groups by a specific characteristic. **4.** A subdivision of a species consisting of populations or individuals that differ from the remainder of the species in certain minor characteristics: *Broccoli is a variety of cabbage.*

variety show *n.* A theatrical performance consisting of a series of unrelated acts, such as songs, dances, and comic skits.

variety store *n.* A retail store carrying a large variety of usually inexpensive merchandise.

var•i•ous (**vâr′**ē əs *or* **văr′**ē əs) *adj.* **1.a.** Of diverse kinds: *unable to go for various reasons.* **b.** Unlike; different: *flowers as various as the rose, the daisy, and the carnation.* **2.** Being more than one; several: *He spoke to various members of the club.* **3.** Being an individual or separate member of a group or class: *The various reports all agreed.* —**var′i•ous•ly** *adv.* —See Note.

var•let (**vär′**lĭt) *n.* A rascal; a knave.

var•mint (**vär′**mĭnt) *n. Informal.* A person or thing that is considered undesirable, obnoxious, or troublesome. [First written down in 1539 in Modern English and spelled *varment,* variant of *vermin.*]

var•nish (**vär′**nĭsh) *n.* **1.** A paint containing a solvent and a binder, used to coat a surface with a hard glossy transparent film. **2.** The smooth coating or gloss that results from the application of this paint. **3.** Something resembling or suggesting a coat of varnish; outward appearance; gloss: *hiding his temper under a varnish of good manners.* —*tr.v.* **var•nished, var•nish•ing, var•nish•es.** To cover or coat with or as if with varnish: *varnish a cabinet; tried to varnish over her lack of experience on her application.*

var•si•ty (**vär′**sĭ tē) *n., pl.* **var•si•ties.** The principal team representing a university, school, or college in sports, games, or other competitions.

var•y (**vâr′**ē *or* **văr′**ē) *v.* **var•ied** (**vâr′**ēd *or* **văr′**ēd), **var•y•ing, var•ies** (**vâr′**ēz *or* **văr′**ēz). —*tr.* **1.** To make changes in or cause to change; modify or alter: *I varied the speed of the drill to get it to work better.* **2.** To give variety to; make diverse: *vary one's diet.* —*intr.* **1.** To undergo or show change: *the temperature varied throughout the day.* **2.** To be different; deviate: *vary from the norm.* [First written down about 1350 in Middle English and spelled *varien,* from Latin *variāre,* from *varius,* various.]

vas•cu•lar (**văs′**kyə lər) *adj.* Of or containing tubes or vessels that carry or circulate liquids such as blood, lymph, or water within an animal or plant.

vas def•er•ens (**văs′** **dĕf′**ə rĕnz′) *n., pl.* **va•sa def•er•en•ti•a** (**vā′**zə dĕf′ə **rĕn′**shē ə). The duct through which sperm passes from a testis to the urethra.

vase (vās *or* vāz *or* väz) *n.* An open container, as of glass or porcelain, used for holding flowers for ornamentation. [First written down in 1563 in Modern English, from Latin *vās,* vessel.]

va•sec•to•my (və **sĕk′**tə mē) *n., pl.* **va•sec•to•mies.** Surgical removal of all or part of the vas deferens, usually as a means of sterilization.

Vas•e•line (**văs′**ə lēn′ *or* văs′ə **lēn′**). A trademark used for a brand of petroleum jelly.

vas•sal (**văs′**əl) *n.* **1.** A person who held land from a feudal lord and received protection in return for homage and allegiance. **2.** One who is a subordinate or dependent.

vas•sal•age (**văs′**ə lĭj) *n.* **1.** The condition of being a vassal. **2.** The service, homage, and fealty required of a vassal. **3.** A position of subordination or subjection.

vast (văst) *adj.* **vast•er, vast•est. 1.** Very great in size, number, amount, or quantity: *sold her collection for a vast sum.* **2.** Very great in area or extent; immense: *the vast expanse of the Pacific Ocean.* **3.** Very great in degree or intensity: *a vast difference between the two policies.* [First written down about 1580 in Modern English, from Latin *vastus.*] —**vast′ly** *adv.* —**vast′ness** *n.*

vat (văt) *n.* A large vessel, such as a tub or barrel, used to hold or store liquids.

Vat•i•can (**văt′**ĭ kən) *n.* **1.** The official residence of the pope in Vatican City. **2.** The papal government; the papacy.

Vatican City. An independent papal state on the Tiber River within Rome, Italy. It was created by a treaty in 1929 and issues its own currency and postage stamps. Population, 736.

vaude•ville (**vôd′**vĭl′) *n.* Stage entertainment offer-

Usage: various

You should not use **various** as a pronoun, as in *He spoke to various of the members.* Instead write *He spoke to various members.*

ing a variety of short acts such as singing and dancing routines and juggling performances.

vault[1] (vôlt) *n.* **1.** An arched structure forming the supporting structure of a ceiling or roof. **2.** A room, such as a cellar, with arched walls and ceiling, especially when underground. **3.** A room or compartment for the safekeeping of valuables. **4.** A burial chamber, especially when underground. —*tr.v.* **vault•ed, vault•ing, vaults.** To build or cover with a vault. [First written down before 1300 in Middle English and spelled *vaute*, from Latin *volūtus*, past participle of *volvere*, to roll.]

vault[2] (vôlt) *tr. & intr.v.* **vault•ed, vault•ing, vaults.** To jump or leap over, especially with the aid of a support such as the hands or a pole. —*n.* The act of vaulting; a leap. [First written down in 1538 in Modern English, from Old Italian *voltare*, from Latin *volvere*, to turn, roll.] —**vault'er** *n.*

vaunt (vônt *or* vŏnt) *tr. & intr.v.* **vaunt•ed, vaunt•ing, vaunts.** To speak boastfully of or brag. —*n.* A boastful remark.

vb. *abbr.* An abbreviation of verb.

VCR (vē'sē är') *n., pl.* **VCR's.** An electronic device for recording and playing back video images and sound on a videocassette.

VD also **V.D.** *abbr.* An abbreviation of venereal disease.

VDT (vē'dē tē') *n., pl.* **VDT's.** A device using the screen of a cathode-ray tube to display computer data and graphic images.

veal (vēl) *n.* The meat of a calf. [First written down about 1395 in Middle English, from Latin *vitellus*, from *vitulus*, calf.]

vec•tor (vĕk'tər) *n.* **1.** In mathematics and physical science, a quantity, such as velocity or change of position, that must be identified by its direction as well as by its measure. **2.** An organism, such as a mosquito or tick, that carries disease-causing microorganisms from one host to another [First written down in 1704 in Modern English, from Latin *vector*, carrier, from *vehere*, to carry.]

veer (vîr) *v.* **veered, veer•ing, veers.** —*intr.* To turn aside from a course, direction, or purpose; swerve: *The plane veered east to avoid the oncoming storm.* —*tr.* To alter the direction of; turn: *He veered the car sharply to the left.* [First written down in 1582 in Modern English, from French *virer.*]

Ve•ga (vē'gə *or* vā'gə) *n.* A bright star seen in the northern sky.

veg•e•ta•ble (vĕj'tə bəl *or* vĕj'ĭ tə bəl) *n.* **1.** A plant of which the roots, leaves, stems, flowers, and in some cases the seeds, pods, or fruit are used as food. **2.** The part of such a plant eaten as food. **3.** A member of the plant kingdom; a plant. **4.** A person who is regarded as dull, passive, or unresponsive.

veg•e•tar•i•an (vĕj'ĭ târ'ē ən) *n.* A person whose diet consists primarily or wholly of plants and plant products and sometimes eggs and dairy products as well. —*adj.* **1.** Of or relating to vegetarians or vegetarianism. **2.** Consisting primarily or wholly of plants and plant products: *a vegetarian meal.*

veg•e•tar•i•an•ism (vĕj'ĭ târ'ē ə nĭz'əm) *n.* The practice of subsisting on a vegetarian diet.

veg•e•tate (vĕj'ĭ tāt') *intr.v.* **veg•e•tat•ed, veg•e•tat•ing, veg•e•tates.** **1.** To grow or sprout as a plant does. **2.** To grow or spread abnormally, as a tumor or other growth. **3.** To be physically inactive and mentally dull: *We vegetated in front of the TV during the storm.*

veg•e•ta•tion (vĕj'ĭ tā'shən) *n.* **1.** The act or process of vegetating. **2.** The plants of an area or a region; plant life.

veg•e•ta•tive (vĕj'ĭ tā'tĭv) *adj.* **1.** Of or relating to plant life. **2.** Of, relating to, or characterized by the biological processes of growth and nutrition rather than sexual reproduction.

ve•he•ment (vē'ə mənt) *adj.* **1.** Marked by forcefulness of expression or intensity of emotion or conviction; fervent: *a vehement critic of his foreign policy.* **2.** Marked by or full of vigor or energy; strong: *vehement applause.* —**ve'he•mence** *n.* —**ve'he•ment•ly** *adv.*

ve•hi•cle (vē'ĭ kəl) *n.* **1.a.** A device or structure for transporting people or things. **b.** A self-propelled conveyance that runs on tires; a motor vehicle. **2.** A medium through which something is transmitted, expressed, or accomplished: *Oral tales are an important vehicle of culture.* **3.** A play, role, or piece of music used to display the special abilities of a performer or group of performers. **4.** A substance, such as oil, into which pigments are mixed in making paint. [First written down in 1612 in Modern English, from Latin *vehiculum*, from *vehere*, to carry.]

ve•hic•u•lar (vē hĭk'yə lər) *adj.* **1.** Of, relating to, or intended for vehicles, especially motor vehicles: *vehicular traffic; vehicular regulations.* **2.** Serving as a vehicle.

veil (vāl) *n.* **1.** A length of cloth worn by women over the head, shoulders, and often the face. **2.** The part of a nun's headdress that frames the face and falls over the shoulders. **3.** Something that covers or conceals like a veil, curtain, or cloak: *a veil of secrecy.* —*tr.v.* **veiled, veil•ing, veils.** **1.** To cover with or as if with a veil: *veil one's face.* **2.** To conceal or disguise.

❑ *These sound alike:* **veil, vale** (valley).

vein (vān) *n.* **1.** Any of a branching system of blood vessels through which blood returns to the heart. **2.** One of the narrow, usually branching tubes of supporting parts forming the framework of a leaf or an insect's wing. **3.** A long, regularly shaped deposit of an ore or a mineral in the earth: *a vein of copper ore; a vein of coal.* **4.** A long wavy strip of a different shade or color, as in marble or wood. **5.** A particular turn of mind: *He spoke in a light playful vein.* —*tr.v.* **veined, vein•ing, veins.** To fill or supply with veins. [First written down before 1300 in Middle English and spelled *veine*, from Latin *vēna.*]

❑ *These sound alike:* **vein, vain** (proud), **vane** (weathervane).

ve•lar (vē'lər) *adj.* **1.** Relating to or involving the soft palate. **2.** Formed with the back of the tongue on or near the soft palate, as the *c* in *cut.*

Vel•cro (vĕl'krō). A trademark used for a fastening tape consisting of a strip of nylon with a surface of minute hooks that fasten to another nylon strip with a surface of uncut pile, used especially on cloth products, such as outerwear and luggage.

veldt also **veld** (vĕlt *or* fĕlt) *n.* An open grazing area of southern Africa.

vel•lum (vĕl'əm) *n.* **1.** A fine parchment made from the skins of calf, lamb, or kid and used for the pages and binding of books. **2.** A heavy paper that looks like this parchment.

ve•loc•i•ty (və lŏs'ĭ tē) *n., pl.* **ve•loc•i•ties.** **1.** The rate at which an object moves in a specified direction. **2.** Speed.

ve•lour (və lo͝or') *n., pl.* **ve•lours** (və lo͝orz'). A closely napped fabric resembling velvet, used chiefly for clothing and upholstery.

vel•vet (vĕl'vĭt) *n.* **1.** A soft fabric, such as silk, rayon, or nylon, having a smooth dense pile on one side and a plain underside. **2.** Something resembling velvet.

vel•vet•een (vĕl'vĭ tēn') *n.* A cotton pile fabric resembling velvet.

vel•vet•y (vĕl'vĭ tē) *adj.* **vel•vet•i•er, vel•vet•i•est.** Having the soft smooth texture of velvet.

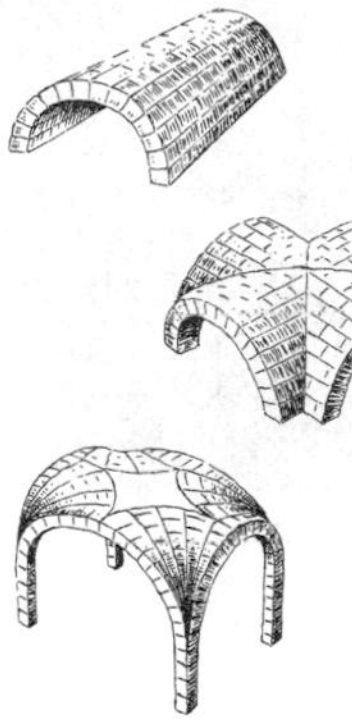

vault[1]
Top: Barrel vault
Center: Groin vault
Bottom: Fan vault

VDT

ă	pat	oi	boy
ā	pay	ou	out
âr	care	o͝o	took
ä	father	o͞o	boot
ĕ	pet	ŭ	cut
ē	be	ûr	urge
ĭ	pit	th	thin
ī	pie	*th*	this
îr	pier	hw	whoop
ŏ	pot	zh	vision
ō	toe	ə	about
ô	paw	N	*French* bon

vender

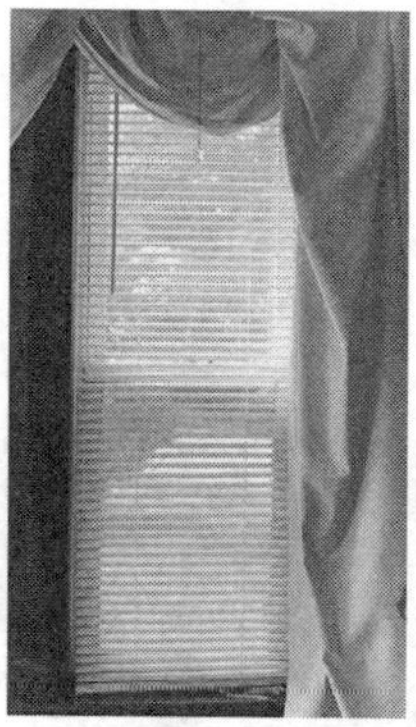

venetian blind

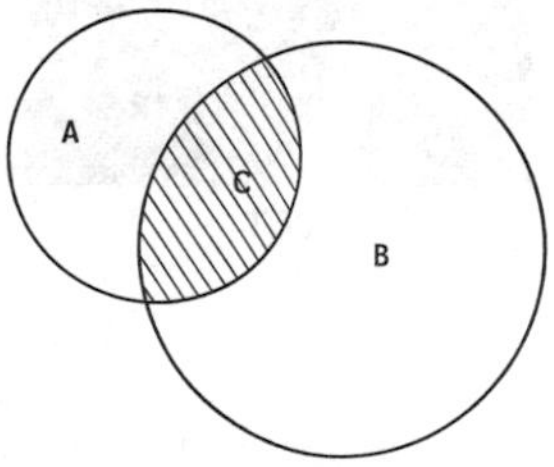

Venn diagram
A. People who like dogs
B. People who like cats
C. People who like dogs and cats

ă	pat	oi	boy
ā	pay	ou	out
âr	care	o͝o	took
ä	father	o͞o	boot
ĕ	pet	ŭ	cut
ē	be	ûr	urge
ĭ	pit	th	thin
ī	pie	*th*	this
îr	pier	hw	whoop
ŏ	pot	zh	vision
ō	toe	ə	about
ô	paw	N	*French* bon

ve•na ca•va (vē′nə kā′və) *n., pl.* **ve•nae ca•vae** (vē′nē kā′vē). Either of two large veins that return blood to the right atrium of the heart.

ve•nal (vē′nəl) *adj.* **1.** Willing to be bribed; mercenary: *a venal police officer.* **2.** Marked by corrupt dealings, especially bribery: *a venal administration.* [First written down in 1652 in Modern English, from Latin *vēnum*, sale.]

ve•na•tion (vē nā′shən *or* vĕ nā′shən) *n.* **1.** Distribution or arrangement of a system of veins, as in a leaf blade or the wing of an insect. **2.** The veins of such a system considered as a group.

vend (vĕnd) *v.* **vend•ed, vend•ing, vends.** —*tr.* **1.** To sell by means of a vending machine. **2.** To sell, especially by peddling. —*intr.* To engage in selling.

vend•er or **ven•dor** (vĕn′dər) *n.* **1.** A person who sells or vends: *a street vender.* **2.** A vending machine.

ven•det•ta (vĕn dĕt′ə) *n.* A feud between two families or clans that arises out of a killing and is perpetuated by acts of revenge.

vend•ing machine (vĕn′dĭng) *n.* A machine operated by coins or bills that dispenses merchandise.

ven•dor (vĕn′dər) *n.* Variant of **vender.**

ve•neer (və nîr′) *n.* **1.** A thin surface layer, as of finely grained wood, glued to a base of inferior material: *a pine cabinet with a mahogany veneer.* **2.** Any of the thin layers glued together to make plywood. **3.** A deceptive superficial show; a façade: *a veneer of friendliness.* —*tr.v.* **ve•neered, ve•neer•ing, ve•neers. 1.** To overlay (a surface) with a thin layer of better or finer material. **2.** To conceal, as something common or crude, with a deceptively attractive outward show.

ven•er•a•ble (vĕn′ər ə bəl) *adj.* **1.** Worthy of respect or reverence by virtue of age, dignity, character, or position: *a venerable senator.* **2.** Deserving of reverence, especially for historic or religious associations: *venerable relics of a saint.* **—ven′er•a•bly** *adv.*

ven•er•ate (vĕn′ə rāt′) *tr.v.* **ven•er•at•ed, ven•er•at•ing, ven•er•ates.** To regard with respect, reverence, or heartfelt deference. **—ven′er•a′tion** *n.*

ve•ne•re•al disease (və nîr′ē əl) *n.* Any of several diseases transmitted by sexual contact, such as syphilis and gonorrhea.

ve•ne•tian blind or **Ve•ne•tian blind** (və nē′shən) *n.* A window blind consisting of a number of thin horizontal adjustable slats that overlap when closed.

Ven•e•zue•la (vĕn′ə zwā′lə *or* vĕn′ə zwē′lə). A country of northern South America on the Caribbean Sea northeast of Colombia. Venezuela was liberated from Spain by Simón Bolívar in 1821, and was formally separated from Colombia in 1830. Capital, Caracas. Population, 14,515,885.

ven•geance (vĕn′jəns) *n.* Infliction of punishment in return for a wrong committed; retribution. —***idiom.* with a vengeance.** With great violence or force: *The snowstorm hit with a vengeance.*

venge•ful (vĕnj′fəl) *adj.* Desiring vengeance; vindictive. **—venge′ful•ly** *adv.*

ve•ni•al (vē′nē əl *or* vēn′yəl) *adj.* Easily excused or forgiven; minor or pardonable. [First written down about 1303 in Middle English, from Latin *venia*, forgiveness.]

Ven•ice (vĕn′ĭs). A city of northeast Italy on islets within a lagoon in the **Gulf of Venice,** a wide inlet of the northern Adriatic Sea. It was founded in the 5th century A.D. Population, 332,775. **—Ve•ne′tian** (və nē′shən) *adj. & n.*

ven•i•son (vĕn′ĭ sən *or* vĕn′ĭ zən) *n.* The flesh of a deer used as food.

Venn diagram (vĕn) *n.* A diagram that uses circles to represent sets. Relations and operations on sets can be shown as overlapping, included, and excluded regions. [First written down in 1918 in Modern English, after John *Venn* (1834–1923), British logician.]

ven•om (vĕn′əm) *n.* **1.** A poisonous substance that is secreted by certain snakes, spiders, scorpions, and insects, and can be transmitted to a victim by a bite or sting. **2.** Malice; spite. [First written down before 1250 in Middle English and spelled *venim*, from Latin *venēnum*, poison.]

ven•om•ous (vĕn′ə məs) *adj.* **1.** Secreting and transmitting venom: *a venomous snake.* **2.** Full of or containing venom: *a venomous substance.* **3.** Malicious; spiteful: *a venomous look.* **—ven′om•ous•ly** *adv.* **—ven′om•ous•ness** *n.*

ve•nous (vē′nəs) *adj.* **1.** Of or contained in the veins: *venous blood.* **2.** Having numerous veins, as a leaf or the wings of an insect.

vent¹ (vĕnt) *n.* **1.** A means of escape or release from confinement; an outlet. **2.** An opening through which a liquid, gas, or vapor can pass or escape. —*tr.v.* **vent•ed, vent•ing, vents. 1.** To give often forceful expression or utterance to: *venting their grievances.* **2.** To release or discharge (steam, for example) through an opening. **3.** To provide with a vent. [First written down in 1508 in Modern English, partly from French *vent* and partly alteration of French *évent* (from Old French *esventer*, to let out air).]

vent² (vĕnt) *n.* A slit in a garment, as in the back seam of a pocket. [First written down about 1430 in Middle English and spelled *vente*, from Old French *fente*, slit.]

ven•ti•late (vĕn′tl āt′) *tr.v.* **ven•ti•lat•ed, ven•ti•lat•ing, ven•ti•lates. 1.** To admit fresh air into (a mine, for example) to replace stale or noxious air. **2.** To provide with a vent, as for airing. **3.** To expose to public discussion or examination; air: *We ventilated our misgivings.*

ven•ti•la•tor (vĕn′tl ā′tər) *n.* A device that circulates fresh air and expels stale or foul air.

ven•tral (vĕn′trəl) *adj.* Related to or located on or near the abdomen; abdominal.

ven•tri•cle (vĕn′trĭ kəl) *n.* A cavity or chamber in an organ, especially either of the chambers of the heart that contract to pump blood into arteries. **—ven•tric′u•lar** (vĕn trĭk′yə lər) *adj.*

ven•tril•o•quism (vĕn trĭl′ə kwĭz′əm) *n.* The art of projecting one's voice so that it seems to come from another source, as from a wooden figure. **—ven•tril′o•quist** *n.*

ven•ture (vĕn′chər) *n.* **1.** An undertaking that is dangerous, daring, or of uncertain outcome. **2.** A business enterprise involving some financial risk. —*v.* **ven•tured, ven•tur•ing, ven•tures.** —*tr.* **1.** To expose to danger or risk: *venturing all his capital on a deal.* **2.** To brave the dangers of: *ventured the high seas in a light boat.* **3.** To dare to say; express at the risk of denial, criticism, or censure: *venture an opinion.* —*intr.* **1.** To take a risk; dare. **2.** To proceed despite possible danger or risk: *ventured into the mountains.*

ven•ture•some (vĕn′chər səm) *adj.* **1.** Given to venturing or taking risks; daring: *venturesome investors.* **2.** Involving risk or danger; hazardous.

ven•tu•ri (vĕn to͝or′ē) *n., pl.* **ven•tu•ris.** A short tube having a narrow section through which a fluid moving through the tube must pass at a higher velocity than at other points. The fluid in the narrow section exerts less pressure than that in the wider parts, allowing the use of the tube as an air speed indicator, as an atomizer, and in rockets. [First written down in 1887 in Modern English, after G.B. *Venturi* (1746–1822), Italian physicist.]

ven•ue (vĕn′yo͞o) *n.* **1.** The locality in which a crime or other cause of legal action occurs. **2.** The locality in which a trial is held. **3.** The scene or setting in which something takes place; a locale.

Ve•nus (vē′nəs) *n.* **1.** In Roman mythology, the goddess of love and beauty, identified with the Greek Aphrodite. **2.** The second planet from the sun at a mean distance of 67 million miles (108 million kilometers), and the sixth largest in the solar system with a mean diameter of 7,600 miles (12,200 kilometers).

Ve•nus's-fly•trap (vē′nəs flī′trăp′ *or* vē′nə sĭz flī′-trăp′) *n.* A plant having leaf ends that are edged with bristles and that can close and trap insects that are then digested and absorbed by the plant.

ve•ra•cious (və rā′shəs) *adj.* **1.** Honest; truthful: *a veracious person.* **2.** Accurate; precise: *a veracious description of the accident.* **—ve•ra′cious•ly** *adv.*

ve•rac•i•ty (və răs′ĭ tē) *n., pl.* **ve•rac•i•ties. 1.** Adherence to the truth; honesty: *doubting the veracity of the witnesses.* **2.** Accuracy; precision: *checking the veracity of his report.*

ve•ran•da or **ve•ran•dah** (və răn′də) *n.* A usually roofed porch or balcony extending along the outside of a building.

verb (vûrb) *n.* **1.** In grammar, a word, such as *be, run,* or *happen,* that expresses existence, action, or occurrence. **2.** A phrase, such as *has been thinking,* that is used as a verb. [First written down before 1397 in Middle English and spelled *verbe,* from Latin *verbum,* word, verb.] —See Note.

ver•bal (vûr′bəl) *adj.* **1.** Of, relating to, or associated with words: *verbal aptitude tests.* **2.** Expressed in spoken rather than written words; oral: *a verbal agreement.* **3.** Word for word; literal: *a verbal translation.* **4.** Relating to, having the nature or function of, or derived from a verb: *verbal constructions.* **5.** Used to form verbs: *a verbal suffix.* *—n.* A noun or adjective derived from a verb. **—ver′bal•ly** *adv.*

ver•bal•ize (vûr′bə līz′) *v.* **ver•bal•ized, ver•bal•iz•ing, ver•bal•iz•es.** *—tr.* To express in words: *verbalized his fears.* *—intr.* To express oneself in words.

ver•ba•tim (vər bā′tĭm) *adj.* Using exactly the same words; corresponding word for word: *a verbatim quotation.* *—adv.* Word for word; in the same words: *He repeated the speech verbatim.*

ver•be•na (vər bē′nə) *n.* Any of various plants grown for their spikes of variously colored, often fragrant flowers.

ver•bi•age (vûr′bē ĭj *or* vûr′bĭj) *n.* An excess of words for the purpose; wordiness.

ver•bose (vər bōs′) *adj.* Using or containing more words than necessary; wordy. **—ver•bose′ly** *adv.* **—ver•bos′i•ty** (vər bŏs′ĭ tē) *n.*

ver•dant (vûr′dnt) *adj.* **1.** Green with growing plants; covered with green growth: *verdant meadows.* **2.** Green in hue: *verdant leaves.*

Ver•di (vâr′dē), **Giuseppe.** 1813–1901. Italian composer whose operas include *Aïda* (1871) and *Otello* (1887).

ver•dict (vûr′dĭkt) *n.* **1.** The decision reached by a jury at the end of a trial. **2.** An expressed conclusion; a judgment or an opinion.

ver•di•gris (vûr′dĭ grēs′) *n.* **1.** A blue or green copper acetate, used as a pigment and as a poison for insects and fungi. **2.** A green coating or crust of copper salts that forms on copper, brass, or bronze that is exposed to air or sea water for a long time.

ver•dure (vûr′jər) *n.* **1.** The lush green color of healthy growing plants. **2.** A growth of green plants.

verge (vûrj) *n.* **1.** The extreme edge or margin of something; a border: *on the verge of the city's industrial section.* **2.** The point beyond which an action, a state, or a condition is likely to begin or occur: *on the verge of tears.* *—intr.v.* **verged, verg•ing, verg•es.** To approach the nature or condition of something specified; come close: *enthusiasm verging on fanaticism.*

Ver•gil (vûr′jəl). Virgil.

ver•i•fi•ca•tion (vĕr′ə fĭ kā′shən) *n.* **1.** The act of verifying or the state of being verified. **2.** A confirmation of truth or authority.

ver•i•fy (vĕr′ə fī′) *tr.v.* **ver•i•fied** (vĕr′ə fīd′), **ver•i•fy•ing, ver•i•fies** (vĕr′ə fīz′). **1.** To prove the truth of by presentation of evidence or testimony: *Astronomers have verified certain findings of the ancient Greeks.* **2.** To test or determine the truth or accuracy of: *verify your hypothesis.* [First written down before 1325 in Middle English and spelled *verifien,* from Latin *vērus,* true.]

ver•i•ly (vĕr′ə lē) *adv.* In fact; in truth.

ver•i•si•mil•i•tude (vĕr′ə sĭ mĭl′ĭ to͞od′ *or* vĕr′-ə sĭ mĭl′ĭ tyo͞od′) *n.* The quality of appearing to be real or true.

ver•i•ta•ble (vĕr′ĭ tə bəl) *adj.* Being truly so called; real or genuine: *a veritable success.*

ver•i•ty (vĕr′ĭ tē) *n., pl.* **ver•i•ties. 1.** The quality or condition of being real, factual, or true: *the verity of his description.* **2.** Something, such as a principle or belief, that is true: *verities proclaimed by the church.*

ver•mi•cel•li (vûr′mĭ chĕl′ē *or* vûr′mĭ sĕl′ē) *n.* Pasta made into long strands thinner than spaghetti.

ver•mi•form (vûr′mə fôrm′) *adj.* Shaped like or resembling a worm.

vermiform appendix *n.* The tubular projection attached to the large intestine near its junction with the small intestine; the appendix.

ver•mil•ion also **ver•mil•lion** (vər mĭl′yən) *n.* **1.** A bright red sulfide of mercury, used as a pigment. **2.** A vivid red to reddish orange. *—adj.* Of a vivid red to reddish orange.

ver•min (vûr′mĭn) *n., pl.* **vermin. 1.** Various small animals or insects, such as rats or cockroaches, that are destructive, annoying, or injurious to health. **2.** A person considered loathsome or highly offensive. **3.** Such people considered as a group. [First written down before 1300 in Middle English, from Latin *vermis,* worm.]

ver•min•ous (vûr′mə nəs) *adj.* **1.** Of, relating to, or caused by vermin. **2.** Infested with vermin.

Ver•mont (vər mŏnt′). A state of the northeast United States west of New Hampshire. It was admitted as the 14th state in 1791. Capital, Montpelier. Population, 564,964. —See Note.

ver•mouth (vər mo͞oth′) *n.* A sweet or dry wine flavored with aromatic herbs and used chiefly in mixed drinks.

ver•nac•u•lar (vər năk′yə lər) *n.* **1.** The ordinary spoken language of a country or locality as distinct from the literary language. **2.** The idiom of a particular trade or profession: *the medical vernacular.* *—adj.* **1.** Native to or commonly spoken by the members of a country or region. **2.** Using the native language of a region, especially as distinct from the literary language: *a vernacular poet.*

ver•nal (vûr′nəl) *adj.* Of, relating to, or occurring in the spring. [First written down in 1534 in Modern English, from Latin *vērnus,* from *vēr,* spring.] **—ver′nal•ly** *adv.*

vernal equinox *n.* The equinox that occurs on or about March 21, when the sun, moving northward, crosses the celestial equator, marking the beginning of spring in the Northern Hemisphere. —See Note.

ver•ni•er (vûr′nē ər) *n.* **1.** A small auxiliary scale attached parallel to a main scale and arranged to indicate fractional parts of the smallest divisions of the main scale. **2.** An auxiliary device that allows

Usage: verb

Many verbs can be used transitively with an object as well as intransitively without an object. Using the verb *hit* as an example, we can say *I hit the ball* with the object *ball* or we can say *I hit hard* without an object. Verbs also are often used both in the active voice (*I hit the ball hard*) and in the passive voice (*The ball was hit hard by me*).

Vermont

The name for the state of **Vermont** comes from a combination of two French words that together mean "green mountain."

Word History: vernal equinox

The term **vernal equinox** is not hard to remember when you know what it means. The adjective **vernal** means "of the spring season," and it first appears in English in the writings of Saint Thomas More in 1534. Our word comes from the Latin adjective *vernālis* (with the same meaning as the English), which comes from the Latin noun *vēr,* "spring (the season)." **Equinox,** "the time at which the sun crosses the celestial equator and the day and night are each 12 hours long," first appears in English in 1391 in the writings of the great poet Geoffrey Chaucer. It comes from the Latin word *equinoxium* or *aequinoctium.* The Latin word is formed from the word roots *aequi–,* "equal," as in **equidistant,** and *noct–* or *nocti–,* "night," as in **nocturnal.** The season opposite **spring** is **autumn,** which in Latin is *autumnus.* The Latin adjective to *autumnus* is *autumnālis,* our **autumnal,** and the corresponding equinox is the **autumnal equinox.**

Amerigo Vespucci
Portrait by an unknown artist

vetch
Cow vetch

fine adjustments or measurements to be made on or with an instrument or device. [First written down in 1766 in Modern English, after Pierre *Vernier* (1580?–1637), French mathematician.]

vernier caliper *n.* A measuring device consisting of a caliper equipped with a vernier scale.

Ver•sailles (vər sī′ *or* vĕr sī′). A city of north-central France west-southwest of Paris. It is best known for its magnificent palace built by Louis XIV. Population, 91,494.

ver•sa•tile (vûr′sə təl *or* vûr′sə tīl′) *adj.* **1.** Capable of doing many things well: *It takes a versatile athlete to do well in the decathlon.* **2.** Having varied uses or functions: *a versatile piece of machinery.* **3.** Variable or inconstant; changeable: *a versatile temperament.* —**ver′sa•til′i•ty** (vûr′sə tĭl′ĭ tē) *n.*

verse (vûrs) *n.* **1.** One line of poetry. **2.** A stanza of a long poem or hymn. **3.** The art or work of a poet; poetry. **4.** A specific type of poetic writing: *elegiac verse.* **5.** One of the numbered subdivisions of a chapter of the Bible.

versed (vûrst) *adj.* Acquainted through study or experience; skilled or knowledgeable: *versed in foreign languages.*

ver•si•fy (vûr′sə fī′) *v.* **ver•si•fied** (vûr′sə fīd′), **ver•si•fy•ing, ver•si•fies** (vûr′sə fīz′). —*tr.* **1.** To change from prose into metrical form **2.** To treat or tell in verse. —*intr.* To write verses.

ver•sion (vûr′zhən) *n.* **1.** A description or an account from a specific point of view: *his version of the accident disagreed with mine.* **2.** A translation of a written work: *the King James version of the Bible.* **3.** A form or variation of an earlier or original type: *a reworked version of the Ford Model T.* **4.** An adaptation of a work of art or literature into another medium or style: *a motion-picture version of a play.*

ver•sus (vûr′səs *or* vûr′səz) *prep.* **1.** Against: *the plaintiff versus the defendant.* **2.** As an alternative to or in contrast with: *studying to be a chemist versus working on a farm.*

vert. *abbr.* An abbreviation of vertical.

ver•te•bra (vûr′tə brə) *n., pl.* **ver•te•brae** (vûr′tə-brā′) or **ver•te•bras.** Any of the bones or segments of cartilage forming the spinal column.

ver•te•bral (vûr′tə brəl) *adj.* **1.** Of or relating to a vertebra. **2.** Having or consisting of vertebrae: *the vertebral column.*

ver•te•brate (vûr′tə brĭt *or* vûr′tə brāt′) *adj.* **1.** Having a backbone: *vertebrate animals.* **2.** Of or characteristic of a vertebrate or vertebrates: *the vertebrate brain.* —*n.* Any of a large group of animals having a backbone, including the fishes, amphibians, reptiles, birds, and mammals.

ver•tex (vûr′tĕks′) *n., pl.* **ver•tex•es** or **ver•ti•ces** (vûr′tĭ sēz′). **1.** The highest point of something; the apex or summit. **2.a.** The point at which the sides of an angle intersect. **b.** The point of a triangle that is opposite to and farthest away from its base. **c.** A point of a polyhedron at which three or more edges intersect. **d.** The point of a cone or pyramid farthest from its base.

ver•ti•cal (vûr′tĭ kəl) *adj.* **1.** Being or situated at right angles to the horizon; directly upright. **2.** Situated at the vertex or highest point; directly overhead. —*n.* **1.** Something vertical, as a line, plane, or circle. **2.** A vertical position: *a post that leans slightly from the vertical.* [First written down in 1559 in Modern English, from Late Latin *verticālis*, overhead, from Latin *vertex*, highest point, vertex.] —**ver′ti•cal•ly** *adv.*

vertical angle *n.* Either of two angles formed by two intersecting lines and lying on opposite sides of the point of intersection.

vertical file *n.* A collection of resource materials, such as clippings from periodicals and photographs, arranged in a library or an archive for easy reference.

ver•ti•ces (vûr′tĭ sēz′) *n.* A plural of **vertex.**

ver•ti•go (vûr′tĭ gō′) *n., pl.* **ver•ti•goes** or **ver•ti•gos. 1.** The sensation of dizziness. **2.** A confused disoriented state of mind.

verve (vûrv) *n.* **1.** Energy and enthusiasm in the expression of ideas: *His plays lack verve.* **2.** Liveliness or vitality; animation.

ver•y (vĕr′ē) *adv.* **1.** In a high degree; extremely: *feeling very happy.* **2.** Truly; absolutely: *the very best advice.* —*adj.* **ver•i•er, ver•i•est. 1.** Absolute; utter: *the very end of the day.* **2.** Being the identical one: *the very dress we saw yesterday.* **3.** Used to emphasize the importance of the thing described: *the very mountains crumbled.* **4.** Being precisely as stated: *the very center of town.* **5.** Mere: *The very thought is frightening.* **6.** Actual: *caught in the very act of stealing.*

very high frequency *n.* A radio-wave frequency lying in the band between 30 and 300 megahertz.

very low frequency *n.* A radio-wave frequency lying in the band between 3 and 30 kilohertz.

ves•i•cle (vĕs′ĭ kəl) *n.* **1.** A small bladder or sac, especially one that contains a body fluid. **2.** A blister.

ve•sic•u•lar (vĕ sĭk′yə lər) *adj.* **1.** Of or relating to vesicles. **2.** Composed of or containing vesicles.

ves•per (vĕs′pər) *n.* **1.** A bell that summons worshipers to vespers. **2. Vesper.** The evening star, especially Venus.

ves•pers also **Ves•pers** (vĕs′pərz) *pl.n. (used with a singular or plural verb).* **1.a.** The sixth of the seven canonical hours. **b.** A Christian worship service held in the late afternoon or evening. **2.** Evensong.

Ves•puc•ci (vĕs po͞o′chē *or* vĕs pyo͞o′chē), **Amerigo.** 1454–1512. Italian navigator and explorer of the South American coast. America was named in his honor.

ves•sel (vĕs′əl) *n.* **1.** A hollow utensil, such as a bowl, pitcher, jar, or tank, used especially as a container for liquids. **2.** A ship, large boat, or similar craft. **3.** A narrow tubular body part or plant part through which a fluid flows or circulates: *Veins and arteries are vessels.*

vest (vĕst) *n.* **1.** A sleeveless garment, often having buttons down the front, worn usually over a shirt or blouse and sometimes as part of a three-piece suit. **2.** A sleeveless protective garment extending to the waist: *a bulletproof vest.* **3.** *Chiefly British.* An undershirt. —*tr.v.* **vest•ed, vest•ing, vests. 1.** To place (authority or power, for example) in the control of a person or group: *Their constitution vests ultimate power in the sovereign.* **2.** To give power or authority to: *vesting the President with executive powers.* **3.** To dress, as in religious robes or vestments. [First written down in 1613 in Modern English, from Latin *vestis*, garment.]

Ves•ta (vĕs′tə) *n.* In Roman mythology, the goddess of the hearth.

ves•tal (vĕs′təl) *adj.* **1.** Of or relating to Vesta. **2.** Chaste; pure. —*n.* In Roman mythology, one of the six virgin women who tend the sacred fire in the temple of Vesta.

vest•ed (vĕs′tĭd) *adj.* Legally settled, fixed, or absolute; being without contingency: *a vested right to the throne.*

ves•ti•bule (vĕs′tə byo͞ol′) *n.* **1.** A small entrance hall or lobby. **2.** An enclosed area at the end of a railroad passenger car. **3.** A chamber, an opening, or a channel of the body that serves as an entrance to another chamber or cavity.

ves•tige (vĕs′tĭj) *n.* **1.** A visible trace or sign of something that once existed: *barely a vestige of col-*

or left in the faded curtains. **2.** An organ or a structure that was present and functioning in an earlier form of an organism and that remains, usually greatly reduced in size, in later forms as a nonfunctioning part. [First written down in 1602 in Modern English, from Latin *vestīgium.*]

ves•tig•i•al (vĕ **stĭj′**ē əl) *adj.* **1.** Of, relating to, or being a vestige. **2.** Occurring or remaining in a related or undeveloped form.

vest•ment (**vĕst′**mənt) *n.* A garment, especially a robe, gown, or other article of dress, worn as an indication of office or state or by a cleric at a religious service.

ves•try (**vĕs′**trē) *n., pl.* **ves•tries. 1.** A room in a church where vestments and sacred objects are stored. **2.** A meeting room in a church. **3.** A committee that manages the temporal affairs of a parish.

ves•try•man (**vĕs′**trē mən) *n.* A man who is a member of a vestry.

ves•try•wom•an (**vĕs′**trē wo͝om′ən) *n.* A woman who is a member of a vestry.

Ve•su•vi•us (vĭ **so͞o′**vē əs), **Mount.** An active volcano, 4,200 feet (1,281 meters) high, of southern Italy. A violent eruption in A.D. 79 destroyed the nearby city of Pompeii.

vet¹ (vĕt) *n. Informal.* A veterinarian.

vet² (vĕt) *n. Informal.* A veteran.

vet. *abbr.* An abbreviation of veteran.

vetch (vĕch) *n.* Any of various climbing plants having feathery leaves and usually purplish flowers.

vet•er•an (**vĕt′**ər ən *or* **vĕt′**rən) *n.* **1.** A person who is long experienced or practiced in a profession or an activity. **2.** A person who has served in the armed forces: *a veteran of the Korean War.* [First written down in 1509 in Modern English, from Latin *veterānus*, from *vetus*, old.]

Vet•er•ans Day (**vĕt′**ər ənz *or* **vĕt′**rənz) *n.* November 11, observed in honor of veterans of the armed services and in commemoration of the armistice ending World War I in 1918.

vet•er•i•nar•i•an (vĕt′ər ə **nâr′**ē ən *or* vĕt′rə **nâr′**ē ən) *n.* A person specially trained and qualified to give medical treatment to animals.

vet•er•i•nar•y (**vĕt′**ər ə nĕr′ē *or* **vĕt′**rə nĕr′ē) *adj.* Of or relating to the medical treatment, diseases, or injuries of animals: *a veterinary college.* —*n., pl.* **vet•er•i•nar•ies.** A veterinarian.

ve•to (**vē′**tō) *n., pl.* **ve•toes. 1.a.** The right or power of a branch of government to reject a bill that has been passed and therefore prevent or delay its enactment into law. **b.** Exercise of this right. **2.** An authoritative prohibition or rejection of a proposed or intended act. —*tr.v.* **ve•toed, ve•to•ing, ve•toes. 1.** To prevent (a legislative bill) from becoming law by exercising the power of veto. **2.** To forbid or prohibit authoritatively: *The board vetoed all wage increases.* [First written down in 1629 in Modern English, from Latin *vetō*, I forbid.]

vex (vĕks) *tr.v.* **vexed, vex•ing, vex•es. 1.** To irritate or annoy; bother. **2.** To cause perplexity in; puzzle. **3.** To bring distress or suffering to; afflict.

vex•a•tion (vĕk **sā′**shən) *n.* **1.** The act of vexing or the condition of being vexed. **2.** A source of irritation or annoyance.

vhf or **VHF** *abbr.* An abbreviation of very high frequency.

vi•a (**vī′**ə *or* **vē′**ə) *prep.* **1.** By way of: *going to Washington via New York.* **2.** By means of: *sent the letter via air mail.*

vi•a•ble (**vī′**ə bəl) *adj.* **1.** Capable of continuing to live, grow, or develop: *viable seeds; a prematurely born but viable infant.* **2.** Capable of success or continuing effectiveness: *a viable national economy.* —**vi′a•bil′i•ty** *n.*

vi•a•duct (**vī′**ə dŭkt′) *n.* A series of spans or arches used to carry a road or railroad over a wide valley or other roads or railroads. [First written down in 1816 in Modern English : Latin *via*, road + English *(aque)duct.*]

vi•al (**vī′**əl) *n.* A small glass container, usually having a closure, used especially for liquids.

❑ *These sound alike:* **vial, viol** (stringed instrument).

vi•and (**vī′**ənd) *n.* **1.** An item of food. **2. viands.** Provisions; victuals.

vi•brant (**vī′**brənt) *adj.* **1.** Pulsing or throbbing with energy or activity. **2.** Vigorous, lively, and vital. **3.** Showing or marked by rapid rhythmic movement; vibrating.

vi•brate (**vī′**brāt′) *v.* **vi•brat•ed, vi•brat•ing, vi•brates.** —*intr.* **1.** To move back and forth or to and fro, especially rhythmically and rapidly. **2.** To produce a sound; resonate. —*tr.* **1.** To cause to tremble or quiver. **2.** To cause to move back and forth rapidly. [First written down in 1616 in Modern English, from Latin *vibrāre.*]

vi•bra•tion (vī **brā′**shən) *n.* **1.a.** The act of vibrating. **b.** The condition of being vibrated. **2.** A rapid motion of a particle or an elastic solid back and forth in a straight line on both sides of a center position. —**vi•bra′tion•al** *adj.* —**vi′bra•to′ry** (**vī′**brə tôr′ē) *adj.*

vi•bra•to (və **brä′**tō) *n., pl.* **vi•bra•tos.** A tremulous or pulsating effect produced in an instrumental or vocal tone by small rapid variations in pitch.

vi•bra•tor (**vī′**brā′tər) *n.* **1.** Something that vibrates. **2.** An electrically operated device used for massage.

vi•bur•num (vī **bûr′**nəm) *n.* Any of various shrubs or trees having rounded clusters of small white or pink flowers.

vic•ar (**vĭk′**ər) *n.* **1.** A salaried priest in charge of a parish. **2.** In the Roman Catholic Church, a priest who acts for or represents another member of the clergy, especially one of higher rank.

vic•ar•age (**vĭk′**ər ĭj) *n.* **1.** The residence of a vicar. **2.** The office or duties of a vicar.

vi•car•i•ous (vī **kâr′**ē əs *or* vĭ **kăr′**ē əs) *adj.* **1.** Felt or undergone as if one were taking part in the experience or feelings of another: *the vicarious thrills provided by reading an adventure story.* **2.** Endured or done by one person substituting for another: *vicarious punishment.* **3.** Acting or serving in place of someone or something else. —**vi•car′i•ous•ly** *adv.*

vice¹ (vīs) *n.* **1.** An evil, degrading, or immoral practice or habit. **2.** A serious moral failing. **3.** Wicked or evil conduct or habits; corruption. **4.** A slight personal failing; a foible. [First written down about 1300 in Middle English, from Latin *vitium.*]

❑ *These sound alike:* **vice¹** (wickedness), **vise** (tool).

vice² (vīs) *n. & v.* Variant of **vise.**

vice admiral *n.* A commissioned officer in the U.S. Navy or Coast Guard, ranking above rear admiral and below admiral.

vice-pres•i•den•cy (vīs **prĕz′**ĭ dən sē) *n.* The office of a vice president or the period during which a vice president is in office.

vice pres•i•dent or **vice-pres•i•dent** (**vīs′prĕz′**ĭ dənt) *n.* An officer ranking next below a president and having authority to take the president's place in case of absence, illness, or death.

vice•roy (**vīs′**roi′) *n.* A man who is the governor of a country, province, or colony, ruling as the representative of a sovereign.

vi•ce ver•sa (vī′sə **vûr′**sə *or* vīs′ **vûr′**sə) *adv.* With the order or meaning reversed; conversely: *adapted themselves to the desires of the dog, rather than vice versa.*

vi•chys•soise (vĭsh′ē **swäz′**) *n.* A creamy potato

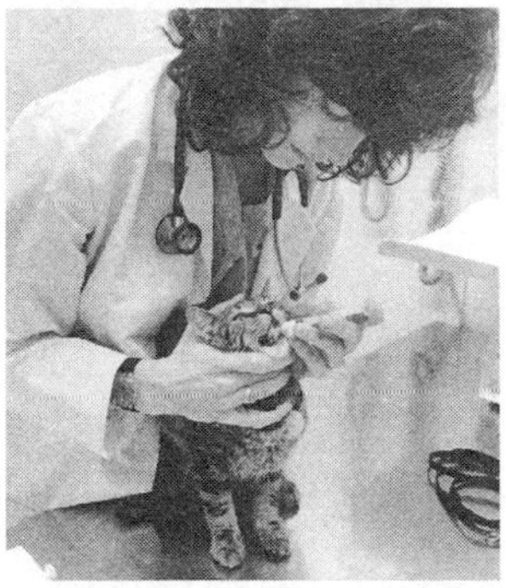

veterinarian

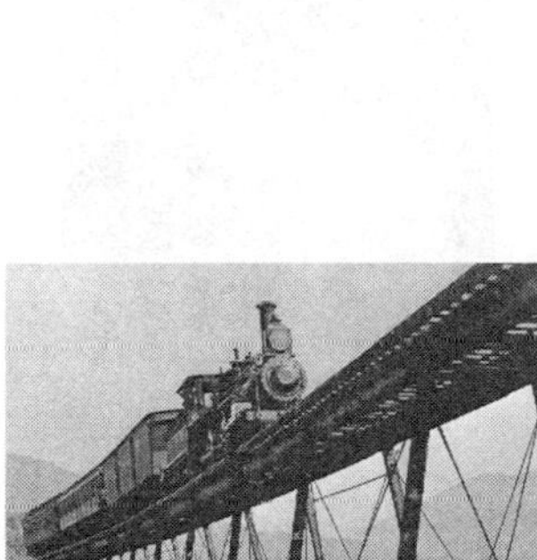

viaduct

ă	**pat**	oi	**boy**
ā	**pay**	ou	**out**
âr	**care**	o͝o	**took**
ä	**father**	o͞o	**boot**
ĕ	**pet**	ŭ	**cut**
ē	**be**	ûr	**urge**
ĭ	**pit**	th	**thin**
ī	**pie**	*th*	**this**
îr	**pier**	hw	**whoop**
ŏ	**pot**	zh	**vision**
ō	**toe**	ə	**about**
ô	**paw**	N	*French* **bon**

victoria
c. 1895 American

Victoria[1]

vicuña

video game

soup flavored with leeks and onions and usually served cold.

Vi•chy water (vĭsh′ē *or* vē′shē) *n.* A naturally effervescent mineral water from the springs at Vichy in central France.

vi•cin•i•ty (vĭ sĭn′ĭ tē) *n., pl.* **vi•cin•i•ties. 1.** The state of being near in space or relationship; proximity. **2.** A nearby or surrounding region or place. **3.** An approximate degree or amount: *houses priced in the vicinity of $100,000.*

vi•cious (vĭsh′əs) *adj.* **1.** Having the nature of vice; evil, immoral, or depraved. **2.** Given to vice, immorality, or depravity. **3.** Spiteful; malicious: *Don't spread such vicious gossip.* **4.** Disposed to or marked by violent or destructive behavior: *a vicious dog.* **—vi′cious•ly** *adv.*

vicious circle *n.* A situation in which the apparent solution of one problem creates a new problem and increases the difficulty of solving the original problem.

vi•cis•si•tude (vĭ sĭs′ĭ to͞od′ *or* vĭ sĭs′ĭ tyo͞od′) *n.* **1.** A change or variation. **2.** One of the sudden or unexpected changes or shifts often encountered in one's life or surroundings. Often used in the plural.

vic•tim (vĭk′tĭm) *n.* **1.** A person who is harmed or killed by another or by an act, an agency, or a condition: *the victim of a burglar; the victims of an epidemic.* **2.** A living creature killed as a religious sacrifice. **3.** A person who is tricked, swindled, or taken advantage of: *the victim of a hoax.* [First written down in 1497 in Middle English, from Latin *victima.*]

vic•tim•ize (vĭk′tə mīz′) *tr.v.* **vic•tim•ized, vic•tim•iz•ing, vic•tim•iz•es. 1.** To subject to swindle or fraud. **2.** To make a victim of.

vic•tor (vĭk′tər) *n.* The winner in a fight, battle, contest, or struggle.

vic•to•ri•a (vĭk tôr′ē ə) *n.* A low, light, four-wheeled carriage for two, with a folding top and a raised seat in front for the driver. [First written down in 1870 in Modern English, after Queen *Victoria.*]

Vic•to•ri•a[1] (vĭk tôr′ē ə). 1819–1901. Queen of Great Britain and Ireland (1837–1901) and empress of India (1876–1901).

Vic•to•ri•a[2] (vĭk tôr′ē ə). **1.** The capital of British Columbia, Canada, on southeast Vancouver Island. It was founded in 1843 and became capital in the late 1860's. Population, 64,379. **2.** The capital of Hong Kong, on the northwest coast of Hong Kong Island. Population, 1,183,621. **3.** The capital of Seychelles, on the Indian Ocean north-northeast of Madagascar. Population, 23,000.

Victoria, Lake. A lake of east-central Africa bordered by Uganda, Kenya, and Tanzania.

Vic•to•ri•an (vĭk tôr′ē ən) *adj.* **1.** Of, relating to, or belonging to the period of the reign of Queen Victoria: *a Victorian novel.* **2.** Relating to or displaying the standards or ideals of morality regarded as typical of the time of Queen Victoria. **—Vic•to′ri•an•ism** *n.*

vic•to•ri•ous (vĭk tôr′ē əs) *adj.* **1.** Being the winner in a contest or struggle: *the victorious team.* **2.** Characteristic of or expressing a sense of victory or fulfillment: *a victorious cheer.* **—vic•to′ri•ous•ly** *adv.*

vic•to•ry (vĭk′tə rē) *n., pl.* **vic•to•ries. 1.** Defeat of an enemy or opponent. **2.** Success in a struggle against difficulties or an obstacle. [First written down about 1340 in Middle English, from Latin *victōria*, from *victor*, victor.]

vict•ual (vĭt′l) *n.* **1.** Food fit for human consumption. **2. victuals.** Food supplies; provisions. [First written down about 1303 in Middle English and spelled *vitaille*, from Late Latin *vīctuālia.*]

vi•cu•ña also **vi•cu•na** (vĭ ko͞on′yə *or* vĭ ko͞o′nə) *n.* **1.** A mammal of the Andes mountains of South America, related to the llama and having a fine silky fleece. **2.a.** The fleece of this mammal. **b.** Cloth made from the fleece of this mammal. [First written down in 1604 in Modern English, from Quechua *wikuña.*]

vid•e•o (vĭd′ē ō′) *n., pl.* **vid•e•os. 1.** The visual part of a television broadcast. **2.** Television: *a star of stage, screen, and video.* **3.** A videocassette or videotape.

vid•e•o•cas•sette (vĭd′ē ō kə sĕt′) *n.* A cassette containing blank or prerecorded videotape.

vid•e•o•disk also **vid•e•o•disc** (vĭd′ē ō dĭsk′) *n.* A recording on optical disk of sounds and images, as of a movie, that can be played back on a television receiver.

video game *n.* An electronic or computerized game played by manipulating images on a display screen.

vid•e•o•tape (vĭd′ē ō tāp′) *n.* A relatively wide magnetic tape used to record visual images and associated sound for later playback or broadcasting. *—tr.v.* **vid•e•o•taped, vid•e•o•tap•ing, vid•e•o•tapes.** To record on videotape: *videotape a wedding.*

videotape recorder *n.* A device for making a videotape recording.

video terminal *n.* A device used to enter and retrieve data in a computer and utilizing a cathode-ray tube to display data on a screen.

vie (vī) *intr.v.* **vied, vy•ing** (vī′ĭng), **vies.** To strive for victory or superiority; contend.

Vi•en•na (vē ĕn′ə). The capital and largest city of Austria, in the northeast part of the country on the Danube River. It was originally a Celtic settlement and became the capital of Austria in 1918. Population, 1,524,510.

Vien•tiane (vyĕn tyän′). The capital and largest city of Laos, in the north-central part of the country on the Mekong River and the Thailand border. Population, 210,000.

Vi•et•cong also **Vi•et Cong** (vē ĕt′kŏng′ *or* vē ĕt′-kông′) *n., pl.* **Vietcong** also **Viet Cong.** A Vietnamese belonging to or supporting the former National Liberation Front of the former country of South Vietnam.

Vi•et•minh also **Vi•et Minh** (vē ĕt′mĭn′) *n., pl.* **Vietminh** also **Viet Minh.** A member of the Vietnamese army that defeated the Japanese and the French between 1941 and 1954.

Vi•et•nam (vē ĕt′näm′ *or* vē′ĭt näm′). A country of southeast Asia in eastern Indochina on the South China Sea. It was partitioned into **North Vietnam** and **South Vietnam** after 1954. The country was reunited in July 1976 after the end of the Vietnam War (1954–1975). Capital, Hanoi. Population, 52,741,766.

Vi•et•nam•ese (vē ĕt′nə mēz′ *or* vē ĕt′nə mēs′) *adj.* Of or relating to Vietnam or its people, language, or culture. *—n., pl.* **Vietnamese. 1.** A native or inhabitant of Vietnam. **2.** The language of Vietnam.

view (vyo͞o) *n.* **1.** An examination or inspection: *picked up the rock for a closer view.* **2.** A systematic survey; coverage. **3.** An opinion; a personal perception: *her views on education.* **4.** Range or field of sight: *The airplane disappeared from view.* **5.** A scene; a vista: *the view from the top of the mountain.* **6.** A way of showing or seeing something, as from a particular position or angle: *a side view of the house.* **7.** An aim; an intention: *These laws were made with the view of providing equal rights for all.* *—tr.v.* **viewed, view•ing, views. 1.** To look at; watch: *viewed the stars through a telescope.* See Synonyms at **see**[1]. **2.** To examine or inspect: *viewed* *the specimen through a microscope.* **3.** To regard; consider: *The President viewed the uprising with alarm.* ***—idioms.* in view of.** Taking into account; in consideration of. **on view.** Placed so as to be seen; exhibited: *The photographs will be on view through next month.* [First written down in 1415 in Middle English and spelled *vewe,* from Anglo-Norman, from Latin *vidēre,* to see.]

view•er (vyōō′ər) *n.* **1.** A person who views something, especially an onlooker or a spectator. **2.** Any of various devices used to magnify photographic images so that they are easily visible.

view•find•er (vyōō′fīn′dər) *n.* A device on a camera that indicates what will appear in the field of view of the lens.

view•point (vyōō′point′) *n.* A position from which something is observed or considered; a point of view.

vig•il (vĭj′əl) *n.* **1.** A watch kept during normal sleeping hours: *a vigil at the bedside of her sick friend.* **2.** The act or a period of observing; surveillance. **3.** The eve of a religious festival. **4. vigils.** Services held on the eve of a religious festival. [First written down before 1200 in Middle English and spelled *vigile,* from Latin *vigilia,* wakefulness, watch.]

vig•i•lance (vĭj′ə ləns) *n.* Alert watchfulness.

vig•i•lant (vĭj′ə lənt) *adj.* On the alert; watchful. **—vig′i•lant•ly** *adv.*

vig•i•lan•te (vĭj′ə lăn′tē) *n.* A member of a group of citizens that without authority assumes such powers as pursuing and punishing those suspected of being criminals or offenders.

vi•gnette (vĭn yĕt′) *n.* **1.** A decorative design near the beginning or end of a chapter or book or along the border of the page. **2.** A picture that shades off into the surrounding color at the edges. **3.** A short literary sketch or scene from a movie.

vig•or (vĭg′ər) *n.* **1.** Physical or mental energy or strength. **2.** The capacity for natural growth and survival, as of plants or animals. **3.** Strong feeling; enthusiasm or intensity: *The opposing party, with great vigor, claimed the disputed votes for their candidate.* [First written down before 1300 in Middle English and spelled *vigour,* from Latin *vigor,* from *vigēre,* to be lively.]

vig•or•ous (vĭg′ər əs) *adj.* **1.** Strong, energetic, and active in mind or body; robust: *a nest of vigorous young birds.* **2.** Marked by or done with force and energy: *vigorous exercise.* **—vig′or•ous•ly** *adv.*

vig•our (vĭg′ər) *n. Chiefly British.* Variant of **vigor.**

Vi•king (vī′kĭng) *n.* One of a seafaring Scandinavian people who plundered the coasts of northern and western Europe from the eighth through the tenth century.

Vi•la (vē′lə). The capital of Vanuatu in the southwest Pacific Ocean. It was a Japanese base during World War II. Population, 13,067.

vile (vīl) *adj.* **vil•er, vil•est. 1.** Hateful; disgusting: *vile language.* **2.** Unpleasant or objectionable: *vile weather.* **3.** Miserable; base; wretched. [First written down before 1300 in Middle English, from Latin *vīlis.*] **—vile′ly** *adv.* **—vile′ness** *n.*

vil•i•fy (vĭl′ə fī′) *tr.v.* **vil•i•fied** (vĭl′ə fīd′), **vil•i•fy•ing, vil•i•fies** (vĭl′ə fīz′). To make vicious and defamatory statements about. **—vil′i•fi•ca′tion** (vĭl′ə fĭ kā′shən) **—vil′i•fi′er** *n.*

vil•la (vĭl′ə) *n.* A large and luxurious country house of a rich person.

vil•lage (vĭl′ĭj) *n.* **1.** A small group of homes and other buildings in a rural area, forming a community smaller than a town. **2.** The inhabitants of a village: *The entire village welcomed the newcomers.* [First written down about 1390 in Middle English, from Latin *vīllāticum,* farmstead.]

vil•lag•er (vĭl′ə jər) *n.* A person who lives in a village.

vil•lain (vĭl′ən) *n.* **1.** A wicked or very bad person; a scoundrel. **2.** A dramatic or fictional character who is typically at odds with the hero. **3.** (*also* **vĭl′-ān′** *or* vĭ **lān′**). Variant of **villein. 4.** Something said to be the cause of particular trouble. [First written down about 1303 in Middle English and spelled *vilein,* feudal serf, from Old French, from Latin *vīlla,* country house.]

❑ *These sound alike:* **villain, villein** (serf).

vil•lain•ous (vĭl′ə nəs) *adj.* **1.** Appropriate to a villain, as in wickedness or depravity. **2.** Highly undesirable or offensive. **—vil′lain•ous•ly** *adv.*

vil•lain•y (vĭl′ə nē) *n., pl.* **vil•lain•ies. 1.** Baseness of mind or character. **2.** Viciousness of conduct or action.

vil•lein also **vil•lain** (vĭl′ən *or* vĭl′ān′ *or* vĭ **lān′**) *n.* One of a class of feudal serfs who held the legal status of freemen in their dealings with all people except their lords.

❑ *These sound alike:* **villein, villain** (scoundrel).

vil•lus (vĭl′əs) *n., pl.* **vil•li** (vĭl′ī). A small projection on the surface of a mucous membrane, especially that of the small intestine.

Vil•ni•us (vĭl′nē əs) or **Vil•na** (vĭl′nə). The capital of Lithuania, in the southeast part of the country. It was founded in the tenth century. Population, 544,000.

vim (vĭm) *n.* Liveliness and energy; enthusiasm.

vin•ai•grette (vĭn′ĭ **grĕt′**) *n.* **1.** A sauce or dressing of vinegar and oil. **2.** A small decorative container with a perforated top, used for holding an aromatic preparation such as smelling salts.

vin•di•cate (vĭn′dĭ kāt′) *tr.v.* **vin•di•cat•ed, vin•di•cat•ing, vin•di•cates. 1.** To clear of accusation, blame, suspicion, or doubt with supporting proof: *He vindicated himself of the charges.* **2.** To justify or support: *vindicate one's claim.* **3.** To defend or maintain (one's rights, for example).

vin•dic•tive (vĭn **dĭk′**tĭv) *adj.* Having or showing a desire for revenge; vengeful. **—vin•dic′tive•ly** *adv.* **—vin•dic′tive•ness** *n.*

vine (vīn) *n.* **1.a.** A plant having a stem that climbs on, creeps along, twines around, or clings to something for support. **b.** The stem of such a plant. **2.** A grapevine. [First written down before 1300 in Middle English, from Latin *vīnea.*]

vin•e•gar (vĭn′ĭ gər) *n.* A dilute solution of acetic acid obtained by fermentation beyond the alcohol stage and used in flavoring and preserving food.

vin•e•gar•y (vĭn′ĭ gə rē *or* vĭn′ĭ grē) also **vin•e•gar•ish** (vĭn′ĭ gər ĭsh *or* vĭn′ĭ grĭsh) *adj.* **1.** Having the taste, smell, or nature of vinegar. **2.** Unpleasant.

vine•yard (vĭn′yərd) *n.* A piece of ground on which grapevines are grown and tended.

vineyard

vin•tage (vĭn′tĭj) *n.* **1.** The grapes or wine produced by a particular vineyard or district in a single season. **2.** The year or place in which a wine is bottled. **3.** *Informal.* A year or period of origin: *drives a car of 1950 vintage.* *—adj.* **1.** Of or relating to a vintage. **2.** Characterized by excellence and maturity; classic.

vint•ner (vĭnt′nər) *n.* A person who makes or sells wine.

vi•nyl (vī′nəl) *n.* **1.** The chemical radical CH_2CH, derived from ethylene and having a valence of 1. **2.** Any of various chemical compounds, typically highly reactive, that contain this radical, used in making plastics. **3.** Any of various plastics, typically tough, flexible, and shiny, often used in upholstery and clothing.

vi•ol (vī′əl) *n.* Any of a family of stringed instruments, chiefly of the 16th and 17th centuries, hav-

ă	pat	oi	boy
ā	pay	ou	out
âr	care	ŏŏ	took
ä	father	ōō	boot
ĕ	pet	ŭ	cut
ē	be	ûr	urge
ĭ	pit	th	thin
ī	pie	*th*	this
îr	pier	hw	whoop
ŏ	pot	zh	vision
ō	toe	ə	about
ô	paw	N	*French* bon

viola

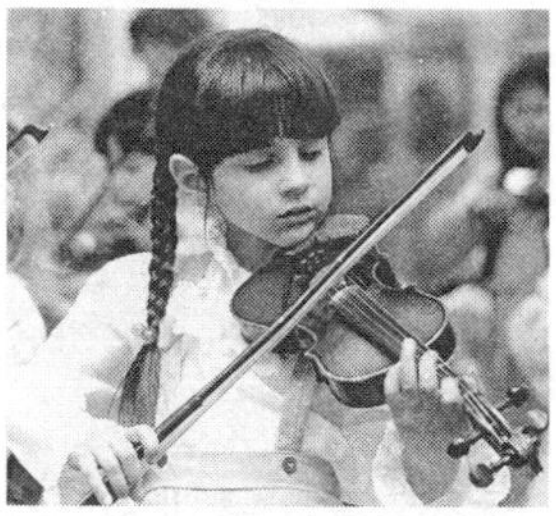

violin

Virginia

The name **Virginia** is a Latin term that was given to the territory in 1584 by Queen Elizabeth I of England, who was known as "the Virgin Queen" because she never married.

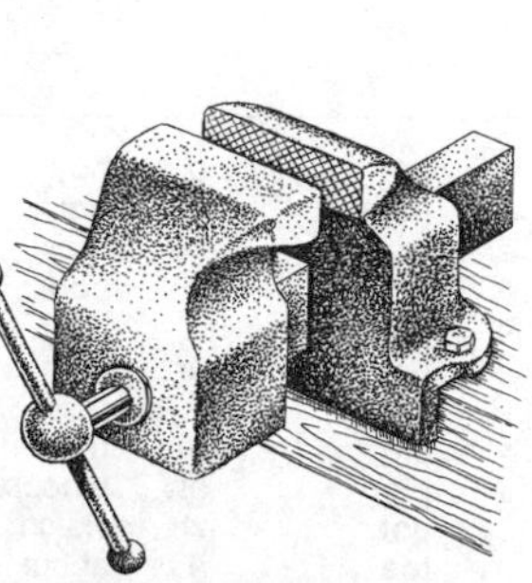

vise

ing a flat back and usually six strings and played with a curved bow.

❑ *These sound alike:* **viol, vial** (glass container).

vi•o•la (vē ō′lə) *n.* A stringed instrument of the violin family, slightly larger than a violin, tuned a fifth lower, and having a deeper tone. **—vi•o′list** *n.*

vi•o•late (vī′ə lāt′) *tr.v.* **vi•o•lat•ed, vi•o•lat•ing, vi•o•lates. 1.** To break or disregard: *violate a law; violate a promise.* **2.** To do harm to (something sacred or highly respected); desecrate or defile: *violate a shrine.* **3.** To assault (a person) sexually. **4.** To disturb rudely or interrupt.

vi•o•la•tion (vī′ə lā′shən) *n.* The act or an instance of violating or the condition of being violated: *the violation of a truce; a traffic violation.*

vi•o•lence (vī′ə ləns) *n.* **1.** Physical force exerted for the purpose of causing damage or injury: *crimes of violence.* **2.** Great force or intensity: *the violence of a hurricane.* **3.** An act or an instance of violent action or behavior: *protests that have led to violence.* **4.** Abuse or injury to meaning, content, or intent: *do violence to a text.*

vi•o•lent (vī′ə lənt) *adj.* **1.** Marked by, acting with, or resulting from great physical force: *a violent attack; violent blows.* **2.** Having or showing great emotional force: *a violent outburst.* **3.** Marked by intensity; severe; harsh: *a violent storm.* **4.** Caused by unexpected force or injury rather than by natural causes: *a violent death.* [First written down about 1340 in Middle English, from Latin *violentus,* from *vīs,* force.] **—vi′o•lent•ly** *adv.*

vi•o•let (vī′ə lĭt) *n.* **1.a.** Any of various low-growing plants having flowers that are usually bluish purple but are sometimes yellow or white. **b.** A flower of such a plant. **2.** A bluish purple. [First written down before 1300 in Middle English, from Old French *violete,* from Latin *viola.*]

vi•o•lin (vī′ə lĭn′) *n.* A stringed instrument played with a bow, having four strings tuned at intervals of a fifth, an unfretted fingerboard, and a greater range than a viol. [First written down in 1579 in Modern English, from Italian *violino,* small viola.] **—vi′o•lin′ist** *n.*

vi•o•lon•cel•lo (vē′ə lən chĕl′ō) *n., pl.* **vi•o•lon•cel•los.** A cello. **—vi′o•lon•cel′list** *n.*

VIP (vē′ī pē′) *n., pl.* **VIPs.** *Informal.* A person of great importance.

vi•per (vī′pər) *n.* **1.** Any of several poisonous snakes of northern Europe and Asia having a single pair of long hollow fangs and a thick heavy body; an adder. **2.** A pit viper. **3.** A person regarded as wicked or hateful. [First written down before 1425 in Middle English and spelled *vipere,* from Latin *vīpera,* snake.]

vi•per•ous (vī′pər əs) *adj.* **1.** Suggestive of or relating to a viper. **2.** Wicked; hateful.

vi•ra•go (və rä′gō *or* və rā′gō) *n., pl.* **vi•ra•goes** or **vi•ra•gos. 1.** A woman regarded as noisy, scolding, or bossy. **2.** A large, strong, courageous woman.

vi•ral (vī′rəl) *adj.* Of, relating to, or caused by a virus: *viral diseases.*

vir•e•o (vîr′ē ō′) *n., pl.* **vir•e•os.** Any of various small insect-eating grayish or greenish songbirds.

Vir•gil also **Ver•gil** (vûr′jəl). 70–19 B.C. Roman poet whose epic poem *Aeneid* tells of the wanderings of Aeneas after the sack of Troy.

vir•gin (vûr′jĭn) *n.* **1.** A person who has not experienced sexual intercourse. **2. Virgin.** The Virgin Mary. *—adj.* **1.** Of, relating to, or being a virgin; chaste. **2.** Being in a pure and natural state; untouched: *virgin snow.* **3.** Unused, uncultivated, or unexplored: *virgin forests.*

vir•gin•al (vûr′jə nəl) *adj.* Of, relating to, or appropriate to a virgin; chaste.

Vir•gin•ia (vər jĭn′yə). A state of the eastern United States on the Atlantic Ocean north of North Carolina. It was admitted as one of the original Thirteen Colonies in 1788. Virginia seceded from the Union in April 1861 and was the scene of many major battles during the Civil War. Capital, Richmond. Population, 6,216,568. —SEE NOTE.

Virginia Algonquian *n.* The extinct Eastern Algonquian language of eastern Virginia.

Virginia creeper *n.* A North American climbing vine having leaves with five leaflets and bluish-black berries.

Virginia reel *n.* An American dance in which two lines of couples face each other and perform various steps together to instructions called out by a leader.

Virgin Islands. 1. A group of islands of the northeast West Indies east of Puerto Rico. They are divided into the **British Virgin Islands** to the northeast and the Virgin Islands of the United States to the southwest. **2.** A United States territory constituting the southwest group of the Virgin Islands. Charlotte Amalie is the capital. Population, 96,569.

vir•gin•i•ty (vər jĭn′ĭ tē) *n., pl.* **vir•gin•i•ties. 1.** The quality or condition of being a virgin. **2.** The state of being pure or untouched.

Virgin Mary *n.* The mother of Jesus.

Vir•go (vûr′gō) *n.* **1.** A constellation near the celestial equator. **2.** The sixth sign of the zodiac in astrology.

vir•ile (vîr′əl *or* vîr′īl′) *adj.* **1.** Of, relating to, or having the characteristics of an adult male. **2.** Having or showing masculine spirit, strength, vigor, or power. **3.** Able to perform sexually as a male; potent. **—vi•ril′i•ty** (və rĭl′ĭ tē) *n.*

vi•rol•o•gy (vī rŏl′ə jē) *n.* The study of viruses and viral diseases. **—vi•rol′o•gist** *n.*

vir•tu•al (vûr′cho͞o əl) *adj.* Existing in effect though not in actual fact, form, or name: *the virtual extinction of the buffalo.*

virtual image *n.* An image, such as one seen in a mirror, from which rays of reflected or refracted light appear to come.

vir•tu•al•ly (vûr′cho͞o ə lē) *adv.* **1.** In fact or to all purposes; practically: *The city was virtually paralyzed by the blizzard.* **2.** Almost but not quite; nearly: *Virtually every household has a TV these days.*

vir•tue (vûr′cho͞o) *n.* **1.a.** Moral excellence and righteousness; goodness. **b.** A particular example or kind of moral excellence: *the virtue of patience.* **2.** Chastity, especially in a woman or girl. **3.** A particularly efficacious, good, or beneficial quality; an advantage: *a plan with the virtue of being practical.* **4.** Effective force or power; ability to produce a definite result: *believing in the virtue of vitamins to fight colds.* ***—idiom.*** **by virtue of** or **in virtue of.** On the grounds or basis of; by reason of: *She has the reputation of being a great writer by virtue of her prize-winning books.*

vir•tu•os•i•ty (vûr′cho͞o ŏs′ĭ tē) *n., pl.* **vir•tu•os•i•ties.** The technical skill or style displayed by a virtuoso.

vir•tu•o•so (vûr′cho͞o ō′sō *or* vûr′cho͞o ō′zō) *n., pl.* **vir•tu•o•sos** or **vir•tu•o•si** (vûr′cho͞o ō′sē). **1.** A musical performer of great excellence, technique, or ability. **2.** A person of great skill or technique in the arts. *—adj.* Exhibiting the ability, technique, or personal style of a virtuoso: *a virtuoso performance.*

vir•tu•ous (vûr′cho͞o əs) *adj.* **1.** Having or showing virtue, especially moral excellence: *virtuous conduct.* **2.** Chaste; pure: *a virtuous person.* **—vir′tu•ous•ly** *adv.*

vir•u•lent (vîr′yə lənt *or* vîr′ə lənt) *adj.* **1.** Extremely infectious, malignant, or poisonous, as a disease or toxin. **2.** Bitterly hostile or malicious: *virulent criticism.* **—vir′u•lence, vir′u•len•cy** *n.*

vi•rus (vī′rəs) *n., pl.* **vi•rus•es.** Any of various very small disease-producing particles that can infect plants, animals, and bacteria and that consist of a segment of RNA or DNA surrounded by a protein coat. Unable to reproduce without a host cell, viruses are typically not considered living organisms. [First written down in 1392 in Middle English and spelled *virus,* venomous substance, from Latin *vīrus,* poison.]

vi•sa (vē′zə) *n.* An official authorization added to a passport, permitting entry into and travel within a particular country or region.

vis•age (vĭz′ĭj) *n.* **1.** The face or facial expression of a person. **2.** Appearance; aspect: *the green visage of spring.*

vis•cer•a (vĭs′ər ə) *pl.n.* The soft internal organs of the body, especially those contained within the abdomen and thorax.

vis•cer•al (vĭs′ər əl) *adj.* **1.** Relating to, situated in, or affecting the viscera. **2.** Coming from the depths of one's being; profound. **3.** Instinctive: *visceral needs.* **—vis′cer•al•ly** *adv.*

vis•cid (vĭs′ĭd) *adj.* Thick and sticky; resembling glue. Used of a fluid. **—vis′cid•ly** *adv.*

vis•cos•i•ty (vĭ skŏs′ĭ tē) *n., pl.* **vis•cos•i•ties. 1.** The condition or property of being viscous. **2.** The degree to which a fluid resists flow when pressure is applied to it.

vis•count (vī′kount′) *n.* A nobleman ranking below an earl or a count and above a baron.

vis•count•ess (vī′koun′tĭs) *n.* **1.** The wife or widow of a viscount. **2.** A noblewoman holding the rank of viscount in her own right.

vis•cous (vĭs′kəs) *adj.* **1.** Tending to resist flow when pressure is applied, as a fluid; having a high viscosity. **2.** Viscid. **—vis′cous•ly** *adv.*

vise also **vice** (vīs) *n.* A clamping device of metal or wood, usually consisting of a pair of jaws that are opened and closed by means of a screw or lever, used in carpentry or metalworking to hold work in position. *—tr.v.* **vised, vis•ing, vis•es** also **viced, vic•ing, vic•es.** To hold or compress in or as if in a vise. [First written down before 1300 in Middle English and spelled *vis,* screwlike device, from Latin *vītis,* vine.]

❑ *These sound alike:* **vise, vice**[1] (wickedness).

Vish•nu (vĭsh′no͞o) *n.* One of the principal Hindu deities, worshiped as a protector and preserver of worlds.

vis•i•bil•i•ty (vĭz′ə bĭl′ĭ tē) *n., pl.* **vis•i•bil•i•ties. 1.** The fact or degree of being visible. **2.** The greatest distance over which it is possible to see without aid from instruments under given weather conditions. **3.** The capability of being easily observed.

vis•i•ble (vĭz′ə bəl) *adj.* **1.** Possible to see; perceptible to the eye: *a visible change of expression on her face.* **2.** Easily noticed; clear; apparent: *no visible solution to the problem.* **—vis′i•bly** *adv.*

Vis•i•goth (vĭz′ĭ gŏth′) *n.* A member of the western Goths that invaded the Roman Empire in the fourth century A.D. and settled in France and Spain.

vi•sion (vĭzh′ən) *n.* **1.** The sense of sight; eyesight. **2.** Unusual discernment; intelligent foresight: *a leader of vision.* **3.** A mental image produced by the imagination: *having visions of warm summer days.* **4.** The experience of seeing, as if with the eyes, the supernatural or a supernatural being. **5.** A person or thing of great beauty: *The mountains were a vision of newly fallen snow.* [First written down about 1300 in Middle English and spelled *visioun,* from Latin *vīsiō,* from *vidēre,* to see.]

vi•sion•ar•y (vĭzh′ə nĕr′ē) *adj.* **1.** Characterized by vision or foresight. **2.** Not practicable; existing only in the imagination: *visionary schemes for getting rich.* **3.** Marked by or given to apparitions, prophecies, or revelations. *—n., pl.* **vi•sion•ar•ies. 1.** A person given to impractical ideas; a dreamer. **2.** A person who has visions; a seer.

vis•it (vĭz′ĭt) *v.* **vis•it•ed, vis•it•ing, vis•its.** *—tr.* **1.** To go or come to see for reasons of business, duty, or pleasure: *visit a dentist; visit one's family.* **2.** To go to see or spend time at (a place) with a certain intent: *visiting Chicago over the weekend.* **3.** To stay with as a guest: *visiting his former classmate in California.* **4.** To afflict or assail: *A plague visited the village.* *—intr.* **1.** To make a visit. **2.** *Informal.* To converse or chat: *I hope you'll be able to stay and visit.* *—n.* The act or an instance of visiting; a brief call or stay. [First written down before 1200 in Middle English and spelled *visiten,* from Latin *vīsitāre.*]

vis•i•tant (vĭz′ĭ tənt) *n.* **1.** A visitor; a guest. **2.** A ghost or other supernatural being. *—adj.* Visiting.

vis•i•ta•tion (vĭz′ĭ tā′shən) *n.* **1.** The act or an instance of visiting, especially an official visit for the purpose of inspection or examination. **2.** A visit of affliction or blessing, regarded as being ordained by God. **3. Visitation.** In the Roman Catholic Church, the visit of the Virgin Mary to her cousin Elizabeth.

vis•i•tor (vĭz′ĭ tər) *n.* A person who visits.

vi•sor also **vi•zor** (vī′zər) *n.* **1.** A piece projecting from the front of a cap to shade and protect the eyes. **2.** A shield against glare attached above the windshield of an automobile. **3.** The front piece of the helmet of a suit of armor that protects the eyes, nose, and forehead.

vis•ta (vĭs′tə) *n.* **1.a.** A distant view, especially one seen through an opening, as between buildings or trees. **b.** A passage or avenue that provides such a view. **2.** A broad mental view or awareness of a series of events or subjects: *a scientific discovery that opens up new vistas of human improvement.* [First written down in 1644 in Modern English, from Italian *vista,* something seen.]

vi•su•al (vĭzh′o͞o əl) *adj.* **1.** Of or relating to the sense of sight. **2.** Seen or able to be seen by the eye; visible. **3.** Done or performed by means of sight alone: *visual navigation.* **4.** Of or relating to a method of instruction involving sight: *visual instruction; visual aids.*

vi•su•al•ize (vĭzh′o͞o ə līz′) *v.* **vi•su•al•ized, vi•su•al•iz•ing, vi•su•al•iz•es.** *—tr.* To form a mental image or vision of: *Try to visualize what our new house will look like.* *—intr.* To form a mental image. **—vi′su•al•i•za′tion** (vĭzh′o͞o ə lĭ zā′shən) *n.*

vi•ta (vī′tə *or* vē′tə) *n., pl.* **vi•tae** (vī′tē *or* vē′tī). A short biographical or autobiographical account.

vi•tal (vīt′l) *adj.* **1.** Of, relating to, or characteristic of life: *vital processes; vital signs.* **2.** Necessary to the continuation of life; life-sustaining: *vital organs; vital functions.* **3.** Having great importance; essential: *Irrigation is vital to successful farming.* **4.** Full of life; animated. [First written down about 1385 in Middle English, from Latin *vīta,* life.] **—vi′tal•ly** *adv.*

vi•tal•i•ty (vī tăl′ĭ tē) *n., pl.* **vi•tal•i•ties. 1.** The capacity to live, grow, or develop. **2.** Physical or intellecutual vigor; energy. **3.** Power to survive: *the vitality of an old tradition.*

vi•tal•ize (vīt′l īz′) *tr.v.* **vi•tal•ized, vi•tal•iz•ing, vi•tal•iz•es. 1.** To fill with life; animate. **2.** To make more lively; invigorate. **—vi′tal•i•za′tion** (vīt′l ĭ zā′shən) *n.*

vi•tals (vīt′lz) *pl.n.* **1.** The vital body organs. **2.** The parts, as of a system, that are essential to continued functioning.

vi•ta•min (vī′tə mĭn) *n.* Any of various complex organic compounds that are needed in small amounts

Vishnu
Tenth-century bronze

visor

ă	pat	oi	boy
ā	pay	ou	out
âr	care	o͝o	took
ä	father	o͞o	boot
ĕ	pet	ŭ	cut
ē	be	ûr	urge
ĭ	pit	th	thin
ī	pie	*th*	this
îr	pier	hw	whoop
ŏ	pot	zh	vision
ō	toe	ə	about
ô	paw	N	*French* bon

vitamin

To help the cells in our bodies work properly, it is essential that we get a daily supply of **vitamins**. This link between vitamins and good health was made in the early 1900's by Polish biochemist Casimir Funk. Funk was studying **beriberi**, a disease that damages nerves, when he discovered an organic compound that prevented this illness. He named the compound *vitamine*, or "life amine," a name that stuck even though most **vitamins** do not include a type of chemical called an **amine**. Today we know that vitamins help prevent a variety of illnesses. But because our bodies cannot produce these compounds, we must get them in the foods we eat as part of a well-balanced diet.

for normal growth and activity of the body and are found naturally in foods obtained from plants and animals. [First written down in 1912 in Modern English and spelled *vitamine* : Latin *vīta*, life + *amine*, a type of organic compound.] —SEE NOTE.

vitamin A *n.* A vitamin or mixture of vitamins, necessary for normal cell growth and development, found in fish-liver oils, milk, and some green and yellow leafy vegetables. A lack of it in humans causes night blindness and damage to the skin and mucous membranes.

vitamin B *n.* **1.** The vitamin B complex. **2.** A member of the vitamin B complex, especially thiamine.

vitamin B_1 *n.* Thiamine.

vitamin B_2 *n.* Riboflavin.

vitamin B_6 *n.* Pyridoxine.

vitamin B_{12} *n.* A vitamin of the B complex that contains cobalt. It is found in liver and yeast and is used to treat anemia.

vitamin B complex *n.* Any of a group of related vitamins including thiamine, riboflavin, pyridoxine, and vitamin B_{12} and other substances such as niacin, biotin, and folic acid.

vitamin C *n.* Ascorbic acid.

vitamin D *n.* Any of various related vitamins produced by exposure of sterols found in milk, fish, and eggs to ultraviolet light. It is necessary for normal bone growth.

vitamin E *n.* A vitamin found chiefly in plant leaves, wheat germ oil, and milk and used to treat sterility and various abnormalities of the muscles, red blood cells, liver, and brain.

vitamin G *n.* Riboflavin.

vitamin H *n.* Biotin.

vitamin K *n.* Any of several related vitamins that are essential for normal clotting of the blood and are found in leafy green vegetables, tomatoes, and egg yolks.

vi•ti•ate (vĭsh′ē āt′) *tr.v.* **vi•ti•at•ed, vi•ti•at•ing, vi•ti•ates. 1.** To reduce the value or quality of. **2.** To make ineffective or worthless; invalidate: *vitiate a contract.* **—vi′ti•a′tion** *n.*

vit•i•cul•ture (vĭt′ĭ kŭl′chər) *n.* The cultivation of grapes.

vit•re•ous (vĭt′rē əs) *adj.* **1.** Of, relating to, resembling, or having the nature of glass; glassy. **2.** Of or relating to the vitreous humor. [First written down in 1646 in Modern English, from Latin *vitrum*, glass.]

vitreous humor *n.* The clear jelly-like substance that fills the eyeball between the retina and the lens.

vit•ri•fy (vĭt′rə fī′) *v.* **vit•ri•fied** (vĭt′rə fīd′), **vit•ri•fy•ing, vit•ri•fies** (vĭt′rə fīz′). *—tr.* To change or make into glass or a similar substance, especially through melting by heat. *—intr.* To become vitreous.

vit•ri•ol (vĭt′rē ōl′) *n.* **1.** Sulfuric acid. **2.** Any of various salts of sulfuric acid, such as ferrous sulfate, zinc sulfate, or copper sulfate. **3.** Bitterly abusive feeling or expression.

vit•ri•ol•ic (vĭt′rē ŏl′ĭk) *adj.* **1.** Of, similar to, or derived from vitriol. **2.** Bitterly scathing; caustic: *a vitriolic remark.*

vi•tu•per•ate (vī to͞o′pə rāt′ *or* vī tyo͞o′pə rāt′) *v.* **vi•tu•per•at•ed, vi•tu•per•at•ing, vi•tu•per•ates.** *—tr.* To criticize harshly or abusively. *—intr.* To use harshly abusive language; rail.

vi•tu•per•a•tion (vī to͞o′pə rā′shən *or* vī tyo͞o′pə rā′shən) *n.* **1.** The act or an instance of criticizing harshly or abusively. **2.** Harshly abusive language.

vi•tu•per•a•tive (vī to͞o′pər ə tĭv *or* vī tyo͞o′pər ə tĭv *or* vī to͞o′pə rā′tĭv *or* vī tyo͞o′pə rā′tĭv) *adj.* Using, containing, or marked by harshly abusive language. **—vi•tu′per•a•tive•ly** *adv.*

vi•va (vē′və) *interj.* An expression used to show approval or applause.

vi•va•cious (vĭ vā′shəs *or* vī vā′shəs) *adj.* Full of animation and spirit; lively: *a charming and vivacious host.* **—vi•va′cious•ly** *adv.* **—vi•vac′i•ty** (vĭ văs′ĭ tē *or* vī văs′ĭ tē) *n.*

viv•id (vĭv′ĭd) *adj.* **viv•id•er, viv•id•est. 1.** Perceived as bright and distinct; brilliant: *a vivid star.* **2.** Having intensely bright color or colors: *a vivid tapestry; a vivid blue.* **3.a.** Evoking realistic images within the mind; heard, seen, or felt as if real: *a vivid description.* **b.** Active in forming realistic images: *a vivid imagination.* **4.** Full of the vigor and freshness of immediate experience. [First written down in 1638, from Latin *vīvidus*, from *vīvere*, to live.] **—viv′id•ly** *adv.* **—viv′id•ness** *n.*

viv•i•fy (vĭv′ə fī′) *tr.v.* **viv•i•fied, viv•i•fy•ing, viv•i•fies. 1.** To give or bring life to; animate. **2.** To make more lively or intense; enliven.

vi•vip•a•rous (vī vĭp′ər əs) *adj.* Giving birth to living young that develop within the mother's body rather than hatching from eggs. Most mammals are viviparous.

viv•i•sect (vĭv′ĭ sĕkt′) *tr.v.* **viv•i•sect•ed, viv•i•sect•ing, viv•i•sects.** To perform vivisection on (an animal).

viv•i•sec•tion (vĭv′ĭ sĕk′shən *or* vĭv′ĭ sĕk′shən) *n.* The act or practice of cutting into or dissecting a living animal, especially for scientific research.

vix•en (vĭk′sən) *n.* **1.** A female fox. **2.** A woman regarded as sharp-tempered or quarrelsome. [First written down about 1150 in Middle English and spelled *fixen*, from Old English *fyxe*.]

viz. *abbr.* An abbreviation of videlicet (namely).

vi•zier (vĭ zîr′ *or* vĭz′yər) *n.* A high official in a Muslim government, especially in the Ottoman Empire. [First written down in 1562 in Modern English, from Arabic *wazīr*, minister.]

vi•zor (vī′zər) *n.* Variant of **visor.**

Vlad•i•vos•tok (vlăd′ə və stŏk′ *or* vlăd′ə vŏs′tŏk′). A city of extreme southeast Russia on an arm of the Sea of Japan. It grew rapidly after the completion of the Trans-Siberian Railroad in the early 1900's. Population, 600,000.

vo•cab•u•lar•y (vō kăb′yə lĕr′ē) *n., pl.* **vo•cab•u•lar•ies. 1.** All the words of a language. **2.** The sum of words used by or understood by a particular person or group: *a writer who uses a very rich vocabulary; the vocabulary of economics.* **3.** A list of words and phrases, usually arranged alphabetically and defined or translated; a lexicon or glossary. [First written down in 1532 in Modern English, from Latin *vocābulum*, word.]

vo•cal (vō′kəl) *adj.* **1.** Of, relating to, or produced by the voice: *vocal quality; vocal organs.* **2.** Of, relating to, or performed by singing: *vocal music.* **3.** Tending to speak often and freely; outspoken: *He is very vocal in his opposition to new taxes.* *—n.* A piece of popular music that features a singer. [First written down before 1396 in Middle English, from Latin *vōx*, voice.] **—vo′cal•ly** *adv.*

vocal cords *pl.n.* Either of two pairs of muscular bands or folds in the larynx, of which the lower pair vibrate when pulled together and when air from the lungs is forced between them, thereby producing the sound of the voice.

vo•cal•ic (vō kăl′ĭk) *adj.* **1.** Containing or consisting of vowels. **2.** Of, relating to, or having the nature of a vowel.

vo•cal•ist (vō′kə lĭst) *n.* A singer.

vo•cal•ize (vō′kə līz′) *v.* **vo•cal•ized, vo•cal•iz•ing, vo•cal•iz•es.** *—tr.* **1.** To produce with the voice. **2.** To give voice to; articulate: *vocalize a popular opinion.* *—intr.* **1.** To use the voice. **2.** To sing.

W w

waders

waffle iron

Richard Wagner
Photographed in 1865

w or **W** (dŭb′əl yo͞o *or* dŭb′əl yo͝o) *n., pl.* **w's** or **W's.** **1.** The 23rd letter of the English alphabet. **2.** The 23rd in a series or group.
W[1] The symbol for the element **tungsten.**
W[2] *abbr.* An abbreviation of: **1.** Watt. **2.** West.
WAC or **Wac** (wăk) *n.* A member of the Women's Army Corps, organized during World War II but now no longer a separate branch.
wack•y (wăk′ē) *adj.* **wack•i•er, wack•i•est.** *Slang.* **1.** Eccentric. **2.** Crazy; silly: *showed up in a wacky outfit.*
wad (wŏd) *n.* **1.** A small mass of soft material, often folded or rolled, used for padding, stuffing, or packing. **2.** A compressed ball, roll, or lump, as of tobacco. **3.** A soft plug or disk used to hold an explosive charge in place in a cartridge or firearm. **4.** *Informal.* A large roll of paper money: *a wad of bank notes.* **5.** *Informal.* A large amount, especially of money. —*tr.v.* **wad•ded, wad•ding, wads. 1.** To squeeze, roll, crumple, or crush into a compact mass: *wad up a sheet of paper.* **2.** To insert a wad into (a firearm).
wad•ding (wŏd′ĭng) *n.* **1.** A wad or wads. **2.** A soft layer of cotton or wool used for padding or stuffing.
wad•dle (wŏd′l) *intr.v.* **wad•dled, wad•dling, wad•dles.** To walk with short steps that tilt the body from side to side. —*n.* A swaying walk.
wade (wād) *v.* **wad•ed, wad•ing, wades.** —*intr.* **1.** To walk in or through water or another substance that makes normal movement difficult. **2.** To make one's way slowly and with difficulty. —*tr.* To cross by wading: *The river was too deep to wade.*
wad•ers (wā′dərz) *pl.n.* Waterproof hip boots or trousers worn while fishing.
wa•di (wä′dē) *n., pl.* **wa•dis** also **wa•dies.** A gully or streambed in northern Africa and southwest Asia that remains dry except during the rainy season.
wad•ing bird (wā′dĭng) *n.* A long-legged bird, such as a crane or stork, that walks about in shallow water, especially in search of food.
wa•fer (wā′fər) *n.* **1.** A small, thin, crisp cake, biscuit, or candy. **2.** A small thin disk of unleavened bread used in the Eucharist. **3.** A small thin disk of material on which an integrated circuit can be formed for use in computers.
waf•fle[1] (wŏf′əl) *n.* A light crisp cake with an indented surface, made by baking batter in a waffle iron. [First written down in 1744 in American English and spelled *wafel,* from Dutch *wafel.*]
waf•fle[2] (wŏf′əl) *intr.v.* **waf•fled, waf•fling, waf•fles.** *Informal.* To speak or write evasively. [First written down in 1701 in Modern English, probably from obsolete *waff,* to yelp.]
waffle iron *n.* An appliance having hinged indented plates that press a grid pattern into waffle batter as it bakes.
waft (wäft *or* wăft) *v.* **waft•ed, waft•ing, wafts.** —*tr.* To cause to go or move gently through the air or over water: *The breeze wafted the fog through the fields.* —*intr.* To float easily and gently, as on the air; drift: *The smell of the ocean wafted in when she opened the door.* —*n.* **1.** Something, such as a scent or sound, carried lightly through the air: *a waft of perfume.* **2.** A light breeze; a rush of air.
wag[1] (wăg) *v.* **wagged, wag•ging, wags.** —*intr.* To move, swing, or wave repeatedly back and forth or up and down: *The puppy's tail wagged as we walked in.* —*tr.* To move (a body part) from side to side or up and down, as in playfulness: *The puppy wagged its tail eagerly.* —*n.* The act or motion of wagging. [First written down before 1200 in Middle English and spelled *waggen.*]
wag[2] (wăg) *n.* A witty humorous person; a wit. [First written down before 1553 in Modern English, perhaps from *wag,* to move back and forth.]
wage (wāj) *n.* **1.** Payment made to a worker for work done or services rendered; salary or earnings. **2.** A suitable return or recompense. Often used in the plural with a singular or plural verb: *The wages of idleness is poverty.* —*tr.v.* **waged, wag•ing, wag•es.** To engage in (a war or campaign, for example). [First written down before 1338 in Middle English, from Old North French, of Germanic origin.]
wage earner *n.* A person who works for wages, especially one whose earnings support or help support a household.
wa•ger (wā′jər) *n.* A bet. —*tr. & intr.v.* **wa•gered, wa•ger•ing, wa•gers.** To bet or make a bet.
wag•gish (wăg′ĭsh) *adj.* Of or resembling a wag; jocular or witty.
wag•gle (wăg′əl) *intr. & tr.v.* **wag•gled, wag•gling, wag•gles.** To move or cause to move with short quick motions; wag or wiggle.
Wag•ner (väg′nər), **Richard.** 1813–1883. German composer whose operas include *Der Ring des Nibelungen* (1853–1874).
wag•on (wăg′ən) *n.* **1.** A four-wheeled, usually horse-drawn vehicle with a large rectangular body, used to transport loads. **2.** A roomy motor vehicle used for a similar purpose, especially: **a.** A station wagon. **b.** A lightweight delivery truck: *a milk wagon.* **c.** A police patrol wagon. **3.** A child's low four-wheeled cart hauled by a long handle that controls the direction of the front wheels. [First written down before 1475 in Middle English and spelled *waggin,* from Middle Dutch *wagen.*]
wag•on•er (wăg′ə nər) *n.* A person who drives a wagon.
wagon train *n.* A line or train of wagons traveling cross-country.
waif (wāf) *n.* A lost or homeless person or animal, especially an orphaned or abandoned child.
wail (wāl) *intr.v.* **wailed, wail•ing, wails. 1.** To grieve or protest loudly and bitterly; lament. **2.** To make a prolonged sound suggesting a cry: *The wind wailed through the trees.* —*n.* A long high-pitched cry or sound: *the lonesome wail of a train whistle.*
❑ *These sound alike:* **wail, wale** (mark on the skin), **whale** (sea mammal).
wain•scot (wān′skət *or* wān′skŏt′) *n.* **1.** Wall paneling or facing, usually of wood. **2.** The lower part of an inside wall when finished in a material different from that of the upper part.
wain•scot•ing (wān′skə tĭng *or* wān′skŏ′tĭng) *n.* **1.**

—**vo′cal•i•za′tion** (vō′kə lĭ zā′shən) *n.* —**vo′cal•iz′er** *n.*
vo•ca•tion (vō kā′shən) *n.* **1.** A profession or an occupation, especially one for which a person is particularly suited or qualified: *plans to make medicine her vocation.* **2.** A strong inclination to do a particular type of work; a calling. —**vo•ca′tion•al** *adj.*
vocational school *n.* A school that offers instruction and training in skilled trades such as mechanics, plumbing, carpentry, and construction; a trade school.
vo•cif•er•ous (vō sĭf′ər əs) *adj.* Making, given to, or marked by a noisy and insistent outcry: *a vociferous crowd; vociferous protests.* —**vo•cif′er•ous•ly** *adv.*
vod•ka (vŏd′kə) *n.* An alcoholic liquor originally distilled from fermented wheat mash, but now also made from a mash of rye, corn, or potatoes.
vogue (vōg) *n.* **1.** The current fashion or style. **2.** Popular acceptance; popularity: *His novels enjoyed a great vogue in the 1930's.*
voice (vois) *n.* **1.a.** The sound produced by the vocal organs of a vertebrate, especially a human being. **b.** The ability to produce such sounds: *He caught a bad cold and lost his voice.* **2.** The condition or quality of a person's vocal sound: *a baritone in excellent voice; had a hoarse voice from coughing.* **3.** A singer. **4.** One of the individual parts in a musical composition: *a fugue for four voices.* **5.** Expression or utterance, as of feelings or thoughts: *give voice to one's feelings.* **6.** The right or opportunity to express a choice or opinion: *The children had no voice in deciding where to spend their vacation.* **7.** A sound resembling or likened to a vocal sound or utterance: *the voice of the wind.* **8.** In grammar, a property of a verb that indicates the relation between the subject and the action expressed by the verb. English has two voices, active and passive. —*tr.v.* **voiced, voic•ing, voic•es. 1.** To give voice to; utter: *had a chance to voice her feelings.* **2.** To pronounce with vibration of the vocal cords. —*idiom.* **with one voice.** In complete agreement; unanimously: *Our group rejected the contract with one voice.* [First written down before 1300 in Middle English, from Latin *vōx.*]
voice box *n.* The larynx.
voiced (voist) *adj.* **1.** Having a voice or a specified kind of voice: *a soft-voiced person.* **2.** Uttered with vibration of the vocal cords, as the consonants *b* and *d.*
voice•less (vois′lĭs) *adj.* **1.** Having no voice; mute. **2.** Uttered without vibration of the vocal cords, as the consonants *p* and *t.*
voice-o•ver or **voice•o•ver** (vois′ō′vər) *n.* In motion pictures and television, the voice of a narrator or character who does not appear on screen.
void (void) *adj.* **1.** Containing no matter; empty. See Synonyms at **empty. 2.** Not occupied; unfilled. **3.** Completely lacking; devoid: *void of all fear.* **4.** Having no legal force or validity: *was able to declare the contract void.* —*n.* An empty space; a vacuum: *the void of outer space.* —*tr.v.* **void•ed, void•ing, voids. 1.** To take out (the contents of something); empty. **2.** To excrete (body wastes). **3.** To leave; vacate. **4.** To make null; invalidate: *void an old passport.* [First written down about 1300 in Middle English, from Latin *vocīvus,* from *vacuus.*]
voile (voil) *n.* A light sheer fabric of cotton, rayon, wool, or silk, used especially for making curtains and dresses.
vol. *abbr.* An abbreviation of volume.
vol•a•tile (vŏl′ə tl *or* vŏl′ə tīl′) *adj.* **1.** Changing to vapor easily or readily at normal temperatures and pressures. **2.** Changeable, especially: **a.** Inconstant; fickle: *the volatile preferences of the public.* **b.** Tending to erupt into violent action; explosive: *a volatile political situation.* [First written down in 1597 in Modern English, from Latin *volātilis,* flying, from *volāre,* to fly.] —**vol′a•til′i•ty** (vŏl′ə tĭl′ĭ tē) *n.*
vol•can•ic (vŏl kăn′ĭk *or* vôl kăn′ĭk) *adj.* **1.** Of, resembling, or caused by a volcano or volcanoes. **2.** Produced or thrown from a volcano. **3.** Powerfully explosive: *a volcanic temper.*
vol•ca•no (vŏl kā′nō) *n., pl.* **vol•ca•noes** or **vol•ca•nos. 1.** An opening in the crust of the earth from which molten rock, dust, ash, and hot gases flow or are thrown out. **2.** A mountain or other elevation formed by the material thrown forth in this way. [First written down in 1613 in Modern English and spelled *vulcano,* ultimately from Latin *Volcānus,* the god Vulcan.]
vole (vōl) *n.* Any of various rodents resembling rats or mice but having a shorter tail and limbs and a heavier body.
Vol•ga (vŏl′gə *or* vôl′gə *or* vōl′gə). A river of western Russia rising northwest of Moscow and flowing about 2,300 miles (3,701 kilometers) generally east and south to the Caspian Sea. It is the longest river of Europe.
Vol•go•grad (vŏl′gə grăd′ *or* vōl′gə grăd′). Formerly **Sta•lin•grad** (stä′lĭn grăd′). A city of southwest Russia on the Volga River. It was besieged and severely damaged during World War II. Population, 974,000.
vo•li•tion (və lĭsh′ən) *n.* **1.** The act or an instance of choosing or deciding. **2.** A conscious choice or decision: *He left of his own volition.*
vol•ley (vŏl′ē) *n., pl.* **vol•leys. 1.a.** The simultaneous discharge of a number of missiles: *The defenders shot off a volley of bullets.* **b.** The missiles thus discharged. **2.** A bursting forth of many things together: *a volley of questions.* **3.** In sports, especially tennis, a shot made by striking the ball before it touches the ground. —*v.* **vol•leyed, vol•ley•ing, vol•leys.** —*tr.* **1.** To discharge in or as if in a volley. **2.** To strike (a tennis ball, for example) before it touches the ground. —*intr.* **1.** To be discharged in or as if in a volley. **2.** To make a volley, especially in tennis.
vol•ley•ball (vŏl′ē bôl′) *n.* **1.** A game played by two teams on a rectangular court divided by a high net, in which a ball is hit back and forth over the net with the hands. **2.** The ball used in this game.
volt (vōlt) *n.* A unit of electric potential or electromotive force, equal to the difference of electric potential measured between the ends of a conductor that has a resistance of one ohm and through which a steady current of one ampere is flowing. [First written down in 1873 in Modern English, after Count Alessandro *Volta* (1745–1827), Italian physicist.]
volt•age (vōl′tĭj) *n.* Electromotive force expressed in volts. A current of high voltage is used in transmitting electric power over long distances.
vol•ta•ic (vŏl tā′ĭk) *adj.* **1.** Of or indicating electricity that is produced as a result of chemical action. **2.** Producing electricity by chemical action: *a voltaic cell.* [First written down in 1813 in Modern English, after Count Alessandro *Volta* (1745–1827), Italian physicist.]
Vol•taire (vōl târ′ *or* vŏl târ′) Pen name of François Marie Arouet. 1694–1778. French philosopher and writer whose works include *Candide* (1759).
volt•am•me•ter (vōl tăm′mē′tər *or* vōlt′ăm′mē′tər) *n.* An instrument for measuring electrical current or potential.
volt•me•ter (vōlt′mē′tər) *n.* An instrument, such as

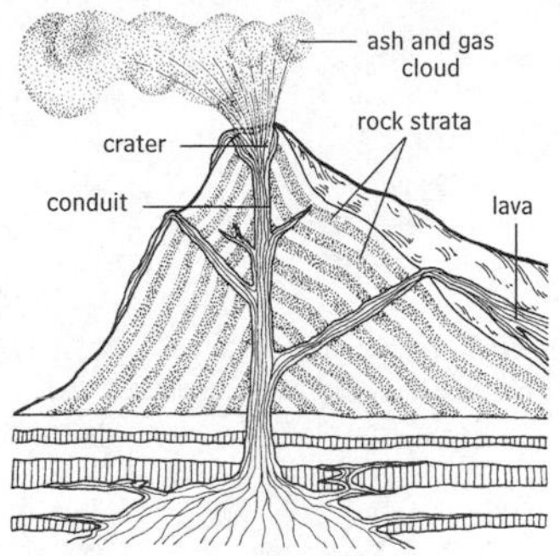

volcano
Cutaway view
of an erupting volcano

vole
Young meadow vole

volleyball

ă	pat	oi	boy
ā	pay	ou	out
âr	care	o͝o	took
ä	father	o͞o	boot
ĕ	pet	ŭ	cut
ē	be	ûr	urge
ĭ	pit	th	thin
ī	pie	*th*	this
îr	pier	hw	whoop
ŏ	pot	zh	vision
ō	toe	ə	about
ô	paw	N	*French* bon

a galvanometer, for measuring potential differences in volts.

vol•u•ble (vŏl′yə bəl) *adj.* Marked by a ready flow of speech; fluent. **—vol′u•bil′i•ty** *n.* **—vol′u•bly** *adv.*

vol•ume (vŏl′yo͞om *or* vŏl′yəm) *n.* **1.a.** A collection of written or printed sheets bound together; a book. **b.** One book of a set: *an encyclopedia published in 16 volumes.* **2.** The amount of space occupied by a three-dimensional object or region of space: *the volume of a cube; a container having a standard volume.* **3.a.** The force or intensity of a sound; loudness. **b.** A control, as on a radio, for regulating loudness: *Don't touch the volume!* **4.** Quantity; amount: *a large volume of mail.* [First written down before 1382 in Middle English, from Latin *volūmen,* roll of writing, from *volvere,* to roll.]

vol•u•met•ric (vŏl′yo͝o mĕt′rĭk) *adj.* Of or relating to measurement by volume. **—vol′u•met′ri•cal•ly** *adv.*

vo•lu•mi•nous (və lo͞o′mə nəs) *adj.* **1.** Having great volume, size, fullness, or number: *a voluminous trunk.* **2.** Filling or capable of filling a large volume or many volumes: *a voluminous court record.* **3.** Ample or lengthy in speech or writing.

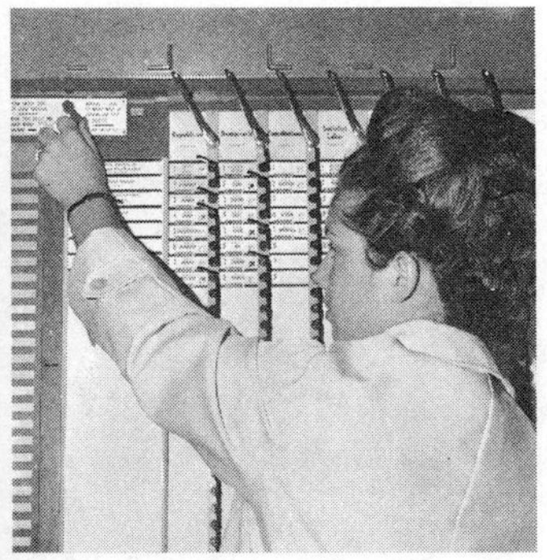

voting machine

vol•un•tar•y (vŏl′ən tĕr′ē) *adj.* **1.** Arising from or acting on one's own free will: *makes a voluntary contribution to the pension fund monthly.* **2.** Acting, serving, or done willingly and without expectation of reward: *voluntary community work.* **3.** Normally controlled by or subject to individual will: *a voluntary muscle.* **4.** Capable of making choices; having free will. **5.** Supported by contributions and donations rather than by government assistance: *voluntary hospitals.* —*n., pl.* **vol•un•tar•ies.** A short solo organ piece, often improvised, played before, during, and after a religious service. **—vol′un•tar′i•ly** (vŏl′ən târ′ə lē) *adv.*

vol•un•teer (vŏl′ən tîr′) *n.* A person who performs or offers to perform a service of his or her own free will. —*adj.* Being, consisting of, or done by volunteers: *volunteer firefighters.* —*v.* **vol•un•teered, vol•un•teer•ing, vol•un•teers.** —*tr.* To give or offer to give voluntarily: *volunteered to give blood.* —*intr.* **1.** To perform or offer to perform a service of one's own free will. **2.** To do charitable or helpful work without pay. [First written down about 1600 in Modern English, from Latin *voluntārius,* voluntary, from *velle,* to wish.]

vo•lup•tu•ar•y (və lŭp′cho͞o ĕr′ē) *n., pl.* **vo•lup•tu•ar•ies.** A person whose life is given over to luxury and sensual pleasures.

vo•lup•tu•ous (və lŭp′cho͞o əs) *adj.* **1.** Marked by, giving, or suggesting sensual pleasure and luxury: *voluptuous sculptural forms.* **2.** Devoted to, indulging in, or arising from sensual pleasures.

vol•vox (vŏl′vŏks′) *n.* Any of various freshwater green algae that form hollow, spherical, many-celled colonies.

vom•it (vŏm′ĭt) *v.* **vom•it•ed, vom•it•ing, vom•its.** —*intr.* To eject or discharge part or all of the contents of the stomach through the mouth, usually in a series of involuntary spasms. —*tr.* To eject (the contents of the stomach) through the mouth. —*n.* Matter discharged from the stomach by vomiting.

voo•doo (vo͞o′do͞o) *n., pl.* **voo•doos.** A religion practiced chiefly in Caribbean countries, characterized by belief in a Supreme God and many other deities and derived from a mixture of African religions and Roman Catholicism. [First written down in 1850 in American English and spelled *voudou,* from Louisiana French, of West African origin.]

voo•doo•ism (vo͞o′do͞o ĭz′əm) *n.* **1.** The practice and beliefs of voodoo. **2.** The practice of sorcery or witchcraft.

vo•ra•cious (və rā′shəs) *adj.* **1.** Eating or eager to eat great amounts of food; ravenous: *a voracious person.* **2.** Having or marked by an insatiable appetite for an activity or occupation: *a voracious reader.*

vor•tex (vôr′tĕks′) *n., pl.* **vor•tex•es** or **vor•ti•ces** (vôr′tĭ sēz′). **1.** A spiral motion of fluid, especially a whirling mass of water that sucks everything near it toward its center. **2.** A place or situation regarded as drawing into its center all that surrounds it.

vo•ta•ry (vō′tə rē) *n., pl.* **vo•ta•ries.** **1.** A person bound by vows to a life of religious worship or service. **2.** A person who is devoted, as to a particular hobby or pastime; an enthusiast.

vote (vōt) *n.* **1.a.** A formal expression of one's preference or choice, made in or as if in an election. **b.** The means by which such choice is made known, such as a raised hand or marked ballot. **2.** The number of votes cast in an election or to resolve an issue: *a heavy vote in favor of the bill.* **3.** A group of voters alike in some way: *the labor vote.* **4.** The result of an election. **5.** The right to participate as a voter; suffrage. —*v.* **vot•ed, vot•ing, votes.** —*intr.* To express one's preference for the resolution of an issue or for a candidate; cast a vote: *voted early.* —*tr.* **1.** To express one's preference for by vote. **2.** To bring into existence or make available by vote: *vote funds for a program.* **3.** To declare or pronounce by general consent: *vote the play a success.* [First written down before 1300 in Middle English, from Latin *vōtum,* vow, from *vovēre,* to vow.]

vot•er (vō′tər) *n.* A person who votes or has the right to vote.

vot•ing machine (vō′tĭng) *n.* A machine that mechanically records and counts votes.

vo•tive (vō′tĭv) *adj.* Given or dedicated in fulfillment of a vow or pledge: *a votive offering.*

vouch (vouch) *v.* **vouched, vouch•ing, vouch•es.** —*intr.* To give or serve as a guarantee; supply assurance or supporting evidence: *I can vouch for her honesty.* —*tr.* To prove or support by supplying evidence: *charges that he could not vouch.*

vouch•er (vou′chər) *n.* A receipt, signed statement, or similar paper that serves as proof or record that something has been paid for, given, or sold.

vouch•safe (vouch sāf′ *or* vouch′sāf′) *tr.v.* **vouch•safed, vouch•saf•ing, vouch•safes.** To condescend to grant or give (a reply or privilege, for example); deign.

vow (vou) *n.* A solemn promise or earnest pledge, especially to live or act in a specified way: *a vow to use his knowledge only for good; take the vows of a nun.* —*v.* **vowed, vow•ing, vows.** —*tr.* **1.** To promise or pledge solemnly: *She vowed that she would return home a success.* **2.** To make a pledge or threat to accomplish or bring about something: *vowing revenge on their persecutors.* —*intr.* To make a vow; promise. [First written down about 1300 in Middle English and spelled *vou,* from Latin *vōtum.*]

Synonyms: vow, promise, pledge, swear. These verbs all mean to declare solemnly that one will perform or avoid a particular course of action. *The protesters vowed they would never give up their cause. I promise to write back soon. Various countries pledged to obey the ban on whale hunting. In those movies, the villain always swears he will seek revenge.*

vow•el (vou′əl) *n.* **1.** A speech sound created by the relatively free passage of the breath through the larynx and mouth, usually forming the most prominent or central part of a syllable. **2.** A letter such as *a, e, i, o, u,* and sometimes *y,* that represents such a sound.

voy•age (voi′ĭj) *n.* **1.a.** A journey by sea to a foreign or distant land. **b.** A journey by land to a distant place. **c.** A journey through outer space. **2.** The events of a voyage of discovery or exploration considered as material for a narrative. Often used in the plural. —*intr.v.* **voy•aged, voy•ag•ing, voy•ag•es.** To make a voyage. **—voy′ag•er** *n.*

VP or **V.P.** *abbr.* An abbreviation of Vice President.

vs. *abbr.* An abbreviation of versus.

VT also **Vt.** *abbr.* An abbreviation of Vermont.

Vul•can (vŭl′kən) *n.* In Roman mythology, the god of fire and metalworking, identified with the Greek Hephaestus.

vul•ca•nite (vŭl′kə nīt′) *n.* A hard rubber produced by vulcanization.

vul•ca•nize (vŭl′kə nīz′) *tr.v.* **vul•ca•nized, vul•ca•niz•ing, vul•ca•niz•es.** To give (rubber or sometimes other materials) greater strength, resistance, and elasticity by combining with sulfur or other additives in the presence of heat and pressure. **—vul′ca•ni•za′tion** (vŭl′kə nĭ zā′shən) *n.*

vul•gar (vŭl′gər) *adj.* **1.** Of or associated with the great masses of people; common. **2.** Lacking good taste, refinement, or elegance; crude; coarse: *vulgar jokes.* **3.** Spoken by or expressed in the language of the common people; vernacular: *"Liverleaf" is the vulgar name for a plant known to botanists as hepatica.* **—vul′gar•ly** *adv.*

vul•gar•ism (vŭl′gə rĭz′əm) *n.* A word or expression used chiefly by uneducated people.

vul•gar•i•ty (vŭl găr′ĭ tē) *n., pl.* **vul•gar•i•ties.** **1.** The quality or condition of being vulgar. **2.** Something, such as an act or expression, that offends good taste or propriety.

vul•gar•ize (vŭl′gə rīz′) *tr.v.* **vul•gar•ized, vul•gar•iz•ing, vul•gar•iz•es.** **1.** To make vulgar; cheapen: *vulgarize a novel with a TV movie.* **2.** To popularize; make generally known. **—vul′gar•i•za′tion** (vŭl′gər ĭ zā′shən) *n.* **—vul′gar•i′zer** *n.*

Vulgar Latin *n.* The common speech of the ancient Romans, the ancestor of the Romance languages.

Vul•gate (vŭl′gāt′ *or* vŭl′gĭt) *n.* The Latin version of the Bible used in the Roman Catholic Church.

vul•ner•a•ble (vŭl′nər ə bəl) *adj.* **1.** Capable of being harmed or injured: *Baby birds are helpless and vulnerable.* **2.** Open to danger and attack; unprotected: *The retreat of the army had left the outlying territories vulnerable.* **3.** Easily affected, as by persuasion or temptation. **—vul′ner•a•bil′i•ty** *n.* **—vul′ner•a•bly** *adv.*

vul•pine (vŭl′pīn′) *adj.* **1.** Of, resembling, or characteristic of a fox. **2.** Cunning.

vul•ture (vŭl′chər) *n.* **1.** Any of various large birds having dark feathers and a bare head and neck and feeding on the flesh of dead animals. **2.** A greedy, grasping, or ruthless person. [First written down about 1380 in Middle English and spelled *voltor,* from Latin *vultur.*]

vul•va (vŭl′və) *n., pl.* **vul•vae** (vŭl′vē). The external female genital organs.

vy•ing (vī′ĭng) *v.* Present participle of **vie.**

vulture
Rüppell's griffon vulture

ă	pat	oi	boy
ā	pay	ou	out
âr	care	o͝o	took
ä	father	o͞o	boot
ĕ	pet	ŭ	cut
ē	be	ûr	urge
ĭ	pit	th	thin
ī	pie	*th*	this
îr	pier	hw	whoop
ŏ	pot	zh	vision
ō	toe	ə	about
ô	paw	N	*French* bon

W w

waders

waffle iron

Richard Wagner
Photographed in 1865

w or **W** (**dŭb′**əl yo͞o *or* **dŭb′**əl yo͞o) *n., pl.* **w's** or **W's. 1.** The 23rd letter of the English alphabet. **2.** The 23rd in a series or group.

W[1] The symbol for the element **tungsten.**

W[2] *abbr.* An abbreviation of: **1.** Watt. **2.** West.

WAC or **Wac** (wăk) *n.* A member of the Women's Army Corps, organized during World War II but now no longer a separate branch.

wack•y (**wăk′**ē) *adj.* **wack•i•er, wack•i•est.** *Slang.* **1.** Eccentric. **2.** Crazy; silly: *showed up in a wacky outfit.*

wad (wŏd) *n.* **1.** A small mass of soft material, often folded or rolled, used for padding, stuffing, or packing. **2.** A compressed ball, roll, or lump, as of tobacco. **3.** A soft plug or disk used to hold an explosive charge in place in a cartridge or firearm. **4.** *Informal.* A large roll of paper money: *a wad of bank notes.* **5.** *Informal.* A large amount, especially of money. *—tr.v.* **wad•ded, wad•ding, wads. 1.** To squeeze, roll, crumple, or crush into a compact mass: *wad up a sheet of paper.* **2.** To insert a wad into (a firearm).

wad•ding (**wŏd′**ĭng) *n.* **1.** A wad or wads. **2.** A soft layer of cotton or wool used for padding or stuffing.

wad•dle (**wŏd′**l) *intr.v.* **wad•dled, wad•dling, wad•dles.** To walk with short steps that tilt the body from side to side. *—n.* A swaying walk.

wade (wād) *v.* **wad•ed, wad•ing, wades.** *—intr.* **1.** To walk in or through water or another substance that makes normal movement difficult. **2.** To make one's way slowly and with difficulty. *—tr.* To cross by wading: *The river was too deep to wade.*

wad•ers (**wā′**dərz) *pl.n.* Waterproof hip boots or trousers worn while fishing.

wa•di (**wä′**dē) *n., pl.* **wa•dis** also **wa•dies.** A gully or streambed in northern Africa and southwest Asia that remains dry except during the rainy season.

wad•ing bird (**wā′**dĭng) *n.* A long-legged bird, such as a crane or stork, that walks about in shallow water, especially in search of food.

wa•fer (**wā′**fər) *n.* **1.** A small, thin, crisp cake, biscuit, or candy. **2.** A small thin disk of unleavened bread used in the Eucharist. **3.** A small thin disk of material on which an integrated circuit can be formed for use in computers.

waf•fle[1] (**wŏf′**əl) *n.* A light crisp cake with an indented surface, made by baking batter in a waffle iron. [First written down in 1744 in American English and spelled *wafel,* from Dutch *wafel.*]

waf•fle[2] (**wŏf′**əl) *intr.v.* **waf•fled, waf•fling, waf•fles.** *Informal.* To speak or write evasively. [First written down in 1701 in Modern English, probably from obsolete *waff,* to yelp.]

waffle iron *n.* An appliance having hinged indented plates that press a grid pattern into waffle batter as it bakes.

waft (wäft *or* wăft) *v.* **waft•ed, waft•ing, wafts.** *—tr.* To cause to go or move gently through the air or over water: *The breeze wafted the fog through the fields.* *—intr.* To float easily and gently, as on the air; drift: *The smell of the ocean wafted in when she opened the door.* *—n.* **1.** Something, such as a scent or sound, carried lightly through the air: *a waft of perfume.* **2.** A light breeze; a rush of air.

wag[1] (wăg) *v.* **wagged, wag•ging, wags.** *—intr.* To move, swing, or wave repeatedly back and forth or up and down: *The puppy's tail wagged as we walked in.* *—tr.* To move (a body part) from side to side or up and down, as in playfulness: *The puppy wagged its tail eagerly.* *—n.* The act or motion of wagging. [First written down before 1200 in Middle English and spelled *waggen.*]

wag[2] (wăg) *n.* A witty humorous person; a wit. [First written down before 1553 in Modern English, perhaps from *wag,* to move back and forth.]

wage (wāj) *n.* **1.** Payment made to a worker for work done or services rendered; salary or earnings. **2.** A suitable return or recompense. Often used in the plural with a singular or plural verb: *The wages of idleness is poverty.* *—tr.v.* **waged, wag•ing, wag•es.** To engage in (a war or campaign, for example). [First written down before 1338 in Middle English, from Old North French, of Germanic origin.]

wage earner *n.* A person who works for wages, especially one whose earnings support or help support a household.

wa•ger (**wā′**jər) *n.* A bet. *—tr. & intr.v.* **wa•gered, wa•ger•ing, wa•gers.** To bet or make a bet.

wag•gish (**wăg′**ĭsh) *adj.* Of or resembling a wag; jocular or witty.

wag•gle (**wăg′**əl) *intr. & tr.v.* **wag•gled, wag•gling, wag•gles.** To move or cause to move with short quick motions; wag or wiggle.

Wag•ner (**väg′**nər), **Richard.** 1813–1883. German composer whose operas include *Der Ring des Nibelungen* (1853–1874).

wag•on (**wăg′**ən) *n.* **1.** A four-wheeled, usually horse-drawn vehicle with a large rectangular body, used to transport loads. **2.** A roomy motor vehicle used for a similar purpose, especially: **a.** A station wagon. **b.** A lightweight delivery truck: *a milk wagon.* **c.** A police patrol wagon. **3.** A child's low four-wheeled cart hauled by a long handle that controls the direction of the front wheels. [First written down before 1475 in Middle English and spelled *waggin,* from Middle Dutch *wagen.*]

wag•on•er (**wăg′**ə nər) *n.* A person who drives a wagon.

wagon train *n.* A line or train of wagons traveling cross-country.

waif (wāf) *n.* A lost or homeless person or animal, especially an orphaned or abandoned child.

wail (wāl) *intr.v.* **wailed, wail•ing, wails. 1.** To grieve or protest loudly and bitterly; lament. **2.** To make a prolonged sound suggesting a cry: *The wind wailed through the trees.* *—n.* A long high-pitched cry or sound: *the lonesome wail of a train whistle.*
❑ *These sound alike:* **wail, wale** (mark on the skin), **whale** (sea mammal).

wain•scot (**wān′**skət *or* **wān′**skōt′) *n.* **1.** Wall paneling or facing, usually of wood. **2.** The lower part of an inside wall when finished in a material different from that of the upper part.

wain•scot•ing (**wān′**skə tĭng *or* **wān′**skō′tĭng) *n.* **1.**

a, e, i, o, u, and sometimes *y,* that represents such a sound.

voy•age (voi′ĭj) *n.* **1.a.** A journey by sea to a foreign or distant land. **b.** A journey by land to a distant place. **c.** A journey through outer space. **2.** The events of a voyage of discovery or exploration considered as material for a narrative. Often used in the plural. *—intr.v.* **voy•aged, voy•ag•ing, voy•ag•es.** To make a voyage. **—voy′ag•er** *n.*

VP or **V.P.** *abbr.* An abbreviation of Vice President.

vs. *abbr.* An abbreviation of versus.

VT also **Vt.** *abbr.* An abbreviation of Vermont.

Vul•can (vŭl′kən) *n.* In Roman mythology, the god of fire and metalworking, identified with the Greek Hephaestus.

vul•ca•nite (vŭl′kə nīt′) *n.* A hard rubber produced by vulcanization.

vul•ca•nize (vŭl′kə nīz′) *tr.v.* **vul•ca•nized, vul•ca•niz•ing, vul•ca•niz•es.** To give (rubber or sometimes other materials) greater strength, resistance, and elasticity by combining with sulfur or other additives in the presence of heat and pressure. **—vul′can•i•za′tion** (vŭl′kə nĭ zā′shən) *n.*

vul•gar (vŭl′gər) *adj.* **1.** Of or associated with the great masses of people; common. **2.** Lacking good taste, refinement, or elegance; crude; coarse: *vulgar jokes.* **3.** Spoken by or expressed in the language of the common people; vernacular: *"Liverleaf" is the vulgar name for a plant known to botanists as* hepatica. **—vul′gar•ly** *adv.*

vul•gar•ism (vŭl′gə rĭz′əm) *n.* A word or expression used chiefly by uneducated people.

vul•gar•i•ty (vŭl găr′ĭ tē) *n., pl.* **vul•gar•i•ties. 1.** The quality or condition of being vulgar. **2.** Something, such as an act or expression, that offends good taste or propriety.

vul•gar•ize (vŭl′gə rīz′) *tr.v.* **vul•gar•ized, vul•gar•iz•ing, vul•gar•iz•es. 1.** To make vulgar; cheapen: *vulgarize a novel with a TV movie.* **2.** To popularize; make generally known. **—vul′gar•i•za′tion** (vŭl′gər ĭ zā′shən) *n.* **—vul′gar•i′zer** *n.*

Vulgar Latin *n.* The common speech of the ancient Romans, the ancestor of the Romance languages.

Vul•gate (vŭl′gāt′ *or* vŭl′gĭt) *n.* The Latin version of the Bible used in the Roman Catholic Church.

vul•ner•a•ble (vŭl′nər ə bəl) *adj.* **1.** Capable of being harmed or injured: *Baby birds are helpless and vulnerable.* **2.** Open to danger and attack; unprotected: *The retreat of the army had left the outlying territories vulnerable.* **3.** Easily affected, as by persuasion or temptation. **—vul′ner•a•bil′i•ty** *n.* **—vul′ner•a•bly** *adv.*

vul•pine (vŭl′pīn′) *adj.* **1.** Of, resembling, or characteristic of a fox. **2.** Cunning.

vul•ture (vŭl′chər) *n.* **1.** Any of various large birds having dark feathers and a bare head and neck and feeding on the flesh of dead animals. **2.** A greedy, grasping, or ruthless person. [First written down about 1380 in Middle English and spelled *voltor,* from Latin *vultur.*]

vul•va (vŭl′və) *n., pl.* **vul•vae** (vŭl′vē). The external female genital organs.

vy•ing (vī′ĭng) *v.* Present participle of **vie.**

vulture
Rüppell's griffon vulture

ă	pat	oi	boy
ā	pay	ou	out
âr	care	o͝o	took
ä	father	o͞o	boot
ĕ	pet	ŭ	cut
ē	be	ûr	urge
ĭ	pit	th	thin
ī	pie	*th*	this
îr	pier	hw	whoop
ŏ	pot	zh	vision
ō	toe	ə	about
ô	paw	N	*French* bon

voting machine

a galvanometer, for measuring potential differences in volts.

vol•u•ble (vŏl′yə bəl) *adj.* Marked by a ready flow of speech; fluent. **—vol′u•bil′i•ty** *n.* **—vol′u•bly** *adv.*

vol•ume (vŏl′yo͞om *or* vŏl′yəm) *n.* **1.a.** A collection of written or printed sheets bound together; a book. **b.** One book of a set: *an encyclopedia published in 16 volumes.* **2.** The amount of space occupied by a three-dimensional object or region of space: *the volume of a cube; a container having a standard volume.* **3.a.** The force or intensity of a sound; loudness. **b.** A control, as on a radio, for regulating loudness: *Don't touch the volume!* **4.** Quantity; amount: *a large volume of mail.* [First written down before 1382 in Middle English, from Latin *volūmen*, roll of writing, from *volvere*, to roll.]

vol•u•met•ric (vŏl′yo͞o mĕt′rĭk) *adj.* Of or relating to measurement by volume. **—vol′u•met′ri•cal•ly** *adv.*

vo•lu•mi•nous (və lo͞o′mə nəs) *adj.* **1.** Having great volume, size, fullness, or number: *a voluminous trunk.* **2.** Filling or capable of filling a large volume or many volumes: *a voluminous court record.* **3.** Ample or lengthy in speech or writing.

vol•un•tar•y (vŏl′ən tĕr′ē) *adj.* **1.** Arising from or acting on one's own free will: *makes a voluntary contribution to the pension fund monthly.* **2.** Acting, serving, or done willingly and without expectation of reward: *voluntary community work.* **3.** Normally controlled by or subject to individual will: *a voluntary muscle.* **4.** Capable of making choices; having free will. **5.** Supported by contributions and donations rather than by government assistance: *voluntary hospitals.* *—n., pl.* **vol•un•tar•ies.** A short solo organ piece, often improvised, played before, during, and after a religious service. **—vol′un•tar′i•ly** (vŏl′ən târ′ə lē) *adv.*

vol•un•teer (vŏl′ən tîr′) *n.* A person who performs or offers to perform a service of his or her own free will. *—adj.* Being, consisting of, or done by volunteers: *volunteer firefighters.* *—v.* **vol•un•teered, vol•un•teer•ing, vol•un•teers.** *—tr.* To give or offer to give voluntarily: *volunteered to give blood.* *—intr.* **1.** To perform or offer to perform a service of one's own free will. **2.** To do charitable or helpful work without pay. [First written down about 1600 in Modern English, from Latin *voluntārius*, voluntary, from *velle*, to wish.]

vo•lup•tu•ar•y (və lŭp′cho͞o ĕr′ē) *n., pl.* **vo•lup•tu•ar•ies.** A person whose life is given over to luxury and sensual pleasures.

vo•lup•tu•ous (və lŭp′cho͞o əs) *adj.* **1.** Marked by, giving, or suggesting sensual pleasure and luxury: *voluptuous sculptural forms.* **2.** Devoted to, indulging in, or arising from sensual pleasures.

vol•vox (vŏl′vŏks′) *n.* Any of various freshwater green algae that form hollow, spherical, many-celled colonies.

vom•it (vŏm′ĭt) *v.* **vom•it•ed, vom•it•ing, vom•its.** *—intr.* To eject or discharge part or all of the contents of the stomach through the mouth, usually in a series of involuntary spasms. *—tr.* To eject (the contents of the stomach) through the mouth. *—n.* Matter discharged from the stomach by vomiting.

voo•doo (vo͞o′do͞o) *n., pl.* **voo•doos.** A religion practiced chiefly in Caribbean countries, characterized by belief in a Supreme God and many other deities and derived from a mixture of African religions and Roman Catholicism. [First written down in 1850 in American English and spelled *voudou*, from Louisiana French, of West African origin.]

voo•doo•ism (vo͞o′do͞o ĭz′əm) *n.* **1.** The practice and beliefs of voodoo. **2.** The practice of sorcery or witchcraft.

vo•ra•cious (və rā′shəs) *adj.* **1.** Eating or eager to eat great amounts of food; ravenous: *a voracious person.* **2.** Having or marked by an insatiable appetite for an activity or occupation: *a voracious reader.*

vor•tex (vôr′tĕks′) *n., pl.* **vor•tex•es** or **vor•ti•ces** (vôr′tĭ sēz′). **1.** A spiral motion of fluid, especially a whirling mass of water that sucks everything near it toward its center. **2.** A place or situation regarded as drawing into its center all that surrounds it.

vo•ta•ry (vō′tə rē) *n., pl.* **vo•ta•ries.** **1.** A person bound by vows to a life of religious worship or service. **2.** A person who is devoted, as to a particular hobby or pastime; an enthusiast.

vote (vōt) *n.* **1.a.** A formal expression of one's preference or choice, made in or as if in an election. **b.** The means by which such choice is made known, such as a raised hand or marked ballot. **2.** The number of votes cast in an election or to resolve an issue: *a heavy vote in favor of the bill.* **3.** A group of voters alike in some way: *the labor vote.* **4.** The result of an election. **5.** The right to participate as a voter; suffrage. *—v.* **vot•ed, vot•ing, votes.** *—intr.* To express one's preference for the resolution of an issue or for a candidate; cast a vote: *voted early.* *—tr.* **1.** To express one's preference for by vote. **2.** To bring into existence or make available by vote: *vote funds for a program.* **3.** To declare or pronounce by general consent: *vote the play a success.* [First written down before 1300 in Middle English, from Latin *vōtum*, vow, from *vovēre*, to vow.]

vot•er (vō′tər) *n.* A person who votes or has the right to vote.

vot•ing machine (vō′tĭng) *n.* A machine that mechanically records and counts votes.

vo•tive (vō′tĭv) *adj.* Given or dedicated in fulfillment of a vow or pledge: *a votive offering.*

vouch (vouch) *v.* **vouched, vouch•ing, vouch•es.** *—intr.* To give or serve as a guarantee; supply assurance or supporting evidence: *I can vouch for her honesty.* *—tr.* To prove or support by supplying evidence: *charges that he could not vouch.*

vouch•er (vou′chər) *n.* A receipt, signed statement, or similar paper that serves as proof or record that something has been paid for, given, or sold.

vouch•safe (vouch sāf′ *or* vouch′sāf′) *tr.v.* **vouch•safed, vouch•saf•ing, vouch•safes.** To condescend to grant or give (a reply or privilege, for example); deign.

vow (vou) *n.* A solemn promise or earnest pledge, especially to live or act in a specified way: *a vow to use his knowledge only for good; take the vows of a nun.* *—v.* **vowed, vow•ing, vows.** *—tr.* **1.** To promise or pledge solemnly: *She vowed that she would return home a success.* **2.** To make a pledge or threat to accomplish or bring about something: *vowing revenge on their persecutors.* *—intr.* To make a vow; promise. [First written down about 1300 in Middle English and spelled *vou*, from Latin *vōtum*.]

Synonyms: **vow, promise, pledge, swear.** These verbs all mean to declare solemnly that one will perform or avoid a particular course of action. *The protesters vowed they would never give up their cause. I promise to write back soon. Various countries pledged to obey the ban on whale hunting. In those movies, the villain always swears he will seek revenge.*

---

vow•el (vou′əl) *n.* **1.** A speech sound created by the relatively free passage of the breath through the larynx and mouth, usually forming the most prominent or central part of a syllable. **2.** A letter such as

—vo′cal•i•za′tion (vō′kə lĭ **zā′**shən) *n.* **—vo′cal•iz′er** *n.*

vo•ca•tion (vō **kā′**shən) *n.* **1.** A profession or an occupation, especially one for which a person is particularly suited or qualified: *plans to make medicine her vocation.* **2.** A strong inclination to do a particular type of work; a calling. **—vo•ca′tion•al** *adj.*

vocational school *n.* A school that offers instruction and training in skilled trades such as mechanics, plumbing, carpentry, and construction; a trade school.

vo•cif•er•ous (vō **sĭf′**ər əs) *adj.* Making, given to, or marked by a noisy and insistent outcry: *a vociferous crowd; vociferous protests.* **—vo•cif′er•ous•ly** *adv.*

vod•ka (**vŏd′**kə) *n.* An alcoholic liquor originally distilled from fermented wheat mash, but now also made from a mash of rye, corn, or potatoes.

vogue (vōg) *n.* **1.** The current fashion or style. **2.** Popular acceptance; popularity: *His novels enjoyed a great vogue in the 1930's.*

voice (vois) *n.* **1.a.** The sound produced by the vocal organs of a vertebrate, especially a human being. **b.** The ability to produce such sounds: *He caught a bad cold and lost his voice.* **2.** The condition or quality of a person's vocal sound: *a baritone in excellent voice; had a hoarse voice from coughing.* **3.** A singer. **4.** One of the individual parts in a musical composition: *a fugue for four voices.* **5.** Expression or utterance, as of feelings or thoughts: *give voice to one's feelings.* **6.** The right or opportunity to express a choice or opinion: *The children had no voice in deciding where to spend their vacation.* **7.** A sound resembling or likened to a vocal sound or utterance: *the voice of the wind.* **8.** In grammar, a property of a verb that indicates the relation between the subject and the action expressed by the verb. English has two voices, active and passive. *—tr.v.* **voiced, voic•ing, voic•es. 1.** To give voice to; utter: *had a chance to voice her feelings.* **2.** To pronounce with vibration of the vocal cords. ***—idiom.* with one voice.** In complete agreement; unanimously: *Our group rejected the contract with one voice.* [First written down before 1300 in Middle English, from Latin *vōx.*]

voice box *n.* The larynx.

voiced (voist) *adj.* **1.** Having a voice or a specified kind of voice: *a soft-voiced person.* **2.** Uttered with vibration of the vocal cords, as the consonants *b* and *d.*

voice•less (**vois′**lĭs) *adj.* **1.** Having no voice; mute. **2.** Uttered without vibration of the vocal cords, as the consonants *p* and *t.*

voice-o•ver or **voice•o•ver** (**vois′**ō′vər) *n.* In motion pictures and television, the voice of a narrator or character who does not appear on screen.

void (void) *adj.* **1.** Containing no matter; empty. See Synonyms at **empty. 2.** Not occupied; unfilled. **3.** Completely lacking; devoid: *void of all fear.* **4.** Having no legal force or validity: *was able to declare the contract void.* *—n.* An empty space; a vacuum: *the void of outer space.* *—tr.v.* **void•ed, void•ing, voids. 1.** To take out (the contents of something); empty. **2.** To excrete (body wastes). **3.** To leave; vacate. **4.** To make null; invalidate: *void an old passport.* [First written down about 1300 in Middle English, from Latin *vocīvus,* from *vacuus.*]

voile (voil) *n.* A light sheer fabric of cotton, rayon, wool, or silk, used especially for making curtains and dresses.

vol. *abbr.* An abbreviation of volume.

vol•a•tile (**vŏl′**ə tl *or* **vŏl′**ə tīl′) *adj.* **1.** Changing to vapor easily or readily at normal temperatures and pressures. **2.** Changeable, especially: **a.** Inconstant; fickle: *the volatile preferences of the public.* **b.** Tending to erupt into violent action; explosive: *a volatile political situation.* [First written down in 1597 in Modern English, from Latin *volātilis,* flying, from *volāre,* to fly.] **—vol′a•til′i•ty** (vŏl′ə **tĭl′**ĭ tē) *n.*

vol•can•ic (vŏl **kăn′**ĭk *or* vôl **kăn′**ĭk) *adj.* **1.** Of, resembling, or caused by a volcano or volcanoes. **2.** Produced or thrown from a volcano. **3.** Powerfully explosive: *a volcanic temper.*

vol•ca•no (vŏl **kā′**nō) *n., pl.* **vol•ca•noes** or **vol•ca•nos. 1.** An opening in the crust of the earth from which molten rock, dust, ash, and hot gases flow or are thrown out. **2.** A mountain or other elevation formed by the material thrown forth in this way. [First written down in 1613 in Modern English and spelled *vulcano,* ultimately from Latin *Volcānus,* the god Vulcan.]

vole (vōl) *n.* Any of various rodents resembling rats or mice but having a shorter tail and limbs and a heavier body.

Vol•ga (**vŏl′**gə *or* **vôl′**gə *or* **vōl′**gə). A river of western Russia rising northwest of Moscow and flowing about 2,300 miles (3,701 kilometers) generally east and south to the Caspian Sea. It is the longest river of Europe.

Vol•go•grad (**vŏl′**gə grăd′ *or* **vōl′**gə grăd′). Formerly **Sta•lin•grad** (**stä′**lĭn grăd′). A city of southwest Russia on the Volga River. It was besieged and severely damaged during World War II. Population, 974,000.

vo•li•tion (və **lĭsh′**ən) *n.* **1.** The act or an instance of choosing or deciding. **2.** A conscious choice or decision: *He left of his own volition.*

vol•ley (**vŏl′**ē) *n., pl.* **vol•leys. 1.a.** The simultaneous discharge of a number of missiles: *The defenders shot off a volley of bullets.* **b.** The missiles thus discharged. **2.** A bursting forth of many things together: *a volley of questions.* **3.** In sports, especially tennis, a shot made by striking the ball before it touches the ground. *—v.* **vol•leyed, vol•ley•ing, vol•leys.** *—tr.* **1.** To discharge in or as if in a volley. **2.** To strike (a tennis ball, for example) before it touches the ground. *—intr.* **1.** To be discharged in or as if in a volley. **2.** To make a volley, especially in tennis.

vol•ley•ball (**vŏl′**ē bôl′) *n.* **1.** A game played by two teams on a rectangular court divided by a high net, in which a ball is hit back and forth over the net with the hands. **2.** The ball used in this game.

volt (vōlt) *n.* A unit of electric potential or electromotive force, equal to the difference of electric potential measured between the ends of a conductor that has a resistance of one ohm and through which a steady current of one ampere is flowing. [First written down in 1873 in Modern English, after Count Alessandro *Volta* (1745–1827), Italian physicist.]

volt•age (**vōl′**tĭj) *n.* Electromotive force expressed in volts. A current of high voltage is used in transmitting electric power over long distances.

vol•ta•ic (vŏl **tā′**ĭk) *adj.* **1.** Of or indicating electricity that is produced as a result of chemical action. **2.** Producing electricity by chemical action: *a voltaic cell.* [First written down in 1813 in Modern English, after Count Alessandro *Volta* (1745–1827), Italian physicist.]

Vol•taire (vōl **târ′** *or* vŏl **târ′**) Pen name of François Marie Arouet. 1694–1778. French philosopher and writer whose works include *Candide* (1759).

volt•am•me•ter (vōl **tăm′**mē′tər *or* **vōlt′**ăm′mē′tər) *n.* An instrument for measuring electrical current or potential.

volt•me•ter (**vōlt′**mē′tər) *n.* An instrument, such as

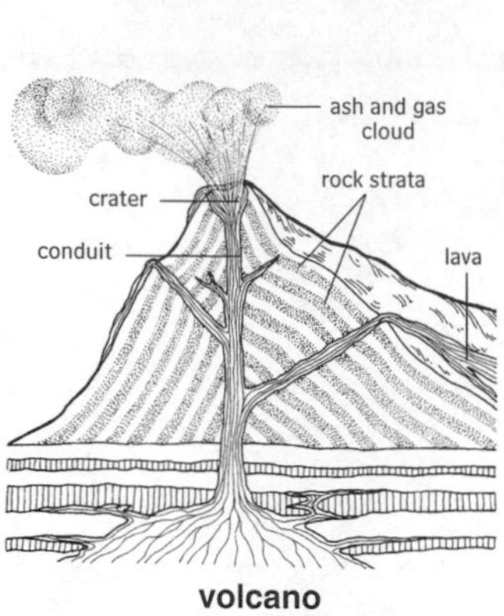

volcano
Cutaway view of an erupting volcano

vole
Young meadow vole

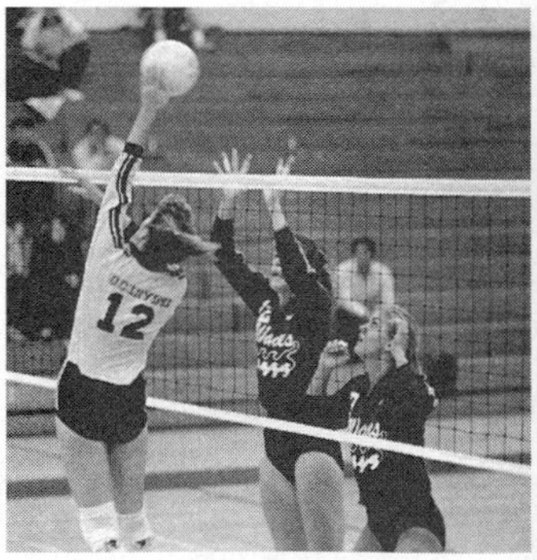

volleyball

ă	pat	oi	boy
ā	pay	ou	out
âr	care	o͝o	took
ä	father	o͞o	boot
ĕ	pet	ŭ	cut
ē	be	ûr	urge
ĭ	pit	th	thin
ī	pie	*th*	this
îr	pier	hw	whoop
ŏ	pot	zh	vision
ō	toe	ə	about
ô	paw	N	*French* bon

wallaby

walrus
Bull walrus

a dramatic production, usually without speaking lines. **2.** A performer playing such a role.

walk•out (wôk′out′) *n.* **1.** A labor strike. **2.** The act of leaving or quitting a meeting, a company, or an organization, especially as a sign of protest.

walk•up (wôk′ŭp′) *n.* **1.** An apartment house or building with no elevator. **2.** An apartment or office in a building with no elevator: *lives in a fourth-floor walkup.*

walk•way (wôk′wā′) *n.* A passage or path for walking.

wall (wôl) *n.* **1.** An upright structure of building material that serves to enclose an area or to separate two areas from each other. **2.** Something that is like a wall in appearance, function, or construction: *the wall of the stomach.* **3.** Something that is like a wall, as in hiding or dividing something: *a wall of fog; a wall of secrecy.* —*tr.v.* **walled, wall•ing, walls. 1.** To enclose, surround, or fortify with or as with a wall. **2.** To divide or separate with or as if with a wall: *wall off compartments.* —***idioms.* off the wall.** *Slang.* **1.** Extremely unconventional; strange: *His outfit is really off the wall.* **2.** Without foundation; ridiculous: *That explanation is really off the wall.* **up the wall.** *Slang.* Into a state of extreme frustration, anger, or distress: *My little brother is driving me up the wall.* [First written down about 725 in Old English and spelled *weall,* from Latin *vallus,* stake.]

wal•la•by (wŏl′ə bē) *n., pl.* **wal•la•bies** or **wallaby.** Any of various Australian mammals related to and resembling the kangaroos but generally smaller.

Wal•la•chi•a also **Wa•la•chi•a** (wŏ lā′kē ə). A historical region of southeast Romania between the Transylvanian Alps and the Danube River. It was united in 1861 with Moldavia to form Romania.

wall•board (wôl′bôrd′) *n.* Plasterboard.

wal•let (wŏl′ĭt) *n.* A small flat folding case, usually made of leather, for holding paper money, cards, or photographs; a billfold.

wall•eye (wôl′ī′) *n.* **1.a.** An eye that is directed out to one side rather than being aligned with the other eye. **b.** An eye having a white or opaque cornea. **2.** A North American freshwater fish having large staring eyes and caught for food.

wall•eyed (wôl′īd′) *adj.* **1.** Having a walleye. **2.** Having large bulging or staring eyes.

wall•flow•er (wôl′flou′ər) *n.* **1.** Any of numerous plants having fragrant yellow or orange flowers. **2.** A person who does not take part in the activities of a social event because of shyness or unpopularity.

wal•lop (wŏl′əp) *Informal. tr.v.* **wal•loped, wal•lop•ing, wal•lops. 1.** To beat soundly or defeat thoroughly: *They walloped their opponents.* **2.** To strike with a hard blow. —*n.* A hard blow or the ability to strike such a blow.

wal•low (wŏl′ō) *intr.v.* **wal•lowed, wal•low•ing, wal•lows. 1.** To roll the body about, as in water or mud: *The rhinoceros wallowed playfully in the mud.* **2.** To luxuriate; revel: *The sultan wallowed in luxury.* **3.** To move with difficulty in a clumsy or rolling manner; flounder. —*n.* **1.** The act or an instance of wallowing. **2.** A pool of water or mud where animals go to wallow.

wall•pa•per (wôl′pā′pər) *n.* Paper often colored and printed with designs and pasted to a wall as a decorative covering. —*tr.v.* **wall•pa•pered, wall•pa•per•ing, wall•pa•pers.** To cover with or as if with wallpaper.

Wall Street *n.* The people who control or influence the finances of the United States economy.

wall-to-wall (wôl′tə wôl′) *adj.* **1.** Completely covering a floor: *wall-to-wall carpeting.* **2.** Present or spreading throughout an entire area: *wall-to-wall people at the party.*

wal•nut (wôl′nŭt′) *n.* **1.** An edible nut having a hard rough shell. **2.** Any of several trees that bear such nuts. **3.** The hard dark-brown wood of any of these trees.

wal•rus (wôl′rəs *or* wŏl′rəs) *n., pl.* **walrus** or **wal•rus•es.** A large sea mammal of Arctic regions, related to the seals and sea lions and having tough wrinkled skin and large tusks. [First written down in 1728 in Modern English, from Dutch, of Scandinavian origin.]

waltz (wôlts *or* wôls) *n.* **1.** A ballroom dance in triple time with a strong accent on the first beat. **2.** A piece of music for this dance. —*intr.v.* **waltzed, waltz•ing, waltz•es.** To dance the waltz.

Wam•pa•no•ag (wäm′pə nō′ăg) *n., pl.* **Wampanoag** or **Wam•pa•no•ags. 1.** A member of a Native American people of eastern Rhode Island and southeast Massachusetts. **2.** The Algonquian language of the Wampanoag, a variety of Massachusett. —**Wam′pa•no′ag** *adj.*

wam•pum (wŏm′pəm *or* wôm′pəm) *n.* **1.** Small beads made from polished shells and strung together into strands or belts, formerly used by certain Native American peoples as money or jewelry or in ceremonies. **2.** *Informal.* Money. [First written down in 1627 in American English and spelled *wampumpeag,* from Massachusett.]

wan (wŏn) *adj.* **wan•ner, wan•nest. 1.** Unnaturally pale, as from physical or emotional distress: *a wan face.* **2.** Suggesting weariness, illness, or unhappiness: *a wan smile.* —**wan′ly** *adv.*

wand (wŏnd) *n.* **1.** A thin supple rod, twig, or stick. **2.** A slender rod carried as a symbol of office; a scepter. **3.** A conductor's baton. **4.** A stick or baton used by a magician, conjurer, or diviner.

wan•der (wŏn′dər) *v.* **wan•dered, wan•der•ing, wan•ders.** —*intr.* **1.** To move about without a destination or purpose. **2.** To go by an indirect route or stroll in a leisurely way. **3.** To follow an irregular winding or rambling course: *The brook wandered through the pasture.* **4.** To go astray: *One hiker wandered away from the others. The speaker's dull drone caused my attention to wander.* —*tr.* To wander across or through: *wander the backwoods.* —**wan′der•er** *n.*

Synonyms: **wander, ramble, roam, meander.** These verbs mean to move about at random or without destination or purpose. **Wander** and **ramble** both mean to move about without a fixed course or goal: *He wandered from room to room looking for something interesting to do. After breakfast we can ramble through the hills.* **Roam** suggests wandering with freedom of movement, especially over a wide area: *Herds of bison once roamed across the Great Plains.* **Meander** suggests wandering leisurely and sometimes aimlessly over an irregular or winding course: *Susie is meandering down to the beach at her own pace.*

wan•der•lust (wŏn′dər lŭst′) *n.* A very strong desire to travel.

wane (wān) *intr.v.* **waned, wan•ing, wanes. 1.** To decrease gradually in size, amount, intensity, or degree. **2.** To show a progressively smaller lighted surface from full moon to new moon. **3.** To approach an end: *The old year was waning.* —*n.* **1.** The period during which the moon wanes. **2.** A time or phase of gradual decrease. —***idiom.* on the wane.** In a period of decline or decrease.

wan•gle (wăng′gəl) *tr. & intr.v.* **wan•gled, wan•gling, wan•gles.** *Informal.* To make, achieve, or get by contrivance: *wangle an invitation to the exclusive party.*

Wan•kel engine (väng′kəl *or* wăng′kəl) *n.* An internal-combustion engine in which a turning triangular rotor carries out the functions performed by the pistons of a conventional engine, resulting in

Wainscot; paneling. **2.** Material, such as wood, used as wainscot or paneling.

waist (wāst) *n.* **1.** The part of the human body between the bottom of the rib cage and the pelvis. **2.** The part of a garment that fits around the waist or that covers the upper body from the neck or shoulders to the waist. **3.** The slender part of the abdomen of various insects, such as wasps, ants, and some flies.

❑ *These sound alike:* **waist, waste** (squander).

waist•band (wāst′bănd′) *n.* A band of material encircling and fitting the waist of a garment, such as trousers.

waist•coat (wĕs′kĭt *or* wāst′kōt′) *n. Chiefly British.* A vest.

waist•line (wāst′līn′) *n.* **1.** A line thought of as encircling the body at the waist. **2.** The point or line at which the skirt and bodice of a dress join.

wait (wāt) *v.* **wait•ed, wait•ing, waits.** *—intr.* **1.** To remain or rest in expectation: *waiting for the guests to arrive.* See Synonyms at **stay**[1]. **2.** To pause or tarry until another catches up: *Wait for me!* **3.** To remain temporarily neglected, unattended to, or postponed: *Dinner will have to wait.* **4.** To work serving tables, as in a restaurant or a private home. *—tr.* **1.** To remain or stay in expectation of; await: *Wait your turn.* **2.** To be waiter or waitress at: *wait tables.* *—n.* The act of waiting or a period of time spent in waiting: *a short wait.* ***—idioms.*** **wait on** or **wait upon. 1.** To serve the needs of; be in attendance on. **2.** To await: *They're waiting on my decision.* **wait up. 1.** To postpone going to bed in anticipation of something or someone: *Let's wait up to watch the late show.* **2.** *Informal.* To stop or pause so that another can catch up: *They got too far ahead, so I yelled to them to wait up.* [First written down before 1200 in Middle English and spelled *waiten,* from Old North French *waitier,* to watch, of Germanic origin.]

❑ *These sound alike:* **wait, weight** (gravity force).

wait•er (wā′tər) *n.* A man who serves at a table, as in a restaurant.

wait•ing (wā′tĭng) *n.* The act of remaining inactive or stationary. ***—idiom.*** **in waiting.** In attendance, especially at a royal court.

waiting list *n.* A list of people waiting, as for an appointment or a table at a restaurant.

waiting room *n.* A room, as in a railroad station or doctor's office, for the use of people waiting.

wait•ress (wā′trĭs) *n.* A woman who serves at a table, as in a restaurant.

waive (wāv) *tr.v.* **waived, waiv•ing, waives. 1.** To give up (a right or claim) by one's own choice: *waive a jury trial.* See Synonyms at **yield. 2.** To set aside, dispense with, or postpone: *Let's waive the formalities and start the discussion.*

❑ *These sound alike:* **waive, wave** (swell).

waiv•er (wā′vər) *n.* **1.** The intentional giving up of a right, claim, or privilege. **2.** A written agreement to give up such a right, claim, or privilege.

❑ *These sound alike:* **waiver, waver** (vacillate).

Wa•kash•an (wä kăsh′ən *or* wô′kə shăn′) *n.* A family of Native American languages spoken by the peoples of Washington and British Columbia.

wake[1] (wāk) *v.* **woke** (wōk) or **waked** (wākt), **waked** or **wok•en** (wō′kən), **wak•ing, wakes.** *—intr.* **1.** To cease to sleep; become awake: *I woke before daybreak.* **2.** To remain awake: *Whether he sleeps or wakes, her little brother hugs his teddy bear.* *—tr.* To rouse from sleep or stir, as from an inactive condition: *Wake me at nine o'clock.* *—n.* A watch or vigil kept over the body of a dead person before the burial. [First written down about 1200 in Middle English and spelled *wakien, waken,* from Old English *wacan,* to wake up, and *wacian,* to be awake, keep watch.] —See Notes.

wake[2] (wāk) *n.* **1.** The visible track of waves, ripples, or foam left behind something moving through water: *the wake of a ship.* **2.** The course, track, or condition left behind something that has passed: *The hurricane left destruction in its wake.* [First written down before 1500 in Middle English, possibly from Middle Low German *wake,* hole in the ice, of Scandinavian origin.]

wake•ful (wāk′fəl) *adj.* **1.** Not sleeping or not able to sleep. **2.** Without sleep; sleepless: *a wakeful night.*

wak•en (wā′kən) *v.* **wak•ened, wak•en•ing, wak•ens.** *—tr.* **1.** To rouse from sleep; awake. **2.** To stir, as from an inactive state. *—intr.* To become awake; wake up. —See Note at **wake**[1].

Wald•heim (wôld′hīm′), **Kurt.** Born 1918. Austrian politician who served as secretary-general of the United Nations (1972–1981) and president of Austria (since 1986) despite his alleged Nazi affiliations during World War II.

wale (wāl) *n.* **1.** A mark raised on the skin, as by a lash or blow; a welt. **2.** One of the parallel ribs or ridges in the surface of a fabric such as corduroy. *—tr.v.* **waled, wal•ing, wales.** To raise marks on (the skin), as by whipping.

❑ *These sound alike:* **wale, wail** (cry), **whale** (sea mammal).

Wales (wālz). A principality of the United Kingdom on the western peninsula of the island of Great Britain. Wales has maintained its own distinct culture and a strong nationalist sentiment. Capital, Cardiff. Population, 2,790,462.

walk (wôk) *v.* **walked, walk•ing, walks.** *—intr.* **1.** To move over a surface by taking steps with the feet at a pace slower than a run: *The baby is just learning to walk.* **2.** To go or travel on foot: *I walked to school.* **3.** To go on foot for pleasure or exercise; stroll: *walk in the park.* **4.** To move in a way that resembles or suggests walking: *an astronaut walking in space.* **5.** In baseball, to go to first base after the pitcher has thrown four balls. *—tr.* **1.** To go or pass over, on, or through by walking: *walking the historic section of the city.* **2.** To cause to walk or go at a walk: *walk a horse uphill.* **3.** To accompany in walking; escort on foot: *We walked her to the bus stop.* **4.** In baseball, to allow (a batter) to go to first base by pitching four balls. *—n.* **1.** The gait of a human being or two-footed animal in which the feet are lifted alternately with one part of a foot always on the ground. **2.** The gait of a four-footed animal in which at least two feet are always touching the ground. **3.** A stroll or journey on foot. **4.** A pathway or sidewalk on which to walk: *shovel snow off the walk.* **5.** An act, way, or speed of walking: *a waddling walk; a brisk walk.* **6.** In baseball, a base on balls. ***—idioms.*** **walk on air.** To feel elated: *I was walking on air after I heard the good news.* **walk out.** To leave suddenly, often as a signal of disapproval. **walk out on.** To desert or abandon. **walk over.** *Informal.* To treat badly or contemptuously.

walk•er (wô′kər) *n.* **1.** A person who walks, especially a contestant in a footrace. **2.** A frame used to support someone while walking, as an infant learning to walk or a person recovering from an injury.

walk•ie-talk•ie (wô′kē tô′kē) *n., pl.* **walk•ie-talk•ies.** A battery-powered portable radio set for sending and receiving messages.

walk•ing stick (wô′kĭng) *n.* **1.** A cane or stick, used as an aid in walking. **2.** Any of several brown to greenish insects that resemble sticks or twigs.

walk-on (wôk′ŏn′ *or* wôk′ôn′) *n.* **1.** A minor role in

Regional Note: wake[1]

People who live in the northern United States seem to favor verb forms that change the internal vowel—hence *dove* for the past tense of **dive** and *woke* for **wake**. Southerners tend to prefer forms that add an *-ed,* hence the forms *dived* and *waked.*

Usage: wake[1]

The pairs **wake/waken** and **awake/awaken** have bewildered people for centuries. All four words have similar meanings, though there are some differences in use. Only **wake** is used in the sense "to be awake," as in expressions such as *every waking hour.* **Wake** is also more common than **waken** when used together with *up.* **Awake** and **awaken** are never used this way: *She woke up* (rarely *wakened up;* never *awakened up* or *awoke up*). In figurative senses *awake* and *awaken* are more common: *awoke to the danger; awakened my memory.*

walkie-talkie

ă	pat	oi	boy
ā	pay	ou	out
âr	care	ŏŏ	took
ä	father	ōō	boot
ĕ	pet	ŭ	cut
ē	be	ûr	urge
ĭ	pit	th	thin
ī	pie	*th*	this
îr	pier	hw	whoop
ŏ	pot	zh	vision
ō	toe	ə	about
ô	paw	N	*French*

lighter weight and fewer moving parts. [First written down in 1961 in Modern English, after Felix *Wankel* (1902–1988), German engineer.]

want (wŏnt *or* wônt) *v.* **want•ed, want•ing, wants.** —*tr.* **1.** To desire greatly; wish for: *They wanted to play outdoors. He wants a guitar.* See Synonyms at **desire. 2.a.** To be in need of; require: *The grass wants cutting.* **b.** To be without; lack: *That speech wants wit.* **3.** To seek with the intent to capture or arrest as a lawbreaker: *The fugitive is wanted by the police.* —*intr.* **1.** To have need: *They want for nothing.* **2.** To be destitute or needy. **3.** To be disposed; wish: *Stop by if you want.* —*n.* **1.** The condition or quality of lacking something usual or necessary. **2.** Pressing need; destitution. **3.** Something desired: *has many wants.* [First written down about 1200 in Middle English and spelled *wanten*, to be lacking, from Old Norse *vanta*.]

want ad *n. Informal.* A classified advertisement.

wan•ton (wŏn′tən) *adj.* **1.** Unnecessarily cruel; merciless: *wanton killing.* **2.** Marked by a disregard for morals or justice; unjust: *wanton destruction.* **3.** Unrestrained; excessive: *wanton luxury.* **4.** Lewd or indecent. **—wan′ton•ly** *adv.* **—wan′ton•ness** *n.*

wap•i•ti (wŏp′ĭ tē) *n., pl.* **wapiti** or **wap•i•tis.** A large North American deer having long branching antlers.

war (wôr) *n.* **1.** A state of open armed conflict carried on between nations, states, or parties. **2.** The techniques or procedures of war; military science. **3.** A serious determined struggle or attack on something considered injurious: *declared a war on poverty.* —*intr.v.* **warred, war•ring, wars. 1.** To wage or carry on warfare. **2.** To struggle, contend, or fight. [First written down before 1121 in Middle English and spelled *wirre*, from Old North French *werre*, of Germanic origin.]

War Between the States *n.* The Civil War.

war•ble (wôr′bəl) *tr. & intr.v.* **war•bled, war•bling, war•bles.** To sing with trills, runs, or other melodic sounds. —*n.* The act or an instance of singing with trills, runs, or quavers.

war•bler (wôr′blər) *n.* Any of various small songbirds, of which those of North America often have brightly colored feathers or markings.

war bonnet *n.* A ceremonial headdress used by some Plains Indians, having a trailing extension decorated with feathers.

war crime *n.* Any of various crimes, such as genocide, committed during a war and considered in violation of the conventions of warfare.

ward (wôrd) *n.* **1.** An administrative division of a city or town, especially an election district. **2.a.** A large hospital room usually shared by six or more patients. **b.** A section of a hospital devoted to the care of a particular group of patients: *a maternity ward.* **3.** A person, especially a minor, placed under the care or protection of a guardian or court. —*tr.v.* **ward•ed, ward•ing, wards.** To guard; protect. ***—idiom.*** **ward off.** To turn aside; repel: *I warded off the bothersome insects by building a fire.* [First written down about 725 in Old English, action of guarding.]

—ward or **—wards** *suff.* A suffix that means: **1.** In a specified direction in time or space: *downward.* **2.** Toward a specified place or position: *homeward.* —SEE NOTE.

war•den (wôr′dn) *n.* **1.** An official in charge of a prison. **2.** An official who enforces certain laws, such as hunting, fishing, or fire regulations: *a game warden; a fire warden.*

ward•er (wôr′dər) *n.* A guard, porter, or watcher of a gate or tower.

ward•robe (wôr′drōb′) *n.* **1.** A cabinet, closet, or small room for holding clothes. **2.** Articles of clothing considered as a group, especially all the pieces of clothing belonging to one person.

—wards *suff.* Variant of **—ward.**

ware (wâr) *n.* **1.** Articles of the same general kind, made of a given material or used in a specific application: *silverware; hardware.* **2.** An article for sale: *people displaying their wares in the market.*
❑ *These sound alike:* **ware, wear** (have on).

ware•house (wâr′hous′) *n.* A place in which goods or articles of merchandise are stored; a storehouse.

war•fare (wôr′fâr′) *n.* **1.** The waging of war against an enemy; armed conflict. **2.** A special type or method of military operation: *guerrilla warfare.* **3.** A state of disharmony or conflict; strife.

war•head (wôr′hĕd′) *n.* A section in the forward part of a bomb, missile, or torpedo that contains the explosive charge.

war•horse (wôr′hôrs′) *n.* **1.** A horse used in combat. **2.** *Informal.* A person who has been through many battles, struggles, or fights.

war•like (wôr′līk′) *adj.* **1.** Belligerent; hostile: *a warlike people.* **2.** Of or relating to war; martial. **3.** Threatening or indicating war: *a warlike call to arms.*

war•lock (wôr′lŏk′) *n.* A male witch, sorcerer, wizard, or demon. [First written down before 900 in Old English and spelled *wǣrloga*, oath-breaker : *wǣr*, pledge + *-loga*, liar.]

war•lord (wôr′lôrd′) *n.* A military leader who has control over a region.

warm (wôrm) *adj.* **warm•er, warm•est. 1.** Moderately hot; neither cool nor very hot: *warm weather; warm air.* **2.** Giving off or keeping in heat: *the warm sun; a warm sweater.* **3.** Having or causing a feeling of unusually high body heat, as from exercise or hard work. **4.** Enthusiastic, friendly, cordial, or sincere: *a warm smile; warm greetings.* **5.** Characterized by liveliness, excitement, or disagreement; heated: *a warm debate.* **6.** Predominantly red or yellow in tone: *a warm sunset.* **7.** In certain games, close to discovering, guessing, or finding something. —*tr. & intr.v.* **warmed, warm•ing, warms.** To make or become warm or warmer; heat up. ***—idiom.*** **warm up. 1.** To prepare for an athletic event by exercising, stretching, or practicing for a short time beforehand. **2.** To make or become ready for an event or operation: *warmed up for her speech by practicing the opening lines.* [First written down before 899 in Old English and spelled *wearm*.] **—warm′ly** *adv.* **—warm′ness** *n.*

warm-blood•ed (wôrm′blŭd′ĭd) *adj.* **1.** Having a relatively warm body temperature that stays about the same regardless of changes in the temperature of the surroundings. Birds and mammals are warm-blooded. **2.** Full of feeling; passionate. **—warm′-blood′ed•ness** *n.*

warm front *n.* A front along which an advancing mass of warm air rises over a mass of cold air.

warm-heart•ed (wôrm′här′tĭd) *adj.* Characterized by kindness, sympathy, and generosity.

warm•ing pan (wôr′mĭng) *n.* A covered metal pan on a long handle, filled with hot coals and used to warm a bed.

war•mon•ger (wôr′mŭng′gər *or* wôr′mŏng′gər) *n.* A person who advocates or tries to stir up war.

warmth (wôrmth) *n.* **1.** The state or quality of being warm; moderate heat. **2.** The sensation of moderate heat. **3.** Friendliness, kindness, or affection: *a person of great warmth.* **4.** Excitement or intensity, as of love or passion: *warmth of feeling.*

warm-up or **warm•up** (wôrm′ŭp′) *n.* **1.** The act or procedure of warming up. **2.** A period spent in warming up.

warn (wôrn) *v.* **warned, warn•ing, warns.** —*tr.* **1.** To make aware in advance of present or approach-

wapiti

Word Building: —ward

The basic meaning of the suffix **—ward** is "having a particular direction or location." Its use dates back to Old English. Thus **inward** means "directed or located inside." Other examples are **outward**, **forward**, **backward**, **upward**, **downward**, **earthward**, **homeward**, **northward**, **southward**, **eastward**, and **westward**. The suffix **—ward** forms adjectives and adverbs. Adverbs ending in **—ward** can also end in **—wards**. Thus *I stepped backward* and *I stepped backwards* are both correct. Only **backward** is an adjective: *a backward glance.*

ă	**pat**	oi	**boy**
ā	**pay**	ou	**out**
âr	**care**	ŏŏ	**took**
ä	**father**	ōō	**boot**
ĕ	**pet**	ŭ	**cut**
ē	**be**	ûr	**urge**
ĭ	**pit**	th	**thin**
ī	**pie**	*th*	**this**
îr	**pier**	hw	**whoop**
ŏ	**pot**	zh	**vision**
ō	**toe**	ə	**about**
ô	**paw**	N	*French* **bon**

wart hog

Washington

The state of **Washington** is named after George Washington, the first President of the United States. It is the only state that is named after a United States President.

Booker T. Washington
c. 1895 photograph
by Elmer Chickering
(d. 1915)

ing danger, harm, or evil: *warned the sailors of bad weather.* **2.** To advise, caution, or counsel: *We warned them to be careful.* —*intr.* To give a warning. [First written down before 1000 in Old English and spelled *warnian.*]

warn•ing (wôr′nĭng) *n.* **1.** A sign, indication, notice, or threat of coming danger: *The dog's low growl was a warning.* **2.** Advice to beware or to stop a given course of action. **3.** Something, such as a signal, that warns: *Without warning the shelf collapsed.*

warp (wôrp) *v.* **warped, warp•ing, warps.** —*tr.* **1.** To turn or twist (wood, for example) out of shape. **2.** To turn from a true or proper course. **3.** To affect unfavorably, unfairly, or wrongly; bias: *The fear of losing his fortune warped his personality.* **4.** To move (a ship) by hauling on a line that is fastened to a piling, an anchor, or a pier. —*intr.* **1.** To become bent or twisted out of shape: *Left in the damp basement, the boards warped.* **2.** To turn aside from a true, correct, or natural course; go astray. **3.** To move a ship by hauling on a line that is fastened to a piling, an anchor, or a pier. —*n.* **1.** A bend or twist, especially in a piece of wood. **2.** A mental or moral twist or quirk. **3.** The threads that run lengthwise in a woven fabric, crossed at right angles to the woof. [First written down about 725 in Old English and spelled *weorpan,* to throw away.]

war•path (wôr′păth′) *n.* A course that leads to battle or warfare.

war•rant (wôr′ənt *or* wŏr′ənt) *n.* **1.** Authorization or certification; sanction: *The school board gave the teachers its warrant to try new methods.* **2.** Justification, as for an action or opinion; grounds: *What warrant does he have for feeling this way?* **3.** A guarantee or proof: *Casting her in the leading role was a warrant of the movie's success.* **4.** An official written order authorizing something, such as an arrest, a search, or a seizure: *a search warrant.* —*tr.v.* **war•rant•ed, war•rant•ing, war•rants.** **1.** To guarantee: *warrant a product.* **2.** To call for, justify, or merit: *There is enough evidence to warrant a trial.*

warrant officer *n.* A military officer, usually a technician, having a rank between a noncommissioned officer and a commissioned officer.

war•ran•ty (wôr′ən tē *or* wŏr′ən tē) *n., pl.* **war•ran•ties.** **1.** Official guarantee, authorization, or justification. **2.** A guarantee given to a buyer by a company stating that the product sold is as represented and that repairs will be made without charge if certain defects are found within a stated period of time. [First written down before 1338 in Middle English and spelled *warantie,* from Old North French, from *warantir,* to guarantee.]

war•ren (wôr′ən *or* wŏr′ən) *n.* **1.** An area where rabbits live in burrows. **2.** An enclosure for small game animals. **3.** An overcrowded place where people live.

War•ren (wôr′ən *or* wŏr′ən), **Earl.** 1891–1974. American jurist who served as the chief justice of the U.S. Supreme Court (1953–1969).

war•ri•or (wôr′ē ər *or* wŏr′ē ər) *n.* A person who is or has been in battle.

War•saw (wôr′sô′). The capital of Poland, in the east-central part of the country southeast of Gdańsk. Founded in the 13th century, it became the capital in 1596. Most of Warsaw's Jewish residents were executed during the German occupation in World War II. Population, 1,649,000.

wart (wôrt) *n.* **1.** A hard rough lump growing on the skin, caused by a virus. **2.** A similar growth, as on a plant.

wart hog *n.* A wild African hog having tusks and growths resembling warts on the face.

war•time (wôr′tīm′) *n.* A period during which a war is in progress.

war•y (wâr′ē) *adj.* **war•i•er, war•i•est.** **1.** On guard; watchful: *We were wary of mistakes in our experiment.* **2.** Characterized by caution: *a wary look.*

was (wŭz *or* wŏz; wəz *when unstressed*) *v.* First and third person singular past tense of **be.**

wash (wŏsh *or* wôsh) *v.* **washed, wash•ing, wash•es.** —*tr.* **1.** To clean by using water or another liquid and often soap or detergent: *wash dishes.* **2.** To soak, rinse out, and remove (dirt or stain) with or as if with water: *wash dirt out of the jeans.* **3.** To flow over and wet with water: *The waves washed the sandy shores.* **4.** To carry or remove or be carried or removed by the action of moving water: *Rain falls and washes the soil downhill.* **5.** To cover (a painting, for example) with a watery layer of paint or other coloring. **6.** To pour or shake water through (gravel, sand, or crushed ore) to separate out valuable material: *wash gravel for gold.* —*intr.* **1.** To clean something in or by means of water or other liquid. **2.** To undergo washing without fading or other damage: *Cotton washes well.* **3.** To flow, sweep, or beat with a lapping sound: *Waves washed over the rocks.* —*n.* **1.** The act or process of washing or cleansing. **2.** A batch of articles washed or intended for washing. **3.a.** A liquid preparation used in cleansing or coating something, as mouthwash or whitewash. **b.** A thin coating, as of water color or whitewash. **4.** A turbulent flow of air or water caused by the passage or action of a boat, aircraft, oar, or propeller. ***—idioms.*** **come out in the wash.** *Slang.* To be revealed eventually. **wash down.** To follow the ingestion of (food, for example) with the ingestion of a liquid: *washed down the chips with some juice.* **wash (one's) hands of.** To refuse to accept responsibility for: *I washed my hands of the problem.* **wash out.** To remove or be removed by washing: *That stain will wash out easily.* **wash up.** To wash one's hands. [First written down in 900 in Old English and spelled *wacsan, wæscan.*]

Wash. *abbr.* An abbreviation of Washington.

wash•a•ble (wŏsh′ə bəl *or* wôsh′ə bəl) *adj.* Capable of being washed without fading or other damage: *a washable skirt.*

wash-and-wear (wŏsh′ən wâr′ *or* wôsh′ən wâr′) *adj.* Treated so as to be easily washed and to require little or no ironing: *a wash-and-wear shirt.*

wash•ba•sin (wŏsh′bā′sən *or* wôsh′bā′sən) *n.* A washbowl.

wash•board (wŏsh′bôrd′ *or* wôsh′bôrd′) *n.* **1.** A board having a ridged surface on which clothes can be rubbed in laundering. **2.** Such a board used as a percussion instrument.

wash•bowl (wŏsh′bōl′ *or* wôsh′bōl′) *n.* A basin that can be filled with water for use in washing oneself; a washbasin.

wash•cloth (wŏsh′klôth′ *or* wŏsh′klŏth′ *or* wôsh′klôth′ *or* wôsh′klŏth′) *n.* A small cloth of absorbent material used for washing the face or body.

washed-out (wŏsht′out′ *or* wôsht′out′) *adj.* **1.** Lacking color or intensity; faded. **2.** Exhausted or tired-looking.

washed-up (wŏsht′ŭp′ *or* wôsht′ŭp′) *adj.* No longer successful or needed; finished.

wash•er (wŏsh′ər *or* wô′shər) *n.* **1.** A person who washes: *a washer of windows.* **2.** A washing machine. **3.** An automatic dishwasher. **4.** A small disk, as of metal or rubber, placed under a nut or at an axle bearing or a joint to relieve friction, prevent leakage, or distribute pressure.

wash•ing (wŏsh′ĭng *or* wô′shĭng) *n.* **1.** The act or process of one that washes. **2.** A batch of clothes or linens washed or intended to be washed at one time.

washing machine *n.* A usually automatic machine for washing clothes and linens.

washing soda *n.* A form of sodium carbonate used as a general cleanser.

Wash•ing•ton (wŏsh′ĭng tən *or* wô′shĭng tən). **1.** A state of the northwest United States on the Pacific Ocean north of Oregon. It was admitted as the 42nd state in 1889. Olympia is the capital and Seattle the largest city. Population, 4,132,204. **2.** The capital of the United States, on the Potomac River between Virginia and Maryland and having the same boundaries as the District of Columbia. It became the capital in 1800. Population, 609,909. —SEE NOTE.

Washington, Booker T(aliaferro). 1856–1915. American educator. Born into slavery, he acquired an education after emancipation and founded Tuskegee Institute (1881), an industrial college for Blacks.

Washington, George. 1732–1799. American military leader and the first President of the United States (1789–1797). Washington served as Commander of the American forces in the Revolutionary War (1775–1783).

Washington, Martha Dandridge Custis. 1731–1802. First Lady of the United States (1789–1797) as the wife of President George Washington.

Wash•ing•ton's Birthday (wŏsh′ĭng tənz *or* wô′shĭng tənz) *n.* February 22, formerly observed to commemorate the birth of George Washington in 1732. This holiday is now included in the observances of Presidents' Day.

wash•out (wŏsh′out′ *or* wôsh′out′) *n.* **1.** Erosion of a relatively soft surface, such as an embankment, by a sudden gush of water. **2.** A total failure or disappointment.

wash•rag (wŏsh′răg′ *or* wôsh′răg′) *n.* A washcloth.

wash•room (wŏsh′ro͝om′ *or* wŏsh′ro͞om′ *or* wôsh′ro͝om′ *or* wôsh′ro͞om′) *n.* A bathroom, especially one in a public place.

wash•stand (wŏsh′stănd′ *or* wôsh′stănd′) *n.* **1.** A stand used to hold a basin and pitcher of water for washing. **2.** A bathroom sink.

wash•tub (wŏsh′tŭb′ *or* wôsh′tŭb′) *n.* A tub used for washing clothes.

was•n't (wŭz′ənt *or* wŏz′ənt). Contraction of *was not.*

wasp (wŏsp *or* wôsp) *n.* Any of numerous insects having a body with a narrow midsection and two pairs of wings and often capable of giving a painful sting. [First written down about 700 in Old English and spelled *wæps, wæsp.*]

Wasp or **WASP** *n.* A white Protestant of Anglo-Saxon ancestry.

wasp•ish (wŏs′pĭsh) *adj.* **1.** Of, relating to, or typical of a wasp. **2.** Easily irritated or annoyed; snappish. **—wasp′ish•ly** *adv.* **—wasp′ish•ness** *n.*

was•sail (wŏs′əl *or* wŏ săl′) *n.* **1.** A toast given in drinking someone's health or as an expression of good will on festive occasions. **2.** The drink used in such toasting, commonly spiced ale or wine. **3.** A festivity with much drinking. *—tr.v.* **was•sailed, was•sail•ing, was•sails.** To drink to the health of; toast.

wast (wŏst; wəst *when unstressed*) *v. Archaic.* A second person singular past tense of **be.**

waste (wāst) *v.* **wast•ed, wast•ing, wastes.** *—tr.* **1.** To spend, consume, use, or expend foolishly or needlessly; squander: *waste food by leaving it out to spoil; wasted energy by leaving the heat on all night.* **2.** To cause to lose strength, energy, or vigor: *Disease wasted his body.* **3.** To fail to take advantage of or use for profit; lose: *wasted my chance.* **4.** To destroy completely. *—intr.* **1.** To lose energy, strength, weight, or vigor: *wasting away with hunger.* **2.** To pass without being put to use: *Time is wasting.* *—n.* **1.** The act or an instance of wasting or the condition of being wasted: *a waste of resources.* **2.** An area, a region, or a land that is uninhabited or uncultivated; a desert or wilderness. **3.** A worthless or useless byproduct, as from a manufacturing process: *industrial wastes.* **4.** Garbage; trash. **5.** The material that remains after food has been digested and that is eliminated from the body. ***—idiom.*** **waste (one's) breath.** To gain or accomplish nothing by speaking: *Don't waste your breath arguing; the decision's been made.* [First written down before 1200 in Middle English and spelled *wasten,* from Latin *vāstāre,* to make empty.]

❑ *These sound alike:* **waste, waist** (body part).

waste•bas•ket (wāst′băs′kĭt) *n.* An open container for rubbish.

waste•ful (wāst′fəl) *adj.* Characterized by or inclined to waste; extravagant: *wasteful use of resources; a wasteful method.* **—waste′ful•ly** *adv.* **—waste′ful•ness** *n.*

waste•land (wāst′lănd′) *n.* Land that is desolate, barren, or ravaged.

waste•pa•per (wāst′pā′pər) *n.* Discarded paper.

wast•ing (wā′stĭng) *adj.* **1.** Gradually deteriorating; declining. **2.** Sapping the energy, strength, or substance of the body: *a wasting disease.*

wast•rel (wā′strəl) *n.* A person who wastes, especially one who wastes money. [First written down about 1589 in Modern English : *wast(e)* + *-rel* (as in *scoundrel*).]

watch (wŏch) *v.* **watched, watch•ing, watch•es.** *—intr.* **1.** To look or observe closely or attentively: *Passers-by stopped to watch as the parade went by.* **2.** To look and wait expectantly or in anticipation: *watch for an opportunity.* **3.** To stay awake at night while serving as a guard, sentinel, or watcher. **4.** To keep vigil. *—tr.* **1.** To look steadily; observe carefully: *watched the pianist's hands as she played.* **2.** To keep a watchful eye on; guard. **3.** To tend (a flock or child, for example). *—n.* **1.** The act or process of keeping awake or mentally alert, especially for the purpose of guarding. **2.** The act of closely observing or the condition of being closely observed; surveillance. **3.** A person or group of people serving to guard or protect. **4.** The post or period of duty of a guard, sentinel, or watcher. **5.** A period of wakefulness, especially one observed as a religious vigil. **6.** A small portable timepiece, especially one worn on the wrist or carried in the pocket. ***—idioms.*** **watch it.** To be careful. **watch (one's) step. 1.** To act or proceed with care and caution. **2.** To behave as it is demanded, required, or appropriate. **watch out.** To be careful or on the alert; take care. **watch over.** To be in charge of; superintend. [First written down about 725 in Old English and spelled *wæccan,* to watch, be awake.]

watch•dog (wŏch′dôg′ *or* wŏch′dŏg′) *n.* **1.** A dog trained to protect people or property. **2.** A person or group who guards or protects against waste, loss, or illegal practices.

watch•er (wŏch′ər) *n.* A person or thing that watches or observes: *a watcher of local politics.*

watch•ful (wŏch′fəl) *adj.* Closely observant or alert. **—watch′ful•ly** *adv.* **—watch′ful•ness** *n.*

watch•mak•er (wŏch′mā′kər) *n.* A person who makes or repairs watches. **—watch′mak′ing** *n.*

watch•man (wŏch′mən) *n.* A man employed to stand guard or keep watch.

watch•tow•er (wŏch′tou′ər) *n.* An observation tower on which a guard or lookout is stationed to keep watch.

watch•word (wŏch′wûrd′) *n.* **1.** A secret word or

George Washington
1795 portrait by Rembrandt Peale (1778–1860)

Martha Washington
Early 19th-century portrait by an unknown artist

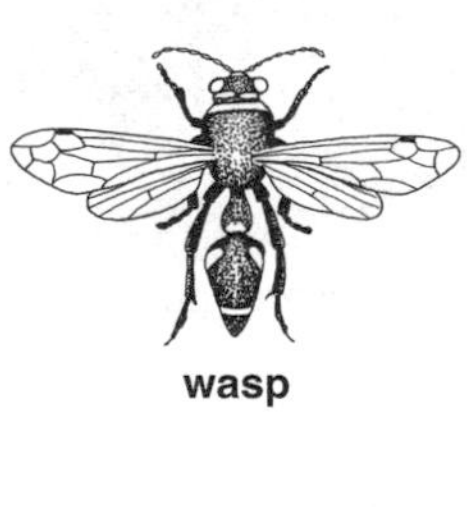

wasp

ă	pat	oi	boy
ā	pay	ou	out
âr	care	o͝o	took
ä	father	o͞o	boot
ĕ	pet	ŭ	cut
ē	be	ûr	urge
ĭ	pit	th	thin
ī	pie	*th*	this
îr	pier	hw	whoop
ŏ	pot	zh	vision
ō	toe	ə	about
ô	paw	N	*French* bon

waterbuck

water polo

phrase that one uses to identify oneself as friendly or accepted; a password. **2.** A motto used as a call for support; a rallying cry.

wa•ter (wô′tər *or* wŏt′ər) *n.* **1.** A compound of hydrogen and oxygen having the formula H_2O, occurring as a liquid that covers about three-quarters of the earth's surface and also in solid form as ice and in gaseous form as steam. Water freezes at 32°F (0°C) and boils at 212°F (100°C). **2.** A body of water such as a sea, lake, river, or stream. **3. waters.** A particular stretch of sea or ocean, especially that of a state or country. **4.** A supply of water: *Turn off the water when you're through.* **5.** Any of various forms of water: *waste water; sparkling water.* **6.** Mineral water. Often used in the plural. **7.** Any of various watery substances or secretions occurring in or discharged from the body, as sweat, saliva, or urine. —*v.* **wa•tered, wa•ter•ing, wa•ters.** —*tr.* **1.** To sprinkle, moisten, or supply with water: *water the garden.* **2.** To give drinking water to: *water the horses.* **3.** To mix or dilute with water: *water the wine.* —*intr.* **1.** To produce or discharge fluid, as from the eyes. **2.** To salivate in anticipation of food: *My mouth watered when I smelled the fresh bread.* —***idioms.*** **water down.** To reduce the strength or effectiveness of: *had to water down the sweet syrup.* **water under the bridge.** A past occurrence, especially something unfortunate, that cannot be undone or made right. [First written down before 899 in Old English and spelled *wæter.*]

water bird *n.* A swimming or wading bird.

wa•ter•borne (wô′tər bôrn′ *or* wŏt′ər bôrn′) *adj.* **1.** Floating on or supported by water; afloat. **2.** Transported by water.

wa•ter•buck (wô′tər bŭk′ *or* wŏt′ər bŭk′) *n., pl.* **waterbuck** or **wa•ter•bucks.** Any of several African antelopes having curved ridged horns and living near bodies of water.

water buffalo *n.* An Asian buffalo having large spreading horns that is often domesticated, especially for pulling or carrying loads.

water bug *n.* **1.** Any of various insects that live in water or wet places. **2.** A large cockroach.

water chestnut *n.* **1.a.** A tropical Asian water plant having a crisp edible underground stem that resembles a bulb. **b.** The underground stem of this plant, used in Asian cookery. **2.** A floating Asian water plant having fruit that resembles a nut.

water closet *n.* A room or booth containing a toilet and often a sink.

wa•ter•col•or (wô′tər kŭl′ər *or* wŏt′ər kŭl′ər) *n.* **1.** A paint in which water instead of oil is mixed with the coloring material before use. **2.** A work done in this paint. **3.** The art of using watercolors.

water cooler *n.* A device for cooling and dispensing drinking water.

wa•ter•course (wô′tər kôrs′ *or* wŏt′ər kôrs′) *n.* A natural or artificial channel through which water flows.

wa•ter•craft (wô′tər krăft′ *or* wŏt′ər krăft′) *n.* **1.** Skill in water-related sports. **2.** A boat or ship. **3.** Water vehicles considered as a group.

wa•ter•cress (wô′tər krĕs′ *or* wŏt′ər krĕs′) *n.* A plant that grows in freshwater ponds and streams and has strong-tasting leaves used in salads and as a garnish.

wa•ter•fall (wô′tər fôl′ *or* wŏt′ər fôl′) *n.* A natural stream of water descending from a height.

wa•ter•fowl (wô′tər foul′ *or* wŏt′ər foul′) *n.* A water bird, especially a swimming bird.

wa•ter•front (wô′tər frŭnt′ *or* wŏt′ər frŭnt′) *n.* **1.** Land that borders a body of water. **2.** The part of a town or city that borders the water, especially a wharf district where ships dock.

water gap *n.* A valley cutting across a mountain ridge through which a stream flows.

water hole *n.* A small natural depression in which water collects, especially a pool where animals come to drink.

wa•ter•ing can (wô′tər ĭng *or* wŏt′ər ĭng) *n.* A watering pot.

watering place *n.* A place where animals find water to drink.

watering pot *pl.n.* A vessel, usually having a long spout with a perforated nozzle, used to water plants.

water lily *n.* Any of various water plants having broad floating leaves and showy variously colored flowers.

water line *n.* **1.** The line on the hull of a ship to which the surface of the water rises. **2.** A mark or stain, as one left on a seawall, indicating the level to which water has risen or may rise.

wa•ter•logged (wô′tər lôgd′ *or* wô′tər lŏgd′ *or* wŏt′ər lôgd′ *or* wŏt′ər lŏgd′) *adj.* **1.** Heavy and slow-moving because it is full of water: *a waterlogged ship.* **2.** Soaked or saturated with water: *a waterlogged field.*

Wa•ter•loo (wô′tər lo͞o′ *or* wŏt′ər lo͞o′). A town of central Belgium near Brussels. Napoleon met his final defeat in the Battle of Waterloo (June 18, 1815).

water main *n.* A principal pipe in a system of pipes for conveying water.

wa•ter•mark (wô′tər märk′ *or* wŏt′ər märk′) *n.* **1.a.** A mark showing the height to which water has risen. **b.** A line indicating the heights of high and low tide. **2.** A design impressed on paper during manufacture and visible when the paper is held up to light.

wa•ter•mel•on (wô′tər mĕl′ən *or* wŏt′ər mĕl′ən) *n.* **1.** An often very large melon having a hard green rind and sweet, watery, pink or reddish flesh. **2.** The vine that bears such fruit.

water mill *n.* A mill with machinery that is driven by water.

water moccasin *n.* A poisonous snake of swampy regions of the southern United States.

water of crystallization *n.* Water combined with other substances to form a crystal, capable of being removed by sufficient heat.

water polo *n.* A water sport played by two teams of swimmers who try to throw a ball into the opponents' goal.

wa•ter•pow•er (wô′tər pou′ər *or* wŏt′ər pou′ər) *n.* The energy produced by falling or running water that is used for driving machinery or generating electricity.

wa•ter•proof (wô′tər pro͞of′ *or* wŏt′ər pro͞of′) *adj.* **1.** Capable of keeping water from coming through. **2.** Made of or treated with a substance to prevent penetration by water. —*n.* **1.** A waterproof material or fabric. **2.** *Chiefly British.* A raincoat. —*tr.v.* **wa•ter•proofed, wa•ter•proof•ing, wa•ter•proofs.** To make waterproof.

wa•ter•proof•ing (wô′tər pro͞o′fĭng *or* wŏt′ər pro͞o′fĭng) *n.* A substance applied to something to prevent the penetration of water.

water rat *n.* **1.** Any of various rodents closely related to and resembling the muskrat that live near bodies of water. **2.** The muskrat.

wa•ter-re•pel•lent (wô′tər rĭ pĕl′ənt *or* wŏt′ər rĭ pĕl′ənt) *adj.* Resistant to penetration by water but not entirely waterproof.

wa•ter•shed (wô′tər shĕd′ *or* wŏt′ər shĕd′) *n.* **1.** A ridge forming the boundary between regions whose water drains into two different systems of rivers. **2.** The region draining into a river, river system, or other body of water. **3.** A turning point in a course of events.

water ski *n.* A broad ski used for skiing on water.

wa•ter-ski (wô′tər skē′ *or* wŏt′ər skē′) *intr.v.* **wa•ter-skied, wa•ter-ski•ing, wa•ter-skis.** To ski on water while being towed by a motorboat.

water snake *n.* Any of various nonpoisonous snakes living in or near freshwater streams and ponds.

wa•ter•spout (wô′tər spout′ *or* wŏt′ər spout′) *n.* A tornado or smaller whirlwind occurring over water and resulting in a funnel-shaped column of air and spray.

water table *n.* The upper limit of the zone of underground rock that is saturated with water.

wa•ter•tight (wô′tər tīt′ *or* wŏt′ər tīt′) *adj.* **1.** So tightly made that no water can enter or escape. **2.** Having no flaws or loopholes: *a watertight excuse.*

water tower *n.* A standpipe or elevated tank used as a reservoir or for maintaining equal pressure in a water system.

water vapor *n.* Water in its gaseous state, especially in the atmosphere and at a temperature below the boiling point.

wa•ter•way (wô′tər wā′ *or* wŏt′ər wā′) *n.* A navigable body of water, such as a river, canal, or channel.

water wheel *n.* A wheel propelled by running or falling water and used to power machinery.

water wings *pl.n.* A pair of inflatable bags that fit under a person's arms and keep a person afloat.

wa•ter•works (wô′tər wûrks′ *or* wŏt′ər wûrks′) *pl.n.* **1.** *(used with a singular or plural verb).* The water system, including reservoirs, tanks, buildings, pumps, and pipes, that supplies water to a city or town. **2.** *(used with a singular verb).* A single unit, such as a pumping station, within such a system.

wa•ter•y (wô′tə rē *or* wŏt′ə rē) *adj.* **wa•ter•i•er, wa•ter•i•est. 1.** Filled with, consisting of, or soaked with water: *watery soil.* **2.** Containing too much water; diluted: *watery soup.* **3.** Resembling water, as in paleness, thinness, or liquidity: *a watery blue sky.*

watt (wŏt) *n.* A unit of power equal to one joule per second or about $\frac{1}{746}$ horsepower. [First written down in 1882 in Modern English, after James *Watt.*]

Watt (wŏt), **James.** 1736–1819. British engineer and inventor whose improvements to the steam engine resulted in the modern steam engine (patented 1769).

watt•age (wŏt′ĭj) *n.* An amount of power, especially electrical power, expressed in watts or kilowatts.

watt-hour (wŏt′our′) *n.* A unit of energy, especially electrical energy, equal to the work done by one watt acting for one hour and equivalent to 3,600 joules.

wat•tle (wŏt′l) *n.* **1.** A structure of poles intertwined with twigs, reeds, or branches, used for walls, fences, and roofs. **2.** A fleshy, often brightly colored fold of skin hanging from the neck or throat, as of chickens or turkeys. [First written down before 899 in Old English and spelled *watol.*]

wave (wāv) *v.* **waved, wav•ing, waves.** *—intr.* **1.** To move freely back and forth or up and down in the air, as branches in the wind: *The weeds waved in the breeze.* **2.** To make a signal with an up-and-down or back-and-forth movement of the hand: *She waved and called "Good-bye!"* **3.** To fall in curves, curls, or swirls, as hair. *—tr.* **1.** To cause to move back and forth or up and down: *She waved a fan before her face.* **2.** To move or swing as in giving a signal: *waved our hands wildly.* **3.** To signal or express by waving the hand: *waved good-bye.* **4.** To arrange into curves, curls, or swirls. *—n.* **1.** A ridge or swell that moves along the surface of a body of water. **2.** A moving curve or succession of curves in or on a surface; an undulation: *waves of wheat across the plain.* **3.** A movement up and down or back and forth: *a wave of the hand.* **4.** A curve or arrangement of curves, as in hair: *a soft wave.* **5.** A widespread persistent weather condition: *a heat wave.* **6.** A disturbance or vibration, such as a sound wave, that passes through a medium or through space. [First written down about 1000 in Old English and spelled *wafian.*]

❑ *These sound alike:* **wave, waive** (give up).

wave•length (wāv′lĕngkth′ *or* wāv′lĕngth′) *n.* The distance between one peak or crest of a wave and the next peak or crest. **—*idiom.* on the same wavelength.** *Informal.* In complete accord; in harmony: *We were on the same wavelength when discussing the class trip.*

wave•let (wāv′lĭt) *n.* A small wave; a ripple.

wa•ver (wā′vər) *intr.v.* **wa•vered, wa•ver•ing, wa•vers. 1.** To move unsteadily back and forth. **2.** To act in a hesitant or indecisive way; vacillate: *We wavered over the purchase of a new couch.* **3.** To become unsteady or unsure; falter: *His resolve began to waver.* **4.** To tremble or flicker, as sound or light. *—n.* The act of wavering. [First written down about 1280 in Middle English and spelled *weiveren.*] **—wa′ver•er** *n.*

❑ *These sound alike:* **waver, waiver** (relinquishment).

WAVES *abbr.* An abbreviation of Women Accepted for Volunteer Emergency Service.

wav•y (wā′vē) *adj.* **wav•i•er, wav•i•est. 1.** Full of or rising in waves: *wavy hair; a wavy sea.* **2.** Having curves that resemble waves: *a wavy line.* **—wav′i•ness** *n.*

wax[1] (wăks) *n.* **1.** Any of various solid or soft sticky substances that melt or soften easily when heated. They are insoluble in water but soluble in most organic liquids. **2.** A waxy substance produced by bees; beeswax. **3.** A waxy substance produced by certain glands in the canal of the external ear. **4.** A solid plastic or very thick liquid material such as paraffin. **5.** A preparation containing wax used for polishing floors and other surfaces. *—tr.v.* **waxed, wax•ing, wax•es.** To coat, treat, or polish with wax: *wax a floor; wax a car.* [First written down about 805 in Old English and spelled *weax.*]

wax[2] (wăks) *intr.v.* **waxed, wax•ing, wax•es. 1.** To increase gradually in size, number, strength, or intensity: *Civilizations have waxed and waned over the centuries.* **2.** To show a progressively larger lighted surface, as the moon does in passing from new to full. [First written down about 725 in Old English and spelled *weaxan.*]

wax bean *n.* A kind of string bean having yellow pods.

waxed paper (wăkst) *n.* Wax paper.

wax•en (wăk′sən) *adj.* **1.** Made of or covered with wax: *a waxen image.* **2.** Pale or smooth as wax: *a waxen face.*

wax myrtle *n.* An evergreen shrub of the southeast United States having small berries with a waxy coating.

wax paper *n.* Paper that has been made moistureproof by treatment with wax, used in cooking and storing foods.

wax•wing (wăks′wĭng′) *n.* Any of several crested brownish birds having waxy red tips on the wing feathers, as the cedar waxwing of North America.

wax•work (wăks′wûrk′) *n.* **1.** The art of modeling in wax. **2.** A figure made of wax, especially a life-size wax likeness of a famous person.

wax•y (wăk′sē) *adj.* **wax•i•er, wax•i•est. 1.** Resembling wax in appearance or texture; pale, pliable, or smooth and lustrous: *a flower with waxy petals.* **2.** Full of, consisting of, or covered with wax.

James Watt

Portrait by Henry Howard (1769–1847)

wattle

Of a rooster

waxwork

Touching up a waxwork figure in a Russian museum

ă	**pat**	oi	**boy**
ā	**pay**	ou	**out**
âr	**care**	o͝o	**took**
ä	**father**	o͞o	**boot**
ĕ	**pet**	ŭ	**cut**
ē	**be**	ûr	**urge**
ĭ	**pit**	th	**thin**
ī	**pie**	*th*	**this**
îr	**pier**	hw	**whoop**
ŏ	**pot**	zh	**vision**
ō	**toe**	ə	**about**
ô	**paw**	N	*French* **bon**

way (wā) *n.* **1.a.** A road, path, or highway affording passage from one place to another. **b.** An opening affording passage: *This door is the only way into the attic.* **2.** Space or opportunity to proceed: *cleared the way for the parade; opened the way to peace.* **3.** A course used in going from one place to another: *the shortest way home.* **4.** Progress or travel along a certain route or in a specific direction: *on his way north.* **5.** A course of conduct or action: *the easy way out.* **6.** A manner or method of doing: *had no way to reach her.* **7.** A usual or habitual manner of being, living, or acting: *the American way of life.* **8.** An individual or personal manner of behaving, acting, or doing: *Have it your own way.* **9.** *Informal.* Distance. Also used in the plural with a singular verb: *It is a long ways from here to Moscow.* **10.** A specific direction: *He glanced my way.* **11.** An aspect, a detail, or a feature: *Our jobs are in no way comparable.* **12.** An ability or a skill: *has a way with words.* **13.** A state or condition: *He is in a bad way financially.* **14.** A neighborhood or an area: *Drop in when you're out our way.* —*adv. Informal.* **1.** By a great distance or to a great degree; far: *way off base; way over budget.* **2.** From this place; away: *Go way.* —***idioms.*** **by way of.** Through; via: *We walked to school by way of the park.* **go out of one's way.** To do something that is inconvenient and beyond what is required: *went out of their way to put me up for the night.* **in the way.** In a position that obstructs, hinders, or interferes: *There's nothing in the way of this project now.* **on (one's) way.** In the process of coming, going, or traveling: *It's getting dark, so I'll be on my way.* **on the way.** On the route of a journey: *stopped at a diner on the way.* **out of the way.** In a position that does not obstruct, hinder, or interfere: *Tell them to keep out of the way while I fix the sink.* [First written down before 800 in Old English and spelled *weg.*]

❑ *These sound alike:* **way, weigh** (measure weight).

way•far•er (wā′fâr′ər) *n.* A person who travels, especially on foot.

way•far•ing (wā′fâr′ĭng) *n.* Traveling, especially on foot.

way•lay (wā′lā′) *tr.v.* **way•laid** (wā′lād′), **way•lay•ing, way•lays.** To lie in wait for and attack from ambush.

way-out (wā′out′) *adj. Slang.* Very unconventional, unusual, or strange: *way-out clothes; way-out ideas.*

–ways *suff.* A suffix that means in a specified way, manner, direction, or position: *sideways.*

way•side (wā′sīd′) *n.* The side or edge of a road, way, path, or highway.

way station *n.* A station between principal stations on a route, as of a railroad.

way•ward (wā′wərd) *adj.* **1.** Stubborn or disobedient; willful or uncontrollable: *a wayward child.* **2.** Tending not to follow a procedure or method; unpredictable.

we (wē) *pron.* **1.** The person who is speaking or writing together with another or others: *We want to go swimming.* **2.** The person who is speaking or writing in an official capacity, especially a monarch or an editor of a magazine or newspaper. [First written down about 725 in Old English and spelled *wē.*] —SEE NOTE.

❑ *These sound alike:* **we, wee** (tiny).

weak (wēk) *adj.* **weak•er, weak•est. 1.** Lacking physical strength, energy, or vigor; feeble. **2.** Likely to fail under pressure, stress, or strain; lacking resistance: *a weak link in a chain.* **3.** Not having the proper or necessary strength, power, or potency: *weak coffee; weak eyesight.* **4.** Lacking aptitude or skill: *weak in math.* **5.** Lacking or resulting from a lack of intelligence: *a weak mind.* **6.** Lacking persuasiveness; unconvincing: *a weak argument.* **7.** Lacking potency or intensity: *weak sunlight.* **8.** Unstressed or unaccented in pronunciation or poetic meter. Used of a word or syllable. [First written down about 1300 in Middle English and spelled *waike*, from Old Norse *veikr*, pliant.]

❑ *These sound alike:* **weak, week** (seven days).

weak•en (wē′kən) *tr. & intr.v.* **weak•ened, weak•en•ing, weak•ens.** To make or become weak or weaker.

weak•fish (wēk′fĭsh′) *n.* A food fish of Atlantic North American waters.

weak•ling (wēk′lĭng) *n.* A person or thing having a weak body or character.

weak•ly (wēk′lē) *adj.* **weak•li•er, weak•li•est.** Delicate in constitution; frail or sickly. —*adv.* With little physical force or strength.

❑ *These sound alike:* **weakly, weekly** (every week).

weak-mind•ed (wēk′mīn′dĭd) *adj.* **1.** Having or showing a lack of judgment or conviction. **2.** Foolish; silly.

weak•ness (wēk′nĭs) *n.* **1.** The condition or quality of being weak: *physical weakness.* **2.** A personal defect or failing: *Concentrate on overcoming your weaknesses.* **3.a.** A special fondness or liking: *a weakness for good talkers.* **b.** Something that one desires and cannot resist: *Ice cream is his weakness.*

weal[1] (wēl) *n.* **1.** Prosperity; happiness. **2.** The welfare of the community; the general good: *the public weal.* [First written down before 899 in Old English and spelled *wela.*]

❑ *These sound alike:* **weal**[1] (prosperity), **weal**[2] (welt), **we'll** (we will), **wheal** (swelling), **wheel** (circular frame).

weal[2] (wēl) *n.* A ridge on the flesh raised by a blow; a welt. [First written down in 1821 in Modern English, alteration of *wale.*]

❑ *These sound alike:* **weal**[2] (welt), **weal**[1] (prosperity), **we'll** (we will), **wheal** (swelling), **wheel** (circular frame).

wealth (wĕlth) *n.* **1.** A great quantity of money or valuable resources; riches. **2.** The state of being rich; affluence. **3.** A great amount; an abundance: *a wealth of information.*

wealth•y (wĕl′thē) *adj.* **wealth•i•er, wealth•i•est. 1.** Having wealth; rich: *a wealthy family.* **2.** Well supplied; abundant: *a region wealthy in wildlife.* **—wealth′i•ly** *adv.* **—wealth′i•ness** *n.*

wean (wēn) *tr.v.* **weaned, wean•ing, weans. 1.** To accustom (a young mammal) to take nourishment other than by suckling. **2.** To detach from something to which one is strongly habituated or devoted: *weaned herself from sweets.*

weap•on (wĕp′ən) *n.* **1.a.** An instrument of attack or defense in combat, as a gun, missile, or sword. **b.** A part of the body, as the horns, teeth, or claws of an animal, used in attack or defense. **2.** A means used to defend against or defeat another: *Logic was her best weapon.* [First written down about 725 in Old English and spelled *wǣpen.*]

weap•on•ry (wĕp′ən rē) *n.* **1.** Weapons considered as a group. **2.** The design and production of weapons.

wear (wâr) *v.* **wore** (wôr), **worn** (wôrn), **wear•ing, wears.** —*tr.* **1.** To carry or have on the person as covering, adornment, or protection. **2.** To display in one's appearance: *wore a smile.* **3.** To bear, carry, or maintain in a certain way: *She wears her hair long.* **4.** To fly or display (colors). Used of a ship, jockey, or knight. **5.a.** To damage, diminish, erode, or use up, as by long or hard use, friction, or exposure: *The wind and rain wore away the top layer of rock.* **b.** To produce by constant friction, pres-

Usage: we

Be sure to write *We students are going* and not *Us students.* In this case the pronoun is part of the subject of the sentence. On the other hand it is correct to say *for us students*, not *for we students.* In this case the pronoun is the object of a preposition.

sure, or erosion: *Wore a hole in the old shoes.* **6.** To fatigue, weary, or exhaust: *Your questions wear my patience.* —*intr.* **1.** To last under continual or hard use: *That fabric wears well.* **2.** To break down or diminish, as through use or friction: *The rear tires began to wear.* **3.** To pass gradually or tediously: *The December day wore on toward night.* —*n.* **1.** The act of wearing or the state of being worn; use: *clothes for evening wear.* **2.** Clothing: *men's wear.* **3.** Damage resulting from use or age: *The rug shows evidence of wear.* **4.** The ability to withstand use; lasting quality: *The suit has plenty of wear left.* —***idioms.*** **wear down.** To break down or exhaust by relentless pressure or resistance: *The child's continual pleading finally wore her parents down.* **wear off.** To diminish gradually in effect: *My mouth hurt after the anesthetic wore off.* **wear out.** **1.** To make or become unusable through long or heavy use: *wore out a pair of hockey skates.* **2.** To exhaust; tire: *Raking the leaves wore me out.* **wear thin.** To become less convincing, acceptable, or popular, as through repeated use: *Oversleeping is an excuse that has worn thin.* [First written down before 899 in Old English and spelled *werian.*] **—wear′er** *n.*

❑ *These sound alike:* **wear, ware** (goods).

wea•ri•some (wîr′ē səm) *adj.* Tiresome or tedious.

wea•ry (wîr′ē) *adj.* **wea•ri•er, wea•ri•est. 1.** Physically or mentally tired. **2.** Showing or caused by tiredness: *a weary sigh.* **3.** Having one's interest, patience, or indulgence worn out: *I am weary of your complaints.* —*tr. & intr.v.* **wea•ried** (wîr′ēd), **wea•ry•ing, wea•ries** (wîr′ēz). To make or become weary; tire. [First written down about 725 in Old English and spelled *wērig.*] **—wea′ri•ly** *adv.* **—wea′ri•ness** *n.*

wea•sel (wē′zəl) *n.* **1.** Any of various mammals having a long narrow body, short legs, and a long tail, and feeding on small animals and birds. **2.** A person regarded as cunning, sneaky, or treacherous. —*intr.v.* **wea•seled, wea•sel•ing, wea•sels** also **wea•selled, wea•sel•ling, wea•sels.** To be evasive in the use of words; equivocate. —***idiom.*** **weasel out.** *Informal.* To back out of a situation or commitment in a sneaky or cowardly manner: *weaseled out of helping us clean up after the dance.*

weath•er (wĕ*th*′ər) *n.* **1.** The condition or activity of the atmosphere at a given time and place, especially as described by variables such as temperature, humidity, wind velocity, and barometric pressure. **2.** Bad, rough, or stormy atmospheric conditions. —*v.* **weath•ered, weath•er•ing, weath•ers.** —*tr.* **1.** To expose to the action of the weather, as for drying, seasoning, or coloring: *weather lumber.* **2.** To affect or change, as in color or condition, by exposure: *Many voyages weathered the ship's hull.* **3.** To pass through (something) safely; survive: *weather a storm.* —*intr.* **1.** To show the effects of exposure to the elements. **2.** To withstand the effects of weather. —***idiom.*** **under the weather.** Somewhat ill. [First written down about 725 in Old English and spelled *weder.*]

❑ *These sound alike:* **weather, wether** (sheep), **whether** (if).

weath•er-beat•en (wĕ*th*′ər bēt′n) *adj.* Worn by exposure to the weather: *a weather-beaten house.*

weath•er•cock (wĕ*th*′ər kŏk′) *n.* A weathervane, especially one in the form of a rooster.

weath•er•glass (wĕ*th*′ər glăs′) *n.* An instrument, such as a barometer, that indicates change in atmospheric conditions.

weath•er•ing (wĕ*th*′ər ĭng) *n.* Any of the chemical or mechanical processes by which rocks exposed to the weather are broken down.

weath•er•proof (wĕ*th*′ər pro͞of′) *adj.* Capable of withstanding exposure to weather without damage. —*tr.v.* **weath•er•proofed, weath•er•proof•ing, weath•er•proofs.** To make weatherproof.

weather station *n.* A place where meteorological data are gathered, recorded, and released.

weath•er-strip (wĕ*th*′ər strĭp′) *tr.v.* **weath•er-stripped, weath•er-strip•ping, weath•er-strips.** To fit or equip with weather stripping.

weather stripping *n.* A narrow piece of material, such as rubber, plastic, or felt, installed around doors and windows to keep out cold or hot air.

weath•er•vane (wĕ*th*′ər vān′) *n.* A device for indicating wind direction.

weave (wēv) *v.* **wove** (wōv), **wo•ven** (wō′vən), **weav•ing, weaves.** —*tr.* **1.** To make (cloth) on a loom by interlacing the threads of the woof and the warp. **2.** To interlace (threads, for example) into a fabric: *weave straw into a mat.* **3.** To make by interlacing or interweaving strands or strips of material: *weave a basket.* **4.** To combine into a whole made up of related parts: *She wove the separate incidents into a story.* **5.** To make or create by joining separate elements in an intricate way: *weave a captivating tale.* **6.** To spin (a web, for example). **7.** *Past tense* **weaved.** To make (a path or way) by winding in and out or from side to side: *The taxi weaved its way through the traffic.* —*intr.* **1.** To engage in weaving; make cloth. **2.** *Past tense* **weaved.** To move in a winding course or sway from side to side. —*n.* The pattern or method of weaving a fabric: *a twill weave; a loose weave.* [First written down about 899 in Old English and spelled *wefan.*] **—weav′er** *n.*

❑ *These sound alike:* **weave, we've** (we have).

weav•er•bird (wē′vər bûrd′) *n.* Any of various African, Asian, or Australian birds that make nests of interwoven leaves and twigs.

web (wĕb) *n.* **1.** A woven fabric, especially one on or just removed from a loom. **2.** A latticed or woven structure: *A web of palm branches formed the roof of the hut.* **3.** A structure of fine silky strands woven by spiders or by certain insect larvae. **4.** Something that traps or snares by or as if by entangling: *a web of deceit.* **5.** A fold of skin or thin tissue connecting the toes of certain water birds or other animals. —*tr.v.* **webbed, web•bing, webs.** To provide with a web or webs. [First written down about 725 in Old English and spelled *webb.*]

webbed (wĕbd) *adj.* **1.** Having the fingers or toes connected by a fold of skin or tissue: *the webbed foot of a seagull.* **2.** Connected by a fold of skin or tissue: *webbed toes.* **3.** Formed by or provided with a web.

web•bing (wĕb′ĭng) *n.* A strong closely woven fabric used especially for seat belts and harnesses or in upholstery.

web-foot•ed (wĕb′fo͝ot′ĭd) *adj.* Having feet with webbed toes.

Web•ster (wĕb′stər), **Daniel.** 1782–1852. American politician. He served as a U.S. representative from New Hampshire (1813–1817) and later as a representative (1823–1827) and senator (1827–1841 and 1845–1850) from Massachusetts.

Webster, Noah. 1758–1843. American lexicographer whose major work, *An American Dictionary of the English Language,* was originally published in 1828.

wed (wĕd) *v.* **wed•ded, wed** or **wed•ded, wed•ding, weds.** —*tr.* **1.** To take as a spouse; marry. **2.** To unite in marriage: *The minister wedded the young couple.* —*intr.* To take a spouse; marry.

Wed. *abbr.* An abbreviation of Wednesday.

weathervane

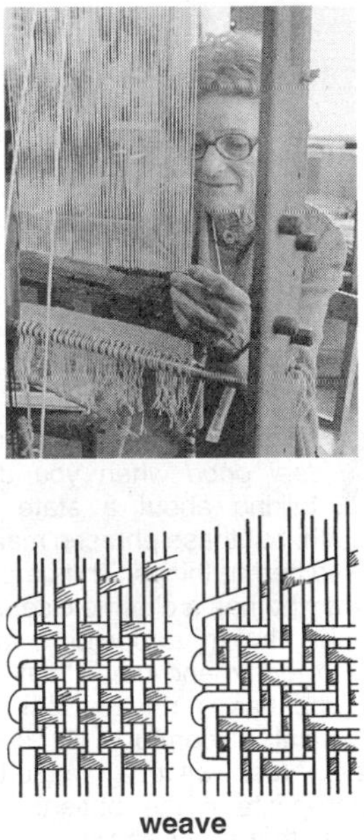

weave

Top: Weaving a tapestry
Bottom: Plain weave design (*left*) and twilled weave design (*right*)

ă	pat	oi	boy
ā	pay	ou	out
âr	care	o͝o	took
ä	father	o͞o	boot
ĕ	pet	ŭ	cut
ē	be	ûr	urge
ĭ	pit	th	thin
ī	pie	*th*	this
îr	pier	hw	whoop
ŏ	pot	zh	vision
ō	toe	ə	about
ô	paw	N	*French* bon

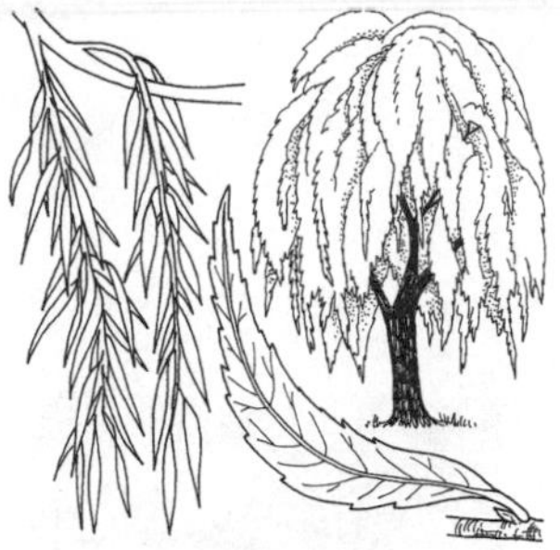

weeping willow

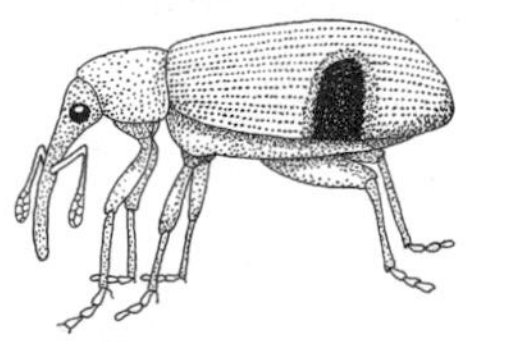

weevil

Usage: well²

You can use *feel well* and *feel good* when you are talking about a state of health, but these phrases mean two different things. Thus a patient who has a chronic disease might say to a doctor *I feel good today*, and mean that he or she has a relative lack of physical discomfort. By contrast, *I feel well today* would be appropriate if the patient believes that he or she no longer has a disease.

we'd (wēd). Contraction of *we had, we should,* or *we would.*
❑ *These sound alike:* **we'd, weed¹** (plant), **weed²** (token of mourning).

wed•ding (**wĕd′**ĭng) *n.* **1.** The act of marrying. **2.** The ceremony or celebration of a marriage. **3.** The anniversary of a marriage: *a golden wedding.*

wedge (wĕj) *n.* **1.** A piece of material, such as metal or wood, tapered in a triangular shape and designed to be inserted into a crack or crevice and used for splitting, tightening, securing, or levering. **2.** Something shaped like a wedge: *cut myself a wedge of pie.* **3.** Something that intrudes and causes division or disruption: *The issue drove a wedge between the party leaders.* —*v.* **wedged, wedg•ing, wedg•es.** —*tr.* **1.** To split or force apart with or as if with a wedge: *wedge open a log; wedge apart the opposition.* **2.** To fix in place or tighten with a wedge: *wedged the window so it fit tightly.* —*intr.* To become lodged or jammed. [First written down before 800 in Old English and spelled *wecg.*]

wed•lock (**wĕd′**lŏk′) *n.* The state of being married; matrimony.

Wednes•day (**wĕnz′**dē *or* **wĕnz′**dā′) *n.* The fourth day of the week.

wee (wē) *adj.* **we•er, we•est. 1.** Very small; tiny: *a wee boy.* See Synonyms at **little. 2.** Very early: *the wee hours.*
❑ *These sound alike:* **wee, we** (you and I).

weed¹ (wēd) *n.* A plant considered troublesome or useless, especially one growing freely where it is not wanted, as in a garden. —*tr. & intr.v.* **weed•ed, weed•ing, weeds.** To rid of or remove weeds. [First written down before 899 in Old English and spelled *wēod*, grass, weed.]
❑ *These sound alike:* **weed¹** (plant), **we'd** (we had), **weed²** (token of mourning).

weed² (wēd) *n.* **1.** A token of mourning, such as a black band worn on the sleeve. **2. weeds.** The black mourning clothes of a widow. [First written down before 899 in Old English and spelled *wǣd*, garment.]
❑ *These sound alike:* **weed²** (token of mourning), **we'd** (we had), **weed¹** (plant).

weed•er (**wē′**dər) *n.* A person, tool, or device that removes weeds.

weed•y (**wē′**dē) *adj.* **weed•i•er, weed•i•est. 1.** Full of or consisting of weeds: *weedy ground; a weedy field.* **2.** Resembling or characteristic of a weed: *a weedy plant.*

week (wēk) *n.* **1.** A seven-day calendar period, especially one that begins on a Sunday and continues through Saturday. **2.** The part of a calendar week devoted to work, school, or business. [First written down in 878 in Old English and spelled *wicu.*]
❑ *These sound alike:* **week, weak** (feeble).

week•day (**wēk′**dā′) *n.* Any day of the week except Sunday, or often except Saturday and Sunday.

week•end (**wēk′**ĕnd′) *n.* The end of the week, especially the period from Friday evening through Sunday evening.

week•ly (**wēk′**lē) *adv.* **1.** Once a week or every week: *She visits us weekly.* **2.** By the week: *I am paid weekly.* —*adj.* **1.** Of or relating to a week. **2.** Done, happening, or coming once a week or every week: *a weekly trip.* **3.** Computed by the week: *weekly earnings.* —*n., pl.* **week•lies.** A newspaper or magazine issued once a week.
❑ *These sound alike:* **weekly, weakly** (frail).

ween•ie (**wē′**nē) *n. Informal.* A wiener.

weep (wēp) *v.* **wept** (wĕpt), **weep•ing, weeps.** —*tr.* To shed (tears) as an expression of emotion; cry. See Synonyms at **cry.** —*intr.* **1.** To express emotion, such as grief or sadness, by shedding tears. **2.** To mourn or grieve. **3.** To emit or run with drops of liquid: *The seams of the tent started to weep.*

weep•ing (**wē′**pĭng) *adj.* **1.** Shedding tears; tearful. **2.** Dropping rain: *weeping clouds.* **3.** Having drooping branches: *a weeping cherry tree.*

weeping willow *n.* A widely cultivated tree native to China and having long, slender, drooping branches and narrow leaves.

wee•vil (**wē′**vəl) *n.* Any of numerous beetles that have a long downward-curving snout and that do great damage to plants and plant products.

weft (wĕft) *n.* The threads running crosswise in weaving; the woof.

weigh (wā) *v.* **weighed, weigh•ing, weighs.** —*tr.* **1.** To determine the weight of by or as if by using a scale or balance. **2.** To consider carefully by balancing in the mind; ponder: *weighed possible alternatives.* **3.** To choose carefully or deliberately: *He weighed his words when answering the question.* —*intr.* **1.** To be of a specific weight. **2.** To have consequence or influence: *That factor weighed heavily in the decision.* **3.** To press heavily: *Guilt weighed on him.* —***idiom.* weigh down. 1.** To cause to bend down with added weight. **2.** To burden or oppress: *I'm weighed down with responsibility right now.* [First written down about 725 in Old English and spelled *wegan.*]
❑ *These sound alike:* **weigh, way** (path).

weight (wāt) *n.* **1.** The measure of the heaviness of an object: *The car has a weight of 2,800 pounds.* **2.** The force with which an object near the earth or another celestial body is attracted toward the center of the body by gravity. **3.a.** A unit used as a measure of gravitational force: *a table of weights and measures.* **b.** A system of such measures: *avoirdupois weight; troy weight.* **4.** An object having a particular weight, used as a standard in weighing: *place a two-pound weight on the scale.* **5.** An object whose principal function is to exert a downward force by means of the action of gravity upon it, such as a paperweight or dumbbell. **6.** A load or burden; oppressiveness: *feeling a heavy weight of worry.* **7.** Influence or importance: *Her opinion has a lot of weight in the medical community.* —*tr.v.* **weight•ed, weight•ing, weights. 1.** To make heavy or heavier with a weight or weights. **2.** To load down, burden, or oppress.
❑ *These sound alike:* **weight, wait** (remain).

weight•less (**wāt′**lĭs) *adj.* **1.** Having little or no weight. **2.** Experiencing a gravitational force that is zero or very nearly zero. —**weight′less•ness** *n.*

weight•lift•ing (**wāt′**lĭf′tĭng) *n.* The lifting of heavy weights as an exercise or in athletic competition.

weight•y (**wā′**tē) *adj.* **weight•i•er, weight•i•est. 1.** Having considerable weight; heavy: *a weighty package.* **2.** Burdensome; oppressive: *weighty responsibilities.* **3.** Very serious or important: *a weighty matter.*

weir (wîr) *n.* **1.** A fence or barrier placed in a stream to catch or hold fish. **2.** A dam placed across a river or canal. [First written down in 839 in Old English and spelled *wer.*]
❑ *These sound alike:* **weir, we're** (we are).

weird (wîrd) *adj.* **weird•er, weird•est. 1.** Of, relating to, or suggesting the supernatural. **2.** Of a strikingly odd or unusual character; strange. [First written down about 1400 in Middle English and spelled *werde*, controlling fate, from Old English *wyrd*, fate.] —**weird′ly** *adv.* —**weird′ness** *n.*

weird•o (**wîr′**dō) *n., pl.* **weird•oes.** *Slang.* A person regarded as being very strange or eccentric.

welch (wĕlch) *v.* Variant of **welsh.**

wel•come (**wĕl′**kəm) *adj.* **1.** Received with pleasure and friendliness into one's company or home: *a welcome guest.* **2.** Giving pleasure or satisfaction: *a* *welcome break from hard work.* **3.** Warmly or willingly permitted or invited: *You are welcome to join us.* **4.** Freely granted one's courtesy. Used to acknowledge an expression of gratitude: *You're welcome.* —*n.* **1.** A friendly greeting or reception. **2.** A reception upon arrival: *gave the stranger an unfriendly welcome.* —*tr.v.* **wel•comed, wel•com•ing, wel•comes. 1.** To greet, receive, or entertain (another or others) cordially or hospitably. **2.** To receive or accept gladly: *We would welcome a little privacy.* —*interj.* An expression used to greet a visitor or recent arrival.

weld (wĕld) *v.* **weld•ed, weld•ing, welds.** —*tr.* **1.** To join (pieces of metal) by heating them until the edges run together or until the edges are soft enough to be hammered or pressed together. **2.** To bring into close association or union: *A lifelong love of music welded their partnership.* —*intr.* To undergo welding or be capable of being welded: *an alloy that welds easily.* —*n.* The joint formed when metal parts are united by welding. **—weld′er** *n.*

wel•fare (wĕl′fâr′) *n.* **1.** Health, happiness, and good fortune; well-being: *The government should promote the general welfare.* **2.** Financial or other aid provided, especially by the government, to people in need. ***—idiom.* on welfare.** Receiving regular assistance from the government or private agencies because of need. [First written down about 1303 in Middle English, from Old English *wel faran,* to fare well.]

welfare state *n.* A social system in which the state assumes primary responsibility for the welfare of its citizens, as in health care, education, employment, and social security.

wel•kin (wĕl′kĭn) *n.* The sky.

well[1] (wĕl) *n.* **1.** A deep hole or shaft dug or drilled into the earth to obtain water, oil, gas, sulfur, or brine. **2.** A container or reservoir used to hold a liquid, as an inkwell. **3.** A spring or fountain serving as a natural source of water. **4.** A source to be drawn upon: *The dictionary is a well of information.* **5.** A vertical opening that passes through the floors of a building, as for ventilation. —*intr.v.* **welled, well•ing, wells.** To rise to the surface, ready to flow: *Tears welled in his eyes.* [First written down before 830 in Old English and spelled *welle.*]

well[2] (wĕl) *adv.* **bet•ter** (**bĕt′ər**), **best** (bĕst). **1.** In a good or proper manner: *The children behaved very well on the trip.* **2.** Skillfully or proficiently: *She plays the piano well.* **3.** Satisfactorily or sufficiently: *Did you sleep well?* **4.** Successfully or effectively: *gets along well with others.* **5.** In a favorable or approving manner: *They spoke well of you.* **6.** Thoroughly; completely: *Blend the ingredients well.* **7.** Perfectly; clearly: *How well do you remember the trip?* **8.** To a considerable degree or extent: *It was well after sunset.* **9.** In a close or familiar manner: *I knew him well.* **10.** With care or attention: *Listen well to what I say.* **11.** With reason or propriety; reasonably: *We cannot well refuse their hospitality.* —*adj.* **better, best. 1.** In a satisfactory condition; right or proper: *All is well.* **2.a.** In good health; not sick. **b.** Cured or healed. —*interj.* **1.** An expression used to show surprise or relief. **2.** An expression used to introduce a remark or fill a pause during conversation: *Well, no one's perfect.* ***—idiom.* as well. 1.** In addition; also: *took another class as well.* **2.** With equal effect: *I might as well go.* [First written down about 725 in Old English and spelled *wel.*] —SEE NOTE.

we'll (wēl). Contraction of *we will* or *we shall.*

❑ *These sound alike:* **we'll** (we will), **weal**[1] (prosperity), **weal**[2] (welt), **wheal** (swelling), **wheel** (circular frame).

well-ap•point•ed (wĕl′ə poin′tĭd) *adj.* Having a full array of suitable equipment or furnishings.

well-bal•anced (wĕl′băl′ənst) *adj.* **1.** Evenly proportioned, balanced, or regulated. **2.** Mentally stable or sound; sane or sensible.

well-be•ing (wĕl′bē′ĭng) *n.* The state of being healthy, happy, or prosperous; welfare.

well•born (wĕl′bôrn′) *adj.* Of good lineage or stock.

well-bred (wĕl′brĕd′) *adj.* **1.** Of good upbringing; polite and refined. **2.** Of good breed. Used of animals.

well-de•fined (wĕl′dĭ fīnd′) *adj.* Having definite and distinct lines or features.

well-done (wĕl′dŭn′) *adj.* Cooked all the way through: *a well-done steak.*

well-fa•vored (wĕl′fā′vərd) *adj.* Handsome; attractive.

well-fed (wĕl′fĕd′) *adj.* **1.** Adequately or properly nourished. **2.** Overfed; fat.

well-fixed (wĕl′fĭkst′) *adj. Informal.* Financially secure; well-to-do.

well-found•ed (wĕl′foun′dĭd) *adj.* Based on sound judgment, reasoning, or evidence.

well-groomed (wĕl′gro͞omd′) *adj.* **1.** Neat and clean in dress and appearance: *well-groomed girls and boys.* **2.** Carefully combed and cared for: *sleek well-groomed horses.*

well-ground•ed (wĕl′groun′dĭd) *adj.* **1.** Familiar with the most important aspect of a subject: *He's well-grounded in physics but not in chemistry.* **2.** Having a sound basis; well-founded.

well•head (wĕl′hĕd′) *n.* **1.** The source of a well or stream. **2.** A structure built over a well.

well-heeled (wĕl′hēld′) *adj.* Having plenty of money; prosperous.

Wel•ling•ton (wĕl′ĭng tən). The capital of New Zealand, on extreme southern North Island. It was founded in 1840. Population, 133,200.

Wellington, First Duke of. 1769–1852. British general and politician whose troops defeated Napoleon at Waterloo (1815).

well-known (wĕl′nōn′) *adj.* **1.** Renowned; famous: *a well-known author.* **2.** Widely or generally known: *well-known facts.*

well-man•nered (wĕl′măn′ərd) *adj.* Polite; courteous.

well-mean•ing (wĕl′mē′nĭng) *adj.* Having or showing good intentions: *well-meaning advice.*

well-nigh (wĕl′nī′) *adv.* Nearly; almost: *well-nigh impossible.*

well-off (wĕl′ôf′ *or* wĕl′ŏf′) *adj.* Wealthy or prosperous.

well-read (wĕl′rĕd′) *adj.* Knowledgeable through extensive reading.

well-round•ed (wĕl′roun′dĭd) *adj.* **1.** Knowing or interested in a wide range or variety of subjects: *a well-rounded person.* **2.** Consisting of a wide range of subjects: *a well-rounded education.*

Wells (wĕlz), **Ida Bell.** 1862–1931. American journalist who led an international antilynching campaign and founded the Negro Fellowship League in 1910. —SEE NOTE.

well-spo•ken (wĕl′spō′kən) *adj.* **1.** Chosen or expressed with aptness or propriety: *well-spoken words.* **2.** Courteous in speech: *a well-spoken young man.*

well•spring (wĕl′sprĭng′) *n.* **1.** The source of a stream or spring. **2.** A source: *She's a wellspring of ideas.*

well-thought-of (wĕl thôt′ŭv′ *or* wĕl thôt′ŏv′) *adj.* Regarded with respect; esteemed.

well-timed (wĕl′tīmd′) *adj.* Occurring or done at an opportune time: *a well-timed remark.*

well-to-do (wĕl′tə do͞o′) *adj.* Prosperous; affluent; well-off.

Ida B. Wells

Ida B. Wells

Born in 1862 in northern Mississippi to parents who were slaves, Ida B. **Wells** spent her life working tirelessly against racial discrimination. In 1891, after several years of teaching students in rural Tennessee, Wells cofounded *Free Speech,* a radical Memphis newspaper she used as a forum for denouncing lynching. Wells's fiery editorials soon gained her recognition and notoriety. While she was on a lecture tour in the North, an angry mob burned her offices. Wells then mounted an international antilynching crusade, taking her lectures to England to gain support. In 1895 she published *A Red Record,* a book giving statistics and an analysis of lynching over a three-year period. Wells went on to help found the NAACP in 1909 and founded on her own the Negro Fellowship League in Chicago in 1910.

ă	pat	oi	boy
ā	pay	ou	out
âr	care	o͝o	took
ä	father	o͞o	boot
ĕ	pet	ŭ	cut
ē	be	ûr	urge
ĭ	pit	th	thin
ī	pie	*th*	this
îr	pier	hw	whoop
ŏ	pot	zh	vision
ō	toe	ə	about
ô	paw	N	*French* bon

Eudora Welty

Word History: werewolf

Unfortunately, **werewolves** are not nice guys, and they are *guys*, not gals. The word first appears in Old English as *werewulf.* The Old English word root *were–* means "a male person, a man"; *wulf* means "wolf." There is a Greek word for the same unpleasant person: *lycanthrope,* which is formed from the Greek word roots *luco–*, "wolf," and *anthrōpo–*, "a human being," as in **anthropology**, "the scientific study of human beings." The *lycanthrope* suffers from *lycanthropy,* which was coined by the Greek physician Galen (A.D. 130?–200?) in his description of a madness in which the patient has the ravenous hunger and other qualities of a wolf.

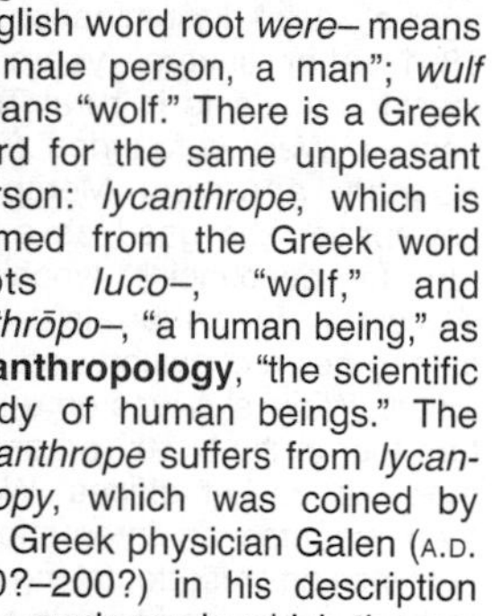

John Wesley

well-wish•er (wĕl′wĭsh′ər) *n.* A person who extends good wishes to another.

well-worn (wĕl′wôrn′) *adj.* **1.** Showing signs of much use or wear. **2.** Repeated too often; trite or hackneyed: *a well-worn phrase.*

welsh (wĕlsh *or* wĕlch) also **welch** (wĕlch) *intr.v.* **welshed, welsh•ing, welsh•es** also **welched, welch•ing, welch•es.** *Informal.* To cheat a person by not paying a debt or bet.

Welsh (wĕlsh) *adj.* Of or relating to Wales or its people, language, or culture. *—n.* **1.** The people of Wales. **2.** The Celtic language of Wales. [First written down about 668 in Old English and spelled *Wælisc,* from *Wealh,* Welshman, Celt.]

Welsh cor•gi (kôr′gē) *n.* Either of two breeds of dog that originated in Wales, having a long body, short legs, and a head like that of a fox.

Welsh•man (wĕlsh′mən) *n.* A man who is a native or inhabitant of Wales.

Welsh rabbit *n.* A dish made of melted cheese, milk or cream, and sometimes ale, served hot over toast or crackers.

Welsh rare•bit (râr′bĭt) *n.* Welsh rabbit.

Welsh•wom•an (wĕlsh′wo͝om′ən) *n.* A woman who is a native or inhabitant of Wales.

welt (wĕlt) *n.* **1.** A strip, as of leather or other material, stitched into a shoe between the upper and the sole. **2.** A ridge or bump raised on the skin by a blow or sometimes by an allergic reaction. [First written down about 1425 in Middle English and spelled *weltte.*]

wel•ter (wĕl′tər) *n.* **1.** A confused mass; a jumble: *a welter of papers and magazines on the table.* **2.** Confusion; turmoil. *—intr.v.* **wel•tered, wel•ter•ing, wel•ters. 1.** To wallow, roll, or toss about, as in mud or high seas. **2.** To lie soaked in a liquid.

wel•ter•weight (wĕl′tər wāt′) *n.* A professional boxer who weighs more than 135 and not more than 147 pounds (approximately 66–66.5 kilograms).

Wel•ty (wĕl′tē), **Eudora.** Born 1909. American writer known for her stories and novels detailing rural Southern life. Her works include *The Ponder Heart* (1954).

wen (wĕn) *n.* A cyst containing oily secretions from the skin.

wench (wĕnch) *n.* **1.** A young woman or girl, especially a peasant. **2.** A woman servant.

wend (wĕnd) *tr.v.* **wend•ed, wend•ing, wends.** To proceed on or along (one's way); go: *People wended their way home after the fireworks.* [First written down about 725 in Old English and spelled *wendan.*]

went (wĕnt) *v.* Past tense of **go.**

wept (wĕpt) *v.* Past tense and past participle of **weep.**

were (wûr) *v.* **1.** Second person singular and plural past tense of **be. 2.** First and third person plural past tense of **be. 3.** Past subjunctive of **be.**

❑ *These sound alike:* **were, whir** (buzz).

we're (wîr). Contraction of *we are.*

❑ *These sound alike:* **we're, weir** (dam).

were•n't (wûrnt *or* wûr′ənt). Contraction of *were not.*

were•wolf (wâr′wo͝olf′ *or* wîr′wo͝olf′ *or* wûr′wo͝olf′) *n.* A person who is transformed into a wolf or capable of assuming the form of a wolf. [First written down about 1000 in Old English and spelled *werewulf* : *wer,* man + *wulf,* wolf.] —See Note.

wert (wûrt) *v. Archaic.* A second person singular past tense of **be.**

Wes•ley (wĕs′lē *or* wĕz′lē), **John.** 1703–1791. British religious leader who founded Methodism (1738). His brother **Charles** (1707–1788) wrote numerous hymns.

west (wĕst) *n.* **1.** The direction from which the sun is seen to set, directly opposite east: *a wind blowing from the west.* **2.** Often **West. a.** A region or part of a country in this direction: *the west of Colombia.* **b.** The western part of the earth, especially Europe and the Western Hemisphere. **c.** The region of the United States west of the Mississippi River. *—adj.* **1.** Of, in, or toward the west: *the west bank of the river.* **2.** From the west: *a west wind.* *—adv.* In, from, or toward the west: *a river flowing west.* [First written down about 725 in Old English.]

West Af•ri•ca (ăf′rĭ kə). A region of western Africa between the Sahara and the Gulf of Guinea.

West Bank. A disputed territory of southwest Asia between Israel and Jordan west of the Jordan River.

west•bound (wĕst′bound′) *adj.* Going toward the west: *a westbound train.*

west•er•ly (wĕs′tər lē) *adj.* **1.** Situated toward the west: *a westerly direction.* **2.** Coming or being from the west: *westerly winds.* *—n., pl.* **west•er•lies.** A wind or storm coming from the west.

west•ern (wĕs′tərn) *adj.* **1.** Situated in, facing, or toward the west: *the western sky.* **2.** Coming from the west: *a western wind.* **3.** Native to or growing in the west. **4.** Often **Western.** Of, relating to, or characteristic of western regions or the West. **5. Western.** Of, relating to, or descended from those Christian churches that use or used Latin as their liturgical language. *—n.* Often **Western.** A book, motion picture, or television or radio program about frontier life in the American West.

west•ern•er also **West•ern•er** (wĕs′tər nər) *n.* A native or inhabitant of the west, especially the western United States.

Western Hemisphere. The half of the earth made up of North America, Mexico, Central America, and South America.

west•ern•ize (wĕs′tər nīz′) *tr.v.* **west•ern•ized, west•ern•iz•ing, west•ern•iz•es.** To cause to adopt the customs of Western civilization.

west•ern•most (wĕs′tərn mōst′) *adj.* Farthest west.

Western Sa•ha•ra (sə hâr′ə *or* sə hăr′ə *or* sə hä′rə). A region of northwest Africa on the Atlantic coast. First visited by Portuguese navigators in 1434, it was claimed as a protectorate by Spain in 1884. The territory was partly annexed in 1976 and partly occupied in 1979 by Morocco.

Western Sa•mo•a (sə mō′ə). An island country of the southern Pacific Ocean made up of the western Samoa Islands. Western Samoa gained its independence from New Zealand in 1962. Capital, Apia. Population, 156,349.

West Germanic *n.* A subdivision of the Germanic languages that includes German, Dutch, Flemish, Yiddish, and English. **—West Ger•man′ic** *adj.*

West Ger•ma•ny (jûr′mə nē). A former country of central Europe on the North Sea east of the Netherlands. It was formed in 1949 from part of Germany and reunified with East Germany in October 1990.

West In•dies (ĭn′dēz). A group of islands between southeast North America and northern South America, including the Greater Antilles, the Lesser Antilles, and the Bahama Islands.

West Point. A U.S. military installation in southeast New York on the western bank of the Hudson River north of New York City. It is the seat of the U.S. Military Academy.

West Vir•gin•ia (vər jĭn′yə). A state of the east-central United States west of Virginia. It was admitted as the 35th state in 1863. Charleston is the capital and the largest city. Population, 1,801,625. —SEE NOTE.

west•ward (wĕst′wərd) *adv. & adj.* Toward, to, or in the west: *sailed westward.* —*n.* A westward direction, point, or region.

wet (wĕt) *adj.* **wet•ter, wet•test. 1.** Covered or soaked with a liquid, such as water: *wet clothes.* **2.** Not yet dry or hardened: *wet paint; wet plaster.* **3.** Rainy, humid, or foggy: *a wet day; a wet climate.* —*n.* **1.** Something that wets; moisture. **2.** Rainy or snowy weather. —*tr. & intr.v.* **wet** or **wet•ted, wet•ting, wets.** To make or become wet. [First written down before 899 in Old English and spelled *wǣt.*] —**wet′ly** *adv.* —**wet′ness** *n.*

Synonyms: wet, moist, damp, humid. These adjectives mean covered with or filled with liquid. **Wet** is the most general: *Marcia hung the wet towels on the clothesline.* **Moist** means slightly wet: *He wiped off the table with a moist sponge.* **Damp** means moist and often also unpleasantly sticky: *The damp cellar had a moldy smell.* **Humid** refers to a disagreeably high degree of water vapor in the atmosphere: *The hot, humid weather made us want to jump in the pond.*

wet blanket *n. Informal.* A person or thing that discourages enjoyment or enthusiasm.

wet cell *n.* A primary electric cell having its electrolyte in the form of a liquid rather than in the form of a paste as in a dry cell.

weth•er (wĕ*th*′ər) *n.* A castrated male sheep.
❑ *These sound alike:* **wether, weather** (state of the atmosphere), **whether** (if).

wet•land (wĕt′lănd′) *n.* A lowland area, such as a marsh or swamp, that is saturated with moisture, especially when regarded as the natural habitat of wildlife.

wet suit *n.* A tight-fitting usually rubber suit worn in cold water, as by scuba divers, to retain body heat.

we've (wēv). Contraction of *we have.*
❑ *These sound alike:* **we've, weave** (make cloth).

whack (wăk) *tr. & intr.v.* **whacked, whack•ing, whacks.** To strike with a sharp blow; slap. —*n.* **1.** A sharp swift blow. **2.** The loud sound made by a sharp swift blow. —***idiom.*** **out of whack.** *Informal.* Out of order; not functioning correctly: *I woke up late this morning because my alarm clock is out of whack.*

whale (wāl) *n.* Any of various often very large sea mammals that resemble fish in form but breathe air. [First written down before 899 in Old English and spelled *hwæl.*]
❑ *These sound alike:* **whale, wail** (cry), **wale** (mark on the skin).

whale•boat (wāl′bōt′) *n.* A long fast-moving rowboat formerly used in the pursuit and harpooning of whales.

whale•bone (wāl′bōn′) *n.* **1.** A flexible horny substance forming plates or strips in the upper jaw of certain kinds of whales; baleen. **2.** An object made of this material.

whal•er (wā′lər) *n.* **1.** A person who hunts whales. **2.** A ship or boat used in whaling.

whal•ing (wā′lĭng) *n.* The business or practice of hunting and killing whales for their meat, oil, and bone.

wharf (wôrf) *n., pl.* **wharves** (wôrvz) or **wharfs.** A landing place or pier where ships may tie up and load or unload.

Whar•ton (wôr′tn), **Edith Newbold Jones.** 1862–1937. American writer whose works include *The House of Mirth* (1905).

wharves (wôrvz) *n.* A plural of **wharf.**

what (wŏt *or* wŭt; wət *when unstressed*) *pron.* **1.a.** Which thing or which particular one of many: *What are you having for dinner? What did she say?* **b.** Which kind, character, or designation: *What are these objects?* **2.a.** That which; the thing that: *Listen to what I tell you.* **b.** Whatever thing that: *come what may.* **3.** *Informal.* Something: *I'll tell you what.* —*adj.* **1.** Which one or ones of several or many: *What movie did you see?* **2.** Whatever: *They soon repaired what damage had been done.* **3.** How great; how astonishing: *What a fool!* —*adv.* How much; in what respect; how: *What does it matter?* —*interj.* An expression used to show surprise, disbelief, or other strong and sudden excitement. —***idioms.*** **what if.** What would occur if; suppose that: *What if everyone who registered to vote went to the polls?* **what it takes.** The necessary expertise or qualities needed for success: *She's young, but she's got what it takes.* [First written down about 725 in Old English and spelled *hwæt.*]

what•ev•er (wŏt ĕv′ər *or* wŭt ĕv′ər) *pron.* **1.** Everything or anything that: *Please do whatever you can to help.* **2.** What amount that; the whole of what: *You may have whatever is left over.* **3.** No matter what: *Whatever you do, come early.* **4.** *Informal.* Which thing or things; what: *Whatever do you mean?* —*adj.* **1.** Of any number or kind; any: *Whatever needs you may have, feel free to call on us.* **2.** All of; the whole of: *He used whatever strength he had left to finish the job.* **3.** Of any kind at all: *He was left with nothing whatever.*

what•not (wŏt′nŏt′ *or* wŭt′nŏt′) *n.* A set of open shelves for holding ornaments.

what•so•ev•er (wŏt′sō ĕv′ər *or* wŭt′sō ĕv′ər) *pron.* Whatever. —*adj.* Whatever: *They have no power whatsoever.*

wheal (wēl) *n.* A small swelling on the skin, as from an insect bite, that usually itches or burns.
❑ *These sound alike:* **wheal, weal**[1] (prosperity), **weal**[2] (welt), **we'll** (we will), **wheel** (circular frame).

wheat (wēt) *n.* **1.** Any of various grain-bearing grasses native to the Mediterranean region and southwest Asia but grown in many parts of the world as an important source of food. **2.** The seeds of any of these plants, usually ground to produce flour. [First written down before 830 in Old English and spelled *hwǣte.*]

wheat•en (wēt′n) *adj.* Of, relating to, or made from wheat.

wheat germ *n.* The embryo of a wheat kernel, rich in vitamins and used as a cereal or food supplement.

Wheat•ley (wēt′lē), **Phillis.** 1753?–1784. African-born American poet considered the first widely recognized Black writer in North America.

whee•dle (wēd′l) *tr.v.* **whee•dled, whee•dling, whee•dles. 1.** To persuade or try to persuade by flattery or deceit; cajole. **2.** To get by flattering or deceit: *He wheedled a promise out of me.*

wheel (wēl) *n.* **1.** A solid disk or a rigid circular frame attached to a hub by spokes, designed to turn around an axle passed through its center. **2.** Something resembling a wheel or having a wheel for its main part, as a steering wheel or a potter's wheel. **3. wheels.** Forces that provide energy, movement, or direction: *the wheels of commerce.* **4. wheels.** *Slang.* A motor vehicle. **5.** *Slang.* A very powerful or influential person: *He's a big wheel in business.* —*v.* **wheeled, wheel•ing, wheels.** —*tr.* **1.** To move, roll, or transport on wheels: *Put the books on the cart and wheel them to the library.* **2.** To cause to turn around or as if around a central axis; rotate or revolve. —*intr.* **1.** To turn around or as if around a central axis; revolve or rotate. **2.** To turn or whirl around in place; pivot: *The bull wheeled and charged.* **3.** To fly in a curving or circular

West Virginia

The state of **West Virginia** was formed in 1863 when 20 loyal counties in northwest Virginia separated from the state of **Virginia** after it seceded from the Union in 1861.

wet suit

Edith Wharton

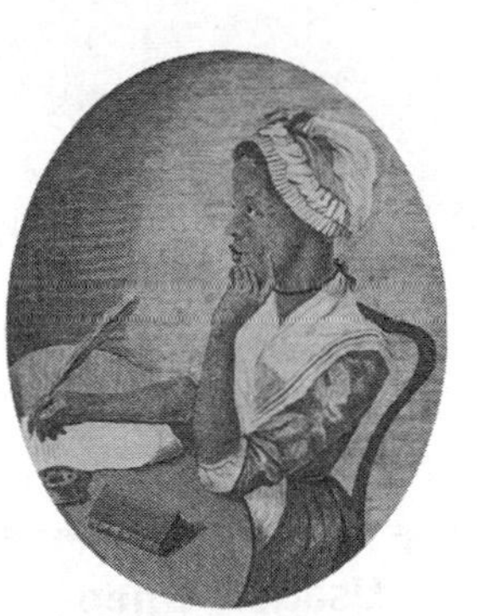
Phillis Wheatley
1773 engraving
by Scipio Moorhead

ă	pat	oi	boy
ā	pay	ou	out
âr	care	o͝o	took
ä	father	o͞o	boot
ĕ	pet	ŭ	cut
ē	be	ûr	urge
ĭ	pit	th	thin
ī	pie	*th*	this
îr	pier	hw	whoop
ŏ	pot	zh	vision
ō	toe	ə	about
ô	paw	N	*French* bon

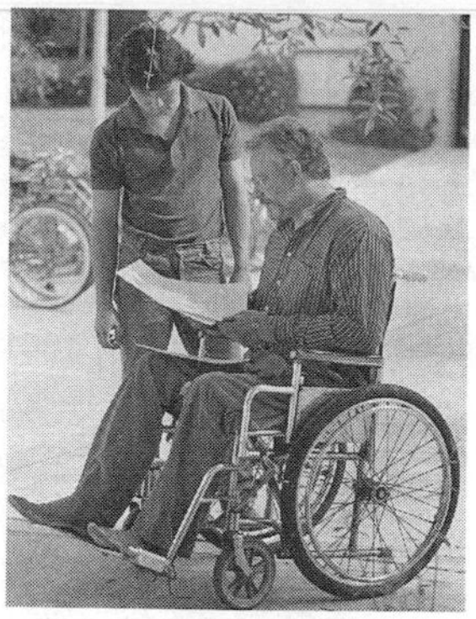

wheelchair

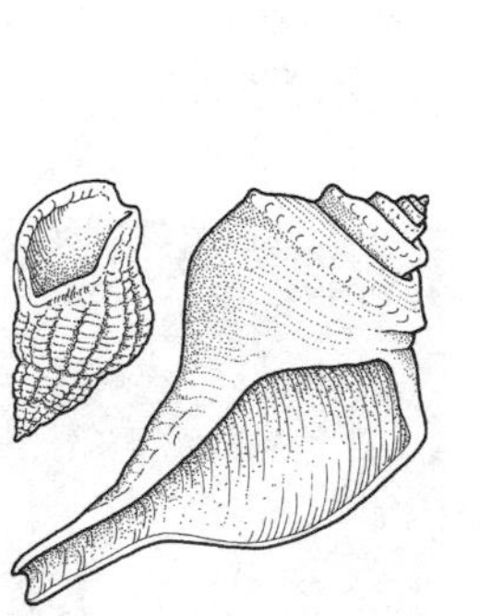

whelk
Left: Waved whelk
Right: Channeled whelk

Usage: when

You should not use **when** in your writing after a form of the verb *to be* in definitions: *A dilemma is when you do not know which way to turn.* Write instead *A dilemma is a situation in which you do not know which way to turn.*

course: *A hawk wheeled over the meadow.* —***idiom.*** **at the wheel** or **behind the wheel.** Operating the steering mechanism of a vehicle; driving. [First written down before 899 in Old English and spelled *hwēol.*]

❑ *These sound alike:* **wheel, weal**[1] (prosperity), **weal**[2] (welt), **we'll** (we will), **wheal** (swelling).

wheel•bar•row (**wēl′**băr′ō) *n.* A vehicle having one or two wheels, with handles at the rear, used to move small loads.

wheel•base (**wēl′**bās′) *n.* The distance from the center of the front wheel to that of the rear wheel in a motor vehicle.

wheel•chair also **wheel chair** (**wēl′**châr′) *n.* A chair mounted on large wheels for the use of a sick or disabled person.

wheeled (wēld) *adj.* Having wheels or a wheel: *a three-wheeled cart.*

wheel•er (**wē′**lər) *n.* **1.** A person or thing that wheels. **2.** A thing that moves on or is equipped with wheels or a wheel: *My nephew can now ride a two-wheeler.*

wheel•er-deal•er (**wē′**lər **dē′**lər) *n. Informal.* A person who is shrewd, aggressive, or unscrupulous, especially in business.

wheel•house (**wēl′**hous′) *n.* A pilothouse.

wheel•wright (**wēl′**rīt′) *n.* A person who builds and repairs wheels.

wheeze (wēz) *intr.v.* **wheezed, wheez•ing, wheez•es. 1.** To breathe with difficulty, producing a hoarse whistling sound. **2.** To make a sound resembling laborious breathing: *The steam engine chugged and wheezed.* —*n.* A wheezing sound. [First written down before 1460 in Middle English and spelled *whesen*, probably from Old Norse *hvæsa*, to hiss.]

wheez•y (**wē′**zē) *adj.* **wheez•i•er, wheez•i•est. 1.** Given to wheezing. **2.** Making a wheezing sound: *a wheezy old car.*

whelk (wĕlk) *n.* Any of various large sea snails having a pointed spiral shell. [First written down about 700 in Old English and spelled *weoloc.*]

whelm (wĕlm) *tr.v.* **whelmed, whelm•ing, whelms. 1.** To cover with water; submerge. **2.** To overwhelm.

whelp (wĕlp) *n.* **1.** The young offspring of a wolf, dog, or similar mammal. **2.** A young person; a child. —*intr.v.* **whelped, whelp•ing, whelps.** To give birth to a whelp or whelps.

when (wĕn) *adv.* At what time: *When did you leave?* —*conj.* **1.** At the time that: *in April, when the snow melts.* **2.** As soon as: *I'll call you when I get there.* **3.** Whenever: *When the wind blows, the windows rattle.* **4.** During the time at which; while: *When I was out, she stopped by for a visit.* **5.** Whereas; although: *He's always reading comic books when he should be studying.* **6.** Considering that; since: *How are you going to make the team when you won't practice?* —*pron.* What or which time: *Since when has this been going on?* —*n.* The time or date: *We knew the when but not the where of it.* [First written down before 899 in Old English and spelled *hwenne.*] —See Note.

whence (wĕns) *adv.* **1.** From where; from what place: *Whence came the traveler?* **2.** From what origin or source: *Whence comes this splendid feast?* —*conj.* **1.** Out of which place; from or out of which. **2.** By reason of which; from which: *The dog was white, whence the name Snowflake.*

when•ev•er (wĕn **ĕv′**ər) *adv.* **1.** At whatever time. **2.** When: *Whenever is she coming?* —*conj.* **1.** At whatever time that: *We can start whenever you're ready.* **2.** Every time that: *I smile whenever I think back on that day.*

when•so•ev•er (wĕn′sō **ĕv′**ər) *adv.* At whatever time at all; whenever. —*conj.* Whenever.

where (wâr) *adv.* **1.a.** At or in what place: *Where is the telephone?* **b.** In what situation or position: *Where would we be without your help?* **2.** From what place or source: *Where did you get that idea?* **3.** To what place or end: *Where does this road lead?* —*conj.* **1.** At what or which place: *I am going to my room, where I can study.* **2.** In a place in which: *She lives where the climate is mild.* **3.** Wherever: *Where there's smoke, there's fire.* **4.** To a place in which: *Let's go where it's quiet.* —*n.* **1.** The place or occasion: *We know the when but not the where of it.* **2.** What place, source, or cause: *Where are you from?* [First written down about 725 in Old English and spelled *hwǣr.*]

where•a•bouts (**wâr′**ə bouts′) *adv.* About where; in, at, or near what location: *Whereabouts do you live?* —*n. (used with a singular or plural verb).* The approximate location of someone or something: *His whereabouts are unknown.*

where•as (wâr **ăz′**) *conj.* **1.** It being the fact that; inasmuch as: *Whereas you have worked hard to help us, so too will we work hard to help you.* **2.** While on the contrary: *We thought the dinner was tonight, whereas it was last night.*

where•at (wâr **ăt′**) *conj.* **1.** Toward or at which. **2.** As a result or consequence of; whereupon.

where•by (wâr **bī′**) *conj.* In accordance with which; by or through which: *I had a plan whereby we could take two hours off our traveling time.*

where•fore (**wâr′**fôr′) *adv.* For what purpose or reason; why: *Wherefore should we fear?* —*n.* A purpose or cause: *I don't know all the whys and wherefores of the decision.*

where•in (wâr **ĭn′**) *adv.* In what way; how: *Wherein have I offended?*

where•of (wâr **ŏv′** *or* wâr **ŭv′**) *conj.* **1.** Of what: *I know whereof I speak.* **2.** Of which: *folk songs whereof many were handed down orally.*

where•on (wâr **ŏn′** *or* wâr **ôn′**) *adv. Archaic.* On which or what.

where•to (**wâr′**to͞o′) *adv.* To what place; toward what end: *Whereto are we heading?* —*conj.* To which.

where•up•on (**wâr′**ə pŏn′ *or* **wâr′**ə pôn′) *conj.* **1.** On which: *the old maple, whereupon we used to build a tree house every summer.* **2.** Closely following which: *The metal cools until it hardens, whereupon it is removed from the sand.*

wher•ev•er (wâr **ĕv′**ər) *adv.* **1.** In or to whatever place; situation: *used red pencil wherever needed.* **2.** Where: *Wherever have you been so long?* —*conj.* In or to whatever place or situation: *My thoughts are with you wherever you go.*

where•with (**wâr′**wĭth′ *or* **wâr′**wĭ*th*′) *pron.* The thing or things with which. —*conj.* By means of which.

where•with•al (**wâr′**wĭth ôl′ *or* **wâr′**wĭ*th* ôl′) *n.* The necessary means, especially financial means: *We haven't the wherewithal to build a new pool.*

whet (wĕt) *tr.v.* **whet•ted, whet•ting, whets. 1.** To sharpen (a knife, for example); hone. **2.** To make more keen; stimulate: *The cooking odors whetted my appetite.* [First written down about 725 in Old English and spelled *hwettan.*]

wheth•er (**wĕ*th*′**ər) *conj.* **1.** Used in indirect questions to introduce one of two alternatives: *We should find out whether the museum is open.* **2.** Used to introduce alternative possibilities: *Whether she wins or whether she loses, this will be her last tournament.* **3.** Either: *He passed the test, whether by skill or luck.*

❑ *These sound alike:* **whether, weather** (state of the atmosphere), **wether** (sheep).

whet•stone (**wĕt′**stōn′) *n.* A hard fine-grained stone used for sharpening tools.

whew (hwyo͞o *or* hwo͞o) *interj.* An expression used to show strong emotion, such as relief or amazement.

whey (wā) *n.* The watery part of milk that separates from the curds, as in the process of making cheese. [First written down before 800 in Old English and spelled *hwæg.*]

which (wĭch) *pron.* **1.** What particular one or ones: *Which is your house?* **2.** The one or ones previously mentioned or implied: *My house, which is near the ocean, stays cool in summer. The nets with which they catch fish need to be repaired.* **3.** Whatever one or ones; whichever: *Choose which of these you want to take with you.* **4.** A thing or circumstance that: *She left early, which was smart.* —*adj.* **1.** What particular one or ones of a number of things or people: *Which part of town do you mean?* **2.** Any one or any number of; whichever: *Use which door you please.* **3.** Being the one or ones previously mentioned or implied: *It started to rain, at which point we ran.* [First written down before 899 in Old English and spelled *hwilc.*] —SEE NOTE at **that.**

which•ev•er (wĭch ĕv′ər) *pron.* Whatever one or ones. —*adj.* Being any one or any number of a group: *Read whichever books you please.*

whiff (wĭf) *n.* **1.** A slight gentle gust of air; a waft. **2.** A brief passing odor carried in the air: *a whiff of popcorn.* **3.** An inhalation, as of air or smoke: *Take a whiff of this perfume.* —*v.* **whiffed, whiff•ing, whiffs.** —*intr.* To be carried in brief gusts; waft: *smoke whiffing from the chimney.* —*tr.* **1.** To blow or convey in whiffs. **2.** To inhale through the nose; sniff.

whif•fle•tree (wĭf′əl trē′) *n.* The crossbar to which the traces of a harness are attached, permitting a draft animal to pull a vehicle or an implement.

Whig (wĭg) *n.* **1.** A member of an 18th- and 19th-century British political party that was opposed to the Tories. **2.** A supporter of the war against England during the American Revolution. **3.** A 19th-century American political party formed to oppose the Democratic party and favoring high tariffs and a loose interpretation of the Constitution.

while (wīl) *n.* **1.** A period of time: *stay for a while; singing all the while.* **2.** The time, effort, or trouble taken in doing something: *It will be worth your while to pay attention.* —*conj.* **1.** As long as; during the time that: *It was great while it lasted.* **2.** At the same time that; although: *Betty is tall while her sisters are short.* **3.** Whereas; and: *The soles of the shoes are leather, while the uppers are canvas.* —*tr. v.* **whiled, whil•ing, whiles.** To spend (time) idly or pleasantly. [First written down about 725 in Old English and spelled *hwīl.*]

whilst (wīlst) *conj. Chiefly British.* While.

whim (wĭm) *n.* A sudden idea; a fancy.

whim•per (wĭm′pər) *v.* **whim•pered, whim•per•ing, whim•pers.** —*intr.* To cry or sob with soft broken sounds. See Synonyms at **cry.** —*tr.* To utter in a whimper. —*n.* A low, broken, sobbing sound.

whim•si•cal (wĭm′zĭ kəl) *adj.* **1.** Determined by, arising from, or marked by whim: *a whimsical notion.* **2.** Erratic in behavior; unpredictable: *Middle English spelling seems whimsical to us now.* —**whim′si•cal•ly** *adv.*

whim•sy (wĭm′zē) *n.* **1.** An odd or fanciful idea; a whim. **2.** A quaint or fanciful quality.

whine (wīn) *v.* **whined, whin•ing, whines.** —*intr.* **1.** To make a mournful high-pitched sound, as in pain or complaint. **2.** To complain or protest in a childish way. —*tr.* To utter with a whine. —*n.* **1.** The act of whining. **2.** A whining sound or complaint. [First written down before 1300 in Middle English and spelled *whinen,* from Old English *hwīnan,* to make a whizzing sound.]

whin•ny (wĭn′ē) *intr.v.* **whin•nied** (wĭn′ēd), **whin•ny•ing, whin•nies** (wĭn′ēz). To neigh, especially in a gentle manner. —*n., pl.* **whin•nies.** The sound made in whinnying; a neigh.

whip (wĭp) *v.* **whipped** or **whipt** (wĭpt), **whip•ping, whips.** —*tr.* **1.** To strike with repeated strokes, as with a strap or rod; lash. **2.** To punish by repeated striking with a strap or rod; flog. **3.** To affect in a manner similar to lashing: *Icy winds whipped my face.* **4.** To beat (cream or eggs, for example) into a froth or foam. **5.** To move, pull, snatch, or remove suddenly: *She whipped her notebook out of her bag.* **6.** *Informal.* To defeat; outdo: *You can't whip our team.* —*intr.* **1.** To move in a sudden quick manner; dart. **2.** To move in a manner similar to a whip; thrash or snap about: *In the storm, branches whipped against the windows.* —*n.* **1.** A flexible rod or thong attached to a handle, used for driving animals on or for striking or beating someone as punishment. **2.** Something that looks, bends, or lashes about like a whip. **3.** A member of a legislature selected by his or her political party to enforce party discipline: *the majority whip in the Senate.* **4.** A dessert made of sugar, whipped cream or stiffly beaten egg whites, and often fruit: *prune whip.* **5.** A lashing motion, stroke, or blow. —*idiom.* **whip up. 1.** To arouse; excite: *The mayor tried to whip up support for new construction projects.* **2.** *Informal.* To prepare quickly: *We whipped up some sandwiches.* [First written down before 1250 in Middle English and spelled *wippen.*]

whip•lash (wĭp′lăsh′) *n.* **1.** The lash of a whip. **2.** An injury to the neck or spine caused by a sudden backward or forward jerk of the head.

whip•per•snap•per (wĭp′ər snăp′ər) *n.* A person regarded as unimportant and pretentious.

whip•pet (wĭp′ĭt) *n.* Any of a breed of slender swift-running dog resembling the greyhound but smaller.

whip•poor•will (wĭp′ər wĭl′ *or* wĭp′ər wĭl′) *n.* A spotted brown North American bird that is active at night and has a call that sounds like its name.

whip•stitch (wĭp′stĭch′) *n.* A stitch made by sewing with overcast stitches, as in binding two pieces of fabric together.

whipt (wĭpt) *v.* A past tense and a past participle of **whip.**

whir (wûr) *intr.v.* **whirred, whir•ring, whirs.** To move so as to make a buzzing or vibrating sound. —*n.* A sound of buzzing or vibration.
❑ *These sound alike:* **whir, were** (existed).

whirl (wûrl) *v.* **whirled, whirl•ing, whirls.** —*intr.* **1.** To revolve rapidly about a center or an axis: *The propeller whirled faster and faster.* See Synonyms at **turn. 2.** To rotate or spin rapidly: *The dancer whirled on stage.* **3.** To turn suddenly, changing direction: *whirled around to face me.* **4.** To move or go quickly: *The bike racers whirled around the curve.* **5.** To have a spinning sensation; reel: *My head is whirling from the news.* —*tr.* **1.** To cause to rotate or turn rapidly: *whirl a baton.* **2.** To move or drive in a circular or curving course: *The wind whirled the leaves.* —*n.* **1.** The act of rotating or revolving rapidly. **2.** Something, such as a cloud of dust, that whirls or is whirled. **3.** A state of confusion; a tumult. **4.** A swift succession or round of events: *the social whirl.* **5.** *Informal.* A short trip or ride: *Let's go for a whirl in the car.* **6.** *Informal.* A brief or experimental try: *I've never skied before, but I'll give it a whirl.*

whirl•i•gig (wûr′lĭ gĭg′) *n.* **1.** Any of various spinning toys. **2.** A merry-go-round. **3.** Something that is always whirling.

whirl•pool (wûrl′po͞ol′) *n.* **1.** A rapidly rotating current of water or other liquid, as one produced by the meeting of two tides; an eddy. **2.** A state of

ă	pat	oi	boy
ā	pay	ou	out
âr	care	o͝o	took
ä	father	o͞o	boot
ĕ	pet	ŭ	cut
ē	be	ûr	urge
ĭ	pit	th	thin
ī	pie	*th*	this
îr	pier	hw	whoop
ŏ	pot	zh	vision
ō	toe	ə	about
ô	paw	N	*French* bon

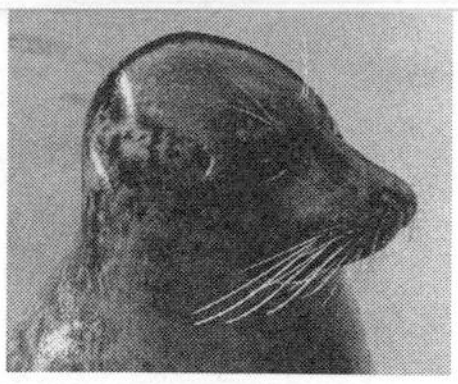

whisker
Whiskers on a sea lion

Walt Whitman

Walt Whitman

Born on Long Island and raised in Brooklyn, Walt **Whitman** was a poet of the people. Largely self-educated, Whitman read widely and spent much time carefully observing the great variety of life in New York City. In 1855 Whitman published *Leaves of Grass,* a volume of 12 poems that were radical in form and content and celebrated the people, democracy, and land of America. Although these poems may seem patriotic to us today, at the time Whitman was denounced for their unconventional style and content. Ten years later, Whitman published *Drum Taps and Sequel,* which deals with his experiences during the Civil War and includes a poem written in commemoration of President Abraham Lincoln. Over the years Whitman expanded *Leaves of Grass* into a volume that included 350 poems when it was republished in 1891. Whitman has since become known as one of the most original and influential of American poets.

confusion; a tumult. **3.** A bathtub or pool having jets of warm water that can be directed at a body part.

whirl•wind (wûrl′wĭnd′) *n.* **1.** A rapidly rotating column of air. **2.** A tumultuous confused rush.

whirl•y•bird (wûr′lē bûrd′) *n. Informal.* A helicopter.

whirr (wûr) *v. & n. Chiefly British.* Variant of **whir.**

whisk (wĭsk) *v.* **whisked, whisk•ing, whisks.** *—tr.* **1.** To cause to move with quick, light, sweeping motions: *whisking the crumbs off the table.* **2.** To whip (eggs or cream). *—intr.* To move lightly, nimbly, and rapidly. *—n.* **1.** A quick, light, sweeping motion: *the whisk of a cow's tail.* **2.** A whiskbroom. **3.** A kitchen tool used for whipping foodstuffs: *a wire whisk.* [First written down about 1410 in Middle English and spelled *wisken,* of Scandinavian origin.]

whisk•broom (wĭsk′bro͞om′ *or* **wĭsk′**bro͝om′) *n.* A small short-handled broom used especially to brush clothes.

whisk•er (wĭs′kər) *n.* **1a. whiskers.** The hair on a man's cheeks and chin. **b.** A single hair of a beard or mustache. **2.** One of the bristles or long hairs growing near the mouth of certain animals, such as cats, rats, or rabbits.

whis•key also **whis•ky** (wĭs′kē) *n., pl.* **whis•keys** also **whis•kies.** An alcoholic liquor distilled from grain, such as corn, rye, or barley. [First written down in 1715 in Modern English and spelled *whiskie,* from Scottish Gaelic *uisge beatha,* water of life.]

whis•per (wĭs′pər) *n.* **1.** Soft speech produced without full voice. **2.** Something uttered very softly. **3.** A low rustling sound: *The whisper of wind in the trees.* *—v.* **whis•pered, whis•per•ing, whis•pers.** *—intr.* **1.** To speak softly. **2.** To make a soft rustling sound: *wind whispering in the leaves.* *—tr.* **1.** To utter very softly. **2.** To say or tell privately or secretly. [First written down in 1599 in Modern English, from Middle English *whisperen,* to whisper, from Old English *hwisprian.*]

whist (wĭst) *n.* A card game played by two teams of two players each that was a forerunner of bridge.

whis•tle (wĭs′əl) *v.* **whis•tled, whis•tling, whis•tles.** *—intr.* **1.** To make a clear musical sound by forcing air through the teeth or through an opening in the lips. **2.** To produce a clear, shrill, sharp musical sound by blowing on or through a device. **3.** To make a shrill sharp cry: *The birds whistled in the trees.* **4.** To move swiftly so as to make a high-pitched sound: *The wind whistled through the trees.* *—tr.* **1.** To produce by whistling: *whistle a tune.* **2.** To summon, direct, or signal by whistling: *whistle down a cab.* *—n.* **1.** A small wind instrument for making whistling sounds by means of the breath. **2.** A device for making whistling sounds by means of forced air or steam. **3.** A sound produced by whistling. **4.** A whistling sound, as of an animal or a projectile. **5.** The act of whistling. ***—idiom.*** **blow the whistle.** *Slang.* To expose wrongdoing in the hope of bringing it to a halt. [First written down about 1000 in Old English and spelled *hwistlian.*]

Whis•tler (wĭs′lər), **James Abbott McNeill.** 1834–1903. American painter whose works include a portrait of his mother, entitled *Arrangement in Grey and Black* (1872).

whit (wĭt) *n.* The least or smallest bit: *doesn't care a whit.* [First written down before 900 in Old English and spelled *wiht,* amount.]

white (wīt) *n.* **1.** The color of maximum lightness, as of milk, for example. **2.** The white or nearly white part, such as the albumen of an egg or the part of an eyeball around the iris. **3.** A thing that is white or nearly white, as a white dye or a white variety of flower. **4. whites.** White trousers or a white outfit of a special nature: *tennis whites.* **5.** Also **White.** A member of a racial group of people having light skin, especially a person of European origin. **4.** A politically conservative or reactionary person. *—adj.* **whit•er, whit•est. 1.** Being of the color white, as new snow. **2.** Approaching the color white, as: **a.** Weakly colored; almost colorless; pale: *white wine.* **b.** Pale gray; silvery and lustrous: *white hair.* **3.** Also **White.** Of, relating to, or belonging to a racial group having light skin, especially one of European origin. **4.** Not written or printed on; blank. **5.** Accompanied by or covered in snow: *a white Christmas.* **6.** Incandescent: *white flames.* **7.** With milk added. Used of tea or coffee. **8.** Politically conservative or reactionary. *—tr.v.* **whit•ed, whit•ing, whites.** To create or leave blank spaces in (printed or illustrated matter). [First written down before 899 in Old English and spelled *hwīt.*] **—white′ness** *n.*

❑ *These sound alike:* **white, wight** (creature).

white ant *n.* A termite.

white blood cell *n.* Any of the white or colorless cells in the blood that have a nucleus and help protect the body against infections.

white•cap (wīt′kăp′) *n.* A wave with a crest of foam.

white-col•lar (wīt′kŏl′ər) *adj.* Of or relating to workers whose work usually does not involve manual labor.

white corpuscle *n.* A white blood cell.

white dwarf *n.* A whitish star having low brightness, small size, and very great density.

white elephant *n.* **1.** A rare expensive possession that is a financial burden to maintain. **2.** Something of doubtful or limited value.

white•fish (wīt′fĭsh′) *n.* Any of various silvery freshwater fishes used as food.

white flag *n.* A white cloth or flag used to signal surrender or truce.

white gold *n.* An alloy of gold and nickel, sometimes also containing palladium or zinc, having a pale color like that of platinum.

white•head (wīt′hĕd′) *n.* A small white or yellowish lump in the skin caused by the buildup of fluid in a sebaceous gland.

white heat *n.* The temperature or physical condition of a white-hot substance.

White•horse (wīt′hôrs′). The capital and largest city of Yukon Territory, Canada, in the southern part of the territory on the Yukon River. It has been the capital since 1952. Population, 14,814.

white-hot (wīt′hŏt′) *adj.* So hot as to glow with a bright white light.

White House *n.* **1.** The executive branch of the U.S. government. **2.** The executive mansion of the President of the United States.

white lie *n.* A lie concerning a trivial matter, often told to prevent someone's feelings from being hurt.

white matter *n.* Whitish nerve tissue, especially of the brain and spinal cord, consisting chiefly of myelin-covered nerve fibers.

whit•en (wīt′n) *tr. & intr.v.* **whit•ened, whit•en•ing, whit•ens.** To make or become white, especially by bleaching. **—whit′en•er** *n.*

white night *n.* A night without full darkness, as during the summer near the Arctic Circle.

white noise *n.* Acoustical or electrical noise in which the intensity is the same at all frequencies within a given band.

white oak *n.* A large oak of eastern North America having heavy, hard, light-colored wood.

white•out (wīt′out′) *n.* A polar weather condition in which the light reflected from the snow blends into the light reflected from the clouds, making any shadows and the horizon invisible and making it impossible to see where one is going.

white pepper *n.* Pepper ground from peppercorns from which the outer black layer has been removed.

white pine *n.* A timber tree of eastern North America, having needles in clusters of five and durable easily worked wood.

white sauce *n.* A sauce made with butter, flour, and milk, cream, or stock, and seasoning, used as a base for other sauces.

white-tailed deer (wīt′tāld′) *n.* A common North American deer having a tail that is white on the underside.

white tie *n.* **1.** A white bow tie worn as part of men's formal evening dress. **2.** Men's formal evening dress.

white•wall tire (wīt′wôl′) *n.* An automobile tire having a white sidewall.

white•wash (wīt′wŏsh′ *or* wīt′wôsh′) *n.* **1.** A mixture of lime and water, often with whiting, size, or glue, that is used to whiten walls, fences, and other structures. **2.** Concealment or glossing over of flaws or failures. —*tr.v.* **white•washed, white•wash•ing, white•wash•es. 1.** To paint or coat with or as if with whitewash. **2.** To conceal or gloss over (a flaw, for example).

white water *n.* Turbulent or frothy water, as in rapids or surf.

whith•er (wĭth′ər) *adv.* To what place, result, or condition: *Whither are we going?*

❑ *These sound alike:* **whither, wither** (shrivel).

whit•ing[1] (wī′tĭng) *n.* A pure white grade of chalk that has been ground and washed for use in paints, ink, and putty. [First written down about 1440 in Middle English and spelled *whityng*, from *whiten*, to whiten.]

whit•ing[2] (wī′tĭng) *n., pl.* **whiting** or **whit•ings. 1.** A food fish of European Atlantic waters, related to the cod. **2.** Any of several silvery ocean fishes of North American coastal waters valued as food. [First written down before 1425 in Middle English and spelled *whitynge*, from Middle Dutch *wijting*.]

whit•ish (wī′tĭsh) *adj.* Somewhat white.

Whit•man (wĭt′mən), **Walt.** 1819–1892. American poet whose *Leaves of Grass* (first published in 1855), celebrates the connections between human life and nature and the greatness of democracy and the United States. —SEE NOTE.

Whit•ney (wĭt′nē), **Eli.** 1765–1825. American inventor and manufacturer who invented the cotton gin (1793), revolutionizing the cotton industry.

Whitney, Mount. A peak, 14,494 feet (4,420.7 meters) high, in the Sierra Nevada of east-central California. It is the highest elevation in the continental United States.

Whit•sun•day (wĭt′sən dē *or* wĭt′sən dā′) *n.* Pentecost.

Whit•sun•tide (wĭt′sən tīd′) *n.* The week beginning on Whitsunday, especially the first three days of this week.

Whit•ti•er (wĭt′ē ər), **John Greenleaf.** 1807–1892. American poet who is best known for his poems about New England, including *Snow-Bound* (1866).

whit•tle (wĭt′l) *v.* **whit•tled, whit•tling, whit•tles.** —*tr.* **1.** To cut small bits or pare shavings from (a piece of wood). **2.** To fashion or shape in this way: *whittle a toy boat.* **3.** To reduce or eliminate gradually, as if by whittling: *He whittled down his debt by making regular payments.* —*intr.* To cut or shape wood with a knife. **—whit′tler** *n.*

whiz also **whizz** (wĭz) *v.* **whizzed, whiz•zing, whiz•zes.** —*intr.* **1.** To make a whirring or hissing sound, as of an object speeding through air. **2.** To move rapidly; rush: *The subway train whizzed by without stopping.* —*tr.* To throw or spin rapidly: *whizzed the ball to me.* —*n.* **1.** A whirring or hissing sound. **2.** *Informal.* A person who has remarkable skill: *He's a whiz at math.*

who (ho͞o) *pron.* **1.** What or which person or persons: *Who is calling?* **2.** Used as a relative pronoun to introduce a clause referring to a human being: *The boy who came yesterday is now gone.* [First written down about 725 in Old English and spelled *hwā*.] —SEE NOTE.

whoa (wō) *interj.* An expression used as a command to stop, as to a horse.

who'd (ho͞od). Contraction of *who would.*

who•dun•it (ho͞o dŭn′ĭt) *n. Informal.* A story dealing with a crime and its solution.

who•ev•er (ho͞o ĕv′ər) *pron.* **1.** Whatever person or persons: *Whoever comes should be welcomed into the house.* **2.** Who: *Whoever could have dreamed of such a thing?*

whole (hōl) *adj.* **1.** Containing all component parts; complete: *a whole formal wardrobe.* **2.** Not divided or disjoined; in one unit: *a whole acre of land.* **3.** Constituting the full amount, extent, or duration: *The baby slept the whole trip home.* **4.** Sound; healthy: *a whole organism.* —*n.* **1.** A number, group, set, or thing lacking no part or element; a complete thing. **2.** An entity or system made up of interrelated parts: *the universe as a whole made up of the sun, planets, satellites, and other celestial bodies.* —*adv. Informal.* Entirely; wholly: *a whole new idea.* ***—idioms.*** **as a whole.** All parts or aspects considered; altogether. **on the whole.** Considering everything: *The damage doesn't look too bad, on the whole.* [First written down about 725 in Old English and spelled *hāl*.]

❑ *These sound alike:* **whole, hole** (opening).

whole•heart•ed (hōl′här′tĭd) *adj.* Marked by full devotion or commitment; sincere: *wholehearted cooperation.* **—whole′heart′ed•ly** *adv.* **—whole′heart′ed•ness** *n.*

whole note *n.* A musical note having the value of four beats in common time.

whole number *n.* Any of the set of numbers including 0 and all negative and positive multiples of 1.

whole•sale (hōl′sāl′) *n.* The sale of goods in large quantities, especially to a retailer. —*adj.* **1.** Of, relating to, or engaged in the sale of goods in large quantities for resale: *a wholesale dealer; wholesale prices.* **2.** Sold in large bulk or quantity, usually at a lower cost: *wholesale merchandise.* **3.** Made or accomplished extensively and indiscriminately: *wholesale destruction.* —*adv.* In large bulk or quantity: *sell wholesale.* **—whole′sal′er** *n.*

whole•some (hōl′səm) *adj.* **whole•som•er, whole•som•est. 1.** Conducive to sound health or well-being; salutary: *a wholesome diet.* **2.** Enjoying or marked by a healthy physical, moral, or mental condition: *a wholesome rosy complexion; a wholesome attitude.* **—whole′some•ly** *adv.* **—whole′some•ness** *n.*

whole-wheat (hōl′wēt′) *adj.* **1.** Made from the entire grain of wheat, including the bran: *whole-wheat flour.* **2.** Made with whole-wheat flour.

who'll (ho͞ol). Contraction of *who will* or *who shall.*

whol•ly (hō′lē) *adv.* Entirely; completely.

❑ *These sound alike:* **wholly, holy** (sacred).

whom (ho͞om) *pron.* The objective case of **who.**

whom•ev•er (ho͞om ĕv′ər) *pron.* The objective case of **whoever.**

whom•so•ev•er (ho͞om′sō ĕv′ər) *pron.* The objective case of **whosoever.**

whoop (ho͞op *or* hwo͞op *or* wo͞op) *n.* **1.** A loud cry, as of exultation or excitement. **2.** A hooting cry, as of a bird. **3.** The gasp characteristic of whooping cough. —*v.* **whooped, whoop•ing, whoops.** —*intr.*

Usage: who

Use **who** as a subject, where a nominative pronoun such as *I* or *he* would be appropriate, and *whom* elsewhere: *The actor who played Hamlet was there.* In this case **who** stands for the subject of *played Hamlet.* But we write *The student whom the teacher called on had no answer.* In this case *whom* is the object of *called on.* It is difficult sometimes to apply the rules correctly, as in the sentence *I met the person whom my friend wanted me to invite.*

ă	pat	oi	boy
ā	pay	ou	out
âr	care	o͝o	took
ä	father	o͞o	boot
ĕ	pet	ŭ	cut
ē	be	ûr	urge
ĭ	pit	th	thin
ī	pie	*th*	this
îr	pier	hw	whoop
ŏ	pot	zh	vision
ō	toe	ə	about
ô	paw	N	*French* bon

whooping crane

Usage: **whose**

It is correct to use **whose** as a possessive form for both persons and things: *The cabinet, whose decoration was very ornate, was filled with china.*

widgeon

wigwam
Birch bark wigwam

Oscar Wilde
Photographed in 1882

1. To utter a loud shout or hooting cry. **2.** To make the gasp characteristic of whooping cough. —*tr.* To utter with a whoop: *The fans whooped their delight.*

❑ *These sound alike:* **whoop, hoop** (circular band).

whoop•ing cough (ho͞o′pĭng *or* **ho͝op′**ĭng) *n.* A bacterial infection of the lungs and respiratory passages that causes spasms of coughing alternating with gasps.

whooping crane *n.* A large long-legged North American bird having white and black feathers and a shrill trumpeting cry. It is now very rare and is in danger of becoming extinct.

whoops (wo͝ops *or* wo͞ops) *interj.* An expression used to show apology or mild surprise.

whop•per (wŏp′ər) *n. Slang.* **1.** Something exceptionally big or remarkable. **2.** A gross untruth; a big lie.

whore (hôr) *n.* A prostitute.

❑ *These sound alike:* **whore, hoar** (frost).

whorl (wôrl *or* wûrl) *n.* **1.** A form that coils or spirals; a curl or swirl. **2.** An arrangement of three or more plant parts, as of leaves or petals, radiating from a single point or part. **3.** One of the turns of a spiral shell. **4.** One of the circular ridges or convolutions of a fingerprint.

who's (ho͞oz). Contraction of *who is* or *who has.*

❑ *These sound alike:* **who's, whose** (possessive of who).

whose (ho͞oz) *adj.* **1.** The possessive form of **who. 2.** The possessive form of **which.** —See Note.

❑ *These sound alike:* **whose, who's** (who is).

who•so•ev•er (ho͞o′sō **ĕv′**ər) *pron.* Whoever.

why (wī) *adv.* For what purpose, reason, or cause: *Why is the door shut?* —*conj.* **1.** The reason, cause, or purpose for which: *I know why you're here.* **2.** On account of which; for which: *The reason why I went swimming yesterday was that it was very hot.* —*n., pl.* **whys.** A cause or reason: *studying the whys of unemployment.* —*interj.* An expression used to show mild surprise, indignation, or impatience: *Why, I'm delighted to help!* [First written down before 899 in Old English and spelled *hwȳ.*]

Wich•i•ta[1] (**wĭch′**ĭ tô′) *n., pl.* **Wichita** or **Wich•i•tas. 1.** A member of a Native American confederacy now living in southwest Oklahoma. **2.** The Caddoan language of the Wichita.

Wich•i•ta[2] (**wĭch′**ĭ tô′). A city of south-central Kansas southwest of Kansas City. It was founded in the 1860's on the site of an earlier Wichita Village. Population, 304,011.

wick (wĭk) *n.* A cord or strand of loosely woven fibers, as in a candle or an oil lamp, that draws up fuel to the flame by capillary action. [First written down about 1000 in Old English and spelled *wēoce.*]

wick•ed (**wĭk′**ĭd) *adj.* **wick•ed•er, wick•ed•est. 1.** Morally bad; evil. **2.** Playfully malicious or mischievous: *played a wicked prank.* **3.** Severe and distressing: *has a wicked cough.* **—wick′ed•ly** *adv.* **—wick′ed•ness** *n.*

wick•er (**wĭk′**ər) *n.* **1.** A flexible plant branch or twig, as of a willow, used in weaving baskets or furniture. **2.** Work made of interlaced plant branches or twigs. [First written down in 1336 in Middle English and spelled *wekirr*, of Scandinavian origin.]

wick•et (**wĭk′**ĭt) *n.* **1.** A small gate or door, especially one built into or near a larger one. **2.** A small window or opening. **3.** In cricket, either of the two sets of three stakes, topped by a crossbar, that forms the target of the bowler. **4.** In croquet, any of the wire arches through which each player tries to hit a ball.

wick•i•up (**wĭk′**ē ŭp′) *n.* A frame hut covered with matting, as of bark or brush, used by nomadic Native Americans of North America.

wide (wīd) *adj.* **wid•er, wid•est. 1.** Extending over a large area from side to side; broad: *a wide street.* **2.** Having a specified extent from side to side: *a ribbon two inches wide.* **3.** Having great range or extent; including much or many: *a wide selection of dresses.* **4.** Fully open or extended: *look with wide eyes.* **5.** Being at a distance from a desired goal or point: *a shot wide of the mark.* —*adv.* **wider, widest. 1.** Over a great distance; extensively: *traveling far and wide.* **2.** To the full extent; completely: *The door was wide open.* **3.** So as to miss the target; astray: *shoot wide.* [First written down about 725 in Old English and spelled *wīd.*] **—wide′ly** *adv.* **—wide′ness** *n.*

wide-a•wake (**wīd′** ə **wāk′**) *adj.* **1.** Completely awake. **2.** Alert; watchful: *a wide-awake sentry.*

wide-eyed (**wīd′**īd′) *adj.* **1.** Having the eyes completely open. **2.** Innocent; naive.

wid•en (**wīd′**n) *tr. & intr.v.* **wid•ened, wid•en•ing, wid•ens.** To make or become wide or wider.

wide•spread (**wīd′sprĕd′**) *adj.* **1.** Spread or scattered over a considerable extent: *widespread damage from last month's storm.* **2.** Occurring or accepted widely: *widespread agreement on the new proposal.*

wid•geon (**wĭj′**ən) *n., pl.* **widgeon** or **wid•geons.** Either of two kinds of wild duck having brownish feathers, a white belly, and a light-colored patch on the top of the head.

wid•ow (**wĭd′**ō) *n.* A woman whose husband has died and who has not remarried. —*tr.v.* **wid•owed, wid•ow•ing, wid•ows.** To make a widow or widower of.

wid•ow•er (**wĭd′**ō ər) *n.* A man whose wife has died and who has not remarried.

wid•ow's peak (**wĭd′**ōz) *n.* A V-shaped point formed by the hair at the middle of the forehead.

wid•ow's walk *n.* A rooftop platform surrounded with a railing and originally built on coastal houses to observe ships at sea.

width (wĭdth *or* wĭth *or* wĭtth) *n.* **1.** The state, quality, or fact of being wide. **2.** The measurement of the extent of something from side to side: *a room ten feet in width.* **3.** A piece of material measured along the crosswise grain; a piece of fabric measured from selvage to selvage.

wield (wēld) *tr.v.* **wield•ed, wield•ing, wields. 1.** To handle (a weapon or tool, for example) with skill and ease. **2.** To exercise (power or influence, for example) effectively.

wie•ner (**wē′**nər) *n.* **1.** Wienerwurst. **2.** A hot dog.

wie•ner•wurst (**wē′**nər wûrst′ *or* **wē′**nər wo͝orst′) *n.* A smoked pork or beef sausage similar to a frankfurter.

wife (wīf) *n., pl.* **wives** (wīvz). A woman who is married to a man.

wife•ly (**wīf′**lē) *adj.* Of or befitting a wife.

wig (wĭg) *n.* An artificial covering of synthetic or human hair worn on the head for adornment, as a way to hide baldness, or as part of a costume. [First written down in 1675 in Modern English, short for *periwig.*]

wig•gle (**wĭg′**əl) *intr. & tr.v.* **wig•gled, wig•gling, wig•gles.** To move or cause to move with short irregular motions from side to side: *She wiggled her toes. The dog's ears wiggled.* —*n.* A wiggling movement or course.

wig•gler (**wĭg′**lər) *n.* **1.** A person or thing that wiggles. **2.** The larva or pupa of a mosquito.

wight (wīt) *n. Obsolete.* A living being; a creature.

❑ *These sound alike:* **wight, white** (color).

wig•wag (**wĭg′**wăg′) *v.* **wig•wagged, wig•wag•ging, wig•wags.** —*intr.* **1.** To move back and forth;

wag: *watched the metronome wigwag.* **2.** To signal or send a message by such motions: *wigwag for help.* —*tr.* **1.** To move (something) back and forth, especially as a means of signaling: *wigwag a flag.* **2.** To send (a message) by moving something back and forth. —*n.* **1.** The act or practice of wigwagging. **2.** A message sent by this method.

wig•wam (wĭg′wŏm′) *n.* A Native American dwelling commonly having an arched or conical framework covered with bark, hides, or mats.

wild (wīld) *adj.* **wild•er, wild•est. 1.** Growing, living, or occurring in a natural state; not cultivated, kept, or tamed by human beings: *wild plants; wild honey.* **2.** Not lived in or cultivated by people: *wild unsettled country.* **3.** Uncivilized; savage. **4.** Lacking discipline or control; unruly: *a wild young boy.* **5.** Full of or suggestive of strong uncontrolled feeling: *wild with joy; wild laughter.* **6.** Very strange or unlikely; outlandish: *a wild idea.* **7.** Far from the intended mark or target: *a wild throw.* **8.** In card games, having a value determined by the cardholder's choice: *playing poker with deuces wild.* —*n.* **1.** A natural or undomesticated state: *Have you ever seen moose in the wild?* **2.** A region not lived in or cultivated by human beings: *the wilds of northern Canada.* [First written down before 800 in Old English and spelled *wilde.*] **—wild′ly** *adv.* **—wild′ness** *n.*

wild boar *n.* A wild pig of Europe, Asia, and northern Africa, having dark dense bristles.

wild•cat (wīld′kăt′) *n.* **1.** Any of various wild small to medium-sized mammals, such as the lynx and the bobcat, related to the domestic cat. **2.** A quick-tempered or fierce person. —*adj.* **1.** Risky or unsound, especially financially. **2.** Of or relating to an oil or natural-gas well drilled in an area not known to be productive. **3.** Carried on without official permission or sanction: *a wildcat strike.*

Wilde (wīld), **Oscar (Fingal O'Flahertie Wills).** 1854–1900. Irish writer known for his plays, including *The Importance of Being Earnest* (1895), and his novel *The Picture of Dorian Gray* (1891).

wil•de•beest (wĭl′də bēst′) *n., pl.* **wil•de•beests** or **wildebeest.** The gnu.

Wil•der (wĭl′dər), **Thornton (Niven).** 1897–1975. American writer whose works include novels and the play *Our Town* (1938).

wil•der•ness (wĭl′dər nĭs) *n.* An unsettled uncultivated region left in its natural condition.

wild•fire (wīld′fīr′) *n.* **1.** A raging rapidly spreading fire. **2.** Something that acts very quickly and intensely. **3.** Lightning that occurs without audible thunder.

wild•flow•er also **wild flow•er** (wīld′flou′ər) *n.* **1.** A flowering plant that grows without cultivation or special care, as distinguished from those specially planted and cared for. **2.** The flower of such a plant.

wild•fowl (wīld′foul′) *n.* A wild game bird, such as a duck, partridge, or quail.

wild-goose chase (wīld′gōōs′) *n.* A futile pursuit or search.

wild•life (wīld′līf′) *n.* Wild vegetation and animals, especially animals living in the wild.

wild oat *n.* A grass related to the cultivated oat.

wild pitch *n.* In baseball, an erratic pitch that the catcher cannot catch and that enables a base runner to advance.

wild rice *n.* **1.** A tall North American water grass having narrow brownish seeds used as food. **2.** The seeds of this plant.

Wild West *n.* The western United States during the 19th and early 20th centuries.

wild•wood (wīld′wŏŏd′) *n.* A forest or wooded area in its natural state.

wile (wīl) *n.* **1.** A plan or trick intended to deceive or ensnare. **2.** A disarming or seductive manner, device, or procedure. —*tr.v.* **wiled, wil•ing, wiles. 1.** To entice; lure: *wiled him into betraying his friends.* **2.** To pass (time) agreeably: *wile away a Sunday afternoon.* [First written down before 1160 in Middle English and spelled *wil,* from Old Norse *vēl,* trick, or of Low German origin.]

wil•ful (wĭl′fəl) *adj.* Variant of **willful.**

will[1] (wĭl) *n.* **1.** The power by which one deliberately chooses or decides upon a course of action: *the freedom of will.* **2.** The act of exercising this faculty; a choice. **3.** Diligent purposefulness; determination: *the will to succeed.* **4.** A desire, purpose, or determination, especially of one in authority: *What is your will in this matter?* **5.** Bearing or attitude toward others; disposition: *a man of good will.* **6.** A legal declaration of how a person wishes his or her possessions to be disposed of after death. —*v.* **willed, will•ing, wills.** —*tr.* **1.** To decide on; choose or determine: *He can finish the race if he wills it.* **2.** To influence or induce by sheer force of will: *The coach seemed to will us to make a comeback.* **3.** To grant in a legal will; bequeath. —*intr.* **1.** To exercise the will. **2.** To make a choice; choose. [First written down about 725 in Old English and spelled *willa.*]

will[2] (wĭl) *aux.v.* Past tense **would** (wŏŏd). **1.** Used to indicate future action or condition: *They will return later.* **2.** Used to indicate likelihood or certainty: *You will regret this.* **3.** Used to indicate willingness: *Will you help me with this package?* **4.** Used to indicate requirement or command: *You will report to me afterward.* **5.** Used to indicate intention: *I will too if I feel like it.* **6.** Used to indicate customary or habitual action: *People will talk.* **7.** Used to indicate capacity or ability: *This metal will not crack.* **8.** Used to indicate probability or expectation: *That will be Bob calling to say he is going to be late.* —*tr. & intr.v.* To wish; desire: *Do what you will. Sit here if you will.* [First written down about 725 in Old English and spelled *willan.*]

Wil•lard (wĭl′ərd), **Emma Hart.** 1787–1870. American educator who was an early advocate of higher education for women.

Willard, Frances Elizabeth Caroline. 1839–1898. American reformer who served as president of the Woman's Christian Temperance Union (1879–1898).

will•ful also **wil•ful** (wĭl′fəl) *adj.* **1.** Said or done on purpose; deliberate: *a willful waste of money.* **2.** Stubbornly bent on having one's own way: *a willful child.* **—will′ful•ly** *adv.* **—will′ful•ness** *n.*

Wil•liam I (wĭl′yəm) Known as **"William the Conqueror."** 1027?–1087. King of England (1066–1087) and duke of Normandy (1035–1087) who led the Norman invasion of England (1066).

Wil•liams (wĭl′yəmz), **Roger.** 1603?–1683. English cleric in America who founded Providence, Rhode Island (1636), after being expelled from Massachusetts for his criticism of Puritanism.

Williams, Tennessee. 1911–1983. American playwright whose works include *Cat on a Hot Tin Roof* (1955).

Williams, William Carlos. 1883–1963. American poet whose verse is marked by a spare style and vivid observations of everyday occurrences and scenes.

Wil•liams•burg (wĭl′yəmz bûrg′). A city of southeast Virginia southeast of Richmond. It was settled in about 1632 and was the capital of Virginia from 1699 to 1779. The city is now home to a restored colonial village. Population, 11,530.

William the Conqueror. William I.

will•ing (wĭl′ĭng) *adj.* **1.** Disposed or inclined; pre-

Emma Willard

William the Conqueror

Tennessee Williams

ă	pat	oi	boy
ā	pay	ou	out
âr	care	ŏŏ	took
ä	father	ōō	boot
ĕ	pet	ŭ	cut
ē	be	ûr	urge
ĭ	pit	th	thin
ī	pie	*th*	this
îr	pier	hw	whoop
ŏ	pot	zh	vision
ō	toe	ə	about
ô	paw	N	*French* bon

Woodrow Wilson

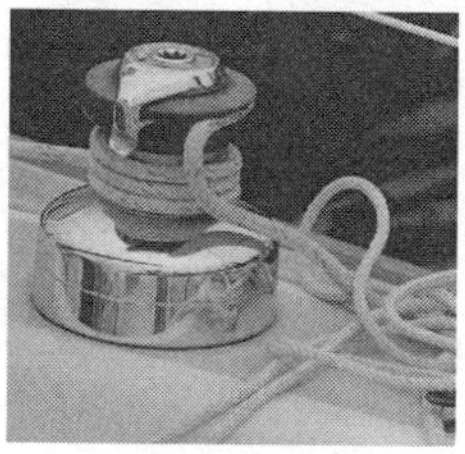

winch

windmill
Top: Water-pumping windmill in Colorado
Bottom: Grain-grinding windmill in La Mancha, Spain

pared: *willing to accept your apology.* **2.** Acting or ready to act gladly: *a willing worker.* **3.** Done, given, accepted, or borne voluntarily or ungrudgingly. **—will′ing•ly** *adv.* **—will′ing•ness** *n.*

will-o'-the-wisp (wĭl′ə *thə* **wĭsp′**) *n.* **1.** A phosphorescent light that flits over swampy ground at night, possibly caused by spontaneous combustion of gases given off by rotting organic matter. **2.** A delusive or misleading hope.

wil•low (wĭl′ō) *n.* **1.** Any of various trees having slender flexible twigs and narrow leaves. **2.** The strong lightweight wood of any of these trees.

wil•low•y (wĭl′ō ē) *adj.* **wil•low•i•er, wil•low•i•est. 1.** Planted with or abounding in willows: *a willowy grove.* **2.** Suggestive of a willow, as in flexibility, slenderness, or gracefulness.

will•pow•er or **will pow•er** (wĭl′pou′ər) *n.* The strength of will to carry out one's decisions, wishes, or plans.

wil•ly-nil•ly (wĭl′ē nĭl′ē) *adv.* **1.** Whether desired or not: *He must do what we've asked, willy-nilly.* **2.** Without order or plan; haphazardly.

Wil•ming•ton (wĭl′mĭng tən). The largest city in Delaware, in the northeast part of the state southwest of Philadelphia, Pennsylvania. It was founded in 1638. Population, 71,529.

Wil•son (wĭl′sən), **(Thomas) Woodrow.** 1856–1924. The 28th President of the United States (1913–1921), whose administration was marked by World War I and the introduction of prohibition. He won the 1919 Nobel Peace Prize.

wilt[1] (wĭlt) *v.* **wilt•ed, wilt•ing, wilts.** *—intr.* **1.** To become limp or flaccid; droop: *plants wilting in the dry heat.* **2.** To feel or show the effects of exhaustion: *We wilted after the long hike in the dunes.* *—tr.* **1.** To cause to droop or lose freshness: *The hot air from the heat vent wilted the flowers.* **2.** To deprive of energy or vigor; fatigue or exhaust. [First written down in 1691 in Modern English, possibly alteration of dialectal *welk,* from Middle English *welken.*]

wilt[2] (wĭlt) *aux.v. Archaic.* A second person singular present tense of **will[2].**

wi•ly (wī′lē) *adj.* **wi•li•er, wi•li•est.** Full of wiles; cunning: *a wily fox.*

wimp (wĭmp) *n. Slang.* A person who is regarded as weak or ineffectual.

wim•ple (wĭm′pəl) *n.* A piece of cloth wound around the head, framing the face, worn by women in medieval times and as part of the habit of certain orders of nuns.

win (wĭn) *v.* **won** (wŭn), **win•ning, wins.** *—intr.* **1.** To achieve victory or finish first in a competition. **2.** To achieve success in an effort or venture. *—tr.* **1.** To achieve victory or finish first in (a race, for example). **2.** To receive as a prize or reward for performance: *won a blue ribbon.* **3.** To obtain or earn: *My grandfather won his livelihood as a train engineer.* **4.** To take in battle; capture: *won the old fort.* **5.** To succeed in gaining the favor or support of; prevail on: *Her speech won over the audience.* **6.** To gain the affection and loyalty of: *The new student won many friends.* *—n.* A victory, especially in a competition. ***—idiom.*** **win out.** To succeed or prevail. [First written down about 725 in Old English and spelled *winnan,* to fight, strive.]

wince (wĭns) *intr.v.* **winced, winc•ing, winc•es.** To shrink or start involuntarily, as in pain, embarrassment, or distress: *She winced as the doctor pricked her finger to draw blood.* *—n.* A shrinking or startled movement or gesture.

winch (wĭnch) *n.* A machine for pulling or lifting, consisting of a drum around which is wound a rope or chain attached to the load being lifted.

wind[1] (wĭnd) *n.* **1.** A current of air, especially a natural one that moves along or parallel to the ground. **2.** A movement of air produced artificially, as by bellows or a fan. **3.** A natural current of air carrying sound or an odor: *The hounds got wind of the bear.* **4.** An influence, a tendency, or a destructive force: *the winds of change; the winds of war.* **5.** Breath, especially normal or adequate breathing: *had the wind knocked out of him.* **6.** Gas produced in the stomach or intestines during digestion. **7. winds. a.** Wind instruments considered as a group. **b.** The players of these instruments forming part of an orchestra. **8.** Rumor or information: *There will be trouble if wind of this gets out.* **9.** Speech or writing empty of meaning; verbiage. *—tr.v.* **wind•ed, wind•ing, winds. 1.** To cause to be out of or short of breath: *The long hill winded the runners.* **2.** To allow (a horse, for example) to rest so as to recover breath. ***—idiom.*** **in the wind.** Likely to occur; in the offing. [First written down about 725 in Old English.]

wind[2] (wīnd) *v.* **wound** (wound), **wind•ing, winds.** *—tr.* **1.a.** To wrap (something) around itself or around something else: *She wound the string into a ball. I wound the line around the pole.* **b.** To wrap or encircle (something) in a series of coils: *wound the spool with thread.* **2.a.** To go along (a curving or twisting course). **b.** To proceed on (one's way) in a coiling or spiraling course: *The brook winds its way through the forest.* **3.** To turn (a crank, for example) in a series of circular motions: *Wind the crank and then release it.* **4.** To coil the spring of (a mechanism) by turning a stem or cord, for example. *—intr.* **1.** To move in or have a curving or twisting course: *The river winds through the hills.* **2.** To be coiled or spiraled: *The vine wound around the trellis.* **3.** To be twisted or whorled into curved forms. *—n.* A single turn, twist, or curve. ***—idioms.*** **wind down.** *Informal.* **1.** To diminish gradually in energy, intensity, or scope: *Tourism really winds down at this time of year.* **2.** To relax; unwind. **wind up. 1.** To come or bring to an end: *The fishing season is winding up. We wound up the school year with a picnic.* **2.** *Informal.* To arrive in a place or situation after or because of a course of action: *My watch was running slow, so I wound up being late.* **3.** In baseball, to swing back the arm and raise the foot in preparation for pitching the ball. [First written down about 725 in Old English and spelled *windan.*] **—wind′er** *n.*

wind•bag (wĭnd′băg′) *n.* **1.** The flexible air-filled chamber of a bagpipe, an accordian, or a similar wind instrument. **2.** *Slang.* A person who talks a lot but does not say anything important or interesting.

wind•break (wĭnd′brāk′) *n.* A hedge, fence, or row of trees serving to lessen or break the force of the wind.

Wind•break•er (wĭnd′brā′kər). A trademark used for a warm outer jacket with close-fitting bands around the waist and cuffs.

wind•burn (wĭnd′bûrn′) *n.* A reddened irritation of the skin caused by long exposure to the wind.

wind-chill factor (wĭnd′chĭl′) *n.* The temperature of windless air that would have the same effect on exposed human skin as a given combination of wind speed and air temperature.

wind•fall (wĭnd′fôl′) *n.* **1.** A sudden unexpected piece of good fortune. **2.** Something, such as a ripened fruit, that has been blown down by the wind.

wind•flow•er (wĭnd′flou′ər) *n.* The anemone.

Wind•hoek (vĭnt′ho͝ok′). The capital of Namibia, in the central part of the country. It was originally the headquarters of an African leader. Population, 88,700.

wind•ing (wīn′dĭng) *n.* **1.** Something wound about a center or an object. **2.** One complete turn of something wound. **3.** A curve or bend, as of a stream or road. *—adj.* **1.** Turning or twisting: *a winding stream.* **2.** Spiral: *a winding staircase.*

wind instrument (wĭnd) *n.* A musical instrument, such as a clarinet or harmonica, in which sound is produced by a current of air, especially the breath.

wind•jam•mer (wĭnd′jăm′ər) *n.* A large sailing ship.

wind•lass (wĭnd′ləs) *n.* Any of various hauling or lifting devices similar to a winch.

wind•mill (wĭnd′mĭl′) *n.* A machine that gets power from a wheel of adjustable blades or slats turned by the wind.

win•dow (wĭn′dō) *n.* **1.** An opening constructed in a wall or roof to admit light or air, usually framed and fitted with one or more panes of glass. **2.** A pane of glass enclosed in such a framework; a windowpane. **3.** An opening or transparent part that resembles a window in function or appearance: *an envelope with a window.* **4.** A period of time during which an activity can or must take place: *a window of opportunity for preserving an unspoiled region.* **5.** A small area on the screen of a computer monitor in which information is displayed. [First written down before 1200 in Middle English, from Old Norse *vindauga* : *vindr*, air, wind + *auga*, eye.]

window box *n.* A long narrow box for growing plants, placed on a windowsill or ledge.

win•dow-dress•ing also **win•dow dress•ing** (wĭn′dō drĕs′ĭng) *n.* **1.** Decorative exhibition of goods for sale in store windows. **2.** A means of improving appearances or creating a falsely favorable impression.

win•dow•pane (wĭn′dō pān′) *n.* A piece of glass in a window.

win•dow-shop (wĭn′dō shŏp′) *intr.v.* **win•dow-shopped, win•dow-shop•ping, win•dow-shops.** To look at merchandise in store windows without making purchases.

win•dow•sill (wĭn′dō sĭl′) *n.* The horizontal member at the base of a window frame or opening.

wind•pipe (wĭnd′pīp′) *n.* The trachea.

wind•row (wĭnd′rō′) *n.* **1.** A row, as of leaves or snow, heaped up by the wind. **2.** A long row of cut hay or grain left to dry in a field before being bundled.

wind•shield (wĭnd′shēld′) *n.* A framed pane of glass or other transparent material located in the front of a vehicle to protect passengers from the wind.

wind•sock (wĭnd′sŏk′) *n.* A large cone-shaped bag that is open at both ends and attached to a stand by a pivot to indicate the direction of the wind blowing through it.

Wind•sor[1] (wĭn′zər). Ruling house of Great Britain (since 1917), including George V and his descendants Edward VIII, George VI, and Elizabeth II.

Wind•sor[2] (wĭn′zər). A city of southeast Ontario, Canada, opposite Detroit, Michigan. It was settled by the French after 1701. Population, 192,083.

Windsor, Duke of. See **Edward VIII.**

Windsor chair *n.* A wooden chair having a high rounded back of spokes and legs sloping outward.

wind•storm (wĭnd′stôrm′) *n.* A storm with high winds or violent gusts but little or no rain.

wind•surf•ing (wĭnd′sûr′fĭng) *n.* The sport of sailing while standing on a sailboard.

wind tunnel (wĭnd) *n.* A chamber through which wind can be forced at controlled speeds so its effect on an object, such as an aircraft, can be studied.

wind-up or **wind•up** (wĭnd′ŭp′) *n.* **1.** The act of bringing something to an end. **2.** A concluding part; a conclusion. **3.** In baseball, the movements of a pitcher, as the bringing back of the arm and raising of the foot, prior to pitching the ball.

wind•ward (wĭnd′wərd) *adj.* Of or moving toward the quarter from which the wind blows: *a windward tide; the windward quarter.* *—adv.* In a direction from which the wind blows; against the wind. *—n.* The direction from which the wind blows.

Wind•ward Islands (wĭnd′wərd). An island group of the southeast West Indies, including the southern group of the Lesser Antilles from Martinique south to Grenada.

wind•y (wĭn′dē) *adj.* **wind•i•er, wind•i•est. 1.** Characterized by or having much wind: *a windy winter month.* **2.** Open to the wind; unsheltered: *the windy side of an apartment.* **3.a.** Given to prolonged talk: *a windy speaker.* **b.** Lacking substance; empty: *a windy speech.*

wine (wīn) *n.* **1.** An alcoholic beverage made of the fermented juice of grapes. **2.** An alcoholic beverage made of the fermented juice of other fruits or plants: *dandelion wine.* **3.** The color of red wine. *—tr.v.* **wined, win•ing, wines.** To provide or entertain with wines. [First written down about 725 in Old English and spelled *wīn*, from Latin *vīnum*.]

wine cellar *n.* A place for storing wine.

wine•press (wīn′prĕs′) *n.* A vat in which the juice is pressed from grapes.

win•er•y (wī′nə rē) *n., pl.* **win•er•ies.** An establishment where wine is made.

Wine•sap (wīn′săp′) *n.* A variety of apple having fruit with dark red skin.

wing (wĭng) *n.* **1.** One of a pair of specialized parts used for flying, as in birds, bats, or insects. **2.** A corresponding part of an animal that does not fly: *the wings of a penguin.* **3.** An extending part resembling a wing, as one of the thin projections on certain plant seeds. **4.** A part extending from the side of an aircraft whose principal purpose is to provide a force that holds the craft aloft. **5. wings.** One of the areas that extend on either side of a stage and are concealed from the audience. **6.** A structure attached to and connected with the side of a building. **7.** A group affiliated with or subordinate to an older or larger organization. **8.** A unit of military aircraft or aviators. *—v.* **winged, wing•ing, wings.** *—intr.* To move on or as if on wings: *birds winging southward.* *—tr.* **1.** To throw (a ball, for example). **2.** To wound slightly, as in the wing or arm. ***—idioms.*** **in the wings. 1.** In the stage wings, unseen by the audience. **2.** Close by in the background; available at short notice. **on the wing.** In flight; flying. **under (one's) wing.** Under one's protection; in one's care. **wing it.** *Informal.* To say or do something without preparation, forethought, or sufficient experience; improvise. [First written down about 1175 in Middle English and spelled *wenge*, of Scandinavian origin.]

wing case *n.* An elytron.

winged (wĭngd *or* wĭng′ĭd) *adj.* **1.** Having wings or parts resembling wings: *winged insects; the winged seeds of the maple.* **2.** Moving on or as if on wings; flying.

wing•less (wĭng′lĭs) *adj.* Having no wings or only undeveloped wings.

wing nut *n.* A nut with projections for enabling the thumb and forefinger to turn it.

wing•span (wĭng′spăn′) *n.* **1.** The distance between the tips of the wings on an aircraft. **2.** Wingspread.

wing•spread (wĭng′sprĕd′) *n.* The distance between the tips of the wings, as of a bird or an insect, when fully extended.

wink (wĭngk) *v.* **winked, wink•ing, winks.** *—intr.* **1.** To close and open the eyelid of one eye deliberately, as to convey a message, signal, or suggestion. **2.** To shine fitfully; twinkle: *A lighthouse winked in the far distance.* *—tr.* **1.** To close and open (an eye or the eyes) rapidly. **2.** To signal or express by wink-

windsurfing

ă	pat	oi	boy
ā	pay	ou	out
âr	care	o͝o	took
ä	father	o͞o	boot
ĕ	pet	ŭ	cut
ē	be	ûr	urge
ĭ	pit	th	thin
ī	pie	*th*	this
îr	pier	hw	whoop
ŏ	pot	zh	vision
ō	toe	ə	about
ô	paw	N	*French* bon

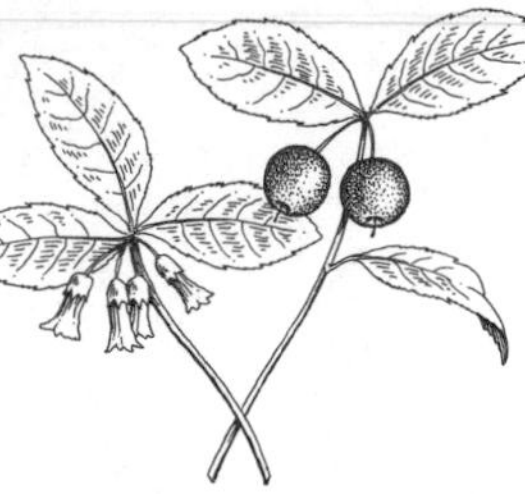

wintergreen

John Winthrop

Wisconsin

The name **Wisconsin** comes from an Algonquian language and was originally applied to the Wisconsin River. The name later passed to the territory and the state. Unfortunately, we do not know exactly what the word *Wisconsin* means.

Word Building: –wise

The suffix **–wise** forms adverbs when it attaches to adjectives or nouns. It comes from the Old English suffix *–wīse*, which meant "in a particular direction or manner." Thus **clockwise** means "in the direction that a clock goes," and **likewise** means "in like manner, similarly." For the last 50 years or so, **–wise** has also meant "with respect to," as in *saleswise*, meaning "with respect to sales," and *taxwise*, meaning "with respect to taxes." This usage is considered to be awkward, however, and should be avoided, especially in writing.

ing. *—n.* **1.a.** The act of winking. **b.** The very brief time required for a wink; an instant. **2.** A gleam or twinkle. **3.** *Informal.* A brief period of sleep. ***—idiom.*** **wink at.** To pretend not to see. [First written down before 899 in Old English and spelled *wincian.*]

win•ner (wĭn′ər) *n.* A person or thing that wins, especially a victor in sports or a notably successful person.

win•ning (wĭn′ĭng) *adj.* **1.** Of or relating to the act of winning: *pulled the winning card.* **2.** Successful; victorious: *the winning team.* **3.** Attractive; charming: *a winning personality.* *—n.* **1.** The act of one that wins; victory. **2.** Something won, especially money. Often used in the plural: *took her winnings to the bank.* **—win′ning•ly** *adv.*

Win•ni•peg (wĭn′ə pĕg′). The capital and largest city of Manitoba, Canada, in the southeast part of the province north of the North Dakota–Minnesota border. Population, 564,473.

win•now (wĭn′ō) *v.* **win•nowed, win•now•ing, win•nows.** *—tr.* **1.** To separate the chaff from (grain) by means of a current of air. **2.** To separate or get rid of (an undesirable part); sort or eliminate. **3.** To sort or select (a desirable part); extract. *—intr.* **1.** To separate grain from chaff. **2.** To separate the good from the bad. **—win′now•er** *n.*

win•some (wĭn′səm) *adj.* Charming, often in a childlike or naive way.

win•ter (wĭn′tər) *n.* The coldest season of the year, occurring between fall and spring. In the Northern Hemisphere, it lasts from the winter solstice to the vernal equinox, or in ordinary usage, from December until March. *—adj.* **1.** Of, occurring in, or appropriate to the season of winter: *a winter storm; winter clothes.* **2.** Grown during the season of winter: *winter wheat.* [First written down about 725 in Old English.]

win•ter•green (wĭn′tər grēn′) *n.* **1.** A low-growing plant having spicy-smelling evergreen leaves and edible red berries. **2.** An oil or a flavoring obtained from this plant.

win•ter•ize (wĭn′tə rīz′) *tr.v.* **win•ter•ized, win•ter•iz•ing, win•ter•iz•es.** To prepare or equip (an automobile or a house, for example) for winter weather.

winter solstice *n.* In the Northern Hemisphere, the solstice that occurs on or about December 22.

winter squash *n.* Any of several kinds of squash that have a thick rind and can be stored for long periods.

win•ter•time (wĭn′tər tīm′) *n.* The season of winter.

Win•throp (wĭn′thrəp), **John.** 1588–1649. English colonial administrator who was the first governor of Massachusetts Bay Colony, serving seven terms between 1629 and 1649.

win•try (wĭn′trē) also **win•ter•y** (wĭn′tə rē) *adj.* **win•tri•er, win•tri•est** also **win•ter•i•er, win•ter•i•est.** **1.** Of or characteristic of winter; cold: *wintry weather.* **2.** Suggestive of winter, as in coldness: *a wintry tone of voice.*

wipe (wīp) *tr.v.* **wiped, wip•ing, wipes.** **1.** To rub, as with a cloth or paper, in order to clean or dry: *wipe the dishes with a towel.* **2.** To remove by or as if by rubbing: *wiping the tears away.* **3.** To spread or apply by or as if by wiping: *wiped furniture polish over the table.* *—n.* The act or an instance of wiping: *giving the table a wipe with a clean cloth.* ***—idiom.*** **wipe out.** **1.** To destroy or be destroyed completely. **2.** To lose one's balance and fall or jump off, as from a surfboard. [First written down about 960 in Old English and spelled *wīpian.*] **—wip′er** *n.*

wire (wīr) *n.* **1.** A usually flexible rod or strand of metal, often covered with an electrical insulator, used to conduct electricity or to support parts of a structure. **2.** A group of wire strands joined or twisted together as a functional unit; a cable. **3.** An active telephone connection: *Please hold the wire.* **4.a.** A telegraph service. **b.** A telegram. **5.** *Slang.* A hidden microphone, as on a person's body or in a building. *—v.* **wired, wir•ing, wires.** *—tr.* **1.** To join, connect, or attach with a wire or wires. **2.** To equip with a system of electrical wires: *wire a house.* **3.** To send by telegraph: *wire congratulations.* **4.** To send a telegram to. *—intr.* To send a telegram. ***—idioms.*** **down to the wire.** *Informal.* At the very end, as in a race. **under the wire.** **1.** At the finish line of a race. **2.** *Informal.* At the last moment. [First written down about 725 in Old English and spelled *wīr.*]

wire•haired (wīr′hârd′) *adj.* Having a coat of stiff wiry hair: *a wirehaired fox terrier.*

wire•less (wīr′lĭs) *adj.* **1.** Having no wire or wires. **2.** *Chiefly British.* Of or relating to radio communication *—n.* **1.** A radio telegraph or radio telephone system. **2.** *Chiefly British.* A radio.

wire•tap (wīr′tăp′) *n.* A concealed listening or recording device connected to a telephone or telegraph circuit. *—v.* **wire•tapped, wire•tap•ping, wire•taps.** *—tr.* **1.** To connect a wiretap to (a telephone circuit, for example). **2.** To monitor (a telephone circuit) by means of a wiretap. *—intr.* To install or use a wiretap.

wire•worm (wīr′wûrm′) *n.* A yellowish hard-bodied larva of certain beetles that feeds on the roots and seedlings of many crop plants.

wir•ing (wīr′ĭng) *n.* **1.** The act of attaching, connecting, or installing electric wires. **2.** A system of electric wires.

wir•y (wīr′ē) *adj.* **wir•i•er, wir•i•est.** **1.** Of or relating to wire. **2.** Resembling wire in form or quality, especially in stiffness: *wiry hair.* **3.** Sinewy and lean: *a basketball player with a wiry physique.* **—wir′i•ness** *n.*

Wis. *abbr.* An abbreviation of Wisconsin.

Wis•con•sin (wĭs kŏn′sĭn). A state of the north-central United States north of Illinois. It was admitted as the 30th state in 1848. Madison is the capital and Milwaukee the largest city. Population, 4,906,745. —See Note.

wis•dom (wĭz′dəm) *n.* **1.** Understanding of what is true, right, or lasting. **2.** Common sense; good judgment. **3.** The sum of scholarly learning through the ages.

wisdom tooth *n.* One of four molars, the last on each side of both jaws in human beings, usually appearing much later than the others.

wise[1] (wīz) *adj.* **wis•er, wis•est.** **1.** Having wisdom; judicious: *a wise leader.* **2.** Showing common sense; prudent: *a wise decision.* **3.** Shrewd; crafty: *a wise move.* **4.** Having great learning; erudite. **5.** Provided with information; informed: *I'm wise to your tricks.* **6.** *Slang.* Rude and disrespectful; impudent. [First written down about 725 in Old English and spelled *wīs.*] **—wise′ly** *adv.*

wise[2] (wīz) *n.* Method or manner of doing: *In no wise would that be fair.* [First written down about 725 in Old English and spelled *wīse.*]

–wise *suff.* A suffix that means in a specified manner, position, or direction: *clockwise.* —See Note.

wise•a•cre (wīz′ā′kər) *n.* *Slang.* A person who is conceited or shows off in a disagreeable way.

wise•crack (wīz′krăk′) *Slang.* *n.* A joking or sarcastic remark. *—intr.v.* **wise•cracked, wise•crack•ing, wise•cracks.** To make or utter a wisecrack.

wise guy *n.* *Slang.* A smart aleck.

wish (wĭsh) *n.* **1.** A desire or longing for a specific thing. **2.** An expression of such a desire or longing:

Give them my best wishes. **3.** Something desired or longed for: *He got his wish.* —*v.* **wished, wish•ing, wish•es.** —*tr.* **1.** To long for; want: *They wish to see you.* See Synonyms at **desire. 2.** To entertain or express wishes for; bid: *Several students wish help with their writing.* **3.** To call or invoke upon: *wish him luck.* **4.** To impose or force; foist: *They wished too much work on him.* —*intr.* **1.** To have or feel a desire: *He wished for a skateboard.* **2.** To make or express a wish. [First written down before 1325 in Middle English and spelled *wiss*, from Old English *wȳscan*, to wish.] —**wish′er** *n.*

wish•bone (**wĭsh′**bōn′) *n.* The forked bone in front of the breastbone in most birds.

wish•ful (**wĭsh′**fəl) *adj.* Having or expressing a wish or longing: *wishful eyes.* —**wish′ful•ly** *adv.*

wish•y-wash•y (**wĭsh′**ē wŏsh′ē *or* **wĭsh′**ē **wô′**shē) *adj.* **wish•y-wash•i•er, wish•y-wash•i•est.** *Informal.* **1.** Thin or watery, as tea or soup. **2.** Lacking in strength of character or purpose.

wisp (wĭsp) *n.* **1.** A small bunch or bundle, as of hair, straw, or grass. **2.** A person or thing that is thin, frail, or slight. **3.** A faint streak, as of smoke or clouds.

wist (wĭst) *v.* Past tense and past participle of **wit²**.

wis•ter•i•a (wĭ **stîr′**ē ə) also **wis•tar•i•a** (wĭ **stâr′**ē ə) *n.* Any of several climbing woody vines having drooping clusters of showy purplish or white flowers. [First written down in 1819 in Modern English, after Caspar *Wistar* (1761–1818), American physician.]

wist•ful (**wĭst′**fəl) *adj.* **1.** Full of wishful yearning. **2.** Pensively sad; melancholy. —**wist′ful•ly** *adv.* —**wist′ful•ness** *n.*

wit¹ (wĭt) *n.* **1.** The natural ability to perceive and understand; intelligence. **2.a.** Resourcefulness; ingenuity. Often used in the plural: *We had to use our wits to find our way back to camp.* **b. wits.** Sound mental faculties; sanity: *I was scared out of my wits.* **3.a.** The ability to make clever and humorous remarks. **b.** A person having this ability. —***idiom.*** **at (one's) wits' end.** At the limit of one's mental resources; utterly at a loss. [First written down about 725 in Old English.]

wit² (wĭt) *v.* **wist** (wĭst), **wit•ting** (**wĭt′**ĭng), first and third person singular present tense **wot** (wŏt). —*tr. & intr.v. Archaic.* To learn or know. —***idiom.*** **to wit.** That is to say; namely. [First written down about 725 in Old English and spelled *witan*.]

witch (wĭch) *n.* **1.** A woman believed to have supernatural powers and practice sorcery. **2.** A follower of a pagan nature religion having its roots in pre-Christian Europe. **3.** A hag. [First written down about 1000 in Old English and spelled *wicce*.]

witch•craft (**wĭch′**krăft′) *n.* Magic; sorcery.

witch doctor *n.* A person believed to be able to cure sickness by means of magic or the ability to drive away evil spirits, especially among African peoples.

witch hazel *n.* **1.** Any of several North American shrubs having yellow flowers that bloom in late fall or winter. **2.** A spicy-smelling liquid made from the bark and leaves of this shrub and rubbed on the skin, especially to relieve soreness.

witch-hunt (**wĭch′**hunt′) *n.* An investigation carried out supposedly to uncover disloyalty or subversive activities, but actually used to harass people with dissenting opinions or gain publicity for the investigators.

with (wĭ*th* *or* wĭth) *prep.* **1.** In the company of; accompanying: *Did you go with her?* **2.** Next to; alongside of: *I sat with my friends.* **3.** Having as a possession, an attribute, or a characteristic: *arrived with good news; just sat there with his mouth open.* **4.a.** In a manner characterized by: *performed with skill.* **b.** In the performance, use, or operation of: *had trouble with the car.* **5.** In the charge or keeping of: *left the cat with the neighbors.* **6.** In the opinion or estimation of: *if it's all right with you.* **7.** Of the same opinion or belief as: *He is with us on that issue.* **8.** In the same group or mixture as; among: *planted onions with the carrots.* **9.** In the membership or employment of: *plays with a band.* **10.a.** By the means or agency of: *eat with a fork.* **b.** By the presence or use of: *a pillow stuffed with feathers.* **11.** In spite of: *With all her experience, she could not get a job.* **12.** In the same direction as: *sail with the wind.* **13.** At the same time as: *gets up with the birds.* **14.** In regard or relation to: *We are pleased with her decision. I spoke with her yesterday.* **15.** Having received: *He went with his parents' permission.* **16.a.** And; plus: *My books, with my brother's, make a sizable library.* **b.** Having as a part; including: *comes to $29.95 with postage and handling.* **17.** As a result or consequence of: *sick with the flu.* **18.** So as to be touching or joined to: *linked arms with their partners.* **19.** In proportion to: *wines that improve with age.* **20.** According to the experience or practice of: *With me, rushing through a job is always a mistake.* [First written down about 725 in Old English and spelled *with*, against.] —SEE NOTE.

with•al (wĭ*th* **ôl′** *or* wĭth **ôl′**) *adv.* Besides; as well: *gentle and soothing withal.*

with•draw (wĭ*th* **drô′** *or* wĭth **drô′**) *v.* **with•drew** (wĭ*th* **dro͞o′** *or* wĭth **dro͞o′**), **with•drawn** (wĭ*th*-**drôn′** *or* wĭth **drôn′**), **with•draw•ing, with•draws.** —*tr.* **1.** To take back or away; remove: *withdraw funds from the bank.* **2.** To remove from participation or consideration: *withdrew her application.* —*intr.* **1.** To move or draw back; retire: *The dinner guests withdrew to the den.* **2.** To remove oneself from active participation: *He withdrew from the tournament.*

with•draw•al (wĭ*th* **drô′**əl *or* wĭth **drô′**əl) *n.* **1.** The act or process of withdrawing. **2.** A removal of something that has been deposited: *a withdrawal from a bank account.* **3.a.** Discontinuation of the use of an addictive substance. **b.** The physiological and mental readjustment that accompanies such discontinuation.

with•drawn (wĭ*th* **drôn′** *or* wĭth **drôn′**) *v.* Past participle of **withdraw.** —*adj.* **1.** Not readily approached; remote. **2.** Socially retiring; shy: *a withdrawn person.*

with•drew (wĭ*th* **dro͞o′** *or* wĭth **dro͞o′**) *v.* Past tense of **withdraw.**

with•er (**wĭ*th*′**ər) *v.* **with•ered, with•er•ing, with•ers.** —*intr.* **1.** To dry up from or as if from lack of moisture; shrivel: *The flowers withered in the vase.* **2.** To lose freshness, vitality, or force: *The proposed tax on energy use withered away and was never adopted.* —*tr.* **1.** To cause to shrivel or fade. **2.** To render speechless or incapable of action; stun: *The principal withered the noisy student with a glance.* [First written down about 1380 in Middle English and spelled *widderen*, perhaps variant of *wederen*, to weather, from *weder*, weather.]

❑ *These sound alike:* **wither, whither** (to where).

with•ers (**wĭ*th*′**ərz) *pl.n.* The highest part of the back of a horse or similar animal, located between the shoulder blades.

with•hold (wĭth **hōld′** *or* wĭ*th* **hōld′**) *tr.v.* **with•held** (wĭth **hĕld′** *or* wĭ*th* **hĕld′**), **with•hold•ing, with•holds. 1.** To keep in check; restrain: *withhold the applause until the end of the act.* **2.** To refrain from giving, granting, or permitting: *Let's withhold judgment until we know the whole story.* See Synonyms at **keep. 3.** To deduct (withholding tax) from an employee's wages or salary.

with•hold•ing tax (wĭth **hōl′**dĭng *or* wĭ*th* **hōl′**-dĭng) *n.* A portion of an employee's wages or salary

wisteria

Word History: with

When you fight **with** someone, are you fighting on his or her side or against him or her? We are often confused by that usage of the word *with* since we nearly always take it to mean "in the company of, alongside of." The word *with* in Old English means "against," and that meaning is still there in the verb **withstand**, "to stand up against, resist." The meaning of *with* progressed this way: "against, up close against, up close, up close together, together with, in the company of." Old English uses the preposition *mid* for our modern sense of *with. Mid* is now obsolete, but it probably occurs in **midwife**, "a woman who is *with* the woman in childbirth."

ă	pat	oi	boy
ā	pay	ou	out
âr	care	o͝o	took
ä	father	o͞o	boot
ĕ	pet	ŭ	cut
ē	be	ûr	urge
ĭ	pit	th	thin
ī	pie	*th*	this
îr	pier	hw	whoop
ŏ	pot	zh	vision
ō	toe	ə	about
ô	paw	N	*French* bon

wok

wolverine

wombat

woodchuck

Regional Note: woodchuck

The woodchuck goes by several names in the United States. The most famous of these is **groundhog**, under which name the animal's annual day is celebrated on February 2. In the Appalachian Mountains the woodchuck is known as a *whistle pig.*

withheld by an employer as an advance payment of the employee's income tax.

with•in (wĭth ĭn′ *or* wĭth ĭn′) *adv.* In or into the inner part; inside: *We stayed within.* —*prep.* **1.** In the inner part or parts of; inside: *within the body.* **2.** Inside the limits or extent of in time or distance: *They arrived within an hour of us. We are within ten miles of home.* **3.** Not exceeding or transgressing: *within the laws of the land.*

with•out (wĭth out′ *or* wĭth out′) *adv.* On the outside: *The structure is sturdy within and without.* —*prep.* **1.** Not having; lacking: *without a car to get home.* **2.** Not accompanied by; in the absence of: *no smoke without fire.*

with•stand (wĭth stănd′ *or* wĭth stănd′) *tr.v.* **with•stood** (wĭth stŏŏd′ *or* wĭth stŏŏd′), **with•stand•ing, with•stands.** To resist or oppose, especially with success: *The troops withstood the attack. The buildings withstood the hurricane.*

wit•less (wĭt′lĭs) *adj.* Lacking intelligence or wit; foolish.

wit•ness (wĭt′nĭs) *n.* **1.** A person who can give a firsthand account of something seen, heard, or experienced: *a witness of the accident.* **2.** Something that serves as evidence; a sign. **3.a.** A person who is called to testify before a court of law. **b.** A person who is called on to be present at a transaction in order to attest to what takes place: *a witness at a wedding.* **4.** One who signs one's name to a document to attest to its authenticity. —*tr.v.* **wit•nessed, wit•ness•ing, wit•ness•es. 1.** To be present at or have personal knowledge of: *witness a volcanic eruption.* **2.** To provide or serve as evidence of: *The child's laughter witnessed her delight.* **3.** To sign (a document) as witness to its legality or authenticity: *witness a will.* [First written down about 950 in Old English and spelled *witnes,* from *wit,* knowledge.]

wit•ti•cism (wĭt′ĭ sĭz′əm) *n.* A witty remark.

wit•ting (wĭt′ĭng) *adj.* **1.** Aware or conscious of something: *a witting bystander to the crime.* **2.** Done intentionally; deliberate: *a witting insult.* —*v.* Present participle of **wit**[2]. —**wit′ting•ly** *adv.*

wit•ty (wĭt′ē) *adj.* **wit•ti•er, wit•ti•est. 1.** Having or showing wit in speech or writing: *a witty person.* **2.** Characterized by or having the nature of wit; funny or jocular: *a witty saying.* —**wit′ti•ly** *adv.* —**wit′ti•ness** *n.*

wives (wīvz) *n.* Plural of **wife.**

wiz•ard (wĭz′ərd) *n.* **1.** A sorcerer or magician. **2.** A skilled or clever person: *a wizard at mathematics.* [First written down before 1425 in Middle English and spelled *wisard,* from *wise,* wise.]

wiz•ard•ry (wĭz′ər drē) *n., pl.* **wiz•ard•ries.** The art, skill, or practice of a wizard; sorcery.

wiz•ened (wĭz′ənd) *adj.* Shriveled; withered.

wk. *abbr.* An abbreviation of: **1.** Week. **2.** Work.

wkly. *abbr.* An abbreviation of weekly.

wob•ble (wŏb′əl) *v.* **wob•bled, wob•bling, wob•bles.** —*intr.* To move unsteadily from side to side: *The old table wobbles.* —*tr.* To cause to wobble. —*n.* The act or an instance of wobbling; unsteady motion: *The top spun with a wobble.*

wob•bly (wŏb′lē) *adj.* **wob•bli•er, wob•bli•est.** Tending to wobble; unsteady.

Wo•den (wōd′n) *n.* An Anglo-Saxon god identified with Odin.

woe (wō) *n.* **1.** Deep distress or misery, as from grief: *yearning for company in her woe.* **2.** A misfortune or difficulty: *What is the cause of their financial woes?* —*interj.* An expression used to show sorrow or dismay. [First written down about 725 in Old English and spelled *wā.*]

woe•be•gone (wō′bĭ gôn′ *or* wō′bĭ gŏn′) *adj.* Affected with or marked by deep sorrow, grief, or wretchedness.

woe•ful (wō′fəl) *adj.* **1.** Affected by or full of woe; mournful. **2.** Causing or involving woe. **3.** Deplorably bad: *woeful wrongs.* —**woe′ful•ly** *adv.*

wok (wŏk) *n.* A metal pan with a rounded bottom, used in Asian cooking for frying and steaming. [First written down in 1952 in Modern English and spelled *wock,* from Chinese (Cantonese) *wok.*]

woke (wōk) *v.* A past tense of **wake**[1].

wok•en (wō′kən) *v.* A past participle of **wake**[1].

wolf (wŏŏlf) *n., pl.* **wolves** (wŏŏlvz). **1.a.** Either of two meat-eating mammals related to the dog and living chiefly in northern regions. **b.** The fur of such a mammal. **2.** A person who is regarded as fierce, cruel, or dangerous. —*tr.v.* **wolfed, wolf•ing, wolfs.** To eat hungrily or greedily: *wolfed down the hamburger.* —***idiom.*** **wolf in sheep's clothing.** A person who pretends to be friendly while actually intending harm. [First written down about 750 in Old English and spelled *wulf.*]

Wolfe (wŏŏlf), **James.** 1727–1759. British general in Canada who defeated the French at Quebec (1759).

wolf•hound (wŏŏlf′hound′) *n.* Any of various large dogs, such as the borzoi, originally trained to hunt wolves or other large game.

wolf•ram (wŏŏl′frəm) *n.* Tungsten.

wolfs•bane (wŏŏlfs′bān′) *n.* Any of several poisonous perennial herbs having broad rounded leaves and light purple flowers.

Woll•stone•craft (wŏŏl′stən krăft′), **Mary.** 1759–1797. British writer and reformer noted for *A Vindication of the Rights of Woman* (1792).

Wo•lof (wō′lŏf′) *n.* **1.** A member of a West African people living in coastal Senegal. **2.** The language of this people.

wol•ver•ine (wŏŏl′və rēn′ *or* wŏŏl′və rēn′) *n.* A meat-eating mammal of northern regions, related to the weasels and having thick dark fur and a bushy tail.

wolves (wŏŏlvz) *n.* Plural of **wolf.**

wom•an (wŏŏm′ən) *n., pl.* **wom•en** (wĭm′ĭn). **1.** An adult female human being. **2.** Women considered as a group; womankind. —***idiom.*** **to a woman.** Without exception among a group of women: *They favored the proposal to a woman.* [First written down before 766 in Old English and spelled *wīfman* : *wīf,* woman + *man,* person.] —See Note at **man.**

wom•an•hood (wŏŏm′ən hŏŏd′) *n.* **1.** The condition of being an adult female person. **2.** The qualities considered appropriate to or representative of women. **3.** Women considered as a group.

wom•an•ish (wŏŏm′ə nĭsh) *adj.* Of, characteristic of, or natural to a woman.

wom•an•kind (wŏŏm′ən kīnd′) *n.* Women considered as a group.

wom•an•ly (wŏŏm′ən lē) *adj.* **wom•an•li•er, wom•an•li•est.** Having qualities generally attributed to a woman. —**wom′an•li•ness** *n.*

womb (wōōm) *n.* **1.** The uterus. **2.** A place where something is generated or begun.

wom•bat (wŏm′băt′) *n.* Any of several Australian mammals that resemble a small bear and feed mainly on grass, leaves, and roots.

wom•en (wĭm′ĭn) *n.* Plural of **woman.**

wom•en•folk (wĭm′ĭn fōk′) also **wom•en•folks** (wĭm′ĭn fōks′) *pl.n.* **1.** Women considered as a group. **2.** The women of a community or family.

wom•en's rights (wĭm′ĭnz) *pl.n.* The political and legal rights of women to opportunities equal to those of men.

won (wŭn) *v.* Past tense and past participle of **win.** ❑ *These sound alike:* **won, one** (single).

won•der (wŭn′dər) *n.* **1.** A person or thing that arouses awe, surprise, or admiration; a marvel. **2.**

Awe, astonishment, or admiration. **3.** An event that cannot be explained by the laws of nature; a miracle. **4.** A feeling of puzzlement or doubt. —*v.* **won•dered, won•der•ing, won•ders.** —*intr.* **1.** To have a feeling of awe or admiration; marvel: *They wondered at the sight of the canyon.* **2.** To be filled with curiosity or doubt: *He wondered about the future.* —*tr.* To feel curiosity or be in doubt about: *I wonder what she is doing.*

Synonyms: **wonder, marvel, miracle, sensation.** These nouns all mean something that causes amazement or admiration in others. *If you want to see wonders of architecture, go see the Egyptian pyramids. That dinner was no marvel. The artificial heart is a miracle of medical science. Her latest book is a sensation; it has already won three literary prizes.*

won•der•ful (wŭn′dər fəl) *adj.* **1.** Capable of causing wonder; astonishing: *A soaring eagle is a wonderful sight.* **2.** Admirable; excellent: *a wonderful idea.* **—won′der•ful•ly** *adv.*

won•der•land (wŭn′dər lănd′) *n.* **1.** A marvelous imaginary realm. **2.** A marvelous real place or scene.

won•der•ment (wŭn′dər mənt) *n.* **1.** Astonishment, awe, or surprise. **2.** Something that produces wonder; a marvel.

won•drous (wŭn′drəs) *adj.* Remarkable or extraordinary; wonderful. **—won′drous•ly** *adv.*

wont (wônt *or* wōnt *or* wŭnt) *adj.* Accustomed, apt, or used: *He was wont to go for long walks on the heath.* —*n.* Customary practice; usage: *jogged every morning, as was her wont.*

won't (wōnt). Contraction of *will not.*

wont•ed (**wôn′**tĭd *or* **wōn′**tĭd *or* **wŭn′**tĭd) *adj.* Accustomed; usual: *He took his wonted meal of toast and tea.*

won ton or **won•ton** (**wŏn′**tŏn′) *n.* A small dumpling typically filled with spiced ground meat.

woo (wo͞o) *v.* **wooed, woo•ing, woos.** —*tr.* **1.** To seek the affection of (someone) with intent to romance. **2.** To seek to get or achieve: *woo money from investors.* **3.** To solicit or seek the favor of; try to persuade: *Advertisers often woo teenagers.* —*intr.* To court a woman. **—woo′er** *n.*

wood (wo͝od) *n.* **1.a.** The tough fibrous substance beneath the bark of trees and shrubs and forming the stems of certain other plants. **b.** This substance, often cut and dried for use as building material and fuel. **2.** A dense growth of trees; a forest. Often used in the plural. **3.** Something made from wood, as a golf club with a wooden head or a woodwind instrument. [First written down about 725 in Old English and spelled *wudu.*]

❑ *These sound alike:* **wood, would** (past tense of will).

wood alcohol *n.* Methanol.

wood•bine (**wo͝od′**bīn′) *n.* Any of various climbing vines having yellowish flowers, especially a European honeysuckle.

wood•carv•ing (**wo͝od′**kär′vĭng) *n.* **1.** The art of creating or decorating wood objects by carving with a tool. **2.** A carved wood object.

wood•chuck (**wo͝od′**chŭk′) *n.* A short-legged burrowing North American rodent having brownish fur; a groundhog. —SEE NOTE.

wood•cock (**wo͝od′**kŏk′) *n., pl.* **woodcock** or **wood•cocks.** Either of two birds having brownish feathers, short legs, and a long bill, often hunted as game.

wood•craft (**wo͝od′**krăft′) *n.* **1.** Skill and experience in things relating to the woods, as hunting, fishing, or camping. **2.** The art of carving or fashioning objects from wood.

wood•cut (**wo͝od′**kŭt′) *n.* **1.** A piece of wood having an engraved design for printing. **2.** A print made from such a piece of wood.

wood•cut•ter (**wo͝od′**kŭt′ər) *n.* A person or thing that cuts wood.

wood duck *n.* A brightly colored American duck that nests in hollow trees and the male of which has a large crest.

wood•ed (**wo͝od′**ĭd) *adj.* Covered with trees or woods.

wood•en (**wo͝od′**n) *adj.* **1.** Made or consisting of wood: *a wooden bridge.* **2.** Stiff and unnatural: *a wooden smile.* **—wood′en•ly** *adv.*

Wood•hull (**wo͝od′**hŭl′), **Victoria Claflin.** 1838–1927. American reformer and suffragist who published the first American translation of Karl Marx's *Communist Manifesto* (1872) and with her sister **Tennessee Claflin** (1845–1923) opened the first Wall Street brokerage house owned by women.

wood•land (**wo͝od′**lənd) *n.* Land covered with trees and shrubs.

wood louse *n.* A sow bug.

wood•man (**wo͝od′**mən) *n.* A woodsman.

wood•peck•er (**wo͝od′**pĕk′ər) *n.* Any of various usually brightly colored birds having strong claws for clinging to and climbing trees and a strong pointed bill for drilling into bark and wood.

wood•pile (**wo͝od′**pīl′) *n.* A pile of wood, especially when intended for use as fuel.

wood pulp *n.* Any of various cellulose pulps ground from wood, treated chemically, and used in making paper, cellophane, and rayon.

wood•shed (**wo͝od′**shĕd′) *n.* A shed in which firewood is stored.

woods•man (**wo͝odz′**mən) *n.* A man who works or lives in the woods or is skilled in woodcraft.

woods•y (**wo͝od′**zē) *adj.* **woods•i•er, woods•i•est.** Of, relating to, suggesting, or typical of the woods.

wood tar *n.* A black syrupy fluid that is a byproduct of the destructive distillation of wood and is used in pitch and medicines.

wood thrush *n.* A large thrush of wooded areas of eastern North America having a reddish-brown head and a spotted breast.

wood•wind (**wo͝od′**wĭnd′) *n.* **1.** A wind instrument, such as a bassoon, clarinet, or flute, consisting of a tube with holes at intervals and producing sound when air is blown into or across a mouthpiece, which in some instruments is fitted with a reed. **2. woodwinds.** The section of an orchestra or a band composed of such instruments.

wood•work (**wo͝od′**wûrk′) *n.* Objects made of or work done in wood, especially wooden interior fittings in a house, as doors, moldings, or windowsills. —***idiom.*** **out of the woodwork.** Out of obscurity or a place of seclusion: *People come out of woodwork to claim the reward money.*

wood•work•ing (**wo͝od′**wûr′kĭng) *n.* The art, act, or trade of working with wood.

wood•y (**wo͝od′**ē) *adj.* **wood•i•er, wood•i•est. 1.** Forming or consisting of wood: *woody tissue.* **2.** Characteristic or suggestive of wood: *a woody smell.* **3.** Abounding in trees; wooded: *a woody hill.*

woof[1] (wo͝of *or* wo͞of) *n.* **1.** The threads that run crosswise in a woven fabric, at a right angle to the warp; the weft. **2.** The texture of a fabric. [First written down before 800 in Old English and spelled *ōwef.*]

woof[2] (wo͝of) *n.* **1.** The characteristically deep gruff bark of a dog. **2.** A sound similar to a woof. —*intr. v.* **woofed, woof•ing, woofs.** To make such a sound. [First written down in 1804 in Modern English and spelled *wouff*, of imitative origin.]

woof•er (**wo͝of′**ər) *n.* A loudspeaker designed to reproduce bass frequencies.

Victoria Woodhull

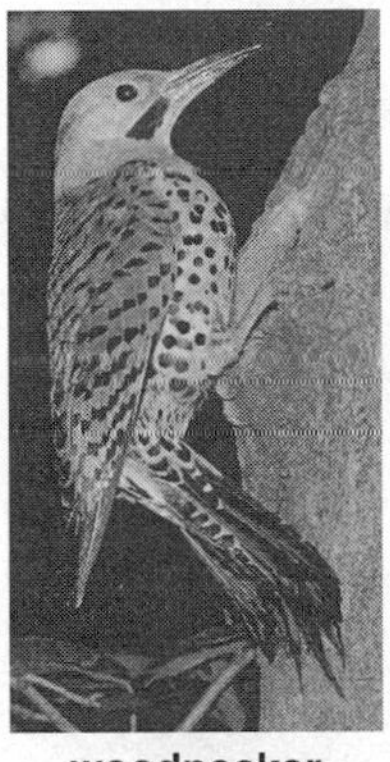
woodpecker
Common flicker

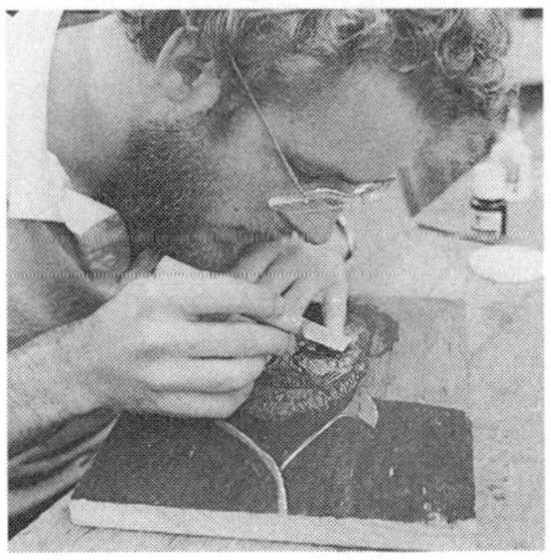
woodworking

ă	pat	oi	boy
ā	pay	ou	out
âr	care	o͝o	took
ä	father	o͞o	boot
ĕ	pet	ŭ	cut
ē	be	ûr	urge
ĭ	pit	th	thin
ī	pie	*th*	this
îr	pier	hw	whoop
ŏ	pot	zh	vision
ō	toe	ə	about
ô	paw	N	*French* bon

Virginia Woolf
Photographed in 1902
by George Charles Beresford
(1864–1938)

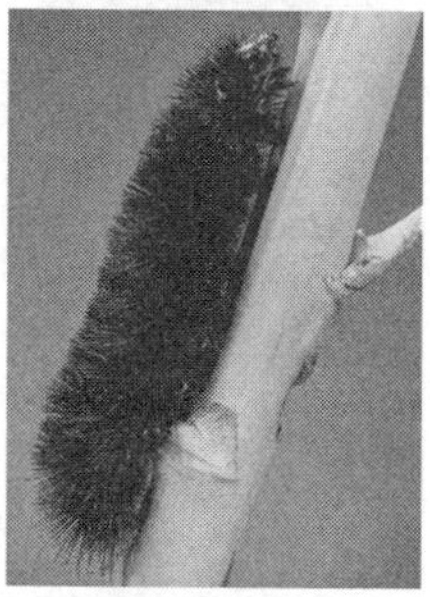

woolly bear
Isabella tiger moth caterpillar

William Wordsworth

wool (wo͝ol) *n.* **1.** The dense, soft, often curly hair of a sheep and certain other animals, used to make yarn and fabric. **2.** Yarn, cloth, or clothing made of this hair. **3.** Something suggesting the texture of wool, as a mass of fine, curled metal strands. [First written down before 800 in Old English and spelled *wull.*]

wool•en also **wool•len** (wo͝ol′ən) *adj.* **1.** Made or consisting of wool: *a woolen blanket.* **2.** Making or dealing in wool cloth or clothing: *a woolen mill.* —*n.* Fabric or clothing made from wool. Often used in the plural.

Woolf (wo͝olf), **(Adeline) Virginia (Stephen).** 1882–1941. British writer whose works include novels, such as *Mrs. Dalloway* (1925), and collections of essays, such as *A Room of One's Own* (1929).

wool•gath•er•ing (wo͝ol′găth′ər ĭng) *n.* The act of daydreaming. **—wool′gath′er•er** *n.*

wool•len (wo͝ol′ən) *adj. & n.* Variant of **woolen.**

wool•ly (wo͝ol′ē) *adj.* **wool•li•er, wool•li•est. 1.** Relating to, consisting of, or covered with wool: *a woolly coat; a woolly lamb.* **2.** Resembling wool: *leaves covered with woolly down.* **3.** Lacking sharp detail or clarity; blurry: *woolly thinking.* **4.** Rough and disorderly; lawless: *a wild and woolly frontier town.* —*n., pl.* **wool•lies.** A garment made of wool, especially an undergarment of knitted wool.

woolly bear *n.* A hairy caterpillar of any of various moths, especially that of the tiger moth of North America, having a reddish-brown middle stripe and being black at either end.

wooz•y (wo͞o′zē *or* wo͝oz′ē) *adj.* **wooz•i•er, wooz•i•est. 1.** Dazed or confused. **2.** Queasy or dizzy. **—wooz′i•ness** *n.*

word (wûrd) *n.* **1.** A spoken sound or group of sounds that communicates a meaning. **2.** A written or printed letter or group of letters representing such a sound or group of sounds. **3.** Something said; an utterance or a comment: *May I have a word with you?* **4. words.** Discourse or talk; speech or writing: *Actions speak louder than words.* **5.** A promise; an assurance: *keeping her word to be on time.* **6.** A direction to do something; an order: *Just say the word, and we'll send up reinforcements.* **7.** News; information: *sent word of her safe arrival.* **8. words.** Hostile or angry remarks made back and forth; a quarrel. **9. Word.** The Bible. —*tr.v.* **word•ed, word•ing, words.** To express in words. ***—idioms.*** **good word. 1.** A favorable comment: *I'll put in a good word for you.* **2.** Favorable news. **in so many words.** In precisely those words; exactly: *wanted us to leave, but wouldn't say it in so many words.* **of few words.** Not talkative; laconic: *a person of few words.* **take (one) at (one's) word.** To be convinced of another's sincerity and act in accord with his or her statement: *We took him at his word that he would lock up when he left.* **upon my word.** Indeed; really. [First written down about 725 in Old English.]

word•book (wûrd′bo͝ok′) *n.* A vocabulary or dictionary.

word for word *adv.* In exactly the same words. **—word′-for-word′** (wûrd′fər wûrd′) *adj.*

word•ing (wûr′dĭng) *n.* The act or style of expressing in words.

word•less (wûrd′lĭs) *adj.* **1.** Not expressed in words; unspoken: *a look that served as a wordless reproach.* **2.** Speechless; silent: *wordless with gratitude.* **—word′less•ly** *adv.* **—word′less•ness** *n.*

word of mouth *n.* Spoken communication: *News of their success spread by word of mouth.*

word processing *n.* The creation and production of documents and texts by means of computer systems.

word processor *n.* A computer system specially designed for or capable of word processing.

Words•worth (wûrdz′wûrth′), **William.** 1770–1850. British poet whose works include "Tintern Abbey" (1798). He was appointed poet laureate in 1843.

word•y (wûr′dē) *adj.* **word•i•er, word•i•est. 1.** Relating to or consisting of words; verbal. **2.** Using or expressed in too many words; verbose. **—word′i•ly** *adv.* **—word′i•ness** *n.*

wore (wôr) *v.* Past tense of **wear.**

work (wûrk) *n.* **1.** Physical or mental effort or activity directed toward the production or accomplishment of something. **2.a.** Employment in a job or profession: *looking for work.* **b.** A trade, profession, or other means of livelihood. **3.** Something that one is doing, making, or performing, especially as an occupation or a duty: *begin the day's work.* **4.a.** The part of a day devoted to an occupation or undertaking: *met her after work.* **b.** One's place of employment: *Should I call you at home or at work?* **5.a.** Something that has been produced or accomplished through a particular kind of effort or activity: *This story is the work of an active imagination.* **b.** An act; a deed: *good works.* **6.** An artistic creation, such as a painting or musical composition. **7. works.** Engineering structures, such as bridges or dams. **8. works.** *(used with a singular or plural verb).* A factory, plant, or similar building where a specific type of business or industry is carried on: *a steelworks.* **9. works.** Internal mechanism: *the works of a watch.* **10.** The manner, style, or quality of working or treatment: *sloppy work.* **11. works.** *Informal.* The full range of possibilities; everything: *ordered a pizza with the works.* —*v.* **worked** also **wrought** (rôt), **work•ing, works.** —*intr.* **1.** To exert oneself physically or mentally in order to do, make, or accomplish something. **2.** To be employed; have a job. **3.** To function; operate: *How does this latch work? The telephone isn't working.* **4.** To have the desired effect or outcome; be successful: *This recipe seems to work.* **5.** To arrive at a specified condition through gradual or repeated movement: *The stitches worked loose.* **6.** To proceed or progress slowly and laboriously: *worked through the underbrush.* —*tr.* **1.** To cause or effect; bring about: *working miracles.* **2.** To cause to operate or function: *worked the controls.* **3.** To shape or forge: *worked the metal into a sculpture.* **4.** To knead, stir, or otherwise manipulate in preparation: *Work the dough before shaping it.* **5.** To bring to a specified condition by gradual or repeated effort or work: *finally worked the window open.* **6.** To make, achieve, or pay for by work or effort: *worked her way through college.* **7.** To solve by reasoning: *work a math problem.* **8.** To make productive; cultivate: *work a farm.* **9.** To cause to work: *works his horses hard.* **10.** To excite or provoke: *The speaker worked the mob into a frenzy.* ***—idioms.*** **in the works.** In preparation; under development: *There's a new movie in the works.* **work off.** To get rid of by work or effort: *worked off some energy at the gym.* **work out. 1.** To find a solution for; solve: *Can you work out these math problems?* **2.** To prove successful, effective, or satisfactory: *Everything worked out in the end.* **3.** To have a specified result: *The arrangements worked out just fine.* **4.** To engage in strenuous exercise for physical conditioning. **work up. 1.** To arouse the emotions of; excite or aggravate. **2.** To develop or produce: *worked up a report; worked up an appetite.* [First written down about 725 in Old English and spelled *weorc.*] —SEE NOTE at **wreak.**

work•a•ble (wûr′kə bəl) *adj.* **1.** Capable of being worked, dealt with, or handled. **2.** Capable of being put into effective operation: *a workable plan.* —**work′a·bil′i·ty, work′a·ble·ness** *n.*

work·a·day (wûr′kə dā′) *adj.* **1.** Relating to or suited for working days; everyday. **2.** Mundane; commonplace.

work·bench (wûrk′bĕnch′) *n.* A sturdy table or bench at which skilled manual work is done, as by a carpenter or machinist.

work·book (wûrk′bo͝ok′) *n.* **1.** A booklet containing problems and exercises that a student may work out directly on its pages. **2.** A manual of instructions, as for running a machine or an appliance.

work·day (wûrk′dā′) *n.* **1.** A day on which work is done. **2.** The part of the day during which one works.

work·er (wûr′kər) *n.* **1.** A person who works: *a fast worker; an office worker.* **2.** A member of the working class. **3.** A member of a colony of ants, bees, or other social insects that does the work of the colony and cannot produce offspring.

work·ers' compensation (wûr′kərz) *n.* Payments made to an employee who is injured at work.

work force or **work·force** (wûrk′fôrs′) *n.* All the people working or available to work, as in a nation or a company.

work·horse (wûrk′hôrs′) *n.* **1.** A person or thing that works tirelessly or under prolonged use. **2.** A horse that is used for labor.

work·house (wûrk′hous′) *n.* A prison in which sentences are served at manual labor.

work·ing (wûr′kĭng) *adj.* **1.** Capable of working; functioning: *a machine in working condition.* **2.** Having a paying job; employed: *a working person.* **3.** Spent in work: *working hours.* **4.** Sufficient or adequate for using: *a working knowledge of a language.*

working class *n.* The part of society made up of those who work for wages, especially manual or industrial laborers.

work·ing·man (wûr′kĭng măn′) *n.* A man who works for wages.

working papers *pl.n.* Legal documents certifying the right to employment of a minor or an alien.

work·ing·wom·an (wûr′kĭng wo͝om′ən) *n.* A woman who works for wages.

work·load (wûrk′lōd′) *n.* The amount of work that can be produced in a specified period of time, as by a worker or a machine.

work·man (wûrk′mən) *n.* A man who performs manual or industrial labor for wages.

work·man·ship (wûrk′mən shĭp′) *n.* **1.** The skill of a craftsperson or an artisan. **2.** The quality of something made, as by an artisan.

work·men's compensation (wûrk′mənz) *n.* Workers' compensation.

work·out (wûrk′out′) *n.* A period of exercise, as to improve fitness or for an athletic competition.

work·shop (wûrk′shŏp′) *n.* **1.** A place where manual or light industrial work is done. **2.** An educational seminar held for a usually small number of participants: *a teachers' workshop.*

work·ta·ble (wûrk′tā′bəl) *n.* A table designed for a specific kind of task or activity, such as needlework or graphic arts.

world (wûrld) *n.* **1.** The earth. **2.** The universe. **3.** The inhabitants of the earth; the human race. **4.** Often **World.** A particular part of the earth: *the Western World.* **5.** A particular part of the earth and its inhabitants as known during a given period of history: *the Renaissance world.* **6.** A field, sphere, group, or realm: *the scientific world.* **7.** Secular life and its concerns: *a man of the world.* **8.** A state of existence: *the next world.* **9.** A large amount. Often used in the plural: *spent worlds of time.* **10.** A planet or other celestial body. —***idioms.*** **in the world.** Used as an intensive: *Where in the world did you find that?* **out of this world.** *Informal.* Extraordinary; superb: *had some pizza that was out of this world.* **the world over.** Throughout the world: *a folk musician famous the world over.* [First written down about 725 in Old English and spelled *worold.*]

world·ly (wûrld′lē) *adj.* **world·li·er, world·li·est.** **1.** Of, relating to, or devoted to the affairs of the world; secular; not spiritual: *worldly concerns.* **2.** Sophisticated; cosmopolitan. —**world′li·ness** *n.*

world·ly-wise (wûrld′lē wīz′) *adj.* Experienced in the ways of the world.

world power *n.* A nation having the power to influence the course of world events.

World Series *n.* In baseball, a series of games played to decide the championship of the major leagues.

World War I *n.* A war fought from 1914 to 1918, in which Great Britain, France, the United States, and their allies defeated Germany, Austria-Hungary, and their allies.

World War II *n.* A war fought from 1939 to 1945, in which Great Britain, France, the Soviet Union, the United States, and their allies defeated Germany, Italy, and Japan.

world·wide (wûrld′wīd′) *adj.* Involving or extending throughout the world. —*adv.* Throughout the world: *distributed worldwide.*

worm (wûrm) *n.* **1.** Any of various animals having a soft, long, often limbless rounded or flattened body and no backbone. **2.** Any of various animals resembling worms, especially a caterpillar, grub, or other insect larva. **3. worms.** Infestation of the intestines or other parts of the body by parasitic worms. **4.** A person regarded as pitiable or contemptible. —*v.* **wormed, worm·ing, worms.** —*tr.* **1.** To make (one's way) or move with or as if with the crawling or twisting motion of a worm. **2.** To get by sly or deceitful means: *The spy wormed the information from the messenger.* **3.** To cure of intestinal worms. —*intr.* **1.** To move in a manner suggestive of a worm. **2.** To make one's way by artful or devious means: *worm out of an obligation.* [First written down about 725 in Old English and spelled *wyrm.*] —**worm′like′** *adj.*

worm gear *n.* A gear made of a spirally threaded shaft and a wheel with teeth that mesh into it.

worm·wood (wûrm′wo͝od′) *n.* Any of several strong-smelling plants that yield a bitter substance used for flavoring certain alcoholic liquors.

worm·y (wûr′mē) *adj.* **worm·i·er, worm·i·est.** Infested with or damaged by worms.

worn (wôrn) *v.* Past participle of **wear.** —*adj.* **1.** Affected or damaged by wear or use: *worn faded trousers.* **2.** Showing the wearing effects of worry, sickness, or strain: *a pale worn face.*

worn-out (wôrn′out′) *adj.* **1.** Used or worn until no longer usable: *worn-out clothes.* **2.** Extremely tired; exhausted.

wor·ri·some (wûr′ē səm *or* wŭr′ē səm) *adj.* **1.** Causing worry or anxiety. **2.** Tending to worry.

wor·ry (wûr′ē *or* wŭr′ē) *v.* **wor·ried** (wûr′ēd *or* wŭr′ēd), **wor·ry·ing, wor·ries** (wûr′ēz *or* wŭr′ēz). —*intr.* **1.** To feel uneasy or concerned about something; be troubled: *worried about his health.* **2.** To pull or tear at something with or as if with the teeth. —*tr.* **1.** To cause to feel anxious, distressed, or troubled: *Don't worry your parents!* **2.** To seize with the teeth and tug at repeatedly: *a kitten worrying a ball of yarn.* —*n., pl.* **wor·ries. 1.** Mental uneasiness or anxiety. **2.** A source of anxiety or uneasiness. [First written down before 800 in Old English and spelled *wyrgan,* to strangle.] —**wor′ri·er** *n.*

wor·ry·wart (wûr′ē wôrt′ *or* wŭr′ē wôrt′) *n.* A

workshop
Woodcraft workshop

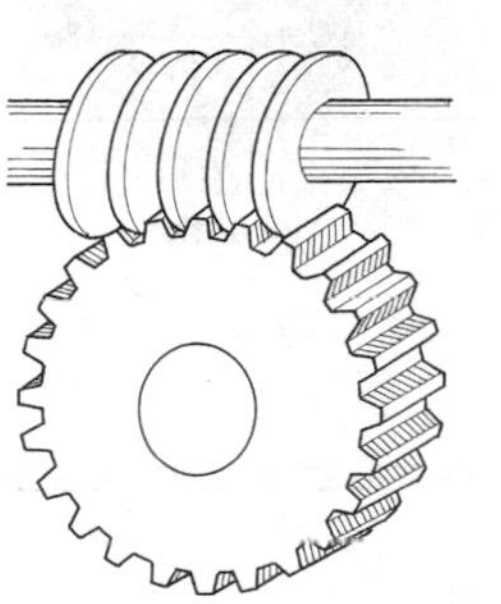

worm gear

ă	pat	oi	boy
ā	pay	ou	out
âr	care	o͝o	took
ä	father	o͞o	boot
ĕ	pet	ŭ	cut
ē	be	ûr	urge
ĭ	pit	th	thin
ī	pie	*th*	this
îr	pier	hw	whoop
ŏ	pot	zh	vision
ō	toe	ə	about
ô	paw	N	*French* bon

Usage: wreak

Sometimes people confuse **wreak** with **wreck**. This confusion may exist because the wreaking of damage may leave a wreck: *The storm wreaked havoc along the coast.* The past tense and past participle of wreak is *wreaked*, not **wrought**. **Wrought** is an alternative past tense and past participle of work: *What hath God wrought?*

wreath

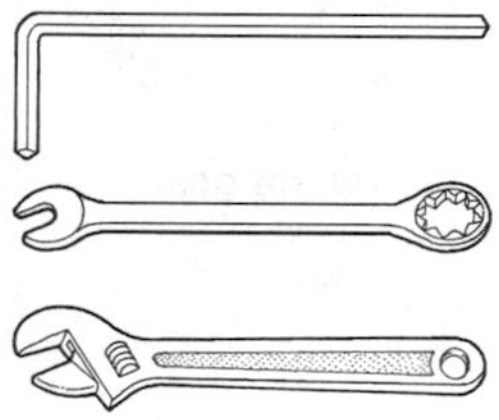

wrench
Top: Allen wrench
Center: Open-end box wrench
Bottom: Adjustable wrench

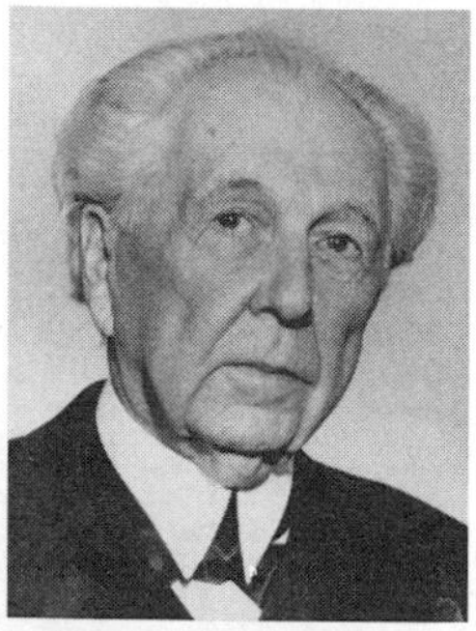

Frank Lloyd Wright

person who worries excessively and needlessly.

worse (wûrs) *adj.* Comparative of **bad[1], ill. 1.** Of a more inferior quality, condition, or effect: *This restaurant is worse than the last one we ate at.* **2.** More severe or unfavorable: *The weather got worse as the night wore on.* **3.** Being in poorer health; more ill. *—n.* Something that is worse: *Of the two cars, the old one is the worse. —adv.* Comparative of **badly, ill.** In a worse manner; to a worse degree: *The team plays worse when we skip a practice.* ***—idiom.* for better or worse.** Whether the situation or consequences be good or ill. [First written down about 725 in Old English and spelled *wyrsa.*]

wors•en (wûr′sən) *tr. & intr.v.* **wors•ened, wors•en•ing, wors•ens.** To make or become worse.

wor•ship (wûr′shĭp) *n.* **1.** The reverent love and devotion given to a deity or an idol. **2.** A set of ceremonies, prayers, or other religious forms by which this love is expressed. **3.** Ardent devotion; adoration. **4.** Often **Worship.** *Chiefly British.* Used as a form of address for certain officials: *Is your Worship ready? —v.* **wor•shiped, wor•ship•ing, wor•ships** or **wor•shipped, wor•ship•ping, wor•ships.** *—tr.* **1.** To honor and love as a deity. **2.** To regard with adoring esteem or devotion. See Synonyms at **revere.** *—intr.* To participate in religious rites of worship. [First written down before 900 in Old English and spelled *weorthscipe*, worthiness, honor: *weorth*, worth + *-scipe*, condition.] **—wor′ship•er, wor′ship•per** *n.*

wor•ship•ful (wûr′shĭp fəl) *adj.* Reverent; pious.

worst (wûrst) *adj.* Superlative of **bad[1], ill. 1.** Of most inferior quality, condition, or effect. **2.** Most severe or unfavorable: *the worst winter in years.* **3.** Least desirable or satisfactory: *the worst piece of land. —adv.* Superlative of **badly, ill.** In the worst manner or degree. *—n.* Something that is worst: *Cold pizza is the worst!* ***—idiom.* in the worst way.** *Informal.* Very much; a great deal: *wanted a kitten in the worst way.* [First written down before 899 in Old English and spelled *wyrresta.*]

wor•sted (wo͝os′tĭd *or* wûr′stĭd) *n.* **1.** Smooth, firmly twisted yarn made from long strands of wool. **2.** Fabric made from such yarn.

worth (wûrth) *n.* **1.** The quality that gives value or usefulness to something: *the worth of a good reputation.* **2.** The value of something expressed in money; market value: *property with a worth of a million dollars.* **3.** The amount that a certain sum of money will buy: *20 dollars' worth of nails.* **4.** Wealth; riches: *the company's net worth. —adj.* **1.** Equal in value to something specified: *a pen worth five dollars.* **2.** Deserving of; meriting: *a plan worth a trial.* **3.** Having wealth amounting to: *a person worth $2,000,000.* ***—idiom.* for what it's worth.** Even though it may not be important or valuable: *Let's listen to the proposal, for what it's worth.* [First written down before 695 in Old English and spelled *weorth.*]

worth•less (wûrth′lĭs) *adj.* Lacking worth; of no use or value: *a worthless promise.* **—worth′less•ly** *adv.*

worth•while (wûrth′wīl′) *adj.* Sufficiently valuable or important to justify the time, effort, or interest involved.

wor•thy (wûr′*th*ē) *adj.* **wor•thi•er, wor•thi•est. 1.** Having worth, merit, or value; useful or valuable: *a worthy cause.* **2.** Honorable; admirable: *a worthy opponent.* **3.** Having sufficient worth; deserving: *worthy to be considered; worthy of praise. —n., pl.* **wor•thies.** An important or distinguished person. **—wor′thi•ness** *n.*

wot (wŏt) *v.* First and third person singular present tense of **wit[2].**

would (wo͝od) *aux.v.* Past tense of **will[2]. 1.** Used in a dependent clause after a statement of desire, request, or advice: *I wish you would stay.* **2.** Used to make a polite request: *Would you like to go with us?* **3.** Used to indicate uncertainty: *His statement would seem to incriminate him.* **4.** Used to indicate preference or willingness: *I would rather stay home tonight.* **5.** Used to indicate intention: *He said that he would take us to the fair.* **6.** Used to indicate customary or habitual behavior in the past: *Every day we would go to the beach.* **7.** Used to indicate probability or likelihood: *We would be there by now if we had taken the train.*

❑ *These sound alike:* **would, wood** (forest).

would-be (wo͝od′bē′) *adj.* Desiring, attempting, or professing to be.

would•n't (wo͝od′nt). Contraction of *would not.*

wouldst (wo͝odst) *v. Archaic.* Second person singular past tense of **will[2].**

wound[1] (wo͞ond) *n.* **1.** An injury, especially one in which skin or tissue is cut, pierced, or broken. **2.** An injury to one's feelings. *—tr.v.* **wound•ed, wound•ing, wounds. 1.** To inflict a wound or wounds on. **2.** To hurt the feelings of (someone). [First written down about 725 in Old English and spelled *wund.*]

wound[2] (wound) *v.* Past tense and past participle of **wind[2].**

wove (wōv) *v.* Past tense of **weave.**

wo•ven (wō′vən) *v.* Past participle of **weave.** *—adj.* Made by weaving: *a woven rag.*

wow (wou) *Informal. interj.* An expression used to show wonder, arrangement, or great pleasure. *—n.* A great success. *—tr.v.* **wowed, wow•ing, wows.** To have a strong and pleasant effect on: *The singer wowed the audience.*

wrack[1] (răk) *n.* **1.** Destruction or ruin. **2.** A remnant or vestige of something destroyed. [First written down about 725 in Old English and spelled *wræc.*]

❑ *These sound alike:* **wrack[1]** (ruin), **rack** (frame), **wrack[2]** (wreckage).

wrack[2] (răk) *n.* **1.** Wreckage, especially of a ship cast ashore. **2.** Dried seaweed. [First written down about 1390 in Middle English and spelled *wrak*, from Middle Dutch.]

❑ *These sound alike:* **wrack[2]** (wreckage), **rack** (frame), **wrack[1]** (ruin).

wraith (rāth) *n.* An apparition or ghost.

wran•gle (răng′gəl) *v.* **wran•gled, wran•gling, wran•gles.** *—intr.* To argue noisily and angrily; bicker. *—tr.* **1.** To win or obtain by argument: *The union wrangled concessions from management.* **2.** To herd (horses or other livestock). *—n.* **1.** The act of wrangling. **2.** An angry noisy dispute.

wrang•ler (răng′glər) *n.* **1.** A person who wrangles. **2.** A cowboy or cowgirl, especially one who tends saddle horses.

wrap (răp) *v.* **wrapped** or **wrapt** (răpt), **wrap•ping, wraps.** *—tr.* **1.** To arrange or fold (something) about as a covering: *She wrapped her shawl about her.* **2.** To enclose within a covering: *wrap one's head in a scarf.* **3.** To enclose, especially in paper, and fasten: *wrap a package.* **4.** To clasp, fold, or coil around something: *She wrapped the line around the post.* **5.** To envelop and obscure: *a plan wrapped in secrecy. —intr.* **1.** To coil or twist about or around something: *The flag wrapped around the pole.* **2.** To put on warm clothing. *—n.* **1.** An outer garment worn for warmth, as a cloak, shawl, or coat. **2.** A wrapping or wrapper. ***—idioms.* under wraps.** *Informal.* Secret or concealed: *Plans for the project are still under wraps.* **wrap up.** To bring to a conclusion; settle finally or successfully. **wrapped up in.** Completely involved in; engrossed: *all wrapped up in a new mystery novel.* [First written down about 1320 in Middle English and spelled *wrappen*.]

❑ *These sound alike:* **wrap, rap**[1] (knock), **rap**[2] (talk).

wrap•per (răp′ər) *n.* **1.** A cover, as of paper, in which something is wrapped: *a candy wrapper.* **2.** A person or device that wraps, as a store employee who wraps parcels.

wrap•ping (răp′ĭng) also **wrap•pings** (răp′ĭngz) *n.* The material used for wrapping something.

wrapt (răpt) *v.* A past tense and a past participle of **wrap.**

❑ *These sound alike:* **wrapt, rapt** (delighted).

wrath (răth) *n.* **1.** Violent anger. **2.** Punishment or vengeance, as for a sin or crime. [First written down about 950 in Old English and spelled *wrǣththu*, from *wrāth*, angry.]

wrath•ful (răth′fəl) *adj.* Full of wrath: *wrathful fury.* **—wrath′ful•ly** *adv.*

wreak (rēk) *tr.v.* **wreaked, wreak•ing, wreaks. 1.** To inflict (vengeance or punishment) upon a person. **2.** To express or gratify (anger or resentment); vent: *The emperor wreaked his anger upon his advisers.* **3.** To bring about; cause: *wreak havoc.* [First written down about 725 in Old English and spelled *wrecan*.] —See Note.

❑ *These sound alike:* **wreak, reek** (smell badly).

wreath (rēth) *n., pl.* **wreaths** (rē*th*z *or* rēths). **1.** A ring or circlet of leaves, flowers, or boughs worn on the head, placed on a memorial, or used as a decoration. **2.** A ring or similar curving form: *a wreath of smoke.* [First written down about 1000 in Old English and spelled *writh*, band.]

wreathe (rē*th*) *tr.v.* **wreathed, wreath•ing, wreathes. 1.** To twist or entwine into a wreath or circular form: *wreathe flowers into a garland.* **2.** To coil so as to encircle something: *The snake wreathed itself around the branch.* **3.** To encircle or decorate with or as if with a wreath: *a poet wreathed with laurel.*

wreck (rĕk) *n.* **1.** The act of wrecking or the state of being wrecked. **2.** Accidental destruction of a ship; a shipwreck. **3.** The remains of something that has been wrecked; wreckage. **4.** A person or thing in a disorderly or worn-out state: *The house was a wreck after the party.* *—tr.v.* **wrecked, wreck•ing, wrecks. 1.** To cause the destruction of in a collision: *He wrecked the car.* See Synonyms at **ruin. 2.** To tear down or dismantle: *The crew wrecked the building in five days.* **3.** To bring to a state of ruin: *A long period of overspending wrecked their finances.* **—wreck′er** *n.*

wreck•age (rĕk′ĭj) *n.* **1.** The act of wrecking or the state of being wrecked. **2.** Something wrecked. **3.** The debris of something wrecked.

wreck•er (rĕk′ər) *n.* **1.** A person or thing that wrecks or destroys: *a wrecker of dreams.* **2.** A person who is in the business of demolishing old buildings. **3.** A person who dismantles junk cars for salvage. **4.** A person or vessel that salvages wrecked ships, planes, or cargo. **5.** A truck with a hoist used to tow broken-down or wrecked cars.

wren (rĕn) *n.* Any of various small brownish songbirds having rounded wings, a slender bill, and a short, often erect tail.

wrench (rĕnch) *n.* **1.** A sudden sharp, forcible twist or turn. **2.** An injury produced by twisting or straining. **3.** A sudden tug at one's emotions; a surge of compassion, sorrow, or anguish. **4.** Any of various tools for gripping and turning objects such as nuts, bolts, or pipes. *—tr.v.* **wrenched, wrench•ing, wrench•es. 1.** To pull or turn suddenly and forcibly: *wrenched the nail out of the board.* **2.** To twist and sprain (a joint or other body part).

wrest (rĕst) *tr.v.* **wrest•ed, wrest•ing, wrests. 1.** To obtain by or as if by pulling and twisting forcefully: *trying to wrest the pen from her grasp.* **2.** To gain or usurp forcefully: *wrested power from the king.*

❑ *These sound alike:* **wrest, rest**[1] (period of inactivity), **rest**[2] (leftover).

wres•tle (rĕs′əl) *v.* **wres•tled, wres•tling, wres•tles.** *—intr.* **1.** To fight by grappling and trying to bring one's opponent to the ground. **2.** To struggle or contend: *wrestle with a problem.* *—tr.* **1.a.** To take part in (a wrestling match). **b.** To take part in a wrestling match with (an opponent). **2.** To move or lift with great effort: *wrestled the box up the stairs.* [First written down before 1250 in Middle English and spelled *wrestlen*, from Old English *wrǣstan*, to twist.]

wres•tler (rĕs′lər) *n.* A person who wrestles, especially as a sport.

wres•tling (rĕs′lĭng) *n.* A sport in which two opponents try to throw or immobilize each other by grappling.

wretch (rĕch) *n.* **1.** A miserable, unfortunate, or unhappy person. **2.** A person regarded as base, mean, or despicable. [First written down about 725 in Old English and spelled *wrecca*.]

wretch•ed (rĕch′ĭd) *adj.* **wretch•ed•er, wretch•ed•est. 1.** Very unhappy or unfortunate; miserable. **2.** Characterized by or causing distress or unhappiness: *wretched working conditions.* **3.** Hateful or contemptible: *a wretched person.* **4.** Inferior in quality: *a wretched performance.* **—wretch′ed•ly** *adv.* **—wretch′ed•ness** *n.*

wri•er (rī′ər) *adj.* A comparative of **wry.**

wri•est (rī′ĭst) *adj.* A superlative of **wry.**

wrig•gle (rĭg′əl) *v.* **wrig•gled, wrig•gling, wrig•gles.** *—intr.* **1.** To turn or twist the body with winding writhing motions; squirm. **2.** To move with writhing motions: *The snake wriggled under the rock.* **3.** To get into or out of a situation by sly or subtle means: *wriggled out of baby-sitting.* *—tr.* To move with a wriggling motion: *wriggle a toe.* *—n.* A wriggling movement.

wright (rīt) *n.* A person who constructs or repairs something: *a playwright.*

Wright (rīt), **Frank Lloyd.** 1869–1959. American architect whose designs include private homes, corporate buildings, and the Guggenheim Museum in New York City (1943–1959).

Wright, Orville. 1871–1948. American aviation pioneer who with his brother **Wilbur** (1867–1912) invented the airplane. Their first flight was made on December 17, 1903, near Kitty Hawk, North Carolina.

Wright, Richard. 1908–1960. American writer whose fiction, including the novel *Native Son* (1940), explores the oppression of Black Americans.

wring (rĭng) *tr.v.* **wrung** (rŭng), **wring•ing, wrings. 1.** To twist, squeeze, or compress, especially to get liquid out: *Wring out the wet clothes.* **2.** To force or squeeze (liquid) out by or as if by twisting or pressing. **3.** To twist forcibly or painfully. **4.** To clasp and twist or squeeze (one's hands), as in distress. **5.** To obtain or extract by force or pressure: *The lawyer wrung the truth out of the witness.* *—n.* A forceful squeeze or twist.

❑ *These sound alike:* **wring, ring**[1] (circle), **ring**[2] (sound a bell).

wring•er (rĭng′ər) *n.* A person or thing that wrings, especially a device in which laundry is pressed between rollers to extract water.

wrin•kle (rĭng′kəl) *n.* A small furrow, ridge, or crease on a normally smooth surface, such as cloth or skin. *—v.* **wrin•kled, wrin•kling, wrin•kles.** *—tr.* **1.** To make a wrinkle or wrinkles in: *Don't*

Wright Brothers
Top: Orville Wright
Bottom: Wilbur Wright

Richard Wright

ă	pat	oi	boy
ā	pay	ou	out
âr	care	o͝o	took
ä	father	o͞o	boot
ĕ	pet	ŭ	cut
ē	be	ûr	urge
ĭ	pit	th	thin
ī	pie	*th*	this
îr	pier	hw	whoop
ŏ	pot	zh	vision
ō	toe	ə	about
ô	paw	N	*French* bon

wrought iron

Wyoming

The name **Wyoming** comes from a Delaware word meaning "at the big river flats" that was first used for a valley in Pennsylvania. The name became popular when it was used in a Romantic poem, and was later proposed for the Wyoming Territory and then for the state of Wyoming.

wrinkle the suit. **2.** To draw up into wrinkles or pucker: *wrinkled her nose.* *—intr.* To form wrinkles: *Linen wrinkles easily.* [First written down in 1392 in Middle English, probably from Old English *gewrinclian*, to wind, crease.]

wrist (rĭst) *n.* **1.** The joint between the hand and the forearm. **2.** The carpus. [First written down before 940 in Old English.]

wrist•band (**rĭst′**bănd′) *n.* A band, as on a sleeve or wristwatch, that encircles the wrist.

wrist•watch (**rĭst′**wŏch′) *n.* A watch worn on a band that fastens about the wrist.

writ¹ (rĭt) *n.* A written court order commanding a person to do or stop doing a specified act. [First written down before 900 in Old English.]

writ² (rĭt) *v.* A past tense and a past participle of **write.**

write (rīt) *v.* **wrote** (rōt) also **writ** (rĭt), **writ•ten** (**rĭt′**n) also **writ, writ•ing, writes.** *—tr.* **1.** To form (letters, symbols, or words) on a surface with an instrument such as a pen. **2.** To form (words or letters) in cursive style. **3.** To compose and set down: *write a poem; write music.* **4.** To draw up in legal form; draft: *write a lease.* **5.** To express in writing; set down: *writing down one's thoughts.* **6.** To communicate by writing: *wrote that she planned to visit.* **7.** To show clearly; mark: *Happiness was written in her smile.* **8.** To fill in the blank spaces of: *write a check.* *—intr.* **1.** To form letters, words, or symbols on a surface. **2.** To produce written material, such as essays or books. **3.** To compose a letter; communicate by mail: *Write to me.* ***—idioms.*** **write in.** To cast a vote by inserting (a name not listed on a ballot). **write off.** To consider as a loss or failure: *He wrote off his first paintings as mere practice.* **write up.** To write a report or description of, as for publication. [First written down about 725 in Old English and spelled *wrītan.*]

❑ *These sound alike:* **write, right** (direction), **rite** (ritual).

write-in (**rīt′**ĭn′) *n.* A vote cast by writing in the name of a candidate not on the ballot.

writ•er (**rī′**tər) *n.* A person who writes, especially as an occupation.

write-up (**rīt′**ŭp′) *n.* A published account, review, or notice, especially a favorable one.

writhe (rīth) *v.* **writhed, writh•ing, writhes.** *—intr.* **1.** To twist, as in pain, struggle, or embarrassment. **2.** To move with a twisting or contorted motion. *—tr.* To cause to twist or squirm; contort.

writ•ing (**rī′**tĭng) *n.* **1.** The act of one who writes. **2.** Written form: *Make the request in writing.* **3.** Meaningful letters or characters that make up readable matter: *Can you make out the writing in this note?* **4.** The occupation or style of a writer. **5.** A written work, especially a literary composition. **6.** **Writings.** *(used with a singular or plural verb).* The third of the three divisions of the Hebrew Scriptures, usually composed of Psalms, Proverbs, Job, Song of Solomon, Ruth, Lamentations, Ecclesiastes, Esther, Daniel, Ezra, Nehemiah, and Chronicles.

writ•ten (**rĭt′**n) *v.* Past participle of **write.**

wrong (rông *or* rŏng) *adj.* **1.** Not correct; erroneous: *a wrong answer.* **2.** Contrary to conscience, morality, or law; immoral or wicked. **3.** Not required, intended, or wanted: *a wrong telephone number; the wrong direction.* **4.** Not fitting or suitable; inappropriate: *said the wrong thing.* **5.** Not in accordance with an established usage, method, or procedure: *the wrong way to make pie crust.* **6.** Not functioning properly; amiss: *What is wrong with this machine?* **7.** Designating the side, as of a garment, that is less finished and not intended to show: *socks worn the wrong side out.* *—adv.* **1.** Mistakenly; erroneously: *told the story wrong.* **2.** Immorally or unjustly: *behave wrong.* *—n.* **1.** An unjust, injurious, or immoral act or circumstance: *felt many wrongs had been committed against them.* **2.** The condition of being mistaken or at fault: *in the wrong.* *—tr.v.* **wronged, wrong•ing, wrongs.** **1.** To treat unjustly, injuriously, or dishonorably. **2.** To discredit unjustly; malign. ***—idiom.*** **go wrong.** **1.** To take a wrong turn or make a wrong move. **2.** To go amiss; turn out badly: *What went wrong with the project?* [First written down before 1200 in Middle English and spelled *wrang*, twisted, awry, of Scandinavian origin.] **—wrong′ly** *adv.* **—wrong′ness** *n.*

wrong•do•er (**rông′**do͞o′ər *or* **rŏng′**do͞o′ər) *n.* A person who does something wrong. **—wrong′do′ing** *n.*

wrong•ful (**rông′**fəl *or* **rŏng′**fəl) *adj.* **1.** Wrong; unjust: *wrongful criticism.* **2.** Unlawful.

wrote (rōt) *v.* Past tense of **write.**

❑ *These sound alike:* **wrote, rote** (routine).

wroth (rôth) *adj.* Wrathful; angry.

wrought (rôt) *v.* A past tense and a past participle of **work.** *—adj.* **1.** Made, formed, or fashioned: *a carefully wrought cabinet.* **2.** Shaped by hammering with tools: *wrought metal.*

wrought iron *n.* A highly purified form of iron that is easily shaped, forged, or welded.

wrung (rŭng) *v.* Past tense and past participle of **wring.**

❑ *These sound alike:* **wrung, rung¹** (rod), **rung²** (sounded).

wry (rī) *adj.* **wri•er** (**rī′**ər), **wri•est** (**rī′**ĭst) or **wry•er, wry•est.** **1.** Funny in an understated or ironic way; dry: *wry humor.* **2.** Temporarily twisted in an expression of distaste or displeasure: *made a wry face.* **3.** Twisted or bent to one side: *a wry nose.* **—wry′ly** *adv.*

❑ *These sound alike:* **wry, rye** (grain).

wt. *abbr.* An abbreviation of weight.

wurst (wûrst *or* wo͝orst) *n.* Sausage.

WV *abbr.* An abbreviation of West Virginia.

W.Va. *abbr.* An abbreviation of West Virginia.

WWI *abbr.* An abbreviation of World War I.

WWII *abbr.* An abbreviation of World War II.

WY *abbr.* An abbreviation of Wyoming.

Wyc•liffe (**wĭk′**lĭf), **John.** 1328?–1384. English theologian and religious reformer whose beliefs anticipated the Protestant Reformation.

Wyo. *abbr.* An abbreviation of Wyoming.

Wy•o•ming (wī **ō′**mĭng). A state of the western United States south of Montana. It was admitted as the 44th state in 1890. Cheyenne is the capital and the largest city. Population, 455,975. —SEE NOTE.

Xx

x or **X** (ĕks) *n., pl.* **x's** or **X's. 1.** The 24th letter of the English alphabet. **2.** The 24th in a series or group. **3.** A mark made to represent the signature of a person who is unable to sign his or her name.

X (ĕks) *n.* A movie rating that allows admission to no one under the age of 17.

Xan•a•du (zăn′ə do͞o′ *or* zăn′ə dyo͞o′) *n.* An idyllic beautiful place.

Xa•vi•er (zā′vē ər), Saint **Francis.** 1506–1552. Spanish missionary who cofounded the Jesuit order (1534) with Ignatius of Loyola.

x-ax•is (ĕks′ăk′sĭs) *n., pl.* **x-ax•es** (ĕks′ăk′sēz). **1.** The horizontal axis of a two-dimensional coordinate system. **2.** One of the three axes of a three-dimensional coordinate system.

X-chro•mo•some (ĕks′krō′mə sōm′) *n.* The chromosome associated with female sex characteristics. In females it is paired with another X-chromosome; in males it is paired with a Y-chromosome.

Xe The symbol for the element **xenon.**

xe•bec (zē′bĕk′) *n.* A small three-masted Mediterranean sailing ship having both square and triangular sails. [First written down in 1756 in Modern English and spelled *xebeck*, from Arabic dialectal *šabbāk*.]

xe•non (zē′nŏn′) *n. Symbol* **Xe** A colorless, odorless, gaseous element that is found in the atmosphere in small amounts and that rarely reacts with other substances. It is used in bubble chambers and in filling flashbulbs and electron tubes. Atomic number 54. See table at **element.** [First written down in 1898 in Modern English, from Greek *xenos*, foreign, strange.]

xen•o•phobe (zĕn′ə fōb′ *or* zē′nə fōb′) *n.* A person who fears or scorns that which is foreign, especially foreign peoples or strangers.

xen•o•pho•bi•a (zĕn′ə fō′bē ə *or* zē′nə fō′bē ə) *n.* Undue scorn toward or fear of foreign peoples or strangers. [First written down in 1909 in Modern English and spelled *xenophoby* : Greek *xenos*, foreign + Greek *phobia*, fear.] **—xen′o•pho′bic** *adj.*

xer•o•graph•ic (zîr′ə grăf′ĭk) *adj.* Of, used in, or produced by xerography: *the xerographic method; xerographic prints.*

xe•rog•ra•phy (zĭ rŏg′rə fē) *n.* A process for producing photographs or photocopies in which an image made up of particles of dry pigment held in place by electric charges on a plate is transferred to a sheet of paper and fixed to the paper by heat. [First written down in 1948 in Modern English : Greek *xēros*, dry + *-graphy*, writing.]

Xer•ox (zîr′ŏks). A trademark used for a photocopying process or machine employing xerography.

Xer•xes I (zûrk′sēz) Known as "Xerxes the Great." 519?–465 B.C. King of Persia (486–465) whose army defeated the Greeks at Thermopylae and destroyed Athens (480).

Xho•sa (kō′sä) *n., pl.* **Xhosa** or **Xho•sas. 1.** A member of a Bantu people of southern Africa. **2.** The language of this people.

xi (zī *or* sī) *n.* The 14th letter of the Greek alphabet, written Χ, χ. In English it is represented as *X, x.*

X•mas (krĭs′məs *or* ĕks′məs) *n.* Christmas.

X-rat•ed (ĕks′rā′tĭd) *adj.* Having the rating X: *an X-rated movie.*

x-ray also **X-ray** (ĕks′rā′) *n.* also **x ray** or **X ray 1.a.** Electromagnetic radiation having a wavelength shorter than that of ultraviolet light but longer than that of a gamma ray and having a correspondingly high energy. **b.** A stream of such radiation. Often used in the plural. **2.** A photograph taken with x-rays. *—tr.v.* **x-rayed, x-ray•ing, x-rays** also **X-rayed, X-ray•ing, X-rays. 1.** To irradiate with x-rays. **2.** To photograph with x-rays.

xy•lem (zī′ləm) *n.* Plant tissue consisting of thick-walled cells that provide support and through which water and dissolved minerals are conducted upward to the various plant parts. [First written down in 1875 in Modern English, from Greek *xulon*, wood.]

xy•lo•phone (zī′lə fōn′) *n.* A percussion instrument consisting of a series of mounted wooden bars of various sizes that sound various tones, played with two small mallets. [First written down in 1866 in Modern English : Greek *xulon*, wood + *-phone*, sound.]

Xerxes I

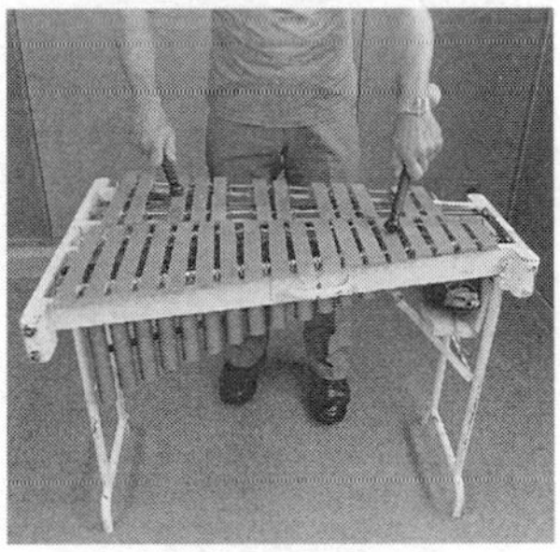

xylophone

ă	pat	oi	boy
ā	pay	ou	out
âr	care	o͝o	took
ä	father	o͞o	boot
ĕ	pet	ŭ	cut
ē	be	ûr	urge
ĭ	pit	th	thin
ī	pie	*th*	this
îr	pier	hw	whoop
ŏ	pot	zh	vision
ō	toe	ə	about
ô	paw	N	*French* bon

Y y

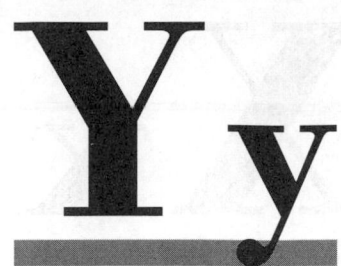

y or **Y** (wī) *n., pl.* **y's** or **Y's. 1.** The 25th letter of the English alphabet. **2.** The 25th in a series or group.
Y The symbol for the element **yttrium.**
–y[1] or **–ey** *suff.* A suffix that means: **1.** Characterized by; consisting of: *moldy.* **2.** Like: *summery.* **3.** To some degree; rather: *chilly.* **4.** Tending toward: *sleepy.*
–y[2] *suff.* A suffix that means: **1.** Condition; state: *jealousy.* **2.** Activity: *cookery.* **3.** Place for an activity: *cannery.* **4.** Result or product of an activity: *laundry.*
–y[3] or **–ie** *suff.* A suffix that means: **1.** Small one: *doggy.* **2.** Dear one: *sweetie.*

yacht

yacht (yät) *n.* Any of various relatively small sailing or motor-driven vessels used for pleasure trips or racing. *—intr.v.* **yacht•ed, yacht•ing, yachts.** To sail, cruise, or race in a yacht.
yacht•ing (**yä′**tĭng) *n.* The activity of sailing in a yacht.
yachts•man (**yäts′**mən) *n.* A man who owns or sails a yacht.
yachts•wom•an (**yäts′**wo͝om′ən) *n.* A woman who owns or sails a yacht.
ya•hoo (**yä′**ho͞o *or* **yā′**ho͞o) *n., pl.* **ya•hoos.** A person regarded as crude or brutish.
Yah•weh (**yä′**wĕ) *n.* A name for God assumed by modern scholars to be a rendering of the pronunciation of the Hebrew name for God in the Hebrew Scriptures.

yak[1]

yak[1] (yăk) *n.* A long-haired ox of the mountains of central Asia, often domesticated and used for pulling and carrying loads or raised for its meat and milk. [First written down in 1795 in Modern English, from Tibetan *gyag.*]
yak[2] (yăk) *intr.v.* **yakked, yak•king, yaks.** *Slang.* To talk persistently and meaninglessly; chatter. [First written down in 1950 in Modern English, of imitative origin.]
y'all (yôl) *pron.* Variant of **you-all.**
yam (yăm) *n.* **1.a.** The starchy root of any of numerous tropical vines, used as food. **b.** A vine that has such roots. **2.** A reddish sweet potato. —SEE NOTE at **goober.**
yam•mer (**yăm′**ər) *intr. & tr.v.* **yam•mered, yam•mer•ing, yam•mers.** To complain or say peevishly or whimperingly; whine. **—yam′mer•er** *n.*
Yan•gon (**yän′gôn′**). Rangoon.
Yang•tze River (**yăng′sē′** *or* **yăng′tsē′**) or **Chang Jiang** (**chäng′ jyäng′**). The longest river of China and of Asia, flowing about 3,450 miles (5,551 kilometers) from Xizang (Tibet) to the East China Sea.

yarmulke

yank (yăngk) *v.* **yanked, yank•ing, yanks.** *—tr.* To pull on with a quick strong movement; jerk: *The baby yanked her bib off and threw it down. —intr.* To pull with a quick strong movement: *I yanked on the rope until the knot gave. —n.* A sudden sharp pull; a jerk.
Yank (yăngk) *n. Informal.* A Yankee.
Yan•kee (**yăng′**kē) *n.* **1.** A native or inhabitant of New England. **2.** A native or inhabitant of a northern U.S. state, especially a Union soldier during the Civil War. **3.** A native or inhabitant of the United States.
Yankee Doodle *n.* A Yankee.
Ya•oun•dé (yä o͞on **dā′**). The capital of Cameroon, in the south-central part of the country. It was founded in 1888. Population, 561,000.
yap (yăp) *intr.v.* **yapped, yap•ping, yaps. 1.** To bark sharply; yelp. **2.** *Slang.* To talk noisily or stupidly; jabber. *—n.* **1.** A sharp high-pitched bark. **2.** *Slang.* The mouth.
Ya•qui (**yä′**kē) *n., pl.* **Yaqui** or **Ya•quis. 1.** A member of a Native American people living in northern Mexico and southern Arizona. **2.** The Uto-Aztecan language of this people.
yard[1] (yärd) *n.* **1.** A unit of length equal to 3 feet or 36 inches (0.9144 meter). See table at **measurement. 2.** A long pole slung to a mast to support the head of a sail. [First written down about 725 in Old English and spelled *gerd.*]
yard[2] (yärd) *n.* **1.** A piece of ground near a building or group of buildings: *our back yard; the school yard.* **2.** An area, often enclosed, used for a particular kind of work, business, or other activity: *a coal yard; a lumber yard.* **3.** An area where railroad cars are switched from track to track, made up into trains, stored, and repaired. [First written down about 725 in Old English and spelled *geard.*]
yard•age (**yär′**dĭj) *n.* **1.** An amount or a length measured in yards: *yardage gained in a game.* **2.** Cloth sold by the yard.
yard•arm (**yärd′**ärm′) *n.* Either end of a yard supporting a square sail.
yard goods *pl.n.* Piece goods.
yard•mas•ter (**yärd′**măs′tər) *n.* An employee in charge of a railroad yard.
yard•stick (**yärd′**stĭk′) *n.* **1.** A graduated measuring stick one yard in length. **2.** A standard used in comparing or judging.
yar•mul•ke (**yär′**məl kə *or* **yä′**məl kə) *n.* A skullcap worn by Jewish men and boys, especially those adhering to Orthodox or Conservative Judaism. [First written down in 1903 in Modern English and spelled *jarmulka,* from Yiddish *yarmulke,* from Polish and Ukranian *yarmulka,* possibly from Turkish *yağmurluk,* rain clothing.]
yarn (yärn) *n.* **1.** A continuous strand of twisted threads of material such as wool or nylon, used in weaving, knitting, or crocheting. **2.** *Informal.* A long, sometimes elaborate story, often made-up or exaggerated. [First written down about 1000 in Old English and spelled *gearn.*]
yar•row (**yăr′**ō) *n.* Any of several plants having narrow feathery leaves and flat-topped clusters of usually white flowers.
yaw (yô) *intr.v.* **yawed, yaw•ing, yaws. 1.** To swerve off course momentarily or temporarily: *The schooner yawed in the rough seas.* **2.** To turn right or left about a vertical axis: *The plane yawed because of the strong wind. —n.* **1.** The act of yawing. **2.** Extent of yawing, measured in degrees: *The pilot corrected for the yaw of the plane.*
yawl (yôl) *n.* A two-masted fore-and-aft rigged sail-

ing boat having the shorter mast far to the stern, aft of the tiller.

yawn (yôn) *v.* **yawned, yawn•ing, yawns.** —*intr.* **1.** To open the mouth wide with a deep inward breath, usually involuntarily, as when sleepy or bored. **2.** To open wide; gape: *The entrance to the tunnel yawned ahead of them.* —*tr.* To say or express wearily, while or as if while yawning: *yawned a few bored remarks.* —*n.* **1.** The act of yawning. **2.** A fatigued or bored response.

yawp (yôp) *intr.v.* **yawped, yawp•ing, yawps.** To utter a sharp cry; yelp. —*n.* A bark; a yelp.

yaws (yôz) *pl.n.* *(used with a singular or plural verb).* A tropical skin disease caused by bacteria in which many reddish pimples appear on the skin.

y-ax•is (wī′ăk′sĭs) *n., pl.* **y-ax•es** (wī′ăk′sēz). **1.** The vertical axis of a two-dimensional coordinate system. **2.** One of the three axes of a three-dimensional coordinate system.

Yb The symbol for the element **ytterbium.**

Y-chro•mo•some (wī′krō′mə sōm′) *n.* The chromosome associated with male sex characteristics, pairing with an X-chromosome in male organisms.

yd *abbr.* An abbreviation of yard[1] (measurement).

ye[1] (*th*ē) *def. art. Archaic.* The. [First written down before 1568 in Modern English, alteration of Middle English þe, the.]

ye[2] (yē) *pron. Archaic.* **1.** *(used with a plural verb).* You. **2.** *(used with a singular verb).* You. [First written down about 725 in Old English and spelled *gē*.]

yea (yā) *adv.* **1.** Yes; aye. **2.** Indeed; truly. —*n.* An affirmative statement or vote.

yeah (yĕ′ə *or* yă′ə *or* yā′ə) *adv. Informal.* Yes.

year (yîr) *n.* **1.a.** The period of time during which the earth makes one complete revolution around the sun, consisting of 365 days, 5 hours, 49 minutes, and 12 seconds. In the Gregorian calendar a year begins on January 1 and ends on December 31 and is divided into 52 weeks and 12 months. **b.** A period approximately equal to a year in other calendars. **2.** The period during which a planet completes a single revolution around the sun: *A year on Mars is longer than a year on Earth.* **3.** The time it takes for the sun to make an apparent journey on the celestial sphere from a given star back to it again. **4.** A period of 12 months: *a year from June.* **5.** A period of time, often shorter than 12 months, used for a special activity or purpose: *the school year.* **6. years.** Age, especially old age: *I'm feeling my years.* **7. years.** A long time: *I haven't seen them in years.* [First written down about 900 in Old English and spelled *gēar*.]

year•book (yîr′bo͝ok′) *n.* **1.** A memorial or historical book published every year, giving information about the year just ended. **2.** A book published at the end of each school or college year, especially as a record of the members and activities of a graduating class.

year•ling (yîr′lĭng) *n.* An animal that is one year old or between one and two years old.

year•ly (yîr′lē) *adj.* Occurring once a year or every year; annual. —*adv.* Once a year; annually: *Maples and oaks shed their leaves yearly.*

yearn (yûrn) *intr.v.* **yearned, yearn•ing, yearns. 1.** To have a strong, often melancholy desire. **2.** To feel deep pity, concern, or tenderness: *yearned over the poor child's fate.*

yearn•ing (yûr′nĭng) *n.* A persistent, often melancholy desire: *a yearning for truth and justice.* **—yearn′ing•ly** *adv.*

year-round (yîr′round′) *adj.* Existing, active, or continuous throughout the year: *year-round ice skating.*

yeast (yēst) *n.* **1.** Any of various one-celled fungi that can cause the fermentation of carbohydrates, producing carbon dioxide and alcohol. **2.** A commercial preparation in either compressed or powdered form, containing yeast cells and used as a leavening agent and a dietary supplement.

Yeats (yāts), **William Butler.** 1865–1939. Irish writer whose poetry is published in collections such as *The Winding Stair* (1929). He won the 1923 Nobel Prize for literature.

yell (yĕl) *v.* **yelled, yell•ing, yells.** —*intr.* To cry out loudly, as in excitement, pain, fright, or surprise: *They yelled and jumped up and down.* See Synonyms at **shout.** —*tr.* To utter or express with a loud cry; shout. —*n.* **1.** A loud shout or cry. **2.** A rhythmic cheer chanted in unison by a group.

yel•low (yĕl′ō) *n.* **1.a.** The color of ripe lemons. **b.** A pigment or dye having this hue. **2.** Something having this color, as the yolk of an egg. —*adj.* **yel•low•er, yel•low•est. 1.** Of the color yellow. **2.** *Slang.* Cowardly. —*tr. & intr.v.* **yel•lowed, yel•low•ing, yel•lows.** To make or become yellow: *Many washings had yellowed the linen tablecloth. The paper yellowed with age.* [First written down about 725 in Old English and spelled *geolu*.] **—yel′low•ness** *n.*

yellow fever *n.* A severe infectious disease of tropical and subtropical regions caused by a virus transmitted by the bite of an infected mosquito. Its symptoms include high fever, jaundice, and dark-colored vomit resulting from internal bleeding.

yel•low•ham•mer (yĕl′ō hăm′ər) *n.* **1.** A flicker having brown feathers with yellow markings on the tail and wings. **2.** A small European bird having yellow and brown feathers.

yel•low•ish (yĕl′ō ĭsh) *adj.* Somewhat yellow.

yellow jack *n.* **1.** Yellow fever. **2.** A yellow flag flown on a ship to request clearance to come into port or indicate that there is disease on board.

yellow jacket *n.* Any of several small wasps having yellow and black markings.

Yel•low•knife (yĕl′ō nīf′). The capital of Northwest Territories, Canada, in the south-central part of the territory. It was founded in 1935 and became the capital in 1967. Population, 9,483.

yel•low•legs (yĕl′ō lĕgz′) *n., pl.* **yellowlegs.** Either of two North American wading birds having yellow legs and a long narrow bill.

Yellow River. Huang He.

Yellow Sea. An arm of the Pacific Ocean between the Chinese mainland and the Korean Peninsula. It connects with the East China Sea to the south.

Yel•low•stone (yĕl′ō stōn′). A river, about 671 miles (1,080 kilometers) long, of northwest Wyoming and southern and eastern Montana. It flows northward through **Yellowstone National Park,** then east and northeast to the Missouri River.

yelp (yĕlp) *tr.v.* **yelped, yelp•ing, yelps.** To utter with a short sharp bark or cry. —*n.* A short sharp bark or cry.

Yel•tsin (yĕlt′sĭn), **Boris.** Born 1931. Russian politician who was elected President in 1991.

Yem•en (yĕm′ən *or* yā′mən). A country of southwest Asia at the southern tip of the Arabian Peninsula. It was formed when Yemen (or North Yemen) merged with Southern Yemen in May 1990. Capital, Sana. Population, 8,959,000.

yen[1] (yĕn) *n.* A strong desire or inclination; a longing. [First written down in 1906 in American English, from Chinese (Cantonese) *yem*.]

yen[2] (yĕn) *n., pl.* **yen.** The basic monetary unit of Japan. [First written down in 1875 in Modern English, from Japanese *en*, from Chinese (Mandarin) *yuán*, dollar.]

yeo•man (yō′mən) *n.* **1.** An attendant, a servant, or a lesser official in a royal or noble household. **2.** A

William Butler Yeats
Photographed in 1932

yellow jacket

Boris Yeltsin
Photographed in the early 1990's

ă	**pat**	oi	**boy**
ā	**pay**	ou	**out**
âr	**care**	o͝o	**took**
ä	**father**	o͞o	**boot**
ĕ	**pet**	ŭ	**cut**
ē	**be**	ûr	**urge**
ĭ	**pit**	th	**thin**
ī	**pie**	*th*	**this**
îr	**pier**	hw	**whoop**
ŏ	**pot**	zh	**vision**
ō	**toe**	ə	**about**
ô	**paw**	N	*French* **bon**

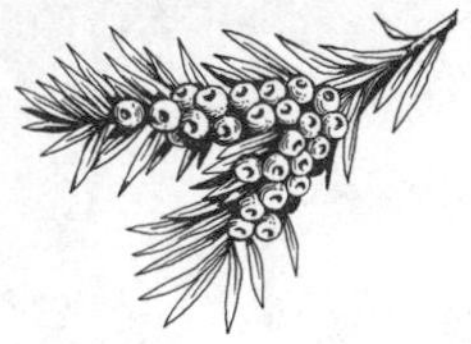

yew

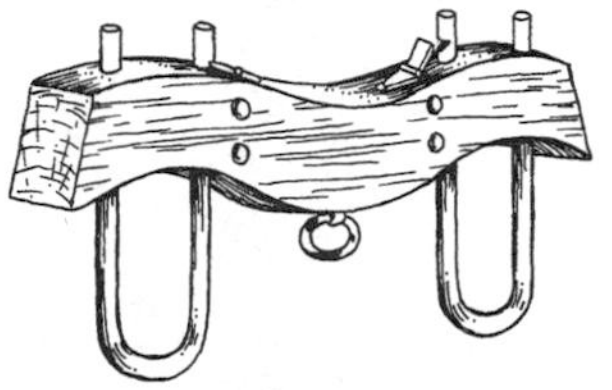

yoke

Regional Note: you-all

The single most famous feature of southern United States dialects is the pronoun **you-all**, probably heard more often in its variant form *y'all.* Southerners often use **you** and **you-all** to make a distinction between one person and more than one person. You used to be able to do this in English by using **thou** for the singular and **you** for the plural.

Brigham Young

petty officer who performs clerical duties in the U.S. Navy. **3.** An assistant, as of a sheriff. **4.** A diligent dependable worker. **5.** A farmer who works his own land, especially in England.

yeo•man•ry (yō′mən rē) *n., pl.* **yeo•man•ries.** Yeomen considered as a group.

yer•ba maté (yâr′bə *or* yûr′bə) *n.* Maté.

Ye•re•van (yĕ′rĭ **vän′**). The capital of Armenia, in the west-central part of the republic. It was founded on the site of a fortress built in the eighth century B.C. Population, 1,133,000.

yes (yĕs) *adv.* It is so; as you say or ask. Used to express affirmation, agreement, or consent. *—n., pl.* **yes•es. 1.** An affirmative or consenting reply: *His suggestion was met with a chorus of yeses.* **2.** An affirmative vote or voter.

ye•shi•va or **ye•shi•vah** (yə **shē′**və) *n.* **1.** A Jewish institute of learning where students study the Talmud. **2.** A Jewish school with a curriculum that includes Jewish religion and culture.

yes•ter•day (**yĕs′**tər dā′ *or* **yĕs′**tər dē) *n.* **1.** The day before the present day: *Yesterday was cold and windy.* **2.** Time in the past, especially the recent past: *The science fiction of yesterday seems quaint today. —adv.* **1.** On the day before the present day: *I mailed the letter yesterday.* **2.** A short while ago.

yes•ter•year (**yĕs′**tər yîr′) *n.* **1.** The year before the present year. **2.** Time past; yore.

yet (yĕt) *adv.* **1.** At this time; for the present: *Dinner isn't ready yet.* **2.** Up to a specified time; thus far: *They have not started yet.* **3.** At a future time: *We may yet decide to go.* **4.** Besides; in addition: *He returned for yet another helping of pie.* **5.** Even; still more: *a yet sadder tale.* **6.** Nevertheless: *young yet wise. —conj.* Nevertheless; and despite this: *She said she would be late, yet she arrived on time.* ***—idiom.* as yet.** Up to the present time; up to now: *I haven't seen any qualified applicants as yet.*

ye•ti (**yĕt′**ē) *n., pl.* **ye•tis.** The abominable snowman.

yew (yo͞o) *n.* **1.** Any of several evergreen trees or shrubs having poisonous, flat, dark-green needles and red berries. **2.** The tough wood of any of these trees, used in making furniture and archery bows.
❑ *These sound alike:* **yew, ewe** (female sheep), **you** (pronoun).

Yid•dish (**yĭd′**ĭsh) *n.* A language derived principally from medieval German dialects and spoken by Jews of Central and Eastern Europe and by their descendants in other parts of the world.

yield (yēld) *v.* **yield•ed, yield•ing, yields.** *—tr.* **1.** To give forth by or as if by a natural process: *The garden yielded a variety of vegetables.* **2.** To provide as return for effort or investment: *an investment that yields high percentages.* **3.** To give over possession of; surrender: *yield the right of way.* **4.** To give up (an advantage, for example) to another; concede. *—intr.* **1.** To give forth a natural product; be productive. **2.** To produce a return for effort or investment. **3.** To give up, as in defeat. **4.** To give way to pressure or force: *The dough yields when pressed with a finger.* **5.** To give way to argument, persuasion, or influence. *—n.* **1.** An amount yielded or produced; a product: *a high yield of corn.* **2.** A profit obtained from an investment. [First written down about 725 in Old English and spelled *geldan,* to pay.]

Synonyms: yield, abandon, surrender, cede, waive. These verbs mean to let something go or to give something up. **Yield** suggests giving way, as to pressure or superior authority: *The diplomat had yielded a lot of ground by the time the conversation with the President was finished.* **Abandon** means to let something go or give something up with no expectation of returning to it or recovering it: *The shipwrecked family slowly abandoned all hope of being rescued.* **Surrender** means to abandon under force or demand: *The passengers surrendered their luggage to the customs agents.* **Cede** suggests giving up something by formal transfer: *Germany ceded the region to France as part of the peace treaty.* **Waive** means voluntarily to do away with something, such as a claim: *The club members waived several of their privileges.*

yield•ing (**yēl′**dĭng) *adj.* Inclined to give way to pressure, argument, or influence.

yip (yĭp) *n.* A short high-pitched bark. *—intr.v.* **yipped, yip•ping, yips.** To make a sharp high-pitched bark.

yip•pee (**yĭp′**ē) *interj. Informal.* An expression used to show elation.

YMCA or **Y.M.C.A.** *abbr.* An abbreviation of Young Men's Christian Association.

YMHA or **Y.M.H.A.** *abbr.* An abbreviation of Young Men's Hebrew Association.

yo•del (**yōd′**l) *v.* **yo•deled, yo•del•ing, yo•dels** or **yo•delled, yo•del•ling, yo•dels.** *—intr.* To sing so that the voice alternates rapidly between the normal voice and a falsetto. *—tr.* To sing (a song) by yodeling. *—n.* A song or cry that is yodeled.

yo•ga (yō′gə) *n.* **1.** Also **Yoga.** A Hindu discipline that trains the mind for a state of perfect spiritual insight and tranquillity. **2.** A system of physical exercises practiced as part of this discipline. [First written down in 1820 in Modern English, from Sanskrit *yogaḥ,* union, joining.]

yo•ghurt (**yō′**gərt) *n.* Variant of **yogurt.**

yo•gi (**yō′**gē) *n., pl.* **yo•gis.** A person who practices yoga.

yo•gurt also **yo•ghurt** (**yō′**gərt) *n.* A tart food similar to custard, made from milk curdled by bacteria and often sweetened or flavored. [First written down in 1625 in Modern English and spelled *yoghurd,* from Turkish *yoğurt.*]

yoke (yōk) *n.* **1.** A crossbar with two U-shaped pieces that fit around the necks of a pair of oxen or other animals working as a team. **2.** *pl.* **yoke** or **yokes.** A pair of draft animals, such as oxen, joined by a yoke. **3.** A frame carried across a person's shoulders with equal loads suspended from each end. **4.** A clamp or vise that controls the motion of a part, holds a part in place, or holds two parts together. **5.** A part of a garment fitting closely around the neck and shoulders or over the hips. **6.** Something that connects or joins; a bond. **7.** The condition of being subjugated by or as if by a conqueror: *the yoke of tyranny. —tr.v.* **yoked, yok•ing, yokes. 1.** To join or harness with a yoke: *yoked the oxen to the cart.* **2.** To join closely as if with a yoke; unite: *The two friends were yoked in a long successful partnership.* [First written down before 899 in Old English and spelled *geoc.*]
❑ *These sound alike:* **yoke, yolk** (egg yellow).

yo•kel (**yō′**kəl) *n.* A country person with little sophistication.

Yo•ko•ha•ma (yō′kə **hä′**mə). A city of southeast Honshu, Japan, south of Tokyo. It was almost entirely destroyed by an earthquake and fire in 1923, but was quickly rebuilt. Population, 2,992,644.

yolk (yōk) *n.* **1.** The yellow, usually round part of an egg of a bird or reptile, surrounded by the albumen and supplying food to the developing young. **2.** The part of the egg of other animals that supplies food to the embryo. [First written down before 1000 in Old English and spelled *geolca,* from *geolu,* yellow.]
❑ *These sound alike:* **yolk, yoke** (crossbar).

Yom Kip•pur (yôm′ **kĭp′**ər *or* yôm′ kē **po͝or′**) *n.* A Jewish holy day observed on the tenth day following Rosh Hashanah and marked by fasting and prayer for the atonement of sins.

yon (yŏn) *adv. & adj.* Yonder.

yon•der (**yŏn′**dər) *adv.* In or at that indicated place: *the village over yonder.* —*adj.* At a distance, but usually within sight: *yonder oak tree.*

yore (yôr) *n.* Time long past: *days of yore.*

York•shire pudding (**yôrk′**shîr *or* **yôrk′**shər) *n.* A soufflélike quick bread made of popover batter baked in meat drippings and served with roast beef.

York•town (**yôrk′**toun′). A village of southeast Virginia southeast of Richmond. It was the site of Charles Cornwallis's surrender of the British forces (1781) in the American Revolution.

you (yo͞o) *pron.* **1.** The one or ones being addressed: *You have very little time left. I'll lend you the book.* **2.** An indefinitely specified person; one: *You can't win them all.* [First written down about 725 in Old English and spelled *ēow*, dative and accusative of *gē*, ye, you.] —See Note at **you-all.**

❑ *These sound alike:* **you, ewe** (female sheep), **yew** (evergreen).

you-all (**yo͞o′ôl′**) also **y'all** (yôl) *pron.* You. Used chiefly in the Southern United States in addressing two or more people. —See Note.

you'd (yo͞od). Contraction of *you had* or *you would.*

you'll (yo͞ol *or* yo͝ol; yəl *when unstressed*) Contraction of *you will* or *you shall.*

❑ *These sound alike:* **you'll, Yule** (Christmas).

young (yŭng) *adj.* **young•er, young•est. 1.** Being in an early stage of life, growth, or development. **2.** Not far advanced; at or near the beginning: *The evening is young.* **3.** Of, belonging to, or suggestive of youth or early life: *He is young for his age.* **4.** Lacking experience or maturity: *a young hand at plowing.* —*n.* **1.** Young persons considered as a group; youth. **2.** Offspring: *a lioness with her young.* —***idiom.*** **with young.** Pregnant. [First written down about 725 in Old English and spelled *geong.*]

Young (yŭng), **Brigham.** 1801–1877. American religious leader who led the Mormons from Illinois to the site of present-day Salt Lake City, Utah, where they established a permanent home for the church (1847).

young•ish (**yŭng′**ĭsh) *adj.* Somewhat young.

young•ster (**yŭng′**stər) *n.* **1.** A child or young person. **2.** A young animal.

your (yo͝or *or* yôr; yər *when unstressed*) *adj.* The possessive form of **you. 1.** Of or belonging to you: *your boots; your achievements.* **2.** A person's; one's: *The light switch is on your right.* [First written down about 725 in Old English and spelled *ēower*, genitive of *gē*, ye, you.]

❑ *These sound alike:* **your, you're** (you are).

you're (yo͝or; yər *when unstressed*) Contraction of *you are.*

❑ *These sound alike:* **you're, your** (of you).

yours (yo͝orz *or* yôrz) *pron.* *(used with a singular or plural verb).* **1.** The one or ones belonging to you: *Use my car if yours hasn't been repaired.* **2.** Used in the complimentary close of a letter: *sincerely yours.* —***idiom.*** **yours truly.** I, myself, or me: *The work was done by yours truly.*

your•self (yo͝or **sĕlf′** *or* yôr **sĕlf′** *or* yər **sĕlf′**) *pron.* **1.** That one that is the same as you. **a.** Used as the direct or indirect object of a verb or as the object of a preposition to show that the action of a verb refers back to the subject: *You should not tire yourself. Give yourself enough time. Keep it for yourself.* **b.** Used to give emphasis: *You yourself admitted it.* **2.** Your normal or healthy condition: *You were not feeling yourself when you did it.*

your•selves (yo͝or **sĕlvz′** *or* yôr **sĕlvz′** *or* yər **sĕlvz′**) *pron.* **1.** Those ones that are the same as you. **a.** Used as the direct or indirect object of a verb or as the object of a preposition to show that the action of a verb refers back to the subject: *Help yourselves. Have yourselves a good time. You should all watch out for yourselves.* **b.** Used to give emphasis: *You'll have to take care of it yourselves.* **2.** Your normal or healthy condition: *Just relax and be yourselves.*

youth (yo͞oth) *n., pl.* **youths** (yo͞oths *or* yo͞o*th*z). **1.** The condition or quality of being young. **2.** An early period of development or existence, especially the time of life before one is an adult. **3.** A young person, especially a young male in late adolescence. **4.** *(used with a singular or plural verb).* Young people considered as a group: *the youth of our city.* [First written down about 725 in Old English and spelled *geoguth.*]

youth•ful (**yo͞oth′**fəl) *adj.* **1.** Characterized by youth; young: *the youthful hero.* **2.** Of, relating to, or characteristic of youth: *youthful impatience.* **3.** Marked by or having characteristics, such as vigor or enthusiasm, that are associated with youth. —**youth′ful•ly** *adv.* —**youth′ful•ness** *n.*

you've (yo͞ov). Contraction of *you have.*

yowl (youl) *intr.v.* **yowled, yowl•ing, yowls.** To make a long, loud, mournful cry; wail. —*n.* A long, loud, mournful cry.

yo-yo (**yō′**yō′) *n., pl.* **yo-yos.** A toy consisting of a flattened spool wound with string that is spun down from and reeled up to the hand by motions of the wrist.

yr. *abbr.* An abbreviation of: **1.** Year. **2.** Your.

yt•ter•bi•um (ĭ **tûr′**bē əm) *n.* *Symbol* **Yb** A soft, bright, silvery rare-earth element that occurs in two different forms and is used in making special alloys. Atomic number 70. See table at **element.** [First written down in 1879 in Modern English, after *Ytterby*, a town in Sweden.]

yt•tri•um (**ĭt′**rē əm) *n.* *Symbol* **Y** A silvery metallic element used to strengthen magnesium and aluminum alloys. Atomic number 39. See table at **element.**

yu•an (yo͞o **än′**) *n., pl.* **yuan** or **yu•ans.** The basic monetary unit of China.

Yu•ca•tán (yo͞o′kə **tăn′**). A peninsula mostly in southeast Mexico between the Caribbean Sea and the Gulf of Mexico. The region includes many Mayan and Toltec sites.

yuc•ca (**yŭk′**ə) *n.* Any of various plants of dry regions of southern and western North America, having stiff pointed leaves and a large cluster of whitish flowers. [First written down in 1664 in Modern English, from Taino *yuca*, cassava.]

Yu•go•sla•vi•a (yo͞o′gō **slä′**vē ə). A country of southeast Europe on the Balkan Peninsula made up of Serbia and Montenegro. It was formed in 1918 as a kingdom and became a Communist-led regime after World War II. Four of Yugoslavia's constituent republics declared independence in 1991. Capital, Belgrade. Population, 12,098,779.

Yu•kon River (**yo͞o′**kŏn′). A river flowing about 2,000 miles (3,218 kilometers) from southern Yukon Territory, Canada, through Alaska to the Bering Sea.

Yukon Territory. A territory of northwest Canada east of Alaska. It joined the Canadian confederacy in 1898. Whitehorse is the capital and the largest city. Population, 23,153. —See Note.

Yukon Time *n.* Alaska Standard Time.

Yule (yo͞ol) *n.* Christmas or the season or feast celebrating Christmas. [First written down before 899 in Old English and spelled *geōl.*]

❑ *These sound alike:* **Yule, you'll** (you will).

yule log *n.* A large log traditionally burned in a fireplace at Christmas.

Yule•tide (**yo͞ol′**tīd′) *n.* Christmastime.

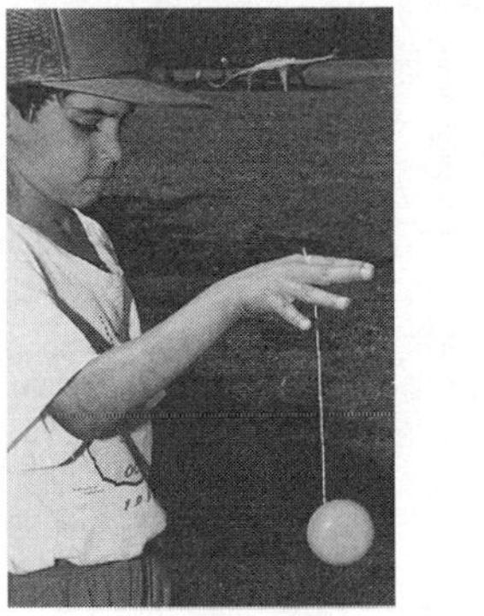

yo-yo

yucca

Yukon Territory

The name **Yukon Territory** comes from the **Yukon River**. The Native American word spelled *yooqana* is translated "big river."

ă	pat	oi	boy
ā	pay	ou	out
âr	care	o͝o	took
ä	father	o͞o	boot
ĕ	pet	ŭ	cut
ē	be	ûr	urge
ĭ	pit	th	thin
ī	pie	*th*	this
îr	pier	hw	whoop
ŏ	pot	zh	vision
ō	toe	ə	about
ô	paw	N	*French* bon

ă	pat	oi	boy
ā	pay	ou	out
âr	care	o͝o	took
ä	father	o͞o	boot
ĕ	pet	ŭ	cut
ē	be	ûr	urge
ĭ	pit	th	thin
ī	pie	*th*	this
îr	pier	hw	whoop
ŏ	pot	zh	vision
ō	toe	ə	about
ô	paw	N	*French* bon

Yu•ma (yo͞o′mə) *n., pl.* **Yuma** or **Yu•mas. 1.** A member of a Native American people living along the lower Colorado River. **2.** The Yuman language of this people.

Yu•man (yo͞o′mən) *n.* A family of Native American languages of the southwest United States and parts of Mexico. **—Yu′man** *adj.*

yum•my (yŭm′ē) *adj.* **yum•mi•er, yum•mi•est.** *Slang.* Delicious; appetizing to the taste or smell.

yup•pie (yup′ē) *n. Informal.* A young city or suburban resident with a well-paid job and expensive tastes.

YWCA *abbr.* An abbreviation of Young Women's Christian Association.

YWHA *abbr.* An abbreviation of Young Women's Hebrew Association.

Zz

z or **Z** (zē) *n., pl.* **z's** or **Z's. 1.** The 26th letter of the English alphabet. **2.** The 26th in a series or group.

Za•greb (zä′grĕb). The capital of Croatia, in the northern part of the republic north-northwest of Belgrade, Yugoslavia. Population, 768,700.

zaire (zī′îr *or* zä îr′) *n.* The basic monetary unit of Zaire.

Zaire (zī′îr *or* zä îr′). A country of central Africa astride the equator east of Congo. It gained its independence from Belgium in 1960. Capital, Kinshasa. Population, 29,671,407.

Zam•be•zi (zăm bē′zē). A river, about 1,700 miles (2,735 kilometers) long, of central and southern Africa rising in northwest Zambia and flowing south and west through Mozambique to an arm of the Indian Ocean.

Zam•bi•a (zăm′bē ə). A country of south-central Africa east of Angola. It gained its independence from Great Britain in 1964. Capital, Lusaka. Population, 5,661,801.

za•ny (zā′nē) *n., pl.* **za•nies. 1.** A buffoonish character in old comedies who attempts to mimic the clown. **2.** An outlandishly comical person. —*adj.* **za•ni•er, za•ni•est.** Ludicrously comical; clownish.

Zan•zi•bar (zăn′zə bär′). A region of Tanzania in eastern Africa, made up of **Zanzibar Island** and several adjacent islands off the northeast coast of Tanzania.

zap (zăp) *Slang. tr.v.* **zapped, zap•ping, zaps. 1.** To destroy or kill with a burst of gunfire, flame, or electric current: *The new gadget zapped bugs effectively.* **2.** To expose to radiation; irradiate: *zap leftovers in a microwave.* —*n.* Something that imparts excitement or great interest.

Za•po•tec (zä′pə tĕk′) *n., pl.* **Zapotec** or **Za•po•tecs. 1.** A member of a Native American people of southern Mexico. **2.** Any of a group of related Native American languages spoken in southern Mexico. —**Za′po•tec′** *adj.*

z-ax•is (zē′ăk′sĭs) *n., pl.* **z-ax•es** (zē′ăk′sēz). One of the three axes of a three-dimensional coordinate system.

zeal (zēl) *n.* Enthusiastic devotion to a cause, an ideal, or a goal. [First written down before 1382 in Middle English and spelled *zele*, from Greek *zēlos*.]

zeal•ot (zĕl′ət) *n.* A person who is zealous, especially excessively so.

zeal•ous (zĕl′əs) *adj.* Filled with or motivated by zeal; fervent: *zealous support of a cause.* —**zeal′ous•ly** *adv.* —**zeal′ous•ness** *n.*

ze•bra (zē′brə) *n.* Any of several African mammals related to the horse, having the entire body strongly marked with black and whitish stripes.

ze•bu (zē′bo͞o *or* zē′byo͞o) *n., pl.* **ze•bus.** A domesticated ox of Asia and Africa having a hump on the back and a large dewlap.

Zech•a•ri•ah (zĕk′ə rī′ə) *n.* **1.** A Hebrew prophet of the sixth century B.C. **2.** A book of the Bible in which Zechariah declares his visions and prophecies.

zed (zĕd) *n. Chiefly British.* The letter *z.*

Zen Buddhism (zĕn) *n.* A Chinese and Japanese form of Buddhism asserting that enlightenment can be reached through meditation and intuition rather than through faith and devotion. —**Zen Buddhist** *n.*

Zeng•er (zĕng′gər *or* zĕng′ər), **John Peter.** 1697–1746. German-born colonial journalist who was acquitted of libel charges in 1735, establishing a legal precedent for freedom of the press.

ze•nith (zē′nĭth) *n.* **1.** The point on the celestial sphere that is directly above the observer. **2.a.** The upper region of the sky. **b.** The highest point above the horizon to which a celestial body, as seen by an observer, rises. **3.** The highest point; peak; acme: *the zenith of success.* [First written down before 1387 in Middle English and spelled *cinit*, from Arabic *samt (ar-ra's)*, path (over the head).]

Zeph•a•ni•ah (zĕf′ə nī′ə) *n.* **1.** A Hebrew prophet of the seventh century B.C. **2.** A book of the Bible in which Zephaniah announces the coming day of judgment of all nations.

zeph•yr (zĕf′ər) *n.* **1.** The west wind. **2.** A gentle breeze.

zep•pe•lin (zĕp′ə lĭn) *n.* A rigid airship with a long cylindrical body, supported by cells containing a gas that is lighter than air. [First written down in 1900 in Modern English, after Count Ferdinand von *Zeppelin* (1838–1917), German inventor.]

ze•ro (zîr′ō *or* zē′rō) *n., pl.* **ze•ros** or **ze•roes. 1.** The numerical symbol 0; a cipher. **2.** A number that when added to another number leaves the original number unchanged; the identity element with respect to addition. **3.** The temperature indicated by the numeral 0 on a thermometer. **4.** *Informal.* Nothing; nil: *We have accomplished zero today.* —*tr.v.* **ze•roed, ze•ro•ing, ze•roes.** To adjust (an instrument or a device) to a setting of zero. —***idiom.*** **zero in. 1.** To aim or concentrate firepower on an exact target location. **2.** To concentrate one's attention; focus: *The boy zeroed in on the toy display in the window.* [First written down in 1604 in Modern English, from Arabic *ṣifr*, nothing, cipher.] —SEE NOTE.

zero gravity *n.* The condition of apparent weightlessness occurring when the centrifugal force on a body exactly counterbalances the gravitational attraction to it.

zero hour *n.* The scheduled time for the start of an operation or action, especially a combat operation.

zero population growth *n.* A condition in which the population remains the same because the number of births equals the number of deaths.

zest (zĕst) *n.* **1.** Flavor or interest: *We can use spices to give zest to simple foods.* **2.** The outermost rind of an orange or a lemon, used as a flavoring. **3.** Spirited enjoyment; relish; gusto: *He ate his oysters with zest.* [First written down in 1674 in Modern English and spelled *zest*, orange or lemon peel, from French.]

zest•ful (zĕst′fəl) *adj.* Full of or showing zest. —**zest′ful•ly** *adv.*

ze•ta (zā′tə) *n.* The sixth letter of the Greek alphabet, written Z, ζ, or in English, *Z, z.*

Zeus (zo͞os) *n.* In Greek mythology, the principal god, ruler of the heavens, and brother and husband of Hera. He is identified with the Roman Jupiter.

zebra
Grevy's zebra

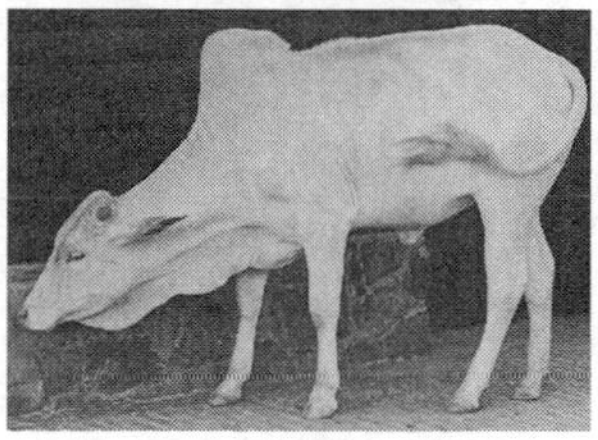

zebu

zero

Zero is not nothing! It is a number that stands for nothing. In many ways, zero is the most important of all numbers. When zero is added to or subtracted from a number, it leaves the number at its original value. Zero thus makes negative numbers possible. Zero is also essential to representing many numbers, such as 203 and 1,024. In these numbers zero serves as a placeholder in the system known as *positional notation.* Thus in 203, there are two hundreds, zero tens, and three ones. In other words, zero indicates that the value of the tens place is zero. In 1,024, zero indicates that the value of the hundreds place is zero. When you think about it, if we didn't have zero, we wouldn't have hundreds, thousands, or millions in our number system.

Zhou Enlai

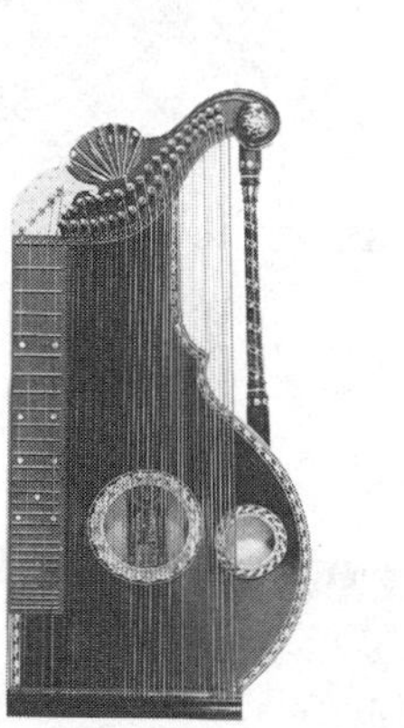
zither

Word Building: zoo–

The prefix **zoo–**, which is pronounced with two syllables, comes from the Greek word *zōion*, meaning "animal, living being." We know this prefix best in the one-syllable word **zoo**. **Zoo** is a popular shortening of the longer, more formal **zoological garden**, which was originally a park where wild animals were kept on display. **Zoological** is the adjective form of the noun **zoology**, which means "the study of animals." **Zoology** is thus part of **biology**, which means "the study of life."

zucchini

Zhou En•lai or **Chou En-lai** (jō′ ĕn lī′). 1898–1976. Chinese politician who was the first prime minister (1949–1976) and foreign minister (1949–1958) of China.

zig•gu•rat (zĭg′ə răt′) *n.* A temple tower of the ancient Assyrians and Babylonians, having the form of a terraced pyramid.

zig•zag (zĭg′zăg′) *n.* **1.** A line or course that proceeds by sharp turns in alternating directions. **2.** One of a series of such sharp turns. **3.** Something, such as a road or a design, shaped like or following the course of a zigzag. *—adj.* Moving in or having a zigzag: *a zigzag path.* *—adv.* In a zigzag manner or pattern: *The blindfolded child went zigzag across the room.* *—intr.v.* **zig•zagged, zig•zag•ging, zig•zags.** To move in or form a zigzag: *The trail zigzagged up the mountain.*

zil•lion (zĭl′yən) *n. Informal.* An extremely large, indefinite number.

Zim•bab•we (zĭm **bäb′**wē *or* zĭm **bäb′**wā). Formerly **Rho•de•sia** (rō **dē′**zhə). A country of southern Africa west of Mozambique. It gained its independence from Great Britain in 1980. Harare is the capital and the largest city. Population, 7,539,000.

zinc (zĭngk) *n. Symbol* **Zn** A shiny bluish-white metallic element widely used as a coating for iron, in alloys such as brass, as a roofing material, and in electric batteries. Atomic number 30. See table at **element.** [First written down in 1651 in Modern English and spelled *zinke*, from German *Zink*.]

zinc oxide *n.* A white or yellowish powdery compound of zinc and oxygen having the formula ZnO. It is used as a pigment and in various medicines and cosmetics for the skin.

zinc white *n.* Zinc oxide.

zing (zĭng) *n.* A high-pitched buzzing sound, such as that made by a taut vibrating string. *—intr.v.* **zinged, zing•ing, zings. 1.** To make a zing. **2.** To move swiftly with or as if with a zing.

zin•ni•a (zĭn′ē ə) *n.* Any of various garden plants native to tropical America and having showy, variously colored flowers. [First written down in 1767 in Modern English, after Johann Gottfried *Zinn* (1727–1759), German botanist.]

Zi•on (zī′ən) *n.* **1.** The historic land of Israel as a symbol of the Jewish people. **2.** The Jewish people; Israel. **3.** A place or community regarded as sacredly devoted to God.

Zi•on•ism (zī′ə nĭz′əm) *n.* A movement that arose in Europe in the late 19th century with the aim of reestablishing a Jewish state in Palestine. **—Zi′on•ist** *adj. & n.*

zip (zĭp) *n.* **1.** A brief, sharp, hissing sound. **2.** Energy; vim. **3.** *Informal.* Nothing; nil. *—v.* **zipped, zip•ping, zips.** *—intr.* **1.** To move with a sharp hissing sound: *The cars zipped by.* **2.** To move or act with a speed that suggests such a sound: *She zipped down the hill on her sled.* *—tr.* To fasten or unfasten with a zipper: *Zip up the dress.*

ZIP code (zĭp). A servicemark used for a system for speeding and simplifying the sorting and delivery of mail by assigning a series of numbers to each delivery area in the United States.

zip•per (zĭp′ər) *n.* A fastener consisting of two rows of interlocking teeth on adjacent edges of an opening that are closed or opened by a sliding tab.

zip•py (zĭp′ē) *adj.* **zip•pi•er, zip•pi•est.** Full of energy; lively.

zir•con (zûr′kŏn′) *n.* A mineral, essentially a silicate of zirconium, that can be heated, cut, and polished to form brilliant blue-white gems. [First written down in 1794 in Modern English and spelled *circon*, ultimately from Persian *āzargūn*, fire color.]

zir•co•ni•um (zûr **kō′**nē əm) *n. Symbol* **Zr** A shiny grayish-white metallic element used in alloys for wires and filaments, in making steel, and in nuclear reactors. Atomic number 40. See table at **element.**

zith•er (zĭth′ər *or* zĭth′ər) *n.* A musical instrument consisting of a flat box with about 30 to 40 strings stretched over it and played with the fingers or with a pick. [First written down in 1850 in Modern English, from German, from Greek *kithara*, cithara (ancient instrument resembling the lyre).]

zlo•ty (zlô′tē) *n., pl.* **zloty** or **zlo•tys.** The basic monetary unit of Poland.

Zn The symbol for the element **zinc.**

zo•di•ac (zō′dē ăk′) *n.* **1.** A band of the celestial sphere extending about eight degrees on both sides of the ecliptic that contains the paths of the sun, moon, and principal planets. **2.** In astrology, the twelve divisions, or signs of the zodiac, into which this band is divided, each having the name of a constellation.

zom•bie (zŏm′bē) *n., pl.* **zom•bies. 1.** According to voodoo belief, a corpse revived by a supernatural power or spell. **2.** A person who looks or behaves like a zombie, as in mechanical movements or aloof manner. [First written down in 1871 in American English, of West African origin.]

zon•al (zō′nəl) *adj.* Of or associated with a zone: *zonal divisions.*

zone (zōn) *n.* **1.** An area or region distinguished from a nearby one by a distinctive characteristic or reason: *a residential zone.* **2.a.** Any of the five regions of the earth that are loosely divided on the basis of climate and latitude, including the Torrid Zone, the North and South Temperate zones, and the North and South Frigid zones. **b.** A similar division of any other planet. **3.** A portion of a sphere cut off by two parallel planes that intersect the sphere. *—tr.v.* **zoned, zon•ing, zones.** To divide or mark off into zones. [First written down in 1393 in Middle English, from Greek *zōnē*, belt.]

zoo (zo͞o) *n., pl.* **zoos. 1.** A park or an institution where living animals are kept and exhibited. **2.** *Slang.* A place or situation marked by confusion or disorder. [First written down about 1847 in Modern English, from *zoological garden.*]

zoo– *pref.* A prefix that means animal or animals: *zoology.* —See Note.

zo•o•log•i•cal (zō′ə lŏj′ĭ kəl) also **zo•o•log•ic** (zō′ə lŏj′ĭk) *adj.* Of or relating to animals or zoology: *a zoological collection.* **—zo′o•log′i•cal•ly** *adv.*

zoological garden *n.* A zoo.

zo•ol•o•gist (zō ŏl′ə jĭst) *n.* A scientist who specializes in zoology.

zo•ol•o•gy (zō ŏl′ə jē) *n., pl.* **zo•ol•o•gies. 1.** The branch of biology that deals with animals. **2.** The animals of a particular area or period: *the zoology of South America.* **3.** The characteristics of a particular animal group or category: *the zoology of mammals.*

zoom (zo͞om) *v.* **zoomed, zoom•ing, zooms.** *—intr.* **1.** To make or move with a low-pitched buzzing or humming sound: *A hornet zoomed past my ear.* **2.** To climb suddenly and sharply. Used of an airplane. **3.** To move about rapidly; swoop. **4.a.** To move a camera lens rapidly toward or away from a photographic subject. **b.** To imitate a movement of this kind, as by means of a zoom lens. *—tr.* To cause to zoom. *—n.* The sound or act of zooming.

zoom lens *n.* A camera lens whose focal length can be changed to allow a rapid change in the size of an image while keeping the image in focus.

zo•o•phyte (zō′ə fīt′) *n.* Any of various animals, such as a sea anemone or sponge, that attach to surfaces and have the general appearance of plants.

Zo•ro•as•ter (zôr′ō ăs′tər). Sixth century B.C. Persian prophet who founded Zoroastrianism.

Zo•ro•as•tri•an (zôr′ō **ăs′**trē ən) *n.* A believer in Zoroastrianism. *—adj.* Of or relating to Zoroaster or Zoroastrianism.

Zo•ro•as•tri•an•ism (zôr′ō **ăs′**trē ə nĭz′əm) *n.* The religious system founded in Persia by Zoroaster, that views the universe as a place of conflict between the forces of good and evil.

zounds (zoundz) *interj.* An expression used to show anger, surprise, or indignation.

Zr The symbol for the element **zirconium.**

zuc•chi•ni (zo͞o **kē′**nē) *n., pl.* **zucchini** or **zuc•chi•nis.** A type of long narrow squash having a thin dark green rind.

Zu•lu (**zo͞o′**lo͞o) *n., pl.* **Zulu** or **Zu•lus. 1.** A member of a Bantu people of southeast Africa. **2.** The language of this people, closely related to Xhosa. **—Zu′lu** *adj.*

Zu•ni (**zo͞o′**nē) also **Zu•ñi** (**zo͞o′**nyē *or* **zo͞o′**nē) *n., pl.* **Zuni** or **Zu•nis** also **Zuñi** or **Zu•ñis. 1.** A member of a Native American people of western New Mexico. **2.** The language of this people.

Zu•rich (**zo͝or′**ĭk). The largest city in Switzerland, in the northeast part of the country at the northern tip of the **Lake of Zurich.** It was founded before Roman times. Population, 354,500.

zwie•back (**swī′**băk′ *or* **zwī′**băk′) *n.* A usually sweetened bread baked first as a loaf and then sliced and toasted.

zy•gote (**zī′**gōt′) *n.* The cell formed by the union of two gametes, especially a fertilized egg cell.

ă	pat	oi	**boy**
ā	**pay**	ou	**out**
âr	**care**	o͝o	**took**
ä	**fa**ther	o͞o	**boot**
ĕ	**pet**	ŭ	**cut**
ē	**be**	ûr	**ur**ge
ĭ	**pit**	th	**th**in
ī	**pie**	*th*	**th**is
îr	**pier**	hw	**wh**oop
ŏ	**pot**	zh	vi**s**ion
ō	**toe**	ə	**a**bout
ô	**paw**	N	*French* bon

Picture Credits

The editorial and production staff wishes to thank the many individuals, organizations, and agencies that have contributed to the art program of the Dictionary.

Credits on the following pages are arranged alphabetically by boldface entry word. In cases where two or more illustrations complement an entry, the sources are separated by slashes and follow the order of the illustrations.

The following abbreviations are used throughout: AA/Animals Animals; AP/WWP/AP-Wide World Photos; AR/Archive Photos; BA/Bettmann Archive, Inc.; CC/Chris Costello; CDB/Cecile Duray-Bito; CP/Culver Pictures, Inc.; EPJCo./E.P. Jones Company; HMCo./©Houghton Mifflin Company-Photograph by Evelyn Shafer; GEP/Gail Piazza; GHP/Grant Heilman Photography, Inc.; GP/Globe Photos, Inc.; HAR/H. Armstrong Roberts; HPSM/Historical Pictures-Stock Montage, Inc.; KAMD/*Knight's American Mechanical Dictionary*; LC/Laurel Cook; LOC/Library of Congress; LRE/Leonard Rue Enterprises; LW/Lightwave; MMA/Metropolitan Museum of Art; NASA/National Aeronautics and Space Administration; NGA/National Gallery of Art, Smithsonian Institution, Washington, D.C.; NMAI/National Museum of the American Indian, Smithsonian Institution; NYZS/NYZS-The Wildlife Conservation Society; PC/The Picture Cube; PE/PhotoEdit; PI/Positive Images; PR/Photo Researchers, Inc.; San Diego Zoo/Zoological Society of San Diego; SB/Stock, Boston; SLAM/The Saint Louis Art Museum; TG/Tech-Graphics (Susan Coons); TSI/Tony Stone Images; USDA/United States Department of Agriculture; WCFTR/Wisconsin Center for Film and Theater Research; ZP/Zephyr Pictures.

aardvark AP/WWP **abacus** BA **Aberdeen Angus** GHP **abscissa** TG **abstract** BA **abutment** CC **accolade** BA **accordion** SB - Jean-Claude Lejeune **acorn** PR - Alvin E. Staffan **Acropolis** BA **activist** BA **acupuncture** SB - Spencer Grant **Abigail Adams** LOC **John Adams** LOC **John Quincy Adams** LOC **Jane Addams** The Granger Collection, New York **addax** PR - Arthur W. Ambler **admiral** GHP **adobe** SB - Elizabeth Hamlin **adrenal gland** CDB **adz** CC **aerialist** HAR **aerobics** TSI - Jon Gray **Aesop** BA **A-frame** HAR **agave** CC **agitator** CC **aileron** LC **air bag** PE **aircraft carrier** AR - Earl Young **Airedale** HMCo. **air pump** PE - Cleo Photography **albatross** PR - Karl W. Kenyon **Louisa May Alcott** Chicago Historical Society, neg. no. ICHi-09394 **Alexander the Great** BA **alimentary canal** LC **Ethan Allen** BA **alley** PE - Dennis MacDonald **alligator** PR - Robert Wright **alluvial fan** Phototake - Edward S. Ross **aloe vera** CC **alpaca** PR - Andrew Rakoczy **altar** EPJCo. - Harold M. Lambert **amaranth** CC **ambulance** PI - Jerry Howard **amphitheater** BA **amphora** MMA, Rogers Fund, 1917 **Roald Amundsen** BA **anaconda** PR - Dade W. Thornton **anchor** LC **Marian Anderson** LOC **aneroid barometer** TG **angelfish** PR - Maurice E. Landre **Angora goat** GHP **anklet** PI - Jerry Howard **Anne** CP **anteater** PR - Jeanne White **anther** LC **Susan B. Anthony** National Portrait Gallery, Smithsonian Institution, Washington, D.C. **anticline** GEP **antimacassar** LW - S.E. Byrne **antler** GEP **anvil** CC **aphelion** CC **apogee** TG **appaloosa** *Appaloosa Journal* and Crown Center Farms, Columbia, Missouri **apricot** LC **apse** LC **aqueduct** HAR **arabesque** Boston Ballet - John Burke **arch[1]** PC - Stanley Rowin **archery** GP - Newton Nelson **arena** SB - Donald Dietz **Aristotle** The Granger Collection, New York **armadillo** CC **armor** MMA, Rogers Fund and Pratt Gift, 1933 (33.164a-x) **Neil Armstrong** AP/WWP **arrowhead** GHP **arroyo** PI - Karen Bussolini **art deco** SB - Joseph Schuyler **artesian well** GEP **Chester A. Arthur** LOC **artichoke** LC **art nouveau** SB - Peter Menzel **ascot** AR **asparagus** LC **aspen** CC **assembly line** PR - Tom McHugh **aster** CC **astigmatism** CDB **astronaut** NASA **atmosphere** TG **atomizer** Phototake **attaché case** EPJCo. **Crispus Attucks** AR **John James Audubon** PR **auk** PR - Gösta Håkansson Visby **auricle** LC **Jane Austen** The Granger Collection, New York **automated teller machine** ZP - Denise DeLuise **avocado** LC **awning** EPJCo. - Kevin Galvin **ax** CC **axle** KAMD **Ayrshire** GHP - John Colwell **Johann Sebastian Bach** LOC **backboard** PI - Jerry Howard **backpack** PE - David Young-Wolff **backstop** PI - Jerry Howard **bagpipe** AP/WWP **Ella Baker** AP/WWP **balalaika** MMA, Gift of Mr. Ustin Smolensky, 1948 (48.146) **bald eagle** AA - Irene Vandermolen **baldric** SB - Peter Southwick **James Baldwin** National Portrait Gallery, Smithsonian Institution, Washington, D.C.; © of 1955 negative, Estate of Carl Van Vechten; © of 1983 photogravure, Eakins Press Foundation **balloon** PC - Stanley Rowin **balsam fir** GEP **balustrade** Image Photos - Clemens Kalischer **bamboo** SB - Mike Mazzaschi **banjo** SB - Jean-Claude Lejeune **baobab** CC **barbel** PR - John Hendry **barbell** BA **P.T. Barnum** CP **baroque** PR **barrel organ** SB - Peter Menzel **Clara Barton** LOC **bass clef** TG **bass drum** PC - Sharon A. Bazarian **basset hound** HMCo. **bassoon** PE - Ulrike Welsch **battering ram** HPSM **battlement** TSI - Robert Frerck **bay window** PI - Jerry Howard **beagle** HMCo. **beaker** Image Photos - Clemens Kalischer **beanie** TSI - Bob Daemmrich **bearskin** PC - Cynthia W. Sterling **Simone de Beauvoir** PR - Gisele Freund **beaver[1]** LRE - Leonard Lee Rue III **Ludwig van Beethoven** LOC **beetle[1]** CC **belfry** BA **Alexander Graham Bell** HPSM **bellows** CC **bellyband** CP **David Ben Gurion** BA **beret** SB - Owen Franken **Mary McLeod Bethune** HPSM **biceps** LC **bicycle** LW - S.E. Byrne **bighorn** AA - Leonard Lee Rue III **big top** SB - Fredrik Bodin **bill[2]** BA **binocular** SB - Gale Zucker **biplane** GP - Ben Ross **birch** CC **bird** CDB **Otto von Bismarck** AP/WWP **bison** AA - C.W. Perkins **black bear** LRE - Leonard Lee Rue III **blackberry** LC **black-eyed Susan** LC **Elizabeth Blackwell** Brown Brothers **black widow** PR - Bucky Reeves **blast furnace** TG **blastoff** NASA **blazer** LW - S.E. Byrne **bleeding heart** LC **blimp** The Goodyear Tire & Rubber Company **block and tackle** GEP **bloodhound** HMCo. **bloomers** LOC **blowhole** PR - Omikron **bluebell** CC **blue whale** CC **bobsled** AP/WWP **Simón Bolívar** LOC **boll weevil** CDB **bongo drums** PC - Frank Siteman **bonsai** SB - Charles Kennard **boomerang** ZP - Denise DeLuise **Daniel Boone** National Portrait Gallery, Smithsonian Institution, Washington, D.C. **John Wilkes Booth** LOC **borzoi** HMCo. **boss[2]** CC **Boston terrier** HMCo. **boutonniere** PI - Jerry Howard **bow tie** SB - Owen Franken **box turtle** CC **William Bradford** CP **Johannes Brahms** BA **Braille** TG/EPJCo. **brain** LC **brant** PR - Niall Rankin **Brazil nut** CDB **breakwater** GHP - Runk & Schoenberger **breastplate** BA **brickwork** PC - Richard Wood **bridge[1]** SB - Jeff Albertson **broadax** CC **brocade** LW - Oscar Palmquist **Brontë** National Portrait Gallery, London **brontosaur** CC **Gwendolyn Brooks** BA **John Brown** BA **Elizabeth Barrett Browning** The Granger Collection, New York **Marcus Junius Brutus** The Granger Collection, New York **James Buchanan** LOC **Pearl Buck** PR - Jack Rosen **budgerigar** PR - Jeanne White **buffalo** GHP - Hal Harrison **bugle** AR **bulldog** HMCo. **bullhorn** EPJCo. - Harold M. Lambert **Bunsen burner** SB - Jeffrey Dunn **buoy** SB - Frank Siteman **burnoose** SB - Frank Siteman **Robert Burns** CP **Aaron Burr** Brown Brothers **burrow** LC **George Bush** The Bush Library, College Station, Texas **bustle[2]** BA **buttress** PI - Ivan Massar **buzzard** PR - Allan D. Cruickshank **Richard E. Byrd** BA **cactus** PR - Jen & Des Bartlett **caduceus** LC **Julius Caesar** CP **caftan** SB - Owen Franken **cairn** Comstock - Richard Harrington **calabash** CC **caldron** EPJCo. - Ewing Galloway **calliope** AP/WWP **camcorder** PI - Candace Cochrane **camel** SB - J. Berndt PR - George Holton **camera** TG **canal** PR - Don Morgan **candytuft** PI - Jerry Howard **canoe** SB - Fredrik Bodin **canopy** EPJCo. **cantilever bridge** TG **cape[1]** PI - Patricia J. Bruno **capuchin** PR - Robert C. Hermes **capybara** PR - John Marinus **carafe** PI - Jerry Howard **carburetor** TG **cardinal** PR - Karl H. Maslowski **caribou** LRE - Len Rue, Jr. **carousel** PR - Spencer Grant **carpus** LC **Kit Carson** Colorado Historical Society **Rachel Carson** AP/WWP **Jimmy Carter** Courtesy, Jimmy Carter Library **George Washington Carver** HPSM **cashew** LC **Mary Cassatt** National Portrait Gallery, Smithsonian Institution, Washington, D.C. **cassowary** PR - Len Rue, Jr. **castle** EPJCo. **catamaran** PR - Frederick Ayer III **catapult** BA **cathedral** EPJCo. **Willa Cather** Brown Brothers **Catherine the Great** CP **cathode-ray tube** TG **cat's cradle** PE - David Young-Wolff **Carrie Chapman Catt** Brown Brothers **C clef** TG **cecropia moth** CDB **celesta** CC **cell** LC **cello** Jeroboam, Inc. - Kent Reno **censer** BA **cerebellum** LC **Cervantes** CP **Paul Cézanne** Giraudon - Art Resource, New York **chain saw** SB - Peter Menzel

chaise longue PE - David Young-Wolff **chameleon** PR - George Porter **chandelier** SB - Peter Southwick **chaps** SB - Lionel J-M Delevingne **chariot** MMA, Rogers Fund, 1903 (03.23.1) **Charlemagne** CP **Charybdis** BA **Chaucer** CP **Cesar Chavez** SB - Jon Chase **cheetah** AA - Leonard Lee Rue III **chela** CC **chevron** PR - Bettye Lane **Chiang Kai-shek** BA **Chihuahua**[2] HMCo. **chimpanzee** AR **chipmunk** AA - Irene Vandermolen **Shirley Chisholm** BA **chock** PI - Martin Miller **Frédéric Chopin** AP/WWP **chow**[1] HMCo. **Agatha Christie** AP/WWP **chrysalis** CC **Winston S. Churchill** BA **churn** New York Public Library **circle** LC **circuit** GEP **circular saw** SB - Donald C. Dietz **civet** San Diego Zoo **clamp** CC **clarinet** Comstock - Russ Kinne **William Clark** Independence National Historical Park **clavichord** Worcester Art Museum, Museum Purchase, 1920.88 **Samuel Clemens** GP **Cleopatra** The Granger Collection, New York **Grover Cleveland** LOC **Bill Clinton** The White House - Bob McNeely **clipper** Peabody Museum of Salem, Massachusetts **cloister** Palmer/Brilliant, Boston, Massachusetts **clotheshorse** PE - Dennis MacDonald **cloverleaf** HPSM **coati** PR - Karl H. & Stephen Maslowski **cobweb** PR - Jeanne White **coccyx** LC **Cochise** Brown Brothers **cockatoo** BA **cockpit** PR - Jeannine Niepce/Rapho **cockscomb** EPJCo. - Harold M. Lambert **William F. Cody** National Portrait Gallery, Smithsonian Institution, Washington, D.C. **coffee** CC **cogwheel** CC **colander** ZP - Denise DeLuise **coliseum** SB - Elizabeth Hamlin **collie** Mrs. Kathy Peters - Gulie Krook **colossus** BA **Christopher Columbus** LOC **combination lock** EPJCo. - Ewing Galloway **combine** HPSM **comet** Lick Observatory Photograph **commencement** PC - Beringer-Dratch **compact disk** LW - Oscar Palmquist **compass** LW - Oscar Palmquist **complementary angles** LC **compote** EPJCo. - Harold M. Lambert **computer** EPJCo. **concave** LC **concertina** CC **conch** PC - Frank Siteman **condor** USDA **Conestoga wagon** Shelburne Museum, Shelburne, Vermont **Confucius** Brown Brothers **conger** CC **conic section** LC **conning tower** PR - Hubertus Kanus **conservatory** PR - Jim Kalett **console**[2] EPJCo. - Ewing Galloway **Constantine I** CP **contact lens** LW - Oscar Palmquist **continental shelf** GEP **control tower** EPJCo. - Ewing Galloway **convection** TG **convex** LC **conveyer** Olof Källström **Calvin Coolidge** LOC **Copernicus** CP **coral** GHP - Runk & Schoenberger **Charlotte Corday** CP **cordon** SB - Jim Anderson **core** LC **cornet** From the collections of Henry Ford Museum & Greenfield Village **cornucopia** PI - Jerry Howard **cosecant** TG **cosine** TG **cotangent** TG **cotter pin** CC **cottonwood** CC **countersink** CC **coupler** PI - Jerry Howard **courtyard** PI - Jerry Howard **covered wagon** Carriage Association of America, New Jersey **cowcatcher** HPSM **coxswain** SB - Arthur Grace **coyote** LRE - Leonard Lee Rue III **crab apple** CC **crampon** LC **crane** AA - Miriam Austerman/PR - Robert A. Isaacs **crazy quilt** PR - Roberta Hershenson **creel** AR **crescent** EPJCo. - Camerique **cresset** BA **crew**[1] PC - Rick Friedman **cricket**[2] AR **crochet** CC **Davy Crockett** LOC **crocodile** NYZS **crocus** CC **Oliver Cromwell** LOC **crossbow** HPSM **crowbar** Phototake **crow's-nest** BA **crust** LC **cuff link** PE - David Young-Wolff **culottes** PI - Jerry Howard **culvert** PR - John Hendry, Jr. **cuneiform** Comstock - Georg Gerster **Marie Curie** BA **currycomb** LW - Oscar Palmquist **cutaway** SB - Jeff Albertson **cuttlefish** CDB **cylinder** TG **cymbal** SB - Cary S. Wolinsky **cypress** CC **Cyrus the Great** CP **dachshund** HMCo. **daffodil** LC **dais** PE - David Young-Wolff **Dalmatian** HMCo. **damselfly** CC **Dante** The Granger Collection, New York **Darius I** Courtesy of The Oriental Institute of the University of Chicago **Charles Darwin** The Granger Collection, New York **date palm** CC **davit** EPJCo. - Ewing Galloway **Dorothy Day** BA **decagon** CC **decal** SB - Owen Franken **decoy** LW - Oscar Palmquist **deer** AA - Len Rue, Jr. **Charles de Gaulle** HPSM **dehumidify** TG **delft** Jewish Museum - Art Resource, New York **delicatessen** SB - David Powers **delphinium** CDB **delta** SB - Peter Vandermark **demolition** AP/WWP **dendrite** PR - G. Tomsich **dentin** LC **dentist** PE - Bill Aron **derby** SB - Jeff Albertson **derrick** GHP - Alan Pitcairn **dervish** Turkish Culture and Information Office **René Descartes** BA **Hernando de Soto** BA **destroyer** GP - Roy Pinney **detector** EPJCo. - Harold M. Lambert **Eamon De Valera** CP **dew** PC - David S. Strickler **diadem** The Granger Collection, New York **diagonal** LC **diamondback rattlesnake** GHP - Hal Harrison **diaphragm** LC **Charles Dickens** BA **Emily Dickinson** HPSM **diesel engine** TG **differential gear** CC **digestive system** LC **dimple** TSI - Cathlyn Melloan **dingo** PR - Des Bartlett **diploma** SB - Jean-Claude Lejeune **dirigible** CP **dirt bike** GP - Mark Stoddard **disc brake** TG **disc jockey** PR - Spencer Grant **discus** SB - Barbara Alper **dish** GHP - Runk & Schoenberger **dislocate** Martin M. Rotker/Martin M. Rotker **dispenser** LW - S.E. Byrne **Benjamin Disraeli** BA **distillation** LC **diver** EPJCo. **Dorothea Dix** The Granger Collection, New York **DNA** LC **Doberman pinscher** HMCo. **Charles Dodgson** HPSM **dodo** TG **dolphin** PR - Omikron **domino**[1] LW - Oscar Palmquist **donkey** PI - Jerry Howard **Doric** LC **dormer** EPJCo. **double bass** Jeroboam, Inc. - Emilio A. Mercado **double-decker** TSI - Michael Bertan **doublet** Yale Center for British Art, Paul Mellon Collection **Frederick Douglass** Sophia Smith Collection, Smith College **dovetail** TG **Arthur Conan Doyle** CP **dragonfly** CDB **Sir Francis Drake** LOC **drawbridge** EPJCo. - Harold M. Lambert **drill**[1] LW - Oscar Palmquist **dromedary** NYZS **drop leaf** From the collections of Henry Ford Museum and Greenfield Village **dry dock** BA **W.E.B. Du Bois** BA **dugout** EPJCo. - Ewing Galloway **dulcimer** LW - Barry Slaven **dune buggy** SB - Virginia L. Blaisdell **Albrecht Dürer** BA **Anton Dvořák** BA **Mary Dyer** Margaret Anne Miles **Amelia Earhart** AP/WWP **earphone** PR - David M. Grossman **easel** SB - Barbara Alper **Easter Island** Comstock - Richard Harrington **eaves** PI - Martin Miller **echelon** EPJCo. - Ewing Galloway **echidna** NYZS **eclipse** SB - Ira Kirschenbaum **edelweiss** LC **Thomas Edison** Snark - Art Resource, New York **Edward VIII** GP - Camera Press **eggplant** CC **egret** GHP - Leonard Lee Rue III **Albert Einstein** HPSM **Dwight D. Eisenhower** Dwight D. Eisenhower Library - U.S. Navy **eland** San Diego Zoo **elbow** GEP **electrocardiograph** SB - Paul Fortin **elephant** AA - Leonard Lee Rue III AA - Irene Vandermolen **George Eliot** Sophia Smith Collection, Smith College **T.S. Eliot** GP - Tony Armstrong Jones **Elizabeth II** GP - H.R.H. Prince Andrew/Camera Press **ellipse** TG **emblem** AP/WWP **embroidery** PI - Patricia J. Bruno **Ralph Waldo Emerson** The Granger Collection, New York **emery** PI - Candace Cochrane **emu** PR - Jeanne White **enamel** LC **endive** CC **endocrine gland** LC **English horn** © Walter Silver - Courtesy of New England Conservatory of Music **engraving** LW - Oscar Palmquist **entablature** CC **eohippus** LC **epaulet** CP **epigraph** PC - Betsy Fuchs **equator** LC **equestrian** SB - Ellis Herwig **Erasmus** LOC **Leif Ericson** AR **ermine** LRE - Irene Vandermolen **eruption** EPJCo. **escalator** TG **escapement** CC **espadrille** PI - Jerry Howard **esplanade** PC - Jeffrey Dunn **eucalyptus** LC **euphonium** PI - Jerry Howard **Mount Everest** TSI - Arnold Crane **ewer** PI - Candace Cochrane **excavation** Comstock - Georg Gerster **Exodus** HPSM **exosphere** TG **expressionism** NGA, Rosenwald Collection **exterior angle** TG **extinguisher** LW - Oscar Palmquist **eye** LC **eyelet** SB - T.A. Rothschild **eyestalk** PR - Jen & Des Bartlett **factory** PE - Ford Motor Co. **fair**[2] GHP - Robert Barclay **falcon** LRE - Mark Wilson **fallow deer** PR - Leonard Lee Rue III **fan**[1] PE - Tony Freeman/TSI - Lawrence Hedges **fang** PR - Leonard Lee Rue III **farm** PC - Dede Hatch **farthingale** MMA, Irene Lewisohn Bequest, 1962 **faucet** GEP **William Faulkner** AP/WWP **fawn**[2] PR - Karl H. Maslowski **fax** LW - Oscar Palmquist **feather** CDB **fedora** SB - Rick Smolan **feeler** PC - David S. Strickler **femur** LC **Ferdinand V** Brown Brothers **Enrico Fermi** Brown Brothers **ferret** AP/WWP **Ferris wheel** Chicago Historical Society, neg. no. ICHi-02442 **festoon** LC **fez** PR - Carl Frank **fibula** LC **field hockey** LW - Ben De Marco **field mouse** CC **fife** SB - Peter Southwick **figurehead** SB - Jeff Albertson **file**[2] LC **Millard Fillmore** LOC **fin** PR - Jen & Des Bartlett **finch** PR - Karl H. Maslowski **finger painting** PR - Myron Papiz **fir** CC **fireboat** EPJCo. - Harold M. Lambert **fire escape** LW - Oscar Palmquist **fish** CDB **fisher** LRE - Leonard Lee Rue III **Ella Fitzgerald** BA **flag**[1] AP/WWP **flagellum** CDB **flamingo** PC - Jaye R. Phillips **flange** CC **flatcar** PE - Tony Freeman **Sir Alexander Fleming** The Granger Collection, New York **fleur-de-lis** CC **flintlock** MMA, Gift of Wilfred Wood, 1956 (42.22) **floppy disk** PI - Jerry Howard **fluke**[2] CDB **flute** SB - Joseph Schuyler **flying buttress** PR - Omikron **flying fish** CC **flying squirrel** LRE - Leonard Lee Rue III **Elizabeth Gurley Flynn** Brown Brothers **folk dance** PR - Renee Lynn **font**[1] Comstock - Russ Kinne **footbridge** Comstock - Michael S. Thompson **forceps** LC **Gerald Ford** LOC **forehand** Frank Siteman **forget-me-not** LC **forked** TSI - Leonard Lee Rue III **forklift** EPJCo. **fortune cookie** PI - Jerry Howard **fossil** GHP - Runk & Schoenberger **Stephen Foster** National Portrait Gallery, Smithsonian Institution, Washington, D.C. - Art Resource, New York **fountain pen** CC **fox** EPJCo. - Ewing Galloway **foxhound** HMCo. **Anne Frank** CP **Benjamin Franklin** National Portrait Gallery, Smithsonian Institution, Washington, D.C., Gift of the Morris and Gwendolyn Cafritz Foundation **Frederick the Great** Brown Brothers **John C. Frémont** CP **French curve** GEP **French horn** PR - John Bova **fret**[2] LW - Oscar Palmquist **Sigmund Freud** HPSM **frigate bird** PR - Jen & Des Bartlett **frog** BA **frond** LW - Oscar Palmquist **Robert Frost** AP/WWP **frustum** LC **Margaret Fuller** Brown Brothers **Robert Fulton** CP **fuse**[2] LC **futon** LW - Oscar Palmquist **gable roof** BA **Yuri Gagarin** LOC **galaxy** Lick Observatory Photograph **Galileo** LOC **galleon** CP **Vasco da Gama** The Granger Collection, New York **Indira Gandhi** BA **Mahatma Gandhi** AP/WWP **gangplank** SB - Dean Abramson **Isabella Stewart Gardner** The Granger Collection, New York **James A. Garfield** LOC **gargoyle** SB - Barbara Alper **Giuseppe Garibaldi** New York Public Library **William Lloyd Garrison** HPSM **gas mask** SB - Lionel J-M Delevingne **gauntlet**[1] BA **gavel** EPJCo. **gazelle** PR - Leonard Lee Rue III **Genghis Khan** The Granger Collection, New York **geodesic dome** Jeroboam, Inc. - Ilka Hartman **Saint George** Yale University Art Gallery, Purchase by the University, from James Jackson Jarves **George III** The Granger Collection, New York

German shepherd HMCo. **Geronimo** National Portrait Gallery, Smithsonian Institution, Washington, D.C. **geyser** Russell A. Thompson **gibbon** PR - Arthur W. Ambler **Gila monster** AA - Miriam Austerman **gill**[1] CDB **Charlotte Perkins Gilman** Brown Brothers **gimlet** LC **giraffe** AA - Leonard Lee Rue III **gladiolus** CC **glass blowing** EPJCo. **John Glenn** NASA **glider** SB - Peter Southwick **glockenspiel** PC - Carol Palmer **gnu** LRE - Leonard Lee Rue III **goatee** SB - Cary S. Wolinsky **goblet** Jewish Museum - Art Resource, New York **Goethe** The Granger Collection, New York **goggles** SB - Jonathan Rawle **goldenrod** CC **Emma Goldman** HPSM **golf** ZP - Michael Yada **Maud Gonne** The Granger Collection, New York **Mikhail Gorbachev** BA **gorilla** PR - Jeanne White **gourd** CC **Martha Graham** HPSM **Grand Canyon** EPJCo. **grandfather clock** Brown Brothers **grand piano** PE - Michael Newman **Ulysses S. Grant** LOC **grape** LC **grapeshot** PE - Robert Brenner **grappling iron** PC - Jeffrey Dunn **grasshopper** LC **Great Wall of China** AP/WWP **greyhound** BA **Edvard Grieg** Brown Brothers **groin** CDB **grommet** PI - Jerry Howard **grouse**[1] PR - Nell Bolen **guanaco** PR - Arthur W. Ambler **guava** CC **Guernsey** GHP **guide dog** PC - Spencer Grant **guinea pig** GHP - Grant Heilman **guitar** PE - Merritt A. Vincent **Johann Gutenberg** LOC **gyroscope** GHP - Runk & Schoenberger **Haile Selassie** AR **halberd** MMA, Gift of Mary Alice Dyckman Dean, in memory of Alexander McMillan Welch, 1949 (49.120.12) **half-mast** AP/WWP **Halley's comet** AP/WWP **Alexander Hamilton** AP/WWP **George Frederick Handel** LOC **handstand** PC - Jaye R. Phillips **hang glider** AP/WWP **Lorraine Hansberry** AP/WWP **hardhat** PC - Robert Finken **Warren G. Harding** LOC **Thomas Hardy** HPSM **harmonica** PI - Jerry Howard **harp** PE - Tony Freeman **harpsichord** LW - Oscar Palmquist **Benjamin Harrison**[2] LOC **William Henry Harrison** LOC **hatchback** EPJCo. - Camerique **Hatshepsut** AP/WWP **hauberk** HPSM **hawk**[1] LRE - Mark Wilson **Nathaniel Hawthorne** LOC **Rutherford B. Hayes** LOC **hazel** CC **headdress** SB - Ira Kirschenbaum/SB - John Running **headphone** PR - Barbara Rios **headstand** PI - Jerry Howard **heart** LC **heat exchanger** CC **hedgehog** PR - Eric Hosking **helicon** SB - Michael Dwyer **helicopter** SB - Peter Vandermark **helix** TG **hellebore** CC **helmet** PC - Paul Nurnberg **Ernest Hemingway** GP - Hy Simon **Henry VIII** LOC **Katharine Hepburn** CP **Hereford** GHP - Grant Heilman **hermit crab** CC **heron** PR - Allan D. Cruickshank **hexagon** CC **hibiscus** CC **hieroglyphics** CP **high jump** SB - Barbara Alper **hinge** GEP **hippopotamus** LRE - Leonard Lee Rue III **Hirohito** BA **Adolf Hitler** HPSM **hive** PR - Stephen Dalton **hobbyhorse** LW - Barry Slaven **hockey** PC - K.L. Kliskey **Dorothy Hodgkin** PR - Mary Evans Picture Library **hoe** LC **Billie Holiday** CP **hollyhock** PE - David Young-Wolff **holly** LC **Oliver Wendell Holmes** Sophia Smith Collection, Smith College **holster** PC - Sarah Putnam **Homer** The Granger Collection, New York **honeycomb** AA - Stephen Dalton **hoop skirt** CP **Herbert Hoover** LOC **horned toad** PR - Verna R. Johnston **hot plate** LW - Aldo Mastrocola **hourglass** PI - Patricia J. Bruno **houseboat** LW - Charlene Blankenship **house sparrow** PR - Peter & Stephen Maslowski **Sam Houston** International Museum of Photography at the George Eastman House **Julia Ward Howe** CP **Henry Hudson** AP/WWP **Victor Hugo** CP **humerus** CC **hummingbird** AA - Len Rue, Jr. **hurdle** AP/WWP **hurdy-gurdy** Courtesy, Museum of Fine Arts, Boston, Mary Smith Fund **Zora Neale Hurston** The Granger Collection, New York **hutch** LW - Ben De Marco **Anne Hutchinson** Brown Brothers **hydrofoil** AP/WWP **hyena** PR - Mark Boulton **hypotenuse** LC **ibis** AA - C.C. Lockwood **Henrik Ibsen** HPSM **iceberg** AR **icebreaker** EPJCo. - Ewing Galloway **ice-skate** SB - Michael Dwyer **identical** PI - Catharine Reeve **ideogram** CC **igloo** EPJCo. - Ewing Galloway **iguana** AA - Len Rue, Jr. **ileum** CC **impala** AA - Len Rue, Jr. **impressionism** EPJCo. **imprint** GHP - Grant Heilman **inauguration** The White House **incandescent lamp** LC **incise** PC - Frank Siteman **inclined plane** PR - Barbara Rios **Indian club** LW - Oscar Palmquist **Indian paintbrush** CC **inflatable** PR - Herman Emmet **inflorescence** GEP **ingot** AP/WWP **inhalator** LW - Oscar Palmquist **initial** BA **inlay** ZP - Denise DeLuise **inlet** SB - Peter Vandermark **inscription** PI - Jerry Howard **insect** LC **insignia** SB - Peter Southwick **instrument** LC **insulation** PC - Steven Baratz **intercom** PE - Tony Freeman **interior angle** CC **internal-combustion engine** LC **intestine** LC **Ionic** LC **iris** LC **Irish terrier** HMCo. **iron** LW - Aldo Mastrocola **ironwork** SB - Mike Mazzaschi **Washington Irving** National Portrait Gallery, Smithsonian Institution, Washington, D.C. **Isabella I** CP **ivy** PI - Jerry Howard **jackal** AA - Leonard Lee Rue III **Andrew Jackson** The Granger Collection, New York **jaguar** San Diego Zoo **jai alai** BA **jasmine** CC **javelin** SB - Jean-Claude Lejeune **Thomas Jefferson** LOC **jerboa** PR - Arthur W. Ambler **jew's-harp** LW - Barry Slaven **jinriksha** Hong Kong Tourist Association **Joan of Arc** Giraudon - Art Resource, New York **jodhpurs** Palmer/Brilliant, Boston, Massachusetts **Andrew Johnson** National Portrait Gallery, Smithsonian Institution, Washington, D.C. **Lady Bird Johnson** GP **Lyndon B. Johnson** BA **Mother Jones** GP **jonquil** LC **Chief Joseph** National Anthropological Archives at the National Museum of Natural History, Smithsonian Institution, Washington, D.C. **Juan Carlos** GP - Richard Open **judo** HPSM **Juliana** AR **juniper** CC **junk**[2] HPSM **Kamehameha I** National Portrait Gallery, Smithsonian Institution, Washington, D.C., Gift of the Bernice Pauahi Bishop Museum **karate** SB - James R. Holland **kayak** SB - Peter Menzel **John Keats** Brown Brothers **Helen Keller** The Schlesinger Library, Radcliffe College **John F. Kennedy** GP **Jomo Kenyatta** AR **kettledrum** Comstock - Russ Kinne **keyboard** PI - Jerry Howard **kickstand** PI - Candace Cochrane **killer whale** EPJCo. - Camerique **kilt** LW - Oscar Palmquist **kimono** PR - Hubertus Kanus **Martin Luther King, Jr.** BA **kingfisher** PR - Ed Cesar **kinkajou** PR - Jen & Des Bartlett **kiwi** PR - R. Van Nostrand **kneepad** PI - Candace Cochrane **knot**[1] TG **koala** HAR **Komodo dragon** ZP - Denise DeLuise **kookaburra** AA - Ann Sanfedele **koto** PE - Gary A. Conner **Kublai Khan** LOC **kumquat** LC **labyrinth** Brown Brothers **lacewing** CC **lacrosse** SB - Bruce M. Wellman **ladder** SB - Daniel S. Brody **ladle** LW - Aldo Mastrocola **ladybug** CDB **lamb** PR - Arthur W. Ambler **landau** Shelburne Museum, Shelburne, Vermont **Dorothea Lange** The Granger Collection, New York **lantern** LW - Ben De Marco **lapel** LW - Aldo Mastrocola **laptop** PI - Jerry Howard **large intestine** LC **larva** GHP - Grant Heilman **La Salle** LOC **laser** LC **lateen** CC **lattice** Image Photos - Clemens Kalischer **launch pad** NASA **laurel** PC - Michael F. Kullen **Antoine Lavoisier** MMA, Purchase, Mr. and Mrs. Charles Wrightsman Gift, 1977 (1977.10) **lawn mower** LW - Oscar Palmquist **leaf** LC **Louis and Mary Leakey** PR - Des Bartlett **lectern** PE - James L. Shaffer **Robert E. Lee** LOC **legging** PR - M. Fennelli **lei** TSI - David Olsen **lemming** CC **lemur** AA - George Roos **Vladimir Lenin** AP/WWP **Leonardo da Vinci** BA **leopard** PR - Leonard Lee Rue III **leotard** PC - Jaye R. Phillips **levee** LOC **Meriwether Lewis** Independence National Historical Park **library** EPJCo. - Harold M. Lambert **lichen** PR - Jack Dermid **life jacket** SB - George Bellerose **life raft** AR **lighthouse** GHP - Hal H. Harrison **lightning** AA - Michael Fredericks, Jr. **lightning rod** Brown Brothers **Liliuokalani** The Granger Collection, New York **lily of the valley** GHP - Barry L. Runk **Abraham Lincoln** LOC **Charles Lindbergh and Anne Morrow Lindbergh** Brown Brothers **Carolus Linnaeus** Brown Brothers **lion** AA - Len Rue, Jr. **Franz Liszt** HPSM **litchi** LC **litter** EPJCo. **David Livingstone** The Granger Collection, New York **llama** HPSM **loblolly pine** CC **locomotive** PC - William A. Todd, Jr. **loganberry** LC **Henry Wadsworth Longfellow** National Portrait Gallery, Smithsonian Institution, Washington, D.C. **longhorn** PR - Clint Grant **long jump** Jeroboam, Inc. - Cheryl A. Traendly **loom**[2] Comstock - Stuart Cohen **loon**[1] LRE - Leonard Lee Rue III **lop-eared** PR - Mary Eleanor Browning **lotus** PI - Jerry Howard **Louis XIV** Giraudon - Art Resource, New York **Amy Lowell** Brown Brothers **Clare Booth Luce** AP/WWP **lungfish** CC **lute** Courtesy, Museum of Fine Arts, Boston, Leslie Lindsey Mason Fund **Martin Luther** Alinari - Art Resource, New York **Rosa Luxemburg** PR - © Archiv **lynx** AA - Leonard Lee Rue III **lyre** CC **lyrebird** PR - John R. Brownlie **macaw** GHP - Larry Lefever **macramé** PC - Frank Siteman **Dolley Madison** LOC **James Madison** LOC **magnetic field** GHP - Runk & Schoenberger **magnolia** CC **maidenhair fern** CDB **maintop** SB - Frances M. Cox **major scale** TG **malamute** HMCo. **Malcolm X** BA **mallet** LC **mammoth** TG **Nelson Mandela** GP - Jan Kopec **mandolin** LW - Oscar Palmquist **mandrill** PR - R. Van Nostrand **mane** EPJCo. **manhole** SB - Rudolph Robinson **mansard** LW - S.E. Byrne **manta** CC **mantis** CDB **mantle** LC **manual alphabet** TG **Mao Zedong** AP/WWP **marabou** PR - Des Bartlett **Maria Theresa** Brown Brothers **Marie Antoinette** Brown Brothers **marina** SB - Peter Menzel **marlin**[1] CC **marmot** Comstock - Phyllis Greenberg **marquee** PI - Martin Miller **Karl Marx** The Granger Collection, New York **mask** PR - Joseph Nettis/PI - Patricia J. Bruno **Mason jar** GHP - John Colwell **Massasoit** Brown Brothers **mastiff** HMCo. **Matterhorn** Swiss National Tourist Office **mattock** LC **mausoleum** SB - Ira Kirschenbaum **Barbara McClintock** AP/WWP **William McKinley** CP **Margaret Mead** AP/WWP **measure** TG **measuring worm** PR - Gordon S. Smith **medal** SB - James R. Holland **megaphone** SB - Arthur Grace **meiosis** CDB **Golda Meir** GP **melon** LC **Herman Melville** BA **memorial** PC - Dennis MacDonald **menorah** Peter Vandermark **meridian** TG **merino** GHP - John Colwell **mess kit** PI - Patricia J. Bruno **metacarpus** LC **metatarsus** LC **metronome** LW - S.E. Byrne **mezuzah** PR - Roberta Hershenson **mezzanine** TSI - Paul Merideth **Michelangelo** BA **microphone** PC - Beringer-Dratch **microscope** AA - George F. Godfrey **microwave oven** GHP - Barry L. Runk **milk snake** PR - Jack Dermid **milkweed** PI - Martin Miller **Edna Saint Vincent Millay** AP/WWP **millipede** PR - Robert C. Hermes **mill wheel** EPJCo. **mine**[1] EPJCo. **mink** LRE - Leonard Lee Rue III **minor scale** TG **minuteman** SB - Lionel J-M Delevingne **mirror** SB - Elizabeth Crews **mission** Russell A. Thompson **mistletoe** LC **Gabriela Mistral** AP/WWP **mitosis** CDB **François Mitterrand** AP/WWP **moat** TSI - Lois Moulton **mobile** The Solomon

R. Guggenheim Foundation, New York, Collection Mary Reynolds, Gift of her brother (FN54.1388) **moccasin** NMAI **molar**[2] LC **mold**[1] PE - Tony Freeman **molt** PR - Leonard Lee Rue III **monarch butterfly** AA - Stan Schroeder **Claude Monet** The Granger Collection, New York **mongoose** PR - Jen & Des Bartlett **monkey wrench** CC **monocle** Ewing Galloway **James Monroe** LOC **Maria Montessori** CP **Montezuma II** LOC **moon** Lick Observatory Photograph/Lick Observatory Photograph/Lick Observatory Photograph **moose** PR - Leonard Lee Rue III **J.P. Morgan** The Granger Collection, New York **morning glory** CC **Morse code** TG **mortarboard** PC - Kindra Clineff **mosaic** PR - Fabio Ponzio/Agenzia Contrasto **motorboat** EPJCo. **Lucretia Mott** The Granger Collection, New York **mountain goat** PR - Harry Engels **mountain laurel** LC **mouth** LC **Wolfgang Amadeus Mozart** GP **muff**[2] CP **muffler** LC **mulberry** CC **mule**[1] PR - Joe Munroe **mummer** SB - Addison Geary **mummy**[1] The Granger Collection, New York **mural** BA **museum** SB - Martha Bates **mushroom** CC **musk ox** AA - Leonard Lee Rue III **Benito Mussolini** BA **mustang** PR - H. Ryden **mute** Peter Vandermark **Mutsuhito** Brown Brothers **myopia** CDB **nail** CC **Napoleon I** NGA - Samuel H. Kress Collection **narcissus** GHP - Barry L. Runk **narwhal** PR - Richard Ellis **nasturtium** LC **Carry Nation** Brown Brothers **nautilus** GHP - Runk & Schoenberger **Martina Navratilova** AP/WWP **nebula** Lick Observatory Photograph **neckerchief** Jeroboam, Inc. - Laimute Druskis **necktie** PC - Kory Addis **needle** LC **Nefertiti** Art Resource, New York **Jawaharlal Nehru** CP **nest** PR - Hal H. Harrison/ Museum of Art, Rhode Island School of Design, Gift of Mrs. Harold Brown **nettle** CC **neuron** LC **Isaac Newton** HPSM **nighthawk** PR - Joe Van Wormer **Florence Nightingale** Brown Brothers **Nike** MMA, Rogers Fund, 1907 **nimbostratus** SB - Fredrik D. Bodin **Richard M. Nixon** GP - Larry Stevens **noisemaker** PE - David Young-Wolff **nose** LC **note** CC **nozzle** SB - Bob Daemmrich **nuclear reactor** CC **nucleus** LC **nut** LC **nuthatch** AA - Leonard Lee Rue III **nutmeg** LC **Annie Oakley** Brown Brothers **oarlock** PE - Tony Freeman **obi** PE - Gary Conner **oboe** Comstock - Russ Kinne **observatory** GHP - Runk & Schoenberger **obtuse angle** LC **ocarina** PI - Martin Miller **ocelot** NYZS **Sandra Day O'Connor** Supreme Court Historical Society **octahedron** TG **octopus** GHP - Runk & Schoenberger **Odysseus** CP **Oedipus** Alinari - Art Resource, New York **okapi** PR - Frank Stevens **Georgia O'Keeffe** AP/ WWP **okra** LC **olive** LC **Eugene O'Neill** AP/ WWP **onion** LC **open-hearth** TG **openwork** SB - William Finch **opera**[1] EPJCo. - Camerique **opera glasses** PC - Robert W. Ginn **opossum** GHP - Runk & Schoenberger **optic nerve** LC **orange** CC **orangutan** AA - Miriam Austerman **orchard** SB - George Bellerose **orchestra** Courtesy of Boston Symphony Orchestra - Christian Steiner **organ** PC - Michael Serino **oriel** SB - Ellis Herwig **origami** PE - Felicia Martinez **oriole** PR - G. Ronald Austing **George Orwell** AP/WWP **oryx** LRE - Leonard Lee Rue IV **osprey** PR - Jen & Des Bartlett **ostrich** AA - Stewart D. Halperin **otter** San Diego Zoo **outboard motor** AR **outrigger** PR - George Holton **ovenbird** PR - Allan D. Cruickshank **overalls** SB - Jeffry W. Myers **overhang** PE - David Young-Wolff **overpass** PE - Tony Freeman **Jesse Owens** BA **owl** PR - Karl H. Maslowski **ox** PR - Tom McHugh **pacemaker** Phototake - Yoav Levy **paddle**[1] LC **paddlefish** CC **pagoda** SCALA - Art Resource, New York **paisley** Allen Moore **palace** EPJCo. - Ewing Galloway **palette** PR - David M. Grossman **palm**[2] CC **panda** GP - Popperfoto **pangolin** AR **Emmeline Pankhurst** The Granger Collection, New York **pannier** PI - Jerry Howard **panpipe** GEP **panther** PR - S. Nagendra **papaya** CC **parabola** LC **parachute** GHP **parallel bars** EPJCo. - Camerique **Rosa Parks** AP/WWP **parquetry** Comstock - Russ Kinne **parrot** EPJCo. - Harold M. Lambert **Parthenon** Marburg - Art Resource, New York **partridge** PR - Arthur W. Ambler **passionflower** LC **Louis Pasteur** HPSM **patchwork** SB - Peter Southwick **patella** LC **Alice Paul** HPSM **pavilion** PI - Jerry Howard **Ivan Pavlov** CP **pawl** LC **peacock** PR - Pierre Berger **pear** LC **pearl** EPJCo. - Harold M. Lambert **peccary** PR - Leonard Lee Rue III **pediment** SB - Owen Franken **Pegasus** National Museum of American History, Smithsonian Institution, Washington, D.C., National Numismatics Collection **Pekingese** HMCo. **pelican** PC - Cynthia W. Sterling **pendant** ZP - Denise DeLuise **pendulum** GEP **penguin** PR - George Holton **William Penn** Historical Society of Pennsylvania **pennant** EPJCo. - Ewing Galloway **pentagon** LC/AP/WWP **pepper** LC **peregrine falcon** PR - G. Ronald Austing **Pericles** Alinari - Art Resource, New York **perihelion** CC **Frances Perkins** HPSM **Persian cat** PR - Ylla **persimmon** LC **peruke** Worcester Art Museum, Worcester, Massachusetts **pestle** BA **Peter the Great** The Granger Collection, New York **petri dish** PC - Tom McHugh **phalanx** LC **Pharaoh** The Granger Collection, New York **pheasant** AA - Robert Maier **King Philip** HPSM **philodendron** CC **phoenix** The Granger Collection, New York **phonograph** EPJCo. - Camerique **photoelectric cell** TG **piano**[1] Steinway & Sons **piazza** PR - Roberto Koch **Pablo Picasso** BA **piccolo** PE - David Young-Wolff **pickax** GEP **picot** ZP - Denise DeLuise **Franklin Pierce** LOC **pika** PR - L & D Klein **pillar** PI - Jerry Howard **pillory** EPJCo. **piñata** PC - Ellis Herwig **pince-nez** BA **pineapple** LC **pinwheel** LW - Barry Slaven **pipeline** GHP **piranha** PR - John H. Gerard **pistil** LC **pitcher plant** CC **pith helmet** PI - Martin Miller **Francisco Pizarro** The Granger Collection, New York **placard** PE - James L. Shaffer **plaque** PE - Tony Freeman **Sylvia Plath** Sophia Smith Collection, Smith College **Plato** BA **platypus** PR - Jen & Des Bartlett **player piano** Marilyn Root **pliers** CC **plinth** PC - Jeffrey Dunn **plow** GHP - Grant Heilman **plum** LC **Pocahontas** Brown Brothers **Edgar Allan Poe** CP **poinsettia** CC **pointer** HMCo. **polar bear** LRE - Leonard Lee Rue III **polecat** LRE - Leonard Lee Rue III **pole vault** SB - George Bellerose **James K. Polk** LOC **polo** SB - Pamela Schuyler **Pomeranian** AA - Paula Wright **pompon** PE - David Young-Wolff **Ponce de León** Brown Brothers **poncho** PR - George Holton **poppy** CC **porcupine** PR - Mark N. Boulton **porpoise** CC **portcullis** CC **Portuguese man-of-war** GHP - Runk & Schoenberger **postage stamp** LW - Oscar Palmquist **potato** LC **potbelly stove** EPJCo. **Beatrix Potter** AP/WWP **potter's wheel** PR - Fritz Henle **powder horn** MMA, Gift of Mrs. J.H. Grenvelle, 1940 (40.105) **prairie dog** AA - Harry Engels **prairie schooner** PR - Omikron **precipice** SB - Roy Bishop **pre-Columbian** MMA, The Michael C. Rockefeller Memorial Collection, Bequest of Nelson A. Rockefeller, 1979 (1979.206.497) **prefab** PI - Jerry Howard **prehensile** AA - Leonard Lee Rue III **press conference** PE - Paul S. Conklin **pressure cooker** AR **pressure suit** NASA **pretzel** LC **prickly pear** GEP **primrose** CC **printed circuit** PR - Robert A. Isaacs **printing press** SB - Donald Dietz **prism** EPJCo. - Camerique **proboscis** AA - Leonard Lee Rue III **profile** NGA **prominence** PR - Science Source **pronghorn** AA - Tom Edwards **propeller** National Center for Atmospheric Research, National Science Foundation **prospector** SB - Peter Southwick **protozoan** GHP - Runk & Schoenberger **protractor** GEP **prow** PI - Jerry Howard **ptarmigan** AA - Charles G. Summers, Jr. **pterodactyl** TG **Ptolemaic system** CC **puffin** AA - Leonard Lee Rue III **pug** HMCo. **Joseph Pulitzer** Brown Brothers **pulley** CC **pump**[1] GEP **pumpkin** PI - Karen Bussolini **punt**[1] Mystic Seaport Museum, Inc. All rights reserved. **pupil** TG **Purple Heart** Official U.S. Navy Photograph **purse** LW - S.E. Byrne **pushcart** SB - David Carmack **pushup** PC - Spencer Grant **pussy willow** LC **putt** LW - Oscar Palmquist **pyramid** SB - Peter Menzel **python** PR - Dade W. Thornton **quail**[1] TSI - Len Rue, Jr. **quarry**[2] PR - Ulrike Welsch **quartz** GHP - Barry L. Runk **Queen Anne's lace** LC **quetzal** PR - Robert Hermes **Quetzalcoatl** HPSM **quill** The Granger Collection, New York **quilt** © 1991 Judith Winters **quirt** LW - Oscar Palmquist **quiver**[2] NMAI **rabbit** GHP **rabbit ears** PI - Jerry Howard **raccoon** American Museum of Natural History, Courtesy Department Library Services, neg. no. 336665 **radial symmetry** GHP - Runk & Schoenberger **radio telescope** National Radio Astronomy Observatory, operated by Associated University, Inc., under cooperative agreement with the National Science Foundation **radish** LC **radius** LC **raft**[1] SB - Michael Weisbrot **railroad** SB - Jean-Claude Lejeune **rain forest** AR **Rameses II** The Granger Collection, New York **ranch** PR - Josephus Daniels **Jeannette Rankin** Sophia Smith Collection, Smith College **Raphael** The Granger Collection, New York **rasp** CC **raspberry** CC **rattlesnake** EPJCo. - Harold M. Lambert **raven** TSI - Leonard Lee Rue III **ravine** GHP - Grant Heilman **ray**[2] © 1991 by Sea World, Inc. **Ronald Reagan** EPJCo. - Camerique **reamer** CC/ © 1991 Judith Winters **rebus** LOC **receiver** CC **receptacle** LC **recorder** SB - Peter Vandermark **Red Cloud** Smithsonian Institution National Anthropological Archives, Bureau of American Ethnology Collection **red deer** LRE - Leonard Lee Rue III **redwood** PE - David Young-Wolff **reef**[1] TSI - Paul Chesley **reel**[1] PE - David Young-Wolff/ EPJCo. - Harold M. Lambert **referee** PC - Henry Horenstein **reflector** PI - Jerry Howard **refracting telescope** LC **refraction** CC **refrigerator** CC **regalia** GP - © Alpha **regatta** PC - Mac Donald **register** EPJCo./EPJCo. **reindeer** NYZS **relay race** PR - Kenneth Murray **relief** Virginia Museum of Fine Arts, Richmond, Purchase, The Williams Fund, 1960 **Rembrandt** BA **remora** CC **Pierre Auguste Renoir** Brown Brothers **reporter** PE - Robert Brenner **reptile** PR - Stephen Dalton/ PR - Jack Dermid/PR - Leonard Lee Rue III **reservoir** EPJCo. - Ewing Galloway **respiratory system** LC **rest**[1] TG **retort**[2] LC **retriever** HMCo. **Paul Revere** Brown Brothers **rhea** PR - Leonard Lee Rue III **rhinoceros** PC - Lynn McLaren **rib** LC **ribbon** SB - Jean-Claude Lejeune **Sally Ride** BA **right angle** LC **ring**[1] AR **rink** SB - Barbara Alper **RNA** LC **roadrunner** PR - Alexander Lowry **roadster** Brown Brothers **robe** PR - Barbara Rios **John D. Rockefeller** The Granger Collection, New York **rock garden** TSI - Lois Moulton **rocking chair** SB - Owen Franken **roller coaster** PC - Stanley Rowin **roller skate** CC **rolling pin** LW - Barry Slaven **Eleanor Roosevelt** CP **Franklin D. Roosevelt** HPSM **Theodore Roosevelt** HPSM **rose**[1] AR **rosemary** CDB **rotunda** BA **rowboat** PI - Jerry Howard **rowel** CC **ruff** PR - Mary Evans Picture Library/ GHP - Larry Lefever **ruffed grouse** TSI - Leonard Lee Rue III **rumble seat** PI - Jerry Howard **running board** SB - Lionel J-M Delevingne **Mount Rushmore** GHP **rutabaga** GEP **Babe Ruth** BA **sabot** BA **sacrum** LC **safety belt** EPJCo. - Harold M. Lambert **saguaro** AA - Leonard Lee Rue III **sailboat** EPJCo. - Harold M. Lambert **Saint Bernard** HMCo. **salamander** GHP - Hal H. Harrison **salmon** The Granger Collection, New York **saltcellar** LW - Oscar Palmquist **salute** SB - Elizabeth Hamlin **Deborah Samspon** The Granger Collection, New York **Carl Sandburg** GP - Nat Dallinger **sand dollar** GHP - Runk & Schoenberger **Antonio López de Santa Anna** Courtesy of The New-York Historical Society **Santa Claus** Courtesy of The New-York Historical Society **sari** PR - Omikron **saw**[1] GEP **sawfish** PR - Karl H. Maslowski **sawhorse** CC **saxophone** PC - J.D. Sloan **scapula** LC **scarecrow** EPJCo. **schnauzer** HMCo. **schooner** SB - Fredrik D. Bodin **Franz Schubert** PR **Albert Schweitzer** HPSM **scissors** LC **scooter** PI - Jerry Howard **scorpion** CDB **Dred Scott** Missouri Historical Society **Sir Walter Scott** CP **Scottish terrier** HMCo. **scrapbook** PE - Tony Freeman **screw** CC **scuba** PE - Tony Freeman **sculptor** SB - Bohdan Hrynewych **scythe** GHP **sea cucumber** CC **sea horse** GHP - Runk & Schoenberger **Elizabeth Seaman** CP **seat belt** PR - Bobbie Kingsley **secant** TG **secretary** The Connecticut Historical Society **secretary bird** PR - Mark Boulton **seesaw** EPJCo. **semitrailer** PC - Beringer-Dratch **sentry box** HAR **sepal** LC **Sequoya** LOC **serape** PR - Carl Frank **Elizabeth Seton** Mount St. Vincent-on-Hudson, Sisters of Charity Center, Bronx, New York **setter** HMCo. **sewing machine** LW - Barry Slaven **sextant** LC **Anne Sexton** AP/WWP **William Shakespeare** The Folger Shakespeare Library, Washington, D.C. **shallot** CC **shark** PR - Tom McHugh **shay** From the collections of Henry Ford Museum & Greenfield Village, neg. no. A2811 **sheet music** SB - Spencer Grant **Mary Wollstonecraft Shelley** National Portrait Gallery, London **Percy Bysshe Shelley** National Portrait Gallery, London **William Tecumseh Sherman** LOC **Shetland pony** EPJCo. **shipyard** AR **shish kebab** PI - Jerry Howard **shock absorber** TG **shofar** LW - Barry Slaven **shot put** PE - Richard Hutchings **shovel** CC **shrew** PR - Karl H. Maslowski **shuttlecock** CC **Siamese cat** PR - Ylla **sickle** CC **sidewinder** PR - Tom McHugh **silhouette** *Silhouettes: A Pictorial Archive of Varied Illustrations* **silo** SB - Daniel Brody **silverfish** CC **sine** TG **single file** SB - Hazel Hankin **sisal** Comstock - Georg Gerster **sitar** PC - Mikki Ansin Ehrenfeld **Sitting Bull** NMAI **skateboard** LW - Oscar Palmquist **skeleton** LC **ski** EPJCo. - Camerique **skin diving** Comstock - Russ Kinne **skull** LC **skunk** PR - Leonard Lee Rue III **skyscraper** SB - Michael Dwyer **sledge** EPJCo. **sledgehammer** CC **sleigh** EPJCo. **slide** PI - Jerry Howard **slide projector** LW - Oscar Palmquist **sloth** PR - Jen & Des Bartlett **sluice** SB - Lionel J-M Delevingne **small intestine** LC **Bessie Smith** The Granger Collection, New York **Joseph Smith** The National Portrait Gallery, Smithsonian Institution, Washington, D.C., Gift of the Reorganized Church of Jesus Christ of Latter-Day Saints, Independence, Missouri **smock** PC - Bob Kramer **smocking** PE - David Young-Wolff **snaffle** GEP **snail** GP **snapdragon** LC **snare drum** PE - Tony Freeman **snorkel** SB - Peter Vandermark **snout** PR - Jeanne White **snowshoe** The Brooklyn Museum, Nathan Sturges Jarvis Collection **soccer** GP **Socrates** HPSM **softball** SB - Ellis Herwig **solarium** PI - Karen Bussolini **solitaire** PC - Susan Van Etten **sombrero** SB - Jean-Claude Lejeune **Sophocles** Alinari - Art Resource, New York **sorrel**[1] *Field Guide to the Wildflowers* by Roger Tory Peterson and Margaret McKenny. © 1986 by Roger Tory Peterson and Margaret McKenny. Reprinted by permission of Houghton Mifflin Company. All rights reserved. **John Philip Sousa** AP/WWP **sousaphone** Brent Jones, Chicago, Illinois **sow**[2] GHP - John Colwell **soybean** LC **space shuttle** NASA **space suit** NASA **spark plug** LC **sparrow** PR - Karl H. Maslowski **spectroscope** TG **Edmund Spenser** CP **sphinx** MMA, Hewitt Fund, 1911, Rogers Fund, 1921, Munsey Fund, 1936, 1938, and Anonymous gift, 1951 (11.185) **sphygmomanometer** PC - Kindra Clineff **spider monkey** PR - S. Nagendra **spinning wheel** PC - Edward Bishop **spire**[1] LW - Barry Slaven **splint** PR - Peter G. Aitken **sponge** GHP - Runk & Schoenberger **spoonbill** GHP **Squanto** The Pilgrim Society, Plymouth, Massachusetts **square dance** SB - Tim Barnwell **squash**[1] LC **squid** GHP - Runk & Schoenberger **squirrel** CC **stagecoach** From the collections of Henry Ford Museum & Greenfield Village, neg. no. A2768 **stalactite and stalagmite** GHP - Runk & Schoenberger **Joseph Stalin** AP/WWP **stamen** LC **Miles Standish** CP **Elizabeth Cady Stanton** Sophia Smith Collection, Smith College **starfish** CC **statehouse** SB - Charles Kennard **station wagon** LW - S.E. Byrne **steam engine** TG **steamroller** SB - Owen Franken **steel band** Comstock - Russ Kinne **steeple** GHP - Alan Pitcairn **Gertrude Stein** AP/WWP **John Steinbeck** GP **stethoscope** CC **Baron von Steuben** CP **Robert Louis Stevenson** The Granger Collection, New York **stilt** EPJCo. **stingray** PR - Tom McHugh **stirrup** GEP **stomach** LC **Lucy Stone** CP **Stonehenge** AP/WWP **stopwatch** Peter Vandermark **stork** SB - Ira Kirschenbaum **Harriet Beecher Stowe** CP **Johann Strauss the Younger** BA **strawberry** LC **stringed instrument** SB - Gale Zucker/LW - Steve Gravano/SB - Elizabeth Crews **stroller** PI - Jerry Howard **sturgeon** PR - Tom McHugh **Peter Stuyvesant** Courtesy of The New-York Historical Society **submarine** AR **subway** GP - Camera Press **suffragist** BA **sugar cane** GHP - Grant Heilman **sugar maple** CC **suitcase** SB - Hazel Hankin **sumac** CDB **sundial** EPJCo. **sunflower** PI - Jerry Howard **Sun Yat-sen** BA **superhighway** SB - Eric Neurath **supertanker** PE - Tony Freeman **surfboard** EPJCo. - Camerique **surveying** The Granger Collection, New York **suspension bridge** SB - Peter Menzel **Bertha von Suttner** CP **swallowtail** LRE - Irene Vandermolen **swan** LRE - Leonard Lee Rue III **sweatpants** LW - S.E. Byrne **sweet William** CC **Jonathan Swift** National Portrait Gallery, London **swimmeret** CDB **swordfish** CC **sycamore** CC **symbiosis** LRE - Leonard Lee Rue III **synagogue** LW - S.E. Byrne **synapse** CC **syncline** GEP **synthesizer** SB - Judy Gelles **tabard** BA **taco** Palmer/Brilliant, Boston, Massachusetts **tadpole** CDB **William Howard Taft** LOC **takeoff** EPJCo. - Harold M. Lambert **talon** CC **tambourine** PI - Martin Miller **tandem bicycle** PI - Jerry Howard **tangent** TG **tangerine** CC **tap dance** The Granger Collection, New York **tapir** PR - Jen & Des Bartlett **target** EPJCo. - Harold M. Lambert **tarsier** PR - Arthur W. Ambler **tarsus** LC **tassel** PR - Steve Kagan **Zachary Taylor** LOC **Peter Ilich Tchaikovsky** BA **teapot** LW - Oscar Palmquist **Tecumseh** CP **tee** LW - Oscar Palmquist **telegraph** PE - Tony Freeman **telescope** LC **Alfred Tennyson** CP **tentacle** PC - Eric A. Roth **tent caterpillar** PR - Jerome Wexler **tepee** American Museum of Natural History, Courtesy Department Library Services, neg. no. 317248 - Rodman Wanamaker **Mother Teresa** GP - Camera Press **terrarium** GP - Victoria Beller-Smith **test tube** SB - Anestis Diakopoulos **tetrahedron** TG **thalamus** LC **Margaret Thatcher** GP - Norman Parkinson **thermograph** GHP - Runk & Schoenberger **thermometer** LC **Theseus** MMA, Bequest of John Cadwalader, 1914 (14.58.131) **thimble** LW - Oscar Palmquist **thistle** CC **Dylan Thomas** The Granger Collection, New York **Henry David Thoreau** Brown Brothers **thrasher** PR - Allan D. Cruickshank **threshing machine** TSI **tiara** Valentine Museum, Richmond, Virginia **tibia** LC **tide** SB - Fredrik D. Bodin/SB - Fredrik D. Bodin **tiger lily** PR - Robert H. Wright **timpani** PE - Tony Freeman **tippet** Courtesy, Museum of Fine Arts, Boston, Gift of Amelia Peabody and William S. Eaton **titmouse** GP **toadstool** CC **toboggan** LC **toggle bolt** CC **Leo Tolstoy** BA **tomahawk** NMAI **tom-tom** EPJCo. - Ewing Galloway **tooth** LC **top hat** SB - Owen Franken **topiary** SB - Harry Wilks **torch** EPJCo. - A. Devaney **tornado** EPJCo. - Ewing Galloway **totem pole** EPJCo. - Harold M. Lambert **toucan** PR - Arthur W. Ambler **tower** SB - Peter Menzel **towhee** PR - Karl H. Maslowski **track and field** PC - Mac Donald/BA **tractor** SB - Cary S. Wolinsky **traffic light** EPJCo. - Camerique **trampoline** PE - Tony Freeman **transformer** TG **transom** © 1981 Walter Silver **trap** GEP **trapeze** PC - Frank Siteman **trapezoid** LC **treadmill** PE - Tony Freeman **treble clef** TG **triangle** LC/Comstock - Russ Kinne **triceps** LC **triceratops** LC **trident** CC **trilobite** CC **tripod** SB - Joseph Schuyler **Triton** Courtesy, Museum of Fine Arts, Boston, Edwin E. Jack Fund **Trojan horse** BA **trombone** PI - Jerry Howard **trophy** PC - Jaye R. Phillips **tropic** LC **Harry S. Truman** Harry S. Truman Library - U.S. Army Photo **trumpet** GP - Leo M. Johnson **Sojourner Truth** National Portrait Gallery, Smithsonian Institution, Washington, D.C. **tsetse fly** CDB **tuatara** PR - Tom McHugh **Harriet Tubman** LOC **tulip** LC **tumbleweed** PR - Joe Munroe **tumbrel** SB - Peter Simon **tuna**[1] CC **tuning fork** LW - Oscar Palmquist **turban** SB - Rick Smolan **turkey vulture** PR - Allan D. Cruickshank **turnstile** SB - Jack Prelutsky **turtle** GHP - Hal H. Harrison **turtleneck** SB - Susie Fitzhugh **tusk** AA - Leonard Lee Rue III **Tutankhamen** MMA - Harry Burton **Desmond Tutu** AR **tuxedo** AR **John Tyler** In the Collection of The Corcoran Gallery of Art, Museum Purchase **typewriter** SB - Ellis Herwig **tyrannosaur** LC **ukulele** PC - Jeffrey Dunn **umbrella** PC - Carolyn Hine **umiak** AR **umpire** PC - Herb Snitzer **Uncle Sam** LOC **underhand** PI - Jerry Howard **unicorn** Courtesy, Winterthur Museum **unicycle** SB - Jean-Claude Lejeune **uniform** PE - David Young-Wolff **Union Jack** EPJCo. **universal joint** LC **upholster** TSI - Chip Henderson **upright piano** PI - Martin Miller **urn** SLAM, Museum Purchase **Saint Valentine** The Granger Collection, New York **valley** TSI - Robert Everts **Martin Van Buren** LOC **Vincent Van Gogh** The Granger Collection, New York **vanilla** CC **vault**[1] CC **VDT** SB - Tim Barnwell **vender** PR - Barbara Rios **venetian blind** LW - Aldo Mastrocola **Venn diagram** CC **Amerigo Vespucci** SCALA - Art Resource, New York **vetch** *Field Guide to the Wildflowers* by Roger Tory Peterson and Margaret McKenny. © 1986 by Roger Tory Peterson and Margaret McKenny. Reprinted by permission of Houghton Mifflin Company. All rights reserved. **veterinarian** SB - David Carmack **viaduct** LOC **victoria** The Shelburne Museum, Shelburne, Vermont **Victoria**[1] BA **vicuña** San Diego Zoo **video game** SB - Jeffry W. Myers **vineyard** SB - Owen Franken **viola** AP/

WWP **violin** SB - Gale Zucker **vise** CC **Vishnu** SLAM, Museum Purchase **visor** Comstock - Georg Gerster **volcano** LC **vole** PR - Jen & Des Bartlett **volleyball** PC - Ellis Herwig **voting machine** EPJCo. - Harold M. Lambert **vulture** AA - Leonard Lee Rue III **waders** Ewing Galloway **waffle iron** PE - Felicia Martinez **Richard Wagner** HPSM **walkie-talkie** AP/WWP **wallaby** NYZS **walrus** PR - Leonard Lee Rue III **wapiti** USDA - Chester F. Fry **wart hog** PR - Clem Haagner **Booker T. Washington** National Portrait Gallery, Smithsonian Institution, Washington, D.C., Transfer from the National Gallery of Art **George Washington** NGA, Gift of Andrew W. Mellon, 1942 **Martha Washington** National Portrait Gallery, Smithsonian Institution, Washington, D.C. **wasp** CDB **waterbuck** SB - Ira Kirschenbaum **water polo** SB - Ellis Herwig **James Watt** The Granger Collection, New York **wattle** GHP **waxwork** GP - Camera Press **weathervane** EPJCo. - Harold M. Lambert **weave** SB - Charles Kennard/GEP **weeping willow** LC **weevil** CDB **Ida B. Wells** The Granger Collection, New York **Eudora Welty** The Granger Collection, New York **John Wesley** CP **wet suit** SB - Mike Mazzaschi **Edith Wharton** AR **Phillis Wheatley** LOC **wheelchair** PC - Spencer Grant **whelk**[1] LC **whisker** TSI - Peter Pearson **Walt Whitman** HPSM **whooping crane** CC **widgeon** PR - Leonard Lee Rue III **wigwam** NMAI **Oscar Wilde** BA **Emma Willard** © 1868 *Eminent Women of the Age* **William the Conqueror** CP **Tennessee Williams** GP **Woodrow Wilson** HPSM **winch** PI - Jerry Howard **windmill** USDA/BA **windsurfing** SB - Peter Menzel **wintergreen** CC **John Winthrop** CP **wisteria** LC **wok** LW - Steve Gravano **wolverine** CC **wombat** NYZS **woodchuck** EPJCo. **Victoria Woodhull** Sophia Smith Collection, Smith College **woodpecker** PR - Leonard Lee Rue III **woodworking** PC - Frank Siteman **Virginia Woolf** BA **woolly bear** GHP **William Wordsworth** AR **workshop** PR - Laimute Druskis **worm gear** LC **wreath** AR **wrench** LC **Frank Lloyd Wright** BA **Wright Brothers** HPSM/HPSM **Richard Wright** GP - Samuel Kravitt **wrought iron** EPJCo. **Xerxes I** CP **xylophone** Comstock - Russ Kinne **yacht** EPJCo. **yak**[1] PR - Russ Kinne **yarmulke** PC - William Thompson **William Butler Yeats** BA **yellow jacket** CDB **Boris Yeltsin** GP - Vario Press and Camera Press **yew** LC **yoke** CC **Brigham Young** Brigham Young University Photoarchives **yo-yo** LW - Oscar Palmquist **yucca** SB - Eric Neurath **zebra** AA - Leonard Lee Rue III **zebu** PR - John Marinus **Zhou Enlai** AR **zither** Smithsonian Institution, Washington, D.C., Division of Musical Instruments **zucchini** LC

ABCDEFGHIJKL—RMT—9987654